The New
Cambridge Bibliography
of English Literature

in five volumes
Volume 1

The New Cambridge Bibliography of English Literature

Edited by

GEORGE WATSON

Volume 1
600–1660

CAMBRIDGE
AT THE UNIVERSITY PRESS
1974

Published by the Syndics of the Cambridge University Press
Bentley House, 200 Euston Road, London NW1 2DB
American Branch: 32 East 57th Street, New York, N.Y.10022

© Cambridge University Press 1974

Library of Congress Catalogue Card Number: 73–82455

ISBN: 0 521 20004 0

Printed in Great Britain
at the University Printing House, Cambridge
(Brooke Crutchley, University Printer)

CONTENTS

THE ANGLO-SAXON PERIOD (TO 1100)

I. Old English Literature

Aldhelm, Alms-giving, Andreas, Azarias, Battle of Brunanburh, Battle of Finnsburh, Battle of Maldon, Bede's death song, Beowulf, Brussels cross, Cædmon, Cædmon's hymn, Christ, Christ and Satan, Creed, Cynewulf, Daniel, Deor, Descent into Hell, Dream of the rood, Durham, Durham proverbs, Elegies, Elene, Exhortation to Christian living, Exodus, Fates of the apostles, Fortunes of men, Fragments of psalms, Franks casket, Genesis, Gifts of men, Gloria I–II, Guthlac, Homiletic fragments I–II, Husband's message, Instructions for Christians, Judgment Day I–II, Judith, Juliana, Kentish hymn, Latin-English proverbs, Leiden riddle, Lord's prayer I–III, Maxims I–II, Menologium, Metres of Boethius, Metrical charms, Metrical epilogue to ms 41 Corpus Cambridge, Metrical epilogue to Pastoral care, Metrical preface to Gregory's Dialogues, Metrical preface to Pastoral care, Order of the world, Paris psalter, Pharaoh, Phoenix, Physiologus, Poems of the Anglo-Saxon chronicle, Prayer, Precepts,

THE MIDDLE ENGLISH PERIOD (1100–1500)

1. Introduction

2. Middle English literature

I. The Middle English romances

CONTENTS

II. Middle English literature to 1400

III. Geoffrey Chaucer

IV. Education

3. The fifteenth century

I. The English Chaucerians

II. Middle Scots poets

III. English prose of the fifteenth century

IV. Miscellaneous and anonymous verse and prose of the fifteenth century

4. Songs and ballads

I. Songs and lyrics

II. Ballads

5. Medieval drama

6. Writings in Latin

THE RENAISSANCE TO THE RESTORATION
(1500–1660)

1. Introduction
I. General works

II. Literary relations with the Continent

CONTENTS

III. Book production and distribution

2. Poetry

I. Introduction

II. Tudor poetry

CONTENTS

III. The Elizabethan sonnet 1073

IV. Minor Tudor poetry

T.A., W. A., Achelley, Adam Bell, Alabaster, Alexander, Alsoppe, Armin, Arthington, Aske, Avale, Averell, R. B., Bacon, Baker, Baldwin, Bale, Banquet of dainties, Barlow, Barnes, Barnfield, Basse, Bastard, Batman, Baxter, Beaumont, Becon, Lady Bessy, Beverley, Bieston, Birchensa, Blenerhasset, Blundeville, Book of a ghostly father, Borde, Bradshaw, Brice, Arthur Broke, Thomas Broke the younger, Bushe, E. C., H. C., J. C. gent., J. C., J. C., T. C. gent., Calendar of shepherds, Carew, Castle of labour, Cavendish, Cavyl (Humphrey Cavell?), Thomas Chaloner the elder, Chapman, Chappell, Chester, Churchyard, Chute, Clapham, Cock Lorrel's boat, Colclough, Colin Blowbols testament, Colse, Combe, Connaissance d'amours, Constable, Copland, Copley, Cotton, Coverdale, Crowley, T. D., Davies, Day, Deloney, Devereux, Dickenson, Dolman, Anne Dowriche, Drant, Drout, Translator of Du Bartas, Dyer, Dymoke, J. G. E. (Egerton?), Richard Edwards, Thomas Edwards, Elderton, Queen Elizabeth I, Elviden, Maid Emlyn, Evans, Fabyan, Fairfax, Fenne, Ferrers, Feylde, Fifteen joys of marriage, Fisher, Fitzgeffrey, Fleming, Giles Fletcher the elder, Flodden field, Forrest, Fraunce, Fulwell, C.G. gent., Gale, Garter, Jeaste of Syr Gawayne, Gifford, God, Golding, Goodwyn, Googe, Gorges, Gosynhyll, Grange, Gray, Greepe, Life of St Gregory's mother, Griffin, Grimald, Grove, Elizabeth Grymeston, Guarini, Guilpin, T. H., T. H., Hake, Arthur Hall, John Hall, Joseph Hall, John Harington the elder, Sir John Harington, Hawes, Hendred, Preservation of Henry VII, Henry VIII, Heraclitus and Democritus, Mary Herbert, Jasper Heywood, John Heywood, Higgins, Hilarie, Hogarde (or Huggarde), Hugh Holland, Robert Holland, Holme, Howard, Howell, Hudson, Hugh of Leicester, Hunnis, Hunting of the Cheviot, Image of hypocrisy, Jacob, Welcome to James I, Jenny, Jenynges, John of Capistrano, Johnson, Joseph of Armathia, Jousts of May and June, Kelton, Kendall, Kethe, Thomas Knell junior, Knight of courtesy, Kyttes, E. L., F. L., R. L. gent, V. or U. L., W. L., Lane, Lewicke, Lisle, Lodowick Lloyd, Richard Lloyd, Lodge, Lok, Lord of Lorn, Lord's Prayer, Lovell, Lyly, Marbeck, Mardeley, St Margaret of Scotland, Markham, Marlowe, Marshall, Marston, Mary the Blessed Virgin, St Mary Magdalene, Christopher Middleton, Thomas Middleton, Miller of Abington, Moffet, Moone, Edward More, Thomas More, Muggins, Mulcaster, Munday, A. N., Nashe, Nevill, Neville, Newbery, Humfrey Newton, Thomas Newton of Cheshire, Thomas Newton gent., Nicholson, Niclas (Christopher Vitell?), Nixon, Norden, Norton, Nuce, Nutbrown maid, Ocland, Ogle, Henry Parker Baron Morley, Matthew Parker, Parry, Partridge, Passions of the spirit, Peele, Peend, Peeris (Pyers), Percy, Petowe, Pett, Phaer, Phillip(s), Pilgrim's tale, Plowman's tale, Powell, Pricket, Procter, Proud wife's paternoster, Pyrrye, Ramsey, Rankins, Remedy of love, Hugh Rhodes, John Rhodes, Robert the devil, Roberts, Robin Conscience, Robin Hood, Clement Robinson, Richard Robinson of Alton, Richard Robinson of London, Roche, Rogers, Rosse, Francis Rous the elder, Richard Rowlands, Samuel Rowlands, R. S. esquire, Sabie, Sackville, Salmacis and Hermaphroditus, Saltwood, Salusbury, Samuel, Schoolhouse of women, Scot, Scott, Scottish Field, Seager, Shakespeare, Sharrock, Shepherd, Skeltonical salutation, Smith that forged a new dame, Sir Thomas Smith, Walter Smith, William Smith, Solomon and Marcolphus, Soowthern, Squire of low degree, Stanley, Stanyhurst, Sternhold, Storer, Studley, Sylvester, F. T., J. T., Terence in English, Translator of Theocritus, St Thomas à Becket, Thynne, Tilney, Tofte, Tourneur, Trussel, Turbervile, Tusser, Twyne, Tye, Tyro, Udall, Underdowne, St Ursula, Vallans, Robert Vaughan, Sir William Vaughan, Vaux, Vennar(d), de Vere,

CONTENTS

xiv

CONTENTS

CONTENTS

VI. The early tragedies

VII. Later Elizabethan drama

VIII. Minor Elizabethan drama (1580–1603)

IX. William Shakespeare

CONTENTS

X. Jacobean and Caroline drama

XI. Minor Jacobean and Caroline drama (1603–60)

XII. University plays (1500–1642)

4. Religion

I. Humanists and reformers

CONTENTS

II. The English Bible

III. The Prayer Book

CONTENTS

5. Popular and miscellaneous prose

I. Pamphleteers and miscellaneous writers

II. Minor popular literature

III. Character-books and essays

IV. Prose fiction

CONTENTS

V. News-sheets and newsbooks

VI. Travel

VII. Translations into English

6. History, philosophy, science and other forms of learning

I. Historians, biographers and antiquaries

CONTENTS

VII. Philosophy

Sir Thomas More, Baldwin, Wilson, Lever, Everard Digby, Temple, Case, Sanderson,
Perkins, Barckley, Davies, Joseph Hall, Selden, Sanderson, Fludd, Crakanthorp,
Carpenter, Fotherby, Lord Herbert of Cherbury, Hakewill, Ames, Flavel, Casaubon,
Greville, Hartlib, John Hall, Henry More, Cudworth, Wallis, Bramhall,
Sir Kenelm Digby, Ross, White, Filmer, Culverwel, Ward, Pordage, Stanley,
Harrington, Lawson, Wren, Pierce, Stubbe, Smith, Boyle, Lucy, Gale, Parker, Tenison,
Legrand, Eachard, Milton, Clarendon, Whitehall, Tyrrell, Dowel, Whichcote

VIII. Science

IX. Education

7. Scottish literature

I. Introduction

II. Poetry and drama

Arbuthnot, Bellenden, Boyd, Burel, Davidson, Fowler, Alexander Hume,
Sir Patrick Hume, James VI of Scotland, Kirkcaldy, Lauder, Lindsay, Sir Richard
Maitland, Andrew Melville, Elizabeth Melville, James Melville, Montgomerie,
Philotus, Rolland Scott, Sempill, Semple, Stewart, Wedderburn

Henry Adamson, John Adamson, Craig, Gardyne or Garden, Gordon, Grahame,
Hannay, Anna Hume, David Hume, Johnston, Kennedy, Lauder, Lithgow, Melville,
Montrose, Mure, Murray, Ramsay

CONTENTS

III. Prose

EDITOR'S PREFACE

This is the final volume of the *New Cambridge Bibliography of English Literature* to appear, apart from volume 5 (*Index*), now in preparation; and like two of its forerunners, volume 2 (1660–1800) and volume 3 (1800–1900), it is based upon a volume of *CBEL* (1940) edited by F. W. Bateson and its *Supplement* of 1957: in this case a total revision of the old volume 1 together with appropriate sections of the 1957 supplement. Once again the original order of the Bibliography has proved too familiar to be abandoned; and little in the general arrangement of these medieval and Renaissance sections has needed to be altered. The General Introduction too remains unchanged in its scope. Apart from the historical aids which appeared in 1940 as Social and Political Background, no section has had to be dropped; and the order of the rest of the volume has been essentially preserved, including the characteristic arrangement of major and minor authors under the great literary kinds such as Poetry, Drama and Prose.

Each volume of *New CBEL* has been designed, if necessary, to be used in isolation from the rest; and much of this preface repeats with variations information in the prefaces to volumes 2, 3 and 4. As before, the task of more than fifty contributors has been to revise and integrate the existing lists of 1940 and 1957, to add materials of the past dozen years and more, to correct and refine the bibliographical details already available, and to reshape the whole according to new conventions. The index in the present volume, like its companions, lists headings and primary authors.

New CBEL is confined to literary authors native to or mainly resident in the British Isles—a definition less troublesome here than in the nineteenth and twentieth centuries. But, as in *Concise CBEL* (1958), no restriction of nationality or language has been imposed on the choice of secondary materials, mainly biography and criticism, concerning the British and Irish authors included here, and writings by such authors in Latin are within the scope of the volume. Celtic literature is excluded. The concept of period remains unchanged: an author who was established before 1660 qualifies, if of sufficient literary interest, for inclusion in this volume. Of the six periods of *New CBEL*, three are collected in this volume: the Anglo-Saxon period (600–1100); the Middle English (1100–1500); and the Renaissance to the Restoration (1500–1660). The remaining three periods (1660–1800, 1800–1900, 1900–50) have already appeared as separate volumes, and an index to the whole of *New CBEL*, which will include among other entries the names of primary authors and certain headings, is already in preparation.

The Bibliography attempts to represent English studies, so far as these concern the literature of the British Isles, both in primary and in secondary materials, 'works by' and 'works about'. The symbols §1 and §2 have again been imposed upon author-sections to mark this distinction, and the canon of an author's works, or the primary section, has usually been merged into a single chronological list, with the object of demonstrating more clearly the shape of his literary career. Author-sections ordinarily begin with bibliographies, where they exist, and collections, followed by the primary section and its subsections, followed in turn by a chronological list of secondary material with works by individual scholars and critics grouped together. In a few instances, for the sake of greater clarity, secondary works have been grouped under the titles of individual primary works, especially in cases of doubtful attribution.

The Bibliography continues to aim at completeness in its own terms. Certain categories of material have as before been excluded, notably unpublished dissertations and their published abstracts, ephemeral journalism, encyclopaedia articles, reviews of secondary works, brief notes of less than crucial interest to scholarship, and sections in general works such as literary histories which are listed at the head of each period or major division. Headnotes to certain sections define their scope in special detail. In general, contributors have been encouraged to drop antiquated articles which are now either superseded or absorbed into later studies and editions; but the history of an author's reputation remains an object of study, and articles which represent it memorably have been retained, even when discredited by later scholarship. Details of format are not normally included except to distinguish between early editions of major primary works.

The location of copies, as before, remains essentially outside the scope of the Bibliography, which cannot undertake to rival the *Short-Title Catalogue* in this respect. But brief headnotes on manuscripts have often been included; and where a unique copy of a work is known to exist outside the British Museum, such information has at times been admitted into the Bibliography, though in neither case has consistency been attempted.

The page has been designed to accommodate about one quarter more than the old *CBEL* page, and a radical attempt has been made to simplify and standardize the existing conventions of the Bibliography. Punctuation has been considerably reduced: colons regularly precede subtitles, semicolons divide titles; and commas rather than semicolons now ordinarily separate the dates of reprints. Capitalization has been reduced to the level of ordinary prose, which has enabled titles within titles to be distinguished by a capital letter. Contractions are expanded. In titles in English, the modern use of u/v and i/j has been followed. Roman numerals have been greatly reduced in favour of arabic. Abbreviations, apart from certain initials representing periodicals, have been moderately used, and it is hoped they are largely self-explanatory. The use of brackets has been much reduced, and headnotes and endnotes which serve as editorial explanations have been allowed to define themselves simply by their position. Titles, as in old *CBEL*, are 'short', and omissions are unmarked; and, as before, the number of volumes is entered unless it is one, and the place of publication unless it is London; for this purpose, books published in England by the Oxford University Press have been entered as 'Oxford'. Such details continue to apply in any given entry until contradicted, and 'I vol' and 'London' may then be used to contradict. In citing periodical-articles, monthlies are normally quoted by the month and quarterlies by volume-number. Translations of primary works have been admitted in summary form only, and commonly without details of translator or place of publication, e.g. 'tr French, 1738'; if no language is specified, the translation is into English. In the case of secondary works, only translations into English have normally been cited.

The scale of bibliographical detail in the primary section is a matter which eludes simple definition: it necessarily varies according to the state of knowledge in the subject and even according to the preoccupations of the contributor. The detail of an entry tends, as before, to be most intense in the early years of the life of a book; late editions are usually cited only when revised or enlarged; and modern reprints may not be included at all unless they justify themselves by reason of an introduction or editorial apparatus. Major authors tend to be more minutely treated than minor, and headnotes to individual sections often define the limits that have been placed. As in other volumes, the proper demands of consistency have not been interpreted as signifying that every author should be treated in precisely the same way.

Annual period bibliographies, now appearing in a number of learned journals and covering the range of English studies, are listed at the head of each period section of *New CBEL*. They will continue to supply indispensable supplements to the Bibliography for recent and future publications.

ACKNOWLEDGEMENTS

My first acknowledgements are due to the fifty and more contributors in Europe and North America who have sacrificed so much to make this volume; many of them have advised far beyond the scope of their own sections. The Advisory Committee of H. S. Bennett (Chairman), P. G. Burbidge, R. W. David, A. N. L. Munby and I. R. Willison, who together initiated the project, have again helped to guide the progress of the volume over three years; and the death of the Chairman in 1972, at a moment when this last volume was nearing completion, was a sad loss after a decade of his friendly counsel. Early advice was received from members of the staff of the British Museum and of the Bodleian Library, to the benefit of the undertaking; and on individual sections from Mr Giles G. Barber, Dr Richard Bauckham, Dr D. S. Brewer, Professor Robert A. Day, Dr M. R. Godden, Mr W. Speed Hill, Professor James Kinsley, Mr J. C. Maxwell, Mr Brian Nellist and Dr Rosemary Woolf. Mr M. Johnson and Mrs Y. Surtees acted as assistants to a contributor. Miss Katharine F. Pantzer, whose editing of the new *Short-Title Catalogue* for the Bibliographical Society has run parallel with this work, has been generous with advice to contributors and editor; the patient skill of the staff of the University Printer has once again proved exemplary; and the Cambridge University Library has continued to allow us the use of an office, where Mrs Phyllis Parsons has completed her seven-year task of typing the entire four-volume Bibliography. It is a service for which no gratitude could ever suffice.

For myself, I lay down with this volume a task on which I have been engaged for twenty years, since I began work on the *Supplement* in 1952. Meanwhile readers will, as I hope, continue to send me corrections both to *New CBEL* *1-3* and to the *Concise CBEL*. The work has made me a host of friendly critics and critical friends throughout Europe and America, and I hope through its good offices to make many more.

GEORGE WATSON

St John's College, Cambridge
August 1972

LIST OF CONTRIBUTORS
TO VOLUME 1

N.J.B.	Nicolas J. Barker	T.F.H.	T. F. Hoad
C.B.L.B.	C. B. L. Barr	J.H.	John Horden
P.J.B.	Priscilla J. Bawcutt	C.H.	Cyrus Hoy
J.A.W.B.	J. A. W. Bennett	P.H.-B.	Peter Hunter-Blair
N.F.B.	Norman F. Blake	E.J.K.	E. J. Kenney
D.S.B.	D. S. Bland	J.L.	Joyce Lorimer
A.J.B.	A. J. Bliss	J.K.M.	J. K. McConica
R.R.B.	R. R. Bolgar	R.E.M.	R. E. Maddison
W.W.S.B.	W. W. S. Breem	W.M.	William Matthews
T.J.B.	T. J. Brown	A.D.M.	A. David Mills
A.C.	Alistair Campbell	J.N.-S.	J. Norton-Smith
G.C.	Gloria Cigman	R.I.P.	R. I. Page
C.C.	Cecily Clark	C.A.P.	C. A. Patrides
P.C.	Peter Clemoes	D.A.P.	Derek A. Pearsall
R.C.	Robert Cockcroft	E.D.P.	Eric D. Pendry
R.L.C.	Rowland L. Collins	H.C.P.	H. C. Porter
J.C.	James Craigie	B.R.	Barbara Raw
J.E.C.	J. E. Cross	W.A.R.	William A. Ringler
R.T.D.	R. T. Davies	J.W.R.	John W. Robinson
T.S.D.	T. S. Dorsch	J.R.-S.	Joy Russell-Smith
R.D.D.	R. D. Dunn	V.J.S.	V. J. Scattergood
N.E.	Norman Endicott	J.S.	Joan Simon
S.B.G.	Stanley B. Greenfield	P.G.S.	Paul G. Stanwood
D.G.	David Greer	J.W.	Joanna Watson
A.C.H.	A. C. Hamilton	C.W.	Charles Webster
H.H.	Henry Hargreaves	J.S.W.	John S. Wilders
B.H.	Bernard Harris	J.W.Y.	John W. Yolton
G.R.H.	G. R. Hibbard	T.Y.	Theodore Yonge

ABBREVIATIONS

Acad	Academy	illustr	illustrated by
addn	addition	Inst	Institute
Amer	American	introd	introduction
anon	anonymous	JEGP	Journal of English and
Archiv	Archiv für das Studium der		Germanic Philology
	neueren Sprachen	JHI	Journal of the History of Ideas
AS	Anglo-Saxon	Jnl	Journal
Assoc	Association	Lang	Language
b.	born	Lib	Library
Bibl	Bibliographical	Lit	Literature
bk	book	MÆ	Medium Ævum
BM	British Museum	Mag	Magazine
Br	British	ME	Middle English
Bull	Bulletin	ML	Muses' Library
BNYPL	Bulletin of New York Public	MLN	Modern Language Notes
	Library	MLQ	Modern Language Quarterly
c.	circa	MLR	Modern Language Review
ch	chapter	MP	Modern Philology
CHEL	Cambridge History of English	ms	manuscript
	Literature	Nat	National
col	column	nd	no date
CQ	Critical Quarterly	N & Q	number
d.	died	no	Notes and Queries
DNB	Dictionary of National	OE	Old English
	Biography	OHEL	Oxford History of English
ed	edited by		Literature
edn	edition	OSA	Oxford Standard Authors
E & S	Essays and Studies	p.	page
et al	and others	pbd	published
EC	Essays in Criticism	pbn	publication
EETS	Early English Text Society	PBSA	Papers of the Bibliographical
EHR	English Historical Review		Society of America
EL	Everyman's Library	PMLA	Publications of the Modern
ELH	Journal of English Literary		Language Association of
	History		America
EML	English Men of Letters	PQ	Philological Quarterly
Eng	English	priv	privately
E Studien	Englische Studien	Proc	Proceedings
E Studies	English Studies	prop	proprietor
facs	facsimile	pt	part
fl.	floruit	ptd	printed
GM	Gentleman's Magazine	Quart	Quarterly
HLQ	Huntington Library Quarterly	REL	Review of English Literature

ABBREVIATIONS

rev	revised by	STS	Scottish Text Society
Rev	Review	Stud	Studies
RES	Review of English Studies	suppl	supplement
rptd	reprinted	TLS	Times Literary Supplement
SB	Studies in Bibliography (University of Virginia)	tr	translated by
		trn	translation
SE	Studies in English (University of Texas)	Univ	University
		unpbd	unpublished
ser	series	UTQ	University of Toronto Quarterly
Sh Jb	Shakespeare Jahrbuch	vol	volume
Soc	Society	WC	World's Classics
SP	Studies in Philology		

GENERAL INTRODUCTION

For bibliographies, literary histories, journals etc wholly or mainly related to a single period see under the period concerned.

I. BIBLIOGRAPHIES

(1) LISTS OF BIBLIOGRAPHICAL SOURCES

Courtney, W. P. A register of national bibliography. 3 vols 1905–12.

Cross, T. P. A list of books and articles designed to serve as an introduction to the bibliography and methods of English literary history. Chicago 1919, 1951 (10th edn rev), 1962 (rev and enlarged D. F. Bond as A reference guide to English studies).

Northup, C. S. A register of bibliographies of the English language and literature. New Haven 1925.

Esdaile, A. The sources of English literature. Cambridge 1928.

Vorstius, J. et al. Internationale Bibliographie des Buch- und Bibliothekswesens mit besonderer Berücksichtigung der Bibliographie. 15 vols Leipzig 1928–41.

Cole, G. W. An index to bibliographical papers published by the Bibliographical Society and the Library Association. London 1877–1932, Chicago 1933.

Van Patten, N. An index to bibliographies and bibliographical contributions relating to the work of American and British authors 1923–32. Stanford 1934.

Coulter, E. M. and M. Gerstenfeld. Historical bibliographies: a systematic and annotated guide. Berkeley 1935.

Bibliographic index: a cumulative bibliography of bibliographies. New York 1937–.

Microfilm (*later* Dissertation) abstracts. Ann Arbor 1938.

Besterman, T. A world bibliography of bibliographies and of bibliographical catalogues, calendars, abstracts, digests, indexes. 2 vols 1939–40, 3 vols 1947–9, 4 vols Geneva 1955–6, 1965 (all rev).

Bohatta, H. and F. Hodes. Internationale Bibliographie der Bibliographien. Frankfurt 1939–50.

Spargo, J. W. A bibliographical manual for students of the language and literature of England and the United States. Chicago 1939, 1941, New York 1956 (rev).

Kennedy, A. G. A concise bibliography for students of English. Stanford 1940, 1945, 1954, 1960 (rev and enlarged D. B. Sands).

Ireland, N. O. An index to indexes: a subject bibliography of published indexes. Boston 1942.

Fleishack, C., E. Rückert and G. Reichardt. Grundriss der Bibliographie. Leipzig 1957.

Watson, G. The concise Cambridge bibliography of English literature 600–1950. Cambridge 1958, 1965 (rev).

Altick, R. D. and A. Wright. Selective bibliography for the study of English and American literature. New York 1960, 1963 (rev).

Bateson, F. W. A guide to English literature. 1965, 1968 (rev).

Black, D. C. Guide to lists of masters' theses. Chicago 1965.

McNamee, L. F. Dissertations in English and American literature: theses accepted by American, British and German universities 1865–1964. New York 1968; Supplement one for 1964–8, New York 1969.

Howard-Hill, T. H. Bibliography of British literary bibliographies. Oxford 1969.

(2) JOURNALS ETC
(in alphabetical order)

Abstracts of English studies. Boulder 1958–.

American book collector (Amateur book collector 1950–5). Chicago 1956–.

Anglia. Halle 1877–1944, Tübingen 1950– (with Beiblatt, 1891–1944).

Anglica. Osaka 1950–.

Annuale mediaevale. Pittsburgh 1960–.

Archiv für das Studium der neueren Sprachen (also known as Herrigs Archiv). Brunswick etc 1846–1942, 1948–.

Ball State University forum. Muncie Ind 1960–.

Bibliographical notes and queries. 1935–9.

Bodleian quarterly record. Oxford 1914–37; superseded by Bodleian Library record, Oxford 1938–.

The book collector. 1952–.

British journal of aesthetics. 1960–.

British Museum quarterly. 1926–.

The bulletin of bibliography. Boston 1897–.

Bulletin of the John Rylands Library. Manchester 1914–.

Bulletin of the New York Public Library. New York 1897–.

The Cambridge quarterly. Cambridge 1965–.

College English (English journal 1912–38). Chicago 1939–.

Comparative drama. Kalamazoo Michigan 1967–.

Comparative literature. Eugene 1949–.

Comparative literature studies. Cardiff 1940–6.

Comparative literature studies. College Park Md 1963–7 Urbana 1967–.

Cornell library journal. Ithaca 1966–.

Critical quarterly. 1959–.

The critical review. Melbourne 1958–.

The critical survey. 1962–. Suppl to Critical quarterly, above.

Criticism. Detroit 1959–.

Dalhousie review. Halifax Nova Scotia 1921–.

The dial. Chicago 1880–1929.

Drama survey. St Paul 1961–.

ELH: a journal of English literary history. Baltimore 1934–.

Englische Studien. Leipzig 1877–1944.

English. 1936–.

English Institute essays (formerly Studies). New York 1940–.

English language notes. Boulder 1963–.

English miscellany. Rome 1950–.

English philological studies (English and Germanic studies 1947–61). Cambridge 1963–.

English studies. Amsterdam 1919–.

English studies in Africa. Johannesburg 1958–.

Essays and studies. Oxford 1910– (Eng Assoc), 1948–9 (as English studies).

Essays by divers hands. 1921–.

Essays in criticism. Oxford 1951–.

Etudes anglaises. Paris 1938–.

Explicator. Fredericksburg Va 1942–7, Lynchburg Va 1947–54, Columbia SC 1954–66, Richmond Va 1966–.

Forum for modern language studies. St Andrews 1965–.

Hartford studies in literature. Hartford Conn 1969–.

Harvard library bulletin. Cambridge Mass 1947–61, 1966–.

Hudson review. New York 1948–.

Hungarian studies in English. Budapest 1963–.

Huntington library quarterly (Huntington library bulletin 1931–7). San Marino 1938–.

Jahrbuch für romanische und englische Literatur. Berlin 1859–76.

The journal of aesthetics and art criticism. New York 1941–4, Cleveland 1945–.

The journal of British studies. Hartford Conn 1961–.

The journal of English and Germanic philology (The journal of Germanic philology, Bloomington 1897–1902). Urbana 1903–.

Journal of the history of ideas. New York 1940–.

Kenyon review. Gambier Ohio 1939–70.

Leeds studies in English. Leeds 1932–.

The library. 1899–1919 (then incorporated with Transactions of Bibliographical Society, below).

The library chronicle of the University of Texas. Austin 1944.

Manuscripta. St Louis 1957–.

Massachusetts studies in English. Amherst 1967–.

MLA abstracts. New York 1972–.

Modern drama. Lawrence Kansas 1958–.

Modern fiction studies. Lafayette Ind 1955–.

Modern language notes. Baltimore 1886–. No English or American material after 1962.

Modern language quarterly. Seattle 1940–.

The modern language review. Cambridge 1905–.

Modern philology. Chicago 1903–.

Mosaic: a journal for the comparative study of literature and ideas. Winnipeg 1967–.

Neophilologus. Groningen 1916–.

Die neueren Sprachen. Frankfurt 1893–.

Neuphilologische Mitteilungen. Helsinki 1899–.

New literary history. Charlottesville 1969–.

Notes and queries. 1849–.

Novel: a forum on fiction. Providence 1967–.

Oxford bibliographical society: proceedings and papers. Oxford 1923–.

The Oxford review. Oxford 1966–.

Papers of the Bibliographical Society of America. New York 1904–.

Papers on language and literature. Carbondale 1965–.

Philological quarterly. Iowa City 1922.

PMLA: publications of the Modern Language Association of America. New York 1886–.

Princeton University library chronicle. Princeton 1939–.

Quarterly review. 1809–1967.

Renaissance and modern studies. Nottingham 1957–.

Renaissance papers. Columbia SC 1954–.

Renaissance quarterly. Hanover NH 1948–53, New York 1954–.

Renascence. Milwaukee 1948–.

Review of English literature. 1960–7.

The review of English studies. Oxford 1925–.

La revue anglo-américaine. Paris 1923–.

Revue de la littérature comparée. Paris 1921–.

Rivista di letterature moderne e comparate. Florence 1963–.

Scottish poetry. Edinburgh 1966–.

Scrutiny. Cambridge 1932–53, 20 vols Cambridge 1963 (with index).

Seventeenth-century news. New York 1942–.

Sewanee review. Sewanee 1892–.

Southern review. Adelaide 1963–.

Sprache und Literatur Englands und Amerikas. Tübingen 1952–.

Studia neophilologica. Upsala 1928.

Studia romanica et anglica Zagrabiensia. Zagreb 1956–.

Studies (formerly Papers) in bibliography. Charlottesville 1948–.

Studies in English. University Mississippi 1960–.

Studies in English literature. Tokyo 1919–.

Studies in English literature 1500–1900. Houston 1961–.

Studies in philology. Chapel Hill 1904–.

Tennessee studies in literature. Knoxville 1956–.

Texas studies in literature. Austin 1959–.

Theatre survey. Waltham Mass 1960–3, Pittsburgh 1963–.

Thoth. Syracuse NY 1959–.

The times literary supplement. 1902–.

Transactions of the Bibliographical Society (incorporated by Library, above, after 1920). 1893–.

Transactions of the Cambridge Bibliographical Society. Cambridge 1949–.

Tri-quarterly. Evanston 1964–.

Tulane studies in English. New Orleans 1949–.

Unisa English studies. Pretoria 1968–.

University of Toronto quarterly. Toronto 1935–.

Uppsala university English institute essays and studies on English language and literature. Upsala and Cambridge 1949–.

Virginia quarterly review. Charlottesville 1925–.

West Virginia philological papers. Morgantown 1936– (since 1963 as Victorian poetry).

Yearbook of comparative and general literature. Chapel Hill 1952–60, Bloomington 1961–.

Zeitschrift für Anglistik und Amerikanistik. East Berlin 1953–.

(3) CURRENT LISTS OF NEW BOOKS

The English catalogue of books from 1835– (with retrospective vol for 1801–36 by R. A. Peddie and Q. Waddington, 1914). 1864– (now annual with a 5-year cumulation).

The publishers' trade list annual (Uniform trade list annual, 1873–7). New York 1873–; Books in print: an index to the publishers' trade list annual, New York 1948–.

British books in print (superseding Reference catalogue of current literature, 1874–1940, 1951, 1961, 1965). 1967– (annual).

The British Museum list of accessions. 1881– (now monthly, formerly fortnightly).

The United States catalog: books in print. New York 1899–1928; Cumulative book index: a world list of books in English supplementing the United States catalog, ed M. Burnham et al, New York 1933–.

The times literary supplement. 1902–.

The booklist and subscription books bulletin: a guide to current books. Boston 1906–10 (Amer Lib Assoc), Chicago 1911–.

Whitaker's cumulative booklist. 1924– (annually and, since 1944, also in 4- or 5-year cumulations).

The British national bibliography: a subject list of new British books. Ed A. J. Wells 1950– (annual).

The library of Congress author catalog 1948–52. 24 vols Ann Arbor 1953; continued as National union catalog: a cumulative author list, 1953–7, 26 vols Ann Arbor 1958; for 1952–5 imprints, 30 vols Ann Arbor 1961; for 1958–62, 50 vols New York 1963; for 1963–7, 59 vols Ann Arbor 1969; for 1968, 12 vols Washington 1969; 1969– (9 issues annually with quarterly and annual cumulations and 5-year cumulations projected).

The Library of Congress catalog, books: subjects 1950–4. 20 vols Ann Arbor 1955; for 1955–9, 22 vols Paterson NJ 1960; for 1960–4, 25 vols Ann Arbor 1965; 1965–

(quarterly with annual cumulations and 5-year cumulations projected).

Paperbound books in print. New York 1955– (semi-annually to 1959; quarterly to 1964; now monthly).

American book publishing record. New York 1960– (monthly, then annual cumulations from Publishers' weekly).

Australian national bibliography. Canberra 1961– (monthly with annual cumulations).

Canadian books in print. Ed G. Simoneau, Toronto 1967– (annual).

National union catalog, pre-1956 imprints: the Mansell catalog. Chicago 1968–.

(4) CURRENT LISTS OF ENGLISH STUDIES

English Association bulletin. 1907–35.

The year's work in English studies. 1919–.

Annual bibliography of English language and literature. Cambridge 1921– (Modern Humanities Research Assoc).

The review of English studies. Oxford 1925– (quarterly lists of articles and periodicals).

Research in progress in the modern languages and literatures. PMLA 63–75 1948–60.

Recent studies. Stud in Eng Lit 1500–1900 1961–. Quarterly issues contain, in turn, annual survey of scholarship in 4 major literary periods.

MLA international bibliography of books and articles on the modern languages and literatures. New York 1963– (replacing Annual bibliography 1956–63, and American bibliography 1922–55).

(5) REFERENCE WORKS

General

Watt, R. Bibliotheca britannica: or a general index to British and foreign literature. 4 vols Edinburgh 1824.

Chambers, R. Cyclopaedia of English literature. 2 vols Edinburgh 1843–4, 4 vols 1857–60 (rev R. Carruthers); ed D. Patrick 3 vols 1901–3; rev J. L. Geddie 3 vols Philadelphia 1938.

Allibone, S. A. A critical dictionary of English literature and British and American authors (suppl by J. F. Kirk). 5 vols Philadelphia 1858–91.

Brewer, E. C. Dictionary of phrase and fable. 1870, 1970 (rev).

Adams, W. D. Dictionary of English literature: a comprehensive guide to English authors and their works. 1878.

Halkett, S., J. Laing et al. A dictionary of the anonymous and pseudonymous literature of Great Britain. 4 vols 1882–8; rev J. Kennedy, W. A. Smith and A. F. Johnson 7 vols Edinburgh 1926–34; vols 8 (for 1900–50) and 9 (addns for vols 1–8) ed D. E. Rhodes and A. E. C. Simoni, Edinburgh 1956–62.

Stephen, L., S. Lee et al. The dictionary of national biography from the earliest times to 1900 [with 6 decennial suppls]. 69 vols 1885–1901, 22 vols 1908–9. See Corrections and additions, cumulated from the Bulletin of the Institute of Historical Research, University of London 1923–63, Boston 1966.

Ryland, F. Chronological outlines of English literature. 1890, 1914 (rev).

Sharp, R. F. A dictionary of English authors. 1897, 1904 (rev).

Moulton, C. W. The library of literary criticism of English and American authors. 8 vols Buffalo 1901–5; rev M. Tucker 4 vols New York 1966.

Cousin, J. W. A short biographical dictionary of English literature. 1910, 1938 (EL) (rev); rev D. C. Browning 1958 (EL).

Stonehill, C. A. and H. W. and A. Black. Anonyma and pseudonyma. 4 vols 1926–7.

Harvey, P. The Oxford companion to English literature. Oxford 1932, 1946 (rev), 1967 (rev D. Eagle).

A list of books quoted in the Oxford English dictionary. Appended to Supplement, Oxford 1933.

The author's and writer's who's who. 1934, 1935, 1948, 1960, 1963.

Riches, P. M. An analytical bibliography of universal collected biography: comprising books published in the English tongue in Great Britain and Ireland, America and the British dominions. 1934.

Ghosh, J. C. and E. G. Withycombe. Annals of English literature 1475–1925. Oxford 1935, 1961 (rev).

Oxford dictionary of quotations. Oxford 1941, 1953 (rev).

Union list of microfilms. 4 vols Philadelphia 1942, Ann Arbor 1951 (rev); suppl 1949–59, Philadelphia 1961.

Shipley, J. T. Dictionary of world literature. New York 1943, 1953 (rev).

— Encyclopaedia of literature. 2 vols New York 1946.

Smith, H. Columbia dictionary of modern literature. New York 1947.

Mayer, A. Annals of European civilization 1501–1900. 1949.

Arms, G. and J. M. Kuntz. Poetry explication: a checklist of interpretation since 1925 of British and American poems. New York 1950, Denver 1962 (rev).

Baldensperger, F., and W. P. Friederich. Bibliography of comparative literature. Chapel Hill 1950.

Matthews, W. British diaries: an annotated bibliography of British diaries written between 1442 and 1942. Berkeley 1950.

— British autobiographies: an annotated bibliography of British autobiographies published or written before 1951. Berkeley 1955.

Spemann, A. Vergleichende Zeittafel der Weltliteratur 1150–1939. Stuttgart 1951.

Steinberg, S. H. Cassell's encyclopaedia of literature. 2 vols 1953, 3 vols 1973 (enlarged).

Contemporary authors: a bio-bibliographical guide to current authors and their works. Detroit 1962– (semi-annual).

Fulghum, W. B. A dictionary of biblical allusions in English literature. 1966.

Bibliography and Bookmanship

Lowndes, W. T. The bibliographer's manual of English literature. 4 vols 1834; rev H. G. Bohn 11 pts 1857–64, 6 vols 1890.

Quaritch, B. General catalogue of books. 17 vols 1882–97.

— Contributions towards a dictionary of English book-collectors. 14 pts 1892–1921, New York 1968.

Bigmore, E. C. and C. W. H. Wyman. A bibliography of printing. 2 vols 1884.

Book-prices current. 1888– (annual, with indexes for 1887–1916 3 vols 1901–20).

American book-prices current. New York 1895– (annual, with indexes every 4 to 9 years).

Book auction records. 26 vols 1903–29.

Livingston, L. S. Auction prices of books. 4 vols New York 1905.

British Museum. List of catalogues of English book sales 1676–1900. 1915.

de Ricci, S The book collector's guide. Philadelphia 1921, New York 1967.

— English collectors of books and mss 1530–1930 and their marks of ownership. Cambridge 1930, New York 1969.

[Holden, J. A.] The bookman's glossary. New York 1925, 1931, 1950 (rev), 1961 (rev M. C. Turner).

McKerrow, R. B. Introduction to bibliography for literary students. Oxford 1927, 1928 (corrected).

Sawyer, C. J., and F. J. H. Darton. English books 1475–1900. 2 vols 1927.

Targ, W. Modern English first editions and their prices. Chicago 1932–.
—— and H. F. Marks. Ten thousand rare books and their prices. New York 1936.

Greenhood, D. and H. Gentry. Chronology of books and printing. New York 1933, 1936 (rev).

Hart, H. Biblioteca typographica. Rochester NY 1933.

Carter, J. New paths in book-collecting. 1934.
—— Taste and technique in book-collecting. 1934.
—— ABC for book-collectors. New York 1951, London 1953, 1961 (both rev), 1967 (corrected).
—— Books and book-collectors. 1956.

Vail, R. W. G. The literature of book-collecting: a selective bibliography. New York 1936.

Ker, N. R. Medieval libraries of Great Britain: a list of surviving books. 1941, 1964 (rev and enlarged).

McMurtrie, D. C. The invention of printing: a bibliography. Chicago 1942, New York 1962.

Ulrich, C. F. and K. Kup. Books and printing: a selected list of periodicals 1800–1942. New York 1943.

Hayward, J. English poetry: a catalogue of first and early editions from Chaucer to the present day, exhibited at the National Book League. 1947, 1950 (rev).

Bowers, F. T. Principles of bibliographical description. Princeton 1949.

Willoughby, E. E. The uses of bibliography to the students of literature and history. Hamden Conn 1957.

Glaister, G. A. An encyclopedia of the book. Cleveland 1960.

Simmons, J. (ed). Bibliography in Britain: a classified list of books and articles published in the United Kingdom. Oxford 1962– (annual).

McGrath, D. F. (ed). Bookman's price index. Detroit 1964– (annual).

Clair, C. A chronology of printing. 1969.

(6) GENERAL LIBRARY CATALOGUES

England

Heber, Richard. A catalogue of Heber's collection of early English poetry. Ed J. P. Collier [1834].
—— Bibliotheca Heberiana. 13 pts in 3 vols 1834–6.

Douce, F. A catalogue of the printed books and manuscripts bequeathed by Francis Douce to the Bodleian Library. Oxford 1840.

Bodleian Library, Oxford. Catalogus librorum impressorum. 4 vols Oxford 1843–51. Omits Douce collection, above.

Corser, T. Collectanea anglo-poetica: or a bibliographical and descriptive catalogue of a portion of a collection of early English poetry. 11 vols Manchester 1860–83 (Chetham Soc).

Dyce collection. A catalogue of the printed books and manuscripts bequeathed [to Victoria and Albert Museum]. 2 vols 1875.

[Ellis, F. S.] The Huth library: a catalogue. 5 vols 1880.

Duff, E. G. Catalogue of the printed books and manuscripts in the John Rylands Library. 3 vols Manchester 1899.

British Museum. Subject index of modern works added to the library (1881–). 1902–. Begun by G. K. Fortescue, and often known by his name.
—— Lists of catalogues of English book sales 1676–1900. 1915.
—— Catalogue of printed books. 1881–1900; suppl, including all books in the library at the end of 1905, 1931–; rptd 58 vols Ann Arbor 1946.
—— General catalogue of printed books to 1955. 263 vols 1959–66; suppl for 1956–65, 50 vols Ann Arbor 1968.

Wright, C. T. H. and C. J. Purnell. Subject-index of the London Library. 3 vols 1909–38.
—— Catalogue of the London Library. 2 vols 1913–14; suppl for 1913–20, 1920; for 1920–8, 1929; for 1928–50, 1953.

Crawford, Earls of. Bibliotheca Lindesiana: the catalogue of the printed books preserved at Haigh Hall, Wigan. 8 vols 1910–13.

A catalogue of the Bradshaw collection of Irish books in the University Library, Cambridge. 3 vols Cambridge 1916.

Wise, T. J. The Ashley library: a catalogue of printed books, manuscripts and autograph letters collected by T. J. Wise. 11 vols 1922–36.

The Britwell handlist: or short-title catalogue of the principal volumes from the time of Caxton to the year 1800 formerly in the library of Britwell Court. 2 vols 1933.

Roupell, M. G. Union catalogue of the periodical publications in the university libraries of the British isles. 1937.

[Canney, M. and J. Hayward]. The Sterling library: a catalogue of the books and manuscripts collected by Sir Louis Sterling. 1954.

British union-catalogue of periodicals in British libraries. 4 vols 1955; suppl to 1960, 1962; monthly issues cumulated annually.

Johnson, D. M. Dr Williams's library catalogue of accessions 1900–50. 1955.

Deed, S. G. and J. Francis. Catalogue of the Plume library. Maldon 1959.

Scotland

National Library of Scotland (formerly Advocates' library). Catalogue of the printed books. 7 vols Edinburgh 1867–79.

Aberdeen University. Catalogue of the library. 3 vols Aberdeen 1873–4 (with suppls for King's College 1887, Marischal College 1897).

Edinburgh University. Catalogue of the printed books in the library. 3 vols Edinburgh 1918–23.

Glasgow University. Catalogus impressorum librorum in bibliotheca universitatis Glasguensis [with 2 suppls]. Glasgow 1791–1836.

St Andrews University. Catalogus librorum. 1826.
—— Catalogue of books added (1867–8 to 1900). St Andrews 1869–1902.

Signet library. Catalogue of the printed books. 2 pts and 2 suppls Edinburgh 1871–91 (annual suppls).

Ferguson, M. The printed books in the library of the Hunterian Museum. Glasgow 1930.

Wales

National Library of Wales. Bibliotheca celtica: a register of publications relating to Wales and the Celtic people and languages (1909–). Aberystwyth 1910–.

Jones, E. G. and J. R. V. Johnston. Catalogue of the Bangor Cathedral library now deposited in the University College of North Wales. Bangor 1962.

Ireland

Dublin, Trinity College. Catalogus librorum impressorum. 9 vols Dublin 1864–87.

Cambridge University. Catalogue of the Bradshaw collection of Irish books. Ed C. E. Sayle 3 vols Cambridge 1916.

United States

[Hoe, R.] A catalogue of books by English authors who lived before the year 1700. 5 vols New York 1903–5.

—— A catalogue of books in English later than 1700. New York 1905. Addns in sale catalogue of 1912.

Rosenbach, A. S. W. A catalogue of the books and manuscripts of H. E. Widener. 2 vols Philadelphia 1918.

Cole, G. W. Huntington Library check lists. New York 1919–20.

Wise, T. J. A catalogue of the library of the late John Henry Wrenn. 5 vols Austin 1920.

Cowan, R. E. The library of William Andrews Clark. 2 vols San Francisco 1922–30.

Gregory, W. Union list of serials in libraries of the US and Canada. New York 1927, 1943, 1965 (rev); suppl 2 vols 1945, 1965.

Haskell, D. C. A check list of cumulative indexes to individual periodicals in the New York Public Library. New York 1942.

A catalog of books represented by Library of Congress printed cards issued to July 31 1942. 167 vols Ann Arbor 1942–6; suppl 42 vols 1948.

Metzdorf, R. F. The Tinker Library. New Haven 1959.

(7) CATALOGUES OF MANUSCRIPTS
General

Bernard, E. Catalogi librorum Angliae et Hiberniae, cum indice [by H. Wanley]. Oxford 1697.

Wanley, H. Antiquae literaturae septentrionalis liber alter: seu librorum vett. septentrionalium in Angliae bibliothecis, nec non multorum alibi catalogus. Oxford 1705. Vol 3 of the Thesaurus of G. Hickes.

Brown, C. A register of Middle English religious and didactic verse. 2 vols 1916–20; completed as The index of Middle English verse, New York 1943; suppl Lexington Kentucky 1965.

Library of Congress. Check list of collections of personal papers in the United States. Washington 1918.

Madan, F. Books in manuscript. 1920, 1927 (rev).

Library of Congress. Manuscripts in public and private collections in the United States. Washington 1924.

Singer, D. W. Catalogue of Latin and vernacular manuscripts in Great Britain and Ireland dating from before the xvi century. 1928–.

de Ricci, S. and W. J. Wilson. Census of medieval and Renaissance manuscripts in the US and Canada. 3 vols New York 1935–40; suppl by C. U. Faye and W. H. Bond, New York 1962.

Guide to depositories of manuscript collections in the United States. Columbus 1938.

Ker, N. R. Catalogue of manuscripts containing Anglo-Saxon. Oxford 1957.

—— Medieval manuscripts in British libraries. Oxford 1969–.

The national union catalog of manuscript collections 1959–. Ann Arbor, Hamden Conn and Washington 1962–.

London
British Museum

Ayscough, S. A catalogue of the manuscripts preserved in the British Museum. 2 vols 1782.

Gilson, J. P. A student's guide to the manuscripts of the British Museum. 1920.

Skeat, T. C. The British Museum: the catalogues of the manuscript collections. 1951, 1962 (rev).

Collections

Arundel and Burney. 2 vols 1834–40.

Ashley, by E. G. Millar. 1937; by T. A. S. Burnett, 1973.

Cotton. 1696, 1802.

Egerton 1829– (after no 606 see Additional).

Hargrave. 1818.

Harleian. 4 vols 1808–12.

Lansdowne. 1819.

Old Royal and King's. 4 vols 1921.

Sloane and Additional. 1830– (acquisitions since 1783).

Stowe. 2 vols 1895–6.

Catalogue of romances by H. L. D. Ward and J. A. Herbert. 3 vols 1883–1910.

Catalogue of Irish manuscripts by S. H. O'Grady and R. Flower. 3 vols 1926–53.

Catalogue of manuscripts relating to Wales by E. Owen. 4 vols 1900–22.

Library of Sir Simonds D'Ewes by A. G. Watson. 1966.

Lambeth Palace

Catalogue of the archiepiscopal manuscripts. Ed H. J. Todd 1812.

Descriptive catalogue of the manuscripts. Ed M. R. James and C. Jenkins 5 pts Cambridge 1930–3.

Other Collections

College of Arms. Catalogue of the Arundel manuscripts. Ed W. H. Black 1829.

Gray's Inn. Catalogue of ancient manuscripts. 1869.

Lincoln's Inn. Catalogue of manuscripts. Ed J. Hunter 1838.

Oxford
Bodley

Catalogus codicum manuscriptorum Bibliothecae Bodleianae. 1845–. Pts containing English mss are: ii, Catalogus codicum laudianorum, ed H. O. Coxe 1858–85; iv, Codices T. Tanneri, ed A. Hackman 1859; v (fasciculi 1–5), Codices R. Rawlinson (A–D), ed W. D. Macray 1862–1900; ix, Codices a K. Digby anno 1654 donati, ed W. D. Macray 1883; x, A descriptive analytical and critical catalogue of the mss bequeathed unto the University of Oxford by E. Ashmole, ed W. H. Black 1845 (index by W. D. Macray, 1886).

A summary catalogue of western manuscripts which have not hitherto been catalogued in the quarto series. Ed F. Madan et al 7 vols Oxford 1895–1953.

Crum, M. First-line index of English poetry 1500–1800 in manuscripts. Oxford 1969.

Colleges

Catalogus codicum manuscriptorum qui in collegiis aulisque Oxonii adservantur. Ed H. O. Coxe 2 vols Oxford 1852.

Catalogus codicum manuscriptorum qui in bibliotheca Aedis Christi apud oxonienses adservantur. Ed G. W. Kitchin, Oxford 1867.

Riley, H. T. Report on manuscripts belonging to Balliol, Corpus Christi, Exeter, Lincoln, St Mary Magdalen, New, Oriel, Pembroke, Queen's, St John's, Trinity, University, Wadham and Worcester colleges. 1871–4 (Historical Mss Commission).

Denholm-Young, N. Cartulary of the mediaeval archives of Christ Church. Oxford 1931.

Powicke, F. M. The medieval books of Merton College. Oxford 1931.

Mynors, R. A. B. Catalogue of the manuscripts of Balliol College. Oxford 1963.

Cambridge

Catalogue of mss in the library of the University of Cambridge. 6 vols Cambridge 1856–67. *See also* A. E. B. Owen, Summary guide to accessions of western manuscripts—other than medieval—since 1867 in the University Library, Cambridge, Cambridge 1966.

Riley, H. T. Report on manuscripts belonging to Christ's, Clare, Corpus Christi, Downing (the Bowtell collection), Emmanuel, Gonville and Caius, Jesus, King's, Magdalene, Pembroke, St Peter's, Queens', St Catharine's, St John's, Sidney Sussex, Trinity and Trinity Hall. 1870–6 (Historical Mss Commission).

Catalogues of western mss in the university and college libraries of Cambridge. Ed M. R. James, Cambridge 1895–1925:

Christ's College. 1905.
Clare College. 1905.
Corpus Christi College. 2 vols 1909–12.
Emmanuel College. 1904.
Fitzwilliam Museum. 1895.
— (McClean collection). 1912.
Gonville and Caius College. 3 vols 1907–14.
Jesus College. 1895.
King's College. 1895.
Magdalene College. 1909.
— Bibliotheca Pepysiana (medieval mss catalogue pt iii). 1923.
Pembroke College. 1905.
Peterhouse. 1899.
Queens' College. 1905.
St Catharine's College. 1925.
St John's College. 1913.
Sidney Sussex College. 1895.
Trinity College. 4 vols 1900–5.
Trinity Hall. 1907.

Scotland

Aberdeen University

A catalogue of the medieval manuscripts in the University Library, Aberdeen. Ed M. R. James, Cambridge 1932.

Edinburgh

Report on the manuscripts in the library of the University of Edinburgh. 1870 (Historical Mss Commission).
A descriptive catalogue of western medieval manuscripts in Edinburgh University library. Ed C. Borland, Edinburgh 1916.
National Library of Scotland: catalogue of manuscripts acquired since 1925. 3 vols Edinburgh 1938–68.

Glasgow

Catalogue of mss in the library of the Hunterian Museum. Glasgow 1908.

Wales

National Library of Wales. Catalogue of manuscripts. Aberystwyth 1921–.
Handlist of manuscripts in the National Library of Wales. 5 pts Aberystwyth 1940–2.

Ireland

Dublin. Catalogue of the manuscripts in the library of Trinity College. Ed T. K. Abbott 1900.

United States

Morgan, J. P. Catalogue of manuscripts from the library of William Morris [et al]. Ed M. R. James, New York 1906–7.
Hoe, R. Catalogue of manuscripts. New York 1909.
Ballard, J. F. A catalogue of the medieval and Renaissance manuscripts and incunabula in the Boston medical library. Boston 1944.
Guide to the manuscript collections in the Duke University library. Durham NC 1947.
Manuscript collections in the Columbia University libraries. New York 1959.
Catalogue of manuscripts in the libraries of the University of Pennsylvania. Philadelphia 1965.
New York Public Library. Dictionary catalog of the manuscript division. 2 vols Boston 1967.

Other Collections

Canterbury Cathedral. Catalogue of the books, both manuscript and printed. 1802.
Durham Cathedral. Codicum manuscriptorum catalogus. Ed T. Rud 1825.
Phillipps, T. Catalogus librorum manuscriptorum in bibliotheca D. Thomae Phillipps. 3 pts 1837–67.
Lincoln Cathedral. Catalogue of the books and manuscripts. Ed S. F. Apthorp 1859.
Catalogue of the manuscripts of Lincoln Cathedral chapter library. Ed R. M. Woolley 1927.
Eton College. Catalogue of manuscripts. Ed M. R. James, Cambridge 1895.
The ancient libraries of Canterbury and Dover. The catalogue of the libraries of Christ Church Priory and St Augustine's Abbey at Canterbury and of St Augustine's Priory at Dover. Ed M. R. James, Cambridge 1903.
Worcester Cathedral. Catalogue of manuscripts. Ed J. K. Floyer and S. G. Hamilton 1906.
Hereford Cathedral. Catalogue of manuscripts. Ed A. T. Bannister, Cambridge 1927.
Hand-list of the collection of English manuscripts. Ed M. Tyson, Manchester 1929.
Young, P. Catalogus librorum manuscriptorum bibliothecae Wigorniensis 1622–3. Ed I. Atkins and N. R. Ker, Cambridge 1944.

(8) PERIODS
See also under the appropriate periods, below.

Old English

See (7) Catalogues of Manuscripts, above.

Petheram, J. An historical sketch of the progress and present state of Anglo-Saxon literature in England. 1840.
Adams, E. N. Old English scholarship in England from 1566–1800. New Haven 1917.
Robinson, F. C. Old English literature: a select bibliography. Toronto 1970.

Middle English

Bale, J. Illustrium majoris Britanniae scriptorum summarium. Ipswich 1548, Basle 1556–9.
Leland, J. Commentarii de scriptoribus britannicis. Ed A. Hall, Oxford 1709.
Kingsford, C. L. English historical literature in the fifteenth century. Oxford 1913.
Gross, C. The sources and literature of English history to 1485. 1915.

Wells, J. E. A manual of the writings in Middle English 1050–1400. New Haven 1916; 9 suppls 1919–52 (complete to 1945); rev J. B. Severs et al, New Haven 1967–.
Loomis, R. S. Introduction to medieval literature chiefly in England: a reading list and bibliography. New York 1939, 1948 (rev).

Modern English

1475–1500

Blades, W. The life and typography of W. Caxton. 2 vols 1861–3, 1 vol 1877 (rev as Biography and typography of W. Caxton), 1882 (rev).
Proctor, R. G. C. An index to the early printed books in the British Museum to the year 1500. 1898–1903; rev as Catalogue of books printed in the xvth century, 10 vols 1908–62.
Abbott, T. K. Catalogue of fifteenth-century books in the library of Trinity College. Dublin 1905.

Duff, E. G. William Caxton. Chicago 1905.
— Fifteenth-century English books. 1917.
de Ricci, S. A census of Caxtons. 1909.
Gesamtkatalog der Wiegendrucke. 8 vols Leipzig 1925–40. Includes English incunabula.
Scholderer, V. Hand-list of incunabula in the National Library of Wales. Aberystwyth 1940.
Stillwell, M. B. Incunabula in American libraries: a second census of fifteenth-century books owned in the US, Mexico and Canada. New York 1940 (Bibl Soc of America; rev F. R. Goff, New York 1964.
Oates, J. C. T. A catalogue of the fifteenth-century printed books in the University Library, Cambridge. Cambridge 1954.
Heilbroner, W. L. Printing and the book in fifteenth-century England. Charlottesville 1967.

1475–1640

Stationers, Company of. A transcript of the registers of the Company 1554–1640. Ed E. Arber 5 vols 1875–94.
Maunsell, A. The first [and the seconde] part of the catalogue of English printed books. 1595. Pt 1 divinity; pt 2 sciences.
Ames, J. Typographical antiquities from 1471 to 1600, augmented by W. Herbert. 3 vols 1785–90. Ames's original edn appeared in 1749; an enlarged edn was begun by T. F. Dibdin, vols 1–4 1810–19.
Brydges, S. E. Censura literaria. 10 vols 1805–9, 1815.
— The British bibliographer. 4 vols 1810–14. With J. Haslewood.
— Restituta. 4 vols 1814–16.
Collier, J. P. A bibliographical and critical account of the rarest books in the English language. 2 vols 1865. Incorporates catalogue of the Bridgewater library.
McKerrow, R. B. et al. A dictionary of printers and booksellers in England, Scotland and Ireland and of foreign printers of English books 1557–1640. 1910 (Bibl Soc).
— Printers' and publishers' devices in England and Scotland 1485–1640. 1913 (Bibl Soc).
Duff, E. G. et al. Hand-lists of books printed by London printers 1501–56. 1913.
Pollard, A. W. and G. R. Redgrave. A short-title catalogue of books printed in England, Scotland and Ireland, and of English books printed abroad 1475–1640. 1926 (Bibl Soc).
Bishop, W. W. A checklist of American copies of STC books. Ann Arbor 1944, 1950 (rev).
Morrison, P. G. Index of printers, publishers and booksellers in STC. Charlottesville 1950.
Ramage, D. et al. A finding-list of English books to 1640 in libraries in the British Isles. Durham NC 1958.
Besterman, T. Early printed books to the end of the sixteenth century: a bibliography of bibliographies. Geneva 1940, 1961 (rev and enlarged).
Greg, W. W. A companion to Arber. Oxford 1967.

British Museum. Catalogue of books in the library of the British Museum printed in England, Scotland and Ireland and of books in English printed abroad to 1640. Ed G. Bullen 3 vols 1884.
Lambeth Palace. An index of English books printed before 1600. Ed S. R. Maitland 1845.
Society of Antiquaries. Catalogue of a collection of printed broadsides. Ed R. Lemon 1866.
Cambridge University Library. Early English printed books in the library 1475–1640. Ed C. E. Sayle 4 vols Cambridge 1900–7.
Pepys Library, Magdalene College, Cambridge. Catalogue: pt II (English books printed to 1558). Ed E. G. Duff 1914.
Cambridge, Emmanuel College. A hand-list of English books printed before 1641. Cambridge 1915.
Cambridge, Trinity College. Catalogue of English books before 1601. Ed R. Sinker, Cambridge 1885.

Oxford, Magdalen College. List of books printed before 1641, of which the Bodleian Library has no copy. Ed G. R. Driver, Oxford 1929. Announced as first instalment of catalogue of early ptd books in Oxford libraries.
Oxford, Wadham College. A short catalogue of books printed in England and English books printed abroad before 1641. Ed H. A. Wheeler 1929.
John Rylands Library, Manchester. Catalogue of books in the John Rylands library printed in England, Scotland and Ireland, and of books in English printed abroad to 1640. Ed E. G. Duff, Manchester 1895.
New York Public Library. Check-list of early English printing 1475–1640 in the library. Ed D. C. Haskell, New York 1925.
Newberry Library, Chicago. English books and books printed in England before 1641. Ed G. L. Woodward, Chicago 1939.

1475–1700

Hazlitt, W. C. Handbook to the popular, poetical and dramatic literature of Great Britain, from the invention of printing to the Restoration. 1867; continued as Bibliographical collections and notes 1474–1700, 6 vols 1876–1903.
Dickson, R. and J. P. Edmond. Annals of Scottish printing from 1507 to the beginning of the seventeenth century. Cambridge 1890.
Dix, E. R. McC. Catalogue of early Dublin-printed books 1601–1700. 3 vols Dublin 1898–1912.
The term catalogues 1668–1709, with a number for Easter term 1711. Ed E. Arber 3 vols 1903–6.
Growoll, A. Three centuries of English book-trade bibliography. New York 1903.
Aldis, H. G. A list of books printed in Scotland before 1700, including those printed furth of the realm for Scottish booksellers. Edinburgh 1904, 1970 (with addns).
Plomer, H. R. A dictionary of the booksellers and printers who were at work in England, Scotland and Ireland from 1641 to 1667. 1907; from 1668 to 1725, 1922; from 1726 to 1775, 1932.
British Museum. Catalogue of the pamphlets, books, newspapers and manuscripts relating to the Civil War, the Commonwealth and Restoration, collected by G. Thomason 1640–61. Ed G. K. Fortescue 2 vols 1908.
Stationers, Company of. A transcript of the registers of the worshipful Company from 1640 to 1708. Ed G. E. Briscoe Eyre, transcribed by H. R. Plomer 3 vols 1913–14 (Roxburghe Club).
Quaritch, B. Catalogue of books in English history and literature 1483–1700. 1922.
Davies, G. Bibliography of British history: Stuart period 1603–1714. Oxford 1928 (Royal Historical Soc), 1970 (rev M. F. Keeler).
Abbott, W. C. A bibliography of Oliver Cromwell. Cambridge Mass 1929.
Johnstone, J. F. K. and A. W. Robertson. Bibliographia Aberdonensis. 2 vols Aberdeen 1929–30.
Read, C. Bibliography of British history: Tudor period 1485–1603. Oxford 1933 (Royal Historical Soc), 1959 (rev).
Wing, D. G. Short-title catalogue of books printed in England, Scotland, Ireland, Wales and British America, and of English books printed in other countries 1641–1700. 3 vols New York 1945–51.
Morrison, P. G. Index of printers, publishers and booksellers in Wing. Charlottesville 1955.
Hiscock, W. G. The Christ Church supplement to Wing's Short-title catalogue 1641–1700. Oxford 1956.
Woodward, G. L. and J. G. McManaway. A check list of English plays 1641–1700. Chicago 1945; suppl by F. T. Bowers, Charlottesville 1949.
Folger Shakespeare library. 28 vols Boston 1970.

18th Century and After

This period is partly covered by R. Watt, Bibliotheca britannica, 1824, but is little served by comprehensive bibliographers.

Martin, J. Bibliographical catalogue of privately printed books. 1834, 1854, New York 1968.

Rowlands, W. Cambrian bibliography from 1546 to the end of the eighteenth century. Ed D. S. Evans, Llanidloes 1869.

Adams, E. N. Old English scholarship in England from 1566–1800. New Haven 1917.

Jones, J. I. History of printing and printers in Wales to 1810 (1823). Cardiff 1925.

Williams, J. B. Guide to the printed materials for English social and economic history 1750–1850. 2 vols New York 1926.

Jessop, T. E. A bibliography of David Hume and of Scottish philosophy from Francis Hutcheson to Lord Balfour. 1938.

Block, A. The English novel 1740–1850: a catalogue including prose romances, short stories and translations of foreign fiction. 1939, 1961 (rev).

Tobin, J. E. Eighteenth-century English literature and its cultural background. New York 1939.

Carty, J. Bibliography of Irish history 1870–1911. Dublin 1940.

Summers, M. A Gothic bibliography. [1941].

Pargellis, S. M. and D. J. Medley. Bibliography of British history: the eighteenth century 1714–89. Oxford 1951.

[Shawyer, N. M. et al]. The Rothschild library: a catalogue of eighteenth-century printed books and manuscripts. 2 vols Cambridge 1955.

McBurney, W. H. A check list of English prose fiction 1700–39. Cambridge Mass 1960.

Eager, A. R. A guide to Irish bibliographical material. 1964.

(9) ENGLISH UNIVERSITIES AND PROVINCES
For Scotland, Wales and Ireland see (6), above.

Gross, C. A bibliography of British municipal history. New York 1897, 1964, Leicester 1966 (with preface by G. H. Martin).

Humphreys, A. L. A handbook to county bibliography. 1917.

Mullins, L. C. Texts and calendars: an analytical guide to serial publication. 1958.

—— A guide to the historical and archaeological publications of societies in England and Wales 1901–33. 1968.

Bedfordshire

Conisbee, L. R. A Bedfordshire bibliography. 2 vols Luton 1962–7.

Berkshire

Reading Public Libraries. Local collection catalogue of books and maps. Reading 1958.

Buckinghamshire

Gough, H. Bibliotheca buckinghamiensis. Aylesbury 1890.

Cambridgeshire

Bowes, R. Catalogue of books printed at or relating to the university, town and county of Cambridge 1521–1893. 2 pts Cambridge 1894 (with index by E. Worman).

Cooper, C. H. and T. Athenae cantabrigienses 1500–1611. 3 vols 1858–1911.

Roberts, S. C. A history of the Cambridge University Press 1521–1921. Cambridge 1921. Bibliography for 1521–1750.

Bartholomew, A. T. Catalogue of the books and papers relating to the university, town and county of Cambridge, bequeathed to the university by John Willis Clark. Cambridge 1912.

Venn, J. and J. A. Alumni cantabrigienses to 1900. Pt 1 to 1751, 4 vols 1922–7; pt 2 1752–1900, 6 vols 1940–54.

Walker, T. A. A Peterhouse bibliography. Cambridge 1924.

Madan, F. and W. M. Palmer. Notes on Bodleian manuscripts relating to Cambridge: pt 1, town and university; pt 2, county. Cambridge 1931.

Birley, R. Some unrecorded Cambridge books in the library of Eton college. Trans Cambridge Bibl Soc 1 1953.

Oates, J. C. T. Cambridge books of congratulatory verses 1603–40. Ibid.

Emden, A. E. A biographical register of the University of Cambridge to 1500. 3 vols 1957–9, 1963.

McKenzie, D. F. The Cambridge University Press 1696–1712. 2 vols Cambridge 1966.

Cheshire

Cooke, J. H. Bibliotheca Cestriensis. Warrington 1904.

See also under Lancashire, below.

Cornwall

Boase, G. C. and W. P. Courtney. Bibliotheca Cornubiensis. 3 vols 1874–82.

See also Devonshire, below.

Cumberland

Sparke, A. A bibliography of the dialect literature of Cumberland and Westmoreland, and Lancashire north-of-the-sands. Kendal 1907.

Derbyshire

Taylor, N. Derbyshire printing and printers before 1800. Derbyshire Archaeological Jnl 1950.

Devonshire

Davidson, J. Bibliotheca Devoniensis. Exeter 1852; suppl 1862.

Dredge, J. I. Devon booksellers and printers in the 17th and 18th centuries. 3 pts Plymouth 1885, 1887.

—— A few sheaves of Devon bibliography. Plymouth 1889–96 (in sheets, from Trans Devonshire Assoc), 1899 (with notes and addns by F. B. Troup).

Brushfield, T. N. The literature of Devonshire up to the year 1640. 1893.

Attwood, J. Booksellers and printers in Devon and Cornwall in the 17th and 18th centuries. Exeter 1917. Addns to Dredge, above.

Dorsetshire

Mayo, C. H. Bibliotheca Dorsetiensis. 1885.

Durham

Botfield, B. Catalogi veteres librorum Ecclesiae Cathedralis Dunelm, including catalogues of the library of the Abbey of Hulm, and of the mss preserved in the library of Bishop Cosin. Durham 1838 (Surtees Soc).

Thompson, A. H. Publications of the Surtees Society. In The Surtees Society 1834–1934, Durham 1939.

East Anglia

East Anglian Master Printers' Alliance. Early print in East Anglia: an exhibition. Eastbourne 1951.

Library Association, Eastern Branch. East Anglian bibliography: a checklist of publications now in British National Bibliography. Norwich 1960.

Essex

Moon, Z. Essex literature: catalogue of books published in or relating to the county. Leyton 1900 (Leyton Public Libraries).

Havering Public Libraries. South Essex authors: a checklist issued for national library week 1966. Romford 1966.

Gloucestershire

Austin, R. Catalogue of the Gloucestershire collection. Gloucester 1928 (Gloucester Public Lib).

Hyett, F. A. and W. Bazeley. The bibliographer's manual of Gloucestershire literature. 5 vols Gloucester 1895–1915.

—— Notes on the first Bristol and Gloucestershire printers. Bristol & Gloucestershire Archaeological Soc Trans 1895–6.

Matthews, E. R. N. Bristol bibliography. Bristol 1916.

Hampshire

Edwards, F. A. Early Hampshire printers. Hampshire Field Club Papers & Proc 1891.

Gilbert, H. M. and G. N. Godwin. Bibliotheca Hamtoniensis. Southampton 1891.

Huntingdonshire

Norris, H. E. Catalogue of the Huntingdonshire books collected by H. E. Norris. Cirencester 1895.

Kent

Smith, J. R. Bibliotheca cantiana. 1837.

Gritten, A. G. Catalogue of books, pamphlets and excerpts dealing with Margate, the Isle of Thanet and the county of Kent in the local collection. Margate 1934 (Margate Public Lib).

Burch, B. Periodicals published in Bromley. In A bibliography of printed material relating to Bromley, Hayes and Keston, in the county of Kent, Bromley 1964.

Lancashire

Fishwick, H. The Lancashire library. 1875.

Sutton, A. Bibliotheca lancastriensis: a catalogue of books on the typography and genealogy of Lancashire, with an appendix of Cheshire books. Manchester 1893, 1898.

Green, J. A. Bibliography of the town of Heywood. Heywood 1902.

Jaggard, W. Liverpool literature: a descriptive bibliography. Liverpool 1905.

Liverpool Public Library. Liverpool prints and documents. Liverpool 1908.

Sparke, A. Bibliographia boltoniensis: being a bibliography with biographical details of Bolton authors and the books written by them from 1550 to 1912; books about Bolton and those printed and published in the town from 1785. Manchester 1913.

Hawkes, A. J. Lancashire printed books: a bibliography of all the books printed in Lancashire down to the year 1800. Wigan 1925 (Wigan Public Lib).

Manchester Public Libraries. The Manchester press before 1801; a list of books, pamphlets and broadsides printed in Manchester in the 18th century. Manchester 1931.

—— Wythenshawe: a bibliography. Manchester 1955.

See also Cumberland, above.

Leicestershire

Kirkby, C. V. Catalogue of the books, pamphlets relating to Leicestershire. Leicester 1893 (Leicester Public Libraries).

Bloom, J. H. English tracts, pamphlets and printed sheets vol 2: Leicestershire, Staffordshire, Warwickshire, Worcestershire (–1680). 1923.

Lincolnshire

Corns, A. R. Bibliotheca Lincolniensis. Lincoln 1904 (Lincoln Public Lib).

Man, Isle of

Cubbon, W. A bibliographical account of works relating to the Isle of Man. 2 vols 1933–9.

Norfolk

Quinton, J. Bibliotheca norfolciensis. Norwich 1896. Catalogue of collection of J. J. Colman.

Northamptonshire

Taylor, J. Bibliotheca northamtoniensis. Northampton [1869?].

Northumberland

Heslop, R. O. A bibliographical list of works illustrative of the dialect of Northumberland. 1896.

Society of Antiquaries, Newcastle-upon-Tyne. A catalogue of the library belonging to the Society. Newcastle 1896.

Welford, R. Early Newcastle typography 1639–1800. Newcastle 1906.

Burman, C. C. An account of the art of typography as practised in Alnwick from 1748 to 1900. Edinburgh [1918].

Newcastle-upon-Tyne Public Library. Local catalogue of material concerning Newcastle and Northumberland. Newcastle 1932.

Nottinghamshire

Creswell, S. F. Collections towards the history of printing in Nottinghamshire. 1863.

Briscoe, J. P. List of books in the reference library, no 14, Nottinghamshire collection. Nottingham 1890 (Nottinghamshire Public Libraries).

Clarke, W. J. Early Nottingham printers and printing. Nottingham 1942, 1953.

Oxfordshire

Madan, F. Oxford books. 3 vols Oxford 1895–1931.

—— A chart of Oxford printing '1468'–1680. Oxford 1904, 1908 (in A brief account of the University Press), 1909.

—— The Oxford press 1650–75: the struggle for a place in the sun. Oxford 1925.

—— A chronological list of Oxford books 1681–1713. Oxford 1954. Transcribed from notebooks by J. S. G. Simmons.

Cordeaux, H. and D. H. Merry. A bibliography of printed works relating to Oxfordshire, excluding the university and city. Oxford 1955; Addenda and corrigenda, Bodleian Lib Record 1958, 1960.

—— A bibliography of printed works relating to the University of Oxford. Oxford 1968.

Briggs, G. M. The William W. Clary Oxford collection: a descriptive catalogue. Claremont Cal 1956 (Honnold Lib).

Somerset

Green, E. Bibliotheca Somersetiensis. 3 vols Taunton 1902.

Shum, F. A catalogue of Bath books from the 16th century to the 20th century. Bath 1913.

Staffordshire

Lawley, G. T. The bibliography of Wolverhampton: a record of local books, authors and booksellers. Bilston 1890.

Simms, R. Bibliotheca Staffordiensis. Lichfield 1894.

Emery, N. and D. R. Beard. Staffordshire directories: a union list of directories relating to Stafford. Stoke-on-Trent 1966 (Stoke Public Libraries).

See also Leicestershire, above.

Suffolk

Bloom, J. H. English tracts, pamphlets and printed sheets vol 1: Suffolk (–1680). 1923.

Sussex

Piper, A. C. Note on the introduction of printing into Sussex up to the year 1850, with a chronology of Sussex printers to that date. Sussex 1914.

Warwickshire

Powell, W. and H. M. Cashmore. A catalogue of the Birmingham collection, including printed books and pamphlets. Birmingham 1918 (Birmingham Public Libraries); suppl 1931.
See also Leicestershire, above

Westmorland

See Cumberland, above.

Worcestershire

Burton, J. R. and F. S. Pearson. A bibliography of Worcestershire. 2 vols Oxford 1898–1903.
See also Leicestershire, above.

Yorkshire

Davies, R. A memoir of the York press. 1868.
Boyne, W. Yorkshire library. 1869.
Dickons, J. N. A catalogue of books, pamphlets etc published at Bradford. Bradford 1895.
Duff, E. G. The printers, stationers and bookbinders of York up to 1600. Trans Bibl Soc 1899.
Freemantle, W. T. A bibliography of Sheffield and vicinity, section 1: to the end of 1700. Sheffield 1911.
Taylor, F. J. Bibliographical list of books, pamphlets and articles connected with Barnsley and the immediate district. Barnsley 1916.
Keighley, M. Whitby writers 1867–1949. Whitby 1957.

(10) RELIGIOUS BODIES

Verneuil, J. A nomenclator of such tracts and sermons as have been printed, or translated into English, upon any place or booke of Holy Scripture. Oxford 1642, 1668 (rev and enlarged).
[Crowe, W.] An exact catalogue of our English writers on the Old and New Testament. 1663, 1668 (incorporated in Verneuil, above).
Wright, C. H. H. and C. Neil. A Protestant dictionary containing articles on the history, doctrines and practices of the Christian Church. 1904; rev and ed C. S. Carter and G. E. A. Weeks 1933.
Burrage, C. The early English dissenters in the light of recent research 1550–1641. 2 vols Cambridge 1912.
Barrow, J. G. A bibliography of bibliographies in religion. Ann Arbor 1955.
American Theological Library Association. Index to religious periodical literature. 1953 (for 1940–52)– (annually).
Metz, R. and J. Schlick. Répertoire bibliographique des institutions chrétiennes. Strasbourg 1969 (for 1968)– (annually).

Anglicans

LeNeve, J. Fasti ecclesiae anglicanae: or a calendar of the principal ecclesiastical dignitaries in England and Wales to 1715. 1716; rev and enlarged T. D. Hardy 3 vols Oxford 1854; for 1066–1300 rev and enlarged D. E. Greenway 2 vols 1968–71; for 1300–1541 rev and enlarged H. P. F. King, J. M. Horn and B. Jones 12 vols 1962–7.
Glover, F. R. A. The fruits of endowments. 1840. List of works by authors who have had non-cure endowments.
Gough, H. A general index to the publications of the Parker Society. Cambridge 1855.
Three centuries of Anglican theology [1500–1800]. Oxford 1858.
Burn, J. S. Registrum ecclesiae parochialis. 1829, 1862.
National Book Council. The Church of England: a selected list of books. 1943.
Owen, D. M. The records of the Established Church in England, excluding parochial records. 1970.
—— Handlists of ecclesiastical records. Archives 10 1971.

Baptists

Haynes, T. W. Baptist cyclopaedia. 1848.
Gould, G. P. Catalogue of the Angus library at Regent's Park College. 1908.
McIntyre, W. E. Baptist authors: a manual of bibliography 1500–1914. Montreal 1914.
Whitley, W. T. A Baptist bibliography. 2 vols 1916–22.

Starr, E. C. A Baptist bibliography: being a register of printed material by and about Baptists. Philadelphia 1947, Rochester NY 1971–.

Catholics

Hunter, J. English monastic libraries: I, A catalogue of the library of the priory of Bretton, in Yorkshire; II, Notices of the libraries belonging to other religious houses. 2 vols 1831.
Oliver, G. Collections towards illustrating the biography of the Scotch, English and Irish members of the Society of Jesus. 1845.
Backer, A. and A. de. Bibliothèque des écrivains de la Compagnie de Jésus. 7 vols Liège 1853–61, 3 vols Paris 1869–76, 10 vols Brussels 1890–1909 (rev C. Sommervogel).
Catalogue Provinciae Angliae Societatis Jesu, ineunte anno mdccclxv. Roehampton 1865.
Sommervogel, C. Dictionnaire des ouvrages anonymes et pseudonymes publiés par des religieux de la Compagnie de Jésus. Paris 1884.
Gillow, J. A bibliographical dictionary of the English Catholics. 5 vols 1885–1902.
Romig, W. The guide to Catholic literature 1888–1940. Detroit 1940– (annual, cumulating every 4 years).
Allison, A. F. and D. M. Rogers. A catalogue of Catholic books in English printed abroad or secretly in England 1558–1640. 2 vols Bognor Regis 1956.

Church of Christ

de Grott, A. T. Literature of the Churches of Christ in Great Britain and Ireland: a design for a catalogue. Fort Worth 1950.

Congregationalists

Dexter, H. M. The Congregationalism of the last three hundred years. New York 1880.
A catalogue of the Congregational library, Memorial Hall, Farringdon St, London. 2 vols 1895.
National Book Council. Congregationalism: a selected list of books. 1936.

Society of Friends

Whiting, J. A catalogue of Friends' books. 1708.
Phillips, J. A catalogue of Friends' books wanted to complete the collection. 1779.
Smith, J. A descriptive catalogue of Friends' books. 2 vols 1867; suppl 1893.
—— Bibliotheca antiquakeriana: or a catalogue of books adverse to the Society of Friends. 1873.
Catalogue of the books and pictures in the Friends' Institute. 1907.
National Book Council. Bibliography: Quakerism. 1929.

Huguenots

Stride, E. E. A bibliography of works relating to Huguenot refugees, reprinted from Proceedings of the Huguenot Society of London. Lymington 1886.

A rough hand-list of the library of the Huguenot Society of London. 1892.

Morand, J. P. M. Catalogue or bibliography of the library of the Huguenot Society of America. New York 1920.

Methodists

[Cavender, C. H.] Catalogue of works in refutation of Methodism. Philadelphia 1846, 1868 (rev).

Osborn, G. Outlines of Wesleyan bibliography. 1869.

Green, R. Anti-Methodist publications issued during the eighteenth century. 1902.

A catalogue of manuscripts and relics, books and pamphlets belonging to the Wesleyan Methodist conference. 1921.

National Book Council. John Wesley and Methodism: a selected list of books. 1938.

Presbyterians

Catalogue of the Divinity hall library of the United Presbyterian Church. Edinburgh 1850.

Catalogue of the Brown library: Glasgow section of the Theological hall library of the United Presbyterian Church. Glasgow 1863.

Scott, H. Fasti ecclesiae scoticanae: the succession of ministers in the Church of Scotland from the Reformation. 3 vols Edinburgh 1866–71, 7 vols Edinburgh 1915–28 (new and rev); vol 8, 1950.

Catalogue of the Theological hall library of the United Presbyterian Church. Edinburgh 1868.

Johnston, J. C. Treasury of the Scottish covenant. Edinburgh 1887.

Cowan, W. A bibliography of the book of common order and psalm book of the Church of Scotland 1556–1644. Edinburgh 1913.

Campbell, A. A. Irish Presbyterian magazines, past and present: a bibliography. Belfast 1919.

R. L. C.

II. HISTORIES AND ANTHOLOGIES

This brief selection is generally confined to surveys and anthologies of the whole of English literature. Works of more limited scope are listed under historical periods, below.

(1) GENERAL HISTORIES

Bale, J. Illustrium majoris Britanniae scriptorum, hoc est Angliae, Cambriae ac Scotiae summarium. Ipswich 1548, Basle 1557–9 (enlarged).
— Index Britanniae scriptorum. Ed R. L. Poole and M. Bateson, Oxford 1902.

Pits, J. Relationum historicarum de rebus anglicis. Vol 1, ed W. Bishop, Paris 1619.

Leland, J. Commentarii de scriptoribus britannicis. Ed A. Hall 2 vols Oxford 1709.

Tanner, T. Bibliotheca britannico-hibernica. Ed D. Wilkins 1748.

Berkenhout, J. Biographia literaria: or a biographical history of literature. 1777 (complete only to 16th century).

Hallam, H. Introduction to the literature of Europe, in the fifteenth, sixteenth and seventeenth centuries. 4 vols 1837–9.

Arnold, T. A manual of English literature. 1862.

Taine, H. Histoire de la littérature anglaise. 4 vols Paris 1863–4; tr 2 vols Edinburgh 1871; tr H. Van Laun 4 vols New York 1965.

Morley, H. A first sketch of English literature. 1873, 1892 (rev).
— English writers: an attempt towards a history of English literature. 11 vols 1887–95. To Shakespeare.

ten Brink, B. Geschichte der englischen Literatur. 2 vols Berlin 1877–93 (vol 1 rev A. Brandl, 1899); tr 3 vols 1883–96. To Renaissance.

Engel, E. Geschichte der englischen Literatur. Leipzig 1883; tr 1902.

Koerting, G. Grundriss der Geschichte der englischen Literatur. Münster 1887, 1910 (5th edn rev).

Jusserand, J. J. Histoire littéraire du peuple anglais. 2 vols Paris 1894–1904; tr 3 vols 1895–1909. To Civil War.

Handbooks of English literature. Ed J. Hales 10 pts 1895–1903. Age of Alfred, Age of Chaucer, Transition age, by F. J. Snell; Age of Shakespeare, 2 vols by J. W. Allen and T. Seccombe; Age of Milton, by J. B. Masterman; Age of Dryden, by R. Garnett; Age of Pope, by J. Dennis; Age of Johnson, by T. Seccombe;

Age of Wordsworth, by C. H. Herford; Age of Tennyson, by H. Walker.

Wülcker, R. Geschichte der englischen Literatur. 2 vols Leipzig 1896, 1906–7.

Gosse, E. A short history of modern English literature. 1897.

Periods of European literature. Ed G. Saintsbury 12 vols Edinburgh 1897–1908. Dark ages, by W. P. Ker; Flourishing of romance, by G. Saintsbury; Fourteenth century, by F. J. Snell; Transition period, by G. Smith; Earlier Renaissance, by G. Saintsbury; Later Renaissance, by D. Hannay; First half of seventeenth century, by H. J. C. Grierson; Augustan ages, by O. Elton; Mid-eighteenth century, by J. H. Millar; Romantic revolt, by C. E. Vaughan; Romantic triumph, by T. S. Omond; Later nineteenth century, by G. Saintsbury.

Saintsbury, G. A short history of English literature. 1898.

Garnett, E. and E. Gosse. English literature: an illustrated record. 4 vols 1903.

Seccombe, T. and W. R. Nicoll. History of English literature. 2 vols 1906.

The Cambridge history of English literature. Ed A. W. Ward and A. R. Waller 14 vols Cambridge 1907–16 (vol 15, Index, 1927), 1932 (without bibliographies).

Mair, G. H. English literature, modern—1450–1910. 1911, 1944 (rev and enlarged to 1939 by A. C. Ward), 1961 (enlarged to 1959 by A. C. Ward).

Schroeer, M. M. A. Grundzüge und Haupttypen der englischen Literaturgeschichte. 2 pts Berlin 1911–14, 1922–7 (rev).

Hudson, W. H. An outline history of English literature. 1913, 1955 (rev A. C. Ward).

Buchan, J., H. Newbolt and E. Baker (ed). A history of English literature. 1923.

Drinkwater, J. (ed). The outline of English literature. [1923–4].

Albert, E. A history of English literature. New York 1924, 1956 (rev J. A. Stone).

Legouis, E. and L. Cazamian. Histoire de la littérature

anglaise. Paris 1924; tr 2 vols 1926–7, 1964 (16th edn rev R. Las Vergnas).

Groom, B. A literary history of England. 1929.

Legouis, E. A short history of English literature. Tr Oxford 1934. Abridged from Legouis and Cazamian, above.

Osgood, C. G. The voice of England: a history of English literature. New York 1935, 1952 (enlarged).

Smith, C. P. Annals of the poets. New York 1935.

Praz, M. Storia della letteratura inglese. Florence 1937, 1960 (7th edn rev and enlarged).

Daiches, D. Literature and society. 1938.

—— A critical history of English literature. 2 vols 1960.

Dobrée, B. (ed). Introductions to English literature. 5 vols 1938–40.

Evans, B. I. A short history of English literature. 1940, 1963, 1964 (rev).

Sampson, G. The concise Cambridge history of English literature. Cambridge 1941, 1961, 1970 (rev).

Entwistle, W. J. and E. Gillett. The literature of England AD 500–1942. 1943, 1962 (enlarged to 1960).

Wilson, F. P. and B. Dobrée (ed). The Oxford history of English literature. Oxford 1945–. Chaucer and the fifteenth century, by H. S. Bennett, 1947; English literature at the close of the Middle Ages, by E. K. Chambers, 1945; English literature in the sixteenth century, by C. S. Lewis, 1954; The English drama 1485–1585, by F. P. Wilson, 1969; English literature in the earlier seventeenth century, by D. Bush, 1945, 1962 (rev); English literature of the late seventeenth century, by J. R. Sutherland, 1969; English literature in the earlier eighteenth century, by B. Dobrée, 1959; English literature 1789–1815, by W. L. Renwick, 1963; English literature 1815–32, by I. R. Jack, 1963; Eight modern writers, by J. I. M. Stewart, 1963.

Zanco, A. Storia della letteratura inglese. 2 vols Turin 1946–7, 1958 (rev).

Mulgan, J. and D. M. Davin. An introduction to English literature. Oxford 1947.

Raith, J. Kleine englische Literaturgeschichte. 1947, 1961 (rev and enlarged).

Baugh, A. C. (ed). A literary history of England. New York 1948 (The OE period, by K. Malone; The ME period, by A. C. Baugh; The Renaissance, by T. Brooke; The Restoration and eighteenth century, by G. Sherburn; The nineteenth century and after, by S. C. Chew), 1967 (The Renaissance rev M. A. Shaaber; The Restoration and eighteenth century rev D. F. Bond; The nineteenth century and after rev R. D. Altick).

Craig, H. (ed). A history of English literature. New York 1950.

Ward, A. C. Illustrated history of English literature. 3 vols 1953–5.

Ford, B. (ed). A guide to English literature. 7 vols 1954–63 (Pelican), 1961 (rev).

Lüdeke, H. Die englische Literatur. Berne 1954.

Schirmer, W. Geschichte der englischen und amerikanischen Literatur von den Anfängen bis zur Gegenwart. Tübingen 1954, 2 vols 1960 (rev).

Schubel, F. Englische Literaturgeschichte. 2 vols Berlin 1954–6.

Ciaramella, M. A short account of English literature from earliest times to 1939. Rome 1958, 1966 (rev).

Birrell, T. A. Geschiednis van de engelse literatur. Utrecht 1961.

Izzo, C. Storia della letteratura inglese. 2 vols Milan 1961–4.

Phelps, G. H. A short history of English literature. 1962, 1965 (rev and enlarged as A survey of English literature).

Parry, J. A guide through English literature. 1963.

Basu, N. K. A history of English literature. Calcutta 1965.

Otis, W. B. and M. H. Needleman. An outline history of English literature. 2 vols 1965.

Rees, R. J. An introduction to English literature. 1966.

Stowell, H. E. An introduction to English literature. 1966.

(2) GENERAL HISTORIES OF SCOTTISH LITERATURE

Dempster, T. Historia ecclesiastica gentis scotorum: sive de scriptoribus scotis. 1627; ed D. Irving 1829 (Bannatyne Club).

Campbell, A. Introduction to the history of poetry in Scotland. 2 vols Edinburgh 1798–9.

Sibbald, J. Chronicle of Scottish poetry. 4 vols Edinburgh 1802.

Irving, D. The lives of the Scotish poets. 2 vols Edinburgh 1804, London 1810 (rev).

—— Lives of Scotish writers. 2 vols Edinburgh 1839.

—— The history of Scottish poetry. Ed J. A. Carlyle, Edinburgh 1861.

Ross, J. M. Scottish history and literature to the Reformation. Glasgow 1884.

Veitch, J. The feeling for nature in Scottish poetry. 2 vols Edinburgh 1887.

—— History and poetry of the Scottish border. 2 vols Edinburgh 1887.

Walker, H. Three centuries of Scottish literature. 2 vols Glasgow 1893.

Henderson, T. F. Scottish vernacular literature. 1898.

Millar, J. H. A literary history of Scotland. 1903.

—— Scottish prose of the seventeenth and eighteenth centuries. Glasgow 1912.

Mackenzie, A. M. An historical survey of Scottish literature to 1714. 1933.

Power, W. Literature and oatmeal: what literature has meant to Scotland. 1935.

Speirs, J. The Scots literary tradition. 1940, 1962 (rev).

Patrick, M. Four centuries of Scottish psalmody. 1949.

Wood, H. H. Scottish literature. 1952.

Kinsley, J. (ed). Scottish poetry: a critical survey. 1955.

Wittig, K. The Scottish tradition in literature. 1958.

Craig, D. Scottish literature and the Scottish people 1680–1830. 1961.

(3) GENERAL HISTORIES OF IRISH LITERATURE

Hyde, D. A literary history of Ireland from earliest times to the present day. 1899, 1967.

Saul, G. B. The shadow of three queens, a handbook: introduction to traditional Irish literature and its backgrounds. Harrisburg 1953.

Mercier, V. and D. H. Greene. 1000 years of Irish prose: the literary revival. New York 1962.

Corney, J. The Irish bardic poet. 1967.

O'Connor, F. The backward look. 1967.

(4) HISTORIES AND CATALOGUES OF LITERARY GENRES

Poetry

Phillips, E. Theatrum poetarum: or a complete collection of the poets. 1674; ed S. E. Brydges 1800.

Winstanley, W. Lives of the most famous English poets. 1687.

Jacob, G. Lives of the English poets. 1720.

Cibber, T. An account of the lives of the poets of Great Britain and Ireland. Ed R. Shiels 5 vols 1753.

Warton, T. The history of English poetry. 3 vols 1774–81; ed W. C. Hazlitt 4 vols 1871; Continuation, ed R. M. Baine, Los Angeles 1953 (Augustan Reprint Soc).

Johnson, S. The lives of the most eminent English poets. 4 vols 1781; ed G. B. Hill 3 vols Oxford 1905.

The English poets. Ed T. H. Ward 5 vols 1880–1918.

Courthope, W. J. A history of English poetry. 6 vols 1895–1910, New York 1962.

Carpenter, F. I. An outline guide to the study of English lyric poetry. Chicago 1897.

Gayley, C. M. and C. C. Young. The principles and progress of English poetry. New York 1904.

Greg, W. W. Pastoral poetry and pastoral drama. 1906.

Saintsbury, G. A history of English prosody. 3 vols 1906–10.

Gummere, F. B. Popular ballad. Boston 1907.

Mackail, J. W. The springs of Helicon. 1909.

Previté-Orton, C. W. Political satire in English poetry. Cambridge 1910.

Dixon, W. M. English epic and heroic poetry. 1912.

Reed, E. B. English lyrical poetry from its origins to the present time. New Haven 1912.

Rhys, E. Lyric poetry. 1913.

Schelling, F. E. The English lyric. Boston 1913.

Crosland, T. W. H. The English sonnet. 1917.

Read, H. Phases of English poetry. 1928, 1950 (rev).

Wolfe, H. Notes on English verse satire. 1929.

Kitchin, G. A survey of burlesque and parody in English. Edinburgh 1931.

Gerould, G. H. The ballad of tradition. Oxford 1932.

Williams, C. The English poetic mind. Oxford 1932.

Eliot, T. S. The use of poetry and the use of criticism. 1933.

Elton, O. The English Muse. 1933.

Bateson, F. W. English poetry and the English language. Oxford 1934.

—— English poetry: a critical introduction. 1950, 1966 (rev).

Empson, W. Some versions of pastoral. 1938.

—— The structure of complex words. 1951.

Bradner, L. Musae anglicanae: a history of Anglo-Latin poetry 1500–1925. New York 1940.

Evans, B. I. Tradition and romanticism in English poetry from Chaucer to W. B. Yeats. 1940.

Shuster, G. N. The English ode from Milton to Keats. New York 1940.

Grierson, H. J. C. and J. C. Smith. A critical history of English poetry. 1944, 1947 (rev).

Brooks, C. The well wrought urn: studies in the structure of poetry. New York 1947.

Bush, D. Science and English poetry: a historical sketch 1590–1950. New York 1950.

—— English poetry: the main currents from Chaucer to the present. New York 1952.

—— Pagan myth and Christian tradition in English poetry. Philadelphia 1968.

Lombardo, A. La poesia inglese dall'estetismo al simbolismo. Rome 1950.

Vivante, L. English poetry and its contributions to the knowledge of a creative principle. 1950 (with preface by T. S. Eliot).

Wells, E. K. The ballad tree. New York 1950.

Miles, J. The continuity of poetic language: studies in English poetry from the 1540's to the 1940's. Berkeley 1951, New York 1965 (rev).

—— Eras and modes in English poetry. Berkeley 1957.

—— Renaissance, eighteenth century and modern language in English poetry. Berkeley 1960.

Opie, I. and P. The Oxford dictionary of nursery rhymes. Oxford 1951, 1952 (corrected).

Thomson, J. A. K. Classical influences on English poetry. 1951.

Bowra, C. M. Heroic poetry. 1952.

Kermode, F. (ed). English pastoral poetry from the beginnings to Marvell. 1952.

Dobrée, B. The broken cistern. 1954.

Mitchell, E. R. The English May lyric: its background and development to the end of the seventeenth century. Ann Arbor 1954.

Tillyard, E. M. W. The English epic and its background. 1954.

Unwin, R. The rural Muse: studies in the peasant poetry of England. 1954.

Davie, D. A. Articulate energy: an enquiry into the syntax of English poetry. 1955.

Groom, B. The diction of poetry from Spenser to Bridges. Toronto 1955.

Sells, A. L. The Italian influence on English poetry from Chaucer to Southwell. Bloomington 1955.

Nettel, R. Seven centuries of popular song. 1956.

Routley, E. The English carol. 1958.

Duncan, J. E. The revival of metaphysical poetry: the history of a style, 1800 to the present. Minneapolis 1959.

Untermeyer, L. Lives of the poets: the story of one thousand years of English and American poetry. New York 1959.

Maddison, C. Apollo and the nine: a history of the ode. Baltimore 1960.

Friedman, A. B. The ballad revival: studies in the influence of popular on sophisticated poetry. Chicago 1961.

Reeves, J. A short history of English poetry 1340–1940. 1961.

Bullough, G. Mirror of minds: changing psychological beliefs in English poetry. 1962.

Haas, R. Wege zur englischen Lyrik in Wissenschaft und Unterricht: Interpretationen. Heidelberg 1962.

Hopkins, K. English poetry: a short history. 1962.

Shepard, L. The broadside ballad: a study in origins and meaning. 1962.

Cohen, J. M. The baroque lyric. 1963.

Green, T. The descent from heaven: a study in epic continuity. New Haven 1963.

Spender, S. and D. Hall (ed). The concise encyclopaedia of English and American poets and poetry. 1963.

Gibbon, J. M. Melody and the lyric from Chaucer to the cavaliers. New York 1964.

Schlüter, K. Die englische Ode: Studien zu ihrer Entwicklung unter dem Einfluss der antiken Hymne. Bonn 1964.

Grant, L. W. Neo-Latin literature and the pastoral. Chapel Hill 1965.

Preminger, A., F. J. Warnke and O. B. Hardison (ed). Encyclopedia of poetry and poetics. Princeton 1965.

Woodhouse, A. S. P. The poet and his faith: religion and poetry in England from Spenser to Eliot and Auden. Chicago 1965.

Bronowski, J. The poet's defence: the concept of poetry from Sidney to Yeats. Cleveland 1966.

Cruttwell, P. The English sonnet. 1966 (Br Council pamphlet).

Baring-Gould, W. S. The lure of the limerick: an un-inhibited history. New York 1967.

Barnes, T. R. English verse: voice and movement from Wyatt to Yeats. Cambridge 1967.

Colby, E. English Catholic poets, Chaucer to Dryden. Freeport NY 1967.

Winters, Y. Forms of discovery: critical and historical essays on the forms of the short poem in English. Chicago 1967.

Buckley, V. Poetry and the sacred. 1968.

Clemen, W. Das Problem des Stilwandels in der englischen Dichtung. Munich 1968.

Fowler, D. C. A literary history of the popular ballad. Durham NC 1968.

Heath-Stubbs, J. F. A. The verse satire. 1969.

Prose

The Novel

Dunlop, J. The history of fiction. 3 vols Edinburgh 1814; rev H. Wilson 2 vols 1888.

Scott, W. Lives of the novelists. 2 vols Paris 1825.

Masson, D. British novelists and their styles. Cambridge 1859.

Raleigh, W. The English novel. 1894. To 1800.

Cross, W. L. The development of the English novel. New York 1899.

Esdaile, A. List of English tales and prose romances printed before 1740. 1912.

Baker, E. A. and J. Packman. A guide to the best fiction, English and American, including translations from foreign languages. 1913, 1932 (rev).

Saintsbury, G. The English novel. 1913.

Baker, E. A. The history of the English novel. 10 vols 1924–39.

Prothero, R. E. (Baron Ernle). The light reading of our ancestors. 1927. To Scott.

Muir, E. The structure of the novel. 1928.

Lovett, R. M. and H. S. Hughes. The history of the novel in England. Boston 1932.

Verschoyle, D. (ed). The English novelists. 1936.

Fox, R. The novel and the people. 1937.

Bentley, P. The English regional novel. 1941.

Gerould, G. H. The patterns of English and American fiction: a history. Boston 1942.

Wagenknecht, E. C. Cavalcade of the English novel: from Elizabeth to George VI. New York 1943, 1954 (rev).

McCullough, B. Representative English novelists, Defoe to Conrad. New York 1946.

Pritchett, V. S. The living novel. 1946, 1964 (rev).

Church, R. The growth of the English novel. 1951.

Kettle, A. An introduction to the English novel. 2 vols 1951–3.

Neill, S. D. A short history of the English novel. 1951, 1964 (rev).

Kondo, I. English novels. Tokyo 1952.

Wölcken, F. Der literarische Mord: eine Untersuchung über die englische und amerikanische Detektivliteratur. Nuremberg 1953.

Allen, W. The English novel: a short critical history. 1954.

— (ed). The novelist as innovator. 1965.

Proctor, M. R. The English university novel. Berkeley 1957.

Varma, D. P. The gothic flame: being a history of the gothic novel in England. 1957.

Watt, I. The rise of the novel. 1957.

Murch, A. E. The development of the detective novel. 1958, 1968 (rev).

Booth, W. C. The rhetoric of fiction. Chicago 1961.

Other Forms of Prose

Gray, W. The origin and progress of English prose literature. 1835.

Minto, W. A manual of English prose literature. 1872.

Earle, J. English prose. 1890.

Gayley, C. M. and F. N. Scott. An introduction to the methods and materials of literary criticism. Boston 1899.

Saintsbury, G. A history of criticism and literary taste in Europe. 3 vols 1900–4.

— A history of English criticism. 1911.

— A history of English prose rhythm. 1912.

Chandler, F. W. Literature of roguery. Boston 1907.

Burr, A. D. The autobiography. Boston 1909.

Merrill, E. The dialogue in English literature. New Haven 1911.

Seth, J. English philosophers and schools of philosophy. 1912.

Walker, H. The English essay and essayist. 1915.

— English satire and satirists. 1925.

Dunn, W. H. English biography. 1916.

Gerould, G. H. Saints legends. Boston 1916.

Gayley, C. M. and B. P. Kurtz. Methods and materials of literary criticism. Boston 1920.

[Muddiman, J. G.] Tercentenary handlist of English and Welsh newspapers, magazines and reviews. 1920.

Kennedy, A. G. A bibliography of writings on the English language. Cambridge Mass 1927.

Nicolson, H. G. The development of English biography. 1927.

Darton, F. J. H. Children's books in England. Cambridge 1932, 1958 (rev).

Smith, W. G. The Oxford dictionary of English proverbs. Oxford 1935, 1948 (rev P. Harvey), 1970 (rev F. P. Wilson).

Barnes, H. E. A history of historical writing. Norman Oklahoma 1937.

Johnson, E. One mighty torrent: the drama of biography. New York 1937.

Smith, E. The history of children's literature. Chicago 1937.

Russell, L. (ed). English wits. 1940.

Smyth, C. H. E. The art of preaching 747–1939. 1940.

Worcester, D. The art of satire. Cambridge Mass 1940.

Wellek, R. The rise of English literary history. Chapel Hill 1941, New York 1966 (with foreword).

Thompson, J. W. and B. J. Holm. A history of historical writing. 2 vols New York 1942.

Atkins, J. W. H. English literary criticism [to 1800]. 3 vols Cambridge (later London) 1943–51.

Dobrée, B. English essayists. 1946.

Cazamian, L. The development of English humor. Durham NC 1952.

Morton, A. L. The English utopia: the 'utopia' tradition throughout English literature. 1952.

Coombes, H. Literature and criticism. 1953.

Crane, R. S. The languages of criticism and the structure of poetry. Toronto 1953.

Gilbert, K. and H. Kuhn. A history of esthetics. Bloomington 1953.

Meigs, C. et al. A critical history of children's literature. New York 1953, 1969 (rev).

Shumaker, W. English autobiography: its emergence, materials and form. Berkeley 1954.

Irving, W. H. The providence of wit in the English letter writers. Durham NC 1955.

Misch, G. Geschichte der Autobiographie. 2 vols Frankfurt 1955.

Thomson, J. A. K. Classical influences on English prose. 1956.

Mayer, T. L'humour anglais. Paris 1961.

Alden, R. M. The rise of formal satire in England under classical influence. New York 1962.

Auden, W. H. and L. Kronenberger (ed). The Viking book of aphorisms. New York 1962.

Ward, M. E. and D. A. Marquardt. Authors of books for young people. New York 1964.

Altick, R. D. Lives and letters: a history of literary biography in England and America. New York 1965.

Townsend, J. R. Written for children: an outline of English children's literature. 1965.

Gordon, I. A. The movement of English prose. 1966.

Whiting, B. J. Proverbs, sentences and proverbial phrases: from English writings mainly before 1500. Cambridge Mass 1968.

— Proverbs in the earlier English drama. New York 1969.

Drama

Langbaine, G. An account of the English dramatic poets. 1691, 1699 (rev C. Gildon as The lives of the poets).

[Baker, D. E.] The companion to the playhouse. 2 vols 1764, 1782 (rev I. Reed as Biographia dramatica), 4 vols 1812 (rev S. Jones as Biographica dramatica).

Ward, A. W. A history of English dramatic literature to the death of Queen Anne. 2 vols 1875, 3 vols 1899 (rev).

Collier, J. P. The history of English dramatic poetry. 3 vols 1879. To the Restoration.

Lowe, R. W. A bibliographical account of English theatrical literature. 1888.

Creizenach, W. Geschichte des neueren Dramas. 5 vols Halle 1895–1916, 1911 (rev).

Bates, K. L. and L. B. Godfrey. English drama. Wellesley 1896.

Adams, W. D. A dictionary of the drama. 1904.

Greg, W. W. Pastoral poetry and pastoral drama. 1906.

Thorndike, A. H. Tragedy. Boston 1908.

— English comedy. New York 1929.

Clarence, R. The stage cyclopedia: a bibliography of [English] plays. 1909.

Craig, E. G. On the art of the theatre. 1911.

Matthews, B. The development of the drama. 1914.

Schelling, F. E. English drama. 1914.

Archer, W. The old drama and the new. 1923.

Nicoll, A. British drama. 1925, 1947 (rev), 1962 (rev).

— The development of the theatre. 1927, 1966 (rev).

— World drama from Aeschylus to the present day. 1949.

— History of English drama 1660–1900. 6 vols Cambridge 1952–9.

Freedley, G. and J. A. Reeves. A history of the theatre. New York 1941.

Ellis-Fermor, U. M. The frontiers of drama. 1945.

Prior, M. E. The language of tragedy. New York 1947.

Downer, A. British drama: a handbook and brief chronicle. New York 1950.

Rossiter, A. P. English drama from early times to the Elizabethans. 1950.

Hartnoll, P. The Oxford companion to the theatre. Oxford 1951, 1967 (rev).

Stamm, R. Geschichte des englischen Theaters. Berne 1951.

Speaight, G. The history of the English puppet theatre. 1955.

Wimsatt, W. K. (ed). English stage comedy. New York 1955.

Henn, T. R. The harvest of tragedy. 1956.

Mander, R. and J. Mitchenson. A picture history of the British theatre. 1957.

Southern, R. The seven ages of the theatre. New York 1961.

Joseph, S. The story of the playhouse in England. 1963.

Sawyer, N. W. The comedy of manners from Sheridan to Maugham. New York 1963.

Bradbrook, M. C. English dramatic form. 1965.

Leaska, M. A. The voice of tragedy. New York 1966.

Sharp, H. S. and M. Z. Index to characters in the performing arts. 2 vols New York 1966.

Taylor, J. R. The Penguin dictionary of the theatre. 1966.

Cheshire, D. Theatre; history, criticism and reference. Melbourne 1967.

Taylor, A. The story of the English stage. Oxford 1967.

Roston, M. Biblical drama in England from the Middle Ages to the present day. Evanston 1968.

(5) ANTHOLOGIES

General

Cunliffe, J. W. et al. Century readings in English literature. New York 1910, 1937 (rev), 1940 (rev).

Woods, G. B. et al. The literature of England. 2 vols Chicago 1936, 1966 (rev).

Grebanier, B. D. et al. English literature and its backgrounds. 2 vols New York 1939, 1949 (rev).

Shafer, R. From Beowulf to Thomas Hardy. 2 vols New York 1939, 1959 (rev and enlarged J. Ball as From Beowulf to modern British writers).

Whiting, B. J. et al. The college survey of English literature. 2 vols New York 1942.

Wood, P. S. and E. M. Masters of English literature. 2 vols New York 1942.

Spencer, H. et al. British literature. 2 vols Boston 1951.

Baugh, A. C. and G. W. McClelland. English literature: a period anthology. New York 1954.

Pratt, R. A. et al. Masters of British literature. 2 vols Boston 1958.

Abrams, M. H. et al. The Norton anthology of English literature. 2 vols New York 1962, 1968 (rev).

Poetry

Johnson, S. The works of the English poets. 68 vols 1779–81, 75 vols 1790.

[Ellis, G.] Specimens of the early English poets. 1790, 3 vols 1801. Supplemented by R. Southey, Specimens of the later English poets, 3 vols 1807.

Anderson, R. The works of the British poets. 14 vols Edinburgh 1792–1807.

Chalmers, A. The works of the English poets. 21 vols 1810. Incorporates and expands Johnson's collection.

Campbell, T. Specimens of the British poets. 7 vols 1819, 1841 (rev P. Cunningham).

Aikin, J. Select works of the British poets. 1824. Supplemented by R. Southey, Select works of the British poets from Chaucer to Jonson, 1831.

Child, F. J. English and Scottish ballads. 8 vols Boston 1857–9, 1864, 8 vols in 4 1880, 1885–6, 5 vols Boston 1883–98 (rev as English and Scottish popular ballads), 5 vols in 3 1956, 1965; ed H. C. Sargent and G. L. Kittredge, Boston 1904, 1922, 1932.

Palgrave, F. T. The golden treasury. 1861, 1891 (rev), Oxford 1954 (suppl by C. D. Lewis), 1964 (suppl by J. Press).

— The treasury of sacred song. Oxford 1889.

Hunt, L. and S. A. Lee. The book of the sonnet. 2 vols 1867.

Locker-Lampson, F. Lyra elegantiarum: a collection of social and occasional verse. 1867; ed C. Kernahan 1891.

Trench, R. C. A household book of English poetry. 1868.

Hales, J. W. Longer English poems. 1872.

Main, D. M. A treasury of English sonnets. 1880.

Ward, T. H. The English poets. 5 vols 1880–1918.

Gosse, E. English odes. 1881.

Caine, T. H. Sonnets of three centuries. 1882.

Arber, E. British anthologies. 10 vols 1899–1901.

Quiller-Couch, A. T. The Oxford book of English verse. Oxford 1900, 1939 (enlarged), 1947 (rev).

— English sonnets. 1910.

Lloyd, M. Elegies ancient and modern. Trenton 1903.

Hadow, G. E. and W. H. The Oxford treasury of English literature. 3 vols 1906–8.

Nicholson, D. H. S. and A. H. E. Lee. The Oxford book of English mystical verse. Oxford 1916.

Auden, W. H. and J. Garrett. The poet's tongue. 2 vols 1935.

Lowry, H. F. and W. Thorp. An Oxford anthology of English poetry. New York 1935, 1956 (rev H. C. Horsford).

Williams, C. The new book of English verse. 1935.

Harrison, G. B. A book of English poetry. 1937, 1950 (enlarged).

Auden, W. H. The Oxford book of light verse. Oxford 1938.

Roberts, D. K. The centuries' poetry. 4 vols 1938–53 (Penguin).

Cecil, David. The Oxford book of Christian verse. Oxford 1940.

Bennett, H. S., C. S. Lewis et al. Fifteen poets. Oxford 1941.

Bottrall, M. and R. Collected English verse. 1946.

Aldington, R. Poetry of the English-speaking world. 1947, 2 vols New York 1958.

Bax, C. and M. Stewart. The distaff Muse: an anthology of poetry written by women. 1949.

Bevington, J. D. The charm of poetry. 1949.

Herron, E. E. The way to poetry. 1949.

Read, H. and B. Dobrée. The London book of English verse. 1949, 1952 (rev).

Auden, W. H. and N. H. Pearson. Poets of the English language. 5 vols New York 1950.

Daiches, D. and W. Charvat. Poems in English 1530–1940. New York 1950.

Holmes, J. A. A little treasury of love poems from Chaucer to Dryden. New York 1950.

Masefield, J. My favorite English poems. 1950.

Smith, A. J. M. The worldly Muse: an anthology of serious light verse. New York 1951.

Cohen, J. M. Comic and curious verse. 1952; More comic and curious verse, 1956; Yet more comic and curious verse, 1959 (Penguin).

Housman, J. E. British popular ballads. 1952.

Legman, G. The limerick. Paris 1953.

Leiper, M. and H. W. Simon. A treasury of hymns. New York 1953.

Leyland, P. and M. A. Pink. The English association book of verse. 1953.

Leach, MacE. The ballad book. New York 1955.

Opie, I. and P. The Oxford nursery rhyme book. Oxford 1955.

Hayward, J. The Penguin book of English verse. 1956 (Penguin), 1958 (as The Faber book of English verse).

Ingram, T. and D. Newton. Hymns as poetry. 1956.

Jeffares, A. N. Seven centuries of poetry. 1956, 1961 (rev).

Betjeman, J. and G. Taylor. English love poems. 1957.

Graves, R. English and Scottish ballads. 1957.

Gregory, H. and M. Zaturenska. The Mentor book of religious verse. New York 1957.

Pinto, V. de S. and A. E. Rodway. The common Muse. 1957.

Adams, C. The worst English poets. 1958.

MacDonagh, D. and L. Robinson. The Oxford book of Irish verse. Oxford 1958.

Williams, G. Presenting Welsh poetry. 1959.

Colum, P. The poet's circuits: collected poems of Ireland. Oxford 1960.

Herbert, D. The Penguin book of narrative verse. 1960 (Penguin).

Peters, D. J. and B. E. Towers. The poetry of history: an anthology of historical verse. 1960.

Scott, R. I. From Barbour to Burns: an anthology of Scots poetry. 1960.

Lewis, C. D. A book of English lyrics. 1961.

Cole, W. Erotic poetry. New York 1963.

Hindley, W. and J. Betjeman. A wealth of poetry. Oxford 1963.

Hodgart, M. J. C. The Faber book of ballads. 1965.

Horne, C. J. and M. O'Brien. The progress of poetry. Melbourne 1965.

Reeves, J. The Cassell book of English poetry. 1965.

Bender, R. M. and C. L. Squier. The sonnet: a comprehensive anthology. New York 1966.

Ehrenpreis, A. H. The literary ballad. 1966.

Johnson, R. B. A book of English ballads. 1966.

MacQueen, J. and T. Scott. The Oxford book of Scottish verse. Oxford 1966.

Eastman, A. et al. The Norton anthology of poetry. New York 1970.

Prose

Chalmers, A. The British essayists. 45 vols 1802–3.

Scoones, W. B. Four centuries of English letters. 1880.

Saintsbury, G. Specimens of English prose style. 1885.

Craik, H. English prose. 5 vols 1893–6.

Hopkins, A. B. and H. S. Hughes. The English novel before the nineteenth century. Boston 1915.

Peacock, W. English prose. 5 vols 1921–2.

Ponsonby, A. English diaries. 1923.

— More English diaries. 1927.

Murphy, G. A cabinet of characters. 1925.

Quiller-Couch, A. T. The Oxford book of English prose. Oxford 1925.

Smith, L. P. A treasury of English aphorisms. 1928.

Read, H. and B. Dobrée. The London book of English prose. 1931.

Francis, J. H. From Caxton to Carlyle. Cambridge 1937.

Bütow, H. Der englische Geist: Meister des Essays von Bacon bis zur Gegenwart. Leipzig 1939.

Walbank, F. A. The English scene in the works of prose writers since 1700. 1941, 1947 (rev).

— England yesterday and today in the works of the novelists 1837 to 1938. 1949.

Davies, R. E. Of youth and age: an anthology of English prose forms. Pretoria 1949.

Vulliamy, C. E. The anatomy of satire. 1950.

Bate, W. J. Criticism: the major texts. New York 1952.

Negley, G. and J. M. Patrick. The quest for utopia. New York 1952.

Sutherland, J. R. The Oxford book of English talk. Oxford 1953.

Collins, V. H. Three centuries of English essays. Melbourne 1954.

Allott, K. and M. et al. The Pelican book of English prose. 5 vols 1956 (Pelican).

James, E. An anthology of English prose 1400–1900. Cambridge 1956.

Kieran, J. Treasury of great nature writing. New York 1957.

Newman, B. English historians. Oxford 1957.

MacDonald, D. Parodies: an anthology from Chaucer to Beerbohm and after. New York 1960.

McPhedran, I. F. and P. Kitchen. Scottish harvest: an anthology of Scottish prose. 1960.

— Scots adventuring: an anthology of Scottish prose. Edinburgh 1961.

Reeves, J. Great English essays. 1961.

Bell, H. Selected English prose: Malory to Joyce. Oxford 1963.

Johnson, E. D. H. The poetry of earth: a collection of English nature writings. New York 1966.

Drama

[Dodsley, R.] A select collection of old plays. 12 vols 1744; ed W. C. Hazlitt 15 vols 1874–6. To Restoration.

Bell's British theatre. 34 vols 1791–7.

Inchbald, E. The British theatre. 25 vols 1808.

[Scott, W.] Ancient British drama. 3 vols 1810. To Restoration.

— Modern British drama. 5 vols 1811. Restoration to 1800.

D[aniel], G. Cumberland's British theatre. 48 vols 1829.

Gayley, C. M. Representative English comedies [to 1642]. 3 vols New York 1903.

Tatlock, J. S. P. and R. G. Martin. Representative English plays. New York 1916, 1938 (rev).

Bentley, G. E. The development of English drama. New York 1950.

R. L. C.

III. PROSODY AND PROSE RHYTHM

(1) GENERAL HISTORIES AND BIBLIOGRAPHIES

Guest, E. A history of English rhythms. 1838; ed W. W. Skeat 1882.

Schipper, J. M. Englische Metrik in historischer und systematischer Entwickelung dargestellt. 3 vols Bonn 1881–8.

— Grundriss der englischen Metrik. Leipzig 1895; tr 1910. An abridgment of his Englische Metrik, above.

Alden, R. M. English verse: specimens illustrating its principles and history. New York 1904.

Saintsbury, G. A history of English prosody from the twelfth century to the present day. 3 vols 1906–10.

— A historic manual of English prosody. 1910.

— A history of English prose rhythm. 1912.

Kaluza, M. Englische Metrik in historischer Entwicklung dargestellt. Berlin 1909; tr 1911.

Shapiro, K. A bibliography of modern prosody. Baltimore 1948.

Schulte, E. Profilo storico della metrica inglese. Naples 1960.

(2) OLD ENGLISH

Schubert, H. De Anglo-Saxonum arte metrica. Berlin 1870.

Rieger, M. Die alt- und angelsächsische Verskunst. Zeitschrift für Deutsche Philologie 7 1876.

Schipper, J. M. Altenglische Metrik. Bonn 1881. Vol 1 of his Englische Metrik.

Trautmann, M. Zur alt- und mittelenglischen Verslehre. Anglia Anzeiger 5 1882.

— Zur Kenntnis des altgermanischen Verses, vornehmlich des altenglischen. Anglia Beiblatt 5 1895.

— Die neuste Beowulfausgabe und die altenglische Verslehre. Bonner Beiträge zur Anglistik 17 1905.

— Zum altenglischen Versbau. E Studien 44 1912.

Kluge, F. Zur Geschichte des Reimes im Altgermanischen. Pauls und Braunes Beiträge 9 1884.

Sievers, E. Zur Rhythmik des germanischen Alliterationsverses. Pauls und Braunes Beiträge 10 1885.

— Der angelsächsische Schwellvers. Pauls und Braunes Beiträge 12 1887.

— Altgermanische Metrik. Halle 1893. Abridged version in Pauls Grundriss 2. 1–2 1893–1905.

— Zu Cynewulf. In Festgabe Karl Luick, Marburg 1925.

Gummere, F. B. The translation of Beowulf, and the relations of ancient and modern English verse. Amer Jnl of Philology 7 1886.

Luick, K. Zur Theorie der Entstehung der Schwellverse. Pauls und Braunes Beiträge 13 1887.

— Zur altenglischen und altsächsischen Metrik. Pauls und Braunes Beiträge 17 1891.

Möller, W. Zur althochdeutschen Alliterationspoesie. Leipzig 1888.

Kauffmann, F. Die sogenannten Schwellverse der alt- und angelsächsischen Dichtung. Pauls und Braunes Beiträge 15 1890.

Bright, J. W. An Anglo-Saxon reader. New York 1891. Appendix 2.

— Proper names in Old English verse. PMLA 14 1899.

Fuhr, K. Die Metrik des westgermanisches Alliterationsverses. Marburg 1892.

Heath, H. F. The Old English alliterative line. Trans of Philological Soc 1893.

Lawrence, J. Chapters on alliterative verse. 1893.

Brenner, O. Zur Verteilung der Reimstäbe in der alliterierende Langzeile. Pauls und Braunes Beiträge 19 1894.

Kaluza, M. Studien zum germanischen Alliterationsvers. Berlin 1894.

— Der altenglische Vers: eine metrische Untersuchung. Berlin 1894.

— Die Schwellverse in der altenglischen Dichtung. E Studien 21 1895.

— Zur Betonungs- und Verslehre des Altenglischen. In Festschrift Oskar Schrade, Königsberg 1896.

Sweet, H. An Anglo-Saxon reader. Oxford 1894 (7th edn). Introd §§356–92.

Morris, J. Sidney Lanier and Anglo-Saxon verse-technic. Amer Jnl of Philology 20 1899.

Schröder, E. Steigerung und Häufung der Alliteration in der westgermanischen Dichtung. Zeitschrift für Deutsches Altertum 43 1899.

Emerson, O. F. Transverse alliteration in Teutonic poetry. JEGP 3 1900.

Huguenin, J. Secondary stress in Anglo-Saxon (determined by metrical criteria). Baltimore 1901.

Clark, J. Early alliterative verse. Proc of Royal Philosophical Soc of Glasgow 1902.

Deutschbein, M. Zur Entwicklung des englischen Alliterationsverses. Halle 1902.

Sokoll, E. Zur Technik des altgermanischen Alliterationsverses. In Beiträge zur neueren Philologie, Jakob Schipper dargebracht, Leipzig 1902.

Setzler, E. B. On Anglo-Saxon versification from the standpoint of Modern-English versification. Baltimore 1904.

Bohlen, A. Zusammengehörige Wortgruppen, getrennt durch Cäsur oder Versschluss, in der angelsächsischen Epik. Berlin 1908.

Krauel, H. Der Haken- und Langzeilenstil im Beowulf. Göttingen 1908.

Morgan, B. Q. Zur Lehre von der Alliteration in der westgermanischen Dichtung. Pauls und Braunes Beiträge 33 1908.

Richter, C. Chronologische Studien zur angelsächsischen Literatur auf Grund sprachlich-metrischer Kriterien. Halle 1910.

Schmitz, T. Die Sechstakter in der altenglischen Dichtung. Anglia 33 1910.

Classen, E. On vowel alliteration in the Old Germanic languages. Manchester 1913.

Fijn van Draat, P. The cursus in Old English poetry. Anglia 38 1914.

Heims, W. Der germanische Allitterationsvers und seine Vorgeschichte. Münster 1914.

Boer, R. C. Studiën over de metriek van het alliteratievers. Amsterdam 1916.

Kock, E. A. Jubilee jaunts and jottings: 250 contributions to the interpretation and prosody of Old West Teutonic alliterative poetry. Lunds Univ Årsskrift new ser 1. 14 1918.

Leonard, W. E. Beowulf and the Niebelungen couplet. Univ of Wisconsin Stud in Lang & Lit 11 1918.

— Four footnotes to papers on Germanic metrics. In F. Klaeber miscellany, Minneapolis 1929.

Bognitz, A. Doppelt-steigende Alliterationsverse (Sievers Typus B) im Angelsächsischen. Berlin 1920.

Neuner, E. Über ein- und dreihebige Halbverse in der altenglischen alliterierenden Poesie. Berlin 1920.

Rankin, J. W. Rhythm and rime before the Norman Conquest. PMLA 36 1921.

Routh, J. E. Anglo-Saxon meter. MP 21 1924.

Greg, W. W. The 'five types' in Anglo-Saxon verse. MLR 20 1925.

Heusler, A. Deutsche Versgeschichte mit Einschluss des altenglischen und altnordischen Stabreimverses. In Pauls Grundriss 8. 1 1915.

Scripture, E. W. Die Grundgesetze des altenglischen Stabreimverses. Anglia 52 1928.

— Experimentelle Untersuchungen über die Metrik in Beowulf. Archiv für die Gesamte Psychologie 66 1928.

Andrew, S. O. The Old English alliterative measure. Croydon 1931.

— Postscript on Beowulf. Cambridge 1948.

Baum, P. F. The character of Anglo-Saxon verse. MP 28 1931.

— The meter of the Beowulf. MP 46 1949.

Kuhn, H. Wortstellung und -betonung im Altgermanischen. Pauls und Braunes Beiträge 57 1933.

Lewis, C. S. The alliterative metre. Lysistrata 2 1935; rptd in his Rehabilitations and other essays, Oxford 1939.

Magoun, F. P. Strophische Überreste in den altenglischen Zaubersprüchen. E Studien 72 1937.

Tolkien, J. R. R. Preface on words and metres. In J. R. Clark Hall, Beowulf translated into modern English prose, 1940.

Vogt, W. H. Altgermanische Druck-'Metrik': recht unbekümmerte Meinungen eines Nicht-Metrikers. Pauls und Braunes Beiträge 64 1940.

Malone, K. Lift patterns in Old English verse. ELH 8 1941.

— Plurilinear units in Old English poetry. RES 19 1943.

— The old tradition: poetic form. In A literary history of England, ed A. C. Baugh, New York 1948.

Travis, J. The relations between Early Celtic and Early Germanic alliteration. Germanic Rev 17 1942.

— Intralinear rhyme and consonance in Early Celtic and Early Germanic poetry. Germanic Rev 18 1943.

Pope, J. C. The rhythm of Beowulf. New Haven 1942, 1966 (with introd). See R. E. Past, MLN 64 1949.

Daunt, M. Old English verse and English speech rhythm. Trans of Philological Soc 1946.

Gradon, P. Cynewulf's Elene and Old English prosody. Eng & Germanic Stud 2 1949.

Kuryłowicz, J. Latin and Germanic metre. Ibid.

Flasdieck, H. M. The phonetic aspect of Old Germanic alliteration. Anglia 69 1950.

Ross, A. S. C. Philological probability problems. Jnl of Royal Statistical Soc B 12 1950. Extra alliteration accidental?

Koziol, H. Zur Alliteration im AE. Anglia 70 1951.

Slay, D. Some aspects of the technique of composition of Old English verse. Trans of Philological Soc 1952.

Timmer, B. J. Expanded lines in Old English poetry. Neophilologus 39 1952.

Touster, E. K. Phonological aspects of the meter of Beowulf. In Essays in honor of Walter Clyde Curry, Nashville 1954.

— Metrical variation as a poetic device in Beowulf. Anglia 73 1955.

Lehmann, W. P. The development of Germanic verse form. Austin 1956.

— Metrical evidence for Old English suprasegmentals. Texas Stud in Lit & Lang 1 1960.

— and T. Tabusa. The alliterations of the Beowulf. Austin 1958.

Le Page, R. B. A rhythmical framework for the five types. Eng & Germanic Stud 6 1957.

— Alliterative patterns as a test of style in Old English poetry. Eng Stud 58 1959.

Bliss, A. J. The metre of Beowulf. Oxford 1958.

— An introduction to Old English metre. Oxford 1962.

— The appreciation of Old English metre. In English and medieval studies presented to J. R. R. Tolkien, 1962.

— Single half-lines in Old English poetry. N & Q Dec 1971.

Funke, O. Zur Rhythmik des altenglischen Alliterationsverses. Anglia 76 1958.

Salmon, P. Anomalous alliteration in Germanic verse. Neophilologus 42 1958.

Wrenn, C. L. On the continuity of English poetry. Anglia 76 1958; rptd with alterations in his A study of Old English literature, 1967.

— Form and style in Anglo-Saxon literature. In his A study of Old English literature, 1967.

Nist, J. A. The structure and texture of Beowulf. São Paulo 1959.

— Metrical uses of the harp in Beowulf. In Old English poetry: fifteen essays, ed R. P. Creed, Providence 1967.

Brinkmann, H. Der Reim im frühen Mittelalter. In Festschrift für Hermann M. Flasdieck, Heidelberg 1960.

Bulst, W. Almus altus agnus aptus. Ibid. On Latin influence in OE verse.

Schabram, H. The seasons for fasting 206f.; mit einem Beitrag zur ae Metrik. Ibid.

Taglicht, J. Beowulf and Old English verse rhythm. RES new ser 12 1961.

Dawson, R. McG. The structure of the Old English gnomic poems. JEGP 61 1962.

Quirk, R. Poetic language and Old English metre. In Studies presented to Hugh Smith, 1963.

Schulze, F. W. Reimstrukturen im Offa-Preislied Æthelwalds und die Entwicklung des altenglischen Alliterationsverses. Zeitschrift für Deutsches Altertum 92 1963.

Greenfield, S. B. Some remarks on the nature and quality of Old English poetry. In his A critical history of Old English literature, New York 1965.

Creed, R. P. A new approach to the rhythm of Beowulf. PMLA 81 1966.

Bazell, C. E. Notes on Old English metre and morphology. In Festschrift zum 60 Geburtstag von Hans Marchand, Hague 1967.

Bessinger, J. B. The Sutton Hoo harp replica and Old English musical verse. In Old English poetry: fifteen essays, ed R. P. Creed, Providence 1967.

Stevick, R. D. The meter of the Dream of the rood. Neuphilologische Mitteilungen 68 1967.

— Suprasegmentals, meter and the manuscript of Beowulf. Hague 1967.

See, K. von. Germanische Verskunst. Stuttgart 1967.

Willard, R. and E. D. Clemons. Bliss's light verses in the Beowulf. JEGP 66 1967.

Cygan, J. A critique of the Sieversian theory of Old Germanic alliterative verse. Germanica Wratislaviensis 12 1968.

Isaacs, N. D. Afterword on the scansion of Old English poetry. In his Structural principles in Old English poetry, Knoxville 1968.

Keyser, S. J. Old English prosody. College Eng Feb 1968. Replies by J. Sledd and Keyser, Oct 1969.

Kim, J. H. Metrical observations of Old English verse. Eng Lang & Lit 31 1969.

Lehman, R. P. M. The metrics and structure of Wulf and Eadwacer. PQ 48 1969.

Cable, T. M. Rules for syntax and metrics in Beowulf. JEGP 69 1970.

— Clashing stress in the metre of Beowulf. Neuphilologische Mitteilungen 72 1971.

— Constraints on anacrusis in Old English metre. MP 69 1971.

Hieatt, C. B. A new theory of triple rhythm in the hypermetric lines of Old English verse. MP 67 1970.

(3) MIDDLE ENGLISH

Rosenthal, F. Die alliterierende englische Langzeile. Anglia 1 1878.

Trautmann, M. Zur alt- und mittelenglischen Verslehre. Anglia Anzeiger 5 1882.

Börsch, J. Ueber Metrik und Poetik der altenglischen Dichtung Owl and Nightingale. Münster 1883.

Schlüter, A. Ueber die Sprache und Metrik der mittelenglischen Lieder der MS 2253. Archiv 71 1884.

Fuhrmann, J. Die alliterierende Sprachformeln. Hamburg 1886.

Wilda, O. Über die örtliche Verbreitung der zwölfzeiligen Schweifreimstrophe in England. Breslau 1887.

Luick, K. Die englische Stabreimzeile im 14, 15 und 16 Jahrhundert. Anglia 11 1889.

— Zur Metrik der mittelenglischen reimend-alliterierenden Dichtung. Anglia 12 1889.

— Zur mittelenglischen Verslehre. Anglia 38 1914.

Kaluza, M. Strophische Gliederung in der mittelenglischen rein alliterirenden Dichtung. E Studien 16 1891.

Wittenbrinck, G. Zur Kritik und Rhythmik des altenglischen Lais von Havelok dem Dänen. Burgsteinfurt 1891.

Kuhnke, B. Die alliterirende Langzeile. Königsberg 1899.

— Die alliterierende Langzeil in Sir Gawayne. Berlin 1900.

Mennicken, F. Versbau und Sprache in Huchowns Morte Arthure. Bonner Beiträge zur Anglistik 5 1900.

Fischer, J. Die stabende Langzeile in den Werken des Gawaindichters. Bonner Beiträge zur Anglistik 11 1901.

Schneider, A. Die mittelenglische Stabzeile. Bonner Beiträge zur Anglistik 12 1902.

McNary, S. J. Studies in Layamon's verse. New York 1904.

Pilch, L. Umwandlung des altenglischen Alliterationsverses in den mittelenglischen Reimvers. Königsberg 1904.

Reicke, C. Untersuchungen über den Stil der mittelenglischen alliterierenden Gedichte. Königsberg 1906.

West, H. S. The versification of King Horn. Baltimore 1907.

Thomas, J. Die alliterierende Langzeile des Gawayn-Dichters. Coburg 1908.

Deakin, M. The alliteration of Piers Plowman. MLR 4 1909.

Brandstädter, K. Stabreim und Endreim. Heidelberg 1912.

Bülbring, K. Untersuchungen zur mittelenglischer Metrik. Studien zur Englischen Philologie 50 1913.

Schumacher, K. Studien über den Stabreim. Studien zur Englischen Philologie 51 1914.

Medary, M. P. and A. C. L. Brown. Stanza-linking in Middle English verse. Romanic Rev 7 1916.

Strandberg, O. The rime-vowels of Cursor mundi. Upsala 1919.

Brink, A. Stab und Wort im Gawain. Studien zur Englischen Philologie 59 1920.

Finsterbusch, F. Der Versbau der mittelenglischen Dichtungen Sir Perceval of Galles und Sir Degravant. Vienna 1920.

Leonard, W. E. The scansion of Middle English alliterative verse. Univ of Wisconsin Stud in Lang & Lit 11 1920.

Liebermann, F. Zu Liedrefrain und Tanz im englischen Mittelalter. Archiv 140 1920.

Emerson, O. F. Imperfect lines in the Pearl and the rhymed parts of Sir Gawain and the Green Knight. MP 19 1921.

Meier, H. Die Strophenform in den englischen Mysterienspielen. Freiburg 1921.

Miller, F. H. Stanzaic division in York Play xxxix. MLN 36 1921.

Fort, M. D. The metres of the Brome and Chester Abraham and Isaac plays. PMLA 41 1926.

Stewart, G. R. The meter of Piers Plowman. PMLA 42 1927.

Scripture, E. W. Der Versrhythmus in King Horn. Anglia 52 1928.

Oakden, J. P. Alliterative poetry in Middle English: the dialectal and metrical survey. Manchester 1930.

— and E. R. Innes. Alliterative poetry in Middle English. Manchester 1935.

Day, M. Strophic division in Middle English alliterative verse. E Studien 66 1931.

Hulbert, J. R. A hypothesis concerning the alliterative revival. MP 28 1931.

— Quatrains in Middle English alliterative poems. MP 48 1951.

Trounce, A. McI. The English tail-rhyme romances. MÆ 1–3 1932–4.

Pyle, F. The place of Anglo-Norman in the history of English versification. Hermathena 24 1935.

Scholte, J. H. Stafrijm en eindrijm. Neophilologus 27 1942.

Reese, J. B. Alliterative verse in the York cycle. SP 48 1951.

Schoeck, R. J. Alliterative assonance in Harley ms 2253. E Studies 32 1951.

Cutler, J. L. The versification of the Gawain epigone in Humfrey Newton's poems. JEGP 51 1952.

Gerhardt, M. I. Metrische schema's van het lange vers. Neophilologus 43 1959.

Standop, E. Der Rhythmus des Layamon-Verses. Anglia 79 1961.

Henry, P. L. A Celtic-English prosodic feature. Zeitschrift für Celtische Philologie 29 1962. On circular concatenation.

Fifield, M. Thirteenth-century lyrics and the alliterative tradition. JEGP 62 1963.

Mitchell, B. The couplet system in Havelok the Dane. N & Q Nov 1963.

Göller, K. H. Stab und Formel im alliterierenden Morte Arthure. Neophilologus 49 1965.

Hilker, W. Der Vers in Layamons Brut: Untersuchungen zu seiner Struktur und Herkunft. Münster 1965.

Salter, E. The alliterative revival. MP 64 1967.

Mitsui, T. Notes on the stanzaic division and the metre of Judas. Stud in Eng Lit (Tokyo) 44 1968.

Moorman, C. The origins of the alliterative revival. Southern Quart 7 1969.

Schöpf, M. Zur Strophenform einiger Carols. Anglia 87 1969.

Blake, N. F. Rhythmical alliteration. MP 67 1970.

(4) CHAUCER TO WYATT

Tyrwhitt, T. An essay on the language and versification of Chaucer. In his Canterbury tales of Chaucer vol 4, 1775.

Lindner, F. The alliteration in Chaucer's Canterbury tales. In Essays on Chaucer, ed F. J. Furnivall 1868–74 (Chaucer Soc).

ten Brink, B. Chaucers Sprache und Verskunst. Strasbourg 1884; tr 1901.

Höfer, P. Alliteration bei Gower. Leipzig 1890.

Hempel, E. Die Silbenmassung in Chaucers fünftaktigen Verse. Halle 1898.

Bischoff, O. Ueber zweisilbige Senkung und epische Cäsur bei Chaucer. E Studien 24–5 1898–9.

Bock, F. Metrische Studien zu Hoccleves Versen. Weilheim 1900.

Smith, M. B. Some remarks on chapter III of ten Brink's Chaucers Sprache und Verskunst. MLQ 5 1902.

Miller, R. D. Secondary accent in Modern English verse (Chaucer to Dryden). Baltimore 1904.

Licklider, A. H. Chapters on the metric of the Chaucer tradition. Baltimore 1910.

Reger, H. Die epische Cäsur in der Chaucer-Schule. Bayreuth 1910.

Seeberger, A. Fehlende Auftakt und fehlende Senkung nach der Cäsur in der Chaucer-Schule. Bayreuth 1911.

Klee, F. Das Enjambement bei Chaucer. Halle 1913.

Shannon, E. Chaucer's use of octosyllabic verse. JEGP 12 1913.

Babcock, C. F. A study of the metrical use of inflectional e in Middle English. PMLA 29 1914.

Vockrodt, G. Die Reimteknik bei Chaucer. Halle 1914.

Joerden, O. Das Verhältnis von Wort-, Satz-, und Vers-Akzent in Chaucers Canterbury Tales. Studien zur Englischen Philologie 55 1915.

Bihl, J. Die Wirkungen des Rhythmus in der Sprache von Chaucer und Gower. Anglistische Forschungen 50 1916.

Emerson, O. F. The Old French diphthong ei (ey) and Middle English metrics. Romanic Rev 8 1917.

Beschorner, F. Verbale Reime bei Chaucer. Studien zur Englischen Philologie 60 1920.

Langhans, V. Der Reimvokal 'e' bei Chaucer. Anglia 45 1921.

Hammond, E. P. The nine-syllabled pentameter line in some post-Chaucerian manuscripts. MP 23 1925.

— English verse between Chaucer and Surrey. Durham NC 1927. Introd.

Cowling, G. H. A note on Chaucer's stanza. RES 2 1926.

Lineberger, J. E. An examination of Professor Cowling's new metrical test. MLN 42 1927.

Buck, H. Chaucer's use of feminine rhyme. MP 26 1928.

Purcell, J. M. The Troilus verse. PQ 12 1933.

Maynard, T. The connection between the ballade, Chaucer's modification of it, rime royal and the Spenserian stanza. Washington 1934.

Pyle, F. A metrical point in Chaucer. N & Q 22 Feb 1936.

— The pedigree of Lydgate's heroic line. Hermathena 25 1936.

— The origins of the Skeltonic. N & Q 21 Nov 1936.

— 'The barbarous metre of Barclay'. MLR 32 1937.

Lewis, C. S. The fifteenth-century heroic line. E & S 24 1938; rptd in his Selected literary essays, Cambridge 1969.

Bernard, J. E. The prosody of the Tudor interlude. New Haven 1939.

McJimsey, R. B. Chaucer's irregular -e. New York 1942.

Everett, D. Chaucer's 'good ear'. RES 23 1947; rptd in her Essays on Middle English literature, Oxford 1955.

Southworth, J. G. Chaucer's final -e in rhyme. PMLA 62 1947. Replies by E. T. Donaldson 63 1948, J. G. Southworth and Donaldson 64 1949.

— Verses of cadence: an introduction to the prosody of Chaucer and his followers. Oxford 1954.

— The prosody of Chaucer and his followers. Oxford 1963.

Swallow, A. The pentameter lines in Skelton and Wyatt. MP 48 1950.

Kinsman, R. S. Skelton's Uppon a deedmans hed: new light on the origin of the Skeltonic. SP 50 1953.

Seronsy, C. C. A Skeltonic passage in Ben Jonson. N & Q 1 Jan 1953.

Watson, M. R. Wyatt, Chaucer and terza rima. MLN 68 1953.

Evans, R. O. Some aspects of Wyatt's metrical technique. JEGP 53 1954.

Malone, K. Chaucer's double consonants and final e. Toronto Mediæval Stud 18 1956.

Harding, D. W. The rhythmical intention in Wyatt's poetry. Scrutiny 14 1957.

Baum, P. F. Chaucer's verse. Cambridge 1960.

Green, A. W. Chaucer's Sir Thopas: meter, rhyme and contrast. Mississippi Stud in Eng 1 1960.

— Meter and rhyme in Chaucer's Anelida and Arcite. Mississippi Stud in Eng 2 1961.

Manzalaoui, M. Lydgate and English prosody. Cairo Stud in Eng 1960.

Mumford, I. L. Sir Thomas Wyatt's verse and Italian musical sources. Eng Miscellany (Rome) 14 1963.

Schwartz, E. The meter of some poems of Wyatt. SP 60 1963.

Christophersen, P. The scansion of two lines in Chaucer. In English studies presented to R. W. Zandvoort, Amsterdam 1964.

Masui, M. The structure of Chaucer's rime words: an exploration into the poetic language of Chaucer. Tokyo 1964.

Halle, M. and S. J. Keyser. Chaucer and the study of prosody. College Eng Dec 1966.

Frankis, P. J. The syllabic value of final -es in English versification about 1500. N & Q Jan 1967.

Spina, E. Skeltonic meter in Elynour Rummyng. SP 64 1967.

Mustanoja, T. F. Chaucer's prosody. In Companion to Chaucer studies, ed B. Rowland, Oxford 1968.

Stanley, E. G. Stanza and ictus: Chaucer's emphasis in Troilus and Criseyde. In Chaucer und seine Zeit, ed. A. Esch, Tübingen 1968.

Sudo, J. Some specific rime-units in Chaucer. Stud in Eng Lit (Tokyo) 45 1969.

(5) MODERN ENGLISH

General Studies

Manwaring, E. Of harmony and numbers, in Latin and English prose, and in English poetry. 1744.

Mason, J. The power of numbers and the principle of harmony in poetic compositions. 1749; rev and rptd with a paper on prose rhythm as Two essays on the power of numbers, 1761.

Gray, T. Observations on English metre [1760]. In his Works, ed T. J. Mathias 1814.

Foster, J. An essay on the different nature of accent and quantity. Eton 1762.

Goldsmith, O. Essay on versification. Br Mag Jan 1763; rptd in his Works as no 18 of Miscellaneous essays.

Steele, J. An essay towards establishing the melody and measure of speech. 1775; rptd with addns as Prosodia rationalis, 1779.

Sayers, F. English metre. In his Disquisitions, 1793; rptd in his Poetic works, 1830.

Smith, A. Of the affinity between certain English and Italian verses. In his Essays of philosophical subjects, 1795.

Fogg, P. W. Dissertations grammatical and philological. In his Elementa anglicana, Stockport 1796. Nos 11–12.

Robertson, J. An essay on the nature of English verse. 1799.

Roe, R. B. The elements of English metre. 1801.

— The principles of rhythm both in speech and music, especially as exhibited in the mechanism of English verse. Dublin 1823.

Odell, J. An essay on the elements, accents and prosody of the English language. 1806.

Bryant, W. C. On the use of trisyllabic feet in iambic verse. North Amer Rev 9 1819; rptd with addns in Works vol 1, New York 1884.

Crowe, W. A treatise on English versification. 1827.

Humphrey, A. The English prosody; with rules deduced from the genius of our language and the examples of the poets. Boston 1847.

Malden, H. On Greek and English versification. Proc of Philological Soc 3 1847.

Everett, E. A system of English versification. New York 1848.

Poe, E. A. The rationale of verse. Southern Literary Messenger 14 1848.

Evans, R. W. A treatise on versification, ancient and modern. 1852.

Patmore, C. English metrical critics. North Br Rev 27 1857; rptd with slight changes as Prefatory study on English metrical law in Amelia, 1878.

Freeman-Mitford, J. T. F. Thoughts on prosody. Oxford 1859.

—— Further thoughts on prosody. Oxford 1859.

Barham, T. F. On metrical time, or the rhythm of verse, ancient and modern. Trans of Philological Soc 1861.

Brewer, R. F. A manual of English prosody. 1869; rptd with addns as Orthometry, 1893.

Wadham, E. English versification. 1869.

Sylvester, J. J. The laws of verse. 1870.

Ellis, A. J. On the physical constituents of accent and emphasis. Trans of Philological Soc 1874.

Mayor, J. B. Dr Guest and Dr Abbott on English metre. Ibid.

—— English metre; together with Mr A. J. Ellis's remarks on Prof Mayor's two papers on rhythm, an appendix by J. B. Mayor, and additional observations by A. J. Ellis. Trans of Philological Soc 1876.

—— English metre. Trans of Philological Soc 1877.

—— Chapters on English metre. Cambridge 1886.

—— A handbook of modern English metre. Cambridge 1903.

Conway, G. A treatise on versification. 1878.

Lanier, S. The science of English verse. Boston 1880.

Ruskin, J. Elements of English prosody. Orpington 1880.

Jenkin, F. Papers on metre. Saturday Rev Feb–March 1883; rptd in Memoir by R. L. Stevenson, Edinburgh 1887.

Stevenson, R. L. On style in literature: its technical elements. Contemporary Rev April 1885; rptd in his Essays in the art of writing, 1905.

[Blake, J. W.] Accent and rhythm explained by the law of mono-pressures. Edinburgh 1888.

Browne, W. H. Certain considerations touching the structure of English verse. MLN 4 1889.

Bateson, H. D. English rhythms. 1891.

—— An introduction to the study of English rhythms. Manchester 1904.

Parsons, J. C. English versification for the use of students. Boston 1891.

Corson, H. A primer of English verse. Boston 1892.

Humphreys, M. W. On the equivalence of rhythmical bars and metrical feet. Trans of Amer Philological Assoc 23 1892.

Bolton, T. L. Rhythm. Amer Jnl of Psychology 6 1894.

Larminie, W. The development of English metres. Contemporary Rev Nov 1894.

Omond, T. S. English verse-structure. Edinburgh 1897.

—— English prosody. GM Feb 1898.

—— English metrists, pt 1. Tunbridge Wells 1903.

—— A study of metre. 1903.

—— Metrical rhythm. Tunbridge Wells 1905.

—— English metrists in the eighteenth and nineteenth centuries. Oxford 1907. Pt 2 of English metrists, above; both pts rptd together, Oxford 1921.

—— Some thoughts about verse. 1923 (Eng Assoc lecture).

Lewis, C. M. The foreign sources of modern English versification. New York 1898.

—— The principles of English verse. New York 1906.

Thomson, W. The basis of English rhythm. Glasgow 1904.

—— The rôle of number in the rhythm of ancient and modern languages. 1907.

—— Rhythm and scansion. 1911.

—— Scansion and rhythm. 1913.

—— The laws of speech-rhythm. 1914.

—— The rhythm of speech. Glasgow 1923.

Luick, K. Englische Metrik. In Pauls Grundriss 2.2 1905.

Rudmose-Brown, T. B. Etude comparée de la versification française et de la versification anglaise. Grenoble 1905.

—— Verrier's Essai sur les principes de la métrique anglaise. MLR 6 1911.

—— English and French metric. MLR 8 1913, 10 1915.

—— The principles of English versification. Dublin Mag Sept 1930.

Andersen, J. C. Metre. Trans of New Zealand Inst 1908–11.

—— The laws of verse. Cambridge 1928.

Brown, W. Time in English verse rhythm. New York 1908.

—— Temporal and accentual rhythm. Univ of California Psychological Rev 18 1911.

Bridges, R. A letter to a musician on English prosody. Musical Antiquary 1 1909.

—— Letter on English prosody and note on neo-Miltonics. In his Collected essays, papers etc, Oxford 1927–30.

Verrier, P. Essai sur les principes de la métrique anglaise. 3 vols Paris 1909–10.

—— Questions de métrique anglaise. Paris 1912.

—— English metric. MLR 7 1912.

—— English and French metric. MLR 9 1914.

Woodraw, H. A quantitative study of rhythm. New York 1909.

Morton, E. P. The technique of English non-dramatic blank verse. Chicago 1910.

Skeat, W. W. On the scansion of English poetry. Trans of Philological Soc 1898.

Alden, R. M. The time element in English verse. MLN 14 1899.

—— The mental side of metrical form. MLR 9 1914.

Hurst, A. S. and J. McKay. Experiments on time relations of poetical metres. Univ of Toronto Stud in Psychology ser 3 1899.

Ker, W. P. Analogies between English and Spanish verse. Trans of Philological Soc 1899.

Harford, F. K. A note on the scansion of the pentameter. Oxford 1900.

Wallin, J. E. W. Researches on the rhythm of speech. Stud from Yale Psychological Laboratory 7 1901.

Bright, J. W. Concerning grammatical ictus in English verse. In An English miscellany presented to Dr [F. J.] Furnivall, Oxford 1901.

—— Rhythmic elements in English. Univ of Texas Bull 1 Jan 1917.

Squire, C. R. A genetic study of rhythm. Amer Jnl of Psychology 12 1901.

Triplett, N. and E. C. Sanford. Studies of rhythm and meter. Amer Jnl of Psychology 12 1901.

Liddell, M. H. An introduction to the scientific study of English poetry. New York 1902.

—— A brief extract of a new English prosody based upon the laws of English rhythm. Lafayette Ind 1914.

van Dam, B. A. P. and C. W. Stoffel. Chapters on English printing, prosody and pronunciation 1550–1700. Heidelberg 1902.

Newman, E. The rationale of English verse-rhythm. Weekly Critical Rev (Paris) 3–24 Sept 1903.

Johnson, C. F. Forms of English poetry. New York 1904.

Miller, R. D. Secondary accent in Modern English verse (Chaucer to Dryden). Baltimore 1904.

Scott, F. N. The most fundamental differentia of poetry and prose. PMLA 19 1904.

Matthews, B. A study of versification. Boston 1911.

MacColl, D. S. Rhythm in English verse, prose and speech. E & S 5 1914.

— Metre. Saturday Rev 6–13 Feb 1926. Reply by E. A. Sonnenschein 6 March 1926.

Odling, W. The technic of versification. Oxford 1916.

Bayfield, M. A. Our traditional prosody and an alternative. MLR 13 1918.

— The measures of the poets: a new system of English prosody. Cambridge 1919.

Crapsey, A. A study in English metrics. New York 1918.

Jacob, C. F. The foundations and nature of verse. New York 1918.

— Rhythm in prose and poetry. Quart Jnl of Speech 13 1927.

Snell, A. L. F. Pause: a study of its nature and its rhythmical function in verse, especially blank verse. Ann Arbor 1918.

Creek, H. L. Rising and falling rhythms in English verse. PMLA 35 1920.

Lowell, A. Some musical analogies in modern poetry. Musical Quart 6 1920.

Saintsbury, G. Some recent studies in English prosody. Proc Br Acad 9 1920.

Sapir, E. The musical foundations of verse. JEGP 20 1921.

Baum, P. F. The principles of English versification. Cambridge Mass 1922.

— Sprung rhythm. PMLA 74 1959.

Jones, L. A principle of prosody. Freeman 26 April 1922.

Lotspeitch, C. M. Poetry, prose and rhythm. PMLA 37 1922.

Russell, C. E. Principles of prosody. Freeman 5 July 1922. Reply by L. Jones 30 Aug 1922.

Stewart, G. R. Modern metrical technique as illustrated by ballad meter 1700–1920. New York 1922.

— A method toward the study of dipodic verse. PMLA 39 1924.

— The meter of the popular ballad. PMLA 40 1925.

— The iambic trochaic theory in relation to musical notation of verse. JEGP 24 1925.

— The technique of English verse. New York 1930.

Strunk, W. English meters. Ithaca 1922.

Abercrombie, L. Principles of English prosody. 1923.

Croll, M. W. Music and metrics: a reconsideration. SP 20 1923.

— The rhythm of English verse. Princeton 1925.

— Style, rhetoric and rhythm. Princeton 1966.

Smith, E. The principles of English metre. Oxford 1923.

Blümel, R. Die Rhytmusarten. Pauls und Braunes Beiträge 48 1924.

Grew, S. A book of English prosody. 1924.

Hall, W. C. Rhythm. Manchester Quart 50 1924.

— Blank verse. Manchester Quart 51 1925.

Robertson, J. M. The evolution of English blank verse. Criterion Feb 1924.

Sonnenschein, E. A. What is blank verse? Contemporary Rev Dec 1924.

— What is rhythm? Oxford 1925.

Arnell, C. J. The art and practice of versification. Exeter 1925.

Legouis, E. A short parallel between French and English versification. 1925 (MHRA Presidential Address).

Morris, A. R. The orchestration of the metrical line: an analytical study of rhythmical form. Boston 1925.

— Liddell's laws of English rhythm. Papers of Michigan Acad of Science, Art & Letters 22 1937.

Routh, J. E. English iambic meter. PMLA 40 1925.

— The theory of verse. Atlanta 1948.

Scott, J. H. Rhythmic verse. Iowa City 1925.

Scripture, E. W. Das Wesen des Verses. In Festschrift für K. Luick, Marburg 1925.

— The choriambus in English verse. PMLA 43 1928.

— Grundzüge der englischen Verswissenschaft. Marburg 1929.

— Besondere Betonungen im englischen Vers. Anglia 55 1931.

Welch, C. Some experimental work in speech-rhythm. Quart Jnl of Speech 11 1925.

Whitmore, C. E. A proposed compromise in metrics. PMLA 41 1926.

Douady, J. La prosodie anglaise. Paris 1928.

Young, G. An English prosody on inductive lines. Cambridge 1928.

Gibbon, J. M. The influence of music on metre. Trans of Royal Soc of Canada 23 1929.

Taig, T. Rhythm and metre. Cardiff 1929.

Wilson, K. M. The real rhythm in English poetry. Aberdeen 1929.

Fairclough, H. R. The influence of Virgil upon the forms of English verse. Classical Jnl 26 1930.

Hamer, E. The metres of English poetry. 1930.

Thieme, H. P. Rhythm. In Mélanges Baldensperger vol 2, Paris 1930.

Timberlake, P. W. The feminine ending in English blank verse in the drama up to 1595. Menasha 1931.

Trevelyan, R. C. Classical and English verse-structure. E & S 16 1931.

Buchanan, V. Versification. Eng Jnl 22 1933.

de Groot, A. W. Le mètre et le rythme du vers. Journal de Psychologie 30 1933.

Jespersen, O. Notes on metre. In his Linguistica, Copenhagen 1933; rptd in Essays on the language of literature, ed S. Chatman and S. R. Levin, New York 1967.

Mégroz, R. L. Modern English poetry 1882–1932: technical developments. 1933.

Sasaki, T. Apocope in Modern English verse. Stud in Eng Lit (Tokyo) 13 1933.

Barkas, P. A critique of Modern English prosody 1880–1930. Studien zur Englischen Philologie 82 1934.

Eichler, A. Taktumstellung und schwebende Betonung. Archiv 165 1934.

Norrie, G. Metrisk statistik: fuldstændige og over-fuldstændige former af den femfodede jambe. Danske Studier 1934.

Richter, W. Der Hiatus im englischen Klassizismus (Milton, Dryden, Pope). Schramberg 1934.

Schramm, W. L. Time and intensity in English tetrameter verse. PQ 13 1934.

— Approaches to a science of English verse. Iowa City 1935.

Allen, G. W. American prosody. New York 1935.

Leathes, S. Rhythm in English poetry. 1935.

Stephens, W. H. The stroke-flick structure of English verse. Poetry Rev Feb 1935.

— Discipline in pattern for English verse. Poetry Rev April 1935.

— New measures in English verse. Poetry Rev June 1935.

— Four-time in English verse. Poetry Rev July, Sept 1937.

Bontoux, G. La chanson en Angleterre au temps d'Elisabeth. Paris 1936.

Fogerty, E. Rhythm. Proc of Second International Congress of Phonetic Sciences 1936.

Hendren, J. W. A study of ballad rhythm, with special reference to ballad music. Princeton 1936.

— Time and stress in English verse; with special reference to Lanier's theory of rhythm. Houston 1959.

—, W. K. Wimsatt and M. C. Beardsley. A word for rhythm and a word for meter. PMLA 76 1961.

Winters, Y. The influence of meter on poetic convention. In his Primitivism and decadence, New York 1937.

Olson, E. General prosody. Chicago 1938.

Pyle, F. The rhythms of the English heroic line: an essay in empirical analysis. Hermathena 28 1939.

— Pyrrhic and spondee: speech stress and metrical accent in English five-foot iambic verse structure. Hermathena 57 1968.

Anderson, J. R. The principle of uniformity in English metre. Durham Univ Jnl 2–3 1940–1.

Gordon, R. Verse and prose technique: a study in rhythm and tone color. New York 1940.

Macdermott, M. M. Vowel sounds in poetry. 1940.

Atkins, H. G. Holding down the trochees. MLR 37 1942.

Eliot, T. S. The music of poetry. Glasgow 1942; rptd in his On poetry and poets, 1957.

Ghiselin, B. Pæonic measures in English verse. MLN 57 1942.

Pyles, T. A new meteorological theory of stress. MLN 60 1945.

Bracher, F. The silent foot in pentameter verse. PMLA 62 1947.

Shapiro, K. English prosody and modern poetry. ELH 14 1947; Baltimore 1947.

—— Prosody as the meaning. Poetry 73 1949.

—— and R. Beum. A prosody handbook. 1965.

Scholl, E. H. English meter once more. PMLA 63 1948.

Cejp, L. Několik slov o rytmu anglického verše. Časopis pro Moderní Filologii 33 1950. On English verse rhythm. In Czech.

Clark, R. W. Some remarks on verse techniques. Poet Lore 56 1951.

Ing, C. M. Elizabethan lyrics: a study of the development of English metres and their relation to poetic effect. 1951.

Patmore, D. Three poets discuss new verse forms: the correspondence of Gerard Manley Hopkins, Robert Bridges and Coventry Patmore. Month Aug 1951.

Blackmur, R. P. Lord Tennyson's scissors 1912–50. Kenyon Rev 14 1952. On modern prosody.

Burklund, C. E. Melody in verse. Quart Jnl of Speech 39 1953.

Fussell, P. A note on Samuel Johnson and the rise of accentual prosodic theory. PQ 33 1954.

—— The meter-making argument. In Essays presented to Howard Mumford Jones, Columbus 1962.

—— Poetic meter and poetic form. New York 1965.

Hamm, V. M. Meter and meaning. PMLA 69 1954.

Kenner, H. A plea for metrics. Poetry 86 1955.

Hemphill, G. Accent, stress and emphasis. College Eng March 1956.

—— The meters of the intermediate poets. Kenyon Rev 19 1957.

Ransom, J. C. The strange music of English verse. Kenyon Rev 18 1956.

Stein, A. A note on meter. Ibid.

Whitehall, H. From linguistics to criticism. Ibid.

Levý, J. Slovo a mluvní takt v anglickém verši. Sbornik Vysoké Školy Pedegogické v Olomouci 4 1957. 'Measure' in English verse. In Czech.

—— A contribution to the typology of accentual-syllabic versification. Poetics 1 1962.

Dudek, L. A note on metrics. Delta Oct 1958.

Schlauch, M. Zarys wersyfikacji angielskieij. Breslau 1958. An outline of English versification. In Polish.

Sutherland, R. Structural linguistics and English prosody. College Eng Oct 1958.

Whiteley, M. Verse and its feet. RES new ser 9 1958. Replies by E. Schanzer 10 1959, M. Whiteley, J. Buxton and Schanzer 10 1959.

Epstein, E. A. and T. Hawkes. Linguistics and English prosody. Stud in Linguistics, Occasional Papers 7 1959.

Smith, H. L. Towards redefining English prosody. Stud in Linguistics 14 1959.

Wimsatt, W. K. and M. C. Beardsley. The concept of meter: an exercise in abstraction. PMLA 74 1959; rptd in Essays on the language of literature, ed S. Chatman and S. R. Levin, Boston 1967.

Chatman, S. Comparing metrical styles. In Style in language, ed T. A. Sebeok, Cambridge Mass 1960; rptd in Essays on the language of literature, ed Chatman and S. R. Levin, Boston 1967.

—— A theory of meter. Janua Linguarum ser minor 36 1965.

Jakobson, R. Linguistics and poetics. In Style and language, ed T. A. Sebeok, Cambridge Mass 1960.

Lewis, C. S. Metre. REL 1 1960; rptd in his Selected literary essays, Cambridge 1969.

Lotz, J. Metric typology. In Style in language, ed T. A. Sebeok, Cambridge Mass 1960.

Kökeritz, H. Elizabethan prosody and historical phonology. Annales Academiæ Regiæ Scientiarum Upsaliensis 5 1961.

Pace, G. B. The two domains: meter and rhythm. PMLA 76 1961.

Thompson, J. The founding of English metre. 1961.

—— Linguistic structure and the poetic line. Poetics 1 1962.

Empson, W. Rhythm and imagery in English poetry. Br Jnl of Aesthetics 2 1962.

Halpern, M. On the two chief metrical modes in English. PMLA 77 1962.

Hammond, M. A new theory of meter. Sewanee Rev 70 1962.

Hawkes, T. The problems of prosody. REL 3 1962.

—— The matter of metre. EC 12 1962. Reply by F. W. B[ateson], ibid.

—— The matter of metre. EC 13 1963. Reply by F. W. Bateson, ibid.

—— New prosodists for old? EC 16 1966.

Hollander, J. Experimental and pseudo-experimental metrics in recent American poetry. Poetics 1 1962.

Levin, S. R. Suprasegmentals and the performance of poetry. Quart Jnl of Speech 48 1962.

Raith, J. Englische Metrik. Munich 1962.

Schwartz, E. Rhythm and 'exercises in abstraction'. PMLA 77 1962. Replies by W. K. Wimsatt and M. C. Beardsley, ibid.

—— Rhythm and meaning in English verse. Criticism 6 1964.

Taylor, C. R. Developments in English prosody. Revue de l'Université de Sherbrooke (Quebec) 4 1962.

Gross, G. The æsthetic function of prosody. Centennial Rev of Arts & Science 7 1963.

Gross, H. S. Sound and form in modern poetry: a study of prosody from Thomas Hardy to Robert Lowell. Ann Arbor 1964.

—— (ed). The structure of verse: modern essays in prosody. Greenwich Conn 1966.

Kurath, H. A phonology and prosody of Modern English. Heidelberg 1964.

Malof, J. The native rhythm of English meters. Texas Stud in Lit & Lang 5 1964.

—— The artifice of scansion. Eng Jnl 54 1965.

Nist, J. The word-group cadence: basis of English metrics. Linguistics 6 1964.

Ridland, J. M. The matter of metre. EC 14 1964. Reply by F. W. Bateson, ibid.

Abercrombie, D. A phonetician's view of verse structure. Linguistics 6 1964; rptd in his Studies in phonetics and linguistics, Oxford 1965.

—— Syllable quantity and enclitics in English. In In honour of Daniel Jones, 1964; rptd in his Studies in phonetics and linguistics, Oxford 1965.

Brown, C. S. Can musical notation help English scansion? Jnl of Aesthetics 23 1965.

Coffin, T. P. Remarks preliminary to a study of ballad meter and ballad singing. Jnl of Amer Folklore 78 1965.

Mussulman, J. S. A descriptive system of musical prosody. Centennial Rev of Arts & Science 9 1965.

Perry, J. O. The relationships between rhythm and meaning. Criticism 7 1965. Reply by E. Schwartz, ibid.

Schneider, E. W. Sprung rhythm: a chapter in the evolution of nineteenth-century verse. PMLA 80 1965.

Towner, A. E. Welsh bardic meters and English poetry. Massachusetts Rev 6 1965.

Fowler, R. 'Prose rhythm' and metre. In his Essays on style and language, 1966.

—— Structural metrics. Linguistics 27 1966; rptd in Essays on the language of literature, ed S. Chatman and S. R. Levin, Boston 1967.

—— What is metrical analysis? Anglia 86 1968.

Kuryłowicz, J. Accent and quantity as elements of rhythm. Poetics 2 1966.

McAuley, J. P. Versification: a short introduction. East Lansing 1966.

—— A primer of English versification. Sydney 1966.

—— Metrical accent and speech stress. Balcony 4 1966.

Minaishi, F. Notes on metre. Onsei no Kenkyū 12 1966.

Tatsuma, M. Rhythm patterns in English poetry: its variety and classification. Ibid.

Cummings, D. W. and J. Herum. Metrical boundaries and rhythm-phrases. MLQ 28 1967.

Lightfoot, M. J. Prosody and performance. Quart Jnl of Speech 53 1967.

Tarlinskaya, M. G. Aktsentiye osobennosti angliiskogo sillabotonischeskogo stikha. Voprosy Yazykoznaniya 3 1967. Peculiarities of syllabo-tonic verse. In Russian.

Beaver, J. C. A grammar of prosody. College Eng Jan 1968.

—— Contrastive stress and metered verse. Lang & Style 2 1969.

Freeman, D. C. On the primes of metrical style. Lang & Style 1 1968.

—— Metrical position constituency and generative metrics. Lang & Style 2 1969.

Guillaume, G. Le verbe, la phrase et les vers. Vol 2 of his Récréations et recherches linguistiques et stylistiques, Paris 1968.

Hascall, D. L. Some contributions to the Halle-Keyser theory of prosody. College Eng Feb 1969.

Herdan, G. The mathematical theory of verse. Zeitschrift für Phonetik, Sprachwissenschaft und Kommunikationsforschung 22 1969.

Spangenberg, D. F. Enjambement en voordrag. Tydskrif vir Letterkunde 7 1969.

Malof, J. A manual of English meters. Bloomington 1970.

Stanza Form

Morton, E. P. The Spenserian stanza before 1700. MP 4 1907.

—— The Spenserian stanza in the eighteenth century. MP 10 1913.

Cohen, H. L. The ballade. New York 1915.

Bullock, W. L. The genesis of the English sonnet form. PMLA 38 1923.

Pope, E. F. The critical background of the Spenserian stanza. MP 24 1926.

Ruhrmann, F. G. Studien zur Geschichte und Charakteristik des Refrains in der englischen Literatur. Heidelberg 1927.

Oliphant, E. H. C. Sonnet structure: an analysis. PQ 11 1932.

Wallerstein, R. C. The development of the rhetoric and metre of the heroic couplet, especially in 1625-45. PMLA 50 1935.

Thompson, E. N. S. The octosyllabic couplet. PQ 18 1939.

Binyon, L. Terza rima in English poetry. English 3 1940.

Wain, J. Terza rima: a foot note on English prosody. Rivista di Letterature Moderne 1 1950.

Levý, J. On the relation of language and stanza pattern in the English sonnet. In Worte und Werte: Bruno Markwardt zum 60 Geburtstag, Berlin 1961.

Boswell, G. W. Stanza form and music-imposed scansion in southern ballads. Southern Folklore Quart 31 1967.

Piper, W. B. The inception of the closed heroic couplet. MP 66 1969.

—— The heroic couplet. Cleveland 1969.

Rhyme, Assonance, Alliteration

Scott, F. N. Vowel alliteration in MnE. MLN 30 1915.

Smith, G. C. M. The use of an unstressed extra-metrical syllable to carry the rime. MLR 15 1920.

Wyld, H. C. Studies in English rhymes from Surrey to Pope. 1923.

Blümel, R. Bedingungen für den Reim. Pauls und Braunes Beiträge 48 1924.

Lanz, H. The physical basis of rime. PMLA 41 1926.

—— The physical basis of rime: an essay on the æsthetics of sound. 1931.

Colum, P. Assonance in English verse. Forum 94 1935.

Schramm, W. L. A characteristic of rime. PMLA 50 1935.

Stephens, W. H. Alliteration in strokes. Poetry Rev Aug 1935.

Herbert, T. W. Near-rhimes and paraphones. Sewanee Rev 45 1937.

Koziol, H. Die Alliteration in der modernen englischen Dichtung. Archiv 184 1943.

Simpson, P. The rhyming of stressed with unstressed syllables in Elizabethan verse. MLR 38 1943.

Shapiro, K. Essay on rime. New York 1945.

Ingalls, J. Chromatic rhyme. Word Study 25 1949.

Bullitt, J. M. The use of rhyme link in the sonnets of Sidney, Drayton and Spenser. JEGP 49 1950.

Draper, J. W. The origin of rhyme. Revue de Littérature Comparée 31 1957.

Kirchner, G. Der Reimklang im Englischen (Nachträge). Zeitschrift für Anglistik und Amerikanistik 7 1959.

Miller, E. S. Rime counterpoint. Annali Istituto Universario Orientale, Napoli, Sezione Germanica 2 1959.

Free Verse

Eliot, T. S. Reflections on vers libre. New Statesman 3 March 1917; rptd in his To criticize the critic, 1965.

Andrews, C. E. The rhythm of prose and of free verse. Sewanee Rev 26 1918.

Lowell, A. The rhythms of free verse. Dial 17 Jan 1918.

van Doorn, W. Vers libre in theory and practice. E Studies 3 1921.

Baldwin, C. S. Which verse is free? Literary Rev 14 Oct 1922.

Bridges, R. Humdrum and harum-scarum: a lecture on free verse. London Mercury Nov 1922, North Amer Rev 216 1922; rptd in his Collected essays, papers etc, Oxford 1927-36.

Maynard, T. The fallacy of free verse. Yale Rev 11 1922.

Burdett, O. Vers libre. New Statesman 20 Jan 1923.

Coppard, A. E. and R. E. Jarvis. Free verse. Mercury Jan 1923.

Hills, E. C. Meter in Anglo-American free verse. Univ of California Chron July 1924.

Allen, C. Cadenced free verse. College Eng Jan 1948.

Folk, B. N. Modern verse: not blank but not free. Classical Weekly Sept 1955.

Hough, G. Free verse. Proc Br Acad 44 1958.

Hrushovski, B. On free rhythms in modern poetry. In Style in language, ed T. A. Sebeok, Cambridge Mass 1960.

Coetzee, A. J. Die ritme van die 'vrye vers': 'n tentatiewe benadering. Standpunte 82 1969.

Quantitative and Syllabic Verse

An introduction of the ancient Greek and Latin measures into British poetry. 1737.

Tillbrook, S. Historical and critical remarks upon the modern hexametrists. Cambridge 1822.

Oxenford, J. The practice of writing English in classical metres. Classical Museum 3 1846.

Cayley, C. B. Remarks and experiments on English hexameters. Trans of Philological Soc 1863.

Monro, C. J. Latin metres in English. Jnl of Philology 4 1872.

Goodell, T. D. Quantity in English verse. Trans of Amer Philological Assoc 16 1885.

Omond, T. S. English hexameters. Edinburgh 1897.

Stone, W. J. On the use of classical metres in English. Oxford 1899; rptd with R. Bridges, Milton's prosody, Oxford 1901.

McKerrow, R. B. The use of so-called classical metres in Elizabethan verse. MLQ 4–5 1901–2.

Snell, A. L. F. An objective study of syllabic quantity in English verse. PMLA 34 1920.

Inge, W. R. Classical metres in English poetry. Essays by Divers Hands 2 1922.

Hollowell, B. M. Elizabethan hexametrists. PQ 3 1924.

Willcock, G. D. Passing pitefull hexameters: a study in quantity and accent in English Renaissance verse. MLR 29 1934.

Hendrickson, G. L. Elizabethan quantitative hexameters. PQ 28 1949.

Hunter, G. K. The English hexameter and the Elizabethan madrigal. PQ 32 1953.

Beum, R. Syllabic verse in English. Prairie Schooner 31 1957.

Baker, S. English meter *is* quantitative. College Eng March 1960.

Allen, W. S. On quantity and quantitative verse. In Papers in honour of Daniel Jones, 1964.

Ghose, Z. A defence of syllabics. TLS 16 Jan 1964. With ensuing correspondence.

Studies of Individual Authors and Works

Forde, W. The true spirit of Milton's versification. 1831.

Walker, W. S. On Shakespeare's versification. 1854.

Bathurst, C. Remarks on the differences in Shakespeare's versification in different periods of his life. 1857.

Abbott, E. A. A Shakespearian grammar. 1869, 1870 (rev).

Symonds, J. A. The blank verse of Milton. Fortnightly Rev Dec 1874; rptd in his Sketches and studies in Italy, 1879, and in his Blank verse, 1895.

Browne, G. H. Notes on Shakspere's versification. Boston 1884.

Bridges, R. Milton's prosody. In his edn of Milton, Oxford 1887; rev and pbd separately, 1889; rptd with W. J. Stone, On the use of classical metres in English, Oxford 1901.

Mead, W. E. The versification of Pope in its relation to the seventeenth century. Leipzig 1889.

Bateson, H. D. The rhythm of Coleridge's Christabel. Manchester Quart 13 1894; rptd with addns, Manchester 1904.

van Dam, B. A. P. and C. W. Stoffel. Shakespeare: prosody and text. Leyden 1900.

Brown, G. D. Syllabification and accent in the Paradise lost. Baltimore 1901.

van Dam, B. A. P. Robert Bridges, Milton's prosody and William Johnson Stone: classical metres in English verse. E Studien 32 1903.

Thomas, W. Milton's heroic line viewed from an historical viewpoint. MLR 2–3 1907–8.

[Eliot, T. S.] Ezra Pound: his metric and poetry. New York 1917; rptd in his To criticize the critic, 1965.

— A note on the verse of John Milton. E & S 21 1935.

Bayfield, M. A. Shakespeare's versification and the early texts. TLS 13 June 1918.

— A study of Shakespeare's versification. Cambridge 1920.

Pyre, J. F. A. The formation of Tennyson's style: a study, primarily of the versification of the early poems. Madison 1921.

Erskine, J. Whitman's prosody. SP 20 1923.

Shipley, J. T. Spenserian prosody: the couplet forms. SP 21 1924.

Banks, T. H. Miltonic rhythm. PMLA 42 1927.

Lindsay, J. The metric of William Blake. In his Poetical sketches by Blake, 1927.

Lotspeich, C. M. The metrical element of Pope's illustrative couplets. JEGP 26 1927.

Scripture, E. W. Der Lear-Vers oder der englische Dochmius. Anglia 51 1927.

— Die Versformen in Mother Goose. Anglia 54 1930.

Hatcher, H. H. The versification of Robert Browning. Columbus 1928.

Snell, A. L. F. The meter of Christabel. In Fred Newton Scott anniversary papers, Chicago 1929.

Boas, C. The metre of the Testament of beauty. London Mercury June 1930.

Wyld, H. C. Observations on Pope's versification. MLR 25 1930.

Hickson, E. C. The versification of Thomas Hardy. Philadelphia 1931.

Werner, W. L. Pope's theories and practice in poetic technique. Amer Lit 2 1931.

Woody, L. Masefield's use of dipodic meter. PQ 10 1931.

Franz, W. Shakespeares Blankvers. Tübingen 1932, 1935 (rev).

Weaver, B. Shelley works out the rhythm of A lament. PMLA 47 1932.

Pettigrew, R. C. Poe's rime. Amer Lit 4 1933.

Propst, L. An analytical study of Shelley's versification. Iowa City 1933.

Diekhoff, J. S. Rhyme in Paradise lost. PMLA 49 1934.

— Terminal pause in Milton's verse. SP 32 1935.

— Milton's prosody in the poems of the Trinity ms. PMLA 54 1939.

Leavis, F. R. Milton's verse. Scrutiny 2 1934.

Bradley, S. The fundamental principle in Whitman's poetry. Amer Lit 10 1939.

Smith, F. M. Mrs Browning's rhymes. PMLA 54 1939.

Stein, A. Donne and the couplet. PMLA 57 1942.

— Donne's prosody. PMLA 59 1944.

— Donne's prosody. Kenyon Rev 18 1956. Reply by S. Chatman, ibid.

— George Herbert's prosody. Lang & Style 1 1968.

Purcell, J. M. Rime in Paradise lost. MLN 59 1944.

Short, R. W. The metrical theory and practice of Thomas Campion. PMLA 59 1944.

Holloway, M. M. The prosodic theory of Gerard Manley Hopkins. Washington 1947.

Hunter, W. B. The sources of Milton's prosody. PQ 28 1949.

Havens, R. P. Structure and prosodic pattern in Shelley's lyrics. PMLA 65 1950.

Moloney, M. F. Donne's metrical practice. PMLA 65 1950.

— The prosody of Milton's Epitaph, L'allegro and Il penseroso. MLN 72 1957.

Welland, D. S. R. Half-rhyme in Wilfrid Owen: its derivation and use. RES new ser 1 1950.

Wilcox, S. C. The prosodic structure of Ode to the west wind. N & Q 18 Feb 1950.

Pitchford, L. W. The curtal sonnets of Gerard Manley Hopkins. MLN 67 1952.

Kellogg, G. A. Bridges' Milton's prosody and Renaissance metrical theory. PMLA 68 1953.

Kermode, F. Samson Agonistes and Hebrew prosody. Durham Univ Jnl 14 1953.

Oras, A. Metre and chronology in Milton's Epitaph on the Marchioness of Winchester, L'allegro and Il penseroso. N & Q Aug 1953.

— Milton's early rhyme schemes and the structure of Lycidas. MP 52 1954.

— Intensified rhyme links in the Faerie Queene: an aspect of Elizabethan rhymecraft. JEGP 54 1955.

— Blank verse and chronology in Milton. Gainesville 1966.

Sprott, S. E. Milton's art of prosody. Oxford 1953.

Prince, F. T. The Italian element in Milton's verse. Oxford 1954.

Applegate, J. Sidney's classical meters. MLN 70 1955.

Simpson, P. Shakespeare's versification: a study of development. In his Studies in Elizabethan drama, Oxford 1955.

Watkins, W. B. C. An anatomy of Milton's verse. Baton Rouge 1955.

Chatman, S. Robert Frost's Mowing: an inquiry into prosodic structure. Kenyon Rev 18 1956.

Fletcher, H. F. A possible origin of Milton's 'counterpoint' or double rhythm. JEGP 55 1956.

Whaler, J. Counterpoint and symbol: an inquiry into the rhythm of Milton's epic style. Copenhagen 1956.

Burke, F. Metrical roughness in Marston's formal satire. Washington 1957.

Hemphill, G. Dryden's heroic line. PMLA 72 1957.

Bludau, D. Sonettstruktur bei Samuel Daniel. Shakespeare Jahrbuch 114 1958.

Standop, E. Bemerkungen zu einer neuen Verslehre mit Analyse von East Coker iv. Anglia 76 1958.

Levy, J. Rhythmical ambivalence in the poetry of T. S. Eliot. Anglia 77 1959.

Mooney, S. Hopkins and counterpoint. Victorian Newsletter no 18 1960.

Manierre, W. R. Versification and imagery in the Fall of Hyperion. Texas Stud in Lit & Lang 3 1961.

Beum, R. The rhyme in Samson Agonistes. Texas Stud in Lit & Lang 4 1962.

— Some observations on Spenser's verse forms. Neuphilologische Mitteilungen 64 1963.

Maveety, S. R. Versification in the Steele glas. SP 60 1963.

Adler, J. H. The reach of art: a study of the prosody of Pope. Gainesville 1964.

Pierson, R. M. The metre of the Listeners. E Studies 45 1964.

Hewitt, E. K. Structure and meaning in T. S. Eliot's Ash Wednesday. Anglia 83 1965.

Ostriker, A. Vision and verse in William Blake. Madison 1965.

— The three modes in Tennyson's prosody. PMLA 82 1967.

Evans, R. O. Milton's elisions. Gainesville 1966.

Wheeler, T. Milton's blank verse couplets. JEGP 66 1967.

Adams, P. G. Pope's concern with assonance. Texas Stud in Lit & Lang 9 1968.

Low, A. A metrical device in the Exequy. MLR 63 1968.

Sipe, D. L. Shakespeare's metrics. 1968.

Mitchell, R. A prosody for Whitman? PMLA 84 1969.

(6) PROSE RHYTHM

Manwaring, E. Of harmony and numbers, in Latin and English prose and in English poetry. 1744.

Mason, J. The power and harmony of prosaic numbers. 1749; rev and rptd with a paper on prosody as Two essays on the power of numbers, 1761.

Steele, J. An essay towards establishing the melody and measure of speech. 1775; rptd with adds as Prosodia rationalis, 1779.

Marbe, K. Über den Rhythmus der Prosa. Giessen 1904.

Scott, F. N. The scansion of prose-rhythm. PMLA 20 1905.

— The accentual structure of isolable English phrases. PMLA 333 1918.

Ritter, O. Rhythmische Prosa im englischen Schauspiel. Archiv 117 1906.

Lipsky, A. Rhythm as a distinguishing characteristic of prose style. New York 1907.

Western, A. On sentence-rhythm and word-order in Modern English. Christiania 1908.

Fijn van Draat, P. Rhythm in English prose. Heidelberg 1910.

— Rhythm in English prose. Anglia 36 1912.

— The place of the adverb: a study in rhythm. Neophilologus 6 1920.

Franz, W. Zum Prosarhythmus im Englischen. Zeitschrift für Französischen und Englischen Unterricht 10 1911.

Shelly, J. Rhythmical prose in Latin and English. Church Quart Rev 74 1912.

Clark, A. C. Prose-rhythm in English. Oxford 1913.

Elton, O. English prose numbers. E & S 4 1913; rptd in his A sheaf of papers, Liverpool 1922.

MacColl, D. S. Rhythm in English verse, prose and speech. E & S 5 1914.

Gropp, F. Zur Ästhetik und statistischen Beschreibung des Prosarhythmus. Würzburg 1915.

Patterson, W. M. The rhythm of prose. Columbia Univ Stud in Eng & Comparative Lit 1916.

Foster, F. M. K. Cadence in English prose. JEGP 16 1917.

Savage, O. M. Rhythm in prose. 1917.

Andrews, C. E. The rhythm of prose and of free verse. Sewanee Rev 26 1918.

Croll, M. W. The cadence of English oratorical prose. SP 16 1919.

Lotspeitch, C. M. Poetry, prose and rhythm. PMLA 37 1922.

Routh, J. E. Prose rhythms. PMLA 38 1923.

Gerould, G. H. Abbot Ælfric's rhythmic prose. MP 22 1925.

Parrish, W. M. The rhythm of oratorical prose. In Studies in honor of James Albert Winans, New York 1925.

Scott, J. H. Rhythmic prose. Iowa City 1925.

— and Z. E. Chandler. Phrasal patterns in English prose. New York 1932.

Jacob, C. F. Rhythm in prose and poetry. Quart Jnl of Speech 13 1927.

Tempest, N. R. Rhythm in the prose of Sir Thomas Browne. RES 3 1927.

— The rhythm of English prose. Cambridge 1930.

Griffith, H. Time patterns in prose. Princeton 1929.

Chambers, R. W. On the continuity of English prose. In Harpsfield's Life of More, 1931 (EETS); rptd separately, 1932, Oxford 1957.

Hayes, J. J. The rhythm of prose. Eng Jnl 25 1936.

Clough, W. O. The rhythm of prose. Univ of Wyoming Pbns 4 1936.

Classe, A. The rhythm of English prose. Oxford 1939.

Gordon, R. Verse and prose technique: a study in rhythm and tone color. New York 1940.

McIntosh, A. Wulfstan's prose. Proc Br Acad 34 1948.

Emden, C. S. Rhythmical features in Dr Johnson's prose style. RES 25 1949.

Schlauch, M. Chaucer's prose rhythms. PMLA 65 1950.

Baum, P. F. The other harmony of prose. Cambridge Mass 1952.

Cooper, L. Certain rhythms in the English Bible. Ithaca 1952.

Morgan, M. M. A treatise in cadence. MLR 47 1952.

Boulton, M. The anatomy of prose. 1954.

Dahl, T. Alliteration in English prose. E Studies 40 1959.

Moloney, M. F. Meter and cursus in Sir Thomas Browne's prose. JEGP 58 1959.

Wilson, R. M. On the continuity of English prose. In Mélanges Fernand Mossé, Paris 1959.

Funke, O. Studien zur alliterierenden und rhythmischen Prosa in der ältern altenglischen Homiletik. Anglia 80 1962.

— Some remarks on Wulfstan's prose rhythm. E Studies 43 1962.

Fowler, R. 'Prose rhythm' and metre. In his Essays on style and language, 1966.

Gordon, I. A. The movement of English prose. 1966.

Lipp, F. R. Ælfric's Old English prose style. SP 66 1969.

A. J. B.

IV. LANGUAGE

A. GENERAL WORKS

(1) BIBLIOGRAPHIES

Gesellschaft für Deutsche Philologie in Berlin. Jahresbericht über die Erscheinungen auf dem Gebiete der germanischen Philologie 1879–. Berlin 1880–. Later pbd by the Deutsche Akademie der Wissenschaften zu Berlin.

Modern Language Association of America. American bibliography. 1921–; International bibliography, vol 3: Linguistics 1969– pbd in General Linguistics 10 1970–.

Horn, W. Die englische Sprachwissenschaft. In Stand und Aufgaben der Sprachwissenschaft: Festschrift für Wilhelm Streitberg, Heidelberg 1924.

—— Englische Sprachforschung. In Germanische Philologie: Festschrift für O. Behagel, Heidelberg 1934.

Kennedy, A. G. A bibliography of writings on the English language from the beginning of printing to the end of 1922. Cambridge Mass 1927.

Comité International Permanent de Linguistes: Permanent International Committee of Linguists. Bibliographie linguistique: linguistic bibliography. Vols 1–2 (1939–47), Utrecht 1949–50; annually thereafter. In progress.

Funke, O. Englische Sprachkunde: ein Überblick ab 1935. Berne 1950.

—— Altenglische Wortgeographie: eine bibliographische Überschau. In Anglistische Studien: Festschrift zum 70 Geburtstag von Friedrich Wild, Vienna 1958.

Stroh, F. Handbuch der germanischen Philologie. Berlin 1952.

Marquardt, H. Bibliographie der Runeninschriften nach Fundorten: erster Teil, die Runeninschriften der britischen Inseln. Göttingen 1961.

Gipper, H. and H. Schwartz. Bibliographisches Handbuch zur Sprachinhaltsforschung. Cologne 1962–. In progress; 1: Schrifttum zur Sprachinhaltsforschung in alphabetischer Folge nach Verfassern mit Besprechungen und Inhaltshinweisen, to pt 14 *Knutsson* 1971.

Scheurweghs, G. Analytical bibliography of writings on Modern English morphology and syntax 1877–1960. 4 vols Louvain 1963–8.

Alston, R. C. A bibliography of the English language from the invention of printing to the year 1800. Leeds 1965–. In progress.

Butte, B. and K. Hansen. Bibliographie sowjetischer Veröffentlichungen zur englischen Sprache 1955–65. Zeitschrift für Anglistik und Amerikanistik 14–20 1966–72.

Bailey, R. W. and D. M. Burton. English stylistics: a bibliography. Cambridge Mass 1968.

(2) DICTIONARIES

General; Modern English

Murray, J. A. H., H. Bradley, W. A. Craigie and C. T. Onions. A new English dictionary on historical principles. 10 vols Oxford 1884–1928; Introduction, supplement and bibliography, Oxford 1933; corrected re-issue as The Oxford English dictionary, with introduction, supplement and bibliography, 13 vols Oxford 1933.

Wright, J. The English dialect dictionary. 6 vols Oxford 1896–1905.

Skeat, W. W. A glossary of Tudor and Stuart words. Ed A. L. Mayhew, Oxford 1914.

Holthausen, F. Etymologisches Wörterbuch der englischen Sprache. Göttingen 1917, 1949 (rev).

Craigie, W. A. and A. J. Aitken. A dictionary of the older Scottish tongue from the twelfth century to the end of the seventeenth. Oxford and Chicago 1931– (from 1970 pbd Chicago only). To pt 25 *natural* (1) 1971; in progress.

Grant, W. and D. D. Murison. The Scottish national dictionary. Edinburgh 1931–. To pt 9.2 *teth* 1972; in progress.

Wyld, H. C. The universal dictionary of the English language. 1932, 1952 (7th impression with appendix by E. Partridge).

Little, W., H. W. Fowler and J. Coulson. The shorter Oxford English dictionary on historical principles. Rev and ed C. T. Onions, Oxford 1933, 1956 (3rd edn with rev addns).

Partridge, E. A dictionary of slang and unconventional English. 1937; vol 1, Dictionary 1961 (5th edn); vol 2, Supplement 1967 (6th edn).

Shipley, S. Dictionary of early English. 1957.

Gove, P. B. Webster's third new international dictionary. Springfield 1961.

Bliss, A. J. A dictionary of foreign words and phrases in current English. 1966.

Klein, E. A comprehensive etymological dictionary of the English language. 2 vols Amsterdam 1966–7.

Onions, C. T., G. W. S. Friedrichsen and R. W. Burchfield. The Oxford dictionary of English etymology. Oxford 1966, 1967 (corrected).

Dolby, J. L. and H. L. Resnikoff. The English word speculum: volume 1, The random word list. Hague 1967. In progress.

Finkenstaedt, T., E. Leisi and D. Wolff. A chronological English dictionary. Heidelberg 1970.

See also M. M. Mathews, A survey of English dictionaries, *Oxford 1933.*

Old English

Dictionaries

Grein, C. W. M. Sprachschatz der angelsächsischen Dichter. Cassel 1861–4; ed F. Holthausen and J. J. Köhler, Heidelberg 1912–14.

Hall, J. R. C. A concise Anglo-Saxon dictionary. Cambridge 1894, 1960 (4th edn with suppl by H. D. Meritt).

Sweet, H. The student's dictionary of Anglo-Saxon. Oxford 1897.

Bosworth, J. and T. N. Toller. An Anglo-Saxon dictionary. Oxford 1898; Supplement by Toller, Oxford 1921.

Napier, A. S. Contributions to Old English lexicography. Trans Philological Soc 1906.

Holthausen, F. Altenglisches etymologisches Wörterbuch. Heidelberg 1934, 1963 (re-issue with rev bibliography). *See also* F. Holthausen, Zum altenglischen Wortschatz, Beiblatt zur Anglia 52–3 1941–2.

Bessinger, J. B. A short dictionary of Anglo-Saxon poetry. Toronto 1960.

Glossaries of Individual Texts (*in alphabetical order of texts*)

Wyatt. A. J. and H. H. Johnson. A glossary to Aelfric's homilies. [1890].

Braasch, T. Vollständiges Wörterbuch zur sog. Caedmonschen Genesis. Heidelberg 1933.

Lindelöf, U. Wörterbuch zur Interlinearglosse des Rituale ecclesiae dunelmensis. Bonn 1901. *See also* Beiblatt zur Anglia 39 1928.

Cook, A. S. A glossary of the Old Northumbrian Gospels. Halle 1894.

Schulte, E. Glossar zu Farmans Anteil an der Rushworth-Glosse (Rushworth 1). Bonn 1904.

Lindelöf, U. Glossar zur altnordhumbrischen Evangelien-übersetzung in der Rushworth-Handschrift. Helsinki 1897.

Wyld, H. C. and P. G. Thomas. A glossary of the Mercian hymns in ms Vespasian A i. Otia Merseiana 4 1904.

Grimm, C. Glossar zum Vespasian-Psalter und den Hymnen. Heidelberg 1906.

Mertens-Fonck, P. A glossary of the Vespasian Psalter and hymns: pt 1, The verb. Paris 1960. In progress.

Harris, M. A. A glossary of the West Saxon Gospels. Boston 1899.

Dodd, L. H. A glossary of Wulfstan's homilies. New York 1908.

Middle English

Coleridge, H. Glossarial index to the printed English literature of the 13th century. 1859, 1863 (as Dictionary of the first, or oldest words).

Mayhew, A. L. and W. W. Skeat. A concise dictionary of Middle English. Oxford 1888.

Stratmann, F. H. and H. Bradley. A Middle-English dictionary. Oxford 1891.

Kurath, H., S. M. Kuhn and J. Reidy. Middle English dictionary. Ann Arbor 1952–. To pt L.3 *leten* 1971; in progress.

(3) HISTORIES OF THE LANGUAGE, HISTORICAL GRAMMARS ETC.

Morris, R. Historical outlines of English accidence. 1872; rev L. Kellner and H. Bradley 1895.

Sweet, H. A history of English sounds. Oxford 1888.

—— A New English grammar: logical and historical. Oxford 1892–8.

—— A short historical English grammar. Oxford 1892.

Kluge, F., D. Behrens and E. Einenkel. Geschichte der englischen Sprache. In H. Paul, Grundriss der germanischen Philologie vol 1, Strasbourg 1891, 1901, 1916 (pt 2 only, Historische Syntax, by Einenkel).

Emerson, O. F. The history of the English language. New York 1894.

Kaluza, M. Historische Grammatik der englischen Sprache. Berlin 1900–1, 1906–7 (rev).

Bradley, H. The making of English. 1904; rev S. Potter 1968.

Jespersen, O. Growth and structure of the English language. Leipzig 1905, Oxford 1948 (9th edn).

Wyld, H. C. The historical study of the mother tongue: an introduction to philological method. 1906.

—— The growth of English. 1907.

—— A short history of English. 1913, 1927 (rev).

—— A history of modern colloquial English. 1920, 1936 (rev), Oxford 1953.

Luick, K. Historische Grammatik der englischen Sprache. Leipzig 1914–29; rptd (with index by R. F. S. Hamer) Oxford and Stuttgart 1964.

Classen, E. Outlines of the history of the English language. 1919.

Thomas, P. G. An introduction to the history of the English language. 1920.

Huchon, R. Histoire de la langue anglaise. 2 vols Paris 1923–30.

McKnight, G. H. and B. Emsley. Modern English in the making. New York 1928.

Weekley, E. The English language. 1928, 1952 (rev).

Baugh, A. C. A history of the English language. 1935, 1959 (rev).

Il'ish, B. A. Istoriya angliĭskogo yazȳka. Moscow 1935, 1958 (rev). History of the English language.

Kennedy, A. G. Current English. Boston 1935.

Robertson, S. The development of Modern English. 1936; rev F. G. Cassidy, New York 1954.

Bøgholm, N. English speech from an historical point of view. Copenhagen 1939.

Wood, F. T. An outline history of the English language. 1941, 1969 (rev).

Marckwardt, A. H. An introduction to the English language. Oxford 1942.

Delcourt, J. Initiation à l'étude historique de l'anglais. Paris 1944.

Mossé, F. Esquisse d'une histoire de la langue anglaise. Lyons 1947.

Onions, C. T. The English language. In The character of England, ed E. Barker, Oxford 1947.

Jungandreas, W. Geschichte der deutschen und der englischen Sprache: Teil III, Geschichte der englischen Sprache. Göttingen 1949.

Wrenn, C. L. The English language. 1949 (Home Study Bks), 1952 (rev).

Brunner, K. Die englische Sprache. Halle 1950–1, 1960–2 (rev).

Potter, S. Our language. 1950 (Pelican).

Moore, S., rev A. H. Marckwardt. Historical outlines of English sounds and inflections. Ann Arbor 1951.

Rota, F. Grammatica storica della lingua inglese. Milan 1951.

Mincoff, M. English historical grammar. Sofia 1955.

Clark, J. W. Early English: a study of Old and Middle English. 1957.

Brook, G. L. A history of the English language. 1958.

Ross, A. S. C. Etymology, with especial reference to English. 1958.

Pinsker, H. E. Historische englische Grammatik. Munich 1959, 1969 (rev).

Schlauch, M. The English language in modern times (since 1400). Warsaw 1959.

Yartseva, V. N. Istoricheskaya morfologiya angliĭskogo yazȳka. Moscow 1960. Historical morphology of English.

—— Razvitie natsional'nogo literaturnogo angliĭskogo yazȳka. Moscow 1969. Development of the English national literary language; with English summary.

Tellier, A. R. Histoire de la langue anglaise. Paris 1962.

Bloomfield, M. W. and L. Newmark. A linguistic introduction to the history of English. New York 1963.

Šimko, J. The origin and development of the Modern English literary language. Philologica Pragensia 6 1963.

Pyles, T. The origins and development of the English language. New York 1964, 1971 (rev).

Francis, W. N. The English language: an introduction. New York 1966.

Myers, L. M. The roots of Modern English. Boston 1966.

Nist, J. A structural history of English. New York 1966.

Koziol, H. Grundzüge der Geschichte der englischen Sprache. Darmstadt 1967.

Peters, R. A. A linguistic history of English. Boston 1968.

Stevick, R. D. English and its history. Boston 1968.

McLaughlin, J. C. Aspects of the history of English. New York 1970.

Strang, B. M. H. A history of English. 1970.

(4) SPECIAL STUDIES
(*on more than one period*)

Luick, K. Untersuchungen zur englischen Lautgeschichte. Strasbourg 1896. 1, Die mittelenglischen Längen in den lebenden Mundarten; 2, Die Entwicklung von ae. *i, u* in offener Silbe.

—— Beiträge zur englischen Grammatik III: die Quantitätsveränderungen im Laufe der englischen Sprachentwicklung. Anglia 20 1898.

Horn, W. Beiträge zur Geschichte der englischen Gutturallaute. Berlin 1901.

—— Sprachkörper und Sprachfunktion. Berlin 1921. *See also* W. Horn, Neue Beobachtungen über Sprachkörper und Sprachfunktion im Englischen, Giessener Beiträge zur Erforschung der Sprache und Kultur Englands und Nordamerikas 1 1923.

—— Schwächung und Stärkung des Sprachkörpers: Zweck und Ausdruck in der Sprachentwicklung, mit Beispielen aus der englischen Sprache. Archiv 186 1949.

—— Eine Lautsubstitution im Englischen: *s*>*š*, *z*>*ž* nach *t, d* und *n*. Ibid.

Wyld, H. C. Contributions to the history of the guttural sounds in English. Trans Philological Soc 1902.

Ekwall, E. Zur Geschichte der stimmhaften interdentalen Spirans im Englischen. Lund 1906.

Hackmann, G. Kürzung langer Tonvokale vor einfachen auslautenden Konsonanten in einsilbigen Wörtern im Alt-, Mittel- und Neuenglischen. Halle 1908.

Roedler, E. Die Ausbreitung des *s*-Plurals im Englischen, 1. Kiel 1911; 2, Anglia 40 1916.

Gevenich, O. Die englische Palatalisierung von *k*> *č* im Lichte der englischen Ortsnamen. Halle 1918.

Lindkvist, H. On the origin and history of the English pronoun *she*. Anglia 45 1921.

Holmqvist, E. On the history of the English present inflections, particularly *-th* and *-s*. Heidelberg 1922.

Langenhove, G. C. van. On the origin of the gerund in English: phonology. Ghent 1925.

Smith, A. H. Some place names and the etymology of *she*. RES 1 1925. *See also* M. B. Ruud, *She* once more, 2 1926.

Gaaf, W. van der. Contributions to the history of English. Neophilologus 12 1927.

Western, A. Aphesis, syncope and apocope in Middle and early Modern English. In A grammatical miscellany offered to Otto Jespersen, Copenhagen 1930.

Zwerina, H. Neuenglisch *o* gesprochen wie *u*. Leipzig 1930.

Wokatsch, W. Unhistorisches *ea* in angelsächsischen und frühmittelenglischen Handschriften. Berlin 1932.

Jespersen, O. Verners Gesetz und das Wesen des Akzents. In his Linguistica, Copenhagen 1933.

—— Voicing of spirants in English. E Studies 19 1937.

Gericke, B. and W. Greul. Das Personalpronomen der 3 Person in spätags. und frühmittelenglischen Texten: ein Beitrag zur altenglischen Dialektgeographie. Leipzig 1934.

Bongartz, J. Die deutsche Mundartforschung in ihrer Bedeutung für den englischen Unterricht. Berlin 1935.

Brook, G. L. Notes on some English sound-changes. Leeds 1935.

Marckwardt, A. H. Origin and extension of the voiceless preterite and the past participle inflections of the English irregular weak verb conjugation. In Essays and studies in English and comparative literature, Ann Arbor 1935.

Ross, A. S. C. The nom. acc. sg. fem. and the nom. acc. pl. of the Anglo-Frisian *hi*-pronoun. Leeds Stud in Eng 4 1935.

Trnka, B. On the phonological development of spirants in English. In Proceedings of Second International Congress of Phonetic Sciences, Cambridge 1936.

—— The phonemic development of spirants in English. E Studies 20 1938.

—— Ke změně středoanglického *-erC*>*-arC* v rané nové angličtině. Slovo a Slovesnost 30 1969. On *-erC*>*-arC* in late ME and early Modern English; with English summary.

West, V. R. Der etymologische Ursprung der neuenglischen Lautgruppe [*sk*]. Heidelberg 1936.

Grosse, E. Die neuenglische *ea*-Schreibung. Leipzig 1937.

Magoun, F. P. Colloquial Old and Middle English. Harvard Stud & Notes in Philology & Lit 19 1937.

Eckhardt, E. Die konsonantische Dissimilation im Englischen. Anglia 62 1938.

Schöffler, H. Zur Kultursoziologie des englischen ablautenden Verbums. Ibid.

Eliason, N. E. and R. C. Davis. The effect of stress upon quantity in dissyllables: an experimental and historical study. Bloomington 1939.

Ellinger, J. Die mit Präpositionen zusammengesetzten Adverbien *here, there, where*. E Studien 73 1939.

Hill, A. A. Early loss of [*r*] before dentals. PMLA 55 1940.

Wilde, H.-O. Aufforderung, Wunsch und Möglichkeit. Anglia 63–4 1939–40.

Rooth, E. Zur Geschichte der englischen Partizip-präsens Form auf *-ing*. Studia Neophilologica 14 1942.

Heltveit, T. Differentiating and unifying tendencies in the ablaut system of strong verbs in English. Oslo 1949.

—— Notes on the development of the personal pronouns in English. Norsk Tidsskrift for Sprogvidenskap 16 1952.

—— Studies in English demonstrative pronouns. Oslo 1953.

Reed, D. W. The history of inflectional *n* in English verbs before 1500. Berkeley 1950.

Dal, I. Zur Entstehung des englischen Participium Praesentis auf *-ing*. Norsk Tidsskrift for Sprogvidenskap 16 1952.

Flasdieck, H. M. Studien zur Laut- und Wortgeschichte. Anglia 70 1952.

—— Die Entstehung des engl. Phonems [ʃ]: zugleich ein Beitrag zur Geschichte der Quantität. Anglia 76 1958.

Vachek, J. Foném *h/χ* ve vývoji angličtiny. Sborník Prací Filosofické Fakulty Brněnské University 1 1952. The phoneme *h/χ* in the development of English; with English summary. *See also* Vachek, Ještě k likvidaci fonému *h/χ* v angličtině [More thoughts on the elimination of the *h/χ*-phoneme in English; with English summary], Časopis pro Moderní Filologii 39 1957; and Brno Stud in Eng 4, below.

—— Notes on the phonological development of the NE pronoun *she*. Sborník Prací Filosofické Fakulty Brněnské University 3 1954; rev in Brno Stud in Eng 4, below.

—— K vývoji anglické psané normy. Časopis pro Moderní Filologii 37 1955. Notes on the development of the English written norm; with English summary.

—— Notes on the English 'possessive case'. Philologica 7 1955; rev in Brno Stud in Eng 3, below.

—— On the phonetic and phonemic problems of the southern English *wh*-sounds. Zeitschrift für Phonetik und Allgemeine Sprachwissenschaft 8 1955; rev in Brno Stud in Eng 4, below.

—— On the interplay of quantitative and qualitative aspects in phonemic development: a contribution to the history of some English consonant phonemes. Zeitschrift für Anglistik und Amerikanistik 5 1957.

—— Notes on the quantitative correlation of vowels in the phonematic development of English. In Mélanges de linguistique et de philologie: Fernand Mossé in memoriam, Paris 1959. *See also* Brno Stud in Eng 3, below, and Prins 1971, col 98, below.

— Two chapters on written English. Spisy University v Brně: Filosofická Fakulta 55 1959 (= Brno Stud in Eng 1).

— The decline of the phoneme /r/ in English. Sborník Prací Filosofické Fakulty Brněnské University 9 1960. *See also* Brno Stud in Eng 4, *below*.

— Some less familiar aspects of the analytical trend of English. Brno Stud in Eng 3 1961.

— On peripheral phonemes of Modern English. Brno Stud in Eng 4 1964.

Stene, A. Hiatus in English: problems of catenation and juncture. Copenhagen 1954.

Bennett, W. H. The southern English development of Germanic [f s þ]. Language 31 1955.

Dieth, E. *Hips*: a geographical contribution to the 'she' puzzle. E Studies 36 1955.

Leisi, E. Das heutige Englisch: Wesenszüge und Probleme. Heidelberg 1955, 1960 (rev).

Nosek, J. Poznámky kvývoji anglických zájmen přivlastnovačích. Časopis pro Moderní Filologii 37 1955. On development of possessive pronouns; with English summary.

Langenfelt, G. Notes on English prepositions and interjections. Studier i Modern Språkvetenskap 19 1956.

Lehnert, M. The interrelation between form and function in the development of the English language. Zeitschrift für Anglistik und Amerikanistik 5 1957.

—- Das Problem von Schreibung und Aussprache im Englischen. Zeitschrift für Anglistik und Amerikanistik 10 1962.

Derolez, R. Periodisierung en continuïteit, of 'when did Middle English begin?' (K. Malone). In Album Edgard Blancquaert, Tongeren 1958. *See col 77, below*.

Levin, S. R. Negative contraction: an Old and Middle English dialect criterion. JEGP 57 1958. *See also Levin 1960, col 64, below*.

McCue, G. S. A graphic history of English stressed vowels. Denver 1958.

Başkan, Ö. Some notes on sound changes in connection with English vowels descending from the Proto-Germanic /a/-phoneme. Litera 6 1959.

Brunner, K. Die Herkunft der anglischen Elemente in der frühen englischen Schriftsprache. In Mélanges de linguistique et de philologie: Fernand Mossé in memoriam, Paris 1959.

Durand, M. La palatalisation en anglais. Ibid.

Malone, K. Diphthong and glide. Ibid.

Wagner, H. Das Verbum in den Sprachen der britischen Inseln: ein Beitrag zur geographischen Typologie des Verbums. Tübingen 1959.

Ball, C. J. E. Old Kentish *wig* and Middle English *owy*. RES new ser 11 1960.

Potter, S. Referential prepositions. In Britannica: Festschrift für Hermann M. Flasdieck, Heidelberg 1960.

Schirmunski, V. Der Umlaut im Englischen und Deutschen: ein historisch-grammatischer Vergleich. Zeitschrift für Anglistik und Amerikanistik 9 1961.

Storms, G. The origin and functions of the definite article in English. Amsterdam 1961.

Bazell, C. E. Six questions of Old and Middle English morphology. In English and medieval studies presented to J. R. R. Tolkien, 1962.

Jacobsson, U. Phonological dialect constituents in the vocabulary of Standard English. Lund 1962.

Pinsker, H. E. Phonologische Studien zum englischen Vokalismus. Moderne Sprachen: Schriftenreihe 7 1962.

Pisani, V. Germanische Miszellen: 1, Zur Endung -*s* der 3. sg. im englischen Verbum. Lingua 11 1962.

Meier, H. H. Constanten in het Engels. Groningen 1963.

Miftakhova, N. Kh. Fonologicheskiĭ analiz rezul'tatov drevneangliĭskogo udlineniya glasnȳkh pered *ld*, *mb*, *nd*, *nl*, *rn* i dr. v sovremennom angliĭskom yazȳke. In Voprosy obshchego i romano-germanskogo yazȳkoznaniya (Uchenȳe Zapiski, Bashkirskiĭ Gosudarstvennȳĭ Universitet, vȳpusk 21, seriya filologicheskikh nauk no 9), Ufa 1964. Phonological analysis of the reflexes in Modern English of vowels lengthened before consonant groups in OE.

Stockwell, R. P. On the utility of an overall pattern in historical English phonology. Proceedings of Ninth International Congress of Linguists, Hague 1964.

— Mirrors in the history of English pronunciation. In Studies in language, literature and culture of the Middle Ages and later, ed E. B. Atwood and A. A. Hill, Austin 1969.

Macháček, J. Complementation of the English verb by the accusative-with-infinitive and the content clause. Prague 1965.

Stemmler, T. Die Entwicklung der englischen Haupttonvokale: eine Übersicht in Tabellenform. Göttingen 1965.

Prins, A. A. A synopsis of the history of English tonic vowels. Leyden 1966.

Ščur, G. S. Some peculiarities of the morphology of the English modal verbs. In Studies in language and literature in honour of Margaret Schlauch, Warsaw 1966.

Braaten, B. Notes on continuous tenses in English. Norsk Tidsskrift for Sprogvidenskap 21 1967.

Eliason, N. E. The origin of irregular -*t* in weak preterits like *sent* and *felt*. In Studies in historical linguistics in honor of George Sherman Lane, Chapel Hill [1967].

Plotkin, V. Ya. Dinamika angliĭskoĭ fonologicheskoĭ sistemȳ. Novosibirsk 1967. Dynamics of the English phonological system; with English summary.

Fisiak, J. Prevocalic consonant clusters in the history of English. Studia Anglica Posnaniensia 1 1968.

Pilch, H. Modelle der englischen Wortbildung. In Wortbildung, Syntax und Morphologie: Festschrift zum 60 Geburtstag von Hans Marchand, Hague 1968.

Reszkiewicz, A. The elimination of the front rounded and back unrounded short vowel phonemes from medieval English: a reinterpretation. Kwartalnik Neofilologiczny 18 1971.

Samuels, M. L. Kent and the Low Countries: some linguistic evidence. In Edinburgh studies in English and Scots, ed A. J. Aitken et al 1971. On OE and ME.

B. PHONOLOGY AND MORPHOLOGY

(1) OLD ENGLISH

General

Sweet, H. Anglo-Saxon primer. Oxford 1882, 1953 (rev N. Davis).

Bright, J. W. An outline of Anglo-Saxon grammar. New York 1894, 1971 (rev F. G. Cassidy and R. N. Ringler as Bright's Old English grammar and reader).

Bülbring, K. D. Altenglisches Elementarbuch, 1 Teil: Lautlehre. Heidelberg 1902.

Wright, J. and E. M. Old English grammar. Oxford 1908, 1925 (3rd edn).

Wardale, E. E. An Old English grammar. 1922, 1936 (rev).

Girvan, R. Angelsaksisch handboek. Haarlem 1931.

Kieckers, E. Altenglische Grammatik. Munich 1935.

Lehnert, M. Altenglisches Elementarbuch. Berlin 1939, 1969 (rev).

Mossé, F. Manuel de l'anglais du Moyen Age, 1: vieil-anglais. 2 vols Paris 1945.

Brunner, K. Altenglische Grammatik, nach der angelsächsischen Grammatik von Eduard Sievers. Halle 1942, Tübingen 1965 (3rd edn).

Ross, A. S. C. The essentials of Anglo-Saxon grammar. Cambridge 1948.
— Tables for Old English sound-changes. Cambridge 1951.
Brook, G. L. An introduction to Old English. Manchester 1955.
Quirk, R. and C. L. Wrenn. An Old English grammar. 1955, 1957 (rev).
Smirnitskiĭ, A. I. Drevneangliĭskiĭ yazȳk. Moscow 1955.
Campbell, A. Old English grammar. Oxford 1959.
Mitchell, B. A guide to Old English. Oxford 1965, 1968 (rev).
Pilch, H. Altenglisch. In L. E. Schmitt (ed), Kurzer Grundriss der germanischen Philologie bis 1500, Band 1: Sprachgeschichte, Berlin 1970.
— Altenglische Grammatik. Munich 1970.

Special Studies

Dieter, F. Über Sprache und Mundart der ältesten englischen Denkmäler, der Epinaler und Cambridger Glossen, mit Berücksichtigung des Erfurter Glossars. Göttingen 1885.
Lindelöf, U. Über die Verbreitung des sogenannten u- (o-) Umlauts in der starken Verbalflexion des Altenglischen. Archiv 89 1892.
Pogatscher, A. Über die Chronologie des altenglischen i-Umlauts. Beiträge zur Geschichte der Deutschen Sprache und Literatur 18 1894.
Bülbring, K. D. Altenglischer Palatalumlaut vor ht, hs und hþ. Anglia: Beiblatt 10 1899.
Chadwick, H. M. Studies in Old English. Trans Cambridge Philological Soc 4 1899.
Sievers, E. Zum angelsächsischen Vokalismus. Leipzig 1900.
Wyld, H. C. West Germanic a in Old English. Otia Merseiana 4 1904.
Weyhe, H. Beiträge zur westgermanischen Grammatik. Beiträge zur Geschichte der Deutschen Sprache und Literatur 30–1 1905–6.
— Zur Palatalisierung von in- und auslautendem sk im Altenglischen. E Studien 39 1908.
Weightman, J. The language and dialect of the later Old English poetry. Liverpool 1907.
Richter, C. Chronologische Studien zur angelsächsischen Literatur auf Grund sprachlich-metrischer Kriterien. Halle 1910.
Schlemilch, W. Beiträge zur Sprache und Orthographie spätaltengl. Sprachdenkmäler der Übergangszeit 1000–1150. Halle 1914.
Kügler, H. ie und seine Parallelformen im Angelsächsischen. Berlin 1916.
Jiriczek, O. L. Tenuis für Media im Altenglischen. Indogermanische Forschungen 38 1920.
Borowski, B. Zum Nebenakzent beim altenglischen Nominalkompositum. Halle 1921.
— Lautdubletten im Altenglischen. Halle 1924.
Ritter, O. Vermischte Beiträge zur englischen Sprachgeschichte: Etymologie, Ortsnamenkunde, Lautlehre. Halle 1922.
Heidemann, G. Die Flexion des verb. subst. im Ags. Archiv 147 1924.
Prokosch, E. The Old English weak preterites without medial vowel. PMLA 42 1927.
Weber, G. Suffixvokal nach kurzer Tonsilbe vor r, n, m, im Angelsächsischen. Leipzig 1927.
Bloomfield, L. Old English plural subjunctives in -e. JEGP 29 1930.
Flasdieck, H. M. Zur Geschichte der femininen ō-Flexion im Westgermanischen. Indogermanische Forschungen 48 1930.
— Die zweite Person des Singulars im ae. Verbalsystem. Anglia 58 1934.
— Untersuchungen über die germanischen schwachen Verben III Klasse (unter besonderer Berücksichtigung des Altenglischen). Anglia 59 1935.
— Die reduplizierenden Verben des Germanischen (unter besonderer Berücksichtigung des Altenglischen). Anglia 60 1936.
— Ae. dōn und gān. Anglia 61 1937.
— Das altgermanische Verbum substantivum unter besonderer Berücksichtigung des Altenglischen. E Studien 71 1937; Nachschrift 72 1938.
— Das Verbum wollen im Altgermanischen (unter besonderer Berücksichtigung des Altenglischen). Anglia 61 1937.
— The phonetic aspect of Old Germanic alliteration. Anglia 69 1950.
Langenhove, G. van. The assibilation of palatal stops in Old English. In A grammatical miscellany offered to Otto Jespersen, Copenhagen 1930.
Seelig, F. Die Komparation der Adjektiva und Adverbien im Altenglischen. Heidelberg 1930.
Barber, C. C. Die vorgeschichtliche Betonung der germanischen Substantiva und Adjektiva. Heidelberg 1932.
Lotspeich, C. M. Germanic strong verbs of class VII. JEGP 32 1933.
Ross, A. S. C. The accusative and dative of the pronouns of the first and second persons in Germanic. JEGP 32 1933.
— The 1st sg. pres. ind. -e in Old English. Neuphilologische Mitteilungen 34 1933.
— The pl. pres. ind. in English and Low German. Neuphilologische Mitteilungen 35 1934.
— Old English æ~a. E Studies 32 1951.
Wrenn, C. L. 'Standard' Old English. Trans Philological Soc 1933.
— The value of spelling as evidence. Trans Philological Soc 1943.
Petersen, W. The dual personal pronouns in Germanic. JEGP 33 1934.
Förster, M. Zur i-Epenthese im Altenglischen. Anglia 59 1935.
Luick, K. Zur Palatalisierung. Ibid.
Rooth, E. Det primära i-omljudet och frågan om muljerade konsonanter och i-epentheser i väst- och nordgermanskan. Vetenskapssocieteten i Lund: Årsbok 1935.
Harl, W. Die überkurzen Vokale in den historischen indogermanischen Sprachen. Zeitschrift für Vergleichende Sprachforschung 63 1936.
Lane, G. S. The labiovelars before ŏ in Germanic. JEGP 35 1936.
— The genesis of the stem-vowel u (o) in the Germanic r stems. JEGP 50 1951.
— Bimoric and trimoric vowels and diphthongs: laws of Germanic finals again. JEGP 62 1963.
Malone, K. The inflexion of OE gar 'spear'. Beiblatt zur Anglia 47 1936.
Sturtevant, A. M. Germanic notes. JEGP 35 1936.
Ångström, M. Studies in Old English mss with special reference to the delabialization of ȳ (ŭ+i) to ĭ. Upsala 1937.
Bazell, C. E. Indo-European final unaccented ē in Germanic. JEGP 36 1937.
— Four West Germanic verbal endings. Neophilologus 24 1939.
— Case-forms in -i in the oldest English texts. MLN 55 1940.
— The phonemic interpretation of the Old English diphthongs. Litera 3 1956.
— Some problems of Old English morphology. In Mélanges de linguistique et de philologie: Fernand Mossé in memoriam, Paris 1959.
— A question of syncretism and analogy. Trans Philological Soc 1960.
— Notes on Old English metre and morphology. In Wortbildung, Syntax and Morphologie: Festschrift zum 60 Geburtstag von Hans Marchand, Hague 1968. 1, A peculiarity of alliteration in the Battle of Maldon; 2, Locative singulars in -um.

Flom, G. T. Breaking in Old Norse and Old English, with special reference to the relations between them. Language 13 1937.

Martinet, A. La gémination consonantique d'origine expressive dans les langues germaniques. Copenhagen 1937.

Mezger, F. Zur Ineinanderbildung der verschiedenen Wurzeln und Formen im Präsens indic. des Verbum substantivum im Westgermanischen. Archiv 171 1937.

Dahl, I. Substantival inflexion in early Old English. Lund 1938.

Berg, B. van den. Het verlies van n voor scherpe spirans in de germaanse talen. Leuvense Bijdragen 31 1939.

Daunt, M. Old English sound changes reconsidered in relation to scribal tradition and practice. Trans Philological Soc 1939.

—— Some notes on Old English phonology. Trans Philological Soc 1952.

Eckhardt, E. Die vokalische Dissimilation im Altenglischen. E Studien 73 1939.

Fourquet, J. Anglo-saxon ēode, dyde et la théorie du prétérit faible. Studia Neophilologica 14 1942.

—— Le système des éléments vocaliques longs en vieilanglais. In Mélanges de linguistique et de philologie: Fernand Mossé in memoriam, Paris 1959.

Schubel, F. Die Aussprache des anlautenden ae. sc. Studia Neophilologica 14 1942.

Slettengren, E. On the development of OE initial sc. Studier i Modern Språkvetenskap 15 1943.

Penzl, H. A phonemic change in early Old English. Language 20 1944. On medial spirants.

—— The phonemic split of Germanic k in Old English. Language 23 1947.

Campbell, A. West Germanic problems in the light of modern dialects. Trans Philological Soc 1947.

Eliason, N. E. Old English vowel lengthening and vowel shortening before consonant groups. SP 45 1948.

Hallqvist, H. Studies in Old English fractured ea. Lund 1948.

Marckwardt, A. H. Verb inflections in late Old English. In Philologica: the [Kemp] Malone anniversary studies, Baltimore 1949.

Bliss, A. J. The Old English long diphthongs ēo and ēa. Eng & Germanic Stud 3 1950.

Quirk, R. On the problem of morphological suture in Old English. MLR 45 1950. Rev as On the problem of inflexional juncture in Old English, in his Essays on the English language: medieval and modern, 1968. On contracted and athematic verbs.

Stockwell, R. P. and C. W. Barritt. Some Old English graphemic-phonemic correspondences: ae, ea and a. Norman Oklahoma 1951. See S. M. Kuhn and R. Quirk 1953, below.

—— The Old English short digraphs: some considerations. Language 31 1955. See S. M. Kuhn and R. Quirk 1955, below.

—— Scribal practice: some assumptions. Language 37 1961. On Hockett, Language 35 1959.

Samuels, M. L. The study of Old English phonology. Trans Philological Soc 1952.

Brosnahan, L. F. Some Old English sound changes: an analysis in the light of modern phonetics. Cambridge 1953.

Brunner, K. The Old English vowel phonemes. E Studies 34 1953.

—— Die altenglische Ebnung. Beiträge zur Geschichte der Deutschen Sprache und Literatur (Tübingen) 77 1955.

Kuhn, S. M. and R. Quirk. Some recent interpretations of Old English digraph spellings. Language 29 1953.

—— The Old English digraphs: a reply. Language 31 1955. On R. P. Stockwell and C. W. Barritt, ibid.

Must, G. The genitive singular of o-stems in Germanic. Language 29 1953.

Reszkiewicz, A. The phonemic interpretation of Old English digraphs. Biuletyn Polskiego Towarzystwa Językoznawczego 12 1953.

Stanley, E. G. The chronology of r-metathesis in Old English. Eng & Germanic Stud 5 1953.

—— Spellings of the waldend group. In Studies in language, literature and culture of the Middle Ages and later, ed E. B. Atwood and A. A. Hill, Austin 1969.

Lehmann, W. P. Old English and Old Norse secondary preterites in -r-. Language 30 1954.

—— Metrical evidence for Old English suprasegmentals. Texas Stud in Lit & Lang 1 1959.

—— Post-consonantal l m n r and metrical practice in Beowulf. In Nordica et anglica: studies in honor of Stefán Einarsson, Hague 1968.

Moulton, W. G. The stops and spirants of early Germanic. Language 30 1954.

Bauer, G. The problem of short diphthongs in Old English. Anglia 74 1956.

Coetsem, F. van. Das System der starken Verba und die Periodisierung im älteren Germanischen. Amsterdam 1956.

Storms, G. The weakening of OE unstressed i to e and the date of Cynewulf. E Studies 37 1956.

Anderson, G. K. The fifth case in Old English. JEGP 57 1958.

Chatman, S. The a/æ opposition in Old English. Word 14 1958.

Stockwell, R. P. The phonology of Old English: a structural sketch. Stud in Linguistics 13 1958.

—— and R. Willard. Further notes on Old English phonology. Stud in Linguistics 14 1959.

Hamp, E. P. Final syllables in Germanic and the Scandinvanian accent system. Studia Linguistica 13 1959.

Hockett, C. F. The stressed syllabics of Old English. Language 35 1959. See R. P. Stockwell and C. W. Barritt, 1961, col 63, above.

Levin, S. R. An Anglo-Frisian morphological correspondence. Orbis 9 1960. On contraction of ne+verb.

—— A reclassification of the Old English strong verbs. Language 40 1964.

Antonsen, E. H. Germanic umlaut anew. Language 37 1961.

—— On the origin of Old English digraph spellings. Stud in Linguistics 19 1967.

Blake, N. F. A note on hw in Old English. N & Q May 1961.

Krupatkin, Y. B. The Anglo-Frisian development of Germanic ē₁. Philologica Pragensia 4 1961.

—— K istorii drevneangliĭskoĭ sistemȳ glasnȳkh. Voprosȳ Yazȳkoznaniya 1962. On the history of the OE vowel system.

—— Germanic ai, au in Old English. Philologica Pragensia 6 1963.

—— Old English breaking: a step to a phonemic approach. Philologica Pragensia 7 1964.

—— Nazalizovannȳe glasnȳe v istorii drevneangliĭskogo yazȳka. Voprosȳ Yazȳkoznaniya 1964. Nasalized vowels in the history of OE.

—— A synchronic problem diachronically solved: the pre-English nasalized vowels. Philologica Pragensia 8 1965.

Kuhn, S. [M.] On the syllabic phonemes of Old English. Language 37 1961.

—— On the consonantal phonemes of Old English. In Philological essays: studies in Old and Middle English language and literature in honour of Herbert Dean Meritt, Hague 1970.

Ivanova, I. P. Sistema soglasnȳkh i eë dinamika v drevneangliĭskom yazȳke. Nauchnȳe Doklady Vȳssheĭ Shkolȳ: Filologicheskie Nauki 1963. The OE consonant system and its dynamics.

—— 'Overlapping' of /ĭ/, /ǯ/ in Old English. Philologica Pragensia 8 1965.

Mȳrkin, V. Ya. Po povodu asimmetrichnoĭ proportsii drevneangliĭskikh ic: mec i drevneislandskikh ek: mik. Nauchnȳe Doklady Vȳsssheĭ Shkolȳ: Filologicheskie Nauki 1964. On the reason for the asymmetrical relationship between OE ic: mec and Old Icelandic ek: mik.

Cowgill, W. The Old English present indicative ending -*e*. In Symbolae linguisticae in honorem Georgii Kuryłowicz (Prace Komisji Językoznawstwa 5), Wrocław 1965.

Peters, R. A. Case-number morphs of Old English nouns. Linguistics 14 1965.

— Phonic and phonemic long consonants in Old English. Stud in Linguistics 19 1967.

— Morphemic classification of Old English adverb subsets. Canadian Jnl of Linguistics 13 1968.

Essen, A. J. van. Some remarks on Old English phonology. Linguistics 32 1967.

Fisiak, J. The Old English ⟨*wr*-⟩ and ⟨*wl*-⟩. Ibid.

Howren, R. The generation of Old English weak verbs. Language 43 1967.

Seebold, E. Die ae. schwundstufigen Präsentien (Aoristpräsentien) der *ei*-Reihe. Anglia 84 1966.

— Die ae. starken Partizipia Praeteriti mit Umlaut. Anglia 85 1967.

Bammesberger, A. Die kurzsilbigen femininen *i*-Stämme im Altenglischen. Die Sprache 15 1969.

Goosens, L. A chronology for the falling together of late Old English *hr* and *r*. E Studies 50 1969.

Ney, J. W. Old English vowel digraph spellings. Linguistics 45 1969.

Pilch, H. The phonemic interpretation of Old English spelling evidence. Acta Linguistica Hafniensia 12 1969.

Anderson, J. 'Ablaut' in the synchronic phonology of the Old English strong verb. Indogermanische Forschungen 75 1970.

Dietz, K. Zur Vokalquantität ae. Wörter des Typus *w(e)alh – w(e)alas*. Anglia 88 1970.

O'Neill, W. A. Explaining vowel gradation in Old English. General Linguistics 10 1970.

Peeters, C. A formal description of the use of some verbal endings in Old English. In Linguistique contemporaine: hommage à Eric Buyssens, Brussels 1970.

Scragg, D. G. Initial *h* in Old English. Anglia 88 1970.

Awedyk, W. Some remarks on the phonology of Old English. Studia Anglica Posnaniensia 3 1971.

Lass, R. Palatals and umlaut in Old English. Acta Linguistica Hafniensia 13 1971.

Speedie, D. C. A note on Old English diphthongization of back vowels after initial *j*. Archivum Linguisticum new ser 2 1971.

Old English Dialects

Hilmer, H. Zur altnordhumbrischen Laut- und Flexionslehre. Beilage zu dem Jahresbericht der Realschule, Goslar 1880.

Cosijn, P. J. Altwestsächsische Grammatik. 2 vols Hague 1883–8.

Wolff, R. Untersuchung der Laute in den kentischen Urkunden. Heidelberg 1893.

Weightman, J. Vowel-levelling in early Kentish and the use of the symbol *ę* in Old English charters. E Studien 35 1905.

Taxweiler, R. Angelsächsische Urkundenbücher von kentischem Lokalcharakter. Berlin 1906.

Köhler, T. Die altenglischen Namen in Baedas Historia ecclesiastica und auf den altnordhumbrischen Münzen. Berlin 1908.

Gabrielson, A. On the late Old Northumbrian (*w*)*æ* for regular (*w*)*e*. Beiblatt zur Anglia 21 1910.

Bryan, W. F. Studies in the dialects of the Kentish charters of the Old English period. Menasha 1915.

Ekwall, E. Contributions to the history of Old English dialects. Lund 1917. On *æ*+*l*+consonant, and *i*-mutation of this group.

— A problem of Old Mercian phonology in the light of West Midland place-names. Namn och Bygd 51 1963. On *e*<*æ*.

Flasdieck, H. M. Zur Charakteristik der sprachlichen Verhältnisse in altengl. Zeit. Beiträge zur Geschichte der deutschen Sprache und Literatur 48 1924.

— Miszellen zur ae. Grammatik. Beiblatt zur Anglia 41 1930. 1, Zur relativen Chronologie des Velarumlauts im Westmittelland; 2, Zu got. *fijands* im Vesp. Psalter; 3, Zu ws. *nam–nāmon*.

— Zur Datierung des ae. Wandels *īǫ* > *ęǫ* im westlichen Mittelland. Ibid.

Ross, A. S. C. The origin of the -*s* endings of the present indicative in English. JEGP 33 1934.

— A hitherto unnoticed Anglo-Saxon sound-change. In Britannica: Festschrift für H. M. Flasdieck, Heidelberg 1960. On **īu* > **ēu* in Northumbrian.

Salmen, H. *w*+westgerm. *ĕ* and *i* im Angelsächsischen. Bottrop 1936.

Campbell, A. An Old English will. JEGP 37 1938. On Kentish.

Linke, G. *Standeð* und *stent* und dergleichen in ags. sicher fixierten Hss. E Studien 73 1939.

Ström, H. Old English personal names in Bede's History. Lund 1939.

Anderson, O. S. Old English material in the Leningrad Manuscript of Bede's Ecclesiastical history. Lund 1941.

Hedberg, J. The syncope of the Old English present endings: a dialect criterion. Lund 1945.

Watson, J. W. Northumbrian Old English *ēo* and *ēa*. Language 22 1946.

— Non-initial *k* in the north of England. Language 23 1947.

— Smoothing and palatal umlaut in Northumbrian. In English studies in honor of J. S. Wilson, Charlottesville 1951.

Kuhn, S. M. From Canterbury to Lichfield. Speculum 23 1948.

Löfvenberg, M. T. On the syncope of the Old English present endings. Upsala 1949; also Studia Neophilologica 21 1949.

Berndt, R. Form und Funktion des Verbums im nördlichen Spätaltenglischen. Halle 1956.

— Zum *s*/*ð*-Problem in der nordhumbrischen Verbalflexion. Zeitschrift für Anglistik und Amerikanistik 6 1958.

DeCamp, D. The genesis of the Old English dialects: a new hypothesis. Language 34 1958.

Penzl, H. Zur Vorgeschichte von westsächsisch *ǣ* und zur Methode des Rekonstruierens. In Anglistische Studien: Festschrift zum 70 Geburtstag von Friedrich Wild, Vienna 1958.

Ball, C. J. E. Mercian 'second fronting'. Archivum Linguisticum 14 1962.

Gradon, P. Studies in late West-Saxon labialization and delabialization. In English and medieval studies presented to J. R. R. Tolkien, 1962.

Steponavičius, A. O razvitii drevneangliiskikh diftongov v kentskom dialekte. Lietuvos TSR Aukštųjų Mokyklų Mokslo Darbai: Kalbotyra 9 1963. On the development of the OE diphthongs in Kentish.

— Suzhenie /*ǣ*/ v kentskom dialekte drevneangliiskogo yazȳka. Lietuvos TSR Aukštųjų Mokyklų Mokslo Darbai: Kalbotyra 13 1965. The narrowing of /*ǣ*/ in the Kentish dialect of OE.

— Sud'ba drevneangliiskikh diftongov /*ĕa*/, /*ĕo*/, /*ĭo*/ v kentskom. Ibid. The fate of the OE diphthongs /*ĕa*/, /*ĕo*/, /*ĭo*/ in Kentish.

Robb, K. A. Some changes in Kentish OE phonology. Lingua 20 1968. On *ĕ*, *ĕ̆*, *y̆*>*ĕ*.

Kirsten, H. Die angelsächsische Besiedlung Britanniens in ihrer Bedeutung für die Herausbildung der altenglischen Sprache und deren Dialektgeographie. Zeitschrift für Anglistik und Amerikanistik 17 1969.

Pak, T.-Y. Position and affrication in Northumbrian Old English. Linguistics 82 1972.

Old English Texts
(in alphabetical order)

Assmann, B. Abt Aelfrics ags. Bearbeitung des Buches Esther. Halle 1885. *See also* Assmann, Anglia 9 1886.

Fischer, F. The stressed vowels of Ælfric's Homilies, vol 1. PMLA 4 1889.

Braunschweiger, M. Flexion des Verbums in Älfrics Grammatik. Marburg 1890.

Tessmann, A. Aelfrics ae. Bearbeitung der Interrogationes Sigewulfi presbyteri in Genesin des Alcuin. Berlin 1891.

Brühl, C. Die Flexion des Verbums in Aelfrics Heptateuch und Buch Hiob. Marburg 1892.

Schwerdtfeger, G. Das schwache Verbum in Aelfrics Homilien. Marburg 1893.

Brüll, H. Die altenglische Latein-Grammatik des Aelfric. Berlin 1900.

Wilkes, J. Lautlehre zu Aelfrics Heptateuch und Buch Hiob. Bonn 1905.

Schüller, O. Lautlehre von Aelfrics Lives of Saints. Bonn 1908.

Glaeser, K. Lautlehre der Aelfricschen Homilien in der Hs Cotton Vespasianus D xiv. Leipzig 1916.

Göhler, T. Lautlehre der altenglischen Hexameron-Homilie des Abtes Aelfric. Weida 1933.

Anderson, G. K. Notes on the language of Aelfric's English Pastoral letters in Corpus Christi College 190 and Bodleian Junius 121. JEGP 40 1941.

See also Cosijn 1883–8, col 65, above.

Karaus, A. Die Sprache der Gesetze des Königs Aethelred. Berlin 1901.

Schiebel, K. Die Sprache der altenglischen Glossen zu Aldhelms Schrift De laude virginitatis. Halle 1907

Hulme, W. H. Die Sprache der altenglischen Bearbeitung der Soliloquien Augustins. Freiburg 1894.

Krawutschke, A. Die Sprache der Boethius-Uebersetzung des K. Alfred. Berlin 1902.

Herold, C. P. The morphology of King Alfred's translation of the Orosius. Hague 1968.

Bauer, H. Über die Sprache und Mundart der altenglischen Dichtungen Andreas, Guðlac, Phoenix, Hl. Kreuz und Höllenfahrt Christi. Marburg 1890.

Cosijn, P. J. De oudste westsaksische Chroniek (Parker ms.). Taalkundige Bijdragen 2 1879.

Flohrschütz, A. Die Sprache der Handschrift D der angelsächsischen Annalen im ms Cotton Tib. B iv. Jena 1909.

Sprockel, C. The language of the Parker Chronicle, volume 1: phonology and accidence. Hague 1965.

Stevick, R. D. Scribal notation of prosodic features in the Parker Chronicle, anno 894 [893]. Jnl of Eng Linguistics 1 1967.

Märkisch, R. Die altenglische Bearbeitung der Erzählung von Appolonius von Tyrus. Berlin 1899.

Deutschbein, M. Dialektisches in der angelsächsischen Übersetzung von Bedas Kirchengeschichte. Beiträge zur Geschichte der Deutschen Sprache und Literatur 26 1901.

Eger, O. Dialektisches in den Flexionsverhältnissen der angelsächsichen Bedaübersetzung. Leipzig 1910.

Linke, G. Zum Velarumlaut in der starken Verbalflexion der Hs T des ags. Beda. Archiv 173 1938.

Hermanns, W. Lautlehre und dialektische Untersuchung der altenglischen Interlinearversion der Benediktinerregel. Bonn 1906.

Rohr, G. Die Sprache der altenglischen Prosabearbeitung der Benediktinerregel. Bonn 1912.

Davidson, C. The phonology of the stressed vowels in Beowulf. PMLA 7 1892.

Thomas, P. G. Notes on the language of Beowulf. MLR 1 1906. On dialect features.

Morsbach, L. Zur Datierung des Beowulfepos. Göttingen 1906.

Hardy, A. K. Die Sprache der Blickling Homilien. Leipzig 1899.

Hein, B. Die Sprache der altenglischen Glosse zu Eadwines Canterbury Psalter. Würzburg 1903.

Wildhagen, K. Der Psalter des Eadwine von Canterbury. Halle 1905.

Kuhn, S. M. The dialect of the Corpus Glossary. PMLA 54 1939.

Groschopp, C. Das angelsächsische Gedicht Crist und Satan. Anglia 6 1883.

Leiding, H. Die Sprache der Cynewulfschen Dichtungen Crist, Juliana und Elene. Göttingen 1887.

Lindelöf, U. Die Sprache des Rituals von Durham. Helsinki 1890.

—— Die neue Ausgabe des Rituale ecclesiae dunelmensis und die Sprache der Glosse. Beiblatt zur Anglia 39 1928.

Ross, A. S. C. Aldrediana xvii: Ritual supplement. Eng Philological Stud 11 1968.

—— Conservatism in the Anglo-Saxon gloss to the Durham Ritual. N & Q Oct 1970. Aldrediana xxii.

Kolkwitz, M. Zum Erfurter Glossar. Anglia 17 1895.

Williams, O. T. The dialect of the text of the Northumbrian Genealogies. MLR 4 1909.

Kamp, A. Die Sprache der altenglischen Genesis: eine Lautuntersuchung. Münster 1913.

Seiffert, F. Die Behandlung der Wörter mit auslautenden ursprünglichen silbischen Liquiden oder Nasalen und mit Kontraktionsvokalen in der Genesis A und im Beowulf. Halle 1913.

Menner, R. J. The date and dialect of Genesis A 852–2936. Anglia 70 1952.

Trilsbach, G. Die Lautlehre der spätwestsächsischen Evangelien. Bonn 1905.

Boll, P. Die Sprache der altenglischen Glossen im ms Harley 3376. Bonn 1904.

Campbell, J. J. The Harley Glossary and 'Saxon patois'. PQ 34 1955.

Brunner, K. Die Sprache der Handschrift Junius 24. Beiblatt zur Anglia 51 1940.

Williams, I. F. The significance of the symbol ę in the Kentish Glosses. Otia Merseiana 4 1904.

—— A grammatical investigation of the Old Kentish glosses. Bonn 1905.

Schmitt, L. Lautliche Untersuchung der Sprache des Læceboc. Bonn 1908.

Sauer, P. R. Zur Sprache des Leidener Glossars cod. Voss. lat. 4°, 69. Munich 1917.

Hellwig, H. Untersuchungen über die Namen des nordhumbrischen Liber vitae: 1. Berlin 1888.

Müller, R. Untersuchungen über die Namen des nordhumbrischen Liber vitae. Berlin 1901.

Lindelöf, U. Beiträge zur Kenntnis des Altnorthumbrischen. Mémoires de la Société Néo-philologique à Helsingfors 1 1893. On Lindisfarne and Rushworth Gospels and Durham Ritual.

Lea, E. M. The language of the Northumbrian gloss to the Gospel of St Mark. Anglia 16 1894.

Füchsel, H. Die Sprache der northumbrischen Interlinearversion zum Johannes-Evangelium. Anglia 24 1901.

Foley, E. H. The language of the Northumbrian gloss to the Gospel of St Matthew. New York 1903.

Kellum, M. D. The language of the Northumbrian gloss to the Gospel of St Luke. New York 1906.

Stolz, W. Der Vokalismus der betonten Silben in der altnordhumbrischen Interlinearversion der Lindisfarner Evangelien. Bonn 1908.

Carpenter, H. C. A. Die Deklination in der northumbrischen Evangelienübersetzung der Lindisfarner Handschrift. Bonn 1910.

Kolbe, T. Die Konjugation der Lindisfarner Evangelien. Bonn 1912.

Ross, A. S. C. The errors in the Old English gloss to the Lindisfarne Gospels. RES 8 1932.

—— 'Scribal preference' in the Old English gloss to the Lindisfarne Gospels. MLN 48 1933.

—— Studies in the accidence of the Lindisfarne Gospels. Leeds 1937.

—— Prolegomena to an edition of the Old English gloss to the Lindisfarne Gospels. JEGP 42 1943.

— Aldrediana XI: The *u*-orthographies. Studia Germanica 1 1959.

— 'This' in the Lindisfarne Gospels and the Durham Ritual. N & Q Aug 1967. Aldrediana XVI; *see also Jones 1969, below.*

— Aldrediana XX: Notes on the preterite-present verbs. Eng Philological Stud 11 1968.

— On some forms of the anomalous and contracted verbs in the Anglo-Saxon glosses to the Lindisfarne Gospels and the Durham Ritual. Trans Philological Soc 1968. Aldrediana XIX.

— Two vestigial distinctions in the late north Northumbrian dialect of Anglo-Saxon. Archivum Linguisticum new ser 2 1971. On 3 sg. pres. ind. vs pl. pres. ind. and inf. vs pres. subj. in Lindisfarne Gospels and Durham Ritual.

Mincoff, M. K. Zur Altersfrage der Lindisfarner Glosse. Archiv 173 1938.

Blakeley, L. Accusative-dative syncretism in the Lindisfarne Gospels. Eng & Germanic Stud 1 1948.

— The Lindisfarne *s*/ð problem. Studia Neophilologica 22 1950.

Brunner, A. A note on the distribution of the variant forms of the Lindisfarne Gospels. Eng & Germanic Stud 1 1948.

Berndt, R. Die Flexion des Verbums im Nordhumbrischen und Mercischen im späten 10 Jahrhundert. Halle 1956. Also pbd as Form und Funktion des Verbums im nördlichen Spätaltenglischen, Halle 1956. On Lindisfarne and Rushworth Gospels and Durham Ritual.

Britton, G. C. Aldrediana IV: The *e*- and *i*- diphthongs. Eng & Germanic Stud 7 1961.

— Aldrediana XII: *æ* ~ *e*. Eng Philological Stud 12 1970.

— and A. S. C. Ross. Aldrediana X: Manifesta. Anglia 78 1960.

Jones, C. A further note on the use of 'this' in the gloss to the Lindisfarne Gospels and the Durham Ritual. N & Q April 1969. *Discusses Ross 1967, above.*

Madert, A. Die Sprache der altenglischen Rätsel des Exeterbuches. Marburg 1900.

Trautmann, M. Sprache und Versbau der altenglischen Rätsel. Anglia 38 1914.

Svensson, J. V. Om språket i den förra (merciska) delen af Rushworth-handskriften, 1: Ljudlära. Gothenburg 1883.

Otten, G. The language of the Rushworth gloss to the Gospel of St Matthew. 2 pts Leipzig 1890–1.

Brown, E. M. Die Sprache der Rushworth Glossen zum Evangelium Matthäus und der mercische Dialekt, 1: Vokale. Göttingen 1891.

— The language of the Rushworth gloss to the Gospel of Matthew and the Mercian dialect, 2: the vowels of other than stem-syllables; consonants; inflection. Göttingen 1892.

Lindelöf, U. Die südnorthumbrische Mundart des 10 Jahrhunderts: die Sprache der sog. Glosse Rushworth². Bonn 1901.

Menner, R. J. Farman vindicatus. Anglia 58 1934.

Scargill, M. H. The earliest example of the West Riding dialect. Trans Yorkshire Dialect Soc pt 40 1940.

Kuhn, S. M. *e* and *æ* in Farman's Mercian glosses. PMLA 60 1945.

Peteson, P. W. Dialect grouping in the unpublished Vercelli Homilies. JEGP 50 1953.

Zeuner, R. Die Sprache des kentischen Psalters (Vespasian A 1). Halle 1881.

Bülbring, K. D. *e* and *æ* in the Vespasian Psalter. In An English miscellany presented to Dr [F. J.] Furnivall, Oxford 1901.

Kuhn, S. M. The Vespasian Psalter and the Old English charter hands. Speculum 18 1943.

Wilson, R. M. The provenance of the Vespasian Psalter gloss: the linguistic evidence. In The Anglo-Saxons: studies presented to Bruce Dickins, 1959.

Ball, C. J. E. The language of the Vespasian Psalter gloss: two caveats. RES new ser 21 1970.

Hecht, H. Die Sprache der altenglischen Dialoge Gregors des Grossen: die Vokale der Stammsilben in den Hss C und O. Berlin 1900. On Wærferth.

Selection of Old English Texts

Readers and Anthologies

Zupitza, J. Altenglisches Übungsbuch. Vienna 1874; rev J. Schipper and A. Eichler as Alt- und mittelenglisches Übungsbuch, 1922; tr G. E. MacLean, The Old and Middle English reader, New York 1893, 1922 (rev).

Sweet, H. An Anglo-Saxon reader in prose and verse. Oxford 1876; rev D. Whitelock, Sweet's Anglo-Saxon reader, Oxford 1967.

— The oldest English texts. 1885 (EETS).

— A second Anglo-Saxon reader: archaic and dialectal. Oxford 1887.

— First steps in Anglo-Saxon. Oxford 1897.

Kluge, F. Angelsächsisches Lesebuch. Halle 1888, 1915 (rev).

Förster, M. Altenglisches Lesebuch für Anfänger. Heidelberg 1913, 1949 (rev).

Wyatt, A. J. An Anglo-Saxon reader. Cambridge 1919.

— The threshold of Anglo-Saxon. Cambridge 1926.

Sedgefield, W. J. An Anglo-Saxon verse book. Manchester 1922.

— An Anglo-Saxon prose book. Manchester 1928.

Krapp, G. P. and A. P. Kennedy. Anglo-Saxon reader. New York 1929.

Flom, G. T. Introductory Old English grammar and reader. Boston 1930.

Anderson, M. and B. C. Williams. Old English handbook. Cambridge Mass 1936.

Raith, J. Altenglisches Lesebuch (Prosa). Munich 1940; Wörterbuch, Munich 1944.

Funke, O. and K. Jost. An Old English reader. Berne 1942.

Langenhove, G. van. Old English reader, pt 1: texts. Bruges 1942.

Mossé, F. Manuel de l'anglais du Moyen Age, 1: vieil-anglais. Paris 1945.

Kaiser, R. Alt- und mittelenglische Anthologie. Berlin 1954; rev as Medieval English: an Old English and Middle English anthology, 1958 (3rd edn).

Lehnert, M. Poetry and prose of the Anglo-Saxons. 2 vols Berlin 1955–6.

Texts Used in Linguistic Studies

Except in the case of unique copies, reference to individual mss is selective.

For further details and bibliography see N. R. Ker, Catalogue of manuscripts containing Anglo-Saxon, *Oxford 1957.*

ASPR 6 = G. P. Krapp, E. V. K. Dobbie, The Anglo-Saxon poetic records: 6, The Anglo-Saxon minor poems, New York 1942;

ASR = H. Sweet. An Anglo-Saxon reader, rev D. Whitelock, above;

OET = H. Sweet, The Oldest English texts, above.

Wright-Wülcker = T. Wright, Anglo-Saxon and Old English vocabularies, 2 vols 1857–73, rev R. P. Wülcker 1884.

Charters and Other Historical Documents

Kemble, J. M. Codex diplomaticus aevi saxonici. 6 vols 1839–48.

Thorpe, B. Diplomatarium anglicum aevi saxonici. 1865.

[Bond, E. A. (ed)]. Facsimiles of ancient charters in the British Museum. 4 vols 1873–8.

[Sanders, W. B. (ed)]. Facsimiles of Anglo-Saxon manuscripts. 3 vols Southampton 1878–84 (Ordnance Survey).

Birch, W. de G. Cartularium saxonicum. 4 vols 1885–99.

Sweet, H. OET.
— A second Anglo-Saxon reader: archaic and dialectal. Oxford 1887.
Earle, J. A hand-book to the land-charters, and other Saxonic documents. Oxford 1888.
Napier, A. S. and W. H. Stevenson. The Crawford collection of early charters and documents. Oxford 1895.
Harmer, F. E. Select English historical documents of the ninth and tenth centuries. Cambridge 1914.
— Anglo-Saxon writs. Manchester 1952.
Ashdown, M. English and Norse documents relating to the reign of Ethelred the Unready. Cambridge 1930.
Whitelock, D. Anglo-Saxon wills. Cambridge 1930.
Robertson, A. J. Anglo-Saxon charters. Cambridge 1939, 1956 (rev).
For further details of charters see P. H. Sawyer, Anglo-Saxon charters: an annotated list and bibliography, *1968.*
Anglo-Saxon Chronicle. Ed B. Thorpe, The Anglo-Saxon Chronicle [all versions except BM ms Cotton Otho B xi], 2 vols 1861 (Rolls ser); ed C. Plummer, Two of the Saxon Chronicles parallel [mss Corpus Christi College Cambridge 173, Bodley Laud misc 636], 2 vols Oxford 1892–9, 1952 (with addns by D. Whitelock); ed E. Classen and F. E. Harmer, An Anglo-Saxon Chronicle [BM ms Cotton Tiberius B iv], Manchester 1926; ed H. A. Rositzke, The C-text of the Old English Chronicles [BM ms Cotton Tiberius B i], Bochum 1940; ed R. Flower and A. H. Smith, The Parker Chronicle and laws [Corpus Christi College Cambridge ms 173], Oxford 1941 (EETS) (facs); ed D. Whitelock and C. Clark, The Peterborough Chronicle [Bodley ms Laud misc 636], Copenhagen 1954 (facs) (Early Eng Mss in Facs 4).

West Saxon Texts

Ælfric. Works. *See col 317, below.*
Anglo-Saxon Chronicle [to 891]. Corpus Christi College Cambridge ms 173 ('Parker'). c. 891. *See above.*
Old English trn of Cura pastoralis. Mss Bodley Hatton 20, BM Cotton Tiberius B xi. c. 900. Ed H. Sweet, King Alfred's West-Saxon version of Gregory's Pastoral care, 1871–2 (EETS); ed N. R. Ker, The pastoral care, Copenhagen 1956 (facs) (Early Eng Mss in Facs 6).
Gospels, late West Saxon. Cambridge Univ Lib ms Ii 2 ii. c. 1000. Ed W. W. Skeat, The four Gospels in Anglo-Saxon, Northumbrian and Old Mercian versions, 4 vols Cambridge 1871–87; ed J. W. Bright, The Gospels in West Saxon, 4 vols Boston 1904–6; ed M. Grünberg, The West-Saxon Gospels, Amsterdam 1967.
Old English trn of Orosius. BM ms additional 47967 ('Lauderdale'). c. 900. Ed H. Sweet, King Alfred's Orosius: pt 1, 1883 (EETS); ed A. Campbell, The Tollemache Orosius, Copenhagen 1953 (facs) (Early Eng Mss in Facs 3).

Mercian Texts

Royal glosses. BM ms Royal 2 A xx. c. 1000. Ed J. Zupitza, Mercisches aus der Hs Royal 2 A 20 im Britischen Museum, Zeitschrift für Deutsches Alterthum und Deutsche Litteratur 33 1889.
Gloss to the Rushworth Gospels [Matthew, Mark 1 i – 2 xv, John 18 i–iii; 'Rushworth¹']. Bodley ms Auct D ii 19. 10th century. Ed W. W. Skeat, The four Gospels in Anglo-Saxon, Northumbrian and Old Mercian versions, 4 vols Cambridge 1871–87.
Gloss to the Vespasian Psalter. *See Psalters, below.*

Northumbrian Texts (*in alphabetical order*)

Bede's death-song. St Gallen, Stiftsbibliothek ms 254. 9th century. Ed H. Sweet, OET, ASR; ed A. H. Smith, Three Northumbrian poems, 1933; ed E. V. K. Dobbie,

ASPR 6. *See* E. V. K. Dobbie, The manuscripts of Cædmon's hymn and Bede's death song, New York 1937; on Hague, Koninklijke Bibliothek ms 70.H.7 *see* N. R. Ker, The Hague manuscript of the Epistola Cuthberti de obitu Bedæ with Bede's song, MÆ 8 1940 and R. Brotanek, Nachlese zu den 'Hss der Epistola Cuthberti und des Sterbespruches Bedas, Anglia 64 1940.
English names in Bede's Historia ecclesiastica. Mss Cambridge Univ Lib Kk 5 xvi ('Moore'), Leningrad Public Lib Lat Q v i 18. 8th century. Ed H. Sweet, OET; ed H. Ström, Old English personal names in Bede's History, Lund 1939; ed O. S. Anderson (Arngart), Old English material in the Leningrad manuscript of Bede's Ecclesiastical history, Lund 1941; ed Arngart, Copenhagen 1952 (facs of Leningrad ms), P. H. Blair and R. A. B. Mynors, Copenhagen 1959 (facs of Moore ms) (Early Eng Mss in Facs 2, 9).
Caedmon's hymn. Mss Cambridge Univ Lib Kk 5 xvi ('Moore'), Leningrad Public Lib Lat Q v i 18 of Bede's Historia ecclesiastica. 8th century. Ed H. Sweet, OET, ASR; ed A. H. Smith, Three Northumbrian poems, 1933; ed E. V. K. Dobbie, ASPR 6; ed O. Arngart (facs of Leningrad ms), P. H. Blair and R. A. B. Mynors (facs of Moore ms), above. *See* E. V. K. Dobbie, The manuscripts of Cædmon's hymn and Bede's death song, New York 1937.
Durham Ritual. Durham cathedral ms A iv 19. 10th century. Ed U. Lindelöf 1927 (Surtees Soc); ed T. J. Brown et al, Copenhagen 1969 (facs) (Early Eng Mss in Facs 16). Collation by A. Squires, N & Q Oct 1971.
Franks casket inscription. 8th century. Ed H. Sweet, OET; ed E. Wadstein, The Clermont runic casket, Skrifter Utgivna av Kungl. Humanistiska Vetenskaps-Samfundet i Uppsala 6 1900; ed A. S. Napier, in An English miscellany presented to Dr [F. J.] Furnivall, Oxford 1901; ed E. V. K. Dobbie, ASPR 6; ed R. W. V. Elliott, Runes, Manchester 1959. *See also* C. J. E. Ball, The Franks casket: right side, E Studies 47 1966; M. Osborn, Two inconsistent letters on the Franks casket, right side, Neuphilologische Mitteilungen 72 1971.
Leiden riddle. Leiden, Rijksuniversiteit ms Vossianus Lat 4° 106. 9th century. Ed H. Sweet, OET, ASR; ed A. H. Smith, Three Northumbrian poems, 1933; ed R. W. Zandvoort, Eng & Germanic Stud 3 1950, rptd with two additional plates in his Collected papers, Groningen 1954; ed E. V. K. Dobbie, ASPR 6; ed J. Gerritsen, The text of the Leiden riddle, E Studies 50 1969.
Liber vitae dunelmensis. BM ms Cotton Domitian A vii. 9th century. Ed H. Sweet, OET; ed A. H. Thompson 1923 (Surtees Soc) (facs). Partial collation by E. Björkman, Zum nordhumbrischen Liber vitæ, Beiblatt zur Anglia 29 1918.
Gloss to the Lindisfarne Gospels. BM ms Cotton Nero D iv. 10th century. Ed W. W. Skeat, The four Gospels in Anglo-Saxon, Northumbrian and Old Mercian versions, 4 vols Cambridge 1871–87; ed T. D. Kendrick et al, Evangeliorum quattuor codex lindisfarnensis, 2 vols Lausanne 1956–60 (facs). Partial collation by D. E. Chadwick, C. B. Judge and A. S. C. Ross, Leeds Stud in Eng 3 1934.
Gloss to the Rushworth Gospels [Except Matthew, Mark 1 i – 2 xv, John 18 i–iii; 'Rushworth²']. Bodley ms Auct D ii 19. 10th century. Ed W. W. Skeat, The four Gospels in Anglo-Saxon, Northumbrian and Old Mercian versions, 4 vols Cambridge 1871–87.
Ruthwell cross inscription. 8th century. Ed H. Sweet, OET, ASR; ed B. Dickins and A. S. C. Ross, The dream of the rood, 1934, 1963 (with addns and corrections); ed E. V. K. Dobbie, ASPR 6; ed R. W. V. Elliott, Runes, Manchester 1959; ed M. Swanton, The dream of the rood, 1970.

Kentish Texts

Kentish glosses. BM ms Cotton Vespasian D vi. 10th century. Ed J. Zupitza, Kentische Glossen des neunten Jahrhunderts, Zeitschrift für Deutsches Alterthum und Deutsche Litteratur 21 1877, corrections 22 1878; ed Wright-Wülcker; ed H. Sweet, A second Anglo-Saxon reader; archaic and dialectal, Oxford 1887.

Kentish hymn. BM ms Cotton Vespasian D vi. 10th century. Ed E. V. K. Dobbie, ASPR 6.

Kentish psalm. BM ms Cotton Vespasian D vi. 10th century. Ed H. Sweet, ASR; ed E. V. K. Dobbie, ASPR 6.

Psalters (in alphabetical order)

Arundel Psalter. BM ms Arundel 60. c. 1050–75. Ed G. Oess, Der altenglische Arundel-Psalter, Heidelberg 1910.

Blickling Psalter. New York, Pierpont Morgan Lib ms 776. 8th and 11th centuries. Ed H. Sweet, OET (8th century glosses); ed E. Brock in R. Morris, The Blickling homilies: pt 3, 1880 (EETS).

Bosworth Psalter. BM ms additional 37517. c. 975–1000. Ed U. Lindelöf, Die altenglischen Glossen im Bosworth-Psalter, Helsinki 1909.

Cambridge Psalter. Cambridge Univ Lib ms Ff 1 xxiii. c. 1025. Ed K. Wildhagen, Der Cambridger Psalter, Hamburg 1910.

Canterbury Psalter. Trinity College Cambridge ms R 17 i. c. 1150. Ed F. Harsley, Eadwine's Canterbury Psalter, 1889 (EETS); ed M. R. James, The Canterbury Psalter, 1935 (facs). See K. Wildhagen, Über die in Eadwine's Canterbury Psalter enthaltene altenglische Psalter-Interlinearversion, Göttingen 1903; Wildhagen 1905, col 67, above; Zum Eadwine- und Regius-Psalter, E Studien 39 1908.

Junius Psalter. Bodley ms Junius 27. c. 925. Ed E. Brenner, Der altenglische Junius-Psalter, Heidelberg 1909.

Lambeth Psalter. Lambeth Palace ms 427. c. 1025. Ed U. Lindelöf, Der Lambeth-Psalter, 2 pts Helsinki 1909–14.

Paris Psalter. Paris, Bibliothèque Nationale ms Latin 8824. c. 1025. Ed B. Thorpe, Libri psalmorum versio antiqua latina cum paraphrasi anglo-saxonica, Oxford 1835; ed J. W. Bright and R. L. Ramsay, Liber psalmorum: the West-Saxon psalms, Boston 1907 (prose only); ed G. P. Krapp, The Paris Psalter and the metres of Boethius, New York 1932 (The Anglo-Saxon poetic records 5) (verse only); ed B. Colgrave, Copenhagen 1958 (facs) (Early Eng Mss in Facs 8).

Royal Psalter. BM ms Royal 2 B v. c. 950. Ed F. Roeder, Der altenglische Regius-Psalter, Halle 1904.

Salisbury Psalter. Salisbury cathedral ms 150. c. 1100. Ed C. and K. Sisam, The Salisbury Psalter, 1959 (EETS).

Vespasian Psalter. BM ms Cotton Vespasian A i. c. 875–900. Ed H. Sweet, OET; ed S. M. Kuhn, The Vespasian Psalter, Ann Arbor [1965]; ed D. H. Wright and A. Campbell, Copenhagen 1967 (facs) (Early Eng Mss in Facs 14). Collations by R. Roberts, Leeds Stud in Eng 1 1932; by S. M. Kuhn, JEGP 40 1941. See also J. Gerritsen, A note on the Vespasian Psalter gloss, E Studies 51 1970 (on origin of gloss).

Vitellius Psalter. BM ms Cotton Vitellius E xviii. c. 1050. Ed J. L. Rosier, Ithaca 1962.

The Psalter in BM ms Stowe 2 (11th century) is ptd in J. Spelman, Psalterium Davidis latino-saxonicum vetus, 1640, also partially in U. Lindelöf 1904, below, and the Canticles from this ms are ed J. L. Rosier, The Stowe Canticles, Anglia 82 1964; the Psalter in BM ms Cotton Tiberius C vi (c. 1050–75) is partially ptd in U. Lindelöf 1904, below; further Psalter fragments are ptd by H. Hargreaves and C. Clark, An unpublished Old English

Psalter-gloss fragment, N & Q Dec 1965 (Paris, Bibliothèque Nationale ms Latin 8846), and by K. Dietz, Dic ae. Psalterglossen der Hs. Cambridge, Pembroke College 312, Anglia 86 1968.

See also U. Lindelöf, Studien zu altenglischen Psalterglossen, Bonn 1904; K. Wildhagen, Studien zum Psalterium romanum in England und zu seinen Glossierungen, in Festschrift für Lorenz Morsbach, Halle 1913, also separately, Halle 1913; Das Psalterium gallicanum in England, E Studien 54 1920; O. Heinzel, Kritische Entstehungsgeschichte des ags. Interlinear-Psalters, Leipzig 1926.

Glossaries (in alphabetical order)

See Wright-Wülcker; W. M. Lindsay, The Corpus, Epinal, Erfurt and Leyden glossaries, Oxford [1921].

Corpus glossary. Corpus Christi College Cambridge ms 144. 8th or 9th century. Ed Wright-Wülcker; ed H. Sweet, OET; ed J. H. Hessels, An eighth-century Latin–Anglo-Saxon glossary preserved in the library of Corpus Christi College, Cambridge, Cambridge 1890; ed W. M. Lindsay, The Corpus glossary, Cambridge 1921.

Epinal glossary. Épinal, Bibliothèque Municipale ms 72. 9th century? Ed H. Sweet, OET; ed H. Sweet 1883 (EETS) (facs); ed O. B. Schlutter, Hamburg 1912 (facs).

Erfurt glossary. Erfurt, Wissenschaftliche Bibliothek ms Amplonianus F 42. 9th century. Ed H. Sweet, OET.

Harley glossary. BM ms Harley 3376. 10th century. Ed Wright-Wülcker; ed R. O. Oliphant, The Harley Latin–Old English glossary, Hague 1966.

Leiden glossary. Leiden, Rijksuniversiteit ms Vossianus Lat 4° 69. 8th century. Ed H. Sweet, OET; ed P. Glogger, Das Leidener Glossar, 3 vols Augsburg 1901–8; ed J. H. Hessels, A late eighth-century Latin–Anglo-Saxon glossary preserved in the library of the Leiden University, Cambridge 1906; ed F. Holthausen, Die Leidener Glossen, E Studien 50 1917 (see O. B. Schlutter, Anglia 44–5 1920–1).

Other Texts

Glosses to Aldhelm, De laudibus virginitatis. Brussels, Bibliothèque Royale ms 1650 (1520). 11th century. Ed F. Mone, Quellen und Forschungen zur Geschichte der teutschen Literatur und Sprache, Aachen 1830; ed [C. W.] Bouterwek, Zeitschrift für Deutsches Alterthum 9 1853 (collation by E. Hausknecht, Anglia 6 1883; see also O. B. Schlutter, Zu den Brüsseler Aldhelmglossen, Anglia 33 1910); ed G. van Langenhove, Bruges 1941 (facs). See also Derolez 1955–60, col 76, below.

Bede glosses. BM ms Cotton Tiberius C ii. c. 900. Ed H. Sweet, OET; ed F. Holthausen, Die altenglischen Beda-Glossen, Archiv 136 1917. Kentish?

Old English trn of Bede's Historia ecclesiastica. Ms Bodley Tanner 10. 10th century. Ed T. Miller 1890–8 (EETS); ed J. Schipper, Leipzig 1899. See F. Klaeber, Zur altenglischen Bedaübersetzung, Anglia 25 1902, 27 1904.

Blickling homilies. Ms in John H. Scheide Lib, Princeton. 10th century. Ed R. Morris 1874–80 (EETS); ed R. Willard, Copenhagen 1960 (facs) (Early English Mss in Facs 10).

The life of St Chad. Bodley ms Hatton 116. 12th century. Ed A. Napier, Anglia 10 1888; ed R. Vleeskruyer, Amsterdam 1953.

Genealogies in BM ms Cotton Vespasian B vi. 9th century. Ed H. Sweet, OET. See K. Sisam, Anglo-Saxon royal genealogies, Proc Br Acad 39 1953.

Old English trn of Gregory's Dialogues. Mss Corpus Christi College Cambridge 322, BM Cotton Otho C i vol 2. 11th century. Ed H. Hecht, Bischof Wærferths von Worcester Übersetzung der Dialoge Gregors des Grossen, Cassel 1900–7.

The following edns of miscellaneous items are arranged in chronological order of pbn:

Zupitza, J. Englisches aus Prudentiushandschriften. Zeitschrift für Deutsches Alterthum und Deutsche Litteratur 20 1876.

— Altenglische Glossen zu Abbos Clericorum decus. Zeitschrift für Deutsches Alterthum und Deutsche Litteratur 31 1887.

Logeman, H. The rule of St Benet: Latin and Anglo-Saxon interlinear version. 1888 (EETS).

Logeman, W. S. De consuetudine monachorum. Anglia 13 1891, 15 1893.

Napier, A. S. Old English glosses: chiefly unpublished. Oxford 1900.

Förster, M. Die altenglische Glossenhandschrift Plantinus 32 (Antwerpen) und Additional 32246 (London). Anglia 41 1917.

— Zu den ae. Texten aus ms Arundel 155. Anglia 66 1942.

Klappenbach, H. Zu altenglischen Interlinearversionen von Paraphrasen lateinischer Hymnen. Leipzig 1930.

Meritt, H. [D.] Old English scratched glosses in Cotton ms Tiberius C ii. Amer Jnl of Philology 54 1933.

— Old English entries in a manuscript at Bern. JEGP 33 1934.

— Old English Sedulius glosses. Amer Jnl of Philology 57 1936.

— Possible elliptical compounds in Old English glosses. Amer Jnl of Philology 59 1938.

— Three studies in Old English. Amer Jnl of Philology 62 1941.

— Old English glosses: a collection. New York 1945.

— Old English Aldhelm glosses. MLN 67 1952.

— Old English glosses to Gregory, Ambrose and Prudentius. JEGP 56 1957.

— The Old English Prudentius glosses at Boulogne-sur-Mer. Stanford 1959.

— Old English glosses, mostly dry point. JEGP 60 1961.

Holthausen, F. Altenglische Interlinearversionen lateinischer Gebete und Beichten. Anglia 65 1941.

— Eine altenglische Interlinearversion des athanasianischen Glaubensbekenntnisses. E Studien 75 1943.

Mustanoja, T. F. Notes on some Old English glosses in Aldhelm's De laudibus virginitatis. Neuphilologische Mitteilungen 51 1950.

Sisam, C. An early fragment of the Old English Martyrology. RES new ser 4 1953. BM ms additional 40, 165A, 9th century.

Stryker, W. G. Old English glossary gleanings. JEGP 52 1953.

Derolez, R. De oudengelse Aldhelmglossen in hs 1650 van de Koninklijke bibliothek te Brussel. Handelingen van de Zuidnederlandse Maatschappij voor Taal-en Letterkunde en Geschiedenis 9 1955. Aldhelmus glosatus 1.

— Zu den brüsseler Aldhelmglossen. Anglia 74 1956. Aldhelmus glosatus 2.

— Aldhelmus glosatus 3. E Studies 40 1959.

— Aldhelmus glosatus 4: some *hapax legomena* among the Old English Aldhelm glosses. Studia Germanica Gandensia 2 1960.

Rosier, J. L. Old English glosses to an epistle of Boniface. JEGP 59 1960.

— Contributions to OE lexicography: some Boethius glosses. Archiv 200 1964.

— Ten Old English Psalter glosses. JEGP 63 1964.

Quinn, J. J. Ghost words, obscure lemmata, and doubtful glosses in a Latin–Old English glossary. PQ 40 1961. On BM ms Cotton Cleopatra A iii.

Hofmann, J. Altenglische und althochdeutsche Glossen aus Würzburg und dem weiteren angelsächsischen Missionsgebiet. Beiträge zur Geschichte der Deutschen Sprache und Literatur (Halle) 85 1963.

Riehle, W. Über einige neuentdeckten altenglischen Glossen. Anglia 84 1966.

(2) MIDDLE ENGLISH

General

Morsbach, L. Mittelenglische Grammatik: 1 Hälfte. Halle 1896.

Wright, J. and E. M. An elementary Middle English grammar. Oxford 1923, 1928 (rev).

Jordan, R. Handbuch der mittelenglischen Grammatik, 1 Teil: Lautlehre. Heidelberg 1925; rev H. C. Matthes with bibliographical addns by K. Dietz 1968.

Wardale, E. E. An introduction to Middle English. 1937.

Brunner, K. Abriss der mittelenglischen Grammatik. Halle 1938, 1962 (rev); tr G. K. W. Johnston, An outline of Middle English grammar, Oxford 1963.

Mossé, F. Manuel de l'anglais du Moyen Age, 2: moyen-anglais. 2 vols Paris 1949, 1959 (rev); tr J. A. Walker, A handbook of Middle English, Baltimore 1952.

Berndt, R. Einführung in das Studium des Mittelenglischen: unter Zugrundelegung des Prologs der Canterbury tales. Halle 1960.

Fisiak, J. Outlines of Middle English grammar, 1: graphics, phonology and morphology. Łódź 1964, Warsaw 1968 (rev as A short grammar of Middle English, Part 1: graphemics, phonemics and morphemics).

Weinstock, H. Mittelenglisches Elementarbuch. Berlin 1968.

Jones, C. An introduction to Middle English. New York 1972.

Special Studies

Maack, R. Die Flexion des englischen Substantivs von 1100 bis etwa 1250. Strasbourg 1888.

Luick, K. Über die Entwicklung von ae. *ŭ-, ĭ-* und die Dehnung in offener Silbe überhaupt. Archiv 102–3 1899.

— Studien zur englischen Lautgeschichte. Vienna 1903. On development of OE *ĭ, ŭ.*

Heuser, W. Die mittelengl. Entwicklung von *ŭ* in offener Silbe. E Studien 27 1900.

Diehn, O. Die Pronomina im Frühmittelenglischen. Heidelberg 1901.

Pogatscher, A. Die englische *æ/ē*-Grenze. Anglia 23 1901.

Wyld, H. C. The history of Old English fronted (palatalized) initial *ʒ* in the Middle and Modern English dialects. Otia Merseiana 2 1901.

— The treatment of OE *ȳ* in the dialects of the Midland and SE counties in ME. E Studien 47 1914.

— Old English *ȳ* in the dialects of the south and south western counties in Middle English. Ibid.

Knapp, O. Die Ausbreitung des flektierten Genitivs auf -s im Mittelenglischen. E Studien 31 1902.

Vogel, E. Zur Flexion des englischen Verbums im xi und xii Jahrhundert. Jena 1902.

Bülbring, K. D. Über Erhaltung des altenglischen kurzen und langen *æ*-Lautes im Mittelenglischen. Bonn 1904.

Cornelius, H. Die altenglische Diphthongierung durch Palatale im Spiegel der mittelenglischen Dialekte. Halle 1907.

Eilers, F. Die Dehnung vor dehnenden Konsonantenverbindungen im Mittelenglischen mit Berücksichtigung der neuenglischen Mundarten. Halle 1907.

Flom, G. T. Contributions to the history of English, 1: the origin of the pronoun *she*. JEGP 7 1908.

Mařík, J. *W*-Schwund im Mittel- und Frühneuenglischen. Vienna 1911.

Gabrielson, A. The influence of *w*- in Old English as seen in the Middle English dialects. Gothenburg 1912.

Ekwall, E. Ortsnamenforschung ein Hilfmittel für das englische Sprachgeschichte. Germanisch-romanische Monatsschrift 5 1913. On OE *ā*, *ȳ* in Lancs.

— The Middle English *ā/ō* boundary. E Studies 20 1938.

Ritter, O. Zur englischen *ǣ/ē* Grenze. Anglia 37 1913.

Brandl, A. Zur Geographie der altenglischen Dialekte. Berlin 1915. On OE *ǣ*, *ȳ*.

Ruud, M. B. A conjecture concerning the origin of Modern English *she*. MLN 35 1920.

Bryan, W. F. The Midland present plural indicative ending -*e(n)*. MP 18 1921.

Marquardt, P. Das starke Participium Praeteriti im Mittelenglischen. Berlin 1922.

Serjeantson, M. S. The dialectal distribution of certain phonological features in Middle English. E Studies 4 1922. On *æ*+*l*+consonant; *i*-mutation of *ēa*; *ēo* in South and West; *ȳ*.

— The development of Old English *ēag*, *ēah* in Middle English. JEGP 26 1927.

— Middle English -*ong* > -*ung*. RES 7 1930.

Kihlbom, A. A contribution to the study of fifteenth-century English. Upsala 1926.

Mackenzie, B. A. A special dialectal development of OE *ēa*. E Studien 61 1927.

Moore, S. Earliest morphological changes in Middle English. Language 4 1928.

Malone, K. When did Middle English begin? In Curme volume of linguistic studies, Baltimore 1930.

Langenfelt, G. Select studies in colloquial English of the late Middle Ages. Lund 1933.

Gaaf, W. van der. The evolution of nasal *a* in Anglo-Norman and in English. E Studies 15 1933.

Wilson, R. M. *ǣ*[1] and *ǣ*[2] in Middle English. Proc Leeds Philosophical & Literary Soc 3 1935.

Buchholz, E. Das Verbum substantivum im Mittelenglischen. Bottrop 1936.

Appel, M. F. von. Zur Schreibung der interdentalen Spirans im Mittelenglischen. E Studien 71 1937.

Koziol, H. Der Abfall des nachtonigen -*e* im Mittelenglischen. Beiblatt zur Anglia 48 1937.

Ekselius, P. A study on the development of the Old English combinations *ǎht/ōht* in Middle English. Upsala 1940.

Prins, A. A. A few early examples of the Great Vowel Shift. Neophilologus 27 1942.

Long, M. M. The English strong verb from Chaucer to Caxton. Menasha 1944.

French, W. H. Dialects and forms in three romances. JEGP 45 1946.

Forsström, G. The verb *to be* in Middle English: a survey of the forms. Lund 1948.

Bliss, A. J. Three Middle English studies. Eng & Germanic Stud 2 1949.

Wittig, K. Über die mittelenglische Dehnung in offener Silbe und die Entwicklung der *ēr* Laute im Frühneuenglischen. Anglia 70 1951.

Pilch, H. Me. *i*- beim Participium Präteriti. Anglia 73 1955.

Kurath, H. The loss of long consonants and the rise of voiced fricatives in Middle English. Language 32 1956.

McIntosh, A. The analysis of written Middle English. Trans Philological Soc. 1956

Sundby, B. Middle English overlapping of *v* and *w* and its phonemic significance. Anglia 74 1956.

Lamberts, J. J. The development of *made*. JEGP 55 1956.

Bazire, J. An examination of rhymes containing Middle English *ē*. Studia Neophilologica 29 1957.

Stockwell, R. P. The Middle English 'long close' and 'long open' mid vowels. Texas Stud in Lit & Lang 2 1961.

Dobson, E. J. Middle English lengthening in open syllables. Trans Philological Soc 1962.

Francis, W. N. Graphemic analysis of late Middle English manuscripts. Speculum 37 1962.

Rennhard, S. Das Demonstrativum im Mittelenglischen 1200–1500. Winterthur 1962.

Stevick, R. D. The morphemic evolution of Middle English *she*. E Studies 45 1964.

Liberman, A. S. K voprosu o sredneangliĭskom udlinenii v otkrytom sloge: iz istorii fonem /e/ i /o/. Vestnik Leningradskogo Universiteta 20 1965: Seriya istorii, yazyka i literatury. On the problem of ME lengthening in open syllables: concerning the history of the phonemes /e/ and /o/.

— K istorii dolgoty v sredneangliĭskom. Nauchnye Doklady Vysshei Shkoly: Filologicheskie Nauki 1965. On the history of length in ME.

— Some notes on the history of Middle English /e/ and /o/ in open syllables. Zeitschrift für Anglistik und Amerikanistik 13 1965.

— On the history of Middle English *ā* and *a*. Neuphilologische Mitteilungen 67 1966.

Yamaguchi, H. On the phonological feature of the feminine personal pronoun *she*. Study of Sounds (Tokyo) 12 1966.

Garcia, E. C. Inflection as a derivational device: the ME Midlands plural endings. Neuphilologische Mitteilungen 71 1970.

Middle English Dialects

Bülbring, K. D. Geschichte des Ablauts der starken Zeitwörter innerhalb des Südenglischen. Strasbourg 1889.

Konrath, M. Zur Laut- und Flexionslehre des Mittelkentischen. Archiv 88–9 1892.

Reeves, W. P. A study in the language of Scottish prose before 1600. Baltimore 1893.

Heuser, W. Zum kent. Dialekt im Mittelenglischen. Anglia 17 1895.

— Die ältesten Denkmäler und die Dialekte des Nordenglischen. Anglia 31 1908.

— Alt-London. Osnabrück 1914.

Ackermann, A. Die Sprache der ältesten schottischen Urkunden. Göttingen 1897.

Danker, O. Die Laut- und Flexionslehre der mittelkentischen Denkmäler. Strasbourg 1897.

Baumann, I. Die Sprache der Urkunden aus Yorkshire im 15 Jahrhundert. Heidelberg 1902.

Gregory Smith, G. Specimens of Middle Scots. Edinburgh 1902. Introd.

Knopff, P. Darstellung der Ablautsverhältnisse in der schottischen Schriftsprache. Berne 1904.

Hanssen, H. Die Geschichte der starken Zeitwörter im Nordenglischen. Kiel 1906.

Lekebusch, J. Die Londoner Urkundensprache von 1430–1500. Halle 1906.

Meyer, W. Flexionslehre der ältesten schottischen Urkunden 1385–1440. Halle 1907.

Jordan, R. Die mittelenglischen Mundarten. Germanisch-romanische Monatsschrift 2 1910.

Dölle, E. Zur Sprache Londons vor Chaucer. Halle 1913.

Wyld, H. C. South-Eastern and South-East Midland dialects in Middle English. E & S 6 1920.

— The Surrey dialect in the xiiith century. E Studies 3 1921.

Hulbert, J. R. The 'West Midland' of the romances. MP 19 1921.

— A thirteenth-century English literary standard. JEGP 45 1946. On 'AB' language.

Menner, R. J. Sir Gawain and the Green Knight and the West Midland dialect. PMLA 37 1922.

— Four notes on the West Midland dialect. MLN 41 1926.

— and H. R. Patch. A bibliography of Middle English dialects. SP 20 1923.

Vikar, A. Contributions to the history of the Durham dialects. Malmö 1922.

Öfverberg, W. The inflections of the East Midland dialects in early Middle English: substantives, adjectives, numerals and pronouns. Lund 1924.

—— The verbal inflections of the East Midland dialects in early Middle English. Lund 1924.

Taylor, A. B. On the history of Old English ēa, ēo in Middle Kentish. MLR 19 1924.

Reaney, P. H. On certain phonological features of the dialect of London in the twelfth century. E Studien 59 1925.

—— The dialect of London in the thirteenth century. E Studien 61 1927.

Serjeantson, M. S. The dialects of the West Midlands in Middle English. RES 3 1927.

Mackenzie, B. A. The early London dialect: contributions to the history of the dialect of London during the Middle English period. Oxford 1928.

Peitz, A. Der Einfluss des nördlichen Dialektes im Mittelenglischen auf die entstehende Hochsprache. Bonn 1933.

Koch, J. Der anglonormannische Traktat des Walter von Bibbesworth in seiner Bedeutung für die Anglistik. Anglia 58 1934.

Rettger, J. F. The development of ablaut in the strong verbs of the East Midland dialects of Middle English. Philadelphia 1934.

Moore, S., S. B. Meech and H. Whitehall. Middle English dialect characteristics and dialect boundaries. In Essays and studies in English and comparative literature, Ann Arbor 1935.

Friederici, H. Der Lautstand Londons um 1400. Jena 1937.

Weber-Liel, B. Die Sprache Winchesters im Spätmittelalter. Jena 1939.

Bohman, H. Studies in the Middle English dialects of Devon and London. Gothenburg 1944.

Arngart, O. S. Middle English dialects. Studier i Modern Språkvetenskap 17 1949.

Rubin, S. The phonology of the Middle English dialect of Sussex. Lund 1951.

Bliss, A. J. A note on 'language AB'. Eng & Germanic Stud 5 1953.

Conner, J. E. Phonemic discrimination of Middle English dialects. In Studies in English honoring George Wesley Whiting, Houston 1958 (Rice Inst).

McIntosh, A. A new approach to Middle English dialectology. E Studies 44 1963.

—— and M. L. Samuels. Prolegomena to a study of mediæval Anglo-Irish. MÆ 37 1968.

Samuels, M. L. Some applications of Middle English dialectology. E Studies 44 1963.

Sundby, B. Studies in the Middle English dialect material of Worcestershire records. Bergen 1963.

—— Present-day trends in Middle English dialectology. Revue des Langues Vivantes 36 1970.

Kristensson, G. Another approach to Middle English dialectology. E Studies 46 1965. Example of Lincolnshire.

—— A survey of Middle English dialects 1290–1350: the six northern counties and Lincolnshire. Lund 1967.

Kohler, K. J. Aspects of Middle Scots phonemics and graphemics: the phonological implications of the sign ⟨i⟩. Trans Philological Soc 1967.

Jacobson, R. The London dialect of the late fourteenth century: a transformational analysis in historical linguistics. Hague 1970.

Aitken, A. J. Variation and variety in written Middle Scots. In Edinburgh studies in English and Scots, ed A. J. Aitken et al 1971.

Macrae-Gibson, O. D. The Auchinleck ms: participles in -and(e). E Studies 52 1971. On -and(e) as a London form.

Ek, K.-G. The development of OE ȳ and ēo in southeastern Middle English. Lund 1972.

See also A. Steponavičius 1963, 1965, col 66, above.

Middle English Texts
(in alphabetical order)

Langer, F. Zur Sprache des Abingdon Chartulars. Berlin 1904.

Glawe, E. Der Sprachgebrauch in den altschottischen Gesetzen der Handschrift Adv. Lib. 25.4.16. Berlin 1908.

Mühe, T. Über den in ms Cotton Titus D xviii enthaltenen Text der Ancren riwle. Göttingen 1902.

Williams, I. F. The language of the Cleopatra ms of the Ancren riwle. Anglia 28 1905.

Ostermann, H. Lautlehre des germanischen Wortschatzes in der von Morton herausgegebenen Handschrift der Ancren riwle. Bonn 1905.

Heuser, W. Die Ancren riwle. Anglia 30 1907.

Serjeantson, M. S. The dialect of the Corpus manuscript of the Ancrene riwle. London Mediæval Stud 1 1939 [1948].

Zettersten, A. Studies in the dialect and vocabulary of the Ancrene riwle. Lund 1965.

Suzuki, S. The language of the Ancrene wisse. Tokyo 1967.

Liedholm, A. A phonological study of the Middle English romance Arthour and Merlin (ms Auchinleck). Upsala 1941.

Rasmussen, J. K. Die Sprache John Audelays. Bonn 1914.

Hooper, A. G. The Awntyrs off Arthure: dialect and authorship. Leeds Stud in Eng 4 1935.

Jensen, H. Die Verbalflexion im Ayenbite of inwyt. Kiel 1908.

Dölle, R. Graphische und lautliche Untersuchung von Aȝenbite of inwit. Bonn 1912.

Senff, H. Die Nominalflexion im Ayenbite of inwyt. Jena 1937.

Henschel, F. H. Darstellung der Flexionslehre in Barbours Bruce. Leipzig 1886.

Mühleisen, F. W. Untersuchungen von Barbours Bruce. Bonn 1913.

Williams, O. T. On OE a, ā and æ in the rimes of Barbour's Brus and in Modern Scotch dialects. Trans Philological Soc 1911–14.

Tachauer, J. Die Laute und Flexionen der 'Winteney-Version' der Regula S. Benedicti. Würzburg 1900.

Hagel, F. Zur Sprache der mittelenglischen Prosaversion der Benediktiner Regel. Anglia 43 1920.

Hallbeck, E. S. The language of the Middle English Bestiary. Christiansund 1905.

Meech, S. B. Nicholas Bishop: an exemplar of the Oxford dialect of the fifteenth century PMLA 49 1934.

Hoofe, A. Lautuntersuchungen zu Osbern Bokenams Legenden. E Studien 8 1885.

Dibelius, W. John Capgrave und die englische Schriftsprache. Anglia 23–4 1901.

Perrin, L. P. Über Thomas Castlefords Chronik. Boston 1890.

Roemstedt, H. Die englische Schriftsprache bei Caxton. Göttingen 1891.

Wiencke, H. Die Sprache Caxtons. Leipzig 1930.

Süssbier, K. Die Sprache der Cely-papers. Berlin 1905.

Daunt, M. A study on the rhymes used by Charles of Orleans in his English poems. Trans Philological Soc 1949.

Brink, B. ten. Chaucers Sprache und Verskunst. Leipzig 1884, 1920 (rev F. Kluge and E. Eckhardt); tr M. B. Smith, The language and metre of Chaucer, 1901.

Frieshammer, J. Die sprachliche Form der Chaucerschen Prosa. Halle 1910.

Wild, F. Die sprachlichen Eigentümlichkeiten der wichtigeren Chaucer-Handschriften und die Sprache Chaucers. Vienna 1915.

Bihl, J. Die Wirkungen des Rhythmus in der Sprache von Chaucer und Gower. Heidelberg 1916.

Langhans, V. Der Reimvokal e bei Chaucer. Anglia 44 1921.

Tolkien, J. R. R. Chaucer as a philologist: the Reeve's tale. Trans Philological Soc 1934.

Crow, M. M. The Reeve's tale in the hands of a North Midland scribe. SE 18 1938.

McJimsey, R. B. Chaucer's irregular -e. New York 1942.

Bradley, R. J. The use of cockney dialect by Chaucer. Quart Jnl of Speech 29 1943.

Southworth, J. G. Chaucer's final -e in rhyme. PMLA 62 1947. See E. T. Donaldson 63-4 1948-9, J. G. Southworth 64 1949.

Kökeritz, H. A guide to Chaucer's pronunciation. Stockholm 1954.

Malone, K. Chaucer's double consonants and the final e. Mediaeval Stud 18 1956.

Storms, G. A note on Chaucer's pronunciation of French u. E Studies 41 1960.

Fisiak, J. Morphemic structure of Chaucer's English. University Al 1965.

Topliff, D. Analysis of singular weak adjective inflection in Chaucer's works. Jnl of Eng Linguistics 4 1970.

Curtis, F. J. An investigation of the rimes and phonology of the Middle-Scotch romance Clariodus. Anglia 16–17 1894–5.

Hörning, W. Die Schreibung der Hs. E des Cursor mundi. Berlin 1906.

Strandberg, O. Rime-vowels of Cursor mundi. Upsala 1919.

Arend, Z. M. Linking in Cursor mundi: a phonological investigation. Trans Philological Soc 1930.

Baildon, H. B. On the rimes in the authentic poems of William Dunbar. Trans Royal Soc of Edinburgh 39 1900; also separately, Edinburgh 1899.

Knigge, F. Die Sprache des Dichters von Sir Gawain and the Green Knight, der sogenannten Early English alliterative poems und De Erkenwalde. Marburg 1886.

Bazire, J. ME ẹ̄ and ę̄ in the rhymes of Sir Gawain and the Green Knight. JEGP 51 1952.

Hilmer, H. Die Sprache von Genesis und Exodus. Sondershausen 1876.

Segelhorst, W. Die Sprache des English register of Godstow nunnery (c. 1450). Marburg 1908.

Fahrenberg, F. Zur Sprache der Confessio amantis. Archiv 89 1892.

Burch, J. C. H. Notes on the language of John Gower. E Studies 16 1934.

Casson, L. F. Studies in the diction of the Confessio amantis. E Studien 69 1934.

Schultz, E. Die Sprache der English Gilds aus dem Jahre 1389. Jena 1891.

Moeller, W. Untersuchungen über Dialekt und Stil des mittelenglischen Guy of Warwick in der Fassung der Auchinleck-Handschrift. Königsberg 1917.

Schlüter, A. Über die Sprache und Metrik der mittelenglischen weltlichen und geistlichen lyrischen Lieder des ms Harl. 2253. Archiv 71 1884.

Brook, G. L. The original dialect of the Harley lyrics. Leeds Stud in Eng 2 1933.

Keller, H. Die me. Rezepte des ms Harley 2253. Archiv 207 1971.

Hohmann, L. Über Sprache und Stil des altenglischen Lai Havelok þe Dane. Marburg 1886.

Schmidt, F. Zur Heimatbestimmung des Havelok. Göttingen 1900.

Britton, G. C. n-plurals in the nouns of Havelok the Dane. Neuphilologische Mitteilungen 60 1959.

—— A note on the word thing in Havelok the Dane. Neuphilologische Mitteilungen 61 1960.

Kirschten, W. Überlieferung und Sprache der mittelenglischen Romanze The lyfe of Ipomedon. Marburg 1885.

Wolderich, W. Über die Sprache und Heimat einiger frühmittelenglischer religiöser Gedichte des Jesus und Cotton ms. Göttingen 1909.

Stodte, H. Über die Sprache und Heimat der Katherine-Gruppe. Göttingen 1896.

Reimann, M. Die Sprache der mittelkentischen Evangelien. Berlin 1883.

Stadlmann, A. Die Sprache der mittelenglischen Predigtsammlung in der Handschrift Lambeth 487. Vienna 1921.

Wilson, R. M. The provenance of the Lambeth homilies with a new collation. Leeds Stud in Eng 4 1935.

Lucht, P. B. Lautlehre der älteren Laȝamonhandschrift. Berlin 1905.

Luhmann, A. Die Überlieferung von Laȝamons Brut. Halle 1905.

Lange, H. Das Zeitwort in den beiden Handschriften von Laȝamons Brut. Strasbourg 1906.

Kühl, O. Der Vokalismus der Laȝamon-Handschrift B. Halle 1913.

Stern, G. Old English ǣ in the earlier text of Laȝamon. Göteborgs Högskolas Årsskrift 47 1941.

Bøgholm, N. The Layamon texts: a linguistical investigation. Copenhagen 1944.

Stanley, E. G. Laȝamon's antiquarian sentiments. MÆ 38 1969.

Brook, G. L. A piece of evidence for the study of Middle English spelling. Neuphilologische Mitteilungen 73 1972. On Laȝamon's Brut.

Kjerrström, B. Studies in the language of the London Chronicles. Upsala 1946.

Kramer, M. Sprache und Heimat des sogen. Ludus Coventriae. Halle 1892.

Hingst, H. Die Sprache John Lydgates aus seinen Reimen. Greifswald 1908.

Sandved, A. O. Studies in the language of Caxton's Malory and that of the Winchester manuscript. Oslo 1968.

Weber, O. The language of the English metrical homilies. Berne 1902.

Duncan, T. G. Notes on the language of the Hunterian ms of the Mirror. Neuphilologische Mitteilungen 69 1968.

Seyferth, P. Sprache und Metrik des mittelenglischen strophischen Gedichtes Le morte Arthur. Berlin 1895.

Mennicken, F. Versbau und Sprache in Huchown's Morte Arthure. Bonn 1900.

Wetzlar, A. Die Sprache (Laut- und Formenlehre) sowie Glossar der nordenglischen Homiliensammlung des Edinburger Royal College of Physicians. Freiburg 1907.

Whitehall, H. Some fifteenth-century spellings from the Nottingham records. Michigan Essays in Comparative Lang & Lit 13 1935.

Vollmer, E. Sprache und Reime des Londoners Hoccleve. Anglia 21 1899.

Fischer, E. Der Lautbestand des südmittelenglischen Octavian verglichen mit seinen Entsprechungen im Lybeaus Desconus und im Launfal. Heidelberg 1927.

Napier, A. S. Notes on the orthography of the Ormulum. Oxford 1893, London 1894 (EETS).

Lambertz, P. Die Sprache des Ormulum nach der lautlichen Seite untersucht. Marburg 1904.

Bülbring, K. D. Die Schreibung eo im Ormulum. Bonn 1905.

Björkman, E. Orrms Doppelkonsonanten. Anglia 37 1913.

Flasdieck, H. M. Die sprachliche Einheitlichkeit des Orrmulums. Anglia 47 1923.

Turville-Petre, J. E. Studies on the Ormulum ms. JEGP 46 1947.

Burchfield, R. W. The language and orthography of the Ormulum ms. Trans Philological Soc 1956.

Stevick, R. D. Plus juncture and the spelling of the Ormulum. JEGP 64 1965.

Breier, W. Eule und Nachtigall. Halle 1910.

Wells, J. E. Accidence in the Owl and the nightingale. Anglia 33 1910.

Sundby, B. The dialect and provenance of the Middle English poem the Owl and the nightingale. Lund 1950.

Struever, C. Die mittelenglische Übersetzung des Palladius: ihr Verhältnis zur Quelle und ihre Sprache. Göttingen 1887.

Blume, R. Die Sprache der Paston letters. Bremen 1882.

Neumann, G. Die Orthographie der Paston letters von 1422–61. Marburg 1904.

Davis, N. A scribal problem in the Paston letters. Eng & Germanic Stud 4 1952.

— The language of the Pastons. Proc Br Acad 40 1955.

Yamaguchi, H. Pasuton shokanshū no onin kenkyū [The phonological study of the Paston letters]. Onsei no Kenkyū (Study of Sounds) 9 1961. In Japanese.

Fick, W. Zum mittelenglischen Gedicht von der Perle: eine Lautuntersuchung. Kiel 1885.

Hoffman, A. Laut- und Formenlehre in Reginald Peacocks Repressor. Greifswald 1900.

Schmidt, F. Studies in the language of Pecock. Upsala 1900.

Behm, O. P. Language of the later part of the Peterborough Chronicle. Upsala 1884.

Meyer, H. Zur Sprache der jüngeren Teile der Chronik von Peterborough. Freiburg 1889.

Teichmann, E. Die Verbalflexion in William Langleys Buche von Peter dem Pflüger. Aachen 1887.

Chambers, R. W. The authorship of Piers plowman. MLR 5 1910. 6: differences of dialect between A, B and C.

— The three texts of Piers plowman and their grammatical forms. MLR 14 1919.

Haworth, R. A. L. Some notes on the dialect and the manuscripts of the Poema morale. Stud in Eng Lit (Tokyo) 14 1934.

Hirst, T. O. The phonology of the London ms of the earliest complete English prose Psalter. Bonn 1907.

Serjeantson, M. S. The dialect of the earliest complete English prose Psalter. E Studies 6 1924.

Wende, E. Überlieferung und Sprache der mittelenglischen Version des Psalters und ihr Verhältnis zur lateinischen Vorlage. Breslau 1884.

Bertram, A. Essay on the dialect, language and metre of Ratis raving. Sondershausen 1896.

Ostermann, L. Untersuchungen zu Ratis raving und dem Gedicht The thewis of gud women. Bonn 1902.

Hellmers, G. H. Über die Sprache Robert Mannyngs of Brunne. Göttingen 1885.

Boerner, O. Die Sprache Roberd Mannyngs of Brunne und ihr Verhältnis zur neuenglischen Mundart. Halle 1904.

— Reimuntersuchung über die Qualität der betonten langen e-Vokale bei Robert of Brunne. In Festschrift für Lorenz Morsbach, Halle 1913.

Pabst, F. Die Sprache der mittelenglischen Reimchronik des Robert von Gloucester, 1: Lautlehre. Berlin 1889.

— Die Flexionsverhältnisse bei Robert von Gloucester. Anglia 13 1891.

Ullmann, J. Studien zu Richard Rolle von Hampole. E Studien 7 1884.

Heuser, W. Die mittelenglischen Legenden von St Editha und St Etheldreda: eine Untersuchung über Sprache und Autorschaft. Erlangen 1887.

Fischer, R. Zur Sprache und Autorschaft der mittelengl. Legenden St Editha und St Etheldreda. Anglia 11 1889.

Williams, I. F. The language of Sawles warde. Anglia 29 1906.

Mohr, F. Sprachliche Untersuchungen zu den mittelenglischen Legenden aus Gloucestershire. Bonn 1888.

Brown, B. D. A study of the Middle English poem known as the Southern passion. Oxford 1926.

Kobayashi, E. The verb forms of the South English legendary. Hague 1964.

Pfeffer, R. Die Sprache des Polychronicons John Trevisas. Bonn 1912. Tiberius ms.

Krüger, A. Sprache und Dialekt der mittelenglischen Homilien in der Handschrift B 14.52 Trinity College, Cambridge. Erlangen 1885.

Strauss, O. Die Sprache der mittelenglischen Predigtsammlung in der Handschrift Trinity College, Cambridge B 14.52. Vienna 1916.

Vogel, B. The dialect of Sir Tristrem. JEGP 40 1941.

Schmidt, G. Über die Sprache und Heimat der Vices and virtues. Leipzig 1899.

Philippsen, M. Die Deklination in den Vices and virtues. Kiel 1911.

Meyerhoff, E. Die Verbalflexion in den Vices and virtues. Kiel 1913.

Neufeldt, E. Zur Sprache des Urkundenbuches von Westminster (Cotton Faustina A iii). Rostock 1907.

Schüddekopf, W. A. Sprache und Dialekt des mittelenglischen Gedichtes William of Palerne. Göttingen 1886.

Davis, N. Two unprinted dialogues in late Middle English and their language. Revue des Langues Vivantes 35 1969. On Winchester College ms 33.

Williams, R. A. Die Vokale der Tonsilben im Codex Wintoniensis. Anglia 25 1902. On BM ms additional 15350.

Gasner, E. Über Wycliffes Sprache. Göttingen 1891.

— Beiträge zum Entwicklungsgang der neuenglischen Schriftsprache auf Grund der mittelenglischen Bibelversionen wie sie auf Wyclif und Purvey zurückgehen sollen. Nuremberg 1891.

Skeat, W. W. On the dialect of Wycliffe's Bible. Trans Philological Soc 1895.

Hudnall, R. H. A presentation of the grammatical inflections in Andrew of Wyntoun's Orygynale cronykil of Scotland. Leipzig 1898.

Kamann, P. Über Quellen und Sprache der York plays. Leipzig 1887.

Lindheim, B. von. Studien zur Sprache des Manuskriptes Cotton Galba E ix: enthaltend eine Darstellung der Sprache des ersten und fünften Schreibers des gennanten Manuskriptes bzw. der Texte Ywain and Gawain, The seven sages of Rome, The pricke of conscience. Vienna 1937.

Taglicht, J. Notes on the language of Ywain and Gawain. In Stud in Eng Lang & Lit: Scripta Hierosolymitana 17, Jerusalem 1966.

Selection of Middle English Texts

Readers and Anthologies

Mätzner, E. Altenglische Sprachproben; nebst einem Wörterbuche. Berlin 1867–1900. 1, Sprachproben; 2, Wörterbuch [A–M].

Zupitza, J. Altenglisches Übungsbuch. Vienna 1874; rev J. Schipper and A. Eichler as Alt- und mittelenglisches Übungsbuch, Vienna 1922; tr G. E. MacLean, The Old and Middle English reader, New York 1893, 1922 (rev).

Morris, R. and W. W. Skeat. Specimens of early English [based on R. Morris, Specimens of early English 1250–1400, Oxford 1867]. pt 1, 1150–1300, Oxford 1882, rev A. L. Mayhew and W. W. Skeat 1885; pt 2, 1298–1393, Oxford 1872, 1894 (rev).

Sweet, H. First Middle English primer. Oxford 1884.

Kluge, F. Mittelenglisches Lesebuch. Halle 1904, 1912 (rev). Glossary by A. Kölbing.

Emerson, O. F. Middle English reader. New York 1905, 1915 (rev).

Brandl, A. and O. Zippel. Mittelenglische Sprach- und Literaturproben. Berlin 1917, 1927 (rev).

Hall, J. Selections from early Middle English. 2 vols Oxford 1920.

Sisam, K. Fourteenth-century verse and prose. Oxford 1921. Glossary by J. R. R. Tolkien.

Morsbach, L. Mittelenglische Originalurkunden von der Chaucer-Zeit bis zur Mitte des xv Jahrhunderts. Heidelberg 1923.

Brown, C. Religious lyrics of the xivth century. Oxford 1924; rev G. V. Smithers, Oxford 1952.

—— English lyrics of the xiiith century. Oxford 1932.
—— Religious lyrics of the xvth century. Oxford 1939.
Flasdieck, H. M. Mittelenglische Originalurkunden 1405–30. Heidelberg 1926.
Lyell, L. A mediæval post-bag. 1934. 15th-century correspondence.
Funke, O. A Middle English reader. Berne 1944.
Mossé, F. Manuel de l'anglais du Moyen Age, 2: moyen-anglais. *See col 75, above.*
Dickins, B. and R. M. Wilson. Early Middle English texts. Cambridge 1951, 1952 (rev).
Kaiser, R. Alt- und mittelenglische Anthologie. Berlin 1954; rev as Medieval English: an Old English and Middle English anthology, Berlin 1958 (3rd edn).
Bennett, J. A. W. and G. V. Smithers. Early Middle English verse and prose. Oxford 1966, 1968 (rev). Glossary by N. Davis.

Glossaries

Anglo-Saxon and Old English vocabularies. Ed T. Wright 2 vols 1857 73; rev R. P. Wülcker 1884.
Promptorium parvulorum. English–Latin. 1440. Ed A. L. Mayhew 1908 (EETS).
Catholicum anglicum: English–Latin. 1483. Ed S. J. Herrtage 1882 (Camden Soc).

Texts Used in Linguistic Studies

The classification is based on that adopted in Kurath, Kuhn and Reidy, Middle English dictionary (*col 56, above*), *Plan and bibliography pp. 11 f., where a fuller list is to be found.*

East Midland

See R. W. Chambers and B. M. Daunt, A book of London English 1384–1425, *Oxford 1931.*
Kyng Alisaunder. Mss Nat Lib of Scotland Advocates 19.2.1 ('Auchinleck'), c. 1330, Bodley Laud miscellany 622, c. 1400. Ed G. V. Smithers 2 vols Oxford 1952–7 (EETS).
Arthour and Merlin. Nat Lib of Scotland ms Advocates 19.2.1 ('Auchinleck'). c. 1330. Ed E. Kölbing, Heilbronn 1890.
Bestiary. BM ms Arundel 292. Late 13th century. Ed R. Morris, An Old English miscellany, 1872 (EETS); ed J. Hall, Selections from early Middle English 1130–1250, 2 vols Oxford 1920.
Osbert Bokenham's Lives of Saints. BM ms Arundel 327. 1447. Ed C. Horstmann 1883; ed M. S. Serjeantson, Oxford 1938 (EETS).
The book of vices and virtues. Mss BM additional 17013, c. 1400, Huntington Lib 147, 15th century. Ed W. N. Francis 1942 (EETS).
Cely papers. PRO. 1472–88. Ed H. E. Malden, The Cely papers: selections from the correspondence and memoranda of the Cely family, Merchants of the Staple AD 1475–1488, 1900 (Camden Soc). *See also* A. Hanham, The text of the Cely papers, MÆ 26 1957.
Chaucer, Geoffrey. Works. *See col 557, below.*
Adam Davy's five dreams about Edward II. Bodley ms Laud miscellany 622. c. 1400. Ed F. J. Furnivall 1878 (EETS).
Emare. BM ms Cotton Caligula A ii. 15th century. Ed E. Rickert 1908 (EETS); ed W. H. French and C. B. Hale, Middle English metrical romances, New York 1930.
Genesis and Exodus. Corpus Christi College Cambridge ms 444. Early 14th century, original c. 1250. Ed R. Morris 1865 (EETS).
Gower, John. *See col 553, below.*
Lay of Havelok. Bodley ms Laud miscellany 108. c. 1300–20. Ed W. W. Skeat 1868 (EETS); Oxford 1902, rev K. Sisam 1915; ed F. Holthausen 1901, 1928 (rev); ed W. H. French and C. B. Hale, Middle English metrical romances, New York 1930.
Hoccleve, Works. 15th century. Ed F. J. Furnivall and I. Gollancz 3 vols 1892–1925 (EETS).

Lambeth homilies. Lambeth Palace ms 487. c. 1200. Ed R. Morris, Old English homilies ser 1, 2 vols 1867–8 (EETS).
Lydgate, John. Works. *See col 639, below.*
Travels of Sir John Mandeville. BM ms Cotton Titus C xvi. c. 1410–20. Ed J. O. Halliwell (-Phillipps) 1866; ed P. Hamelius 2 vols 1916 (EETS). *See also col 471, below.*
Mannyng, Robert, of Brunne. Works. *See col 465, below.*
Norfolk guild returns. c. 1389. Ed T. and L. T. Smith 1870 (EETS).
Ormulum. Bodley ms Junius 1. c. 1200. Ed R. M. White 2 vols Oxford 1852, 1878 (with addns by R. Holt). *See* N. R. Ker, Unpublished parts of the Ormulum printed from ms Lambeth 783, MÆ 9 1940; R. W. Burchfield 1956, *col 82, above*; Burchfield, Ormulum: Words copied by Jan van Vliet from parts now lost, English and medieval studies presented to J. R. R. Tolkien, 1962.
Parlement of the thre ages. BM ms additional 31,042. 15th century, original later 14th century. Ed I. Gollancz, Oxford 1915 (Select early English poems 2); ed M. Y. Offord, Oxford 1959 (EETS).
Paston letters. Ed J. Gairdner, The Paston letters 1422–1509, 3 vols 1872–5, 4 vols 1901, 6 vols 1904; ed N. Davis, Paston letters and papers of the fifteenth century, Oxford 1971– (pt 1 1971; in progress). *See also* N. Davis, The text of Margaret Paston's letters, MÆ 18 1949.
Peterborough chronicle [annals for 1122–54]. Bodley ms Laud miscellany 636. c. 1154. *See* B. Thorpe 1861, C. Plummer 1892–9, D. Whitelock and C. Clark 1954, *under* Anglo-Saxon Chronicle, *col 71, above.* Also C. Clark, The Peterborough chronicle 1070–1154, Oxford 1958, 1970 (rev).
The prisoner's prayer. Guildhall ms. 13th century. Ed E. Ekwall, An early London text, Studier i Modern Språkvetenskap 17 1949.
Proclamation of Henry III. 1258. Ed O. F. Emerson, Middle English reader, New York 1905.
The seven sages of Rome. Nat Lib of Scotland ms Advocates 19.2.1 ('Auchinleck'). c. 1330. Ed H. Weber, Metrical romances, 3 vols 1810; ed K. Brunner, Oxford 1933 (EETS).
Trinity homilies. Trinity College Cambridge ms B. 14. 15. Early 13th century. Ed R. Morris, Old English homilies ser 2, 1873 (EETS).
Vices and virtues. BM ms Stowe 240. c. 1200. Ed F. Holthausen 2 vols 1888–1921 (EETS).
William of Palerne. King's College Cambridge ms 13. c. 1375. Ed W. W. Skeat 1867 (EETS).
Wynnere and Wastoure. BM ms additional 21,042. c. 1450, original c. 1353. Ed I. Gollancz, Oxford 1920, rev M. Day 1930 (Select early English poems 3).

South Eastern

Aʒenbite of inwyt. BM ms Arundel 57. 1340. Ed R. Morris 1866, 1965 (with corrections by P. Gradon) (EETS).
Kentish sermons. Bodley ms Laud miscellany 471. c. 1275. Ed R. Morris, An Old English miscellany, 1872 (EETS); ed J. Hall, Selections from early Middle English 1130–1250, 2 vols Oxford 1920.
Vespasian homilies. BM ms Cotton Vespasian A xxii. 1200–25. Ed R. Morris, Old English homilies ser 1, 2 vols 1867–8 (EETS).
William of Shoreham, poems. BM ms additional 17,376. c. 1350. Ed M. Konrath 1902 (EETS).

South Western, including South West Midland

Ancrene wisse (*see also* Ancrene riwle, *col 498, below*). Corpus Christi College Cambridge ms 402. Early 13th century. Ed J. R. R. Tolkien, Oxford 1962 (EETS).
Winteney version of the Rule of St Benedict. BM ms Cotton Claudius D iii. Early 13tl century. Ed M. M. A. Schröer, Halle 1888.

Chertsey cartulary. BM ms Cotton Vitellius A xiii. c. 1260–80. Ed J. M. Kemble 1839, *col 70, above*.

Short English metrical chronicle. Mss BM Royal 12 C xii, Nat Lib of Scotland Advocates 19.2.1 ('Auchinleck'), c. 1330, BM additional 19,677, c. 1400, Cambridge Univ Lib Dd 14 ii, Ff 5 xlviii, 15th century. Ed J. Ritson, Ancient Engleish metrical romanceës, 3 vols 1802; rev E. Goldsmid as Ancient English metrical romances, 3 vols Edinburgh 1884–5 (Royal ms); ed E. Zettl, Oxford 1935 (EETS) (Additional ms, with variants).

St Editha. BM ms Cotton Faustina B iii. c. 1420. Ed C. Horstmann, Heilbronn 1883.

St Etheldreda. BM ms Cotton Faustina B iii. c. 1420. Ed C. Horstmann, Altenglische Legenden: neue Folge, Heilbronn 1878–81.

Sir Firumbras. Ms Bodley 25166–67. c. 1380. Ed S. J. Herrtage 1879 (EETS).

Hali meiðhad. Mss Bodley 34, BM Cotton Titus D xviii. Early 13th century. Ed O. Cockayne 1866, re-ed F. J. Furnivall, Oxford 1922 (EETS); ed A. F. Colborn, Copenhagen 1940.

English poems of BM ms Harley 2253. c. 1325. Ed K. Boeddeker, Altenglische Dichtungen des ms Harley 2253, Berlin 1878; ed G. L. Brook, The Harley lyrics, Manchester 1948, 1968 (rev).

Herebert, William. Poems. BM ms additional 46,919. Early 14th century. Ed C. Brown, Religious lyrics of the xivth century, Oxford 1924, rev G. V. Smithers, Oxford 1952; ed H. Gneuss, William Hereberts Übersetzungen, Anglia 78 1960.

St Juliana. Mss Bodley 34, BM Royal 17 A xxvii. Early 13th century. Ed S. R. T. O. d'Ardenne, Paris 1936, Oxford 1961 (EETS).

St Katherine. Mss Bodley 34, BM Royal 17 A xxvii, BM Cotton Titus D xviii. Early 13th century Ed E. Einenkel 1884 (EETS).

Laȝamon's Brut. Mss BM Cotton Caligula A ix, BM Cotton Otho C xiii. 13th century. Ed F. Madden 1847; ed G. L. Brook and R. F. Leslie, Oxford 1963– (EETS) (in progress).

South English lengendary. Mss Bodley Laud 108, BM Harley 2277, Corpus Christi College Cambridge 145. c. 1300. Ed C. Horstmann 1887 (EETS) (Laud ms); C. d'Evelyn and A. J. Mill 3 vols Oxford 1956–9 (EETS) (Harley and Corpus mss).

St Marherete. Mss Bodley 34, BM Royal 17 A xxvii. Early 13th century. Ed O. Cockayne 1862; ed F. M. Mack 1934 (EETS).

Mum and the sothsegger. Mss Cambridge Univ Lib Ll 4 xiv, BM additional 41,666. 15th century. Ed M. Day and R. Steele, Oxford 1936 (EETS).

The owl and the nightingale. Mss BM Cotton Caligula A ix, Jesus College Oxford 29. c. 1250. Ed J. E. Wells 1907; ed J. W. H. Atkins, Cambridge 1922; ed J. H. G. Grattan and G. F. H. Sykes 1935 (EETS); ed E. G. Stanley 1960.

Robert of Gloucester's Chronicle. BM ms Cotton Caligula A xi. c. 1325. Ed T. Hearne 2 vols Oxford 1724; ed W. A. Wright 2 vols 1887 (Rolls ser).

Sawles warde. Mss Bodley 34, BM Royal 17 A xxvii, BM Cotton Titus D xviii. Early 13th century. Ed R. Morris, Old English homilies ser 1, 2 vols 1867–8 (EETS); ed R. M. Wilson, Leeds 1938; ed J. A. W. Bennett and G. V. Smithers, Early Middle English verse and prose, Oxford 1966, 1968 (rev).

A talkyng of þe loue of God. Ms Bodley 3938 ('Vernon'). c. 1390. Ed M. S. Westra, Hague 1950.

Trevisa. Trn of Higden's Polychronicon. St John's College Cambridge ms H 1. c. 1375. Ed C. Babington and J. R. Lumby 4 vols 1865–86 (Rolls ser).

Usages of Winchester. Guildhall, Winchester mss 24–5. 15th century. Ed K. W. Engeroff, Bonn 1914.

Brunner, K. Zwei Gedichte aus der Handschrift Trinity College Cambridge 323. E Studien 70 1936.

Serjeantson, M. S. The index of the Vernon manuscript. MLR 32 1937. Early 15th century.

Whitehall, H. A most ancient petition [1344] (PRO. SC 8, 192/9580). PQ 18 1939.

Stanley, E. G. An inedited Nativity sermon from Worcester. Eng & Germanic Stud 7 1961. Worcester Cathedral Lib ms Q 29. c. 1200.

West Midland

Alexander and Dindimus. Ms Bodley 264. c. 1450, original c. 1350. Ed W. W. Skeat 1878 (EETS); ed F. P. Magoun, The gests of King Alexander of Macedon, Cambridge Mass 1929.

Alisaunder of Macedoine. Bodley ms Greaves 60. c. 1600, original c. 1350. Ed W. W. Skeat, The romance of William of Palerne, 1867 (EETS); ed F. P. Magoun, The gests of King Alexander of Macedon, Cambridge Mass 1929.

Audelay, John. Poems. Ms Bodley 21,876. c. 1426. Ed E. K. Whiting, Oxford 1931 (EETS).

Boke of curtasye. BM ms Sloane 1986. c. 1460. Ed F. J. Furnivall, Early English meals and manners, 1868 (EETS).

Cleanness. BM ms Cotton Nero A x. c. 1400. Ed R. Morris, Early English alliterative poems, 1864 (EETS); ed I. Gollancz and M. Day 2 vols 1921–33 (Select early English poems 7, 9); ed R. J. Menner, Purity, New Haven 1920.

Compassio Mariae. Bodley ms Tanner 169*. c. 1250. Ed A. S. Napier, in History of the holy rood-tree, 1894 (EETS).

The conflict of wit and will. Cambridge Univ Lib ms Res b 162. c. 1400. Ed B. Dickins, Leeds 1938.

St Erkenwald. BM ms Harley 2250. 15th century, original c. 1386. Ed I. Gollancz 1922 (Select early English poems 4); ed H. L. Savage, New Haven 1926.

Sir Gawain and the Green Knight. BM ms Cotton Nero A x. c. 1400. Ed R. Morris, Early English alliterative poems, 1864 (EETS); ed J. R. R. Tolkien and E. V. Gordon, Oxford 1925, rev N. Davis, Oxford 1967; ed I. Gollancz, Oxford 1938 (EETS).

Romances in the Ireland ms. 15th century. (a) Awntyrs off Arthure; (b) The avowynge of King Arthur; (c) Sir Amadace. Ed J. Robson, Three early English metrical romances, 1842 (Camden Soc); The avowing of Arthur, ed W. H. French and C. B. Hale, Middle English metrical romances, New York 1930; Sir Amadace and the Avowing of Arthur, ed C. Brookhouse, Copenhagen 1968.

Lay folk's mass-book. Mss BM Royal 17 B xvii, c. 1400, Caius College Cambridge 84, c. 1450. Ed T. F. Simmons 1879 (EETS).

Liber cure cocorum. BM ms Sloane 1986. c. 1460. Ed R. Morris 1862 (Trans Philological Soc suppl).

Mirk, John. Works. *See Index*.

Patience. BM ms Cotton Nero A x. c. 1400. Ed R. Morris, Early English alliterative poems, 1864 (EETS); ed H. Bateson, Manchester 1912, 1918 (rev); ed I. Gollancz 1913, 1924 (rev) (Select early English poems 1); ed J. J. Anderson, Manchester 1969.

Pearl. BM ms Cotton Nero A x. c. 1400. Ed R. Morris, Early English alliterative poems, 1864 (EETS); ed I. Gollancz 1921 (Select early English poems 8, also separately); ed E. V. Gordon, Oxford 1953.

Gest historiale of the destruction of Troy. Glasgow, Hunterian Museum ms. c. 1450. Ed G. A. Panton and D. Donaldson 2 vols 1869–74 (EETS).

Meech, S. B. An early treatise in English concerning Latin grammar. In Essays and studies in English and comparative literature, Ann Arbor 1935. Trinity College Cambridge ms O.5.4. 15th century.

Northern

Northern prose version of the Rule of St Benedict. BM ms Lansdowne 378. Early 15th century. Ed E. A. Knock 1902 (EETS).

Thomas Castleford's Chronicle. Göttingen Univ Lib ms Hist. 740. Early 15th century, original early 14th century. Ed F. Behre, Göteborgs Högskolas Årsskrift 46 1940 (in part).

Cursor mundi. BM ms Cotton Vespasian A iii. c. 1400. Ed R. Morris 7 vols 1874–92 (EETS).

Liber de diversis medicinis. Lincoln Cathedral ms 91 (A.5.2) ('Thornton'). c. 1440. Ed M. S. Ogden, Oxford 1938 (EETS).

Minot, Laurence. Poems. BM ms Cotton Galba E ix. Early 15th century, original 14th century. Ed J. Hall, Oxford 1887, 1914 (rev).

Northern homily cycle. Edinburgh, Royal College of Physicians ms. Late 14th century, original c. 1300. Ed J. Small, English metrical homilies, Edinburgh 1862.

Sir Perceval of Galles. Lincoln Cathedral ms 91 (A.5.2) ('Thornton'). c. 1440, original 14th century. Ed. J. O. Halliwell(-Phillipps), The Thornton romances, 1844 (Camden Soc); ed J. Campion and F. Holthausen, Heidelberg 1913; ed W. H. French and C. B. Hale, Middle English metrical romances, New York 1930.

Metrical chronicle of Robert of Knaresborough. BM ms Egerton 3143. 15th century. Ed J. Bazire, Oxford 1953 (EETS).

Rolle, Richard. Works. *See col 517, below.*

Brunner, K. Mittelenglische Marienstunden. E Studien 70 1936. BM ms Arundel 285. 16th century.

Scottish

Andrew of Wyntoun's Orygynale cronykil. Mss BM Royal 17 D xx, BM Cotton Nero D xi, 15th century, St Andrews Univ T.T.6.6, Wemyss Castle, Fife, 16th century. Ed F. J. Amours 6 vols 1903–14 (STS).

Barbour's Bruce. Mss St John's College Cambridge G 23, 1487, Nat Lib of Scotland, 1489. Ed W. W. Skeat 4 vols 1870–89 (EETS); ed W. M. Mackenzie 1909.

Lancelot of the laik. Cambridge Univ Lib ms Kk 1 v. 15th century. Ed W. W. Skeat 1865, 1905 (rev) (EETS).

Ratis raving. Cambridge Univ Lib ms Kk 1 v. 15th century. Ed J. R. Lumby 1870 (EETS).

Taill of Rauf Coilyear. Original c. 1475–1500, ptd text of 1572. Ed S. J. Herrtage, The English Charlemagne romances vol 6, 1882 (EETS).

(3) MODERN ENGLISH

General
Modern English Grammars etc

Onions, C. T. An advanced English syntax. 1904, 1971 (rev B. D. H. Miller as Modern English syntax).

Jespersen, O. A Modern English grammar on historical principles. 7 vols Heidelberg 1909–49.

— Essentials of English grammar. 1933.

Poutsma, H. A. A grammar of late Modern English. 5 vols Groningen 1914–26. Pt 1, The sentence, 1928–9 (2nd edn).

Kruisinga, E. A handbook of present-day English. 2 vols Groningen 1909–11. Pt 1, English sounds 1925 (4th edn); pt 2, English accidence and syntax 3 vols 1931–2 (5th edn).

— and P. A. Erades. An English grammar. Groningen 1953–. 1, Accidence and syntax, 1st pt 1953 (8th edn); 2nd pt 1967 (9th edn). First pbd 1911 as An English grammar for Dutch students.

Kurath, H. and G. O. Curme. A grammar of the English language. Boston 1931–5. 2, Parts of speech and accidence [by Curme], 1935; 3, Syntax [by Curme], 1931; vol 1 unpbd.

Zandvoort, R. W. A handbook of English grammar. Groningen 1944; rev R. W. Zandvoort and J. A. van Ek 1972 (6th edn).

Fries, C. C. The structure of English. New York 1952.

Trager, G. L. and H. L. Smith. An outline of English structure. Washington 1951.

Hill, A. A. An introduction to linguistic structures. New York 1958.

Scheurweghs, G. Present-day English syntax. 1959.

Sledd, J. A short introduction to English grammar. Chicago 1959.

Nida, E. A. A synopsis of English syntax. Norman 1960, Hague 1966 (rev).

Mathesius, V. Obsahový rozbor současné angličtiny na základě obecně lingvistickém. Ed J. Vachek, Prague 1961. Functional analysis of present-day English; with English summary.

Strang, B. M. H. Modern English structure. 1962, 1968 (rev).

Gleason, H. A. Linguistics and English grammar. New York 1965.

Il'ish, B. A. Stroĭ sovremennogo angliĭskogo yazȳka. Moscow 1965. In English; cover bears title The structure of Modern English.

Schibsbye, K. A Modern English grammar. Oxford 1965, 1970 (rev).

Leech, G. N. Towards a semantic description of English. 1969.

Modern English Phonology and Morphology

Ellis, A. J. On early English pronunciation. 5 pts 1867–89 (EETS). *See* S. S. Eustace, The meaning of the palaeotype in A. J. Ellis's On early English pronunciation, Trans Philological Soc 1969.

Morsbach, L. Über den Ursprung der neuenglischen Schriftsprache. Heilbronn 1888.

Luick, K. Beiträge zur englischen Grammatik. Anglia 14 1891, 16 1894, 20 1898, 29–30 1906–7, 45 1921.

Rudolf, E. Die englische Orthographie von Caxton bis Shakespeare. Marburg 1904.

Diehl, L. Englische Schreibung und Aussprache im Zeitalter Shakespeares. Anglia 29 1906; also Giessen 1906.

Horn, W. Historische neuenglische Grammatik, 1: Lautlehre. Strasbourg 1908.

— Probleme der neuenglischen Lautgeschichte. Studia Neophilologica 14 1942.

— and M. Lehnert. Laut und Leben: englische Lautgeschichte der neueren Zeit 1400–1950. Berlin 1954.

Jones, D. The pronunciation of English. Cambridge 1909, 1956 (rev).

— An English pronouncing dictionary. 1917. Later as Everyman's English pronouncing dictionary; 13th edn rev A. C. Gimson 1967.

— An outline of English phonetics. Leipzig 1918, Cambridge 1960 (rev).

Zachrisson, R. E. Pronunciation of English vowels 1400–1700. Gothenburg 1913.

— A contribution to the history of early New English pronunciation. E Studien 52 1918.

Ekwall, E. Historische neuenglische Laut- und Formenlehre. Berlin 1914, 1965 (rev).

Kruisinga, E. An introduction to the study of English sounds. Groningen 1914; rev C. Hedeman and J. J. Westerbeek 1966.

— The phonetic structure of English words. Berne 1942.

Flasdieck, H. M. Forschungen zur Frühzeit der neuenglischen Schriftsprache: Teil 1. Halle 1922.

Wyld, H. C. Studies in English rhymes from Surrey to Pope. 1923.

Wright, J. and E. M. An elementary historical New English grammar. Oxford 1924.

Trnka, B. A phonological analysis of present-day Standard English. Práce z Vědeckých Ústavů 37; 1935 rev

T. Kanekiyo and T. Koizumi, Tokyo 1966 (also pbd University Al 1968). *See* K. Malone, E Studies 18 1936.

Malone, K. The phonemes of current English. In Studies for William A. Read, University Louisiana 1940; rev in his Studies in heroic legend and in current speech, Copenhagen 1959.

Funke, O. Zur Charakteristik des englischen Sprach-systems: Versuch eines Aufrisses einer Strukturlehre. E Studien 1944; rptd in his Wege und Ziele, Berne 1945.

Cohen, A. The phonemes of English. Hague 1952.

Smirnitskiĭ, A. I. Morfologiya angliĭskogo yazȳka. Moscow 1959.

Nordhjem, B. The phonemes of English. Copenhagen 1960.

Gimson, A. C. An introduction to the pronunciation of English. 1962, 1970 (rev).

Barber, C. Linguistic change in present-day English. 1964.

Kurath, H. A phonology and prosody of modern English. Heidelberg 1964.

Pierce, J. E. The phonemes of English. Linguistics 17 1965.

Kohler, K. Modern English phonology. Lingua 19 1967.

Chomsky, N. and M. Halle. The sound pattern of English. New York 1968.

See also Dobson 1956, 1968, col 95, below.

16th–18th-century Works on the English Language
Modern Editions of Individual Grammars, Dictionaries etc

See also Kennedy 1927, Alston 1965–, *cols 53–4, above. For Johnson's Dictionary see vol 2, col 1130. For the works listed below the date of the first edn only is given.*

Palsgrave, J. Lesclaircissement de la langue francoise. 1530; ed F. Genin, Paris 1852.

Du Wes, G. An introductorie. 1532; ed F. Genin, with Palsgrave, above.

Salesbury, W. A dictionary in Englyshe and Welshe. 1547; ed R. C. Alston, Menston 1969 (facs). Section on pronunciation in A. J. Ellis 1867–89, *col 90, above* (Welsh text, with English trn).

— A plain and a familiar introduction, teaching how to pronounce the letters in the Brytishe tongue, now commonly called Welshe. 1567; in A. J. Ellis 1867–89, *col 90, above.*

Hart, J. Works. Ed B. Danielsson 1955–63, *col 95, below.*

— An orthographie. 1569; ed R. C. Alston, Menston 1969 (facs). *See* O. Jespersen, John Hart's pronunciation of English 1569–70, Heidelberg 1907.

Smith, Sir T. De recta et emendata linguae anglicae scriptione dialogus. 1568; ed O. Deibel, Halle 1913.

Bellot, J. Le maistre d'escole anglois. 1580; ed T. Spira, Halle 1912.

Bullokar, W. Works. Ed B. Danielsson and R. C. Alston, Leeds 1966–. 1, A short introduction or guiding 1580–1, ed B. Danielsson and R. C. Alston 1966 (facs); 3, Booke at large 1580, ed J. R. Turner 1970 (facs); 4, Aesopś fablź 1585, ed J. R. Turner 1969 (facs). In progress.

— Booke at large for the amendment of orthographie for English speech. 1580; ed M. Plessow, Geschichte der Fabeldichtung in England bis zu John Gay (1726): nebst Neudruck von Bullokars Fables of Æsop 1585, Booke at large 1580, Bref grammar for English 1586, und Pamphlet for grammar 1586, Berlin 1806. *See also preceding entry.*

Mulcaster, R. The first part of the elementarie. 1582; ed E. T. Campagnac, Oxford 1925; ed R. C. Alston, Menston 1970 (facs).

Gr[eaves?], P. Grammatica anglicana. 1594; ed O. Funke, Vienna 1938; ed R. C. Alston, Menston 1969 (facs).

Coote, E. The English school-master. 1596. *See* E. Horn, Coote's Bemerkungen über englische Aussprache, Anglia 28 1905.

Brinsley, J. The posing of the parts. 1612; ed R. C. Alston, Menston 1967 (facs).

Bullokar, J. An English expositor. 1616; ed R. C. Alston, Menston 1967 (facs).

Robinson, R. The art of pronunciation. 1617; ed E. J. Dobson, The phonetic writings of Robert Robinson, Oxford 1957 (EETS) (with Robinson's phonetic transcriptions); ed R. C. Alston, Menston 1969 (facs).

Gil, A. Logonomia anglica. 1619; ed O. Jiriczek, Strasbourg 1903; ed R. C. Alston, Menston 1968 (facs of 2nd edn of 1621).

Mason, G. Grammaire angloise. 1622; ed R. Brotanek, Halle 1905.

Cockeram, H. The English dictionarie. 1623; ed R. C. Alston, Menston 1968 (facs).

Butler, C. English grammar. 1634; ed A. Eichler, Halle 1910.

Daines, S. Orthoepia anglicana. 1640; ed M. Rösler and R. Brotanek, Halle 1908; ed R. C. Alston, Menston 1967 (facs).

Jonson, B. English grammar. 1640; ed S. Gibson 1928; in Ben Jonson's Works vol 8, ed C. H. Herford, P. and E. M. Simpson, Oxford 1947.

Hodges, R. A special help to orthography. 1643; ed C. C. F[ries], Ann Arbor 1932 (facs).

— The English primrose. 1644; ed H. Kauter, Heidelberg 1930; ed R. C. Alston, Menston 1969 (facs).

Poole, J. The English accidence. 1646; ed R. C. Alston, Leeds 1967 (facs).

Wallis, J. Grammatica linguae anglicanae. 1653; ed R. C. Alston, Menston 1969 (facs); 6th edn (1765) ed J. A. Kemp 1972. *See* L. Morel, De Johannis Wallisii Grammatica linguae anglicanae, Paris 1895.

Wharton, J. The English grammar. 1654; ed R. C. Alston, Menston 1970 (facs).

Walker, W. A treatise of English particles. 1655; ed R. C. Alston, Menston 1970 (facs).

Blount, T. Glossographia. 1656; ed R. C. Alston, Menston 1969 (facs).

Phillips, E. The new world of English words. 1658; ed R. C. Alston, Menston 1969 (facs).

Coles, E. The compleat English schoolmaster. 1674; ed R. C. Alston, Menston 1967 (facs).

— An English dictionary. 1676; ed R. C. Alston, Menston 1971 (facs).

Ray, J. A collection of English words. 1674; ed R. C. Alston, Menston 1969 (facs of 2nd edn of 1691).

Cooper, C. Grammatica linguae anglicanae. 1685; ed J. D. Jones, Halle 1912; ed R. C. Alston, Menston 1968 (facs).

— The English teacher. 1687; ed B. Sundby, Lund 1953.

Miege, G. The English grammar. 1688; ed R. C. Alston, Menston 1969 (facs).

Gazophylacium anglicanum. 1689; ed R. C. Alston, Menston 1969 (facs).

Aickin, J. The English grammar. 1693; ed R. C. Alston, Menston 1967 (facs).

The writing scholar's companion. 1695; ed E. Ekwall, Halle 1911.

Browne, R. The English school reformed. 1700; ed R. C. Alston, Menston 1969 (facs).

Lane, A. A key to the art of letters. 1700; ed R. C. Alston, Menston 1969 (facs).

Jones, J. Practical phonography. 1701; ed E. Ekwall, Halle 1907; ed R. C. Alston, Menston 1969 (facs).

K[ersey], J. A new English dictionary. 1702; ed R. C. Alston, Menston 1969 (facs).

— Dictionarium anglo-britannicum. 1708; ed R. C. Alston, Menston 1969 (facs).

Dyche, T. A guide to the English tongue. 1707; ed R. C. Alston, Menston 1968 (facs).

Gildon, C. and J. Brightland. A grammar of the English tongue. 1711; ed R. C. Alston, Menston 1967 (facs).

Greenwood, J. An essay towards a practical English grammar. 1711; ed R. C. Alston, Menston 1968 (facs).

Maittare, M. The English grammar. 1712; ed R. C. Alston, Menston 1967 (facs).

[Oldmixon, J.] Reflections on Dr Swift's letter. 1712; ed R. C. Alston, Menston 1970 (facs).

Swift, J. A proposal for correcting, improving and ascertaining the English tongue. 1712; ed R. C. Alston, Menston 1969 (facs).

Jones, H. An accidence to the English tongue. 1724; ed R. C. Alston, Menston 1967 (facs).

Lediard, T. Grammatica anglicana critica. 1725; in A. J. Ellis 1867–89, col 90, above.

Duncan, D. A new English grammar. 1731; ed R. C. Alston, Menston 1967 (facs).

Collyer, J. The general principles of grammar. 1735; ed R. C. Alston, Menston 1968 (facs).

Dilworth, T. A new guide to the English tongue. 1740; ed R. C. Alston, Leeds 1967 (facs of 13th edn of 1751).

The Irish spelling book. 1740; ed R. C. Alston, Menston 1969 (facs).

Fisher, A. A new grammar. 1750; ed R. C. Alston, Menston 1968 (facs).

Bertram, C. The Royal English–Danish grammar. Copenhagen 1753.

Gough, J. A practical grammar of the English tongue. 1754; ed R. C. Alston, Menston 1967 (facs).

Buchanan, J. Linguae britannicae vera pronunciatio: or a new English dictionary. 1757; ed R. C. Alston, Menston 1967 (facs).

— The British grammar. 1762; ed R. C. Alston, Menston 1968 (facs).

Ward, J. Four essays upon the English language. 1758; ed R. C. Alston, Menston 1967 (facs).

Priestley, J. The rudiments of English grammar. 1761; ed R. C. Alston, Menston 1969 (facs).

White, J. The English verb. 1761; ed R. C. Alston, Menston 1969 (facs).

Lowth, R. A short introduction to English grammar. 1762; ed R. C. Alston, Menston 1967 (facs).

Ash, J. Grammatical institutes. 1763; ed R. C. Alston, Leeds 1967 (facs of 4th edn of 1763).

Johnston, W. A pronouncing and spelling dictionary. 1764; ed R. C. Alston, Menston 1969 (facs).

Elphinston, J. The principles of the English language 1765. See E. Müller, Englische Lautlehre nach James Elphinston, 1765, 1787, 1796, Heidelberg 1914.

Ward, W. An essay on grammar. 1765; ed R. C. Alston, Menston 1967 (facs).

Trusler, J. The difference between words esteemed synonymous. 2 vols 1766; ed R. C. Alston, Menston 1970 (facs).

Baker, R. Reflections on the English language. 1770; ed R. C. Alston, Menston 1968 (facs).

Bayly, A. The English accidence. 1771.

— A plain and complete grammar of the English language; to which is prefixed the English accidence. 1772; ed R. C. Alston, Menston 1969 (facs).

Fenning, D. A new grammar of the English language. 1771; ed R. C. Alston, Menston 1967 (facs).

Peyton, V. J. The history of the English language. 1771; ed R. C. Alston, Menston 1970 (facs).

The English accidence. 1773; ed R. C. Alston, Leeds 1967 (facs). Anon.

Tucker, A. ('Edward Search'). Vocal sounds. 1773; ed R. C. Alston, Menston 1969 (facs).

Spence, T. The grand repository of the English language. 1775; ed R. C. Alston, Menston 1969 (facs).

Steele, J. An essay towards establishing the melody and measure of speech. 1775; ed R. C. Alston, Menston 1969 (facs).

Burn, J. A pronouncing dictionary of the English language. 1777; ed R. C. Alston, Menston 1969 (facs of 2nd edn of 1786).

Harrison, R. Institutes of English grammar. 1777; ed R. C. Alston, Menston 1967 (facs).

Sheridan, T. A general dictionary of the English language. 2 vols 1780; ed R. C. Alston, Menston 1967 (facs). Contains A rhetorical grammar of the English language, also pbd separately (rev) 1781; ed R. C. Alston, Menston 1969 (facs of 1781).

— Elements of English. 1786; ed R. C. Alston, Menston 1968 (facs).

Fell, J. An essay towards an English grammar. 1784; ed R. C. Alston, Menston 1967 (facs).

Nares, R. Elements of orthoepy. 1784. See W. Bendix, Englische Lautlehre nach Nares, Darmstadt 1921.

Webster, N. A grammatical institute of the English language: pt 2, containing a plain and comprehensive grammar. Hartford 1784; ed R. C. Alston, Menston 1968 (facs).

— Dissertations on the English language. Boston 1789, Gainesville 1951 (facs); ed R. C. Alston, Menston 1967 (facs).

Ussher, G. N. The elements of English grammar. 1785; ed R. C. Alston, Menston 1967 (facs).

Walker, J. A critical pronouncing dictionary. 1791; ed R. C. Alston, Menston 1968 (facs).

Murray, L. English grammar. 1795; ed R. C. Alston, Menston 1968 (facs).

Smith, W. An attempt to render the pronunciation of the English language more easy to foreigners. 1795; ed R. C. Alston, Menston 1969 (facs).

A pronouncing dictionary of the English language. 1796; ed R. C. Alston, Menston 1969 (facs).

A vocabulary of such words in the English language as are of dubious or unsettled pronunciation. 1797; ed R. C. Alston, Menston 1967 (facs).

Mackintosh, D. A plain, rational essay on English grammar. Boston 1797; ed R. C. Alston, Menston 1969 (facs).

[Sedger, J.] The structure of the English language. 1798; ed R. C. Alston, Menston 1970 (facs).

Angus, W. A pronouncing vocabulary of the English language. 1800; ed R. C. Alston, Menston 1969 (facs).

Bachelor, T. Orthoepical analysis of the English language. 1809.

Studies on 16th–18th-century Writers on the English Language

Viëtor, W. Aussprache des Englischen nach englischdeutschen Grammatiken vor 1750. Marburg 1886.

Holthausen, F. Die englische Aussprache bis zum Jahre 1750 nach dänischen und schwedischen Zeugnissen. Göteborgs Högskolas Årsskrift 1–2 1895–6.

Hauck, E. Systematische Lautlehre Bullokars: Vokalismus. Marburg 1906.

Horn, J. Das englische Verbum nach den Zeugnissen von Grammatikern des 17 und 18 Jahrhunderts. Darmstadt 1911.

Spira, T. Die englische Lautentwicklung nach französischen Grammatikerzeugnissen. Strasbourg 1912.

Eichler, A. Schriftbild und Lautwert in Charles Butler's English grammar 1633, 1634 und Feminin' monarchi' 1634. Halle 1913.

Kaffenberger, E. Englische Lautlehre nach Thomas Sheridans Dictionary of the English language 1780. Giessener Beiträge zur Erforschung der Sprache und Kultur Englands und Nordamerikas 3 1927.

Zachrisson, R. E. The English pronunciation at Shakespeare's time as taught by William Bullokar, with wordlists from all his works. Skrifter Utgivna av Kungl. Humanistiska Vetenskapssamfundet i Uppsala 22 1927.

Cardim, L. Portuguese–English grammarians and eighteenth-century spoken English. Porto 1930.

Gabrielson, A. Edward Bysshe's Dictionary of rhymes 1702 as a source of information on early Modern English pronunciation. Upsala 1930.

— Elisha Coles's Syncrisis 1675 as a source of information on seventeenth-century English. E Studien 70 1936.

—— A few notes on Gill's Logonomia anglica 1619. Studia Neophilologica 14 1942.

Kökeritz, H. English pronunciation as described in shorthand systems of the 17th and 18th centuries. Studia Neophilologica 7 1935.

—— Guy Miege's pronunciation. Language 19 1943.

—— Mather Flint on early eighteenth-century English pronunciation. Skrifter Utgivna av Kungl. Humanistiska Vetenskapssamfundet i Uppsala 37 1944.

—— John Hart and early Standard English. In Philologica: the [Kemp] Malone anniversary studies, Baltimore 1949.

Fiedler, H. G. A contemporary of Shakespeare on phonetics and on the pronunciation of English and Latin. 1936.

Lehnert, M. Die Grammatik des englischen Sprachmeisters John Wallis 1616–1703. Breslau 1936.

—— Die Abhängigkeit frühneuenglischer Grammatiker. E Studien 72 1938.

Matthews, W. William Tiffin: an eighteenth-century phonetician. E Studies 18 1936.

Funke, O. William Bullokars Bref grammar for English 1586. Anglia 62 1938.

—— Ben Jonson's English grammar 1640. Anglia 64 1940.

—— Die Frühzeit der englischen Grammatik. Berne 1941.

—— Sprachphilosophie und Grammatik in englischen Sprachbüchern des 17 und 18 Jahrhunderts. In his Wege und Ziele, Berne 1945.

Mackie, W. S. Gill's account of English 'long a'. MLR 33 1938.

Read, A. W. The motivation of Lindley Murray's grammatical work. JEGP 38 1939.

Meyer, E. Der englische Lautstand in der zweiten Hälfte des 18 Jahrhunderts nach James Buchanan 1766. Würzburg 1940.

Ong, W. J. Historical backgrounds of Elizabethan and Jacobean punctuation theory. PMLA 59 1944.

Scholl, E. H. New light on seventeenth-century pronunciation from the English school of Lutenist song writers. Ibid.

Firth, J. R. The English school of phonetics. Trans Philological Soc 1946.

Sheldon, E. K. Pronouncing systems in eighteenth-century dictionaries. Language 22 1946.

—— Walker's influence on the pronunciation of English. PMLA 62 1947.

Dobson, E. J. Robert Robinson and his phonetic transcripts of early seventeenth-century English pronunciation. Trans Philological Soc 1947.

—— English pronunciation 1500–1700. Oxford 1956, 1968 (rev).

Abercrombie, D. Forgotten phoneticians. Trans Philological Soc 1948.

Poldauf, I. On the history of some problems of English grammar before 1800. Práce z Vědeckých Ústavů 55 1948.

Sundby, B. A case of seventeenth-century plagiarism. E Studies 33 1952. Borrowing by the Writing scholar's companion 1695 from Cooper's Grammatica linguae anglicanae 1685 and English teacher 1687.

Jones, R. F. The triumph of the English language. Stanford 1953.

Elliott, R. W. V. Isaac Newton as phonetician. MLR 49 1954.

Bergström, F. John Kirkby 1746 on English pronunciation. Studia Neophilologica 27 1955. Includes ch 1 of Kirkby's A new English grammar: or guide to the English tongue, 1746.

Danielsson, B. John Hart's works on English orthography and pronunciation 1551, 1569, 1570. 2 pts Stockholm 1955–63. Pt 1, Biographical and bibliographical introductions, texts and index verborum; pt 2, Phonology.

Holmberg, B. James Douglas on English pronunciation. Lund 1956.

Tucker, S. I. Some notes on William Walker's Treatise of English particles. N & Q Aug 1957.

Vallins, G. H. The Wesleys and the English language. 1957.

Watanabe, S. Studien zur Abhängigkeit der frühneuenglischen Grammatiken von den mittelalterlichen Lateingrammatiken. Münster 1958.

Salmon, V. Thomas Hayward, grammarian. Neophilologus 43 1959.

—— James Shirley and some problems of 17th-century grammar. Archiv 197 1961.

—— The evolution of Dalgarno's Ars signorum. In Studies in language and literature in honour of Margaret Schlauch, Warsaw 1966.

Scheurweghs, G. and E. Vorlat. Problems of the history of English grammar. E Studies 40 1959. Notes on Greaves' Grammatica anglicana, Brightland's or Steele's Grammar, Ash's Grammatical institutes.

Vorlat, E. The sources of Lindley Murray's The English grammar. Leuvense Bijdragen 48 1959.

—— Progress in English grammar 1585–1735: a study of the development of English grammar and of the interdependence among the early English grammarians. 4 vols Louvain 1963.

Scheurweghs, G. English grammars in Dutch and Dutch grammars in English in the Netherlands before 1800. E Studies 41 1960. Suppl by R. C. Alston 45 1964.

Kaiser, R. Eine englische Ausspracheliste des späten xvii Jahrhunderts. In Festschrift für Walter Hübner, Berlin 1964.

Söderlind, J. The attitude to language expressed by or ascertainable from English writers of the 16th and 17th centuries, Studia Neophilologica 36 1964.

Sugg, R. S. The mood of eighteenth-century English grammar. PQ 43 1964.

Vorlat, M. Case in the early English grammars from William Bullokar 1586 to Ben Jonson 1640. Leuvense Bijdragen 56 1967.

Harlow, C. G. An unnoticed observation on the expansion of sixteenth-century Standard English. RES new ser 21 1970. On R. Ryece, The breviary of Suffolk (1603).

Michael, I. English grammatical categories and the tradition to 1800. Cambridge 1970.

Melchior, A. B. Sir Thomas Smith and John Wallis: the problem of early Modern English [y] re-examined. E Studies 53 1972.

Special Studies

Spies, H. Studien zur Geschichte des englischen Pronomens im xv und xvi Jahrhundert. Halle 1897.

Luick, K. Der Ursprung der neuenglischen ai- und au- Diphthonge. E Studien 27 1899, 29 1901.

—— Über die neuenglische Vokalverschiebung. E Studien 45 1912.

—— Über Vokalverkürzung in abgeleiteten und zusammengesetzten Wörtern. E Studien 54 1920.

—— Gab es im Frühneuenglischen einen ü-Laut? Anglia 45 1921.

Blach, S. Die Schriftsprache in der Londoner Paulsschule zu Anfang des xvi Jahrhunderts. Halberstadt 1905.

Horn, W. Untersuchungen zur neuenglischen Lautgeschichte. Strasbourg 1905.

—— Grundsätzliches zur neuenglischen Lautlehre. Archiv 159 1931.

—— Der Lautwandel von sj zu š im Neuenglischen. Beiblatt zur Anglia 51 1940.

—— Neuere Erscheinungen in der Lautgebung des Englischen. Archiv 177 1940.

—— Vom Einfluss des Schriftbildes auf die Aussprache im Englischen. Anglia 64 1940.

—— Probleme der neuenglischen Lautgeschichte. Studia Neophilologica 14 1942.

—— Eine Lautsubstitution im Englischen. Archiv 186 1949.

Price, H. T. A history of ablaut in the strong verbs from Caxton to the end of the Elizabethan period. Bonn 1910.

—— Grammar and the compositor in the sixteenth and seventeenth centuries. JEGP 38 1939.

Eckhardt, E. Die neuenglische Verkürzung langer Tonsilbenvokale in abgeleiteten und zusammengesetzten Wörten. E Studien 50 1917.
—— Die Quantität einfacher Tonvokale in offener Silbe bei zwei- oder dreisilbigen Wörtern französischer Herkunft im heutigen Englisch. Anglia 60 1936.
Tietjens, E. Englische Zahlwörter des 15 und 16 Jahrhunderts. Greifswald 1922.
Weiss, A. Die Mundart im englischen Drama von 1642–1800. Giessen 1924.
Mackie, W. S. On the independent development of the Middle English vowels in early New English. MLR 24 1929.
Zachrisson, R. E. The early English loan-words in Welsh and the chronology of the English sound-shift. In Studies in English philology: a miscellany in honor of Frederick Klaeber, Minneapolis 1929.
Morsbach, L. Probleme der neuenglischen Schriftsprache in ihrer Frühzeit. In A grammatical miscellany offered to Otto Jespersen, Copenhagen 1930.
Flasdieck, H. M. Studien zur schriftsprachlichen Entwicklung der neuenglischen Velarvokale in Verbindung mit r. Anglia 56 1932; Halle 1932.
—— Zum Lautwert von me. ē im 18 Jahrhundert. Anglia 60 1936.
—— Zur Lautgeschichte von me. ī im Frühneuenglischen. Beiblatt zur Anglia 49 1938.
Matthews, W. Two notes upon seventeenth-century pronunciation. JEGP 32 1933.
—— Some eighteenth-century phonetic spellings. RES 12 1936.
—— Polite speech in the eighteenth century. English 1 1937.
—— Variant pronunciations in the seventeenth century. JEGP 37 1938.
—— English pronunciation and shorthand in the early modern period. Berkeley 1943.
Vachek, J. Über die phonologische Interpretation der Diphthonge mit besonderer Berücksichtigung des Englischen. Práce z Vědeckých Ústavů 33 1933.
—— Phonemic remarks on the short mixed vowel of Modern English. Sborník Prací Filosofické Fakulty Brněnské University 5 1956; rev in Brno Stud in Eng 4 1964.
—— The phonematic status of Modern English long vowels and diphthongs. Philologica Pragensia 6 1963.
—— Notes on the phonematic value of the Modern English [ŋ] sound. In In honour of Daniel Jones, 1964; rev in Brno Stud in Eng 4 1964.
—— Phonemic remarks on the long mixed vowel of Modern English. Sborník Prací Filosofické Fakulty Brněnské University 14 1965.
—— The English Great Vowel Shift again. Acta Universitatis Carolinae (Philologica 3) 1965.
—— The place of [ɔi] in the phonic pattern of Southern British English. Linguistics 14 1968.
—— Some phonological problems of Modern English sonant sounds. Acta Universitatis Carolinae (Philologica 3) 1969.
Buyssens, E. On some rare instances of distributed stress. Neophilologus 19 1934.
Reinhold, C. A. Neuenglisch ou (ow) und seine Geschichte. Leipzig 1934.
Allen, D. C. A note on sixteenth-century vernacular English. Language 11 1935.
Barnouw, A. J. How English was taught in Jan van Hout's Leyden. E Studies 17 1935.
Brown, H. The modern development of Middle-English -ly, -lie in rhyme. Harvard Stud & Notes in Philology and Lit 17 1935.
Schubiger, M. The role of intonation in spoken English. Cambridge 1935.
—— English intonation and syntax. In Proceedings of Second International Congress of Phonetic Sciences, Cambridge 1936.
—— Intonation—word-order—provisional it. E Studies 27 1946.

—— The intonation of interrogative sentences. E Studies 30 1949, 32 1951.
—— Notes on the intonation of coordinate sentences and syntactic groups. E Studies 34 1953.
—— The expanded form of the verb and intonation. E Studies 40 1959.
—— The interplay and co-operation of word-order and intonation in English. In In honour of Daniel Jones, 1964.
—— A note on two notional functions of the low-falling nuclear tone in English. E Studies 48 1967.
Umpfenbach, H. Die oa-Schreibung im Englischen. Leipzig 1935.
Abercrombie, D. Two early transcriptions. Le Maître Phonétique 59 1937.
—— Syllable quantity and enclitics in English. In In honour of Daniel Jones, 1964.
—— Some functions of silent stress. In Edinburgh studies in English and Scots, ed A. J. Aitken et al 1971.
Gerring, H. The pronunciation of adjectives and attributive past participles in -ed. Studier i Modern Språkvetenskap 13 1937.
Koziol, H. Wertungsbedingte Lautwandlungen im Neuenglischen. E Studien 71 1937.
—— Die Artikulation der englischen h-Laute. Phonetica 1 1957.
—— Zur Aussprache des Englischen im 18 und 19 Jahrhundert. In Studies in English language and literature presented to Karl Brunner, Vienna 1957.
Schmidt, W. Satzsinn und Tonfall: Modus der betonten Tatsächlichkeit und intensive Aktionsart im Ne. Anglia 61 1937.
Lehnert, M. Die Anfänge der wissenschaftlichen und praktischen Phonetik in England. Archiv 173–4 1938.
—— Schreibung und Aussprache im Englischen. Berlin 1963.
Baader, T. 'The Great Vowel Shift': einige Bemerkungen zur Chronologie der sog. 'mittelenglischen' Lautveränderungen. Tijdschrift voor Taal en Letteren 27 1939.
Dittes, R. Zu einigen Lautwandlungen in der südenglischen Hochsprache der letzten sechzig Jahre. E Studien 73 1939.
Franck, M. Englische Schreibung und Aussprache im Zeitalter der Tudors und Stuarts (nach Briefen). Bottrop 1939.
Hultzén, L. S. Seventeenth-century intonation. Amer Speech 14 1939.
—— System status of obscured vowels in English. Language 37 1961.
Penzl, H. 'Kompromissvokal' und Lautwandel. Anglia 63 1939.
Buchmann, E. Der Einfluss des Schriftbildes auf die Aussprache im Neuenglischen. Würzburg 1940.
Dunlap, A. R. 'Vicious' pronunciations in eighteenth-century English. Amer Speech 15 1940.
Prins, A. A. The Great Vowel-shift. Groningen 1940.
—— The Great Vowel-shift reconsidered. E Studies 24 1942.
—— The Great Vowel Shift: a refutation. Neophilologus 55 1971. On Trnka 1959, below, and Vachek 1959[1], col 58, above.
Whitehall, H. The historical status of Modern English [ɪ]. Language 16 1940.
—— and T. Fein. The development of ME ŭ in early Modern British and American English. JEGP 40 1941.
Braaksma, M. H. Has Modern English a genitive plural? E Studies 23 1941.
Hockett, C. F. English verb inflection. Stud in Linguistics 1 1942. See Hidalgo 1967, col 102, below.
Rooth, E. Zur Geschichte der englischen Partizip-Präsens-Form auf -ing. Studia Neophilologica 14 1942.
Sturzen-Becker, A. Some notes on English pronunciation about 1800. Ibid.
Bodelsen, C. A. The two English intonation tunes. E Studies 25 1943.

Lindelöf, U. On some phonetic tendencies at work in present-day Standard English. Neuphilologische Mitteilungen 44 1943.

Onions, C. T. The plural of nouns ending in *th*. Oxford 1943 (Soc for Pure Eng).

Kökeritz, H. The reduction of initial *kn* and *gn* in English. Language 21 1945.

Newman, S. S. On the stress system of English. Word 2 1946.

Trnka, B. Fonologická poznámka k posunutí dlouhých samohlásek v pozdní střední angličtině. Časopis pro Moderní Filologii 29 1946. Phonological note on the Great Vowel Shift in late ME.

— A phonemic aspect of the Great Vowel Shift. In Mélanges de linguistique et de philologie: Fernand Mossé in memoriam, Paris 1959. *See Prins 1971, col 98, above.*

— On foreign phonological features in present-day English. In In honour of Daniel Jones, 1964.

Bambas, R. C. Verb forms in -*s* and -*th* in early Modern English prose. JEGP 46 1947.

Bloch, B. English verb inflection. Language 23 1947. *See Heltveit 1959, Hidalgo 1967, below, Castagna 1968, col 137, below.*

Swadesh, M. On the analysis of English syllabics. Ibid.

Bolinger, D. [L.] The intonation of accosting questions. E Studies 29 1948.

— English stress: the interpenetration of strata. Study of Sounds (Tokyo) 1957.

— On certain features of accents A and B. Litera 4 1957.

— A theory of pitch accent in English. Word 14 1958.

— Contrastive accent and contrastive stress. Language 37 1961.

— Binomials and pitch accent. Lingua 11 1962.

Brunner, K. Neuenglisch *break, great* und *broad*. In Studien zur Sprach- und Kulturgeschichte: Festschrift zu Ehren von Josef Schatz, Innsbruck 1948.

— Zum Problem der britischen Gemeinsprache in *calf, half, calm* und dgl. In Festschrift zum 75 Geburtstag von Theodor Spira, Heidelberg 1961.

Hinman, C. *Nether* and *neither* in the seventeenth century. MLN 63 1948.

Svartengren, H. The *s*-genitive of non-personal nouns in present-day English. Studier i Modern Språkvetenskap 17 1949.

Sieberer, A. Die grosse englische Langvokalverschiebung: ihr Mechanismus und ihre Gründe. Die Sprache 2 1950.

Merlingen, W. Zur Phonologie der englischen Diphthonge und langen Vokale. Acta Linguistica 6 1951.

Christophersen, P. The glottal stop in English. E Studies 33 1952.

Jassem, W. Intonation of colloquial English (educated southern British). Wrocław 1952.

— Regular changes of vocalic quantity in early New English. Biuletyn Polskiego Towarzystwa Językoznawczego 12 1953.

Berger, M. D. Vowel distribution and accentual prominence in Modern English. Word 11 1955.

Dobson, E. J. Early Modern Standard English. Trans Philological Soc 1955.

— Notes on sound-change and phoneme theory. Brno Stud in Eng 8 1969.

O'Connor, J. D. The intonation of tag questions in English. E Studies 36 1955.

— and G. F. Arnold. Intonation of colloquial English: a practical handbook. 1961.

— and O. M. Tooley. The perceptibility of certain word-boundaries. In In honour of Daniel Jones, 1964.

Chomsky, N., M. Halle and F. Lukoff. On accent and juncture in English. In For Roman Jakobson, Hague 1956.

Danielsson, B. Erasmus Roterodamus and Tudor pronunciation. Studier i Modern Språkvetenskap 19 1956.

Dietrich, G. Die Akzentverhältnisse im Englischen bei Adverb und Präposition in Verbindung mit einem Verb und Verwandtes. In Strena anglica: Otto Ritter zum 80 Geburtstag, Halle 1956.

Krámský, J. On the quantitative phonemic analysis of English mono- and disyllables. Philologica [suppl to Časopis pro Moderní Filologii] 8 1956.

Lee, W. R. English intonation: a new approach. Lingua 5 1956.

— Fall-rise intonations in English. E Studies 37 1956. Replies by M. Schubiger and W. R. Lee, ibid.

Sigurd, B. English diphthongs from a structural point of view. Studia Linguistica 10 1956.

Sledd, J. Superfixes and intonation patterns. Litera 3 1956.

— Some questions of English phonology. Language 34 1958. On Kurath 1957, below; reply by Kurath 34 1958.

Arnold, G. F. Stress in English words. Lingua 6 1957; rptd Amsterdam 1957.

Bowman, E. On the analysis of syllabic resonants in English. Stud in Linguistics 12 1957.

Holmberg, B. Notes on the Modern English development of ME *ŭ* in stressed position compared with the neutral vowel /ə/. Studia Linguistica 11 1957.

Kurath, H. The binary interpretation of English vowels: a critique. Language 33 1957. *See Sledd 1958, above.*

Hagen, S. On the pronunciation of the sequence *ow* in English. Bergen 1958.

— The pronunciation of the spellings *ow* and *ou* in English. Bergen 1959.

Sharp, A. E. Falling-rising intonation patterns in English. Phonetica 2 1958.

— The analysis of stress and juncture in English. Trans Philological Soc 1960.

Spencer, J. Received pronunciation: some problems of interpretation. Lingua 7 1958.

Adamus, M. Traitement phonologique des diphtongues de la langue anglaise. Uniwersytet Wrocławski im. Bolesława Bieruta: Zeszyty Naukowe seria A nr 12 1959.

Andrésen, B. S. The glottal stop in the received pronunciation of English: an attempt at an acoustic analysis of the sequences -*tl*-, -*tr*-, -*tn*-, -*tj*-, and -*tw*-. Bergen 1959.

— Pre-glottalization in English standard pronunciation. Oslo 1968.

Davis, N. Scribal variation in late fifteenth-century English. In Mélanges de linguistique et de philologie: Fernand Mossé in memoriam, Paris 1959.

Heltveit, T. The linguistic status of irregular verbal forms in English. E Studies 40 1959. *Discusses Bloch 1947, above.*

Pilch, H. Neue Wege der englischen Phonetik. Anglia 77 1959.

— The elementary intonation contour of English: a phonemic analysis. Phonetica 22 1970.

Plotkin, V. Ya. O prichinakh sdviga glasnÿkh v angliĭskom yazÿke. Uchenÿe Zapiski Karel'skogo Pedagogicheskogo Instituta 9 1959. On causes of Great Vowel Shift.

Low, D. M. Contemporary trends in English pronunciation. E & S new ser 13 1960.

Lutstorf, H. T. The stressing of compounds in Modern English: a study in experimental phonetics. Berne 1960.

Stockwell, R. P. The place of intonation in a generative grammar of English. Language 36 1960.

Torsuev, G. P. Voprosÿ aktsentologii sovremennogo angliĭskogo yazÿka. Moscow 1960.

— Voprosÿ foneticheskoĭ strukturÿ slova: na materiale angliĭskogo yazÿka. Moscow 1962.

Malone, K. Glides, diphthongs and boundaries. E Studies 42 1961.

Meinecke, F. Die Akzentfaktoren im Englischen. In Festschrift zum 75 Geburtstag von Theodor Spira, Heidelberg 1961.

Doodkorte, A. C. J. and R. W. Zandvoort. On the stressing of prepositions. E Studies 43 1962. *See J. Posthumus, ibid; M. Schubiger, E Studies 44 1963.*

Faure, G. Recherches sur les caractères et le rôle des éléments musicaux dans la prononciation anglaise. Paris 1962.

Householder, F. W. The distributional determination of English phonemes. Lingua 11 1962.

Shen, Y. and G. C. Peterson. Isochronism in English. Buffalo 1962.

Stubelius, S. The *you will* request: a study on intonation. In Contributions to English syntax and philology by C. L. Barber [et al], Gothenburg 1962. *See* F. Behre, ibid.

Conner, J. E. Old French dissyllables and the Great Vowel Shift. E Studies 44 1963.

Ellegård, A. English, Latin and morphemic analysis. Gothenburg 1963.

Fu, Y.-C. The phonemic structure of English words. Taipei 1963.

Halliday, M. A. K. Intonation in English grammar. Trans Philological Soc 1963.

— The tones of English. Archivum Linguisticum 15 1963.

— Intonation and grammar in British English. Hague 1967. Includes 2 papers above.

Pinsker, H. E. Zur Phonologie der neuenglischen Sonanten. Moderne Sprachen 7 1963.

Standop, E. Strukturelle Überlagerungen im Englischen. Anglia 81 1963.

Bertrand, G. L'accentuation lexicale des polysyllabes anglais: finales à accentuation fixe. In In honour of Daniel Jones, 1964.

Brekle, H. E. Statistical correlation between typographical data and spelling-variants in 16th and 17th century English books: a contribution to diachronic English morphographemics. Linguistics 9 1964.

Castelo, L. M. The phonetic and phonemic treatment of English /h/. Phonetica 11 1964.

Crystal, D. and R. Quirk. Systems of prosodic and paralinguistic features in English. Hague 1964.

Fries, C. C. On the intonation of 'yes-no' questions in English. In In honour of Daniel Jones, 1964.

Gimson, A. C. Phonetic change and the RP vowel system. Ibid.

— A note on the variability of the phonemic components of English words. Brno Stud in Eng 8 1969.

Higginbottom, E. Glottal reinforcement in English. Trans Philological Soc 1964.

Holmberg, B. On the concept of Standard English and the history of Modern English pronunciation. Lund 1964.

Pierce, J. E. Phonemic theory and the analysis of English syllabic nuclei. Linguistics 7 1964.

— Phonemic composition of English morphemes. Linguistics 20 1966.

— The supra-segmental phonemes of English. Linguistics 21 1966.

— The morphemes of English: morphemic theory. Linguistics 23 1966.

— The morphemes of English: major morpheme stem classes. Linguistics 36 1967.

— A look at the so-called *ing*-forms of English verbs. Linguistics 50 1969.

— The morphemes of English: theme formers. Linguistics 45 1969.

— The morphemes of English: unbound minor morphemes. Linguistics 47 1969.

— The morphemes of English: structural outline. Linguistics 64 1970.

— Word vs. morpheme levels of analysis in English grammar. Linguistics 68 1971.

— A look at the so-called past tenses and participial forms of English verbs. Linguistics 71 1971.

Quirk, R. [et al]. Studies in the correspondence of prosodic to grammatical features in English. In Proceedings of 9th International Congress of Linguistics, Hague 1964.

Graband, G. Die Entwicklung der frühneuenglischen Nominalflexion. Tübingen 1965.

Hartvigson, H. A specific case of terminal juncture and syntactic cohesion. Phonetica 13 1965.

Kuryłowicz, J. A remark on the Great Vowel Shift. Word 21 1965.

Lejnieks, V. The phonemic code of English. Linguistics 14 1965.

— The system of English suffixes. Linguistics 29 1967.

Macháček, J. Segmentation of a Modern English corpus. Philologica Pragensia 8 1965.

Peters, R. A. Linguistic differences between early and late Modern English. Studia Neophilologica 37 1965.

Wells, J. C. The phonological status of syllabic consonants in English RP. Phonetica 13 1965.

Guierre, L. Eléments pour une étude linguistique de l'accentuation en anglais. Les Langues Modernes 60 1966.

— Accent secondaire et segmentation en anglais. Ibid.

— Accentuation, dérivation et syllabation. Ibid.

Hoard, J. E. Juncture and syllable structure in English. Phonetica 15 1966.

— Aspiration, tenseness and syllabication in English. Language 47 1971.

Wode, H. Englische Satzintonation. Phonetica 15 1966.

Hidalgo, C. A. English verb inflection. Lingua 18 1967. Discusses Hockett 1942 and Bloch 1947, above.

Scott, C. T. On the dating of NE *ee* and *ea* spellings from ME *ẹ̄* and *ę̄*. In Approaches in linguistic methodology, ed I. Rauch and C. T. Scott, Madison 1967.

Trager, G. L. A componential morphemic analysis of English personal pronouns. Language 43 1967.

Firbas, J. On the prosodic features of the Modern English finite verb as a means of functional sentence perspective. Brno Stud in Eng 7 1968.

— On the prosodic features of the Modern English finite verb-object combination as [a] means of functional sentence perspective. Brno Stud in Eng 8 1969.

Mulder, J. W. F. and H. A. Hurren. The English vowel phonemes from a functional point of view and a statement of their distribution. La Linguistique 1968.

Wang, W. S.-Y. Vowel features, paired variables and the English vowel shift. Language 44 1968.

Crystal, D. Prosodic systems and intonation in English. Cambridge 1969.

Davidsen-Nielsen, N. English stops after initial /s/. E Studies 50 1969.

Lehto, L. English stress and its modification by intonation. Helsinki 1969.

Lipka, L. Assimilation and dissimilation as regulating factors in English morphology. Zeitschrift für Anglistik und Amerikanistik 17 1969.

Luelsdorff, P. A. On the phonology of English inflection. Glossa 3 1969.

Poldauf, I. Some notes on the signalization of the plural in English nouns. Brno Stud in Eng 8 1969.

Shen, Y. Two intonations in eight types of English questions. Jnl of Eng Linguistics 3 1969.

Cruttenden, A. On the so-called grammatical nature of intonation. Phonetica 21 1970.

Cygan, J. English vowels and syllable peaks. Studia Anglica Posnaniensia 2 1970.

— Consonant clusters and distinctive features. Ibid.

— Distinctive features and final consonant clusters in English. Studia Anglica Posnaniensia 3 1971.

Foley, J. A systematic phonological interpretation of the English vowel shift. Glossa 4 1970.

Kivimaa, K. and L. Lehto. The Great Vowel Shift: a combinatory change? Univ of Helsinki: Pbns of Inst of Phonetics 23 1970.

Bresnan, J. W. Sentence stress and syntactic transformations. Language 47 1971. *See A. Berman and M. Szamosi 1972, G. Lakoff 1972, below.*

Delack, J. B. English morphology and linguistic universals. Glossa 5 1971.

Engler, L. F. and R. G. Hilyer. Once again: American and British intonation tunes. Acta Linguistica Hafniensia 13 1971.

Halle, M. and S. J. Keyser. English stress: its form, its growth and its role in verse. New York 1971.

Krohn, R. Contradictory feature specifications and the front vowels of English. General Linguistics 11 1971.

Magnusson, W. L. Stages of linguistic changes in Modern English. Linguistics 71 1971.

Sloat, C. and J. E. Hoard. The inflectional morphology of English. Glossa 5 1971.

Sørensen, K. On the stressing of be, been and as. E Studies 52 1971.

Berman, A. and M. Szamosi. Observations on sentential stress. Language 48 1972. See J. W. Bresnan, Stress and syntax: a reply, ibid.

Lakoff, G. The global nature of the nuclear stress rule. Ibid. See J. W. Bresnan, Stress and syntax: a reply, ibid.

Dialects

For Yorkshire dialects see Trans Yorkshire Dialect Soc ; for Lancashire dialects Jnl of Lancashire Dialect Soc ; for Devon dialects Reports on Devonshire verbal provincialisms in Reports & Trans of Devonshire Assoc ; for Cumberland dialects Jnl of Lakeland Dialect Soc.

See A. J. Ellis 1867–89, col 90, above.

Halliwell (-Phillipps), J. O. A dictionary of archaic and provincial words. 2 vols 1847, 1881 (rev).

Dickinson, W. A glossary of the words and phrases of Cumberland. 1859, [1899] (rev E. W. Prevost); suppl by Prevost 1905; 2nd suppl by Prevost 1924.

Murray, J. A. H. The dialect of the southern counties of Scotland. 1873.

Wright, J. A grammar of the dialect of Windhill in the West Riding. 1892.

— The English dialect grammar. In vol 6 of his English dialect dictionary, col 53, above; also separately 1905.

Wall, A. A contribution towards the study of the Scandinavian elements in the English dialects. Anglia 20 1897.

Grüning, B. Schwund und Zusatz von Konsonanten in den neuenglischen Dialekten. Strasbourg 1904.

Hargreaves, A. A grammar of the dialect of Adlington (Lancashire). Heidelberg 1904.

Kruisinga, E. A grammar of the dialect of West Somerset: descriptive and historical. Bonn 1905.

Franzmeyer, F. Studien über den Konsonantismus und Vokalismus der neuenglischen Dialekte. Strasbourg 1906.

Hirst, T. O. A grammar of the dialect of Kendal (Westmorland). Heidelberg 1906.

Kjederqvist, J. The dialect of Pewsey (Wiltshire). Trans Philological Soc 1903–6.

Mutschmann, H. A phonology of the north-eastern Scotch dialect on an historical basis. Bonn 1909.

Binzel, A. Die Mundart von Suffolk in frühneuenglischer Zeit. Darmstadt 1912.

Sixtus, J. Der Sprachgebrauch des Dialekt-Schriftstellers Frank Robinson zu Bowness in Westmorland. Berlin 1912.

Brilioth, B. A grammar of the dialect of Lorton (Cumberland). Oxford 1913.

Wilson, J. The dialect of the New Forest in Hampshire (as spoken in the village of Burley). Oxford [1913].

— Lowland Scotch. Oxford 1915.

— The dialects of central Scotland. Oxford 1926.

Grant, W. The pronunciation of English in Scotland. Cambridge 1914.

— and J. M. Dixon. Manual of Modern Scots. Cambridge 1921.

Klein, W. Der Dialekt von Stokesley in Yorkshire. Berlin 1914.

Cowling, G. H. The dialect of Hackness (north-east Yorkshire). Cambridge 1915.

Gepp, E. A contribution to an Essex dialect dictionary. 1920, 1923 (as An Essex dialect dictionary), Wakefield 1969 (with addn and biography by J. S. Appleby).

Vikar, A. Contribution to the history of the Durham dialects. Malmö 1922.

Watson, G. The Roxburghshire word-book. Cambridge 1923.

— Dialect survivals of Anglo-Saxon inflection. JEGP 35 1936.

Zachrisson, R. E. Notes on the Essex dialect and the origin of vulgar London speech. E Studien 59 1925.

Brandl, A. Englische Dialekte. Berlin 1927.

— Lebendige Sprache: Beobachtungen an Lautplatten englischer Dialektsätze. Sitzungsberichte der Preussischen Akademie der Wissenschaften (Berlin) 1928.

Heldmann, A. Lautlehre der schottischen Mundart im südöstlichen Perthshire. Giessener Beiträge zur Erforschung der Sprache und Kultur Englands und Nordamerikas 3 1927.

Reaney, P. H. A grammar of the dialect of Penrith. Manchester 1927.

Guilford, E. L. A list of words illustrating the Nottinghamshire dialect. Trans Thoroton Soc 32–53 1928–49.

Haigh, W. E. A new glossary of the dialect of the Huddersfield district. Oxford 1928.

Orton, H. The medial development of ME ōi (tense), Fr. ü (= [ȳ]) and ME eu (OE ēow) in the dialects of the north of England. E Studien 63 1929.

— The dialects of Northumberland. Trans Yorkshire Dialect Soc pt 31 1930.

— The phonology of a south Durham dialect. 1933.

— The isolative treatment in living north-Midland dialects of OE e lengthened in open syllables in Middle English. Leeds Stud in Eng 7–8 1952.

— Remarks upon field work for an English linguistic atlas for England. E Studies 34 1953.

— and E. Dieth. Survey of English dialects. Leeds 1962–. In progress; A: Introduction, by H. Orton, 1962; B: The basic material; vol 1, The six northern counties and the Isle of Man, ed H. Orton and W. J. Halliday 3 pts 1962–3; vol 2, The west Midland counties, ed H. Orton and M. V. Barry 3 pts 1969–71; vol 3, The east Midland counties and East Anglia, ed H. Orton and P. M. Tilling 3 pts 1969–71; vol 4, The southern counties, ed H. Orton and M. F. Wakelin 3 pts 1967–8.

Kökeritz, H. The phonology of the Suffolk dialect. Upsala 1932.

— Alexander Gill (1621) on the dialects of south and east England. Studia Neophilologica 11 1939.

— A record of late eighteenth-century cockney. Language 25 1949.

Dieth, E. A grammar of the Buchan dialect (Aberdeenshire). Vol 1, Cambridge 1933.

— A new survey of English dialects. E & S 32 1946.

— Whose little lad are you? E Studies 38 1957. On history of owe, ought with reference to Scots and Northern English.

Ehrmann, L. and H. Scherer. Die Dialekte von Norfolk und von Lanarkshire–Glasgow. Leipzig 1933.

Mann, S. E. Dialect words of Nottingham and district. N & Q 30 Sept 1933.

Flom, G. T. Vowel-harmony in Old Norse and northern Aberdeenshire Scotch. JEGP 33 1934.

Gill, W. W. Manx dialect: words and phrases. Bristol 1934.

— Dialect words of south Somerset. N & Q 16 March 1935.

— A glossary of Somerset dialect. N & Q 1 Feb–28 March, 23 May 1936.

— Somerset dialect words and provincialisms. N & Q 8–15 July, 16 Sept 1939.

— Wiltshire and Somerset words. N & Q 22 June 1940.

— Cheshire and Dorset words. N & Q 3 Aug 1940.

— Manx dialect words. N & Q 4–18 Oct 1941.

Brooks, C. The relation of the Alabama–Georgia dialect to the provincial dialects of Great Britain. Baton Rouge 1935.

Clarke, E. D. *Obthrust* in north Lincolnshire. Leeds Stud in Eng 4 1935.

Craigie, W. A. Older Scottish and English: a study in contrasts. Trans Philological Soc 1935.

— Northern words in Modern English. Oxford 1937 (Soc for Pure Eng).

— Pure English of the soil. Oxford 1945 (Soc for Pure Eng).

Dorow, K.-G. Die Beobachtungen des Sprachmeisters James Elphinston über die schottische Mundart 1787. Weimar 1935.

Matthews, W. Sailors' pronunciation in the second half of the seventeenth century. Anglia 59 1935.

— The Lincolnshire dialect in the eighteenth century. N & Q 7 Dec 1935.

— Sailors' pronunciation 1770–83. Anglia 61 1937.

— Some contributions to English dialects. N & Q 5 June 1937.

— Some eighteenth-century vulgarisms. RES 13 1937.

— The vulgar speech of London in the fifteenth to seventeenth centuries. N & Q 2 Jan–3 April 1937.

— Cockney past and present: a short history of the dialect of London. 1938.

— South-western dialect in the early modern period. Neophilologus 24 1939.

Munderloh, H. Die Sprache der Lincoln diocese documents 1450–1544. Oldenburg 1935.

Wratzke, W. Die gegenwärtigen Lautverhältnisse im heutigen Englisch mit gelegentlichen Ausblicken auf die Mundart. Bottrop 1935.

Delatte, F. Somerset dialect. N & Q 9 May 1936.

Huscher, H. Das Anglo-irische und seine Bedeutung als sprachkünstlerisches Ausdrucksmittel. In Englische Kultur in sprachwissenschaftlicher Deutung: M. Deutschbein zum 60 Geburtstage, Leipzig 1936.

Müller, A. and K.-H. Borgis. Der Sprachgebrauch in den Dialektgebieten von Südost-Yorkshire und Nord-Durham. Leipzig 1936.

Partridge, E. Some Romany words. TLS 26 Dec 1936.

Saxe, J. Bernard Shaw's phonetics: a comparative study of cockney sound-changes. Copenhagen 1936.

Smith, A. H. English dialects. Trans Philological Soc 1936.

Forster, L. The coalman's cry. E Studien 71 1937.

Lamprecht, A. Der Sprachgebrauch im südwestlichen Yorkshire. Leipzig 1937.

Nehls, W. Der Sprachgebrauch der Dialektgegend von Aberdeen. Leipzig 1937.

Sheldon, E. K. The vulgar speech of London in the fifteenth to seventeenth centuries. N & Q 4 Dec 1937.

Thielke, K. Arbeiten über Mundart und Slang. Zeitschrift für Neusprachlichen Unterricht 36 1937.

Westergaard, E. Gaelic influences on lowland Scottish. Anglia 61 1937.

Wijk, A. The orthography and pronunciation of Henry Machyn the London diarist: a study of the south-east Yorkshire dialect in the early 16th century. Upsala 1937.

Büttner, K., K. Frank and G. Kozmiensky. Intonation und Vokalqualität in englischen Mundarten. Breslau 1938.

Hohenstein, R. Intonation und Vokalqualität in den englischen Mundarten von Norfolk und Suffolk. Berlin 1938.

Keller, M. Die Frau und das Mädchen in den englischen Dialekten. Zürich 1938.

Wilde, H.-O. Der Industrie-Dialekt von Birmingham. Halle 1938.

Schubel, F. Zur neueren englischen Dialektforschung. E Studien 73 1939.

Oxley, J. E. The Lindsey dialect. Leeds 1940.

Hulme, H. M. Derbyshire dialect in the seventeenth century. Jnl of Derbyshire Archaeological Soc new ser 15 1941.

— A Warwickshire word list. MLR 46 1951.

Urwin, K. Northern English *mardy*. MLR 39 1944.

Sheard, J. A. Dialect studies. Trans Philological Soc 1945.

Livingston, C. H. Eng. *searce*, *search*, 'sieve, strainer'. MLN 62 1947.

Marckwardt, A. H. An unnoted source of English dialect vocabulary. JEGP 46 1947. On Laurence Nowell's Vocabularium saxonicum.

Kirkham, N. Derbyshire lead-mining glossary. Cave Research Group Pbn no 2 1949.

Löfvenberg, M. T. English dialectal *slait*, *sleight* 'a sheep pasture'. Studier i Modern Språkvetenskap 17 1949.

Widén, B. Studies on the Dorset dialect. Lund 1949.

Wood, F. T. Dialect words not found in Wright's dictionary. N & Q 12 Nov 1949.

Carr, B. M. H. Neglected sources for the vocabulary of Kentish and some neighbouring dialects in the eighteenth and nineteenth centuries. Trans Philological Soc 1950.

Visser, F. T. Cockney *what are you doing of?* E Studies 32 1951.

Jones, W. E. The definite article in living Yorkshire dialect. Leeds Stud in Eng 7–8 1952.

Langenfelt, G. *She* and *her* instead of *it* and *its*. Anglia 70 1952.

McIntosh, A. An introduction to a survey of Scottish dialects. Edinburgh 1952.

Thorson, P. A new etymology for *sheal* and *shealing*. JEGP 51 1952.

Wright, P. Parasitic syllabic nasals at Marshside, Lancashire. Leeds Stud in Eng 7–8 1952.

— Coal-mining language: a recent investigation. In Patterns in the folk speech of the British Isles, ed M. F. Wakelin 1972.

Traynor, M. The English dialect of Donegal: a glossary. Dublin 1953.

Catford, J. C. Vowel-systems of Scots dialects. Trans Philological Soc 1957.

Henry, P. L. An Anglo-Irish dialect of North Roscommon: phonology, accidence, syntax. Dublin 1957.

— A linguistic survey of Ireland: preliminary report. In Lochlan: a review of Celtic studies 1 (Norsk Tidsskrift for Sprogvidenskap suppl 5) 1958.

Gregg, R. J. Notes on the phonology of a County Antrim Scotch-Irish dialect. 2 pts Orbis 7–8 1958–9.

— The Scotch-Irish boundaries in Ulster. In Patterns in the folk speech of the British Isles, ed M. F. Wakelin 1972.

Cawley, A. C. (ed). George Meriton's A Yorkshire dialogue 1683. Ptd Kendal 1959.

Kolb, E. The icicle in English dialects. E Studies 40 1959.

— Phonological atlas of the northern region: the six northern counties, north Lincolnshire and the Isle of Man (Linguistic atlas of England). Berne 1966.

— Die Infiltration der Hochsprache in die nordenglischen Dialekte. Anglia 86 1968.

Quirk, R. 'Dialects' within Standard English. Trans Yorkshire Dialect Soc 10 1960.

Sivertsen, E. Cockney phonology. Oslo 1960. See J. Vachek, Some thoughts on the phonology of cockney English, Philologica Pragensia 5 1962.

Francis, W. N. Some dialectal verb forms in English. Orbis 10 1961.

— Modal *daren't* and *durstn't* in dialectal English. Leeds Stud in Eng new ser 2 1968.

Dean, C. The dialect of George Meriton's A Yorkshire dialogue 1683. Ptd Kendal 1962.

— Some consonantal elements in Northern English dialects. Canadian Jnl of Linguistics 12 1967.

Brook, G. L. English dialects. 1963.

Plant, D. The dialect of north Staffordshire. Istituto Orientale di Napoli: Annali (sezione germanica) 6 1963.

Wilson, R. M. The orthography and provenance of Henry Machyn. In Early English and Norse studies presented to Hugh Smith, 1963.

[Adams, G. B., J. Braidwood and R. J. Gregg (ed)]. Ulster dialects: an introductory symposium. Holywood 1964.

Viereck, W. Der English dialect survey und der Linguistic survey of Scotland: Arbeitsmethoden und bisherige Ergebnisse. Zeitschrift für Mundartforschung 31 1964.
— Zur Entstehung und Wertung des uvularen r unter besonderer Berücksichtigung der Situation in England. Phonetica 13 1965.
— Phonematische Analyse des Dialekts von Gateshead-upon-Tyne, Co Durham. Hamburg 1966.
— A diachronic-structural analysis of a Northern English urban dialect. Leeds Stud in Eng new ser 2 1968. On Gateshead dialect.
— Englische Dialektologie. In Germanische Dialektologie: Festschrift für Walther Mitzka zum 80 Geburtstag, Wiesbaden 1968.
— Britische und amerikanische Sprachatlanten. Zeitschrift für Dialektologie und Linguistik 38 1971.
Wölck, W. Phonematische Analyse der Sprache von Buchan [Aberdeenshire]. Heidelberg 1965.
Kohler, K. A late eighteenth-century comparison of the 'provincial dialect' of Scotland and the 'pure dialect'. Linguistics 23 1966.
Adams, G. B. Phonemic systems in collision in Ulster English. In Verhandlungen des zweiten internationalen Dialektologenkongresses, 1 (Zeitschrift für Mundartforschung: Beihefte 3 1967).
Hedevind, B. The dialect of Dentdale in the West Riding of Yorkshire. Upsala 1967.
Murison, D. A survey of Scottish language studies. Forum for Modern Lang Stud 3 1967.
Harris, M. Demonstrative adjectives and pronouns in a Devonshire dialect. Trans Philological Soc 1968. On South Zeal dialect.
— Relationships of place in a Devonshire dialect. Archivum Linguisticum new ser 2 1971. On South Zeal dialect.
Sandred, K. I. Notes on the distribution of some plough terms in Modern English dialects. Studia Neophilologica 40 1968.
Ščur, G. S. On the non-finite forms of the verb can in Scottish. Acta Linguistica Hafniensia 11 1968.
Speitel, H.-H. and J. Y. Mather. Schottische Dialektologie. In Germanische Dialektologie: Festschrift für Walther Mitzka zum 80 Geburtstag, Wiesbaden 1968.
Strang, B. [M. H.] The Tyneside linguistic survey. In Verhandlungen des zweiten internationalen Dialektologenkongresses, 2 (Zeitschrift für Mundartforschung: Beihefte 4 1968).
Wakelin, M. F. and M. V. Barry. The voicing of initial fricative consonants in present-day dialectal English. Leeds Stud in Eng new ser 2 1968.
Widdowson, J. D. A. The dialect of Filey (Yorkshire, East Riding): the vowels of stressed syllables. Ibid.
— Proverbs and sayings from Filey. In Patterns in the folk speech of the British Isles, ed M. F. Wakelin 1972.
Braidwood, J. The Ulster dialect lexicon. Belfast 1969.
Speitel, H.-H. An areal typology of isoglosses: isoglosses near the Scottish-English border. Zeitschrift für Dialektologie und Linguistik 36 1969.
Wakelin, M. F. A dialect note: South-Western breakfast in the Survey of English dialects. Orbis 19 1970.
— Names for the cow-house in Devon and Cornwall. Studia Neophilologica 42 1970.
— Dialect and place-names: the distribution of kirk. In Patterns in the folk speech of the British Isles, ed M. F. Wakelin 1972.
Weissmann, E. Phonematische Analyse des Stadtdialektes von Bristol. Phonetica 21 1970.
Wells, J. C. Local accents in England and Wales. Jnl of Linguistics 6 1970.
Fashola, J. B. Structural and non-structural factors in linguistic interference: a study of the influence of Received Pronunciation on a speaker of English provincial standard from Workington, Cumberland. Zeitschrift für Dialektologie und Linguistik 38 1971.

Barry, M. V. The morphemic distribution of the definite article in contemporary regional English. In Patterns in the folk speech of the British Isles, ed M. F. Wakelin 1972.
Duncan, P. Forms of the feminine pronoun in Modern English dialects. Ibid.
Mather, J. Y. Linguistic geography and the traditional drift-net fishery of the Scottish East Coast. Ibid.
Påhlsson, C. The Northumbrian burr. Lund 1972.
Parry, D. R. Anglo-Welsh dialects in South-East Wales. In Patterns in the folk speech of the British Isles, ed M. F. Wakelin 1972.

Individual Authors and Texts
(*in alphabetical order*)

Wille, J. Die Orthographie in Roger Aschams Toxophilus und Scholemaster. Marburg 1889.
Sommer, I. Die frühneuenglische Orthographie und Lautlehre in Lord Bacons englischen Werken. Heidelberg 1937.
Prins, A. A. The booke of common prayer 1549: an enquiry into its language. Amsterdam 1933.
Brook, S. The language of the Book of common prayer. 1965.
Wilson, J. The dialect of Robert Burns as spoken in central Ayrshire. 1923.
Harder, B. Die Reime von Butlers Hudibras. Königsberg 1900.
Swearingen, G. F. Die englische Schriftsprache bei Coverdale. Berlin 1904.
Horten, F. Studien über die Sprache Defoes. Bonn 1914.
David Copperfield and dialect. TLS 30 April 1949.
Gerken, H. Die Sprache des Bischofs Douglas von Dunkeld. Strasbourg 1898.
Larue, J. L. Das Pronomen in den Werken des schottischen Bischofs Gavin Douglas. Strasbourg 1908.
Dierberger, J. John Drydens Reime. Freiburg 1895.
Wyld, H. C. The best English: a claim for the superiority of received Standard English; together with notes on Mr Gladstone's pronunciation. Oxford 1934 (Soc for Pure Eng).
Fuhr, K. Lautuntersuchungen zu Stephen Hawes Gedicht The pastime of pleasure. Marburg 1891.
Partridge, A. C. The accidence of Ben Jonson's plays. Cambridge 1953.
Pennanen, E. V. Notes on the grammar in Ben Jonson's dramatic works. Acta Academiae Socialis A 3, Tampere 1966.
Sprotte, O. Zum Sprachgebrauch bei John Knox. Berlin 1906.
Schau, K. Sprache und Grammatik der Dramen Marlowes. Leipzig 1901.
Whiting, G. W. Milton's rules for -ed. MLN 49 1934.
— The significance of -'n and -en in Milton's spelling. E Studien 70 1936.
Grünzinger, M. Die neuenglische Schriftsprache in den Werken des Sir Thomas More. Freiburg 1909.
Dalcourt, J. Essai sur la langue de Sir Thomas More d'après ses œuvres anglaises. Paris 1914.
Mead, W. H. The versification of Pope. 1889.
McLean, L. M. The riming-system of Alexander Pope. PMLA 6 1891.
Erämetsä, E. Notes on Richardson's language. Neuphilologische Mitteilungen 53 1952.
Abbott, E. A. Shakespearian grammar. 1869, 1870 (rev).
Lummert, A. Die Orthographie der ersten Folio-Ausgabe der Shakespere'schen Dramen. Halle 1883.
Franz, W. Shakespeare-Grammatik. Halle 1898, Heidelberg 1924; rev as Die Sprache Shakespeares in Vers und Prosa, Halle 1939.
— Orthographie, Lautgebung und Wortbildung in den Werken Shakespeares. Heidelberg 1905.
Viëtor, W. Shakespeare's pronunciation. Marburg 1906.

Zachrisson, R. E. Shakespeares uttal. Studier i Modern Språkvetenskap 5 1914.

Horn, W. Zur englischen Bühnensprache. Archiv 166 1935.

Mackie, W. S. Shakespeare's English, and how far it can be investigated with the help of the New English dictionary. MLR 31 1936.

Kökeritz, H. Shakespeare's use of dialect. Trans Yorkshire Dialect Soc pt 51 1951.

—— Shakespeare's pronunciation. New Haven 1953.

Cercignani, F. ME *ou* in Shakespeare. Studia Neophilologica 43 1971.

—— The status of ME *ěr*, *ǐr* and *ǔr* in Shakespeare. Studia Neophilologica 44 1972.

Whitehall, H. A short study of the vowels in the language of the Shuttleworth accounts 1582–1621. PQ 10–11 1931–2.

Schoeneberg, G. Die Sprache John Skeltons in seinen kleineren Werken. Marburg 1888.

Düring, H. Über die Pronomina bei Spenser. Halle 1891.

Bauermeister, K. Zur Sprache Spensers auf Grund der Reime in der Faerie Queene. Freiburg 1896.

Boehm, K. Spensers Verbalflexion. Berlin 1909.

Millican, C. B. The northern dialect of the Shepheardes calendar. ELH 6 1939.

Sugden, H. W. The grammar of Spenser's Faerie Queene. Philadelphia 1936.

Neumann, J. H. Jonathan Swift and English spelling. SP 41 1944.

Strang, B. M. H. Swift and the English language: a study in principles and practice. In To honor Roman Jakobson, Hague 1967.

Tilling, P. M. Local dialect and the poet: a comparison of the findings in the Survey of English dialects with dialect in Tennyson's Lincolnshire poems. In Patterns in the folk speech of the British Isles, ed M. F. Wakelin 1972.

Steuerwald, K. Die Londoner Vulgärsprache in Thackerays Yellowplush papers. Leipzig 1930.

Hoelper, F. Die englische Schriftsprache in Tottels Miscellany (1557) und in Tottels Ausgabe von Brookes Romeus and Juliet (1562). Strasbourg 1894.

Sopp, W. Orthographie und Aussprache der ersten neuenglischen Bibelübersetzung des William Tyndale. Anglia 12 1889.

Bogenschneider, H.-J. Die englische Lautentwicklung im 17 Jahrhundert nach den Briefen der Familie Verney. Ohlau 1936.

Wyld, H. C. The spoken English of the early eighteenth century. Modern Lang Teaching 11 1915. Wentworth papers.

Palmer, R. E. Thomas Whythorne's speech: the phonology of a sixteenth-century native of Somerset in London. Copenhagen 1969.

Kökeritz, H. Dialectal traits in Sir Thomas Wyatt's poetry. In Medieval and linguistic studies in honor of Francis Peabody Magoun jr, 1965.

Selection of Texts Written in the Early Modern English Period

Readers and Anthologies

Skeat, W. W. Specimens of English literature from the Ploughmans crede to the Shepheardes calender AD 1394–AD 1579. Oxford 1871, 1884 (rev).

Flügel, E. Neuenglisches Lesebuch, 1 Band: die Zeit Heinrichs VIII. Halle 1895. No more pbd.

Davies, C. English pronunciation from the fifteenth to the eighteenth century.

Local Documents (*in alphabetical order*)

The great red book of Bristol. Ed E. W. W. Veale 5 vols 1931–53 (Bristol Record Soc).

Bury wills and inventories 1463–1569. Ed S. Tymms 1850 (Camden Soc).

Records of the guild of the Holy Trinity, Coventry. Ed G. Templeman 1944 (Dugdale Soc).

Wills and inventories from the registry at Durham [16th century]. [Ed J. Raine, W. Greenwell and J. C. Hodgson] 3 vols 1835–1906 (Surtees Soc).

Lambeth churchwardens' accounts 1504–1645 and Vestry book 1610. Ed C. Drew and H. Jenkinson 4 vols 1940–50 (Surrey Record Soc).

Lancashire deeds vol 1: Shuttleworth deeds. Ed J. Parker 1934 (Chetham Soc).

The town book of Lewes 1542–1701. Ed L. F. Salzman 1946 (Sussex Record Soc).

The records of the Commissioners of Sewers in the parts of Holland 1547–1603. Ed A. M. Kirkus and A. E. B. Owen 1959– (Lincoln Record Soc). In progress.

Norfolk lieutenancy journal 1676–1701. Ed B. Cozens-Hardy 1961 (Norfolk Record Soc).

Minutes of the Norwich court of mayoralty 1630–5. Ed W. L. Sachse 2 vols 1942–67 (Norfolk Record Soc).

Records of the guild of St George in Norwich 1389–1547. Ed M. Grace 1937 (Norfolk Record Soc).

Nottinghamshire household inventories [1512–68]. Ed P. A. Kennedy 1963 (Thoroton Soc).

Some Oxfordshire wills [1393–1510]. Ed J. R. H. Weaver and A. Beardwood 1958 (Oxfordshire Record Soc).

The churchwardens' accounts of Prescot, Lancashire 1523–1607. Ed F. A. Bailey 1953 (Lancashire & Cheshire Record Soc).

Surveys of the manors of Robertsbridge, Sussex and Michelmarsh, Hampshire and of the demesne lands of Halden in Rolvenden, Kent 1567–70. Ed R. H. D'Elboux 1944 (Sussex Record Soc).

Somerset assize orders 1629–40. Ed T. G. Barnes 1959 (Somerset Record Soc).

The Admiralty court book of Southampton 1566–85. Ed E. Welch 1968 (Southampton Records ser).

The third book of remembrance of Southampton 1514–1602. Ed A. L. Merson 1952– (Southampton Records ser). To vol 3 [1573–89], 1965; in progress.

Transcripts of Sussex wills up to the year 1560 by R. Garraway Rice. Ed W. H. Godfrey 3 vols 1935–41 (Sussex Record Soc).

Ecclesiastical terriers of Warwickshire parishes, vol 1: parishes *A* to *Li* [1585–1753]. Ed D. M. Barratt 1955 (Dugdale Soc).

York civic records. Ed A. Raine 8 vols 1939–53 (Yorkshire Archaeological Soc).

Other Texts (*in chronological order*)

[*See also* W. Matthews, British diaries: an annotated bibliography of British diaries written between 1442 and 1942, Berkeley 1950.]

Letters and papers of the Verney family 1478–1639. Ed J. Bruce 1853 (Camden Soc).

Memorials of the Holles family 1493–1656. Ed A. C. Wood 1937 (Royal Historical Soc).

Sir John Eliot and the Vice-Admiralty of Devon. Ed H. Hulme, in Camden miscellany vol 17, 1940 (Royal Historical Soc).

Clifford letters of the sixteenth century. Ed A. G. Dickins 1962 (Surtees Soc).

Valentine and Orson translated by Henry Watson [1503–5?]. Ed A. Dickson, Oxford 1937 (EETS).

Lord Berners' translation of Froissart [1520]. Ed W. P. Ker 6 vols 1901–3.

Rede me and be not wrothe [1528]. Ed E. Arber 1871.

Boece, Hector. The chronicles of Scotland translated by J. Bellenden. 1531. Ed R. W. Chambers, E. C. Batho and H. W. Husbands, 2 vols 1936–41 (STS).

The Mar Lodge translation of the History of Scotland by Hector Boece. Ed G. Watson 1946 (STS).

The comedy of Acolastus translated by John Palsgrave [1540]. Ed P. L. Carver, Oxford 1937 (EETS).

Forty-six lives, translated from Boccaccio's De claris mulieribus by Henry Parker, Lord Morley [c. 1540]. Ed H. G. Wright, Oxford 1943 (EETS).

The letters of Queen Elizabeth [1544–1603]. Ed G. B. Harrison 1935.

Ascham, R. Toxophilus. 1545; ed E. Arber 1868.
—— The scholemaster. 1570; ed E. Arber 1870.
Latimer, H. Seven sermons. 1549; ed E. Arber 1869.
Diary of Henry Machyn 1550–63. Ed J. G. Nichols 1848 (Camden Soc).
John Isham, mercer and merchant adventurer: two account books of a London merchant in the reign of Elizabeth I [1558–72]. Ed G. D. Ramsay 1962 (Northamptonshire Record Soc).
Darrell–Hungerford letters [1560 etc]. In H. Hall, Society in the Elizabethan age, 1887.
Proceedings of the Company of Soapmakers 1562–1642. Ed H. E. Matthews 1939 (Bristol Record Soc).
The life, letters and writings of John Hoskyns 1566–1638. Ed L. B. Osborn, New Haven 1937.
Letter book of Gabriel Harvey 1573–80. Ed E. J. L. Scott 1884 (Camden Soc).
The letters of Sir Francis Hastings 1574–1609. Ed C. Cross 1969 (Somerset Record Soc).
The autobiography of Thomas Whythorne [c. 1576]. Ed J. M. Osborn, Oxford 1961.
Alleyne papers 1580–1661. Ed J. P. Collier 1843 (Shakespeare Soc).
Letters of Queen Elizabeth and James VI of Scotland [1582–1602]. Ed J. Bruce 1849 (Camden Soc).
Thomas Hudson's History of Judith [1584]. Ed J. Craigie 1940 (STS).
Mr Harrie Cavendish his journey to and from Constantinople 1589, by Fox his servant. Ed A. C. Wood, in Camden miscellany vol 17, 1940 (Royal Historical Soc).
The Stockwell papers 1590–1614. Ed J. Rutherford 2 vols 1932–3 (Southampton Record Soc).
A seventeenth-century doctor and his patients: John Symcotts 1592?–1662. Ed F. N. L. Poynter and W. J. Bishop 1951 (Bedfordshire Historical Record Soc).
The notebook of John Penry 1593. Ed A. Peel 1944 (Royal Historical Soc).
Queen Elizabeth's englishings [1593–8]. Ed C. Pemberton 1899 (EETS).
Memoirs of Edward Alleyne 1593–1626. Ed J. P. Collier 1841 (Shakespeare Soc).
James VI. Basilicon doron. 1598; ed J. Craigie 2 vols 1942–4 (STS).
The records of King Edward's School, Birmingham. Ed W. F. Carter, E. A. B. Barnard and P. B. Chatwin 5 vols 1924–63 (Dugdale Soc).
The Tusmore papers. Ed L. G. Wickham-Legg 1939 (Oxfordshire Record Soc).
Tudor treatises. Ed A. G. Dickins 1959 (Yorkshire Archaeological Soc). Includes Sir Francis Bigod, A treatise concerning impropriations of benefices; Robert Parkyn, Devotional treatises; Michael Sherbrook, The fall of religious houses.
The Earl of Hertford's lieutenancy papers 1603–12. Ed W. P. D. Murphy 1969 (Wiltshire Record Soc).
The correspondence of Lady Katherine Paston 1603–27. Ed R. Hughey 1941 (Norfolk Record Soc).
Robert Loder's farm accounts 1610–20. Ed G. E. Fussell 1936 (Royal Historical Soc).

The Knyvett letters 1620–44. Ed B. Schofield 1949 (Norfolk Record Soc).
Letters of the Lady Brilliana Harley [1625–43]. Ed T. T. Lewis 1854 (Camden Soc).
Correspondence of Dr Basire 1634–75. Ed W. M. Darnell 1831.
Memoirs of Sir John Reresby [1634–89]. Ed A. Browning, Glasgow 1936.
Memoirs of the Verney family during the Civil War. Ed F. P. Verney 4 vols 1892–9; 3rd edn entitled Memoirs of the Verney family during the seventeenth century, ed F. P. and M. M. Verney 1925.
The Oxinden and Peyton letters 1642–70. Ed D. Gardiner 1937.
The Tower of London letter-book of Sir Lewis Dyve 1646–7. Ed H. G. Tibbutt 1958 (Bedfordshire Historical Record Soc).
The correspondence of Bishop Brian Duppa and Sir Justinian Isham 1650–60. Ed G. Isham 1955 (Northamptonshire Record Soc).
The letter-book of John Viscount Mordaunt 1658–60. Ed M. Coate 1945 (Royal Historical Soc).
The diurnal of Thomas Rugg 1659–61. Ed W. L. Sachse 1961 (Royal Historical Soc).
The diary of Roger Lowe of Ashton-in-Makerfield, Lancashire 1663–74. Ed W. L. Sachse 1938.
An early seventeenth-century calendar of records preserved in Westminster Palace Treasury. Ed F. Taylor, Bull John Rylands Lib 23 1939.
Charges to the grand jury at quarter sessions 1660–1677, by Sir Peter Leicester. Ed E. M. Halcrow 1953 (Chetham Soc).
The correspondence of Thomas Corie, town clerk of Norwich 1664–87. Ed R. H. Hill 1956 (Norfolk Record Soc).
The autobiography of William Stout of Lancaster 1665–1752. Ed J. D. Marshall 1967 (Chetham Soc).
Letters of John Pinney 1679–99. Ed G. F. Nuttall 1939.
Diana Astry's recipe book c. 1700. Ed B. Stitt 1957 (Bedfordshire Historical Record Soc).
Ramblin' Jack: the journal of Captain John Cremer 1700–74. Ed R. R. Bellamy 1936.
The great diurnal of Nicholas Blundell of Little Crosby, Lancashire. Ed F. Tyrer and J. J. Bagley 2 vols 1968–70 (Lancashire & Cheshire Record Soc). Vol 1, 1702–11; vol 2, 1712–19.
The letters and papers of the Banks family of Revesby Abbey 1704–60. Ed J. W. F. Hill 1952 (Lincoln Record Soc).
The correspondence of Sir James Clavering 1705–41. Ed H. T. Dickinson 1967 (Surtees Soc).
The Wentworth papers 1705–39. Ed J. J. Cartwright 1883.
Correspondence of the Reverend Joseph Greene 1712–90. Ed L. Fox 1965 (Dugdale Soc).
The diary of Richard Kay 1716–51 of Baldingstone, near Bury: a Lancashire doctor. Ed W. Brockbank and F. Kenworthy 1968 (Chetham Soc).
The Williamson letters 1748–65. Ed F. J. Manning 1954 (Bedfordshire Historical Record Soc).

C. SYNTAX

(1) GENERAL STUDIES; STUDIES DEALING WITH MORE THAN ONE PERIOD

Jespersen, O. Studier over engelske kasus. Copenhagen 1891.
—— Negation in English and other languages. Copenhagen 1917.
—— Analytic syntax. 1937.
Kellner, L. Historical outlines of English syntax. 1892.
Ross, C. H. The absolute participle in Middle and Modern English. PMLA 8 1893.

Einenkel, E. Geschichte der englischen Sprache II: historische Syntax. In H. Paul, Grundriss der germanischen Philologie vol 1, Strasbourg 1901 (2nd edn), 1916 (3rd edn).
—— Das englische Indefinitum. Anglia 26–7 1903–4; Nachträge 29–31 1906–8, 33–36 1910–12.
—— Die englische Verbalnegation. Anglia 35 1912.

—— Zur Geschichte des englischen Gerundiums. Anglia 37 1913.

—— Die Entwicklung des englischen Gerundiums. Anglia 38 1914. *See* G. O. Curme and E. Einenkel, ibid.

Bødtker, A. T. Critical contributions to early English syntax. 2 sers Christiania 1908–10.

Püttmann, A. Die Syntax der sogenannten progressiven Form im Alt- und Frühmittelenglischen. Anglia 31 1908.

Åkerlund, A. On the history of the definite tenses in English. Lund 1911.

Curme, G. O. A history of the English relative constructions. JEGP 11 1912.

—— History of the English gerund. E Studien 45 1912. *See* E. Einenkel, Anglia 37–8 1913–14.

Morsbach, L. Grammatisches und psychologisches Geschlecht im Englischen. Berlin 1913, 1926 (rev).

Kreickemeier, H. Die Wortstellung im Nebensatz des Englischen. Giessen 1915.

Stoelke, H. Die Inkongruenz zwischen Subjekt und Prädikat im Englischen und in den verwandten Sprachen. Heidelberg 1916.

Steadman, J. M. The origin of the historical present in English. SP 14 1917.

Aronstein, P. Die periphrastische Form im Englischen. Anglia 42 1918.

Sundén, K. F. The predicational categories in English. Uppsala Universitets Årsskrift 1918.

—— A category of predicational change in English. Ibid. On transitive verbs used in active form with passive sense.

Düringer, H. Die Analyse im Formenbau des englischen Nomens. Giessener Beiträge zur Erforschung der Sprache und Kultur Englands und Nordamerikas 1 1923.

Gutheil, H. Form und Funktion in der englischen Verbalflexion. Ibid.

Jäger, E. Die Konjunktionen *for* und *for that* im Englischen. Ibid.

Small, G. W. The comparison of inequality. Baltimore 1924.

—— The Germanic case of comparison, with a special study of English. Philadelphia 1929.

Trnka, B. Příspěvky k syntaktickému a fraseologickému vývoji slovesa *to have*. Prácc z Vědeckých Ústavů 5 1924. Studies in the syntactical and phraseological history of the verb *to have*; with English summary.

Stahl, L. Der adnominale Genetiv und sein Ersatz im Mittelenglischen und Frühneuenglischen. Giessener Beiträge zur Erforschung der Sprache und Kultur Englands und Nordamerikas 3 1927.

Bøgholm, N. Outstanding features of English grammatical number. In A grammatical miscellany offered to Otto Jespersen, Copenhagen 1930.

Gaaf, W. van der. The passive of a verb accompanied by a preposition. E Studies 12 1930.

—— The absolute genitive. E Studies 14 1932.

—— The connection between verbs of rest (*lie, sit* and *stand*) and another verb, viewed historically. E Studies 16 1934.

Karpf, F. Some minor points of English syntax. In A grammatical miscellany offered to Otto Jespersen, Copenhagen 1930.

Knispel, E. Der altenglische Instrumental bei Verben und Adjektiven und sein Ersatz im Verlaufe der englischen Sprachgeschichte. Ohlau 1932.

Bliemel, W. Die Umschreibung des Personalpronomens im Englischen. Breslau 1933.

Steinki, J. Die Entwicklung der englischen Relativpronomina in spätmittelenglischer und frühneuenglischer Zeit. Ohlau 1933.

Winkler, G. Das Relativum bei Caxton und seine Entwicklung von Chaucer bis Spenser. Saalfeld 1933.

Haislund, N. Abstrakter og konkreter og artikelbrug på engelsk. In Studier tilegnede Verner Dahlerup, Copenhagen 1934.

Hoffmann, G. Die Entwicklung des umschriebenen Perfektums im Altenglischen und Frühmittelenglischen. Ohlau 1934.

Weber, G. Der Bau der englischen Sprache. Leipzig 1934.

Süsskand, P. Geschichte des unbestimmten Artikels im Alt- und Frühmittelenglischen. Halle 1935.

Dahl, T. Form and function: studies in Old and Middle English syntax. Copenhagen 1936.

Roberts, M. H. The antiquity of the Germanic verb-adverb locution. JEGP 35 1936.

Dekker, A. The pseudo-pronoun *so*. Neophilologus 23 1938.

Engblom, V. On the origin and early development of the auxiliary *do*. Lund 1938.

Gehse, H. Die Kontaminationen in der englischen Syntax. Breslau 1938.

Marchand, H. Remarks about English negative sentences. E Studies 20 1938.

—— The syntactical change from inflectional to word order system and some effects of this change on the relation 'verb/object' in English. Anglia 70 1952.

Mossé, F. Histoire de la forme périphrastique *être+participe présent* en germanique. 2 pts Paris 1938.

—— Réflexions sur la genèse de la 'forme progressive'. In Studies in English language and literature presented to Karl Brunner, Vienna 1957.

Reuter, O. On continuative relative clauses in English. Helsinki 1938.

Brose, B. Die englischen Passivkonstruktionen vom Typus *I am told a story* und *I am sent for*: ein Beitrag zur englischen Syntax des 14 bis 16 Jahrhunderts. Würzburg 1939.

Christophersen, P. The articles: a study of their theory and use in English. Copenhagen 1939.

Kihlbom, A. Concerning the present subjunctive in conditional clauses. Studia Neophilologica 11 1939.

Burnham, J. M. The presentative sentence. In Studies in English in honor of Raphael Dorman O'Leary and Selden Lincoln Whitcomb, Lawrence Kansas 1940 (Univ Kansas Pbns, humanistic ser 6).

Yartseva, V. N. Razvitie slozhnopodchinennogo predlozheniya v angliiskom yazyke. Leningrad 1940. Development of the complex sentence in English.

—— Istoricheskaya sintaksis angliiskogo yazyka. Moscow 1961. Historical syntax of English.

Zandvoort, R. W. 'Pregnant' *one*. E Studies 22 1940.

—— Varia syntactica. In Language and society: essays presented to Arthur M. Jensen, Copenhagen 1961. 1: The split genitive; 2: Grammatical discord.

Ekwall, E. Studies on the genitive of groups in English. Kungl. Humanistiska Vetenskapssamfundet i Lund: Årsberättelse 1943.

Ohlander, U. Omission of the object in English. Studia Neophilologica 16 1944.

Ahlgren, A. On the use of the definite article with 'nouns of possession' in English. Upsala 1946.

Fridén, G. Studies on the tenses of the English verb from Chaucer to Shakespeare, with special reference to the late sixteenth century. Upsala 1948.

—— On the use of auxiliaries to form the perfect and the pluperfect in late Middle English and early Modern English. Studia Linguistica 11 1957. *See* T. Johannisson 12 1958.

Visser, F. T. Enige opmerkingen betreffende de studie van de historische syntaxis van het Engels. Nijmegen 1948.

—— Two or more auxiliaries with a common verbal complement. E Studies 31 1950.

—— The terms 'subjunctive' and 'indicative'. E Studies 36 1955.

—— A historical syntax of the English language. Leyden 1963–. In progress; 1–2, Syntactical units with one verb, 1963–6; 3, Syntactical units with two verbs (first half), 1969.

Funke, O. On the use of the attributive adjective in OE prose and early ME. E Studies 30 1949.

Grad, A. Prispevek k problemu infinitivnih konstrukcij v angleščini. Zbornik Filozofske Fakultete (Ljubljana) 1 1950. A contribution to the problem of the infinitive constructions in English; with English summary.

— A contribution to the problem of word-order in Old and Middle English. Slavistična Revija 8 1955.

— Notes about the origin of the '*for*+subject+infinitive' construction in English. Slovenska Akademija Znanosti in Umetnosti (Razred za Filološke in Literarne Vede): Razprave 2 1956.

— Notes on the causative use of intransitive verbs in English. Zbornik Filozofske Fakultete (Ljubljana) 3 1960.

Mann, G. Die Entstehung des finalen Infinitivs im Englischen. Archiv 187 1950.

— Die Entstehungsgeschichte des englischen Konditionalsatzes. Archiv 197 1961.

Ellegård, A. The auxiliary *do*: the establishment and regulation of its use in English. Stockholm 1953.

Langenfelt, G. The type *a Talbot!* Studier i Modern Språkvetenskap 18 1953. Addns 19 1956. *See* C. T. Onions, The type *a Talbot*, MÆ 26 1957.

Potter, S. The expression of reciprocity. E Studies 34 1953.

— Attributes and attributive adjectives. Brno Stud in Eng 8 1969.

Karlberg, G. The English interrogative pronouns: a study of their syntactic history. Stockholm 1954.

Suter, K. Das Pronomen beim Imperativ im Alt- und Mittelenglischen. Aarau 1955.

Graband, G. Neuenglisches *them* als Demonstrativum. Zeitschrift für Anglistik und Amerikanistik 4 1956.

Jud-Schmid, E. Der indefinite Agens von Chaucer bis Shakespeare: die Wörter und Wendungen für 'man'. Berne 1956. *See also Fröhlich 1951, Meier 1953, cols 118, 123, below.*

Lindheim, B. von. Zur Problematik der grammatischen Kategorien im Englischen. Die Neueren Sprachen new ser 5 1956.

Sørensen, K. Substantive with two epithets. E Studies 37 1956.

Vallins, G. H. The pattern of English. 1956.

Firbas, J. Some thoughts on the function of word-order in Old English and Modern English. Sborník Prací Filosofické Fakulty Brněnské University 6 1957.

Sundby, B. The independent genitive in English. Vetenskapssocieteten i Lund: Årsbok 1957.

Heltveit, T. Attribute and anaphora in the gender-system of English. Norsk Tidsskrift for Sprogvidenskap 18 1958.

— The Old English appositional construction exemplified by *sume his geferan*: a forerunner of the modern construction *a friend of mine*? E Studies 50 1969.

Mustanoja, T. F. The English syntactical type *one the best man*, and its occurrence in other Germanic languages. Helsinki 1958.

— Shakespeare's *a Talbot*. Neuphilologische Mitteilungen 60 1959.

Schlauch, M. The generic singular in English: a supplement. Kwartalnik Neofilologiczny 5 1958.

Whitehall, H. Structural essentials of English. 1958.

Crowell, T. L. *Have got*: a pattern preserver. Amer Speech 34 1959.

Kirch, M. S. Scandinavian influence on English syntax. PMLA 74 1959.

Spitzbardt, H. Some remarks on the syntax of comparison. Philologica Pragensia 2 1959.

— 'Bestimmende' und 'erweiternde' Relativsätze im Englischen. Zeitschrift für Anglistik und Amerikanistik 8 1960.

Behre, F. 'It cannot be; it is impossible': a study in diachronic grammar. In Frank Behre: papers on English vocabulary and syntax, Gothenburg 1961. On *should* in *that*-clauses.

Il'ish, B. A. Razvitie sposobov vyrazheniya smyslovogo predikata v angliiskom yazyke. In Voprosy germanskogo yazykoznaniya: materialy vtoroi nauchnoi sessii po voprosam germanskogo yazykoznaniya, Moscow 1961. Ways of expressing the sense predicate in English (historical outline); with English summary.

Koziol, H. Zum Gebrauch des Demonstrativums anstelle des bestimmten Artikels. Neuphilologische Mitteilungen 62 1961.

Carstensen, B. Die Testationsformel: eine umstrittene englische Infinitivkonstruktion. Anglia 80 1962.

Tellier, A. Les verbes perfecto-présents et les auxiliaires de mode en anglais ancien (viiie s.–xvie s.). Paris 1962.

Finkenstaedt, T. *You* und *thou*: Studien zur Anrede im Englischen. Berlin 1963. *See also Kisbye 1964, col 120, below.*

Kisbye, T. An historical survey of English syntax. Århus 1963–5. 1, The non-finite forms of the verb, 1963; 2, Pronouns, adjectives and adverbs, 1964; 3, Articles, numerals, gender and case, the finite forms of the verb, 1965.

— On the so-called imperative with preposed pronominal subject (1489–1695). Archiv 203 1967.

Harris, D. P. The development of word-order patterns in twelfth-century English. In Studies in languages and linguistics in honor of Charles C. Fries, Ann Arbor 1964.

Rankova, M. On the development of periphrastic auxiliary *do* in Modern English. Godishnik na Sofiĭskiya Universitet: Filologicheski Fakultet 58 1964.

Closs [Traugott], E. Diachronic syntax and generative grammar. Language 41 1965.

— A history of English syntax: a transformational approach to the history of English sentence structure. New York 1972.

Meier, H. H. The lag of relative *who* in the nominative. Neophilologus 51 1967.

Rissanen, M. The uses of *one* in Old and early Middle English. Helsinki 1967.

— The use of *one* and the indefinite article with plural nouns in English. Neophilologische Mitteilungen 73 1972.

Fries, U. Demonstrativum und bestimmter Artikel. Neuphilologische Mitteilungen 69 1968.

Harsh, W. The subjunctive in English. University Al 1968.

Mutt, O. The use of substantives as premodifiers in early English. Neuphilologische Mitteilungen 69 1968.

Hladký, J. A note on the quantitative evaluation of the verb in English. Brno Stud in Eng 8 1969.

Macháček, J. Historical aspect of the accusative with infinitive and the content clause in English. Ibid.

Šimko, J. A few notes concerning the interpretation and classification of the English verb. Ibid.

Marckwardt, A. H. *Much* and *many*: the historical development of a Modern English distributional pattern. In Philological essays: studies in Old and Middle English language and literature in honour of Herbert Dean Meritt, Hague 1970.

Baron, N. S. A reanalysis of English grammatical gender. Lingua 27 1971.

Brorström, S. A historical survey of prepositions expressing the sense 'for the duration of'. E Studies 52 1971.

(2) OLD ENGLISH

General

See also Sweet 1882, 1953, Mossé 1945, Brook 1955, Quirk and Wrenn 1955, 1957, Mitchell, 1965, 1968, Pilch 1970, cols 59–61, above.

Chase, F. H. A bibliographical guide to Old English syntax. Leipzig 1896.

Small, G. W. On the study of Old English syntax. PMLA 51 1936

Andrew, S O. Syntax and style in Old English. Cambridge 1940. See Andrew 1948, col 121, below.

Special Studies

Lichtenheld, A. Das schwache Adjektiv im Ags. Zeitschrift für Deutsches Alterthum 16 1873.

Lüttgens, C. Über Bedeutung und Gebrauch der Hilfsverba im frühen Altenglischen: sculan und willan. Wismar 1888.

Callaway, M. The absolute participle in Anglo-Saxon. Baltimore 1889.

— Statistics of the appositive participle in Anglo-Saxon. PMLA 16 1901.

— The infinitive in Anglo-Saxon. Washington 1913.

— The temporal subjunctive in Old English. Austin 1931.

— The consecutive subjunctive in Old English. Boston 1933.

Smith, C. A. The order of words in Anglo-Saxon prose. PMLA 8 1893.

Henshaw, A. N. The syntax of the indicative and subjunctive moods in the Anglo-Saxon Gospels. Leipzig 1894.

Gorrell, J. H. Indirect discourse in Anglo-Saxon. PMLA 10 1895.

Pessels, C. The present and past periphrastic tenses in Anglo-Saxon. Strasbourg 1896.

Barnouw, A. J. Textkritische Untersuchungen nach dem Gebrauch des bestimmten Artikels und des schwachen Adjektivs in der altenglischen Poesie. Leyden 1902.

Shearin, H. G. The expression of purpose in Old English prose. New York 1903.

Shipley, G. The genitive case in Anglo-Saxon poetry. Baltimore 1903.

Henk, O. Die Frage in der altenglischen Dichtung. Kiel 1904.

Kromer, W. Altenglisch in und on. Berlin 1904.

Grossmann, H. Das angelsächsische Relativ. Weimar 1906.

Adams, A. The syntax of the temporal clause in Old English prose. New York 1907.

Benham, A. R. The clause of result in Old English prose. Anglia 31 1908.

Riggert, G. Der syntaktische Gebrauch des Infinitivs in der altenglischen Poesie. Kiel 1909.

Burnham, J. M. Concessive constructions in Old English prose. New York 1911.

Sorg, W. Zur Syntax und Stilistik des Pronominalgebrauches in der älteren angelsächsischen Dichtung. Breslau 1912.

Hübener, G. Zur Erklärung der Wortstellungsentwicklung im Ags. Anglia 39 1916.

Nadler, H. Studien zum attributiven Genetiv des Angelsächsischen. Berlin 1916.

Trnka, B. Syntaktická charakteristika řeči anglosaských památek básnických. Práce z Vědeckých Ústavů 10 1925. A syntactical analysis of the language of Anglo-Saxon poetry; with English summary.

Frary, L. G. Studies in the syntax of the Old English passive with special reference to the use of wesan and weorðan. Baltimore 1929.

Glunz, H. Die Verwendung des Konjunktivs im Altenglischen. Leipzig 1929.

Bloomfield, L. OHG eino, OE ana 'solus'. In Curme volume of linguistic studies, Baltimore 1930.

Ericson, E. E. The use of Old English swa in negative clauses. In Studies in honor of Hermann Collitz, Baltimore 1930.

— Old English swa in worn-down correlative clauses. E Studies 65 1931.

— The use of Old English swa as a pseudo-pronoun. JEGP 30 1931.

— The use of swa in Old English. Göttingen 1932.

Vogt, A. Beiträge zum Konjunktivgebrauch im Altenglischen. Leipzig 1930.

Gaaf, W. van der. Beon and habban connected with an inflected infinitive. E Studies 13 1931.

Kuhn, H. Zur Wortstellung und -betonung im Altgermanischen. Beiträge zur Geschichte der Deutschen Sprache und Literatur 57 1933.

Andrew, S. O. Some principles of Old English word-order. MÆ 3 1934.

— Relative and demonstrative pronouns in Old English. Language 12 1936.

Behre, F. The subjunctive in Old English poetry. Gothenburg 1934.

Klaeber, F. Zwei Anmerkungen zur Wortstellung im Altenglischen. In Studia germanica tillägnade E. A. Kock, Lund 1934.

— Eine Randbemerkung zur Nebenordnung und Unterordnung im Altenglischen. Beiblatt zur Anglia 52 1941.

Johansen, H. Zur Entwicklungsgeschichte der altgermanischen Relativsatzkonstruktionen. Copenhagen 1935.

Maisenhelder, K. Die altenglische Partikel and. Königsfeld 1935.

Schlachter, W. Zur Stellung des Adverbs im Germanischen. Leipzig 1935.

Klingebiel, J. Die Passivumschreibungen im Altenglischen. Bottrop 1937.

Möllmer, H. Konjunktionen und Modus im Temporalsatz des Altenglischen. Breslau 1937.

Fourquet, J. L'ordre des éléments de la phrase en germanique ancien. Paris 1938.

Meritt, H. D. The construction ἀπόκοινοῦ in the Germanic languages. Stanford 1938.

Schneider, K. Die Stellungstypen des finiten Verbs im urgermanischen Haupt- und Nebensatz. Heidelberg 1938.

Mann, G. Konjunktionen und Modus im konsekutiven und finalen Nebensatz des Altenglischen. Breslau 1939.

Hermann, E. Jeder einzelne in den germanischen Sprachen. Nachrichten von der Gesellschaft der Wissenschaften zu Göttingen (philologisch-historische Klasse) new ser 3 1940.

Meroney, H. Old English ðær 'if'. JEGP 41 1942.

— The early history of down as an adverb. JEGP 44 1945.

Gray, L. H. Man in Anglo-Saxon and Old High German Bible-texts. Word 1 1945.

Cobb, G. W. The subjunctive mood in Old English poetry. In Philologica: the [Kemp] Malone anniversary studies, Baltimore 1949.

Fröhlich, J. Der indefinite Agens im Altenglischen: unter besonderer Berücksichtigung des Wortes man. Berne 1951. See also Jud-Schmid 1956, col 115, above, Meier 1953, col 123, below.

Quirk, R. Expletive or existential there. London Mediæval Stud 2 1951.

— The concessive relation in Old English poetry. New Haven 1954.

Raith, J. Untersuchungen zum englischen Aspekt 1: grundsätzliches Altenglisch. Munich 1951.

Hermodsson, L. Reflexive und intransitive Verba im älteren Westgermanischen. Upsala 1952.

Rynell, A. Parataxis and hypotaxis as a criterion of syntax and style especially in Old English poetry. Lund 1952.

Schaubert, E. von. Vorkommen, gebietsmässige Verbreitung und Herkunft altenglischer absoluter Partizipialkonstruktionen in Nominativ und Akkusativ. Paderborn 1954.

Funke, O. Some remarks on late OE word-order: with special reference to Ælfric and the Maldon poem. E Studies 37 1956.

Dam, J. van. The causal clause and causal prepositions in early Old English prose. Groningen 1957.

Standop, E. Syntax und Semantik der modalen Hilfsverben im Altenglischen: *magan, motan, sculan, willan*. Bochum 1957.

Page, R. I. Northumbrian *æfter* (= in memory of)+ accusative. Studia Neophilologica 30 1958.

Peltola, N. On the 'identifying' *swa (swa)* phrase in Old English. Neuphilologische Mitteilungen 60 1959.

— On appositional constructions in Old English prose. Neuphilologische Mitteilungen 61 1960.

Liggins, E. M. The clause of 'denied reason' in Old English. JEGP 59 1960.

Scheler, M. Altenglische Lehnsyntax: die syntaktischen Latinismen im Altenglischen. Berlin 1961.

Bacquet, P. La structure de la phrase verbale à l'époque Alfrédienne. Paris 1962. *See* B. Mitchell, Neuphilologische Mitteilungen 67 1966.

Zatočil, L. Zur Stellung des adnominalen Genetivs im Althochdeutschen und Altenglischen. Sborník Prací Filosofické Fakulty Brněnské University 11 1962.

Bauer, G. Über Vorkommen und Gebrauch von ae. *sin*. Anglia 81 1963.

Carlton, C. Word order of noun modifiers in Old English prose. JEGP 62 1963.

— Descriptive syntax of the Old English charters. Hague 1970.

Mitchell, B. Adjective clauses in Old English poetry. Anglia 81 1963.

— Old English syntactical notes. N & Q Sept 1963.

— Pronouns in Old English poetry: some syntactical notes. RES new ser 15 1964.

— Some problems of mood and tense in Old English. Neophilologus 49 1965.

— The status of *hwonne* in Old English. Ibid.

— An Old English syntactical reverie: the Wanderer, lines 22 and 34–36. Neuphilologische Mitteilungen 68 1967.

— More musings on Old English syntax. Neuphilologische Mitteilungen 69 1968.

— Some syntactical problems in the Wanderer. Ibid.

— Five notes on Old English syntax. Neuphilologische Mitteilungen 70 1969.

Khomiakov, V. A. A note on the so-called 'passive participles with active meaning' in Old English. JEGP 63 1964.

Smushkevich, E. S. K istorii formirovaniya vozvratnogo zaloga v angliiskom yazyke (na materiale drevneangliiskogo perioda). In Voprosy obshchego i romano-germanskogo yazykoznaniya (Uchenye Zapiski, Bashkirskii Gosudarstvennyi Universitet, vypusk 21, seriya filologicheskikh nauk no 9), Ufa 1964. On the history of the formation of the reflexive voice in English (OE material).

Tengstrand, E. A special use of Old English *oþer* after *swilce*. Studia Neophilologica 30 1958.

Nickel, G. Die expanded form im Altenglischen: Vorkommen, Funktion und Herkunft der Umschreibung *beon/wesan*+Partizip präsens. Neumünster 1966.

Reszkiewicz, A. Ordering of elements in late Old English prose in terms of their size and structural complexity. Wrocław 1966.

— Split constructions in Old English. In Studies in language and literature in honour of Margaret Schlauch, Warsaw 1966.

Makovskii, M. M. O 'leksicheskom' vyrazhenii vidovoi dikhotomii v germanskikh yazykakh. Nauchnye Doklady Vysshei Shkoly: Filologicheskie Nauki 1967. On the 'lexical' expression of aspectual dichotomy in the Germanic languages.

Pillsbury, P. W. Descriptive analysis of discourse in late West Saxon texts. Hague 1967.

Rissanen, M. OE *þæt an* 'only'. Neuphilologische Mitteilungen 68 1967.

Wagner, K. H. Generative grammatical studies in the Old English language. Heidelberg 1969.

Campbell, A. Verse influences in Old English prose. In Philological essays: studies in Old and Middle English language and literature in honour of Herbert Dean Meritt, Hague 1970.

Hess, H. H. Old English nominals. Papers on Lang & Lit 6 1970.

Pilch, H. Matrix der altenglischen Satztypen. In Linguistique contemporaine: hommage à Eric Buyssens, Brussels 1970.

Roberts, J. Traces of unhistorical gender congruence in a late Old English manuscript. E Studies 51 1970. On Life of St Guthlac in BM ms Cotton Vespasian D xxi.

Millward, C. M. Imperative constructions in Old English. Hague 1971.

Enkvist, N. E. Old English adverbial *þa*—an action marker? Neuphilologische Mitteilungen 73 1972.

Joly, A. La négation dite 'explétive' en vieil anglais et dans d'autres langues indo-européennes. Etudes Anglaises 25 1972.

Old English Texts

(in alphabetical order)

Wohlfart, T. Die Syntax des Verbums in Aelfric's Übersetzung des Heptateuch und des Buches Hiob. Munich 1886.

Schrader, B. Studien zur Aelfricschen Syntax. Jena 1887.

Kühn, P. T. Die Syntax des Verbums in Aelfrics Heiligenleben. Leipzig 1889.

Ropers, K. Zur Syntax und Stilistik des Pronominalgebrauchs bei Aelfric. Kiel 1918.

Barrett, C. R. Studies in the word-order of Ælfric's Catholic homilies and Lives of the saints. Cambridge 1953.

Kisbye, T. Zur pronominalen Anrede bei Ælfric: Anmerkung zu Th. Finkenstaedts *You und Thou*. Archiv 201 1964.

Fujiwara, H. On the infinitive in the interlinear gloss of Ælfric's Colloquy. Anglica (Osaka) 5 1965.

Bock, K. Die Syntax der Pronomina und Numeralia in König Alfreds Orosius. Göttingen 1887.

Hüllweck, A. Über den Gebrauch des Artikels in den Werken Alfreds des Grossen. Dessau 1887.

Haarstrick, A. Untersuchungen über die Präpositionen bei Alfred dem Grossen. Kiel 1890.

Lehmann, A. Der syntaktische Gebrauch des Genitivs in Ælfreds Orosius. Leipzig 1891.

Wülfing, J. E. Die Syntax in den Werken Alfreds des Grossen. 3 vols Bonn 1894–1901.

Rauert, M. Die Negation in den Werken Alfreds. Kiel 1910.

Brown, W. H. A syntax of King Alfred's Pastoral care. Hague 1970.

Holtbuer, F. Der syntaktische Gebrauch des Genitives in Andreas, Guðlac, Phönix, dem Heiligen Kreuz und Höllenfahrt. Anglia 8 1885.

Reussner, H. A. Untersuchungen über die Syntax in dem angelsächsischen Gedichte vom heiligen Andreas. Leipzig 1889.

Kube, E. Die Wortstellung in der Sachsenchronik. Jena 1886. Parker ms.

Robertson, W. A. Tempus und Modus in der altenglischen Chronik: Hss A und E (C.C.C.C. 173, Laud 636). Marburg 1906.

Shannon, A. A descriptive syntax of the Parker manuscript of the Anglo-Saxon Chronicle from 734 to 891. Hague 1964.

Nader, E. Dativ und Instrumental im Beowulf. Vienna 1883.

— Tempus und Modus im Beowulf. Anglia 10–11 1888–9.

Köhler, K. Der syntaktische Gebrauch des Infinitivs und Particips im Beowulf. Münster 1886.

Schücking, L. L. Die Grundzüge der Satzverknüpfung im Beowulf: 1 Teil. Halle 1904.

Ries, J. Die Wortstellung im Beowulf. Halle 1907.

Schuchardt, R. Die Negation im Beowulf. Berlin 1910.

Woolf, H. B. Subject-verb agreement in Beowulf. MLQ 4 1943.

Andrew, S. O. Postscript on Beowulf. Cambridge 1948.

Mitchell, B. Two syntactical notes on Beowulf. Neophilologus 52 1968. On Beowulf 1141 and 2035.

Cable, T. M. Rules for syntax and metrics in Beowulf. JEGP 69 1970.

Flamme, J. Syntax der Blickling Homilien. Bonn 1884.

Hofer, O. Der syntaktische Gebrauch des Dativs und Instrumentals in den Cædmon beigelegten Dichtungen. Anglia 7 1884.

Meyer, E. Darstellung der syntaktischen Erscheinungen in dem angelsächsischen Gedicht Crist und Satan. Rostock 1898.

Schürmann, A. Darstellung der Syntax in Cynewulfs Elene. Münster 1884.

Conradi, B. Darstellung der Syntax in Cynewulfs Gedicht Juliana. Leipzig 1886.

Prollius, M. Über den syntaktischen Gebrauch des Conjunktivs in den Cynewulfschen Dichtungen Elene, Juliana und Crist. Marburg 1888.

Rose, A. Darstellung der Syntax in Cynewulfs Crist. Leipzig 1890.

Kopas, W. Die Grundzüge der Satzverknüpfung in Cynewulfs Schriften. Breslau 1900.

Dethloff, R. Darstellung der Syntax im angelsächsischen Gedicht Daniel. Rostock 1907.

Kempf, E. Darstellung der Syntax in der sogenannten Caedmonschen Exodus. Leipzig 1888.

Seyfarth, H. Der syntaktische Gebrauch des Verbums in dem Cædmon beigelegten angelsächsischen Gedicht von der Genesis. Leipzig 1891.

Halfter, O. Die Satzverknüpfung in der älteren Genesis. Kiel 1915.

Capek, M. J. The nationality of a translator: some notes on the syntax of Genesis B. Neophilologus 55 1971.

Scherer, P. Aspect in the Old English of the Corpus Christi ms. Language 34 1958. On West-Saxon Gospels.

Furkert, M. Der syntaktische Gebrauch des Verbums in dem angelsächsischen Gedichte vom heiligen Guthlac. Leipzig 1889.

Foster, T. G. Judith: studies in metre, language and style. Strasbourg 1892.

Oldenburg, K. Untersuchungen über die Syntax in dem altenglischen Gedicht Judith. Rostock 1907.

Bale, C. The syntax of the genitive case in the Lindisfarne Gospels. Iowa City 1907.

Callaway, M. Studies in the syntax of the Lindisfarne Gospels. Baltimore 1918.

Anderson, G. K. Some irregular uses of the instrumental case in Old English. PMLA 50 1935. Mostly on Lindisfarne and Rushworth Gospels and Durham Ritual.

Ross, A. S. C. Sex and gender in the Lindisfarne Gospels. JEGP 35 1936.

Samuels, M. L. The Elder Edda and the Lindisfarne gloss: a syntactic parallel. Eng & Germanic Stud 3 1950.

Jones, C. The functional motivation of linguistic change. E Studies 48 1967. On gender in Lindisfarne Gospels and Durham Ritual.

— Some features of determiner usage in the Old English glosses to the Lindisfarne Gospels and the Durham Ritual. Indogermanische Forschungen 75 1970.

Lange, F. Darstellung der syntaktischen Erscheinungen im angelsächsischen Gedichte von Byrhtnoþs Tod. Rostock 1906.

Ahrens, J. Darstellung der Syntax im angelsächsischen Gedicht Phoenix. Rostock 1904.

Madert, A. Die Sprache der altenglischen Rätsel des Exeterbuches. Marburg 1900.

Schneider, R. Satzbau und Wortschatz der altenglischen Rätsel des Exeterbuches. Breslau 1913.

Tilley, M. P. Zur Syntax Wærferths. Leipzig 1903.

Timmer, B. J. Studies in Bishop Wærferth's translation of the Dialogues of Gregory the Great. Wageningen 1934.

— The place of the attributive noun-genitive in Anglo-Saxon, with special reference to Gregory's Dialogues. E Studies 21 1939.

Fraatz, P. Darstellung der syntaktischen Erscheinungen in den angelsächsischen Waldere-Bruchstücken. Rostock 1908.

Jacobsen, R. Darstellung der syntaktischen Erscheinungen im angelsächsischen Gedicht vom Wanderer. Rostock 1901.

Daniels, A. J. Kasussyntax zu den (echten und unechten) Predigten Wulfstans. Leyden 1904.

(3) MIDDLE ENGLISH

General

See also Brunner 1938, 1962, Mossé 1949, 1959, col 75, above.

Einenkel, E. Streifzüge durch die mittelenglische Syntax unter besonderer Berücksichtigung der Sprache Chaucers. Münster 1887.

Dubislav, G. Studien zur mittelenglischen Syntax. Anglia 40 1915, 44 1921, 46 1922.

Mustanoja, T. F. A Middle English syntax. Helsinki 1960–. In progress; pt 1, Parts of speech, 1960.

Special Studies

Einenkel, E. Das persönliche Pronomen im Mittelenglischen. Neuphilologisches Centralblatt 3 1889.

— Der Infinitiv im Mittelenglischen. Anglia 12 1891.

Wichers, P. Über die Bildung der zusammengesetzten Zeiten der Vergangenheit im Frühmittelenglischen. Kiel 1889.

Bearder, J. W. Über den Gebrauch der Präpositionen in der altschottischen Poesie. Halle 1894.

Böhme, W. Die Temporalsätze in der Übergangszeit vom Angelsächsischen zum Altenglischen. Halle 1903.

Ausbüttel, E. Das persönliche Geschlecht unpersönlicher Substantiva einschliesslich der Tiernamen im Mittel-Englischen. Halle 1904.

Gaaf, W. van der. The transition from the impersonal to the personal construction in Middle English. Heidelberg 1904.

— A friend of mine. Neophilologus 12 1927.

— The split infinitive in Middle English. E Studies 15 1933.

Swane, W. Studien zur Casussyntax des Frühmittelenglischen. Kiel 1904.

Rossmann, B. Zum Gebrauch der Modi und Modalverba in Adverbialsätzen im Frühmittelenglischen. Kiel 1908.

Janus, R. Der syntaktische Gebrauch des Numerus im Frühmittelenglischen. Kiel 1913.

Sanders, H. Der syntaktische Gebrauch des Infinitivs im Frühmittelenglischen. Heidelberg 1915.

Glahn, N. von. Zur Geschichte des grammatischen Geschlechts im Mittelenglischen vor dem völligen Erlöschen des aus dem Altenglischen ererbten Zustandes. Heidelberg 1918.

Zilling, O. Das Hilfsverb *do* im Mittelenglischen. Halle 1918.

Moore, S. Grammatical and natural gender in Middle English. PMLA 36 1921.

Funke, O. Die Fügung *ginnen* mit dem Infinitiv im Mittelenglischen. E Studien 56 1922.

Gebhardt, L. Das unausgedrückte Subjekt im Mittelenglischen. Giessen 1922.

Häusermann, H. W. Studien zu den Aktionsarten im Frühmittelenglischen. Vienna 1930.

Koziol, H. Grundzüge der Syntax der mittelenglischen Stabreimdichtungen. Vienna 1932.

— Die Entstehung der Umschreibung mit *to do*. Germanisch-romanische Monatsschrift 24 1936.

— Zur Syntax der englischen Urkundensprache des 14 und 15 Jahrhunderts. Anglia 62 1938.

Paschke, E. Der Gebrauch des bestimmten Artikels in der spätmittelenglischen Prosa 1380–1500. Emsdetten 1934.

Hittmair, R. Zu den Aktionsarten im Mittelenglischen. E Studien 70 1935.

Ohlander, U. Studies on coordinate expressions in Middle English. Lund 1936.

— A study on the use of the infinitive sign in Middle English. Studia Neophilologica 14 1942.

Peters, G. Der syntaktische Gebrauch des unbestimmten Artikels im Zentral- und Spätmittelenglischen. Göttingen 1937.

Reuter, O. Some notes on the origin of the relative construction *the which*. Neuphilologische Mitteilungen 38 1937.

Roberts, W. F. J. Ellipsis of the subject pronoun in Middle English. London Mediæval Stud 1 1939 [1948].

Urwin, K. The progressive tense in early English and Old French. Comparative Lit Stud 3 1941.

McIntosh, A. The relative pronouns *þe* and *þat* in early Middle English. Eng & Germanic Stud 1 1948.

Smithers, G. V. A Middle English idiom and its antecedents. Ibid. On *bidde* = 'wish'.

Behre, F. The origin and early history of meditative-polemic *should* in *that*-clauses. In Symbolae philologicae gotoburgenses, Gothenburg 1950. *See Behre 1955, col 130, below.*

Mossé, F. Un cas d'ambiguité syntactique en moyen-anglais: le type *I was wery forwandred*. Etudes Anglaises 5 1952.

Meier, H. H. Der indefinite Agens im Mittelenglischen 1050–1350: die Wörter und Wendungen für 'man'. Berne 1953. *See also Jud-Schmid 1956, Fröhlich 1951, cols 115, 118, above.*

Phillipps, K. C. Contamination in late Middle English. E Studies 35 1954, 37 1956.

— Asyndetic relative clauses in late Middle English. E Studies 46 1965.

— Absolute constructions in late Middle English. Neuphilologische Mitteilungen 67 1966.

— Adverb clauses in the fifteenth century. E Studies 47 1966.

Spitzer, L. Le type moyen anglais *I was wery for wandred* et ses parallèles romans. Neuphilologische Mitteilungen 55 1954. *See Samuels 1955, below.*

Mustanoja, T. F. Middle English *wery of wandred*: a variant of *wery for wandred*. Neuphilologische Mitteilungen 56 1955.

— Troilus and Criseyde iv 607: *of fered.* Ibid.

— The Middle English syntactical type *his own hand(s)* 'with his own hands, himself', with reference to other similar expressions. Neuphilologische Mitteilungen 60 1959.

Samuels, M. L. Middle English *wery forwandred*: a rejoinder. E Studies 36 1955.

Kaartinen, A. and T. F. Mustanoja. The use of the infinitive in A book of London English 1384–1425. Neuphilologische Mitteilungen 59 1958.

Rynell, A. On Middle English *take(n)* as an inchoative verb. Studier i Modern Språkvetenskap new ser 1 1960.

— On alleged constructions like *did wrote*. Studier i Modern Språkvetenskap new ser 2 1964.

Appenzeller-Gassmann, V. Mittelenglische Bekräftigungsformeln. Zürich 1961.

Rantavaara, I. On the development of the periphrastic dative in late Middle English prose. Neuphilologische Mitteilungen 63 1962.

Rennhard, S. Das Demonstrativum im Mittelenglischen 1200–1500. Winterthur 1962.

Visser, F. T. The 'historical present' in Middle English verse narratives. In English studies presented to R. W. Zandvoort, Amsterdam 1964 (suppl to E Studies 45 1964).

Brorström, S. Studies on the use of the preposition *of* in 15th-century correspondence. Stockholm 1965. *See also Brorström 1963, col 133, below.*

Stevick, R. D. Historical selection of relative *þat* in early Middle English. E Studies 46 1965.

Kivimaa, K. *Þe* and *þat* as clause connectives in early Middle English. Helsinki 1966.

Jones, C. The grammatical category of gender in early Middle English. E Studies 48 1967.

Nagucka, R. An interpretation of the *because* construction in Middle English. Studia Anglica Posnaniensia 1 1968.

MacLeish, A. The Middle English subject-verb cluster. Hague 1969.

Sundby, B. A note on causative verbs in 15th century English. Neuphilologische Mitteilungen 71 1970.

Utley, F. L. Syntactical problems in Middle English. Neuphilologische Mitteilungen 73 1972.

Middle English Texts
(in alphabetical order)

Dahlstedt, A. The word-order of the Ancren riwle. Sundsvall 1903.

Dieth, E. Flexivisches und Syntaktisches über das Pronomen in der Ancren riwle. Zürich 1919.

Ladd, C. A. A note on the language of the Ancrene riwle. N & Q Aug 1961.

Kolkwitz, M. Das Satzgefüge in Barbours Bruce und Henrys Wallace. Halle 1893.

Pirkhofer, A. Zum syntaktischen Gebrauch des bestimmten Artikels bei Caxton. E Studien 70 1935.

Schrader, A. Das altenglische Relativpronomen mit besonderer Berücksichtigung der Sprache Chaucers. Kiel 1880.

Graef, A. Das Perfectum bei Chaucer. Frankenhausen 1888.

— Die präsentischen Tempora bei Chaucer, 1 Teil: das Praesens. Anglia 12 1889.

— Das Futurum und die Entwicklung von *schal* und *wil* zu futurischen Tempusbildnern bei Chaucer. Flensburg 1893.

Kent, C. W. On the use of the negative by Chaucer. PMLA 5 1890.

Wilson, L. R. Chaucer's relative constructions. SP 1 1906.

Kenyon, J. S. The syntax of the infinitive in Chaucer. 1909.

Borst, E. Zur Stellung des Adverbs bei Chaucer. E Studien 42 1910.

Eitle, H. Die Satzverknüpfung bei Chaucer. Heidelberg 1914.

Hittmair, R. Das Zeitwort *do* in Chaucers Prosa. Vienna 1923.

Karpf, F. Zur Kontamination bei Chaucer. E Studien 64 1929.

—— Studien zur Syntax in den Werken Geoffrey Chaucers: 1 Tcil. Vienna 1930.

Heuer, H. Studien zur syntaktischen und stilistischen Funktion des Adverbs bei Chaucer und im Rosenroman. Heidelberg 1932.

Walcott, C. C. The pronoun of address in Troilus and Criseyde. PQ 14 1935.

Schlauch, M. Chaucer's colloquial English: its structural traits. PMLA 67 1952.

Homann, E. R. Chaucer's use of *gan*. JEGP 53 1954.

Benson, L. D. Chaucer's historical present: its meaning and uses. E Studies 42 1961.

Dean, C. Chaucer's use of function words with substantives. Canadian Jnl of Linguistics 9 1964.

Kerkhof, J. Studies in the language of Geoffrey Chaucer. Leyden 1966.

Kivimaa, K. The pleonastic *that* in relative and interrogative constructions in Chaucer's verse. Helsinki 1966.

—— Clauses in Chaucer introduced by conjunctions with appended *that*. Helsinki 1969.

Bauer, G. Historisches Präsens und Vergegenwärtigung des epischen Geschehens: ein erzähltechnischer Kunstgriff Chaucers. Anglia 85 1967.

—— Studien zum System und Gebrauch der 'Tempora' in der Sprache Chaucers und Gowers. Vienna 1970.

Smyser, H. M. Chaucer's use of *gin* and *do*. Speculum 42 1967.

Miura, T. Arrangement of two or more attributive adjectives in Chaucer (1). Anglica (Osaka) 6 1968.

Nagucka, R. The syntactic component of Chaucer's Astrolabe. Zeszyty Naukowe Uniwersytetu Jagiellońskiego 199: Prace Językoznawcze 23, Cracow 1968.

Svartvik, J. and R. Quirk. Types and uses of non-finite clause in Chaucer. E Studies 51 1970.

Fries, U. Zur Syntax der Chester plays. Vienna 1968.

Eichhorn, E. Das Partizipium bei Gower im Vergleich mit Chaucers Gebrauch. Kiel 1912.

Wolff, A. Zur Syntax des Verbums im altenglischen Lay of Havelok the Dane. Leipzig 1909.

Nilsson, E. E. The syntax of the homilies and homiletic treatises of the xii and xiii centuries edited by R. Morris. Lund 1900.

Azzalino, W. Die Wortstellung im King Horn. Halle 1915.

Reszkiewicz, A. Main sentence elements in the Book of Margery Kempe. Warsaw 1962.

Lichtsinn, P. Der syntaktische Gebrauch des Infinitivs im Laȝamons Brut. Kiel 1913.

Courmont, A. Studies on Lydgate's syntax in the Temple of Glas. Paris 1912.

Hüttmann, E. Das Partizipium Präsentis bei Lydgate im Vergleich mit Chaucers Gebrauch. Kiel 1914.

Juhl, H. Der syntaktische Gebrauch des Infinitivs bei John Lydgate. Kiel 1921.

Baldwin, C. S. The inflections and syntax of the Morte d'Arthur of Sir Thomas Malory. Boston 1894.

Dekker, A. Some facts concerning the syntax of Malory's Morte d'Arthur. Amsterdam 1932.

Šimko, J. Word-order in the Winchester manuscript and in William Caxton's edition of Sir Thomas Malory's Morte d'Arthur 1485: a comparison. Halle 1957.

Pervaz, D. Neki aspekti sintakse glagola *do* u delima ser Tomasa Malorija. Godišnjak Filozofskog Fakulteta u Novom Sadu 13 1970. On the syntax of *do* in Malory; with English summary.

Meer, H. J. van der. Main facts concerning the syntax of Mandeville's Travels. Utrecht 1929.

Buchtenkirch, E. Der syntaktische Gebrauch des Infinitivs in Occleve's De regimine principum. Jena 1889.

Weyel, F. Der syntaktische Gebrauch des Infinitivs im Ormulum. Meiderich 1896.

Funke, O. Kasus-Syntax bei Orm und Laȝamon. Munich 1907.

Zenke, W. Synthesis und Analysis des Verbums im Orrmulum. Halle 1910.

Laeseke, B. Ein Beitrag zur Stellung des Verbums in Orrmulum. Kiel 1917.

Weinmann, P. Über den Gebrauch des Artikels im Orrmulum. Kiel 1920.

Lehnert, M. Sprachform und Sprachfunktion im Orrmulum (um 1200): die Deklination. Berlin 1953.

Palmatier, R. A. A descriptive syntax of the Ormulum. Hague 1969.

Ebisch, W. Zur Syntax des Verbs im altenglischen Gedicht Eule und Nachtigall. Leipzig 1905.

Breier, W. Synthesis und Analysis des Konjunktivs in dem frühmittelenglischen Streitgedicht Eule und Nachtigall. In Festschrift für Lorenz Morsbach, Halle 1913.

Carstensen, B. Studien zur Syntax des Nomens, Pronomens und der Negation in den Paston Letters. Bochum 1959.

Davis, N. Margaret Paston's uses of *do*. Neuphilologische Mitteilungen 73 1972.

Zickner, B. Syntax und Stil in Reginald Pecocks Repressor. Greifswald 1900.

Rothstein, E. Die Wortstellung in der Peterborough Chronik. Halle 1922.

Clark, C. Gender in the Peterborough Chronicle 1070–1154. E Studies 38 1957.

Mitchell, B. Syntax and word-order in the Peterborough Chronicle 1122–54. Neuphilologische Mitteilungen 65 1964.

Shores, D. L. The subject-noun object-verb pattern in the Peterborough Chronicle. Neuphilologische Mitteilungen 70 1969. Reply by B. Mitchell 71 1970.

—— A descriptive syntax of the Peterborough Chronicle from 1122 to 1154. Hague 1971.

—— Morphosyntactic relations in the Peterborough Chronicle 1122–1154. E Studies 52 1971.

Way, A. Old English prenominal modifiers in noun-headed objects of prepositions in the first and second continuations of the Peterborough Chronicle (1122–54). Jnl of Eng Linguistics 4 1970.

Wandschneider, W. Zur Syntax des Verbs in Langleys Vision of William. Kiel 1887.

Świeczkowski, W. Word order patterning in Middle English: a quantitative study based on Piers plowman and Middle English sermons. Hague 1962.

Preusler, W. Syntax im Poema morale. Breslau 1914.

Reuter, O. Instances of the *which* in the glossed prose Psalter and their relation to the French original as represented by ms Bibl. Nat. fr. 6260. Neuphilologische Mitteilungen 40 1939.

Henningsen, H. Über die Wortstellung in den Prosaschriften Richard Rolles of Hampole. Erlangen 1911.

Pitschel, E. H. Zur Syntax des mittelenglischen Gedichtes William of Palerne. Marburg 1890.

Smith, H. Syntax der Wycliffe-Purveyschen Übersetzung und der Authorised version der vier Evangelien. Anglia 30 1907.

Thamm, W. Das Relativpronomen in der Bibelübersetzung Wyclifs und Purveys. Berlin 1908.

(4) MODERN ENGLISH

(For general accounts see Modern English grammars, cols 89f., above.)

Special Studies

Kellner, L. Zur Syntax des englischen Verbums mit besonderer Berücksichtigung Shakespeares. Vienna 1885.

Franz, W. Zur Syntax des älteren Neuenglisch. E Studien 17–18 1892–3, 20 1895.

Spies, H. Studien zur Geschichte des englischen Pronomens im xv und xvi Jahrhundert: Flexionslehre und Syntax. Halle 1897.

— Der *split infinitive*. Anglia 65 1941.

Knecht, J. Die Kongruenz zwischen Subjekt und Prädikat und die 3 Person Pluralis Präsentis auf -*s* im Elisabethanischen Englisch. Heidelberg 1911.

Fries, C. C. The periphrastic future with *shall* and *will* in Modern English. PMLA 40 1925.

— The rules of Common School grammars 1586–1825. PMLA 42 1927.

— Some notes on the inflected genitive in present-day English. Language 14 1938.

— On the development of the structural use of word order in Modern English. Language 16 1940.

Krüger, A. Studien über die Syntax des englischen Relativpronomens zu Beginn der spätneuenglischen Zeit. Giessen 1929.

Brusendorff, A. The relative aspect of the verb in English. In A grammatical miscellany offered to Otto Jespersen, Copenhagen 1930.

Collinson, W. E. Some expressions of quantity in spoken English. Ibid.

Kruisinga, E. Contributions to English syntax xix: The verbal -*ing* in living English. E Studies 12 1930.

— On some uses of *one*. RES 10 1934.

— Zur Wortstellung im Englisch. Beiblatt zur Anglia 47 1936. On postponed adjectives.

— Die Fürwörter *who*, *what* und *which* in Fragesätzen. Beiblatt zur Anglia 48 1937.

— Die persönlichen Fürwörter auf -*self*. Ibid.

— *Each other* und *one another*. Beiblatt zur Anglia 49 1938.

— Die Wortfolge in den englischen Substantivgruppen. Ibid.

Swaen, A. E. H. The elliptical genitive. In A grammatical miscellany offered to Otto Jespersen, Copenhagen 1930.

Trnka, B. On the syntax of the English verb from Caxton to Dryden. Prague 1930.

— Conversion in English. Brno Stud in Eng 8 1969.

Buyssens, E. The place of *never* and *ever* in present-day English prose. E Studies 15 1933.

— L'aspect verbal en anglais. Revue Belge 36 1958.

— Les deux aspectifs de la conjugaison anglaise au xxe siècle: étude de l'expression de l'aspect. Brussels 1968.

Ellinger, J. Substantivsätze mit oder ohne *that* in der neueren englischen Literatur. Anglia 57 1933.

— Über die mit *that* zusammengesetzten Bindewörter im neueren Englisch. Anglia 58 1934.

— Die konjunktionale Verwendung von substantivischen Wortgruppen mit oder ohne *that* im neueren Englisch. E Studien 71 1937.

— Die Gerundialfügung mit und ohne Präposition im neueren Englisch. E Studien 72 1938.

Kühner, G. Die Intensiv-Adverbien des Frühneuenglischen. Ludwigshafen-am-Rhein 1934.

Stene, A. The animate gender in modern colloquial English. Norsk Tidsskrift for Sprogvidenskap 7 1934.

Fiedler, F. Zum Gebrauch der Zeiten im Englischen 1: Praeteritum und Perfekt im heutigen Englisch. Zeitschrift für Neusprachlichen Unterricht 34 1935.

— Glossen zur Syntax des heutigen Englisch. Neuphilologische Monatsschrift 9–10 1938–9.

— Versuch einer Deutung der Modalbegriffe *can*, *may*, *must* im heutigen Englisch. Neuphilologische Monatsschrift 9 1938.

— Das Vorstellungsbild der Begriffe *some-any each-every all-whole*; *both-the two*. Neuphilologische Monatsschrift 11 1940.

— Glossen zur neuenglischen Syntax. Anglia 71 1953. 1 *ought to*; 2 Hervorhebung durch *or*+Frage.

— and W. Maurice. Grundsätzliches zum Gebrauch der Relativpronomina *who*, *which*, *that* im gegenwärtigen Englisch und zu seiner Darstellung in der Schulgrammatik. Neuphilologische Monatsschrift 8 1937.

Kirchner, G. Praesensgebrauch statt Perfekt bis Kontinuität des Vorgangs. Zeitschrift für Neusprachlichen Unterricht 34 1935.

— *To feed* (tr. v.) construed with various objects and prepositions. E Studies 17 1935.

— The verbs with direct and indirect object re-examined. E Studies 18–19 1936–7.

— (*To be*) *due* as a (passive) verb-equivalent. E Studies 22 1940.

— *To want* as an auxiliary of modality. Ibid.

— *Across* und *over* in moderner Verbindung mit Hauptverben, insbesondere *put*. Zeitschrift für Neusprachlichen Unterricht 40 1941.

— The road to standard English: two more cases in point, 'The conclusive perfect' and *To be for*+-*ing*. E Studies 23 1941.

— A few sidelights on 'appended questions'. E Studies 31 1950.

— A special case of the object of result. E Studies 32 1951.

— Die zehn Hauptverben des Englischen im Britischen und Amerikanischen: eine semasiologisch-syntaktische Darstellung ihrer gegenwärtigen Funktionen mit sprachgeschichtlichen Rückblicken. Halle 1952.

— Direct transitivation. E Studies 36 1955.

— Gradadverbien: Restriktiva und Verwandtes im heutigen Englisch (britisch und amerikanisch). Halle 1955.

— *Of*-Fügung+Personalpronomen—oder Possessivpronomen. Die Neueren Sprachen new ser 4 1955.

— Recent American influence on Standard English: the syntactical sphere. Zeitschrift für Anglistik und Amerikanistik 5 1957. *See* H. Kirsten, Bemerkungen zu *to prevent*+Gerundium, ibid; G. Kirchner, *Prevent* +Gerundium, 6 1958.

— Der Ausrufsatz im Neuenglischen. Anglia 76 1958.

— 'Neue Synthese' im Gegenwartsenglisch. In Festschrift für Walther Fischer, Heidelberg 1959.

— Zur transitiven und intransitiven Verwendung des englischen Verbums. Zeitschrift für Anglistik und Amerikanistik 7 1959.

— Verbal *ing* resumed by an auxiliary. E Studies 43 1962.

Volbeda, R. The 'definite forms'. Neophilologus 20 1935.

Bryan, W. F. The preterite and perfect tense in present-day English. JEGP 35 1936.

Friedrich, H. Gibt es eine intensive Aktionsart im Neuenglischen? Leipzig 1936.

Heuer, H. Beobachtungen zur Syntax und Stilistik des Adverbs im Neuenglischen. Anglia 60 1936.

Koziol, H. Bemerkungen zum Gebrauch einiger neuenglischen Zeitformen. E Studien 70 1936.

— Zum Gebrauch der englischen Tempora. E Studien 71 1937.

— Consecutio Temporum und subjektive Stellungnahme im Englischen. Orbis 8 1959.

Schibsbye, K. Om de udvidede verbalformers begreb og anvendelse i moderne engelsk. Copenhagen 1936.

Åkerlund, A. *I go a-fishing*. Studia Neophilologica 9 1937.

Behrens, W. Lateinische Satzformen im Englischen: Latinismen in der Syntax der englischen Übersetzungen des Humanismus. Münster 1937.

Bodelsen, C. A. The expanded tenses in Modern English: an attempt at an explanation. E Studien 71 1937.

— The system governing the use of the futuric *shall* and *will*. Studia Neophilologica 14 1942.

— Tense and aspect. In Essays and papers presented to C. A. Bodelsen, Copenhagen 1964.

Cassidy, F. G. 'Case' in Modern English. Language 13 1937.

Ericson, E. E. Noun clauses in *because*. Anglia 61 1937.

— Observations on New English syntax. Anglia 63 1939.

Mulder, G. The infinitive after *to dare*. Neophilologus 22 1937.

Knorrek, M. Der Einfluss des Rationalismus auf die englische Sprache: Beiträge zur Entwicklungsgeschichte der englischen Syntax im 17 und 18 Jahrhundert. Breslau 1938.

Barts, E. Der umschriebene Konjunktiv im Neuenglischen. Zeitschrift für Neusprachlichen Unterricht 37 1939.

Deutschbein, M. Aspekte und Aktionsarten im Neuenglischen. Neuphilologische Monatsschrift 10 1939.

Marchand, H. Syntaktische Homonymie: das umschreibende *do*. E Studien 73 1939.

Satchell, T. Expanded tenses. E Studies 21 1939.

Dennis L. The progressive tense: frequency of its use in English. PMLA 55 1940.

Mulder, H. Demonstrative pronouns: Dutch and English compared. E Studies 22 1940.

Charleston, B. M. Studies on the syntax of the English verb. Berne 1941.

— A reconsideration of the problem of time, tense and aspect in Modern English. E Studies 36 1955.

Holthausen, F. Zur neuenglischen Syntax. Archiv 179 1941.

Kihlbom, A. The use of *should* plus infinitive in subordinate clauses of time. Studia Neophilologica 14 1942.

Zandvoort, R. W. On the relative frequency of the forms and functions of *to do*. E Studies 24 1942.

— Note on 'inorganic *for*'. E Studies 30 1949.

— Is 'aspect' an English verbal category? In Contributions to English syntax and philology by C. L. Barber [et al], Gothenburg 1962.

— Varia syntactica. Revue des Langues Vivantes 35 1969.

Erades, P. A. On alternative repeated questions. E Studies 25 1943.

— The case against 'provisional' *it*. Ibid.

— On identifying and classifying sentences. E Studies 30 1949.

Hatcher, A. G. *Mr Howard amuses easy*. MLN 58 1943.

— *To get/be invited*. MLN 64 1949.

— The English construction *a friend of mine*. Word 6 1950.

— The use of the progressive form in English. Language 27 1951.

Calver, E. The uses of the present tense forms in English. Language 22 1946. *See also Bolinger 1947, below*.

Hall, R. A. A note on bound forms. JEGP 45 1946.

Langenfelt, G. The roots of the propword *one*. Studier i Modern Språkvetenskap 16 1946.

Visser, F. T. Two remarkable constructions in Shakespeare. Neophilologus 30 1946.

— *I had heard her cried*. E Studies 28 1947.

— Two or more auxiliaries with a common verbal complement. E Studies 31 1950.

— Celtic influence in English. Neophilologus 39 1955.

Bolinger, D. L. More on the present tense in English. Language 23 1947.

— Adjective comparison: a semantic scale. Jnl of Eng Linguistics 1 1967.

— Adjectives in English: attribution and predication. Lingua 18 1967.

— The imperative in English. In To honor Roman Jakobson, Hague 1967.

— The phrasal verb in English. Cambridge Mass 1971.

Bosker, A. Some aspects of the study of English syntax. Neophilologus 31 1947.

Hulbert, J. R. On the origin of the grammarians' rules for the use of *shall* and *will*. PMLA 62 1947.

Poldauf, I. Some points on negation in colloquial English. Práce z Vědeckých Ústavů 51 1947.

— Infinitiv v angličtině. Časopis pro Moderní Filologii 36 1954. The infinitive in English; with English summary.

— O konkurenci infinitivu a gerundu v angličtině. Časopis pro Moderní Filologii 37 1955. On the rivalry between the infinitive and the gerund in English; with English summary.

— The so-called medio-passive in English. Acta Universitatis Carolinae (Philologica 3) 1969.

Bolbjerg, A. *Between* and *among*: an attempt at an explanation. E Studies 30 1949.

Dietrich, G. Die Syntax der *do*-Umschreibung bei *have*, *be*, *ought* and *used* (*to*) auf sprachgeschichtlicher Grundlage dargestellt. Brunswick 1949.

— Erweiterte Form, Präteritum und Perfektum im Englischen: eine Aspekt- und Tempusstudie. Munich 1955.

— Adverb oder Präposition? Halle 1960.

Svartengren, H. The -'s genitive of non-personal nouns in present-day English. Studier i Modern Språkvetenskap 17 1949.

Jacobsson, B. Inversion in English with special reference to the early Modern English period. Upsala 1951.

— On the use of *that* in non-restrictive relative clauses. Moderna Språk 57 1963.

Wood, F. T. *Shall you? or will you?* E Studies 32 1951.

— *Fairly, rather* and *pretty* as adverbs of degree. Moderna Språk 53 1959.

— Some aspects of conditional clauses in English. Moderna Språk 54 1960.

Azzalino, W. Präposition+nominale Verbform im Englischen. Die Neueren Sprachen new ser 1 1952.

Charnley, M. B. The eventuative relation. Studia Neophilologica 26 1954.

Karlberg, G. and P. A. Erades. Classifying *which*. E Studies 35 1954.

Nosek, J. Několik poznámek k polovětným vazbám v angličtině xvii století. Acta Universitatis Carolinae 7 Philologica et Historica) 1954. Some remarks concerning 'semi-sentence' constructions in xviith century English; with English summary.

— Adverbial subclauses in Modern English. Philologica Pragensia 1 1958.

— Studies in post-Shakespearian English: adverbial clauses. Acta Universitatis Carolinae (Philologica 2) 1959.

— Relative clauses in Modern English. Philologica Pragensia 3 1960.

— Notes on syntactic condensation in Modern English. Travaux Linguistiques de Prague 1 1964.

— Overlapping predications in Modern English. Acta Universitatis Carolinae (Philologica 3) 1965.

— Contributions to the syntax of the New English complex sentence. Acta Universitatis Carolinae (Philologica monographia 13) 1966.

— English colloquial metaphor and the syntax. Philologica Pragensia 10 1967.

Behre, F. Meditative-polemic *should* in Modern English *that*-clauses. Stockholm 1955. *See Behre 1950, col 123, above*.

— A question of linguistic predictability. In Language and society: essays presented to Arthur M. Jensen, Copenhagen 1961. On the sequence initial *that+should*.

—— On the principle of connecting elements of speech in contemporary English. In English studies today: 2nd series, Berne 1961.

—— *That this quality should have survived*. . .: a study in synchronic grammar. In Frank Behre: papers on English vocabulary and syntax, Gothenburg 1961.

—— Notes on indicative clauses of condition. In Contributions to English syntax and philology by C. L. Barber [et al], Gothenburg 1962.

—— The *you will* request: a syntactical study. Ibid. *See S. Stubelius, ibid.*

—— Some criteria of non-conditional *if*. In English studies presented to R. W. Zandvoort, Amsterdam 1964 (suppl to E Studies 45 1964).

—— Variation and change in the distribution of *lot(s)*, *deal*, *much*, *many*, etc. E Studies 50 1969.

Brunner, K. Expanded verbal forms in early Modern English. E Studies 36 1955.

Frei, H. A note on Bloomfield's limiting adjectives. Ibid.

Grad, A. Affectivity and inversion in Modern English. Zbornik Filozofske Fakultete (Ljubljana) 2 1955.

Link, F. H. *And* oder *with*+Partizipium. Anglia 73 1955.

Vachek, J. Some thoughts on the so-called complex condensation in Modern English. Sborník Prací Filosofické Fakulty Brněnské University 4 1955; rev in Brno Stud in Eng 3 1961.

—— Notes on gender in Modern English. Sborník Prací Filosofické Fakulty Brněnské University 13 1964.

Dahl, T. Linguistic studies in some Elizabethan writings 2: the auxiliary *do*. Copenhagen 1956. *See also Dahl 1951, col 140, below.*

Firbas, J. Poznámky k problematice anglického slovního pořádku s hlediska aktuálního členění větného. Sborník Prací Filosofické Fakulty Brněnské University 5 1956. Some notes on the problem of English word order from the point of view of actual sentence analysis: with English summary.

—— K otázce nezákladových podmetů v současné angličtině. Časopis pro Moderní Filologii 39 1957. On the problem of non-thematic subjects in contemporary English; with English summary.

—— More thoughts on the communicative function of the English verb. Sborník Prací Filosofické Fakulty Brněnské University 8 1959.

—— On the communicative value of the Modern English finite verb. Brno Stud in Eng 3 1961.

—— Non-thematic subjects in contemporary English. Travaux Linguistiques de Prague 2 1966.

—— *It was yesterday that*. . . Sborník Prací Filosofické Fakulty Brněnské University 16 1967.

Francis, W. N. Resolution of structural ambiguity by lexical probability: the English double object. Amer Speech 31 1956.

Carstensen, B. *Ich* im Englischen. Anglia 75 1957.

—— Zur Struktur des englischen Wortverbandes. Die Neueren Sprachen new ser 13 1964.

Haas, H. Studien zur Adverbfunktion von Adjektivformen in frühneuenglischer Zeit. Cologne 1957.

Long, R. B. Paradigms for English verbs. PMLA 72 1957.

—— The clause patterns of contemporary English. Amer Speech 32 1957.

—— The function of the complement in the English sentence. Texas Stud in Eng 37 1958.

—— Imperative and subjunctive in contemporary English. Amer Speech 41 1966.

—— Expletive *there* and the *there* transformation. Jnl of Eng Linguistics 2 1968.

—— The grammar of English proper names. Names 17 1969.

Müller, D. Studies in Modern English syntax: two aspects of synthesis. Winterthur 1957. Pt 1, Anticipatory word-order; pt 2, Deferment of the preposition: a phenomenon of condensation.

Müller-Schotte, H. Zur typisch-englischen Kürze und Bündigkeit des Ausdrucks. Die Neueren Sprachen new ser 6 1957.

Quirk, R. Relative clauses in educated spoken English. E Studies 38 1957.

—— Aspect and variant inflection in English verbs. Language 46 1970. On verbs with past tense forms in *-ed* and *-t*.

—— Taking a deep smell. Jnl of Linguistics 6 1970.

—— and A. P. Duckworth. Co-existing negative preterite forms of *dare*. In Language and society: essays presented to Arthur M. Jensen, Copenhagen 1961.

—— and J. Mulholland. Complex prepositions and related sequences. In English studies presented to R. W. Zandvoort, Amsterdam 1964 (suppl to E Studies 45 1964).

Spitzbardt, H. Negationsverstärkungen im Englischen. Die Neueren Sprachen new ser 6 1957.

—— On the grammatical categories of present participle and gerund in English. Zeitschrift für Anglistik und Amerikanistik 6 1958.

Akhmanova, O. S. Lexical and syntactical collocation in contemporary English. Zeitschrift für Anglistik und Amerikanistik 6 1958.

—— Nekotorȳe zakonomernosti postroeniya angliĭskoĭ rechi. Nauchnȳe Okladȳ Vȳssheĭ Shkolȳ: Filologicheskie Nauki 1961. On 'split verbs'.

Fischer, W. Britisch/amerikanisch *on* 'zu Ungunsten von', 'gegen' und verwandte Wendungen unter anglo-irischem Einfluss. Anglia 76 1958.

Lehnert, M. Die Entstehung des neuenglischen *its*. Zeitschrift für Anglistik und Amerikanistik 6 1958.

Schlauch, M. Early Tudor colloquial English. Philologica Pragensia 1 1958.

Sørensen, H. S. Word-classes in Modern English, with special reference to proper names. Copenhagen 1958.

—— The function of the definite article in Modern English. E Studies 40 1959.

—— The meaning of proper names. Copenhagen 1963.

—— On the semantic unity of the perfect tense. In English studies presented to R. W. Zandvoort, Amsterdam 1964 (suppl to E Studies 45 1964).

Karlsen, R. Studies in the connection of clauses in current English: zero, ellipsis and explicit form. Bergen 1959.

Maclay, M. and C. E. Osgood. Hesitation phenomena in spontaneous English speech. Word 15 1959.

Olsson, Y. The English verb in its contexts. E Studies 40 1959.

—— On the syntax of the English verb, with special reference to *have a look* and similar complex structures. Gothenburg 1961. *See* M. Renský, A syntax based on concretes, Philologica Pragensia 6 1963.

Smith, W. M. The split infinitive. Anglia 77 1959.

Spalatin, L. Verbal aspect in English. Filologija 2 1959.

Chatman, S. Pre-adjectivals in the English nominal phrase. Amer Speech 35 1960.

—— English sentence connectors. In Studies in languages and linguistics in honor of Charles C. Fries, Ann Arbor 1964.

Lees, R. B. A multiply ambiguous adjectival construction in English. Language 36 1960.

—— The grammar of English nominalizations. Bloomington 1960.

—— Grammatical analysis of the English comparative construction. Word 17 1961.

—— The constituent structure of noun phrases. Amer Speech 36 1961.

—— Analysis of the 'cleft sentence' in English. Zeitschrift für Phonetik, Sprachwissenschaft und Kommunikationsforschung 16 1963.

—— and E. S. Klima. Rules for English pronominalization. Language 39 1963.

Leisi, E. Die progressive form im Englischen. Die Neueren Sprachen new ser 9 1960.

Levin, S. R. Homonyms and English form-class analysis. Amer Speech 35 1960.

Mikhailović, L. Lexical context of the Modern English verbs *can* and *may*. Godišnjak Filozofskog Fakulteta u Novom Sadu 5 9160.

— The syntactic and semantic development of the English verbs *can* and *may*. Godišnjak Filozofskog Fakulteta u Novom Sadu 6 1961.

— Diferentsijalna analiza gramatichkog konteksta engleskikh glagola *can* i *may*. Anali Filoloshkog Fakulteta (Belgrade) 3 1963. A differential analysis of the grammatical context of the English verbs *can* and *may*; with English summary.

Söderlind, J. On the preposition *over*. E Studies 41 1960.

Twaddell, W. F. The English verb auxiliaries. Providence 1960, 1963 (rev). *See Palmer 1967, col 135, below.*

Gleitman, L. R. Pronominals and stress in English conjunctions. Language Learning 11 1961.

— Coordinating conjunctions in English. Language 41 1965.

Ivanova, I. P. Vid i vremya v sovremennom angliĭskom yazyke. Leningrad 1961. Aspect and tense in present-day English; with English summary.

Kanekiyo, T. The conjunction-headed phrase. E Studies 42 1961.

— Notes on gender in English. Philologica Pragensia 8 1965.

Potter, S. Problems of word order. In English studies today: 2nd series, Berne 1961.

— English phrasal verbs. Philologica Pragensia 8 1965.

Smith, C. S. A class of complex modifiers in English. Language 37 1961.

— Determiners and relative clauses in a generative grammar of English. Language 40 1964. *See Rydén 1970, col 137, below.*

Adamus, M. On the participles, finite verbs and adjectives of the Germanic languages. Warsaw 1962.

Gräf, G. Konjunktionen und konjunktionale Wendungen mit und ohne *that*. Die Neueren Sprachen new ser 11 1962.

— Nebensätze ohne *that* im heutigen Englisch. Zeitschrift für Anglistik und Amerikanistik 10 1962.

Juilland, A. and A. Macris. The English verb system. Hague 1962. *See Castagna 1968, col 137, below.*

Osselton, N. E. and C. J. Osselton-Bleeker. The plural attributive in contemporary English. E Studies 43 1962. *See* F. T. Wood, The plural attributive in contemporary English 44 1963.

Penttilä, E. Advertising English. Helsinki 1962.

Salmon, V. Early seventeenth-century punctuation as a guide to sentence structure. RES new ser 13 1962.

— Sentence-types in Modern English. Anglia 81 1963.

Sroka, K. A. Critique of the traditional syntactic approach to adverb/preposition words in Modern English. Biuletyn Polskiego Towarzystwa Językoznawczego 21 1962.

Diver, W. The chronological system of the English verb. Word 19 1963.

— The modal system of the English verb. Word 20 1964.

Bowman, E. The classification of imperative sentences in English. Stud in Linguistics 17 1963.

— The minor and fragmentary sentences of a corpus of spoken English. Bloomington 1966.

Brorström, S. The increasing frequency of the preposition *about* during the Modern English period: with special reference to the verbs *say*, *tell*, *talk* and *speak*. Stockholm 1963. *See also Brorström 1965, col 124, above.*

Kirsten, H. Gerundium und Halbgerundium nach *to prevent* und *to hinder* bei englischen Prosaschriftstellern zwischen 1650 und 1900. Wissenschaftliche Zeitschrift der Martin-Luther-Universität Halle-Wittenberg 12 1963.

Mikhailović, L. Pasiv kod engleskog glagola kao formalno oznachena kategorija i kao pojmovna kategorija. Anali Filoloshkog Fakulteta (Belgrade) 3 1963. The passive voice of verbs in English as a formally marked category and as a notional category; with English summary.

— Passive and pseudopassive verbal groups in English. E Studies 48 1967.

Osselton, N. E. Anaphoric *this* expressing shared experience. E Studies 44 1963.

— Introductory *this*. E Studies 48 1967.

Reszkiewicz, A. Internal structure of clauses in English. Warsaw 1963.

Schopf, A. *He is being clever*: die einfache und umschriebene Form in der prädikativen Formel. Anglia 81 1963.

— Untersuchungen zur Wechselbeziehung zwischen Grammatik und Lexik im Englischen. Berlin 1969.

Hirtle, W. H. The English present subjunctive. Canadian Jnl of Linguistics 9 1964.

— Auxiliaries and voice in English. Les Langues Modernes 59 1965.

— The simple and progressive forms: an analytical approach. Quebec 1967.

Jacobson, S. Adverbial positions in English. Upsala 1964. *See* E. Uhlenbeck, Facts and theory in the study of so-called adverbs and adverbials in present-day English, in Linguistique contemporaine: hommage à Eric Buyssens, Brussels 1970.

— Studies in English transformational grammar. Stockholm 1971.

Joly, A. Esquisse d'une théorie de la forme progressive. Les Langues Modernes 58 1964.

Joos, M. The English verb: form and meanings. Madison 1964, 1968 (rev). *See Palmer 1967, Castagna 1968, cols 135, 137, below.*

Khlebnikova, I. B. Binary relations in morphology (with special reference to the English verb). Philologica Pragensia 7 1964.

— Homonymy and the subjunctive mood in English. Philologica Pragensia 8 1965.

Klima, E. S. Negation in English. In J. A. Fodor and J. J. Katz, The structure of language, Englewood Cliffs NJ 1964.

Lejnieks, V. The English predicate constituent. Linguistics 3 1964.

Noël, G. *May* and *might*: meanings, tenses and usage. Revue des Langues Vivantes 30–1 1964–5. *See* R. W. Zandvoort, *May* and *might*: a critical comment, 31 1965.

Renský, M. English verbo-nominal phrases: some structural and stylistic aspects. Travaux Linguistiques de Prague 1 1964.

— Nominal tendencies in English. Philologica Pragensia 7 1964.

Salus, P. H. Syntactic compounds in Modern English. E Studies 45 1964.

Storms, G. The subjective and the objective form in Mdn English. In English studies presented to R. W. Zandvoort, Amsterdam 1964 (suppl to E Studies 45 1964).

— *That*-clauses in Modern English. E Studies 47 1966.

Arnold, R. Zur Entwicklung der Sprachgebrauchsebene des *split infinitive*. Zeitschrift für Anglistik und Amerikanistik 13 1965.

— *Them* als demonstratives Adjektiv. Zeitschrift für Anglistik und Amerikanistik 15 1967.

— *Lesser* und *worser*: Form und Funktion bei der Entwicklung eines Typs der doppelten Steigerung. Zeitschrift für Anglistik und Amerikanistik 18 1970.

Bately, J. M. *Who* and *which* and the grammarians of the 17th century. E Studies 46 1965.

Danchev, A., A. Pavlova, M. Nalchadjan and O. Zlatareva. The construction *going to*+ inf. in Modern English. Zeitschrift für Anglistik und Amerikanistik 13 1965.

Dušková, L. On some disputed points in the use of pronouns in present-day English. Philologica Pragensia 8 1965.

— Some remarks on the syntax of the *ing*-form in present-day English. Philologica Pragensia 12 1969.

Fillmore, C. J. Indirect object constructions in English and the ordering of transformations. Hague 1965.
—— A proposal concerning English prepositions. Monograph Ser on Languages and Linguistics (Georgetown Univ) 19 1966.
—— On the syntax of preverbs. Glossa 1 1967.
Fowler, R. Sentence and clause in English. Linguistics 14 1965.
—— The design of rules for 'Det'. Archivum Linguisticum new ser 2 1971.
Grady, M. The medio-passive voice in Modern English. Word 21 1965.
—— A note on the theory of the primary IC cut in English. Glossa 1 1967.
—— On the essential nominalizing function of English -ing. Linguistics 34 1967.
—— An analysis of some English multi-possessives. Linguistics 50 1969.
—— Varieties of the English middle voice and mediopassive. Linguistics 54 1969.
—— Syntax and semantics of the English verb phrase. Hague 1970.
Groot, A. W. de. The construction subject-predicate in English: primary and secondary semantic functions. In Symbolae linguisticae in honorem Georgii Kuryłowicz (Prace Komisji Językoznawstwa 5), Wrocław 1965.
Jindra, M. Function word *there*: its special features and whims. Philologica Pragensia 8 1965.
Lebrun, Y. *Can* and *may* in present-day English. Brussels 1965.
—— A note on *can* and *could*. Revue des Langues Vivantes 32 1966.
Lee, W. R. Preliminary notes on *Also* and *too*. Philologica Pragensia 8 1965.
—— A point about 'in' and 'into'. Brno Stud in Eng 8 1969.
Live, A. H. The discontinuous verb in English. Word 21 1965.
Palmer, F. R. A linguistic study of the English verb. 1965. *See Castagna 1968, col 137, below.*
—— The semantics of the English verb. Lingua 18 1967. *Discusses Twaddell 1960, Joos 1964, above, Crystal 1966, below.*
Pilch, H. Comparative constructions in English. Language 41 1965.
Vorlat, E. About the use of gerund and infinitive with certain verbs. Leuvense Bijdragen 54 1965.
Watanabe, T. On the aspect of the English verb. Stud in Eng Lit (Tokyo) 41 1965. In Japanese; with English summary.
Boguslavskaya, G. P. Adverbial modifier of subsequent events and its syntactical synonyms. Zeitschrift für Anglistik und Amerikanistik 14 1966.
Brekle, H. E. Syntaktische Gruppe (Adjektiv + Substantiv) vs Kompositum im modernen Englisch: Versuch einer Deutung auf Klassen- und Relationslogischer Basis. Linguistics 23 1966.
—— On the syntax of adjectives determining agent nouns in present-day English. In Wortbildung, Syntax und Morphologie: Festschrift zum 60 Geburtstag von Hans Marchand, Hague 1968.
Caton, C. E. On the general structure of the epistemic qualification of things said in English. Foundations of Language 2 1966.
Crystal, D. Specification and English tenses. Jnl of Linguistics 2 1966. *See Palmer 1967, above.*
—— Word classes in English. Lingua 17 1967.
Ek, J. A. van. Four complementary structures of predication in contemporary British English. Groningen 1966.
—— A grammatical description of the accusative with infinitive and related structures in English. E Studies 48 1967.
—— The 'progressive' reconsidered. E Studies 50 1969.
Johnson, A. C. The pronoun of direct address in seventeenth-century English. Amer Speech 41 1966.

Koskenniemi, I. On the use of 'figurative negation' in English Renaissance drama. Neuphilologische Mitteilungen 67 1966.
Langendoen, D. T. The syntax of the English expletive *it*. Monograph Ser on Languages and Linguistics (Georgetown Univ) 19 1966.
Leech, G. N. English in advertising. 1966.
—— Meaning and the English verb. 1971.
Mitchell, T. F. Some English phrasal types. In In memory of J. R. Firth, 1966.
McIntosh, A. Predictive statements. Ibid.
Postal, P. M. On so-called 'pronouns' in English. Monograph Ser on Languages and Linguistics (Georgetown Univ) 19 1966. *See Delorme and Dougherty 1972, col 142, below.*
Raïkhel', G. M. Vyrazhenie otnosheniya k klassu odnorodnȳkh predmetov sushchestvitel'nȳmi sovremmenogo angliĭskogo yazȳka. Voprosȳ Yazȳkoznaniya 15 1966. The expression of relation to a class of homogeneous objects by the nouns of Modern English.
Strang, B. M. H. Some features of s-v concord in present-day English. In English studies today: 4th series, Rome 1966.
Svartvik, J. On voice in the English verb. Hague 1966. *See Castagna 1968, col 137, below.*
—— Plotting divided usage with *dare* and *need*. Studia Neophilologica 40 1968.
Thorne, J. P. English imperative sentences. Jnl of Linguistics 2 1966.
Bach, E. *Have* and *be* in English syntax. Language 43 1967.
Davies, E. C. Some notes on English clause types. Trans Philological Soc 1967.
Doherty, P. C. and A. Schwartz. The syntax of the compared adjective in English. Language 43 1967.
Foster, D. W. Ejemplos de la ambigüedad estructural en ingles producidos por la estructura de la frase y transformaciones opcionales. Universidad (Santa Fe) 73 1967.
Halliday, M. A. K. Notes on transitivity and theme in English. Jnl of Linguistics 3–4 1967–8.
—— Options and functions in the English clause. Brno Stud in Eng 8 1969.
—— Functional diversity in language as seen from a consideration of modality and mood in English. Foundations of Lang 6 1970.
Huddleston, R. [D.] More on the English comparative. Jnl of Linguistics 3 1967.
—— Some observations on tense and deixis in English. Language 45 1969.
—— The sentence in written English: a syntactic study based on an analysis of scientific texts. Cambridge 1971.
Hudson, R. A. Constituency in a systemic description of the English clause. Lingua 18 1967.
—— On clauses containing conjoined and plural noun-phrases in English. Lingua 24 1970.
—— English complex sentences: an introduction to systemic grammar. Amsterdam 1971.
Live, A. H. Subject-verb inversion (in English). General Linguistics 7 1967.
Malone, J. L. A transformational re-examination of English questions. Language 43 1967.
Quinn, J. J. An additional subordinate clause transformation. Jnl of Eng Linguistics 1 1967.
Rosenbaum, P. S. Phrase structure principles of English complex sentence formation. Jnl of Linguistics 3 1967.
—— The grammar of English predicate complement constructions. Cambridge Mass 1967.
Ross, J. R. On the cyclic nature of English pronominalization. In To honor Roman Jakobson, Hague 1967.
Vouk, V. Comparison of speech forms used in utterances and references to utterances. E Studies 48 1967.
Anderson, J. Ergative and nominative in English. Jnl of Linguistics 4 1968.

—— Some proposals concerning the modal verb in English. In Edinburgh studies in English and Scots, ed A. J. Aitken et al 1971.

Bennett, D. C. English prepositions: a stratificational approach. Jnl of Linguistics 4 1968.

Bladon, R. A. W. Selecting the *to-* or *-ing* nominal after *like, love, hate, dislike* and *prefer*. E Studies 49 1968. *See also* R. D Eagleson, Selecting the *to-* and *-ing* nominal after *prefer*, E Studies 53 1972; R. A. W. Bladon, Postscript, ibid.

Bowers, F. A transformational description of the Elizabethan *be*+V-*ing*. Orbis 17 1968. Material from novels of Thomas Deloney.

—— English complex sentence formation. Jnl of Linguistics 4 1968.

Breithutová, H. The function of tenses used in Modern English temporal clauses. Brno Stud in Eng 7 1968.

Bugarski, R. On the interrelatedness of grammar and lexis in the structure of English. Lingua 19 1968.

Castagna, A. Le verbe anglais vu à travers quelques ouvrages récents. La Linguistique 1968. *Discusses Bloch 1947, col 99, above, Juilland and Macris 1962, Joos 1964, Palmer 1965, Svartvik 1966, above.*

Corder, S. P. Double-object verbs in English. Studia Anglica Posnaniensia 1 1968.

Frischknecht, H. Syntaktische Elemente zwischen Prädikat und direktem Objekt im Neuenglischen. Zürich 1968.

Golková, E. On the English infinitive of purpose in functional sentence perspective. Brno Stud in Eng 7 1968.

Goyvaerts, D. L. An introductory study on the ordering of a string of adjectives in present-day English. Philologica Pragensia 11 1968.

—— Towards a theory of the expanded form in English. La Linguistique 1968.

Hasegawa, K. The passive construction in English. Language 44 1968.

Jackendoff, R. S. Quantifiers in English. Foundations of Lang 4 1968.

—— Les constructions possessives en anglais. Langages 14 1969.

Jacobsson, B. A note on common-number *they/them/their* and *who*. Studia Neophilologica 40 1968.

Jones, C. Aspects of English indirect strings. Lingua 20 1968.

Kalogjera, D. *Shall*—future and time specification. Studia Romanica and Anglica Zagrabiensia 25–6 1968.

Koutsoudas, A. On *wh-* words in English. Jnl of Linguistics 4 1968.

Kuroda, S.-Y. English relativization and certain related problems. Language 44 1968.

Nickel, G. The contrast *he is reading-he is interesting* and related problems. In Wortbildung, Syntax und Morphologie: Festschrift zum 60 Geburtstag von Hans Marchand, Hague 1968.

Nilsen, D. L. F. English infinitives. Canadian Jnl of Linguistics 13 1968.

—— The expletive *there* from a transformational point of view. Glossa 3 1969.

Ono, H. The structure of clause-sequency in early eighteenth-century prose. Anglica (Osaka) 6 1968.

Pocheptsov, G. G. Indispensable attributive adjuncts in English. Lingua 20 1968.

Putseys, Y. Gebruik van het hulpwerkwoord *do* in de transformationele generatieve grammatica. Koninklijke Zuidnederlandse Maatschappij voor Taal- en Letterkunde en Geschiedenis: Handelingen 22 1968.

Robbins, B. L. The definite article in English transformations. Hague 1968.

Roggero, J. La substitution en anglais. La Linguistique 1968.

Rydén, M. On concord in relative clauses. Studia Neophilologica 40 1968. On 16th-century English.

—— Determiners and relative clauses. E Studies 51 1970.

Svoboda, A. The hierarchy of communicative units and fields as illustrated by English attributive constructions. Brno Stud in Eng 7 1968.

—— A note on N+Adj. Sborník Prací Filosofické Fakulty Brněnské University 19 1970.

Teyssier, J. Notes on the syntax of the adjective in Modern English. Lingua 20 1968.

Watt, W. C. English reduplication. Jnl of Eng Linguistics 2 1968.

Aarts, F. G. A. M. On the use of the progressive and non-progressive present with future reference in present-day English. E Studies 50 1969.

—— On the distribution of noun-phrase types in English clause-structure. Lingua 26 1971.

Arbini, R. Tag-questions and tag-imperatives in English. Jnl of Linguistics 5 1969.

Bellert, I. On certain syntactical properties of the English connectives *and* and *but*. Biuletyn Fonograficzny 10 1969.

Boyd, J. and J. P. Thorne. The semantics of modal verbs. Jnl of Linguistics 5 1969.

Braun, F. Studien zu Konstituentenstruktur und Merkmalanalyse englischer Sätze. Hamburg 1969.

Brisau, A. Complex sentence structure in headlines. E Studies 50 1969.

Campbell, R. N. and R. J. Wales. Comparative structures in English. Jnl of Linguistics 5 1969.

Coppieters, R. A survey of sentence patterns with '*to*+ infinitive'. Revue des Langues Vivantes 35 1969.

Cygan, J. On the functions of syntactical operators in English. Acta Universitatis Wratislaviensis 110: Germanica Wratislaviensia 13 1969.

Fiehler, R. Regional influence on *shall* and *will*. In Studies in language, literature and culture of the Middle Ages and later, ed E. B. Atwood and A. A. Hill, Austin 1969.

Froehlich, P. A. The logeme and the syntagmeme in English. Linguistics 45 1969.

Greenbaum, S. Studies in English adverbial usage. 1969.

—— Verb-intensifier collocations in English: an experimental approach. Hague 1970.

Hartvigson, H. H. On the intonation and position of the so-called sentence modifiers in present-day English. Odense 1969.

Hofmann, T. R. La transformation de remplacement du constituant 'passé' et ses rapports avec le système modal de l'anglais. Langages 14 1969.

Huang, S. F. A note on English quantifiers. Linguistics 48 1969.

Il'ish, B. A. Prepositions and conjunctions in present-day English. Brno Stud in Eng 8 1969.

King, H. V. Punctual versus durative as covert categories. Lang Learnings 19 1969.

Kirkwood, H. W. Aspects of word order and its communicative function in English and German. Jnl of Linguistics 5 1969.

Lakoff, R. Some reasons why there can't be any *some-any* rule. Language 45 1969.

Levenston, E. A. Imperative structures in English. Linguistics 50 1969.

Lockwood, D. G. Pronoun concord domains in English. Linguistics 54 1969.

Norwood, J. E. Notes on some aspects of the preposition. Philologica Pragensia 12 1969.

Oller, J. W. and B. D. Sales. Conceptual restrictions on English: a psycholinguistic study. Lingua 23 1969.

Partridge, A. C. Tudor to Augustan English: a study in syntax and style from Caxton to Johnson. 1969.

Roey, J. A. van. The order of post-nominal modifiers in present-day English. E Studies 50 1969.

—— A note on the coordination of adjectives in English. In Linguistique contemporaine: hommage à Eric Buyssens, Brussels 1970.

Scott, R. I. Two ways to determine the most useful kernel for English. Linguistics 45 1969.

Sloat, C. Proper nouns in English. Language 45 1969.

Sundby, B. Coordination and word-order. Studia Germanica Gandensia 11 1969. On coordinative expressions using *-ing* forms.

— Front-shifted *ing* and *ed* groups in present-day English. Lund 1970.

Traugott, E. C. and J. Waterhouse. *Already* and *yet*: a suppletive set of aspect-markers? Jnl of Linguistics 5 1969.

Tuyn, H. Semantic and unconscious influences in tense usage. Studia Neophilologica 41 1969.

— Semantics and the notion of transitivity in passive conversion. Studia Neophilologica 42 1970.

Baker, C. L. Notes on the description of English questions: the role of an abstract question morpheme. Foundations of Lang 6 1970.

Bauer, G. The English 'perfect' reconsidered. Jnl of Linguistics 6 1970.

Burlakova, V. V. Word-combinations in Modern English. Zeitschrift für Anglistik und Amerikanistik 18 1970.

Carls, U. Zum Gebrauch der Relativpronomen in den 'close relative clauses' im modernen Englisch. Ibid.

Dierickx, J. Why are plural attributives becoming more frequent? In Linguistique contemporaine: hommage à Eric Buyssens, Brussels 1970.

Dougherty, R. C. A grammar of coördinate conjoined structures. Language 46–7 1970–1.

Gough, J. and L. Chiaraviglio. On the base referential structure of the English noun phrase. Foundations of Lang 6 1970.

Hansen, K. Zur Kategorie des Kasus im modernen Englisch. Zeitschrift für Anglistik und Amerikanistik 18 1970.

Kakietek, P. Some observations on the modals *will* and *shall*. Studia Anglica Posnaniensia 2 1970.

Lascelles, M. Some problems of base to surface development in English. Linguistics 64 1970.

Lehrer, A. Verbs and deletable objects. Lingua 25 1970.

Lord, J. B. Sequence in clusters of pre-nominal adjectives and adjectivals in English. Jnl of Eng Linguistics 4 1970.

McCawley, J. D. English as a *VSO* language. Language 46 1970.

Rutherford, W. E. Some observations concerning subordinate clauses in English. Ibid.

Shen, Y. Vocabulary participation and co-existent grammatical formulas. Jnl of Eng Linguistics 4 1970.

Taglicht, J. The genesis of the conventional rules for the use of *shall* and *will*. E Studies 51 1970.

— A new look at English relative constructions. Lingua 29 1972.

Wonder, J. P. Ambiguity and the English gerund. Lingua 25 1970.

Yotsukura, S. The articles in English. Hague 1970.

Bald, W.-D. The scope of negation and copula sentences in English. Jnl of Eng Linguistics 5 1971.

Caldwell, S. J. G. Classes of modification of the headword of the nominal group in English. Neuphilologische Mitteilungen 72 1971.

Dahl, L. The *s*-genitive with non-personal nouns in Modern English journalistic style. Ibid.

Dingwall, W. O. On so-called anaphoric *to* and the theory of anaphora in general. Jnl of Eng Linguistics 5 1971.

Nagucka, R. Some remarks on genitival relations in English. Studia Anglica Posnaniensia 3 1971.

Newmeyer, F. J. The source of derived nominals in English. Language 47 1971.

Seppänen, A. Proper names in a transformational grammar of English. Neuphilologische Mitteilungen 72 1971.

Starosta, S. Some lexical redundancy rules for English nouns. Glossa 5 1971.

Szwedek, A. The English finite verb system. Studia Anglica Posnaniensia 3 1971.

Delorme, E. and R. C. Dougherty. Appositive NP constructions: *we, the men*; *we men*; *I, a man*; etc. Foundations of Lang 8 1972.

Hoffmann, A. Die verbo-nominale Konstruktion: eine spezifische Form der nominalen Ausdrucksweise im modernen Englisch. Zeitschrift für Anglistik und Amerikanistik 20 1972.

Juul, A. The category of number in Modern English. E Studies 53 1972.

Nixon, G. Corporate-concord phenomena in English. Studia Neophilologica 44 1972.

Individual Authors and Texts
(*in alphabetical order*)

Riikonen, E. The gerundial constructions in Jane Austen's novels. Neuphilologische Mitteilungen 36 1935.

Raybould, E. Of Jane Austen's use of expanded verbal forms. In Studies in English language and literature presented to Karl Brunner, Vienna 1957.

Phillipps, K. C. Jane Austen's English. Neuphilologische Mitteilungen 70 1969.

— Jane Austen's English. 1970.

Rohs, A. Syntaktische Untersuchungen zu Bacons Essays. Marburg 1889.

Tarselius, R. *Would* as an exhortative auxiliary: a contribution to the syntax of Francis Bacon. Studier i Modern Språkvetenskap 18 1953.

— *Will* as an exhortative auxiliary: another contribution to the syntax of Francis Bacon. Studier i Modern Språkvetenskap 19 1956.

Klausmann, G. Formenlehre und Syntax des Verbums in der Froissart-Übersetzung von Lord Berners. Greifswald 1919.

Behre, F. Studies in Agatha Christie's writings: the behaviour of *a good* (*great*) *deal, a lot, lots, much, plenty, many, a good* (*great*) *many*. Gothenburg 1967. *See also Behre 1969, col 131, above.*

Dahl, T. Linguistic studies in some Elizabethan writings 1: an inquiry into aspects of the language of Thomas Deloney. Copenhagen 1951. *See also Dahl 1956, Bowers 1968, cols 131, 137, above.*

Söderlind, J. Verb syntax in John Dryden's prose. 2 pts Upsala 1951–8.

Simon, I. Dryden's revision of the Essay of dramatic poesy. RES new ser 14 1963.

Bately, J. M. Dryden's revisions in the Essay of dramatic poesy: the preposition at the end of the sentence and the expression of the relative. RES new ser 15 1964.

Ire, K. The auxiliary *do* in John Dryden's plays. Anglica (Osaka) 5 1965.

Rydén, M. Relative constructions in early sixteenth-century English, with special reference to Sir Thomas Elyot. Upsala 1966.

Partridge, A. C. The periphrastic auxiliary verb *do* and its use in the plays of Ben Jonson. MLR 43 1948.

— Studies in the syntax of Ben Jonson's plays. Cambridge 1953.

Jungnell, T. Notes on the language of Ben Jonson. Studier i Modern Språkvetenskap new ser 1 1960.

Craigie, W. A. The language of the Kingis quair. E & S 25 1939.

Emma, R. D. Milton's grammar. Hague 1964.

Chatman, S. Milton's participial style. PMLA 83 1968.

Musacchio, G. L. Milton's feminine pronouns with neuter antecedents. Jnl of Eng Linguistics 2 1968.

Visser, F. T. A syntax of the English language of St Thomas More: A, The verb. 3 pts Louvain 1946–56.

Scheurweghs, G. The relative pronouns in the xvith [century] plays Roister Doister and Respublica. In English studies presented to R. W. Zandvoort, Amsterdam 1964 (suppl to E Studies 45 1964).

Harz, H. Die Umschreibung mit *do* in Shakespeares Prosa. Cöthen 1918.

Biese, Y. M. Notes on the compound participle in the works of Shakespeare and his contemporaries. Helsinki 1950.

— Notes on the use of the ingressive auxiliaries in the works of William Shakespeare. Neuphilologische Mitteilungen 53 1952.

Jackson, MacD. P. Affirmative particles in Henry VIII. N & Q Oct 1962.

Salmon, V. Sentence structures in colloquial Shakespearian English. Trans Philological Soc 1965.

Schlauch, M. Asyndeton in Shakespeare and Webster: a comparative note. In Symbolae linguisticae in honorem Georgii Kuryłowicz (Prace Komisji Językoznawstwa 5), Wrocław 1965.

Millward, C. Pronominal case in Shakespearean imperatives. Language 42 1966.

Mulholland, J. *Thou* and *you* in Shakespeare: a study in the second person pronoun. E Studies 48 1967.

Kakietek, P. *May* and *might* in Shakespeare's English. Linguistics 64 1970.

See also Kellner 1885, col 127, above.

D. VOCABULARY AND WORD FORMATION

(1) GENERAL STUDIES

Skeat, W. W. Principles of English etymology. Ser 1, Oxford 1887, 1892 (rev).

— Notes on English etymology. Oxford 1901.

Greenough, J. B. and G. L. Kittredge. Words and their ways in English speech. New York 1901.

Smith, L. P. The English language. 1912 (Home Univ Lib), Oxford 1966 (rev).

— Words and idioms in the English language. 1925.

Weekley, E. The romance of words. 1912, 1961 (rev).

— Words ancient and modern. 2 sers 1926–7.

— Words and names. 1932.

— Something about words. 1935.

McKnight, G. H. English words and their background. New York 1923.

Aronstein, P. Englische Wortkunde. Leipzig 1925.

Barfield, O. History in English words. 1926.

Stern, G. Meaning and change of meaning, with special reference to the English language. Gothenburg 1931.

Groom, B. A short history of English words. 1934.

Behr, U. L. A. Wortkontaminationen in der neuenglischen Schriftsprache. Würzburg 1935.

Koziol, H. Handbuch der englischen Wortbildungslehre. Heidelberg 1937.

— Zur englischen Bedeutungslehre. In Festschrift zum 75 Geburtstag von Theodor Spira, Heidelberg 1961.

— Beiträge zur englischen Bezeichnungslehre. Moderne Sprachen: Schriftenreihe 9 1963.

— Grundzüge der englischen Semantik. Vienna 1967.

Partridge, E. The world of words. 1938, 1948 (rev).

Ullmann, S. The range and mechanism of changes of meaning. JEGP 41 1942.

— The principles of semantics. Glasgow 1951.

— Semantics: an introduction to the science of meaning. 1962.

Menner, R. J. Multiple meaning and change of meaning in English. Language 21 1945.

Spitzer, L. Essays in historical semantics. New York 1948.

Firth, J. R. Modes of meaning. E & S new ser 4 1951.

Horn, W. Beiträge zur englischen Wortgeschichte. Wiesbaden 1951.

Leisi, E. Der Wortinhalt: seine Struktur im Deutschen und Englischen. Heidelberg 1953, 1967 (rev).

Sheard, J. A. The words we use. 1954.

Sprachwissenschaftliches Colloquium (Bonn). Europäische Schlüsselwörter. Munich 1963–. In progress; 1, Humor und Witz, 1963; 2, Kurzmonographien 1: Wörter im geistigen und sozialen Raum, 1964; 3, Kultur und Zivilisation, 1967.

Waldron, R. A. Sense and sense development. 1967.

Pisani, V. Lezioni sul lessico inglese. Brescia 1968.

(2) SPECIAL STUDIES

(on more than one period)

Stoffel, C. Intensives and down-toners: a study in English adverbs. Heidelberg 1901.

Draat, P. F. van. The loss of the prefix *ge-* in the English verb. E Studien 31–2 1902–3, 36 1906.

Palmgren, C. English gradation-nouns in their relation to strong verbs. Upsala 1904.

Campbell, C. D. The names of relationship in English. Strasbourg 1905.

Hemken, E. Das Aussterben alter Substantiva im Verlaufe der englischen Sprachgeschichte. Kiel 1906.

Oberdörffer, W. Das Aussterben altenglischer Adjektive und ihr Ersatz im Verlaufe der englischen Sprachgeschichte. Kiel 1908.

Offe, J. Das Aussterben alter Verba und ihr Ersatz im Verlaufe der englischen Sprachgeschichte. Kiel 1908.

Bechler, K. Das Präfix *to* im Verlaufe der englischen Sprachgeschichte. Königsberg 1909.

Efvergren, C. Names of places in a transferred sense in English. Lund 1909.

Bergsten, N. A study on compound substantives in English. Upsala 1911.

Weick, F. Das Aussterben des Präfixes *ge-* im Englischen. Darmstadt 1911.

Teichert, F. Über das Aussterben alter Wörter im Verlaufe der englischen Sprachgeschichte. Erlangen 1912.

Spielmann, M. H. Slang: modern–antique. TLS 7 Nov 1918; rptd English 12 1958.

Bengtsson, E. Studies on passive nouns with a concrete sense in English. Lund 1927.

Beysel, K. Die Namen der Blutverwandtschaft im Englischen. Giessener Beiträge zur Erforschung der Sprache und Kultur Englands und Nordamerikas 3 1927.

Bergener, C. A contribution to the study of the conversion of adjectives into nouns in English. Lund 1928.

Schreuder, H. Pejorative sense development in English. Groningen 1929.

— On some cases of restriction of meaning. E Studies 37 1956.

Jaeschke, K. Beiträge zur Frage des Wortschwundes im Englischen. Breslau 1931.

Raith, J. Die englischen Nasalverben. Leipzig 1931.

Dike, E. B. Obsolete words. PQ 12 1933.

— Our obsolete vocabulary: some historical views. PQ 13 1934.

— Obsolete English words: some recent views. JEGP 34 1935.

Lindelöf, U. English agent-nouns with a suffixed adverb. Neuphilologische Mitteilungen 36 1935.

Malone, K. Herlekin and Herlewin. E Studies 17 1935.

Menner, R. J. The conflict of homonyms in English. Language 12 1936.

Einarsson, S. Old and Middle English notes. JEGP 36 1937.

Flasdieck, H. M. Harlekin: germanischer Mythos in romanischer Wandlung. Anglia 61 1937, 66 1942.
— *Boxen*. Anglia 70 1951.
— *Pall Mall*: Beiträge zur Etymologie und Quantitätstheorie. Anglia 72 1955.
Swaen, A. E. H. An essay in blue. E Studien 71 1937.
— Greenery gallery. E Studien 72 1938.
— The palette set. E Studien 74 1941.
Zessin, H. Der Begriff 'Bauer' im Englischen im Spiegel seiner Bezeichnungsgeschichte und Bedeutungsgeschichte. Halle 1937.
Lotspeich, C. M. The type OE *lōca hwā*, ME *looke who*. JEGP 37 1938.
Downs, L. G. Notes on the intensive use of Germanic *te, *to, *'to*: *too*. JEGP 38 1939.
Jespersen, O. The history of a suffix. Acta Linguistica 1 1939. On *-en* in verbs.
Wilhelmsen, L. J. On the verbal prefixes *for-* and *fore-* in English. Oslo 1939.
Bertschinger, M. *To want*: an essay in semantics. Berne 1941.
Biese, Y. M. Origin and development of conversions in English. Helsinki 1941.
Prins, A. A. On the loss and substitution of words in Middle English. Neophilologus 26–7 1941–2.
Whitehall, H. Interim etymologies: *L.* PQ 20 1941.
Mann, G. Die Entstehung von nebensatzeinleitenden Konjunktionen im Englischen. Archiv 180 1942.
Marquardt, H. Der englische Wortschatz als Spiegel englischer Kultur. Germanisch-romanische Monatsschrift 30 1942.
Sundén, K. F. A new etymological group of Germanic verbs and their derivatives: a study on semantics. Gothenburg 1943.
Williams, E. R. The conflict of homonyms in English. New Haven 1944.
McClean, R. J. Germanic nursery words. MLR 42 1947.
Lee, D. W. Functional change in early English. Menasha 1948.
Muir, A. L. Some observations on the early English Psalters and the English vocabulary. MLQ 9 1948.
Lindheim, B. von. OE *dream* and its subsequent development. RES 25 1949.
Visser, F. T. Some causes of verbal obsolescence. Nijmegen 1949.
Holthausen, F. Beiträge zur englischen Etymologie. Anglia 70 1951.
Smithers, G. V. Some English ideophones. Archivum Linguisticum 6 1954.
Pilch, H. Der Untergang des Präverbs *ʒe-* im Englischen. Anglia 73 1955.
Kirchner, G. Der Reimklang im Englischen. Zeitschrift für Anglistik und Amerikanistik 4 1956.
Alanne, E. Observations on the development and structure of English wine-growing terminology. Helsinki 1957.
Penttilä, E. A sense-development of verbs denoting emission of light. Neuphilologische Mitteilungen 59 1958.
Genzel, P. Die Lebensfunktionen der Menschen und Säugetiere im Spiegel der englischen Sprache. Halle 1959.

Marchand, H. The negative verbal prefixes in English. In Mélanges de linguistique et de philologie: Fernand Mossé in memoriam, Paris 1959.
— On a question of contrary analysis with derivationally connected but morphologically uncharacterised words. E Studies 44 1963.
Spitzbardt, H. Etymologische Betrachtungen zu ne. *heal*, *whole*, *holy*. Lingua 8 1959.
— Präfigierte Verstärkungselemente im Englischen. Wissenschaftliche Zeitschrift der Friedrich-Schiller-Universität Jena: gesellschafts- und sprachwissenschaftliche Reihe 11 1962.
Pareigytė, E. Priesagos *-ment* anglų kalboje atsiradimo klausimu. Vilniaus Valstybnis V. Kapsuko Vardo Universitetas Mokslo Darbai 30: Kalbotyra 2 1960. On development of suffix *-ment*; with Russian summary.
Ufimzewa, A. A. Zur Geschichte der semantischen Entwicklung des Wortes *land*. Zeitschrift für Anglistik und Amerikanistik 8 1960.
Frolova, T. I. Protsess vychleneniya prefiksov romanskogo proiskhozhdeniya v angliĭskom yazyke. Nauchnye Doklady Vysshei Shkoly: Filologicheskie Nauki 1963. On prefixes of Romance origin.
Ross, A. S. C. Three lexicographic notes. Eng Philological Stud 8 1963. 1: Some obscure 'Grocers'' words; 2: An early occurrence of the word *kerbing*?; 3: *ac bȳð . . . flæsces fodor*.
Thun, N. Reduplicative words in English: a study of formations of the types *tick-tick*, *hurly-burly* and *shilly-shally*. Upsala 1963.
White, B. Decline and fall of interjections. Neuphilologische Mitteilungen 64 1963.
Majut, R. Die Libelle im deutschen und englischen Sprachgebrauch: ein Beitrag zur vergleichenden Wortgeschichte. Germanisch-romanische Monatsschrift 45 1964.
Mutt, O. The adjectivization of nouns in English. Zeitschrift für Anglistik und Amerikanistik 12 1964.
Pocheptsov, G. G. De-etymologization in English. Zeitschrift für Anglistik und Amerikanistik 13 1965.
Nickel, G. Operational procedures in semantics, with special reference to Medieval English. Monograph Ser on Languages and Linguistics (Georgetown Univ) 19 1966.
Pennanen, E. V. Contributions to the study of back-formation in English. Acta Academiae Socialis A 4, Tampere 1966.
Potter, S. Limits of functional shift. In Studies in language and literature in honour of Margaret Schlauch, Warsaw 1966.
Sandred, K. I. On the terminology of the plough in England. Studia Neophilologica 38 1966.
Habicht, W. Zur Bedeutungsgeschichte des englischen Wortes *countenance*. Archiv 203 1967.
Marckwardt, A. H. Lexical redistribution in Modern English *say* and *tell*. In Papers in linguistics in honor of Léon Dostert, Hague 1967.
Peltola, N. Contributions to the study of intensives. Neuphilologische Mitteilungen 70 1969.
Strang, B. M. H. Aspects of the history of the *-er* formative in English. Trans Philological Soc 1969.

(3) OLD ENGLISH

General

Bode, W. Die Kenningar in der angelsächsischen Dichtung. Strasbourg 1886.
Stevenson, W. H. Some Old English words omitted or imperfectly explained in dictionaries. Trans Philological Soc 1895.
Swaen, A. E. H. Contributions to Anglo-Saxon lexicography. E Studien 26, 32–3, 35, 37–8, 40, 43, 49, 53–4 1899–1920.

Jordan, R. Eigentümlichkeiten des anglischen Wortschatzes. Heidelberg 1906.
Förster, M. Beiträge zur altenglischen Wortkunde aus ungedruckten volkskundlichen Texten. E Studien 39 1908.
— Ae. *hrider*, *hriddern* und *hriddel* im Lichte altbritischer Entlehnungen. Anglia 61 1937.
— König Eadgars Tod (†975). E Studien 72 1938. On *gewealc* in Lambeth Palace ms 204.
— Die spätae. deiktische Pronominal-form *þæʒe* und ne. *they*. Beiblatt zur Anglia 52 1941.

— Die Bedeutung von ae. *gebisceopian* und seiner Sippe. Anglia 66 1942.

— Die liturgische Bedeutung von ae. *traht*. Beiblatt zur Anglia 53 1942.

— Nochmals ae. *þæze*. Ibid.

— Zu ae. *beard* und *bearm*. Ibid.

Rankin, J. W. A study of the kennings in Anglo-Saxon poetry. JEGP 8–9 1909–10.

Schlutter, O. B. Weitere Beiträge zur altenglischen Wortforschung. Anglia 37–40, 42–6 1913–22.

Schücking, L. L. Untersuchungen zur Bedeutungslehre der angelsächsischen Dichtersprache. Heidelberg 1915.

Keiser, A. The influence of Christianity on the vocabulary of Old English poetry. Urbana 1919.

Grundy, G. B. On the meanings of certain terms in the Anglo-Saxon charters. E & S 8 1922.

Langenhove, G. C. van. De etymologie van *ontberen*, ohd. *inbëran*, ags. *onberan* en *oðberan*. Verslagen en Mededeelingen van de Koninklijke Vlaamsche Academie voor Taal en Letterkunde 1923.

Craigie, W. A. The meaning of *ambyre wind*. Philologica 2 1924.

Wyld, H. C. Diction and imagery in Anglo-Saxon poetry. E & S 11 1925.

Malone, K. Old English (*ge*)*hȳdan* 'heed'. In A grammatical miscellany offered to Otto Jespersen, Copenhagen 1930.

— Old English *beagas*. Beiblatt zur Anglia 52 1941.

— Old English *gar* 'storm'. E Studies 28 1947.

Pedersen, H. Oldengelsk *fǣmne*. In A grammatical miscellany offered to Otto Jespersen, Copenhagen 1930.

— Angl. *wife* et *woman*. Studia Neophilologica 14 1942.

Langenfelt, G. The OE Paradise lost. Anglia 55 1931. On *neorxnawang*.

— The OE Paradise lost: *neorxnawang*. Anglia 60 1936.

Flasdieck, H. M. Ae. *ēow*. Anglia 57 1933.

— OE *nefne*: a revaluation. Anglia 69 1950.

— Nochmals ae. *nefne*. Anglia 70 1951.

Grandinger, M. M. Die Bedeutung des Adjektivs *good* in der religiösen Literatur der Angelsachsen. Landshut 1933.

Krogmann, W. Ae. *dyde*. Anglia 57 1933.

— Ae. *gang*. Ibid.

— Ae. *neorx(e)nawang* 'Paradies'. Anglia 58 1934.

— Ae. *strosle* 'Drossel'. Ibid.

— Ae. *tosocnung*. Anglia 59 1935.

— Ae. *georman-leaf* und der Name der Germanen. E Studien 69 1935.

— Ae. *georman- geormen-*. E Studien 70 1936.

— Ae. *defu*. Ibid.

— Ae. Wortdeutungen. Anglia 60 1936.

— Zwei ae. Wortdeutungen. Ibid.

— Altenglisches. Anglia 61 1937.

— Altenglisches. Anglia 63 1939.

— Ae. (*n*)*eorx(e)nawang*. E Studien 74 1941.

— *Neorxna wang* und *iða vǫllr*. Archiv 191 1954.

Lane, G. S. Two Germanic etymologies. JEGP 32 1933. [2] OE *mētan* ['paint'], Ilcel *mót*, *móta*, etc.

Vočadlo, O. Anglo-Saxon terminology. Práce z Vědeckých Ústavů 33 1933.

Dike, E. B. Our oldest obsoletisms. E Studien 68 1934.

Ross, A. S. C. OE *weofod*. Leeds Stud in Eng 3 1934.

— *Give*. Studia Neophilologica 41 1969.

— *Whilom*. N & Q Feb 1969.

— and II. W. Bailcy. OE *afigen*: Ossctc *fëzōnäg*. Lccds Stud in Eng 3 1934.

Stern, G. Old English *fuslic* and *fus*. E Studien 68 1934.

Haessler, L. Old English *bebeodan* and *forbeodan*. Language 11 1935.

Mezger, F. Ae. *tintreg(a)* < **tind-treg(a)*? Archiv 167 1935.

— Gehört ae. *earwunga* 'gratis', got. *arwjō*, ahd. *arw(ing)un* zu got. *arjan* 'pflügen'? Archiv 173 1938.

— OE *gehygd*, *hyht*, *hlyst*, *geþyld*. Arkiv for Nordisk Filologi 54 1939.

— Ae. *genæstan* 'streiten': ae. *hæst* 'Heftigkeit', 'Streit'. Archiv 175 1939.

— OE *tān*: Idg. *dⱴōu; *dⱴoi? JEGP 40 1941.

— Two etymologies. Language 19 1943. 1, Old English *swicn*.

— Heth. *kiššan*: ae. *hislīc*. Zeitschrift für Vergleichende Sprachforschung 77 1961.

Horn, W. Altenglische *hwæþere* 'dennoch'. E Studien 70 1936.

Bloomfield, L. Notes on Germanic compounds. Acta Jutlandica 9 1937.

Linke, G. Zu ae. *blægettan* = 'blöken', 'schreien'. Archiv 172 1937.

Holmes, U. T. Old French *mangon*, Anglo-Saxon *mancus*, late Latin *mancussus*, *mancosus*, *mancessus* etc. PMLA 53 1938.

Marquardt, H. Die altenglischen Kenningar. Halle 1938.

Harder, H. Zur Herkunft von ahd. *thuris*, ags. *þyrs*, aisl. *þurs*. Archiv 175 1939.

Martz, O. Die Wiedergabe biblischer Personenbezeichnungen in der altenglischen Missionssprache. Bochum 1939.

Schwentner, E. Alts. *dref*, ags. *drep*, *dreb*. Zeitschrift für Vergleichende Sprachforschung 66 1939.

— Ags. *wuducocc*, altind. *vanakukkuta*. Indogermanische Forschungen 57 1940.

Oehl, W. Ags. *mamor* 'Schlaf' und Elementar-Paralleles. Ibid.

Lotspeich, C. M. Old English etymologies. JEGP 40 1941.

Weber, E. Zu dem Wort *rune*. Archiv 178 1941.

Anderson, O. S. An etymological note. Studia Neophilologica 14 1942. On OE *lȳþre*.

Bennett, J. A. W. Old English *hrohian*. MÆ 11 1942.

Holthausen, F. Zur altenglischen Wortkunde. Beiblatt zur Anglia 53–4 1942–3.

Johannisson, T. Altenglisch *incuð* und *oncyð(ð)*. Studia Neophilologica 14 1942.

Meyer, W. Die Bedeutung des altenglischen Wortes *huru*. Beiblatt zur Anglia 53 1942.

Ekwall, E. Old English *ambyrne wind*. In Mélanges de philologie offerts à M. Johan Melander, Upsala 1943.

— Old English *forræpe*. Studia Neophilologica 16 1944.

Mincoff, M. K. Zur angelsächsischen Dichtersprache. Sofia 1943.

Fischer, W. Zur Etymologie von ae. *docga*, ne. *dog* und einigen anderen Tiernamen. Anglia 67–8 1944.

Menner, R. J. Two Old English words: 1 Old Anglian (*ge*)*strynd*; 2 OE *gullisc*. MLN 59 1944.

Löfvenberg, M. T. An etymological note. Studia Neophilologica 17 1945. On OE *cȳte*, *cēte* 'hut'.

— Old English *twicele*. Studier i Modern Språkvetenskap 19 1956.

Derolez, R. L. M.—and that difficult word *garsecg*. MLQ 7 1946.

Meritt, H. D. Studies in Old English vocabulary. JEGP 46 1947.

— Twenty hard Old English words. JEGP 49 1950.

— Fact and lore about Old English words. Stanford 1954.

— The Leiden gloss to *histrionibus*. Anglia 80 1962. On OE *ðocrere 'runner-about'.

— Some of the hardest glosses in Old English. Stanford 1968.

— Old English *hünsporan*. In Studies in language, literature and culture of the Middle Ages and later, ed. E. B. Atwood and A. A. Hill, Austin 1969.

Magoun, F. P. OE *ealle prage*. MLN 63 1948.

Carr, C. T. OE *fitel*, OLG *fitil*, OHG *fizzel*, ON *-fjǫtli*. Eng & Germanic Stud 2 1949.

Schaubert, E. von. Bedeutung und Herkunft von altenglischem *feormian* und seiner Sippe. Göttingen 1949.

Lindheim, B. von. Traces of colloquial speech in OE. Anglia 70 1951.

— Problems of Old English semantics. In English studies today: 3rd series, Edinburgh 1964.

Hurnard, N. D. The Anglo-Norman franchises. EHR 64 1949. On OE *grithbryce forstal, hamsocn* etc.

Willard, R. OE *oma* 'rust'. MLN 66 1951.

Einarsson, S. Old English *ent*: Icelandic *enta*. MLN 67 1952.

— *Kyning-wuldor* and *mann-skratti*. MLN 75 1960.

Walker, W. S. The *bruneeg* sword. MLN 67 1952.

Brooks, K. R. Old English *ēa* and related words. Eng & Germanic Stud 5 1953.

Wolf-Rottkay, W.-H. Zur Etymologie von ae. *bāt*. Anglia 71 1953.

Temple, W. M. OE *hlædfæt*—Welsh *lletwad*. RES new ser 6 1955.

Wüst, W. Zur Deutung und Herkunft des ae. *bāt* m.f. 'Boot, Schiff'. Anglia 73 1955.

Schabram, H. Zur Bedeutung von ae. *cēne*. Anglia 74 1956.

— Zur Bedeutung und Etymologie von ae. *rōf*. Anglia 75 1957.

— Ae. *þ(r)istra* 'coniuncla'. Anglia 76 1958.

— Die Bedeutung von *ʒāl* und *ʒalscipe* in der ae. Genesis B. Beiträge zur Geschichte der Deutschen Sprache und Literatur (Tübingen) 82 1960.

— Ae. *beohata*, Exodus 253. In Wortbildung, Syntax und Morphologie: Festschrift zum 60 Geburtstag von Hans Marchand, Hague 1968.

— Kritische Bemerkungen zu Angaben über die Verbreitung altenglischer Wörter. In Festschrift für Edgar Mertner, Munich 1969.

McLintock, D. R. OE *wīs* and *(ge)wiss*. Archivum Linguisticum 11 1959.

Ball, C. [J. E.] *Incge* Beow. 2577. Anglia 78 1960.

Cowgill, W. Gothic *iddja* and Old English *ēode*. Language 36 1960.

Must, G. English *holy*, German *heilig*. JEGP 59 1960.

Forsberg, R. Old English *scipsteall*. Studia Neophilologica 33 1961.

Gillam, D. M. E. The connotations of OE *fæge*, with a note on Beowulf and Byrhtnoth. Studia Germanica Gandensia 4 1962.

— A method for determining the connotations of OE poetic words. Studia Germanica Gandensia 6 1964.

Kuhn, H. Angelsächsisch *cōp* 'Kappe' und seinesgleichen. In Festgabe für L. L. Hammerich aus Anlass seines siebzigsten Geburtstags, Copenhagen 1962.

Makovskiĭ, M. M. Problema 'geografii slov' v drevneangliĭskikh dialektakh. Voprosȳ Yazȳkoznaniya 1962. The problem of 'word geography' in OE dialects.

— Variantnost' leksem v drevneangliĭskikh glossakh kak priznak dialektnoĭ prinadlezhnosti slovarya. In Étimologiya: issledovaniya po russkomu i drugim yazȳkam, Moscow 1963. On dialectal significance of lexical variation in OE glosses.

— Sravnitel'no-istoricheskaya dialektografiya anglskoĭ leksik v predelakh germanskoĭ yazykovoĭ oblasti, 1: o metodakh analiza. In Étimologiya [1964]: printsipȳ rekonstruktsii i metodika issledovaniya, Moscow 1965. On Anglian vocabulary within the Germanic area: methods of analysis.

— Étimoloa i problema filologicheskoĭ dostovernosti slova. In Étimologiya 1966: problemȳ lingvogeografii i mezh"yazȳkovȳkh kontaktov, Moscow 1968. Etymology and the problem of the philological reliability of words.

Hille, A. OE *Seoluini* and ON *Sjóli*. E Studies 44 1963.

Kökeritz, H. The Anglo-Saxon unicorn. In Early English and Norse studies presented to Hugh Smith, 1963.

Oliphant, R. O. *Ætnes* and *ytend*: two rare Old English glossary words. PQ 42 1963.

Peters, R. A. OE *ælf, -ælf, ælfen, -ælfen*. Ibid.

Salus, P. H. OE *eoletes*. Lingua 12 1963. See P. B. Taylor and P. H. Salus 13 1965.

Wilbur, T. H. The Germanic interrogatives of the *how* type. Word 19 1963.

Århammar, N. Altsächs. *skion* m. 'Wolke' und altengl. *scēo* (?) Jahrbuch des Vereins für Niederdeutsche Sprachforschung 87 1964.

Rauch, I. A problem in historical synonymy. Linguistics 6 1964. On *ofermōd, ofermēde, oferhygd, ofermētto* in Genesis B.

Bammesberger, A. Old English *gycer* and Gothic *jukuzi*. Language 41 1965.

— Old English *brecþa* and *-brecþ*. Language 43 1967.

Dick, E. S. Ae. *dryht* und seine Sippe. Münster 1965.

Mitchell, B. Bede's *habere* = Old English *magan*? Neuphilologische Mitteilungen 66 1965.

Robinson, F. C. Old English lexicographical notes. Philologica Pragensia 8 1965.

— The significance of names in Old English literature. Anglia 86 1968.

— Lexicography and literary criticism: a caveat. In Philological essays: studies in Old and Middle English language and literature in honour of Herbert Dean Meritt, Hague 1970.

Daunt, M. Some modes of Anglo-Saxon meaning. In In memory of J. R. Firth, 1966.

Gardner, T. [J.]. Old English *gārsecg*. Archiv 202 1966.

— Semantic patterns in Old English substantival compounds. Hamburg 1968.

— *Þreaniedla* and *þreamedla*: notes on two Old English abstracta in *-la(n)*. Neuphilologische Mitteilungen 70 1969.

— The Old English kenning: a characteristic feature of Germanic poetical diction? MP 67 1970.

Rosier, J. L. *Icge gold* and *incge lafe* in Beowulf. PMLA 81 1966.

Whitbread, L. Old English *unbleoh*. Neophilologus 50 1966. See Cameron 1969, below.

Erades, P. A. A Romance congener of OE *symbel*. E Studies 48 1967.

Lehmann, W. P. *Atertanum fah*. In Studies in historical linguistics in honor of George Sherman Lane, Chapel Hill [1967].

Kühlwein, W. Modell einer operationellen lexicologischen Analyse: altenglisch 'Blut'. Heidelberg 1968.

— Entropie und Redundanz in der angelsächsischen Poesie. Linguistics 68 1971.

Seebold, E. Ae. *twegen* und ahd. *zwēne* 'zwei'. Anglia 86 1968.

Cameron, A. F. Old English *unbleoh* again. Neophilologus 53 1969.

Kristensson, G. Old English **gēol, *golu*. Studia Neophilologica 41 1969.

— An etymological note: Old English *drȳgan* 'to make dry'. Studia Neophilologica 43 1971.

Stanley, E. G. Old English *-calla, ceallian*. In Medieval literature and civilization: studies in memory of G. N. Garmonsway, 1969.

— Studies in the prosaic vocabulary of Old English verse. Neuphilologische Mitteilungen 72 1971.

Štech, S. A few remarks on the etymology of OE *ædre* 'vein'. Brno Stud in Eng 8 1969.

Hallander, L.-G. Contributions to Old English lexicography, 1: *hwamm ~ hwemm*. E Studies 51 1970.

Cooke, W. G. *Hronas* and *hronfixas*. N & Q July 1971.

Peltola, N. Observations on intensification in Old English poetry. Neuphilologische Mitteilungen 72 1971.

Brown, A *Heifer*. Neophilologus 56 1972.

Klegraf, J. Beowulf 769: *ealuscerwēn*. Archiv 208 1972.

Special Studies

Word Formation

Storch, T. Angelsächsische Nominalcomposita. Strasbourg 1886.

Harrison, T. P. The separable prefixes in Anglo-Saxon. Baltimore 1892.

Thiele, O. Die konsonantischen Suffixe der Abstrakta des Altenglischen. Darmstadt 1902.

Eckhardt, E. Die angelsächsischen Deminutivbildungen. E Studien 32 1903.

Krackow, O. Die Nominalcomposita als Kunstmittel im altenglischen Epos. Berlin 1903.

Best, K. Die persönlichen Konkreta des Altenglischen nach ihren Suffixen geordnet. Strasbourg 1905.

Schön, E. Die Bildung des Adjektivs im Altenglischen. Kiel 1905.

Schuldt, C. Die Bildung der schwachen Verba im Altenglischen. Kiel 1905.

Lehmann, W. Das Präfix uz-, besonders im Altenglischen. Kiel 1906.

Nicolai, O. Die Bildung des Adverbs im Altenglischen. Kiel 1907.

Both, M. Die konsonantischen Suffixe altenglischer Konkreta und Kollektiva. Kiel 1909.

Lenze, J. Das Praefix bi- in der ae. Nominal- und Verbalkomposition mit gelegentlicher Berücksichtigung der anderen germanischen Dialekte. Kiel 1909.

Siemerling, O. Das Präfix for(e)- in der altenglischen Verbal- und Nominalkomposition. Kiel 1909.

Lüngen, W. Das Praefix on(d)- in der ae. Verbalkomposition mit einem Anhang über das Praefix oð- (uð-). Kiel 1911.

Weyhe, H. Zu den altenglischen Verbalabstrakten auf -nes und -ing -ung. Halle 1911.

Hohenstein, C. Das altengl. Präfix wið(er)- im Verlauf der engl. Sprachgeschichte mit Berücksichtigung der andern germ. Dialekte. Kiel 1912.

Jensen, J. Die I und II Ablautsreihe in der ae. Wortbildung. Kiel 1913.

Röhling, M. Das Präfix ofer- in der ae. Verbal- und Nominalkomposition mit Berücksichtigung der übrigen germanischen Dialekte. Kiel 1914.

Kärre, K. Nomina Agentis in Old English. Upsala 1915.

Uhler, K. Die Bedeutungsgleichheit der altenglischen Adjektiva und Adverbia mit und ohne -lic (-lice). Heidelberg 1926.

Mezger, F. Der germanische Kult und die ae. Feminina auf -icge und -estre. Archiv 168 1935.

— The formation of OHG diorna, Old Saxon thiorna, Gothic widuwairna and Old English niwerne. MLN 57 1942.

Carr, C. T. Nominal compounds in Germanic. Oxford 1939.

Johannisson, T. Verbal och postverbal partikelkomposition i de germanska språken. Lund 1939.

Shook, L. K. A technical construction in Old English: translation loans in -lic. Mediaeval Stud 2 1940.

Meritt, H. D. Some minor ways of word formation in Old English. Stanford Stud in Lang & Lit 1941.

Marckwardt, A. H. The verbal suffix -ettan in Old English. Language 18 1942.

Hendrickson, J. R. Old English prepositional compounds in relationship to their Latin originals. Baltimore 1948.

Walker, J. A. The rank-number relationship of adjectival suffixes in Old English. PQ 27 1948.

Brady, C. The Old English nominal compounds in -rad. PMLA 67 1952.

Pilch, H. Das ae. Präverb ge-. Anglia 71 1953.

Trnka, B. K staroanglické deminutivní příponě -incel. Časopis pro Moderní Filologii 38 1956. Old English diminutive suffix -incel; with English summary.

Lindheim, B. von. Die weiblichen Genussuffixe im Altenglischen. Anglia 76 1958. Korrekturen und Nachträge 87 1969. See Schabram 1970, below.

— Das altenglische Deminutivsuffix -incel. Beiträge zur Geschichte der Deutschen Sprache und Literatur (Tübingen) 92 1970.

— Das Suffix -bære im Altenglischen. Archiv 208 1972.

Hofmann, D. K-Diminutiva im Nordfriesischen und in verwandten Sprachen. Niederdeutsche Studien 7 1961.

Iarovici, E. Conversiunea în engleza veche. Revista de Filologie Romanică şi Germanică 6 1962. Conversion in Old English; with English summary.

Lindemann, J. W. R. Old English preverbal ge-: a reexamination of some current doctrines. JEGP 64 1965.

— Old English preverbal ge-: its meaning. Charlottesville 1970.

Hallander, L.-G. Old English verbs in -sian. Stockholm 1966.

Joly, A. Ge- préfixe lexical en vieil anglais. Canadian Jnl of Linguistics 12 1967.

Schabram, H. Bemerkungen zu den ae. Nomina Agentis auf -estre und -icge. Anglia 88 1970. Supplements von Lindheim 1958, 1969, above.

Special Classes of Words

Hoops, J. Über die altenglischen Pflanzennamen. Freiburg 1889.

Whitman, C. H. The birds of Old English literature. JEGP 2 1898. See also Swaen 1907, below.

— The Old English mammal names. JEGP 6 1906.

— The Old English animal names. Anglia 30 1907.

Padelford, F. M. Old English musical terms. Bonn 1899.

Willms, J. E. Eine Untersuchung über den Gebrauch der Farbenbezeichnungen in der Poesie Altenglands. Münster 1902.

Jordan, R. Die altenglischen Säugetiernamen. Heidelberg 1903.

Ströbe, L. L. Die altenglischen Kleidernamen. Leipzig 1904.

Cortelyou, J. van Z. Die altenglischen Namen der Insekten, Spinnen- und Krustentiere. Heidelberg 1906.

Geldner, J. Untersuchungen einiger altenglischer Krankheitsnamen. 1, Würzburg 1906; 2–3, Augsburg 1907–8.

Keller, M. L. The Anglo-Saxon weapon names. Heidelberg 1906.

Köhler, J. J. Die altenglischen Fischnamen. Heidelberg 1906.

Swaen, A. E. H. Some Old English bird names. Archiv 118 1907.

Garrett, R. M. Precious stones in Old English literature. Leipzig 1908.

Klump, W. Die altenglischen Handwerkernamen. Heidelberg 1908.

Schnepper, H. Die Namen der Schiffe und Schiffsteile im Altenglischen. Kiel 1908.

Fehr, B. Die Sprache des Handels in Altengland. St Gallen 1909.

Graf, L. Landwirtschaftliches im altenglischen Wortschatz. Breslau 1909.

Jacobs, H. Die Namen der profanen Wohn- und Wirtschaftsgebäude und Gebäudeteile im Altenglischen. Kiel 1911.

Kross, T. Die Namen der Gefässe bei den Angelsachsen. Kiel 1911.

Thöne, F. Die Namen der menschlichen Körperteile bei den Angelsachsen. Kiel 1912.

Hansen, A. Angelsächsische Schmucksachen und ihre Bezeichnungen. Kiel 1913.

Matzerath, J. Die altenglischen Namen der Geldwerte, Masse und Gewichte. Bonn 1913.

Wolf, A. Die Bezeichnungen für 'Schicksal' in der angelsächsischen Dichtersprache. Breslau 1919.

Jente, R. Die mythologischen Ausdrücke im altenglischen Wortschatz: ein kulturgeschichtlich-etymologische Untersuchung. Heidelberg 1921.

Szogs, A. Die Ausdrücke für 'Arbeit' und 'Beruf' im Altenglischen. Heidelberg 1931.

Mincoff, M. K. Die Bedeutungsentwicklung der ags. Ausdrücke für 'Kraft' und 'Macht'. Leipzig 1933.

Weman, B. Old English semantic analysis and theory with special reference to verbs denoting locomotion. Lund 1933.

Bäck, H. The synonyms for 'child', 'boy', 'girl' in Old English: an etymological-semasiological investigation. Lund 1934.

Stibbe, H. 'Herr' und 'Frau' und verwandte Begriffe in ihren altenglischen Äquivalenten. Heidelberg 1935.

Gramm, W. Die Körperpflege der Angelsachsen. Heidelberg 1938.

Beer, H. Führen und Folgen, Herrschen und Beherrschtwerden im Sprachgut der Angelsachsen. Breslau 1939.

Juzi, G. Die Ausdrücke des Schönen in der altenglischen Dichtung. Zürich 1939.

Lambert, C. The Old English medical vocabulary. Proc Royal Soc of Medicine 33 1940.

Bonser, W. Anglo-Saxon medical nomenclature. Eng & Germanic Stud 4 1952.

Schubel, F. Zur Bedeutungskunde altenglischer Wörter mit christlichem Sinngehalt. Archiv 189 1953.

Stolzmann, P. Die angelsächsischen Ausdrücke für 'Tod' und 'Sterben': ihr Vorstellungsgehalt und dessen Ursprung. Erlangen 1953.

König, G. Die Bezeichnungen für 'Farbe', 'Glanz' und 'Helligkeit' im Altenglischen. Mainz 1957.

Bähr, D. Ae. *œðele* und *freo*: ihre Ableitungen und Synonyma im Ae. und Me. Berlin 1959.

Benning, H. A. 'Welt' und 'Mensch' in der altenglischen Dichtung. Bochum 1961.

Ostheeren, K. Studien zum Begriff der 'Freude' und seinen Ausdrucksmitteln in altenglischen Texten. Heidelberg 1964.

Schabram, H. Superbia: Studien zum altenglischen Wortschatz, Teil 1: die dialektale und zeitliche Verbreitung des Wortguts. Munich 1965.

Weimann, K. Der Friede im Altenglischen: eine bezeichnungsgeschichtliche Untersuchung. Bonn 1966.

Kühlwein, W. Die Verwendung der Feindseligkeitsbezeichnungen in der altenglischen Dichtersprache. Neumünster 1967.

Büchner, G. Vier altenglische Bezeichnungen für Vergehen und Verbrechen (*firen, gylt, man, scyld*). Berlin 1968.

Old English Texts
(in alphabetical order)

See also Loan-Words, col 163, below.

Meissner, P. Studien zum Wortschatz Aelfrics. Archiv 165–6 1934–5. *See Schabram 1969, col 150, above.*

Lenz, P. Der syntaktische Gebrauch der Partikel *ge* in den Werken Alfreds des Grossen. Darmstadt 1886.

Bloomfield, L. Notes on the preverb *ge-* in Alfredian English. In Studies in English philology: a miscellany in honor of Frederick Klaeber, Minneapolis 1929.

Schlepper, E. Die Neubildung von Substantiven in den Übersetzungen König Alfreds, mit einem Ausblick auf Chaucer. Gütersloh 1936.

Linke, G. Zur Präposition *betweoh* und zum Zahlwort *tuwa* im ags. Beda. Archiv 173 1938.

—— Grammatische und phraseologische Tautologie im ae. Beda. Archiv 175 1939.

Kuhn, S. M. Synonyms in the Old English Bede. JEGP 46 1947.

Campbell, J. J. The dialect vocabulary of the Old English Bede. JEGP 50 1951.

Bammesberger, A. Zu altenglisch *-faerae* in Bedas Sterbespruch. Zeitschrift für Vergleichende Sprachforschung 85 1971.

Schemann, K. Die Synonyma im Beowulfsliede. Münster 1882.

Banning, A. Die epischen Formeln im Beowulf, 1 Teil: die verbalen Synonyma. Marburg 1886.

Sonnefeld, G. Stilistisches und Wortschatz im Beowulf. Strasbourg 1893.

Kistenmacher, R. Die wörtlichen Wiederholungen im Beowulf. Greifswald 1898.

Scheinert, M. Die Adjektiva im Beowulfepos als Darstellungsmittel. Beiträge zur Geschichte der Deutschen Sprache und Literatur 30 1905.

Menner, R. J. The Anglian vocabulary of the Blickling Homilies. In Philologica: the [Kemp] Malone anniversary studies, Baltimore 1949.

Collins, R. L. Six words in the Blickling Homilies. In Philological essays: studies in Old and Middle English language and literature in honour of Herbert Dean Meritt, Hague 1970.

Ziegler, H. Der poetische Sprachgebrauch in den sogennannten Cædmonischen Dichtungen. Münster 1883.

Jansen, G. Beiträge zur Synonymik und Poetik der Dichtungen Cynewulfs. Münster 1883.

Simons, R. Cynewulfs Wortschatz. Bonn 1899.

Faiss, K. 'Gnade' bei Cynewulf und seiner Schule: semasiologisch-onomasiologische Studien zu einem semantischen Feld. Tübingen 1967.

Ross, A. S. C. Notes on some words in the Anglo-Saxon gloss to the Durham Ritual. N & Q Nov 1968. Aldrediana 11A.

—— Notes on some further words in the Anglo-Saxon gloss to the Durham Ritual. Neuphilologische Mitteilungen 73 1972. Aldrediana 11B.

Faiss, K. 'Gnade' und seine Kontexte in der altenglischen Genesis: ein Beitrag zum Problem der altenglischen Dichtersprache. Linguistics 56 1970.

Cross, J. E. Lexicographical notes on the Old English Life of St Giles and the Life of St Nicholas. N & Q Oct 1971.

Rauh, H. Der Wortschatz der altenglischen Übersetzungen des Matthaeus-Evangeliums. Berlin 1936.

Tuso, J. F. An analysis and glossary of dialectal synonymy in the Corpus, Lindisfarne and Rushworth Gospels. Linguistics 43 1968.

Lefèvre, P. Das altenglische Gedicht vom heiligen Guthlac. Anglia 6 1883. 2, Wortschatz und Phraseologie.

Geisel, I. Sprache und Wortschatz der altenglischen Guthlac-Übersetzung [prose]. Basle 1915.

Menner, R. J. The vocabulary of the Old English poems on Judgment Day. PMLA 62 1947.

Ross, A. S. C. Notes on some words in the Lindisfarne Gospels. MLR 27 1932. On *arg, draga, lufu, pinn, snīwa, givixla*.

—— Notes on some Old English words. E Studien 67 1933. On **ancum, -spere, fǽger, gedeða* in Lindisfarne gospels.

—— Notes on the method of glossing employed in the Lindisfarne Gospels. Trans Philological Soc 1933. On imitation of Latin compounds etc.

—— Aldrediana III: *sniueð*. Neuphilologische Mitteilungen 58 1957.

—— Aldrediana I: three suffixes. Moderna Språk: Language Monographs 3 1959.

—— Aldrediana II: Observations upon certain words of the Lindisfarne gloss. Zeitschrift für Vergleichende Sprachforschung 77 1961.

—— Aldrediana XIV: *felle-read*. Neuphilologische Mitteilungen 62 1961.

—— Aldrediana XV: on the vowel of nominal composition. Neuphilologische Mitteilungen 69 1968.

—— Aldrediana XXI: the correspondent of West Saxon *wunian*. Neuphilologische Mitteilungen 71 1970.

Samuels, M. L. The *ge-* prefix in the Old English gloss to the Lindisfarne Gospels. Trans Philological Soc 1949.

Hill, B. Four Anglo-Saxon compounds. RES new ser 8 1957. *all-efne, fifteig-dæg, hwit-corn, larcnæht* in Lindisfarne Gospels.

Boyd, W. J. P. Aldrediana VII: Hebraica. Eng Philological Stud 10 1967.

Hüttenbrenner, F. Probe eines metrischen Wörterbuchs für das Altenglische. E Studien 56 1922. On the Phoenix.

Tinkler, J. D. Vocabulary and syntax of the Old English version in the Paris Psalter. Hague 1971.

Schlutter, O. B. Zum Wortschatz des Regius und Eadwine Psalters. E Studien 38 1907.

Gneuss, H. Lehnbildungen und Lehnbedeutungen im Altenglischen. Berlin 1955. On Vespasian Psalter.

Scherer, G. Zur Geographie und Chronologie des angelsächsischen Wortschatzes im Anschluss an Bischof Wærferths Übersetzung der Dialoge Gregors. Berlin 1928.

Menner, R. J. Anglian and Saxon elements in Wulfstan's vocabulary. MLN 63 1948.

(4) MIDDLE ENGLISH

General

Hein, J. Über die bildliche Verneinung in der mittelenglischen Poesie. Anglia 15 1893.

Mendenhall, J. C. Aureate terms: a study in the literary diction of the 15th century. Philadelphia 1917.

Sundén, K. F. The etymology of the ME verbs *rope*, *ropele* and *rupe*. In A grammatical miscellany offered to Otto Jespersen, Copenhagen 1930.

Gerould, G. H. New evidence for Middle English *pef*. MLN 48 1933.

Krebs, K. Der Bedeutungswandel von me. *clerk* und damit zusammenhängende Probleme. Bonn 1933.

Mezger, F. Middle English *run*. PMLA 48 1933.

Fettig, A. Die Gradadverbien im Mittelenglischen. Heidelberg 1934.

Stewart, G. R. The meaning of *bacheler* in Middle English. PQ 13 1934.

Hulbert, J. R. English in manorial documents of the thirteenth and fourteenth centuries. MP 34 1936.

Adams, G. C. S. French *aumusse*, English *amice*. SP 34 1937.

Hammerschlag, J. Dialekteinflüsse im frühneuenglischen Wortschatz, nachgewiesen an Caxton und Fabyan. Bonn 1937.

Kaiser, R. Zur Geographie des mittelenglischen Wortschatzes. Leipzig 1937. *See Heltveit 1964, col 156, below.*

Behre, F. A Middle English noun *lede*. E Studies 20 1938.

— Middle English *rochine*. Studia Neophilologica 11 1938.

Whitehall, H. The etymology of Middle English *myse*. PQ 18 1939.

Wyld, H. C. Aspects of style and idiom in fifteenth-century English. E & S 26 1940.

Ekwall, E. Lexicographical and etymological notes. E Studien 23 1941.

— A twelfth-century Lollard? E Studies 28 1947. On *le Lollere* in a personal name.

— Two Middle English etymologies. In Philologica: the [Kemp] Malone anniversary studies, Baltimore 1949. On *fōn* '(a) few', *sen* Genesis & Exodus 298, 1923.

Löfvenberg, M. T. Notes on Middle English *aubel* and English dialectal *ebble*. Studia Neophilologica 14 1942.

— Contributions to Middle English lexicography and etymology. Lund 1946.

Ross, A. S. C. German *dirne*: Icelandic *perna*: Middle English *perne*. Proc Leeds Philosophical & Literary Soc: Literary and Historical Section 5 1943.

Russell, J. C. *Buzones*: an English-Latin hybrid? SP 42 1945. *See* D. W. Robertson, ibid.

Finberg, H. P. R. What is a *farleu*? N & Q 21 Feb 1948.

Donaldson, E. T. Middle English *seint*, *seinte*. Studia Neophilogica 21 1949.

Tengstrand, E. Three Middle English *bahuvrihi* adjectives. Studier i Modern Språkvetenskap 17 1949.

Rynell, A. On the origin of Middle English *rinnen*. Studier i Modern Språkvetenskap 18 1953.

Mustanoja, T. F. Middle English *with an o and an i*, with a note on two Shakespearean 'o-i' puns. Neuphilologische Mitteilungen 56 1955.

Prins, A. A. *As fer as last Ytaille*. E Studies 37 1956.

— *Loke who, what, how, when.* E Studies 43 1962.

Arngart, O. S. Middle English *wold*, *awold*. E Studies 40 1959.

Baugh, A. C. Two Middle English lexical notes. Language 27 1961. On *embose*; *double worstede*.

Bloomfield, M. W. Middle English *gladly*: an instance of linguisticism. Neuphilologische Mitteilungen 63 1962.

Oliphant, R. Middle English *bāner*. PQ 41 1962.

Hille, A. Exit Middle English *micclelic* 'multitude'—enter *þe miccle lic* 'leprosy'. E Studies 50 1969.

Scheler, M. Zur Etymologie des me. *burde*. Archiv 205 1969.

Tilander, G. Moyen anglais *gauntycule* (écrit *gountykule*). In Mélanges de philologie offerts à Alf Lombard (Etudes Romanes de Lund 18), Lund 1969.

Hoffman, D. L. *Renischsche renkes* and *runisch sauez*. N & Q Dec 1970.

Nevanlinna, S. On the origin of the Middle English adverbs *bedene* and *albedene*. Neuphilologische Mitteilungen 73 1972.

Special Studies

Word Formation

Höge, O. Die Deminutivbildungen im Mittelenglischen. Heidelberg 1906.

Booker, J. M. The French 'inchoative' suffix -*ss* and the French -*ir* conjugation in Middle English. SP 9 1912.

Jessen, T. Über die Bildung des Adverbs im Mittelenglischen. Kiel 1922.

Wehrle, O. Die hybriden Wortbildungen des Mittelenglischen 1050–1400. Freiburg 1935.

Special Classes of Words

Earle, J. English plant-names from the 10th to the 15th century. Oxford 1880.

Voltmer, B. Die mittelenglische Terminologie der ritterlichen Verwandtschafts- und Standesverhältnisse nach den höfischen Epen und Romanzen des 13 und 14 Jahrhunderts. Kiel 1911.

Snell, B. S. Some ancient building terms. Trans Philological Soc 1930.

Döll, H. Mittelenglische Kleidernamen im Spiegel literarischer Denkmäler des 14 Jahrhunderts. Giessen 1932.

Källner, R. Die Bezeichnungen für Geldwerte im Mittelenglischen. Ohlau 1934.

Fransson, G. Middle English surnames of occupation 1100–1350. Lund 1935.

Kalb, H. Die Namen der Säugetiere im Mittelenglischen. Bottrop 1937.

Serjeantson, M. S. The vocabulary of cookery in the fifteenth century. E & S 23 1937.

Arngart, O. English *cræft* 'a vessel' and some other names for vessels. E Studies 25 1943.

Thuresson, B. Middle English occupational terms. Lund 1950.

Sundby, B. Some ME occupational terms. E Studies 33 1951.

Sandahl, B. Middle English sea terms; 1, The ship's hull. Upsala 1951; 2, Masts, spars and sails, Upsala 1958.

Käsmann, H. Studien zum kirchlichen Wortschatz des Mittelenglischen 1100–1350. Tübingen 1961.

Corner, R. More fifteenth-century 'terms of association'. RES new ser 13 1962.

Mills, A. D. Some Middle English occupational terms. N & Q July 1963.

— Notes on some Middle English occupational terms. Studia Neophilologica 40 1968.

Rickenbach, M. Die Dimensionalwörter im Mittelenglischen 1250–1500. Winterthur 1963.

Norwood, J. E. Lexical changes in the preposition during the Middle English period as related to modern problems of definition. Philologica Pragensia 11 1968.

Wallner, B. A note on some Middle English medical terms. E Studies 50 1969.

Kjellmer, G. Context and meaning: a study of distributional and semantic relations in a group of Middle English words. Gothenburg 1971. On ME *folk, leod, man, nation, people, þeod.*

Ostheeren, K. Toposforschung und Bedeutungslehre: die Glanzvorstellung im Schönheitskatalog und die mittelenglischen Farbadjektive *blak* und *brown.* Anglia 89 1971.

Middle English Texts
(in alphabetical order)

See also Loan-Words, cols 163f, below.

Wallner, B. The distribution and frequency of Scandinavian and native synonyms in Kyng Alisaunder and Arthour and Merlin. E Studies 40 1959.

Bøgholm, N. Vocabulary and style of the Middle English Ancrene riwle. E Studies 19 1937.

Zettersten, A. Middle English word studies. Lund 1964. On Ancrene riwle. *See also Zettersten 1965, col 80, above.*

Turville-Petre, J. Two etymological notes: Ancrene wisse *eskibah, hond þet ilke.* Studia Neophilologica 41 1969.

Wallenberg, J. K. The vocabulary of Dan Michel's Ayenbite of inwyt. Upsala 1923.

Leisi, E. Die tautologischen Wortpaare in Caxtons Eneydos. Cambridge Mass 1947.

Brekle, H. E. Semantische Analyse von Wertadjektiven als Determinanten persönlicher Substantive in William Caxtons Prologen und Epilogen. Tübingen [1963].

Blake, N. F. Caxton's language. Neuphilologische Mitteilungen 67 1966.

Donner, M. The infrequency of word borrowings in Caxton's original writings. Eng Lang Notes 4 1967.

Kennedy, A. G. On the substantivation of adjectives in Chaucer. Lincoln Nebraska 1905.

Gross, E. von. Bildung des Adverbs bei Chaucer. Berlin 1921.

Huppe, B. F. The translation of technical terms in the Middle English Romaunt of the rose. JEGP 47 1948.

Potter, S. Chaucer's untransposable binomials. Neuphilologische Mitteilungen 73 1972.

See also under Loan-Words (French), below.

Barth, C. Der Wortschatz des Cursor mundi. Königsberg 1903.

Kivimaa, K. *Bitwix and* in Cursor mundi. Neuphilologische Mitteilungen 73 1972.

Conley, J. William Dunbar: additions to and corrections of OED and DOST. N & Q May 1968.

Foster, F. A. Some English words from Fasciculus morum. In Essays and studies in honor of Carleton Brown, New York 1940.

Kullnick, M. Studien über den Wortschatz in Sir Gawayne and the Grene Knight. Berlin 1902.

Schmittbetz, K. Das Adjektiv in Sir Gawayn and the Grene Kny3t. Anglia 32 1909.

Clark, J. W. Observations on certain differences in vocabulary between Cleanness and Sir Gawain and the Green Knight. PQ 28 1949.

— Paraphrases for 'God' in the poems attributed to the Gawain-poet. MLN 65 1950.

— The Gawain-poet and the substantival adjective. JEGP 49 1950.

Yamaguchi, H. A lexical note on the language of Sir Gawain and the Green Knight. Philologica Pragensia 8 1965. On combination of native and foreign elements.

Linke, G. Der Wortschatz des mittelengl. Epos Genesis und Exodus, mit grammatischer Einleitung. Leipzig 1935.

Tiete, G. Zu John Gowers Confessio amantis: 1, Lexikalisches. Breslau 1889.

Ross, A. S. C. The vocabulary of the records of the Grocers' company. Eng & Germanic Stud 1 1948. *See also Ross 1963, col 144, above.*

Wallner, B. Lexical matter in the Middle English translation of Guy de Chauliac. In English studies presented to R. W. Zandvoort, Amsterdam 1964 (suppl to E Studies 45 1964).

Brook, G. L. The recipes of ms Harley 2253. Leeds Stud in Eng 3 1934.

Webster, M. The vocabulary of An holy medytacion. PQ 17 1938.

Tatlock, J. S. P. Epic formulas, especially in La3amon. PMLA 38 1923.

Wyld, H. C. Studies in the diction of Layamon's Brut. Language 6 1930, 9–10 1933–4, 13 1937.

Sundén, K. F. Notes on the vocabulary of Layamon's Brut. Studia Neophilologica 14 1942.

Wülfing, J. E. Das Bild und die bildliche Verneinung im Laud-Troy-book. Anglia 27–8 1904–5.

Tilgner, E. Die aureate terms als Stilelement bei Lydgate. Berlin 1936.

Rioux, R. N. Sir Thomas Malory créateur verbal. Etudes Anglaises 12 1959.

Fife, R. H. Der Wortschatz des englischen Maundeville nach der Version des Cotton-ms Titus C xvi. Leipzig 1902.

McIntosh, A. Some words in the Northern Homily collection. Neuphilologische Mitteilungen 73 1972.

Ross, A. S. C. The rare words of the Ormulum. Eng Philological Stud 12 1970.

Clark, C. Studies in the vocabulary of the Peterborough Chronicle 1070–1154. Eng & Germanic Stud 5 1953.

Dobson, M. The vocabulary of the A-text of Piers the plowman. Anglia 33 1910.

Kittner, H. Studien zum Wortschatz William Langlands. Würzburg 1937.

Dareau, M.-G. and A. McIntosh. A dialect word in some West Midland manuscripts of the Prick of conscience. In Edinburgh studies in English and Scots, ed A. J. Aitken et al 1971. On *goben* 'stem of a tree'.

Bazire, J. The vocabulary of the metrical Life of St Robert of Knaresborough. Leeds Stud in Eng 7–8 1952.

Rynell, A. A note on *lynde(s)* in Robert Mannyng's Chronicle. Studier i Modern Språkvetenskap 19 1956.

Schneider, J. P. The prose style of Richard Rolle of Hampole. Baltimore 1906.

Dunlap, A. R. The vocabulary of the Middle English romances in tail-rhyme stanza. Delaware Notes 14th ser 36 1941.

Heltveit, T. Dialect words in The seven sages of Rome. In English studies presented to R. W. Zandvoort, Amsterdam 1964 (suppl to E Studies 45 1964). *Supplements Kaiser 1937, col 153, above.*

Bishop, H. The vocabulary of the English translation of Speculum humanae salvationis. E Studies 53 1972.

Hargreaves, H. The vocabulary of the Surtees Psalter. MLQ 17 1956.

Rynell, A. On the meaning of *foyn* and *fo* in the Towneley plays. E Studies 40 1959.

Trusler, M. The language of the Wakefield playwright. SP 33 1936.

(5) MODERN ENGLISH

General

Gerloff, W. Über die Veränderungen im Wortgebrauch in den englischen Bibelübersetzungen der Hexapla 1388–1611. Berlin 1902.

Reuning, K. Das Altertümliche im Wortschatz der Spenser-Nachahmungen des 18 Jahrhunderts. Strasbourg 1912.

Platt, J. The development of English colloquial idiom during the eighteenth century. RES 2 1926.

Jenkins, T. A. Word-studies in French and English. Philadelphia 1933.

Funke, O. Englische Sprachphilosophie im späteren 18 Jahrhundert. Berne 1934.

Reuter, O. Verb doublets of Latin origin in English. Helsinki 1936.

Branys, E. Homonyme Substantive im Neuenglischen. Bottrop 1938.

Onions, C. T. The phrase *end of one's kin*. MÆ 7 1938.
— *Die and live*. RES new ser 7 1956.

Austin, W. M. The etymology of English *big*. Language 15 1939.

Ekwall, E. English *fond* : an etymological and semasiological study. Studia Neophilologica 11 1939.

Dobson, E. J. The etymology and meaning of *boy*. MÆ 9 1940. *See also Bliss 1952, col 166, below.*
— Middle English and Middle Dutch *boye*. MÆ 12 1943.
— The word *feud*. RES new ser 7 1956.

Rubel, V. L. Poetic diction in the English renaissance. New York 1941.

Hand, W. D. A dictionary of words and idioms associated with Judas Iscariot. Berkeley 1942.

Holthausen, F. Zur neuenglischen Wortkunde. Beiblatt zur Anglia 53 1942.

Kökeritz, H. Elizabethan *che vore ye* 'I warrant you'. MLN 57 1942.

Malone, K. On the etymology of *runt*. Language 20 1944.
— On the etymology of *filch*. MLN 70 1955.
— On the etymology of *scarf*. In Papers in linguistics in honor of Léon Dostert, Hague 1967.

Behre, F. English *gal(e)*, *gol*, *goal*. Studia Neophilologica 17 1945.

Hulme, H. Manuscript material for the study of Tudor and Stuart English. MLR 41 1946.

Miles, J. Major adjectives in English poetry from Wyatt to Auden. Berkeley 1946.
— The primary language of poetry in the 1640's. Berkeley 1948.
— The primary language of poetry in the 1740's and 1840's. Berkeley 1950.
— The primary language of poetry in the 1940's. Berkeley 1951.
The last 3 reissued as The continuity of poetic language, New York 1965.

Neumann, J. H. Coleridge on the English language. PMLA 63 1948.

Partridge, E. Name into word. 1949, 1950 (rev).

Lindkvist, K. G. Studies on the local sense of the prepositions *in*, *at*, *on*, and *to* in Modern English. Lund 1950.

Erämetsä, E. A study of the word *sentimental* and of other linguistic characteristics of the eighteenth-century sentimentalism in England. Helsinki 1951.

Noyes, G. E. The beginnings of the study of synonyms in England. PMLA 66 1951.

Rudskoger, A. *Fair*, *foul*, *nice*, *proper* : a contribution to the study of polysemy. Stockholm 1952.

Nordhagen, R. *Kusmyre*, *kodriver*, *cowslip* og *paigle*. Oslo 1954.

Spies, H. Englische Geisteshaltung und sprachlicher Formgebung (snobbery, swank, cant, innuendo). In Anglo-Americana: Festschrift zum 70 Geburtstag von Leo Hibler-Lebmannsport, Vienna 1955.

— Moral, Sex und Euphemismus im neuesten Englisch. In Studies in English language and literature presented to Karl Brunner, Vienna 1957.

Flasdieck, H. M. Elisab. *faburden* 'fauxbourdon' und ne. *burden* 'refrain'. Anglia 74 1956.

Sandhagen, H. Studies on the temporal senses of the prepositions *at*, *on*, *in*, *by*, and *for* in present-day English. Upsala 1956.

Smirnitskiĭ, A. I. Leksikologiya angliĭskogo yazȳka. Moscow 1956. Lexicology of English.

Gowers, E. Some thoughts on new words. E & S new scr 10 1957.

Swensen, F. M. Zur Herkunft des engl. *gun*. Leuvense Bijdragen 46 1957.

Zimmer, W. Die neuenglische Interjektionen. Zeitschrift für Anglistik und Amerikanistik 5 1957.

Hietsch, O. Moderne englische Wortbildungselemente. In Anglistische Studien: Festschrift zum 70 Geburtstag von Friedrich Wild, Vienna 1958.

Osselton, N. E. Branded words in English dictionaries before Johnson. Groningen 1958.
— Early bi-lingual dictionaries as evidence for the status of words in English: Willem Sewel's Volkomen woordenboek der engelsche en nederduitsche taalen, revised Egbert Buys, 1766. In English studies presented to R. W. Zandvoort, Amsterdam 1964 (suppl to E Studies 45 1964).

Stubelius, S. *Airship*, *aeroplane*, *aircraft* : studies in the history of terms for aircraft in English. Gothenburg 1958.
— *Balloon*, *flying-machine*, *helicopter* : further studies in the history of terms for aircraft in English. Göteborgs Universitets Årsskrift 66 1960; also separately, Gothenburg 1960.

Sundby, B. Old English *gumstōl* > Modern English *gumble-stool*. E Studies 39 1958.

Carstensen, B. Semantische Genusdifferenzierungen im Neuenglischen. Anglia 77 1959.

Simon, I. Saxonism and the hard-words dictionaries. Revue des Langues Vivantes 26 1960.
— Saxonism old and new. Revue Belge 39 1961.

Bailey, H. W. and A. S. C. Ross. *Path*. Trans Philological Soc 1961. *See Binyon 1966, below.*

Koskenniemi, I. Studies in the vocabulary of English drama 1550–1600, excluding Shakespeare and Ben Jonson. Turku 1962.

Nosek, J. Semantic features of modern colloquial English. Zeitschrift für Anglistik und Amerikanistik 11 1963.

Utz, H. Das Bedeutungsfeld 'Leid' in der englischen Tragödie vor Shakespeare. Berne 1963.

Dolby, J. L. and H. L. Resnikoff. On the structure of written English words. Language 40 1964.

Koziol, H. Zur Entstehung von Synonymen im britischen und im amerikanischen Englisch. Orbis 13 1964.

Lehmann, W. P. On the etymology of *black*. In Taylor Starck Festschrift, Hague 1964.

Potter, S. On the etymology of *plough*. Prace Filologiczne 18 1964.

Nickel, G. Sprachlicher Kontext und Wortbedeutung im Englischen. Germanisch-romanische Monatsschrift 46 1965.

Yamada, J. Sources of the vocabulary of older Scots. Anglica (Osaka) 5 1965.

Binyon, T. Concerning the etymology of English *path*. Trans Philological Soc 1966.

Hansen, K. Rhyming slang und Reimformen im Slang. Zeitschrift für Anglistik und Amerikanistik 14 1966.

Thun, N. *Chevin*, *chavender* and *chub* : notes on English fish-names. Studia Neophilologica 38 1966.

Robinson, F. C. Advancing clothing names and the etymology of *girl*. In Studies in historical linguistics in honor of George Sherman Lane, Chapel Hill [1967]. On derivation from OE *gyrela* 'dress'.

Tucker, S. I. Protean shape: a study in eighteenth-century vocabulary and usage. 1967.
— *Enthusiasm*: a study in semantic change. Cambridge 1972.
Bliss, A. J. *Shanty* and *bother*. N & Q Aug 1968.
— *Bridge*. N & Q Nov 1969.
Foster, B. The changing English language. 1968.
Kohler, K. J. An etymological note on *ay(e)* 'yes'. Trans Philological Soc 1968.
Ross, A. S. C. *Pize-ball*. Proc Leeds Philosophical & Literary Soc: Literary and Historical Section 13 1968.
Sandahl, B. *Bittern*. Studia Neophilologica 40 1968.
Caluwé-Dor, J. de. Towards an etymology of the verb *to lie*. E Studies 50 1969.
Lockwood, W. B. Etymological miscellany. Zeitschrift für Anglistik und Amerikanistik 17 1969. On *cod*, *halibut*, *herring*, *garefowl*, *penguin*.
Bald, W.-D. and R. Quirk. A case study of multiple meaning. E & S new ser 23 1970. On *become*.
Givón, T. Notes on the semantic structure of English adjectives. Language 46 1970.
Bolinger, D. Semantic overloading: a restudy of the verb *remind*. Language 47 1971.

Special Studies

Word Formation

Gerber, E. Die Substantivierung des Adjektivs im 15 und 16 Jahrhundert. Göttingen 1895.
Rotzoll, E. Die Deminutivbildungen im Neuenglischen unter besonderer Berücksichtigung der Dialekte. Heidelberg 1910.
Müller, L. Neuenglische Kurzformbildungen. Giessener Beiträge zur Erforschung der Sprache und Kultur Englands und Nordamerikas 1 1923.
Deter, H. Alte Partizipia auf *-en*, *-ed* und *-ate*, die im modernen Englisch zu Adjektiven geworden sind. Saalfeld 1934.
Reuter, O. On the development of English verbs from Latin and French past participles. Helsinki 1934.
Behr, U. Wortkontaminationen in der neuenglischen Schriftsprache. Würzburg 1935.
Lindelöf, U. English agent-nouns with a suffixed adverb. Neuphilologische Mitteilungen 36 1935.
— English verb-adverb groups converted into nouns. Helsinki 1937.
— Some observations on the English adjective formations in *-ative* and *-atory*. Helsinki 1942.
Houtzager, M. E. Unconscious sound- and sense-assimilations. Amsterdam 1935.
Jespersen, O. A few back-formations. E Studien 70 1936.
Dike, E. B. The suffix *-ess* etc. JEGP 36 1937.
Hittmair, R. Wortbildende Kräfte im heutigen Englisch. Leipzig 1937.
Eckhardt, E. Reim und Stabreim im Dienste der neuenglischen Wortbildung. E Studien 72 1938.
Zandvoort, R. W. A note on *cacti*. E Studies 20 1938.
— On two collective functions of the nominal *s*-suffix. In Philologica: the [Kemp] Malone anniversary studies, Baltimore 1949.
Chapman, R. W. Adjectives from proper names. Oxford 1939 (Soc for Pure Eng).
Koziol, H. Imperativbildungen und Wahlspruchwörter. Germanisch-romanische Monatsschrift 27 1939.
— Zu den Reim- und Ablautbildungen im Englischen. E Studien 73 1939.
— Zur Wortbildung im Englischen. Anglia 65 1941.
— Förderung und Hemmung analoger Wortbildungen im Englischen. In Anglo-Americana: Festschrift zum 70 Geburtstag von Leo Hibler-Lebmannsport, Vienna 1955.
Thielke, K. Neuenglische Kose- und Spitznamen auf *-s*. E Studien 73 1939.
Draat, P. F. van. Reduplicatory emphasis. E Studien 74 1941.

Kirchner, G. Silbenverdoppelung ohne Vokaländerung. Anglia 65 1941.
Wentworth, H. The allegedly dead suffix *-dom* in Modern English. PMLA 56 1941.
Kruisinga, E. Diminutieve en affektieve suffixen in de germaanse talen. Mededeelingen der Nederlandsche Akademie van Wetenschappen new ser 5: Afdeeling Letterkunde pt 9 1942.
Langenfelt, G. The hypocoristic English suffix *-s*. Studia Neophilologica 14 1942.
— *Land* and *country* and equivalents. In Language and society: essays presented to Arthur M. Jensen, Copenhagen 1961.
Hatcher, A. G. Bahuvrihi in Sears-Roebuck. MLN 59 1944.
— *Twilight splendour, shoe colors, bolero brilliance*. MLN 61 1946.
— Modern English word-formation and neo-Latin. Baltimore 1951.
— An introduction to the analysis of English noun compounds. Word 16 1960.
Read, A. W. English words with constituent elements having independent semantic value. In Philologica: the [Kemp] Malone anniversary studies, Baltimore 1949.
Marchand, H. Notes on English suffixation. Neuphilologische Mitteilungen 54 1953.
— Notes on English prefixation. Neuphilologische Mitteilungen 55 1954.
— Notes on nominal compounds in present-day English. Word 11 1955.
— Compounds with locative particles as first elements in present-day English. Word 12 1956.
— Compound and pseudo-compound verbs in present-day English. Amer Speech 32 1957.
— Phonetic symbolism in English word-formation. Indogermanische Forschungen 64 1959.
— Die Länge englischer Komposita und die entsprechenden Verhältnisse im Deutschen. Anglia 78 1960.
— The categories and types of present-day English word formation: a synchronic-diachronic approach. Wiesbaden 1960, Munich 1969 (rev). *See* H. Galinsky, Gedanken zu einer neuen Darstellung der englischen Wortbildung, Die Neueren Sprachen new ser 11 1962.
— Das Wortbildungstypus *anti-aircraft* (*battery*) und Verwandtes. In Festschrift zum 75 Geburtstag von Theodor Spira, Heidelberg 1961.
— Die Ableitung desubstantivischer Verben mit Nullmorphem im Englischen, Französischen und Deutschen. Die Neueren Sprachen new ser 13 1964.
— On the analysis of substantive compounds and suffixal derivatives not containing a verbal element. Indogermanische Forschungen 70 1966. *See* R. B. Lees 1966, *below*.
— The analysis of verbal nexus substantives. Ibid.
Wölcken, F. *Skim-milk*. Anglia 73 1955.
— Entwicklungsstufen der Wortbildung aus Initialen. Anglia 75 1957.
Poldauf, I. Die Bildung der englischen Adjektiva auf *-ble*: ein Beitrag zur Theorie der synchronen Wortbildungslehre. Zeitschrift für Anglistik und Amerikanistik 7 1959.
Hansen, K. Makkaronische Sprachformen—hybride Wortbildungen. Zeitschrift für Anglistik und Amerikanistik 9 1961.
— Wortverschmelzungen. Zeitschrift für Anglistik und Amerikanistik 11 1963.
— Reim- und Ablautverdoppelungen. Zeitschrift für Anglistik und Amerikanistik 12 1964.
— Zur Analyse englischer Komposita. In Wortbildung, Syntax und Morphologie: Festschrift zum 60 Geburtstag von Hans Marchand, Hague 1968.
Ikeya, A. [A description of English derivational suffixes]. Stud in Eng Lit (Tokyo) 37 1961. In Japanese; with English summary.

Morciniec, N. Attributive word-groups in English. Kwartalnik Neofilologiczny 8 1961.

Trager, F. H. English -sion, -tion nouns. Canadian Jnl of Linguistics 7 1962.

Castelo, L. M. An inquiry into compounds and syntactic phrases. Zeitschrift für Anglistik und Amerikanistik 11 1963.

Olsson, Y. Implications and complications of the stressed suffix -el. In English studies presented to R. W. Zandvoort, Amsterdam 1964 (suppl to E Studies 45 1964).

Roey, J. van. A note on noun+noun combinations in Modern English. E Studies 45 1964.

Zimmer, K. E. Affixal negation in English and other languages. New York 1964. Suppl to Word 20: Monograph no 5.

Bareš, K. On the transformation of morphemes in present-day English. Philologica Pragensia 8 1965. On noun suffixes.

— Semantic features of quantitative prefixes in technical English. Philologica Pragensia 12 1969.

Lubbers, K. The development of -ster in Modern British and American English. E Studies 46 1965.

Lees, R. B. On a transformational analysis of compounds: a reply to Hans Marchand. Indogermanische Forschungen 71 1966.

Birenbaum, Y. English compound adjectives consisting of a noun stem plus an adjective stem. Zeitschrift für Anglistik und Amerikanistik 15 1967.

Leïzerson, O. D. Otgranichenie slozhnikh slov so vtorým komponentom 'ved' ot vneshne skhodnýkh obrazovaniĭ s substantivnými osnovami: na materiale angliĭskogo yazýka. Izvestiya Akademii Nauk SSSR: Seriya Literatury i Yazýka 26 1967. On compound adjectives with past tense forms of verbs as second elements.

Pervaz, D. Agentivni sufiks -er u savremenom engleskom jeziku. Godišnjak Filozofskog Fakulteta u Novom Sadu 12 1969. Agentive suffix -er in Modern English; with English summary.

Wojtasiewicz, O. A. A type of compound adjective in present-day English. Kwartalnik Neofilologiczny 16 1969. On compounds of noun+adjective.

Ljung, M. English denominal adjectives. Gothenburg 1970.

Gunter, R. English derivation. Jnl of Linguistics 8 1972.

Pennanen, E. Current views of word-formation. Neuphilologische Mitteilungen 73 1972.

Special Classes of Words

Fehr, B. Beiträge zur Sprache des Handels in England im 16 und 17 Jahrhundert. E Studien 42 1910.

Partridge, E. H. Slang today and yesterday. 1933, 1950 (rev).

— (ed). A dictionary of Forces slang 1939–45. 1948.

— Slang. Oxford 1940 (Soc for Pure Eng).

— A dictionary of RAF slang. 1945.

— A dictionary of the underworld. 1949 [1950].

Kühner, G. Die Intensiv-Adverbien des Frühneuenglischen. Ludwigshafen-am-Rhein 1934.

Allen, H. E. Influence of superstition on vocabulary: two related examples. PMLA 50–1 1935–6.

Matthews, W. London slang at the beginning of the xviii century. N & Q 15–29 June 1935.

— Some eighteenth-century vulgarisms. RES 13 1937.

Allen, H. B. Lay and law. JEGP 35 1936.

Dienst, A. Untersuchungen zur akademischen Berufssprache in England. Giessen 1937.

Thielke, K. Slang und Umgangssprache in der englischen Prosa der Gegenwart 1919–37. Emsdetten 1938.

Biese, Y. M. J. Some additions to the Oxford dictionary. Neuphilologische Mitteilungen 40 1939.

Burke, W. J. The literature of slang. New York 1939.

Hare, C. E. The language of field sports. 1939, 1949 (rev).

Gill, W. W. Some additions to the slang dictionaries. N & Q 1 June 1940. Replies by St V. Troubridge, 29 June 1940; by W. Jaggard, 28 Sept 1940.

Marples, M. Public school slang. 1940.

— University slang. 1950.

Philipson, U. Political slang 1750–1850. Lund 1941.

Chase, G. D. Sea terms come ashore. Maine Univ Stud 56 1942.

Taylor, A. M. The language of World War II. New York 1944, 1948 (rev).

Irving, J. Royal Navalese. 1946.

Bullock, H. Chimney-sweeping terms. N & Q 30 Oct 1948.

Phillips, G. L. Glossary of terms pertaining to the trade of chimney-sweeping. N & Q 7, 21 Aug, 18 Sept 1948, 24 June 1950.

Arthos, J. The language of natural description in eighteenth-century poetry. Univ Michigan Pbns in Lang & Lit 24 1949.

Granville, W. P. Sea slang of the twentieth century. 1949; rev as A dictionary of sailors' slang, 1962.

Hatchmann, G. H. Chimney-sweepers' terms. N & Q 16 April 1949.

— Nineteenth-century London slang. N & Q 14 Oct 1950.

Langenfelt, G. Hurly-burly, hallaloo, hullabaloo. Neuphilologische Mitteilungen 51–2 1950–1.

Tempest, P. Lag's lexicon. 1950.

Zandvoort, R. W. Wartime English. In Studies in English language and literature presented to Karl Brunner, Vienna 1957.

— [et al]. Wartime English: materials for a linguistic history of World War II. Groningen 1957.

Haschka, H. 'Actie' – 'share': eine wirtschaftslinguistische Studie. In Anglistische Studien: Festschrift zum 70 Geburtstag von Friedrich Wild, Vienna 1958.

Wirl, J. Das Affektleben des Wertpapiermarktes im Spiegel der englischen Sprache. Ibid.

Müller-Schotte, H. Nahrung und Essen im idiomatischenglischen Sprachgebrauch. Die Neueren Sprachen new ser 9 1960.

Hall, R. Some new seventeenth-century words and antedatings. N & Q Feb 1963.

— The language of logic: some unrecorded uses. N & Q May 1963.

— Some antedatings in Kantian philosophy. N & Q Aug 1970.

— Antedatings in logic. N & Q Sept 1970.

— Unnoticed terms in logic i–iii. N & Q April–June 1972.

Schneeberger, M. Das Wortfeld des Lachens und Lächelns im modernen Englisch. Winterthur 1964.

Jacobsson, U. Notes on further dialect words in Standard English. E Studies 46 1965.

Spitzbardt, H. English adverbs of degree and their semantic fields. Philologica Pragensia 8 1965.

Wagner, G. 'Frech' im heutigen Englisch. Zürich 1967.

Chiţoran, D. The semantic field of English factitive verbs. Revue Roumaine de Linguistique 14 1969.

Individual Authors and Texts
(in alphabetical order)

See also Loan-Words, cols 163f., below.

Jacobs, W. D. William Barnes: linguist. Albuquerque 1952.

Ludwig, H.-W. Die self-Komposita bei Thomas Carlyle, Matthew Arnold und Gerard Manly Hopkins: Untersuchungen zum geistlichen Gehalt einer sprachlichen Form. Tübingen 1963.

Meritt, H. [D.] The vocabulary of Sir John Cheke's partial version of the Gospels. JEGP 39 1940.

Rynell, A. Defoe's Journal of the plague year, the Lord Mayor's Orders and OED. E Studies 50 1969.

Legouis, P. Some lexicological notes and queries on Donne's Satires. Studia Neophilologica 14 1942.

Sullens, Z. R. Neologisms in Donne's English poems. Istituto Orientale di Napoli: Annali (sezione germanica) 7 1964.

Bawcutt, P. Lexical notes on Gavin Douglas's Eneados. MÆ 40 1971.

Tillotson, K. The language of Drayton's Shepheards garland. RES 13 1937.

Bately, J. M. Dryden and branded words. N & Q April 1965.

Mark, H. Die Verwendung der Mundart und des Slang in den Werken von John Galsworthy. Breslau 1936.

Wimsatt, W. K. Philosophic words: a study of style and meaning in the Rambler and Dictionary of Samuel Johnson. New Haven 1948.

Krishnamurti, S. Frequency-distribution of nouns in Dr Johnson's prose works. Bombay Univ Jnl 20 1951.

King, A. H. The language of satirized characters in Poëtaster. Lund 1941.

Pennanen, E. V. Chapters on the language in Ben Jonson's dramatic works. Turku 1951.

Rosier, J. L. The vocabulary of Ralph Lever's Arte of reason. Anglia 76 1958.

Hall, R. The diction of John Stuart Mill. N & Q Jan, March, May-June, Aug, Oct-Nov 1964, Feb, May, July, Nov 1965, Jan, Oct 1970.

Oras, A. Notes on some Miltonic usages. Tartu 1938.

Hulme, H. M. Milton's use of colloquial language in Paradise lost, with a new interpretation of drugd as oft (x, 568). MLR 64 1969.

Delcourt, J. Some aspects of Sir Thomas More's English. E & S 21 1935.

Roberts, P. Sir Walter Scott's contributions to the English vocabulary. PMLA 68 1953.

Schmidt, A. Shakespeare-Lexicon. 2 vols Berlin 1874-5; rev G. Sarrazin, 2 vols Berlin 1902.

Ekwall, E. Shakespeare's vocabulary: its etymological elements, 1. Upsala 1903.

Onions, C. T. A Shakespeare glossary. Oxford 1911, 1949 (with addns and corrections).

Kellner, L. Shakespeare-Wörterbuch. Leipzig 1922.

Schultz, J. H. A glossary of Shakespeare's hawking language. SE 18 1938.

Wilson, F. P. Shakespeare and the diction of common life. Proc Br Acad 27 1941; rptd in his Shakespearian and other studies, Oxford 1969.

Hart, A. Vocabularies of Shakespeare's plays. RES 19 1943.

— Growth of Shakespeare's vocabulary. Ibid.

Becker, D. Shakespeares Englisch und seine Erforschbarkeit mit Hilfe des New English dictionary. Sh Jb 84-6 1950.

Kökeritz, H. Shakespeare's use of dialect. Trans Yorkshire Dialect Soc pt 51 1951.

Stahl, H. Schöpferische Wortbildung bei Shakespeare? Sh Jb 90 1954.

Hulme, H. M. Shakespeare and the Oxford English dictionary: some supplementary glosses. RES new ser 6 1955.

— Explorations in Shakespeare's language: some problems of lexical meaning in the dramatic text. 1962.

Monsarrat, G. Notes sur le vocabulaire astronomique et astrologique de Shakespeare. Etudes Anglaises 13 1960.

Falconer, A. F. A glossary of Shakespeare's sea and naval terms including gunnery. 1965.

Böse, P. 'Wahnsinn' in Shakespeares Dramen: eine Untersuchung zu Bedeutungsgeschichte und Wortgebrauch. Tübingen 1966.

Salter, F. M. John Skelton's contribution to the English language. Trans Royal Soc of Canada 3rd ser 39 1945.

Padelford, F. M. Spenser's use of stour. MLQ 2 1941.

Rosier, J. L. Richard Stanyhurst and 16th-century lexical usage. Studia Neophilologica 33 1961.

Gray, M. M. Surrey's vocabulary. TLS 3 Oct 1936.

Söderlind, J. The word Lilliput. Studia Neophilologica 40 1968.

Strang, B. M. H. Swift's agent-noun formations in -er. In Wortbildung, Syntax und Morphologie: Festschrift zum 60 Geburtstag von Hans Marchand, Hague 1968.

Swaen, A. H. Walton's bockerel, bockeret. MLR 31 1936.

DeMott, B. The source and development of John Wilkins' philosophical language. JEGP 57 1958.

Funke, O. On the sources of John Wilkins' philosophical language. E Studies 40 1959.

Davis, N. The epistolary usages of William Worcester. In Studies in medieval literature and civilization: studies in memory of G. N. Garmonsway, 1969.

Miles, J. Wordsworth and the vocabulary of emotion. Berkeley 1942.

(6) LOAN-WORDS

General

Pogatscher, A. Zur Lautlehre der griechischen, Lateinischen und romanischen Lehnworte im Altenglischen. Strasbourg 1888.

Skeat, W. W. Principles of English etymology, 2nd ser: the foreign element. Oxford 1891.

Serjeantson, M. S. A history of foreign words in English. 1935.

Mathesius, V. Zur synchronischen Analyse fremden Sprachguts. E Studien 70 1936.

Craigie, W. A. The critique of pure English from Caxton to Smollet. Oxford 1946 (Soc for Pure Eng).

Price, H. T. Foreign influences on Middle English. Univ Michigan Contributions in Modern Philology 10 1947.

Danielsson, B. Studies on the accentuation of polysyllabic Latin, Greek and Romance loan-words in English with special reference to those ending in -able, -ate, -ator, -ible, -ic, -ical and -ize. Stockholm 1948.

— Native, classical or Romance? Studier i Modern Språkvetenskap 17 1949.

Sledd, J. A footnote on the inkhorn controversy. SE 28 1949.

Thorson, P. English long vowels rendering foreign short: a distinctive class of sound substitutions. JEGP 50 1951.

Ross, A. S. C. Ginger: a loan-word study. Oxford 1952.

Haschka, H. Die fremdsprachlich beeinflussten Bezeichnungsweisen in der englischen Wirtschaftsterminologie (doppelte Buchhaltung und Wechsel). Vienna 1960.

Kloss, H. Dem germanischen Erbgut freundliche Strömungen in der englischen Sprachgeschichte. Leuvense Bijdragen 50 1961.

Sekirin, V. P. Zaimstvovaniya v angliĭskom yazȳke. Kiev 1964. Loan-words in English.

Celtic

Schlutter, O. B. Altenglische Entlehnung aus dem Keltischen. Anglia 36 1912.

Ekwall, E. Zu zwei keltischen Lehnwörter im Altenglischen. E Studien 54 1920. On OE funta (in place-names), torr.

Förster, M. Keltisches Wortgut im Englischen. In Texte und Forschungen zur englischen Kulturgeschichte: Festgabe für Felix Liebermann, Halle 1921; also separately, Halle 1921.

— Englisch-keltisches. E Studien 56 1922.

— Altenglisch stōr : ein altirisches Lehnwort. E Studien 70 1936.

— Der Flussname Themse und seine Sippe: Studien zur Anglisierung keltischer Eigennamen und zur Lautchronologie des Altbritischen. Munich 1941.

Preusler, W. Keltischer Einfluss im Englischen. Indogermanische Forschungen 56-7 1938-40; Anglia 66 1942; Revue des Langues Vivantes 22 1956.

Jackson, K. Language and history in early Britain. Edinburgh 1953.

Lewy, E. Zu den irisch-englischen Beziehungen. Neuphilologische Mitteilungen 57 1956.

Thomson, R. L. Aldrediana V: Celtica. Eng & Germanic Stud 7 1961.
—— The Celtic element in the English vocabulary. Univ of Leeds Rev 8 1963.
Lockwood, W. B. On Celtic loan words in Modern English 1–2. Zeitschrift für Anglistik und Amerikanistik 13 1965, 16 1968.
Wakelin, M. F. *Crew, cree* and *crow*: Celtic words in English dialect. Anglia 87 1969.

Dutch

Bense, J. F. A dictionary of the Low-Dutch element in the English vocabulary. Hague and Oxford 1926–39.
Toll, J. M. Niederländisches Lehngut im Mittelenglischen. Halle 1926.
Logeman, H. Low-Dutch elements in English. Neophilologus 16 1931.
Clark, G. N. The Dutch influence on the English vocabulary. Oxford 1935 (Soc for Pure Eng).
Llewellyn, E. C. The influence of Low Dutch on the English vocabulary. 1936.
Frankis, P. J. Flemish words in a fifteenth-century English poem. N & Q Jan 1963.
Blake, N. F. Some Low Dutch loan-words in fifteenth-century English. N & Q July 1969.
Murison, D. The Dutch element in the vocabulary of Scots. In Edinburgh studies in English and Scots, ed A. J. Aitken et al 1971.

French

Behrens, D. Beiträge zur Geschichte der französischen Sprache in England, 1: zur Lautlehre der französischen Lehnwörter im Mittelenglischen. Französische Studien (Heilbronn) 5 1886.
—— Französische Elemente im Englischen. In H. Paul, Grundriss der germanischen Philologie vol 1, Strasbourg 1891.
Sykes, F. H. French elements in Middle English. Oxford 1899.
Vising, J. Franska språket i England. 3 pts Gothenburg 1900–2.
Hoevelmann, K. Zum Konsonantismus der altfranzösischen Lehnwörter in der mittelenglischen Dichtung des 14 und 15 Jahrhunderts. Kiel 1903.
Remus, H. Die kirchlichen und speziellwissenschaftlichen romanischen Lehnworte Chaucers. Halle 1906.
Faltenbacher, H. Die romanischen, speziell französischen und lateinischen (bezw. latinisierten) Lehnwörter bei Caxton. Munich 1907.
Mettig, R. Die französischen Elemente im Alt- und Mittelenglischen 800–1258. E Studien 41 1910; also separately, Marburg 1910.
Reismüller, G. Romanische Lehnwörter (Erstbelege) bei Lydgate. Leipzig 1911.
Brüll, H. Untergegangene und veraltete Worte des Französischen im heutigen Englisch. Halle 1913.
Noejd, R. The vocalism of Romanic words in Chaucer. Upsala 1919.
Funke, O. Zur Wortgeschichte der französischen Elemente im Englischen. E Studien 55 1921.
Luick, K. Über die Betonung der französischen Lehnwörter im Mittelenglischen. Germanisch-romanische Monatsschrift 9 1921.
Bush, S. H. Old Northern French loan-words in Middle English. PQ 1 1922.
Slettengren, E. Contributions to the study of French loan-words in Middle English. Örebro 1932–. Only Pt 1: O.F. *ö* < *ue* and its variants in Anglo-French and Middle English.
Ksoll, A. Die französischen Lehn- und Fremdwörter in der englischen Sprache der Restaurationszeit. Breslau 1933.
Feist, R. Studien zur Rezeption des französischen Wortschatzes im Mittelenglischen. Leipzig 1934.

Baugh, A. C. The chronology of French loan-words in English. MLN 50 1935.
Eckhardt, E. Die Quantität einfacher Tonvokale in offener Silbe bei zwei- oder dreisilbigen Wörtern französischer Herkunft im heutigen Englisch (Typus x́x oder x́xx). Anglia 60 1936.
—— Der Übergang zur germanischen Betonung bei den Wörtern französischer Herkunft im Frühneuenglischen. E Studien 75 1943.
—— Der Übergang zur germanischen Betonung bei den Wörtern französischer Herkunft im Mittelenglischen. Ibid.
Koszul, A. Note sur la courbe des emprunts de l'anglais au français. Bulletin de la Faculté des Lettres de Strasbourg 15 1937.
Mersand, J. Chaucer's Romance vocabulary. New York 1937.
Reuter, O. A study of the French words in the earliest complete English prose Psalter. Helsinki 1938.
Eliason, E. The short vowels in French loan words like *city*. Anglia 63 1939.
Mackenzie, F. Les relations de l'Angleterre et de la France d'après le vocabulaire. 2 vols Paris 1939.
Brunner, K. Die Wiedergabe von französischem *ü* (*u*) im Englischen. Beiblatt zur Anglia 52 1941.
Koziol, H. Die französischen Lehnwörter in Chaucers Werken. E Studien 74 1941.
Leidig, P. Französische Lehnwörter und Lehnbedeutungen im Englischen des 18 Jahrhunderts. Bochum 1941.
Mossé, F. On the chronology of French loan-words in English. E Studies 25 1943.
Onions, C. T. The fate of French *é* in English. Oxford 1943 (Soc for Pure Eng).
Wilson, R. M. English and French in England 1100–1300. History 28 1943.
Malkiel, Y. Three Old French sources of the English *arriv-al, withdraw-al* type. JEGP 43 1944.
Pope, M. K. The Anglo-Norman element in our vocabulary. Manchester 1944.
Livingston, C. H. French *tréteau*: English *trestle*. MP 43 1946.
—— Dialectal English *pie*. MLN 73 1958. On derivation from Old Norman *pie*.
—— Old French *essüer, ressüer* in English. Romance Philology 11 1958.
—— Etymology of English *haggis*. Romance Philology 12 1959. On derivation from Old Norman *haguier*.
—— Two Anglo-French etymologies. Romance Philology 15 1962. On English *rush*, Old French *roissier*; dialectal English *douce* 'chaff'.
Hulbert, J. R. Chaucer's Romance vocabulary. PQ 26 1947.
Suggett, H. The use of French in England in the later Middle Ages. Trans Royal Historical Soc 28 1946.
Orr, J. The impact of French upon English. Oxford 1948.
—— Words and sounds in English and French. Oxford 1953.
—— Old French and Modern English idiom. Oxford 1962.
Horsman, E. A. Dryden's French borrowings. RES 26 1950.
Laugesen, A. T. Om de germanske folks kendskab til fransk sprog i middelelderen. Copenhagen 1951.
Prins, A. A. French phrases in English. Neophilologus 32 1948.
—— Two notes to the prologue of Chaucer's Canterbury tales. E Studies 30 1949. *in chyvachie* A 85; *pace* A 175.
—— Further notes on the Canterbury tales. E Studies 32 1951. *in muwe, in stuwe* A 349f.
—— French influence in English phrasing. Leyden 1952.
—— French influence in English phrasing: a supplement. E Studies 40–1 1959–60.
Bliss, A. J. Three etymological notes. Eng & Germanic Stud 4 1952. 1, *lure* and *fur*; 2, *boy* and *toy*; 3, *gyves*.

—— Vowel-quantity in Middle English borrowing from Anglo-Norman. Archivum Linguisticum 4–5 1952–3.

—— Quantity in Old French and Middle English. Archivum Linguisticum 7 1955.

—— Imparisyllabic nouns in English. Eng Philological Stud 8 1963.

Sørensen, K. On the pronunciation of recent French loan-words. E Studies 37 1956.

Käsmann, H. Zur Rezeption französischer Lehnwörter im Mittelenglischen. Anglia 76 1958.

Kökeritz, H. English *i* for Old French *ü*. In Mélanges de linguistique et de philologie: Fernand Mossé in memoriam, Paris 1959.

Storms, G. A note on Chaucer's pronunciation of French *u*. E Studies 41 1960.

Kenyon, B. A note on two expressions contained in the manuscript BM Royal 13 A xviii: *en le mene temps, en poynt devis*. MLR 56 1961.

Schmidt, U. Die Rezeption des *a*-nasalis romanischer Lehnwörter im Mittelenglischen und seine Weiterentwicklung in Standard u. Dialekten. Heidelberg 1963.

Lüdtke, H. Zur Etymologie von engl. *to dash* (afrz. *dachier*) und *to squash* (afrz. *escachier*). Archiv 200 1964.

Berndt, R. The linguistic situation in England from the Norman Conquest to the loss of Normandy 1066–1204. Philologica Pragensia 8 1965.

Clark, C. Ancrene wisse and Katherine group: a lexical divergence. Neophilologus 50 1966.

Dietz, K. Die Rezeption des vorkonsonantischen *l* in romanischen Lehnwörtern des Mittelenglischen und seine Reflexe im neuenglischen Standard. 2 vols Munich 1968.

Derolez, R. A chronic case of linguistic indigestion? Revue des Langues Vivantes 35 1969.

Kristensson, G. Studies on Middle English local surnames containing elements of French origin. E Studies 50 1969.

Zettersten, A. French loan-words in the Ancrene riwle and their frequency. In Mélanges de philologie offerts à Alf Lombard (Etudes Romanes de Lund 18), Lund 1969.

Foster, B. English *jaw*: a borrowing from French. Neuphilologische Mitteilungen 71 1970. Footnote by B. Woledge, ibid. On derivation from Old French *joe* 'cheek'.

Muir, M. A. and P. J. C. Field. French words and phrases in Sir Thomas Malory's Le morte Darthur. Neuphilologische Mitteilungen 72 1971.

Pennanen, E. V. On the introduction of French loan-words into English. Acta Universitatis Tamperensis A 38 1971.

Latin

MacGillivray, H. S. The influence of Christianity on the vocabulary of Old English: pt 1 (first half). Halle 1902.

Dellit, O. Über lateinische Elemente im Mittelenglischen. Marburg 1905.

Metzger, E. Zur Betonung der lateinisch-romanischen Wörter im Mittelenglischen. Heidelberg 1908.

Pogatscher, A. Zur Behandlung von lat. *ų* in altenglischen Lehnwörtern. In Untersuchungen und Quellen zur germanischen und romanischen Philologie Johann von Kelle dargebracht, 1 (Prager Deutsche Studien 8), Prague 1908.

Luick, K. Zu den lateinischen Lehnwörtern im Altenglischen. Archiv 126 1911.

Kern, J. H. Zum Vokalismus einiger Lehnwörter im Altenglischen. Anglia 37 1913. 1, Zur Vertretung von lat. *ǫ*; 2, Zu ae. *Crīst*.

Funke, O. Die gelehrten lateinischen Lehn- und Fremdwörter in der altenglischen Literatur von der Mitte des x Jahrhunderts bis um des Jahr 1066. Halle 1914.

Trnka, B. Germánský přízvuk a anglická slova přejatá z latiny. Sborník Filologický 10 1935. Germanic stress and Latin loan-words in English; with English summary.

Fowler, G. H. Notes on the pronunciation of medieval Latin in England. History 22 1937.

Pyles, T. The pronunciation of Latin learned loan-words and foreign words in Old English. PMLA 58 1943.

Johnson, F. R. Latin versus English: the sixteenth-century debate over scientific terminology. SP 41 1944.

Ross, A. S. C. A note on 'philological Lautersatz'. Studia Neophilologica 30 1958. Discusses OE *mæsse*.

Ericson, E. E. English assumed singulars from Latin borrowings. Duquesne Stud: Philological Ser 5 1964.

Gamillscheg, E. Zur Geschichte der lateinischen Lehnwörter im Westgermanischen. In Wortbildung, Syntax und Morphologie: Festschrift zum 60 Geburtstag von Hans Marchand, Hague 1968.

Stuckert, K. Untersuchungen über das Verhältnis von Präfix und postverbaler Partikel bei lateinischen Lehnverben im Englischen, dargestellt an den Gruppen der *ad*- und *dis*-Komposita. Zürich 1968.

Scandinavian

Brate, E. Nordische Lehnwörter im Ormulum. Halle 1884.

Sarrazin, G. Altnordisches im Beowulfliede. Beiträge zur Geschichte der Deutschen Sprache und Literatur 11 1886.

Wall, A. A contribution towards the study of the Scandinavian element in the English dialects. Anglia 20 1898.

Björkman, E. Scandinavian loan-words in Middle English. Halle 1900–2.

Ekwall, E. How long did the Scandinavian language survive in England? In A grammatical miscellany offered to Otto Jespersen, Copenhagen 1930.

—— Middle English *o bon*. Meijerbergs Arkiv för Svensk Ordforskning 2 1939.

Olszewska, E. S. Illustrations of Norse formulas in English. Leeds Stud in Eng 2 1933.

—— Types of Norse borrowing in Middle English. Sagabook 11 1935.

—— Legal borrowings from Norse in Old and Middle English. Ibid.

—— Some English and Norse alliterative phrases. Sagabook 12 1945.

Thorson, P. Anglo-Norse studies: an inquiry into the Scandinavian elements in the Modern English dialects. Amsterdam 1936.

Behre, F. Middle English *hāk*, a Scandinavian loan-word. Meijerbergs Arkiv för Svensk Ordforskning 2 1939.

—— Two Middle English words of Scandinavian origin. Studia Neophilologica 14 1942. On *stoke* 'flee', *in waght* 'in suspense, doubt' in Thomas Castleford's Chronicle.

—— A Middle English rhyme-pair: further studies in Scandinavian origins. E Studies 40 1959. On *ouse* 'empty': *trouse* 'cup, ladle' in Thomas Castleford's Chronicle.

—— Three dialect words in Middle English verse. In Septentrionalia et orientalia: studia Bernhardo Karlgren dedicata (Kungl. Vitterhets Historie och Antikvitets Akademiens Handlingar 91), Stockholm 1959. On *in state* 'got, fell into', *ga of* 'give heed to', *etheer* 'in a more lordly way' in Thomas Castleford's Chronicle.

Ross, A. S. C. Four examples of Norse influence in the Old English gloss to the Lindisfarne Gospels. Trans Philological Soc 1940.

—— Old Norse diphthongs in English. Acta Philologica Scandinavica 14 1940.

Onions, C. T. Middle English *wrabbe, wrobbe*. MÆ 10 1941. On connection with Icelandic and Norwegian *rabba* 'babble'.

—— Middle English *gawne*. MÆ 21–2 1952–3. On derivation of *gawne* in Towneley plays from Old Norse *gagna* 'be of use, avail', and on English derivatives of Old Norse *gagn*(-), *gegn*.

Rynell, A. The rivalry of Scandinavian and native synonyms in Middle English, especially *taken* and *nimen*. Lund 1948.

Sperber, H. Etymology of the verb *sock*. Language 28 1952. On derivation from Old Norse *søkkva*.

Hofmann, D. Nordisch-englische Lehnbeziehungen der Wikingerzeit. Copenhagen 1955.

Kalugina, E. I. K voprosu ob assimilatsii skandinavskikh zaimstvovanii v angliiskom yazýke: na materiale sredneangliiskogo perioda. Uchenýe Zapiski Leningradskogo Ordena Lenina Gosudarstvennogo Universiteta im. A. A. Zhdanova 262 1958. On assimilation of Scandinavian loan-words in ME.

Kolb, E. English light on the Scand. assimilation of *ht* > *tt*. E Studies 43 1962. *See Roe 1967, below*.

— Skandinavisches in den nordenglischen Dialekten. Anglia 83 1965.

— The Scandinavian loanwords in English and the date of the West Norse change *mp* > *pp*, *nt* > *tt*, *nk* > *kk*. E Studies 50 1969.

Sandahl, B. On Old Norse *jó*, *jú* in English. Studia Neophilologica 36 1964.

Roe, H. A. A note on loanwords from Old Norse. E Studies 48 1967. On OE *ht* for Old Norse *tt*.

Kristensson, G. Middle English *scuter signe*. Neuphilologische Mitteilungen 71 1970.

Other Languages

Praz, M. The Italian element in English. E & S 15 1929.

Taylor, W. Arabic words in English. Oxford 1933 (Soc for Pure Eng).

— Arabic words in Ben Jonson. Leeds Stud in Eng 3 1934.

Bensly, E. Scientific words from the Greek. N & Q 20 Jan 1934.

Carr, C. T. The German influence on the English vocabulary. Oxford 1934 (Soc for Pure Eng).

— Some notes on German loan-words in English. MLR 35 1940.

Dayrush, A. A. Persian words in English. Oxford 1934 (Soc for Pure Eng). Includes R. C. Goffin, Some notes on Indian English.

Gatenby, E. V. Additions to Japanese words in English. Stud in Eng Lit (Tokyo) 14 1934.

Taube, E. German influence on the English vocabulary in the nineteenth century. JEGP 39 1940.

Barfield, O. Greek thought in English words. E & S new ser 3 1950.

Simpson, P. The Elizabethan pronunciation of accented Greek words. MLR 45 1950.

Subba Rao, G. Indian words in English. Oxford 1954.

Krumpelmann, J. T. *Spoon = Löffel*. Archiv 191 1955.

Marcus, H. Orientalisches Wortgut im Englischen. Ibid.

Panten, G. Die Amerikanismen im Manchester Guardian Weekly 1948–54. Munich 1959.

Enkvist, N. E. New words in Roger Barlow's Brief summe of geographie (1541). Eng Philological Stud 8 1963.

Dziedzic, Z. A. English borrowings from the terminology of Greek rhetoric: a supplement to the Oxford English dictionary. Kwartalnik Neofilologiczny 15 1968.

Stanforth, A. W. Deutsch-englischer Lehnwortaustausch. In Wortgeographie und Gesellschaft [Festgabe für Ludwig Erich Schmitt], Berlin 1968.

T. F. H.

E. PLACE AND PERSONAL NAMES

(1) BIBLIOGRAPHIES

Roberts, R. J. Bibliography of writings on English place- and personal names. Onoma 8 1959. To 1959.

Roberts, R. J., K. Jackson and W. F. H. Nicolaisen. Bibliographia onomastica 1960–1: Great Britain. Onoma 10–11 1963–4.

Jackson, K., W. F. H. Nicolaisen and M. Richards. Bibliographia onomastica 1962: Great Britain. Onoma 12 1967.

Jackson, K. and W. F. H. Nicolaisen. Bibliographia onomastica 1963: Great Britain. Onoma 13 1968.

Mills, A. D., K. Jackson and W. F. H. Nicolaisen.

Bibliographia onomastica 1964–5: Great Britain. Onoma 14 1969.

Mills, A. D. Bibliography for 1967–8. Jnl of Eng Place-Name Soc 1–2 1969–70.

— Bibliographia onomastica 1966–8: English (a) British English. Onoma 15 1970.

Jameson, J. and M. E. Traylen. Bibliography for 1969. Jnl of Eng Place-Name Soc 3 1971.

Hubble, J. and M. E. Traylen. Bibliography for 1970. Jnl of Eng Place-Name Soc 4 1972.

(2) PLACE-NAMES

General Studies

Leo, H. A treatise on the local nomenclature of the Anglo-Saxons. 1852.

Taylor, I. Words and places. 1864.

Wagner, L. Names and their meaning: a book for the curious. 1892.

— More about names. 1893.

Binz, G. Zeugnisse zur germanischen Sage in England. Beiträge zur Geschichte der Deutschen Sprache und Literatur 20 1895.

Miller, T. Place-names in the English Bede. Strasbourg 1896.

Jellinghaus, H. Englische und niederdeutsche Ortsnamen. Anglia 20 1898.

Middendorf, H. H. B. Altenglisches Flurnamenbuch. Halle 1902.

Stolze, M. Zur Lautlehre der altenglischen Ortsnamen im Domesday Book. Berlin 1902.

Zachrisson, R. E. A contribution to the study of Anglo-Norman influence on English place-names. Lund 1909.

— Some instances of Latin influence on English place-nomenclature. Lund 1910.

— The French definite article in English place-names. Anglia 34 1911.

— Two instances of French influence on English place-names. Studier i Modern Språkvetenskap 5 1914.

— English place-names in *-ing* of Scandinavian origin. Upsala 1924.

— English place-names and river-names containing the primitive Germanic roots *vis, *vask. Upsala 1926.

— Five years of English place-name study 1922–7: a critical survey. E Studien 62 1927.

— Romans, Kelts and Saxons in Ancient Britain. Upsala 1927.

— English place-name puzzles: a methodical investigation into the question of personal names or descriptive words in English place-names. Studia Neophilologica 5 1933.

— The meaning of English place-names in the light of the terminal theory. Studia Neophilologica 6 1934.

— English place-name compounds containing descriptive nouns in the genitive. E Studien 70 1935.

— Some identifications of place-names in Old English charters. Namn och Bygd 23 1935.

— Engelska ortnamn och engelsk historia. Ortnamns-sällskapets i Upsala Årsskrift 1 1936.

— Full-names and short-names in Old English place-names. Studia Neophilologica 8 1936.

— The non-Germanic element in Old English place-names. In Actes du quatrième Congrès International de Linguistes, Prague 1936.

— Studies in the -ing suffix in Old English place-names. Studia Neophilologica 9 1937.

Bradley, H. Dialect in English place-names. E & S 1 1910; in his Collected papers, Oxford 1928.

McClure, E. British place-names in their historical setting. 1910.

Alexander, H. The particle -ing in place-names. E & S 2 1911.

Lindkvist, H. Middle English place-names of Scandinavian origin. Uppsala 1912.

Cornelius, H. Die englischen Ortsnamen auf -wick, -wich. Studien zur Englischen Philologie 50 1913.

Ekwall, E. Die Ortsnamenforschung ein Hilfsmittel für das Studium der englischen Sprachgeschichte. Germanisch-romanische Monatsschrift 5 1913.

— Contributions to the study of Old English dialects, Lund 1917.

— Scandinavians and Celts in the North West of England. Lunds Universitets Årsskrift new ser 14 1918.

— English place-names in -ing. Lund 1923, 1962 (rev).

— An Old English sound change and some English forest names. Anglia Beiblatt 36 1925.

— Ablaut in Flussnamen. Ibid.

— English river names. Oxford 1928.

— Studies on English place and personal names. Lund 1931.

— The English place-names Drayton, Draycot, Dran etc. Namn och Bygd 20 1932.

— Names of trades in English place-names. In Historical essays in honour of James Tait, Manchester 1933.

— Grim's ditch. In Studia germanica tillägnade E. A. Kock, Lund 1934.

— Some notes on English place-names containing names of heathen deities. E Studien 70 1935.

— Some notes on English place-names containing tribal names. Namn och Bygd 24 1936.

— Studies on English place-names. Stockholm 1936.

— Some English place-name etymologies. Studia Neophilologica 10 1938.

— The place-name Lingfield. Anglia 63 1939.

— Some notes on place-names in Middle English writings. In Studies for William A. Read, Baton Rouge 1940.

— Nordiska ord belysta av engelska ortnamn. Meijerbergs Arkiv för Svensk Ordforskning 3 1941.

— Comparative place-name study. In Proceedings of third International Congress of Toponymy and Anthroponymy, Louvain 1951.

— Tribal names in English place-names. Namn och Bygd 41 1953.

— English place-name elements. Namn och Bygd 45 1957.

— Etymological notes on English place-names. Lund 1959.

— Variation and change in English place-names. Lund 1962.

— A problem of Old Mercian phonology in the light of West Midland place-names. Namn och Bygd 51 1963.

— Selected papers. Lund 1963. 21 rptd articles, many on place-names.

— Old English wīc in place-names. Lund 1964.

— Some cases of variation and change in English place-names. E Studies 45 1964.

— A note on OE bece 'brook, valley' in place-names. Namn och Bygd 53 1965.

Mawer, A. Some unconsidered elements in English place-names. E & S 4 1913.

— Animal and personal names in Old English place-names. MLR 14 1919.

— Early Northumbrian history in the light of place-names. Archaeologia Aeliana 18 1921.

— Place-names and history. Liverpool 1922.

— The chief elements used in English place-names. Cambridge 1924.

— Problems of place-name study. Cambridge 1929.

— The Scandinavian settlements in England as reflected in English place-names. Acta Philologica Scandinavica 7 1932.

— The study of field-names in relation to place-names. In Historical essays in honour of James Tait, Manchester 1933.

— English place-names and English philology. Trans Philological Soc 1937.

— Place-names and archaeology. Antiquity 1 1937.

— Place-names and history. Lincolnshire Mag 4 1939.

Moorman, F. W. English place-names and Teutonic sagas. E & S 5 1914.

Brandl, A. Zur Geographie der altenglischen Dialekt. Berlin 1915.

Walker, B. Interchange and substitution of second elements in place-names. E Studien 51 1918.

Crawford, O. G. S. Celtic place-names in England. Archaeological Jnl 77 1920.

— Place-names. Archaeological Jnl 78 1921.

Langenfelt, G. Toponymics or derivations from local names in English. Upsala 1920.

— De engelska grevskapens namn. Namn och Bygd 39 1951.

— The OE suffix ingas in non-Germanic folknames. Namn och Bygd 46 1958.

— Foreign names in Old English: a comparison between Alfred's 'Orosius' and 'Widsith'. Neuphilologische Mitteilungen 72 1961.

— Some Widsith names and the background of Widsith. Kongressberichte München 3 1961.

Bugge, A. The Norse settlements in the British Islands. Trans Royal Historical Soc 4th ser 4 1921.

Ritter, O. Vermischte Beiträge zur englischen Sprachgeschichte. Halle 1922.

Förster, M. Keltisches Wortgut im Englischen. Halle 1921.

— Die Etymologien des Namens Edinburgh. Anglia 64 1940.

— Der Flussname Themse und seine Sippe. Munich 1941.

Mawer, A. and F. M. Stenton. Introduction to the survey of English place-names: I, W. J. Sedgefield, Methods of place-name study; II, E. Ekwall, The Celtic element; III, F. M. Stenton, The English element; IV, E. Ekwall, The Scandinavian element; V, R. E. Zachrisson, The French element; VI, J. Tait, The Feudal element; VII, H. C. Wyld: Place-names and English linguistic studies; VIII, O. G. S. Crawford, Place-names and archaeology; IX, F. M. Stenton, Personal names in English place-names. Cambridge 1924.

Anglica: Untersuchungen zur englischen Philologie, Alois Brandl überreicht. Leipzig 1925.

Smith, A. H. Some place-names and the etymology of 'she'. RES 1 1925.

— Danes and Norwegians in Yorkshire. Saga-book 10 1929.

— Analogical development of -ing and the interpretation of Patrington. Leeds Stud in Eng 5 1936.

— Stress-shifting in place-names. London Mediaeval Stud 1 1937.

— The surveys of English place-names. In Proceedings of third International Congress of Toponymy and Anthroponymy, Louvain 1951.

— The preparation of county place-name surveys. 1954.

— English place-name elements. 2 vols Cambridge 1956.

— Place-names and the Anglo-Saxon settlement. 1957.

— The Hwicce? In Medieval and linguistic studies in honor of F. P. Magoun jr, New York 1965.

— Whelter. Saga-book 17 1966.

— Some place-names of the West Riding. Trans of Yorkshire Dialect Soc 1967.

Karlström, S. Old English compound place-names in -ing. Upsala 1927.

Weekley, E. Words and names. 1932.

Dickins, B. English names and Old English heathenism. E & S 19 1933.

— Latin additions to place- and parish-names of England and Wales. Proc Leeds Philosophical & Literary Soc (literary & historical section) 3 1935.

— The progress of English place-name studies since 1901. Antiquity 35 1961.

Anderson (Arngart), O. S. The English hundred-names. Lund 1934.

— The English hundred-names: the south-eastern counties. Lund 1939.

— The English hundred-names: the south-western counties. Lund 1939.

— Old English material in the Leningrad manuscript of Bede's Ecclesiastical history. Lund 1941.

— Aktuella tendenser och problem i engelsk namn-forskning. Namn och Bygd 33 1945.

— Some aspects of the relation between the English and the Danish element in the Danelaw. Studia Neophilologica 20 1948.

Magoun, F. P. Place-names in the Parker Chronicle. Harvard Stud 18 1935.

— Territorial, place- and river-names in OE Annals D-text. Harvard Stud 20 1937.

Whitehall, H. Scaitcliffe: a place-name derivation. Essays & Stud in Eng & Comparative Lit 13 1935.

Darby, H. C. (ed.) An historical geography of England before 1800. Cambridge 1936.

— Place-names and the geography of the past. In Early English and Norse studies presented to Hugh Smith, 1963.

Marcus, H. Der gegenwärtige Stand der englischen Ortsnamenforschung. Archiv 169 1936.

Charles, B. G. The substitution of Welsh sounds in place-names of English origin in the border counties of Wales. London Mediaeval Stud 1 1937.

Elmer, H. Die sächsischen Siedlungen auf dem französischen Litus saxonicum. Halle 1937.

Bestmann, F. Die lautliche Gestaltung englischer Ortsnamen im Altfranzösischen und Anglonormannischen. Zürich 1938.

Jackson, K. Nennius and the twenty-eight Cities of Britain. Antiquity 12 1938.

— On some Romano-British place-names. Jnl of Roman Stud 38 1948.

— Language and history in early Britain: a chronological survey of the Brittonic languages first to twelfth century AD. Edinburgh 1953.

— Angles and Britons in Northumbria and Cumbria. In Angles and Britons: O'Donnell lectures, Cardiff 1963.

— On the Northern British section in Nennius. In Celt and Saxon: studies in the early British border, ed N. K. Chadwick, Cambridge 1963.

— Addenda and corrigenda to the Celtic vocabulary in English Place-Name Society volumes 25 and 26: English place-name elements, parts 1 and 2. Jnl of Eng Place-Name Soc 1 1969.

— Romano-British names in the Antonine Itinerary. Britannia 1 1970.

Stenton, F. M. The historical bearing of place-name studies: England in the sixth century. Trans Royal Historical Soc 4th ser 21 1939.

— The historical bearing of place-name studies: the English occupation of Southern Britain. Trans Royal Historical Soc 4th ser 22 1940.

— The historical bearing of place-name studies: Anglo-Saxon heathenism. Trans Royal Historical Soc 4th ser 23 1941.

— The historical bearing of place-name studies: the Danish settlement of Eastern England. Trans Royal Historical Soc 4th ser 24 1942.

— The historical bearing of place-name studies: the place of women in Anglo-Saxon society. Trans Royal Historical Soc 4th ser 25 1943.

Tengstrand, E. A contribution to the study of genitival composition in Old English place-names. Upsala 1940.

— Det fornengelska ortnamnselementet wīc. Namn och Bygd 53 1965.

Forsberg, R. Topographical notes on some Anglo-Saxon charters. Namn och Bygd 30 1942.

— A contribution to a dictionary of Old English place-names. Uppsala 1950.

— English wormsteall. Namn och Bygd 48 1960.

— Hurn. Studia Neophilologica 40 1968.

— On Old English ǣd in English place-names. Namn och Bygd 58 1970.

Löfvenberg, M. T. Studies on Middle English local surnames. Lund 1942.

— Contributions to Middle English lexicography and etymology. Lund 1946.

Wainwright, F. T. Field names. Antiquity 17 1945.

— Danes and Norwegians in England. In Quatrième Congrès International de Sciences Onomastiques, Upsala 1952.

— Archaeology and place-names and history: an essay on problems of co-ordination. 1962, 1967 (rev).

Hallqvist, H. Studies in Old English fractured ea. Lund 1948.

Stokes, H. G. English place-names. 1948.

Blenner-Hassett, R. A study of the place-names in Lawman's Brut. Stanford 1950.

Rubin, S. The phonology of the Middle English dialect of Sussex. Lund 1951.

Gelling, M. Place-names as clues to history. Amateur Historian 1 1952.

— The gumstool. MLR 48 1953.

— The element hamm in English place-names: a topographical investigation. Namn och Bygd 48 1960.

— Place-names and Anglo-Saxon paganism. Univ Birmingham Historical Jnl 8 1961.

— English place-names derived from the compound wīchām. Medieval Archaeology 11 1967.

Robins, F. W. Stories in street-names. Amateur Historian 1 1954.

Dieth, E. Hips: a geographical contribution to the 'she' puzzle. E Studies 36 1955.

Munslow, F. W. Field names. Amateur Historian 2 1956.

Sawyer, P. H. The place-names of the Domesday manuscripts. Bull John Rylands Lib 38 1956.

— The density of the Danish settlement in England. Univ Birmingham Historical Jnl 6 1957.

Dodgson, J. McN. The background of Brunanburh. Saga-book 14 1956-7.

— The significance of the distribution of the English place-name in -ingas, -inga- in South-East England. Medieval Archaeology 10 1966.

— The -ing- in English place-names like Birmingham and Altrincham. Beiträge zur Namenforschung new ser 2 1967.

— Various forms of Old English -ing in English place-names. Ibid.

— Cheshire field-name elements. N & Q April 1968.

— Various English place-name formations containing Old English -ing. Beiträge zur Namenforschung new ser 3 1968.

Nicolaisen, W. F. H. Der Alteuropäischen Gewässernamen der Britischen Hauptinsel. Beiträge zur Namenforschung new ser 8 1957.

— Aspects of Scottish mountain names. In Disputationes ad montium vocabula vol 1, Vienna 1969.

—— Norse settlement in the Northern and Western Isles: some place-name evidence. Scottish Historical Rev 48 1969.

—— Some problems of chronology in southern Scotland. Onoma 14 1969.

Lehiste, I. Names of Scandinavians in the Anglo-Saxon Chronicle. PMLA 73 1958.

Sundby, B. Old English gumstōl > Modern English gumblestool: an etymological-semasiological problem. E Studies 39 1958.

—— Notes on names. E Studies 40 1959.

Cameron, K. A note on the Celtic element in English place-names. Jnl Derbyshire Archaeological Soc 79 1959.

—— English place-names. 1961.

—— Scandinavian settlement in the territory of the Five Boroughs: the place-name evidence. Nottingham 1965.

—— Eccles in English place-names. In Christianity in Britain 300–700, Leicester 1968.

—— Addenda and corrigenda to English Place-Name Society volumes 25 and 26: English place-name elements parts 1 and 2. Jnl of Eng Place-Name Soc 1 1969.

—— The two Viking ages of Britain, a discussion: linguistic and place-name evidence. Mediaeval Scandinavia 2 1969.

—— Maps and the study of place-names. Bull Soc of Univ Cartographers 4 1970.

—— Scandinavian settlement in the territory of the Five Boroughs: the place-name evidence, part II, place-names in Thorp. Mediaeval Scandinavia 3 1970.

—— Scandinavian settlement in the territory of the Five Boroughs: the place-name evidence, part III, the Grimston-hybrids. In England before the Conquest, Cambridge 1971.

Cawley, A. C. Hippological proper names. Trans Yorkshire Dialect Soc 10 1959.

Wrenn, C. L. Saxons and Celts in South-west Britain. Trans Hon Soc of Cymmrodorion 1959.

Janzén, A. Are there so-called inversion compounds in Yorkshire place-names? Namn och Bygd 48 1960.

—— Scandinavian place-names in England i–vii. Names 5–8 1957–60, 10–12 1962–4.

—— The Viking colonization of England in the light of place-names. Names 20 1972.

Reaney, P. H. The origin of English place-names. 1960.

Jensen, K. B. Altindogermanische Ortsnamen in Südengland. Kongressberichte München 2 1961.

—— The blending of languages in the place-names of the north-east of England. Onoma 14 1969.

Pearsall, W. H. Place-names as clues in the pursuit of ecological history. Namn och Bygd 49 1961.

Roberts, R. J. Some early uses and abuses of English onomastics. Kongressberichte München 3 1961.

Tolstoy, N. Nennius, chapter fifty-six. Bull Board of Celtic Stud 19 1961.

Jensen, G. F. Some observations on Scandinavian personal names in English place-names. Saga-book 16 1962.

—— The scribe of the Lindsey Survey. Namn och Bygd 57 1969.

—— The Domesday Book account of the Bruce Fief. Jnl of Eng Place-Name Soc 2 1970.

Copley, G. J. Names and places. 1963.

—— English place-names and their origins. Newton Abbot 1968.

Sandred, K. I. English place-names in -stead. Upsala 1963.

—— En fornengelsk gränsbeskrivning. Namn och Bygd 53 1965.

—— Strövtåg bland engelska, särskilt-kentiska ägonamn. Ortnamnssällskapets i Uppsala Årsskrift 1965.

—— Notes on English compound place-names in -hamstede. Namn och Bygd 55 1967.

—— The derivative suffix -et, -ett(e). Namn och Bygd 55 1967.

—— Äkta och oäkta sta-namn, Sta-namnens förleder, Den ursprungliga innebörden av ortnamnselementet -sta. In En diskussion om sta-namnen, ed G. Holm, Lund 1967.

—— Beachampstead: a complicated place-name in Huntingdonshire. E Studies 50 1969.

Sørensen, H. S. The meaning of proper names, with a definiens formula for proper names in modern English. Copenhagen 1963.

Hamlin, R. Les éléments français dans la toponymie anglaise. Revue Internationale d'Onomastique 16 1964.

Hogg, A. H. A. The survival of Romano-British place-names in Southern Britain. Antiquity 38 1964.

Laur, W. Ortsnamen in England und in den festländischen Stammlanden der Angelsachsen. In Namenforschung: Festschrift Adolf Bach, Heidelberg 1964.

—— Namenübertragungen im Zuge der angelsächsischen Wanderungen. Beiträge zur Namenforschung 15 1964.

Olsson, I. Om engelska ortnamn på -stead och gotländska på -städe. Ortnamnssällskapets i Uppsala Årsskrift 1964.

Hill, B. Problems in the 'Clee' place-names of Shropshire. N & Q July 1965.

Matley, I. M. Elements of Celtic place-names. Names 13 1965.

Meaney, A. L. Woden in England: a reconsideration of the evidence. Folklore 77 1966.

Ogden, T. L. Coldharbours and Roman roads. Durham Univ Jnl 1966.

Franzen, G. Sv. Gertre och eng. Gartree. Namn och Bygd 55 1967.

Hekket, B. J. A reconsideration of the etymologies of Daventry and Deventer. Mededelingen van de Vereniging voor Naamkunde te Leuven en de Commissie voor Naamkunde te Amsterdam 43 1967.

Ramsey, I. A. R. J. The history of technology in place-names. Amateur Historian 7 1967, Local Historian 8 1968.

Cox, J. S. Identification of fictitious place-names in Hardy's works. St Peter Port 1968.

Ejder, B. Modern field-name research. Onoma 13 1968.

Zabeeh, F. What is in a name? Hague 1968.

Adams, J. H. Bos and Lan names. Devon & Cornwall N & Q 31 1969.

Hamp, E. P. Early Welsh names, suffixes and phonology. Onoma 14 1969.

Hutton, K. Streets called '-gate'. Local Historian 8 1969.

Kristensson, G. Studies on Middle English local surnames containing elements of French origin. E Studies 50 1969.

—— Studies on Middle English topographical terms. Lund 1970.

Long, R. B. The grammar of English proper names. Names 17 1969.

Zinkin, V. The syntax of place-names. Ibid.

Davies, C. S. and J. Levitt. What's in a name? 1970.

Fraser, I. Place-names from oral tradition: an informant's repertoire. Scottish Stud 14 1970.

Wakelin, M. F. Names for the cow house in Devon and Cornwall. Studia Neophilologica 42 1970.

Dunkling, L. English house names. 1971.

Field, J. Discovering place-names. Tring 1971.

Harley, J. B. Place-names on the early Ordnance Survey maps of England and Wales. Cartographic Jnl 8 1971.

Miller, G. M. BBC pronouncing dictionary of British names. 1971.

Seppänen, A. Proper names in a transformational grammar of English. Neuphilologische Mitteilungen 72 1971.

Hart, C. Shoelands. Jnl of Eng Place-Name Soc 4 1972.

Kirk, S. A distribution pattern: -ingas in Kent. Jnl of Eng Place-Name Soc 4 1972.

Countries and Regions
(in alphabetical order)

Gelling, M., W. F. H. Nicolaisen and M. Richards. The names of towns and cities in Britain. 1970.

Johnston, J. B. The place-names of England and Wales. 1914.

Ekwall, E. The concise Oxford dictionary of English place-names. Oxford 1936, 1960 (rev).

Reaney, P. H. Some extinct Fenland rivers. Studia Neophilologica 14 1942.

Schram, O. K. Fenland place-names. In Early cultures of north-west Europe, ed C. F. Fox and B. Dickins, Cambridge 1950.

Hogan, E. Onomasticon Goedelicum. Dublin 1910.

Joyce, P. W. Irish names of places. 2 vols Dublin 1910–13.

Flanagan, D. Ecclesiastical nomenclature in Irish texts and place-names: a comparison. In Disputationes ad montium vocabula vol 1, Vienna 1969.

Johnston, J. B. Place-names of Scotland. Edinburgh 1892, 1903, London 1934.

MacBain, A. Place-names of the Highlands and Islands of Scotland. Stirling 1922.

Watson, W. J. The history of Celtic place-names of Scotland. Edinburgh 1926.

Nicolaisen, W. F. H. Notes on Scottish place-names 1–32. Scottish Stud 2–13 1958–69.

—— The story behind the name. Scots Mag 1960–8. Monthly articles on Scottish place-names.

—— Norse place-names in south-west Scotland. Scottish Stud 4 1960.

—— Celts and Anglo-Saxons in the Scottish border counties and place-name evidence. Scottish Stud 8 1964.

—— Early spellings of Scottish place-names. In Edinburgh studies in English and Scots, ed A. J. Aitken, A. McIntosh and H. Pálsson, 1971.

Barrow, G. W. S. Rural settlement in central and eastern Scotland: the medieval evidence. Scottish Stud 6 1962.

Oftedal, M. Norse place-names in Celtic Scotland. Proc International Congress of Celtic Stud 1962.

Whittington, G. and J. H. Soulsby. A preliminary report of an investigation into pit place-names. Scottish Geographical Mag 84 1968.

Charles, B. G. Non-Celtic place-names in Wales. 1938.

Thomas, R. J. Enwau Afonydd a Nentydd Cymru. Cardiff 1938.

Davies, E. A gazetteer of Welsh place-names. Cardiff 1957, 1958 (rev).

Williams, I. Enwau Lleoedd. Liverpool 1962.

Richards, M. Some medieval township and hamlet names [in Wales]. Bull Board of Celtic Stud 20 1963.

—— The distribution of some Welsh place-names. Lochlann 3 1965.

Counties, Parts of Counties, Islands
(in alphabetical order)

Will, C. P. Place-names of north-east Angus. Arbroath 1964.

Mawer, A. and F. M. Stenton. The place-names of Bedfordshire and Huntingdonshire. Cambridge 1926.

Hutchings, J. B. Milton Ernest: a field survey. Bedfordshire Archaeological Jnl 4 1969.

Skeat, W. W. The place-names of Berkshire. Oxford 1911.

Stenton, F. M. Place-names of Berkshire. Reading 1911.

Gelling, M. The charter bounds of Æscesbyrig and Ashbury [Berkshire]. Berkshire Archaeological Jnl 63 1968.

Mawer, A. and F. M. Stenton. The place-names of Buckinghamshire. Cambridge 1925.

Reaney, P. H. The place-names of Cambridgeshire and the Isle of Ely. Cambridge 1943.

Potter, S. Cheshire place-names. Liverpool 1955.

Barnes, G. The evidence of place-names for the Scandinavian settlements in Cheshire. Trans Lancashire & Cheshire Antiquarian Soc 63 1953.

Richards, M. The River Wheelock: Cheshire Wheelock= Welsh Chwilog. Trans Historical Soc of Lancashire & Cheshire 111 1960.

Dodgson, J. McN. The English arrival in Cheshire. Trans Historical Soc of Lancashire & Cheshire 119 1967.

—— The place-names of Cheshire. 5 vols Cambridge 1970–.

Dexter, T. F. G. Cornish names. 1926.

Gover, J. E. B. Cornish place-names. Antiquity 2 1928.

—— The element ros in Cornish place-names. London Mediaeval Stud 1 1938.

Quentel, P. Quelques traits de la toponymie maritime de la Cornouaille britannique. Annales de Bretagne 57 1950.

—— Étude de toponymie cornique. Revue Internationale d'Onomastique 11 1959.

Nance, R. M. A guide to Cornish place-names, with a list of words contained in them. St Ives 1955, 1961 (rev).

Armstrong, A. M., A. Mawer, F. M. Stenton and B. Dickins. The place-names of Cumberland. 3 vols Cambridge 1950–2.

Fraser, W. Field-names in South Derbyshire. Ipswich 1947.

Wainwright, F. T. Early Scandinavian settlement in Derbyshire. Derbyshire Archaeological Soc Jnl 67 1947.

Cameron, K. The Scandinavians in Derbyshire: the place-name evidence. Nottingham Mediaeval Stud 2 1958.

—— The place-names of Derbyshire. 3 vols Cambridge 1959.

Cockerton, R. W. P. Celtic influence in Derbyshire place-names. Jnl of Derbyshire Archaeological Soc 79 1959.

Blomé, B. The place-names of North Devonshire. Upsala 1929.

Gover, J. E. B., A. Mawer and F. M. Stenton. The place-names of Devon. 2 vols Cambridge 1931–2.

Finberg, H. P. R. The place-names of Devon. Devon & Cornwall N & Q 25 1953.

Ellis, D. M. and L. E. A. Liptrott. Field names in Ilsington [Devon]. Devon & Cornwall N & Q 31 1969.

O'Kane, J. Place-names of Inniskeel and Kilteevoge [Donegal]. Zeitschrift für Celtische Philologie 31 1970.

Fägersten, A. The place-names of Dorset. Upsala 1933.

Zachrisson, R. E. The meaning of the place-names of Dorset in the light of the terminal rule. Studia Neophilologica 6 1934.

Damoney, C. R. Some Dorset place-names. Dorset Year Book 1965.

Kerr, B. Dorset field-names and the agricultural revolution. Proc Dorset Natural Historical & Archaeological Soc 82 1960.

—— Dorset fields and their names. Proc Dorset Natural Historical & Archaeological Soc 89 1967.

Taylor, C. C. Lost Dorset place-names. Proc Dorset Natural Historical & Archaeological Soc 88 1966.

Mawer, A. The place-names of Northumberland and Durham. Cambridge 1920.

—— The river-names of Northumberland and Durham. Archaeologia Aeliana 4th ser 6 1929.

Watts, V. E. The place-names of county Durham. Architectural & Archaeological Soc of Durham & Northumberland Trans 9 1965.

Reaney, P. H. The place-names of Essex. Cambridge 1935.

O'Leary, J. G. Dagenham [Essex] place-names. Dagenham 1958.

Chance, S. W. Place-names of Harlow [Essex]. Harlow 1968.

Britton, A. J. Some Chingford [Essex] field names. Trans Essex Archaeological Soc 3rd ser 2 1970.

Davies, E. Flintshire place-names. Cardiff 1959.

Pierce, G. O. The place-names of Dinas Powys Hundred [Glamorgan]. Cardiff 1968.

Smith, A. H. The place-names of Gloucestershire. 4 vols Cambridge 1964.

Ståhl, H. Ortnamnen i Gloucestershire. Namn och Bygd 53 1965.

Harris, H. C. W. Housing nomenclature in Bristol [Gloucestershire]. Bristol 1969.

Oftedal, M. Norse *steinn* in Hebridean place-names. Froðskaparrit 13 1964.

Fraser, I. A. Place-names from oral tradition in the Scottish Outer Hebrides. In Disputationes ad montium vocabula vol 1, Vienna 1969.

Taylor, A. B. The name St Kilda [Hebrides]. Scottish Stud 13 1969.

Bannister, A. T. Place-names of Herefordshire. Cambridge 1916.

Baddeley, W. St C. Herefordshire place-names. Trans Bristol & Gloucester Archaeological Soc 39 1916.

Tonkin, J. W. Early street-names of Hereford. Woolhope Naturalists' Field Club Trans 38 1966.

Gover, J. E. B., A. Mawer and F. M. Stenton. The place-names of Hertfordshire. Cambridge 1938.

Mawer, A. and F. M. Stenton. The place-names of Bedfordshire and Huntingdonshire. Cambridge 1926.

Wallenberg, J. K. Kentish place-names: a topographical and etymological study of the place-name material in Kentish charters dated before the Conquest. Upsala 1931.

— The place-names of Kent. Upsala 1934.

Reaney, P. H. A survey of Kent place-names. Archaeologia Cantiana 73 1960.

Ritter, O. Über einige Ortsnamen aus Lancashire. E Studien 54 1920.

Wyld, H. C. and T. O. Hirst. The place-names of Lancashire. 1911.

Ekwall, E. The place-names of Lancashire. Manchester 1921.

Schram, O. K. The meaning of Rochdale [Lancashire] place-names. Trans Rochdale Literary & Scientific Soc 19 1937.

Wainwright, F. T. Field-names of Amounderness Hundred [Lancashire]. Trans Historical Soc of Lancashire & Cheshire 92 1945.

— The Scandinavians in Lancashire. Trans Lancashire & Cheshire Antiquarian Soc 58 1946.

Wood, A. C. Leicestershire place-names. Trans Philological Soc 1917–20, 1932.

Hoskins, W. G. The place-names of Leicestershire. Trans Leicestershire Archaeological Soc 18 1935.

Ekwall, E. Etymological notes: 3, Some Lincolnshire place-names. Studia Neophilologica 2 1929.

Payling, L. W. H. Geology and place-names in Kesteven [Lincolnshire]. Leeds Stud in Eng & Kindred Languages 4 1935.

Hald, K. Danes and Frisians in Lincolnshire. In Proceedings of third International Congress of Toponymy and Anthroponymy, Louvain 1951.

Cameron, K. Work on place-names in Lincolnshire: a preliminary discussion. Lincolnshire Historian 2 1956.

Ekwall, E. Street-names of the City of London. Oxford 1954.

Smith, A. Dictionary of City of London street names. New York 1970.

Moore, A. W. Manx names: or the surnames and place-names of the Isle of Man. 1890, 1903 (rev).

Kneen, J. J. The place-names of the Isle of Man, with their origin and history. 2 vols Douglas 1925–9.

Gelling, M. The place-names of the Isle of Man. Jnl of Manx Museum 7 1971.

Gover, J. E. B., A. Mawer and F. M. Stenton (with S. J. Madge). The place-names of Middlesex, apart from the City of London. Cambridge 1942.

Ekwall, E. Notes on some Middlesex place-names. Studia Neophilologica 17 1945.

Curle, B. R. Kensington and Chelsea street-names [Middlesex]. 1968.

Gover, J. E. B., A. Mawer, and F. M. Stenton. The place-names of Northamptonshire. Cambridge 1933.

Karlström, S. Notes on the place-names of Northamptonshire. Namn och Bygd 22 1934.

Mawer, A. The place-names of Northumberland and Durham. Cambridge 1920.

— Early Northumbrian history in the light of its place-names. Archaeologia Aeliana 3rd ser 18 1921.

— The river-names of Northumberland and Durham. Archaeologia Aeliana 4th ser 6 1929.

Watson, G. Goodwife Hot and others [Northumberland]. Newcastle 1970.

Gover, J. E. B., A. Mawer and F. M. Stenton. The place-names of Nottinghamshire. Cambridge 1940.

Marwick, H. The place-names of Rousay [Orkney]. Kirkwall 1947.

— Orkney farm-names. Kirkwall 1952.

— The place-names of Birsay [Orkney]. Ed W. F. H. Nicolaisen, Aberdeen 1970.

Gelling, M. The place-names of Oxfordshire. 2 vols Cambridge 1953–4.

Forsberg, R. Notes on the place-names of Oxfordshire. Namn och Bygd 44 1956.

Stewart, J. Shetland farm names. In The fourth Viking Congress (York 1961), Edinburgh 1965.

Bowcock, A. B. Shropshire place-names. Shrewsbury 1923.

Hobbs, J. L. Shrewsbury street-names. Shrewsbury 1954.

Finberg, H. P. R. Three Anglo-Saxon boundaries in Shropshire. Trans Shropshire Archaeological Soc 56 1958.

Hill, J. S. The place-names of Somerset. Bristol 1914.

Turner, A. G. C. Notes on some Somerset place-names. Somerset Archaeological & Natural History Soc Proc 95 1950.

— A selection of North Somerset place-names. Somerset Archaeological & Natural History Soc Proc 96 1951.

— Some aspects of Celtic survival in Somerset. Somerset Archaeological & Natural History Soc Proc 97 1952.

Duignan, W. H. Staffordshire place-names. 1902.

— Notes on Staffordshire place-names. Oxford 1912. *See Oakden, below.*

Thompson, H. V. Scandinavian place-names in North Staffordshire. North Staffordshire Field Club Trans 51 1917.

Smith, W. Place-names of the Staffordshire-Cheshire border. North Staffordshire Field Club Trans 67 1933.

Oakden, J. P. Duigan's Notes on Staffordshire place-names: a reassessment. South Staffordshire Archaeological & Historical Soc Trans 9 1968.

Skeat, W. W. The place-names of Suffolk. Cambridge 1913.

Gover, J. E. B., A. Mawer and F. M. Stenton. The place-names of Surrey. Cambridge 1934.

Zachrisson, R. E. Descriptive words or personal names in Old English place-name compounds: a survey of some Surrey place-names. Studia Neophilologica 7 1935.

Rumble, A. R. The Merstham (Surrey) charter-bounds AD 947. Jnl of Eng Place-name Soc 3 1971.

— The medieval boundary of Coulsdon (Surrey). Jnl of Eng Place-name Soc 4 1972.

Mawer, A. and F. M. Stenton (with J. E. B. Gover). The place-names of Sussex. 2 vols Cambridge 1929–30.

Davey, L. S. The street-names of Lewes [Sussex]. Lewes 1961.

Gover, J. E. B., A. Mawer and F. M. Stenton (with F. T. S. Houghton). The place-names of Warwickshire. Cambridge 1936.

Gelling, M. Some notes on the place-names of Birmingham and the surrounding districts [Warwickshire]. Birmingham Archaeological Soc Trans 72 1956.

Harley, J. B. The settlement geography of early medieval

Warwickshire. Trans & Papers Inst of Br Geographers 1964.

Macdonald, A. The place-names of West Lothian. Edinburgh 1941.

Smith, A. H. The place-names of Westmorland. 2 vols Cambridge 1967.

Kökeritz, H. The place-names of the Isle of Wight. Upsala 1940.

Gover, J. E. B., A. Mawer and F. M. Stenton. The place-names of Wiltshire. Cambridge 1939.

Brentnall, H. C. Wiltshire place-names. Antiquity 15 1941.

Mawer, A. Some notes from Wiltshire. Studia Neophilologica 14 1942.

Thomson, T. R. Notes on the place-names of Wiltshire. Wiltshire Archaeological & Natural Historical Mag 57 1960.

— The place-names of Wiltshire. Wiltshire Archaeological & Natural Historical Mag 58 1961.

Bonney, D. J. Two tenth-century Wiltshire charters concerning lands at Avon and at Collingbourne. Wiltshire Archaeological & Natural History Mag 65 1970.

Thomson, T. R. The northern county boundary. Wiltshire Archaeological & Natural Historical Mag 65 1970.

Mawer, A. and F. M. Stenton (with F. T. S. Houghton). The place-names of Worcestershire. Cambridge 1927.

Gelling, M. A note on the name Worcester. Worcestershire Archaeological Soc Trans 3rd ser 2 1969.

Smith, A. H. The place-names of the North Riding of Yorkshire. Cambridge 1928.

— The place-names of the East Riding of Yorkshire and York. Cambridge 1937.

Hedevind, B. Scandinavian elements in the dialect and place-names of Dent in the West Riding of Yorkshire. Trans Yorkshire Dialect Soc 10 1958.

Smith, A. H. The place-names of the West Riding of Yorkshire. 8 vols Cambridge 1961–2.

Ekwall, E. Some notes on West Riding place-names. Namn och Bygd 52 1964.

Smith, A. H. Some aspects of Irish influence on Yorkshire. Revue Celtique 44 1927.

Thomson, R. L. Celtic place-names in Yorkshire. Trans Yorkshire Dialect Soc 11 1965.

Ejder, B. Notes on Yorkshire place-names. E Studies 46 1965.

Dodgson, J. McN. and P. Khaliq. Addenda and corrigenda to the Survey of English place-names. Jnl of Eng Place-name Soc 2 1970.

Dodgson, J. McN. Addenda and corrigenda to the Survey of English place-names. Jnl of Eng Place-name Soc 3 1971.

(3) PERSONAL NAMES

Arthur, W. An etymological dictionary of Family and Christian names. New York 1857, Detroit 1969.

Lower, M. A. Patronymica britannica. 1860.

— English surnames. 1875, Detroit 1968.

Sims, C. S. The origin and signification of Scottish surnames, with a vocabulary of Christian names. Albany 1862, Baltimore 1968.

Yonge, C. M. History of Christian names. 1863.

Thomas, R. Handbook of fictitious names. 1868, Detroit 1969.

Bardsley, C. W. English surnames: their sources and significations. 1873, 1897, 1968.

— Curiosities of Puritan nomenclature. 1880.

— A dictionary of English and Welsh surnames, with special American instances. 1901, Baltimore 1967.

Solly, E. An index of hereditary English, Scottish and Irish titles of honour. 1880, Baltimore 1968.

Long, H. A. Personal names and family names. Glasgow 1883, Detroit 1968.

Guppy, H. B. Homes of family names in Great Britain. 1890, Baltimore 1968.

Moore, A. W. Manx names: or the surnames and place-names of the Isle of Man. 1890, 1903 (rev).

Nicholson, E. W. B. The pedigree of 'Jack' and of various allied names. 1892.

Searle, W. G. Onomasticon anglo-saxonicum: a list of Anglo-Saxon proper names from the time of Beda to that of King John. Cambridge 1897.

Müller, R. Die Namen des nordhumbrischen Liber vitae. Berlin 1901.

Barber, H. British family names: their origin and meaning. 1903, Baltimore 1968.

Köhler, T. Die altenglischen Namen in Baedas Historia ecclesiastica und auf den altnordhumbrischen Münzen. Berlin 1908.

Köpke, J. Altnordische Personennamen bei den Angelsachsen. Berlin 1909.

Matheson, R. E. Special report on surnames in Ireland; Varieties and synonyms of surnames and Christian names in Ireland. Dublin 1909, Baltimore 1968.

Baring-Gould, S. Family names and their story. 1910, Detroit 1969.

Björkman, E. Nordische Personennamen in England in alt- und frühmittelenglischen Zeit. Halle 1910.

— Zur englischen Namenkunde. Halle 1912.

— Studien über die Eigennamen im Beowulf. Halle 1920.

Hitching, F. K. and S. References to English surnames in 1601 and 1602. 1910, 1911, Baltimore 1968.

Chambers, R. W. Widsith. Cambridge 1912.

Harrison, H. Surnames of the United Kingdom: a concise etymological dictionary. 2 vols 1912–18, Baltimore 1968.

Weekley, E. The romance of names. 1914, 1928 (rev).

— Surnames. 1916, 1936 (rev).

— Jack and Jill: a study in our Christian names. 1939, 1948 (rev).

Forssner, T. Continental-Germanic personal names in England in Old and Middle English times. Upsala 1916.

— Beiträge zum Studium der neuenglischen Familiennamen. Göttingen 1920.

— De l'influence française sur les noms propres anglais. Skövde 1920.

— Imitative alterations in modern English personal nomenclature. Skövde 1920.

— Deutsche und englishe Imperativnamen. Östersund 1922.

Zachrisson, R. E. Notes on early English personal names. Studier i Modern Språkvetenskap 6 1917.

Hackenberg, E. Die Stammtafeln der angelsächsischen Königsreiche. Berlin 1918.

Redin, M. Studies on uncompounded personal names in Old English. Upsala 1919.

Johnston, J. B. The Scottish Macs. Paisley 1922.

Förster, M. Proben eines Eigennamenwörterbuches. Germanisch-romanische Monatsschrift 11 1923.

— Die Französierung des englischen Personennamenschatzes. In Germanica: Eduard Sievers zum 75, Halle 1925.

— The Breton name of St Budoc. Devon & Cornwall N & Q 19 1937.

Woulfe, P. Sloinnte Gaedheal is Gall. Dublin 1923.

Böhler, M. Die altenglischen Frauennamen. Berlin 1930.

Loomis, R. S. Some names in Arthurian romance. PMLA 45 1930.

Bowman, W. D. The story of surnames. 1931, Detroit 1968.

— What is your surname?: surnames, their origin and history. 1932.

Ewen, C. L. A history of surnames of the British Isles 1931, Baltimore 1968.

— A guide to the origin of British surnames. 1938, Detroit 1969.

—— Early surnames of Devonshire from the Exchequer Subsidy Roll 1332. Paignton 1947.

Hofmann, M. Die Französierung des Personennamenschatzes im Domesday Book der Grafschaften Hampshire und Sussex. Murnau 1934.

Meier, A. Die alttestamentliche Namengebung in England. Leipzig 1934.

Smith, A. H. Early northern nick-names and surnames. Saga-book 11 1934.

Fransson, G. Middle English surnames of occupation 1100–1350. Lund 1935.

Gordon, E. V. Wealhþeow and related names. MÆ 4 1935.

Spiegelhalter, C. Surnames of Devon. Devonshire Assoc Reports & Trans 68–72 1936–40, 79 1947.

Feilitzen, O. von. The pre-Conquest personal names of Domesday Book. Upsala 1937.

—— Notes on Old English bynames. Namn och Bygd 27 1940.

—— Some unrecorded Old and Middle English personal names. Namn och Bygd 33 1945.

—— Old Welsh Enniaun and the Old English personal name element wen. MLN 62 1947.

—— Some continental Germanic personal names in England. In Early English and Norse studies, ed A. Brown and P. Foote 1963.

—— Notes on some Scandinavian personal names in English 12th-century records. Anthroponymica Suecana 6 1965.

—— Some Old English uncompounded personal names and bynames. Studia Neophilologica 40 1968.

—— and C. Blunt. Personal names on the coinage of Edgar. In England before the Conquest: studies presented to Dorothy Whitelock, Cambridge 1971.

Kneen, J. J. The personal names of the Isle of Man. Oxford 1937.

Krause, K. Sonderformen und Kurzformen englischer Vornamen. Sprachkunde 5 1937.

Kökeritz, H. Notes on the pre-Conquest personal names of Domesday Book. Namn och Bygd 26 1938.

—— Punning names in Shakespeare. MLN 65 1950.

—— Shakespeare's names: a pronouncing dictionary. New Haven 1959.

Tengvik, G. Old English bynames. Upsala 1938.

Ström, H. Old English personal names in Bede's history: an etymological-phonological investigation. Lund 1939.

Woolf, H. B. The Old Germanic principles of name giving. Baltimore 1939.

—— The personal names in the Battle of Maldon. MLN 53 1938.

—— The naming of women in Old English times. MP 36 1939.

Gardiner, A. H. The theory of proper names. Oxford 1940, 1954 (rev).

Hutson, A. E. British personal names in the Historia regum Britanniae. Berkeley 1940.

Langenfelt, G. Family names as English font-names and other name problems. Studier i Modern Språkvetenskap 14 1940.

Whitelock, D. Scandinavian personal names in the Liber vitae of Thorney Abbey. Saga-book 12 1940.

Deutschbein, M. Geographie der Wortbildung der germanischen Völkernamen nach angelsächsischer Überlieferung. Zeitschrift für Mundartforschung 16 1941.

Hoops, J. Shakespeares Name und Herkunft. Heidelberg 1941.

Löfvenberg, M. T. Studies on Middle English local surnames. Lund 1942.

Murray, M. A. The divine King in Northumbria. Folk-Lore 53 1942.

Pâsche, F. Aethelstan-Adalstein. Studia Neophilologica 14 1942.

Friesen, O. von. Personal names of the type 'Bótolfr'. Studia Neophilologica 14 1942.

Ekwall, E. Studies on the genitive of groups in English. Lund 1943.

—— Variation in surnames in medieval London. Lund 1945.

—— Early London personal names. Lund 1947.

—— Two early London subsidy rolls. Lund 1951.

—— Studies on the population of medieval London. Stockholm 1956.

—— Some cases of initial variation in mediaeval London surnames. Moderna Språk 51 1957.

—— Some early London bynames and surnames. E Studies 46 1965.

Anderson (Arngart), O. S. The calendar of St Willibrord: a little-used source of Old English personal names. Studia Neophilologica 16 1944.

Withycombe, E. G. The Oxford dictionary of English Christian names. Oxford 1945, 1951 (rev).

Black, G. F. The surnames of Scotland. New York 1946, 1962 (rev).

Horn, W. Der Name Shakespeare. Archiv 185 1948.

Nitze, W. A. Arthurian names: Arthur. PMLA 64 1949.

—— Additional note on Arthurian names. PMLA 65 1950.

—— An Arthurian crux: Viviane or Niniane? Romance Philology 7 1954.

Smith, E. C. The story of our names. New York 1950.

—— Smith compound names. Kongressberichte München 3 1961.

—— Treasury of name-lore. 1967.

—— American surnames. Philadelphia 1969.

Sundby, B. The dialect and provenance of the Middle English poem the Owl and the nightingale. Lund 1950.

—— Some Middle English occupational terms. E Studies 33 1952.

—— Studies in the Middle English dialect material of Worcestershire records. Bergen and Oslo 1963.

Thuresson, B. Middle English occupational terms. Lund 1950.

Chapman, C. O. An index of names in Pearl, Purity, Patience and Gawain. Ithaca 1951.

Partridge, E. Name this child: a dictionary of modern British and American given names or Christian names. 1951.

—— Name your child. 1959, 1968 (rev).

Reaney, P. H. Notes on Christian names. N & Q May 1951.

—— Onomasticon essexiense: a proposal for the systematic collection of the personal names and surnames of Essex. Essex Rev 61 1952.

—— Pedigrees of villeins and freemen. N & Q May 1952.

—— Three unrecorded Old English personal names of a late type. MLR 47 1952.

—— Notes on the survival of Old English personal names in Middle English. Studier i Modern Språkvetenskap 18 1953.

—— A dictionary of British surnames. 1958.

—— The origin of English surnames. 1967.

Ackerman, R. W. An index of Arthurian names in Middle English. Stanford 1952.

Bloom, E. A. Symbolic names in Johnson's periodical essays. MLQ 13 1952.

Davies, T. R. A book of Welsh names. 1952.

Bain, R. The clans and tartans of Scotland. 1953.

Malone, K. Royal names in Old English poetry. Names 1 1953.

—— Epithet and eponym. Names 2 1954.

—— Meaningful fictive names in English literature. Names 5 1957.

Ramsay, R. L. Scyldings and shields. Names 1 1953.

Boillot, F. La proportion de noms de métiers dans les noms de famille à Paris et à Londres. Revue Internationale d'Onomastique 6 1954.

George, F. and G. Alexander. The meaning of Christian names. 1954.

Hughes, J. P. On H for R in English proper names. JEGP 53 1954.

Johansson, B. Något om puritanska personnamn i engelskan. Moderna Språk 48 1954.

Kilian, D. Eigennamen als Normalsubstantive im Englischen. Die Neueren Sprachen new ser 3 1954.

Maidbury, L. English Christian names in Latin. Amateur Historian 1 1954.
— English surnames in Latin. Ibid.
Mercer, A. C. B. Scandinavian surnames in Britain. Norseman 12 1954.
Pine, L. G. They came with the Conqueror. 1954.
— The story of surnames. 1965.
— The genealogist's encyclopaedia. 1969.
— The story of titles. 1969.
Smith, R. M. Swift's little language and nonsense names. JEGP 53 1954.
Williams, F. B. Renaissance names in masquerade. PMLA 69 1954.
Hamp, E. P. Viviane or niniane: a comment from the Celtic side. Romance Philology 8 1955.
— Early Welsh names, suffixes and phonology. Onoma 14 1969.
Harder, K. B. The names of Thomas Dekker's devils. Names 3 1955.
— Charles Dickens names his characters. Names 7 1959.
Kellogg, A. B. Nicknames and nonce-names in Shakespeare's comedies. Names 3 1955.
Turner, E. A. The Welsh element in Shropshire surnames. Trans Caradoc & Severn Valley Field Club for 1947–50 1956.
MacLysaght, E. Irish families. Dublin 1957.
— More Irish families. Galway and Dublin 1960.
— The surnames of Ireland. New York 1970.
Turville-Petre, J. E. Hengest and Horsa. Saga-book 14 1957.
Storms, G. Compounded names of peoples in Beowulf: a study in the diction of a great poet. Utrecht-Nijmegen 1957.
Weintraub, S. 'Humors' names in Shaw's prentice novels. Names 5 1957.
Bliss, A. J. The hero's name in the Middle English version of Lanval. MÆ 27 1958.
Lehiste, I. Names of Scandinavians in the Anglo-Saxon Chronicle. PMLA 73 1958.
Hughes, J. P. How you got your name: the origin and meaning of surnames. 1959.
— Is thy name Wart? 1965.
— Your book of surnames. 1967.
Nightingale, J. L. Puritans at the font. History Today March 1959.
Niva, W. N. Significant character names in English drama to 1603. Names 8 1960.
Power, W. Middleton's way with names. N & Q Jan 1960.
Dawe, P. N. Alias surnames. N & Q Somerset & Dorset 28 1962.
— Christian name Izzot. Ibid.
Foster, B. 'Familial S': a further note. E Studies 42 1961.
Simmonds, J. D. More's use of names in Book II of Utopia. Die Neueren Sprachen new ser 10 1961.
Thomson, C. C. Names for every child. 1961.
Franklyn, J. A dictionary of nicknames. 1962.
Jensen, G. F. Some observations on Scandinavian personal names in English place-names. Saga-book 16 1962.
— Scandinavian personal names in Lincolnshire and Yorkshire. Copenhagen 1968.
— Scandinavian personal names in Lincolnshire and Yorkshire. Onoma 14 1969.
Sleigh, L. and C. Johnson. The book of girls' names. 1962.
— The Pan book of boys' names. 1965.
— The Pan book of girls' names. 1965.
Voitl, H. Die englische Personennamenkunde: ein Forschungsbericht. Archiv 199–200 1962–3.
— Die englischen Familiennamen in sprachwissenschaftlicher Sicht. Archiv 202 1965.
— Schreibung und Aussprache bei englischen Familiennamen als methodisches Problem. In Disputationes ad montium vocabula vol 1, Vienna 1969.
Ashley, L. R. N. French surnames and the English. Names 11 1963.

Mills, A. D. Some Middle English occupational terms. N & Q July 1963.
— The Christian names of women in fourteenth-century Dorset. Proc Dorset Natural History & Archaeological Soc 88 1966.
— Notes on some Middle English occupational terms. Studia Neophilologica 40 1968.
Sørensen, H. S. The meaning of proper names. Copenhagen 1963.
Evans, D. E. Some Celtic personal names in the Commentaries on the Gallic War. Bull Board of Celtic Stud 21 1964.
— Gaulish personal names. Oxford 1967.
Hourahane, P. Names for the Welsh: five hundred Welsh Christian names. Merthyr Tydfil 1964.
Kristensson, G. Another approach to Middle English dialectology. E Studies 46 1965.
— A survey of Middle English dialects 1290–1350. Lund 1967.
— Studies on Middle English local surnames containing elements of French origin. E Studies 50 1969.
— Studies on Middle English topographical terms. Lund 1970.
Seltén, B. Some notes on Middle English bynames. E Studies 46 1965.
— Early East-Anglian nicknames: 'Shakespeare' names. Lund 1969.
Bethers, R. How did we get our names? 1966.
Matthews, C. M. English surnames. 1966.
— How surnames began. 1967.
Cottle, B. The Penguin dictionary of surnames. 1967.
Devereux, L. The story of surnames. Oxford 1967.
Dodgson, J. McN. Hodge and Dodge. N & Q Feb 1967.
Foreman, J. B. (ed). Gem dictionary of first names. 1967.
Hassall, W. O. History through surnames. Oxford 1967.
Adams, G. B. A new survey of Ulster surnames. Ulster Folklife 14 1968.
— The distribution of surnames in an Irish county. In Disputationes ad montium vocabula vol 2, Vienna 1969.
Freeman, J. W. Discovering surnames: their origins and meanings. Tring 1968.
Hanning, R. W. Uses of names in medieval literature. Names 16 1968.
Rennick, R. M. Obscene names and naming in folk tradition. Names 16 1968.
Robinson, F. C. Some uses of name-meanings in Old English poetry. Neuphilologische Mitteilungen 69 1968.
— The significance of names in Old English literature. Anglia 86 1968.
— Personal names in medieval narrative and the name of Unferþ in Beowulf. Birmingham-Southern College Bull 63 1970.
Rogers, P. B. The names of the Canterbury pilgrims. Names 16 1968.
McKinley, R. A. Norfolk surnames in the 16th century. Leicester 1969.
— The survey of English surnames. Local Historian 8 1969.
Thewes, R. Name your daughter. 1969.
— Name your son. 1969.
Richards, M. Arthurian onomastics. Trans Honourable Soc of Cymmrodorion, session 1969, pt 2 1970.
— The population of the Welsh Border. Trans Honourable Soc of Cymmrodorion, session 1970, pt 1 1971.
— Places and persons of the early Welsh church. Welsh History Rev 5 1971.
Davies, C. S. and J. Levitt. What's in a name? 1970.
Dorian, N. C. East Sutherland by-naming. Scottish Stud 14 1970.
Miller, G. M. BBC pronouncing dictionary of British names. 1971.
Okasha, E. Hand-list of Anglo-Saxon non-runic inscriptions. Cambridge 1971.

A. D. M.

THE ANGLO-SAXON PERIOD
(TO 1100)

I. OLD ENGLISH LITERATURE

A. GENERAL WORKS: *Bibliographies; Histories; Anthologies; Studies; Dictionaries; Collections; Ancillary studies: Germanic background; History; Palaeography.*

B. POETRY: *Dictionaries; Collections and anthologies; Manuscript studies; General criticism; Individual poems and authors.*

C. PROSE: *Collections and anthologies; General criticism; Major translators of King Alfred's reign; Major writers of the later period; Other religious prose; The chronicle; Laws, charters etc; Science, medicine and magic, and folklore; Other secular prose.*

A. GENERAL WORKS

(1) BIBLIOGRAPHIES

Wülcker, R. Grundriss zur Geschichte der angelsächsischen Litteratur. Leipzig 1885.

Koerting, G. Grundriss der Geschichte der englischen Litteratur. Münster 1887, 1910 (5th edn).

Edwardes, M. A summary of the literature of modern Europe from the origins to 1400. 1907.

Ayres, H. M. A bibliographical sketch of Anglo-Saxon literature. New York 1910.

Kennedy, A. G. A bibliography of writings on the English language. Cambridge Mass 1927, 1961.

— and D. G. Sands. A concise bibliography for students of English. Stanford 1940, 1960 (4th edn).

Lawrence, W. W. Selected bibliography of medieval literature in England. New York 1930.

Heusinkveld, A. H. and E. J. Bashe. A bibliographical guide to Old English. Iowa City 1931.

Loomis, R. S. Introduction to medieval literature chiefly in England: a reading list and bibliography. New York 1939, 1948 (rev).

Renwick, W. L. and H. Orton. The beginnings of English literature to Skelton, 1509. 1939, 1952 (rev); rev M. F. Wakelin 1966.

Farrar, C. P. and A. P. Evans. Bibliography of English translations from medieval sources. New York 1946.

Springer, O. Germanic bibliography 1940–5. JEGP 45 1946.

Williams, H. F. An index of medieval studies published in Festschriften 1865–1946. Berkeley 1951.

Mummendey, R. Language and literature of the Anglo-Saxon nations as presented in German doctoral dissertations 1885–1950. Bonn 1954.

Ker, N. R. Catalogue of manuscripts containing Anglo-Saxon. Oxford 1957. *See also OE poetry and Manuscript studies, below.*

Bonser, W. An Anglo-Saxon and Celtic bibliography 450–1087. 2 vols Oxford 1957.

Anderson, G. K. Beowulf, Chaucer and their backgrounds. In Contemporary literary scholarship: a critical review, ed L. Leary, New York 1958.

— Old English literature. In The medieval literature of Western Europe, ed J. H. Fisher, New York 1966.

Greenfield, S. B. An Old English bibliographical guide. In D. M. Zesmer, Guide to English literature from Beowulf through Chaucer and medieval drama, New York 1961.

Robinson, F. C. Old English research in progress. Neuphilologische Mitteilungen 66– 1965–.

— Old English literature: a select bibliography. Toronto 1970.

Matthews, W. Old and Middle English literature. New York 1968.

See also bibliographies in R. W. Chambers, Beowulf: an introduction, Cambridge 1921, 1959 (3rd edn with suppl by C. L. Wrenn); and in Beowulf, ed F. Klaeber, Boston 1922, 1941 (with suppl), 1950 (3rd edn with suppl).

(2) HISTORIES

General

Twisden, R. Historiae anglicanae scriptores. 1652.

Wharton, H. Anglia sacra. 2 vols 1692.

Hickes, G. Linguarum veterum septentrionalium thesaurus grammatico-criticus et archaeologicus. Vol 1, pt i, Institutiones grammaticae anglo-saxonicae et moesogothicae; pt 2, Institutiones franco-theotiscae; vol 2, pt i, Grammaticae islandicae rudimenta; pt 2, De literaturae septentrionalis utilitate: sive de linguarum veterum septentrionalium usu dissertatio epistolaris, cum numismatibus saxonicis; vol 3, Antiquae literaturae septentrionalis liber alter: seu Humphredi Wanleii librorum veterum septentrionalium catalogus. Oxford 1703–5.

Wright, T. Biographia britannica literaria. Vol 1, 1842, Detroit 1968.

Behnsch, O. Geschichte der englischen Sprache und Literatur von den ältesten Zeiten bis zur Einführung der Buchdruckerkunst. Breslau 1853.

Taine, H. Histoire de la littérature anglaise. Paris 1863–4, 1881 (5th edn).

Morley, H. English writers. Vol 1, 1864, 1891 (3rd edn).

Ebert, A. Allgemeine Geschichte der Literatur des Mittelalters im Abendlande. 3 vols Leipzig 1874–87, 1889 (new edn of vol 1).

ten Brink, B. Geschichte der englischen Literatur. Vol 1, Berlin 1877; ed A. Brandl, Strasbourg 1899; tr 1883.

Azarias, Brother. The development of English literature: Old English period. New York 1879, 1890 (3rd edn).

Grein, C. W. M. Übersicht der angelsächsischen Litteratur. In Kurzgefasste angelsächsische Grammatik, Cassel 1880.

Earle, J. Anglo-Saxon literature. 1884.

Wülcker, R. Grundriss zur Geschichte der angelsächsischen Litteratur. Leipzig 1885.

— Geschichte der englischen Litteratur von den Anfängen bis zur Gegenwart. Leipzig 1896, 1907.

Koerting, G. Grundriss der Geschichte der englischen Litteratur. Münster 1887, 1910 (5th edn).

Brooke, S. A. History of early English literature to the accession of King Alfred. 2 vols 1892.

— English literature from the beginning to the Norman Conquest. 1898.

Koegel, R. Geschichte der deutschen Literatur. Vol 1, pt i, Strasbourg 1894.

Jusserand, J. J. Histoire littéraire du peuple anglais. Vol 1, Paris 1894, 1896.

Griffin, W. H. A handbook of English literature. 1897.

Ker, W. P. Epic and romance. 1897, 1931.

— The Dark Ages. Edinburgh 1904.

— Medieval English literature. Oxford 1912 (Home Univ Lib).

CHEL vol 1. Cambridge 1907.

Dale, E. National life and character in the mirror of early English literature. Cambridge 1907.

Brandl, A. Geschichte der altenglischen Literatur. Strasbourg 1908. Rptd from H. Paul, Grundriss der germanischen Philologie.

Snell, F. J. The age of Alfred 664–1154. 1912.

Benham, A. R. English literature from Widsith to the death of Chaucer. New Haven 1916.

Legouis, E. and L. Cazamian. Histoire de la littérature anglaise. Paris 1924; tr 2 vols 1926–7.

Thomas, P. G. English literature before Chaucer. 1924.

Routh, H. V. God, man and epic poetry. Vol 2 (medieval), Cambridge 1927.

Schroeer, M. M. A. Grundzüge und Haupttypen der englischen Literaturgeschichte. Pt 1, 1927 (3rd edn) (Sammlung Göschen).

Schücking, L. L. Die angelsächsische und frühmittelenglische Dichtung. In Handbuch der literaturwissenschaft, ed O. Walzel, Berlin-Potsdam.

Wardale, E. E. Chapters on Old English literature 1935.

Schirmer, W. F. Geschichte der englischen Literatur von den Anfängen bis zur Gegenwart. Halle 1937.

— Kurze Geschichte. Halle 1945. From preceding.

Malone, K. The Old English period to 1100. In A literary history of England, ed A. C. Baugh, New York 1948, 1967 (rev).

Anderson, G. K. The literature of the Anglo-Saxons. Princeton 1949, 1966 (rev).

— Old and Middle English literature from the beginnings to 1485. New York 1950.

Whitelock, D. The beginnings of English society. 1952 (Pelican), 1965 (rev).

Schubel, F. Englische Literaturgeschichte: I, Die alt- und mittelenglische Periode. Berlin 1954 (Sammlung Göschen), 1967.

Schlauch, M. English medieval literature and its social foundations. Warsaw 1956, Warsaw and London 1967.

Blair, P. H. An introduction to Anglo-Saxon England. Cambridge 1956.

Zesmer, D. M. Guide to English literature from Beowulf through Chaucer and medieval drama. New York and London 1961.

Basu, N. K. History of English literature from the beginning to Chaucer. Calcutta 1961.

Dubois, M.-M. La littérature anglaise du Moyen Age 500–1500. Paris 1962.

Greenfield, S. B. A critical history of Old English literature. New York 1965.

Stanley, E. G. (ed). Continuations and beginnings: studies in Old English literature. 1966.

Wrenn, C. L. A study of Old English literature. 1967.

Cross, J. E. Old English literature. In The Middle Ages, ed W. F. Bolton 1970.

(3) ANTHOLOGIES

See also under OE Poetry, Prose, below.

In Old English

Thorpe, B. Analecta anglo-saxonica. 1834, 1846.

Leo, H. Altsächsische und angelsächsische Sprachproben. Halle 1838.

Wright, T. and J. O. Halliwell (-Phillipps). Reliquiae antiquae. 2 vols 1841–3.

Ebeling, F. W. Angelsächsisches Lesebuch. Leipzig 1847.

Klipstein, L. F. Analecta anglo-saxonica. 2 vols New York 1849.

Ettmüller, E. Engla and Seaxna Scopas and Boceras. Quedlinburg 1850.

Rieger, M. Alt- und angelsächsisches Lesebuch. Giessen 1861.

Zupitza, J. Altenglisches Übungsbuch. Vienna 1874, 1882 (as Alt- und mittelenglisches Übungsbuch); rev J. Schipper 1897; rev A. Eichler 1922; rev 1932.

Sweet, H. An Anglo-Saxon reader. Oxford 1876; rev C. T. Onions, Oxford 1922–59; rev D. Whitelock, Oxford 1967 (15th edn).

— An Anglo-Saxon primer. Oxford 1882; rev N. Davis 1953 (9th edn).

— The oldest English texts. 1885 (EETS).

— A second Anglo-Saxon reader: archaic and dialectal. Oxford 1887.

— First steps in Anglo-Saxon. Oxford 1897.

Körner, K. Angelsächsische Texte. Heilbronn 1880.

Kluge, F. Angelsächsisches Lesebuch. Halle 1888, 1915.

Bright, J. W. An Anglo-Saxon reader. New York 1891; rev J. R. Hulbert 1935; rev Hulbert and B. C. Monroe 1965.

MacLean, G. E. The Old and Middle English reader on the basis of Prof Julius Zupitza's Alt- und mittelenglisches Übungsbuch. New York 1893, 1922.

Cook, A. S. A first book in Old English. Boston 1894, 1903 (3rd edn rev).

Wyatt, A. J. An elementary Old English reader (early West Saxon). Cambridge 1901.

— An Anglo-Saxon reader. Cambridge 1919.

— The threshold of Anglo-Saxon. Cambridge 1926.

Warren, K. M. A treasury of English literature: origins to eleventh century. 1908.

Williams, O. T. Short extracts from Old English poetry, chiefly for unseen translations. Bangor 1909.

Förster, M. Altenglisches Lesebuch für Anfänger. Heidelberg 1913, 1963 (7th edn).

Schücking, L. L. Kleines angelsächsisches Dichterbuch. Köthen 1919, Leipzig 1933.

Moore, S. and T. A. Knott. The elements of Old English. Ann Arbor 1919, 1940 (rev).

Sedgefield, W. J. An Anglo Saxon verse book. Manchester 1922.

— An Anglo-Saxon prose book. Manchester 1928.

— An Anglo-Saxon book of verse and prose. Manchester 1928.

Kershaw, N. Anglo-Saxon and Norse poems. Cambridge 1922.

Craigie, W. A. Easy readings in Anglo-Saxon. Edinburgh 1927.

— Specimens of Anglo-Saxon prose. 3 vols Edinburgh 1923–9.

— Specimens of Anglo-Saxon poetry. 3 vols Edinburgh 1923–31.

Turk, M. H. An Anglo-Saxon reader. New York 1927, 1931 (rev).

Krapp, G. P. and A. G. Kennedy. An Anglo-Saxon reader. New York 1929.

Flom, G. T. Introductory Old English grammar and reader. Boston 1930 (2nd edn).

Anderson, M. and B. C. Williams. Old English handbook. Boston 1935, 1938.

Lehnert, M. Altenglisches Elementarbuch. Berlin 1939, 1950 (rev), 1959 (7th edn rev).

— Poetry and prose of the Anglo-Saxons: 1, texts. Berlin 1955, London 1957, 1960 (rev); 2, dictionary, Berlin 1956, Halle 1969 (rev).

Raith, J. Altenglisches Lesebuch: Prosa. Munich 1940, 1958 (rev).

Funke, O. and K. Jost. An Old English reader. 2 vols Berne 1942.

van Langenhove, G. Old English reader: part 1, texts. Bruges 1942.

Mossé, F. Manuel de l'anglais du Moyen Age des origines au xive siècle: 1, vieil-anglais: 1, grammaire et textes; 2, notes et glossaire. Paris 1945, 1950 (rev).

Ardern, P. S. First readings in Old English. Wellington 1948, 1951 (rev), Cambridge 1953.

Kaiser, R. Alt- und mittelenglische Anthologie. Berlin 1954, London 1958 (3rd edn rev as Medieval English: an Old and Middle English anthology), 1961 (5th impression rev).

Brook, G. L. An introduction to Old English. Manchester 1955.

Bolton, W. F. An Old English anthology. 1963, Evanston 1966 (rev).

Blakeley, L. Teach yourself Old English. London and New York 1964.

Fowler, R. Old English prose and verse. 1966.

Magoun, F. P., jr. The Anglo-Saxon poems in Bright's Anglo-Saxon reader. Cambridge Mass 1967.

In Translation

Sampson, G. The Cambridge book of prose and verse from the beginnings to the cycles of romance. Cambridge 1924.

Williams, M. Word-hoard: passages from Old English literature from the sixth to the eleventh centuries, translated and arranged. New York 1940.

Magoun, F. P. and J. A. Walker. An Old-English anthology: translation of Old-English prose and verse. Dubuque 1950.

Whitelock, D. English historical documents: 1, c. 500–1042. 1955.

(4) STUDIES

See also Old English Poetry : General Criticism, below.

Gummere, F. B. On the symbolic use of black and white in Germanic tradition. Haverford College Stud 2 1889.

Hunt, T. W. Ethical teachings in Old English literature. New York 1892.

Whitman, C. H. The birds in Old English literature. JEGP 2 1898.

MacGillivray, H. S. Der Einfluss des Christentums auf den Wortschatz des Altenglischen. Halle 1898.

Becker, C. J. A contribution to the comparative study of the material visions of Heaven and Hell. Baltimore 1899.

Jordan, R. Die altenglischen Säugetiernamen. Anglistische Forschungen 12 1902.

Stevens, W. O. The cross in the life and literature of the Anglo-Saxons. New Haven 1904.

Keller, M. The Anglo-Saxon weapon names. Anglistische Forschungen 15 1905.

Köhler, J. J. Die altenglischen Fischnamen. Anglistische Forschungen 21 1906.

Pfändler, W. Die Vergnügungen der Angelsachsen. Anglia 29 1906.

Klump, W. Die altenglischen Handwerkernamen. Anglistische Forschungen 24 1908.

Garrett, R. M. Precious stones in Old English literature. Munich 1909.

Mosher, J. A. The exemplum in early religious and didactic literature of England. New York 1911.

Brotanek, R. Texte und Untersuchungen zur altenglischen Literatur- und Kirchengeschichte. Halle 1913.

Jente, R. Die mythologische Ausdrücke im altenglischen Wortschatz. Anglistische Forschungen 56 1922.

Kirtlan, E. J. The relation of sin and fate in Anglo-Saxon literature. London Quart Rev 23 1922.

Chambers, R. W. The lost literature of medieval England. Library 2nd ser 6 1925.

Neusprachliche Studien: Festgabe Karl Luick zu seinem 60 Geburtstage. Marburg 1925.

Phillpotts, B. S. Wyrd and providence in Anglo-Saxon thought. E & S 13 1927.

Faverty, F. E. Legends of Joseph in Old and Middle English. PMLA 43 1928.

Ricci, A. The Anglo-Saxon eleventh-century crisis. RES 5 1929.

Boehler, M. Die altenglischen Frauennamen. Berlin 1931.

Laistner, M. L. W. Thought and letters in Western Europe AD 500 to 900. 1931, 1957 (rev).

— The intellectual heritage of the Early Middle Ages. Ithaca 1957.

Rose-Troup, F. The ancient monastery of St Mary and St Peter at Exeter [680–1050]. Report & Trans of Devonshire Assoc 63 1931.

Chadwick, H. M. and N. K. The ancient literature of Europe. Cambridge 1932 (vol 1 of The growth of literature).

Cravens, M. J. Designations and treatment of the Holy Eucharist in Old and Middle English before 1300. Washington 1932.

Wilson, R. M. Lost literature in Old and Middle English. Leeds Stud no 2 1933.

— Some lost Saints' lives in Old and Middle English. MLR 36 1941.

— The lost literature of medieval England. 1952.

Mincoff, M. K. Die Bedeutungsentwicklung der ags. Ausdrücke für Kraft und Macht. Palaestra 188 1933.

Brandl, A. Zur Entstehung der germanischen Heldensage, gesehen vom angelsächsischen Standpunkt. Archiv 162 1933.

— Vom kosmologischen Denken des heidnisch-christlichen Germanentums: der früh-ags Schicksalsspruch der Handschrift Tiberius B. xiii und seine Verwandheit mit Boethius. Sitzungsberichte der Preussischen Akademie der Wissenschaften (phil-hist Klasse) 1937.

Dickins, B. English names and Old English heathenism. E & S 19 1933.

— J. M. Kemble and Old English scholarship. Proc Br Acad 25 1939.

Schneider, H. Englische und nordgermanische Heldensage. Berlin 1933 (Sammlung Göschen).

— Englische Heldensage. Berlin 1934 (vol 2.2 of Germanische Heldensage (Pauls Grundriss 10, 3)).

Schücking, L. L. Heldenstolz und Würde im Angelsächsischen. Abhandlungen der Sächsischen Akademie der Wissenschaften, phil-hist Klasse 42 1933.

Stephens, G. R. The knowledge of Greek in England in the Middle Ages. Philadelphia 1933.

Crawford, S. J. Anglo-Saxon influence on Western Christendom 600–800. Oxford 1933.

Tatlock, J. S. P. The dragons of Wessex and Wales. Speculum 8 1933.

Wehrle, W. O. The macaronic hymn tradition in medieval English literature. Washington 1933.

Bonser, W. Survivals of Paganism in Anglo-Saxon England. Trans Birmingham Archaeological Soc 56 1934.

— The medical background of Anglo-Saxon England: a study in history, psychology and folklore. 1963.

Einarsson, S. Old English 'beot' and Old Icelandic 'heitstrenging'. PMLA 49 1934.

Judge, C. B. Anglo-Saxonica in Hereford Cathedral Library. Harvard Stud in Philology 16 1934.

Klaeber, F. Zwei Anmerkungen zur Wortstellung im Altenglischen. In Studia germanica tillägnade E. A. Kock, Lund 1934.

— Eine Randbemerkungen zur Nebenordnung und Unterordnung im Altenglischen. Beiblatt zur Anglia 52 1941.

— Zum germanischen Sprachstil: das Nomen. Archiv 183 1943.

— Der Reliquienkultus in Altengland. Archiv 189 1953.

Stibbe, H. Herr und Frau und verwandte Begriffe in ihren altenglischen Äquivalenten. Anglistische Forschungen 80 1935.

Flower, R. Laurence Nowell and the discovery of England in Tudor times. Proc Br Acad 21 1935.

Ogilvy, J. D. A. Books known to Anglo-Latin writers from Aldhelm to Alcuin. Cambridge Mass 1936.

— Books known to the English 597–1096. Cambridge Mass 1967.

Pfeilstücker, S. Spätantikes und germanisches Kunstgut in der frühangelsächsischen Kunst, nach lateinischen und altenglischen Schriftquellen. Berlin 1936.

Rosenthal, C. L. The 'Vitae patrum' in Old and Middle English Literature. Philadelphia 1936.

Serjeantson, M. S. The vocabulary of folk-lore in Old and Middle English. Folk-lore 47 1936.

Smith, A. H. The early literary relations of England and Scandinavia. Saga-book 11 1936.

Birney, E. English irony before Chaucer. UTQ 6 1973.

Griffiths, M. E. Early vaticination in Welsh with English parallels. Ed T. Gwynn Jones, Cardiff 1937.

Gramm, W. Die Körperpflege der Angelsachsen: eine kulturgeschichtliche etymologische Untersuchung. Anglistische Forschungen 80 1938.

McNeill, J. T. and H. M. Gamer. Medieval handbooks of penance: a translation of the principal Libri poenitentiales and selections from related documents. New York 1938.

Woolf, H. B. The naming of women in Old English times. MP 36 1938.

— The old Germanic principles of name-giving. Baltimore 1939.

— Longfellow's interest in Old English. In Philologica: the [Kemp] Malone anniversary studies, Baltimore 1949.

Bressie, R. Libraries of the British Isles in the Anglo-Saxon period. In The medieval library, ed J. W. Thompson, Chicago 1939.

Tuve, R. Ancients, moderns and Saxons. ELH 6 1939.

Wright, C. E. The cultivation of saga in Anglo-Saxon England. Edinburgh 1939.

— Sir Edward Dering: a seventeenth-century antiquary and his 'Saxon' charters. In The early cultures of north-west Europe, ed C. Fox and B. Dickins, Cambridge 1950.

— The dispersal of the monastic libraries and the beginnings of Anglo-Saxon studies. Trans Cambridge Bibl Soc 1 1951.

Brown, C. 'Poculum mortis' in Old English. Speculum 15 1940.

Colgrave, B. (ed). Two lives of Saint Cuthbert. Cambridge 1940.

— The earliest saints' lives written in England. Proc Br Acad 44 1958.

Heningham, E. K. Old English precursors of the Worcester fragments. PMLA 55 1940.

Ker, N. R. An eleventh-century Old English legend of the cross before Christ. MÆ 9 1940.

— Old English notes signed 'Coleman'. MÆ 18 1949.

Levison, W. An eighth-century poem on St Ninian. Antiquity 14 1940.

— England and the Continent in the eighth century. Oxford 1946.

Anderson, O. S. Old English material in the Leningrad manuscript of Bede's Ecclesiastical history. Lund 1941.

Chadwick, H. M. The study of Anglo-Saxon. Cambridge 1941, 1955 (rev).

Glunz, H. H. Nationale Eigenart im mittelalterlichen Schrifttum Englands. In Grundformen der englischen Geistesgeschichte, ed P. Meissner, Stuttgart 1941.

Timmer, B. J. Wyrd in Anglo-Saxon prose and poetry. Neophilologus 26 1941.

Wild, F. Odin und Euemeros: Spiegelung germanischer Göttersage im englischen Schrifttum. Vienna 1941.

Förster, M. Zur Liturgik der angelsächsischen Kirche. Anglia 66 1942.

— Zu den ae Texten aus ms Arundel 155. Ibid.

— Zur Geschichte des Reliquienkultus in Altengland. Sitzungsberichte der Bayerischen Akademie der Wissenschaften (phil-hist Abteilung) 1943.

Deutschbein, M. Germanisches Heldentum in der angelsächsischen Zeit. In Mannestum und Heldenideal, ed T. Mayer, Marburg 1942.

Liljegren, S. B. and J. Melander (ed). A philological miscellany presented to E. Ekwall. 2 vols Upsala 1942.

Brady, C. The legends of Ermanaric. Berkeley 1943.

— The Old English nominal compounds in -rad. PMLA 67 1952.

Schröder, E. Die nordhumbrische Königsgenealogie. In his Deutsche Namenkunde, Göttingen 1944.

Adamson, J. W. The illiterate Anglo-Saxon and other essays. Cambridge 1946.

Magoun, F. P. On some survivals of pagan belief in Anglo-Saxon England. Harvard Theological Rev 40 1947.

— On the Old-Germanic altar- or oath-ring (Stallahringr). Acta Philologica Scandinavica 20 1949.

Duckett, E. S. Anglo-Saxon saints and scholars. New York 1947.

— Alcuin, friend of Charlemagne: his world and his work. New York 1951.

Jones, C. W. Saints' lives and chronicles in early England. Ithaca 1947.

— Medieval literature in translation. New York 1950.

— The Saint Nicholas liturgy and its literary relationships (ninth to twelfth centuries). Berkeley 1963.

Martin-Clarke, D. E. Culture in early Anglo-Saxon England. Baltimore 1947.

Curtius, E. R. Europäische Literatur und lateinisches Mittelalter. Berne 1948; tr 1953.

Buck, C. D. et al. A dictionary of selected synonyms in the principal Indo-European languages: a contribution to the history of ideas. Chicago 1949.

Loomis, L. H. The Saint Mercurius legend in medieval England and in Norse saga. In Philologica: the [Kemp] Malone anniversary studies, Baltimore 1949.

— The holy relics of Charlemagne and King Athelstan: the Lances of Longinus and St Mauritius. Speculum 25 1950.

Savage, D. J. Grundtvig: a stimulus to Old English scholarship. In Philologica: the [Kemp] Malone anniversary studies, Baltimore 1949.

Schaubert, E. von. Bedeutung und Herkunft von altenglischen 'feormian' und seiner Sippe. Göttingen 1949.

Lohr, E. Patristic demonology in Old English literature. New York 1949.

Davidson, H. R. E. The hill of the dragon: Anglo-Saxon burial mounds in literature and archaeology. Folk-lore 61 1950.

Harmer, F. E. The English contribution to the epistolary usages of early Scandinavian Kings. Saga-book 13 1950.

Patch, H. R. The other world according to descriptions in medieval literature. Cambridge Mass 1950.

White, B. M. Fact and fancy in medieval English literature. Essays by Divers Hands new ser 25 1950.

— Medieval mirth. Anglia 78 1960.

Zink, G. Les légendes héroiques de Dietrich et d'Ermrich dans les littératures germaniques. Lyons 1950.

Lerner, L. D. Colour words in Anglo-Saxon. MLR 46 1951.

Bloomfield, M. W. The seven deadly sins. Ann Arbor 1952.

Clemoes, P. Liturgical influence on punctuation in late OE and early ME mss. Cambridge 1952.

— Rhythm and cosmic order in OE Christian literature. Cambridge 1970.

Marckwardt, A. H. (ed). Laurence Nowell's Vocabularium saxonicum. Ann Arbor 1952.

Mezger, F. Self-judgment in Old English documents. MLN 67 1952.

Helm, K. Die Westgermanen. Heidelberg 1953. Vol 2.2 of his Altgermanische Religionsgeschichte.

Sisam, K. Studies in the history of Old English literature. Oxford 1953.

— Anglo-Saxon royal genealogies. Proc Br Acad 39 1953.

Southern, R. W. The making of the Middle Ages. 1953.

Davis, N. 'Hippopotamus' in Old English. RES new ser 4 1953.

Talbot, C. H. The Anglo-Saxon missionaries in Germany. 1954.

Hatto, A. T. The lime-tree in early German, Goliard and English poetry. MLR 49 1954.

Wahrig, G. Das Lachen im Altenglischen und Mittelenglischen. Zeitschrift für Anglistik und Amerikakunde 3 1955.

Stallbaumer, V. R. The Canterbury School of St Gregory's disciples. Amer Benedictine Rev 6 1956.

— Lessons the Anglo-Saxon libraries teach. Benedictine Rev 15 1960.

— The Canterbury School of Theodore and Hadrian. Amer Benedictine Rev 22 1971.

— St Benedict Biscop's Wearmouth-Jarrow monastic school Benedictine Rev 17 1962.

Cross, J. E. *Ubi sunt* passages in Old English: sources and relationships. Vetenskaps-Societetens i Lund Årsbok 1956.

— Aspects of microcosm and macrocosm in Old English literature. Comparative Lit 14 1962; rptd in Studies in honor of Arthur G. Brodeur, Eugene 1963.

— Latin themes in Old English poetry. Bristol 1962.

— The elephant to Alfred, Ælfric, Aldhelm and others. Studia Neophilologica 37 1965.

— The ethic of war in Old English. In England before the Conquest; studies presented to Dorothy Whitelock, Cambridge 1971.

— The literate Anglo-Saxon: on sources and dissemination. Proc Br Acad 58 1972.

König, G. Die Bezeichnungen für Farbe, Glanz und Helligkeit im Altenglischen. Mainz 1957.

Tucker, S. I. The Anglo-Saxon poet considers the heavens. Neophilologus 41 1957.

— Laughter in Old English literature. Neophilologus 43 1959.

Utley, F. L. Jaica: the city of sunrise. Names 5 1957.

Enkvist, N.-E. The seasons of the year: chapters on a motif from Beowulf to the Shepherd's calendar. Copenhagen and Helsinki 1957.

Stenton, D. M. The English woman in history. 1957.

Thompson, E. A. Christianity and the Northern Barbarians. Nottingham Mediaeval Stud 1 1957.

Albertson, C. Anglo-Saxon literature and Western culture. Thought 33 1958.

Poole, A. L. (ed). Medieval England. 2 vols 1958.

Whitelock, D. Changing currents in Anglo-Saxon studies. Cambridge 1958.

Wormald, F. The monastic library. In The English library before 1700, ed Wormald and C. E. Wright 1959.

Habicht, W. Die Gebärde in englischen Dichtungen des Mittelalters. Munich 1959.

Chaney, W. A. Paganism to Christianity. Harvard Theological Rev 53 1960; rptd in Early medieval society, ed S. L. Thrupp, New York 1967.

Sturzl, E. Die christliche Elemente in den altenglischen Zaubersagen. Sprache 6 1960.

Leslie, R. F. Analysis of stylistic devices and effects in Anglo-Saxon literature. Stil- und Formprobleme 5 1960.

Temple, W. The song of the angelic hosts. Annuale Mediaevale 2 1961.

Benning, H. A. 'Welt' und 'Mensch' in der altenglischen Dichtung. Münster 1958; rptd in Beiträge zur Englischen Philologie (Bochum) 44 1961.

Gelling, M. Place-names and Anglo-Saxon paganism. Univ of Birmingham Historical Jnl 8 1961.

Derolez, R. Anglo-Saxon literature: Attic or Asiatic? Old English poetry and its Latin background. In English studies today; second series, ed G. Bonnard, Berne 1961.

Bouman, A. C. Patterns in Old English and Old Icelandic literature. Leyden 1962.

Crawford, J. Evidence for witchcraft in Anglo-Saxon England. MÆ 32 1963.

Fuss, K. 'Der Held': Versuch einer Wesenbestimmung. Zeitschrift für Deutsche Philologie 82 1963.

Chadwick, N. K. The Celtic background of early Anglo-Saxon England. In Celt and Saxon, ed N. K. Chadwick, Cambridge 1963.

Kökeritz, H. The Anglo-Saxon unicorn. In Early English and Norse studies presented to Hugh Smith, 1963.

Stanley, E. G. The search for Anglo-Saxon paganism. N & Q 1964, 1965.

— Laʒamon's antiquarian sentiments. MÆ 38 1969.

Brunner, K. Überlieferungsgeschichte der alt- und mittelenglischen Literatur. In Geschichte der Textüberlieferung vol 2, Zürich 1964.

Wolpers, T. Die englische Heiligenlegende des Mittelalters: eine Formgeschichte des Legendenerzählens von der spätantiken lateinischen Tradition bis zur Mitte des 16 Jhdts. Tübingen 1964.

Grinda, K. Einige Handwerke in der ae Dichtung und in zeitgenössischen Inschriften. In Festschrift für Walter Hübner, Berlin 1964.

Ostheeren, K. Studien zum Begriff der 'Freunde' und seinem Ausdrucksmitteln in altenglischen Texten. Heidelberg 1964.

Dick, E. S. Altenglisch 'Dryht' und seine Sippe: eine wortkundliche, kultur- und religionsgeschichtliche Betrachtung zur altgermanischen Glaubensvorstellung vom wachstümlichen Heil. Münster 1965.

Garmonsway, G. N. Anglo-Saxon heroic attitudes. In Franciplegius: medieval and linguistic studies in honor of Francis Peabody Magoun jr, New York 1965.

Morrell, M. C. A manual of Old English Biblical materials. Knoxville 1965.

Trier, J. Wortgeschichten aus alten Gemeinden. Cologne 1965.

Page, R. I. Anglo-Saxon episcopal lists. Nottingham Medieval Stud 9–10 1965–6.

Schabram, H. Superbia: Studien zum altenglischen Wortschatz. Munich 1965.

Campbell, J. J. Learned rhetoric in Old English poetry. MP 63 1966.

—— Knowledge of rhetorical figures in Anglo-Saxon England. JEGP 66 1967.

Katzenellenbogen, A. The image of Christ in the early Middle Ages. In Life and thought in the early Middle Ages, ed R. S. Hoyt, Minneapolis 1967.

Gneuss, H. Hymnar und Hymnen im englischen Mittelalter. Tübingen 1968.

Robinson, F. C. The significance of names in Old English literature. Anglia 86 1968.

—— Some uses of name-meanings in Old English poetry. Neuphilologische Mitteilungen 69 1968.

Green, D. H. OE dryht: a new suggestion. MLR 63 1968.

Murphy, M. Religious polemics in the genesis of Old English studies. HLQ 32 1969.

Chaney, W. A. The cult of kingship in Anglo-Saxon England. Manchester 1969.

Gatch, M. McC. Death: meaning and mortality in Christian thought and contemporary culture. New York 1969. Ch 5.

Shepherd, G. English versions of the scriptures before Wyclif. In The Cambridge history of the Bible vol 2, ed G. W. H. Lampe, Cambridge 1969.

England before the Conquest: studies in primary sources presented to Dorothy Whitelock. Ed P. Clemoes and K. Hughes, Cambridge 1971.

J. E. C.

(5) ANCILLARY STUDIES

(a) GERMANIC BACKGROUND

Grimm, W. Die deutsche Heldensage. Göttingen 1829, 1889 (3rd edn).

Grimm, J. Deutsche Mythologie. Göttingen 1835, 1875 (4th edn); tr 1883.

—— Über das Verbrennen der Leichen. In his Kleinere Schriften vol 2, Berlin 1865.

Mone, F. J. Untersuchungen zur Geschichte der teutschen Heldensage. Quedlinburg 1936.

Zeuss, J. C. Die Deutschen und die Nachbarstämme. Munich 1837.

Simrock, F. Deutsche Mythologie. Bonn 1853.

Müllenhoff, K. Zeugnisse und Excurse zur deutschen Heldensage. Zeitschrift für Deutsches Alterthum 12 1860.

—— Deutsche Altertumskunde. Berlin 1870, 1890 (rev M. Roediger).

Müller, W. Mythologie der deutschen Heldensage. Heilbronn 1886.

Bradley, H. The Goths. 1888.

Rydberg, V. Teutonic mythology. Tr B. Anderson 1889.

Gummere, F. B. Germanic origins: a study in primitive culture. New York 1892.

Sijmons, B. Heldensage. In Pauls Grundriss vol 3, Strasbourg 1893.

Jonsson, F. Den oldnorske og oldislandske litteraturs historie. 3 vols Copenhagen 1893–1902.

Jiriczek, O. L. Die deutsche Heldensage. Leipzig 1894; tr M. Bentinck Smith 1902 (as Northern hero legends).

—— Deutsche Heldensagen. Vol 1, Strasbourg 1898.

Binz, G. Zeugnisse zur germanischen Sage in England. Paul and Braune, Beiträge zur Geschichte der Deutschen Sprache und Literatur 20 1895.

Golther, W. Handbuch der germanischen Mythologie. Leipzig 1895.

Kluge, F. Zeugnisse zur germanischen Sage in England. E Studien 21 1895.

Schauffler, T. Zeugnisse zur Germania des Tacitus aus der altnordischen und angelsächsischen Dichtung. Vol 1, Ulm 1898.

Heyne, M. Fünf Bücher deutscher Hausaltertümer. 3 vols Leipzig 1899–1903.

Mogk, E. Deutsche Mythologie. In Pauls Grundriss, Strasbourg 1900 (2nd edn).

John, I. B. Popular studies in mythology, romance and folklore. Vol 11, 1901.

Schrader, O. Reallexikon der indogermanischen Altertumskunde. Vol 1, Strasbourg 1901, 1917.

Herrmann, P. Erläuterungen zu den neun ersten Büchern des Saxo Grammaticus. 2 pts Leipzig 1901–22.

Chantepie de la Saussaye, P. D. The religion of the Teutons. 4 vols Boston 1902.

Kauffmann, F. Northern mythology. Tr M. Steele Smith 1903.

—— Deutsche Altertumskunde. Vol 1, Munich 1913.

Heusler, A. Lied und Epos in germanischer Sagendichtung. Dortmund 1905.

—— Geschichtliches und Mythisches in der germanischen

Heldensage. Sitzungsberichte der Königlichen Preussischen Akademie der Wissenschaften 37 1909.

—— Die altgermanische Dichtung. Berlin 1923.

Groenbech, V. Vor folkeæt i oldtiden. 4 vols Copenhagen 1909–12; tr 2 vols 1931 (The culture of the Teutons); tr German, 2 vols Hamburg 1937–9.

Meyer, R. M. Altgermanische Religionsgeschichte. Leipzig 1910.

Clarke, M. G. Sidelights on Teutonic history during the migration period. Cambridge 1911.

Hoops, J. Reallexikon der germanischen Altertumskunde. Strasbourg 1911–.

Maurus, P. Die Wielandsage in der Literatur. Munich 1911.

Schoenfeld, M. Wörterbuch der altgermanischen Personen- und Völkernamen. Heidelberg 1911.

Chadwick, H. M. The heroic age. Cambridge 1912.

Widsith. Ed R. W. Chambers, Cambridge 1912.

von der Leyen, F. Die deutschen Heldensagen. Munich 1912, 1923.

Helm, K. Altgermanische Religionsgeschichte. 2 vols Heidelberg 1913–53.

—— Gaut. Beiträge zur Geschichte der Deutschen Sprache und Literatur 62 1938.

—— Wodan, Ausbreitung und Wanderung seines Kultes. Giessen 1946.

Moorman, F. W. English place-names and Teutonic sagas. E & S 5 1914.

Neckel, G. Adel und Gefolgschaft: ein Beitrag zur germanischen Altertumskunde. Beiträge zur Geschichte der Deutschen Sprache und Litteratur 41 1916.

Flom, G. T. Alliteration and variation in old Germanic name-giving. MLN 32 1917.

Jente, R. Die mythologischen Ausdrücke im altenglischen Wortschatz. Heidelberg 1921.

Wolters, F. and C. Petersen. Die Heldensagen der germanischen Frühzeit. Breslau 1921.

Larsen, H. Wudga: a study in the Theoderic legends. PQ 1 1922.

Krappe, A. H. The legend of Roderick, last of the Visigothic kings, and the Ermanarich cycle. Heidelberg 1923.

—— Etudes de mythologie et de folklore germaniques. Paris 1929.

—— Les dieux jumeaux dans la religion germanique. Acta Philologica Scandinavica 6 1931.

Malone, K. The literary history of Hamlet, 1: the early tradition. Anglistische Forschungen 59 1923.

Major, A. F. Ship burials in Scandinavian lands and the beliefs that underlie them. Folk-lore 25 1924.

Singer, S. Stil und Weltanschauung der altgermanischen Poesie. In Festschrift für Oskar Walzel, Wildpark-Potsdam 1924.

Wadstein, E. Norden och Västeuropa i gammal tid. Stockholm 1925.

Philippson, E. A. Germanisches Heidentum bei den Angelsachsen. Leipzig 1929.

—— Neuere Forschung auf dem Gebiet der germanischen Mythologie. Germanic Rev 11 1936.

—— Die agrarische Religion der Germanen nach den Ergebnissen der nordischen Ortsnamenforschung. PMLA 51 1936.

—— Der germanische Mütter- und Matronen-kult am Niederrhein. Germanic Rev 19 1944.

—— Die Genealogie der Götter in germanischer Religion, Mythologie und Theologie. Urbana 1953.

Schütte, G. Our forefathers. Tr 2 vols Cambridge 1929–33.

Ashdown, M. (ed). English and Norse documents relating to the reign of Ethelred the Unready. Cambridge 1930.

Hermannson, H. (ed). Islendingabók: the book of the Icelanders. Ithaca 1930. With trn.

—— The problem of Wineland. New York 1936.

—— The sagas of the kings and the mythical-heroic sagas: two bibliographical supplements. Ithaca 1937.

Hübener, G. England und die Gesittungsgrundlage der europäischen Frühgeschichte. Frankfurt 1930.

Liestøl, K. The origin of the Icelandic family sagas. Oslo 1930.

MacCulloch, J. A. Eddic. 1930 (vol 2 of The mythology of all races).

—— The Celtic and Scandinavian religions. 1948.

Olrik, A. Viking civilization. Rev H. Ellekilde 1930.

Christiansen, R. T. The Viking and the Viking wars in Irish and Gaelic traditions. Oslo 1931.

Indrebø, G. Gamal norsk homiliebok. Oslo 1931.

Karsten, T. E. Les anciens Germains. Tr F. Mossé, Paris 1931.

Koht, H. The Old Norse sagas. 1931.

Munn, W. A. Wineland voyages. St John's Newfoundland 1931.

Naumann, H. (ed). Frühgermanisches Dichterbuch. Berlin 1931.

—— Germanischer Schicksalsglaube. Jena 1934.

—— Der germanische König und seine Dichter. Zeitschrift für Deutsche Bildung 15 1939.

Nerman, B. The poetic Edda in the light of archaeology. Coventry 1931.

Phillpotts, B. F. Edda and saga. 1931.

Borchling, C. and R. Muuss (ed). Die Friesen. Breslau 1931. Essays.

Birkeli, E. Høgsætet: det gamle ondvege i religionshistorisk belysning. Stavanger 1932.

Cawley, F. S. (ed). Hrafnkels saga Freysgoða. Cambridge Mass 1932.

—— The figure of Loki in Germanic mythology. Harvard Theological Rev 32 1939.

van Hamel, A. G. Oðinn hanging on the tree. Acta Philologica Scandinavica 7 1932.

—— The mastering of the mead. In Studia germanica tillägnade E. A. Kock, Lund 1934.

—— Gods, skalds and magic. Saga-book 11 1936.

—— The conception of fate in early Teutonic and Celtic religion. Ibid.

Heimskringla: or the lives of the Norse kings, by Snorre Sturlason. Ed E. Monsen, tr A. H. Smith, Cambridge 1932.

Strasser, K. T. Sachsen und Angelsachsen. Hamburg 1932, 1941 (rev).

Baesecke, G. Der Vocabularius Sti Galli in der angelsächsischen Mission. Halle 1933.

—— Vor- und Frühgeschichte des deutschen Schrifttums. 2 vols Halle 1940–53.

Jordans, W. Der germanische Volksglaube von den Toten und Dämonen im Berg: die Spuren in England. Bonner Studien 17 1933.

Mitteis, H. Lehnrecht und Staatsgewalt. Weimar 1933.

—— Der Staat des hohen Mittelalters. Weimar 1941, 1953 (rev).

—— Die Krise des deutschen Königwahlerechts. Sitzungsberichte der Bayerischen Akademie der Wissenschaften (philologisch-historische Klasse) 1950.

Mossé, F. La saga de Grettir. Paris 1933. A French trn.

—— Bibliographia gotica: a bibliography of writings on the Gothic language to the end of 1940. Mediaeval Stud 12 1950; suppl 15 1953.

Schneider, H. Germanische Heldensage. 3 vols Berlin 1928–34.

—— Das germanische Epos. Tübingen 1936.

—— Über die ältesten Götterlieder der Nordgermanen. Sitzungsberichte der Bayerischen Akademie der Wissenschaften (philologisch-historische Abteilung) 1936.

—— et al. Germanische Altertumskunde. Munich 1938, 1951. Includes H. de Boor, Dichtung; H. Schneider, Glauben, etc.

—— Germanic mythological poetry. Tr M. O. Walshe, London Medieval Stud 1 1938.

Schröder, F. R. Quellenbuch zur germanischen Religionsgeschichte. Berlin 1933.

—— Germanische Heldendichtung. Tübingen 1935.

—— Untersuchungen zur germanischen und vergleichenden Religionsgeschichte. 2 vols Tübingen 1941.

Schütte, G. The problem of the Hraid-Goths. Acta Philologica Scandinavica 8 1933.

—— Die Wohnsitze der Angeln und Kimbern. Acta Philologica Scandinavica 14 1940.

—— Skjǫldungsagnene i ny Læsemaade. Danske Studier 39 1942.

—— Anglian legends in Danish traditions. Acta Philologica Scandinavica 16 1943.

—— 'Gothonic': the most neutral denomination for the Germanic nations. In Philologica: the [Kemp] Malone anniversary studies, Baltimore 1949.

Shetelig, H. Vikingeminner i Vest-Europa. Oslo 1933.

Shetelig, H. and H. Falk. Scandinavian archaeology. Tr E. V. Gordon, Oxford 1937.

—— Arkeologi, historie, kunst, kultur: mindre avhandlinger. Bergen 1947.

—— Classical impulses in Scandinavian art from the migration period to the Viking age. Oslo 1949.

Bretschneider, A. Die Heliandheimat und ihre sprachgeschichtliche Entwicklung. Marburg 1934.

Clemen, C. C. Altgermanische Religionsgeschichte. Bonn 1934.

Gamillscheg, E. Romania germanica: Sprach- und Siedlungsgeschichte der Germanen auf dem Boden des alten Römerreichs. 3 vols Berlin 1934–6 (Pauls Grundriss vol 11, 1–3).

—— Germanische Siedlung in Belgien und Nordfrankreich. Abhandlung der Preussischen Akademie der Wissenschaften (philologisch-historische Klasse) 1937.

Helgason, J. Norrön litteraturhistorie. Copenhagen 1934.

—— Íslenzk miðaldakvæði: islandske digte fra senmiddelalderen. 2 vols Copenhagen 1936–8.

—— and S. Nordal. Litteraturhistorie: Norge og Island. Stockholm 1953.

Jeffrey, M. The discourse in seven Icelandic sagas. Bryn Mawr 1934.

Ludwig, W. Untersuchungen über den Entwicklungsgang und die Funktion des Dialogs in der isländischen Saga. Halle 1934.

Malone, K. The votaries of Nerthus. Namn och Bygd 22 1934.

Rooth, E. G. T. Zum Heliandproblem. In Studia germanica tillägnade E. A. Kock, Lund 1934.

—— Saxonica: Beiträge zur niedersächsischen Sprachgeschichte. Lund 1949.

—— Nordseegermanische Beiträge. Stockholm 1957 (Filologiskt Arkiv 5).

Schlauch, M. Romance in Iceland. 1934.

—— The women of the Icelandic sagas. Amer-Scandinavian Rev 31 1943.

—— and M. H. Scargill. Three Icelandic sagas. New York 1950. Tr from Icelandic.

Thórólfsson, B. K. Rímur fyrir 1600. Copenhagen 1934.

de Vries, J. De skaldenkenningen met mythologischen inhoud. Haarlem 1934.
— Odin am Baume. In Studia germanica tillägnade E. A. Kock, Lund 1934.
— Die Welt der Germanen. Leipzig 1934.
— Altgermanische Religionsgeschichte. 2 vols Berlin 1935–7 (Pauls Grundriss vol 12, 1–2), 1956–7 (rewritten).
— De Godsdienst der Germanen. In G. van der Leeuw, De Godsdiensten der Wereld vol 2, Amsterdam 1941.
— Altnordische Literaturgeschichte. 2 vols Berlin 1941–2 (Pauls Grundriss vols 15–16), 1964–7.
— Die geistige Welt der Germanen. Halle 1943.
— Betrachtungen zum Wielandabschnitt in der þiðrekssaga. Arkiv för Nordisk Filologi 65 1950.
— Der heutige Stand der germanischen Religionsforschung. Germanisch-romanische Monatsschrift 33 1951.
— Kimbren und Teutonen. In Erbe der Vergangenheit: Festgabe für K. Helm, Tübingen 1951.
— Über das Verhältnis von Óðr und Óðinn. Zeitschrift für Deutsche Philologie 73 1954.
— Kelten und Germanen. Berne and Munich 1960.
— Heroic song and heroic legend, translated by B. J. Timmer. Oxford 1963.
Arndt, J. Germanische Kunst: von der altnordischen Kunst bis zur Kunst der Wikingzeit. Leipzig 1935.
Barger, E. The problem of Roman survivals in Germany. EHR 50 1935.
Jones, G. Four Icelandic sagas. Princeton 1935. Tr from Icelandic.
— Mabinogi and Edda. Saga-book 13 1946.
— History and fiction in the sagas of the Icelanders. Saga-book 13 1953.
Kelchner, G. D. Dreams in Old Norse literature and their affinities in folklore, with an appendix containing the Icelandic texts and translations. Cambridge 1935.
Larson, L. M. The earliest Norwegian laws. New York 1935. Tr from Norwegian.
von der Leyen, F. Das Reich deutscher Volksdichtung: Märchen, Sage, Legende, Zauberspruch, Segen, Rätsel und Volkslied. Berlin 1935.
— Die Götter der Germanen. Munich 1938.
Lot, F. Les invasions germaniques. Paris 1935.
Turville-Petre, G. The cult of Freyr in the evening of Paganism. Proc Leeds Philosophical Soc 3 1935.
— (ed). Víga-Glúms saga. Oxford 1940.
— and E. S. Olszewska. The life of Guðmund the Good, Bishop of Holar. Coventry 1942. Tr from Norse.
Turville-Petre, G. Notes on the intellectual history of the Icelanders. History 27 1942.
— The heroic age of Scandinavia. 1951.
— Origins of Icelandic literature. Oxford 1953.
— Myth and religion of the North. 1964.
Gutenbrunner, S. Die germanischen Götternamen der antiken Inschriften. Halle 1936.
— Germanische Frühzeit in den Berichten der Antike. Halle 1939.
— Schleswig-Holsteins älteste Literatur von der Kimbernzeit bis zur Gudrundichtung. Kiel 1949.
— Heldenleben und Heldendichtung. Zeitschrift für Deutsche Philologie 73 1954.
Hollander, L. M. Old Norse poems. New York 1936.
— Litotes in Old Norse. PMLA 53 1938.
— The Skalds: a selection of their poems. Princeton 1945.
— The translation of Skaldic poetry. Scandinavian Stud 18 1945.
— The sagas of Kormák and the Sworn Brothers. New York 1949. Tr from Norse.
— The Old Norse God Óðr. JEGP 49 1950.
Holtsmark, A. En islandsk scholasticus fra det 12 århundre. Oslo 1936.

Kjær, H. St Canute and St Olaf in the Church of the Nativity, Bethlehem. Saga-book 11 1936.
Lehmann, P. Skandinaviens Anteil an der lateinischen Literatur und Wissenschaft des Mittelalters. Sitzungsberichte der Bayerischen Akademie der Wissenschaften 1936–7.
— Erforschung des Mittelalters: ausgewählte Abhandlungen und Aufsätze. Leipzig 1941.
Nørlund, P. Viking settlers in Greenland. Cambridge 1936.
Smith, A. H. The sons of Ragnar Lothbrok. Saga-book 11 1936.
— The early literary relations of England and Scandinavia. Ibid.
Tellenbach, G. Libertas, Kirche und Weltordnung im Zeitalter des Investiturstreites. Stuttgart 1936; tr Oxford 1940.
Vasiliev, A. A. The Goths in the Crimea. Cambridge Mass 1936.
Anderson, W. Nordische Bildkunst des ersten Jahrtausends. Annales de l'Institut Kondakov (Seminarium Kondakovianum) 9 1937.
Bennett, J. A. W. The beginnings of Norse studies in England. Saga-book 12 1937.
Craigie, W. A. The art of poetry in Iceland. Oxford 1937.
— The romantic poetry of Iceland. Glasgow 1950.
— (ed). Sýnisbók islenzkra rimna. 3 vols 1952. Specimens of the Icelandic metrical romances.
Freeden, H. von and G. Smolka. Auswanderer: Bilder und Skizzen aus der Geschichte der deutschen Auswanderung. Leipzig 1937.
Krogmann, W. Loki. Acta Philologica Scandinavica 12 1937.
— Die Heimatfrage des Heliand im Lichte des Wortschatzes. Wismar 1937.
— Der Name Germanen. Archiv 175 1939.
Much, R. (ed). Die Germania des Tacitus. Heidelberg 1937.
Sveinsson, E. Ó. The Icelandic family sagas and the period in which their authors lived. Acta Philologica Scandinavica 12 1937.
— The age of the Sturlungs: Icelandic civilization in the thirteenth century. Tr Ithaca 1953.
Anderson, J. G. C. (ed). Cornelii Taciti de origine et situ Germanorum. Oxford 1938.
Arbman, H. et al. Vendel i fynd och forskning: skrift utgiven upplands fornminnesförening. Stockholm 1938.
de Boor, H. Dichtung. In Germanische Altertumskunde, ed H. Schneider, Munich 1938, 1951 (rev).
— and R. Newald. Geschichte der deutschen Literatur von den Anfängen bis zur Gegenwart. Vol 1, Die deutsche Literatur von Karl dem Grossen bis zum Beginn der höfischen Dichtung 770–1170, Munich 1949.
Brady, C. Becca of the Banings. JEGP 37 1938.
— The date and metre of the Hamðismál. JEGP 38 1939.
— The legends of Ermanaric. Berkeley 1943.
Hashagen, J. Der Einfluss der angelsächsischen Kultur auf das deutsche Mittelalter. Germanisch-romanische Monatsschrift 26 1938.
Ljungberg, H. Den nordiska religionen och kristendomen: studier över det nordiska religionsskiftet under vikingatiden. Upsala 1938.
— Tor. Upsala 1947.
Mohr, W. Entstehungsgeschichte und Heimat der jüngeren Eddalieder südgermanischen Stoffes. Zeitschrift für Deutsches Altertum 75 1938.
Wattenbach, W. Deutschlands Geschichtsquellen im Mittelalter. Vol 1, Deutsche Kaiserzeit, by R. Holtzmann, Berlin 1938; 2 i, Die Vorzeit, by W. Levison, Weimar 1952; 2 ii, Die Karolinger, by W. Levison and H. Löwe, Weimar 1953; Beiheft, Die Rechtsquellen, by R. Büchner, Weimar 1953.

Dumézil, G. Mythes et dieux des Germains. Paris 1939.
— Loki. Paris 1948.
— Les dieux des Indo-européens. Paris 1952.
— La Saga de Hadingus (Saxo Grammaticus I, v–viii). Paris 1953.
Hempel, H. Matronenkult und germanischer Mütterglaube. Germanisch-romanische Monatsschrift 27 1939.
Kern, F. Kingship and law in the Middle Ages. Tr Oxford 1939.
Kuhn, H. Zur Worstellung und -Betonung im Altgermanischen. Beiträge zur Geschichte der Deutschen Sprache und Literatur 57 1933.
— Westgermanisches in der altnordischen Verskunst. Beiträge zur Geschichte der Deutschen Sprache und Literatur 63 1939.
— König und Volk in der germanischen Bekehrungsgeschichte. Zeitschrift für Deutsches Altertum 77 1940.
— Das nordgermanische Heidentum in den ersten christlichen Jahrhunderten. Zeitschrift für Deutsches Altertum 79 1942.
— Zur Gliederung der germanischen Sprachen. Zeitschrift für Deutsches Altertum 68 1956.
— Zur Geschichte der Walthersage. In Festgabe für Ulrich Pretyel, Berlin 1963.
Picton, H. Early German art and its origins, from the beginnings to about 1050. 1939.
Schmidt, K. D. Die Bekehrung der Ostgermanen zum Christentum (der ostgermanische Arianismus). Göttingen 1939.
Schultze, A. Zum altnordischen Eherecht. Leipzig 1939.
Schuster, M. (ed). Das Germanentum bei Cäsar und Tacitus. Vienna 1939.
Seaver, E. I. Some examples of Viking figure representation in Scandinavia and the British Isles. In Medieval studies in memory of A. K. Porter vol 2, Cambridge Mass 1939.
Springer, O. The style of the Old Icelandic family sagas. JEGP 38 1939.
— Medieval pilgrim routes from Scandinavia to Rome. Mediaeval Stud 12 1950.
Wolff, L. Das deutsche Schrifttum bis zum 1939–51. Vol 1 of Handbuch des deutschen Schrifttums, ed F. Koch.
— (ed). Erbe der Vergangenheit: Festgabe für K. Helm. Tübingen 1951.
Woolf, H. B. The Old Germanic principles of name-giving. Baltimore 1939.
— The naming of women by the continental Germans. In Studies for W. A. Read, Baton Rouge 1940.
Berron, G. Der Heliand als Kunstwerk. Würzburg 1940.
Dickins, B. The cult of St Olave in the British Isles. Saga-book 12 1940.
Eckhardt, K. A. Ingwi und die Ingwaeonen in der Überlieferung des Nordens. Weimar 1939.
— Nordische Chronologie. Bonn 1940.
Reinerth, H. et al. Vorgeschichte der deutschen Stämme. 3 vols Leipzig 1940.
Beissner, F. Geschichte der deutschen Elegie. Berlin 1941 (Pauls Grundriss vol 14).
Kralik, D. von. Die Sigfrid-trilogie im Nibelungenlied und in der Thidrekssaga. Vol 1, Halle 1941.
Smyser, H. M. and F. P. Magoun. Survivals in Old Norwegian of medieval English, French and German literature, together with the Latin version of the heroic legend of Walter of Aquitaine. Baltimore 1941.
Baetke, W. Das Heilige im Germanischen. Tübingen 1942.
— Die Götterlehre der Snorra-Edda. Berlin 1950.
— Christliches Lehngut in der Sagareligion; has Svǫldr-Problem: zwei Beiträge zur Saga-kritik. Berlin 1952.
Campbell, A. The opponents of Haraldr at Hafrsfjǫrðr. Saga-book 12 1942.

— Saxo Grammaticus and Scandinavian historical tradition. Saga-book 13 1946.
— West Germanic problems in the light of modern dialects. Trans of Philological Soc 1947.
Ellis, H. R. Sigurd in the art of the Viking Age. Antiquity 16 1942.
Fiedler, H. G. The oldest study of Germanic proper names. MLR 37 1942.
Flasdieck, H. M. England und die altgermanische Welt: sprachwissenschaftliche Ergebnisse und Ausgabe. Neuphilologische Monatsschrift 13 1942.
Maurer, F. Nordgermanen und Alemannen: Studien zur germanischen und frühdeutschen Sprachgeschichte, Stammes- und Volkskunde. Strasbourg 1942, Berne 1952 (rev).
Mayer, T. (ed). Mannestum und Heldenideal. Marburg 1942. Includes F. Müller, Das griechische und das nordische Heldenideal; M. Deutschbein, Germanisches Heldentum in der angelsächsischen Zeit, etc.
Boberg, I. M. Die Sage von Vermund und Uffe. Acta Philologica Scandinavica 16 1943.
Lukman, N. C. Skjǫldunge und Skilfinge: Hunnen- und Herulerkönige in ostnordischer Überlieferung. Copenhagen 1943.
Mezger, F. Did the institution of marriage by purchase exist in Old Germanic law? Speculum 18 1943.
— The publication of slaying in the saga and in the Nibelungenlied. Arkiv för Nordisk Filologi 61 1946.
Frings, T. Herbort: Studien zur Thidrekssaga. Vol 1, Leipzig 1943.
— Die Stellung der Niederlande im Aufbau des Germanischen. Halle 1944.
Heusler, A. Kleine Schriften. Ed H. Reuschel, Berlin 1943.
Pipping, R. Den fornsvenska litteraturen. Stockholm 1943.
Askeberg, F. Norden och Kontinenten i gammal tid. Upsala 1944.
Collinder, B. The name Germani. Arkiv för Nordisk Filologi 59 1944.
Genzmer, F. Germanische Seefahrt und Seegeltung. Munich 1944.
— Vorzeitsaga und Heldenlied. In Festschrift P. Kluckhohn und H. Schneider, Tübingen 1948.
— Heliand und die Bruchstücke der Genesis aus dem Altsächsischen und Angelsächsischen übertragen. Leipzig 1948.
— Germanische Zaubersprüche. Germanisch-romanische Monatsschrift 32 1951.
— Das Waltharilied und die Waldhere-Bruchstücke. Stuttgart 1953. Trn.
— Haben die Germanen vergiftete Schwerter verwendet? Arkiv för Nordisk Filologi 68 1953.
Magoun, F. P. A note on old west Germanic poetic unity. MP 43 1945. Includes trn of Hildebrandslied into OE.
— The Praefatio and Versus associated with some Old-Saxon Biblical poems. In Medieval studies in honor of J. D. M. Ford, Cambridge Mass 1948.
— On the Old-Germanic Altar- or Oath-ring (Stallahringr). Acta Philologica Scandinavica 20 1949.
— and H. M. Smyser. Walter of Aquitaine: materials for the study of his legend. New London Conn 1950.
Cross, S. H. The Scandinavian infiltration into early Russia. Speculum 21 1946.
Jørgensen, P. Über die Herkunft der Nordfriesen. Copenhagen 1946.
Kock, E. A. (ed). Den norsk-isländska skaldediktningen. 2 vols Lund 1946–9.
Leach, H. G. (ed). A pageant of Old Scandinavia. Princeton 1946. Anthology with trns.
Ensslin, W. Theoderich der Grossa. Munich 1947.
Swanton, J. R. The Wineland voyages. Washington 1947 (Smithsonian Inst).

Einarsson, S. Hvat megi fótr foeti veita? Scandinavian Stud 20 1948. Hamðismal, Athelstan legend, Godwin legend.

Levison, W. Aus rheinischer und fränkischer Frühzeit: ausgewählte Aufsätze. Ed W. Holtzmann, Düsseldorf 1948.

Mattingly, H. Tacitus on Britain and Germany: a new translation. 1948 (Penguin).

Paasche, F. Hedenskap og kristendom: studier i norrøn middelalder. Oslo 1948.

Stengel, E. E. Die Reichsabtei Fulda in der deutschen Geschichte. Weimar 1948.

Vleeskruyer, R. A. Campbell's views on Inguaeonic. Neophilologus 32 1948.

Drögereit, R. Sachsen und Angelsachsen. Niedersächsisches Jahrbuch für Landesgeschichte 21 1949.

—— Werden und der Heliand. Essen 1951.

Trillmich, W. and H. Aubin (ed). Kleine Bücherkunde zur Geschichtswissenschaft. Hamburg 1949.

Foerste, W. Untersuchungen zur westfälischen Sprache des 9 Jahrhunderts. Marburg 1950.

Folz, R. Le souvenir et la légende de Charlemagne dans l'Empire germanique médiéval. Paris 1950.

—— Etudes sur le culte liturgique de Charlemagne dans les églises de l'Empire. Paris 1951.

Harmer, F. E. The English contribution to the epistolary usages of early Scandinavian kings. Saga-book 13 1950.

Jones, C. W. Medieval literature in translation. New York 1950.

Meier, J. Ahnengrab und Rechtsstein. Berlin 1950.

Schieffer, T. Angelsachsen und Franken: zwei Studien zur Kirchengeschichte des 8 Jahrhunderts. Akademie der Wissenschaften und der Literatur in Mainz (Abhandlungen der geistes- und sozialwissenschaftlichen Klasse), Wiesbaden 1950.

Young, J. I. A note on the Norse occupation of Ireland. History 35 1950.

Wartburg, W. von. Umfang und Bedeutung der germanischen Siedlung in Nordgallien im 5 und 6 Jahrhunderten. Berlin 1950.

Schwarz, E. Goten, Nordgermanen, Angelsachsen: Studien zur Ausgliederung der germanischen Sprachen. Berne and Munich 1951.

Bowra, C. M. Heroic poetry. 1952.

Brown, U. (ed). Þorgils saga ok Hafliða. Oxford 1952.

Edda, Skalden. Saga: Festschrift zum 70 Geburtstag von F. Genzer. Ed H. Schneider, Heidelberg 1952.

Höfler, O. Zur Bestimmung mythischer Elemente in der geschichtlichen Überlieferung. In Festschrift für O. Scheel, Schleswig 1952.

Kaspers, W. Germanische Götternamen. Zeitschrift für Deutsches Altertum 83 1952.

Rosenfeld, H. Buck, Schrift und lateinische Sprachkenntnis bei den Germanen vor der christlichen Mission. Rheinisches Museum für Philologie new ser 95 1952.

Brøgger, A. W. and H. Shetelig. The Viking ships: their ancestry and evolution. Oslo 1953.

Paulsen, P. Schwertortbänder der Wikingerzeit: ein Beitrag zur Frühgeschichte Osteuropas. Stuttgart 1953.

Thomas, R. G. Some exceptional women in the sagas. Saga-book 13 1953.

Gautries, J. A. des. Les noms de personnes scandinaves en Normandie de 911 à 1066. Upsala 1954.

van Haeringen, C. B. Netherlandic language research. Leyden 1954.

Kolb, E. Alemannisch-nordgermanisches Wortgut. Frauenfeld 1956.

Rösel, L. Die Gliederung der germanischen Sprachen nach dem Zeugnis ihrer Flexionsformen. Nuremberg 1962.

Schlaug, W. Die altsächsischen Personenamen vor dem Jahre 1000. Lund 1962.

Davidson, H. R. E. Gods and myths of northern Europe. 1964 (Pelican).

Frings, T. and G. Lerchner. Niederländisch und Niederdeutsch. Berlin 1966.

A. C.

(b) HISTORY

For fuller lists see W. Bonser, An Anglo-Saxon and Celtic bibliography, Oxford 1957, on material pbd to 1953; and D. P. Kirby, The making of early England, 1967, with select bibliography to 1966.

General Studies

Kemble, J. M. The Saxons in England. 1849, 1876 (rev).

Freeman, E. A. The history of the Norman Conquest of England. Vol 1, 1867, 1877 (rev); vol 2, 1868, 1877 (rev); vol 3, 1869, 1875 (rev); vol 4, 1871, 1876 (rev); vol 5, 1876; vol 6, index 1879 (rev).

Chadwick, H. M. The origin of the English nation. Cambridge 1907.

Stenton, F. M. William the Conqueror. 1908.

—— Anglo-Saxon England. Oxford 1943, 1970 (rev).

Chambers, R. W. England before the Norman Conquest. 1928.

Kendrick, T. D. A history of the Vikings. 1930.

—— British antiquity. 1950.

Hodgkin, R. H. A history of the Anglo-Saxons. Oxford 1935, 1952 (rev).

Collingwood, R. G. and J. N. L. Myres. Roman Britain and the English settlements. Oxford 1936, 1937 (rev).

Levison, W. England and the Continent in the eighth century. Oxford 1946.

Sayles, G. O. The medieval foundations of England. 1948, 1964 (rev).

Poole, A. L. From Domesday book to Magna Carta. Oxford 1951, 1955 (rev).

Wallace-Hadrill, J. M. The barbarian West 400–1000. 1952, 1957 (rev).

Whitelock, D. The beginnings of English society. 1952 (Pelican), 1965 (rev).

—— (ed). English historical documents vol 1: c. 500–1042. 1955.

Douglas, D. C. and G. W. Greenaway (ed). English historical documents vol 2: 1042–1189. 1953.

Wainwright, F. T. The problem of the Picts. Edinburgh 1955.

Hunter Blair, P. An introduction to Anglo-Saxon England. Cambridge 1956.

—— Roman Britain and early England 55 BC–AD 871. 1963.

Duckett, E. S. Alfred the Great and his England. 1957.

Arbmann, H. The Vikings. 1961.

Brooke, C. N. L. From Alfred to Henry III 871–1272. 1961.

—— The Saxon and Norman kings. 1963.

Loyn, H. R. Anglo-Saxon England and the Norman Conquest. 1962.

—— Alfred the Great. Oxford 1967.

Sawyer, P. H. The age of the Vikings. 1962.

Richardson, H. G. and G. O. Sayles. The governance of medieval England. Edinburgh 1963.

Douglas, D. C. William the Conqueror. 1964.

Kirby, D. P. The making of early England. 1967.

Jones, G. A history of the Vikings. Oxford 1968.

Barlow, F. Edward the Confessor. 1970.

Foote, P. G. and D. M. Wilson. The Viking achievement. 1970.

Page, R. I. Life in Anglo-Saxon England. 1970.

Wilson, D. The Vikings and their origins. 1970.

The Church

Bright, W. Chapters of early English church history. Oxford 1878, 1897 (rev).

Stenton, F. M. The early history of the abbey of Abingdon. 1913.

Robinson, J. A. The times of St Dunstan. Oxford 1923.

Allison, T. English religious life in the eighth century. 1929.

— Pioneers of English learning. Oxford 1932.

Clapham, A. W. English romanesque architecture before the Conquest. Oxford 1930.

Crawford, S. J. Anglo-Saxon influence on western Christendom 600–800. Oxford 1933.

Thompson, A. H. (ed). Bede: his life, times and writings. Oxford 1935.

Pfeiffer, E. Bonifatius: sein Leben und Wirken. Munich 1936.

Moore, W. J. The Saxon pilgrims to Rome and the Schola saxonum. Fribourg 1937.

Ryan, A. M. A map of old English monasteries and related ecclesiastical foundations AD 400–1066. Ithaca 1939.

Verbist, G. H. Saint Willibrord. Louvain 1939.

Emerton, E. The letters of Saint Boniface. New York 1940.

Brechter, S. Die Quellen zur Angelsachsenmission Gregors des Grossen. Münster 1941.

Duckett, E. S. Anglo-Saxon saints and scholars. New York 1947.

— Alcuin. New York 1951.

— Saint Dunstan of Canterbury. 1955.

— The wandering saints. 1959.

Jones, C. W. Saints' lives and chronicles in early England. Ithaca 1947.

Michael, J. P. Bonifatius und die apostolische Sukzession. Paderborn 1954.

Raabe, C. et al. Sankt Bonifatius. Fulda 1954.

Talbot, C. H. (ed). The Anglo-Saxon missionaries in Germany. 1954.

Chadwick, N. K. (ed). Studies in the early British Church. Cambridge 1958.

Deanesley, M. The pre-Conquest Church in England. 1961, 1963 (rev).

— Sidelights on the Anglo-Saxon Church. 1962.

Godfrey, J. The Church in Anglo-Saxon England. Cambridge 1962.

Fisher, E. A. The greater Anglo-Saxon churches. 1962.

— Introduction to Anglo-Saxon architecture and sculpture. 1964.

Barlow, F. The English Church 1000–66. 1963.

Taylor, H. M. and J. Anglo-Saxon architecture. Cambridge 1965.

Barley, M. M. and R. P. C. Hanson (ed). Christianity in Britain 300–700. Leicester 1968.

Hunter Blair, P. The world of Bede. 1970.

Thomas, C. Britain and Ireland in early Christian times. 1971.

Constitutional, Social and Economic

Seebohm, F. The English village community. 1883.

— Tribal custom in Anglo-Saxon law. 1902.

Maitland, F. W. Domesday book and beyond. Cambridge 1897.

Larson, L. M. The King's household in England before the Norman Conquest. Madison 1904.

Chadwick, H. M. Studies on Anglo-Saxon institutions. Cambridge 1905.

Vinogradoff, P. The growth of the manor. 1904, 1911 (rev).

— English society in the eleventh century. Oxford 1908.

Stenton, F. M. Types of manorial structure in the northern Danelaw. Oxford 1910.

— The Latin charters of the Anglo-Saxon period. Oxford 1955.

Liebermann, F. The national assembly in the Anglo-Saxon period. Halle 1913.

Ekwall, E. Scandinavians and Celts in the north-west of England. Lund 1918.

Jolliffe, J. E. A. Pre-feudal England: the Jutes. Oxford 1933.

Tait, J. The medieval English borough. Manchester 1936.

Schramm, P. E. Geschichte des englischen Königtums im Lichte der Krönung. Weimar 1937; tr Oxford 1937.

Orwin, C. S. and C. S. The open fields. Oxford 1938.

Sutherland, C. H. V. Anglo-Saxon gold coinage in the light of the Crondall hoard. Oxford 1948.

Finberg, H. P. R. Tavistock abbey. Cambridge 1951.

— Lucerna. 1964.

Chrimes, S. B. An introduction to the administrative history of medieval England. Oxford 1952.

Darby, H. C. The Domesday geography of eastern England. Cambridge 1952, 1957 (rev).

— and I. B. Terrett. The Domesday geography of midland England. Cambridge 1954.

— The Domesday geography of south-east England. Cambridge 1962.

— The Domesday geography of northern England. Cambridge 1962.

— and R. W. Finn. The Domesday geography of south-west England. Cambridge 1967.

Grattan, J. H. G. and C. Singer. Anglo-Saxon magic and medicine. Oxford 1952.

Oleson, T. The Witenagemot in the reign of Edward the Confessor. Toronto 1955.

Sylloge of coins in the British isles. 1958– (Br Acad).

John, E. Land tenure in early England. Leicester 1960.

— Orbis Britanniae. Leicester 1966.

Dolley, R. H. M. (ed). Anglo-Saxon coins. 1961.

— Anglo-Saxon pennies. 1964 (BM).

— Viking coins of the Danelaw and Dublin. 1965 (BM).

Warren Hollister, C. W. Anglo-Saxon military institutions. Oxford 1962.

Bonser, W. The medical background to Anglo-Saxon England. 1965.

Petersson, H. B. A. Anglo-Saxon currency. Lund 1969.

Wallace-Hadrill, J. M. Early Germanic kingship in England and on the Continent. Oxford 1971.

Art and Archaeology

Brown, G. Baldwin. The arts in early England. 6 vols 1903–37.

Leeds, E. T. The archaeology of the Anglo-Saxon settlements. Oxford 1913.

— Celtic ornament in the British isles down to AD 700. Oxford 1933.

— Early Anglo-Saxon art and archaeology. Oxford 1936.

— A corpus of early Anglo-Saxon great square-headed brooches. Oxford 1949.

Brøndsted, J. Early English ornament. 1924.

— The Vikings. 1960.

Åberg, N. The Anglo-Saxons in England. 1927.

— The occident and the orient in the art of the seventh century: the British Isles. Stockholm 1943.

Collingwood, W. G. Northumbrian crosses of the pre-Norman age. 1927.

Wheeler, R. E. M. London and the Saxons. 1935.

Pfeilstucker, S. Spätantikes und germanisches Kunstgut in der frühangelsächsischen Kunst. Berlin 1936.

Ehmer, H. Die sächsischen Siedlungen auf dem französischen Litus saxonicum. Halle 1936.

Kendrick, T. D. Anglo-Saxon art to AD 900. 1938.

— Late Saxon and Viking art. 1949.

Maclagan, E. The Bayeux tapestry. 1943.

Shetelig, H. et al. Viking antiquities in Great Britain and Ireland. 6 vols Oslo 1940–54.

Bruce-Mitford, R. L. S. The Sutton Hoo ship-burial. 1947 (BM), 1972 (rev).

Rice, D. T. The Byzantine element in late Saxon art. Oxford 1947.
—— English art 871–1100. Oxford 1952.
Kirk, J. R. The Alfred and Minister Lovel jewels. Oxford 1948, 1971 (rev).
Saxl, F. and R. Wittkower. British art and the Mediterranean. Oxford 1948.
Jessop, R. Anglo-Saxon jewellery. 1950.
Oakeshott, W. F. The sequence of English medieval art. 1950.
Copley, G. T. The conquest of Wessex in the sixth century. 1954.
Fox, C. Offa's dyke. 1955.
Battiscombe, C. F. (ed). The relics of St Cuthbert. Oxford 1956.
Harden, D. B. (ed). Dark-Age Britain. 1956.
Stenton, F. M. (ed). The Bayeux tapestry. 1957, 1965 (rev).
Wilson, D. M. The Anglo-Saxons. 1950.
—— Catalogue of antiquities of the later Saxon period vol 1. 1964 (BM).
—— and O. Klindt-Jensen. Viking art. 1966.
Davidson, H. R. E. The sword in Anglo-Saxon England. Oxford 1962.
Wainwright, F. T. Archaeology and place-names and history. 1962.
Green, C. Sutton Hoo. 1963.
Meaney, A. Gazetteer of early Anglo-Saxon burial sites. 1964.
Evison, V. I. The fifth-century invasions south of the Thames. 1965.
Werckmeister, O.-K. Irisch-northumbrische Buchmalerei des 8 Jahrhunderts und monastische Spiritualität. Berlin 1967.
Myres, J. N. L. Anglo-Saxon pottery and the settlement of England. Oxford 1969.
Okasha, E. Hand-list of Anglo-Saxon non-runic inscriptions. Cambridge 1971.

Collected Studies

Poole, R. L. (ed). Studies in chronology and history. Oxford 1934.

Fox, C. F. and B. Dickins (ed). The early cultures of north-west Europe. Cambridge 1950.
Charlesworth, M. P. et al. The heritage of early Britain. 1952.
Chadwick, N. K. (ed). Studies in early British history. Cambridge 1954.
—— (ed). Celt and Saxon: studies in the early British border. Cambridge 1963.
Clemoes, P. (ed). The Anglo-Saxons. Cambridge 1959.
—— and K. Hughes. England before the Conquest: studies in primary sources presented to Dorothy Whitelock. Cambridge 1971.
Whitelock, D. et al. The Norman Conquest. 1966.
Stenton, D. M. (ed). Preparatory to Anglo-Saxon England: being the collected papers of F. M. Stenton. Oxford 1970.

Various

Searle, W. G. Anglo-Saxon bishops, kings and nobles. Cambridge 1899.
Laistner, M. L. W. Thought and letters in west Europe AD 500–900. 1931, Ithaca 1957 (rev).
—— The intellectual heritage of the early Middle Ages. New York 1957.
Map of Britain in the Dark Ages: ordnance survey. South sheet. 1935; north sheet, 1938; single sheet, 1966 (rev).
Ekwall, E. The concise Oxford dictionary of English place-names. Oxford 1936, 1960 (rev).
Wright, C. E. The cultivation of saga in Anglo-Saxon England. Edinburgh 1939.
Whitelock, D. The audience of Beowulf. Oxford 1951.
Jackson, K. H. Language and history in early Britain. Edinburgh 1953.
—— The Gododdin. Edinburgh 1969.
Reaney, P. H. The origin of English place-names. 1960.
Cameron, K. English place-names. 1961.
Korner, S. The battle of Hastings. Lund 1964.
Greenfield, S. B. A critical history of old English literature. New York 1965.

P. H. B.

(c) PALAEOGRAPHY

A. LATIN PALAEOGRAPHY: *Periodicals; Bibliographies; Handbooks; Facsimiles; Latin mss to c. 1100; Latin mss after c. 1100; Humanistic mss; Abbreviations etc; Codicological studies.*

B. INSULAR MSS TO 1100: *Irish and Welsh mss; Anglo-Saxon mss; Anglo-Saxon documents; Anglo-Saxon script on the Continent; Complete facsimiles of insular mss; Insular illuminated mss.*

C. ENGLISH MSS AFTER C. 1100: *English mss to c. 1500; Mss in Middle English; Complete facsimiles of mss in Middle English; English illuminated mss; English handwriting after c. 1500.*

D. RUNIC SCRIPT: *Bibliographies; Collections of runic inscriptions mainly outside the English tradition; General studies; Anglo-Saxon runes and runic mss.*

A. Latin Palaeography

(1) Periodicals

Palaeographia latina. Ed W. M. Lindsay. Vols 1–6, 1922–9.
Scriptorium: revue internationale des études relatives aux mss. 1947– (in progress).

(2) Bibliographies

Bieler, L. Insular palaeography: present state and problems. Scriptorium 3 1949.
Perrat, C. Paléographie romaine. B. Bischoff, Paläographie der abendländischen Buchschriften vom v bis zum xii Jahrhundert; G. Post, A general report: suggestions for future studies in late medieval and Renaissance Latin palaeography, in Relazioni del x congresso internazionale di scienze storiche vol 1, Rome 1955.
Brown, T. J. Latin palaeography since Traube. Trans Cambridge Bibl Soc 3 1959–63.

Kristeller, P. O. Latin ms books before 1600: a list of the printed catalogues and unpublished inventories of extant collections. New York 1960, 1965 (rev).
University of London Library. The palaeography collection. [Ed J. Gibbs] 2 vols Boston 1968.
Bischoff, B. Paläographie. In Dahlmann-Waitz Quellenkunde der deutschen Geschichte vol 1, Stuttgart 1969.

(3) Handbooks

Reusens, E. H. J. Eléments de paléographie. Louvain 1899.
Steffens, F. Lateinische Paläographie. Freiburg 1903, Trier 1909 (rev); tr French, ed R. Coulon, Trier and Paris 1910.
Prou, M. Manuel de paléographie latine et française. Paris 1904, 1924 (rev A. de Boüard).
Thompson, E. M. Introduction to Greek and Latin palaeography. Oxford 1912.
Lowe, E. A. Handwriting. In The legacy of the Middle Ages, ed C. G. Crump and E. F. Jacob, Oxford 1926; Rome 1969 (pbd separately, rev).

Ullman, B. L. Ancient writing and its influence. New York 1932, Cambridge Mass 1969 (with introd and supplementary bibliography).

Battelli, G. Lezioni di paleografia. Vatican 1936, 1949 (rev).

Dain, A. Les manuscrits. Paris 1949, 1964 (rev).

Fairbank, A. F. A book of scripts. 1949, 1968 (rev).

Foerster, H. Abriss der lateinischen Paläographie. Berne 1949, Stuttgart 1963 (rev).

Bischoff, B. Paläographie; mit besonderer Berücksichtigung des deutschen Kulturgebiets. Berlin 1952, 1957 (rev). Rptd from Deutsche Philologie im Aufriss ed W. Stammler vol 1.

Bischoff, B., G. I. Lieftinck and G. Battelli. Nomenclature des écritures livresques du ixe au xvie siècle. Paris 1954.

Cencetti, G. Lineamenti di storia della scrittura latina. Bologna 1954.

Denholm-Young, N. Handwriting in England and Wales. Cardiff 1954.

(4) Facsimiles

Delisle, L. V. Le cabinet des mss de la Bibliothèque Nationale. 4 vols Paris 1868–81.

Palaeographical Society: facsimiles of mss and inscriptions. Ed E. A. Bond et al 1873–94.

Recueil des fac-similés à l'usage de l'Ecole des Chartes. 4 vols Paris 1880–7.

Archivio paleografico italiano. Ed E. Monaci et al, Rome 1882–.

Chatelain, E. Paléographie des classiques latins. 2 vols Paris 1884–1900.

Thompson, E. M. and G. F. Warner. Catalogue of ancient mss in the BM: vol 2, Latin. 1884.

Flammeront, J. Album paléographique du nord de la France. Lille 1896.

Kenyon, F. G. Facsimiles of royal, historical, literary and other autographs in the BM. 1899.

— Facsimiles of biblical mss in the BM. 1900.

Chroust, A. Monumenta palaeographica. Munich (later Leipzig) 1902–40.

New Palaeographical Society: facsimiles of ancient mss. Ed E. M. Thompson et al 1903–30.

Petzet, E. and O. Glauning. Deutsche Schrifttafeln des xi bis xvi Jahrhunderts aus Handschriften der K. Hof- und Staatsbibliothek in München. 5 pts Munich (later Leipzig) 1910–30.

Crous, E. and J. Kirchner. Die gotischen Schriftarten. Leipzig 1928.

Katterbach, B., A. Pelzer and C. Silva-Tarouca. Codices latini saeculi xiii. 1930 (Exempla scripturarum).

Katterbach, B. and C. Silva-Tarouca. Epistolae et instrumenta saeculi xiii. 1930 (Exempla scripturarum).

Battelli, G. Acta pontificum. 1933, 1965 (rev) (Exempla scripturarum).

Federici, V. La scrittura delle cancellerie italiane dal secolo xii al xviii. Rome 1934.

Lowe, E. A. Codices latini antiquiores. 12 pts Oxford 1934–71.

Bruckner, A. Scriptoria medii aevi helvetica. Geneva 1935.

Mallon, J., R. Marichal and C. Perrat. L'écriture latine de la capitale romaine à la minuscule. Paris 1939.

Foerster, H. Mittelalterliche Buch- und Urkundenschriften. Berne 1946.

Bruckner, A. and R. Marichal. Chartae latinae antiquiores. Olten and Lausanne 1954–.

Kirchner, J. Scriptura latina libraria. Munich 1955.

— Scriptura gothica libraria. Munich and Vienna 1966.

Catalogue des mss en écriture latine portant des indications de date, de lieu ou de copiste. Ed C. M. D. Samaran and R. Marichal. Pt 1, Musée Condé et bibliothèques parisiennes, 2 vols Paris 1959; pt 2, Bibliothèque Nationale, fonds latin, nos 1 à 8,000, 2 vols 1962; pt 5, Est de la France, 2 vols 1965; pt 6,

Bourgogne, centre, sud-est et sud-ouest de la France, 2 vols 1968– (in progress).

Lieftinck, G. I. Mss datés conservés dans les Pays-Bas: catalogue paléographique. Pt 1, Les mss d'origine étrangère, 816–c. 1550. 2 vols Amsterdam 1964– (in progress).

Thomson, S. H. Latin bookhands of the Middle Ages 1100–1500. Cambridge 1969.

Unterkircher, F. Katalog der datierten Handschriften in lateinischer Schrift in Österreich. Pt 1, Die datierten Handschriften der österreichischen Nationalbibliothek bis zum Jahre 1400, 2 vols Vienna 1969– (in progress).

Mss datés conservés en Belgique. Ed F. Masai and M. Wittek. Pt 1 819–1400, Ghent 1970– (in progress).

(5) Latin Mss to c. 1100

Traube, L. Vorlesungen und Abhandlungen. 3 vols Munich 1909–20.

Loew, E. A. The Beneventan script. Oxford 1914.

Schiaparelli, L. La scrittura latina nell' età romana. Como 1921.

Lowe, E. A. and E. K. Rand. A 6th-century fragment of the letters of Pliny the younger. Washington 1922.

Lowe, E. A. A hand-list of half-uncial mss. In Miscellanea Ehrle vol 4, 1924 (Studi e testi).

— Scriptura Beneventana. 2 vols Oxford 1929.

— Palaeographical papers 1907–65. 2 vols Oxford 1972.

Millares Carlo, A. Tratado di paleografia española. Barcelona and Buenos Aires 1929, Madrid 1932 (rev).

Koehler, W. Die karolingischen Miniaturen. Berlin 1930–.

Rand, E. K. A survey of the mss of Tours. 2 vols Cambridge Mass 1929.

Jones, L. W. The script of Cologne from Hildebald to Hermann. Cambridge Mass 1932.

— The script of Tours in the 10th century. Speculum 14 1939.

— The art of writing at Tours from 1000 to 1200 AD. Speculum 15 1940.

Rand, E. K. and L. W. Jones. The earliest book of Tours. Cambridge Mass 1934.

Carey, F. M. The scriptorium of Reims during the archbishopric of Hincmar. In Classical and medieval studies in honor of E. K. Rand, New York 1938.

Lehmann, P. J. G. Erforschung des Mittelalters. 5 vols Leipzig (later Stuttgart) 1941–62.

Marichal, R. De la capitale romaine à la minuscule. In M. Audin, Somme typographique vol 1, Paris 1947.

Mallon, J. Paléographie romaine. Madrid 1952.

Tjäder, J. O. Die nichtliterarischen Papyri Italiens aus der Zeit 445–700. Lund 1954 (Svenska Institut i Rom).

Bischoff, B. Die karolingische Minuskel. In Karl der Grosse: Werk und Wirkung: exhibition at Aachen, 1965.

— Panorama der Handschriftenüberlieferung aus der Zeit Karls des Grossen. In Karl der Grosse vol 2, ed W. Braunfels, Stuttgart 1965.

— Mittelalterliche Studien. 2 vols Stuttgart 1966–7.

— Frühkarolingische Handschriften und ihre Heimat. Scriptorum 22 1968.

Petrucci, A. L'onciale romana. Studi Medievali 3rd ser 12 1971.

(6) Latin Mss after c. 1100

Meyer, W. Die Buchstaben-Verbindungen der sogenannten gothischen Schrift. Abhandlungen der Gesellschaft der Wissenschaften zu Göttingen new ser 6 1897.

Hill, G. F. The development of Arabic numerals in Europe. Oxford 1915.

Wehmer, C. Die Namen der 'gotischen' Buchschriften. Zentralblatt für Bibliothekswesen 49 1932.

Kruitwagen, B. Laat-middeleeuwsche paleografica. Hague 1942.

Steinberg, S. H. Medieval writing-masters. Library 4th ser 22 1942.

Wehmer, C. Die Schreibmeisterblätter des späten Mittelalters. In Miscellanea Giovanni Mercati vol 6, 1946 (Studi e testi).

Boussard, J. Influences insulaires dans la formation de l'écriture gothique. Scriptorium 5 1951.

Van Dijk, S. J. P. An advertisement sheet of an early 14th-century writing master at Oxford. Scriptorium 10 1956.

Vreese, W. L. de. Over handschriften en handschriftenkunde. Zwolle 1962.

Petrucci, A. La scrittura di Francesco Petrarca. Vatican 1967 (Studi e testi).

— Francesco Petrarca, Epistole autografe. Padua 1968.

(7) Humanistic Mss

Hessel, A. Die Entstehung der Renaissanceschriften. Archiv für Urkundenforschung 13 1933.

Morison, S. Early humanistic script and the first Roman type. Library 4th ser 24 1944.

Mardersteig, G. Leon Battista Alberti e la rinascita del carattere lapidario romano nel quattrocento. Italia Medioevale e Umanistica 2 1959.

Ullman, B. L. The origin and development of humanistic script. Rome 1960.

Fairbank, A. J. and R. W. Hunt. Humanistic script of the 15th and 16th centuries. Oxford 1960.

Meiss, M. Towards a more comprehensive Renaissance palaeography. Art Bull 42 1960.

Wardrop, J. The script of humanism. Oxford 1963.

Ogg, O. Three classics of Italian calligraphy. New York 1963.

Calligraphy and palaeography: essays presented to A. J. Fairbank. Ed A. S. Osley 1965.

Casamassima, E. Trattati di scrittura del cinquecento italiano. Milan 1966.

Alexander, J. J. G. and A. C. de la Mare. The Italian mss in the library of Major J. R. Abbey. 1969.

(8) Abbreviations etc

Cappelli, A. Lexicon abbreviaturarum. Milan 1889, 1961 (6th edn).

Martin, C. T. The record interpreter. 1892, 1910 (rev).

Traube, L. Nomina sacra. Munich 1907.

Lindsay, W. M. Notae latinae. Cambridge 1915.

Schiaparelli, L. Avviamento allo studio delle abbreviature latine nel medioevo. Florence 1926.

Bains, D. Supplement to Notae latinae. Cambridge 1936.

Laurent, M. H. De abbreviationibus et signis scripturae gothicae. Rome 1939.

Mentz, A. Die tironischen Noten. Berlin 1944.

— Geschichte der Kurzschrift. Wolfenbüttel 1949.

Bischoff, B. Übersicht über die nichtdiplomatischen Geheimschriften des Mittelalters. Graz and Cologne 1954.

Pelzer, A. Abréviations latines médiévales. Louvain and Paris 1964.

(9) Codicological Studies

Wattenbach, W. Das Schriftwesen im Mittelalter. Leipzig 1871, 1896 (rev).

Johnston, E. Writing and illuminating, and lettering. 1906.

Schubart, W. Das Buch bei den Griechen und Römern. Berlin and Leipzig 1907, 1921 (rev), Heidelberg 1962 (rev).

Kenyon, F. G. Books and readers in ancient Greece and Rome. Oxford 1932, 1951 (rev).

Destrez, J. La pecia dans les mss universitaires du xiiie et du xive siècle. Paris 1935.

Lesne, E. Les libres, 'scriptoria' et bibliothèques du commencement du viiie à la fin du xie siècle. In Histoire de la propriété ecclésiastique en France vol 4, Lille 1938.

Santifaller, L. Beiträge zur Geschichte der Beschreibstoffe im Mittelalter vol 1. Graz and Cologne 1953.

Roberts, C. H. The codex. Proc Br Acad 40 1954.

— Books in the Graeco-Roman world and in the New Testament. In Cambridge history of the Bible vol 1, ed P. R. Ackroyd and C. F. Evans, Cambridge 1970.

Dondaine, A. Secrétaires de Saint Thomas. Rome 1956.

Delaissé, L. M. J. La miniature flamande: le mécénat de Philippe le Bon. 1959. Exhibition in Brussels etc.

Bühler, C. F. The 15th-century book: the scribes, the printers, the decorators. Philadelphia 1960.

Ker, N. R. From 'Above top line' to 'Below top line': a change in scribal practice. Celtica 5 1960.

— Medieval mss in British Libraries: vol 1, London. Oxford 1969.

McGurk, P. M. J. Latin Gospel books from AD 400 to AD 800. 1961 (Pbn de Scriptorium).

Stevenson, A. Paper as bibliographical evidence. Library 5th ser 17 1962.

Turner, E. G. Greek papyri. Oxford 1968.

— Greek mss of the ancient world. Oxford 1971.

Skeat, T. C. Early Christian book-production: papyri and mss. In Cambridge history of the Bible vol 2, ed G. W. H. Lampe, Cambridge 1969.

See also Book Production and Distribution, col 927f, below: C–E, H.

B. Insular Mss to c. 1100

(1) Irish and Welsh Mss

Lindsay, W. M. Early Irish minuscule script. Oxford 1910.

— Early Welsh script. Oxford 1912.

Schiaparelli, L. Note paleografiche: intorno all' origine e ad alcuni caratteri della scrittura e del sistema abbreviativo irlandese. Archivio Storico Italiano 74 1916.

Nash-Williams, V. E. The Early Christian monuments of Wales. Cardiff 1950.

McGurk, P. M. J. The Irish pocket Gospel book. Sacris Erudiri 8 1956.

Hughes, K. The distribution of Irish scriptoria and centres of learning from 730 to 1111. In Studies in the early British Church, ed N. K. Chadwick, Cambridge 1958.

Dold, A., L. Einzelhöfer and D. H. Wright. Das irische Palimpsestsakramentar im CLM 14429 der Staatsbibliothek München. Beuron 1964 (Texte und Arbeiten).

(2) Anglo-Saxon Mss

Wanley, H. Librorum vett. septentrionalium catalogus. In G. Hickes, Linguarum vett. septentrionalium thesaurus vol 2, Oxford 1705.

Skeat, W. W. Twelve facsimiles of Old English mss. Oxford 1892.

Forbes-Leith, W. The Gospel book of St Margaret. Edinburgh 1896.

Kuypers, A. B. The book of Cerne. Cambridge 1902.

Keller, W. Angelsächsische Palaeographie. 2 vols Berlin 1906.

— Über die Akzente in den angelsächsischen Handschriften. Prager Deutsche Studien 8 1908.

Gasquet, F. A. and E. Bishop. The Bosworth psalter. 1908.

Greg, W. W. Facsimiles of twelve early English mss in the Library of Trinity College, Cambridge. Cambridge 1913.

Turner, C. H. Early Worcester mss of the 8th century. Oxford 1916.

Hessel, A. Studien zur Ausbreitung der karolingischen Minuskel: 2, Grossbritannien und Italien. Archiv für Urkundenforschung 8 1923.

Gilson, J. P. Description of the Saxon ms of the four Gospels in the library of York Minster. York 1925.

Mynors, R. A. B. Durham Cathedral mss to the end of the 12th century. Oxford 1939.

Kuhn, S. M. The Vespasian Psalter and the Old English charter hands. Speculum 18 1943.

Ker, N. R. Aldred the scribe. E & S 28 1943.
— Hemming's cartulary: descriptions of the two Worcester cartularies in Cotton Tiberius A. xiii. In Studies in mediaeval history presented to F. M. Powicke, Oxford 1948.
— A palimpsest in the National Library of Scotland. Trans Edinburgh Bibl Soc 3 1948–55.
— Catalogue of mss containing Anglo-Saxon. Oxford 1957.
— The handwriting of Archbishop Wulfstan. In England before the Conquest: studies presented to Dorothy Whitelock, Cambridge 1971.
Clemoes, P. A. M. Liturgical influence on punctuation in late Old English and early Middle English mss. 1952 (Dept of Anglo-Saxon, Cambridge, Occasional Papers).
Bishop, T. A. M. Notes on Cambridge mss 1–7. Trans Cambridge Bibl Soc 1–4 1953–68 (in progress).
— A charter of King Edwy. Bodleian Lib Record 6 1957–61.
— An early example of the square minuscule. Trans Cambridge Bibl Soc 4 1964–8.
— The Corpus Martianus Capella. Ibid.
— An early example of Insular-Caroline. Ibid.
— The Copenhagen Gospel book. Nordisk Tidskrift för Bok- och Biblioteksväsen 54 1967.
— Lincoln Cathedral ms 182. Lincolnshire History & Archaeology 2 1967.
— English Caroline miniscule. Oxford 1971.
Derolez, R. Runica manuscripta: the English tradition. [Bruges 1954].
Wormald, F. The insular script in late 10th-century English Latin mss. In Atti del x congresso internazionale di scienze storiche, Rome 1955.
Natale, A. R. Esercizi di calligrafia insulare in codici del secolo viii. Archivio Storico Italiano 116 1958.
Lowe, E. A. English uncial. Oxford 1960.
Wright, D. H. Some notes on English uncial. Traditio 17 1961.
Colgrave, B. and A. Hyde. Two recently discovered leaves from Old English mss. Speculum 37 1962.
McGurk, P. M. J. An Anglo-Saxon Bible fragment of the late 8th century: Royal 1 E. VI. Jnl of Warburg & Courtauld Inst 25 1962.
Okasha, E. The non-runic scripts of Anglo-Saxon inscriptions. Trans Cambridge Bibl Soc 4 1964–8.
— Hand-list of Anglo-Saxon non-runic inscriptions. Cambridge 1971.
Vezin, J. Mss des xe et xie siècles copiés en Angleterre en minuscule caroline et conservés à la Bibliothèque Nationale de Paris. In Humanisme actif: mélanges offerts à Julien Cain, Paris 1968.
Brown, T. J. Northumbria and the Book of Kells. Anglo-Saxon England 1 1972.

(3) Anglo-Saxon Documents

Facsimiles of ancient charters in the BM. Ed E. A. Bond 4 pts 1873–8.
Facsimiles of Anglo-Saxon mss. Ed W. B. Saunders 3 pts Southampton 1878–85.
Bishop, T. A. M. and P. T. V. M. Chaplais. Facsimiles of English royal writs to AD 1100. Oxford 1957.
Chaplais, P. T. V. M. The origin and authenticity of the royal Anglo-Saxon diploma. Jnl of Soc of Archivists 3 1965–9.
— The Anglo-Saxon chancery: from the diploma to the writ. Ibid.
— Some early Anglo-Saxon diplomas on single sheets: originals or copies? Ibid.
— Who introduced charters into England? the case for Augustine. Ibid.
Sawyer, P. H. Anglo-Saxon charters: an annotated list and bibliography. 1968 (Royal Historical Soc).
Whitelock, D., N. R. Ker and Lord Rennell. The will of Æthelgifu. Oxford 1968 (Roxburghe Club).

(4) Anglo-Saxon Script on the Continent

Gallée, J. H. Old-Saxon texts: facsimiles of mss. Leyden 1895.
Enneccerus, M. Die ältesten deutschen Sprach-Denkmäler in Lichtdrucken. Frankfurt 1897.
Baesecke, G. Der deutsche Abrogans und die Herkunft des deutschen Schrifttums. Halle 1930.
— Der Vocabularius Sti Galli in der angelsächsischen Mission. Halle 1933.
— Vor- und Frühgeschichte des deutschen Schrifttums. 2 vols Halle 1940–53.
— Das Hildebrandlied. Halle 1945.
Bischoff, B. Die südostdeutschen Schreibschulen und Bibliotheken in der Karolingerzeit: vol 1, Die bayrischen Diözesen. Leipzig 1940, Wiesbaden 1960 (rev).
— Lorsch im Spiegel seiner Handschriften. In Die Reichsabtei Lorsch: Festschrift zum Bedenken an ihre Stiftung 764, Darmstadt 1973.
——and J. Hofmann. Libri sancti Kyliani: die Würzburger Schreibschule und die Dombibliothek im viii und ix Jahrhundert. Würzburg 1952.
Lieftinck, G. I. Le ms d'Aulu-Gelle à Leeuwarden exécuté à Fulda en 836. Bulletino dell'Archivio Paleografico Italiano new ser 1 1955.
Hofmann, J. Altenglische und althochdeutsche Glossen aus Würzburg und dem weiteren angelsächsischen Missionsgebiet. Beiträge zur Geschichte der deutschen Sprache und Literatur (Halle) 85 1963.

(5) Complete Facsimiles of Insular Mss

Zupitza, J. Beowulf. 1882, 1959 (rev N. Davis) (EETS).
Sweet, H. and W. Griggs. The Epinal glossary. 1883 (EETS).
Warren, F. E. The Antiphonary of Bangor. 2 vols 1893–5 (Bradshaw Soc).
Dewick, E. S. Facsimiles of Horae de beata Maria virgine from English mss of the 11th century. 1902 (Bradshaw Soc).
Warner, G. F. and H. A. Wilson. The Benedictional of St Æthelwold. Oxford 1910 (Roxburghe Club).
Schlutter, O. B. Das Epinaler und Erfurter Glossar: 1, Faksimile und Translitteration des Epinaler Glossars. 1912 (Bibliothek der angelsächsischen Prosa).
Foerster, M. Il codice vercellese. Rome 1913.
Breul, K. The Cambridge songs. Cambridge 1915.
Wilson, H. A. The Calendar of Saint Willibrord. 1918 (Bradshaw Soc).
Liber vitae ecclesiae Dunelmensis. 1923 (Surtees Soc).
Gunther, R. T. The herbal of Apuleius Barbarus. Oxford 1925 (Roxburghe Club).
Gollancz, I. The Cædmon ms. 1927.
James, M. R. Marvels of the East. 1929 (Roxburghe Club).
— The Canterbury psalter. 1935.
Chambers, R. W., M. Förster and R. Flower. The Exeter book of Old English poetry. 1933.
The Parker Chronicle and Laws. Ed R. Flower and A. H. Smith 1941 (EETS).
Langenhove, G. van. Aldhelm's De laudibus virginitatis. Bruges 1941.
Alton, E. H. and P. Meyer. Evangeliorum quattuor codex Cennanensis. 3 vols Berne 1950.
Early English mss in facsimile. Ed B. Colgrave, later P. A. M. Clemoes, Copenhagen 1951–.
  1. The Thorkelin transcripts of Beowulf. Ed K. Malone 1951.
  2. The Leningrad Bede. Ed O. Arngart 1952.
  3. The Tollemache Orosius. Ed A. Campbell 1953.
  4. The Peterborough Chronicle. Ed D. Whitelock and C. Clark 1954.
  5. Bald's Leechbook. Ed C. E. Wright 1955.
  6. The Pastoral care: King Alfred's translation of St Gregory's Regula pastoralis. Ed N. R. Ker 1956.
  7, 11. Textus Roffensis. Ed P. Sawyer 1957–62.

8. The Paris Psalter. Ed B. Colgrave et al 1958.

9. The Moore Bede. Ed P. H. Blair and R. A. B. Mynors 1959.

10. The Blickling Homilies. Ed R. Willard 1960.

12. The Nowell Codex. Ed K. Malone 1963.

13. Aelfric's first series of Catholic homilies. Ed N. Eliason and P. A. M. Clemoes 1966.

14. The Vespasian Psalter. Ed D. H. Wright and A. Campbell 1967.

15. The Rule of St Benedict. Ed D. H. Farmer 1968.

16. The Durham Ritual. Ed T. J. Brown, F. Wormald, A. S. C. Ross and E. G. Stanley 1969.

Kendrick, T. D., T. J. Brown, R. L. S. Bruce-Mitford, H. Roosen-Runge, A. S. C. Ross, E. G. Stanley and A. E. A. Werner. Evangeliorum quattuor codex Lindisfarnensis. 2 vols Olten and Lausanne 1956–60.

Luce, A. A., G. O. Simms, P. Meyer and L. Bieler. Evangeliorum quattuor codex Durmachensis. 2 vols Olten 1960.

Hunt, R. W. Saint Dunstan's classbook from Glastonbury. 1961 (Umbrae codicum occidentalium).

Bishop, T. A. M. Aethici Istri Cosmographia Vergilio Salisburgensi rectius adscripta. 1966 (Umbrae codicum occidentalium).

Brown, T. J., R. Powell and P. Waters. The Stonyhurst Gospel of St John. 1969 (Roxburghe Club).

(6) Insular Illuminated Mss

Westwood, J. O. Facsimiles of the miniatures and ornaments of Anglo-Saxon and Irish mss. 1868.

Salin, B. Die altgermanische Thierornamentik. Stockholm 1904.

Homburger, O. Die Anfänge der Malschule von Winchester im x Jahrhundert. 1912 (Studien über christliche Denkmäler).

Zimmermann, E. H. Vorkarolingische Miniaturen. 5 vols Berlin 1916.

Brøndsted, T. Early English ornament. London and Copenhagen 1924.

Millar, E. G. English illuminated mss from the 10th to the 13th century. Paris and Brussels 1926.

Saunders, O. E. English illumination. 2 vols Florence and Paris 1928.

Tolhurst, J. B. L. An examination of two Anglo-Saxon mss of the Winchester school. Archaeologia 83 1933.

Kendrick, T. D. Anglo-Saxon art to AD 900. 1938.

— Late Saxon and Viking art. 1949.

Niver, C. The psalter in the BM Harley 2904. In Medieval studies in memory of A. K. Porter vol 2, Cambridge Mass 1939.

Micheli, G. L. L'enluminure du haut Moyen Age et les influences irlandaises. Brussels 1939.

Henry, F. Irish art in the early Christian period, to 800 AD. 1940, 1965 (rev).

— Les débuts de la miniature irlandaise. Gazette des Beaux-Arts 6th ser 37 1950.

— An Irish ms in the BM (Add 40618). Jnl Royal Soc of Antiquaries of Ireland 87 1957.

— Irish art during the Viking invasions 800–1020 AD. 1967.

— Irish art in the romanesque period 1020–1170 AD. 1970.

Åberg, N. The Occident and the Orient in the art of the 7th century: vol 1, British Isles. Stockholm 1943.

Wormald, F. The survival of Anglo Saxon illumination after the Norman Conquest. Proc Br Acad 30 1944.

— Decorated initials in English mss from AD 900 to 1100. Archaeologia 91 1945.

— English drawings of the 10th and 11th centuries. 1952.

— The miniatures in the Gospels of St Augustine: Corpus Christi College ms 286. Cambridge 1954.

— The Benedictional of Saint Ethelwold. 1959.

— An English 11th-century psalter with pictures: Cotton Tiberius C. vi. Walpole Soc 38 1962.

— Anglo-Saxon initials in a Paris Boethius ms. Gazette des Beaux-Arts 6th ser 62 1963.

— The 'Winchester School' before St Æthelwold. In England before the Conquest: studies presented to Dorothy Whitelock, Cambridge 1971.

Nordenfalk, C. Before the Book of Durrow. Acta Archaeologica 18 1947.

Masai, F. Essai sur les origines de la miniature dite irlandaise. 1947 (Pbn de Scriptorium).

Oakeshott, W. The sequence of English medieval art. 1950.

Paecht, O. Hugo pictor. Bodleian Lib Record 3 1951.

Duft, J. and P. Meyer. The Irish miniatures in the abbey library of St Gall. Olten 1953.

Dodwell, C. R. The Canterbury school of illumination. Cambridge 1954.

— L'originalité iconographique de plusieurs illustrations anglo-saxonnes de l'Ancien testament. Cahiers de Civilisation Médiévale 14 1971.

Rickert, M. Painting in Britain: the Middle Ages. 1954, 1965 (rev).

Schapiro, M. The decoration of the Leningrad ms of Bede. Scriptorium 12 1958.

Henderson, G. Late antique influences in some English mediaeval illustrations of Genesis. Jnl Warburg & Courtauld Inst 25 1962.

Heimann, A. Three illustrations from the Bury St Edmunds Psalter and their prototypes. Jnl Warburg & Courtauld Inst 29 1966.

Bruce-Mitford, R. L. S. The art of the Codex Amiatinus. Jnl of Archaeological Assoc 3rd ser 32 1969.

Alexander, J. J. G. Norman illumination at Mont St Michel 966–1100. Oxford 1970.

— Anglo-Saxon illumination in Oxford libraries. Oxford 1970.

Koehler, W. Buchmalerei des frühen Mittelalters: Fragmente und Entwürfe aus dem Nachlass. Munich 1972.

C. English Mss after c. 1100

(1) English Mss to c. 1500

Warner, G. F. and H. J. Ellis. Facsimiles of royal and other charters in the BM: vol 1, William I–Richard I. 1903.

Delisle, L. V. Rouleau mortuaire du B. Vital, abbé de Savigny. Paris 1909.

Johnson, C. and C. H. Jenkinson. English court hand, AD 1066 to 1500. 2 pts Oxford 1915.

Jenkinson, C. H. The later court hands in England from the 15th to the 17th century. 2 pts Cambridge 1927.

Salter, H. E. Facsimiles of early charters in Oxford muniment rooms. Oxford 1929.

Pollard, H. G. The Company of Stationers before 1557. Library 4th ser 18 1938.

Ker, N. R. William of Malmesbury's handwriting. EHR 59 1944.

— English mss in the century after the Norman Conquest. Oxford 1960.

Mynors, R. A. B. A 15th-century scribe: T. Werken. Trans Cambridge Bibl Soc 1 1949–53.

Vaughan, R. The handwriting of Matthew Paris. Ibid.

— Matthew Paris. Cambridge 1958.

Grieve, H. E. P. Examples of English handwriting 1150–1750. 1954 (Essex Record Office).

Parkes, M. B. A 15th-century scribe: Henry Mere. Bodleian Lib Record 6 1957–61.

Hector, L. C. The handwriting of English documents. 1958, 1966 (rev).

Bishop, T. A. M. Scriptores regis. Oxford 1961.

Parkes, M. B. English cursive bookhands 1250–1500. Oxford 1969.

Duke Humfrey and English humanism in the fifteenth century: catalogue of an exhibition held in the Bodleian Library. Oxford 1970.

Chaplais, P. T. V. M. Master John de Branketre and the office of notary in Chancery 1355–75. Jnl Soc of Archivists 4 1971.

(2) Mss in Middle English

Deanesly, M. Vernacular books in England in the 14th and 15th centuries. MLR 15 1920.

Crawford, S. J. The Worcester marks and glosses of the Old English mss in the Bodleian. Anglia 52 1928.

Schramm, W. L. The cost of books in Chaucer's time. MLN 48 1933.

Bell, H. E. The price of books in medieval England. Library 4th ser 17 1937.

Cawley, A. C. Punctuation in the early versions of Trevisa. London Mediaeval Stud 1 1939.

Ker, N. R. The date of the 'tremulous' Worcester hand. Leeds Stud in Eng 6 1937.

Schulz, H. C. Thomas Hoccleve, scribe. Speculum 12 1937.

Bühler, C. F. Sir John Paston's Grete Boke: a 15th-century best-seller. MLN 56 1941.

Loomis, L. H. The Auchinleck ms and a possible London bookshop of 1330–40. PMLA 57 1942.

Bennett, H. S. The production and dissemination of vernacular mss in the 15th century. Library 5th ser 1 1947.

Turville-Petre, J. E. Studies on the Ormulum ms. JEGP 46 1947.

Bliss, A. J. Notes on the Auchinleck ms. Speculum 26 1951.

Davis, N. A scribal problem in the Paston letters. Eng & Germanic Stud 4 1954.

Burchfield, R. W. A source of scribal error in early Middle English mss. MÆ 22 1953.

Doyle, A. I. Books connected with the Vere family and Barking Abbey. Trans of Essex Archaeological Soc new ser 25 1955–60.

— The work of a late 15th-century English scribe, William Ebesham. Bull John Rylands Lib 39 1957.

— An unrecognised piece of Piers the Ploughman's Creed and other work by its scribe. Speculum 34 1959.

— More light on John Shirley. MÆ 30 1961.

Zeeman, E. Punctuation in an early ms of Love's Mirror. RES new ser 7 1956.

Wright, C. E. English vernacular hands from the 12th to the 15th centuries. Oxford 1960.

Smith, K. L. A 15th-century vernacular ms reconstructed. Bodleian Lib Record 7 1962–7.

Lucas, P. J. John Capgrave OSA (1393–1464): scribe and 'publisher'. Trans Cambridge Bibl Soc 5 1969.

(3) Complete Facsimiles of Mss in Middle English

Facsimiles [of Chaucer mss]. Ed F. J. Furnivall 1876–85 (Chaucer Soc).

Carysfort, W., Earl of. The pageants of Richard Beauchamp Earl of Warwick. Oxford 1908 (Roxburghe Club).

The Ellesmere Chaucer. 2 vols Manchester 1911.

The mss of Chaucer's Troilus. Ed R. K. Root 1914 (Chaucer Soc).

Gollancz, I. Pearl, Cleanness, Patience and Sir Gawain. 1923 (EETS).

Pintelon, P. Chaucer's treatise on the astrolabe, ms 4862–4869 of the Royal Library in Brussels. Antwerp 1940.

Vallese, T. Un ignoto ricettario medico inglese del xiv secolo trovato nella Biblioteca Nazionale di Napoli. Naples 1940.

Price, D. J. The equatorie of the planetis, edited from Peterhouse ms 75.1. Cambridge 1955.

Ker, N. R. Facsimile of ms Bodley 34: St Katherine etc. 1960 (EETS).

— The owl and the nightingale. 1963 (EETS).

— Facsimile of BM ms Harley 2253. 1965 (EETS).

The Metamorphoses of Ovid translated by William Caxton 1480. 2 vols New York 1968.

(4) English Illuminated Mss

Millar, E. G. English illuminated mss of the 14th and 15th centuries. Paris and Brussels 1928.

Manly, J. M. and E. Rickert. The text of the Canterbury tales vol I: description of the mss, with a chapter on illuminations by M. Rickert. Chicago 1940.

Rickert, M. The reconstructed Carmelite Missal. 1952.

Paecht, O., C. R. Dodwell and F. Wormald. The St Albans Psalter. 1960 (Warburg Inst).

Paecht, O. The rise of pictorial narrative in 12th-century England. Oxford 1962.

Turner, D. H. Early Gothic illuminated mss in England. 1965.

Scott, K. L. A mid-15th-century English illuminating shop and its customers. Jnl Warburg & Courtauld Inst 31 1968.

(5) English Handwriting after c. 1500

Greg, W. W. English literary autographs 1550–1650. 2 vols Oxford 1925–32.

— Dramatic documents from the Elizabethan playhouses. 2 vols Oxford 1931.

Heal, A. and S. Morison. The English writing-masters and their copybooks 1570–1800. 1931.

Tannenbaum, S. A. The handwriting of the Renaissance. London and New York 1931.

Judge, C. B. Specimens of 16th-century English handwriting. Cambridge Mass 1935.

Flower, D. J. N. and A. N. L. Munby. English poetical autographs from Sir Thomas Wyat to Rupert Brooke. 1938.

Morison, S. American copybooks. Philadelphia 1951.

Brown, T. J. English literary autographs [1650–1950]. Book Collector 1–13 1952–64.

Fairbank, A. J. and B. Wolpe. Renaissance handwriting. 1960.

Fairbank, A. J. and B. Dickins. The italic hand in Tudor Cambridge. 1962 (Cambridge Bibl Soc).

Dawson, G. E. and L. Kennedy-Skipton. Elizabethan handwriting 1500–1650. New York 1966, London 1968 (rev).

See also Book Production and Distribution, cols 933–6, below : D (2)–(4).

For medieval and later libraries and private collections of mss see cols 985–96, below, III, Printing and Bookselling U–V.

T. J. B.

D. Runic Script

(1) Bibliographies

Arntz, H. Bibliographie der Runenkunde. Leipzig 1937. Nachträge und Ergänzungen 1 in his Berichte zur Runenforschung, Giessen 1939.

Marquardt, H. Bibliographie der Runeninschriften nach Fundorten 1: die Runeninschriften der britischen Inseln. Göttingen 1961.

(2) Collections of Runic Inscriptions mainly outside the English Tradition

Stephens, G. The Old-Northern runic monuments of Scandinavia and England. 4 vols London, Copenhagen and Lund 1866–1901.

— Handbook of the Old-Northern runic monuments of Scandinavia and England. London and Copenhagen 1884.

Bugge, S. and M. Olsen. Norges indskrifter med de ældre runer. 4 vols Oslo 1891–1924.

Söderberg, S. et al. Sveriges runinskrifter. Stockholm 1900–.

Marstrander, C. J. S. De gotiske runeminnesmerker. Norsk Tidsskrift for Sprogvidenskap 3 1929.

— De nordiske runeinnskrifter i eldre alfabet. Viking 16 1953.

Arntz, H. and H. Zeiss. Die einheimischen Runendenkmäler des Festlandes. Leipzig 1939.

Olsen, M. et al. Norges innskrifter med de yngre runer. 5 vols Oslo 1941-60.

Jacobsen, L. et al. Danmarks runeindskrifter. 3 vols Copenhagen 1941-2.

Bæksted, A. Islands runeindskrifter. Copenhagen 1942.

Royal Commission on the ancient monuments of Scotland: twelfth report. 3 vols Edinburgh 1946. On Maeshowe.

Olsen, M. Runic inscriptions in Great Britain, Ireland and the Isle of Man. In Viking antiquities in Great Britain and Ireland vol 6, ed H. Shetelig, Oslo 1954.

Jansson, S. B. F. The runes of Sweden. 1962.

Liestøl, A. Runer frå Bryggen. Viking 27 1964.

Krause, W. and H. Jankuhn. Die Runeninschriften im älteren Futhark. 2 vols Göttingen 1966.

(3) General Studies

Grimm, W. Über deutsche Runen. Göttingen 1821.

— Zur Litteratur der Runen. Wiener Jahrbücher der Literatur 43 1828.

Liljegren, J. G. Run-Lära. Stockholm 1832.

Wimmer, L. F. A. Runeskriftens Oprindelse og Udvikling i Norden. Aarbøger for Nordisk Oldkyndighed og Historie 1874.

— Die Runenschrift. Berlin 1887.

Thorsen, P. G. Om Runernes Brug til skrift udenfor det Monumentale. Copenhagen 1877.

Olsen, B. M. Runerne i den oldislandske literatur. Copenhagen 1883.

Friesen, O. v. Om runskriftens härkomst. Upsala 1904.

— et al. Runorna. Stockholm 1933.

Cahen, M. L'écriture runique chez les Germains. Scientia 1923.

— Origine et développement de l'écriture runique. Mémoires de la Société Linguistique de Paris 23 1923.

Marstrander, C. J. S. Om runene og runenavnenes oprindelse. Norsk Tidsskrift for Sprogvidenskap 1 1928.

Hammarström, M. Om runskriftens härkomst. Studier i Nordisk Filologi 20 1930.

Baesecke, G. Die Herkunft der Runen. Germanisch-romanische Monatsschrift 22 1934.

Schlottig, K. H. Beiträge zur Runenkunde und nordischen Sprachwissenschaft. Leipzig 1938.

Blomfield, J. Runes and the Gothic alphabet. Saga-book 12 1942.

Krause, W. Was man in Runen ritzte. Halle 1935, 1943 (rev).

— Untersuchungen zu den Runennamen. Nachrichten der Akademie der Wissenschaften in Göttingen 1947-8.

— Runen. Berlin 1970.

Bæksted, A. Runerne. Copenhagen 1943.

— Målruner og troldruner. Copenhagen 1952.

Arntz, H. Handbuch der Runenkunde. Halle 1935, 1944 (rev).

Moltke, E. Er runeskriften opstået i Danmark? Fra Nationalmuseets Arbejdsmark 1951.

Elliott, R. W. V. Runes. Manchester 1959.

Musset, L. Introduction à la runologie. Paris 1965.

Düwel, K. Runenkunde. Stuttgart 1968.

(4) Anglo-Saxon Runes and Runic Manuscripts

See also Cynewulf, Husband's message, Poetical dialogues of Solomon and Saturn, Exeter Book riddles and the Runic Poem, below.

Hickes, G. Linguarum vett. septentrionalium thesaurus. Oxford 1705.

Kemble, J. M. On Anglo-Saxon runes. Archaeologia 28 1840.

Grienberger, T. von. Die angelsächsischen Runenreihen und die s.g. Hrabanischen Alphabete. Arkiv för Nordisk Filologi 15 1899.

— Das ags. Runengedicht. Anglia 45 1921.

Hempl, G. Hickes's additions to the Runic poem. MP 1 1904.

Dickins, B. Runic and heroic poems. Cambridge 1915.

— A system of transliteration for Old English runic inscriptions. Leeds Stud in Eng 1 1932.

— Runic rings and Old English charms. Archiv 167 1935.

Klaeber, F. Die Ing-Verse im angelsächsischen Runengedicht. Archiv 142 1921.

Sisam, K. Cynewulf and his poetry. Proc Br Acad 18 1932; rptd in his Studies in the history of Old English literature, Oxford 1953.

Wrenn, C. L. Late Old English rune-names. MÆ 1 1932.

Wright, C. E. A postscript to 'Late Old English rune-names'. MÆ 5 1936.

— Robert Talbot and Domitian A. ix. MÆ 6 1937.

Keller, W. Zum altenglischen Runengedicht. Anglia 60 1936.

— Zur Chronologie der ae. Runen. Anglia 62 1938.

Raucq, E. Die Runen des Brüsseler Codex no 9565-9566. Mededeelingen van de Koninklijke Vlaamsche Academie voor Wetenschappen, Letteren en Schoone Kunsten van België 3 1941.

Dobbie, E. v. K. The Anglo-Saxon minor poems. New York 1942.

Krause, W. Ing. Nachrichten der Akademie der Wissenschaften in Göttingen 1944.

Arntz, H. Runen und Runennamen. Anglia 67-8 1944.

Bennett, J. A. W. The beginnings of runic studies in England. Saga-book 13 1951.

Derolez, R. Runica manuscripta. Bruges 1954; addn in E Studies 45 suppl 1964.

— Anglo-Saxon runes in Switzerland. E Studies 43 1962.

Elliott, R. W. V. Runes, yews and magic. Speculum 32 1957.

Page, R. I. Language and dating in OE inscriptions. Anglia 77 1959.

— The Old English rune ear. MÆ 30 1961.

— The use of double runes in Old English inscriptions. JEGP 61 1962.

— Anglo-Saxon runes and magic. Jnl of Br Archaeological Assoc 3rd ser 27 1964.

— The Old English rune eoh, ih, 'yew-tree'. MÆ 37 1968.

— Runes and non-runes. In Medieval literature and civilisation, ed D. A. Pearsall and R. A. Waldron 1969.

Goetz, H. G. Geschichte des Wortes rūn (rune) und seiner Ableitungen im englischen. Göttingen 1964.

The Ruthwell and Bewcastle Crosses

Letter from R. Bainbrigg c. 1600. In F. Haverfield, Cotton Iulius F. vi, Trans Cumberland Westmorland Antiquarian & Archaeological Soc new ser 11 1911, and in R. I. Page, An early drawing of the Ruthwell cross, Medieval Archaeology 3 1959.

Letter from N. Roscarrock 1607. In V. Cl. Gulielmi Camdeni epistolae, ed T. Smith 1691.

Nicolson, W. A letter concerning a runic inscription at Beaucastle. Philosophical Trans Royal Soc 15 1685.

— A report dated 1703-4. In R. S. Ferguson, Miscellany accounts of the diocese of Carlisle 1877, and in Bishop Nicolson's diaries, Trans Cumberland Westmorland Antiquarian & Archaeological Soc new ser 2 1902.

Hickes, G. Linguarum vett. septentrionalium thesaurus. Oxford 1705.

Gordon, A. Itinerarium septentrionale. 1727.

Smith, G. The explanation of the runic obelisk. GM June-July 1742.

Pennant, T. A tour in Scotland. Chester 1774.

Cardonnel, A. de. Vetusta monumenta. 1789.

Hutchinson, W. History of the county of Cumberland. Carlisle 1794.

Sinclair, J. The statistical account of Scotland. Edinburgh 1794.

Howard, H. Observations on Bridekirk font and on the runic column at Bewcastle. Archaeologia 14 1803.

Lysons, D. and S. Magna Britannia: Cumberland. 1816.

Kemble, J. M. On Anglo-Saxon runes. Archaeologia 28 1840.

— Additional observations on the runic obelisk at Ruthwell. Archaeologia 30 1844.

Maughan, J. The Maiden Way. Archaeological Jnl 11 1854.

— A memoir on the Roman station and runic cross at Bewcastle. 1857.

Duncan, H. An account of the remarkable monument in the shape of a cross preserved in the garden of Ruthwell Manse. Archaeologia Scotica 4 1857.

Haigh, D. H. The Saxon cross at Bewcastle. Archaeologia Aeliana new ser 1 1857.

Dietrich, F. Disputatio de cruce Ruthwellensi. Marburg 1865.

Pococke, R. Tours in Scotland 1760. Edinburgh 1887.

Ferguson, R. S. Report on injury to the Bewcastle obelisk. Trans Cumberland Westmorland Antiquarian & Archaeological Soc 12 1893.

Calverley, W. S. Notes on the early sculptured crosses, shrines and monuments in the diocese of Carlisle. Ed W. G. Collingwood, Kendal 1899.

Cook, A. S. Notes on the Ruthwell cross. PMLA 17 1902.

— The Bewcastle cross. MLN 18 1903.

— The date of the Ruthwell and Bewcastle crosses. Trans Connecticut Acad of Arts & Sciences 17 1912.

— Some accounts of the Bewcastle cross between the years 1607 and 1861. New Haven 1914.

Forbes, M. S. and B. Dickins. The inscriptions of the Ruthwell and Bewcastle crosses and the Bridekirk font. Burlington Mag 25 1914.

— The Ruthwell and Bewcastle crosses. MLR 10 1915.

Collingwood, W. G. The Ruthwell cross in its relation to other monuments of the early Christian age. Trans Dumfriesshire & Galloway Natural History & Antiquarian Soc 3rd ser 5 1916–18.

— Northumbrian crosses of the pre-Norman age. 1927.

Browne, G. F. The ancient cross-shafts at Bewcastle and Ruthwell. Cambridge 1916.

Brown, G. B. The arts in early England vol 5. 1921.

Royal Commission on the ancient monuments of Scotland: seventh report. Edinburgh 1920.

Ross, A. S. C. The linguistic evidence for the date of the Ruthwell cross. MLR 28 1933.

Dickins, B. and A. S. C. Ross. The dream of the rood. 1934, 1963 (rev).

Collingwood, R. G. The Bewcastle cross. Trans Cumberland Westmorland Antiquarian & Archaeological Soc new ser 35 1935.

Dahl, I. Substantival inflexion in early Old English. Lund 1938.

Kendrick, T. D. Anglo-Saxon art to AD 900. 1938.

Dobbie, E. v. K. The Anglo-Saxon minor poems. New York 1942.

Saxl, F. The Ruthwell cross. Jnl Warburg & Courtauld Inst 6 1943.

Schapiro, M. The religious meaning of the Ruthwell cross. Art Bull 26 1944.

Willett, F. The Ruthwell and Bewcastle crosses. Memoirs & Proc Manchester Literary & Philosophical Soc 98 1957.

Page, R. I. The Bewcastle cross. Nottingham Medieval Stud 4 1960.

Mercer, E. The Ruthwell and Bewcastle crosses. Antiquity 38 1964.

Swanton, M. The dream of the rood. Manchester 1970.

Franks (Auzon) Casket

Franks, A. W. On an ancient casket, formed of bone of the whale. Archaeological Jnl 16 1859.

Hofmann, C. Ueber die Clermonter Runen. Sitzungsberichte der Königlichen Bayerischen Akademie der Wissenschaften zu München 1871.

Sweet, H. Old English etymologies II: gársecg. E Studien 2 1879.

Notes and news. Academy 38 1890.

Wadstein, E. The Clermont runic casket. Upsala 1900.

Napier, A. S. Contributions to Old English literature 2: the Franks casket. In An English miscellany presented to Dr [F. J.] Furnivall, Oxford 1901.

Vietor, W. Das angelsächsische Runenkästchen aus Auzon bei Clermont-Ferrand. Marburg 1901.

Grienberger, T. von. Schriften über das ags Runenkästchen. Zeitschrift für Deutsche Philologie 33 1901.

— Zu den Inschriften des Clermonter Runenkästchens. Anglia 27 1904.

Holthausen, F. Zur altenglischen Literatur 3: zum Clermonter Runenkästchen. Anglia Beiblatt 16 1905.

— Nochmals zum Clermonter Runenkästchen. Anglia Beiblatt 18 1907.

Dalton, O. M. Catalogue of the ivory carvings of the Christian era. 1909.

Boer, R. C. Über die rechte Seite des angelsächsischen Runenkästchens. Arkiv för Nordisk Filologi 27 1911.

Brown, G. B. The arts in early England. Vol 3, 1915; vol 6, 1930.

Smith, R. A. A guide to the Anglo-Saxon and foreign Teutonic antiquities in the British Museum. 1923.

Souers, P. W. The top of the Franks casket. Harvard Stud 17 1935.

— The Franks casket: left side. Harvard Stud 18 1935.

— The magi on the Franks casket. Harvard Stud 20 1937.

— The Wayland scene on the Franks casket. Speculum 18 1943.

Kendrick, T. D. Anglo-Saxon art to AD 900. 1938.

Dahl, I. Substantival inflexion in early Old English. Lund 1938.

Dobbie, E. v. K. The Anglo-Saxon minor poems. New York 1942.

Davidson, H. R. E. Sigurd in the art of the Viking age. Antiquity 16 1942.

Krogmann, W. Die Verse vom Wal auf dem Runenkästchen von Auzon. Germanisch-romanische Monatsschrift new ser 9 1959.

Krause, W. Erta, ein anglischer Gott. Die Sprache 5 1959.

Bouman, A. C. The Franks casket's right side and lid. Neophilologus 49 1965.

Ball, C. J. E. The Franks casket: right side. E Studies 47 1966.

D'Ardenne, S. R. T. O. Does the right side of the Franks casket represent the burial of Sigurd? Etudes Germaniques 21 1966.

Other Anglo-Saxon Runic Inscriptions

Vietor, W. Die northumbrischen Runensteine. Marburg 1895.

Collingwood, W. G. A rune-inscribed Anglian cross-shaft at Urswick church. Trans Cumberland Westmorland Antiquarian & Archaeological Soc new ser 11 1911.

Brown, G. B. The Hartlepool tombstones and the relation between Celtic and Teutonic art in the early Christian period. Proc Soc of Antiquaries of Scotland 53 1919.

Peers, C. R. The inscribed and sculptured stones of Lindisfarne. Archaeologia 74 1924.

Cahen, M. and M. Olsen. L'inscription runique du coffret de Mortain. Paris 1930.

Olsen, M. Notes on the Urswick inscription. Norsk Tidsskrift for Sprogvidenskap 4 1930.

Harder, H. Zur Deutung von ags. 'kiismeel'. Archiv 161 1932.

Dickins, B. A system of transliteration for Old English runic inscriptions. Leeds Stud in Eng 1 1932.

— Runic rings and Old English charms. Archiv 167 1935.

— The Sandwich runic inscription 'Ræhæbul'. In Beiträge zur Runenkunde und nordischen Sprachwissenschaft, ed K. H. Schlottig, Leipzig 1938.

— and A. S. C. Ross. The Alnmouth cross. JEGP 39 1940.

Ross, A. S. C. Notes on the runic stones at Holy Island. E Studien 70 1936.

Sutherland, C. H. V. Anglo-Saxon gold coinage in the light of the Crondall hoard. Oxford 1948.

Hill, P. V. Saxon sceattas and their problems. Br Numismatic Jnl 26 1951.

Battiscombe, F. C. The relics of St Cuthbert. Oxford 1956.

Scott, F. S. The Hildithryth stone and other Hartlepool name-stones. Archaeologia Aeliana 4th ser 34 1956.

Radford, C. A. R. and G. Donaldson. Whithorn and Kirk Madrine Wigtownshire. Edinburgh 1957.

Fink, A. Zum gandersheimer Runenkästchen. In Karolingische und ottonische Kunst, Wiesbaden 1957.

Lyon, C. S. S. A reappraisal of the sceatta and styca coinage of Northumbria. Br Numismatic Jnl 28 1957.

Taralon, J. Note technique sur le coffret de Mortain. Les Monuments Historiques de la France new ser 4 1958.

Wilson, D. M. A group of Anglo-Saxon amulet rings. In The Anglo-Saxons, ed P. Clemoes 1959.

— Anglo-Saxon ornamental metalwork 700–1100. 1964. On the Thames scramasax, the Greymoor Hill ring, the Lancashire ring and the Thames mount.

Elliott, R. W. V. Two neglected English runic inscriptions: Gilton and Overchurch. In Mélanges de linguistique et de philologie, Paris 1959.

— A runic fragment at Leek. Medieval Archaeology 8 1964.

Evison, V. I. and J. M. Bately. The Derby bone piece. Medieval Archaeology 5 1961.

— The Dover ring-sword and other swords. Archaeologia 101 1967.

Rigold, S. E. The two primary series of sceattas. Br Numismatic Jnl 30 1961. See also 35 1966.

Blunt, C. E. The coinage of Offa. In Anglo-Saxon coins, ed R. H. M. Dolley 1961.

— The coinage of southern England 796–840. Br Numismatic Jnl 32 1964.

— and G. van der Meer. A new type for Offa. Br Numismatic Jnl 38 1969.

Davidson, H. R. E. The sword in Anglo-Saxon England. Oxford 1962.

Cramp, R. A name-stone from Monkwearmouth. Archaeologia Aeliana 4th ser 42 1964.

Evison, V. I. The Dover rune brooch. Antiquaries Jnl 44 1964.

Page, R. I. Ralph Thoresby's runic coins. Br Numismatic Jnl 34 1965.

— The Whitby runic comb. Whitby Literary & Philosophical Soc Report 1966.

— The runic solidus of Schweindorf, Ostfriesland, and related runic solidi. Medieval Archaeology 12 1968.

— and S. C. Hawkes. Swords and runes in south-east England. Antiquaries Jnl 47 1967.

Page, R. I. How long did the Scandinavian language survive in England? the epigraphical evidence. In England before the Conquest: studies presented to Dorothy Whitelock, Cambridge 1971.

Berghaus, P. and K. Schneider. Anglo-friesische Runensolidi im Lichte des Neufundes von Schweindorf (Ostfriesland). Cologne and Opladen 1967.

Pagan, H. E. A new type for Beonna. Br Numismatic Jnl 37 1968.

R. I. P.

B. POETRY

For bibliographies, dictionaries and collections including both prose and poetry, and literary histories, see General Works, above.

(1) DICTIONARIES

Grein, C. W. M. Sprachschatz der angelsächsischen Dichter. Cassel and Göttingen 1861–4, Heidelberg 1912 (rev J. J. Köhler).

Bessinger, J. B. A short dictionary of Anglo-Saxon poetry. Toronto 1960, 1961 (rev).

(2) COLLECTIONS AND ANTHOLOGIES

Only collections of 6 or more poems are included; for others, see individual poems, below. For ms collections and edns, see Manuscript Studies, below.

In Old English

Conybeare, J. J. Illustrations of Anglo-Saxon poetry. 1826. Contains Bede's death song, Deor, Cædmon's hymn, Finnsburh, Maldon, Riming poem, Ruin, Widsith, Wife's lament; parts of Christ, Exodus, Genesis, Maxims, Phoenix, Riddles, Solomon and Saturn, Soul and body. With English or Latin trns.

Grein, C. W. M. Bibliothek der angelsächsischen Poesie. Göttingen 1857–8. See next item.

Wülcker, R. P. Bibliothek der angelsächsischen Poesie. 3 vols Cassel 1881–98, Hamburg 1922. An extensive revision of Grein; comprehensive. For notes on this edn, see P. J. Cosijn, Anglo-Saxonica, Beiträge zur Geschichte der Deutschen Sprache und Literatur 19–21 1894–6, 23 1898.

— Kleinere angelsächsische Dichtungen. Halle 1882. Contains Deor, Durham, Finnsburh, Husband's message, Maldon, Maxims, Precepts, Ruin, Rune poem, Seafarer, Waldere, Wanderer, Widsith, Wife's lament.

Schücking, L. L. Kleines angelsächsisches Dichterbuch. Cöthen 1919. Contains Brunanburh, Deor, Finnsburh, Husband's message, Maldon, Resignation (78b–118), Riming poem, Ruin, Seafarer, Waldere, Wanderer, Wife's lament, Wulf and Eadwacer.

Sedgefield, W. J. An Anglo-Saxon verse book. Manchester 1922. Contains Bede's death song, Brunanburh, Cædmon's hymn, Deor, Finnsburh, Fortunes of men, Gifts of men, Husband's message, Maldon, Precepts, Riming poem, Seafarer, Vainglory (1–50a), Waldere, Wanderer, Widsith, Wife's lament, Wulf and Eadwacer, 10 riddles and selections from longer poems.

Krapp, G. P. and E. V. K. Dobbie. The Anglo-Saxon poetic records. 6 vols New York 1931–53. 1, The Junius manuscript, ed Krapp 1931; 2, The Vercelli book, ed Krapp 1932; 3, The Exeter book, ed Krapp and Dobbie 1936; 4, Beowulf and Judith, ed Dobbie 1953; 5, The Paris psalter and the Meters of Boethius, ed Krapp 1933; 6, The Anglo-Saxon minor poems, ed Dobbie 1942. A comprehensive collection.

Campbell, J. J. and J. L. Rosier. Poems in Old English. New York 1962. Contains Death of Edgar, Deor, Dream of the rood, Epilogue to the Pastoral care, Fortunes of men, Maldon, Wanderer, selections from Andreas, Christ, Genesis, Guthlac, Maxims and Riddles.

Magoun, F. P. The Anglo-Saxon poems in Bright's Anglo-Saxon reader, done in a normalized orthography. Cambridge Mass 1965.

Pope, J. C. Seven Old English poems. Indianapolis 1966. Contains Brunanburh, Cædmon's hymn, Deor, Dream of the rood, Maldon, Seafarer, Wanderer.

Hamer, R. F. S. A choice of Anglo-Saxon verse. 1970. With trns.

In Translation

Grein, C. W. M. Dichtungen der Angelsachsen stabreimend übersetzt. 2 vols Göttingen 1857-9, 1930. A comprehensive collection.

Steineck, H. Altenglische Dichtungen in wortgetreuer Übersetzung. Leipzig 1898. Contains Bede's death song, Beowulf, Cædmon's hymn, Elene, Waldere, Widsith.

Cook, A. S. and C. B. Tinker. Select translations from Old English poetry. Boston 1902, Cambridge Mass 1926 (rev). Contains Bede's death song, Brunanburh, Cædmon's hymn, Deor, Dream of the rood, Husband's message, Judith, Maldon, Phoenix, Ruin, Seafarer. Wanderer, Wife's lament, selections from longer poems.

Olivero, F. Traduzioni dalla poesia anglo-sassone. Bari 1915. Contains Brunanburh, Dream of the rood, Maldon, Ruin, Seafarer, Wanderer, Widsith, Wife's lament; selections from Christ, Elene and Phoenix.

Faust, C. and S. Thompson. Old English poems. Chicago and New York 1918. Contains Bede's death song, Brunanburh, Cædmon's hymn, Deor, Dream of the rood, Finnsburh, Fortunes of men, Husband's message, Judith, Maldon, Phoenix, Ruin, Seafarer (1–64a), Waldere, Wanderer, Widsith, Wife's lament; selections from maxims, charms, riddles and longer poems.

Spaeth, J. D. Old English poetry: translations into alliterative verse. Princeton 1922 (for 1921). Contains parts of many poems.

Thomas, W. L'épopée anglo-saxonne. Paris [1924]. Contains Brunanburh, Deor, Finnsburh, Judith, Maldon, Waldere; selections from longer poems.

Gordon, R. K. Anglo-Saxon poetry. 1926, 1954 (rev), 1964. Contains most of the poetry in prose trn.

Malone, K. Ten Old English poems put into modern alliterative verse. Baltimore 1941. Contains Brunanburh, Deor, Dream of rood, Finnsburh, Maldon, Seafarer, Wanderer, Widsith, Wife's lament, Wulf and Eadwacer.

Bone, G. Anglo-Saxon poetry: an essay with specimen translations in verse. Oxford 1943. Contains Deor, Dream of the rood, Fortunes of men, Gifts of men, Husband's message, Judith, Maldon, Maxims, Ruin, Seafarer, Wanderer, Whale, Wife's lament, 2 riddles and a charm.

Kennedy, C. W. Early English Christian poetry translated into alliterative verse. 1952, Gloucester Mass 1965. Contains Andreas, Christ (entire), Christ and Satan (1–364), Dream of the rood, Elene, Genesis (1–964), Judgment Day II, Physiologus.

—— An anthology of Old English poetry. Oxford 1960. Contains portions of the above, with Brunanburh, Deor, Finnsburh, Fortunes of men, Husband's message, Maldon, Ruin, Seafarer, Waldere, Wanderer, Widsith, Wife's lament and some riddles and charms.

Raffel, B. Poems from the Old English; foreword by R. P. Creed. Lincoln Nebraska 1960, 1964 (2nd edn). The 2nd edn contains Bede's death song, Brunanburh, Cædmon's hymn, Christ I, Death of Edgar, Deor, Dream of the rood, Husband's message, Judith, Maldon, Phoenix (1–423), Ruin, Seafarer, Wanderer, Wife's lament, Wulf and Eadwacer; 15 riddles, a metrical charm, and part of Genesis (Abraham and Isaac).

Crossley-Holland, K. The battle of Maldon and other Old English poems. Ed B. Mitchell 1965. Also contains Brunanburh, Brussels cross, Cædmon's hymn, Deor, Dream of the rood, Finnsburh, Husband's message, Physiologus, Ruin, Seafarer, Wanderer, Wife's lament, 27 riddles and 3 charms.

Alexander, M. The earliest English poems. 1966 (Penguin). Contains Deor, Dream of the rood, Finnsburh, Husband's message, Maldon, Maxims, Seafarer, Wanderer, Widsith, Wife's lament, Wulf and Eadwacer, some riddles and parts of Beowulf.

Hieatt, C. B. Beowulf and other Old English poems. New York 1967. Also contains Brunanburh, Deor, Dream of the rood, Judith, Maldon, Seafarer (tr E. Pound), Wanderer.

(3) MANUSCRIPT STUDIES

General

Sievers, E. Collationen angelsächsischer Gedichte. Zeitschrift für Deutsches Altertum 15 1872.

Bradley, H. The numbered sections in Old English manuscripts. 1916. Also in Proc Br Acad 7 1916.

Sisam, K. The authority of Old English poetical manuscripts. RES 22 1946; rptd in his Studies in the history of OE literature, Oxford 1953.

Timmer, B. J. Sectional divisions of poems in Old English manuscripts. MLR 47 1952.

Ker, N. R. Catalogue of manuscripts containing Anglo-Saxon. Oxford 1957.

Individual

Cotton Vitellius A. xv (Beowulf ms)

Holder, A. Beowulf 1: Abdruck der Handschrift. Freiburg 1881, 1895 (3rd edn).

Wülker, R. P. Beowulf: Text nach der Handschrift. In his Bibliothek vol 1, 1881.

Zupitza, J. Beowulf: autotypes of the unique Cotton ms Vitellius A. xv, with a transliteration and notes. 1882 (EETS), 1959 (with introd by N. Davis).

Davidson, C. Differences between the scribes of Beowulf.

MLN 5 1890. Answer by C. F. McClumpha, ibid; response by Davidson, ibid.

Sisam, K. The Beowulf manuscript. MLR 11 1916; rptd in his Studies in the history of OE literature, Oxford 1953.

—— The compilation of the Beowulf manuscript. In his Studies in the history of OE literature, Oxford 1953.

Förster, M. Die Beowulf-Handschrift. Berichte über die Verhandlungen der Sächsischen Akademie der Wissenschaften zu Leipzig 61 1919.

Rypins, S. I. The Beowulf codex. MP 17 1920.

—— A contribution to the study of the Beowulf codex. PMLA 36 1921.

—— The Beowulf codex. Colophon 10 1932.

Hoops, J. Die Foliierung der Beowulf-Handschrift. E Studien 63 1928.

Hulbert, J. R. The accuracy of the B-scribe of Beowulf. PMLA 43 1928.

Keller, W. Zur Worttrennung in den angelsächsischen Handschriften. In Britannica: M. Förster zum 60 Geburtstage, Leipzig 1929.

Prokosch, E. Two types of scribal errors in the Beowulf ms. In Studies in English philology in honor of F. Klaeber, Minneapolis 1929.

Smith, A. H. The photography of manuscripts. London Medieval Stud 1 1938.

Malone, K. Thorkelin's transcripts of Beowulf. Studia Neophilologica 14 1942.

— Readings from the Thorkelin transcripts of Beowulf. PMLA 64 1949.

— The text of Beowulf. Proc Amer Philosophical Soc 93 1949.

— The Thorkelin transcripts of Beowulf in facsimile. Copenhagen 1951 (Early Eng Mss in Facs).

— The Nowell codex. Copenhagen 1963 (Early Eng Mss in Facs).

Stevick, R. D. Suprasegmentals, meter and the manuscript of Beowulf. Hague 1968.

Taylor, P. B. and P. Salus. The compilation of Cotton Vitellius A. xv. Neuphilologische Mitteilungen 69 1968.

See also Krapp-Dobbie 4, col 226 above.

Exeter Book

Conybeare, J. J. Account of a Saxon ms preserved in the Cathedral Library at Exeter. Archaeologia 17 1814.

[Chambers, R. ?]. British Museum transcripts of the Exeter Book, BM Add 9067. 1831–2.

Thorpe, B. Codex exoniensis. 1842 (Soc of Antiquaries). Text and trn.

Schipper, J. Zum Codex exoniensis. Germania 19 1874.

Gollancz, I. The Exeter book part I. 1895 (EETS). Text and trn.

Chambers, R. W. The British Museum transcript of the Exeter book (Add ms 9067). Anglia 36 1912.

Tupper, F., jr. The British Museum transcript of the Exeter book (Add ms 9067). Ibid.

The Exeter book of Old English poetry, with introductory chapters by R. W. Chambers, M. Förster, and R. Flower. 1933 (facs).

Mackie, W. S. The Exeter book part II. 1934 (EETS). Text and trn.

Dickins, B. The beheaded manumission in the Exeter book. In The early cultures of north-west Europe, ed C. Fox and B. Dickins, Cambridge 1950.

Sisam, K. In his Studies in the History of OE literature, Oxford 1953.

Coveney, D. K. The ruling of the Exeter book. Scriptorium 12 1958.

Blake, N. F. The scribe of the Exeter book. Neophilologus 46 1962.

See also Krapp-Dobbie 3, above.

Junius Ms (Bodley, Junius xi)

Ellis, H. Account of Cædmon's metrical paraphrase of Scripture history. Archaeologia 24 1832; 1833 (separately). With engravings in facs.

Sievers, E. Zu Codex Junius xi. Beiträge zur Geschichte der Deutschen Sprache und Literatur 10 1885.

Stoddard, F. H. The Cædmon poems in Ms Junius xi. Anglia 10 1888.

Lawrence, J. On Codex Junius xi. Anglia 12 1889.

Gollancz, I. The Cædmon manuscript of Anglo-Saxon biblical poetry. Oxford 1927 (facs).

Clubb, M. D. The second book of the Cædmonian manuscript. MLN 43 1928.

— Report of progress on a census of Junius. JEGP 61 1962.

— Grimm's transcript of Cædmon. PQ 44 1965.

— Junius, Marshall, Madden, Thorpe—and Harvard. In Studies in language and literature in honour of M. Schlauch, Warsaw 1966.

Hulbert, J. R. On the text of the Junius manuscript. JEGP 37 1938.

Timmer, B. J. The history of a manuscript. Book Collector 1 1952.

Thornley, G. C. The accents and points of ms Junius Eleven. Trans of Philological Soc 1954.

Larès, M.-M. Echos d'un rite hiérosolymitain dans un manuscrit du haut Moyen Age anglais. Revue de l'Histoire des Religions 165 1964.

See also Krapp-Dobbie 1, above and under Cædmon, below.

Vercelli Book

[Thorpe, B.] Appendix B to Mr Cooper's Report on Rymer's Foedera. 1869 (ptd 1836).

Kemble, J. M. The poetry of the Codex Vercellensis. 2 pts 1843–6. Text and trn.

Wülcker, R. P. Über das Vercellibuch. Anglia 5 1882.

— Codex Vercellensis: die angelsächsische Handschrift zu Vercelli in getreuer Nachbildung. Leipzig 1894 (facs).

Cook, A. S. Cardinal Guala and the Vercelli Book. Univ of California Lib Bull 10 1888. Supplementary note, MLN 4 1889.

Napier, A. S. Collation der altenglischen Gedichte im Vercellibuch. Zeitschrift für Deutsches Altertum 33 1889.

Krapp, G. P. The first transcript of the Vercelli Book. MLN 17 1902.

Förster, M. Il Codice Vercellese con omelie e poesie in lingua anglosassone. Rome 1913 (facs).

Herben, S. J. The Vercelli book: a new hypothesis. Speculum 10 1935.

Ker, N. R. C. Maier's transcript of the Vercelli book. MÆ 19 1950.

Sisam, K. Marginalia in the Vercelli book. In his Studies in the history of OE literature, Oxford 1953.

Halsall, M. Benjamin Thorpe and the Vercelli book. Eng Lang Notes 6 1969.

— Vercelli and the Vercelli book. PMLA 84 1969.

— More about C. Maier's transcript of the Vercelli book. Eng Lang Notes 8 1970.

Scragg, D. G. Accent marks in the Vercelli book. Neuphilologische Mitteilungen 72 1971.

See also Krapp-Dobbie 2, above.

(4) GENERAL CRITICISM

Only major works on metrics are recorded here: for others, see section on English Prosody; for linguistic items, including primarily semantic studies, see English Language, above.

Conybeare, J. J. Illustrations of Anglo-Saxon poetry. 1826.

Köhler, A. Über den Stand berufsmässiger Sänger im nationalen Epos germanischer Völker. Germania 15 1870.

Hammerich, F. Älteste christliche Epik der Angelsachsen, Deutschen und Nordländer. Gütersloh 1874. Tr from Danish.

Heinzel, R. Über den Stil der altgermanischen Poesie. Strasbourg 1875.

Gummere, F. B. The Anglo-Saxon metaphor. Halle 1881.

Merbach, H. Das Meer in der Dichtung der Angelsachsen. Breslau 1884.

Tolman, A. H. The style of Anglo-Saxon poetry. PMLA 3 1887.

Kail, J. Über die Parallelstellen in der angelsächsischen Poesie. Anglia 12 1889.

Meyer, R. M. Die altgermanische Poesie nach ihren formelhaften Elementen beschrieben. Berlin 1889.

Deering, W. The Anglo-Saxon poets on the judgment day. Halle 1890.

Abbey, C. J. Religious thought in Old English verse. 1892.

Holthausen, F. [Various textual notes on OE poems in] Beiträge zur Geschichte der Deutschen Sprache und Literatur 16 1892; Indo-germanische Forschungen 4

1894; Beiblatt zur Anglia 9 1898, 18 1907, 31 1920, 32 1921, 34–5 1923–4; E Studien 37 1906, 51 1918; Anglia 44 1920, 46 1922, 73 1956; Archiv 188 1951; Germanisch-romanische Monatsschrift new ser 3 1953.

Sarrazin, G. Parallelstellen in altenglischer Dichtung. Anglia 14 1892.

— Von Kädmon bis Kynewulf. Berlin 1913.

Douglas-Lithgow, R. A. Anglo-Saxon alliterative poetry. Trans of Royal Soc of Lit 2nd ser 15 1893.

Sievers, E. Altgermanische Metrik. Halle 1893.

Wülcker, R. P. Die Entstehung der christlichen Dichtung bei den Angelsachsen. Berichte über die Verhandlungen der Königlich Sächsischen Gesellschaft der Wissenschaften, philologisch-historische Klasse 45 1893.

Abegg, D. Zur Entwicklung der historischen Dichtung bei den Angelsachsen. Strasbourg 1894.

Burton, R. Nature in Old English poetry. Atlantic Monthly April 1894.

— Woman in Old English poetry. Sewanee Rev 4 1895.

Price, M. B. Teutonic antiquities in the generally acknowledged Cynewulfian poetry. Leipzig 1896.

Becker, C. J. A contribution to the comparative study of the medieval visions of heaven and hell. Baltimore 1899.

Mead, W. E. Color in Old English poetry. PMLA 14 1899.

Roeder, F. Die Familie bei den Angelsachsen. Halle 1899.

Heusler, A. Der Dialog in der altgermanischen erzählenden Dichtung. Zeitschrift für Deutsches Altertum 46 1902.

Otto, E. Typische Motive in dem weltlichen Epos der Angelsachsen. Berlin 1902.

Abbetmeyer, C. Old English poetical motives derived from the doctrine of sin. New York 1903.

Anderson, L. F. The Anglo-Saxon scop. Toronto 1903.

Krackow, O. Die Nominalcomposita als Kunstmittel im altenglischen Epos. Berlin 1903.

Panzer, F. Das altdeutsche Volksepos. Halle 1903.

Hanscom, E. D. The feeling for nature in Old English poetry. MLN 20 1905.

Krapp, G. P. The parenthetic exclamation in Old English poetry. MLN 20 1905.

Moorman, F. W. The interpretation of nature in English poetry from Beowulf to Shakespeare. Strasbourg 1905.

Skemp, A. R. The transformation of scriptural story, motive and conception in Anglo-Saxon poetry. MP 4 1906.

Barnouw, A. J. Schriftuurlijke poëzie der Angelsaken. Hague 1907; tr as Anglo-Saxon Christian poetry, 1914.

Grau, G. Quellen und Verwandtschaften der älteren germanischen Darstellungen des jüngsten Gerichtes. Halle 1908.

Schücking, L. L. Das angelsächsische Totenklagelied. E Studien 39 1908.

— Untersuchungen zur Bedeutungslehre der angelsächsischen Dichtersprache. Heidelberg 1915.

Ehrismann, G. Religionsgeschichtliche Beiträge zum germanischen Frühchristentum. Beiträge zur Geschichte der Deutschen Sprache und Literatur 35 1909.

Olrík, A. Epische Gesetze der Volksdichtung. Zeitschrift für Deutsches Altertum 51 1909–10.

Rankin, J. W. A study of the kennings in Anglo-Saxon poetry. JEGP 8–9 1909–10.

Smithson, G. A. The Old English Christian epic. Berkeley 1910.

Tupper, F., jr. Textual criticism as a pseudo-science. PMLA 25 1910.

Bartels, A. Rechtsaltertümer in der angelsächsischen Dichtung. Kiel 1913.

Paetzel, W. Die Variationen in der altgermanischen Alliterationspoesie. Berlin 1913.

Kock, E. A. Jubilee jaunts and jottings: 250 contributions to the interpretation and prosody of Old West Teutonic

alliterative poetry. Lunds Univ Årsskrift, new ser (1) 14 1918.

— Interpretations and emendations of early English texts v–xi. Anglia 43–7 1919–23.

— Plain points and puzzles: sixty notes on Old English poetry. Lunds Univ Årsskrift, new ser (1) 17 1922.

Keiser, A. The influence of Christianity on the vocabulary of Old English poetry. Urbana 1919.

Imelmann, R. Forschungen zur altenglischen Poesie. Berlin 1920.

Pons, E. Odoacre dans la poésie anglo-saxonne. Revue Germanique 13 1922.

— Le thème et le sentiment de la nature dans la poésie anglo-saxonne. Strasbourg 1925.

Wolff, L. Über den Stil der altgermanischen Poesie. Deutsche Vierteljahrsschrift für Literaturwissenschaft und Geistesgeschichte 1 1923.

Singer, S. Stil und Weltanschauung der altgermanischen Poesie. In Festschrift für O. Walzel, Wildpark-Potsdam 1924.

Wyld, H. C. Diction and imagery in Anglo-Saxon poetry. E & S 11 1925; rptd in Essential articles for the study of OE poetry, ed J. B. Bessinger and S. J. Kahrl, Hamden Conn 1968.

Emerson, O. F. Originality in Old English poetry. RES 2 1926.

Kissack, R. A. The sea in Anglo-Saxon and Middle English poetry. Washington Univ Stud 13 1926.

Treneer, A. The sea in English literature from Beowulf to Donne. 1926.

van der Merwe Scholtz, H. The kenning in Anglo-Saxon and Old Norse poetry. Utrecht 1927.

Routh, H. V. God, man and epic poetry. Vol 1, Cambridge 1927.

Buckhurst, H. Terms and phrases for the sea in Old English poetry. In Studies in English philology in honor of F. Klaeber, Minneapolis 1929.

Ricci, A. The chronology of Anglo-Saxon poetry. RES 5 1929.

Baum, P. F. The character of Anglo-Saxon verse. MP 28 1930.

Olivero, F. Echi d'Italia nella poesia anglosassone. In his Studi britannici, Turin 1931.

Mohr, W. Kenningstudien. Stuttgart 1933.

Bartlett, A. C. The larger rhetorical patterns in Anglo-Saxon poetry. New York 1935.

Einarsson, S. Old English 'beot' and Old Icelandic 'heitstrenging'. PMLA 49 1934; rptd in Essential articles for the study of OE poetry, ed J. B. Bessinger and S. J. Kahrl, Hamden Conn 1968.

Kuriyagawa, F. A study of Old English poetry. Stud in Eng Lit (Tokyo) 15 1935.

Bracher, F. Understatement in Old English poetry. PMLA 52 1937; rptd in Essential articles for the study of OE poetry, ed J. B. Bessinger and S. J. Kahrl, Hamden Conn 1968.

Marquardt, H. Die altenglischen Kenningar. Halle 1938.

Reuschel, H. Kenningar bei Alkuin: zur Disputatio Pippini cum Albino. Beiträge zur Geschichte der Deutschen Sprache und Literatur 62 1938.

Hotchner, C. A. Wessex and Old English poetry, with special consideration of the Ruin. New York 1939.

Juzi, G. Die Ausdrücke des Schönen in der altenglischen Dichtung. Zürich 1939.

Andrew, S. O. Syntax and style in Old English. Cambridge 1940.

Brown, C. 'Poculum mortis' in Old English. Speculum 15 1950.

Gross, E. Das Wunderbare im altenglischen geistigen Epos. Frankfurt 1940.

Galinsky, H. Sprachlicher Ausdrück und künstlerische Gestalt germanischer Schicksalsauffassung in der angelsächsischen Dichtung. E Studien 74 1941.

Timmer, B. J. Wyrd in Anglo-Saxon prose and poetry. Neophilologus 26 1941; rptd in Essential articles for the

study of OE poetry, ed J. B. Bessinger and S. J. Kahrl, Hamden Conn 1968.
—— Irony in Old English poetry. E Studies 24 1942.
—— The elegiac mood in Old English poetry. Ibid.
—— Heathen and Christian elements in Old English poetry. Neophilologus 29 1944.
—— Expanded lines in Old English poetry. Neophilologus 35 1951.
Pope, J. C. The rhythm of Beowulf: an interpretation of the normal and hypermetric verse forms in Old English poetry. New Haven 1942, 1966 (rev).
Bone, G. Anglo-Saxon poetry: an essay. Oxford 1943.
Brady, C. The legends of Ermanaric. Berkeley 1943.
Kennedy, C. W. The earliest English poetry. 1943.
Mincoff, M. Zur angelsächsischen Dichtersprache. Godšinik na Sofiiskiya Universitet, Istoriko-filologičeski Fakultet 39 1943.
Magoun, F. P. A note on Old West Germanic poetic unity. MP 43 1945.
—— A brief plea for a normalization of Old-English poetical texts. Les Langues Modernes 45 1951.
—— Oral-formulaic character of Anglo-Saxon narrative poetry. Speculum 28 1953; rptd in Essential articles for the study of OE poetry, ed J. B. Bessinger and S. J. Kahrl, Hamden Conn 1968, and in Beowulf essay collections.
—— Abbreviated titles for the poems of the Anglo-Saxon poetic corpus. Etudes Anglaises 8 1955.
—— The theme of the beasts of battle in Anglo-Saxon poetry. Neuphilologische Mitteilungen 56 1955.
—— Conceptions and images common to Anglo-Saxon poetry and the Kalevala. In Britannica: Festschrift für H. M. Flasdieck, Heidelberg 1960.
—— Some notes on Anglo-Saxon poetry. In Studies in medieval literature in honor of A. C. Baugh, Philadelphia 1961.
Sisam, K. Notes on Old English poetry: on the authority of Old English poetical manuscripts. RES 22 1946; rptd as The authority etc in his Studies in the history of OE literature, Oxford 1953.
—— Dialect origins of the earlier Old English verse. In his Studies in the history of OE literature, Oxford 1953; rptd in Essential articles for the study of OE poetry, ed J. B. Bessinger and S. J. Kahrl, Hamden Conn 1968.
Brooks, K. R. Old English 'wopes hring'. Eng & Germanic Stud 2 1949.
Kashiwakura, S. Old English lyrics. Literature (Japan) 1 1949.
von Schaubert, E. Zur Erklärung Schwierigkeiten bietender altenglischer Textstellen. In Philologica: the [Kemp] Malone anniversary studies, Baltimore 1949.
Whitelock, D. Anglo-Saxon poetry and the historian. Trans Royal Historical Soc 4th ser 31 1949.
Willard, R. The Exeter book Alms: styles in printing Old English verse. SE 28 1949.
Kliger, S. The neo-classical view of Old English poetry. JEGP 49 1950.
Young, J. I. Glæd wæs ic gliwum: ungloomy aspects of Old English poetry. In The early cultures of northwest Europe, ed C. Fox and B. Dickins, Cambridge 1950.
Anderson, O. J. Once more: the Old English simile. West Virginia Univ Bull, Philological Papers 8 1951.
Girvan, R. The medieval poet and his audience. In English studies today, ed C. L. Wrenn, Oxford 1951.
Lerner, L. D. Colour words in Anglo-Saxon. MLR 46 1951; rptd in Essential articles for the study of OE poetry, ed J. B. Bessinger and S. J. Kahrl, Hamden Conn 1968.
Bowra, C. M. In his Heroic poetry, 1952.
Mezger, F. Self-judgment in Old English documents. MLN 67 1952.
Slay, D. Some aspects of the technique of composition of Old English verse. Trans of Philological Soc 1952.

Borges, J. L. Las kenningar. In his Historia de la eternidad, Buenos Aires 1953, 1966 (with suppls).
Madden, J. F. A frequency word-count of Anglo-Saxon poetry. Mediaeval Stud 15 1953.
—— and F. P. Magoun. A grouped frequency word-list of Anglo-Saxon poetry. Cambridge Mass 1954.
Scargill, M. H. Gold beyond measure: a plea for Old English poetry. JEGP 52 1953.
Woolf, H. B. The earliest printing of Old English poetry. E Studies 34 1953.
Woolf, R. E. The Devil in Old English poetry. RES new ser 4 1953; rptd in Essential articles for the study of OE poetry, ed J. B. Bessinger and S. J. Kahrl, Hamden Conn 1968.
—— Saints lives. In Continuations and beginnings, ed E. G. Stanley 1966.
Derolez, B. Runica manuscripta: the English tradition. Bruges 1954. Addn in E Studies 45 1964.
—— Anglo-Saxon literature: Attic or Asiatic? Old English poetry and its Latin background. In English studies today: 2nd series, ed G. H. Bonnard, Berne 1961; rptd in Essential articles for the study of OE poetry, ed J. B. Bessinger and S. J. Kahrl, Hamden Conn 1968.
Frye, R. M. Christ and Ingeld. Theology Today 11 1954.
Greenfield, S. B. The formulaic expression of the theme of 'exile' in Anglo-Saxon poetry. Speculum 30 1955; rptd in Essential articles for the study of OE poetry, ed J. B. Bessinger and S. J. Kahrl, Hamden Conn 1968.
—— Syntactic analysis and Old English poetry. Neuphilologische Mitteilungen 64 1963.
—— Some remarks on the nature and quality of Old English poetry. In his A critical history of OE literature, New York 1965.
—— The canons of Old English criticism. ELH 34 1967.
—— The interpretation of Old English poems. 1972.
Mittner, L. Wurd: das Sakrale in der altgermanischen Epik. Berne 1955.
Wahrig, G. Das Lachen im Altenglischen und Mittelenglischen. Zeitschrift für Anglistik und Amerikanistik 3 1955.
Lehmann, W. P. The development of Germanic verse form. Austin 1956.
Schaar, C. On a new theory of Old English poetic diction. Neophilologus 40 1956.
Stanley, E. G. Old English poetic diction and the interpretation of the Wanderer, the Seafarer and the Penitent's prayer. Anglia 73 1956; rptd in Essential articles for the study of OE poetry, ed J. B. Bessinger and S. J. Kahrl, Hamden Conn 1968.
—— The search for Anglo-Saxon paganism. N & Q June 1964–Sept 1965.
—— Studies in the prosaic vocabulary of Old English verse. Neuphilologische Mitteilungen 72 1971.
Bessinger, J. B. Oral to written: some implications of the Anglo-Saxon transition. Explorations 8 1957.
—— Computer techniques for an Old English concordance. Amer Documentation 12 1961.
—— The Sutton Hoo harp replica and Old English musical verse. In Old English poetry: fifteen essays, ed R. P. Creed, Providence 1967.
Creed, R. P. The andswarode system in Old English poetry. Speculum 32 1957.
—— The making of an Anglo-Saxon poem. ELH 26 1959; rptd in Essential articles for the study of OE poetry, ed J. B. Bessinger and S. J. Kahrl, Hamden Conn 1968, and in Fry, below, with addns.
—— On the possibility of criticizing OE poetry. Texas Stud in Lit & Lang 3 1961.
—— The art of the singer: three OE tellings of the Offering of Isaac. In Old English poetry: fifteen essays, ed R. P. Creed, Providence 1967.
Enkvist, N. E. The seasons of the year: chapters on a motif from Beowulf to the Shepheardes calendar. Copenhagen 1957.

Irving, E. B. Latin prose sources for Old English verse. JEGP 56 1957.

Tucker, S. I. The Anglo-Saxon poet considers the heavens. Neophilologus 41 1957.

— Laughter in Old English literature. Neophilologus 43 1959.

Bliss, A. J. The metre of Beowulf. 1958.

— The appreciation of Old English metre. In English and medieval studies presented to J. R. R. Tolkien, 1962.

— An introduction to Old English metre. Oxford 1962.

— Single half-lines in Old English poetry. N & Q Dec 1971.

Wrenn, C. L. On the continuity of English poetry. Anglia 76 1958; rptd in his Word and symbol, 1967.

— Anglo-Saxon poetry and the amateur archaeologist. 1962 (Chambers Memorial lecture).

— Two Anglo-Saxon harps. Comparative Lit 14 1962. rptd in Studies in OE literature in honor of A. G. Brodeur, Eugene 1963.

Collins, D. C. Kennings in Anglo-Saxon poetry. E & S new ser 12 1959.

Colosimo, C. Anglo-Saxon poetry. Naples 1959.

Elliott, R. W. V. Runes: an introduction. Manchester 1959.

Habicht, W. Die Gebärde in englischen Dichtungen des Mittelalters. Munich 1959.

Hofman, D. Die altsächsische Bibelepik ein Ableger der angelsächsischen geistlichen Epik? Zeitschrift für Deutsches Altertum 89 1959.

Huppé, B. F. Doctrine and poetry: Augustine's influence on Old English poetry. New York 1959.

— The web of words. Albany NY 1970.

Kranz, G. Lyrik der Angelsachsen. Antaios 1 1959.

LePage, R. B. Alliterative patterns as a test of style in Old English poetry. JEGP 58 1959.

Leslie, R. F. Analysis of stylistic devices and effects in Anglo-Saxon literature. In Stil- und Form-probleme in der Literatur, ed P. Böckmann, Heidelberg 1959; rptd in Essential articles for the study of OE poetry, ed J. B. Bessinger and S. J. Kahrl, Hamden Conn 1968, and with supplementary footnotes in Old English literature: twenty-two analytical essays, ed M. Stevens and J. Mandel, Lincoln Nebraska 1968.

Malone, K. Studies in heroic legend and in current speech. Copenhagen 1959.

Barnes, R. Horse colors in Anglo-Saxon poetry. PQ 39 1960.

Shuman, R. B. and H. C. Hutchings. The un-prefix: a means of Germanic irony in Beowulf. MP 57 1960.

Diamond, R. E. Theme as ornament in Anglo-Saxon poetry. PMLA 76 1961; rptd in Essential articles for the study of OE poetry, ed J. B. Bessinger and S. J. Kahrl, Hamden Conn 1968.

Bloomfield, M. W. Patristics and Old English literature. Comparative Lit 14 1962; rptd in Studies in OE literature in honor of A. G. Brodeur, Eugene 1963, and in Essential articles for the study of OE poetry, ed J. B. Bessinger and S. J. Kahrl, Hamden Conn 1968.

— Understanding Old English poetry. Annuale Mediaevale 9 1968, rptd in his Essays and explorations, Cambridge Mass 1970.

Campbell, A. The Old English epic style. In English and medieval studies presented to J. R. R. Tolkien, 1962.

— Verse influences in Old English prose. In Philological essays in honour of H. D. Meritt, Hague 1970.

Cross, J. E. Aspects of microcosm and macrocosm in Old English literature. Comparative Lit 14 1962; rptd in Studies in OE literature in honor of A. G. Brodeur, Eugene 1963.

— Latin themes in Old English poetry. Bristol 1962.

— The Old English poetic theme of the gifts of men. Neophilologus 46 1962.

— The ethic of war in Old English. In England before the Conquest: studies presented to Dorothy Whitelock, Cambridge 1971.

Gillam, D. M. E. The connotations of OE fæge, with a note on Beowulf and Byrhtnoð. Studia Germanica Gandensia 4 1962.

— A method for determining the connotations of Old English poetic words. Studia Germanica Gandensia 6 1964.

Stevick, R. D. The oral-formulaic analyses of Old English verse. Speculum 37 1962; rptd in Essential articles for the study of OE poetry, ed J. B. Bessinger and S. J. Kahrl, Hamden Conn 1968.

Frey, L. H. Exile and elegy in Anglo-Saxon Christian epic poetry. JEGP 62 1963.

Hill, D. M. Romance as epic. E Studies 44 1963.

Mitchell, B. Adjective clauses in Old English poetry. Anglia 81 1963.

— Pronouns in Old English poetry: some syntactical notes. RES new ser 15 1964.

Nicholson, L. E. Oral techniques in the composition of expanded Anglo-Saxon verses. PMLA 78 1963.

Quirk, R. Poetic language and Old English metre. In Early English and Norse studies presented to Hugh Smith, 1963.

Schulze, F. W. Reimstrukturen im Offa-preislied Æthilwalds und die Entwicklung des altenglischen Alliterationsverses. Zeitschrift für Deutsches Altertum 92 1963.

Bessai, F. Comitatus and exile in Old English poetry. Culture 6 1964.

Grinda, K. R. Einige Handwerke in der altenglischen Dichtung und in zeitgenössischen Inschriften: Gesichtspunkte der Darstellung und soziale Wertung. In Festschrift für W. Hübner, Berlin 1964.

Cassidy, F. G. How free was the Anglo-Saxon scop? In Franciplegius: medieval and linguistic studies in honor of F. P. Magoun, New York 1965.

Clark, G. The traveler recognizes his goal: a traditional theme in Anglo-Saxon poetry. JEGP 64 1965.

Kellogg, R. L. The South Germanic oral tradition. In Franciplegius: medieval and linguistic studies in honor of F. P. Magoun, New York 1965.

Manganella, G. Gli animali nella poesia anglosassone. Annali Istituto Universitario Orientale, Napoli: Sezione Germanica 8 1965.

Benson, L. The literary character of Anglo-Saxon formulaic poetry. PMLA 81 1966.

Campbell, J. J. Learned rhetoric in Old English poetry. MP 63 1966.

— Knowledge of rhetorical figures in Anglo-Saxon England. JEGP 66 1967.

Daunt, M. Some modes of Anglo-Saxon meaning. In In memory of J. R. Firth, 1966.

Dietrich, G. Ursprünge des Elegischen in der altenglischen Literatur. In Literatur-Kultur-Gesellschaft in England und Amerika, ed G. Müller-Schwefe and K. Tuzinski, Frankfurt 1966.

Henry, P. L. The early English and Celtic lyric. 1966.

Rogers, H. L. The crypto-psychological character of the oral formula. E Studies 47 1966.

Shepherd, G. Scriptural poetry. In Continuations and beginnings, ed E. G. Stanley 1966.

Bullard, M. Some objections to the formulaic theory of the composition of Anglo-Saxon narrative poetry. Bull Rocky Mountain Modern Lang Assoc 21 1967.

Curschmann, M. Oral poetry in medieval English, French, and German literature: some notes on recent research. Speculum 42 1967.

Fry, D. K. Old English formulas and systems. E Studies 48 1967.

— Old English formulas and type-scenes. Neophilologus 52 1968.

— Some aesthetic implications of a new definition of the formula. Neuphilologische Mitteilungen 69 1968.

Old English poetry: fifteen essays. Ed R. P. Creed, Providence 1967.

Whitbread, L. The doomsday theme in Old English poetry. Beiträge zur Geschichte der Deutschen Sprache und Literatur (Halle) 89 1967.

Essential articles for the study of Old English poetry. Ed J. B. Bessinger and S. J. Kahrl, Hamden Conn 1968.

Hill, T. D. The tropological context of heat and cold imagery in Anglo-Saxon poetry. Neuphilologische Mitteilungen 69 1968.

Isaacs, N. D. Structural principles in Old English poetry. Knoxville 1968.

Kühlwein, W. Die Verwendung der Feindseligkeitsbezeichnungen in der altenglischen Dichtersprache. Neumünster 1968.

Robinson, F. C. The significance of names in Old English literature. Anglia 86 1968.

— Some uses of name-meanings in Old English poetry. Neuphilologische Mitteilungen 69 1968.

— Lexicography and literary criticism: a caveat. In Philological essays in honour of H. D. Meritt, Hague 1970.

Gardner, T. The Old English kenning: a characteristic feature of Germanic poetical diction? MP 67 1969.

Jabbour, A. Memorial transmission in Old English poetry. Chaucer Rev 3 1969.

Keyser, S. J. Old English prosody. College Eng Feb 1969.

Martin, B. K. Aspects of winter in Latin and Old English poetry. JEGP 68 1969.

Norman, F. The early German background of Old English verse. In Medieval literature and civilization: studies in memory of G. N. Garmonsway, 1969.

O'Brien, M. Poetic diction in Old English poetry. Eng Lit & Lang (Tokyo) 6 1969.

Sonderegger, S. Erscheinungsformen der Variation im Germanischen. In Festschrift für K. Reichardt, Berne and Munich 1969.

Watts, A. C. The lyre and the harp: a comparative reconsideration of oral tradition in Homer and Old English epic poetry. New Haven 1969.

Weber, G. W. Wyrd: Studien zum Schicksalsbegriff der altenglischen und altnordischen Literatur. Bad Homburg 1969.

Whallon, W. Formula, character, and context: studies in Homeric, Old English and Old Testament poetry. Cambridge Mass 1969.

Capek, M. J. A note on formula development in Old Saxon. MP 67 1970.

Clemoes, P. Rhythm and cosmic order in Old English Christian literature. Cambridge 1970.

Crépin, A. Récentes études sur le style formulaire de la poésie vieil-anglaise. Etudes Anglaises 23 1970.

Fakundiny, L. The art of Old English verse composition. RES new ser 21 1970.

Opland, J. The oral origins of early English poetry. Univ of Cape Town Stud in Eng 1 1970.

— Scop and imbongi: Anglo-Saxon and Bantu oral poets. Eng Stud in Africa 14 1971.

Pilch, H. Syntactic prerequisites for the study of Old English poetry. Lang & Style 3 1970.

Rollinson, P. Some kinds of meaning in Old English poetry. Annuale Mediaevale 11 1970.

Starr, D. Metrical changes: from Old to Middle English. MP 68 1970.

Mandel, J. Contrast in Old English poetry. Chaucer Rev 6 1971.

Peltola, N. Observations on intensification in Old English poetry. Neuphilologische Mitteilungen 72 1971.

Duncan, E. H. Short fiction in medieval English: a survey. Stud in Short Fiction 9 1972.

Frank, R. Some uses of paronomasia in Old English scriptural verse. Speculum 47 1972.

Shippey, T. A. Old English verse. 1972.

(5) INDIVIDUAL POEMS AND AUTHORS

Poems are listed alphabetically with titles assigned by Krapp-Dobbie, above, with a few other cross-referenced titles assigned by modern critics, and with additional entries for Cædmon, Cynewulf and Elegies. There are no references to general collections, anthologies or ms edns, above, except Krapp-Dobbie. Purely linguistic, textual and metrical items are usually omitted, especially in the earlier years.

ADVENT LYRICS

See Christ, *col 269, below.*

ALDHELM

Ms : Corpus Christi College Cambridge 326, pp. 5-6.
Krapp-Dobbie 6 1942.

ALMS-GIVING

Ms : Exeter book 121b-2b.

§1

Krapp-Dobbie 3 1936.

§2

Whitbread, L. The Old-English poem Almsgiving. N & Q 14 July 1945.

Willard, R. The Exeter book Alms: styles in printing OE verse. SE 28 1949.

Trahern, J. B. The Old English Almsgiving. N & Q Feb 1969.

ANDREAS

Ms : Vercelli book 29b-52b.

§1

Grimm, J. Andreas und Elene. Cassel 1840.

Baskerville, W. M. Andreas: a legend of St Andrew. Boston 1885.

Krapp, G. P. Andreas and the Fates of the apostles. Boston 1906.

Krapp-Dobbie 2 1932.

Brooks, K. R. Andreas and the Fates of the apostles. Oxford 1961.

Translations

Root, R. K. Andreas: the legend of St Andrew. New York 1899.

Kennedy, C. W. The poems of Cynewulf. 1910.

Hall, J. L. Judith, Phoenix and other Anglo-Saxon poems. New York 1912.

Olivero, F. Andreas e i Fati degli apostoli. Turin 1927.

§2

Fritzsche, A. Das angelsächsische Gedicht Andreas und Cynewulf. Halle 1879. Also in Anglia 2 1879.

Ramhorst, F. Das altenglische Gedicht vom heiligen Andreas und der Dichter Cynewulf. Leipzig 1886.

Zupitza, J. Zur Frage nach der Quelle von Cynewulfs Andreas. Zeitschrift für Deutsches Altertum 30 1886.

Kent, C. W. Teutonic antiquities in Andreas and Elene. Halle 1887.

Trautmann, M. Wer hat die Schicksale der Apostel zuerst für den Schluss des Andreas erklärt? Beiblatt zur Anglia 7 1897.

Buttenwieser, E. Studien über die Verfasserschaft des Andreas. Heidelberg 1899.

Bourauel, J. Zur Quellen- und Verfasserfrage von Andreas, Crist und Fata. Bonner Beiträge zur Anglistik 11 1901.

Skeat, W. W. Andreas and Fata apostolorum. In An English miscellany presented to Dr [F. J.] Furnivall, Oxford 1901.

Cook, A. S. The authorship of the Old English Andreas. MLN 34 1919.

— The Old English Andreas and Bishop Acca of Hexham. Trans Connecticut Acad 26 1924.

— Bitter beer-drinking. MLN 40 1925.

Hamilton, G. L. The sources of the Fates of the apostles and Andreas. MLN 35 1920.

Holthausen, F. Die Quelle der altenglischen Andreas-Legenden. Beiblatt zur Anglia 44 1933.

Schaar, C. Notes on Andreas and Elene. Studia Neophilologica 19 1947.

— The Old English Andreas and scholarship past and present: a review of a review. E Studies 45 1969.

Peters, L. J. The relationship of the Old English Andreas to Beowulf. PMLA 66 1951.

Willard, R. Andreas and the Fates of the apostles. MP 62 1964.

Schabram, H. Andreas und Beowulf: Parallelstellen als Zeugnis für literarische Abhängigkeit. Nachrichten der Giessener Hochschulgesellschaft 34 1965.

Hill, T. D. Two notes on patristic allusion in Andreas. Anglia 34 1965.

— Figural narrative in Andreas: the conversion of the Mermedonians. Neuphilologische Mitteilungen 70 1969.

Stanley, E. G. Beowulf. In Continuations and beginnings, ed Stanley 1966.

Brodeur, A. G. A study of diction and style in three Anglo-Saxon narrative poems. In Nordica et Anglica: studies in honor of S. Einarsson, Hague 1968.

Grosz, O. J. H. The island of exiles: a note on Andreas 15. Eng Lang Notes 7 1970.

Trahern, J. B. Joshua and Tobias in The Old English Andreas. Studia Neophilologica 42 1970.

See also under Cynewulf, *below.*

AZARIAS

Ms : Exeter book 53a–5b.

§1

Schmidt, W. Die altenglischen Dichtungen Daniel und Azarias. Bonner Beiträge zur Anglistik 23 1907.

Krapp-Dobbie 3 1936.

§2

Jones, A. Daniel and Azarias as evidence for the oral-formulaic character of Old English poetry. MÆ 35 1966.

See also under Daniel, *below.*

BATTLE OF BRUNANBURH

Mss : in 4 mss of the Anglo-Saxon Chronicle : Corpus Christi College Cambridge 173, Cotton Tiberius A vi, Cotton Tiberius B i, Cotton Tiberius B iv.

§1

Crow, C. L. Maldon and Brunanburh: two Old English songs of battle. Boston 1897.

Sedgefield, W. J. The battle of Maldon and short poems from the Saxon chronicle. Boston 1904.

Kershaw, N. Anglo-Saxon and Norse poems. Cambridge 1912.

Campbell, A. The battle of Brunanburh. 1938.

Krapp-Dobbie 6 1942.

See also edns of the Chronicle, *below.*

Translations

Tennyson, H. The song of Brunanburh. Contemporary Rev Nov 1876. In prose, by the Laureate's son.

Tennyson, A. Battle of Brunanburh. In Ballads and other poems, 1880. In verse.

Garnett, J. M. Elene, Judith, Brunanburh and Maldon. Boston 1889.

Brown, A. R. The battle of Brunanburh. Poet-lore 3 1891.

Hall, J. L. Judith, Phoenix and other Anglo-Saxon poems. New York 1912.

Garmonsway, G. N. In his Anglo-Saxon chronicle, 1953 (EL).

Whitelock, D. In her English historical documents c. 500–1042 vol 1, 1955; rptd in her Anglo-Saxon chronicle: a revised translation, 1962.

§2

Abegg, D. Zur Entwicklung der historischen Dichtung bei den Angelsachsen. Strasbourg 1894.

Tupper, F. Notes on Old English poems: 3, A field of blood. JEGP 11 1912.

Klaeber, F. A note on the Battle of Brunanburh. In Anglica: Festschrift für A. Brandl, Leipzig 1925.

Ashdown, M. Notes on two passages of Old English verse. RES 5 1929.

Cockburn, J. H. The battle of Brunanburh and its period elucidated by place-names. 1931.

Hollander, L. M. The battle on the vin-heath and the battle of the Huns. JEGP 32 1938.

Crawford, O. G. S. The battle of Brunanburh. Antiquity 8 1934.

Angus, W. S. The battlefield of Brunanburh. Antiquity 11 1937.

Smith, A. H. The site of the Battle of Brunanburh. London Medieval Stud 1 1937.

Varah, W. E. The battlefield of Brunanburh. N & Q 18 Dec 1937.

Magoun, F. P. Zu Etzeln burc, Finns buruh und Brunan burh. Zeitschrift für Deutsches Altertum 77 1940.

Hampson, C. P. New light on the Battle of Brunanburh AD 937. Trans Lancs & Cheshire Antiquarian Soc 58 1946. *See also* F. W. Hogarth, ibid.

Dodgson, J. McN. The background of Brunanburh. Saga-book 14 1957.

Isaacs, N. D. Battlefield tour: Brunanburg. Neuphilologische Mitteilungen 63 1962; rev in his Structural principles, Knoxville 1969.

— The battle of Brunanburh 13b–17a. N & Q July 1963.

Bolton, W. F. Variation in the Battle of Brunanburh. RES new ser 19 1968.

Johnson, A. S. The rhetoric of Brunanburh. PQ 47 1968.

Lipp, F. R. Contrast and point of view in the Battle of Brunanburh. PQ 48 1969.

Taylor, P. B. Heroic ritual in the Old English maxims. Neuphilologische Mitteilungen 70 1969.

BATTLE OF FINNSBURH

Ms not known. Transcript by G. Hickes in his Linguarum veterum septentrionalium thesaurus *vol 1, Oxford 1705.*

Bibliographies

Fry, D. K. Beowulf and the Fight at Finnsburh: a bibliography. Charlottesville 1969.

§1

Möller, H. Das altenglische Volksepos in der ursprünglichen strophischen Form. Kiel 1883.

Trautmann, M. Finn und Hildebrand. Bonner Beiträge zur Anglistik 7 1903.

Dickins, B. Runic and heroic poems of the old Teutonic peoples. Cambridge 1915. With trn.
Mackie, W. S. The fight at Finnsburg. JEGP 16 1917.
Krapp-Dobbie 6 1942.

Translations
Uhland, L. Finnsburg. Germania 2 1857.
Gummere, F. B. The oldest English epic. New York 1909.
Dixon, W. M. English epic and heroic poetry. 1912.
Scott-Moncrieff, C. K. Widsith, Beowulf, Finnsburgh, Waldere, Deor. 1921.
Brandl, A. Der Saalkampf im Finns Burg. In Britannica: M. Förster zum 60 Geburtstage, Leipzig 1929.
Kalma, D. Kening Finn. Frisia-Tige 3 1937. Into Frisian alliterative verse.
Williams, M. Word-hoard. New York 1940.
Lattimore, R. Finnsburg. Hudson Rev 16 1963.
See also edns and trns of Beowulf, *below.*

§2
Schilling, H. The Finnsburg-fragment and the Finn-episode. MLN 2 1887.
Jellinek, M. H. Zum Finnsburgfragment. Beiträge zur Geschichte der Deutschen Sprache und Literatur 15 1891.
Boer, R. C. Finnsage und Nibelungensage. Zeitschrift für Deutsches Altertum 47 1903.
Swiggett, G. L. Notes on the Finnsburg fragment. MLN 20 1905.
Lawrence, W. W. Beowulf and the tragedy of Finnsburg. PMLA 30 1915.
Aurner, N. S. An analysis of the interpretations of the Finnsburg documents. Iowa City 1917.
Scott-Thomas, H. F. The fight at Finnsburg: Guthlaf and the son of Guthlaf. JEGP 30 1931.
Klaeber, F. Garulf, Guðlafs Sohn, im Finnsburg-Fragment. Archiv 162 1932.
—— Drei Anmerkungen zur Texterklärung. E Studien 70 1936.
Girvan, R. Finnsburuh. Proc Br Acad 26 1940.
Magoun, F. P. Zu Etzeln burc, Finns Buruh und Brunanburh. Zeitschrift für Deutsches Altertum 77 1940.
Kökeritz, H. Two interpretations. Studia Neophilologica 14 1942; rptd in MLN 58 1943.
Meyer, W. Zum Finnsburg Fragment, Vers 6–8a. Beiblatt zur Anglia 54–5 1943–4.
de Vries, J. Die beide Hengeste. Zeitschrift für Deutsche Philologie 72 1953.
Berry, F. A suppressed aposiopesis in the Fight at Finnsburgh. N & Q May 1954.
Laur, W. Die Heldensage vom Finnsburgkampf. Zeitschrift für Deutsches Altertum 85 1954.
Lehmann, W. P. The Finnsburg fragment 34a: 'hwearflacra hrær'. SE 34 1955.
Henry, P. L. The opening of the Finnsburg fragment. Die Sprache 8 1962; rptd in his Early English and Celtic lyric, 1966.
Fuss, K. Der Held: Versuch einer Wesensbestimmung. Zeitschrift für Deutsche Philologie 82 1963.
Fry, D. K. The hero on the beach in Finnsburh. Neuphilologische Mitteilungen 67 1966.
—— Finnsburh 34a: 'hwearflicra hwær'. Eng Lang Notes 6 1969.
Osborn, M. The Finnsburg raven and 'guðrinc astah'. Folklore 81 1970.
Greenfield, S. B. 'Folces hyrde', Finnsburh 46b. Neuphilologische Mitteilungen 73 1972.
See also under Beowulf, *below.*

BATTLE OF MALDON

Ms: Cotton Otho A. xii 57a–62b, burnt in library fire 1731. Transcript by J. Elphinston in Bodley Rawlinson B 203, from which T. Hearne ptd the earliest extant record in his Johannis Glastoniensis chronica, 2 vols Oxford 1726.

§1
Crow, C. L. Maldon and Brunanburh: two Old English songs of battle. Boston 1897.
Sedgefield, W. J. The battle of Maldon and short poems from the Saxon chronicle. Boston 1904.
Ashdown, M. English and Norse documents relating to the reign of Ethelred the Unready. Cambridge 1930. With trn.
Rowles, H. J. The battle and song of Maldon. Colchester 1930.
Laborde, E. D. Byrhtnoth and Maldon. 1936.
Gordon, E. V. The battle of Maldon. 1937, 1957 (corrected).
Krapp-Dobbie 6 1942.

Translations
Hickey, E. H. Academy 27 1885.
Lumsden, H. W. The song of Maldon. Macmillan's Mag March 1887.
Garnett, J. M. Elene, Judith, Brunanburh and Maldon. Boston 1889.
Sims, W. R. The battle of Maldon. MLN 7 1892.
Hall, J. L. Judith, Phoenix and other Anglo-Saxon poems. New York 1912.
Rowles, H. J. The song of Maldon. Essex Rev 38 1929.
Koziol, H. Byrhtnoths Tod, aus dem Altenglischen übersetzt. Vienna and Stuttgart 1960.

§2
Zernial, U. Das Lied von Byrhtnoths Fall. Berlin 1882. Contains trn.
Abegg, D. Zur Entwicklung der historischen Dichtung bei den Angelsachsen. Strasbourg 1894.
Liebermann, F. Zur Geschichte Byrhtnoths, des Helden von Maldon. Archiv 101 1898.
Laborde, E. D. The style of the Battle of Maldon. MLR 19 1924.
—— The site of the Battle of Maldon. EHR 40 1925.
Phillpotts, B. S. The battle of Maldon: some Danish affinities. MLR 24 1929.
Dickins, B. The day of Byrhtnoth's death and other obits from a twelfth-century Ely kalendar. Leeds Stud in Eng 6 1937.
Gordon, E. V. The date of Æthelred's treaty with the Vikings: Olaf Tryggvason and the Battle of Maldon. MLR 32 1937.
Woolf, H. B. The personal names in the Battle of Maldon. MLN 53 1938.
Klaeber, F. Zu dem altenglischen Gedicht auf die Schlacht bei Maldon. Archiv 179 1941.
Tolkien, J. R. R. The homecoming of Beorhtnoth Beorhthelm's son. E & S new ser 6 1953.
Whitehead, F. 'Ofermod' et desmesure. Cahiers de Civilisation Médiévales 3 1960.
Irving, E. B. The heroic style in the Battle of Maldon. SP 58 1961.
Bessinger, J. B. Maldon and the Óláfsdrápa: an historical caveat. Comparative Lit 14 1962; rptd in Studies in OE literature in honor of A. G. Brodeur, Eugene 1963.
Bloomfield, M. W. Patristics and Old English literature. Ibid.
—— Beowulf, Byrhtnoth and the judgment of God: trial by combat in Anglo-Saxon England. Speculum 44 1969.
Elliott, R. W. V. Byrhtnoth and Hildebrand: a study in heroic technique. Comparative Lit 14 1962; rptd in Studies in OE literature in honor of A. G. Brodeur, Eugene 1963.
Gillam, D. M. E. The connotations of OE 'fæge', with a note on Beowulf and Byrhtnoth. Studia Germanica Gandensia 4 1962.
Samouce, W. A. General Byrhtnoth. JEGP 57 1963.

Battaglia, F. J. Notes on Maldon: toward a definitive 'ofermod'. Eng Lang Notes 2 1965.

Blake, N. F. The battle of Maldon. Neophilologus 49 1965.

Britton, G. C. The characterization of the Vikings in the Battle of Maldon. N & Q March 1965.

Cross, J. E. Oswald and Byrhtnoth: a Christian saint and a hero who is a Christian. E Studies 46 1965.

Mills, A. D. Byrhtnoð's mistake in generalship. Neuphilologische Mitteilungen 67 1966.

Clark, C. Byrhtnoth and Roland: a contrast. Neophilologus 51 1967.

Clark, G. The battle in the Battle of Maldon. Neuphilologische Mitteilungen 69 1968.

— The battle of Maldon: a heroic poem. Speculum 43 1968.

Hale, D. G. Structure and theme in the Battle of Maldon. N & Q July 1968.

Isaacs, N. D. Maldon and magnetic action. In his Structural principles, Knoxville 1968.

Swanton, M. J. The battle of Maldon: a literary caveat. JEGP 67 1968.

Bolton, W. F. Byrhtnoð in the wilderness. MLR 64 1969.

Campbell, B. R. The 'superne gar' in the Battle of Maldon. N & Q Feb 1969.

Anderson, E. R. Flyting in the Battle of Maldon. Neuphilologische Mitteilungen 71 1970.

Hill, T. D. History and heroic ethic in Maldon. Neophilologus 54 1970.

Macrae-Gibson, O. D. Maldon: the literary structure of the later part. Neuphilologische Mitteilungen 71 1970.

Metcalf, A. A. 'West' in Maldon. Papers on Lang & Lit 6 1970.

BEDE'S DEATH SONG

Mss: 29 known to exist, of which 11 give the song in the Northumbrian dialect, 17 in West Saxon, and one (Hague ms 70.H.7) in a mixed Northumbrian-West Saxon. See Krapp-Dobbie 6 pp. ci-civ.

§1

Smith, A. H. Three Northumbrian poems. 1933.

Dobbie, E. V. K. The manuscripts of Cædmon's hymn and Bede's death song. New York 1937.

Brotanek, R. Nachlese zu den Hss. der Epistola Cuthberti und des Sterbespruches Bedas. Anglia 64 1940.

Krapp-Dobbie 6 1942.

§2

Brotanek, R. Zur Überlieferung des Sterbegesanges Bedas. In his Texte und Untersuchungen zur altenglischen Literatur, Halle 1913. Addn, Beiblatt zur Anglia 25 1914.

Bulst, W. Bedas Sterbelied. Zeitschrift für Deutsches Altertum 75 1938.

Ker, N. R. The Hague ms of the Epistola Cuthberti de obitu Bedae, with Bede's song. MÆ 8 1939.

Ross, A. S. C. Miscellaneous notes on Cædmon's Hymn and Bede's death song. Eng & Germanic Stud 3 1950.

Huppé, B. F. Doctrine and poetry: Augustine's influence on Old English poetry. New York 1959.

BENEDICTINE OFFICE POEMS

See Creed, Gloria I, Lord's Prayer III.

BEOWULF

Ms : BM Cotton Vitellius A. xv 132a–201b (new foliation).

Concordances

Cook, A. S. A concordance to Beowulf. Halle 1911 Detroit 1969.

Bessinger, J. B. with P. H. Smith. A concordance to Beowulf. Ithaca 1969.

Bibliographies

Tinker, C. B. The translations of Beowulf: a critica bibliography. New Haven 1903.

Magoun, F. P. The Sutton Hoo ship-burial: a chronological bibliography. Speculum 29 1954. Part 2 by J. B. Bessinger 33 1958.

Fry, D. K. Beowulf and the Fight at Finnsburh: a bibliography. Charlottesville 1969.

See also Klaeber's edn, 1922, 1950, and in R. W. Chambers, Beowulf: an introduction, 1921, 1959 (3rd edn with suppl by C. L. Wrenn).

§1

Thorkelin, G. J. De Danorum rebus gestis seculis III et IV poema danicum dialecto anglosaxonica. Copenhagen 1815. With Latin trn.

Kemble, J. M. The Anglo-Saxon poems of Beowulf, the Traveller's song and the Battle of Finnesburh I. 1833, 1835.

Schaldemose, F. Beo-Wulf og Scopes widsið to angelsaxiske digte. Copengahen 1847, 1851.

Thorpe, B. The Anglo-Saxon poems of Beowulf, the Scop or gleeman's tale, and the Fight at Finnsburg. Oxford 1855, 1875 (with trn); ed V. F. Hopper, Great Neck NY 1963.

Grundtvig, N. F. S. Beowulfes beorh eller Bjovulfs-drapen. Copenhagen 1861.

Heyne, M. Beowulf. Paderborn 1863, 1888 (5th edn rev A. Socin), 1908 (8th edn rev L. L. Schücking), 1940 (15th edn rev E. von Schaubert), 3 vols 1946–9, 1961–3 (18th edn).

Grein, C. W. M. Beovulf nebst den Fragmenten Finnsburg und Valdere. Cassel and Göttingen 1867.

Ettmüller, L. Carmen de Beovulfi. Zürich 1875.

Arnold, T. Beowulf. 1876. With trn.

Harrison, J. A. and R. Sharp. Beowulf; The fight at Finnsburh. Boston 1883, 1894 (4th edn).

Möller, H. Das altenglische Volksepos in der ursprünglichen strophischen Form. Kiel 1883.

Holder, A. Beowulf IIa. Freiburg 1884, 1899.

Wyatt, A. J. Beowulf. Cambridge 1894, 1898.

Trautmann, M. Das Beowulflied als Anhang das Finn-Bruchstück und die Waldhere-Bruchstücke. Bonner Beiträge zur Anglistik 16 1904. With trn.

Holthausen, F. Beowulf nebst dem Finnsburg-Bruchstück Heidelberg 1905–6, 1948 (8th edn); addns and errata to 8th edn in Archiv 187 1950; 2, Heidelberg 1906, 1929 (5th edn).

Sedgefield, W. J. Beowulf. Manchester 1910, 1935 (3rd edn).

Chambers, R. W. Beowulf with the Finnsburg Fragment. Cambridge 1914, 1920. Nominally a revision of Wyatt, above, but really a new edn.

Klaeber, F. Beowulf and the Fight at Finnsburg. Boston 1922, 1936 (3rd edn), 1941, 1950 (both with suppls).

Krapp-Dobbie 4 1953.

Wrenn, C. L. Beowulf with the Finnsburg fragment. 1953, 1958.

Magoun, F. P. The poems of British Museum ms Cotton Vitellius A.xv. Cambridge Mass 1955, 1959 (expanded as Beowulf and Judith, done in a normalized orthography), 1966 (rev J. B. Bessinger).

Perez, O. V. Beowulf. Madrid 1959. With trn.

Translations

Grundtvig, N. F. S. Bjowulfs drape. Copenhagen 1820, 1865.

Kemble, J. M. In Vol 2 of 2nd edn of his text.

Ettmüller, L. Beowulf. Zürich 1840.

Wackerbarth, A. D. Beowulf. 1849.

Simrock, K. Beowulf übersetzt und erläutert. Stuttgart and Augsburg 1859. Inserts Battle of Finnsburh after line 1124.

Heyne, M. Beowulf, angelsächsisches Heldengedicht. Paderborn 1863, 1915 (3rd edn).

Wolzogen, H. von. Beovulf aus dem Angelsachsen. Leipzig 1872.

Botkine, L. Beowulf, épopée anglo-saxonne. Le Havre 1877.

Lumsden, H. W. Beowulf: an Old English poem. 1881, 1883.

Garnett, J. M. Beowulf: an Anglo-Saxon poem and the Fight at Finnsburg. Boston 1882, 1900 (4th edn).

Grion, G. Beovulf: poema epico anglosassone del VII secolo. Lucca 1883. First Italian trn.

Wickberg, R. Beovulf, en fornengelsk hjältedikt. Westervik 1889, Upsala 1914. First Swedish trn.

Earle, J. The deeds of Beowulf. Oxford 1892.

Hall, J. L. Beowulf: an Anglo-Saxon epic poem. Boston 1892.

Hoffmann, P. Beowulf: ältestes deutsches Heldengedicht. Züllichau 1893, Hanover 1900.

Morris, W. and A. J. Wyatt. The tale of Beowulf. Hammersmith 1895, London 1898.

Simons, L. Beowulf: angelsaksisch Volksepos. Ghent 1896. First Dutch trn.

Hall, J. R. Clark. Beowulf and the Fight at Finnsburg. 1901, 1950 (rev C. L. Wrenn, with prefatory remarks by J. R. R. Tolkien).

— Beowulf: a metrical translation. Cambridge 1914.

Tinker, C. B. Beowulf. New York 1902.

Child, C. G. Beowulf and the Finnesburh fragment. Boston 1904.

Vogt, P. Beowulf: altenglisches Heldengedicht. Halle 1905.

Gering, H. Beowulf nebst dem Finnsburg-bruchstück. Heidelberg 1906, 1914.

Huyshe, W. Beowulf: an Old English epic. 1907.

Gummere, F. B. The oldest English epic. New York 1909.

Hansen, A. Bjovulf. Ed V. J. von H. Rathlou, Copenhagen and Christiania 1910.

Pierquin, H. Le poème anglo-saxon de Beowulf. Paris 1912.

Kirtlan, E. J. B. The story of Beowulf. 1913.

Benedetti, A. La canzone di Beowulf. Palermo 1916.

Thomas, W. Beowulf et les premiers fragments épiques anglo-saxons. Paris 1919.

Rytter, H. Beowulf og Striden um Finnsborg. Oslo 1921. Norwegian landsmaal.

Scott-Moncrieff, C. K. Beowulf translated. 1921; rptd in his Widsith, Beowulf, Finnsburgh, Waldere, Deor, 1921.

Gordon, R. K. The song of Beowulf. 1923.

Leonard, W. E. Beowulf: a new verse translation. 1923.

Munn, J. B. Beowulf. In Ideas and forms in English and American literature, ed H. A. Watt and J. B. Munn, Chicago 1925.

Strong, A. Beowulf translated into modern English rhyming verse. 1925.

Crawford, D. H. Beowulf translated into English verse. 1926.

Kuriyagawa, F. Beowulf and the Fight at Finnsburg. Tokyo 1932. Tr into Japanese.

Olivero, F. Beowulf. Turin 1934; tr French by C. Monnet, Turin 1937.

Green, A. W. Beowulf, literally translated. Boston 1935.

Kennedy, C. W. Beowulf: the oldest English epic. New York 1940.

Bone, G. Beowulf in modern verse. Oxford 1945.

Waterhouse, M. E. Beowulf in modern English. Cambridge 1949.

Genzmer, F. Beowulf und das Finnsburgbruchstück. Leipzig 1951.

Morgan, E. Beowulf: a verse translation into modern English. Aldington Kent 1952, Berkeley and Los Angeles 1962.

Collinder, B. Beowulf översatt i originalets versmått. Stockholm 1954, 1955 (rev).

Wright, D. Beowulf: a prose translation. 1957 (Penguin Classics).

Cecioni, C. G. Beowulf: poema eroico anglosassone. Bologna 1959.

Alfred, W. Beowulf. In Medieval epics, New York 1963 (Modern Lib).

Raffel, B. Beowulf. New York 1963, 1963 (Mentor paperback with Afterword by R. P. Creed).

Pearson, L. D. Beowulf. Bloomington 1965.

Donaldson, E. T. Beowulf. New York 1966.

Nagano, M. The Beowulf. Tokyo 1966.

Hieatt, C. B. Beowulf and other Old English poems. New York 1967. Introd by A. K. Hieatt.

Crossley-Holland, K. Beowulf. 1968. Introd by B. Mitchell.

Garmonsway, G. N. and J. Simpson. Beowulf and its analogues. 1968.

§2

Leo, H. Beowulf: das älteste deutsche, in angelsächsischer Mundart erhaltene Heldengedicht. Halle 1839.

Müllenhoff, K. Der Mythus von Beóvulf. Zeitschrift für Deutsches Altertum 7 1849.

— Sceáf und seine Nachkommen. Ibid.

— Die innere Geschichte des Beovulfs. Zeitschrift für Deutsches Altertum 14 1869.

Brynjulfsson, G. Oldengelsk og Oldnordisk. Antikuarisk Tidsskrift (Copenhagen) 1852–4.

Bouterwek, K. W. Das Beowulflied: eine Vorlesung. Germania 1 1856.

— Zur Kritik des Beowulfliedes. Zeitschrift für Deutsches Altertum 11 1859.

Rieger, M. Ingväonen, Istväonen, Herminonen. Zeitschrift für Deutsches Altertum 11 1859.

— Zum Beowulf. Zeitschrift für Deutsche Philologie 3 1871.

Vollmer, W. Über das Beowulflied. In Album des literarischen Vereins in Nürnberg für 1861.

Grein, C. W. M. Die historischen Verhältnisse des Beowulfliedes. Jahrbuch für Romanische und Englische Literatur 4 1962.

Holtzmann, A. Zu Beowulf. Germania 8 1863.

Heyne, M. Ueber die Lage und Construction der Halle Heorot. Paderborn 1864.

Köhler, A. Germanische Alterthümer im Beóvulf. Germania 13 1868.

— Die beiden Episoden von Heremod im Beowulfliede. Zeitschrift für Deutsche Philologie 2 1870.

— Die Einleitung des Beovulfliedes: ein Beitrag zur Frage über die Liedertheorie. Ibid.

Bugge, S. Spredte iagttagelser vedkommende de oldengelske digte om Beówulf og Waldere. Tidskrift for Philologi og Pædagogik 8 1869.

— Studien über das Beowulfepos. Beiträge zur Geschichte der Deutschen Sprache und Literatur 12 1887.

— and A. Olrik. Røveren ved Gråsten og Beowulf. Dania 1 1891.

Schrøder, L. Om Bjovulfs-drapen. Copenhagen 1875.

Dederich, H. Historische und geographische Studien zum angelsächsischen Beovulfliede. Cologne 1877.

Schultze, M. Altheidnisches in der angelsächsischen Poesie, speziell im Beowulfsliede. Berlin 1877.

Suchier, H. Über die Sage von Offa und Ðryðo. Beiträge zur Geschichte der Deutschen Sprache und Literatur 4 1877.

Müller, N. Die Mythen im Beówulf. Leipzig 1878.

Gering, H. Der Beówulf und die isländische Grettissaga. Anglia 3 1880.

March, F. A. The world of Beowulf. Proc of Amer Philological Assoc 13 1882.

Schemann, K. Die Synonyma im Beówulfsliede, mit Rücksicht auf Composition und Poetik des Gedichtes. Hagen 1882.

Hoffmann, A. Der bildliche Ausdruck im Beowulf und in der Edda. E Studien 6 1883.

Rönning, F. Beovulfs-kvadet: en literær-historisk undersøgelse. Copenhagen 1883.

Sievers, E. Beiträge zur Geschichte der Deutschen Sprache und Literatur 9 1883, 12 1886, 29 1904, 36 1910, 55 1931; Anglia 14 1892. Notes.

— Die Heimat des Beowulfdichters. Beiträge zur Geschichte der Deutschen Sprache und Literatur 11 1886.

— Beowulf und Saxo. Berichte über die Verhandlungen der Königlich Sächsischen Gesellschaft der Wissenschaften zu Leipzig, philologisch-historische Klasse 47 1895.

Harrison, J. A. Old Teutonic life in Beowulf. Overland Monthly July–Aug 1884.

Hertz, W. Beowulf, das älteste germanische Epos. Nord und Süd 29 1884.

Hornburg, J. Die Komposition des Beowulf. Archiv 72 1884.

Krüger, T. Über Ursprung und Entwicklung des Beowulfliedes. Archiv 71 1884.

Lehmann, H. Brünne und Helm im angelsächsischen Beowulfliede. Leipzig 1885.

— Über die Waffen im angelsächsischen Beowulfliede. Germania 31 1886.

Gummere, F. B. The translation of Beowulf and the relations of ancient and modern English verse. Amer Jnl of Philology 7 1886.

Sarrazin, G. Die Beowulfsage in Dänemark; Beowa und Böthvar; Beowulf und Kynewulf. Anglia 9 1886.

— Der Schauplatz des ersten Beowulfliedes und die Heimat des Dichters. Beiträge zur Geschichte der Deutschen Sprache und Literatur 11 1886.

— Beowulf-Studien. Berlin 1888.

— Die Abfassungszeit des Beowulfliedes I. Anglia 14 1892.

— Neue Beowulf-Studien. E Studien 23 1896, 35 1905, 42 1910.

— Die Hirschhalle; Der Balder-Kultus in Lethra. Anglia 19 1897.

— Rolf Krake und sein Vetter im Beowulfliede. E Studien 24 1897.

Skeat, W. W. On the signification of the monster Grendel in the poem of Beowulf; with a discussion of lines 2076–2100. Jnl of Philology 15 1886.

Schilling, H. The Finnsburg-fragment and the Finnepisode. MLN 2 1887.

ten Brink, B. Beowulf: Untersuchungen. Strasbourg 1888.

Miller, T. The position of Grendel's arm in Heorot. Anglia 12 1889.

Klöpper, C. Heorot-Hall in the Anglo-Saxon poems of Beowulf. In Festschrift für K. E. Krause, Rostock 1890.

Jellinek, M. H. and C. Kraus. Die Widersprüche im Beowulf. Zeitschrift für Deutsches Altertum 35 1891.

Cook, A. S. MLN 7–9 1892–4, 17–18 1902–3, 22 1907, 39–40 1924–5; Archiv 103 1899; JEGP 22 1923. Notes.

— The possible begetter of the Old English Beowulf and Widsith. Trans Connecticut Acad of Arts & Sciences 25 1922.

— Beowulfian and Odyssean voyages. Trans Connecticut Acad of Arts & Sciences 28 1926.

— The Beowulfian maðelode. JEGP 25 1926.

— Greek parallels to certain features of the Beowulf. PQ 5 1926.

— Hellenic and Beowulfian shields and spears. MLN 41 1926.

— Béowulf 1039 and the Greek ἀρχι-. Speculum 3 1928.

Cosijn, P. J. Aanteekeningen op den Beowulf. Leyden 1891–2.

Holthausen, F. [Textual notes from 1892 absorbed in his edn, except the last, Germanisch-romanische Monatsschrift new ser 3 1953.]

Sonnefeld, G. Stilistisches und Wortschatz im Beówulf. Würzburg 1892.

McNary, S. J. Beowulf and Arthur as English ideals. Poet-lore 6 1894.

Kluge, F. Der Beowulf und die Hrolfs Saga Kraka. E Studien 22 1896.

Ker, W. P. In his Epic and romance, 1897.

Blackburn, F. A. The Christian coloring in the Beowulf. PMLA 12 1897; rptd in Nicholson, below.

— Note on Beowulf 1591–1617. MP 9 1911.

Henning, R. Sceaf und die westsächsische Stammtafel. Zeitschrift für Deutsches Altertum 41 1897.

Arnold, T. Notes on Beowulf. 1898.

Trautmann, M. Berichtungen, Vermutungen und Erklärungen zum Beowulf. Bonner Beiträge zur Anglistik 2 1899.

— Finn und Hildebrand. Bonner Beiträge zur Anglistik 7 1903, 17 1905.

Klaeber, F. [Textual and interpretative notes from 1900 absorbed in his edn and its suppls, except 3 in Archiv 187–8 1950–1, 191 1955, Beiträge zur Geschichte der Deutschen Sprache und Literatur 72 1950.]

— Die ältere Genesis und der Beowulf. E Studien 42 1910.

— Aeneis und Beowulf. Archiv 126 1911.

— Die christlichen Elemente im Beowulf. Anglia 35–6 1911–12.

— Observations on the Finn episode. JEGP 14 1915.

— Concerning the relation between Exodus and Beowulf. MLN 33 1918.

— Der Held Beowulf in deutscher Sagenüberlieferung. Anglia 46 1922.

— Attila's and Beowulf's funeral. PMLA 42 1927.

— Unferðs Verhalten im Beowulf. Beiblatt zur Anglia 53 1942.

Lehmann, E. Fandens Oldemor. Dania 8 1901; tr as Teufels Grossmutter in Archiv für Religionswissenschaft 8 1905.

Uhlenbeck, C. C. Het Beowulf-Epos als Geschiedbron. Tijdschrift voor Nederlandsche Taal-en Lietterkunde 20 1901.

Boer, R. C. Die Béowulfsage. Arkiv för Nordisk Filologi 19 1902.

— Finnsage und Nibelungensage. Zeitschrift für Deutsches Altertum 47 1904.

— Die altenglische Heldendichtung I: Beowulf. Halle 1912.

— Studier over Skjoldungedigtningen. Aarbøger for Nordisk Oldkyndighed of Historie 3 1922.

Olrik, A. Danmarks heltedigtning I: Rolf Krake og den ældre Skjoldungrække; II: Starkad den gamle og den yngre Skjoldungrække. Copenhagen 1903–10. Pt I tr as The heroic legends of Denmark, New York 1919.

— Nogle grundsætninger for sagnforskning. Copenhagen 1921.

Stjerna, K. [Archaeological papers pbd in Swedish 1903–8.] Tr and ed J. R. C. Hall as Essays on questions connected with the Old English poem of Beowulf, Coventry 1912.

Abbott, W. C. Hrothulf. MLN 19 1904. Reply by F. Klaeber 20 1905.

Hagen, S. N. Classical names and stories in the Beowulf. MLN 19 1904.

Kock, E. Interpretations and emendations of Early English texts. Anglia 27 1904, 42 1918, 44–6 1920–2. Textual notes and comments.

Rickert, E. The Old English Offa saga. MP 2 1904.

Schücking, L. L. Die Grundzüge der Satzverknüpfung im Beowulf part 1. Halle 1904.

— Beowulfs Rückkehr. Halle 1905.

— Das angelsächsische Totenklagelied. E Studien 39 1908.

— Wann entstand der Beowulf? Glossen, Zweifel und Fragen. Beiträge zur Geschichte der Deutschen Sprache und Literatur 42 1917.

— Wiðergyld (Beowulf 2051). E Studien 53 1920.

— Die Beowulfdatierung: eine Replik. Beiträge zur Geschichte der Deutschen Sprache und Literatur 47 1923.

— Das Königsideal im Beowulf. E Studien 67 1932. Tr in Nicholson, below.

— Heldenstolz und Würde im Angelsächsischen: Anhang, zur Charakterisierungstechnik im Beowulfepos. Abhandlungen der Sächsischen Akademie der Wissenschaften, philologisch-historische Klasse 42, no 5 1933.

Routh, J. E. Two studies on the ballad theory of the Beowulf. Baltimore 1905.

Scheinert, M. Die Adjektiva im Beowulfepos als Darstellungsmittel. Beiträge zur Geschichte der Deutschen Sprache und Literatur 30 1905.

Heusler, A. Zur Skiöldungendichtung. Zeitschrift für Deutsches Altertum 48 1906.

— Zeitrechnung im Beowulfepos. Archiv 124 1910.

Emerson, O. F. Legends of Cain, especially in Old and Middle English. PMLA 21 1906.

— Grendel's motive in attacking Heorot. MLR 16 1921.

— The punctuation of Beowulf and literary interpretation. MP 23 1926.

Morsbach, L. Zur Datierung des Beowulf-epos. Nachrichten der Königl Gesellschaft der Wissenschaften zu Göttingen, philologisch-historische Klasse 1906.

Ries, J. Die Wortstellung im Beowulf. Halle 1907.

Schück, H. Folknamnet Geatas id en fornengelska dikten Beowulf. Upsala 1907.

— Studier i Beowulfsagen. Upsala 1909.

Björkman, E. [Articles on names in Beowulf 1908–20, culminating in] Studien über die Eigennamen im Beowulf. Halle 1920.

— Beowulf och Sveriges historia. Nordisk Tidskrift 7 1917.

— Beowulfforskning och mytologi. Finsk Tidskrift 84 1918.

Weyhe, H. König Ongentheows Fall. E Studien 39 1908.

Deutschbein, M. Die sagenhistorischen und literarischen Grundlagen des Beowulfepos. Germanisch-romanische Monatsschrift 1 1909.

— Beowulf der Gautenkönig. In Festschrift für L. Morsbach, Halle 1913.

Lawrence, W. W. Some disputed questions in Beowulf-criticism. PMLA 24 1909.

— The haunted mere in Beowulf. PMLA 27 1912.

— The Breca episode in Beowulf. In Anniversary papers [for] G. L. Kittredge, Boston 1913.

— Beowulf and the tragedy of Finnsburg. PMLA 30 1915.

— The dragon and his lair in Beowulf. PMLA 33 1918.

— Beowulf and epic tradition. Cambridge Mass 1928, London and New York 1963.

— Beowulf and the saga of Samson the fair. In Studies in English philology in honor of F. Klaeber, Minneapolis 1929.

— The battle of Ravenswood. Amer Scandinavian Rev 22 1934.

— Grendel's lair. JEGP 38 1939.

Grienberger, T. von. Bemerkungen zum Beowulf. Beiträge zur Geschichte der Deutschen Sprache und Literatur 36 1910.

Panzer, F. Studien zur germanischen Sagengeschichte 1: Beowulf. Munich 1910.

Sedgefield, W. J. MLR 5 1910, 16 1921, 18 1923, 27–8 1932–3. Textual notes.

— The Finn episode in Beowulf. MLR 28 1933.

— The scenery in Beowulf. JEGP 35 1936.

Smithson, G. A. The Old English Christian epic. Berkeley 1910.

Chambers, R. W. Six thirteenth-century drawings illustrating the story of Offa and of Thryth (Drida) from ms Cotton Nero D.i. 1912.

— The shifted leaf in Beowulf. MLR 10 1915.

— Beowulf: an introduction to the study of the poem with a discussion of the stories of Offa and Finn. Cambridge 1921, 1959 (3rd edn, with suppl by C. L. Wrenn).

— Beowulf and the heroic age. Foreword to Strong's trn, 1925; rptd in his Man's unconquerable mind, 1939.

— Beowulf's fight with Grendel and its Scandinavian parallels. E Studien 11 1929.

Schütte, G. The Geats of Beowulf. JEGP 11 1912.

— Vor Folkegruppe: Gottjod. Copenhagen 1926; tr J. Young as Our forefathers the Gothonic nations, 2 vols Cambridge 1929–33.

— Ethnische Prunknamen. Zeitschrift für Deutsches Altertum 67 1930.

— Geatersporgsmaalet. Danske Studier 27 1930.

— Episoderne med Hygelac og Ongentheow. Danske Studier 37 1940.

— Skjoldungsagnene i ny Læsemaade. Danske Studier 39 1942.

— Anglian legends in Danish traditions. Acta Philologica Scandinavica 16 1943.

— Offa I reduced ad absurdum. Acta Philologica Scandinavica 19 1947.

Stefanovič, S. Ein Beitrag zur angelsächsischen Offa-Sage. Anglia 35 1912; rewritten as Epizoda o Ofl i Dridi u Beowulfu, Strani Pregled 1927.

— Zur Offa-Thryðo-Episode im Beowulf. E Studien 69 1934.

Belden, H. M. Onela the Scylding and Ali the bold. MLN 28 1913.

Berendsohn, W. A. Drei Schichten dichterischer Gestaltung im Beowulf-Epos. Münchener Museum für Philologie 2 1913.

— Die Gelage am Dänenhof zu Ehren Beowulfs. Münchener Museum für Philologie 3 1914.

— Hrólfssaga Kraka und Beowulf-Epos. In Niederdeutsche Studien: Festschrift C. Borchling, Neumünster 1932.

— Healfdenes Vater. Arkiv för Nordisk Filologi 50 1934.

— Zur Vorgeschichte des Beowulf. Copenhagen 1935.

— Stilkritik am Beowulf-Epos. Arkiv för Nordisk Filologi 54 1939.

Nerman, B. Studier över Svärges bedna litteratur. Upsala 1913.

— Vilke konungar ligga i Uppsala högar? Upsala 1913.

— Otta Vendelkråka och Ottarshögen i Vendel. Upplands Fornminnesförnings Tidskrift 7 1917.

— Ynglingasagan i arkeologisk belysning. Fornvännen 12 1917.

Thomas, P. G. Beowulf and Daniel A. MLR 8 1913.

Müller, J. Das Kulturbild des Beowulfepos. Halle 1914

Olson, O. L. Beowulf and the feast of Bricriu. MP 11 1914.

— The relation of the Hrólfs Saga Kraka and the Bjarkarímur to Beowulf. Urbana 1916.

von Sydow, C. W. Grendel i anglosaxiska ortnamn. Namn och Bygd 2 1914.

— Irisches in Beowulf. In Verhandlungen der 52 Versammlung deutscher Philologen und Schulmänner in Marburg 1913, Leipzig 1914.

— Beowulf och Bjarke. Studier i Nordisk Filologi 14 1923.

—— Beowulfskalden och nordisk tradition. Yearbook of New Soc of Letters at Lund, Årsbok 1923.

—— Hur mytforskningen tolkat Beowulfdikten. Folkminner och Folktankar 11 1924.

—— Scyld Scefing. Namn och Bygd 12 1924.

Kier, C. Beowulf: et bidrag til nordens oldhistorie. Copenhagen 1915.

Green, A. The opening of the episode Finn of in Beowulf. PMLA 31 1916.

—— An episode in Ongentheow's fall (Beowulf, ll. 2957–60). MLR 12 1917.

Pizzo, E. Zur Frage der ästhetischen Einheit des Beowulf. Anglia 39 1916.

Aurner, N. S. An analysis of the interpretations of the Finnsburg documents. Iowa City 1917.

—— Hengest: a study in early English hero legend. Iowa City 1921.

Ayres, H. M. The tragedy of Hengest in Beowulf. JEGP 16 1917.

Fog, R. Trolden Grendel i Bjovulf: en hypothese. Danske Studier 14 1917.

Mead, G. W. Wiðergyld of Beowulf 2051. MLN 32 1917.

Rooth, E. G. T. Der Name Grendel in der Beowulfsage. Beiblatt zur Anglia 28 1917.

Brandl, A. Die Urstammtafel der Westsachsen und das Beowulf-Epos. Archiv 137 1918.

—— Hercules und Beowulf. Sitzungsberichte der Preussischen Akademie der Wissenschaften, philologisch-historische Klasse 1928.

—— Beowulf und die Merowinger. In Studies in English philology in honor of F. Klaeber, Minneapolis 1929; expanded in Sitzungsberichte der Preussischen Akademie der Wissenschaften 1929.

—— Einige Tatsachen betreffend Scyld Scefing. In A grammatical miscellany offered to O. Jespersen, Copenhagen 1930.

—— Zur Entstehung der germanischen Heldensage, gesehen vom angelsächsischen Standpunkt. Archiv 162 1932.

—— Das Beowulfepos und die mercische Königskrisis um 700. Forschungen und Fortschritte 12 1936; tr as The Beowulf epic and the crisis in the Mercian dynasty about the year AD 700, Research & Progress 2 1936.

—— Beowulf-Epos und Aeneis in systematischer Vergleichung. Archiv 171 1937.

Brown, C. F. Beowulf 1080–1106. MLN 34 1919.

—— Beowulf and the Blickling homilies, and some textual notes. PMLA 53 1938.

—— 'Poculum mortis' in Old English. Speculum 15 1940.

Mogk, E. Altgermanische Spukgeschichten; zugleich ein Beitrag zur Erklärung der Grendel-episode im Beowulf. Neue Jahrbücher für das Klassische Altertum 43 1919.

Hoops, J. Das Verhüllen des Haupts bei Toten, ein angelsächsisch-nordischer Brauch. E Studien 54 1920.

—— War Beowulf König von Dänemark? In Britannica: M. Förster zum 60 Geburtstage, Leipzig 1929; rptd in his Beowulfstudien, below.

—— Das Preislied auf Beowulf und die Sigemund-Heremod-Episode. Beiträge zur Neueren Literaturgeschichte (Heidelberg) 16 1930; rptd in his Beowulfstudien, below.

—— Altenglisch 'ealuscerwen', 'meoduscerwen'. E Studien 65 1931. Replies by F. Klaeber, Hoops and K. Krogmann, E Studien 66 1931.

—— Beowulfstudien. Heidelberg 1932.

—— Kommentar zum Beowulf. Heidelberg 1932.

Hubbard, F. G. The plundering of the hoard in Beowulf. Univ of Wisconsin Stud in Lang & Lit 11 1920.

Imelmann, R. Forschungen zur altenglischen Poesie. Berlin 1920.

—— E Studien 66–8 1932–3. Textual and interpretative notes.

La Cour, V. Lejrestudier. Danske Studier 17 1920. *See also* 18 1921, 21 1924.

—— Skjoldungefejden. Dansk Studier 23 1926.

Liebermann, F. Ort und Zeit der Beowulfdichtung. Nachrichten von der Königlicher Gesellschaft der Wissenschaften zu Göttingen, philologisch-historische Klasse 1920.

Noreen, A. Yngve, Inge, Inglinge. Namn och Bygd 8 1920.

Gaidoz, H. Cûchulainn, Beowulf et Hercule. Paris 1921.

Schreiner, K. Die Sage von Hengest und Horsa. Berlin 1921.

Herrmann, P. Die Heldensagen des Saxo Grammaticus. Leipzig 1922.

Meyer, W. Wēalhþēo(w). Beiblatt zur Anglia 33 1922.

Patzig, H. Zur Episode von Þryð im Beowulf. Anglia 46 1922.

Laborde, E. D. Grendel's glove and his immunity from weapons. MLR 18 1923.

Malone, K. The literary history of Hamlet I: the early tradition. Heidelberg 1923, New York 1964.

—— King Alfred's Geats. MLR 20 1925. *See* 23 1928.

—— Danes and Half-Danes. Arkiv för Nordisk Filologi 42 1926.

—— The Finn episode in Beowulf. JEGP 25 1926.

—— Hrethric. PMLA 42 1927.

—— Hunlafing. MLN 43 1928.

—— The daughter of Healfdene. In Studies in English philology in honor of F. Klaeber, Minneapolis 1929; rptd in his Studies in heroic legend, Copenhagen 1959.

—— The identity of the Geatas. Acta Philologica Scandinavica 4 1929.

—— Ingeld. MP 27 1930; rptd and rev as part of Tale of Ingeld in his Studies in heroic legend, Copenhagen 1959.

—— The votaries of Nerthus. Namn och Bygd 22 1934.

—— Healfdene. E Studien 70 1936.

—— The burning of Heorot. RES 13 1937.

—— Young Beowulf. JEGP 36 1937.

—— Swerting. Germanic Rev 14 1939; rptd as part of Tale of Ingeld in his Studies in heroic legend, Copenhagen 1959.

—— Hygelac. E Studies 21 1939.

—— Humblus and Lotherus. Acta Philologica Scandinavica 13 1939; rptd in his Studies in heroic legend, Copenhagen 1959.

—— Ecgtheow. MLQ 1 1940; rptd ibid.

—— Freawaru. ELH 7 1940; rptd ibid.

—— Hagbard and Ingeld. In Essays and studies in honor of C. Brown, New York 1940; rptd ibid.

—— Time and place in the Ingeld episode of Beowulf. JEGP 39 1940; rptd as part of Tale of Ingeld, ibid.

—— Grundtvig as Beowulf critic. RES 17 1941.

—— Hygd. MLN 56 1941.

—— Grendel and Grep. PMLA 57 1942.

—— Hildeburg and Hengest. ELH 10 1943.

—— Finn's stronghold. MP 43 1945.

—— Beowulf. E Studies 29 1948; rptd in Nicholson, below.

—— Royal names in Old English poetry. Names 1 1953. Replies by R. L. Ramsay, Scyldings and shields, ibid, and by K. Malone, Epithets and eponym, 2 1954.

—— Coming back from the mere. PMLA 69 1954.

—— Grendel and his abode. In Studia philologica et litteraria in honorem L. Spitzer, Berne 1958.

—— The Finn episode once again. In Festschrift für W. Fischer, Heidelberg 1959.

—— Words of wisdom in Beowulf. In Humaniora: essays honoring A. Taylor, Locust Valley NY 1960.

—— Symbolism in Beowulf: some suggestions. In English studies today: 2nd series, ed G. A. Bonnard, Berne 1961.

— Widsith, Beowulf and Bravellir. In Festgabe für L. L. Hammerich, Copenhagen 1962.
— Conybeare and Thorkelin. E Studies 50 1969.
— A reading of Beowulf 3169–82. In Medieval literature and folklore studies: essays in honor of F. L. Utley, New Brunswick NJ 1970.
— MLN 41 1926, 68 1953; PQ 8 1929; MLR 24–5 1929–30, 56 1961; Anglia 53–4 1929–30, 56–7 1932–3, 63 1939, 65 1941, 69 1950; Beiblatt zur Anglia 52 1941; JEGP 27 1928, 29 1930, 50 1951; MÆ 2 1933; RES 21 1945; in Britannica: Festschrift für H. M. Flasdieck, Heidelberg 1960; in Franciplegius: medieval and linguistic studies in honor of F. P. Magoun, New York 1965. Textual notes.
Williams, R. A. The Finn episode in Beowulf. Cambridge 1924.
Trnka, B. Dnešní stav badání o Beowulfovi. Časopis pro Moderni Filologii 12 1925. On state of the Beowulf problem.
Wadstein, E. Beowulf, Etymologie und Sinn des Namens. In Germanica: E. Sievers zum 75 Geburtstage, Halle 1925.
— The Beowulf poem as an English national epos. Acta Philologica Scandinavica 8 1934.
Crawford, S. J. MLR 21 1926, 23–4 1928–9; RES 7 1931. Notes.
Hübener, G. Beowulf und die Psychologie der Standesentwicklung. Germanisch-romanische Monatsschrift 14 1926.
— Beowulf und nordische Dämonenaustreibung. E Studien 62 1928.
— Beowulf und Germanic exorcism. RES 11 1935.
— Beowulf's seax, the Saxons and an Indian exorcism. RES 12 1936; also as Beowulf: ein indisches Messer-exorzismus und die Sachsen, in Englische Kultur in sprachwissenschaftlicher Deutung: Festschrift für M. Deutschbein, Leipzig 1936.
Strömholm, D. Försök över Beowulfdikten och Ynglingasagan. Edda 25 1926.
Cornelius, R. D. Palus inambilis. Speculum 2 1927.
Magoun, F. P. The burning of Heorot: an illustrative note. MLN 42 1927.
— Recurring first elements in different nominal compounds in Beowulf and in the Elder Edda. In Studies in English philology in honor of F. Klaeber, Minneapolis 1929.
— Zum heroischen Exorcismus des Beowulfepos. Arkiv för Nordisk Fililogi 54 1939.
— Danes, North, South, East and West, in Beowulf. In Philologica: the [Kemp] Malone anniversary studies, Baltimore 1949.
— The geography of Hygelác's raid on the lands of the West Frisians and the Hætt-ware, ca. 530 AD. E Studies 34 1953.
— Oral-formulaic character of Anglo-Saxon narrative poetry. Speculum 28 1953; rptd in Essential articles for the study of OE poetry, ed J. B. Bessinger and S. J. Kahrl, Hamden Conn 1968, and in Nicholson and Fry, below.
— Béowulf and King Hygelác in the Netherlands. E Studies 35 1954.
— Béowulf A': a folk-variant. Arv: Tidskrift för Nordisk Folkminnesforskning 14 1958.
— Béowulf B: a folk-poem on Beowulf's death. In Early English and Norse studies presented to Hugh Smith, 1963.
Wessén, E. De nordiska Folkstammarna i Beowulf. Kungl Vitterhets Historie och Antikivitets Akademiens Handlingar 36 Stockholm 1927.
— Nordiska Namnstudier. Uppsala Universitets Årsskrift 1927.
Dehmer, H. Die Grendelkämpfe Beowulfs im Lichte moderner Märchenforschung. Germanisch-romanische Monatsschrift 16 1928.

Bryan, W. F. Epithetic compound folk-names in Beowulf. In Studies in English philology in honor of F. Klaeber, Minneapolis 1929.
— The Wægmundings—Swedes or Geats? MP 34 1936.
van Hamel, A. G. Hengest and his namesake. In Studies in English philology in honor of F. Klaeber, Minneapolis 1929.
Hulbert, J. R. A note on the psychology of the Beowulf poet. Ibid.
— A note on compounds in Beowulf. JEGP 31 1932.
— Beowulf and the classical epic. MP 44 1946.
— The genesis of Beowulf: a caveat. PMLA 66 1951.
— Surmises concerning the Beowulf poet's source. JEGP 50 1951.
Schick, J. Die Urquelle der Offa-Konstanze-Sage. In Britannica: M. Förster zum 60 Geburtstage, Leipzig 1929.
Steadman, J. M. The Ingeld episode in Beowulf: history or prophecy? MLN 45 1930.
Work, J. A. Odyssean influence on the Beowulf. PQ 9 1930.
Zachrisson, R. E. Grendel in Beowulf and in local names. In A grammatical miscellany offered to O. Jespersen, Copenhagen 1930.
Chapman, C. O. Beowulf and Apollonius of Tyre. MLN 46 1931.
Haber, T. B. A comparative study of the Beowulf and the Aeneid. Princeton 1931, New York 1968. See MLN 48 1933.
Henel, H. 'Stanboga' im Beowulf. Anglia 55 1931.
Langenfelt, G. Notes on the Anglo-Saxon pioneers vii: Beowulf problems. E Studien 66 1931.
— Beowulf och Fornsverige: ett försök till datering av den fornengelska hjältediken. Ortnamnssällskapets i Uppsala Årsskrift 1962.
Weber, E. Seelenmörder oder Unholdtöter? Neuphilologische Monatsschrift 2 1931.
— Die Halle Heorot als Schlafsaal. Archiv 162 1932.
— Der Germanenglaube im Beowulf. Germanien (Leipzig) 6 1934.
— Zur gemeingermanischen Ritterlichkeit im Beowulfslied. Neuphilologische Monatsschrift 10 1940.
Krogmann, W. Anglia 56–8 1932–4, 61 1937, 63 1939; E Studien 66–8 1932–3, 70 1935–6. Notes on words.
— 'Ealuscerwen' und 'meoduscerwen'. E Studien 67 1932.
O'Neill, Sr M. A. Elegiac elements in Beowulf. Washington 1932.
Schröder, E. Beowulf. Anglia 56 1932. See 57 1933.
— Der Name Healfdene. Anglia 58 1934.
Beaty, J. O. The echo-word in Beowulf with a note on the Finnsburg fragment. PMLA 49 1934.
Dickins, B. English names and Old English heathenism. E & S 19 1934.
Du Bois, A. E. The unity of Beowulf. PMLA 49 1934.
— Beowulf 1107 and 2577: hoards, swords and shields. E Studien 69 1935.
— MLN 50 1935, 69–70 1954–5. Notes on cruxes.
— Stod on stapole. MLQ 16 1955.
— The dragon in Beowulf. PMLA 72 1957.
Fischer, W. Von neuerer deutscher Beowulf-Forschung. In Germanische Philologie: Festschrift für O. Behagel, Heidelberg 1934.
Hintz, H. W. The Hama reference in Beowulf 1197–1201. JEGP 33 1934.
Keller, W. Beowulf der riesige Vorkämpfer. E Studien 68 1934. Replies by G. Hübner, Richtigstellung, E Studien 69 1935 and Keller, ibid.
Peter, I. S. Beowulf and the Rāmāyana: a study in epic poetry. 1934.
Bouman, A. C. The heroes of the fight at Finnsburg. Acta Philologica Scandinavica 10 1935.
— Beowulf's song of sorrow. In Mélanges de linguistique et de philologie: F. Mossé in memoriam, Paris 1959.

Eliason, N. E. Wulfhliŏ (Beowulf l. 1358). JEGP 34 1935.
— The improvised lay in Beowulf. PQ 31 1952.
— Beowulf notes. Anglia 71 1953.
— The þyle and scop in Beowulf. Speculum 38 1963.
— The Thryth-Offa digression in Beowulf. In Franciplegius: medieval and linguistic studies in honor of F. P. Magoun, New York 1965.
— The arrival at Heorot. In Studies in language, literature and culture, ed E. B. Atwood and A. A. Hill, Austin 1969.
Girvan, R. Beowulf and the seventh century. 1935, 1971 (with new ch by R. Bruce-Mitford).
— Finnsburuh. Proc Br Acad 26 1940.
Gordon, E. V. Wealhþeow and related names. MÆ 4 1935.
Herben, S. J. Heorot. PMLA 50 1935.
— A note on the helm in Beowulf. MLN 52 1937.
— Beowulf, Hrothgar and Grendel. Archiv 173 1938.
Krappe, A. H. Der blinde König. Zeitschrift für Deutsches Altertum 72 1935.
— The Offa-Constance legend. Anglia 61 1937.
Clarke, D. E. M. The office of thyle in Beowulf. RES 12 1936.
Lindqvist, S. Uppsala högar och Ottarshögen. Stockholm 1936.
— Sutton Hoo och Béowulf. Forvännen 43 1948; tr as Sutton Hoo and Beowulf, Antiquity 22 1948.
— Beowulf dissectus. Upsala 1958. With English summary.
Marquardt, H. Fürsten und Kriegerkenning im Beowulf. Anglia 60 1936.
— Zur Entstehung des Beowulf. Anglia 64 1940.
Tolkien, J. R. R. Beowulf: the monsters and the critics. Proc Br Acad 22 1936; 1937 (separately); rptd in Nicholson and Fry, below.
de Vries, J. Een nieuwe Beowulf-Theorie. Neophilologus 21 1936.
— Die beiden Hengeste. Zeitschrift für Deutsche Philologie 72 1953.
Batchelor, C. C. The style of the Beowulf: a study of the composition of the poem. Speculum 12 1937.
Woolf, H. B. The name of Beowulf. E Studien 72 1937.
— A note on the hoard in Beowulf. MLN 58 1943.
— Subject-verb agreement in Beowulf. MLQ 4 1943.
— Beowulf and Grendel: an analogue from Burma. MLN 62 1947.
— On the characterization of Beowulf. ELH 15 1948.
— Unferth. MLQ 10 1949.
— Hrothgar. Louisiana State Univ Stud humanities ser 5 1954.
Blomfield, J. The style and structure of Beowulf. RES 14 1938; rptd in Fry, below.
Mackie, W. S. The demons' home in Beowulf. JEGP 37 1938.
— Notes upon the text and the interpretation of Beowulf. MLR 34 1939, 36 1941.
von Schaubert, E. Zur Gestaltung und Erklärung des Beowulftextes. Anglia 62 1938.
Huppé, B. F. A reconsideration of the Ingeld passage in Beowulf. JEGP 38 1939.
Schröbler, L. Beowulf und Homer. Beiträge zur Geschichte der Deutschen Sprache und Literatur 63 1939.
Whitelock, D. Beowulf 2444–71. MÆ 8 1939.
— The audience of Beowulf. Oxford 1951.
Andrew, S. O. Syntax and style in Old English. Cambridge 1940.
— Postscript on Beowulf. Cambridge 1948.
Bonjour, A. The use of anticipation in Beowulf. RES 16 1940; rptd in his Twelve Beowulf papers, 1962.
— Genèse et unité de Beowulf. Etudes de Lettres no 64 1946.
— Weohstan's slaying of Eanmund (Beowulf 2611–25). E Studies 27 1946.

— Grendel's dam and the composition of Beowulf. E Studies 30 1949; rptd in his Twelve Beowulf papers, 1962.
— The digressions in Beowulf. Oxford 1950.
— The technique of parallel descriptions in Beowulf. RES new ser 2 1951; rptd in his Twelve Beowulf papers, 1962.
— Beowulf and Heardred. E Studies 32 1951; rptd in his Twelve Beowulf papers, 1962.
— The problem of Daeghrefn. JEGP 51 1952; rptd in his Twelve Beowulf papers, 1962.
— Young Beowulf's inglorious period. Anglia 70 1952; rptd in his Twelve Beowulf papers, 1962.
— Monsters crouching and critics rampant: or the Beowulf dragon debated. PMLA 68 1953; rptd in his Twelve Beowulf papers, 1962.
— On sea images in Beowulf. JEGP 54 1955; rptd in his Twelve Beowulf papers, 1962.
— Beowulf and the beasts of battle. PMLA 72 1957; rptd in his Twelve Beowulf papers, 1962.
— Beowulf and the snares of literary criticism. Etudes Anglaises 10 1957; rptd in his Twelve Beowulf papers, 1962.
— Poésie héroique du Moyen Age et critique littéraire. Romania 78 1957; rptd in his Twelve Beowulf papers, 1962.
— Beowulf et l'épopée anglo-saxonne. La Table Ronde no 132 1958.
— Beowulf et le démon de l'analogie. In his Twelve Beowulf papers, 1962.
— Twelve Beowulf papers 1940–60, with additional comments. Neuchâtel 1962.
— The Beowulf poet and the tragic muse. In Studies in OE literature in honor of A. G. Brodeur, Eugene 1963.
— Jottings on Beowulf and the aesthetic approach. In Old English poetry: fifteen essays, ed R. P. Creed, Providence RI 1967.
Brown, C. S. Beowulf's arm-lock. PMLA 55 1940.
— On reading Beowulf. Sewanee Rev 50 1942.
Caldwell, J. R. The origin of the story of Boðvar-Bjarki. Arkiv för Nordisk Filologi 55 1940.
Cooley, F. D. Early Danish criticism of Beowulf. ELH 7 1940.
— Grundtvig's first translation from Beowulf. Scandinavian Stud 16 1941.
— Contemporary reaction to the identification of Hygela. In Philologica: the [Kemp] Malone anniversary studies, Baltimore 1949.
Niederstenbruch, A. Germanisch-heidenische und christlich-kirchliche Elemente im Beowulf. Weltanschauung und Schule 3 1940.
Pirkhofer, A. Figurengestaltung im Beowulf-Epos. Heidelberg 1940.
Whitbread, L. Grendel's abode: an illustrative note. E Studies 22 1940.
— Beowulfiana. MLR 37 1942.
— Beowulf and Grendel's mother: two minor parallels from folklore. MLN 57 1942.
— Three Beowulf allusions. N & Q July 1945.
— The hand of Æschere: a note on Beowulf 1343. RES 25 1949.
— Beowulf and archaeology: two footnotes. Neuphilologische Mitteilungen 68 1967. See 69–70 1968–9.
Heraucourt, W. Figurengestaltung im Beowulf-Epos. Die Neueren Sprachen 49 1941.
Pope, J. C. The rhythm of Beowulf: an interpretation of the normal and hypermetric verse-forms in Old English poetry. New Haven 1942, 1966 (rev).
— Three notes on the text of Beowulf. MLN 67 1952.
— Beowulf 3150–1: Queen Hygd and the word 'geomeowle'. MLN 70 1955.
— The emendation 'oreðes ond attres', Beowulf 2523. MLN 72 1957.
— Beowulf's old age. In Philological essays in honour of H. D. Meritt, Hague 1970.

Boberg, I. M. Die Sage von Vermund und Uffe. Acta Philologica Scandinavica 16 1943.
— Er Skjoldungerne Hunnerkinger? Acta Philologica Scandinavica 18 1945.
Bond, G. Links between Beowulf and Mercian history. SP 40 1943.
Brady, C. The legends of Ermanaric. Berkeley 1943.
— The synonyms for 'sea' in Beowulf. In Studies in honor of A. M. Sturtevant, Lawrence Kansas 1952.
Brodeur, A. G. The climax of the Finn episode. Univ of California Pbns in Eng 3 1943.
— Design and motive in the Finn episode. Essays & Studies, Univ of California Pbns in Eng 14 1943.
— The structure and unity of Beowulf. PMLA 68 1953.
— Design for terror in the purging of Heorot. JEGP 53 1954.
— The art of Beowulf. Berkeley 1959.
— Beowulf: one poem or three? In Medieval literature and folklore studies: essays in honor of F. L. Utley, New Brunswick NJ 1970.
Gadde, F. Viktor Rydberg and some Beowulf questions. Studia Neophilologica 15 1943.
Kuhn, S. M. The sword of Healfdene. JEGP 42 1943.
— Beowulf and the life of Beowulf: a study in epic structure. In Studies in language, literature and culture, ed E. B. Atwood and A. A. Hill, Austin 1969.
Lukman, N. C. Skjoldunge und Skilfinge, Hunnen- und Herulerkönige in ostnordischer Überlieferung. Copenhagen 1943.
Estrich, R. M. The throne of Hrothgar: Beowulf ll. 168–9. JEGP 43 1944.
Derolez, R. L. M. 'And that difficult word, garsecg' (Gummere). MLQ 7 1946.
— Filologie en oudheidkunde: de Beowulf voor en na de ontdekking van Sutton Hoo. Handelingen van de Koninklijke Zuidnederlandse Maatschappij voor Taal en Letterkunde en Geschiedenis 15 1961.
— Beowulfiana. Revue Belge 40 1962.
Hamilton, M. P. The religious principle in Beowulf. PMLA 61 1946; rptd in Nicholson, below.
Berry, F. The modernity of Beowulf. Life & Letters April 1947.
Johansson, G. Beowulfsagans Hronesnæsse, Lekmannafunderingar angående det gamla Götland. Gothenberg 1947.
— Beowulfsagans historiska fragment. Gothenberg 1964.
— The making of Beowulf and place-names in Beowulf. Gothenberg 1967.
Splitter, H. W. Note on a Beowulf passage. MLN 63 1948.
— The relation of Germanic folk custom and ritual to 'ealuscerwen' (Beowulf 769). MLN 67 1952.
Timmer, B. J. Beowulf: the poem and the poet. Neophilologus 32 1948.
— A note on Beowulf, ll. 2526b–7a and l. 2295. E Studies 40 1959.
Baum, P. F. The meter of the Beowulf. MP 46 1948–9.
— The Beowulf poet. PQ 39 1960; rptd in Nicholson, below.
Lumiansky, R. M. The contexts of Old English 'ealuscerwen' and 'meoduscerwen'. JEGP 48 1959.
— The dramatic audience in Beowulf. JEGP 51 1952; rptd in Fry, below.
— Wiglaf. College Eng Jan 1953.
Ward, G. Hengest. Archaeologia Cantiana 61 1949; 1949 (separately).
Davidson, H. R. E. The hill of the dragon: Anglo-Saxon burial mounds in literature and archaeology. Folk-lore 61 1950.
— The sword in Anglo-Saxon England; its archaeology and literature. Oxford 1962.
— Archaeology and Beowulf. In Beowulf and its analogues, tr G. N. Garmonsway and J. Simpson 1968.

Donahue, C. Grendel and the Clanna Cain. Jnl of Celtic Stud 1 1950.
— Beowulf, Ireland and the natural good. Traditio 7 1951.
— Beowulf and Christian tradition: a reconsideration from a Celtic stance. Traditio 21 1965.
Genzmer, F. Die skandinavischen Quellen des Beowulfs. Arkiv för Nordisk Filologi 55 1950.
Zink, G. Les légendes héroïques de Dietrich et d'Ermanrich dans les littératures germaniques. Lyons and Paris 1950.
Bloomfield, M. W. Beowulf and Christian allegory: an interpretation of Unferth. Traditio 7 1951; rptd in Nicholson and Fry, below.
— Patristics and Old English literature: notes on some poems. Comparative Lit 14 1962; rptd in Studies in OE literature in honor of A. G. Brodeur, Eugene 1963; in Essential articles for the study of OE poetry, ed J. B. Bessinger and S. J. Kahrl, Hamden Conn 1968; and in Nicholson and Fry, below.
— Beowulf, Byrhtnoth and the judgment of God: trial by combat in Anglo-Saxon England. Speculum 44 1969.
— Episodic motivations and marvels in epic and romance. In his Essays and explorations, Cambridge Mass 1970.
Colgrave, B. A Mexican version of the Bear's son folk tale. Jnl of Amer Folklore 64 1951.
Ochs, E. Healfdenes Tochter. Neuphilologische Mitteilungen 52 1951.
Peters, L. J. The relationship of the Old English Andreas to Beowulf. PMLA 66 1951.
Robertson, D. W. The doctrine of charity in medieval literary gardens: a topical approach through symbolism and allegory. Speculum 26 1951; rptd in Nicholson, below.
Gang, T. M. Approaches to Beowulf. RES new ser 3 1952.
O'Loughlin, J. L. N. Beowulf: its unity and purpose. MÆ 21 1952.
— Sutton Hoo: the evidence of the documents. Mediaeval Archaeology 8 1964.
Smithers, G. V. Five notes on Old English texts. Eng & Germanic Stud 4 1952.
— The making of Beowulf. Durham 1962. Inaugural lecture 1961.
— Four cruxes in Beowulf. In Studies in language and literature in honour of M. Schlauch, Warsaw 1966.
— Destiny and the heroic warrior in Beowulf. In Philological essays in honour of H. D. Meritt, Hague 1970.
— The Geats in Beowulf. Durham Univ Jnl 63 1971.
Taylor, A. R. Two notes on Beowulf. Leeds Stud in Eng 7 1952.
Walker, W. S. The 'brunecg' sword. MLN 67 1952.
Engelhart, G. J. On the sequence of Beowulf's geogoð. MLN 68 1953.
— Beowulf 3150. MLN 68 1953.
— Beowulf: a study in dilatation. PMLA 70 1955.
Leisi, E. Gold und Manneswert im Beowulf. Anglia 71 1953.
Matthes, H. C. Beowulfstudien. Ibid.
— Hygd. In Festschrift zum 75 Geburtstag von T. Spira, Heidelberg 1961.
Moore, A. K. Beowulf's dereliction in the Grendel episode. MLN 68 1953.
— Medieval English literature and the question of unity. MP 65 1968.
Sisam, K. Anglo-Saxon royal genealogies. Proc Br Acad 39 1953.
— Liber monstrorum and English heroic legend. In his Studies in the history of OE literature, Oxford 1953.
— Beowulf's fight with the dragon. RES new ser 9 1958.
— The structure of Beowulf. Oxford 1965.

Brunner, K. Why was Beowulf preserved? Etudes Anglaises 7 1954.

Collinder, B. Beowulfskolier. In Festskrift tillägnade E. Wessén, Lund 1954.

Friend, J. H. The Finn episode climax: another suggestion. MLN 69 1954.

— A new reading of a Beowulf crux. MLN 74 1959.

Laur, W. Die Heldensage vom Finnsburgkampf. Zeitschrift für Deutsches Altertum 85 1954.

Moorman, C. Suspense and foreknowledge in Beowulf. College Eng April 1954.

— The essential paganism of Beowulf. MLQ 28 1967.

Tillyard, E. M. W. In his English epic and its background, 1954.

Woodward, R. H. 'Swanrad' in Beowulf. MLN 69 1954.

Beare, W. Pollicis ictus, the Saturnian and Beowulf. Classical Philology 50 1955.

Cabaniss, A. Beowulf and the liturgy. JEGP 54 1955.

Carney, J. The Irish elements in Beowulf. In his Studies in Irish literature and history, Dublin 1955.

van Meurs, J. C. Beowulf and literary criticism. Neophilologus 39 1955.

Pepperdene, M. W. Grendel's geis. Jnl Royal Soc of Antiquaries of Ireland 85 1955.

— Beowulf and the coast-guard. E Studies 47 1966.

Rogers, H. L. Beowulf's three great fights. RES new ser 6 1955.

— The crypto-psychological character of the oral formula. E Studies 47 1966.

Sander, G. Gliederung und Komposition des Beowulfs. Mainz 1955.

Sutherland, R. C. The meaning of eorlscipe in Beowulf. PMLA 70 1955.

— The celibate Beowulf, the Gospels and the liturgy. Atlanta 1964.

Touster, E. K. Metrical variation as a poetic device in Beowulf. Anglia 73 1955.

Chapman, R. L. Alas, poor Grendel. College Eng March 1956.

Einarsson, S. Bjolfur and Grendill in Iceland. MLN 71 1956.

— Beowulfian place names in East Iceland. MLN 76 1961.

Howren, R. A note on Beowulf 168–9. MLN 71 1956.

Jelinek, V. Three notes on Beowulf. MLN 71 1956.

Orrick, A. H. 'Reðes and hattres', Beowulf 2523. MLN 71 1956.

— Beowulf's fight with Grendel. In Essays in literary history presented to J. M. French, New Brunswick NJ 1960.

Piper, W. B. The case for 'weard Scildinga' (Beowulf 305b–6a). PQ 35 1956.

Szöverffy, J. From Beowulf to the Arabian nights (preliminary notes on Aarne-Thompson 301). Midwest Folklore 6 1956.

Cramp, R. Beowulf and archaeology. Medieval Archaeology 1 1957; rptd in Fry, below.

Emerson, E. H. On translating Beowulf. South Atlantic Quart 56 1957.

Enkvist, N. E. The seasons of the year: chapters on a motif from Beowulf to the Shepheardes calendar. Copenhagen 1957.

Hatto, A. T. Snake-swords and bow-helms in Beowulf. E Studies 38 1957.

Nist, J. A. Textual elements in the Beowulf manuscript. Papers of Michigan Acad 42 1957.

— The structure of Beowulf. Papers of Michigan Acad 43 1958.

— Alliterative patterns in Beowulf: a key to authorship. Papers of Michigan Acad 44 1959.

— The structure and texture of Beowulf. São Paulo 1959.

— Beowulf and the classical epics. College Eng Jan 1963.

— Metrical uses of the harp in Beowulf. In Old English poetry: fifteen essays, ed R. P. Creed, Providence RI 1967.

Storms, G. Compounded names of peoples in Beowulf: a study in the diction of a great poet. Utrecht-Nijmegen 1957.

— The figure of Beowulf in the OE epic. E Studies 40 1959.

— The subjectivity of the style of Beowulf. In Studies in OE literature in honor of A. G. Brodeur, Eugene 1963.

— The significance of Hygelac's raid. Nottingham Medieval Stud 14 1970.

— Grendel the terrible. Neuphilologische Mitteilungen 73 1972.

Wright, H. G. Good and evil; light and darkness; joy and sorrow in Beowulf. RES new ser 8 1957; abridged in Nicholson, below.

Anderson, G. K. Beowulf, Chaucer and their backgrounds. In Contemporary literary scholarship: a critical review, ed L. Leary, New York 1958.

Bessinger, J. B. Beowulf and the harp at Sutton Hoo. UTQ 27 1958.

— A concordance to Beowulf. In Computers and OE concordances, ed A. Cameron et al, Toronto 1970.

Bliss, A. J. The metre of Beowulf. Oxford 1958.

Cohen, H. Beowulf 86–98. Explicator 16 1958.

Fanger, D. Three aspects of Beowulf and his God. Neuphilologische Mitteilungen 59 1958.

Fisher, P. F. The trials of the epic hero in Beowulf. PMLA 73 1958.

Harding, E. Språkvetenskapliga problem: om Beowulf's gætas och några andra problem. Lund 1958.

Isshiki, M. The kennings in Beowulf. In Studies in English grammar and linguistics in honour of T. Otsuka, Tokyo 1958.

Kaske, R. E. Sapientia et fortitudo as the controlling theme of Beowulf. SP 55 1958; rptd in Nicholson, below.

— Weohstan's sword. MLN 75 1960.

— Hygelac and Hygd. In Studies in OE literature in honor of A. G. Brodeur, Eugene 1963.

— The eotenas in Beowulf. In Old English poetry: fifteen essays, ed R. P. Creed, Providence RI 1967.

— Beowulf. In Critical approaches to six major English works: Beowulf through Paradise lost, ed R. M. Lumiansky and H. Baker, Philadelphia 1968.

— Beowulf and the book of Enoch. Speculum 46 1971.

Lehmann, W. P. and T. Tabusa. The alliterations of the Beowulf. Austin 1958.

Lehmann, W. P. Beowulf 33, 'isig'. MLN 74 1959.

— Beowulf 2298. In Festschrift für L. Wolff, Neumünster 1962.

— Post-consonantal l, m, n, r, and metrical practice in the Beowulf. In Nordica et anglica: studies in honor of S. Einarrson, Hague 1968.

— On posited omissions in Beowulf. In Studies in language, literature and culture, ed E. B. Atwood and A. A. Hill, Austin 1969.

Chadwick, N. K. The monsters and Beowulf. In The Anglo-Saxons: studies presented to B. Dickins, 1959.

Creed, R. P. The making of an Anglo-Saxon poem. ELH 26 1959; rptd in Essential articles for the study of OE poetry, ed J. B. Bessinger and S. J. Kahrl, Hamden Conn 1968; in Fry, below, with addns.

— On the possibility of criticising Old English poetry. Texas Stud in Lang & Lit 3 1961.

— The singer looks at his sources. Comparative Lit 14 1962; rptd in Studies in OE literature in honor of A. G. Brodeur, Eugene 1963.

— A new approach to the rhythm of Beowulf. PMLA 81 1966.

— '. . . Wél-hwelĉ gecwæþ . . .': the singer as architect. Tennessee Stud in Lit 11 1966.

Daunt, M. Minor realism and contrast in Beowulf. In Mélanges de linguistique et de philologie: F. Mossé in memoriam, Paris 1959.

Edwards, P. The horse-races in Beowulf. Folklore 70 1959.

Frankis, P. J. Beowulf and the one that got away. Neuphilologische Mitteilungen 60 1959.

Garbáty, T. J. Feudal linkage in Beowulf. N & Q Jan 1959.

—— The fallible sword: inception of a motif. Jnl of Amer Folklore 75 1962.

McElroy, D. D. England's first poet-critic? N & Q Sept 1959.

Stevick, R. D. Emendation of Old English poetic texts: Beowulf 2523. MLQ 20 1959.

—— The oral-formulaic analyses of Old English verse. Speculum 37 1962; rptd in Essential articles for the study of OE poetry, ed J. B. Bessinger and S. J. Kahrl, Hamden Conn 1968.

—— Christian elements and the genesis of Beowulf. MP 61 1963.

Wrenn, C. L. Sutton Hoo and Beowulf. In Mélanges de linguistique et de philologie: F. Mossé in memoriam, Paris 1959.

Culbert, T. The narrative functions of Beowulf's swords. JEGP 59 1960.

—— Narrative technique in Beowulf. Neophilologus 47 1963.

Goldsmith, M. E. The Christian theme of Beowulf. MÆ 29 1960.

—— The Christian perspective in Beowulf. Comparative Lit 14 1962; rptd in Studies in OE literature in honor of A. G. Brodeur, Eugene 1963; and in Nicholson, below.

—— The choice in Beowulf. Neophilologus 48 1964.

—— The mode and meaning of Beowulf. 1970.

Kee, K. Beowulf 1408ff: a discussion and a suggestion. MLN 75 1960.

Lord, A. B. The singer of tales. Cambridge Mass 1960.

—— Homer and other epic poetry. In A companion to Homer, ed A. J. B. Wace and F. H. Stubbings 1963.

—— Beowulf and Odysseus. In Franciplegius: medieval and linguistic studies in honor of F. P. Magoun, New York 1965.

McNamee, M. B. Beowulf: an allegory of salvation? JEGP 59 1960; rptd in Nicholson, below.

—— Honor and the epic hero. New York 1960.

Utley, F. L. Folklore, myth, and ritual. In Critical approaches to medieval literature, ed D. Bethurum, New York 1960.

Wild, F. Beowulf und Phokas. Annali Istituto Universitario Orientale, Napoli, Sezione Germanica 3 1960.

—— Beowulf und die Waegmundinge. Die Modernen Sprachen, Schriftenreihe 6 1961.

—— Drachen im Beowulf und andere Drachen. Vienna 1962.

Wood, C. 'Nis þæt seldguma': Beowulf 249. PMLA 75 1960.

Ball, C. J. E. 'Incge' Beow. 2577. Anglia 78 1961.

—— Beowulf 987. Archiv 201 1964.

—— Beowulf 99–101. N & Q May 1971.

Gillam, D. M. E. The use of the term 'æglæca' in Beowulf at lines 813 and 2592. Studia Germanica Gandensia 3 1961.

—— The connotations of OE 'fæge', with a note on Beowulf and Byrhtnoð. Studia Germanica Gandensia 4 1962.

Hahn, E. A. Wæs Hrunting nama. Language 37 1961.

Henry, P. L. Beowulf cruces. Zeitschrift für Vergleichende Sprachforschung 77 1961.

Markland, M. F. The craven comitatus. College Eng Feb 1961.

Reiman, D. H. Folklore and Beowulf's defense of Heorot. E Studies 42 1961.

Shimizu, T. Pleonasm in Beowulf. In Essays in English and American literature [for] T. Nakayama, Tokyo 1961.

Standop, E. Zum Tempus der Ingeld-Episode im Beowulf. Archiv 197 1961.

Taglicht, J. Beowulf and Old English verse rhythm. RES new ser 12 1961.

Takayanagi, S. Beowulf and Christian tradition. Stud in Eng Lit (Tokyo) 37 1961.

Whallon, W. The diction of Beowulf. PMLA 76 1961.

—— The Christianity of Beowulf. MP 60 1962.

—— Formulas for heroes in the Iliad and in Beowulf. MP 63 1965.

—— The idea of God in Beowulf. PMLA 80 1965.

—— Formula, character and context: studies in Homeric, Old English and Old Testament poetry. Cambridge Mass 1969.

Willard, R. Beowulf 2672b: 'lig yðum for'. MLN 76 1961.

—— and E. D. Clemons. Bliss's light verses in the Beowulf. JEGP 66 1967.

Blake, N. F. The Heremod digressions in Beowulf. JEGP 51 1962.

Chaney, W. A. Grendel and the gifstol: a legal view of monsters. PMLA 77 1962.

Durant, J. The function of joy in Beowulf. Tennessee Stud in Lit 7 1962.

Greenfield, S. B. Beowulf and epic tragedy. Comparative Lit 14 1962; rptd in Studies in OE literature in honor of A. G. Brodeur, Eugene 1963.

—— Geatish history: poetic art and epic quality in Beowulf. Neophilologus 47 1963.

—— Beowulf 207b–28: narrative and descriptive art. N & Q March 1966.

—— The canons of Old English criticism. ELH 34 1967.

—— Grammar and meaning in poetry. PMLA 82 1967.

—— Grendel's approach to Heorot: syntax and poetry. In Old English poetry: fifteen essays, ed R. P. Creed, Providence RI 1967.

McGalliard, J. C. The complex art of Beowulf. MP 59 1962.

—— Beowulf and Bede. In Life and thought in the early Middle Ages, ed R. S. Hoyt, Minneapolis 1967.

Renoir, A. Point of view and design for terror in Beowulf. Neuphilologische Mitteilungen 63 1962; rptd in Fry, below.

—— The heroic oath in Beowulf, the Chanson de Roland and the Nibelungenlied. In Studies in OE literature in honor of A. G. Brodeur, Eugene 1963.

—— Originality, influence, imitation: two mediaeval phases. In Proceedings of the 4th Congress of the International Comparative Literature Association vol 2, ed F. Jost, Hague 1966.

Roper, A. H. Boethius and the three fates of Beowulf. PQ 41 1962.

Rosier, J. L. Design for treachery: the Unferth intrigue. PMLA 77 1962.

—— The uses of association: hands and feasts in Beowulf. PMLA 78 1963.

—— A textual ambiguity in Beowulf: 'stod on stapole'. MÆ 34 1965.

—— 'Icge gold' and 'incge lafe' in Beowulf. PMLA 81 1966.

—— The 'unhlitm' of Finn and Hengest. RES new ser 17 1966.

—— Heafod and helm: contextual composition in Beowulf. MÆ 37 1968.

Brooke, C. The world of Beowulf. History Today Feb 1963.

Evans, D. R. The sequence of events in Beowulf, ll. 207–16. MÆ 32 1963.

Fuss, K. Der Held: Versuch einer Wesensbestimmung. Zeitschrift für Deutsche Philologie 82 1963.

Horgan, A. D. Beowulf, lines 224–5. Eng Philological Stud 8 1963.

Isaacs, N. D. Six Beowulf cruces. JEGP 62 1963.

—— The convention of personification in Beowulf. In Old English poetry: fifteen essays, ed R. P. Creed, Providence RI 1967.

Metcalf, A. Ten natural animals in Beowulf. Neuphilologische Mitteilungen 64 1963.

Mitchell, B. Until the dragon comes: some thoughts on Beowulf. Neophilologus 47 1963.

— Two syntactical notes on Beowulf. Neophilologus 52 1968.

Nicholson, L. E. An anthology of Beowulf criticism. Notre Dame Ind 1963.

— The literal meaning and symbolic structure of Beowulf. Classica et Medievalia 25 1964.

Stanley, E. G. 'Hæthenra hyht' in Beowulf. In Studies in OE literature in honor of A. G. Brodeur, Eugene 1963.

— The search for Anglo-Saxon paganism. N & Q Sept 1964.

— Beowulf. In Continuations and beginnings, ed E. G. Stanley 1966.

Taylor, C. Narrative technique in Beowulf. Neophilologus 47 1963.

Taylor, P. B. 'Heofon riece swealg': a sign of Beowulf's state of grace. PQ 42 1963.

— Snorri's analogue to Beowulf's funeral. Archiv 201 1965.

— Heorot, earth and Asgard: Christian poetry and pagan myth. Tennessee Stud in Lit 11 1966.

— Some vestiges of ritual charm in Beowulf. Jnl of Popular Culture 1 1967.

— Themes of death in Beowulf. In Old English poetry: fifteen essays, ed R. P. Creed, Providence RI 1967.

Candelaria, F. 'Gārsecg' in Beowulf. Eng Lang Notes 1964.

Clark, G. Beowulf and Bear's Son in the Vishnu purana. PQ 43 1964.

— Beowulf's armor. ELH 32 1965.

— The traveller recognizes his goal: a theme in Anglo-Saxon poetry. JEGP 64 1965.

Higgins, W. Dramatic function of the Unferth incident. Iowa Eng Yearbook 9 1964.

Meigs, C. Beowulf, mythology and ritual: a common-reader exploration. Xavier Univ Stud 3 1964.

Ogilvy, J. D. A. Unferth: foil to Beowulf? PMLA 79 1964.

Puhvel, M. 'Lices feorm', l. 451, Beowulf. Eng Lang Notes 1 1964.

— Beowulf and Celtic under-water adventure. Folklore 76 1965.

— Beowulf's slaying of Dæghræfn: a connection with Irish myth? Folklore 77 1967.

— Beowulf and Irish battle rage. Folklore 79 1968.

— The melting of the giant-wrought sword in Beowulf. Eng Lang Notes 7 1969.

— The might of Grendel's mother. Folklore 80 1969.

Robinson. F. C. Is Wealhtheow a prince's daughter? E Studies 45 1964.

— Beowulf's retreat from Frisia: some textual problems in ll. 2361–2. SP 62 1965.

— Beowulf 1917–19. N & Q Nov 1966.

— Two non-cruces in Beowulf. Tennessee Stud in Lit 11 1966.

— The significance of names in Old English literature. Anglia 86 1968.

— The American element in Beowulf. E Studies 49 1969.

— Personal names in medieval narrative and the name of Unferth in Beowulf. In Essays in honor of R. G. McWilliams, Birmingham Ala 1970.

Rumble, T. C. The hyran-gefrignan formula in Beowulf. Annuale Mediaevale 5 1964.

Bevis, R. W. Beowulf: a restoration. Eng Lang Notes 2 1965.

Byers, J. R. On the decorating of Heorot. PMLA 80 1965.

— A possible emendation of Beowulf 461b. PQ 46 1967.

— The last of the Waegmundings and a possible emendation of Beowulf. MP 66 1968.

Fadda, A. M. L. Sul problema dei rapporti fra il Beowulf e il mondo culturale anglosassone. Annali della Facoltà di Lettere, Filosofia e Magistero del Università di Cagliari 29 1961–5.

Garmonsway, G. N. Anglo-Saxon heroic attitudes. In Franciplegius: medieval and linguistic studies in honor of F. P. Magoun, New York 1965.

Haarder, A. Et gammelt indlaeg i en ny debat: Grundtvigs vurdering af Beowulf som kunstværk. In Grundtvig studier, Copenhagen 1965. With English summary.

Hoffmann, R. L. 'Guðrinc astah': Beowulf 1118b. JEGP 64 1965.

Leyerle, J. Beowulf the hero and the King. MÆ 34 1965.

— The interlace structure of Beowulf. UTQ 37 1967.

Oshitari, K. In F. Nakajima Festschrift, Tokyo 1965. On Beowulf criticism; in Japanese.

Schabram, H. Andreas und Beowulf: Parallelstellen als Zeugnis für literarische Abhängigkeit. Nachrichten der Giessener Hochschulgesellschaft 34 1965.

— Zu einer neuen Deutung von Beowulf 1011f. Indogermanische Forschungen 73 1968.

— Zur Interpretation von Beowulf 2697ff. In Fachliteratur des Mittelalters: Festschrift für G. Eis, Stuttgart 1968.

Smyser, H. M. Ibn Fadlān's account of the Rūs with some commentary and allusions to Beowulf. In Franciplegius: medieval and linguistic studies in honor of F. P. Magoun, New York 1965.

Sowa, H. Beowulf no Ingeld episode ni tsuite [The Ingeld episode in Beowulf]. Acta Litterarum: Kenkyu Ronshu (Nagoya Univ) 37 1965.

Baird, J. L. Grendel the exile. Neuphilologische Mitteilungen 67 1966.

— The uses of ignorance: Beowulf 435, 2330. N & Q Jan 1967.

— For metode: Beowulf 169. E Studies 49 1968.

— The happy hurt: Beowulf 2697–9. MP 66 1969.

— Unferth the þyle. MÆ 39 1970.

Buchloch, P. G. Unity and intention in Beowulf. In English studies today 4, ed I. Cellini and G. Melchiori 1966.

Eremeeva, E. A. Xudozestvennye funcii istoriceskix otstuplenij v Beovul'fe [On the artistic function of historical digressions in Beowulf]. Filologiceskie Nauki 9 1966.

Halverson, J. Beowulf and the pitfalls of piety. UTQ 35 1966.

— The world of Beowulf. ELH 36 1969.

Irving, E. B. 'Ealuscerwen': wild party at Heorot. Tennessee Stud in Lit 11 1966.

— A reading of Beowulf. New Haven 1968.

— Introduction to Beowulf. Englewood Cliffs NJ 1969.

Lawrence, R. F. The formulaic theory and its application to English alliterative poetry. In Essays on style and language, ed R. Fowler 1966.

McClelland, C. B. Horses in Beowulf: a horse of a different color. Tennessee Stud in Lit 11 1966.

Milosh, J. Sisam's Structure of Beowulf and realism in criticism: a review essay. Cithara 5 1966.

— A supplement for teaching Beowulf. Eng Jnl 59 1970.

Pearce, T. M. Beowulf and the Southern sun. Amer N & Q 4–5 1966–7.

— Beowulf's moment of decision in Heorot. Tennessee Stud in Lit 11 1966.

Pickering, J. D. The conversion of the Haugbui. Timarit Þjóðrǽknisfelags Islendinga i Vesturheimi 47 1966.

Reiss, E. Nationalism and cosmopolitanism as subject and theme in medieval narratives. In Proceedings of the 4th Congress of the International Comparative Literature Association, Fribourg 1964, Hague 1966.

Ringler, R. N. Him sēo wēn gelēah: the design for irony in Grendel's visit to Heorot. Speculum 41 1966.

Whitesell, J. E. Intentional ambiguities in Beowulf. Tennessee Stud in Lit 11 1966.

Witke, C. Béowulf 2069b–199: a variant? Neuphilologische Mitteilungen 67 1966.

Barakat, R. A. John of the Bear and Beowulf. Western Folklore 26 1967.

Benson, L. D. The pagan coloring of Beowulf. In Old English poetry: fifteen essays, ed R. P. Creed, Providence RI 1967.

—— The originality of Beowulf. Harvard Eng Stud 1 1970.

Carlson, S. M. The monsters of Beowulf: creations of literary scholars. Jnl of Amer Folklore 80 1967.

Carrigan, E. Structure and thematic development in Beowulf. Proc of Royal Irish Acad 66 1967.

Crawford, J. 'Scirwered': Beowulf 496a. N & Q June 1967.

Leake, J. A. The Geats of Beowulf: a study in the geographical mythology of the Middle Ages. Madison 1967.

Mustanoja, T. F. The unnamed woman's song of mourning over Beowulf and the tradition of ritual lamentation. Neuphilologische Mitteilungen 68 1967.

Norton, J. Tolkien, Beowulf and the poet: a problem in point of view. E Studies 48 1967.

Rissanen, M. Two notes on Old English poetic texts: Beowulf 2461, Ruthwell Cross III 3. Neuphilologische Mitteilungen 68 1967.

Rose, N. Hrothgar, Nestor, and religiosity as a mode of characterization in heroic poetry. Jnl of Popular Culture 1 1967.

Tripp, R. P. Beowulf and the motion of monsters: a thematic inquiry. Pennsylvania Council of Teachers of Eng Bull 14 1967.

Westphalen, T. Beowulf 3150–5: Textkritik und Editionsgeschichte. Munich 1967.

Wright, T. L. Hrothgar's tears. MP 65 1967.

Cherniss, M. D. The progress of the hoard in Beowulf. PQ 47 1968.

—— Beowulf: oral presentation and the criterion of immediate rhetorical effect. Genre 3 1970.

Delasanta, R. and J. Slevin. Beowulf and the hypostatic union. Neophilologus 52 1968.

Evans, D. A. H. The lake of the monsters in Beowulf. Studia Neophilologica 40 1968.

Fry, D. K. Variation and economy in Beowulf. MP 65 1968.

—— (ed). The Beowulf poet. Englewood Cliffs NJ 1968.

—— 'Wið earm gesæt' and Beowulf's hammerlock. MP 67 1970.

—— The location of Finnsburh: Beowulf 1125–9a. Eng Lang Notes 8 1970.

Helterman, J. Beowulf: the archetype enters history. ELH 35 1968.

Kiessling, N. K. Grendel: a new aspect. MP 65 1968.

Ringbom, H. Studies in the narrative technique of Beowulf and Lawman's Brut. Acta Academiae Aboensis ser A 36 1968.

Starcke, V. Jyder eller Göter: hvem var Geaterne, Beowulf's folk? Berlingske Tidendes Kronik 6 June 1968.

Tuso, J. Beowulf 461B and Thorpe's 'wara'. MLQ 29 1968.

Arent, A. M. The heroic pattern: Old Germanic helmets, Beowulf, and Grettis saga. In Old Norse literature and mythology, ed E. C. Polomé, Austin 1969.

Cameron, A. F. Saint Gildas and Scyld Scefing. Neuphilologische Mitteilungen 70 1969.

Campbell, A. P. The time element of interlace structure in Beowulf. Ibid.

Dronke, U. Beowulf and Ragnarǫk. Saga-book 17 1969.

Hardy, A. The Christian hero Beowulf and Unferð þyle. Neophilologus 53 1969.

Hart, T. E. A tectonic consideration of the Eotenas in Beowulf. Thoth 10 1969.

—— Ellen: tectonic relationships in Beowulf and their formal resemblance to Anglo-Saxon art. Papers on Lang & Lit 6 1970.

Hume, K. The function of the hrefn blaca: Beowulf 1801. MP 67 1969.

Kühlwein, W. Andreascrux 1241 und Beowulfscrux 849. Beiträge zur Geschichte der Deutschen Sprache und Literatur (Tübingen) 91 1969.

Lee, A. A. Heorot and the guest-hall of Eden. Mediaeval Scandinavia 2 1969; rptd in his Guest-hall of Eden: four essays on the design of Old English poetry, New Haven 1972.

McDavid, R. I. Hroþulf, Hengest and Beowulf: two structural parallels. In Studies in language, literature and culture, ed E. B. Atwood and A. A. Hill, Austin 1969.

Osborn, M. Laying the Roman ghost of Beowulf 320 and 725. Neuphilologische Mitteilungen 70 1969.

—— Some uses of ambiguity in Beowulf. Thoth 10 1969.

Page, A. and V. H. Cassidy. Beowulf: the Christologers and the mythic. Orbis Litterarum 24 1969.

Rosenberg, B. A. The necessity of Unferth. Jnl of Folklore Inst 6 1969.

Shippey, T. A. The fairy-tale structure of Beowulf. N & Q Jan 1969.

Trahern, J. B. A defectione potus sui: a sapiential basis for 'ealuscerwen' and 'meoduscerwen'. Neuphilologische Mitteilungen 70 1969.

Travis, J. Hiberno-Saxon Christianity and the survival of Beowulf. Lochlann: Rev of Celtic Stud 4 1969.

Tremaine, H. P. Beowulf's 'ecg brun' and other rusty relics. PQ 48 1969.

Watts, A. C. The lyre and the harp: a comparative reconsideration of oral tradition in Homer and Old English epic poetry. New Haven 1969.

Ziegelmaier, G. God and nature in the Beowulf poem. Amer Benedictine Rev 20 1969.

Barnes, D. R. Folktale morphology and the structure of Beowulf. Speculum 45 1970.

Bruce-Mitford, R. and M. The Sutton Hoo lyre, Beowulf and the origins of the frame harp. Antiquity 44 1970.

Cable, T. M. Rules for syntax and metrics in Beowulf. JEGP 69 1970.

——Clashing stress in the meter of Beowulf. Neuphilologische Mitteilungen 72 1971.

Cassidy, F. G. A symbolic word-group in Beowulf. In Medieval literature and folklore studies: essays in honor of F. L. Utley, New Brunswick NJ 1970.

Cox, B. S. Cruces of Beowulf. Hague 1970.

Crane, J. K. To thwack or be thwacked: an analysis of available translations and editions of Beowulf. College Eng Dec 1970.

Dow, J. Beowulf and the walkers in darkness. Connecticut Rev 4 1970.

Gardner, J. Fulgentius's Expositio Vergiliana continentia and the plan of Beowulf: another approach to the poem's style and structure. Papers on Lang & Lit 6 1970.

Murray, A. C. The lending of Hrunting and the Anglo-Saxon laws. N & Q March 1970.

Sklute, L. M. 'Freoðuwebbe' in Old English poetry. Neuphilologische Mitteilungen 71 1970.

Britton, G. C. Unferth, Grendel and the Christian meaning of Beowulf. Neuphilologische Mitteilungen 72 1971.

Cooke, W. G. 'Hronas' and 'hronfixas'. N & Q July 1971.

Hill, T. D. 'Hwyrftum scriþað': Beowulf, line 163. Mediaeval Stud 33 1971.

Klegraf, J. Beowulf 760: 'ealuscerwen'. Archiv 208 1971.

Lehmann, R. P. M. Six notes on Beowulf. Neuphilologische Mitteilungen 72 1971.

Ramsey, L. C. The sea voyages in Beowulf. Ibid.

Wentersdorf, K. P. Beowulf's withdrawal from Frisia: a reconsideration. SP 68 1971.

Anderson, E. R. A submerged metaphor in the Scyld episode. MHRA Yearbook of Eng Stud 2 1972.

Calder, D. G. Setting and ethos: the pattern of measure and limit in Beowulf. SP 69 1972.

Kahrl, S. J. Feuds in Beowulf: a tragic necessity? MP 69 1972.

Morgan, G. The treachery of Hrothulf. E Studies 53 1972.

Nickel, G. Problems of Beowulf-research with special reference to editorial questions. Neuphilologische Mitteilungen 73 1972.

Peltola, N. Grendel's descent from Cain reconsidered. Ibid.

See also Manuscript Studies, Individual, above.

BRUNANBURH

See Battle of Brunanburh, *above.*

BRUSSELS CROSS

Inscription in roman letters on cross reliquary in Cathedral of SS. Michel and Gudule at Brussels.

§1

Krapp-Dobbie 6 1942.

§2

Logeman, H. L'inscription anglo-saxonne du reliquaire de la vraie croix au trésor de l'église des SS-Michel-et-Gudule à Bruxelles. Mémoires couronnés publiés par l'Académie Royale de Belgique 45 1891.

Cook, A. S. The date of the Old English inscription on the Brussels Cross. MLR 10 1915.

Hensen, A. Het Egmonder Kruis. Het Gildeboek 8 1925.

d'Ardenne, S. T. R. O. The Old English inscription on the Brussels Cross. E Studies 21 1939.

See also Dream of the rood, ed Cook, Dickins and Ross, below.

CÆDMON

The poems of the Junius ms, as well as the Hymn, were once thought to be by Cædmon; a certain body of literature developed around this misconception.

§1

Junius, F. Cædmonis monachi paraphrasis poetica Genesios. Amsterdam 1655.

Thorpe, B. Cædmon's metrical paraphrase of parts of the Holy Scriptures in Anglo-Saxon. 1832 (Soc of Antiquaries). With trn.

Bouterwek, K. W. Cædmons des Angelsachsen biblische Dichtungen. Vol 1, Gütersloh 1854; vol 2, Elberfeld 1851.

Krapp-Dobbie 1 1931.

Kennedy, C. W. The Cædmon poems. 1916, Gloucester Mass 1965.

§2

Bouterwek, K. W. De Cedmone poeta anglo-saxonum vetustissimo brevis dissertatio. Elberfeld 1845.

— Über Cædmon, den ältesten Dichter, und desselben metrische Paraphrase der heiligen Schrift. Elberfeld 1845.

Dietrich, F. Zu Cädmon. Zeitschrift für Deutsches Altertum 10 1856.

Sandras, S. G. De carminibus anglo-saxonicis Cædmoni adjudicatis disquisitio. Paris 1859.

Götzinger, E. Über die Dichtungen des Angelsachsen Cædmon und deren Verfasser. Göttingen 1860.

Watson, R. S. Cædmon: the first English poet. 1875.

Balg, H. Der Dichter Cædmon und seine Werke. Bonn 1882.

Ziegler, H. Der poetische Sprachgebrauch in den sogenannten Cædmonschen Dichtungen. Münster 1883.

Wülker, R. P. Der Name Cædmon. Beiblatt zur Anglia 2 1891.

Graz, F. Die Metrik der sogenannten Cædmonschen Dichtungen mit Berücksichtigung der Verfasserfrage. Weimar 1894.

Crawford, S. J. The Cædmon poems. Anglia 49 1926.

Klaeber, F. Analogues of the story of Cædmon. MLN 42 1927.

— Bede's story of Cædmon again. MLN 53 1938.

Chappell, L. W. The Cædmon story. E Studien 69 1934.

Whitbread, L. An analogue of the Cædmon story. RES 15 1939.

— The Cædmon story: bibliography. N & Q 10 Oct 1942.

Wrenn, C. L. The poetry of Cædmon. Proc Br Acad 32 1946; rptd in Essential articles for the study of OE poetry, ed J. B. Bessinger and S. J. Kahrl, Hamden Conn 1968.

Shepherd, G. The prophetic Cædmon. RES new ser 5 1954.

— Scriptural poetry. In Continuations and beginnings, ed E. G. Stanley 1966.

Malone, K. Cædmon and English poetry. MLN 76 1961.

Fritz, D. W. Cædmon: a traditional Christian poet. Mediaeval Stud 31 1969.

See also under Junius ms above, under Cædmon's Hymn, Christ and Satan, Daniel, Exodus and Genesis.

CÆDMON'S HYMN

Mss: 17 known to exist, ranging in date from the eighth to the fifteenth centuries; 4 in the Northumbrian dialect, 13 in West Saxon; of the latter, 8 in Latin mss of Bede's Ecclesiastical history, and 5 in OE trns of Bede. See Krapp-Dobbie 6 pp. xcv–xcvii for an account.

§1

Smith, A. H. Three Northumbrian poems. 1933.

Dobbie, E. V. K. The manuscripts of Cædmon's hymn and Bede's death song. New York 1937.

Krapp-Dobbie 6 1942.

Arngart [Anderson], O. S. The Leningrad Bede. Copenhagen 1952 (facs).

Kroll, J. Translations from Old English. Cambridge Quart 4 1969.

The text is included in most OE readers as part of the story of Cædmon.

§2

Wülker, R. P. Über den Hymnus Cædmons. Beiträge zur Geschichte der Deutschen Sprache und Literatur 3 1876.

Zupitza, J. Über den Hymnus Cädmons. Zeitschrift für Deutsches Altertum 22 1878.

Schröer, A. Über den Hymnus Cædmons. Archiv 115 1905.

Wüst, P. Zwei neue Handschriften von Cædmons Hymnus. Zeitschrift für Deutsches Altertum 48 1906.

Frampton, M. G. Cædmon's Hymn. MP 22 1925.

Cook, A. S. King Oswy and Cædmon's Hymn. Speculum 2 1927.

Pound, L. Cædmon's dream song. In Studies in English philology in honor of F. Klaeber, Minneapolis 1929.

Judge, C. B. Anglo-saxonica in Hereford Cathedral Library. Harvard Stud 16 1934.

Anderson, O. S. Old English material in the Leningrad ms of Bede's Ecclesiastical history. Lund 1941.

Ross, A. S. C. Miscellaneous notes on Cædmon's hymn and Bede's death song. Eng & Germanic Stud 3 1950.

Magoun, F. P. Bede's story of Cædman: the case history of an Anglo-Saxon oral singer. Speculum 30 1955.

Huppé, B. F. Doctrine and poetry: Augustine's influence on Old English poetry. New York 1959.

Blake, N. F. Cædmon's hymn. N & Q July 1962.

Bloomfield, M. W. Patristics and Old English literature. Comparative Lit 14 1962; rptd in Studies in OE literature in honor of A. G. Brodeur, Eugene 1963; and in Essential articles for the study of OE poetry, ed J. B. Bessinger and S. J. Kahrl, Hamden Conn 1968.

Henry, P. L. The early English and Celtic lyric. 1966.

Mitchell, B. Swa in Cædmon's Hymn line 3. N & Q June 1967.

Golden, J. An onomastic allusion in Cædmon's Hymn. Neuphilologische Mitteilungen 70 1969.

See also under Cædmon, above.

CAPTURE OF THE FIVE BOROUGHS

See under Poems of the Anglo-Saxon Chronicle, *below.*

CHRIST

The 3 pts of this poem are no longer considered to be a unity, but are treated together here for convenience.

Ms: Exeter Book 8a–32b.

§1

Gollancz, I. Cynewulf's Christ. 1892. With trn.

Cook, A. S. The Christ of Cynewulf: a poem in three parts, the Advent, the Ascension and the Last Judgment. Boston 1900.

Krapp-Dobbie 3 1936.

Campbell, J. J. The Advent lyrics of the Exeter book. Princeton 1959. With trn.

Whitman, C. H. The Christ of Cynewulf. Boston 1900. Trn.

§2

Dietrich, F. Cynewulfs Christ. Zeitschrift für Deutsches Altertum 9 1853.

Cook, A. S. Cynewulf's principal sources for the third part of Christ. MLN 4 1889.

— Bemerkungen zu Cynewulfs Christ. In Philologische Studien: Festgabe für E. Sievers, Halle 1896.

— Alfred's Soliloquies and Cynewulf's Christ. MLN 17 1902.

Trautmann, M. Der sogenannte Crist. Anglia 18 1896.

Blackburn, F. A. Is the Christ of Cynewulf a single poem? Anglia 19 1897.

Bourauel, J. Zur Quellen- und Verfasserfrage von Andreas, Crist und Fata. Bonner Beiträge zur Anglistik 11 1901.

Grüters, O. Über einige Beziehungen zwischen altsächsischer und altenglischer Dichtung. Bonner Beiträge zur Anglistik 17 1905.

Schwartz, F. Cynewulfs Anteil am Crist: eine metrische Untersuchung. Königsberg 1905.

Binz, G. Untersuchungen zum altenglischen sogenannten Christ. In Festschrift zur 49 Versammlung deutscher Philologen und Schulmänner, Basle 1907; Leipzig 1907 (separately).

Gerould, G. H. Studies in the Christ. E Studien 41 1909.

— Carpenter or athlete? Christ vv. 678–9. JEGP 28 1929.

Mason, L. Christ 779–886. Archiv 129 1912.

Moore, S. Notes on the Old English Christ. Archiv 131 1914.

— The source of Christ 416ff. MLN 29 1914.

— The Old English Christ: is it a unit? JEGP 14 1915.

Jenney, A. M. A note on Cynewulf's Christ. MLN 31 1916.

Burgert, E. The dependence of Part 1 of Cynewulf's Christ upon the antiphonary. Washington 1921.

Willard, R. Vercelli Homily viii and the Christ. PMLA 42 1927.

Howard, E. J. Cynewulf's Christ 1665–93. PMLA 45 1930.

— Old English tree climbing: Christ vv. 678–9. JEGP 30 1931. *See* B. J. Whiting 31 1932.

Philip, Brother A. The Exeter scribe and the unity of the Christ. PMLA 55 1940.

Meritt, H. D. Beating the oaks: an interpretation of Christ 678–9. Amer Jnl of Philology 66 1945.

Jost, K. Crist 558–85. E Studies 27 1946.

Mildenberger, K. Unity of Cynewulf's Christ in the light of iconography. Speculum 23 1948.

Kuhn, S. M. A damaged passage in the Exeter book. JEGP 50 1951.

Greenfield, S. B. Of locks and keys: line 19a of the Old English Christ. MLN 67 1952.

— The theme of spiritual exile in Christ 1. PQ 32 1953.

Elliott, R. W. V. Cynewulf's runes in Christ 11 and Elene. E Studies 34 1953.

Campbell, J. J. Structural patterns in the Old English Advent lyrics. ELH 23 1956.

Hofmann, D. Die altsächsische Bibelepik ein Ableger der angelsächsischen geistlichen Epik? Zeitschrift für Deutsches Altertum 89 1959.

Schubel, F. Bedeutungsnuancen von bealu in Christ 1–111. In Festschrift zum 75 Geburtstag T. Spira, Heidelberg 1961.

Krogmann, W. Crist 111 und Heliand. In Festschrift für L. Wolff, Neumünster 1962.

Cross, J. E. The coeternal beam in the Old English Advent poem (Christ 1) ll. 104–29. Neophilologus 48 1964.

— 'Halga hyht' and poetic stimulus in the Advent poem (Christ 1) 50–70. Neophilologus 53 1969.

Isaacs, N. D. Who says what in Advent lyric vii? Papers on Lang & Lit 2 1966; rev in his Structural principles, Knoxville 1968.

Lass, R. Poem as sacrament: transcendence of time in the Advent sequence from the Exeter book. Annuale Mediaevale 7 1966.

Shepherd, G. Scriptural poetry. In Continuations and beginnings, ed E. G. Stanley 1966.

Whitbread, L. The doomsday theme in Old English poetry. Beiträge zur Geschichte der Deutschen Sprache und Literatur (Halle) 89 1967.

Burlin, R. B. The Old English Advent: a typological commentary. New Haven 1968.

Hill, T. D. Fiat lux and the generation of the son: Christ 1. 214–48. N & Q July 1969.

— Notes on the eschatology of the Old English Christ 111. Neuphilologische Mitteilungen 70 1969. Addn 72 1971.

— The seven joys of heaven in Christ 111 and Old English homiletic texts. N & Q May 1969.

— Notes on the imagery and structure of The Old English Christ 1. N & Q March 1972.

Pope, J. C. The lacuna in the text of Cynewulf's Ascension (Christ 11. 556b). In Studies in language, literature and culture, ed E. B. Atwood and A. A. Hill, Austin 1969.

Grosz, O. J. H. Man's imitation of the Ascension: the unity of Christ 11. Neophilologus 54 1970.

Tugwell, S. Advent lyrics 348–77 (lyric no. x). MÆ 39 1970.

Anderson, E. R. Mary's role as eiron in Christ 1. JEGP 70 1971.

Clemoes, P. Cynewulf's image of the Ascension. In England before the Conquest: studies presented to Dorothy Whitelock, Cambridge 1971.

See also under Cynewulf, below.

CHRIST AND SATAN

Ms: Bodley, Junius xi, numbered pp. 213–29.

§1

Clubb, M. D. Christ and Satan. New Haven 1925.

Krapp-Dobbie 1 1931.

See also under Manuscripts, above, and under Cædmon, above.

§2

Groschopp, F. Das angelsächsische Gedicht Crist und Satan. Anglia 6 1883.
Kühn, A. Über die angelsächsischen Gedichte von Christ und Satan. Halle 1883.
Bright, J. W. Jottings on the Cædmonian Christ and Satan. MLN 18 1903.
Frings, T. Christ und Satan. Zeitschrift für Deutsche Philologie 45 1914.
Greene, R. L. A rearrangement of Christ and Satan. MLN 43 1928.
Huppé, B. F. Doctrine and poetry: Augustine's influence on Old English poetry. New York 1959.
Manganella, G. Cristo e Satana. Annali Istituto Universitario Orientale, Napoli: Sezione Germanica 7 1964.
Isaacs, N. D. The one-man band of Christ and Satan. In his Structural principles, Knoxville 1968.
Hill, T. D. Apocryphal cosmography and the 'stream uton sæ': a note on Christ and Satan, lines 4–12. PQ 48 1969.
—— 'Byrht word' and 'hælendes heafod': Cristological allusion in the Old English Christ and Satan. Eng Lang Notes 8 1970.
—— Satan's fiery speech: Christ and Satan 78–9. N & Q Jan 1972.
Finnegan, R. E. Two notes on ms Junius Christ and Satan: lines 19–20, lines 319 and 384. PQ 49 1970.
See also under Cædmon, above.

CORONATION OF EDGAR

See under Poems of the Anglo-Saxon Chronicle, below.

CREED

Ms: Bodley, Junius 121, 46a–7a.

§1

Feiler, E. Das Benedikter-Offizium. Heidelberg 1901.
Krapp-Dobbie 6 1942.
Ure, J. M. The Benedictine office: an old English text. Edinburgh 1957.

§2

Sisam, K. Seasons of fasting. In his Studies in the history of OE literature, Oxford 1953.
Whitbread, L. The Old English poems of the Benedictine Office and some related questions. Anglia 80 1962.

CYNEWULF

§1

Kennedy, C. W. The poems of Cynewulf, translated into English prose. 1910, 1949.

§2

Leo, H. Quae de se ipso Cynevulfus poeta anglosaxonicus tradiderit. Halle 1857.
Dietrich, F. Commentatio de Kynewulf poetae aetate. Marburg 1859.
Rieger, M. Über Cynevulf. Zeitschrift für Deutsche Philologie 1 1869.
Wülker, R. P. Über den Dichter Cynewulf. Anglia 1 1878.
—— Cynewulfs Heimat. Anglia 17 1895.
D'Ham, O. Der gegenwärtige Stand der Cynewulffrage. Limburg 1883.
Sarrazin, G. Beowulf und Kynewulf. Anglia 9 1886.

Cosijn, P. J. Cynewulf's Runenverzen. Verslagen en Mededeelingen der Koninklijke Akademie van Wetenschappen, Afdeeling Letterkunde ser 3 pt 7 1890.
Sievers, E. Zu Cynewulf. Anglia 13 1891.
—— Zu Cynewulf. Neusprachliche Studien (Die Neueren Sprachen Beiheft 6) 1925.
Mather, F. J. The Cynewulf question from a metrical point of view. MLN 7 1892.
Price, M. B. Teutonic antiquities in the generally acknowledged Cynewulfian poetry. Leipzig 1896.
Trautmann, M. Kynewulf der Bischof und Dichter. Bonner Beiträge zur Anglistik 1 1898.
—— Zu Cynewulfs Runenstellen. Bonner Beiträge zur Anglistik 2 1899.
—— Berichtungen, Erklärungen und Vermutungen zu Cynewulfs Werken. Bonner Beiträge zur Anglistik 23 1907.
Simons, R. Cynewulfs Wortschatz. Bonner Beiträge zur Anglistik 3 1899.
Bourauel, J. Zur Quellen- und Verfasserfrage von Andreas, Crist und Fata. Bonner Beiträge zur Anglistik 11 1901.
Brown, C. F. Cynewulf and Alcuin. PMLA 18 1903.
—— The autobiographical element in the Cynewulfian rune passages. E Studien 38 1907.
—— Irish-Latin influences in Cynewulfian texts. E Studien 40 1909.
Jansen, K. Die Cynewulf-Forschung von ihren Anfängen bis zur Gegenwart. Bonner Beiträge zur Anglistik 24 1908.
von der Warth, J. J. Metrisch-sprachliches und Textkritisches zu Cynewulfs Werken. Bonn 1908.
Tupper, F. The philological legend of Cynewulf. PMLA 26 1911.
—— The Cynewulfian runes of the religious poems. MLN 27 1912.
Lindeman, J. M. A note on Cynewulf. MLN 39 1924.
Cook, A. S. Cynewulf's part in our Beowulf. Trans of Connecticut Acad 27 1925.
Sisam, K. Cynewulf and his poetry. Proc Br Acad 18 1932; rptd in his Studies in the history of OE literature, Oxford 1953.
Das, S. K. Cynewulf and the Cynewulf canon. Calcutta 1942.
Dubois, M. M. Les éléments latins dans la poésie religieuse de Cynewulf. Paris 1942.
Schaar, C. Critical studies in the Cynewulf group. Lund 1949.
Elliott, R. W. V. Cynewulf's runes in Christ II and Elene. E Studies 34 1953.
—— Cynewulf's runes in Juliana and Fates of the apostles. Ibid.
Derolez, R. Runica manuscripta: the English tradition. Bruges 1954.
Schneider, K. Die germanischen Runennamen: Versuch einer Gesamtdeutung. Meisenheim-am-Glan 1956.
Storms, G. The weakening of OE unstressed i to e and the date of Cynewulf. E Studies 37 1956.
Diamond, R. E. The diction of the signed poems of Cynewulf. PQ 38 1959.
Faiss, K. Gnade bei Cynewulf und seiner Schule: semasiologisch-onomasiologische Studien zu einem semantischen Feld. Tübingen 1967.
See also under Manuscripts, above: Exeter and Vercelli books; and under Andreas, Christ, above, and Elene, Fates of the Apostles and Juliana, below.

DANIEL

Ms: Bodley, Junius xi, numbered pp. 173–212.

§1

Hunt, T. W. Cædmon's Exodus and Daniel. Boston 1883.

Blackburn, F. A. Exodus and Daniel. Boston 1907.

Schmidt, W. Die altenglische Dichtung Daniel. Halle 1907.

—— Die altenglischen Dichtungen Daniel und Azarias. Bonner Beiträge zur Anglistik 23 1907.

Krapp-Dobbie 1 1931.

See also under Manuscripts, and Cædmon, above.

§2

Hofer, O. Über die Entstehung des angelsächsischen Gedichtes Daniel. Anglia 12 1889.

Steiner, G. Über die Interpolation im angelsächsischen Gedichte Daniel. Leipzig 1889.

Dethloff, R. Daniel. Rostock 1907.

Thomas, P. G. Beowulf and Daniel A. MLR 8 1913.

Jones, A. Daniel and Azarias as evidence for the oral-formulaic character of Old English poetry. MÆ 35 1966.

Farrell, R. T. The unity of Old English Daniel. RES new ser 18 1967.

—— The structure of Old English Daniel. Neuphilologische Mitteilungen 69 1968.

—— A possible source of Old English Daniel. Neuphilologische Mitteilungen 70 1969.

Isaacs, N. D. Daniel and the change of pace. In his Structural principles, Knoxville 1968.

See also under Cædmon, above.

DEATH OF ALFRED

See under Poems of the Anglo-Saxon Chronicle, *below.*

DEATH OF EDGAR

See under Poems of the Anglo-Saxon Chronicle, *below.*

DEOR

Ms: Exeter book 100.

§1

Dickins, B. Runic and heroic poems of the Old Teutonic peoples. Cambridge 1915. With trn.

Malone, K. Deor. 1933, 1966 (rev).

Krapp-Dobbie 3 1936.

Translations

Scott-Moncrieff, C. K. Widsith, Beowulf, Finnsburgh, Waldere, Deor. 1921.

Davis, L. M. Deor: a new verse translation. West Virginia Bull Philological Papers 14 1963.

Kroll, J. Translations from Old English. Cambridge Quart 4 1969.

Also in many readers and collections, including those of the Elegies, as well as in edns of the Exeter book. See below for some other trns.

§2

Müllenhoff, K. Sängernamen. Zeitschrift für Deutsches Altertum 7 1849.

—— Zur Kritik des angelsächsischen Volksepos 1: Deors Klage. Zeitschrift für Deutsches Altertum 11–12 1859.

[Haigh, D. H.] The oldest English lyric. Atlantic Monthly Feb 1891. With trn.

Burton, R. The oldest English lyric. Poet-lore 5 1893. With trn.

Bugge, S. The Norse lay of Wayland and its relation to English tradition. Saga-book 2 1900.

Klaeber, F. Zu Deors Klage, 15ff. Beiblatt zur Anglia 17 1906.

—— The first line of Deor. Beiblatt zur Anglia 32 1921.

—— Ein paar Anmerkungen zu den altenglischen Deorversen. Archiv 185 1948.

Stefanovič, S. Zu Deor, v. 14–17. Anglia 33 1910, 36–7 1912–13.

Lawrence, W. W. The song of Deor. MP 9 1912.

Tupper, F. The song of Deor. Ibid.

—— The third strophe of Deor. Anglia 37 1913.

Grienberger, T. von. Déor. Anglia 45 1921.

Ashdown, M. Notes on two passages of Old English verse. RES 5 1929.

Malone, K. [Articles from 1934, subsumed in his later edns. One of these, MP 40 1942, rptd in his Studies in heroic legend, Copenhagen 1959.]

Forster, L. Die Assoziation in Deors Klage. Anglia 61 1937.

Norman, F. Deor: a criticism and an interpretation. MLR 32 1937.

—— Deor and modern Scandinavian ballads. London Medieval Stud 1 1938.

—— Problems in the dating of Deor and its allusions. In Franciplegius: medieval and linguistic studies in honor of F. P. Magoun, New York 1965.

Bouman, A. C. Vǫlundr as an aviator. Arkiv för Nordisk Filologi 55 1940.

—— Leodum is minum: Beadohild's complaint. Neophilologus 33 1949.

Whitbread, L. MLN 55 1940, 58 1943, 62 1947; MP 38 1941; MÆ 25 1956. Notes.

—— The pattern of misfortune in Deor and other Old English poems. Neophilologus 54 1970.

Magoun, F. P. Deors Klage und Guðrúnarkviða. E Studien 75 1942.

Brady, C. The legends of Ermanaric. Berkeley 1943.

Zink, G. Les légendes héroïques de Dietrich et d'Ermanrich dans les littératures germaniques. Lyons and Paris 1950.

Jost, K. Welund und Samson: ein Beitrag zur Erklärung der 1 Deor-Strophe. In Festschrift zum 75 Geburtstag von T. Spira, Heidelberg 1961.

Frankis, P. J. Deor and Wulf and Eadwacer: some conjectures. MÆ 31 1962.

Kaske, R. E. Weland and the Wurmas in Deor. E Studies 44 1963.

Bloomfield, M. W. The form of Deor. PMLA 79 1964.

Eliason, N. E. The story of Geat and Mæðhild in Deor. SP 62 1965.

—— Two Old English scop poems. PMLA 81 1966.

—— Deor: a begging poem? In Medieval literature and civilization: studies in memory of G. N. Garmonsway, 1969.

Isaacs, N. D. Structure and excellence: Deor and the critics. In his Structural principles, Knoxville 1968.

Markland, M. F. Boethius, Alfred and Deor. MP 66 1968.

Schibsbye, K. þæs ofereode, þisses swā mæg. E Studies 50 1969.

Stephens, J. Weland and a little restraint: a note on Deor 5–6. Studia Neophilologica 41 1969.

Bolton, W. F. Beothius, Alfred and Deor again. MP 69 1972.

See also under Elegies, below.

DESCENT INTO HELL

Ms: Exeter book 119b–21b.

§1

Cramer, J. Quelle, Verfasser und Text des altenglischen Gedichtes Christi Höllenfahrt. Anglia 19 1897.

Krapp-Dobbie 3 1936.

§2

Kirkland, J. H. A study of the Anglo-Saxon poem Harrowing of Hell. Halle 1885.

Crotty, G. The Exeter Harrowing of Hell: a re-interpretation. PMLA 54 1939.

Trask, R. M. The descent into Hell of the Exeter book. Neuphilologische Mitteilungen 72 1971.

DREAM OF THE ROOD

Ms: Vercelli book 104b–6a.

§ 1

Pacius, A. Das heilige Kreuz. Gera 1873. With trn.

Cook, A. S. The dream of the rood. Oxford 1905.

Ricci, A. Il sogno della Croce-Cristo. Florence 1926.

Dickins, B. and A. S. C. Ross. The dream of the rood. 1934, 1963 (rev.).

Krapp-Dobbie 2 1932.

Bütow, H. Das altenglische Traumgesicht vom Kreuz. Heidelberg 1935.

Swanton, M. J. The dream of the rood. Manchester 1970.

Translations

Hickey, E. H. Academy 21 1882.

Brown, A. R. Poet-lore 2 1890.

Garnett, J. M. Elene, Judith, Brunanburh, Maldon, Dream of the rood. Boston 1901 (2nd edn).

Roy, J. A. The dream of the rood. 1912.

Brooks, H. F. The dream of the rood. Dublin 1942.

§ 2

Ebert, A. Über das angelsächsische Gedicht: der Traum vom heiligen Kreuz. Berichte über die Verhandlungen der Königlich Sächsischen Gesellschaft der Wissenschaften, philologisch-historische Klasse 36 1884; Leipzig 1884 (separately).

Brandl, A. Zum angelsächsischen Gedichte Traumgesicht vom Kreuze Christi. Sitzungsberichte der Königlich Preussischen Akademie der Wissenschaften 1905; tr and rev as On the early Northumbrian poem A vision of the Cross of Christ, Scottish Historical Rev 9 1912.

Patch, H. R. Liturgical influence in the Dream of the rood. PMLA 34 1919.

Schlauch, M. The dream of the rood as prosopopoeia. In Essays and studies in honor of C. Brown, New York 1940; rptd in Essential articles for the study of OE poetry, ed J. B. Bessinger and S. J. Kahrl, Hamden Conn 1968.

Diamond, R. E. Heroic diction in the Dream of the rood. In Studies in honor of J. Wilcox, Detroit 1958.

Woolf, R. Doctrinal influences on the Dream of the rood. MÆ 27 1958.

Burrow, J. A. An approach to the Dream of the rood. Neophilologus 43 1959.

Bolton, W. F. Connectives in the Seafarer and the Dream of the rood. MP 57 1960.

— Tatwine's De cruce Christi and the Dream of the rood. Archiv 200 1963.

— The dream of the rood 9b: engel=nuntius? N & Q May 1968.

Fleming, J. V. The dream of the rood and Anglo-Saxon monasticism. Traditio 22 1966.

Shepherd, G. Scriptural poetry. In Continuations and beginnings, ed E. G. Stanley 1966.

Britton, G. C. 'Bealuwara weorc' in the Dream of the rood. Neuphilologische Mitteilungen 68 1967.

Farina, D. P. 'Wædum geweorðod' in the Dream of the rood. N & Q Jan 1967.

Leiter, L. H. The dream of the rood: patterns of transformation. In Old English poetry: fifteen essays, ed R. P. Creed, Providence RI 1967.

Stevick, R. D. The meter of the Dream of the rood. Neuphilologische Mitteilungen 68 1967.

Burlin, R. B. The Ruthwell Cross, the Dream of the rood and the vita contemplativa. SP 65 1968.

Isaacs, N. D. Progressive identifications: the structural principle of the Dream of the rood. In his Structural principles, Knoxville 1968.

Patten, F. H. Structure and meaning in the Dream of the rood. E Studies 49 1968.

Scragg, D. G. 'Hwæt/þæt' in the Dream of the rood line 2. N & Q May 1968.

Canuteson, J. The crucifixion and the second coming in the Dream of the rood. MP 66 1969.

Macrae-Gibson, O. D. Christ the victor-vanquished in the Dream of the rood. Neuphilologische Mitteilungen 70 1969.

Swanton, M. J. Ambiguity and anticipation in the Dream of the rood. Ibid.

Edwards, R. R. Narrative technique and distance in the Dream of the rood. Papers on Lang & Lit 6 1970.

Huppé, B. F. The web of words. Albany NY 1970. With text and trn.

Raw, B. C. The dream of the rood and its connections with early Christian art. MÆ 39 1970.

Wolf, C. J. Christ as hero in the Dream of the rood. Neuphilologische Mitteilungen 71 1970.

Hieatt, C. B. Dream frame and verbal echo in the Dream of the rood. Neuphilologische Mitteilungen 72 1971.

DURHAM

Mss: Cambridge Univ Lib Ff.i.27, p. 202 (col 101b); formerly also in Cotton Vitellius D.xx, destroyed in fire of 1731, but ptd by G. Hickes in his Thesaurus 1703–5.

§ 1

Krapp-Dobbie 6 1942.

§ 2

Holthausen, F. Gedicht auf Durham. Beiblatt zur Anglia 31 1920.

Schlauch, M. An Old English ecomium urbis. JEGP 40 1941.

Offler, H. S. The date of Durham (Carmen de situ Dunelmi). JEGP 61 1962.

Robinson, F. C. The royal epithet 'Engle leo' in the Old English Durham poem. MÆ 37 1968.

DURHAM PROVERBS

Ms: Durham Cathedral B.III.32.

§ 1

Arngart, O. S. The Durham proverbs. Lund 1956. Not in Krapp-Dobbie.

ELEGIES

§ 1

Kershaw, N. Anglo-Saxon and Norse poems. Cambridge 1922. With trn.

Translations

Kennedy, C. W. Old English elegies, translated into alliterative verse. Princeton 1936.

Brugger, I. M. de. Las elegías anglo-sajonas. Buenos Aires 1954.

See also under individual elegies: Deor, *above;* Husband's message, Resignation, Ruin, Seafarer, Wanderer, Wife's lament, Wulf and Eadwacer, *below.*

§ 2

Imelmann, R. Die altenglische Odoaker-Dichtung. Berlin 1907.

—— Forschungen zur altenglischen Poesie. Berlin 1920.

Sieper, E. Die altenglische Elegie. Strasbourg 1915. With trn.

Ricci, H. L'elegia pagana anglosassone. Florence 1923.

Idelmann, T. Das Gefühl in den altenglischen Elegien. Bochum-Langendreer 1932.

Jackson, K. Studies in early Celtic nature poetry. Cambridge 1936.

Reuschel, H. Ovid und die angelsächsischen Elegien. Beiträge zur Geschichte der Deutschen Sprache und Literatur 62 1938.

Rosteutscher, J. Germanischer Schicksalsglaube und angelsächsische Elegiendichtung. E Studien 73 1938.

Timmer, B. J. The elegiac mood in Old English poetry. E Studies 34 1942.

Grubl, E. D. Studien zu den angelsächsischen Elegien. Marburg 1948.

Greenfield, S. B. The formulaic expression of the theme of exile in Anglo-Saxon poetry. Speculum 30 1955; rptd in Essential articles for the study of OE poetry, ed J. B. Bessinger and S. J. Kahrl, Hamden Conn 1968.

—— The Old English elegies. In Continuations and beginnings, ed E. G. Stanley 1966.

Elliott, R. W. V. Form and image in the Old English lyrics. EC 11 1961.

Göller, K. H. Die angelsächsischen Elegien. Germanisch-romanische Monatsschrift new ser 14 1964.

Pilch, H. The elegiac genre in Old English and Old Welsh poetry. Zeitschrift für Celtische Philologie 29 1964.

Stanley, E. G. The search for Anglo-Saxon paganism. N & Q Dec 1964.

Dietrich, G. Ursprünge des Elegischen in der altenglischen Literatur. In Literatur-Kultur-Gesellschaft in England und Amerika: Festgabe für F. Schubel, Frankfurt 1966.

Henry, P. L. The early English and Celtic lyric. 1966.

Irving, E. B. Image and meaning in the elegies. In Old English poetry: fifteen essays, ed R. P. Creed, Providence RI 1967.

Suzuki, S. Old English poetry: elegy. Tokyo 1967.

Whitbread, L. The pattern of misfortune in Deor and other Old English poems. Neophilologus 54 1970.

ELENE

Ms: Vercelli book 121a–33b.

§1

Grimm, J. Andreas und Elene. Cassel 1840.

Zupitza, J. Cynewulf's Elene. Berlin 1877, 1899 (rev).

Kent, C. W. Elene. Boston 1889.

Holthausen, F. Cynewulf's Elene. Heidelberg 1905, 1936 (rev).

Cook, A. S. The Old English Elene, Phoenix and Physiologus. New Haven 1919.

Krapp-Dobbie 2 1932.

Lupi, S. Sant' Elena. Naples 1951. With trn.

Gradon, P. Cynewulf's Elene. 1958.

Translations

Weymouth, R. F. A literal translation of Cynewulf's Elene. 1888.

Garnett, J. M. Elene, Judith, Brunanburh and Maldon. Boston 1889, 1901.

Menzies, J. Cynewulf's Elene. Edinburgh 1894.

Holt, L. H. The Elene of Cynewulf. New York 1904.

§2

Glöde, O. Untersuchung über die Quelle zu Cynewulfs Elene. Anglia 9 1886.

Kent, C. W. Teutonic antiquities in Andreas and Elene. Halle 1887.

Cook, A. S. The date of the Old English Elene. Anglia 15 1893.

Holthausen, F. Zur Quelle von Cynewulfs Elene. Zeitschrift für Deutsche Philologie 37 1905; Archiv 125 1910; Beiblatt zur Anglia 45 1934, 49 1938.

Arngart [Anderson], O. Some notes on Cynewulf's Elene. E Studies 27 1946.

Sisam, K. Notes on Old English poetry. RES 22 1946.

Gradon, P. Constantine and the barbarians: a note on the Old English Elene. MLR 42 1947.

—— Cynewulf's Elene and Old English prosody. Eng & Germanic Stud 2 1949.

Schaar, C. Notes on Andreas and Elene. Studia Neophilologica 19 1947.

Elliott, R. W. V. Cynewulf's runes in Christ II and Elene. E Studies 34 1953.

Muinzer, L. A. Maier's transcript and the conclusion of Cynewulf's Fates of the apostles. JEGP 56 1957.

Wolpers, T. Die englische Heiligenlegende des Mittelalters. Tübingen 1964.

Woolf, R. Saints' lives. In Continuations and beginnings, ed E. G. Stanley 1966.

Fry, D. K. Themes and type-scenes in Elene 1–113. Speculum 44 1969.

Stepsis, R. and R. Rand. Contrast and conversion in Cynewulf's Elene. Neuphilologische Mitteilungen 70 1969.

Gardner, J. Cynewulf's Elena: sources and structure. Neophilologus 54 1970.

Hill, T. D. Sapiential structure and figural narrative in the Old English Elene. Traditio 27 1971.

See also under Cynewulf, above.

EXHORTATION TO CHRISTIAN LIVING

Ms: Corpus Christi College Cambridge 201, numbered pp. 165–6.

§1

Lumby, J. R. Be domes dæge. 1876 (EETS).

Krapp-Dobbie 6 1942.

§2

Whitbread, L. Two notes on minor Old English poems. Studia Neophilologica 20 1948.

—— The Old English Exhortation to Christian living: some textual problems. MLR 44 1949.

—— Notes on the Old English Exhortation to Christian living. Studia Neophilologica 22 1951, 29 1957.

EXODUS

Ms: Bodley, Junius xi, numbered pp. 143–71.

§1

Hunt, T. W. Cædmon's Exodus and Daniel. Boston 1883, 1888 (rev).

Blackburn, F. A. Exodus and Daniel. Boston 1907.

Krapp-Dobbie 1 1931.

Irving, E. B. The Old English Exodus. New Haven 1953.

Johnson, W. S. Translation of the Old English Exodus. JEGP 5 1903.

§2

Strobl, J. Angelsächsische Studien 1: zur sogenannten Cædmonschen Exodus. Germania 20 1875.

Groth, E. Composition und Alter der altenglischen (ags.) Exodus. Göttingen 1883.

Rau, M. Germanische Altertümer in der angelsächsischen Exodus. Leipzig 1890.

Mürkens, G. Untersuchungen über das altenglische Exoduslied. Bonner Beiträge zur Anglistik 2 1899.

Bright, J. W. Notes on the Cædmonian Exodus. MLN 17 1902.
— The relation of the Caedmonian Exodus to the liturgy. MLN 27 1912.
Holthausen, F. Zur Quellenkunde der altenglischen Exodus. Archiv 115 1905.
Moore, S. On the sources of the Old English Exodus. MP 9 1911.
Napier, A. S. The Old English Exodus, ll. 63–134. MLR 6 1911.
Sisam, K. Notes on Old English poetry. RES 22 1946.
Hofmann, D. Untersuchungen zu den altenglischen Gedichten Genesis und Exodus. Anglia 75 1957.
Irving, E. B. On the dating of the Old English poems Genesis and Exodus. Anglia 77 1959.
Cross, J. E. and S. I. Tucker. Allegorical tradition and the Old English Exodus. Neophilologus 44 1960. See Appendix on Exodus ll. 289–90, ibid.
Robinson, F. C. Notes on the Old English Exodus. Anglia 80 1962.
— The significance of names in Old English literature. Anglia 86 1968.
Wehrli, M. Sacra poesis: Biblelepik als europäische Tradition. In Die Wissenschaft von deutscher Sprache und Dichtung: Festschrift für F. Maurer, Stuttgart 1963.
Farrell, R. T. Eight notes on Old English Exodus. Neuphilologische Mitteilungen 67 1966.
— A reading of Old English Exodus. RES new ser 20 1969.
Creed, R. P. The art of the singer: three Old English tellings of the offering of Isaac. In Old English poetry: fifteen essays, ed R. P. Creed, Providence RI 1967.
Mirsky, A. On the sources of the Anglo-Saxon Genesis and Exodus. E Studies 48 1967.
Brodeur, A. G. A study of the diction and style in three Anglo-Saxon narrative poems. In Nordica et Anglica: studies in honor of S. Einarsson, Hague 1968.
Isaacs, N. D. Exodus and the essential digression. In his Structural principles, Knoxville 1968.
Wall, Sr C. Stylistic variation in the Old English Exodus. Eng Lang Notes 6 1968.
Lucas, P. J. N & Q June, Oct 1969, Aug 1971. Notes on ll. 46–53, 265, 480.
— The cloud in the interpretation of the Old English Exodus. E Studies 51 1970.
McLoughlin, E. OE Exodus and the Antiphonary of Bangor. Neuphilologische Mitteilungen 70 1969.
Earl, J. W. Christian tradition in the Old English Exodus. Neuphilologische Mitteilungen 71 1970.
Keenan, H. T. Exodus 312: the green street of Paradise. Ibid.
Kossick, S. J. The Anglo-Saxon Exodus. Eng Stud in Africa 14 1971.
See also under Cædmon, above.

FATES OF THE APOSTLES

Ms: Vercelli book 52b–4a.

§1

Thorpe, B. Appendix B to Cooper's report on Rymer's Foedera. 1869 (ptd 1836).
Krapp, G. P. Andreas and the Fates of the apostles. Boston 1906.
Krapp-Dobbie 2 1932.
Brooks, K. R. Andreas and the Fates of the apostles. Oxford 1961.
Olivero, F. The Fates of the apostles: translation and critical commentary. Milan 1927. See also under Andreas, above.

§2

Cook, A. S. The affinities of the Fata apostolorum. MLN 4 1889.
Sarrazin, G. Die Fata apostolorum und der Dichter Kynewulf. Anglia 12 1889.
Trautmann, M. Wer hat die Schicksale der Apostel zuerst für den Schluss des Andreas erklärt? Beiblatt zur Anglia 7 1897.
Brandl, A. Zu Cynewulfs Fata apostolorum. Archiv 100 1898.
Bourauel, J. Zur Quellen- und Verfasserfrage von Andreas, Crist und Fata. Bonner Beiträge zur Anglistik 11 1901.
Holthausen, F. Zur Quelle der altenglischen Fata apostolorum. Archiv 106 1901.
Barnouw, A. J. Die Schicksale der Apostel doch ein unabhängiges Gedicht. Archiv 108 1902.
Hamilton, G. L. The sources of the Fates of the apostles and Andreas. MLN 35 1920.
Elliott, R. W. V. Cynewulf's runes in Juliana and Fates of the apostles. E Studies 34 1953.
Muinzer, L. A. Maier's transcript and the conclusion of Cynewulf's Fates of the apostles. JEGP 56 1957.
Woolf, R. Saints' lives. In Continuations and beginnings, ed E. G. Stanley 1966.
Boren, J. L. Form and meaning in Cynewulf's Fates of the apostles. Papers on Lang & Lit 5 1969.
See also under Cynewulf, above.

FINNSBURG FRAGMENT
See under Battle of Finnsburh, above.

FORTUNES OF MEN

Ms: Exeter book 87a–8b.

§1

Krapp-Dobbie 3 1936.

§2

Rieger, M. Über Cynewulf. Zeitschrift für Deutsche Philologie 1 1868.
Bradley, H. Two corruptions in Old English mss. Academy 28 Jan 1893.
Cross, J. E. On the wanderer lines 80–4: a study of a figure and a theme. Vetenskaps-societen i Lund Årsbok 1959.

FRAGMENTS OF PSALMS

Ms: Bodley, Junius 121, 43b, 45a–b, 47a–50b, 51a, 52a, 53b.

§1

Krapp-Dobbie 6 1942.
See also under Creed, above.

§2

See under Paris psalter, below.

FRANKS CASKET
Bibliographies
Marquardt, H. Die Runeninschriften der britischen Inseln. In Bibliographie der Runeninschriften nach Fundorten pt 1, Göttingen 1961.
Front panel and right side have poetic inscriptions in runes.

§1

Stephens, G. Handbook of the Old-Northern Runic monuments. 1884.

Wadstein, E. The Clermont runic casket. Upsala 1900.

Napier, A. S. The Franks casket. In An English miscellany presented to Dr [F. J.] Furnivall, Oxford 1901.

Viëtor, W. Das angelsächsische Runenkästchen aus Auzon bei Clermont-Ferrand: the Anglo-Saxon runic casket. Marburg 1901. In German and English.

Krapp-Dobbie 6 1942.

§2

Hofmann, K. Über die Clermonter Runen. Sitzungsberichte der Philosophisch-Philologischen und Historischen Classe der Königlich Bayerischen Akademie der Wissenschaften 1–2 1871–2.

Hempl, G. The variant runes on the Franks casket. Trans of Amer Philological Assoc 32 1901.

Grienberger, T. von. Zu den Inschriften des Clermonter Runenkästchens. Anglia 27 1904.

Boer, R. C. Über die rechte Seite des angelsächsischen Runenkästchens. Arkiv för Nordisk Filologi 27 1911.

Walker, F. C. Fresh light on the Franks casket. Washington Univ Stud 2 1915.

Imelmann, R. Die Hos-Inschrift des Franks Casket. In his Forschungen zur altenglischen Poesie, Berlin 1920.

Clark, E. G. The right side of the Franks casket. PMLA 45 1930.

Spiess, K. Das angelsächsische Runenkästchen (die Seite mit der Hos-Inschrift). In J. Strzygowski Festschrift, Klagenfurt 1932.

Souers, P. W. The Magi on the Franks casket. Harvard Stud 19 1937.

—— The Wayland scene on the Franks casket. Speculum 18 1943.

Elliott, R. W. V. Runes. Manchester 1959.

Krause, W. Erta: ein anglischer Gott. Die Sprache 5 1959.

Schneider, K. Zu den Inschriften und Bilden des Franks Casket und einer ae. Version des Mythos von Balders Tod. In Festschrift für W. Fischer, Heidelberg 1959.

Bouman, A. C. The Franks casket's right side and lid. Neophilologus 49 1965.

Ball, C. J. E. The Franks casket: right side. E Studies 47 1966.

D'Ardenne, S. T. R. O. Does the right side of the Franks casket represent the burial of Sigurd? Etudes Germaniques 21 1966.

Wolf, A. Franks Casket in literarhistorischer Sicht. Frühmittelalterliche Studien 3 1969.

Osborn, M. Two inconsistent letters in the inscription on the Franks casket, right side. Neuphilologische Mitteilungen 72 1971.

GENESIS

Ms: Bodley, Junius xi, numbered pp. 1–142. Genesis A (The older Genesis) consists of ll. 1–234, 852–2936; Genesis B (The later Genesis) of ll. 235–851.

Concordance

Braasch, T. Vollständiges Wörterbuch zur sogenannten Cædmonschen Genesis. Heidelberg 1933.

§1

Sievers, E. Der Heliand und die angelsächsische Genesis. Halle 1875.

Behagel, O. Heliand und Genesis. Halle 1903, 1922 (rev).

Klaeber, F. The later Genesis and other Old English and Old Saxon texts relating to the fall of man. Heidelberg 1913.

Holthausen, F. Die ältere Genesis. Heidelberg 1914. Addns and errata in Anglia 46 1922.

Krapp-Dobbie 1 1931.

Timmer, B. J. The later Genesis. Oxford 1948, 1954 (rev).

Translations

Greverus, J. P. E. Cædmon's Schöpfung und Abfall der bösen Engel. Oldenburg 1852.

—— Cædmon's Sündenfall. Oldenburg 1854.

Mason, L. Genesis A. New York 1915.

Genzmer, F. Heliand und die Bruchstücke der Genesis. Leipzig 1948.

See also under Manuscripts and Cædmon, above.

§2

Windisch, W. O. E. Der Heliand und seine Quellen. Leipzig 1868.

Sievers, E. Der Heliand und die angelsächsische Genesis. Halle 1875. See Anglia 5 1882.

—— Cædmon und Genesis. In Britannica: M. Förster zum 60 Geburtstage, Leipzig 1929.

Wülker, R. P. Cædmon und Milton. Anglia 4 1881.

—— Die Bedeutung einer neuen Entdeckung für die angelsächsische Literaturgeschichte. Berichten über die Verhandlungen der Königlich Sächsischen Gesellschaft der Wissenschaften, philologisch-historische Klasse 1884.

Ebert, A. Zur angelsächsischen Genesis. Anglia 5 1882.

Fritzsche, A. Ist die altenglische Story of Genesis and Exodus das Werk eines Verfassers? Anglia 5 1882.

Hönncher, E. Studien zur angelsächsischen Genesis. Anglia 7–8 1884–5.

Heinze, A. Zur altenglischen Genesis. Berlin 1889.

Merrill, K. and C. F. McClumpha. The parallelisms of the Anglo-Saxon Genesis. MLN 5 1890.

Ferrell, C. C. Teutonic antiquities in the Anglo-Saxon Genesis. Halle 1893.

Zangemeister, K. F. W. and W. Braune. Bruchstücke der altsächsischen Bibeldichtung. Heidelberg 1894.

Gurteen, V. H. The epic of the fall of man: a comparative study of Cædmon, Dante and Milton. New York 1896.

Graz, F. Beiträge zur Textkritik der sogenannten Cædmonschen Genesis. Königsberg 1896.

Agard, A. F. Poetic personifications of evil: Cædmon, Marlowe, Milton, Goethe. Poet-lore 9 1897.

Jovy, H. Untersuchungen zur altenglischen Genesisdichtung. Bonner Beiträge zur Anglistik 5 1900.

Behagel, O. Der Heliand und die angelsächsische Genesis. Giessen 1902, Halle 1910.

Grüters, O. Über einige Beziehungen zwischen altsächsischer und altenglischer Dichtung. Bonner Beiträge zur Anglistik 17 1905.

Emerson, O. F. Legends of Cain, especially in Old and Middle English. PMLA 21 1906.

Klaeber, F. Die ältere Genesis und der Beowulf. E Studien 42 1910.

—— Anglia 37 1913, 49 1926, 55 1931; PQ 19 1940; Archiv 178 1941. Notes.

Gajšek, S. von. Milton und Cædmon. Vienna 1911.

Gerould, G. H. The transmission and date of Genesis B. MLN 26 1911.

Bradley, H. The Cædmonian Genesis. E & S 6 1920.

McKillop, A. D. Illustrative notes on Genesis B. JEGP 20 1921.

Crawford, S. J. A Latin parallel for part of the Later Genesis? Anglia 48 1924.

Berthold, L. Die Quellen für die Grundgedanken von v. 235–851 der altsächsisch-angelsächsischen Genesis. In Germanica: E. Sievers zum 75 Geburtstage, Halle 1925.

Dustoor, P. E. Legends of Lucifer in early English and in Milton. Anglia 54 1930.

Bruckner, W. Zu den Versen 564–7, 599–620, 666–77, 772f. der angelsächsischen Genesis B und zu Frage nach der Heimat des Dichters. Beiträge zur Geschichte der Deutschen Sprache und Literatur 56 1932.

Sisam, K. Notes on Old English poetry. RES 22 1946, new ser 2 1951.

Lever, J. W. Paradise lost and the Anglo-Saxon tradition. RES 23 1947.

Michel, L. Genesis A and the Praefatio. MLN 62 1947.

Menner, R. J. The date and dialect of Genesis A 852–2936. Anglia 70 1952.

Woolf, R. E. The Devil in Old English poetry. RES new ser 4 1953.

—— The fall of man in Genesis B and the Mystère d'Adam. In Studies in OE literature in honor of A. G. Brodeur, Eugene 1963.

Stanley, E. G. A note on Genesis B, 328. RES new ser 5 1954.

Hofmann, D. Untersuchungen zu den altenglischen Gedichten Genesis und Exodus. Anglia 75 1957.

Renoir, A. 'Romigan ures rices': a reconsideration. MLN 72 1957.

—— The self-deception of temptation: Boethian psychology in Genesis B. In Old English poetry: fifteen essays, ed R. P. Creed, Providence RI 1967.

Creed, R. P. Genesis 1316. MLN 73 1958.

—— The art of the singer: three Old English tellings of the offering of Isaac. In Old English poetry: fifteen essays, ed R. P. Creed, Providence RI 1967.

Huppé, B. F. Doctrine and poetry: Augustine's influence on Old English poetry. New York 1959.

Irving, E. B. On the dating of the Old English poems Genesis and Exodus. Anglia 77 1959.

Young, J. I. Two notes on the Later Genesis. In The Anglo-Saxons, presented to B. Dickins, 1959.

Schabram, H. Die Bedeutung von 'gal' und 'galschipe' in der altenglischen Genesis B. Beiträge zur Geschichte der Deutschen Sprache und Literatur 82 1960.

Evans, J. M. Genesis B and its background. RES new ser 14 1963.

Malone, K. Satan's speech: Genesis 347–440. Emory Univ Quart 19 1963.

Salmon, P. The site of Lucifer's throne. Anglia 81 1963.

Utley, F. L. The flood narrative in the Junius ms and in Baltic literature. In Studies in OE literature in honor of A. G. Brodeur, Eugene 1963.

Wehrli, M. Sacra poesis: Bibelepik als europäische Tradition. In Die Wissenschaft von deutscher Sprache und Dichtung: Festschrift für F. Maurer, Stuttgart 1963.

Århammar, N. Altsächsische skion m. Wolke und altenglische sceo (?), mit einem Beitrag zur Textkritik von Genesis 16ff und des altenglischen Rätsels vom Gewittersturm. Jahrbuch des Vereins für Niederdeutsche Sprachforschung 87 1964.

Rosier, J. L. God on the warpath: Genesis A 2112. Archiv 202 1965.

—— 'Hrincg' in Genesis A. Anglia 88 1970.

Vickrey, J. F. 'Selfsceaft' in Genesis B. Anglia 83 1965.

—— An emendation to 'l[æ]nes' in Genesis B line 258. Archiv 204 1967.

—— The vision of Eve in Genesis B. Speculum 44 1969.

—— A note on Genesis lines 242–4. Neuphilologische Mitteilungen 71 1970.

—— The 'micel wundor' of Genesis B. SP 68 1971.

Mirsky, A. On the sources of the Anglo-Saxon Genesis and Exodus. E Studies 48 1967.

Robinson, F. C. Notes and emendations to Old English poetic texts. Neuphilologische Mitteilungen 67 1966.

—— The Old English Genesis, lines 1136–7. Archiv 204 1967.

—— The significance of names in Old English literature. Anglia 86 1968.

Cherniss, M. D. Heroic ideals and the moral climate of Genesis B. MLQ 30 1969.

Hill, T. D. Some remarks on the site of Lucifer's throne. Anglia 87 1969.

Faiss, K. Gnade und seine Kontexte in der altenglischen Genesis. Linguistics 56 1970.

Lucas, P. J. Genesis B 623–5: part of the speech to Eve? N & Q July 1970.

Sklute, L. M. 'Freoðuwebbe' in Old English poetry. Neuphilologische Mitteilungen 71 1970.

Benskin, M. An argument for an interpolation in the Old English Later Genesis. Neuphilologische Mitteilungen 72 1971.

Capek, M. J. The nationality of a translator: some notes on the syntax of Genesis B. Neophilologus 55 1971.

See also under Cædmon, above.

GIFTS OF MEN

Ms: Exeter book 78a–80a.

§1

Krapp-Dobbie 3 1936.

Whitelock, D. In her English historical documents vol 1, c. 500–1042, Oxford 1955. Trn.

§2

Rieger, M. Über Cynewulf. Zeitschrift für Deutsche Philologie 1 1869.

Cross, J. E. The Old English poetic theme of the Gifts of men. Neophilologus 46 1962.

GLORIA I

Mss: Bodley, Junius 121, 43b–44b; Corpus Christi College Cambridge 201, numbered pp. 169–70.

§1

Lumby, J. R. Be domes dæge. 1876 (EETS). With trn.

Krapp-Dobbie 6 1942.

See also under Creed, above.

§2

Whitbread, L. The Old English poems of the Benedictine Office and some related questions. Anglia 80 1962.

—— Notes on two minor Old English poems. Eng Lang Notes 4 1967.

GLORIA II

Ms: BM Cotton Titus D. xxvii, 56a–b.

§1

Krapp-Dobbie 6 1942.

GUTHLAC

Ms: Exeter book 33a–52b. Guthlac I (or A) consists of ll. 1–818; Guthlac II (or B), of ll. 819–1379.

§1

Krapp-Dobbie 3 1936.

Olivero, F. Sul poemetto anglosassone Guthlac. Memorie della Reale Accademia delle Scienze di Torino, 2nd ser 70 1942. With trn.

For other edns and trns see under Manuscripts and Cynewulf, above.

§2

Charitius, F. Über die angelsächsischen Gedichte vom heiligen Guthlac. Anglia 2 1879.

Lefèvre, P. Das altenglische Gedicht vom heiligen Guthlac. Anglia 6 1883.

Forstmann, H. Untersuchungen zur Guthlac-legende. Bonner Beiträge zur Anglistik 12 1902.

Gerould, G. H. The Old English poems on St Guthlac and their Latin source. MLN 32 1917.

Shook, L. K. The burial mound in Guthlac A. MP 58 1960.

— The prologue of the Old English Guthlac A. Mediaeval Stud 23 1961.

Bolton, W. F. The background and meaning of Guthlac. JEGP 61 1962.

Cross, J. E. Aspects of microcosm and macrocosm in Old English literature. Comparative Lit 14 1962; rptd in Studies in OE literature in honor of A. G. Brodeur, Eugene 1963.

Wolpers, T. Die englische Heiligenlegende des Mittelalters. Tübingen 1964.

Woolf, R. Saints' lives. In Continuations and beginnings, ed E. G. Stanley 1966.

Robinson, F. C. The significance of names in Old English literature. Anglia 86 1968.

Roberts, J. An inventory of early Guthlac materials. Mediaeval Stud 32 1970.

Rosier, J. L. Death and transfiguration: Guthlac B. In Philological essays in honour of H. D. Meritt, Hague 1970.

Lipp, F. R. Guthlac A: an interpretation. Mediaeval Stud 33 1971.

HOMILETIC FRAGMENT I

Ms: Vercelli book 104a–b.

§1

Krapp-Dobbie 2 1932.

§2

Hill, T. D. The hypocritical bee in the Old English Homiletic fragment I lines 18–30. N & Q April 1968.

Isaacs, N. D. The Old English Taste of honey. In his Structural principles, Knoxville 1968.

HOMILETIC FRAGMENT II

Ms: Exeter book 122a–b.

§1

Krapp-Dobbie 3 1936.

§2

Witting, J. S. Homiletic fragment II and the Epistle to the Ephesians. Traditio 25 1969.

HUSBAND'S MESSAGE

Ms: Exeter book 123a–b.

§1

Krapp-Dobbie 3 1936.

Leslie, R. F. Three Old English elegies: The Wife's lament, The husband's message, The ruin. Manchester 1961.

See also under Elegies, above.

§2

Hicketier, F. Klage der Frau, Botschaft des Gemahls und Ruine. Anglia 11 1889.

Trautmann, M. Zur Botschaft des Gemahls. Anglia 16 1894.

Roeder, F. Die Familie bei den Angelsachsen. Halle 1899.

Blackburn, F. A. The Husband's message and the accompanying riddles of the Exeter book. JEGP 3 1901. With trn.

Brunner, K. Hero und Leander und die altenglischen Elegien. Archiv 142 1921.

Holthausen, F. Zur Botschaft des Gemahls. Beiblatt zur Anglia 34 1923.

Elliott, R. W. V. The runes in the Husband's message. JEGP 54 1955.

Schneider, K. Die germanischen Runennamen: Versuch einer Gesamtdeutung. Meisenheim-am-Glan 1956.

Bouman, A. C. The OE poems the Wife's lament and the Husband's message. In his Patterns in OE and Old Icelandic literature, Leyden 1962.

Kaske, R. E. The reading 'genyre' in the Husband's message, line 49. MÆ 33 1964.

— A poem of the Cross in the Exeter book: Riddle 60 and the Husband's message. Traditio 23 1967.

Swanton, M. J. The wife's lament and The husband's message: a reconsideration. Anglia 82 1964.

Bolton, W. F. The wife's lament and the Husband's message: a reconsideration revisited. Archiv 205 1969.

See also under Elegies, above.

INSTRUCTIONS FOR CHRISTIANS

Ms: Univ Lib Cambridge Ii.1.33, 224b–7b.

§1

Rosier, J. L. Instructions for Christians: a poem in Old English. Anglia 82 1964; addns 84 1966.

Not in Krapp-Dobbie.

JUDGMENT DAY I

Ms: Exeter book 115b–7b.

§1

Krapp-Dobbie 3 1936.

§2

Deering, G. The Anglo-Saxon poets on the Judgment Day. Halle 1990. With trn.

Menner, R. J. The vocabulary of the Old English poems on the Judgment Day. PMLA 62 1947.

Whitbread, L. The doomsday theme in Old English poetry. Beiträge zur Geschichte der Deutschen Sprache und Literatur (Halle) 89 1967.

JUDGMENT DAY II

Ms: Corpus Christi College Cambridge 201, numbered pp. 161–5.

§1

Lumby, J. R. Be domes dæge. 1876 (EETS). With trn.

Löhe, H. Be domes dæge. Bonner Beiträge zur Anglistik 22 1907. With trn.

Krapp-Dobbie 6 1942.

§2

Deering, G. The Anglo-Saxon poets on the Judgment Day. Halle 1890. With trn.

Menner, R. J. The vocabulary of the Old English poems on Judgment Day. PMLA 62 1947.

Holthausen, F. Zur Textkritik alt- und mittelenglischer Gedichte. Archiv 188 1951.

Huppé, B. F. Doctrine and poetry: Augustine's influence on Old English poetry. New York 1959.

Whitbread, L. Old English and Old High German: a note on Judgment Day II 292–3. SP 60 1963.

— The Old English poem Judgment Day II and its Latin source. PQ 45 1966. A further article, Zeitschrift für Deutsches Altertum 95 1966, deals only with the Latin.

—— Text-notes on the Old English poem Judgment Day II. E Studies 48 1967.

Hoffman, R. L. Structure and symbolism in the Judgment Day II. Neophilologus 52 1968.

—— The theme of Judgment Day II. Eng Lang Notes 6 1969.

JUDITH

Ms: BM Cotton Vitellius A. xv, 199a–206.

§1

Nilsson, L. G. Judith. Copenhagen 1858. With Swedish trn.

Cook, A. S. Judith: an Old English epic fragment. Boston 1888.

Timmer, B. J. Judith. 1952, 1961 (rev).

Krapp-Dobbie 4 1953.

Translations

Elton, O. Judith [ll. 1–121]. In An English miscellany presented to Dr [F. J.] Furnivall, Oxford 1901.

Hall, J. L. Judith, Phoenix and other Anglo-Saxon poems. New York 1912.

§2

Luick, K. Über den Versbau des angelsächsischen Gedichtes Judith. Beiträge zur Geschichte der Deutschen Sprache und Literatur 11 1886.

Cook, A. S. Notes on a Northumbrianized version of Judith. Trans Amer Philological Assoc 20 1889.

—— Notes on Judith. JEGP 5 1903.

Foster, T. G. Judith: studies in metre, language and style. Strasbourg 1892.

Neumann, M. Über das altenglische Gedicht von Judith. Kiel 1892.

Brincker, F. Germanische Altertümer in dem angelsächsischen Gedicht Judith. Hamburg 1898.

Smyth, E. The numbers in the ms of the Old English Judith. MLN 20 1905.

Tupper, F. Notes on Old English poems 1: the home of the Judith. JEGP 11 1912.

Woolf, R. E. The lost opening to the Judith. MLR 50 1955.

Malone, K. Some Judith readings. In Festschrift zum 75 Geburtstag von T. Spira, Heidelberg 1961.

Renoir, A. Judith and the limits of poetry. E Studies 43 1962.

Enzensberger, C. Das altenglische Judith-Gedicht als Stilgebilde. Anglia 82 1964.

Fry, D. K. The heroine on the beach in Judith. Neuphilologische Mitteilungen 68 1967.

—— Imagery and point of view in Judith 206–31. Eng Lang Notes 5 1968.

Brodeur, A. G. A study of diction and style in three Anglo-Saxon narrative poems. In Nordica et Anglica: studies in honor of S. Einarsson, Hague 1968.

Heinemann, F. J. Judith 236–291a: a mock heroic approach-to-battle type scene. Neuphilologische Mitteilungen 71 1970.

Huppé, B. F. The web of words. Albany NY 1970. With text and trn.

Campbell, J. J. Schematic technique in Judith. ELH 38 1971.

Doubleday, J. F. The principle of contrast in Judith. Neuphilologische Mitteilungen 72 1971.

JULIANA

Ms: Exeter book 65b–76a.

§1

Strunk, W. Juliana. Boston 1904.

Krapp-Dobbie 3 1936.

Woolf, R. E. Juliana. 1955, New York 1966 (corrected with addns).

Translations

Murch, H. S. Translation of Cynewulf's Juliana. JEGP 5 1904.

Kennedy, C. W. The legend of St Juliana, translated from the Latin of the Acta sanctorum and the Anglo-Saxon of Cynewulf. Princeton 1906.

See also under Cynewulf, above.

§2

Glöde, O. Cynewulf's Juliana und ihre Quelle. Anglia 11 1889.

Backhaus, O. Über die Quelle der mittelenglischen Legende von der heiligen Juliana und ihr Verhältnis zu Cynewulfs Juliana. Halle 1899.

Garnett, J. M. The Latin and the Anglo-Saxon Juliana. PMLA 14 1899.

Brunöhler, E. Über einige lateinische, englische, französische und deutsche Fassungen der Julianalegende. Bonn 1912.

Elliott, R. W. V. Cynewulf's runes in Juliana and Fates of the apostles. E Studies 34 1953.

Wolpers, T. Die englische Heiligenlegende des Mittelalters. Tübingen 1964.

Woolf, R. Saints' lives. In Continuations and beginnings, ed E. G. Stanley 1966.

Bleeth, K. A. Juliana. MÆ 38 1969.

Doubleday, J. F. The allegory of the soul as fortress in Old English poetry. Anglia 88 1970

See also under Cynewulf, above.

KENTISH HYMN

Ms: BM Cotton Vespasian D. vi, 68b–9b.

§1

Krapp-Dobbie 6 1942.

§2

Shepherd, G. The sources of the Old English Kentish hymn. MLN 67 1952.

LATIN-ENGLISH PROVERBS

Ms: BM Cotton Faustina A. x, 100b; Royal 2 B. v, 6a.

§1

Krapp-Dobbie 6 1942.

LEIDEN RIDDLE

Ms: Univ Lib Leyden, Voss. Q. 106, 25b.

§1

Bethmann, L. C. Zeitschrift für Deutsches Altertum 5 1845.

Kietrich, F. Kynewulfi poetae aetas aenigmatum fragmento e codice Lugdunensi. Marburg 1860.

Schlutter, O. Das Leidener Rätsel. Anglia 32 1909.

Smith, A. H. Three Northumbrian poems. 1933.

Krapp-Dobbie 6 1942.

§2

Kern, J. H. Das Leidener Rätsel. Anglia 33 1910. *See* 38 1914.
Schlutter, O. Zum Leidener Rätsel. Anglia 33 1910.
Gerritsen, J. Þurh þreata ʒeþræcu. E Studies 35 1954.
—— The text of the Leiden riddle. E Studies 50 1969.
Zandvoort, R. W. In his Collected papers, Groningen 1954.
Anderson, G. K. Aldhelm and the Leiden Riddle. In Old English poetry: fifteen essays, ed R. P. Creed, Providence RI 1967.
See also under Riddles, *below.*

LORD'S PRAYER I

Ms: Exeter book 122a.

§1

Krapp-Dobbie 3 1936.

LORD'S PRAYER II

Ms: Corpus Christi College Cambridge 201, numbered pp. 167–9.

§1

Lumby, J. R. Be domes dæge. 1876 (EETS). With trn.
Krapp-Dobbie 6 1942.

§2

Whitbread, L. The Old English poems of the Benedictine office and some related questions. Anglia 80 1962.
—— Notes on two minor OE poems. Eng Lang Notes 4 1967.

LORD'S PRAYER III

Ms: Bodley, Junius 121, 45.

§1

Krapp-Dobbie 6 1942.
See also under Creed, *above.*

§2

Whitbread, L. The Old English poems of the Benedictine Office and some related questions. Anglia 80 1962.

MALDON

See Battle of Maldon, *above.*

MAXIMS I

Ms: Exeter book 88b–90a (I or A); 90a–1a (II or B); 91a–2b (III or C).

§1

Williams, B. C. Gnomic poetry in Anglo-Saxon. New York 1914.
Krapp-Dobbie 3 1936.

§2

Rieger, M. Über Cynewulf. Zeitschrift für Deutsche Philologie 1 1868.
Strobl. J. Zur Spruchdichtung bei den Angelsachsen. Zeitschrift für Deutsches Altertum 31 1887.
Müller, H. Über die angelsächsische Versus Gnomici. Jena 1893.
Malone, K. Notes on Gnomic poem B of the Exeter book. MÆ 12 1943.

Whitbread, L. The Frisian sailor passage in the Old English gnomic verses. RES 22 1946.
Dawson, R. M. The structure of the Old English gnomic poems. JEGP 61 1962.
Henry, P. L. The early English and Celtic lyric. 1966.
Taylor, P. B. Heroic ritual in the Old English maxims. Neuphilologische Mitteilungen 70 1969.
Hill, T. D. Notes on the Old English Maxims I and II. N & Q Dec 1970–.

MAXIMS II

Ms: BM Cotton Tiberius B. i, 115a–b.

§1

Fox, S. Menologium seu calendarium poeticum. 1830. With trn.
Williams, B. C. Gnomic poetry in Anglo-Saxon. New York 1914.
Krapp-Dobbie 6 1942.

§2

Whitbread, L. Two notes on minor Old English poems. Studia Neophilologica 20 1948.
See Rieger, Strobl, Müller, Dawson, Henry, Taylor, Hill, *under* Maxims I, *above.*

MENOLOGIUM

Ms: BM Cotton Tiberius B. i, 112a–4b.

§1

Fox, S. Menologium seu calendarium poeticum. 1830. With trn.
Bouterwek, K. W. Calendecwide, i.e. Menologium ecclesiae anglo-saxonicae poeticum. Gütersloh 1857. With Latin trn.
Imelmann, R. Das altenglische Menologium. Berlin 1902.
Krapp-Dobbie 6 1942.
Malone, K. The Old English Calendar poem. In Studies in language, literature and culture, ed E. B. Atwood and A. A. Hill, Austin 1969. Trn.

§2

Piper, F. Die Kalendarien und Martyrologien der Angelsachsen. Berlin 1862.
Liebermann, F. Zum angelsächsischen Menologium. Archiv 110 1903.
Fritsche, P. Darstellung der Syntax in dem ae. Menologium. Berlin 1907.
Henel, H. Studien zum altenglischen Computus. Leipzig 1934.
Hennig, J. The Irish counterparts of the Anglo-Saxon Menologium. Mediaeval Stud 14 1952.

METRES OF BOETHIUS

Ms: BM Cotton Otho A. vi, 1a–129b (alternating with prose); paper transcript, Junius 12 (17th century).

§1

Fox, S. King Alfred's Anglo-Saxon version of the Metres of Boethius. 1835. With trn.
—— King Alfred's Anglo-Saxon version of Boethius De consolatione philosophiæ. 1864. With verse trns of Metres by M. F. Tupper.
Sedgefield, W. J. King Alfred's version of Boethius De consolatione philosophiæ. Oxford 1899.
Krämer, E. Die altenglischen Metra des Boetius. Bonner Beiträge zur Anglistik 8 1902.
Krapp-Dobbie 5 1932.

Translations

Sedgefield, W. J. King Alfred's version of the Consolations of Boethius, done into modern English. Oxford 1900.

§2

Hartmann, K. A. M. Ist König Ælfred Verfasser der alliterierenden Übertragung der Metra des Boetius? Anglia 5 1882.

Zimmermann, O. Über den Verfasser der altenglischen Metren des Boetius. Greifswald 1882.

Leicht, A. Ist König Ælfred der Verfasser der alliterierenden Metra des Boetius? Anglia 6 1883. Addn, 7 1884.

Kern, J. H. A few notes on the Metra of Boethius in Old English. Neophilologus 8 1923.

Schmidt, K. H. König Alfreds Boethius-Bearbeitung. Göttingen 1934.

Sisam, K. Authorship of the verse translation of Boethius' Metra. In his Studies in the history of Old English literature, Oxford 1953.

Otten, K. König Alfreds Boethius. Tübingen 1964.

Benson, L. D. The literary character of Anglo-Saxon formulaic poetry. PMLA 81 1966.

Payne, F. A. King Alfred and Boethius: an analysis of the Old English version of the Consolation of philosophy. Madison 1969.

Conlee, J. W. A note on verse composition in the Meters of Boethius. Neuphilologische Mitteilungen 71 1970.

Metcalf, A. A. On the authorship and originality of the Meters of Boethius. Ibid.

See further under Alfredian Prose: Boethius, below.

METRICAL CHARMS

Edns, trns and criticism of individual charms to 1948, and general works on magic, medicine and religion are not listed here. See full discussion and bibliography in Storms, 1948, and see also under Prose: Science and Medicine, Charms, below.

  Mss: BM Cotton Caligula A. vii (for unfruitful land), 176a–8a.
  BM Harley 585 (nine herbs), 160a–3b; (against a dwarf), 167a–7b; (for a sudden stitch), 175a–6a; (for loss of cattle), 180b–1a; (for delayed birth), 185a–b.
  BM Royal ms 12D. xvii (for the water-elf disease), 125a–b.
  Corpus Christi College Cambridge 41 (for a swarm of bees), numbered p. 182; (for theft of cattle), numbered p. 206; (for loss of cattle), ibid; (a journey charm), numbered pp. 350–3.
  BM Royal ms 4A. xiv (against a wen), 106b.

§1

Cockayne, O. Leechdoms, wortcunning and starcraft of early England. 3 vols 1864–6. With trn.

Grendon, F. The Anglo-Saxon charms. Jnl of Amer Folklore 22 1909; New York 1909 (separately). With trn.

Krapp-Dobbie 6 1942.

Storms, G. Anglo-Saxon magic. Hague 1948. With trn.

Grattan, J. H. G. and C. Singer. Anglo-Saxon magic and medicine. New York 1952. Pt 2 is an edn of Lacnunga (in Harley 585), containing 5 metrical charms.

§2

Helm, K. Der angelsächsische Flursegen. Hessische Blätter für Volkskunde 41 1950.

Schröder, F. R. Erce und Fjorgyn. In Erbe der Vergangenheit: Festgabe für K. Heml, Tübingen 1951.

Stürzl, E. Die christliche Elemente in den altenglischen Zaubersegen. Die Sprache 6 1960.

Schneider, K. Die strophischen Strukturen und heidnisch-religiösen Elemente der ae. Zauberspruchgruppe wið þeofðe. In Festschrift zum 75 Geburtstag von T. Spira, Heidelberg 1961.

Fife, A. F. Christian swarm charms from the ninth to the nineteenth centuries. Jnl of Amer Folklore 77 1964.

Hill, T. D. An Irish-Latin analogue for the blessing of the sods in the Old English Æcerbot charm. N & Q Oct 1968.

METRICAL EPILOGUE TO MS 41 CORPUS CHRISTI COLLEGE CAMBRIDGE

Holthausen, F. Altenglische Schreiberverse. Beiblatt zur Anglia 38 1927.

Sievers, E. Altenglische Schreiberverse. Beiträge zur Geschichte der Deutschen Sprache und Literatur 52 1928.

Krapp-Dobbie 6 1942.

METRICAL EPILOGUE TO THE PASTORAL CARE

Mss: Bodley, Hatton 20, 98a–b; Corpus Christi College Cambridge 12.

§1

Sweet, H. King Alfred's West-Saxon version of Gregory's Pastoral care. 1871 (EETS). With trn.

Holthausen, F. Die Gedichte in Ælfreds Übersetzung der Cura pastoralis. Archiv 106 1901.

Krapp-Dobbie 6 1942.

§2

Isaacs, N. D. Still waters run undiop. PQ 44 1965; rev in his Structural principles, Knoxville 1968.

Cross, J. E. The metrical epilogue to the Old English version of Gregory's Cura pastoralis. Neuphilologische Mitteilungen 70 1969.

METRICAL PREFACE TO GREGORY'S DIALOGUES

Ms: BM Cotton Otho C. i, pt 2, 1a.

§1

Holthausen, F. Die alliterierende Vorrede zur altenglischen Übersetzung von Gregors Dialogen. Archiv 105 1900. See Anglia 41 1917.

Cook, A. S. An unsuspected bit of Old English verse. MLN 17 1902.

Krapp-Dobbie 6 1942.

§2

Sisam, K. An Old English translation of a letter from Wynfrith to Eadburga (AD 716–17) in Cotton ms Otho C 1. MLR 18 1923; rptd in his Studies in the history of OE literature, Oxford 1953.

— Addendum: the verses prefixed to Gregory's Dialogues. In his Studies in the history of OE literature, Oxford 1953. With trn.

METRICAL PREFACE TO THE PASTORAL CARE

Mss: Bodley, Hatton 20, 2b; Bodley, Junius 53, numbered p. 4; Corpus Christi College Cambridge 12; Trinity College Cambridge R.5.22, 72a.

§1

Sweet, H. King Alfred's West-Saxon version of Gregory's Pastoral care. 1871 (EETS).
Körner, K. Einleitung in das Studium des Angelsächsischen II. Heilbronn 1880.
Holthausen, F. Die Gedichte in Alfreds Übersetzung der Cura pastoralis. Archiv 106 1901.
Krapp-Dobbie 6 1942.

§2

Sisam, K. The publication of Alfred's Pastoral care. In his Studies in the history of Old English literature, Oxford 1953.

ORDER OF THE WORLD

Ms: Exeter book 92b–4a.

§1

Krapp-Dobbie 3 1936.

§2

Isaacs, N. D. The exercise of art, part II: the order of the world. In his Structural principles, Knoxville 1968.
Huppé, B. F. The web of words. Albany NY 1970. With text and trn.

PANTHER

See Physiologus, *below.*

PARIS PSALTER

Ms: Bibliothèque Nationale, Paris, Fonds Latin 8824, 64a–175b. For prose see col 323, below.

§1

Thorpe, B. Libri psalmorum versio antiqua latina; cum paraphrasi anglo-saxonica. Oxford 1835.
Krapp-Dobbie 5 1932.
Bromwich, J. The Paris psalter. Copenhagen 1958 (facs).

§2

Bartlett, H. The metrical division of the Paris psalter. Baltimore 1896.
Holthausen, F. Zur altenglischen metrischen Psalmenübersetzung. Beiblatt zur Anglia 31 1920, 43 1932.
Diamond, R. E. The diction of the Anglo-Saxon metrical psalms. Hague 1963.
Morrell, M. C. A manual of Old English biblical materials. Knoxville 1965.

PARTRIDGE

See Physiologus, *below.*

PENITENT'S PRAYER

See Resignation, *below.*

PHARAOH

Ms: Exeter book 122a.

§1

Krapp-Dobbie 3 1936.

§2

Whitbread, L. The Old English poem Pharaoh. N & Q 9 Feb 1946.
Trahern, J. B. The Ioca monachorum and the Old English Pharaoh. Eng Lang Notes 7 1970.

PHOENIX

Ms: Exeter book 55b–65b.

§1

Grundtvig, N. F. S. Phenix-Fuglen. Copenhagen 1840. With Danish trn.
Schlotterose, O. Die altenglische Dichtung Phoenix. Bonner Beiträge zur Anglistik 25 1908. With trn.
Cook, A. S. The Old English Elene, Phoenix and Physiologus. New Haven 1919.
Krapp-Dobbie 3 1936.
Blake, N. F. The Phoenix. Manchester 1964.

Translations

Stephens, G. The King of birds: or the lay of the phoenix. Archaeologia 30 1844. Also pbd separately.
Grein, C. W. M. Der Vogel Phönix. Rinteln 1854.
Hall, J. L. Judith, Phoenix and other Anglo-Saxon poems. New York 1912.

§2

Gäbler, H. Über die Autorschaft des angelsächsischen Gedichtes vom Phoenix. Anglia 3 1880.
Bradshaw, M. R. The versification of the Old English Phoenix. Amer Jnl of Philology 15 1894.
Fulton, E. On the authorship of the Anglo-Saxon poem Phoenix. MLN 11 1896.
Holthausen, F. Zum Schluss der altenglischen Phönix. Archiv 112 1904.
Emerson, O. F. Originality in Old English poetry. RES 2 1926.
Hietsch, O. On the authorship of the Old English Phoenix. In Anglo-Americana: Festschrift für L. Hibler-Lebmannsport, Vienna 1955.
Blake, N. F. Originality in the Phoenix. N & Q Sept 1961.
— Some problems of interpretation and translation in the Old English Phoenix. Anglia 70 1962.
Cassidy, F. G. The edged teeth. In Studies in OE literature in honor of A. G. Brodeur, Eugene 1963.
Kantrowitz, J. S. The Anglo-Saxon Phoenix and tradition. PQ 43 1964.
Cross, J. E. The conception of the Old English Phoenix. In Old English poetry: fifteen essays, ed R. P. Creed, Providence RI 1967.
Thormann, J. Variations on the theme of 'the hero on the beach' in the Phoenix. Neuphilologische Mitteilungen 71 1970.
See also under Cynewulf, above.

PHYSIOLOGUS

Ms: Exeter book 95b–6b (Panther); 96b–7b (Whale); 97b–8b (Partridge).

§1

Cook, A. S. The Old English Elene, Phoenix and Physiologus. New Haven 1919. Text of Physiologus alone rptd 1922, with verse trn by J. H. Pitman.
Krapp-Dobbie 3 1936 (as 3 poems).

§2

Ebert, A. Der angelsächsische Physiologus. Anglia 6 1883.
Cook, A. S. The Old English Whale. MLN 9 1894.
Mann, M. F. Zur Bibliographie des Physiologus. Beiblatt zur Anglia 10 1900, 12–13 1902–3.
Sokoll, E. Zum angelsächsischen Physiologus. Marburg 1900.
Holthausen, F. Zum Physiologus. Beiblatt zur Anglia 12 1901.

Peebles, R. J. The Anglo-Saxon Physiologus. MP 8 1911.
Tupper, F. Notes on Old English poems 2: the Physiologus of the Exeter book. JEGP 11 1912.
Cordasco, F. The Old English Physiologus: its problems. MLQ 10 1949.

POEMS OF THE ANGLO-SAXON CHRONICLE

Here are considered the Capture of the Five Boroughs, Coronation of Edgar, Death of Edgar, Death of Alfred *and* Death of Edward. *See also* Battle of Brunanburh, *above.*

Mss: in 4 mss of the Chronicle: Corpus Christi College Cambridge 173, Cotton Tiberius A. vi, Cotton Tiberius B. i, Cotton Tiberius B. iv. The 2 poems on Edgar are not found in Cambridge ms; those on Alfred and Edward appear only in last 2. See under respective dates: 942, 973, 975, 1036, 1065.

§ 1

Sedgefield, W. J. The battle of Maldon and short poems from the Saxon Chronicle. Boston 1904.
Craigie, W. A. Specimens of Anglo-Saxon poetry III. Edinburgh 1931.
Krapp-Dobbie 6 1942.
See also under Prose: Anglo-Saxon Chronicle, *below, for edns and trns. Individual poems appear in many readers.*

§ 2

Abegg, J. D. Zur Entwicklung der historischen Dichtung bei den Angelsachsen. Strasbourg 1894.
Neuendorff, B. Das Gedicht auf den Tod Eadweards des Martyres. Archiv 128 1912.
Mawer, A. The redemption of the five boroughs. EHR 38 1923.
Holthausen, F. Zu dem ae. Gedichte von Ælfreds Tode (1036). Beiblatt zur Anglia 50 1939.
Isaacs, N. D. The death of Edgar (and others). Amer N & Q 4 1965; rev in his Structural principles, Knoxville 1968.

A PRAYER

Mss: BM Cotton Julius A. ii, 136a–7a; Lambeth Palace Lib 427, 183b.

§ 1

Junius, F. Cædmonis monachi paraphrasis poetica Genesios. Amsterdam 1655.
Thomson, E. Select monuments of the doctrine and worship of the Catholic Church in England before the Norman Conquest. 1849. With trn.
Bouterwek, K. W. Cædmons des Angelsachsen biblische Dichtungen. Vol 1, Gütersloh 1854. With trn.
Nilsson, L. G. Några fornengelska andeliga qväden på grundspråket. Lund 1857. With trn.
Krapp-Dobbie 6 1942.

§ 2

Cook, A. S. New texts of the Old English Lord's Prayer and hymns. MLN 7 1892.
Holthausen, F. Beiblatt zur Anglia 5 1895, 31 1920.

PRECEPTS

Ms: Exeter book 80a–1b.

§ 1

Krapp-Dobbie 3 1936.

§ 2

Bright, J. W. Notes on Fæder larcwidas. MLN 10 1895.

A PROVERB FROM WINFRID'S TIME

Ms: Nationalbibliothek, Vienna 751 (letters of St Boniface) 34b–5a.

§ 1

Kemble, J. M. Anglo-Saxon proverb. GM June 1836.
Krapp-Dobbie 6 1942.

§ 2

Holthausen, F. Der altenglische Spruch aus Winfrids Zeit. Archiv 106 1901.
Williams, B. C. Gnomic poetry in Anglo-Saxon. New York 1914.

PSALM 50

Ms: BM Cotton Vespasian D. vi, 70a–3b.

§ 1

Krapp-Dobbie 6 1942.

RESIGNATION

Ms: Exeter book 117b–19b.

§ 1

Krapp-Dobbie 3 1936.

§ 2

Rieger, M. Über Cynevulf IV. Zeitschrift für Deutsche Philologie 1 1868.
Klæber, F. Zu altenglischen Dichtungen. Archiv 167 1935.
Stanley, E. G. Old English poetic diction and the interpretation of the Wanderer, the Seafarer and the Penitent's prayer. Anglia 73 1956; rptd in Essential articles for the study of OE poetry, ed J. B. Bessinger and S. J. Kahrl, Hamden Conn 1968.
Prins, A. A. The Wanderer (and the Seafarer). Neophilologus 48 1964.
Henry, P. L. The early English and Celtic lyric. 1966.
See other general discussions under Elegies, *above.*

RIDDLES

Ms: Exeter book 101a–15a, 122b–3a, 124a–130b.

§ 1

Tupper, F. The riddles of the Exeter book. Boston 1910.
Wyatt, A. J. Old English riddles. Boston 1912.
Trautmann, M. Die altenglischen Rätsel. Heidelberg 1915.
Krapp-Dobbie 3 1936.

Translations

Baum, P. F. The Anglo-Saxon riddles of the Exeter book. Durham NC 1963 (complete).
Abbott, H. H. The riddles of the Exeter book. Cambridge 1968.
Crossley-Holland, K. Storm and other Old English riddles, 1970.
See also under Exeter book, *above. Selected riddles and trns appear in many readers and literary histories; some recent trns by B. Raffel, in his Poems from the Old English, Lincoln Nebraska 1960, 1964 (rev and enlarged), and by K. Crossley-Holland, in his Battle of Maldon and other Old English poems, 1965.*

§2

Dietrich, [F.] Die Räthsel des Exeterbuchs. Zeitschrift für Deutsches Altertum 11–12 1859–65.

Müller, E. Die Rätsel des Exeterbuches. Cöthen 1861.

Grein, C. W. M. Kleine Mittheilungen 2: zu den Rätseln des Exeterbuches. Germania 10 1865.

Ebert, A. Die Rätsel-Poesie der Angelsachsen. Berichte über die Verhandlung der Königlich Sächsischen Gesellschaft der Wissenschaft, philologisch-historische Klasse 29 1877.

Prehn, A. Komposition und Quellen der Rätsel des Exeterbuches. Neuphilologische Studien no 3, Paderborn 1883.

Trautmann, M. Cynewulf und die Rätsel. Anglia Anzeiger 6 1883.

— Zum 89 (95) Rätsel. Anglia Anzeiger 7 1884.

— Die Auflösungen der altenglischen Rätsel. Beiblatt zur Anglia 5 1894. Further solutions 25 1914; Anglia 17 1895, 36 1912, 42–3 1918–19; Bonner Beiträge zur Anglistik 17, 19 1905.

— Das Geschlecht in den altenglischen Rätseln. Beiblatt zur Anglia 25 1914.

— Die Quelle der altenglischen Rätsel; Sprache und Versbau; Zeit, Heimat und Verfasser. Anglia 38 1914.

Hicketier, F. Fünf Rätsel des Exeterbuches. Anglia 10 1888.

Nuck, R. Zu Trautmanns Deutung des ersten und neunundachtzigen Rätsels. Ibid.

Herzfeld, G. Die Räthsel des Exeterbuches und ihr Verfasser. Acta Germanica 11, pt i, Berlin 1890.

Cook, A. S. Recent opinion concerning the riddles of the Exeter book. MLN 7 1892.

Walz, J. Notes on the Anglo-Saxon riddles. Harvard Stud 5 1896.

Madert, A. Die Sprache der altenglischen Rätsel des Exeterbuches und die Cynewulf-frage. Marburg 1900.

Blackburn, F. A. The husband's message and the accompanying riddles of the Exeter book. JEGP 3 1901.

Erlemann, E. Zu den altenglischen Rätseln. Archiv 111 1903. See 115 1903.

Tupper, F. The comparative study of riddles: originals and analogues of the Exeter book riddles. MLN 18 1903.

— Solutions of the Exeter book riddles. MLN 21 1906.

Holthausen, F. Anglia 24 1901, 35 1912, 38 1914; Beiblatt zur Anglia 16 1905, 30 1919, 36 1925; E Studien 36 1906, 51 1917, 74 1941; Germanisch-romanische Monatsschrift 15 1927; Archiv 188 1951. Textual notes.

Liebermann, F. Das angelsächsische Rätsel 56: 'Galgen' als Waffenständer. Archiv 114 1905.

Sonke, E. Zu dem 25 Rätsel des Exeterbuches. E Studien 37 1907.

Bradley, H. Two riddles of the Exeter book. MLR 6 1911.

Lowenthal, F. Studien zum germanischen Rätsel. Heidelberg 1914.

Wood, G. A. The Anglo-Saxon riddles. Aberystwyth Stud 1–2 1912–14.

Swaen, A. E. H. Het 18ᵉ oudengelsche raadsel. Neophilologus 4 1918.

— Het angelsaksische raadsel 58. Neophilologus 13 1928.

— Riddle XIII (XVI). Neophilologus 26 1941.

— The Anglo-Saxon horn riddles. Ibid.

— Riddle 63 (60, 62). Neophilologus 27 1942.

— Riddle 9 (6, 8). Studia Neophilologica 14 1942.

— Riddle 9 (12) and 8 (10, 11). Neophilologus 30 1946.

— Notes on Anglo-Saxon riddles. Neophilologus 31 1947.

Patch, H. R. Anglo-Saxon riddle 56. MLN 35 1920.

Erhardt-Siebold, E. von. Die lateinischen Rätsel der Angelsachsen. Heidelberg 1925.

— History of the bell in a riddle's nutshell. E Studien 69 1934.

— Old English riddle no 4. PMLA 61 1946.

— Old English riddle no 39. Ibid.

— The Anglo-Saxon riddle 74 and Empedokles' fragment 117. MÆ 15 1946. Addn, 21 1952.

— Old English riddle no 57. PMLA 62 1947.

— Old English riddle no 95. MLN 62 1947.

— The Old English hunt riddles. PMLA 63 1948.

— The Old English storm riddles. PMLA 64 1949.

— The Old English loom riddles. In Philologica: the [Kemp] Malone anniversary studies, Baltimore 1949.

— Old English riddle 13. MLN 65 1950.

— Old English Riddle 23, bow, OE boga. Ibid.

Crotch, W. J. B. An Old English riddle. TLS 17 June 1926.

Colgrave, B. and B. M. Griffiths. A suggested solution of riddle 61. MLR 31 1936.

Colgrave, B. Some notes on riddle 21. MLR 32 1937.

Konick, M. Exeter book riddle 41 as a continuation of riddle 40. MLN 54 1939.

Young, J. I. Riddle 8 of the Exeter book. RES 18 1942.

— Riddle 15 of the Exeter book. RES 20 1944.

Brodeur, A. G. The man, the horse and the canary. California Folklore Quart 2 1943.

Klaeber, F. Das 9 [ste] altenglische Rätsel. Archiv 182 1943.

White, B. Three notes on Old and Middle English 2: the barnacle goose legend. MLR 40 1945.

Shook, L. K. Old-English riddle 1: fire. Mediaeval Stud 8 1946.

— Old-English riddle 28: testudo (tortoise-lyre). Mediaeval Stud 20 1958.

— Old English riddle no 20: heoruswealwe. In Franciplegius: medieval and linguistic studies in honor of F. P. Magoun, New York 1965.

Eliason, N. E. Riddle 68 of the Exeter book. In Philologica: the [Kemp] Malone anniversary studies, Baltimore 1949.

— Four Old English cryptographic riddles. SP 49 1952.

Derloez, R. Runica manuscripta: the English tradition. Bruges 1954.

Blakely, L. Riddles 22 and 58 of the Exeter book. RES new ser 9 1958.

Århammar, N. Altsächsische skion m. Wolke und altenglische scēo (?), mit einem Beitrag zur Textkritik von Genesis 16ff und des altenglischen Rätsels vom Gewittersturm. Jahrbuch des Vereins für Niederdeutsche Sprachforschung 87 1964.

Adams, J. F. The Anglo-Saxon riddle as lyric mode. Criticism 7 1965.

Hacikyan, A. The Exeter manuscript: riddle 19. Eng Lang Notes 3 1965.

— A linguistic and literary analysis of Old English riddles. Montreal 1966.

— The literary and the social aspects of the Old English riddles. Revue de l'Université d'Ottawa 36 1966.

— Emendations for Codex Exoniensis, folios 101a–15a; 122b–3a; 124b–30b. Revue de l'Université d'Ottawa 37 1967.

— The modern English readings of Codex Exoniensis, folios 101a–15a; 122b–3a; 124b–30b. Revue de l'Université d'Ottawa 39 1969.

Garvin, K. Nemnað hy sylfe: a note on riddle 57, Exeter book. Classica et Mediaevalia 27 1966.

Blauner, D. G. The early literary riddle. Folklore 78 1967.

Kaske, R. E. A poem of the Cross in the Exeter book: riddle 60 and the Husband's message. Traditio 23 1967.

Kay, D. Riddle 20: a revaluation. Tennessee Stud in Lit 13 1968.

Kossick, S. Old English riddles. Unisa 1968.

Leslie, R. F. The integrity of riddle 60. JEGP 67 1968.

Whitman, F. H. Old English riddle 74. Eng Lang Notes 6 1968.

—— The origin of Old English riddle LXV. N & Q June 1968.
—— The Christian background to two riddle motifs. Studia Neophilologica 41 1969.
—— Medieval riddling. Neuphilologische Mitteilungen 71 1970.
—— Riddle 60 and its source. PQ 50 1971.
Reisner, T. A. Riddle 75 (Exeter book). Explicator 28 1970.

RIMING POEM

Ms: Exeter book 94a–5b.

§1

Mackie, W. S. The Old English rhymed poem. JEGP 21 1922. With trn.
Holthausen, F. Das altenglische Reimlied. E Studien 65 1931. With trn.
—— Das altenglische Reimlied. Germanisch-romanische Monatsschrift new ser 3 1953. Another edn, with trn.
Krapp-Dobbie 3 1936.
Lehmann, R. P. M. The Old English Riming poem: interpretation, text and translation. JEGP 69 1970.

§2

Grein, C. W. M. Kleine Mitteilungen: das Reimlied des Exeterbuches. Germania 10 1865. With Latin trn.
Rieger, M. Über Cynevulf iv. Zeitschrift für Deutsche Philologie 1 1869.
Sievers, E. Zum angelsächsischen Reimlied. Beiträge zur Geschichte der Deutschen Sprache und Literatur 11 1886.
Holthausen, F. Beiblatt zur Anglia 20–1 1909–10, 31 1920, 41 1930, 46 1935; Studien zur Englischen Philologie 50 1913; E Studien 74 1941. Notes.
Cross, J. E. Aspects of microcosm and macrocosm in Old English literature. Comparative Lit 14 1962; rptd in Studies in OE literature in honor of A. G. Brodeur, Eugene 1963.
Schaar, C. Brondhord in the Old English rhyming poem. E Studies 43 1962.
Lehmann, R. P. M. A lacuna in the Riming poem of the Exeter book. Eng Lang Notes 3 1965.
Goldsmith, M. E. Corroding treasure: a note on the Old English Rhyming poem lines 45–50. N & Q May 1967.
Isaacs, N. D. The exercise of art, part 1: the Rhyming poem. In his Structural principles, Knoxville 1968.

RUIN

Ms: Exeter book 123b–4b.

§1

Leo, H. Carmen anglosaxonicum in codice exoniensi servatum quod vulgo inscribitur Ruinæ. Halle 1865.
Earle, J. An ancient Saxon poem of a city in ruins, supposed to be Bath. Proc of Bath Natural History Club 2 1871. With trn.
Krapp-Dobbie 3 1936.
Leslie, R. F. Three Old English elegies: the Wife's lament, the Husband's message, the Ruin. Manchester 1961.

Translations

Earle, J. The ruined city. Academy 26 1884.
Abbott, C. C. Three Old English elegies. Durham Univ Jnl 36 1944.
Massingham, H. The ruin (after the Anglo-Saxon). TLS 18 Aug 1966.
See also under Elegies, *above.*

§2

Wülcker, R. P. Ruine. Anglia 2 1879.
Kirkland, J. H. A passage in the Anglo-Saxon poem the Ruin critically discussed. Amer Jnl of Philology 7 1886.
Hicketier, F. Klage der Frau, Botschaft des Gemahls, und Ruine. Anglia 11 1889.
Nenninger, J. Die altenglische Ruine. Limburg 1938.
Herben, S. J. The ruin. MLN 54 1939. Addn, 59 1944.
Hotchner, C. A. Wessex and Old English poetry, with special consideration of the Ruin. New York 1939.
Cross, J. E. Notes on Old English texts. Neophilologus 39 1955.
—— On Sievers-Brunner's interpretation of the Ruin, line 7, 'forweorone geleorene'. Eng & Germanic Stud 6 1957.
Dunleavy, G. W. A De excidio tradition in the Old English Ruin? PQ 38 1959.
—— Colum's other island: the Irish at Lindisfarne. Madison 1960.
Baker, S. A. 'Weal' in the Old English Ruin. N & Q Sept 1963. Reply by E. G. Stanley, Nov 1963.
Keenan, H. T. The ruin as Babylon. Tennessee Stud in Lit 11 1966.
Calder, D. G. Perspective and movement in the Ruin. Neuphilologische Mitteilungen 72 1971.
See also under Elegies, *above.*

RUNE POEM

Ms: BM Cotton Otho B. x, 165a–5b, burnt in 1731, but ptd in Hickes's Thesaurus, 1705.

§1

Botkine, L. La chanson des runes. Le Havre 1879. With trn.
Dickins, B. Runic and heroic poems. 1915. With trn.
Krapp-Dobbie 6 1942.

§2

Hempl, G. Hickes's additions to the Runic poem. MP 1 1904.
Grienberger, T. von. Das ags. Runengedicht. Anglia 41 1921.
Klaeber, F. Die Ing-Verse im angelsächsischen Runengedicht. Archiv 142 1921.
Keller, W. Zum altenglischen Runengedicht. Anglia 60 1936.
—— Zur Chronologie der ae. Runen. Anglia 42 1938.
Krappe, A. H. Le char d'Ing. Revue Germanique 24 1933.
Arntz, H. Handbuch der Runenkunde. Halle 1935, 1944 (rev). With edn and trn.
Redbond, W. J. Notes on the word Eolhx. MLR 31 1936.
Krause, W. Ing. Nachrichten von der Akademie der Wissenschaften in Göttingen, philologisch-historische Klasse 1944.
Derolez, R. Runica manuscripta: the English tradition. Bruges 1954.
Elliott, R. W. V. Runes. Manchester 1959.

RUTHWELL CROSS

Bibliographies

Marquardt, H. Die Runeninschriften der britischen Inseln. In Bibliographie der Runeninschriften nach Fundorten pt 1, Göttingen 1961.
Runic inscriptions on east and west faces of lower shaft.

§1

Viëtor, W. Die northumbrischen Runensteine. Marburg 1895.

Cook, A. S. The dream of the rood. Oxford 1905.

Brown, G. B. The arts in early England V. 1921.

Dickins, B. and A. S. C. Ross. The dream of the rood. 1934.

Bütow, H. Das altenglische Traumgesicht vom Kreuz. Heidelberg 1935.

Krapp-Dobbie 6 1942.

§2

Kemble, J. M. On Anglo-Saxon runes. Archaeologia 28 1840.

— Additional observations on the runic obelisk at Ruthwell. Archaeologia 30 1844.

[MacFarlan, J.] The Ruthwell Cross. Edinburgh 1885, Dumfries 1896.

Cook, A. S. The date of the Ruthwell Cross. Academy 37 1890.

— Notes on the Ruthwell Cross. PMLA 17 1902.

— The date of the Ruthwell and Bewcastle Crosses. Trans of Connecticut Acad of Arts & Sciences 17 1912.

Rousseau, H. La Ruthwell Cross. Annales de la Société d'Archéologie de Bruxelles 16 1902.

Hewison, J. K. The runic roods of Ruthwell and Bewcastle. Glasgow 1914.

Forbes, M. D. and B. Dickins. The inscriptions of the Ruthwell and Bewcastle crosses and the Bridekirk font. Burlington Mag 25 1914.

— The Ruthwell and Bewcastle crosses. MLR 10 1915.

Browne, G. F. The ancient cross shafts at Bewcastle and Ruthwell. Cambridge 1916.

Dinwiddie, J. L. The Ruthwell Cross and its story. Dumfries 1927.

Keller, W. Zur Chronologie der ae. Runen. Anglia 62 1938.

Elliott, R. W. V. Runes. Manchester 1959.

Rissanen, M. Two notes on Old English poetic texts: Beowulf 2461, Ruthwell Cross III, 3. Neuphilologische Mitteilungen 68 1967.

Burlin, R. B. The Ruthwell Cross, the Dream of the rood and the vita contemplativa. SP 65 1968.

See also under General Works: Paleography, Runic Script, above.

SEAFARER

Ms: Exeter book 81b–3a.

§1

Krapp-Dobbie 3 1936.

Gordon, I. L. The seafarer. 1960.

Translations

Pound, E. The seafarer from the Anglo-Saxon. In his Personae, New York 1926.

Bone, G. The seafarer. MÆ 3 1934; rptd in his Anglo-Saxon poetry, Oxford 1943.

Abbott, C. C. The seafarer. Durham Univ Jnl 35 1943.

Whitelock, D. In her English historical documents vol I, c. 500–1042, 1955.

See also under Elegies, above.

§2

Rieger, M. Seefahrer als Dialog hergestellt. Zeitschrift für Deutsche Philologie 1 1869. With text.

Kluge, F. Zu altenglischen Dichtungen 1: der Seefahrer. E Studien 6 1883. Addn, 8 1885.

Hönncher, E. Zur Dialogeinteilung im Seefahrer (A) und zur zweiten homiletischen Partie (B) dieses Gedichtes. Anglia 9 1886.

Ferrell, C. C. Old Germanic life in the Anglo-Saxon Wanderer and Seafarer. MLN 9 1894.

Lawrence, W. W. The Wanderer and the Seafarer. JEGP 4 1902.

Boer, R. C. Wanderer und Seefahrer. Zeitschrift für Deutsche Philologie 35 1903.

Imelmann, R. Wanderer und Seefahrer im Rahmen der altenglischen Odoaker-Dichtung. Berlin 1908.

Ehrismann, G. Religionsgeschichtliche Beiträge zum germanischen Frühchristentum II: das Gedicht vom Seefahrer. Beiträge zur Geschichte der Deutschen Sprache und Literatur 35 1909.

Daunt, M. The Seafarer ll. 97–102. MLR 11 1916.

— Some difficulties of the Seafarer reconsidered. MLR 13 1918.

Schücking, L. L. Heroische Ironie im angelsächsischen Seefahrer. In Englische Kultur in sprachwissenschaftlicher Deutung: Festschrift für M. Deutschbein, Leipzig 1936.

Anderson [Arngart], O. S. The seafarer: an interpretation. Kungliga Humanistiska Vetenskapssamfundets i Lund Årsberättelse 1 1938.

Liljegren, S. B. Some notes on the Old English poem the Seafarer. Studia Neophilologica 14 1942.

Sisam, K. The seafarer lines 97–102. RES 21 1945.

Whitelock, D. The interpretation of the Seafarer. In The early cultures of north-west Europe, ed C. Fox and B. Dickins, Cambridge 1950; rptd in Essential articles for the study of OE poetry, ed J. B. Bessinger and S.J. Kahrl, Hamden Conn 1968.

Goldsmith, M. E. The seafarer and the birds. RES new ser 5 1954.

Gordon, I. L. Traditional themes in the Wanderer and the Seafarer. Ibid.

Greenfield, S. B. Attitudes and values in the Seafarer. SP 51 1954.

— Min, sylf and dramatic voices in the Wanderer and the Seafarer. JEGP 68 1969.

Cross, J. E. Ubi sunt passages in Old English: sources and relationships. Vetenskaps-societeten i Lund Årsbok 1956.

— On the allegory in the Seafarer: illustrative notes. MÆ 28 1959.

— Aspects of microcosm and macrocosm in Old English literature. Comparative Lit 14 1962; rptd in Studies in OE literature in honor of A. G. Brodeur, Eugene 1963.

Stanley, E. G. Old English poetic diction and the interpretation of the Wanderer, the Seafarer and the Penitent's prayer. Anglia 73 1956; rptd in Essential articles for the study of OE poetry, ed J. B. Bessinger and S. J. Kahrl, Hamden Conn 1968.

Smithers, G. V. The meaning of the Seafarer and the Wanderer. MÆ 26 1957, 28 1959.

Bolton, W. F. Connectives in the Seafarer and the Dream of the rood. MP 57 1960.

Campbell, J. J. Oral poetry in the Seafarer. Speculum 35 1960.

Denny, N. Image and symbol in the Seafarer. Theoria (Natal Univ College) 14 1960.

Dunleavy, G. W. Colum's other island: the Irish at Lindisfarne. Madison 1960.

O'Neil, W. A. Another look at oral poetry in the Seafarer. Speculum 35 1960.

Salmon, V. The Wanderer and the Seafarer, and the Old English conception of the soul. MLR 55 1960.

Bessinger, J. B. The oral text of Ezra Pound's the Seafarer. Quart Jnl of Speech 47 1961.

Blake, N. F. The seafarer lines 48–9. N & Q May 1962.

Rigby, M. The seafarer, Beowulf l. 769 and a Germanic conceit. N & Q July 1962.

Prins, A. A. The Wanderer (and the Seafarer). Neophilologus 48 1964.

Pheifer, J. D. The seafarer 43–5. RES new ser 16 1965.

Pope, J. C. Dramatic voices in the Wanderer and the Seafarer. In Franciplegius: medieval and linguistic studies in honor of F. P. Magoun, New York 1965; rptd in Essential articles for the study of OE poetry, ed J. B. Bessinger and S. J. Kahrl, Hamden Conn 1968.

Stevick, R. D. The text and the composition of the Seafarer. PMLA 80 1965.

Isaacs, N. D. Image, metaphor, irony, allusion and moral: the shifting perspective of the Seafarer. Neuphilologische Mitteilungen 67 1966; rev in his Structural principles, Knoxville 1968.
—— The seafarer 109–15a. E Studies 48 1967.
Cherniss, M. D. The meaning of the Seafarer, lines 97–102. MP 66 1968.
Whittier, P. G. Spring in the Seafarer 48–50. N & Q Nov 1968.
Clemoes, P. A. M. Mens absentia cogitans in the Seafarer and the Wanderer. In Medieval literature and civilization: studies in memory of G. N. Garmonsway, 1969.
Calder, D. G. Setting and mode in the Seafarer and the Wanderer. Neuphilologische Mitteilungen 72 1971.
Diekstra, F. N. M. The seafarer 58–66a: the flight of the exiled soul to its fatherland. Neophilologus 55 1971.
See also under Elegies, above.

SEASONS FOR FASTING

Ms: BM additional ms 43,703 (transcript by Laurence Nowell, 1562, of Cotton Otho B. xi, destroyed in fire of 1731).

§ 1

Krapp-Dobbie 6 1942.
Holthausen, F. Ein altenglisches Gedicht über die Fastenzeiten. Anglia 71 1953.

§ 2

Flower, R. Laurence Nowell and a recovered Anglo-Saxon poem. BM Quart 8 1934.
Whitbread, L. Notes on the Seasons for fasting. N & Q 14 Dec 1946.
Leslie, R. F. Textual notes on the Seasons for fasting. JEGP 52 1953.
Sisam, K. Seasons of fasting. In his Studies in the history of OE literature, Oxford 1953.
Schabram, H. The seasons for fasting 206f. In Britannica: Festschrift für H. M. Flasdieck, Heidelberg 1960.
Heyworth, P. E. The Old English Seasons for fasting. Mediaeval Stud 26 1964.

SOLOMON AND SATURN

Mss: Corpus Christi College Cambridge 422, pp. 1–26 (1–13); from middle p. 6 to p. 12 is a fragment of a prose dialogue between Solomon and Saturn.
Corpus Christi College Cambridge 41, pp. 196–8 (98b–9b). Contains only ll. 1–94.

§ 1

Kemble, J. M. The dialogue of Salomon and Saturnus. 1848. With trn.
Schipper, J. Salomo und Saturn. Germania 22 1877.
Menner, R. J. The poetical dialogues of Solomon and Saturn. New York 1941.
Krapp-Dobbie 6 1942.
Wild, F. Salomon und Saturn. Sitzberichte der Österreichischen Akademie der Wissenschaften in Wien, philologisch-historische Klasse 243 1964. German verse trn of Menner text, with introd and notes.

§ 2

Schaumberg, W. Untersuchungen über das deutsche Spruchgedicht Salomo und Marolf. Beiträge zur Geschichte der Deutschen Sprache und Literatur 2 1876.
Vogt, F. Die deutschen Dichtungen von Salomon und Markolf 1. Halle 1880.
Holthausen, F. Anglia 23 1901, 35 1911; E Studien 37

1907, 51 1917; Beiblatt zur Anglia 21 1910, 27–8 1916–17, 31 1920; Archiv 188 1951. Textual notes.
Vincenti, A. R. von. Die altenglischen Dialoge von Salomon und Saturn. Leipzig 1904.
Larsen, H. Kemble's Salomon and Saturn. MP 26 1929.
Menner, R. J. The vasa mortis passage in the Old English Salomon and Saturn. In Studies in English philology in honor of F. Klaeber, Minneapolis 1929.
—— Nimrod and the wolf in the Old English Solomon and Saturn. JEGP 37 1938.
Derolez, R. Runica manuscripta: the English tradition. Bruges 1954.
Schneider, K. Die germanischen Runennamen: Versuch einer Gesamtdeutung. Meisenheim-am-Glan 1956.
Hopkins, R. H. A note on Solomon and Saturn II, 449 (Menner edition). N & Q June 1959.
Page, R. I. A note on the text of ms CCCC 422 (Solomon and Saturn). MÆ 34 1965.
Hill, T. D. The falling leaf and buried treasure: two notes on the imagery of Solomon and Saturn 314–22. Neuphilologische Mitteilungen 71 1970.
—— Two notes on Solomon and Saturn. MÆ 40 1971.

SOUL AND BODY I AND II

Mss: Vercelli book 101b–3b (I); Exeter book 98a–100a (II).

§ 1

Krapp-Dobbie 2–3 1932–6.

§ 2

Rieger, M. Addresses of soul and body. Germania 3 1858. Addn, Zeitschrift für Deutsche Philologie 1 1868.
Varnhagen, H. Addresses of soul and body. Anglia 2 1879.
Kleinert, G. Über den Streit zwischen Leib und Seele. Halle 1880.
Bruce, J. D. A contribution to the study of the body and soul poems in England. MLN 5 1890.
Kurtz, B. P. Gifer the worm: an essay toward the history of an idea. Univ of California Pbns in Eng 2 1929.
Willard, R. The address of the soul to the body. PMLA 50 1935.
Heningham, E. K. Old English precursors of the Worcester fragments. PMLA 55 1940.
Smetana, C. Second thoughts on Soul and body I. Mediaeval Stud 29 1967.
Whitbread, L. The doomsday theme in Old English poetry. Beiträge zur Geschichte der Deutschen Sprache und Literatur (Halle) 89 1967.
Gyger, A. The Old English Soul and body as an example of oral transmission. MÆ 38 1969.
Hill, T. D. Punishment according to the joints of the body in the Old English Soul and body II. N & Q Nov 1968. Addn, July 1969.
Ferguson, M. H. The structure of the soul's address to the body in Old English. JEGP 69 1970.

SUMMONS TO PRAYER

Ms: Corpus Christi College Cambridge 201, numbered pp. 166–7.

§ 1

Lumby, J. R. Be domes dæge. 1876 (EETS). With trn.
Krapp-Dobbie 6 1942.
Holthausen, F. Eine altenglische Aufforderung zum Gebet um Fürbitte. E Studien 75 1943.

§ 2

Förster, M. Zur Liturgik der angelsächsischen Kirche. Anglia 66 1946.
Whitbread, L. Notes on two minor Old English poems. Studia Neophilologica 29 1957.

THURETH

Ms: BM Cotton Claudius A. iii, 31b.

§ 1

Krapp-Dobbie 6 1942.

VAINGLORY

Ms: Exeter book 83a–4b.

§ 1

Krapp-Dobbie 3 1936.

§ 2

Doubleday, J. F. The allegory of the soul as fortress in Old English poetry. Anglia 88 1970.
Huppé, B. F. The web of words. Albany NY 1970. With text and trn.
Regan, C. A. Patristic psychology in the Old English Vainglory. Traditio 26 1970.

WALDERE

Ms: 2 leaves in the Royal Library at Copenhagen, Ny kgl. saml. 167b.

§ 1

Stephens, G. Two leaves of King Waldere's lay. Copenhagen 1860. With trn.
Dietrich, F. and K. Müllenhoff. Waldere. Zeitschrift für Deutsches Altertum 12 1865.
Möller, H. Das altenglische Volksepos in der ursprünglichen strophischen Form. Kiel 1883.
Learned, M. D. The saga of Walter of Aquitaine. PMLA 7 1892.
Holthausen, F. Die altenglischen Waldere-Bruchstücke. Gothenburg 1899. With facs.
Trautmann, M. *See under §2, 1900, below.*
Norman, F. Waldere. 1933, 1949 (rev).
Dickins, B. Runic and heroic poems of the old Teutonic peoples. Cambridge 1915. With trn.
Krapp-Dobbie 6 1942.
Schwab, U. Waldere: testo e commento. Messina 1967. With facs and Italian trn.
Also in many edns of Beowulf *and in many collections.*

Translations

Gummere, F. B. The oldest English epic. New York 1909.
Scott-Moncrieff, C. K. Widsith, Beowulf, Finnsburgh, Waldere, Deor. 1921.
Magoun, F. P. and H. M. Smyser. Walter of Aquitaine: materials for the study of his legend. New London 1950.
Genzmer, F. Das Waltharilied und die Waldere-Bruchstücke. Stuttgart 1953.

§ 2

Fischer, J. Zu den Waldere-Fragmenten. Breslau 1886.
Dieter, F. Die Walderefragmente und die ursprüngliche Gestalt der Walthersage. Anglia 10–11 1888–9.
Heinzel, R. Über die Walthersage. Vienna 1889.
Cosijn, P. J. De Waldere-Fragmenten. Verslagen en Mededeelingen der Koninklijke Akademie van Wetenschappen, Afd. Letterkunde 3rd ser 12 1896.
Althof, H. Über einige Stellen im Waltharius und die angelsächsischen Waldere-Fragmente. Bericht über das 43 Schuljahr des Realgymnasiums zu Weimar 1899.
Trautmann, M. Zur Berichtigung und Erklärung der Waldhere-Bruchstücke. Bonner Beiträge zur Anglistik 5 1900. With text and trn.
—— Zum zweiten Waldhere-Bruchstück. Bonner Beitrage zur Anglistik 11 1901.

Seemüller, J. Lieder von Walther und Hildegund. In Mélanges Godefroid Kurth vol 2, Liège 1908.
Simons, L. Waltharius en de Walthersage: Waldere. Leuvensche Bijdragen 12 1914.
Leitzmann, A. Walther und Hiltgunt bei den Angelsachsen. Halle 1917.
Neckel, G. Das Gedicht von Waltharius manu fortis: Waltharius und Waldere. Germanisch-romanische Monatsschrift 9 1921.
Krappe, A. H. The legend of Walther and Hildegund. JEGP 22 1923.
Schücking, L. L. Waldere und Waltharius. E Studien 60 1925.
Wolff, L. Zu den Waldere-Bruchstücken. Zeitschrift für Deutsches Altertum 62 1925.
Klaeber, F. Zu den Waldere-Bruchstücken. Anglia 51 1927. Addn, E Studien 70 1936.
Miller, D. C. The sequence of the Waldhere fragments. MÆ 10 1941.
Smyser, H. M. and F. P. Magoun. Survivals in Old Norwegian of medieval English, French and German literature, together with the Latin version of the heroic legend of Walter of Aquitaine. Baltimore 1941. *See also Magoun and Smyser under §1, above.*
Carroll, B. H. An essay on the Walther legend. Florida State Univ Stud no 5, 1952.
—— On the lineage of the Walther legend. Germanic Rev 28 1953.
Magoun, F. P. Two verses in the Old-English Waldere characteristic of oral poetry. Beiträge zur Geschichte der Deutschen Sprache und Literatur (Tübingen) 80 1958.
Eis, G. Waltharius-Probleme: Bemerkungen zu dem lateinische Waltharius, dem angelsächsischen Waldere und dem voralthochdeutschen Walthari. In Britannica: Festschrift für H. M. Flasdieck, Heidelberg 1960.
Pheifer, J. D. Waldere 1. 29–31. RES new ser 11 1960.
Kuhn, H. Zur Geschichte der Walthersaga. In Festgabe für U. Pretzel, Berlin 1963.
Berschin, W. Ergebnisse der Waltharius-Forschung seit 1951. Deutsches Archiv für Erforschung des Mittelalters 24 1968.
Norman, F. The evidence for the Germanic Walter lay. Acta Germanica 3 1968.

WANDERER

Ms: Exeter book 76b–8a.

§ 1

Krapp-Dobbie 3 1936.
Leslie, R. F. The wanderer. Manchester 1966.
Dunning, T. P. and A. J. Bliss. The wanderer. 1969.

Translations

Hickey, E. H. The wanderer. Academy 19 1881.
Sims, W. R. The wanderer. MLN 5 1890.
Brown, A. R. The wanderer's lament. Poet-lore 3 1891.
Fulton, E. On translating Anglo-Saxon poetry. PMLA 13 1898.
Abbott, C. C. Three Old English elegies. Durham Univ Jnl 36 1944.
Davison, D. Theoria (Natal Univ College) 8 1954.
Whitelock, D. In her English historical documents vol 1, c. 500–1042, 1955.
Stewart, J. T. The wanderer: a translation and interpretation. Furman Stud new ser 4 1957.
See also under Elegies, *above, and in most collections, both in Old English and in trn.*

§ 2

Rieger, M. Über Cynevulf v. Zeitschrift für Deutsche Philologie 1 1869.
Ferrell, C. Old Germanic life in the Anglo-Saxon Wanderer and Seafarer. MLN 9 1894.

Bright, J. W. The wanderer 78–84. MLN 13 1898.

Lawrence, W. W. The Wanderer and the Seafarer. JEGP 4 1902.

Boer, R. C. Wanderer und Seefahrer. Zeitschrift für Deutsche Philologie 35 1903.

Imelmann, R. Wanderer und Seefahrer im Rahmen der altenglischen Odoaker-Dichtung. Berlin 1908.

Ashdown, M. The wanderer ll. 41–3. MLR 22 1927.

Fischer, W. Wanderer, v. 25 und v. 6–7. Anglia 59 1935.

Huppé, B. F. The wanderer: theme and structure. JEGP 42 1943.

Lumiansky, R. M. The dramatic structure of the Old English Wanderer. Neophilologus 34 1950.

Owen, W. J. B. Wanderer lines 50–7. MLN 65 1950. Addn, 68 1953.

Greenfield, S. B. The wanderer: a reconsideration of theme and structure. JEGP 50 1951.

— Syntactic analysis and Old English poetry. Neuphilologische Mitteilungen 64 1963.

— Min, sylf and dramatic voices in the Wanderer and the Seafarer. JEGP 68 1969.

Robertson, D. W. Historical criticism. Eng Inst Essays 1950.

Brewer, D. S. Wanderer lines 50–7. MLN 67 1952.

French, W. H. The wanderer 98: wyrmlicum fah. MLN 67 1952.

Smithers, G. V. Five notes on Old English texts. Eng & Germanic Stud 4 1952.

— The meaning of the Seafarer and the Wanderer. MÆ 26 1957, 28 1959.

Gordon, I. L. Traditional themes in the Wanderer and the Seafarer. RES new ser 5 1954.

Suddaby, E. Three notes on Old English texts. MLN 69 1954.

Bowen, R. O. The wanderer 98. Explicator 13 1955.

Cross, J. E. Ubi sunt passages in Old English: sources and relationships. Vetenskaps-societeten i Lund Årsbok 1956.

— On the Wanderer lines 80–4: a study of a figure and a theme. Vetenskaps-societeten i Lund Årsbok 1959.

— On the genre of the Wanderer. Neophilologus 45 1961; rptd in Essential articles for the study of OE poetry, ed J. B. Bessinger and S. J. Kahrl, Hamden Conn 1968.

Stanley, E. G. Old English poetic diction and the interpretation of the Wanderer, the Seafarer and the Penitent's prayer. Anglia 73 1956; rptd in Essential articles for the study of OE poetry, ed J. B. Bessinger and S. J. Kahrl, Hamden Conn 1968.

Stewart, J. T. See under trns 1957, above.

Elliott, R. W. V. The wanderer's conscience. E Studies 39 1958.

Rumble, T. C. From eardstapa to snottor on mode: the structural principle of the Wanderer. MLQ 19 1958.

Tucker, S. I. Return to the Wanderer. EC 8 1958.

Midgely, G. The wanderer lines 49–55. RES new ser 10 1959.

Salmon, V. The Wanderer and the Seafarer, and the Old English conception of the soul. MLR 55 1960.

Erzgräber, W. Der Wanderer: eine Interpretation von Aufbau und Gehalt. In Festschrift zum 75 Geburtstag von T. Spira, Heidelberg 1961.

Prins, A. A. The Wanderer (and the Seafarer). Neophilologus 48 1964.

Rosier, J. L. The literal-figurative identity of the Wanderer. PMLA 79 1964.

Burrow, J. A. The wanderer lines 73–87. N & Q May 1965.

Dean, C. 'Weal wundrum heah, wyrmlicum fah' and the narrative background of the Wanderer. MP 63 1965.

Gottlieb, S. A. The metaphors of Wanderer. Neuphilologische Mitteilungen 66 1965.

Pope, J. C. Dramatic voices in the Wanderer and the Seafarer. In Franciplegius: medieval and linguistic studies in honor of F. P. Magoun, New York 1965; rptd in Essential articles for the study of OE poetry, ed J. B. Bessinger and S. J. Kahrl, Hamden Conn 1968.

Anthony, M. Aesthetic balance in the Wanderer. Lock Haven Rev no 8 1966.

Fowler, R. A theme in the Wanderer. MÆ 36 1967.

Mitchell, B. An Old English syntactical reverie: the Wanderer lines 22 and 34–6. Neuphilologische Mitteilungen 68 1967.

— Some syntactical problems in the Wanderer. Neuphilologische Mitteilungen 69 1968.

Rohrberger, M. A psychoanalytical reading of the Wanderer. Cimmaron Rev (Oklahoma) 1967.

Isaacs, N. D. Association and guilt: motive and structure in the Wanderer. In his Structural principles, Knoxville 1968.

Bolton, W. F. The dimensions of the Wanderer. Leeds Stud in Eng new ser 3 1969.

Clemoes, P. Mens absentia cogitans in the Sea-farer and the Wanderer. In Medieval literature and civilization: studies in memory of G. N. Garmonsway, 1969.

Doubleday, J. The three faculties of the soul in the Wanderer. Neophilologus 53 1969.

Malmberg, L. The Wanderer: waþema gebind. Neuphilologische Mitteilungen 71 1970.

Calder, D. G. Setting and mode in the Seafarer and the Wanderer. Neuphilologische Mitteilungen 72 1971.

Diekstra, F. N. M. The wanderer 65b–72: the passions of the mind and the cardinal virtues. Neophilologus 55 1971.

Taylor, P. B. Charms of 'wynn' and fetters of 'wyrd' in the Wanderer. Neuphilologische Mitteilungen 73 1972.

See also under Elegies, *above.*

WHALE

See Physiologus, *above.*

WIDSITH

Ms: Exeter book 84b–7a.

§1

Ettmüller, L. Scôpes vîdsidh: Sängers Weitfahrt. Zürich 1839. With trn.

Möller, H. Das altenglische Volksepos in der ursprünglichen strophischen Form. Kiel 1883.

Chambers, R. W. Widsith: a study in Old English heroic legend. Cambridge 1912. With trn.

Krapp-Dobbie 3 1936.

Malone, K. Widsith. 1936, Copenhagen 1962 (rev).

Also in many edns of Beowulf and in readers and collections.

Translations

Gummere, F. B. Widsith: a translation, with brief commentary. MLN 4 1889.

— The oldest English epic. New York 1909.

Scott-Moncrieff, C. K. Widsith, Beowulf, Finnsburgh, Waldere, Deor. 1921.

§2

Müllenhoff, K. Die deutschen Völker in Nord- und Ostsee in ältester Zeit. Nordalbingische Studien 1 1844.

— Zur Kritik des angelsächsischen Volksepos 2: Widsith. Zeitschrift für Deutches Altertum 11 1859.

Haigh, D. H. The Anglo-Saxon sagas. 1861.

Anderson, L. F. The Anglo-Saxon scop. Toronto 1903.

Lawrence, W. W. Structure and interpretation of Widsith. MP 4 1906.

Siebs, T. Wîdsîð. Die Neueren Sprachen (suppl) 1910.

Anscombe, A. Widsith. Anglia 34 1911.

— N & Q 1912–15. Notes.

— The historical side of the Old English poem of Widsith. Trans Royal Historical Soc 3rd ser 9 1915. Replies by R. W. Chambers and Anscombe, ibid.

Marquart, J. Studien zum Widsið. In Festschrift für V. Thomsen, Leipzig 1912.

Berendsohn, W. A. Widsiþ. Münchener Museum für Philologie 3 1916; rptd in his Zur Vorgeschichte des Beowulf, Copenhagen 1935.

Sievers, E. Zum Widsith. In Texte und Forschungen zur englischen Kulturgeschichte: Festgabe für F. Liebermann, Halle 1921.

Grienberger, T. von. Widsið. Anglia 46 1922.

Malone, K. Widsith and the Hervararsaga. PMLA 40 1925.

— Ealhild. Anglia 55 1935.

— The Frumtings of Widsith. E Studies 14 1932.

— Ic wæs mid Eolum. E Studien 67 1933.

— The suffix of appurtenance in Widsith. MLR 28 1933.

— Secca and Becca. In Studia germanica tillägnade E. A. Kock, Lund 1934; rptd in Studies in heroic legend, ed S. Einarsson and N. E. Eliason, Copenhagen 1959.

— The Theodoric of the Rök inscription. Acta Philologica Scandinavica 9 1934.

— Alliteration in Widsith. ELH 2 1935.

— Herlekin and Herlewin. E Studies 17 1935.

— The Lidwicings of Widsith. MÆ 6 1937.

— Mid Moidum ic wæs. Anglia 61 1937.

— Widsith and the critic. ELH 5 1938; rptd in Essential articles for the study of OE poetry, ed J. B. Bessinger and S. J. Kahrl, Hamden Conn 1968.

— Becca and Seafola. E Studien 73 1939; rptd in Studies in heroic legend, ed S. Einarsson and N. E. Eliason, Copenhagen 1959.

— Humblus and Lotherus. Acta Philologica Scandinavica 13 1939.

— The Myrgingas of Widsith. MLN 55 1940.

— The With-Myrgings of Widsith. MLR 39 1944.

— Variation in Widsith. JEPG 45 1946.

— Royal names in Old English poetry. Names 1 1953; rptd in Studies in heroic legend, ed S. Einarsson and N. E. Eliason, Copenhagen 1959.

— Widsith, Beowulf and Bravellir. In Festgabe für L. L. Hammerich, Copenhagen 1962.

— Qmð and Hinn. Islensk Tunga 6 1965.

— The Franks casket and the date of Widsith. In Nordica et Anglica: studies in honor of S. Einarsson, Hague 1968.

Much, R. Widsith: Beiträge zu einem Commentar. Zeitschrift für Deutsches Altertum 62 1925.

Sundén, K. F. Den fornengelska dikten Widsið. Gothenburg 1929. With Swedish trn.

Langenfelt, G. Notes on the Anglo-Saxon pioneers VI: the Widsith folk-names. E Studien 66 1931.

— Païens et héros dans le Widsith. Vetenskaps-Societeten i Lund Årsbok 1935.

— Studies on Widsith. Namn och Bygd 47 1959.

— Some Widsith names and the background of Widsith. In VI Internationaler Kongress für Namenforschung vol 3, ed G. Rohlfs and K. Puchner, Munich 1961.

Schlauch, M. Wīdsīth, Vīðförull and some other analogues. PMLA 46 1931.

Smith, A. H. Þeodric in Widsith and the Rök inscription. MLR 26 1931.

Johannson, A. ÞiaurikR miR hraiþkutum. Acta Philologica Scandinavica 7 1932.

Lintzel, M. Myrgingas und Mauringa. Beiträge zur Kultur-geographie: Petermanns Mittheilungen 214 (Festschrift für O. Schlüter) 1932.

Schütte, G. The problem of the Hraid-Goths. Acta Philologica Scandinavica 8 1933.

— Die Nationalität der Báninger. Beiträge zur Geschichte der Deutschen Sprache und Literatur 57 1933.

— Die umstrittenen Baininge. Beiträge zur Geschichte der Deutschen Sprache und Literatur 62 1938.

— Offa 1 reduced ad absurdum. Acta Philologica Scandinavica 19 1947.

Einarsson, S. Wídsíð: Víðförull. Skírnir 110 1936.

— Alternate recital by twos in Widsith (?), Sturlunga, and Kalevala. Arv, Jnl of Scandinavian Folklore 7 1951. Also in Icelandic in Skírnir 125 1951.

Gutenbrunner, S. Die Herkunft der Baininge. Beiträge zur Geschichte der Deutschen Sprache und Literatur 60 1936.

— Die Deanas im Widsith. Zeitschrift für Deutches Altertum 77 1940.

Brady, C. The Eormanric of the Widsīð. Univ of California Pbns in Eng 3 1937.

— Becca of the Banings. JEGP 37 1938.

— Innweorud Earmanrices. Speculum 15 1940.

— The legends of Ermanaric. Berkeley 1943.

Woolf, H. B. Three notes on Widsith. JEGP 36 1937.

Abercrombie, L. Widsith as art. Sewanee Rev 46 1938.

Magoun, F. P. Fifeldor and the name of the Eider. Namn och Bygd 28 1940.

Whitbread, L. N & Q 1942-3, 1944, 1946. Notes.

Boberg, I. M. Die Sage von Vermund und Uffe. Acta Philologica Scandinavica 16 1943.

— Er Skjoldungerne Hunnerkonger? Acta Philologica Scandinavica 18 1945.

French, W. H. Widsith and the scop. PMLA 60 1945.

Zink, G. Les légendes héroïques de Dietrich et d'Ermanrich dans les littératures germaniques. Lyons and Paris 1950.

Reynolds, R. L. Le poème anglo-saxon Widsith: réalité et fiction. Le Moyen Age 59 1953.

— Eadhild, duchesse de la Francia et Ealhild, patronne du scop de Widsith. Le Moyen Age 61 1955.

— Reconsideration of the history of the Suevi. Revue Belge 35 1957.

Meindl, R. J. The artistic unity of Widsith. Xavier Univ Stud 3 1964.

Eliason, N. E. Two Old English scop poems. PMLA 81 1966.

WIFE'S LAMENT

Ms: Exeter book 115a–b.

§1

Krapp-Dobbie 3 1936.

Leslie, R. F. Three Old English elegies: the Wife's lament, the Husband's message, the Ruin. Manchester 1961.

Translations

Abbott, C. C. Three Old English elegies. Durham Univ Jnl 36 1944.
See also under Elegies, above.

§2

Hicketier, F. Klage der Frau, Botschaft des Gemahls. Beiblatt zur Anglia 11 1889.

Roeder, F. Die Familie bei den Angelsachsen. Studien zur Englischen Philologie 4 1899.

Rickert, E. The Wife's complaint. MP 2 1905.

Schücking, L. L. Das angelsächsische Gedicht von der Klage der Frau. Zeitschrift für Deutsches Altertum 48 1906.

Lawrence, W. W. The banished wife's lament. MP 5 1908.

Stefanovič, S. Das angelsächsische Gedicht Die Klage der Frau. Anglia 32 1909.

Brunner, K. Hero und Leander und die altenglischen Elegien. Archiv 142 1921.

Greenfield, S. B. The Wife's lament reconsidered. PMLA 68 1953.

Dunleavy, G. W. Possible Irish analogues for the Wife's lament. PQ 35 1956.

— Colum's other island: the Irish at Lindisfarne. Madison 1960.

Stevick, R. D. Formal aspects of the Wife's lament. JEGP 59 1960.

Ward, J. A. The Wife's lament: an interpretation. Ibid.

Bouman, A. C. Patterns in Old English and Old Icelandic literature. Leyden 1962.

Malone, K. Two English Frauenlieder. Comparative Lit 14 1962; rptd in Studies in OE literature in honor of A. G. Brodeur, Eugene 1963. With trn.

Bambas, R. C. Another view of the Old English Wife's lament. JEGP 62 1963.

Fitzgerald, R. P. The Wife's lament and the Search for the lost husband. Ibid.

Swanton, M. J. The Wife's lament and the Husband's message: a reconsideration. Anglia 82 1964.

Davis, T. M. Another view of the Wife's lament. Papers on Lang & Lit 1 1965. With trn.

Curry, J. L. Approaches to a translation of the Anglo-Saxon the Wife's lament. MÆ 35 1966. With trn.

Doane, A. N. Heathen form and Christian function in the Wife's lament. Mediaeval Stud 28 1966.

Schulze, F. W. Die altenglische Klage der Frau. In Festschrift für E. Mertner, Munich 1968.

Stevens, M. The narrator of the Wife's lament. Neuphilologische Mitteilungen 69 1968.

Bolton, W. F. The Wife's lament and the Husband's message: a reconsideration revisited. Archiv 205 1969.

Lucas, A. M. The narrator of the Wife's lament reconsidered. Neuphilologische Mitteilungen 70 1969.

Rissanen, M. The theme of exile in the Wife's lament. Ibid.

Lench, E. The Wife's lament: a poem of the living dead. Comitatus 1 1970.

Patrick, M. D. The Wife's lament 24–41. Explicator 28 1970.

Rountree, T. J. The Wife's lament 25b–6. Explicator 29 1970.

Short, D. D. The Old English Wife's lament: an interpretation. Neuphilologische Mitteilungen 71 1970.

Wentersdorf, K. P. The situation of the narrator's lord in the Wife's lament. Ibid.

Johnson, L. A. The narrative structure of the Wife's lament. E Studies 52 1971.

Mitchell, B. The narrator of the Wife's lament. Neuphilologische Mitteilungen 73 1972.

See also under Elegies, *above.*

WULF AND EADWACER

Ms: Exeter book 100b.

§ 1

Krapp-Dobbie 3 1936.
Also in many edns of Riddles; see also under Elegies, *above.*

§ 2

Rieger, M. Über Cynevulf 1. Zeitschrift für Deutsche Philologie 1 1869.

Bradley, H. The first riddle of the Exeter book. Academy 33 1888; rptd in his Collected papers, 1928.

Gollancz, I. Wulf and Eadwacer: an Anglo-Saxon monodrama in five acts. Athenaeum 23 Dec 1893. With text and trn.

Holthausen, F. Zu alt- und mittelenglischen Denkmälern: Klage um Wulf. Anglia 15 1893. Reply by H. Bradley, ibid.

Cook, A. S. The Christ of Cynewulf. Boston 1900. With text and trn.

Lawrence, W. W. The first riddle of Cynewulf. PMLA 17 1902.

Schofield, W. H. Signy's lament. Ibid.

Imelmann, R. Die altenglische Odoaker-Dichtung. Berlin 1907.

Tupper, F. The Cynewulfian runes of the first riddle. MLN 25 1910.

Trautmann, M. Das sogenannte erste Rätsel. Anglia 36 1912.

Budjuhn, G. Leodum is minum: ein altenglischer Dialog. Anglia 40 1916.

Brunner, K. Hero und Leander und die altenglischen Elegien. Archiv 142 1921.

Patzig, H. Zum ersten Rätsel des Exeterbuchs. Archiv 145 1923.

Sedgefield, W. J. Old English notes 1: Wulf und Eadwacer. MLR 26 1931.

Whitbread, L. A note on Wulf and Eadwacer. MÆ 10 1941.

Bouman, A. C. Leodum is minum: Beadohild's complaint. Neophilologus 33 1949; rptd in his Patterns in OE and Old Icelandic literature, Leyden 1962.

Adams, J. F. Wulf and Eadwacer: an interpretation. MLN 73 1958.

Frankis, P. J. Deor and Wulf and Eadwacer: some conjectures. MÆ 31 1962.

Malone, K. Two English Frauenlieder. Comparative Lit 14 1962; rptd in Studies in OE literature in honor of A. G. Brodeur, Eugene 1963. With trn.

Renoir, A. Wulf and Eadwacer: a noninterpretation. In Franciplegius: medieval and linguistic studies in honor of F. P. Magoun, New York 1965.

Isaacs, N. D. A negative note on Wulf and Eadwacer. In his Structural principles, Knoxville 1968.

Lehmann, R. P. M. The metrics and structure of Wulf and Eadwacer. PQ 48 1969.

Fry, D. K. Wulf and Eadwacer: a wen charm. Chaucer Rev 5 1971.
See also under Elegies *and* Riddles, *above.*

S. B. G.

C. PROSE

See J. R. Bennet, English prose style from Alfred to More: a bibliography, *Mediaeval Stud 5 1969.*
For a description of all the mss and their contents and for a list of the main edns and the mss on which they draw, see N. R. Ker, Catalogue of manuscripts containing Anglo-Saxon, *Oxford 1957.*

(1) COLLECTIONS AND ANTHOLOGIES

Bibliothek der angelsächsischen Prosa. Ed C. W. M. Grein, R. Wülcker and H. Hecht 13 vols Cassel, Leipzig and Hamburg 1872–1933. *Some vols rptd with supplementary material; see individual texts below.*

Sweet, H. Anglo-Saxon primer. Oxford 1882, 1953 (9th edn, rev N. Davis).

Craigie, W. A. Specimens of Anglo-Saxon prose. 2 pts Edinburgh 1923–5.

Sedgefield, W. J. An Anglo-Saxon prose book. Manchester 1928.

Raith, J. Altenglisches Lesebuch (Prosa). Munich 1940, 1958 (rev).

Translations

Cook, A. S. and C. B. Tinker. Select translations from Old English prose. Boston 1908.

For trns of numerous OE prose texts see D. Whitelock, English historical documents c. 500–1042, *1955.*

(2) GENERAL CRITICISM

Tupper, J. W. Tropes and figures in Anglo-Saxon prose. Baltimore 1897.

Chambers, R. W. On the continuity of English prose from Alfred to More and his school. In Nicholas Harpsfield, Life of Sir Thomas Moore, ed E. V. Hitchcock and R. W. Chambers 1932 (EETS); rptd separately 1966.

Wright, C. E. The cultivation of saga in Anglo-Saxon England. Edinburgh 1939.

Campbell, A. Verse influences in Old English prose. In Philological essays in honour of H. D. Meritt, Hague 1970.

(3) MAJOR TRANSLATORS OF KING ALFRED'S REIGN (871-99)

KING ALFRED
849–99

§ 1

Pastoral Care

King Alfred's West Saxon version of Gregory's Pastoral care. Ed H. Sweet 2 vols 1871–2 (EETS). With trn.

The metrical preface and epilogue to the Pastoral care. In The Anglo-Saxon minor poems, ed E. V. K. Dobbie, New York 1942. *See also under Poetry, col 292, above.*

The pastoral care. Ed N. R. Ker, Early English mss in facsimile vol 6, Copenhagen 1956. Facs of mss Hatton 20, Cotton Tiberius B. xi and Kassel.

Boethius

King Alfred's Old English version of Boethius De consolatione philosophiae. Ed W. J. Sedgefield, Oxford 1899.

Die altenglischen Metra des Boethius. Ed E. Krämer, Bonner Beiträge zur Anglistik 8 1902.

The meters of Boethius. In The Paris Psalter and the meters of Boethius, ed G. P. Krapp, New York 1932.

Tr W. J. Sedgefield, Oxford 1900.

Soliloquies

King Alfred's Old English version of St Augustine's Soliloquies. Ed H. L. Hargrove, New York 1902.

König Alfreds des Grossen Bearbeitung der Soliloquien des Augustinus. Ed W. Endter, Bibliothek der angelsächsischen Prosa vol 11, 1922.

King Alfred's version of St Augustine's Soliloquies. Ed T. A. Carnicelli, Cambridge Mass 1969.

Tr H. L. Hargrove, New York 1904.

For Paris psalter, perhaps by Alfred in its prose part, see col 323, below. For trns of Orosius and Bede, formerly thought to be by Alfred, see below.

§ 2

Wülcker, R. Über die angelsächsische Bearbeitung der Soliloquien Augustins. Beiträge zur Geschichte der Deutschen Sprache und Literatur 4 1877.

Hartmann, M. Ist König Alfred der Verfasser der alliterierenden Übertragung der Metra des Boetius? Anglia 5 1882.

Zimmermann, O. Über den Verfasser der altenglischen Metren des Boethius. Greifswald 1882.

Leicht, A. Ist König Alfred der Verfasser der alliterierenden Metra des Boetius? Anglia 6 1883.

—Zur angelsächsischen Bearbeitung des Boetius. Anglia 7 1884.

Fleischhauer, W. Über den Gebrauch des Conjunctivs in Alfreds altenglischer Übersetzung von Gregors Cura pastoralis. Erlangen 1885.

Cossack, A. H. Über die altenglische metrische Bearbeitung von Boethius De consolatione philosophiae. Leipzig 1889.

Dewitz, A. Untersuchungen über Alfreds des Grossen westsächsische Übersetzung der Cura pastoralis Gregors. Bunzlau 1889.

Wack, G. Über das Verhältnis von König Aelfreds Übersetzung der Cura pastoralis zum Original. Greifswald 1889.

Kern, J. H. Zur Cura pastoralis. Beiträge zur Geschichte der Deutschen Sprache und Literatur 16 1892.

— Zur Cura pastoralis. Anglia 33 1910.

— A few notes on the Metra of Boethius in Old English. Neophilologus 8 1923.

Hubbard, F. G. The relation of the Blooms of King Alfred to the Anglo-Saxon translation of Boethius. MLN 9 1894.

Schepss, G. Zu König Alfreds Boethius. Archiv 94 1895.

Brooke, S. A. King Alfred as educator of his people and man of letters. 1901.

Förster, M. Zum altenglischen Boethius. Archiv 106 1901.

Klaeber, F. Notes on Old English prose texts 1. MLN 18 1903. On the Boethius.

— Zu König Alfreds Vorrede zu seiner Übersetzung der Cura pastoralis. Anglia 47 1923.

Asser's Life of King Alfred. Ed W. H. Stevenson, Oxford 1904, 1959 (with addn by D. Whitelock).

Koeppel, E. Zur Chronologie der Übersetzungen des Königs Alfred. Anglia Beiblatt 19 1908.

Fehlauer, F. Die englischen Übersetzungen von Boethius' De consolatione philosophiae 1: die alt- und mittelenglischen Übersetzungen. Berlin 1909.

Jost, K. Zu den Handschriften der Cura pastoralis. Anglia 37 1913.

— Zur Textkritik der altenglischen Soliloquienbearbeitungen. Anglia Beiblatt 31–2 1920–1.

Holthausen, F. Zur altenglischen Metra-Übersetzung. Anglia Beiblatt 31 1931.

Borinski, L. Der Stil König Alfreds: eine Studie zur Psychologie der Rede. Leipzig 1934.

Schmidt, K. H. König Alfreds Boethius-Bearbeitung. Göttingen 1934.

Flasdieck, H. M. Das Kasseler Bruchstück der Cura pastoralis. Anglia 62 1938.

— Weiteres zum Kasseler Bruchstück der Cura pastoralis. Anglia 66 1942.

Grierson, P. Grimbald of St Bertin's. EHR 55 1940.

Potter, S. The Old English Pastoral care. Trans of Philological Soc 1947.

— King Alfred's last preface. In Philologica: the [Kemp] Malone anniversary studies, Baltimore 1949.

Zandvoort, R. W. Three notes on King Alfred's Boethius. E Studies 28 1947.

Magoun, F. P. Some notes on King Alfred's circular letter on educational policy addressed to his bishops. Mediaeval Stud 10 1948.

— King Alfred's letter on educational policy according to the Cambridge manuscripts. Mediaeval Stud 11 1949.

Sisam, K. The publication of Alfred's Pastoral care. In his Studies in the history of Old English literature, Oxford 1953.

— The authorship of the verse translation of Boethius's Metra. Ibid.

Donaghey, B. S. The sources of King Alfred's translation of Boethius's De consolatione philosophiae. Anglia 82 1964.

Otten, K. König Alfreds Boethius. Tübingen 1964.

Cross, J. E. The elephant to Alfred, Ælfric, Aldhelm and others. Studia Neophilologica 37 1965.

—— The metrical epilogue to the Old English version of Gregory's Cura pastoralis. Neuphilologische Mitteilungen 70 1969.

Bately, J. M. Grimbald of St Bertin's. MÆ 35 1966.

Whitelock, D. The prose of Alfred's reign. In Continuations and beginnings, ed E. G. Stanley 1966.

—— William of Malmesbury on the works of King Alfred. In Medieval literature and civilization: studies in memory of G. N. Garmonsway, 1969.

Payne, F. A. King Alfred and Boethius: an analysis of the Old English version of the Consolation of philosophy. 1968.

Brown, W. H. Method and style in the Old English Pastoral care. JEGP 68 1969.

Davis, R. H. C. Alfred the Great: propaganda and truth. History 56 1971.

WÆRFERTH
d. by 915

Gregory's Dialogues

§1

Bischofs Wærferth von Worcester Übersetzung der Dialoge Gregors des Grossen. Ed H. Hecht, Bibliothek der angelsächsischen Prosa vol 5, 1900–7.

The metrical preface to Wærferth's translation of Gregory's Dialogues. In The Anglo-Saxon minor poems, ed E. V. K. Dobbie, New York 1942.

§2

Krebs, H. Die angelsächsische Übersetzung der Dialoge Gregors. Anglia 2–3 1879–80.

Timmer, B. J. Studies in Bishop Wærferth's translation of the Dialogues of Gregory the Great. Wageningen 1934.

Harting, P. N. U. The text of the Old English translation of Gregory's Dialogues. Neophilologus 22 1937.

Sisam, K. The verses prefixed to Gregory's Dialogues. In his Studies in the history of Old English literature, Oxford 1953.

Whitelock, D. *See under Alfred, above.*

ANONYMOUS TRANSLATORS
Orosius

§1

King Alfred's Anglo-Saxon version of Orosius. Ed J. Bosworth 1859. With trn.

King Alfred's Orosius. Ed H. Sweet 1883 (EETS).

The Tollemache Orosius: BM additional ms 47967. Ed A. Campbell, Early English mss in facsimile vol 3, Copenhagen 1953.

Tr B. Thorpe in R. Pauli, The life of Alfred the Great, 1853.

§2

Purely geographical studies are excluded.

Schilling, H. König Aelfred's angelsächsische Bearbeitung der Weltgeschichte des Orosius. Halle 1886.

Geidel, H. Alfred der Grosse als Geograph. Munich 1904.

Napier, A. S. Two fragments of Alfred's Orosius. MLR 8 1913.

Laborde, E. D. King Alfred's system of geographical description in his version of Orosius. Geographical Jnl 62 1923.

Craigie, W. A. The nationality of King Alfred's Wulfstan. JEGP 24 1925.

Hübener, G. Alfred und Osteuropa. E Studien 60 1925.

—— König Alfreds Geografie. Speculum 6 1931.

Malone, K. King Alfred's 'Geats'. MLR 20 1925.

—— King Alfred's north: a study in mediaeval geography. Speculum 5 1930.

—— On King Alfred's geographical treatise. Speculum 8 1933.

—— The date of Ohthere's voyage to Hæthum. MLR 25 1930.

—— On Wulfstan's Scandinavia. SP 28 1931.

Kirkman, A. Proper names in the Old English Orosius. MLR 25 1930.

Cross, S. H. Notes on King Alfred's north: Osti, Este. Speculum 6 1931.

Ross, A. S. C. OWN Bjarmar: Russian Perm. Leeds Stud in Eng 6 1937.

—— The Terfinnas and Beormas of Ohthere. Leeds 1940.

—— Ohthere's cwenas and lakes. Geographical Jnl 120 1954.

Potter, S. The Old English Orosius. Trans of Philological Soc 1939.

—— Commentary on King Alfred's Orosius. Anglia 71 1953.

Ekblom, R. Ohthere's voyage from Skiringssal to Hedeby. Studia Neophilologica 12 1940.

—— Der Volksname 'Osti' in Alfreds des Grossen Orosius-Übersetzung. Studia Neophilologica 13 1941.

—— Alfred the Great as geographer. Studia Neophilologica 14 1942; rptd in A philological miscellany presented to E. Ekwall, Upsala 1942.

—— King Alfred, Ohthere and Wulfstan. Studia Neophilologica 32 1960. Reply by A. Ellegard, The old Scandinavian system of orientation, ibid.

Whiting, B. J. Ohthere (Óttar) and Egilssaga. PQ 24 1945.

Koutaissoff, E. Ohtheriana 1: Kuznetsov on Biarmia. Eng & Germanic Stud 2 1949.

Brewer, D. S. Sixteenth-, seventeenth- and eighteenth-century references to the voyage of Ohthere. Anglia 71 1953.

Mossé, F. Another lost ms of the Old English Orosius? E Studies 36 1955.

Stokoe, W. C. On Ohthere's 'steorbord'. Speculum 32 1957.

Bately, J. M. Alfred's Orosius and Les empereors de Rome. SP 57 1960.

—— King Alfred and the Latin mss of Orosius' history. Classica et Mediaevalia 22 1961.

—— The Vatican fragment of the Old English Orosius. E Studies 45 1964.

—— The Old English Orosius: the question of dictation. Anglia 84 1966.

—— The relationship between the mss of the Old English Orosius. E Studies 48 1967.

—— King Alfred and the Old English Orosius. Anglia 88 1970.

—— The classical additions to the Old English Orosius. In England before the Conquest: studies presented to Dorothy Whitelock, Cambridge 1971.

Binns, A. L. Ohtheriana VI: Ohthere's northern voyage. Eng & Germanic Stud 7 1961.

Linderski, J. Alfred the Great and the tradition of ancient geography. Speculum 39 1964.

Whitelock, D. 1966. *See under Alfred, above.*

Liggins, E. M. The authorship of the Old English Orosius. Anglia 88 1970.

Derolez, R. The orientation system in the Old English Orosius. In England before the Conquest: studies presented to Dorothy Whitelock, Cambridge 1971.

The Old English Bede

§1

The Old English version of Bede's Ecclesiastical history. Ed T. Miller 4 pts 1890–8 (EETS). With trn.

König Alfreds Übersetzung von Bedas Kirchengeschichte. Ed J. Schipper, Bibliothek der angelsächsischen Prosa vol 4, 1899.

The metrical epilogue to ms 41, Corpus Christi College, Cambridge. In The Anglo-Saxon minor poems, ed E. V. K. Dobbie, New York 1942.

§2

Miller, T. Place-names in the English Bede and the localisation of the mss. Quellen und Forschungen zur Sprach- und Culturgeschichte 78 1896.

Schipper, J. Die Geschichte und der gegenwärtiger Stand der Forschung über König Alfreds Übersetzung von Bedas Kirchengeschichte. Sitzungsberichte der Philosophisch-historischen Klasse der Kaiserlichen Akademie der Wissenschaften (Vienna) 138 1898.

Hart, J. M. Rhetoric in the translation of Bede. In An English miscellany presented to Dr [F. J.] Furnivall, Oxford 1901.

Klaeber, F. An emendation in the Old English version of Bede IV 24. JEGP 3 1901.

— Zur altenglischen Bedaübersetzung. Anglia 25 1902, 27 1904.

Fijn van Draat, P. The authorship of the Old English Bede: a study in rhythm. Anglia 39 1916.

Malone, K. King Alfred's 'Geats'. MLR 20 1925.

Förster, M. Ae. 'bam handum twam awritan'. Archiv 162 1932.

Kuhn, S. M. Synonyms in the Old English Bede. JEGP 46 1947.

Campbell, J. J. The dialect vocabulary of the Old English Bede. JEGP 50 1951.

— The Old English Bede: book III, chapters 16 to 20. MLN 67 1952.

Whitelock, D. The Old English Bede. Proc Br Acad 48 1963. *See also under Alfred, above.*

For Anglo-Saxon Chronicle, first compiled in Alfred's reign, see below.

(4) MAJOR WRITERS OF THE LATER PERIOD

ÆLFRIC
c. 955–c. 1010(?)

For the Ælfric canon see P. Clemoes, The chronology of Ælfric works, in The Anglo-Saxons: studies presented to Bruce Dickins, 1959.

§1

Catholic Homilies

The homilies of the Anglo-Saxon church: the first part, containing the Sermones catholici or Homilies of Ælfric. Ed B. Thorpe 2 vols 1844–6 (Ælfric Soc). With trn.

Ælfric: selected homilies. Ed H. Sweet, Oxford 1885.

Ælfric's first series of Catholic homilies: BM Royal 7 C. xii. Ed N. Eliason and P. Clemoes, Early English mss in facsimile vol 13, Copenhagen 1966.

Early English homilies from the 12th century ms Vespasian D. xiv. Ed R. D.-N. Warner 1917 (EETS). Contains mainly items from the Catholic homilies but also other works by Ælfric and some anon pieces.

Other Homilies

De duodecim abusivis. Ed R. Morris, Old English homilies: first series, 1867–8 (EETS), p. 299 line 1–p. 304.

Wulfstan: Sammlung der ihm zugeschriebenen Homilien. Ed A. S. Napier, Berlin 1883. Nos viii, xxxi and the Latin part of no vii are by Ælfric.

Angelsächsische Homilien und Heiligenleben. Ed B. Assmann, Bibliothek der angelsächsischen Prosa vol 3, 1889; rptd with supplementary introd by P. Clemoes, Darmstadt 1964. Nos i–ix are by Ælfric.

Twelfth-century homilies in ms Bodley 343. Ed A. O. Belfour 1909 (EETS). With trn. Items i–iv, vii–ix, xiii and xiv are by Ælfric, but i–ii have been re-ed Pope, below, and xiii–xiv are extracts from Catholic homilies II xxx and Pope no vi respectively.

Zwei Homilien des Ælfric. Ed R. Brotanek, Texte und Untersuchungen, Halle 1913. Only the first by Ælfric.

Exameron anglice. Ed S. J. Crawford, Bibliothek der angelsächsischen Prosa vol 10, 1921. With trn.

Ælfric's Old English homily De doctrina apostolica. Ed W. Braekman, Studia Germanica Gandensia 5 1963. Same as Pope no xix.

Wyrdwriteras: an unpublished Ælfrician text in ms

Hatton 115. Ed W. Braekman, Revue Belge de Philologie 44 1966. Same as Pope no xxii.

Homilies of Ælfric: a supplementary collection. Ed J. C. Pope 2 vols 1967–8 (EETS).

Lives of Saints

Lives of saints. Ed W. W. Skeat 4 pts 1881–1900 (EETS). With trn. Nos xxiii, xxiiib, xxx and xxxiii are not by Ælfric.

Gloucester fragments. Ed J. Earle 1861. With facs and trn. Includes fragments of Skeat no xxi, St Swithun, and xxiiib, St Mary of Egypt (latter not by Ælfric).

Lives of three English saints. Ed G. I. Needham 1966. SS Oswald, Edmund, Swithun; Skeat nos xxvi, xxxii, xxi.

Letters

Die Hirtenbriefe Ælfrics. Ed B. Fehr, Bibliothek der angelsächsischen Prosa vol 9, 1914; rptd with suppl by P. Clemoes to introd, Darmstadt 1966.

Letter to the monks of Eynsham (Latin). Ed M. Bateson as Excerpta ex institutionibus monasticis, in Compotus rolls of the obedientiaries of St Swithun's priory, ed G. W. Kitchin 1892.

Fragment eines angelsächsischen Briefes (De sanguine prohibito). Ed F. Kluge, E Studien 8 1885.

Items i–ii in Assmann's collection, above, and Ælfric's treatise on the Old and New testaments, below, are also letters.

Other Works

Admonitio ad filium spiritualem. Ed H. W. Norman 1849 (with Hexameron) (with trn).

Ælfric's version of Alcuini Interrogationes Sigewulfi in Genesin. Ed G. E. MacLean, Halle 1883. Also in Anglia 6–7 1883–4.

The Old English Heptateuch, Ælfric's treatise on the Old and New testament, and his preface to Genesis. Ed S. J. Crawford 1922 (EETS); rptd with text of two additional mss 1969. The Heptateuch is only partly by Ælfric.

Colloquy. Ed G. N. Garmonsway 1939, 1947 (rev). Only the Latin is by Ælfric.

Grammatik und Glossar: Text und Varianten. Ed J. Zupitza, Berlin 1880; rptd with preface by H. Gneuss, Berlin 1966.

De temporibus anni. Ed H. Henel 1942 (EETS).

Vita, S. Æthelwoldi. Ed J. Stevenson, Chronicon monasterii de Abingdon, 1858 (Rolls ser); tr S. H. Gem 1912, below, and D. Whitelock, English historical documents vol 1, 1955.

Ely charter. Ed J. Pope, England before the Conquest: studies presented to Dorothy Whitelock, Cambridge 1971.

§2

Dietrich, E. Abt Ælfrik. Zeitschrift für Historische Theologie 25–6 1855–6.

Holthaus, E. Ælfric's Lives of saints. Anglia 6 1883.

Menthel, E. Zur Geschichte des Otfridischen Verses im Englischen. Anglia 8 1885.

Zupitza, J. Bemerkungen zu Ælfrics Lives of Saints. Zeitschrift für Deutsches Altertum 29 1885.

— Die ursprüngliche Gestalt von Ælfrics Colloquium. Zeitschrift für Deutsches Altertum 31 1887.

Reum, A. De temporibus: ein echtes Werk des Abtes Ælfric. Anglia 10 1888.

Ott, J. H. Über die Quellen der Heiligenleben in Ælfrics Lives of saints 1. Halle 1892.

Förster, M. Ælfric's s.g. Hiob-Übersetzung. Anglia 15 1893.

— Über die Quellen von Ælfrics Homiliae catholicae 1: Legenden. Berlin 1892.

— Über die Quellen von Ælfrics exegetischen Homiliae catholicae. Anglia 16 1894.

— Altenglische Predigtquellen 1: 2, Pseudo-Augustin und Ælfric (Skeat no xvii). Archiv 116 1906.

Liebermann, F. Aus Ælfrics Grammatik und Glossar. Archiv 92 1894.

— Ein staatsrechtlicher Satz Ælfrics aus lateinischer Quelle. Archiv 139 1919.

Schroeder, E. Colloquium Ælfrici. Zeitschrift für Deutsches Altertum 41 1897.

Napier, A. S. A fragment of Ælfric's Lives of saints (ms Cotton Otho B. x). MLN 2 1887.

— Fragments of an Ælfric ms (from Catholic homilies 1. i). MLN 8 1893.

— Nachträge zu Cooks Biblical quotations in Old English prose writers. Archiv 101–2 1898–9. Prints biblical quotations omitted in Thorpe's edn of Catholic homilies.

Zimmermann, O. Die beiden Fassungen des dem Abte Ælfric zugeschriebenen ags Traktats über die siebenfältige Gabe des Heiligen Geistes. Leipzig 1888.

Herzfeld, G. Bruchstücke von Ælfrics Lives of Saints (ms BM Royal 8 c vii). E Studien 16 1891.

Klaeber, F. Notes on Old English prose texts ii. MLN 18 1903.

Brandeis, A. Die Alliteration in Ælfrics metrischen Homilien. Vienna 1897. In Jahresbericht der K.K. Staatsrealschule im vii Bezirke in Wien für 1896–7.

White, C. L. Ælfric: a new study of his life and writings. New Haven 1898.

Stephan, A. Eine weitere Quelle von Ælfrics Gregorhomilie. Anglia Beiblatt 14 1903.

Gerould, G. H. Ælfric's legend of St Swithin. Anglia 32 1909.

— Ælfric's lives of St Martin of Tours. JEGP 24 1925.

— Abbot Ælfric's rhythmic prose. MP 22 1925.

Gem, S. H. An Anglo-Saxon abbot: Ælfric of Eynsham. Edinburgh 1912.

Fehr, B. Über einige Quellen zu Ælfrics Homiliae catholicae. Archiv 130 1913.

Crawford, S. J. The Lincoln fragment of the Old English version of the Heptateuch. MLR 15 1920.

Jost, K. Unechte Ælfrictexte. Anglia 51 1927. On authorship of OE Heptateuch.

— Wulfstanstudien. Berne 1950.

— The legal maxim in Ælfric's homilies. E Studies 36 1955.

Loomis, G. Further sources of Ælfric's saints' lives. Harvard Stud 13 1931.

— The growth of the Saint Edmund legend. Harvard Stud 14 1932.

Sisam, K. Mss Bodley 340 and 342: Ælfric's Catholic homilies. RES 7–9 1931–3; rptd in his Studies in the history of OE literature, Oxford 1953.

— The order of Ælfric's early books. In his Studies in the history of Old English literature, Oxford 1953.

Bethurum, D. The form of Ælfric's Lives of saints. SP 29 1932.

Halvarson, N. O. Doctrinal terms in Ælfric's homilies. Iowa City 1932.

Meissner, P. Studien zum Wortschatz Ælfrics. Archiv 165–6 1934–5.

Rosenthal, C. L. The Vitae patrum in Old and Middle English literature. Philadelphia 1936.

Wright, C. E. Two Ælfric fragments. MÆ 7 1938.

Prins, A. A. Some remarks on Ælfric's Lives of saints and his translations from the Old Testament. Neophilologus 25 1940.

Davis, C. R. Two new sources for Ælfric's Catholic homilies. JEGP 41 1942.

— A note on Ælfric's translation of Job i. 6. MLN 60 1945.

Dubois, M. M. Ælfric, sermonnaire, docteur et grammairien. Paris 1943.

Whitbread, L. Notes on Ælfric's Colloquy. N & Q 30 Jan 1943.

Whitelock, D. Two notes on Ælfric and Wulfstan 1: the date of Ælfric's death. MLR 38 1943.

Loomis, L. H. The Saint Mercurius legend in medieval England and in Norse saga. In Philologica: the [Kemp] Malone anniversary studies, Baltimore 1949.

Willard, R. The punctuation and capitalization of Ælfric's homily for the first Sunday in Lent. SE 29 1950.

Fisher, D. J. V. The early biographers of St Ethelwold. EHR 67 1952.

Raith, J. Ælfric's share in the Old English Pentateuch. RES new ser 3 1952.

Barrett, C. R. Studies in the word-order of Ælfric's Catholic homilies and Lives of saints. Dept of Anglo-Saxon Occasional Papers 3 (Cambridge) 1953.

Meyer, R. T. Isidorian Glossae collectae in Ælfric's vocabulary. Traditio 12 1956.

Raynes, E. M. Ms Boulogne-sur-Mer 63 and Ælfric. MÆ 26 1957.

Cross, J. E. A source for one of Ælfric's Catholic homilies. E Studies 39 1958.

— Ælfric and the medieval homiliary: objection and contribution. Scripta Minora Lundensis 4 1962.

— Bundles for burning: a theme in two of Ælfric's Catholic homilies with other sources. Anglia 81 1963.

— Gregory, Blickling homily x and Ælfric's Passio S. Mauricii on the world's youth and age. Neuphilologische Mitteilungen 66 1965.

— Oswald and Byrhtnoth. E Studies 46 1965.

— More sources for two of Ælfric's Catholic homilies. Anglia 86 1968.

— Ælfric: mainly on memory and creative method in two Catholic homilies. Studia Neophilologica 41 1969.

— Source and analysis of some Ælfrician passages. Neuphilologische Mitteilungen 72 1971.

Clemoes, P. The chronology of Ælfric's works. In The Anglo-Saxons: studies presented to Bruce Dickins, 1959.

— The Old English Benedictine Office, CCCC 190, and the relations between Ælfric and Wulfstan: a reconsideration. Anglia 78 1960.

— In Continuations and beginnings, ed E. G. Stanley 1966.

Garmonsway, G. N. The development of the colloquy. In The Anglo-Saxons: studies presented to Bruce Dickins, 1959.

Harlow, C. G. Punctuation in some mss of Ælfric. RES new ser 10 1959.

Smetana, C. L. Ælfric and the early medieval homiliary. Traditio 15 1959.
— Ælfric and the homiliary of Haymo of Halberstadt. Traditio 17 1961.
Williams, E. R. Ælfric's grammatical terminology. PMLA 73 1958.
Collins, R. L. An Ælfric ms fragment (Indiana University ms Poole 10: Lives of saints). TLS 2 Sept 1960.
— Two fragments of Ælfric's Grammar: the kinship of Ker 384 and Ker 242. Annuale Mediaevale 5 1964.
Schelp, H. Die Deutungstradition in Ælfrics Homiliae catholicae. Archiv 196 1960.
Turville-Petre, J. Sources of the vernacular homily in England, Norway and Iceland. Arkiv för Nordisk Filologi 75 1960.
Colledge, E. An allusion to Augustine in Ælfric's Colloquy. RES new ser 12 1961.
Temple, W. The song of the angelic hosts. Annuale Mediaevale 2 1961.
Colgrave, B. and A. Hyde. Two recently discovered leaves from Old English mss. Speculum 37 1962. One leaf is from item iv in Assmann's edn.
Ker, N. R. The Bodmer fragment of Ælfric's homily for Septuagesima Sunday. In English and medieval studies presented to J. R. R. Tolkien, 1962.
Nichols, A. E. 'Awendan': a note on Ælfric's vocabulary. JEGP 63 1964.
— Ælfric's prefaces: rhetoric and genre. E Studies 49 1968.
— Ælfric and the brief style. JEGP 70 1971.
Hargreaves, H. From Bede to Wiclif: medieval English Bible translations. Bull John Rylands Lib 48 1965.
Kisbye, T. Zur pronominalen Anrede bei Ælfric. Archiv 201 1965.
Gatch, M. McC. Ms Boulogne-sur-Mer 63 and Ælfric's first series of Catholic homilies. JEGP 65 1966.
Pearce, T. M. Name patterns in Ælfric's Catholic homilies. Names 14 1966.
Clark, C. Ælfric and Abbo. E Studies 49 1968.
Godden, M. R. The sources for Ælfric's homily on St Gregory. Anglia 86 1968.
Lipp, F. R. Ælfric's Old English prose style. SP 66 1969.
Taylor, A. Hauksbok and Ælfric's De falsis diis. Leeds Stud in Eng new ser 3 1969.
Wrenn, C. L. Some aspects of Anglo-Saxon theology. In Studies in language, literature and culture of the Middle Ages and later, ed E. B. Atwood and A. A. Hill, Austin 1969. Refers to Ælfric's homily on Easter sacrifice.
Hurt, J. R. A note on Ælfric's Lives of saints no. xvi. E Studies 51 1970.
Meaney, A. L. Æthelweard, Ælfric, the Norse Gods and Northumbria. Jnl of Religious History 1970.
Ross, A. S. C. Some alliterative phrases in the Bodley homilies. N & Q 17 Feb 1970.

WULFSTAN
d. 1023

§1

Wulfstan: Sammlung der ihm zugeschriebenen Homilien. Ed A. S. Napier, Berlin 1883; rptd with bibliographical suppl by K. Ostheeren, 1967. Not all by Wulfstan; see K. Jost, Wulfstanstudien, below.
Sermo Lupi ad Anglos. Ed D. Whitelock 1939, 1963 (rev); tr D. Whitelock in her English historical documents vol 1, 1955.
Homilies. Ed D. Bethurum, Oxford 1957.
Die Institutes of polity, civil and ecclesiastical. Ed K. Jost, Berne 1959.
A Wulfstan ms containing institutes, laws and homilies: BM Cotton Nero A.i. Ed H. R. Loyn, Early English mss in facsimile vol 17, Copenhagen 1971.

Wulfstan was probably the author of various legal writings included in the edns of Liebermann and Thorpe, below, of the prose part of the Benedictine Office, *below, and of 2 passages in a version of the* Anglo-Saxon Chronicle. *For details see* Sermo Lupi, *ed D. Whitelock, above.*

§2

Napier, A. S. Über die Werke des altenglischen Erzbischofs Wulfstan. Weimar 1882.
Zimmermann, O. 1888. *See under Ælfric, above.*
Kinard, J. P. A study of Wulfstan's homilies, their style and sources. Baltimore 1897.
Liebermann, F. Wulfstan and Cnut. Archiv 103 1899.
— Die Abfassungszeit von 'Rectitudines' und ags. 'aferian'. Archiv 109 1902.
Feiler, E. Das Benediktiner-Offizium: ein Beitrag zur Wulfstanfrage. Anglistische Forschungen 4 1900.
Förster, M. Altenglische Predigtquellen 1: 3, Adso und Wulfstan. Archiv 116 1906.
Dodd, L. II. A glossary of Wulfstan's homilies. New York 1908.
Becher, C. F. Wulfstans Homilien. Leipzig 1910.
Fehr, B. Das Benediktiner-Offizium und die Beziehungen zwischen Ælfric und Wulfstan. E Studien 46 1913.
Jost, K. Wulfstan und die angelsächsische Chronik. Anglia 47 1923.
— Einige Wulfstantexte und ihre Quellen. Anglia 56 1932.
— Wulfstanstudien. Berne 1950.
Whitelock, D. A note on the career of Wulfstan the homilist. EHR 52 1937.
— Wulfstan and the so-called Laws of Edward and Guthrum. EHR 56 1941.
— Archbishop Wulfstan, homilist and statesman. Trans Royal Historical Soc 4th ser 24 1942.
— Two notes on Ælfric and Wulfstan 2: Gildas, Alcuin and Wulfstan. MLR 38 1943.
— Wulfstan and the laws of Cnut. EHR 63 1948.
— Wulfstan's authorship of Cnut's laws. EHR 70 1955.
— Wulfstan at York. In Franciplegius: medieval and linguistic studies in honor of F. P. Magoun, New York 1965, London 1965 (as Medieval and linguistic studies).
Bethurum, D. Archbishop Wulfstan's commonplace book. PMLA 57 1942.
— A letter of protest from the English bishops to the Pope. In Philologica: the [Kemp] Malone anniversary studies, Baltimore 1949.
— Six anonymous Old English codes. JEGP 49 1950.
— Episcopal magnificence in the eleventh century. In Studies in OE literature in honor of A. G. Brodeur, Eugene 1963.
— In Continuations and beginnings, ed E. G. Stanley 1966.
— (D. Bethurum Loomis). Regnum and sacerdotium in the early eleventh century. In England before the Conquest: studies presented to Dorothy Whitelock, Cambridge 1971.
Ker, N. R. Hemming's cartulary. In Studies in medieval history presented to F. M. Powicke, Oxford 1948.
— The handwriting of Archbishop Wulfstan. In England before the Conquest: studies presented to Dorothy Whitelock, Cambridge 1971.
Menner, R. J. Anglian and Saxon elements in Wulfstan's vocabulary. MLN 63 1948.
McIntosh, A. Wulfstan's prose. Proc Br Acad 35 1949.
Whitbread, L. Ms CCCC 201: a note on its character and provenance. PQ 38 1959.
Clemoes, P. 1960. *See under Ælfric, above.*
Levin, S. R. On the authenticity of five 'Wulfstan' homilies. JEGP 60 1961.
Strang, B. M. H. Two Wulfstan expressions ('bec' and 'stric'). N & Q May 1961.

Funke, O. Some remarks on Wulfstan's prose rhythm. E Studies 43 1962.

Fowler, R. G. 'Archbishop Wulfstan's commonplace-book' and the Canons of Edgar. MÆ 32 1963.

— Some stylistic features of the Sermo Lupi. JEGP 65 1966.

Stuart, C. I. J. M. Wulfstan's use of 'Leofan men'. E Studies 45 1964.

(5) OTHER RELIGIOUS PROSE

TRANSLATIONS OF THE BIBLE

General

Cook, A. S. Biblical quotations in Old English prose writers. Sers 1–2, 1898–1903.

Hargreaves, H. From Bede to Wiclif: medieval English Bible translations. Bull John Rylands Lib 48 1965.

Shepherd, G. English versions of the scriptures before Wyclif. In The Cambridge history of the Bible vol 2, ed G. W. H. Lampe, Cambridge 1969.

West Saxon Gospels

§ 1

Ða halgan godspel on englisc. Ed B. Thorpe 1842.

The Gothic and Anglo-Saxon gospels, with the versions of Wyclif and Tyndale. Ed J. Bosworth 1865.

The gospels in Anglo-Saxon, Northumbrian and Old Mercian versions. Ed W. W. Skeat 4 vols Cambridge 1871–87.

The gospel of St Luke in Anglo-Saxon. Ed J. W. Bright, Oxford 1893.

The gospels in West Saxon. Ed J. W. Bright 4 vols Boston 1904–6.

The West-Saxon gospels: a study of the gospel of St Matthew with text of the four gospels. Ed M. Grünberg, Amsterdam 1967.

§ 2

Napier, A. S. Bruchstücke einer altenglischen Evangelien-Handschrift. Archiv 87 1891.

Drake, A. The authorship of the West Saxon gospels. New York 1894.

Harris, L. M. Studies in the Anglo-Saxon version of the gospels 1: the form of the Latin original and mistaken renderings. Baltimore 1901.

Glunz, H. Die lateinische Vorlage der westsächsischen Evangelien-version. Leipzig 1928.

Rauh, H. Der Wortschatz der altenglischen Übersetzungen des Matthäus-Evangeliums untersucht auf seine dialektische und zeitliche Gebundenheit. Berlin 1936.

Paris Psalter

§ 1

Liber psalmorum: the West Saxon psalms being the prose portion of the Paris Psalter. Ed J. W. Bright and R. L. Ramsay, Boston 1907.

The Paris Psalter: Bibliothèque Nationale Paris Lat. 8824. Ed J. Bromwich et al, Early English mss in facsimile vol 8, Copenhagen 1958.

§ 2

Wichmann, J. König Aelfreds angelsächsische Übertragung der Psalmen i–li excl. Anglia 11 1889.

Bruce, J. D. Immediate and ultimate source of the rubrics and introductions to the psalms in the Paris Psalter. MLN 8 1893.

— The Anglo-Saxon version of the book of psalms, commonly known as the Paris Psalter. PMLA 9 1894.

Grattan, J. H. G. On the text of the prose portion of the Paris Psalter. MLR 4 1909.

Bright, J. W. and R. L. Ramsay. Notes on the introductions of the West Saxon psalms. Jnl of Theological Stud 13 1912.

Ramsay, R. L. The Latin text of the Paris Psalter. Amer Jnl of Philology 41 1920.

Bromwich, J. Who was the translator of the prose portion of the Paris Psalter? In The early cultures of northwest Europe: H. M. Chadwick memorial studies, Cambridge 1950.

For trns of the Old testament (The Old English Heptateuch which is partly by Ælfric, Skeat nos xviii and xxv, and items viii–ix in Assmann's collection), see under Ælfric, above. For Old English glosses in Latin gospels, psalters etc see Language, col 73, above.

HOMILIES

§ 1

Blickling

The Blickling homilies. Ed R. Morris 3 pts 1874–80 (EETS). With trn.

The Blickling homilies. Ed R. Willard, Early English mss in facsimile vol 10, Copenhagen 1960.

Vercelli

Förster, M. Der Vercelli-Codex cxvii nebst Abdruck einiger altenglischer Homilien der Handschrift (nos ix, xv, xxii). Studien zur Englischen Philologie 50 1913.

Die Vercelli-Homilien i–viii. Ed M. Förster, Bibliothek der angelsächsischen Prosa vol 12, 1932.

Il codice vercellese riprodotto in fototipia. Ed M. Förster, Rome 1913.

Others

An Old English homily on the observance of Sunday. Ed A. S. Napier, An English miscellany presented to Dr [F. J.] Furnivall, Oxford 1901. From ms CCCC 162.

A new version of the Apocalypse of Thomas in Old English. Ed M. Förster, Anglia 73 1955.

Three Old English texts in a Salisbury pontifical, Cotton Tiberius C. i. Ed N. R. Ker, The Anglo-Saxons: studies presented to Bruce Dickins, 1959.

For other anon homilies see collections of Assmann, Belfour, Brotanek, Morris and Warner, under Ælfric, above; Napier's collection, under Wulfstan, above; §2 below and under Gospel of Nicodemus, below; also index to N. R. Ker, Catalogue of mss containing Anglo-Saxon, Oxford 1957.

§ 2

Zupitza, J. Blickling homilies. Anzeiger für Deutsches Altertum 1 1876.

— Kritische Beiträge zu den Blickling homilies und Blickling glosses. Zeitschrift für Deutsches Altertum 26 1882.

Wülcker, R. P. Über das Vercellibuch. Anglia 5 1882. Includes text of homily xiii.

Holthausen, F. Beiträge zur Erklärung und Textkritik. E Studien 14 1890.

Förster, M. Zu den Blickling homilies. Archiv 91 1893.

— Zur vierten Blickling homily. Archiv 103 1899.

— Altenglische Predigtquellen 1: 1, Pseudo-Augustin und die 7 Blickling homily. Archiv 116 1906.

— Altenglische Predigtquellen 11: 6, Petrus Chrysologus und die 14 Blickling homily. Archiv 122 1909.

— Altenglische Predigtquellen 11: 7, Augustin und Be Gecyrrednysse; 8, Defensor und Be Ðurhwununge (both with text from ms Cotton Tiberius A. iii). Ibid.

Priebsch, R. The chief sources of some Anglo-Saxon homilies (on the 'Sunday letter'). Otia Merseiana 1 1899. Includes text of homily in ms CCCC 140.

Klaeber, F. Notes on Old English prose texts III. MLN 18 1903.

Napier, A. S. Notes on the Blickling homilies. MP 1 1904.

Mosher, J. A. The exemplum in the early religious and didactic literature of England. New York 1911.

Willard, R. Vercelli homily viii and the Christ. PMLA 42 1927.

— The address of the soul to the body. PMLA 50 1935.

— Two apocrypha in Old English homilies. Leipzig 1935.

— On Blickling homily xiii: the Assumption of the Virgin. RES 12 1936.

— The two accounts of the Assumption in Blickling homily xiii. RES 14 1938.

— An Old English Magnificat. SE 1940.

— The Blickling-Junius tithing homily and Caesarius of Arles. In Philologica: the [Kemp] Malone anniversary studies, Baltimore 1949.

— Vercelli homily xi and its sources. Speculum 24 1949. Includes text of homily.

Schlutter, O. B. Some remarks on M. Förster's print of some Old English homilies in Vercelli codex cxvii. Neophilologus 15 1930.

Brown, C. Beowulf and the Blickling homilies. PMLA 53 1938.

Swaen, A. E. H. Notes on the Blickling homilies. Neophilologus 25 1940.

Menner, R. J. The Anglian vocabulary of the Blickling homilies. In Philologica: the [Kemp] Malone anniversary studies, Baltimore 1949.

Peterson, P. W. Dialect grouping in the unpublished Vercelli homilies. SP 50 1953.

Cross, J. E. 'Ubi sunt' passages in Old English: sources and relationships. Årsbok Vetenskaps-societetens i Lund 1956.

— 'The dry bones speak': a theme in some Old English homilies. JEGP 56 1957.

— Aspects of microcosm and macrocosm in Old English literature. Comparative Lit 14 1962.

— See under Ælfric, above.

— On the Blickling homily for Ascension Day. Neuphilologische Mitteilungen 70 1969.

Turville-Petre, J. Sources of the vernacular homily in England, Norway and Iceland. Arkiv for Nordisk Filologi 75 1960.

— Translations of a lost penitential homily. Traditio 19 1963.

Funke, O. Studien zur alliterierenden und rhythmisierenden Prosa in der älteren altenglischen Homiletik. Anglia 80 1962.

Whitbread, L. 'Wulfstan' homilies xxix, xxx and some related texts. Anglia 81 1963.

Gatch, M. McC. Two uses of apocrypha in Old English homilies. Church History 33 1964.

— Eschatology in the anonymous Old English homilies. Traditio 21 1965.

Dawson, R. MacG. Two new sources for Blickling homilies (viii and xi). N & Q April 1967.

Dalbey, M. A. A textual crux in the third Blickling homily. Eng Lang Notes 5 1968.

— Hortatory tone in the Blickling homilies. Neuphilologische Mitteilungen 70 1969.

Ryan, W. M. Word-play in some Old English homilies and a late Middle English poem. In Studies in language, literature and culture of the Middle Ages and later, ed E. B. Atwood and A. A. Hill, Austin 1969.

Collins, R. L. Six words in the Blickling homilies. In Philological essays in honour of H. D. Meritt, Hague 1970.

Szarmach, P. E. Caesarius of Arles and the Vercelli homilies. Traditio 26 1970.

Scragg, D. G. Accent marks in the Old English Vercelli Book. Neuphilologische Mitteilungen 72 1971.

SAINTS' LIVES

St Chad

Ein altenglisches Leben des heiligen Chad. Ed A. S. Napier, Anglia 10 1888.

The life of St Chad: an Old English homily. Ed R. Vleeskruyer, Amsterdam 1953.

St Christopher

Brüchstuck einer ae. Legende. Ed G. Herzfeld, E Studien 13 1889.

Three Old English prose texts. Ed S. Rypins 1924 (EETS).

The Nowell Codex: BM Cotton Vitellius A. xv, second ms. Ed K. Malone, Early English mss in facsimile vol 12, Copenhagen 1963.

Sisam, K. The compilation of the Beowulf ms. In his Studies in the history of OE literature, Oxford 1953.

For other studies of the ms see under Poetry, col 244, above.

St Guthlac

Das angelsächsische Prosa-Leben des heiligen Guthlac. Ed P. Gonser, Anglistische Forschungen 27 1909.

Klaeber, F. Notes on Old English prose texts IV. MLN 18 1903.

Kern, J. H. Altenglische Varia 1: zum Prosa-Guthlac. E Studien 51 1917.

Bolton, W. F. The ms source of the Old English prose life of St Guthlac. Archiv 197 1961.

See also under verse lives of St Guthlac, col 284, above.

St Margaret

Ed O. Cockayne, Narratiunculae, 1861. Version from ms Cotton Tiberius A. iii. Another version, from ms CCCC 303, is no xv in Assmann's collection, col 317, above.

St Mildred

Ed O. Cockayne, Leechdoms, wort-cunning and star-craft, 3 vols 1864–6 (Rolls ser).

For other anon saints' lives and homilies on saints see collections of Assmann, Skeat and Warner, under Ælfric, above, and the Blickling homilies, above; also index to N. R. Ker, Catalogue of mss containing Anglo-Saxon, Oxford 1957.

MARTYROLOGY

§1

An Old English martyrology. Ed G. Herzfeld 1900 (EETS).

§2

Liebermann, F. Zum Old English martyrology. Archiv 105 1900.

Klaeber, F. Notes on Old English prose texts VI. MLN 18 1903.

Sisam, C. An early fragment of the Old English martyrology (BM add ms 40, 165 A). RES new ser 4 1953.

Cross, J. E. De signis et prodigiis in Versus Sancti Patricii episcopi de mirabilibus Hibernie. Proc Royal Irish Acad 71 1971.

APOCRYPHA AND LEGENDS

Gospel of Nicodemus

The Old English version of the gospel of Nicodemus. Ed W. H. Hulme, PMLA 13 1898.

Wülcker, R. Das Evangelium Nicodemi in der abendländischen Literatur. Paderborn 1872.

Förster, M. Zum altenglischen Nicodemus-Evangelium. Archiv 107 1901.

Hulme, W. H. The Old English gospel of Nicodemus. MP 1 1904. Includes text of homily in ms CCCC 41 and of piece in Cotton Vespasian D. xiv.

Crawford, S. J. The gospel of Nicodemus. Edinburgh 1927.

Jamnes and Mambres

A fragment of the Penitence of Jamnes and Jambres [sic]. Ed M. R. James, Jnl Theological Stud 2 1901. Ms Cotton Tiberius B. v.

Marvels of the East. Ed M. R. James, Oxford 1929. Facs.

Förster, M. Das lateinisch-altenglische Fragment der Apokryphe von Jamnes und Mambres. Archiv 108 1902.

Legends of the Cross

Legends of the holy rood. Ed R. Morris 1871 (EETS). Includes OE text from ms Bodley Auct. F.4.32.

History of the holy rood-tree. Ed A. S. Napier 1894 (EETS). Ms Bodley 343.

Ker, N. R. An eleventh-century Old English legend of the cross before Christ. MÆ 9 1940. Fragment from ms CCCC 557 of text ed Napier, above.

Colgrave, B. and A. Hyde. Two recently discovered leaves from Old English mss. Speculum 37 1962. Another fragment of text ed Napier, above.

Leofric

An Old English vision of Leofric, Earl of Mercia. Ed A. S. Napier, Trans of Philological Soc 1909.

Silverstein, H. T. The vision of Leofric and Gregory's Dialogues. RES 9 1933.

Phoenix (prose version)

Kluge, F. Zum Phoenix. E Studien 8 1885. With text from mss CCCC 198 and Cotton Vespasian D. xiv.

Larsen, H. Notes on the Phoenix. JEGP 41 1942.

Text also ptd in Warner 1917 (col 317, above). See also edns of verse Phoenix by Cook and Blake, col 294, above. For apocrypha see also under Homilies, above.

RULES

General

Tupper, F. History and texts of the Benedictine reform of the tenth century. MLN 8 1893.

Bateson, M. Rules for monks and secular canons after the revival under King Edgar. EHR 9 1894.

Benedictine Rule

Die angelsächsischen Prosabearbeitungen der Benediktinerregel. Ed A. Schröer, Bibliothek der angelsächsischen Prosa vol 2, 1885–8; rptd with appendix by H. Gneuss, Darmstadt 1964.

Caro, G. Die Varianten der Durhamer Hs. und des Tiberius-fragments der ae. Prosa-version der Benedictinerregel. E Studien 24 1898.

Old English Regularis Concordia

De consuetudine monachorum. Ed A. Schröer, E Studien 9 1886.

Ein weiteres Bruchstück der Regularis concordia in altenglischer Sprache (CCCC 201). Ed J. Zupitza, Archiv 84 1890.

Fragment of Ælfric's translation of Æthelwold's De consuetudino monachorum and its relation to other mss. Ed E. Breck, Leipzig 1887. Not by Ælfric.

Regularis concordia. Ed T. Symons 1953. Latin text with modern Eng trn.

Rule of Chrodegang

The Old English rule of Chrodegang and the capitula of Theodulf. Ed A. S. Napier 1914 (EETS).

PENITENTIAL TEXTS

Ancient laws and institutes of England. Ed B. Thorpe 2 vols 1840. With trn.

Das altenglische Bussbuch (sog. Confessionale Pseudo-Egberti). Ed R. Spindler, Leipzig 1934; tr J. T. McNeill and H. M. Gamer, Medieval handbooks of penance, New York 1938.

Die altenglische Version des Halitgar'schen Bussbuches (sog. Poenitentiale Pseudo-Ecgberti). Ed J. Raith, Bibliothek der angelsächsischen Prosa vol 13, 1933, Darmstadt 1964 (with new introd).

Fowler, R. A late Old English handbook for the use of a confessor. Anglia 83 1965. With text.

LITURGY AND PRAYERS

Benedictine Office

Das Benediktiner-Offizium. Ed E. Feiler, Anglistische Forschungen 4 1901.

The Benedictine Office: an Old English text. Ed J. M. Ure, Edinburgh 1957.

Ure, J. M. The Benedictine Office and the metrical paraphrase of the Lord's Prayer in ms CCCC 201. RES new ser 4 1953.

Clemoes, P. 1960. *See under Ælfric, above.*

For the poems in the Benedictine Office (The Creed, Gloria I, Lord's Prayer III and fragments of psalms) see cols 271, 284, 289 and 296, above.

Prayers

Logeman, H. Anglo-Saxonica minora. Anglia 11–12 1889.

Förster, M. Zur Liturgik der angelsächsischen Kirche. Anglia 66 1942.

Banks, R. A. Some Anglo-Saxon prayers from BM ms Cotton Galba A. xiv. N & Q June 1965.

Braekman, W. Some minor Old English texts 1: Prayers from ms Galba A. xiv. Archiv 202 1966.

Hallander, L.-G. Two Old English confessional prayers. Studier i Modern Språkvetenskap new ser 3 1968.

For prayers by Ælfric see Catholic homilies vol 2, ed Thorpe, under Ælfric, above.

MISCELLANEOUS

Æthelwold's account of the monastic revival. Ed O. Cockayne, Leechdoms, wort-cunning and starcraft, 3 vols 1864–6 (Rolls ser), vol 3, 432–44 (with trn); partly tr D. Whitelock, English historical documents vol 1, 1955.

Liebermann, F. Æthelwolds Anhang zur Benedictinerregel. Archiv 108 1902.

Whitelock, D. The authorship of the account of King Edgar's establishment of the monasteries. In Philological essays in honour of H. D. Meritt, Hague 1970.

Indicia monasterialia. Ed F. Kluge, Internationale Zeitschrift für Allgemeine Sprachwissenschaft 2 1885.

Übersetzung von Alcuins De virtutibus et vitiis liber. Ed B. Assmann, Anglia 11 1889.

Die Heiligen Englands. Ed F. Liebermann, Hanover 1889.

Ein altenglisches Prosa-Menologium. Ed H. Henel, Studien zum altenglischen Computus, Halle 1934.

An Old English translation of a letter from Wynfrith to Eadburga in Cotton ms Otho C. i. Ed K. Sisam, MLR 18 1923; rptd in his Studies in the history of OE literature, Oxford 1953.

(6) THE CHRONICLE

Versions

A Corpus Christi College Cambridge 173 (Parker; to 1070)
B BM Cotton Tiberius A. vi (to 977)
C BM Cotton Tiberius B. i (to 1066)
D BM Cotton Tiberius B. iv (to 1079)
E Bodley, Laud Miscellaneous 636 (Peterborough; to 1154)
F BM Cotton Domitian A. viii (bilingual; to 1058)
G BM Cotton Otho B. xi (fragments of a copy of A to 1001)
H BM Cotton Domitian A. ix (fragment; 1113–14).

§1

Venerabilis Bedae Historia ecclesiastica. Ed A. Whelock, Cambridge 1640. Includes text of G copied from the ms before it was burnt.
The Anglo-Saxon chronicle. Ed B. Thorpe 2 vols 1861 (Rolls ser). With trn.
Zupitza, J. Fragment einer englischen Chronik von 1113 und 1114. Anglia 1 1878.
Liebermann, F. Ungedruckte anglo-normannische Geschichtsquellen. Strasbourg 1879. Includes text of annals from ms Cotton Caligula A xv.
Two of the Saxon chronicles parallel (A and E). Ed C. Plummer on the basis of an edn by J. Earle 2 vols Oxford 1892–9, 1952 (with addns by D. Whitelock).
An Anglo-Saxon chronicle from BM Cotton ms Tiberius B. iv. Ed E. Classen and F. E. Harmer, Manchester 1926.
The Anglo-Saxon chronicle (C), annals 978–1017. Ed M. Ashdown, English and Norse documents relating to the reign of Ethelred the Unready, Cambridge 1930. With trn.
The Parker chronicle 832–900. Ed A. H. Smith 1935.
The C-text of the Old English chronicles. Ed H. A. Rositzke, Bochum 1940.
The Parker chronicle and laws: a facsimile. Ed R. Flower and H. Smith 1941 (EETS).
Annales Domitiani Latini. Ed F. P. Magoun, Mediaeval Stud 9 1947.
The genealogical preface to the Anglo-Saxon chronicle: four texts edited to supplement Earle-Plummer. Ed B. Dickins, Cambridge 1952.
The Peterborough chronicle. Ed D. Whitelock, Early English mss in facsimile vol 4, Copenhagen 1955. With appendix by C. Clark.
The Peterborough chronicle 1070–1154. Ed C. Clark, Oxford 1958, 1970 (rev).

Translations

Rositzke, H. A. The Peterborough chronicle translated with an introduction. New York 1951.
Garmonsway, G. N. The Anglo-Saxon chronicle. 1953 (EL).
Tucker, S. I. The Anglo-Saxon chronicle 1042–1154. In English historical documents vol 2, ed D. C. Douglas and G. W. Greenaway 1953.
Whitelock, D. The Anglo-Saxon chronicle 60 BC–AD 1042. In her English historical documents vol 1, 1955.
—— The Anglo-Saxon chronicle: a revised translation. 1961. With D. C. Douglas and S. I. Tucker. Based on 2 preceding items, with full bibliography.
Hoffmann-Hirtz, M. Une chronique anglo-saxonne traduite d'après le manuscrit 173 de Corpus Christi College Cambridge. Strasbourg 1933.
Dahl, T. Den oldengelske krönike i udvalg. Copenhagen 1936.

§2

Purely historical studies are excluded. For poems in the Chronicle see under Poetry, col 295, above.

Grubitz, E. Kritische Untersuchung über die angelsächsischen Annalen bis zum Jahre 893. Göttingen 1868.
Howorth, H. H. Notes on the Anglo-Saxon chronicle. EHR 15 1900.
—— The Anglo-Saxon chronicle: its origin and history. Archaeological Jnl 65 1908.
Poole, R. L. The beginning of the year in the Anglo-Saxon chronicles. EHR 16 1901.
Donald, G. C. Zur Entwicklung des Prosastils in der Sachsenchronik. Marburg 1914.
Rübens, G. Parataxe und Hypotaxe in dem ältesten Teil der Sachsenchronik (Parker HS bis zum Jahre 891). Göttingen 1915.
Beaven, M. L. R. The regnal dates of Alfred, Edward the Elder and Athelstan. EHR 32 1917.
—— The beginning of the year in the Alfredian chronicle 866–87. EHR 33 1918.
Viglione, F. Studio critico-filologico su l'Anglo-Saxon chronicle. Pavia 1922.
Jost, K. Wulfstan und die angelsächsische Chronik. Anglia 47 1923.
Hodgkin, R. H. The beginning of the year in the English chronicle. EHR 39 1924.
Stenton, F. M. The south-western element in the Old English chronicle. In Essays presented to T. F. Tout, Manchester 1925.
Magoun, F. P. Cynewulf, Cyneheard and Osric. Anglia 57 1933.
—— Territorial place- and river-names in the Old English chronicle A-text. Harvard Stud 18 1935.
—— Territorial place- and river-names in the Old English annals D-text. Harvard Stud 20 1938.
—— The Domitian bilingual of the Old English annals: notes on the F-text. MLQ 6 1945.
—— The Domitian bilingual of the Old English annals: the Latin preface. Speculum 20 1945.
—— Brutus and English politics. ELH 14 1947.
—— King Æthelwulf's biblical ancestors. MLR 46 1951.
Thorogood, A. J. The Anglo-Saxon chronicle in the reign of Ecgberht. EHR 48 1933.
Johannson, A. Die erste Westrwiking. Acta Philologica Scandinavica 9 1934.
Fernquist, C. H. Study on the Old English version of the Anglo-Saxon chronicle in Cotton Domitian A. viii. Studier i Modern Sprakvetenskap 13 1937.
Angus, W. S. The chronology of the reign of Edward the Elder. EHR 53 1938.
—— The eighth scribe's dates in the Parker manuscript of the Anglo-Saxon chronicle. MÆ 10 1941.
Atkins, I. The origin of the later part of the Saxon chronicle known as D. EHR 55 1940.
Dickins, B. The late addition to ASC 1066 C. Proc Leeds Philosophical Soc 5 1940.
Wrenn, C. L. A saga of the Anglo-Saxons. History 25 1941. Reply by G. Turville-Petre 27 1942.
Kökeritz, H. Wihtgaraburh. MLN 58 1943.
Wainwright, F. T. Cledemutha. EHR 65 1950.
Clark, C. Studies in the vocabulary of the Peterborough chronicle 1070–1154. Eng & Germanic Stud 5 1953.
—— Notes on ms Laud Misc 636. MÆ 23 1954.
—— Gender in the Peterborough chronicle. E Studies 38 1957.
—— Early Middle English prose: three essays in stylistics. EC 18 1968. Partly on Peterborough chronicle.
—— 'France' and 'French' in the Anglo-Saxon chronicle. Leeds Stud in Eng new ser 3 1969.

— The narrative mode of the Anglo-Saxon chronicle before the Conquest. In England before the Conquest: studies presented to Dorothy Whitelock, Cambridge 1971.

Moorman, C. The Anglo-Saxon chronicle for 755. N & Q March 1954.

Vaughan, R. The chronology of the Parker chronicle 890–970. EHR 69 1954.

Wynn, J. B. The beginning of the year in Bede and the Anglo-Saxon chronicle. MÆ 25 1956.

Whitbread, L. Æthelweard and the Anglo-Saxon chronicle. EHR 74 1959.

Lehiste, I. Names of Scandinavians in the Anglo-Saxon chronicle. PMLA 73 1958.

Towers, T. H. Thematic unity in the story of Cynewulf and Cyneheard. JEGP 62 1963.

Kirby, D. P. Problems of early West Saxon history. EHR 80 1965.

Battaglia, F. J. Anglo-Saxon chronicle for 755: the missing evidence for a traditional reading. PMLA 81 1966.

Derolez, R. An epitome of the Anglo-Saxon chronicle in Lambert of St-Omer's Liber Floridus. E Studies 48 1967.

Waterhouse, R. The theme and structure of 755 Anglo-Saxon chronicle. Neuphilologische Mitteilungen 70 1969.

Davis, R. H. C. Alfred the Great: propaganda and truth. History 56 1971.

Harrison, K. Early Wessex annals in the Anglo-Saxon chronicle. EHR 86 1971.

(7) LAWS. CHARTERS etc

Laws

§1

Ancient laws and institutes of England. Ed B. Thorpe 2 vols 1840. With trn.

Gerefa. Ed F. Liebermann, Anglia 9 1886.

The legal code of Ælfred the Great. Ed M. H. Turk, Halle 1893.

Gesetze der Angelsachsen. Ed F. Liebermann 3 vols Halle 1903–16.

The laws of the earliest English kings. Ed F. L. Attenborough, Cambridge 1922. With trn.

The laws of the kings of England from Edmund to Henry I. Ed A. J. Robertson, Cambridge 1925. With trn.

Textus Roffensis part I: Rochester Cathedral library A.3.5 ff. 1–118. Ed P. Sawyer, Early English mss in facsimile vol 7, Copenhagen 1957.

The Parker Chronicle and laws: a facsimile. Ed R. Flower and H. Smith 1941 (EETS).

A Wulfstan ms. Ed H. R. Loyn 1970. *See under Wulfstan, above.*

For trns of several codes see D. Whitelock, English historical documents c. 500–1042, *1955*.

§2

Studies of Old English law rather than of legal writings are excluded.

Liebermann, F. Die angelsächsische Verordnung über die Dunsæte. Archiv 102 1899.

— Ist Lambardes Text der Gesetze Æthelstans neuzeitliche Fälschung? Anglia Beiblatt 35 1924.

Sisam, K. The authenticity of certain texts in Lambard's Archaionomia 1568. MLR 18 1926; rptd in his Studies in the history of OE literature, Oxford 1953.

— The relationship of Æthelred's codes v and vi. In his Studies in the history of OE literature, Oxford 1953.

Bethurum, D. Stylistic features of the Old English laws. MLR 27 1932.

See also under Wulfstan, above.

Charters

Bibliographies

Sawyer, P. H. Anglo-Saxon charters: an annotated list and bibliography. 1968 (Royal Historical Soc).

§1

Codex diplomaticus aevi saxonici. Ed J. M. Kemble 6 vols 1839–48 (Eng Historical Soc).

Diplomatarium anglicum. Ed B. Thorpe 1865. With trn.

Cartularium saxonicum. Ed W. de G. Birch 3 vols 1885–93.

Birch, W. de G. Index saxonicus: an index to all the names of persons in the Cartularium saxonicum. 1899.

A handbook to the land charters and other Saxonic documents. Ed J. Earle, Oxford 1888.

The Crawford collection of early charters and documents. Ed A. S. Napier and W. H. Stevenson, Oxford 1895.

Select English historical documents of the ninth and tenth centuries. Ed F. E. Harmer, Cambridge 1914. With trn.

Anglo-Saxon charters. Ed A. J. Robertson, Cambridge 1939. With trn.

Textus Roffensis part II: Rochester Cathedral library A.3.5 ff. 119–235. Ed P. Sawyer, Early English mss in facsimile vol 11, Copenhagen 1962.

§2

Ker, N. R. Hemming's cartulary. In Studies in medieval history presented to F. M. Powicke, Oxford 1948.

For numerous studies of individual charters see Sawyer, above.

Other Documents

Anglo-Saxon wills. Ed D. Whitelock, Cambridge 1930. With trn.

An Old English will (of Badanoth Beotting, from ms Cotton Augustus II 42). Ed A. Campbell, JEGP 37 1938.

The will of Æthelgifu. Ed Lord Rennell, Oxford 1968 (Roxburghe Club). With discussion and trn by D. Whitelock, notes by N. Ker and facs.

Anglo-Saxon writs. Ed F. E. Harmer, Manchester 1952. With trn.

Facsimiles of royal writs to AD 1100 presented to V. H. Galbraith. Ed T. A. M. Bishop and P. Chaplais, Oxford 1957.

For trns of many charters, wills etc see D. Whitelock, English historical documents c. 500–1042, *1955*.

(8) SCIENCE, MEDICINE AND MAGIC, AND FOLKLORE

Byrhtferth's Manual

§ 1

Byrhtferth's manual. Ed S. J. Crawford 1929 (EETS).
Byrhtferth's preface. Ed G. F. Forsey, Speculum 3 1928. With trn.

§ 2

Classen, C. M. Über das Leben und die Schriften Byrhtferths. Leipzig 1896.
Singer, C. and D. Byrhtferth's diagram of the physical and physiological fours. Bodleian Quart Record 2 1919.
Crawford, S. J. Byrhtferth of Ramsey and the anonymous life of St Oswald. In Speculum religionis: essays presented to C. G. Montefiore, Oxford 1929.
Ker, N. R. Two notes on ms Ashmole 328. MÆ 4 1935.
Henel, H. Planetenglaube in Ælfrics Zeit. Anglia 58 1934.
— Ein Bruchstück aus Byrhtferths Handbuch. Anglia 61 1937.
— Notes on Byrhtferth's manual. JEGP 41 1942.
— Byrhtferth's preface: the epilogue of his manual? Speculum 18 1943.
Jones, C. W. The Byrhtferth glosses. MÆ 7 1938.
Whitbread, L. Byrhtferth's hexameters. N & Q 30 Oct 1948.
Murphy, J. J. The rhetorical lore of the 'boceras' in Byrhtferth's manual. In Philological essays in honour of H. D. Merritt, Hague 1970.

Medicine and Magic

§ 1

Leechdoms, wort-cunning and starcraft. Ed O. Cockayne 3 vols 1864–6 (Rolls ser).
Peri Didaxeon: eine Sammlung von Rezepten. Ed M. Löweneck, Erlangen 1896.
Herbarium Apuleii. Ed H. Berberich, Heidelberg 1902.
Das Læcceboc; die Lacnunga. Ed G. Leonhardi, Kleinere angelsächsische Denkmäler, Bibliothek der angelsächsischen Prosa vol 6, 1905.
The Anglo-Saxon charms. Ed F. Grendon, Jnl Amer Folklore 22 1909.
Medicina de quadrupedibus. Ed J. Delacourt, Heidelberg 1914. With trn.
Cotton ms Vitellius C. iii of the Herbarium Apulcii. Ed A. J. G. Hilbelink, Amsterdam 1930.
Storms, G. Anglo-Saxon magic. Hague 1948.
Bald's leechbook: BM Royal 12 D. xvii. Ed C. E. Wright, Early English mss in facsimile vol 5, Copenhagen 1955.
Braekman, W. Some minor Old English texts II: various herb recipes (from Nowell transcript of ms Cotton Otho B. xi). Archiv 202 1966.

§ 2

Zupitza, J. Ein verkannter englischer und zwei bisher ungedruckte lateinische Bienensegen. Anglia 1 1878.
— Ein Zauberspruch. Zeitschrift für Deutsches Altertum 31 1887.
Bradley, H. The song of the nine magic herbs. Archiv 113 1904.
Payne, J. F. English medicine in the Anglo-Saxon times. Oxford 1904.
McBryde, J. M. Charms to recover stolen cattle. MLN 21 1906.
Skemp, A. R. The Old English charms. MLR 6 1911.
Meissner, R. Die Zunge des grossen Mannes. Anglia 40 1916.

Singer, C. Early English magic and medicine. Proc Br Acad 9 1920.
Horn, W. Der altenglische Zauberspruch gegen den Hexenschuss. In Probleme der englischen Sprache und Kultur: Festschrift J. Hoops, Heidelberg 1925.
Grattan, J. H. G. Three Anglo-Saxon charms from the Lacnunga. MLR 22 1927.
Holthausen, F. Zu den altenglischen Zaubersprüchen und Segen. Anglia Beiblatt 31 1920.
— Die altenglischen Neunkräutersegen. E Studien 69 1934.
— Zur Textkritik alt- und mittelenglischer Gedichte. Archiv 188 1951.
Magoun, F. P. Zu den ae. Zaubersprüchen. Archiv 171 1937.
— Strophische Überreste in den altenglischen Zaubersprüchen. E Studien 72 1937.
— Old English charm A 13: butan heardan beaman. MLN 58 1943.
Lambert, C. The Old English medical vocabulary. Proc Royal Soc of Medicine 33 1940.
Shook, L. K. Notes on the Old English charms. MLN 55 1940.
Flom, G. T. On the Old English Herbal of Apuleius, Vitellius C. iii. JEGP 40 1941.
Meroney, H. The nine herbs. MLN 59 1944.
— Irish in the Old English charms. Speculum 20 1945.
Storms, G. An Anglo-Saxon prescription from the Lacnunga. E Studies 28 1947.
Helm, K. Der angelsächsische Flursegen. Hessische Blätter für Volkskunde 41 1950.
Schröder, F. R. Erce und Fjorgyn. In Erbe der Vergangenheit: Festgabe für K. Helm, Tübingen 1951.
Bonser, W. Anglo-Saxon medical nomenclature. Eng & Germanic Stud 4 1952.
— General medical practice in Anglo-Saxon England. In Science, medicine and history: essays in honour of C. Singer, Oxford 1953.
— The medical background of Anglo-Saxon England. 1963.
Grattan, J. H. G. and C. Singer. Anglo-Saxon magic and medicine, illustrated specifically from the semi-pagan text Lacnunga. 1952.
Matthiessen, C. C. Et oldengelsk Middel mod Marepine. Danske Studier 1959.
Stürzl, E. Die christlichen Elemente in den altenglischen Zaubersegen. Die Sprache 6 1960.
Fife, A. E. Christian swarm charms. Jnl of Amer Folklore 77 1964.
Talbot, C. H. Some notes on Anglo-Saxon medicine. Medical History 9 1965.
— Anglo-Saxon medicine. In his Medicine in medieval England, 1967.
Rosenberg, B. A. The meaning of Æcerbot. Jnl of Amer Folklore 79 1966.
Hill, T. D. An Irish-Latin analogue for the blessing of the sods in the Old English Æcerbot charm. N & Q Oct 1968.
Scheider, K. Zu den ae. Zaubersprüchen Wiþ wennum and Wiþ wætcrælfadlc. Anglia 87 1969.

Folklore

Assmann, B. Eine Regel über den Donner. Anglia 10 1888.
— Prophezeiung aus dem 1 Januar für das Jahr. Anglia 11 1889.
Förster, M. Die Kleinliteratur der Aberglaubens im Altenglischen. Archiv 110 1903.
— Beiträge zur mittelalterlichen Volkskunde I–IX. Archiv 120–1, 125, 128–9, 134 1908–18.

—— Die altenglischen Traumlunare. E Studien 60 1926.
—— Vom Fortleben antiker Samellunare im Englischen und in anderen Volkssprachen. Anglia 67-8 1944.
Old English lapidary. Ed J. Evans and M. S. Serjeantson, English mediaeval lapidaries, 1933 (EETS).

Henel, H. Altenglischen Mönchsaberglaube. E Studien 69 1935.
—— Planetenglaube in Ælfrics Zeit. Anglia 58 1934.

(9) OTHER SECULAR PROSE

Apollonius of Tyre

§ 1

Die altenglische Bearbeitung der Erzählung von Apollonius von Tyrus. Ed J. Zupitza, Archiv 97 1896.
Die alt- und mittelenglischen Apollonius-Bruchstücke. Ed J. Raith, Munich 1956.
The Old English Apollonius of Tyre. Ed P. Goolden, Oxford 1958.

§ 2

Zupitza, J. Welcher Text liegt der altenglischen Bearbeitung der Erzählung von Apollonius von Tyrus zu Grunde? Romanische Forschungen 3 1886.
Singer, S. Apollonius von Tyrus. Halle 1895.
Klebs, E. Die Erzählung von Apollonius aus Tyrus. Berlin 1899.
Märkisch, R. Die altenglische Bearbeitung der Erzählung von Apollonius von Tyrus. Berlin 1899.
Chapman, C. O. Beowulf and Apollonius of Tyre. MLN 46 1931.
Goepp, P. H. The narrative material of Apollonius of Tyre. ELH 5 1938.

Letter of Alexander to Aristotle

§ 1

Ed S. Rypins, Three Old English prose texts, 1924 (EETS).
For facs and studies of the ms, see under St Christopher, col 326 above, and under Poetry, col 244, above.

§ 2

Klaeber, F. Notes on Old English prose texts v. MLN 18 1903.
Bradley, H. and K. Sisam. Textual notes on the Old English Epistola Alexandri. MLR 14 1919.
Hamilton, G. L. Quelques notes sur l'histoire de la légende d'Alexandre en Angleterre au Moyen Age. In Mélanges offerts à Antoine Thomas, Paris 1927.

Pfister, F. Auf den Spuren Alexanders des Grossen in der alteren englischen Literatur. Germanisch-romanische Monatsschrift 16 1928.
Butturff, D. R. A note on the Old English translation of the Epistola Alexandri ad Aristotelem. Eng Lang Notes 8 1970.

Wonders of the East

Die Wunder des Ostens. Ed R. Knappe, Berlin 1906.
Three Old English prose texts. Ed S. Rypins 1924 (EETS).
Facs of both mss and of Latin versions in Marvels of the East, *ed M. R. James, Oxford 1929. For facs of ms Vitellius A. xv and studies of this ms, see under* St Christopher, *col 326 above and under* Poetry, *col 244, above.*
Förster, M. Zur altenglischen Mirabilien-Version. Archiv 117 1906.

Salomon and Saturn (prose version)

§ 1

Analecta anglo-saxonica. Ed B. Thorpe 1834.
The prose Salomon and Saturn. Ed J. M. Kemble, Anglo-Saxon dialogues of Salomon and Saturn, 3 pts 1845-8.
There is also a prose section in the poetical Solomon and Saturn; *see col 303, above.*

§ 2

Utley, F. L. The prose Salomon and Saturn and the tree called Chy. Mediaeval Stud 19 1957.
Evans, J. M. Microcosmic Adam. MÆ 35 1966.

Adrian and Ritheus

Ed J. M. Kemble, Anglo-Saxon dialogues of Salomon and Saturn, 3 pts 1845-8.
Förster, M. Zu Adrian und Ritheus. E Studien 23 1897.

Distichs of Cato

Der altenglische Cato. Ed J. Nehab, Berlin 1879.

P. C.

II. WRITINGS IN LATIN

GENERAL WORKS: *Collections of Sources; Literary Histories; British Celtic Writers; Early Irish Writers; Early Old English Writers; Later Old English Writers; Later Irish Writers.*

A. GENERAL WORKS

(1) COLLECTIONS OF SOURCES

Acta sanctorum. Antwerp 1643–.
Mabillon, J. Acta sanctorum ordinis Sancti Benedicti. 9 vols Paris 1668-1701, Venice 1733–.
Patrologia latina. Ed J. P. Migne 221 vols Paris 1844-64.
Rees, W. J. Lives of the Cambro-British Saints. Llandovery 1854 (Welsh Mss Soc).
Keil, H. Grammatici latini. 7 vols Leipzig 1857–.
Rerum britannicarum medii aevi scriptores (Chronicles and Memorials of Great Britain and Ireland during the Middle Ages). 1858– (Rolls Ser).

Raine, J. The historians of the church of York and its archbishops. 3 vols 1879-94 (Rolls ser).
Stubbs, W. Memorials of Saint Dunstan. 1874 (Rolls ser).
Monumenta Germaniae historica: poetae latini aevi carolini. 4 vols Berlin 1881-1923.
Analecta hymnica medii aevi. Ed G. M. Dreves, C. Blume and H. M. Bannister 55 vols Leipzig 1886-1922.
Plummer, C. Vitae sanctorum Hiberniae. 2 vols Oxford 1910.

(2) LITERARY HISTORIES ETC

Wright, T. Biographia britannica literaria (Anglo-Saxon period). 1842.

Hauréau, B. Les écoles d'Irlande. In Singularités historiques et littéraires, Paris 1861.

Haddan, A. W. and W. Stubbs. Councils and ecclesiastical documents relating to Great Britain and Ireland. 4 vols Oxford 1869–78.

Warren, F. E. The liturgy and ritual of the Celtic Church. Oxford 1881.

Zimmer, H. Über die Bedeutung des irischen Elements für die mittelalterliche Kultur. Preussische Jahrbücher 59 1887.

Hauck, A. Kirchengeschichte Deutschlands. 5 vols Leipzig 1887–1920, 1904 (4th edn of vol 1).

Ebert, A. Allgemeine Geschichte der Literatur des Mittelalters im Abendlande bis zum Beginne des XI Jahrhunderts. Vols 1–2, Leipzig 1889 (2nd edn); vol 3, 1887; tr French 3 vols Paris 1883–9.

Bellesheim, A. Geschichte der katholischen Kirche in Irland. 3 vols Mainz 1890–1.

Manitius, M. Geschichte der christlichlateinischen Poesie bis zur Mitte des viii Jahrhunderts. Stuttgart 1891.

— Geschichte der lateinischen Literatur des Mittelalters. 3 vols Munich 1911–31.

Gross, C. Sources and literature of English history from the earliest times to about 1485. Cambridge Mass 1897, London 1915.

Stephens, W. R. W. and W. Hunt. History of the English Church. Vol 1 (597–1066), 1899.

Zimmer, H. The Celtic Church in Britain and Ireland. 1902.

Roger, M. L'enseignement des lettres classiques d'Ausone à Alcuin. Paris 1905.

Esposito, M. The Latin writers of mediaeval Ireland. Hermathena 14 1907; suppl 1908.

Turner, W. Irish teachers in the Carolingian revival of learning. Catholic Univ Bull 13 1907.

Gougaud, L. Les Chrétientés celtiques. Paris 1911; tr 1932 (enlarged).

— L'œuvre des Scotti dans l'Europe continentale. Revue d'Histoire Ecclésiastique 9 1908.

— Etude sur les Loricae celtiques et sur les prières qui s'en rapprochent. Bulletin d'Ancienne Littérature et d'Archéologie Chrétiennes 1 1911.

— The achievement and influence of Irish monks. Studies 20 1931.

— Les surnuméraires de l'émigration scottique (vie–viiie siècles). Revue Bénédictine 43 1931.

— Les scribes monastiques d'Irlande au travail. Revue d'Histoire Ecclésiastique 27 1931.

The Cambridge medieval history. Ed J. B. Bury et al 8 vols Cambridge 1911–36.

Raby, F. J. E. A history of Christian-Latin poetry from the beginnings to the end of the Middle Ages. Oxford 1927.

— A history of Christian-Latin poetry from the beginnings to the end of the Middle Ages. Oxford 1927, 1953 (rev).

Ueberweg, F. Grundriss der Geschichte der Philosophie.

Vol 2, Berlin 1928. Die patristische und scholastische Philosophie, ed B. Geyer.

Kenney, J. F. The sources for the early history of Ireland: an introduction and guide. Vol 1, Ecclesiastical, New York 1929. Also on some English writers, e.g. Gildas, Nennius, Aldhelm, Bede.

Messenger, R. E. Ethical teachings in the Latin hymns of medieval England. New York 1930.

Laistner, M. L. W. Thought and letters in Western Europe AD 500 to 900. 1931.

MacNeill, E. Beginnings of Latin culture in Ireland. Studies 20 1931.

Wright, F. A. and T. A. Sinclair. A history of later Latin literature. 1931.

Baxter, J. H., C. Johnson and J. F. Willard. An index of British and Irish Latin writers AD 400–1520. Archivum Latinitatis Medii Aevi 7 1932.

Crawford, S. J. Anglo-Saxon influence on Western Christendom. Oxford 1933.

Ogilvy, J. D. A. Anglo-Saxon scholarship 597–780. Univ of Colorado Stud 22 1935.

— Books known to Anglo-Latin writers from Aldhelm to Alcuin 670–804. Cambridge Mass 1936.

See F. van Steenberghen, Philosophie des Mittelalters: bibliographische Einführungen in das Studium der Philosophie vol 17, Berne 1950.

Sarton, G. Introduction to the history of science. Vols 1–3, Baltimore 1927–48.

Vignaux, P. La pensée au Moyen Age. Paris 1938.

Ghellinck, J. de. Littérature latine au Moyen Age. 2 vols Paris 1939.

Ker, N. R. Medieval libraries of Great Britain. 1941 (Royal Historical Soc).

Levison, W. England and the Continent in the eighth century. Oxford 1946.

Jones, C. W. Saints' lives and chronicles in early England. Ithaca 1947.

Martin-Clarke, D. E. Culture in early Anglo-Saxon England. Oxford 1947.

Duckett, E. S. Anglo-Saxon saints and scholars. New York 1947.

Hélin, M. A history of medieval Latin literature. New York 1949.

Forest, A., F. van Steenberghen and M. de Gandillac. Le mouvement doctrinal du ixe au xive siècle. In Histoire de l'Eglise, ed A. Fliche and V. Martin, vol 13, Paris 1951.

Crombie, A. C. Augustine to Galileo: the history of science AD 400–1650. 1952.

Chadwick, N. K. Intellectual contacts between Britain and Gaul in the fifth century. In Studies in early British history, ed Chadwick, Cambridge 1954.

Colgrave, B. The earliest saints' lives written in England. Proc Br Acad 44 1959.

Morrel, M. C. A manual of Old English Biblical materials. Knoxville 1965.

Hanning, R. W. The vision of history in early Britain. New York 1966.

Bolton, W. F. A history of Anglo-Latin literature 597–1066. Vol 1: 597–740, Princeton 1967.

B. BRITISH CELTIC WRITERS

GILDAS
d. c. 570

§ 1

De excidio et conquestu Britanniae. Ed J. Stephenson 1838 (Eng Historical Soc) (=Migne, Patrologia latina vol 69); ed T. Mommsen, Chronica minora vol 3, pt i,

Monumenta Germaniae historica, Auctores antiquiores vol 13; ed H. Williams 1899 (as Gildas, The ruin of Britain) (text and trn) (Hon Soc of Cymmrodorion).

Poems abscribed to Gildas:

Lorica. Analecta hymnica vol 51, p. 159; Irish liber hymnorum vol 1, 1898, p. 206; F. J. H. Jenkinson, Hisperica famina, Cambridge 1908, p. 52. Both

Mommsen and Wilhelm Meyer doubt whether Gildas is the author: against H. Zimmer, Nennius vindicatus, Berlin 1893, pp. 301 f.

[Prayer] pro itineris et navigii prosperitate. W. Meyer, Gildae oratio rythmica, Nachrichten der Königlichen Gesellschaft der Wissenschaften zu Göttingen, 1912, pp. 48 f. Probably by Gildas.

§2

de la Borderie, A. La date de la naissance de Gildas. Revue Celtique 6 1883.

— L'Historia britonum attribuée à Nennius et l'Historia britannica avant Geoffroi de Monmouth. Paris 1883.

Wade-Evans, A. W. Notes on the Excidium Britanniae. Celtic Rev 1 1905.

— The ruin of Britannia. Celtic Rev 2 1905. Reply by E. W. B. Nicholson, The ruin of history, ibid.

— The Scotti and Picti in the Excidium Britanniae. Archaeologia Cambrensis ser 6 10 1910.

— The Saxones in the Excidium Britanniae. Archaeologia Cambrensis ser 6 11 1911.

— The Picti and Scotti in the Excidium Britanniae. Celtic Rev 9 1914.

— The Romani in the Excidium Britanniae. Ibid.

— The Saxones in the Excidium Britanniae. Celtic Rev 10–11 1915–16.

— Some insular sources of the Excidium Britanniae. Y Cymmrodor 27 1917.

— Gildas and modern professors. Y Cymmrodor 31 1921.

— Further remarks on the De excidio. Archaeologia Cambrensis 98 1944.

Fonssagrives, J. S. Gildas de Ruis et la société bretonne au vie siècle. Paris 1908.

Thurneysen, R. Zum Geburtsjahr des Gildas. Zeitschrift für Keltische Philologie 14 1923.

Wheeler, G. H. Gildas de Excidio Britanniae, chapter 26. EHR 41 1926.

Lot, F. De la valeur historique du De excidio et conquestu Britanniae de Gildas. In Mediæval studies in memory of Gertrude S. Loomis, Paris 1927.

— Bretons et Anglais au 5e et 6e siècles. Proc Br Acad 16 1930.

Ernault, E. Sur le nom breton de Gildas. Revue Celtique 48 1931.

Burkitt, F. C. The Bible of Gildas. Revue Bénédictine 46 1934.

Stevens, C. E. Gildas sapiens. EHR 56 1941.

Johnstone, P. K. Dual personality of St Gildas. Antiquity 30 1946.

HISTORIA BRITONUM AND NENNIUS

The problems which this complex of writings presents are summarized in Manitius, Geschichte der lateinischen Literatur des Mittelalters vol 1, Munich 1911; in Kenney, Sources for the early history of Ireland, New York 1929; and in F. Lot, Nennius et l'Historia britonum, 2 vols Paris 1934–6 (with text). The contents of the collection (the individual members of which are, for the most part, composite in character; see Kenney, p. 154) are, according to one arrangement (BM Harleian ms 3859): Computus and De sex aetatibus mundi; Historia britonum (description of Britain; Brutus legend; Irish events; sons of Noah; Roman conquest of Britain; legend of the Christian King Lucius; end of Roman dominion; coming of Saxons; St Germanus; Ambrosius; Vortigern and his descendants; Vita Patricii; Arthur legend; Genealogies of Saxon kings and computus; Annales Cambriae; Welsh genealogies; list of British cities; mirabilia Britanniae.

§1

Historia britonum. Ed J. Stevenson 1838 (Historical Soc); ed A. Schulz (San-Marte), Berlin 1844; ed T. Mommsen, Chronica minora vol 3, Monumenta Germaniae historica, Auctores antiquiores vol 13; ed F. Lot, Paris 1934.

Nennius's History of the Britons. Tr A. W. Wade-Evans 1938.

§2

Zimmer, H. Nennius vindicatus. Berlin 1893.

Duchesne, L. Nennius retractatus. Revue Celtique 15 1894.

Howorth, H. Nennius and the Historia britonum. Archaeologia Cambrensis ser 6 17 1917.

Liebermann, F. Nennius the author of the Historia brittonum. In Essays in mediaeval history presented to T. F. Tout, Manchester 1925. Regards Nennius as the true compiler of the collection.

Loth, J. Remarques à l'Historia britonum dite de Nennius. Revue Celtique 49 1932.

Thurneysen, R. Nochmals Nennius. Zeitschrift für Keltische Philologie 20 1935.

Nitze, W. A. Note on the Arthuriana of Nennius. MLN 58 1943.

Jackson, K. On the Northern British section in Nennius. In Celt and Saxon, ed N. Chadwick, Cambridge 1963.

HISPERICA FAMINA

A composition in a mysterious speech (Geheimsprache), composed of a mixture of Hebrew, Greek and Vulgar Latin along with words of no known origin. It was probably written in Britain in the 6th century, and not in Ireland as Jenkinson and others have supposed. This speech has some affinity with that used by Virgilius Maro, the grammarian of Toulouse. His works are ed H. Huemer, Virgilii Maronis grammatici opera, Leipzig 1886; see D. Tardi, Les Epitomae de Virgile de Toulouse, Paris 1928, and Huemer, Die Epitomae des Grammaticus Virgilius Maro nach dem Fragmentum Vindobonese 19556, Wiener Sitzungsberichte 99 1882; H. Zimmer, Über direkte Handelsverbindungen Westgalliens mit Irland, Berliner Sitzungsberichte 1909, thinks Virgil came to Ireland at the end of the 5th century.

§1

Ed A. Mai, Classici auctores vol 5, Rome 1833 (=Migne, Patrologia latina, vol 90); ed J. M. Stowasser, Incerti auctoris Hisperica famina, Vienna 1887; ed F. J. H. Jenkinson, The Hisperica famina, Cambridge 1908.

Luxemburg and Paris fragments. F. J. Mone, Die gallische Sprache und ihre Brauchbarkeit, Karlsruhe 1851 (Institut de Luxembourg, 1896); H. Zimmer, Neue Fragmente von Hisperica famina, Nachrichten der Königlichen Gesellschaft der Wissenschaften zu Göttingen, 1895; H. Bradshaw, Collected papers, Cambridge 1889.

§2

Geyer, P. Die Hisperica famina. Archiv für Lateinische Lexikographie und Grammatik 2 1885.

Stowasser, J. M. Zu den Hisperica famina. Archiv für Lateinische Lexikographie und Grammatik 3 1886. Reply by R. Thurneysen, ibid.

— Das Luxemburger Fragment. Wiener Studien 9 1887.

— De quarto quodam scoticae latinitatis specimine. Fünfzehnter Jahresbericht über das Franz-Joseph-Gymnasium in Wien 1889.

Rhys, J. The Luxembourg folio. Revue Celtique 1 1870.

— The Luxembourg fragment. Revue Celtique 13 1892.

Zimmer, H. Nennius vindicatus. Berlin 1893. Pp. 291 f.

Goetz, G. Über Dunkel- und Geheimsprache im späten und mittelalterlichen Latein. Leipziger Sitzungsberichte 1896.

Ellis, R. Notes on mss of Catullus and Hisperica famina. Hermathena 12 1902.

— On the Hisperica famina. Jnl of Philology 28 1903.

Polheim, K. Die lateinische Reimprosa. Leipzig 1925. The Hisperica famina are not simple rimed prose, but have a structure that suggests verse.

Rand, E. K. The Irish flavour of Hisperica famina. In Ehrengabe für Karl Strecker, Dresden 1931.

Damon, P. W. The meaning of the Hisperica famina. Amer Jnl of Philology 79 1953.

Winterbottom, M. On the Hesperica famina. Celtica 8 1969.

Pieces Related to Hisperica Famina

(a) Lorica of Gildas. *See under Gildas, above.*
(b) Rubrisca, alphabetical poem (? by Olimbrianus; *see* verse 78). Text in Jenkinson, pp. 55 f.
(c) Alphabetical hymn, Adelphus Adelpha meter. Text in Jenkinson, pp. 61 f; *see also* R. Thurneysen, Gloses bretonnes, Revue Celtique 11 1890; bibliography in Manitius, Geschichte der lateinischen Literatur des Mittelalters vol 1, Munich 1911.

C. IRISH WRITERS, FIRST PERIOD

IRISH HYMNS

See Kenney, col 338, above.

Hymnodia hiberno-celtica. Ed C. Blume, Analecta hymnica vol 5. A *corpus* of Irish-Celtic Latin hymns, including those in the Liber hymnorum, Bangor antiphonary and Book of Cerne.

The Irish liber hymnorum. Ed J. H. Bernard and R. Atkinson 2 vols 1898 (Henry Bradshaw Soc).

The antiphonary of Bangor (with facsimile of ms). Ed F. E. Warren 2 vols 1893–5 (Henry Bradshaw Soc). Not an Antiphonary, but a collection of hymns, prayers etc from end of 7th century.

IRISH LITURGICAL BOOKS

See Kenney, pp. 689 f. for full bibliography and reference to fragments.

(a) The Bobbio Missal. 3 vols 1917–24 (Henry Bradshaw Soc).
(b) The Stowe Missal. 2 vols 1906–15 (Henry Bradshaw Soc).
(c) The Antiphonary of Bangor. *See* under Irish Hymns, above.

ST PATRICK
d. 463

Confessio etc. Ed N. J. D. White. In Libri sancti Patricii: the Latin writings of St Patrick, Proc Royal Irish Acad 23 1905; also in Libri sancti Patricii, 1918. For further bibliography, *see* Kenney, p. 166.

Bury, J. B. Life of St Patrick and his place in history. 1905.

Müller, K. Der heilige Patrick. Nachrichten der Königlichen Gesellschaft der Wissenschaften zu Göttingen 1931.

Meissner, J. L. C. The British tradition of St Patrick's Life. Proc Royal Irish Acad 40 1932.

Hitchcock, F. H. M. The Confessio and Epistola of Patrick of Ireland and their literary affinities in Irenaeus, Cyprian and Orientius. Hermathena 47,1932.

Macneill, E. St Patrick. 1934.

Wheeler, G. H. St Patrick's birthplace. EHR 50 1935.

Oulton, J. E. L. The Credal statements of St Patrick as contained in the fourth chapter of his confession: a study of their sources. Dublin 1940.

Bieler, L. The life and legend of St Patrick. Dublin 1949.

— The place of St Patrick in Latin language and literature. Vigiliae Christianae 6 1952.

COLUMBA or COLUM-CILLE
d. 597

Among the poems ascribed to him, 2 have the best claim:
(i) Altus prosator, Analecta hymnica vol 51; Liber

hymnorum vol 1, 1898; ed C. Cuissard, La prose de S. Columba, Revue Celtique 5 1881; *for mss and bibliography see Kenney, pp. 263 f.*; (ii) Noli Pater, Analecta hymnica vol 51; Liber hymnorum vol 1, 1898.

Menzies, L. St Columba of Iona. 1920.

Anderson, A. O. In his Early sources of Scottish history vol 1, 1922.

Lindsay, W. M. Columba's Altus and the Abstrusa glossary. Classical Quart 17 1923.

Simpson, W. D. The historical Saint Columba. Aberdeen 1927.

COLUMBANUS
d. 615

§1

Letters and poems. In Migne, Patrologia latina vol 80; ed W. Gundlach, Monumenta Germaniae historica, epistolae vol 3. 4 of these are poems, which Gundlach regards as authentic; *see* Über die Columban-Briefe, Neues Archiv 13 1888.

Seebass, O. Über die Handschriften der Sermonen und Briefe Columbas von Luxeuil. Neues Archiv 17 1892. Reply by Gundlach, Zu den Columbanbriefen: eine Entgegnung, *ibid.*

Sermons: or homilies. In Migne, Patrologia latina vol 80. 4 of these may be by Columbanus: nos 3, 11, 14, 17 ed O. Seebass, Zeitschrift für Kirchengeschichte 14 1894.

The Rule of Columbanus and the Penitential. *See* Kenney, pp. 197 f.; and G. Domenici, Rivista Storica Benedettina 11 1920.

Columbanus may be the author of A boating song, ed E. Dümmler, *Neues Archiv 6 1881.*

§2

Martin, E. S. Columban. Paris 1905.

Metlake, G. The life and writings of S. Columban. Philadelphia 1914.

Domenici, G. S. Colombano. La Civiltà Cattolica 1916.

Lugnano, P. S. Columbano: monaco e scrittore. Rivista Storica Benedettina 7 1916.

Laux, J. J. Der heilige Kolumban. Freiburg 1919.

Pellizzari, A. S. Colombano e le lettere. Scuola Cattolica 15 July 1923.

Krusch, B. Zur Mönchsregel Columbans. Neues Archiv 46 1925.

Morin, G. Le 'Liber S. Columbani in psalmos' et le ms Ambros. C. 101. inf. Revue Bénédictine 38 1926.

Roussel, J. Saint Columban. 2 vols Paris 1941–2.

ADAMNAN, Abbot of Iona
d. 704

Vita Sancti Columbae. Ed W. Reeves, The life of St Columba, from a ms of the eighth century, Edinburgh

1857 (with notes etc); ed W. F. Skene, The historians of Scotland vol 6, Edinburgh 1874; ed W. M. Metcalfe, Pinkerton's lives of the Scottish saints vol 1, Paisley 1889; ed J. T. Fowler, Adamni vita S. Columbae, Oxford 1894. For mss see Kenney, pp. 429 f. On the shorter recension (in Migne, Patrologia latina vol 88), see Kenney, p. 431.

Huyshe, W. The life of S. Columba. Tr 1906.

De locis sanctis. Ed T. Tobler, Itinera hierosolymitana vol 1, Geneva 1879; ed P. Geyer, Corpus scriptorum ecclesiasticorum latinum vol 39, Vienna 1898. Used by Bede in his treatise on the Holy Places. Adamnan got his information from Arculf, a Gallic bishop who was wrecked on his return from Palestine and came to Iona.

Commentary on Virgil. Adamnan may be the original compiler of a collection of scholia on the Eclogues and Georgics. For bibliography and discussion see Kenney, pp. 286 f.

Cook, A. S. Possible begetter of Old English Beowulf and Widsið. Trans Connecticut Acad of Arts & Sciences 25 1922.

— Who was the Elfrid of Aldhelm's letter? Speculum 2 1927.

Meritt, H. Old English Aldhelm glosses. MLN 67 1952.

MINOR IRISH LATIN WRITERS

(a) Augustine (an Irishman, fl. 655). De mirabilibus sanctae scripturae. In Migne, Patrologia latina vol 35. See L. Gougaud, Christianity in Celtic lands, 1932, p. 266, and W. Reeves, On Augustine: an Irish writer of the seventh century, Proc Royal Irish Acad 7 1861, and Kenney, pp. 275 f.

(b) Lathcen (d. 661). Abridgement of Gregory's Moralia. See L. Gougaud, Christianity in Celtic lands, 1932, p. 276, and Kenney, pp. 278 f.

(c) Aileran the Wise (d. 664). (i) Interpretatio mystica progenitorum domini Jesu Christi. In Migne, Patrologia latina vol 80, completed in C. MacDonnell, Proc Royal Irish Acad 8 1857–61, pp. 369 f; (ii) Poems on the Canons of Eusebius, in Migne, Patrologia latina vol 101. See Kenney, p. 280, and D. de Bruyne, Une poésie inconnue d'Aileran le Sage, Revue Bénédictine 29 1911.

ANONYMOUS IRISH LATIN WRITERS

(a) Versus cuiusdam Scotti de Alfabeto. Ed E. Baehrens in Poetae latini minores vol 5, Leipzig 1883. Riddles on the letters of the alphabet, c. 650.

Müller, L. Versus Scoti cuiusdam de alphabeto. Rheinisches Museum 20 1865.

— Zu den versus Scoti cuiusdam de alphabeto. Rheinisches Museum 22 1867.

Wagner, W. Zu den versus Scoti cuiusdam de Alphabeto. Ibid.

Grosse, E. Zu den versus Scoti cuiusdam de alphabeto. Rheinisches Museum 24 1869.

Klein, J. Zu den versus Scoti cuiusdam de alphabeto. Rheinisches Museum 31 1876.

Buecheler, F. Coniectanea. Rheinisches Museum 36 1881.

Manitius, M. Geschichte der christlichlateinischen Poesie, p. 484; Geschichte der lateinischen Literatur des Mittelalters vol 1, pp. 190 f.

(b) The Berne collection of riddles. Ed A. Riese, Anthologica latina, 1869–70, no 481 (Aenigmata codicis Bernensis, 611).

Shenkl, K. Handschriftliches zur lateinischen Anthologie. Wiener Studien 2 1880.

Meyer, W. Anfang und Ursprung der lateinischen und griechischen rythmischen Dichtung. Abhandlungen der Bayerischen Akademischen 17 1886.

(c) Vere novo florebat. Ed A. Riese, Anthologia latina, 1869–70, no 941.

(d) Perge carina. Ed J. B. Pitra, Spicilegium solesmense vol 3, 1855.

(e) Rauca sonora languida voce. Ed A. Riese, Anthologia latina, 1869–70, no 739.

(f) Incipit de signis et prodigiis et de quibusdam Hyberniae admirandis. Ed A. Riese, Anthologica latina, 1869–70, no 791 (31 verses); ed T. Mommsen, Monumenta Germaniae historica, Auctores antiquiores vol 13.

On the last 4 poems, see Kenney, pp. 733 f.

(g) De duodecim abusivis saeculi. Ed W. Hartel, Cypriani opera vol 3, pp. 152 f, Corpus Scriptorum ecclesiasticorum latinorum vol 3, Vienna 1868; ed S. Hellmann, Pseudo-Cyprianus de xii abusivis saeculi, Texte und Untersuchungen vol 34, pt i, Leipzig 1909. Anon, c. 650, written in south-east Ireland, attributed to Cyprian, Augustine and Isidore, and very popular.

D. ANGLO-SAXON WRITERS, FIRST PERIOD

ALDHELM
d. 709

§ 1

Opera. Ed J. A. Giles, Oxford 1844 (=Migne, Patrologia latina vol 89); ed R. Ehwald, Monumenta Germaniae historica, Auctores antiquiae vol 15 1919 (critical edn).

De laudibus virginitatis. Ed G. van Langenhove, Bruges 1941 (facs).

§ 2

Müller, L. Zu Aldhelmus. Rheinisches Museum 22 1867.

Manitius, M. Zu Aldhelm und Beda. Wiener Sitzungsberichte 113 1886. On the authors quoted by Aldhelm and Bede.

Zupitza, J. Eine Conjectur zu Aldhelm. Romanische Forschungen 3 1887.

Zimmer, H. Keltische Beiträge, I. Zeitschrift für Deutsches Alterthum 32 1887. On the date of Aldhelm's letter Ealfrid; before 690.

Bönhoff, L. Aldhelm von Malmesbury. Dresden 1894.

Browne, G. F. Aldhelm. 1903.

Mazzoni, D. Aldhelmiana: studio critico letterario su Aldhelmo di Sherborne. Rome 1916. From Rivista Storica Benedettina 1915.

Strecker, K. Aldhelms Gedichte in Tegernsee. Archiv 143 1922.

Cook, A. S. Aldhelm's legal studies. JEGP 7 1924.

— Aldhelm and the source of Beowulf 2523. MLN 40 1926.

Pitman, J. H. The riddles of Aldhelm. New Haven 1925.

von Ehrhardt-Siebold, E. Aldhelm's Chrismal. Speculum 10 1935.

Anderson, G. K. Aldhelm and the Leiden riddle. In Old English poetry, ed R. P. Creed 1967.

ÆTHELWALD

Author of some of a group of rhythmical Latin poems which were formerly ascribed to Aldhelm; see Raby, Christian-Latin poetry, pp. 144 f.

Poems. In Ehwald's edn of Aldhelm, pp. 519 f; also in
P. Jaffé, Monumenta Moguntina, Bibliotheca rerum
germanicarum vol 3, Berlin 1866.
Traube, L. Karolingische Dichtungen. Berlin 1888.
Bradley, H. Some poems ascribed to Aldhelm. EHR 15
1900.
Brandl, A. Zu dem angeblichen Schreiben des alt-
mercischen Königs Æthelwæld an Aldhelm. Archiv
171 1937.
Schröbler, I. Zu den Carmina rhythmica. Beiträge zur
Geschichte der Deutschen Sprache und Literatur 79
1957.
Schulze, F. W. Reimstrukturen im Offa-Preislied
Aethilwalds und die Entwicklung des altenglischen
Alliterations verses. Zeitschrift für Deutsches
Alterthum 92 1963.

THE MONK OF WHITBY
fl. c. 710

The life of Gregory the Great. Ed F. A. Gasquet,
Westminster 1904; ed B. Colgrave, Lawrence Kansas
1968.

FELIX, Monk of Croyland
fl. 730

Life of S. Guthlac. Ed J. Mabillon, Acta SS. ordinis
S. Benedicti vol 3 pt i; Acta SS. April vol 2; ed R.
Gough, The history and antiquities of Croyland
Abbey, 1783; ed C. W. Goodwin 1848 (with Old Eng-
lish version); ed B. Colgrave, Cambridge 1956.

EDDIUS STEPHANUS
fl. 711-31

The life of Bishop Wilfrid. Ed B. Colgrave, Cambridge
1927. Also ed W. Levison in Monumenta Germaniae
historica, Script Rerum Merov vol 6; and J. Raine,
Historians of the Church of York, vol 1.
Wells, B. W. Eddi's Life of Wilfrid. EHR 6 1891.

TATWINE, Archbishop of Canterbury
d. 734

De octo partibus orationis. Ms Rome codex palatinus,
1746, folios 99 f. Ed in part A. Wilmanns, Der
Katalog der Lorscher Klosterbibliothek aus dem
zehnten Jahrhundert, Rheinisches Museum 23 1868.
See Roger, L'enseignement des lettres classiques,
p. 338.
— Aenigmata. Ed T. Wright, Anglo-Latin satirical
poets of the twelfth century, 1872 (Rolls ser).

EUSEBIUS or HWAETBERHT
fl. 730

Aenigmata. Ed T. Wright, Anecdota Bedae, Lanfranci
et aliorum, 1851 (Caxton Soc).
Buecheler, F. Coniectanea. Rheinisches Museum 36
1881.

BEDE
673-735
Bibliographies

Beda Venerabilis: Bibliographie. Deutscher Gesamtkatalog (Sonderheft). Berlin 1938.
Laistner, M. L. W. and H. H. King. A handlist of Bede
manuscripts. Ithaca 1943.
Bolton, W. F. A Bede bibliography 1935-60. Traditio 18
1962.

Collections

Opera. Paris 1544, Basle 1563, Cologne 1612, 1688;
ed J. A. Giles 12 vols 1843-4 (=Migne, Patrologia
latina vols 90-5).
Bedae opera historica. Ed C. Plummer 2 vols Oxford
1896; ed J. E. King 2 vols 1930 (Loeb edn).

§1
Grammatical Works

De metrica arte. Ed H. Keil, Grammatici latini vol 7.
De schematibus et tropis. Ed C. Halm, Rhetores latini
minores, Leipzig 1863.
De orthographia. Ed H. Keil, Grammatici latini vol 7.
See R. B. Palmer, Bede as a textbook writer: a study of
his De arte metrica. Speculum 34 1959; G. H. Tanen-
hous, Bede's De schematibus et tropis: a translation,
Quart Jnl of Speech 48 1962.
See Roger, L'enseignement des lettres classiques, pp. 331-
2, for Cunabula grammaticae artis Donati (Migne,
Patrologia latina vol 90; doubtfully attributed to Bede).

Scientific Works

De natura rerum. Giles and Migne.
De temporibus liber. Giles and Migne. The Chronicle is
in Bedae chronica minora, ed T. Mommsen, Monumenta Germaniae historica, Auctores antiquiores vol 13.
De ratione temporum. Giles and Migne. The Chronicle
is in Monumenta Germaniae historica, Auctores
antiquiores vol 13. The De ratione computi (Migne,
vol 90) is not by Bede, but is an abstract. *See* C. T.
Fordyce, A rhythmical version of Bede's De ratione
temporum, Archivum Latinatis Medii Aevi 1927.
Opera de temporibus. Ed C. W. Jones, New York 1943.
See C. W. Jones, Bedae pseudepigraphica: scientific
writings falsely attributed to Bede, Ithaca 1939;
F. Strunz, Beda Venerabilis in der Geschichte der
Naturbetrachtung, Scientia 33 1939; M. Förster,
Die Weltzeitalter bei den Angelsachsen, Neusprachliche
Studien, Festgabe K. Luick, Marburg 1925; J. B.
Wynn, The beginning of the year in Bede and the Anglo-
Saxon Chronicle, MÆ 25 1956; D. P. Kirby, Bede and
Northumbrian chronology, EHR 78 1963.

Historical Works

Historia ecclesiastica gentis Anglorum. Strasbourg
[c. 1475], Antwerp 1550, Cologne 1601, Cambridge
1643-4, Paris 1681; ed J. Smith, Cambridge 1722;
ed J. Stevenson 1838; vols 3-4 ed J. E. B. Mayor and
J. R. Lumby, Cambridge 1881; ed A. Holder, Freiburg
1890 (2nd edn); ed B. Colgrave and R. A. B. Mynors,
Oxford 1969 (with trn).
On mss see Manitius, Geschichte der lateinischen Literatur
des Mittelalters vol 1, pp. 70 f.; Plummer vol 1,
pp. lxxx f.; E. A. Lowe, A new ms fragment of Bede's
Historia ecclesiastica, EHR 41 1926, pp. 244 f.;
O. Dobiache-Rojdestvensky, Un manuscrit de Bède à
Leningrad, Speculum 3 1928; O. Arngart, The Lenin-
grad Bede: early English mss in facsimile ii, Copen-
hagen 1952; P. H. Blair, The Moore Bede, 1959;
D. H. Wright, The date of the Leningrad Bede,
Revue Bénédictine 71 1961. *For King Alfred's trn of
the* Historia ecclesiastica, *see col 317, above.*
Jones, P. F. A concordance to the Historia ecclesiastica
of Bede. Cambridge Mass 1929.
Poole, R. L. The chronology of Bede's Historia
ecclesiastica and the Councils of 679-680. Oxford 1934.
Vita b. Abbatum Benedicti, Ceolfridi, Eosterwini, Sigfridi
atque Hwaeberhti. Plummer.
Vita Sancti Cudbercti
Metrical life and prose life. Giles and Migne. These
are based on the anon Life, ed Acta SS. Mart. vol 3,
pp. 117 f.

Jaager, W. Bedas metrische Vita Sancti Cuthberti. Leipzig 1935.

Vita Sancti Felicis. Giles and Migne. A paraphrase in prose of Paulinius of Nola's verse-life.

De locis sanctis. Ed T. Tobler, Itinera hierosolymitana vol 1, Geneva 1879; ed P. Geyer, Corpus scriptorum ecclesiasticorum latinorum vol 39, Vienna 1898.

Chronica majora et Chronica minora. Ed T. Mommsen, Monumenta Germaniae historica auctores antiquiores vol 13.

Historia ecclesiastica
Druhan, D. R. The syntax of Bede's Historia ecclesiastica. Stud in Medieval & Renaissance Latin 8 1938.
For the Old English version see col 317, above.

Vita Sancti Cudbercti
Two lives of St Cuthbert: a life by an anonymous monk of Lindisfarne and Bede's prose life. Ed B. Colgrave, Cambridge 1940. Text and trn.

Theological Works
Commentaries. Giles and Migne.
Bruyne, A. de. Note sur les mss et les editions du commentaire de Bède sur les Proverbes. Jnl of Theological Stud 28 1927.
Morin, G. Notes sur plusieurs écrits attribués à Bède le Vénérable. Revue Bénédictine 11 1894.
— Le Pseudo-Bède sur les Psaumes et l'Opus super Psalterium de Maître Manegold de Lautenbach. Revue Bénédictine 28 1911.
Schönbach, A. F. Über einige Evangelienkommentare des Mittelalters. Wiener Sitzungsberichte 147 1903.
Lehmann, P. Wert und Echtheit einer Beda abgesprochen Schrift. Abhandlungen der Bayerischen Akademie 4 1919. The Liber quaestionum.
Sutcliffe, E. F. Some footnotes to the Fathers. Biblica 6 1925.
— Quotations in the Venerable Bede's commentary on St Mark. Biblica 7 1926.
— The Venerable Bede's knowledge of Hebrew. Biblica 16 1935.
Wilmart, A. La collection de Bède le Vénérable sur l'apôtre. Revue Bénédictine 38 1926.
Laistner, M. L. W. Source-marks in Bede mss. Jnl of Theological Stud 34 1933, pp. 350 f.
Jones, C. W. In Genesim. Corpus Christianorum vol 118, 1967.

Homilies on the Gospel
Morin, G. La liturgie de Naples au temps de S. Grégoire, d'après deux Evangeliaires du viie siècle. Revue Bénédictine 8 1891.
— Le recueil primitif des homélies de Bède sur l'évangile. Revue Bénédictine 9 1892.
Ahrens, E. Das ursprüngliche Homiliar Bedas und sein Einfluss auf Aelfrics Homiliae catholicae. Münster 1923.

Martyrology. Act. SS. Mart. vol 2.
Quentin, H. Les martyrologes historiques du Moyen Age. Paris 1908.
— 'Bède le Vénérable'. In F. Cabrol, Dictionnaire d'archéologie chrétienne, Paris 1903.

Expositiò actuum apostolorum et retractatio. Ed M. L. W. Laistner, Cambridge Mass 1939.
Capella, B. Le rôle théologique de Bède le Vénérable. Studia Anselmiana (Rome) 6 1936.
Laistner, M. L. W. Was Bede the author of a Penitential? Harvard Theological Rev 31 1938.
Hablitzel, J. Bedas Expositio in proverbia Salomonis und seine Quellen. Biblische Zeitschrift 24 1939.
Carroll, Sr M. The Venerable Bede: his spiritual teachings. Washington 1946.
Leclerq, J. Le iiie livre des homélies de Bède le Vénérable. Recherches de Théologie Ancienne et Médiévale 14 1947.

Bedae Venerabilis opera ii, 2–3, iii. Ed D. Hurst, Corpus christianorum, 1955–62. Theological works and homilies.

Poetry
Bede's Liber hymnorum is lost (Historia ecclesiastica bk 5, 24); but some hymns may have survived. Dreves prints 16 in Analecta hymnica vol 50 pp. 96 f. The text of the hymn to Etheldreda is in Historia ecclesiastica 4, 20. Poems in Giles and Migne.
Lehmann, P. Die Erstveröffentlichung von Bedas Psalmen-Gedichten. Zeitschrift für Kirchengeschichte 34 1913.
Meyer, W. Bedae oratio ad Deum. Nachrichten von der Königlichen Gesellschaft der Wissenschaften zu Göttingen 1912.
— Poetische Nachlese aus dem sogenannten Book of Cerne in Cambridge und aus der Londoner Codex Regius 29 xx. Nachrichten von der Königlichen Gesellschaft der Wissenschaften zu Göttingen 1917.
Raby, F. J. E. Christian-Latin poetry. Oxford 1927.
Fraipoint, J. Opera rhythmica (Bedae Venerabilis opera iv, 1955).
Whitbread, L. After Bede, the influence and dissemination of his Doomsday Verses. Archiv 204 1967, pp. 250 f.

§2
Gehle, H. De Baedae Venerabilis vita et scriptis. Leyden 1838.
Werner, K. Beda der Ehrwürdige und seine Zeit. Vienna 1875.
Mommsen, T. Die Papstbriefe bei Beda. Neues Archiv 17 1892.
Zimmer, H. Zur Orthographie des Namens Beda. Neues Archiv 27 1902.
Browne, G. F. The Venerable Bede. 1919.
Cook, A. S. Bede and Gregory of Tours. PQ 6 1927.
Canter, H. V. The Venerable Bede and the Colosseum. Trans of Amer Philological Assoc 61 1930.
Jones, C. W. Bede and Vegetius. Classical Rev 46 1932.
Davis, R. Bede's early reading. Speculum 8 1933.
Laistner, M. L. W. Bede as a classical and a patristic scholar. Trans Royal Historical Soc 1933.
— The Spanish archetype of ms Harley 4980 (Bede's Exposition of Acts). Jnl of Theological Stud 27 1936.
— An addition to Bede in ms Balliol 177. Jnl of Theological Stud 43 1942.
Macdonald, G. Bede and Vegetius. Classical Rev 37 1933.
Raby, F. J. E. Bède le Vénérable. In Dictionnaire d'histoire et de géographie ecclésiastiques vol 7, 1934.
— Bede 735–1925. Laudate 13 1935.
Maycock, A. L. Bede and Alcuin 735–1935. Hibbert Jnl 33 1935.
Thompson, A. H. et al. Bede: his life, times and writings, Oxford 1935. W. Levison, Bede as historian, includes a bibliography; also M. L. W. Laistner, The library of the Venerable Bede.
Chambers, R. W. Bede. Proc Br Acad 22 1936; rptd in his Man's unconquerable mind, 1939.
See also the articles on Bede in DNB (C. Plummer); Wetzer und Weltes Kirchenlexikon, Freiburg 1903; Hauck's Realencyclopädie für protestantische Theologie, Leipzig 1896–.
Jones, C. W. The 'lost' Sirmond ms of Bede's Computus. EHR 52 1937.
Ker, N. R. The Hague ms of the Epistola Cuthberti de obitu Bedae, with Bede's Song. MÆ 8 1939.
Whitbread, L. A study of Bede's Versus de die iudicii. PQ 23 1944.
Loomis, C. G. The miracle traditions of the Venerable Bede. Speculum 21 1946.
Colgrave, B. The Venerable Bede and his times. Jarrow 1958.

Whitelock, D. After Bede. Jarrow 1960.
Campbell, J. Bede. In Latin historians, ed T. A. Dorey 1966.
Kirby, D. P. Bede's native sources for the Historia ecclesiastica. Bull John Rylands Lib 47 1966.

BIBLES AND PRAYER BOOKS

The book of Cerne. Ed A. B. Kuypers, Cambridge 1902. A private prayer book with strong Irish elements, and Irish hymns; see E. Bishop, Liturgica historica, Oxford 1918.
Chapman, J. Notes on the early history of the Vulgate Gospels. Oxford 1908.
Gasquet, F. A. and E. Bishop. The Bosworth Psalter. 1908.

E. ANGLO-SAXON WRITERS, SECOND PERIOD

BONIFACE or WYNFRITH
d. 755
§ I

De partibus orationis. Ed A. Mai, Classici auctores vol 7, Rome 1835.
See Roger, L'enscignement des lettres classiques, pp. 334 f.; and, for additional fragment, W. N. Du Rien, Schedae Vaticanae, Leyden 1860, p. 141. See also K. Bursian, Die Grammatik des Winfried-Bonifacius, Münchener Sitzungsberichte 1873.
[Treatise] De caesuris. Ed T. Gaisford, Scriptores latini rei metricae, Oxford 1837; ed A. Wilmanns, Der Katalog der Lorscher Bibliothek aus dem 10 Jahrhundert, Rheinisches Museum 23 1868 (in part). See also Roger, L'enseignement des lettres classiques, pp. 364 f.
Letters. Ed J. A. Giles 2 vols 1844 (=Migne, Patrologia latina vol 89); ed P. Jaffé, Bibliotheca rerum germanicarum vol 3, 1866 (in part); ed E. Dümmler, Monumenta Germaniae historica: epistolae vol 3; ed M. Tangl, Die Briefe des heiligen Bonifatius und Lull, Monumenta Germaniae historica: epistolae selectae vol 1, Berlin 1916.
Poems. Besides the poems included in his Letters, Boniface wrote poetical riddles. The Aenigmata Bonifatii are in E. Dümmler, Monumenta Germaniae historica: poetae latini aevi carolini vol 1.

§ 2

Müller, L. Zu den Räthseln des heiligen Bonifacius. Rheinisches Museum 22 1966.
Bishop, E. St Boniface and his correspondence. Proc Devonshire Assoc 8 1876.
Hahn, H. Bonifaz und Lul. Leipzig 1883.
Kurth, G. S. Boniface. Paris 1902.
Traube, L. Die älteste Handschrift der Aenigmata Bonifatii. Neues Archiv 27 1902.
Koch, H. Stellung des heiligen Bonifaz zu Bildung und Wissenschaft. Pastoralblatt für die Diözese Ermland 1905.
Hauck, A. Kirchengeschichte Deutschlands. Vol 1, Leipzig 1906.
Browne, G. F. Boniface of Crediton. 1910.
James, M. R. S. Boniface's Poem to Nithardus. EHR 29 1914.
Tangl, M. Bonifatiusfragen. Abhandlungen der Berliner Akademie 1919.
Laux, J. J. Der heilige Bonifatius. Freiburg 1922.
Lehmann, P. Die Grammatik aus Aldhelms Kreise. Historische Vierteljahrsschrift 27 1932.
Fickermann, N. Der Widmungsbrief des hl Bonifatius. Neues Archiv 50 1933.
See also Bibliography on Boniface in Cambridge medieval history vol 2, pp. 794 f.

AETHELWULF
fl. 802

Poem on the Abbots and miracles of the Church of Lindisfarne. Ed T. Arnold, Symeonis monachi opera

vol 1, 1882 (Rolls ser); ed E. Dümmler, Monumenta Germaniae historica: poetae latini aevi carolini vol 1; ed A. Campbell, Æthelwulf: De abbatibus, Oxford 1967. See T. Wright, Biographia britannica literaria vol 1, pp. 370 f.; L. Traube, Karolingische Dichtungen, Berlin 1888.

ALCUIN
d. 804
Collections

Opera. Regensburg 1777; Migne, Patrologia latina vols 100–1.

§ I

Poems. In Monumenta Germaniae historica: poetae latini aevi carolini vol 1.
Hymns. Analecta hymnica vol 50.
Strecker, K. Drei Rhythmen Alkuins. Neues Archiv 43 1921.
See Monumenta Germaniae historica: poetae latini aevi carolini vol 4.
> Winterfeld, P. von. Wie sah der Codex Blandinus vetustissimus des Horaz aus? Rheinisches Museum 40 1905. Alciun had not read Horace, and was not the author of Conflictus veris et hiemis.
Grammar. Migne, Patrologia latina vol 101; ed E. Putsche, Grammaticae latinae auctores antiqui, Hanover 1605.
Frees, J. De Alcuini arte grammatica commentatio. Münster 1886.
De orthographia. Ed H. Kiel, Grammatici latini vol 7.
De rhetorica. Ed C. Halm, Rhetores latini minores, Leipzig 1863.
De dialectica. In Migne, Patrologia latina vol 101.
Disputatio regalis et nobilissimi iuvenis Pippini cum Albino scholastico. Ed W. Wilmanns, Zeitschrift für Deutsches Altertum 14 1867.
Letters. Ed P. Jaffé, Monumenta Alcuiniana: bibliotheca rerum germanicarum vol 6, Berlin 1873; ed E. Dümmler, Monumenta Germaniae historica: epistolae vol 4.
On Alcuin's mathematical and astronomical interests and his Propositiones ad acuendos iuvenes and De saltu lunae ac bissexto, see Manitius, Geschichte der lateinischen Literatur des Mittelalters vol 1.

§ 2

Monnier, F. Alcuin et Charlemagne. Paris 1864.
Sickel, T. Alcuinstudien I. Wiener Sitzungsberichte 79 1875.
Werner, K. Alcuin und sein Jahrhundert. Vienna 1881.
Dümmler, E. Alchvinstudien. Berliner Sitzungsberichte 1891.
—— Zur Lebensgeschichte Alchvins. Neues Archiv 18 1893.
West, A. F. Alcuin. 1893.
Ditscheid, H. Alkuins Leben und Bedeutung für den religiösen Unterricht. Coblenz 1902.
Gaskoin, C. J. B. Alcuin: his life and his work. Cambridge 1904.

Wilmot-Buxton, E. M. Alcuin. New York 1922.

Taylor, P. The construction 'habere with infinitive' in Alcuin as expression of the future. Romanic Rev 15 1924.

Sanford, E. Alcuin and the classics. Classical Jnl 20 1925.

Delius, W. War Alchvin Mönch? Theologische Studien und Kritiken 103 1931.

Ramackers, J. Eine unbekannte Handschrift der Alcuin-briefe. Neues Archiv 50 1933.

Boas, M. Alcuin and Cato. Brill 1937.

Howell, W. S. The rhetoric of Alcuin and Charlemagne. Princeton 1941.

Moé, E.-A. van. Textes inédits d'Alcuin. Bibliothèque de l'Ecole des Chartes 102 1941.

Kleinclausz, A. Alcuin. Paris 1948.

Duckett, E. S. Alcuin, friend of Charlemagne. New York 1951. With bibliography.

Wallach, L. Charlemagne's De litteris colendis and Alcuin. Speculum 26 1951.

— Charlemagne and Alcuin: studies in Carolingian epistolography. Traditio 9 1953.

— Alcuin and Charlemagne. Cornell Stud in Classical Philology 32 1959.

— The Libri Carolini and patristics, Latin and Greek. In The classical tradition, ed Wallach, Ithaca 1966.

Grosjean, P. Le De excidio chez Bède et chez Alcuin. Analecta Bollandiana 65 1957.

Mombello, G. A propos d'un 'traité' sur les commande-ments de Dieu attribué à Alcuin. Romania 89 1968.

Alcuin and the Liturgy

Bishop, E. Liturgica historica. Oxford 1918. The Gregorian Sacramentary, sent to Charles the Great by Pope Hadrian, was enlarged and edited by Alcuin who, for this purpose, drew largely on the 'Gelasian' Sacramentary. The resultant Sacramentary is the foundation of the present Roman missal.

Alfonso, P. Alcuino e il Sacramentario Gregoriano. Rivista Liturgica 1924.

Lietzmann, H. Handschriftliches zu Alkuins Ausgabe und Sakramentarium. Jahrbuch für Liturgiewissen-schaft 5 1925.

Capelle, B. Alcuin et l'histoire du symbole de la messe. Recherches de Théologie Ancienne et Mediévale 6 1934.

Ellard, G. Master Alcuin, liturgist. Chicago 1956.

For Alcuin's liturgical writings generally, see under Alcuin in F. Cabrol, Dictionnaire d'archéologie chrétienne, Paris 1903.

ASSER, Bishop of Sherborne
d. 910

Life of King Alfred. Ed W. H. Stevenson, Oxford 1904, 1959 (rev D. Whitelock). See D. Whitelock, The genuine Asser, Reading 1967 (Stenton Lecture).

FRITHEGODE or FRIDEGODUS
fl. 950

Life of Wilfrid. Mabillon, Acta SS. vol 3, i, p. 150 (= Migne, Patrologia latina vol 133). A versification of Eddius. Ed J. Raine, The historians of the Church of York vol 1, pp. 105 f. The Vita Audoeni, in Acta SS. Aug. vol 4, pp. 810 f. is probably not by Frithegode: see Manitius, Geschichte der lateinischen Literatur des Mittelalters vol 2, pp. 501.

Breviloquium vitae beati Wilfridi et Wulfstani Cantoris narratio metrica de sancto Swithuno. Ed A. Campbell, Zürich 1950.

Young, D. C. C. Authors variants and interpretations in Frithegod. Archivum Latinitatis Medii Ævi 25 1955.

WULFSTAN of Winchester
fl. 965

Vita Ethelwoldi. Mabillon, Acta SS. vol 5, pp. 606 (= Migne, Patrologia latina vol 137).

Vita S. Swithuni. Mabillon, Acta SS. vol 5 pp. 628 (= Migne, Patrologia latina vol 137). This is a versifica-tion of Lantfred's Life of S. Swithin, which is in Acta SS. Jul. vol 1, pp. 328 f. Part only is ptd; the prologue in Mabillon, Acta SS.; extracts also in Wright, Bio-graphia britannica literaria vol 1, pp. 472 f.; Ebert, Allgemeine Geschichte der Literatur des Mittelalters vol 3, pp. 498. See also under Frithegode, above.

Hymns, Analecta hymnica vol 48, pp. 9 f.; vol 51, pp. 164 f.

Sequences. Analecta hymnica vol 40, pp. 180 f., 154 f., 288 f.; vol 37, pp. 265 f., 138 f.

Blume, C. Wolstan von Winchester und Vital von Saint-Evroult: Dichter der drei Lobgesänge auf die heiligen Aethelwold, Birin und Swithun. Wiener Sitzungberichte 146 1903.

Fisher, D. J. V. The early biographies of St Ethel-wold. EHR 67 1952. Confirms attribution of Vita Ethelwoldi to Wulfstan.

Whitelock, D. Wulfstan Cantor and Anglo-Saxon law. In Nordica et anglica: studies in honor of S. Einarsson, Hague 1968.

F. IRISH WRITERS, SECOND PERIOD

JOSEPHUS SCOTTUS
d. after 791
(friend of Alcuin)

Poems. Ed E. Dümmler, Monumenta Germaniae his-torica: poetae latini aevi carolini vol 1.

DUNGAL
fl. 787
(Hibernicus Exul; came from Ireland to S. Denis: friend of Charlemagne)

Letters, including astronomical work addressed to Charles. Ed E. Dümmler, Monumenta Germaniae historica: epistolae vol 4 pp. 570 f.

Responsa [against Claudius of Turin]. Migne, Patrologia latina vol 105. Prologue only in Monumenta Ger-maniae historica: epistolae vol 4.

Poems. Ed E. Dümmler, Monumenta Germaniae his-torica: poetae latini aevi carolini vol 1.

On the various Dungals, see L. Traube, Dungali, Abhand-lung der Bayerischen Akademie 19 1891; also L. Gougaud, L'œuvre des Scotti dans l'Europe con-tinentale, Revue d'Histoire Ecclésiastique 19 1908; but M. Esposito, The poems of Colmanus Nepos Cracavist; and Dungalus Praecipuus Scottorum, Jnl Theological Stud 33 1932, rejects (p. 125) the identifica-tion of Dungal with Hibernicus Exul, whom he prefers to identify with Dicuil. This article also contains an account of Donatus, the Irish bishop of Fiesole (d. 876), whose poems are in Monumenta Germaniae historica: poetae latini aevi carolini vol 3. Esposito (p. 129) thinks that Donatus was the author of the poem printed in K. Strecker, Ein neues Dungal? Zeitschrift für Romanische Philo-logie 41 1921. Colmanus was a 9th-century Irishman settled on the Continent.

SMARAGDUS of St Mihiel
fl. 800
(perhaps Irish; a grammarian)

Expositio libri comitis [on Epistles and Gospels for Sundays]. In Migne, Patrologia latina vol 102.
Via regia (to Charles). In Migne, Patrologia latina vol 102.
Diadema monochorum. In Migne, Patrologia latina vol 102.
Expositio in regula S. Benedicti. In Migne, Patrologia latina vol 102. See E. Bishop, Liturgica historica, Oxford 1918, pp. 214 f.
Liber in partibus Donati. In H. Keil, De grammaticis quibusdam latinis infimae aetatis commentatio, Erlangen 1868, pp. 19 f. (in part). For other references see Manitius, Geschichte der lateinischen Literatur des Mittelalters vol 1, p. 467; Kenney, p. 544.
Poems. Ed E. Dümmler, Monumenta Germaniae historica: poetae latini aevi carolini vol 1–2.
Laistner, M. L. W. The date and the recipient of Smaragdus' Via regia. Speculum 3 1928.

DICUIL
d. c. 825
(grammarian at Carolingian Court)

§ 1

Astronomical work (dedicated to Louis the Pious; written in prose and verse). For mss, see Kenney, p. 546; ed E. Dümmler, Neues Archiv 4 1879 (poems only); ed K. Strecker, Monumenta Germaniae historica: poetae latini aevi carolini vol 4.
Esposito, M. An unpublished astronomical treatise by the Irish monk Dicuil. Proc Royal Irish Acad 26 1907.
Liber de mensura orbis terrae. Ed J. A. Letronne, Recherches géographiques et critiques sur le Livre de mensura orbis terrae, Paris 1814; ed G. Parthey, Dicuili liber de mensura orbis terrae, Berlin 1870; some verses in E. Dümmler, Monumenta Germaniae historica; poetae latini aevi carolini vol 2. See bibliography in Kenney, p. 547.
Poem: De arte grammatica. Ed H. Keil, Grammatici latini vol 3; ed E. Dümmler Monumenta Germaniae historica: poetae latini aevi carolini vol 2.

§ 2

Esposito, M. Dicuil: an Irish monk in the 9th century. Dublin Rev 1905.
— An Irish teacher at the Carolingian Court: Dicuil. Studies 3 1914.
van der Vyver, A. Dicuil et Micon de Saint-Riquier. Revue Belge 14 1935.

CLEMENS SCOTTUS
fl. 826
(grammarian at Court of Charles the Great)

Ars grammatica. For mss, see Kenney, p. 537. Ed H. Keil, Grammatici latini vol 1 and De grammaticis quibusdam latinis infimae aetatis commentatio, Erlangen 1868; ed M. Esposito, Hiberno-Latin mss in the Libraries of Switzerland, Proc Royal Irish Acad 30 1912. See B. Hauréau, Singularités historiques et littéraires, Paris 1861.

MALSACHANUS
8th or 9th century

Ars Malsachani. Ed M. Roger, Traité du verbe publié d'après le ms lat. 13026 de la Bibliothèque Nationale, Paris 1905.

CRUINDMELUS
first half of 9th century
(Irishman in Frankish Empire)

Ars metrica. Ed J. Heumer, Vienna 1883. See Kenney, p. 552 and Manitius, Geschichte der lateinischen Literatur des Mittelalters vol 1.

SEDULIUS SCOTTUS
fl. 850
(an Irish scholar who settled at Liège)

§ 1

Poems. Ed L. Traube, Monumenta Germaniae historica: poetae latini aevi carolini vol 3; ed E. Dümmler, Sedulii Scoti carmina quadraginta, Halle 1869 (incomplete).
Levillain, L. Date et interprétation d'un poème de Sedulius Scottus. Moyen Âge 6 1935.
Hymns. In Analecta hymnica 50. Commentary on Eutyches. Ed H. Hagen, Anecdota helvetica, Leipzig 1870.
See M. Roger, Le commentariolum in artem Eutychii de Sedulius Scottus, Revue de Philologie 30 1906.
Theological works. The Collectaneum in omnes beati Pauli epistolas is in Migne, Patrologia latina vol 103; Collectaneum in Mattheum is not ptd; see Kenney, p. 565 and Manitius, Geschichte der lateinischen Literatur des Mittelalters, vol 1. On the former, see A. Souter, The sources of Sedulius Scottus' Collectaneum on the Epistles of St Paul, Jnl of Theological Stud 18 1917. Other theological works are in Migne, Patrologia latina vol 103.
Liber de rectoribus christianis. Ed S. Hellmann, Sedulius Scottus, Munich 1906.
Tiralla, H. Das augustinische Idealbild der christlichen Obrigkeit als Quelle des Fürstenspiegels des Sedulius Scottus und Hincmar von Reims. Greifswald 1916.
Martini, G. Un Codice sconosciuto del De rectoribus Christianis di Sedulio Scoto. Bull Istituto Storico Italiano Archeologico Murator 50 1935.
Collektaneum. A collection of extracts made by Sedulius in the course of his reading. See Kenney, p. 566; Manitius, Geschichte der lateinischen Literatur des Mittelalters vol 1, pp. 320 f.; and L. Traube, Die Excerptensammlung der Handschrift C 14 in der Bibliothek des Hospitals Cues, in Abhandlungen der Bayerischen Akademie 29 1891.

§ 2

Hellmann, S. Sedulius Scottus. Munich 1906.
Pirenne, H. Sedulius de Liège. Mémoires Couronnés et Autres Mémoires Publiés par l'Académie Royale de Belgique 33 1882.
Traube, L. Sedulius Scottus. Abhandlungen der Bayerischen Akademie 19 1891.

JOHANNES SCOTUS ERIGENA
d. 860

For full bibliography and mss, see Kenney, pp. 569 f.; also Ueberweg-Geyer, Grundriss der Geschichte der Philosophie vol 2, pp. 693 f.

Collections

Opera. In Migne, Patrologia latina vol 120.

§ 1

Excerpta Macrobii etc. Ed H. Keil, Grammatici latini vol 5.

Commentary on Martianus Capella. Extracts in B. Hauréau, Notices et extraits des mss, xx, pt ii, Paris 1862; M. Manitius, Didaskaleion vols 1–2, 1912.

Laistner, M. L. W. Martianus Capella and his ninth-century commentators. Bull John Rylands Lib 9 1925.

Narducci, M. Bollettino di Bibliografia e di Storia delle Scienze Matematiche e Fisiche 15 1882.

Commentary on Boethius, Opuscula sacra. Ed E. K. Rand, Johannes Scotus, Munich 1906. There is also a life of Boethius attributed to John; see Kenney, p. 585; ed R. Peiper, De consolatione, Leipzig 1871.

Translation of the Solutiones of Priscianus Lydus. Ed I. Bywater, Prisciani Lydi quae extant, Berlin 1886.

Esposito, M. Priscianus Lydus and Johannes Scotus. Classical Rev 32 1918.

De praedestinatione. In Migne, Patrologia latina vol 122; the dedication is in E. Dümmler, Monumenta Germaniae historica: epistolae vol 5. Prudentius of Troyes answered this; Migne, 115.

Περὶ φύσεων μεριόμοῦ: de divisione naturae. In Migne, Patrologia latina vol 122.

Schmitt, A. Zwei noch unbenützte Handschriften des Johannes Scotus Erigena. Bamberg 1900.

Dräseke, J. Johannes Scotus Erigena und dessen Gewährmänner in seinem Werke, De divisione naturae libri v. Studien zur Geschichte der Theologie und der Kirche 9 1902.

Lehmann, P. Johannes Scotus über die Kategorien. Philologische Wochenschrift 41 1921.

Translation of works of the Pseudo-Dionysius. In Migne, Patrologia latina vol 122.

Grabmann, M. Pseudo-Dionysius Areopagita in lateinischen Übersetzungen des Mittelalters. In Festgabe Ehrhard, Bonn 1922.

Lehmann, P. Zur Kenntnis der Schriften des Dionysius Areopagita im Mittelalter. Revue Bénédictine 35 1923.

Commentary on the Pseudo-Dionysius. In Migne, Patrologia latina vol 122.

Translation of the Ambigua of Maximus Confessor. Ed T. Gale, Appendix to De divisione naturae, Oxford 1681; in Migne, Patrologia latina vol 122.

Poems. Ed L. Traube, Monumenta Germaniae historica: poetae latini aevi carolini vol 3.

For Homily on prologue to Gospel of S. John, *fragments of commentary on that Gospel, and* Commentary on Old Testament, *see* Kenney pp. 585 f.

Annotationes in Marcianum. Ed C. E. Lutz, Cambridge Mass 1939.

§2

Hermens, O. Das Leben des Scotus Erigena. Jena 1868.

Dräseke, J. Zu Johannes Scotus Erigena. Zeitschrift für Wissenschaftliche Theologie 46–7 1903–4.

Brilliantoff, A. Zu Maximus Confessor. Zeitschrift für Wissenschaftliche Theologie 47 1904. On influence of Maximus on John.

— Der Einfluss der orientalischen Theologie auf die occidentalische in der Werken des Johannes Scotus Erigena. St Petersburg 1908.

Rand, E. K. Johannes Scotus. Munich 1906.

Baldini, P. Scoto Erigena e la filosofia religiosa nel ix secolo. Rivista Storica Critica delle Scienze Teologiche 2 1906.

Jacquin, M. Le néo-platonisme de Jean Scot. Revue des Sciences Philosophiques et Théologiques 1 1907. *See* J. Dräseke, Zum Neuplatonismus Erigenas, Zeitschrift für Kirchengeschichte 33 1912.

Esposito, M. Latin writers of mediaeval Ireland: supplement. Hermathena 15 1908.

Lehmann, P. Zur Kenntnis und Geschichte einiger Joh. Scotus zugeschriebener Werke. Hermes 52 1917.

Schneider, A. Die Erkenntnislehre des Johannes Erigena im Rahmen ihrer metaphysischen und anthropologischen Voraussetzungen. 2 vols Berlin 1921–3.

Bett, H. Johannes Scotus Erigena. Cambridge 1925.

Doerries, H. Zur Geschichte der Mystik: Erigena und der Neoplatonismus. Tübingen 1925.

Théry, G. Scot Erigène, traducteur de Denys. Archivum Latinitatis Medii Aevi 6 1931.

— Scot Erigène, introducteur de Denys. New Scholasticism 5 1933.

— Jean Sarrazin, 'traducteur' de Scot Erigène. In Studia mediaevalia in honorem Raymundi J. Martin, Bruges 1948.

Cappuyns, M. Jean Scot Erigène: sa vie, son oeuvre, sa pensée. Louvain 1933.

— Le plus ancien commentaire des Opuscula sacra et son origine. Recherches de Théologie Ancienne et Médiévale 3 1931. Attributed to Remi of Auxerre.

Mélandre, M. Iepa ou Scot Erigène. Archives d'Histoire Doctrinale et Littéraire du Moyen Age 6 1931.

Rand, E. K. The supposed commentary of John the Scot on the Opuscula sacra of Boethius. Revue Néo-scolastique 36 1934.

— How much of the Annotationes in Marcianum is the work of John the Scot? Trans Amer Philological Soc 61 1940.

Silk, E. T. Saeculi noni auctoris in Boetii Consolationem philosophiae commentarius. Papers of Amer Acad in Rome 9 1935. Attributed to Scotus.

Ehrhardt-Siebold, E. von and R. von Ehrhardt. The astronomy of Johannes Scotus Erigena. Baltimore 1950.

— Cosmology in the Annotationes in Marcianum. Baltimore 1940.

Prau, M. del. Scoto Eriugena ed il platonismo medievale. Milan 1941.

— Scoto Eriugena. Milan 1951.

Pittenger, W. N. The Christian philosophy of John Scotus Erigena. Jnl of Religion 24 1944.

Bonafede, G. Saggi sul pensiero di Scoto Erigena. Atti dell' Accademia di Scienze, Lettere e Arte di Palermo 4th ser 10 1950.

Silvestre, H. Le commentaire inédit de Jean Scot Erigène au mètre ix du livre iii du De consolatione philosophiae de Boèce. Revue d'Histoire Ecclésiastique 47 1952.

OTHER IRISH WRITINGS

(a) Anonymous commentary on Donatus. *See* Kenney, p. 553.

(b) Dunchad's writings. *See* Kenney, p. 573.

(c) Anonymous poems by Irishmen. Ed L. Traube, Carmina Scottorum latina et graecanica in Monumenta Germaniae historica: poetae latini aevi carolini vols 3–4. *See* Kenney, pp. 603 f.

A. C.

THE MIDDLE ENGLISH PERIOD (1100–1500)

1. INTRODUCTION

(1) BIBLIOGRAPHIES

Revue d'Histoire Ecclésiastique 1– 1900–.

Geddie, W. Bibliography of Middle Scots poets. Edinburgh 1912 (Scottish Text Soc).

Wells, J. E. Manual of the writings in Middle English 1050–1400. New Haven 1916; 9 suppls to 1951; Manual 1050–1500, ed J. B. Severs, New Haven 1967– (rev and enlarged).

Willard, J. F. et al. Progress of medieval (and Renaissance) studies in the United States (and Canada). Nos 1–25, Boulder 1923–60.

Tucker, L. L. and A. R. Benham. Bibliography of fifteenth-century literature. Seattle 1928.

Announcements of books received. Speculum 3– 1928–; Bibliography of American periodical literature, 9– 1934–.

Lawrence, W. W. Selected bibliography of medieval literature in England. New York 1930.

Russell, J. C. Dictionary of writers of thirteenth-century England. Bull Inst of Historical Research suppl 3 1936. Occasional suppls 1939–.

Loomis, R. S. Introduction to medieval literature, chiefly in England. New York 1939.

Renwick, W. L. and H. Orton. The beginnings of English literature to Skelton. 1939, 1952 (enlarged).

Brown, C. and R. H. Robbins. Index of Middle English verse. New York 1943; suppl ed Robbins and J. L. Cutler, Lexington Kentucky 1965.

Farrar, C. P. and A. P. Evans. Bibliography of English translations from medieval sources. New York 1946.

Williams, H. F. Index of mediaeval studies published in Festschriften 1865–1946. Berkeley 1951.

Zesmer, D. M. and S. B. Greenfield. Guide to English literature from Beowulf through Chaucer and medieval drama. New York 1961.

Matthews, W. Old and Middle English literature. New York 1968.

Sawyer, P. H. et al. International medieval bibliography. Leeds 1968–.

(2) HISTORICAL SOURCE-MATERIAL

For fuller bibliographies, see

Gross, C. A bibliography of British municipal history. New York 1897; ed G. H. Martin, Leicester 1966.

—— Sources and literature of English history to about 1485. 1900, 1915 (rev).

Davis, G. R. C. Medieval cartularies of Great Britain. 1958.

Mullins, E. L. C. Texts and calendars: an analytical guide to serial publication. 1958 (Royal Historical Soc).

Also vols of the Oxford history of England, English historical documents, and Bibliographical handbooks issued by the Conference on British Studies, Cambridge 1969–.

Texts are pbd in the Rolls ser, by the Pipe Roll and Selden Socs and by the County Record socs. Calendars, and some texts, of the Close Rolls, Patent Rolls, Fine Rolls and Feet of Fines, Liberate Rolls, Charter Rolls, Treaty Rolls, Chancery Rolls and Chancery Warrants, and Inquisitions etc, are pbd by the Record Commission and the Public Record Office.

In the following sections the material is arranged in this order: narrative sources, administrative documents, legal and ecclesiastical documents, local and miscellaneous materials by topic.

General

Descriptive catalogue of materials relating to the history of Great Britain and Ireland. Ed T. D. Hardy 3 vols in 4 1862–71 (Rolls ser).

Calendar of entries in the papal registers relating to Great Britain etc. Ed W. H. Bliss et al. Letters, 14 vols in 15 1893–1960; Petitions, 1896.

Concilia magnae Britanniae et Hiberniae. Ed D. Wilkins 4 vols 1737.

List of ancient correspondence. Ed C. T. Martin 1902 (Public Record Office); Index, New York 1969 (for PRO).

Foedera, conventiones, litterae, etc. Ed T. Rymer et al 20 vols 1727–35. Syllabus, ed T. D. Hardy 3 vols 1869–85 (Rolls ser).

English historical documents. Vol 2 1042–1189, ed and tr D. C. Douglas and G. W. Greenaway 1953; vol 3 1189–1327, ed and tr H. Rothwell 1972; vol 4 1327–1485, ed and tr A. H. Thompson 1969.

Anglo-Scottish relations 1174–1328: some selected documents. Ed and tr E. L. G. Stones, Oxford 1970.

Select charters of English constitutional history. Ed W. Stubbs, rev H. W. C. Davis 1913.

Documents illustrative of English history in the 13th and 14th centuries. Ed H. Cole 1844.

English royal documents 1199–1416. Ed P. Chaplais, Oxford 1970. With plates.

Parliamentary writs and writs of military summons etc. Ed F. Palgrave 2 vols 1827–34.

Rotuli parliamentorum. Ed J. Strachey et al 6 vols and index 1783–1832.

Chartes des libertés anglaises. Ed C. Bémont, Paris 1902.

Statutes of the realm. Ed A. Luders et al 11 vols 1810–28.

Year books [i.e. law reports]. Edw I, ed and tr A. J. Horwood 5 vols 1866–79 (Rolls ser); Edw II, ed and tr F. W. Maitland et al 25 vols [to 1970] 1903– (Selden Soc); Edw III, ed and tr A. J. Horwood and L. O. Pike 15 vols 1883–1911 (Rolls ser); 11, 12, 13 Richard II, ed T. F. T. Plucknett et al, Cambridge Mass 1914– (Ames Foundation); 1422, ed C. H. Williams 1933 (Selden Soc); 1470, ed N. Neilson 1931 (Selden Soc). Others in 16th- and 17th-century edns.

Select cases concerning the law merchant. Ed and tr C. Gross and H. Hall 3 vols 1908–32 (Selden Soc).

Public works in mediaeval law. Ed and tr C. T. Flower 2 vols 1915–23 (Selden Soc).

Proceedings before the Justices of the Peace. Ed B. H. Putnam 1938 (Ames Foundation).

The Court baron. Ed and tr F. W. Maitland and W. P. Baildon 1891 (Selden Soc).

Anglia sacra. Ed H. Wharton 2 vols 1691.

Monasticon anglicanum. Ed W. Dugdale 3 vols 1655–73; rev. J. Stevens 5 vols 1722–3; rev J. Cley et al 6 vols in 8 1817–30, 1846.

Annales monastici. Ed H. R. Luard 5 vols 1864–9 (Rolls ser).

Documents illustrating the activities of the general and provincial chapters of the English black monks 1215–1540. Ed W. A. Pantin 3 vols 1931–7 (Camden Soc).

English Benedictine kalendars after AD 1100. Ed F. Wormald 2 vols 1939–46 (Henry Bradshaw Soc).

Chapters of the Augustinian canons. Ed H. E. Salter 1922 (Oxford Historical Soc).

Select documents of the English lands of the abbey of Bec. Ed M. Chibnall 1951 (Camden Soc).

Letters from the English abbots to the chapter at Cîteaux. Ed C. H. Talbot 1967 (Camden Soc).

The Cellarers' rolls of Battle abbey 1275–1513. Ed E. Searle and B. Ross 1967 (Sussex Record Soc), Sydney 1967.

Memorials of St Edmund's abbey. Ed T. Arnold 3 vols 1890–6 (Rolls ser).

Liber vitæ ecclesiæ dunelmensis. Ed J. Stevenson 1841 (Surtees Soc).

Historia et cartularium monasterii Sancti Petri Gloucestriæ. Ed W. H. Hart 3 vols 1863–7 (Rolls ser).

Registrum antiquissimum of the cathedral church of Lincoln. Ed C. W. Foster and K. Major 9 vols 1931–68 (Lincoln Record Soc).

Documents illustrating the history of St Paul's Cathedral. Ed W. S. Simpson 1880 (Camden Soc).

Cartulary of the monastery of St Frideswide at Oxford. Ed S. R. Wigram 2 vols 1895–6 (Oxford Historical Soc).

Gesta abbatum monasterii Sancti Albani a Thoma Walsingham compilata. Ed H. T. Riley 3 vols 1867–9 (Rolls ser).

Chronicle of St Mary's abbey, York. Ed H. H. E. Craster and M. E. Thornton 1934 (Surtees Soc).

British borough charters. Ed A. Ballard et al 3 vols Cambridge 1913–43.

Borough customs. Ed and tr M. Bateson 2 vols 1904–6 (Selden Soc).

Beverley town documents. Ed and tr A. F. Leach 1900 (Selden Soc).

Great red book of Bristol. Ed E. W. W. Veale 5 vols 1931–53 (Bristol Record Soc).

Little red book of Bristol. Ed F. B. Bickley 1900 (Bristol Record Soc).

Calendar of the letter-books of the City of London. Ed R. R. Sharpe 1901–7.

Munimenta Gildhallae londoniensis. Ed H. T. Riley 3 vols in 4 1859–62 (Rolls ser).

Mamecestre: being chapters from the early recorded history of Manchester. Ed J. Harland 3 vols 1861–2 (Chetham Soc).

Cartulaire de l'ancienne Estaplede Bruges. Ed L. Gilliodts van Severen 4 vols Bruges 1904–6.

Original statutes of the University of Cambridge. Ed M. B. Hackett, Cambridge 1970.

Statuta antiqua universitatis oxoniensis. Ed S. Gibson, Oxford 1931.

Medieval archives of the University of Oxford. Ed H. E. Salter 2 vols 1920–1 (Oxford Historical Soc).

Educational charters and documents 598–1909. Ed A. F. Leach, Cambridge 1911.

Documents illustrating education in Worcester 685–1700. Ed A. F. Leach 1913 (Worcestershire Historical Soc).

Early Yorkshire schools. Ed A. F. Leach 2 vols 1899–1903 (Yorkshire Archæological Soc).

Percy chartulary. Ed M. T. Martin 1911 (Surtees Soc).

Honor and forest of Pickering. Ed R. B. Turton 4 vols 1894–7 (North Riding Record Soc).

Sherwood Forest book. Ed H. E. Boulton 1965 (Thoroton Soc).

Documents relating to the law and custom of the sea. Ed R. G. Marsden 2 vols 1915–16 (Navy Records Soc).

Catalogue of English mediaeval rolls of arms. Ed A. R. Wagner 1950 (Harleian Soc).

Manners and household expenses of England in the 13th and 15th centuries. Ed B. Botfield 1841 (Roxburghe Club).

English mediaeval lapidaries. Ed J. Evans and M. S. Serjeantson 1933 (EETS).

Anglo-Norman political songs. Ed I. S. T. Aspin, Oxford 1953 (Anglo-Norman Text Soc).

Twelfth Century

Anglo-saxon chronicle. Ed and tr B. Thorpe 2 vols 1861 (Rolls ser); ed C. Plummer and J. Earle 2 vols Oxford 1892–9 (in part), 1952; 1070–1154, ed C. Clark, Oxford 1958, 1970 (rev); tr 1953, 1961.

Chronicles of the reigns of Stephen, Henry II and Richard I. Ed R. Howlett 4 vols 1884–9 (Rolls ser). Includes Wm of Newburgh, Richd of Hexham, Jordan Fantosme, Robt of Torigni.

Chronicle of the reigns of Henry II and Richard I. Ed W. Stubbs 2 vols 1867 (Rolls ser). 'Benedict of Peterborough'.

Chronicles and memorials of the reign of Richard I. Ed W. Stubbs 2 vols 1864–5 (Rolls ser).

Carmen de Hastingae proelio. Ed and tr C. Morton and H. Muntz, Oxford 1971.

Eadmeri historia novorum in Anglia. Ed M. Rule 1884 (Rolls ser); tr 1964 (in part).

Florentii wigorniensis monachi chronicon ex chronicis. Ed B. Thorpe 2 vols 1848–9.

L'estorie des Engles solum la translacion Geffrei Gaimar. Ed and tr T. D. Hardy and C. T. Martin 2 vols 1888–9 (Rolls ser) (with Gesta Herwardi); ed A. Bell, Oxford 1960 (Anglo-Norman Text Soc).

Historical works of Gervase of Canterbury. Ed W. Stubbs 2 vols 1879–80 (Rolls ser).

Gesta Stephani. Ed and tr K. R. Potter 1955.

Giraldi Cambrensis opera. Ed J. S. Brewer et al 8 vols 1861–91 (Rolls ser); Autobiography, tr 1937.

Hugh the Chantor: history of the church of York 1066–1127. Ed and tr C. Johnson 1961.

Henrici archidiaconi huntendunensis historia Anglorum. Ed T. Arnold 1879 (Rolls ser).

Chronica de Mailres. Ed J. Stevenson, Edinburgh 1835; ed A. O. and M. O. Anderson 1936 (facs).

Orderici Vitalis historiæ ecclesiasticæ libri tredecim. Ed A. Le Prévost 5 vols Paris 1838–55; ed and tr M. Chibnall 1969–.

Radulphi de Diceto opera historica. Ed W. Stubbs 1876 (Rolls ser).

Chronicle of Richard of Devizes. Ed and tr J. T. Appleby 1963.

Chronica Magistri Rogeri de Houedene. Ed W. Stubbs 4 vols 1868–71 (Rolls ser).

Symeonis monachi opera omnia. Ed T. Arnold 2 vols 1882–5 (Rolls ser).

Willelmi malmesbiriensis monachi de gestis pontificum Anglorum libri quinque. Ed N. E. S. A. Hamilton 1870 (Rolls ser).

Willelmi malmesbiriensis monachi de gestis regum Anglorum libri quinque. Ed W. Stubbs 2 vols 1887–9 (Roll ser).

Historia novella by William of Malmesbury. Ed and tr K. R. Potter 1955.

Calendar of documents preserved in France illustrative of the history of Great Britain. Ed J. H. Round 1899.

Ancient charters, royal and private, prior to 1200. Ed J. H. Round 1888 (Pipe Roll Soc).

Regesta regum anglo-normannorum. Ed H. W. C. Davis et al 4 vols Oxford 1913–69. Plates.

Facsimiles of English royal writs to AD 1100. Ed T. A. M. Bishop and P. Chaplais, Oxford 1957.

Royal writs in England from the Conquest to Glanvill. Ed and tr R. C. van Caenegem 1959 (Selden Soc).

Domesday book. Ed A. Farley and H. Ellis 4 vols 1783–1816, Southampton 1861–4 (facs). Trns in Victoria County History.

Inquisitio comitatus cantabrigiensis. Ed N. E. S. A Hamilton 1876 (Royal Soc of Lit).

Dialogus de Scaccario. Ed and tr C. Johnson 1950.

Great roll of the Pipe. 31 Henry I, ed J. Hunter 1833, 1929; 2, 3, 4 Henry II, ed J. Hunter 1844, 1931; 1 Richard I, ed J. Hunter 1844; 1158– various dates and editors (Pipe Roll Soc).

Receipt roll of the Exchequer, Michaelmas 1183. Ed H. Hall 1899.

Chancellor's roll, Michaelmas 1196. Ed D. M. Stenton 1930 (Pipe Roll Soc).

Memoranda roll 1199–1200. Ed H. G. Richardson 1943 (Pipe Roll Soc).

Rotuli de dominabus et pueris et puellis 1185. Ed J. H. Round 1913 (Pipe Roll Soc).

Documents illustrative of the social and economic history of the Danelaw. Ed F. M. Stenton, Oxford 1920 (Br Acad).

Earldom of Gloucester charters to 1217. Ed R. B. Patterson, Oxford 1971.

Herefordshire domesday, circa 1160–70. Ed V. H. Galbraith and J. Tait 1950 (Pipe Roll Soc).

Charters of the earldom of Hereford 1095–1201. Ed D. Walker, Camden Miscellany 22 1964.

Charters of the honour of Mowbray 1107–1191. Ed D. E. Greenway, Oxford 1972 (Br Acad).

Lincolnshire Domesday and the Lindsey survey. Ed C. W. Foster et al 1924 (Lincoln Record Soc).

Early Yorkshire charters. Ed W. Farrer and C. T. and E. M. Clay 12 vols 1914–65.

Die Gesetze der Angelsachsen. Ed F. Liebermann 3 vols Halle 1903–16.

Leges Henrici Primi. Ed and tr L. J. Downer, Oxford 1972.

Treatise on the laws and customs of the realm of England commonly called Glanvill. Ed and tr G. D. G. Hall 1965.

Placita anglo-normannica: law cases from William I to Richard I. Ed M. M. Bigelow, Boston 1879.

Rotuli curiae regis. Ed F. Palgrave 2 vols 1835.

Three rolls of the King's Court 1194–5. Ed F. W. Maitland 1891 (Pipe Roll Soc).

Curia regis rolls. Ed C. T. Flower, vol 1 1922.

Chronicon monasterii de Abingdon. Ed J. Stevenson 2 vols 1858 (Rolls ser).

Chronicon monasterii de Bello. 1896 (Anglia Christiana).

Burton abbey twelfth-century surveys. Ed C. G. O. Bridgeman 1916 (William Salt Archaeological Soc).

Chronicle of Jocelin of Brakelond. Ed and tr H. E. Butler 1949.

Kalendar of Abbot Samson of Bury St Edmunds. Ed R. H. C. Davis 1954 (Camden Soc).

Feudal documents from the abbey of Bury St Edmunds. Ed D. C. Douglas, Oxford 1932 (Br Acad).

An eleventh-century inquisition of St Augustine's, Canterbury. Ed A. Ballard, Oxford 1920 (Br Acad).

Domesday monachorum of Christ Church, Canterbury. Ed D. C. Douglas 1944. With plates.

Boldon buke: a survey of the possessions of the see of Durham 1183. Ed W. Greenwell 1852 (Surtees Soc).

Liber eliensis. Ed E. O. Blake 1962 (Camden Soc).

Adami de Domerham historia de rebus gestis glastoniensibus. Ed T. Hearne 2 vols Oxford 1727.

Liber Henrici de Soliaco abbatis Glaston. Ed J. E. Jackson 1882 (Roxburghe Club).

Eleventh- and twelfth-century sections of the cartulary of St Benet of Holme. Ed J. R. West 2 vols 1932 (Norfolk Record Soc).

Papal decretals relating to the diocese of Lincoln in the twelfth century. Ed W. Holtzmann and E. W. Kemp 1954 (Lincoln Record Soc).

Chronicle of Hugh Candidus, a monk of Peterborough. Ed W. T. Mellows, Oxford 1949; tr 1941.

Textus roffensis. Ed T. Hearne, Oxford 1720; ed P. Sawyer 2 vols Copenhagen 1957–62 (facs).

Records of the Templars in England in the twelfth century. Ed B. A. Lees, Oxford 1935.

Hemingi chartularium ecclesiae wigorniensis. Ed T. Hearne 2 vols Oxford 1723.

Life of Ailred of Rievaulx by Walter Daniel. Ed and tr F. M. Powicke 1950.

Life of St Anselm. Ed and tr R. W. Southern 1962.

Life of Christina of Markyate. Ed and tr C. H. Talbot, Oxford 1959.

Le livre de saint Gilbert de Sempringham. Ed R. Foreville, Paris 1943.

Libellus de vita et miraculis S. Godrici. Ed J. Stevenson 1847 (Surtees Soc).

Magna vita S. Hugonis. Ed and tr D. L. Douie and H. Farmer 2 vols 1961–2.

Materials for the history of Thomas Becket. Ed J. C. Robertson 7 vols 1875–85 (Rolls ser).

Guernes de Pont-Sainte-Maxence: la vie de Saint Thomas Becket. Ed E. Walberg, Paris 1936.

Life and miracles of Saint William of Norwich. Ed A. Jessopp and M. R. James, Cambridge 1896.

Wulfric of Haselbury. Ed M. Bell 1933 (Somerset Record Soc).

Vita Wulfstani of William of Malmesbury. Ed R. R. Darlington 1928 (Camden Soc).

Alexandri Neckam de naturis rerum libri duo. Ed T. Wright 1863 (Rolls ser).

Anselmi omnia opera. Ed F. S. Schmitt 6 vols Edinburgh 1946–61; Memorials of St Anselm, ed R. W. Southern and Schmitt, Oxford 1969.

Letters of Arnulf of Lisieux. Ed F. Barlow 1939 (Camden Soc).

Geoffrey of Monmouth's Historia regum Britanniae. Ed A. Griscom 1929; tr 1912, 1966.

Letters and charters of Gilbert Foliot. Ed A. Morey and C. N. L. Brooke, Cambridge 1967.

John of Salisbury. Policraticus. Ed C. C. J. Webb 2 vols Oxford 1909, tr 1927, 1938 (complementary and partial trns); Metalogicon, ed C. C. J. Webb, Oxford 1929, tr 1955; Historia pontificalis, ed and tr M. Chibnall 1956; Letters, ed and tr C. N. L. Brooke et al 1955–.

Monastic constitutions of Lanfranc. Ed and tr M. D. Knowles 1951.

Letters of Osbert of Clare. Ed E. W. Williamson 1929.

Serlon de Wilton: poèmes latins. Ed J. Öberg, Stockholm 1965.

Walter Map: de nugis curialium. Ed M. R. James, Oxford 1914; tr 1923.

William FitzStephen's description of London. Ed F. M. Stenton 1934 (Historical Assoc).

Anglo-Latin satirical poets and epigrammatists of the twelfth century. Ed T. Wright 2 vols 1872 (Rolls ser); Speculum stultorum, tr 1963.

Marie de France. Die Fabeln. Ed K. Warnke, Halle 1898; Lais, ed J. Rychner, Paris 1966.

Philippe de Thaun. Li cumpoz, ed E. Mall, Strasbourg 1873; Le bestiaire, ed E. Walberg, Paris 1900.

Bayeux tapestry. Ed F. M. Stenton et al 1957, 1965. With plates.

Canterbury psalter. Ed M. R. James 1935 (facs).

St Albans psalter. Ed O. Pächt et al 1960 (facs).

Thirteenth Century

Chronicles of the reigns of Edward I and Edward II. Ed W. Stubbs 2 vols 1882–3 (Rolls ser).

Bartholomei de Cotton historia anglicana. Ed H. R. Luard 1859 (Rolls ser).

Chronicle of Bury St Edmunds 1212–1301. Ed and tr A. Gransden 1964.

Chronicon Henrici de Silegrave. Ed C. Hook 1849 (Caxton Soc).

Johannis de Trokelowe et Henrici de Blaneforde chronica et annales. Ed H. T. Riley 1866 (Rolls ser).

Chronicon de Lanercost. Ed J. Stevenson, Edinburgh 1839 (Bannatyne Club).

Matthaei Parisiensis chronica majora. Ed H. R. Luard 7 vols 1872–83 (Rolls ser); Historia Anglorum, ed F. H. Madden 3 vols 1866–9 (Rolls ser); Four maps of Great Britain, ed J. P. Gilson and H. Poole 1928.

F. Nicholai Triveti annales. Ed T. Hog 1845 (Eng Historical Soc).

Chronicle of Pierre de Langtoft. Ed T. Wright 2 vols 1866–8 (Rolls ser); tr Robert Mannyng 1338, ed T. Hearne 2 vols Oxford 1725.

Radulphi de Coggeshall chronicon anglicanum. Ed J. Stevenson 1875 (Rolls ser).

Metrical chronicle of Robert of Gloucester. Ed W. A. Wright 2 vols 1887 (Rolls ser).

Rogeri de Wendover chronica sive flores historiarum. Ed H. O. Coxe 5 vols 1841–4 (Eng Historical Soc); ed H. G. Hewlett 3 vols 1886–9 (Rolls ser).

Memoriale Fratris Walteri de Coventria. Ed W. Stubbs 2 vols 1872–3 (Rolls ser).

Chronicle of Walter of Guisborough, previously edited as of Walter of Hemingford or Hemingburgh. Ed. H. Rothwell 1957 (Camden Soc).

Chronicle of William de Rishanger. Ed H. T. Riley 1865 (Rolls ser).

Histoire de Guillaume le Maréchal. Ed P. Meyer 3 vols Paris 1891–1901.

Song of Lewes. Ed C. L. Kingsford, Oxford 1890.

Red book of the Exchequer. Ed H. Hall 3 vols 1896 (Rolls ser).

Great roll of the Pipe. See above; 1241–2, ed H. L. Cannon, New Haven 1918.

Memoranda rolls. 1207–8, ed R. A. Brown 1957 (Pipe Roll Soc); 1230–1, ed C. Robinson 1933 (Pipe Roll Soc).

Cartæ antiquæ rolls 1–20. Ed L. Landon and J. C. Davies 2 vols 1939–60 (Pipe Roll Soc).

Liber feodorum: testa de Nevill. Ed H. C. Maxwell-Lyte 2 vols in 3 1920–31.

Royal and other historical letters. Ed W. W. Shirley 2 vols 1862–6 (Rolls ser).

Building accounts of Henry III. Ed H. M. Colvin, Oxford 1971.

Henry of Bracton. De legibus et consuetudinibus Angliae. Ed G. E. Woodbine 2 vols New Haven 1915–22; Bracton's note book, ed F. W. Maitland 3 vols 1887.

Fleta. Ed and tr H. G. Richardson and G. O. Sayles 1955– (Selden Soc).

Mirror of justices. Ed and tr W. J. Whittaker and F. W. Maitland 1895 (Selden Soc).

Brevia placitata. Ed and tr G. J. Turner and T. F. T. Plucknett 1951 (Selden Soc.)

Curia regis rolls 1201–32. Ed C. T. Flower et al 13 vols 1925–61; Introduction by C. T. Flower 1943 (Selden Soc).

Pleas before the King etc. Ed D. M. Stenton 4 vols 1953–67 (Selden Soc).

Select pleas of the crown 1200–25. Ed and tr F. W. Maitland 1888 (Selden Soc).

Select cases in the court of King's Bench under Edward I. Ed and tr G. O. Sayles 3 vols 1936–9.

State trials of the reign of Edward the First. Ed T. F. Tout and H. Johnstone 1906 (Camden Soc).

Select civil pleas 1200–3. Ed and tr W. P. Baildon 1890 (Selden Soc).

Calendar of the plea rolls of the Exchequer of the Jews. Ed J. M. Rigg and H. Jenkinson 3 vols 1905–29 (Jewish Historical Soc of England).

Rolls of the justices in eyre. Ed and tr D. M. Stenton 3 vols 1934–40 (Selden Soc).

Select pleas in manorial and other seignorial courts. Ed and tr F. W. Maitland 1889 (Selden Soc).

Select pleas of the forest. Ed and tr G. J. Turner 1901 (Selden Soc).

Court roll of Chalgrave Manor 1278–1313. Ed M. K. Dale, Streatley 1950 (Bedfordshire Historical Record Soc).

Calendar of the county court etc of Chester 1259–97. Ed R. Stewart-Brown 1926 (Chetham Soc).

A Lincolnshire assize roll for 1298. Ed W. S. Thomson 1944 (Lincoln Record Soc).

Somersetshire pleas. Ed C. E. H. Chadwyck-Heeley 1897 (Somerset Record Soc).

Three Yorkshire assize rolls. Ed C. T. Clay 1911 (Yorkshire Archæological Soc).

Councils and synods 1205–1313. Ed F. M. Powicke and C. R. Cheney 2 vols Oxford 1964.

Letters of Pope Innocent III: a calendar. Ed C. R. and M. G. Cheney, Oxford 1967; Selected letters of Pope Innocent II, ed and tr C. R. Cheney and W. H. Semple 1953.

Interdict documents. Ed P. M. Barnes and W. R. Powell 1960 (Pipe Roll Soc).

Thomas of Eccleston, De adventu Fratrum Minorum in Anglia. Ed A. G. Little, Paris 1904, Manchester 1951.

Transcripts of charters relating to Gilbertine houses. Ed F. M. Stenton 1922 (Lincoln Record Soc).

C. H. Lawrence, St Edmund of Abingdon, Oxford 1960. Includes texts.

Custumals of Battle Abbey 1283–1312. Ed S. R. Scargill-Bird 1887 (Camden Soc).

Acta Stephani Langton, cantuariensis archiepiscopi AD 1207–28. Ed K. Major 1950 (Canterbury & York Soc).

Register of St Augustine's abbey Canterbury. Ed G. J. Turner and H. E. Salter 2 vols 1915–24 (Br Acad).

Records of Antony Bek, Bishop and Patriarch [of Durham] 1283–1311. Ed C. M. Fraser 1953 (Surtees Soc).

Durham annals and documents of the thirteenth century. Ed F. Barlow 1945 (Surtees Soc).

A roll of the household expenses of Richard de Swinfield, Bishop of Hereford. Ed J. Webb 2 vols 1853–5 (Camden Soc).

Rotuli Roberti Grosseteste, episcopi lincolniensis. Ed F. N. Davis 1913 (Canterbury & York Soc).

Early charters of the cathedral church of St Paul. Ed M. Gibbs 1939 (Camden Soc).

Domesday of St Paul's of the year 1222. Ed W. H. Hale 1858 (Camden Soc).

Cartulary of St Mary Clerkenwell. Ed W. O. Hassall 1949 (Camden Soc).

Registrum malmesburiense. Ed J. S. Brewer and C. T. Martin 2 vols 1879–80 (Rolls ser).

Vetus registrum sarisberiense. Ed W. H. R. Jones 2 vols 1883–4 (Rolls ser).

Documents illustrating the rule of Walter de Wenlok, Abbot of Westminster 1283–1307. Ed B. F. Harvey 1965 (Camden Soc).

Pipe roll of the bishopric of Winchester 1208–9. Ed H. Hall 1903.

Cartulary of Worcester Cathedral Priory. Ed R. R. Darlington 1968 (Pipe Roll Soc).

Chronicles of the mayor and sheriffs of London. Ed H. T. Riley 1863.

Two early London subsidy rolls. Ed E. Ekwall, Lund 1951.

Early rolls of Merton College. Ed J. R. L. Highfield 1964 (Oxford Historical Soc).

Medieval customs of the manors of Taunton and Bradford-on-Tone. Ed T. J. Hunt 1962 (Somerset Record Soc).

Walter of Henley and other treatises on estate management and accounting. Ed D. Oschinsky, Oxford 1970.

Le traité de Walter de Bibbesworth sur la langue française. Ed A. Owen, Paris 1929.

Robert Grosseteste. Writings [a catalogue], ed S. Harrison Thomson, Cambridge 1940; Epistolæ, ed H. R. Luard 1861 (Rolls ser).

Political songs of England. Ed T. Wright 1839 (Camden Soc).

Thirteenth-century bestiary in the library of Alnwick Castle. Ed E. G. Millar 1958 (Roxburghe Club) (facs).

Thirteenth-century York psalter. Ed E. G. Millar 1952 (Roxburghe Club) (facs).

Fourteenth Century

Chronicon Angliae. Ed E. M. Thompson 1874 (Rolls ser).

Anonimalle chronicle 1333–81. Ed V. H. Galbraith, Manchester 1927.

The Brut or the chronicles of England. Ed F. W. D. Brie 2 vols 1906–8 (EETS).

Chronicles of the reigns of Edward I and Edward II. *As above.*

Eulogium historiarum. Ed F. S. Haydon 3 vols 1858–63 (Rolls ser).

Flores historiarum. Ed H. R. Luard 3 vols 1890 (Rolls ser).

Chronicon de Lanercost. *As above.*

Vita Edwardi Secundi. Ed N. Denholm-Young 1957.

Robertus de Avesbury de gestis mirabilibus Edwardi Tertii. Ed E. M. Thompson 1889 (Rolls ser).

Herald of Chandos. Life of the Black Prince. Ed M. K. Pope and E. C. Lodge, Oxford 1910.

Historia vitae et regni Ricardi Secundi. Ed T. Hearne, Oxford 1729.

Chronique de la traïsun et mort de Richart Deux. Ed B. Williams 1846 (English Historical Soc).

Chronicon Galfridi le Baker de Swynbroke. Ed E. M. Thompson, Oxford 1889.

Johannis de Fordun Scotichronicon. Ed W. Goodall 2 vols Edinburgh 1759; Continuatio, ed T. Hearne, Oxford 1722.

Chroniques de Jean Froissart. Ed Kervyn de Lettenhove 25 vols Brussels 1870–7; tr Lord Berners 4 vols 1523–5; ed W. P. Ker 6 vols 1901–3.

Sir Thomas Gray of Heton; Scalachronica. Ed J. Stevenson, Edinburgh 1836 (Maitland Club).

Polychronicon Rannulphi Higden. Ed C. Babington and J. R. Lumby 9 vols 1865–86 (Rolls ser). Includes trn by John Trevisa 1387.

Chronicon Henrici Knighton monachi leycestrensis. Ed J. R. Lumby 2 vols 1889–95 (Rolls ser).

Adae Murimuth continuatio chronicarum. Ed E. M. Thompson 1889 (Rolls ser).

Johannes de Trokelowe et Henrici de Blaneforde chronica. *As above.*

Chronicon Adae de Usk 1377–1421. Ed E. M. Thompson 1904 (Royal Soc of Lit).

Thomæ Walsingham historia anglicana. Ed H. T. Riley 2 vols 1863–4 (Rolls ser); Annales Ricardi Secundi et Henrici Quarti, ed H. T. Riley 1886 (Rolls ser).

Memoranda de parliamento, 1305. Ed F. W. Maitland 1893 (Rolls ser).

Proceedings and ordinances of the Privy Council. Ed N. H. Nicolas 7 vols 1834–7.

Issue roll of Thomas de Brantingham, Lord High Treasurer of England. Ed and tr F. Devon 1835.

Letters of Edward, Prince of Wales 1304–5. Ed H. Johnstone 1931 (Roxburghe Club).

Diplomatic correspondence of Richard II. Ed E. Perroy 1933 (Camden Soc).

Select cases in the Court of King's Bench under Edward II and Edward III. Ed and tr G. O. Sayles 6 vols 1936–65 (Selden Soc).

Placita de quo warranto etc. Ed W. Illingworth 1818.

Select bills in Eyre 1292–1333. Ed W. C. Bolland 1914 (Selden Soc).

Eyre of London 1321. Ed and tr H. Cam 2 vols 1968–9 (Selden Soc).

Select cases from the coroners' rolls 1265–1413. Ed and tr C. Gross 1896 (Selden Soc).

Halmota prioratus dunelmensis, Ed W. H. Longstaffe and J. Booth 1889 (Surtees Soc).

Kent keepers of the peace 1316–17. Ed B. Putnam, Ashford 1933.

Some sessions of the peace in Lincolnshire. 1360–75, ed R. Sillem 1937 (Lincoln Record Soc); 1381–96, ed E. G. Kimball 2 vols 1955–62 (Lincoln Record Soc).

Leet jurisdiction in Norwich. Ed W. Hudson 1892 (Selden Soc).

Yorkshire sessions of the peace 1361–4. Ed B. H. Putnam 1939 (Yorkshire Archaeological Soc).

Records of the trial of Walter Langeton, Bishop of Coventry and Lichfield 1307–12. Ed A. Beardwood 1969 (Camden Soc).

A contemporary narrative of the proceedings against Dame Alice Kyteler, prosecuted for sorcery in 1324. Ed T. Wright 1843 (Camden Soc).

The Knights Hospitallers in England. Ed L. B. Larking and J. M. Kemble 1857 (Camden Soc).

Customary of the Benedictine monasteries of Saint Augustine, Canterbury and Saint Peter, Westminster. Ed E. M. Thompson 2 vols 1902–4 (Bradshaw Soc).

Memorials of Beverley Minster 1286–1347. Ed A. F. Leach 2 vols 1898–1903 (Surtees Soc).

Pinchbeck Register [of Bury St Edmunds]. Ed Lord F. Hervey, Brighton 1925.

Registrum palatinum dunelmense. Ed T. D. Hardy 4 vols 1873–8 (Rolls ser).

A terrier of Fleet. Ed N. Neilson, Oxford 1920 (Br Acad).

Great chartulary of Glastonbury. Ed A. Watkin 3 vols 1947–56 (Somerset Record Soc).

Henry of Pytchley's book of fees. Ed and tr W. T. Mellows 1927 (Northamptonshire Record Soc).

Fabric rolls of York minster. Ed J. Raine 1859 (Surtees Soc).

English gilds. Ed T. and L. T. Smith 1870 (EETS).

Accounts of the county of Chester 1301–60. Ed R. Stewart-Brown 1910 (Lancashire & Cheshire Record Soc).

Chroniques de London. Ed G. J. Aungier 1844 (Camden Soc).

Memorials of London. Ed and tr H. T. Riley 1868.

Chaucer's world. Ed and tr E. Rickert et al, New York 1948.

Register of Daniel Rough, common clerk of Romney 1352–80. Ed K. M. E. Murray 1945 (Kent Archæological Soc).

Oak book of Southampton. Ed and tr P. Studer 2 vols and suppl 1910–11 (Southampton Record Soc).

John of Gaunt's register. Ed S. Armitage-Smith et al 4 vols 1911–37 (Camden Soc).

Indentures of retinue with John of Gaunt. Ed N. B. Lewis, Camden Miscellany 22 1964.

Register of Edward the Black Prince. Ed M. C. B. Dawes 4 vols 1930–3.

Estate book of Henry de Bray. Ed D. Willis 1916 (Camden Soc).

Expeditions to Prussia and the Holy Land made by Henry, Earl of Derby [Henry IV]. Ed L. T. Smith 1894 (Camden Soc).

The Scrope and Grosvenor controversy 1385–90. Ed N. H. Nicholas 2 vols 1832 (priv ptd).

Missale ad usum ecclesie westmonasteriensis. Ed J. Wickham Legg 3 vols 1891–7 (Bradshaw Soc). With music.

Sermons of Thomas Brinton, Bishop of Rochester 1373–89. Ed Sr M. A. Devlin 2 vols 1954 (Camden Soc).

Richard of Bury. Philobiblon. Ed and tr E. C. Thomas, Oxford 1960; Liber epistolaris of Richard de Bury, ed N. Denholm-Young 1950 (Roxburghe Club).

The monk of Farne: the meditations of a fourteenth-century monk. Ed H. Farmer 1961.

Poems of John of Hovedene. Ed F. J. E. Raby 1939 (Surtees Soc).

Le livre de seyntz medicines of Henry of Lancaster. Ed E. J. Arnould, Oxford 1940 (Anglo-Norman Text Soc).

Political poems and songs. Ed T. Wright 2 vols 1859–61 (Rolls ser).

John Wyclif, Catalogue of extant Latin works. Ed W. W. Shirley 1925 (Wyclif Soc); Select English works, ed T. Arnold 3 vols Oxford 1869–71. For English writings *see below.* Many Latin works pbd by Wyclif Soc.

Lanfrank's science of cirurgie. Ed R. von Fleischhacker 1894 (EETS).

The Gough map. Ed E. J. S. Parsons and F. M. Stenton, Oxford 1958.

Holkham Bible picture book. Ed W. O. Hassall 1954 (facs).

A Peterborough psalter and bestiary of the fourteenth century. Ed M. R. James, Oxford 1921 (Roxburghe Club) (facs).

The Luttrell psalter. Ed E. G. Millar 1932 (facs).

Fifteenth Century

An English chronicle 1377–1461. Ed J. S. Davies 1856 (Camden Soc).

Chronicon Angliae, temporibus Ricardi II, Henrici IV, Henrici V et Henrici VI. Ed J. A. Giles 1848.

Three fifteenth-century chronicles. Ed J. Gairdner 1880 (Camden Soc).

The Brut. *As above.*

St Albans chronicle 1406–20. Ed V. H. Galbraith, Oxford 1937.

John Capgrave's chronicle of England. Ed F. C. Hingeston 1858 (Rolls ser).

Robert Fabyan: the new chronicles of England and France. Ed H. Ellis 1811.

Hall's chronicle. Ed H. Ellis 1809.

Chronicles of London. Ed C. L. Kingsford, Oxford 1905.

Great chronicle of London. Ed A. H. Thomas and I. D. Thornley 1938.

Historical collections of a citizen of London in the fifteenth century. Ed J. Gairdner 1876 (Camden Soc).

Six town chronicles. Ed R. Flenley, Oxford 1911.

Chronicon Adae de Usk. *As above.*

Anglica historia of Polydore Vergil 1485–1537. Ed and tr D. Hay 1950 (Camden Soc).

Recueil des croniques par Jehan de Wavrin. Ed and partly tr W. and E. L. C. P. Hardy 8 vols 1864–91 (Rolls ser).

Chronicles of the White Rose of York. Ed J. A. Giles 1845.

Narratives of the expulsion of the English from Normandy. Ed J. Stevenson 1863 (Rolls ser).

Journal d'un bourgeois de Paris 1405–49. Ed A. Tuekey, Paris 1881; tr 1968.

First English life of Henry V. Ed C. L. Kingsford, Oxford 1911.

Memorials of Henry V. Ed C. A. Cole 1858 (Rolls ser).

Henrici Quinti Angliae regis gesta. Ed B. Williams 1850 (Eng Historical Soc).

Historie of the arrivall of Edward IV in England. Ed J. Bruce 1838 (Camden Soc).

La révolte du conte de Warwick contre le roi Edward IV. Ed J. A. Giles 1849 (Caxton Soc).

Sir Thomas More, History of King Richard III. 1544; ed J. R. Lumby, Cambridge 1883.

Official correspondence of Thomas Bekynton, secretary to Henry VI. Ed G. Williams 2 vols 1872 (Rolls ser).

Letters of Queen Margaret of Anjou. Ed C. Monro 1863 (Camden Soc).

Black book of the Admiralty. Ed T. Twiss 4 vols 1871–6 (Rolls ser).

Readings and moots at the Inns of Court in the fifteenth century. Ed and tr S. E. Thorne 1954– (Selden Soc).

Select cases in the Court of Chancery 1364–1471. Ed and tr W. P. Baildon 1896 (Selden Soc).

Coventry leet book 1420–1555. Ed M. D. Harris 4 vols 1907–13 (EETS).

Calendar of the plea and memoranda rolls of London, 1413–37. Ed A. H. Thomas, Cambridge 1943.

Register of Henry Chichele, Archbishop of Canterbury 1414–43. Ed E. F. Jacob, Oxford 1947.

English register of Godstow nunnery. Ed A. Clark 3 vols 1905–11 (EETS).

Lincoln diocese documents 1450–1544. Ed A. Clark 1914 (EETS).

Visitations of religious houses in the diocese of Lincoln. Ed A. H. Thompson 3 vols 1914–29 (Lincoln Record Soc).

Medieval records of a London City church. Ed H. Littlehales 1905 (EETS).

English register of Oseney abbey. Ed A. Clark 2 vols 1913 (EETS).

Ordinale Sarum. Ed W. Cook and C. Wordsworth 2 vols 1901–2 (Bradshaw Soc).

Bristol charters 1378–1499. Ed H. A. Cronne, Bristol 1946.

Accounts of John Balsall, purser of the Trinity of Bristol 1480–1. Ed T. F. Reddaway and A. W. Ruddock, Camden Miscellany 23 1968.

A book of London English. Ed R. W. Chambers and M. Daunt, Oxford 1931. Mainly local records.

Port books of Southampton. 1427–30, ed and tr P. Studer 1913 (Southampton Record Soc); 1469–71, 1477–81, ed and tr D. B. Quinn 2 vols 1937–8 (Southampton Record Soc).

Building accounts of Tattershall Castle 1434–72. Ed W. D. Simpson 1960 (Lincoln Record Soc).

A small household of the fifteenth century. Ed K. Wood-Legh, Manchester 1956.

Household book of Dame Alice de Bryene 1412–13. Ed V. B. Redstone and tr M. K. Dale, Ipswich 1931 (Suffolk Inst of Archaeology & Natural History).

Black book of the household of Edward IV. Ed A. R. Myers, Manchester 1959.

Household books of John Duke of Norfolk and Thomas Earl of Surrey temp. 1481–90. Ed J. P. Collier 1842 (Roxburghe Club).

Two fifteenth-century cookery books. Ed T. Austin 1888 (EETS).

Early English meals and manners. Ed F. J. Furnivall 1868 (EETS).

Caxton's book of curtesye. Ed F. J. Furnivall 1868 (EETS).

Book of nurture by John Russell. Ed F. J. Furnivall 1867 (Roxburghe Club).

A fifteenth-century courtesy-book and two fifteenth-century Franciscan rules. Ed R. W. Chambers and W. W. Seton 1914 (EETS).

The master of game. Ed W. A. and F. Baillie-Grohman 1909.

The book of St Albans. Ed W. Blades 1881 (facs).

A leechbook of the fifteenth century. Ed W. R. Dawson 1934.

Liber de diversis medicinis. Ed M. S. Ogden 1938 (EETS).

Cyrurgie of Guy de Chauliac. Ed M. S. Ogden 1971 (EETS).

A fifteenth-century school book. Ed W. Nelson, Oxford 1956.

Catholicon anglicum. Ed S. J. H. Herrtage and H. B. Wheatley 1881 (EETS).

Manipulus vocabulorum. Ed H. B. Wheatley 1869 (Camden Soc).

Promptorium parvulorum. Ed A. L. Mayhew 1908 (EETS).

Sir John Fortescue. Works. Ed Thomas Lord Clermont 2 vols 1869; The governance of England, ed C. Plummer, Oxford 1885; De laudibus legum Anglie, ed S. B. Chrimes, Cambridge 1949.

Thomas Gascoigne. Loci e libro veritatum. Ed J. E. T. Rogers, Oxford 1881.

Book of Margery Kempe. Ed S. B. Meech and H. E. Allen 1940 (EETS).

Libelle of English polycye. Ed G. Warner, Oxford 1926.

Reginald Pecock. The repressor of overmuch blaming of the clergy. Ed C. Babington 2 vols 1860 (Rolls ser); Donet, ed E. V. Hitchcock 1918 (EETS); Folewer to the Donet, ed Hitchcock 1923 (EETS); Reule of Cristen religioun, ed W. C. Greet 1926 (EETS).

A commonplace book of the fifteenth century. Ed L. T. Smith, Norwich 1886.

Cely papers. Ed H. E. Malden 1900 (Camden Soc).

Paston letters. Ed N. Davis, Oxford 1970–; Selections, ed N. Davis, Oxford 1958.

Plumpton correspondence. Ed T. Stapleton 1839 (Camden Soc).

Letters and papers of John Shillingford. Ed S. A. Moore 1872 (Camden Soc).

Stonor letters and papers. Ed C. L. Kingsford 2 vols 1919 (Camden Soc); addns in Camden Miscellany 13 1924.

William Worcestre. Itineraries. Ed and tr J. H. Harvey, Oxford 1969.

(3) MANUSCRIPTS, INCUNABULA, MEDIEVAL LIBRARIES ETC

Ward, H. L. D. and J. A. Herbert. Catalogue of romances in the Department of Manuscripts of the British Museum. 3 vols 1883–1910.

Dillon, Viscount and W. H. St J. Hope. Inventory of Thomas, Duke of Gloucester 1397. Archaeological Jnl 54 1897. With book list.

Skeat, W. W. Twelve facsimiles of Old English manuscripts. Oxford 1892.

Duff, E. G. Early printed books. 1893. With plates.

— Early English printing. 1896. With plates.

— A century of the English book trade. 1905 (Bibl Soc).

— The printers, stationers and bookbinders of Westminster and London from 1476 to 1535. Cambridge 1906 (Sandars lectures).

— The English provincial printers, stationers and bookbinders to 1557. Cambridge 1912 (Sandars lectures).

— Fifteenth-century English books. Oxford 1917 (Bibl Soc). A bibliography, with facs.

Madan, F. Books in manuscript. 1893, 1920.

— Handwriting. In Mediaeval England, ed H. W. C. Davis, Oxford 1924.

— The localization of manuscripts. In Essays in history presented to R. L. Poole, Oxford 1927.

Thompson, E. M. The history of English handwriting AD 700–1400. Trans Bibl Soc 5 1900.

James, M. R. The ancient libraries of Canterbury and Dover. Cambridge 1903.

— The Chaundler manuscripts. 1916 (Roxburghe Club). With plates.

— The wanderings and homes of manuscripts. 1919 (SPCK); largely rptd in G. Watson, The literary thesis, 1970.

— A Peterborough psalter and bestiary. Oxford 1921 (Roxburghe Club) (facs).

— The Royal manuscripts of the British Museum. Library 4th ser 2 1922.

— Lists of manuscripts formerly in Peterborough Abbey library. Oxford 1926 (Bibl Soc).

— and S. C. Cockerell. Two East Anglian psalters. 1926 (Roxburghe Club) (facs).

— The bestiary. Oxford 1928 (Roxburghe Club) (facs).

— The Canterbury psalter. 1935 (facs).

— and E. G. Millar. The Bohun manuscripts. Oxford 1936 (Roxburghe Club). With plates.

Hammond, E. P. Ashmole 59 and other Shirley manuscripts. Anglia 30 1907.

Greg, W. W. Facsimiles of twelve early English manuscripts in the library of Trinity College, Cambridge. Oxford 1913.

Hibbard (Loomis), L. A. The books of Sir Simon de Burley 1387. MLN 30 1915.

— The Auchinleck manuscript and a possible London bookshop of 1330–40. PMLA 67 1942.

Jenkinson, H. Palaeography and the practical study of court hand. Cambridge 1915. With plates.

— and C. Johnson. English court hand AD 1066 to 1500. 2 pts Oxford 1915. With plates.

— The teaching and practice of handwriting in England. History new ser 11 1927.

Brown, C. F. Register of Middle English religious and didactic verse. 2 vols 1916–20 (Bibl Soc).

— A thirteenth-century ms at Maidstone. MLR 21 1926.

— A thirteenth-century manuscript from Llanthony Priory. Speculum 3 1928.

— Texts and the man. Bull of Modern Humanities Research Assoc 2 1928.

Deanesley, M. Vernacular books in England in the fourteenth and fifteenth centuries. MLR 15 1920.

Gollancz, I. (ed). Facsimile of ms Cotton Nero A x. 1922 (EETS).

Wilson, J. M. Worcester Cathedral library. Library 4th ser 2 1922.

Lathrop, H. B. The first English printers and their patrons. Library 4th ser 3 1923.

Chambers, R. W. The lost literature of medieval England. Library 4th ser 5 1925.

Millar, E. G. English illuminated manuscripts from the xth to the xiiith century. Paris and Brussels 1926. With plates.

— English illuminated manuscripts of the xivth and xvth centuries. Paris and Brussels 1928. With plates.

— A thirteenth-century bestiary. 1958 (Roxburghe Club) (facs).

Brett, C. Two newly found Middle English texts. MLR 22 1927.

Cumming, W. P. A Middle English ms in the Bibliothèque Ste Geneviève. PMLA 42 1927.

Rickert, E. A leaf from a fourteenth-century letter book. MP 25 1927.

— King Richard II's books. Library 4th ser 13 1932.

Warner, G. (ed). The Guthlac roll. Oxford 1928 (Roxburghe Club) (facs).

Plomer, H. R. The importation of Low Country and French books into England 1480 and 1502–3. Library 4th ser 9 1929.

Clarke, M. V. Henry Knighton and the library catalogue of Leicester Abbey. EHR 45 1930.

Pantin, W. A. A mediæval collection of Latin and English proverbs and riddles from the Rylands Latin ms 394. Bull John Rylands Lib 14 1930.

Andrews, H. C. Books in a late fifteenth-century will. N & Q 23 May 1931.

Bone, G. Extant manuscripts printed from by W. de Worde. Library 4th ser 12 1931.

Allen, H. E. The localization of Bodl. ms 34. MLR 28 1933.

Dickins, B. The date of the Ireland manuscript. Leeds Stud in Eng 2 1933.

— The Ireland-Blackburne manuscript. Leeds Stud in Eng 3 1934.

Irwin, P. J. The lost Loscombe manuscript. Anglia 57 1933.

Oakden, J. P. The scribal errors of the ms Cotton Nero A x. Library 4th ser 14 1933.

Schramm, W. L. The cost of books in Chaucer's time. MLN 48 1933.

Wilson, R. M. Lost literature in Old and Middle English. Leeds Stud in Eng 2 1933.

— More lost literature. Leeds Stud in Eng 5–6 1936–7.

— The lost literature of medieval England. 1952, 1970 (rev).

Ker, N. R. Some notes on the Peterborough Chronicle. MÆ 3 1934.

— Ms Cotton Galba A xix. MÆ 5 1936.

— The mediæval pressmarks of St Guthlac's priory, Hereford, and of Roche abbey, Yorks. Ibid.

— The date of the 'tremulous' Worcester hand. Leeds Stud in Eng 6 1937.

— Medieval libraries of Great Britain: a list of surviving books. 1941, 1964.

— The migration of manuscripts from the English medieval libraries. Library 4th ser 23 1943.

— William of Malmesbury's handwriting. EHR 59 1944.

— Fragments of medieval manuscripts used as pastedowns in Oxford bindings. Oxford 1954 (Oxford Bibl Soc).

— The chaining, labelling and inventory numbers of manuscripts belonging to the old University Library. Bodleian Lib Record 5 1955.

— English manuscripts in the century after the Norman Conquest. Oxford 1960.

— (ed). Facsimile of ms Bodley 34. 1960 (EETS).

— (ed). The owl and the nightingale. 1963 (EETS) (facs).

— (ed). Facsimile of British Museum ms Harley 2253. 1965 (EETS).

—— Middle English verses and a Latin letter in a manuscript at Stanbrook Abbey. MÆ 34 1965.
—— Medieval manuscripts in British libraries. Oxford 1969–.
Bressie, R. The Leicester Abbey catalogue. TLS 24 Oct 1935.
—— Ms Sloane 3548, folio 158. MLN 54 1939.
—— Modern textual corruption in ms Cambridge additional 3470. MLN 60 1945.
Flower, R. The manuscript of the poem of Roberte the deuyll. BM Quart 9 1935.
—— Lost manuscripts. Essays by Divers Hands new ser 18 1940.
Haselden, R. B. Scientific aids for the study of manuscripts. Oxford 1935 (Bibl Soc).
—— A scribe and printer in the fifteenth century. HLQ 2 1939.
de Ricci, S. Census of medieval and Renaissance manuscripts in the United States and Canada. 3 vols New York 1935–40; Supplement, ed C. U. Faye and W. H. Bond 1962; S. A. Ives, Corrigenda and addenda to the description of the Plimpton mss, Speculum 17 1942.
Richardson, E. C. A list of printed catalogues of manuscripts. New York 1935 (pt 3 of Union world catalogue of manuscript books).
Thompson, D. V. Medieval parchment-making. Library 4th ser 16 1936.
Bell, H. E. The price of books in medieval England. Library 4th ser 17 1937.
Bühler, C. F. A Middle English prayer roll. MLN 52 1937.
—— Sir John Paston's ¦grete booke: a fifteenth-century 'best-seller'. MLN 56 1941.
—— A note on fifteenth-century printing technique. Lib Chron 11 1949.
—— Incunabula. In Bühler et al, Standards of bibliographical description, Philadelphia 1949.
—— Fifteenth-century books and the twentieth century. New York 1952 (Grolier Club).
—— The Middle English texts of Morgan ms 861. PMLA 69 1954.
—— Watermarks and the dates of fifteenth-century books. SB 9 1957.
—— The fifteenth-century book: the scribes, the printers, the decorators. Philadelphia 1960.
—— Three Middle English prose charms from ms Harley 2389. N & Q Feb 1962.
—— Middle English apophthegms in a Caxton volume. Eng Lang Notes 1 1963.
—— Prayers and charms in certain Middle English scrolls. Speculum 39 1964.
—— Dates in incunabular colophons. SB 22 1969.
——Chainlines versus imposition in incunabula. SB 23 1970.
Harrison, F. English manuscripts of the fourteenth century. 1937. With plates.
Morison, S. J. The art of printing. Proc Br Acad 33 1937.
Serjeantson, M. S. The index of the Vernon manuscript. MLR 23 1937.
T[aylor], F. A recently acquired Middle English manuscript. Bull John Rylands Lib 21 1937.
Ullman, B. L. Manuscripts of Duke Humphrey of Gloucester. EHR 52 1937.
Thomson, S. H. The criteria of Latin paleography in the study of Anglo-Norman documents. Romanic Rev 29 1938.
—— Latin bookhands of the later Middle Ages 1100–1500. Cambridge 1969.
Weiss, R. The library of John Tiptoft, Earl of Worcester. Bodleian Quart Record 8 1938.
—— Piers de Monte, John Whethamstede and the library of St Albans Abbey. EHR 60 1945.
Bennett, J. A. W. A Middle English inscription. N & Q 3 June 1939.

Dean, R. J. An essay in Anglo-Norman palaeography. In Studies in French language and medieval literature presented to M. K. Pope, Manchester 1939.
—— The science and art of paleography. In Literature and science: proceedings of the 6th triennial congress of the International Federation for Modern Languages and Literatures, Oxford 1955.
Leach, MacE. Some problems in editing Middle English manuscripts. Eng Inst Annual 1 1939.
Mead, H. R. Fifteenth-century schoolbooks. HLQ 3 1939.
Thompson, J. W. et al. The medieval library. Chicago 1939, New York 1957 (with suppl by B. Boyer, rptd from Lib Quart 10 1940).
Vinaver, E. Principles of textual emendation. In Studies presented to M. K. Pope, Manchester 1939.
Wrenn, C. L. Curiosities in a medieval manuscript. E & S 25 1939.
Boyer, B. B. The medieval library. Lib Quart 10 1940.
Laird, C. A fourteenth-century scribe. MLN 55 1940.
Meech, S. B. A collection of proverbs in Rawlinson ms D. 328. MP 38 1940.
Schulz, H. C. Middle English texts from the 'Bement' manuscript. HLQ 3 1940.
—— Manuscript printer's copy for a lost early English book. Library 4th ser 22 1942.
—— et al. Ten centuries of manuscripts in the Huntington Library. San Marino 1962.
—— A Middle English manuscript used as printer's copy. HLQ 29 1966.
Winship, G. P. Printing in the fifteenth century. 1940.
Brunner, K. Der Inhalt der me Handschriften und die Literaturgeschichte. Anglia 65 1941.
—— Die Überlieferung der alt- und mittelenglischen Literaturwerke. Anzeiger der Österreichischen Akademie der Wissenschaften (philologische-historische klasse) 95 1958.
Chaytor, H. J. The medieval reader and textual criticism. Bull John Rylands Lib 26 1941.
—— From script to print. Cambridge 1945.
Egbert, D. D. The Western European manuscripts [in the Garrett Collection]. Princeton Univ Lib Chron 3 1942.
Schubel, F. Die gedruckte Wiedergabe mittelenglischer Handschriften. Anglia 66 1942.
Steinberg, S. H. Medieval writing-masters. Library 4th ser 22 1942. See also Speculum 16 1941.
Goldschmidt, E. P. Medieval texts and their first appearance in print. Oxford 1943 (Bibl Soc). Corrections in Library 4th ser 25 1944.
Walpole, R. N. The source ms of Charlemagne and Roland and the Auchinleck bookshop. MLN 60 1945.
Bennett, H. S. Medieval English mss and contemporary taste. Edinburgh Bibl Soc Trans 2 1946.
—— The production and dissemination of vernacular manuscripts in the fifteenth century. Library 5th ser 1 1946.
—— Printers, authors and readers 1475–1557. Library 5th ser 4 1950.
—— English books and readers 1475 to 1557. Cambridge 1952.
Kibre, P. Intellectual interests reflected in the libraries of the fourteenth and fifteenth centuries. JHI 7 1946.
Smyser, H. M. Charlemagne and Roland and the Auchinleck ms. Speculum 21 1946.
—— The list of Norman names in the Auchinleck ms (Battle Abbey roll). In Medieval studies in honor of J. D. M. Ford, Cambridge Mass 1948.
Grieve, H. E. P. Some examples of English handwriting. Chelmsford 1949. With plates.
—— More examples of English handwriting. Chelmsford 1950. With plates.
Pratt, R. A. The importance of manuscripts for the study of medieval education. Progress of Medieval & Renaissance Stud Bull 20 1949.

Smithers, G. V. Two newly-discovered fragments from the Auchinleck ms. MÆ 18 1949.
— Another fragment of the Auchinleck ms. In Medieval literature and civilization: studies in memory of G. N. Garmonsway, 1969.
Binns, A. L. A manuscript source of the Book of St Albans. Bull John Rylands Lib 33 1950.
d'Ardenne, S. The editing of Middle English texts. In English studies today, ed C. L. Wrenn and G. Bullough, Oxford 1951.
— On Middle English textual criticism. Etudes Anglaises 7 1954.
Bliss, A. H. Notes on the Auchinleck manuscript. Speculum 26 1951.
Mitchner, R. W. Wynkyn de Worde's use of the Plimpton manuscript of De proprietatibus rerum. Library 5th ser 6 1951.
Wright, C. E. Late Middle English parerga in a school collection. RES new ser 2 1951.
— The Rous roll: the English version. BM Quart 20 1956.
— and F. Wormald (ed). The English library before 1700. 1958. With plates.
— English vernacular hands from the twelfth to the fifteenth centuries. Oxford 1960. With plates.
Rickert, M. The reconstructed Carmelite missal. 1952. See also Speculum 16 1941.
Schofield, B. The manuscript of a fourteenth-century Oxford Franciscan. BM Quart 16 1952.
Burchfield, R. W. A source of scribal error in early Middle English manuscripts. MÆ 22 1953.
Klinefelter, R. A. A newly discovered fifteenth-century English manuscript. MLQ 14 1953.
Kurvinen, A. Ms Porkington 10. Neuphilologische Mitteilungen 54 1953.
Pafort, E. Notes on the Wynkyn de Worde editions of the Boke of St Albans. SB 5 1953.
Read, B. Manuscript illumination and poetry. Boston Public Lib Quart 5 1953.
Brewer, D. S. Observations on a fifteenth-century manuscript. Anglia 72 1954.
Clark, C. Notes on ms Laud Misc. 636. MÆ 23 1954.
Denholm-Young, N. Handwriting in England and Wales. Cardiff 1954. With plates and bibliography.
Robbins, R. H. The Findern anthology. PMLA 69 1954.
— Five Middle English verse prayers from Lambeth ms 541. Neophilologus 38 1954.
— Good gossips reunited. BM Quart 27 1964.
— Wall verses at Launceston Priory. Archiv 200 1964.
— Mirth in manuscripts. E & S new ser 21 1968.
Whitelock, D. (ed). The Peterborough chronicle (the Bodleian manuscript Laud Misc. 636). Copenhagen 1954 (facs).
Kerling, N. J. M. Caxton and the trade in printed books. Book Collector 8 1955.
Avis, F. C. English printers' marks of the incunabula period. Gutenberg-Jahrbuch 1956.
Dijk, S. J. P. van. An advertisement sheet of an early fourteenth-century writing master at Oxford. Scriptorium 10 1956.
Seaton, M. E. The Devonshire manuscript and its medieval fragments. RES new ser 7 1956.
Skeat, T. C. Use of dictation in ancient book-production. Proc Br Acad 42 1956. Includes Middle Ages.
Winger, H. W. Regulations relating to the book trade in London from 1357 to 1586. Lib Quart 26 1956.
Blaess, M. L'abbaye de Bordesley et les livres de Guy de Beauchamp. Romania 78 1957.
Doyle, A. I. The work of a late fifteenth-century English scribe, William Ebesham. Bull John Rylands Lib 39 1957. With plates.
— Date of a ms in Bibliotheca Bodmeriana. Book Collector 8 1959.

— Books connected with the Vere family and Barking Abbey. Trans Essex Archæological Soc new ser 25 1960.
Pafford, J. H. P. University of London Library ms 278. In Studies presented to Sir Hilary Jenkinson, Oxford 1957.
Febvre, L. and H.-J. Martin et al. L'apparition du livre. Paris 1958.
Galbraith, V. H. Handwriting. In Medieval England, ed A. L. Poole 2 vols Oxford 1958.
Gibson, S. Printed books, the book-trade and libraries. Ibid.
Hector, L. C. The handwriting of English documents. 1958, 1966 (rev). With plates.
Jennett, S. In his Pioneers in printing, 1958.
Luttrell, C. A. Three north-west midland manuscripts. Neophilologus 42 1958.
MacFarlane, L. William Elphinstone's library. Aberdeen Univ Rev 37 1958.
Watson, A. G. An identification of some manuscripts owned by Dr John Dee and Sir Simonds d'Ewes. Library 5th ser 13 1958.
Davis, N. Scribal variation in late fifteenth-century England. In Mélanges de linguistique et de philologie Fernand Mossé in memoriam, Paris 1959.
Dodgson, J. McN. A library at Pott Chapel (Pott Shrigley, Cheshire) c. 1493. Library 5th ser 15 1960.
Harrier, R. C. A printed source for 'the Devonshire manuscript'. RES new ser 11 1960.
Parkes, M. B. A fifteenth-century scribe: Henry Mere. Bodleian Lib Record 6 1961.
— English cursive book hands 1250–1500. Oxford 1969. With plates.
Pearsall, D. A. Notes on the manuscript of Generydes. Library 5th ser 16 1961.
Francis, W. N. Graphemic analysis of late Middle English manuscripts. Speculum 37 1962.
Pollard, G. The construction of English twelfth-century bindings. Library 5th ser 17 1962.
— The names of some English fifteenth-century binders. Library 5th ser 25 1970.
Rasmussen, B. H. The transition from manuscript to printed book. Oxford 1962.
Richardson, F. E. A Middle English fragment from the First book of Kilkenny. N & Q Feb 1962.
Stemmler, T. Zur Datierung des ms Harley 2253. Anglia 80 1962.
Barber, M. J. The books and patronage of learning of a 15th-century prince. Book Collector 12 1963.
Fox, D. Some scribal alterations of dates in the Bannatyne ms. PQ 42 1963.
Hill, B. The history of Jesus College Oxford ms 29. MÆ 32 1963.
— A collation of the Robert of Gloucester fragments: British Museum ms add 50848. N & Q Feb 1965.
— Cambridge Fitzwilliam Museum ms McClean 123. N & Q March 1965.
Miller, B. D. H. The early history of Bodleian ms Digby 86. Annuale Mediaevale 4 1963.
Mills, M. A mediæval reviser at work. MÆ 32 1963.
Russell, G. H. Editorial theory and Middle English texts. Australasian Univs Lang & Lit Assoc 8th Congress 1963.
Arngart, O. Two Middle English textual notes. E Studies 45 (suppl) 1964.
Roth, C. Pledging a book in medieval England. Library 5th ser 19 1964.
Turner, D. H. The Evesham psalter. Jnl Warburg & Courtauld Inst 27 1964.
— The Penwortham breviary. BM Quart 28 1964.
Blakey, B. The scribal process. In Medieval miscellany presented to Eugène Vinaver, Manchester 1965.
Hudson, A. British Museum ms additional 50848. N & Q Nov 1965.
— Tradition and innovation in some Middle English manuscripts. RES new ser 17 1966.

Moe, P. A fifteenth-century manuscript: new words and antedatings. N & Q Dec 1965.

Moran, J. The Book of St Albans. Coat of Arms 8 1965.

Asher, J. A. Truth and fiction: the text of medieval manuscripts. Jnl of Australasian Univs Lang & Lit Assoc 25 1966.

Donaldson, E. T. The psychology of editors of Middle English texts. In English studies today: 4th series, ed I. Cellini and G. Melchiori, Rome 1966.

McLaughlin, J. C. A graphemic-phonemic study of a Middle English manuscript. Hague 1966.

Macrae-Gibson, O. D. Walter Scott, the Auchinleck ms and ms Douce 124. Neophilologus 50 1966.

Nevanlinna, S. A note on the Robartes ms of the Northern homily collection. Neuphilologische Mitteilungen 67 1966.

Rigg, A. G. Some notes on Trinity College, Cambridge ms 0.9.38. N & Q Sept 1966.

Zettersten, A. Further notes on the Robartes manuscripts. Neuphilologische Mitteilungen 67 1966.

— The Lambeth manuscript of the Boke of huntyng. Neuphilologische Mitteilungen 70 1969.

— On some Middle English acquisitions to the Bodleian Library. Neuphilologische Mitteilungen 72 1971.

Blake, N. F. The Mirror of the World and ms Royal 19 A ix. N & Q June 1967.

— Caxton and his world. 1969.

Gray, D. A Middle English verse at Warkworth. N & Q April 1967.

Hands, R. Juliana Berners and the Book of St Albans. RES new ser 18 1967.

Heilbronner, W. L. Printing and the book in fifteenth-century England. Charlottesville 1967. Bibliography.

Hirsch, R. Printing, selling and reading 1450–1550. Wiesbaden 1967.

Humphrey, K. Distribution of books in the English West Midlands in the later Middle Ages. Libri 17 1967.

Hunt, R. W. A dismembered manuscript. Bodleian Lib Record 7 1967.

Pritchard, V. English medieval graffiti. Cambridge 1967.

Sajavaara, K. The relationship of the Vernon and Simeon manuscripts. Neuphilologische Mitteilungen 68 1967.

Smith, K. L. A fifteenth-century vernacular manuscript reconstructed. Bodleian Lib Record 7 1967.

Duncan, T. G. Notes on the language of the Hunterian ms of the Mirror. Neuphilologische Mitteilungen 69 1968.

Seymour, M. C. A fifteenth-century East Anglian scribe. MÆ 37 1968.

Hargreaves, H. The Mirror of Our Lady: Aberdeen University Library ms 134. Aberdeen Univ Rev 42 1968.

— Middle English lyrics in an Aberdeen University Library manuscript. Aberdeen Univ Rev 43 1970.

Kane, G. Conjectural emendation. In Medieval literature and civilization: studies in memory of G. N. Garmonsway, 1969.

Lowe, E. A. Handwriting: our medieval legacy. Rome 1969. With plates.

Payen, J. C. De la tradition à l'écriture. Le Moyen Age 75 1969.

Pollak, M. Production costs in fifteenth-century printing. Lib Quart 39 1969.

Scattergood, V. J. Two medieval book lists. Library 5th ser 23 1969.

Sinclair, K. V. Descriptive catalogue of medieval and Renaissance Western manuscripts in Australia. Sydney 1969.

Weiss, J. The Auchinleck ms and the Edwardes mss. N & Q Dec 1969.

Sands, D. B. Orthographic changes in Middle English verse: hazards and virtues. Neuphilologische Mitteilungen 71 1970. On editorial principles.

Kekewich, M. Edward IV, William Caxton and literary patronage in Yorkist England. MLR 66 1971.

Ackerman, R. W. Sir Frederic Madden and medieval scholarship. Neuphilologische Mitteilungen 73 1972.

See also Caxton, col. 667 below.

(4) LITERARY HISTORY AND CRITICISM

Warton, Thomas (the younger). History of English poetry. 3 vols 1774–81; ed W. C. Hazlitt 4 vols 1871.

Ritson, Joseph. Bibliographia poetica. 1802.

Morley, H. English writers [to Dunbar]. 2 vols 1864–7.

— English writers. 11 vols 1887–95. Vols 3–7.

Brink, B. ten. Geschichte der englischen Literatur. 2 vols Berlin 1877–93 (vol 1 rev A. Brandl, Strasbourg 1899); tr 3 vols 1883–96.

Jusserand, J. J. La vie nomade et les routes d'Angleterre au xive siècle. Paris 1884; tr 1889, 1920, 1925.

— Histoire littéraire du peuple anglais. Paris 1894; tr 3 vols 1895–1909, 1926 (rev). Vol 1.

Koerting, G. Grundriss der Geschichte der englischen Litteratur. Münster 1887.

Brandl, A. Mittelenglische Literatur. In vol 2 of Pauls Grundriss der germanischen Philologie, 2 vols in 3 Strasbourg 1891–3.

Courthope, W. J. History of English poetry. 6 vols 1895–1910. Vol 1.

Wülcker, R. P. Geschichte der englischen Literatur. Leipzig 1896, 1906–7.

Ker, W. P. Epic and romance. 1897.

— Essays on medieval literature. 1905.

— English literature, medieval. 1912 (Home Univ Lib).

Saintsbury, G. The flourishing of romance and the rise of allegory. Edinburgh 1897.

— Short history of English literature. 1898. Bks 2–4.

— History of criticism. 3 vols 1900–4. Vol 1.

— History of English prosody. 3 vols 1906–10, 1923. Vol 1.

Snell, F. J. The fourteenth century. 1899.

— Age of Chaucer. 1901.

— Age of transition. 2 vols 1905.

Smith, G. G. The transition period. 1900.

Pollard, A. W. Middle English literature. In Chambers's Cyclopædia of English literature, 3 vols 1901–3. Vol 1.

Schofield, W. H. English literature from the Norman Conquest to Chaucer. 1906.

— Chivalry in English literature. Cambridge Mass 1912.

Edwardes, M. Summary of the literatures of modern Europe to 1400. 1907.

Cambridge history of English literature vols 1–2. Cambridge 1907–8.

Lawrence, W. W. Medieval story. New York 1911.

Kingsford, C. L. English historical literature of the fifteenth-century. Oxford 1913.

— Prejudice and promise in xvth-century England. Oxford 1925.

Baldwin, C. S. Introduction to English medieval literature. 1914.

— Medieval rhetoric and poetic (to 1400). 1928.

— Three mediæval centuries of literature in England 1100–1400. Boston 1932.

Krapp, G. P. The rise of English literary prose. New York 1915.

Huizinga, J. Herfsttij der middeleeuwen. Haarlem 1919, 1921; tr 1924; tr French, 1932; tr Italian, 1944.

Berdan, J. M. Early Tudor poetry 1485–1547. New York 1920.

Chaytor, H. J. The troubadours and England. Cambridge 1923.

— From script to print. Cambridge 1945.

Holzknecht, K. J. Literary patronage in the Middle Ages. Philadelphia 1923.

Faral, E. Les arts poétiques du xiie et du xiiie siècle. Paris 1924.

Legouis, E. H. and L. Cazamian. Histoire de la littérature anglaise. Paris 1924; tr 2 vols 1926-7.

Thomas, P. G. English literature before Chaucer. 1924.

Patch, H. R. Desiderata in Middle English research. MP 22 1925.

— Characters in medieval literature. MLN 40 1925.

— The goddess Fortuna in mediaeval literature. Cambridge Mass 1927.

— The tradition of Boethius. New York 1935.

— The other world. Cambridge Mass 1950.

Traver, H. The four daughters of God. PMLA 40 1925.

Crosland, J. The conception of 'mesure' in some medieval poets. MLR 21 1926.

Haskins, C. H. The spread of ideas in the Middle Ages. Speculum 1 1926.

Tupper, F. Types of society in medieval literature. New York 1926.

— Twelfth-century scholarship and satire. In Essays and studies in honor of Carleton Brown, New York 1940.

Audiau, J. Les troubadours et l'Angleterre. Paris 1927.

Cooke, J. D. Euhemerism: a mediæval interpretation of classical paganism. Speculum 2 1927.

Thorndike, L. Some thirteenth-century classics. Ibid.

Rand, E. K. The classics in the thirteenth century. Speculum 4 1929.

Tout, T. F. Literature and learning in the English Civil Service in the fourteenth century. Speculum 4 1929.

Cornelius, R. D. The figurative castle. Bryn Mawr 1930.

Griffith, D. D. The origin of the Griselda story. Seattle 1931.

Schirmer, W. F. Der englische Frühhumanismus: ein Beitrag zur englischen Literaturgeschichte des 15 Jahrhunderts. Leipzig 1931, Tübingen 1963.

— Geschichte der englischen Literatur von den Anfängen bis zur Gegenwart. Halle 1937.

— and U. Broich. Studien zum literarischen Patronat im England des 12 Jahrhunderts. Cologne 1962.

Chambers, R. W. On the continuity of English prose. Oxford 1932 (EETS).

— Man's unconquerable mind. 1939.

Campbell, J. M. Patristic studies and the literature of mediaeval England. Speculum 8 1933.

Lippmann, C. F. Das ritterliche Persönlichkeitsideal. Meerane 1933.

Mohl, R. The three estates in medieval and Renaissance literature. New York 1933.

Coffmann, G. R. Old age from Horace to Chaucer. Speculum 9 1934.

— Some recent trends in English literary scholarship, with special reference to medieval backgrounds. SP 35 1938.

Krappe, A. H. Mediaeval literature and the comparative method. Speculum 10 1935.

— The hero champion of animals. MLQ 4 1943.

Slover, C. H. Glastonbury Abbey and the fusing of English literary culture. Speculum 10 1935.

Smith, Sr M. F. Wisdom and personification of wisdom occurring in Middle English literature before 1500. Washington 1935.

Arnould, E.-J. Taine et le Moyen-Age anglais. Revue de Littérature Comparée 16 1936.

Crosby, R. Oral delivery in the Middle Ages. Speculum 11 1936.

Lewis, C. S. The allegory of love. Oxford 1936.

— The anthropological approach. In English and medieval studies presented to J. R. R. Tolkien, 1962.

— The discarded image. Cambridge 1964.

— Studies in medieval and Renaissance literature. Ed W. Hooper, Cambridge 1966.

— Selected literary essays. Ed W. Hooper, Cambridge 1969.

Rosenthal, C. L. The Vitae Patrum in Old and Middle English literature. Philadelphia 1936.

Bennett, H. S. The author and his public in the fourteenth and fifteenth centuries. E & S 23 1937.

— Science and information in English writings in the fifteenth century. RES 39 1944.

— Medieval literature and the modern reader. E & S 31 1945.

— Chaucer and the fifteenth century. Oxford 1947 (OHEL).

Birney, E. English irony before Chaucer. UTQ 6 1937.

Brie, F. W. D. Die nationale Literatur Schottlands von den Anfängen bis zur Renaissance. Halle 1937.

Bühler, C. F. Greek philosophers in the literature of the later Middle Ages. Speculum 12 1937.

Glunz, H. H. Die Literarästhetik des europäischen Mittelalters. Bochum 1937, Frankfurt 1963.

— Nationale Eigenart im mittelalterlichen Schrifttum Englands. In Grundformen der englischen Geistesgeschichte, ed K. W. P. Meissner, Stuttgart 1941.

Tatlock, J. S. P. Interpreting literature by history. Speculum 12 1937.

— Medieval laughter. Speculum 21 1946.

Hopper, V. F. Medieval number symbolism. New York 1938.

Whitbread, L. A medieval English metaphor. PQ 17 1938.

Thompson, J. W. The literacy of the laity in the Middle Ages. New York 1939.

Wilson, R. M. Early Middle English literature. 1939, 1968 (rev).

— The lost literature of medieval England. 1952, 1970 (rev).

Wyld, H. C. Aspects of style and idiom in fifteenth-century English. E & S 26 1940.

Olson, C. G. The minstrels at the Court of Edward III. PMLA 56 1941.

Reinhard, J. R. Setting adrift in mediæval law and literature. PMLA 56 1941.

— Burning at the stake in mediaeval law and literature. Speculum 16 1941.

Smyser, H. M. The Middle English and Old Norse story of Olive. PMLA 56 1941. See MLN 61 1946.

Weiss, R. Humanism in England during the fifteenth century. Oxford 1941.

Buttenwiser, H. Popular authors of the Middle Ages. Speculum 17 1942.

McKeon, R. Rhetoric in the Middle Ages. Speculum 17 1942.

— Poetry and philosophy in the twelfth century. MP 43 1946.

Stewart, H. L. Literature and learning five centuries ago. Queen's Quart 48 1942.

Atkins, J. W. H. English literary criticism: the medieval phase. Cambridge 1943.

Russell, J. C. An introduction to the study of medieval biography. MLQ 4 1943.

Sanford, E. M. The study of ancient history in the Middle Ages. JHI 5 1944.

Utley, F. L. The crooked rib. Columbus 1944.

Chambers, E. K. English literature at the close of the Middle Ages. Oxford 1945 (OHEL).

White, B. Three notes on Old and Middle English. MLR 40 1945.

— Fact and fancy in medieval English literature. Essays by Divers Hands 25 1950.

— Medieval animal lore. Anglia 72 1954.

— Medieval mirth. Anglia 78 1960.

— Medieval beasts. E & S new ser 18 1965.

— Saracens and Crusaders. In Medieval literature and civilization: studies in memory of G. N. Garmonsway, 1969.

Auerbach, E. Mimesis. Berne 1946; tr 1953.

— Literatursprache und Publikum in der lateinischen Spätantike und im Mittelalter. Berne 1958; tr 1965.

Adolf, H. On medieval laughter. Speculum 22 1947.

Closs, H. M. M. Courtly love in literature and art. Symposium 1 1947.

Purdy, R. R. The Platonic tradition in Middle English literature. Vanderbilt Univ Bull 67 1947.
— The friendship motif in Middle English literature. Vanderbilt Stud in Humanities 1 1951.
Sherwood, M. Magic and mechanics in medieval fiction. SP 44 1947.
Whitesell, F. R. Fables in mediaeval exampla. JEGP 46 1947.
Arbusow, L. Colores rhetorici. Göttingen 1948, 1963.
Boas, G. Essays on primitivism and related ideas in the Middle Ages. Baltimore 1948.
Curtius, E. R. Europäische Literatur und lateinisches Mittelalter. Berne 1948; tr 1953.
Loomis, L. H. The Saint Mercurius legend. In Philologica: the [Kemp] Malone anniversary studies, Baltimore 1949.
— The Athelstan gift story. PMLA 67 1952.
Baugh, A. C. and K. Malone. The Middle Ages. In Literary history of England, ed Baugh, New York 1950.
Clark, J. M. The dance of death in medieval literature. MLR 45 1950.
Bloom, E. A. The allegorical principle. ELH 18 1951.
Girvan, R. The medieval poet and his public. In English studies to-day, ed C. L. Wrenn and G. Bullough, Oxford 1951.
Kane, G. Middle English literature. 1951.
Robertson, D. W. Some medieval literary terminology. SP 48 1951.
— The doctrine of charity. Speculum 26 1951.
Bloomfield, M. W. The seven deadly sins. East Lansing 1952.
— Symbolism in medieval literature. MP 56 1958.
— A grammatical approach to personification allegory. MP 61 1963.
— Essays and explorations. Cambridge Mass 1970.
Telfer, J. M. Evolution of a mediaeval theme. Durham Univ Jnl 14 1952.
Artz, F. B. The mind of the Middle Ages AD 200–1500. New York 1953.
Frank, R. W. The art of reading medieval personification allegory. ELH 20 1953.
Ford, B. (ed). The age of Chaucer. 1954 (Pelican Guide to Eng Lit).
Brewer, D. S. The ideal of feminine beauty in medieval literature. MLR 50 1955.
Chastel, A. Arts et littérature au xvᵉ siècle. In Actes du 5ᵉ Congrès International des Langues et Littératures Modernes, Florence 1955.
Cutler, J. L. A Middle English acrostic. MLN 70 1955.
Everett, D. Essays on Middle English literature. Oxford 1955.
Cejp, L. The fourteenth-century allegory and its methods. Philologica: suppl to Časopis pro Moderní Filologii 8 1956.
Jones, G. F. Sartorial symbols in mediaeval literature. MÆ 25 1956.
Peter, J. P. Complaint and satire in early English literature. Oxford 1956.
Schlauch, M. English medieval literature and its social foundations. Warsaw 1956.
— Realism and convention in medieval literature. Kwartalnik Neofilologiczny 11 1964.
Clark, J. W. Early English. 1957, 1967 (rev).
Speirs, J. Medieval English poetry: the non-Chaucerian tradition. 1957.
Hussey, M. The petitions of the Paternoster in mediaeval English literature. MÆ 27 1958.
Isaacs, N. D. Constance in fourteenth-century England. Neuphilologische Mitteilungen 59 1958.
Adams, R. P. Bold bawdry and open manslaughter. HLQ 23 1959.
Bethurum, D. (ed). Critical approaches to medieval literature. Eng Inst Essays 1959.
Clark, D. L. Rhetoric and the literature of the English Middle Ages. Quart Jnl of Speech 45 1959.

Kinghorn, A. M. The mediaeval makars. Texas Stud in Lit & Lang 1 1959.
Klenke, Sr M.A. The 'Christus Domini' concept in mediaeval art and literature. SP 56 1959.
Moody, P. The problems of medieval criticism. Melbourne Critical Rev 3 1960.
Baker, D. C. Gold coins in medieval English literature. Speculum 36 1961.
Damon, P. Modes of analogy in ancient and medieval verse. Berkeley 1961.
Elliott, R. W. V. Landscape and rhetoric in Middle-English alliterative poetry. Melbourne Critical Rev 4 1961.
Jackson, W. T. H. The literature of the Middle Ages. New York 1961.
— Allegory and allegorization. Research Stud 32 1964.
— Medieval literature. New York 1966.
Johnston, G. Medieval criticism: a comment. Melbourne Critical Rev 4 1961.
Lawrence, N. G. and J. A. Reynolds. A Chaucerian puzzle and other medieval essays. Coral Glades 1961.
Murphy, J. J. The arts of discourse 1050–1400. Mediaeval Stud 23 1961.
— The medieval arts of discourse: an introductory bibliography. Speech Monographs 19 1962.
— Rhetoric in fourteenth-century Oxford. MÆ 34 1965.
— A fifteenth-century treatise on prose style. Newberry Lib Bull 6 1966.
— The literary implications of instruction in the verbal arts in fourteenth-century England. Leeds Stud in Eng new ser 1967.
Robson, C. A. The technique of symmetrical composition in medieval narrative poetry. In Studies in medieval French presented to Alfred Ewert, Oxford 1961.
Salmon, P. B. The 'three voices' of poetry in mediaeval literary theory. MÆ 30 1961.
Dubois, M.-M. La littérature anglaise du Moyen-Age 500–1500. Paris 1962.
Kritzeck, J. Moslem-Christian understanding in mediaeval times. Comparative Stud in Society & History 4 1962.
Luttrell, C. A. The mediaeval tradition of the pearl virginity. MÆ 31 1962.
Wenzel, S. Sloth in Middle English devotional literature. Anglia 79 1962.
— Acedia 700–1200. Traditio 22 1966.
— The sin of sloth. Chapel Hill 1967.
— The three enemies of man. Mediaeval Stud 29 1967.
— The seven deadly sins: some problems of research. Speculum 43 1968.
Woolf, R. The theme of Christ the lover-knight in medieval English literature. RES new ser 13 1962.
Holdsworth, C. J. Visions and visionaries in the Middle Ages. History 48 1963.
Leyerle, J. The text and the tradition. UTQ 32 1963.
McAlindon, T. The devil and giant as buffoon. Anglia 81 1963.
— Comedy and terror in Middle English literature: the diabolical game. MLR 60 1965.
— Magic, fate and providence in mediaeval narrative. RES new ser 16 1965.
Muscatine, C. Locus of action in medieval narrative. Romance Philology 17 1963.
Ogilvy, J. D. A. Mimi, scurrae, histriones: entertainers of the early Middle Ages. Speculum 38 1963.
Pickford, C. E. Fiction and the reading public in the fifteenth century. Bull John Rylands Lib 45 1963.
Gerhardt, M. I. Two wayfarers: some medieval stories on the theme of good and evil. Utrecht 1964.
Greaves, M. The blazon of honour. 1964.
Sachs, A. Religious despair in mediaeval literature and art. Mediaeval Stud 26 1964.
Spearing, A. C. Criticism and mediaeval poetry. 1964, 1972 (rev and enlarged).

Varty, K. The pursuit of Reynard in mediaeval English literature and art. Nottingham Mediaeval Stud 8 1964.
— Reynard the fox. Leicester 1967.
Vinaver, E. From epic to romance. Bull John Rylands Lib 46 1964.
— Critical approaches to medieval romance. In Acta of the 9th Congress of the International Federation for Modern Languages and Literatures, New York 1964.
Barron, W. R. J. 'Luf-daungere'. In Medieval miscellany presented to Eugène Vinaver, Manchester 1965.
Bennett, J. A. W. The humane medievalist. Cambridge 1965.
Bromwich, R. The Celtic inheritance of medieval literature. MLQ 26 1965.
Dieter, O. A. Arbor picta: the medieval tree of preaching. Quart Jnl of Speech 51 1965.
Matthews, W. (ed). Medieval secular literature: four essays. Berkeley 1965.
Snyder, S. The left hand of God. Stud in Renaissance 12 1965.
Tade, G. T. Rhetorical aspects of the spiritual exercises in the medieval tradition of preaching. Quart Jnl of Speech 51 1965.
Vasta, E. (ed). Middle English survey: critical essays. Notre Dame Ind 1965.
Ackermann, R. W. Backgrounds to medieval English literature. New York 1966.
Fisher, J. H. (ed). The medieval literature of Western Europe: a review of research, mainly 1930–60. New York 1966.
Hinton, N. Anagogue and archetype. Annuale Medievale 7 1966.
Howard, D. R. The three temptations: medieval man in search of the world. Princeton 1966.
Kahrl, S. J. Allegory in practice: a study of narrative styles in medieval example. MP 63 1966.
Kelly, D. The scope of the treatment of composition in twelfth- and thirteenth-century arts of poetry. Speculum 41 1966.
— Theory of composition in medieval narrative poetry and Geoffrey of Vinsauf's Poetria nova. Mediaeval Stud 31 1969.
Lawlor, J. (ed). Patterns of love and courtesy: essays in memory of C. S. Lewis. 1966.
Owen, D. D. R. False attitudes in medieval literary criticism. Forum for Modern Lang Stud 2 1966.
Pascal, P. Mediaeval uses of antiquity. Classical Jnl 61 1966.
Richmond, V. B. Laments for the dead in mediaeval narrative. Pittsburgh 1966.
Tuve, R. Allegorical imagery: some mediaeval books and their posterity. Princeton 1966.
Alston, R. C. and J. L. Rosier. Rhetoric and style: a bibliographical guide. Leeds Stud in Eng new ser 1 1967.
Beichner, P. The allegorical interpretation of medieval literature. PMLA 82 1967.
Curschmann, M. Oral poetry in medieval English, French and German literature. Speculum 42 1967.

Egbert, V. W. The medieval artist at work. Princeton 1967.
Evans, W. O. Cortaysye in Middle English. Mediaeval Stud 27 1967.
Hieatt, C. B. The realism of dream visions.Hague 1967.
Kinter, W. L. and J. R. Keller. The sibyl: prophetess of antiquity and medieval fay. Philadelphia 1967.
Moorman, C. A knyght there was. Lexington Kentucky 1967.
Raymo, R. R. Quod the devill to the frier. Eng Lang Notes 4 1967.
Robbins, R. H. Middle English misunderstood. Anglia 85 1967.
Silverstein, T. Allegory and literary form. PMLA 82 1967.
Fox, D. Chaucer's influence on fifteenth-century poetry. In Companion to Chaucer studies, ed B. Rowland, Toronto 1968.
Hanning, R. W. Use of names in medieval literature. Names 16 1968.
Holmes, U. T. The mediaeval minstrel. In Medieval and Renaissance studies, ed J. L. Lievsay, Durham NC 1968.
Moore, A. K. Medieval English literature and the question of unity. MP 65 1968.
Newman, F. X. (ed). The meaning of courtly love. Albany 1968.
Salter, E. Medieval poetry and the figural view of reality. Proc Br Acad 54 1968.
— Medieval poetry and the visual arts. E & S new ser 22 1969.
Schoek, R. J. On rhetoric in fourteenth-century Oxford. Mediaeval Stud 30 1968.
Aartz, F. G. A. M. The paternoster in medieval English literature. Papers on Lang & Lit 5 1969.
Braekman, W. L. and P. S. Macaulay. The story of the cat and the candle in Middle English literature. Neuphilologische Mitteilungen 70 1969.
Cottle, B. The triumph of English 1350–1400. 1969.
Duncan, T. G. Reading Middle English. Forum for Modern Lang Stud 5 1969.
Keller, J. R. The triumph of vice. Annuale Mediaevale 10 1969.
Blake, N. F. The fifteenth century reconsidered. Neuphilologische Mitteilungen 71 1970.
— Rhythmical alliteration. MP 67 1970.
Caplan, H. Of eloquence: studies in ancient and mediaeval rhetoric. Ed A. King and N. North, Ithaca 1970.
Friedman, J. B. Orpheus in the Middle Ages. Cambridge Mass 1970.
Whitman, F. H. Medieval riddling. Neuphilologische Mitteilungen 71 1970.
Gradon, P. O. E. Form and style in early English literature. 1971.
Kekewich, M. Edward iv, William Caxton and literary patronage in Yorkist England. MLR 66 1971.
Piehler, P. The visionary landscape: a study of medieval allegory. 1971.
Starr, D. Metrical changes: from Old to Middle English. MP 68 1971.

(5) COLLECTIONS

Original Texts

Hartshorne, C. H. Ancient metrical tales. 1829.
Mätzner, E. Altenglische Sprachproben. 2 pts Berlin 1867. Also Wörterbuch A—MISB, Berlin 1878–1900 (German trns).
Morris, R. Specimens of early English 1250–1400. Oxford 1867.
Skeat, W. W. Specimens of English literature 1394–1579. Oxford 1871.
Morris, R. and W. W. Skeat. Specimens of early English. 2 pts Oxford 1872–82.

Wülcker, R. P. Altenglisches Lesebuch. 2 vols in 3 Halle 1874.
Zupitza, J. Altenglisches Übungsbuch. Vienna 1874, 1882 (as Alt- und mittelenglisches Lesebuch).
Sweet, H. First Middle English primer. Oxford 1884, 1938.
— Second Middle English primer. Oxford 1886.
MacLean, G. E. Old and Middle English reader. New York 1893. Based on Zupitza, above.
Kluge, F. Mittelenglisches Lesebuch. Halle 1904.
Emerson, O. F. Middle English reader. New York 1905.
Cook, A. S. Literary Middle English reader. Boston 1915.

Brandl, A. and O. Zippel. Mittelenglische Sprach- und Literaturproben. Berlin 1917.

Segar, M. G. Some minor poems of the Middle Ages. 1917.

Hall, J. Selections from early Middle English 1130–1250. 2 pts Oxford 1920.

Sisam, K. Fourteenth-century verse and prose. Oxford 1921, 1922 (with vocabulary by J. R. R. Tolkien).

Morsbach, L. Mittelenglische Originalurkunden. Heidelberg 1923. Charters etc.

Sampson, G. Cambridge book of prose and verse. Cambridge 1924. With trns.

Flasdieck, H. M. Mittelenglische Originalurkunden 1405–30. Heidelberg 1926. Charters etc.

Hammond, E. P. English verse between Chaucer and Surrey. Durham NC 1927.

Brunner, C. and R. Hittmair. Mittelenglisches Lesebuch für Anfänger. Heidelberg 1929.

Chambers, R. W. and M. Daunt. A book of London English 1384–1425. Oxford 1931. Mainly local records.

Patterson, R. F. Six centuries of English literature. 6 vols 1933. Vol 1, Chaucer to Spenser.

Funke, O. A Middle English reader. Berne 1944.

Mossé, F. Manuel de l'anglais du Moyen Age. Paris 1949; tr 1952.

Dickins, B. and R. M. Wilson. Early Middle English reader. Cambridge 1951.

Kaiser, R. Alt- und mittelenglische Anthologie. Berlin 1954.

Bennett, J. A. W. and G. V. Smithers. Early Middle English verse and prose. Oxford 1966, 1968 (rev).

Stevick, R. D. Five Middle English narratives. Indianapolis 1967.

Modernized Texts

Pollard, A. W. Fifteenth-century verse and prose. 1903.

Rickert, E. (ed and tr). Early English romances in verse. 2 vols 1908.

Weston, J. L. (ed and tr). Romance, vision and satire. 1912.

— Chief Middle English poets. [1914].

Shackford, M. H. (ed and tr). Legends and satires from mediæval literature. Boston 1913.

Segar, M. G. (ed and tr). A medieval anthology. 1915.

Benham, A. R. (ed and tr). English literature from Widsith to the death of Chaucer. New Haven 1916.

Neilson, W. A. and K. G. T. Webster. Chief British poets of the 14th and 15th centuries. [1916].

Watts, N. (ed and tr). Love songs of Sion. 1924.

Adamson, M. R. (ed and tr). Treasury of Middle English verse. 1930.

Lyell, L. A mediæval postbag. 1934.

Reinhard, J. R. (ed and tr). Medieval pageant. 1939.

Matthews, W. Later medieval English prose. 1962.

Stone, B. (ed and tr). Medieval English verse. 1965 (Penguin).

C. C.

2. MIDDLE ENGLISH LITERATURE

I. THE MIDDLE ENGLISH ROMANCES

References

Index The index of Middle English verse, ed C. Brown and R. H. Robbins, New York 1943; Supplement, ed R. H. Robbins and J. L. Cutler, Lexington Kentucky 1965.

Severs A manual of the writings in Middle English 1050–1500, ed J. B. Severs, fascicule 1: Romances, by M. J. Donovan et al, New Haven 1967.

For Ritson, Weber, Madden, Hales and Furnivall, Sisam, French and Hale, Dickins and Wilson, Mossé, Ford, Rumble, Sands, Gibbs, Stevick, Bennett and Smithers, see under Collections, below.

(1) General (Bibliographies and summaries, Collections, Modern versions, General studies, Special studies)
(2) Arthurian romance: the matter of Britain (Bibliographies, General studies, the 'historical' Arthur, Merlin and the youth of Arthur, Lancelot and the death of Arthur, Gawain, Perceval, the Grail, Tristram)
(3) Charlemagne romances: the matter of France (General studies, Firumbras group, Otuel group, Others)
(4) The matter of Antiquity (Alexander, Troy, Thebes)
(5) The cycle of Godfrey of Bouillon
(6) The 'matter of England'
(7) 'Breton lays'
(8) Romances based on legends of the Eustace-Constance-Florence type
(9) Composites of courtly romance
(10) 'Ancestral' romances
(11) Didactic legends
(12) Miscellaneous romances

Individual romances are numbered consecutively throughout.

(1) GENERAL

Bibliographies and Summaries

Ward, H. L. D. and J. A. Herbert. Catalogue of romances in the department of manuscripts of the British Museum. 3 vols 1883–1910.

Billings, A. H. Guide to the Middle English metrical romances. New York 1901.

Spence, L. Dictionary of medieval romance and romance writers. 1913.

Wells, J. E. Manual of the writings in Middle English. New Haven 1916; Supplements 1–9, 1919–51.

Hibbard, L. A. Medieval romance in England: a study of the sources and analyses of the non-cyclic metrical romances. New York 1924.

Thompson, S. Motif-index of folk literature: a classification of narrative elements in folk-tales, ballads, myths, fables, mediaeval romances etc. Bloomington 1932.

Renwick, W. L. and H. Orton. The beginnings of English literature to Skelton 1509. 1939, 1952 (rev).

Brown, C. and R. H. Robbins. The index of Middle English verse. New York 1943; Supplement by R. H. Robbins and J. L. Cutler, Lexington Kentucky 1965.

Farrar, C. P. and A. P. Evans. Bibliography of English translations from medieval sources. New York 1946.

Cabeen, D. C. Critical bibliography of French literature vol 1: the medieval period. Ed U. T. Holmes, Syracuse NY 1949.

Bossuat, R. Manuel bibliographique de la littérature française du Moyen Age. Paris 1951; Supplément, 1955.

Bordman, G. Motif-index of the English metrical romances. Helsinki 1963.

Severs, J. B. A manual of the writings in Middle English 1050-1500. Fascicule 1: Romances, by M. J. Donovan, C. W. Dunn, L. Hornstein, R. M. Lumiansky, H. Newstead, H. M. Smyser. New Haven 1967.

Collections

Ritson, J. Ancient English metrical romances. 3 vols 1802.

Weber, H. Metrical romances of the xiii, xiv and xv centuries. 3 vols Edinburgh 1810.

Utterson, R. Select pieces of early popular poetry. 2 vols 1817.

Laing, D. Select remains of the ancient popular poetry of Scotland. 1822, 1885 (rev).

— Early metrical tales. 1826, 1889 (rev).

— Early popular poetry of Scotland and the Northern border. Rev W. C. Hazlitt 1895.

Thoms, W. J. Collection of early prose romances. 3 vols 1828, 1907 (rev).

Hartshorne, C. H. Ancient metrical tales. 1829.

Madden, F. Sir Gawayne. 1839 (Bannatyne Club).

Robson, J. Three early English metrical romances. 1842 (Camden Soc).

Halliwell(-Phillipps), J. O. Thornton romances. 1844 (Camden Soc).

Hazlitt, W. C. Remains of the early popular poetry of England. 4 vols 1864-6.

Hales, J. W. and F. J. Furnivall. Percy folio manuscript. 4 vols 1867-9.

McKnight, G. H. Middle English humorous tales in verse. Boston 1913.

Sisam, K. Fourteenth-century verse and prose. Oxford 1921, 1937 (rev).

French, W. E. and C. B. Hale. Middle English metrical romances. New York 1930.

Dickins, B. and R. M. Wilson. Early Middle English texts. 1951.

Mossé, F. A handbook of Middle English. Tr J. A. Walker, Baltimore 1952.

Ford, B. (ed). The age of Chaucer. 1954 (Pelican).

Rumble, T. C. The Breton lays in Middle English. Detroit 1965.

Bennett, J. A. W. and G. V. Smithers. Early Middle English verse and prose. Oxford 1966, 1968 (rev).

Gibbs, A. C. Middle English romances. 1966 (York Medieval Texts).

Sands, D. B. Middle English verse romances. New York 1966.

Stevick, R. D. Five Middle English narratives. Indianapolis 1967.

Modern Versions

Ellis, G. Specimens of early English metrical romances. 3 vols 1805, 1848 (rev).

Ashton, J. Romances of chivalry. 1890.

Darton, F. J. H. Wonder book of old romance. New York 1907.

Rickert, E. Early English romances in verse. 2 vols 1908.

Hibbard, L. A. Three Middle English romances. New York 1911.

Weston, J. L. Romance, vision and satire. Boston 1912.

— Chief Middle English poets. Boston 1914.

Loomis, R. S. and R. Willard. Medieval English verse and prose. New York 1948.

Loomis, R. S. and L. H. Medieval romances. New York 1957.

Brengle, R. L. Arthur King of Britain: history, romance, chronicle and criticism, with texts in modern English from Gildas to Malory. New York 1964.

General Studies

Saintsbury, G. The flourishing of romance. Edinburgh 1897.

Ker, W. P. Epic and romance. 1897, 1908 (rev).

Lawrence, W. W. Medieval story. New York 1911, 1931 (rev).

Leach, H. G. Angevin Britain and Scandinavia. Cambridge Mass 1921.

Baker, E. A. History of the English novel vol 1: the age of romance. 1924.

Barrow, S. F. Medieval society romances. New York 1924.

Thomas, W. The epic cycles of medieval England and their relative importance. French Quart 10 1928.

Weston, J. L. Legendary cycles of the Middle Ages. Cambridge 1929 (Cambridge medieval history vol 6).

Taylor, A. B. An introduction to medieval romance. 1930.

Oakden, J. P. Alliterative poetry in Middle English. 2 vols Manchester 1930-5.

Trounce, A. McI. The English tail-rhyme romances. MÆ 1-3 1932-4.

Fisher, F. Narrative art in medieval romances. Cleveland 1939.

Wilson, R. M. Early Middle English literature. 1939.

— Lost literature of medieval England. 1952.

Doutrepont, G. Les mises en prose des épopées et des romans chevaleresques du 14e au 15e siècle. Brussels 1939.

Chaytor, H. J. From script to print. Cambridge 1945.

Bezzola, R. R. Le sens de l'aventure et de l'amour. Paris 1947.

Hatzfeld, H. Esthetic criticism applied to medieval romance literature. Romance Philology 1 1947.

Kane, G. Middle English literature. 1951.

Southern, R. W. The making of the Middle Ages. 1953.

Ford, B. (ed). The age of Chaucer. 1954 (Pelican).

Schlauch, M. English medieval literature. Warsaw 1956.

— Antecedents of the English novel 1400-1600. Warsaw and London 1963.

Speirs, J. Medieval English poetry: the non-Chaucerian tradition. 1957.

Heer, F. Mittelalter. Zürich 1961; tr 1962 (as The medieval world: Europe 1100-1350).

Pearsall, D. A. The development of Middle English romance. Mediaeval Stud 27 1965.

Schelp, H. Exemplarische Romanzen im Mittelelenglischen. Göttingen 1967.

Rosenberg, B. A. The morphology of the Middle English metrical romance. Jnl of Popular Culture 1 1967.

Mehl, D. Die mittelenglischen Romanzen des 13 und 14 Jahrhunderts. Heidelberg 1967; tr 1969.

Loomis, R. S. Studies in medieval literature. 1970.

Special Studies

Wilda, O. Über die zwölfzeiligen Schweifreimstrophe in England. Breslau 1887.

Söchtig, P. Zur Technik altenglischer Spielmannsepen. Leipzig 1903.

Nutt, A. The influence of Celtic upon mediaeval romance. 1904.

Comfort, W. W. The essential difference between a chanson de geste and a roman d'aventure. PMLA 19 1904.

Grossmann, W. Frühmittelenglische Zeugnisse über Minstrels. Brandenburg 1906.

Kahle, R. Der Klerus im mittelenglischen Versroman. Strasbourg 1906.

Deutschbein, M. Studien zur Sagengeschichte Englands. Cöthen 1906.

Strong, C. History and relations of the tail-rhyme. PMLA 22 1907.

Geissler, O. Religion und Aberglaube in den mittelenglischen Versromanzen. Halle 1908.

Ker, W. P. Romance. Oxford 1909, 1913 (rev).

Hübner, W. Die Frage in einigen mittelenglischen Versromanen. Kiel 1910.

Faral, E. Les jongleurs en France au Moyen Age. Paris 1910.

Voltmer, B. Die mittelenglische Terminologie der ritterlichen Verwandtschaft und Standesverhältnisse. Kiel 1911.

Creek, H. Character in the 'matter of England' romances. JEGP 10 1911.

Witter, E. Das bürgerliche Leben im mittelenglischen Versroman. Kiel 1912.

Borchers, K. H. Die Jagd in den mittelenglischen Romanzen. Kiel 1912.

Deters, F. Die englischen Angriffswaffen zur Zeit der Einführung der Feuerwaffen 1300–50. Anglistische Forschungen 38 1913.

Steenstrup, J. C. H. R. The medieval popular ballad. Tr E. G. Cox, Boston 1914, Seattle 1968 (with addns).

Curry, W. C. Medieval ideal of personal beauty in metrical romances. Baltimore 1916.

Medary, M. P. Stanza-linking in English alliterative verse. Romanic Rev 7 1916.

Brown, L. Origins of stanza-linking in English alliterative verse. Ibid.

Willson, E. Middle English legends of visits to the Under-world and their relations to metrical romances. Chicago 1917.

Crane, R. S. The vogue of medieval chivalric romances during the English Renaissance. Menasha Wis 1919.

Ashdown, M. Single combat in English and Scandinavian tradition and romance. MLR 17 1922.

Griffin, N. E. Definition of romance. PMLA 38 1922.

Sparnaay, H. Verschmelzung legendarischer und weltlicher Motive in der Poesie des Mittelalters. Groningen 1922.

Brunner, K. Romanzen und Volksballaden. Palaestra 148 1925.

—— Der Inhalt der mittelenglischen Handschriften und die Literaturgeschichte. Anglia 65 1941.

—— Die Überlieferung der mittelenglischen Versromanzen. Anglia 76 1958.

—— Middle English metrical romances and their audiences. In Studies in medieval literature for A. C. Baugh, Philadelphia 1961.

Holthausen, F. Zur Textkritik mittelenglischen Romanzen. In Neusprachliche Studien: Festgabe K. Luick, Marburg 1925.

Patch, H. R. Chaucer and medieval romance. In Essays in memory of B. Wendell, Cambridge Mass 1926.

—— The adaptation of Otherworld motifs to medieval romance. In Philologica: the [Kemp] Malone anniversary studies, Baltimore 1949.

—— The other world. Cambridge Mass 1950.

Harris, A. E. Heroine of the Middle English romances. Western Reserve Univ Stud 2 1928.

Prestage, E. (ed). Chivalry. 1928.

Everett, D. Characterization of the English medieval romances. E & S 15 1929.

Hoops, R. Der Begriff 'Romance' in der mittelenglischen und frühneuenglischen Literatur. Anglistische Forschungen 68 1929.

Eagleson, H. Costume in the Middle English metrical romances. PMLA 47 1932.

Wilcox, J. French courtly love in English composite romances. Papers of Michigan Acad 18 1932.

Lippmann, K. Das ritterliche Persönlichkeitsideal in der mittelenglischen Literatur des 13 und 14 Jahrhunderts. Leipzig 1933.

Reinhard, R. The survival of Geis in medieval romance. Halle 1933.

Tuve, R. Seasons and months. Paris 1933.

—— Allegorical imagery: some medieval books and their posterity. Princeton 1966.

Whiting, B. J. Proverbs in certain Middle English romances in relation to their French sources. Harvard Stud 15 1933.

Crosby, R. Oral delivery in the Middle Ages. Speculum 11 1936.

Smithers, G. V. Notes on Middle English texts. London Medieval Stud 1 1938.

Van de Voort, D. Love and marriage in the English medieval romance. Nashville 1938.

West, C. B. Courtoisie in Anglo-Norman literature. 1938.

Ackerman, R. W. Armor and weapons in the Middle English romances. State College of Washington Research Stud 7 1939.

—— 'Dub' in the Middle English romances. State College of Washington Research Stud 9 1941.

—— The knighting ceremonies in the Middle English romances. Speculum 19 1944.

Loomis, L. H. Chaucer and the Auchinleck ms. In Essays and studies in honor of C. Brown, New York 1940.

—— Chaucer and the Breton lays of the Auchinleck ms. SP 38 1941.

—— The Auchinleck ms and a possible London bookshop of 1330–40. PMLA 57 1942.

For the Auchinleck ms see also under (30) Roland and Vernagu and (70) Sir Orfeo, below.

Painter, S. French chivalry. Baltimore 1940.

Webster, K. G. T. Galloway and the romances. MLN 55 1940.

Dunlap, A. R. The vocabulary of the Middle English romances in tail-rhyme stanza. Delaware Notes 14 1941.

Reinhard, J. R. Setting adrift in mediaeval law and literature. PMLA 56 1941.

—— Burning at the stake in mediaeval law and literature. Speculum 16 1941.

Olson, C. C. The minstrels at the court of Edward III. PMLA 56 1941.

Norbert, Mother M. The reflection of religion in English medieval verse romances. Bryn Mawr 1941.

Levy, H. L. 'As myn auctour seyth'. MÆ 12 1943.

Cline. R. The influence of romances upon tournaments of the Middle Ages. Speculum 20 1945.

Bennett, H. S. Production and dissemination of vernacular mss in the 15th century. Library 5th ser 1 1947.

Gist, M. A. Love and war in the Middle English romances. Philadelphia 1947.

Sherwood, M. Magic and mechanics in medieval fiction. SP 44 1947.

Mathew, G. Marriage and amour courtois in late 14th-century England. In Essays presented to Charles Williams, Oxford 1947.

—— Ideals of knighthood in late 14th-century England. In Studies in medieval history presented to F. M. Powicke, Oxford 1948.

Spence, L. The fairy tradition in Britain. 1948.

Baugh, A. C. The authorship of the Middle English romances. Modern Humanities Research Assoc Annual Bull 22 1950.

—— Improvisation in the Middle English romances. Proc of Amer Philosophical Soc 103 1959.

—— The Middle English romance: some questions of creation, presentation and preservation. Speculum 42 1967.

Bernheimer, R. Wild men in the Middle Ages. Cambridge Mass 1952.

Owings, M. A. The arts in the Middle English romances. New York 1952.

Auerbach, E. Mimesis. Tr W. Trask, Princeton 1953.

Muscatine, C. The emergency of psychological allegory in Old French romance. PMLA 68 1953.

Reinhold, H. Humoristische Tendenzen in der englischen Dichtung des Mittelalters. Tübingen 1953.

Moore, A. K. Sir Thopas as criticism of 14th-century minstrelsy. JEGP 53 1954.

Enkvist, N. E. The seasons of the year. Copenhagen 1957.

Waldron, R. A. Oral-formulaic technique in Middle English alliterative poetry. Speculum 32 1957.

Habicht, W. Die Gebärde in englischen Dichtungen des Mittelalters. Munich 1959.

Kuhn, H. Dichtung und Welt im Mittelalter. Stuttgart 1959.

Utley, F. L. Folklore, myth and ritual. In Critical approaches to medieval literature, ed D. Bethurum, New York 1960.

Lord, A. B. The singer of tales. Harvard Stud in Comparative Lit 24 1960.

Fourrier, A. Le courant réaliste dans le roman courtois au Moyen Age. Paris 1961.

Robson, C. A. The technique of symmetrical composition in medieval narrative poetry. In Studies in medieval French presented to A. Ewert, Oxford 1961.

McAlindon, T. The emergence of a comic type in Middle English narrative: the devil and giant as buffoon. Anglia 81 1963.

—— Comedy and terror in Middle English literature: the diabolical game. MLR 60 1965.

Hill, D. M. Romance as epic. E Studies 44 1963.

Mehl, D. 'Point of view' in mittelenglischen Romanzen. Germanisch-romanische Monatsschrift 45 1964.

—— Die kürzeren mittelenglischen 'Romanzen' und die Gattungsfrage. Deutsche Vierteljahrsschrift für Literaturwissenschaft und Geistgeschichte 38 1964.

Bumke, J. Studien zum Ritterbegriff im 12 und 13 Jahrhundert. Heidelberg 1964.

Lazar, M. Amour courtois et 'fin amors' dans la littérature du xiie siècle. Strasbourg 1964.

Lewis, C. S. The discarded image. Cambridge 1964.

Vinaver, E. From epic to romance. Bull John Rylands Lib 16 1964.

—— Form and meaning in medieval romance. Cambridge 1966.

—— The rise of romance. 1971.

Brewer, D. S. The relationship of Chaucer to the English and European tradition. In Chaucer and Chaucerians, ed Brewer 1966.

Horrent, J. Chanson de geste et roman courtois. Romance Philology 20 1966.

Kratins, O. Treason in Middle English metrical romances. PQ 45 1966.

Moorman, C. A knyght ther was: the evolution of the knight in literature. Lexington Kentucky 1967.

Nygard, H. O. Popular ballad and medieval romance. In Folklore international: essays in honor of W. D. Hand, Hatboro Pa 1967.

Payen, M. Les origines de la courtoisie dans la littérature française médiévale: tome 2, le roman. Paris 1967.

Ruh, K. Höfische Epik des deutschen Mittelalters. Berlin 1967.

Holmes, U. T. The mediaeval minstrel. In Mediaeval and Renaissance studies, ed J. L. Lievsay, Durham NC 1968.

Fowler, D. C. A literary history of the popular ballad. Durham NC 1968.

Newman F. X. (ed). The meaning of courtly love. Albany NY 1968.

Thiébaux, M. The mouth of the boar as a symbol in medieval literature. Romance Philology 22 1969.

White, B. Saracens and Crusaders: from fact to allegory. Medieval literature and civilisation: studies in memory of G. N. Garmonsway, 1969.

Ménard, P. Le rire et le sourire dans le roman courtois en France au Moyen Age. Geneva 1969.

Dorfman, E. The narreme in the medieval romance-epic: an introduction to narrative structures. Toronto 1969.

Kelly, D. Theory of composition in medieval poetry and Geoffrey of Vinsauf's Poetria nova. Mediaeval Stud 31 1969.

Green, D. H. Irony and the medieval romance. Forum for Modern Lang Stud 6 1970.

Barber, R. The knight and chivalry. New York 1970.

(2) ARTHURIAN ROMANCES: THE MATTER OF BRITAIN

Bibliographies

Parry, J. J. A bibliography of critical Arthurian literature 1922–9. 2 vols New York 1931–6. Annually in MLQ 1940–.

Nitze, W. A. The Newberry collection of Arthuriana. MP 30 1932.

Utley, G. Newberry Library report of trustees for 1931. Chicago 1932.

Harding, J. The Arthurian legend: a check list of books in the Newberry Library. Chicago 1933; suppl 1938.

Northup, C. S. and J. J. Parry. The Arthurian legends, modern retellings of the old stories: an annotated bibliography. JEGP 43 1944, 49 1950.

Ackerman, R. W. et al. Arthurian bibliography for 1948. Bulletin Bibliographique de la Société Internationale Arthurienne 1– 1949– (annually).

See also Malory, col 674, below.

General Studies

Paris, P. Romans de la Table Ronde. 5 vols Paris 1868–77.

Rhys, J. Arthurian legend. Oxford 1891.

Puetz, F. R. Zur Geschichte der Entwicklung der Arthursage. Bonn 1892.

Hoeppner, A. B. Arthurs Gestalt in der Literatur Englands. Leipzig 1892.

Wülcker, R. P. Die Arthursage in der englischen Literatur. Leipzig 1895.

Lot, F. Etudes sur la provenance du cycle arthurien. Romania 25 1896, 28 1899, 30 1901.

Newell, W. W. King Arthur and the Table Round. Boston 1897.

Weston, J. L. King Arthur and his knights. 1899, 1905 (rev).

Brown, A. C. L. The Round Table before Wace. Harvard Stud 7 1900.

Dickinson, W. H. King Arthur in Cornwall. New York 1900.

Kittredge, G. L. Arthur and Gorlagon. Harvard Stud 8 1903.

Paton, L. A. Fairy mythology of the Arthurian romances. Radcliffe Monographs 13 1903.

Fletcher, R. H. Arthurian material in the chronicles. Harvard Stud 10 1906; New York 1966 (rev).

Maynadier, G. H. Arthur of the English poets. Boston 1907.

Sommer, H. O. Vulgate version of the Arthurian romances. 8 vols Washington 1908–16.

—— Structure of the Livre d'Artus and its function in the evolution of the Arthurian prose romances. Paris and London 1914.

Jones, W. L. King Arthur in history and legend. Cambridge 1911.

Loth, J. Contributions à l'étude des romans de la Table Ronde. Paris 1912.

Bruce, J. D. Evolution of Arthurian romance to 1300. 2 vols Göttingen 1923–4, 1928 (rev).

—— Mordred's incestuous birth. In Medieval studies in memory of G. S. Loomis, Paris and New York 1927.

Plesner, K. F. Engelsk Arthur-digtning. Copenhagen 1925.

Ven-ten Bensel, E. van der. Character of Arthur in English literature. Amsterdam 1925.

Loomis, R. S. Medieval iconography and the question of Arthurian origins. MLN 40 1925.

—— Celtic myth and Arthurian romance. New York 1927.

—— Some names in Arthurian romance. PMLA 45 1930.

—— The scientific method in Arthurian studies. Studi Medievali 3 1931.
—— The visit to the Perilous Castle. PMLA 48 1933.
—— By what route did the romantic tradition of Arthur reach the French? MP 33 1936.
—— The Modena sculpture and Arthurian romance. Studi Medievali 9 1936. Replies by G. H. Gerould, Speculum 10 1935, Loomis 13 1938.
—— Chivalric and dramatic imitations of Arthurian romance. In Medieval studies in memory of A. K. Porter, Cambridge 1939.
—— The Arthurian legend before 1139. Romanic Rev 32 1941.
—— King Arthur and the Antipodes. MP 38 1941.
—— The spoils of Annwn: an early Arthurian poem. PMLA 56 1941.
—— Morgain la Fée and the Celtic goddesses. Speculum 20 1945.
—— Arthurian tradition and Chrétien de Troyes. New York 1949.
—— The Fier Baiser in Mandeville's Travels, Arthurian romance and Irish saga. Studi Medievali 17 1951.
—— Edward I: Arthurian enthusiast. Speculum 28 1953.
—— Wales and the Arthurian legend. Cardiff 1956.
—— Objections to the Celtic origin of the matière de Bretagne. Romania 79 1958.
—— Scotland and the Arthurian legend. Proc Soc of Antiquaries of Scotland 89 1958.
—— (ed). Arthurian literature in the Middle Ages. Oxford 1959.
—— Morgain la Fée in oral tradition. Romania 80 1959.
—— The development of Arthurian romance. 1963.
—— Did Gawain, Perceval and Arthur hail from Scotland? Etudes Celtiques 11 1965.
Singer, S. Die Artussage. Berne 1926.
Robinson, J. A. Two Glastonbury legends, King Arthur and St Joseph of Arimathea. Cambridge 1926.
Gerould, G. H. King Arthur and politics. Speculum 1–2 1926–7.
Loomis, L. H. Arthur's Round Table. PMLA 41 1926.
—— The Round Table again. MLN 44 1929.
—— Arthurian tombs and megalithic monuments. MLR 26 1931.
Chambers, E. K. Arthur of Britain. 1927.
Faral, E. La légende arthurienne: études et documents. 3 vols Paris 1929.
Northup, C. S. King Arthur, the Christ and some others. In Miscellany in honor of F. Klaeber, Minneapolis 1929.
Gardner, E. G. The Arthurian legend in Italian literature. New York 1930.
Lewis, C. B. Classical mythology and Arthurian romance. Oxford 1932.
Brinkley, R. F. Arthurian legend in the 17th century. Baltimore 1932.
Loomis, C. G. King Arthur and the Saints. Speculum 8 1933.
Krappe, A. H. Arthur and Charlemagne. E Studien 68 1934.
—— Arturus Cosmocrator. Speculum 20 1945.
Nitze, W. A. The exhumation of King Arthur at Glastonbury. Speculum 9 1934.
—— The 'beste glatissant' in Arthurian romance. Zeitschrift für Romanische Philologie 56 1936.
—— Arthurian romance and modern poetry and music. Chicago 1940.
—— Arthurian names: 'Arthur'. PMLA 64–5 1949–50.
—— Arthurian problems. Bulletin Bibliographique de la Société Internationale Arthurienne 5 1953.
Newstead, H. The 'joie de la cort' episode in Erec and the Horn of Bran. PMLA 51 1936.
—— Bran the Blessed in Arthurian romance. New York 1939.
—— The besieged ladies in Arthurian romance. PMLA 63 1948.
—— King Mark of Cornwall. Romance Philology 11 1958.

Tatlock, J. S. P. The traditional Arthur before Geoffrey. PMLA 52 1936.
—— The dates of the Arthurian saints' legends. Speculum 14 1939.
Praz, M. The Arthurian legend in Italy. In his Studi e svaghi inglesi, Florence 1937.
Baker, Sr I. The King's household in the Arthurian court. Washington 1937.
Bennett, R. E. Arthur and Gorlagon, the Dutch Lancelot and St Kentigern. Speculum 13 1938.
Loomis, R. S. and L. H. Arthurian legends in medieval art. 1938.
Reid, M. J. C. Arthurian legend: comparison of treatment in medieval and modern literature. Edinburgh 1938.
Nitze, W. A. and A. Taylor. Some recent Arthurian studies. MP 36 1939.
Sparnaay, H. De Weg van Koning Arthur. Groningen 1942.
Sandoz, E. Tourneys in the Arthurian tradition. Speculum 19 1944.
Cross, T. P. Early Irish literature in its relation to Arthurian romance. PMLA 59 1944.
—— Motif-index of early Irish literature. Bloomington 1952.
Scherer, M. About the Round Table. New York 1945.
Gruffydd, W. J. The Arthurian legend and the Mabinogion. Welsh Rev 6 1947.
Housman, J. E. Higden, Trevisa, Caxton and the beginnings of Arthurian romance. RES 23 1947.
Jones, G. and T. Jones. The Mabinogion: a new translation. 1948 (EL).
Williams, M. Eleanor of Aquitaine and the Arthurian romances. Durham Univ Jnl 42 1949.
Parry, J. J. Arthur dans le poésie galloise ancienne. Bulletin Bibliographique de la Société Internationale Arthurienne 3 1951.
Ackerman, R. W. An index of the Arthurian names in Middle English. Stanford 1952.
—— Arthur's Wild man knight. Romance Philology 9 1955.
—— The English rimed and prose romances. In Arthurian literature in the Middle Ages, ed R. S. Loomis, Oxford 1959.
Loomis, R. S. and J. J. Parry. Arthur's Round Table and Bran the Blessed. MLQ 14 1953.
Bromwich, R. The character of the early Welsh tradition. In Studies in early British history, ed N. K. Chadwick, Cambridge 1954.
—— Scotland and the Arthurian tradition. Bulletin Bibliographique de la Société Internationale Arthurienne 15 1963.
—— The Celtic inheritance of medieval literature. MLQ 26 1965.
Köhler, E. Ideal und Wirklichkeit in der höfischen Epik: Studien zur Form und frühen Artus- und Graldichtung. Zeitschrift für Romanische Philologie 72 1956.
Harward, V. J. The dwarfs of Arthurian romance and Celtic tradition. Leyden 1958.
Schirmer, W. F. Die frühen Darstellungen des Arthurstoffes. Cologne 1958.
O'Loughlin, J. L. N. The English alliterative romances. In Arthurian literature in the Middle Ages, ed R. S. Loomis, Oxford 1959.
Williams, H. F. Apocryphal gospels and Arthurian romance. Zeitschrift für Romanische Philologie 75 1959.
Morton, A. L. The matter of Britain: the Arthurian cycle and the development of feudal society. Zeitschrift für Anglistik und Amerikanistik 8 1960.
Barber, R. W. Arthur of Albion: an introduction to the Arthurian literature and legends of England. 1961.
Cross, J. E. King Arthur and the Old Swedish legendary. MÆ 30 1961.
Bliss, A. J. Celtic myth and Arthurian romance. Ibid. Reply by V. Harward 31 1962.

Göller, K. H. König Arthur in den schottischen Chroniken. Anglia 80 1962.
— König Arthur in der englischen Literatur des späten Mittelalters. Palaestra 238 1963.
Stiennon, J. and R. Lejeune. La légende arthurienne dans la sculpture de la cathédrale de Modène. Cahiers de Civilisation Médiévales 6 1963.
Fourquet, J. La littérature arthurienne au Moyen Age. Etudes Anglaises 16 1963.
Utley, F. L. Arthurian romance and international folk-tale method. Romance Philology 17 1964.
Misrahi, J. Symbolism and allegory in Arthurian romance. Ibid.
Brengle, R. L. Arthur King of Britain: history, romance, chronicle and criticism. New York 1964.
Marx, J. Nouvelles recherches sur la littérature arthurienne. Paris 1965.
Muses, C. Celtic origins and the Arthurian cycle: Arthur, the chain of evidence. Celticum 12 1965.
Bullock-Davies, C. Professional interpreters and the matter of Britain. Cardiff 1966.
Adolf, H. The concept of original sin as reflected in Arthurian romance. In Studies in language and literature in honour of M. Schlauch, Warsaw 1966.
Cosman, M. P. The education of the hero in Arthurian romance. Chapel Hill 1966.
Lejeune, R. La légende du roi Arthur dans l'iconographie religieuse médiévale. Archeologia 14 1967.
Ashe, G. All about King Arthur. 1969.
Bogdanow, F. Morgain's role in the 13th-century prose romances of the Arthurian cycle. MÆ 38 1969.
Frappier, J. Le motif du 'don contraignant' dans la littérature du Moyen Age. Travaux de Linguistique et de Littérature (Strasbourg) 7 1969.
Payen, J. C. La destruction des mythes courtois dans le roman arthurien: la femme dans le roman en vers après Chrétien de Troyes. Revue des Langues Romanes 78 1969.
West G. D. Index of proper names in French Arthurian verse romances 1150–1300. Toronto 1969.
Hunt, T. The rhetorical background to the Arthurian prologue. Forum for Modern Lang Stud 6 1970.
Jackson, W. H. Status of the narrator in Hartmann von Aue's Erec and Iwein. Ibid.
Ménard, P. La déclaration amoureuse dans la littérature arthurienne au xiie siècle. Cahiers de Civilisation Médiévale 13 1970.
Owen, D. D. R. (ed). Arthurian romance: seven essays. 1970.

The Historical Arthur: Gildas, Nennius, Geoffrey of Monmouth, Wace

Giles, J. A. (tr). Six Old English chronicles. 1848, 1901 (rev).
Mommsen, T. (ed). Nennius, Historia Britonum. In Monumenta Germaniae historica vol 13, Berlin 1898.
Fletcher, R. H. Arthurian materials in the chronicles. Harvard Stud 10 1906; New York 1966 (rev).
Mason, E. (tr). Arthurian chronicles represented by Wace and Layamon. 1912.
Hopkins, A. B. The influence of Wace on the Arthurian romances of Crestien de Troiies. Menasha Wis 1913.
Waldner, L. Waces Brut und seine Quellen. Karlsruhe 1914.
Greulich, E. F. Die Arthur-Sage in der Historia regum Britanniae. Halle 1916.
Brandenburg, H. Galfrid von Monmouth und die frühmittelenglischen Chronisten. Berlin 1918.
Matter, H. Englische Grundungssagen von Geoffrey of Monmouth bis zur Renaissance. Anglistische Forschungen 58 1922.
Gordon, G. Trojans in Britain. E & S 9 1923.
Malone, K. Historicity of Arthur. JEGP 23 1924.
— Artorius. MP 22 1925.

Parry, J. J. Celtic tradition and the Vita Merlini. PQ 4 1925.
— (ed). Vita Merlini. Illinois Univ Stud 10 1925.
— A variant version of Geoffrey of Monmouth's Historia. In Miscellany of studies presented to L. E. Kastner, Cambridge 1932.
— Geoffrey of Monmouth and the paternity of Arthur. Speculum 13 1938.
— The historical Arthur. JEGP 58 1959.
Chambers, E. K. Arthur of Britain. 1927.
Lot, F. De la valeur historique de De excidio. In Medieval studies in memory of G. S. Loomis, New York 1927.
— Nennius et l'Historia Britonum. Bibliographie de l'Ecole des Hautes Etudes 263 1934.
Nitze, W. A. Geoffrey of Monmouth's King Arthur. Speculum 2 1927.
— Bédier's epic theory and the 'Arthuriana' of Nennius. MP 39 1941.
— More on the Arthuriana of Nennius. MLN 58 1943.
Loomis, R. S. Geoffrey of Monmouth and Arthurian origins. Speculum 3 1928.
— Geoffrey of Monmouth and the Modena Archivolt. Speculum 13 1938.
— The Arthurian legend before 1139. Romanic Rev 32 1941.
Anscombe, A. King Arthur in Gildas. N & Q 18 Aug 1928.
Griscom, A. (ed). Historia regum Britanniae. New York 1929.
Arnold, I. Wace et l'Historia regum Britanniae de Geoffroi de Monmouth. Romania 57 1931.
— (ed). Le Roman de Brut. 2 vols Paris 1938–40.
Pelan, M. L'influence du Brut de Wace sur les romanciers français de l'époque. Paris 1931.
Crawford, O. G. S. King Arthur's last battle. Antiquity 5 1931.
Anderson, A. O. Nennius's chronological chapter. Antiquity 6 1932.
Williams, M. The Brut tradition in the English mss. In Miscellany of studies presented to L. E. Kastner, Cambridge 1932.
Brugger, E. Zu Galfrid von Monmouths Historia. Zeitschrift für Französische Sprache und Literatur 57 1933.
Hammer, J. Note on a ms of Geoffrey of Monmouth's Historia. PQ 12 1933.
— A commentary on the Prophetia Merlini. Speculum 10 1935, 15 1940.
— Some additional mss of Geoffrey's Historia. MLQ 3 1942.
— Sources and textual history of Geoffrey's Historia. Quart Bull of Polish Inst 2 1944.
— Les sources de Geoffrey, Historia. Latomus 4–5 1946.
— Geoffrey of Monmouth's use of the Bible. Bull John Rylands Lib 30 1947.
— (ed). Geoffrey of Monmouth: a variant version. Cambridge Mass 1951.
— Notes on Geoffrey's History. Scriptorium 6–7 1952–3.
Tatlock, J. S. P. Geoffrey and King Arthur in Normannicus Draco. MP 31 1933.
— Geoffrey of Monmouth's motives for writing his Historia. Proc Amer Philosophical Soc 79 1938.
— Geoffrey of Monmouth's Vita Merlini. Speculum 18 1943.
— The lunatic lover. Univ of California Pbns in Eng 14 1943.
— The legendary history of Britain: Geoffrey of Monmouth's History and its early vernacular versions. Berkeley 1950.
Johnstone, P. K. and H. Askew. The victories of Arthur. N & Q 2–16 June, 28 July 1934.
Williams, I. Notes on Nennius. Bull Board of Celtic Stud 7 1935, 9 1937.

Jackson, K. Nennius and the 28 cities of Britain. Antiquity 12 1938.
— Once again Arthur's battles. MP 43 1945.
— Language and history in early Britain. Edinburgh 1953.
— The Britons in southern Scotland. Antiquity 29 1955.
— The site of Mt Badon. Jnl of Celtic Stud 2 1958.
— The Arthur of history. In Arthurian literature in the Middle Ages, ed R. S. Loomis, Oxford 1959.
Wade-Evans, L. History of the Britons. 1938.
Hutson, A. E. British personal names in the History of Geoffrey. Berkeley 1940.
Jones, E. V. Geoffrey of Monmouth's account of the establishment of episcopacy in Britain. JEGP 40 1941.
Piggott, S. The sources of Geoffrey of Monmouth. Antiquity 15 1941.
Griffin, M. E. Cadwalader, Arthur and Brutus in the Wigmore ms. Speculum 16 1941.
Houck, M. Sources of the Roman de Brut of Wace. Berkeley 1941.
Blenner-Hassett, R. Geoffrey of Monmouth's 'Mons Agned' and 'Castellum Puellarum'. Speculum 17 1942.
Lloyd, J. E. Geoffrey of Monmouth. EHR 56 1942.
Paton, L. A. Notes on Merlin in the Historia of Geoffrey. MP 41 1943.
Zumthor, P. Merlin le prophète. Lausanne 1943.
Keeler, L. Geoffrey of Monmouth and the late Latin chronicles 1300–1500. Berkeley 1946.
— The Historia and four medieval chroniclers. Speculum 21 1946.
Gerould, G. H. A text of Merlin's Prophecies. Speculum 23 1948.
Kendrick, T. D. British antiquity. 1950.
Williams, S. Geoffrey of Monmouth and the canon law. Speculum 27 1952.
Delbouille, M. Le témoignage de Wace sur la légende arthurienne. Romania 74 1953.
Caldwell, R. A. Geoffrey of Monmouth, Wace and the Stour. MLN 69 1954.
— The history of the kings of Britain in College of Arms ms Arundel xxii. PMLA 69 1954.
— Wace's Brut and the variant version of Geoffrey's Historia. Speculum 31 1956.
Pilch, H. Zu den Quellen des Roman de Brut. Zeitschrift für Celtische Philologie 27 1957.
Fowler, D. C. Some biblical influences on Geoffrey of Monmouth's historiography. Traditio 14 1958.
Dunn, C. W. (tr). Geoffrey of Monmouth's History of the kings of Britain. New York 1958.
Pähler, H. Strukturuntersuchungen zur Historia des Geoffrey. Bonn 1958.
Parry, J. J. and R. A. Caldwell. Geoffrey of Monmouth. In Arthurian literature in the Middle Ages, ed R. S. Loomis, Oxford 1959.
Foulon, C. Wace. Ibid.
Lukman, N. The Viking nations and King Arthur in Geoffrey of Monmouth. Classica et Mediaevalia 20 1959.
Tolstoy, N. Nennius chap 56. Bull Board of Celtic Stud 19 1961.
Arnold, I. and M. Pelan. La partie arthurienne du Roman de Brut de Wace. Paris 1962.
Jones, T. The early evolution of the legend of Arthur. Nottingham Medieval Stud 8 1964.
Holmes, U. T. Norman literature and Wace. In Medieval secular literature, ed W. Matthews, Berkeley 1965.
Emanuel, H. D. Geoffrey's Historia: a second variant version. MÆ 35 1966.
Gallais, P. La variant version de l'Historia et le Brut de Wace. Romania 87 1966.
Thorpe, L. (tr). Geoffrey of Monmouth's History of the Kings of Britain. 1966.
Hanning, R. W. The vision of history in early Britain from Gildas to Geoffrey of Monmouth. New York 1966.

Lindsay, J. Arthur and his times: Britain in the Dark Ages. New York 1966.
Ashe, G. The quest for Arthur's Britain. 1968.
— Camelot and the vision of Albion. 1971.
Muir, L. King Arthur's northern conquests in the Leges Anglorum. MÆ 37 1968.
See also Laȝamon, *below, and, for the ballad of* The legend of King Arthur, *C. B. Millican, PMLA 46 1931 and A. Friedman 69 1954. For Geoffrey see col 755, below.*

(1) Arthur
Index 1113. 642 lines in short couplets.
Ms: Longleat 55.

§1
Ed F. J. Furnivall 1864 (EETS), 1869 (rev).

§2
Finlayson, J. The source of Arthur, an early 15th-century verse chronicle. N & Q Feb 1960.

(2) Morte Arthure
Index 2322. 4346 alliterative long lines.
Ms: Lincoln Cathedral 91 (Thornton).

§1
Ed J. O. Halliwell (-Phillipps), The alliterative romance of the death of King Arthur, 1847; ed G. G. Perry 1865 (EETS), rev E. Brock 1871; ed M. M. Banks 1900; ed E. Björkman, Heidelberg 1915; ed J. Finlayson 1967 (York Medieval Texts) (extracts; about half the text).
Selections in Mossé; modern version by A. Boyle 1912 (EL).

§2
For dialect and authorship etc see under (8) Gawain, below.
Branscheid, P. Quellen. Anglia Anzeiger 8 1885.
Mennicken, F. Versbau und Sprache. Bonner Beiträge 5 1900.
Banks, M. M. Notes on glossary. MLQ 6 1903.
Griffith, R. H. Malory, Morte Arthure and Fierabras. Anglia 32 1909.
Björkman, E. Morte Arthure and its vocabulary. In Minneskrift tillägnad Axel Erdmann, Upsala 1913.
— Zum alliterierenden Morte Arthure. Anglia 39 1915.
Holthausen, F. Notes. Beiblatt zur Anglia 24 1913, Anglia 34 1923, 36 1925.
Bruce, J. D. Development of the Morte Arthure theme. Romanic Rev 4 1913.
Andrew, S. O. Dialect. RES 4 1928.
Brown, C. Somer Soneday. In Miscellany in honor of F. Klaeber, Minneapolis 1929.
O'Loughlin, J. L. N. The Middle English alliterative Morte Arthure. MÆ 4 1935.
Schröder, E. Zur Datierung der Morte Arthure. Anglia 60 1936.
Gordon, E. V. and E. Vinaver. New light on the text of the alliterative Morte Arthure. MÆ 6 1937.
Vorontzoff, T. Malory's story of Arthur's Roman campaign. Ibid. Reply by I. Arnold 7 1938.
Hammerle, K. Das Fortunamotiv von Chaucer bis Bacon. Anglia 65 1941.
Parks, G. D. King Arthur and the roads to Rome. JEGP 45 1946.
Wilson, R. H. How many books did Malory write? SE 30 1951.
Everett, D. The alliterative revival. In her Essays on Middle English literature, Oxford 1955.
Waldron, R. A. Oral-formulaic technique and alliterative poetry. Speculum 32 1957.
Höltgen, K. J. Konig Arthur und Fortuna. Anglia 75 1957.
Matthews, W. The tragedy of Arthur. Berkeley 1960.

Finlayson, J. Two minor sources for the alliterative Morte Arthure. N & Q April 1962.
— Formulaic technique in the Morte Arthure. Anglia 81 1963.
— Rhetorical 'descriptio' of place in the alliterative Morte Arthure. MP 61 1963.
— Arthur and the giant of St Michael's Mount. MÆ 33 1964.
— Morte Arthure: the date and a source for the contemporary references. Speculum 42 1967.
— The concept of the hero in Morte Arthure. In Chaucer und seine Zeit: Symposium für W. F. Schirmer, Tübingen 1968.
McIntosh, A. The textual transmission of the alliterative Morte Arthure. In English and medieval studies presented to J. R. R. Tolkien, 1962.
Göller, K. H. Stab und Formel im alliterierenden Morte Arthure. Neophilologus 49 1965.
Clark G. Gawain's fall: the alliterative Morte Arthure and Hastings. Tennessee Stud in Lit 11 1966.
Benson, L. D. The alliterative Morte Arthure and medieval tragedy. Ibid.
Gross, L. The meaning and oral-formulaic use of 'riot' in the alliterative Morte Arthure. Annuale Mediaevale (Duquesne) 9 1968.
Lumiansky, R. M. The alliterative Morte Arthure, the concept of medieval tragedy and the cardinal virtue Fortitude. In Medieval and Renaissance studies, ed J. L. Lievsay, Chapel Hill 1968.
Schelp, H. Gestaltung und Funktion des Auftakts in der mittelenglischen alliterierenden Morte Arthure. Archiv 207 1971.

Merlin and the Youth of Arthur

See also under the Historical Arthur, above.
Paris, G. and J. Ulrich. Huth Merlin. Paris 1886 (Société des Anciens Textes Français).
Mead, W. E. Outlines of the history of the legend of Merlin. 1899 (EETS).
Lot, F. Etudes sur Merlin. Paris 1900.
Sommer, H. O. Le roman de Merlin. 1904.
Brugger, E. L'enserrement Merlin: Studien zur Merlinsage. Zeitschrift für Französische Sprache und Literatur 29–31 1906–8, 33–5 1910–12.
Taylor, R. Political prophecy in England. New York 1911.
Paton, L. A. Prophécies de Merlin. 2 vols New York 1926–7.
— Notes on Merlin in Geoffrey's Historia. MP 41 1943.
Eyre-Todd, G. Scottish battles of King Arthur. Scots Mag 15 1931.
Schiprowski, P. Merlin in der deutschen Dichtung. Breslau 1933.
Weiss, A. M. Merlin in German literature. Washington 1933.
Krappe, A. H. L'enserrement de Merlin. Romania 60 1934.
Crawford, O. G. S. Arthur and his battles. Antiquity 9 1935.
Brodeur, A. G. Arthur dux bellorum. Berkeley 1939.
Jackson, K. The motif of the three-fold death. In Feil-Sgribhinn Eoin MhicNeill, Dublin 1940.
Giffin, M. E. Cadwalader, Arthur and Brutus in the Wigmore ms. Speculum 16 1941.
— A reading of Robert de Boron. PMLA 80 1965.
Zumthor, P. La délivrance de Merlin. Zeitschrift für Romanische Philologie 62 1942.
— Merlin le prophète. Lausanne 1943.
Nitze, W. A. The Esplumoir Merlin. Speculum 18 1943.
Wierusowski, H. King Arthur's Round Table: an 'Academic Club' in 13th-century Tuscany. Traditio 2 1944.
Brown, A. C. L. The Esplumoir and Viviane. Speculum 20 1945.
Smith, R. M. King Lear and the Merlin tradition. MLQ 7 1946.

Adolf, H. The Esplumoir Merlin. Speculum 21 1946.
Russell, J. C. Arthur and the Romano-Celtic frontier. MP 48 1951.
Denomy, A. J. The Round Table and the Council of Rheims 1049. Mediaeval Stud 14 1952.
Wilson, R. H. The rebellion of the Kings in Malory and in the Cambridge Suite du Merlin. SE 31 1952. Replies by F. Bogdanow 34 1955, Wilson 36 1957.
Vinaver, E. The dolorous stroke. MÆ 25 1956.
Micha, A. Les mss du Merlin en prose de Robert de Boron. Romania 79 1958.
— The Vulgate Merlin. In Arthurian literature in the Middle Ages, ed R. S. Loomis, Oxford 1959.
Bogdanow, F. Essai de classement des mss de la Suite du Merlin. Romania 81 1960.
— Pellinor's death in the Suite du Merlin and the Palamedes. MÆ 29 1960.
— Quelques fragments inconnus de la mise en prose du Merlin de Robert de Boron. Romania 90 1969.
Vielhauer, I. Einleitung in die Vita Merlini. Castrum Peregrini 72–3 1964.
Zimmer, H. Merlin. Ibid.
Payen, J.-C. L'art du récit dans le Merlin de Robert de Boron, le Didot Perceval et le Perlesvaus. Romance Philology 17 1964.
Marx, J. Le thème du coup félon et le roman de Balain. Le Moyen Age 72 1966.
Colin, P. Un nouveau manuscrit du Merlin en prose et de la Suite-Vulgate. Romania 88 1967.

(3) Arthour and Merlin, A and B

Index 1675 (A). 9938 lines in short couplet.
Index 1162 (B). 2490 lines in short couplet.
Mss: A. Nat Lib of Scotland 19.2.1 (Auchinleck); B. Bodley 21,880 (Douce 236); Harley 6223; BM additional 27,879 (Percy Folio); Lincoln's Inn 150.

§1

Ed W. B. D. Turnbull, Edinburgh 1838 (Abbotsford Club) (B); ed J. W. Hales and F. J. Furnivall, Percy Folio ms 1867–9, 1905–10 (rev) (B); ed E. Kölbing, Leipzig 1890 (A and B).

§2

Gaster, M. Jewish sources of and parallels to Arthur and Merlin. 1887.
Holthausen, F. Textual notes. Beiblatt zur Anglia 31 1920.
Liedholm, A. Phonological study of Arthour and Merlin. Upsala 1941.
French, W. H. Dialects and forms in three romances. JEGP 45 1946. With Kyng Alisaunder and Richard Coeur de Lion.
Loomis, R. S. Vandeberes, Wandlebury and de l'Espine. Romance Philology 9 1955.

(4) Henry Lovelich's Merlin

Index 2312. 27,852 lines in short couplet.
Ms: Corpus Christi College Cambridge 80.

§1

Ed E. A. Kock 3 vols 1904–32 (EETS).

§2

Kölbing, E. (ed). Arthour and Merlin. Leipzig 1890. Introd.
Ackerman, R. W. Herry Lovelich's Merlin. PMLA 67 1952.
— Henry Lovelich's name. MLN 67 1952.
See also under (22) Lovelich's Grail, below.

(5) Prose Merlin

Mss: Cambridge Univ Ff.3.11; Rawlinson Miscellany 1370 (formerly 1262). Fragment.

§1

Ed H. B. Wheatley and W. E. Mead 1865–99 (EETS); ed L. Cranmer-Byng, Selections, 1930.

§2

Richter, G. and G. Stecher. Erklärung und Textkritik. E Studien 20 1895, 28 1900.
Workman, S. B. 15th-century translations as an influence on English prose. Princeton Univ Stud in Eng 18 1940.

Lancelot and the Death of Arthur

Weston, J. L. The legend of Sir Lancelot du Lac. 1901.
—— The three days' tournament. 1902.
Sommer, H. O. (ed). French Vulgate Lancelot. 3 vols Washington 1910–12.
Bruce, J. D. (ed). Mort Artu. Halle 1910.
—— Development of the Mort Arthur theme. Romanic Rev 4 1913.
—— The composition of the Prose Lancelot. Romanic Rev 9–10 1918–19.
Lot, F. Étude sur le Lancelot en prose. Paris 1916, 1954 (rev).
—— L'origine du nom de Lancelot. Romania 51 1925.
—— Sur la date du Lancelot en prose. Romania 57 1931.
Cross, T. P. The passing of Arthur. In J. M. Manly anniversary studies, Chicago 1923.
App, A. J. Lancelot in English literature. Washington 1929.
Paton, L. A. (tr). Sir Lancelot of the Lake. New York 1929.
Cross, T. P. and W. A. Nitze. Lancelot and Guenevere: a study in the origins of courtly love. Chicago 1930.
Winters, D. A new source for Lancelot's madness. SP 31 1934.
Frappier, J. (ed). La mort le roi Artu. Paris 1936, 1954 (rev).
—— Etude sur la Mort le roi Artu. Paris 1936, 1961 (rev).
—— Le personnage de Galehaut dans le Lancelot en prose. Romance Philology 17 1964.
Thompson, J. W. On the date of the Lancelot. MLN 52 1937.
Brown, A. C. L. Arthur's loss of Queen and kingdom. Speculum 15 1940
Webster, K. G. T. Walter Map's French things. Ibid.
—— Guinevere: a study of her abductions. Milton Mass 1951.
—— (tr). Ulrich van Zatzikhoven: Lanzelot. New York 1951.
Krappe, A. H. Avallon. Speculum 18 1943.
Southward, E. C. Arthur's Dream. Ibid.
Adler, A. Problems of aesthetic versus historical criticism in La mort le roi Artu. PMLA 65 1950.
Loomis, R. S. The descent of Lancelot from Lug. Bulletin Bibliographique de la Société Internationale Arthurienne 3 1951.
Kennedy, E. The two versions of the false Guinevere episode in the Old French prose Lancelot. Romania 77 1956.
—— Social and political ideas in the French prose Lancelot. MÆ 26 1957.
—— King Arthur in the first part of the prose Lancelot. In Medieval miscellany presented to E. Vinaver, Manchester 1965.
Micha, A. Les manuscrits du Lancelot en prose. Romania 81 1960, 84–7 1963–6.
—— Etudes sur le Lancelot en prose. Romania 82 1961.
Grisward, J. H. Le motif de l'épée jetée au lac: la mort d'Artur et la mort de Batradz. Romania 90 1969.

Noble, P. Some problems in La mort le roi Artu. MLR 65 1970.
Carman, J. N. The Conquests of the Grail Castle and Dolorous Guard. PMLA 85 1970.

(6) Lancelot of the Laik

Index 3466. 3486 lines in heroic couplet.
Ms: Cambridge Univ Kk.1.5.

§1

Ed J. Stevenson 1839 (Maitland Club); ed W. W. Skeat 1865 (EETS), 1870 (rev); ed M. M. Gray 1911 (STS).

§2

Weston, J. L. The three days' tournament. 1902.
Hubert, H. The Kingis quhair, the Quare of jelusy and Lancelot of the Laik. Jahrbuch der Philosophischen Fakultät der Deutschen Universität in Prag 1926–7.
Vogel, B. Secular politics and the date of Lancelot of the Laik. SP 40 1943.
Scheps, W. The thematic unity of Lancelot of the Laik. Stud in Scottish Lit 5 1968.

(7) Le Morte Arthur

Index 1994. 3834 lines in 8-line stanza.
Ms: BM Harley 2252.

§1

Ed G. A. Panton 1819 (Roxburghe Club); ed F. J. Furnivall 1864; ed J. D. Bruce 1903 (EETS); ed S. B. Hemingway, New York 1912.
Modern version by L. A. Paton 1912 (EL).

§2

Bruce, J. D. Sources and relation to Malory. Anglia 23 1900. Replies by H. O. Sommer 29 1906, Bruce 30 1907.
Seyferth, P. Sprache und Metrik. Bonner Beiträge 8 1902.
Wilson, R. H. Malory, the stanzaic Morte Arthur and the Mort Artu. MP 37 1939.
Donaldson, E. T. Malory and the stanzaic Morte Arthur. SP 47 1950.
See also Malory, below.
For the ballads of Sir Lancelot du Lake and King Arthur's Death, see Hales and Furnivall, Severs 237–8, and C. B. Millican, PMLA 46 1931.

Gawain

Weston, J. L. The legend of Sir Gawain. 1897.
—— (tr). Sir Gawain at the Grail castle. 1903.
Maynadier, G. H. The wife of Bath's tale. 1901.
Heller, E. K. Studies on the story of Gawain in Chrestien and Wolfram. JEGP 24 1925.
Ray, B. K. Character of Gawain. Dacca Univ Bull 11 1926.
Loomis, R. S. Gawain in the Squire's tale. MLN 52 1937.
Whiting, B. J. The wife of Bath's tale. In Sources and analogues of Chaucer's Canterbury tales, ed W. F. Bryan and G. Dempster, Chicago 1941.
—— Gawain: his reputation, his courtesy and his appearance in Chaucer's Squire's tale. Mediaeval Stud 9 1947.
Nitze, W. A. The character of Gauvain in the romances of Chrétien de Troyes. MP 50 1952.
Bogdanow, F. The character of Gauvain in the 13th-century prose romances. MÆ 27 1958.
Taylor, P. B. Icelandic analogues to the northern English Gawain cycle. Jnl of Popular Culture 4 1970.
Kelly, D. Gauvin and fin' amors in the poems of Chrétien de Troyes. SP 67 1970.

(8) Sir Gawain and the Green Knight

Index 3144. 2530 lines in unrhymed alliterative stanza with bob and wheel.
Ms: *BM Cotton Nero A.x;* ed I. Gollancz 1923 (EETS) (facs).
Kottler, B. and A. M. Markman. Concordance to five Middle English poems. Pittsburgh 1966.

§1

Ed R. Morris 1864, 1869, 1897 (both rev); ed J. R. R. Tolkien and E. V. Gordon, Oxford 1925, rev N. Davis 1967; ed I. Gollancz, M. Day and M. S. Serjeantson 1938 (EETS); ed A. C. Cawley 1962 (EL) (with Pearl); ed R. A. Waldron 1970 (York Medieval Texts).
Also in Madden and Ford; selections in Sisam and Mossé; modern versions by E. J. B. Kirtlan 1912; K. Hare 1918, 1948 (rev); S. O. Andrew, New York 1929; G. H. Gerould, New York 1929; M. R. Ridley, Leicester 1944; E. Pons, Paris 1946 (French); G. Jones 1953; J. L. Rosenberg, New York 1959; B. Stone 1959; J. Gardner, Chicago 1965; M. Borroff 1968.

§2

For minor textual notes see Severs 239–41. There are important textual notes by C. T. Onions, N & Q March–April 1924; E. M. Wright, JEGP 34–5 1935–6, 38 1939; C. A. Luttrell, Neophilologus 39–40 1955–6, N & Q Dec 1962.

Language and Versification

Rosenthal, F. Die alliterierende englische Langzeile im 14 Jahrhundert. Anglia 1 1878.
Knigge, F. Die Sprache des Dichters von Sir Gawain. Marburg 1885.
Fuhrmann, J. Die alliterierenden Sprachformeln. Kiel 1886.
Luick, K. Die englische Stabreimzeile im 14, 15 und 16 Jahrhundert. Anglia 11 1888.
Kuhnke, B. Die alliterierende Langzeile. Königsberg 1899.
Kaluza, M. Studien zum germanischen Alliterationsvers. Berlin 1900.
Fischer, J. Die stabende Langzeile in den Werken des Gawaindichters. Bonner Beiträge 11 1901.
Fischer, J. and F. Mennicken. Zur mittelenglischen Stabzeile. Ibid.
Kullnick, M. Studien über den Wortschatz in Sir Gawayne. Berlin 1902.
Thomas, J. Die alliterierende Langzeile des Gawayn-dichters. Jena 1908.
Schmittbetz, K. Das Adjektiv in Sir Gawayn. Anglia 32 1909.
Schumacher, K. Studien über den Stabreim in der mittelenglischen Alliterationsdichtung. Bonner Studien 11 1914.
Brink, A. Stab und Wort im Gawain. Halle 1920.
Oakden, J. P. Alliterative poetry in Middle English. 2 vols Manchester 1930–5.
Day, M. Strophic division in Middle English alliterative verse. E Studien 66 1931.
Koziol, H. Grundzüge der Syntax der mittelenglischen Stabreimdichtungen. Wiener Beiträge 58 1932.
Hulbert, J. R. Quatrains in Middle English alliterative poems. MP 48 1950.
Clark, J. W. Paraphrases for God in the Gawain-poet. MLN 65 1950.
— The Gawain-poet and the substantival adjective. JEGP 49 1950.
— On certain alliterative and poetic words in the Gawain-poet. MLQ 12 1951.
Waldron, R. A. Oral-formulaic technique and alliterative poetry. Speculum 32 1957.

Schiller, A. The Gawain rhythm. Lang & Style 1 1968.
Blake, N. F. Rhythmical alliteration. MP 67 1970.

Dialect and Authorship

Neilson, G. Huchown of the Awle Ryale. Glasgow 1900.
Brown, J. T. T. Huchown of the Awle Ryale. Glasgow 1902.
Reicke, C. Untersuchungen über den Stil der mittelenglischen Gedichte Morte Arthur, the Destruction of Troy, the Wars of Alexander, the Siege of Jerusalem, Sir Gawain. Königsberg 1906.
Hulbert, J. R. The West Midland of the Romances. MP 19 1921.
— A hypothesis concerning the alliterative revival. MP 28 1930.
Menner, R. J. Sir Gawain and the West Midland. PMLA 37 1922.
— Four notes on the West Midland dialect. MLN 41 1926.
Serjeantson, M. S. The dialects of the West Midlands in Middle English. RES 3 1927.
Andrew, S. O. Huchown's works. RES 5 1928.
Koziol, H. Zur Frage der Verfasserschaft einiges mittelenglischen Stabreimdichtungen. E Studien 67 1932.
Greg, W. W. The continuity of the alliterative tradition. MLR 27 1932.
Oakden, J. P. The continuity of the alliterative tradition. MLR 28 1933.
Clark, J. W. Observations on certain differences in vocabulary between Cleanness and Sir Gawain. PQ 28 1949.
Everett, D. The alliterative revival. In her Essays on Middle English literature, Oxford 1955.
Salter, E. The alliterative revival. MP 64 1967.
Blake, N. F. Chaucer and the alliterative romances. Chaucer Rev 3 1969.
Moorman, C. The origins of the alliterative revival. Southern Quart 7 1969.
Shepherd, G. T. The nature of alliterative poetry in late medieval England. Proc Br Acad 56 1970.
See also Pearl, Patience, Cleanness, col 549, below.

Interpretative Studies etc

Thomas, M. C. Sir Gawayne and the Green Knight. Zürich 1883.
Bruce, J. D. The breaking of the deer. E Studien 32 1903.
Jackson, I. Sir Gawain as a Garter poem. Anglia 37 1913.
Kittredge, G. L. Gawain and the Green Knight. Cambridge Mass 1916.
Hulbert, J. R. The name of the Grene Knight. In J. M. Manly anniversary studies, Chicago 1923.
von Schaubert, E. Der englische Ursprung von Syr Gawayn. E Studien 57 1923.
Förster, M. Name des Green Knight. Archiv 147 1924.
Garrett, R. M. The lay of Sir Gawayne. JEGP 24 1925.
Loomis, R. S. Gawain, Gwri and Cuchulainn. PMLA 43 1928.
— More Celtic elements in Gawain. JEGP 42 1943.
Savage, H. L. Significance of hunting-scenes. JEGP 27 1928.
— Notes. MLN 46 1931, PMLA 46 1931, 49 1934, MLN 49 1934, MÆ 4 1935, MLN 52 1937, 55 1940, 58 1943, 60 1945, JEGP 47 1948.
— Sir Gawain and the Order of the Garter. ELH 5 1938.
— Enguerrand de Coucy VII and the campaign of Nicopolis. Speculum 14 1939.
— Historical background of Gawain. Year Book of Amer Philosophical Soc 1939.
— The Green Knight's Molaynes. In Philologica: the [Kemp] Malone anniversary studies, Baltimore 1949.
— Hunting terms in Middle English. MLN 66 1951.
— The feast of fools in Gawain. JEGP 51 1952.
— The Gawain-poet: studies in his personality and background. Chapel Hill 1956.

Plessow, G. L. Gotische Tektonik im Wortkunstwerk. Munich 1931.

Buchanan, A. The Irish framework. PMLA 47 1932.

Gerould, G. H. Beowulf and Sir Gawain. New York 1934.

—— The Gawain-poet and Dante: a conjecture. PMLA 51 1936.

Nitze, W. A. Is the Green Knight story a vegetation myth? MP 33 1936.

Magoun, F. P. Sir Gawain and medieval football. E Studies 19 1937.

Colgrave, B. Sir Gawayne's Green Chapel. Antiquity 12 1938.

Krappe, A. H. Who was the Green Knight? Speculum 13 1938.

Löhmann, O. Die Sage von Gawain. Königsberg 1938.

Obrecht, D. Le thème et la langue de la chasse dans Gawain. Bulletin de la Faculté des Lettres de Strasbourg 17 1938.

Vogel, H. Etude du personnage de Gauvain. Ibid 18 1939.

Robbins, R. H. A Gawain Epigone. MLN 58 1943.

Coomaraswamy, A. K. Gawain: Indra and Namuci. Speculum 19 1944.

Chapman, C. O. Virgil and the Gawain-poet. PMLA 60 1945.

—— Chaucer and the Gawain-poet: a conjecture. MLN 68 1953.

Hill, L. L. Madden's divisions of Sir Gawain and the large initial capitals of Cotton Nero A.x. Speculum 21 1946.

Smith, R. M. Guinganbresil and the Green Knight. JEGP 45 1946.

Brewer, D. S. Gawain and the Green Chapel. N & Q 10 Jan 1948. Reply by R. T. Davies 1 May 1948.

—— Courtesy and the Gawain-poet. In Patterns of love and courtesy: essays in memory of C. S. Lewis, 1966.

—— The Gawain-poet: a general appreciation of four poems. EC 17 1967. Reply by A. Samson 18 1968.

Dowden, P. J. Sir Gawayne and the Green Knight. MLR 64 1949.

Eagan, J. F. The import of color symbolism in Sir Gawayn. St Louis Univ Stud ser A 1 1949.

Watson, M. R. The chronology of Gawain. MLN 64 1949.

Baughan, D. E. The role of Morgan le Fay in Gawain. ELH 17 1950.

Ong, W. J. The Green Knight's harts and bucks. MLN 65 1950.

Speirs, J. Sir Gawain and the Green Knight. Scrutiny 16–17 1949–50. Replies by J. Bayley, Speirs and Q. D. Leavis, ibid.

Braddy, H. Sir Gawain and Ralph Holmes the Green Knight. MLN 67 1952.

Cutler, J. L. The versification of the Gawain epigone in Humfrey Newton's poems. JEGP 51 1952.

Highfield, J. R. L. The Green Squire. MÆ 22 1953.

Berry, F. Sir Gawayne and the Green Knight. In The age of Chaucer, ed B. Ford 1954 (Pelican).

Everett, D. The alliterative revival. In her Essays on Middle English literature, Oxford 1955.

Clark, C. The Green Knight Shoeless: a reconsideration. RES new ser 6 1955.

—— Sir Gawain: characterization by syntax. EC 16 1966.

—— Sir Gawain: its artistry and its audience. MÆ 40 1971.

Pearsall, D. A. Rhetorical 'descriptio' in Gawain. MLR 50 1955.

Engelhardt, G. J. The predicament of Gawain. MLQ 16 1955.

Moorman, C. Myth and medieval literature: Sir Gawain. Mediaeval Stud 18 1956.

—— The Pearl-poet. New York 1968.

Markman, A. M. The meaning of Sir Gawain and the Green Knight. PMLA 72 1957.

Ackerman, R. W. Gawain's shield: penitential doctrine. Anglia 76 1958.

—— Sir Gawain and its interpreters. In On stage and off: essays for E. L. Avery, Pullman 1968.

Ebbs, J. D. Stylistic mannerisms of the Gawain-poet. JEGP 57 1958.

Renoir, A. Descriptive technique in Gawain. Orbis Litterarum 13 1958.

—— An echo to the sense: the patterns of sound in Gawain. Eng Miscellany (Rome) 13 1962.

Burrow, J. The two confession scenes in Gawain. MP 57 1959.

—— A reading of Sir Gawain and the Green Knight. 1965.

—— In his Ricardian poetry, 1971.

Loomis, L. H. Sir Gawain and the Green Knight. In Arthurian literature in the Middle Ages, ed R. S. Loomis, Oxford 1959.

d'Ardenne, S. R. T. O. 'The Green Count' in Sir Gawain. RES new ser 10 1959.

Schnyder, H. Aspects of kingship in Sir Gawain. E Studies 40 1959.

—— Sir Gawain and the Green Knight: an essay in interpretation. Berne 1962.

Randall, D. B. J. Was the Green Knight a fiend? SP 57 1960.

Friedman, A. B. Morgan le Fay in Sir Gawain. Speculum 35 1960.

Bloomfield, M. W. Sir Gawain and the Green Knight: an appraisal. PMLA 76 1961.

Frankis, P. J. Sir Gawain, line 35: 'with lel letteres loken'. N & Q Sept 1961.

Kiteley, J. F. The De arte honeste amandi of Andreas Capellanus and the concept of courtesy in Gawain. Anglia 79 1961.

—— The knight who cared for his life. Anglia 80 1962.

Benson, L. D. The source of the beheading episode in Gawain. MP 59 1961.

—— Art and tradition in Sir Gawain. New Brunswick NJ 1965.

Borroff, M. Sir Gawain and the Green Knight: a stylistic and metrical study. New Haven 1962.

Green, R. H. Gawain's shield and the quest for perfection. ELH 29 1962.

Carson, A. Morgain la Fée as the principle of unity in Sir Gawain. MLQ 23 1962.

—— The Green Chapel: its meaning and function. SP 60 1963.

—— The Green Knight's name. Eng Lang Notes 1 1963.

Solomon, J. The lesson of Sir Gawain. Papers of Michigan Acad 48 1963.

Cook, R. G. The play-element in Sir Gawain. SE 13 1963.

Smithers, G. V. What Sir Gawain is about. MÆ 32 1963.

Hills, D. F. Gawain's fault. RES new ser 14 1963. Reply by J. Burrow 15 1964.

Bowers, R. H. Gawain as entertainment. MLQ 24 1963.

Silverstein, T. The art of Sir Gawain. UTQ 33 1964.

—— Sir Gawain, Dear Brutus etc: a study in comedy and convention. MP 62 1965.

Dodgson, J. M. Sir Gawain's arrival in Wirral. In Early English and Norse studies presented to Hugh Smith, 1963.

Howard, D. R. Structure and symmetry in Sir Gawain. Speculum 39 1964.

—— The three temptations: medieval man in search of the world. Princeton 1966.

Spearing, A. C. Criticism and medieval poetry. 1964.

—— Patience and the Gawain-poet. Anglia 84 1966.

—— The Gawain-poet: a critical study. Cambridge 1971.

Manning, S. A psychological interpretation of Sir Gawain. Criticism 6 1964.

Malarkey, S. and J. B. Toelken. Gawain and the green girdle. JEGP 63 1964.

White, R. B. A note on the Green Knight's red eyes. Eng Lang Notes 1 1965.

White, B. The Green Knight's classical forebears. Neuphilologische Mitteilungen 66 1965.

Moon, D. M. Clothing symbolism. Ibid.

—— The role of Morgan la Fee. Neuphilologische Mitteilungen 67 1966.

Mills, M. Christian significance and romance tradition in Sir Gawain. MLR 60 1965.

McAlindon, T. Magic, fate and providence in medieval narrative and Sir Gawain. RES new ser 16 1965.

Delany, P. The role of the guide in Sir Gawain. Neophilologus 49 1965.

Donner, M. Tact as a criterion of reality in Sir Gawain. Papers on Eng Lang & Lit 1 1965.

Broes, A. T. Sir Gawain: romance as comedy. Xavier Univ Stud 4 1965.

Nickel, G. Die Begleiterepisode in Sir Gawain. Germanisch-romanische Monatsschrift 15 1965.

Bercovitch, S. Romance and anti-romance in Sir Gawain. PQ 44 1965.

Levy, B. S. Gawain's spiritual journey: imitation of Christ in Sir Gawain. Annuale Mediaevale (Duquesne) 6 1965.

Blanch, R. J. (ed). Sir Gawain and Pearl: critical essays. 1966. Reprints.

Tuttleton, J. W. The ms divisions of Sir Gawain. Speculum 41 1966.

Scott, P. G. A note on the paper castle in Sir Gawain. N & Q April 1966.

Lass, R. Man's heaven: the symbolism of Gawain's shield. Mediaeval Stud 28 1966.

Salter, E. The alliterative revival. MP 64 1967.

Champion, L. S. Grace versus merit in Sir Gawain. MLQ 28 1967.

Shedd, G. M. Knight in tarnished armour: the meaning of Sir Gawain. MLR 62 1967.

Evans, W. W. Dramatic use of the second-person singular pronoun in Sir Gawain. Studia Neophilologica 39 1967.

Pace, G. B. Physiognomy in Sir Gawain. Eng Lang Notes 4 1967.

Johnston, E. C. The signification of the pronoun of address in Sir Gawain. Lang Quart 5 1967.

Newstead, H. Chaucer and his contemporaries: essays on medieval literature and thought. Greenwich Conn 1968.

Pierle, R. C. Sir Gawain: a study in moral complexity. Southern Quart 6 1968.

Lucas, P. J. Gawain's anti-feminism. N & Q Sept 1968.

Hieatt, A. K. Pentangle, luf-lace, numerical structure. Papers in Lang & Lit 4 1968.

Hussey, S. S. Sir Gawain and romance-writing. Studia Neophilologica 40 1968.

Mills, D. An analysis of the temptation scenes in Gawain. JEGP 67 1968.

—— The rhetorical function of Gawain's antifeminism? Neuphilologische Mitteilungen 71 1970.

Owen, D. D. R. Burlesque tradition and Gawain. Forum for Modern Lang Stud 4 1968.

Howard, D. R. and C. K. Zacher (ed). Critical studies of Sir Gawain. 1968. Reprints.

David, A. Gawain and Aeneas. E Studies 49 1968.

Eadie, J. Morgain la Fée and the conclusion of Sir Gawain. Neophilologus 52 1968.

Fox, D. (ed). 20th-century interpretations of Sir Gawain. Englewood Cliffs NJ 1968. Reprints.

Crane, J. K. The four levels of time in Sir Gawain. Annuale Mediaevale (Duquesne) 10 1969.

Gross, L. Telescoping in time in Sir Gawain. Orbis Litterarum 24 1969.

Halverson, J. Template criticism: Sir Gawain and the Green Knight. MP 67 1969.

Jones, E. T. The sound of laughter in Sir Gawain. Mediaeval Stud 31 1969.

Mertens-Fonck, P. Morgan, fée et déesse. In Mélanges offerts à R. Lejeune vol 2, Gembloux 1969.

Tamplin, R. The saints in Sir Gawain. Speculum 44 1969.

Taylor, P. B. Nature and ritual in Sir Gawain. E Studies 50 1969.

Carrière, J. L. Sir Gawain as a Christmas poem. Comitatus 1 1970.

Davis, N. Line 2073. N & Q May 1970.

Gallant, G. The three beasts: symbols of temptation in Sir Gawain. Annuale Mediaevale (Duquesne) 11 1970.

Tester, S. K. The use of the word 'lee' in Sir Gawain. Neophilologus 54 1970.

Thiébaux, M. Sir Gawain, the fox hunt and Henry of Lancaster. Neuphilologische Mitteilungen 71 1970.

Haines, V. Y. Morgan and the missing day in Sir Gawain. Mediaeval Stud 33 1971.

Hughes, D. W. The problem of reality in Sir Gawain. UTQ 40 1971.

Reichardt, P. A. A note on structural symmetry in Sir Gawain. Neuphilologische Mitteilungen 72 1971.

Shippey, T. A. The uses of chivalry: 'Erec' and 'Gawain'. MLR 66 1971.

(9) The Grene Knight

Index 1908. 528 lines in 6-line tail-rhyme stanza.
Ms: BM additional 27,879 (Percy Folio).

§ 1

Ed F. J. Child, English and Scottish popular ballads, Boston 1857.
Also in Madden, Hales and Furnivall.

§ 2

Hulbert, J. R. Syr Gawayn and the Grene Knight. MP 13 1915.

Kittredge, G. L. Gawain and the Green Knight. Cambridge Mass 1916.

Day, M. (ed). Sir Gawain and the Green Knight. 1938 (EETS). Introd.

(10) The Turke and Gowin

Index 1886. 337 lines in 6-line tail-rhyme stanza.
Ms: BM additional 27,879 (Percy Folio).

§ 1

In Madden, Hales and Furnivall.

§ 2

Hulbert, J. R. Syr Gawayn and the Grene Knight. MP 13 1915.

Kittredge, G. L. Gawain and the Green Knight. Cambridge Mass 1916.

Walpole, R. N. The Pelerinage de Charlemagne. Romance Philology 8 1954.

Simpson, J. Otherworld adventures in an Icelandic saga. Folklore 77 1966.

Lyle, E. B. The Turk and Gawain as a source of Thomas of Erceldoune. Forum for Modern Lang Stud 6 1970.

(11) Syre Gawane and the Carle of Carelyle

Index 1888. 660 lines in short couplet.
Ms: Nat Lib of Wales, Porkington 10.

§ 1

Ed R. W. Ackerman, Ann Arbor 1947; ed A. Kurvinen, Helsinki 1951.
Also in Madden, Sands.

§ 2

Hulbert, J. R. Syr Gawayn and the Grene Knyght. MP 13 1915.

Kittredge, G. L. Gawain and the Green Knight. Cambridge Mass 1916.

Kurvinen, A. Ms Porkington 10, description with abstracts. Neuphilologische Mitteilungen 54 1953.

Holthausen, F. Textual notes. Archiv 190 1954.

For the ballad of The Carle off Carlile, *see Madden, Hales and Furnivall, Kurvinen above, Severs 244.*

(12) The Awntyrs off Arthure at the Terne Wathelyne

Index 1566. 715 lines in 13-line alliterative stanza.
Mss: Bodley 21,898 (Douce 324); Lambeth 491; Lincoln Cathedral 91 (Thornton); Bibliotheca Bodmeriana, Geneva (formerly Ireland Blackburn).

§1

Ed J. Pinkerton, Scottish poems vol 3, 1792; ed D. Laing, Ancient popular poetry of Scotland, Edinburgh 1822, 1885, 1895 (both rev); ed J. Robson, Three early English metrical romances, 1842; ed F. J. Amours, Scottish alliterative poems, 1897 (STS); ed R. J. Gates, Philadelphia 1969.
Also in Madden.

§2

For dialect and authorship etc see under (8) Sir Gawain, above.
Lübke, H. The Aunters of Arthur. Berlin 1883.
Luick, K. Zur Metrik der mittelenglischen reimend-alliterierenden Dichtung. Anglia 12 1889.
Pilch, L. Umwandlung des altenglischen Alliterationsverses in den mittelenglischen Reimvers. Königsberg 1904.
Brown, L. Stanza-linking in English alliterative verse. Romanic Rev 7 1916. Also M. P. Medary, ibid.
Holthausen, F. Textual notes. Beiblatt zur Anglia 36 1925.
Dickins, B. The Ireland Ms. Leeds Stud in Eng 2–3 1933–4; TLS 21 Dec 1933 (reply to A. E. Schmidt).
Hooper, A. G. The Lambeth Palace ms. Leeds Stud in Eng 3 1934.
— The Awntyrs off Arthure: dialect and authorship. Leeds Stud in Eng 4 1935.
Webster, K. G. T. Galloway and the romances. MLN 55 1940.
Matthews, W. The tragedy of Arthur. Berkeley 1960.
Hanna, R. The Awntyrs off Arthure: an interpretation. MLQ 31 1970.

(13) Golagrus and Gawain

Index 1567. 1362 lines in 13-line alliterative stanza.
No ms extant. Print by Chepman and Myllar, Edinburgh 1508, Edinburgh 1827 (facs).

§1

Ed J. Pinkerton, Scottish poems vol 3, 1792; ed M. Trautmann, Anglia 2 1879; ed F. J. Amours, Scottish alliterative poems, 1897 (STS).
Also in Madden.

§2

For dialect and versification etc see also under (8) Sir Gawain and (12) The Awntyrs off Arthure, above.
Noltemeyer, O. Über die Sprache. Marburg 1889.
Neilson, G. History in Golagrus and Gawain. Proc Philosophical Soc of Glasgow 1902.
Holthausen, F. Textual notes. Beiblatt zur Anglia 36 1925.
Kettrick, P. J. The relation of Golagros and Gawaine to the Old French Perceval. Washington 1931.
Lascelles, M. M. Alexander and the Earthly Paradise in medieval English writings. MÆ 5 1936.
Craigie, W. The Scottish alliterative poems. Proc Br Acad 28 1942.
Matthews, W. The tragedy of Arthur. Berkeley 1960.

(14) The Avowynge of King Arthur, Sir Gawan, Sir Kaye, Sir Bawdewyn of Bretan

Index 1161. 1152 lines in 16-line tail-rhyme stanza.
Ms: Bibliotheca Bodmeriana, Geneva (formerly |Ireland Blackburn).

§1

Ed J. Robson, Three early English metrical romances, 1842; ed C. Brookhouse, Sir Amadace and the Avowing of Arthur, Copenhagen 1968.
Also edited in French and Hale.

§2

Greenlaw, E. The vows of Baldwin. PMLA 21 1906.
Bülbring, K. D. Untersuchungen zur Metrik. Studien zur Englischen Philologie 50 1913.
Luick, K. Zur Verslehre. Anglia 38–9 1914–15.
Reinhard, J. R. Some illustrations of the medieval Gab. Essays & Stud in Eng & Comparative Lit (Michigan) 8 1932.
For dialect, see under (8) Sir Gawain, above; for notes on the ms, under (12) The Awntyrs off Arthure, above.

(15) The Weddynge of Sir Gawen and Dame Ragnell

Index 1916. 853 lines in 6-line tail-rhyme stanza.
Ms: Bodley 11,951 (Rawlinson c. 86).

§1

Ed L. Sumner, Smith College Stud in Modern Langs 5 1924; rptd by B. J. Whiting, The wife of Bath's tale, in Sources and analogues of Chaucer's Canterbury tales, ed W. F. Bryan and G. Dempster, Chicago 1941.
Also edited in Madden, Sands; modern versions by G. B. Saul, New York 1934; J. R. Reinhard, Mediaeval pageant, New York 1939.

§2

Maynadier, G. The wife of Bath's tale. 1901.
Kittredge, G. L. Gawain and the Green Knight. Cambridge Mass 1916.
Whiting, B. J. The Wife of Bath's tale. Bryan and Dempster, above.
Coomaraswamy, A. K. On the Loathly bride. Speculum 20 1945.
For the ballad of The marriage of Sir Gawaine, see Ritson, Madden, Hales and Furnivall, Whiting above, Severs 247, and F. Görbing, Anglia 23 1900.

(16) The Jeaste of Syr Gawayne

*Index *13. 541 lines in 6-line tail-rhyme stanza.*
Ms: Bodley 21,835 (Douce 261); Harley 5927, Arts 32 (ptd fragment).

§1

In Madden.

§2

Bennett, R. E. The sources of the Jeaste of Syr Gawayne. JEGP 33 1934.
For the ballad of King Arthur and King Cornwall, see Severs 247–8.

(17) Ywain and Gawain

Index 259. 4032 lines in short couplet.
Ms: Cotton Galba E.ix.

§1

Ed G. Schleich, Leipzig 1887; ed A. B. Friedman and N. T. Harrington 1964 (EETS).
Also edited in Ritson, Stevick.

§2

Steinbach, G. P. Der Einfluss des Crestien de Trois auf die altenglische Literatur. Leipzig 1886.

Schleich, G. Verhältnis zu ihrer altfranzösischen Quelle. Berlin 1889. Reply by M. Kaluza, E Studien 15 1891.

Weston, J. L. Ywain and Gawain and Le Chevalier au Lion. MLQ 2–3 1899–1900.

Brown, A. C. L. Iwain: a study in the origins of Arthurian romance. Harvard Stud 8 1903.

— The Knight of the Lion. PMLA 20 1905.

Zenker, R. Ivainstudien. Halle 1921.

Brodeur, A. B. Grateful lion. PMLA 39 1924.

Chotzen, T. M. Le lion d'Owein et ses prototypes celtiques. Neophilologus 18 1933.

Hutchings, G. Gawain and the abduction of Guenevere. MÆ 4 1935.

Lindheim, B. von. Sprachliche Studien zu Texten des Ms Cotton Galba E.ix. Anglia 61 1937.

Lister, W. Textual notes. MLR 35 1940.

Brugger, E. Yvain and his lion. MP 38 1941.

Foerster, W. and T. Reid (ed). Chrétien de Troyes, Yvain. Manchester 1942.

Adler, A. Sovereignty in Chrétien's Yvain. PMLA 62 1947.

Loomis, R. S. Arthurian tradition and Chrétien de Troyes. New York 1949.

Harris, J. The role of the lion in Chrétien's Yvain. PMLA 64 1949.

Frappier, J. Le roman breton: Yvain ou le Chevalier au Lion. Paris 1952.

Nitze, W. A. Yvain and the myth of the fountain. Speculum 30 1955.

Reason, J. H. Structural style and originality of Chrestien's Yvain. Washington 1958.

Whitehead, F. Yvain's wooing. In Medieval miscellany presented to E. Vinaver, Manchester 1695.

Taglicht, J. Notes on the language of Ywain and Gawain. Stud in Eng Lang & Lit (Hebrew Univ) 17 1966.

— Notes. Neuphilologische Mitteilungen 71 1970.

Luria, M. The storm-making spring and the meaning of Chrétien's Yvain. SP 64 1967.

Cook, R. G. The ointment in Chrétien's Yvain. Mediaeval Stud 31 1969.

Finlayson, J. Ywain and Gawain and the meaning of Adventure. Anglia 87 1969.

Uitti, K. D. Chrétien's Yvain: fiction and sense. Romance Philology 22 1969.

Zaddy, Z. P. The structure of Chrétien's Yvain. MLR 65 1970.

Lacy, N. J. The organic structure of Yvain's expiation. Romanic Rev 61 1970.

Harrington, N. T. The problem of the lacunae in Ywain and Gawain. JEGP 69 1970.

Cornbellack, C. R. B. Yvain's guilt. SP 68 1971.

(18) Libeaus Desconus

Index 1690. 2250 lines in 12-line tail-rhyme stanza.
Mss: Bodley 6922 (Ashmole 61); Cotton Caligula A.ii; BM additional 27,879 (Percy Folio); Lambeth 306; Lincoln's Inn 150; Royal Lib Naples XIII B 29.

§1

Ed C. Hippeau, Le bel inconnu, Paris 1860; ed M. Kaluza, Leipzig 1890; ed M. Mills 1969 (EETS).
Also edited in Ritson, Hales and Furnivall; modern version by J. L. Weston 1902.

§2

See also (71) Sir Launfal, (82) Octavian.

Sarrazin, G. (ed). Octavian. Heilbronn 1885.

Mennung, A. Der Bel Inconnu des Renaut de Beaujeu in seinem Verhältnis zum Lybeaus Desconus, Carduino und Wigalois. Halle 1890.

Kaluza, M. Thomas Chestre, Verfasser des Launfal, Libeaus Desconus und Octavian. E Studien 18 1893.

Schofield, W. H. Studies on the Libeaus Desconus. Boston 1895.

Fischer, E. Der Lautbestand des Octavian, Lybeaus Desconus und Launfal. Heidelberg 1927.

Magoun, F. P. The source of Sir Thopas. PMLA 42 1927.

Williams, G. P. (ed). Renaud de Beaujeu, Le bel inconnu. Paris 1929.

Everett, D. The relation of Chestre's Launfal and Lybeaus Desconus. MÆ 7 1938.

Wilson, R. H. The Fair Unknown in Malory. PMLA 58 1943.

McHugh, S. J. The lay of the Big Fool: its Irish and Arthurian sources. MP 42 1945.

Loomis, R. S. From Segontium to Sinadon: the legends of a Cité Gaste. Speculum 22 1947.

Mills, M. Composition and style of the 'southern' Octavian, Sir Launfal and Libeaus Desconus. MÆ 31 1962.

— A mediaeval reviser at work. MÆ 32 1963.

— The huntsman and the dwarf in Erec and Libeaus Desconus. Romania 87 1966.

Schmidz, C. C. D. Sir Gareth of Orkney: Studien zum siebenten Buch von Malorys Morte Darthur. Groningen 1963.

Boiron, F. and J. C. Payen. Structure et sens du Bel Inconnu de Renaut de Beaujeu. Le Moyen Age 76 1970.

Sturm, S. The Bel Inconnu's enchantress and the intent of Renaut de Beaujeu. French Rev 44 1971.

— The love-interest in Le Bel Inconnu: innovation in the roman courtois. Forum for Modern Lang Stud 7 1971.

Perceval

See also under The Holy Grail, *below.*

Hertz, W. Die Sage vom Parzival und dem Gral. Breslau 1882.

— Die Sage vom Parzival. Stuttgart 1884.

Golther, W. Ursprung und Entwicklung der Sage vom Parzival. Bayreuther Blätter 7 1891.

— Parzival und der Gral in der Dichtung des Mittelalters. Stuttgart 1925.

Newell, W. W. The legend of the Holy Grail and the Perceval of Crestien of Troyes. Cambridge Mass 1902.

Weston, J. L. The legend of Sir Perceval. 2 vols 1906–9.

Woods, G. B. Reclassification of the Perceval romances. PMLA 27 1912.

Nitze, W. A. and T. A. Jenkins. Le haut livre du Graal: Perlesvaus. 2 vols Chicago 1932–7.

Weinberg, B. The magic chessboard in the Perlesvaus: an example of medieval literary borrowing. PMLA 50 1935.

Robinson, H. L. The sword of John the Baptist in the Perlesvaus. MLN 51 1936.

Carman, J. N. The relation of the Perlesvaus and the Queste del Saint Greal. Lawrence Kansas 1936.

— The symbolism of the Perlesvaus. PMLA 61 1946.

Williams, M. Notes on Perlesvaus. Speculum 14 1939.

Brugger, E. 'Der schöne Feigling' in der arthurischen Literatur. Zeitschrift für Romanische Philologie 61 1941, 63 1943, 65 1949, 67 1951.

Roach, W. Eucharistic tradition in the Perlesvaus. Zeitschrift für Romanische Philologie 59 1939.

— The Didot Perceval according to the mss of Modena and Paris. Philadelphia 1941.

— The continuations of the Perceval of Chrétien de Troyes. 3 vols Philadelphia 1949–55.

— Le roman de Perceval: ou le Conte du Graal. Geneva 1956, 1959 (rev).

— Transformations of the Grail theme in the first two continuations of the Old French Perceval. Proc Amer Philosophical Soc 110 1966.

Adolf, H. A historical background for Chrétien's Perceval. PMLA 63 1943.

— Studies in the Perlesvaus: the historical background. SP 42 1945.

— New light on Oriental sources for Wolfram's Parzival and other Grail romances. PMLA 62 1947.

Ham, E. B. Notes on the Didot Perceval. MLQ 5 1944.

Loomis, R. S. The combat at the ford in the Didot Perceval. MP 43 1945.

Newstead, H. Perceval's father and Welsh tradition. Romanic Rev 36 1945.

Brown, A. C. L. Irish fabulous history and Chrétien's Perceval. MLQ 8 1947.

Nitze, W. A. Perceval and the Holy Grail. Berkeley 1949.

Zeydel, E. H. (tr). Wolfram's Parzival. Chapel Hill 1951.

Thompson, A. W., O. Springer, P. le Gentil and W. A. Nitze. In Arthurian literature in the Middle Ages, ed R. S. Loomis, Oxford 1959. Chs 17–20.

Owen, D. D. R. The development of the Perceval story. Romania 80 1959.

Fowler, D. C. Prowess and charity in the Perceval of Chrétien. Washington 1959.

Haidu, P. Aesthetic distance in Chrétien: irony and comedy in Cliges and Perceval. Geneva 1968.

(19) Sir Perceval of Galles

Index 1853. 2288 lines in 16-line tail-rhyme stanza.
Ms: Lincoln Cathedral 91 (Thornton).

§1

Ed J. O. Halliwell (-Phillipps), The Thornton romances, 1844; ed F. S. Ellis 1895 (Kelmscott Press) (reprint of Halliwell); ed J. Campion and F. Holthausen, Heidelberg 1913.
Also edited in French and Hale.

§2

Steinbach, G. P. Über den Einfluss des Crestien de Trois auf die altenglische Literatur. Leipzig 1885.

Ellinger, J. Über die sprachlichen und metrischen Eigentümlichkeiten. Troppau 1889.

— Syntaktische Untersuchungen. Troppau 1893.

Golther, W. Chrestiens Conte del Graal in seinem Verhältnis zum englischen Sir Perceval. Sitzungsberichte der Münchener Akademie, philologische-historische Klasse 2 1890.

Strucks, C. Der junge Parzival in Wolfram's Parzival, Crestiens Conte del Gral, Sir Perceval und Carduino. Leipzig 1910.

Griffith, R. H. Sir Perceval of Galles. Chicago 1911.

Pace, R. B. Sir Perceval and the boyish exploits of Finn. PMLA 32 1917.

Brown, A. C. L. The Grail and the English Sir Perceval. MP 16–18 1918–20, 22 1924.

Finsterbusch, F. Der Versbau der Sir Perceval und Sir Degrevant. Vienna 1919.

McHugh, S. J. Sir Percyvelle: its Irish connections. Ann Arbor 1946.

Levy, R. The quest for biographical evidence in Perceval. Medievalia et Humanistica 6 1950.

The Holy Grail

See also under Perceval, above.

Birch-Hirschfeld, A. Die Sage vom Gral. Leipzig 1877.

Nutt, A. Studies on the legend of the Holy Grail. 1888.

— Legends of the Holy Grail. 1902.

Wechssler, E. Die Sage vom Heiligen Gral. Halle 1898.

Kempe, D. The legend of the Holy Grail. 1905 (EETS).

Peebles, R. The legend of Longinus. Bryn Mawr 1911.

Weston, J. L. The quest of the Holy Grail. 1913.

— From ritual to romance. Cambridge 1920.

Rosenberg, A. Longinus in England. Berlin 1917.

Nitze, W. A. On the chronology of the Grail romances. MP 17 1919; rptd in J. M. Manly anniversary studies, Chicago 1923.

— (ed). Robert de Boron, Le roman de l'Estoire dou Graal. Paris 1927.

— Who was the Fisher King: a note on Halieutics. Romanic Rev 33 1942.

— The home of Robert de Boron. MP 40 1942.

— What did Robert de Boron write? MP 41 1943.

— Count Philip's book and the Graal. MLN 59 1944.

— Spitzer's Grail etymology. Amer Jnl of Philology 66 1945.

— The waste land: a Celtic Arthurian theme. MP 43 1945.

— The Fisher King and the Grail in retrospect. Romance Philology 6 1952.

— The Siege Perilleux and the Lia Fail, or 'Stone of Destiny'. Speculum 31 1956.

Pauphilet, A. (ed). La queste del Saint Graal. Paris 1923.

— Au sujet du Graal. Romania 66 1941.

Golther, W. Parzival und der Gral in der Dichtung des Mittelalters. Stuttgart 1925.

Comfort, W. W. (tr). The quest of the Holy Grail. 1926.

Brown, A. C. L. The Irish element in King Arthur and the Grail. In Medieval studies in memory of G. S. Loomis, New York 1927.

— Another analogue to the Grail story. In Miscellany presented to L. E. Kastner, Cambridge 1932.

— The origin of the Grail legend. Cambridge Mass 1943.

Jaffray, R. King Arthur and the Holy Grail. 1928.

Lot-Borodine, M. Autour du Saint Graal. Romania 56–7 1930–1.

— Le symbolisme du Graal dans l'Estoire del Saint Graal. Neophilologus 34 1950.

Lot, F. Les auteurs du Conte de Graal. Romania 57 1931.

Morgan, M. L. Galahad in English literature. Washington 1932.

Waite, A. E. The Holy Grail: its legends and symbolism. 1933.

Loomis, R. S. The Irish origin of the Grail legend. Speculum 8 1933.

— From Segontium to Sinadon: legends of a Cité Gaste. Speculum 22 1947.

— Grail problems. Romanic Rev 45 1954.

— The Grail story of Chrétien as ritual and symbolism. PMLA 71 1956.

— The origin of the Grail legends. In Arthurian literature in the Middle Ages, ed R. S. Loomis, Oxford 1959.

— The Grail: from Celtic myth to Christian symbol. Cardiff and New York 1963.

Carman, J. N. The sword withdrawal in Robert de Boron's Merlin and the Queste del Saint Graal. PMLA 53 1938.

Burdach, K. Der Graal: Forschungen über seinen Ursprung und seinen Zusammenhang mit den Longinuslegende. Stuttgart 1938.

Krappe, A. H. The Fisher King. MLR 39 1944.

— The Grail messenger. PQ 26 1948.

Spitzer, L. The name of the Holy Grail. Amer Jnl of Philology 65 1944.

Swinscow, D. The Holy Grail: qui on en servoit? Folklore 55–6 1944–5.

Newstead, H. The Grail legend and Celtic tradition. New York 1945.

Adolf, H. Oriental sources for Grail romances. PMLA 62 1947.

— Studies in Chrétien's Conte del Graal. MLQ 8 1947.

— Studien zur Gralssaga. Archiv 188 1951.

— Visio Pacis: Holy City and Grail. University Park Pa 1960.

Holmes, U. T. A new interpretation of Chrétien's Conte del Graal. SP 44 1947.

Hatto, A. T. On Wulfram's conception of the Graal. MLR 43 1948.

Marx, J. La légende arthurienne et le Graal. Paris 1952.

— Sur l'origine du Graal. Le Moyen Age 63 1957.

— Origines et développement de la légende du Graal. Paris 1965.

Emmel, H. Formprobleme des Artusromans und der Graldichtung. Berne 1952.

Tucker, P. E. The place of the quest of the Holy Grail in Malory. MLR 48 1953.

Frappier, J. Le Graal et la chevalerie, Romania 75 1954.
— Sur la composition du Conte du Graal. Le Moyen Age 64 1958; Romania 81 1960.
— Le Conte du Graal est-il une allégorie judéo-chrétienne? Romance Philology 16 1963, 20 1966.
— Le Graal et ses feux divergents. Romance Philology 24 1971.

Hofer, S. Les romans du Graal dans la littérature des xiie et xiiie siècles. Colloques Internationaux du Centre National de la Recherche Scientifique 3 1956.

Barb, A. A. Mensa Sacra: the Round Table and the Holy Grail. Jnl Warburg & Courtauld Inst 19 1956.

Köhler, E. Ideal und Wirklichkeit in der höfischen Epik: Studien zur Form der frühen Artus- und Graldichtung. Tübingen 1956.

Séchelles, D. de. L'évolution et la transformation du mythe arthurien dans le thème du Graal. Romania 78 1957.

Holmes, U. T. and M. A. Klenke. Chrétien de Troyes and the Grail. Chapel Hill 1959.

Locke, F. W. The Quest for the Holy Grail: a literary study of a 13th-century French romance. Stanford 1960.

Riquer, M. de. Interpretación cristiana de li contes del Graal. In Miscelanea filológica dedicada à A. Griera vol 2, Barcelona 1960.

Olschki, L. Il castello del Re Pescatore e i soui misteri nel Conte del Graal di Chrétien di Troyes. Rome 1961; tr Manchester 1966.

Owen, D. D. R. The radiance in the Grail castle. Romania 83 1962.
— From Grail to Holy Grail. Romania 89 1968.
— The evolution of the Grail legend. Edinburgh 1968.

Whitehead, F. Lancelot's redemption. In Mélanges offerts à M. Delbouille, Gembloux 1964.

Bogdanow, F. The Romance of the Grail: a study of the structure and genesis of a 13th-century Arthurian prose romance. Manchester 1966.

Fourquet, J. Wolfram d'Eschenbach et le Conte del Graal. Paris 1966.

Fiore, S. Les origines orientales de la légende du Graal. Cahiers de Civilisation Médiévale 10 1967.

Pollmann, L. Chrétien und der Conte del Graal. Tübingen 1967.

Delbouille, M. Chrétien de Troyes et le Livre del Graal. Travaux de Linguistique et de Littérature (Strasbourg) 6 1968.

Micha, A. 'Matiere' et 'sen' dans l'Estoire dou Graal de Robert de Boron. Romania 89 1968.

O'Gorman, R. Ecclesiastical tradition and the Holy Grail. Australian Jnl of French Stud 1 1969.

Carman, J. N. The conquests of the Grail castle and Dolorous Guard. PMLA 85 1970.

(20) Joseph of Arimathie
*Index *49. 709 alliterative long lines.*
Ms: Bodley 3938 (Vernon ms).

§1
Ed W. W. Skeat 1871 (EETS).

§2
Robinson, J. A. Two Glastonbury legends, King Arthur and Joseph of Arimathea. New York 1926.

Gazay, J. Etudes sur les légendes de Sainte Marie-Madeleine et de Joseph d'Arimathie. Annales du Midi 51 1937.

Viscardi, A. Il Gral, Giuseppe d'Arimatea, l'abbazzia di Glastonbury e le origini cristiane della Britania. Cultura Neolatina 2 1941.

Roach, W. The Modena text of the prose Joseph d'Arimathie. Romance Philology 9 1956.

Marx, J. Le lai de Joseph d'Arimathie. Le Moyen Age 69 1963.

Barron, W. R. J. Joseph of Arimathie and the Estoire del Saint Graal. MÆ 33 1964.

O'Gorman, R. The legend of Joseph of Arimathea and the Old French Huon de Bordeaux. Zeitschrift für Romanische Philologie 80 1964.
— The prose version of Robert de Boron's Joseph d'Arimathie. Romance Philology 23 1970.

Treharne, R. F. The Glastonbury legends: Joseph of Arimathea, the Holy Grail and King Arthur. 1967.

Carter, H. H. (ed). The Portuguese book of Joseph of Arimathea. Chapel Hill 1967.

Lagorio, V. M. The evolving legend of St Joseph of Glastonbury. Speculum 46 1971.

For dialect and authorship see under (8) Sir Gawain, above.

(21) Lovelich's History of the Holy Grail
*Index *29. 23,932 lines in short couplet.*
Ms: Corpus Christi Cambridge 80.

§1
Ed F. J. Furnivall 1861–3 (Roxburghe Club) (with French original); ed Furnivall and D. Kempe 1874–1905 (EETS).

§2
Bradley, H. Henry Lonelich the Skinner. Athenaeum 1 Nov 1902.

Skeat, W. W. The translator of the Graal. Athenaeum 22 Nov, 6 Dec 1902.

See also under (4) Lovelich's Merlin, above.

(22) The Lyfe of Joseph of Arimathia
Index 1778. 456 lines in 8-line stanza.
No ms. Print by Pynson 1520.

§1
Ed W. W. Skeat 1871 (EETS).

§2
Hucher, E. (ed). Le saint Graal: ou le Joseph d'Arimathie. 3 vols Le Mans 1875–8.

Weidner, G. (ed). Der Prosaroman von Joseph von Arimathea. Oppeln 1881.

See also under (20) Joseph of Arimathie, above.

For the short ptd prose lives of Joseph of Arimathea, A treatyse of Ioseph of Arimathy, 1511 (de Worde), De Sancto Joseph ab Arimathia, 1516 (Pynson), A praysing to Joseph, 1520 (Pynson), see Skeat above, Severs 253.

Tristram
Michel, F. (ed). Recueil des poèmes. 3 vols 1835–9.

Golther, W. Die Sage von Tristan und Isolde. Munich 1887.
— Tristan und Isolde in den Dichtungen des Mittelalters und der neuen Zeit. Leipzig 1907.

Bédier, J. (ed). Le roman de Tristan par Thomas. 2 vols Paris 1902–5.

Bossert, A. La légende chevaleresque de Tristan et Iseult. Paris 1902.

Muret, E. (ed). Le roman de Tristan par Béroul. Paris 1903, 1947 (rev).

Schoepperle, G. Tristan and Isolt: a study of sources. Frankfurt 1913.

Kelemina, J. Geschichte der Tristansage. Vienna 1923.

Ranke, F. Gottfried von Strassburgs Tristan und Isold. Munich 1925.
— Isoldes Gottesurteil. In Medieval studies in memory of G. S. Loomis, New York 1927.

Vinaver, E. Etudes sur le Tristan en prose. Paris 1925.

—— The love potion in the primitive Tristan romance. In Medieval studies in memory of G. S. Loomis, New York 1927.

—— The prose Tristan. In Arthurian literature in the Middle Ages, ed R. S. Loomis, Oxford 1959.

—— Le caractère de Dinadan dans le Tristan en prose. In Mélanges offerts à M. Delbouille, Gembloux 1964.

Lot-Borodine, M. Tristan et Lancelot. In Medieval studies in memory of G. S. Loomis, New York 1927.

Aitken, D. F. The voyage à l'aventure in the Tristan of Thomas. MLR 23 1928.

Loomis, R. S. (tr). The romance of Tristram by Thomas. New York 1931, 1951 (rev).

Remigereau, F. Tristan maître de vénerie dans la tradition anglaise et dans le roman de Tristan. Romania 58 1932.

Ehrentreich, A. Neue Variationen zum Tristanthema. E Studien 70 1936.

Ewert, A. The romance of Tristan by Béroul. Oxford 1939.

Küpper, H. Bibliographie zur Tristansage. Jena 1941.

Adams, R. D. A. A Tristan bibliography. Los Angeles 1943.

Frank, G. Marie de France and the Tristram legend. PMLA 63 1948.

Sharpe, R. C. Tristram of Lyonesse. New York 1949.

Newstead, H. Kaherdin and the enchanted pillow: an episode in the Tristan legend. PMLA 65 1950.

—— The tryst beneath the tree: an episode in the Tristan legend. Romance Philology 9 1955.

—— King Mark of Cornwall. Romance Philology 11 1958.

—— The origin and growth of the Tristan legend. In Arthurian literature in the Middle Ages, ed R. S. Loomis, Oxford 1959.

—— The Enfances of Tristan and English tradition. In Studies in medieval literature in honor of A. C. Baugh, Philadelphia 1961.

—— Isolt of the White Hands and Tristan's marriage. Romance Philology 19 1965.

—— The harp and the rote: an episode in the Tristan legend. Romance Philology 22 1969.

—— The equivocal oath in Tristan legend. In Mélanges offerts à R. Lejeune vol 2, Gembloux 1969.

Panvini, B. La leggenda di Tristano e Isotta. Florence 1951.

Bivar, A. D. H. Lyonnesse: the evolution of a fable. MP 50 1953.

Denomy, A. J. Tristan and Morholt: David and Goliath. Mediaeval Stud 18 1956.

Fisher, J. H. Tristan and courtly adultery. Comparative Lit 9 1957.

Whitehead, F. The early Tristan poems. In Arthurian literature in the Middle Ages, ed R. S. Loomis, Oxford 1959.

Wind, B. (ed). Les fragments du roman de Tristan. Geneva and Paris 1960.

—— Les versions françaises du Tristan et les influences contemporaines. Neophilologus 45 1961.

Hatto, A. T. (tr). Gottfried von Strassburg's Tristan. 1960 (Penguin).

Lejeune, R. Les influences contemporaines dans les romans français de Tristan au xiie siècle. Le Moyen Age 66 1960.

Delbouille, M. Le premier roman de Tristan. Cahiers de Civilisation Médiévale 5 1962.

Frappier, J. Structure et sens du Tristan: version commune, version courtoise. Cahiers de Civilisation Médiévale 6 1963.

Nichols, S. G. Ethical criticism and medieval literature. In Medieval secular literature, ed W. Matthews, Berkeley 1965.

Stone, D. (tr). Tristan et Iseut. Englewood Cliffs NJ 1966.

Caulkins, J. H. and G. R. Mermier (tr). The Tristan and Iseult of Béroul. Paris 1967.

Fedrick, A. The account of Tristan's birth and childhood in the French prose Tristan. Romania 89 1968.

Blanch, R. J. The history and progress of the Tristan legend: Drust to Malory. Revue des Langues Vivantes 35 1969.

Bogdanow, F. Sur la composition du roman en prose de Tristan. In Mélanges offerts à R. Lejeune vol 2, Gembloux 1969.

Brault, G. J. Le Coffret de Vaunes et la légende de Tristan au xiie siècle. Ibid.

Curtis, R. L. Tristan studies. Munich 1969.

Eisner, S. The Tristan legend: a study in sources. Evanston 1969.

Legge, M. D. Place-names and the date of Béroul. MÆ 38 1969.

Noble, P. L'influence de la courtoisie sur le Tristan de Béroul. Le Moyen Age 75 1969.

York, E. C. Isolt's ordeal: English legal customs in the medieval Tristan legend. SP 68 1971.

(23) Sir Tristrem

Index 1382. 3344 lines in 11-line stanza.
Ms: Nat Lib of Scotland 19.2.1 (Auchinleck).

§1

Ed W. Scott, Edinburgh 1804; ed E. Kölbing 2 vols Heilbronn 1878–82 (with Norse version); ed G. P. McNeill 1886 (STS).

§2

Skeat, W. W. The romance of Sir Tristrem. Scottish Historical Rev 6 1908.

Henderson, T. F. Scottish vernacular literature. Edinburgh 1910.

Holthausen, F. Textual notes. Anglia 39 1915, 58 1934; Beiblatt zur Anglia 39 1928.

Medary, M. P. Stanza-linking. Romanic Rev 7 1916.

Vogel, B. The dialect of Sir Tristrem. JEGP 40 1941.

—— Wortgeographische Belege und Sir Tristrem. JEGP 41 1942.

Smith, R. M. Gernemuþe and the benighted geography of the minstrels. MLN 64 1949.

Rumble, T. C. The Middle English Sir Tristrem: toward a reappraisal. Comparative Lit 11 1959.

(3) CHARLEMAGNE ROMANCES: THE MATTER OF FRANCE

General Studies

Gautier, L. Les épopées françaises. 4 vols Paris 1878–92.

—— Bibliographie des chansons de geste. Paris 1897.

Lee, S. The Charlemagne romances in France and England. 1882 (EETS).

Lot, F. Etudes sur les légendes épiques françaises. Romania 27 1898, 52–4 1926–8, 66 1940–1, 70 1948–9. Collected with introd by R. Bossuat, Paris 1958. Reply by E. Healey, SP 36 1939.

Weston, J. L. The romance cycle of Charlemagne. 1901.

Paris, G. Histoire poétique de Charlemagne. Paris 1905.

Ker, W. P. Epic and romance. 1908.

Bédier, J. Les légendes épiques. 4 vols Paris 1909–13.

Bullfinch, T. (tr). Legends of Charlemagne. 1911 (EL).

Kirchhoff, J. Zur Geschichte der Karlssage in der englischen Literatur. Marburg 1913.

Smyser, H. M. The engulfed Lucerna of the Pseudo-Turpin. Harvard Stud 15 1933.

—— (ed). The Pseudo-Turpin. Cambridge Mass 1937.

—— The Middle English and Old Norse story of Olive. PMLA 56 1941.

—— Olive again. MLN 61 1946.

Thoron, W. (ed). Chronicle of the Pseudo-Turpin. Boston 1934.

Lehmann, P. Das literarische Bild Karls des Grossen, vornehmlich im lateinischen Schriftum des Mittelalters. Sitzungsberichte der Bayerischen Akademie der Wissenschaft, philologisch-historische Abteilung 1935-6.

Meredith-Jones, C. (ed). Historia Karoli Magni et Rotholandi ou Chronique du Pseudo-Turpin. Paris 1936. Note by R. N. Walpole, Speculum 22 1947.

— The conventional Saracen of the songs of geste. Speculum 17 1942.

Larsen, H. Olive and Landres. JEGP 40 1941.

Lambert, E. Pseudo-Turpin et le Pèlerinage de Compostelle. Romania 69 1947.

Walpole, R. N. Philip Mouskés and the Pseudo-Turpin Chronicle. Berkeley 1948.

— The Pèlerinage de Charlemagne: poem, legend and problem. Romance Philology 8 1955.

— Sur la chronique du Pseudo-Turpin. Travaux de Linguistique et de Littérature (Strasbourg) 3 1965.

Crosland, J. The Old French epic. Oxford 1951.

Siciliano, I. Les origines des chansons de geste. Paris 1951.

— Les chansons de geste et l'épopée. Turin 1968.

Loomis, L. H. The Athelstan gift-story: its influence on English chronicles and Carolingian romances. PMLA 67 1952.

Burger, A. Sur les relations de la chanson de Roland avec le récit du faux Turpin et celui du Guide du Pèlerin. Romania 73 1952.

Rychner, J. Les chansons de geste. Geneva 1955, 1968 (rev).

Holmes, U. T. The post-Bédier theories on the origins of the chansons de geste. Speculum 30 1955.

Riquer, M. de. Les chansons de geste françaises. Paris 1957.

Tonguç, S. The Saracens in the Middle English Charlemagne romances. Litera 5 1958.

Menéndez Pidal, R. La Chanson de Roland et la tradition épique des Francs. Paris 1960.

de Mandach, A. Naissance et développement de la chanson de geste en Europe. Geneva 1961.

McMillan, D., E. von Richthofen and J. Wathelet-Willem. In Mélanges offerts à M. Delbouille, Gembloux 1964.

le Gentil, P. Le traditionalisme et l'étude des chansons de geste. La Revue Nouvelle 42 1965.

Aebischer, P. Rolandiana et Oliveriana: recueil d'études sur les chansons de geste. Geneva 1967.

White, B. Saracens and Crusaders: from fact to allegory. In Medieval literature and civilisation: studies in memory of G. N. Garmonsway, 1969.

van Emden, W. G. 'La bataille est aduree endementres': traditionalism and individualism in chanson de geste studies. Nottingham Medieval Stud 13 1969.

Short, I. The Pseudo-Turpin chronicle: some unnoticed versions and their sources. MÆ 38 1969.

The Firumbras Group

Kroeber, A. and G. Servois (ed). Fierabras. Paris 1860.

Gröber, G. Die handschriftlichen Gestaltungen der chanson de geste Fierabras. Leipzig 1869.

Bédier, J. La composition de Fierabras. Romania 17 1888.

Jarnik, H. Studien über Fierebrasdichtungen. Halle 1903.

Smyser, H. M. A new ms of the Destruction de Rome and Fierabras. Harvard Stud 14 1932.

Brandin, L. La destruction de Rome et Fierabras. Romania 64 1938.

Mehnert, R. Neue Beitrage zum Handschriftenverhältnis der Fierabras. Göttingen 1938.

— Alte und neue Fierabras-Fragen. Zeitschrift für Romanische Philologie 60 1940.

Adler, A. Thematic development of Oliver's duel with Fierabras. Romanische Forschungen 70 1958.

(24) The Ashmole Firumbras

*Index *23. 7130 lines in long couplet and 6-line tail-rhyme stanza.*
Ms: Bodley 25,166 (Ashmole 33).

§ 1

Ed S. J. Herrtage 1879 (EETS).

§ 2

Carstens, B. H. Zur Dialektbestimmung. Kiel 1884.

Hausknecht, E. Textual notes. Anglia 7 1884.

Reichel, C. Sir Fyrumbras und ihr Verhältnis zum altfranzösischen und provenzalischen Fierabras. Breslau 1892.

— Textual notes. E Studien 18 1900.

Fischer, W. Das Verhältnis des ersten Entwurfs [lines 331–759] zur Reinschrift. Archiv 142 1921.

(25) The Fillingham Firumbras

*Index *33. 1842 lines in short couplet.*
Ms: BM additional 37,492 (Fillingham).

§ 1

Ed M. I. O'Sullivan 1935 (EETS).

§ 2

O'Sullivan, M. I. Study of the Fillingham text of Firumbras and Otuel and Roland. Bryn Mawr 1927.

(26) The Sowdone of Babylone

Index 950. 3274 lines in quatrains.
Ms: Garrett (Baltimore) 140, on deposit at Princeton.

§ 1

Ed anon 1854 (Roxburghe Club); ed E. Hausknecht 1881 (EETS).
Selections in French and Hale.

§ 2

Hausknecht, E. Über Sprache und Quelle. Berlin 1879.

Holthausen, F. Textual notes. Anglia 15 1893.

Smyser, H. M. The Sowdon of Babylon and its author. Harvard Stud 13 1931.

(27) Charles the Grete

Prose. Print by Caxton 1485.

§ 1

Ed S. J. Herrtage 2 vols 1880-1 (EETS).

§ 2

Doutrepont, G. Les mises en prose des épopées et des romans chevaleresques du 14e au 16e siècles. Brussels 1939.

The Otuel Group

Guessard, G. and H. Michelant (ed). Otinel. Paris 1859.

Treutler, H. Die Otinelsage. E Studien 5 1882.

Rajna, P. Contributi alla storia dell' epopea. Romania 18 1889.

Loomis, L. H. The Auchinleck ms and a possible London bookshop of 1330–40. PMLA 57 1942.

Walpole, R. N. Charlemagne and Roland: a study of the source of two Middle English metrical romances, Roland and Vernagu and Otuel and Roland. Univ of California Pbns in Modern Philology 26 1944.

— The source ms of Charlemagne and Roland and the Auchinleck bookshop. MLN 60 1945.

Smyser, H. M. Charlemagne and Roland and the Auchinleck ms. Speculum 21 1946.

Aebischer, P. Etudes sur Otinel. Berne 1960.

Weiss, J. The Auchinleck ms and the Edwardes mss. N & Q Dec 1969.

(28) The Auchinleck Otuel

Index 1103. 1738 lines in short couplet.
Ms: Nat Lib of Scotland 19.2.1 (Auchinleck).

§ I

Ed A. Nicholson, Edinburgh 1836 (Abbotsford Club); ed S. J. Herrtage 1882 (EETS).

§ 2

Wächter, W. Untersuchungen über Roland and Vernagu und Otuel. Berlin 1885.

Holthausen, F. Textual notes. Anglia 21 1889.

Gragger, J. Zur mittelenglischen 'Sir Otuel' Dichtung. Graz 1896.

Koeppel, E. Eine historische Anspielung in Otuel. Archiv 107 1901.

O'Sullivan, M. I. (ed). Firumbras and Otuel and Roland. 1935 (EETS). Introd.

(29) The Fillingham Otuel and Roland

Index 1106. 2786 lines in 12-line tail-rhyme stanza.
Ms: BM additional 37,492 (Fillingham).

§ I

Ed M. I. O'Sullivan 1935 (EETS).

§ 2

O'Sullivan M. I. Study of the Fillingham text of Firumbras and Otuel and Roland. Bryn Mawr 1927.

Walpole, R. N. Charlemagne and Roland: a study of the source of Roland and Vernagu and Otuel and Roland. Univ of California Pbns in Modern Philology 26 1944.

— Syr Bertram the Baner in Otuel and Roland. MLN 62 1947.

(30) Roland and Vernagu

*Index *28. 880 lines in 12-line tail-rhyme stanza.*
Ms: Nat Lib of Scotland 19.2.1 (Auchinleck).

§ I

Ed A. Nicholson, Edinburgh 1836 (Abbotsford Club); ed S. J. Herrtage 1882 (EETT).

§ 2

Wächter, W. Untersuchungen über Roland and Vernagu und Otuel. Berlin 1885.

Holthausen, F. Textual notes. Anglia 21 1889.

O'Sullivan, M. I. (ed). Fillingham Firumbras and Otuel and Roland. 1935 (EETS).

Walpole, R. N. Charlemagne and Roland; a study of the source of Roland and Vernagu and Otuel and Roland. Berkeley 1944.

— Stanzas 26 and 27 of Roland and Vernagu. MÆ 20 1951.

Loomis, L. H. The Auchinleck Roland and Vernagu and the Short Chronicle. MLN 60 1945.

(31) Duke Rowlande and Sir Ottuell

Index 1996. 1596 lines in 12-line tail-rhyme stanza.
Ms: BM additional 31,042 (Thornton).

§ I

Ed S. J. Herrtage 1880 (EETS).

§ 2

Engler, H. Quelle und Metrik. Königsberg 1901.

Holthausen, F. Textual Notes. Anglia 40 1916.

(32) The Sege of Melayne

Index 234. 1602 lines in 12-line tail-rhyme stanza.
Ms: BM additional 31,042 (Thornton).

§ I

Ed S. J. Herrtage 1880 (EETS).

§ 2

Kölbing, E. Textual notes. E Studien 5 1882.

Bülbring, K. D. Textual notes. E Studien 13 1889.

Dannenberg, B. Metrik und Sprache. Göttingen 1890.

Holthausen, F. Textual notes. Anglia 40 1916.

Other Charlemagne Romances

(33) The Song of Roland

*Index *35. 1049 lines in couplet-rhymed semi-alliterative verse.*
Ms: BM Lansdowne 388.

§ I

Ed S. J. Herrtage 1879 (EETS).

§ 2

Schleich, G. Prolegomena ad Carmen de Rolando Anglicanum. Burg 1879.

— Beiträge zum mittelenglischen Roland. Anglia 4 1881.

Wichmann, C. A. Das Abhängigkeitsverhältnis des altenglischen Roland zur altfranzösischen Dichtung. Münster 1889.

Holthausen, F. Textual notes. Anglia 51 1927.

Faral, E. La chanson de Roland: étude et analyse. Paris 1933.

Mortier, R. (ed). Les textes de la Chanson de Roland vol 1. Paris 1940. Introd.

Le Gentil, P. La Chanson de Roland. Paris 1955; tr Cambridge Mass 1969.

(34) The Taill of Rauf Coilyear

Index 1541. 975 lines in 13-line alliterative stanza.
No extant ms. Print by Robert Lekpreuik 1572.

§ I

Ed D. Laing, Select remains of the ancient popular poetry of Scotland, Edinburgh 1821, 1882, 1895 (both rev); ed S. J. Herrtage 1882 (EETS); ed M. Tonndorf, Berlin 1894; ed F. J. Amours, Scottish alliterative poems, 1892-7 (STS); ed W. H. Browne, Baltimore 1903.

Selections in W. H. Browne, Selections from early Scottish poets, *Baltimore 1896; modern version by B. J. Whiting as* Ralph the Collier, College Survey of English, *New York 1942.*

§ 2

Tonndorf, M. Rauf Coilyear. Halle 1893.

Henderson, T. F. Scottish vernacular literature. Edinburgh 1910.

Oakden, J. P. Alliterative poetry in Middle English. 2 vols Manchester 1930-5.

Smyser, H. M. The Taill of Rauf Coilyear and its sources. Harvard Stud 14 1932.
For versification see under (8) Sir Gawain, (12) The Awntyrs off Arthure, above.

(35) The Foure Sonnes of Aymon
Prose. No extant ms. Print by Caxton 1489–91.

§ 1

Ed O. Richardson 2 vols 1880–1 (EETS).
Modern version, abridged, by R. Steele as Renaud of Montauban, 1897.

§ 2

Castets, F. (ed). Les quatre fils Aymon. Revue des Langues Romanes 49–52 1908–12; Montpellier 1909.
Besch, E. Les adaptations en prose des chansons de geste au 15e et au 16e siècle. Revue du Seizième Siècle 3 1915.
Doutrepont, G. Les mises en prose des épopées. Brussels 1939.
See under Caxton, col 667, below.

(36) Huon of Burdeux
Prose (a trn by Lord Berners). No extant ms. Print by de Worde 1534.

§ 1

Ed S. Lee 4 vols 1882–7 (EETS).
Modern version by R. Steele, 1895.

§ 2

Besch, E. Les adaptations en prose des chansons de geste au 15e et au 16e siècle. Revue du Seizième Siècle 3 1915.
Ebert, W. Vergleich der beiden Versionen von Lord Berners Huon of Bordeaux. Halle 1917.
Krappe, A. H. Über die Quellen des Huon de Bordeaux. Zeitschrift für Romanische Philologie 54 1934.
Doutrepont, G. Les mises en prose des épopées. Brussels 1939.
Owen, D. D. R. The principal source of Huon de Bordeaux. French Stud 7 1953.
Ruelle, P. (ed). Huon de Bordeaux. Paris 1961.
Calin, W. The epic quest: studies in four Old French chansons de geste. Baltimore 1966.
See under Berners, col 678, below.

(4) THE MATTER OF ANTIQUITY

Alexander
Ausfeld, A. Die Orosius-Recension der Historia de preliis und Babiloths Alexanderchronik. Festschrift der Badischen Gymnasien 1886.
Meyer, P. Alexandre le Grand dans la littérature du Moyen Age. 2 vols Paris 1886.
Budge, E. A. W. History of Alexander the Great. Cambridge 1889.
—— The life and exploits of Alexander the Great. 1896.
Becker, H. Die Bramahnen in der Alexandersage. Leipzig 1889.
Herz, W. Aristoteles in den Alexanderdichtungen des Mittelalters. Munich 1889.
Pfister, F. Der Alexanderroman des Archipresbyters Leo. Heidelberg 1913.
—— Studien zum Alexanderroman. Würzburger Jahrbücher 1 1946.
—— Eine neue Handschrift des Alexanderromans des Archpresbyters Leo. Classica et Mediaevalia 21 1961.
Hilka, A. Der altfranzösische Prosa-Alexanderroman nebst dem lateinischen Original des Historia de preliis. Halle 1920.
Ogle, M. B. The perilous bridge and human automata. MLN 35 1920.
Müller, H. E. (ed). Die Werke des Pfaffen Lamprecht. Munich 1923.
Kroll, W. (ed). Historia Alexandri Magni (Pseudo-Callisthenes). Berlin 1926; tr H. E. Haight as The life of Alexander of Macedon, New York 1955.
Hamilton, G. L. A new redaction of the Historia de preliis and the date of redaction J³. Speculum 2 1927.
—— La légende d'Alexandre en Angleterre. In Mélanges offerts à M. A. Thomas, Paris 1927.
Magoun, F. P. (ed). Gests of King Alexander of Macedon. Cambridge Mass 1929.
—— The Harvard Epitome of the Historia de preliis, recension J². Harvard Stud 14 1932.
—— The Prague Epitome of the Historia de preliis, recension J². Harvard Stud 16 1934.
Hilka, A. and F. P. Magoun. A list of mss containing texts of the Historia de preliis. Speculum 9 1934.
Lascelles, M. M. Alexander and the Earthly Paradise in medieval English writings. MÆ 5 1936.
Armstrong, E. C. et al (ed). The medieval French Roman d'Alexandre. 5 vols Princeton 1937–55.

Thomson, S. H. An unnoticed abridgement of the Historia de preliis. Colorado Stud Ser B: Stud in Humanities 1 1939–41.
Maurer, F. (ed). Das Alexanderlied des Pfaffen Lamprecht. Leipzig 1940.
Ham, E. B. Branch 2 of the French Alexander. MP 42 1944.
Robinson, C. A. Alexander the Great. New York 1947.
—— The history of Alexander the Great. Brown Univ Stud 16 1953.
Tarn, W. W. Alexander the Great. 2 vols Cambridge 1948.
Merkelbach, R. Die Quellen des griechischen Alexander-Romans. Munich 1954.
Savill, A. F. Alexander the Great and his time. 1955.
Cary, G. The medieval Alexander. Cambridge 1956.
Matthews, W. The tragedy of Arthur. Berkeley 1960.
Ross, D. J. A. The J³ Historia de preliis and the Fuerre de Gadres. Classica et Mediaevalia 22 1961.
—— Alexander Historiatus: a guide to medieval illustrated Alexander literature. Warburg Inst Surveys 1 1963.
Michael, I. The treatment of classical material in the Libro de Alexandre. Manchester 1970.

(37) Kyng Alisaunder
Index 683. 8034 lines in short couplet.
Mss : Bodley 1414 (Laud miscellany 622); Lincoln's Inn 150; Nat Lib of Scotland 19.2.1 (Auchinleck) (fragment); Univ of St Andrews (2 fragments); Univ of London Lib 593 (fragment); BM (Bagford ballads) (6 ptd leaves).

§ 1

Ed J. W. Ebsworth, The Bagford ballads vol 1, 1878 (BM ptd fragment); ed G. V. Smithers 2 vols 1952–7 (EETS).
Also edited in Weber; selections in French and Hale, Bennett and Smithers.

§ 2

Bülbring, K. D. Vier neue Alexanderbruchstücke. E Studien 13 1889. Reply by G. L. Kittredge 14 1890.
Kölbing, E. Textual notes. E Studien 13 1899, 17 1892.
—— (ed). Arthour and Merlin. Leipzig 1890. Introd.
Searles, C. Boiardo's version of the Alexander-sagas. MLN 15 1900.

Hildenbrand, T. Die altfranzösische Roman de toute chevalerie und Kyng Alisaunder. Bonn 1911.

French, W. H. Dialects and forms in three romances. JEGP 45 1946.

Smithers, G. V. Two newly-discovered fragments from the Auchinleck ms in the library of the University of St Andrews. MÆ 18 1949.

— Another fragment of the Auchinleck ms. In Medieval literature and civilisation: studies in memory of G. N. Garmonsway, 1969.

(38) Alexander, fragment A

Index 4262. 1247 alliterative long lines.
Ms: Bodley 3832 (Greaves 60).

§ 1

Ed W. W. Skeat 1867 (EETS); ed F. P. Magoun, The Gests of King Alexander of Macedon, Cambridge Mass 1929.

§ 2

For language and versification, dialect and authorship, see (8) Sir Gawain, above.

(39) Alexander, fragment B (Alexander and Dindimus)

Index 4262. 1139 alliterative long lines.
Ms: Bodley 2464 (Bodley 264).

§ 1

Ed J. Stevenson 1849 (Roxburghe Club); ed W. W. Skeat 1878 (EETS); ed F. P. Magoun, The Gests of King Alexander of Macedon, Cambridge Mass 1929; ed M. R. James, Oxford 1933 (facs).

§ 2

For language and versification, dialect and authorship, see under (8) Sir Gawain, above.

(40) The Wars of Alexander

*Index *74. c. 5800 alliterative long lines.*
Mss: Bodley 6925 (Ashmole 44); Trinity College Dublin 213.

§ 1

Ed J. Stevenson 1849 (Roxburghe Club); ed W. W. Skeat 1886 (EETS).

§ 2

Bradley, H. The Gawain-poet and the Wars of Alexander. Academy 14 Jan 1888.

Hennemann, J. B. Untersuchungen über das Gedicht Wars of Alexander. Berlin 1889.

— Textual notes. MLN 5 1890.

Steffens, H. Versbau und Sprache. Bonner Beiträge 9 1901.

Hamilton, G. L. A new redaction of the Historia de preliis. Speculum 2 1927.

Andrew, S. O. The Wars of Alexander and the Destruction of Troy. RES 5 1929.

Lawrence, R. F. The formulaic theory and its application to English alliterative poetry. In Essays on style and language, ed R. Fowler 1966.

— Formula and rhythm in the Wars of Alexander. E Studies 51 1970.

For language and versification, dialect and authorship, see under (8) Sir Gawain, above.

(41) Alexander-Cassamus fragment

*Index *22. 566 lines in 8-line stanza (trn of vv. 1604–1977 of Les voeux du paon).*
Ms: Cambridge Univ Lib Ff.1.6.

§ 1

Ed K. Rosskopf, Munich 1911.

§ 2

Holthausen, F. Textual notes. E Studien 51 1917.

Seaton, E. Sir Richard Roos c. 1410–82: Lancastrian poet. 1961. Pp. 238–40.

(42) The Prose Alexander

Ms: Lincoln Cathedral 91 (Thornton).

§ 1

Ed J. S. Westlake 1913 (EETS).

§ 2

Halliwell (-Phillipps), J. O. The Thornton romances. 1844 (Camden Soc). Introd.

Hamilton, G. L. A new redaction of the Historia de preliis. Speculum 2 1927.

(43) The Scottish Alexander Buik

Index 3923. 14,442 lines in short couplet.
No extant ms. Print by Alexander Arbuthnet 1580.

§ 1

Ed D. Laing 1831 (Bannatyne Club) (rptd from Arbuthnet, above, with French); ed R. L. G. Ritchie 4 vols 1921–9 (STS).

§ 2

Hermann, A. Untersuchungen über das schottische Alexanderbuch. Berlin 1893.

Ham, E. B. Three neglected mss of Les voeux du paon. MLN 46 1931.

Whiting, B. J. Proverbs in relation to French source. Harvard Stud 15 1933.

Smith, J. M. French background of middle Scots literature. 1934.

(44) Gilbert Hay's Buik of King Alexander

*Index *55. c. 20,000 lines in couplet.*
Mss: BM additional 40,732 (formerly Taymouth castle); 41,063 (formerly Taymouth castle).

§ 1

Ed A. Hermann, The forraye of Gadderis, The vows: extracts from Sir Gilbert Hay's Buik of King Alexander, Ostern 1900.

§ 2

Hermann, A. The Taymouth ms. Berlin 1898.

Stevenson, J. H. Gilbert of the Haye's prose ms. 1901 (STS). Introd.

Ritchie, R. L. G. (ed). The buik of Alexander. 1925–9 (STS). Introd and notes.

Smith, J. M. The French background of middle Scots literature. 1934.

(45) The Dublin Epitome

Prose. Fragment of a copy of the Alexander section in a Caxton print (1477) of Earl Rivers's trn of The dicts and sayings of the philosophers.

§ 1

Ed W. W. Skeat, The wars of Alexander, 1886 (EETS) (introd); ed F. Pfister, Eine orientalische Alexander-geschichte in mittelenglischer Prosabearbeitung, E Studien 74 1940.

§2

Bühler, C. F. The dicts and sayings of the philosophers. 1941 (EETS). P. 358.

(46) Amoryus and Cleopes
See John Metham, below.

Troy
See also Chaucer, Troilus and Criseyde, col 562, below.

Körting, G. Dares und Dictys. Halle 1874.
Greif, W. D. Die mittelalterlichen Bearbeitungen der Trojanersage: ein neuer Beitrag zur Dares- und Dictys-frage. Marburg 1886.
Heeger, G. Über die Trojanersage der Britten. Munich 1886.
Taylor, H. O. The classical heritage of the Middle Ages. New York 1901.
Constans, L. (ed). Le roman de Troie par Benoît de Sainte-Maure. 6 vols 1904–12.
Griffin, N. E. Dares and Dictys: introduction to the study of the medieval versions. Baltimore 1907.
—— Un-Homeric elements in the medieval story of Troy. JEGP 7 1907–8.
—— (ed). Guido de columnis, Historia destructionis Troiae. Cambridge Mass 1936.
Tatlock, J. S. P. The siege of Troy in Elizabethan literature. PMLA 30 1915.
—— The legendary history of Britain. Berkeley 1950.
Curry, W. C. The judgment of Paris. MLN 31 1916.
Gordon, G. The Trojans in Britain. E & S 9 1923.
Root, R. K. (ed). Chaucer's Troilus and Criseyde. Princeton 1926. Introd.
Parsons, A. E. The Trojan legend in England. MLR 24 1929.
Sedgwick, W. B. The Bellum Troianum of Joseph of Exeter. Speculum 5 1930.
Atwood, E. B. The Rawlinson Excidium Troie. Speculum 9 1934.
—— The Excidium Troie and medieval Troy literature. MP 35 1937.
—— Robert Mannyng's version of the Troy story. SE 18 1938.
Oldfather, W. A. Notes on the Excidium Troie. Speculum 11 1936.
Atwood, E. B. and V. K. Whitaker (ed). The Excidium Troiae. Cambridge Mass 1944.
Riddehough, G. B. A forgotten poet: Joseph of Exeter. JEGP 46 1947.
—— Joseph of Exeter: the Cambridge ms. Speculum 24 1949.
Young, A. M. Troy and her legend. Pittsburgh 1948.
Highet, G. The classical tradition. 1949.
Preston, R. K. Shakespeare's Troilus and Cressida and the legends of Troy. Madison 1953.
Adler, A. Militia et Amor in the Roman de Troie. Romanische Forschungen 72 1960.
Scherer, M. R. Legends of Troy in art and literature. New York 1963.
Frazer, R. M. (tr). The Trojan war: the chronicles of Dictys of Crete and Dares the Phrygian. Bloomington 1966.
Marcello, G. (ed). Dares Phrygius, De excidio Troiae. Rome 1967.
Schneider, K. Der trojanische Krieg im späten Mittelalter. Berlin 1968.
Stohlmann, J. Anonymi Historia troyana Daretis Frigii: Untersuchungen und kritische Ausgabe. Wuppertal 1968.
Lumiansky, R. M. Dares' Historia and Dictys' Ephemeris: a critical comment. In Studies in the language, literature and culture of the Middle Ages and later, Austin 1969.
Strohm, P. Storie, spelle, geste, romaunce, tragedie: generic distinctions in the Middle English Troy narratives. Speculum 46 1971.

(47) The Gest Historiale of the Destruction of Troy
Index 2129. 14,044 alliterative long lines.
Ms: Univ of Glasgow, Hunterian 388.

§1

Ed G. A. Panton and D. Donaldson 1866–74 (EETS). Selections in Sisam, French and Hale, Gibbs.

§2

Bock, W. Sprach- und Quellenuntersuchung. Halle 1883.
Brandes, H. Quelle. E Studien 8 1885.
Andrew, S. O. The Wars of Alexander and the Destruction of Troy. RES 5 1929.
Kölbing, E. and M. Day (ed). The Siege of Jerusalem. 1932 (EETS). Introd.
Wood, G. R. Note on the ms. MLN 67 1952.
For language and versification, dialect and authorship, see also (8) Sir Gawain, above.

(48) The Seege of Troye
Index 3139. 1988 lines in short couplet.
Mss: BM Egerton 2862; BM Harley 525; College of Arms Arundel XXII; Lincoln's Inn 150.

§1

Ed A. Zeitsch, Archiv 72 1884; ed C. H. A. Wager, New York 1899; ed M. E. Barnicle 1927 (EETS); ed L. Hibler-Lebmannsport 2 vols Graz 1928.

§2

Zeitsch, A. Quelle und Sprache. Cassel 1883.
Kölbing, E. Vier Romanzen-Handschriften. E Studien 7 1884.
Granz, E. T. Über die Quellengemeinschaft des Seege of Troye und des mittelhochdeutschen Gedichtes vom trojanischen Kriege des Konrad von Würzburg. Leipzig 1888.
Fick, W. Zur Seege of Troye. Breslau 1894.
Hibler, L. Methodisches zur Ermittlung des Schreiber-individualität dargestellt an der Seege of Troye. Anglia 51 1927.
—— Die Individualität des A-Schreibers (Arundel XXII). Anglia 60 1936.
Hofstrand, G. A study in the intertextual relations of the Seege or Batayle of Troye. Lund Stud in Eng 4 1936.
Atwood, E. B. The youth of Paris in the Seege of Troye. SE 21 1941.
—— The story of Achilles in the Seege of Troye. SP 39 1942.
—— The judgment of Paris in the Seege of Troye. PMLA 57 1942.
Caldwell, R. A. Joseph Holland: collector and antiquary. MP 40 1942.

(49) The Laud Troy-Book
Index 249. 18,664 in lines in short couplet.
Ms: Bodley 1502 (Laud 595).

§1

Ed J. E. Wülfing 2 vols 1902–3 (EETS).

§2

Kempe, D. A Middle English tale of Troy. E Studien 29 1901. Reply by J. E. Wülfing, ibid.
Wülfing, J. E. Das Bild und die bildliche Verneinung im Laud Troy-book. Anglia 27–8 1904–5.

(50) Lydgate's Troy-Book

See John Lydgate, col 639, below.

(51) Scottish Troy Fragments

*Index *8. 2 fragments, of 596 and 1562 lines, inserted in mss of Lydgate's Troy-book.*
Mss: Cambridge Univ Lib Kk.5.30; Bodley 21,722 (Douce 148).

§1

Ed C. Horstmann, Barbours Legendensammlung vol 2, Heilbronn 1881.

§2

Bradshaw, H. On two hitherto unknown poems by John Barbour. Cambridge Antiquarian Soc 3 1865; rptd in his Collected papers, Cambridge 1889.
Buss, P. Authorship. Anglia 9 1886.
Koeppel, E. Authorship. E Studien 10 1887.
Wülfing, J. E. Das Laud Troy-book. E Studien 29 1901.
Ritchie, R. L. G. (ed). The buik of Alexander. 1925 (STS). Introd.
Farish, J. Some spellings and rhymes in the Scots Sege of Troy. E Studies 38 1957.
See also John Barbour, col 466, below.

(52) The Rawlinson prose Siege of Troy

Ms: Bodley 12,908 (Rawlinson miscellany d. 82).

§1

Ed N. E. Griffin, PMLA 22 1907; ed F. Brie, Archiv 130 1913 (with prose Siege of Thebes).

§2

Combellack, C. R. B. The composite catalogue of the Seege of Troye. Speculum 26 1951.

Benson, C. D. Chaucer's influence on the prose Sege of Troy. N & Q April 1971.

(53) Recuyell of the Histories of Troye

Prose. Print by Caxton; ed H. O. Sommer 2 vols 1894.
See under Caxton, col 667, below.

Thebes

Constans, L. (ed). La légende d'Oedipe. Paris 1881.
—— (ed). Roman de Thèbes. Paris 1890. *See P. Meyer, Romania 21 1892; reply by Constans, Revue des Langues Romanes 35 1894.*
Fisher, F. Narrative art in medieval romances. Cleveland 1939.
Adler, A. The Roman de Thèbes, a Consolatio philosophiae. Romanische Forschungen 72 1960.
Ripley, D. P. The genesis of the Roman de Thèbes: individual and collective literary creation. In Medieval studies in honor of U. T. Holmes, Chapel Hill 1965.
Renoir, A. The poetry of John Lydgate. 1967.
Grout, P. B. Contemporary life and society in the Roman de Thèbes. MÆ 38 1969.
Micha, A. Couleur épique dans le Roman de Thèbes. Romania 91 1970.
Payen, J. C. Structure et sens du Roman de Thèbes. Le Moyen Age 76 1970.

(54) Lydgate's Siege of Thebes

See John Lydgate, col 639, below.

(55) The Rawlinson prose Siege of Thebes

Ms: Bodley 12,908 (Rawlinson miscellany d. 82).

§1

Ed F. Brie, Archiv 130 1913 (with prose Siege of Troy).

(5) THE CYCLE OF GODFREY OF BOUILLON

Pigeonneau, H. Le cycle de la Croisade. St Cloud 1877.
Lot, F. Le mythe des Enfants-Cygnes. Romania 21 1892.
Blöte, J. F. D. Der historische Schwanritter. Zeitschrift für Romanische Philologie 21 1897.
—— Das Aufkommen des Clevischen Schwanritters. Zeitschrift für Deutsches Alterthum 42 1898.
—— Die Sage vom Schwanritter in der Brogner Chronik. Zeitschrift für Deutsches Alterthum 44 1900.
—— Der Ursprung von Schwanrittertradition in englischen Adelsfamilien. E Studien 29 1901.
—— Mainz in der Sage vom Schwanritter. Zeitschrift für Romanische Philologie 27 1903.
Paris, G. Mayence et Nimègue dans le Chevalier au Cygne. Romania 30 1901.
Huet, G. Sur quelques formes de la légende du Chevalier au Cygne. Romania 34 1905.
Jaffray, R. The two knights of the Swan. New York 1910.
Sparnaay, H. Verschmelzung legendarischer und weltlicher Motive in der Poesie des Mittelalters. Groningen 1922.
Frey, A. L. The Swan-knight legend. Nashville 1931.
Boekenoogen, G. J. (ed). Historie van den Ridder metter Swane. Leyden 1931.
Krüger, A. G. Die Quellen der Schwanritterdichtungen. Hanover 1936.
Krogmann, W. Die Schwanrittersage. Archiv 171 1937.
Andressohn, J. C. The ancestry and life of Godfrey of Bouillon. Bloomington 1947.
Wagner, A. R. The swan badge and the swan knight. Archaeologia 97 1959.

(56) Chevalere Assigne

Index 272. 370 alliterative long lines.
Ms: BM Cotton Caligula A.ii.

§1

Ed R. Utterson 1820 (Roxburghe Club); ed H. H. Gibbs 1868 (EETS), rev Aldenham.
Also in French and Hale.

§2

Krüger, A. Zur mittelenglischen Chevalere Assigne. Archiv 77 1887.
Todd, H. A. La naissance du Chevalier au Cygne. PMLA 4 1889.
Holthausen, F. Textual notes. Anglia 21 1899.
Liebermann, F. Chevalier au Cygne in England. Archiv 107 1901.
Loomis, C. G. Two miracles in the Chevalere Assigne. E Studien 73 1939.
Barron, W. R. Chevalere Assigne and the Naissance du Chevalier au Cygne. MÆ 36 1967.
—— Versions and texts of the Naissance du Chevalier au Cygne. Romania 89 1968.
For dialect and authorship, language and versification, see also (8) Sir Gawain, above.

(57) Helyas, the Knight of the Swan

Prose. No extant ms. Prints by R. Copland 1504 and de Worde 1512, New York 1901 (Grolier Club facs).

Ed W. J. Thoms, Collection of early printed romances vol 3, 1828, 1904 (rptd from Copland); ed J. Ashton, Romances of chivalry, New York 1887 (rptd from Copland).

(58) Godefroy of Boloyne

Prose. Print by Caxton 1481 ; ed M. Colvin 1893 (EETS). See under Caxton, col 667, below.

(6) THE 'MATTER OF ENGLAND'

Deutschbein, M. Studien zur Sagengeschichte Englands. Cöthen 1906.
Creek, H. Character in the 'matter of England' romances. JEGP 10 1911.
Noack, G. Sagehistorische Untersuchungen zu den Gesta Herewardi. Halle 1914.
Leach, H. G. Angevin Britain and Scandinavia. Cambridge Mass 1921.
Vising, J. Anglo-Norman language and literature. 1923.
Hibbard, L. Medieval romance in England. New York 1924.
de Lange, J. The relation and development of English and Icelandic outlaw traditions. Haarlem 1935.
Wright, C. E. The cultivation of saga in Anglo-Saxon England. Edinburgh 1939.
Wilson, R. M. Early Middle English literature. 1939.
— Lost literature of medieval England. 1952.
Smyser, H. M. and F. P. Magoun. Survivals in Old Norwegian of medieval English, French and German literature. Baltimore 1941.
Bell, A. (ed). Gaimar's Estoire des Engleis. Oxford 1960.
Keen, M. The outlaws of medieval legend. Toronto 1961.
Legge, M. D. Anglo-Norman literature and its background. Oxford 1963.

(59) King Horn

Index 166. 1569 lines in irregular short couplet.
Mss: Bodley 1486 (Laud miscellany 108); Cambridge Univ Lib Gg.4.27 (11); BM Harley 2253.

§ 1

Ed F. Michel, Horn et Rimenhild, Paris 1845 (Bannatyne Club); ed J. R. Lumby 1866 (EETS), rev G. H. McKnight 1901; ed E. Mätzner, Altenglische Sprachproben vol 1, Berlin 1867; ed C. Horstmann, King Horn nach Laud 108, Archiv 50 1872; ed T. Wissman, Quellen und Forschungen 16 1876, 45 1881; ed J. Hall, Oxford 1901; ed W. H. French, Essays on King Horn, Ithaca 1940 (reconstructed text).
Also in Ritson, French and Hale, Sands; selections in Dickins and Wilson, Mossé, Gibbs; modern version by J. S. P. Tatlock, Berkeley 1948.

§ 2

Wissmann, T. Untersuchungen. Quellen und Forschungen 16 1876.
— Studien zu King Horn. Anglia 4 1881.
McKnight, G. H. Germanic elements. PMLA 15 1900.
Hartenstein, O. Studien zur Hornsage. Kieler Studien 4 1902.
Morsbach, L. Die angebliche Originalität des King Horn. In Festgabe für W. Förster, Halle 1902.
Northup, C. S. Recent texts and studies. JEGP 4 1902.
Schofield, W. H. Horn and Rimenhild. PMLA 18 1903.
West, H. S. Versification of King Horn. Baltimore 1907.
Heuser, W. Horn und Rigmel. Anglia 31 1908.
Deutschbein, M. Beiträge zur Horn- und Haveloksage. Beiblatt zur Anglia 20 1909.
Schipper, J. History of English versification. Oxford 1910.
Breier, W. Zur Lokalisierung des King Horn. E Studien 42 1910.
Kaluza, M. Short history of English versification. Tr A. C. Dunstan 1911.
Azzalino, W. Die Wortstellung im King Horn. Halle 1915.

Funke, O. Zum Verkleidungsmotiv im King Horn. Beiblatt zur Anglia 31 1920.
Töpperwien, A. Sprache und Heimat des King Horn. Jahrbuch der Philosophischen Fakultät, Göttingen 1921.
Krappe, A. H. Legends of Amicus and Amelius and of King Horn. Leuvensche Bijdragen 16 1924.
Leidig, P. Studien zu King Horn. Leipzig 1927.
Scripture, E. W. Der Versrhythmus in King Horn. Anglia 52 1928.
Oliver, W. King Horn and Suddene. PMLA 46 1931.
McKeehan, I. P. The book of the nativity of St Cuthbert. PMLA 48 1933.
West, C. B. Courtoisie in Anglo-Norman literature. 1938.
French, W. H. Essays on King Horn. Ithaca 1940.
Everett, D. Laȝamon and the earliest English alliterative verse. In her Essays on Middle English literature, Oxford 1955.
Pope, M. K. (ed). The romance of Horn by Thomas. 2 vols Oxford 1955–64.
— The romance of Horn and King Horn. MÆ 25 1956.
Hill, D. M. An interpretation of King Horn. Anglia 75 1957.
Christmann, H. H. Über das Verhältnis zwischen dem anglonormannischen und dem mittelenglischen Horn. Zeitschrift für Französische Sprache und Literatur 70 1960.
Gellinek, C. The romance of Horn: a structural survey. Neuphilologische Mitteilungen 66 1965.
Nimchinsky, H. Orfeo, Guillaume and Horn. Romance Philology 22 1969.

(60) Horn Childe

Index 2253. 1136 lines in 12-line tail-rhyme stanza.
Ms: Nat Lib of Scotland 19.2.1 (Auchinleck).

§ 1

Ed F. Michel, Horn et Rimenhild, Paris 1845 (Bannatyne Club); ed J. Caro, Kleine Publicationen aus der Auchinleck-Hs, E Studien 12 1889; ed J. Hall, King Horn, Oxford 1901.
Also in Ritson.

§ 2

See under (59) King Horn, above.
Brunner, K. Romanzen und Volksballaden. Palaestra 148 1925.
Casson, T. E. Horn Childe and the battle of Stainmoor. Trans Cumberland & Westmoreland Antiquarian & Archaeological Soc 37 1937.
For the ballad of Hind Horn, see W. C. Nelles, Jnl of Amer Folklore 22 1909, J. J. MacSweeney, MLR 14 1919, Severs 210, and King Horn above.

(61) King Ponthus and the fair Sidone

Prose. Mss: Bodley 1786 (Digby 185); 1959 (Digby 384).
Prints by de Worde 1505 (fragment); 1510 (fragment), 1511.

§ 1

Ed F. J. Mather, PMLA 12 1897 (text-notes by F. Holthausen, Beiblatt zur Anglia 8 1897 and G. Paris, Romania 26 1897); ed F. Brie, Zwei frühneuenglische Prosaromane, Archiv 118 1907, Zu Surdyt, Archiv 121 1908 (from de Worde 1510).

§2

Wüst, P. Die deutschen Prosaromane von Pontus und Sidonia. Marburg 1903.

Thomas, A. Ponthis de la Tour-Laundri. Romania 34 1905.

Dalbanne, C. and E. Droz. Ponthus et la belle Sidoine. Lyons 1926.

Rickard, P. Britain in medieval French literature. Cambridge 1956.

(62) Havelok

Index 114. 3001 lines in short couplet.
Mss: Bodley 1486 (Laud misc 108); Cambridge Univ Lib additional 4407 (19) (4 fragments).

§1

Ed F. Madden 1828 (Roxburghe Club) (with French); ed W. W. Skeat 1868 (EETS), Oxford 1902, rev K. Sisam, Oxford 1915; ed Skeat, A new Havelok ms, MLR 6 1911 (Cambridge fragments); ed F. Holthausen, Heidelberg 1901, 1910, 1928 (both rev).
Also in French and Hale, Sands; selections in Dickins and Wilson, Mossé, Gibbs, Bennett and Smithers; modern versions by A. J. Wyatt 1889, 1913 (rev), E. Hickey 1902, L. A. Hibbard 1911, R. Montagu, Leicester 1954.

§2

Ludorff, F. Über die Sprache des Havelok. Münster 1874.

Kupferschmidt, M. Die Haveloksage bei Gaimar. Romanische Studien 4 1880.

Storm, G. Havelok and the Norse King Olaf Kuaran. E Studien 3 1880.

Hohmann, L. Sprache und Stil. Marburg 1886.

Wohlfeil, P. Lay of Havelok. Leipzig 1890.

Peacock, M. Havelok the Dane, bygone Lincolnshire. Hull 1891.

Wittenbrinck, G. Zur Kritik und Rhythmik des Havelok. Burgsteinfurt 1891.

Gollancz, I. Hamlet in Iceland. 1898.

Putnam, E. K. The Lambeth version of Havelok. PMLA 15 1900.

— The Scalacronica version. Trans Amer Philological Assoc 34 1903.

Schmidt, F. Zur Heimatbestimmung des Havelok. Göttingen 1900.

Heyman, H. Studies on the Havelok tale. Upsala 1903.

Brie, F. Zum Fortleben der Havelok-Sage. E Studien 35 1905.

Zenker, R. Boeve-Amlethus. Berlin 1905.

Björkman, E. Nordiska Vikingasagor in England. Nordisk Tidsskrift 1906.

— Zur Haveloksage. Beiblatt zur Anglia 28 1917.

Wolff, A. K. Zur Syntax des Verbums im Havelok. Leipzig 1909.

Deutschbein, M. Beiträge zur Horn- und Haveloksage. Beiblatt zur Anglia 20 1909.

Bugge, A. Havelok and Olaf Tryggvason. Saga-book 6 1910.

Creek, H. The author of Havelok. E Studien 48 1915.

Fahnestock, E. Study of the sources and composition of the lai d'Haveloc. Jamaica NY 1915.

Holthausen, F. Textual notes. Anglia 42 1918, Beiblatt zur Anglia 49–50 1938–9.

Bell, A. Single combat in the Lai d'Haveloc. MLR 18 1923.

— (ed). Le lai d'Haveloc and Gaimar's Haveloc episode. Manchester 1926.

— (ed). Gaimar's Estoirc des Engleis. Oxford 1960.

Liebermann, G. Havelok and Anlaf. Archiv 146 1923.

Smithers, G. V. Textual notes. RES 13 1937, Eng & Germanic Stud 2 1951.

McIntosh, A. Note. RES 16 1940.

Dickins, B. The names of Grim's children. Studia Neophilologica 14 1942.

Whitbread, L. Notes on Havelok. N & Q 19 Dec 1942, 13 Jan 1943, 22 April 1944, 10 March 1945.

Hill, J. W. F. Medieval Lincoln. Cambridge 1948.

Britton, G. C. The *n*-plurals in nouns. Neuphilologische Mitteilungen 60 1959.

— The word 'thing'. Neuphilologische Mitteilungen 61 1960.

Mitchell, B. The couplet system in Havelok. N & Q Nov 1963.

Dunn, C. W. Havelok and Anlaf Cuaran. In Franciplegius: medieval and linguistic studies in honor of F. P. Magoun, New York 1965.

Reiss, E. Havelok and Norse mythology. MLQ 27 1966.

Hanning, R. W. Havelok the Dane: structure, symbols, meaning. SP 64 1967.

Mills, M. Havelok and the brutal fisherman. MÆ 36 1967.

Meyer-Lindenberg, H. Zur Datierung des Havelok. Anglia 86 1968.

Weiss, J. Structure and characterisation in Havelok. Speculum 44 1969.

(63) Guy of Warwick, A, B and C

A *(tripartite version): Index 3145. 7306 lines in short couplet with 3588 lines in 12-line tail-rhyme stanza (Index 946) and 1534 lines in 12-line tail-rhyme stanza (Index 1754), separately entitled Reinbrun Gy sone of Warwicke.*

B *(early couplet version): Index 3145. 11,095 lines in short couplet.*

C *(15th-century version): Index 3146. 11,976 lines in short couplet.*

Mss: Nat Lib of Scotland 19.2.1 (Auchinleck) (A); Caius College Cambridge 107 (B); Sloane 1044 (B fragment); Cambridge Univ Lib Ff.2.38 (C); BM additional 14,408 (Phillipps) (C fragment).

Prints by Pynson 1500, de Worde 1500 (fragments), W. Copland 1560.

§1

Ed T. Phillipps, Middlehill Worcs 1838 (C fragment); ed W. B. Turnbull, Edinburgh 1840 (Abbotsford Club) (A, C fragments); ed J. Zupitza, Zur Literaturgeschichte des Guy von Warwick, Sitzungsberichte der Wiener Akademie der Wissenschaften: philosophische Klasse 74 1873 (B fragment); 2 vols 1875–6 (EETS) (C); 3 vols 1883–91 (EETS) (A–B); ed G. Schleich, Palaestra 139 1923 (Copland).

§2

Zupitza, J. Zur Literaturgeschichte des Guy von Warwick. Vienna 1873.

Tanner, A. Die Sage von Guy von Warwick. Heilbronn 1877.

Reeves, W. The so-called prose version of Guy. MLN 11 1896.

Liebermann, F. Guy of Warwick Einfluss. Archiv 107 1901.

Weyrauch, M. Die mittelenglischen Fassungen der Sage von Guy. Breslau 1901.

Crane, R. S. The vogue of Guy of Warwick. PMLA 30 1915.

Hibbard, L. A. Guy of Warwick and Jean Louvet. MP 13 1915.

Möller, W. Dialekt und Stil und Verhältnis zu Amis and Amiloun. Königsberg 1917.

Ewert, A. (ed). Gui de Warewic. 2 vols Paris 1932–3.

Loomis, L. H. Chaucer's 'Jewes werk' and Guy of Warwick. PQ 14 1935.

— Chaucer and the Auchinleck ms: Thopas and Guy of Warwick. In Essays and studies in honor of Carleton Brown, New York 1940.

Ackerman, R. W. Two scribal errors in Guy of Warwick. Washington State College Research Stud 8 1940.

Todd, W. B. (tr). Guy of Warwick. Austin 1968. Trn of French prose version of 1525.

For Lydgate's Guy of Warwick see John Lydgate; for the Speculum Guidonis de Warwyk see edn by G. L. Morrill 1898 (EETS); for the ballad of Guy and Colbrond see Hales and Furnivall, Severs 220; for the song of Guy and Phillis see Hales and Furnivall, Severs 219.

(64) Bevis of Hampton

*Index 1993 and *58. 4620 lines in 12-line tail-rhyme (1–474) and short couplet.*
Mss: Cambridge Univ Lib Ff.2.38; Caius College Cambridge 175; BM Egerton 2862; Nat Lib of Scotland 19.2.1 (Auchinleck); Royal Lib Naples XIII.B.29; Chetham Manchester 8009; Trinity College Cambridge 1117 (IV)(fragment).
Prints by de Worde 1500 (fragments), Pynson 1503, W. Copland 1565.

§ 1

Ed W. B. Turnbull, Edinburgh 1838 (Maitland Club); ed F. Kölbing 3 vols 1885–94 (EETS).
Modern versions by L. A. Hibbard 1911, A. Sampson, Southampton 1963.

§ 2

Schmirgel, C. Stil und Sprache. Breslau 1886.
Kölbing, E. Die Alliteration in Sir Beues. E Studien 19 1894.
Robinson, F. N. Celtic versions of Sir Beves. E Studien 24 1898.
Stimming, A. (ed). Der anglonormannische Boeve de Haumtoune. Halle 1899.
— (ed). Der festländische Bueve de Hantone. 5 vols Dresden 1911–20.
Gerould, G. H. The Eustace legend. PMLA 19 1904. *See also (8), below.*
Zenker, R. Boeve-Amlethus. Berlin 1905.
Jordan, L. Orientalische Verwandten. Archaeologia 121 1908.
Boje, C. Über den altfranzösischen Roman von Beuve de Hamtonc. Zeitschrift für Romanische Philologie 19 1909.
Matzke, J. E. The oldest form of the Beves legend. MP 10 1912.
Crawford, S. J. Sir Bevis of Hamtoun. Wessex 1 1930.
Rickard, P. Britain in medieval French literature. Cambridge 1956.

(65) Richard Coeur de Lyon

Index 1979. 7136 lines in short couplet.
Mss: Bodley 21,802 (Douce 228); Caius College Cambridge 175; BM Egerton 2862; BM Harley 4690; BM additional 31,042; College of Arms HDN 58 (Arundel); Nat Lib of Scotland 19.2.1 (Auchinleck)(fragment); Univ of Edinburgh 218, div 56 (2 fragments of Auchinleck); Univ of St Andrews fragment 2 (fragment of Auchinleck); Badminton (Duke of Beaufort) 704.1.16 (fragment).
Prints by de Worde 1509, 1528.

§ 1

Ed D. Laing and W. B. Turnbull, Owen Miles and other inedited fragments of ancient English poetry, Edinburgh 1837 (Auchinleck); ed E. Kölbing, Kleine Publicationen aus der Auchinleck-Hs, E Studien 8 1885; ed K. Brunner, Vienna 1913.
Also in Weber; modern version by B. B. Broughton, New York 1966.

§ 2

Kölbing, E. (ed). Arthour and Merlin. Leipzig 1890. On authorship.

Needler, G. H. Richard Coeur de Lion in literature. Leipzig 1890.
Jentsch, F. Quellen. E Studien 15 1891.
Paris, G. Le roman de Richard Coeur de Lion. Romania 26 1897.
— (ed). Ambroise, L'estoire de la guerre sainte. Paris 1897; tr M. J. Hubert as The crusade of Richard the Lion-hearted, New York 1951.
Loomis, R. S. Richard Coeur de Lion and the Pas Saladin in medieval art. PMLA 30 1915.
Cartellieri, A. Richard Löwenherz. In Probleme der englischen Sprache und Kultur: Festschrift J. Hoops, Heidelberg 1925.
Wilkinson, C. Richard Coeur de Lion. New York 1933.
Chambers, F. M. Some legends concerning Eleanor of Aquitaine. Speculum 16 1941.
French, W. H. Dialects and forms in three romances. JEGP 45 1946.
Smithers, G. V. Two newly-discovered fragments from the Auchinleck ms. MÆ 18 1949.
— (ed). Kyng Alisaunder. 1957 (EETS). On authorship etc.
Kelly, A. Eleanor of Aquitaine and the four kings. Cambridge Mass 1950.
Chapman, R. L. A note on the demon Queen Eleanor. MLN 70 1955.
Broughton, B. B. The legends of King Richard Coeur de Lion: a study of sources and variations to the year 1600. Hague 1966.
Davis, N. Another fragment of Richard Coer de Lyon. N & Q Dec 1969. On Badminton fragment.

(66) Athelston

Index 1973. 811 lines in 12-line tail-rhyme stanza.
Ms: Caius College Cambridge 175.

§ 1

Ed C. H. Hartshorne, Ancient metrical tales, 1829; ed T. Wright and J. O. Halliwell (-Phillipps), Reliquiae antiquae vol 2, 1843; ed J. Zupitza, E Studien 13–14 1889–90; ed F. Hervey, Corolla Sancti Eadmundi, 1907; ed A. McI. Trounce, Pbns of Philological Soc 11 1933; 1951 (EETS) (rev).
Also in French and Hale, Sands.

§ 2

Gerould, G. H. Social and historical reminiscences in Athelston. E Studien 36 1906.
Hibbard, L. Athelston a Westminster legend. PMLA 36 1921.
Beug, K. Die Sage von König Athelstan. Archiv 148 1925.
Baugh, A. C. A source for Athelston. PMLA 44 1929.
Taylor, G. Notes. Leeds Stud in Eng 3–4 1934–5.
Onions, C. T. The phrase 'end of one's kin'. MÆ 7 1938.
Loomis, L. H. The Athelstan gift story: its influence on English chronicles and Carolingian romances. PMLA 67 1952.

(67) Gamelyn

Index 1913. 902 lines in long couplet.
Mss: Included in 26 mss of the Canterbury tales. See Severs 220–1 and J. M. Manly and E. Rickert, The text of the Canterbury tales, 8 vols Chicago 1940.

§ 1

Frequently edited in the older edns of Chaucer up to Skeat's Oxford Chaucer vol 4, 1894; also independently by Skeat, Oxford 1884, 1893 (rev), and in French and Hale, Sands.

§ 2

Lindner, F. The tale of Gamelyn. E Studien 2 1879.
Björkman, E. Personennamen. Archiv 119 1907, 123 1909.

Kaluza, M. A short history of English versification. Tr A. C. Dunstan 1911.

Leonard, W. E. The scansion of Middle English alliterative verse. Univ of Wisconsin Stud in Lang & Lit 11 1920.

Brusendorff, A. The Chaucer tradition. Copenhagen 1925.

Holthausen, F. Textual notes. Beiblatt zur Anglia 40 1929.

Tatlock, J. S. P. The Canterbury tales in 1400. PMLA 50 1935.

de Lange, J. Relation and development of English and Icelandic outlaw traditions. Haarlem 1935.

Shannon, E. F. Medieval law in the tale of Gamelyn. Speculum 26 1951.

Bullough, G. Narrative and dramatic sources of Shakespeare vol 2. 1958. On As You Like It.

Rogers, F. R. The tale of Gamelyn and the editing of the Canterbury tales. JEGP 58 1959.

Keen, M. The outlaws of medieval legend. Toronto 1961.

Mankin, E. Z. Comic irony and the sense of two audiences in the tale of Gamelyn. Thoth (S. B. Meech issue) 10 1969.

(68) William of Palerne

Index *54. 5540 alliterative long lines.
Ms: King's College Cambridge 13.

§1

Ed F. Madden, The ancient English romance of William and the Werwolf, 1832 (Roxburghe Club); ed W. W. Skeat 1867 (EETS).

§2

Asklöf, I. Essay on William and the Werwolf. Upsala 1872.

Michelant, H. (ed). Guillaume de Palerne. Paris 1876.

Kaluza, M. Französische Quelle. E Studien 4 1881.

Stratmann, F. H. Textual notes. Ibid.

Schüddekopf, A. Sprache und Dialekt. Erlangen 1886.

Pitschel, E. Zur Syntax. Marburg 1890.

Browne, W. H. Textual notes. MLN 7 1892.

Smith K. F. Historical study of the Werwolf in literature. PMLA 9 1894.

Kock, E. A. Textual notes. Anglia 26 1903.

Tibbals, K. Magic in William of Palerne. MP 1 1904.

Brie, F. (ed). Zwei frühneuenglische Prosaromane. Archiv 118 1907. 16th-century prose version.

McKeehan, I. P. Guillaume de Palerne: a medieval bestseller. PMLA 41 1926.

Williams, H. F. Les versions de Guillaume de Palerne. Romania 73 1952.

Dunn, C. W. The foundling and the werwolf: a literary-historical study of Guillaume de Palerne. Toronto 1960.

For dialect, versification etc, see under (8) Sir Gawain, above.

(7) 'BRETON LAYS'

Foulet, L. Marie de France et les lais bretons. Zeitschrift für Romanische Philologie 29 1905.

— Le prologue du Franklin's Tale et les lais bretons. Zeitschrift für Romanische Philologie 30 1906.

Mason, E. (tr). French mediaeval romances from the lays of Marie de France and other French legends. 1911 (EL).

Ahlström, A. Marie de France et les lais narratifs. Gothenburg 1925.

Grimes, E. M. (ed). The lays of Desiré, Graelent and Melion. New York 1928.

Damon, S. F. Marie de France: psychologist of courtly love. PMLA 44 1929.

Spitzer, L. Marie de France: Dichterin von Problemmärchen. Zeitschrift für Romanische Philologie 50 1930.

Schürr, F. Komposition und Symbolik in den Lais der Marie de France. Ibid.

Hoepffner, E. Lais et romans bretons. Revue des Cours et Conférences 34 1933.

— (ed). Les lais de Marie de France. Paris 1935.

— The Breton lais. In Arthurian literature in the Middle Ages, ed R. S. Loomis, Oxford 1959.

Loomis, L. H. Chaucer and the Breton lays of the Auchinleck ms. SP 38 1941.

Foulon, C. Les voyages merveilleux dans les romans bretons. Paris 1943.

Ewert, A. (ed). Marie de France, Lais. Oxford 1944.

Brereton, G. E. A 13th-century list of French lays and other narrative poems. MLR 45 1950.

Francis, E. A. Marie de France et son temps. Romania 72 1951.

Smithers, G. V. Story-patterns in some Breton lays. MÆ 22 1953.

Bromwich, R. A note on the Breton lays. MÆ 26 1957.

Reaney, G. Concerning the origins of the medieval lai. Music & Letters 39 1958.

Lods, J. (ed). Les lais de Marie de France. Paris 1959.

Stemmler, T. Die mittelenglischen Bearbeitungen zweier Lais der Marie de France. Anglia 80 1962.

Wind, B. H. L'idéologie courtoise dans les lais de Marie de France. In Mélanges offerts à M. Delbouille, Gembloux 1964.

Rumble, T. C. (ed). The Breton lays in Middle English. Detroit 1965.

Stevens, J. The granz biens of Marie de France. In Patterns of love and courtesy: essays in memory of C. S. Lewis, 1966.

Rychner, J. (ed). Les lais de Marie de France. Paris 1966.

Baum, R. Recherches sur les oeuvres attribués à Marie de France. Heidelberg 1968.

— Les troubadours et les lais. Zeitschrift für Romanische Philologie 85 1969.

Donovan, M. J. The Breton lay: a guide to varieties. Notre Dame 1969.

Mickel, E. J. A reconsideration of the lais of Marie de France. Speculum 46 1971.

Emare

See (8), below.

(69) Lai le Freine

Index 3869. 320 lines in short couplet.
Ms: Nat Lib of Scotland 19.2.1 (Auchinleck).

§1

Ed H. Varnhagen, Anglia 3 1880; ed F. J. Child, English and Scottish popular ballads vol 2, Boston 1886; ed M. Wattie, Smith College Stud in Modern Langs 10 1929.
Also in Weber, Rumble, Sands.

§2

Laurin, A. An essay on the language of Lai le Freine. Upsala 1869.

Zupitza, J. Zum Lay le Freine. E Studien 10 1887.

Guillaume, G. The prologues of Lay le Freine and Sir Orfeo. MLN 36 1921.

Brugger, E. Eigennamen in den Lais der Marie de France. Zeitschrift für Französische Sprache und Literatur 49 1927.

Küchler, W. Schön Annie, Fraisne und Griselda. Die Neueren Sprachen 35 1927. See also under (8), below.

Adler, A. Höfische Dialektik im Lai du Fresne. Germanisch-romanische Monatsschrift 42 1956.

Hirsch, J. C. Providential concern in Lay le Freine. N & Q March 1969.

(70) Sir Orfeo

Index 3868. 604 lines in short couplet.
Mss: Nat Lib of Scotland 19.2.1 (Auchinleck); Bodley 6922 (Ashmole 61); BM Harley 3810.

§ 1

Ed D. Laing, Selected remains of the ancient popular poetry of Scotland, 1822, rev W. C. Hazlitt 1895; ed J. O. Halliwell (-Phillipps), Illustrations of the fairy mythology of A midsummer night's dream, 1845, ed W. C. Hazlitt 1875; ed O. Zielke, Breslau 1880; ed A. S. Cook, A literary Middle English reader, Boston 1915; ed A. J. Bliss, Oxford 1954, 1966 (rev).
Also in Ritson, Sisam, French and Hale, Ford, Rumble, Sands, Gibbs, Stevick; modern versions by E. E. Hunt 1910, F. Montagu 1954.

§ 2

Auchinleck ms. See also The Otuel Group *and* (30) Roland and Vernagu, *above.*

Kölbing, E. Vier Romanzen-Handschriften. E Studien 7 1884.

Carr, M. B. Notes on a Middle English scribe's methods. Univ of Wisconsin Stud in Lang & Lit 2 1918.

Loomis, L. H. Chaucer and the Auchinleck ms. In Essays and studies in honor of Carleton Brown, New York 1940.

— Chaucer and the Breton lays of the Auchinleck ms. SP 38 1941.

— The Auchinleck ms and a possible London bookshop of 1330–40. PMLA 57 1942.

— The Auchinleck Roland and Vernagu and the Short Chronicle. MLN 60 1945.

Smyser, H. M. Charlemagne and Roland and the Auchinleck ms. Speculum 21 1946.

Smithers, G. V. Two newly-discovered fragments from the Auchinleck ms in the library of the University of St Andrews. MÆ 18 1949.

— Another fragment of the Auchinleck ms. In Medieval literature and civilisation: studies in memory of G. N. Garmonsway, 1969.

Bliss, A. J. Notes on the Auchinleck ms. Speculum 26 1951.

— (ed). Sir Orfeo. Oxford 1954. Introd.

Brunner, K. Middle English metrical romances and their audience. In Studies in medieval literature for A. C. Baugh, Philadelphia 1961.

Weiss, J. The Auchinleck ms and the Edwardes mss. N & Q Dec 1969.

Macrae-Gibson, O. D. The Auchinleck ms: participles in —and(e). E Studies 52 1971.

Interpretative Studies etc

Child, F. J. (ed). English and Scottish popular ballads vol 1. Boston 1857. On ballad of King Orfeo.

Kittredge, G. L. Sir Orfeo. Amer Jnl of Philology 7 1886.

Foulet, L. The prologue of Sir Orfeo. MLN 21 1906.

Marshall, L. E. Greek myths in modern English poetry. Studi di Filologia Moderne 5 1912.

Wirl, J. Orpheus in der englischen Literatur. Vienna 1913.

Guillaume, G. The prologues of the Lai le Freine and Sir Orfeo. MLN 36 1921.

Brunner, K. Romanzen und Volksballaden. Palaestra 148 1925.

Davies, C. Notes on the sources of Sir Orfeo. MLR 31 1936.

Loomis, R. S. Sir Orfeo and Walter Map's De Nugis. MLN 51 1936. Reply by C. Davies, ibid.

Patch, H. R. The other world. Cambridge Mass 1950.

Tucker, S. Note on line 514. Eng & Germanic Stud 2 1951.

Donovan, M. J. Herodis in the Auchinleck Sir Orfeo. MÆ 27 1958.

Rota, F. Echi di miti e leggende in un poemetto medievale inglese. Letterature Moderne 8 1958.

Hill, D. The structure of Sir Orfeo. Mediaeval Stud 23 1961.

Severs, J. B. The antecedents of Sir Orfeo. In Studies in medieval literature in honor of A. C. Baugh, Philadelphia 1961.

Gray, D. Note on line 565. Archiv 198 1961.

Bullock-Davies, C. Classical threads in Orfeo. MLR 56 1961.

— Ympe tre and Nemeton. N & Q Jan 1962.

Heitmann, K. Orpheus im Mittelalter. Archiv für Kulturgeschichte 45 1963.

— Typen der Deformierung antiker Mythen im Mittelalter: am Beispiel der Orpheussage. Romanistisches Jahrbuch 14 1963.

Mitchell, B. The faery world of Sir Orfeo. Neophilologus 48 1964.

Allen, D. Orpheus and Orfeo: the dead and the taken. MÆ 33 1964.

Kinghorn, A. M. Human interest in Sir Orfeo. Neophilologus 50 1966.

Heydon, P. N. Chaucer and the Sir Orfeo prologue of the Auchinleck ms. Papers of Michigan Acad 51 1966.

Gros Louis, K. R. R. Henryson's Orpheus and Eurydice and the Orpheus tradition of the Middle Ages. Speculum 41 1966.

— The significance of Sir Orfeo's self-exile. RES new ser 18 1967.

Friedman, J. B. Eurydice, Heurodis and the noonday dream. Speculum 41 1966.

— Orpheus in the Middle Ages. Cambridge Mass 1970.

Wright, D. A. Sir Orfeo: a note on 'in ich ways'. N & Q Feb 1967.

Knapp, J. K. The meaning of Sir Orfeo. MLQ 29 1968.

Nimchinsky, H. Orfeo, Guillaume and Horn. Romance Philology 22 1969.

Bristol, M. D. The structure of Sir Orfeo. Papers on Lang & Lit 6 1970.

(71) Sir Launfal

Index 567. 1044 lines in 12-line tail-rhyme stanza.
Ms: BM Cotton Caligula A.ii.

§ 1

Ed J. O. Halliwell (-Phillipps), Illustrations of the fairy mythology of A midsummer night's dream, 1845, ed W. C. Hazlitt 1875; ed L. Erling, Li lais de Lanval, Kempten 1883; ed M. Kaluza, E Studien 18 1893; ed A. J. Bliss 1960.
Also in Ritson, French and Hale, Rumble, Sands.

§ 2

Sarrazin, G. (ed). Octovian. Heilbronn 1855. Introd.

Münster, K. L. C. Untersuchungen zu Thomas Chestres Launfal. Kiel 1886.

Kolls, A. F. H. Zur Lanvalsage. Berlin 1886.

Kaluza, M. (ed). Libeaus Desconus. Leipzig 1890. Introd.

— Thomas Chestre, Verfasser des Launfal, Libeaus Desconus und Octovian. E Studien 18 1893.

Schofield, W. H. The lays of Graelent and Launfal. PMLA 15 1900.

Cross, T. P. The Celtic Fée in Launfal. In G. L. Kittredge anniversary studies, Boston 1913.

— The Celtic elements in the lais of Lanval and Graelent. MP 12 1915.

Fischer, E. Die Lautbestand des Octovian, Lybeaus Desconus und Launfal. Heidelberg 1927.

Harris, J. A note on Thomas Chestre. MLN 46 1931.

Everett, D. The relationship of Chestre's Launfal and Lybeaus Desconus. MÆ 7 1938.

Francis, E. A. The trial scene in Lanval. In Studies in French language and mediaeval literature presented to M. K. Pope, Manchester 1939.

Stokoe, W. C. The sources of Sir Launfal: Lanval and Graelent. PMLA 63 1948.

Hoepffner, E. Graelent ou Lanval? In Recueil de travaux offerts à M. C. Brunel, Paris 1955.

Bliss, A. J. The spelling of Sir Launfal. Anglia 75 1957.

—— The hero's name in the Middle English versions of Lanval. MÆ 27 1958.

—— Thomas Chestre: a speculation. Litera 5 1958.

Rychner, J. (ed). Marie de France, Le lai de Lanval. Paris 1958.

Mills, M. Composition and style of the 'southern' Octavian, Sir Launfal and Libeaus Desconus. MÆ 31 1962.

—— A note on lines 743–4. MÆ 35 1966.

Stemmler, T. Die mittelenglischen Bearbeitungen zweier Lais der Marie de France. Anglia 80 1962.

Martin, B. K. Sir Launfal and the folktale. MÆ 35 1966.

Hirsh, J. C. Pride as theme in Sir Launfal. N & Q Aug 1967.

Edwards, A. S. G. Unknightly conduct in Sir Launfal. N & Q Sept 1968.

Knight, S. T. The oral transmission of Sir Launfal. MÆ 38 1969.

Lucas, P. J. Towards an interpretation of Sir Launfal, with particular reference to line 683. MÆ 39 1970.

(72) Sir Landeval

Index 3203. 535 lines in short couplet.
Ms: Bodley 11,951 (Rawlinson c. 86).

§1

Ed G. L. Kittredge, Sir Launfal, Amer Jnl of Philology 10 1889; ed R. Zimmermann, Königsberg 1900; ed A. J. Bliss, Sir Launfal, 1960.

§2

Williams, E. Lanval and Sir Landevale: a medieval translator and his methods. Leeds Stud in Eng new ser 3 1969.
See (71) Sir Launfal, above.

(73) Sir Lambewell

Index 689. 632 lines in short couplet.
Ms: BM additional 27,879 (Percy Folio).

§1

Ed A. F. H. Kolls, Zur Lanvalsage, Berlin 1886.
Also in Hales and Furnivall.

§2

See (71) Sir Launfal, above.

(74) Sir Lamwell

*Index *37. Fragments in short couplet.*
Ms: Cambridge Univ Lib Kk.v.30 (fragment).
Fragments of 2 prints in the Bodley, Malone 941 and Douce e.40.

§1

Ed F. J. Furnivall, Captain Cox, his ballads and books, 1871 (Ballad Soc); Robert Laneham's letter 1890 (New Shakspere Soc); ed A. F. H. Kolls, Zur Lanvalsage, Berlin 1886.
Also in Hales and Furnivall.

§2

See (71) Sir Launfal, above.

(75) Sir Degare

Index 1895. 1066 lines in short couplet.
Mss: Bodley 14,528 (Rawlinson F.34); Bodley 21,835 (Douce 261) (4 fragments); Cambridge Univ Lib Ff.2.38; BM Egerton 2862 (2 fragments); BM additional 27,879 (Percy Folio); Nat Lib of Scotland 19.2.1 (Auchinleck).
Prints by de Worde c. 1502–34, Copland c. 1548–68, John King 1560.

§1

Ed E. V. Utterson, Select pieces of early popular poetry vol 1, 1817; ed D. Laing, Edinburgh 1849 (Abbotsford Club); ed G. Schleich, Heidelberg 1929.
Also in Hales and Furnivall, French and Hale, Rumble.

§2

Slover, C. H. Sire Degarre: a study in a mediaeval hack writer's methods. SE 11 1931.

Faust, G. P. Sir Degare: a study of the texts and narrative structure. Princeton 1935.

Smithers, G. V. Story-patterns in some Breton lays. MÆ 22 1953.

Donovan, M. J. Lines 992–7. Mediaeval Stud 15 1953.

Stokoe, W. C. The double problem of Sir Degare. PMLA 70 1955.

Kozicki, H. Critical methods in the literary evaluation of Sir Degare. MLQ 29 1968.

Jacobs, N. Two corrections in the Auchinleck Sir Degarre. N & Q June 1969.

—— Old French 'degaré' and Middle English 'degarre' and 'deswarre'. N & Q May 1970.

—— The Egerton fragment of Sir Degarre. Neuphilologische Mitteilungen 72 1971.

(76) Sir Gowther

Index 973. 757 lines in 12-line tail-rhyme stanza.
Mss: BM Royal 17.B.xliii; Nat Lib of Scotland 19.3.1.

§1

Ed E. V. Utterson, Select pieces of early popular poetry vol 1, 1817; ed K. Breul, Oppeln 1886.
Also in Rumble.

§2

Thoms, W. J. (ed). Collection of early prose romances. 1828, 1904, 1906. Rptd from de Worde's Robert the Devil.

Hazlitt, W. C. (ed). Remains of the early popular poetry of England vol 1. 1864. Rptd from De Worde.

Löseth, E. (ed). Robert le Diable. Paris 1902.

Meyer, P. L'enfant voué au diable. Romania 33 1904.

Ravenal, F. L. Tydorel and Sir Gowther. PMLA 20 1905.

Ogle, M. The orchard scene in Tydorel and Sir Gowther. Romanic Rev 13 1914.

Flower, R. The ms of Roberte the Deuyll. BM Quart 9 1934.

Lancaster, C. M. (tr). Saints and sinners in old romance: poems of feudal France and England. Nashville 1942. Modern version of 16th-century print.

(77) The Earl of Toulous

Index 1681. 1224 lines in 12-line tail-rhyme stanza.
Mss: Bodley 6922 (Ashmole 61); 6926 (Ashmole 45); Cambridge Univ Lib Ff.2.38; Lincoln Cathedral 91 (Thornton).

§1

Ed G. Lüdtke, Berlin 1881.
Also in Ritson, French and Hale, Rumble.

§2

Paris, S. Le roman du Comte de Toulouse. Annales du
Midi 12 1900.

Bolte, J. Graf von Toulouse. Tübingen 1901.
Siefken, O. Das geduldige Weib. Leipzig 1904.
Thomas, A. Le roman de Goufier de Lastours. Romania
34 1905.
Holthausen, F. Textual notes. Beiblatt zur Anglia 27
1916.
Christophersen, P. (ed). The ballad of Sir Aldingar.
Oxford 1952.

(8) ROMANCES BASED ON LEGENDS OF THE EUSTACE–CONSTANCE–FLORENCE TYPE

Westenholz, F. Die Griseldis-Sage in der Literatur-
geschichte. Heidelberg 1888.
Lücke, E. Das Leben der Constance bei Trivet, Gower und
Chaucer. Anglia 14 1891.
Gough, A. B. The Constance-Saga. Palaestra 23 1902.
Siefken, O. Das geduldige Weib in der englischen
Literatur. Leipzig 1904.
— Der Konstanze-Griseldistypus in der englischen
Literatur bis auf Shakspere. Rathenow 1904.
Gerould, G. H. Forerunners, Congeners and derivatives
of the Eustace legend. PMLA 19–20 1904–5.
Däumling, H. Studie über den Typus des Mädchens ohne
Hände innerhalb des Konstanzezyklus. Munich 1912.
Petersen, H. Les origines de la légende de S. Eustache.
Neuphilologische Mitteilungen 26 1925.
Murray, J. The Eustace legend in medieval England. Bull
Modern Humanities Research Assoc 1 1927.
Schlauch, M. Chaucer's Constance and the accused
queens. New York 1927.
— Historical precursors of Chaucer's Constance. PQ 29
1950.
Laserstein, K. Der Griseldis-Stoff in der Weltliteratur.
Weimar 1926.
Griffith, D. D. Origin of the Griselda story. Univ of
Washington Stud in Lang & Lit 8 1931.
Cate, W. A. The problem of the origin of the Griselda
story. SP 29 1932.
Krappe, A. H. The Offa-Constance legend. Anglia 61
1937.
— Florent et Octavien. Romania 65 1939.
Severs, J. B. The literary relationships of Chaucer's
Clerk's tale. New Haven 1942.
Wickert, M. Chaucer's Konstanze und die Legende der
guten Frauen. Anglia 69 1950.
Christophersen, P. (ed). The ballad of Sir Aldingar.
Oxford 1952.
Isaacs, N. D. Constance in 14th-century England.
Neuphilologische Mitteilungen 59 1958.
See also Chaucer's Man of Law's tale *and* Clerk's tale,
col 579, 583, below.

(78) Emare
Index 1766. 1035 lines in 12-line tail-rhyme stanza.
Ms: BM Cotton Caligula A.ii.

§1

Ed A. B. Gough, Old and Middle English texts, 1901; ed
E. Rickert 1906 (EETS).
Also in Ritson, French and Hale, Rumble; selections in Gibbs.

§2

Gough, A. B. On the Middle English Emare. Kiel 1900.
— The Constance Saga. Palaestra 23 1902.

(79) Sir Isumbras
Index 1184. 794 lines in 12-line tail-rhyme stanza.
Mss: Bodley 6922 (Ashmole 61); Univ College Oxford 142
(fragment); Caius College Cambridge 175; BM Cotton
Caligula A.ii; Nat Lib of Scotland 19.3.1; Gray's Inn 20

(fragment); Lincoln Cathedral 91 (Thornton); Royal Lib
Naples XIII.B.29 (fragment).
For fragments of 6 prints see Index, Severs 279.

§1

Ed E. V. Utterson, Select pieces of early popular poetry
vol 1, 1817 (fragment); ed T. Wright and J. O. Halliwell
(-Phillipps), Reliquiae antiquae vol 2, 1843 (Naples
fragment); ed J. O. Halliwell (-Phillipps), Thornton
romances, 1844 (Camden Soc); ed E. Kölbing, Das
Neapler Fragment, E Studien 3 1880; ed J. Zupitza,
Archiv 88 1892, 90 1893 (ptd fragment); ed F. S. Ellis
1897 (Kelmscott Press) (rptd from Halliwell); ed G.
Schleich and J. Zupitza, Palaestra 15 1901; ed C. Brown,
E Studien 48 1915 (Univ College Oxford fragment);
ed C. D'Evelyn, E Studien 52 1918 (Gray's Inn fragment).

§2

Ostermann, L. Entstehungszeit des Isumbras. Bonner
Beiträge 12 1902.
Gerould, G. H. The grateful dead. Folklore Soc 60 1908.
Krappe, A. H. An oriental theme in Sir Ysumbras. E
Studien 67 1932.
Braswell, L. Sir Isumbras and the legend of St Eustace.
Mediaeval Stud 27 1965.

(80) Sir Eglamour of Artois
Index 1725. 1341 lines in 12-line tail-rhyme stanza.
Mss: Cambridge Univ Lib Ff.2.38; BM Cotton Caligula
A.ii; BM Egerton 2862 (fragment); BM additional
27,879 (Percy Folio) (copy of print); Lincoln Cathedral
91 (Thornton).
For fragments of 6 prints see Index, Severs 281.

§1

Ed D. Laing, The knightly tale of Gologros and Gawane,
Edinburgh 1827 (Chepman and Myllar print); ed J. O.
Halliwell (-Phillipps), Thornton romances 1844 (Camden Soc); ed E. Kölbing, E Studien 7 1884 (Egerton
fragment); ed G. Schleich, Palaestra 53 1906; ed A. S.
Cook, New York 1911; ed W. Beattie, The Chepman
and Myllar prints, Edinburgh 1950; ed F. E. Richardson
1965 (EETS).
Also edited in Hales and Furnivall.

§2

Child, F. J. (ed). English and Scottish popular ballads.
5 vols Boston 1882–98. Ballads of Lionel, Cawline and
Eglamore.
Adam, E. (ed). Sir Torrent of Portyngale. 1887 (EETS).
Introd.
Zielke, A. Untersuchungen über Sir Eglamour. Kiel 1889.
Schleich, G. Über die Beziehungen von Eglamour und
Torrent. Archiv 92 1894.
Baskerville, C. R. Some new evidence for early romantic plays
in England. MP 14 1917.
— An Elizabethan Eglamour play. Ibid.

Rank, O. Das Inzest-Motiv in Dichtung und Sage. Leipzig 1926.

Lüthi, M. Das europäische Volksmärchen: Form und Wesen. Berne 1947.

(81) Sir Torrent of Portyngale

Index 983. 2668 lines in 12-line tail-rhyme stanza.
Ms: Chetham Lib Manchester 8009.
For fragments of 2 prints see Index, Severs 283.

§ 1

Ed J. O. Halliwell (-Phillipps) 1842; ed E. Adam 1887 (EETS).

§ 2

Adam, E. Über Sir Torrent of Portyngale. Breslau 1887. Rptd as EETS introd, above.

Schleich, G. Über die Beziehungen von Eglamour und Torrent. Archiv 92 1894.

Holthausen, F. Textual notes. Anglia 42 1918.

(82) Octavian, A and B

A ('*Northern*' version): Index 1918. 1731 lines in 12-line tail-rhyme stanza. Mss: Cambridge Univ Lib Ff.2.38; Lincoln Cathedral 91 (Thornton).

B ('*Southern*' version, also titled Octovian): Index 1774. 1962 lines in unique 6-line stanza.

Ms: BM Cotton Caligula A.ii.

Fragment of print by de Worde 1504–6.

§ 1

Ed J. O. Halliwell (-Phillipps) 1848 (Percy Soc) (A); ed G. Sarrazin, Heilbronn 1885 (A and B).
Also edited by Weber (B).

§ 2

See also under (18) Libeaus Desconus, (71) Sir Launfal, above.

Conybeare, J. J. The romance of Octavian. Oxford 1809. Abridged trn of Old French version. Rptd E. M. Goldsmid, Edinburgh 1882.

Vollmöller, K. (ed). Octavian. Heilbronn 1885. Old French version.

Streve, P. Die Octaviansage. Erlangen 1884.

Eule, R. Untersuchungen über die nordenglische Version. Halle 1889.

Kaluza, M. (ed). Libeaus Desconus. Leipzig 1890.
— Thomas Chestre. E Studien 18 1893.

Settegast, F. Floovent und Julian. Halle 1906.

Brockstedt, G. Floovent-Studien. Kiel 1907.

Fischer, E. Der Lautbestand des südmittelenglischen Octavian, Lybeaus Desconus und Sir Launfal. Heidelberg 1927.

Kessler, L. (ed). Der Prosaroman vom Kaiser Oktavian. Frankfort 1932.

Bateson, F. H. Le chanson de Floovant. Paris 1938.

Krappe, A. H. Florent et Octavien. Romania 65 1939.

Andolf, S. Floovant: chanson de geste du 12e siècle. Upsala 1941.

Bossuat, R. Florent et Octavian: chanson de geste du 14e siècle. Romania 73 1952.

Mills, M. Composition and style of the 'southern' Octavian, Sir Launfal and Libeaus Desconus. MÆ 31 1962.

(83) Sir Triamour

Index 1177. 1719 lines in 12-line tail-rhyme stanza.
Mss: Cambridge Univ Lib Ff.2.38; BM additional 27,879 (Percy Folio); Bodley Rawlinson fragment (now missing).

Prints by W. Copland c. 1561, c. 1565; for fragments of 3 other prints by Pynson see Index, Severs 287.

§ 1

Ed E. V. Utterson, Select pieces of early English popular poetry vol 1, 1817 (Copland print); ed J. O. Halliwell (-Phillipps) 1846 (Percy Soc); ed A. J. Erdman-Schmidt, Utrecht 1937.
Also edited in Hales and Furnivall.

§ 2

Köhler, R. Zu der altspan. Erzählung von Karl und Sibille. Jahrbuch für Romanische und Englische Sprache und Literatur 12 1871.

Baugart, F. Die Tiere in altfranzösische Epos. Marburg 1885.

Bauszus, H. Die Romanze Sir Triamour. Königsberg 1902.

Baker, A. T. Fragments de la chanson de la reine Sibile. Romania 44 1917.

Malone, K. Rose and cypress. PMLA 43 1928.

Viscardi, J. Le chien de Montargis. Paris 1932.

(84) The King of Tars

Index 1108. 1228 lines in 12-line tail-rhyme stanza.
Mss: Bodley 3938 (Vernon); BM additional 22,283 (Simeon); Nat Lib of Scotland 19.2.1 (Auchinleck).

§ 1

Ed F. Krause, E Studien 11 1888.
Also edited in Ritson.

§ 2

Holthausen, F. Textual notes. Anglia 15 1893.

Hornstein, L. H. New historical sources for the King of Tars. PMLA 53 1938.
— Trivet's Constance and the King of Tars. MLN 55 1940.
— A folklore theme in the King of Tars. PQ 20 1941.
— The historical background of the King of Tars. Speculum 16 1941.
— New analogues to the King of Tars. MLR 36 1941.

Geist, R. J. On the genesis of the King of Tars. JEGP 42 1943.
— Notes. JEGP 47 1948.

Smyser, H. M. Charlemagne and Roland and the Auchinleck ms. Speculum 21 1946.

Bliss, A. J. Notes. N & Q Nov 1955.

(85) Le Bone Florence of Rome

Index 334. 2189 lines in 12-line tail-rhyme stanza.
Ms: Cambridge Univ Lib Ff.2.38.

§ 1

Ed W. Viëtor, Marburg 1893.
Also edited in Ritson.

§ 2

Wenzel, R. Die Fassungen der Sage von Florence de Rome. Marburg 1890.

Knobbe, A. Über die mittelenglische Dichtung Le Bone Florence. Marburg 1899.

Wallensköld, A. (ed). Florence de Rome, chanson d'aventure du 13e siècle. 2 vols Paris 1907–9.
— L'origine et l'évolution du conte de la Femme Chaste (Légende de Crescentia). Neuphilologische Mitteilungen 14 1912.

Stefanović, S. Die Crescentia-Florence Sage. Romanische Forschungen 29 1911.

Holthausen, F. Textual notes. Anglia 41 1917.

Chaytor, H. J. A fragment of the chanson d'aventure Florence de Rome. Modern Humanities Research Assoc Bull 1 1927.

Fahlin, C. La femme innocente exilée dans une forêt. In Mélanges offerts à K. Michaëlsson, Gothenburg 1952.

(9) COMPOSITES OF COURTLY ROMANCE

Barrow, S. F. The medieval society romances. New York 1924.

Wilcox, J. French courtly love in English composite romances. Papers of Michigan Acad 18 1932.

(86) Ipomadon, A, B and C

A *Index 2635. 8890 lines in 12-line tail-rhyme stanza.*
Ms: Chetham Lib Manchester 8009.
B *Index 2142. 2345 lines in short couplet.*
Ms: BM Harley 2252.
Prints by de Worde, c. 1522 (fragment), c. 1530 (impertfect).
C *Prose*
Ms: Longleat (Marquis of Bath) 257.

§ 1

Ed K. D. Bülbring, Vier neue Alexanderbruchstücke, E Studien 13 1889 (B ptd fragment); ed E. Kölbing, Breslau 1889 (A, B and C).
Also edited in Weber (B); selections in French and Hale (A).

§ 2

Kirschten, W. Überlieferung und Sprache. Marburg 1885. On B.

Kölbing, E. and E. Koschwitz (ed). Hue de Rotelande's Ipomedon: ein französischer Abenteuerroman des 12 Jahrhundert. Breslau 1889.

Köppel, E. and G. L. Kittredge. Textual notes. E Studien 14 1890.

Seyferth, P. Sprache und Metrik des strophischen Gedichtes Le Morte Arthur und sein Verhältnis zu Ipomydon. Berliner Beiträge 8 1895.

Weston, J. L. The three days' tournament. 1902.

Carter, C. H. Ipomedon: an illustration of romance origins. In Haverford essays: studies in modern literature, Haverford 1909.

Webster, K. G. T. The 12th-century tourney. In G. L. Kittredge anniversary papers, Boston 1913.

Holthausen, F. Textual notes. Anglia 40–1 1916–17.

Gay, L. M. Hue de Rotelande's Ipomedon and Chrétien de Troyes. PMLA 32 1917.

Muchnic, H. The coward knight and the damsel of the cart. PMLA 43 1928.

Cline, R. H. The influence of romances on tournaments. Speculum 20 1945.

Legge, M. D. Anglo-Norman literature and its background. Oxford 1963.

(87) Sir Degrevant

Index 1953. 1904 lines in 16-line tail-rhyme stanza.
Mss: Cambridge Univ Lib Ff.1.6 (Findern); Lincoln Cathedral 91 (Thornton).

§ 1

Ed J. O. Halliwell (-Phillipps), Thornton romances, 1844 (Camden Soc); ed F. S. Ellis 1896 (Kelmscott Press) (rptd from Halliwell); ed K. Luick, Wiener Beiträge 47 1917; ed L. F. Casson 1949 (EETS).
Selections in Gibbs.

§ 2

Bülbring, K. Untersuchungen zu mittelenglischer Metrik. Studien zur Englischen Philologie 50 1913.

Medary, M. P. and A. C. L. Brown. Stanza-linking. Romanic Rev 7 1916.

Finsterbusch, F. Der Versbau der Sir Perceval of Gales und Sir Degrevant. Wiener Beiträge 49 1919. *See also* (14) The Avowynge, *above*.

Tolkien, J. R. R. The Devil's coach-horses. RES 1 1925.

Robbins, R. H. The Findern anthology. PMLA 69 1954.

(88) The Squyr of Lowe Degre, A and B

A *Index 1644. 1132 lines in short couplet.*
No ms extant. Print by W. Copland c. 1560, and fragments of print by de Worde c. 1520.
B *Index 1644. Shortened version in 170 lines.*
Ms: BM additional 27,879 (Percy Folio).

§ 1

Ed T. F. Dibdin, Reminiscences of a literary life vol 2, 1836 (fragment); ed W. C. Hazlitt, Remains of early popular poetry of England vol 2, 1866 (A); ed W. E. Mead, Boston 1904 (A and B); ed J. D. McCallum, English literature: the beginnings to 1500, New York 1929 (A).
Also edited in Ritson (A), Hales and Furnivall (B), French and Hale (A), Sands (A).

§ 2

Tunk, P. Studien zur The Squyr of Lowe Degre. Breslau 1900.

Weyrauch, M. Zur Komposition, Entstehungszeit und Beurteilung. E Studien 31 1902.

Jefferson, B. L. Note. MLN 28 1913.

Lüthi, M. Das europäische Volksmärchen: Form und Wesen. Berne 1947.

(89) Generydes, A and B

A *Index 70. 10,086 lines in short couplet.*
Ms: Pierpont Morgan Lib M876 (Helmingham-Tollemache).
3 fragments of 2 prints by Pynson, c. 1500, 1510.
B *Index 1515. 6995 lines in rhyme royal.*
Ms: Trinity College Cambridge 1283 (Gale O.5.2).

§ 1

Ed F. J. Furnivall 1866 (Roxburghe Club) (A and ptd fragments); ed W. A. Wright 2 vols 1873–8 (EETS) (B).

§ 2

Zupitza, J. Textual notes. Anglia 1 1878.

Zirwer, O. Untersuchungen zu den beiden mittelenglischen Generydes Romanzen. Breslau 1889.

—— Textual notes. E Studien 17 1892.

Kölbing, E. Textual notes. Ibid.

Holthausen, F. Beiträge zur Textkritik. In Festskrift tillägnad O. Ekman, Gothenburg 1898.

Settegast, F. Quellenstudien zur galloromanischen Epik. Leipzig 1904.

Faverty, F. E. The story of Joseph and Potiphar's wife in medieval literature. Harvard Stud 13 1932.

Pearsall, D. A. Notes on the ms (Trinity) of Generydes. Library 5th ser 16 1961.

—— The Assembly of Ladies and Generydes. RES new ser 12 1961.

(90) Partonope of Blois, A and B

A *Index 4132. 12,195 lines in heroic couplet.*
Mss: Bodley 14,507 (Rawlinson Eng poet F.14); 30,516 (Rawlinson Eng poet C.3); Univ College Oxford c. 188; BM additional 35,288; Bodley Latin miscellany b.17 (Clifden Robartes) (fragments).
B *Index 4081. 308 lines in 12-line stanza.*
Ms: Penrose 6 (Delamere-Vale Royal).

§1

Ed W. E. Buckley 1862 (Roxburghe Club) (A); ed R. C. Nichols 1873 (Roxburghe Club) (B); ed R. Wülcker Anglia 12 1890 (Clifden Robartes fragments); ed A. T. Bödtker 1911 (EETS) (A and B).

§2

Robert, A. C. M. (ed). Partonopeus de Blois. 2 vols Paris 1834.

Kölbing, E. Beiträge zur vergleichenden Geschichte der romantischen Poesie und Prosa des Mittelalters. Breslau 1876.

Weingartner, F. Die mittelenglischen Fassungen der Partonopeus-Sage und ihr Verhältniss zum altfranzösischen Originale. Breslau 1888.

Leach, H. G. Is Gibbonssaga a reflection of Partonopeus? In Medieval studies in memory of G. S. Loomis, New York 1927.

Moret, A. L'originalité de Conrad de Wurzbourg dans son poème Partonopier und Meliur. Lille 1933.

Smith, R. M. Three notes on the Knight's tale. MLN 51 1936.

Robbins, R. H. The Speculum misericordie. PMLA 54 1939. Penrose ms.

Wright, H. G. An allusion to Partonope in Guiscardo and Ghismonda. MLR 38 1943.

Parr, J. Chaucer and Partonope of Blois. MLN 60 1945.

Whiting, B. J. A 15th-century English Chaucerian: the translator of Partonope of Blois. Mediaeval Stud 7 1945.

Newstead, H. The traditional background of Partonopeus de Blois. PMLA 61 1946.

Uri, S. P. Some remarks on Partonopeus de Blois. Neophilologus 37 1953.

Swahn, J. O. The tale of Cupid and Psyche. Lund 1955.

Fourrier, A. Le courant réaliste dans le roman courtois en France au Moyen-Age. Paris 1960.

Smith, L. P. A newly-discovered ms fragment of the Old French Partonopeus de Blois. MP 59 1961.

Gildea, J. (ed). Partonopeu de Blois: a French romance of the 12th century. 2 vols Villanova Pa 1967–70.

(91) Eger and Grime
Index 1624. 1474 lines in short couplet.
Ms: BM additional 27,879 (Percy Folio).
Prints by Robert Sanders, Glasgow 1669, 1687, Aberdeen 1711.

§1

Ed D. Laing, Early metrical tales, Edinburgh 1826 (rptd from 1711), Glasgow 1889; rev W. C. Hazlitt, Early popular poetry of Scotland, 1895; ed J. R. Caldwell, Cambridge Mass 1933.
Also edited in Hales and Furnivall, French and Hale (Percy).

§2

Reichel, G. Studien zu der schottischen Romanze Sir Eger, Sir Grime and Sir Gray-Steel. Breslau 1893; rptd E Studien 19 1894.

Basilius, H. A. The rhymes in Eger and Grime. MP 35 1937.

Christophersen, P. (ed). The ballad of Sir Aldingar. Oxford 1952.

Van Duzee, M. A medieval romance of friendship: Eger and Grime. New York 1963.

(92) Roswall and Lillian
Not in Index. 846 lines in short couplet.
No extant ms. Early prints, 1663, 1663, Newcastle nd, c. 1700. See Severs 309.

§1

Ed D. Laing, Select remains of the ancient popular poetry of Scotland, Edinburgh 1822, 1882 (separately); Early metrical tales, Edinburgh 1826; ed W. C. Hazlitt, Early popular poetry of Scotland, 1895 (rev from Laing); ed O. Lengert, E Studien 16–17 1892.

§2

Child, F. J. (ed). English and Scottish popular ballads vol 5. Boston 1896.

(93) Valentine and Orson
Prose. No extant ms. For 2 prints by W. Copland and fragments of 2 others, see Severs 312.

§1

Ed A. Dickson 1936 (EETS).

§2

Child, F. J. (ed). English and Scottish popular ballads 5 vols Boston 1882–98. Valentine and Ursine, Sir Aldingar, Sir Cawline.

Littlewood, S. R. Valentine and Orson: the twin-knights of France. 1919.

Dickson, A. Valentine and Orson: a study in late medieval romance. New York 1929.

Dieperink, G. J. Studien zum Valentin und Namelos. Haarlem 1933.

(94) Clariodus
Not in Index. Supplement *548.5. 11,845 lines in heroic couplet.
Ms: Nat Lib of Scotland 19.2.5.

§1

Ed D. Irving, Edinburgh 1830 (Maitland Club).

§2

Curtis, F. J. Rimes and Phonology. Anglia 16–17 1895–6.

Smith J. M. The French background of Middle Scots literature. Edinburgh 1934.

(10) 'ANCESTRAL' ROMANCES

Legge, M. D. Anglo-Norman literature and its background. Oxford 1963.

Guy of Warwick
See under (6) (63), above.

(95) Melusine
Prose. Ms: BM Royal XVIII.B.2.
Ptd fragment of c. 1510.

§1

Ed A. K. Donald 1895 (EETS).

§2

De Saivre, L. Le mythe de la Mère Lusine. Niort 1885.

Nowack, M. Die Melusinasage. Freiburg 1886.

Köhler, J. Der Ursprung der Melusinensage. Leipzig 1895.

Bourdillon, F. W. Notes on two early romances: Huon de Bordeaux and Melusine. Library 4th ser 1 1920.

Marchand, J. La légende de Mélusine. Paris 1927.

Hoffrichter, L. Die ältesten französischen Bearbeitungen der Melusine-Sage. Halle 1928.

Stouff, L. Essai sur Mélusine: roman du xive siècle. Publications de l'Université de Dijon, fascicule 3 1930.

—— (tr). Mélusine: ou la Fée de Lusignan. Ibid, fascicule 5 1932.

MacCulloch, J. A. Medieval faith and fable. 1932.

Albrecht, W. P. The Loathly Lady in Thomas of Erceldoune. Univ of New Mexico Pbns in Lang & Lit 11 1954.

Painter, S. The houses of Lusignan and Châtellérault. Speculum 30 1955.

Schneider, K. (ed). Thüring von Ringoltingen, Melusine. Berlin 1958.

See also (96) Partenay, below.

(96) The Romauns of Partenay (Lusignan)

*Index *27. 6615 lines in rhyme royal.*
Ms: Trinity College Cambridge 597 (R.3.17).

§1

Ed W. W. Skeat 1866 (EETS), 1899 (rev).

§2

Michel, F. (ed). Mellusine par Couldrette. Niort 1854.
Hattendorff, W. Sprache und Dialekt. Leipzig 1887.
See (95) Melusine, *above*.

(97) The Knight of Curtesy and the Fair Lady of Faguell

Index 1486. 504 lines in quatrains.
No extant ms. Print by W. Copland [1568?].

§1

Ed W. C. Hazlitt, Remains of early popular poetry of England vol 2, 1866; ed E. McCausland, Smith College Stud 4 1922.
Also edited in Ritson; modern version by A. Kemp-Welch, The Chatelaine of Vergi, *1903.*

§2

Lorenz, E. Die Kastellanin von Vergi in der Literatur Frankreichs, Italiens &c. Halle 1909.

Raynaud, G. (ed). La Chastelaine de Vergi. Paris 1910, 1912, 1921 (both rev).

Matzke, J. E. The legend of the eaten heart. MLN 26 1911.

—— The roman du Châtelain de Coucy and Fauchet's Chronique. In Studies for A. M. Elliott, Baltimore 1913.

Matzke, J. E. and M. Delbouille (ed). Le roman du Castelain de Couci et de la Dame de Fauel. Paris 1936.

Whitehead, F. (ed). La Chastelaine de Vergi. Manchester 1944.

Frappier, J. (ed). La Chastelaine de Vergi. Strasbourg 1945.

—— Études littéraires. Paris 1946.

(11) DIDACTIC LEGENDS

Schelp, H. Exemplarische Romanzen im Mittelenglischen. Palaestra 246 1967.

(98) Amis and Amiloun

Index 821. 2395 lines in 12-line tail-rhyme stanza.
Mss: Bodley 21,900 (Douce 326); BM Egerton 2862; Harley 2386; Nat Lib of Scotland 19.2.1 (Auchinleck).

§1

Ed E. Kölbing, Heilbronn 1884; ed M. Leach 1937 (EETS).
Also edited in Weber; selections in Gibbs; modern version by B. B. Broughton, Richard the Lion-hearted and other medieval romances, *New York 1966.*

§2

Hofmann, K. Amis et Amiles und Jourdains de Blaivies. Erlangen 1852, 1882 (rev).

—— Erster Nachtrag zur Einleitungen in Amis et Amiles. Romanische Forschungen 1 1883.

Schweiger, P. Die Sage von Amis und Amiles. Berlin 1885; rptd in Zeitschrift für Romanische Philologie 9 1885.

Potter, M. A. Ami et Amile. PMLA 23 1908.

Ayres, H. M. The Faerie Queene and Amis and Amiloun. MLN 30 1915.

Möller, W. Untersuchungen über Dialekt und Stil des Guy of Warwick und Amis and Amiloun. Königsberg 1917.

Krappe, A. H. The legend of Amicus and Amelius. MLR 18 1923.

—— The legends of Amicus and Amelius and of King Horn. Leuvensche Bijdragen 16 1924.

Bar, F. Les épitres latines de Raoul le Tourtier, études des sources: la légende d'Ami et Amile. Paris 1937.

—— Le Mabinogi et la légende d'Ami et Amile. Romania 68 1944.

Woledge, B. Ami et Amile: les versions en prose française. Romania 65 1939.

Bauerfeld, W. Die Sage von Amis und Amiles. Halle 1941.

Asher, J. A. Amis et Amiles: an exploratory survey. Auckland Univ Modern Lang Stud 1 1952.

Goetinck, G. W. La légende d'Ami et Amile et le Mabinogi de Pwyll. Romania 86 1965.

Calin, W. The epic quest: studies in 4 Old French chansons de geste. Baltimore 1966.

Kratins, O. The Middle English Amis and Amiloun: chivalric romance or secular hagiography? PMLA 81 1966.

Mathew, G. Ideals of friendship. In Patterns of love and courtesy: essays in memory of C. S. Lewis, 1966.

Kramer, D. Structural artistry in Amis and Amiloun. Annuale Mediaevale (Duquesne) 9 1968.

Hume, K. Structure and perspective: romance and hagiographic features in the Amicus and Amelius story. JEGP 69 1970.

(99) Sir Amadace

*Index *62. 852 lines in 12-line tail-rhyme stanza.*
Mss: Nat Lib of Scotland 19.3.1; Bibliotheca Bodmeriana, Geneva (formerly Ireland-Blackburn).

§1

Ed J. Robson, Three early English metrical romances, 1847; ed G. Stephens, Ghost-Thanks, or the Grateful Unburied: a mythic tale in its oldest European form, Sir Amadace, Copenhagen 1860; ed C. Brookhouse, Sir Amadace and the Avowing of Arthur, Copenhagen 1968.
Also edited in Weber.

§2

Hippe, M. Untersuchungen zur Sir Amadace. Archiv 81 1888.

Dutz, H. Der Dank der Todten in der englischen Literatur. Jahresbericht der Staats-Oberrealschule, Troppau 1894.

Gerould, G. H. The grateful dead. Folklore Soc 60
1907.
Tatlock, J. S. P. Leuvenoth and the Grateful Dead. MP
22 1925.
Reinhard, J. R. Amadas et Ydoine. Paris 1926, Durham
NC 1927.
Dickins, B. The Ireland ms. Leeds Stud in Eng 2–3
1933–4; TLS 21 Dec 1933.

(100) Sir Cleges

Index 1890. 564 lines in 12-line tail-rhyme stanza.
*Mss: Bodley 6922 (Ashmole 61); Nat Lib of Scotland
19.1.11.*

§ 1

Ed H. Morley, Shorter English poems, 1876; ed A.
Treichel, E Studien 22 1896; ed G. H. McKnight,
Middle English humorous tales in verse, Boston
1913.
*Also edited in Weber, French and Hale; modern version by
J. L. Weston 1902.*

§ 2

Reinhard, J. R. Strokes shared. Jnl of Amer Folklore 36
1925.
Loomis, C. G. Sir Cleges and unseasonable growth in
hagiology. MLN 53 1938.

(101) Roberd of Cisyle

Index 2780. 444 lines in short couplet.
*Mss: Bodley 3938 (Vernon); Trinity College Oxford D.57;
Cambridge Univ Lib Ff.2.38; Ii.4.9; Caius College
Cambridge 174; BM Harley 525; Harley 1701; BM
additional 22,283 (Simeon); BM additional 34,801
(fragment); Trinity College Dublin 432B.*

§ 1

Ed E. V. Utterson 1839; ed J. O. Halliwell (-Phillipps),
Nugae poeticae, 1844; ed W. C. Hazlitt, Remains of
early English popular poetry vol 1, 1864; ed C. Horstmann, Altenglische Legenden, Heilbronn 1878; Nachträge zu den Legenden, Archiv 62 1879; ed R. Nuck,
Berlin 1887; ed R. Brotanek, Mittelenglische Dichtungen
aus der Hs 432 des Trinity College in Dublin, Halle
1940; ed L. H. Hornstein, King Robert of Sicily: a new
ms, PMLA 78 1963.
Also edited in French and Hale, Ford.

§ 2

Gerould, G. H. Saints' legends. Boston 1916.
Kapp, R. Heilige und Heiligenlegenden. Halle 1934.
Janson, H. W. Apes and ape lore in the Middle Ages and
the Renaissance. 1952 (Warburg Inst).
Hornstein, L. H. King Robert of Sicily: analogues and
origins. PMLA 79 1964.

(12) MISCELLANEOUS ROMANCES

(102) Floris and Blauncheflur

Index *45. 1083 lines in short couplet.
*Mss: Cambridge Univ Lib Gg.4.27 (II); BM Cotton
Vitellius D.3 (fragment); BM Egerton 2862; Nat Lib of
Scotland 19.2.1 (Auchinleck).*

§ 1

Ed C. H. Hartshorne, Ancient metrical tales, 1829; ed
D. Laing, A penni worth of witte, Edinburgh 1857
(Abbotsford Club); ed J. R. Lumby 1866 (EETS), rev
G. H. McKnight 1901; ed E. Hausknecht, Berlin 1885;
ed A. B. Taylor, Oxford 1927; ed F. C. de Vries,
Utrecht 1966.
*Also edited in French and Hale, Sands, Stevick; selections
in Dickins and Wilson, Gibbs, Bennett and Smithers;
modern version by B. B. Broughton, Richard the Lion-
hearted and other medieval romances, New York 1966.*

§ 2

Huet, G. Sur l'origine de Floire et Blanchefleur. Romania
28 1899, 35 1906.
Reinhold, J. Floire et Blanchefleur: études de littérature
comparée. Paris 1906.
Johnstone, A. M. The description of the Emir's orchard
in Floire et Blanchefleur. Zeitschrift für Romanische
Philologie 32 1908.
— The origin of the legend of Floire and Blanchefleur.
In [J. E.] Matzke memorial volume, Stanford 1911.
Singer, S. Arabische und europäische Poesie im Mit-
telalter. Zeitschrift für Deutsches Alterthum 52
1910.
Spargo, J. W. The basket incident in Floire and Blanche-
flor. Neuphilologische Mitteilungen 28 1927.
Pelan, M. (ed). Floire et Blanchefleur. Paris 1937, 1956
(rev).
Wirtz, W. Flore et Blancheflor. Frankfurter Quellen und
Forschungen 15 1937.
Krüger, F. Li romanz de Floire et Blancheflor. Roman-
ische Studien 45 1938.

Delbouille, M. La patrie et la date de Floire et Blanche-
fleur. In Mélanges offerts à M. Roques vol 4, Paris 1952.
François, C. Floire et Blancheflor: du chemin de Compo-
stelle au chemin de la Mecque. Revue Belge de Philo-
logie et d'Histoire 44 1966.
Hubert, M. J. (tr). The romance of Floire and Blanche-
fleur: a French idyllic poem of the 12th century.
Chapel Hill 1967.
Britton, G. C. Three notes on Floris and Blancheflour.
N & Q Oct 1970.

(103) The Siege of Jerusalem

Index 1583. 1334 alliterative long lines.
*Mss: Bodley 1059 (Laud miscellany 656); Cambridge Univ
Lib Mm.5.14; BM Cotton Caligula A.ii; Cotton
Vespasian E.xvi (fragment); BM additional 31,042
(Thornton); Lambeth 491; Huntington HM 128
(formerly Ashburnham 130).*

§ 1

Ed G. Steffler, Marburg 1891; ed E. Kölbing and M. Day
1932 (EETS).

§ 2

Kopka, F. M. The destruction of Jerusalem. Breslau 1887.
Dobschütz, E. von. Christusbilder: Untersuchungen zur
christlichen Legende. Leipzig 1899.
Suchier, W. Über das altfranzösische Gedicht La venjance
Nostre Seigneur. Halle 1899; rptd Zeitschrift für
Romanische Philologie 24–5 1900–1.
Hulbert, J. R. The text of the Siege of Jerusalem. SP 28
1931.
Duparc-Quioc, S. Les manuscrits de La conquête de
Jérusalem. Romania 65 1939.
Kellogg, A. B. The language of the alliterative Siege of
Jerusalem. Chicago 1943.
Gryting, L. A. T. La venjance Nostre Seigneur. Univ of
Michigan Contributions in Modern Philology 19 1952.
— The Venjance Nostre Seigneur as a medieval com-
posite. Modern Lang Jnl 38 1954.
— The flowering of an epic. In Romance studies in
memory of E. B. Ham, Hayward Cal 1967.

Benson, L. D. The 'rede wynde' in the Siege of Jerusalem. N & Q Oct 1960.

Moe, P. The French source of the alliterative Siege of Jerusalem. MÆ 39 1970.
For language and versification, dialect and authorship, see under (8) Sir Gawain, above.

(104) Titus and Vespasian, or The Destruction of Jerusalem

Index 1881. 5166 lines in short couplet.
Mss: Bodley 1414 (Laud miscellany 622); 1831 (Digby 240); 21,652 (Douce 78); 21,700 (Douce 126); Magdalene College Cambridge Pepys 2014 (formerly Pepys 37); BM Harley 4733; BM additional 10,036; BM additional 36,523; BM additional 36,983 (Bedford); Pierpont Morgan Lib Morgan M898; Osborn, New Haven (formerly Derby, Knowsley Hall) (Osborn 32, deposited at Yale); Coventry Corporation Record Office (fragment).

§ 1

Ed R. Fischer, Vindicta salvatoris: the vengeaunce of Goddes deth or Bataile of Jerusalem, Archiv 111–12 1903–4; ed J. A. Herbert 1905 (Roxburghe Club).

§ 2

Bergau, F. Untersuchungen über Quelle und Verfasser. Königsberg 1901.
Arvidson, J. M. The language of ms Pepys 37. Lund 1916.
Bühler, C. F. The new Morgan ms of Titus and Vespasian. PMLA 76 1961.
For the legend see (103) The Siege of Jerusalem, above.

(105) The Prose Titus and Vespasian

Ms: Cleveland Public Lib W q091.92-C468, John G. White collection (formerly Aldenham).

§ 1

Ed A. Kurvinen, The siege of Jerusalem in prose, Mémoires de la Société Néophilologique de Helsinki 34 1969.

§ 2

For the legend see (103) The Siege of Jerusalem, above.

(106) The Three Kings' Sons

Prose. Ms: BM Harley 326.

§ 1

Ed F. J. Furnivall 1895 (EETS).

§ 2

Schlauch, M. Antecedents of the English novel 1400–1600. 1963.

(107) The Seven Sages of Rome

Index 3187. Not in Severs. 3974 lines in short couplet.
Mss:
A *Nat Lib of Scotland 19.2.1 (Auchinleck); BM Egerton 1995; Arundel 140; Cambridge Univ Lib Ff.2.38; Balliol College Oxford 354.*
B *Cambridge Univ Lib Dd.1.17.*
C *BM Cotton Galba E.ix; Bodley 14,667 (Rawlinson poet. 175).*
D *Asloan (Scottish version).*

§ 1

Ed D. Laing 1837 (Bannatyne Club) (C); ed T. Wright 1845 (Percy Soc) (B); ed H. Varnhagen, E Studien 25

1898 (D); ed K. Campbell, Boston 1907 (C); ed W. Craigie, The Asloan ms vol 2, 1924 (STS) (D); ed K. Brunner 1933 (EETS) (A).
Also edited in Weber (A, part of C).

§ 2

Paris, G. Deux rédactions des Sept Sages. Paris 1876.
Petras, P. Über die mittelenglischen Fassungen der Sage von den Sieben weisen Meistern. Grünberg 1885.
Buchner, G. Historia septem sapientum. Erlangen 1889.
—— Beiträge zur Geschichte der Sieben weisen Meister. Archiv 113 1904.
Campbell, K. A study of the romance of the Seven Sages of Rome. Baltimore 1898; PMLA 14 1899.
—— The sources of the story of Sapientes. MLN 23 1908.
—— Notes. MLR 17 1922.
Fischer, H. Beiträge zur Literatur der Sieben weisen Meister. Greifswald 1902.
Tuttle, A. H. Rimes and language. MLR 16 1921.
Brunner, K. Die Reimsprache der sogennanten kentischen Fassung der Sieben weisen Meister. Archiv 140 1920.
Krappe, A. H. Studies in the Seven Sages of Rome. Archivum Romanicum 8–9 1924–5, 11 1927, 16 1932, 19 1936.
Black, G. F. (ed). J. Rolland's The seuin seages. 1932 (STS). Scottish version of c. 1560.
Lindheim, B. von. Studien zur Sprache des Ms Cotton Galba E.ix. Wiener Beiträge 59 1937.
Crosland, J. Dolopathos and the Seven sages of Rome. MÆ 25 1956.
Smithers, G. V. (ed). Kyng Alisaunder. 1957 (EETS). Introd.
Lumiansky, R. M. Thematic antifeminism in the Middle English Seven sages of Rome. Tulane Stud in Eng 7 1957.
Heltveit, T. Dialect words in the Seven sages of Rome. E Studies 45 1964.

(108) Apollonius of Tyre

*Index *51. 140 lines in quatrains.*
Ms: Bodley 21,790 (Douce 216).

§ 1

Ed J. O. Halliwell (-Phillipps), A new boke about Shakespeare and Stratford-on-Avon, 1850; ed A. H. Smyth, Shakespeare's Pericles and Apollonius of Tyre, Philadelphia 1898; ed J. Raith, Die alt- und mittelenglischen Apollonius-Bruchstücke, Munich 1956.

§ 2

Singer, S. Apollonius von Tyrus: Untersuchungen über das Fortleben des antiken Romans in spätern Zeiten. Halle 1895.
Klebs, E. Die Erzählung von Apollonius aus Tyrus. Berlin 1899.
Lewis, C. B. (ed). Die altfranzösischen Prosaversionen des Apollonius-Romans. Breslau 1912; Romanische Forschungen 34 1915.
Goepp, P. H. The narrative material in Apollonius of Tyre. ELH 5 1938.
Goolden, P. (ed). The Old English Apollonius of Tyre. Oxford 1958.
Delbouille, M. Apollonius de Tyr et les débuts du roman français. In Mélanges offerts à R. Lejeune vol 2, Gembloux 1969.

D. A. P.

II. MIDDLE ENGLISH LITERATURE TO 1400

Tales; Chronicles; Travel; Prophecies; Versions of the Bible; Sermons; John Wyclif and Wycliffite writings; Other religious writings; Saints' legends; William Langland and associated poems; The Pearl poet; John Gower.

(1) TALES

Bibliographies

Wells *pp. 164, 778, 955, 1006, 1051, 1107, 1169, 1211, 1302, 1345, 1390, 1492, 1608, 1706, 1899.*

Renwick, W. L. and H. Orton. In their Beginnings of English literature to Skelton, 1939, 1952 (enlarged).

Brown, C. F. and R. H. Robbins. Index to Middle English verse. New York 1943; Supplement, Lexington Kentucky 1965.

Matthews, W. In his Old and Middle English literature, New York 1968.

General Studies

Plessow, M. Geschichte der Fabeldichtung in England. Berlin 1906.

Canby, H. S. The English fabliau. PMLA 21 1906.

— The short story in English. New York 1909.

Hart, W. M. The fabliau and popular literature. PMLA 23 1908.

Ker, W. P. In his English literature medieval, 1912. Ch 6.

McKnight, G. H. ME humorous tales in verse. Boston 1913.

Wilson, R. M. In his Early ME literature, 1939. Ch 10.

— In his Lost literature of medieval England, 1952. Ch 7.

White, B. Medieval mirth. Anglia 78 1960.

Individual Tales
Dame Siriʒ

Wells *pp. 178, 790, 1108, 1211, 1302, 1346, 1390, 1608, 1707.*
Ms: *Bodley Digby 86.*

§1

Brydges, E. and J. Haslewood. British bibliographer vol 4. 1814.

Wright, T. Anecdota literaria. 1844.

Mätzner, E. Altenglische Sprachproben pt 1. Berlin 1867.

Zupitza, J. Übungsbuch. Vienna 1874.

McKnight, G. H. ME humorous tales in verse. Boston 1913.

Cook, A. S. Literary ME reader. Boston 1915.

Brandl, A. and O. Zippel. Mittelenglische Sprach- und Literaturproben. Berlin 1917.

Sampson, G. Cambridge book of prose and verse. Cambridge 1924.

Kaiser, R. Medieval English, translated from the German. Berlin 1958.

Bennett, J. A. W. and G. V. Smithers. Early ME prose and verse. 1966, 1968 (rev).

§2

Schipper, J. In his Englische Metrik, Bonn 1881. Section 168.

Elsner, W. Untersuchungen zu Dame Siriʒ. Berlin 1887.

Hauser, W. Das Interludium de Clerico et Puella und das Fabliau von Dame Siriʒ. Anglia 30 1907.

Schröder, E. Dame Sirith, Nachrichten von der Gesellschaft der Wissenschaften zu Göttingen. Philologisch-historische Klasse Fachgruppe 4, 1 1936.

Miller, B. D. H. Two notes. MÆ 28 1959.

— Dame Siriʒ and the OED. N & Q April 1961.

— Three notes. N & Q Oct 1961.

— 'Word in hand'. N & Q Feb–April 1963.

The Vox and the Wolf

Wells *pp. 183, 791, 1108, 1211, 1390.*
Ms: *Bodley Digby 86.*

§1

Wright, T. and J. O. Halliwell (-Phillipps). Reliquae antiquae vol 2. 1843.

Hazlitt, W. C. Remains of the early popular poetry of England vol 1. 1864.

Mätzner, E. Altenglische Sprachproben pt 1. Berlin 1869.

McKnight, G. H. ME humorous tales in verse. Boston 1913.

Cook, A. S. Literary ME reader. Boston 1915.

Brandl, A. and O. Zippel. Mittelenglische Sprach- und Literaturproben. Berlin 1917.

Sampson, G. Cambridge book of prose and verse. Cambridge 1924. Selections.

Dickins, B. and R. M. Wilson. Early ME texts. 1951.

Mossé, F. Handbook of ME, translated from the French. Baltimore 1952. Omits lines 1–70.

Kaiser, R. Medieval English, translated from the German. Berlin 1958.

Bennett, J. A. W. and G. V. Smithers. Early ME prose and verse. Oxford 1966, 1968 (rev).

Sisam, C. and K. Sisam. Oxford book of medieval English verse. Oxford 1970.

Translation

Weston, J. L. Chief ME poets. Boston 1914.

§2

McKnight, G. H. The ME Vox and Wolf. PMLA 23 1908.

Brett, C. Notes on passages of Old and ME. MLR 14 1919.

Mossé, F. Le Roman de Renart dans l'Angleterre du Moyen Age. Langues Modernes 45 1951.

Flinn, L. Le Roman de Renart dans la littérature française et dans les littératures étrangères au Moyen Age. Paris 1963.

Varty, K. The pursuit of Reynard in medieval English literature and art. Nottingham Medieval Stud 8 1964.

Bercovitch, S. Clerical satire in the Vox and the Wolf. JEGP 65 1966.

Von Kreisler, N. Satire in the Vox and the Wolf. JEGP 69 1970.

How the Psalter of Our Lady Was Made

Wells *pp. 168, 789, 955–6, 1006, 1107.*
Mss: *1, Bodley Digby 86; 2, Nat Lib of Scotland 19.2.1; 3, Bodley Laud Lat. 95 (lacks a beginning); 4, Trinity College Cambridge R.3.21.*

§1

Ed D. Laing, A peniworth of witte, 1857 (Abbotsford Club) (ms 2); ed C. Horstmann, Altenglische Legenden, Heilbronn 1881 (1 with variants of 2); ed A. S. Napier, Odds and ends 1, MLN 4 1889 (ms 3).

Land of Cockaygne

Wells *pp. 228, 798, 1009, 1213, 1304, 1393, 1495.*
Ms: *BM Harley 913 (Kildare ms).*

§ I

Hickes, G. Linguarum veterum septentrionalium thesaurus grammatico-criticus et archaeologicus vol I. Oxford 1743.

Ellis, G. Specimens of the early English poets vol I. 1801.

Haupt, M. and A. H. Hoffman. Altdeutsche Blättern vol I. Leipzig 1836.

Furnivall, F. J. Early English poems and lives of saints. Berlin 1862.

Mätzner, E. Altenglische Sprachproben pt I. Berlin 1867.

Morley, H. Shorter English poems. 1876.

Heuser, W. Die Kildare Gedichte. Bonn 1904.

Cook, A. S. Literary ME reader. Boston 1915. Selections.

Sampson, G. Cambridge book of prose and verse. Cambridge 1924.

Kaiser, R. Medieval English, translated from the German. Berlin 1958.

Robbins, R. H. Historical poems of the 14th and 15th centuries. New York 1959.

Bennett, J. A. W. and G. V. Smithers. Early ME prose and verse. Oxford 1966, 1968 (rev).

Sisam, C. and K. Sisam. Oxford book of medieval English verse. Oxford 1970. Selection.

Translations

Shackford, M. H. Legends and satires. Boston 1913.

Weston, J. L. Chief ME poets. Boston 1914.

Kuriyagawa, F. Eigo Seinen. CI, nos 5–8 (with Japanese trn).

§ 2

Barbazan, A. and M. Meon. Fabliaux et contes vol 4. Paris 1808. For the French source.

Wright, T. St Patrick's Purgatory. 1844.

Graf, A. Miti, leggende e superstizioni del Medio Evo. Turin 1878.

Holthausen, F. Zu den Kildare-Gedichten. Anglia 40 1916.

Lascelles, M. Alexander and the earthly paradise in mediaeval English writings. MÆ 5 1936.

Väänänen, V. Le fabliau de Cocagne. Neuphilologische Mitteilungen 48 1947.

Patch, H. R. The other world. Cambridge Mass 1950.

Morton, A. L. The English utopia. 1952.

Garbáty, T. J. Studies in the Franciscan the Land of Cockaygne in the Kildare ms. Franziscanische Studien 45 1963.

Howard, I. The folk origins of the Land of Cockaygne. Humanities Assoc Bull 18 1967.

A Peniworþ of Witte

Wells pp. 179, 790, 1108, 1492.

Version I (A peniworþ of witte)

Ms : Nat Lib of Scotland 19.2.1.

Laing, D. A peniworth of witte. 1857 (Abbotsford Club).

Kölbing, E. Kleine Publicationen aus der Auchinleck – ms. E Studien 7 1884.

Version II (How a merchande dyd hys wyfe betray)

Mss: 1, Cambridge Univ Lib Ff.2.38; 2, BM Harley 5396; 3, Porkington 10.

Ed J. Ritson, Pieces of ancient poetry, 1791 (ms I); ed J. Sibbald, Chronicle of Scottish poetry vol 1, Edinburgh 1802 (ms I); ed W. C. Hazlitt, Remains of the early popular poetry of England vol 1, 1864 (ms I); ed E. Kölbing, Kleine Publicationen aus der Auchinleck-hs, E Studien 7 1884 (mss 1–2).

Masters, J. E. Rymes of the minstrels. Shaftesbury 1933.

For French analogues, see A. Montaiglon and G. Raynaud, Recueil général et complet des fabliaux, Paris 1876.

The Clerk Who Would See the Virgin

Wells pp. 169, 789, 1108.

Ms: Nat Lib of Scotland 19.2.1.

§ I

Horstmann, C. Altenglische Legenden. Heilbronn 1881.

Boyd, B. ME miracles of the Virgin. San Marino 1964.

The Gast of Gy

Wells pp. 170, 789, 956, 1007, 1108, 1346, 1390, 1608, 1706, 1899.

Version I (couplets)

Mss: 1, BM Cotton Tiberius E 7; 2, Bodley Rawlinson poet. 175; 3, Penrose 6.

Ed G. Schleich, Palaestra 1 1898 (ms 1–2); ed C. Horstmann, Yorkshire writers vol 2, 1896 (ms 1). For ms 3 *see* R. H. Robbins, The Speculum Misericorde, PMLA 54 1939.

Version II (prose)

Mss: 1, Bodley 3938 (Vernon); 2, Caius Cambridge 175 (35 line fragment); 3, Queen's College Oxford 383.

Ed G. Schleich, Palaestra 1 1898 (ms 2); ed R. H. Bowers, The Gast of Gy, Beiträge zur Englischen Philologie 1938 (ms 3 with variants of 1).

Version III (quatrains)

Mss: 1, Pepys 2125; 2, Univ of Leeds, Brotherton Collection 501.

Ed J. Lightbown, A shorter metrical version of the Gast of Gy. MLR 47 1952 (extracts from ms 1–2).

See E. P. Goldschmidt, Medieval texts and their first appearance in print, *1943 (Bibl Soc).*

Trentalle Sancti Gregorii

Wells pp. 172, 789, 956, 1007, 1051, 1108.

§ I

Version I

Mss: 1, BM Cotton Caligula A2; 2, Nat Lib of Wales, Peniarth 394.

Ed F. J. Furnivall, Political, religious and love poems. 1886 (EETS) (ms 1); ed C. Horstmann, Minor poems of the Vernon ms (vol 1), 1892 (EETS).

Version II

Mss: 1, Bodley 3938 (Vernon), 2 texts f. 231r col 1 and f. 303r col 3; 2, Balliol College Oxford 354; 3, Lambeth 306; 4, Princeton Univ Lib, Garrat ms 143.

Ed C. Horstmann, Mittheilungen aus ms Vernon, E Studien 8 1885 (ms 1); ed Horstmann, Minor poems of the Vernon ms pt 1, 1892 (EETS) (ms 1); ed A. Kaufmann, Trentalle Sancti Gregorii, Erlanger Beiträge 3 1889 (ms 3); ed R. K. Root, Poems from the Garrat ms, E Studien 41 1910 (ms 4).

Version III

Mss: 1, Nat Lib of Scotland 19.2.1; 2, Cambridge Univ Lib Kk 1.6; 3, BM Harley 3810; 4, Porkington 20.

[c. 1500] (Pynson); 1515 (de Worde); [c. 1548] (Mychell); ed W. D. B. Turnbull, Vision of Tundale, Edinburgh 1843 (ms 1); ed A. Kaufmann, Trentalle Sancti Gregorii, Erlanger Beiträge 3 1889 (ms 2); ed K. D. Bulbring, Das Trentalle Sancti Gregorii in der Edinburgher Handschrift, Anglia 13 1891 (ms 1); ed R. Jordan, Das Trentalle Gregorii in der Handschrift Harley 3810, E Studien 40 1909.

§2

Bulbring, K. D. Das Trentalle Sancti Gregorii in der Edinburgher Handschrift. Anglia 13 1891.
Gerould, G. H. Saints' legends. Boston 1916.
Hulbert, J. R. The sources of St Erkenwald and the Trental of Gregory. MP 16 1919.

The Smith and his Dame

Wells pp. 174, 789.
No surviving mss; modern edns are based on the early print of Robert Copland, nd.

§1

Halliwell, J. O. Contributions to early English poetry. 1849.
Hazlitt, W. C. Remains of early popular poetry of England vol 3. 1866.
Horstmann, C. Altenglische Legenden. Heilbronn 1881.

Vernon Miracles of Mary (9 stories)

Wells pp. 166, 788, 1169, 1211, 1390, 1492, 1706, 1899.
Ms: Bodley 3938 (Vernon).

§1

Ed C. Horstmann, Archiv 56 1876; ed Horstmann, Minor poems of the Vernon ms, 1892 (EETS); ed W. F. Bryan and G. Dempster, Sources and analogues of Chaucer's Canterbury tales, Chicago, 1941 (one only); ed R. D. French, Chaucer handbook, New York 1947 (one only); ed B. Boyd, Miracles of the Virgin, San Marino 1964 (4 only).

Translations

Segar, M. G. Medieval anthology. New York 1915. Extracts.

§2

Tryon, R. W. Miracles of Our Lady in ME verse. PMLA 38 1923.

Southern, R. W. The English origins of the Miracles of the Virgin. Medieval & Renaissance Stud 4 1958. Reply by J. C. Jennings 6 1968.

The Eremyte and the Outlaw

Wells pp. 174, 789, 906, 1107, 1302, 1390, 1609.
Mss 1, BM additional 37,492; 2, BM additional 22,577 (copy of 1).

§1

Ed T. Park in E. Brydges, Restituta vol 4, 1816 (ms 1); ed M. Kaluza, Kleinere Publicationen aus ME Handschriften, E Studien 14 1890 (ms 2).

§2

Barbazan, A. and M. Meon. Fabliaux et contes vol 1. Paris 1808.
de la Marche, A. Légendes et apologues d'Etienne de Bourbon. Paris 1877. Nos 26, 284.
Crane, T. F. Exempla of Jacques de Vitry. 1890. Nos 72, 165.
Kittredge, G. L. The hermit and the outlaw. E Studien 19 1894.

The Childe of Bristowe

Wells pp. 175, 789, 1007, 1211, 1608, 1708, 1899.

§1

Mss: 1, BM Harley 2382 (version 1); 2, Cambridge Univ Lib Ff.2.38 (version 2: The merchant and his son).
Ed T. Wright, Retrospective Rev new ser 2 1832 (ms 1); ed J. O. Halliwell (-Phillipps), Nugae poeticae, 1844 (ms 2); ed C. Hopper, The Camden miscellany vol 4, 1859 (ms 1) (Camden Soc); ed W. C. Hazlitt, Remains of the early popular poetry of England vol 1, 1864 (ms 1–2); ed C. Horstmann, Altenglische Legenden, Heilbronn 1881; ed F. J. Child, English and Scottish popular ballads, Cambridge Mass 1886.

V. J. S.

(2) CHRONICLES

Bibliographies

Wells pp. 190, 792, 956, 1007, 1052, 1107, 1169, 1211, 1262, 1303, 1346, 1391, 1493, 1609, 1707, 1900. See also under Tales, above.

General Studies

Gross, C. The sources and literature of English history from the earliest times to about 1485. 1900, 1915 (rev and enlarged).
Bruce, H. English history in contemporary poetry: the fourteenth century. 1914.
Curry, W. C. ME ideal of personal beauty in the chronicles. Baltimore 1916.
Tout, T. F. The study of medieval chronicles. Bull John Rylands Lib 6 1922.
Poole, R. L. Chronicles and annals: a brief outline of their origins and growth. Oxford 1926.
Starke, F. J. Populäre englische Chroniken des 15 Jahrhunderts: eine Untersuchung über ihre literarische Form. Berlin 1935.
Edwards, A. C. Knaresborough Castle and the Kynges moodres court. PQ 19 1940.
Douglas, D. C. The Norman Conquest and British historians. Glasgow 1946.
Schlauch, M. Historical precursors of Chaucer's Constance. PQ 29 1950.
Wilson, R. M. The lost literature of medieval England. 1952. Ch 2.
Bagley, J. J. Historical interpretation. 1965 (Pelican).

Taylor, J. The use of medieval chronicles. 1965.
Kellogg, A. L. Chronicles of England. Jnl of Rutgers Univ Lib 29 1966.

Laȝamon's Brut

Wells pp. 32, 191, 792, 1007, 1109, 1169, 1212, 1262, 1303, 1346, 1391, 1493, 1609, 1707, 1900. See R. M. Estrich, The present state of Lawman studies, PMLA 60 1945.
Mss: 1, BM Cotton Caligula A 9; 2, BM Cotton Otho c 13.

§1

Laȝamon's Brut or Chronicle of England. Ed F. Madden 3 vols 1847 (ms 1–2).
Laȝamon's Brut. Ed G. L. Brook and R. F. Leslie vol 1 1963 (EETS). Lines 1–8020.

Selections

Morris, R. and W. W. Skeat. Specimens of early English vol 1. Oxford 1885.
Kluge, F. Mittelenglisches Lesebuch. Halle 1904.
Emerson, O. F. ME reader. New York 1905.
Cook, A. S. Literary ME reader. Boston 1915.
Brandl, A. and O. Zippel. Mittelenglische Sprach- und Literaturproben. Berlin 1917.
Hall, J. Selections from early ME. Oxford 1924.
Sampson, G. Cambridge book of prose and verse. Cambridge 1924.
Dickins, B. and R. M. Wilson. Early ME texts. 1951.

Mossé, F. Handbook of ME translated from the French. Baltimore 1952.

Kaiser, R. Medieval English, translated from the German. Berlin 1958.

Brook, G. L. Selections from Laȝamon's Brut. Oxford 1963 (long extracts).

Bennett, J. A. W. and G. V. Smithers. Early ME prose and verse. Oxford 1966, 1968 (rev).

Funke, O. A ME reader. In Bibliotheca anglicana 7, Berne 1966 (3rd edn rev).

Sisam, C. and K. Sisam. Oxford book of medieval English verse. Oxford 1970.

Mss and Text

Stratmann, F. H. Verbesserungen zu altenglischen Schriftstellern. E Studien 3–5 1880–2.

Zessach, A. Die beiden Handschriften von Layamons Brut und ihr Verhältnis zu einander. Breslau 1888.

Kellner, L. V. Archiv 114 1905.

Monroe, B. S. In Studies in language and literature in celebration of the 70th birthday of J. M. Hart, New York 1911.

Bartels, L. Die Zuverlässigkeit der Handschriften von Layamons Brut. Studien zur Englischen Philologie 49 1913.

Stroud, J. A. Scribal editing in Lawman's Brut. JEGP 51 1952.

Keith, W. J. Laȝamon's Brut: the literary differences between the two texts. MÆ 29 1960.

Versification

Trautmann, M. Über den Vers Laȝamons. Anglia 2 1879.

Schipper, J. In his Englische Metrik, Bonn 1881. Section 67.

— In his Grundriss der englischen Metrik, Vienna 1899. Section 34.

Guest, E. In his History of English rhythms, ed W. W. Skeat 1882.

McNary, S. J. Studies in Layamon's verse. New York 1904.

Brandstadter, K. Stabreim und Endreim. Heidelberg 1912.

Language

Stratmann, F. H. æ in Layamon. E Studien 2 1878.

— Nachträge zu englische Studien. E Studien 3 1880.

— Das paragogische n. Anglia 3 1880.

Luhmann, A. Die Überlieferung von Layamons Brut. Göttingen 1905.

— Überlieferung nebst einer Darstellung der lateinischen Vokale und Diphthonge. Studien zur Englischen Philologie 2 1906.

Bohnke, M. Die Flexion des Verbums. Berlin 1906.

Lange, H. Das Zeitwort in den beiden Handschriften. Strasbourg 1906.

Funke, P. Kasussyntax bei Orm und Layamon. Munich 1907.

Monroe, B. S. French words in Laȝamon. MP 4 1907.

Hoffmann, P. Das grammatische Genus. Studien zur Englischen Philologie 36 1909.

Kühl, O. Der Vokalismus der Layamonhandschrift B [Cotton Otho C 13]. Halle 1913.

Lichtsinn, P. Der syntaktische Gebrauch des Infinitivs. Kiel 1913.

Macmillan, M. Wunder ane. MLR 13 1918.

Funke, O. Zur Wortgeschichte der französischen Elemente im Englischen. E Studien 55 1921.

Meissgeier, E. Grammatisches Geschlecht. E Studien 56 1922.

Serjeantson, M. S. The dialects of the West Midlands in ME. RES 3 1927.

Stern, G. OE æ in the early text of Layamon. Gothenburg 1941.

Sunden, K. F. Notes on the vocabulary of Layamon's Brut. Studia Neophilologica 14 1942.

Bøgholm, N. The Layamon texts: a linguistical investigation. Copenhagen 1944.

Dobson, E. J. Some notes on ME texts. Eng & Germanic Stud 1 1947.

Sources

Krautwald, H. Layamon's Brut verglichen mit Wace's Roman de Brut. Breslau 1887.

Brown, A. C. L. Welsh traditions in Layamon's Brut. MP 1 1903.

— The round table before Wace. Harvard Stud 7 1900.

Fletcher, R. H. Did Layamon make any use of Geoffrey's Historia? PMLA 18 1903.

— Arthurian material in the chronicles. Boston 1906.

Inmelmann, R. Layamon: Versuch über seine Quellen. Berlin 1906.

Bruce, J. D. Proper names. MLN 26 1911.

— Arthur matter. Romanic Rev 4 1913.

Cook, A. S. Layamon's knowledge of runic inscriptions. Scottish Historical Rev 11 1914.

Pilch, H. Layamon und die kynrische Literatur. Zeitschrift für Celtische Philologie 39 1962.

Blanchet, M. C. Layamon et l'Ecosse. Bulletin Bibliographique de la Société Arthurienne, no 15.

Literary etc

Kolbe, M. Schild, Helm und Panzer zur Zeit Layamons und ihre Schilderung in dessen Brut. Breslau 1891.

Hamelius, P. Rhetorical structure. In Mélanges G. Kurth, Liège 1908.

Seyger, R. Beiträge zu Layamons Brut. Halle 1912.

Gillespy, F. L. Layamon's Brut: a comparative study of narrative art. Univ of California Pbns in Modern Philology 3 1916.

Cross, T. P. Passing of Arthur. In J. M. Manly anniversary studies, Chicago 1923.

Gordon, G. The Trojans in Britain. E & S 9 1923.

Tatlock, J. S. P. Epic formulas. PMLA 38 1923.

— Layamon's poetic style. In J. M. Manly anniversary studies, Chicago 1923.

— Irish costume in Lawman. SP 28 1931.

— Greater Irish saints in Lawman and in England. MP 43 1945.

— The legendary history of Britain. Berkeley 1950. Ch 23.

Wyld, H. C. Laȝamon as an English poet. RES 6 1930.

— Studies in the diction of Layamon's Brut. Language 6 1930, 9–10 1933–4, 13 1937.

Hinckley, H. B. The date of of Laȝamon's Brut. Anglia 56 1932.

Loomis, R. S. Notes on Laȝamon. RES 10 1934.

— Arthurian literature in the Middle Ages. Oxford 1959. Ch 10.

Visser, G. H. Laȝamon: an attempt at vindication. Assen 1935.

Heather, P. J. Laȝamon's Brut. Folklore 48 1937.

— Gleanings from Laȝamon's Brut. Folklore 53 1942.

— Seven planets. Folklore 54 1943.

Blenner-Hassett, R. The English river names in Lawman's Brut. MLN 55 1940.

— Gernemuðe: a place name puzzle in Lawman's Brut. MLN 57 1942.

— A nature name puzzle in Lawman's Brut. Studia Neophilologica 14 1942.

— Lawman's London. Mediaeval Stud 10 1948.

— Two ON motifs in Lawman's Brut. Studia Neophilologica 21 1949.

— A study of the place names in Lawman's Brut. Stanford 1950.

— and F. P. Magoun. The Italian campaign of Belin and Brenne in the Bruts of Wace and Lawman. PQ 12 1942.

Smith, R. M. Lawman's Gernemuðe. MLN 60 1945.

— Gernemuðe and the benighted geography of the minstrels. MLN 64 1949.

Willard, R. Laʒamon in the seventeenth and eighteenth centuries. SE 27 1948.

Everett, D. Laʒamon and the earliest ME alliterative verse. In her Essays on ME literature, Oxford 1955.

Schirmer, W. F. Die frühen Darstellungen des Arthurstoffes. Arbeitsgemeinschaft für Forschung des Nordrhein-Westfalen 73 1958.

Pilch, H. Laʒamon's Brut: eine literarische Studie. Heidelberg 1960.

Kirby, R. J. Angles and Saxons in Laʒamon's Brut. Studia Neophilologica 36 1964.

Swart, J. Laʒamon's Brut. In Studies in language and literature in honour of Margaret Schlauch, Warsaw 1966.

Ringbom, A. Studies in the narrative technique of Beowulf and Lawman's Brut. Acta Academica Aboensis Humaniora ser A 36 1968.

Stanley, E. G. The date of Laʒamon's Brut. N & Q March 1968.

—— Laʒamon's antiquarian sentiments. MÆ 38 1969.

Baumann, W. Pound and Laʒamon's Brut. JEGP 68 1969.

Robert of Gloucester's Chronicle

Wells pp. 195, 794, 1008, 1109, 1169, 1212, 1347, 1391, 1609, 1901.
Mss:

Version I

1, BM Cotton Caligula A 11 ; 2, BM Harley 201 ; 3, BM additional 19,677; 4, Balliol College, Oxford, ptd book, 575 (fragments in the binding) ; 5, BM additional 18,631 ; 6, Hunterian, 415 ; 7, BM additional 50,848.

Version II

8, Trinity College, Cambridge R.4.26 ; 9, Bodley Digby 205 ; 10, Cambridge Univ Lib Ee 4 31 ; 11, London Univ 728 ; 12, Magdalene College Cambridge, Pepys 2014 ; 13, Bodley 1806 ; 14, BM Sloane 2027 ; 15, Huntington HM 126.

Version III

16, College of Arms 58 (with prose insertions).

§ 1

Hearne, T. Robert of Gloucester's Chronicle. 2 vols Oxford 1724, 1810 (ms 1–2).

Wright, W. A. The metrical chronicle of Robert of Gloucester. 2 vols 1897 (Rolls ser) (ms 1).

Selections

Mätzner, E. Altenglische Sprachproben. 2 pts Berlin 1869–1900.

Wülcker, R. Lesebuch. 2 pts Halle 1874–9.

Morris, R. and W. W. Skeat. Specimens of early English vol 2. Oxford 1894.

Kluge, F. Mittelenglisches Lesebuch. Halle 1904.

Hervey, F. Corolla S. Eadmundi. 1907.

Brandl, A. and O. Zippel. Mittelenglische Sprach- und Literaturproben. Berlin 1917.

Sampson, G. Cambridge book of prose and verse. Cambridge 1924.

Dickins, B. and R. M. Wilson. Early ME texts. 1951.

Kaiser, R. Medieval English, translated from the German. Berlin 1958.

Bennett, J. A. W. and G. V. Smithers. Early ME prose and verse. Oxford 1966, 1968 (rev).

Sisam, C. and K. Sisam. Oxford book of medieval English verse. Oxford 1970.

§ 2

Schipper, J. Englische Metrik. Bonn 1881. Section 114.

Ellmer, W. Über die Quellen der Reimchronik Roberts von Gloucester. Halle 1886. *See* Anglia 10 1888.

Pabst, F. Die Sprache der mittelenglischen Reimchronik des Robert von Gloucester. Berlin 1889.

Strohmeyer, H. Der Stil der mittelenglischen Reimchronik Roberts von Gloucester. Berlin 1891.

Liebermann, F. Archiv 146 1923.

Brown, B. D. Robert of Gloucester and the life of Kenelm. MLN 41 1926.

Hill, B. A collation of the Robert of Gloucester fragments in BM add. 50848. N & Q Feb 1965.

Hudson, A. BM ms additional 50848: fragments of Robert of Gloucester's Chronicle. N & Q Nov 1965.

—— Robert of Gloucester and the antiquaries 1550–1800. N & Q Sept 1969.

Short Metrical Chronicle

Wells pp. 198, 794, 1262, 1303, 1347, 1391, 1493, 1609, 1901.
Mss:

Version I

1, BM Royal 12 C 12.

Version II

2, Cambridge Univ Lib Ff 5 48.

Version III

3, BM additional 19,677; 4, Nat Lib of Scotland 19.2.1 ; 5, Cambridge Univ Lib Dd.14.2 ; 6, College of Arms 57 ; 7, Bodley 15,432; 8, BM Cotton Caligula A 9 (a single leaf).

§ 1

Ritson, J. Ancient English metrical romances vol 2. 1802 (ms 1).

Carroll, M. C. and Tuve, R. Two mss of the ME anonymous riming chronicle. PMLA 46 1931 (mss 4, 7).

Zettl, E. A short English metrical chronicle. 1934 (EETS) (all mss).

§ 2

Sternberg, R. Ueber eine versificirte mittelenglische Chronik. E Studien 18 1893.

Serjeantson, M. S. The dialects of the West Midlands in ME. RES 3 1927.

Loomis, L. H. The Auchinleck Roland and Vernagu and the Short Chronicle. MLN 60 1945.

Legge, M. D. The Brut abridged: a query. MÆ 16 1947.

Thomas Castleford's Chronicle

Wells pp. 199, 794, 1391, 1609, 1901.
Ms: Göttingen Lib Codex ms Histor. 740.

§ 1

Behre, F. Castleford's Chronicle. Gothenburg 1940 (part).

Kaiser, R. In Festschrift für Ernst Otto, Berlin 1957 (extracts).

—— Medieval English, translated from the German. Berlin 1958 (extracts).

§ 2

Perrin, M. L. Über Thomas Castlefords Chronik. Göttingen 1890.

Blach, S. Ist Thomas Bek der Verfasser der Göttinger Reimchronik? E Studien 64 1929.

Sunden, K. F. The ME verb Nuyse. Göteborgs Högskolas Aarsskrift 39 1933.

Behre, F. ME noun 'lede'. E Studies 20 1938.

—— ME Rochine. Studia Neophilologica 11 1939.

—— Two words of Scandinavian origin. Studia Neophilologica 14 1942.

—— English 'gal(e)', 'gol', 'goal'. Studia Neophilologica 17 1945.

McIntosh, A. ME 'gannokes' and some place name problems. RES 17 1940.

Brut or the Chronicles of England

Wells pp. 206, 795, 1008, 1052, 1110, 1170, 1212, 1303, 1392, 1494, 1610, 1708, 1902.
Mss: 1, Bodley Rawlinson B 171; 2, Bodley Douce 323; 3, Trinity College Dublin 490. For the details of many others see Brie, below.

§ 1

Brie, F. The Brut or the Chronicles of England. 2 vols 1906–8 (EETS) (ms 1 with collation of 2–3).

§ 2

Madden, F. Prose chronicles of England called the Brute. N & Q 5 Jan 1856.
Brie, F. Geschichte und Quellen der mittelenglischen Prosachronik. In his Brute of England, Marburg 1905.
Arnold, I. The Brut tradition in the English mss. In Miscellany of studies presented to L. E. Kastner, Cambridge 1932.
Brereton, G. E. Des grantz geanz. Oxford 1937.
von Scherling, E. History of King Lear in an early 15th-century ms. Rotulus 4 1937.
Powell, E. O. The Brute or the Chronicle of England. Folklore 48 1937. On Jesus College Oxford ms.

Robert Mannyng of Brunne's Story

Wells pp. 199, 794, 1008, 1109, 1212, 1391, 1493, 1901.
Mss: 1, Inner Temple Lib Petyt no 511, no 7; 2, Lambeth 131; 3, Lincoln Cathedral ms; 4, Bodley Rawlinson Miscellany 1370. See Legge, below.

§ 1

Hearne, T. Peter Langtoft's Chronicles as illustrated and improved by Robert of Brunne. 2 vols Oxford 1725.
Zetsche, A. Chronik des Robert von Brunne. Anglia 9 1886 (ms 2).
Furnivall, F. J. The story of England by Robert Mannyng. 2 vols 1887 (Rolls ser).
Kölbing, E. Ein Fragment von Robert Mannings Chronik. E Studien 17 1892 (ms 4).

Selections

Mätzner, E. Altenglische Sprachproben. 2 pts Berlin 1867–1900.
Wülcker, R. Lesebuch. 2 pts Halle 1874–9.
Zupitza, J. Übungsbuch. Vienna 1874.
Hervey, F. Corolla S. Eadmundi. 1907.
Brandl, A. and O. Zippel. Mittelenglische Sprach- und Literaturproben. Berlin 1917.
Sampson, G. Cambridge book of prose and verse. Cambridge 1924.
Kaiser, R. Medieval English, translated from the German, Berlin 1958.

§ 2

Hellmers, G. H. Über die Sprache von Mannyng. Göttingen 1885.
Preussner, O. Mannyngs Übersetzung von Pierre de Langtofts Chronicle und ihr Verhältniss zum Originale. Breslau 1891.
—— Zur Textkritik von Mannyngs Chronik. E Studien 17 1892.
Thümmig, M. Über die altenglische Übersetzung der Reimchronik Peter Langtofts durch Manning von Brunne. Leipzig 1891. Also Anglia 14 1891.
Boerner, O. Die Sprache Robert Mannyngs of Brunne. Studien zur Englischen Philologie 12 1904. *See also* 50 1913.
Moore, S. Mannyng's use of *do* as auxiliary. MLN 33 1918.

Wyld, H. C. South Eastern and South East Midland dialects in ME. E & S 6 1920.
Beard, C. R. Armour terminology. TLS 26 May 1932.
Legge, M. D. A list of Langtoft mss. MÆ 4 1935.
Atwood, E. B. Mannyng's version of the Troy story. SE 18 1938.
Crosby, R. Mannyng of Brunne: a new biography. PMLA 57 1942.
Seaton, E. Mannyng of Brunne in Lincoln. MÆ 12 1943.
Stepsis, R. The mss of Mannyng of Brunne's Chronicle. Manuscripta 13 1969.

Barbour's Bruce

Wells pp. 202, 795, 1008, 1110, 1212, 1303, 1392, 1493, 1610, 1708, 1901.
Mss: 1, St John's College, Cambridge G 23; 2, Nat Lib of Scotland 19.2.2.

§ 1

Pinkerton, J. The Bruce of the history of Robert I. 1790.
Jamieson, J. The Bruce and Wallace. Edinburgh 1820.
Innes, C. The Brus. Aberdeen 1856 (Spalding Club).
Skeat, W. W. Barbour's Bruce. 4 vols 1870–89 (EETS); rptd 2 vols 1894 (STS), 1968 (EETS).
MacKenzie, W. M. The Bruce. 1909.

Selections

Mätzner, E. Altenglische Sprachproben. 2 pts Berlin 1867–1900.
Zupitza, J. Übungsbuch. Vienna 1874.
Wülcker, R. Lesebuch. 2 pts Halle 1874–9.
Todd, G. E. Early Scottish poetry. Glasgow 1891.
MacLean, G. E. Reader. New York 1893.
Morris, R. and W. W. Skeat. Specimens of early English vol 2. Oxford 1894.
Browne, W. H. Early Scottish poets. Baltimore 1896.
Kluge, F. Mittelenglisches Lesebuch. Halle 1904.
Dixon, W. M. The Edinburgh book of Scottish verse. Edinburgh 1910.
Metcalfe, W. M. Specimens of Scottish literature. 1913.
Emerson, O. F. ME reader. New York 1915.
Cook, A. S. Literary ME reader. Boston 1915.
Neilson, W. A. and K. G. T. Webster. Chief British poets. Boston 1916.
Brandl, A. and O. Zippel. Mittelenglische Sprach- und literaturproben. Berlin 1917.
Sisam, K. Fourteenth-century verse and prose. Oxford 1921.
Gray, M. N. Scottish poetry from Barbour to James VI. 1935.
Mossé, F. Handbook of ME, translated from the French. Baltimore 1952.
Kaiser, R. Medieval English, translated from the German. Berlin 1958.
Kinghorn, A. The Bruce: a selection. Edinburgh 1960.
Douglas, A. N. The Bruce. Glasgow 1964.
MacQueen, J. and T. Scott. The Oxford book of Scottish verse. Oxford 1966.
Sisam, C. and K. Sisam. Oxford book of medieval English verse. Oxford 1970.

Translations

Todd, G. E. The Bruce. Glasgow 1907.
MacMillan, M. The Bruce of Bannockburn. Stirling 1914.
Weston, J. E. Chief ME poets. Boston 1914.

§ 2

Regel, E. Inquiry into phonetic pecularities of Barbour's Bruce. Gera 1877.
Baudisch, U. Ueber die Charactere. Marburg 1886.
Henschel, F. H. Darstellung des Flexionslehre. Leipzig 1886.

Craigie, W. A. Barbour and Blind Harry. Scottish Rev 22 1893.

Kolkwitz, K. P. M. Die Satzgefüge in Barbours Bruce. Halle 1893.

Bearder, J. W. Ueber den Gebrauch der Praepositionen. Halle 1894.

Brown, J. T. T. The Wallace and the Bruce restudied. Bonn 1900.

Neilson, G. J. John Barbour. 1900.

N[eilson], G. Barbour's Bruce: two errors. Scottish Historical Rev 14 1917.

Heuser, W. *Ai* und *ei* in der Cambridger Hanschrift des Bruce. Anglia 17 1904.

Williams, O. T. Old English *a*, *ā*, *æ*. Trans of Philological Soc 1911.

Mühleisen, F. W. Verwantschaft der Überlieferungen von Barbours Bruce. Bonn 1912.

— Textkritische, metrische und grammatische Unter-suchungen von Barbours Bruce. Bonn 1912.

Maxwell, H. The battle of Bannockburn. Scottish Historical Rev 11 1914.

Peter, W. Syntaktischer Gebrauch des Artikels. Kiel 1923.

Wilson, S. C. Scottish Canterbury pilgrims. Scottish Historical Rev 24 1927.

Morris, J. E. The battle of Bannockburn. History 17 1932.

Brie, F. Die nationale Literatur Schottlands. Halle 1937.

Sledd, J. Three textual notes on 14th-century poetry. MLN 55 1940.

Koht, H. Medieval liberty poems. Amer Historical Rev 48 1943.

Legge, M. D. 'In fere of werre'. Scottish Historical Rev 35 1956.

Balfour-Melville, E. W. M. Two John Crabbs. Scottish Historical Rev 39 1960.

Sisam, C. Notes on ME texts. RES new ser 13 1962.

Walker, I. C. Barbour, Blind Harry and Sir William Craigie. Stud in Scottish Lit 1 1964.

Goedhals, B. John Barbour, the Bruce and Bannockburn. Unisa Eng Stud 2 1968.

Trace, J. The supernatural element in Barbour's Bruce. Massachusetts Stud in Eng 1 1968.

Utz, H. Freedom in John Barbour's Bruce. E Studies 50 1969.

Kinghorn, A. M. Scottish historiography in the 14th century. Stud in Scottish Lit 6 1969.

JOHN TREVISA
c. 1330–1402

Wells pp. 204, 795, 957, 1008, 1110, 1170, 1212, 1303, 1392, 1493, 1610, 1708, 1901.
Mss: 1, St John's College, Cambridge H.1 ; 2, BM additional 24,194 ; 3, BM Harley 1900 ; 4, Cotton Tiberius D.7.

§1

Babington, C. and J. R. Lumby. Polychronicon Ranulphi Higden. 9 vols 1865–8 (Rolls ser). Tr Trevisa from Higden's Latin.

Selections

Mätzner, E. Altenglische Sprachproben. 2 pts Berlin 1867–1900.

Wülcker, R. Lesebuch. 2 pts Halle 1874–9.

Morris, R. and W. W. Skeat. Specimens of Early English vol 2. Oxford 1894.

Emerson, O. F. ME reader. New York 1905.

Kluge, F. Mittelenglisches Lesebuch. Halle 1904.

Hervey, F. Corolla S. Eadmundi. 1907.

Sisam, K. Fourteenth-century verse and prose. Oxford 1921.

Mossé, F. Handbook of ME, translated from the French. Baltimore 1952.

Kaiser, R. Medieval English, translated from the German. Berlin 1958.

Minor Pieces by Trevisa

Dialogue between master and clerk. Ed J. Maclean in J. Smyth, Lives of the Berkeleys vol 1, Gloucester 1883; rptd in Fifteenth-century verse and prose, ed A. W. Pollard 1899.

Dialogus inter militem et clericum. Ed A. J. Perry 1924 (EETS).

De proprietatibus rerum. Extracts in R. Steele, Medieval lore, 1893.

§2

Pfeffer, B. Die Sprache des Polychronicons Trevisas. Bonn 1912. On ms Cotton Tiberius D.7.

Wilkins, E. H. Was John Wycliffe a negligent pluralist?; also John de Trevisa his life and work. New York 1915; Appendix, New York 1916.

Perry, A. J. Notes on Trevisa. MLN 33 1918.

— Trevisa: 14th-century translator. In Manitoba essays, ed R. C. Lodge, Toronto 1938.

Cawley, A. C. Punctuation in the early versions of Trevisa. London Medieval Stud 1 1937.

— The relationships of the Trevisa mss and Caxton's Polychronicon. London Medieval Stud 2 1947.

Housman, J. E. Higden, Trevisa, Caxton and the beginnings of Arthurian criticism. RES 23 1947.

Fowler, D. C. Trevisa and the English Bible. MP 58 1960.

— New light on Trevisa. Traditio 18 1962.

— Trevisa: scholar and translator. Trans Bristol & Gloucester Archaeological Soc 89 1970.

— More about Trevisa. MLQ 32 1971.

Taylor, J. The development of the Polychronicon continuation. EHR 76 1961.

Dwyer, R. A. Some readers of Trevisa. N & Q Aug 1967.

V. J. S.

(3) TRAVEL

General Works

Freeling, G. H. (ed). Informacōn for pylgrymes unto the Holy Londe. 1824 (Roxburghe Club); facs of De Worde's 1498 edn ed E. G. Duff 1893.

Wright, T. (ed). Early travels in Palestine. 1848. Includes modernized version of Mandeville's travels.

Ellis, H. (ed). The pylgrymage of Sir Richard Guylforde to the Holy Land. 1851 (Camden Soc).

Grotefend, C. L. Die Edelherren von Boldensele. Hanover 1855. Rptd from Zeitschrift des Historischen Vereins für Niedersachsen 2 1852.

Williams, G. (ed). The itineraries of William Wey, Fellow of Eton College, to Jerusalem AD 1458 and AD 1462; and to Saint James of Compostella AD 1456. 1857

(Roxburghe Club). Also facs of companion map 1867 (Roxburghe Club).

La Grange, Marquis de (ed). Voyaige d'oultremer en Jhérusalem par le Seigneur de Caumont, l'an mccccxviii. Paris 1958.

Chabaille, P. (ed). Li livres dou tresor par Brunetto Latini. Paris 1863.

Laurent, J. C. M. (ed). Peregrinatores medii aevi quatuor. Leipzig 1864.

Bonnardot, F., and A. Longnon (ed). Le saint voyage de Jhérusalem du Seigneur d'Anglure 1395. Paris 1878 (Société des Anciens Textes Français).

Alberti Aquensis historia hierosolymitana. In Recueil des historiens des Croisades: historiens occidentaux vol 4, Paris 1879, 1967.

Michelant, H. and G. Reynaud (ed). Itinéraires à Jérusalem etc. Geneva 1882.

Prutz, H. Kulturgeschichte der Kreuzzüge. Berlin 1883.

Library of Palestine Pilgrims' Text Society. 13 vols and index 1887–97. Especially vol 6 pt 3, Guide-book to Palestine (c. 1350 AD), tr J. H. Bernard; vol 6 pt 4, John Poloner's description of the Holy Land (c. 1421 AD), tr A. Stewart; vol 11 pt 2, The history of Jerusalem, AD 1180, by Jacques de Vitry, tr A. Stewart.

Röhricht, R. Bibliotheca geographica Palaestinae. Berlin 1890, Jerusalem 1963 (with addns).

Cordier, H. (ed). Les voyages en Asie au xive siècle du bienheureux Frère Odoric de Pordenone. Paris 1891.

—— (ed). The book of Ser Marco Polo etc. 2 vols 1903; Notes and addenda, 1920.

—— (ed). Cathay and the way thither etc. 4 vols 1913–16 (Hakluyt Soc).

Schefer, C. (ed). Le voyage d'outremer de Bertrandon de la Broquière. Paris 1892.

Beazley, C. R. The dawn of modern geography. 3 vols 1897–1906.

—— Directorium ad faciendum passagium transmarinum. Amer Historical Rev 12–13 1906–8.

Rockhill, W. W. (ed and tr). The journey of William of Rubruck, with two accounts of the earlier journey of John of Pian de Carpine. 1900 (Hakluyt Soc).

Hayton: La flor des estoires de la terre d'Orient. In Recueil des historiens des Croisades: documents arméniens vol 2, Paris 1906, 1967.

Hallberg, I. L'extrême Orient dans la littérature et la cartographie de l'Occident des xiiie, xive, et xve siècles. Gothenburg 1907.

Le livre des merveilles: manuscrit français 2810 de la Bibliothèque Nationale. 2 vols (portfolios) Paris [1908] (facs).

Stretton, G. Some aspects of medieval travel. Trans Royal Historical Soc 4th ser 7 1924.

Wyngaert, A. v. d. Jean de Mont Corvin. Lille 1924.

—— (ed). Sinica Franciscana vol 1: itinera et relationes fratrum minorum saeculi xiii et xiv. Florence 1929.

Wright, J. K. The geographical lore of the time of the Crusades. New York 1925.

Andrews, M. C. The study and classification of medieval mappae mundi. Archaeologia 75 1926.

Letts, M. (ed and tr). Pero Tafur: travels and adventures 1435–9. 1926.

Letts, M. Prester John. Trans Royal Historical Soc 4th ser 29 1947.

Newton, A. P. (ed). Travel and travellers of the Middle Ages. 1926.

Benedetto, L. F. (ed). Marco Polo: il milione. Florence 1928. Plates.

Komroff, M. (ed). Contemporaries of Marco Polo. 1928.

Le Strange, G. (ed and tr). Clavijo: embassy to Tamerlane 1403–6. 1928.

James, M. R. (ed). Marvels of the East. 1929 (Roxburghe Club) (facs).

Anderson, A. R. Alexander's gate, Gog and Magog, and the inclosed nations. Cambridge Mass 1932.

Rice, W. G. Early English travelers to Greece and the Levant. Univ of Michigan Pbns in Lang & Lit 10 1933.

Woodruff, C. E. (ed and tr). A xvth-century guide-book to the principal churches of Rome. 1933.

Joranson, E. The Palestine pilgrimage of Henry the Lion. In Medieval and historiographical essays in honor of J. W. Thompson, Chicago 1938.

Kimble, G. H. T. Geography in the Middle Ages. 1938.

Moule, A. C. and P. Pelliot. Marco Polo: the description of the world. 2 vols 1938.

Olschki, L. Marco Polo's precursors. Baltimore 1943.

—— L'Asia di Marco Polo. Venice and Rome 1957; tr 1960.

Crone, G. R. The Hereford world map. 1948 (Royal Geographical Soc).

Monneret de Villard, U. (ed). Liber peregrinationis di Jacopo da Verona. Rome 1950 (Il nuovo Ramusio vol 1).

Beer, E. S. de. The development of the guide-book. Jnl of Br Archaeological Assoc 3rd ser 15 1952.

Penrose, B. Travel and discovery in the Renaissance 1420–1620. Cambridge Mass 1952.

Carus-Wilson, E. M. English merchant venturers. 1954.

Parks, G. B. The English traveler to Italy: vol 1, The Middle Ages (to 1525). Rome 1954.

Dawson, C. (ed). The Mongol mission. 1955.

Barber, M. J. The Englishman abroad in the fifteenth century. Medievalia et Humanistica 11 1957.

Helleiner, K. F. Prester John's letter: a mediaeval Utopia. Phoenix: Jnl Classical Assoc of Canada 13 1959.

Slessarev, V. (ed). Prester John: the letter and the legend. Minneapolis 1959.

Travels of Marco Polo. 1959. 25 plates.

T'Serstevens, A. Les précurseurs de Marco Polo. Paris 1959.

Jewkes, W. T. The literature of travel and the mode of romance in the Renaissance. BNYPL April 1963.

Parry, J. H. The age of reconnaissance. 1963.

Mitchell, R. J. The spring voyage: the Jerusalem pilgrimage in 1458. 1964.

Skelton, R. A. et al. The Vinland map and the Tartar relation. 1965. Plates; with bibliography.

Hyde, J. K. Medieval descriptions of cities. Bull John Rylands Lib 48 1966.

Rachewiltz, I. de. Papal envoys to the Great Khans. 1971.

Stations of Rome

§1

Ms 1, Vernon ms (ms Bodley 3938); ms 2, BM additional ms 22,283; with prologue; ed F. J. Furnivall 1867 (EETS) and, prologue only, 1901 (EETS).

Ms 3, BM ms Cotton Caligula A ii; ms 4, Lambeth ms 306; ed F. J. Furnivall 1866 (EETS).

Ms 5, BM additional ms 37,787 (incomplete). Ed N. S. Baugh, A Worcestershire miscellany, Philadelphia 1956.

Ms 6, Public Record Office ms SC 6/956/5 (roll). See Scattergood, below.

Ms 7, BM ms Cotton Vespasian D ix (incomplete).

Ms 8, Newberry Library ms Gen add 12 (roll; formerly Condover Hall ms).

Ms 9, National Library of Wales Porkington ms 10 (prose); ed F. J. Furnivall 1867 (EETS).

[Ms 10, Canterbury Cathedral additional ms 68, formerly Z.8.33, Ingilby ms, contains not this text but the Latin one of William Brewyn, ed and tr Woodruff 1933 above].

§2

Hulbert, J. R. Some medieval advertisements of Rome. MP 20 1923.

de Beer, E. S. The stacions of Rome. N & Q 27 Feb 1943.

—— An English xv-century pilgrimage poem. N & Q 2 Dec 1944.

Kurvinen, A. Ms Porkington 10. Neuphilologische Mitteilungen 54 1953.

Scattergood, V. J. An unpublished Middle English poem. Archiv 203 1967.

—— An inedited ms of the Stacions of Rome. Eng Philological Stud 11 1968.

Stations of Jerusalem
See also General Works on the Holy Land, above.

§ 1

Ms 1, Bodley ms Ashmole 61; ed C. Horstmann, Altenglische Legenden, Heilbronn 1881.

Ms 2, Bodley 565; pbd in The itineraries of William Wey, above.

Ms 3, Huntington Library ms HM 144 (formerly Huth ms); not pbd; see Ricci Census p. 58, and Manly and Rickert, Text of the Canterbury tales vol 1, pp. 289 f.

§ 2

Brown, J. T. T. The poems of David Rate etc. Scottish Antiquary 11 1897.

Dunlap, A. R. A pilgrimage to the Holy Land. MLN 63 1948. See de Beer, N & Q 1944, above.

Travels of Sir John Mandeville

There are some 250 mss in most West European languages; see Bennett, Rediscovery, below. For the 40 English mss, see Seymour, Edinburgh Bibl Soc Trans 4 1966, below.

§ 1

Ms 1, BM ms Cotton Titus C xvi; ed P. Hamelius 2 vols Oxford 1919–23 (EETS); ed M. C. Seymour, Oxford 1967 (with bibliography). Modernized edns: A. W. Pollard 1901, 1923; M. C. Seymour, Oxford 1968 (WC). Selections in R. Morris and W. W. Skeat, Specimens of early English pt 2, Oxford 1894; K. Sisam, 14th-century verse and prose, Oxford 1921; W. Matthews, Later medieval English prose, 1962 (modernized).

Ms 2, BM ms Egerton 1982; ed G. F. Warner 1889 (Roxburghe Club) (with French text, plates). Modernized version ed M. Letts 2 vols 1953 (Hakluyt Soc) (with French text, bibliography etc; see also below). Selections in A. S. Cook, Reader, Boston 1915.

Ms 3, Bodley ms Rawlinson D 99; ed M. Letts above.

Ms 4, Bodley ms e Musæo 116; ed M. C. Seymour, Oxford 1963 (EETS) (with Latin text).

Also the defective version, represented by 32 mss and a collection of extracts; pbd in pre-18th-century edns and in modernized form ed J. Bramont 1928 (EL).

Ms 5, The epitome, in BM additional ms 37049; see Seymour, Anglia 84, below.

Ms 6, The metrical version, in a Coventry Record Office ms; unpbd.

Ms 7, The stanzaic fragment, in Bodley ms e Musæo 160. *See Seymour, Jnl of Australasian Univs, below.*

§ 2

See also the edns by Warner, Hamelius, Letts and Seymour, above. For edns of sources see under General Works, above.

Vogels, J. Die ungedruckten lateinischen Versionen Mandevilles. Programm des Gymnasiums zu Crefeld 1885–6.

— Handschriftliche Untersuchungen über die englische Version Mandevilles. Crefeld 1891.

Bovenschen, A. Untersuchungen über Johann von Mandeville und die Quellen seiner Reisebeschreibung. Zeitschrift der Gesellschaft für Erdkunde zu Berlin 23 1888.

Cordier, H. Jean de Mandeville. T'oung pao: archives de l'Asie orientale 2 1891.

Toynbee, P. Christine de Pisan and Sir John Mandeville. Romania 21 1892.

Fife, R. H. Der Wortschatz des englischen Maundeville nach der Version der Cotton Handschrift etc. Leipzig 1902.

Brown, C. F. Note on the dependence of Cleanness on the Book of Mandeville. PMLA 19 1904.

Lowes, J. L. The dry sea and the Carrenare. MP 3 1905.

Singer, D. W. Note on Sir John Mandeville. Library 3rd ser 9 1918.

Munro, J. J. Sir John Mandeville's Egypt. Egypt & Sudan Diocesan Rev 3 1924.

Jackson, I. Who was Sir John Mandeville? a fresh clue. MLR 23 1928.

Steiner, A. The date of composition of Mandeville's travels. Speculum 9 1934.

Meer, H. J. v. d. Main facts concerning the syntax of Mandeville's travels. Utrecht 1929.

Cameron, K. W. A discovery in John de Mandevilles. Speculum 11 1936.

Lascelles, M. Alexander and the earthly paradise in mediæval English writing. MÆ 5 1936.

Braaksma, M. Travel and literature. Groningen 1938.

Lange, H. Chaucer und Mandevilles travels. Archiv 174 1938.

— Die Paradiesvorstellung in Mandevilles Travels im Lichte mittelalterlicher Dichtung: zur Lösung der Legendenprologfrage bei Chaucer. E Studien 72 1938.

Bennett, H. S. Science and information in English writings of the fifteenth century. MLR 39 1944.

Letts, M. The dry tree; the liver sea; the ark on Mount Ararat; Sir John Mandeville, the man; truth or fiction? N & Q 13 July, 10 Aug, 5 Oct, 16 Nov, 28 Dec 1946.

— The sources; manuscripts and printed editions; Jean d'Outremeuse; the earliest manuscript; the Libri-Barrois scandal. N & Q 8 Feb, 5 April, 31 May, 15 Nov 1947.

— The Ogier passages again; the transformations of place-names and errors in translation. N & Q 7 Feb, 15 May 1948.

— Mandeville: the man and his book. 1949.

— The source of the woodcuts in Wynkyn de Worde's edition of Mandeville's travels. Library 5th ser 6 1951.

Fazy, R. Jehan de Mandeville: ses voyages et son séjour discuté en Egypte. Etudes Asiatiques 4 1950.

Haraszti, Z. The travels of Sir John Mandeville. Boston Public Lib Quart 2 1950.

Bennett, J. W. Chaucer and Mandeville's travels. MLN 68 1953.

— The woodcut illustrations in the English editions of Mandeville's travels. PBSA 47 1953.

— The rediscovery of Sir John Mandeville. New York 1954. Lists mss and early edns.

Mourin, L. Les lapidaires attribués à Jean de Mandeville et à Jean à la Barbe. Romanica Gandensia 4 1955.

Poerck, G. de. La tradition manuscrite des Voyages de Jean de Mandeville. Romanica Gandensia 4 1955.

— Le corpus mandevillien du ms Chantilly 699. In Fin du Moyen Age et Renaissance: mélanges de philologie française offerts à Robert Guiette, Antwerp 1961.

Cawley, A. C. A Ripon fragment of Mandeville's travels. E Studies 38 1957.

Thomas, J. D. The date of Mandeville's travels. MLN 72 1957.

Yorke, E. C. Nashe and Mandeville. N & Q April 1957.

Seymour, M. C. Secundum Iohannem Maundvyle. Eng Stud in Africa 4 1961.

— A medieval redactor at work. N & Q May 1961.

— The origin of the Egerton version of Mandeville's travels. MÆ 30 1961.

— The early English editions of Mandeville's travels. Library 5th ser 19 1964.

— The scribal tradition of Mandeville's travels: the insular version. Scriptorium 18 1964.

— Mandeville and Marco Polo: a stanzaic fragment. Jnl of Australasian Universities' Lang & Lit Assoc 21 1964.

— The English manuscripts of Mandeville's travels. Edinburgh Bibl Soc Trans 4 1966.

— The English epitome of Mandeville's travels. Anglia 84 1966.

— A fifteenth-century East Anglian scribe. MÆ 37 1968.

Schepens, L. Quelques observations sur la tradition manuscrite du Voyage de Mandeville. Scriptorium 18 1964.

Kock, J. de. Quelques copies aberrantes des Voyages de Jean de Mandeville. Le Moyen Age 71 1965.

Moseley, C. W. R. D. Stitched ships and loadstone rocks. N & Q Sept 1968. Addn by B. Foster, Nov 1969.

— The lost play of Mandeville. Library 5th ser 25 1970.

— Richard Head's The English rogue: a modern Mandeville? MLR 65 1970.

— Mandeville's visit to the Pope: the implications of an interpolation. Neophilologus 54 1970.

C. C.

(4) PROPHECIES

Wells pp. 220, 797, 957, 1008, 1111, 1170, 1213, 1304, 1347, 1392, 1495, 1709.

General Studies

Taylor, R. Political prophecy in England. New York 1911.

Griffiths, M. E. Early vaticination. Cardiff 1937.

Here Prophecy

Wells pp. 221, 797.

§ 1

Hales, J. W. Folia literaria. 1893.

Morley, H. English writers vol 3. 1889.

Stubbs, W. Chronicle of Benedict of Peterborough vol 2. 1867 (Rolls ser).

Riley, H. T. Roger of Hoveden vol 2. 1853.

Saintsbury, G. A history of English prosody vol 1. 1906.

Taylor, R. Political prophecy in England. New York 1911.

Adam Davy's Five Dreams

Wells pp. 221, 797, 1008, 1111, 1213.
Ms: Bodley Laud 622.

§ 1

Furnivall, F. J. Adam Davie's Five Dreams about Edward II. 1878 (EETS).

Emerson, O. F. ME Reader. New York 1915.

Selections

Kluge, F. Mittelenglisches Lesebuch. Halle 1904.

Brandl, A. and O. Zippel. Mittelenglische Sprach- und Literaturproben. Berlin 1917.

§ 2

Emerson, O. F. The date of Adam Davy's Dreams. MLR 21 1926.

Heather, P. J. Seven planets. Folklore 54 1943.

Scattergood, V. J. Adam Davy's Dreams and Edward II. Archiv 206 1969.

Prophecy of the Six Kings

Wells pp. 222, 797, 1304.
Mss: 1, BM Cotton Galba E 9; 2, Bodley 4062; 3, BM Harley 559.

§ 1

Laing, D. Ancient Scottish prophecies. Edinburgh 1833 (Bannatyne Club).

Hall, J. Poems of Minot. Oxford 1907 (ms 1). Appendix 2.

Brie, F. The Brut or the Chronicle of England. 1906 (EETS) (ms 2).

Earliest Scottish Prophecy

('When Alisandre our King was deid . . .')

Mss: at the end of Bk 7 of Andrew Wintoun's Chronicle of Scotland. 1, BM Cotton Nero D 11; 2, BM Lansdowne 197; 3, BM Royal 17 D 20; 4, Nat Lib of Scotland 19.2.3; 5, Nat Lib of Scotland 19.2.4; 6, Nat Lib of Scotland 651; 7, St Andrews Univ T.T. 66; 8, Colville; 9, Wemyss.

§ 1

Ellis, G. Specimens of the early English poets vol 1. 1790.

Laing, D. The Orygynale cronykil of Scotland by Andrew of Wyntoun. Edinburgh 1872.

Eyre-Todd, G. Early Scottish poetry. Glasgow 1891 (Abbotsford ser).

Murray, J. A. H. Dialects of the southern counties of Scotland. 1873.

Amours, F. J. The original chronicle of Andrew of Wyntoun. 6 vols 1903–14 (STS).

Brandl, A. and O. Zippel. Mittelenglische Sprach- und Literaturproben. Berlin 1917.

Wilson, R. M. More lost literature in Old and ME. Leeds Stud in Eng 5 1936.

MacQueen, J. and T. Scott. Oxford book of Scottish verse. Oxford 1966.

First Scottish Prophecy

'When the cocke in the Northe . . .'

Wells pp. 226, 798, 1347, 1393, 1495, 1611.
Mss: 1, Bodley Lyell, 35 ; 2, Cambridge Univ Lib Kk 1.5 ; 3, Caius College Cambridge 249 ; 4, BM Cotton Rolls 2.23 ; 5, BM Harley 559 ; 6, BM Harley 1717 ; 7, BM Lansdowne 762 ; 8, BM Sloane 1802 ; 9, BM Sloane 2578 ; 10, BM Sloane 4031 ; 11, BM additional 24663 ; 12, Nat Lib of Wales, Peniarth 26 ; 13, Nat Lib of Wales, Peniarth 50 ; 14, Nat Lib of Wales, Peniarth 58 ; 15, Trinity College, Dublin 516 ; 16, Westminster Abbey 27 ; 17, Porkington 10.

§ 1

Laing, D. Ancient Scottish prophecies. Edinburgh 1833 (Bannatyne Club).

Lumby, J. R. Bernardus de cura rei famuliaris. 1870 (EETS) (ms 2).

Robbins, R. H. Historical poems of the 14th and 15th centuries. New York 1959 (ms 4).

Composite texts have been edited by A. Brandl, Sitzungberichte der Königlichen Preussischen Akademie der Wissenschaften, Berlin 1909; and by Haferkorn, Eine politische Prophezeiung des 14 Jahrhunderts, Beiträge zur Englischen Philologie 19 1932.

Second Scottish Prophecy

'Qwhen Rome is removyde . . .'

Wells pp. 226, 798, 1347, 1393, 1495, 1611.
Mss:

Version I

1, Bodley Lyell 35 ; 2, Cambridge Univ Lib Kk 1.5 ; 3, Nat Lib of Wales, Peniarth 26 ; 4, Nat Lib of Wales, Peniarth 50 ; 5, Nat Lib of Wales, Peniarth 94 ; 6, Nat Lib of Wales additional 441 C ; 7, Llanstephen 119 ; 8, Public Record Office, State papers of Henry VIII ; 9, Westminster Abbey 27 ; 10, Mostyn 133.

Fragments of this version appear in BM Harley 559 and BM Sloane 2578.

Version II

11, Cotton Vespasian E 8 ; 12, BM Sloane 1802.

Version III

13, BM Cotton Cleopatra C.4; 14, BM Royal 7 A 9; 15, Nat Lib of Wales, Peniarth 26 ; 16, Nat Lib of Wales, Peniarth 94; 17, Llanstephen 119.

§1

Laing, D. Ancient Scottish prophecies. Edinburgh 1833 (Bannatyne Club).

Stevenson, J. Lancelot du Lak. Glasgow 1839 (Maitland Club) (ms 2).

Wright, T. Political poems and songs vol 2. 1861 (Rolls ser) (ms 13).

Furnivall, F. J. Ballads from mss. 1868 (Ballad Soc) (ms 8).

Lumby, J. R. Bernardus de cura rei famuliaris. 1870 (EETS) (ms 2).

Robbins, R. H. Historical poems of the 14th and 15th centuries. New York 1959 (mss 2, 14).

Most mss and fragments are ptd by Haferkorn, Eine politische Prophezeiung des 14 Jahrhunderts. Beiträge zur Englischen Philologie 19 1932.

§2

Taylor, R. Political prophecy in England. New York 1911.

Oakden, J. P. Alliterative poetry in ME vol 1. Manchester 1930.

Thomas A Becket's Prophecy

Wells pp. 1392, 1611.
Mss: 1, Bodley 4062; 2, Cambridge Univ Lib Kk 1.5.

§1

Stevenson, J. Lancelot du Lak. Glasgow 1839 (Maitland Club) (ms 2).

Lumby, J. R. Bernardus de cura rei famuliaris. 1870 (EETS) (ms 2).

Taylor, R. Political prophecy in England. New York 1911 (30 lines only of ms 1).

Thomas of Ersseldoune

Wells pp. 224, 798, 1009, 1111, 1213, 1611, 1902.
Mss: 1, Bodley 13814; 2, Cambridge Univ Lib Ff.5.48; 3, BM Cotton Vitellius E 10 ; 4, BM Lansdowne, 762 ; 5, BM Sloane 2578 ; 6, Lincoln Cathedral 91 (Thornton).
Fragments appear in Bodley 4062, 6683, 8258, BM Harley 559, BM additional 6702.

§1

Jamieson, R. Popular ballads and songs vol 2. 1806 (ms 2).

Halliwell, J. O. Illustrations of the fairy mythology of Shakespear's Midsummer night's dream. 1845 (ms 2).

Murray, J. A. H. The romance and prophecies of Thomas of Erceldoune. 1875 (EETS) (ms 2-6).

Brandl, A. Sammlung englischer Denkmäler vol 2. Berlin 1880 (ms 2).

Child, F. J. English and Scottish popular ballads vols 1, 4. Boston 1883-98 (ms 6).

Laing, D. Early popular poetry of Scotland vol 1. Rev W. C. Hazlitt 1895 (ms 6).

Scott, W. Minstrelsy of the Scottish border vol 4. Rev T. F. Henderson, Edinburgh 1902 (ms 3).

Selections

Wright, T. and J. O. Halliwell. Reliquae antiquae vol 1. 1840.

Cook, A. S. Literary ME reader. Boston 1915.

Brandl, A. and O. Zippel. Mittelenglische Sprach- und Literaturproben. Berlin 1917.

Sampson, G. Cambridge book of prose and verse. Cambridge 1924.

§2

Holthausen, F. Alt- und mittelenglischen Dichtungen. Anglia 14 1892.

Burnham, J. M. A study of Thomas of Erceldoune. PMLA 23 1908.

Taylor, R. Political prophecy in England. New York 1911.

Saalbach, A. Entstehungsgeschichte der schottischen Volksballade T. Rymer. Halle 1913.

Medary, M. P. Stanza linking in ME verse. Romanic Rev 7 1916.

Flasdieck, H. M. Tom der Reimer: von keltischen Feen und politischen Propheten. Breslau 1934.

Schmidt, W. Die Volksballaden von Tom dem Reimer. Anglia 61 1939.

Albrecht, W. P. The loathly lady in Thomas of Erceldoune, with a text of the poem printed in 1652. Albuquerque 1954.

—— A seventeenth-century text of Thomas of Erceldoune. MÆ 23 1954.

Nelson, C. E. The origin and tradition of the ballads of Thomas the Rhymer. In New voices in American studies, ed R. B. Browne et al, Lafayette Ind 1966.

Lyle, E. B. A comment on the rhyme-scheme of two stanzas in Thomas of Erceldoune. N & Q Feb 1969.

—— A reconsideration of the place-names in Thomas the Rhymer. Scottish Stud 13 1969.

—— The Turk and Gawain as a source for Thomas of Erceldoune. Forum for Modern Lang Stud 6 1970.

—— The relationship between Thomas the Rhymer and Thomas of Erceldoune. Leeds Stud in Eng new ser 4 1970.

—— The Celtic affinities of the gift in Thomas of Erceldoune. Eng Lang Notes 8 1971.

—— The visions of St Patrick's Purgatory: Thomas of Erceldoune, Thomas the Rhymer and the Demon Lover. Neuphilologische Mitteilungen 72 1971.

'To ny3t is boren a barn in Kærnervam . . .'

Ms: Arundel 57.

§1

Brandl, A. and O. Zippel. Mittelenglische Sprach- und Literaturproben. Berlin 1917.

Morris, R. Dan Michel's A3enbite of Inwyt. 1866 (EETS); rev P. Gradon 1965. Preface.

'When man as mad a kyng of capped man . . .'

Ms: Harley 2253.

§1

Pinkerton, J. Ancient Scottish poems vol 1. 1786.

Murray, J. A. H. The romance and prophecies of Thomas of Erceldoune. 1875 (EETS).

Laing, D. Select remains of the ancient popular and romance poetry of Scotland. Rev J. Small, Edinburgh 1885.

Brandl, A. and O. Zippel. Mittelenglische Sprach- und Literaturproben. Berlin 1917.

Scott, W. Minstrelsy of the Scottish border vol 4. Rev Henderson, Edinburgh 1932.

Robbins, R. H. Historical poems of the 14th and 15th centuries. New York 1959.

Merlin's Prophecy

*Mss: 1, Bodley 6943; 2, Bodley 8113; 3, Bodley 9914;
4, Bodley 14526; 5, Bodley Latin Miscellany C.66;
6, Cambridge Univ Lib Gg.4.27; 7, Cambridge Univ
Lib Ii.3.26; 8, Cambridge Univ Lib Ii.6.11; 9, Pepys 1236;
10, Trinity College, Cambridge 595; 11, BM Harley
1337; 12, BM Royal 17.A.16; 13, BM additional
24,663; 14, Fitzwilliam Museum 355 (a); 15, John
Rylands Lib Latin 201; 16, Trinity College Dublin 516;
17, Illuminated Missal (location unknown).*

§ 1

Todd, H. J. Illustrations of the lives and writings of
Gower and Chaucer. 1810 (ms 10).

Brydges, E. and J. Haslewood. The British bibliographer
vol 2. 1863 (ms 17).

Blades, W. Life and typography of William Caxton vol 2.
1863 (ms 17).

Furnivall, F. J. and G. Kingsley. Francis Thynne's
Animadversions. 1865 (EETS) (ms 16).

Skeat, W. W. Complete works of Chaucer vols 1, 7.
Oxford 1894–7 (ms 1).

Fawtier, E. C. and R. From Merlin to Shakespeare:
adventures of an English prophecy. Bull John Rylands
Lib 5 1920 (ms 15).

James, M. R. Bibliotheca Pepysiana: medieval mss vol 3.
1923 (ms 9).

D'Evelyn, C. Peter Idley's Instructions to his son.
Cambridge Mass 1935 (ms 9).

Robbins, R. H. Poems of Humfrey Newton esq 1466–
1536. PMLA 65 1950 (ms 8).

— Historical poems of the 14th and 15th centuries.
New York 1959 (ms 16).

§ 2

Paton, L. Les prophécies de Merlin. New York 1926.

— Notes on Merlin in the Historia regum Britanniae of
Geoffrey of Monmouth. MP 41 1943.

Millican, C. B. The first English translations of the
Prophecies of Merlin. SP 28 1931. On a 17th-century
version.

Hammer, J. A commentary on the Prophetia Merlini.
Speculum 10 1935, 15 1940.

Gerould, G. H. A text of Merlin's prophecies. Speculum
23 1948. On Geoffrey of Monmouth's version.

Geoffrey of Monmouth's Prophecy

Ms: Bodley 15165 (Rawlinson K.42).

§ 1

Robbins, R. H. Geoffrey of Monmouth: an English
fragment. E Studies 38 1957.

— Historical poems of the 14th and 15th centuries.
New York 1959.

'And xl yen barons ful bolde shall be brittend to dethe . . .'

Ms: Cambridge Univ Lib Ll.1.18.

§ 1

Day, M. Fragment of an alliterative political prophecy.
RES 15 1939.

A Political Prophecy by the Dice

Mss:

Version I

*1, Bodley 13814; 2, Trinity College Cambridge 1157;
3, BM Cotton Cleopatra C. 4; 4, BM Harley 559;
5, BM Harley 7332; 6, BM Lansdowne 762; 7, BM
Sloane 2578 (several texts); 8, Trinity College Dublin
516.*

Version II (with introductory lines)

*9, Cambridge Univ Lib Ii.6.11; 10, BM Cotton Rolls 2.23;
11, BM Harley 559.*

§ 1

Furnivall, F. J. Ballads from mss. 1868 (Ballad Soc)
(mss 5, 9).

— and G. Kingsley. Thynne's Animadversions. 1865
(EETS) (ms 8).

Robbins, R. H. Historical poems of the 14th and 15th
centuries. New York 1959 (ms 8).

V. J. S.

(5) VERSIONS OF THE BIBLE

Severs pp. 381, 534; for Wycliffite versions see (7), below.

Paues, A. C. A fourteenth-century English biblical
version. Cambridge 1902. Introd, omitted from later
edns.

Deanesly, M. The Lollard Bible and other medieval
biblical versions. Cambridge 1920, 1966 (with note).

Craigie, W. A. The English versions (to Wyclif). In The
Bible in its ancient and English versions, ed H. W.
Robinson, Oxford 1940.

Butterworth, C. C. The literary lineage of the King James
Bible. Philadelphia 1941.

Grierson, H. J. C. The English Bible. 1943.

Smalley, B. The study of the Bible in the Middle Ages.
1941, 1952 (rev).

Hargreaves, H. From Bede to Wyclif: medieval English
Bible translations. Bull John Rylands Lib 48 1966.

— The Mirror of our Lady: Aberdeen Univ Lib ms 134.
Aberdeen Univ Rev 42 1968.

Shepherd, G. English versions of the scriptures before
Wyclif. In The Cambridge history of the Bible vol 2,
Cambridge 1969.

Metrical Paraphrase of the Old Testament

Severs pp. 382, 535; Index 944.

§ 1

Ed H. Kalen, A ME paraphrase of the Old Testament,
Göteborgs Högskolas Arsskrift 28 1923 (first 6,000
lines); continued in U. Ohlander, A ME metrical
paraphrase of OT, Gothenburg Stud in Eng 5 1955,
11 1961, 16 1963.

Selections: C. Horstmann, Nachträge zu den Legenden,
Archiv 79 1887; ed W. Heuser, Die alttestamentlichen
Dichtungen des Ms Seld Supra 52, Anglia 31 1908.

§ 2

Ohlander, U. Old French parallels to a ME metrical
paraphrase of OT. Gothenburg Stud in Eng 14 1961.

Genesis and Exodus

Severs pp. 381, 535; Index 2072.

§ 1

Ed R. Morris 1865 (EETS), 1873 (rev); ed O. Arngart,
Lund Stud in Eng 36 1968.

Selections: J. Hall, Selections from early ME, Oxford
1920.

§2

Caro, J. Zur mittelenglischen Genesis und Exodus. E Studien 68 1933.

Linke, G. Der Wortschatz des ME Epos Genesis und Exodus. Palaestra 197 1935.

— Zur Textkritik von ME Genesis und Exodus. Archiv 171 1937.

Arngart, O. Notes on the ME Genesis and Exodus. E Studies 38 1957.

— Two ME textual notes. In English studies presented to R. W. Zandvoort, Amsterdam 1964.

Jacob and Josep

Severs pp. 382, 536; Index 4172.

§1

Ed W. Heuser, Das fruhmittelenglische Josephlied, Bonner Beiträge zur Anglistik 17 1905; ed A. S. Napier, Oxford 1916.

§2

Sherwin, O. Art's spring-birth: the ballad of Jacob and Josep. SP 42 1945.

Faverty, F. E. Legends of Joseph in Old and Middle English. PMLA 43 1928.

Commentary on Psalms 90-1 (Vulgate)

Severs pp. 389, 541. For mss see Wallner, below.

B. Wallner, An exposition of Qui habitat and Bonum est in English. Lund Stud in Eng 23 1954.

Midland Prose Psalter

Severs pp. 385, 537; mss BM additional 17376, Magdalene College Cambridge Pepys 2498, Trinity College Dublin A4.4.

§1

Ed K. Bülbring, The earliest complete English prose psalter, 1891 (EETS).

§2

Logeman, H. The ME WM prose psalter Ps. 90 10. Archiv 134 1916. Reply by O. F. Emerson, MP 16 1918.

Sergeantson, M. S. The dialect of the earliest complete English prose psalter. E Studies 6 1924.

Dodson, S. The glosses in the earliest complete English prose psalter. SE 12 1932.

Reuter, O. A study of the French words in the earliest complete English prose psalter. Societas Scientiarum Fennica Commentationes Humanarum Litterarum 9 1938.

Reuter, O. Instances of 'the which' in the glossed prose psalter and their relation to the French original. Neuphilologische Mitteilungen 40 1939.

Muir, A. L. Some observations on the early English psalters and the English vocabulary. MLQ 9 1948.

Hargreaves, H. The vocabulary of the Surtees psalter. MLQ 17 1956.

Richard Rolle's English Psalter

See under Richard Rolle, col 517, below.

Surtees Psalter

Severs pp. 385, 537; Index 3103.

§1

Ed J. Stevenson, Early English psalter, 2 vols 1843–7 (Surtees Soc); ed C. Horstmann, Library of early English writers: Yorkshire writers vol 2, 1896.

§2

Wende, E. Überlieferung und Sprache der ME Versions des Psalters. Breslau 1884.

Everett, D. The ME prose psalter of Richard Rolle part 2. MLR 17 1922.

Muir, A. L. Some observations on the early English psalters and the English vocabulary. MLQ 9 1948.

Hargreaves, H. The vocabulary of the Surtees psalter. MLQ 17 1956.

Maydestone's Penitential Psalms

Severs pp. 388, 540; Index 1961, 2157, 3755.

§1

Ed M. Kaluza, Studien zu Richard Rolle de Hampole, E Studien 10 1887; ed F. S. Ellis 1894 (Kelmscott Press); ed M. Day, The Wheatley manuscript, 1917 (EETS); [Psalm 51 only] ed F. J. Furnivall, Political, religious and love poems, 1866 (EETS); ed C. Horstmann, Minor poems of the Vernon ms, 1892 (EETS).

Bühler, C. F. The Kelmscott edition of the Psalmi penitentiales and Morgan ms 99. MLN 60 1945.

Kreuzer, J. R. Richard Maidstone's version of the fifty-first psalm. MLN 66 1951.

Brampton's Penitential Psalms

Sever :pp. 388, 541; Index 355, 1591.

Ed J. R. Kreuzer, Traditio 7 1949.

Susannah or the Pistill of Susan

Severs pp. 390, 542; Index 3553.

§1

Ed D. Laing, Select remains of the ancient popular poetry of Scotland, 1822; rev W. C. Hazlitt 1895; ed C. Horstmann, Die Legenden von Celestin und Susanna, Anglia 1 1878; Nachträge zu den Legenden, Archiv 62 1879; Nachtrage zu den Legenden, Archiv 74 1885; ed F. J. Amours, Scottish alliterative poems, 1892 (STS); ed H. Köster, Quellen und Forschungen 76 1895; ed F. J. Furnivall, Minor poems of the Vernon manuscript, 1901 (EETS); ed A. Miskimin, New Haven 1969.

§2

Brade, G. Ueber Huchowns Pistil of suet Susane. Breslau 1892.

Mozley, J. M. Susannah and the elders: three medieval poems. Studi Medievali 3 1930.

Kellogg, A. L. Susannah and the Merchant's tale. Speculum 35 1960.

Paues New Testament Version

Severs pp. 398, 546; mss Selwyn College Cambridge 108 L 1, Corpus Christi College Cambridge Parker 434, Cambridge Univ Lib Dd xii 39, Bodley Douce 250, Bodley Holkham miscellany 40.

Ed A. C. Paues, A fourteenth-century English biblical version, Cambridge 1902, 1904 (with shortened introd).

Prose Life of Jesus

Severs pp. 393, 544; ms Magdalene College Cambridge Pepys 2498.

Ed M. Goates, The Pepysian gospel harmony, 1922 (EETS).

The Women of Samaria

Severs pp. 397, 546; Index 3704.

Ed R. Morris, An Old English miscellany, 1872 (EETS).

The Passion of our Lord

Severs pp. 393, 544; Index 1441.

Ed R. Morris, An Old English miscellany, 1872 (EETS).

Stanzaic Life of Christ

Severs pp. 392, 543; Index 1755.

§1

Ed F. A. Foster 1926 (EETS).

§2

Wilson, R. H. The stanzaic life of Christ and the Chester plays. SP 28 1931.

Bodley NT Verse Passages

Severs pp. 396, 545; Index 1474, 1535, 1536, 4022 with cross-references.

Ed W. Heuser, Eine vergessene Hs des Surtees psalters, Anglia 29 1906. *See also under Northern Homily Cycle in (9), below.*

Rawlinson NT Strophic Passages

Severs pp. 396, 545; Index 876, 2021, 2022, 4002 with cross-references.

§1

Ed W. Heuser, With an O and an I, Anglia 27 1904.

§2

Hammerle, K. With an O and an I. Anglia 54 1930.
Mustanoja, T. F. ME with an O and an I. Neuphilologische Mitteilungen 56 1956.
Greene, R. L. A ME love poem and the O and I refrain phrase. MÆ 30 1961.
See also under Northern Homily Cycle in (9), below.

Pauline Epistles

Severs pp. 399, 546; ms Corpus Christi College Cambridge Parker 32.

Ed M. J. Powell 1915 (EETS).

Apocalypse

Severs pp. 400, 546; for mss see Fridner, below.

Ed E. Fridner, A fourteenth-century Apocalypse version with a prose commentary, Lund Stud in Eng 29 1961.

Gospel of Nicodemus

Severs pp. 448, 640; Index 512; for mss of prose versions, see Hulme, below.

§1

Ed C. Horstmann, Evangelium Nicodemi in altschottischer Mundart, Archiv 53 1874 (*see also* 57 1877); Nachträge zu den Legenden, Archiv 68 1882; ed W. H. Hulme 1907 (EETS); ed F. Klotz, Königsberg 1913.

§2

Wülcker, R. Evangelium Nicodemi. Paderborn 1872.
Straub, F. Lautlehre der jungen Nicodemusversion. Würzburg 1908.
Craigie, W. A. The Gospel of Nicodemus and the York plays. In An English miscellany presented to F. J. Furnivall, Oxford 1901.
Miller, F. H. The Northern passion and the mysteries. MLN 34 1919.
Clark, E. G. The York plays and the Gospel of Nicodemus. PMLA 43 1928.

Harrowing of Hell

Severs pp. 449, 641; Index 185, 1258.

§1

Ed J. P. Collier, Five miracle plays, 1836; ed D. Laing, Edinburgh 1837; ed J. O. Halliwell (-Phillipps), 1840; ed E. Mall, Breslau 1871; ed K. Böddeker, Altenglische Dichtungen des Ms Harley 2253, Berlin 1878; ed H. Varnhagen, Erlangen 1898; ed W. H. Hulme 1907 (EETS); ed A. W. Pollard, English miracle plays, 1927 (8th edn).

§2

Becker, E. J. Die Sage von der Höllenfahrt Christi. Göttingen 1912.
Schmidt, K. W. C. Die Darstellung von Christi Höllenfahrt. Marburg 1915.
MacCulloch, J. A. The harrowing of Hell: a comparative study of an early Christian doctrine. Edinburgh 1931.
Curtiss, C. G. The York and Towneley plays on the harrowing of Hell. SP 30 1933.

Bible Summary

Severs pp. 401, 547.

Ker, N. R. A ME summary of the Bible. MÆ 29 1960.
Fowler, D. C. A ME Bible commentary (Oxford Trinity College ms 93). Manuscripta 12 1968.

H. H.

(6) SERMONS

A. General Studies

See Wells ch 5 and suppls.

Neale, J. M. Mediaeval preachers and mediaeval preaching. 1856.
Crane, T. F. Medieval sermon-books and stories. Proc Amer Philosophical Soc 21 1883.
—— Exempla or illustrative stories [from the sermones of Jacques de Vitry]. 1890.
—— Medieval story books. MP 9 1912.
—— Recent collections of exempla. Romanic Rev 6 1916.
—— Medieval sermon-books and their study since 1883. Proc Amer Philosophical Soc 56 1917.
Lecoy de la Marche, A. La chaire française au Moyen Age. Paris 1856.
Smith, L. T. English popular preaching in the 14th century. EHR 7 1892.
Boucher, E. L'éloquence de la chaire. Lille 1894.
Petit-Dutaillis, C. Les prédications populaires. In Etudes dédiées à G. Monod, Paris 1896.

Mosher, J. A. The exemplum in the early religious and didactic literature of England. New York 1911.
Cutts, E. L. Parish priests and their peoples in the Middle Ages in England. 1914. Ch 14.
Little, A. G. Studies in English Franciscan history. Manchester 1917. Pp. 123–57.
Croll, M. W. The cadence of English oratorical prose. SP 16 1919; rptd in his Style, rhetoric and rhythm, Princeton 1966.
Manning, B. The people's faith in the age of Wyclif. Cambridge 1919. Pp. 17–28.
Deanesly, M. The Lollard Bible. Cambridge 1920, 1966 (with prefatory note).
Gilson, E. Michel Menot et la technique du sermon médiéval. Revue d'Histoire Franciscaine 2 1925.
Caplan, H. A late medieval tractate on preaching. In Studies in rhetoric and public speaking in honor of James Albert Winans, New York 1925.
—— Rhetorical invention in some medieval tractates on preaching. Speculum 2 1927.

— Four senses of scriptural interpretation and the medieval theory of preaching. Speculum 4 1929.
— Classical rhetoric and the medieval theory of preaching. Classical Philology 28 1933.
— Henry of Hesse, On the art of preaching. PMLA 48 1933.
— Medieval Artes praedicandi: a hand-list. Ithaca 1934; Supplement, 1936.
Owst, G. R. Preaching in medieval England. Cambridge 1926.
— Literature and pulpit in medieval England. Cambridge 1933, Oxford 1961 (rev).
— 'Sortilegium' in English homilectic literature of the 14th century. In Studies presented to Sir Hilary Jenkinson, 1957.
Chapman, C. O. The Pardoner's tale: a medieval sermon. MLN 41 1926.
— The Parson's tale: a medieval sermon. MLN 43 1928.
— Chaucer on preachers and preaching. PMLA 44 1929.
Baldwin, C. S. Medieval rhetoric and poetic to 1400. New York 1928.
Zawart, A. History of Franciscan preaching. New York 1928.
Cornelius, R. D. The figurative castle: a study in medieval allegory with especial reference to religious writings. Bryn Mawr 1930.
Charland, T. M. Les auteurs d'artes praedicandi au xiiie siècle d'après les manuscrits. Etudes d'Histoire Littéraire et Doctrinale du xiiie Siècle 1 1932.
— Artes praedicandi. Paris 1936.
Smalley, B. Stephen Langton and the four senses of Scripture. Speculum 6 1931.
— Robert Bacon and the early Dominican school at Oxford. Trans of Royal Historical Soc 4th ser 30 1948.
— English friars and antiquity in the early 14th century. Oxford 1960. Chs 2, 5 iv, 7 ii, 10–11.
Brown, C. Sermons and miracle plays. MLN 49 1934.
Pfander, H. G. The medieval friars and some alphabetical reference books for sermons. MÆ 3 1934.
— Some medieval manuals of religious instruction in England, and observations on Chaucer's Parson's tale. JEGP 35 1936.
— The popular sermons of the medieval friar in England. New York 1937.
Devlin, Sr M. A. The chronology of Bishop Brunton's sermons. PMLA 51 1936.
Hopper, V. F. Medieval number symbolism. New York 1938.
Smyth, C. The art of preaching. 1940.
Westermann, E. J. A comparison of some of the sermons and dicta of Robert Grosseteste. Medievalia et Humanistica 3 1945.
Douie, D. L. Archbishop Pecham's sermons and collations. In Studies in medieval history presented to F. M. Powicke, Oxford 1948.
Robertson, D. W. Frequency of preaching in 13th-century England. Speculum 24 1949.
Bowers, R. H. A ME treatise on hermeneutics: Harley ms 2276, 32v–35v. PMLA 65 1950.
Hinnebusch, W. A. The early English friars preachers. Rome 1951. Ch 16.
Robson, C. A. Maurice of Sully and the medieval vernacular homily. Oxford 1952.
Sweet, J. Some 13th-century sermons and their authors [with appendix listing mss. containing sermons]. Jnl of Ecclesiastical History 4 1953.
Pantin, W. A. The English church in the 14th century. Cambridge 1955.
Shain, C. E. Pulpit eloquence in three Canterbury tales. MLN 70 1955.
Murphy, J. J. The arts of discourse 1050–1400. Mediaeval Stud 23 1961.
—Rhetoric in 14th-century Oxford. MÆ 34 1965.

Świeczkowski, W. Word order patterning in ME: a quantitative study based on Piers Plowman and ME sermons. Hague 1962.
Yunck, J. A. The lineage of Lady Meed. Notre Dame 1963.
Blench, J. W. Preaching in England. Oxford 1964.
Auerbach, E. 'Sermo humilis'. In his Literary language and its public in late Latin antiquity and in the Middle Ages, 1965.
Leclerq, J. L'art de la composition dans les sermons de S. Bernard. Studi Medievali 7 1966.
— Sur la caractère littéraire des sermons de S. Bernard. Ibid.
Wenzel, S. The three enemies of man. Mediaeval Stud 29 1967.
— The source for the Remedia of the Parson's tale. Traditio 27 1971.
Oberman, H. A. and J. A. Weisheipl. The Sermo epicinius ascribed to Thomas Bradwardine (1346). Archives d'Histoire Doctrinale et Littéraire au Moyen Age 25 1958.
Erb, P. C. Vernacular material for preaching in ms Univ Lib Cambridge Ii.III.8. Mediaeval Stud 33 1971.
See also Terasawa, col 496 below.

B. Sermon Collections
Bodley Homilies
Wells pp. 277, 804, 1499.

§1

Ms: Bodley 343.

Ed A. O. Belfour, Twelfth-century homilies, 1909 (EETS) (text and trn).

§2

Ross, A. C. Some alliterative phrases in the Bodley homilies. N & Q Feb 1970.

Lambeth Homilies
Wells pp. 278, 804, 1010, 1114, 1214, 1266, 1306, 1396, 1499, 1571, 1904.

§1

Ms: Lambeth 487.

Ed R. Morris, Old English homilies, 1867 (EETS). *See* E Studien 14 1890.
Selections: J. Zupitza, Übungsbuch, Vienna 1874; R. Morris and W. W. Skeat, Specimens of early English vol 1, Oxford 1885; G. E. MacLean, Reader, New York 1893; J. Hall, Selections from early ME, Oxford 1920; G. Sampson, Cambridge book of prose and verse, Cambridge 1924.

§2

Skeat, W. W. MLQ 2 1899.
Mosher, J. A. The exemplum in the early religious and didactic literature of England. New York 1911.
Stadlmann, A. Die Sprache der mittelenglischen Predigtsammlung in der Handschrift Lambeth 487. Vienna 1921.
Funke, O. E Studien 55 1921. On French words.
Allen, H. E. PMLA 44 1929. On authorship.
Wilson, R. M. The provenance of the Lambeth homilies, with a new collation. Leeds Stud in Eng 4 1935.
Sisam, C. The scribal tradition of the Lambeth homilies. RES new ser 2 1951.

Trinity Homilies
Wells pp. 280, 804, 1010, 1058, 1114, 1266, 1306, 1449, 1499.

§1

Ms: Trinity College Cambridge B 14 52.

Ed R. Morris, Old English homilies, 1873 (EETS). *See* E Studien 14 1890.

Selections: R. Morris and W. W. Skeat, Specimens of early English vol 1, Oxford 1885; T. Wright and J. O. Halliwell (-Phillipps), Reliquiae antiquae vol 1, 1845; E. Matzner, Altenglische Sprachproben pt 2, Berlin 1900; J. Hall, Selections from early ME, Oxford 1920.

§2

E Studien 15 1891.
Mosher, J. A. The exemplum in the early religious and didactic literature of England. New York 1911.
Strauss, O. Die Sprache der mittelenglischen Predigt-sammlung in der Handschrift B 14 52 Trinity College Cambridge. Vienna 1916.
Beiblatt zur Anglia 29 1918.
E Studien 51 1918.
Funke, O. E Studien 55 1921. On French words.
Ker, N. R. The scribes of the Trinity homilies. MÆ 1 1932.

Ormulum

Wells pp. 282, 804, 1010, 1058, 1114, 1214, 1306, 1396, 1449, 1499, 1571, 1614, 1699, 1905.

§1

Ms: Junius I (Bodley).

Ed R. M. White, Oxford 1852; rev R. Holt, Oxford 1878. *See* E Studien 1 1877.
Selections: J. Zupitza, Übungsbuch, Vienna 1874; H. Sweet, First ME primer, Oxford 1884; R. Morris and W. W. Skeat, Specimens of early English, Oxford 1885; G. E. MacLean, Reader, New York 1893; O. F. Emerson, Reader, Boston 1915; A. Brandl and O. Zippel, Mittelenglische Sprach- und Literatur-proben, Berlin 1917; J. Hall, Selections from early ME, Oxford 1920; J. A. W. Bennett and G. V. Smithers, Early ME verse and prose, Oxford 1966, 1968 (rev).

§2

Callenberg, C. Layamon und Orm nach ihren Laut-verhältnissen verglichen. Jena 1876.
Henrici, E. Orm's brother. Zeitschrift für Deutsches Alterthum 22 1878.
Kaphengst, C. Essay on the Ormulum. Rostock 1879.
Sachse, R. Die unorganische e. Halle 1881.
Schipper, J. Englische Metrik. Bonn 1881.
Blackburn, F. A. Þ to t. Amer Jnl of Philology 3 1882.
Effer, H. Einfache und doppelte Konsonanten. Berlin 1885.
Menze, E. Der östmittel-landische Dialekt. Cöthen 1889.
Napier, A. S. Academy 15 March 1890.
—— History of the holy rood-tree. 1894.
Kluge, F. Das französische Element. E Studien 22 1896.
Weyel, F. Der syntaktische Gebrauch des Infinitivs. Meiderich 1896.
McKnight, G. H. Double consonants. E Studien 26 1899.
Holthausen, F. Wel and Well. Beiblatt zur Anglia 13 1902.
Lambertz, P. Die Sprache. Marburg 1904.
Bülbring, Die Schreibung eo. Bonner Beiträge zur Anglistik 17 1905; Beiblatt zur Anglia 17 1906.
Bradley, H. and J. Wilson. Athenaeum 10 May, 14–28 July 1906.
Reichmann, Die Eigennamen. Studien zur Englischen Philologie 25 1906.
Saintsbury, G. In his History of English prosody vol 1, 1906.
Funke, O. Kasus-syntax. Munich 1907.
Thuns, B. Das Verbum. Leipzig 1909.
Zenke, W. Syntax und Analyse des Verbums. Studien zur Englischen Philologie 40 1910.
Deutschbein, M. Quantity signs. Archiv 126–7 1911.
Bjorkmann, E. Doppelkonsonanten. Anglia 37 1913. Pp. 351, 494.

Laeseke, B. Beitrage zur Stellung des Verbums. Berlin 1917.
Deanesly, M. In her Lollard Bible, Cambridge 1920, 1966 (with prefatory note).
Weinmann, P. Ueber den Gebrauch des Artikels. Berlin 1920.
Holm, S. Corrections and additions in Ormulum ms. Upsala 1922.
Oldendorf, H. Syntax und Analyse des Nomens und Pronomens. Jahrbuch der Philosophischen Fakultät Göttingen 1 1922.
Flasdieck, H. M. Sprachliche Einheitlichkeit. Anglia 47 1923.
Sisam, K. Mss Bodley 340 and 342: Ælfric's Catholic homilies. RES 7–9 1931–3.
Matthes, H. C. Die Einheitlichkeit des Ormulum. Heidelberg 1933; Anglia 59 1935.
—— Zum literarischen Charakter und zu den Quellen des Orrmulum. Beiblatt zur Anglia 46 1935.
—— Das Orrmulum: sein Gehalt und sein Verfasser. Germanisch-romanische Monatsschrift 26 1938.
—— Die Orrmulum-korrecturen. JEGP 50 1951.
Hinckley, H. B. The riddle of the Ormulum. PQ 14 1935.
Glunz, H. H. Zur Orrmulumfrage. Beiblatt zur Anglia 46 1935.
—— Die Literarästhetik des europäischen Mittelalters. Bochum 1937.
Ker, N. R. More of the Ormulum. TLS 14 Nov 1936.
—— Unpublished parts of the Ormulum printed from ms Lambeth 783. MÆ 9 1940.
Olszewska, E. S. Alliterative phrases in the Ormulum. Leeds Stud in Eng 5 1936.
—— Alliterative phrases in the Ormulum: some Norse parallels. In English and medieval studies presented to J. R. R. Tolkien, 1962.
Russell, J. C. Dictionary of writers of 13th-century England. Bull Inst of Historical Research, special suppl 3 1936.
Turville-Petre, J. E. Studies in the Ormulum ms. JEGP 46 1947.
Burchfield, R. W. Two misreadings of the Ormulum ms. MÆ 21 1953.
—— The language and orthography of the Ormulum ms. Trans Philological Soc 1956.
—— Ormulum: words copied by Jan van Vliet from parts now lost. In English and medieval studies presented to J. R. R. Tolkien, 1962.
Eis, G. Die Quelle für den Eingang des Orrmulums. Archiv 189 1952.
Lehnert, M. Sprachform und Sprachfunktion im Orrmu-lum. Zeitschrift für Anglistik und Amerikanistik Beiheft 1 1953.

Kentish Sermons

Wells pp. 283, 805, 1010, 1114.

§1

Ms: Laud 471 (Bodley).

Ed R. Morris 1872 (EETS); J. Zupitza, Übungsbuch, Vienna 1874; R. Morris and W. W. Skeat, Specimens of early English vol 1, Oxford 1885; G. E. MacLean, Reader, New York 1893; O. F. Emerson, Reader, New York 1905; F. Kluge, Lesebuch, Halle 1912; J. Hall, Selections from early ME, Oxford 1920; J. A. W. Bennett and G. V. Smithers, Early ME verse and prose, Oxford 1966, 1968 (rev).

§2

Danker, O. Die Laut- und Flexionslehre der mittel-kentischen Denkmäler. Strasbourg 1879.
Reimann, M. Die Sprache der Mittelkentischen Evangelien. Berlin 1883.
Bülbring, K. Quellen und Forschungen 63 1889. On verbs.

Heuser, W. Anglia 17 1894.
Glahn, N. von. Zur Geschichte des grammatischen Geschlechts im Mittelenglischen. Anglistische Forschungen 53 1918.
Funke, O. E Studien 55 1921.
Robson, C. A. Maurice of Sully and the medieval vernacular homily. Oxford 1952.

Cotton Vespasian Homilies

Wells pp. 284, 805, 1010, 1058, 1114, 1499, 1905.

§ 1

Ms: Cotton Vespasian A 22.

Ed R. Morris 1868 (EETS) p. 217. *See* E Studien 14 1890 p. 396; R. Morris and W. W. Skeat, Specimens of early English vol 1, Oxford 1885; J. Hall, Selections from early ME, Oxford 1920.

§ 2

Vollhardt, H. Einfluss der lateinischen geistlichen Literatur. Leipzig 1888. *See* E Studien 13 1889.
Glahn, N. von. Zur Geschichte des grammatischen Geschlechts im Mittelenglischen. Anglistische Forschungen 53 1918.

Worcester Sermons

Wells pp. 1571, 1615, 1669, 1711.
Ms: Worcester Chapter F 10.

Ed D. M. Grisdale, Kendal 1939.

Gloucester Sermons

Ms: Gloucester Cathedral 22, Press no 1. See D. S. Brewer, Observations on a 15th-century ms, Anglia 72 1954.

Royal Sermons

Wells pp. 1669, 1711.

§ 1

Ms: BM Royal 18 B XXIII.
Ed W. O. Ross 1940 (EETS).

§ 2

Świeczkowski, W. Word order patterning in ME: a quantitative study based on Piers Plowman and ME sermons. Janua Linguarum 19 1962.
Braekman, W. L. and P. S. Macaulay. Two unpublished ME exempla. Neuphilologische Mitteilungen 27 1971.

Sidney Sussex Lollard Sermons

Ms: Sidney Sussex College Cambridge 74 △ 4 12. See E. W. Talbert, A 15th-century Lollard sermon cycle, SE 1939.

Bodley Wycliffite Sermons

Wells pp. 468f, 1363, 1583.

§ 1

Ms: Bodley 788 etc; see Arnold, below.

Ed T. Arnold, Selected English works of John Wiclif, Oxford 1869–71.

§ 2

Talbert, E. W. The date and composition of the English Wycliffite collection of sermons. Speculum 12 1937.
Hudson, A. A Lollard sermon-cycle and its implications. MÆ 40 1971.
Knapp, P. A. John Wyclif as Bible translator: the texts for the English sermons. Speculum 46 1971.
See also (7), John Wyclif and Wycliffite Writings, col 491, below.

BM Lollard (?) Sermons

Wells pp. 1669, 1711.

§ 1

Ms: BM additional 41,321; see also Bodley Rawlinson C 751.

§ 2

BM Quart 1 1926.
Owst, G. R. In his Literature and pulpit in medieval England, Cambridge 1933, Oxford 1961 (rev).

Festial (John Mirk)

Wells pp. 168–9, 301–3, 307, 311, 313–14, 319, 329, 807, 961, 1500, 1670, 1712, 1817; Brown-Robbins Index and Suppl item 462.

§ 1

Mss: BM Cotton Claudius A II; Gough Eccl Top 4 (Bodley); Caius College Cambridge 168/89; BM Harley 1288; Harley 2247; Harley 2250; Harley 2371; Harley 2391; Harley 2403; Harley 2417; Royal 18 B XXV; Lansdowne 392; Douce 60 (Bodley); Douce 108 (Bodley); Hatton 96 (Bodley); Rawlinson A 381 (Bodley); Univ College Oxford 102 (Bodley); Univ Lib Cambridge Dd 10 50; Univ Lib Cambridge Ee 2 15; Univ Lib Cambridge Ff 2 38; Univ Lib Cambridge Nn 3 10; St John's College Cambridge G 19; Southwell Minister; Brotherton (Univ Leeds); Durham Univ Lib Cosin V III 5; New College London Z c 19.

Ed T. Erbe 1905 (EETS). *See* C. Horstmann, Altenglische Legenden, Heilbronn 1881, Anglia 3 1880.
On early ptd edns see W. Blades, The biography and typography of William Caxton, *1882; N. S. Aurner,* Caxton, *1926.*

§ 2

Mosher, J. A. The exemplum in the early religious and didactic literature of England. New York 1911.
Owst, G. R. In his Preaching in medieval England, Cambridge 1926.
— In his Literature and pulpit in medieval England, Cambridge 1933, Oxford 1961 (rev).
Young, K. Instructions for parish priests. Speculum 11 1936.
Steckman, L. L. A late 15th-century revision of Mirk's Festial. SP 34 1937.
Cronin, G. Mirk on bonfires, elephants and dragons. MLN 57 1942.
Long, M. Undetected verse in Mirk's Festial. MLN 70 1955.
Pantin, W. The English church in the 14th century. Cambridge 1955.
Wakelin, M. F. The mss of Mirk's Festial. Leeds Stud in Eng new ser 1 1967.
Poteet II, D. Avoiding women in times of affliction: an analogue for the Miller's tale A3589–91. N & Q March 1972.

Speculum Sacerdotale

§ 1

Ms: BM additional 36, 791.
Ed E. H. Weatherly 1936 (EETS).

§ 2

Owst, G. R. In his Preaching in medieval England, Cambridge 1926.
— In his Literature and pulpit in medieval England, Cambridge 1933, Oxford 1961 (rev).

Mirrur

Prose homilies from Robert de Gretham's Anglo-Norman 'Miroir' (?).
Wells pp. 959, 1010.

§2

Deanesly, M. In her Lollard Bible and other medieval biblical versions, Cambridge 1920, 1966 (with prefatory note).

Owst, G. R. In his Preaching in medieval England, Cambridge 1926.

Laird, C. G. Five new Gretham sermons and the ME 'Mirrur'. PMLA 57 1942.

Duncan, T. G. Notes on the language of the Hunterian ms of the 'Mirror'. Neuphilologische Mitteilungen 69 1968.

The Miroir of Robert of Gretham. MÆ 39 1970.

Northern Homily Cycle

See (9), Saints' Legends, col 528, below.

C. Particular Sermons

A Lutel Soth Sermun

Wells pp. 274, 803, 1396, 1498.

§1

Mss: BM Cotton Caligula A IX; Jesus College Oxford 29 (Bodley).

Ed T. Wright 1843 (Percy Soc); R. Morris 1872 (EETS).

A Sarmun

Wells pp. 274, 803, 1396.
Ms: Harley 913.

Ed F. J. Furnivall, Early English poems and lives of saints, Berlin 1862; E. Mätzner, Altenglische Sprachproben pt 1, Berlin 1867; W. Heuser, Bonner Beiträge zur Anglistik 14 1904.

Speculum Gy de Warewyke

Wells pp. 275, 803, 1350, 1396, 1614, 1711.

§1

Mss: Auchinleck (Nat Lib of Scotland 19 2 1); Royal 17 B XVII; Harley 525; Harley 1731; Arundel 140; Univ Lib Cambridge Dd XI 89.

Ed G. L. Morrill 1898 (EETS); C. Horstmann, Yorkshire Writers vol 2, 1896.

Weyrauch, M. Die mittelenglischen Fassungen Guy de Warwick. Breslau 1899.

Sermo in Festo Corporis Christi

Wells pp. 276, 803, 1498, 1614.

§1

Mss: Vernon (Bodley 3938); Univ Lib Cambridge Dd I 1; Harley 4196.

Ed C. Horstmann, Archiv 82 1889; C. Horstmann 1892 (EETS); see 1903 (EETS).

§2

Harley, M. Holy Eucharist in ME homilectic and devotional verse. Washington 1936.

A Luytel Sarmoun of Good Edificacioun

Wells pp. 275, 803, 1351, 1396.
Ms: Vernon (Bodley 3938).

Ed F. J. Furnivall 1901 (EETS).

A Sermon against Miracle Plays

Wells pp. 483, 843.

§1

Ms: BM additional 24,202.

Ed T. Wright and J. O. Halliwell (-Phillipps), Reliquiae antiquae vol 1, 1841; E. Mätzner, Altenglische Sprachproben pt 2, Berlin 1900.

Selections: A. S. Cook, Reader, Boston 1915; W. Matthews, Later medieval English prose, 1962.

§2

Chambers, E. K. In his Medieval stage vol 2, Oxford 1903.

Cook, A. S. Nation (New York) 27 May 1915.

Kolve, V. A. In his Play called Corpus Christi, Stanford 1966.

Speculum Christiani

Wells pp. 968, 993, 1015, 1452, 1454, 1503, 1574, 1715, 1909

Ed G. Holmstedt 1933 (EETS); 1, A prose sermon, pp. 74–123; 2, A verse sermon, pp. 132–59.

Redde Racionem (Thomas Wimbledon)

Wells pp. 1057, 1170, 1266, 1306, 1449, 1499, 1500, 1571, 1614, 1669, 1711.

§1

Mss: Hatton 57 (Bodley); BM Royal 18 A XVII; Royal 18 B XXIII; Harley 2398; Sidney Sussex College Cambridge 74 △ 4 12; Corpus Christi College Cambridge 357; BM additional 37,677; Brotherton 501 (Univ of Leeds); Laud Miscellaneous 524 (Bodley); Hunter 15 (Durham Cathedral Lib); etc: see N. H. Owen under §2, below. See A. G. Watson, The mss of Henry Savile of Banke, 1969 (pp. 78 f).

Ed N. H. Owen, Thomas Wimbledon's sermon, Mediaeval Stud 28 1966; Ione Kemp Knight, Wimbledon's sermon, Duquesne Stud, Philological ser 9 1967.

§2

Owen, N. H. Thomas Wimbledon. Mediaeval Stud 24 1962.

A Nativity Sermon

§1

Ms: Worcester Cathedral Q 29.

§2

Wallner, B. A commentary on the 'Benedictus'. Lund 1957.

Stanley, E. G. An inedited nativity sermon from Worcester. Eng & Germanic Stud 7 1961.

Dan Jon Gaytryge's Sermon

Wells pp. 348, 453, 483, 817, 843.

Ed G. G. Perry 1867 (EETS); C. Horstmann, Yorkshire writers vol 1, 1895.

G. C.

(7) JOHN WYCLIF AND WYCLIFFITE WRITINGS

c. 1325–84

Bibliographies

Severs pp. 354, 517.

Shirley, W. W. A catalogue of the original works by Wyclif. Oxford 1865, London 1924 (as Catalogue of the extant works) (rev J. Loserth).

§ 1

This section is concerned only with English works by Wyclif and his supporters, not distinguished. For his Latin works see col 789, below.

Wycklyffes wycket. 1546; ed T. P. Pantin, Oxford 1828.
The last age of the Church. Ed J. H. Todd, Dublin 1840.
Treatise of miraclis pleyinge. Ed T. Wright and J. O. Halliwell (-Phillipps), Reliquiae antiquae vol 1, 1841.
An apology for Lollard doctrines. Ed J. H. Todd 1842 (Camden Soc).
Three treatises by Wyclif. Ed J. H. Todd, Dublin 1851.
Thirty-seven conclusions of the Lollards. Ed J. Forshall, Remonstrance against Romish corruptions, 1851.
— Ed H. F. B. Compston, EHR 26 1911.
Select English works of Wyclif. Ed T. Arnold 3 vols Oxford 1869–71.
English works of Wyclif hitherto unprinted. Ed F. D. Matthew 1880 (EETS).
Twelve conclusions of the Lollards. Ed H. S. Cronin, EHR 22 1907.
The recluse. Ed J. Pahlsson, Lunds Univ Årsskrift new ser 6 1910.
The holi prophete Dauid seith. Ed M. Deanesly, Lollard Bible, Cambridge 1920.
Aჳens hem that seyn that hooli wriჳt schulde not or may not be drawun into Englische. Ed M. Deanesly, ibid.
— Ed C. F. Bühler, MÆ 7 1938.
Select English writings. Ed H. E. Winn, Oxford 1929.
A Lollard chronicle of the papacy. Ed E. W. Talbert, JEGP 41 1942.
The two ways: an unpublished religious treatise by Sir John Clanvowe. Ed V. J. Scattergood, Eng Philological Stud 10 1967.
Jack Upland, Friar Daw's reply and Upland's rejoinder. Ed P. L. Heyworth, Oxford 1968.

§ 2

Lewis, J. The history of the life and sufferings of Wicliffe. 1720, Oxford 1820.
Vaughan, R. Life and opinions of John de Wycliffe DD. 1828.
Shirley, W. W. Fasciculi zizaniorum magistri Johannis Wyclif cum tritico. 1858 (Rolls ser).
Lechler, G. V. Wiclif und die Vorgeschichte der Reformation. Leipzig 1873; tr 1878, 1884 (rev).
Fischer, H. Ueber die Sprache Wycliffs. Halle 1880.
Loserth, J. Hus und Wiclif. Prague 1884; tr 1884.
Buddensieg, R. J. Wicklif: patriot and reformer. 1884.
— Wiclif und seine Zeit. Gotha 1885.
Vattier, V. Wyclyff: sa vie, ses oeuvres, sa doctrine. Paris 1886.
Gasner, E. Ueber Wyclifs Sprache. Göttingen 1891.
Sergeant, L. Wyclif, schoolman and reformer. 1893.
Petit-Dutaillis, C. Les prédications populaires. In Etudes dédiées à G. Monod, Paris 1896.
Trevelyan, G. M. England in the age of Wycliffe. 1899, 1909 (rev).
Fürstenau, H. Johann von Wiclifs Lehren von der Einteilung der Kirche und von der Stellung der weltlichen Gewalt. Berlin 1900.

Rosenkranz, A. E. Wycliffes ethisch-sozialische Anschauung. Barmen 1901.
Heine, D. Wiclifs Lehre vom Güterbesitz. Erlangen 1903.
Siebert, G. Untersuchungen über An apology. Charlottenburg 1906.
Jones, E. D. On the authenticity of some English works ascribed to Wycliffe. Anglia 30 1907.
Carrick, J. C. Wycliffe and the Lollards. Edinburgh 1908.
Gairdner, J. Lollardry and the reformation in England. 1908.
Dakin, A. Die Beziehungen Wycliffes und der Lollarden zu den Bettelmönchen. 1911.
Wilkins, H. J. Was Wycliffe a negligent pluralist? 1915, Bristol 1916 (with appendix).
Krapp, J. P. In his Rise of English literary prose, New York 1916.
Loserth, J. Wiclif und Guilelmus Peraldus. Sitzungsberichte der Königlichen Akademie der Wissenschaften, philosophisch-historische Klasse (Vienna) 180 1917.
— Wiclif und Robert Grosseteste. Sitzungsberichte der Königlichen Akademie der Wissenschaften, philosophisch-historische Klasse (Vienna) 186 1921.
Taylor, H. O. In his Thought and expression in the sixteenth century vol 2, New York 1920.
Shettle, G. T. John Wycliffe of Wycliffe. Leeds 1922.
Hearnshaw, F. J. C. In his Social and political ideas of some great medieval thinkers, 1923.
Workman, H. B. Wyclif: a study of the English medieval Church. Oxford 1926.
McNeill, J. T. Some emphases in Wyclif's teaching. Jnl of Religion 7 1927.
Cumming, W. P. A Middle English manuscript in Bibliothèque Ste Geneviève, Paris. PMLA 42 1927.
Irvine, A. S. The participle in Wycliffe with especial reference to his original English works. SE 9 1929.
— The 'to comynge(e)' construction in Wyclif. PMLA 45 1930.
Thomson, S. H. The philosophical basis of Wyclif's theology. Jnl of Religion 11 1931.
— Wyclif or Wyclyf. EHR 53 1938.
Manning, B. L. In Cambridge medieval history vol 7, Cambridge 1932.
Pressfield, H. Wyclif and the common law. Bibliotheca Sacra 90 1933.
Smith, H. M. Lollardry. Church Quart Rev 119 1935.
Odložilík, O. Wyclif and Bohemia. Prague 1937.
Talbert, E. W. The composition date of the English Wycliffite sermons. Speculum 12 1937.
Colledge, E. The Recluse: a Lollard interpolated version of the Ancrene riwle. RES 15 1939.
Gwynn, A. The English Austin friars in the time of Wyclif. 1940.
Dahmus, J. H. Further evidence for the spelling 'Wyclyf'. Speculum 16 1941.
— Did Wyclyf recant? Catholic Historical Rev 29 1943.
— The prosecution of Wyclyf. New Haven 1952.
— Wyclif was a negligent pluralist. Speculum 28 1953.
— Wyclif and the English government. Speculum 35 1960.
Cutts, C. The Croxton play: an anti-Lollard piece. MLQ 5 1944.
Utley, F. L. The layman's complaint and the friar's answer. Harvard Theological Rev 38 1945.
Russell, H. G. Lollard opposition to oaths by creatures. Amer Historical Rev 51 1946.
Ransom, M. W. The chronology of Wyclif's English sermons. Washington State College Research Stud 16 1948.

Towne, F. Wyclif and Chaucer on the contemplative life. In Essays dedicated to Lily B Campbell, Berkeley 1950.

McFarlane, K. B. Wycliffe and the beginnings of English nonconformity. 1952.

— Lancastrian kings and Lollard knights. Oxford 1972. On Clanvowe.

Bühler, C. F. The Middle English texts of Morgan ms 861. PMLA 69 1954.

Parkes, M. B. Manuscript fragments of English sermons attributed to Wyclif. MÆ 24 1955.

Schlauch, M. A Polish vernacular eulogy of Wycliff. Jnl of Ecclesiastical History 8 1957.

Hanrahan, T. J. Wyclif's political activity. Mediaeval Stud 20 1958.

Cannon, W. R. Wyclif and John Hus. Emory Univ Quart 15 1959.

Stacey, J. The character of Wyclif. London Quart 184 1959.

— Wyclif and reform. 1964.

Boyd, B. Wiclif and the Sarum ordinal. MÆ 28 1959.

Kellogg, A. L. and E. W. Talbert. The Wycliffite Paternoster and Ten Commandments. Bull John Rylands Lib 42 1960.

Aston, M. Lollardy and sedition 1381–1431. Past & Present 17 1960.

— Lollardy and the Reformation: survival or revival? History 49 1964.

— Wyclif's Reformation reputation. Past & Present 30 1965.

Hurley, M. Scriptura sola: Wyclif and his critics. Traditio 16 1960; New York 1963 (separately).

Greene, R. L. A Middle English love poem and the 'o-and-i' refrain. MÆ 30 1961.

Mallard, W. Wyclif and the tradition of biblical authority. Church History 30 1961.

— Dating the Sermones quadraginta of Wyclif. Medievalia et Humanistica 17 1966.

Fisher, J. H. Wyclif, Langland, Gower and the Pearl poet on aristocracy. In Studies in medieval literature in honor of A. C. Baugh, Philadelphia 1961.

Robson, J. A. Wyclif and the Oxford Schools. Cambridge 1961.

Block, E. A. Wyclif, radical dissenter. San Diego 1962.

Daly, L. J. The political theory of Wyclif. Chicago 1962.

Smalley, B. The Bible and eternity: Wyclif's dilemma. Jnl Warburg & Courtauld Inst 27 1964.

McIntosh, A. Some linguistic reflections of a Wycliffite. In Franciplegius: medieval and linguistic studies in honor of F. P. Magoun, New York 1965.

Parker, G. H. W. The morning star: Wycliffe and the dawn of the Reformation. Exeter 1965.

Leff, G. Wyclif: the path to dissent. Proc Br Acad 52 1966.

— Wyclif and Hus: a doctrinal comparison. Bull John Rylands Lib 50 1968.

Davidson, C. Wyclif and the Middle English sermon. Universitas 3 1966.

Benrath, G. Wyclifs Bibelkommentar. Berlin 1966.

Hargreaves, H. Wyclif's prose. E & S new ser 19 1966.

Dyson, T. Wyclif reviewed. Church Quart Rev 168 1967.

Terasawa, Y. A rhetorical spoken style of Middle English: the case of Wyclif's sermon translation. Stud in Eng Lit (Tokyo), Eng no 1968.

Hudson, A. A Lollard sermon-cycle and its implications. MÆ 40 1971.

— A Lollard quaternion. RES new ser 22 1971.

— A Lollard compilation and the dissemination of Wycliffite thought. Jnl of Theological Stud 23 1972.

Wycliffite Translations of the Bible

Severs pp. 402, 547. See also general works listed at head of (5), above.

§ 1

The New testament translated out of the Latin Vulgat by Wiclif about 1378. Ed J. Lewis 1731.

The New testament translated from the Latin in the year 1380 by Wiclif. Ed H. H. Baber 1810.

The English Hexapla, exhibiting the six important English translations of the New testament scriptures. [1841].

The New testament in English, translated by Wycliffe circa mccclxxx. Ed Lea Wilson 1848.

The Holy Bible translated by Wycliffe and his followers. Ed J. Forshall and F. Madden 4 vols Oxford 1850.

The New testament in English. Ed W. W. Skeat, Oxford 1879.

The books of Job, Psalms, Ecclesiastes, Song of songs. Ed W. W. Skeat, Oxford 1881.

The New testament in Scots. Ed T. G. Law and J. Hall 3 vols 1901–4 (STS).

Ms Bodley 959: Genesis–Baruch 3.20 in the earlier version of the Wycliffite Bible. Ed C. Lindberg 5 vols Stockholm 1959–69.

§ 2

Grimm, F. Das syntaktische Gebrauch der Praepositionen bei Wyclif und Purvey. Marburg 1891.

Moulton, W. F. In his A history of the English Bible, 1895.

Gasquet, F. A. In his Old English Bible and other essays, 1897.

Carr, J. W. Ueber das Verhältnis der Wiclifitischen und der Purvey'schen Bibelübersetzungen zur Vulgata. Leipzig 1902.

Ortmann, F. J. Formen und Syntax des Verbums bei Wyclif und Purvey. Weimar 1902.

Hollack, E. Vergleichende Studien zu der Hereford, Wyclif und Purvey Bibelübersetzung und der lateinischen Vulgata. Leipzig 1903.

Thamm, W. Das Relativpronomen in der Bibelübersetzung Wyclifs und Purveys. Berlin 1908.

Pollard, A. W. In his Records of the English Bible, Oxford 1911.

Kox, M. Studien zur Syntax des Artikels Wyclifs und Purveys. Kiel 1922.

Gray, M. M. The prose of Wyclif's Bible. London Quart 159 1934.

Cammack, M. M. Wyclif and the English Bible. New York 1938.

Talbert, E. W. A note on the Wyclyfite Bible translation. SE 20 1940.

Menner, R. J. A manuscript of the first Wycliffite translation of the Bible. Yale Univ Lib Gazette 19 1945.

Harrison, F. A hitherto-unnoticed Biblical manuscript in the library of the Dean and Chapter of York. Bull John Rylands Lib 29 1946.

Deanesly, M. The significance of the Lollard Bible. 1951.

Fristedt, S. L. The Wycliffe Bible pt 1: the principal problems. Stockholm Stud in Eng 4 1953.

— The authorship of the Lollard Bible. Stockholm Stud in Modern Philology 19 1956.

— The dating of the earliest manuscript of the Wycliffite Bible. Stockholm Stud in Modern Philology new ser 1 1960.

— A weird manuscript enigma in the British Museum. Stockholm Stud in Modern Philology new ser 2 1964.

— New light on Wycliffe and the first full English Bible. Stockholm Stud in Modern Philology new ser 3 1968.

— The Wycliffe Bible pt 2: the origin of the first revision. Stockholm Stud in Eng 21 1969.

Hargreaves, H. The Latin text of Purvey's psalter. MÆ 24 1955.

— The Middle English primers and the Wycliffite Bible. MLR 51 1956.

— An intermediate version of the Wycliffite Old testament. Studia Neophilologica 28 1956.

—— The marginal glosses to the Wycliffite New testament. Studia Neophilologica 33 1961.
—— The Wycliffite versions. In The Cambridge history of the Bible vol 2, ed G. W. H. Lampe, Cambridge 1969.
Frederick, P. W. H. Wyclif and the first English Bible. Fremont 1957.
Fowler, D. C. John Trevisa and the English Bible. MP 58 1960.

Terasawa, Y. A rhetorical spoken style of Middle English: the case of Wyclif's sermon translation. Stud in Eng Lit (Tokyo), Eng no 1968.
Lindberg, C. The manuscripts and versions of the Wycliffite Bible. Studia Neophilologica 42 1970.
Knapp, P. A. Wyclif as Bible translator. Speculum 46 1971.

H. H.

(8) OTHER RELIGIOUS WRITINGS

A. GENERAL STUDIES.
B. PARTICULAR WORKS: *Religious information and instruction, Aids to Church services; Allegorical works; Proverbs, precepts and monitory works; Dialogues and debates; Miscellaneous.*
C. SHORTER PIECES IN PROSE AND VERSE.
D. DEVOTIONAL AND CONTEMPLATIVE WRITINGS.

A. General Studies

Mosher, J. A. The exemplum in the early religious and didactic literature of England. New York 1911.
Manning, B. L. The people's faith in the age of Wyclif. Cambridge 1919.
Welter, J. T. L'exemplum dans la littérature religieuse et didactique du Moyen Age. Paris 1927.
Deanesly, M. The Lollard Bible. Cambridge 1920, 1966 (with prefatory note).
—— Vernacular books in the 14th and 15th centuries. MLR 12 1920.
Owst, G. R. Preaching in medieval England. Cambridge 1926.
—— Literature and pulpit in medieval England. Cambridge 1933, Oxford 1961 (rev).
—— The Destructorium viciorum of Alexander Carpenter: a 15th-century sequel to Literature and pulpit in Medieval England. 1952.
Cornelius, R. D. The figurative castle: a study in mediaeval allegory with especial reference to the religious writings. Bryn Mawr 1930.
Campbell, J. M. Patristic studies and the literature of medieval England. Speculum 8 1933.
Pflaum, H. Die religiöse Disputation in der europäische Dichtung des Mittelalters. Geneva 1935.
Harley, M. Holy eucharist in ME homilectic and devotional verse. Washington 1936.
Pfander, H. G. Some medieval manuals of religious instruction in England and observations on Chaucer's Parson's tale. JEGP 35 1936.
McNeill, J. T. and H. M. Gamer. Medieval handbooks of penance. New York 1938.
Hopper, V. F. Mediaeval number symbolism. New York 1938.
Schlauch, M. The allegory of church and synagogue. Speculum 14 1939.
Bloomfield, M. W. The origin and concept of the seven cardinal sins. Harvard Theological Rev 34 1941.
—— The seven deadly sins: an introduction to the history of a religious concept, with special reference to medieval English literature. East Lansing 1952.
Smalley, B. The study of the Bible in the Middle Ages. Oxford 1941, 1952 (rev).
—— English friars and antiquity in the early 14th century. Oxford 1960.
Whitesell, F. R. Fables in medieval exempla. JEGP 46 1947.
Morgan, M. M. 'A talking of the love of God' and the continuity of stylistic tradition in ME prose meditations. RES new ser 3 1952.
Pantin, W. A. The English Church in the 14th century. Cambridge 1955.
Robbins, R. H. On dating a ME moral poem. MLN 70 1955.
Zeeman, E. Continuity in ME devotional prose. JEGP 55 1956.
—— Continuity and change in ME versions of the Meditationes vitae Christi. MÆ 26 1957.

Doyle, A. I. Books connected with the Vere family and Barking Abbey. Essex Archaeological Soc Trans 25 new ser pt 2 1958.
Hussey, M. The petitions of the paternoster in medieval English literature. MÆ 27 1958.
Wenzel, S. Sloth in ME devotional literature. Anglia 79 1961.
—— Acedia 700–1200. Traditio 22 1966.
—— The sin of sloth. Chapel Hill 1967.
—— The three enemies of man. Mediaeval Stud 29 1967.
—— The seven deadly sins: some problems of research. Speculum 43 1968.
Yunck, J. A. The lineage of Lady Meed: the development of mediaeval venality satire. Notre Dame 1963.
Sachs, A. Religious despair in mediaeval literature and art. Mediaeval Stud 26 1964.
Kahrl, S. J. Allegory in practice: a study of narrative styles in medieval exempla. MP 63 1965.
Howard, D. H. The three temptations: medieval man in search of the world. Princeton 1966.
Aarts, F. G. A. M. Þe Pater Noster of Richard Ermyte. Nijmegen 1967.

B. Particular Works

(Religious Information and Instruction, Aids to Church Services)

Lay-Folks' Mass-Book

Wells pp. 355, 818, 970, 1061, 1120, 1269, 1309; see also C. Brown Register vol 2, Oxford 1920, items 806, 2256; and Brown-Robbins Index and suppl, items 1323, 3507.

§ I

Mss: 1, Nat Lib of Scotland 19 3 1; 2, BM Royal 17 B XIII; 3, Corpus Christi College Oxford 155; 4, Univ Lib Cambridge Gg V 31; 5, Caius College Cambridge 84; 6, Newnham College Cambridge.

Ed W. D. B. Turnbull, Visions of Tundale, Edinburgh 1843; E Studien 35 1905 (ms 1); 2–6, T. F. Simmons 1879 (EETS); 2, C. Horstmann, Yorkshire writers vol 2, 1896; 2 pieces from 2, F. A. Patterson, ME penitential lyric, New York 1911; 3, E Studien 33 1904.
Wordsworth, C. and H. Littlehales. Old service books of the English Church. 1904.
Deanesly, M. In her Lollard Bible, Cambridge 1920, 1966 (with prefatory note).

Lay-Folks' Catechism

Wells pp. 348, 355, 817–18, 967, 970, 1015, 1120, 1269, 1309, 1353, 1399; C. Brown, Register vol 2, Oxford 1920, item 263; see Brown-Robbins Index and suppl item 409.

Gaystek or Gaytryge version

Mss: 1, Thornton (Lincoln Cathedral Lib A 5 2); 2, Rawlinson C 285 (Bodley).
Ed G. G. Perry 1867 (EETS) 1913 (rev) (ms 1); 2, C. Horstmann, Yorkshire writers vol 1, 1895; 2, T. F. Simmons and H. E. Nolloth 1901 (EETS).

Wycliffite version

Mss: Lambeth 408; York Minster XVI L 12.

Ed T. F. Simmons and H. E. Nolloth 1901 (EETS).

§2

Wordsworth, C. and H. Littlehales. Old service books of the English Church. 1904.
Deanesly, M. In her Lollard Bible, Cambridge 1920, 1966 (with prefatory note).
Owst, G. R. In his Preaching in medieval England, Cambridge 1926.

Primer, or Lay-Folks' Prayer Book

Wells pp. 356, 399, 819, 826, 970, 1015, 1062, 1065, 1120, 1124.

§1

Mss: 1, Univ Lib Cambridge Dd XI 82; 2, BM additional 17,010; 3, St John's College Cambridge G 24; 4, Digby 102 (Bodley); 5, BM additional 39,574; etc.

Ed H. Littlehales 2 pts 1895–7 (EETS) (ms 1); *see also* 1903 (EETS); 2, W. Maskell, Monumenta ritualia vol 3, 1882; 3, H. Littlehales, The prymer (with collation of other mss), 2 vols 1891–2; 4, J. Kail, Dirige, 1904 (EETS); 5, M. Day 1917 (EETS).

§2

Brown, C. Chaucer Soc 2nd ser 45 1910. P. 126.
— Chaucer and the Prymer. MLN 30 1915.
Deanesly, M. In her Lollard Bible, Cambridge 1820, 1966 (with prefatory note).
Birchenough, E. The Prymer in English. Library 4th ser 18 1938.
Hennig, J. Primer-versions of liturgical prayers. MLR 39 1944.
Hargreaves, H. The ME primers and the Wycliffite Bible. MLR 51 1956.

Instructions to Parish Priests (Mirk)

Wells pp. 361, 819; C. Brown, Register vol 2, Oxford 1920, items 302, 599; and Brown-Robbins Index, item 961.

§1

Ed E. Peacock 1868 (EETS).

§2

Mosher, J. A. The exemplum in the early religious and didactic literature of England. New York 1911.
Deanesly, M. In her Lollard Bible, Cambridge 1920, 1966 (with prefatory note).
Owst, G. R. Preaching in medieval England. Cambridge 1926.
— Literature and pulpit in medieval England. Cambridge 1933, Oxford 1961 (rev).
Pantin, W. In his English Church in the 14th century, Cambridge 1955.

Doctrinal of Sapience

§1

Tr from French and ptd by Caxton 1489.

§2

Blades, W. In his Biography and typography of William Caxton, 1882. Pp. 324–8.
Duff, E. G. William Caxton. Chicago 1905. Pp. 76, 93.
Aurner, N. S. Caxton: a study of the literature of the first English press. 1926. Pp. 101–4, 105.

Rule of St Benedict

Wells pp. 365, 820, 1016, 1063, 1121, 1399; C. Brown, Register vol 2, Oxford 1920, item 141.

§1

Mss: 1, Common version, Corpus Christi College Cambridge 178; Corpus Christi College Oxford 197; BM Cotton Tiberius A III; Durham Cathedral Lib B 4 24; Cotton Tiberius A IV; Cotton Faustina A X; 2, Wells version, Loose leaves in Chapter Lib Wells Cathedral; 3, Interlinear version, Cotton Tiberius A III; 4, Winteney version, Cotton Claudius D III; 5, Northern Prose and Ritual, Lansdowne 378; VI, Northern metre, Cotton Vespasian A XXV.

Ed R. Wülcker, Bibliothek der angelsächsischen Prosa vol 2, Cassel 1885; E Studien 24 1898, p. 161; 2, R. Wülcker, Bibliothek der angelsächsischen Prosa vol 2, Cassel 1885; 2 and 4, A. Schröer, Halle, 1888; 3, H. Logemann 1888 (EETS); 4, *see* Schröer above, also collation E Studien 16 1892, p. 152; 5, E. A. Kock 1902 (EETS); 6, E Studien 1870; and *see* Anglia 14 1892; E Studien 23 1897; E. A. Kock 1902 (EETS).

§2

Böddeker, K. Über die Sprache der Benediktinerregel. E Studien 2 1878. On version 6.
Tachauer, J. Die Laute und Flexionen. Würzburg 1900. On version 4.
Hermanns, W. Lautlehre und Dialektische. Bonn 1906. On version 3.
Heuser, W. Die Prosaversion der Benediktinerregel. Anglia 31 1908. On version 5.
Fehr, B. Das Benediktiner-offizium und die Beziehungen zwischen Aelfric und Wulstan. E Studien 46 1913.
Rohr, G. Die Sprache der altenglischen Prosabearbeitungen. Bonn 1912.
Deanesly, M. In her Lollard Bible, Cambridge 1920, 1966 (with prefatory note).
Hagel, F. Zur Sprache der nordenglischen Prosaversion der Benediktinerregel. Anglia 44 1920.
Funke, O. Zur Wortgeschichte der französischen Element im Englischen. E Studien 55 1921.

Ancrene Riwle and Wisse [AR] [AW]

Wells pp. 361, 820, 972, 1015, 1062, 1120, 1172, 1217, 1269, 1309, 1353, 1399, 1504; Brown-Robbins Index and suppl, item 3568.

§1

Mss: English 1, Corpus Christi College Cambridge 402; 2, BM Cotton Titus D XVIII; 3, Cotton Nero A XIV; 4, Cotton Cleopatra C VI; 5, Caius College Cambridge 234; see Anglia 3 1880, E Studien 3 1880, 9 1886, 19 1894; 6, Vernon (Bodley 3938); 7, Magdalene College Cambridge Pepys 2498; |8, Lord Robartes – one leaf, Bodmin Cornwall; 9, Royal 8 C I; French, 1, Cotton Vitellius F VII; 2, Trinity College Cambridge R 14 7; 3, Bibliothèque Nationale F.Fr. 6276; 4, Bodley 90; Latin, 1, Magdalen College Oxford 67; 2, Cotton Vitellius E VII (fragments); see also H. E. Allen, MLR 14 1919, 17 1922.

Ed J. R. R. Tolkien, The English text of the AR, AW, 1962 (EETS); G. Shepherd, AW, pts 6–7, 1959; 2, F. M. Mack, The English text of the AR, together with the Lanhydrock fragment (ms Bodley Eng. th. c. 70) ed A. Zettersten 1963 (EETS); 3, with some variants of 2 and 4, J. Morton 1853 (Camden Soc) (collation in Jahrbuch für Romanische und Englische Sprache 15 1876); M. Day and J. A. Herbert 1952 (EETS); 5, R. M. Wilson, The English text of AR, 1954 (EETS); 7, Påhlsson, The recluse, Lund 2 pts 1911–18; 8, JEGP 2 1898; 9, A. C. Baugh 1956 (EETS); Modern

English, The AR (from ms 1) tr M. B. Salu, introd by Dom G. Sitwell, preface by J. R. R. Tolkien 1956; French, 1, J. A. Herbert 1944 (EETS); 2, W. H. Trethewey 1958 (EETS); Latin, C. d'Evelyn 1944 (EETS).
Selections: J. Hall, Selections from early ME, 2 vols Oxford 1920; J. A. W. Bennett and G. V. Smithers, Early ME verse and prose, Oxford 1966, 1968 (rev).

§2

Mosher, J. A. The exemplum in the early religious and didactic literature of England. New York 1911.
Macaulay, G. C. The AR. MLR 9 1914.
Allen, H. E. The origin of the AR. PMLA 33 1918.
— The mystical lyrics of the Manuel de pechiez. Romanic Rev 9 1918.
— Some 14th-century borrowings from the AR. MLR 18–19 1923–4; Further borrowings from the AR, MLR 24 1929.
— On the author of the AR. PMLA 44 1929.
— The localisation of ms Bodley 34. MLR 28 1933.
— Eleanor Cobham. TLS 22 March 1934.
— The AR and Geoffrey of Monmouth. MLR 29 1934.
— The three daughters of Deorman. PMLA 50 1935.
— The Torlington chartulary. TLS 14 Feb 1935.
— Mss of the AR. TLS 8 Feb 1936.
— The AR. TLS 24 Oct 1936.
— Wynkyn de Worde and a second French compilation from the AR with a description of the first. In Essays and studies in honor of Carleton Brown, New York 1940.
Deanesly, M. The Lollard Bible. Cambridge 1920, 1966 (with prefatory note).
McNabb, V., H. E. Allen and G. G. Coulton. On the origin. MLR 15–17 1920–2.
Deith, E. Flexivisches und Syntaktisches über das Pronomen. Zürich 1920.
Funke, O. Zur Wortgeschichte der französischen Elemente im Englischen. E Studien 55 1921.
Zeise, A. Die Wortschatz. Jena 1923.
Dymes, D. M. E. The original language of the AR. E & S 9 1923. See Beiblatt zur Anglia 35 1924.
Chambers, R. W. Recent research upon the AR. RES 1 1925.
—, V. McNabb and F. H. Thurston. Further research upon the AR. RES 2 1926.
Owst, G. R. Preaching in medieval England. Cambridge 1926.
— Literature and pulpit in medieval England. Cambridge 1933, Oxford 1961 (rev).
Sergeantson, M. S. The dialect of Nero. RES 3 1927.
— The dialect of the Corpus ms of the AR. London Medieval Stud 1 1938.
Knowles, D. In his English mystics, 1928.
Tolkien, J. R. R. AW and Hali Maiðhad. E & S 14 1928.
Crawford, S. E. The influence of AR in the late 14th century. MLR 25 1930.
Coleman, T. W. The AR: the beginnings of English mysticism. London Quart 159 1934.
Ives, D. V. The proverbs in the AR. MLR 29 1934.
Whiting, B. J. Proverbs in the AR and the Recluse. MLR 30 1935.
McNabb, V. The authorship of the AR. In Archivum fratrum praedicatorum vol 4, Rome 1935.
Russell, J. C. In his Dictionary of writers in 13th-century England, 1936. P. 118.
Bögholm, N. Vocabulary and style of the ME AR. E Studies 19 1937.
Magoun, F. P. Ancrene Wisse vs Ancren Riwle. ELH 4 1937.
Colledge, E. The hours of the planets: an obscure passage in the Recluse. MLN 54 1939.
— The Recluse: a Lollard interpolated version of the AR. RES 15 1939.

Darwin, F. D. In his English medieval recluse, 1944.
Humbert, Sr A. M. Verbal repetition in the AR. Washington 1944.
Utley, F. L. The crooked rib. Columbus 1944.
White, B. M. I. The date of the AR. MLR 40 1945.
— Whale-hunting, the barnacle goose and the date of the AR. MLR 40 1945.
Hulbert, J. R. A 13th-century English literary standard. JEGP 45 1946.
d'Evelyn, C. Notes on some interrelations between the Latin and English texts of the AR. PMLA 64 1949.
Fisher, J. H. Continental association for the AR. PMLA 64 1949.
— (ed). The Treatyse of loue. 1951 (EETS).
— Seven variants in the Treatyse of loue. PBSA 46 1952.
— The French versions of the AR. Univ of North Carolina Stud in the Germanic Languages & Literatures 26 1959.
Shepherd, G. All the wealth of Croesus...: a topic in the AR. MLR 51 1956.
Shuman, R. Baird. Educational materials in the AR. N & Q May 1957.
— Concerning the authorship of the AR. N & Q Oct 1957.
Russell-Smith, J. Ridiculosae sternutationes (o nore in AW). RES new ser 8 1957.
Bennett, J. A. W. Lefunge o swefne o nore. RES new ser 9 1958.
Käsmann, H. Zur Frage der ursprünglichen Fassung der AR. Anglia 75 1957.
Kaske, R. E. Eve leaps in the AR. MÆ 29 1960.
Ladd, C. A. A note on the language of the AR. N & Q Aug 1961.
Stevens, W. The titles of the mss AB. MLN 76 1961.
Dobson, E. J. The affiliation of the mss of AW. In English and medieval studies presented to J. R. R. Tolkien, 1962.
— The date and composition of AW. Proc Br Acad 52 1966.
Miller, B. D. H. She who hath drunk any potion. MÆ 31 1962.
Smithers, G. V. Two typological terms in the AR. MÆ 34 1965.
Zettersten, A. Studies in the dialect and vocabulary of the AR. Lund Stud in Eng 34 1965.
Suzuki, S. The language of the AW. Tokyo 1967.
— Linguistic features in AW. Anglica 6 1967.
Wilson, E. The four doves in AW. RES new ser 19 1968.
Clark, C. Early ME prose. EC 18 1968.
Turville-Petre, J. Two etymological notes. Studia Neophilologica 41 1969.
Waldron, R. A. Enumeration in AW. N & Q March 1969.

Cursor Mundi

Wells pp. 339, 415, 517, 816, 1014, 1119, 1179, 1180, 1216, 1308, 1398, 1618; C. Brown, Register vol 2, Oxford 1920, item 1349; Brown-Robbins Index, items 694, 780, 1029, 1775, 1786, 1885, 2153, 3208, 3976.

§1

Mss: BM Cotton Vespasian A III etc. See above, and BM catalogue of additions 1900–5 p. 266.
Ed R. Morris 7 vols 1874–93 (EETS).
Selections: R. Morris and W. W. Skeat, Specimens of early English vol 2, Oxford 1894; J. Zupitza, Übungsbuch, Vienna 1922; O. F. Emerson, Reader, New York 1915; A. Brandl and O. Zippel, Mittelenglische Sprach- und Literaturproben, Berlin 1917; C. Brown, Religious lyrics of the 14th century, Oxford 1924, 1952 (rev); G. Sampson, Cambridge book of prose and verse, Cambridge 1924; J. A. W. Bennett and G. V. Smithers, Early ME verse and prose, Oxford 1966, 1968 (rev).

§2

Hänisch, H. C. W. On sources. Breslau 1884.

Hupe, H. Genealogie und Überlieferung der Handschriften des mittelenglischen Gedichtes Cursor mundi. Altenburg 1886.

Cook, A. S. A literary motive. MLN 7 1892.

Crow, C. L. On metre. Göttingen 1892.

Napier, A. S. In his History of the holy rood-tree, 1894 (EETS).

Brown, C. The Cursor mundi and the Southern passion. MLN 26 1911.

Mosher, J. A. In his Exemplum in the early religious and didactic literature of England, New York 1911.

Brunner, K. On BM additional ms 31,042. Archiv 132 1914.

Gerould, G. H. In his Saints' legends, Boston 1916.

d'Evelyn, C. The revelations of Methodius. PMLA 33 1918.

Strandberg, O. The rime-vowels of Cursor mundi. Upsala 1919.

Durrschmidt, H. Die Sage von Kain. Bayreuth 1919.

Deanesly, M. In her Lollard Bible, Cambridge 1920, 1966 (with prefatory note).

Frank, G. Vernacular sources and an Old French passion play. MLN 35 1920.

Arend, Z. M. Linking in Cursor mundi. Trans Philological Soc 1925–30.

Owst, G. R. In his Preaching in medieval England, Cambridge 1926.

— In his Literature and pulpit in medieval England, Cambridge 1933, Oxford 1961 (rev).

Menner, J. R. Two notes on mediaeval euhemerism. Speculum 3 1928.

Borland, L. Herman's Bible and the Cursor mundi. SP 30 1933.

Kaiser, R. Zur Geographie des mittelenglischen Wortschatzes. Palaestra 205 1937.

Larsen, H. Origi crucis. In If by your art: a testament to Percival Hunt, Pittsburgh 1948.

— Cursor mundi 1291. In Philologica: the [Kemp] Malone anniversary studies, Baltimore 1949.

Beichner, P. E. The Cursor mundi and Petrus Riga. Speculum 24 1949.

Lazar, M. La légende de l'arbre de paradis ou bois de la croix. Zeitschrift für Romanische Philologie 76 1960.

Quinn, E. C. The quest of Seth for the oil of life. Chicago 1962.

Lamberts, J. J. The Noah story in Cursor mundi vv 1625–1916. Mediaeval Stud 24 1962.

Buehler, P. The Cursor mundi and Herman's Bible: some additional parallels. SP 61 1964.

Sajavaara, K. The use of Robert Grosseteste's Chateau d'Amour as a source of the Cursor mundi. Neuphilologische Mitteilungen 68 1967.

Vices and Virtues

A 14th-century trn of the Somme des vices et des virtues, or Somme le Roi, of Lorens d'Orléans. A parallel text to Dan Michel's Ayenbite, below, and Caxton's Royal book.

Wells pp. 345, 346, 413, 830, 1019, 1068, 1125, 1219, 1311, 1714, 1823, 1908.

§1

Mss: Stowe 240 etc; see Wells.

Ed F. Holthausen 1920 (EETS); W. N. Francis 1942 (EETS). From mss BM additional 17,013, 22,283, Huntington Lib HM 147; The Royal book, or book for a King, tr and ptd Caxton, c. 1486; see Blades and Aurner under §2, below.

Selections: J. Hall, Selections from early ME, Oxford 1920.

§2

Blades, W. In his Biography and typography of William Caxton, 1882.

Schmidt, G. In his Ueber die Sprache und Heimat, Leipzig 1899.

Traver, H. E. Four daughters of God. Philadelphia 1907.

Merrill, E. In his Dialogue in English literature, New Haven 1911.

Mosher, J. A. In his Exemplum in the early religious and didactic literature of England, New York 1911.

Philippsen, M. Die Deklination. Erlangen 1911.

Meyerhoff, E. Die Verbalflexion. Kiel 1913.

Glahn, N. von. Zur Geschichte des grammatischen Geschlechts. Anglistische Forschungen 53 1918.

Funke, O. Zur Wortgeschichte der französichen Elemente im Englischen. E Studien 55 1921.

Flasdieck, H. M. On the language. E Studien 58 1924.

Aurner, N. S. In his Caxton, 1926.

Owst, G. R. In his Preaching in medieval England, Cambridge 1926.

— In his Literature and pulpit in medieval England, Cambridge 1933, Oxford 1961 (rev).

Cravens, Sr M. J. In her Designations and treatment of the holy eucharist in Old and ME before 1300, Washington 1932.

Thomson, S. H. A 13th-century Oure Fader in a Pavia ms. MLN 49 1934.

Pantin, W. In his English church in the 14th century, Cambridge 1955.

Ayenbite of Inwyt (Dan Michel)

Wells pp. 345, 817, 966, 1015, 1120, 1216, 1308, 1399; Brown-Robbins Index, items 1227, 2034, 2331, 3579.

§1

Ms: Arundel 57.

Ed J. Stevenson 1885 (Roxburghe Club); R. Morris 1866 (EETS), 1965 (rev P. Gradon).

Selections: E. Mätzner, Altenglische Sprachproben, Berlin 1867–1900; R. Wülcker, Lesebuch, Halle 1874–9; J. Zupitza, Übungsbuch, Vienna 1904; G. E. MacLean, Reader, New York 1915; F. Kluge, Lesebuch, Halle 1904; R. Morris and W. W. Skeat, Specimens of early English vol 2, Oxford 1894; A. Brandl and O. Zippel, Mittelenglische Sprach- und Literaturproben, Berlin 1917; C. Brown, Religious lyrics of the 14th century, Oxford 1924, 1952 (rev).

§2

Varnhagen, J. E Studien 1–2 1877–8.

Petersen, K. O. Sources of the Parson's tale. Radcliffe College Monographs 12 1901.

Förster, M. Die Bibliothek des Dan Michel. Archiv 115 1905.

Jensen, H. Die Verbalflexion. Kiel 1908.

Mosher, J. A. In his Exemplum in the early religious and didactic literature of England, New York 1911.

Dolle, R. Graphische und lautliche Untersuchung. Bonn 1912.

Glahn, N. von. Zur Geschichte des grammatischen Geschlechts. Anglistische Forschungen 53 1918.

Wallenberg, J. K. On vocabulary. Upsala 1923.

Flasdieck, H. Kentish ordinalia. Beiblatt zur Anglia 39 1928.

Owst, G. R. In his Literature and pulpit in medieval England, Cambridge 1933, Oxford 1961 (rev).

Francis, W. N. The original of the Ayenbite of inwyt. PMLA 52 1937.

Senff, H. Die Nominalinflexion. Jena 1937.

O'Connor, M. C. The art of dying well: the development of the Ars moriendi. New York 1942.

Schwede, I. Die Bezeichnungen der Numeri, Kasus und Genera des Nomens. Berlin 1942.

Pantin, W. In his English church in the 14th century, Cambridge 1955.

Pricke of Conscience

Wells pp. 447, 838, 1020, 1129, 1275, 1313, 1361, 1407, 1513, 1628, 1721, 1916; C. Brown, Register vol 2, Oxford 1920, items 314, 723, 2206–7; Brown-Robbins Index, items 484, 672, 790, 812, 1166, 1193, 1657, 3429, 3561.

§1

Mss: see above; also H. E. Allen, Writings ascribed to Rolle, New York 1927 pp. 374–83; and Trans Philological Soc 1890; Archiv 86 1891 p. 283; MLN 20 1905 p. 210; P. Andrae, Mss of the Pricke of conscience, Berlin 1888; H. E. Allen, On Latin mss, MP 13 1916 p. 745.

Ed R. Morris, Berlin 1863 (Philological Soc); G. Horstmann, Yorkshire writers vol 1, 1895 pp. 129, 372; vol 2, 1896 pp. 36, 67, 70.
Selections: E. Mätzner, Altenglische Sprachproben pt 1, Berlin 1867; R. Wülcker, Lesebuch, Halle 1874–9; R. Morris and W. W. Skeat, Specimens of early English vol 2, Oxford 1894; A. Brandl and O. Zippel, Mittelenglische Sprach- und Literaturproben, Berlin 1917.

§2

Köhler, R. Jahrbuch für Romanische und Englische Sprache 6 1864.
—— In his Kleinere Schrifte vol 3, Berlin 1900. No 26.
Ullman, J. Studien zu Richard Rolle. E Studien 7 1884.
Bülbring, K. D. Handschriften. E Studien 23 1887.
Hahn, A. Quellenuntersuchungen zu Rolle, Englische Schriften. Berlin 1900; and Archiv 106 1901 p. 349.
Allen, H. E. The authorship. Radcliffe College Monographs 15 1910.
—— Speculum vitae. PMLA 32 1917.
—— Writings ascribed to Richard Rolle. New York 1927.
Deanesly, M. In her Lollard Bible, Cambridge 1920, 1966 (with prefatory note).
Comper, F. M. M. The life of Richard Rolle. 1928.
d'Evelyn, C. An east midland recension of the Pricke of conscience. PMLA 45 1930.
Coffman, G. R. Old age from Horace to Chaucer. Speculum 9 1934.
Lightbown, J. The Pricke of conscience: a collation of mss Galba E IX and Harley 4196. Leeds Stud in Eng 4 1935.
Linn. I. Dean Swift, Pope Innocent and Oliver Wendell Holmes. PQ 16 1937.
Lindheim, B. von. Studien zur Sprache des ms Cotton Galba E IX. Vienna 1937.

Robert Mannyng

For Mannyng's Chronicle see (2), Chronicles, col 465, above.

Handlyng Synne

Wells pp. 14, 177, 185, 200–1, 276, 342–4, 352, 358, 374, 447, 449, 543, 595, 816, 966, 1015, 1060, 1119, 1308, 1399, 1618–19; C. Brown, Register vol 2, Oxford 1920, items 340, 486, 583.

§1

Mss: 1, BM Harley 1701; 2, Bodley 415; 3, Univ Lib Cambridge Ii IV 9; 4, Dulwich College XXIV.

Ed F. J. Furnivall 1862 (Roxburghe Club); 1901 (EETS), 1903 (EETS).
Selections: A story from ms Ashmole 61, in C. Horstmann, Altenglische Legenden, Heilbronn 1881, p. 339; R. Morris and W. W. Skeat, Specimens of early English vol 2, Oxford 1894; A. S. Cook, Reader, Boston 1915; O. F. Emerson, Reader, New York 1915; W. A. Neilson and K. G. T. Webster, Chief ME poets, Boston 1916; K. Sisam, Fourteenth-century verse and prose, Oxford 1921.

§2

CHEL 1 1907 p. 344.
Allen, H. E. Mystical lyrics of the Manuel de Péchiez. Romanic Rev 9 1912.
Kunz, A. Mannyng of Brunne's Handlyng synne compared with the French. Königsberg 1913.
Schlutter, O. B. Anglia 37–8 1913–14.
Welter, J. T. L'exemplum dans la littérature religieuse et didactique du Moyen Age. Paris 1927.
Arnould, E. J. Un manuscrit partiel du Manuel de péchés. Romania 63 1937.
—— Le manuel de péchés. Paris 1940.
Laird, C. G. Mss of the Manuel de Pechiez. In Stanford studies in language and literature, ed H. Craig, Stanford 1941.
—— Palatinus latinus: a composite ms. MLR 38 1943.
Crosby, R. Mannyng: a new biography. PMLA 57 1942.
Seaton, E. Mannyng in Lincoln. MÆ 12 1943.
Robertson, D. W. The Manuel de péchés and an English episcopal decree. MLN 60 1945.
—— The Manuel de péchés. MLN 61 1946.
—— Certain theological conventions in Mannyng's treatment of the commandments. MLN 61 1946.
—— The cultural tradition of Handlyng synne. Speculum 22 1947.

Septem Miracula
A Southern version of Handlyng synne

Wells pp. 273, 344, 804.

§1

Ed C. Horstmann 1892 (EETS); F. J. Furnivall 1903 (EETS); C. Horstmann, Altenglische Legenden, Heilbronn 1881, pp. lxviii, lxxiii, lxxxii.

Meditations on the Supper of Our Lord

Wells pp. 358, 819, 1269, 1309.

Ed J. M. Cowper 1875 (EETS).

Prose Version of the Manuel

Wells pp. 966, 1015. See H. E. Allen, Two ME translations from the Anglo-Norman, MP 13 1916; Romanic Rev 8 1917.
See also Peter Idley's Instructions, below.

Peter Idley's Instructions to His Son

Book 2 based on Mannyng's Handlyng synne, see above, with addns from Lydgate's Falls of Princes.

Ed C. d'Evelyn, Boston 1935 (on mss see pp. 58–61); W. Heuser, Bonner Beiträge zur Anglistik 14 1904 (part).

A Litil Tretys on the Seven Deadly Sins (Lavynham)

Ed J.P.W. M. van Zutphen from ms Harley 211 and 13 other mss (details pp. xxxiii f), Rome 1956.

The Two Ways

§1

Ed V. J. Scattergood, The two ways: an unpublished religious treatise by Sir John Clanvowe from ms Univ College Oxford 97, Eng Philological Stud 10 1967.

§2

Wilson, E. A supplementary note to an edition of Sir John Clanvowe's treatise the Two ways. Eng Philological Stud 11 1968.

The Book of the Craft of Dying

Wells pp. 360, 1824, 1908, 1910.

§ 1

Mss: Bodley 423; Rawlinson C 894 (Bodley); Douce 322 (Bodley); Laud Miscellaneous 99 (Bodley); Marley 1706; Royal 17 C XVIII; BM additional 10,596; Univ Lib Cambridge Kk I 5; Univ Lib Cambridge Ff 5 45; Corpus Christi College Cambridge 494; Corpus Christi College Oxford 220; etc.

Ed Caxton, Ars moriendi, 1491, Wynkyn de Worde 1497; The art and craft to know well to die, Caxton 1490; Pynson (before 1501?); and *see* Short title catalogue, items 791–3; R. Girvan, Ratis raving (summary in English of a portion of the Latin Ars Moriendi pp. xiv–xviii and 166–74) 1939 (Scottish Text Soc); parts: W. N. Francis 1942 (EETS) pp. xlii–xliii and 68–71; tr F. M. M. Comper, The book of the craft of dying, 1917.

§ 2

O'Connor, M. C. The art of dying well: the development of the Ars moriendi. New York 1942.

Allegorical Works
Charters of Christ

Wells pp. 369, 821, 1016, 1121, 1217, 1400; C. Brown, Register vol 2, Oxford 1920 items 716, 1049, 1130, 2644, 2659; Brown-Robbins Index items 1174, 1718, 1740, 1828, 4154, 4184.

§ 1

Ed Archiv 79 1887; F. J. Furnivall 1901 (EETS); B. Fehr, Archiv 106 1901; N & Q 21 Sept 1901; M. C. Spalding, Bryn Mawr 1914; M. Förster, Anglia 42 1918.

§ 2

Thien, U. Über die englischen Marienklagen. Kiel 1906.
Perrow, E. C. The last will and testament as a form. Trans Wisconsin Acad 17 1914.

Abbey of the Holy Ghost

Wells pp. 368, 821, 1121, 1270, 1309, 1400, 1621, 1716, 1911.

§ 1

Mss: 1, Laud 210 (Bodley); 2, Vernon (Bodley 3938); 3, Thornton (Lincoln Cathedral Lib A 5 2); 4, Lambeth 432; etc.

Ed G. G. Perry 1867 (ms 3) (EETS); C. Horstmann, Yorkshire writers vol 1, 1895 (ms 3 and variants from others).
Selections: W. Matthews, Later medieval English prose, 1962.

§ 2

Traver, H. The four daughters of God. Philadelphia 1907.
Mosher, J. A. In his Exemplum in the early religious and didactic literature of England, New York 1911.
Deanesly, M. In her Lollard Bible, Cambridge 1920, 1966 (with prefatory note).
Owst, G. R. In his Preaching in medieval England, Cambridge 1926.
—— In his literature and pulpit in medieval England, Cambridge 1933, Oxford 1961 (rev).
Allen, H. E. In her Writings ascribed to Richard Rolle, New York 1927.
Bühler, C. The first edition of the Abbey of the Holy Ghost. SB 6 1954.

Charter of the Abbey of the Holy Ghost

Wells pp. 369, 370, 821.

§ 1

Ed C. Horstmann, Yorkshire writers vol 1, 1895.

§ 2

Brook, S. The charter of the Abbey of the Holy Ghost. MLR 44 1959.

The Castel of Love

Wells pp. 366, 820, 1016, 1121, 1217, 1309, 1400; and see C. Brown, Register vol 2, Oxford 1920: items 1016, 2092, 2637; and Brown-Robbins Index, items 1677, 3270, 4145.

§ 1

Mss: A Version, 1, Vernon (Bodley 3938); 2, BM additional 22,283; 3, Bodley additional B 107; B Version, Bodley 6922; C Version, Egerton 927.

Edns: A Version, 1–2, 1892 (EETS); 1901 (EETS); A Version, 3, J. O. Halliwell (-Phillipps), Castel of love, Brixton Hill 1849; and see C. Horstmann 1892 (EETS); B Version, C. Horstmann, Altenglische Legenden, Heilbronn 1881; C Version, M. Cooke, R. Grosseteste, Carmina anglo-normanica, 1852 (Caxton Soc); and see Anglia 14 1892, and C. Horstmann 1892 (EETS); R. F. W. Weymouth, Castel off loue, 1864; J. Murray 1918; K. Sajavaara, The ME translations of Robert Grosseteste's Chateau d'Amour, Mémoires de la Société Néophilologique de Helsinki 32 1967.

§ 2

Weymouth, R. E. Trans Philological Soc 8 1863.
Haase, E. Altenglische Bearbeitungen von Grossetestes Chasteau d'Amour. Anglia 12 1890.
Owst, G. R. In his Preaching in medieval England, Cambridge 1926.
—— In his Literature and pulpit in medieval England, Cambridge 1933, Oxford 1961 (rev).
Bühler, C. F. Sources of the Court of Sapience. Beiträge zur Englischen Philologie 23 1932.
Van Os, A. B. Religious visions. Amsterdam 1932.
Langfors, A. Notice et extraits des mss de la Bibliothèque Nationale 52 1933.
Brunner, K. Der Streit der vier Himmelstöchter. E Studien 68 1934.
Pantin, W. In his English Church in the 14th century, Cambridge 1955.

Myrour of Lewed Men

Another version of Castel of Love, above.
Wells pp. 1576, 1621.
Ms: BM Egerton 927.

Edn: Mémoires de la Société Néophilologique de Helsinki 32 1967. Pp. 165f, 320f.

Testament of Love (Thomas Usk)

Wells pp. 370, 821, 1121, 1270, 1309, 1353, 1400; E. P. Hammond, Chaucer: a bibliographical manual, New York 1908.

§ 1

Ed W. Thynne, Workes of Chaucer, 1532; W. W. Skeat, Complete works of Chaucer vol 7, Oxford 1897.

§ 2

Morley, H. In his English writers vol 5, 1890.
Skeat, W. W. In Complete works of Chaucer vol 5, Oxford 1894; vol 7, 1897.
—— Usk and Ralph Higden. N & Q 26 March 1904.
Krapp, G. P. In his Rise of English literary prose, New York 1916.
Bressie, R. The date of Usk's Testament of love. MP 26 1928.
—— A study of Usk's Testament of love as an autobiography. Chicago Univ Humanistic Ser 7 1931.

Tuve, R. Seasons and months. Paris 1933.

Lewis, C. S. In his Allegory of love, Oxford 1936.

Sanderlin, G. Usk's Testament of love and St Anselm. Speculum 17 1942.

Schaar, C. Notes on Usk's Testament of love. Lund 1950.

—— Usk's 'knot in the hert'. E Studies 37 1956.

Heninger, S. K., jr. The margarite-pearl allegory in Usk's Testament of love. N & Q June 1964.

Canley, J. The Lord's day as the eighth day. N & Q Oct 1970.

Quatrefoil of Love

Ed I. Gollancz and M. M. Weale 1934 (EETS).

B. Particular Works
(Proverbs, Precepts and Monitory Works)

Proverbs of Alfred

Wells pp. 375, 822, 1016, 1064, 1122, 1183, 1217, 1310, 1354, 1400, 1506; and C. Brown, Register vol 2, Oxford 1920; item 285; and Brown-Robbins, Index and suppl, items 433 and 2093.

§1

Mss: 1, Jesus College Oxford 29 (Bodley); 2, Trinity College Cambridge B 14 39; 3, BM Cotton Galba A XIX (fragments); 4, Bodley James 6 (complete copy of 3); 5, Maidstone Museum A 13.

Ed J. Hall, Selections from early ME, Oxford 1920 (ms 1); T. Wright and J. O. Halliwell (-Phillipps), Reliquiae antiquae vol 1, 1841 (mss 1–2); R. Morris, 1872 (EETS); W. W. Skeat, Oxford 1907; J. M. Kemble, Dialogue of Salomon and Saturnus, 1848 (ms 2); E. Borgström, Lund 1908, 1911 (ms 3); A. Brandl and O. Zippel, Mittelenglische Sprach- und Literaturproben, Berlin 1917; C. Brown, MLR 21 1926 (mss 4–5); O. S. Anderson Arngart, Lund 1955 (mss 4–5); tr J. L. Weston, Chief ME poets, Boston 1914; M. G. Segar, A medieval anthology, 1916 (selected).

Selections: R. Morris and W. W. Skeat, Specimens of early English vol 1, Oxford 1885; J. Zupitza, Übungsbuch, Vienna 1922; G. Sampson, Cambridge book of prose and verse, Cambridge 1924.

§2

Greg, W. W. The troubles of a Norman scribe. MLR 5 1910.

Brown, C. A 13th-century ms at Maidstone. MLR 21 1926.

South, H. P. The proverbs of Alfred. New York 1931.

Ker, N. R. Ms Cotton Galba A XIX: the proverbs of Alfred. MÆ 5 1936.

[Anderson]-Arngart, O. S. The proverbs of Alfred I: a study of the texts. Lund 1942.

—— On some readings in the proverbs of Alfred. E Studies 30 1949.

—— 'Seiʒe þu it noht þe areʒe' PA (M) 204. E Studies 42 1961.

Storms, G. 'Ne say þu hit þin areʒe' PA (T) 204. Ibid.

Proverbs of Hendyng

Wells pp. 377, 822, 973, 1016, 1122, 1217, 1271, 1310; and C. Brown, Register vol 2, Oxford 1920; items 383, 1009, 1298, 1732, 2636; and Anglia 5 1882, and Archiv 115 1905.

§1

Mss: 1, Digby 86 (Bodley); 2, BM Harley 2253; 3, Univ Lib Cambridge Gg I 1; 4 (parts), Univ Lib Cambridge 4407 (19); 5, St John's College Cambridge F 8 (145); 6, Worcester Cathedral Lib F 19; 7, Bodley 410; 8, Rawlinson C 670 (Bodley); 9, Eton College 34; 10–11, Laud 111 and 213 (Bodley).

Ed J. M. Kemble, Salomon and Saturnus, 1848 (appendix) (ms 2); K. Böddeker, Altenglische Dichtungen des ms Harley 2253, Berlin 1878 (ms 2); E. Mätzner, Altenglische Sprachproben pt 1, Berlin 1867 (ms 2); R. Morris and W. W. Skeat, Specimens of early English vol 2, Oxford 1894 (ms 2); T. Wright and J. O. Halliwell (-Phillipps), Reliquiae antiquae vol 1, 1841 (ms 2); H. Varnhagen, Anglia 4 1881 (1 and 3, with comparison of 2); W. W. Skeat, MLR 7 1912 (ms 4); C. Brown, Register vol 1, Oxford 1916, pp. 450–1 (ms 6); G. Schleich, Anglia 51 1927; tr J. L. Weston, Chief ME poets, Boston 1914.

Selection: G. Sampson, Cambridge book of prose and verse, 1924.

§2

Wright, T. In his Essays on literature of the Middle Ages vol 1, 1846.

Meyer, P. Romania 15 1886.

Kneuer, K. Die Sprichwörter Hendyngs. Leipzig 1901.

Schleich, G. Zu den Sprichwörtern Hendings. Anglia 52 1928.

Singer, S. Die Sprichwörter Hendings. Studia Neophilologica 14 1942.

—— In his Sprichwörter des Mittelalters vol 1, Berne 1944.

Distichs of Cato

Wells pp. 378, 822, 973, 1122, 1173, 1217, 1622, 1716; and Brown-Robbins Index and suppl: items 169, 247, 558, 820, 854, 1539, 1629, 3955, 3957.

§1

Mss: I, Old English, BM Cotton Junius A II etc (col 336, above); II, Northern couplet version, 1, Rawlinson G 59 (Bodley); 2, Sidney Sussex College Cambridge LXIII; III, Four-line stanza version: Little Cato, Great Cato, 1, Vernon (Bodley 3938); 2, BM additional 22,283; IV, Six-line stanza version, 1, Bodley 3894; 2, Bodley 29,003; V, Burgh's rime royal (a) Cato major: 30 mss, see Brown, Register vol 2 item 533; (b) Cato minor: 19 mss, see Brown, Register vol 2 item 2533; VI, Latin version: see Brown, Register vol 2 items 103, 159, 533, 558, 2533, 2534; also 1901 (EETS) p. 553, 1878 (EETS) p. 99. Archiv 95 1895 p. 163, E Studien 7 1884 p. 197.

Edns: II.2, M. Förster, E Studien 36 1906; III.1, M. O. Goldberg, Anglia 7 1884; F. J. Furnivall 1901 (EETS) p. 553; IV.1, R. Morris 1878 (EETS) p. 1667; IV.2, M. Förster, Archiv 115–16 1905–6 (from ms Univ Lib Cambridge Hh IV 12); Caxton's edn Cambridge 1906 (facs); VI, tr W. J. Chase, Madison 1922.

§2

Grober, G. Grundriss der romanischen Philologie vol 2. Strasbourg 1902 (2nd edn). Pp. 381, 383, 482, 863, 1066, 1187.

Schanz, M. Geschichte der römischen Literatur. Munich 1905 (2nd edn p. 38).

Paul, H. Grundriss der germanischen Philologie vol 2. Strasbourg 1909 (2nd edn). Pp. 1072, 1128.

Brusendorff, A. 'He knew nat Catoun...' In A miscellany in honor of F. Klaeber, Minneapolis 1929.

Whiting, B. J. Notes on the fragmentary Fairfax version of the Disticha Catonis. Mediaeval Stud 10 1948.

Hazelton, R. The christianization of 'Cato': the Disticha Catonis in the light of late mediaeval commentaries. Mediaeval Stud 19 1957.

Ruhe, E. Untersuchungen zu den altfranzösischen Übersetzungen. Beiträge zur Romanischen Philologie des Mittelalters 2 1968.

Brunner, I. A. On some of the vernacular translations of Cato's Distichs. In Helen Adolf Festschrift, New York 1968.

Poema Morale

*Wells pp. 385, 823, 1017, 1064, 1122, 1173, 1218, 1356,
1401; C. Brown, Register vol 2, Oxford 1920 item 786;
Brown-Robbins, Index and suppl items 1272 and 3246;
and MLR 21 1926.*

§ 1

Mss: 1, *Digby A 4 (Bodley)*, see *Archiv* 115 1905; 2, *Jesus
College Oxford 29 (Bodley)*; 3, *Trinity College Cambridge
B 14 52*; 4, *Fitzwilliam Museum Cambridge McClean
123*; 5–6, *Egerton 613 (2 texts)*; 7, *Lambeth 487.*

Edns: 1, Anglia 1 1878; 2–3, R. Morris and W. W. Skeat,
Specimens of early English vol 1, Oxford 1885; 2, R.
Morris 1872 (EETS); 3, R. Morris 1873 (EETS);
4, A. C. Paues, Anglia 30 1907; 5, R. Morris 1868
(EETS); O. F. Emerson, Reader, New York 1915;
5–6, F. J. Furnivall, Early English poems and lives of
saints, Berlin 1862; 6, J. Zupitza, Übungsbuch, Leipzig
1915; G. E. MacLean, Reader, 1894; 3 and 7 and parts
of 5–6, J. Hall, Selections from early ME, Oxford 1920;
7, R. Morris 1867 (EETS); and critical edns: H. Lewin,
Halle 1881; H. Marcus, Palaestra 194 1934.

§ 2

Suchier, H. On analogues: Reimpredigt. Halle 1879.
Schipper, J. In his Englische Metrik, Bonn 1881.
Krüger, A. In his Sprache und Dialekt, Erlangen 1885.
On ms 3.
Paul, H. In his Grundriss der germanischen Philologie
vol 2, Strasbourg 1892.
Paues, A. C. A newly discovered ms of the Poema morale.
Anglia 30 1907.
Gabrielson, A. Le sermon de Guischart de Beauliu.
Upsala 1909.
—— Guischart de Beauliu's debt. Archiv 128 1912.
Jordan, R. On the dialect of ms 7. E Studien 42 1910.
Preusler, W. On syntax. Breslau 1914.
Allen, H. E. Romanic Rev 9 1918.
Stegen, L. Die Sprachformen und Schreibungen. Jahr-
buch der Philosophischen Fakultät Göttingen 1 1921.
Walberg, E. Neuphilologische Mitteilungen 26 1925.
Moore, S. Anglia 44 1930.
Ker, N. R. The scribes of the Trinity homilies. MÆ 1
1932.
Haworth, R. A. L. Some notes on the dialect and mss
the Poema morale. Tokyo Univ Stud in Eng 14
1934.
Hill, B. Notes on the Egerton e text of the Poema morale.
Neophilologus 50 1966.

The Sayings of St Bernard

§ 1

Ms: Bodley additional E 6 etc.

§ 2

Cross, J. E. The sayings of Saint Bernard and ubi scount
qui ante nos fuerount. RES new ser 9 1958.
Monda, J. B. The sayings of Saint Bernard. Mediaeval
Stud 32 1970.

B. Particular Works
(Dialogues and Debates)

The Owl and the Nightingale [ON]

*Wells pp. 418, 831, 1019, 1069, 1126, 1219, 1273, 1311,
1358, 1404, 1719.*

§ 1

Mss: 1, *BM Cotton Caligula A IX*; 2, *Jesus College Oxford
29 (Bodley)*.

Ed J. Stevenson 1838 (Roxburghe Club); T. Wright 1843
(Percy Soc); F. H. Stratmann, Krefeld 1867, and *see*
E Studien 1 1877; J. E. Wells, Boston and London 1907
(parallel texts); W. Gadow, Das mittelenglische Streit-
gedicht Eule und Nachtigall, Palaestra 65 1909; J. H. G.
Grattan and G. F. H. Sykes 1935 (EETS); J. W. H.
Atkins, Cambridge 1922 (with trn); G. Eggers 1955
(trn); E. G. Stanley 1960; N. R. Ker 1963 (EETS) (ms
facs with introd).
Selections: E. Mätzner, Altenglische Sprachproben, Berlin
1867–1900; R. Morris and W. W. Skeat, Specimens of
early English vol 1, Oxford 1885, and *see* E. A. Kock in
Anglia 25 1902; A. S. Cook, Reader, Boston 1915;
A. Brandl and O. Zippel, Mittelenglische Sprach- und
Literaturproben, Berlin 1917; J. Hall, Selections from
early ME, Oxford 1920; G. Sampson, Cambridge book
of prose and verse, 1924.

§ 2

Walther, H. Das Streitgedicht in der lateinischen Literatur
des Mittelalters. Quellen und Untersuchungen zur
Lateinischen Philologie des Mittelalters 5 1920.
Owen, A. (ed). Le traité de Walter de Bibbesworth. Paris
1929.
Whiting, B. J. On v.816. Anglia 58 1934.
Dickins, B. ON and the S William window in York
Minster, with plate of panel 53. Leeds Stud in Eng 5
1936.
Onions, C. T. An experiment in textual reconstruction.
E & S 22 1936.
—— 'Gaping against an oven'. MÆ 9 1940.
—— Two notes on ME texts. MÆ 17 1948.
Chandler, A. R. Larks, nightingales and poets: an essay
and an anthology. Columbus 1937.
Huganir, K. Further notes on the date of ON. Anglia 63
1939.
Kunstmann, J. G. The Hoopoe: a study in European folk-
lore. Chicago 1938.
—— The bird that fouls its nest. Southern Folklore Quart
3 1939.
Wrenn, C. L. Curiosities in a medieval ms. E & S 25 1939.
Atkins, J. W. H. A note on ON. MLR 35 1940.
—— English literary criticism: the medieval phase. Cam-
bridge 1943.
Utley, F. L. The crooked rib. Columbus 1944.
Magoun, F. P. ON and the tale of the cat and the fox.
California Folklore Quart 4 1945.
Chapman, R. Noreweie and galeweie in ON. MLR 41 1946.
d'Ardenne, S. R. T. O. 'Ine so gode kinges londe.' E
Studies 30 1949.
—— The editing of ME texts. In English studies today,
ed C. L. Wrenn and G. Bullough, Oxford 1951.
—— 'Smithes' in ON. RES new ser 9 1958.
Sundby, B. The dialect and provenance of the ME poem
ON. Lund Stud in Eng 18 1950.
Cawley, A. C. Astrology in ON. MLR 46 1951.
Stanley, E. G. Some notes on ON. Eng & Germanic Stud
6 1951.
Lumiansky, R. M. Concerning ON. PQ 32 1953.
Gordon, I. A. ON 258. The semantic development of
'spell' (= 'rest'). MLN 70 1955.
Peterson, D. L. ON and Christian dialectic. JEGP 55
1956.
Donovan, M. J. The owl as religious altruist in ON.
Mediaeval Stud 18 1956.
Sisam, C. Notes on ME texts. RES new ser 13 1962.
Bruten, A. The cessation of the nightingale's song: ON.
N & Q Nov 1966.
Colgrave, B. ON and 'the good man from Rome'. Eng
Lang Notes 4 1966.
Gardner, J. ON: a burlesque. Papers in Lang & Lit 2
1966.
Gottschalk, J. ON: lay preachers to a lay audience. PQ 45
1966.

Baldwin, A. W. Henry II and ON. JEGP 66 1967.

Kinneavy, G. B. Fortune, providence and the owl. SP 64 1967.

Carson, M. A. Rhetorical structure in ON. Speculum 42 1967.

Hieatt, G. The subject of the mock-debate between the owl and the nightingale. Studia Neophilologica 40 1968.

de Vries, F. C. A note on ON 951, 1297. N & Q Dec 1969.

Russell, J. C. The patrons of the owl and the nightingale. PQ 48 1969.

Finkelstein, D. On the motion of the heart in ON. Neuphilologische Mitteilungen 71 1970.

Martin, B. K. Notes on ON. N & Q Nov 1971.

The Thrush and the Nightingale

Wells pp. 421, 831, 1126, 1404; and see Brown-Robbins, Index item 3222.

§ I

Mss: 1, *Auchinleck (Nat Lib of Scotland 19.2.1)* ; 2, *Digby 86 (Bodley).*

Ed T. Wright and H. O. Halliwell (-Phillipps), Reliquiae antiquae vol 1, 1841 (ms 1); W. C. Hazlitt, Remains of the early popular poetry of England vol 1, 1864; E. M. Stengel, Codicem manu scriptum Digby 86, Halle 1871 (collation); 2, Anglia 4 1881, 43 1919, and *see* 44 1920; C. Brown, English lyrics of the 13th century, Oxford 1932 (lyric 52).

§ 2

Heider, O. Untersuchungen zur mittelenglischen erotischen Lyrik. Halle 1905.

Le jardin de plaisance et fleur de réthorique. Société des Anciens Textes Français 60 1910 (facs of 1501).

Hagman, L. W. Youth and crabbed thrush. Stud in Medieval Culture, Univ Western Michigan 2 1966.

Owen, L. J. The thrush and the nightingale: the speaker in lines 94-6. Eng Lang Notes 7 1969.

The Boke of Cupide, or Cuckoo and Nightingale

Wells, pp. 423, 831, 1273, 1311, 1404; and Brown-Robbins, Index item 3361.

§ I

Mss: 1, *Fairfax 16 (Bodley)* ; 2, *Bodley 638; 3, Univ Lib Cambridge Ff I 6; 4, Tanner 346 (Bodley); 5, Selden B 24 (Bodley).*

Ed E. Vollmer, Berlin 1898; W. W. Skeat, Complete works of Chaucer, vol 3, Oxford 1897; V. J. Scattergood, Eng Philological Stud 9 1965.

§ 2

Kittredge, G. L. MP 1 1903.

Cook, A. S. Trans Connecticut Acad 20 1916.

Ward, C. E. The authorship of the Cuckoo and the nightingale. MLN 44 1929.

Utley, F. L. The crooked rib. Columbus 1944.

Robbins, R. H. The Findern anthology. PMLA 69 1954.

Scattergood, V. J. The authorship of the Boke of Cupide. Anglia 82 1964.

Lampe, D. E. Tradition and meaning in the Cuckoo and the nightingale. Univ of Illinois Papers on Lang & Lit 3 (suppl) 1967.

The Body and the Soul

Wells pp. 411, 829, 980, 1018, 1068, 1125, 1272, 1311, 1358, 1404; and C. Brown, Register vol 2, Oxford 1920 items 228, 883, 1429, and Brown-Robbins, Index items 351, 1461, 2336, 3967.

§ I

Mss: Version 1, Exeter Book (Cathedral Lib Exeter) ; Version 2, Worcester Cathedral Lib (fragments) ; Version 3, Bodley 343 (25vv) ; Version 4a, Laud 108 (Bodley) ; b, Auchinleck (Nat Lib of Scotland 19.2.1) ; c, Royal 18 A X; d, Vernon (Bodley 3938) ; e, BM additional 22,283 ; f, Digby 102 (Bodley) ; g, BM additional 37,787 ; Version 5a, Digby 86 (Bodley) ; b, Trinity College Cambridge B.14.39 ; c, Harley 2253 ; Version 6, Trinity College Cambridge B.14.39 (f27r.22vv).

Ed C. W. M. Grein, Bibliothek der angelsächsischen Poesie vol 1, Göttingen 1857 (version 1); R. Wülcker, Leipzig 1894 (version 1); T. Phillipps, Fragment of Aelfric's grammar, 1838 (version 2); S. W. Singer, Departing soul's address to the body, 1845 (version 2); E. Haufe, Greifswald 1880 (version 2); R. Buchholz, Erlanger Beiträge 6 1890 (version 2); J. Hall, Selections from early ME, Oxford 1920 (version 2); Archaeologia 17 1814 (version 3); T. Thorpe, Analecta anglosaxonica, 1846 (version 3); F. L. M. Rieger, Alt- und angelsächsisches Lesebuch, Giessen 1861 (version 3); A. Schröer, Anglia 5 1882 (version 3); R. Buchholz, Erlanger Beiträge 6 1890 (version 3); (with Latin and French), T. Wright, Latin poems attributed to W. Mapes 1841 (Camden Soc) (version 4a, d); 1-2, W. Linow, Erlanger Beiträge 1 1889 (version 4a, b, d, f with variants of e); E. Mätzner, Altenglische Sprachproben pt 1, Berlin 1867 (version 4a); O. F. Emerson, Reader, New York 1915 (4a); D. Laing, Owain Miles, Edinburgh 1837 (version 4b); H. Varnhagen, Anglia 2 1879 (version 4c); E. M. Stengel, Codicem manu scriptum, Digby 86, Halle 1871 (version 5a); T. Wright, Latin poems attributed to W. Mapes, 1841 (Camden Soc) (5c); K. Böddeke, Altenglische Dichtungen der Handschrift Harley 2253, Berlin 1878 (version 5c); T. Wright, Latin poems attributed to W. Mapes, 1841 (Camden Soc) (version 6); H. Varnhagen, Anglia 3 1880 (version 6); tr C. G. Child, Boston 1908; J. L. Weston, Chief ME poets, Boston 1914.

§ 2

Heesch, G. Über Sprache und Versbau. Kiel 1884.

Wülcker, R. Grundriss zur Geschichte der angelsächsischen Literatur. Leipzig 1885.

Bruce, J. D. MLN 5 1890.

Batiouchkof, T. Le débat de l'âme et du corps. Romania 20 1891.

Holthausen, F. On version 2. Anglia 14 1892.

Kunze, O. þe desputisoun bitwen þe bodi and þe soule. Berlin 1892.

Dudley, L. JEGP 8 1909.

Glahn, N. von. Anglistische Forschungen 53 1918.

Allen, B. On version III.6. MLR 22 1927.

Allison, T. E. Castell of perseverance. MLN 42 1927.

Oakden, J. P. Alliterative poetry in ME. Manchester 1930.

Willard, R. The address of the soul to the body. PMLA 50 1935.

Heningham, E. K. An early Latin debate of the body and the soul, preserved in ms Royal 7 A III in the BM. New York 1939.

— Old English precursors of the Worcester fragments. PMLA 55 1940.

Vogel, Sr M. U. Some aspects of the horse and rider analogy in the debate of the body and soul. Washington 1948.

Ackerman, R. W. The debate of the body and the soul and parochial Christianity. Speculum 37 1962.

Smetana, C. Second thoughts on Soul and body 1. Mediaeval Stud 29 1967.

Hill, T. D. Punishment according to the joints of the body in the Old English Soul and body 2. N & Q Nov 1968.

Ferguson, M. H. The structure of the soul's address to the body in OE. JEGP 69 1970.

The Good Man and the Devil
Wells pp. 423, 831.

§ 1

Mss: 1, Vernon (Bodley 3938); 2, BM additional 22,283.

Ed E Studien 8 1885; C. Horstmann 1892 (EETS); F. J. Furnivall 1901 (EETS).

Ypotis, or L'Enfant Sage
Wells pp. 425, 832, 981, 1019, 1126, 1358, 1404; and C. Brown, Register vol 2, Oxford 1920 item 140, and Brown-Robbins, Index and suppl item 220.

§ 1

Mss: 1, Vernon (Bodley 3938); 2, BM additional 22,283; 3, Cotton Caligula A II; 4, Cotton Titus A XXVI; 5, Arundel 140; 6, Brome (at Brome Hall); 7, English Poetry C 3 (Bodley); 8, Rawlinson Q b 4 (Bodley); 9, St John's College Cambridge 29; 10, BM additional 36,983; 11, Ashmole 750 (Bodley); 12, Douce 323 (Bodley); 13, Trinity College Cambridge B 2 18 etc.

Ed C. Horstmann, Altenglische Legenden, Heilbronn 1881 (ms 1 with variants from 2); ibid (3 with variants from 4–5, 11); L. T. Smith, A commonplace book of the 15th century, Norwich 1886, and Anglia 7 1884 (6); J. Sutton, PMLA 31 1916 (7–10, 13); H. Gruber, Berlin 1887 (11–12); W. Suchier, L'enfant sage, Dresden 1910 (10, 13).

§ 2

See edns Sutton, Gruber, Suchier, above.

Gruber, H. Anglia 18 1895.
Förster, M. Anglia 42 1918.

Miscellaneous
Bestiary
Wells pp. 182, 791, 1007, 1052, 1108, 1211, 1302, 1391; and see under Physiologus, Bestiaries, Bestiary matter; also Brown-Robbins, Index items 3353, 3412.

§ 1

Ms: Arundel 292.

Ed T. Wright, Altdeutsche Blätter vol 2, 1837; T. Wright and J. O. Halliwell (-Phillipps), Reliquiae antiquae vol 1, 1841; R. Morris, 1872 (EETS), and Archiv 88 1891; E. Mätzner, Altenglische Sprachproben pt 1, Berlin 1867; J. Hall, Selections from early ME, Oxford 1920; J. A. W. Bennett and G. V. Smithers, Early ME verse and prose, Oxford 1968; tr M. H. Shackford, Legends and satires, Boston 1913; J. L. Weston, Chief ME poets, Boston 1914.

§ 2

Thetbaldus. Liber Fisiologus. Ed R. Morris 1872 (EETS).
Mosher, J. A. In his Exemplum in the early religious and didactic literature of England, New York 1911.
Druce, G. C. The mediaeval bestiaries and their influence on ecclesiastical decorative art. Jnl Br Archaeological Assoc new ser 25–6 1919–20.
Owst, G. R. In his Preaching in medieval England, Cambridge 1926.
—— In his Literature and pulpit in medieval England, Cambridge 1933, Oxford 1961 (rev).
James, M. R. In his Bestiary, 1928 (Roxburghe Club).
Rendell, A. W. Physiologus: a metrical bestiary by Bishop Theobald. 1928.
Carmody, F. J. Physiologus latinus: versio B. Paris 1939.

—— Versio Y. Univ of California Pbns in Classical Philology 12 1941.
Cronin, G. The bestiary and the medieval mind. MLQ 2 1941.
Ives, S. A. and H. H. Lehmann-Haupt. An English 13th-century bestiary: a new discovery in the technique of medieval illumination. New York 1942.
Krappe, A. H. The historical background of Philippe de Thäun's bestiare. MLN 59 1944.
White, B. Medieval animal lore. Anglia 72 1954.
White, T. H. In his Book of beasts, 1954.
Emory, O. J. Hall's edition of the ME bestiary. MLN 72 1957.
Matthes, H. C. Bestiary 345f. Anglia 74 1956. In German.
McCulloch, F. In his Medieval Latin and French bestiaries, Chapel Hill 1960.

Caligula-Jesus Poems
1, Hwon Holy Chireche is vnder Uote; 2, Duty of Christians (Deo supe luue); 3, On Serving Christ (Hwi ne serue we crist?); 4, Doomsday; 5, Death; 6, Long Life; 7, Signs of Death; 8, Saws of St Bede (Sinners Beware); 9, Will and Wit.
Wells pp. 227, 383, 387, 390–2, 395, 504, 798, 823–5, 848, 1402; and C. Brown, Register vol 1, Oxford 1916, pp. 18, 144–5, 266, 354–5.
Mss: 1–8, Jesus College Oxford 29 (Bodley); 4–6, 9, BM Cotton Caligula A.IX; 7, Harley 7322; 8, Digby 86 (Bodley).
Ed R. Morris 1872 (EETS) (mss 1–9); 5, T. Wright, Percy Soc 11 1843; 6, Anglia 1–3 1878–80; 7, T. Wright and J. O. Halliwell (-Phillipps), Reliquiae antiquae vol 1, 1841; 8, G. Horstmann 1901 (EETS), Altenglische Legenden, Heilbronn 1881.

C. Shorter Pieces in Prose [P] and Verse [V]
A ME Diatribe against Backbiting [V]
Ms: BM Royal 18.A.X.

Ed R. H. Bowers, MLN 69 1954.

A ME Rake's Progress Poem [V]
Ms: BM Harley 7578.

Ed R. H. Bowers, MLN 70 1955; ed R. H. Robbins as A warning against lechery, PQ 35 1956. The 2 editors disagree in their readings.

Poem on the Seven Gifts of the Holy Ghost [V]
Ms: Univ Lib Cambridge Ii.IV.9.

Ed R. H. Bowers, MLN 70 1955.

A ME Mnemonic Poem on Usury [V] [P]
Ms: Harley 45.

Ed R. H. Bowers, Mediaeval Stud 17 1955.

Three ME Poems on the Apostles [V]
Mss: Corpus Christi College Oxford 155; BM additional 39,996; BM additional 32,578.

Ed R. H. Bowers, PMLA 70 1955.

Life of Adam and Eve [V]
Ms: Auchinleck.

Ed A. J. Bliss, RES new ser 7 1956.

ME Verses against Thieves [V]

§ 1

Ms: Sloane 2457.

Ed C. F. Bühler, Speculum 33 1958.

§ 2

Vann, J. D. ME verses against thieves: a postscript. Speculum 34 1959.

Two ME Versions of a Prayer to the Sacrament
(*part of Suso's Horologium Sapiential*) [P]
Ed E. Zeeman, Archiv 194 1958.

William Flete's De Remediis Contra Temptaciones [P]

§ 1

Ms: Univ Lib Cambridge Hh.I.11 and 8 others.
Ed E. Colledge and N. Chadwick, Archivio Italiano per la Storia della Pietà 5 1968.

§ 2

Hackett, B., E. Colledge and N. Chadwick. Flete's De remediis contra temptaciones in its Latin and English recensions: the growth of a text. Mediaeval Stud 26 1964.

Prayers and Charms in Certain ME Scrolls [P] [V]
Mss: BM Harley Rot 43 A 14; Harley Rot T 11; Wellcome 632; Glazier 39.
Ed C. F. Bühler, Speculum 39 1964.

A ME Anti-Mendicant Squib [V]
Ms: Harley 2252.
Ed R. H. Bowers, Eng Lang Notes 1 1964.

Three ME Cautionary Lyrics [V]
Ms: Yale University.
Ed R. Lass, Anglia 83 1965.

A ME Treatise on the Nature of Man [P]
Ms: Garret 143 Princeton.
Ed J. V. Fleming, N & Q July 1967.

Two ME Devotional Poems of the 15th Century [V]
Ms: Douce I (Bodley).
Ed J. C. Hirsh, N & Q Jan 1968.

A Good Lesson of Nine Vertewis [V]
Ms: Univ Lib Cambridge Dd.1.1.
Ed R. H. Bowers, Southern Folk-lore Quart 31 1967.

The Gast of Gy [P]
Ms: Queen's College Oxford 383.
See col 458, above.

Cur Mundus Militat [V]
Ms: Cleveland Public Lib W q091. 92-C468.
Ed P. Moe, Eng Lang Notes 7 1970.

A Fifteenth-century Didactic Poem [V]
Ms: BM additional 29,729.
Ed A. S. G. Edwards, Neuphilologische Mitteilungen 70 1969.

Ihesu for Thy Holy Name [V]
Ms: Douce 54 (Bodley).
Ed J. C. Hirsh, A fifteenth-century commentary, N & Q Feb 1970.

Debate between Nurture and Kynd [V]
Ms: BM Harley 541.
Ed V. J. Scattergood, N & Q July 1970.

Miraculum Beatae Mariae with ME Verses [V]
Ms: Eton College 34.
Ed S. Wenzel, Neuphilologische Mitteilungen 72 1971.
G. C.

D. Devotional and Contemplative Writings

On ureisun of oure Louerde [early 13th century]. Ed R. Morris, Old English homilies, 1868 (EETS); ed W. M. Thompson 1958 (EETS). *See* M. Konrath, Eine übersehene Fassung der Ureisun, Anglia 42 1918.

On wel swuð egod ureisun of God almihti [early 13th century]. Ed R. Morris, Old English homilies, 1868 (EETS); ed W. M. Thompson 1958 (EETS). *See* M. Konrath, Anglia 42 1918.

The wohunge of ure Lauerde [early 13th century]. Ed R. Morris, Old English homilies 1868 (EETS); ed W. M. Thompson 1958 (EETS). *See* M. Konrath, Anglia 42 1918.

A talkyng of þe loue of God [14th century]. Ed C. Horstman, Yorkshire writers vol 2, 1896, p. 345; ed M. S. Westra, Hague 1950. *See* M. Konrath, Anglia 42 1918; M. M. Morgan, A talking of the love of God and the continuity of stylistic tradition in ME prose meditations, RES new ser 10 1952.

Meditatio de passione domini [14th century, perhaps by Rolle]. *See under Richard Rolle, below.*

De passione secundum Ricardum: possibly a new work by Richard Rolle. Ed F. Wormald, Laudate 13 1935.

The goad of loue [14th-century trn, perhaps by Walter Hilton from Ps Bonaventure, Stimulus amoris]. *See under Walter Hilton, below.*

Contemplations of the dread and loue of God [14th century]. 1506 (de Worde); rptd G. Horstman, Yorkshire writers vol 2, 1896, p. 72.

The privity of the passion [14th-century trn from Ps Bonaventure]. Ed C. Horstman, Yorkshire writers vol 1, 1895, p. 198. *See* E. Zeeman, Continuity and change in ME versions of the Meditationes vitae Christi, MÆ 26 1957.

The Revelation of the hundred pater nosters: a fifteenth-century meditation. Ed F. Wormald, Laudate 14 1936.

The myrrour of the blessed lyf of Iesu Crist [early 15th-century trn from Ps Bonaventure]. Ed L. F. Powell, Oxford 1911; ed a monk of Parkminster 1926 (modernized). *See* E. Zeeman (Salter), Nicholas Love: a fifteenth-century translator, RES new ser 6 1955; Continuity and change in ME versions of the Meditationes vitae Christi, MÆ 26 1957; Continuity in ME devotional prose, JEGP 55 1956; Two ME versions of a prayer to the sacrament, Archiv 194 1958.

Informacio Alredi [14th-century trn of Aelred of Rievaulx's letter to his sister]. Vernon ms, ed C. Horstman, E Studien 7 1884.

The myrrour of the chyrche [14th- or 15th-century trn from St Edmund Rich]. 1521 (de Worde); Thornton ms, ed G. Perry, Religious pieces in prose and verse, 1867 (EETS); Thornton and Vernon mss, ed C. Horstman, Yorkshire writers vol 1, 1895, p. 219, ed F. M. Steel 1905 (modernized); Cambridge ms, ed H. W. Robbins, PMLA 40 1925.

A deuout treatyse called the tree and xii frutes of the holy ghost [14th or 15th century]. 1534 (R. Coplande); ed J. J. Vaissier, Groningen 1960.

A number of short devotional pieces and excerpts, not otherwise available in print, were modernized by C. Kirchberger in Life of the spirit *4–10, 1949–56, and in her* Coasts of the country, *1952.*

A ladder of four rungs [ME trn of Scala claustralium]. Ed J. McCann, Ampleforth Jnl 30 1925 (modernized); 1926; Worcester 1963; ed P. Hodgson 1955 (EETS) (with Deonise his diuinite). *See* P. Hodgson, A ladder of four rungs: a study of the prose style, MLR 44 1949.

The mirror of simple souls [14th- or 15th-century trn from Margaret Porete]. Ed C. Kirchberger 1927 (modernized); ed M. Doiron, Archivio Italiano per la Storia della Pieta 5 1968 (with appendix by E. Colledge and R. Guarnieri). *See* E. Underhill, Fortnightly Rev Feb 1911; M. Doiron, The Middle English translation of Le mirouer des simples ames, in Dr L. Reypens-Album, Antwerp 1964.

The seven poyntes of trewe loue [late 14th-century trn of Suso's Horologium sapientiae]. In The book of divers ghostly matters, 1491 (Caxton); ed C. Horstman, Anglia 10 1866 (from BM ms Douce 114). *See* W. Wichgraf, Susos Horologium sapientiae in England, Anglia 53–4 1929–30, Archiv 169 1936 (on mss), G. Schleich, Über die me Bearbeitung von Susos Horologium, Archiv 157 1930; E. Zeeman, Two ME versions of a prayer to the sacrament, Archiv 194 1958.

The chastising of God's children [c. 1382–1408, largely derived from Ruysbroek]. 1493 (de Worde); ed J. Bazire and E. Colledge, Oxford 1957. *See* C. F. Bühler, Seven variants in the Chastising, PBSA 43 1949; J. Bazire, The dialects of the manuscripts of the Chastising, Eng & Germanic Stud 6 1957; G. B. de Soer, The relationships of the Latin versions of Ruysboek's Die Geestelike Brulocht to the Chastising, Mediaeval Stud 21 1959.

The treatise of perfection of the sons of God [early 15th-century trn from Ruysbroek]. Ed J. Bazire and E. Colledge, Oxford 1957 (with Chastising, above). *See* Colledge, The treatise of perfection of the sons of God: a fifteenth-century translation, E Studies 33 1952.

The orcherd of Syon [trn after 1415 from Catherine of Siena]. 1519 (de Worde); ed P. Hodgson and C. M. Liegey 1966 (EETS). *See* P. Hodgson, The orcherd of Syon and the English mystical tradition, Proc Br Acad 50 1964.

The revelations of Saint Birgitta [tr before 1450?]. Ed W. P. Cumming 1929 (EETS). Another trn (long excerpts) ptd with Epistle of Saunt Bernard, [1535?] (T. Godfrey).

De imitatione Christi [trn c. 1440–82]. Ed J. K. Ingram 1893 (EETS). *See* R. Lovatt, The imitation of Christ in late medieval England, Trans of Royal Historical Soc 5th ser 18 1968.

A text attributed to Ruusbroec circulating in England. Ed A. I. Doyle, Dr L. Reypens-Album, Antwerp 1964.

RICHARD ROLLE
c. 1300–49
Bibliographies

Freemantle, W. T. A bibliography of Sheffield and vicinity. Sheffield 1911.

Allen, H. E. Writings ascribed to Rolle and materials for his biography. New York 1927.

Brown, C. and R. H. Robbins. Index of ME verse 1943; suppl 1965.

Marzac, N. Richard Rolle de Hampole. Paris 1968.

Collections
Latin Works

De emendatione peccatoris. Antwerp 1533.
De emendatione peccatoris opusculum cum aliis aliquot appendicibus. Cologne 1535.
In psalterium davidicum atque alia quaedam sacrae scripturae monumenta. Cologne 1536.
M. de la Bigne, Magna bibliotheca vol 15. Cologne 1622.
M. de la Bigne, Maxima bibliotheca vol 26. Lyons 1677.

English Works

English prose treatises. Ed G. G. Perry 1866 (EETS), 1921 (rev).
Yorkshire writers: Rolle and his followers. Ed C. Horstman 2 vols 1895–6.
Some minor works. Ed G. E. Hodgson 1923 (modernized).
Selected works. Ed G. C. Heseltine 1930 (modernized).
English writings. Ed H. E. Allen, Oxford 1931.

§1
Latin Works

Canticum amoris. Ed A. Wilmart, Revue d'Ascétique et de Mystique 21 1940; ed G. M. Liegey, Traditio 12 1956.
Melos amoris. Ed E. J. F. Arnould, Oxford 1957.
Super lectiones Job in officium mortuorum. Oxford 1483, Paris 1510; in Cologne 1536, above.
Super aliquos versus cantici canticorum. Excerpt in collections, 1533, 1535, 1536, 1622, 1677 above; ed Y. Madon, Mélanges de Science Religieuse 7 1950; medieval English version ed G. G. Perry, English prose treatises of Rolle, 1866 (EETS); ed C. Horstman, Yorkshire writers vol 1, 1895, p. 186.
Super Threnos Jeremiae. In Cologne 1536, above; Paris 1542.
Super Apocalypsim. Ed N. Marzac, Paris 1968.
Super orationem dominicam. In collections 1535, 1536, 1622, 1677, above.
Super symbolum apostolorum. Ibid.
Commentary on the psalter. In Cologne 1536, above.
Super psalmum xx. Ibid.
Contra amatores mundi. Ed P. F. Theiner, Berkeley 1968.
Incendium amoris. Ed M. Deanesly, Manchester 1915. R. Misyn's ME trn The fire of love ed R. Harvey 1896 (EETS); ed D. Harford 1913 (modernized); ed F. M. M. Comper 1914 (modernized); ed G. C. Heseltine 1935 (modernized); tr French, 1928.
Emendatio vitae. Ptd with Speculum spiritualium, Paris 1510. In collections 1533, 1535, 1536, 1622, 1677, above. R. Misyn's ME trn The amending of life, ed D. Harford 1913 (modernized); ed F. M. M. Comper 1914 (with Fire of love); ed H. L. Hubbard 1912 (modernized); ed G. C. Heseltine, Selected works, 1930. Another ME trn ed W. H. Hulme, Western Reserve Univ Bull new ser 21 1918. An English verse trn cd C. Horstman, Yorkshire writers vol 2, p. 283 (*see under William of Nassyngton, below*); tr French, 1926.

English Works

Commentary on the psalter. Ed H. R. Bramley, Oxford 1884; commentary on canticles ed G. C. Heseltine, Selected works 1930; ed H. E. Allen, English writings of Rolle, Oxford 1931 (excerpts).
Ego dormio. Ed C. Horstman, Yorkshire writers vol 1, p. 5; ed R. H. Benson 1904 (modernized); ed G. C. Hodgson, Some minor works, 1923; ed G. C. Heseltine, Selected works, 1930; ed H. E. Allen, English writings, Oxford 1931; ed E. Colledge, The mediaeval mystics of England, 1962 (modernized).
The commandment. Ed C. Horstman, Yorkshire writers vol 1, p. 61; ed G. E. Hodgson, Some minor works, 1923; ed G. C. Heseltine, Selected works, 1930; ed H. E. Allen, English writings, Oxford 1931.
The form of living. Ed C. Horstman, Yorkshire writers vol 1, p. 3; ed G. E. Hodgson 1910 (modernized); ed G. C. Heseltine, Selected works, 1930; ed H. E. Allen, English writings, Oxford 1931.
Short prose pieces. Ed C. Horstman, Yorkshire writers vol 1, p. 193, p. 81; ed G. C. Heseltine, Selected works, 1930; ed H. E. Allen, English writings, Oxford 1931.
Meditations on the passion. [Shorter version], ed J. Ullman, E Studien 7 1884; [longer version], ed C. Horstman vol 1, p. 92; ed H. Lindqvist, Upsala 1917; ed C. Horstman, Yorkshire writers vol 1, p. 83; ed E. Burton 1906 (modernized); ed G. C. Heseltine, Selected works, 1930; ed H. E. Allen, English writings, Oxford 1931.
Lyrics. Ed C. Horstman, Yorkshire writers vol 1 pp. 72–81, 363, 367, 370; vol 2 p. 247; ed F. M. M. Comper, Life and lyrics of Rolle, 1928 (modernized); ed H. E. Allen, English writings, Oxford 1931.
Our daily work [authorship uncertain]. Ed G. E. Hodgson 1910 (with The form of perfect living); Rolle and Our daily work, 1929 (modernized).

§2

The English martyrologe, by a Catholicke priest. 1608.

The English martyrologe. [St Omer] 1672.

Officium de sancto Ricardo de Hampole. Ed G. G. Perry, English prose treatises of Rolle, 1866 (EETS); ed F. Proctor, Breviarium ad usum ecclesie eboracensis, ed S. W. Lawley, Durham 1883 (Surtees Soc); ms fragment ed H. Lindqvist in his edn of Meditatio de passione domini, Upsala 1917; ed R. M. Woolley 1919; tr F. M. M. Comper 1914 (with Fire of love).

Middendorf, H. Studien über Rolle. Magdeburg 1888. On sources of psalm commentaries.

Paves, A. C. A fourteenth-century English biblical version. Cambridge 1902.

Hahn, A. Quellenuntersuchungen zu Rolles englischen Schriften. Berlin 1900.

Inge, W. In his Studies of English mystics, 1906.

Schneider, J. P. The prose style of Rolle. Baltimore 1906.

Allen, H. E. The authorship of the Prick of conscience. Boston 1910.

— The mystical lyrics of the Manuel des pechiez. Romanic Rev 9 1918.

— Writings ascribed to Rolle. New York 1927.

Henningsen, H. Über die Wortstellung in den Prosaschriften Rolles. Erlangen 1911.

Spurgeon, C. F. E. In her Mysticism in English literature, Cambridge 1913.

Clay, R. M. Hermits and anchorites of England. 1914.

Underhill, E. Introd to F. Comper's edn of Fire of love, 1914.

— Ricardus heremita. Dublin Rev 183 1928; rptd in her Mixed pasture, 1933.

Deanesly, M. Incendium amoris. EHR 29 1914.

— In her Lollard Bible, Cambridge 1920.

— Vernacular books in England. MLR 15 1920.

Hodgson, G. E. In her English mystics, 1922.

— In her Sanity of mysticism, 1926.

Everett, D. The Middle English prose psalter of Rolle. MLR 17–18 1922–3.

Noetinger, M. The biography of Rolle. Month Jan 1926.

Knowles, D. In his English mystics, 1927.

— In his English mystical tradition, 1961.

Comper, F. M. M. The life of Rolle. 1928.

Elwin, V. Rolle: a Christian Sannyasi. Madras 1930.

Schnell, E. Die Traktate des Rolle Incendium amoris und Emendatio vitae und deren Übersetzung durch Richard Misyn. Leipzig 1932.

Peitz, A. Der Einfluss des nordlichen Dialektes. Bonner Studien 20 1933.

Olmes, A. Sprache und stil der englischen Mystik des Mittelalters. Halle 1933.

Muir, L. Influence of the Rolle and Wycliffite psalters upon the psalter of the Authorized version. MLR 30 1935.

Wormald, F. De passione secundum Ricardum: possibly a new work by Rolle. Laudate 13 1935.

Lehman, M. Untersuchungen zur mystischen Terminologie Rolles. Jena 1936.

Niederstenbruch, A. Die geistige Haltung Rolles. Archiv 175 1939.

Arnould, E. J. F. On Rolle's patrons. MÆ 6 1937.

— Rolle and a Bishop: a vindication. Bull John Rylands Lib 21 1937; rptd in his edn of Melos amoris, 1957.

— Rolle and the Sorbonne. Bull John Rylands Lib 23 1939.

— Melos amoris. Oxford 1957.

— Richard Rolle. Month Jan 1960; rptd in Pre-reformation English spirituality, ed J. Walsh [1965].

Coleman, T. W. In his English mystics of the fourteenth century, 1938.

Wilmart, A. Le cantique d'amour de Rolle. Revue d'Ascétique et de Mystique 21 1940.

Whiting, C. E. Richard Rolle. Yorkshire Archaeological Jnl 37 1948–51.

Morgan, M. M. Versions of the meditations on the passion ascribed to Rolle. MÆ 22 1953.

Liegey, G. M. The Canticum amoris of Rolle. Traditio 12 1956.

— Rolle's Carmen prosaicum. Mediaeval Stud 19 1957.

Gilmour, J. Notes on the vocabulary of Rolle. N & Q March 1956.

Wilson, R. M. Three middle English mystics. E & S new ser 10 1956.

Pepler, C. In his English religious heritage, 1958.

— Richard Rolle. Clergy Rev Feb 1959; rptd in English spiritual writers, ed C. Davis 1961.

Thornton, M. In his English spirituality, 1963.

Wilson, S. The Longleat version of Love is life. RES new ser 10 1959.

Emden, A. B. In his A biographical register of the University of Oxford, Oxford 1959.

Woolf, R. In her English religious lyric in the Middle Ages, Oxford 1968.

WILLIAM OF NASSYNGTON
d.c. 1359

§1

Tractatus Willelmi Nassyngtone quondam advocati curiae Eboraci. Ed G. G. Perry, Religious pieces in prose and verse, 1867 (EETS).

The mirror of life. Lines 1–370 ed J. Ullman, E Studien 7 1884; fragment ed C. Wordsworth, Horae eboracenses, Durham 1920 (Surtees Soc).

Metrical version of Richard Rolle's Form of living. Ed C. Horstman, Yorkshire writers vol 2 p. 283, 1896. Authorship uncertain.

§2

Allen, H. E. The authorship of the Prick of conscience, Boston 1910.

— The Speculum vitae: addendum. PMLA 32 1917.

— Writings ascribed to Richard Rolle. New York 1927.

Watson, G. N & Q Nov 1924.

Pantin, W. A. In his English church in the fourteenth century, Cambridge 1955.

Emden, A. B. In his A biographical register of the University of Oxford, Oxford 1958.

AUTHOR OF THE CLOUD OF UNKNOWING
late 14th century

Bibliographies

Hodgson, P. In edn of Cloud of unknowing, 1958 (EETS).

Collections

Deonise hid divinite and other treatises. Ed P. Hodgson 1955 (EETS).

§1

The cloud of unknowing. Ed H. Collins 1871 (modernized); ed E. Underhill 1912 (modernized); ed J. McCann 1924 (modernized), 1952 (rev); ed P. Hodgson 1944 (EETS), 1958 (rev); ed L. Progroff 1959 (modernized); ed C. Wolters 1961; tr French 1925 (by M. Noetinger); German, 1958 (by E. Strakosch).

Epistle of privy counselling. Ed J. McCann 1924 (with Cloud, above); ed P. Hodgson 1944 (with Cloud); ed E. Colledge, The mediaeval mystics of England, 1962 (modernized); ed J. Walsh, Verona 1963 (modernized); tr French, 1925 (with Cloud).

Deonise hid divinite. Ed J. McCann 1924 (with Cloud, above); ed P. Hodgson 1955 (EETS).

A veray devoute treatyse named Benyamyn, A pistle of preier, A pistle of discrecioun of stirings, A tretis of discrescyon of spirites. 1521 (H. Pepwell); ed J. E. G. Gardner, The cell of self-knowledge, 1910 (modernized); ed P. Hodgson 1955 (with Deonise hid diuinite); tr French, 1925 (with Cloud, above); A tretyse that men clepen Beniamyn, ed C. Horstman, Richard Rolle vol 1 p. 162, 1895.

§2

Baker, A. (1575–1641). Commentary (1629). Ed J. McCann 1924 (with Cloud).
M'Intyre, D. M. The cloud of unknowing. Expositor Oct 1907.
Knowles, D. In his English mystics, 1927.
— The excellence of the Cloud. Downside Rev 52 1934.
— In his English mystical tradition, 1961.
Chambers, R. W. On the continuity of English prose. In N. Harpsfield, Life of More, 1932 (EETS).
Gardner, H. L. Walter Hilton and the authorship of the Cloud of unknowing. RES 9 1933.
Elwin, H. V. H. Christian dhyana: a study of the Cloud of unknowing. 1930.
Hort, G. Sense and thought. 1936.
Hodgson, P. Walter Hilton and the Cloud of unknowing. MLR 50 1955.
— In her Three fourteenth-century mystics, 1967.
Pepler, C. In his English religious heritage, 1958.
Graef, H. In her Light and the rainbow, 1959.
Sitwell, G. The cloud of unknowing. Clergy Rev July 1960; rptd in English spiritual writers, ed C. Davis 1961.
Thornton, M. In his English spirituality, 1963.
Walsh, J. The cloud of unknowing. Month Dec 1963; rptd in Pre-reformation English spirituality, ed J. Walsh [1965].
Nieva, C. This transcending God. 1971.

WALTER HILTON
d. 1396
Bibliographies
Hughes, A. C. In Hilton's direction to contemplatives, Rome 1962.
Collections
Minor works. Ed D. Jones 1929 (modernized).

§1

The scale of perfection. 1494 (de Worde), 1507 (Notary), 1519 (de Worde), 1525, 1533, 1659 (de Worde edn rev); ed E. Guy 1869; ed J. B. Dalgairns 1870 (modernized); ed E. Underhill 1923 (BM ms Harley 6579) (modernized); tr G. Sitwell 1953; ed L. Sherley-Price 1957 (Penguin) (modernized); tr French, 1923; German, 1966; ed E. Colledge, The mediaeval mystics of England, 1962 (excerpts).
Epistle to a devout man in temporal estate. 1494 (de Worde) (shorter text with Scale of perfection, above), 1507 (Notary) (longer text with Scale of perfection), 1519 (de Worde), 1525, 1533; 1516 (Pynson) (with Kalendre of the newe legende of England), [1531] (Wyer), 1659 (with Scale of perfection), 1869, 1870; ed G. G. Perry, English prose treatises of Richard Rolle, 1866 (EETS); ed C. Horstman, Yorkshire writers vol 1 p. 264, 1895; ed D. Jones, Minor works, 1929; tr German, Augustiniana 17 1967.
The song of angels. In A veray deuoute treatyse named Benyamyn, 1521 (H. Pepwell); ed G. G. Perry, English prose treatises of Richard Rolle, 1866 (EETS); ed C. Horstman, Yorkshire writers vol 1 p. 175, 1895; ed E. G. Gardner, The cell of self-knowledge, 1910 (modernized); tr French, Vie Spirituelle 9 1923; tr German, Augustiniana 17 1967.

Eight chapters on perfection. Ed D. Jones, Minor works, 1929; ed F. Kuriyagawa, Tokyo 1967.
Qui habitat and Bonum est. Ed D. Jones, Minor works, 1929; ed B. Wallner, Lund 1954.
Benedictus. Ed D. Jones, Minor works, 1929; ed B. Wallner, Lund 1957.
The goad of love. Ed C. Kirchberger 1952 (modernized). Trn of Stimulus amoris.
Epistola ad solitarium [in Latin]. Tr Way July 1966.

§2

Dalgairns, J. B. An essay on the spiritual life of medieval England. In his edn of Scale, 1870.
Inge, W. R. In his Studies of English mystics, 1906.
Noetinger, M. La contemplation d'après Hilton. Vie Spirituelle 4 1921.
— The modern editions of Hilton's Scala perfectionis. Downside Rev June 1923.
Knowles, D. In his English mystics, 1927.
— In his English mystical tradition, 1961.
Underhill, E. In her Mixed pasture, 1933.
Chambers, R. W. The continuity of English prose. In N. Harpsfield, Life of More, 1932 (EETS).
Gardner, H. L. Hilton and the authorship of the Cloud of unknowing. RES 9 1933.
— The text of the Scale of perfection. MÆ 5 1936.
— Hilton and the mystical tradition in England. E & S 22 1936.
Coleman, T. W. Hilton's Scale of perfection. London Quart 160 1935.
— In his English mystics of the fourteenth century, 1938.
White, V. Hilton: an English spiritual guide. 1944.
Sitwell, G. Contemplation in the Scale of perfection. Downside Rev 67–8 1949–50.
— Walter Hilton. Clergy Rev June 1959; rptd in English spiritual authors, ed C. Davis 1961.
Russell-Smith, J. Hilton and a tract in defence of the veneration of images. Dominican Stud 7 1954.
— Walter Hilton. Month Sept 1959; rptd in Pre-reformation English spirituality, ed J. Walsh [1965].
Hodgson, P. Hilton and the Cloud of unknowing. MLR 50 1955.
— In her Three Middle English mystics, 1967.
Zeeman, E. Continuity in ME devotional prose. JEGP 55 1956.
Colledge, E. Recent work on Hilton. Blackfriars June 1956.
Hussey, S. S. Langland, Hilton and the three lives. RES new ser 7 1956.
— The text of the Scale of perfection. Neuphilologische Mitteilungen 65 1964.
Pepler, C. In his English religious heritage, 1958.
Croft, P. J. In his Lady Margaret Beaufort, 1958.
Hughes, A. C. Hilton's direction to contemplatives. Rome 1962.
Thornton, M. In his English spirituality, 1963.
Emden, A. B. In his A biographical register of the University of Cambridge to 1500, Cambridge 1963.
Milosh, J. E. The scale of perfection and the English mystical tradition. Madison 1966.
Lawler, T. M. C. Some parallels between Hilton's Scale and St John Fisher's Penitential psalms. Moreana 3 1966.

JULIAN OF NORWICH
c. 1343–c. 1413
Bibliographies
Molinari, P. In his Julian of Norwich, 1958.

§1

Sixteen revelations of divine love. Ed R. F. S. Cressy 1670 (longer version, Paris ms); ed G. H. Parker 1843; ed G. Tyrrell 1902; ed J. Walsh 1961 (modernized);

ed H. Collins 1877 (longer version, Sloan ms) (modernized); ed G. Warrack 1901 (modernized), 1949 (rev); ed R. Hudleston 1927 (modernized); ed G. Wolters 1966 (modernized); ed D. Harford 1911 (shorter version, Amherst ms); ed A. M. Reynolds 1958. 15th-century excerpts ed J. Walsh and E. Colledge, The knowledge of our self and God, 1961 (modernized); ed P. F. Chambers 1955 (excerpts); ed Colledge, The medieval mystics of England 1962 (modernized excerpts); tr French, 1910, 1926; Italian, 1932; German, 1960.

§2

Tersteegen, G. Auserlesene Lebensbeschreibungen heiliger Seelen vol 3. Essen 1784.
Blomefield, F. Essay towards a topographical history of Norfolk vol 2 p. 546. 1739.
Dalgairns, J. B. An essay on the spiritual life of medieval England. In his edn of Scale of perfection, 1870.
Tyrrell, G. In his Faith of the millions, 1901.
Inge, W. R. In his Studies of English mystics, 1907.
Goyau, L. F. Visions mystiques. Revue des Deux Mondes 15 Aug 1913.
Spurgeon, C. F. E. In her Mysticism in English literature, Cambridge 1913.
Clay, R. M. In her Hermits and anchorites of England, 1914.
Hodgson, G. E. In her English mystics, 1922.
Maw, M. Buddhist mysticism: a study based upon a comparison with the mysticism of St Theresa and Julian of Norwich. Bordeaux 1924.
Thouless, R. H. The lady Julian: a psychological study. 1924.
Knowles, D. In his English mystics, 1927.
—— In his English mystical tradition, 1961.
Vann, G. Mother Julian of Norwich. Month Dec 1932.
Watkin, E. I. Dame Julian of Norwich. In The English way, ed M. Ward 1933; rptd in E. I. Watkin, Poets and mystics, 1953.
Flood, R. H. A description of St Julian's church and an account of Dame Julian's connection with it. Norwich 1936.
Coleman, T. W. In his English mystics of the fourteenth century, 1938.
Lawlor, J. A note on the revelations of Julian of Norwich. RES new ser 2 1951.
Reynolds, A. M. Some literary influences in the Revelations of Julian of Norwich. Leeds Stud in Eng 7–8 1952.
—— Julian of Norwich. Month Sept 1960; rptd in Pre-reformation English spirituality, ed J. Walsh [1965].

Chambers, P. F. Juliana of Norwich. 1955.
Wilson, R. M. Three Middle English mystics. E & S new ser 10 1956.
Walsh, J. God's homely loving. Month March 1958.
Molinari, P. Julian of Norwich: the teaching of a fourteenth-century mystic. 1958.
Pepler, C. In his English religious heritage, 1958.
Graef, H. The light and the rainbow. 1959.
Benedictine of Stanbrook, DSH. Julian of Norwich. Clergy Rev Dec 1959; rptd in English spiritual writers, ed C. Davis 1961.
Thornton, M. In his English spirituality, 1963.

MARGERY KEMPE
c. 1373–c. 1439

§1

A short treatyse of contemplacyon taken out of the boke of Margerie Kempe of Lyn. [1501] (de Worde), 1521 (with A veray deuote treatyse named Beniamyn) (H. Pepwell); ed J. E. G. Gardner, The cell of self knowledge, 1910 (modernized).
The book of Margery Kempe. Ed W. Butler-Bowden 1936 (modernized); ed S. B. Meech and H. E. Allen 1940 (EETS); ed E. Colledge, The medieval mystics of England, 1962 (modernized excerpts).

§2

Knowles, D. In his English mystics, 1927.
—— In his English mystical tradition, 1961.
Chambers, R. W. Introd to Butler-Bowden edn, 1936.
Coleman, T. W. In his English mystics of the fourteenth century, 1938.
Watkin, E. I. In defence of Margery Kempe. Downside Rev 40 1941; rptd in his Poets and mystics, 1953.
Cholmeley, K. Margery Kempe. 1947.
Thurston, H. In Surprising mystics, ed J. Crehan 1955.
Wilson, R. M. Three Middle English mystics. E & S new ser 10 1956.
Thornton, M. Margery Kempe. 1960.
Colledge, E. Margery Kempe. Month July 1962; rptd in Pre-reformation English spirituality, ed J. Walsh [1965].
Reskiewicz, A. Main sentence elements in the Book of Margery Kempe. Warsaw 1962.
Collis, L. The apprentice saint. 1964.

J. R.-S.

(9) SAINTS' LEGENDS

Wells ch 5 and suppls; Severs vol 2 ch 5.

Alliterative Katherine Group
General Studies
Gerould, G. H. Saints' legends. Boston 1916.
Funke, O. E Studien 55 1921. On French words.
Serjeantson, M. S. Dialects of the West Midlands. RES 3 1927.
Tolkien, J. R. R. Ancrene wisse and Hali meiðhad. E & S 14 1928.
Allen, H. E. Localisation of Bodl ms 34. MLR 28 1933.
Bethurum, D. Connection of the Katherine group with OE prose. JEGP 34 1935.
Furuskog, R. Collation of the Katherine group. Studia Neophilologica 19 1947.
d'Ardenne, S. T. R. O. and J. R. R. Tolkien. Ms Bodley 34 (recollection). Studia Neophilologica 20 1948.
Bliss, A. J. Note on 'language AB'. MLN 76 1961.
McAlindon, T. Emergence of a comic type in ME narrative. Anglia 61 1963.

Clark, C. Ancrene wisse and the Katherine group. Neophilologus 50 1966.

Hali Meidenhad
Wells pp. 272 etc.
Mss: 1, Bodley 34; 2, BM Cotton Titus D. XVIII.

§1

1 and 2. Ed O. Cockayne 1866 (EETS); re-ed F. Furnivall 1922 (EETS); ed A. F. Colborn, Copenhagen 1940; ed N. R. Ker, Facsimile of ms Bodley 34, 1960 (EETS).

§2

Wilson, R. M. Note on the authorship of the Katherine group. Leeds Stud 1 1932.

Sawles Warde
Wells, pp. 272 etc.
Mss: 1, Bodley 34; 2, BM Cotton Titus D. XVIII; Royal 17 A. XXVII.

§1

1, Ed R. Morris 1868 (EETS); ed J. Hall, Selections from early ME, Oxford 1920 (part of 3); ed N. R. Ker 1960 (EETS); ed J. A. W. Bennett and G. V. Smithers, Early ME verse and prose, Oxford 1966; 3, ed W. Wagner, Bonn 1908; 1–3, ed R. M. Wilson, Leeds 1936. *See also* R. Morris, Ayenbite of inwit, 1886 (EETS) p. 263 (Kentish: ms Arundel LVII, College of Arms).

§2

Konrath, M. Die lateinische Quelle. E Studien 12 1889. Kentish.
Powell, C. L. Castle of the body. SP 16 1919.
Southern, R. W. St Anselm and his English pupils. Mediaeval & Renaissance Stud 1 1943.
d'Ardenne, S. T. R. O. and J. R. R. Tolkien. 'iþþlen' in Sawles warde. E Studies 28 1947.
Russell-Smith, J. *Keis* in Sawles warde. MÆ 22 1953.
Clark, C. Sawles warde and Herefordshire. N & Q April 1954.
Johnston, G. K. W. Two passages in Sawles warde. MLR 52 1957.
De custodia interioris hominis. In Memorials of St Anselm, ed R. W. Southern and F. S. Schmitt 1969. Attribution to Hugh of St Victor refuted.

Katherine

Severs vol 2 pp. 440, 599.
Mss: 1, Bodley 34; 2, BM Cotton Titus D. XVIII; 3, Royal 17 A. XXVII.

§1

1, Ed N. R. Ker 1960 (EETS) (facs); 2, ed J. Morton 1841 (Abbotsford Club); ed C. Hardwick 1849 (Cambridge Antiquarian Soc); ed J. Hall, Selections from early ME, Oxford 1920; 3, ed E. Einenkel 1884 (EETS).

§2

Schipper, J. In his Englische Metrik, Bonn 1881.
Einenkel, E. Ueber den Verfasser. Anglia 5 1882.
Bülbring, K. Verbs. Quellen und Forschungen 63 1889.
Hilka, A. Zur Katharinenlegende. Archiv 140 1920.
On other Katherine pieces, see Wells, C. Brown, Register, and Index; Severs.

Juliana

Severs vol 2 pp. 440, 597.
Mss: 1, Bodley 34; 2, BM Royal 17 A. XXVII.

§1

1, Ed N. R. Ker 1960 (EETS) (facs); 1–2, ed O. Cockayne and E. Brock 1872 (EETS); ed J. Hall, Selections from early ME, Oxford 1920; ed S. T. R. O. d'Ardenne 1961 (EETS).

§2

Backhaus, O. Über die Quelle. Halle 1899.
Kennedy, C. W. Legend of St Juliana. Princeton 1906.
Brünohler, E. Über einige lateinische, englische, französische Fassungen der Julianalegende. Bonn 1912.
Hotchner, C. A. Note on Dux vitae and Lifes lattiow. PMLA 57 1942.
Niwa, Y. Notes on compound verbs. Anglica 5 1963. In Japanese.
On other Juliana pieces, see Wells, C. Brown, Register and Index; Severs.

Seinte Marherete

Severs vol 2 pp. 440, 606.
Mss: 1, Bodley 34; 2, BM Royal 17 A. XXVII.

§1

1, Ed N. R. Ker 1960 (EETS) (facs); 2, ed O. Cockayne 1886 (EETS); 1–2, ed F. M. Mack 1934 (EETS).

§2

Krahl, E. Untersuchungen über vier Versionen der mittelenglischen Margaretenlegende. Berlin 1889.
Spencer, F. Development of the legend of St Margaret. MLN 4–5 1889–90.
Gerould, G. H. PMLA 39 1924. On sources and related matter.
On other Margaret pieces, see Wells, C. Brown, Register and Index; Severs.

General Studies

Severs vol 2 ch 5 ; for separate entries on legends of the cross p. 637 ; on legends of Adam and Eve p. 635.

Morris, R. Legends of the Holy Rood. 1871 (EETS).
Horstmann, C. Leben Jesu. Münster 1873. Introd.
— Altenglische Legenden. Paderborn 1875.
— Sammlung altenglischer Legenden. Heilbronn 1878.
— Altenglische Legenden: neue Folge. Heilbronn 1881. Introds.
Horstmann, C. 1887 (EETS). Introd.
Meyer, W. Vita Adae et Evae. Munich 1878.
— Die Geschichte des Kreuzholzes von Christus. Munich 1882.
Zupitza, J. Zwei mittelenglische Legendenhandschriften. Anglia 1 1878.
Bachmann, F. Die beiden Versionen des me Canticum de creatione. Hamburg 1891.
Napier, A. S. History of the Holy Rood Tree. 1894 (EETS).
Lovewell, B. E. Life of St Cecilia. New Haven 1898. Bibliography.
Gerould, G. H. Forerunners of the Eustace legend. PMLA 19 1904.
— Saints' legends. Boston 1916. Bibliography.
Emerson, O. F. Legends of Cain. PMLA 21 1906.
Mosher, J. A. The exemplum in early religious and didactic literature of England. New York 1911.
Foster, F. A. Northern Passion. 1912–13 (EETS); suppl 1930 (EETS).
Clay, R. M. The hermits and anchorites of England. 1914.
Baum, P. F. Medieval legend of Judas. PMLA 31 1916.
Day M. The Wheatley ms. 1921 (EETS). Legend of Adam and Eve.
Peebles, R. J. The dry tree. New Haven 1923. Cross legend.
Bonnell, J. R. Cain's jawbone. PMLA 39 1924.
Owst, G. R. Preaching in medieval England. Cambridge 1926.
— Literature and pulpit in medieval England. Cambridge 1933, Oxford 1961 (rev).
Brown, B. Southern Passion. 1927 (EETS).
Herolt, J. Promptuarium discipuli de miraculis BMV. Tr C. Bland 1928.
Mozley, J. H. The Vita Adae. Jnl of Theological Stud 30 1929.
Brown, P. A. The development of the legend of Thomas Becket. Philadelphia 1930.
Dunstan, A. C. The ME Canticum de creatione and the Latin Vita Adae et Evae. Anglia 55 1931.
Faverty F. E. The story of Joseph and Potiphar's wife in medieval literature. SP 13 1931.
— Legends of Joseph in Old and Middle English. PMLA 43 1928.
Ford, J. D. M. The saint's life in the vernacular literature of the Middle Ages. Catholic Historical Rev 17 1931.
Budge, E. W. One hundred and ten miracles of Our Lady Mary. Oxford 1933.

McKeehan, I. P. The book of the nativity of St Cuthbert. PMLA 48 1933.

Kapp, R. Heilige und Heiligenlegenden in England. Halle 1934.

Lascelles, M. Alexander and the Earthly Paradise in mediaeval English writings. MÆ 5 1936.

Rosenthal, C. L. The Vitae patrum in Old and Middle English literature. Philadelphia 1936.

Fornelli, G. Visioni medievali d'oltretomba in Inghilterra. Leghorn 1937.

Hausel, H. Die Maria-Magdalena Legende. Bottrop 1937.

Pfander, H. G. The popular sermon of the medieval friar in England. New York 1937.

Denomy, A. J. The Old French lives of St Agnes and other vernacular versions of the Middle Ages. [Cambridge Mass 1938.

Attwater, D. A dictionary of saints. 1939.

Ryan, G. and H. Ripperger. The Golden Legend of Jacobus de Voragine. New York 1941.

Wilson, R. M. Some lost saints' lives in Old and Middle English. MLR 36 1941.

Moore, G. E. The ME verse life of Edward the Confessor. Philadelphia 1942.

Misrahi, J. A Vita Sanctae Mariae Magdelenae (BHL 5456) in an eleventh-century ms. Speculum 18 1943.

Learned, M. R. Some saints' lives attributed to Nicholas Bozon. Franciscan Stud 25 1944.

Fallandy, Y. M. A reexamination of the rôle of the Blessed Virgin in the Miracles de Nostre Dame par personnages. PQ 43 1946.

Jeremy, Sr M. Caxton's Golden Legend and Voragine's Legenda Aurea. Speculum 21 1946.

Klenke, Sr M. A. Three saints' lives by Nicholas Bozon. New York 1947 (Franciscan Stud).

Loomis, C. G. White Magic: an introduction to the folklore of Christian legend. Cambridge Mass 1948.

Garth, H. M. St Mary Magdalene in medieval literature. Baltimore 1950.

Patch H. R. The other world according to descriptions in medieval literature. Cambridge 1950.

Hinnebusch, W. A. The early English friars preachers. Rome 1951.

Greenhill, E. S. The child in the tree. Traditio 10 1954. Cross legend.

Hennig, J. The place of Irish saints in late mediaeval English hagiography. Mediaeval Stud 16 1954.

Bliss, A. J. The Auchinleck St Margaret and St Katherine. N & Q May 1956.

—— The Auchinleck Life of Adam and Eve. RES new ser 7 1956.

Boyd, B. The Rawlinson version of Theophilus. MLN 71 1956.

—— The Middle English Miracles of the Virgin. San Marino 1964.

Williams, E. C. Mural paintings of St Catherine in England. Br Archaeological Assoc Jnl 19 1957.

Southern, R. W. The English origins of the Miracles of the Virgin. Mediaeval & Renaissance Stud 4 1958.

Garmondsway, G. N. and R. R. Raymo. A ME prose life of St Ursula. RES new ser 9 1958.

Saxer, V. Le culte de Marie Madeleine en Occident des origins à la fin du Moyen Age. Paris 1959.

Bolton, W. F. Parable, allegory and romance in the legend of Barlaam and Josaphat. Traditio 14 1958.

—— A note on hagiological healing. Medievalia et Humanistica 13 1960.

Kurvinen, A. The source of Capgrave's Life of St Katherine of Alexandria. Neuphilologische Mitteilungen 61 1960.

—— Two sixteenth-century editions of the Life of St Catherine of Alexandria. In English and mediaeval studies presented to J. R. R. Tolkien, 1962.

Lawrence, C. H. St Edmund of Abingdon: a study in hagiography and history. Oxford 1960.

Russell, J. C. Notes on the biography of St Edmund of Abingdon. Harvard Theological Rev 54 1961.

Quinn, E. C. The quest of Seth. Chicago 1962. Cross legend.

Püschel, B. Thomas à Becket in der Literatur. Bochum-Langendreer 1963.

Holdsworth, C. J. Visions and visionaries in the Middle Ages. History 48 1963.

Huttar, C. A. Old Testament sainthood. N & Q March 1964.

Wolpers, T. Die englische Heiligenlegende des Mittelalters. Tübingen 1964.

Braswell, L. Sir Isumbras and the legend of Eustace. Mediaeval Stud 27 1965.

Hill, B. The fifteenth-century prose Legend of the Cross before Christ. MÆ 34 1965.

Dorn, E. Der sündige Heilige in der Legende des Mittelalters. Philologische Studien (Munich) 10 1967.

Treharne, R. F. The Glastonbury legends. 1967.

Jennings, J. C. The origins of the 'Elements series' of the Miracles of the Virgin. Mediaeval & Renaissance Stud 6 1968.

McAlindon, T. Hagiography into art: a study of St Erkenwald. SP 67 1970.

Robertson, H. S. La vie de St Alexis: meaning and manuscript. Ibid.

Runnalis, G. A. The Miracles de Notre Dame par personnages. PQ 49 1970.

Lagorio, V. M. The evolving legend of St Joseph of Glastonbury. Speculum 46 1971.

Particular Collections

Northern Homily Cycle

Wells ch 5 p. 287 etc.

Mss: See Register, *and* Index, *appendix 4; G. H. Gerould,* Northern homily collection, *Lancaster Pa 1902, and* Saints' legends, *Boston 1916; Ward, vol 3, pp. 331, 714; Wells as above, Nevanlinna and Zettersten, below.*

§ I

Ed J. Small, English metrical homilies, Edinburgh 1862 (ms Edinburgh Royal College of Physicians); ed E. Mätzner, Altenglische Sprachproben pt i, Berlin 1877, p. 278 (2 items); ed R. Morris and W. W. Skeat, Specimens of early English vol 2, Oxford 1894, p. 83 (2 items); Signs of doom, ed O. F. Emerson, Reader, New York 1915; Northern Passion 1912–13 (EETS), suppl 1930 (EETS); ed R. Morris 1871 (EETS) (Cross story only).

Legends from various mss as follows:

Alexius. Ed C. Horstmann, Altenglische Legenden, Heilbronn 1881.

Andrew. Selection ed O. F. Emerson, Reader, New York 1915.

Barlaam and Josaphat. Ed C. Horstmann, Altenglische Legenden, Paderborn 1875.

Cecilia. Ed B. E. Lovewell, New Haven 1898; E Studien 1 1877.

Erasmus. Archiv 62 1879.

In festo Corporis Christi. 1892 (EETS); Archiv 82 1889.

Miracles of the Virgin. Ed R. W. Tryon, PMLA 38 1923.

Nativity. Ed A. Brandl and O. Zippel, Mittelenglische Sprach- und Literaturproben, Berlin 1917.

Peter and Paul. Ed C. Horstmann, Altenglische Legenden, Heilbronn 1881.

Proprium sanctorum. Archiv 81 1888.

Theophilus. E Studien 1 1877.

Selections. Ed W. Heuser, Anglia 27 1904.

Vernon narrationes. Archiv 57 1877.

For other edns, see Wells, and Index.

§2

Horstmann, C. Altenglische Legenden. Paderborn 1875.
— Sammlung altenglischer Legenden. Heilbronn 1881.
Retzlaff, O. Untersuchungen über den nordenglischen Legendencyclus. Berlin 1888.
Weber, O. Language. Berne 1902. On Small's edn.
Gerould, G. H. Hermit; Oswald. PMLA 20 1905.
— Sources. MLN 22 1907; E Studien 47 1913.
Foster, F. A. Northern Passion. 1913 (EETS). Introd.
— A study of the Northern Passion. 1914.
Lyle, M. C. Original identity of the York and Towneley Cycles. Minneapolis 1919. *See also under* York and Towneley Plays *in Wells, and col 734 f., below.*
Miller, F. H. The Northern Passion and the Mysteries. MLN 34 1919.
Deanesly, M. The Lollard Bible. Cambridge 1920. P. 148 on source.
Frank, G. MLN 35–6 1920–7; PMLA 35 1920. On French passion play.
Aitken, Y. H. Etude sur le Miroir ou les Evangiles des Domnées de Robert de Gretham. Paris 1922. With extracts.
Baker, A. T. A fragment of the Miroir or Evangiles des Domnées of Robert de Gretham. Modern Humanities Research Assoc Bull 1 1928.
Carver, J. E. The Northern Homily Cycle and missionaries to the Saracens. MLN 53 1938.
— The Northern homily cycle: an abridgement. New York 1941.
Nevanlinna, S. A note on the Robartes ms. Neuphilologische Mitteilungen 67 1966.
Zettersten, A. Further notes on the Robartes ms. Ibid.
On French narrative passion, see E. Roy, Le mystère de la passion, Dijon 1903; H. Theben, Die altfranzösische Passion, Greifswald 1909; Foster, above; G. Frank, MLN 35 1920.

Southern Legend Collection

Severs vol 2 pp. 413, 556.
Mss: See Register *col 2, index ;* Index; C. Horstmann, *Altenglische Legenden, Paderborn 1875, p. i ; Heilbronn 1881, p. xliv ; 1887 (EETS), p. vii ; C. d'Evelyn and A. J. Mill 1959 (EETS) ; Severs, above.*

§1

Ed F. J. Furnivall, Early English poems and lives of saints, Berlin 1862 (various items from BM ms Harley 2277).
Ed C. Horstmann, 1887 (EETS) (Laud 108); Archiv 82 1889, pp. 307, 369 (Bodley 779, later addns).
d'Evelyn, C. and A. J. Mill. 1956–9 (EETS) (Corpus Christi College, Cambridge 154, Harley 2277, with variants from Bodley Ashmole 43 and BM Cotton Julius D. IX).

Legends from various mss as follows:

Advent and Christmas Gospels. Ed C. Horstmann, Altenglische Legenden, Paderborn 1875.
Alexius. Archiv 51 1873, 56 1876.
Barlaam and Josaphat. Ed C. Horstmann, Altenglische Legenden, Paderborn 1875.
Becket. Ed H. Thiemke, Palaestra 131 1919; W. H. Black 1845 (Percy Soc).
Birth of Jesus. Ed C. Horstmann, Altenglische Legenden, Paderborn 1875; prologue, 1878 (EETS); with Marriage of Virgin, ed A. Brandl and O. Zippel, Mittelenglische Sprach- und Literaturproben, Berlin 1917.
Brandan. Ed M. Bälz, Die mittelenglische Brandan-Legende des Gloucesters-Legendars, Berlin 1909; G. Sampson, Cambridge book of prose and verse, 1924.
Cecilia. Ed B. E. Lovewell, New Haven 1898.
Celestyn. Anglia 1 1878.

Childhood of Jesus. Ed C. Horstmann, Altenglische Legenden, Paderborn 1875; Archiv 82 1889.
Christopher, Dunstan. E. Mätzner, Altenglische Sprachproben vol 1, Berlin 1867; Jahrbuch für Romische und Englische Sprache und Literatur 14 1875.
Cuthbert. 1891 (Surtees Soc).
Dunstan. Ed R. Morris and W. W. Skeat, Specimens of early English vol 2, Oxford 1894.
Edmund. Ed Lord F. Hervey, Corolla S. Eadmundi, 1907.
Eleven thousand virgins. Ed S. B. Liljegren, E Studien 57 1923.
Gregory. Archiv 55 1876.
Guthlac. Bonner Beiträge zur Anglistik 12 1902.
Juliana. 1872 (EETS); ed G. Schleich, Archiv 151 1927.
Katherine, Judas. Ed R. Wülcker, Lesebuch pt i, Halle 1874.
Kenelm. Ed J. A. W. Bennett and G. V. Smithers, Early Middle English verse and prose, Oxford 1966.
Magdalen. Ed C. Horstmann, Altenglische Legenden, Heilbronn 1877; Archiv 68 1882.
Margaret. 1866 (EETS); Archiv 79 1887.
Michael. Ed T. Wright, Popular treatises on science, 1841. *See* Wells, p. 835 (34).
Miracles of Virgin. Ed R. W. Tryon, PMLA 38 1923.
Purgatory of St Patrick. Ed C. Horstmann, Altenglische Legenden, Paderborn 1875. *See* St Patrick's Purgatory, below.
Southern Passion. Ed C. Horstmann, Leben Jesu, Münster 1873; B. D. Brown 1925 (EETS).
Susanna. Anglia 1 1878.
For other edns of individual items, see Wells *and* Index; Severs vol 2 p. 561.

§2

Rickert, E. The OE Offa saga. MP 2 1905. On Kenelm, pp. 9–10, 335–7.
Brown, C. The Cursor mundi and the Southern Passion. MLN 26 1911.
Hartland, E. S. The Legend of St Kenelm. Trans of Bristol & Gloucestershire Archaeological Soc 39 1916.
Gerould, G. H. Saints' legends. Boston 1916. Pp. 151, 223, 360.
Holthausen, F. Childhood of Jesus. Archiv 87 1918.
Brown, B. Kenelm, Gloucester's Chronicle: origin of collection. MLN 41 1926. *See* EETS 1925, introd.
Plenzat, K. Die Theophiluslegende in den Dichtungen des Mittelalters. Berlin 1926.
Serjeantson, M. S. Dialect. RES 3 1927.
Wells, M. E. The South English Legendary in its relation to the Legenda aurea. PMLA 51 1936.
— The structural development of the South English legendary. JEGP 41 1942.
Schubel, F. Die Südenglische Legende von den elftausend Jungfrauen. Greifswald 1938.
— Die heilige Pinnosa. Anglia 65 1941.
Walberg, E. Sur le nom de l'auteur du Voyage de Saint Brendan. Studia Neophilologica 12 1940.
Selmer, C. The beginnings of the St Brendan legend on the Continent. Catholic Historical Rev 29 1944.
— The Irish St Brendan legend in lower Germany and on the Baltic Coast. Traditio 4 1947.
Manning, W. F. The ME verse life of St Dominic: date and source. Speculum 31 1956.
Boyd, B. New light on the South English Legendary. SE 37 1958.
— A new approach to the South English legendary. PQ 47 1968.
Davis, N. The earliest Do Not. N & Q Feb 1961. On Laud 108.
Antropoff, R. von. Die Entwicklung der mittelenglischen Kenelm Legende. Bonn 1962.
Kobayashi, E. Verb forms in the South English legendary. Hague 1964.

d'Evelyn, C. The legend of the Seven sleepers. In Studies in language and literature in honour of M. Schlauch, Warsaw 1966.

Brooke, C. N. L. St Dominic and his first biographer. Trans of Royal Historical Soc 17 1967.

For further general studies on individual saints, see Wells; Severs vol 2 p. 561.

Smaller Vernon Collection (Golden Legend)

Severs vol 2 pp. 430, 559.
Ms: Vernon (Bodley 3938).

§1

Items 1–7 with Latin. Ed C. Horstmann, Altenglische Legenden, Heilbronn 1878; Barlaam and Josaphat, ed C. Horstmann, Altenglische Legenden, Paderborn 1875; Eufrosyne, ed C. Horstmann, E Studien 1 1877 and Altenglische Legenden, Heilbronn 1878.

§2

Horstmann, C. Altenglische Legenden. Heilbronn 1881, p. lxxxix; Paderborn 1875, p. xxiv.

Gerould, G. H. Saints' legends. Boston 1916. Pp. 229, 367.

Hill, R. T. Romanic Rev 10 1920, 12 1922. Edn of French Euphrosyne.

Serjeantson, M. S. The Index of the Vernon ms. MLR 32 1937.

For Golden legend see under Caxton, col 667, below.

Scottish Collection

Severs vol 2 pp. 419, 557.
Ms: Univ Lib Cambridge Gg.II.6.

§1

Ed C. Horstmann, Barbours des schottischen National-dichters Legendensammlung, 2 vols Heilbronn 1881, (item 29, ptd Altenglische Legenden, Heilbronn 1881, p. 189); W. M. Metcalfe 3 vols 1896 (Scottish Text Soc); Alexius, Archiv 62 1879; Machor, Altenglische Legenden, Heilbronn 1881, p. 189; Cecilia, ed B. E. Lovewell, New Haven 1898; Ninian and Machor, ed W. M. Metcalfe, Paisley 1906.

§2

Horstmann, C. Altenglische Legenden. Heilbronn 1881. P. lxxxix.

Buss, P. Anglia 9 1886. On author.

Koeppel. E. E. Studien 10 1887. On author.

Baudisch, J. Ein Beitrag zur Kenntnis der früher Barbour zugeschreibenen Legendensammlung. In Program der öffentlichen Unterrealschule in Wien, 1903.

Gerould, G. H. Saints' legends. Boston 1916. Pp. 176, 182, 363.

Baum, P. J. Medieval legend of Judas. PMLA 31 1916.

See also under Barbour's Bruce, col 466, above and Huchown Discussion, under Morte Arthure, col 396, above.

John Mirk's Festial

This collection contains several saints' legends. See col 488, above.

Particular Legends

Assumption of Mary

Severs vol 2 pp. 450, 642.
Mss: See Severs above, and Index 315, 1092, 2165, 2191, 2683, 2972, 2991, 3976 (Cursor mundi).

§1

I. 1, Univ Lib Cambridge Dd.I.1; 2, Univ Lib Cambridge Ff.II.38; 3, Univ Lib Cambridge Gg.IV.2; 4, BM Harley 2382; 5, BM additional 10,036; 6, Chetham 8009 (Manchester).

3, 5, Ed J. R. Lumby 1866 (EETS), rev G. H. McKnight 1905; 3, ed E. Hackauf, Zu der altesten me version der Assumptio Mariae, Heidelberg 1902 (critical text).

II. Auchinleck (Nat Lib of Scotland 19.2.1); ed M. Schwarz, E Studien 8 1885.

III. Southern Legend Collection (Index 2991). *See* Southern legend collection, B 2(b), above. *See also* McKnight 1877 (EETS), 1905 (rev) p. liii; ed C. Horstmann, Altenglische Legenden, Paderborn 1875, Heilbronn 1881 (introds); ed M. Schwartz, E Studien 8 1885; Hackauf, above.

IV. Northern Homily Collection (Index 2638, with 2972). *See* Northern homily collection, above.

BM Harley 4196 and Cotton Tiberius E VII. Ed C. Horstmann, Altenglische Legenden, Heilbronn 1881 (*see also* p. lxxviii); Bodley 3938 and BM additional 22,283, ed Horstmann, Archiv 81 1882 (expanded version).

V. Cursor mundi, vv. 20,065f. (Index 3976). Ed R. Morris 1877 (EETS).

VI. BM additional 39,996 (Index 315).

VII. Lambeth 223 (Index 1092).

For other legends of Mary see Severs vol 2 pp. 450, 644.

§2

Gierth, F. Über die älteste mittelenglische Version der Assumptio Mariae. Breslau 1881; rptd E Studien 7 1884.

Swarz, M. Die Assumptio Mariae in der Fassung des ms Bodl 779. E Studien 8 1885.

Leendertz, P. Die Quellen der ältesten me version der Assumptio Mariae. E Studien 35 1905.

Gerould, G. H. Saints' legends. Boston 1916. Pp. 312, 365.

Ryan, N. J. The assumption in the early English pulpit. Theological Stud 11 1950.

Childhood of Christ

Severs vol 2 pp. 447, 639.

§1

I. 1, BM Harley 3954; 2, Harley 2399; 3, BM additional 31,042; ed E. Kölbing, E Studien 2 1878; 1–2, ed C. Horstmann, Altenglische Legenden, Heilbronn 1878; 3, ed Horstmann, Archiv 84 1885.

II. Southern legend collection. Ed C. Horstmann, Altenglische Legenden, Paderborn 1875 (ms Laud 108). *See* Southern legend collection, above.

§2

Reinsch, R. Die Pseudo-Evangelien von Jesus und Marias Kindheit. Halle 1879.

Landshoff, H. Kindheit Jesus. Berlin 1889.

Meyer, P. French sources. Romania 18 1889.

Gast, E. Die beiden Redaktionen. Greifswald 1909.

Holthausen, F. Zum mittelenglischen Kindheit Jesu (Laud 108). Archiv 127 1911.

Gerould, G. H. Saints' legends. Boston 1916. Pp. 215, 226, 365.

James, M. R. The apocryphal New testament. Oxford 1926.

Vision of St Paul: or Eleven Pains of Hell

Severs vol 2 pp. 452, 645.
Mss: See Severs above, and Index 1898, 3089, 3481, 3828. 1, Bodley Laud 108; 2, Jesus College Oxford 29 (Bodley); 3, Bodley Digby 86; 4, Vernon (Bodley 3983); 5, Simeon (BM additional 22,283); 6, Douce 302; 7, Lambeth 487 (homily 4); 8, BM additional 10,036.

§1

1, Archiv 52 1874; 2, ed R. Morris 1872 (EETS); 3, Archiv 62 1879; 4–5, ed C. Horstmann 1892, 1901 (EETS); 4, 1872 (EETS), E Studien 1 1877; 6, 1872 (EETS); 7, 1867 (EETS); 8, E Studien 22 1896.
See also T. Silverstein, Visio Sancti Pauli, 1935 (Latin texts).

§2

Meyer, P. Romania 6 1877, 14 1895. On French versions.
— Notices et extraits des manuscrits de la Bibliothèque Nationale 35. Paris 1897. On French versions.
Brandes, H. Visio S. Pauli. Halle 1885.
— E Studien 7 1884. On sources.
James, M. R. In his Texts and studies vol 2, Cambridge 1893. On source.
Becker, E. Medieval visions of heaven and hell. Baltimore 1899.
Gerould, G. H. Saints' legends. Boston 1916. Pp. 222, 229, 366, 367, 370.
Willson, E. Medieval English legends of visits to the other-world. Chicago 1917.
Patch, H. R. Some elements in medieval descriptions of the other-world. PMLA 33 1918.
King, G. G. Vision of Thurkill. Romanic Rev 10 1919.
Hall, J. Selections from early ME vol 2. Oxford 1920. P. 413.
Voigt, W. Beiträge zur Geschichte der Visionsliteratur im Mittelalter. Palaestra 146 1924.
Os, A. B. van. Religious visions. Amsterdam 1932.
Silverstein, T. Visio Sancti Pauli, above.
Willard, R. The Latin texts of the Three utterances of the soul. Speculum 12 1937.
Stanley, E. G. Die anglonormannischen Verse in dem mittelenglischen Gedicht Die elf Höllenpeinen. Archiv 192 1956.
Silverstein, T. Date of the Apocalypse of Paul. Mediaeval Stud 24 1962.
Tveitane, M. En nörron versjon av Visio Pauli. Arbok (Bergen) humanistic ser 1964. With English summary.

St Patrick's Purgatory
Severs vol 2 pp. 453, 646.
Mss: See Severs, above, and Index 3037–9; also several mss of the Southern Legend collection, including:
1, Bodley Laud 108; 2, BM Cotton Julius D. IX; 4, Bodley Ashmole 43; 5, Univ Lib Cambridge additional 3039; 6, Corpus Christi College Cambridge 145 and cognate Southern legendary mss; 7, Nat Lib of Scotland 19.2.1 (Owain Miles); 8, BM Cotton Caligula A. II; 9, Brome Hall, Suffolk.

§1

1, Ed C. Horstmann 1887 (EETS); 1–2, 4, variants of 3, ed Horstmann, Altenglische Legenden, Paderborn 1875; 6, ed C. D'Evelyn and A. J. Mill 1959 (EETS); 7, ed D. Laing, Owain Miles, Edinburgh 1837; 7–8, E Studien 1 1877; 9, E Studien 9 1886; L. T. Smith, Commonplace book of the 15th century, Norwich 1886; Latin text: Romanische Forschungen 6 1889.

Koelbing, E. E Studien 1 1877. On author.
Krapp, J. P. Legend of St Patrick's Purgatory: its later literary history. Baltimore 1900.
Félice, P. de. L'autre monde. Paris 1906.
Verdeyen, R. and J. Endepols. Tondalus' visioen en St Patricius' Vagevuur. Hague 1914, 1917.
Gerould, G. H. Saints' legends. Boston 1916. Pp. 158, 216–18, 231–2, 248, 284.
Hamel, A. G. van Tondalus' Visioen en Patricius' Vagevuur. Neophilologus 4 1919.
Stanford, M. A. The sumner's tale and St Patrick's Purgatory. JEGP 19 1920.
Zanden, C. M. van der. Etude sur le Purgatoire de Saint Patrice. Amsterdam 1927.
Hammerich, L. L. Visiones Georgii: visiones quas in purgatorio Sancti Patricii vidit Georgius miles de Ungarra AD MCCCLIII. Copenhagen 1931.
Leslie, J. R. S. Saint Patrick's Purgatory. 1932.
McAlindon, T. Comedy and terror in ME literature. MLR 60 1965.
Locke, F. W. A new date for the composition of the Tractatus de Purgatorio Sancti Patricii. Speculum 40 1965.
See also Becker Voigt, van Os, under Vision of St Paul, above.

Vision of Tundale
Severs vol 2 pp. 455, 648.
Mss: See Severs, above, and Index 1724.
1, Nat Lib of Scotland 19.3 1; 2, BM Cotton Caligula A. II; 3, Royal 17 B. XLIII; 4, Ashmole 1491 (Bodley, 2 fragments).

§1

1–4, Composite text. Ed A. Wagner, Halle 1883; 2, Selection, ed R. Wülcker, Lesebuch pt 2, Halle 1879; 3, ed W. D. B. Turnbull, Edinburgh 1843; French texts, ed Friedel and Meyer, Paris 1907.

§2

Wagner, A. Visio Tungdali. Erlangen 1882.
— Zu Tungdalusvision. Anglia 20 1897.
Peters, E. Die Vision des Tangdalus. In Program des Dorotheenstadt Realgymnasiums, Berlin 1895.
Becker, E. Medieval visions. Baltimore 1899. P. 81.
Gerould, G. H. Saints' legends. Boston 1916. Pp. 248, 369.
See also Verdeyen and Endepols, van Hamel, under St Patrick's Purgatory, above. For other legends of afterlife see Severs vol 2, p. 648.

St Robert of Knaresborough
Severs vol 2, above and Index 1724.
Ms: See Severs, above, and Index 1724.

§1

1, Egerton 3134; ed J. Bazire 1953 (EETS).

§2

Bazire, J. Vocabulary of the metrical life of St Robert of Knaresborough. Leeds Stud in Eng 7 1952.

J. W.

(10) WILLIAM LANGLAND AND ASSOCIATED POEMS
c. 1332–1400

General Studies
See Wells pp. 240, 800, 1053, 1112, 1263, 1304, 1349, 1394, 1496, 1612, 1709.

Rosenthal, F. Die alliterierende englische Langzeile im 14 Jahrhundert. Anglia 1 1878.
Schröer, A. Excurs über die Metrik. Anglia 5 1882.

Menthel, E. Die siebentreffige Langzeile nach Orm bis in das 15 Jahrhundert. Anglia 10 1888.
Luick, K. Die englische Stabreimzeile im xiv, xv und xvi Jahrhundert. Anglia 11 1890.
— Zur Metrik der mittelenglischen reimendalliterierenden Dichtung. Anglia 12 1889.
Kaluza, M. Strophische Gliederung in der mittelenglischen rein alliterierenden Dichtung. E Studien 16 1892.
— Englische Metrik in historischer Entwicklung. Berlin 1909.
Lawrence, J. Chapters on alliterative verse. 1893.
Trautmann, M. Zur Kenntniss und Geschichte der mittelenglischen Stabzeile. Anglia 18 1896.
Fischer, J. and F. Mennicken. Zur mittelenglischen Stabzeile. Bonner Beiträge zur Anglistik 11 1901.
Deutschbein, M. Zur Entwicklung des englischen Alliterationsverses. Halle 1902.
Schneider, A. Die mittelenglische Stabzeile im 15 und 16 Jahrhundert. Bonner Beiträge zur Anglistik 12 1902.
Pilch, L. Umwandlung des altenglischen Alliterationsverses. Königsberg 1904.
Reicke, C. Untersuchungen über den Stils der mittelenglischen alliterierenden Gedichte. Königsberg 1906.
Schumacher, K. Studien über den Stabreim. Bonner Studien 11 1914.
Leonard, W. E. The scansion of Middle English alliterative verse. Wisconsin Univ Stud 11 1920.
Oakden, J. P. Alliterative poetry in Middle English. 2 vols Manchester 1930–5.
— The survival of a stylistic feature of Indo-European poetry in Germanic, especially in Middle English. RES 9 1933.
— The continuity of alliterative tradition. MLR 28 1933.
Day, M. Strophic division in Middle English alliterative verse. E Studien 66 1931.
Hulbert, J. R. A hypothesis concerning the alliterative revival. MP 28 1931.
— Quatrains in Middle English alliterative poems. MP 48 1950.
Greg, W. W. The continuity of alliterative tradition. MLR 27 1932.
Koziol, H. Grundzüge der Syntax der mittelenglischen Stabreimdichtungen. Vienna 1932.
— Zur Frage der Verfasserschaft einiger mittelenglischer Stabreimdichtungen. E Studien 67 1932.
Olszewska, E. S. Illustrations of Norse formulas in English. Leeds Stud in Eng 2 1933.
— Norse alliterative tradition in Middle English. Leeds Stud in Eng 6 1937.
Stobie, M. M. R. The influence of morphology on Middle English alliterative poetry. JEGP 39 1940.
Waldron, R. A. Oral-formulaic technique and Middle English alliterative poetry. Speculum 32 1957.
Elliott, R. W. V. Landscape and rhetoric in Middle English alliterative poetry. Melbourne Critical Rev 4 1961.
Salter, E. The alliterative revival. MP 64 1966.

Piers Plowman

See Wells pp. 244, 800, 958, 1009, 1055, 1112, 1170, 1213, 1264, 1304, 1349, 1394, 1447, 1496, 1569, 1612, 1668, 1709, 1809, 1903.
Mss:
A-text: 17 mss. Listed and described in G. Kane, Piers Plowman: the A version, 1960.
B-text: 17 mss. Listed and classified in E. Blackman, Notes on the B-text mss of Piers Plowman, JEGP 17 1918.
C-text: 19 mss. Listed and classified in E. T. Donaldson, Piers Plowman: the C-text and its poet, New Haven 1949.
See also C. Brown, Register of Middle English verse vol 2, Oxford 1920, items 880–1; R. H. Robbins, Index of Middle English verse, New York 1943, items 745, 1458, 1459.

§1
A-text: ed W. W. Skeat, 1867 (EETS); ed T. A. Knott and D. C. Fowler, Baltimore 1952; ed G. Kane 1960.
B-text: ed R. Crowley 1550; ed O. Rogers 1561; ed T. Wright 1842, 1856 (rev), 1895; ed W. W. Skeat 1869 (EETS).
C-text: ed T. D. Whitaker 1813; ed W. W. Skeat 1873 (EETS); ed R. B. Haselden and H. C. Schulz, The Huntington Library ms (HM 143), San Marino 1936 (facs) (introd by R. W. Chambers).
Notes to A-, B- and C-texts by W. W. Skeat, 1885 (EETS); ed Skeat, Oxford 1886 (parallel texts), 1954 (with bibliography); ed Skeat 1886 (EETS) (parallel extracts).
Selections: Ed W. W. Skeat, Oxford 1869, 1923 (B Prologue, i–vii); ed E. Wülcker, Altenglisches Lesebuch, Halle 1874–9; ed R. Morris and Skeat, Specimens of early English vol 2, Oxford 1894 (parts of Visio); ed J. F. Davis 1896 (B Prologue, i–vii); ed H. M. O'Kane, New Rochelle 1901; ed F. Kluge, Mittelenglisches Lesebuch, Halle 1904, 1912 (A Prologue, i); ed A. S. Cook, A literary Middle English reader, Boston 1915 (B, parts of Visio); ed C. M. Drennan 1915 (B Prologue, i); ed A. Brandl and O. Zippel, Mittelenglische Sprach- und Literaturproben, Berlin 1917, tr 1947 (parts of Visio); ed K. Sisam, Fourteenth-century verse and prose, Oxford 1921, 1937 (corrected), (part of vi); ed C. D. Pamely 1928 (B Prologue, v–vii); ed F. A. R. Carnegy 1934 (C ii–iv); ed F. Mossé, Manuel de l'anglais du Moyen Age, Paris 1945, tr Baltimore 1952 (parts of Visio); ed C. Wilcockson 1965; ed E. Salter and D. Pearsall 1967 (selections from C i–xxiii); ed J. A. W. Bennett, Oxford 1972 (B Prologue, i–vii).

Translations
A-text: W. A. Neilson and G. K. T. Webster, Chief British poets of the fourteenth and fifteenth centuries, Boston 1916 (Prologue, i–vii); J. L. Weston, Romance, vision and satire, Boston 1912 (with Prologue of B-text).
B-text: K. M. Warren 1895, 1899 (rev), 1913 (Prologue, i–vii); W. W. Skeat 1905; A. Burrell 1912 (EL); D. Attwater 1907 (Prologue, i–vii) (EL); W. Klett, Bonn 1935 (German); H. W. Wells, 1935; N. Coghill, 1949 (selections in verse); D. Attwater and R. Attwater 1957 (EL); J. F. Goodridge, 1959 (Penguin), 1966 (rev).

§2
Bernard, E. Langland: a grammatical treatise. Bonn 1874.
Kölbing, E. Kleine Beiträge zur Erklärung und Textkritik englischer Dichter [B.v.327 ff]. E Studien 5 1882.
Kron, R. Langley's Buch. Erlangen 1885.
Wandschneider, W. Zur Syntax des Verbums in Langleys Vision of William concerning Piers the Plowman. Leipzig 1887.
Gunther, E. Englische Leben im 14 Jahrhundert nach The vision. Leipzig 1889.
Klapprott, L. Das End-e in W. Langlands Buch von Peter dem Pflüger. Göttingen 1890.
Teichmann, E. Zur Stabreimzeile in Langlands Buch von Peter dem Pflüger. Anglia 13 1891.
— Zum Texte von Langlands Vision. Anglia 15 1893.
Bellezza, P. Langland and Dante. N & Q Aug 1894.
— Langlands Figure des Plowman in der neuesten englischen Litteratur. E Studien 21 1895.
Hanscom, E. D. The argument of the Vision of Piers Plowman. PMLA 9 1894.
Hopkins, E. M. The character and opinions of Langland. Kansas Univ Quart 3 1894.
— The education of Langland. Princeton College Bull 7 1895.
— Who wrote Piers Plowman? Kansas Univ Quart 7 1898.
— Notes on Piers Plowman. Kansas Univ Quart 8 1899.

Jusserand, J. J. L'épopée mystique de Langland. Paris 1893; tr and rev 1894.
— Piers Plowman: the work of one or of five? MP 6–7 1909–10. Reply by J. M. Manly 7 1910; rptd 1910 (EETS).
— et al. The Piers Plowman controversy. 1910 (EETS). Essays by Jusserand, Manly, Chambers and Bradley.
B., A. Zu W. Langland. Archiv 100 1898. Reference of 1396 to a ms of the poem.
Shute, H. W. Piers Plowman B.i.40–1. Archiv 100 1898.
Mensendieck, O. H. L. Charakterentwicklung und ethisch-theologische Anschauungen des Verfassers von Piers the Plowman. 1900.
— Die Verfasserschaft der drei Texte des Piers the Plowman. Zeitschrift für Vergleichende Literatur 18 1910.
— The authorship of Piers Plowman. JEGP 9 1910.
Jack, A. S. The autobiographical elements in Piers the Plowman. JEGP 3 1901.
Sellert, F. Das Bild in Piers the Plowman. Rostock 1904.
Bradley, H. The misplaced leaf of Piers the Plowman. Athenaeum 21 April 1906.
— The word Moillere in Piers the Plowman. MLR 2 1907.
— The lost leaf of Piers the Plowman. Nation (New York) 29 April 1909.
— Some cruces in Piers Plowman. MLR 5 1910.
— The authorship of Piers the Plowman. Ibid.
— Who was John But? MLR 8 1913.
Manly, J. M. The lost leaf of Piers the Plowman. MP 3 1906.
— Piers the Plowman and its sequence. 1908 (EETS). Rptd from CHEL 2.
— The authorship of Piers the Plowman. MP 14 1917.
Traver, H. The four daughters of God. Philadelphia 1907.
— The four daughters of God: a mirror of changing doctrine. PMLA 40 1925.
Fisher, A. W. A note on Piers the Plowman [B.v.28–9]. MLN 23 1908.
Flom, G. T. A note on Piers Plowman [C.i.215]. Ibid.
Onions, C. T. An unrecorded reading in Piers Plowman [C.i.215]. MLR 3 1908.
Deakin, M. The alliteration of Piers the Plowman. MLR 4 1909.
Hall, T. D. Was Langland the author of the C-text of Piers Plowman? Ibid.
— The misplaced lines in Piers Plowman. MP 7 1910.
Koellreuter, M. Das Privatleben in England nach den Dichtungen von Chaucer, Gower und Langland. Zürich 1908.
Brown, C. The lost leaf of Piers the Plowman. Nation (New York) 25 March 1909. Reply by T. A. Knott 13 May 1909.
Chambers, R. W. The authorship of Piers Plowman. MLR 5 1910; rptd 1910 (EETS).
— The original form of the A-text of Piers Plowman. MLR 6 1911.
— The three texts of Piers Plowman and their grammatical forms. MLR 14 1919.
— Long Will, Dante and the righteous heathen. E & S 9 1923.
— The manuscripts of Piers Plowman in the Huntington Library and their value for fixing the text of the poem. Huntington Lib Bull 8 1935.
— Incoherencies in the A- and B-texts of Piers Plowman and their bearing on the authorship. London Mediaeval Stud 1 1937.
— Piers Plowman: a comparative study. In his Man's unconquerable mind, 1939.
— Poets and their critics: Milton and Langland. Proc Br Acad 27 1941.
— A Piers Plowman manuscript [Nat Lib of Wales ms 773]. Nat Lib of Wales Jnl 2 1942.
— Robert or William Longland? London Mediaeval Stud 1 1948.

Chambers, R. W. and J. H. G. Grattan. The text of Piers Plowman: the A-text. MLR 4 1909.
— The text of Piers Plowman: critical methods. MLR 11 1916.
— The text of Piers Plowman. MLR 26 1931.
Dobson, M. An examination of the vocabulary of the A-text of Piers the Plowman. Anglia 33 1910.
Macaulay, G. C. The name of the author of Piers Plowman. MLR 5 1910.
Gebhard, H. Langlands und Gowers Kritik der kirchlichen Verhältnisse ihrer Zeit. Strasbourg 1911.
Keiller, M. M. The influence of Piers Plowman on the Macro play of Mankind. PMLA 26 1911.
Coulton, G. G. Piers Plowman: one or five? MLR 7 1912.
Owen, D. L. Piers Plowman: a comparison with some earlier and contemporary French allegories. 1912.
Cazamian, L. In his Etudes de psychologie littéraire, Paris 1913.
Jones, H. S. V. Imaginatif in Piers Plowman. JEGP 13 1914.
Moore, S. Studies in Piers the Plowman. MP 11 12 1914–15.
Rickert, E. John But: messenger and maker. MP 11 1914.
Görnemann, G. Zur Verfasserschaft und Entstehungsgeschichte von Piers the Plowman. Anglistische Forschungen 48 1915.
Kott, T. A. An essay towards the critical text of the A-version of Piers the Plowman. MP 12 1915. Reply by R. W. Chambers and J. H. G. Grattan, MLR 11 1916.
— Observations on the authorship of Piers the Plowman. MP 14–15 1917–18. Contains a list of contributions to the authorship controversy.
Eberhard, O. Der Bauernaufstand vom Jahre 1381 in der englischen Poesie. Anglistische Forschungen 51 1917.
Hemingway, S. B. The two St Pauls. MLN 32 1917.
Tristram, E. W. Piers Plowman in English wall painting. Burlington Mag 31 1917.
Hanford, J. H. Dame Nature and Lady Life. MP 15 1918. On relation between Piers Plowman and Death and liffe.
Baum, P. F. The fable of belling the cat. MLN 34 1919.
Knowlton, E. C. Nature in Middle English. JEGP 20 1921.
Bannister, A. T. Langland's birthplace. TLS 7 Sept 1922.
Chadwick, D. Social life in the days of Piers Plowman. Cambridge 1922.
Day, M. The alliteration of the versions of Piers Plowman in its bearing on their authorship. MLR 17 1922.
— Duns Scotus and Piers Plowman. RES 3 1927.
— The revisions of Piers Plowman. MLR 23 1928.
— Mele tyme of seintes, Piers Plowman B.v.500. MLR 27 1932.
— Piers Plowman and poor relief. RES 8 1932.
Döring, G. Personennamen in Langland. Leipzig 1922.
Bright, A. H. Langland's birthplace. TLS 12 March 1925.
— Langland's early life. TLS 5 Nov 1925, 9 Sept 1926.
— New light on Piers Plowman. Oxford 1928. Preface by R. W. Chambers.
— Langland and the seven deadly sins. MLR 25 1930.
— Sources of Piers Plowman. TLS 24 April 1930.
Iijima, I. Langland and Chaucer: a study of the two types of genius in English poetry. Boston 1925.
Owst, G. R. The angel and the goliardeys of Langland's prologue. MLR 20 1925.
Burdach, K. Der Dichter des Ackermann aus Böhmen. Berlin 1926 (vol 3 pt 3 of Vom Mittelalter zur Reformation).
Fairchild, H. N. Leyde here legges aliri. MLN 41 1926.
Adams, M. R. The use of the Vulgate in Piers Plowman. SP 24 1927.
Brett, C. Notes on Old and Middle English [A.vii.117; B Prologue 123]. MLR 22 1927.
K., A. R. Parked [C.vii.143–4]. Amer Speech 2 1927.

Stewart, G. R. The meter of Piers Plowman. PMLA 42 1927.

Thomas, G. A. A study of the influence of Piers Plowman. Ithaca 1927.

Withycombe, E. G. The name Robin Hood. TLS 7 April 1927.

Krog, F. Studien zu Chaucer und Langland. Anglistische Forschungen 65 1928.

— Autobiographische oder typische Zahlen in Piers Plowman? Anglia 58 1934.

von Bonsdorff, I. Hankyn or Haukyn? MP 26 1929.

Wells, H. W. The construction of Piers Plowman. PMLA 44 1929; rptd in Vasta, below.

— The philosophy of Piers Plowman. PMLA 53 1938; rptd in Vasta, below.

Hall, B. G. Sources of Piers Plowman. TLS 1 May 1930.

Gaffney, W. The allegory of the Christ-knight in Piers Plowman. PMLA 46 1931.

Marx, K. Das Nachleben von Piers Plowman bis zu Bunyans The pilgrim's progress. Königsberg 1931.

Byrne, M. The tradition of the nun in mediaeval England. Washington 1932.

Cargill, O. The date of the A-text of Piers the Ploughman. PMLA 47 1932.

— The Langland myth. PMLA 50 1935.

Coghill, N. Langland, the Naket, the Nauȝty and the dole. RES 8 1932.

— The sexcentenary of Langland. London Mercury May 1932.

— The character of Piers Plowman considered from the B-text. MÆ 2 1933; rptd in Vasta, below.

— Two notes on Piers Plowman. MÆ 4 1935.

— The pardon of Piers Plowman. Proc Br Acad 30 1944; partly rptd in Blanch, below.

— God's wenches and the light that spoke. In English and mediaeval studies presented to J. R. R. Tolkien, 1962.

— Langland: Piers Plowman. 1964 (Br Council pamphlet).

Cornelius, R. Piers Plowman and the Roman de Fauvel. PMLA 47 1932.

Haselden, R. B. The fragment of Piers Plowman in Ashburnham no cxxx. MP 29 1932.

Haselden, R. B. and H. C. Schulz. Note on the inscription in HM 128. Huntington Lib Bull 8 1935.

James, S. B. The mad poet of Malvern. Month 159 1932.

— Back to Langland. 1935.

— The neglect of Langland. Dublin Rev 196 1935.

Sullivan, C. The Latin inscriptions and the macaronic verse in Piers Plowman. Washington 1932.

Troyer, H. W. Who is Piers Plowman? PMLA 47 1932; rptd in Blanch, below.

Kirk, R. References to the law in Piers the Plowman. PMLA 48 1933.

Carnegy, F. A. R. An attempt to approach the C-text of Piers the Plowman. 1934.

— The relations between the social and divine order in Langland's Vision of William concerning Piers the Plowman. Breslau 1934.

Dawson, C. The vision of Piers Plowman. In his Mediaeval religion, 1934, and Mediaeval essays, 1953.

Kellogg, E. H. Bishop Brunton and the fable of the rats. PMLA 50 1935.

Devlin, M. A. The chronology of Bishop Brunton's sermons. PMLA 51 1936.

Dunning, T. P. Piers Plowman: an interpretation of the A-text. Dublin 1937; partly rptd in Vasta, below.

— Langland and the salvation of the heathen. MÆ 12 1943.

— The structure of the B-text of Piers Plowman. RES new ser 7 1956; rptd in Blanch, below.

— Action and contemplation in Piers Plowman. In Piers Plowman: critical approaches, ed S. S. Hussey 1969.

Kittner, H. Studien zum Wortschatz Langlands. Würzburg 1937.

Traversi, D. A. The vision of Piers Plowman. Scrutiny 5 1937.

— Langland's Piers Plowman. In The age of Chaucer, ed B. Ford 1954 (Pelican).

Ashton, J. W. Rymes of Randolf, Erl of Chestre [C.viii.9–12]. ELH 5 1938.

Hort, G. Piers Plowman and contemporary religious thought. 1938.

Marcett, M. E. Uhtred de Boldon, Friar William Jordan and Piers Plowman. New York 1938.

Stone, G. W. An interpretation of the A-text of Piers Plowman. PMLA 53 1938.

Bloomfield, M. W. Present state of Piers Plowman Studies. Speculum 14 1939; rptd in Blanch, below.

— Was Langland a Benedictine monk? MLQ 4 1943.

— The pardons of Pamplona and the pardoner of Rounceval: Piers Plowman B.xvii.252 (C.xx.218). PQ 35 1956.

— Piers Plowman and the three grades of chastity. Anglia 76 1958.

— Piers Plowman as a fourteenth-century apocalypse. Centennial Rev of Arts & Science 5 1961; rptd in Vasta, below.

— Piers Plowman as a fourteenth-century apocalypse. New Brunswick NJ 1962.

Durkin, J. T. Kingship in the Vision of Piers Plowman. Thought 14 1939.

Huppé, B. F. The A-text of Piers Plowman and the Norman wars. PMLA 54 1939.

— The authorship of the A- and B-texts of Piers Plowman. Speculum 22 1947.

— Petrus id est Christus: word play in Piers Plowman, the B-text. ELH 17 1950.

Klett, W. Wörter im Sinnbereich der Gemeinschaft bei Langland. Bonn 1939.

Mitchell, A. G. The text of Piers Plowman, C Prologue 215. MÆ 8 1939.

— A newly-discovered manuscript of the C-text of Piers Plowman. MLR 36 1941.

— Notes on the C-text of Piers Plowman. London Mediaeval Stud 1 1948.

— Lady Meed and the art of Piers Plowman. 1956; rptd in Blanch, below.

Mitchell, A. G. and G. H. Russell. The three texts of Piers the Plowman. JEGP 52 1953.

Richardson, M. E. Piers Plowman [Rose the regratour, A.v.140]. TLS 11 March 1939.

— Characters in Piers Plowman. TLS 13 Jan 1940.

— The characters in Piers Plowman: the Bishop of Bethlehem. N & Q Feb 1941.

Sledd, J. Three textual notes on 14th-century poetry [Piers Plowman C.vi.1–104]. MLN 55 1940.

Bayley, A. R. Langland at Great Malvern. N & Q Sept 1941.

Petrushevsky, D. V. The vision of Piers Plowman. Moscow 1941.

Sanderlin, G. The character Liberum Arbitrium in the C-text of Piers Plowman. MLN 56 1941.

Kent, M. A fourteenth-century poet surveys the English scene. Hibbert Jnl 40 1942.

Rauch, R. W. Langland and mediaeval functionalism. Annual Report of Amer Historical Assoc 3 1942.

Bennett, J. A. W. The date of the A-text of Piers Plowman. PMLA 58 1943.

— The date of the B-text of Piers Plowman. MÆ 12 1943.

— Lombards' letters (Piers Plowman B.v.251). MLR 40 1945.

— A new collation of a Piers Plowman manuscript (HM 137). MÆ 17 1948.

— Sum rex sum princeps etc (Piers Plowman B Prologue 132–8). N & Q Oct 1960.

— Chaucer's contemporary. In Piers Plowman: critical approaches, ed S. S. Hussey 1969.

Gwynn, A. The date of the B-text of Piers Plowman. RES 19 1943.

Spencer, H. Worth both his ears [Piers Plowman B Prologue 78]. MLN 58 1943.

Coffmann, G. R. The present state of a critical edition of Piers Plowman. Speculum 20 1945.

Burton, D. J. The compact with the Devil in the Middle English vision of Piers the Plowman, B.ii. California Folklore Quart 5 1946.

Grattan, J. H. G. The text of Piers Plowman. SP 44 1947.

— The text of Piers Plowman: a newly-discovered manuscript and its affinities [Chaderton ms]. MLN 42 1947.

Cassidy, F. G. The merit of Malkyn. MLN 63 1948.

Donna, R. B. Despair and hope: a study in Langland and Augustine. Washington 1948.

Gerould, G. H. The structural integrity of Piers Plowman B. SP 45 1948.

Hulbert, J. R. Piers the Plowman after forty years. MP 45 1948.

Kane, G. Piers Plowman: problems and methods of editing the B-text. MLR 43 1948.

— Textual criticism of Piers Plowman. TLS 17 March 1950.

— Piers Plowman. In his Middle English literature, 1951; partly rptd in Vasta, below.

— Piers Plowman: the evidence for authorship. 1965.

— The autobiographical fallacy in Chaucer and Langland studies. 1965.

Kellogg, A. L. Satan, Langland and the North. Speculum 24 1949.

— Langland and two scriptural texts. Traditio 14 1958.

— Langland and the Canes Muti. In Essays in literary history presented to J. Milton French, New Brunswick NJ 1960.

Maguire, S. The significance of Haukyn, Activa Vita, in Piers Plowman. RES 25 1949; rptd in Blanch, below.

Stroud, T. A. Manly's marginal notes on the Piers Plowman controversy. MLN 64 1949.

Frank, R. W. The conclusion of Piers Plowman. JEGP 49 1950.

— The number of visions in Piers Plowman. MLN 66 1951.

— The pardon scene in Piers Plowman. Speculum 26 1951.

— The art of reading mediaeval personification-allegory. ELH 20 1953; rptd in Vasta, below.

— Piers Plowman and the scheme of salvation. New Haven 1957; partly rptd in Vasta, below.

Lawlor, J. Piers Plowman: the pardon reconsidered. MLR 45 1950.

— The imaginative unity of Piers Plowman. RES new ser 8 1957; rptd in Vasta and Blanch, below.

— Piers Plowman: an essay in criticism. 1962.

— Two scenes from the vision of Piers Plowman. In To Nevill Coghill from friends, 1966.

Meroney, H. The life and death of Longe Wille. ELH 17 1950.

Brooks, E. St J. The Piers Plowman manuscripts in Trinity College, Dublin. Library 5th ser 6 1951.

Eliason, M. The peasant and the lawyer. SP 48 1951.

Fowler, D. C. Contamination in manuscripts of the A-text of Piers the Plowman. PMLA 66 1951.

— The forgotten pilgrimage in Piers the Plowman. MLN 67 1952.

— The relationship of the three texts of Piers the Plowman. MP 50 1953.

— Piers the Plowman: literary relations of the A- and B-texts. Seattle 1961.

Kaske, R. E. The use of simple figures of speech in Piers Plowman B: a study in the figurative expression of ideas and opinions. SP 48 1951.

— A note on Bras in Piers Plowman, A.iii.189, B.iii.195. PQ 31 1952.

— Gigas the Giant in Piers Plowman. JEGP 56 1957.

— Langland and the Paradisus claustralis. MLN 72 1957.

— Langland's walnut-simile. JEGP 58 1959.

— The speech of Book in Piers Plowman. Anglia 77 1959.

— Patristic exegesis in the criticism of mediaeval literature: the defence. In Critical approaches to mediaeval literature, ed D. Bethurum, New York 1960.

— Ex vi transicionis and its passage in Piers Plowman. JEGP 62 1963; rev in Blanch, below.

Robertson, D. W. and B. F. Huppé. Piers Plowman and scriptural tradition. Princeton 1951.

Smith, A. H. Piers Plowman and the pursuit of poetry. 1951; rptd in Blanch, below.

Donaldson, E. T. The texts of Piers Plowman: scribes and poets. MP 50 1953.

— Mss R and F in the B-tradition of Piers Plowman. Trans Connecticut Acad of Arts & Sciences 39 1955.

— Piers Plowman: the C-text and its poet. New Haven 1949.

— The grammar of Book's speech in Piers Plowman. In M. Brahmer et al, Studies in language and literature in honour of Margaret Schlauch, Warsaw 1966; rev in Blanch, below.

Maisack, H. Langlands Verhältnis zum Zisterzienschen Mönchtum. Balingen 1953.

Quirk, R. Langland's use of Kind Wit and Inwit. JEGP 52 1953.

— Vis Imaginativa. JEGP 53 1954.

Tillyard, E. M. W. In his English epic and its background, 1954.

Cejp, L. An interpretation of Piers the Plowman. Philologica, suppl to Časopis pro Moderni Filologii 7 1955.

— Some general meanings of Langland's fundamental concepts. Philologica Pragensia 2 1959.

— The methods of mediaeval allegory and Langland's Piers the Plowman. Statni Pedagogické Nakladatelství (Prague) 5 1961. In Czech with English summary.

Erzgräber, W. Langlands Piers Plowman im Lichte der mittelalterlichen Philosophie und Theologie. Anglia 73 1955.

— Langlands Piers Plowman: eine Interpretation des C-textes. Frankfurter Arbeiten aus dem Gebiete der Anglistik und der Amerika-Studien (Heidelberg) 3 1957.

Suddaby, E. The poem Piers Plowman. JEGP 54 1955.

Hussey, S. S. Langland, Hilton and the three lives. RES new ser 7 1956; rptd in Vasta, below.

— (ed). Piers Plowman: critical approaches. 1969. Articles listed separately.

Orrick, A. H. Declynede [A.iv.133]. PQ 35 1956.

Burrow, J. A. The audience of Piers Plowman. Anglia 75 1957.

— The action of Langland's second vision. EC 15 1965; rptd in Blanch, below.

— Words, works and will: theme and structure in Piers Plowman. In Piers Plowman: critical approaches, ed S. S. Hussey 1969.

Colledge, E. Aliri. MÆ 27 1958.

Colledge, E. and W. O. Evans. Piers Plowman. Month 32 1964.

Hamilton, A. C. Spenser and Langland. SP 55 1958.

Moe, H. A. The vision of Piers Plowman and the law of foundation. Proc Amer Philosophical Soc 102 1958.

— The power of poetic vision. PMLA 74 1959.

Zeeman, E. Piers Plowman and the pilgrimage to Truth. E & S new ser 11 1958; rptd in Blanch, below.

— (E. Salter). Piers Plowman: an introduction. Oxford 1962.

— Piers Plowman and the Simonie. Archiv 203 1967.

Bowers, R. H. Piers Plowman and the literary historians. College Eng Oct 1959.

— Foleuyles lawes (Piers Plowman C.xxii.247). N & Q Sept 1961.

Hall, G. D. G. The abbot of Abingdon and the tenants of Winkfield. MÆ 28 1959.

Johnston, G. K. W. Piers Plowman, B Prologue 78–9. N & Q July–Aug 1959.
—— A reading of Piers Plowman. Amer N & Q Nov 1962.
Oiji, T. Why did Piers rend his pardon asunder? Liberal Arts Rev 5 1960.
Oliphant, R. Langland's Sire Piers of Pridie. N & Q May 1960.
Spearing, A. C. The development of a theme in Piers Plowman. RES new ser 11 1960.
—— Verbal repetition in Piers Plowman B and C. JEGP 62 1963.
—— The art of preaching and Piers Plowman. In his Criticism and mediaeval poetry, 1964.
Strang, B. M. H. Piers Plowman B Prologue 132–8. N & Q Nov 1960.
—— Piers Plowman B.v.491–2. N & Q Aug 1963.
Fisher, J. H. Wyclif, Langland, Gower and the Pearl poet on the subject of aristocracy. In Studies in mediaeval literature in honor of A. C. Baugh, Philadelphia 1961.
Fuller, A. H. Scripture in Piers Plowman B. Mediaeval Stud 23 1961.
Orsten, E. M. The ambiguities in Langland's rat parliament. Ibid.
Smith, B. H. Patience's riddle, Piers Plowman B.xiii. MLN 76 1961.
—— Traditional imagery of charity in Piers Plowman. Hague 1966.
Adams, J. F. Piers Plowman and the three ages of man. JEGP 61 1962.
Martin, J. Wil as fool and wanderer in Piers Plowman. Texas Stud in Lang & Lit 3 1962.
Russell, G. H. The evolution of a poem: some reflections on the textual tradition of Piers Plowman. Arts 2 1962.
—— The salvation of the heathen: the exploration of a theme in Piers Plowman. Jnl Warburg & Courtauld Inst 29 1966.
—— Some aspects of the process of revision in Piers Plowman. In Piers Plowman: critical approaches, ed S. S. Hussey 1969.
Russell, G. H. and V. Nathan. A Piers Plowman manuscript in the Huntington Library [HM 114]. HLQ 26 1963.
Swieczkowski, W. Word order patterning in Middle English: a quantitative study based on Piers Plowman and Middle English sermons. Hague 1962.
Woolf, R. Some non-mediaeval qualities of Piers Plowman. EC 12 1962.
—— The tearing of the pardon. In Piers Plowman: critical approaches, ed S. S. Hussey 1969.
Bruneder, H. Personifikation und Symbol in Langlands Piers Plowman. Vienna 1963.
Gupta, J. S. Piers Plowman. EC 13 1963.
Kratins, O. Piers Plowman and Arthurian romance. EC 13 1963.
Muscatine, C. Locus of action in mediaeval narrative. Romance Philology 17 1963.
Samuels, M. L. Some applications of Middle English dialectology. E Studies 44 1963. On places of origin of Piers Plowman mss.
Yunck, J. A. The lineage of Lady Meed: the development of mediaeval venality satire. Notre Dame 1963.
D'Ardenne, S. T. R. O. Me bi-fel a ferly, A feyrie me þouhte (A prologue 6). E Studies 45 1964 (suppl).
Hoffmann, R. L. The burning of Boke in Piers Plowman. MLQ 25 1964.
Jachums, M. C. The legend of the voice from heaven. N & Q Feb 1964.
Jeremy, M. Leggis A-lery, Piers Plowman A.vii.114. Eng Lang Notes 1 1964.
Kean, P. M. Love, law and lewte in Piers Plowman. RES new ser 15 1964; rptd in Blanch, below.
—— Justice, kingship and the good life in the second part of Piers Plowman. In Piers Plowman: critical approaches, ed S. S. Hussey 1969.

Longo, J. A. Piers Plowman and the tropological matrix: passus xi and xii. Anglia 82 1964.
Reidy, J. Piers the Ploughman, whiche a pardoun he hadde. Papers of Michigan Acad 50 1965.
Vasta, E. The spiritual basis of Piers Plowman. Hague 1965.
—— Truth, the best treasure in Piers Plowman. PQ 44 1965.
—— (ed). Interpretations of Piers Plowman. Notre Dame 1968. Reprints of articles and parts of books, listed separately.
Walker, M. Piers Plowman's pardon: a note. Eng Stud in Africa 8 1965.
Wilkes, G. L. The Castle of Unite in Piers Plowman. Mediaeval Stud 27 1965.
Holleran, J. V. The role of the dreamer in Piers Plowman. Annuale Medievale 7 1966.
Howard, D. R. The body politic and the lust of the eyes: Piers Plowman. In his The three temptations: mediaeval man in search of the world, Princeton 1966.
Kinney, T. L. The temper of fourteenth-century verse of complaint. Annuale Medievale 7 1966.
Mroczkowski, P. Piers and his pardon: a dynamic analysis. In Studies in language and literature in honour of Margaret Schlauch, Warsaw 1966.
Risse, R. G. The Augustinian paraphrase of Isaiah xiv 13–14 in Piers Plowman and the Commentary on the Fables of Avianus. PQ 45 1966.
Hieatt, C. The realism of dream vision: the poetic exploitation of the dream experience in Chaucer and his contemporaries. Hague 1967.
St Jacques, R. Langland's Christ-knight and the liturgy. Revue de l'Université d'Ottawa 37 1967.
Schmidt, A. V. C. A note on the A-text of Piers Plowman (x.91–4). N & Q Oct 1967.
—— A note on the phrase Free wit in the C-text of Piers Plowman (xi.51). N & Q May 1968.
—— A note on Langland's conception of Anima and Inwit. N & Q Oct 1968.
—— Langland and scholastic philosophy. MÆ 38 1969.
Jones, F. Dickens and Langland in adjudication upon Meed. Victorian Newsletter no 33 1968.
Newstead, H. Chaucer and his contemporaries: essays on mediaeval literature and thought. Greenwich Conn 1968.
Strange, W. C. The willful trope: some notes on personification with illustrations from Piers A. Annuale Medievale 9 1968.
Wesling, D. Eschatology and the language of satire in Piers Plowman. Criticism 10 1968.
Blanch, R. J. (ed). Style and symbolism in Piers Plowman. Knoxville 1969. Reprints; articles listed separately.
Elliott, R. W. V. The Langland country. In Piers Plowman: critical approaches, ed S. S. Hussey 1969.
Evans, W. O. Charity in Piers Plowman. Ibid.
Jenkins, P. Conscience: the frustration of allegory. Ibid.
Knight, S. T. Satire in Piers Plowman. Ibid.
Mills, D. The rôle of the dreamer in Piers Plowman. Ibid.
Raw, B. Piers and the image of God in man. Ibid.
Schroeder, M. C. The character of Conscience in Piers Plowman. SP 67 1970.
Smith, R. F. Inwit and the Castle of Caro in Piers Plowman. Neuphilologische Mitteilungen 71 1970.
Davlin, M. C. Kynde knowyng as a major theme in Piers Plowman B. RES new ser 22 1971.

The following poems have in the past been associated with Langland:

Pierce the Ploughman's Crede

See Wells pp. 268, 802, 1009, 1113, 1214, 1395, 1497, 1613, 1710.
Mss: BM Royal 18 B.xvii; Trinity College Cambridge R.3.15.

§1

Ed R. Wolfe 1553, 1814; ed T. Wright in Piers Plowman, 1842, 1856 (rev), 1895; ed W. W. Skeat 1867 (EETS); ed Skeat, Specimens of English literature 1394–1579, Oxford 1879, (2nd edn rev); ed A. S. Cook, Literary Middle English reader, Boston 1915.

§2

Williams, W. H. Pierce the Plowman's Crede 372. MLR 4 1909.

Skeat, W. W. Christ-cross [Pierce the Plowman's Crede 1]. N & Q May 1867.

Jones, G. F. Twey mytenes, as mete. MLN 67 1952.

Doyle, A. I. An unrecognised piece of Piers the Ploughman's Creed and other work by its scribe. Speculum 34 1959.

Fleming, J. Gestes of Rome (Pierce the Ploughman's Crede 45). N & Q June 1964.

Richard the Redeless, or Mum and the Sothsegger

See Wells pp. 269, 803, 1010, 1056, 1113, 1265, 1305, 1395, 1498, 1570, 1613, 1710, 1814, 1904.
Mss: Cambridge, Univ Lib Ll.4.14; BM additional 41,666. Both fragmentary.
See also R. Steele, TLS 6 Dec 1928.

§1

Ed T. Wright 1838 (Camden Soc); ed T. Wright, Political poems and songs vol 1, 1859 (Rolls ser); ed W. W. Skeat 1873 (EETS); ed Skeat, Piers Plowman vol 1, Oxford 1886; ed M. Day and R. Steele 1936 (EETS).

Tr A. R. Benham, English literature from Widsith to the death of Chaucer, New Haven 1916 (in part).

§2

Ziepel, C. The reign of Richard II and comments upon an alliterative poem on the deposition of that monarch. Berlin 1874.

Bradley, H. Richard the Redeless, iii.105–6. MLR 12 1917.

Eberhard, O. Der Bauernaufstand vom Jahre 1381 in der englischen Poesie. Anglistische Forschungen 51 1917.

Mohl, R. Theories of monarchy in Mum and the Sothsegger. PMLA 59 1944.

Complaint of the Ploughman or Plowman's Tale

See Wells pp. 267, 802, 1448, 1497, 1570, 1613, 1710;
E. P. Hammond, Chaucer: a bibliographical manual, New York 1908, pp. 444, 540.
For mss see Wells p. 1613; S. de Ricci and W. J. Wilson, Census of mediaeval and Renaissance mss, Washington 1937, vol 2, p. 2157 (Univ of Texas 8).

§1

Ed W. Thynne, Workes of Chaucer, 1542 (2nd edn); ed T. Wright, Political poems and songs vol 1, 1859 (Rolls ser); ed W. W. Skeat, Complete works of Chaucer vol 7, Oxford 1897.

§2

Bradley, H. The plowman's tale. Athenaeum 12 July 1902.

Irvine, A. S. A manuscript of the Plowman's tale. SE 12 1932.

Williams, F. B. Unnoted Chaucer allusions 1550–1650. PQ 16 1937.

Wawn, A. N. The genesis of the Plowman's tale. Yearbook of Eng Stud 2 1972.

Jack Upland

See Wells pp. 268, 802, 1395.
No ms extant.

§1

Ed J. Gough [c. 1540 or c. 1536]; ed T. Wright, Political poems and songs vol 2, 1861 (Rolls ser); ed W. W. Skeat, Complete works of Chaucer vol 7, Oxford 1897; ed P. L. Heyworth, Oxford 1968.

§2

Utley, F. L. How Judicare came into the Creed. Mediaeval Stud 8 1946.

Reply of Friar Daw Thopias; Rejoinder of Jack Upland

See Wells pp. 268, 802.
Ms: Bodley Digby 41.

§1

Ed T. Wright, Political poems and songs vol 2, 1861 (Rolls ser); ed A. S. Cook, Literary Middle English reader, Boston 1915 (Daw only); ed P. L. Heyworth, Oxford 1968.

§2

Heyworth, P. L. Jack Upland's rejoinder: a Lollard interpolator and Piers Plowman B.x.249ff. MÆ 36 1967.

Crowned King

See Wells pp. 268, 802, 1395.
Ms: Bodley Douce 95.

§1

Ed W. W. Skeat 1873 (EETS); ed R. H. Robbins, Historical poems of the 14th and 15th centuries, New York 1959.

Death and Liffe

See Wells pp. 268, 802, 1009, 1113, 1214, 1350, 1395.
Ms: BM additional 27,879 (Percy Folio).

§1

Ed J. W. Hales and F. J. Furnivall, Percy Folio manuscript vol 3, 1868; ed J. H. Hanford and J. M. Steadman, SP 15 1918; ed I. Gollancz 1930; ed E. Arber, Dunbar anthology, Oxford 1901 (modernized).

§2

Scammon, E. The alliterative poem: Death and life. Radcliffe College Monographs 15 1910.

Holthausen, F. Zu Death and life. Beiblatt zur Anglia 23 1912, 32 1921. Annotations.

Hanford, J. H. Dame Nature and Lady Life. MP 15 1918. On relationship with Piers Plowman.

Knowlton, E. C. Nature in Middle English. JEGP 20 1921.

Harrington, D. V. The personifications in Death and life. Neuphilologische Mitteilungen 68 1967.

Scottish Feilde

See Wells pp. 268, 802, 1113, 1305, 1350, 1395, 1448.
Ms: BM additional 27,879 (Percy Folio).

§1

Ed J. W. Hales and F. J. Furnivall, Percy Folio manuscript vol 1, 1867; ed J. Robson, Chetham Society Remains vol 37, 1856; ed J. P. Oakden, Chetham Society Remains new ser 94, 1935.

§2

Mackenzie, W. M. The secret of Flodden. Edinburgh 1931.

Other Alliterative Poems
Parlement of the Thre Ages

See Wells pp. 241, 800, 957, 1009, 1054, 1112, 1170, 1213, 1263, 1304, 1394, 1496, 1612, 1709.
Ms: BM additional 31,042; imperfect copy in 33,994.

§1

Ed I. Gollancz 1897 (Roxburghe Club), 1915; ed F. Berry, The age of Chaucer, ed B. Ford 1954 (Pelican), 1959 (rev); ed M. Y. Offord 1959 (EETS).
Tr H. S. Bennett, England from Chaucer to Caxton, 1928 (in part) and Life on the English manor, 1937 (in part).

§2

Loomis, R. S. Verses on the nine worthies. MP 15 1918.
Hulbert, J. R. The problems of authorship and date of Wynnere and Wastoure. MP 18 1921. Includes discussion of Parlement.
Steadman, J. M. The authorship of Wynnere and Wastoure and the Parlement of the Thre Ages. MP 21 1924.
Serjeantson, M. S. The dialects of the West Midlands in Middle English. RES 3 1927.
Savage, H. L. A note on the Parlement of the Thre Ages 38. MLN 43 1928.
— Notes on the prologue of the Parlement of the Thre Ages. JEGP 29 1930.
— A note on the Parlement of the Thre Ages 220. MLN 45 1930.
Oakden, J. P. Wynnere and Wastoure and the Parlement of the Thre Ages. RES 10 1934.
Spiers, J. Wynnere and Wastoure and the Parlement of the Thre Ages. Scrutiny 17 1950.
Hieatt, C. Winner and Waster and the Parliament of the Three Ages. Amer N & Q 4 1966.
Lewis, R. E. The date of the Parlement of the Thre Ages. Neuphilologische Mitteilungen 69 1968.

Wynnere and Wastoure

See Wells pp. 241, 800, 1054, 1112, 1170, 1213, 1263, 1304, 1394, 1496, 1612, 1809, 1903.
Ms: BM additional 31,042.

§1

Ed I. Gollancz 1897 (Roxburghe Club), 1920, 1930 (for 1931) (with trn); ed F. Berry, The age of Chaucer, ed B. Ford 1954 (Pelican), 1959 (rev); ed R. Kaiser, Mediaeval English, Berlin 1958 (3rd edn of Alt- und mittelenglische Anthologie, rev and enlarged) (in part).

§2

N., G. A note on Wynnere and Wastoure. Athenaeum 3 Aug, 7 Sept 1901. Replies by I. Gollancz 24 Aug, 14 Sept 1901. On date of poem.
Hulbert, J. R. The problems of authorship and date of Wynnere and Wastoure. MP 18 1921.
Steadman, J. M. The date of Wynnere and Wastoure. MP 19 1922.
— The authorship of Wynnere and Wastoure and the Parlement of the Thre Ages. MP 21 1924.
— Notes on Wynnere and Wastoure. MLN 38 1923.
Serjeantson, M. S. The dialects of the West Midlands in Middle English. RES 3 1927.
Anderson, J. M. A note on the date of Winnere and Wastoure. MLN 43 1928.
Oakden, J. P. A note on the unity of authorship of Wynnere and Wastoure and the Parlement of the Thre Ages. RES 10 1934.
Stillwell, G. Wynnere and Wastoure and the Hundred Years War. ELH 8 1941.
James, J. D. The undercutting of conventions in Wynnere and Wastoure. MLQ 25 1964.
Hieatt, C. Winner and Waster and the Parliament of the Three Ages. Amer N & Q 4 1966.
Oiji, T. An essay on Wynnere and Wastoure with special reference to the political, economic and religious attitudes of the poet. Stud in Eng (Tokyo) 43 1966.
Elliott, R. W. V. The topography of Wynnere and Wastoure. E Studies 48 1967.

B. R.

(11) THE PEARL POET

See Wells pp. 578, 863, 993, 1026, 1082, 1138, 1185, 1229, 1283, 1319, 1370, 1418, 1469, 1525, 1586, 1638, 1682, 1729, 1853, 1923; Huchown Discussion, under Morte Arthure, col 396, above; and Langland: General Studies col 533, above, on alliterative verse.
Ms: BM Cotton Nero A.x + 4 (once A.x); ed I. Gollancz 1923 (EETS)(facs). See W. W. Greg, MLR 19 1925.

Indexes and Concordances

Chapman, C. O. An index of names in Pearl, Purity, Patience and Gawain. Ithaca 1951.
Markman, A. A computer concordance to Middle English texts. SB 17 1964.
Kottler, B. and A. M. Markman. A concordance to five Middle English poems: Cleanness, St Erkenwald, Sir Gawain and the Green Knight, Patience, Pearl. Pittsburgh 1966.

Collections

Ed R. Morris 1864 (EETS), 1869 (rev); The Pearl poet: his complete works, ed M. Williams, New York 1967.
Tr J. Gardner, Complete works of the Gawain poet in a modern English version, Chicago 1965.

General Studies

Trautmann, M. Über Verfasser und Entstehungszeit einiger alliterierenden Gedichte. Halle 1876.

Thomas, M. C. Sir Gawayne and the Grene Knight. Zürich 1883. Includes discussion of the other works.
Knigge, F. Die Sprache des Dichters von Sir Gawain and the Green Knight, der sogenannten Early English Alliterative poems und De Erkenwalde. Marburg 1885.
Fuhrmann, J. Die alliterierenden Sprachformeln in Morris's Early English Alliterative Poems und in Sir Gawayne and the Green Knight. Hamburg 1886.
Fisher, J. Die stabende Langzeile in den Werken des Gawaindichters. Bonner Beiträge zur Anglistik 11 1901.
Brown, C. The author of Pearl. PMLA 19 1904.
Reicke, C. Untersuchungen über den Stil der mittelenglischen alliterierenden Gedichte. Königsberg 1906.
Thomas, J. Die alliterierende Langzeile des Gawayn-Dichters. Coburg 1908.
MacCracken, H. N. Concerning Huchown. PMLA 25 1910.
Day, M. The weak verb in the works of the Gawain poet. MLR 14 1919.
Hulbert, J. R. The West Midlands of the romances. MP 19 1922.
Menner, R. J. Sir Gawain and the Green Knight and the West Midlands. PMLA 37 1922.
Serjeantson, M. S. The dialects of the West Midlands in Middle English. RES 3 1927.
Chapman, C. O. The musical training of the Pearl poet. PMLA 46 1931.

—— The authorship of the Pearl. PMLA 47 1932.

Koziol, H. Zur Frage der Verfasserschaft einiger mittelenglischer Stabreimdichtungen. E Studien 67 1932.

Greg, W. W. A bibliographical paradox. Library 4th ser 13 1933. On the transmission of the 4 poems.

Oakden, J. P. The scribal errors of ms Cotton Nero A.x. Library 4th ser 14 1934.

Clark, J. W. Observations on certain differences in vocabulary between Cleanness and Sir Gawain and the Green Knight. PQ 28 1949.

—— The Gawain poet and the substantival adjective. JEGP 49 1950.

—— Paraphrases for God in the poems attributed to the Gawain poet. MLN 65 1950.

—— On certain alliterative and poetic words in the poems attributed to the Gawain poet. MLQ 12 1951.

Everett, D. Patience, Purity and Sir Gawain and the Green Knight. In her Essays on Middle English literature, Oxford 1955.

Luttrell, C. A. The Gawain group: cruxes, etymologies, interpretations. Neophilologus 39–40 1955–6.

—— A Gawain group miscellany. N & Q Dec 1962.

Savage, H. L. The Gawain poet: studies in his personality and background. Chapel Hill 1956.

Ebbs, J. D. Stylistic mannerisms of the Gawain poet. JEGP 57 1958.

Elliott, R. W. V. Landscape and rhetoric in Middle English alliterative poetry. Melbourne Critical Rev 4 1961.

McLaughlin, J. C. A graphemic-phonemic study of a Middle English manuscript. Hague 1963.

Brewer, D. S. Courtesy and the Gawain poet. In Patterns of love and courtesy: essays in memory of C. S. Lewis, 1966.

—— The Gawain poet: a general appreciation of the four poems. EC 17 1967.

Spearing, A. C. Patience and the Gawain poet. Anglia 84 1966.

—— The Gawain-poet: a critical study. Cambridge 1970.

Pearl

See Wells pp. 579, 864, 993, 1026, 1082, 1138, 1185, 1229, 1283, 1320, 1418, 1469, 1525, 1586, 1638, 1729, 1853, 1923.

§ I

Ed R. Morris 1864 (EETS), 1869 (rev); ed I. Gollancz 1891 (with trn), 1897 (rev), 1907, 1921 (rev with trn of Olympia); ed C. G. Osgood, Boston 1906; ed F. Olivero, Turin 1926, Bologna 1936 (both with Italian trn); ed S. P. Chase et al, Boston 1932; ed E. V. Gordon, Oxford 1953; ed M. V. Hillman, New York 1961 (with trn); ed A. C. Cawley 1962 (EL); ed S. de Ford, New York 1967 (with trn).

Selections: Ed A. Brandl and O. Zippel, Mittelenglische Sprach- und Literaturproben, Berlin 1917, 1927, tr 1947, 1949; ed K. Sisam, Fourteenth-century verse and prose, Oxford 1921, 1937 (corrected); ed G. Sampson, Cambridge book of prose and verse, Cambridge 1924; ed F. Mossé, Manuel de l'anglais du Moyen Age, Paris 1945, tr Baltimore 1952.

Translations: G. G. Coulton 1906 (in original metre); C. G. Osgood, Princeton 1907 (prose); S. O. Jewett, New York 1908 (in original metre), rptd in R. S. Loomis, Medieval English verse and prose, New York 1948; S. W. Mitchell, New York 1908 (selection in verse); J. L. Weston, Romance, vision and satire, Boston 1912 (in original metre); W. A. Neilson and K. G. T. Webster, Chief British poets of the 14th and 15th centuries, Boston 1916 (prose); I. Gollancz 1918 (and in his edns above); E. Kirtlan 1918 (verse); S. P. Chase, Oxford 1932 (verse); B. Stone, Medieval English verse, 1964 (Penguin).

§ 2

Fick, W. Zum mittelenglischen Gedicht von der Perle. Kiel 1885.

Northup, C. S. The metrical structure of Pearl. PMLA 12 1897.

Neilson, G. Crosslinks between Pearl and the Awntyrs. Scottish Antiquary 16 1902.

Brown, C. The author of the Pearl considered in the light of his theological opinions. PMLA 19 1904.

Schofield, W. H. The nature and fabric of the Pearl. PMLA 19 1904.

—— Symbolism allegory and autobiography in the Pearl. PMLA 24 1909.

Coulton, G. G. In defence of the Pearl. MLR 2 1906.

Garrett, R. M. The Pearl: an interpretation. Seattle 1918.

Tuttle, E. H. Notes on the Pearl. MLR 15 1920.

Fletcher, J. The allegory of the Pearl. JEGP 20 1921.

Emerson, O. F. Imperfect lines in Pearl and the rimed parts of Sir Gawain and the Green Knight. MP 19 1922.

—— Some notes on the Pearl. PMLA 37 1922.

—— More notes on Pearl. PMLA 42 1927.

Greene, W. H. The Pearl: a new interpretation. PMLA 40 1925.

Madeleva, M. Pearl: a study in spiritual dryness. New York 1925.

Hart, E. Heaven of virgines. MLN 42 1927.

Cargill, O. and M. Schlauch. The Pearl and its jeweler. PMLA 43 1928.

Heather, P. Precious stones in the Middle English verse of the fourteenth century. Folklore 42 1931.

Gordon, E. V. and C. T. Onions. Notes on the text and interpretation of Pearl. MÆ 1–2 1932–3.

Billour, H. La xiv egloga del Boccaccio: Olympia e la Perla. Estratto dall' Annuario del R. Ginnasio-Liceo Piazzi di Sondrio 1933.

Ueno, N. On the Pearl. Stud in Eng Lit (Tokyo) 13 1933.

Wellek, R. Pearl: an interpretation of the Middle English poem. Prague Stud 4 1933; rptd in Blanch, below.

Day, M. Two notes on Pearl [140, 210]. MÆ 3 1934.

Hammerle, K. The Castle of Perseverance and Pearl. Anglia 50 1936.

Bone, G. A note on Pearl and the Buke of the Howlat [140]. MÆ 6 1937.

Thomas, P. G. Notes on the Pearl. London Mediaeval Stud 1 1938.

Chapman, C. O. Numerical symbolism in Dante and the Pearl. MLN 54 1939.

Wright, E. M. Additional notes on Sir Gawain and the Green Knight. JEGP 38 1939. Entirely on Pearl.

—— Additional notes on the Pearl. JEGP 39 1940.

Sledd, J. Three textual notes [604]. MLN 55 1940.

Hillman, M. V. Pearl: inlyche and rewarde [603–4]. MLN 56 1941.

—— The Pearl: west ernays [307] and fasor [432]. MLN 58 1943.

—— Pearl: lere leke [210]. MLN 59 1944.

—— Some debatable words in Pearl and its theme [51–6, 1182–6, 1201–12]. MLN 60 1945.

—— Pearl 382 mare rez mysse? MLN 68 1953.

Hamilton, M. P. The orthodoxy of Pearl 603–4. MLN 58 1943.

—— The meaning of the Middle English Pearl. PMLA 70 1955; rptd in Blanch, below.

Wrenn, C. L. On re-reading Spenser's Shepheardes Calender. E & S 29 1943.

Everett, D. and N. D. Hurnand. Legal phraseology in a passage in Pearl [679–708]. MÆ 16 1947.

Everett, D. In her Essays on Middle English literature, Oxford 1955.

Wintermute, E. The Pearl's author as herbalist. MLN 64 1949.

Robertson, D. W. The Pearl as a symbol. MLN 65 1950.

—— The heresy of the Pearl. Ibid.

Elliott, R. W. V. Pearl and the mediaeval garden: convention or originality? Langues Modernes 45 1951.

Holman, C. H. Marerez mysse in the Pearl [381–4]. MLN 66 1951.

Hoshiga, G. Sir Gawain and Pearl. Rising Generation 97 1951.

Johnson, W. S. The imagery and diction of the Pearl: towards an interpretation. ELH 20 1953.

Le Grelle, L. La Perle: essai d'interprétation nouvelle. Etudes Anglaises 6 1953.

Conley, J. Pearl and a lost tradition. JEGP 54 1955.

Rupp, H. R. Word-play 277–8. MLN 70 1955.

Stern, M. R. An approach to the Pearl. JEGP 54 1955.

Moorman, C. The role of the narrator in Pearl. MP 53 1956.

—— Some notes on Patience and Pearl. Southern Quart 4 1965.

—— The Pearl poet. New York 1968.

Bishop, I. The significance of the garlande gay in the allegory of Pearl. RES new ser 8 1957.

—— Pearl in its setting. Oxford 1968.

Visser, F. M. Pearl 609–11. E Studies 39 1958.

Fowler, D. C. Pearl 558: waning. MLN 74 1959.

—— On the meaning of Pearl 139–40. MLQ 21 1960.

Kaske, R. E. Two cruxes in Pearl: 596 and 601–10. Traditio 15 1959.

Johnston, G. K. W. Northern idiom in Pearl. N & Q Oct 1960.

Fisher, J. H. Wyclif, Langland, Gower and the Pearl poet on the subject of aristocracy. In Studies in mediaeval literature in honor of A. C. Baugh, Philadelphia 1961.

Hoffman, S. de V. The Pearl: notes for an interpretation. MP 58 1961.

Knightley, W. J. Pearl: the hyȝ seysoun. MLN 76 1961.

Oiji, T. The Middle English Pearl and its theology. Stud in Eng Lit (Tokyo) 1961.

Luttrell, C. A. The mediaeval tradition of the pearl virginity. MÆ 31 1962.

—— Pearl: symbolism in a garden setting. Neophilologus 49 1965; rptd in Blanch, below.

Revard, C. A note on stonden, Pearl 113. N & Q Jan 1962.

—— A note on at the fyrst fyne, Pearl 635. Eng Lang Notes 1 1964.

Richardson, F. E. The Pearl: a poem and its audience. Neophilologus 46 1962.

Rathbone, I. E. New light on Pearl 690. Traditio 19 1963.

Spearing, A. C. Symbolic and dramatic development in Pearl. MP 60 1963; rptd in Blanch, below.

Watts, V. E. Pearl as a consolatio. MÆ 32 1963.

Ackerman, R. W. The Pearl maiden and the penny. Romance Philology 18 1964.

Mitchell, B. Pearl 609–10. N & Q Feb 1964.

Pilch, H. Das mittelenglische Perlengedicht: sein Verhältnis zum Rosenroman. Neuphilologische Mitteilungen 65 1964.

Barron, W. J. Luf-daungere. In Mediaeval miscellany presented to Eugene Vinaver, Manchester 1965.

Blanch, R. J. Precious metal and gem symbolism in Pearl. Lock Haven Rev 7 1965; rptd below.

—— (ed). Sir Gawain and Pearl: critical essays. Bloomington 1966. Reprints; articles listed separately.

Carson, A. Aspects of elegy in the Middle English Pearl. SP 62 1965.

Heiserman, A. R. The plot of Pearl. PMLA 80 1965.

Hieatt, C. Pearl and the dream vision tradition. Studia Neophilologica 37 1965.

—— The realism of dream vision: the poetic exploitation of the dream experience in Chaucer and his contemporaries. Hague 1967.

Kean, P. M. Numerical composition in Pearl. N & Q Feb 1965.

—— The Pearl: an interpretation. 1967.

Manzalaoui, M. English analogues to the Liber Scalae. MÆ 34 1965.

Davis, N. A note on Pearl [1208]. RES new ser 17–18 1966–7.

Guidi, A. Il meglio di Pearl. Annali Istituto Universitario Orientale, Napoli: Sezione Germanica 9 1966.

Mahl, M. R. The Pearl as the Church. Eng Record 17 1966.

McIntosh, A. Middle English upon schore and some related matters. In Studies in language and literature in honour of Margaret Schlauch, Warsaw 1966.

Rostvig, M-S. Numerical composition in Pearl. E Studies 48 1967.

Vasta, E. Pearl: immortal flowers and the Pearl's decay. JEGP 66 1967.

Blenkner, L. The theological structure of Pearl. Traditio 24 1968.

—— The pattern of traditional images in Pearl. SP 68 1971.

Macrae-Gibson, O. D. Pearl: the link-words and the thematic structure. Neophilologus 52 1968.

Wilson, E. The gostly drem in Pearl. Neuphilologische Mitteilungen 69 1968.

—— Gromylyoun (Gromwell) in Pearl. N & Q Feb 1971.

—— Word play and the interpretation of Pearl. MÆ 40 1971.

Milroy, J. Pearl: the verbal texture and the linguistic theme. Neophilologus 55 1971.

Murtaugh, D. M. Pearl 462: þe mayster of myste. Neophilologus 55 1971.

Nolan, B. and D. Farley-Hills. The authorship of Pearl: two notes. RES new ser 22 1971.

Patience

See Wells pp. 583, 864, 1026, 1138, 1229, 1283, 1320, 1370, 1418, 1525, 1638, 1729, 1923.

§1

Ed R. Morris 1864 (EETS), 1869 (rev); ed H. Bateson, Manchester 1912, 1918 (rev); ed I. Gollancz 1913, 1924 (rev); ed J. J. Anderson, Manchester 1969.

Selections: Ed J. Zupitza, Altenglisches Übungsbuch, Vienna 1874; ed R. Wülcker, Altenglisches Lesebuch pt 2, Halle 1879; ed G. E. MacLean, Old and ME reader, New York 1893; ed F. Kluge, Mittelenglisches Lesebuch, Halle 1904, 1912; ed G. Sampson, Cambridge book of prose and verse, Cambridge 1924.

Translations: J. L. Weston, Romance, vision and satire, Boston 1912 (selection); B. Stone, Mediaeval English verse, 1964 (Penguin).

§2

Emerson, O. F. A parallel between the Middle English poem Patience and an early Latin poem attributed to Tertullian. PMLA 10 1895.

—— A note on the poem Patience [185]. E Studien 47–8 1914–15. Reply by C. T. Onions 47 1914.

—— Two notes on Patience [1, 231]. MLN 29 1914.

—— More notes on Patience. MLN 31 1916.

Ekwall, E. Some notes on the text of the alliterative poem Patience. E Studien 44 1912.

—— Another note on the poem Patience. E Studien 47 1914.

—— Patience 143. E Studien 49 1916.

Callender, G. Patience. Mariner's Mirror 4 1914.

Laughton, L. G. C. Patience. Ibid.

Liljegren, S. B. Has the poet of Patience read the De Jona? E Studien 48 1915.

Eberhard, O. Die Bauernaufstand vom Jahre 1381 in der englischen Poesie. Anglistische Forschungen 51 1917.

Day, M. A note on Patience 54. MLR 33 1938.

Berlin, N. Patience: a study in poetic elaboration. Studia Neophilologica 33 1961.

Moorman, C. F. The role of the narrator in Patience. MP 61 1964.

—— Some notes on Patience and Pearl. Southern Quart 4 1965.

Anderson, J. J. The prologue of Patience. MP 63 1966.

Spearing, A. C. Patience and the Gawain poet. Anglia 84 1966.

Hill, O. G. The late Latin De Jona as a source for Patience. JEGP 66 1967.

—— The audience of Patience. MP 66 1969.

Kelly, E. M. Parallels between the Middle English Patience and Hymnus Ieiunantium of Prudentius. Eng Lang Notes 4 1967.

Stedman, J. W. The genesis of Patience. MP 66 1969.

Schleusener, J. Patience 35–40. MP 67 1970.

—— History and action in Patience. PMLA 86 1971.

Szarmach, P. E. Two notes on Patience. N & Q April 1971.

Williams, D. The point of Patience. MP 68 1971.

Purity or Cleanness

See Wells pp. 584, 864, 1026, 1139, 1229, 1283, 1320, 1370, 1418, 1469, 1525, 1638.

§ 1

Ed R. Morris 1864 (EETS), 1869 (rev); ed R. J. Menner, Yale Stud 61 1920; ed I. Gollancz 1921.

Selections: Ed R. Morris and W. W. Skeat, Specimens of early English vol 2, Oxford 1894.

Translations: J. L. Weston, Romance, vision and satire, Boston 1912 (selections); B. Stone 1971 (Penguin).

§ 2

Holthausen, F. Zu dem mittelenglischen Gedicht Cleanness. Archiv 106 1901. Petrus Comestor as source?

Brown, C. Notes on the dependence of Cleanness on the Book of Mandeville. PMLA 19 1904.

Bödtker, A. T. Covacle not conacle. MLN 26 1911.

Brett, C. Notes on Cleanness and Sir Gawayne [1413]. MLR 10 1915.

Emerson, O. F. A note on the ME Cleanness [817–28]. Ibid.

—— ME Clannesse. PMLA 34 1919.

Bateson, H. The text of Cleanness. MLR 13 1918.

—— Three notes on the ME Cleanness [599, 982–3]. MLR 19 1924.

—— Looking over the left shoulder [981–2]. Folklore 34 1923.

Gollancz, I. The text of Cleanness. MLR 14 1919.

Thomas, P. G. Notes on Cleanness. MLR 17 1922, 24 1929.

Ohlander, U. A passage in Cleanness: a note on ME construction change. Göteborgs Högstolas Årsskrift 56 1950.

Ackerman, R. W. Pared out of paper: Gawain 802 and Purity 1408. JEGP 56 1957.

Luttrell, C. A. Baiting of bulls and bears in the ME Cleanness. N & Q Jan 1952.

—— Cleanness and the Knight of La Tour Landry. MÆ 29 1960.

Sir Gawayne and the Grene Knight

See under Arthurian Romances, col 401, above.

Erkenwald

See Wells pp. 310, 810, 1012, 1059, 1117, 1215, 1268, 1307, 1351, 1397, 1451, 1501, 1617, 1906.
Ms: BM Harley 2250.

§ 1

Ed C. Horstmann, Altenglische Legenden, Heilbronn 1881; ed I. Gollancz 1922 (with trn); ed H. L. Savage, New Haven 1926; tr B. Stone 1971 (Penguin).

§ 2

Knigge, F. Die Sprache des Dichters von Sir Gawain und De Erkenwalde. Marburg 1885.

Gerould, G. H. Saints' legends. Boston 1916.

Hulbert, J. R. The sources of St Erkenwald and the Trental of Gregory. MP 16 1919.

Hibbard, L. A. Erkenbald the Belgian. MP 17 1920.

Benson, L. D. The authorship of St Erkenwald. JEGP 64 1965.

Petronella, V. A. St Erkenwald: style as the vehicle for meaning. JEGP 66 1967.

McAlindon, T. Hagiography into art: a study of St Erkenwald. SP 67 1970.

B. R.

(12) JOHN GOWER

1330?–1408?

Bibliographies

Macaulay, G. C. In his edn of Complete works, 1899–1902, below.

Collections

Complete works. Ed G. C. Macaulay 4 vols Oxford 1899–1902. *See* Wells p. 865.

Selections. Ed J. A. W. Bennett, Oxford 1968.

§ 1

Confessio amantis. 1483 (Caxton); ed R. Pauli 3 vols 1857; The English works in Complete works, ed G. C. Macaulay 2 vols 1901; ed R. A. Peck, New York 1968; tr Spanish, ed A. Birsh-Hirschfield, Leipzig 1909; Selections, ed H. Morley 1889; ed M. W. Easton, Halle 1896 (as Readings in Gower); ed Macaulay, Oxford 1903; ed T. Tiller 1968 (modernized). In English. At least 60 mss; *see* Macaulay, Complete works, above vol 2 p. cxxxviii; H. Spies, E Studien 28 1900, JEGP 4 1902, E Studien 32 1903, 34 1904; Archiv 110 1903; J. H. Fisher, Gower, New York 1964, appendix A (omits Christ Church Oxford ms, unknown to Macaulay).

Vox clamantis. Ed H. O. Coxe 1850 (Roxburghe Club); tr E. W. Stockton, Seattle 1962 (in Major Latin works of Gower). In Latin.

Mirour de l'omme. In Complete works, ed Macaulay, above. In French.

The minor French and Latin poems were ed H. O. Coxe with Vox clamantis, above ; see also Political poems and songs, ed T. Wright 1859 (Rolls ser) and E. Stengel, Ausgaben und Abhandlungen (*Marburg*) 64 1886.

In praise of peace. In Wright, above.

For Balade moral of gode counsayle *see* M. Forster, Archiv 102 1899.

Un traité: Quixley's translation. Ed H. N. MacCracken, Yorkshire Archaeological Jnl 20 1909.

§ 2

On Gower's tomb in Southwark Cathedral, see Berthelette's edn of Confessio, 1532–4; *also* J. Stow, Survey of London, 1633 p. 450; R. Gough, Sepulchral monuments vol 2, 1786 p. 24.

Thynne, F. In his Animadversions, 1599.

Leland, J. In his Commentarii de scriptoribus britannicis, Oxford 1709.

Todd, H. J. Illustrations of Gower and Chaucer. 1810.

Nicolas, H. N. Gower the poet. Retrospective Rev 2nd ser 2 1827.

Child, F. J. Observations on the language of Gower's Confessio amantis. Memoirs of Amer Acad of Arts & Sciences 8 1867–73.

Hales, J. W. The Confessio amantis. Athenaeum 24 Dec 1881. *See also* DNB.

Bech, L. Das Verhältnis der Confessio amantis zur Legende of goode women. Anglia 5 1882.

Meyer, K. Gowers Beziehungen zu Chaucer und Richard II. Bonn 1889.

Tiete, G. Zu Gowers Confessio amantis: lexicalisches. Breslau 1889.

Flügel, E. Pyramus und Thisbe. Anglia 12 1889.

— Gowers Mirour de l'homme und Chaucers Prologue. Anglia 24 1901.

Höfer, P. Alliteration bei Gower. Leipzig 1890.

Rumbaur, O. Die Geschichte von Appius und Virginia. Breslau 1890.

Lücke, E. Das Leben der Constanze bei Trivet, Gower und Chaucer. Anglia 14 1892.

Easton, M. W. The rhymes of Gower's Confessio amantis. Philadelphia 1895.

Koeppel, E. Ballades and Chaucer. E Studien 20 1895.

Eichinger, J. Die Troja Sage als Stoffquelle. Munich 1900.

Stollreither, E. Quellen-Nachweise. Munich 1901.

Fowler, R. E. Une source française des poèmes de Gower. Mâcon 1905.

Hamilton, G. L. Gower's use of the enlarged Roman de Troie. PMLA 20 1905.

— Some sources of the seventh book of Gower's Confessio amantis. MP 9 1912.

— Studies in the sources of Gower. JEGP 26 1927.

Ker, W. P. In his Essays on medieval literature, 1905.

Spies, H. Wörterbucharbeit. Archiv 116 1906.

Koellreuter, M. In his Das Privatleben in England, Zürich 1908.

Tatlock, J. S. P. and L. Kittredge. The date of Chaucer's Troilus: development and chronology of Chaucer's works, Chaucer Soc 2nd ser 37 1907, 42 1909.

Gebhard, H. Langlands und Gowers Kritik der kirchlichen Verhältnisse. Homburg 1911.

Dodd, W. G. Courtly love in Chaucer and Gower. Boston 1913.

Lowes, J. L. Spenser and Gower's Mirour. PMLA 29 1914.

Cohen, H. L. The Ballade. New York 1915.

Eberhard, O. Der Bauernaufstand vom Jahre 1381 in der englischen Poesie. Anglistische Forschungen 51 1917.

Knowlton, E. C. The allegorical figure Genius. Classical Philology 15 1920. *See also* MLN 39 1924.

Berndt, E. Nature in Gower. Palaestra 90 1923.

Garratt, R. M. Confessio amantis and the Legend of good women. JEGP 22 1923.

Pietsch, K. Zur Frage nach der portugiesischen Übersetzung von Gowers Confessio amantis. In The [J. M.] Manly anniversary studies, Chicago 1923.

Welter, J. T. L'exemplum dans la littérature religieuse et didactique du Moyen Age. Paris 1927.

Gilbert, A. H. Notes on the influence of the secretum secretorum: the seventh book of Gower's Confessio amantis. Speculum 3 1928.

Naunin, T. In his Der Einfluss der mittelalterlichen Rhetorik auf Chaucers Dichtung, Bonn 1929.

Manly, J. M. On the question of the Portuguese translation of Gower's Confessio amantis. MP 27 1930.

Bone, G. Extant mss printed by Wynkyn de Worde. Library 4th ser 12 1931. *See* N. F. Blake, Anglia 85 1967.

Fox, G. G. The mediaeval sciences in the works of Gower. Princeton 1931.

Kaplan, T. H. Gower's vocabulary. JEGP 31 1932.

Krappe, A. H. Le thème de la science stérile chez Gower et chez Goethe. Revue de Littérature Comparée 12 1932.

Kar, G. In his Thoughts on the medieval lyric, Oxford 1933.

Mohl, R. In her Three estates in medieval and Renaissance literature, New York 1933.

Casson, L. F. Studies in the diction of the Confessio amantis. E Studies 69 1934.

Horton, B. J. C. Notes on the language of Gower. E Studies 16 1934.

Daniels, R. B. Rhetoric in Gower's In praise of peace. SP 32 1935.

Lewis, C. S. In his Allegory of love, Oxford 1936.

Coffman, G. R. Gower in his most significant role. In Elizabethan studies in honor of G. F. Reynolds, Boulder 1945; rptd in Middle English survey, ed E. Vasta, Notre Dame 1965.

— Gower: mentor for royalty. PMLA 69 1954.

Bland, D. S. The poetry of Gower. English 6 1947.

Sitwell, G. Gower and the last years of Edward III. SP 45 1948.

Thorpe, L. A source of the Confessio amantis. MLR 43 1948.

Bennett, J. A. W. Caxton and Gower. MLR 45 1950.

— Gower's 'honeste love'. In Patterns of love and courtesy: essays in memory of C. S. Lewis, 1966.

Seaton, E. Le songe vert. MÆ 19 1950.

Wickert, M. Studien zu Gower. Cologne 1953.

Beicher, P. E. Use of Aurora in Vox clamantis. Speculum 30 1955.

Raymo, R. R. Vox clamantis and Speculum stultorum. MLN 70 1955.

Fison, P. The poet in Gower. EC 8 1958.

Russell, P. E. Robert Payn and Juan de Cuenca: translators of Gower's Confessio amantis. MÆ 30 1961.

Legge, M. D. In her Anglo-Norman literature and its background, Oxford 1963.

Murphy, J. J. Confessio amantis and the first discussion of rhetoric in the English language. PQ 41 1963.

Fisher, J. H. Gower: moral philosopher and friend of Chaucer. New York 1964.

McNally, J. J. The penitential and courtly tradition in Gower's Confessio amantis. In Studies in medieval culture, ed J. R. Sommerfeldt, Western Univ Michigan 1964.

Ferguson, A. B. In his Articulate citizen and the English Renaissance, Durham NC 1965.

Weber, E. Gower: Dichter einer ethisch-politischen Reformation. Seulberg 1965.

— Gower: zur literarischen Form seiner Dichtung. Seulberg 1966.

Pearsall, D. A. Gower's narrative art. PMLA 81 1966.

Lawlor, J. On romanticism in the Confessio amantis. In Patterns of love and courtesy: essays in memory of C. S. Lewis, 1966.

Schueler, D. The age of the lover in Gower's Confessio amantis. MÆ 36 1967.

— Some comments on the structure of the Confessio amantis. In Explorations of literature, ed R. D. Dreck, Baton Rouge 1966.

Esch, A. Gowers Erzählkunst. In Chaucer in seiner Zeit: Symposium für Walter F. Schirmer, Tübingen 1968.

J. A. W. B.

GEOFFREY CHAUCER
c. 1343–1400

BIBLIOGRAPHIES etc;

COLLECTIONS: *complete works, selections, modernizations;*

MAJOR POEMS: (i) *Romaunt of the rose;* (ii) *Book of the Duchess;* (iii) *Hous of fame;* (iv) *Parlement of foules;* (v) *Troilus and Criseyde;* (vi) *Legend of good women;* (vii) *Canterbury tales: editions, selections, translations, studies;* (a) *General prologue;* (b) *Knight's tale;* (c) *Miller's tale;* (d) *Reeve's tale;* (f) *Man of law's tale;* (g) *Prioress's tale;* (h) *Sir Thopas;* (i) *Tale of Melibee;* (j) *Monk's tale;* (k) *Nun's priest's tale;* (l) *Wife of Bath's tale;* (m) *Friar's tale;* (n) *Summoner's tale;* (o) *Clerk's tale;* (p) *Merchant's tale;* (q) *Squire's tale;* (r) *Franklin's tale;* (s) *Physician's tale;* (t) *Pardoner's tale;* (u) *Shipman's tale;* (v) *Second nun's tale;* (w) *Canon's yeoman's tale;* (x) *Manciple's tale;* (y) *Parson's tale;* (z) *Chaucer's retraction;*

PROSE: (i) *Astrolabe;* (ii) *Boethius;*

MINOR POEMS;

DOUBTFUL OR SUPPOSITIOUS WORKS;

SOURCES, ANALOGUES AND LITERARY RELATIONS;

LANGUAGE, STYLE AND VERSIFICATION;

MANUSCRIPTS, CHRONOLOGY AND TEXT;

LIFE AND BACKGROUND: *biography; historical, religious and social background;*

INFLUENCE.

(1) BIBLIOGRAPHIES ETC

Cook, A. S. A bibliography of Chaucer compiled from various sources. Berkeley 1886.

Hammond, E. P. Chaucer: a bibliographical manual. New York 1908.

Corson, H. Index to proper names and subjects to Chaucer's Canterbury tales. 1911 (Chaucer Soc).

Jewett, S. English literature: Chaucer: selected references. Wellesley 1911, 1916 (rev M. H. Shackford).

Spurgeon, C. F. E. Five hundred years of Chaucer criticism and allusion. 7 pts 1914–24 (Chaucer Soc), 3 vols Cambridge 1925, New York 1960.

French, R. D. A Chaucer handbook. New York 1927, 1947 (rev).

Tatlock, J. S. P. and A. G. Kennedy. A concordance to the complete works of Chaucer and to the Romaunt of the rose. Washington 1927, Gloucester Mass 1963.

Ruud, M. B. Chaucer studies 1928. PQ 8 1929.
— Chaucer studies 1929. MLN 45 1930.

Martin, W. E. A Chaucer bibliography 1925–33. Durham NC 1935.

Bunn, O. S. A bibliography of Chaucer in English and American belles-lettres since 1900. Bull of Bibliography 19 1949.

Griffith, D. D. Bibliography of Chaucer 1908–53. Seattle 1955. Includes his earlier bibliography 1908–24.

Anderson, W. L. A check-list of supplements to Spurgeon's Chaucer allusions. PQ 32 1953.

Magoun, F. P., jr. A Chaucer gazetteer. Upsala and Chicago 1961.

Crawford, W. R. Bibliography of Chaucer 1954–63. Seattle and London 1967.

Kirby, T. A. Chaucer research 1966. Chaucer Rev 1–1967–. Annual bibliography.

Baugh, A. C. Chaucer. New York 1968. Select bibliography.

(2) COLLECTIONS

Complete Works

Ed R. Pynson 3 vols 1526; ed W. Thynne 1532, 1542, [1545?], 1561, ed W. W. Skeat 1905 (facs), D. S. Brewer, Menston 1970 (facs); ed J. Stow 1561; ed T. Speght 1598, 1602, 1687; ed J. Urry 1721; 1810; 5 vols Chiswick 1822; 1843; 6 vols 1845, rev R. Morris 1866; New York [1880]; ed A. Gilman 3 vols Boston 1880; ed W. W. Skeat 7 vols Oxford 1894–7, 1 vol Oxford 1895, 3 vols Oxford 1909; ed F. S. Ellis 1896 (Kelmscott), ed J. T. Winterich, Cleveland 1958 (facs); ed A. W. Pollard et al 1898; 2 vols New York 1901; 1903; 1906; ed A. W. Pollard 8 vols Oxford 1928–9; 2 vols Oxford 1929–30; Boston 1930; ed F. N. Robinson, Boston 1933, 1957 (rev); ed K. Malone, Baltimore 1953.

Selections

Ed F. N. Paton 1888; ed J. L. Robertson, Edinburgh 1902; ed E. A. Greenlaw, Chicago 1907; ed W. W. Skeat, Oxford 1907; ed C. G. Child, Boston 1912; ed O. F. Emerson, New York 1911; ed H. N. MacCracken, New Haven 1913; ed M. Kaluza, Leipzig 1915, 1927 (rev); ed W. A. Neilson and H. R. Patch, New York 1921; ed E. Legouis, Paris 1923; ed J. Koch, Heidelberg 1928; ed L. J. Lloyd 1952; ed C. W. Dunn, New York 1952; ed R. A. Jeliffe, New York 1952; ed E. T. Donaldson, New York 1958; ed A. C. Baugh, New York 1963; ed R. A. Pratt, Boston 1966; ed K. Kee 1967; ed L. O. Coxe, New York 1969.

Modernizations

Ed J. S. P. Tatlock and P. MacKaye, New York 1912; ed T. Morrison, New York 1949.

(3) MAJOR POEMS

§1

(i) Romaunt of the Rose

Ed F. J. Furnivall 1911 (Chaucer Soc; Thynne's text); ed R. Sutherland, Oxford 1967; ed S. G. Nichols 1967.

Kittredge, G. L. The authorship of the English Romaunt of the rose. Harvard Stud 1 1892.

Kaluza, M. Chaucer und der Rosenroman. Berlin 1893.

Schoch, A. D. The differences in the Middle English Romaunt of the rose and their bearing upon Chaucer's authorship. MP 3 1906.

Lange, H. Rettungen Chaucers: neue Beiträge zur Echtheitsfrage von Fragment A des mittelenglischen Rosenromans. Anglia 35–8 1912–14.

Walter, J. H. Astrophel and Stella and the Romaunt of the rose. RES 15 1939.

Sutherland, R. The Romaunt of the rose and source manuscripts. PMLA 74 1959.

Fleming, J. V. The Roman de la rose: a study in allegory and iconography. Princeton 1969.

(ii) Book of the Duchess

Ed F. J. Furnivall 1871 (Chaucer Soc), Lexington Kentucky 1954.

Torraca, F. Un passo oscuro di Chaucer. Jnl of Comparative Lit 1 1903.

Lowes, J. L. The dry sea and the Carrenare. MP 3 1906.

Nadal, T. W. Spenser's Daphaida and Chaucer's Book of the Duchess. PMLA 23 1908.

Cushman, L. W. Chaucer's Book of the Duchess. Univ of California Chron 11 1909.

Harrison, B. S. Medieval rhetoric in the Book of the Duchesse. PMLA 49 1934.

Stearns, M. W. A note on Chaucer's attitude toward love. Speculum 17 1942.

Galway, M. Chaucer's hopeless love. MLN 60 1945.

French, W. H. Medieval chess and the Book of the Duchess. MLN 64 1949.

— The man in black's lyric. JEGP 56 1957.

Kreuzer, J. P. The dreamer in the Book of the Duchess. PMLA 66 1951.

Bronson, B. H. The Book of the Duchess re-opened. PMLA 67 1952; rptd in Chaucer: modern essays in criticism, ed E. Wagenknecht, New York 1959.

— Concerning houres twelve. MLN 68 1953.

Schoenbaum, S. Chaucer's black Knight. MLN 68 1953.

Baker, D. C. The dreamer again in the Book of the Duchess. PMLA 70 1955.

— Imagery and structure in Chaucer's Book of the Duchess. Studia Neophilologica 30 1958.

Lawlor, J. The pattern of consolation in the Book of the Duchess. Speculum 31 1956; rptd in Chaucer criticism vol 2, ed R. J. Schoeck and J. Taylor, Notre Dame 1961.

Manning, S. That dreamer once more. PMLA 71 1956.

— Chaucer's good fair white: woman and symbol. Comparative Lit 10 1958.

Steadman, J. M. Chaucer's whelp: a symbol of marital fidelity. N & Q Sept 1956.

Lumiansky, R. M. The beareaved narrator in Chaucer's The book of the Duchess. Tulane Stud in Eng 9 1959.

Rowland, B. W. The chess problem in Chaucer's Book of the Duchess. Anglia 80 1962.

— A round tour of yvoyre (The book of the Duchess 946). N & Q Jan 1963.

— The whelp in Chaucer's Book of the Duchess. Neuphilologische Mitteilungen 66 1965.

— Chaucer as a pawn in the Book of the Duchess. Amer N & Q 6 1968.

Crampton, G. R. Transitions and meaning in the Book of the Duchess. JEGP 62 1963.

Moreton, R. L. Literary convention in the Book of the Duchess. Univ of Mississippi Stud in Eng 4 1963.

Grennen, J. E. Hert-huntyng in the Book of the Duchess. MLQ 25 1964.

Severs, J. B. Chaucer's self-portrait in the Book of the Duchess. PQ 43 1964.

Stevens M. Narrative focus in the Book of the Duchess: a critical revaluation. Annuale Medievale 7 1966.

Berlin, N. Chaucer's Book of the Duchess and Spenser's Daphnaida: a contrast. Studia Neophilologica 38 1966.

Carson, M. A. Easing of the hert in the Book of the Duchess. Chaucer Rev 1 1967.

— The sovereignty of Octovyen in the Book of the Duchess. Annuale Medievale 8 1967.

Wimsatt, J. I. The apotheosis of Blanche in the Book of the Duchess. JEGP 66 1967.

Ebel, J. G. Chaucer's The book of the Duchess: a study in medieval iconography and literary structure. College Eng Dec 1967.

Friedman, J. B. The dreamer, the whelp and consolation in the Book of the Duchess. Chaucer Rev 3 1969.

Cherniss, M. D. The Boethian dialogue in Chaucer's Book of the Duchess. JEGP 68 1969.

Delasanta, R. Christian affirmation in the Book of the Duchess. PMLA 84 1969.

Eldredge, L. The structure of the Book of the Duchess. Revue de l'Université d'Ottawa 39 1969.

Gardner, J. Style as meaning in the Book of the Duchess. Lang & Style 2 1969.

Peck, R. A. Theme and number in Chaucer's Book of the Duchess. In Silent poetry, ed A. Fowler 1969.

Brown, J. N. Narrative poems and function in the Book of the Duchess. Massachusetts Stud in Eng 2 1970.

Sadler, L. V. Chaucer's Book of the Duchess and the law of kinde. Annuale Medievale 11 1970.

Condreu, E. I. The historical context of the Book of the Duchess: a new hypothesis. Chaucer Rev 5 1971.

(iii) Hous of Fame

Ed W. Caxton [1484]; ed H. Willert, Berlin 1888; ed W. W. Skeat 1893, 1896; ed C. M. Drennan 1921; tr Skeat 1908.

Sypherd, W. O. Studies in Chaucer's Hous of fame. 1907 (Chaucer Soc).

— The completeness of Chaucer's Hous of fame. MLN 30 1915.

Imelmann, R. Chaucers Haus der Fama. E Studien 45 1912.

Manly, J. M. What is Chaucer's Hous of fame? In Anniversary papers by colleagues and pupils of G. L. Kittredge, Boston 1913.

Cook, A. S. Skelton's Garland of laurel and Chaucer's Hous of fame. MLR 11 1916.

Koch, J. Nochmals die Bedeutung von Chaucers Hous of fame. E Studien 50 1916.

Patch, H. R. Chaucer's desert. MLN 34 1919.

— Precious stones in the Hous of fame. MLN 50 1935.

Tatlock, J. S. P. Chaucer's Elcanor. MLN 36 1921.

Riedel, F. C. The meaning of Chaucer's House of fame. JEGP 27 1928.

Miller, A. H. Chaucer's secte Saturnyn. MLN 47 1932.

Teager, F. E. Chaucer's eagle and the rhetorical colours. PMLA 47 1932.

Bronson, B. H. Chaucer's Hous of fame: another hypothesis. Univ of California Papers in Eng 3 1934.

Baum, P. F. Chaucer's House of fame. ELH 8 1941.

Besser, I. Chaucers Hous of fame: eine Interpretation. Hamburg 1941.

Smyser, H. M. Chaucer's two-mile pilgrimage. MLN 56 1941.

Goffin, R. C. Quiting by tidinges in the House of fame. MÆ 12 1943.

Pratt, R. A. Chaucer borrowing from himself. MLQ 7 1946.

Williams, J. T. Words into images in Chaucer's House of fame. MLN 62 1947.

Ziegler, J. Two notes on J. T. Williams' Words into images in Chaucer's House of fame. MLN 64 1949.

Brunner, K. Chaucer's Hous of fame. Rivista di Letterature Moderne 2 1951.

Ruggiers, P. G. The unity of Chaucer's House of fame. SP 50 1953; rptd in Chaucer: modern essays in criticism, ed E. Wagenknecht, New York 1959; and in Chaucer criticism vol 2, ed R. J. Schoeck and J. Taylor, Notre Dame 1961.

—— Words into images in Chaucer's Hous of fame: a third suggestion. MLN 69 1954.

Schoeck, R. J. A legal reading of Chaucer's Hous of fame. UTQ 23 1954.

Allen, R. J. A recurring motif in Chaucer's House of fame. JEGP 55 1956.

Stillwell, G. Chaucer's O sentence in the Hous of fame. E Studies 37 1956.

Baker, D. C. Recent interpretations of Chaucer's Hous of fame and a new suggestion. Univ of Mississippi Stud in Eng 1 1960. On Allen and Ruggiers, above.

David, A. Literary satire in the House of fame. PMLA 75 1960.

Steadman, J. M. Chaucer's eagle: a contemplative symbol. PMLA 75 1960.

Bevington, D. M. The obtuse narrator in Chaucer's House of fame. Speculum 36 1961.

Cawley, A. C. Chaucer, Pope and fame. REL 3 1962.

Wilson, W. S. The eagle's speech in Chaucer's Hous of fame. Quart Jnl of Speech 50 1964.

—— Exegetical grammar in Hous of fame. Eng Lang Notes 1 1964.

—— Scholastic logic in Chaucer's Hous of fame. Chaucer Rev 1 1967.

Koonce, B. G. Chaucer and the tradition of fame: symbolism in the House of fame. Princeton 1966.

Simmons, J. L. The place of the poet in Chaucer's House of fame. MLQ 27 1966.

Grennen, J. E. Science and poetry in Chaucer's Hous of fame. Annuale Medievale 8 1967.

Sanders, B. R. Love's crack-up: the Hous of fame. Papers in Eng Lang & Lit 3 1967.

Zucker, D. H. The detached and judging narrator in Chaucer's Hous of fame. Thoth 8 1967.

Delany, S. Phantom and House of fame. Chaucer Rev 2 1968.

Bennett, J. A. W. Chaucer's Book of fame: an exposition of the House of fame. Oxford 1968.

Newton, J. M. One of the great English poems? CQ 11 1969.

Eldredge, L. Chaucer's Hous of fame and the via moderna. Neuphilologische Mitteilungen 71 1970.

Leyerle, J. Chaucer's windy eagle. UTQ 40 1971.

(iv) Parlement of Foules

Ed W. Caxton [1477]; ed W. de Worde [1530]; ed [J. Rastell 1525]: ed T. R. Lounsbury, Boston 1877; ed J. Koch, Berlin 1904; ed C. M. Drennan 1911; ed D. S. Brewer 1960; tr W. W. Skeat 1908.

Cook, A. S. The Parlement of foules 353. MLN 21–2 1906–8.

Emerson, O. F. The suitors in the Parlement of foules. MP 8 1911.

—— The suitors in the Parlement of foules again. MLN 26 1911.

—— What is the Parlement of foules? JEGP 13 1914.

Moore, E. A further note on the suitors in the Parlement of foules. MLN 26 1911.

Manly, J. M. What is the Parlement of foules? In Festschrift für L. Morsbach, Halle 1913.

Lange, H. What is the Parlement of foules? Anglia 40 1916.

—— Zu Chaucers Vogelparlament. Anglia 60 1936.

—— Die Nordwest-Stellung der Venus und der Nordwestwind in Chaucers Vogelparlament. Anglia 64 1940.

Farnham, W. E. The fowls in Chaucer's parlement. Univ of Wisconsin Stud in Lang & Lit 2 1918.

—— The contending lovers. PMLA 35 1920.

Rickert, E. A new interpretation of the Parlement of foules. MP 18 1921.

Douglas, T. W. What is the Parlement of foules? MLN 43 1928.

Langhans, V. Altes und neues zu Chaucers Parlement of foules. Anglia 54 1930.

Patrick, D. The satire in Chaucer's parliament of birds. PQ 9 1930.

Braddy, H. The Parlement of foules: a new proposal. PMLA 46 1931.

—— Chaucer's comic Valentine. MLN 68 1953.

Bronson, B. H. In appreciation of Chaucer's Parlement of foules. Univ of California Pbns in Eng 3 1935.

—— Parlement of foules revisited. ELH 15 1948.

Goffin, R. C. Heaven and earth in the Parlement of foules. MLR 31 1936.

Lumiansky, R. M. Chaucer's Parlement of foules: a philosophical interpretation. RES 24 1948.

Stillwell, G. Unity and comedy in Chaucer's Parlement of foules. JEGP 49 1950.

—— Chaucer's eagles and their choice on February 14. JEGP 53 1954.

Bethurum, D. The center of the Parlement of foules. In Essays in honor of W. C. Curry, Nashville 1954.

Emslie, M. Codes of love and class distinctions. EC 5 1955.

Everett, D. Chaucer's love visions, with particular reference to the Parlement of foules. In her Essays on Middle English literature, ed P. Kean, Oxford 1955.

McDonald, C. O. An interpretation of Chaucer's Parlement of foules. Speculum 30 1955; rptd in Chaucer: modern essays in criticism, ed E. Wagenknecht, New York 1959; and in Chaucer criticism vol 2, ed R. J. Schoeck and J. Taylor, Notre Dame 1961.

Clark, C., D. S. Brewer and M. Emslie. Natural love in the Parlement of foules. EC 5–6 1955–6.

Frank, R. W., jr. Structure and meaning in the Parlement of foules. PMLA 71 1956.

Harrison, T. P. They tell of birds: Chaucer, Spenser, Milton, Drayton. Austin 1956.

Bennett, J. A. W. The Parlement of foules: an interpretation. Oxford 1957.

Brewer, D. S. The genre of the Parlement of foules. MLR 53 1958.

Silverstein, T. Chaucer's modest and homely poem: the Parlement. MP 56 1959.

Baker, D. C. The poet of love and the Parlement of foules. Univ of Mississippi Stud in Eng 2 1961.

Manzalaoui, M. Ars longa, vita brevis. EC 12 1962.

Rowland, B. Chaucer's throstil old and other birds. Mediaeval Stud 24 1962.

Selvin, R. H. Shades of love in the Parlement of foules. Studia Neophilologica 37 1965.

Casieri, S. Osservazioni su Parlement of foules. In Studi e ricerche di letteratura inglese e americana, ed A. Lombardo, Milan 1967.

Morris, F. J. Platonic elements in the Parlement of foules. Pennsylvania Council of Teachers of Eng Bull 14 1967.

Wilhelm, J. J. The narrator and his narrative in Chaucer's Parlement. Chaucer Rev 1 1967.

Uphaus, R. W. Chaucer's Parlement of foules: aesthetic order and individual experience. Texas Stud in Lit & Lang 10 1968.

Eldredge, L. Poetry and philosophy in the Parliament of fowls. Revue de l'Université d'Ottawa 40 1970.

Chamberlain, D. S. The music of the spheres and the Parlement of foules. Chaucer Rev 5 1971.

McCall, J. P. The harmony of Chaucer's Parliament. Ibid.

von Kreisler, N. The locus amoenus and eschatological love in the Parlement of foules 204–10. PQ 50 1971.

(v) Troilus and Criseyde

Ed W. Caxton [1484]; ed W. de Worde 1517; ed R. Pynson [1526?]; ed W. S. McCormick and R. K. Root 1914 (Chaucer Soc) (incomplete); ed R. K. Root, Princeton 1926; ed R. C. Goffin 1935 (selections); ed G. Bonnard, Berne 1943 (selections); ed J. Warrington 1953 (EL) (modernized); ed D. Cook, Garden City NY 1966 (selections); ed D. S. and L. E. Brewer 1969 (selections); tr F. Kynaston, Oxford 1635 (Latin); G. P. Krapp, New

York 1932; R. M. Lumiansky, Columbia SC 1952; M. Stanley-Wrench 1965; tr Dutch, A. J. Barnouw, Haarlem 1955; French, J. R. Simon, Paris 1970 (selections).

Price, T. R. Troilus and Criseyde: a study in Chaucer's narrative method. PMLA 11 1896.

McCormick, W. S. Another Chaucer stanza? In An English miscellany presented to Dr [F. J.] Furnivall, Oxford 1901.

Cook, A. S. Archiv 119 1907. On III. 1-38.

— The character of Criseyde. PMLA 22 1907.

Wilkins, E. H. Criseida. MLN 24 1909.

— Cantus Troili. ELH 16 1949.

Patch, H. R. Troilus on predestination. JEGP 17 1918; rptd in Chaucer: modern essays in criticism, ed E. Wagenknecht, New York 1959.

— Troilus on determinism. Speculum 6 1931; rptd in Chaucer criticism vol 2, ed R. J. Schoeck and J. Taylor, Notre Dame 1961.

— Two notes on Chaucer's Troilus. MLN 70 1955.

Young K. Aspects of the story of Troilus and Criseyde. Univ of Wisconsin Stud in Lang & Lit 2 1918.

— Chaucer's renunciation of love in Troilus. MLN 40 1925.

— Chaucer's Troilus and Criseyde as romance. PMLA 53 1938.

Griffin, N. E. Chaucer's portrait of Criseyde. JEGP 20 1921.

Tatlock, J. S. P. The epilog of Chaucer's Troilus. MP 18 1921.

— The people in Chaucer's Troilus. PMLA 56 1941; rptd in Chaucer: modern essays in criticism, ed E. Wagenknecht, New York 1959.

Curry, W. C. Fortuna maior. MLN 38 1923.

— Destiny in Chaucer's Troilus. PMLA 45 1930; rptd in Chaucer criticism vol 2, ed R. J. Schoeck and J. Taylor, Notre Dame 1961.

Murry, J. M. Troilus and Criseyde. Adelphi July 1923.

French, J. M. Defense of Troilus. PMLA 44 1929.

Graydon, J. S. Defense of Criseyde. Ibid. Reply by J. M. Beatty, SP 26 1929.

Del Re, A. In his Secret of the Renaissance and other essays and studies, Tokyo 1930.

Lewis, C. S. What Chaucer really did to Il Filostrato. E & S 17 1932; rptd in his Selected literary essays, Cambridge 1969. *See Sharrock, below.*

de Selincourt, E. In his Oxford lectures on poetry, Oxford 1934.

Prokosch, F. In The English novelists, ed D. Verschoyle 1936.

Haselmayer, L. A., jr. The portraits in Troilus and Criseyde. PQ 17 1938.

Boughner, D. C. Elements of epic grandeur in the Troilus. ELH 6 1939; rptd in Chaucer criticism vol 2, ed R. J. Schoeck and J. Taylor, Notre Dame 1961.

Mizener, A. Character and action in the case of Criseyde. PMLA 64 1939; rptd in Chaucer: modern essays in criticism, ed E. Wagenknecht, New York 1959.

Shanley, J. L. The Troilus and Christian love. ELH 6 1939; rptd ibid and in Chaucer criticism vol 2, ed R. J. Schoeck and J. Taylor, Notre Dame 1961.

Wager, W. J. Fleshly love in Chaucer's Troilus. MLR 34 1939.

Kirby, T. A. Chaucer's Troilus: a study in courtly love. University Louisiana 1940.

Sams, H. W. The dual time-scheme in Chaucer's Troilus. MLN 56 1941; rptd in Chaucer criticism vol 2, ed R. J. Schoeck and J. Taylor, Notre Dame 1961.

apRoberts, R. P. Notes on Troilus and Criseyde IV 1397-1414. MLN 57 1942.

— The central episode in Chaucer's Troilus. PMLA 77 1962.

— Criseyde's infidelity and the moral of the Troilus. Speculum 44 1969.

— The Boethian god and the audience of the Troilus. JEGP 69 1970.

Mayo, R. D. The Trojan background of the Troilus. ELH 9 1942.

Speirs, J. Chaucer: (i) Troilus and Criseyde. Scrutiny 11 1942; rev in his Chaucer the maker, 1951, 1960 (rev).

Neff, S. B. Chaucer's Cressida, lufsom lady dere. In Elizabethan studies in honor of G. F. Reynolds, Boulder 1945.

— Chaucer's Pandarus. Western Humanities Rev 4 1950.

Whiting, B. J. Troilus and pilgrims in wartime. MLN 60 1945.

Pratt, R. A. A geographical problem in Troilus and Criseyde. MLN 61 1946.

— Chaucer's natal Jove and seint Jerome agayn Jovinian. JEGP 61 1962.

van Doren, M. In his Noble voice, New York 1946.

Muscatine, C. The feigned illness in Chaucer's Troilus and Criseyde. MLN 63 1948.

Slaughter, E. E. Chaucer's Pandarus: virtuous uncle and friend. JEGP 48 1949.

— Love and grace in Chaucer's Troilus. In Essays in honor of W. C. Curry, Nashville 1955.

Denomy, A. J. The two moralities of Chaucer's Troilus and Criseyde. Proc & Trans of Royal Soc of Canada 3rd ser 44 1950; rptd in Chaucer criticism vol 2, ed R. J. Schoeck and J. Taylor, Notre Dame 1961.

Lumiansky, R. M. The function of the proverbial monitory element in Chaucer's Troilus and Criseyde. Tulane Stud in Eng 2 1950.

Hagopian, J. V. Explicator Oct 1951. On III. 1744-71.

— Chaucer as psychologist in Troilus and Criseyde. Lit & Psychology 5 1955.

Meech, S. B. Figurative contrasts in Chaucer's Troilus and Criseyde. Eng Inst Essays 1950.

— Design in Chaucer's Troilus. Syracuse NY 1959.

Robertson, D. W., jr. Chaucerian tragedy. ELH 19 1952; rptd in Chaucer criticism vol 2, ed R. J. Schoeck and J. Taylor, Notre Dame 1961.

Schaar, C. Troilus' elegy and Criseyde's. Studia Neophilologica 24 1952.

Hutson, A. E. Troilus' confession. MLN 69 1954.

Joseph, B. Troilus and Criseyde: a most admirable and inimitable epicke poeme. E & S new ser 7 1954.

Saintonge, C. In defense of Criseyde. MLQ 15 1954.

Everett, D. In her Essays on Middle English literature, Oxford 1955.

d'Evelyn, C. Pandarus a devil? PMLA 71 1956.

Jelliffe, R. A. Troilus and Criseyde: studies in interpretation. Tokyo 1956.

Kleinstück, J. Chaucer's Troilus und die höfische Liebe. Archiv 193 1956.

Scott, F. S. The seventh sphere: a note on Troilus and Criseyde. MLR 51 1956.

Smyser, H. M. The domestic background of Troilus and Criseyde. Speculum 31 1956.

Green, M. N. Christian implications of knighthood and courtly love in Chaucer's Troilus. Delaware Notes 30 1957.

Bloomfield, M. W. Distance and predestination in Troilus and Criseyde. PMLA 72 1957; rptd in his Essays and explorations, Cambridge Mass 1970, and in Chaucer criticism vol 2, ed R. J. Schoeck and J. Taylor, Notre Dame 1961.

— The eighth sphere: a note on Chaucer's Troilus and Criseyde V. 1809. MLR 53 1958.

— Troilus' paraclausithryson and its setting. Neuphilologische Mitteilungen 73 1972. On v. 519-602.

Mudrick, M. Chaucer's nightingales. Hudson Rev 10 1957.

Owen, C. A., jr. Chaucer's method of composition. MLN 72 1957.

— The significance of Chaucer's revisions of Troilus and Criseyde. MP 55 1958.

— Significance of a day in Troilus and Criseyde. Mediaeval Stud 22 1960.

— Mimetic form in the central love scene of Troilus and Criseyde. MP 67 1970.

Steadman, J. M. The age of Troilus. MLN 72 1957.

Jordan, R. M. The narrator in Chaucer's Troilus. ELH 25 1958.

Sharrock, R. Second thoughts: C. S. Lewis on Chaucer's Troilus. EC 8 1958; rptd in Chaucer's mind and art, ed A. C. Cawley 1969.

Williams, G. G. Who were Troilus, Criseyde and Pandarus? Rice Inst Pamphlet 44 1958.

Moran, T. The testament of Cresseid and the Book of Troilus. Litera 6 1959.

Bayley, J. Love and the code: Troilus and Criseyde. In his Characters of love, 1960.

Gill, Sr A. B. Paradoxical patterns in Chaucer's Troilus: an explanation of the palinode. Washington 1960.

Renoir, A. Thebes, Troy, Criseyde and Pandarus: an instance of Chaucerian irony. Studia Neophilologica 32 1960.

— Criseyde's two half-lovers. Orbis Litterarum 16 1961.

Wright, H. G. A seventeenth-century modernisation of the first three books of Chaucer's Troilus and Criseyde. Berne 1960.

Bass, E. The jewels of Troilus. College Eng Nov 1961.

Borthwick, Sr M. C. Antigone's song as mirour in Chaucer's Troilus and Criseyde. MLQ 22 1961.

Gaylord, A. T. Uncle Pandarus as Lady Philosophy. Papers of Michigan Acad 46 1961.

— Chaucer's tender trap: the Troilus and the yonge, fresshe folkes. Eng Miscellany (Rome) 15 1964.

— Gentilesse in Chaucer's Troilus. SP 61 1964.

— Friendship in Chaucer's Troilus. Chaucer Rev 3 1969.

Kaske, R. E. The aube in Chaucer's Troilus. In Chaucer criticism vol 2, ed R. J. Schoeck and J. Taylor, Notre Dame 1961.

Longo, J. A. The double time scheme in book II of Chaucer's Troilus and Criseyde. MLQ 22 1961.

McCall, J. P. Chaucer's May 3. MLN 76 1961.

— The Trojan scene in Chaucer's Troilus. ELH 29 1962.

— Five-book structure in Chaucer's Troilus. MLQ 23 1962.

Utley, F. L. Scene-division in Chaucer's Troilus and Criseyde. In Studies in medieval literature in honor of A. C. Baugh, Philadelphia 1961.

David, A. The hero of the Troilus. Speculum 37 1962.

Dunning, T. P. God and man in Troilus and Criseyde. In English and medieval studies presented to J. R. R. Tolkien, 1962.

Edmunds, P. E. A defense of Chaucer's Diomede. Classical Folia 16 1962.

Adams, J. F. Irony in Troilus' apostrophe to the vacant house of Criseyde. MLQ 24 1963.

Bechtel, R. B. The problem of Criseide's character. Susquehanna Univ Stud 7 1963.

Donaldson, E. T. The ending of Chaucer's Troilus. In Early English and Norse studies presented to H. Smith, 1963; rptd in his Speaking of Chaucer, 1970.

Lever, K. The Christian classicist's dilemma. Classical Jnl 58 1963.

Malarkey, S. The corones tweyne: an interpretation. Speculum 38 1963.

Nagarajan, S. The conclusion to Chaucer's lus Troiand Criseyde. EC 13 1963.

Dronke, P. The conclusion of Troilus and Criseyde. MÆ 33 1964.

Erzgräber, W. Tragik und Komik in Chaucers Troilus and Criseyde. In Festschrift für W. Hübner, Berlin 1964.

Kean, P. M. Chaucer's dealings with a stanza of Il Filostrato and the epilogue of Troilus and Criseyde. MÆ 33 1964.

Miller, R. N. Pandarus and Procne. In Studies in mediaeval culture, ed J. R. Sommerfeldt, Kalamazoo Michigan 1964.

Siddiqui, M. N. Troilus and Cressida: treatment of the theme by Chaucer and Shakespeare. Osmania Jnl of Eng Stud (India) 4 1964.

Wenzel, S. Chaucer's Troilus of book IV. PMLA 79 1964.

Bartel, N. A. Child of night. Ball State Univ Forum 6 1965.

Brenner, G. Narrative structure in Chaucer's Troilus and Criseyde. Annuale Mediaevale 6 1965.

Davis, N. The litera Troili and English letters. RES new ser 16 1965.

Gordon, I. L. The narrative function of irony in Chaucer's Troilus and Criseyde. In Medieval miscellany presented to E. Vinaver, Manchester 1965.

— The double sorrow of Troilus. Oxford 1970.

Markland, M. F. Pilgrims errant: the doubleness of Troilus and Criseyde. Research Stud (Washington State) 33 1965.

— Troilus and Criseyde: the inviolability of the ending. MLQ 31 1970.

Mogan, J. J., jr. Further aspects of mutability in Chaucer's Troilus. Papers in Eng Lang & Lit 1 1965.

— Free will and determination in Chaucer's Troilus and Criseyde. Western Stud in Lang & Lit (Ankara) 2 1969.

Schelp, H. Die Tradition der Alba und die Morgenszene in Chaucers Troilus and Criseyde III. 1415 ff. Germanisch-romanische Monatsschrift 46 1965.

Corsa, H. Is this a mannes herte? Lit & Psychology 16 1966.

— Dreams in Troilus and Criseyde. Amer Imago 27 1970.

Howard, D. R. Courtly love and the lust of the flesh: Troilus and Criseyde. In his Three temptations, Princeton 1966.

— Literature and sexuality: book III of Chaucer's Troilus. Massachusetts Rev 8 1967.

— Experience, language and consciousness: Troilus and Criseyde II. 597–931. In Medieval literature and folklore: essays in honor of F. L. Utley, New Brunswick NJ 1970.

Masui, M. The development of mood in Chaucer's Troilus. In Studies in language and literature in honour of M. Schlauch, Warsaw 1966.

McNally, J. J. Chaucer's topsy-turvy Dante. In Studies in medieval culture vol 2, ed J. R. Summerfeldt, Kalamazoo Michigan 1966.

Russell, N. Characters and crowds in Chaucer's Troilus. N & Q July 1966.

Salter, E. Troilus and Criseyde: a reconsideration. In Patterns of love and courtesy: essays in memory of C. S. Lewis, 1966.

Bolton, W. F. Treason in Troilus. Archiv 203 1967.

Elbow, P. Two Boethian speeches in Troilus and Criseyde and Chaucerian irony. In Literary criticism and historical understanding: selected papers from the English Institute, New York 1967.

Farnham, A. E. Chaucerian irony and the ending of the Troilus. Chaucer Rev 1 1967.

Greenfield, S. B. The role of Calkas in Troilus and Criseyde. MÆ 36 1967.

Kelly, E. H. Myth as paradigm in Troilus and Criseyde. Papers in Eng Lang & Lit 3 1967.

Robbie, M. G. Three-faced Pandarus. California Eng Jnl 3 1967.

Berryman, C. The ironic design of fortune in Troilus and Criseyde. Chaucer Rev 2 1968.

Covella, F. D. Audience as determinant of meaning in the Troilus. Ibid.

Heidtmann, P. Sex and salvation in Troilus and Criseyde. Ibid.

Käsmann, H. I wolde excuse hire yit for routhe: Chaucers Einstellung zu Criseyde. In Chaucer und seine Zeit, ed A. Esch, Tübingen 1968.

Reiss, E. Troilus and the failure of understanding. MLQ 29 1968.

Sommer, G. J. The attitudes of the narrator in Chaucer's Troilus and Criseyde. New York–Pennsylvania MLA Newsletter 1 1968.

Bessent, R. R. The puzzling chronology of Chaucer's Troilus. Studia Neophilologica 41 1969.

Corrigan, M. Chaucer's failure with woman: the inadequacy of Criseyde. Western Humanities Rev 23 1969.

Durham, L. J. Love and death in Troilus and Criseyde. Chaucer Rev 3 1969.

Reilly, R. The narrator and his audience: a study of Chaucer's Troilus. Univ of Portland Rev 21 1969.

Rowland, B. Pandarus and the fate of Tantalus. Orbis Litterarum 24 1969.

Sims, D. An essay at the logic of Troilus and Criseyde. Cambridge Quart 4 1969.

Braddy, H. Chaucer's playful Pandarus. Southern Folklore Quart 34 1970.

Cook, P. G. Chaucer's Pandarus and the medieval ideal of friendship. JEGP 69 1970.

di Pasquale, P., jr. Sikernesse and fortune in Troilus and Criseyde. PQ 49 1970.

Frank, R. W., jr. Troilus and Criseyde: the art of amplification. In Medieval literature and folklore studies: essays in honor of F. L. Utley, New Brunswick NJ 1970.

Masi, M. Troilus: a medieval psychoanalysis. Annuale Mediaevale 11 1970.

Adamson, J. Chaucer's Troilus and Criseyde. Critical Rev (Melbourne) 14 1971.

Freiwald, L. R. Swych love of frendes: Pandarus and Troilus. Chaucer Rev 6 1972.

(vi) Legend of Good Women

Ed H. Corson, Philadelphia 1864; ed F. J. Furnivall 3 vols 1871–90 (Chaucer Soc); ed W. W. Skeat, Oxford 1889; tr Skeat 1907.

Legouis, E. Quel fut le premier composé des deux prologues? Le Havre 1900.

Bilderbeck, J. B. Chaucer's Legend of good women. 1902.

French, J. C. The problem of the two prologues to Chaucer's Legend of good women. Baltimore 1905.

Goddard, H. C. Chaucer's Legend of good women. JEGP 7–8 1908–9.

Kittredge, G. L. Chaucer's Alceste. MP 6 1909.

Lowes, J. L. Is Chaucer's Legend of good women a travesty? JEGP 8 1909.

—— The two prologues of the Legend of good women: a new test. In Anniversary papers by colleagues and pupils of G. L. Kittredge, Boston 1913.

Root, R. K. Chaucer's legend of Medea. PMLA 24 1909.

Schofield, W. H. The sea-battle in Chaucer's legend of Cleopatra. In Anniversary papers by colleagues and pupils of G. L. Kittredge, Boston 1913.

Lange, H. Zur Datierung des GC-Prologs zu Chaucers Legende von den guten Frauen: eine heraldische Studie. Deutsche Literaturzeitung 37 1916.

—— Über die Farben König Richards II von England in Beziehung zur Chaucer-Dichtung: eine heraldische Studie, zugleich ein weiterer Beitrag zur Legendenprologfrage. Anglia 42 1918.

—— Die Legendenprologfrage: zur Steuer der Wahrheit. Anglia 44 1920.

—— Zur Priorität des F-Textes in Chaucers Legendenprolog und zur Interpretation von F 531/2 = Gg 519/20. Ibid.

—— Die Sonnen- und die Lilienstelle in Chaucers Legendenprolog: ein neuer Beweis für die Priorität des F-Redaktion. Ibid.

—— Neue Beiträge zu einer endgültigen Lösung der Legendenprologfrage bei Chaucer. Anglia 49 1926.

—— Viktor Langhans und die Unechtheit des F-Prologs in Chaucers Legende von guten Frauen. Anglia 51 1927.

—— Neue Wege zur Lösung der Legendenprologfrage bei Chaucer. Anglia 52 1928.

—— Nochmals die Legendenprologfrage: eine Entgegnung an V. Langhans. Anglia 55 1931.

—— Die Ähnlichkeitstheorie in Chaucers Legendenprolog F. E Studien 69 1935.

Langhans, V. Der Prolog zu Chaucers Legende von guten Frauen. Anglia 41 1917.

—— Zu Chaucers Legendenprolog. Anglia 43 1919.

—— Hugo Langes Artikel in Anglia N.F. 32, S. 213. Anglia 44 1920.

—— Zur F-Fassung von Chaucers Legendenprolog. E Studien 56 1922.

—— Hugo Lange und die Lösung der Legendenprologfrage bei Chaucer. Anglia 50 1926.

—— Nochmals Chaucers Legendenprolog und kein Ende? Anglia 54 1930.

Tupper, F. Chaucer's lady of the daisies. JEGP 21 1922.

Garrett, R. M. Cleopatra the martyr and her sisters. JEGP 22 1923.

Griffith, D. D. An interpretation of Chaucer's Legend of good women. In J. M. Manly anniversary studies, Chicago 1923; rptd in Chaucer: modern essays in criticism, ed E. Wagenknecht, New York 1959.

Holthausen, F. Die Ballade in Chaucers Legendenprolog. Archiv 147 1924.

Einenkel, E. Bemerkung zu dem Streit über Chaucers Legendenprolog. Anglia 50 1926.

Koch, J. Nochmals zur Frage des Prologs in Chaucers Legend of good women. Ibid.

—— Nachtrag zu meinem letzten Aufsatz über Chaucers Legendenprolog. Ibid.

Manly, J. M. Chaucer's lady of the daisies. MP 24 1927.

Webster, K. G. T. Two notes on Chaucer's sea-fight. MP 25 1928.

Ghosh, P. C. Cleopatra's death in Chaucer's Legende of gode wommen. MLR 26 1931.

Tatlock, J. S. P. Chaucer's Bernard the monk. MLN 46 1931.

Kant, T. Chaucer's age and the prologues to the Legend. MLN 49 1934.

Estrich, R. M. Chaucer's maturing art in the prologues to the Legend of good women. JEGP 36 1937.

Galway, M. Chaucer's sovereign lady; a study of the prologue to the Legend and related poems. MLR 33 1938.

—— Cancelled tributes to Chaucer's sovereign lady. N & Q Jan 1948.

Young, K. Chaucer's appeal to the platonic deity. Speculum 19 1944.

Baum, P. F. Chaucer's glorious Legende. MLN 60 1945.

MacDonald, C. Drayton's tydy and Chaucer's tidif. RES new ser 21 1945.

Smith, R. M. The limited vision of St Bernard. MLN 61 1946.

—— Bernard the monk: nota amplificata. MLN 62 1947.

Lumiansky, R. M. Chaucer and the idea of unfaithful men. Ibid.

Hulbert, J. R. A note on the prologues to the Legend of good women. MLN 65 1950.

Malone, K. A poet at work: Chaucer revising his verses. Proc Amer Philosophical Soc 94 1950.

Koonce, B. G. Satan the fowler. Mediaeval Stud 21 1959.

Baker, D. C. Dreamer and critic: the poet in the Legend of good women. Univ of Colorado Stud in Lang & Lit 9 1963.

LaHood, M. J. Chaucer's The legend of Lucrece. PQ 43 1964.

Frank, R. W., jr. The legend of the Legend of good women. Chaucer Rev 1 1967.

Gardner, J. The two prologues to the Legend of good women. JEGP 67 1968.

Overbeck, P. T. Chaucer's good woman. Chaucer Rev 2 1968.

(vii) Canterbury Tales

Ed W. Caxton [1478], [1484]; ed R. Pynson 1492; ed W. de Worde 1498; ed T. Morell 1737; ed T. Tyrwhitt 5 vols 1775–8, 2 vols Oxford 1798; ed T. Wright 3 vols 1847–51 (Percy Soc); ed F. J. Furnivall 36 pts 1868–79 (Chaucer Soc, 6-text edn), 1901–2 (Chaucer Soc, Cambridge ms); ed A. W. Pollard 2 vols 1886–7, 1894; ed J. S. P. Tatlock 1907 (Chaucer Soc); ed A. Burrell 1908, 1912 (EL); ed W. W. Skeat 1908 (Chaucer Soc, 8-text edn); 2 vols Manchester 1911 (Ellesmere ms facs); ed J. Koch, Heidelberg 1915; ed J. M. Manly, New York 1928; Boston 1930; ed W. van Wyck 2 vols 1930; ed J. M. Manly and E. Rickert 8 vols Chicago 1940; ed I. A. Kashkin and O. B. Runner, Moscow 1943; ed A. C. Cawley 1958 (EL); Major tales, ed M. Hoy and M. Stevens 1970; ed N. Coghill 1972.

Selections

Ed R. Morris, Oxford 1867 (General prologue, Knight's tale, Nun's priest's tale), 1889 (rev W. W. Skeat); ed S. H. Carpenter, Boston 1873 (General prologue, Knight's tale); ed Skeat, Oxford 1874 (Clerk's tale, Squire's, Prioress's, Summoner's, Monk's); ed Skeat, Oxford 1877 (Man of law's tale, Pardoner's, second nun's, Canon's yeoman's); ed A. W. Pollard 1886 (General prologue, Knight's tale, Man of law's, Clerk's, Prioress's); ed A. J. Wyatt, Cambridge 1895 (General prologue, Knight's tale); ed H. Corson, New York 1896; ed F. J. Mather, Boston 1898 (General prologue, Knight's tale, Nun's priest's); ed M. H. Liddell, New York 1901 (General prologue, Knight's tale, Nun's priest's); ed A. Ingraham 1902 (General prologue, Knight's tale, Nun's priest's); ed A. J. Wyatt 1903 (General prologue, Squire's tale); ed M. B. Smith, Cambridge 1908 (General prologue, Knight's tale); ed L. Winstanley, Cambridge 1908 (Clerk's tale, Squire's); ed A. M. van Dyke 1909 (General prologue, Knight's tale); ed L. Winstanley, Cambridge 1922 (Prioress's tale, Summoner's); ed G. Boas 1926 (General prologue Knight's tale, Clerk's, Monk's, Nun's priest's); ed A. J. Wyatt 1930; ed C. M. Drennan and Wyatt 1933 (Prioress's tale, Summoner's, Monk's); ed G. H. Cowling 1934 (General prologue, Prioress's tale, Nun's priest's, Pardoner's); ed G. H. Gerould 1935; ed anon, Edinburgh 1938 (General prologue, Squire's tale, Nun's priest's); ed E. J. Howard and G. D. Wilson, Oxford Ohio 1942; ed J. Delacourt, Paris 1946; ed R. D. French 1948; ed C. W. Dunn, New York 1952; ed N. H. Wallis 1957; ed M. J. Barber 1961; ed D. Cook, Garden City NY 1961; ed D. R. Howard and J. Dean, New York 1969; ed F. King and B. Steele, Melbourne 1969.

Modernizations and Translations

Tr F. E. Hill 1935; J. U. Nicholson, New York 1935; H. L. Hitchins 1946; V. F. Hopper, Brooklyn 1948; R. M. Lumiansky, New York 1948; N. Coghill 1952 (Penguin); D. Wright 1964; tr French by E. Legouis, Paris 1908; Italian by G. Chiarini, Florence 1912, by T. Vallese 3 vols Milan 1926–31; Spanish by M. Perez y del Rio-Cosa 2 vols Madrid 1921; German by W. Hertzberg, Berlin 1925.

Studies

Bradshaw, H. The skeleton of Chaucer's Canterbury tales: an attempt to distinguish the several fragments of the work as left by the author. 1868; rptd in his Collected papers, Cambridge 1889.

Furnivall, F. J. A temporary preface to the Chaucer Society's six-text edition of Chaucer's Canterbury tales. 1868 (Chaucer Soc).

Cromie, H. Rhyme-index to the Ellesmere manuscript of Chaucer's Canterbury tales. 2 pts 1875–96 (Chaucer Soc).

Littlehales, H. Some notes on the road from London to Canterbury in the Middle Ages. 1898 (Chaucer Soc).

Hammond, E. P. On the order of the Canterbury tales. MP 3 1906.

Tatlock, J. S. P. The duration of the Canterbury pilgrimage. PMLA 21 1906.

Hinckley, H. B. Notes on Chaucer: a commentary on the prologue and six Canterbury tales. Northampton Mass 1907.

—— The debate on marriage in the Canterbury tales. PMLA 32 1917; rptd in Chaucer: modern essays in criticism, ed E. Wagenknecht, New York 1959.

—— The framing tale. MLN 48 1934.

Skeat, W. W. The evolution of the Canterbury tales. 1907 (Chaucer Soc).

Nadal, T. Spenser's Muiopotmos in relation to Chaucer's Sir Thopas and Nun's priest's tale. PMLA 25 1910.

Markert, E. Chaucer's Canterbury-Pilger und ihre Tracht. Würzburg 1911.

Kittredge, G. L. Chaucer's discussion of marriage. MP 9 1912; rptd in Chaucer: modern essays in criticism, ed E. Wagenknecht, New York 1959; and in Chaucer criticism vol 1, ed R. Schoeck and J. Taylor, Notre Dame 1960.

Tupper, F. Saint Venus and the Canterbury pilgrims. Nation 1913.

—— The quarrels of the Canterbury pilgrims. JEGP 14 1915.

Lawrence, W. W. The marriage group in the Canterbury tales. MP 11 1914.

—— Chaucer and the Canterbury tales. New York and Toronto 1950.

Young, K. The plan of the Canterbury tales. In Anniversary papers by colleagues and pupils of G. L. Kittredge, Boston 1913.

Montgomery, F. The musical instruments in the Canterbury tales. PMLA 30 1915.

Moore, S. The position of group C in the Canterbury tales. Ibid.

Hemingway, S. B. Chaucer's monk and nun's priest. MLN 31 1916.

Jones, H. S. V. The plan of the Canterbury tales. MP 13 1916.

Kenyon, J. S. Further notes on the marriage group in the Canterbury tales. JEGP 15 1916.

Baum, P. F. Notes on Chaucer. MLN 32 1917.

Schultze, K. Zu Chaucers Weib von Bath und Shakespeares Kaufmann von Venedig. Germanisch-romanische Monatsschrift 8 1920.

Knowlton, E. C. Chaucer's man of law. JEGP 23 1924.

Bennett, J. O. In his Much loved books, New York 1927.

Erskine, J. In his Delight of great books, Indianapolis 1928.

Engel, H. Structure and plot in Chaucer's Canterbury tales. Bonn 1931.

Manly, J. M. Tales of the homeward journey. SP 28 1931.

Work, J. A. The position of the tales of the manciple and the parson on Chaucer's Canterbury pilgrimage. JEGP 31 1932.

—— Chaucer's sermon and retractions. MLN 47 1932.

Brown, C. The evolution of the Canterbury marriage group. PMLA 48 1933.

—— The squire and the number of the Canterbury pilgrims. MLN 49 1934.

—— The man of law's head-link and the prologue of the Canterbury tales. SP 34 1937.

—— Author's revision in the Canterbury tales. PMLA 57 1942.

Lyons, C. P. The marriage debate in the Canterbury tales. ELH 2 1935.

Piper, E. F. Canterbury pilgrims. Iowa City 1935.

Baugh, A. C. The original teller of the Merchant's tale. MP 35 1938.

Haselmayer, L. A. The portraits in Chaucer's fabliaux. RES 14 1938.

Mariella, Sr. The parson's tale and the marriage group. MLN 53 1938.

Dempster, G. The original teller of the Merchant's tale. MP 36 1939.

Coffman, G. R. Chaucer's library and literary heritages for the Canterbury tales. SP 38 1941.

Sleeth, C. R. The friendship of Chaucer's summoner and pardoner. MLN 56 1941.

Speirs, J. Chaucer: the Canterbury tales. Scrutiny 11–12 1942–4; rev in his Chaucer the maker, 1951, 1960 (rev).

Braddy, H. Chaucerian minutiae. MLN 58 1943.

— Two Chaucer notes. MLN 42 1947.

Praz, M. Chaucer e i racconti di Canterbury. Rome 1947.

Hulbert, J. R. The Canterbury tales and their narrators. SP 45 1948.

— Chaucer's pilgrims. PMLA 64 1949.

Moore, A. K. The pardoner's interruption of the wife of Bath's prologue. MLQ 10 1949.

Sherbo, A. Chaucer's nun's priest again. PMLA 64 1949.

Owen, C. A., jr. The plan of the Canterbury pilgrimage. PMLA 66 1950.

— The crucial passages in five of the Canterbury tales: a study in irony and symbol. JEGP 52 1953; rptd in Chaucer: modern essays in criticism, ed E. Wagenknecht, New York 1959.

— Chaucer's Canterbury tales: aesthetic design in stories of the first day. E Studies 35 1954.

— Morality as a comic motif in the Canterbury tales. College Eng Jan 1956.

— The relationship between the Physician's tale and the Parson's tale. MLN 71 1956.

— The development of the Canterbury tales. JEGP 57 1958.

— The earliest plan of the Canterbury tales. Mediaeval Stud 21 1959.

— (ed). Discussions of the Canterbury tales. Boston 1962.

Clawson, W. H. The framework of the Canterbury tales. UTQ 20 1951; rptd in Chaucer: modern essays in criticism, ed E. Wagenknecht, New York 1959.

Holman, H. C. Courtly love in the Merchant's and Franklin's tales. ELH 18 1951; rptd ibid.

Neville, M. The function of the Squire's tale in the Canterbury scheme. JEGP 50 1951.

Pratt, R. A. The order of the Canterbury tales. PMLA 66 1951.

Dempster, G. The clerk's endlink. PMLA 67 1952.

Nathan, N. The number of the Canterbury pilgrims. MLN 67 1952.

Stokoe, W. G. Structure and intention in the first fragment of the Canterbury tales. UTQ 21 1952.

Greenfield, S. B. Sittingbourne and the order of the Canterbury tales. MLR 48 1953.

Kimpel, B. The narrator of the Canterbury tales. ELH 20 1953.

Lumiansky, R. M. The nun's priest in the Canterbury tales. PMLA 68 1953.

— Of sondry folk: the dramatic principle in the Canterbury tales. Austin 1955.

— Chaucer's retraction and the degree of completeness of the Canterbury tales. Tulane Stud in Eng 6 1956.

— Two notes on the Canterbury tales. In Studies in language and literature in honour of M. Schlauch, Warsaw 1966.

Shumaker, W. Chaucer's Manciple's tale as part of a Canterbury group. UTQ 22 1953.

Donaldson, E. T. Chaucer the pilgrim. PMLA 69 1954; rptd in his Speaking of Chaucer, 1971 and in Chaucer criticism vol 1, ed R. Schoeck and J. Taylor, Notre Dame 1960.

— The ordering of the Canterbury tales. In Medieval literature and folklore studies: essays in honor of F. L. Utley, New Brunswick NJ 1970.

Gibbons, R. F. Does the nun's priest's epilogue contain a link? SP 51 1954.

Severs, J. B. Author's revision in block C of the Canterbury tales. Speculum 29 1954.

Baldwin, R. The unity of the Canterbury tales. Anglistica 5 1955; rptd in Chaucer criticism vol 1, ed R. Schoeck and J. Taylor, Notre Dame 1960.

Savage, J. E. The marriage problems in the Canterbury tales. Mississippi Quart 9 1955.

Shain, C. E. Pulpit rhetoric in three Canterbury tales. MLN 70 1955.

Stillwell, G. The language of love in Chaucer's Miller's and Reeve's tale and in the Old French fabliaux. JEGP 54 1955.

Bradley, Sr R. The wife of Bath's tale and the mirror tradition. JEGP 55 1956.

Ruggiers, P. G. The form of the Canterbury tales: respice fines. College Eng May 1956.

— The art of the Canterbury tales. Madison and Milwaukee 1965.

Cawley, A. C. Chaucer's summoner, the friar's summoner and the Friar's tale. Proc Leeds Philosophical & Lit Soc 8 1957.

Kaske, R. E. The knight's interruption of the Monk's tale. ELH 24 1957.

Spector, R. D. Chaucer's The manciple's tale. N & Q Jan 1957.

Mroczowski, P. Medieval art and aesthetics in the Canterbury tales. Speculum 33 1958.

Wordsworth, J. A link between the Knight's tale and the Miller's. MÆ 27 1958.

Howard, D. R. The conclusion of the marriage group: Chaucer and the human condition. MP 57 1960.

— The Canterbury tales: memory and form. ELH 38 1971.

Major, J. M. The personality of Chaucer the pilgrim. PMLA 75 1960.

Whittock, T. The marriage debate. Theoria 14–15 1960–1.

— A reading of the Canterbury tales. Cambridge 1968.

Baker, D. C. Witchcraft in the dispute between Chaucer's friar and summoner. South Central Bull (Tulsa) 21 1961.

— Exemplary figures as characterizing devices in the Friar's tale and the Summoner's tale. Univ of Mississippi Stud in Eng 3 1962.

— Chaucer's clerk and the wife of Bath on the subject of gentilesse. SP 59 1962.

— The Bradshaw order of the Canterbury tales: a dissent. Neuphilologische Mitteilungen 63 1962.

Brosnahan, L. Does the nun's priest's epilogue contain a link? SP 58 1961.

Jordan, R. M. Chaucer's sense of illusion: roadside drama reconsidered. ELH 29 1962.

Linke, H. Szenischer Bildwechsel in Chaucers Canterbury tales. Die Neueren Sprachen new ser 11 1962.

Pace, G. B. Physiognomy and Chaucer's summoner and Alisoun. Traditio 18 1962.

Salter, E. Chaucer: Knight's tale and Clerk's tale. 1962.

Simmonds, J. D. Hende Nicholas and his clerk. N & Q Dec 1962.

Beck, R. J. Educational expectation and rhetorical result in the Canterbury tales. E Studies 44 1963.

Boothman, J. Who hath no wyf, he is no cokewold: a study of John and January in Chaucer's Miller's and Merchant's tales. Thoth 4 1963.

Craik, T. W. The comic tales of Chaucer. 1963.

Dudek, L. Art, entertainment and religion. Queen's Quart 70 1963.

Sudo, J. The order of the Canterbury tales reconsidered. Hiroshima Stud in Lang & Lit 10 1963.

Harrington, D. V. Chaucer's Merchant's tale. N & Q May 1964.

Holbrook, D. Chaucer's debate on marriage. In his Quest for love, 1964.

Huppé, B. F. A reading of the Canterbury tales. Binghampton NY 1964.

MacLaine, A. H. The student's comprehensive guide to the Canterbury tales. Great Neck NY 1964.

Penninger, F. E. Chaucer's Knight's tale and the theme of appearance and reality in the Canterbury tales. South Atlantic Quart 63 1964.

Rowland, B. Chaucer's swallow and dove sittynge on a berne (Miller's tale I. 3258, Pardoner's prol VI. 397). N & Q Feb 1964.

Watson, C. S. The relationship of the Monk's tale and the Nun's priest's tale. Stud in Short Fiction 1 1964.

Wood, C. The April date as a structural device in the Canterbury tales. MLQ 25 1964.

Hodge, J. L. The marriage group: precarious equilibrium. E Studies 46 1965.

Josipovici, G. D. Fiction and game in the Canterbury tales. CQ 7 1965.

Knox, N. The satire pattern of the Canterbury tales. In Six satirists, ed A. F. Sochatoff, Pittsburgh 1965.

Moorman, C. The philosophical knights of the Canterbury tales. South Atlantic Quart 64 1965.

Mulvey, M. The Canterbury tales: analytic notes. New York 1965.

Silvia, D. S., jr. Glosses to the Canterbury tales from St Jerome's Epistola adversus Jovinianum. SP 62 1965. Argues for Chaucer's authorship.

— Chaucer on the subject of men, women, marriage and gentilesse. Revue des Langues Vivantes 33 1967.

Turner, W. A. Biblical women in the Merchant's tale and the Tale of Melibee. Eng Lang Notes 3 1965.

Bartholomew, B. Fortuna and Natura: a reading of three Chaucer narratives. Hague 1966.

Elliott, R. W. V. The Nun's priest's tale and the Pardoner's tale. New York 1966.

Grennen, J. E. Saint Cecilia's chemical wedding: the unity of the Canterbury tales, fragment VIII. JEGP 65 1966.

MacDonald, D. Proverbs, sententiae and exempla in Chaucer's comic tales: the function of comic misapplication. Speculum 41 1966.

Cox, L. S. A question of order in the Canterbury tales. Chaucer Rev 1 1967.

Gaylord, A. T. Sentence and solaas in fragment VII of the Canterbury tales: Harry Bailly as horseback editor. PMLA 82 1967.

Hatton, T. J. Chauntecleer and the monk, two false knights. Papers in Lang & Lit 3 1967.

Robinson, I. Chaucer's religious tales. Critical Rev 10 1967.

Stevens, M. Malkyn in the man of law's headlink. Leeds Stud in Eng new ser 1 1967.

Bookhouse, C. The confessions of three pilgrims. Laurel Rev (West Virginia Wesleyan College) 8 1968.

Delasanta, R. K. Namoore of this: Chaucer's priest and monk. Tennessee Stud in Lit 13 1968.

— The horsemen of the Canterbury tales. Chaucer Rev 3 1969.

— The theme of judgment in the Canterbury tales. MLQ 31 1970.

Griffith, R. R. A critical study guide to Chaucer's Canterbury tales. Totowa NJ 1968.

Hoffman, R. L. In Critical approaches to six major English works, ed R. M. Lumiansky and H. Baker, Philadelphia 1968.

Jamais, C. Chaucer, Canterbury tales: forever England. World Lit 13 1968.

Mehl, D. Erscheinungsformen des Erzählers in Chaucers Canterbury tales. In Chaucer und seine Zeit, ed A. Esch, Tübingen 1968.

Rosenburg, B. A. The contrary tales of the second nun and the canon's yeoman. Chaucer Rev 2 1968.

Burkhart, R. E. Chaucer's Absolon: a sinful parody of the miller. Cithara 9 1969.

Dean, C. Imagery in the Knight's tale and the Miller's tale. Mediaeval Stud 31 1969.

Keen, W. To doon yow ese: a study of the host in the General prologue of the Canterbury tales. Topic 9 1969.

Williams, C. A. The host: England's first tour director. Eng Jnl 57 1969.

Beidler, P. G. The pairing of the Franklin's tale and the Physician's tale. Chaucer Rev 4 1970.

Garbaty, T. J. The monk and the Merchant's tale: an aspect of Chaucer's building process in the Canterbury tales. MP 67 1970.

Mogan, J. Chaucer and the Bona matrimonii. Chaucer Rev 4 1970.

Page, B. Concerning the host. Ibid.

Spencer, W. Are Chaucer's pilgrim's keyed to the Zodiac. Ibid.

Nist, J. Chaucer's apostrophic mode in the Canterbury tales. Tennessee Stud in Lit 15 1970.

Reiss, E. The pilgrimage narrative and the Canterbury tales. SP 67 1970.

Richardson, J. Blameth not me: a study of imagery in Chaucer's fabliaux. Hague 1970.

Woo, C. and W. Matthews. The spiritual purpose of the Canterbury tales. Comitatus 1 1970.

Berndt, D. E. Monastic acedia and Chaucer's characterization of Daun Piers. SP 68 1971.

Booker Thro, A. Chaucer's creative comedy: a study of the Miller's tale and the Shipman's tale. Chaucer Rev 5 1971.

Duncan, C. F. Straw for youre gentilesse: the gentle franklin's interruption of the squire. Ibid.

Joseph, G. Chaucerian game-earnest and the argument of herbergage in the Canterbury tales. Ibid.

Murtaugh, D. M. Women and Chaucer. ELH 38 1971.

Strohm, P. Some generic distinctions in the Canterbury tales. MP 68 1971.

White, R. B., jr. Chaucer's Daun Piers and the rule of St Benedict: the failure of an ideal. JEGP 70 1971.

Clark, J. W. This litel tretys again. Chaucer Rev 6 1972.

Fisher, J. H. Chaucer's last revision of the Canterbury tales. MLR 67 1972.

(a) General Prologue

Ed W. McLeod 1871; ed B. ten Brink, Marburg 1871; ed J. Zupitza, Marburg 1871, Berlin 1882, 1920; ed A. Monfries, Edinburgh 1875; ed E. F. Willoughby 1881, Chicago 1907, London 1940; ed J. M. D. Meiklejohn 1882; ed W. W. Skeat, Oxford 1891; ed A. J. Wyatt 1900, 1927; ed A. W. Pollard 1903, 1920; ed C. T. Onions 1904; ed H. van Dyke, New York 1909; ed M. B. Smith 1929; ed A. Burrell, Portland Oregon 1937; ed R. F. Patterson 1940; ed F. W. Robinson 1940, 1054 (rev); ed R. T. Davies 1953; ed J. Winny, Cambridge 1965; ed P. Hodgson 1969; tr Skeat 1907.

Flügel, E. Some notes on Chaucer's prologue. Jnl of Germanic Philology 1 1898.

Emerson, O. F. Some of Chaucer's lines on the monk. MP 1 1904.

Giles, E. Prologue to the Canterbury tales. Jnl of Education 73 1911.

Barnouw, A. J. De prolog tot de Kantelberg-vertelligen. Onze Eeuw 12 1912.

Harper, G. H. Chaucer's big prioress. PQ 12 1933.

Wainwright, B. B. Chaucer's prioress again: an interpretive note. MLN 48 1933.

Lynch, J. J. The prioress's gems. MLN 57 1942.

Madeleva, Sr M. Chaucer's nuns. In Century of Catholic essays, ed R. H. Gross, New York 1946.

Malone, K. Style and structure in the prologue to the Canterbury tales. ELH 13 1946; rptd in his Chapters on Chaucer, Baltimore 1951.

— Harry Bailly and Godelief. E Studies 31 1950.

Bowden, M. A commentary on the general prologue to the Canterbury tales. New York 1948.

Kellogg, A. L. and L. A. Haselmayer. Chaucer's satire of the pardoner. PMLA 66 1951.

Cunningham, J. V. The literary form of the prologue to the Canterbury tales. MP 49 1952.

— Convention as structure: the prologue to the Canterbury tales. In his Tradition and poetic structure, Denver 1960.

Duncan, E. H. Narrator's points of view in the portrait-sketches: prologue to the Canterbury tales. In Essays in honor of W. C. Curry, Nashville 1954.

Hoffman, A. W. Chaucer's prologue to pilgrimage: the two voices. ELH 21 1954; rptd in Chaucer: modern essays in criticism, ed E. Wagenknecht, New York 1959.

Swart, J. The construction of Chaucer's General prologue. Neophilologus 38 1954.

Lumiansky, R. M. Chaucer's cook-host relationship. Mediaeval Stud 17 1955.

Whitesell, J. E. Chaucer's lisping friar. MLN 71 1956.

Hyams, C. B. and K. H. Reichert. The month of April in English poetry, with special reference to Chaucer and T. S. Eliot. Die Neueren Sprachen new ser 6 1957.

Woolf, R. Chaucer as a satirist in the General prologue to the Canterbury tales. CQ 1 1959.

Berndt, R. Einführung in das Studium des Mittelenglischen unter Zugrundlegung des Prologs der Canterbury tales. Halle 1960.

Danby, J. F. Eighteen lines of Chaucer's prologue. CQ 2 1960.

Elliott, R. W. V. Chaucer's prologue to the Canterbury tales. Oxford 1960.

Owen, C. A., jr. The twenty-nine pilgrims and the three priests. MLN 76 1961.

Steadman, J. M. Chaucer's thirty pilgrims and activa vita. Neophilologus 45 1961.

Brooks, H. F. Chaucer's pilgrims: the artistic order of the portraits in the prologue. 1962.

Hart, J. A. The droghte of March: a common misunderstanding. Texas Stud in Lit & Lang 4 1962.

Reidy, J. Grouping of pilgrims in the General prologue to the Canterbury tales. Papers of Michigan Acad 47 1962.

Nevo, R. Chaucer: motif and mask in the General prologue. MLR 58 1963.

Mitchell, C. The worthiness of Chaucer's knight. MLQ 25 1964.

Presson, R. K. The aesthetic of Chaucer's art of contrast. Eng Miscellany (Rome) 15 1964.

Rowland, B. Animal imagery and the pardoner's abnormality. Neophilologus 48 1964.

Courtney, N. Chaucer's poetic vision. Melbourne Critical Rev 8 1965.

Scott, K. L. Sow-and-bagpipe imagery in the miller's portrait. RES new ser 18 1967.

Ussery, H. E. How old is Chaucer's clerk? Tulane Stud in Eng 15 1967.

Zietlow, P. N. In defense of the summoner. Chaucer Rev 1 1967.

Reiss, E. The symbolic surface of the Canterbury tales: the monk's portrait. Chaucer Rev 2–3 1967–9.

Adams, G. R. Sex and clergy in Chaucer's General prologue. Lit & Psychology 18 1968.

Grennen, J. E. Chaucerian portraiture: medicine and the monk. Neuphilologische Mitteilungen 69 1968.

Kelly, E. H. By mouth of innocentz: the prioress vindicated. Papers in Lang & Lit 5 1959.

Lenaghan, R. T. Chaucer's General prologue as history and literature. Comparative Stud in History & Philosophy 12 1969.

Raymond, R. W. The physician: Chaucer's neglected pilgrim. Icarus 19 1969.

Watkins, C. A. Chaucer's sweete preest. ELH 36 1969.

Knoepflmacher, U. C. Irony through scriptural allusion: a note on Chaucer's prioresse. Chaucer Rev 4 1970.

Jeffrey, D. L. The prior's rent. JEGP 70 1971.

Wood, C. The significance of jousting and dancing as attributes of Chaucer's squire. E Studies 52 1971.

(b) Knight's Tale

Ed W. and R. Chambers 1896; ed A. W. Pollard 1903; ed P. Chubb, New York 1908; ed A. M. van Dyke, New York 1909; ed R. J. Cunliffe 1915; ed J. A. W. Bennett 1954, 1958; ed F. W. Robinson 1960; ed A. C. Spearing, Cambridge 1966.

Tatlock, J. S. P., F. J. Mather and G. Hempl. Palamon and Arcite. MLN 23 1908.

Egg, W. Chaucer, the Knight's tale: eine literarische Skizze. Leipzig 1912.

Petersen, O. The two noble kinsmen. Anglia 38 1914.

Williams, W. H. Palamon and Arcite and the Knight's tale. MLR 9 1914.

Robertson, S. Elements of realism in the Knight's tale. JEGP 14 1915.

Curry, W. C. Astrologizing the gods. Anglia 47 1923.

— Arcite's intellect. JEGP 29 1930.

Dustoor, P. E. Notes on the Knighte's tale. MLR 22 1927.

Fairchild, H. N. Active Arcite, contemplative Palamon. JEGP 26 1927.

Hulbert, J. R. What was Chaucer's aim in the Knight's tale? SP 26 1929.

Baum, P. F. Characterization in the Knight's tale. MLN 46 1931.

Wager, W. J. The so-called prologue to the Knight's tale. MLN 50 1935.

Marckwardt, A. H. Characterization in Chaucer's Knight's tale. Ann Arbor 1947.

Webb, H. J. A reinterpretation of Chaucer's Theseus. RES 23 1947.

French, W. H. The lovers in the Knight's tale. JEGP 48 1949.

Frost, W. An interpretation of Chaucer's Knight's tale. RES 25 1949; rptd in Chaucer criticism vol 1, ed R. Schoeck and J. Taylor, Notre Dame 1960.

Ham, E. B. Knight's tale 38. ELH 17 1950.

Muscatine, C. Form, texture and meaning in Chaucer's Knight's tale. PMLA 65 1950; rptd in Chaucer: modern essays in criticism, ed E. Wagenknecht, New York 1959.

Lumiansky, R. M. Chaucer's philosophical knight. Tulane Stud in Eng 3 1952.

Parr, J. Chaucer's cherles rebellyng. MLN 69 1954.

Pratt, R. A. Joye after wo in the Knight's tale. JEGP 57 1958.

Ruggiers, P. G. Some philosophical aspects of the Knight's tale. College Eng April 1958.

Lloyd, M. A defence of Arcite. Eng Miscellany (Rome) 10 1959.

Underwood, D. The first of the Canterbury tales. ELH 26 1959.

Whittock, T. G. Chaucer's Knight's tale. Theoria 13 1959.

Halverson, J. Aspects of order in the Knight's tale. SP 57 1960.

Madden, W. A. Some philosophical aspects of the Knight's tale: a reply. College Eng March 1960.

Nakatani, K. A perpetual prison: the design of Chaucer's The knight's tale. Hiroshima Stud in Eng Lang & Lit 9 1962.

Neuse, R. The knight: the first mover in Chaucer's human comedy. UTQ 31 1962.

Herz, J. S. Chaucer's elegiac knight. Criticism 6 1964.

Hoffman, R. L. The felaweshipe of Chaucer's love and lordship. Classica et Medievalia 25 1964.

Penninger, F. E. Chaucer's Knight's tale and the theme of appearance and reality in the Canterbury tales. South Atlantic Quart 63 1964.

Rumble, T. C. Chaucer's Knight's tale 2680–3. PQ 43 1964.

Westlund, J. The Knight's tale as an impetus for pilgrimage. PQ 43 1964.

Markland, M. F. The order of the Knight's tale and the Tempest. Research Stud (Washington State Univ) 33 1965.

Vann, J. D. A character reversal in Chaucer's Knight's tale. Amer N & Q 3 1965.

Dean, C. The place in the Knight's tale. N & Q March 1966.

Fletcher, P. C. B. The role of destiny in the Knight's tale. Theoria 26 1966.

Bolton, W. F. The topic of the Knight's tale. Chaucer Rev 1 1967.

Haller, R. S. The Knight's tale and the epic tradition. Ibid.

Hargest-Gorzelak, A. A brief comparison of the Knight's tale and Sir Gawain and the Green Knight. Roczniki Humanistyczne 15 1967.

Harrington, D. V. Rhetoric and meaning in Chaucer's Knight's tale. Papers in Eng Lang & Lit 3 1967.

Biedler, P. G. Chaucer's Knight's tale and its teller. Eng Record 18 1968.

Cameron, A. B. The heroine in the Knight's tale. Stud in Short Fiction 5 1968.

Cozart, W. R. Chaucer's Knight's tale: a philosophical reappraisal of a medieval romance. In Medieval theater to the epic theater of Brecht, ed R. P. Armato and J. Spalek, Los Angeles 1968.

Loomis, D. B. Saturn in Chaucer's Knight's tale. In Chaucer und seine Zeit, ed A. Esch, Tübingen 1968.

Thurston, P. T. Artistic ambivalence in Chaucer's Knight's tale. Gainesville 1968.

Benson, C. D. The Knight's tale as history. Chaucer Rev 3 1969.

Delasanta, R. Uncommon commonplaces in the Knight's tale. Neuphilologische Mitteilungen 70 1969.

Fifield, M. The Knight's tale: incident, idea, incorporation. Chaucer Rev 3 1969.

Foster, E. E. Humor in the Knight's tale. Ibid.

Hatton, T. J. Chaucer's crusading knight: a slanted ideal. Ibid.

Meier, T. K. Chaucer's knight as persona: narration as control. Eng Miscellany (Rome) 20 1969.

Schmidt, A. V. C. The tragedy of Arcite. EC 19 1969.

Van, T. A. Second meanings in Chaucer's Knight's tale. Chaucer Rev 3 1969.

Brooks, D. and A. Fowler. The meaning of Chaucer's Knight's tale. MÆ 29 1970.

Helteman, J. The dehumanizing metamorphoses of the Knight's tale. ELH 38 1971.

Tripp, A. R. The Knight's tale and the limitations of language. Jnl of Arts & Letters (Idaho) 6 1971.

(c) Miller's Tale

Ed C. B. Hieatt, New York 1970; ed J. Winny, Cambridge 1971.

Barnouw, A. J. Miller's tale van Chaucer. Handelingen van het Zesde Nederlandse Philologencongres 1910.

Brusendorff, A. He knew nat Catoun for his wit was rude. In Studies in English philology: a miscellany in honor of F. Klaeber, Minneapolis 1929.

Pratt, R. A. Was Robyn the miller's youth misspent? MLN 59 1944.

Beichner, P. E. Absolon's hair. Mediaeval Stud 12 1950.

— Chaucer's hende Nicholas. Mediaeval Stud 14 1952.

— Characterization in the Miller's tale. In Chaucer criticism vol 1, ed R. Shoeck and J. Taylor, Notre Dame 1960.

Donaldson, E. T. Idiom of popular poetry in the Miller's tale. Eng Inst Essays 1950; rptd in his Speaking of Chaucer, 1970.

Parker, R. E. Pilate's voys. Speculum 25 1950.

Albrecht, W. P. Chaucer's Miller's tale. Explicator Feb 1951.

Coffman, G. R. The Miller's tale 3187–215: Chaucer and the seven liberal arts in burlesque vein. MLN 67 1952.

Owen, C. A., jr. One Robin or two? Ibid.

Kreuzer, J. A. The swallow in Chaucer's Miller's tale. MLN 73 1958.

Birney, E. The inhibited and the uninhibited: ironic structure in the Miller's tale. Neophilologus 44 1960.

Siegel, P. N. Comic irony in the Miller's tale. Boston Univ Stud in Eng 4 1960.

Bolton, W. F. The Miller's tale: an interpretation. Mediaeval Stud 24 1962.

Reed, M. B. Chaucer's sely carpenter. PQ 41 1962.

Cline, R. H. Three notes on the Miller's tale. HLQ 26 1963.

Olson, P. A. Poetic justice in the Miller's tale. MLQ 24 1963.

Mullany, P. F. Chaucer's miller and Pilates voys. Amer N & Q 3 1964.

Reiss, E. Chaucer's miller, pilate and the devil. Annuale Mediaevale 5 1964.

— Daun Gervase in the Miller's tale. Papers in Lang & Lit 6 1970.

Rowland, B. Alison identified (Miller's tale 3234). Amer N & Q 3 1964.

— The play of the Miller's tale: a game within a game. Chaucer Rev 5 1971.

Bentley, J. Chaucer's fatalistic miller. South Atlantic Quart 64 1965.

Brown, W. J. Chaucer's double apology for the Miller's tale. Univ of Colorado Stud 10 1966.

Biggins, D. Sym(e)kyn/Simia: the ape in Chaucer's miller. SP 65 1968.

Novelli, C. Absolon's freend so deere: a pivotal point in the Miller's tale. Neophilologus 52 1968.

Burkhart, R. E. Chaucer's Absolon. Cithara 8 1969.

Bloomfield, M. W. The Miller's tale: an unBoethian interpretation. In Medieval literature and folklore studies: essays in honor of F. L. Utley, New Brunswick NJ 1970.

Miller, R. P. The Miller's tale as a complaint. Chaucer Rev 5 1971.

(d) Reeve's Tale

Hart, W. M. The Reeve's tale: a comparative study of Chaucer's narrative art. PMLA 23 1908.

Forehand, B. Old age and Chaucer's reeve. PMLA 69 1954.

Turner, W. A. Chaucer's lusty Malyne. N & Q June 1954.

Block, A. A. ...and it is half-wey pryme. Speculum 32 1957.

Emerson, K. T. The question of lusty Malyne. N & Q July 1957.

Kaske, R. E. An aube in the Reeve's tale. ELH 26 1959.

Pratt, R. A. Symkyn coude turne coppes: the Reeve's tale 3928. JEGP 59 1960.

Copland, M. The Reeve's tale: harlotrie or sermonyng? MÆ 31 1962.

McLaine, A. H. Chaucer's wine-cask image: word play in the reeve's prologue. MÆ 31 1962.

Olson, P. A. The Reeve's tale: Chaucer's Measure for measure. SP 59 1962.

Correale, R. M. Chaucer's parody of compline in the Reeve's tale. Chaucer Rev 1 1967.

Delany, S. Clerks and quiting in the Reeve's tale. Mediaeval Stud 29 1967.

Harvey, R. W. The reeve's polemic. Wascana Rev 3 1967.

Friedman, J. B. A reading of Chaucer's Reeve's tale. Chaucer Rev 2 1968.

Baird, J. L. Law and the Reeve's tale. Neuphilologische Mitteilungen 70 1969.

Brewer, D. S. The Reeve's tale and the King's Hall, Cambridge. Chaucer Rev 5 1971.

(f) Man of Law's Tale

Ed W. and R. Chambers, Edinburgh 1883, 1888; ed N. Coghill and C. Tolkien 1969.

Knowlton, E. C. Chaucer's man of law. JEGP 23 1924.
Marie, Sr R. Chaucer and his mayde bright. Commonweal 33 1940.
Duffey, B. I. The intention and the art of the Man of law's tale. ELH 14 1947.
Beichner, P. E. Chaucer's man of law and disparitas cultus. Speculum 23 1948.
Baum, P. F. The man of law's tale. MLN 64 1949.
Block, E. A. Originality, controlling purpose and craftsmanship of Chaucer's Man of law's tale. PMLA 68 1953.
Sullivan, W. L. Chaucer's man of law as a literary critic. MLN 68 1953.
Bowen, R. O. Chaucer, the man of law's introduction and tale. MLN 71 1956.
Yunck, J. A. Religious elements in Chaucer's Man of law's tale. ELH 27 1960.
Jones, C. E. Chaucer's Custance. Neuphilologische Mitteilungen 64 1963.
Kadambi, S. The man of law's Constance. Eng Miscellany (Delhi) 3 1965.
Hamilton, M. P. The dramatic suitability of the Man of law's tale. In Studies in language and literature in honour of M. Schlauch, Warsaw 1966.
David, A. The man of law vs Chaucer: a case in poetics. PMLA 82 1967.
Harrington, D. V. Chaucer's Man of law's tale: rhetoric and emotion. Moderna Språk 61 1967.
Wood, C. Chaucer's man of law as interpreter. Traditio 23 1967.
Bloomfield, M. W. Il racconto dell'uomo di legge: la tragèdia di una vittima e la commèdia cristiana. Strumenti Critici 9 1969.
Norman, A. In Studies in language, literature and culture of the Middle Ages and later, ed E. B. Atwood and A. Hill, Austin 1969.
Farrell, R. T. Chaucer's use of the theme of the help of God in the Man of law's tale. Neuphilologische Mitteilungen 71 1970.
Labriola, A. C. The doctrine of charity and the use of homiletic figures in the Man of law's tale. Texas Stud in Lit & Lang 12 1970.
Delasanta, R. And of great reverence: Chaucer's man of law. Chaucer Rev 5 1971.
Paull, M. R. The influence of the saint's legend genre in the Man of law's tale. Ibid.

(g) Prioress's Tale

Ed C. M. Drennan 1914; ed L. Winstanley, Cambridge 1922.

Brown, C. A study of the miracle of our Lady told by Chaucer's prioress. 1910 (Chaucer Soc).
Boyd, B. Young Hugh of Lincoln and Chaucer's The prioress's tale. Radford Rev 14 1960.
Yunck, J. A. Lucre of vileyne: Chaucer's prioress and the canonists. N & Q May 1960.
Beichner, P. E. The grain of paradise. Speculum 36 1961.
Preston, R. Chaucer, his prioress, the Jews and Professor Robinson. N & Q Jan 1961.
Cohen, M. Chaucer's prioress and her tale: a study of anal character and anti-semitism. Psychoanalytic Quart 31 1962.
Gaylord, A. T. The unconquered tale of the prioress. Papers of Michigan Acad 47 1962.
Bratcher, J. T. The greyn in the Prioress's tale. N & Q Dec 1963.
Hawkins, S. Chaucer's prioress and the sacrifice of praise. JEGP 63 1964.
Ridley, F. H. The prioress and the critics. Berkeley 1965.

Lee, D. A. Chaucer's prioress and St Venus. Mankato State College Stud 3 1968.
Russell, G. H. In Medieval literature and civilisation: studies in memory of G. N. Garmonsway, 1969.

(h) Sir Thopas

Snyder, F. B. A note on Sir Thopas. MP 6 1909.
Knott, T. A. A bit of Chaucer mythology. MP 8 1911.
Moore, G. F. Ciclatoun scarlet. In Anniversary papers by colleagues and pupils of G. L. Kittredge, Boston 1913.
Manly, J. M. Sir Thopas: a satire. E & S 13 1928.
Camden, C., jr. The physiognomy of Thopas. RES 11 1935.
Lawrence, W. W. Satire in Sir Thopas. PMLA 50 1935.
Linn, I. The arming of Sir Thopas. MLN 51 1936.
Lumiansky, R. M. The meaning of Chaucer's prologue to Sir Thopas. PQ 26 1947.
Moore, A. K. Sir Thopas as criticism of fourteenth-century minstrelsy. JEGP 53 1954.
Melton, J. L. Sir Thopas' charbocle. PQ 25 1956.
Bliss, A. J. Thomas Chestre: a speculation. Litera 5 1958. On relation of Sir Launfal to Sir Thopas.
Tucker, S. I. Sir Thopas and the wild beasts. RES new ser 10 1959.
Rowland, B. Bihoold the murye wordes of the hoost to Chaucer. Neuphilologische Mitteilungen 64 1963.
Scheps, W. Sir Thopas: the bourgeois knight, the minstrel and the critics. Tennessee Stud in Lit 11 1966.
Greene, R. L. The hunt is up, Sir Thopas: irony, pun and ritual. N & Q May 1966.
Burrow, J. A. Sir Thopas: an agony in three fits. RES new ser 22 1971.
Eddy, E. R. Sir Thopas and Sir Thomas Norny: romance parody in Chaucer and Dunbar. Ibid.
Stanley, E. G. The use of bob-lines in Sir Thopas. Neuphilologische Mitteilungen 73 1972.

(i) Tale of Melibee

Lawrence, W. W. In Essays and studies in honor of Carleton Brown, New York 1940.
Stillwell, G. The political meaning of Chaucer's Tale of Melibee. Speculum 19 1944.
Kreuzer, J. R. A note on Chaucer's Tale of Melibee. MLN 63 1948.
Konagaya, Y. The Tale of Melibee and Chaucer. Stud in Eng Lit (Tokyo) 42 1965.
Strohm, P. The allegory of the Tale of Melibee. Chaucer Rev 2 1968.

(j) Monk's Tale

Gelbach, M. On Chaucer's version of the death of Croesus. JEGP 6 1907.
Crawford, S. J. Croesus' dream. TLS 26 June 1924.
Babcock, R. W. The medieval setting of Chaucer's Monk's tale. PMLA 46 1931.
Silverstein, H. T. Chaucer's Brutus Cassius. MLN 47 1932.
Jones, C. The Monk's tale: a medieval sermon. MLN 52 1937.
Seaton, E. Goode lief my wife. MLR 41 1946.
Savage, H. Chaucer and the piteous deeth of Petro glorie of Spayne. Speculum 24 1949.
Socola, E. M. Chaucer's development of fortune in the Monk's tale. JEGP 49 1950.
Braddy, H. Chaucer's Don Pedro and the purpose of the Monk's tale. MLQ 12 1952.
Pratt, R. A. Chaucer and the pillars of Hercules. In Studies in honor of [B. L.] Ullman, St Louis 1960.
Brown, J. O. Chaucer's Daun Piers: one monk or two? Criticism 6 1964.
Oruch, J. B. Chaucer's worldly monk. Criticism 8 1966.
Strange, W. C. The Monk's tale: a generous view. Chaucer Rev 1 1967.
Taylor, E. W. Chaucer's Monk's tale: an apology. College Lang Assoc Jnl 13 1969.

(k) Nun's Priest's Tale

Ed A. W. Pollard 1907, 1924; ed L. Winstanley, Cambridge 1915; ed A. J. Wyatt 1915; ed R. F. Patterson 1920; ed K. Sisam, Oxford 1926, 1940; ed N. Coghill and J. R. R. Tolkien 1959; ed M. Hussey, Cambridge 1965.

Grandgent, C. H. Chanticleer. In Anniversary papers by colleagues and pupils of G. L. Kittredge, Boston 1913.

Brown, C. Mulier est hominis confusio. MLN 35 1920.

Hotson, J. L. Colfox vs Chauntecleer. PMLA 39 1924; rptd in Chaucer: modern essays in criticism, ed E. Wagenknecht, New York 1959.

Greiner, F. J. Form and sources of the Nun's priest's tale. Catholic Education Rev 36 1938.

Severs, J. B. Chaucer's originality in the Nun's priest's tale. SP 43 1946.

Boone, L. P. Chauntecleer and Partlet identified. MLN 64 1949.

Pratt, R. A. The classical lamentations in the Nun's priest's tale. Ibid.

Donovan, M. J. The moralite of the nun's priest's sermon. JEGP 52 1953.

Lumiansky, R. M. The nun's priest in the Canterbury tales. PMLA 68 1953.

Hamm, V. M. Chaucer's heigh ymaginacioun. MLN 69 1954.

Steadman, J. M. Flattery and the moralitas of the Nonne preestes tale. MÆ 28 1959.

Maveety, S. R. An approach to the Nun's priest's tale. College Lang Assoc Jnl 4 1960.

Standop, E. Zur allegorischen Deutung der Nonnes preestes tale. In Festschrift für T. Spira, Heidelberg 1961.

Broes, A. T. Chaucer's disgruntled cleric: the Nun's priest's tale. PMLA 78 1963.

Grennen, J. E. Chauntecleer's venymous cathartics. N & Q Aug 1963.

Lenaghan, R. T. The nun's priest's fable. PMLA 78 1963.

Brindley, D. J. The mixed style of the Nun's priest's tale. Eng Stud in Africa 7 1964.

Joselyn, M. Aspects of form in the Nun's priest's tale. College Eng May 1964.

Harrington, D. V. The undramatic character of Chaucer's nun's priest. Discourse 8 1965.

Rowland, B. Owles and apes in Chaucer's Nun's priest's tale 3092. Mediaeval Stud 27 1965.

Perez Martin, J. El tono de voz en Nun's priest's tale de Chaucer. Filologia Moderna 6 1966.

Levy, B. S. and G. R. Adams. Chauntecleer's paradise lost and regained. Mediaeval Stud 29 1967.

Pearcy, R. J. The epilogue to the Nun's priest's tale. N & Q Feb 1968.

Allen, J. B. The ironic fruyt: Chauntecleer as figura. SP 66 1969.

Kauffman, C. E. Dame Pertelote's parlous parle. Chaucer Rev 4 1970.

Hieatt, C. B. The moral of the Nun's priest's tale. Studia Neophilologica 42 1970.

Meredith, P. Chauntecleer and the mermaids. Neophilologus 54 1970.

Chamberlain, D. S. The Nun's priest's tale and Boethius's De musica. MP 68 1971.

(l) Wife of Bath's Tale

Ed anon 1929; ed R. J. Beck 1964 (expurgated); ed J. Winny, Cambridge 1965.

Jones, R. F. A conjecture on the wife of Bath's prologue. JEGP 24 1925.

Rutter, G. M. The wife of Bath. Western Reserve Univ Bull 34 1931.

Slaughter, E. E. Allas! allas! that ever love was sinne. MLN 49 1934.

— Clerk Jankyn's motive. MLN 65 1950.

Coffman, G. R. Chaucer and courtly love once more: the Wife of Bath's tale. Speculum 20 1945.

Schlauch, M. The marital dilemma in the Wife of Bath's tale. PMLA 61 1946.

Huppé, B. F. Rape and woman's sovereignty in the Wife of Bath's tale. MLN 63 1948.

Albrecht, W. P. The sermon on gentilesse. College Eng April 1951.

Roppolo, J. P. The converted knight in Chaucer's Wife of Bath's tale. College Eng Feb 1951.

Shumaker, W. Alisoun in wander-land: a study in Chaucer's mind and literary method. ELH 18 1951.

Salter, F. M. The tragic figure of the wyf of Bath. Proc & Trans Royal Soc of Canada 3rd ser 48 1954.

Townsend, F. G. Chaucer's nameless knight. MLR 49 1954.

Pratt, R. A. The development of the wife of Bath. In Studies in medieval literature in honor of A. C. Baugh, Philadelphia 1961.

— Saint Jerome in Jankyn's book of wikked wyves. Criticism 5 1962.

Silverstein, T. The wife of Bath and the rhetoric of enchantment: or how to make a hero see in the dark. MP 58 1961.

Malone, K. The Wife of Bath's tale. MLR 57 1962.

Margulies, C. S. The marriages and the wealth of the wife of Bath. Mediaeval Stud 24 1962.

Hoffman, R. L. The wife of Bath as student of Ovid. N & Q Aug 1964.

Mahoney, J. Alice of Bath: her secte and gentil text. Criticism 6 1964.

Albertini, V. R. Chaucer's artistic accomplishment in molding the Wife of Bath's tale. Northwest Missouri State College Stud 28 1964.

Steinberg, A. The Wife of Bath's tale and her fantasy of fulfillment. College Eng Dec 1964.

Haller, R. S. The wife of Bath and the three estates. Annuale Mediaevale 6 1965.

Miller, R. P. The Wife of Bath's tale and medieval exempla. ELH 32 1965.

Duncan, E. H. Bear on hand in the wife of Bath's prologue. Tennessee Stud in Lit 11 1966.

Zimbardo, R. A. Unity and duality in the wife of Bath's prologue and tale. Ibid.

Curtis, P. Chaucer's wyf of Bath. Critical Rev 10 1967.

Holland, N. N. Meaning as transformation: the Wife of Bath's tale. College Eng Jan 1967.

Schmidt, A. V. C. The wife of Bath's marital state. N & Q June 1967.

Silvia, D. S., jr. The wife of Bath's marital state. N & Q Jan 1967.

Garbaty, T. J. Chaucer's weaving wife. Jnl of Amer Folklore 81 1968.

Cotter, J. F. The wife of Bath and the conjugal debt. Eng Lang Notes 6 1969.

Slade, T. Irony in the Wife of Bath's tale. MLR 64 1969.

Allen, J. B. and P. Gallacher. Alisoun through the looking glass: or every man his own Midas. Chaucer Rev 4 1970.

Levy, B. S. The wife of Bath's queynte fantasye. Ibid.

Reid, D. S. Crocodilian humor: a discussion of Chaucer's wife of Bath. Ibid.

Parker, D. Can we trust the wife of Bath? Ibid.

Koban, C. Hearing Chaucer out: the art of persuasion in the Wife of Bath's tale. Chaucer Rev 5 1971.

Rowland, B. Chaucer's Dame Alys: critics in blunderland. Neuphilologische Mitteilungen 73 1972.

— The wife of Bath's unlawfull philtrum. Neophilologus 56 1972.

Shapiro, G. K. Dame Alice as deceptive narrator. Chaucer Rev 6 1972.

(m) Friar's Tale

Ed anon, Pittsburgh 1931; ed P. Hodgson 1960.

Birney, E. After his ymage: the central ironies of the Friar's tale. Mediaeval Stud 21 1959.

Beichner, P. E. Baiting the summoner. MLQ 22 1961.

Bonjour, A. Aspects of irony in the Friar's tale. EC 11 1961.

Mroczkowski, P. The Friar's tale and its pulpit background. In English studies today vol 2, ed G. A. Bonnard, Berne 1961.

Richardson, J. Hunter and prey: functional imagery in Chaucer's Friar's tale. Eng Miscellany (Rome) 12 1961; rptd in Chaucer's mind and art, ed A. C. Cawley 1969.
— An ambiguous reference in Chaucer's Friar's tale. Archiv 198 1962.

Correale, R. M. St Jerome and the conclusion of the Friar's tale. Eng Lang Notes 2 1965.

Hatton, T. Chaucer's friar's old rebekke. JEGP 67 1968.

Passon, R. H. Entente in Chaucer's Friar's tale. Chaucer Rev 2 1968.

Paird, J. L. The Devil's privitee. Neuphilologische Mitteilungen 70 1969.

Hennedy, H. L. The friar's summoner's dilemma. Chaucer Rev 5 1971.

(n) Summoner's Tale

Kellogg, A. L. The fraternal kiss in Chaucer's Summoner's tale. Scriptorium 7 1953.

Birney, E. Structural irony within the Summoner's tale. Anglia 78 1960.

Adams, J. F. The structure of irony in the Summoner's tale. EC 12 1962.

Merrill, T. F. Wrath and rhetoric in the Summoner's tale. Texas Stud in Lit & Lang 4 1962.

Levy, B. S. Biblical parody in the Summoner's tale. Tennessee Stud in Lit 11 1966.

Fleming, J. V. The antifraternalism of the Summoner's tale. JEGP 65 1966.
— The summoner's prologue: an iconographic adjustment. Chaucer Rev 2 1968.

Hartung, A. E. Two notes on the Summoner's tale. Eng Lang Notes 4 1966.

Zietlow, P. In defense of the summoner. Chaucer Rev 1 1967.

Haskell, A. S. St Simon in the Summoner's tale. Chaucer Rev 5 1971.

Levitan, A. The parody of pentecost in Chaucer's Summoner's tale. UTQ 40 1971.

Kaske, R. E. Horn and ivory in the Summoner's tale. Neuphilologische Mitteilungen 73 1972.

(o) Clerk's Tale

Ed W. and R. Chambers, Edinburgh 1883, 1888; ed L. S. Sheppard, C. M. Barrow and E. Winkler, Madras 1900; ed K. Sisam 1923; ed J. Vallese, Naples 1939; ed J. Winny, Cambridge 1966.

Farnham, W. E. Chaucer's Clerk's tale. MLN 33 1918.

Malone, K. Patient Griseldus. Romanic Rev 20 1929.

Severs, J. B. The Job passage in the Clerke's tale. MLN 49 1934.
— Did Chaucer revise the Clerk's tale? Speculum 21 1946.
— Did Chaucer rearrange the clerk's envoy? MLN 69 1954.

Fessia, L. Sul nome Panik nel racconto del chierico di Chaucer. Anglica 2 1948.

Sledd, J. The Clerk's tale: the monsters and the critics. MP 51 1953; rptd in Chaucer: modern essays in criticism, ed E. Wagenknecht, New York 1959 and in Chaucer criticism vol 1, ed R. Schoeck and J. Taylor, Notre Dame 1960.

Rowen, R. O. Chaucer: the clerk's prologue. MLN 71 1956.

Heninger, S. K. The concept of order in Chaucer's Clerk's tale. JEGP 56 1957.

Morse, J. M. The philosophy of the clerk of Oxenford. MLQ 19 1958.

Jeffrey, L. N. Chaucer's Walter: a study in emotional immaturity. Jnl of Humanistic Psychology 3 1963.

Reiman, D. H. The real Clerk's tale: or patient Griselda exposed. Texas Stud in Lang & Lit 5 1963.

Cook, J. W. Augustinian neurosis and the therapy of orthodoxy. Universitas 2 1964.

Lavers, N. Freud, the Clerk's tale and literary criticism. College Eng Dec 1964.

Lanham, R. A. Chaucer's Clerk's tale: the poem not the myth. Lit & Psychology 16 1966.

McCall, J. P. The Clerk's tale and the theme of obedience. MLQ 27 1966.

Cunningham, J. V. Ideal fiction: the Clerk's tale. Shenandoah 19 1968.

Morrow, P. The ambivalence of truth: Chaucer's Clerk's tale. Bucknell Rev 16 1968.

Grennen, J. E. Science and sensibility in Chaucer's clerk. Chaucer Rev 6 1972.

(p) Merchant's Tale

Ed M. Hussey, Cambridge 1966; ed R. J. Blanch, Columbus 1970.

Tatlock, J. S. P. The marriage service in Chaucer's Merchant's tale. MLN 32 1917.
— Chaucer's Merchant's tale. MP 33 1936; rptd in Chaucer criticism vol 1, ed R. Schoeck and J. Taylor, Notre Dame 1960.

Farnham, W. E. The Merchant's tale in Chaucer junior. MLN 41 1926.

Schlauch, M. Chaucer's Merchant's tale and courtly love. ELH 4 1937.

Kirby, T. A. A note on the irony of the Merchant's tale. PQ 21 1942.

McGalliard, J. C. Chaucerian comedy: the Merchant's tale, Jonson and Molière. PQ 25 1946.

Sedgewick, G. G. The structure of the Merchant's tale. UTQ 17 1948.

Miller, M. The heir in the Merchant's tale. PQ 29 1950.

Burrow, J. A. Irony in the Merchant's tale. Anglia 75 1957.

Donovan, M. J. The image of Pluto and Proserpine in the Merchant's tale. PQ 36 1957.

Kaske, R. E. January's aube. MLN 75 1960.

Bronson, B. H. Afterthoughts on the Merchant's tale. SP 58 1961.

Olson, P. A. Chaucer's merchant and January's heuene in erthe heere. ELH 28 1961.
— The merchant's Lombard knight. Texas Stud in Lit & Lang 3 1961.

Jordan, R. M. The non-dramatic disunity of the Merchant's tale. PMLA 78 1963.

Elliott, J. R. The two tellers of the Merchant's tale. Tennessee Stud in Lit 9 1964.

Pace, G. B. The scorpion of Chaucer's Merchant's tale. MLQ 26 1965.

Wentersdorf, K. P. Theme and structure in the Merchant's tale: the function of the Pluto episode. PMLA 80 1965.

White, G. M. Hoolynesse or dotage: the merchant's January. PQ 44 1965.

Blanch, R. J. Irony in Chaucer's Merchant's tale. Lock Haven Rev 8 1966.

Mukherjee, M. The Merchant's tale: a study in multiple meaning. Indian Jnl of Eng Stud 7 1966.

Crane, J. K. An honest debtor?: a note on Chaucer's merchant. Eng Lang Notes 4 1967.

Pittock, M. The Merchant's tale. EC 17 1967.

Brown, E. L., jr. The Merchant's tale: why is May called Mayus? Chaucer Rev 2 1968.

—— Hortus inconclusus: the significance of Priapus and Pyramus and Thisbe in the Merchant's talc. Chaucer Rev 4 1970.

Taylor, W. P. Chaucer's technique in handling anti-feminist material in the Merchant's tale: an ironic portrayal of the senex-amans and jealous husband. College Lang Assoc Jnl 13 1969.

Field, P. J. C. Chaucer's merchant and the sin against nature. N & Q April 1970.

Schroeder, M. C. Fantasy in the Merchant's tale. Criticism 12 1970.

Shores, D. L. The Merchant's tale: some lay observations. Neuphilologische Mitteilungen 71 1970.

Harrington, N. T. Chaucer's Merchant's tale: another swing of the pendulum. PMLA 86 1971.

Otten, C. F. Proserpine: liberatrix suae gentis. Chaucer Rev 5 1971.

Rosenberg, B. A. The cherry-tree carol and the Merchant's tale. Ibid.

von Kreisler, N. A. An Aesopic allusion in the Merchant's tale. Chaucer Rev 6 1972.

Biedler, P. G. The climax in the Merchant's tale. Ibid.

(q) Squire's Tale

Ed W. and R. Chambers, Edinburgh 1882; ed A. W. Pollard 1899; ed W. J. Goodrich, Madras 1899; ed A. D. Innes 1905; ed D. Bethurum, Oxford 1965.

Jones, H. S. V. Some observations upon the Squire's tale. PMLA 20 1905.

Lowes, J. L. The Squire's tale and the land of Prester John. Washington Univ Stud 1 1913.

Braddy, H. The genre of Chaucer's Squire's tale. JEGP 41 1942.

Osgerby, J. R. Chaucer's Squire's tale. Use of Eng 11 1959.

Pearsall, D. A. The squire as storyteller. UTQ 34 1964.

Greene, R. L. Foules of ravyne and foules smale in Chaucer's Squire's tale. N & Q Dec 1965.

Haller, R. S. Chaucer's Squire's tale and the uses of rhetoric. MP 62 1965.

Berger, H., jr. The F-fragment of the Canterbury tales: part 1. Chaucer Rev 1 1967.

McCall, J. P. The squire in wonderland. Ibid.

Göller, K. H. Chaucer's Squire's tale: the knotte of the tale. In Chaucer und seine Zeit, ed A. Esch, Tübingen 1968.

Petersen, J. E. The finished fragment: a reassessment of the Squire's tale. Chaucer Rev 5 1971.

(r) Franklin's Tale

Ed anon, Pittsburgh 1931; ed A. C. Spearing, Cambridge 1966.

Schofield, W. H. Chaucer's Franklin's tale. PMLA 16 1901.

Hart, W. M. In Haverford essays in honor of F. B. Gummere, Haverford 1909.

Aman, A. Die Filiation der Franklin's tale in Chaucers Canterbury tales. Erlangen 1912.

Tatlock, J. S. P. The scene of the Frankeleynes tale visited. 1914 (Chaucer Soc).

Harrison, B. S. The rhetorical inconsistency of Chaucer's franklin. SP 32 1935.

Dempster, G. Chaucer at work on the complaint in the Franklin's tale. MLN 52 1937, 54 1939.

Bøgholm, N. A rash promise. Studia Neophilologica 15 1942.

Sledd, J. Dorigen's complaint. MP 45 1947.

Lumiansky, R. M. The character and performance of Chaucer's franklin. UTQ 20 1951.

Parks, E. W. Haynes's adaptation of the Franklin's tale. In Essays in honor of W. C. Curry, Nashville 1954.

Benjamin, E. B. The concept of order in the Franklin's tale. PQ 38 1959.

Baker, D. C. A crux in Chaucer's Canterbury tales: Dorigen's complaint. JEGP 60 1961.

Mallikarjunan, S. On three interpretations of Chaucer's The franklin's tale. Indian Jnl of Eng Stud 3 1962.

Gaylord, A. T. The promises in the Franklin's tale. ELH 31 1964.

David, A. Sentimental comedy in the Franklin's tale. Annuale Mediaevale 6 1965.

Gray, P. E. Synthesis and the double standard in the Franklin's tale. Texas Stud in Lang & Lit 7 1965.

Mann, L. A. Gentilesse and the Franklin's tale. SP 63 1966.

Severs, J. B. Appropriateness of character to plot in the Franklin's tale. In Studies in language and literature in honour of M. Schlauch, Warsaw 1966.

Wood, C. Of time and tide in the Franklin's tale. PQ 45 1966.

Berger, M., jr. The F-fragment of the Canterbury tales: part 2. Chaucer Rev 2 1967.

Burlin, R. B. The art of Chaucer's franklin. Neophilologus 51 1967.

Hatton, T. J. Magic and honor in the Franklin's tale. Papers in Lang & Lit 3 1967.

Howard, R. R. Appearance, reality and the ideal in Chaucer's Franklin's tale. Ball State Univ Forum 8 1967.

Joseph, G. The Franklin's tale: Chaucer's theodicy. Chaucer Rev 2 1967.

Peck, R. A. Sovereignty and the two worlds of the Franklin's tale. Ibid.

Boker, U. Studien zu Chaucers Franklin's tale. Regensburg 1968.

Milosh, J. Chaucer's too-well-told Franklin's tale: a problem in characterization. Wisconsin Stud in Lit 5 1968.

Kearney, A. M. Truth and illusion in the Franklin's tale. EC 19 1969.

—— The Franklin's tale. EC 21 1971.

Colmer, D. The Franklin's tale: a palimpsest reading. EC 20 1970.

Golding, M. R. The importance of keeping trouthe in the Franklin's tale. MÆ 39 1970.

Knight, S. Rhetoric and poetry in the Franklin's tale. Chaucer Rev 4 1970.

(s) Physician's Tale

Ussery, H. E. The appropriateness of the Physician's tale to its teller. Papers of Michigan Acad 50 1965.

(t) Pardoner's Tale

Ed C. M. Drennan and A. J. Wyatt 1911; ed A. W. Pollard and M. M. Barber 1929; ed C. Brown, Oxford 1935; ed A. C. Spearing, Cambridge 1965.

Kittredge, G. L. Chaucer's pardoner. Atlantic Monthly 1893; rptd in Chaucer: modern essays in criticism, ed E. Wagenknecht, New York 1959.

Tupper, F. The pardoner's tavern. JEGP 13 1914.

Curry, W. C. The secret of Chaucer's pardoner. JEGP 18 1919.

Sedgwick, W. B. Chaucer's pardoner's prologue. MLR 19 1924.

Chapman, C. O. The Pardoner's tale: a medieval sermon. MLN 41 1926.

Hamilton, M. P. Death and old age in the Pardoner's tale. SP 36 1939.

Henkin, L. J. Jacob and the hooly Jew. MLN 55 1940.

Sedgewick, G. G. The progress of Chaucer's pardoner 1880–1940. MLQ 1 1940; rptd in Chaucer: modern essays in criticism vol 1, ed R. Schoeck and J. Taylor, Notre Dame 1960.

Lumiansky, R. M. A conjecture concerning Chaucer's pardoner. Tulane Stud in Eng 1 1949.

Kellogg, A. L. An Augustinian interpretation of Chaucer's pardoner. Speculum 26 1951.

Owen, W. J. B. The old man in the Pardoner's talc. RES new ser 2 1951; rptd in Chaucer: modern essays in criticism, ed E. Wagenknecht, New York 1959.

Swart, J. Chaucer's pardoner. Neophilologus 36 1952.

Gross, S. L. Conscious verbal repetition in the pardoner's prologue. N & Q Oct 1953.

Miller, R. P. Chaucer's pardoner, the scriptural eunuch and the Pardoner's tale. Speculum 30 1955; rptd in Chaucer criticism vol 1, ed R. Schoeck and J. Taylor, Notre Dame 1960.

Duino, R. The tortured pardoner. Eng Jnl 46 1957.

Friend, A. C. The dangerous theme of the pardoner. MLQ 18 1957.

Ethel, G. Chaucer's worste shrew: the pardoner. MLQ 20 1959.

Strang B. M. H. Who is the old man in the Pardoner's tale? N & Q June 1960.

McNamara, L. F. The astounding performance of Chaucer's pardoner. Papers of Michigan Acad 46 1961.

Stockton, E. W. The deadliest sin in the Pardoner's tale. Tulane Stud in Eng 6 1961.

Evanoff, A. The pardoner as huckster: a dissent from Kittredge. Brigham Young Univ Stud 4 1962.

Kantor, B. The sin of pride in the Pardoner's tale. Stanford 1962.

Beichner, P. E. Chaucer's pardoner as entertainer. Mediaeval Stud 25 1963.

Calderwood, J. L. Parody in the Pardoner's tale. E Studies 45 1964.

Elliott, C. and R. G. Thomas. Two points of view: the Pardoner's prologue and tale. Anglo-Welsh Rev 14 1964.

Reiss, E. The final irony of the Pardoner's tale. College Eng Jan 1964.

Rowland, B. Animal imagery and the pardoner's abnormality. Neophilologus 48 1964.

Steadman, J. M. Old age and contemptus mundi in the Pardoner's tale. MÆ 33 1964.

David, A. Criticism and the old man in Chaucer's Pardoner's tale. College Eng Jan 1965.

Roache, J. Treasure trove in the Pardoner's tale. JEGP 64 1965.

Todd, R. E. The magna mater archetype in the Pardoner's tale. Lit & Psychology 15 1965.

Elliott, R. W. V. Our host's triacle: some observations on Chaucer's Pardoner's tale. REL 6 1966.

Mitchell, C. The moral superiority of Chaucer's pardoner. College Eng May 1966.

Schmidt, P. Reexamination of Chaucer's old man of the Pardoner's tale. Southern Folklore Quart 30 1966.

Stewart, D. C. Chaucer's perplexing pardoner. CEA Critic 29 1966.

Bishop, I. The narrative art of the Pardoner's tale. MÆ 36 1967.

Kiehl, J. Dryden's Zimri and Chaucer's pardoner: a comparative study of verse portraiture. Thoth 7 1965.

Nichols, R. E., jr. The pardoner's ale and cake. PMLA 82 1967.

O'Neal, C. M. The syndrome of masochism in Chaucer's pardoner: synopsis of the pardoner. Conference of College Teachers of Eng of Texas 32 1967.

Owen, N. H. The pardoner's introduction, prologue and tale: sermon and fabliau. JEGP 66 1967.

Schweitzer, E. C., jr. Chaucer's pardoner and the hare. Eng Lang Notes 4 1967.

Curtis, P. Prologue and tale in the pardoner's jape. Critical Rev 2 1968.

Dean, C. Salvation, damnation and the role of the old man in the Pardoner's tale. Chaucer Rev 3 1969.

Harrington, D. V. Narrative speed in the Pardoner's tale. Ibid.

Taitt, P. S. Harry Bailly and the Pardoner's tale. Studia Neophilologica 42 1969.

Toole, W. B. Chaucer's Christian irony: the relationship of character and action in the Pardoner's tale. Chaucer Rev 3 1969.

Halverson, J. Chaucer's pardoner and the progress of criticism. Chaucer Rev 4 1970.

(u) Shipman's Tale

Spargo, J. W. Chaucer's Shipman's tale: the lover's gift regained. Helsinki 1930.

Tupper, F. The bearings of the shipman's prologue. JEGP 33 1934.

Silverman, A. H. Sex and money in Chaucer's Shipman's tale. PQ 32 1953.

Appleman, P. The Shipman's tale and the wife of Bath. N & Q Sept 1956.

Chapman, R. L. The Shipman's tale was meant for the shipman. MLN 71 1956.

Lawrence, W. W. The wife of Bath and the shipman. MLN 72 1957.

— Chaucer's Shipman's tale. Speculum 33 1958.

Richardson, J. The façade of bawdry: image patterns in Chaucer's Shipman's tale. ELH 32 1965.

Levy, B. S. The quaint world of the Shipman's tale. Stud in Short Fiction 4 1967.

McClintock, M. W. Games and the players of games: Old French fabliaux and the Shipman's tale. Chaucer Rev 5 1971.

(v) Second Nun's Tale

Brown, C. The prologue of Chaucer's Lyf of Seint Cecile. MP 9 1912.

Jones, C. The Second nun's tale: a medieval sermon. MLR 32 1937.

Gardner, W. B. Chaucer's unworthy sone of Eve. SE 26 1947.

Reilly, C. A. Chaucer's Second nun's tale: Tiburce's visit to Pope Urban. MLN 69 1954.

Peck, R. A. The ideas of entente and translation in Chaucer's Second nun's tale. Annuale Mediaevale 8 1967.

(w) Canon's Yeoman's Tale

Ed M. Hussey, Cambridge 1965.

Kittredge, G. L. The canon's yeoman's prologue and tale. Trans Royal Soc of Lit 2nd ser 30 1910.

Baum, P. F. The Canon's yeoman's tale. MLN 40 1925.

Herz, J. S. The canon's yeoman's prologue and tale. MP 58 1961.

Baldwin, R. G. The yeoman's canons: a conjecture. JEGP 61 1962.

Grennen, J. E. The canon's yeoman and the cosmic furnace: language and meaning in the Canon yeoman's tale. Criticism 4 1962.

— Chaucer's characterization of the canon and his yeoman. JHI 25 1964.

Rosenburg, B. A. Swindling alchemist, antiChrist. Centennial Rev 6 1962.

Harrington, D. V. Dramatic irony in the Canon's yeoman's tale. Neuphilologische Mitteilungen 66 1965.

— The narrator of the Canon's yeoman's tale. Annuale Medievale 9 1968.

Reidy, J. Chaucer's canon and the unity of the Canon's yeoman's tale. PMLA 80 1965.

Whittock, T. G. Chaucer's Canon's yeoman's tale. Theoria 24 1965.

Gardner, J. The canon's yeoman's prologue and tale: an interpretation. PQ 46 1967.

Grenberg, B. L. The Canon's yeoman's tale: Boethian wisdom and the alchemists. Chaucer Rev 1 1967.

Olmert, K. M. The Canon's yeoman's tale: an interpretation. Annuale Medievale 8 1967.

Duncan, E. H. The literature of alchemy and Chaucer's Canon's yeoman's tale: framework, theme and characters. Speculum 43 1968.

O'Reilly, W. M., jr. Irony in the Canon's yeoman's tale. Greyfriar 10 1968.

Adams, G. R. The canon's yeoman, confidence man, arti st. Eng Notes 3 1969.

McCracken, S. Confessional prologue and the topography of the canon's yeoman. MP 68 1971.

(x) Manciple's Tale

Plessow, G. Des Haushälters Erzählung aus den Canterbury Geschichten Chaucers. Berlin 1929.

Root, R. K. The manciple's prologue. MLN 44 1929.

Work, J. A. The manciple's prologue. SP 29 1932.

Severs, J. B. Is the Manciple's tale a success? JEGP 51 1952.

Elliott, J. D. The moral of the Manciple's tale. N & Q Dec 1954.

Donner, M. The unity of Chaucer's manciple fragment. MLN 70 1955.

Birney, E. Chaucer's gentil manciple and his gentil tale. Neuphilologische Mitteilungen 61 1960.

Hazelton, R. The Manciple's tale: parody and critique. JEGP 62 1963.

Cadbury, W. Manipulation of sources and the meaning of the Manciple's tale. PQ 43 1964.

(y) Parson's Tale

Chapman, C. O. The Parson's tale: a medieval sermon. MLN 43 1928.

Ives, D. S. A man of religion. MLR 27 1932.

Johnson, D. R. Homicide in the Parson's tale. PMLA 57 1942.

Friend, A. C. Sampson, David and Solomon in the Parson's tale. MP 46 1949.

Kellogg, A. L. Seith Moyses by the Devel: a problem in Chaucer's Parson's tale. Revue Belge 31 1953.

Fox, R. C. Chaucer and Aristotle. N & Q Dec 1958.

— The philosophre of Chaucer's parson. MLN 75 1960.

Dunning, T. P. Chaucer's Icarus-complex: some notes on his adventures in theology. In English studies today: series 3, ed G. I. Duthie, Edinburgh 1964.

Peck, R. A. Number symbolism in the prologue to Chaucer's Parson's tale. E Studies 48 1967. Donaldson, E. T. In his Speaking of Chaucer, 1970.

Finlayson, J. The satiric mode and the Parson's tale. Chaucer Rev 6 1972.

(z) Chaucer's Retraction

Spies, M. Chaucer's retractio. In Festschrift für A. Tobler, Brunswick 1905.

Tatlock, J. S. P. Chaucer's retractions. PMLA 28 1913.

James, S. B. The repentance of Chaucer. Month 163 1934.

Madden, W. A. Chaucer's retraction and the medieval canons of seemliness. Mediaeval Stud 17 1955.

Gordon, J. D. Chaucer's retraction: a review of opinion. In Studies in medieval literature in honor of A. C. Baugh, Philadelphia 1961.

Campbell, A. P. Chaucer's retraction: who retracted what? Humanities Assoc Bull (Canada) 16 1965.

Sayce, O. Chaucer's retractions: the conclusion of the Canterbury tales and its place in literary tradition. MÆ 40 1971.

(4) PROSE

(i) Astrolabe

Ed A. E. Brae 1870; ed W. W. Skeat 1872 (Chaucer Soc), 1928 (EETS); ed R. T. Gunther, Oxford 1930.

Willoughby, E. F. Chaucer's treatise on the Astrolabe: ms 4862–9 of the Royal Library in Brussels. Antwerp 1940.

Elmquist, K. E. An observation on Chaucer's Astrolabe. MLN 56 1941.

Pintelon, P. Chaucer's treatise on the Astrolabe, ms 4862–9 of the Royal Library in Brussels. Antwerp and Hague 1941.

Wilson, W. G. Chaucer's Astrolabe. Life & Letters 13 1943.

(ii) Boethius

Ed W. Caxton 1478; ed R. Morris, Oxford 1868; ed F. J. Furnivall 1886 (Chaucer Soc).

Witcutt, W. P. Chaucer's Boethius. Amer Rev 8 1936.

Hollander, J. Moedes or prolaciouns in Chaucer's Boece. MLN 71 1956.

(5) MINOR POEMS

Ed W. Caxton [1477] (Anelida, Empty purse, Envoy to the King), rptd F. Jenkinson, Cambridge 1905 (facs); ed Caxton 1477 (Envoy to Scogan, Good counceyl, Gentilesse); ed J. Notary [1500?] (Mars and Venus); ed F. J. Furnivall 5 vols 1868–91 (Chaucer Soc; minor poems); ed J. Koch, Berlin 1883, Heidelberg 1925 (minor poems), E Studien 53 1919 (Against women); ed W. W. Skeat, Oxford 1883 (minor poems); Berkeley 1936 (Merciles beaute); tr Skeat 1909; German by Koch, Heidelberg 1928.

Furnivall, F. J. Trial-forewords to my parallel-text edition of Chaucer's minor poems. 1871 (Chaucer Soc).

Holt, L. M. Chaucer's Lac of stedfastnesse. JEGP 6 1907.

Hammond, E. P. Lament of a prisoner against fortune. Anglia 32 1909.

Kittredge, G. L. Chaucer's Envoy to Bukton. MLN 24 1909.

Tatlock, J. S. P. Notes on Chaucer: earlier or minor poems. MLN 29 1914.

Langhans, V. Chaucer's Anelida and Arcite. Anglia 44 1920.

Renwick, W. L. Chaucer's triple roundel: Merciles beaute. MLR 16 1921.

Goffin, R. C. Lenvoy de Chaucer a Scogan. MLR 20 1925.

Vogt, G. M. Generositas virtus. JEGP 24 1925.

Cowling, G. H. Chaucer's complaintes of Mars and of Venus. RES 2 1926.

Bush, D. Chaucer's Corinne. Speculum 4 1929.

French, W. C. The meaning of Chaucer's Envoy to Scogan. PMLA 48 1933.

Robertson, D. W., jr. Historical criticism. Eng Inst Essays 1950. On Trouthe.

Pace, G. B. Chaucer's Lak of stedfastnesse. SB 4 1952.

Legge, M. D. The gracious conqueror. MLN 68 1953.

Ragan, J. F. The hevenlich mede in Chaucer's Truth. Ibid.

Brewer, D. S. Chaucer's Complaint of Mars. N & Q Nov 1954.

Chewning, H. The text of the Envoy to Alison. SB 5 1955.

Stillwell, G. Convention and individuality in Chaucer's Complaint of Mars. PQ 35 1956.

Williams, G. G. What is the meaning of Chaucer's Complaint of Mars? JEGP 57 1958.

Pittock, M. Chaucer: the Complaint unto pity. Criticism 1 1959.

Carter, T. H. The shorter poems of Chaucer. Shenandoah 11 1960.

Grenn, A. W. Structure of three minor poems by Chaucer. Univ of Mississippi Stud in Eng 4 1963. On Truth, Gentilnesse, Lak of stedfastnesse.

Norton-Smith, J. Chaucer's Etas prima. MÆ 32 1963.

Hoffman, R. L. The felawshipe of Chaucer's Love and lordshipe. Classica et Medievalia 25 1964.

Scott, F. R. A new look at the Complaint of Chaucer to his empty purse. Eng Lang Notes 2 1964.

Cross, J. E. The Old Swedish Trohetsvisan and Chaucer's Lak of stedfastnesse. Saga-book 16 1965.

Pace, G. B. The Chaucerian proverbs. SB 18 1965.

Reiss, E. Dusting off the cobwebs: a look at Chaucer's lyrics. Chaucer Rev 1 1967. On ABC and To Rosamunde.

Hutlin, N. C. Anti-courtly elements in Chaucer's Complaint of Mars. Annuale Medievale 9 1968.

David, A. Chaucer's Good counsel to Scogan. Chaucer Rev 3 1969.

Cherniss, M. D. Chaucer's Anelida and Arcite: some conjectures. Chaucer Rev 5 1971.

Wimsatt, J. I. Anelida and Arcite: a narrative of complaint and comfort. Ibid.

(6) DOUBTFUL OR SUPPOSITIOUS WORKS

The equatorie of the planetis. Ed D. J. Price, Cambridge 1955 (from ms Peterhouse Cambridge 75.i).

Brown, C. An holy meditacioun: by Lydgate? MLN 40 1925.

— Chaucer's Wreched engendrynge. PMLA 50 1935.

— An affirmative reply. MLN 51 1936.

Langhans, V. Chaucers Book of the leoun. Anglia 52 1928.

Bashe, E. J. The prologue of the tale of Beryn. PQ 12 1933.

Dempster, G. Did Chaucer write An holy medytacion? MLN 51 1936.

— Chaucer's Wretched engendering and An holy medytacion. MP 35 1937.

§2

For early scholarship see E. P. Hammond, Chaucer: a bibliographical manual, New York 1908.

Essays on Chaucer, his words and works. 6 pts 1868–92 (Chaucer Soc).

Koch, J. Ein Beitrag zur Kritik Chaucers. E Studien 1 1877.

— Die Chaucer-Forschung seit 1900. Germanisch-romanische Monatsschrift 1 1909.

— Neuere Chaucer-Literatur. Anglia Beiblatt 22 1911; E Studien 46–8 1912–14.

— Neuere Beiträge zur Chaucer-Literatur aus Amerika. Anglia Beiblatt 25 1914.

— Neuere amerikanische Chaucer-Schriften. Anglia Beiblatt 28 1917.

— Alte Chaucer-Probleme und neue Lösungsversuche. E Studien 55 1921.

— Der gegenwärtige Stand der Chaucer-Forschung. Anglia 49 1926.

Würzner, A. Ueber Chaucers lyrische Gedichte. Steyr 1879.

Lounsbury, T. R. Studies in Chaucer. 3 vols New York 1892, 1962.

Pollard, A. W. A Chaucer primer. 1893, 1903 (rev).

— Chaucer. 1893.

— The development of Chaucer's genius. Academy March 1906.

Ames, P. W. Chaucer memorial lectures. 1900.

Björkmann, E. Chaucer: Englands storste medeltida skald. Stockholm 1900.

Capone, G. I poemi minori di Chaucer: saggio critico. Modica 1900.

Root, R. K. The poetry of Chaucer. Boston 1906, 1922 (rev), Gloucester Mass 1957.

Hamilton, G. L. Chauceriana. MLN 23 1908.

Mackail, J. W. In his Springs of Helicon, 1909.

Kittredge, G. L. Chauceriana. MP 8 1911.

— Chaucer and his poetry. Cambridge Mass 1915.

Knott, T. A. A bit of Chaucer mythology. MP 8 1911.

de Montmorency, J. E. G. Gardens in Chaucer and Shakespeare. Contemporary Rev Jan 1911.

Spurgeon, C. F. E. Chaucer devant la critique en Angleterre et en France. Paris 1911.

Northup, C. S. Chaucer in prose. Dial 53 1912.

McCully, B. Chivalry in Chaucer. Trans Amer Philological Assoc 44 1913.

Meyer, E. Die Charakterzeichnung bei Chaucer. Halle 1913.

Newbolt, H. The poetry of Chaucer. Eng Rev 15 1913.

Tatlock, J. S. P. Has Chaucer's Wretched engendering been found? MLN 51 1936.

Brown, B. D. Chaucer's Wreched engendrynge. MP 35 1938.

Dear, F. M. Chaucer's Book of the lion. MÆ 7 1938.

Shannon, E. F., jr. Medieval law in the Tale of Gamelyn. Speculum 26 1951.

Price, D. J. The equatorie of the planetis. Jnl of South-West Technical College & School of Art 3 1952.

Robbins, R. H. A love epistle by Chaucer. MLR 49 1954.

Kennedy, E. S. A horoscope of Messehalla in the Chaucer Equatorium manuscript. Speculum 34 1959.

Lewis, R. E. What did Chaucer mean by Of the wreched engendrynge of mankynde? Chaucer Rev 2 1968.

Snell, A. L. F. Chaucer's comments on his methods of composition. Eng Jnl 2 1913.

Edmunds, E. W. Chaucer and his poetry. 1915.

Monroe, H. Chaucer als Kritiker. Berlin 1916.

Cook, A. S. Chauceriana. Romanic Rev 8 1917.

— Chaucerian papers. Trans Connecticut Acad of Arts & Sciences 23 1919.

Drinkwater, J. Chaucer: the poet of spring. In his Prose papers, 1917.

Hayes, J. A study in Chaucer: an English poet's nature lore. Cork 1917.

Langhans, V. Untersuchungen zu Chaucer. Halle 1918.

— Zu J. Kochs Artikel in Anglia 37, 193. Anglia 49 1926.

— Zu Chaucers Traumgedichten und deren Auffassung durch A. Brusendorff. Anglia 51 1927.

Hinckley, H. B. Chauceriana. MP 16 1919.

Kaluza, M. Chaucer Handbuch. Leipzig 1919.

Emerson, O. F. Science in Chaucer. MP 17 1920.

— Chaucer essays and studies. Cleveland 1929.

Huxley, A. Chaucer. London Mercury June 1920; rptd EC 15 1965.

Jack, A. A. A commentary on the poetry of Chaucer and Spenser. Glasgow 1920.

Benham, A. R. Three Chaucer studies. South Atlantic Quart 21 1921.

Cox, S. H. Chaucer's cheerful cynicism. MLN 36 1921.

Bregy, K. The inclusiveness of Chaucer. Catholic World June 1922.

Quiller-Couch, A. T. A gossip on Chaucer; After Chaucer. In his Studies in English literature: 2nd series, Cambridge 1922.

Grey, P. W. In her Shepherd's crown, New York 1923.

Iijima, I. Langland and Chaucer. Boston 1925.

Madeleva, Sr M. Chaucer's nuns and other essays. New York 1925.

— A lost language and other essays on Chaucer. New York 1951.

Woolf, V. Pastons and Chaucer. In her Common reader, 1925.

Boas, G. Chaucer and Spenser contrasted as narrative poets. 1926.

Manly, J. M. Some new light on Chaucer: lectures delivered at the Lowell Institute. New York 1926.

Raleigh, W. A. In his On writings and writers, 1926.

Wilson, G. P. Chaucer and oral reading. South Atlantic Quart 25 1926.

Cowling, G. H. Chaucer. 1927.

Hill, M. A. Rhetorical balance in Chaucer's poetry. PMLA 42 1927.

Patch, H. R. Chaucer and Lady Fortune. MLR 22 1927.

— Chauceriana. E Studien 65 1921.

— On rereading Chaucer. Cambridge Mass 1939.

— Chaucer and youth. College Eng Oct 1949.

— The subjects of Chaucer's poetry. In Franciplegius: medieval and linguistic studies in honor of F. P. Magoun, New York 1965.

Thompson, N. M. A new way with Chaucer. Univ of California Chron 29 1927.

Kellett, E. E. Chaucer and his influence. In his Reconsiderations, Cambridge 1928.

Krog, F. Studien zu Chaucer und Langland. Heidelberg 1928.

Lüdeke, H. Die Funktionen des Erzählers in Chaucers epischer Dichtung. Halle 1928.

Schirmer, W. F. Das Bild Chaucers in der Forschung der letzten Jahre. Die Neueren Sprachen 36 1928.

— Chaucer. Die Literatur 39 1937.

Stewart, G. R., jr. The moral Chaucer. In Essays in criticism by members of the Department of English, University of California, Berkeley 1928.

Chapman, C. O. Chaucer on preachers and preaching. PMLA 44 1929.

Getty, A. K. Chaucer's changing conception of the humble lover. PMLA 44 1929.

— The medieval-modern conflict in Chaucer's poetry. PMLA 47 1932.

Martin, D. A first book about Chaucer. 1929.

Noyes, A. Chaucer. Bookman 76 1929, 78 1930.

— In his Pageant of letters, 1946.

Canby, H. S. Chaucer renewed. Saturday Rev of Lit 6 1930.

Hall, J. N. Flying with Chaucer. New York 1930.

Lowes, J. L. The art of Chaucer. Proc Br Acad 16 1930.

— Chaucer and the development of his genius. Boston 1934.

Vallese, T. Chaucer visto da un Italiano. Rome 1930.

— La poesia di Chaucer. Naples 1941.

Ellis, C. B. The humour of Chaucer. Holborn Rev 22 1931.

Langenfelt, G. Englands Boccaccio. Finsk Tidskrift 110 1931.

Masefield, J. Chaucer. Cambridge 1931.

— In his Recent prose, 1933.

Brown, C. Three Chaucer studies. New York 1932.

Dempster, G. Dramatic irony in Chaucer. Stanford 1932.

Chesterton, G. K. Chaucer. 1932.

— On Mr Chaucer. In his All I survey: a book of essays, 1933.

Herrick, J. B. Why I read Chaucer at seventy. Annals of Medical History 5 1933.

Strahan, S. The largeness of Chaucer. Catholic Educational Rev 31 1933.

McNabb, Fr V. Chaucer: a study in genius and ethics. 1934.

Manly, J. M. Three recent Chaucer studies. RES 10 1934.

— A defense of his criticism of three Chaucer studies. RES 11 1935.

Goffin, R. C. Chaucer and elocution. MÆ 4 1935.

Connolly, T. L. Chaucer. Bronx 1936.

Herben, S. J., jr. Arms and armor in Chaucer. Speculum 12 1937.

Marcus, H. Chaucer: der Freund des einfachen Mannes. Archiv 171-2 1937.

Tuve, R. Spring in Chaucer and before him. MLN 52 1937.

Whitmore, Sr M. E. Medieval English domestic life and amusements in the works of Chaucer. Washington 1937.

Clemen, W. Der junge Chaucer: Grundlagen und Entwicklung seiner Dichtung. Bochum-Langendreer 1938, Göttingen 1963 (enlarged as Chaucers frühe Dichtung); tr 1963.

Crosby, R. Chaucer and the custom of oral delivery. Speculum 13 1938.

Haselmayer, L. A. The portraits in Chaucer's fabliaux. RES 14 1938.

Birney, E. The beginnings of Chaucer's irony. PMLA 54 1939.

— The two worlds of Chaucer. Manitoba Arts Rev 4 1941.

— Is Chaucer's irony a modern discovery? JEGP 41 1942.

Lange, H. Die Adler in Liebesvisionen Chaucers. Archiv 175 1939.

Chambers, R. W. Chaucer: springtide of English poetry. TLS 21 April 1940.

Shelly, P. V. D. The living Chaucer. Philadelphia 1940.

Braddy, H. Three Chaucer notes. In Essays and studies in honor of Carleton Brown, New York 1940.

— Chaucer: realism or obscenity? Arlington Quart 2 1969.

Alexander, H. Chaucer after six centuries. Queen's Quart 47 1940.

Bronson, B. H. Chaucer's art in relation to his audience. In his Five studies in literature, Berkeley 1940.

— In search of Chaucer. Toronto 1960.

Kashkeen, I. Chaucer. International Lit (USSR) pts 5-6 1940.

— The realism of Chaucer. Literary Critic (USSR) 1940.

Pratt, R. A. Chaucer: the works. Progress of Medieval & Renaissance Stud in US & Canada 15 1940.

— Chaucer borrowing from himself. MLQ 7 1946.

Tupper, F. Chaucer and the Cambridge edition. JEGP 39 1940.

Heraucourt, W. Chaucers Vorstellung von den geistigseelischen Kräften des Menschen. Anglia 65 1941.

Jelliffe, R. A. Chaucer 1340-1940. College Eng May 1941.

Davids, E. I. G. A fourteenth-century Dickens. Dickensian 39 1943.

Long, E. H. Chaucer as a master of the short story. Delaware Notes 16 1943.

Schlauch, M. Chaucer's doctrine of kings and tyrants. Speculum 20 1945.

Baum, P. F. Chaucer's metrical prose. JEGP 45 1946.

— Chaucer: a critical appreciation. Durham NC 1958.

Castelli, A. Chaucer. Brescia 1946.

Slaughter, E. E. Love and the virtues and vices in Chaucer. Nashville 1946.

— Virtue according to love in Chaucer. New York 1957.

Bennett, H. S. In his Chaucer and the fifteenth century, Oxford 1947 (OHEL).

Bland, D. S. Chaucer and his critics. Jnl of South-West Essex Technical College & School of Art Dec 1947.

— Chaucer and the art of narrative verse. English 7 1949.

Lumiansky, R. M. Chaucer and unfaithful man. MLN 62 1947.

Cawley, A. C. Chaucer's prioress and Criseyde. MLR 43 1948.

— (ed). Chaucer's mind and art. Edinburgh 1969.

Stillwell, G. Chaucer in Tartary. RES 24 1948.

Moore, A. K. Chaucer's lost songs. JEGP 48 1949.

— Chaucer's use of lyric as an ornament of style. Comparative Lit 3 1951.

Smith, F. M. Chaucer's prioress and Criseyde. West Virginia Univ Bull Philological Papers 6 1949.

Chute, M. Chaucer and Shakespeare. College Eng Oct 1950.

— On the pleasure of meeting Chaucer. Eng Jnl 45 1956.

Everett, D. Some reflections on Chaucer's art poetical. Proc Br Acad 36 1950; rptd in her Essays on ME literature, Oxford 1955; and in Chaucer's mind and art, ed A. C. Cawley 1969.

Tatlock, J. S. P. The mind and art of Chaucer. Syracuse NY 1950.

Willy, M. Life was their cry. 1950.

Baugh, A. C. Fifty years of Chaucer scholarship. Speculum 26 1951.

Malone, K. Chapters on Chaucer. Baltimore 1951.

Speirs, J. Chaucer the maker. 1951, 1960 (rev).

Swart, J. Het problem van Chaucers poëzie. Groningen 1951.

Bloomfield, M. W. Chaucer's sense of history. JEGP 51 1952; rptd in his Essays and explorations, Cambridge Mass 1970.
— Authenticating realism and the realism of Chaucer. Thought 39 1964; rptd ibid.
Gerould, G. H. Chaucerian essays. Princeton 1952.
Purdy, R. R. Chaucer scholarship in England and America: a review of recent trends. Anglia 70 1952.
Preston, R. Chaucer. 1952.
Stephenson, H. Chaucer explored. Use of Eng 4 1952.
Miller, M. Definition by comparison: Chaucer, Lawrence and Joyce. EC 3 1953.
Block, E. A. Chaucer's millers and their bagpipes. Speculum 29 1954.
Ford, B. (ed). The age of Chaucer. 1954 (Penguin).
Schaar, C. Some types of narrative in Chaucer's poetry. Lund 1954.
— The golden mirror: studies in Chaucer's descriptive technique and its literary background. Lund 1955.
— A postscript to Chaucer studies. E Studies 42 1961.
Brewer, D. S. The ideal of feminine beauty in medieval literature. MLR 50 1955.
— The humour of Chaucer: the artist as insider. In his Proteus: studies in English literature, Tokyo 1958.
— Children in Chaucer. REL 5 1964.
— (ed). Chaucer and Chaucerians: critical studies in Middle English literature. 1966.
— Class-distinction in Chaucer. Speculum 43 1968.
Coghill, N. Geoffrey Chaucer. 1956 (Br Council pamphlet).
— The poet Chaucer. Oxford 1949 (Home Univ Lib), 1960 (corrected), 1967 (with addns).
Kleinstück, J. W. Chaucers Stellung in der mittelalterlichen Literatur. Hamburg 1956.
Muscatine, C. Chaucer and the French tradition: a study in style and meaning. Berkeley 1957.
— Chaucer in an age of criticism. MLQ 25 1964.
Stavrou, C. N. Some implications of Chaucer's irony. South Atlantic Quart 56 1957.
Bessinger, J. B. Chaucer: a parliament of critics. UTQ 29 1959.
Bethurum, D. Chaucer's point of view as narrator in the love poems. PMLA 74 1959.
Mudrick, M. Chaucer as librettist. PQ 38 1959.
Wagenknecht, E. (ed). Chaucer: modern essays in criticism. New York 1959.
Dent, A. A. Pictures from Chaucer. History Today 10 1960.
Jordan, R. M. The limits of illusion: Faulkner, Fielding and Chaucer. Criticism 2 1960.
— Chaucer and the shape of creation: the aesthetic possibilities of inorganic structure. Cambridge Mass 1967.
Masui, M. The language of love in Chaucer. Stud in Eng Lit (Tokyo) 36 1960.
— A study of Chaucer. Tokyo 1962.
— Chaucer's tenderness and the theme of consolation. Neuphilologische Mitteilungen 73 1972.
Moorman, C. Courtly love in Chaucer. ELH 27 1960.
Schoeck, R. J. and J. Taylor (ed). Chaucer criticism. 2 vols Notre Dame 1960-1.
Fisher, J. H. Chaucer's horses. South Atlantic Quart 60 1961.
Kee, K. Two Chaucerian gardens. Mediaeval Stud 23 1961.
Lawrence, N. G. and J. A. Reynolds. A Chaucerian puzzle and other essays. Coral Gable Miami 1961.
Mahoney, J. F. Chaucer tragedy and the Christian tradition. Annuale Medievale 3 1962.
Thompson, W. M. Chaucer's translation of the Bible. In English and medieval studies presented to J. R. R. Tolkien, 1962.
Robertson, D. W., jr. A preface to Chaucer: studies in medieval perspectives. Princeton 1962.
Rowland, B. Chaucer and the unnatural history of animals. Mediaeval Stud 25 1963.
— Aspects of Chaucer's use of animals. Archiv 201 1964.

— The horse and the rider figure in Chaucer's works. UTQ 35 1966.
— (ed). Companion to Chaucer studies. Toronto 1968.
Dunleavy, G. W. Natural law as Chaucer's ethical absolute. Trans Wisconsin Acad of Sciences, Arts & Letters 52 1963.
— The wound and the comforter: the consolations of Chaucer. Papers in Eng Lang & Lit 3 1967.
Farrell, W. J. Chaucer's use of the catalogue. Texas Stud in Lit & Lang 5 1963.
Huppé, B. F. and D. W. Robertson jr. Fruyt and chaf: studies in Chaucer's allegories. Princeton 1963.
Kaske, R. E. Chaucer and medieval allegory. ELH 30 1963.
Payne, R. O. The key of remembrance: a study of Chaucer's poetics. New Haven 1963.
Renoir, A. Tradition and moral realism: Chaucer's conception of the poet. Studia Neophilologica 35 1963.
Stambusky, A. A. Chaucer and Molière: kindred patterns of the dramatic impulse in human comedy. Lock Haven Rev 5 1963.
Corsa, H. S. Chaucer: poet of mirth and morality. Notre Dame 1964.
Enkvist, N. E. Chaucer. Stockholm 1964.
Howard, E. J. Chaucer. New York 1964.
Presson, R. K. The aesthetic of Chaucer's art of contrast. Eng Miscellany (Rome) 15 1964.
Rhys, B. A preface to Chaucer. Sewanee Rev 62 1964.
Bowden, M. A. A reader's guide to Chaucer. 1965.
Brookhouse, C. Chaucer's impossibilia. MÆ 34 1965.
Hussey, M., A. C. Spearing and J. Winny. An introduction to Chaucer. Cambridge 1965.
Knight, S. Chaucer: a modern writer? Balcony 2 1965.
Sharma, G. N. Dreams in Chaucer. Indian Jnl of Eng Stud 6 1965.
Utley, F. L. Robertsonianism redivivus. Romance Philology 19 1965; rptd in Chaucer's mind and art, ed A. C. Cawley 1969.
Williams, G. A new view of Chaucer. Durham NC 1965.
Adams, G. R. and B. S. Levy. Good and bad Fridays and May 3 in Chaucer. Eng Lang Notes 3 1965.
Ando, S. Some problems in Chaucer's description of women. Stud in Eng Lit (Tokyo) 43 1966.
Mills, J. Chaucer's low seriousness. Paunch 27 1966.
Markmann, A. The concern of Chaucer's poetry. Annuale Medievale 7 1966.
Nist, J. R. The art of Chaucer: pathedy. Tennessee Stud in Lit 11 1966.
Wentersdorf, K. P. Chaucer and the lost tale of Wade. JEGP 65 1966.
Wilson, W. S. Days and months in Chaucer's poems. Amer N & Q 4 1966.
Yoshida, S. Chaucer. Tokyo 1966.
Gardner, J. and N. Joost. Papers on the art and age of Chaucer. Edwardsville Ill 1967.
Grose, M. W. Chaucer. 1967.
Hieatt, C. B. The realism of dream visions: the poetic exploitation of the dream-experience in Chaucer and his contemporaries. Hague and Paris 1967.
Lehnert, M. Shakespeare und Chaucer. Sh Jb 103 1967.
Lanham, R. A. Game, play and high seriousness in Chaucer's poetry. E Studies 48 1967.
Owen, C. A., jr. The problem of free will in Chaucer's narratives. PQ 46 1967.
Bright, J. C. and P. M. Birch. Four essays in Chaucer. Sydney 1968.
DeNeef, A. L. Robertson and the critics. Chaucer Rev 2 1968.
Esch, A. (ed). Chaucer und seine Zeit: Symposion für W. F. Schirmer. Tübingen 1968.
Hira, T. Two phases of Chaucer: moral and mortal. In Maekawa Shunichi Kyoju Kanreki Kinen-rontunshu, Tokyo 1968.
Lawlor, J. Chaucer. 1968.
Newstead, H. Chaucer and his contemporaries. Greenwich Conn 1968.

Thompson, M. Current and recurrent fallacies in Chaucer criticism. In Essays in American and English literature presented to B. R. McElderry jr, Columbus 1968.

West, M. D. Dramatic time, setting and motivation in Chaucer. Chaucer Rev 2 1968.

Burrow, J. A. Chaucer. 1969 (Penguin). An anthology of Chaucer criticism.

— In his Ricardian poetry, 1971.

Crawford, W. R. The house of Chaucer's fame. Chaucer Rev 3 1969.

Deligiorgis, S. Structuralism and the study of poverty: a parametric analysis of Chaucer's Shipman's tale and the Parlement of foules. Neuphilologische Mitteilungen 70 1969.

Mogan, J. J. Chaucer and the theme of mutability. Hague and Paris 1969.

North, J. D. Kalenders enlumyned ben they: some astronomical themes in Chaucer. RES new ser 20 1969.

Raizis, M. B. Nikos Katantzakis and Chaucer. Comparative Lit Stud 6 1969.

Whitman, F. H. Exegesis and Chaucer's dream visions. Chaucer Rev 3 1969.

Alderson, W. L. and A. C. Henderson. Chaucer and Augustan scholarship. Berkeley 1970.

Badendyck, J. L. Chaucer's portrait technique and the dream vision tradition. Eng Record 21 1970.

Donaldson, E. T. Speaking of Chaucer. 1970.

— Chaucer and the elusion of clarity. E & S new ser 25 1972.

Sullivan, S. (ed). Critics on Chaucer. 1970.

Taylor, W. P. Supposed anti-feminism in Chaucer's Troilus and Criseyde and its retraction in the Legend of good women. Xavier Univ Stud 9 1970.

Tripp, R. P., jr. Chaucer's psychologizing of Virgil's Dido. Bull Rocky Mountain Modern Lang Assoc 24 1970.

Wood, C. Chaucer and the country of the stars: poetic use of astrological imagery. Princeton 1970.

Hill, B. On reading Chaucer. Proc Leeds Philosophical & Literary Soc 14 1971.

Holbrook, S. E. Thirteen ways of looking at a garden: the kinds, traditions and meanings of Chaucer's gardens. Comitatus 2 1971.

Hussey, S. S. Chaucer: an introduction. 1971.

von Kreisler, N. A recurrent expression of devotion in Chaucer's Book of the Duchess, Parliament of fowls and Knight's tale. MP 68 1971.

Robinson, I. Chaucer and the English tradition. Cambridge 1971.

Strohm, P. Jean of Angouleme: a fifteenth-century reader of Chaucer. Neuphilologische Mitteilungen 72 1971.

Kean, P. M. Chaucer and the making of English poetry. 2 vols 1972.

Smith, J. Chaucer, Boethius and recent trends in criticism. EC 22 1972.

(7) SOURCES, ANALOGUES AND LITERARY RELATIONS

Furnivall, F. J. et al. Originals and analogues of Chaucer's Canterbury tales. 1872–88 (Chaucer Soc).

— and R. E. G. Kirk. Analogues of Chaucer's Canterbury pilgrimage. 1903 (Chaucer Soc).

Rossetti, W. M. A detailed comparison of the Troylus and Cryseyde with Boccaccio's Filostrato. 2 vols 1873–83 (Chaucer Soc).

Clouston, W. A. On the magical elements in Chaucer's Squire's tale, with analogues. 1890 (Chaucer Soc).

Koeppel, E. Chaucer und Innocenz des dritten Traktat De contemptu mundi sive de miseria conditionis humanae. Archiv 84 1890.

— Chaucer und Albertanus Brixiensis. Archiv 86 1891.

— Chaucer und Alanus de Insulis. Archiv 90 1893.

— Zu Chaucers Erzählung des Millers. Zeitschrift für Vergleichende Literaturgeschichte 12 1898.

— Chaucer and Cicero's Laelius de amicitia. Archiv 126 1911.

Holthausen, F. Zu Chaucers Cecilien-Legende. Archiv 87 1891.

— Zu Chaucers Squieres tale. Anglia 14 1892.

— Die Quelle von Chaucers Merchants tale. E Studien 43 1910.

Manly, J. M. Marco Polo and the Squire's tale. PMLA 11 1896.

Broatch, J. W. The indebtedness of Chaucer's Troilus to Benoît's Roman. JEGP 2 1898.

Petersen, K. O. On the sources of the Nonne prestes tale. Boston 1898.

— The sources of the Parson's tale. Boston 1901.

Kittredge, G. L. Chaucer and Froissart (with a discussion of the date of the Meliador). E Studien 26 1899.

— Chauceriana. MP 7 1910.

— The pillars of Hercules and Chaucer's Trophee. In Putnam anniversary studies, New York 1909.

— Guillaume de Machaut and the Book of the Duchess. PMLA 30 1915.

— Chaucer's Lollius. Harvard Stud in Classical Philology 28 1917.

Liddell, M. H. A new source of the Parson's tale. In An English miscellany presented to Dr [F. J.] Furnivall, Oxford 1901.

Maynadier, G. H. The wife of Bath's tale: its sources and analogues. 1901.

Mead, W. The prologue of the Wife of Bath's tale. PMLA 16 1901.

Chiarini, C. Di una imitazione inglese della Divina commedia: la casa della fama di Chaucer. Bari 1902.

Rodeffer, J. D. Chaucer and the Roman de Thebes. MLN 17 1902.

Hamilton, G. L. The indebtedness of Chaucer's Troilus and Criseyde to Guido delle Colonne's Historia trojana. New York 1903.

Rajna, P. Le origini della novella narrata dal Frankeleyn nei Canterbury tales del Chaucer. Romania 32 1903.

Robinson, F. N. Chaucer and Dante. Jnl of Comparative Lit 1 1903.

Lowes, J. L. The prologue to the Legend of good women as related to the French Marguerite poems and the Filostrato. PMLA 19 1904.

— The Chaucerian Merciles beaute and three poems of Deschamps. MLR 5 1910.

— Chaucer's Etik. MLN 25 1910.

— Chaucer and the Miroir de mariage. MP 8 1911.

— The corones two of the Second nun's tale. PMLA 26 1911, 29 1914.

— The dragon and his brother. MLN 28 1913.

— Chaucer's Friday. MLR 9 1914.

— The prioress' oath. Romanic Rev 5 1914.

— Chaucer and Dante's Convivio. MP 13 1916.

— Chaucer and Dante. MP 14 1917.

— Chaucer's Boethius and Jean de Meun. Romanic Rev 8 1917.

— The franklin's tale, the Teseide and the Filocolo. MP 15 1918.

— The second nun's prologue, Alanus, and Macrobius. Ibid.

— Chaucer and the Ovide moralisé. PMLA 33 1918.

Canby, H. S. Some comments on the sources of Chaucer's Pardoner's tale. MP 2 1905.

Brown, C. F. Chaucer's Prioress's tale and its analogues. PMLA 21 1906.

Hinckley, H. B. Chaucer and Ywaine and Gawin. Academy 71–2 1906–7.

— Chauceriana. MP 14–16 1917–19.

—— Chauceriana. PQ 6 1927. On Chaucer and Roman literature.

Tatlock, J. S. P. Chaucer and Dante. MP 3 1906.

—— Boccaccio and the plan of the Canterbury tales. Anglia 37 1913.

—— Notes on Chaucer: the Canterbury tales. MLN 29 1914.

—— The source of the Legend, and other Chauceriana. SP 18 1921.

—— Chaucer and the Legenda aurea. MLN 45 1930.

—— St Cecilia's garlands and their Roman origins. PMLA 45 1930.

Capone, G. La novella del cavaliere—Knight's tale—di Chaucer e la Teseida di Giovanni Boccaccio. 2 vols Sassari 1907–9.

—— Marginalia a la novella del cavaliere di Chaucer: la concepzione de la storia nel Petrarca e nel Chaucer. Sassari 1912.

Dargan, E. P. Cock and fox: a critical study of the history and sources of the medieval fable. MP 4 1907.

Hendrickson, G. L. Chaucer and Petrarch: two notes on the Clerk's tale. Ibid.

Young, K. Chaucer's use of Boccaccio's Filocolo. MP 4 1907.

—— The origin and development of the story of Troilus and Criseyde. 1908 (Chaucer Soc), 1968.

—— Chaucer and Peter Riga. Speculum 12 1937.

—— Chaucer's aphorisms from Ptolemy. SP 34 1937.

—— Chaucer and Aulus Gellius. MLN 52 1937.

—— The maidenly virtues of Chaucer's Virginia. Speculum 16 1941.

—— The Dit de la harpe of Guillaume de Machaut. In Essays in honor of A. Feuillerat, New Haven 1943. On Legend of good women.

—— Chaucer and Geoffrey of Vinsauf. MP 41 1944.

—— Chaucer's appeal to the platonic deity. Speculum 19 1944.

Jones, H. S. V. The Cleomedes and related folktales. PMLA 23 1908.

—— Chaucer and Cleomedes. MLN 24 1909.

Strong, C. Sir Thopas and Sir Guy. MLN 23 1908.

Forsmann, J. Einiges über französisches Einflüsse in Chaucers Werken. Annenschule 1909.

Sypherd, W. O. Le songe vert and Chaucer's dream-poems. MLN 24 1909.

Bushnell, A. J. de H. Names and sources of Chaucer's Squire's tale. Blackwoods Mag May 1910.

Gildersleeve, V. C. Chaucer and Sir Aldingar. MLN 25 1910.

Morsbach, L. Chaucers Plan der Canterbury tales und Boccaccios Decamerone. E Studien 42 1910.

—— Chaucers Canterbury tales und das Decameron. Nachrichten aus der Neueren Philologie und Literaturgeschichte 1 1937.

Bardelli, M. Qualche contributo agli studi sulle relazione del Chaucer col Boccaccio. Florence 1911.

Wise, B. A. The influence of Statius upon Chaucer. Baltimore 1911.

Barnouw, A. J. Chaucer's Miller's tale. MLR 7 1912.

Hathaway, C. M. Chaucer's Lollius. E Studien 44 1912.

Root, R. K. Chaucer and the Decameron. E Studien 44 1912.

—— Chaucer's Dares. MP 15 1918.

Shannon, E. F. The source of Chaucer's Anelida and Arcite. PMLA 27 1912.

—— Chaucer and Lucan's Pharsalia. MP 16 1919.

—— Chaucer and the Roman poets. Cambridge Mass 1929.

Dodd, W. G. Courtly love in Chaucer and Gower. Boston 1913.

Fansler, D. S. Chaucer and the Roman de la rose. New York 1914.

Cummings, H. M. The indebtedness of Chaucer's works to the Italian works of Boccaccio. Menasha 1916.

Emerson, O. F. Seith Trophee. MLN 31 1916.

—— Saint Ambrose and Chaucer's Life of St Cecilia. PMLA 41 1926.

Lange, H. Chaucers Sir Thopas, Ritter Honiggold: ein Beitrag zur Kenntnis Chaucers und Froissarts. Deutsche Literaturzeitung 37 1916.

—— Chaucer and Mandeville's Travels. Archiv 174 1938.

—— Die Paradiesvorstellung in Mandevilles Travels im Lichte mittelalterlicher Dichtung: zur Lösung der Legendenprologfrage bei Chaucer. E Studien 72 1938.

—— Der heliakische Aufgang der Fixsterne bei Dante und Chaucer. Deutsches Dante-Jahrbuch 21 1939.

Farnham, W. E. The sources of Chaucer's Parlement of foules. PMLA 32 1917.

—— England's discovery of the Decameron. PMLA 39 1924.

Jefferson, B. L. Chaucer and the Consolation of philosophy of Boethius. Princeton 1917.

Lecompte, I. C. Chaucer's Nonne prestes tale and the Roman de Renart. MP 14 1917.

Ayres, H. M. Chaucer and Seneca. Romanic Rev 10 1919.

Steele, R. Chaucer and the Almagest. Library 3rd ser 10 1919.

Korten, H. Chaucers literarische Beziehungen zu Boccaccio: die künstlerische Konzeption der Canterbury tales und das Lolliusproblem. Rostock 1920.

Stanford, M. The sumner's tale and Saint Patrick's purgatory. JEGP 19 1920.

Baskerville, C. R. English songs on the night visit. PMLA 36 1921.

Kellett, E. E. Chaucer as a critic of Dante. London Mercury July 1921.

Taylor, A. The Devil and the advocate. PMLA 36 1921.

—— Der Richter und der Teufel. In Studies in honor of H. Collitz, Baltimore 1930.

Hart, W. M. Some Old French miracles of Our Lady and Chaucer's Prioresses tale. In The C. M. Gayley anniversary papers, Berkeley 1922.

Kitchel, A. T. Chaucer and Machaut's Dit de la fortune amoreuse. In Vassar medieval studies, New Haven 1923.

Koch, J. Chaucers Belesenheit in den römischen Klassikern. E Studien 57 1923.

Trigona, F. P. Chaucer imitatore del Boccaccio: saggio di letteratura comparata. Catania 1923.

Wrenn, C. L. Chaucer's knowledge of Horace. MLR 18 1923.

Connelly, W. Imprints of the Heroides of Ovid on Chaucer's The legend of good women. Classical Weekly 13 Oct 1924.

Landrum, G. W. Chaucer's use of the Vulgate. PMLA 39 1924.

Schirmer, W. F. Boccaccios Werke als Quelle Chaucers. Germanisch-romanische Monatsschrift 12 1924.

—— Chaucer, Shakespeare und die Antike. In England und die Antike, Berlin and Leipzig 1931.

Looten, C. Chaucer et Dante. Revue de Littérature Comparée 5 1925.

—— Chaucer: ses modèles, ses sources, sa religion. Lille 1931.

Schlauch, M. Studies in the sources of the Man of law's tale. New York 1925.

—— Chaucer's Constance and accused queens. New York 1927.

Magoun, F. P., jr. Chaucer and the Roman de la rose vv. 16096–105. Romanic Rev 17 1926.

—— The source of Chaucer's Rime of Sir Thopas. PMLA 42 1927.

—— Chaucer's Sir Gawain and the OFr Roman de la rose. MLN 67 1952.

—— Chaucer's summary of Statius' Thebaid II–XII. Traditio 11 1955.

Patch, H. R. Chaucer and medieval romance. In Essays in memory of Barrett Wendell, Cambridge Mass 1926.

—— Chauceriana. E Studien 65 1930.

—— Two notes on Chaucer's Troilus. MLN 70 1955.

Rand, E. K. Chaucer in error. Speculum 1 1926.

Praz, M. Chaucer and the great Italian writers of the trecento. Monthly Criterion 1927; rptd in his Flaming heart, Garden City NY 1958.

Spencer, T. Chaucer's hell: a study in mediaeval convention. Speculum 2 1927.

— The story of Ugolino in Dante and Chaucer. Speculum 9 1934.

Langhans, V. Chaucers angebliche Übersetzung des Traktates De contemptu mundi von Innocenz III. Anglia 52 1928.

Torraca, F. The Knight's tale e la Teseide. Societate Reale di Napoli: atti della reale Accademia di Archeologia, Lettere e Belle Arti new ser 10 1928.

Dempster, G. On the source of the Reeve's tale. JEGP 29 1930.

— On the source of the deception story in the Merchant's tale. MP 34 1937.

— Chaucer's daughter of Cupid. MLR 45 1950.

Meech, S. B. Chaucer and an Italian translation of the Heroides. PMLA 45 1930.

— Chaucer and the Ovide moralisé: a further study. PMLA 46 1931.

Bushnell, N. S. The Wandering Jew and the Pardoner's tale. SP 28 1931.

Griffith, D. D. The origin of the Griselda story. Seattle 1931.

MacCallum, M. W. Chaucer's debt to Italy. Sydney 1931.

McPeek, J. A. S. Did Chaucer know Catullus? MLN 46 1931.

Hamilton, M. P. Chaucer's Marcia Catoun. MP 30 1932.

Hill, A. A. Diomede: the traditional development of a character. Essays and Stud in Eng & Comparative Lit (Michigan) 8 1932.

Severs, J. B. Chaucer's source manuscript for the Clerkes tale. PMLA 47 1932.

— The source of Chaucer's Melibeus. PMLA 50 1935.

— The literary relationships of Chaucer's Clerkes tale. New Haven 1942.

— The sources of the Book of the Duchess. Mediaeval Stud 25 1963.

Rosenthal, C. L. A possible source for Chaucer's Booke of the Duchesse: Li regret de Guillaume by Jehan de la Mote. MLN 48 1933.

Gordon, R. K. (ed and tr). The story of Troilus as told by Benoît de Sainte-Maure, Giovanni Boccaccio, Chaucer and Robert Henryson. 1934.

Hankins, J. E. Chaucer and the Pervigilium Veneris. MLN 49 1934.

Lange, M. Vom Fabliau zu Boccaccio und Chaucer: ein Vergleich zweier Fabliaux mit Boccaccios Decamerone (IX.8) und mit Chaucers Reeves tale. Hamburg 1934.

Whiting, B. J. The Hous of fame and Renaud de Beaujeu's Le biaus descouneüs. MP 31 1934.

— Gawain: his reputation, his courtesy and his appearance in Chaucer's Squire's tale. Mediaeval Stud 9 1947.

Aiken, P. Vincent of Beauvais and Pertelote's knowledge of medicine. Speculum 10 1935.

— The summoner's malady. SP 33 1936.

— Arcite's illness and Vincent of Beauvais. PMLA 51 1936.

— Chaucer's Legend of Cleopatra and the Speculum historiale. Speculum 13 1938.

— Vincent of Beauvais and the green yeoman's lecture on demonology. SP 35 1938.

— Vincent of Beauvais and Chaucer's Monk's tale. Speculum 17 1942.

— Vincent of Beauvais and Chaucer's knowledge of alchemy. SP 41 1944.

Harvey, S. W. Chaucer's debt to Sacrobosco. JEGP 34 1935.

Loomis, L. H. Chaucer's jewes werk and Guy of Warwick. PQ 14 1935.

— Sir Thopas and David and Goliath. MLN 51 1936.

— Chaucer and the Auchinleck ms: Thopas and Guy of Warwick. In Essays and studies in honor of Carleton Brown, New York 1940; rptd in her Adventures in the Middle Ages, New York 1962.

— Chaucer and the Breton lays of the Auchinleck ms. SP 38 1941; rptd ibid.

Train, L. Chaucer's ladys foure and twenty. MLN 50 1935.

Weatherley, E. H. A note on Chaucer's Pardoner's tale. Ibid.

Bennett, J. A. W. Concerning Wade... MLR 31 1936.

— Chaucer, Dante and Boccaccio. MÆ 22 1936.

Cline, J. M. Chaucer and Jean de Meun: De consolatione philosophiae. ELH 3 1936.

Tillotson, K. The friar's lisp. TLS 25 April 1936.

Wentworth, C. L. The prioress' oath. Romanic Rev 27 1936.

Wilson, W. J. An alchemical manuscript by Arnoldus de Bruxella. Osiris 2 1936.

Braddy, H. Chaucer's Book of the Duchess and two of Graunson's complaintes. MLN 52 1937.

— Chaucer and Graunson: the Valentine tradition. PMLA 54 1939.

— Chaucer and the French poet Graunson. Baton Rouge 1947.

Dédeck-Héry, V. L. Jean de Meun et Chaucer: traducteurs de la Consolation de Boèce. PMLA 52 1937.

— Le Boèce de Chaucer et les manuscrits français de la Consolatio de J. de Meun. PMLA 59 1944.

Immaculate, Sr M. Fiends as servant unto man in the Friar's tale. PQ 21 1937.

Loomis, R. S. Gawain in the Squire's tale. MLN 52 1937.

Ruska, J. Chaucer und das Buch Senior. Anglia 61 1937.

Wimsatt, W. K. Vincent of Beauvais and Chaucer's Cleopatra and Croesus. Speculum 12 1937.

Atwood, E. B. Two alterations of Virgil in Chaucer's Dido. Speculum 13 1938.

Dieckmann, E. M. Moore feelynge than had Boece. MLN 53 1938.

McNeal, T. H. Chaucer and the Decameron. Ibid.

Estrich, R. M. Chaucer's prologue to the Legend of good women and Machaut's Le jugement dou roy de Navarre. SP 36 1939.

Sanderlin, G. Quotations from St Bernard in the Parson's tale. MLN 54 1939.

Guinagh, K. Source of the quotation from Augustine in the Parson's tale 985. MLN 55 1940.

Hornstein, L. H. Trivet's Constance and the king of Tars. MLN 55 1940.

— Petrarch's Laelius Chaucer's Lollius? PMLA 63 1948.

Pratt, R. A. Chaucer's Shipman's tale and Sercambi. MLN 55 1940.

— Chaucer's use of the Teseida. PMLA 62 1947.

— Chaucer's Claudian. Speculum 22 1947.

— A note on Chaucer and the Policraticus of John of Salisbury. MLN 65 1950.

— A note on Chaucer's Lollius. MLN 65 1950.

— Chaucer and Le roman de Troyle et de Criseida. SP 53 1956.

— Chaucer and Isidore on why men marry. MLN 74 1959.

— Chaucer and the hand that fed him. Speculum 41 1966.

— Chaucer and Les cronicles of Nicholas Trevet. In Studies in language, literature and culture of the Middle Ages and later, ed E. B. Atwood and A. Hill, Austin 1969.

Bryan, W. F. and G. Dempster (ed). Sources and analogues of the Canterbury tales. Chicago 1941. The standard collection.

Henkins, L. J. The apocrypha and Chaucer's House of fame. MLN 56 1941.

Dilts, D. A. Observations on Dante and the Hous of fame. MLN 57 1942.

Duncan, E. H. Chaucer and Arnold of the newe toun. Ibid.

— Chaucer's wife of Bath's prologue, lines 193–828, and Geoffrey of Vinsauf's Documentum. MP 66 1969.

Epstein, H. J. The identity of Chaucer's Lollius. MLQ 3 1942.

Lessing, M. The prologue to the Legend of good women and the Lai de franchise. SP 39 1942.

Stearns, M. W. Chaucer mentions a book. MLN 57 1942.

— A note on Chaucer's use of Aristotelian psychology. SP 43 1946.

Levy, H. L. As myn auctor seith. MÆ 12 1943.

Savage, H. Seint Julian he was. MLN 58 1943.

Samuel, I. Semiramis in the Middle Ages: the history of a legend. Medievalia et Humanistica 2 1944.

Kuhl, E. P. Chaucer's Madame Eglantine. MLN 60 1945.

Parr, J. Chaucer and the Partonope of bliss. Ibid.

— Chaucer's Semiramis. Chaucer Rev 5 1971.

Callan, N. Thyn owne book: a note on Chaucer, Gower and Ovid. RES 22 1946.

McGalliard, J. C. Chaucer's Merchant's tale and Deschamps' Miroir de mariage. PQ 25 1946.

Francis, W. N. Chaucer's airish beasts. MLN 64 1949.

Smith, R. M. The six gifts. Jnl of Celtic Stud 1 1949.

— Five notes on Chaucer and Froissart. MLN 66 1951.

Wilson, H. S. The Knight's tale and the Teseida again. UTQ 18 1949.

Archer, J. W. On Chaucer's source for Arveragus in the Franklin's tale. PMLA 65 1950.

Heist, W. W. Folklore study and Chaucer's fabliau-like tales. Papers of Michigan Acad 36 1950.

Ruggiers, P. G. Tyrants of Lombardy in Dante and Chaucer. PQ 29 1950.

Statler, M. H. The analogues of Chaucer's Prioress's tale: the relation of group C to group A. PMLA 65 1950.

Wickert, M. Chaucers Konstanze und die Legende der guten Frauen. Anglia 69 1950.

Anderson, G. K. Die Silberlinge des Judas and the accursed treasure. SP 48 1951.

— The legend of the Wandering Jew. Providence 1965.

Clark, J. W. Dante and the epilogue of the Troilus. JEGP 50 1951.

Cordie, G. Chaucer e Giovanni da Legnano. Letterature Moderne 2 1951.

Johnson, D. R. The biblical characters of Chaucer's monk. PMLA 66 1951.

Preston, R. Chaucer and the ballades notées of Guillaume de Machaut. Speculum 26 1951.

Damon, P. W. The Parlement of foules and the Pavo. MLN 67 1952.

Davies, R. T. Chaucer's Madame Eglantine. MLN 67 1952.

Kellogg, A. L. St Augustine and the Parson's tale. Traditio 8 1952.

— Seith Moyses by the Devel: a problem in Chaucer's Parson's tale. Revue Belge 31 1953.

— Susannah and the Merchant's tale. Speculum 35 1960.

— On the tradition of Troilus's vision of little earth. Mediaeval Stud 22 1960.

Bennett, J. W. Chaucer and Mandeville's Travels. MLN 68 1953.

Francis, W. N. Chaucer shortens a tale. PMLA 68 1953.

Friend, A. C. Chaucer's version of the Aeneid. Speculum 28 1953.

Makarewicz, Sr M. R. The patristic influence on Chaucer. Washington 1953.

Schaar, C. The Merchant's tale, Amadas et Ydoine and Guillaume au faucon. Køngliga Humanistiska Vetenskapssamfundet i Lund: Årsberättelse 1953.

Lumiansky R. M. Aspects of the relationship of Boccaccio's Il filostrato with Benoît's Roman de Troie and Chaucer's Wife of Bath's tale. Italica 31 1954.

— Benoît's portraits and Chaucer's General prologue. JEGP 55 1956.

Robertson, D. W., jr. Why the Devil wears green. MLN 69 1954. On Reeve's tale.

Muscatine, C. The name of Chaucer's friar. MLN 70 1955.

— The wife of Bath and Gautier's La veuve. In Romance studies in memory of E. B. Ham, Hayward Cal 1967.

Reid, T. B. W. The she-wolf's mate. MÆ 24 1955.

Wenk, J. C. On the sources of the Prioress's tale. Mediaeval Stud 17 1955.

Bloomfield, M. W. The pardons of Pamplona and the pardoner of Rounceval: Piers Plowman B.xvii.252. PQ 35 1956.

Donovan, M. J. Sir Thopas 772–4. Neuphilologische Mitteilungen 57 1956.

— The Anticlaudian and three passages in the Franklin's tale. JEGP 56 1957.

Harder, K. B. Chaucer's use of the mystery plays in the Miller's tale. MLQ 17 1956.

Mathews, W. Eustache Deschamps and Chaucer's Merchant's tale. MLR 51 1956.

Mitchell, E. R. The two Mayings in Chaucer's Knight's tale. MLN 71 1956.

O'Connor, J. J. The astrological background of the Miller's tale. Speculum 31 1956.

Solari, M. S. Sources of the invocation in the House of fame. Revista de Literaturas Modernas 1 1956.

Boyd, B. The little clergeon's Alma redemptoris mater. N & Q July 1957.

Eisner, A. A tale of wonder: a source of the Wife of Bath's tale. Wexford 1957.

Paffard, M. K. Pertelote's prescription. N & Q Sept 1957.

Wilkins, E. H. Descriptions of pagan divinities from Petrarch to Chaucer. Speculum 32 1957.

Wright, W. H. Boccaccio in England from Chaucer to Tennyson. 1957.

Dédéyan, C. Dante en Angleterre. Les Lettres Romanes 12–13 1958–9.

Birney, E. The franklin's sop in wyn. N & Q Oct 1959.

Steadman, J. M. The book-burning episode in the Wife of Bath's prologue: some additional analogues. PMLA 74 1959.

— Venus' citole in Chaucer's Knight's tale and Berchorius. Speculum 34 1959.

— The Prioress's tale and Granella of Paradiso. Mediaeval Stud 24 1962.

— Chaucer's pardoner and the Thesaurus meritorium. Eng Lang Notes 3 1965.

Thomson, P. The Canticus Troili: Chaucer and Petrarch. Comparative Lit 11 1959.

Baugh, A. C. Chaucer and the Panthere d'Amours. In Britannica: Festschrift für H. M. Flasdieck, Heidelberg 1960.

— and E. T. Donaldson. Chaucer's Troilus IV.1585: a biblical allusion? MLN 76 1961.

Bradley, D. R. Fals Eneas and sely Dido. PQ 39 1960.

Hazleton, R. Chaucer and Cato. Speculum 35 1960.

— Chaucer's Parson's tale and the Moralium dogma philosophorum. Traditio 16 1960.

Pratt, R. A. Chaucer and the pillars of Hercules. In Studies in honor of [B. L.] Ullman, St Louis 1960.

Schless, H. Chaucer and Dante. In Critical approaches to medieval literature, ed D. Bethurum, New York 1960.

Burrow, J. A maner Latyn corrupt. MÆ 30 1961.

Cigada, S. Il tema arturiano del Chateau tournant: Chaucer's Christine de Pisan. Studi Medievali 2 1961.

Craig, H. From Gorgias to Troilus. In Studies in medieval literature in honor of A. C. Baugh, Philadelphia 1961.

Lewis, R. W. B. On translating the Aeneid: yif that I can. Yearbook of Comparative & General Lit 10 1961. On Hous of fame.

Bode, E. L. The source of Chaucer's rusted gold. Mediaeval Stud 24 1962.

Fish, S. E. The Nun's priest's tale and its analogues. College Lang Assoc Jnl 5 1962.

Kaske, R. E. The Canticum canticorum in the Miller's tale. SP 59 1962.

McDermott, W. C. Chaucer and Virgil. Classica et Medievalia 23 1962.

Pace, G. B. Physiognomy and Chaucer's summoner and Alisoun. Traditio 18 1962.

— Adam's hell. PMLA 78 1963.

Daly, S. R. Criseyde's blasphemous aube. N & Q Dec 1963.

Grennen, J. E. Chaucer's secree of screes: an alchemical topic. PQ 42 1963.
— The canon's yeoman's alchemical mass. SP 62 1965.
— Sampsoun in the Canterbury tales: Chaucer adapting a source. Neuphilologische Mitteilungen 67 1966.
— Another French source for the Merchant's tale. Romance Notes 8 1967.
Hall, L. B. Chaucer and the Dido-and-Aeneas story. Mediaeval Stud 25 1963.
Moreton, R. L. Literary convention in the Book of the Duchess. Univ of Mississippi Stud in Eng 4 1963.
Quinn, B. N. Venus, Chaucer and Peter Bersuire. Speculum 38 1963.
Reiss, E. Chaucer's friar and the man in the moon. JEGP 62 1963.
Bawcutt, P. Dunbar's Tretis of the twa mariit wemen and the wedo 185–7 and Chaucer's Parson's tale. N & Q Sept 1964.
Cadbury, W. Manipulation of sources and the meanings of the Manciple's tale. PQ 43 1964.
Cartier, N. R. Froissart, Chaucer and Enclimpostair. Revue de Littérature Comparée 38 1964.
— Le bleu chevalier de Froissart et le Livre de la Duchesse de Chaucer. Romania 88 1967.
Clark, C. Chauntecleer and Deduit. Eng Lang Notes 2 1964.
Clogan, P. M. Chaucer and the Thebaid scholia. SP 61 1964.
— Chaucer's Legend of good women. Explicator April 1965.
— Chaucer's Cybele and the Liber imaginum deorum. PQ 43 1964.
— Chaucer's use of the Thebaid. Eng Miscellany (Rome) 18 1967.
Fleming, J. V. Chaucer's clerk and John of Salisbury. Eng Lang Notes 2 1964.
— Chaucer's squire, the Roman de la rose and the Romaunt. N & Q Feb 1967.
Economou, G. D. Januarie's sin against nature: the Merchant's tale and the Roman de la rose. Comparative Lit 17 1965.
Huber, J. Troilus' predestination soliloquy: Chaucer's changes from Boethius. Neuphilologische Mitteilungen 66 1965.
Levy, B. S. Chaucer's wife of Bath, the loathly lady, and Dante's siren. Symposium 19 1965.
McCall, J. P. Chaucer and John of Legnano. Speculum 40 1965.
Copland, M. The Shipman's tale: Chaucer and Boccaccio. MÆ 35 1966.
Dean, N. Ovid's elegies from exile and Chaucer's House of fame. Hunter College Stud 3 1966.
Dronke, P. Chaucer and Boethius' De musica. N & Q March 1966.
Francon, M. Note on Chaucer's roundels and his French

models. Annali Instituto Universitario Orientale (Napoli), Sezione Germanica 9 1966.
Heydon, P. N. Chaucer and the Sir Orfeo prologue of the Auchinleck ms. Papers of Michigan Acad 51 1966.
Hoffman, R. L. Ovid and the Canterbury tales. Philadelphia 1966.
— Jephthah's daughter and Chaucer's Virginia. Chaucer Rev 2 1968.
Johnston, E. C. The medieval versions of the Reynard-Chanticleer episode. Lang Quart 4 1966.
Lewis, R. E. Chaucer's artistic use of Pope Innocent III's De miseria humane conditionis in the Man of law's prologue and tale. PMLA 81 1966.
— Glosses to the Man of law's tale from Pope Innocent III's De miseria humane conditionis. SP 64 1967.
Norton-Smith, J. Chaucer's epistolary style. In Essays on style and language, ed R. Fowler 1966.
Robbins, R. H. The physician's authorities. In Studies in language and literature in honour of M. Schlauch, Warsaw 1966.
Baird, J. L. The Devil in green. Neuphilologische Mitteilungen 68 1967.
Delany, P. Constantinus Affricanus and Chaucer's Merchant's tale. PQ 46 1967.
Hartung, A. E. The non-comic Merchant's tale, Maximianus and the sources. Mediaeval Stud 29 1967.
Sarno, R. A. Chaucer and the satirical tradition. Classical Folia 21 1967.
Wimsatt, J. I. The sources of Chaucer's Seys and Alcyone. MÆ 36 1967.
— Chaucer and the French love poets: the literary background of the Book of the Duchess. Chapel Hill 1968.
Wood, C. Chaucer's clerk and Chalcidius. Eng Lang Notes 5 1967.
Delany, S. Chaucer's House of fame and the Ovide moralisé. Comparative Lit 20 1968.
Peltola, N. Chaucer's summoner: fyr-reed cherubynnes face. Neuphilologische Mitteilungen 69 1968.
Schmidt, A. V. C. Chaucer's philosophre: a note on the Parson's tale. N & Q Sept 1968.
Walker, I. C. Chaucer and Il filostrato. E Studies 49 1968.
Blake, N. F. Chaucer and the alliterative romances. Chaucer Rev 3 1969.
von Kreisler, N. A. Bird lore and the Valentine's day tradition in Chaucer's Parlement of foules. Ibid.
Cary, M. Sovereignty and old wife. Papers in Lang & Lit 5 1969.
Olson, G. The Reeve's tale and Gombert. MLR 64 1969.
Finkelstein, D. The code of Chaucer's secree of secrees: Arabic alchemical terminology in the Canon's yeoman's tale. Archiv 207 1970.
Fry, D. K. Chaucer's Zanzis and a possible source for Troilus and Criseyde iv. 407–13. Eng Lang Notes 9 1971.
Wood, C. The sources of Chaucer's summoner's 'garleek, onyons, and eek lekes'. Chaucer Rev 5 1971.

(8) LANGUAGE, STYLE AND VERSIFICATION

Child, F. J. Observations on the language of Chaucer. Memoirs of Amer Acad of Arts & Sciences new ser 8 1863.
Weymouth, R. F. On early English pronunciation, with especial reference to Chaucer. 1874.
ten Brink, B. Chaucer's Sprache und Verskunst. Strasbourg 1884, Leipzig 1920 (rev E. Eckhardt); tr 1901.
Marshall, I. and L. Porter. Rhyme index to the manuscript texts of Chaucer's minor poems. 1887 (Chaucer Soc).
McClumpha, C. F. The alliteration of Chaucer. Leipzig 1888.
Petzold, E. Über Alliteration in den Werken Chaucers, mit Ausschluss der Canterbury tales. Marburg 1889.

Kittredge, G. L. Observations on the language of Chaucer's Troilus. 1891–4 (Chaucer Soc).
Skeat, W. W. A rhyme-index to Chaucer's Troilus and Criseyde. 1892 (Chaucer Soc).
Manly, J. M. Observations on the language of Chaucer's Legend of good women. Stud & Notes in Philology & Lit 2 1893.
— The stanza-form of Sir Thopas. MP 8 1911.
Hempel, E. Die Silbermassung in Chaucer's fünftaktigen Verse. Halle 1898.
Bischoff, O. Über zweisilbige Senkung und epische Cäsur bei Chaucer. E Studien 24–5 1898.
Ford, H. C. Observations on the language of Chaucer's House of fame. Lexington Va 1899, 1908.

Remus, H. Untersuchungen über den romanischen Wortschatz Chaucers. Halle 1903.

— Die kirchlichen und speziell-wissenschaftlichen romanischen Lehnwörter Chaucers. Halle 1906.

Wilson, L. R. Chaucer's relative construction. SP 1 1906.

Kenyon, J. S. The syntax of the infinitive in Chaucer. 1909 (Chaucer Soc).

Noyes, G. R. Analyses of the sources of the accented vowels in Chaucer's Canterbury tales: B4011–60. Berkeley 1909.

Borst, E. Zur Stellung des Adverbs bei Chaucer. E Studien 42 1910.

Frieshammer, J. Die sprachliche Form des Chaucerschen Prosa: ihr Verhältnis zur Reimtechnik des Dichters sowie zur Sprache der älteren Londoner Urkunden. Halle 1910.

Licklider, A. H. Chapters on the metre of the Chaucerian tradition. Baltimore 1910.

Lowes, J. L. Simple and coy: a note on fourteenth-century poetic diction. Anglia 33 1910.

— The loveres maladye of Hereos. MP 11 1914.

— Hereos again. MLN 31 1916.

Mayhew, A. L. Dulcarnon in Chaucer. N & Q June 1910.

Brown, C. Shul and shal in Chaucer manuscripts. PMLA 26 1911.

Flügel, E. Benedicitee. In [J.E.] Matzke memorial volume, Stanford 1911.

— Prologomena and side-notes of the Chaucer dictionary. Anglia 34 1911.

— Specimen of the Chaucer dictionary: letter E. Anglia 37 1913.

Foster, C. H. Chaucer's pronunciation of ai, ay, ei, ey. MLN 26 1911.

Gerike, E. Das Partizipium Präsentis bei Chaucer. Kiel 1911.

Eichhorn, E. Partizipium bei Gower im Vergleich mit Chaucers Verbrauch. Kiel 1912.

Klee, F. Das Enjambement bei Chaucer. Halle 1913.

Helmeke, T. Beteuerungen und Verwünschungen bei Chaucer. Kiel 1913.

Shannon, E. F. Chaucer's use of the octosyllabic verse in the Book of the Duchess and the Hous of fame. JEGP 12 1913.

Babcock, C. F. A study of the metrical use of the inflectional e in Middle English, with particular reference to Chaucer and Lydgate. PMLA 29 1914.

Eitle, H. Die Satzverknüpfung bei Chaucer. Heidelberg 1914.

— Die Unterordnung der Sätze bei Chaucer. Tübingen 1914.

Hüttmann, E. Das Partizipium Präsentis bei Lydgate im Vergleich mit Chaucers Verbrauch. Kiel 1914.

Vockrodt, G. Die Reimtechnik bei Chaucer. Halle 1914.

Joerden, O. Das Verhältnis von Wort-, Satz-, und Vers-Akzent in Chaucers Canterbury tales. Halle 1915.

Wild, F. Die sprachlichen Eigentümlichkeiten der wichtigeren Chaucer-Handschriften und die Sprache Chaucers. Vienna 1915.

Bihl, J. Die Wirkungen des Rhythmus in der Sprache von Chaucer und Gower. Heidelberg 1916.

Tatlock, J. S. P. Puns in Chaucer. In [E.] Flügel memorial volume, Stanford 1916.

— The Chaucer concordance. MLN 38 1923.

Hinckley, H. B. Chauceriana. MP 14–16 1917–19.

Sauerbrey, G. Die innere Sprachform bei Chaucer. Halle 1917.

Nöjd, R. The vocalism of Romance words in Chaucer. Upsala 1919.

Beschorner, O. Verbale Reime bei Chaucer. Halle 1920.

von Gross, E. Bildung des Adverbs bei Chaucer. Weimar 1921.

Langhans, V. Der Reimvokal e bei Chaucer. Anglia 45 1921.

Read, W. A. On Chaucer's Troilus and Criseyde. JEGP 20 1921.

Hittmair, R. Das Zeitwort do in Chaucers Prosa. Vienna 1923.

Cowling, G. H. A note on Chaucer's stanza. RES 2 1926.

Gerould, G. H. The social status of Chaucer's franklin. PMLA 41 1926.

Goffin, R. C. Chaucer and reason. MLR 21 1926.

Hammond, E. P. The nine-syllabled pentameter line in some post-Chaucerian manuscripts. MP 23 1926.

Royster, J. F. Chaucer's Colle tregetour. SP 23 1926.

Lineberger, J. E. An examination of Professor Cowling's new metrical test. MLN 42 1927.

Jenkins, T. A. Vitremyte: mot latin-français employé par Chaucer. In Mélanges de linguistique et de littérature offerts à Alfred Jeanroy, Paris 1928.

Robertson, S. Old English verse in Chaucer. MLN 43 1928.

Wyatt, A. J. Chaucer's in termes. RES 4 1928.

Buck, H. Chaucer's use of feminine rhyme. MP 26 1929.

Frost, G. L. Chaucer's man of law at the Parvis. MLN 44 1929.

— That precious corpus Madrian. MLN 57 1942.

Karpf, F. Zur Kontamination bei Chaucer. E Studien 64 1929, 66 1931.

— Studien zur Syntax in den Werken Chaucers. Pt 1, Vienna 1930.

Ross, W. O. A possible significance of the name Thopas. MLN 45 1930.

Malone, K. The freres contree. MLN 26 1931.

— Chaucer's double consonants and the final -e. Mediaeval Stud 18 1956.

— Chaucer's Book of the Duchess: a metrical study. In Chaucer und seine Zeit, ed A. Esch, Tübingen 1968.

Slaughter, E. E. Every vertu at his reste. MLN 46 1931.

Cloyd, M. G. Chaucer's Romance element. PQ 11 1932.

Heuer, H. Studien zur syntaktischen und stilistischen Funktion des Adverbs bei Chaucer und im Rosenroman. Heidelberg 1932.

Webster, C. Chaucer's Turkish bows. MLN 47 1932.

Norris, D. M. Harry Bailey's corpus Madrian. MLN 48 1933.

Trounce, A. McI. Chaucer's imperative with as. MÆ 2 1933.

Brooks, C. Chaucer: Saturn's daughter. MLN 49 1934.

Grauls, J. and J. F. Vanderheijden. Two Flemish proverbs in Chaucer's Canterbury tales. Revue Belge 13 1934.

Maynard, T. The connection between the ballade, Chaucer's modification of it, rime royal and the Spenserian stanza. Washington 1934.

Tolkien, J. R. R. Chaucer as a philologist: the Reeve's tale. Trans Philological Soc 1934.

Whiting, B. J. Chaucer's use of proverbs. Cambridge Mass 1934.

Walcutt, C. C. The pronoun of address in Troilus and Criseyde. PQ 14 1935.

Héraucourt, W. What is trouthe or soothfastnesse? In Englische Kultur in sprachwissenschaftlicher Deutung: M. Deutschbein zum 60 Geburtstage, Leipzig 1936.

— Das Hendiadyoin als Mittel zur Hervorhebung des Werthaften bei Chaucer. E Studien 73 1938.

— Das sprachliche Feld der goodes und seine Gliederung bei Chaucer. Neuphilologische Monatsschrift 11 1940.

Mersand, J. Chaucer's Romance vocabulary. Brooklyn 1937.

Nakayama, T. On some features of Chaucer's language. Stud in Eng Lit (Tokyo) 18 1938.

Webster, M. The vocabulary of An holy medytacion. PQ 17 1938.

Koziol, H. Die romanischen Lehnwörter in Chaucers Werken. E Studien 74 1940–1.

— Die Anredeform bei Chaucer. E Studien 75 1943.

Stevenson, S. W. Chaucer's ferses twelve. ELH 7 1940.

Immaculate, Sr M. Sixty as a conventional number and other Chauceriana. MLQ 2 1941.

McJimsey, R. B. Chaucer's irregular -*e*: a demonstration among monosyllabic nouns of exceptions to grammatical and metrical harmony. New York 1942.

Pyles, T. Dan Chaucer. MLN 57 1942.

Bradley, R. J. The use of Cockney dialect by Chaucer. Quart Jnl of Speech 29 1943.

Starr, H. W. Oaths in Chaucer's poems. West Virginia Univ Philological Papers 4 1943.

Young, K. The secree of secrees of Chaucer's canon's yeoman. MLN 58 1943.

Mather, F. J., jr. Pesen at Actium: an alliterative crux in Chaucer (He poureth pesen upon the haches slidere— Legend of good women 648). JEGP 44 1945.

Baum, P. F. Chaucer's metrical prose. JEGP 45 1946.

— Chaucer's nautical metaphors. South Atlantic Quart 49 1950.

— Chaucer's puns. PMLA 71 1956, 73 1958.

— Chaucer's verse. Durham NC 1961.

Braddy, H. The cook's mormal and its cure. MLQ 7 1946.

— Chaucer's bawdy tongue. Southern Folklore Quart 30 1966.

— Chaucer's bilingual idiom. Southern Folklore Quart 32 1968.

Everett, D. Chaucer's good ear. RES 23 1947; rptd in her Essays in ME literature, Oxford 1955.

Hulbert, J. R. Chaucer's Romance vocabulary. PQ 26 1947.

Kökeritz, H. The wyf of Bathe and al hire secte. Ibid.

— A guide to Chaucer's pronunciation. Stockholm and New Haven 1954.

— Rhetorical word-play in Chaucer. PMLA 69 1954.

Moore, A. K. The eyen greye of Chaucer's prioress. PQ 26 1947.

Southworth, J. G. Chaucer's final -*e* in rhyme. PMLA 62 1947, 64 1949. *See* Donaldson, below.

— Verses of cadence: an introduction to the prosody of Chaucer and his followers. Oxford 1954.

— The prosody of Chaucer and his followers: supplementary chapters to Verses of cadence. Oxford 1962.

— Chaucer: a plea for a reliable text. College Eng Dec 1964; rptd in Chaucer's mind and art, ed A. C. Cawley 1969.

Donaldson, E. T. Chaucer's final -*e*. PMLA 63 1948.

Huppé, B. F. The translation of the technical terms in the Middle English Romaunt of the rose. JEGP 47 1948.

Smithers, G. V. A Middle English idiom and its antecedents. Eng & Germanic Stud 1 1948.

Bloomfield, M. W. Chaucer's summoner and the girls of the diocese. PQ 28 1949.

Griffith, D. D. On word-studies in Chaucer. In Philologica: the [Kemp] Malone anniversary studies, Baltimore 1949.

Severs, J. D. Two irregular Chaucerian stanzas. MLN 64 1949.

Develin, J. C. Gummere and the Chaucerian short *e*. 1950 (priv ptd).

Schlauch, M. Chaucer's prose rhythms. PMLA 65 1950.

— Chaucer's colloquial English: its structural traits. PMLA 67 1952.

Fisher, J. H. Chaucer's use of swete and swote. JEGP 50 1951.

Hendrikson, D. W. The pardoner's hair—abundant or sparse? MLN 66 1951.

Lumiansky, R. M. Chaucer's for the nones. Neophilologus 35 1951.

Gross, S. I. Conscious verbal repetition in the pardoner's prologue. N & Q Oct 1953.

Johnson, O. E. Was Chaucer's merchant in debt? a study in Chaucerian syntax and rhetoric. JEGP 52 1953.

Watson, M. R. Wyatt, Chaucer and terza rima. MLN 68 1953.

Woolf, H. B. The summoner and his concubine. Ibid.

Homann, E. R. Chaucer's use of gan. JEGP 53 1954.

Beichner, P. E. Non alleluia ructare. Mediaeval Stud 18 1956.

Eliason, N. E. Some word-play in Chaucer's Reeve's tale. MLN 71 1956.

Hamp, E. P. St Ninian/Ronyan again. Celtica 3 1956.

Herdan, G. Chaucer's authorship of the Equatorie of the planetis: the use of Romance vocabulary as evidence. Language 32 1956.

Nathan, N. Pronouns of address in the Friar's tale. MLQ 17 1956.

— Pronouns of address in the Canterbury tales. Mediaeval Stud 21 1959.

Nault, C. A., jr. Foure and twenty yer again. MLN 71 1956.

Brown, C. S. Yet once more for the nones. Boston Univ Stud in Eng 3 1957.

Evans, R. O. Whan that Aprill(e)? N & Q June 1957.

Montgomery, M. For the nones once more. Boston Univ Stud in Eng 3 1957.

Novelli, C. The demonstrative adjective this: Chaucer's use of a colloquial narrative device. Mediaeval Stud 19 1957.

Murata, Y. The swearings in Chaucer. In Studies in English grammar and linguistics: a miscellany in honour of T. Otsuka, Tokyo 1958.

Dent, A. A. Chaucer and the horse. Proc Leeds Philosophical & Literary Soc 9 1959.

Berndt, R. Einführung in das Studium des Mittelalters, unter Zugrundlegung des Prologs der Canterbury tales. Halle 1960.

Green, A. W. Chaucer's Sir Thopas: meter, rhyme and contrast. Univ of Mississippi Stud in Eng 1 1960.

— Meter and rhyme in Chaucer's Anelida and Arcite. Univ of Mississippi Stud in Eng 2 1961.

— Chaucer's complaints: stanzaic arrangement, meter and rhyme. Univ of Mississippi Stud in Eng 3 1962.

Storms, G. A note on Chaucer's pronunciation of French *u*. E Studies 41 1960.

Benson, L. D. Chaucer's historical present: its meaning and uses. E Studies 42 1961.

Johnston, E. C. The pronoun of address in Chaucer's Troilus. Language Quart (Univ of S. Florida) 1 1962.

Dean, C. Chaucer's use of function words with substantives. Canadian Jnl of Linguistics 9 1964.

Hankey, C. T. Defining-context, association sets and glossing Chaucer. In Studies in medieval culture, ed J. Sommerfeldt, Kalamazoo Michigan 1964.

Masui, M. The structure of Chaucer's rime words: an exploration into the poetic language of Chaucer. Tokyo 1964.

— A mode of word-meaning in Chaucer's language of love. Stud in Eng Lit (Tokyo) 43 1967.

Fisiak, J. Morphemic structure of Chaucer's English. University Alabama 1965.

Byers, J. R. Harry Bailey's St Madrian. Eng Lang Notes 4 1966.

Gage, P. C. Syntax and poetry in Chaucer's Prioress's tale. Neophilologus 50 1966.

Miura, T. Arrangement of two or more attributive adjectives in Chaucer. Anglica 6 1966.

Owen, C. A., jr. Thy drasty rymyng... SP 63 1966.

Halle, M. and S. J. Keyser. Chaucer and the study of prosody. College Eng Dec 1966.

Kerkhof, J. Studies in the language of Chaucer. Leyden 1966. On syntax.

Kivimaa, K. The pleonastic that in relative and interrogative constructions in Chaucer's verse. Commentationes Humanarum Litterarum, Societas Scientiarum Fennica 41 1966.

— Clauses in Chaucer introduced by conjunctions with appended that. Commentationes Humanarum Litterarum, Societas Scientiarum Fennica 43 1969.

Frey, E. Die Verben des Transportfeldes bei Chaucer und König Alfred dem Grossen. Zürich 1967.

Smyser, H. M. Chaucer's use of 'gin' and 'do'. Speculum 42 1967.

Bauer, G. Historisches Präsens und Vergegenwärtigung des epischen Geschehens: ein erzähltechnischer Kunstgriff Chaucers. Anglia 85 1967.

— Studien zum System und Gebrauch der Tempora in der Sprache Chaucers und Gowers. Vienna 1970.

Kolinsky, M. Pronouns of address and the status of pilgrims in the Canterbury tales. Papers in Lang & Lit 3 1967.

Baird, J. L. The secte of the Wife of Bath. Chaucer Rev 2 1968.

— Secte and suit again: Chaucer and Langland. Chaucer Rev 6 1972.

Haskell, A. S. The host's precious corpus Madrian. JEGP 67 1968.

Nagucka, R. The syntactic component of Chaucer's Astrolabe. Cracow 1968.

Rogers, P. B. The names of the Canterbury pilgrims. Names 16 1968.

Shimose, M. On the rivalry between the inflectional and the periphrastic subjunctives in Chaucer's Troilus and Criseyde. In Maekawa Shunicki Kyoju Kanreki Kinenronbunshu, Tokyo 1968.

Stanley, E. G. Stanza and ictus: Chaucer's emphasis in Troilus and Criseyde. In Chaucer und seine Zeit, ed A. Esch, Tübingen 1968.

Hornstein, L. H. The wyf of Bathe and the merchant: from sex to secte. Chaucer Rev 3 1969.

Deligiorgis, S. Structuralism and the study of poetry. Neuphilologische Mitteilungen 70 1969.

Hascall, D. L. Some contributions to the Halle-Keyser theory of prosody. College Eng Feb 1969.

Ito, M. Gower's use of rime riche in Confessio amantis as compared with his practice in Mirour de l'omme and with the case of Chaucer. Stud in Eng Lit (Tokyo) 45 1969.

Ono, S. Chaucer's variants and what they tell us: fluctuation in the use of modal auxiliaries. Ibid.

Sudo, J. Some specific rime-units in Chaucer. Ibid.

— A preliminary note on the language of Chaucer's House of fame. Kobe City Univ Jnl 19 1969.

Ando, S. The language of the Romaunt of the rose (fragment A), with particular reference to Chaucer's relationship to Middle English provincial poetry. Stud in Eng Lit (Tokyo) 46 1970.

Quirk, R. and J. Svartvik. Types and uses of non-finite clauses in Chaucer. E Studies 51 1970.

Wimsatt, W. K. The rule and the norm: Halle and Keyser on Chaucer's meter. College Eng May 1970.

Topliff, D. E. Analysis of singular weak adjective inflections in Chaucer's works. Jnl of Eng Lang 4 1970.

Robinson, I. Chaucer's prosody. Cambridge 1971.

Burnley, J. D. Chaucer's art of verbal allusion: two notes. Neophilologus 56 1972.

Potter, S. Chaucer's untransposable binomials. Neuphilologische Mitteilungen 73 1972.

(9) MANUSCRIPTS, CHRONOLOGY AND TEXT

ten Brink, B. Chaucer: Studien zur Geschichte seiner Entwicklung und zur Chronologie seiner Schriften. Münster 1870.

— Zur Chronologie von Chaucers Schriften. E Studien 17 1892.

Furnivall, F. J. Autotype specimens of the chief Chaucer manuscripts. 1877–86 (Chaucer Soc).

Kellner, L. Zur Textkritik von Chaucers Boethius. E Studien 14 1890.

Koch, J. The chronology of Chaucer's writings. 1890 (Chaucer Soc).

— A detailed comparison of the eight manuscripts of the Canterbury tales as printed by the Chaucer Society, second series 43. 1913, Amsterdam 1967.

— Textkritische Bemerkungen zu Chaucers Canterbury tales. E Studien 47 1913.

— Textkritische Bemerkungen zu Chaucers Hous of fame. Anglia Beiblatt 27 1916.

— Das Handschriftenverhältnis in Chaucers Legend of good women. Anglia 43–4 1919–20.

— Chaucers Boethiusübersetzung: ein Beitrag zur Bestimmung der Chronologie seiner Werke. Anglia 46 1922.

— Ein neues Datum für Chaucers Quene Anelida and fals Arcite. E Studien 56 1922.

— Berichtungen. E Studien 69 1934. Readings of Naples ms of Clerk's tale.

Hales, J. W. The date of the Canterbury tales. Athenaeum 8 April 1893.

Skeat, W. W. The Chaucer canon. Oxford 1900.

— The eight-text edition of the Canterbury tales; with remarks upon the classification of the manuscripts and upon the Harleian manuscript 7334. 1909.

— Chaucer: the Shipman's prologue. MLR 5 1910.

— Chaucer: a curious misplacement. N & Q March 1910. Canterbury tales D. 1294.

Mather, F. J. On the date of the Knight's tale. In An English miscellany presented to Dr [F. J.] Furnivall, Oxford 1901.

Tatlock, J. S. P. The dates of Chaucer's Troilus and Criseyde and Legend of good women. MP 1 1904.

— The development and chronology of Chaucer's works. 1907 (Chaucer Soc), Gloucester Mass 1964.

— The Harleian ms 7334 and the revision of the Canterbury tales. 1909 (Chaucer Soc).

— Notes on Chaucer. MLN 29 1914. On Plimpton fragment.

— The Canterbury tales in 1400. PMLA 50 1935.

— The date of the Troilus and minor Chauceriana. MLN 50 1935.

Lowes, J. L. The prologue to the Legend of good women considered in its chronological relations. PMLA 20 1905.

— The date of Chaucer's Troilus. PMLA 23 1908.

— The date of the Envoy to Bukton. MLN 27 1912.

Hammond, E. P. On the order of the Canterbury tales. MP 3 1906.

— On the editing of Chaucer's minor poems. MLN 23 1908.

— A Burgundian copy of Chaucer's Troilus. MLN 26 1911.

— Chaucer and Dante and their scribes. MLN 31 1916.

— A scribe of Chaucer. MP 27 1930.

— Chaucer's book of the twenty-five ladies. MLN 48 1933.

Flügel, E. A new collation of the Ellesmere ms. Anglia 30 1907.

Hamilton, G. L. Chauceriana 1: the date of the Clerk's tale and Chaucer's Petrak. MLN 23 1908.

McCracken, H. N. Notes suggested by a Chaucer codex. Ibid.

— A new manuscript of Chaucer's Monk's tale. Ibid.

— More odd texts of Chaucer's Troilus. MLN 25 1910.

— An odd text of Chaucer's Purse. MLN 27 1912.

Prescott, E. P. On the editing of Chaucer's minor poems. MLN 23 1908.

Kittredge, G. L. The date of Chaucer's Troilus and other matters. 1909 (Chaucer Soc), New York 1969.

— Chaucer's Medea and the date of the Legend of good women. PMLA 24 1909.

Emerson, O. F. A new note on the date of Chaucer's Knight's tale. In Studies in language and literature presented to J. M. Hart, New York 1910.

Root, R. K. The date of Chaucer's Medea. PMLA 25 1910.

— The manuscripts of Chaucer's Troilus, with collotype facsimiles of the various handwritings. 1914 (Chaucer Soc).

— The textual tradition of Chaucer's Troilus. 1916 (Chaucer Soc).

— The text of the Canterbury tales. SP 38 1941.

— Chaucer's summoner. TLS 23 Jan 1943.

— and H. N. Russell. A planetary date for Chaucer's Troilus. PMLA 39 1924.

Moore, S. The date of Chaucer's marriage group. MLN 26 1911.

— On the date of Chaucer's Astrolabe. MP 10 1913.

— The position of group C in the Canterbury tales. PMLA 30 1915.

Brown, C. Prologue to Chaucer's Lyf of Seint Cecile. MP 9 1912.

— The text of the Canterbury tales. MLN 55 1940.

— Three notes on the text of the Canterbury tales. MLN 56 1941.

— Author's revision in the Canterbury tales. PMLA 57 1942.

— The date of prologue F to the Legend of good women. MLN 58 1943.

Greg, W. W. Chaucer attributions in ms R.3.19 in the library of Trinity College, Cambridge. MLR 8 1913.

— The early printed editions of the Canterbury tales. PMLA 39 1924.

— The ms source of Caxton's second edition of the Canterbury tales. PMLA 44 1929.

Spies, H. Chaucers religiöse Grundstimmung und die Echtheit der Parsons tale: eine textkritische Untersuchung. In Festschrift für L. Morsbach, Halle 1913.

Campbell, G. H. Chaucer's prophecy in 1586. MLN 29 1914.

Vockrodt, G. Die Reimtechnik Chaucers als Mittel zur chronologischen Bestimmung seiner in Reimpaar geschriebenen Werke. Halle 1914.

Kenyon, J. S. Further notes on the marriage group in the Canterbury tales. JEGP 15 1916.

— Wife of Bath's tale 1159–62. MLN 54 1939.

Shackford, M. H. The date of Chaucer's House of fame. MLN 31 1916.

Amy, E. F. The text of Chaucer's Legend of good women. Princeton 1918.

— The manuscripts of the Legend of good women. JEGP 21 1922.

Lange, H. Chaucers Myn auctour called Lollius und die Datierung des Hous of fame. Anglia 42 1918.

Science, M. A suggested correction of the text of Chaucer's Boethius. TLS 29 March 1923.

Piper, E. F. The miniatures of the Ellesmere manuscript. PQ 3 1924.

— The royal boar and the Ellesmere Chaucer. PQ 5 1926.

Brusendorff, A. The Chaucer tradition. London and Copenhagen 1925; 1967.

Marburg, C, Notes on the Cardigan Chaucer manuscript. PMLA 41 1926.

Conrad, B. R. The date of Chaucer's prologue. N & Q May 1927.

Looten, C. Les portraits dans Chaucer: leurs origines. Revue de Littérature Comparée 7 1927.

Kilgour, M. The manuscript source of Caxton's second edition of the Canterbury tales. PMLA 44 1929.

Langhans, V. Die Datierung der Prosastücke Chaucers. Anglia 53 1929.

Everett, D. Another collation of the Ellesmere manuscript of the Canterbury tales. MÆ 1 1932.

McCormick, W. and J. E. Heseltine. The manuscripts of Chaucer's Canterbury tales: a critical description of their contents. Oxford 1933.

Vine, G. The Miller's tale: a study of an unrecorded manuscript in the John Rylands Library in relation to the first printed text. Bull John Rylands Library 17 1933.

Braddy, H. The two Petros in the Monk's tale. PMLA 50 1935.

— The date of Chaucer's Lak of stedfastnesse. JEGP 36 1937.

Crow, M. M. Corrections in the Paris manuscript of Chaucer's Canterbury tales: a study in scribal collaboration. SE 15 1935.

— Unique variants in the Paris manuscript of Chaucer's Canterbury tales. SE 16 1936.

— The Reeve's tale in the hands of a north Midlands scribe. SE 18 1938.

— John of Angoulême and his Chaucer manuscript. Speculum 17 1942.

Brittain, R. E. A textual note on Chaucer: Gentilesse 20. MLN 51 1936.

Bühler, C. F. A new Lydgate-Chaucer manuscript. MLN 52 1937.

— Notes on the Campsall manuscript of Chaucer's Troilus and Criseyde now in the Pierpont Morgan Library. Speculum 20 1945.

— Chaucer's House of fame: another Caxton variant. PBSA 42 1948.

Lossing, M. L. S. The order of the Canterbury tales: a fresh relation between a and b types of manuscripts. JEGP 37 1938.

Thompson, W. D'A. Archaungel as a bird-name in Chaucer. N & Q Nov 1938.

Manly, J. M. and E. Rickert. The Hengwrt manuscript of the Canterbury tales. Nat Lib of Wales Jnl 1 1939.

— The text of the Canterbury tales. 8 vols Chicago 1940.

Robbins, R. H. The Speculum misericordie. PMLA 54 1939. On Delamere-Penrose ms.

Brotanek, R. Me Dichtungen aus der Hs 432 Trinity College in Dublin. Halle 1940.

Dunn, T. F. The manuscript sources of Caxton's second edition of the Canterbury tales. Chicago 1940.

Kunstmann, J. G. Chaucer's archaungel. MLN 55 1940.

Tupper, F. Chaucer and the Cambridge edition. JEGP 39 1940.

Eliason, N. E. Chaucer's second nun? MLQ 3 1942.

Caldwell, R. Joseph Holand collector and antiquary. MP 40 1943.

— The scribe of the Chaucer ms, Cambridge Univ Lib Gg.4.27. MLQ 5 1944.

Dempster, G. Chaucer's manuscript of Petrarch's version of the Griselda story. MP 41 1944.

— Manly's conception of the early history of the Canterbury tales. PMLA 61 1946.

— A chapter of the manuscript history of the Canterbury tales: the ancestor of group D, the origin of its texts, tale-order and spurious links. PMLA 63 1948.

— On the significance of Hengwrt's change of ink in the Merchant's tale. MLN 63 1948.

— The fifteenth-century editors of the Canterbury tales and the problem of tale order. PMLA 64 1949.

— A period in the development of the Canterbury tales marriage group and of blocks B² and C. PMLA 68 1953.

Coffman, G. R. Canon's yeoman's prologue G.ll.563–5: horse or man? MLN 59 1944.

Parr, J. The date and revision of Chaucer's Knight's tale. PMLA 60 1945.

Pratt, R. A. Conjecture regarding Chaucer's manuscript of the Teseida. SP 42 1945.

— Was Chaucer's Knight's tale extensively revised after the middle of 1390? PMLA 63 1948.

— The order of the Canterbury tales. PMLA 66 1951.

Jones, H. L., jr. The date of Chaucer's House of fame. Delaware Notes 19 1946.

Kökeritz, H. Chaucer's Rosemounde. MLN 63 1948.

Pace, G. B. Four unpublished Chaucer manuscripts. Ibid.

— The text of Chaucer's Purse. SB 1 1948.

— Otho A.xviii. Speculum 26 1951.

— The true text of the Former age. Mediaeval Stud 23 1961.

— Speght's Chaucer and ms Gg.4.27. SB 21 1968.

Seaton, E. That Scotch copy of Chaucer. JEGP 47 1948.

Stroud, T. A. A Chaucer scribe's concern with page format. Speculum 23 1948.

—— The ms Fitzwilliam: an examination of Miss Rickert's hypothesis. MP 46 1949.

—— Scribal errors in Manly and Rickert's text. MLN 68 1953.

Weese, W. E. Vengeance and pleyn correccioun, Knight's tale 2461. MLN 63 1948.

Galway, M. The Troilus frontispiece. MLR 44 1949.

Friedman, A. B. Chaucer and Robin Hood. N & Q May 1950.

Hench, A. L. Printer's copy for Tyrwhitt's Chaucer. SB 3 1950.

O'Leary, J. G. The Urswyck Chaucer. TLS 13 Oct 1950.

Bliss, A. J. Notes on the Auchinleck ms. Speculum 26 1951.

Bonner, F. W. The genesis of the Chaucer apocrypha. SP 48 1951.

Chewning, H. The text of the Envoy to Alison. SB 5 1952.

Hartung, A. E. The clerk's endlink in the D manuscripts. PMLA 67 1952.

—— Inappropriate pointing in the Canon's yeoman's tale G. 1236-9. PMLA 77 1962.

—— Two notes on the Summoner's tale: hosts and swans. Eng Lang Notes 4 1966.

Doyle, A. I. Unrecorded Chaucerian manuscripts. Durham Philobiblon 1 1953.

—— and G. B. Pace. A new Chaucer manuscript. PMLA 83 1968. On Coventry ms.

Donaldson, E. T. Chaucer's Miller's tale A. 3483-6. MLN 69 1954; rptd in his Speaking of Chaucer, 1970.

—— Chaucer, Canterbury tales D. 117: a critical edition. Speculum 40 1965; rptd ibid.

McKenzie, J. J. A Chaucerian emendation. N & Q Nov 1954.

Schaar, C. An emendation in Chaucer's Book of the Duchess. E Studies 35 1954.

Severs, J. B. Did Chaucer rearrange the clerk's envoy? MLN 69 1954.

—— Author's revision in block C of the Canterbury tales. Speculum 29 1954.

Magoun, F. P., jr. Canterbury tales F. 1541-4. MLN 70 1955.

Owen, C. A., jr. The Canterbury tales: early manuscripts and relative popularity. JEGP 54 1955.

O'Connor, J. J. The astronomical dating of Chaucer's Troilus. JEGP 55 1956.

Campbell, J. J. A new Troilus fragment. PMLA 73 1958. On Cecil fragment.

Emerson, F. W. Cambalus in the Squire's tale. N & Q Nov 1958.

McLaughlin, J. C. The honour and the humble obeysaunce: prologue to the Legend of good women l. 135, G-text. PQ 38 1959.

Rogers, F. R. The tale of Gamelyn and the editing of the Canterbury tales. JEGP 58 1959.

Williams, G. The Troilus and Criseyde frontispiece again. MLR 67 1962.

Campbell, J. H. Chaucer's Canterbury tales: Princeton acquisition of Tollemache ms. Princeton Univ Lib Chron 26 1964.

Elliott, C. The reeve's prologue and tale in the Ellesmere and Hengwrt manuscripts. N & Q May 1964.

Hetherington, J. R. Chaucer 1532-1602: notes and facsimile text. Birmingham 1964 (priv ptd).

Silvia, D. S., jr. Chaucer's friars: swans or swains? Summoner's tale D. 1930. Eng Lang Notes 1 1964.

Dunleavy, G. W. The Chaucer ascription in Trinity College Dublin ms D.2.8. Ambix 13 1965.

Schulz, H. C. The Ellesmere manuscript of Chaucer's Canterbury tales. San Marino 1965.

Gardner, J. The case against the Bradshaw shift: or the mystery of the manuscript in the trunk. Papers in Eng Lang & Lit 3 1967.

Davis, N. Chaucer's Gentilesse: a forgotten manuscript, with some proverbs. RES new ser 20 1969.

Nichols, R. E., jr. Chaucer's Fortune, Truth and Gentilesse: the last unpublished manuscript traditions. Speculum 44 1969.

Rand, G. I. The date of the Nun's priest's tale. Amer N & Q 8 1969.

(10) LIFE AND BACKGROUND

Biography

Nicolas, N. H. The life of Chaucer. In Poetical works of Chaucer, 1845.

Ward, A. W. Chaucer. 1879 (EML).

Furnivall, F. J., W. D. Selby, E. A. Bond and R. E. G. Kirk. Life-records of Chaucer. 4 pts 1871-1900 (Chaucer Soc).

Spielmann, M. H. The portraits of Chaucer. 1900 (Chaucer Soc).

—— A portrait of Chaucer. TLS 5 April 1934.

Kirk, R. E. G. A Chaucer tragedy. N & Q Dec 1905.

Kern, A. A. New Chaucer records. MLN 21 1906.

—— The ancestry of Chaucer. Baltimore 1906.

—— Chaucer's sister. MLN 23 1908.

Coulton, G. G. Chaucer's captivity. MLR 4 1908.

Legouis, E. Chaucer. Paris 1910; tr 1913.

Tout, T. F. Mission to Calais: 1360. EHR 25 1910.

Emerson, O. F. A new Chaucer item. MLN 26 1911.

—— Chaucer's first military service: a study of Edward the Third's invasion of France in 1359-60. Romanic Rev 3 1912.

—— Chaucer's testimony as to his age. MP 11 1914.

Hulbert, J. R. Chaucer's official life. Menasha 1912.

—— Chaucer and the Earl of Oxford. MP 10 1913.

—— A Chaucer item. MLN 36 1921.

Moore, S. The new Chaucer item. MLN 27 1912.

—— Studies in the life-records of Chaucer. Anglia 37 1913.

—— New life-records of Chaucer. MP 16 1919, 18 1921.

—— The new Chaucer items. MLR 22 1927.

Kuhl, E. P. Index to the life-records of Chaucer. MP 10 1913.

—— Chaucer and fowle ok. MLN 36 1921.

—— My maistre Bukton. PMLA 38 1923.

—— Chaucer and Aldgate. PMLA 39 1924.

—— New Chaucer items. MLN 40 1925.

—— Why was Chaucer sent to Milan in 1378? MLN 62 1947.

Tatlock, J. S. P. The duration of Chaucer's visits to Italy. JEGP 12 1913.

—— Chaucer and Wyclif. MP 14 1917.

Hadow, G. E. Chaucer and his times. New York 1914.

Rye, W. Chaucer: a Norfolk man. Norwich 1915 (priv ptd).

—— New light on Chaucer. TLS 24 Feb 1927.

Cook, A. S. The last months of Chaucer's earliest patron. Trans Connecticut Acad of Arts & Sciences 21 1916.

Tupper, F. Chaucer and Richmond. MLN 31 1916.

—— Chaucer and Lancaster. MLN 32 1917.

—— Chaucer in Ireland. PMLA 36 1921.

Kittredge, G. L. Lewis Chaucer or Lewis Clifford? MP 14 1917.

Hutton, E. Did Chaucer meet Petrarch and Boccaccio? Anglo-Italian Rev 1 1918.

—— Chaucer and Italy. Nineteenth Century July 1940.

Liebermann, F. Zu Chaucers Stellung in Hofämtern. Archiv 140 1920.

Rickert, E. Was Chaucer a student at the Inner Temple? In J. M. Manly anniversary studies in language and literature, Chicago 1923.

—— Extracts from a fourteenth-century account book. MP 24 1927.

—— Chaucer's debt to Walter Bukholt. Ibid.

—— Chaucer at the funeral of the Princess of Wales. TLS 11 Aug 1927.

—— Chaucer's debt to John Churchman. MP 25 1928.

—— More payments to Chaucer. TLS 27 Oct 1927.

—— Chaucer abroad in 1368. MP 25 1928.

—— More life-records of Chaucer. TLS 27 Sept–4 Oct 1928.

—— Chaucer at school. MP 29 1932.

—— Chaucer called to account. TLS 8 Dec 1932.

—— Chaucer and the treasurer of Calais. TLS 17 Nov 1932.

—— Chaucer's grandfather in action. TLS 6 April 1933.

Jusserand, J. J. On the possible meeting of Chaucer and Petrarch. In his School for ambassadors and other essays, 1924.

Lawrence, C. E. The personality of Chaucer. Quart Rev 242 1924.

Ruud, M. D. Thomas Chaucer. Univ of Minnesota Stud in Lang & Lit 9 1926.

A note about the oath of the comptroller of the petty customs and memoranda about Chaucer's appointment of deputies. N & Q June 1927.

Looten, C. Les portraits de Chaucer: leurs origines. Revue de Littérature Comparée 7 1927.

Manly, J. M. Chaucer as controller. TLS 9 June 1927.

—— Litel Lewis my sone. TLS 7 June 1928.

—— Thomas Chaucer, son of Geoffrey. TLS 3 Aug 1933.

—— Chaucer's mission to Lombardy: reply to Haldeen Braddy. MLN 49 1934.

—— A portrait of Chaucer. TLS 9 March 1934.

—— Mary Chaucer's first husband. Speculum 9 1934.

—— and E. Rickert. Chaucer in a new setting. TLS 19 Aug 1926.

Pollard, A. W. Chaucer's pensions in April 1385. RES 4 1928.

Wyatt, A. J. Chaucer's pensions in April 1385. Ibid.

Brooks, E. St J. Chaucer's mother. New England Historical & Genealogical Register 83 1929; TLS 14 March 1929.

—— Chaucer and the Duchess of Suffolk. N & Q May 1933.

—— The descendants of Chaucer. N & Q Oct 1941.

Langhans, V. Chaucers Heirat. Anglia 54 1930.

Baugh, A. C. Kirk's life-records of Thomas Chaucer. PMLA 47 1932.

—— Thomas Chaucer: one man or two? PMLA 48 1933.

—— The background of Chaucer's mission to Spain. In Chaucer und seine Zeit, ed A. Esch, Tübingen 1968.

Krauss, P. Notes on Thomas, Geoffrey and Philippa Chaucer. MLN 47 1932.

—— William Chaumbre: kinsman of Thomas Chaucer. PMLA 49 1934.

Braddy, H. New documentary evidence concerning Chaucer's mission to Lombardy. MLN 48 1933.

—— Froissart's account of Chaucer's embassy in 1377. RES 14 1938.

—— Chaucer and Dame Alice Perrers. Speculum 21 1946.

—— Chaucer's Philippa, daughter of Panneto. MLN 64 1949.

Chaucer and Henry Yevele. Ars Quatuor Coronatorum 44 1934.

Sedgwick, H. D. Dan Chaucer: an introduction to the poet, his poetry and his times. Indianapolis 1934.

Lange, H. Die Kenntnis der Missweisung oder magnetischen Deklination bei dem Londoner Chaucer (1380); zugleich ein Beitrag zur Lösung einiger Chaucerprobleme. Forschungen und Fortschritte 11 1935.

—— Die Bedeutung der Heraldik für die Erklärung eines mittelalterlichen Dichters. Forschungen und Fortschritte 13 1937.

—— Chaucer und Michael de la Pole. Archiv 172 1938.

Stevenson, H. A. A possible relation between Chaucer's long lease and the date of his birth. MLN 50 1935.

Thompson, C. H. A note on Nicholas Chaucer. PQ 14 1935.

Whitford, H. C. A new document concerning Robert Chaucer. Ibid.

Thompson W. H. Chaucer and his times. 1936.

Salter, F. M. Chaucer: a character analysis. Univ Rev (Univ of Kansas City) 4 1938.

Bressie, R. Was Chaucer at the siege of Paris? JEGP 39 1940.

Lamborn, E. A. G. The arms on the Chaucer tomb at Ewelme. Oxoniensia 5 1940.

—— The descendants of Chaucer. N & Q Sept 1941, May 1942.

Loomis, R. S. Was Chaucer a Laodicean? In Essays and studies in honor of Carleton Brown, New York 1940; rptd in Chaucer criticism vol 1, ed R. Schoeck and J. Taylor, Notre Dame 1960.

—— Was Chaucer a free thinker? In Studies in medieval literature in honor of A. C. Baugh, Philadelphia 1961.

Savage, H. L. Chaucer: the life. Progress of Medieval & Renaissance Stud 15 1940.

Shelly, P. v. D. Chaucer 1340?–1400. Scientific Monthly Nov 1940.

Galway, M. Chaucer JP and MP. MLR 36 1941.

—— Chaucer among thieves. TLS 29 April 1946.

—— Pullesdon in the life-records of Chaucer. N & Q Sept 1957.

—— Chaucer's journeys in 1368. TLS 4 April 1958.

—— Philippa Pan, Philippa Chaucer. MLR 55 1960.

Ross, A. S. C. Nicholas Chaucer. TLS 23 May 1942.

Scott, F. R. Chaucer and the Parliament of 1386. Speculum 18 1943.

Anderson, M. Alice Chaucer and her husbands. PMLA 60 1945.

Carpenter, N. C. A note on Chaucer's mother. MLN 60 1945.

Chute, M. Chaucer of England. New York 1946.

Call, R. The Plimpton Chaucer and other problems of Chaucerian portraiture. Speculum 22 1947.

Watts, P. R. The strange case of Chaucer and Cecilia Chaumpaigne. Law Quart Rev 63 1947.

Plucknet, T. F. T. Chaucer's escapade. Law Quart Rev 64 1948.

Brett-James, N. G. Introducing Chaucer. 1949.

Parks, G. B. The route of Chaucer's first journey to Italy. ELH 16 1949.

Pratt, R. A. Chaucer and Sir John Hawkwood. ELH 16 1949.

Crow, M. M. Materials for a new edition of the Chaucer life-records. SE 31 1952.

—— and C. C. Olson (ed). Chaucer life-records. Oxford and Austin 1966.

Bland, D. S. Chaucer and the Inns of Court: a re-examination. E Studies 33 1952.

—— When was Chaucer born? TLS 26 April 1957.

Kelly, R. Z. Young Chaucer. New York 1952.

Brewer, D. S. Chaucer. 1953, 1960 (rev).

—— Chaucer in his time. 1963.

Howard, D. R. Chaucer the man. PMLA 80 1965; rptd in Chaucer's mind and art, ed A. C. Cawley 1969.

Honoré-Duvergé, S. Chaucer en Espagne? (1366). In Recueil de travaux offerts à Clovis Brunel, 2 vols Paris 1955.

Zanco, A. Chaucer e il suo mondo. Turin 1955.

Kane, G. The autobiographical fallacy in Chaucer and Langland studies. 1965.

Mitchell, J. Hoccleve's supposed friendship with Chaucer. Eng Lang Notes 4 1966.

Fifield, M. Chaucer the theater-goer. Papers in Eng Lang & Lit 3 1967.

Garbaty, T. J. Chaucer in Spain 1366: soldier of fortune or agent of the crown? Eng Lang Notes 5 1967.

Serraillier, I. Chaucer and his world. 1967.
Stanley-Wrench, M. Teller of tales: the life of Chaucer Tadsworth Surrey 1967.
Halliday, F. E. Chaucer and his world. 1968.
Wagenknecht, E. The personality of Chaucer. Norman Oklahoma 1968.

Historical, Religious and Social Background

Browne, M. Chaucer's England. 2 vols 1869.
Brandl, A. Über einige historische Anspielungen in den Chaucer-Dichtungen. E Studien 12 1889.
— Geographie der Chaucerzeit. Archiv 165 1934.
Kittredge, G. L. Supposed historical allusions in the Squire's tale. E Studien 13 1889.
— Chaucer and some of his friends. MP 1 1904.
Morris, E. E. The physician in Chaucer. In An English miscellany presented to Dr [F. J.] Furnivall, Oxford 1901.
Snell, F. J. The age of Chaucer. 1901.
Lowes, J. L. The tempest at hir hoom-cominge. MLN 19 1904.
— The dry sea and the Carrenare. MP 3 1906.
— Illustrations of Chaucer, drawn chiefly from Deschamps. Romanic Rev 2 1911.
— Chaucer and the seven deadly sins. PMLA 30 1915.
Sypherd, W. O. Chaucer's eight years' sickness. MLN 20 1905.
Brown, C. F. Chaucer's litel clergeon. MP 3 1906.
— Another contemporary allusion in Chaucer's Troilus and Criseyde. MLN 26 1911.
— Chaucer and the hours of the Blessed Virgin. MLN 30 1915.
Cook, A. S. Chaucer's prol. 466. MLN 22 1907.
— Beginning the board in Prussia. JEGP 14 1915.
— The historical background of Chaucer's knight. New Haven 1916.
Manly, J. M. A knight there was. Trans Amer Philosophical Soc 38 1907; rptd in Chaucer: modern essays in criticism, ed E. Wagenknecht, New York 1959.
— Chaucer and the rhetoricians. Proc Br Acad 12 1926; rptd in Chaucer criticism vol 1, ed R. Schoeck and J. Taylor, Notre Dame 1960.
Browne, W. H. Notes on Chaucer's astrology. MLN 23 1908.
Coulton, G. Chaucer and his England. 1908, 1963 (with bibliography by T. W. Craik).
Kollreuter, M. Das Privatleben in England nach Chaucer, Gower und Langland. Halle 1908.
Boynton, P. H. Chaucer's London. Chautauquan 60 1910.
Snyder, F. B. Sir Thomas Norray and Sir Thopas. MLN 25 1910.
Jones, H. S. V. The clerk of Oxenford. PMLA 27 1912.
Moore, S. The prologue to Chaucer's Legend of good women in relation to Queen Anne and Richard. MLR 7 1912.
— Chaucer's pardoner of Rounceval. MP 25 1928.
Tatlock, J. S. P. Astrology and magic in Chaucer's Franklin's tale. In Anniversary papers by colleagues and pupils of G. L. Kittredge, Boston 1913.
— Is Chaucer's monk a monk? MLN 56 1941.
Tupper, F. Chaucer's doctour of phisik. Nation (New York) Sept 1913.
— Chaucer and the seven deadly sins. PMLA 29 1914.
— The pardoner's tavern. JEGP 13 1914.
— Chaucer's bed's head. MLN 30 1915.
— Chaucer's sinners and sins. JEGP 15 1916.
— Chaucer's tale of Ireland. PMLA 36 1921. Anelida and Arcite.
Jefferson, B. L. Queen Anne and Queen Alcestis. JEGP 13 1914.
Kuhl, E. P. Some friends of Chaucer. PMLA 29 1914.
— Chaucer's burgesses. Trans Wisconsin Acad of Sciences, Arts & Letters 18 1916.
— Notes on Chaucer's prioress. PQ 2 1923.
— Chaucer and the Church. MLN 40 1925.

— Chaucer's monk. MLN 55 1940.
— Chaucer and the red rose. PQ 24 1945.
— Chaucer the patriot. PQ 25 1946.
— Chaucer and Westminster Abbey. JEGP 45 1946.
— and H. J. Webb. Chaucer's squire. ELH 6 1939.
Rickert, E. Thou Vache. MP 11 1914.
— A leaf from a fourteenth-century letter book. MP 25 1928.
— Goode lief, my wyf. Ibid.
— Some English personal letters of 1402. RES 8 1932.
— Chaucer's Hodge of Ware. TLS 20 Oct 1932.
—, M. M. Crow and C. C. Olson (ed). Chaucer's world. 1948.
Young, K. Chaucer and the liturgy. MLN 30 1915.
— A note on Chaucer's friar. MLN 50 1935.
Savage, H. W. Chaucer's long castel. MLN 31 1916.
Hughes, D. Illustrations of Chaucer's England. 1918.
Curry, W. C. The secret of Chaucer's pardoner. JEGP 18 1919.
— Chaucer's reeve and miller. PMLA 35 1920.
— More about Chaucer's wife of Bath. PMLA 37 1922.
— The malady of Chaucer's summoner. MP 19 1923.
— O Mars, O Atazir. JEGP 22 1923.
— Chaucer's science and art. Texas Rev 8 1923.
— Chauntecleer and Pertelote on dreams. E Studien 58 1924.
— Chaucer's doctor of phisyk. PQ 4 1925.
— Chaucer and the medieval sciences. New York 1926, 1960 (rev).
Grimm, F. M. Astronomical lore in Chaucer. Lincoln Nebraska 1919.
Beatty, J. M. A companion of Chaucer. MLN 35 1920.
Emerson, O. F. Chaucer's opie of Thebes fyn. MP 17 1920.
— Science in Chaucer. Ibid.
— Chaucer and medieval hunting. Romanic Rev 13 1922.
Baum, P. F. Chaucer's faste by the Belle, Canterbury tales A.719. MLN 36 1921.
Farnham, W. E. John (Henry) Scogan. MLR 16 1921.
— The days of the mone. SP 20 1923.
Hotson, J. L. The Tale of Melibeus and John of Gaunt. SP 18 1921.
Knott, T. A. Chaucer's anonymous merchant. PQ 1 1922.
Liebermann, F. Theseus Herzogstitel bei Chaucer. Archiv 145 1923.
Mossé, F. Chaucer et la liturgie. Revue Germanique 14 1923.
— Chaucer et le métier de l'écrivain. Etudes Anglaises 7 1954.
Reid, M. E. The historical interpretations of the Parlement of foules. Univ of Wisconsin Stud in Lang & Lit 18 1923.
Walker, A. S. Note on Chaucer's prologue. MLN 38 1923.
Brendon, J. A. The age of Chaucer. 1924.
Damon, S. F. Chaucer and alchemy. PMLA 39 1924.
Maxfield, E. K. Chaucer and religious reform. Ibid.
Power, E. Madame Eglentyne: Chaucer's prioress in real life. In her Medieval people, 1924.
Wells, W. H. Chaucer as a literary critic. MLN 39 1924.
Fischer, W. Die französische Sprachkenntnisse von Chaucers Priorin. In Probleme der englischen Sprache und Kultur: Festschrift J. Hoops, Heidelberg 1925.
Moffett, H. Y. Oswald the reeve. PQ 4 1925.
Quiller-Couch, A. T. The age of Chaucer. 1926.
Curtiss, J. T. The horoscope in Chaucer's Man of law's tale. JEGP 26 1927.
Bashford, H. H. Chaucer's physician and his forebears. Nineteenth Century Aug 1928.
Camden, C., jr. Query on Chaucer's burgesses. PQ 7 1928.
Wood-Legh, K. L. The franklin. RES 4 1928.
Naunin, T. Der Einfluss der mittelenglischen Rhetorik auf Chaucers Dichtung. Bonn 1929.
White, F. E. Chaucer's shipman. MP 26–7 1929–30.

Clark, T. B. The forehead of Chaucer's prioress. PQ 9 1930.

Evans, J. Chaucer and decorative art. RES 6 1930.

Looten, C. Chaucer et la dialectique. Revue Anglo-américaine 7 1930.

Montgomery, F. A note on the Reeve's prologue. PQ 10 1931.

— The musical instruments in the Canterbury tales. Musical Quart 17 1931.

Ives, D. V. A man of religion. MLR 27 1932.

Lange, H. Chaucer als Hof- und Gelegenheitsdichter. Archiv 157 1930.

— Ein neuer Chaucerfund: zu John Kochs Richard-Anna-Theorie (Vogelparlament). E Studien 68 1934.

— Chaucer und das Wilton House Diptychon. Nachricht von der Gesellschaft der Wissenschaften zu Göttingen: philologische-historische Klasse 1 1934.

— Hat Chaucer den Kompass gekannt und benützt? Anglia 58 1934.

— and A. Nippoldt. Die Deklination am 20 Mai 1380 in London. Quellen und Studien zur Geschichte der Naturwissenschaften und der Medizin 5 1936.

Patch, H. R. Chaucer and the common people. JEGP 29 1930.

Hamilton, M. P. Notes on Chaucer and the rhetoricians. PMLA 47 1932.

— Echoes of childermas in the tale of the prioress. MLR 34 1939; rptd in Chaucer: modern essays in criticism, ed E. Wagenknecht, New York 1959.

— The clerical status of Chaucer's alchemist. Speculum 16 1941.

— The credentials of Chaucer's pardoner. JEGP 40 1941.

— The summoner's psalm of Davit. MLN 57 1942.

— The convent of Chaucer's prioress and her priests. In Philologica: the [Kemp] Malone anniversary studies, Baltimore 1949.

Miller, A. H. Chaucer's secte Saturnyn. MLN 47 1932.

Nicholls, A. G. Medicine in Chaucer's day. Dalhousie Rev 12 1932.

Powley, E. B. Chaucer's reeve. TLS 14 July 1932.

Richardson, M. E. The clerk of Oxenford. TLS 5 May 1932.

Work, J. A. Echoes of the anathema in Chaucer. PMLA 47 1932.

Boldaun, N. W. Chaucer and matters medical. New England Jnl of Medicine 208 1933.

Collins, F., jr. The Kinges note: the Miller's tale line 31: Ave rex gentis Anglorum. Speculum 8 1933. Reply by G. L. Frost, ibid.

Horton, O. E. The neck of Chaucer's friar. MLN 48 1933.

Norris, D. M. Chaucer's Pardoner's tale and Flanders. PMLA 48 1933.

Schramm, W. L. The cost of books in Chaucer's time. MLN 48 1933.

Graham, H. Chaucer's educational background. Thought 9 1934.

Houseman, P. A. Science in Chaucer. Scientific Monthly June 1934.

Myers, L. M. A line in the reeve's prologue. MLN 49 1934.

Braddy, H. The historical background of the Parlement of foules. RES 11 1935.

— Sir Peter and the Envoy to Bukton. PQ 14 1935.

— Cambyuskan's flying horse and Charles VI's cerf volant. MLR 33 1938.

Krauss, R. John Heyron of Newton Plecy, Somerset. Speculum 10 1935.

Maynard, T. Chaucer's monk. Month Feb 1935.

Plimpton, G. A. The education of Chaucer, illustrated from the school-books in use in his time. 1935.

Pfander, H. G. Some medieval manuals of religious instruction and observations on Chaucer's Parson's tale. JEGP 35 1936.

Thurston, H. Conversion of Boccaccio and Chaucer. Studies 25 1936.

Coffman, G. R. Old age in Chaucer's day. MLN 52 1937.

— Chaucer's library and literary heritage for the Canterbury tales. SP 38 1941.

Haselmayer, L. A. The apparitor and Chaucer's summoner. Speculum 12 1937.

Hench, A. L. On the subtly creeping wine of Chaucer's pardoner. MLN 52 1937.

Lewis, N. B. The anniversary service for Blanche, Duchess of Lancaster, 12 September 1374. Bull John Rylands Lib 21 1937.

Lyon, E. D. Roger de Ware, cook. MLN 52 1937.

McKenna, Sr M. B. Liturgy of the Canterbury tales. Catholic Education Rev 35 1937.

Redstone, V. B. and J. L. The Heyrons of London: a study in the social origins of Chaucer. Speculum 12 1937.

Fink, Z. S. Another knight ther was. PQ 17 1938.

Homans, G. C. Free bull. RES 14 1938.

Kirby, T. A. The haberdasher and his companions. MLN 53 1938.

Philip, Br C. A further note on old age in Chaucer's day. Ibid.

Bressie, R. A governour wily and wys. MLN 54 1939.

— Chaucer's monk again. MLN 56 1941.

Galway, M. Chaucer's shipman in real life. MLR 34 1939.

— Chaucer's hopeless love. MLN 60 1945.

— Joan of Kent and the order of the garter. Univ of Birmingham Historical Jnl 1 1947.

— Chaucer, Graunson and Isabel of France. RES 24 1948.

— Cancelled tributes to Chaucer's sovereign lady. N & Q Jan 1948.

— The history of Chaucer's miller. N & Q Nov 1950.

Héraucourt, W. Die Wertwelt Chaucers: die Wertwelt einer Zeitwende. Heidelberg 1939.

— Chaucers Vorstellung von den geistigseelischen Kräften des Menschen. Anglia 65 1941.

Horrell, J. Chaucer's symbolic plowman. Speculum 14 1939; rptd in Chaucer criticism vol 1, ed R. Schoeck and J. Taylor, Notre Dame 1960.

Pratt, R. A. Chaucer and the Visconti libraries. ELH 6 1939.

— Karl Young's work on the learning of Chaucer. In A memorial of Karl Young, New Haven 1946 (priv ptd).

— The importance of manuscripts for the study of medieval education as revealed by the learning of Chaucer. Progress of Medieval & Renaissance Stud 20 1949.

— Chaucer and the holy cross of Bromholm. MLN 70 1955.

— Jankyn's book of wikked wives: medieval antimatrimonial propaganda in the universities. Annuale Mediaevale 3 1962.

Stillwell, G. Chaucer's plowman and the contemporary English peasant. ELH 6 1939.

— Chaucer's sad merchant. RES 20 1944.

— Chaucer's shipman and the shipman's gild. N & Q May 1947.

— Chaucer's merchant: no debts? JEGP 57 1958.

— and H. J. Webb. Chaucer's knight and the Hundred Years' War. MLN 55 1940.

Brown, C. S. and R. H. West. As by the whelp chastised is the leon. MLN 55 1940.

Duncan, E. H. The yeoman's canon's silver citrinacioun. MP 37 1940.

Edwards, A. C. Knaresborough castle and the Kynges moodres court. PQ 19 1940; rptd in Chaucer: modern essays in criticism, ed E. Wagenknecht, New York 1959.

Kirby, T. A. The French of Chaucer's prioress. In Studies for W. A. Read, University Louisiana 1940.

Rosenfeld, M.-V. Chaucer and the liturgy. MLN 55 1940.

Savage, H. Arcite's maying. Ibid.

Schmidt, W. Die Wertwelt Chaucers. Die Neueren Sprachen 48 1940.

Spargo, J. W. Chaucer's love-days. Speculum 15 1940.

— Questio quid iuris. MLN 62 1947.

Veazie, W. B. Chaucer's text-book of astronomy: Johannes de Sacrobosco. Univ of Colorado Stud in Humanities 1 1940.

Henkin, L. J. The pardoner's sheep bone and lapidary lore. Jnl History of Medicine 10 1941.

Olson, C. C. Chaucer and the music of the fourteenth century. Speculum 16 1941.

Stearns, M. W. A note on Chaucer's attitude towards love. Speculum 17 1942.

— A note on Chaucer's of Aristotelian philosophy. SP 43 1946.

Call, R. Whan he his papir soghte (Chaucer's Cook's tale A.4404). MLQ 4 1943.

'Bombardier'. Chaucer: ornithologist. Blackwood's Mag Aug 1944.

Lam, G. L. and W. H. Smith. George Vertue's contributions to Chaucerian iconography. MLQ 5 1944.

Loomis, R. S. Chaucer's eight-years' sickness. MLN 59 1944.

— A mirror of Chaucer's world. Princeton 1965.

Cline, R. H. Four Chaucer saints. MLN 60 1945.

Fullerton, A. B. The five craftsmen. MLN 61 1946.

Huppé, B. Historical allegory in the prologue to the Legend of good women. MLR 43 1948.

— and M. Galway. Chaucer: a criticism and a reply. Ibid.

Smith, R. M. Chaucer's Man of law's tale and Constance of Castile. JEGP 47 1948.

Weese, W. E. Alceste and Joan of Kent. MLN 63 1948.

Wretlind, D. E. The wife of Bath's hat. Ibid.

Brennan, M. J. Speaking of the prioress. MLQ 10 1949.

Sherbo, A. Chaucer's nun's priest again. PMLA 64 1949.

Stobie, M. R. Chaucer's shipman and the wine. Ibid.

Boyd, B. Chaucer's prioress: her green gauds. MLQ 11 1950.

— Chaucer and the liturgy. Philadelphia 1967.

Hulbert, J. R. A note on the prologues to the Legend of good women. MLN 65 1950.

Thomas, M. E. Medieval skepticism and Chaucer. New York 1950.

Towne, F. Wyclif and Chaucer on the contemplative life. In Essays critical and historical dedicated to L. B. Campbell, Berkeley 1950.

Eliason, M. The peasant and the lawyer. SP 48 1951.

Kellogg, A. and L. A. Haselmayer. Chaucer's satire of the pardoner. PMLA 66 1951.

Green, A. W. Chaucer's clerks and the medieval scholarly tradition as represented by Richard de Bury's Philobiblon. ELH 18 1951.

McCarthy, Sr B. Chaucer's pilgrim-prioress. Benedictine Rev 61 1951.

McPeek, J. A. S. Chaucer and the goliards. Speculum 26 1951.

Sledd, J. Canterbury tales C.310, 320; by Seint Ronyan. Mediaeval Stud 13 1951.

Herndon, S. Chaucer's five gildsmen. Florida State Univ Stud 5 1952.

Pearsall, R. B. Chaucer's Panik (Clerk's tale 590). MLN 67 1952.

Price, D. J. Chaucer's astronomy. Nature 20 Sept 1952.

Blenner-Hassett, R. Autobiographical aspects of Chaucer's franklin. Speculum 28 1953.

Frank, R. W., jr. Chaucer and the London bell-founders. MLN 68 1953.

Williams, A. Chaucer and the friars. Speculum 28 1953; rptd in Chaucer criticism vol 1, ed R. Schoeck and J. Taylor, Notre Dame 1960.

— Two notes on Chaucer's friar. MP 54 1957.

— The limitour of Chaucer's time and his limitacioun. SP 57 1960.

Magoun, F. P., jr. Chaucer's ancient and biblical world. Mediaeval Stud 15–16 1953–4.

— Chaucer's Great Britain. Mediaeval Stud 16 1954.

— Canterbury tales B.1761–3, 1839. MLN 71 1956.

— Chaucer's medieval world outside Great Britain. Mediaeval Stud 17 1965.

Block, E. A. Chaucer's millers and their bagpipes. Speculum 29 1954.

Dahlberg, C. Chaucer's cock and fox. JEGP 53 1954.

Forehand, B. Old age and Chaucer's reeve. PMLA 69 1954.

Bloomfield, M. W. The magic of In principio. MLN 70 1955.

Donovan, M. J. Chaucer's shipman and the integrity of his cargo. MLR 50 1955.

Jones, G. F. Chaucer and the medieval miller. MLQ 16 1955.

Lisca, P. Chaucer's gildsmen and their cook. MLN 70 1955.

Candelaria, F. H. Chaucer's fowle ok and the Pardoner's tale. MLN 71 1956.

Giffin, M. Studies on Chaucer and his audience. Quebec 1956 (priv ptd).

Neville, M. Chaucer and St Clare. JEGP 55 1956.

O'Connor, J. J. The astrological background of the Miller's tale. Speculum 31 1956.

Schoeck, R. J. Chaucer's prioress: mercy and tender heart. Bridge 2 1956; rptd in Chaucer criticism vol 1, ed Schoeck and J. Taylor, Notre Dame 1960.

Seaton, E. The parlement of foules and Lionel of Clarence. MÆ 25 1956.

Steadman, J. M. The prioress' dogs and Benedictine discipline. MP 54 1957.

— Chauntecleer and medieval natural history. Isis 50 1959.

— Hir gretteste ooth: the prioress, St Eligius and St Godebertha. Neophilologus 43 1959.

— The prioress' brooch and St Leonard. E Studies 44 1963.

Lynch, J. J. The prioress's greatest oath, once more. MLN 72 1959.

Williams, G. G. The Hous of fame and the house of the musicians. Ibid.

Isaacs, N. D. Constance in fourteenth-century England. Neuphilologische Mitteilungen 59 1958.

Loomis, L. H. Secular dramatics in the Royal Palace, Paris 1378, 1389 and Chaucer's tregetoures. Speculum 33 1958.

Ueno, N. The religious view of Chaucer in his Italian period. Tokyo 1958.

Beichner, P. E. Daun Piers: monk and business administrator. Speculum 34 1959; rptd in Chaucer criticism vol. 1, ed R. Schoeck and J. Taylor, Notre Dame 1960.

Friedman, W. F. and E. S. Acrostics, anagrams and Chaucer. PQ 38 1959.

Koch, R. A. Elijah the prophet: founder of the Carmelite order. Speculum 34 1959. On Summoner's tale.

McCall, J. P. and G. Rudisill jr. The Parliament of 1386 and Chaucer's Trojan parliament. JEGP 58 1959.

McCutchan, J. W. A solempne and a greet fraternitee. PMLA 74 1959.

Manley, F. Chaucer's rosary and Donne's bracelet: ambiguous coral. MLN 74 1959.

Birney, E. The squire's yeoman. REL 1 1960.

Garbáty, T. J. Chaucer's guildsmen and their fraternity. JEGP 59 1960.

— Chaucer's summoner: an example of the assimilation lag in scholarship. Papers of Michigan Acad 47 1962.

— The summoner's occupational disease. Medical History 7 1963.

Gaylord, A. T. A.85–8: Chaucer's squire and the glorious campaign. Papers of Michigan Acad 45 1960.

Manning, S. The nun's priest's morality and the medieval attitude towards fables. JEGP 59 1960.

Hira, T. Chaucer's gentry in the historical background. In Essays in English and American literature in commemoration of T. Nakayama's sixty-first birthday, Tokyo 1961.

Schaut, Q. L. Chaucer's pardoner and indulgences. Grey-friar 3 1961.

Bassan, M. Chaucer's cursed monk, Constantinus Affricanus. Mediaeval Stud 24 1962.

Gnerro, M. L. Ye haselwodes shaken: Pandarus and divination. N & Q May 1962.

Keen, M. Brotherhood in arms. History 47 1962.

Mahoney, J. F. Chaucerian tragedy and the Christian tradition. Annuale Mediaevale 3 1962.

Wilks, M. Chaucer and the mystical marriage in medieval political thought. Bull John Rylands Lib 44 1962.

Malarkey, S. Chaucer's yeoman again. College Eng Jan 1963.

Park, B. A. The character of Chaucer's merchant. Eng Lang Notes 1 1963.

Biggins, D. Chaucer's summoner's wel loved he garleek, onyons and eek lekes. N & Q Feb 1964.

MacDonald, A. Absalon and St Neot. Neophilologus 48 1964.

Murphy, J. J. A new look at Chaucer and the rhetoricians. RÉS new ser 15 1964. *See Manly, col 619 above.*

Grennen, J. E. Chaucer and the commonplaces of alchemy. Classica et Medievalia 26 1965.

— Chaucer's monk: baldness, venery, embonpoint. Amer N & Q 6 1968.

Crane, J. K. An honest debtor?: a note on Chaucer's merchant, line A.276. Eng Lang Notes 4 1966.

Robertson, D. W., jr. The historical setting of Chaucer's Book of the Duchess. In Medieval studies in honor of U. T. Holmes jr, Chapel Hill 1966.

— Chaucer's London. New York 1968.

Rowland, B. Chaucer's mistake: Book of the Duchess line 455. Amer N & Q 4 1966.

— Chaucer's she-ape (the Parson's tale 424). Chaucer Rev 2 1968.

Shugrue, M. The Urry Chaucer (1721) and the London uprising of 1384: a phase in Chaucerian biography. JEGP 65 1966.

Hinton, N. D. The Black Death and the Book of the Duchess. In His firm estate: essays in honor of F. J. Eikenberry, Tulsa 1967.

Hussey, M. Chaucer's world: a pictorial companion. Cambridge 1967.

Silvia, D. S. The wife of Bath's marital state. N & Q Jan 1967.

Drucker, T. Some medical allusions in the Canterbury tales. New York State Jnl of Medicine 68 1968.

Ferris, S. J. The date of Chaucer's final annuity and of the Complaint to his empty purse. MP 65 1968.

Gillmeister, H. Chaucers Mönch und die Reule of Seint Maure or of Seint Beneit. Neuphilologische Mitteilungen 69 1968.

Simons, R. D. The prioress's disobedience of the Benedictine rule. College Lang Assoc Jnl 12 1968.

O'Neill, Y. V. Chaucer and medicine. Jnl Amer Medical Assoc 208 1969.

Taylor, D. Chaucer's England. 1969.

Ussery, H. E. The status of Chaucer's monk: clerical, official, social and moral. Tulane Stud in Eng 17 1969.

— Fourteenth-century logicians: possible models for Chaucer's clerks. Tulane Stud in Eng 18 1970.

Baugh, A. C. Chaucer's serjeant of the law and the year books. In Mélanges de langue et de littérature du Moyen Age et de la Renaissance offerts à J. Frappin vol 1, Geneva 1970.

Daley, A. S. Chaucer's droghte of March in medieval farm lore. Chaucer Rev 4 1970.

Friedman, J. B. The prioress's beads of smal coral. MÆ 39 1970.

Lambkin, M. D. Chaucer's man of law as a purchasour. Comitatus 1 1970.

Loomis, D. R. The Venus of Alanus de Insulis and the Venus of Chaucer. In Philological essays in honour of H. D. Meritt, Hague 1970.

Pearcy, R. J. The marriage costs of Chaucer's friar. N & Q April 1970.

Smyser, H. M. A view of Chaucer's astronomy. Speculum 45 1970.

Gellrich, J. M. Nicholas' kynges noote and melodye. Eng Lang Notes 8 1971.

White, R. B., jr. Chaucer's Daun Piers and the rule of St Benedict: the failure of an ideal. JEGP 70 1971.

(11) INFLUENCE

Tobler, A. Chaucer's influence on English literature. Berlin 1905.

Hertwig, D. Der Einfluss von Chaucers Canterbury tales auf die englische Literatur. Marburg 1908.

Rosenthal, B. Spensers Verhältniss zu Chaucer. Berlin 1911.

Brown, C. Lydgate and the Legend of good women. E Studien 47 1913.

Long, P. W. From Troilus to Euphues. In Anniversary papers by colleagues and pupils of G. L. Kittredge, Boston 1913.

Schultz, J. R. Sir Walter Scott and Chaucer. MLN 28 1913.

Cook, A. S. Skelton's Garland of laurel and Chaucer's House of fame. MLR 11 1916.

Rollins, H. E. The Troilus story from Chaucer to Shakespeare. PMLA 32 1917.

Patch, H. R. Notes on Spenser and Chaucer. MLN 33 1918.

Root, R. K. Shakespeare misreads Chaucer. MLN 38 1923.

Graves, T. S. Some Chaucer allusions 1561-1700. SP 20 1923.

Berkelman, R. G. Chaucer and Masefield. Eng Jnl 16 1927.

Bond, R. P. Some eighteenth-century Chaucer allusions. SP 25 1928.

Wright, L. B. A character from Chaucer in a seventeenth-century satire. MLN 44 1928.

— William Painter and the vogue of Chaucer as a moral teacher. MP 31 1934.

Hunter, A. C. Le conte de la femme de Bath en français au xviiie siècle. Revue de Littérature Comparée 9 1929.

Bond, R. P., J. W. Bowyer, C. B. Millican and G. H. Smith. A collection of Chaucer allusions. SP 28 1931.

Boswell, E. Chaucer, Dryden and the laureateship: a seventeenth-century tradition. RES 7 1931.

McNeal, T. H. The clerk's tale as a possible source for Pandosto. PMLA 47 1932.

Purcell, J. M. The Troilus verse. PQ 12 1933.

Gebhardt, F. R. Ben Jonson's appreciation of Chaucer as evidenced in the English grammar. MLN 49 1934.

Shaver, C. L. Two eighteenth-century modernizations of Chaucer. Harvard Stud 16 1934.

Atkinson, D. F. Some notes on heraldry and Chaucer. MLN 51 1936.

— Some further Chaucer allusions. MLN 55 1940, 59 1944.

Williams, F. B., jr. Unnoted Chaucer allusions 1550-1650. PQ 16 1937.

Atwood, E. B. Some minor sources of Lydgate's Troy book. SP 35 1938.

Boys, R. C. Some Chaucer allusions 1705-99. PQ 17 1938.

Oliver, A. M. Chaucer allusions in xviii-century minor poetry. N & Q March 1938.

Harris, B. Some seventeenth-century Chaucer allusions. PQ 18 1939.

Walter, J. H. Astrophel and Stella and the Romaunt of the rose. RES 15 1939.

Caldwell, R. A. An Elizabethan Chaucer glossary. MLN 58 1943.

Mounts, C. E. The place of Chaucer and Spenser in the genesis of Peter Bell. PQ 23 1944.

Priestley, F. E. L. Keats and Chaucer. MLQ 5 1944.

Stearns, M. W. Henryson and Chaucer. MLQ 6 1945.

Whiting, B. J. A fifteenth-century English Chaucerian: the translator of Partonope of Blois. Mediaeval Stud 7 1945.

— Emerson, Chaucer and Thomas Warton. Amer Lit 17 1945.

— Some Chaucer allusions 1923–42. N & Q Dec 1944.

Zimansky, C. A. Chaucer and the school of Provence: a problem in eighteenth-century literary history. PQ 25 1946.

Seaton, E. That Scotch copy of Chaucer. JEGP 47 1948.

Long R. A. John Heywood, Chaucer and Lydgate. MLN 64 1949.

Smith, R. M. Chaucer allusions in the letters of Sir Walter Scott. MLN 65 1950.

Lyles. A. M. A note on Sidney's use of Chaucer. N & Q March 1953.

Owen, J. A euphemistic allusion to the Reeve's tale. MLN 69 1954.

Ruffin, D. Browning's Childe Roland and Chaucer's Hous of fame. In Essays in honor of W. C. Curry, Nashville 1954.

Renoir, A. Chaucerian character names in Lydgate's Siege of Thebes. MLN 71 1956.

Spector, R. D. Dryden's translation of Chaucer: a problem in neo-classical diction. N & Q Jan 1956.

Bowers. R. H. The suttell and dissayvabull world of Chaucer's Troilus. N & Q July 1957.

— Impingham's borrowings from Chaucer. MLN 73 1958.

— Chaucer's Troilus as an Elizabethan wanton book. N & Q Oct 1960.

Dobbins, A. C. Chaucer allusions 1619–1732. MLQ 18 1957.

Ayres, R. W. Medieval history, moral purpose and the structure of Lydgate's Siege of Thebes. PMLA 73 1958.

Bradbrook, M. C. What Shakespeare did to Chaucer's Troilus and Criseyde. Shakespeare Quart 9 1958.

Coghill, N. Shakespeare's reading in Chaucer. In Elizabethan and Jacobean studies presented to F. P. Wilson, Oxford 1959.

Kinghorn, A. M. The medieval makars. Texas Stud in Lit & Lang 1 1959.

Moran, T. The testament of Cresseid and the Book of Troylus. Litera 6 1960.

Schanzer, E. Antony and Cleopatra and the Legend of good women. N & Q Sept 1960.

Singer, A. E. Chaucer and Don Juan. West Virginia Univ Philological Papers 13 1961.

Grennen, J. E. Chaucer in a chapel perilous: the Waste land 1–18 and 230–42. Eng Record 13 1962.

Buxton, J. The Elizabethan appreciation of Chaucer. In his Elizabethan taste, 1963.

d'Ardenne, S. R. T. O. Troilus and Criseyde and the Tragic comedians. E Studies 44 1963.

Muscatine, C. The book of Chaucer: an account of the publication of Chaucer's works from the fifteenth century to modern times. San Francisco 1963.

Lyons, J. O. James Joyce and Chaucer's prioress. Eng Lang Notes 2 1964.

Maxwell, J. C. An echo of Chaucer in the Kingis quair. N & Q May 1964.

Thomson, P. Wyatt's Boethian Ballade. RES new ser 15 1964.

Dorris, G. E. The first Italian criticism of Chaucer and Shakespeare. Romance Notes 6 1965.

Kiehl, J. M. Dryden's Zimri and Chaucer's pardoner: a comparative study of verse portraiture. Thoth 7 1965.

Taylor, E. F. The knight's tale: a new source for Spenser's Muiopotmos. Renaissance Papers 1966.

Blake, N. F. Caxton and Chaucer. Leeds Stud in Eng new ser 1 1967.

MacDonald, D. Henryson and Chaucer: cock and fox. Texas Stud in Lit & Lang 8 1967.

— Chaucer's influence on Henryson's fables: the use of proverbs and sententiae. MÆ 39 1970.

Miner, E. R. Chaucer in Dryden's Fables. In Studies in criticism and aesthetics 1660–1800; essays in honor of S. H. Monk, Minneapolis 1967.

Robbins, R. H. A late-sixteenth-century Chaucer allusion (Douce ms 290). Chaucer Rev 2 1968.

Rohr, M. R. Gascoigne and My master Chaucer. JEGP 67 1968.

Stafford, T. J. Middleton's debt to Chaucer in the Changeling. Bull Rocky Mountain Modern Lang Assoc 22 1968.

Middleton, A. The modern art of fortifying: Palamon and Arcite as Epicurean epic. Chaucer Rev 3 1969.

Bawcutt, P. Gavin Douglas and Chaucer. RES new ser 21 1970.

Golden, S. A. Chaucer in Minsheu's Guide into the tongues. Chaucer Rev 4 1970.

Schlauch, M. The doctrine of vera nobilitas as developed after Chaucer. Kwartalrik Neofilologiczny (Warsaw) 17 1970.

Benson, C. D. Chaucer's influence on the prose Sege of Troy. N & Q April 1971.

N. F. B.

IV. EDUCATION

(1) BIBLIOGRAPHIES AND GENERAL STUDIES

For bibliographies and general studies covering the history of education, see Education 1500–1660, col 2381, below.

Bibliographies

Dictionnaire de théologie catholique. 15 vols Paris 1903–50. For chief medieval writers on education, with bibliographies.

Manitius, M. Geschichte der lateinischen Literatur des Mittelalters. 3 vols Munich 1911–31.

Paetow, L. J. Guide to the study of medieval history. New York 1917, 1931 (rev). Pt 3.

Caplan, H. Medieval artes praedicandi: a hand-list. Ithaca 1934; Supplement, Ithaca 1936.

Farrar, C. P. and A. P. Evans. Bibliography of English translations from medieval sources. New York 1946.

Boyce, G. C. American studies in medieval education. Progress in Medieval & Renaissance Stud 19 1947.

Emden, A. B. Biographical register of the University of Oxford to 1500. 3 vols Oxford 1957–9. Corrections, Bodleian Lib Record 6–7 1957–67. Includes biographical material.

— Biographical register of the University of Cambridge to 1500. Cambridge 1963.

Murphy, J. T. The medieval arts of discourse: an introductory bibliography. Speech Monographs 29 1962.

General Studies

Drane, A. D. Christian schools and scholars from the Christian era to the council of Trent. 1881.

Adamson, J. W. In Medieval contributions to modern civilisation, ed F. T. C. Hearnshaw 1921.

— In Legacy of the Middle Ages, ed C. G. Crump and E. F. Jacob, Oxford 1926.

— 'The illiterate Anglo-Saxon' and other essays. 1946.

Deanesly, M. Education to c. 1300. In Cambridge medieval history vol 5, Cambridge 1929.

Potter, G. R. Education in the 14th and 15th centuries. In Cambridge medieval history vol 8, Cambridge 1936.

Powicke, F. M. The Christian life in the Middle Ages. Oxford 1935.

Artz, F. B. The mind of the Middle Ages 200–1500. 1953.

Bolgar, R. R. The classical heritage and its beneficiaries. Cambridge 1954.

Emden, A. B. In Medieval England vol 2, ed A. L. Poole, Oxford 1959.

Knowles, D. The evolution of medieval thought. 1962.

(2) PRIMARY SOURCES

(in alphabetical order)

The following selective lists—with emphasis on available trns and edns with introductory material—may be supplemented by reference to Other Religious Writings, col 495 above, Writings in Latin col 743 below, Scholarship col 2285 below, and individual authors.

Treatises and Textbooks

Early Middle Ages

Abelard, Peter. Historia calamitatum. Ed and tr J. T. Muckle, Toronto 1954, 1964 (rev).

Ad Herennium. Ed and tr H. Caplan 1959 (Loeb Classical Lib).

Adamietz, J. Cicero's De inventione und die Rhetorik ad Herennium. Marburg 1960.

Calboli, G. In his Studi grammaticali, Bologna 1962.

Aelfric, grammaticus. Colloquy. Ed G. M. Garmonsway 1939.

Aesop. Der lateinische Äsop des Romulus und die Prosafassungen des Phädrus. Ed G. Thiele, Heidelberg 1910.

— Babrius and Phaedrus. Ed and tr B. E. Perry, Cambridge Mass 1964.

— Steinhöwels Äsop. Ed H. Osterley, Tübingen 1873; tr French by J. Macho, Lyons 1480; tr William Caxton, The book of the fables of Esope, 1484, ed R. T. Lenaghan, Cambridge Mass 1967.

Alcuin. The rhetoric of Alcuin and Charlemagne. Ed and tr W. S. Howell, Oxford 1941.

Alexander de Villa-Die. Das Doctrinale. Ed D. Reichling, Berlin 1893.

— The 'Costerian' Doctrinale. Ed F. Gaselee 1938 (Roxburghe Club).

Delisle, L. V. Alexandre de Villedieu. Paris 1894.

Alfonso, Pedro. Die disciplina clericalis. Ed A. Hilka and W. Söderhjelm, Heidelberg 1911; ed and tr R. J. Jones and J. E. Keller, The scholar's guide, Toronto 1969.

Alfred, King. West Saxon version of Gregory's Pastoral care. Ed H. Sweet 1871 (EETS). Preface.

Ancren riwle: a treatise on the rules and duties of monastic life. Ed J. Morton 1853 (Camden Soc) (with trn). Anon manual of 12th century.

Aquinas, Thomas. De magistro. Tr in Philosophy and teaching of Aquinas, ed M. H. Mayer, New York 1929; in The teacher and the mind, ed J. V. McGlynn, Chicago 1953.

— On the division and methods of the sciences. Ed and tr A. A. Maurer 1963.

Augustine of Hippo. Basic writings vol 1. Ed W. J. Oates, New York 1947.

— De magistro. Tr R. P. Russell, Washington 1968.

Howie, G. Educational theory and practice in St Augustine. 1969.

Basil, of Caesaria. Address to young men on reading Greek literature. In St Basil: the letters vol 4, ed R. J. Deferrari 1934.

— Essays on the study and use of poetry by Plutarch and Basil the great. Ed and tr E. M. Padelford 1902.

Bede. Ecclesiastical history of the English people. Ed and tr B. Colgrave and R. Mynors, Oxford 1969. On schools.

Boethius. The consolation of philosophy with the English translation of 'I.T.' 1609. Ed and rev H. F. Stewart 1926 (Loeb Classical Lib).

Book of vices and virtues. Ed W. N. Francis 1942 (EETS).

Cassiodorus. An introduction to divine and human reading. Ed and tr L. W. Jones, New York 1946.

Catalogus translationum et commentariorum. In Medieval and Renaissance commentaries, ed P. O. Kristeller, Washington 1960.

Cato. Tr W. J. Chase, The distichs of Cato, Madison 1922.

Chrysostom, John. Address on vainglory and the way to bring up children. Tr M. R. W. Laistner, Christianity and pagan culture in the later Roman Empire, New York 1951.

d'Andeli, Henri. The battle of the seven arts. Ed L. J. Paetow, Berkeley 1927.

Dictes and sayings of the philosophers. Ed C. F. Bühler 1941 (EETS).

Donatus. Tr W. J. Chase, The ars minor of Donatus, Madison 1926.

Eberhard of Bethune. Graecismus. Ed J. Wrobel, Bratislava 1887.

Florilegium morale oxoniense. Ed P. Delhaye and C. H. Talbot. Analecta Mediaevalia Namurcensia 5–6 1955–6. 12th century.

Garland, John of. Morale scolarium. In Two medieval satires on the university of Paris, ed L. J. Paetow, Berkeley 1927.

— The Stella maris. Ed E. F. Wilson, Cambridge Mass 1946.

Gerald of Wales. De principis instructione. Tr in Church historians of England vol 5, ed J. Stevenson 1858.

Grammatici latini. Ed H. G. T. Keil 7 vols and suppl Leipzig 1855–80. Vols 2–3 Priscian, vol 4 Donatus.

Gregory the great. Dialogues translated by P[hilip] W[oodward] in 1608. Ed E. G. Gardner 1911.

Hermogenes. Progymnasmata. Tr C. S. Baldwin, Medieval rhetoric and poetic, New York 1928.

Hervieux, L. Les fabulistes latins depuis le siècle d'Auguste jusqu'à la fin du Moyen Age. 5 vols Paris 1893–9. Many extracts.

Hugh of St Victor. The Didascalicon: a medieval guide to the arts. Ed and tr J. Taylor, New York 1961.

Isidore of Seville. Etymologiarum sive originum. Ed W. M. Lindsay, Oxford 1911.

— De natura rerum. Tr and ed J. Fontaine, Traité de la nature, Bordeaux 1960.

Jerome. Select letters. Ed and tr F. A. Wright 1933.

John of Salisbury. Metalogicon. Ed C. C. J. Webb, Oxford 1931; tr D. D. McGarry, Berkeley 1962.

— Policraticus. Ed C. J. Webb, Oxford 1909; tr J. Dickinson, The statesman's book (bks 4–8), New York 1927.

—— Letters vol 1. Ed and tr W. J. Millor and H. E. Butler, rev C. N. L. Brooke 1955.

Le manuel des péchés. Ed E. J. Arnould, Paris 1940. On education of clergy.

Les arts poétiques du xiie et xiiie siècle. Ed E. Faral, Paris 1924. On Matthieu de Vendôme.

Manuale scholarium: an original account of life in the medieval university. Tr R. F. Seybolt, Cambridge Mass 1921.

Martianus Capella. Ed A. Dick, Leipzig 1925.
Stahl, W. H. Speculum 40 1965.

Maximianus. Elegies. Ed R. Webster, Princeton 1900.

Poetae latini minores. Ed P. H. E. Baehrens 3 vols Leipzig 1879–86.

Rabanus Maurus. Education of the clergy. Tr in Great pedagogical essays, ed F. V. N. Painter, New York 1905.

Ranieri of Perugia. Ars notaria. Ed A. Gaudenzi, Bologna 1890.

Rhetores latini minores. Ed C. F. Halm, Leipzig 1863.

Richard of Bury. Philobiblon. Tr H. C. Thomas 1902; ed M. Maclagan, Oxford 1960.

Scholia in Horatium. Ed H. Botschuyver, Amsterdam 1942.

Strabo, Walahfrid. The school-life of Strabo. Tr J. D. Butler, Bibliotheca Sacra 40 1883.

Theodulus. Ecloga. Ed J. Osternacher 1902.
Osternacher, J. Quos auctores Theodulus imitatus esse videatur. Urfahr 1907.

Twelfth-century logic: texts and studies. Ed L. Minio-Paluello 2 vols Rome 1956–8.
Minio-Paluello, L. The Ars disserendi (1132) of Adam of Balsham. Medieval & Renaissance Stud 3 1954.

Vincent of Beauvais. De eruditione filiorum nobilium. Ed A. Steiner, Cambridge Mass 1938.

William of Tournai. De instructione puerorum. Ed J. A. Corbett, Notre Dame 1955.

Later Middle Ages: England

A book of precedence. Ed F. J. Furnivall 1869 (EETS). Includes essays on early Italian and German courtesy books by W. M. Rossetti and E. Oswald.

A fifteenth-century courtesy book. Ed R. W. Chambers 1914 (EETS).

A fifteenth-century schoolbook. Ed E. Nelson, Oxford 1956.

Bartholomew of Glanville. Medieval lore from Bartholomew Anglicus. Ed R. Steele 1893. Trevisa's 14th-century trn modernized.

Berners, Juliana. Boke of St Albans. Ed E. Blades 1881 (facs).

Buonaccorso da Montemagno. Tr John Tiptoft, The declamacion of noblesse, in R. J. Mitchell, John Tiptoft, 1938.

Chaucer, Geoffrey. Treatise on the astrolabe. In Works vol 3, ed W. W. Skeat Oxford 1894. Preface, to his son.

Fortescue, John. De laudibus legum Anglie. Ed and tr S. B. Chrimes, Cambridge 1942. On legal education.

Horae Beatae Maria virginis: or Sarum and York primers. Ed E. Hoskins 1901.

La Tour-Landry, Geoffrey de. Book of the knight of La Tour-Landry for instruction of his daughters. Ed T. Wright 1868 (EETS). Abridged from Caxton's trn, G. B. Rawlings 1902.

Lull, Ramón. Book of the ordre of chyvalry. In Caxton's trn, ed A. T. P. Byles 1926 (EETS).

Peter Idle's instructions to his son. Ed C. D'Evelyn, Boston 1935.

The babees book. Ed F. J. Furnivall 1868 (EETS), 1894 (as Early English meals and manners); abridged and modernized E. Rickert 1908. Tracts from 1430.

The earliest arithmetics in English. Ed R. Steele 1922 (EETS).

The good wife taught her daughter. Ed T. F. Mustanuja, Helsinki 1948. Introd.

Vegetius, Renatus Flavius. Knythode and bataile: a xvth-century verse paraphrase of De re militari. Ed R. Dyboski and Z. M. Arend 1935 (EETS).

Vulgaria quadem abs Terentio in Anglicam linguam traducta. In John Anwykyll, Compendium totius grammaticae, Oxford 1483.
Shaw, E. A. Earliest Latin grammars in English. Trans Bibl Soc 4 1899.

For European material see

Butzbach, J. Autobiography. Ed and tr R. F. Seybolt and P. Monroe, Ann Arbor 1933.

Il pensiero pedagogico del umanesimo. Ed E. Garin, Florence 1958.

Vittorino da Feltre and other humanist educators. Ed and tr W. H. Woodward, Cambridge 1897, New York 1963 (with introd by E. F. Rice jr). *See* A. Gambara, Vittorino da Feltre, Turin 1964.

Documents

University

The medieval student. Ed D. C. Munro 1897. On Paris to 1300.

University records and life in the Middle Ages. Ed L. Thorndike, New York 1944.

Acta facultatis artium universitatis Sanctiandree 1413–1588. Ed A. I. Dunlop, Edinburgh 1964.

Medieval statutes of the faculty of arts of the University of Freiburg-in-Breisgau. Ed H. Ott and J. M. Fletcher, Notre Dame 1964.

The medieval university: masters, students, learning. Ed H. Wieruszowski, Princeton 1966.

The original statutes of Cambridge University. Ed M. B. Hackett, Cambridge 1970. With full bibliography.

See also

Cambridge Antiquarian Society Communications 1863–91. Proceedings 1892–.

Oxford Historical Society Publications 1884–. Listed in E. L. C. Mullins, Texts and calendars, 1958.

Peake, H. and C. P. Hall. Archives of the University of Cambridge. Cambridge 1962.

Cordeaux, E. H. and D. H. Merry. Bibliography of printed works relating to the University of Oxford. Oxford 1968.

Craigie, J. Bibliography of Scottish education. 1970.

General

A medieval garner: human documents for the four centuries preceding the Reformation. Ed and tr G. G. Coulton 4 vols 1910, 1928–30 (rev as Life in the Middle Ages).

Educational charters and documents 598–1909. Ed A. F. Leach, Cambridge 1911.

Fitzstephen, William, Description of London [and its schools c. 1180]. Tr F. M. Stenton, Norman London, 1934 (Historical Assoc). In Documents illustrating the history of civilisation in medieval England, ed R. T. Davies 1926.

The Eton choirbook. Ed F. L. Harrison. Musica Britannica 20 1956.

The household of Edward IV. Ed A. R. Myers, Manchester 1959. Includes a bibliography.

Educational records. Ed J. W. Purvis, York 1959.

(3) SECONDARY WORKS

Organization, Preservation and Transmission of Knowledge

Clerval, A. Les écoles de Chartres du vᵉ au xviᵉ siècle. Paris 1895.

Scherer, H. Die Pädagogik in ihrer Entwicklung im Zusammenhange mit dem Kultur- und Geistesleben. 2 vols Leipzig 1897–1907.

Sandys, J. History of classical scholarship. 3 vols Cambridge 1903–8, 1921 (vol 2 rev).

Grabmann, M. Geschichte der scholastischen Methode. 2 vols Freiburg 1909–11.

Haskins, C. H. Studies in the history of medieval science. New York 1924.

— Studies in medieval culture. Oxford 1929.

Klibansky, R. The continuity of the Platonic tradition. 1939.

Thompson, J. W. The medieval library. Chicago 1939.

— The literacy of the laity in the Middle Ages. New York 1939.

Southern, R. W. The making of the Middle Ages. 1953.

Bolgar, R. R. The classical heritage and its beneficiaries. Cambridge 1954.

Parks, G. B. The English traveller to Italy. Rome 1954. Vol 1, to 1525.

Gilson, E. History of Christian philosophy in the Middle Ages. Tr 1955. With bibliographical information.

van Steenberghen, F. Aristotle in the West. Louvain 1955.

Nardi, B. Il pensiero pedagogico del medioevo. Florence 1957.

Leclercq, J. The love of learning and the desire for God: a study of monastic culture. New York 1962.

Auerbach, E. Literary language and its public in the late Latin antiquity and the Middle Ages. 1965.

Ong, W. J. The presence of the word: some prolegomena for cultural and religious history. New Haven 1967.

Colish, M. L. The mirror of language: a study of the medieval theory of knowledge. 1968.

Shelby, L. R. Education of medieval master masons. Mediaeval Stud 32 1970.

Classical influences on European culture 500–1500. Ed R. R. Bolgar, Cambridge 1971.

Up to 1100

Maitre, L. Les écoles épiscopales et monastiques en occident avant les universités 768–1180. Paris 1886, 1924 (rev).

Roger, M. L'enseignement des lettres classiques d'Ausone à Alcuin: les écoles carolingiennes. Paris 1905.

Rand, E. K. Founders of the Middle Ages. Cambridge Mass 1928.

Laistner, M. L. W. Thought and letters in western Europe 500–900. 1932, 1957 (rev).

— Intellectual heritage of the early Middle Ages. 1961.

van der Eynde, D. Les normes de l'enseignement chrétien dans la littérature patristique des trois premiers siècles. Paris 1933.

Bezzola, R. Les origines et la formation de la littérature courtoise en occident 500–1200. 2 vols Paris 1944–60.

Courcelle, P. Les lettres grecques en occident de Macrobe à Cassiodore. Paris 1948; tr Oxford 1969.

Marrou, H. History of education in antiquity. 1955.

Hagendahl, H. The Latin fathers and the classics. Gothenburg 1958.

Jaeger, W. Early Christianity and Greek paideia. Oxford 1962.

Riché, P. Education et culture dans l'occident barbare viᵉ–viiiᵉ siècle. Paris 1962.

British Isles

James, M. R. Two ancient English scholars. 1931. On Aldhelm.

Crawford, S. Anglo-Saxon influence on western Christendom. 1933.

Bede: his life, time and writings. Ed A. H. Thompson 1935.

Dubois, H. M. Aelfric. Paris 1943.

Stenton, F. M. Place of women in Anglo-Saxon society. Trans Royal Historical Soc 4th ser 25 1943.

Levison, W. England and the Continent in the eighth century. 1946.

Knowles, D. The monastic order in England 943–1216. Cambridge 1949, 1963 (rev).

Lancaster, L. Kinship in Anglo-Saxon society. Br Jnl of Sociology 9 1958.

Bieler, K. Ireland: harbinger of the Middle Ages. Oxford 1963.

Ogilvy, J. D. A. Books known to the English 597–1066. Cambridge Mass 1967.

1100–1350

Haskins, C. H. The rise of universities. New York 1923.

— The renaissance of the twelfth century. Cambridge Mass 1927.

Waddell, H. The wandering scholars. 1927, 1932 (rev).

Limmer, R. Bildungzustände und Bildungsideen des 13 Jahrhunderts. Munich and Berlin 1928.

Born, L. K. The perfect prince: thirteenth- and fourteenth-century ideals. Speculum 3 1928.

Paré, G., A. Brunet and P. Tremblay. La renaissance du xiiᵉ siècle: les écoles et l'enseignement; refonte de l'ouvrage de G. Robert. Paris and Ottawa 1933.

Liebeschütz, H. Medieval humanism in the life and writings of John of Salisbury. 1950.

Tusquets, J. Ramón Lull: pedagogo de la Cristiandad. Madrid 1955.

Gabriel, A. L. Educational ideas of Vincent de Beauvais. Notre Dame 1956.

MacKinney, L. C. Bishop Fulbert and education at the school of Chartres. Notre Dame 1957.

Clagett, M., G. Post and R. Reynolds. Twelfth-century Europe and the foundations of modern society. Madison 1961.

Heer, F. The medieval world: Europe 1100–1350. 1962.

Duby, G. The Europe of the cathedrals 1140–1280. 1966.

Luscombe, D. E. The school of Peter Abelard: influence of his thought in the early scholastic period. Cambridge 1969.

Brooke, C. The twelfth-century renaissance. 1969.

Southern, R. W. Medieval humanism and other studies. 1970.

See Universities, below.

British Isles

Owst, G. R. Preaching in medieval England c. 1350–1450. Cambridge 1926.

— Literature and pulpit in medieval England. Cambridge 1933, Oxford 1961 (rev).

David, C. W. Claim of Henry I to be called learned. In Haskins anniversary essays, Boston and New York 1929.

Parsons, H. R. Anglo-Norman books of courtesy and nurture. PMLA 44 1929.

Russell, J. C. Alexander Neckham in England. EHR 47 1932.

Gibbs, M. and J. Lang. Bishops and reform 1215–72. 1934.

Galbraith, V. H. Literacy of medieval English kings. Proc Br Acad 21 1935.

— Nationalism and language in medieval England. Trans Royal Historical Soc 4th ser 23 1941.

Hunt, R. W. English learning in the late twelfth century. Trans Royal Historical Soc 4th ser 19 1936.

Kleineck, W. Englische Fürstenspiegel vom Policraticus Johannes von Salisbury bis zum Basilikon doron

Königs Jakobs I. Studien zur Englischen Philologie 90 1937.

Edwards, K. Bishops and learning in the reign of Edward II. Church Quart Rev 138 1944.

Smalley, B. English friars and antiquity in the early fourteenth century. Oxford 1960.

Southern, R. W. Place of England in the twelfth-century renaissance. History 45 1960.

Painter, S. The family and the feudal system in 12th-century England. Speculum 35 1960.

Labarge, M. A baronial household of the thirteenth century. 1965.

1350–1500

Woodward, W. H. Studies in education during the Renaissance 1400–1600. Cambridge 1924.

Kibre, P. Intellectual interests as reflected in libraries of the 14th and 15th centuries. JHI 7 1946.

Gabriel, A. L. Educational ideas of Christine de Pisan. JHI 16 1955.

Garin, E. L'educazione in Europa 1400–1600. Bari 1957.

Davis, C. T. Education in Dante's Florence. Speculum 40 1965.

England

Wright, T. Feudal manuals of English history compiled for the gentry and nobility. 1872. On 13th–15th century.

Fischer, R. How the wyse man taught hys sone. Erlangen 1889.

Dunlop, O. English apprenticeship and child labour. 1912.

Deanesly, M. The Lollard Bible and other medieval biblical versions. Cambridge 1920, 1966 (with note).

— The significance of the Lollard Bible. 1951.

Unwin, G. Medieval gilds and education. In his Studies in economic history, ed R. H. Tawney 1927.

Adamson, J. W. Extent of literacy in England in the 15th and 16th centuries. Library 4th ser 20 1932; rptd in his Illiterate Anglo-Saxon, 1946.

Weiss, R. Humanism in England in the fifteenth century. Oxford 1941, 1957 (rev).

Suggett, U. Use of French in England in the later Middle Ages. Trans Royal Historical Soc 4th ser 28 1946.

McMahon, C. Education in fifteenth-century England. Baltimore 1947.

Thrupp, S. L. The merchant class of medieval London 1300–1500. 1948.

Bennett, H. S. English books and readers 1475–1557. Cambridge 1952.

Mitchell, R. J. John Free. 1958.

Universities and Colleges

Europe

Rashdall, H. Universities of Europe in the Middle Ages. 3 vols 1895, Oxford 1936 (rev F. M. Powicke and A. B. Emden). Vol 2 Scotland, vol 3 England, bibliographies to 1934.

Boyce, G. C. The English–German nation in the University of Paris. Bruges 1927.

d'Irsay, S. Histoire des universités françaises et étrangères des origines à nos jours vol i. Paris 1933.

Mitchell, R. J. English law students at Bologna in the fifteenth century. EHR 51 1936.

— English students at Padua 1460–75. Trans Royal Historical Soc 4th ser 19 1937.

— English students at Ferrara in the fifteenth-century. Italian Stud 1 1938.

Toulouse. M. La nation anglaise–allemande de l'Université de Paris à la fin du xvᵉ siècle. Paris 1939.

Kibre, P. Nations in the medieval unversities. Cambridge Mass 1948.

— Scholarly privileges in the Middle Ages at Bologna, Padua, Paris, Oxford. 1961.

Aspects de l'Université de Paris. Ed L. Halphen, Paris 1949.

Gabriel, A. L. English masters and students in Paris in the thirteenth century. Analecta Praemonstratensia 25 1949.

— Garlandia: studies in the history of the medieval university. Notre Dame 1969.

Powicke, F. M. Ways of medieval life and thought. 1950. On problems of university history.

Stelling-Michaud, S. L'histoire des universités au Moyen Age et à la Renaissance au cours des vingt-cinq dernières années. In Rapports xiᵉ Congrès International des Sciences Historiques vol i, Stockholm 1960.

Hargreaves-Mawdsley, W. H. History of academical dress in Europe. Oxford 1963. With full university bibliography.

Leff, G. Paris and Oxford universities in the thirteenth and fourteenth centuries. New York 1968. With bibliography.

Curricula

Paetow, L. J. The arts course at medieval universities with special reference to grammar and rhetoric. Champaign 1910.

Pietsch, G. Die Musik im Erziehungs- und Bildungsideal des ausgehenden Altertums und frühen Mittelalters. Halle 1922.

Welter, J. T. L'exemplum dans la littérature religieuse et didactique du Moyen Age. Paris 1927.

Baldwin, C. S. Medieval rhetoric and poetic. New York 1928.

Ullmann, E. K. Classical authors in medieval florilegia. Classical Philology 23–7 1928–32.

Rand, E. K. The classics in the thirteenth century. Speculum 4 1929.

Ghisalberti, F. Arnolfo d'Orléans: un cultore d'Ovidio nel secolo xii. Memorie del R. Istituto Lombardo di Scienze e Lettere 24 1932.

d'Irsay, G. Les sciences de la nature et les universités médiévales. Archeion 15 1933.

Caplan, H. Classical rhetoric and the medieval theory of preaching. Classical Philology 28 1933.

Hajdu, H. Das mnemotechnische Schriftum des Mittelalters. Vienna 1936.

Smalley, B. Study of the Bible in the Middle Ages. 1941, 1957 (rev).

McKeon, R. Rhetoric in the Middle Ages. Speculum 17 1942.

— Poetry and philosophy in the twelfth century. MP 43 1946.

Both rptd in Critics and criticism ancient and modern, ed R. S. Crane, Chicago 1952.

Wieruszowski, H. Ars dictaminis in the time of Dante. Mediaevalia et Humanistica 1 1943.

Hunt, R. W. Introductions to the 'arts' in the twelfth century. In Studia in honorem R. J. Martin, Bruges 1948.

Thorndike, L. The Sphera of Sacrobosco. Chicago 1949.

Thouzellier, C. L'enseignement et les universités. In La Chrétienté romaine 1198–1274, ed A. Fliche et al, Paris 1950.

Boehner, P. Medieval logic: an outline 1250–1400. Chicago and Toronto 1952.

Huygens, R. B. C. Accessus ad auctores. Latomus 12 1953.

Hajnal, I. L'enseignement de l'écriture aux universités médiévales. Budapest 1954.

Delhaye, P. L'organisation scolaire au xiiᵉ siècle. Traditio 5 1957.

— Grammatica et ethica au xiiᵉ siècle. Recherches de Théologie Ancienne et Médiévale 25 1958.

Carpenter, F. C. Music in the medieval and Renaissance universities. Norman Oklahoma 1958.

Koch, J. Artes liberales von der antiken Bildung zur Wissenschaft des Mittelalters. Leyden 1959.

Crombie, A. C. Medieval and early modern science. 2 vols 1959.

Fuhrmann, M. Das systematische Lehrbuch. Göttingen 1960. On Cato, Ad Herennium, Cicero, Varro etc.

Jeauneau, E. Deux rédactions des gloses de Guillaume de Conches sur Priscien. Recherches de Théologie Ancienne et Médiévale 27 1960.

Studium generale: studies for A. L. Gabriel. Ed L. S. Domonkos and R. J. Schneider, Notre Dame 1967.

Dickey, M. Some commentaries on the De inventione and Ad Herennium of the 11th and early 12th centuries. Medieval & Renaissance Stud 11 1968.

Essays in medieval history for B. Wilkinson. Ed M. R. Powicke and T. A. Sanquist, Toronto 1969. On teaching in Paris, commentaries on Aristotle.

Oxford and Cambridge

Munimenta academica oxoniensis. Ed H. Anstey 2 vols 1868 (Rolls ser).

Poole, R. L. Early lives of Robert Pullen and Nicholas Breakspear. In Essays presented to T. F. Tout, 1925.

Little, A. G. Educational organisation of the friars in medieval England. Trans Royal Historical Soc new ser 8 1894.

— The Franciscan school at Oxford in the 13th century. Archivum Franciscanum Historicum 19 1926.

— Theological schools in medieval England. EHR 55 1940.

Oxford theology and theologians c. 1282–1307. Ed A. G. Little and F. Pelster 1934.

Gumbley, W. The Cambridge Dominicans. Oxford 1938.

Richardson, H. G. An Oxford teacher in the 15th century. Bull John Rylands Lib 23 1939.

— Business training in medieval Oxford. Amer Historical Rev 46 1940.

— The schools of Northampton in the 12th century. EHR 56 1941.

Callus, D. The condemnation of St Thomas at Oxford. 1946.

Smalley, B. Robert Bacon and the early Dominican school at Oxford. Trans Royal Historical Soc 4th ser 30 1948.

Moorman, J. R. H. The Grey Friars in Cambridge. Cambridge 1952.

Duhamel, P. A. The Oxford lectures of John Colet. JHI 14 1952.

Robert Grosseteste: scholar and bishop. Ed D. Callus, Oxford 1953.

Oxford: Victoria County history, Oxfordshire vol 3. Ed H. E. Salter and M. D. Lobel 1954.

Cambridge. Victoria County history: Cambridgeshire vol 3. Ed J. P. C. Roach 1959.

Oxford studies presented to D. Callus. Oxford 1963 (Oxford Historical Soc). On grammar masters, faculty of canon law, halls etc.

Weisheipl, J. A. Curriculum of the faculty of arts at Oxford in the early 14th century. Mediaeval Stud 26 1964, 28 1966.

Murphy, J. J. Rhetoric in fourteenth-century Oxford. MÆ 34 1965.

Jacob, E. F. Essays in later medieval history. Manchester 1967. On university clerks.

Fletcher, J. M. The teaching of arts at Oxford 1400–1520. Paedagogica Historica 7 1967.

Schoeck, R. J. On rhetoric in 14th-century Oxford. Mediaeval Stud 30 1968.

Cobban, A. B. The King's Hall Cambridge in the later Middle Ages. Cambridge 1969. With bibliography.

Inns of Court

Essays in legal history. Ed P. Vinogradoff, Oxford 1913.

Putnam, B. H. Early treatises in the practice of the justices of the peace in the fifteenth and sixteenth centuries. Oxford 1924.

Pollock, F. Origins of the Inns of Court. Oxford 1931.

Readings and moots at the inns of court in the fifteenth century. Ed S. E. Thorne 1952 (Selden Soc).

Thorne, S. E. Early history of the inns of court. Graya 50 1959.

Roxburgh, R. Origins of Lincoln's Inn. Cambridge 1963.

See also Law, col 2277, below.

Schooling

Tuer, A. W. History of the hornbook. 2 vols 1896.

Chambers, E. K. The medieval stage. 2 vols Oxford 1903.

Evelyn White, C. H. The boy-bishop of medieval England. Jnl Br Archaeological Assoc new ser 11 1905.

Varnhagen, H. Parvula: ein lateinisches Lehrbuch in englischen Sprache. In Festschrift deutschen Neuphilologenhage, Pfingsten 1906.

— Th. Rood's fragment of a Latin grammar written in English (Oxford 1481). Erlangen 1906.

Watson, F. English grammar schools to 1660: their curriculum and practice. Cambridge 1908.

— The old grammar schools. Cambridge 1916.

Leach, A. F. Schools of medieval England. 1915. See A. G. Little, EHR 30 1915.

Bernard, F. P. The casting counter and the casting board. Oxford 1916.

Knight, L. S. Welsh monasteries and the education of later medieval Wales. Archaeologia Cambrensis 6th ser 20 1920.

Parry, A. W. Education in England in the Middle Ages. 1920.

Yeldham, F. Story of reckoning in the Middle Ages. 1926.

Morgan, A. Rise and progress of Scottish education. 1927.

Edgar, J. History of early Scottish education. 1927.

Coulton, G. G. Ten medieval studies. Cambridge 1930.

Hajdú, H. Lesen und Schreiben in Spätmittelalter. Pécs 1931.

Plimpton, G. A. The education of Chaucer. Oxford 1935.

Robertson, D. H. Sarum close: education of the cathedral choristers for 700 years. 1938.

Mead, M. R. Fifteenth-century school books. HLQ 3 1940.

Thorndike, L. Elementary and secondary education in the Middle Ages. Speculum 15 1940.

Steinberg, S. H. Medieval writing masters. Library 4th ser 22 1941.

Thompson, A. H. Song schools in the Middle Ages. Church Music Soc Occasional Papers 14 1942.

Jones, E. J. Education in Wales during the later Middle Ages. Swansea [1949].

Lobel, M. D. The grammar schools of the medieval university. In Victoria County history: Oxfordshire vol 3, 1954.

Bonaventure, B. Teaching of Latin in later medieval England. Mediaeval Stud 23 1961.

Ariès, P. Centuries of childhood. 1962.

Lawson, J. Medieval education and the Reformation. 1966.

For individual schools

Victoria County history of England.

Wallis, P. J. Histories of old schools (before 1700): list for England and Wales. Newcastle 1966.

Craigie, J. Bibliography of Scottish education. 1970.

Institutions responsible for schools

Bateson, M. The Huntingdon song school and the school of St Gregory's Canterbury. EHR 18 1903.

Clay, R. M. Medieval hospitals of England. 1909.

Power, E. Medieval nunneries. Cambridge 1922.

Knowles, D. The monastic order in England 943–1216. Cambridge 1940, 1963 (rev).

Thompson, A. H. The English clergy and their organisation in the later Middle Ages. Oxford 1947.

Edwards, K. English secular cathedrals in the Middle Ages. Manchester 1949.

— The religious orders in England. 3 vols Cambridge 1948–59.

Harrison, F. Life in a medieval college: the vicars choral of York minster. 1952.

Knowles, D. and R. N. Hadcock. Medieval religious houses: England and Wales. 1953. Corrections, EHR 52 1957.

Easson, D. E. Medieval religious houses: Scotland. 1957.

Tierney, B. Medieval poor law: canonical theory and its application in England. 1959.

Jordan, W. K. The charities of London 1480–1660. 1960.

Thomson, J. A. F. Piety and charity in late medieval London. Jnl Ecclesiastical History 16 1965.

Gwynn, A. and R. N. Hadcock. Medieval religious houses: Ireland. 1970.

See also biographies of episcopal founders and administrators, e.g.

Douie, D. M. Archbishop Pecham. Oxford 1952.

Saltman, A. Theobald, Archbishop of Canterbury. 1956.

Jacob, E. F. Archbishop Chichele. 1967.

And from parish level

Cutts, F. L. Parish priests and their people in the Middle Ages in England. 1898.

Ditchfield, P. H. The parish clerk. 1907.

Westlake, H. P. Parish gilds of medieval England. 1919.

Moorman, J. R. H. Church life in England in the thirteenth century. 1955.

Pantin, W. A. The English Church in the fourteenth century. 1955.

Williams, G. The Welsh Church from Conquest to Reformation. Cardiff 1962.

Hughes, K. The Church in early Irish society. 1966.

Godfrey, J. The English parish 600–1300. 1969.

Heath, P. The English parish clergy on the eve of the Reformation. 1969.

J. S.

3. THE FIFTEENTH CENTURY

I. THE ENGLISH CHAUCERIANS: LYDGATE, HOCCLEVE, HAWES AND OTHERS

References

Index   Brown, C. and R. H. Robbins, The index of ME verse, 1943;

Index Supplement   Robbins, R. H. and J. L. Cutler, Supplement to the index of ME verse, 1966.

JOHN LYDGATE
1370?-1449
Manuscripts

A full discussion of the mss will be found in the Lydgate canon appended to (1) H. N. MacCracken's edn of Minor poems, 1911; (2) W. F. Schirmer, John Lydgate, 1961. Complete lists are in Index *and* Index Supplement. *Much incidental information on mss containing Lydgate items is included in E. Seaton, Sir Richard Roos, 1961.*

Clarke, D. E. M. A new Lydgate manuscript. MLR 44 1929. On Exeter Miscellany Rolls 59 containing a fragment of the Life of St Edmund. With text.

Bone, G. Extant manuscripts printed from W. de Worde. Library 4th ser 12 1932. Establishes ownership of 3 Lydgate mss by Roger Thorney fl. 1450–98. With brief biography.

Bowers, R. H. The churl and the bird, ms Harley 2407, and Elias Ashmole. MLN 49 1934. With text.

Bühler, C. F. A new Lydgate-Chaucer manuscript. MLN 52 1937. On the Pierpont Morgan ms 4 containing Siege of Thebes; Lenvoy to all princes; Letter to Gloucester; with a text of the last. J. M. Manly and E. Rickert's edn of the Text of the Canterbury tales, Chicago 1940, also contains many references to Lydgate mss.

Klinefelter, R. A. A newly discovered fifteenth-century manuscript. MLQ 14 1953. On Venerable English College Rome ms 1306 containing Life of our lady; King Henry's triumphal entry into London; A pageant of knowledge: Four thinges that make a man to falle; Ballad of good counsel; Pain and sorrow of evil marriage; Dietary; Daunce Machabre and 7 other items.

Van Dorsten, J. A. The Leyden Lydgate manuscript. Scriptorium 14 1960. On Vossius Germ Gall Q.9. Tentatively identifies anon On fortune (ed K. Brunner, Archiv 161 1932) with De fortuna attributed to Lydgate by Bale.

Rigg, A. G. Some notes on Trinity College Cambridge ms O.9.38. N & Q Sept 1966. Beware the blind (f. 28a) rightly attributed by scribe to Lydgate.

Davis, N. Review of Index Supplement. RES new ser 18 1967. On Bodley ms Astor 2, containing Stans puer ad mensam.

Bloomfield, M. Review of Index Supplement. Speculum 42 1967. Index 2696 based on stanzas from Fall of princes 1–11.

Robbins, R. H. A new Lydgate fragment. Eng Lang Notes 5 1968. Trinity College Dublin ms 423 contains Life of our lady III. 1–7.

Doyle, A. I. and G. B. Pace. A new Chaucer manuscript. PMLA 83 1968. On Coventry corp ms, including Dance of death and Siege of Thebes.

Gray, D. A copy of Lydgate's Dietary at Lille. N & Q July 1968. Univ of Lille ms 204 contains Dietary. With text.

Jones, H. G. An unedited ms of Lydgate's Life of our lady: book 5, vv. 344–64, 372–92. Eng Lang Notes 6 1969. F. 178 of Fragmenta Manuscripta (Univ of Missouri Lib) presents one leaf of a ?15th-century copy of Life of our lady (42 lines). With text.

Edwards, A. S. G. Lydgate's Siege of Thebes: a new fragment. Neuphilologische Mitteilungen 71 1971. On mutilated f. 1 of ms now in Cambridge Univ Lib additional ms 2707 (2) (BB). With text.

Selections

Minor poems. Ed J. O. Halliwell (-Phillipps) 1840 (Percy Soc). Includes London lackpenny; Moral of horse, goose and sheep; Bycorne and Chichevache; Churl and the bird; Testament etc.

Einige religiöse Gedichte. Ed O. Maher, Oberfalz 1910, Berlin 1914.

Minor poems. Ed H. N. MacCracken 2 pts 1911–34 (EETS). Includes St Margaret; St Giles; Testament etc.

Poems. Ed J. Norton-Smith, Oxford 1966. Includes Letter to Gloucester; As a mydsomer rose; A complaynt of a loveres lyfe; Temple of glas etc.

Other poems are in T. Wright, Political poems and songs vol 2, 1861; W. W. Skeat, Complete works of Chaucer vol 7, Oxford 1897; E. P. Hammond, English verse between Chaucer and Surrey, *Durham NC 1927;* R. H. Robbins, Historical poems of the xivth and xvth centuries, *New York 1959; C. and K. Sisam*, The Oxford book of medieval verse, *Oxford 1970*.

§ I

Aesop. Ed P. Sauerstein, Anglia 9 1885 (from BM Harley ms 225); ed J. Zupitza, Archiv 85 1890 (from other mss); ed H. N. MacCracken, Minor poems, 1934.

[Assembly of the gods]. The interpretacion of the names of goddis and goddises. [1498] (de Worde), nd (de Worde), [1500?] (de Worde), nd (Pynson), [after 1529] (Redman), 1540; ed O. L. Triggs, Chicago 1895, 1896 (EETS) (from Trinity College Cambridge ms); ed F. Jenkinson, Cambridge 1906 (facs of 2nd edn). But *see* C. F. Bühler, The assembly of gods and Christine de Pisan, Eng Lang Notes 4 1967, who dates it after 1475.

A calendar. Ed C. Horstmann, Archiv 80 1888; ed H. N. MacCracken, Minor poems, 1911; ed A. Clark, The English register of Godstow nunnery, 1911 (EETS).

Chichevache and Bycorne. In Old plays vol 12, R. Dodsley 1780; ed J. O. Halliwell (-Phillipps), Minor poems, 1840; ed E. P. Hammond, English verse between Chaucer and Surrey, Durham NC 1927; ed H. N. MacCracken, Minor poems, 1934.

The chorle and the birde. [1477?] (Caxton), [nd] (Caxton), [1493] (Pynson), nd (de Worde), [1520] (de Worde), [1550?] (Mychel), [after 1561] (Copland), 1652 (in Ashmole's Theatrum chemicum britannicum); ed M. M. Sykes 1822 (Roxburghe Club); ed F. Jenkinson, Cambridge 1906 (facs of first edn), 1929; ed E. P. Hammond, English verse between Chaucer and Surrey, Durham NC 1927; ed H. N. MacCracken, Minor poems, 1934.

[The complaint of the black knight]. The complainte of a lovers lyfe. nd (de Worde), 1508 (as The maying or disport of Chaucer in The knightly tale of Golagrus and Gawane), 1532 (in Thynne's Works of Chaucer and subsequent edns until discovered to be Lydgate's by Shirley's testimony); ed K. Krausser, Anglia 19 1896; ed W. W. Skeat, Complete works of Chaucer vol 7, Oxford 1897; ed G. Stevenson 1918 (STS) (from 1508 edn); ed H. N. MacCracken, Minor poems, 1934; ed J. Norton-Smith, Poems, Oxford 1966.

[Danse macabre]. The daunce machabree. 1554 (in Fall of princes); rptd in W. Dugdale, History of St Paul's Cathedral, 1658, and in Hans Holbein's Alphabet of death, 1856; ed E. P. Hammond, English verse between Chaucer and Surrey, Durham NC 1927; ed F. Warren and B. White 1931 (EETS).

The departing of Thomas Chaucer. Ed E. P. Hammond, MP 1 1903; ed H. N. MacCracken, Minor poems, 1934; ed J. Norton-Smith, Oxford 1966.

Fabula duorum mercatorum. Ed J. Zupitza and G. Schleich, Quellen und Forschungen 83 1897; ed H. N. MacCracken, Minor poems, 1934.

The falle of princis. 1494 (Pynson), 1527 (Pynson), 1554 (Tottell), [1555?] (Wayland); ed H. Bergen, Washington 1923–4, 1924–7 (EETS). E. P. Hammond, English verse between Chaucer and Surrey, Durham NC 1927 contains extracts. *See also* Proverbs of Lydgate, below, which contains extracts.

Flour of curtesye. 1532 (in Thynne's Chaucer and later edns to Chalmers); ed W. W. Skeat, Complete works of Chaucer vol 7, 1897; ed H. N. MacCracken, Minor poems, 1934.

Of Gloucester's wedding, and Complaint for my lady of Gloucester. Ed E. P. Hammond, Anglia 27 1904; ed H. N. MacCracken, Minor poems, 1934; ed E. P. Hammond, English verse between Chaucer and Surrey, Durham NC 1927.

The governance of kings and princes. *See* Secrets of old philosophers, below.

The grateful dead. Ed A. Beatty, A new ploughman's tale, 1902 (Chaucer Soc).

Guy of Warwick. Ed J. Zupitza, Sitzungsberichte der Königlichen Akademie der Wissenschaften (philologische-historische Klasse) 74 1873; ed F. N. Robinson, Harvard Stud 5 1896; ed H. N. MacCracken, Minor poems, 1934.

The hystorye, sege and dystruccyon of Troye. 1513 (Pynson), 1555 (Marshe), 1614 (modernized by T. Heywood as The life and death of Hector); ed H. Bergen 4 pts 1906–35 (EETS). *See also under* Romances of Troy, *col 425, above.*

The horse the ghoos and the sheep. 1477 (Caxton), [1477–8] (Caxton), [1500] (de Worde), [1500?] (de Worde), 1500 (de Worde); ed M. M. Sykes 1822 (Roxburghe Club); ed M. Degenhart 1900; ed F. J. Furnivall 1903 (in Political, religious and love poems) (EETS); ed F. Jenkinson, Cambridge 1906 (facs of 1500 edn); ed H. N. MacCracken, Minor poems, 1934; ed C. F. Bühler, MLN 55 1940 (additional stanzas in Huntington ms HM 144).

King Henry's triumphal entry in London. Ed H. N. MacCracken, Archiv 126 1911; ed H. N. MacCracken, Minor poems, 1934.

On the kings of England. Ed J. Gairdner, The historical collections of a citizen of London in the fifteenth century, 1876 (Camden Soc); ed R. H. Robbins, Historical poems, New York 1959.

The lyf of our lady. [1484] (2 issues) (Caxton), 1531 (Redman); ed C. E. Tame, Early English religious literature 1871–9; ed J. A. Lauritis, R. A. Klinefelter and V. F. Gallagher, Duquesne Stud: Philological ser 2 1961.

The lyfe of Seint Albon and the lyfe of Saint Amphabel. St Albans 1534; ed C. Horstmann, Festschrift der Realschule zu Berlin, Berlin 1882.

Merita missae. Ed T. F. Simmons, Lay folks mass book, 1879 (EETS). Also contains Venus mass and extracts from Virtutes missarum, not to be confused with Virtue of the mass.

Mummings. Ed E. P. Hammond, Mumming at Hertford, Anglia 22 1900; ed R. Brotanek, Die englischen Maskenspiele, Vienna 1902; ed H. N. MacCracken, Minor poems, 1934; ed J. Norton-Smith, Mumming at Bishopswood, Poems, Oxford 1966.

New year's valentine. Ed E. P. Hammond, Anglia 32 1909; ed H. N. MacCracken, Minor poems, 1934.

Two nightingale poems. Ed O. Glauning 1900 (EETS).

The pilgrimage of the life of man. Ed F. J. Furnivall 1899–1904 (EETS); ed F. J. Furnivall and K. B. Locock 1905 (Roxburghe Club). On Deguileville, see edn by J. J. Sturzinger 1893 (Roxburghe Club).

The puerbes [proverbs] of Lydgate. [1515?] (de Worde), [1520?] (de Worde), 1526 (Pynson). Extracts from Fall of princes; Loke in thy merour; Consulo quisquis eris; and Chaucer's Fortune and Truth.

Queen Margaret's entry into London. Ed C. Brown, MLR 7 1912; ed R. Withington, MP 13 1915 (additional stanzas in BM ms Harley 542).

Reason and sensuality. Ed E. Sieper 1901–3 (EETS).

St Edmund and Fremund. Ed C. Horstmann, Altenglische Legenden, Heilbronn 1881; ed F. Harvey, Corolla sancti Eadmundi, 1907.

St Giles. Ed C. Horstmann, Altenglische Legenden, Heilbronn 1881; ed H. N. MacCracken, Minor poems, 1911.

[Secrets of old philosophers]. The governaunce of kynges and prynces. 1511 (Pynson); ed R. Steele 1894 (EETS) (from Sloane ms). T. Prosiegel, The book of the governaunce of kynges and prynces, 1903, corrects this edn and collates with other mss.

The serpent of division. nd (fragment) (Treverys), 1559 (Rogers), 1590 (with Gorboduc); ed H. N. MacCracken, New Haven 1911.

[Siege of Thebes]. The storye of Thebes. [1495?] (de Worde), [1500?] (de Worde), 1561 (in Stow's Chaucer and later edns to Chalmers); pt 1 ed A. Erdmann 1911 (Chaucer Soc and EETS); pt 2 ed Erdmann and E. Ekwall 1930 (EETS); Prologue, ed E. P. Hammond,

Anglia 36 1912. *See also under* Romances of Thebes, *col 428, above.*

Stans puer ad mensam. nd (Caxton), [1545?] (appended to Hugh Rhodes, Book of nurture); ed W. C. Hazlitt, Remains of the early popular poetry of England vol 3, 1866; ed F. J. Furnivall, The Babees Book, 1868 (EETS); ed H. N. MacCracken, Minor poems, 1934.

Two tapestry poems: (a) The life of St George; (b) The falls of seven princes. Ed E. P. Hammond, E Studien 43 1910.

The temple of glass. [1477–8] (Caxton), nd (de Worde), [1500] (de Worde), nd (de Worde), [1505?] (Pynson), [1530?] (Berthelet); ed J. Schick 1891 (EETS); ed F. Jenkinson, Cambridge 1905 (facs of first edn); ed J. Norton-Smith, Poems, Oxford 1966.

The testament of J. Lydgate. [1515?] (Pynson); rptd in Halliwell's and MacCracken's edns of Minor poems.

Troy book. *See* History of Troy, *col 642, above.*

The vertue of the masse. nd (de Worde); rptd in Fugitive tracts vol 3, 1875; ed H. N. MacCracken, Minor poems, 1911.

Works attributed to Lydgate

Cartae versificatae. In Memorials of St Edmund's abbey vol 3, ed T. Arnold 1896. Attributed on internal evidence by Arnold, MacCracken and Index.

The child of Bristow. Ed C. Hopper, Camden Miscellany vol 4, 1859; ed T. Burke, The charm of the West Country, 1913. Attributed by Ritson. *See also under* Tales, *col 460, above.*

The complaint of Mary Magdalen. 1526 (Pynson), 1561 (in Stow's Chaucer); ed C. E. Tame [1871] (as The lamentation of St Mary Magdalene). Attributed in Harleian catalogue.

[The Court of Sapience]. De curia sapiencie. [1490] (Caxton), 1510 (de Worde); ed R. Spindler, Leipzig 1927; [selections] ed E. P. Hammond, English verse between Chaucer and Surrey, Durham NC 1927. Really by author of The babees book? *See,* however, C. F. Bühler, The sources of the Court of Sapience, Leipzig 1932 and Notes on the Plimpton manuscript of the Court of Sapience, MLN 59 1944.

The lamentation of our lady. [before 1519] (de Worde); ed C. E. Tame [1871]. Attributed by Ritson and Tanner.

London lickpenny. Ed E. P. Hammond, Anglia 20 1898; ed F. Holthausen, Anglia 43 1919. Attributed by Stow, Tanner and Ritson.

The medicine of the stomach. In The governayle of helthe, [c. 1491] (Caxton), nd (de Worde), [c. 1491] (Caxton); ed W. Blades 1858. Attributed in BM Harley ms 116, which contains nothing but Lydgate's work.

[The pilgrimage of the soul]. The boke of the pylgremage of the sowle. 1483 (Caxton); [selections] ed K. I. Cust 1859. For facs of several pages of 1483 edn *see* Apollo 14 1931.

The seven virtues. [1500?].

A treatise of a gallant. [1516?] (de Worde). In W. C. Hazlitt, Remains of the early popular poetry of England vol 3, 1866 and F. H. Furnivall, Academy 29 Aug 1896. Attributed by Bishop John Alcock.

A treatise of the smith. nd (Copland). In W. C. Hazlitt, Remains of the early popular poetry of England vol 3, 1866. Attributed by Bale, Ritson.

The verse trn of a Latin prayer (*Brown,* Religious lyrics of the fifteenth century *336*), 'O Lord allmyghty blissid thou be' (Index 2, 483) *in Bodley ms Hatton 73 f. 121a (and in Lambeth ms 344) in Margaret of Anjou's copy of Lydgate's Life of our lady, is probably his.*

§2

Warton, T. In his History of English poetry, 3 vols 1774–81. *See* vol 2 pp. 51–100.

Koeppel, E. Lydgate's Story of Thebes: eine Quellen-untersuchung. Munich 1884.

— Laurents de Premierfait und Lydgates Bearbeitung von Boccaccios De casibus virorum illustrium. Munich 1885.

Gattinger, E. Die Lyrik Lydgates. Vienna 1896.

Robinson, F. N. On two mss of Lydgate's Guy of Warwick. Harvard Stud 5 1896.

Schick, J. Kleine Lydgate-studien: Reason and sensuality. Anglia Beiblatt 8 1897.

Sieper, E. Les échecs amoureux und ihre englische Über-tragung [Reason and sensuality]. Weimar 1898.

Rey, A. Skelton's satirical poems in their relation to Lydgate's Order of fools. Berne 1899.

Emmerig, O. The bataile of Agyncourt im Lichte ge-schichtlicher Quellenwerke. Nuremburg 1906. Attributes it to Lydgate.

MacCracken, H. N. Additional light on the Temple of glas. PMLA 23 1908.

— In despite of the Flemings. Anglia 33 1910.

Reuss, F. Das Naturgefühl bei Lydgate. Archiv 122 1909.

Rudolf, A. Lydgate und die Assembly of gods. Berlin 1909.

Hammond, E. P. A reproof to Lydgate. MLN 26 1911. Reprint of poem censuring passages in Fall of princes.

— Chaucer and Lydgate notes. MLN 27 1912.

— Lydgate's prologue to the story of Thebes. Anglia 36 1912.

— Poet and patron in the Fall of princes. Anglia 38 1914.

— The texts of Lydgate's Danse macabre. MLN 36 1921.

— Lydgate and Coluccio Salutati. MP 25 1927. Passage in the Fall of princes.

Reismüller, G. Romanische Lehnwörter bei Lydgate. Leipzig 1911.

Moore, S. Patrons of letters in Norfolk and Suffolk c. 1450. PMLA 27 1912. On some of Lydgate's patrons.

Courmont, A. Studies in Lydgate's syntax in the Temple of glass. Paris 1912.

Brown, C. Lydgate and the Legend of good women. E Studien 47 1913.

— An holy medytacion—by Lydgate? MLN 40 1925.

— Chaucer's Wretched engendring. PMLA 50 1935. Identifies Chaucer's lost work as An holy medytacion (hitherto attributed to Lydgate).

Withington, R. Queen Margaret's entry into London. MP 13 1915.

— English pageantry, vol 1. Cambridge Mass 1918.

Werner, F. Ein Sammelkapitel aus Lydgates Fall of princes. Münchener Archiv 5 1916.

Royster, J. F. A note on Lydgate's use of the *do* auxiliary. SP 13 1916.

Juhl, H. Der syntaktische Gebrauch des Infinitivs bei Lydgate. Kiel 1921.

— Lydgates Quelle zu seinen Guy of Warwick. Archiv 146 1923. On the Latin chronicle of Gerardus Cornubiensis.

Brie, F. Mittelalter und Antike bei Lydgate. E Studien 64 1929.

Nichols, P. H. Dunbar as a Scottish Lydgatian. PMLA 46 1931.

— Lydgate's influence on the aureate terms of the Scottish Chaucerians. PMLA 47 1932.

Brunner, K. Lydgatiana. Archiv 161 1932.

Bühler, C. F. A note on Lydgate's Verses on the kings of England. RES 9 1933.

— Lydgate's Rules of health in ms Lansdowne 699. MÆ 3 1934.

— Lydgate's Horse, sheep and goose and Huntington ms HM 144. MLN 55 1941. Restated PBSA 46 1952; *see also* 43 1949.

— JEGP 40 1941. The churl and the bird, st 24.

— The churl and the bird and the Dites and sayings of the old philosophers. Library 4th ser 21 1941. On the textual source of Caxton's first edn.

Oakden, J. P. A note on Lydgate's Verses on the kings of England. RES 9 1933.

Wehrle, W. O. The macaronic hymn tradition in medieval English literature. Washington 1933. *See* pp. 129–41 for Lydgate's religious verse.

Lewis, C. S. In his Allegory of love, Oxford 1936.

Pyle, F. The pedigree of Lydgate's heroic line. Hermathena 25 1936.

Tilgner, E. Die aureate terms als Stilelement bei Lydgate. Berlin 1936.

Koch, H. Zu Lydgate, Troy book I. 591: the fyry cat. Archiv 171 1937.

Webster, M. The vocabulary of Holy medytacyon. PQ 17 1938.

Atwood, E. B. Some minor sources of Lydgate's Troy book. SP 35 1938.

Bennett, H. S. In his Chaucer and the fifteenth century, Oxford 1947 (OHEL).

Bowers, R. H. Iconography in Lydgate's Dance of death. Southern Folklore Quart 12 1948.

— Lydgate's Order of fools in Harley ms 374. MLN 67 1952. No 1135 in Index is not an independent poem but 5 stanzas from Lydgate.

Mullett, C. F. Lydgate: a mirror of medieval medicine. Bull History of Medicine 22 1948.

Marquardt, W. F. A source for the passage on the origin of chess in Lydgate's Troy book. MLN 64 1949.

Klinefelter, R. A. Lydgate's Life of our lady and the Chetham ms 6709. PBSA 46 1952.

Parr, J. Astronomical dating for some of Lydgate's poems. PMLA 67 1952.

— The horoscope of Edippus in Lydgate's Siege of Thebes. In Essays in honor of Walter Clyde Curry, Nashville 1954.

— Astronomical date of Lydgate's Life of our lady. PQ 50 1971.

Schirmer, W. F. Lydgate: ein Kulturbild aus dem 15 Jahrhundert. Tübingen 1952; tr and rev as Lydgate: a study in the culture of the 15th century, 1961.

Hyde, I. Lydgate's halff chongyd Latyne: an illustration. MLN 70 1955.

Trapp, J. B. Verses by Lydgate at Long Melford. RES new ser 6 1955.

Renoir, A. Chaucerian character names in Lydgate's Siege of Thebes. MLN 71 1956.

— A note on Saintsbury's criticism of Lydgate. Neuphilologische Mitteilungen 58 1957.

— The binding knot: three uses of one image in Lydgate's poetry. Neophilologus 41 1957.

— On the date of Lydgate's Mumming at Hertford. Archiv 198 1961.

— Attitudes towards women in Lydgate's poetry. E Studies 42 1961.

— The immediate source of Lydgate's Siege of Thebes. Studia Neophilologica 33 1961.

— The poetry of Lydgate. 1967.

Boyd, B. The literary background of Lydgate's The legend of dan Joos. MLN 72 1957.

Wright, H. G. In his Boccaccio in England from Chaucer to Tennyson, 1957.

Ayers, R. W. Medieval history, moral, purpose and the structure of Lydgate's Siege of Thebes. PMLA 73 1958.

Norton-Smith, J. Lydgate's changes in the Temple of glas. MÆ 27 1958.

— Lydgate's metaphors. E Studies 42 1961.

Wickham, G. In his Early English stages vol 1, 1959. *See* pp. 191–207 on Mumming poems.

Dédéyan, C. Dante en Angleterre: Lydgate. Lettres Romanes 13 1959.

Leech, E. Lydgate's The dolorous pyte of Cristes passioun. N & Q Nov 1960.

Rossi, S. In his Poesia cavalleresca e poesia religiosa inglese nel Quattrocento, Milan 1960.

Manzalaoui, M. Lydgate and English prosody. Cairo Stud in Eng 1960.

Seaton, E. In her Sir Richard Roos, 1961.

Ringler, W. Lydgate's Serpent of division 1559, edited by John Stow. SB 14 1961.

Chew, S. C. In his Pilgrimage of life, New Haven 1962.

Wolpers, T. In his Die englische Heiligenlegende des Mittelalters, Tübingen 1964.

Lauritis, J. A. Second thoughts on style in Lydgate's Life of our lady. Duquesne Stud 1964.

Daniel, B. L. A note on Lydgate's corious flour of rhetorik. Emporia State Stud 14 1965.

McKenna, S. W. Henry VI of England and the dual monarchy. Jnl Warburg & Courtauld Inst 28 1965.

Pearsall, D. A. The English Chaucerians. In Chaucer and Chaucerians, ed D. S. Brewer 1966.

— John Lydgate. 1970.

Gathercole, P. Lydgate's Fall of princes and the French version of Boccaccio's De casibus. In Miscellanea sul Quattrocento francese, ed F. Simone, Turin 1966.

Schlauch, M. Stylistic attributes in Lydgate's prose. In To honor Roman Jakobson, Janua Linguarum (Hague) (ser maior 31) 3 1967.

Mathew, G. In his Court of Richard II, 1968.

Edwards, A. S. G. Lydgate's Fall of princes: unrecorded readings. N & Q May 1969.

— Lydgate's attitudes towards women. E Studies 51 1970.

— Lydgate's Tyed with a line and the 'question of Halsam'. Ibid.

— Some borrowings by Cavendish from Lydgate's Fall of princes. N & Q June 1971.

THOMAS HOCCLEVE
1368?–1426?

Manuscripts

For complete lists see Index *and* Index Supplement; *for addns etc,* M. C. Seymour, RES new ser 20 1969. *Since* Index *the Corpus Christi ms 237 has been refoliated.*

Doyle, A. I. and G. B. Pace. A new Chaucer manuscript. PMLA 83 1968. Coventry corp ms contains Hoccleve's complaint and The regiment of princes.

Collections

Poems. Ed G. Mason 1796.

Works. Vol 1: The minor poems, ed F. J. Furnivall 1892; vol 2: The minor poems in the Ashburnham ms [now Huntington HM 144], ed I. Gollancz 1925; vol 3: The regiment of princes and 14 minor poems, ed F. J. Furnivall 1897 (EETS). Other poems are in E. P. Hammond, English verse between Chaucer and Surrey, Durham NC 1927; C. and K. Sisam, The Oxford book of medieval English verse, Oxford 1970.

§I

Address to Sir John Oldcastle. Ed L. T. Smith, Anglia 5 1882; cd F. J. Furnivall, Minor poems vol 1, 1892 (EETS).

Balade au tres honourable compaignie du garter. 1542 (in Thynne's Chaucer); ed W. W. Skeat, Complete works of Chaucer vol 7, Oxford 1897.

Balade au tres noble Henry le quint. 1542 (in Thynne's Chaucer); ed W. W. Skeat, Complete works of Chaucer vol 7, Oxford 1897.

Balade to my Lord Chancellor. Ed R. H. Robbins, Secular lyrics of the 14th and 15th centuries, Oxford 1952.

The letter of Cupid. 1532, [1545?] (in Thynne's Chaucer), 1561 (in Stow's Chaucer); ed E. Arber, An English garner vol 4, 1882; ed W. W. Skeat, Complete works of Chaucer vol 7, Oxford 1897. For Christian de Pisan herself *see* Roy, Oeuvres poétiques vol 2, Paris 1888–96.

The mother of God. In edns of Chaucer from 1532; ed J. Leyden, The complaynt of Scotland, Edinburgh 1801; re-ed 1872 (EETS); ed F. J. Furnivall, Minor poems vol 1, 1892 (EETS).

De regimine principium. Ed T. Wright 1869 (Roxburghe Club).

Tale of Jonathas. In W. Browne, The shepherds pipe, 1614. Modernized and abridged.

Of the virgin and her sleeveless garment. Ed A. Beatty, A new ploughman's tale, 1902 (Chaucer Soc); ed I. Gollancz, Minor poems vol 2, 1925 (EETS); ed B. Boyd, ME miracles of the Virgin, San Marino 1964.

§2

Vollmer, E. Sprache und Reime des Londoners Hoccleve. Anglia 21 1899.

Bock, F. Metrische Studien zu Hoccleves Versen. Weilheim 1900.

MacCracken, H. N. Hoccleve and the poems from Deguilleville. Nation (New York) 26 Sept 1907.

— Another poem by Hoccleve? MLN 24 1909.

Williams, W. H. De regimine principium. MLR 4 1909.

Kern, J. H. Zum Texte einiger Dichtungen Hoccleves. Anglia 39 1916.

— Hoccleves Verszeile. Anglia 40 1916.

— Die Datierung von Hoccleves Dialog. Ibid.

Hulbert, J. R. An Hoccleve item. MLN 36 1921.

Sandison, H. E. The original of Hoccleve's Balade to the Virgin and Christ. In Vassar mediaeval studies, ed C. F. Fiske, New Haven 1923.

Kurtz, B. P. The source of Occleve's Lerne to dye. MLN 38 1923.

— The prose of Occleve's Lerne to dye. MLN 39 1924.

— The relation of Occleve's Lerne to dye to its source. PMLA 40 1925.

Schulz, H. C. Thomas Hoccleve, scribe. Speculum 12 1937. An earlier date of death confirmed by H. S. Bennett, TLS 25 Dec 1953. A. L. Brown, RES new ser 8 1957, gives an earlier probable date as March or April 1426.

Adams, R. P. Pre-Renaissance courtly propaganda for peace in English literature. Papers of Michigan Acad 32 1946.

Bennett, H. S. In his Chaucer and the fifteenth century, Oxford 1947 (OHEL).

— In his Six medieval men and women, Cambridge 1955.

Boyd, B. Hoccleve's Miracle of the Virgin. SE 35 1956.

Rossi, S. In his Poesia cavalleresca e poesia religiosa inglese nel Quattrocento, Milan 1960.

Howarth, R. A rakish rhymer. In his A pot of gillyflowers, Cape Town 1965.

Pearsall, D. A. The English Chaucerians. In Chaucer and Chaucerians, ed D. S. Brewer 1966.

Mitchell, J. Hoccleve's supposed friendship with Chaucer. Eng Lang Notes 4 1966.

— Autobiographical element in Hoccleve. MLQ 28 1967.

— Hoccleve: a study in early 15th-century English poetic. Urbana 1968.

— Hoccleve's tribute to Chaucer. In Chaucer und seine Zeit, ed A. Esch, Tübingen 1968.

Thornley, E. M. The ME penitential lyric and Hoccleve's autobiographical poetry. Neuphilologische Mitteilungen 68 1967.

Mathew, G. In his Court of Richard II, 1968.

Rigg, A. G. Hoccleve's Complaint and Isidore of Seville. Speculum 45 1970.

Fleming, J. V. Hoccleve's Letter of Cupid and the 'quarrel' over the Roman de la rose. MÆ 40 1971.

BENEDICT BURGH
d. 1483

Manuscripts
For complete lists see Index *and* Index Supplement.

Klinefelter, R. A. A newly discovered fifteenth-century manuscript. MLQ 14 1953. On Venerable English College Rome ms 1306 containing Parvus Cato and Cato major.

§1

The ABC of Aristotle. Ed F. J. Furnivall, The babees book, 1868 (EETS).

A Christemasse game. Ed T. Wright, Specimens of old Christmas carols, 1841 (Percy Soc); ed F. J. Furnivall, N & Q 16 May 1868; ed E. Flügel, Anglia 14 1892.

[Distichs of Cato]. Parvus Catho and Magnus Catho. [1477?] (Caxton), [1477] (Caxton), [1478?] (Caxton), [1480?] (Caxton); ed F. Jenkinson, Cambridge 1906 (facs of 1477 edn).

Parvus Cato and Magnus Cato [Latin and English]. [1481?] (Caxton), 1557.

The boke of Cato. 1558 (Copland). Contains extra verses.

Parvus Cato. Ed M. Förster, Archiv 115 1905. From Cambridge Univ Library ms Hh.iv.12.

Cato major. Ed E. Flügel, Anglia 14 1892 (from Royal ms 18 D.11); ed M. Förster, Archiv 115–16 1905–6 (from Cambridge Univ Lib ms Hh.iv.12).

In praise of Lydgate. Ed R. Steele, Secrees of old philosoffres, 1894 (EETS); ed E. P. Hammond, English verse between Chaucer and Surrey, Durham NC 1927.

Continuation of Lydgate's Secrees of old philisoffres, 11. 1492–2730 [Gouernaunce of kynges and prynces]. 1511 (Pynson); ed R. Steele 1894 (EETS); ed T. Prosiegel as The book of the governaunce of kynges and prynces, 1903.

§2

Material for a biography is contained in (1) R. Steele's edn of Lydgate's Secrees of old philisoffres, *1894 (EETS) xvii–xviii; (2) A. B. Emden, A biographical register of the University of Oxford to 1500 vol 1, Oxford 1957.*

GEORGE ASHBY
d. 1475

Manuscripts
Trinity College Cambridge R.3.19; Cambridge Univ Lib Mm.iv.42.

§1

Poems. Ed M. Bateson 1899 (EETS).

Prisoner's reflections. Ed M. Förster, Anglia 20 1898; ed M. Bateson 1899 (EETS); ed F. Holthausen, Anglia 45 1921.

§2

Warton, T. In his History of English poetry, 3 vols 1774–81.

Holthausen, F. Ashbys Trost in Gefangenschaft. Anglia 43 1919.

— Active policy of a Prince. Anglia 45 1921.

Bühler, C. F. The Liber de dictis philosophorum antiquorum and common proverbs in Ashby's poems. PMLA 65 1950.

HENRY BRADSHAW
d. 1513

§1

Lyfe of St Radegunde. [1521?] (Pynson); ed F. Brittain, Cambridge 1926.
The lyfe of Saynt Werburge. 1521 (Pynson); E. Hawkins (facs) 1848 (Chetham Soc); ed C. Horstmann 1887 (EETS).
Anthony Wood mentions 2 Latin works, De antiquitate et magnificentia urbis Cestriæ *and* Chronicon.

§2

Warton, T. In his History of English poetry, 3 vols 1774–81.
Wolpers, T. In his Die englische Heiligenlegende des Mittelalters, Tübingen 1964.

GEORGE RIPLEY
d. 1490?

THOMAS NORTON
fl. 1477

AND OTHER ALCHEMISTS
Manuscripts

Ripley's mss are in (1) E. P. Hammond, English verse between Chaucer and Surrey, Durham NC 1927, p. 252; (2) Index: items 4017, 595; (3) Index Supplement. Mss of Norton's Ordinall of alchemy are in Index: item 3772 (see Index Supplement for revision); Index Supplement: item 3581.5 and col 692 below.

Collections

Theatrum chemicum britannicum. Ed E. Ashmole 1652; Holmyard 1928. The Preface and Prohibicio of Ripley's Compound of alchemy are ed E. P. Hammond, English verse between Chaucer and Surrey, Durham NC 1927.

§1

[Accurtationes et practicae Raymundinae]. The bosome book of Sir G. Ripley. 1683.
The componde of alkemye (Ripley). 1591 (Rabbards), 1591 (Orwin).
Opera omnia chemica (Ripley). Ed Combachius, Cassel 1649.
Saturnus saturatus (Ripley). 1630, 1667.
Tractatus chymicus dictus Crede mihi seu Ordinale (Norton). Ed Maierys, Tripus aureus, 1618 etc.

OSBERN BOKENHAM
1393–1464?

Mss: BM Arundel 327; Harley 4011; Additional ms 11,814.

§1

Legendys of hooly wummen [Lyvys of seynts]. 1835 (Roxburghe Club); ed C. Horstmann, Osbern Bokenhams Legenden, Heilbronn 1883; ed M. S. Serjeantson 1938 (EETS).
Mappula Angliae. Ed C. Horstmann, E Studien 10 1887.
Verse translation of Claudian's De consulatu Stiliconis (ll. 1–413). Ed E. Flügel, Anglia 28 1905. Identified as Bokenham's by Toner on grounds of style, date and provenance.

Verses on the genealogy of the House of York. In J. Weever, Ancient funerall monuments, 1631 p. 734; in W. Dugdale, Monasticon anglicanum vol 6, 1830; ed C. Horstmann, Bokenhams Legenden, Heilbronn 1883.

§2

Material for a biography is contained in (1) F. Roth, Sources for a history of the English Austin friars, *suppl to* Augustiana, *Louvain 1958–61; (2) A. B. Emden,* A biographical register for the University of Cambridge to 1500, *Cambridge 1963; (3) N. Toner,* Augustinian spiritual writers of the English provinces in the 15th and 16th centuries, *Settimana Internazionale di Spiritualità Agostiniana (Rome) 22–7 Oct 1956,* Sanctus Augustinae vitae spiritualis magister *vol 2, Rome 1959. Canon discussed by Toner, who mentions also a doubtful Latin work* Liber de angelis, annulis characteribus et imaginibus planetarum *in Cambridge Univ Lib ms Dd.xi.45. Bokenham (Legendys 2082) refers to himself as the author of a rhythmical Latin poem on St Anne.*

Hoofe, A. Lautuntersuchungen zu Bokenhams Legenden. E Studien 8 1885.
Willenberg, G. Die Quellen von Bokenhams Legenden. E Studien 12 1889.
Moore, S. Patrons of letters in Norfolk and Suffolk c. 1450. PMLA 27–8 1912–13. On some of Bokenham's patrons and friends.
Jeremy, M. The English prose translations of the Legenda aurea. MLN 59 1944. See also Caxton and the synfull wretche, Traditio 4 1946. Argues for Bokenham's authorship of 1438 trn of the Golden legend.
Hackett, M. B. A note on Bokenham. N & Q July 1961.
Barnardison, K. W. Clare priory: seven centuries of a Suffolk house. Cambridge 1962.
Wolpers, T. In his Die englische Heiligenlegende des Mittelalters, Tübingen 1964.

STEPHEN HAWES
fl. 1503–11

New bibliographical material is in Index Supplement. *For possible identification with Hawes, a commoner of Magdalen College Oxford, see A. B. Emden,* A biographical register of the University of Oxford to 1500 *vol 2, Oxford 1958.*

Manuscripts

Scammell, G. V. and H. L. Rogers. An elegy on Henry VII. RES new ser 8 1957. Complete version of contemporary elegy in Registrum parvum (Durham), formerly attributed by Farmer, Douce to Skelton (see Dyce's edn 1843 vol 2, pp. 399–400) is here attributed to Hawes on stylistic grounds. With text.

Selections

Select works of the British poets from Chaucer to Jonson with biographical sketches. Ed R. Southey 1831. Contains selections from Pastyme of pleasure. Text from Wayland's edn of 1554. E. P. Hammond, English verse between Chaucer and Surrey, Durham NC 1927 also contains extracts from Pastyme.

§1

Comfort of lovers. [1512?] (de Worde), [1515?].
The convercyon of swerers. 1509 (de Worde), [1510? de Worde?], [c. 1530] (Butler), 1551 (Copland); ed D. Laing 1865 (Abbotsford Club).
The example of vertu. [1504?] (de Worde), [1510?] (de Worde), [1520?] (de Worde), 1530.
A joyfull medytacyon to all Englande of the coronacyon of Kynge Henry the Eyght. [1509] (de Worde);

ed D. Laing 1865 (Abbotsford Club); ed E. Flügel, Neuenglisches Lesenbuch, Halle 1895 (Prologue only).
The pastyme of pleasure (otherwise titled the Historie of graunde amoure and la bel pucel). [1509] (de Worde), 1517 (de Worde), 1554 (adds 3 verses) (Wayland), 1555 (Tottell), 1555 (Waley); ed T. Wright 1845 (Percy Soc) (from Tottell's 1555 edn); ed W. E. Mead 1928 (EETS).

§2

Wood, A. In his Athenae oxonienses vol 1, ed P. Bliss 1813.

Warton, T. In his History of English poetry, 3 vols 1774–81.

Ames, J. In his Typographical antiquities, 1785. See remarks by W. Herbert, vol 1 p. 194.

Minto, W. In his Characteristics of English poets, 1874.

Fuhr, K. Lautuntersuchungen zu Stephen Hawes The pastime of pleasure. Marburg 1891.

Morley, H. In his English writers vol 7, 1891.

ten Brink, B. In his History of English literature vol 3, 1896.

Burkart, E. A. The pastime of pleasure: critical introduction to a proposed new edition of the text. 1899.

Zander, F. Stephen Hawes Passetyme of pleasure verglichen mit Spensers Faerie Queene. Rostock 1905.

Saintsbury, G. In his A history of English prosody vol 1, 1906.

Natter, H. Untersuchung der Quellen von Stephen Hawes allegorischen Gedichte Pastime of pleasure. Passau 1911.

Berdan, J. M. In his Early Tudor poetry, New York 1920.

Lemmi, C. W. The influence of Boccaccio on Hawes's Pastime of pleasure. RES 5 1929.

Wells, W. Hawes and the Court of Sapience. RES 6 1930.

Bühler, C. F. Kyng Melyzylus and the Pastime of pleasure. RES 10 1934.

Lewis, C. S. In his Allegory of love, Oxford 1936.

Sellers, H. Two poems by Hawes and an early medical tract. BM Quart 13 1939.

Church, M. The first English pattern poems. PMLA 61 1946. On Convercyon of swerers.

Chew, S. C. In his Pilgrimage of life, New Haven 1962.

Pearsall, D. A. The English Chaucerians. In Chaucer and Chaucerians, ed D. S. Brewer 1966.

Morgan, A. The convercyon of swerers: another edition. Library 5th ser 24 1969.

PSEUDO-CHAUCERIAN PIECES

The following are the most important 15th-century poems, other than works by Lydgate and Hoccleve, that were included in the early edns of Chaucer. They have been rptd in Skeat's Complete works of Chaucer vol 7, Oxford 1897, and summaries of criticism are in E. P. Hammond, Chaucer: a bibliographical manual, New York 1908—referred to as Skeat and Hammond respectively. More recent criticism is contained in E. P. Hammond, English verse between Chaucer and Surrey, Durham NC 1927; C. S. Lewis, The allegory of love, Oxford 1936; E. Seaton, Sir Richard Roos, 1961; D. A. Pearsall, The English Chaucerians, in Chaucer and Chaucerians, ed D. S. Brewer 1966.

The assembly of ladies. 1532 (in Thynne's Chaucer); Skeat pp. 380–404; ed D. A. Pearsall, Edinburgh 1962. Hammond pp. 408–9.

[Roos, Sir Richard]. La belle dame sans mercy. [1526?] (in Pynson's Boke of fame, Chaucer); extracts ed R. Southey in Select works of the British poets from Chaucer to Jonson, 1831; Skeat pp. 299–326. Hammond pp. 432–3. For biography, criticism and anagrammatical evidence for new canon, see E. Seaton, Sir Richard Roos, 1961.

The Court of Love. 1561 (in Stow's Chaucer); Skeat pp. 409–47. Hammond pp. 418–19. See W. A. Neilson, The origins and sources of the Court of Love, Harvard Stud 6 1899.

The floure and the leaf. 1598 (in Speght's Chaucer); ed J. Dryden, Fables ancient and modern, 1700 etc (modernized); Skeat; ed D. A. Pearsall, Edinburgh 1962. Hammond pp. 423–4. See D. V. Harrington, The function of allegory in the Flower and the leaf, Neuphilologische Mitteilungen 71 1970.

[Scogan, Henry]. A moral ballade. [1477?] (in Caxton, Temple of glas), [1478?] (in Caxton, Temple of glas), 1532 (in Thynne's Chaucer); Skeat pp. 237–44. Hammond p. 455. See W. E. Farnham, John (Henry) Scogan, MLR 16 1921; A. B. Emden, A biographical register of the University of Oxford to 1500 vol 3, Oxford 1959.

The tale of Beryn. 1561 (in Stow's Chaucer), 1721 (in Urry's Chaucer); ed F. J. Furnivall and W. G. Stone 1876 (Chaucer Soc) (EETS). Hammond p. 412.

J. N.-S.

II. MIDDLE SCOTS POETS

JAMES I, HENRYSON, DUNBAR, GAVIN DOUGLAS AND OTHERS

(1) MIDDLE SCOTS ANTHOLOGIES

Manuscript Collections

Arundel ms 285 and Harleian ms 6919 [BM]. Ed J. A. W. Bennett, Devotional pieces in verse and prose from ms Arundel 285 and ms Harleian 6919, 1955 (STS).

Asloan ms [written c. 1515 by John Asloan, formerly in possession of the Boswell family at Auchinleck; now in Nat Lib of Scotland]. Ed W. A. Craigie 2 vols 1923–5 (STS). See C. C. van Buuren-Veenenbos, John Asloan an Edinburgh scribe, E Studies 47 1966.

Bannatyne ms [said to be compiled 1568, now in Nat Lib of Scotland]. Ed J. B. Murdoch 6 vols 1873–1901 (Hunterian Club); ed W. T. Ritchie 4 vols 1928–34 (STS). See Memorials of George Bannatyne, 1829 (Bannatyne Club); J. T. T. Brown, The Bannatyne

manuscript: a sixteenth-century poetic miscellany, Scottish Historical Rev 1 1904; D. Fox, Some scribal alterations of dates in the Bannatyne ms, PQ 42 1963.

Gray ms [written c. 1500 by James Gray: the Scots pieces are interpolated; now in Nat Lib of Scotland]. Ed G. Stevenson, Pieces from the Makculloch and the Gray mss together with the Chepman and Myllar prints, 1918 (STS).

Maitland folio ms [compiled c. 1580 by Sir Richard Maitland of Lethington, now in Pepys Lib, Magdalene College Cambridge]. Ed W. A. Craigie 2 vols 1919–27 (STS).

Maitland quarto ms [written by Sir Richard's daughter in 1586; also in Pepys Lib]. Ed W. A. Craigie 1920 (STS).

Makculloch ms [a collection of lecture notes in Latin, the Scots pieces being written on blank pages; written after 1477; now in Edinburgh Univ Lib]. Ed G. Stevenson 1918 (STS).

Bibliographies

Geddie, W. A bibliography of Middle Scots poets. 1912 (STS).

Heidtmann, P. A bibliography of Henryson, Dunbar and Douglas 1912–68. Chaucer Rev 5 1970.

Ridley, F. H. A check-list 1956–68 for the study of the Kingis quair, the poetry of Henryson, Douglas and Dunbar. Stud in Scottish Lit 8 1971.

The year's work in Scottish literary studies: (1) medieval to 1660. Scottish Literary News 1– 1970–.

Printed Collections

Chepman and Myllar prints. Edinburgh 1508 (unique copy in Nat Lib of Scotland); ed D. Laing, Edinburgh 1827 (facs); ed G. Stevenson 1918 (STS); ed W. Beattie 1950 (facs) (Edinburgh Bibl Soc).

Ramsay, Allan. The ever green: being a collection of Scots poems wrote by the ingenious before 1600. 2 vols Edinburgh 1724, 1761. Mainly from Bannatyne ms.

Dalrymple, D., Lord Hailes. Ancient Scottish poems, published from the ms of George Bannatyne. Edinburgh 1770, [1815].

Pinkerton, J. Ancient Scotish poems never before in print but now published from the ms collections of Sir Richard Maitland. 2 vols 1786.

—— Scotish poems reprinted from scarce editions. 3 vols 1792.

Dalyell, J. G. Scottish poems of the sixteenth century. Edinburgh 1801.

Sibbald, J. Chronicle of Scottish poetry. 4 vols Edinburgh 1802.

Laing, D. Select remains of the ancient popular and romance poetry of Scotland. Edinburgh 1822; ed J. Small, Edinburgh 1885.

—— Early Scottish metrical tales. Edinburgh 1826, 1889.

—— Early popular poetry of Scotland and the northern border, re-arranged and revised by W. C. Hazlitt. 2 vols 1895.

Ross, J. The book of Scottish poems. Edinburgh 1878, Paisley 1882.

Ward, T. H. The English poets vol 1. 1880.

Morley, H. English writers vol 6 (James I, Henryson). 1890; vol 7 (Dunbar, Douglas), 1891.

Eyre-Todd, G. Mediaeval Scottish poetry. Glasgow 1892.

Amours, F. J. Scottish alliterative poems in riming stanzas. 1892–7 (STS).

Gregory Smith, G. Specimens of Middle Scots. Edinburgh 1902.

Dixon, W. M. The Edinburgh book of Scottish verse 1300–1900. 1910.

Henderson, T. F. A Scots garland. Edinburgh 1931.

Mackie, R. L. A book of Scottish verse. 1934; rev M. Lindsay 1967.

Gray, M. M. Scottish poetry from Barbour to James VI. 1935.

Girvan, R. Ratis raving and other early Scots poems on morals. 1939 (STS).

MacQueen, J. and T. Scott. The Oxford book of Scottish verse. Oxford 1966.

MacQueen, J. Ballatis of lufe. Edinburgh 1970.

Scott, T. Late medieval Scots poetry. 1967.

—— The Penguin book of Scottish verse. 1970.

Kinghorn, A. M. The Middle Scots poets. 1970.

(2) GENERAL STUDIES

Warton, T. The history of English poetry. 3 vols 1774–81; ed W. C. Hazlitt 4 vols 1871; ed R. Wellek 1970 (facs).

Irving, D. The lives of the Scotish poets. 2 vols Edinburgh [1803], 1810 (rev).

—— The history of Scotish poetry. Ed J. A. C[arlyle], Edinburgh 1861.

Lives of the Scottish poets, by the Society of Ancient Scots. Edinburgh 1822.

Wilson, J. G. The poets and poetry of Scotland. 2 vols in 4 1876.

Ross, J. M. Scottish history and literature to the period of the Reformation. Ed J. Brown, Glasgow 1884.

Veitch, J. The feeling for nature in Scottish poetry vol 1. Edinburgh 1887.

Walker, H. Three centuries of Scottish literature. 2 vols Glasgow 1893.

Henderson, T. F. Scottish vernacular literature. 1898, 1900, 1910.

Neilson, W. A. The origins and sources of the Court of Love. Harvard Stud 6 1899.

Gregory Smith, G. The transition period. Edinburgh 1900.

—— Specimens of Middle Scots. Edinburgh 1902.

—— Scottish literature: character and influence. 1919.

Millar, J. H. A literary history of Scotland. 1903.

Kreitz, E. Die Tiere in den Hauptwerken der älteren schottischen Literatur. Bad Lauchstadt 1932.

Nichols, P. H. Lydgate's influence on the aureate terms of the Scottish Chaucerians. PMLA 47 1932.

Mackenzie, A. M. An historical survey of Scottish literature to 1714. 1933.

Smith, J. M. The French background of Middle Scots literature. Edinburgh 1934.

Lewis, C. S. In his Allegory of love, Oxford 1936.

—— In his English literature in the sixteenth century, Oxford 1954 (OHEL).

Brie, F. Die nationale Literatur Schottlands von den Anfängen bis zur Renaissance. Halle 1937.

Speirs, J. The Scots literary tradition. 1940, 1962 (rev).

Craigie, W. A. The Scottish alliterative poems. Proc Br Acad 28 1942.

Whiting, B. J. Proverbs and proverbial sayings from Scottish writings before 1600. Mediaeval Stud 11 1949, 13 1951.

Wood, H. H. Scottish literature. 1952.

Durkan, J. The beginnings of humanism in Scotland. Innes Rev 4 1953.

—— The cultural background in sixteenth-century Scotland. In Essays on the Scottish Reformation, ed D. McRoberts, Glasgow 1962.

Kinsley, J. (ed). Scottish poetry: a critical survey. 1955.

Wittig, K. The Scottish tradition in literature. Edinburgh 1958.

Kinghorn, A. M. The medieval makars. Texas Stud in Lit & Lang 1 1959.

Fox, D. The Scottish Chaucerians. In Chaucer and Chaucerians, ed D. S. Brewer 1966.

MacQueen, J. Some aspects of the early Renaissance in Scotland. Forum for Modern Lang Stud 3 1967.

Aitken, A. J., A. McIntosh and H. Palsson (ed). Edinburgh studies in English and Scots. 1971.

JAMES I, King of Scotland
1394–1437

Collections

Poetical remains of James the First, King of Scotland. [Ed W. Tytler], Edinburgh 1783.

The works of James I, King of Scotland. Perth 1786 (ptd R. Morison).

Poetic remains of some of the Scotish Kings. Ed G. Chalmers 1824.

The works of James the First, King of Scotland. [Ed W. Tytler], Glasgow 1825.

Poetical remains of King James I of Scotland. Ed C. Rogers, Edinburgh 1873.

§ 1

Kingis quair

There is one late fifteenth-century ms, Bodley Arch. Selden B 24.

Chronicle of Scottish poetry vol 1. Ed J. Sibbald, Edinburgh 1802.

The King's quair. Ed E. Thomson, Ayr 1815, 1824, Glasgow 1877.

The Kingis quair, together with a ballad of good counsel. Ed W. W. Skeat 1884 (STS), 1911 (rev).

The Kingis quair, modernised by W. Mackean. 1886, Paisley 1908.

Heirefter followis the quair maid be King James of Scotland the first. Ed R. Steele [1903].

The King's quair. Chiswick 1906 (Caradoc press).

The Kingis quair and the quare of jelusy. Ed A. Lawson 1910.

The Kingis quair. Ed W. M. Mackenzie 1939.

Le livre du roi (the Kingis quair). Ed J. R. Simon, Paris 1967.

The Kingis quair. Ed J. Norton-Smith, Oxford 1971.

Other Poems Attributed to James I

1. *For W. W. Skeat's ascription to James I of fragment B of the* Romaunt of the rose (*ll. 1706–5810*), *see his introd to* Oxford Chaucer, *pp. 3–6;* The Chaucer canon, *Oxford 1900, pp. 75–89; and correspondence in Athenaeum 8, 22 July 1899.*

2. Ballad of good counsel (Sen throw vertew incressis dignitie). Attributed to James I in Ane compendious buik of godly and spirituall songis, 1578, 1600, 1621; ed D. Laing, Edinburgh 1868; ed A. F. Mitchell 1897 (STS). 2 other versions are extant in the Bannatyne ms and ms Cambridge Univ Lib Kk.1.5, ed R. Girvan, Ratis raving and other early Scots poems on morals 1939 (STS). For collation and discussion, *see* Skeat, The Kingis quair, together with a ballad of good counsel, 1911 (STS).

3. Peblis to the play, Christis kirk on the green. Early texts of these poems are in Maitland folio. Another text of Christis kirk occurs in the Bannatyne ms, where it is attributed to James I. Peblis to the play was first ptd in Select Scottish ballads, ed J. Pinkerton 1783. In the seventeenth and eighteenth centuries Christis kirk was very popular, and there are numerous edns and imitations.

A merrie ballad, called Christ's kirk on the green. 1643. Single folio sheet.

A ballad of a country wedding. 1660. Single folio sheet.

Polemo-middinia [by William Drummond of Hawthornden?]; accedit cantilena rustica vulgo inscripta Christs kirk on the green. Ed E.G[ibson], Oxford 1691.

Christ's kirk on the green, in three cantos [cantos 2–3 by A. Ramsay]. Edinburgh 1718. *See also* Poems by A. Ramsay, 1720, 1722, 1723.

Christ's kirk on the green: poems in the Scottish dialect. 1748, [1750], Glasgow 1768.

Two ancient Scottish poems: the gaberlunzie man and Christ's kirk on the green, with notes by J. Callander. Edinburgh 1782, Glasgow 1794, Stirling [1820?], Falkirk [1821].

Chryste-kirk on the green, supposed to be written by King James I: attempted in Latin heroic verse [with text; by John Skinner]. In Carminum rariorum macaronicorum delectus, Edinburgh 1801, 1813.

§ 2

Memoirs relating to the restoration of King James I. 1716; Scotia redivivia vol 1, [1826]; Tracts illustrative of the antiquities of Scotland vol 1, 1836.

Life and death of King James the First of Scotland. [Ed J. Stevenson] 1837 (Maitland Club).

Wood, H. Chaucer's influence upon King James I of Scotland as poet. Anglia 3 1880.

Wischmann, W. Untersuchungen über das Kingis Quair Jakobs I von Schottland. Wismar 1887.

Bierfreund, T. Palemon og Arcite. Copenhagen 1891. On Boccaccio's Teseide, Chaucer's Knight's tale and Kingis quair.

Callaghan, J. The King's quair. Scots Mag 14 1894.

Jusserand, J. J. Le roman d'un roi d'Ecosse. Paris 1895; tr 1896 (with addns).

— Jacques Ier d'Ecosse fut-il poète? Paris 1897. Rptd from Revue Historique 64 1897.

Brown, J. T. T. The authorship of the Kingis quair. Glasgow 1896.

Rait, R. S. The Kingis quair and the new criticism. Aberdeen 1898.

Neilson, G., A. H. Millar and W. A. Craigie. The scribe of the Kingis quair. Athenaeum 16–30 Dec 1899.

Thomson, A. S. Christ's kirk on the green. Scottish N & Q 3 1925.

Balfour-Melville, E. W. M. James the First at Windsor in 1423. Scottish Historical Rev 25 1928.

— The English captivity of James I, King of Scots. 1929 (Historical Assoc).

— James I, King of Scots. 1936.

Macdonald, A. The Kingis quair. TLS 20 March 1937.

— Notes on the Kingis quair. MLR 34 1939.

Weiss, R. The earliest account of the murder of James I of Scotland. EHR 52 1937.

Craigie, W. A. The language of the Kingis quair. E & S 25 1939.

Craigie, J. The Kingis quair. TLS 20 April 1940.

Cronin, G. Two bibliographical notes on the Kingis quair. N & Q Dec 1941.

Jones, G. F. Christis kirk, Peblis to the play and the German peasant-brawl. PMLA 68 1953.

Preston, J. 'Fortunys exiltree': a study of the Kingis quair. RES new ser 7 1956.

Markland, M. F. The structure of the Kingis quair. Research Stud of State College of Washington 25 1957.

Renoir, A. A note on stanza 107 of the Kingis quair. Archiv 197 1960.

Rohrberger, M. The Kingis quair: an evaluation. Texas Stud in Lit & Lang 2 1960.

Slabey, R. M. Art poetical in the Kingis quair. N & Q June 1960.

Bain, C. E. The Kingis quair: two emendations. N & Q May 1961.

— The nightingale and the dove in the Kingis quair. Tennessee Stud in Lit 9 1964.

— The Kingis quair 155.2. E Studies 47 1966.

MacQueen, J. Tradition and the interpretation of the Kingis quair. RES new ser 12 1961.

Bessai, F. A crux in the Kingis quair. N & Q Feb 1962.

Hendy, A. von. The free thrall: a study of the Kingis quair. Stud in Scottish Lit 2 1965.

Maclaine, A. H. The Christis kirk tradition: its evolution in Scots poetry to Burns. Ibid.

Brown, I. The mental traveller: a study of the Kingis quair. Stud in Scottish Lit 5 1968.

Regan, C. L. Joan Beaufort and Mackenzie's error. Amer N & Q 8 1969.

Norton-Smith, J. The Kingis quair. TLS 4 June 1971.

Scheps, W. Chaucerian synthesis: the art of the Kingis quair. Stud in Scottish Lit 8 1971.

RICHARD HOLLAND
fl. c. 1450

The Buke of the howlat *is preserved in the Asloan and Bannatyne mss; fragments of an early edn survive. See F. J. Amours,* Scottish alliterative poems, *1892–7 (STS).*

§1

The buke of the howlat. [Ed D. Laing] 1823 (Bannatyne Club); rptd D. Donaldson, Paisley 1882.
Holland's buke of the houlate published from the Bannatyne ms. Ed A. Diebler, Chemnitz 1893.

§2

Gutmann, J. Untersuchungen über das mittelenglische Gedicht the Buke of the houlate. Halle 1892.
McDiarmid, M. P. Holland's Buke of the howlat: an interpretation. MÆ 38 1969.

BLIND HARY (or HARRY)
c. 1440?–92?

The earliest extant text of the Wallace *is a ms written in 1488 by John Ramsay, now in Nat Lib of Scotland. Fragments of an edn ptd c. 1509 are preserved in the Mitchell Lib at Glasgow and Cambridge Univ Lib. The Wallace was extremely popular; numerous edns and modernized versions appeared in the seventeenth, eighteenth and nineteenth centuries, of which only a selection is listed here; see under Miller and McDiarmid, below.*

§1

The actis and deidis of the illuster and vailzeand campioun schir William Wallace. Edinburgh 1570 (unique copy in BM); ed W. A. Craigie 1940 (STS) (facs).
The lyfe and actis of William Wallace. Edinburgh 1594 (unique copy in Huntington), 1601.
The life and acts of William Wallace. Edinburgh 1611.
The metrical history of Sir William Wallace. 3 vols Perth 1790 (ptd by R. Morison).
Wallace: or the life and acts of Sir William Wallace. Ed J. Jamieson, Edinburgh 1820, Glasgow 1869.
The actis and deidis of the illustere and vailzeand campioun schir William Wallace. Ed J. Moir 3 vols 1885–9 (STS).
Hary's Wallace. Ed M. P. McDiarmid 2 vols 1968–9 (STS).

§2

Craigie, W. A. Barbour and blind Harry as literature. Scottish Rev 22 1893.
Skeat, W. W. Chaucer and blind Harry. MLQ 1 1897.
Brown, J. T. T. The Wallace and the Bruce restudied. Bonn 1900.
Heyne, H. Die Sprache in Henry the Minstrels Wallace. Kiel 1910.
Neilson, G. On blind Harry's Wallace. E & S 1 1910.
Miller, J. F. Blind Harry's Wallace. Records of Glasgow Bibl Soc 3 1914.
—— Some additions to the bibliography of blind Harry's Wallace. Records of Glasgow Bibl Soc. 6 1920.
Schofield, W. H. Mythical bards and the life of William Wallace. Cambridge Mass 1920.
McDiarmid, M. P. The date of the Wallace. Scottish Historical Rev 34 1955.
Scheps, W. William Wallace and his 'buke'. Stud in Scottish Lit 6 1969.
—— Middle English poetic usage and blind Harry's Wallace. Chaucer Rev 4 1970.

ROBERT HENRYSON
1425?–1506?

Henryson's poems survive in a number of mss and prints, most later than his lifetime. The minor poems attributed to him survive almost entirely in the ms collections (Bannatyne, Maitland folio, Makculloch and Gray). 2 short poems and an incomplete version of his Orpheus and Eurydice *are found in the Chepman and Myllar prints. The most important ms collection of the fables is that in the Bannatyne ms; other mss containing one or more of the fables are Harley ms 3865 (BM), the Makculloch ms and the Asloan ms. No authoritative complete ms of the* Testament of Cresseid *survives; it is listed in the Asloan ms table of contents, but the leaves on which it was written have been lost. 2 late English mss (Kinaston in Bodley, and that in St John's College Cambridge) are thought to derive from the version of the poem ptd in Speght's edn of Chaucer.*

Collections

Poems and fables. Ed D. Laing, Edinburgh 1865.
Poems. Ed G. Gregory Smith 3 vols 1906–14 (STS).
Poems: a revised text. Ed W. M. Metcalfe [assisted by T. D. Robb], Paisley 1917.
Selected fables, the Testament of Cresseid, and Robene and Makyne. Ed H. M. R. Murray 1930.
Poems and fables. Ed H. Harvey Wood, Edinburgh 1933, 1958 (rev).
Selections from the poems. Ed D. Murison, Edinburgh 1952.
Poems. Ed C. Elliott, Oxford 1963.

§1

Moral Fables

The morall fabillis of Esope the Phrygian compylit in eloquent and ornate Scottis meter. Edinburgh 1570 (unique copy in BM), Amsterdam 1970 (facs).
The morall fabillis of Esope. Edinburgh 1571. Unique copy in Nat Lib of Scotland.
The fabulous tales of Esope now lately englished. 1577. Unique copy in Nat Lib of Scotland.
The morall fables of Esope the Phrygian. Edinburgh 1621 (unique copy in Nat Lib of Scotland); rptd for Maitland Club, 1832, with unsigned preface by D. Irving.
Henrisones Fabeln. Ed A. R. Diebler, Anglia 9 1886. Edn of Harley ms.

Testament of Cresseid

In Workes of Geoffrey Chaucer, ed W. Thynne 1532.
The testament of Cresseid. Edinburgh 1593 (unique copy in BM); rptd with Robene and Makyne, ed G. Chalmers 1824 (Bannatyne Club); Amsterdam 1969 (facs).
The testament of Cresseid printed in the year 1663. Unique copy in Trinity College Cambridge. Rptd in D. Fox, The 1663 Anderson edition of Henryson's Testament of Cresseid, Stud in Scottish Lit 8 1971.
In Chaucerian and other pieces. Ed W. W. Skeat, Oxford 1897.
The testament of Cresseid. Ed B. Dickins 1925, 1931, 1943 (rev).
The testament of Cresseid. Ed A. Attwater, Cambridge 1926.
The story of Troilus. Ed R. K. Gordon 1934.
A modernization of Henryson's testament of Cresseid, by M. W. Stearns. Bloomington 1945.
The testament of Cresseid. Tr F. Cogswell, Toronto 1957.
The testament of Cresseid. Ed D. Fox 1968.

§2

Diebler, A. R. Henrisones Fabeldichtungen. Halle 1885.

Oliphant, F. R. Robert Henryson. Blackwood's Mag Oct 1890.

Marshall, L. E. Henryson e la Griseida. Milan 1910.

Bullett, G. The fortunes of Cressida. New Statesman 30 June 1923.

Dickins, B. Contributions to the interpretation of Middle Scots texts. TLS 21 Feb 1924.

Jones, W. P. A source for Henryson's Robene and Makyne? MLN 46 1931.

Wood, H. H. In Edinburgh essays on Scots literature, Edinburgh 1933.

—— Two Scots Chaucerians [Henryson and Dunbar]. 1967.

Bone, G. The source of Henryson's fox, wolf and cadger. RES 10 1934.

Grierson, H. J. C. Robert Henryson. Modern Scot 4 1934.

Parr, J. Cresseid's leprosy again. MLN 60 1945.

Whiting, B. J. A probable allusion to Henryson's Testament of Cresseid. MLR 40 1945.

Moore, A. K. Robene and Makyne. MLR 43 1948.

Tillyard, E. M. W. In his Five poems 1470–1870, 1948, 1955 (as Poetry and its background). Contains ch on Testament of Cresseid.

Muir, E. In his Essays on literature and society, 1949, 1965 (rev).

Stearns, M. W. Robert Henryson. New York 1949.

Kinsley, J. Robert Henryson. TLS 14 Nov 1952. Reply by J. Gray 13 March 1953.

Cruttwell, P. Two Scots poets: Dunbar and Henryson. In The age of Chaucer, ed B. Ford 1954 (Pelican).

Elliott, C. Two notes on Henryson's Testament of Cresseid. JEGP 54 1955.

—— Sparth, glebard and bowranbane. N & Q March 1962.

Rossi, S. L'annunciazione di Henryson. Aevum 29 1955.

—— Robert Henryson. Milan 1955.

Moran, T. The Testament of Cresseid and the book of Troylus. Litera 6 1959.

—— The meeting of the lovers in the Testament of Cresseid. N & Q Jan 1963.

Rowlands, M. The fables of Henryson. Dalhousie Rev 39 1960.

—— Henryson and the Scottish courts of law. Aberdeen Univ Rev 39 1962.

Duncan, D. Henryson's Testament of Cresseid. EC 11 1961. Reply by S. J. Harth, ibid.

Crowne, D. K. A date for the composition of Henryson's fables. JEGP 61 1962.

Fox, D. Henryson's fables. ELH 29 1962.

—— Henryson and Caxton. JEGP 67 1968.

—— A Scoto-Danish stanza, Wyatt, Henryson and two mice. N & Q June 1971.

Bauman, R. The folktale and oral tradition in the fables of Henryson. Fabula 6 1963.

MacQueen, J. The text of Henryson's morall fabillis. Innes Rev 14 1963.

—— Henryson: a study of the major narrative poems. Oxford 1967.

McMillan, D. J. Classical tale plus folk tale. Amer N & Q 1 1963.

Cresseid in Scotland. TLS 9 April 1964.

Rowland, B. The 'seiknes incurabill' in Henryson's Testament of Cresseid. Eng Lang Notes 1 1964.

Spearing, A. C. Conciseness and the Testament of Cresseid. In his Criticism and medieval poetry, 1964.

Hyde, I. Poetic imagery: a point of comparison between Henryson and Dunbar. Stud in Scottish Lit 2 1965.

Kinghorn, A. M. The minor poems of Henryson. Stud in Scottish Lit 3 1966.

Toliver, H. E. Henryson: from moralitas to irony. E Studies 46 1965.

Jamieson, I. W. A. Henryson's fabillis: an essay towards a revaluation. Words, Wai-te-Atu Stud in Eng 2 1966.

—— A further source for Henryson's fabillis. N & Q Nov 1967.

—— Henryson's taill of the wolf and the wedder. Stud in Scottish Lit 6 1969.

Louis, K. R. G. Henryson's Orpheus and Eurydice and the Orpheus traditions of the Middle Ages. Speculum 41 1966.

Macdonald, D. Narrative art in Henryson's fables. Stud in Scottish Lit 3 1966.

—— Henryson and the Thre prestis of peblis. Neophilologus 51 1967.

—— Henryson and Chaucer: cock and fox. Texas Stud in Lit & Lang 8 1967.

—— Chaucer's influence on Henryson's fables: The use of proverbs and sententiae. MÆ 39 1970.

Aswell, E. D. The role of fortune in the Testament of Cresseid. PQ 46 1967.

Friedman, J. B. Henryson, the friars and the Confessio Reynardi. JEGP 66 1967.

Jenkins, A. W. Henryson's The fox, the wolf and the cadger again. Stud in Scottish Lit 4 1967.

McDermott, J. J. Henryson's Testament of Cresseid and Heywood's A woman killed with kindness. Renaissance Quart 20 1967.

Chessell, D. Henryson's Testament of Cresseid. Critical Rev 12 1969.

Craik, T. W. An emendation in Henryson's fables. N & Q March 1969.

Hume, K. Leprosy or syphilis in Henryson's Testament of Cresseid? Eng Lang Notes 6 1969.

Stevens, J. Devotion and wit in Henryson's The annunciation. E Studies 51 1970.

Wright, D. A. Henryson's Orpheus and Eurydice and the tradition of the Muses. MÆ 40 1971.

WILLIAM DUNBAR
1460?–1513?

Apart from the 6 poems in the Chepman and Myllar prints, 1508, there are no early ptd texts of Dunbar's poems. The two most important sources are the Bannatyne ms (with 60 poems attributed to Dunbar) and the Maitland folio (with 61 poems attributed to him). Other mss which contain poems by or attributed to Dunbar are the Asloan ms, the Makculloch ms, Arundel ms 285 and the Aberdeen Register of Sasines. During the eighteenth century selections from his poems were ptd in the collections of Ramsay, Dalrymple, Pinkerton and Sibbald, col 653–4, above.

Collections

Select poems of Will Dunbar: part I. Perth 1788 (ptd R. Morison).

Poems. Ed D. Laing 2 vols Edinburgh 1834; Supplementary vol, 1865.

The life and poems of Dunbar. Ed J. Paterson, Edinburgh 1860.

Poems. Ed J. Small 3 vols 1884–93 (STS). With contributions by A. J. G. Mackay and W. Gregor.

Poems. Ed J. Schipper, Denkschriften der kaiserlichen Akademie der Wissenschaften 40–3, Vienna 1892–4.

Selections from the poems of an old makar adapted for modern readers. Ed H. Haliburton [J. L. Robertson] 1895.

The Dunbar anthology 1401–1508 [Dunbar and his contemporaries]. Ed E. Arber 1901.

Poems. Ed H. B. Baildon, Cambridge 1907.

Poems. Ed W. M. Mackenzie, Edinburgh 1932, 1960 (rev).

Selections from the poems. Ed 'Hugh MacDiarmid' (C. M. Grieve), Edinburgh 1952.

Selected poems. Ed 'Hugh MacDiarmid' (C. M. Grieve), Glasgow 1955.

Poems. Ed J. Kinsley, Oxford 1958.

§ 1

Chepman and Myllar prints. Edinburgh 1508. *See* headnote.

The thistle and the rose: a poem in honour of Margaret, Queen to James IV King of Scots, with a poem address to James V by J. Bellentyne. Glasgow 1750.

Two married women and the widow, translated into English verse. Edinburgh 1840.

§ 2

Kaufmann, J. Traité de la langue du poète écossais Dunbar. Bonn 1873.

Schipper, J. Dunbar: sein Leben und seine Gedichte. Berlin 1884.

Mackay, A. J. G. William Dunbar 1460–1520. Edinburgh 1889.

Oliphant, F. R. William Dunbar. Blackwood's Mag Sept 1893.

Smeaton, W. H. O. William Dunbar. Edinburgh 1898. *See* J. W. Baxter, below.

Baildon, H. B. Dissertation on the rimes in the authentic poems of Dunbar. Freiburg 1899; rptd in Trans Royal Soc of Edinburgh 39 1900.

Nelson, A. S. William Dunbar. GM July 1899.

Mebus, F. Studien zu Dunbar. Breslau 1902.

Steinberger, C. Etude sur Dunbar. Paris 1908.

Snyder, F. B. Sir Thomas Norray and Sir Thopas. MLN 25 1910.

Ayres, H. M. Theodolus in Scots. MP 15 1918. On the Ecloga Theoduli.

Dickins, B. Contributions to the interpretation of Middle Scots texts. TLS 21 Feb 1924.

—— Middle Scots texts. TLS 10 July 1924.

—— The flyting of Dunbar and Kennedy. TLS 14 Dec 1935.

—— The flyting of Dunbar and Kennedy. TLS 20 Jan 1945.

William Dunbar. TLS 10 April 1930.

Nichols, P. H. Dunbar as a Scottish Lydgatian. PMLA 46 1931.

Taylor, R. A. Dunbar: the poet and his period. 1932.

Mackenzie, W. M. In Edinburgh essays on Scots literature, Edinburgh 1933.

Bühler, C. F. 'London thow art the flowre of cytes all'. RES 13 1937.

Speirs, J. William Dunbar. Scrutiny 7 1938.

Baxter, J. W. William Dunbar. TLS 8 April 1939.

—— Dunbar: a biographical study. Edinburgh 1952.

Abenheimer, K. M. and J. L. Halliday. The treatise of the two married women and the widow. Psychoanalytic Rev 31 1944.

Moore, A. K. In his Secular lyric in Middle English, Lexington Kentucky 1951.

—— The setting of Tua mariit wemen and the wedo. E Studies 32 1951.

Morgan, E. Dunbar and the language of poetry. EC 2 1952.

Cruttwell, P. Two Scots poets: Dunbar and Henryson. In The age of Chaucer, ed B. Ford 1954 (Pelican).

Jones, G. F. Dunbar's 'Steidis'. MLN 69 1954.

Kinsley, J. The Tretis of the tua mariit wemen and the wedo. MÆ 23 1954.

Hyde, I. Primary sources and associations of Dunbar's aureate imagery. MLR 51 1956.

—— Poetic imagery: a point of comparison between Henryson and Dunbar. Stud in Scottish Lit 2 1965.

Milner, I. Some aspects of satire in the poetry of Dunbar. Philologica [suppl to Časopis pro Moderní Filologii] 38 1956.

Bennett, J. A. W. Dunbar's Birth of Antichrist 31–2. MÆ 26 1957.

Fox, D. Dunbar's The golden targe. ELH 26 1959.

—— The chronology of Dunbar. PQ 39 1960.

Wordsworth, J. Dunbar's Quod cinis es. MLR 54 1959. Reply by I. Hyde, ibid.

Leyerle, J. The two voices of Dunbar. UTQ 31 1962.

Shire, H. M. The thrissil, the rois and the flour-de-lys. Ninth of May (Cambridge) 3 1962.

Rigg, A. G. Dunbar: the 'fenyeit freir'. RES new ser 14 1963.

Bawcutt, P. J. Dunbar's Tretis of the tua mariit wemen and the wedo, 185–7, and Chaucer's Parson's tale. N & Q Sept 1964.

Smith, R. The poetry of Dunbar. Theoria 22 1964.

Scott, T. Dunbar: a critical exposition of the poems. Edinburgh 1966.

Dobson, E. J. and P. Ingham. Three notes on Dunbar's The tua mariit wemen and the wedo. MÆ 36 1967.

Kinghorn, A. M. Dunbar and Villon: a comparison and contrast. MLR 62 1967.

Wood, H. H. Two Scots Chaucerians [Henryson and Dunbar]. 1967.

Dorsch, T. S. Of discretioun [in asking; Dunbar's petitionary poems. In Chaucer und seine Zeit: Symposion für Walter Schirmer, Tübingen 1968.

Brookhouse, C. Deschamps and Dunbar: two elegies. Stud in Scottish Lit 7 1970.

Hope, A. D. A midsummer eve's dream: variations on a theme by Dunbar. Canberra 1970. On The tua mariit wemen and the wedo.

Eddy, E. R. Sir Thopas and Sir Thomas Norny: romance parody in Chaucer and Dunbar. RES new ser 22 1971.

WALTER KENNEDY
1460?–1508?

Poems attributed to Kennedy are found in the Maitland folio, the Bannatyne ms and Arundel ms 285.

§ 1

Poems. Ed J. Schipper, Denkschriften der kaiserlichen Akademie der Wissenschaften vol 48, Vienna 1902.

§ 2

Holthausen, F. Kennedy-Studien. Archiv 110, 112–13 1903–4.

Because of his presumed share in the Flyting of Dunbar and Kennedy, *edns and studies of Dunbar, above, often contain discussions of Kennedy.*

GAVIN DOUGLAS
1474?–1522

No ms survives of Douglas's Palice of honour (c. 1501). For the fragments of an early edn (c. 1530–40) see D. Laing, Adversaria 1867 (Bannatyne Club), p. 19; W. Beattie, Fragments of the Palyce of honour, Edinburgh Bibl Soc Trans 3 1951 (pt 1). Douglas's trn of the Aeneid, 1513, is extant in 5 mss, of which the earliest and most authoritative is that in Trinity College Cambridge; 2 other mss are in Edinburgh Univ Library, one in Lambeth Palace Library, and another the property of the Marquess of Buth. 2 poems King Hart and Conscience have been attributed to Douglas; they are extant only in the Maitland folio ms. King Hart was first ptd by Pinkerton, Ancient Scotish poems vol 1, 1786.

Collections

Select works of Gawin Douglas: containing memoirs of the author, the Palace of honour, prologues to the Aeneid and a glossary. Perth 1787 (ptd by R. Morison).

Poetical works of Gavin Douglas, Bishop of Dunkeld. Ed J. Small 4 vols Edinburgh 1874.
A selection from his poetry. Ed S. Goodsir Smith, Edinburgh 1959.
Selections. Ed D. F. C. Coldwell, Oxford 1964.
Shorter poems. Ed P. J. Bawcutt 1967 (STS).

§ 1

Palice of Honour

The palis of honoure compyled by Gawyne Dowglas. [1553?], Amsterdam 1969 (facs).
Ane treatise callit the palice of honour. Edinburgh 1579 (2 copies extant, one in Edinburgh Univ Lib, the other in the Nat Lib of Scotland); ed J. G. Kinnear 1827 (facs) (Bannatyne Club).

Aeneid

The xiii bukes of Eneados of the famose poete Virgill translatet into Scottish metir. 1553.
Virgil's Aeneis translated into Scottish verse. Edinburgh 1710. The editor was Thomas Ruddiman. *See* D. Duncan, Thomas Ruddiman, Edinburgh 1965.
The Aeneid of Virgil translated into Scottish verse. [Ed G. Dundas] 2 vols 1839 (Bannatyne Club).
Virgil's Aeneid translated into Scottish verse by Gavin Douglas. Ed D. F. C. Coldwell 4 vols 1957–64 (STS).
The prologues have often been anthologized (see Collections, col 662, above) and some have been rptd separately, e.g. by Francis Fawkes, 1752, 1754, Edinburgh 1885 (Aungervyle Soc), and in Original poems and translations, 1761.

§2

Hunter, W. An Anglo-saxon grammar, with an analysis of the style of Douglas. 1832.
Lange, P. Chaucers Einfluss auf die Originaldichtungen des Schotten Douglas. Halle 1882; rptd in Anglia 6 1883.
Gerken, H. Die Sprache des Bischofs Douglas von Dunkeld. Strasbourg 1898.
Schmidt, E. Die schottische Aeneisübersetzung von Douglas. Leipzig 1910.
Schumacher, A. Des Bischofs Douglas Übersetzung der Aeneis Vergils. Strasbourg 1910.
Watt ,L. M. Douglas's Aeneid. Cambridge 1920.

Hofmann, J. Die nordischen Lehnwörter bei Douglas. Munich 1925.
Brinton, A. C. Maphaeus Vegius and his thirteenth book of the Aeneid: a chapter on Virgil in the Renaissance. Stanford 1930. With bk 13 by Douglas.
Gray, M. M. Surrey's vocabulary. TLS 3 Oct 1936 [on Surrey's debt to Douglas]. Reply by E. Bannister 24 Oct 1936.
Gordon, I. A. Variations on a theme of Maro. In Essays in literature, ed J. Murray, Edinburgh 1936.
Beattie, W. Douglas's Palice of honour. TLS 23 Feb 1946.
Bennett, J. A. W. The early fame of Douglas's Eneados. MLN 61 1946.
Goodsir Smith, S. The Aeneid of Douglas. Life & Letters 55 1947.
Dearing, B. Douglas's Eneados: a reinterpretation. PMLA 67 1952.
Tillyard, E. M. W. In his English epic and its background, 1954.
Preston (later Bawcutt), P. J. Did Douglas write King Hart? MÆ 28 1959.
— The sources of Douglas's Eneados IV, prologue 92–9. N & Q Oct 1969.
— Douglas and Chaucer. RES new ser 21 1970.
— Lexical notes on Douglas's Eneados. MÆ 40 1971.
Ridley, F. Did Douglas write King Hart? Speculum 34 1959.
— Surrey's debt to Douglas. PMLA 76 1961.
Hall, L. B. An aspect of the Renaissance in Douglas's Eneados. Stud in Renaissance 7 1960.
Käsmann, H. Douglas' Aeneis-übersetzung. In Festschrift für Walter Hübner, Berlin 1964.
Fulton, R. Douglas and Virgil. Stud in Scottish Lit 2 1965.
Rossi, S. Il tredicesimo libro dell 'Eneide nella versione di Gavin Douglas. In Studi di letteratura, storia e filosofia in onore di Bruno Revel, Florence 1965.
Kineavy, G. B. The poet in the Palice of honour. Chaucer Rev 3 1969.
Blyth, C. R. Douglas's prologues of natural description. PQ 49 1970.
Gordon, C. D. Douglas's Latin vocabulary. Phoenix 24 1970.
Delany, S. M. King Hart: rhetoric and meaning in a Middle Scots allegory. Neophilologus 55 1971.

P. J. B.

III. ENGLISH PROSE OF THE FIFTEENTH CENTURY

CAPGRAVE, PECOCK, FORTESCUE, CAXTON, MALORY, BERNERS

JOHN CAPGRAVE OSA
1393–1464

Bibliographies

de Meijer, A. Capgrave OESA: bibliography. Augustiniana 7 1957. Contains the most comprehensive list of works by Capgrave.

§ 1

Nova legenda Angliae. 1516 (de Worde); tr 1516 (abridged, Pynson); ed C. Horstmann 2 vols Oxford 1901. Capgrave is at best an editor of this collection of saints' lives, originally compiled by John of Tynemouth.
The chronicle of England. Ed F. C. Hingeston 1858

(Rolls ser). With biography and account of Capgrave's works; Cambridge Univ Lib ms Gg.iv.12 (holograph).
Liber de illustribus Henricis. Tr F. C. Hingeston 1858 (Rolls ser).
The life of St Katharine of Alexandria. Ed C. Horstmann (forewords by F. J. Furnivall) 1893 (EETS). Verse; mss Bodley Rawlinson poetry 118 (holograph) and BM Arundel 396.
The life of St Augustine; The life of St Gilbert of Sempringham; A treatise of the orders under the rule of St Augustine. Ed J. J. Munro 1910 (EETS). BM ms 36704 (holograph).
Ye solace of pilgrimes. Ed C. A. Mills (introductory note by H. M. Bannister) 1911 (Br & Amer Soc of Rome). Guide to antiquities and curiosities of Rome; ms Bodley 423 (holograph).
For lost works see de Meijer, above.

§2

Leland, J. In his Commentarii de scriptoribus britannicis vol 2, ed A. Hall, Oxford 1709. Pp. 453–4.

Dibelius, W. Capgrave und die englische Schriftsprache. Anglia 23–4 1900–1.

Arbesmann, R. Jordanus of Saxony's Vita S Augustini, the source for Capgrave's Life of St Augustine. Traditio 1 1943.

Sanderlin, G. Capgrave speaks up for hermits. Speculum 18 1943. Sources for life of St Augustine.

Parks, G. B. The English traveler to Italy vol 1. Rome 1954. On Solace of pilgrims.

de Meijer, A. Capgrave OESA. Augustiniana 5 1955.

Toner, N. Augustinian spiritual writers of the English province in the fifteenth and sixteenth centuries. In Sanctus Augustinus vitae spiritualis magister vol 2, Rome 1959. Pp. 493–521.

Kurvinen, A. The source of Capgrave's life of St Katherine. Neuphilologische Mitteilungen 61 1960.

Emden, A. B. In his A biographical register of the University of Cambridge, Cambridge 1963.

Wolpers, T. Die englische Heiligenlegende des Mittelalters. Tübingen 1964. See pp. 330–42, 404–8.

Roth, F. English Austin friars 1249–1538. New York 1966.

Lucas, P. J. Capgrave OSA: scribe and publisher. Trans Cambridge Bibl Soc 5 1969.

— Capgrave and the Nova legenda Anglie: a survey. Library 5th ser 25 1970.

— Sense-units and the use of punctuation-markers in Capgrave's Chronicle. Archivum Linguisticum 23 1971.

REGINALD PECOCK
1390/5–c. 1460

§1

[The book of faith]. Ed H. Wharton 1688 (incomplete); ed J. L. Morison, Glasgow 1909. Trinity College Cambridge ms B. 14. 45 (unfinished).

The repressor of over much blaming of the clergy. Ed C. Babington 2 vols 1860 (Rolls ser). Camb Univ Lib ms Kk.iv.26 (incomplete). Edn includes sermon Abbrevatio Reginaldi Pecok.

The reule of Crysten religioun. Ed W. C. Greet 1927 (EETS). Pierpont Morgan ms 519 (incomplete).

The donet. Ed E. V. Hitchcock 1921 (EETS). Bodley ms 916 collated with Poore mennis myrrour (BM ms additional 37,788), a slighter edn of the Donet.

The folower to the donet. Ed E. V. Hitchcock 1924 (EETS). BM ms Royal 17.D.IX.

For lost works see Green, below.

§2

An English chronicle. In Three fifteenth-century English chronicles, ed J. Gairdner 1880 (Camden Soc), under 1457.

Chronicle of the Grey Friars. In Monumenta franciscana, ed J. S. Brewer and R. Howlett vol 2 1882 (Rolls ser), under 1457.

Registrum abbatiæ Johannis Whethamstede. Ed H. T. Riley 2 vols 1872–3 (Rolls ser). Vol 1 pp. 279–98.

Bale, J. In his Illustrium maioris Britanniæ scriptorum summarium, Ipswich 1548; ed R. L. Poole and M. Bateson, Oxford 1902. Pp. 337–9.

Wharton, H. A treatise proving Scripture to be the rule of faith. 1668.

Lewis, J. The life of Reynold Pecock. 1744, Oxford 1820.

Pecock, his character and fortunes. Dublin Rev new ser 24 1875.

Historical Manuscripts Commission. 12th report appendix 9 1891.

Wager, C. H. A. Pecock's Repressor and the Wiclif Bible. MLN 9 1894.

Schmidt, F. Studies in the language of Pecock. Upsala 1900.

Gairdner, J. Lollardy and the reformation in England: an historical survey. 4 vols 1908–13. Vol 1 pp. 202–42.

Blackie, E. M. Pecock. EHR 26 1911.

Krapp, G. P. In his Rise of English literary prose, Oxford 1915.

Hannick, F. A. Reginald Pecock. Washington 1922.

Nuttall, G. Pecock and the Lollard movement. Trans Congregational Historical Soc 13 1939.

Pronger, W. A. Thomas Gascoigne. EHR 54 1939.

Green, V. H. H. Pecock and the English Bible. Church Quart Rev 129 1940.

— Bishop Reginald Pecock. Cambridge 1945. The standard biography.

Sellery, G. C. In his Renaissance: its nature and origins, Madison 1950.

Jacob, E. F. Pecock Bishop of Chichester. Proc Br Acad 37 1951; rptd in his Essays in late medieval history, Manchester 1968.

Emerson, E. H. Pecock: Christian rationalist. Speculum 31 1956.

Emden, A. B. In his A biographical register of the University of Oxford to AD 1500 vol 3, Oxford 1959.

Ferguson, A. B. Pecock and the Renaissance sense of history. Stud in Renaissance 13 1966.

SIR JOHN FORTESCUE
c. 1394–c. 1476

Collections

The works of Sir John F[ortescue]. Ed Thomas [Fortescue] Lord Clermont 2 vols 1869 (priv ptd). Contains all Latin and English works attributed to Fortescue, though the attribution of some is now questioned.

§1

[De laudibus legum Angliæ]. Prenobilis militis cognomento Forescu de politica administratione et legibus civilibus florentissimi regni Angliæ commentarius. [1546]; 1567 (Latin, and tr R. Mulcaster as A learned commendation of the politique lawes of Englande); 1573, 1599; ed and tr J. Selden 1616; ed and tr F. Gregor 1737, 1741, 1775, Cincinnati 1874, London 1917 (trn only); ed and tr S. B. Chrimes, Cambridge 1942, 1949. Chrimes's edn has a full introd.

Sir John Fortescue on the governance of England: the difference between an absolute and limited monarchy. Ed J. Fortescue-Aland 1714; ed C. Plummer, Oxford 1885, 1926; rptd in Complaint and reform in England 1436–1714, ed W. H. Dunham and S. Pargellis, New York 1938. Plummer's edn contains a biography, historical study and fragments of works attributed to Fortescue.

§2

Waterhous, E. Fortescutus illustratus or a commentary on that nervous treatise De laudibus legum Angliæ. 1663.

Gilson, J. P. A defence of the proscription of the Yorkists in 1459. EHR 26 1911. Possibly by Fortescue.

Scofield, C. Fortescue in February 1461. EHR 27 1912.

Skeel, C. A. J. The influence of the writings of Fortescue. Trans Royal Historical Soc 3rd ser 10 1916.

Levett, A. E. In The social and political ideas of some great thinkers of the Renaissance and Reformation, ed F. J. C. Hearnshaw 1925.

d'Entreves, A. P. San Tommaso d'Aquino e la costituzione inglese nell'opera di Fortescue. Atti della Reale Accademia delle Scienze di Torino 62 1927.

McIlwain, C. H. In his Growth of political thought in the West, New York 1932.

Jacob, E. F. Fortescue and the law of nature. Bull John Rylands Lib 18 1934; rptd in his Essays in the conciliar epoch, Manchester 1953.

— In his Fifteenth century 1399–1485, Oxford 1961.

Chrimes, S. B. Fortescue and his theory of dominion. Trans Royal Historical Soc 4th ser 17 1934.

— English constitutional ideas in the fifteenth century. Cambridge 1936.

Arrowood, C. F. Fortescue on the education of rulers. Speculum 10 1935.

Shepherd, M. A. The political and constitutional theory of Fortescue. In Essays in history and political theory in honor of Charles Howard McIlwain, Cambridge Mass 1936.

Holdsworth, W. S. In his A history of English law vol 2, 1936.

— In his Some makers of English law, Cambridge 1938.

Carlyle, R. W. and A. L. In his A history of medieval political theory in the West vol 6, Cambridge 1936.

Heyman, E. Fortescues Laudes legum Angliæ. Zeitschrift der Savigny-Stiftung für Rechtsgeschichte 71 1938.

Gilbert, F. Fortescue's dominum regale et politicum. Medievalia et Humanistica 2 1944.

Mosse, G. L. Fortescue and the problem of papal power. Medievalia et Humanistica 7 1952.

Blayney, M. S. Fortescue and Alain Chartier's Traité de l'espérance. MLR 48 1953.

Ferguson, A. B. Fortescue and the Renaissance. Stud in Renaissance 6 1959.

Hinton, R. W. K. English constitutional theories from Fortescue to Sir John Eliot. EHR 75 1960.

Archambault, P. The analogy of the body in Renaissance political literature. Bibliothèque d'Humanisme et Renaissance 29 1967.

WILLIAM CAXTON
1415/24–1490/1

Bibliographies

de Ricci, S. A census of Caxtons. 1909 (Bibl Soc).

Wilson, R. H. In A manual of the writings in Middle English 1050–1500 vol 3, ed A. E. Hartung, New Haven 1972.

Collections

Prologues and epilogues. Ed W. J. B. Crotch 1928 (EETS).

Selections from Caxton. Ed N. F. Blake, Oxford 1973.

§ I

Texts are arranged chronologically under the author or translator, where known. For works by English authors other than Caxton only Caxton's edns or direct reprints are listed; further details of these works will be found elsewhere in the bibliography. Many texts not tr Caxton have addns by him.

Caxton, W. The recuyell of the historyes of Troye. [Bruges 1473/4], 1502 (de Worde), [1503] (de Worde), 1553 (Copland), 1596 (Creede), 1607, 1617, 1636, 1663, 1670, [1676], 1680, 1684, 1702, 1708, 1738, 1802, [1810], 2 vols 1892 (priv ptd); ed H. O. Sommer 2 vols 1894.

Caxton, W. The game and play of the chess. [Bruges 1475/6], [1483]; ed V. Figgins 1855 (facs of 1483 edn); 1860; [1857] (phonetic spelling); 1860; ed W. E. A. Axon 1883.

d'Ailly, P. Septenuaire de pseaulmes de penitence. [Bruges 1475/6].

Lefèvre, R. Le recueil de histoires de Troyes. [Bruges 1475/6].

Lefèvre, R. Les fais et proesses du Jason. [Bruges 1475/6].

Mielot, J. Les quatre choses derrenieres. [Bruges 1475/6].

Russell, J. Propositio clarissimi oratoris magistri Johannis Russell. [Bruges or Westminster 1476]; ed H. Guppy, Manchester 1909 (facs).

Caxton, W. The advertisement. [1477].

Burgh, B. Parvus Cato; Magnus Cato. [1477], [1477], 1481; ed F. Jenkinson, Cambridge 1906 (facs).

Chaucer, G. Anelida and the false Arcite; The complaint of Chaucer to his purse: Th'envoy of Chaucer. [1477]; ed F. J. Furnivall 1868–80 (Chaucer Soc); ed F. Jenkinson, Cambridge 1905 (facs).

Chaucer, G. The parliament of fowls (ptd as Temple of brass); A treatise which John Scogan sent; The good counsel of Chaucer; Balade of a village; Th'envoy of Chaucer. [1477]; ed F. J. Furnivall 1868–80 (Chaucer Soc).

Horae. [1477], [1480], [1489], [1490].

Infantia salvatoris. [1477]; ed F. Holthausen, Halle 1891.

Caxton, W. Jason. [1479], Antwerp 1492 (Leeu); ed J. Munro 1912 (EETS).

Lydgate, J. The churl and the bird. [1477], [1477]; ed F. Jenkinson, Cambridge 1906 (facs).

Lydgate, J. The horse, sheep and goose. [1477], [1477].

Lydgate, J. Stans puer ad mensam; An holy salve regina in English. [1477]. The latter not by Lydgate.

Ordinale secundum usum Sarum. [1477]; ed C. Wordsworth 1894 (Bradshaw Soc).

Woodville, A. The dicts or sayings of the philosophers. 1477, 1479, [1489]; ed W. Blades 1877 (facs).

The book of courtesy. [1477/8]; ed F. J. Furnivall, Oxford 1868 (EETS); ed F. Jenkinson, Cambridge 1907 (facs).

Chaucer, G. Boethius de consolatione philosophiae. [1478].

Chaucer, G. The Canterbury tales. [1478], [1484].

Woodville, A. The moral proverbs of Christine. 1478; ed W. Blades 1859 (facs).

Woodville, A. The cordial. 1479; ed J. A. Mulders, Nijmegen [1962].

Traversagni, L. G. Nova rhetorica. [1479]; ed R. H. Martin and J. E. Mortimer, Proc Leeds Philosophical & Literary Soc 14 1971.

Caxton, W. The metamorphoses of Ovid. Ed G. Hibbert 1819 (Roxburghe Club); ed S. Gaselee and H. F. B. Brett-Smith, Oxford 1924; 2 vols New York and Cambridge 1968 (facs). Survives only in ms (Pepys 2124 and the Phillipps ms, both in Magdalene College Cambridge).

Chronicles of England. 1480, 1482.

De curia sapienciae. [1480]; ed R. Spindler, Leipzig 1927.

Festum visitationis beatae virginis Mariae. [1480].

Psalter. [1480].

Traversagni, L. G. Epitoma sive isagogicum margarite castigate eloquentie. [1480].

Trevisa, J. Description of Britain. 1480. An extract from Trevisa's trn of Higden's Polychronicon.

[Vocabulary in French and English]. [1480]; ed H. Bradley, Oxford 1900 (EETS); ed J. C. T. Oates and L. C. Harmer, Cambridge 1964 (facs).

Caxton, W. Godfrey of Boloyne. 1481; ed W. Morris 1892; ed M. N. Colvin, Oxford 1893 (EETS).

Caxton, W. The mirror of the world. [1481], [1490], 1527 (Andrewe); ed O. H. Prior, Oxford 1913 (EETS).

Caxton, W. Reynard the Fox. [1481], [1489], [1500] (Pynson), [1515] (de Worde), 1550 (Gaultier), 1620, 1629, 1640, 1640, 1656, 1667, 1681, 1694, 1701; ed W. J. Thoms 1844 (Percy Soc); ed E. Arber 1878, 1895; ed E. Goldsmid 1884; ed H. Morley 1889; ed H. H. Sparling, Edinburgh 1892; ed F. S. Ellis 1897; ed W. S. Stallybrass 1924; ed D. B. Sands, Cambridge Mass 1960; ed N. F. Blake, Oxford 1970

(EETS). All modern edns except Blake's are modernized.

Tiptoft, J. Of old age; Of friendship; The declamation of noblesse. 1481, 1530 (Rastell, Of friendship only); ed E. G. Duff 1912 (Of old age and Of friendship); ed H. Susebach, Halle 1933 (Of old age); ed R. Mitchell 1938 (The declamation). The first text is not a Tiptoft trn.

[Deathbed prayers]. [1482].

Trevisa, J. Polychronicon. [1482]. With a continuation added by Caxton.

Carmeliano, P. Sex epistolae. [1483]; ed G. Bullen and J. Hieatt 1892 (facs).

Caxton, W. Caton. [1483].

Caxton, W. The golden legend. [1483], [1487], 1493 (de Worde) (abridged), 1498 (de Worde), 1503 (Notary), [1510] (de Worde), 1512 (de Worde), 1527 (de Worde); ed A. Aspland 1878; ed F. S. Ellis 3 vols 1892; ed G. V. O'Neill 1914 (selection).

Chaucer, G. The book of fame. [1483]; ed F. J. Furnivall 1868-80 (Chaucer Soc).

Chaucer, G. Troilus and Criseyde. [1483]; ed W. S. McCormick and R. K. Root 1914 (Chaucer Soc).

Gower, J. Confessio amantis. 1483.

Lydgate, J. The pilgrimage of the soul. 1483; ed K. I. Cust 1859.

Mirk, J. The festial. [1483], [1491], 1883 (Roxburghe Club).

Caxton, W. Fables of Aesop. 1484, [1497] (Pynson), [1500] (Pynson), 1550 (Myddelton), 1551 (Powell), [1560] (Walley), [1570] (Wykes), 1585 (Bollifant), 1596 (Adams), 1625, 1634, 1647, 1658; ed J. Jacobs 2 vols 1889; San Francisco 1930; Newtown 1931; ed P. M. Zall, Lincoln Nebraska 1963 (selection); ed R. T. Lenaghan, Cambridge Mass 1967.

Caxton, W. The curial. [1484]; ed P. Mayer and F. J. Furnivall, Oxford 1888 (EETS).

Caxton, W. The knight of the tower. 1484; ed G. B. Rawlings 1902 (selection); ed M. Y. Offord, Oxford 1971 (EETS).

Caxton, W. The order of chivalry. [1484]; ed F. S. Ellis 1892; ed A. T. P. Byles, Oxford 1926 (EETS).

Caxton, W. The royal book. 1484?

Lydgate, J. The life of Our Lady. [1484].

Caxton, W. The life of Charles the Great. 1485; ed S. J. H. Herrtage, Oxford 1880-1 (EETS).

Caxton, W. Paris and Vienne. 1484, Antwerp 1492 (Leeu), [1510] (de Worde), 1621, [1628], [1632], 1650; ed W. C. Hazlitt 1868 (Roxburghe Club); ed M. Leach, Oxford 1957 (EETS).

Caxton, W. The life of St Winifred. [1485]; ed C. Horstmann, Anglia 3 1890.

Malory, Sir T. Le morte d'Arthur. 1485; ed H. O. Sommer 2 vols 1889-1900.

The mirror of the life of Christ. [1486], [1490], 1494 (de Worde); ed L. F. Powell 1908 (Roxburghe Club) (from ms).

Caxton, W. The book of good manners. 1487.

Commemoratio lamentationis sive compassionis beatae Mariae. [1487]; ed E. G. Duff, Oxford 1901 (facs) (Bibl Soc of Lancs).

[Image of pity]. [1487], [1490]; ed W. Cooke and C. Wordsworth 2 vols 1900-1 (Bradshaw Soc).

Mancinello, A. Donatus. [1487].

Maydeston, C. Directorium sacerdotum. [1487], [1489]; ed W. Cooke and C. Wordsworth 2 vols 1900-1 (Bradshaw Soc).

Caxton, W. Blanchardin and Eglantine. [1489]; ed L. Kellner, Oxford 1890 (EETS).

Caxton, W. Doctrinal of sapience. [1489].

Caxton, W. Feats of arms. 1489-90; ed A. T. P. Byles, Oxford 1932 (EETS).

Caxton, W. [Four sons of Aymon]. [1489], 1504 (de Worde), 1554 (Copland); ed O. Richardson, Oxford 1884-5 (EETS).

Governal of health; Medicina stomachi. [1489]; ed W. Blades 1858 (facs).

Statutes of Henry VII. [1489]; ed J. Rae 1869 (facs).

Caxton, W. The art and craft to know well to die. [1490], 1875 (facs).

Caxton, W. Eneydos. [1490]; ed M. T. Culley and F. J. Furnivall, Oxford 1890 (EETS).

[The book of divers ghostly matters]. Horologium sapientiae; The twelve profits of tribulation; The rule of St Benedict. [1491]; ed C. Horstmann, Anglia 10 1888 (Horologium); ed C. Horstmann, 1895-6 (Twelve profits); ed E. A. Kock, Oxford 1902 (EETS) (The rule).

Caxton, W. (?) The craft for to die for the health of a man's soul. [1491]; ed E. W. B. Nicholson 1891 (facs); ed F. M. M. Comper 1917.

Festum transfigurationis Jesu Christi. [1491].

Fifteen oes. [1491]; ed S. Ayling 1869 (facs).

Caxton, W. Vitas patrum. 1495 (de Worde). Tr in 1491 from French.

§2

Middleton, C. A dissertation concerning the origin of printing. 1735.

Lewis, J. The life of mayster Wyllyam Caxton of the Weald of Kent. 1737.

Ames, J., W. Herbert and T. F. Dibdin. In their Typographical antiquities vol 1, 1810.

Knight, C. Caxton: the first English printer. 1844, 1877.

Le Roux de Lincy, A. J. V. La vie et les ouvrages de Caxton. Paris 1844.

Jones, J. W. Upon the discovery of two rare tracts in the library of the British Museum hitherto unknown from the press of Caxton. Archaeologia 31 1846.

Blades, W. The life and typography of Caxton. 2 vols London and Strasbourg 1861-3, 1 vol 1882 (as The biography and typography of Caxton); ed J. Moran 1971. First edn contains prologues and epilogues and Liber ultimus of Polychronicon.

— How to tell a Caxton. 1870.

Koennecke, G. Ein unbekannter Druck von Caxton aus dem Jahre 1483. Marburg 1874.

Butt, A. N. Caxton: mercer and courtier, author and printer. 1878 (priv ptd).

Noble, T. C. A Caxton memorial: extracts from the churchwardens' accounts of the parish of St Margaret, Westminster. 1880.

Bradshaw, H. In his Collected papers, Cambridge 1889.

Römstedt, H. Die englische Schriftsprache bei Caxton. Göttingen 1891.

Butler, P. Legenda aurea—Légende dorée—Golden legend: a study of Caxton's Golden legend with special reference to its relations to the earlier English prose translation. Baltimore 1899.

de Reul, P. The language of Caxton's Reynard the Fox: a study in historical English syntax. London and Ghent 1901.

Blades, R. H. Who was Caxton? Library 2nd ser 4 1903.

Gasquet, F. A. The bibliography of some devotional books printed by the earliest English printers. Trans Bibl Soc 7 1904.

Pollard, A. W. Recent Caxtonia. Library 2nd ser 6 1904-5.

— William Blades and Caxton's work at Cologne. In Gutenbergfestschrift, ed A. Ruppel, Mainz 1925.

The new Caxton indulgence. Library 4th ser 9 1929.

Duff, E. G. Caxton. Chicago 1905 (Caxton Club).

— Horae beate virginis Marie secondum usum Sarum: the unique copy printed at Westminster by Caxton circa 1477. 1908.

— The first edition of the Sarum primer. 1908.

— Fifteenth-century English books. 1909 (Bibl Soc).

Peartree, S. M. A portrait of Caxton. Burlington Mag 7 1905.

Winship, G. P. Caxton. Chicago 1909, 1937 (rev).

Lawrence, W. W. Medieval story. New York 1911. On Reynard the fox.

Magnien, C. Une page de l'histoire anglo-belge 1441–72? Annuaire de la Société d'Archéologie de Bruxelles 23 1912.

Moore, S. Caxton reproductions: a bibliography. MLN 25 1910.

Cunnington, S. The story of Caxton. 1917.

Lathrop, H. B. The first English printers and their patrons. Library 4th ser 3 1923.

— Translations from the classics into English from Caxton to Chapman. Univ of Wisconsin Stud in Eng Lang & Lit 35 1933.

Aurner, R. R. Caxton and the English sentence. Univ of Wisconsin Stud in Eng Lang & Lit 18 1923.

Birch, J. G. Caxton's stay at Cologne. Library 4th ser 4 1924.

Greg, W. W. The early printed editions of the Canterbury tales. PMLA 39 1924.

Plomer, H. R. William Caxton 1424–91. London and Boston 1925.

Aurner, N. S. Caxton, mirrour of fifteenth-century letters: a study of the literature of the first English press. 1926, New York 1965. Includes Caxton's prologues and epilogues.

Crotch, W. J. B. Caxton on the continent. Library 4th ser 7 1927.

— Caxton documents. Library 4th ser 8 1928.

— Caxton's son-in-law. Library 4th ser 9 1929.

— An Englishman of the fifteenth century. Economica 10 1930.

Colville, K. N. Caxton: man of letters. Quart Rev 248 1927.

Thomas, H. Wilh. Caxton uyss Engelant: evidence that the first English printer learned his craft at Cologne. Cologne 1928 (priv ptd).

Byles, A. T. P. Caxton's Book of the ordre of chyualry: a French manuscript in Brussels. RES 6 1930.

— Caxton as a man of letters. Library 4th ser 15 1935.

Roberts, W. W. Caxton: writer and critic. Bull John Rylands Lib 14 1930.

Wiencke, H. Die Sprache Caxtons. Leipzig 1930.

Hittmair, R. Caxton: Englands erster Drucker und Verleger. Innsbruck 1931.

— Aus Caxtons vorreden und nachworten. Leipzig 1934.

— Earl Rivers' Einleitung zu seiner Übertragung der Weisheitssprüche der Philosophen. Anglia 59 1955. On Rivers' relations with Caxton.

Bone, G. L. Extant manuscripts printed from by W. de Worde, with notes on the owner Roger Thorney. Library 4th ser 12 1932. On Caxton's edn of Confessio amantis based on ms Magdalen College Oxford 213.

Jackson, H. Caxton. 1933.

d'Israeli, I. The first English printer: being an essay from Amenities of literature. [1933].

Winkler, G. Das relativum bei Caxton. Saalfeld [1933].

Clark, J. W. A new copy of Caxton's indulgence. Speculum 9 1934.

Bühler, C. F. The dictes and sayings of the philosophers. Library 4th ser 15 1935.

— Caxton variants. Library 4th ser 17 1937.

— Three notes on Caxton. Ibid.

— Caxton's History of Jason. PBSA 34 1940.

— Two Caxton problems. Library 4th ser 20 1940.

— The binding of books printed by Caxton. PBSA 38 1944.

— Caxton's Blanchardin and Eglantine. PBSA 39 1945.

— The British Museum's fragment of Lydgate's Horse, sheep and goose printed by Caxton. PBSA 43 1949.

— The Fasciculus temporum and Morgan manuscript 801. Speculum 27 1952. Contains a list of mss made from Caxton prints.

— Yale's new Caxton. Yale Univ Lib Gazette 27 1952.

— Corrections in Caxton's Cordiale. PBSA 48 1954.

— In his Fifteenth-century book: the scribes, the printers, the decorators, Philadelphia 1960.

— Caxton and his critics. Syracuse 1960.

— Middle English apophthegms in a Caxton volume. Eng Lang Notes 1 1964.

Oakeshott, W. F. Caxton and Malory's Morte d'Arthur. Gutenberg-Jahrbuch 1935.

Pirkhofer, A. Zum syntaktischen Gebrauch des bestimmten Artikels bei Caxton. E Studien 70 1936.

Hammerschlag, J. Dialekteinflüsse im frühneuenglischen Wortschatz nachgewiesen an Caxton und Fabyan. Bonn 1937.

Cousland, C. W. The hand of Caxton? Penrose Annual 39 1937.

Cawley, A. C. Relationships of the Trevisa manuscripts and Caxton's Polycronycon. London Medieval Stud 1 1939.

Winship, C. P. Caxton and the first English press: a bio-bibliographical essay. New York 1938.

MacGibbon, D. Elizabeth Woodville 1437–92. 1938. An important patron of Caxton's.

Povey, K. The Caxton indulgence of 1476. Library 4th ser 19 1939.

Dunn, T. A. The manuscript source of Caxton's second edition of the Canterbury tales. Chicago 1940 (priv ptd).

Workman, S. K. Fifteenth-century translation as an influence on English prose. Princeton 1940.

— Versions by Skelton, Caxton and Berners of a prologue by Diodorus Siculus. MLN 56 1941.

McCusker, H. A book from Caxton's library. More Books 15 1940.

Bennett, H. S. Caxton and his public. RES 19 1943.

— In his Chaucer and the fifteenth century, Oxford 1947 (OHEL vol 2 pt i). With bibliography of Caxtoniana.

— In his English books and readers 1475 to 1557, Cambridge 1952, 1969 (rev).

Jeremy, M. Caxton's Golden legend and de Vignai's Légende dorée. Mediaeval Stud 8 1946.

— Caxton's Golden legend and Varagine's Legenda aurea. Speculum 21 1946.

— Caxton and the synfulle wretche. Traditio 4 1946.

— Caxton's original additions to the Legenda aurea. MLN 64 1949.

— Caxton's life of S. Rocke. MLN 67 1952.

Leisi, E. Die tautologischen Wortpaare in Caxtons Eneydos. Cambridge Mass 1947.

Wilson, R. H. Caxton's Chess book. MLN 62 1947.

— The poggiana in Caxton's Esope. PQ 30 1951.

Housman, J. E. Higden, Trevisa, Caxton and the beginnings of Arthurian criticism. RES 23 1947.

Legman, G. A word on Caxton's Dictes. Library 5th ser 3 1949.

Munby, A. N. L. Jacob Bryant's Caxtons: some additions to de Ricci's census. Ibid.

Dempster, G. The fifteenth-century editors of the Canterbury tales and the problem of tale order. PMLA 64 1949.

Kaplan, M. Ovid and fifteenth-century English literature, with especial reference to Caxton's translation: an abridgement. New York 1950.

Bennett, J. A. W. Caxton and Gower. MLR 45 1950.

— Caxton's Ovid. TLS 24 Nov 1966.

Sheppard, L. A. A new light on Caxton and Colard Mansion. Signature new ser 15 1952.

Mortimer, J. E. An unrecorded Caxton at Ripon cathedral. Library 5th ser 8 1953.

Ruysschaert, J. Les manuscrits autographes de deux oeuvres de Lorenzo Guglielmo Traversagni imprimées chez Caxton. Bull John Rylands Lib 36 1954.

Knowles, C. Caxton and his two French sources. MLR 49 1954.

Kerling, N. J. M. Caxton and the trade in printed books. Book Collector 4 1955.

Morgan, P. and G. D. Painter. The Caxton Legenda at St Mary's, Warwick. Library 5th ser 12 1957.

Tanner, L. E. Caxton's houses at Westminster. Ibid.

Sands, D. B. Caxton as a literary critic. PBSA 51 1957.

Simko, J. Word-order in the Winchester manuscript and in Caxton's edition of Thomas Malory's Morte d'Arthur: a comparison. Halle 1957.

Jennett, S. In his Pioneers in printing, 1958.

Kurvinen, A. Caxton's Golden legend and the manuscript of the Gilte legende. Neuphilologische Mitteilungen 60 1959.

Wells, J. Caxton. Chicago 1960 (Caxton Club).

Moran, J. Wynkyn de Worde. 1960 (Wynkyn de Worde Soc).

Stuart, D. M. Caxton: mercer, translator and master printer. History Today April 1960.

Hall, L. B. Caxton's Eneydos and the redactions of Vergil. Mediaeval Stud 22 1960.

Larken, H. W. At the sign of the red pale: a short account of the life and work of Caxton. Maidstone [1960] (priv ptd).

Markland, M. F. The role of Caxton. Research Stud (Washington State Univ) 28 1960.

Wilkinson, A. M. The Ripon Caxtons. Ripon 1960.

Lenaghan, R. T. The variants in Caxton's Esope. PBSA 55 1961.

—— Bytwene playn rude and curyous: a note on Caxton's use of park. PQ 42 1963.

Williams, M. G. Caxton and literary taste. Black Art 1 1962.

Blake, N. F. Caxton and Suffolk. Proc Suffolk Inst of Archaeology 29 1962.

—— Caxton's Reynard the fox and his Dutch original. Bull John Rylands Lib 46 1964.

—— Caxton and Suffolk: a supplement. Proc Suffolk Inst of Archaeology 30 1964.

—— English versions of Reynard the fox in the fifteenth and sixteenth centuries. SP 62 1965.

—— Caxton: his choice of texts. Anglia 83 1965.

—— Caxton's language. Neuphilologische Mitteilungen 67 1966.

—— Some observations on Caxton and the Mercers' Company. Book Collector 15 1966.

—— The vocabulary in French and English printed by Caxton. Eng Lang Notes 3 1966.

—— Investigations into the prologues and epilogues by Caxton. Bull John Rylands Lib 49 1967.

—— Caxton's copytext of Gower's Confessio amantis. Anglia 85 1967.

—— Two new Caxton documents. N & Q March 1967.

—— Caxton and Chaucer. Leeds Stud in Eng new ser 1 1967.

—— Caxton and courtly style. E & S new ser 21 1968.

—— Word borrowings in Caxton's original writings. Eng Lang Notes 6 1968.

—— Caxton and his world. 1969. With list of ptd works and bibliography.

—— The biblical additions in Caxton's Golden legend. Traditio 25 1969.

Brekle, H. E. Semantische Analyse von Wertadjektiven als Determinanten persönlicher Substantive in Caxtons Prologen und Epilogen. Stuttgart 1963.

Nørgaard, H. Sankt Ovid: tekstligt og billedmaessigt om Metamorfosernes forvandling. Fund og Forskning i det Kongelige Biblioteks Samlinger 10 1963. On Caxton's Ovid.

Painter, G. D. Caxton through the looking-glass. Gutenberg Jahrbuch 1963.

Schlauch, M. In her Antecedents of the English novel 1400–1600, Warsaw and Oxford 1963. On Reynard the fox.

Wolpers, T. In his Die englische Heiligenlegende des Mittelalters, Tübingen 1964. On Caxton's Golden legend.

Skeat, T. C. The Caxton deeds. BM Quart 28 1964.

Uden, G. The knight and the merchant. 1965. On Ear Rivers and Caxton.

Gallagher, J. E. The sources of Caxton's Ryal book and the Doctrinal of sapience. SP 62 1965.

Nixon, H. M. A binding from the Caxton bindery. Book Collector 13 1965.

Hellinga, W. and L. The fifteenth-century printing types of the Low Countries. 2 vols Amsterdam 1966. On Caxton's continental work.

Donner, M. The infrequency of word borrowings in Caxton's original writings. Eng Lang Notes 4 1966.

Finlayson, J. The source of Caxton's Paris and Vienne. PQ 46 1967.

Moran, J. Caxton and the origins of English publishing. Gutenberg-Jahrbuch 42 1967.

Rossi, S. Il significato di Caxton. Eng Miscellany (Rome) 18 1967.

Sandved, A. O. Studies in the language of Caxton's Malory. Oslo and New York 1968.

Fox, D. Henryson and Caxton. JEGP 67 1968.

Antin, D. Caxton's The game and the playe of the chesse. JHI 29 1968.

Matthews, W. Caxton and Malory: a defense. In Medieval literature and folklore studies: essays in honor of F. L. Utley, New Brunswick NJ 1970.

Cusak, B. Not wreton with penne and ynke: problems of selection facing the first English printer. In Edinburgh studies in English and Scots, ed A. J. Aitken et al 1971.

Kekewich, M. Edward IV, Caxton and literary patronage in Yorkist England. MLR 66 1971.

Meier-Ewart, C. A Middle English version of the Fifteen oes. MP 68 1971.

Murphy, J. J. Caxton's two choices. Medievalia et Humanistica new ser 3 1972.

SIR THOMAS MALORY
fl. c. 1470

§1

Le morte Darthur reduced in to Englysshe. 1485 (Caxton), 1498 (de Worde), 1529 (de Worde), 1557 (Copland), 1585? (East), 1634; [ed J. Haslewood] 1816; ed R. Southey 1817; ed T. Wright 3 vols 1865–6; ed E. Strachey 1884; ed H. O. Sommer 3 vols 1889–91 (diplomatic edn); ed F. J. Simmons 3 vols 1893–4; ed J. Rhys 1893–4; ed I. Gollancz 1897; ed A. W. Pollard 2 vols 1900; [1913] (priv ptd); [1923] (abridged); ed C. R. Sanders and C. E. Ward, New York 1931 (abridged); ed E. Vinaver 3 vols Oxford 1947, 1 vol Oxford 1954 (OSA), 3 vols Oxford 1967 (rev), 1 vol Oxford 1969 (OSA); ed E. Vinaver, Oxford 1955 (8th bk), New York 1956 (selection); ed R. T. Davies 1967 (selection); ed D. S. Brewer 1968 (bks 7–8); ed J. Cowen 2 vols 1969 (Penguin) (Caxton's text modernized). All texts before Vinaver's 1947 edn were based on Caxton's; Vinaver's and subsequent texts have been based on the Winchester ms, discovered in 1934, which showed the work to be 8 narratives. Vinaver's 1967 edn is now standard.

§2

Baldwin, C. S. The inflexions and syntax of the Morte d'Arthur of Malory. Boston 1894.

Saintsbury, G. In his Flourishing of romance and the rise of allegory, Edinburgh 1897.

—— In his A history of English prose rhythm, 1912.

Kittredge, G. L. Who was Malory? Boston 1897.

—— Malory. Barnstaple 1925 (priv ptd).

Schüler, M. Malorys Le morte d'Arthur und die englische Arthurdichtung des xix Jahrhunderts. Strasbourg 1900.

Gregory Smith, G. In his Transition period, Edinburgh 1900.

Bruce, J. D. The Middle-English metrical romance Le morte Arthur: its sources and its relation to Malory's Morte Darthur. Anglia 23 1901. Replies by H. O. Sommer 29 1906; by Bruce 30 1907.

Williams, T. W. Malory and the Morte Darthur. Bristol 1909.

Schofield, W. H. In his Chivalry in English literature, Cambridge Mass 1912.

Fromm, C. Ueber den verbalen Wortschatz in Malorys Roman Le morte Darthur. Marburg 1914.

Scudder, V. D. The Morte d'Arthur of Malory: a study of the book and its sources. 1917.

Lot, F. Etude sur le Lancelot en prose. Paris 1918.

Chambers, E. K. Malory. 1922 (Eng Assoc); rptd and rev in his Sir Thomas Wyatt and some collected studies, 1933.

Cooksey, C. F. The Morte d'Arthur. Nineteenth Century June 1924.

Vinaver, E. Le roman de Tristan et Iseult dans l'oeuvre de Malory. Paris 1925.

— Malory. Oxford 1929.

— A romance of Gaheret. MÆ 1 1932.

— The legend of Wade in the Morte Darthur. MÆ 2 1933.

— Malory's Morte D'Arthur. Bull John Rylands Lib 19 1935.

— A note on the earliest printed texts of Malory's Morte D'Arthur. Bull John Rylands Lib 23 1939.

— Le manuscrit de Westminster. Bulletin Bibliographique de la Société Internationale Arthurienne 3 1951.

— Epic and tragic patterns in Malory. In Friendship's garland: essays presented to Mario Praz on his seventieth birthday, Rome 1966.

Van der Ven Ten-Bensch, E. F. W. M. The character of King Arthur in English literature. Amsterdam 1925.

Loomis, L. H. Arthur's round table. PMLA 46 1926.

Ray, B. K. The character of Gawain. Dacca Univ Bull 11 1926.

Robinson, F. W. A commentary and a questionnaire on selections from Malory. Ed H. Wragg 1927. On style and characterization.

Hibbard, L. A. Malory's Book of Balin. In Medieval studies in memory of G. S. Loomis, New York 1927; rptd in her Adventures in the Middle Ages, New York 1962.

Hicks, E. Malory, his turbulent career: a biography. Cambridge Mass 1928.

Fox, M. D. Malory and the piteous history of the morte of King Arthur. Arthuriana 1 1929.

Dekker, A. Some facts concerning the syntax of Malory's Morte Darthur. Amsterdam 1932.

Wilson, R. H. Malory and the Perlesvaus. MP 30 1932.

— Characterization in Malory: a comparison with his sources. Chicago 1934 (priv ptd).

— Malory, the stanzaic Morte Arthur and the Mort Artu. MP 37 1940.

— Malory's naming of minor characters. JEGP 42 1943.

— The fair unknown in Malory. PMLA 58 1943.

— Malory in the Connecticut Yankee. SE 27 1948.

— Malory's French book again. Comparative Lit 2 1950.

— Malory's early knowledge of Arthurian romance. SE 29 1950.

— How many books did Malory write? SE 30 1951.

— Notes on Malory's sources. MLN 66 1951.

— The rebellion of the kings in Malory and in the Cambridge Suite de Merlin. SE 31 1952.

— The prose Lancelot in Malory. SE 32 1953.

— Malory's early knowledge of Arthurian romance. Ibid.

— Some minor characters in the Morte Darthur. MLN 71 1956.

— Addenda on Malory's minor characters. JEGP 55 1956.

Aurner, N. S. Malory: historian? PMLA 48 1933.

Baugh, A. C. Documenting Malory. Speculum 8 1933.

Whitehead, F. On certain episodes in the fourth book of Malory's Morte Darthur. MÆ 2 1933.

Oakeshott, W. F. The text of Malory. TLS 27 Sept 1934. First detailed account of Winchester ms, by its discoverer.

— Caxton and Malory's Morte Darthur. Gutenberg-Jahrbuch 1935.

Stewart, G. R. English geography in Malory's Morte D'Arthur. MLR 30 1935.

Thornton, M. M. Malory's Morte Darthur as a Christian epic. Urbana 1936.

Vorontzoff, T. Malory's story of Arthur's Roman campaign. MÆ 6 1937.

Reid, M. J. C. The Arthurian legend: comparison of treatment in modern and medieval literature. Edinburgh and London 1938.

Arnold, I. D. O. Malory's story of Arthur's Roman campaign. MÆ 7 1938.

Loomis, R. S. Malory's Beaumains. PMLA 54 1939.

— Onomastic riddles in Malory's The book of King Arthur and his knights. MÆ 25 1956.

— In his Arthurian literature in the Middle Ages, Oxford 1959.

— In his Development of Arthurian romance, 1963.

— The structure of Malory's Gareth. In Studies in language and literature in honour of Margaret Schlauch, Warsaw 1966.

Bühler, C. F. Two Caxton problems. Library 4th ser 20 1940.

Williams, C. Malory and the Grail legend. Dublin Rev 429 1944.

Parsons, C. O. A Scottish Father of courtesy and Malory. Speculum 20 1945.

Chambers, E. K. In his English literature at the close of the Middle Ages, Oxford 1945 (OHEL vol 2 pt 2). With bibliography.

Williams, C. Arthurian torso. Ed C. S. Lewis 1948.

Dubois, M. M. Le Roman d'Arthur et des chevaliers de la table ronde. Paris 1948.

Altick, R. D. The quest of the knight prisoner. In his Scholar adventurers, New York 1950.

Dichmann, M. E. Characterization in Malory's Tale of Arthur and Lucius. PMLA 65 1950.

Donaldson, E. T. Malory and the stanzaic La morte Arthur. SP 47 1950.

Brewer, D. S. Form in the Morte Darthur. MÆ 21 1952.

— The present study of Malory. In Arthurian romance, ed D. D. R. Owen 1970.

Lumiansky, R. M. The relationship of Lancelot and Guenevere in Malory's Tale of Lancelot. MLN 68 1953.

— The question of unity in Malory's Morte Darthur. Tulane Stud in Eng 5 1955.

— Tristram's first interview with Mark in Malory's Morte Darthur. MLN 70 1955.

— Gawain's miraculous strength: Malory's use of Le morte Arthur and Mort Artu. Etudes Anglaises 10 1957.

— Two notes on Malory's Morte Darthur: Sir Urry in England—Lancelot's burial vow. Neuphilologische Mitteilungen 58 1957.

— Malory's Tale of Lancelot and Guinevere as suspense. Mediaeval Stud 19 1957.

— Malory's steadfast Bors. Tulane Stud in Eng 8 1958.

— Arthur's final companions in Malory's Morte Darthur. Tulane Stud in Eng 11 1961.

— Malory's originality: a critical study of Le morte Darthur. Baltimore 1964.

Tucker, P. E. The place of the Quest of the Holy Grail in the Morte Darthur. MLR 48 1953.

— A source for the healing of Sir Urry in the Morte Darthur. MLR 50 1955.

Bogdanow, F. The rebellion of the kings in the Cambridge ms of the Suite du Merlin. SE 34 1955.

Davies, R. T. Malory's Lancelot and the noble way of the world. RES new ser 6 1955.
—— Malory's vertuouse love. SP 53 1956.
—— The worshipful way in Malory. In Patterns of love and courtesy: essays in memory of C. S. Lewis, 1966.
Muecke, D. C. Some notes on Vinaver's Malory. MLN 70 1955.
Moorman, C. Malory's treatment of the Sankgreall. PMLA 71 1956.
—— The relation of books I and III of Malory's Morte Darthur. Mediaeval Stud 22 1960.
—— Courtly love in Malory. ELH 27 1960.
—— Internal chronology in Malory's Morte Darthur. JEGP 60 1961.
—— Lot and Pellinore: the failure of loyalty in Malory's Morte Darthur. Mediaeval Stud 25 1963.
—— The book of Kyng Arthur: the unity of Malory's Morte Darthur. Lexington Kentucky 1965.
—— Malory's tragic knights. Mediaeval Stud 27 1965.
—— A knyght there was: the evolution of the knight in literature. Lexington Kentucky 1967.
Rumble, T. C. The first explicit in Malory's Morte Darthur. MLN 71 1956.
—— Malory's Works and Vinaver's comments: some inconsistencies resolved. JEGP 59 1960.
—— Malory's Balin and the question of unity in the Morte Darthur. Speculum 41 1966.
Šimko, H. Word-order in the Winchester manuscript and William Caxton's edition of Malory's Morte Darthur 1485: a comparison. Halle 1957.
—— Malory's creed. In Studies in language and literature in honour of Margaret Schlauch, Warsaw 1966.
Bradbrook, M. C. Malory. 1958 (Br Council pamphlet).
Rioux, R. N. Malory créateur verbal. Etudes Anglaises 12 1959.
Ferguson, A. B. The Indian summer of English chivalry. Durham NC 1960.
Angelescu, V. The relationship of Gareth and Gawain in Malory's Morte D'Arthur. N & Q Jan 1961.
Noguchi, S. Malory's English: an aspect of its syntax. Hiroshima Stud in Eng Lang & Lit 7 1961.
Barber, R. W. Arthur of Albion. 1961.
Bennett, J. A. W. (ed). Essays on Malory. Oxford 1963. With bibliographical note.
Bartholomew, B. G. The thematic function of Malory's Gawain. College Eng Jan 1963.
Göller, K. H. König Arthur in der englischen Literatur des späten Mittelalters. Göttingen 1963.
Schmidz, C. C. D. Sir Gareth of Orkeney: Studien zum siebenten Buch von Malorys Morte Darthur. Groningen 1963.
Ackerman, R. W. Malory's Ironsyde. Research Stud (Washington State Univ) 32 1964.
Morgan, H. G. The role of Morgan le Fay in Malory's Morte Darthur. Southern Quart 2 1964.
Davis, G. R. Malory's Tale of Sir Lancelot and the question of unity in the Morte Darthur. Pbns of Michigan Acad 49 1964.
Quinn, E. C. The quest of Seth, Solomon's ship and the Grail. Traditio 21 1965.
Matthews, W. The ill-framed knight: a skeptical inquiry into the identity of Malory. Berkeley 1966.
—— Caxton and Malory: a defense. In Medieval literature and folklore studies: essays in honor of F. L. Utley, New Brunswick NJ 1970.
Reiss, E. Malory. 1966.
Miko, S. T. Malory and the chivalric order. MÆ 35 1966.
Lundie, R. S. Divided allegiance in the last two books of Malory. Theoria 26 1966.
Lewis, C. S. The Morte Darthur. In his Studies in medieval and Renaissance literature, ed W. Hooper, Cambridge 1966.
Starr, N. C. The moral problem in Malory. Dalhousie Rev 47 1967.

Bennett, W. K. Malory's Gawain: the noble villain. West Virginia Univ Philological Papers 16 1967.
Hampsten, E. A reading of Malory's Morte Arthur. North Dakota Quart 35 1967.
Noguchi, S. The paradox of the character of Malory's language. Hiroshima Stud in Eng Lang & Lit 13 1967.
Olstead, M. Morgan Le Fay in Malory's Morte Darthur. Bulletin Bibliographique de la Société Internationale Arthurienne 19 1967.
Sandved, A. O. Studies in the language of Caxton's Malory and that of the Winchester manuscript. Oslo and New York 1968.
Benson, L. D. Le morte Darthur. In Critical approaches to six major English works, ed R. M. Lumiansky, Philadelphia 1968.
DiPasquale, P. Malory's Guinevere: epic queen, romance heroine and tragic mistress. Bucknell Rev 15 1968.
Field, P. J. C. Description and narration in Malory. Speculum 43 1968.
—— Romance and chronicle: a study of Malory's prose style. 1971.
Schueler, D. G. The Tristram section in Malory's Morte Darthur. SP 65 1968.
Dillon, B. Formal and informal pronouns of address in Malory's Le morte Darthur. Annuale Mediaevale 10 1969.
York, E. C. The duel of chivalry in Malory's book xix. PQ 48 1969.
Kennedy, E. D. Malory's use of Harding's chronicle. N & Q May 1969.
—— Arthur's rescue in Malory and the Spanish Tristan. N & Q Jan 1970.
—— Malory and the marriage of Edward IV. Texas Stud in Lit & Lang 12 1970.
—— Two notes on Malory. N & Q Jan 1972.
Olefsky, E. Chronology, factual consistency and the problem of unity in Malory. JEGP 68 1969.
McCarthy, T. Malory's King of Wales: some notes on the text of book 2. N & Q Sept 1971.
—— Order of composition in the Morte Darthur. Yearbook of Eng Stud 1 1971.
Pochoda, E. T. Arthurian propaganda. Chapel Hill 1971. With annotated bibliography.

JOHN BOURCHIER,
BARON BERNERS
1467–1533

Collections

Berners: a selection from his works. Ed V. de Sola Pinto 1937.

§1

The first volum [the third and fourthe boke] of Sir Johan Froyssart: of the cronycles of Englande, Fraunce, Spayne, Portyngale, Scotlande, Bretayne, Flaunders; and other places adioynynge. 2 vols 1523–5 (Pynson), [1545]; ed G. C. Macaulay 1895 (modernized and abridged); ed W. P. Ker 6 vols 1901–3, 8 vols Oxford 1927–8. Trn from French; see Chroniques de J. Froissart, ed S. Luce 10 vols Paris 1869–97.
The boke of Duke Huon of Burdeux. [1534?] (de Worde?), [possible 2nd edn by Copland 1570 not extant], 1601 (Purfoot; rev); ed S. Lee 4 pts 1882–7 (EETS); ed R. Steele 1895 (modernized). Trn of French edn by Michel Lenoir 1513.
The golden boke of Marcus Aurelius. 1535 (Berthelet), 1537 (colophon, 1536 title-page), 1539, 1542, 1546, 1553, 1557, 1559, 1566, 1573, 1586; ed J. M. Galvez, Berlin 1916. Trn from French version of Guevara's Spanish.
The castell of love. [1549] (Turke), [1550] (Wyer), [1560]; ed W. G. Crane, Gainesville 1950 (facs).

Trn of Diego de San Pedro's Spanish, probably via French.

The hystory of Arthur of lytell Brytayne. [1555] (Copland), [1582]; ed E. V. Utterson 1814. Trn from French.

Ordinances for watch and ward at Calais. Ed J. G. Nichols 1846 (in Chronicle of Calais) (Camden Soc) from ms Cotton Faustina E vii. Often attributed to Berners, doubtfully.

Bale attributed Ite in vineam, De officijs Calesianorum, *a trn from Italian, and other texts to Berners; none is identified.*

§2

Bale, John. In his Index Britanniæ scriptorum, ed R. L. Poole and M. Bateson, Oxford 1902.

Wood, Anthony. In his Athenæ oxonienses, 2 vols 1691–2; ed P. Bliss 1813. Includes references to ms letter collections.

Utterson, E. V. Sir J. Froissart's Chronicles. 1812. With a memoir of Berners.

Ker, W. P. In his Essays on medieval literature, 1905. Reprints introd to Ker's edn of Berners' Froissart, above.

Krapp, G. P. In his Rise of English literary prose, New York 1915.

Smith, R. M. Froissart and the English chronicle play. New York 1915.

McDill, J. H. The life of Berners. TLS 17 April 1930.

Schleich, G. Lesefrüchte aus Übersetzungen von Berners. Archiv 160 1931.

—— Berners' Froissart-Übersetzung in ihren Beziehungen zum Original. Archiv 166–7 1935.

—— Beiträge zur Textkritik von Berners' Froissart-Übersetzung. Archiv 170 1936.

Crane, W. G. Berners' translation of Diego de San Pedro's Carcel de amor. PMLA 39 1934.

Workman, S. K. Versions by Skelton, Caxton and Berners of a prologue by Diodorus Siculus. MLN 56 1941.

Benson, L. D. The use of a physical viewpoint in Berners' Froissart. MLQ 20 1959.

Schlauch, M. In her Antecedents of the English novel 1400–1600 (from Chaucer to Deloney), Warsaw and London 1963.

Blake, N. F. Berners: a survey. Medievalia et Humanistica new ser 2 1971.

N. F. B.

IV. MISCELLANEOUS AND ANONYMOUS VERSE AND PROSE OF THE FIFTEENTH CENTURY

This section includes works which do not fit into other sections, and makes no claim to be comprehensive. The limits of the fifteenth century are interpreted broadly.

(1) COLLECTIONS AND ANTHOLOGIES

Select pieces of early popular poetry, republished principally from early printed copies. Ed E. V. Utterson 2 vols 1817.

Original letters, illustrative of English history. Ed H. Ellis 3 sers 11 vols 1825–46.

Excerpta historica: or illustrations of English history. Ed S. Bentley 1833.

Nugae poeticae: select pieces of old English popular poetry, illustrating manners and arts of the fifteenth century. Ed J. O. Halliwell (-Phillipps) 1844.

Letters of the Kings of England. Ed J. O. Halliwell(-Phillipps) 2 vols 1848.

Contributions to early English literature. Ed J. O. Halliwell(-Phillipps) 1849. Poems and prose 15th–17th centuries.

Early English miscellanies in prose and verse. Ed J. O. Halliwell(-Phillipps) 1855 (Warton Club). Porkington ms.

Early English prose romances. Ed W. J. Thoms 3 vols 1858 (2nd edn enlarged).

Political songs and poems relating to English history composed during the period from the accession of Edward III to that of Richard III. Ed H. Wright 1861 (Rolls ser).

Letters and papers illustrative of the reigns of Richard III and Henry VII. Ed J. Gairdner 2 vols 1861–3 (Rolls ser).

Old English jest-books. Ed W. C. Hazlitt 3 vols 1964.

Remains of the early popular poetry of England. Ed W. C. Hazlitt 4 vols 1864–6.

Political, religious and love poems. Ed F. J. Furnivall 1866, 1903 (rev) (EETS).

Hymns to the Virgin and Christ; The parliament of devils; and other religious pieces. Ed F. J. Furnivall 1867 (EETS). Lambeth ms 853 c. 1430.

Religious pieces in prose and verse. Ed G. G. Perry 1867, 1889 (rev) (EETS). Thornton ms c. 1440.

The stacions of Rome; The pilgrims sea-voyage; Clene maidenhood. Ed F. J. Furnivall 1867 (EETS). Vernon and Porkington mss, and Trinity College Cambridge ms R.3.19.

The babees book. Ed F. J. Furnivall 1868 (EETS). Mainly 15th–16th-century books of instruction and etiquette.

Ratis raving and other moral and religious pieces, in prose and verse. Ed J. R. Lumby 1870 (EETS). Cambridge Univ Lib ms Kk.1.5.

Fugitive tracts, written in verse, which illustrate the condition of religious and social feeling in England and the state of society there during two centuries. Ed W. C. Hazlitt, preface by H. Huth 1875 (priv ptd).

The historical collections of a citizen of London. Ed J. Gairdner 1876 (Camden Soc), New York 1965. BM ms Egerton 1995.

Christ Church letters. Ed J. B. Sheppard 1877 (Camden Soc).

Three fifteenth-century chronicles. Ed J. Gairdner 1880 (Camden Soc).

Literae cantuarienses: the letter books of the monastery of Christ Church, Canterbury. Ed J. B. Sheppard 3 vols 1887–9.

Early prose romances. Ed H. Morley 1889.

English carols of the fifteenth century. Ed J. A. Fuller Maitland [1891]. Ed from a Trinity College Cambridge ms roll.

English prose selections, 1: Fourteenth to sixteenth century. Ed H. Craik 1893. With short biographies of authors.

A book of English prose: character and incident 1387–1649. Ed W. E. Henley and C. Whibley 1894.

Epistolae academicae oxon: a collection of letters and other miscellaneous documents illustrative of academical life at Oxford in the fifteenth century. Ed H. Anstey 2 vols Oxford 1898 (Oxford Historical Soc).

Fifteenth-century prose and verse. Ed A. W. Pollard 1903. Modernized.

Twenty-six political and other poems. Ed J. Kail 1904 (EETS). Bodley mss Digby 102, Douce 322.

Chronicles of London. Ed C. L. Kingsford, Oxford 1905. BM Cotton mss Julius B ii, Cleopatra C iv, Vitellius A xvi.

Early English prose romances. Ed H. Morley and W. J. Thoms 1907. An amalgam of Morley's and Thoms' collections, above.

Six town chronicles of England. Ed R. Flenley, Oxford 1911.

English historical literature in the fifteenth century. Ed C. L. Kingsford, Oxford 1913, New York [1963].

English history in contemporary poetry, 2: Lancaster and York 1399 to 1485. Ed C. L. Kingsford 1913, 1933 (Historical Assoc).

Five hundred years of Chaucer criticism and allusion 1357–1900. Ed C. F. E. Spurgeon 7 pts 1914–24 (Chaucer Soc), 3 vols Cambridge 1925.

Letters of the 15th and 16th centuries. Ed R. C. Anderson, Southampton 1921 (Southampton Record Soc).

The Wheatley manuscript. Ed M. Day 1921 (EETS). BM ms additional 39,574.

Mittelenglische Originalurkunde von der Chaucer-zeit bis zur Mitte des xv Jahrhunderts. Ed L. Morsbach, Heidelberg 1923.

Mittelenglische Originalurkunde 1405–30. Ed H. M. Flasdieck, Heidelberg 1926.

English verse between Chaucer and Surrey. Ed E. P. Hammond, Durham NC 1927, New York 1965.

The Middle English stanzaic versions of the Life of St Anne. Ed R. E. Parker 1928 (EETS).

A book of London English 1384–1425. Ed R. W. Chambers and M. Daunt, with an appendix on English documents in the Record Office by M. M. Weale, Oxford 1931, 1967.

A mediæval post-bag. Ed L. Lyell 1934.

The early English carols. Ed R. L. Greene, Oxford 1935.

English constitutional documents 1307–1485. Ed E. C. Lodge and G. A. Thornton, Cambridge 1935.

Die Historie von den vier Kaufleuten (Frederyke of Jennen); Die Geschichte von der vertauschten Wiege (The mylner of Abyngton). Ed J. Raith, Leipzig 1936. Ed from early prints.

The chief British poets of the fourteenth and fifteenth centuries: selected poems. Ed W. W. Neilson and K. G. T. Webster, Boston 1936. Trns.

Religious lyrics of the fifteenth century. Ed C. Brown, Oxford 1939, 1962.

The thought and culture of the English Renaissance: an anthology of Tudor prose 1487–1555. Ed E. M. Nugent, Cambridge 1955.

Secular lyrics of the xivth and xvth centuries. Ed R. H. Robbins, Oxford 1952, 1955.

Bowers, R. H. Three Middle English poems on the Apostles Creed. PMLA 70 1955.

Historical poems of the xivth and xvth centuries. Ed R. H. Robbins, New York 1959.

Poesia cavalleresca e poesia religiosa inglese nel Quattrocento. Ed S. Rossi, Milan 1960.

Select documents of English constitutional history 1307–1485. Ed S. B. Chrimes and A. L. Brown 1961.

Early English Christmas carols. Ed R. H. Robbins, New York 1961.

A selection of English carols. Ed R. L. Greene, Oxford 1962.

Three Middle English religious poems. Ed R. H. Bowers, Gainesville 1963.

A hundred merry tales and other English jestbooks of the fifteenth and sizteenth centuries. Ed P. M. Zall, Lincoln Nebraska 1963. Modernized.

Later medieval English prose. Ed W. Matthews, New York and London [1963]. Modernized.

The constitutional history of England in the fifteenth century 1399–1485, with illustrative documents. Ed B. Wilkinson 1965. Trns and modernizations.

English historical documents 1327–1485. Ed A. R. Myers 1969. Trns and modernizations.

English poetry 1400–1580. Ed W. Tydeman 1970.

(2) CHRONICLES IN ENGLISH

Richard Arnold (d. 1521). A chronicle of London from 1089 to 1483 and the Customs of London, otherwise called Arnold's chronicle. Antwerp [1501]; [ed F. Douce] 1811.

The Brut: or the Chronicles of England. Ed F. W. D. Brie 2 pts 1906–8 (EETS).

Powell, E. O. The Brute of the chronicle of England. Folklore 48 1937. 2 extracts from Jesus College Oxford ms v.

Brie, F. W. D. Geschichte und Quellen der mittelenglischen Prosachronik—The Brute of England oder The chronicles of England. Marburg 1905.

Thomas Castleford's chronicle. Ed F. Behre, Gothenburg 1940. Göttingen Univ Lib ms History 740; probably late 14th-century.

The coronation of Elizabeth Wydeville, Queen Consort of Edward IV, on May 26th 1465. Ed G. Smith 1935.

An English chronicle of the reigns of Richard II, Henry IV, Henry V and Henry VI written before the year 1471. Ed J. S. Davies 1856 (Camden Soc).

Robert Fabyan (d. 1512). The new chronicles of England and France, in two parts. 1516 (Pynson), 1533 (Rastell), 1542 (Reynes), 1559; ed H. Ellis 1811.

The first life of Henry V, written in 1513 by the translator of Livius. Ed C. L. Kingsford, Oxford 1911.

John Hardyng (1378–1465?). English chronicle in metre fro the first begynning of Englande unto the reigne of Edwarde the fourth. 1543 (Grafton); ed H. Ellis 1912.

Kingsford, C. L. Extracts from the first version of Hardyng's chronicle. EHR 27 1912.

Historie of the arrivall of King Edward IV. Ed J. Bruce 1838 (Camden Soc).

Chronicle of the rebellion in Lincolnshire 1470. Ed J. G. Nichols 1847 (Camden Soc).

A chronicle of London. Ed N. H. Nicolas and E. Tyrell 1829.

The great chronicle of London. Ed A. H. Thomas and I. D. Thornley 1938 (priv ptd).

John Page (fl. 1430). The siege of Rouen. Ed J. J. Conybeare, Archaeologia 21 1827; ed F. Madden, Archaeologia 22 1829; ed H. Huscher, Leipzig 1927.

A remarkable fragment of an old English chronicle or history of the affairs of King Edward the Fourth (Hearne's fragment). Ed T. Hearne, Oxford 1719 (in Thomae Sprotti Chronica).

John Rows (1411?–91). This rol was laburd and finished by Master J. Rows, of Warrewyk. Ed W. Courthope 1845.

John Warkworth (d. 1500). A chronicle of the first thirteen years of the reign of Edward IV. Ed J. O. Halliwell(-Phillipps) 1839 (Camden Soc).

(3) CORRESPONDENCE

Thomas Bekynton
c. 1390–1465

Official correspondence of Bekynton, secretary to Henry VI and Bishop of Bath and Wells. Ed G. Williams 2 vols 1872 (Rolls ser). Lambeth ms 211.

Judd, A. F. The episcopate of Bekynton, Bishop of Bath and Wells 1443–65. Jnl of Ecclesiastical History 8 1957. *See also col 802, below.*

Cely Papers

The Cely papers: selections from the correspondence and memoranda of the Cely family merchants of the Staple AD 1475–88. Ed H. E. Malden 1900 (Camden Soc).

Hanham, A. The text of the Cely letters. MÆ 26 1957.

—— The musical studies of a fifteenth-century wool merchant. RES new ser 8 1957.

—— The Cely papers and the Oxford English dictionary. E Studies 42 1961.

—— A fifteenth-century merchant family. History Today Dec 1963.

Paston Letters

Paston letters. Ed J. Fenn 5 vols 1787–1823; rev J. Gairdner 3 vols 1872–5, 4 vols 1901, 6 vols 1904, 1965; ed M. D. Jones 1909 (selection; modernized); ed A. Greenwood 1920 (selection); ed M. Archer-Hind 1924 (selection, modernized); ed H. Pettit, Boulder 1947 (selection, modernized; priv ptd); ed A. H. R. Bell 1949 (selection, modernized); ed J. Warrington 2 vols 1956; ed N. Davis 1958 (selection), 1963 (selection, modernized), 3 vols Oxford 1971– (standard edn).

Neumann, G. Die Orthographie des Paston letters von 1422–61. Marburg 1904.

Bennett, H. S. The Pastons and their England. Cambridge 1922.

Stevenson, E. C. Margaret Paston. Dublin Rev 189 1931.

Robbins, E. C. William Paston, justice: founder of the Paston family 1378–1444. Norwich 1932.

Sykes, W. J. The Paston letters. Dalhousie Rev 16 1936.

Bühler, C. F. Some new Paston documents. RES 14 1938.

—— Sir John Paston's grete booke: a fifteenth-century best-seller. MLN 56 1941.

Davis, N. The text of Margaret Paston's letters. MÆ 18 1949.

—— A scribal problem in the Paston letters. Eng & Germanic Stud 4 1952.

—— A Paston hand. RES new ser 3 1952.

—— The letters of William Paston. Neophilologus 37 1953.

—— The language of the Pastons. Proc Br Acad 40 1954.

—— Margaret Paston's use of *do*. Neuphilologische Mitteilungen 73 1972.

Marshall, K. N. The Pastons 1378–1732. Norwich 1956.

Carstensen, B. Studien zur Syntax des Nomens, Pronomens und der Negativen in den Paston letters. Bochum 1959.

Keen, M. The first English family letters. History Today May 1959.

Faurot, R. M. From records to romance: Stevenson's The black arrow and the Paston letters. Stud in Eng Lit 1500–1900 5 1965.

Plumpton Correspondence

The Plumpton correspondence. Ed T. Stapleton 1839 (Camden Soc).

John Shillingford
fl. 1447–50

Letters and papers of Shillingford, Mayor of Exeter 1447–50. Ed S. H. Moore 1871 (Camden Soc).

Stonor Letters

The Stonor letters and papers 1290–1483. Ed C. L. Kingsford 2 vols 1919 (Camden Soc); Supplementary Stonor letters and papers 1313–1482, ed Kingsford, Camden Miscellany 13 1924.

Various

Letters of Queen Margaret of Anjou and Bishop Beckington and others. Ed C. Monro 1863 (Camden Soc).

Some English personal letters of 1402. Ed E. Rickert, RES 8 1932.

(4) OTHER VERSE

John Audelay
fl. 1426

The poems of Audelay: a specimen of the Shropshire dialect in the fifteenth century. Ed J. O. Halliwell(-Phillipps) 1844 (Percy Soc). Bodley ms Douce 302.

Der Dichter Audelay und sein Werk. Ed J. E. Wülfing, Anglia 18 1896.

Fifteenth-century carols by Audelay. Ed E. K. Chambers and F. Sidgwick, MLR 5–6 1910–11.

The poems of Audelay. Ed E. K. Whiting 1931 (EETS).

Dickins, B. The rhyme in ms Douce 302, 53 and 54. Proc Leeds Philosophical Soc 2 1935.

Copley, J. Audelay's carols and music. E Studies 39 1958.

Boccaccio's Tales of Guiscardo etc

Guystarde and Sygysmonde. 1532 (de Worde). Tr William Walter.

The statly tragedy of Guistard and Sismond. 1597, Edinburgh 1812.

Early English versions of the tales of Guiscardo and

Ghismonda and Titus and Gisippus from the Decameron. Ed H. G. Wright 1937 (EETS). Includes 4 versions.

Thomas Brampton
fl. 1414

A paraphrase on the seven penitential psalms in English verse. Ed W. H. Black 1842 (Percy Soc).

Charles Duke of Orleans
1394–1465

Poems, written in English by Charles d'Orléans. Ed G. W. Taylor 1827 (Roxburghe Club).

Vier Gedichte von Charles d'Orléans. Ed E. Hausknecht, Anglia 17 1895. From Bodley Hearne's Diary no 38 1712.

The English poems of Charles of Orléans. Ed R. Steele and M. Day 2 vols 1941–6 (EETS), rptd 1 vol with new bibliography by C. Clark 1970. BM ms Harley 682.

Some Charles d'Orléans fragments. Ed R. H. Robbins, MLN 66 1951.

Charles d'Orléans. Ed J. Charpier, Paris 1958. Modernized selection.

Un poème mystique de Charles d'Orléans: le Canticum amoris. Ed G. Ouy, Studi Francesi 3 1959.

L'opera poetica di Charles d'Orléans. Ed S. Cigada, Milan 1960.

Croft, T. Early English poetry. Retrospective Rev 2 1827.

Bullrich, G. Über Charles d'Orleans und ihm zugeschriebene englische Übersetzungen seiner Gedichte. Berlin 1893.

Sauerstein, P. Charles d'Orléans und die englische Übersetzung seiner Dichtungen. Halle 1899.

Champion, P. Vie de Charles d'Orléans. Paris 1911.

MacCracken, H. N. An English friend of Charles of Orléans. PMLA 26 1911. Identifies English translator as Duke of Suffolk.

Hammond, E. P. Charles of Orléans and Anne Molyneux. MP 22 1924.

Urwin, K. The 59th English ballade of Charles d'Orléans. MLR 38 1943.

Tardieu, J. Charles d'Orléans. Cahiers de la Pléiade 1946.

Ouy, G. Recherches sur la librairie de Charles d'Orléans et de Jean d'Angoulême pendant leur captivité en Angleterre. Comptes-rendus de l'Académie des Inscriptions et Belles-Lettres 1955.

— A propos des manuscrits autographes de Charles d'Orléans identifiés en 1955 à la Bibliothèque Nationale. Bibliothèque de l'École des Chartes 118 1960.

Seaton, E. Studies in Villon, Vaillant and Charles d'Orléans. 1957.

Poiron, D. Création poétique et composition romanesque dans les premiers poèmes de Charles d'Orléans. Revue des Sciences Humaines 1958.

— Le poète et le prince: l'évolution du lyrisme courtois de Guillaume de Machaut à Charles d'Orléans. Paris 1965.

— Le lexique de Charles d'Orléans dans les ballades. Geneva 1967.

Cigada, S. Christine de Pisan e la traduzione inglese delle poesie di Charles d'Orléans. Aevum 32 1958.

— Studi su Charles d'Orléans e François Villon relativi al ms BN fr. 25458. Studi Francesi 4 1960.

Nardi, L. de. Charles d'Orléans: divagazioni e spunti critici. Marsia 2 1958.

Vàrvaro, A. Realtà e poesia in Charles d'Orléans. In Saggi e ricerche in memoria Ettore Li Gotti vol 3, Palermo 1963.

Goodrich, N. L. Charles Duke of Orleans: a literary biography. New York 1963.

– Charles d'Orléans: a study of theme in his French and in his English poetry. Geneva 1967.

Starobinski, J. L'encre de la mélancolie. Nouvelle Revue Française 21 1963.

Stemmler, T. Zur Verfasserfrage der Charles d'Orléans zugeschriebenen englischen Gedichte. Anglia 82 1964. English trns by professional minstrel.

Watson, H. Charles d'Orléans. Romanic Rev 56 1965.

Fox, J. Charles d'Orléans: poète anglais? Romania 86 1965.

— The lyric poetry of Charles d'Orléans. Oxford 1969.

de Angulo, L. Charles and Jean d'Orléans: an attempt to trace the contacts between them during their captivity in England. In Miscellanea di studi e ricerche sul Quattrocento francese, Turin 1966.

Cellini, B. Le poesie inglese di Charles d'Orléans. In Studi in onore di Itali Siciliano vol 1, Florence 1966.

Ménard, P. Je meurs de soif auprés de la fontaine: d'un mythe antique à une image lyrique. Romania 87 1966.

Foffano, T. Charles d'Orléans e un gruppo di umanisti lombardi in Normandia. Aevum 41 1967.

Choffel, J. Le duc Charles d'Orléans: chronique d'un prince des fleurs de lys. Paris 1968.

Simmons, A. A contribution to the Middle English dictionary: citations from the English poems of Charles duc d'Orléans. Jnl of Eng Linguistics 2 1968.

McLeod, E. Charles of Orleans, Prince and poet. 1969.

Clark, C. Charles d'Orléans: some English perspectives. MÆ 40 1971.

John Gardener
fl. 1440–50

A fifteenth-century treatise on gardening by Mayster Ion Gardener with remarks by the Honourable Alicia M. Tyssen Amherst. Ed Lady Alicia M. T. Amherst, Archaeologia 54 1894. Ed from a Trinity College Cambridge ms.

W. Hichecoke

Hichecoke's This world is but a vanyte (HM 183). Ed R. H. Bowers, MLN 67 1952.

Historical Poems

A siege of Calais: a new text. PMLA 67 1952. Ed R. A. Klinefelter, PMLA 67 1952. Eng College Rome ms 1306.

A song for victory in France 1492. Ed R. H. Robbins, Neuphilologische Mitteilungen 55 1954. BM ms Cotton Domit xviii.

A Middle English diatribe against Philip of Burgundy. Ed Robbins, Neophilologus 39 1955. Eng College Rome ms 1306.

An epitaph for Duke Humphrey 1447. Ed Robbins, Neuphilologische Mitteilungen 56 1955. BM ms Harley 2251.

God amende wykkyd cownsell 1464. Ed Robbins, Neuphilologische Mitteilungen 56 1955.

Victory at Whitby AD 1451. Ed Robbins, SP 67 1970.

Peter Idley
d. 1474?

Kleine Mitteilungen zur mittelenglischen Lehrdichtung. Ed M. Förster, Archiv 104 1900.

Instructions to his son. Ed F. Miessner, Greifswald 1903.

Instructions to his son. Ed C. D'Evelyn 1935. Cambridge Univ Lib ms Ee.4.37.

Brooks, E. St. John Idley. TLS 12 Sept 1935.

Libel of English Policy
1436

The libell of Englishe policye 1436. Ed W. Hertzberg, Leipzig 1878. With introd by R. Pauli.

The libelle of Englyshe polycye: a poem on the use of sea-power 1436. Ed G. F. Warner, Oxford 1926.

Taylor, F. Some manuscripts of the Lybelle of Englysshe polycye. Bull John Rylands Lib 24 1940.

Holmes, C. A. The libel of English policy. EHR 76 1961.

William Lichfield
d. 1447

The complaint of God to sinful man and the answer of man. Ed E. Borgström, Anglia 34 1911. Caius College Cambridge ms 174.

Brown, C. Manuscripts of Lichfield's Complaint of God. E Studien 47 1913.

Henry Lovelich
fl. 1450

The history of the Holy Grail. Ed F. J. Furnivall 2 vols 1861–3 (Roxburghe Club).

The history of the Holy Grail. Ed F. J. Furnivall and D. Kempe 5 vols 1874–1905 (EETS).

Merlin. Ed A. E. Koch 3 vols 1904–30 (EETS).
Ackerman, R. W. Lovelich's name. MLN 67 1952.
—— Lovelich's Merlin. PMLA 67 1952.

John Metham
fl. 1450?

The works of Metham. Ed H. Craig 1916 (EETS). Princeton Univ Lib ms Garrett 142.

John Midwinter
fl. 1450?

Bowers, R. H. Middle-English poems by Mydwynter. MLN 64 1949. BM ms Harley 2383.

John Mirk
fl. 1405

Instructions for parish priests by Myrc. Ed E. Peacock 1868; rev F. J. Furnivall 1902 (EETS). BM ms Cotton Claudius A 2; trn of William de Pagula, Pupilla oculi.

Humfrey Newton
1466–1536

The poems of Newton esquire. Ed R. H. Robbins, PMLA 65 1950.

Palladius

Palladius on husbondrie. Ed B. Lodge and S. J. H. Herrtage 2 vols 1873–9 (EETS). Trn c. 1420.
The Middle English translation of Palladius De re rustica. Ed M. Liddell, Berlin 1896.

J. Quixley
fl. 1402

Quixley's ballades royal (?1402). Ed H. N. MacCracken, Yorkshire Archaeological Jnl 20 1909. BM ms Stowe 951; trn of Gower's Traitie pour essampler les amantz marietz, c. 1440.

The Tournament of Tottenham

The turnament of Totenham and the Feest: two early ballads printed from a ms preserved in the Public Library of the University of Cambridge. [Ed T. Wright] 1836. Cambridge Univ Lib ms Ff.5.48.
Cargill, O. The authorship of Secunda pastorum. PMLA 41 1926. Gilbert Pilkington the author of the Tournament and Secunda pastorum.
Frampton, M. G. Gilbert Pilkington once more. PMLA 47 1932. Rejects Pilkington's authorship.
Jones, G. F. The tournaments of Tottenham and Lappenhausen. PMLA 66 1951.

Jack Upland
early 15th century

Upland, Friar Daw's reply and Upland's rejoinder. Ed P. L. Heyworth, Oxford 1968. Mss BM Harley 6641, Cambridge Univ Lib Ff. vi. 2 and Bodley Digby 41; ptd as both verse and prose.

Heyworth, P. L. Upland's rejoinder: a Lollard interpolator and Piers Plowman B x 249f. MÆ 36 1967.
—— The earliest black-letter editions of Upland. HLQ 30 1967.
—— ME alumnere and snowcrie: two ghosts. Eng Philological Stud 10 1967.
—— Notes on two uncollected Middle English proverbs. N & Q March 1970.

John Walton
fl. 1410

The boke of comfort. 1525 (T. Rychard).
Boethius, De consolacione philosophiæ. Ed M. Science 1925 (EETS). Lincoln Cathedral ms A 4 11.
Schümmer, C. Waltons metrische Übersetzung der Consolatio philosophiæ: Untersuchung des Handschriftenverhältnisses und Probe eines kritischen Textes. Bonn 1914.
Greene, R. L. The port of peace: not death but God. MLN 69 1954. Poems based on Walton's trn of Boethius.

The Wright's Chaste Wife
c. 1462

The wright's chaste wife. Ed F. J. Furnivall 1865 (EETS), 1891 (rev).
Clouston, W. A. The wright's chaste wife: additional analogues. 1866 (EETS).
Llewellyn, R. H. The wright's chaste wife disinterred. Southern Folklore Quart 16 1952.

Various

The lovers' mass. Ed E. P. Hammond, JEGP 7 1908. A parody of the Mass.
Vegetius in English. Ed H. N. MacCracken, Anniversary papers by colleagues and pupils of G. L. Kittredge, Boston 1913.
ME disticha (aus Hs Add 37049). Ed K. Brunner, Archiv 159 1931.
Knyghthode and bataile: a xvth-century verse paraphrase of Flavius Vegetius Renatus' treatise De re militari. Ed R. Dyboski and Z. M. Arend 1936 (EETS). 1458, Pembroke College Cambridge ms 243.
The speculum misericordie. Ed R. H. Robbins, PMLA 54 1939.
The fraternity of drinkers. Ed Robbins SP 47 1950. Nat Lib of Wales ms Peniarth 53.
The complaint against hope. Ed K. G. Wilson, Ann Arbor 1957.
Patience in adversity. Ed C. F. Bühler, Anglia 78 1960. Bodley add B 60.
A Middle English metrical life of Job. Ed G. N. Garmonsway and R. R. Raymo, Early English and Norse studies presented to Hugh Smith, 1963. Huntington Lib ms HM 140 c. 1473.
A fifteenth-century didactic poem in British Museum additional ms 29729. Ed A. S. G. Edwards, Neuphilologische Mitteilungen 70 1969.
Conuertimi: a Middle English refrain poem. Ed Robbins, Neuphilologische Mitteilungen 73 1972.
Mercy and righteousness. Ed A. Kurvinen, ibid.

(5) OTHER PROSE

Alexander

The prose life of Alexander from the Thornton ms. Ed J. S. Westlake 1913 (EETS). Trn from Latin c. 1430.
Hamilton, G. L. A new redaction (J3a) of the Historia de preliis and the date of redaction J3. Speculum 2 1927.

Alphabet of Tales

An alphabet of tales: an English 15th-century translation of Alphabetum narrationum of Etienne de Besançon. Ed M. M. Banks 2 vols 1904–5 (EETS). BM ms additional 25719 c. 1420.
Herbert, J. A. The authorship of the Alphabetum narrationum. Ed J. A. Herbert, Library 2nd ser 6 1905. Dismisses attribution to Etienne de Besançon.

Juliana Berners etc
d. 1388?

The book of hawking, hunting and blasing of arms.
St Albans 1486, London 1496 (de Worde; includes The
treatyse of fysshynge wyth an angle), 1540 (Tab),
[1561] (Copland), [1563] (Vele), 1586, 1595 etc.

The book of hawking, hunting, coat-armour, fishing and
blasing of arms, as printed at Westminster by Wynkyn
de Worde. Ed J. Haslewood 1810 (facs).

The treatyse of fysshynge. Ed M. G. Watkins 1880
(facs).

The boke of St Albans by Dame Juliana Berners 1486.
Ed W. Blades 1881 (facs).

An older form of the treatyse of fysshynge wyth an angle.
Ed T. Satchell 1883.

The treatyse of fysshynge. Ed 'Piscator', Edinburgh 1885
(facs).

The book of hawking, hunting and blasing of arms. Ed
W. Blades [1905] (facs).

The booke of hawkyng after Prince Edwarde Kyng of
Englande and its relation to the Book of St Albans.
Ed A. E. H. Swaen, Studia Neophilologica 16 1944.
BM ms Harley 2340.

The book of St Albans and the origins of its treatise on
hawking. Ed N. J. S. Leggatt, Studia Neophilologica
22 1950. BM ms Sloane 3488 xviii F.

Julians Barnes: boke of huntyng. Ed G. Tilander,
Karlshamn 1964 (Cynegetica 11). Bodley ms Rawlinson
poetry 143.

Hodgkin, J. Proper terms: an attempt at a rational
explanation of the meanings of the collection of phrases
in the Book of St Albans 1486. Trans Philological Soc
1907–10.

Allen, H. E. The fifteenth-century associations of beasts,
of birds and of men: the earliest text with language
for carvers. PMLA 51 1936.

Jacob, E. F. The book of St Albans. Bull John Rylands
Lib 28 1944; rptd in his Essays in later medieval
history, Manchester 1968.

Binns, A. L. A manuscript source of the Book of St
Albans. Bull John Rylands Lib 33 1951. Discusses
Lambeth 491 and Bodley Rawlinson poetry 143.

Wynne, M. G. The boke of St Albans. Yale Lib Gazette
26 1951.

Pafort, E. Notes on the Wynkyn de Worde editions of
the Boke of St Albans and its separates. SB 5 1953.

Corner, R. More fifteenth-century terms of association.
RES new ser 13 1962.

Moran, J. The book of St Albans and the schoolmaster
printer. Black Art 2 1963.

—— The book of St Albans. Coat of Arms 8 1965.

Hands, R. Juliana Berners and the Boke of St Albans.
RES new ser 18 1967.

Zettersten, A. The Lambeth manuscript of the Boke of
huntyng. Neuphilologische Mitteilungen 70 1969.
Lambeth ms 491.

Thomas Betson
fl. 1500

A ryght profytable treatyse. [1500] (de Worde); ed F.
Jenkinson, Cambridge 1905 (facs).

Nicholas Bishop
fl. 1432

Bishop: an exemplar of the Oxford dialect of the fifteenth
century. Ed S. B. Meech, PMLA 49 1934. Camb Univ
Lib ms Dd.xiv.2.

John Blount
fl. 1500

The essential portions of Nicholas Upton's De studio
militari before 1446, translated by Blount c. 1500. Ed
F. P. Barnard, Oxford 1931.

Robert Copland
fl. 1508–33

The romance of Kynge Apollyn of Thyre. 1510 (de Worde);
ed E. W. Ashbee 1870 (priv ptd) (facs).

Gyl of Braintfords testament. 1560 (Copland), 1562 (Copland); ed F. J. Furnivall 1871 (from 2nd edn) (priv ptd).

Helyas, Knight of the Swan. 1512 (de Worde), 1550
(Copland); ed R. Hoe, New York 1901 (facs).

The kalendar and comport of shepeherdes. 1508 (de
Worde), 1518 (Notary, rev); [ed G. C. Heseltine] 1930
(facs).

Plomer, H. R. Copland. Trans Bibl Soc 3 1896.

Klebs, E. Die Erzählung von Apollonius aus Tyrus.
Berlin 1899.

Moore, W. G. Copland and his Hye way. RES 7 1931.

White, B. Three rare books about women. Huntington
Lib Bull No. 2 1931. 2 by Copland.

Francis, F. C. Copland: sixteenth-century printer and
translator. Glasgow 1961.

Dicts and Sayings of the Philosophers
There are at least 3 separate trns of this French text.

The dicts and sayings of the philosophers: a Middle
English version by Stephen Scrope. Ed M. E. Schofield,
Philadelphia 1936 (priv ptd). Bodley ms 943.

Dictes and sayings of the philosophers: the translations by
Stephen Scrope, William Worcester and an anonymous
translator. Ed C. F. Bühler 1941 (EETS).

Brandl, A. On the Dictes and sayings of the philosophers. In An English miscellany presented to Dr
[F. J.] Furnivall, Oxford 1901.

Hittmair, R Earl Rivers Einleitung zu seiner Übertragung der Weisheitssprüche der Philosophen.
Anglia 59 1935.

Bühler, C. F. A survival from the Middle Ages:
William Baldwin's use of the Dictes and sayings.
Speculum 23 1948.

—— New manuscripts of the Dictes and sayings of the
philosophers. MLN 63 1948.

—— The Liber de dictis philosophorum antiquarum
and common proverbs in George Ashby's poems.
PMLA 65 1950.

—— The Newberry Library manuscript of the Dictes
and sayings of the philosophers. Anglia 74 1956.
Ms f. 36, Ry 20.

Dives and Pauper
c. 1405–10

Dives and pauper. 1493 (Pynson), 1496 (de Worde), 1536
(Berthelet).

Richardson, H. G. Dives and pauper. N & Q 21–8 Oct,
30 Dec 1911.

—— Dives et pauper. Library 4th ser 15 1935.

Pfander, H. G. Dives et pauper. Library 4th ser 14
1934.

Slatter, A. Dives and pauper: orthodoxy and liberalism.
Jnl of Rutgers Univ Lib 31 1967.

Edward Duke of York
fl. 1406

The master of game. Ed W. A. and F. Baillie-Groham
1904, 1909 (modernized).

Epistle of Othea
There are at least 2 trns of this French text.

Epistle of Othea to Hector: or the Boke of Knyghthode.
Ed G. F. Warner 1904 (Roxburghe Club).

The epistle of Othea to Hector. Ed J. D. Gordon, Philadelphia 1942. BM ms Harley 838.

The epistle of Othea to Hector. Ed C. F. Bühler 1970
(EETS).

Bühler, C. F. Sir John Fastolf's manuscripts of the Epître d'Othéa and Stephen Scrope's translation of this text. Scriptorium 3 1949.
— The revisions and dedications of the Epistle of Othea. Anglia 76 1958.
MacCracken, H. N. An unknown Middle English translation of L'épître d'Othéa. MLN 24 1909. Identifies version in BM ms Harley 838 by Anthony Babynton (fl. 1470).

Gesta Romanorum
c. 1450
Gesta Romanorum. 1510 (de Worde); several later trns by different hands.
The olde English versions of the Gesta romanorum. Ed F. Madden 1838 (Roxburghe Club).
The gesta romanorum. Ed C. Swan 1824, 1827, 1887 (selections); rev W. Hooper 1905. Modernized.
The early English versions of the Gesta romanorum. Ed S. J. H. Herrtage 1879 (EETS). BM Harley 7333 and additional 9066; Cambridge Univ Lib Kk.1.6.
Oesterley, H. Gesta romanorum. Berlin 1872.
Immaculate, Sr M. The four daughters of God in the Gesta Romanorum and the Court of sapience. PMLA 57 1942.
Brewer, D. S. Observations on a fifteenth-century manuscript. Anglia 72 1954. Gloucester Cathedral ms 22 press no 1.
Kahrl, S. J. The medieval origins of the sixteenth-century English jestbooks. Stud in Renaissance 13 1966.

Gilte Legende
1438
Wells, M. E. The South English legendary in its relation to the Legenda aurea. PMLA 51 1936.
Jeremy, Sr M. The English prose translation of the Legenda aurea. MLN 59 1944. Suggests by Bokenham.
— Caxton and the synfulle wretche. Traditio 4 1946.
Seybolt, R. F. The Legenda aurea, the Bible and the Historia scholastica. Speculum 21 1946.
— Fifteenth-century editions of the Legenda aurea. Speculum 21 1946.
— The Adriatic port in the Legenda aurea. Speculum 21 1946.
Kaiser, L. M. Das Väterbuch and the Legenda aurea. MLN 68 1953.
Kurvinen, A. Caxton's Golden legend and the manuscript of the Gilte legende. Neuphilologische Mitteilungen 60 1959.

Medical and Scientific Texts
Lanfrank's Science of Cirurgie. Ed R. von Fleischhacker 1894 (EETS).
Treatises of fistula in ano, haemorrhoids and clysters by John Arderne. Ed D'Arcy Power 1910 (EETS). BM ms Sloane 6.
The earliest arithmetics in English. Ed R. Steele 1916 (EETS).
Aus mittelenglischen Medizintexten. Ed G. Müller, Leipzig 1929. Stockholm ms Misc X.90.
The Liber de diversis medicinis in the Thornton manuscript (Ms Lincoln Cathedral A 5.2). Ed M. S. Ogden 1938 (EETS).
Agnus castus: a Middle English herbal. Ed G. Brodin, Upsala 1950. Stockholm ms X 90.
An old palmistry: being the earliest known book of palmistry in English, from Bodleian ms Digby roll iv. Ed D. J. Price, Cambridge and New York 1953.
A fifteenth-century text on astronomy. Ed J. R. Russell, Univ of Rochester Lib Bull 12 1957.
The Middle English translation of Guy de Chauliac's Anatomy; with Guy's essay on the history of medicine. Ed B. Wallner, Lund 1964.

The cyrurgie of Guy de Chauliac. Ed M. S. Ogden 1971 (EETS).

John Mirk
fl. 1405
Mirk's festial: a collection of homilies. Ed T. Erbe 1905 (EETS). Bodley ms Gough Eccl Top 4.
Instructions for parish priests. Ed K. Young, Speculum 11 1936. Prose tract from BM ms Harley 2250.
A late fifteenth-century revision of Mirk's festial. Ed L. L. Steckman, SP 34 1937. BM mss Harley 2247, Royal 18 B xxv.
Long, M. Undetected verse in Mirk's festial. MLN 70 1955.
Wakelyn, M. F. The manuscripts of Mirk's festial. Leeds Stud in Eng new ser 1 1967.

Thomas Norton
fl. 1477
The ordinall of alchemy. Ed E. Ashmole 1652 (in Theatrum chemicum); ed E. J. Holmyard 1928 (facs).

George Ripley
d. 1490?
The compende of alkemye. Ed R. Rabbard 1591; ed E. Cassel 1649; ed E. Ashmole 1652 (in Theatrum chemicum).

Saints' Lives and Legends
The life of St Ursula, Guiscard and Sigismund. 1818 (Roxburghe Club).
A merveylous revelation by sent Nycholas to a monke of Enyshamme. 1482 (Machlinia); ed E. Arber 1869 (in English reprints).
The lyf of Seint Jerome. [1501] (de Worde); ed C. Horstmann, Anglia 3 1880 (from Lambeth ms 432).
The myracles of oure blessyd lady. [1496], 1514, 1530 (all de Worde); ed C. Horstmann, Anglia 3 1880 (from Lambeth ms 432).
The life and martyrdom of Saint Katherine of Alexandria. Ed H. H. Gibbs 1884 (Roxburghe Club).
The lyfe of Seint Cristyn the merueylous. Ed C. Horstmann, Anglia 8 1885. Bodley ms Douce 114.
A letter touchynge the lyfe of Seint Kateryn of Senys. Ed C. Horstmann, ibid.
The lyf of Saint Katheryn of Senis. [1493] (de Worde); ed C. Horstmann, Archiv 76 1886.
The revelations of St Elizabeth. [1493] (de Worde); ed C. Horstmann, ibid.
The revelations of Saint Birgitta edited from the fifteenth-century ms in the Garrett collection in the Library of Princeton University. Ed W. P. Cumming 1929 (EETS).

School Books
John Drury and his English writings (Cambridge additional ms 2830). Ed S. B. Meech, Speculum 9 1934.
Early application of Latin grammar to English. Ed S. B. Meech, PMLA 50 1935. St John's College Cambridge ms 163 and Bodley ms Douce 103.
An early treatise in English concerning Latin grammar. Ed S. B. Meech, Essays & Stud in Eng & Comparative Lit (Michigan) 13 1935. Trinity College Cambridge O.5.4.
Late Middle English parerga in a school collection. Ed C. E. Wright, RES new ser 2 1951. BM ms Harley 1002.
A fifteenth-century school book from a manuscript in the British Museum (ms Arundel 249). Ed W. Nelson, Oxford 1956.
Bonaventure, B. The teaching of Latin in later medieval England. Mediaeval Stud 23 1961.
Davis, N. and G. S. Ivy. Ms Walter Rye and its French Grammar. MÆ 31 1962.

Secreta Secretorum

Three prose versions of the Secreta secretorum. Ed R. Steele 1898 (EETS).

Gilbert, A. H. Notes on the influence of the Secretum secretorum. Speculum 3 1928.

Sermon Literature

A famous Middle English sermon (ms Hatton 57, Bodleian Library). Ed K. F. Sundén, Gothenburg 1925. By Robert Wimbledon.

Speculum sacerdotale, edited from British Museum ms additional 36791. Ed E. H. Weatherly 1936 (EETS).

Three Middle English sermons from the Worcester chapter manuscript F. 10. Ed D. M. Grisdale, Leeds School of Eng Lang Texts 5 1939.

Middle English sermons edited from British Museum ms Royal 18B XXIII. Ed W. O. Ross 1940 (EETS).

A Middle English treatise on hermeneutics: Harley ms 2276. Ed R. H. Bowers, PMLA 65 1950.

Caplan, H. A late medieval treatise on preaching. In Studies in rhetoric and public speaking in honor of J. A. Wynans, New York 1925.

Talbert, E. W. The date of the composition of the English Wycliffite collections of sermons. Speculum 12 1937.

— A fifteenth-century Lollard sermon cycle. SE 1939.

John Shirley
c. 1366–1456

Gaertner, O. Shirley: sein Leben und Werken. Halle 1904.

Hammond, E. P. Ashmole 59 and other Shirley manuscripts. Anglia 30 1907.

Doyle, A. I. More light on Shirley. MÆ 30 1961.

Treatise of Love
c. 1493

The tretyse of love. [1493/4] (de Worde); ed J. H. Fisher 1951 (EETS).

Fisher, J. H. Seven variants in the Tretyse of love. PBSA 46 1952.

Henry Watson
fl. 1503–9

Valentyne and Orson. [1503–5] (de Worde), [c. 1548] (Copland), [1565?] (Copland), 1637; ed A. Dickson 1937 (EETS).

The hystorye of Olyver of Castylle. 1518 (de Worde); ed R. E. Graves 1898 (Roxburghe Club).

Dickson, A. Valentine and Orson: a study of late medieval romance. New York 1929.

William Wey
fl. 1458–62

Itineraries to Jerusalem 1458–62 and to Saint James of Compostella 1456. [Ed G. Williams] 1857 (Roxburghe Club).

William Worcester (Botoner)
1582–41?

Letters and papers illustrative of the wars of the English in France during the reign of Henry VI, King of England. Ed J. Stevenson 2 vols 1861–4 (Rolls ser).

Gasquet, F. A. The note books of William Worcester, a fifteenth-century antiquary. In his Old English Bible and other essays, 1908.

Rowe, B. J. H. A contemporary account of the hundred years' war from 1415 to 1429. EHR 41 1926.

Lathrop, H. B. The translations of John Tiptoft. MLN 41 1926.

Kendrick, T. D. British antiquity. 1950.

McFarlane, K. B. Worcester: a preliminary survey. In Studies presented to Sir Hilary Jenkinson, Oxford 1957.

— Worcester and a present of lampreys. MÆ 30 1961.

Davis N. The epistolary usages of Worcester. In Medieval literature and civilisation: studies in memory of G. N. Garmonsway, 1969.

Various

Merlin. Ed H. B. Wheatley 4 vols 1865–99 (EETS).

The book of quinte essence: or the fifth being, that is to say, man's heaven. Ed F. J. Furnivall 1866 (EETS).

The book of the knight of La Tour-Landry. Ed T. Wright 1868; rev J. J. Munro 1906 (EETS). BM ms Harley 1764.

The pilgrimage of the lyf of manhode from the French of G. de Deguileville. Ed W. A. Wright 1869 (Roxburghe Club). Cambridge Univ Lib ms Ff.5.30.

The history of the seven wise masters of Rome. 1493 (Pynson), 1520 (de Worde), [1555] (Copland), 1633; ed G. L. Gomme 1885 (Villon Soc) (from 1520).

The lyfe of the thre kynges of Coleyn. [1496], [1499], 1511 (all de Worde); ed C. Horstmann 1886 (EETS) (from mss). Trn of John of Hildesheim, Historia trium regum.

Two fifteenth-century cookery-books. Ed T. Austin 1888 (EETS). BM mss Harley 279, 4016.

The dyalogus of communyng betw[i]xt Salomon and Marcolphus. Antwerp 1492 (Leeu); ed E. G. Duff 1892 (facs).

Informacion for pylgrymes unto the holy londe. [1498], 1515, 1524 (all de Worde); ed E. G. Duff 1893 (facs).

The English conquest of Ireland AD 1166–85. Ed F. J. Furnivall 1896 (EETS). Trn of Expugnatio hibernica by Giraldus Cambrensis; mss Trinity College Dublin E2.31 and Bodley Rawlinson B 490.

King Ponthus and the fair Sidone. Ed F. J. Mather, PMLA 12 1897. Bodley ms Digby 185; 2 extant prints by de Worde (1501, 1511) of a different version.

Melusine. 1510 (de Worde); ed A. K. Donald 1895 (EETS). Trn from French of Jean d'Arras; BM ms Harley 4418.

The three kings' sons. Ed F. J. Furnivall 1895 (EETS). Trn from French by David Aubert; BM ms Harley 326.

Jacob's well: an English treatise on the cleansing of man's conscience. Ed A. Brandeis, pt 1, 1900 (EETS). Salisbury Cathedral ms 103.

The English register of Godstow Nunnery, near Oxford written about 1450. Ed A. Clark 1905–6 (EETS).

Zwei frühneuenglische Prosaromane. Ed F. Brie, Archiv 118 1907. William of Palerne and Surdyt.

The English register of Oseney Abbey by Oxford written about 1460. Ed A. Clark 1907–13 (EETS).

A fifteenth-century courtesy book and two Franciscan rules. Ed R. W. Chambers and W. W. Seton 1914 (EETS).

The lanterne of light edited from ms Harley 2324. Ed L. M. Swinburn 1915 (EETS).

Peter Alphonse's Disciplina clericalis: English translation from the fifteenth-century Worcester Cathedral manuscript F 172. Ed W. H. Hulme, Cleveland 1919.

The book of the Knight of La Tour-Landry. Ed G. S. Taylor 1930. Modernized.

Mary of Nimmegen. Ed H. M. Ayres and A. J. Barnouw, Cambridge Mass and London 1932 (facs). From Doesborgh's text c. 1518.

English medieval lapidaries. Ed J. Evans and M. S. Serjeantson 1933 (EETS).

Acts of Court of the Mercers' Company 1453–1527. Ed L. Lyell and F. D. Watney, Cambridge 1936.

A Lollard tract: on translating the Bible into English. Ed C. F. Bühler, MÆ 7 1938.

A Lollard chronicle of the papacy. Ed E. W. Talbert, JEGP 41 1942. Emmanuel College Cambridge ms 1.4.6.

The book of vices and virtues. Ed W. N. Francis 1942 (EETS). Huntington Lib ms HM 147.

Ignorancia sacerdotum: a fifteenth-century discourse of the Lambeth constitutions. Ed P. Hodgson, RES 24 1948. Bodley ms Eng Th C. 57.

The four daughters of God: a new version. Ed R. A. Klinefelter, JEGP 52 1953. Trinity College Dublin ms 423.

The Middle English texts of Morgan ms 861. Ed C. F. Bühler, PMLA 69 1954. Prints a commentary on the Decalogue.

A devout treatyse called the tree and xii frutes of the holy goost. Ed J. J. Vaissier, Groningen 1960. Fitzwilliam Museum Cambridge ms McClean 132.

Mary of Nijmeghen (the female Faust) in an English prose version of the Tudor period. Ed M. Schlauch, Philologica Pragensia 6 1963.

The fifteenth-century prose Legend of the cross before Christ. Ed B. Hill, MÆ 34 1965. Worcester Cathedral Lib F.172.

Þe pater noster of Richard Ermyte: a late Middle English exposition of the Lord's prayer. Ed F. G. Aarts, Hague 1967. Westminster School Lib ms 3.

A dialogue between reason and adversity: a late Middle English version of Petrarch's De remediis. Ed F. N. M. Diekstra, Assen 1968. Cambridge Univ Lib ms Ii.vi.39.

A Middle English version of the Epistola Luciferi ad cleros. Ed R. R. Raymo, Medieval literature and civilisation: studies in memory of G. N. Garmonsway, 1969. Huntington Lib ms HM 114.

(6) MISCELLANEOUS

Steele, R. What fifteenth-century books are about. Library 2nd ser 4–6 1903–5, 8 1907.

Brie, F. Die erste Übersetzung einer italienischen Novelle ins Englische. Archiv 124 1910.

Peddie, R. A. Fifteenth-century books. 1913.

Duff, E. G. Fifteenth-century English books. 1917 (Bibl Soc).

Allen, H. E. The speculum vitae: addendum. PMLA 32 1917.

— Wynkyn de Worde and a second French compilation from the Ancrene Riwle with a description of the first (Trinity College Cambridge ms 883). In Essays and studies in honor of Carleton Brown, New York 1940.

Berdan, J. M. Early Tudor poetry. New York 1920.

Deanesly, M. Vernacular books in England in the fourteenth and fifteenth centuries. MLR 15 1920.

Plomer, H. R. Wynkyn de Worde and his contemporaries from the death of Caxton to 1535. 1925.

Campbell, P. G. C. Christine de Pisan en Angleterre. Revue de Littérature Comparée 5 1925.

Adamson, J. W. The extent of literacy in England in the fifteenth and sixteenth centuries: notes and conjectures. Library 4th ser 10 1930.

Schutt, J. H. A guide to English studies: the period of transition between Middle English and Elizabethan literature 1400–1560. E Studies 12 1930.

Schirmer, W. F. Der englische Frühhumanismus. Tübingen 1931, 1963.

— Dichter und Publikum zu Ende des 15 Jahrhunderts in England. Zeitschrift für Ästhetik und Allgemeine Kunstwissenschaft 28 1934.

— Das Ende des Mittelalters in England. In his Kleine Schriften, Tübingen 1950.

Baugh, A. C. Osbert of Clare, the Sarum breviary and the Middle-English Saint Anne in Rime Royal. Speculum 7 1932.

Bone, G. Extant manuscripts printed from by W. de Worde with notes on the owner Roger Thorney. Library 4th ser 12 1932.

Jacob, E. F. Florida verborum venustas: some early examples of Euphuism in England. Bull John Rylands Lib 17 1933.

Geary, B. H. N. A study of 15th-century English lyric verse from manuscripts and printed editions, with special attention to metrical form. Oxford 1934.

Starke, F. J. Populäre englische Chroniken des 15 Jahrhunderts. Berlin 1935.

Brentano, M. T. Relationship of the Latin facetus literature to the medieval English courtesy poems. Univ of Kansas Humanistic Stud 2 1935.

Weiss, R. The library of John Tiptoft, Earl of Worcester. Bodleian Quart Record 8 1935–7.

— Humanism in England during the fifteenth century. Oxford 1941.

— Portrait of a bibliophile. Book Collector 13 1964. Humphrey Duke of Gloucester.

Francis, F. C. Three unrecorded English books of the sixteenth century. Library 4th ser 17 1937.

Bennett, H. S. The author and his public in the fourteenth and fifteenth centuries. E & S 23 1937.

— Science and information in English writings of the fifteenth century. MLR 39 1944.

— Fifteenth-century secular prose. RES 21 1945.

— The production and dissemination of vernacular manuscripts in the fifteenth century. Library 5th ser 1947.

Lewis, C. S. The fifteenth-century heroic line. E & S 24 1938; rptd in his Selected literary essays, ed W. Hooper, Cambridge 1969.

Haselden, R. B. A scribe and printer in the fifteenth century. HLQ 2 1939.

Robbins, R. H. The arma Christi rolls. MLR 34 1939.

— The Findern anthology. PMLA 69 1954.

— Middle English carols as processional hymns. SP 56 1959.

— John Crophill's ale-pots. RES new ser 20 1969.

— Medical manuscripts in Middle English. Speculum 45 1970.

Schulz, H. C. Middle English texts from the Bement manuscript. HLQ 3 1940.

— Manuscript printer's copy for a lost early English book. Library 4th ser 22 1942. Huntington Lib ms HM 130.

— A Middle English manuscript used as printer's copy. HLQ 29 1966.

Workman, S. K. Fifteenth-century translation as an influence on English prose. Princeton 1940.

McCusker, H. The chronicles of England. More Books 16 1941.

O'Connor, Sr M. C. The art of dying well: the development of the Ars moriendi. New York 1942.

Munsterberg, M. The myrrour of the worlde. More Books 17 1942.

Grophill, John. The notebook of a fifteenth-century practising physician. Ed E. W. Talbert, SE 1942.

Goldschmidt, E. P. Medieval texts and their first appearance in print. 1943 (Bibl Soc).

de Beer, E. S. An English xv-century pilgrimage poem. N & Q 2 Dec 1944.

Kibre, P. The intellectual interests of the fourteenth and fifteenth centuries. JHI 7 1946.

Dunlap, A. R. A pilgrimage to the Holy Land. MLN 63 1948.

Clark, J. M. The dance of death in the Middle Ages and the Renaissance. Glasgow 1950.

Bühler, C. F. A fifteenth-century list of recommended books. New Colophon 3 1950.

— The first edition of the Abbey of the holy ghost. SB 6 1953.

— Prayers and charms in certain Middle English scrolls. Speculum 39 1964.

Chesney, K. Notes on some treatises of devotion intended for Margaret of York (ms Douce 365). MÆ 20 1951.

Owst, G. R. The Destructiorum viciorum of Alexander Carpenter: a fifteenth-century sequel to Literature and pulpit in medieval England. 1952.

Mead, H. A. A new title from de Worde's press. Library 5th ser 9 1954.

Prescott, H. F. M. Jerusalem journey: pilgrimage to the Holy Land in the fifteenth century. 1954.

Berry, F. A medieval poem and its secular derivative. EC 5 1955.

Doyle, A. I. The work of a late fifteenth-century English scribe, William Ebesham. Bull John Rylands Lib 39 1957.

Barbare, M. J. The Englishman abroad in the fifteenth century. Medievalia et Humanistica 11 1957.

Zeeman, E. Continuity and change in Middle English versions of the Meditationes vitae Christi. MÆ 26 1957.

Parkes, M. B. A fifteenth-century scribe: Henry Mere. Bodleian Lib Record 6 1961.

Davis, N. Scribal variation in late fifteenth-century English. In Mélanges de linguistique et de philologie, Paris 1959.

— Styles in English prose in the late Middle and early Modern period. Langue et Littérature: les Congrès et Colloques de l'Université de Liège 21 1961.

Wilson, R. M. On the continuity of English prose. In Mélanges de linguistique et de philologie, Paris 1959.

Silverstein, T. On the source of an English thunder-treatise of the fifteenth century. In Middle Ages—Reformation—Volkskunde: Festschrift for John G. Kunstmann, Chapel Hill 1959.

Moran, J. Wynkyn de Worde. 1960 (Wynkyn de Worde Soc).

Bushnell, G. H. Portrait of a book collector, William Schevez, Archbishop of St Andrews, d. 1497. Book Collector 9 1960.

Seaton, E. Sir Richard Roos c. 1410–82: Lancastrian poet. 1961.

Sajavaara, K. The two English prose texts of Robert the devil printed by Wynkyn de Worde. Neuphilologische Mitteilungen 63 1962.

Kurvinen, A. Two sixteenth-century editions of the Life of St Catherine of Alexandria. In English and medieval studies presented to J. R. R. Tolkien, 1962.

Pickford, C. E. Fiction and the reading public in the fifteenth century. Bull John Rylands Lib 45 1963.

Smith, K. I. A fifteenth-century vernacular manuscript reconstructed. Bodleian Lib Record 7 1967.

O'Sullivan, W. John Manyngham: an early Oxford humanist. Ibid.

Schlauch, M. Antecedents of the English novel 1400–1600. Warsaw and London 1963.

— English short fiction in the fifteenth and sixteenth centuries. Stud in Short Fiction 3 1966.

Barber, M. J. The books and patronage of learning of a fifteenth-century prince. Book Collector 12 1963. John Duke of Bedford.

Tuve, R. Notes on the vices and virtues, 1: Two fifteenth-century lines of dependence on the thirteenth and twelfth centuries. Jnl Warburg & Courtauld Inst 26 1963.

Boyd, B. The Middle English miracles of the Virgin. San Marino 1964.

Mitchell, R. J. The spring voyage: the Jerusalem pilgrimage in 1458. 1964.

Balu, J. L. An unpublished English translation of Justinian's life of Columbus. Columbia Lib Columns 13 1964.

Matthews, W. Medieval secular literature: four essays. Berkeley 1965.

Rigg, A. G. Some notes on Trinity College Cambridge ms O.9.38. N & Q Sept 1966.

Moe, P. Cleveland manuscript W q091.92–C468 and the Veronica legend. BNYPL Sept 1966.

Dickison R, Didacticism in the fifteenth-century novella and folktale. Southern Folklore Quart 30 1966.

Murphy, J. J. A fifteenth-century treatise on prose style. Newberry Lib Bull 6 1966. On Merke, De moderno dictamine.

Hirsch, R. Printing, selling and reading 1450–1550. Wiesbaden 1967.

Christian, Sr M. A study in fifteenth-century flamboyant style. Bull Pennsylvania Council of Teachers of Eng 15 1967.

Seymour, M. C. A fifteenth-century East Anglian scribe. MÆ 37 1968.

Dickins, B. The nine unworthies. In Medieval literature and civilization: studies in memory of G. N. Garmonsway, 1969.

Blake, N. F. Wynkyn de Worde and the Quatrefoil of love. Archiv 206 1969.

— Wynkyn de Worde: the early years. Gutenberg-Jahrbuch 1971.

— Wynkyn de Worde: the later years. Gutenberg-Jahrbuch 1972.

Scattergood, V. J. Politics and poetry in the fifteenth century. 1971.

N. F. B.

4. SONGS AND BALLADS

I. SONGS AND LYRICS

Index The index of ME verse ed C. Brown and R. H. Robbins, and Supplement ed Robbins and J. L. Cutler, below.

(1) BIBLIOGRAPHIES

Wells, J. E. A manual of the writings in ME 1050–1400. New Haven 1916; 8 suppls 1919, 1923, 1926, 1929, 1932, 1935, 1938, 1941.

Brown, C. Register of religious and didactic verse. 2 vols Oxford 1916–20. On 1200–1500. Vol 1, list of mss and contents; vol 2, index of first lines (with ptd edns) and index of subjects and titles. Expanded below.

Brown, C. and R. H. Robbins. The index of ME verse. New York 1943. Alphabetical list of first lines of all verse till about 1500 with mss and edns.

Robbins, R. H. and J. L. Cutler. Supplement to the Index of ME verse. Lexington Kentucky 1965. Corrections and addns.

Chambers, E. K. In his English literature at the close of the Middle Ages, Oxford 1945 (OHEL).

(2) EDITIONS

Ritson, J. A select collection of English songs. 3 vols 1783.
— Ancient songs. 1790 (probably for 1792).
Hamper, W. Sarcastic verses written in the time of Richard II. Archaeologia 21 1827.
Sandys, W. Christmas carols, ancient and modern. 1833. Mainly from BM additional mss 5465, 5665.
— Festive songs, principally of the 16th and 17th centuries. 1848 (Percy Soc).
— Christmas tide. 1852.
Wright, T. Songs and carols. 1836. Sloane ms 2593.
— The political songs of England from the reign of John to that of Edward II. 1839 (Camden Soc).
— Specimens of old Christmas carols. 1841 (Percy Soc).
— Specimens of lyric poetry composed in the reign of Edward the First. 1842 (Percy Soc). Harley ms 2253.
— Religious songs [with Owl and nightingale]. 1843 (Percy Soc).
— Songs and carols, from a ms of the 15th century. 1847 (Percy Soc). Bodley ms Eng poets E I.
- Songs and carols. 1856 (Warton Club). Sloane ms 2593.
— Political poems and songs. 2 vols 1859–61 (Rolls ser). Edward III–Richard III.
Madden, F. Political poems of the reigns of Henry VI and Edward IV. Archaeologia 29 1842.
Fairholt, F. W. Satirical songs. 1842 (Percy Soc).
Wright, T. and J. O. Halliwell(-Phillipps). Reliquiae antiquae. 2 vols 1845.
Halliwell(-Phillipps), J. O. Early English miscellanies in prose and verse. 1855 (Warton Club). Brogynton (Porkington) ms 10.
Furnivall, F. J. Early English poems and lives of saints. Berlin 1862.
— Political, religious and love poems. 1866 (EETS), 1903 (rev). Mainly from Lambeth ms 306.
— Hymns to the Virgin and Christ, the Parliament of Devils etc. 1867 (EETS), 1895 (rev). Lambeth ms 853.
— Religious poems from ms Digby 2. Archiv 97 1896. See also 86 1891.
— Minor poems of the Vernon ms part II. 1901 (EETS). Also includes poems from mss Digby 2, 86.
Hazlitt, W. C. Remains of the early popular poetry of England. 4 vols 1864–6.
Perry, G. G. Religious pieces in prose and verse. 1867 (EETS), 1913 (rev). Thornton ms.
Morris, R. Old English homilies. 2 pts 1867–8 (EETS).
— OE miscellany. 1872 (EETS).
Böddeker, K. Altenglische Dichtungen des ms Harleian 2253. Berlin 1878.
Flügel, E. Liedersammlungen des 16 Jahrhunderts, besonders aus der Zeit Heinrichs VIII. Anglia 12 1889, 26 1903. Mss: Balliol 354, BM additional 31,922, Royal App 58 etc.
— Kleinere Mitteilungen aus Handschriften. Anglia 14 1891.
— Englische Weihnachtslieder aus einer Handschrift des Balliol College zu Oxford. In Forschungen zur deutschen Philologie: Festgabe für Rudolf Hildebrand, Leipzig 1894. Balliol College ms 354.
— Neuenglisches Lesebuch. Halle 1895.
Jacoby, M. Vier mittelenglische geistliche Gedichte. Berlin 1890.
Songs and madrigals of the 15th century. 1891 (Plain-song Soc).
Fuller-Maitland, J. A. and W. S. Rockstro. English carols of the 15th century. 1891. Trinity College Cambridge ms O.3.58.
Horstmann, C. Minor poems of the Vernon ms part I. 1892 (EETS).
— Yorkshire writers. 2 vols 1895–6. R. Rolle et al.
Napier, A. S. A ME Compassio Mariae. 1894 (EETS).

Hall, J. Short pieces from ms Cotton Galba E IX. E Studien 21 1895.
— Selections from early ME 1130–1250. 2 vols Oxford 1920.
Fehr, B. Die Lieder des Fairfax Ms. Archiv 106 1901. BM ms additional 5465.
— Die Lieder des Ms additional 5665. Archiv 106 1901.
— Weitere Beiträge zur englischen Lyrik des 15 und 16 Jahrhunderts. Archiv 107 1901. Mss Sloane 2593, 1212, 3501; Harley 541, 367, 7578.
— Die Lieder der Ms Sloane 2593. Archiv 109 1902.
Stainer, J. Early Bodleian music. 2 vols Oxford 1901. Bodley ms Selden B. 26.
Pollard, A. W. 15th-century prose and verse. 1903.
Kail, J. Twenty-six political and other poems. 1904 (EETS). Mss Digby 102, Douce 322.
Heuser, W. With an O and an I. Anglia 27 1904. Index 2021, 2663, 1001, 3921, 701, 412.
— Ave Maria. Ibid. Index 1024.
— Die Kildare-gedichte. Bonner Beiträge zur Anglistik 14 1904. Ms Harley 913.
— Die Katherinenhymne des Ricardus Spaldyng und eine Marienhymne derselben Pergamentrolle. Anglia 30 1907. See Holthausen 59 1935, 60 1936. Index 1813, 2171.
— Fragmente von unbekannten Spielmannsliedern des 14 Jahrhunderts, aus Ms Rawl. D 913. Anglia 30 1907.
Padelford, F. M. Early 16th-century lyrics. Boston 1907.
— The songs in ms Rawlinson C 813. Anglia 31 1908.
— English songs in ms Selden B 26. Anglia 36 1912.
Chambers, E. K. and F. Sidgwick. Early English lyrics. 1907 etc. Introduction rptd in Chambers, Sir Thomas Wyatt and some collected studies, 1933.
Dyboski, R. Songs, carols and other miscellaneous pieces from Balliol ms 354. 1907 (EETS).
Quiller-Couch, A. T. Early English lyrics. Oxford 1908.
Root, R. K. Poems from the Garrett ms. E Studien 41 1910.
Jordan, R. Kleinere Dichtungen der Handschrift Harley 3810. E Studien 41 1910.
Patterson, F. A. The ME penitential lyric. New York 1911.
— Hymnal from BM ms additional 34,193. In Medieval studies in memory G. S. Loomis, New York 1927.
15th-century metrical trns of Latin hymns.
Hurry, J. B. Sumer is icumen in. 1913, 1914 (rev).
James, M. R. and G. C. Macaulay. 15th-century carols and other pieces. MLR 8 1913. St John's Cambridge ms S. 54.
MacCracken, H. N. Unprinted texts from the ms Trinity College Cambridge R.3.21. Archiv 130 1913.
Rickert, E. Ancient English Christmas carols 1400–1700. 1914.
Segar, M. G. Some minor poems of the Middle Ages. 1917.
Day, M. Poems of the Wheatley ms (BM additional 39,574). 1917 (EETS).
D'Evelyn, C. Meditations on the life and passion of Christ. 1919 (EETS); corrected in Essays and studies in honor of Carleton Brown, New York 1940. Index 1034.
Sisam K. 14th-century verse and prose. Oxford 1921, 1937 (rev).
Brown, C. Religious lyrics of the xivth century. Oxford 1924; rev G. V. Smithers, Oxford 1952.
— English lyrics of the xiiith century. Oxford 1932.
— Religious lyrics of the xvth century. Oxford 1939.
Holthausen, F. Ein mittelenglischer Hymnus auf Maria und Christus und seine kymrische Umschrift. Archiv 140 1920. Index 2514.
— Ein mittelenglischer Hymnus auf Maria und Christus. In Anglica: Brandl Festschrift, Leipzig 1925. Addn to preceding entry. Notes in Anglia Beiblatt 50 1939.

—— Ein mittelenglisches Gedicht über die fünf Freuden Marias. Anglia 59 1935. Index 2171. *See* Heuser 30 1907.

—— Ein mittelenglischer Katharinenhymnus von Richard Spalding. Anglia 60 1936. *See* Heuser 30 1907.

Masters, J. E. Rymes of the minstrels: selected from a ms of the 15th century. Shaftesbury 1927. Bodley ms Eng poets e. i.

Dearmer, P. and R. Vaughan Williams. The Oxford book of carols. Oxford 1928.

Bullock, C. The enemies of man. RES 5 1929. Index 3462.

Brown, B. D. Religious lyrics in ms Don C. 13. Bodleian Quart Record 7 1932. Index 1320, 1733.

Reed, E. B. Christmas carols printed in 16th century. Cambridge Mass 1932.

Greene, R. L. A ME timor mortis poem. MLR 28 1933. Index 3743.

—— The early English carols. Oxford 1935.

—— A ME love poem and the O- and -I refrain-phrase. MÆ 30 1961. Index 3098.5.

—— A selection of English carols. Oxford 1962. Selects from and adds to his Early English carols, above.

Brunner, K. Mittelenglische Marienstunden. E Studien 70 1935. Index 3904.

—— Mittelenglische Todesgedichte. Archiv 167 1935. Index 491, 1563, 2589.

—— Ein typisches Bussgedicht aus dem 15 Jahrhundert. Anglia 59 1935. Index 532.

—— Kirchenlieder aus dem 15 Jahrhundert. Anglia 61 1937. Index 1073, 1048, 1079, 3240, 236, 1892.

Brunner, K. and K. Hammerle. With an O and an I. Anglia 54 1930.

Dickins, B. Worcester fragments of the ME secular lyric. Leeds Stud in Eng 4 1935.

Hammerle, K. Verstreute me und frühne Lyrik. Archiv 166 1935. Index *69, 4116, 4083, 2902, 2683, 2343.

Saltmarsh, J. Two medieval love-songs set to music. Antiquaries Jnl 15 1935. Index 521, 2293.5.

Bennett, H. S. Quia amore langueo. 1937.

Bühler C. F. A ME prayer roll. MLN 52 1937. Index 2470.

—— A ME versified prayer to the Trinity. MLN 66 1951. Index 246.

—— ME verses against thieves. Speculum 33 1958. Index 4154.8 is distinct from herbal, Index 2627. Also prints Index 1952.5. *See* J. D. Vann 34 1959 (Index 242.5) and Bühler's addn.

—— A ME stanza on the Commonwealth and the need for wisdom. Eng Lang Notes 2 1965. Prints verse similar to Index 2820 which is part of another poem.

Hayes, G. King's music: an anthology. 1937.

Kreuzer, J. R. Some earlier examples of the rhetorical device in Ralph Roister Doister. RES 14 1938. Includes punctuation verses.

Robbins, R. H. English almanacks of the 15th century. PQ 18 1939. Reply by M. Förster 19 1940. Index 3265.

—— The Arma Christi rolls. MLR 34 1939. Index 2577.

—— Gurney series of religious lyrics. PMLA 54 1939. Index 271, 3882 etc.

—— Popular prayers in ME verse. MP 36 1939. Index 1704, 1687, 1586 etc.

—— Private prayers in ME verse. SP 36 1939. Index 2119, 1703, 241 etc.

—— Punctuation poems: a further note. RES 15 1939.

—— Two 14th-century mystical poems. MLR 35 1940. Index 8, 1747.

—— Levation prayers in ME verse. MP 40 1942. Index 2512, 1052 etc.

—— Two ME satiric love epistles. MLR 37 1942. Index 3832, 2437.

—— A Gawain epigone. MLN 58 1943. Form of verse; disputed by J. L. Cutler, JEGP 51 1952. Index 2682.

—— Two new carols, Hunterian ms 83. MLN 58 1943. Index 889, 182.

—— Secular lyrics of the 14th and 15th centuries. Oxford 1952, 1955 (rev).

—— A late 15th-century love lyric. MLN 69 1954. Index 3707.8.

—— Consilium Domini in eternum manet (Harley ms 2252). Studia Neophilologica 26 1954. Index 2521.

—— A song for victory in France 1492. Neuphilologische Mitteilungen 55 1954. Index 306.8.

—— Five ME verse prayers from Lambeth ms 541. Neophilologus 38 1954. Index 874, 1666, 1736, 1947, 3454.

—— A late 15th-century love lyric. MLN 69 1954. Index 3707.8.

—— ME versions of Christe qui lux es et dies. Harvard Theological Rev 47 1954. Index 616 etc.

—— A love epistle by Chaucer. MLR 49 1954. Index 1838 not by Chaucer.

—— The world upside down: a ME amphibole. Anglia 72 1954. Index 2805.

—— An unkind mistress. MLN 69 1954. Index 2599.

—— The Findern anthology. PMLA 69 1954. Catalogues contents of Cambridge Univ Lib ms Ff.1.6 and prints Index 4059, 3917, 2279, 2568, 3878, 3125, 159, 657, 853, 3613, 3948, 4241.5, 4272.5.

—— An epitaph for Duke Humphrey 1447. Neuphilologische Mitteilungen 56 1955. Index 3206.

—— God amende wykkyd cownscell 1464. Ibid. Index 372.

—— A warning against lechery. PQ 35 1956. Index 551. *See* R. H. Bowers, MLN 70 1955.

—— Historical poems of the 14th and 15th centuries. New York 1959.

—— An early rudimentary carol. MLR 54 1959. Index 3662.

—— Isabel: a riddling mistress. Eng Lang Notes 1 1963. Riddling name poems. Index 597.5.

—— Wall verses at Launceston Priory. Archiv 200 1963. Index 3088, 4135.5 etc.

—— Good gossips reunited. BM Quart 27 1963. Index *32.

—— An English nativity song from a Latin processional. Amer N & Q 2 1964. Index 2348.

—— The Bradshaw carols. PMLA 81 1966. Index 3328.5, 2635.5, 3443.5, 1344.5.

Schulz, H. C. ME texts from the Bement ms. HLQ 3 1940. Index 2469, 2473, 2306, 2118, 1831.

Copley, J. Seven English songs and carols of 15th century. Leeds 1940. Index 670, 3806, 2381, 925, 3259, 353, 753.

Menner, R. J. Three fragmentary English ballades in the Mellon Chansonnier. MLQ 6 1945.

Utley, F. L. When nettles in winter bring forth roses red. PMLA 60 1945.

—— The choristers' lament. Speculum 21 1946. Index 3819.

Schofield, B. A newly discovered 15th-century ms of the English Chapel Royal—pt 1. Musical Quart 32 1946. Egerton ms 3307 includes music and words of some unique carols. Article has thematic index but full text of Index 4229.5 only.

Brook, G. L. The Harley lyrics [2253]. Manchester 1948, 1956 (rev).

Bowers, R. H. ME poems by Mydwynter. MLN 64 1949. Index 2063, 2079.

—— Palden's ME prayer. N & Q 31 March 1951. Index 1750. *See* note by K. Sisam 9 June 1951.

—— The ME Oon sleth the deer wyth an hookid arwe. Southern Folklore Quart 15 1951. Index 2696.

—— Hichecoke's This worlde is but a vanyte (Huntington ms 183). MLN 67 1952. Index 1261.

—— Advice resented: a ME court of love poem (Corpus Christi College ms 61). PQ 31 1952. Index 2594.

—— The ME The fox and the goose. JEGP 51 1952. Index 1622.

—— A ME mnemonic poem on usury. Mediaeval Stud 17 1955. Index 2671.

—— A ME Rake's progress poem. MLN 70 1955. Index 551. *See* R. H. Robbins, PQ 35 1956.

—— A ME poem on the seven gifts of the Holy Ghost. MLN 70 1955. Index 215.

—— When cuckow time cometh oft so soon: a ME animal prophecy. Anglia 73 1955. Index 3375.

—— Three ME poems on the Apostle's creed. PMLA 70 1955. Index 1374, 311, 2700.

—— Versus compositi de Roger Belers. JEGP 56 1957. Index 2172.

—— A ME wheel of fortune poem. E Studies 41 1960. Index *4267.5.

—— Three ME religious poems. Gainesville 1963.

Cawley, A. C. A York fragment of ME secular lyric. Speculum 26 1951. 4 lines from no extant poem?

Dickins, B. and R. M. Wilson. Early ME texts. Cambridge 1951.

Kane, G. The ME verse in ms Wellcome 1493. London Mediaeval Stud 2 1951. Index 3985, 3120; cf 576.

Smith A. H. The ME lyrics in Additional ms 45,896. London Mediaeval Stud 2 1951. Index 2614.5, 2012; cf 2020-2.

Wright, C. E. Late ME parerga in a school collection. RES new ser 2 1951. Index 4028.6.

Stevens, J. Musica britannica IV: medieval carols. 1952. English, Latin and macaronic carols chiefly from mss Trinity College, Cambridge O.3.58; Bodley, Selden b.26 and Ashmole 1393; and BM Egerton 3307 and additional mss 5665-6.

Kurvinen, A. Ms Porkington 10: description with extracts. Neuphilologische Mitteilungen 54 1953.

Person, H. A. Cambridge ME lyrics. Seattle 1953, 1962 (rev). 70 lyrics from Cambridge Univ and College library mss.

Wilson, K. G. Five fugitive pieces of 15th-century secular verse. MLN 69 1954. Index 2412, 2440, 588, 1170, 4060.

—— The lay of sorrow and the lufaris complaynt: an edition. Speculum 29 1954. Index 482, 564. Further linguistic and textual notes by P. J. Frankis. Neuphilologische Mitteilungen 61 1960.

—— Five unpublished secular love poems from ms Trinity College Cambridge 599. Anglia 72 1954. Index 2384.8, 2588.5, 190.5, 2478.5, 1838.

—— The complaint against hope. Ann Arbor 1957. Index 370.

Bennett, J. A. W. Devotional pieces in verse and prose from mss Arundel 285 and Harleian 6919. 1955.

Cutler, J. L. A ME acrostic. MLN 70 1955. Index 2136.

Frankis, P. J. Some late ME lyrics in the Bodleian library. Anglia 73 1955. Index 2535.5, 1864.5, 4284.3.

Ross, T. W. Five 15th-century emblem verses from BM additional ms 37,049. Speculum 32 1957. Index 2507, 38, 269, 637, 149.

—— On the evil times of Edward II: a new version from ms Bodley 48. Anglia 75 1957. Index 4165, 1992.

Frankis, P. J. Two minor French lyric forms in English. Neuphilologische Mitteilungen 60 1959. Index 1470.

Stanley, E. G. An inedited scrap of ME verse from the W. Midlands. Neuphilologische Mitteilungen 60 1959. Index 1531.5.

Wilson, S. The Longleat version of Love is life. RES new ser 10 1959. Index 2007. 3 poems not one?

Mead, E. V. Cristene man þu lerne of love: a medieval lyric. MLR 55 1960. Index 631.5.

Dronke, P. The Rawlinson lyrics. N & Q July 1961. New ms readings.

Gray, D. Two songs of death. Neuphilologische Mitteilungen 64 1963. In 17th-century mss; survival of Dance of Death.

Davies R. T. Medieval English lyrics: a critical anthology. 1963.

Ker, N. R. Facsimile of BM ms Harley 2253: the Harley lyrics. 1964 (EETS).

—— ME verses and a Latin letter in a ms at Stanbrook Abbey. MÆ 34 1965. Index 1793.6, 4242.5.

Stevick, R. D. One hundred ME lyrics. Indianapolis 1964.

Lass, R. Three ME cautionary lyrics from a Yale Univ ms. Anglia 83 1965. Index 2820, 2371 and 8 lines beginning The wyse man his sone for bede/Masons crafte, not in Index.

Wilson, E. An unpublished late ME poem. N & Q Sept 1965. 7 lines beginning Fayr laydis I pray yow tillme, unpbd and not in Index.

Bennett, J. A. W. and G. V. Smithers. Early ME verse and prose. Oxford 1966, 1968 (rev).

Scattergood, V. J. An unpublished ME poem. Archiv 203 1967. 70 lines beginning Ffro this worlde be gynyng, unpbd and not in Index.

Hirsch, J. C. Two English devotional poems of the 15th century. N & Q Jan 1968. Index 2577, 3443.

Hargreaves, H. ME lyrics in an Aberdeen University library ms. Aberdeen Univ Rev 43 1969. Index 4038, 3902, 4129.

Hodder, K. Two unpublished ME carol-fragments. Archiv 205 1969. Variants of Index 1471, 2036, 2111 etc in BM ms additional 31,042.

Modern Renderings

See also under Rolle, col 517, above.

Weston, J. L. The chief ME poets. Boston 1914.

Segar, M. G. A medieval anthology. 1915.

Adamson, M. R. A treasury of ME verse. 1930.

Comper, F. M. M. Spiritual songs from English mss of 14th to 16th centuries. 1936.

Loomis, R. S. and R. Willard. Medieval English verse and prose in modernized versions. New York 1948. Includes select lyrics from 13th century to 15th.

Robbins, R. H. Early English Christmas carols. 1961.

Stone, B. ME verse. 1964 (Penguin).

(3) STUDIES

Many edns above include important studies.

Warton, T. The history of English poetry. 3 vols 1774-81; rev W. C. Hazlitt et al 4 vols 1871.

Stengel, E. Codicem manu scriptum Digby 86. Halle 1871.

Grove, G. Dictionary of music and musicians. 4 vols 1878-89.

Schröder, E. Zur Marienlyrik. Zeitschrift für Deutsches Althertum 25 1881.

Schipper, J. Englische Metrik in historischer und systematischer Entwickelung dargestellt. 2 vols Bonn 1881-8.

—— A history of English versification. Oxford 1910.

Schlüter, A. Ueber die Sprache und Metrik der mittelenglischen Lieder der ms 2253. Archiv 71 1884.

Aust, J. Beiträge zur Geschichte der mittelenglischen Lyrik. Archiv 70 1884.

Vollhardt, W. Einfluss der lateinischen geistlichen Literatur auf einige kleinere Schöpfungen der englischen Übergangsperiode. Leipzig 1888.

Koelbing, E. Kleine Beiträge. E Studien 17 1892.

Lauchert, F. Über das englische Marienlied im 13 Jahrhundert. E Studien 16 1892.

Crowest, F. J. The story of British music. 1896.

Weichardt, C. Die Entwicklung des Naturgefühls. Kiel 1900.

Gummere, F. B. The beginnings of poetry. New York 1901.

Crowne, J. V. ME poems on the Virgin Mary. Catholic Univ Bull 8 1901.

Mayor, J. B. Chapters on English metre. Cambridge 1901. The Oxford history of music. Oxford 1901.

Fröhlich, W. De lamentatione S. Marie. Leipzig 1902.

Chambers, E. K. The medieval stage. 2 vols Oxford 1903. On minstrels etc.

Heider, O. Untersuchungen zum mittelenglischen erotischen Gedichte. Halle 1905.

Haessner, M. Die Goliardendichtung und die Satire im 13 Jahrhundert in England. Leipzig 1905.

Holthausen, F. Beiträge zur Quellenkunde der mittelenglischen geistlichen Lyrik. Archiv 116 1906.

Thien, H. Über die mittelenglischen Marienklagen. Kiel 1906.

Saintsbury, G. A history of English prosody. 1906.

Manitius, M. Die englische Satire des 12 Jahrhunderts. Allgemeine Zeitung, Beilage 1906.

Grossmann, W. Fruhmittelenglische Zeugnisse über Minstrels. Berlin 1906.

Duncan, E. The story of minstrelsy. New York 1907.

Marufke, W. Der älteste englische Marienhymnus. Breslau 1907.

Taylor, G. C. The English planctus Mariae. MP 4 1907.
— The relations of the English Corpus Christi play to the ME religious lyric. MP 5 1907.

Tucker, S. M. Verse satire in England before the Renaissance. New York 1908.

Wolderich, W. Über die Sprache und Heimat einiger frühmittelenglischen religiösen Gedichte der Jesus und Cotton mss. Halle 1909.

Previté-Orton, C. W. Political satire in English poetry. Cambridge 1910.

Müller, A. Mittelenglische geistlichen und weltlichen Lyrik des 13 Jahrhunderts. Studien zur Englischen Philologie 44 1911.

Taylor, R. Political prophecy in England. New York 1911.

Brandl, A. Spielmannsverhältnisse im Frühmittelenglischen. Berlin 1911.

Chaytor, H. J. The troubadours. Cambridge 1912.
— Troubadours and England. Cambridge 1923.

Corsdress, H. Die Motive der mittelenglischen geistlichen Lyrik. Weimar 1913.

Sandison, H. E. Chanson d'aventure in ME. Bryn Mawr 1913.

Spalding, M. C. ME charters of Christ. Bryn Mawr 1914.

Benson, L. F. The English hymn. 1915.

Cohen, H. L. The ballade. New York 1915.

Dodds, M. H. Political prophecy in the reign of King John. MLR 11 1916.

Medary, M. P. and A. C. L. Brown. Stanza-linking. Romanic Rev 7 1916.

Eberhard, O. Der Bauernaufstand vom Jahre 1381 in der englischen Poesie. Anglistische Forschungen 51 1917.

Allen, H. E. Mystical lyrics of Manuel des péchiez. Romanic Rev 9 1918.

Osmond, M. Mystical poets of the English church. New York 1919.

Audiau, J. Les troubadours et l'Angleterre. Tulle 1920.

Liebermann, F. Zu Liedrefrain und Tanz im englischen Mittelalter. Archiv 140 1920.

Berdan, J. M. Early Tudor poetry 1485–1547. New York 1920.

Phillips, W. J. Carols: their origin, music and connection with mystery plays. 1921.

Werner, H. Die Ursprünge der Lyrik. Munich 1924.

Walker, H. English satire and satirists. 1925.

Foerster, M. Datierung und Charakter des kymrisch-englischen Marienhymnus. Archiv 150 1926.

Gillman, F. J. The evolution of the English hymn. 1927.

Allen, B. The debate of the soul and the body in ms Digby 86. MLR 22 1927.

Reed, E. B. Wynter wakeneth al my care. MLN 43 1928. Index 4177.

Jones, W. P. The pastourelle: a study of the origins and tradition. Cambridge Mass 1931.

Hammerle, K. Die mittelenglische Hymnodie. Anglia 55 1931.

Holthausen, F. Zu mittelenglischen Dichtungen. Anglia 56 1932. Adds to Heuser's Die Katherinenhymne etc 30 1907.

Singer, S. Die religiöse Lyrik des Mittelalters. Berne 1933. Psalms and the lyric.

Owst, G. R. Literature and pulpit in medieval England. Cambridge 1933, Oxford 1961 (with addns).

Brook, G. L. The original dialects of the Harley lyrics. Leeds Stud in Eng 2 1933.

Kar, G. Thoughts on the medieval lyric. Oxford 1933.

Wehrle, W. O. The macaronic hymn tradition in medieval English literature. Washington 1933.

Little, A. G. The Lamport fragment of Eccleston and its connections. EHR 49 1934.

Malone, K. Notes on ME lyrics. ELH 2 1935. On C. Brown's 13th-century lyrics.
— Further notes on ME lyrics. ELH 23 1956. On Brown's 14th-century religious lyrics rev G. V. Smithers. See Smithers, Eng Philological Stud 9 1965.

Raby, F. J. E. A ME paraphrase of John of Hoveden's Philomena and the text of his Viola. MLR 30 1935. Source of Meditations on life and passion of Christ: see D'Evelyn, below.

Thomson, S. H. The date of the early English translation of the Candet nudatum pectus. MÆ 4 1935.

Pearson, L. E. Isolable lyrics of the Mystery plays. ELH 3 1936.

McGarry, L. The Holy Eucharist in ME homiletic and devotional verse. Washington 1937.

Ericson, E. E. Bullock sterteþ, bucke verteþ. MLN 53 1938.

Robbins, R. H. The earliest carols and the Franciscans. Ibid.
— The authors of the ME religious lyrics. JEGP 39 1940.
— The burden in the carols. MLN 57 1942.
— On dating a ME moral poem. MLN 70 1955. Index 884 dated 1456.
— Friar Herebert and the carol. Anglia 75 1957.
— The ME carol corpus: some additions. MLN 74 1959. List of carols, mostly ptd.
— ME carols as processional hymns. SP 56 1959.
— ME poems of protest. Anglia 78 1960.
— ME lyrics: handlist of new texts. Anglia 83 1965. Over 100 unpbd lyrics with Index nos.
— A highly critical approach to the ME lyric. College Eng Oct 1968.

Brown, C. See myche, say lytell and lerne to soffer in tyme. MLN 54 1939. Authorship. Index 3083.
— The temptation and the fall: additional notes to religious lyrics of the 15th century. TLS 6 Jan 1940. Reply by W. Bliss 20 Jan 1940.

D'Evelyn, C. Meditations on the life and passion of Christ, In Essays and studies in honor of Carleton Brown, New York 1940. Corrects her EETS 1919 edn of Index 1034, 1761.

Greene, R. L. The traditional survival of two medieval carols. ELH 7 1940. Index 30, 22.
— The Maid of the Moor in the Red Book of Ossory. Speculum 27 1952.
— The port of peace: not death but God. MLN 69 1954. Index 1254.
— Two medieval musical mss: Egerton 3307 and some University of Chicago fragments. Jnl of Amer Musicological Soc 7 1954.
— The meaning of the Corpus Christi carol. MÆ 29 1960.
— The burden and the Scottish variant of the Corpus Christi carol. MÆ 33 1964.

—— If I sing, tie up your cows. N & Q March 1964. Index 1417; on meaning of line 8.

Heningman, E. K. Old English precursors of the Worcester fragments. PMLA 55 1940. Address of soul to body.

Menner, R. J. Notes on ME lyrics. MLN 55 1940. On C. Brown's collections of 13th- and 14th-century lyrics.

—— The man in the moon and hedging. JEGP 48 1949. Index 2066.

Mary Immaculate, Sr. Note on A song of the five joys. MLN 55 1940. Index 359.

Collins, A. J. ME devotional pieces. BM Quart 14 1940. Those in Egerton ms 3245 (= Gurney ms).

Sahlin, M. Etude sur la carole médiévale: l'origine du mot et ses rapports avec l'église. Upsala 1940.

Reese, G. Music in the Middle Ages. 1941.

Olson, C. C. The minstrels at the Court of Edward III. PMLA 56 1941.

Meroney, H. Man must fight three foes. MLN 58 1943. Index 2166.

—— Line notes on the early English lyric. MLN 62 1947.

Bukofzer, M. F. 'Sumer is icumen in': a revision. Univ of California Pbns in Music 2 1944. Written 1300–25.

—— Some sources of 15th-century English music. Renaissance News 2 1949.

—— Studies in medieval and Renaissance music. New York 1950.

Cutler, J. L. Nou goth sonne under wod. Explicator 4 1945.

Hoepfner, T. C. 'Sumer is icumen in'. Explicator 3 1945. See also H. Brown and J. S. Kenyon, ibid.

Arngart, O. Al hende ase hak in chete. E Studies 28 1947.

Onions, C. T. Two notes on ME texts. MÆ 17 1948. Index 360.

Schofield, B. The provenance and date of Sumer is icumen in. Music Rev 9 1948.

Miller, C. K. The early English carol. Renaissance News 3 1950.

Wolpers, T. Geschichte der englischen Marienlyrik im Mittelalter. Anglia 69 1950.

Robertson, D. W. Historical criticism. New York 1950. Includes an analysis of Maiden in the mor lay.

Schoeck, R. J. The maid of the moor. TLS 8 June 1951.

—— Alliterative assonance in Harley ms 2253. E Studies 32 1951.

Spitzer, L. Explication de texte applied to three great ME poems. Archivum Linguisticum 3 1951. Index 1367, 1395, 1893.

—— Emendations proposed to De amico ad amicam and Responcio. MLN 67 1952.

Opie, I. and P. The Oxford dictionary of nursery rhymes. Oxford 1951, 1952 (rev).

Ing, C. Elizabethan lyrics: a study in development of English metres. 1951.

Kane, G. ME literature: a critical study of romances, religious lyrics, Piers Plowman. 1951.

Moore, A. K. The secular lyric in ME. Lexington Kentucky 1951.

Wright, C. E. Late ME parerga in a school collection. RES new ser 2 1951. Scribbled nature-notes in verse.

Telfer, J. M. The evolution of a medieval theme. Durham Univ Jnl 14 1952. On the nightingale.

Bazire, J. The fox and the goose. E Studies 34 1953. On Robbins, Secular lyrics, and R. H. Bowers, JEGP 51 1952.

Kurvinen, A. Ms Porkington [Brogynton] 10. Neuphilologische Mitteilungen 54 1953.

Thayer, C. G. Nou goth sonne under wod. Explicator 11 1953.

Hodgart, M. J. C. Medieval lyrics and the ballads. In The age of Chaucer, ed B. Ford 1954 (Pelican).

Copley, J. The 15th-century carol and Christmas. N & Q June 1954.

—— Two notes on early English carols. N & Q June 1958. On clerical and pagan elements.

—— A popular 15th-century carol. N & Q Nov 1959 Index 21.

—— I syng of a myden. N & Q April 1962.

Stuart, H. L. D. A wayle whyt ase whalles bon reconstructed. JEGP 53 1954.

Hughes, Dom A. The motet and allied forms. In New Oxford history of music vol 2, Oxford 1954. Includes Sumer is icumen in.

Westrup, J. A. Medieval song. Ibid.

Berry, F. A medieval poem and its secularized derivative. EC 5 1955; rptd in his Poet's grammar, 1958. Index 1132.

Mustanoja, T. F. ME With an O and an I. Neuphilologische Mitteilungen 56 1955.

Frankis, P. J. The erotic dream in medieval English lyrics. Neuphilologische Mitteilungen 57 1956.

—— Notes on two 15th-century Scots poems. Neuphilologische Mitteilungen 61 1960. Index 482, 564.

Peter, J. D. Complaint and satire in early English literature. Oxford 1956.

Cutts, J. P. The second Coventry carol and a note on the Maydes metamorphosis. Renaissance News 10 1957. Reply by R. L. Greene, ibid.

Hanham, A. The musical studies of a 15th-century wool merchant. RES new ser 8 1957. Evidence in his accounts.

Speirs, J. Medieval English poetry: the non-Chaucerian tradition. 1957. Includes songs, lyrics, carols.

Cross, J. E. The sayings of St Bernard and Ubi sount qui ante nos fuerount. RES new ser 9 1958.

Friedman, A. B. The late mediaeval ballade and the origin of broadside balladry. MÆ 27 1958.

Harrison, F. L. Music in medieval Britain. 1958.

Johnstone, G. K. W. The interpretation of poems by Mydwynter. N & Q July–Aug 1959. See R. H. Bowers, MLN 64 1949.

Manning, S. Nou goth sonne under wod. MLN 74 1959.

—— I sing of a myden. PMLA 75 1960.

—— Wisdom and number: toward a critical appraisal of the ME religious lyric. Lincoln Nebraska 1962.

—— Game and earnest in the ME and Provencal love lyrics. Comparative Lit 18 1966.

Zumthor, P. Recherches sur les topiques dans la poésie lyrique des xiie et xiiie siècles. Cahiers de Civilisation Médiévale 2 1959.

Gray, D. In what estate so euer I be... N & Q Nov 1960. Supports Greene's note to his carol 370.

—— A ME epitaph. N & Q April 1961. Farewell, this world is but a cherry fair.

—— The five wounds of our Lord. N & Q Feb–May 1963. Index 1011 etc.

—— A ME verse at Warkworth. N & Q April 1967. Cf Index 1703.

Hughes, Dom A. and G. Abraham. Ars nova and the Renaissance 1300–1540. In New Oxford history of music vol 3, Oxford 1960.

Raw, B. C. As dew in Aprille. MLR 55 1960.

Rossi, S. Poesia cavalleresca e poesia religiosa inglese nel Quattrocento. Milan 1960.

Dronke, P. The Rawlinson lyrics. N & Q July 1961.

—— Medieval Latin and the rise of European love-lyric. 2 vols Oxford 1965–6.

—— The medieval lyric. 1968.

Einarsson, S. A burde of blod ant of bon. MLN 76 1961.

Lockwood, W. B. A note on the ME Sunset on Calvary. Zeitschrift für Anglistik und Amerikanistik 9 1961.

Perkins, G. A medieval carol survival: the Fox and the goose. Jnl of Amer Folklore 74 1961.

Ackerman, R. W. The debate of the body and the soul and parochial Christianity. Speculum 37 1962.

Bennett, J. A. W. Why men cry Seynt Barbara. RES new ser 13 1962. Index 2524 lines 20–1.

Stemmler, T. Zur Datierung des Ms Harley 2253. Anglia 80 1962.

— Die englischen Liebesgedichte des Ms Harley 2253. Bonn 1962.
— Interpretation des mittelenglischen Gedichts God that al this myhtes may. Anglia 82 1964. Index 968.
Woolf, R. The theme of Christ the lover-knight in medieval English literature. RES new ser 13 1962.
— The English religious lyric in the Middle Ages. Oxford 1968.
— The construction of In a fryht as I con fare fremede. MÆ 38 1969. Index 1449.
Fifield, M. 13th-century lyrics and the alliterative tradition. JEGP 62 1963.
Jammers, E. Ausgewählte Melodien des Minnesangs. Tübingen 1963. On music of lyrics and especially its relation to words.
Bühler, C. F. Prayers and charms in certain ME scrolls. Speculum 39 1964. Index 2300.3.
Hill, B. The luue-ron and Thomas de Hales. MLR 59 1964.
Sikora, R. The structural simplicity of the early ME lyric: three examples. Kwartalnik Neofilologiczny 11 1964.
Hatto, A. T. Eos: an enquiry into the theme of lovers' meetings and partings at dawn in poetry. Hague 1965.
Manzalaoui, M. Maiden in the mor lay and the Apocrypha. N & Q March 1965.
Sisam, C. Ne saltou neuer, leuedi. N & Q July 1965. Explains verses in B. Dickins, Leeds Stud in Eng 4 1935.
Smithers, G. V. Some textual problems in religious lyrics of 14th century. Eng Philological Stud (Birmingham) 9 1965. See K. Malone, ELH 23 1956.
Wilhelm, J. J. The cruelest month: spring, nature and love in classical and medieval lyrics. New Haven 1965.
Reiss, E. A critical approach to the ME lyric. College Eng Feb 1966.
Stevick, R. D. The criticism of ME lyrics. MP 64 1966.
Riddy, F. The provenance of Quia amore langueo. RES new ser 18 1967.
Zettersten, A. The ME lyrics in the Wellcome Library. Neuphilologische Mitteilungen 68 1967.
Peterson, D. L. The English lyric from Wyatt to Donne: a history of the plain and eloquent styles. Princeton 1967. Considers late medieval lyric.
Wolpers, T. Zum Andachtsbild in der mittelenglischen religiösen Lyrik. In Chaucer und seine Zeit: Symposion für W. F. Schirmer, Tübingen 1968.
Weber, S. A. Theology and poetry in the ME lyric: a study of sacred history and aesthetic form. Columbus 1969.

AUTHORS

See also Rolle, Audelay, Charles of Orleans and J. Ryman, above.

St Godric

Mss: BM Royal 5 F.VII, Harley 153, 322, 1620, Otho B V, Nero D.V, Bodley Laud Miscellany 413, Douce 207, Cambridge Corpus Christi College 26, Univ Lib Mm.IV. 28.

§1

Zupitza, J. Cantus beati Godric. E Studien 11 1888.
Patterson, F. A. The ME penitential lyric. New York 1911.
Hall, J. Selections from early ME. 2 vols Oxford 1920.
Davies, R. T. Medieval English lyrics. 1963.

§2

Ritson, J. Bibliographia poetica: a catalogue of English poets. 1802.
Archer, T. A. A note on St Godric. EHR 17 1902. Life.
Rankin, J. W. The hymns of St Godric. PMLA 38 1923.
McKeehan, I. P. The first biography of an English poet. Univ of Colorado Stud ser B 1941.

Laurence Minot

Ms: BM Cotton Galba E.IX.

§1

Ritson, J. Poems on interesting events in the reign of Edward III. 1795.
Wright, T. Political poems and songs vol 1. 1859 (Rolls ser).
Mätzner, E. Altenglische Sprachproben. Berlin 1867.
Morris, R. Specimens of E.E. Oxford 1867; pt 2 rev Morris and W. W. Skeat 1872.
Wülcker, R. P. Altenglisches Lesebuch. 2 vols Halle 1874–80.
Scholle, W. Minots Lieder (Quellen und Forschungen 52). Strasbourg 1884.
Hall, J. The poems of Minot. Oxford 1887.
Stedman, D. C. The war ballads of Minot. Dublin 1917.
Sisam, K. 14th-century verse and prose. Oxford 1921, 1937 (rev).
Davies, R. T. Medieval English lyrics. 1963.

§2

Bierbaum, F. J. Über Minot und seine Lieder. Halle 1876.
Dangel, M. Minots Gedichte. Königsberg 1888.
Moore, S. Laurence Minot. MLN 35 1920.
Snyder, E. C. The wild Irish. MP 17 1920
Parker, R. E. On Badding. PMLA 37 1922.
Oakden, J. P. Alliterative poetry in ME vol 1. Manchester 1930.

William of Shoreham

Ms: BM additional 17,376.

§1

See Mätzner, Morris, Wülcker, above.

Wright, T. The religious poems of William of Shoreham. 1849 (Percy Soc).
Konrath, M. Poems. 1902 (EETS).
Brown, C. Religious lyrics of the 14th century. Oxford 1924; rev G. V. Smithers, Oxford 1952.
Davies, R. T. Medieval English lyrics. 1963.

§2

Konrath, M. Beiträge zur Erklärung und Textkritik des William von Schorham. Berlin 1878.
Danker, O. Die Laut- und Flexions-lehre der mittelkentischen Denkmäler. Strasbourg 1879.
Varhargen, H. Zu William de Shoreham. Anglia 4 1881.
Kölbing, E. Textkritische Bemerkungen zu William von Schorham. E Studien 21 1895.
Holthausen, F. Zur Textkritik der Dichtungen William von Schorham. E Studien 42 1910.
— Zu William of Shoreham. E Studien 57 1923.
Konrath, M. Zur Textkritik der Dichtungen William von Schorham. E Studien 43 1910.
Virginia, Sr Mary. William of Shoreham's A song to Mary. Explicator 25 1966.

William Herebert

Ms: BM (once Phillipps 8336) additional 46,919.

§1

Wright, T. and J. O. Halliwell(-Phillipps). Reliquiae antiquae. 1841.
Jacoby, M. Vier mittelenglische geistliche Gedichte. Berlin 1890.
Patterson, F. A. The ME penitential lyric. New York 1911.

Brown, C. Religious lyrics of the 14th century. Oxford
1924; rev G. V. Smithers, Oxford 1952.
Kaiser, R. Alt- und mittelenglische Anthologie. Berlin
1954.
—— Medieval English. Berlin 1958.
Davies, R. T. Medieval English lyrics. 1963.

§2

Robbins, R. H. Friar Herebert and the carol. Anglia 75
1957.
Gneuss, H. William Hereberts Übersetzungen. Anglia 78
1960.

II. BALLADS

This section is chiefly concerned with the traditional or popular ballad.

Child   The English and Scottish popular ballads, ed F. J. Child (with number in collection).

(1) BIBLIOGRAPHIES

Holmes, T. J. and G. W. Thayer. English ballads and
songs in the Cleveland Public Library's John G. White
collection of folk-lore and orientalia, and in the Library
of Western Reserve University Cleveland. Cleveland
1931.
Gable, J. H. Bibliography of Robin Hood. Lincoln
Nebraska 1939.
Simeone, W. E. More Robin Hood bibliography. N & Q
6 Jan 1951. See also 17 Feb, 17 March, 1 Sept 1951.
Dean-Smith, M. and E. A. White. An index of English
songs contributed to the Journal of the Folk-song
Society 1899–1931. 1951.
Dean-Smith, M. A guide to English folk-song collections
1822–1952. Liverpool 1954. Descriptive list of collections with index of songs in them.

Millar, B. P. The American ballad list—1952: the survival
of Child ballads in America. Southern Folk-lore Quart
17 1953.
Montgomerie, W. A bibliography of the Scottish ballad
mss 1730–1825. Stud in Scottish Lit 4–7 1966–9.
*See also E. K. Chambers, Popular narrative poetry and the
ballad (for introductory bibliography); F. J. Child, in
particular for lists of mss sources and books containing
ballads; MacE. Leach, The ballad book, for American
sources; T. P. Coffin, The British traditional ballad in
N. America; S. B. Hustvedt, M. E. Sears and P. Crawford, for song and tune indexes, below.*

(2) EDITIONS

[Philips, A. ?] A collection of old ballads. 3 vols 1723–5.
See M. Segar, TLS 3 March 1932.
Ramsay, A. The ever green. 2 vols Edinburgh 1724.
—— The tea-table miscellany. 3 vols 1724–7.
Percy, T. Reliques of ancient English poetry. 3 vols 1765
etc.
[Herd, D.] The ancient and modern Scots songs. Edin-
burgh 1769, 2 vols 1776.
Evans, T. Old ballads. 2 vols 1777–84.
Pinkerton, J. Scottish tragic ballads. 1781.
—— Select Scotish ballads. 2 vols 1783.
Ritson, J. A select collection of English songs. 3 vols 1783.
—— Ancient songs. 1790 (probably for 1792).
—— Pieces of ancient popular poetry. 1791.
—— Scotish song. 2 vols 1794.
—— Robin Hood. 2 vols 1795.
Johnson, J. The Scots musical museum. 6 vols Edinburgh
1787–1803.
Scott, Sir W. Minstrelsy of the Scottish border. 3 vols
Kelso 1802–3 etc.
Jamieson, D. Popular ballads and songs. 2 vols Edinburgh
1806.
Finlay, J. Scottish historical and romantic ballads. 2 vols
Edinburgh 1808.
Laing, D. Select remains of the ancient popular poetry of
Scotland. Edinburgh 1822.
—— Early metrical tales. Edinburgh 1826.
Sharpe, C. K. A ballad book. Edinburgh 1823.
Gilbert, D. Some ancient Christmas carols with tunes,
together with two ancient ballads. 1823. Child 1, 11.
Maidment, J. A north countrie garland. Edinburgh 1824.
—— Reliquiae scoticae. 1828.
—— A new book of old ballads. 1844.
—— Scottish ballads and songs. 1859.

Cunningham, A. The songs of Scotland, ancient and
modern. 4 vols 1825.
Buchan, P. Gleanings of Scotch, English and Irish ballads.
Peterhead 1825.
—— Ancient ballads and songs of the north of Scotland
hitherto unpublished. Edinburgh 1828.
Chambers, R. The popular rhymes of Scotland. 1826.
—— Scottish ballads and Scottish songs. 3 vols Edinburgh
1829.
Kinloch, G. Ancient Scottish ballads. 1827.
Chappell, W. A collection of national English airs. 1840.
With essay on English minstrelsy.
—— Popular music of the olden time. 2 vols 1855–9.
Chappell, W. and J. W. Ebsworth. The Roxburghe ballads.
27 pts 1871–99.
Whitelaw, A. The book of Scottish ballads. Glasgow 1844.
Dixon, J. H. Scottish traditional versions of ancient
ballads. 1845 (Percy Soc).
—— Ancient poems, ballads and songs of the peasantry of
England. 1846 (Percy Soc). See R. Bell, below.
Gutch, J. M. A lytyll geste of Robin Hode. 2 vols 1847.
Bell, R. Ancient poems, ballads, and songs of the peasantry
of England. 1857. Rev and enlarged from J. H. Dixon,
above.
Child, F. J. The English and Scottish popular ballads.
8 vols Boston 1857–9, 10 pts in 5 vols Boston 1882–98,
New York 1956. The 10-pt edn is the standard collection
and includes in pt 10, ed G. L. Kittredge, Sources of
the texts, Index of published airs, Bibliography (Child).
The Students' Cambridge edn, in one vol ed H. C.
Sargent and G. L. Kittredge, Boston 1904 etc, includes
one or more versions of the 305 ballads in the standard
edn and has an introd by Kittredge.
Aytoun, W. E. The ballads of Scotland. 2 vols 1858.

Allingham, W. The ballad book. 1864.

Hales, J. W. and F. J. Furnivall. Bishop Percy's folio manuscript. 3 vols and suppl 1867–8.

Veitch, J. History and poetry of the Scottish border. 1878, 2 vols Glasgow 1893.

Bruce, J. C. and J. Stokoe. Northumbrian minstrelsy. 1882.

Tomson, G. R. Ballads of the north countrie. 1888.

Baring-Gould, S. and H. F. Sheppard. Songs and ballads of the West. 4 pts [1889–92], 1891–5 (rev).

— A garland of country song. 1895.

Eyre-Todd, G. Abbotsford series of the Scottish poets: Scottish ballad poetry. Glasgow 1893.

Fuller-Maitland, J. A. and L. E. Broadwood. English county songs. 1893.

Gummere, F. B. Old English ballads. Boston 1894.

Lang, A. Border ballads. 1895.

— A collection of ballads. 1897.

Sidgwick, F. Popular ballads of the olden time. 4 vols 1903–12.

— The bitter withy. N & Q 29 July 1905. Ballad not in Child.

— The bitter withy. Folklore 19 1908.

Gerould, G. H. The ballad of the Bitter withy. PMLA 23 1908. Ballad not in Child.

Sharp, C. J. and C. L. Marson. Folk-songs from Somerset. 5 vols 1904–19.

Sharp, C. J. et al. Folksongs of England. 5 vols 1908–12.

Sharp, C. J. and O. D. Campbell. English folk-songs from the Southern Appalachians. 1917; rev M. Karpeles 2 vols Oxford 1932.

Quiller-Couch, A. T. The Oxford book of ballads. Oxford 1910.

Hart, W. M. English popular ballads. Chicago 1916.

Stempel, G. H. A book of ballads. New York 1917.

Williams, A. Folksongs of the upper Thames. 1923.

Greig, G. and A. Keith. Last leaves of traditional ballads and ballad airs. Aberdeen 1925.

[Whiting, B. J.?] The ballad of Lord Randal. Jnl of Amer Folk-lore 39 1926.

Henry, M. E. American survivals of an old English ballad. Ibid. Child 84.

— Ballads and songs of the Southern Highlands. Jnl of Amer Folk-lore 42 1929. Child 4, 7, 12, 53, 73, 81, 84, 95, 99, 243, some with music.

— King Henry Fifth's conquest of France (Child 164), not hitherto found in America. PMLA 48 1933.

Hudson, P. A. Ballads and songs from Mississippi. Jnl of Amer Folk-lore 39 1926. Child 13, 73, 79, 84–5, 95, 105, 155, 277.

Pound, L. American text of Robin Hood and Little John. Amer Speech 2 1926.

Rinker, B. F. The ballad of the Jew's daughter. Jnl of Amer Folk-lore 39 1926. Child 155.

Graves, R. The English ballad. 1927.

— English and Scottish ballads. 1957.

Wimberley, L. C. Two traditional ballads. Amer Speech 3 1927. Child 4, 68.

Barry, P., F. H. Eckstorm and M. W. Smyth. British ballads from Maine. New Haven 1929.

Taylor, A. Edward and Sven i Rosengård: a study in the dissemination of a ballad. Chicago 1931.

Cornelius, R. D. A new text of an old ballad. PMLA 46 1931. Child 45.

Pettigrew, H. P. Little Musgrave and Lady Barnard (Child 81). West Virginia Univ Stud 3 1937.

Goss, J. Ballads of Britain. 1937.

Flanders, H. H., E. F. Ballard, G. Brown and P. Barry. The new Green Mountain songster: traditional folk songs of Vermont. New Haven 1939.

Flanders, H. H. Blue mountain lake and Barbara Allen. New York Folk-lore Quart 2 1946.

— Ancient ballads traditionally sung in New England. Philadelphia 1960.

Flanders, H. H. and M. Olney. Ballads migrant in New England. New York 1953.

Bayard, S. P. The Johnny Collins version of Lady Alice. Jnl of Amer Folk-lore 58 1945. Child 85.

Lowrimore, B. S. A California version of Edward. California Folklore Quart 5 1946.

— Some English and Scottish ballads from California. Ibid. Versions of Child 73, 75, 200 etc.

Leach, MacE. and H. P. Beck. Songs from Rappahannock County, Virginia. Jnl of Amer Folk-lore 63 1950. Child 295, 73, 74, 84, with music.

Leach, MacE. The ballad book. New York 1955. Bibliography and list of recordings.

Owens, W. A. Texas folk-song. Dallas 1950. Includes British ballads.

Gant, R. A book of ballads. 1950.

Beckwith, M. W. The Jew's garden. Jnl of Amer Folk-lore 64 1951. Child 155.

Davis, A. K. The unquiet grave: a new-old ballad from Virginia. Univ of Virginia Stud 4 1951. Child 78.

Davis, A. K. and P. C. Worthington. A new traditional ballad from Virginia. Southern Folk-lore Quart 21 1957. Child 27.

— Another new traditional ballad from Virginia: Child 90. Southern Folk-lore Quart 22 1958.

Hubbard, L. A. and LeR. J. Robertson. Traditional ballads from Utah. Jnl of Amer Folk-lore 64 1951. Text and music of Child 4, 43, 45, 62, 155, 243, 250, 277, 286.

Harrison, R. M. Folk-songs from Oregon. Western Folk-lore 11 1952. Child 277, 167.

Housman, J. E. British popular ballads. 1952.

Creighton, H. The songs of Nathan Hatt. Dalhousie Rev 32 1953. Child 4, 49 etc?

Friedman, A. B. A new version of Musselburgh field. Jnl of Amer Folk-lore 66 1953.

— The Viking book of folk ballads of the English-speaking world. New York 1956.

— Chaucer and Robin Hood. N & Q 13 May 1950.

Wycoco-Moore, R. A version of Lord Lovel (Child 75). Jnl of Amer Folk-lore 67 1954.

Campbell, M. A study of twenty-five versions of Little Musgrave and Lady Barnard in ballad collections of N. America. Tennessee Folk-lore Soc Bull 21 1955.

Brewster, P. G. and G. Tarsouli. Two English ballads and their Greek counterparts. Jnl of Amer Folk-lore 69 1956. Child 246, 268.

Pinto, V. de S. and A. E. Rodway. The common Muse: an anthology of popular British ballad poetry 15th–20th century. 1957.

Boswell, G. W. Kentucky folk-songs in the Tennessee archives. Kentucky Folk-lore Record 4 1958. Child 10, 84.

Powers, D. C. The American variants of Earl Brand, Child 7. Western Folk-lore 17 1958.

Stamper, F. C. and W. H. Jansen. Water birch: an American variant of Hugh of Lincoln. Jnl of Amer Folk-lore 71 1958. Child 155.

Bronson, B. H. The traditional tunes of the Child ballads. Princeton 1959.

Hand, W. D. Two Child ballads in the West. Western Folk-lore 18 1959. Child 81, 243.

Collinson, F. Four songs remembered by Miss Margaret Eyre. Jnl of Folk Dance & Song Soc 9 1962. Child 3, 9.

Henderson, H. and F. Collinson. New Child ballad variants from oral tradition. Scottish Stud 9 1965. Child 2–3, 46, 11, 14, 39, 155.

Beck, T. T. A variant of Lord Randal. N & Q Jan 1964.

Glassie, H. H. The gypsy laddie (Child 200): two new texts with tunes. Tennessee Folk-lore Soc Bull 30 1964.

Coffin, T. P. Six unusual texts from Mildred Haun's Cocke County ballads and songs. Southern Folk-lore Quart 29 1965. Child 26, 76, 95, 99, 200.

Hodgart, M. J. C. The Faber book of ballads. 1965.

Sweeney, M. Mrs Ernest Shope: a memorable informant. Kentucky Folk-lore Record 11 1965. Child 10, 20, 49.

Fowke, E. The King and the tinker. Jnl of Amer Folk-lore 79 1966. Child 273.

Toelken, J. B. Riddles wisely expounded. Western Folk-lore 25 1966.

Wilgus, D. K. The oldest (?) text of Edward. Ibid.

Kinsley, J. The Oxford book of ballads. Oxford 1969. With tunes.

(3) STUDIES

Many edns above include important studies.

Chambers, R. The romantic Scottish ballads: their epoch and authorship. Edinburgh 1859.

Lemcke, L. Die traditionellen schottischen Balladen. Jahrbuch für Romanische und Englische Literatur 4 1862.

Fränkel, L. Zur Geschichte von Robin Hood. E Studien 17 1887.

Child, F. J. In Johnson's Cyclopaedia vol 1, New York 1893.

Gummere, F. B. The ballad and communal poetry. Harvard Stud 5 1896.

— The beginnings of poetry. 1901.

— Primitive poetry and the ballad. MP 1 1904.

— The popular ballad. 1907.

Flügel, E. Zur Chronologie der englischen Balladen. Anglia 21 1899.

Görbing, F. Beispiele von realisierten Mythen in den englischen und schottischen Balladen. Anglia 23 1900.

Fehr, B. Die formelhaften Elemente in den alten englischen Balladen. Basle 1900.

Lang, A. In Chambers's Cyclopaedia of English literature vol 1, 1901.

Heusler, A. Lied und Epos. Dortmund 1905.

— Über die Balladendichtung des Spätmittelalters namentlich im skandinavischen Norden. Germanisch-romanische Monatsschrift 10 1922.

Hecht, H. Neuere Literatur zur englisch-schottischen Balladendichtung. E Studien 36 1906.

— Schottische Balladensammler aus dem Kreise F. J. Childs. Nachrichten der Geschichte der Wissenschaften zu Göttingen, philologisch-historische Klasse 1930.

Hart, W. M. Professor Child and the ballad. PMLA 21 1906.

— Ballad and epic. Harvard Stud 11 1907.

— English popular ballads. Chicago 1916.

Schütte, P. Die Liebe in den englischen und schottischen Balladen. Halle 1906.

Rüdiger, G. Zauber und Aberglaube in den englisch-schottischen Volksballaden. Halle 1907.

Duncan, E. The story of minstrelsy. 1907.

Sharp, C. J. English folk-song: some conclusions. 1907; rev M. Karpeles 1954.

Ker, W. P. On the history of the ballads 1100–1500. Proc Br Acad 4 1909; rptd in his Form and style in poetry, 1928.

— Collected essays. 2 vols 1925. Includes Spanish and English ballads, Danish ballads etc.

Barry, P. The origin of folk-melodies. Jnl of Amer Folk-lore 23 1910.

— The transmission of folk-song. Jnl of Amer Folk-lore 27 1914.

— The bridge of sunbeams. Ibid.

Belden, H. M. The relation of balladry to folk-lore. Jnl of Amer Folk-lore 24 1911.

Nessler, K. Geschichte der Ballade Chevy Chase. Berlin 1911.

Henderson, T. F. The ballad in literature. Cambridge 1912.

Bryant, F. E. A history of English balladry. Boston 1913.

Beatty, A. Ballad, tale and tradition. PMLA 29 1914.

Steenstrup, J. C. H. R. The mediaeval popular ballad. Tr Boston [1914].

Sidgwick, F. The ballad. 1914.

Ehrke, K. Das Geistermotiv in den schottisch-englischen Volksballaden. Marburg 1914.

Kidson, F. and M. Neal. English folk-song and dance. 1915.

Baum, P. F. The English ballad of Judas Iscariot. PMLA 31 1916. Child 23.

Hustvedt, S. B. Ballad criticism in Scandinavia and Great Britain during 18th century. New York 1916.

— Ballad books and ballad men. Cambridge Mass 1930.

— A melodic index of Child's ballad tunes. Berkeley 1936.

Moore, J. R. The influence of transmission on English ballads. MLR 11 1916.

Jahn, J. Die mittelenglische Spielmannsballade von Simon Fraser. Bonn 1921.

Pound, L. Poetic origins and the ballad. New York 1921.

— The term Communal. PMLA 39 1924.

— On the dating of the English and Scottish ballads. PMLA 47 1932.

McCutcheon, R. P. Two 18th-century emendations to Chevy Chase. MLN 37 1922.

Batho, E. C. The life of Christ in the ballads. E & S 9 1923.

Watt, L. M. The Scottish ballads and ballad writing. Paisley 1923.

Gerould, G. H. The making of ballads. MP 21 1923.

— The ballad of tradition. Oxford 1932.

— An Irish version of the False knight upon the road. MLN 53 1938.

Brunner, K. Romanzen und Volksballaden. In Anglica, A. Brandl überreicht, Leipzig 1925.

Grierson, H. J. C. Foreword. In Border ballads selected by D. P. Bliss, 1925.

Smith, R. The traditional ballad and its South Carolina survivals. Columbia SC 1925.

Stewart, G. R. The meter of the popular ballad. PMLA 40 1925.

Eicker, H. Die historische Volksballade der Engländer und Schotten. Leipzig 1926.

Ford, W. C. The Isaiah Thomas collection of ballads. Proc Amer Antiquarian Soc 33 1924.

Keith, A. Scottish ballads: their evidence of authorship and origin. E & S 12 1926.

Sears, M. E. and P. Crawford. Song index to more than 12,000 songs in 177 song collections. New York 1926.

Woods, M. L. Ballads. Trans Royal Soc of Lit 6 1926.

Haworth, P. English hymns and ballads and other studies in popular literature. Oxford 1927.

Stack, L. Ballads. Eng Rev 45 1927.

Taylor, A. Das Schloss in Österreich. MLN 42 1927. Cf Child 72.

— The English, Scottish and American versions of the Twa sisters. Jnl of Amer Folk-lore 42 1929.

— The texts of Edward in Percy's Reliques and Motherwell's Minstrelsy. MLN 45 1930.

— A contamination in Lord Randal. MP 29 1931.

— The themes common to English and German balladry. MLQ 1 1940.

— The English riddle ballads. In Studies in language and literature in honour of M. Schlauch, Warsaw 1966.

Tolman, A. H. Mary Hamilton and group authorship of ballads. PMLA 42 1927.

Wimberley, L. C. Death and burial lore in the English and Scottish popular ballads. Lincoln Nebraska 1927.

— Folk-lore in the English and Scottish ballads. Chicago 1928.

Davis, A. K. Some problems of ballad publication. Musical Quart 14 1928.

Dickson, A. The Earl of Westmoreland and Bueve de Hantone. PMLA 43 1928.

Brill, O. J. Der Schäfer und der Edelmann. PQ 9 1930.

Millican, C. B. The original of the ballad Kinge Arthurs death in the Percy folio ms. PMLA 46 1931.

Humbert, G. Literarische Einflüsse in schottischen Volksballaden: Versuch einer kritischen Variantenvergleichung. Halle 1932.

Schmidt, W. Die Entwicklung der englisch-schottischen Volksballaden. Anglia 57 1933.

— Die Entwicklungsgeschichte der Edward-ballade. Ibid.

— Die englischen und schottischen Volksballaden I. Zeitschrift für Neusprachlichen Unterricht 35 1936.

— Der Anlass zum Streit in der Edward-Ballade. Anglia 61 1937.

— Die Volksballade von den Drei Raben. Neuphilologische Monatsschrift 8 1937.

— Die Volksballaden von Tom dem Reimer. Anglia 61 1937.

— Die schottischen Volksballaden von Sir Patrick Spens. E Studien 74 1940.

Flasdieck, H. M. Tom der Reimer: von keltischen Feen und politischen Propheten. Breslau 1934.

Whiting, B. J. Proverbial material in the popular ballad. Jnl of Amer Folk-lore 47 1934.

Speirs, J. The Scottish ballads. Scrutiny 4 1935; rptd in his Scots literary tradition, 1940.

Panke, F. Die schottischen Liebesballaden: ein Beitrag zur Entstehung von Variantenbildung. Berlin 1935.

Becker, H. Die Ballade von Johnie Cock. In Englische Kultur in sprachwissenschaftlicher Deutung, M. Deutschbein zum 60 Geburtstage, Leipzig 1936.

Jordan, H. S. The old French chansons d'histoire as a possible origin of the English popular ballad. Revue de Littérature Comparée 16 1936.

Hendren, J. W. A study of ballad rhythm. Princeton 1936.

Neumann, F. W. Die schottische Volksballade von den Drei Raben in Russland. Neuphilologische Monatsschrift 8 1937.

Firth, C. H. Ballads and broadsides. In his Essays historical and literary, Oxford 1938.

Entwistle, W. J. European balladry. Oxford 1939, 1951 (rev).

— Notation for ballad melodies. PMLA 55 1940.

Greene, R. L. The traditional survival of two medieval carols. ELH 7 1940.

Burns, M. The folk ballad. Dalhousie Rev 22 1943.

Owen, L. V. D. Robin Hood. TLS 13 May 1944.

Chambers, E. K. Popular narrative poetry and the ballad. In his English literature at the close of the Middle Ages, Oxford 1945 (OHEL). With bibliography.

Cutting, E. E. The cherry tree carol. New York Folk-lore Quart 1 1945.

— The joys of Mary. New York Folk-lore Quart 3 1947.

Locke, L. G. The three ravens. Explicator 4 1946. See T. Hillway 5 1947 and S. Lainoff 17 1959.

Richmond, W. E. Ballad place names. Jnl of Amer Folk-lore 59 1946.

Hamer, D. The twa corbies. RES 23 1947.

Heltzel, V. Fair Rosamond: a study of the development of a literary theme. Evanston 1947.

Baldi, S. Studi sulla poesia popolare d'Inghilterra e di Scozia. Rome 1949.

Coffin, T. P. The murder motive in Edward. Western Folk-lore 8 1949.

— The British traditional ballad in N. America. Philadelphia 1950, 1963 (rev). With bibliography.

— The braes of Yarrow tradition in America. Jnl of Amer Folk-lore 63 1950. Child 214–15.

— Mary Hamilton and the Anglo-American ballad as an art form. Jnl of Amer Folk-lore 70 1957.

Parker, H. The scobs was in her lovely mouth. Jnl of Amer Folk-lore 71 1958. Child 91.

Coffin, T. P. and MacE. Leach. The critics and the ballad: selected readings. Carbondale 1961.

Coffin, T. P. The folk ballad and the literary ballad: an essay in classification. Midwest Folk-lore 9 1959, and in Folk-lore in action, Philadelphia 1962.

— Remarks preliminary to a study of ballad meter and ballad singing. Jnl of Amer Folk-lore 78 1965.

Laws, G. M. The British ballad tradition in America. In his Native American balladry: a descriptive study and a bibliographical syllabus. Philadelphia 1950.

Hodgart, M. J. C. The ballads. 1950.

— Medieval lyrics and the ballads. In The age of Chaucer, ed B. Ford 1954 (Pelican).

Wells, E. K. The ballad tree: a study of British and American ballads, their folk-lore, verse and music, together with sixty traditional ballads and their tunes. New York 1950.

Parker, H. The two sisters—going which way? Jnl of Amer Folk-lore 64 1951. To Britain from Norway or Faroes.

Bland, D. S. The evolution of 'Chevy Chase' and 'The Battle of Otterburn'. N & Q 14 April 1951.

Simeone, W. E. Still more about Robin Hood. Jnl of Amer Folk-lore 64 1951.

— The historic Robin Hood. Jnl of Amer Folk-lore 66 1953.

— Robin Hood ballads in N. America. Midwest Folk-lore 7 1957.

Bronson, B. H. On the union of words and music in the Child ballads. Western Folk-lore 11 1952.

— About the commonest British ballads. Jnl of International Folk-music Council 9 1957.

— All this for a song? In Literary views, ed C. Camden, Chicago 1964. On folk songs.

Nygard, H. O. Narrative change in the European tradition of the Lady Isabel and the Elf Knight ballad. Jnl of Amer Folk-lore 65 1952.

— Ballad source study: Child ballad no 4 as exemplar. Jnl of Amer Folk-lore 68 1955.

— The ballad of Heer Halewijn. Helsinki and Knoxville 1958.

— Ballads and the Middle Ages. Tennessee Stud in Lit 5 1960.

— Popular ballad and medieval romance. In Folk-lore international, ed D. K. Wilgus, Hatboro Pa 1967.

Taylor, D. S. The lineage and birth of Sir Aldingar. Jnl of Amer Folk-lore 65 1952.

Williams, J. More about Robin Hood. Ibid.

Christopherson, P. The ballad of Sir Aldingar. Oxford 1952. See A. L. Poole, TLS 21 Aug 1953.

Abrahamsen, S. The English-Scottish and the Scandinavian ballads. Edda 54 1954.

Beard, A. Lord Thomas in America. Southern Folk-lore Quart 19 1955. Child 73.

Harris, R. Lord Thomas and Fair Ellinor: a preliminary study of the ballad. Midwest Folk-lore 5 1955.

Lowe, B. Robin Hood in the light of history. Jnl of Eng Folk Dance & Song Soc 7 1955.

Montgomerie, W. The twa corbies. RES new ser 6 1955.

Woodall, J. R. Sir Hugh: a study in balladry. Southern Folk-lore Quart 19 1955. Child 155.

Fergusson, J. The ballads. In Scottish poetry, ed J. Kinsley 1955.

Kirtley, B. F. Theories and fantasies concerning Robin Hood. Southern Folk-lore Quart 20 1956.

Lowe, B. The final truth about Robin Hood. Folk-lore 67 1956.

Sellers, W. E. Kinship in the British ballads: the historical evidence. Southern Folk-lore Quart 20 1956.

Blum, M. M. Edward and the folk tradition. Southern Folk-lore Quart 21 1957.

Dober, V. The marital status of Child ballad heroines. Ibid.

Hyman, S. E. The Child ballad in America: some aesthetic criteria. Jnl of Amer Folk-lore 70 1957.

Ingham, P. The world of the ballad. RES new ser 8 1957.

Read, H. The writer and his region. In his Tenth muse: essays in criticism, 1957. Regional ethos of ballads.

Sellers, W. E. Kindred and clan in the Scottish border ballads. Boston Univ Stud in Eng 3 1957.

Friedman, A. B. The late mediaeval ballade and the origin of broadside balladry. MÆ 27 1958.

—— The ballad revival: studies in the influence of popular on sophisticated poetry. Chicago 1961. Chiefly of 18th-century interest.

Matthäi, S. Rittertum und Adel in den englischen und schottischen Volksballaden. Berlin 1958.

Moore, A. K. The literary status of the English popular ballad. Comparative Lit 10 1958.

Rountree, T. J. Ethnological implications in the Gypsy laddie. Tennessee Folk-lore Soc Bull 24 1958.

Wilgus, D. K. Shooting fish in a barrel: the Child ballad in America. Jnl of Amer Folk-lore 71 1958.

—— Anglo-American folk-song scholarship since 1898. New Brunswick NJ 1959.

Hoffman, D. G. The unquiet graves. Sewanee Rev 67 1959. On difference between ballad theories of Robert Graves and MacE. Leach.

Hopkins, R. H. A note on Johnie Cock (Child 114, Percy no 5). N & Q Jan 1959.

Ives, E. D. The bonny Earl of Murray: the ballad as history. Midwest Folk-lore 9 1959.

Rennick, R. M. The disguised lover theme and the ballad. Southern Folk-lore Quart 23 1959.

Knoblock, J. A. The gypsy laddie (Child 200); an unrecognized child of medieval romance. Western Folk-lore 19 1960.

Jones, J. H. Commonplace and memorization in the oral tradition of the English and Scottish popular ballads. Jnl of Amer Folk-lore 74 1961. Reply by A. B. Friedman, ibid.

Keen, M. The outlaws of medieval legend. 1961.

Perkins, G. A medieval carol survival: the Fox and the goose. Jnl of Amer Folk-lore 74 1961.

Schmidt-Hidding, W. Edward, Edward in der Balladenwelt. In Festschrift zum 75 Geburtstag von Theodor Spira, Heidelberg 1961.

Chatman, V. V. The three ravens explicated. Midwest Folk-lore 13 1963.

Crawford, T. Scottish popular ballads and lyrics of the 18th and early 19th centuries: some preliminary conclusions. Stud in Scottish Lit 1 1963.

Elder, M. Ballad country. Edinburgh 1963.

Montgomerie, W. William Macmath and the Scott ballad mss. Stud in Scottish Lit 1 1963.

Brunvand, J. H. Child 277: ballad and tale. Western Folklore 23 1964.

McMillan, D. J. A survey of theories concerning the oral transmission of the traditional ballad. Southern Folklore Quart 28 1964.

—— Folk projection and historic truth. Amer N & Q 2 1964. Child 159, 161–3, 168.

—— Some popular views of four mediaeval battles. Southern Folk-lore Quart 30 1966. Durham, Otterburn, Cheviot, Harlaw.

Hatto, A. T. Eos: an enquiry into the theme of lovers' meetings and partings at dawn in poetry. Hague 1965.

Mackenzie, M. L. The great ballad collectors: Percy, Herd and Ritson. Stud in Scottish Lit 2 1965.

Muir, W. Living with ballads. 1965.

Wiatt, W. H. The twa corbies again. Keystone Folk-lore Quart 10 1965.

Bessinger, J. B. Robin Hood: folk-lore and historiography 1377–1500. Tennessee Stud in Lit 11 1966.

Fowler, D. C. The hunting of the Cheviot and the Battle of Otterburn. Western Folk-lore 25 1966.

—— A literary history of the popular ballad. Durham NC 1968.

Nelson, C. E. The origin and tradition of the ballad of Thomas Rhymer. In New voices in American studies, ed R. B. Browne et al, Lafayette Ind 1966.

Urcia, I. The gallows and the golden ball (Child 95). Jnl of Amer Folk-lore 79 1966.

Winkelman, D. M. Some rhythmic aspects of the Child ballad. In New voices in American studies, ed R. B. Brown et al, Lafayette Ind 1966.

Titland, W. J. The bitter withy and its relationship to the Holy well. Jnl of Amer Folk-lore 80 1967.

Graves, J. M. The holy well: a medieval religious ballad. Western Folk-lore 26 1967. On Bitter withy.

R. T. D.

5. MEDIEVAL DRAMA

(1) BIBLIOGRAPHIES; (2) HISTORIES; (3) COLLECTIONS; (4) LITURGICAL DRAMA; (5) ANGLO–NORMAN DRAMA; (6) CORNISH AND WELSH DRAMA; (7) ENGLISH MYSTERY AND MIRACLE PLAYS; (8) SPECTACLES AND MINSTRELSY TO 1485; (9) FOLK DRAMA

For Morality plays see col 1401, below.

(1) BIBLIOGRAPHIES

Chambers, E. K. The mediaeval stage. 2 vols Oxford 1903.

Wells, J. E. A manual of the writings in Middle English 1050–1400. New Haven 1916; 9 suppls 1919–51.

Harbage, A. Annals of English drama 975–1700. Philadelphia 1940, London 1964 (rev S. Schoenbaum); 2 suppls 1966–70.

Brown, C. and R. H. Robbins. The index of Middle English verse. New York 1943.

Farrar, C. P. and A. P. Evans. Bibliography of English translations from medieval sources. New York 1946.

Henshaw, M. A survey of studies in medieval drama 1933–50. Progress of Medieval & Renaissance Stud in US & Canada 21 1951.

Stratman, C. J. Bibliography of medieval drama. Berkeley and Los Angeles 1954, New York 1972 (rev).

Robbins, R. H. and J. L. Cutler. Supplement to the Index of Middle English verse. Lexington Kentucky 1965.

Fisher, J. H. (ed). The medieval literature of Western Europe. New York 1966.

Current projects: medieval. Research Opportunities in Renaissance Drama 10– 1967–. In progress.

(2) HISTORIES

Hone, W. Ancient mysteries described. 1823.

Ward, A. W. A history of English dramatic literature to the death of Queen Anne. 2 vols 1875, 1899 (rev).

Petit de Julleville, L. Histoire du théâtre en France [au Moyen Age]. 5 vols Paris 1880–6.

Cloetta, W. Beiträge zur Litteraturgeschichte des Mittelalters und der Renaissance. 2 vols Halle 1890–2.

Creizenach, W. Geschichte des neueren Dramas. 5 vols Halle 1893–1916; vol 1, 1911 (rev).

Mantzius, K. Skuespilkunstens historie. 6 vols Copenhagen 1897–1916; tr 6 vols 1903–21.

Chambers, E. K. The mediaeval stage. 2 vols Oxford 1903.

—— English literature at the close of the Middle Ages. Oxford 1945 (OHEL), 1947 (corrected).

Gayley, C. M. Plays of our forefathers. New York 1907.

Wells, J. E. A manual of the writings in Middle English 1050–1400. New Haven 1916; 9 suppls 1919–51.

Baskervill, C. R. Some evidence for early romantic plays in England. MP 14 1917.

Mill, A. J. Mediaeval plays in Scotland. Edinburgh and London 1927.

Nicoll, A. The development of the theatre. 1927.

—— Masks, mimes and miracles. 1931.

Withington, R. Ancestry of the 'Vice'. Speculum 7 1932.

D'Amico, S. Storia del teatro drammatico vol 1. Milan 1939, 1968 (rev).

Loomis, R. S. and G. Cohen. Were there theatres in the twelfth and thirteenth centuries? Speculum 20 1945. Replies by D. Bigongiari, Romanic Rev 37 1946; M. H. Marshall, Symposium 4 1950; K. Huganir, Theatre Annual 23 1967.

Marshall, M. H. Boethius' definition of persona and mediaeval understanding of the Roman theatre. Speculum 25 1950.

Rossiter, A. P. English drama from early times to the Elizabethans. 1950.

Stamm, R. Geschichte des englischen Theaters. Berne 1951.

Henshaw, M. The attitude of the Church toward the stage to the end of the Middle Ages. Medievalia et Humanistica 7 1952.

Kindermann, K. Theatergeschichte Europas vol 1. Salzburg 1957.

Wickham, G. Early English stages 1300 to 1660 vol 1. 1959.

Jackson, W. T. H. The literature of the Middle Ages. New York 1960. Ch 9.

Kernodle, G. R. Seven medieval theatres in one social structure. Theatre Research 2 1960.

Tobin, T. The beginnings of drama in Scotland. Theatre Survey 8 1967.

Kinghorn, A. M. Mediaeval drama. 1968.

Fifield, M. Quod quaeritis, o discipuli. Comparative Drama 5 1972.

Sticca, S. (ed). The medieval drama. Albany NY 1972.

Taylor, J. and A. H. Nelson (ed). Medieval English drama: essays critical and contextual. Chicago 1972.

(3) COLLECTIONS

The anthologies are later referred to by the names of the editors.

Hawkins, T. The origin of the English drama. 3 vols 1773. *Hawkins.*

Collier, J. P. Five miracle plays. 1836. *Collier.*

Marriott, W. A collection of English miracle-plays or mysteries. Basle 1838. *Marriott.*

Pollard, A. W. English miracle plays moralities and interludes. Oxford 1890, 1927 (rev). *Pollard.*

Manly, J. M. Specimens of the pre-Shaksperean drama. 2 vols Boston 1897. *Manly.*

Hemingway, S. B. English nativity plays. New York 1909. *Hemingway.*

Adams, J. Q. Chief pre-Shakespearean dramas. Cambridge Mass 1924. *Adams.*

Cohen, G. La 'comédie' latine en France au xii⁰ siècle. 2 vols Paris 1931.

Loomis, R. S. and H. W. Wells. Representative medieval and Tudor plays. New York 1942 (tr and modernized). *Loomis.*

Cawley, A. C. Everyman and medieval miracle plays. 1956 (EL), 1957 (rev). *Cawley.*

Browne, E. M. Religious drama 2: mystery and morality plays. New York 1958 (modernized). *Browne.*

Franceschini, E. Teatro latino medievale. Milan 1960. *Franceschini.*

Franklin, A. Seven miracle plays. Oxford 1963 (adapted). *Franklin.*

Gassner, J. Medieval and Tudor drama. New York 1963 (modernized). *Gassner.*

Thomas, R. G. Ten miracle plays. 1966. *Thomas.*

Robertson, D. W. The literature of medieval England. 1970. *Robertson.*

(4) LITURGICAL DRAMA

Surveys and Special Studies

See also Chambers, Creizenach, Mantzius, Mill, Petit de Julleville and Rossiter, above.

Méril, E. du. Origines latines du théâtre moderne. Paris 1849.

Sepet, M. Les prophètes du Christ. Paris 1878.

Gautier, L. Histoire de la poésie liturgique au Moyen Age: les tropes. Paris 1886.

Cohen, G. Histoire de la mise en scène dans le théâtre religieux français du Moyen Age. 1906, 1926 (rev), 1951 (rev).

Coffman, G. R. A new theory concerning the origin of the miracle play. Menasha 1914.

—— A new approach to medieval Latin drama. MP 22 1925.

—— The miracle play: notes and queries. PQ 20 1941.

Brooks, N. C. The sepulchre of Christ in art and liturgy. Urbana 1921.

Mâle, E. L'art religieux du xii⁰ siècle en France. Paris 1922, 1928 (rev).

Muller, H. F. Pre-history of the mediaeval drama: the antecedents of the tropes and the conditions of their appearance. Zeitschrift für Romanische Philologie 44 1925.

Schwietering, J. Über den liturgischen Ursprung des mittelalterlichen geistlichen Spiels. Zeitschrift für Deutsches Altertum 62 1925.

Brinkmann, H. Zum Ursprung des liturgischen Spieles. Xenia Bonnensia 1929.

—— Das religiöse Drama im Mittelalter: Arten und Stufen. Wirkendes Wort 9 1959.

Liuzzi, F. L'espressione musicale nel dramma liturgico. Studi Medievali 2 1929.

Cargill, O. Drama and liturgy. New York 1930.

Hilka, A. and O. Schumann. Carmina burana. 2 vols Heidelberg 1930–41.

Niedner, H. Die deutschen und französischen Osterspiele bis zum 15 Jahrhundert. Berlin 1932.

Young, K. The drama of the medieval church. 2 vols Oxford 1933, 1962 (corrected).

Kamlah, W. Der Ludus de Antichristo. Historische Vierteljahrsschrift 28 1934.

La Piana, G. The Byzantine theater. Speculum 11 1936.

—— The Byzantine iconography of the Presentation of the Virgin Mary to the Temple and a Latin religious pageant. In Late classical and mediaeval studies in honor of A. M. Friend jr, Princeton 1955.

Wright, E. A. The dissemination of the liturgical drama in France. Bryn Mawr 1936.

Hartl, E. Das Drama des Mittelalters. 2 vols Leipzig 1937.

De Vito, M. S. L'origine del dramma liturgico. Milan 1938.

Steigleder, P. Das Spiel vom Antichrist. Würzburg 1938.

Rava, A. Teatro medievale: l'apparato scenico nella Visita delle Marie al sepolcro. Rome 1939.

Smits van Waesberghe, J. Muziek en drama in de Middeleeuwen. Amsterdam 1939.

— Das Maastrichter Osterspiel. Kongressbericht, Basle 1949 (International Musicological Soc).

— Das gegenwärtige Geschichtsbild der mittelalterlichen Musik. Kirchenmusikalisches Jahrbuch 46– 1962–.

Marshall, M. H. The dramatic tradition established by the liturgical plays. PMLA 56 1941.

— Aesthetic values of the liturgical drama. English Inst Essays 1950.

Pascal, R. On the origins of the liturgical drama of the Middle Ages. MLR 36 1941.

Smoldon, W. L. The Easter Sepulchre music-drama. Music & Letters 27 1946.

— Liturgical drama. In Early medieval music up to 1300, ed A. Hughes, Oxford 1954.

— The music of the medieval church drama. Musical Quart 48 1962.

— Medieval lyrical melody and the Latin church dramas. Musical Quart 51 1965.

— The melodies of the medieval church-dramas and their significance. Comparative Drama 2 1969.

— The origins of the Quem Quaeritis trope and the Easter sepulchre music-dramas as demonstrated by their musical settings. In The medieval drama, ed S. Sticca, Albany NY 1972.

Woerdeman, J. The source of the Easter play. Orate Fratres 20 1946.

Liegey, G. M. Faith and the origin of liturgical art. Thought 22 1947.

Lipphardt, W. Die Weisen der lateinischen Osterspiele des 12 und 13 Jahrhunderts. Cassel 1948.

— Liturgische Dramen des Mittelalters. In Die Musik in Geschichte und Gegenwart vol 8, 1960.

von den Steinen, W. Notker der Dichter und seine geistige Welt. 2 vols Berne 1948.

Reichert, G. Strukturprobleme der älteren Sequenz. Deutsche Vierteljahrsschrift für Literaturwissenschaft und Geistesgeschichte 23 1949.

Marichal, R. Les drames liturgiques du 'Livre de la tresorerie' d'Origny-Sainte-Benoite. In Mélanges offerts à Gustave Cohen, Paris 1950.

Mellot, J. A propos du théâtre liturgique à Bourges. Ibid.

Schuler, E. A. Die Musik der Osterfeiern, Osterspiele und Passionen des Mittelalters. Cassel 1951.

Corbin, S. Le Cantus Sibyllae: origine et premiers textes. Revue de Musicologie 34 1952.

— Le manuscrit 201 d'Orléans. Romania 74 1953.

— La déposition liturgique du Christ au Vendredi Saint. Paris 1960.

Hauk, K. Zur Genealogie und Gestalt des Staufischen Ludus de Antichristo. Germanisch-romanische Monatsschrift 2 1952.

Vecchi, G. Innodia e dramma sacro. Studi Mediolatini e Volgari 1 1953.

Handschin, J. Trope, sequence and conductus. In Early medieval music up to 1300, ed A. Hughes, Oxford 1954.

Chailley, J. Le drame liturgique médiéval à Saint-Martial de Limoges. Revue d'Histoire du Théâtre 7 1955.

Toschi, P. In his Le origini del teatro italiano, Turin 1955. Ch 15.

Donovan, R. B. The liturgical drama in medieval Spain. Toronto 1958.

Wagenaar-Nolthenius, H. Sur la construction musicale du drame liturgique. Cahiers de Civilisation Médiévale 3 1960.

— Structuur en melodiek van het Daniel-spel. In Organicae voces: Festschrift Joseph Smits van Waesberghe, Amsterdam 1963.

Sticca, S. The priority of the Montecassino Passion play. Latomus 20 1961.

— The Latin Passion play: its origins and development. Albany NY 1970.

— The literary genesis of the Latin Passion play and the Planctus Mariae. In The medieval drama, ed S. Sticca, Albany NY 1972.

Weakland, R. The rhythmic modes and medieval Latin drama. Jnl of Amer Musicological Soc 14 1961.

Boor, H. de. Der Salbenkauf in den lateinischen Osterspielen des Mittelalters. In Festgabe für L. L. Hammerich, Copenhagen 1962.

— Die Textgeschichte der lateinischen Osterfeiern. Tübingen 1967.

Pächt, O. The rise of pictorial narrative in twelfth-century England. Oxford 1962.

Velimirović, M. Liturgical drama in Byzantium and Russia. Dumbarton Oaks Papers 16 1962.

Jones, C. W. The Saint Nicholas liturgy and its literary relationships. Berkeley and Los Angeles 1963.

Elders, W. Gregorianisches in liturgischen Dramen der Hs Orléans 201. Acta Musicologica 36 1964.

Falvy, Z. Un Quem queritis en Hongrie au xiie siècle. Studia Musicologica 3 1964.

Modzelewski, Z. Estetyka średniowiecznego dramatu liturgicznego. Rocznik Humanistyczny Polski 12 1964.

Gamer, H. M. Mimes, musicians and the origin of the mediaeval religious play. Deutsche Beiträge zur Geistigen Überlieferung 5 1965.

Hardison, O. B., jr. Christian rite and Christian drama in the Middle Ages. Baltimore 1965.

Sletsjöe, L. Quelques réflexions sur la naissance du théâtre religieux. In Actes du Xe Congrès International de Linguistique et Philologie Romanes, 3 vols Paris 1965.

Brandel, R. Some unifying devices in the religious music drama of the Middle Ages. In Aspects of medieval and Renaissance music: a birthday offering to Gustave Reese, New York 1966.

Guiette, R. Réflexions sur le drame liturgique. In Mélanges René Crozet vol 1, Poitiers 1966.

Kaltenbach, C. Evidence for a Quem Quaeritis Easter matins trope in the Divine Office at Poitiers, c. 800? Emporia Kansas 1968.

Stevens, J. Music in some early medieval plays. In Studies in the arts: proceedings of the St Peter's College Literary Society, New York 1968.

Mathieu, M. Distanciation et émotion dans le théâtre liturgique au Moyen Age. Revue d'Histoire du Théâtre 21 1969.

Stemmler, T. Liturgische Feiern und geistliche Spiele. Tübingen 1970.

Warning, R. Ritus, Mythos und geistliches Spiel. Poetica 3 1970.

Göllner, T. The three-part gospel reading and the medieval magi play. Jnl of Amer Musicological Soc 24 1971.

Dunn, E. C. Voice structure in the liturgical drama: Sepet reconsidered. In Medieval English drama, ed J. Taylor and A. H. Nelson, Chicago 1972.

Texts

The standard edn of the corpus is The drama of the medieval Church, *ed K. Young, Oxford 1933, which prints no music. Edns with music are indicated below.*
One or more plays in the following anthologies, above:
Pollard, Manly, Adams (16 plays), Loomis, Franceschini, Gassner.

Coussemaker, E. de. Drames liturgiques du Moyen Age. Rennes 1860. With music.

Fuller, J. B. Hilarii versus et ludi. New York 1929.

Young, K. The drama of the medieval Church. 2 vols Oxford 1933, 1962 (corrected).

Albrecht, O. E. Four Latin plays of St Nicholas. Philadelphia 1935.

Inguanez, D. M. Un dramma della passione del secolo xii. Montecassino 1936, 1939 (rev).

— Il 'Quem quaeritis' pasquale nei Codici Cassinesi. Studi Medievali 14 1941.

Sievers, H. Die lateinischen liturgischen Osterspiele der Stiftskirche St Blasien zu Braunschweig. Berlin 1936. With music.

Thomas, L.-P. Le Sponsus. Paris 1951. Text, trn, music.

Hartl, E. Das Benediktbeurer Passionsspiel; Das St Galler Passionsspiel. Halle 1952.

Smits van Waesberghe, J. A Dutch Easter play. Musica Disciplina 7 1953. With music.

— Das Nürnberger Osterspiel. In Festschrift Joseph Schmidt-Görg, Bonn 1957. With music.

Vecchi, G. Uffici drammatici padovani. Florence 1954. With texts, music, Italian trns.

Cohen, G. Anthologie du drame liturgique en France au Moyen-Age. Paris 1955. Texts and trns.

Kaff, L. Mittelalterliche Oster- und Passionsspiele aus Oberösterreich. Linz 1956. With music.

Krieg, E. Das lateinische Osterspiel von Tours. Würzburg 1956. With music.

Donovan, R. B. The liturgical drama in medieval Spain. Toronto 1958.

Tintori, G. Sacre rappresentazioni nel manoscritto 201 della Bibliothèque Municipale di Orléans. Cremona 1958. With music.

Greenberg, N. The play of Daniel: a thirteenth-century musical drama. New York 1959. Text, trn, music.

— and W. L. Smoldon. The play of Herod. New York 1965. Text, trn, music.

Gégou, F. Fragment de drame liturgique (?) découvert dans le Manuscrit La Vallière de la Bibliothèque Nationale. Revue de Musicologie 45 1960. With music.

Smoldon, W. L. Herod: a medieval nativity play. 1960. With music.

— The play of Daniel. 1960. With text, trn, music.

— Visitatio sepulchri: an acting version, from the Fleury playbook. Oxford 1964. With text, trn, music.

— Peregrinus: an acting version, from Beauvais. Oxford 1965. With music, trn, text.

— Planctus Mariae: an acting version. Oxford 1965. With music, trn, text.

— Officium pastorum: an acting version. Oxford 1967. With music, trn and text.

Sterne, C. C. The son of Getron. Pittsburgh 1962. With music, trn, text.

Lipphardt, W. Das Herodesspiel von Le Mans nach den Handschriften Madrid, Bibl. Nac. 288 und 289 (11. und 12. Jhd.). In Organicae voces: Festschrift Joseph Smits van Waesberghe, Amsterdam 1963. With music.

Bailey, T. The Fleury play of Herod. Toronto 1965. Text, trn, music.

Bernard, M. L'Officium stellae nivernais. Revue de Musicologie 51 1965. With music.

Lewański, J. Dramat i dramatyzacje liturgiczne w średniowieczu Polskim. Musica Medii Aevi 1 1965.

Stäblein, B. Zur Musik des Ludus de Antichristo. In Zum 70 Geburtstag von Joseph Müller-Blattau, Cassel 1966.

Bischoff, B. Carmina burana. 2 vols Munich 1967 (facs).

Wright, J. The play of Antichrist. Toronto 1967. Trn.

Boor, H. de. Das holländische Osterspiel. Acta Germanica 3 1968.

Stenzl, J. Die Sittener Osterfeier. Kirchenmusikalisches Jahrbuch 52 1968. With music.

de Mézières, P. Figurative representation of the presentation of the Virgin Mary in the Temple, ed R. S. Haller and M. C. Rupp. Lincoln Nebraska 1971. With text and trn.

(5) ANGLO-NORMAN DRAMA

Surveys and Special Studies

Frank, G. The medieval French drama. Oxford 1954.

Legge, M. D. Anglo-Norman literature and its background. Oxford 1963. Ch 12.

Hardison, O. B., jr. Christian rite and Christian drama in the Middle Ages. Baltimore 1965. Ch 7.

Jodogne, O. Recherches sur les débuts du théâtre religieux en France. Cahiers de Civilisation Médiévale 8 1965.

— La tonalité des mystères français. In Studi in onore di Italo Siciliano, Florence 1966.

Sinclair, K. V. Anglo-Norman studies: the last twenty years. Australian Jnl of French Stud 2 1965.

Texts and Criticism
Le Mystère d'Adam, or Ordo representacionis Ade, or Le Jeu d'Adam

§1

Ed K. Grass, Halle 1891, 1907, 1928 (rev); ed P. Studer, Manchester 1918; tr S. F. Barrow and W. H. Hulme, Cleveland 1925; tr E. N. Stone, Seattle 1926; ed G. Cohen, Paris 1936 (abridged and modernized); tr Norwegian by L. Sletsjöe, Oslo 1961; ed P. Aebischer, Geneva 1963; ed U. Ebel, Munich 1968; ed Sletsjöe, Paris 1968; Robertson (extract); tr L. R. Muir, Leeds Philosophical & Literary Soc, Literary & Historical Section 13 1970.

§2

Breuer, H. Untersuchungen zum lateinisch-altfranzösischen Adamsspiel. Zeitschrift für Romanische Philologie 51-2 1931-2.

Frank, G. The genesis and staging of the Jeu d'Adam. PMLA 59 1944.

Auerbach, E. In his Mimesis, Berne 1946; tr 1953. Ch 7.

Calin, W. C. Structural and doctrinal unity in the Jeu d'Adam. Neophilologus 46 1962.

— Cain and Abel in the Mystère d'Adam. MLR 63 1963.

Woolf, R. The fall of man in Genesis B and the Mystère d'Adam. In Studies in Old English literature in honor of Arthur G. Brodeur, Eugene 1963.

Kaske, R. E. The character of 'figura' in Le Mystère d'Adam. In Mediaeval studies in honor of U. T. Holmes jr, Chapel Hill 1965.

Sletsjöe, L. Histoire d'un texte: les vicissitudes qu'a connues le Mystère d'Adam 1854–1963. Studia Neophilologica 37 1965.

Vincent, P. R. Adam's lament in the Jeu d'Adam. L'Esprit Créateur 5 1965.

Mathieu, M. La mise en scène du Mystère d'Adam. Marche Romane 16 1966.

Noomen, W. Le 'Jeu d'Adam': étude descriptive et analytique. Romania 89 1968.

La Seinte Resureccion

§1

Ed T. Jenkins, J. Manly, M. Pope and J. Wright, Oxford 1943; tr Norwegian by L. Sletsjöe, Oslo 1961.

§2

Wright, J. G. A study of the themes of the Resurrection in the mediaeval French drama. Bryn Mawr 1935.

Pope, M. K. Variant readings to three Anglo-Norman poems. In Studies in French language, literature and history presented to R. L. G. Ritchie, Cambridge 1949.

Noomen, W. Passages narratifs dans les drames médiévaux français. Revue Belge de Philologie et d'Histoire 36 1958.

The Cambridge Prologue
See under English Mystery and Miracle Plays, below.

The Rickinghall (Bury St Edmunds) Fragment
See under English Mystery and Miracle Plays, below.

(6) CORNISH AND WELSH DRAMA

Surveys and Special Studies

Le Braz, A. Le théâtre celtique. Paris [1905].

Jenner, H. The Cornish drama. Celtic Rev 3–4 1907–8.

Cuillandre, J. Contributions à l'étude des textes corniques. Revue Celtique 48–9 1931–2.

Nance, R. M. The plen an gwary or Cornish playing-place. Jnl Royal Institution of Cornwall 24 1935.

Parry, R. W. Cyfieithwyr y dramâu Cernyweg. Bull Board of Celtic Stud 8 1937.

Jones, G. A study of three Welsh religious plays. [Bala] 1939.

Holman, T. Cornish plays and playing places. Theatre Notebook 4 1950.

Williams, N. J. A. Four textual notes on the Middle Cornish drama. Bull Board of Celtic Stud 22 1968.

Texts and Criticism
The Cornish Ordinalia

§ 1

Ed and tr E. Norris, The ancient Cornish drama, 2 vols Oxford 1859; tr F. E. Halliday, The legend of the rood, 1955 (abridged and adapted); Cawley (extract); ed and tr J. Earthy, M. Merchant and R. Muscatt in Translations of Cornish, Old Welsh, Anglo-Saxon, Exeter 1967 (extract); tr M. Harris, Washington 1969.

§ 2

[Stokes, W.] (ed and tr). The passion: a Middle-Cornish poem. Trans of Philological Soc 1860–1.

— A collation of Norris' Ancient Cornish drama. Archiv für Celtische Lexikographie 1 1900.

Loth, J. Etudes corniques. Revue Celtique 26 1905.

Fowler, D. C. The date of the Cornish Ordinalia. Mediaeval Stud 23 1961.

Longsworth, R. The Cornish ordinalia: religion and dramaturgy. Cambridge Mass 1967.

Meyer, R. T. The liturgical background of mediaeval Cornish drama. Trivium 3 1968.

The Creation of the World (Gwreans an bys)

Ed and tr D. Gilbert and J. Keigwin 1827; ed and tr W. Stokes, Trans of Philological Soc 1864. *See* P. Neuss, Memorial reconstruction in a Cornish miracle play, Comparative Drama 5 1972.

The Life of St Meriasek (Beunans Meriasek)

§ 1

Ed and tr W. Stokes 1872; ed and tr R. M. Nance and A. S. D. Smith 1966 (rev) (extract).

§ 2

Stokes, W. A glossary to the Cornish drama Beunans Meriasek. Archiv für Celtische Lexikographie 1 1900.

Meyer, R. T. The Middle-Cornish play Beunans Meriasek. Comparative Drama 3 1970.

Cornish Fragments (of a drama?)

Ed H. Jenner, Athenaeum 1 Dec 1877; ed and tr W. S[tokes], Revue Celtique 4 1880; ed and tr H. Jenner, Jnl of Royal Institution of Cornwall 20 1915; ed E. Campanile, Studi e saggi linguistici (suppl to L'Italia Dialettale) 3 1964.

The Three Kings of Cologne (Y Tri Brenin o Gwlen)

Ed and tr G. Jones, Study of three Welsh religious plays, [Bala] 1939.

The Passion (Y Dioddefaint)

Ed and tr G. Jones, ibid.

(7) ENGLISH MYSTERY AND MIRACLE PLAYS

Surveys and Special Studies

See also Chambers, Creizenach, Gayley, Kinghorn, Mill, Nicoll, Rossiter, Stemmler, Ward, Wells and Wickham, above.

Sharp, T. Dissertation on the pageants or dramatic mysteries anciently performed at Coventry. Coventry 1825.

Collier, J. P. The history of English dramatic poetry. 3 vols 1831, 1879 (rev).

Ebert, A. Die englischen Mysterien. Jahrbuch für Romanische und Englische Literatur 1 1859.

Symonds, J. A. Shakspere's predecessors in the English drama. 1884, 1900 (rev). Ch 3.

Hohlfeld, A. Die altenglischen Kollektivmisterien. Anglia 11 1889.

Pollard, A. W. English miracle plays moralities and interludes. Oxford 1890, 1927 (rev). Introd.

Davidson, C. Studies in the English mystery plays. New Haven 1892.

Bates, K. L. The English religious drama. New York 1893.

Cushman, L. W. The Devil and the Vice in English dramatic literature before Shakespeare. Halle 1900.

Leach, A. F. Some English plays and players 1220–1548. In [F. J.] Furnivall miscellany, Oxford 1901.

Eckhardt, E. Die lustige Person im älteren englischen Drama. Berlin 1902.

Emerson, O. F. Legends of Cain, especially in Old and Middle English verse. PMLA 21 1906.

v. d. Gaaf, W. Miracles and mysteries in south-east Yorkshire. E Studien 36 1906.

Thien, U. Über die englischen Marienklagen. Kiel 1906.

Crowley, T. J. Character-treatment in the mediaeval drama. Notre Dame 1907.

Hulme, W. H. (ed). The Middle-English Harrowing of Hell and Gospel of Nicodemus. 1907 (EETS).

Manly, J. M. Literary forms and the new theory of the origin of species. MP 4 1907.

— The miracle play in mediaeval England. Trans Royal Soc of Lit new ser 7 1927.

Moore, E. H. English miracle plays and moralities. 1907.

Taylor, G. C. The English Planctus Mariae. MP 4 1907.

—— The relation of the English Corpus Christi play to the Middle English lyric. MP 5 1908.

Mâle, E. L'art religieux de la fin du Moyen Age en France. Paris 1908, 1931 (rev).

Greene, A. An index to the non-Biblical names in the English mystery plays. In Studies in language and literature in celebration of the seventieth birthday of James Morgan Hart, New York 1910.

Spencer, M. L. Corpus Christi pageants in England. New York 1911.

Cron, B. Zur Entwicklungsgeschichte der englischen Misterien Alten Testaments. Marburg 1913.

Foster, F. A. (ed). The Northern Passion. 3 vols 1913–30 (EETS).

Campbell, E. M. Satire in the early English drama. Columbus 1914.

Dodds, M. H. The Northern stage. Archaeologia Aeliana 3rd ser 11 1914.

Duriez, G. La théologie dans le drame religieux en Allemagne au Moyen Age. Paris and Lille 1914.

Greg, W. W. Bibliographical and textual problems of the English miracle cycles. Library 3rd ser 5 1914; pbd separately 1914.

Pierson, M. The relation of the Corpus Christi procession to the Corpus Christi play in England. Trans Wisconsin Acad of Sciences, Arts & Letters 18 1915.

Coffman, G. R. The miracle play in England: nomenclature. PMLA 31 1916.

—— The miracle play in England. SP 16 1919.

—— A plea for the study of the Corpus Christi plays as drama. SP 26 1929.

Kretzmann, P. E. The liturgical element in the earliest forms of the medieval drama. Minneapolis 1916.

Bonnell, J. K. The serpent with a human head in art and in mystery play. Amer Jnl of Archaeology 21 1917.

Craig, H. The Lincoln cordwainers' pageant. PMLA 32 1917.

—— English religious drama of the Middle Ages. Oxford 1955.

Thomas, C. B. C. The miracle play at Dunstable. MLN 32 1917.

Frank, G. Revisions in the English mystery plays. MP 15 1918.

—— Popular iconography of the Passion. PMLA 46 1931.

Miller, F. H. The Northern Passion and the mysteries. MLN 34 1919.

Meier, H. Die Strophenformen in den englischen Misterienspielen. Freiburg 1921.

Witty, J. The Beverley plays. Trans Yorkshire Dialect Soc 4 1922.

Allison, T. E. The paternoster play and the origin of the Vices. PMLA 39 1924.

Dustoor, P. E. The origin of the play of Moses and the tables of the law. MLR 19 1924.

Vriend, J. The blessed Virgin Mary in the medieval drama of England. Purmerend 1928.

Adrian, G. Die Bühnenanweisungen in den englischen Mysterien. Bochum 1931.

Brown, C. An early mention of a St Nicholas play in England. SP 28 1931.

Tergau, D. Die sozialen Typen im Drama des englischen Mittelalters. Göttingen 1932.

Luke, C. The role of the Virgin Mary in the Coventry, York, Chester and Towneley cycles. Washington 1933.

Owst, G. R. Literature and pulpit in medieval England. Cambridge 1933, Oxford 1961 (rev). Ch 8.

Parker, R. E. The reputation of Herod in early English literature. Speculum 8 1933.

—— 'Pilates voys'. Speculum 25 1950. Suppl by L. Ellinwood 26 1951.

Young, K. An interludium for a gild of Corpus Christi. MLN 48 1933.

Mepham, W. A. Village plays at Dunmow, Essex, in the sixteenth century. N & Q 19–26 May 1934.

—— A xvi-century village play at Heybridge, Essex. N & Q 4 Aug 1934.

—— A general survey of mediaeval drama in Essex. Essex Rev 54 1945.

—— Mediaeval drama in Essex, Dunmow. Essex Rev 55 1946.

—— Mediaeval plays in the 16th century at Heybridge and Braintree. Ibid.

—— The Chelmsford plays of the sixteenth century. Essex Rev 56 1947.

—— Municipal drama at Maldon in the sixteenth century. Essex Rev 55–6 1946–7.

Tomlinson, W. E. Der Herodes-Charakter im englischen Drama. Leipzig 1934.

Radford, C. Early drama in Exeter. Report & Trans of Devonshire Assoc for Advancement of Science, Lit & Art 67 1935.

Deasy, C. P. St Joseph in the English mystery plays. Washington 1937.

Shull, V. Clerical drama in Lincoln cathedral, 1318 to 1561. PMLA 52 1937.

Hassall, W. O. Plays at Clerkenwell. MLR 33 1938.

Melchers, P. Kulturgeschichtliche Studien zu den mittelenglischen Misterienspielen. Würzburg 1938.

Mill, A. J. The Hull Noah play. MLR 33 1938.

—— Noah's wife again. PMLA 56 1941.

—— The Perth Hammermen's play: a Scottish Garden of Eden. Scottish Historical Rev 49 1970.

—— The Edinburgh Hammermen's Corpus Christi Herod pageant. Innes Rev 21 1970.

Whiting, B. J. Proverbs in the earlier English drama. Cambridge Mass 1938.

Wells, H. W. Style in the English mystery plays. JEGP 38 1939.

Blair, L. A note on the relation of the Corpus Christi procession to the Corpus Christi play in England. MLN 55 1940.

Wood, F. T. The comic elements in the English mystery plays. Neophilologus 25 1940.

Sullivan, J. A study of the themes of the sacred passion in the medieval cycle plays. Washington 1943.

Gardiner, H. C. Mysteries' end: an investigation of the last days of the medieval religious stage. New Haven 1946.

Aquin, M. The Vulgate and the Eve-concept in the English cycles. Catholic Biblical Quart 9 1947.

Hildburgh, W. L. English alabaster carvings as records of the medieval religious drama. Archaeologia 93 1949.

Craddock, L. G. Franciscan influences on early English drama. Franciscan Stud 10 1950.

Garth, H. M. Saint Mary Magdalene in mediaeval literature. Baltimore 1950.

Loomis, R. S. Lincoln as a dramatic centre. In Mélanges offerts à Gustave Cohen, Paris 1950.

—— Was there a play on the martyrdom of Hugh of Lincoln? MLN 69 1954.

McNeir, W. F. The Corpus Christi Passion plays as dramatic art. SP 48 1951.

Brown, A. Folklore elements in the medieval drama. Folklore 63 1952.

—— The study of English medieval drama. In Franciplegius: studies in honor of F. P. Magoun, New York 1965.

Wilson, R. M. The lost literature of medieval England. 1952. Ch 11.

Boughner, D. C. The braggart in Renaissance comedy. Minneapolis 1954. Ch 7.

Pantin, W. A. The English Church in the fourteenth century. Cambridge 1955. Pt 3.

Salter, F. M. Mediaeval drama in Chester. Toronto 1955.

Harder, K. B. Chaucer's use of the mystery plays in the Miller's tale. MLQ 17 1956.

Ingram, R. W. The use of music in English miracle plays. Anglia 75 1957.

Lombardo, A. Il dramma pre-shakespeariano. Venice 1957.

Southern, R. The medieval theatre in the round: a study of the staging of the Castle of Perseverance and related matters. 1957. Reply by N. C. Schmitt, Theatre Notebook 23–4 1969–70.

Speirs, J. Medieval English poetry. 1957. Reply by T. Fry, Amer Benedictine Rev 9 1959.

Swart, J. The insubstantial pageant. Neophilologus 41 1957.

Woolf, R. The effect of typology on the English mediaeval plays of Abraham and Isaac. Speculum 32 1957.

Stevens, J. Music in mediaeval drama. Proc of Royal Musical Assoc 84 1958.

Bowles, E. A. The role of musical instruments in medieval sacred drama. Musical Quart 45 1959.

Dunn, E. C. The medieval 'cycle' as history play: an approach to the Wakefield plays. Stud in Renaissance 7 1960.

Wolff, E. Die Terminologie des mittelalterlichen Dramas in bedeutungsgeschichtlicher Sicht. Anglia 78 1960.

Prosser, E. Drama and religion in the English mystery plays: a re-evaluation. Stanford 1961.

Williams, A. The drama of medieval England. East Lansing 1961.

— Typology and the cycle plays: some criteria. Speculum 43 1968.

Jacquot, J. Théâtre médiéval et tragédie élisabéthaine. In Le théâtre tragique, ed Jacquot, Paris 1962.

Janicka, I. The comic elements in the English mystery plays. Poznan 1962.

Anderson, M. D. Drama and imagery in English medieval churches. Cambridge 1963.

Browne, E. M. Producing the mystery plays for modern audiences. Drama Survey 3 1963.

Campbell, A. P. The mediaeval mystery cycle liturgical in impulse. Revue de l'Université d'Ottawa 33 1963.

Morgan, M. M. 'High fraud': paradox and double-plot in the English shepherds' plays. Speculum 39 1964.

Taylor, J. The dramatic structure of the Middle English Corpus Christi or cycle plays. In Literature and society, ed B. Slote, Lincoln Nebraska 1964.

Tribby, W. L. The medieval prompter: a reinterpretation. Theatre Survey 5 1964.

Hurrell, J. D. The figural approach to medieval drama. College Eng May 1965.

McAlindon, T. Comedy and terror in Middle English literature: the diabolical game. MLR 60 1965.

Robinson, J. W. The late medieval cult of Jesus and the mystery plays. PMLA 80 1965.

Kolve, V. A. The play called Corpus Christi. Stanford 1966.

Macaulay, P. S. The play of the Harrowing of Hell as a climax in the English mystery cycles. Studia Germanica Gandensia 8 1966.

Wiemann, R. Platea und locus im Misterienspiel: zu einem Grundprinzip vorshakespearescher Dramaturgie. Anglia 84 1966.

— Die furchtbare Komik des Herodes. Archiv 204 1968.

— Shakespeare und die Tradition des Volkstheaters. Berlin 1967.

Kahrl, S. J. Medieval drama in Louth. Research Opportunities in Renaissance Drama 10 1967.

Margeson, J. M. R. The origins of English tragedy. Oxford 1967. Ch 1.

Carpenter, N. C. Music in the English mystery plays. In Music in English Renaissance drama, ed J. H. Long, Lexington Kentucky 1968.

Roston, M. Biblical drama in England from the Middle Ages to the present day. 1968. Ch 1.

Selz, W. A. (ed). Medieval drama. Vermillion South Dakota 1968.

Stemmler, T. Entstehung und Wesen der englischen Fronleichnamszyklen. In Chaucer und seine Zeit: Symposion für Walter F. Schirmer, Tübingen 1968.

Elliott, J. R. The sacrifice of Isaac as comedy and tragedy. SP 66 1969.

Mills, D. Approaches to medieval drama. Leeds Stud in Eng new ser 3 1969.

Schmitt, N. C. Was there a medieval theatre in the round? Theatre Notebook 23–4 1969–70.

Walsh, M. M. The judgment plays of the English cycles. Amer Benedictine Rev 20 1969.

Wickham, G. In his Shakespeare's dramatic heritage, 1969. Ch 1.

— The staging of saint plays in England. In The medieval drama, ed S. Sticca, Albany 1972.

Leigh, D. J. The Doomsday mystery play: an eschatological morality. MP 67 1970.

Rendall, T. Liberation from bondage in the Corpus Christi plays. Neuphilologische Mitteilungen 71 1970.

Blackburn, R. Biblical drama under the Tudors. Hague 1971.

Hosley, R. Three kinds of outdoor theatre before Shakespeare. Theatre Survey 12 1971.

Stevens, M. Illusion and reality in the medieval drama. College Eng Jan 1971.

Nelson, A. H. Some configurations of staging in medieval English drama. In Medieval English drama, ed J. Taylor and A. H. Nelson, Chicago 1972.

Texts and Criticism
The Cycles

The Chester Plays

§1

Ed T. Wright 2 vols 1843–7 (Shakespeare Soc); ed H. Deimling and Dr Matthews 2 pts 1892–1916 (EETS); ed I. and O. Bolton King 1930 (abridged and modernized); ed M. Hussey 1957 (16 plays modernized).

One or more plays: Ed J. H. Markland 1818 (Noah, Innocents) (Roxburghe Club); Collier; Marriott; Pollard; Manly; Hemingway; Adams; ed P. E. Dustoor, Allahabad 1930 (Fall of Lucifer); ed W. W. Greg, Oxford 1935 (Antichrist); ed F. M. Salter, Oxford 1935 (Trial and flagellation) (Malone Soc); ed W. W. Greg in Trial and flagellation, Oxford 1935 (Malone Soc) (fragment of the Resurrection and banns); Cawley; Browne; Franklin; Gassner; Thomas.

§2

See also Brome Abraham, below.

Deimling, H. W. E. Text-Gestalt und Text-Kritik der Chester plays. Berlin 1890.

Ungemach, H. Die Quellen der fünf ersten Chester plays. Erlangen and Leipzig 1890.

Utesch, H. Die Quellen der Chester plays. Kiel 1909.

Baugh, A. C. The Chester plays and French influence. In [F. E] Schelling anniversary papers, New York 1923.

Foster, F. A. A stanzaic life of Christ. 1926 (EETS).

Wilson, R. H. The stanzaic life of Christ and the Chester plays. SP 28 1931.

[Salter, F. M. and W. W. Greg]. The trial and flagellation with other studies in the Chester cycle. Oxford 1935 (Malone Soc).

Crocker, S. F. The production of the Chester plays. West Virginia Univ Stud 1 1936.

Salter, F. M. The banns of the Chester plays. RES 15–16 1939–40.

— Mediaeval drama in Chester. Toronto 1955.

Lucken, L. U. Antichrist and the prophets of Antichrist in the Chester cycle. Washington 1940.

Bryant, J. A. Chester's sermon for catechumens. JEGP 53 1954.

Lumiansky, R. M. Comedy and theme in the Chester Harrowing of Hell. Tulane Stud in Eng 10 1960.

Carpenter, N. C. Music in the Chester plays. Papers on Eng Lang & Lit 1 1965.

Stemmler, T. Zur Datierung der Chester plays. Germanisch-romanische Monatsschrift 18 1968.

Brownstein, O. L. Revision in the Deluge of the Chester cycle. Speech Monographs 36 1969.

Powlick, L. The staging of the Chester cycle: an alternate theory. Theatre Survey 12 1971.

Martin, L. Comic eschatology in the Chester Coming of Antichrist. Comparative Drama 5 1972.

The Coventry Plays (or True-Coventry Plays)

§ 1

Shearmen and tailors' play. [Ed T. Sharp], Coventry 1817; ed T. Sharp, A dissertation on the Coventry mysteries, Coventry 1825; Marriott; Manly; ed A. W. Pollard, Fifteenth-century prose and verse, 1903 (modernized); Browne; Gassner.
Weavers' play. [Ed J. B. Gracie? and T. Sharp], Edinburgh 1836 (Abbotsford Club).
[Both plays]. Ed H. Craig 1902, 1957 (rev) (EETS).

§ 2

Sharp, T. A dissertation on the pageants or dramatic mysteries anciently performed at Coventry. Coventry 1825.

Flower, R. The Coventry mysteries. BM Quart 8 1934.

Cutts, J. P. The second Coventry carol. Renaissance News 10 1957.

Ludus Coventriae (or Hegge Plays or N-Town Cycle)

§ 1

Ed J. O. Halliwell 1841 (Shakespeare Soc); ed K. S. Block 1922 (EETS); ed R. T. Davies 1972 (abridged and modernized).
One or more plays: Collier; Marriott; Pollard; Manly; Hemingway; ed W. W. Greg, Oxford 1915 (Assumption of the Virgin); Adams; Loomis; Cawley; Browne; Thomas.

§ 2

Hone, W. Ancient mysteries described. 1823.

Kramer, M. Sprache und Heimat des sogen[annten] Ludus Coventriae. Halle 1892.

Traver, H. The four daughters of God. Bryn Mawr 1907.

Falke, E. Die Quellen des sog[enannten] Ludus Coventriae. Leipzig 1908.

Bonnell, J. K. The source in art of the so-called Prophets Play in the Hegge Collection. PMLA 29 1914.

Dodds, M. H. The problem of the Ludus Coventriae. MLR 9 1914.

Swenson, E. L. An inquiry into the composition and structure of Ludus Coventriae. Minneapolis 1914.

Patch, H. R. The Ludus Coventriae and the Digby Massacre. PMLA 35 1920.

Taylor, G. C. The Christus Redivivus of Nicholas Grimald and the Hegge Resurrection plays. PMLA 41 1926.

Parker, R. E. The Middle English stanzaic versions of the life of Saint Anne. 1928 (EETS). Ch 4.

Benkovitz, M. J. Some notes on the Prologue of Demon of Ludus Coventriae. MLN 60 1945.

Fry, T. The unity of the Ludus Coventriae. SP 48 1951.

Bryant, J. A. The function of Ludus Coventriae 14. JEGP 52 1953.

Forrest, M. P. Apocryphal sources of the St Anne's day plays in the Hegge cycle. Medievalia et Humanistica 17 1966.

— The role of the expositor Contemplacio in the St Anne's day plays of the Hegge cycle. Mediaeval Stud 28 1966.

Cameron, K. and S. J. Kahrl. Staging the N-town cycle. Theatre Notebook 21 1967.

Meredith, P. 'Nolo mortem' and the Ludus Coventriae play of the Woman taken in adultery. MÆ 38 1969.

Griffin, J. R. The Hegge Pilate: a tragic hero? E Studies 51 1970.

Eccles, M. Ludus Coventriae: Lincoln or Norfolk? MÆ 40 1971.

The Towneley Plays (or Wakefield Plays)
See also the Wakefield Master's plays, below.

§ 1

[Ed J. Gordon and J. Hunter] 1836 (Surtees Soc); ed G. England and A. W. Pollard 1897 (EETS); ed M. Rose 1961 (modernized).
One or more plays: [Ed F. Douce] 1822 (Judicium, Roxburghe Club); Marriott; Manly; Hemingway; Adams; Loomis; Gassner; Thomas.

§ 2

Bunzen, A. Ein Beitrag zur Kritik de Wakefielder Mysterien. Kiel 1903.

Brown, C. The Towneley play of the Doctors and the Speculum Christiani. MLN 31 1916.

Wann, L. A new examination of the manuscript of the Towneley plays. PMLA 43 1928.

Smith, J. H. The date of some Wakefield borrowings from York. PMLA 53 1938.

Clark, E. M. Liturgical influences in the Towneley plays. Orate Fratres 16 1941.

— The Towneley Peregrini. MLN 61 1946.

Frampton, M. G. The Towneley Harrowing of Hell. PMLA 56 1941.

— Towneley XX: the conspiracio (et capcio). PMLA 58 1943.

— The processus talentorum (Towneley xxiv). PMLA 59 1944.

Kökeritz, H. Some marginal notes to the Towneley Resurrection. MLN 61 1946.

Williams, A. The characterization of Pilate in the Towneley plays. East Lansing 1950.

Speirs, J. In his Medieval English poetry, 1957.

Stevens, M. The accuracy of the Towneley scribe. HLQ 22 1959.

— The composition of the Towneley Talents play: a linguistic examination. JEGP 58 1959.

— The dramatic setting of the Wakefield Annunciation. PMLA 81 1966.

— The staging of the Wakefield plays. Research Opportunities in Renaissance Drama 11 1968.

— The missing parts of the Towneley cycle. Speculum 45 1970.

Dunn, E. C. Lyrical form and the prophetic principle in the Towneley plays. Mediaeval Stud 23 1961.

— The literary style of the Towneley plays. Amer Benedictine Rev 20 1969.

Maltman, N. Pilate os malleatoris. Speculum 36 1961.

Crewe, J. V. The Wakefield play of the Crucifixion. Theoria 22 1964.

Munson, W. F. Typology and the Towneley Isaac. Research Opportunities in Renaissance Drama 11 1968.

Altieri, J. S. The ironic structure of the Towneley Fflagellacio. Drama Survey 7 1969.

Davidson, C. An interpretation of the Wakefield Judicium. Annuale Mediaevale 10 1969.

Brawer, R. A. The dramatic function of the Ministry group in the Towneley cycle. Comparative Drama 4 1970.

Meyers, W. A figure given: typology in the Wakefield plays. Pittsburgh 1970.

The 'Wakefield Master's' Plays
(plays 2–3, 12–13, 16 and 21 in the Towneley cycle)

§1

Ed A. C. Cawley, Manchester 1958.
One or more plays: Collier; Marriott; Pollard; Manly; Hemingway; Adams; Loomis; Cawley; Browne; Franklin; Gassner; Thomas; Robertson.

§2

For criticism of other plays written partly in the 'Wakefield Master's' stanzaic form (plays 20, 22–4, 27, 29–30) see above.

Hamelius, P. The character of Cain in the Towneley plays. Jnl of Comparative Lit 1 1903.

Carey, M. The Wakefield group in the Towneley cycle. Göttingen 1930.

Frampton, M. G. The date of the flourishing of the 'Wakefield Master'. PMLA 50 1935.
— The date of the 'Wakefield Master': bibliographical evidence. PMLA 53 1938. Reply by J. H. Smith, ibid.

Trusler, M. The language of the Wakefield playwright. SP 33 1936.

Watt, H. A. The dramatic unity of the Secunda pastorum. In Essays and studies in honor of Carleton Brown, New York 1940.

Cosbey, R. C. The Mak story and its folklore analogues. Speculum 20 1945.

Chidamian, C. Mak and the tossing in the blanket. Speculum 22 1947.

Thompson, F. J. Unity in the Second shepherds' tale. MLN 64 1949.

Carpenter, N. C. Music in the Secunda pastorum. Speculum 26 1951.

Cawley, A. C. The Wakefield first shepherds' play. Proc of Leeds Philosophical Soc (Literary & Historical Section) 7 1953.

Zumwalt, E. E. Irony in the Towneley Shepherds' plays. Research Stud of State College of Washington 26 1958.

Peel, D. F. The allegory in the Secunda pastorum. Northwest Missouri State College Stud 24 1960.

Schless, H. H. The comic element in the Wakefield Noah. In Studies in medieval literature in honor of A. C. Baugh, Philadelphia 1961.

Bernbrock, J. E. Notes on the Towneley cycle Slaying of Abel. JEGP 62 1963.

Manly, W. M. Shepherds and prophets: religious unity in the Towneley Secunda pastorum. PMLA 78 1963.

Dunn, E. C. The prophetic principle in the Towneley Prima pastorum. In Linguistic and literary studies in honor of Helmut A. Hatzfeld, Washington 1964.

Nelson, A. H. 'Sacred' and 'secular' currents in the Towneley play of Noah. Drama Survey 3 1964.

Diller, H.-J. The craftsmanship of the 'Wakefield Master'. Anglia 83 1965.

Gardner, J. Theme and irony in the Wakefield Mactacio Abel. PMLA 80 1965.
— Structure and tone in the Second Shepherds' play. Educational Theatre Jnl 19 1967.
— Imagery and allusion in the Wakefield Noah play. Papers on Lang & Lit 4 1968.

Cantelupe, E. B., and R. Griffith. The gifts of the shepherds in the Wakefield 'Secunda pastorum': an iconographical interpretation. Mediaeval Stud 28 1966.

Johnson, W. H. The origin of the Second shepherds' play: a new theory. Quart Jnl of Speech 52 1966.

Davidson, C. The unity of the Wakefield 'Mactacio Abel'. Traditio 23 1967.

Sachs, A. The raven and the dove: an iconographic comparison between the Holkham and Towneley Noahs. In Studies in the drama, ed A. Sachs, Jerusalem 1967.

Weimann, R. Realismus und Simultankonvention im Misteriendrama: Mimesis, Parodie und Utopie in den Towneley-Hirtenszenen. Sh Jb 103 1967.

Elliott, C. Language and theme in the Towneley Magnus Herodes. Mediaeval Stud 30 1968.

Ross, L. J. Symbol and structure in the Secunda pastorum. Comparative Drama 1 1968.

Sanders, B. Who's afraid of Jesus Christ? Comparative Drama 2 1969.

Longo, J. A. Symmetry and symbolism in the Secunda Pastorum. Nottingham Mediaeval Stud 13 1969.

Cutts, J. P. The shepherds' gifts in the Second shepherds' play and Bosch's Adoration of the Magi. Comparative Drama 4 1970.

Steinberg, C. Kemp towne in the Towneley Herod play. Neuphilologische Mitteilungen 71 1970.

Remly, L. Deus caritas: the Christian message of the Secunda pastorum. Neuphilologische Mitteilungen 72 1971.

The York Plays

§1

Ed L. T. Smith, Oxford 1885; ed J. S. Purvis 1957 (modernized).
One or more plays: Pollard; Manly; Hemingway; Adams; ed A. C. Cawley, Leeds 1952 (Sykes ms of the Scriveners' play); Cawley; Browne; Franklin; Gassner; Thomas.

§2

Herttrich, O. Studien zu den York plays. Breslau 1886.

Holthausen, F. Beiträge zur Erklärung und Textkritik der York plays. Archiv 85–6 1890–1.

Coblentz, H. E. A rime-index to the parent cycle of the York mystery plays and of a portion of the Woodkirk Conspiracio et capito. PMLA 10 1895.

Kölbing, E. Beiträge zur Erklärung und Textkritik der York plays. E Studien 20 1895.

Craigie, W. A. The Gospel of Nicodemus and the York mystery plays. In An English miscellany presented to Dr [F. J.] Furnivall, Oxford 1901.

Lyle, M. C. The original identity of the York and Towneley cycles. Minneapolis 1919. Replies by E. G. Clark, PMLA 43 1928; F. A. Foster, ibid; G. Frank 44 1929; M. C. Lyle, ibid; F. W. Cady, SP 26 1929.

Frank, G. St Martial of Limoges in the York plays. MLN 44 1929.

Young, K. The records of the York play of the Pater noster. Speculum 7 1932.

Trusler, M. The York Sacrificium Cayme and Abell. PMLA 49 1934.

Mill, A. J. The York Bakers' play of the Last Supper. MLR 30 1935.
— The York plays of the dying, assumption and coronation of Our Lady. PMLA 65 1950.
— The stations of the York Corpus Christi play. Yorkshire Archaeological Jnl pt 148 1951.

Frampton, M. G. The Brewbarret interpolation in the York play The sacrificium Cayme and Abell. PMLA 52 1937.
— The date of the 'Wakefield Master': bibliographical evidence. PMLA 53 1938.
— The York play of Christ led up to Calvary (play xxxiv). PQ 20 1941.

Hoffman, C. F., jr. The source of the words to the music in York 46. MLN 65 1950.

Reese, J. B. Alliterative verse in the York cycle. SP 48 1951.

Brown, A. Some notes on medieval drama in York. In Early English and Norse studies presented to Hugh Smith, 1963.
— York and its plays in the Middle Ages. In Chaucer und seine Zeit: Symposion für Walter F. Schirmer, Tübingen 1968.

Robinson, J. W. The art of the York Realist. MP 60 1963.
— A commentary on the York play of the birth of Jesus. JEGP 70 1971.

Young, M. J. The York pageant wagon. Speech Monographs 34 1967.

Wolff, E. Proculas Traum: der Yorker Misterienzyklus und die epische Tradition. In Chaucer und seine Zeit: Symposion für Walter F. Schirmer, Tübingen 1968.

Leiter, L. H. Typology, paradigm, metaphor and image in the York Creation of Adam and Eve. Drama Survey 7 1969.

Purvis, J. S. From Minster to market place. York [1969].

Nelson, A. H. Principles of processional staging: York cycle. MP 67 1970.

Wall, C. The apocryphal and historical backgrounds of the Appearance of Our Lady to Thomas. Mediaeval Stud 32 1970.

Other Plays and Fragments; Sermon against Miracle Plays

The Digby plays. Ed F. J. Furnivall 1882 (New Shakspere Soc), 1896 (EETS). *Furnivall.*

Non-cycle plays and fragments. Ed N. Davis 1970 (EETS). *Davis.*

Most of the English plays not so far listed are in these 2 collections; the few remaining pieces are listed below.

The Shrewsbury Fragments

§ 1

Ed W. W. Skeat, Academy 37 1890; ed K. Young, The drama of the medieval Church, Oxford 1933; Manly; Adams. No 1 in Davis.

§ 2

Miller, F. M. Metrical affinities of the Shrewsbury Officium pastorum and its York correspondent. MLN 33 1918.

The Norwich Grocers' Play (The Creation, Texts 'A' and 'B')

§ 1

Ed R. Fitch, Norfolk Archaeology 5 1859; Manly; Adams ('B' Text only); Franklin ('B' Text only). No 2 in Davis.

§ 2

Harrod, H. A few particulars concerning early Norwich pageants. Norfolk Archaeology 3 1852.

Nelson, A. H. On recovering the lost Norwich Corpus Christi cycle. Comparative Drama 4 1972.

The Newcastle Play (Noah's Ark)

Ed H. Bourne, The history of Newcastle upon Tyne, Newcastle 1736; ed F. Holthausen, Göteborgs Högskolas Arsskrift 1897; ed R. Brotanek, Anglia 21 1899. No 3 in Davis.

The Northampton (or 'Dublin') Abraham

Collier; ed R. Brotanek, Anglia 21 1899. No 4 in Davis.

The Brome Abraham

§ 1

Ed L. T. Smith, Anglia 7 1884; Manly; Adams, Cawley, Browne; Franklin; Gassner. No 5 in Davis.

§ 2

Harper, C. A. A comparison between the Brome and Chester plays of Abraham and Isaac. In Studies in English and comparative literature presented to Agnes Irwin, 1910.

Fort, M. D. The metres of the Brome and Chester Abraham and Isaac plays. PMLA 41 1926.

Dustoor, P. E. The Chester mss and the Brome play. Allahabad Univ Stud 5 1930.

Severs, J. B. The relationship between the Brome and Chester plays of Abraham and Isaac. MP 42 1945.

The Croxton Play of the Sacrament

§ 1

Ed W. S[tokes], Trans of Philological Soc 1860–1, appendix; Manly; Adams. No 6 in Davis.

§ 2

Cutts, C. The Croxton Play: an anti-Lollard piece. MLQ 5 1944.

Dux Moraud

§ 1

Ed W. Heuser, Anglia 30 1907; Adams. No 8 in Davis.

§ 2

Hieatt, C. B. A case for Duk Moraud as a play of the miracles of the Virgin. Mediaeval Stud 32 1970.

The Cambridge Prologue

Ed R. H. Robbins, MLN 65 1950. No 9 in Davis.

The Rickinghall (Bury St Edmunds) Fragment

Ed J. P. Gilson, TLS 26 May 1921. No 10 in Davis.

The Durham Prologue

Ed J. Cooling, RES 38 1959. No 11 in Davis.

The Ashmole Fragment, or Fragment from a (Caesar Augustus?) Play

Ed R. H. Robbins, Anglia 72 1955. No 12 in Davis.

The Reynes Extracts, or Norfolk Epilogue

Ed I. G. Calderhead, MP 14 1916. No 13 in Davis.

Diabolus' Speech (from a play?) quoted in some notes for a sermon

Ed C. Brown, MLN 49 1934.

The Digby Plays

§ 1

Ed [T. Sharp], Edinburgh 1835 (Abbotsford Club); Furnivall.

§ 2

Schmidt, K. Die Digby-Spiele. Berlin 1884.

—— Die Digby-Spiele. Anglia 8 1885.

Baker, D. C. and J. L. Murphy. The late medieval plays of ms Digby 133: scribes, dates and early history. Research Opportunities in Renaissance Drama 10 1967.

Herod's killing of the children. Hawkins; Marriott; Furnivall.

The conversion of St Paul. Furnivall; Manly; Adams. *See* M. Villar, The staging of the Conversion of St Paul, Theatre Notebook 25 1971.

Mary Magdalene. Furnivall; Pollard (abridged); Adams (abridged).

On Mary Magdalene see

Ritchie, H. M. A suggested location for the Digby Mary Magdalene. Theatre Survey 4 1963.

Bowers, R. H. The tavern scene in the Middle English Digby play of Mary Magdalene. In All these to teach: essays in honor of C. A. Robertson, Gainesville 1965.

Velz, J. W. Sovereignty in the Digby Mary Magdalene. Comparative Drama 2 1969.

Christ's Burial and Resurrection

§1

Ed T. Wright and J. O. Halliwell, Reliquiae antiquae vol 2, 1843; ed F. J. Furnivall, The Digby plays, 1882, 1896.

§2

Abel, P. Grimald's Christus redivivus and the Digby Resurrection play. MLN 70 1955.

Baker, D. C. and J. L. Murphy. The Bodleian ms E Mus. 160 Burial and Resurrection and the Digby plays. RES new ser 19 1968.

Woolf, R. The English religious lyric in the Middle Ages. Oxford 1968. Ch 7.

The Stonyhurst Pageants

§1

Ed C. Brown, Göttingen 1920 (Hesperia).

§2

Craig, H. Terentius Christianus and the Stonyhurst Pageants. PQ 2 1923.

Processus Satanae

[Ed W. W. Greg], Collections vol 2 pt 3, 1931 (Malone Soc).

The Resurrection of Our Lord (c. 1530–60)

Ed J. D. Wilson and B. Dobell 1912 (Malone Soc).

A Sermon against Miracle Plays

See col 490, above.

(8) SPECTACLES AND MINSTRELSY TO 1485

Surveys and Special Studies

See also Chambers, Kernodle, Mill, Nicoll and Wickham under (2), above. For the Tudor period see col 1361, below.

Strutt, J. The sports and pastimes of the people of England. 1801, 1903 (rev J. C. Cox).

Legg, L. G. Wickham. English coronation records. Westminster 1901.

Brotanek, R. Die englischen Maskenspiele. Vienna 1902.

Reich, H. Der Mimus. Berlin 1903.

Allen, P. S. The mediaeval mimus. MP 7–8 1910–11.

— Medieval Latin lyrics. Chicago 1931. Ch 7.

Faral, E. Les jongleurs en France au Moyen Age. Paris 1910.

Webster, K. The twelfth-century tourney. In Anniversary papers by colleagues and pupils of George Lyman Kittredge, Boston 1913.

Withington, R. The early 'Royal Entry'. PMLA 32 1917.

— English pageantry. 2 vols Cambridge Mass 1918–20.

Cripps-Day, F. H. History of the tournament in England and in France. 1918.

Clephan, R. C. The tournament: its periods and phases. 1919.

Chaytor, H. J. The troubadours and England. Cambridge 1923.

Welsford, E. The Court masque. Cambridge 1927.

— The fool. 1935.

Mead, W. The English medieval feast. Boston 1931. Ch 6.

Warren, F. (ed). The dance of death. 1931 (EETS).

Sandberger, D. Studien über das Rittertum in England. Berlin 1937.

Schramm, P. E. A history of the English coronation. Oxford 1937.

Loomis, R. S. Chivalric and dramatic imitations of Arthurian romance. In Medieval studies in memory of A. Kingsley Porter vol 1, Cambridge Mass 1939.

— Edward I, Arthurian enthusiast. Speculum 28 1953.

Wagner, A. R. Heralds and heraldry in the Middle Ages. Oxford 1939.

Olson, C. The minstrels at the Court of Edward III. PMLA 56 1941.

Kernodle, G. R. From art to theatre. Chicago 1944.

Cline, R. H. The influence of romances on tournaments of the Middle Ages. Speculum 20 1945.

Denholm-Young, N. The tournament in the thirteenth century. In Studies in medieval history presented to F. M. Powicke, Oxford 1948.

Clark, J. M. The dance of death. Glasgow 1950.

Bernheimer, R. Wild men in the Middle Ages. Cambridge Mass 1952.

Loomis, L. H. Secular dramatics in the Royal Palace, Paris 1378, 1379 and Chaucer's Tregetoures. Speculum 33 1958.

Poole, A. L. (ed). Medieval England. 2 vols Oxford 1958. Chs 11, 19.

Bowles, E. A. Musical instruments in civic processions during the Middle Ages. Acta Musicologica 33 1961.

— Musical instruments in the medieval Corpus Christi procession. Jnl Amer Musicological Soc 17 1964.

Anglo, S. Financial and heraldic records of the English tournament. Jnl Soc of Archivists 2 1962.

— Anglo-Burgundian feats of arms: Smithfield, June 1467. Guildhall Miscellany 2 1968.

— The great tournament roll of Westminster. 2 vols Oxford 1968. Ch 2.

— Spectacle, pageantry and early Tudor policy. Oxford 1969.

Ogilvy, J. D. A. Mimi, scurrae, histriones: entertainers of the early Middle Ages. Speculum 38 1963.

Fifield, M. Chaucer the theatre-goer. Papers on Lang & Lit 3 (suppl) 1967.

Texts and Criticism

References to contemporary descriptions of spectacles are contained in the works listed above, and in Brown and Robbins and Robbins and Cutler (indexed as Mummings). Minstrels are associated with much medieval literature, especially Romances and Lyrics; see cols 383, 697, above.

Caiaphas' Speech (a Palm Sunday sermon)

Ed T. Wright and J. O. Halliwell(-Phillipps), Reliquiae antiquae vol 2, 1843; ed C. Brown, Anniversary papers by colleagues and pupils of George Lyman Kittredge, Boston 1913.

Maister Benet's Cristemasse Game

Ed F. J. Furnivall, N & Q 16 May, 6 June 1868; ed [E.] Flügel, Anglia 14 1892.

John Lydgate's Mummings and Disguisings

§1

Ed H. N. MacCracken, Minor poems of Lydgate vol 2, 1934 (EETS).

§2

Renoir, A. On the date of Lydgate's Mumming at Hertford. Archiv 193 1961.

See also Lydgate, Poems, ed J. Norton-Smith, Oxford 1966.

Speeches by the Nine Worthies

Ed H. H. Furness, Loves labour's lost, Philadelphia 1904 (New Variorum Shakespeare); ed I. Gollancz, The Parlement of the three ages, Oxford 1915 (appendix 13).

A Mumming of the Seven Philosophers for the 'King of Christmas'

Ed R. H. Robbins, Secular lyrics of the xivth and xvth centuries, Oxford 1952.

A Dramatic Monologue by Law

Ed R. H. Robbins, ibid.

Speeches at Royal Entries

Henry VI, London 1432. Ed E. Gattinger, Die Lyrik Lydgates, Vienna 1896; ed H. N. MacCracken, Minor poems of John Lydgate pt 2, Oxford 1934 (EETS).

Queen Margaret, London 1445. Ed C. Brown, MLR 7 1912; ed R. Withington, MP 13 1916.

Queen Margaret, Coventry 1456, and Prince Edward, Coventry 1474. Ed H. Craig, Two Coventry Corpus Christi plays, 1902, 1957 (rev) (EETS); ed M. D. Harris, The Coventry Leet book pt 2, Oxford 1908 (EETS).

Interludium de Clerico et Puella
(a dramatized fabliau performed by minstrels?)

Ed T. Wright and J. O. Halliwell(-Phillipps), Reliquiae antiquae vol 1, 1841; ed G. V. Smithers, Early Middle English verse and prose, ed J. A. W. Bennett, Smithers and N. Davis, Oxford 1966, 1968 (rev).

(9) FOLK DRAMA

Surveys and Special Studies

See also Chambers, Mill, Withington and Rossiter under (2), above.

Ordish, T. F. Folk drama. Folklore 2 1891, 4 1893.

Beatty, A. The St George or mummers' plays: a study in the protology of the drama. Trans of Wisconsin Acad of Science, Arts & Letters 15 1907.

Moorman, F. W. A Yorkshire folk-play and its analogues. E & S 2 1911.

Smart, W. K. Mankind and the mumming plays. MLN 32 1917.

Baskervill, C. R. Dramatic aspects of medieval folk festivals in England. SP 17 1920.

— Mummers' wooing plays in England. MP 21 1924.

Steadman, J. The dramatization of the Robin Hood ballad. MP 17 1920.

Tiddy, R. J. E. The mummers' play. Oxford 1923.

Chambers, E. K. The English folk-play. Oxford 1933.

Alford, V. and R. Gallop. The traditional dance. 1935.

Simeone, W. E. The May games and the Robin Hood legend. Jnl of Amer Folklore 64 1951. Reply by J. Williams 65 1952.

Dean-Smith, M. Folk-play origins of the English masque. Folklore 65 1954.

— The life-cycle play or folk play. Folklore 69 1958.

— An unromantic view of the mummers' play. Theatre Research 8 1966.

Morse, J. M. The unity of the Revesby sword play. PQ 33 1954.

Barley, M. W. Plough plays in the East Midlands. Jnl Eng Folk Dance & Song Soc 7 1955.

Mares, F. H. The origin of the figure called 'the Vice' in Tudor drama. HLQ 22 1959.

Parker, R. E. Some records of the 'Somyr play'. In Studies in honor of John C. Hodges and Alwin Thaler, Knoxville 1961.

Alford, V. Sword dance and drama. 1962.

Cawte, E. C. et al. A geographical index of the ceremonial dance in Great Britain. Jnl Eng Folk Dance & Song Soc 9 1963.

—, A. Helm and N. Peacock. English ritual drama: a geographical index. 1967.

Happé, P. The Vice and the folk-drama. Folklore 75 1964.

Gailey, A. The folk-play in Ireland. Studia Hibernica 6 1966.

— Irish folk drama. Cork 1969.

Abrahams, R. D. 'Pull out your purse and pay'. Folklore 79 1968.

— British West Indian folk drama and the 'life cycle' problem. Folklore 81 1970.

Green, R. J. Some notes on the St George play. Theatre Survey 9 1968.

Halpert, H. and G. Story (ed). Christmas mumming in Newfoundland. Toronto 1969.

Helm, A. The chapbook mummers' plays. Leicester 1969.

Robinson, J. W. 'As small as flesh to pot'. Folklore 80 1969.

Spears, J. E. A note on the Shetland sword dance. Southern Folklore Quart 33 1969.

Brody, A. The English mummers and their plays: traces of ancient mystery. Philadelphia 1971.

Texts and Criticism
Robin Hood and the Sheriff of Nottingham

Ed F. J. Child, The English and Scottish popular ballads vol 3, Boston 1889; Manly; ed W. W. Greg, Malone Society collections vol 1 pt 2, Oxford 1908; Adams.

A Play of Robin Hood for May-Games (Robin Hood and the Friar, Robin Hood and the Potter)

Ed in A mery geste of Robyn Hoode and of hys lyfe with a newe play, [c. 1560]; ed F. J. Child, The English and Scottish popular ballads vol 3, Boston 1889; Manly; ed W. W. Greg, Malone Society collections vol 1, Oxford 1908; Adams.

[William Dunbar ?], The Dwarf's Part of the Play (or The Manner of the Crying of a Play)

§ I

Ed J. Small, Poems of Dunbar, 3 vols 1893; ed W. M. Mackenzie, Poems of Dunbar, 1932.

§ 2

Jones, G. F. Dunbar's 'Steidis'. MLN 69 1954.

Mummers' Plays (or Ritual Drama, or Men's Dramatic Ceremonies: St George Plays, Wooing Plays and Sword Dances)

For texts of mummers' plays see above: Tiddy (33 plays), Chambers (5 plays), Baskervill, Mummers' wooing plays (5 plays), Cawte (5 plays). One or more plays also in Marriott, Manly, Adams, Gassner. Cawte, Helm and Peacock list all texts known to them.

J. W. R.

6. WRITINGS IN LATIN

This section, which is selective, covers Latin works by authors who lived, either permanently or for a substantial period, in the dominions ruled by the kings of England and Scotland, and also Latin works by authors of British origin resident abroad.

(1) PRINCIPAL COLLECTIONS OF SOURCES;

(2) BIBLIOGRAPHIES AND LITERARY HISTORIES;

(3) ANTHOLOGIES;

(4) SECONDARY WORKS: (*i*) *medieval Latin culture in general and the history of particular periods or groups;* (*ii*) *literacy, the production and dissemination of manuscripts;* (*iii*) *the organization of education where it affected the spread of ideas;* (*iv*) *the study of ancient literatures;* (*v*) *poetry, literary criticism and belles lettres;* (*vi*) *philosophy and theology;* (*vii*) *sermon books and biblical exegesis;* (*viii*) *science, political theory and law;*

(5) ANGLO-NORMAN PERIOD 1066–1154;

(6) EARLY PLANTAGENET PERIOD TO 1200;

(7) THIRTEENTH CENTURY;

(8) FOURTEENTH CENTURY;

(9) FIFTEENTH CENTURY.

Authors appear in the period which includes the date of their death or, where this is not known, the last recorded date in their life. They are listed in alphabetical order: by Christian names up to 1400 and by surnames (where these are commonly used) for the 15th century.

(1) PRINCIPAL COLLECTIONS OF SOURCES

(in alphabetical order)

Bäumker, C. et al. Beiträge zur Geschichte der Philosophie des Mittelalters: Texte und Untersuchungen. Münster 1891.

Brown, E. Fasciculus rerum expetendarum et fugiendarum. 2 vols 1690. Contains works of Fitzralph, Grosseteste, Wyclif et al.

Dreves, G. M., C. Blume and H. M. Bannister. Analecta hymnica medii aevi. 55 vols Leipzig 1866–1922.

Dreves, G. M. and C. Blume. Ein Jahrtausend lateinischer Hymnendichtung. 2 vols Leipzig 1909.

Du Méril, E. Poésies populaires latines du Moyen Age. Paris 1847.

Hauréau, B. Notices et extraits de quelques manuscrits latins de la Bibliothèque Nationale. 6 vols Paris 1890–6.

Hervieux, L. Les fabulistes latins. 5 vols Paris 1893–9.

Martène, E. and W. Durand. Thesaurus novus anecdotorum. 5 vols Paris 1717.

Migne, J. P. Patrologiae cursus completus: series latina. 221 vols Paris 1844–64. For corrections *see* P. Glorieux, Pour revaloriser Migne: tables rectificatives, Mélanges de science religieuse: supplément, 1952.

Plummer, C. Vitae sanctorum Hiberniae. 2 vols Oxford 1910.

Potthast, A. Bibliotheca historica medii aevi. 2 vols Berlin 1862–8, 1896, Rome 1962 (as Repertorium fonticum historiae medii aevi).

Rerum britannicarum medii aevi scriptores: chronicles and memorials of Great Britain and Ireland during the Middle Ages. 1858–96 (Rolls ser).

Shirley, W. W. Fasciculi zizaniorum. 1858 (Rolls ser).

Thurot, C. Notices et extraits de divers manuscrits latins pour servir à l'histoire des doctrines grammaticales du Moyen Age. In Notices et extraits des mss de la Bibliothèque Impériale (Nationale) vol 22.

Wright, T. Early mysteries and other Latin poems of the 12th and 13th centuries. 1838.

— Latin poems commonly attributed to Walter Mapes. 1841.

— The political songs of England from the reign of John to that of Edward II. 1839 (Camden Soc).

— Political poems and songs from the accession of Edward III to that of Richard III. 1859–61.

— Anglo-Latin satirical poets and epigrammatists of the 12th century. 2 vols 1872 (Rolls ser).

(2) BIBLIOGRAPHIES AND LITERARY HISTORIES

Bale, John. Scriptorum illustrium maioris Brytanniae summarium. Basle 1559.

— Index Britanniae scriptorum. Ed R. L. Poole and M. Bateson, Oxford 1902.

Pits, J. De illustribus Angliae scriptoribus. Paris 1619.

Wadding, L. Scriptores ordinis minorum. Rome 1650, 1906. *See also* J. H. Sbarelea, Supplementum ad scriptores a Waddingo aliisve descriptos, Rome 1806, 1921.

Quétif, J. and J. Echard. Scriptores ordinis praedicatorum. 2 vols Paris 1719–23.

Tanner, T. Bibliotheca britannico-hibernica: sive de scriptoribus qui in Anglia, Scotia et Hibernia ad seculi 17 initium floruerunt. 1748.

Wright, T. Biographia britannica literaria vol 2. 1846.

Hardy, T. D. Descriptive catalogue of materials relating to the history of Great Britain and Ireland. 3 vols 1862.

Gottlieb, T. Über mittelalterliche Bibliotheken. Leipzig 1890. *See Beddie, below.*

Gross, C. Sources and literature of English history from the earliest times to about 1485. Cambridge Mass 1892, 1915 (rev).

Hurter, H. Nomenclator literarius theologiae catholicae. 5 vols Leipzig 1903–13 (3rd edn rev and enlarged).

Herbert, J. A. A catalogue of romances in the Manuscript Dept of the British Museum vol 3. 1910.

Bannister, H. M. Some mss of the Cambridge friars now in the Vatican library. Collectanea franciscana 1 1914 (Br Soc of Franciscan Stud vol 5).

Little, A. G. The grey friars in Oxford. Oxford 1922. Contains lists of Franciscan scholars and their works. *See* his Studies in English franciscan history, Manchester 1917.

Manitius, M. Geschichte der lateinischen Literatur des Mittelalters. Vols 2–3, 1923–31. Bibliographies for each author.

Glorieux, P. La littérature quodlibétique de 1260 à 1320. 2 vols Paris 1925–35.

— Répertoire des maîtres en théologie de Paris au 13e siècle. 2 vols Paris 1933–4. Continued in V. Doucet, Maîtres franciscains à Paris, Archivum Franciscanum Historicum 27 1934. See also P. Glorieux, Maîtres franciscains régents à Paris, Recherches Théologiques 18 1951.

Singer, D. W. Catalogue of alchemical mss in Great Britain and Ireland dating from before the 16th century. 2 vols Brussels 1928–31.

Überweg, F. Grundriss der Geschichte der Philosophie vol 2: Die patristische und scholastische Philosophie. Ed B. Geyer, Berlin 1928.

Beddie, J. S. The ancient classics in medieval libraries. Speculum 5 1930. Supplements T. Gottlieb, above.

Paetow, L. J. A guide to the study of medieval history. Ed D. C. Munro and G. C. Boyce, New York 1931.

Powicke, F. M. The medieval books of Merton College. Oxford 1931.

Baxter, J. H., C. Johnson and J. F. Willard. An index of British and Irish Latin writers AD 400–1520. Archivum Latinitatis Medii Aevi 7 1932.

Caplan, H. Medieval artes praedicandi: a handlist. 2 vols Ithaca 1934–6.

Russell, J. C. Dictionary of writers of 13th-century England. 1936.

Halphen, L. and J. B. Mahn. Initiation aux études d'histoire du Moyen Age. Paris 1940.

Riedl, J. O. Catalogue of Renaissance philosophers 1350–1650. Milwaukee 1940.

Stegmüller, F. Repertorium biblicum medii aevi. 5 vols Madrid 1940 (for 1950–5).

— Repertorium commentariorum in Sententias Petri Lombardi. 2 vols Würzburg 1947.

Farrar, C. P. and A. P. Evans. Bibliography of English translations from medieval sources. New York 1946.

Talbot, C. H. A list of Cistercian mss in Great Britain. Traditio 8 1952.

Gilson, E. Christian philosophy in the Middle Ages. 1955. Bibliography to April 1953.

Walther, H. Alphabetisches Verzeichnis der Versenanfänge mittellateinischer Dichtungen. Göttingen 1959.

Grundmann, H. Bibliographie zur Ketzergeschichte des Mittelalters 1900–66. Rome 1967.

Altschul, M. Anglo-Norman England 1066–1154. Cambridge 1969.

Schneyer, J. B. Repertorium der lateinischen Sermones des Mittelalters 1150–1350. 3 vols (A–J) Münster 1969–71. In progress.

Bullough, D. A. and R. L. Storey (ed). The study of medieval records. Oxford 1971.

See also bibliographies in:

Bulletin de Théologie Ancienne et Médiévale (Louvain).

Bulletin Thomiste (Montreal).

Progress of medieval and Renaissance studies in the United States and Canada. Ed J. H. Thomson etc, Boulder 1952–.

Répertoire bibliographique de la philosophie. Louvain 1949–.

Speculum (Medieval Acad of America). Cambridge Mass.

(3) ANTHOLOGIES

McKeon, R. (tr). Selections from medieval philosophers. 2 vols New York 1923–30.

Lindsay, J. Medieval Latin poets. 1934.

Pegis, A. C. The wisdom of Catholicism. New York 1949.

Brown, R. A. British Latin AD 500–1400. 1950.

Jones, C. W. Medieval literature in translation. 1950.

Raby, F. J. E. The Oxford book of medieval Latin verse.

Oxford 1958. *See also* earlier edn by S. Gaselee, Oxford 1937, which contains many poems omitted by Raby.

Waddell, H. Medieval Latin lyrics. 1929. With trns.

Brittain, F. The Penguin book of Latin verse. 1962. With trns.

Whicher, G. F. The goliard poets: medieval Latin songs and satires. New York 1965. With trns.

(4) SECONDARY WORKS

General Studies; Studies of Periods or Groups

Poole, R. L. Illustrations of the history of medieval thought. 1884, 1920 (rev).

Stubbs, W. Learning and literature at the Court of Henry II. In his Seventeen lectures on the study of medieval and modern history, Oxford 1886.

Little, A. G. The grey friars in Oxford. Oxford 1892.

— Studies in English Franciscan history. Manchester 1917.

— The Franciscan school at Oxford in the 13th century. Archivum Franciscanum Historicum 19 1926.

— Theological schools in medieval England. EHR 55 1940.

— Franciscan papers: lists and documents. Manchester 1943.

Clerval, A. Les écoles de Chartres au Moyen Age. Chartres 1895.

Felder, H. Geschichte der wissenschaftlichen Studien im Franziskanerorden bis um die Mitte des 13 Jahrhunderts. Freiburg 1904; tr French, Paris 1908.

Taylor, H. O. The medieval mind. 2 vols 1911 (4th edn).

Kingsford, C. L. English historical literature in the 15th century. Oxford 1913.

Power, E. E. Medieval English nunneries c. 1250–1585. Cambridge 1922.

Coulton, G. G. Five centuries of religion. 4 vols Cambridge 1923–50.

Waddell, H. The wandering scholars. 1927, 1932 (new and enlarged).

Haskins, C. H. The renaissance of the 12th century. Cambridge Mass 1928, 1957.

— Studies in medieval culture. Oxford 1929.

Tout, T. F. Literature and learning in the English civil service in the 14th century. Speculum 4 1929.

Thompson, E. H. The Carthusian order in England. 1930.

Xiberta, B. M. De scriptoribus scholasticis seculi XIV ex ordine carmelitarum. Louvain 1931. On English writers.

Lechner, J. Beiträge zum mittelalterlichen Franziskanerschriftum, vornehmlich der Oxforder Schule des 13 und 14 Jahrhunderts. Franziskanische Studien 19 1932.

— Kleine Beiträge zur Geschichte der englischen Franziskanerschriftums in Mittelalter. Philosophisches Jahrbuch (Fulda) 53 1940.

Swain, B. Fools and folly during the Middle Ages and the Renaissance. New York 1932.

Wilmart, A. Auteurs spirituels et textes dévots du Moyen Age latin. Paris 1932. Extracts from Thomas Bradley, Bishop of Dromore.

Paré, G., A. Brunet and P. Tremblay. La renaissance du 12e siècle. Paris 1933.

Lagarde, G. de. La naissance de l'esprit laïque. 2 vols Saint-Paul-Trois-Châteaux 1934.

Powicke, M. The Christian life in the Middle Ages. Oxford 1935.

— Ways of medieval life and thought. 1950.

Hunt, R. W. English learning in the late 12th century. Trans Royal Historical Soc 19 1936.

Gumbley, W. The Cambridge Dominicans. Oxford 1938.

Gwynn, A. The English Austin friars at the time of Wyclif. Oxford 1940.

Knowles, D. The monastic order in England. Cambridge 1940.

— The religious orders in England. 2 vols Cambridge 1948–55.

— Saints and scholars. Cambridge 1963.

— The English mystical tradition. Cambridge 1963.

Reese, G. Music in the Middle Ages. 1941.

Monneret de Villard, U. Lo studio del Islam in Europa nel 12 e nel 13 secolo. Rome 1944.

Ghellinck, J. de. L'essor de la littérature latine au 12e siècle. 2 vols Brussels 1946.

Chailley, J. Histoire musicale du Moyen Age. Paris 1950.

Colvin, H. M. The white canons in England. Oxford 1951.

Forest, A., F. Van Steenberghen and M. de Gaudillac. Le mouvement intellectuel du 11e au 13e siècle. Paris 1951.

Hinnebusch, W. A. The early English friar preachers. 1951.

Kuttner, S. and E. Rathbone. Anglo-Norman canonists of the 12th century. Traditio 7 1951.

Moorman, J. R. H. The grey friars in Cambridge. Cambridge 1952.

— A history of the Franciscan order. Oxford 1968.

Southern, R. W. The making of the Middle Ages. 1953.

— The place of England in the 12th-century renaissance. History 45 1960.

— Medieval humanism and other studies. New York 1970.

Artz, F. B. The mind of the Middle Ages. 2nd edn with rev bibliography New York 1954.

Pantin, W. A. The English church in the 14th century. Cambridge 1955.

Saltman, A. Archbishop Theobald of Canterbury. 1956.

Le Goff, J. Les intellectuels au Moyen Age. Paris 1957.

Roth, F. English Austin friars. 2 vols 1961–6.

Utley, F. L. (ed). The forward movement of the 14th century. Columbus 1961.

Colledge, E. The medieval mystics of England. 1962.

Oxford studies presented to Daniel Callus. Oxford 1963.

Thomson, J. A. F. The later Lollards 1414–1520. Oxford 1965.

Hoyt, R. S. Life and thought in the early Middle Ages. Minneapolis 1967.

Brooke, C. N. L. The 12th-century Renaissance. 1968.

Lewis, C. E. Canonists and law clerks in the household of Hubert Walter 1193–1205. Colloquia Germanica 1970.

Foundations of Intellectual Life: Literacy, the Production and Collecting of Mss and Books

Lehmann, P. Bücherliebe und Bücherpflege bei den Karthäusern. In Miscellanea Ehrle vol 5, Rome 1924.

Streeter, B. H. The chained library. 1931.

Adamson, J. W. Extent of literacy in England in the 15th and 16th centuries. Library 4th ser 10 1932; rptd in his Illiterate Anglo-Saxon, Cambridge 1946.

Destrez, J. L'outillage des copistes du 13e et du 14e siècle. In Aus der Geisteswelt des Mittelalters: Festgabe M. Grabmann, Münster 1935.

— La Pecia dans les manuscrits universitaires du 13e et 14e siècles. Paris 1935.

Galbraith, V. M. The literacy of the medieval English kings. Proc Br Acad 21 1935.

Thompson, J. W. The literacy of the laity in the Middle Ages. Berkeley 1936.

— The medieval library. Chicago 1939.

Mitchell, R. J. John Tiptoft. 1938.

Gwynn, A. The fate of the English monastic libraries. Dublin Rev 206 1940.

Milkau, F. and G. Leyh. Geschichte der Bibliotheken. 2 vols Leipzig 1940.

Ker, N. R. Medieval libraries of Great Britain. 1941 (Royal Historical Soc) (rev).

Buttenwieser, H. Popular authors in the Middle Ages: the testimony of the mss. Speculum 17 1942.

Edwards, K. Bishops and learning in the reign of Edward II. Church Quart Rev 138 1944.

Denholm-Young, N. Handwriting in England and Wales. Cardiff 1954.

Parks, G. B. The English traveller to Italy vol 1: the Middle Ages. Rome 1954.

Kerling, N. J. M. Caxton and the trade in printed books. Book Collector 4 1955.

Auerbach, E. Literatursprache und Publikum in der lateinischen Spätantike und im Mittelalter. Berne 1958; tr 1965.

Wormald, F. and C. E. Wright. The English library before 1700. 1958.

Schirmer, W. F. and U. Broich. Studien zur literarischen Patronat im England des 12 Jahrhunders. Cologne 1962.

Daly, L. W. Contributions to a history of alphabetization in antiquity and the Middle Ages. Brussels 1967.

Van Thiel, H. Mittellateinische Texte: ein Handschriften-lesebuch. Göttingen 1972. Includes English writers.

Education

Little, A. G. The educational organisation of the mendicant friars in England. Trans Royal Historical Soc 8 1894.

— Theological schools in medieval England. EHR 55 1940.

Abelson, P. The seven liberal arts. New York 1906.

Paetow, L. J. The arts course at the medieval universities. Champaign Ill 1910.

Mandonnet, P. La crise scolaire au début du 13e siècle et la fondation de l'ordre des fréres prêcheurs. Revue d'Histoire Ecclésiastique 15 1914.

Parry, A. W. Education in England in the Middle Ages. 1920.

Boyce, G. C. The English-German nation in the University of Paris. Bruges 1927.

Mitchell, R. J. English law students at Bologna in the 15th century. EHR 51 1936.

— English students at Padua 1460–75. Trans Royal Historical Soc 4th ser 19 1936.

— English students at Ferrara. Italian Stud 6 1937.

Rashdall, H. The universities of Europe in the Middle Ages. Ed F. M. Powicke and A. B. Emden 3 vols Oxford 1936.

Toulouse, M. La nation anglaise-allemande de l'université de Paris des origines à la fin du 15e siècle. Paris 1939.

Lesne, E. Les écoles de la fin du 8e siècle à la fin du 12e. In Histoire de la propriété ecclésiastique en France vol 5, Lille 1940.

Delhaye, P. L'organisation scolaire au 12e siècle. Traditio 5 1947.

McMahon, C. P. Education in 15th-century England. Baltimore 1947.

Kibre, P. The nations in the medieval universities. Cambridge Mass 1948.

Gabriel, A. L. English masters and students in Paris during the 13th century. Analecta Praemonstratensiana 25 1949.

Haskins, C. H. The rise of the universities. Ithaca 1957.

Hunt, R. W. Oxford grammar master in the Middle Ages. In Oxford studies presented to Daniel Callus, Oxford 1963.

Bultot, R. La Chartula et l'enseignement du mépris du monde dans les écoles et les universités médiévales. Studi Medievali 8 1967.

Leff, G. Paris and Oxford universities in the 13th and 14th centuries. 1968.

Study of Ancient Literatures

Norden, E. Die antike Kunstprosa. 2 vols Leipzig 1898.

Sandys, J. E. A history of classical scholarship. Vols 1–2 Cambridge 1908–21.

Krusman, V. E. Early humanism in England. Odessa 1916. In Russian.

Rand, E. K. The classics in the 13th century. Speculum 4 1929.

Schirmer, W. F. Der englische Frühhumanismus. Leipzig 1931.

Jacob, E. F. Some aspects of classical influence in medieval England. Vorträge der Bibliothek Warburg (Hamburg) 9 1932.

Caplan, M. Classical rhetoric and medieval theory of preaching. Classical Philology 28 1933.

Stephens, G. R. The knowledge of Greek in England in the Middle Ages. Philadelphia 1933.

Weiss, R. Humanism in England during the 15th century. Oxford 1941, 1957 (rev).

— New light on humanism in England during the 15th century. Jnl Warburg & Courtauld Inst 14 1951.

— The study of Greek in England during the 14th century. Rinascimento 2 1951.

— Il debito degli umanisti inglesi verso l'Italia. Lettere Italiane 7 1955.

Sanford, E. M. Study of ancient history in the Middle Ages. JHI 5 1944.

Quain, E. A. Medieval accessus ad auctores. Traditio 3 1945.

Robins, R. H. Ancient and mediaeval grammatical theory. 1951.

Huygens, R. B. C. Accessus ad auctores. Latomus 12 1953.

Bolgar, R. R. The classical heritage and its beneficiaries. Cambridge 1954.

— (ed). Classical influences on European culture AD 500–1500. Cambridge 1971.

Murphy, J. J. Rhetoric in 14th-century Oxford. MÆ 34 1965.

Fackovec, W. S. M. The rise and fall of Ciceronianism. Univ of Dayton Rev 4 1967.

Schoeck, R. J. On rhetoric in 14th-century Oxford. Mediaeval Stud 30 1968.

Poetry, Literary Criticism and Belles Lettres

Leyser, P. Historia poetarum et poematum medii aevi. Halle 1721.

Maitland, F. W. A song on the death of Simon de Montfort. EHR 11 1896.

Walter, H. Das Streitgedicht in der lateinischen Literatur des Mittelalters. Munich 1920.

Poole, R. L. Verses on the Exchequer in the 15th century 1398–1410. EHR 36 1921.

Faral, E. Les arts poétiques du 12e et 13e siècle. Paris 1924. See W. B. Sedgwick, Notes and emendations on Faral's Les arts poétiques, Speculum 2 1927.

Baxter, J. H. Four 'new' Scottish authors. Scottish Historical Rev 25 1925. On Thomas Rossy, Laurence of Lindores, William Croyser and Thomas Livingstone.

Polheim, K. Die lateinische Reimprosa. Leipzig 1925.

Raby, F. J. E. A history of Christian-Latin poetry. Oxford 1927, 1953 (rev).

— A history of secular Latin poetry. 2 vols Oxford 1934, 1957 (rev).

Baldwin, C. S. Medieval rhetoric and poetic. New York 1928.

Sedgwick, W. B. The style and vocabulary of the Latin arts of poetry in the 12th and 13th centuries. Speculum 3 1928.

Strecker, K. Einführung in das Mittellatein. Berlin 1929; tr Berlin 1957 (as Introduction to medieval Latin).

Osgood, C. G. Boccaccio on poetry. Princeton 1930.

Allen, P. S. Medieval Latin lyrics. Chicago 1931.

Lobel, E. The medieval Latin poetics. Oxford 1932.

Jacob, E. F. Florida verborum venustas. Manchester 1933.

Young, K. The drama of the medieval Church. 2 vols Oxford 1933.

Denholm-Young, N. The cursus in England. In Oxford essays in medieval history presented to H. E. Salter, Oxford 1934.

Curtius, E. R. Dichtung und Rhetorik im Mittelalter. Halle 1938.

— Europäische Literatur und lateinisches Mittelalter. Berne 1948; tr 1953.

McKeon, R. Rhetoric in the Middle Ages. Speculum 17 1942.

— Poetry and philosophy in the 12th century. MP 43 1946.

Both rptd in R. S. Crane (ed), Critics and criticism, ancient and modern, Chicago 1952.

Atkins, J. W. English literary criticism: the medieval phase. Cambridge 1943.

Russell, J. C. An introduction to the study of medieval biography. MLQ 1943.

Leclercq, J. Le genre épistolaire au Moyen Age. Revue du Moyen Age Latin 2 1946.

Hunt, R. W. The introductions to the Artes in the 12th century. In Studia medievalia (in honorem R. J. Martin), Bruges [1948].

Craig, H. The English religious drama of the Middle Ages. Oxford 1954.

Loomis, R. S. (ed). Arthurian literature in the Middle Ages. Oxford 1959.

Szövérffy, J. Die Annalen der lateinischen Hymnendichtung. 2 vols Berlin 1964.

Dronke, E. P. M. Medieval Latin and the rise of the European love-lyric. 2 vols Oxford 1965–6.

Creuss, H. Hymner and Hymnen im englischen Mittelalter. Tübingen 1968.

Philosophy and Theology

Prantl, C. von. Geschichte der Logik im Abendlande. 4 vols Leipzig 1855–70. Vol 2.

Wulf, M. de. Histoire de la philosophie médiévale. Louvain 1900, 1924; tr 2 vols 1935–8.

Grabmann, M. Die Geschichte der scholastischen Methode. Freiburg 1907.

— Kurze Mitteilungen über ungedruckte englische Thomisten des 13 Jahrhunderts. Divus Thomas (Freiburg) 3 1925.

— Mittelalterliches Geistesleben. 2 vols Munich 1926–36.

— Die Geschichte der katholischen Theologie. Freiburg 1933.

Ghellinck, J. de. Le mouvement théologique du xiie siècle. Paris 1914, Bruges 1948 (rev).

Webb, C. C. J. Studies in the history of natural theology. Oxford 1915.

Gilson, E. Etudes de la philosophie médiévale. Strasbourg 1921.

— L'esprit de la philosophie médiévale. Paris 1932, 1944 (rev); tr 1936.

— History of Christian philosophy in the Middle Ages. 1955.

Ehrle, F. L'agostinismo e l'aristotelismo nella scolastica del secolo 13. Rome 1925.

Michalski, K. Les courants critiques et sceptiques dans la philosophie du 14e siècle. Bulletin de l'Académie Polonaise, 1925.

— Le problème de la volonté à Oxford et à Paris au 14e siècle. Commentariorum Societatis Philosophicae Polonorum (Lemberg) 2 1937.

— La philosophie au 14e siècle: six études. Frankfurt 1968.

Assenmacher, J. Die Geschichte des Individuationsprinzip in der Scholastik. Leipzig 1926.

Egenter, R. Die Lehre von der Gottesfreundschaft in der Scholastik und Mystik des 12 and 13 Jahrhunderts. Augsburg 1928.

Sharp, D. E. Franciscan philosophy at Oxford in the 13th century. Oxford 1930.

Xiberta, B. M. Le thomisme de l'école carmélitaine. In Mélanges Mandonnet vol 1, Paris 1930. On Baconthorpe and other English writers.

Betzendörfer, W. Glauben und Wissen bei den grossen Denkern des Mittelalters. Gotha 1931.

Bréhier, E. Histoire de la philosophie vol 3: le Moyen Age et la Renaissance. Paris 1931; tr Chicago 1965 (with rev bibliography).

Van Steenberghen, F. Aristote en occident: les origines de l'aristotélisme parisien. Louvain 1931.

Taylor, A. E. Platonism and its influence. New York 1932.

Little, A. G. and F. Pelster. Oxford theology and theologians c. 1282–1302. Oxford 1934.

Glorieux, P. Aux origines du quodlibet. Divus Thomas (Piacenza) 38 1935.

Chenu, M.-D. Grammaire et théologie au 12e et 13e siècles. Archives d'Histoire Doctrinale et Littéraire du Moyen Age 10 1935–6.
— La théologie comme science au 13e siècle. Paris 1943.
— La théologie au 12e siècle. Paris 1957; tr as Nature, man and society in the 12th century, Chicago 1968.

Landgraf, A. M. Einführung in die Geschichte der theologischen Literatur der Frühscholastik. Regensburg 1938.

Parent, J. M. La doctrine de la création dans l'école de Chartres. Paris 1938.

Vignaux, P. La pensée au Moyen Age. Paris 1938.

Klibansky, R. The continuity of the Platonic tradition. 1939.

Carré, M. H. Realists and nominalists. Oxford 1941.

Lottin, O. Psychologie et morale aux 12e et 13e siècles. 7 vols Louvain 1942–54.

Callus, D. A. The introduction of Aristotelian learning to Oxford. Proc Br Acad 29 1943.
— The condemnation of S. Thomas at Oxford. 1949.

Smalley, B. Robert Bacon and the Dominican school in Oxford. Trans Royal Historical Soc 4th ser 30 1948.

Boehner, P. Medieval logic: an outline of its development from 1250 to c. 1400. Chicago 1952.

Copleston, F. History of philosophy vols 2–3. 1952–3.

Nardi, B. Soggetto e oggetto del conoscere nella filosofia antica e medievale. Rome 1952.

Leff, G. Medieval thought from Augustine to Ockham. 1958 (Pelican).
— The changing pattern of thought in the earlier 14th century. Bull John Rylands Lib 43 1961.
— Heresy in the later Middle Ages. 2 vols Manchester 1967.

Knowles, D. The evolution of medieval thought. Cambridge 1962.

Oberman, M. A. (ed). Forerunners of the Reformation. New York 1966.

Colish, M. L. The mirror of language: a study in the medieval theory of knowledge. New Haven 1968.

Luscombe, D. E. The school of Peter Abelard. Cambridge 1969.

Sermon Books and Biblical Exegesis

Mosher, J. H. The exemplum in the early religious and didactic literature of England. New York 1911.

Owst, G. R. Preaching in medieval England c. 1350–c. 1450. Cambridge 1926.
— Literature and pulpit in medieval England. Cambridge 1933, Oxford 1961 (rev).

Welter, J. T. L'exemplum dans la littérature religieuse et didactique du Moyen Age. Paris 1927.

Glunz, H. H. History of the Vulgate in England from Alcuin to Roger Bacon. Cambridge 1933.

Charland, T. M. Artes praedicandi. Paris 1936.

Smalley, B. The study of the Bible in the Middle Ages. Oxford 1941, 1952 (rev).
— Which William of Nottingham? Medieval & Renaissance Stud 3 1954.
— The Bible in the medieval schools. In Cambridge history of the Bible vol 2, Cambridge 1969.

Spicq, C. Esquisse d'une histoire de l'exégèse latine au Moyen Age. Paris 1944.

Sweet, J. Some 13th-century sermons and their authors. Jnl of Ecclesiastical History 4 1953.

Blench, J. W. Preaching in England in the late 15th and early 16th centuries. Oxford 1964.

Scientific Thought, Politics, Law etc

Pollock, F. and F. W. Maitland. The history of English law before Edward I. 2 vols Cambridge 1898.

Duhem, P. Etudes sur Léonard de Vinci: ceux qu'il a lus, ceux qui l'ont lu. Paris 1909.
— Le système du monde. 5 vols Paris 1913–17.

Thorndike, L. History of magic and experimental science. New York 1923.
— Science and thought in the 15th century. New York 1929.

Haskins, C. H. Studies in the history of medieval science. Cambridge Mass 1924.

Sarton, G. Introduction to the history of science. Vols 1–2, Baltimore 1927.

McIlwain, C. H. The growth of political thought in the West. New York 1932.

Ullmann, W. The medieval idea of law. 1946.

Maier, A. Studien zur Naturphilosophie der Spätscholastik. Rome 1949.

Crombie, A. C. Augustine to Galileo. 1952.
— Medieval and early modern science. 2 vols New York 1959.

Morrall, J. B. Political thought in medieval times. 1960.

Boyle, L. The curriculum of the faculty of canon law at Oxford in the 14th century. In Oxford studies presented to Davis Callus, Oxford 1963.

Wallace, W. A. Mechanics from Bradwardine to Galileo. JHI 32 1971.

(5) ANGLO-NORMAN PERIOD 1066–1154

Adelard of Bath
fl. c. 1120

Tractatus de eodem et diverso. Ed H. Willner, Münster 1903.

Quaestiones naturales. Ed M. Müller, Münster 1934.

Thorndike, L. Adelard of Bath and the continuity of universal nature. Nature 94 1915.

Haskins, C. H. Adelard of Bath. In Studies in the history of medieval science, Cambridge Mass 1924, 1960. With list of works and mss on scientific subjects.

Bliemetzrieder, F. Adelard von Bath. Munich 1935.

Silverstein, T. Adelard, Aristotle and the De natura deorum. Classical Philology 47 1952.

Anonymous

De expugnatione urbis lisbonniensis. Ed W. Stubbs 1864 (Rolls ser); ed C. Wendell, The conquest of Lisbon, Columbia Missouri 1936. See C. W. David and C. R. Cheney, Speculum 7 1932.

Anselm of Canterbury
d. 1102

Opera omnia. Ed Migne, Patrologia latina vols 158–9; ed F. S. Schmitt, vol 1 Seckau 1938, Edinburgh 1946; vol 2 Rome 1940; vols 3–4 Edinburgh 1946–9; vol 5 London 1951; vol 6 Edinburgh 1961.

Proslogion, Monologion, Libellus pro insipiente, Liber apologeticus. Tr S. N. Deane, Chicago 1903; tr French by A. Koyré, Paris 1932 (as Fides quaerens intellectum).
Oeuvres philosophiques. Tr French by A. Rousseau, Paris 1945.
S. Anselm's Proslogion with a reply on behalf of the fool by Gaunilo etc. Tr M. J. Charlesworth, Oxford 1965.

Individual works:

Cur deus homo? Ed F. S. Schmitt, Bonn 1929.
Libri S. Anselmi Cur deus homo: prima forma inedita. Ed E. Druwé, Rome 1933; ed R. Roques, Paris 1963 (with French trn).
De incarnatione verbi. Ed F. S. Schmitt, Bonn 1931.
[De potestate et impotentia]. Ein neues unvollendetes Werk des hl. Anselm von Canterbury. Ed F. S. Schmitt, Münster 1936.
De veritate. Ed R. McKeon, Selections from medieval philosophers vol 1, New York 1923.
Monologion. Ed F. S. Schmitt, Bonn 1929.
[Orationes sive meditationes]. Méditations et prières. Tr French, D. A. Castel, Paris 1923; Prayers and meditations selected by a religious of CSMV [R. P. Lawson], 1952.
Proslogion. Ed F. S. Schmitt, Bonn 1929; Stuttgart 1962 (new edn with German trn); ed A. C. Pegis, The wisdom of Catholicism, New York 1949.
Levasti, A. Sant' Anselmo: cita e pensiero. Bari 1929. With substantial bibliography.
Van der Plass, G. Des hl Anselms Cur deus homo auf dem Boden der jüdisch-christlichen Polemik des Mittelalters. Divus Thomas (Freiburg) 7-8 1929-30.
Abbagnano, N. L'argomento ontologico di Anselmo di Aosta. Gubbia 1929.
Druwé, E. La première redaction du Cur deus homo de S. Anselme. Recherches de Science Religieuse 20 1930. Reply J. Rivière, Un premier jet du Cur deus homo? Revue de Sciences Religieuses 14 1934.
Barth, K. Fides querens intellectum: Anselms Beweis der Existenz Gottes. Munich 1931; tr 1960.
Wilmart, A. Le premier ouvrage de S. Anselme contre le trithéisme de Roscelin. Recherches de Théologie Ancienne et Mediévale 3 1931.
— La tradition des lettres de S. Anselme. Revue Bénédictine 43 1931.
— Auteurs spirituels et textes dévots du Moyen Age. Paris 1932.
— Textes attribués à S. Anselme et récemment édités. Revue Bénédictine 48 1936.
Antweiler, A. Anselmus von Canterbury, Monologion und Proslogion. Scholastik 8 1933.
Clayton, J. S. Anselm. Milwaukee 1933.
Cappuyns, M. L'argument de Saint Anselme. Recherches de Théologie Ancienne et Médiévale 6 1934.
Gilson, E. Sens et nature de l'argument de Saint Anselme. Archives d'Histoire Doctrinale et Littéraire du Moyen Age 9 1934.
Schmitt, F. Eine dreifache Gestalt der Epistola de sacrificio azimi et fermentati des hl Anselm. Revue Bénédictine 47 1935.
— Zur Entstehungsgeschichte von Anselms Cur deus homo? Theologische Revue 34 1935.
— Zur Entstehungsgeschichte der handschriftlichen Sammlungen der Briefe des hl. Anselm von Canterbury. Revue Bénédictine 48 1936.
— Les corrections de S. Anselme à son Monologion. Revue Bénédictine 50 1938.
— Cinq recensions de L'epistola de incarnatione verbi de S. Anselme. Revue Bénédictine 51 1939.
— Die Chronologie der Briefe des hl Anselm von Canterbury. Revue Bénédictine 64 1954.
— La Meditatio redemptionis humanae di S. Anselmo in relazione al Cur Deus homo. Benedictina 9 1955.

— Die echten und unechten Stücke der Korrespondenz des hl Anselm von Canterbury. Revue Bénédictine 65 1955.
— Die unter Anselm veranstaltete Ausgabe seiner Werke und Briefe. Scriptorium 9 1955.
Allers, R. Anselm von Canterbury. Vienna 1936.
Stolz, A. Anselm von Canterbury. Munich 1937.
Kølping, A. Anselms Proslogion: Beweis der Existenz Gottes in Zusammenhang seines spekulativen Programs. Bonn 1939.
Simone, L. de. S. Anselmo d'Aosta e la formazione della scolastica. Naples 1941.
Southern, R. W. St Anselm and his English pupils. Medieval & Renaissance Stud 1 1941.
— S. Anselm and Gilbert Crispin. Medieval & Renaissance Stud 3 1954.
— S. Anselm and his biographer. Cambridge 1962.
Sanderlin, G. Usk's Testament of love and St Anselm. Speculum 17 1942.
Combes, A. Un inédit de S. Anselme?: le traité De unitate divinae essentiae et pluralitate creaturarum. Paris 1944.
Ceriani, G. S. Anselmo. Brescia 1947.
Vignaux, P. Structure et sens du Monologion. Revue des Sciences Philosophiques 31 1947.
Rovighi, S. V. Anselmo e la filosofia del secolo 11. Milan 1949.
Wolz, H. G. The empirical basis of Anselm's arguments. Philosophical Rev 60 1951.
Cicchetti, A. L'agostinismo nel pensiero di Anselmo d'Aosta. Rome 1951.
Moretti-Costanzi. T. L'ascesi di coscienza e l'argomento di S. Anselmo. Rome 1951.
Dal Pra, M. Studi sul problema logico del linguaggio nella filosofia medievale. Filosofia 9 1955.
Pächt, O. The illustrations of S. Anselm's prayers and meditations. Jnl Warburg & Courtauld Inst 19 1956.
Crouse, R. D. The Augustinian background of S. Anselm's concept of Justitia. Canadian Jnl of Theology 9 1958.
McIntyre, J. S. Anselm and his critics. 1959.
Malcolm, N. Anselm's ontological arguments. Philosophical Rev 69 1960.
Phelan, G. B. The wisdom of S. Anselm. 1960.
Mazzarella, P. Il pensiero speculativo di S. Anselmo d'Aosta. 1962.
Henry, D. P. S. Anselm's Rustici. MÆ 33 1964.
Pouchet, R. La rectitudo chez S. Anselm. Paris 1964.
Hartshorne, C. Anselm's discovery: a re-examination of the ontological proof of God's existence. 1965.
Gauss, J. Anselm von Canterbury. Sacculum 17 1966.
Schurr, A. Die Begründung der Philosophie durch Anselm von Canterbury. Stuttgart 1966.
Pegis, A. C. St Anselm and the argument of the Proslogion. Medieval Stud 28 1966.
Hick, J. and A. C. McGill (ed). The many-faced argument: recent studies on the ontological argument for the existence of God. New York 1967.
Platinga, A. (ed). The ontological argument: from S. Anselm to contemporary philosophers. Detroit 1968.
Armstrong, C. S. Anselm and his critics. Downside Rev 86, 1968.
Van Steenberghen, F. Pour ou contre l'insensé. Revue Philosophique de Louvain 66 1968.
Javelet, R. Image et ressemblance au 12e siècle de S. Anselme à Alain de Lille. 2 vols Strasbourg 1968.
Southern, R. W. and F. S. Schmitt (ed). Memorials of S. Anselm. Oxford 1969.

Dominic of Evesham
d. c. 1145

Jennings, J. C. The writings of Prior Dominic of Evesham. EHR 77 1962.

Eadmer, monk of Canterbury
d. 1142

Opera. Ed Migne, Patrologia latina vol 159.
Historia novorum in Anglia. Ed M. Rule 1884 (Rolls ser); History of recent events in England, tr G. Bosanquet 1964.
Nova opuscula de sanctorum veneratione et obsecratione. Ed A. Wilmart, Revue des Sciences Religieuses 15 1935.
Tractatus de conceptione S. Mariae. Ed H. Thurston and T. Slater, Freiburg 1904; tr German, 1954.
Vita Anselmi. Ed R. W. Southern 1962.
Vita Bregvini. Ed B. W. Scholz, Traditio 22 1966.
Vita Oswaldi, Vita Wilfredi. Ed J. Raine, The historians of the Church of York vol 1, 1879 (Rolls ser).
    La Chapelle, M. L. de. Le mystère de la pureté de Marie selon Eadmer. Revue d'Ascétique et de Mystique 38 1962.
    Southern, R. W. S. Anselm and his biographer. Cambridge 1962.

Florence of Worcester
d. 1118

Chronicon ex chronicis. Ed B. Thorpe 2 vols 1848-9 (Eng Historical Soc); tr T. Forester 1854; ed and tr T. Stevenson, The Church historians of England vol 2 (i), 1853-6 (in part).

Geoffrey of Monmouth
d. 1154

Historia regum Britanniae. Ed J. A. Giles 1844; ed San-Marte (A. Schulz), Halle 1954; ed A. Griscom 1929; ed E. Faral, La légende arthurienne vol 3, pt 1, Paris 1929; tr S. Evans 1903, rev C. W. Dunn 1963; History of the Kings of Britain, tr L. Thorpe 1966 (Penguin).
Historia regum Britanniae: a variant version. Ed J. Hammer, Cambridge Mass 1951 (from ms).
Vita Merlini. Ed F. Michel and T. Wright, Paris 1837; ed J. J. Parry, Illinois Univ Stud 10 1925; ed E. Faral, La légende arthurienne vol 3 pt 1, Paris 1929.
    Griscom, A. The date of composition of Geoffrey of Monmouth's Historia. Speculum 1 1926.
    Nitze, W. A. Geoffrey of Monmouth's King Arthur. Speculum 2 1927.
    Loomis, R. S. Geoffrey of Monmouth and Arthurian origins. Speculum 3 1928.
    Parry, J. J. The chronology of Geoffrey of Monmouth's Historia bks I and II. Speculum 4 1929.
    — The Welsh texts of Geoffrey of Monmouth's Historia. Speculum 5 1930.
    — The triple death in the Vita Merlini. Ibid.
    — A variant version of Geoffrey of Monmonth's Historia. In A miscellany of studies presented to Leon E. Kastner, Cambridge 1932.
    — Geoffrey of Monmouth and the date of Regnum Scotorum. Speculum 9 1934.
    Loomis, L. H. Geoffrey of Monmouth and Stonehenge. PMLA 45 1930.
    Tatlock, J. S. P. Certain contemporaneous matters in Geoffrey of Monmouth. Speculum 6 1931.
    — The origin of Geoffrey of Monmouth's Estildis. Speculum 11 1936.
    — Geoffrey of Monmouth's Vita Merlini. Speculum 18 1943.
    — The legendary history of Britain: Geoffrey's Historia and its early vernacular versions. Berkeley 1950.
    Brugger, E. Zu Galfrid von Mon Monmouths Historia regum Britanniae. Zeitschrift für Französische Sprache und Literatur 57 1933.
    Hammer, J. Some leonine summaries of Geoffrey of Monmouth's Historia regum Britanniae. Speculum 6 1931.

    — Note on a ms of Geoffrey of Monmouth's Historia regum Britanniae. PQ 12 1933.
    — A commentary on the Prophetia Merlini. Speculum 10 1935.
    — The poetry of Johannes Beverus with extracts from his Tractatus de Bruto abbreviato. MP 34 1937.
    — Une version métrique de l'Historia regum Britanniae. Latomus 2 1938.
    — Geoffrey's use of the Bible in the Historia. Ibid.
    — A note on Geoffrey of Monmouth's Historia regum Britanniae 2 (4). Scriptorium 7 1953.
    — Galfridiana. Ibid.
    Hutson, A. E. British personal names in the Historia regum Britanniae. California Univ Pbns in Eng 5 1940.
    Jones, E. Geoffrey of Monmouth: account of the establishment of episcopacy in Britain. JEGP 40 1941.
    — Geoffrey of Monmouth 1640–1800. Berkeley 1944.
    Blenner-Hassett, R. Geoffrey of Monmouth's 'Mons Agned' and 'Castellum Puellarum'. Speculum 17 1942.
    Lloyd, J. E. Geoffrey of Monmouth. EHR 57 1942.
    Levison, W. A combined ms of Geoffrey of Monmouth and Henry of Huntingdon. EHR 58 1943.
    Southward, E. C. Arthur's dream. Speculum 18 1943.
    Paton, L. A. Notes on Merlin in the Historia regum Britanniae. MP 41 1944.
    Keeler, L. Geoffrey of Monmouth and the Late Latin chroniclers 1300–1500. Berkeley 1946.
    Newstead, H. About Geoffrey of Monmouth. Latomus 10 1951.
    Smith, L. F. Geoffrey of Monmouth and Orosius: at third hand? MLN 67 1952.
    Williams, C. Geoffrey of Monmouth and the Canon Law. Speculum 27 1952.
    Caldwell, R. A. Geoffrey of Monmouth, Wace and the Stow. MLN 69 1954.
    — Wace's Roman de Brut and the variant version of Geoffrey of Monmouth's Historia regum Britanniae. Speculum 31 1956.
    Pähler, H. Die 'leges Molmutinae': ein Betracht zum Problem der historischen Absicht bei Geoffrey von Monmouth. Anglia 73 1955.
    Pulch, H. Galfrids Historia: Studien zur ihrer Stellung in der Literaturgeschichte. Germanisch-romanische Monatsschrift 7 1957.
    Parry, J. J. and R. A. Caldwell. Geoffrey of Monmouth. In Arthurian literature in the Middle Ages, ed R. S. Loomis, Oxford 1959.
    Jarman, A. O. H. Geoffrey of Monmouth. Cardiff 1966.
    Hanning, R. W. The vision of history in early Britain. New York 1966.
    Schlauch, M. Geoffrey of Monmouth and early Polish historiography. Speculum 44 1969.

Gilbert Crispin
d. 1117

De monachatu. Ed J. Leclerq, Analecta monastica vol 2, 1953.
Disputatio Judaei cum Christiano. Ed C. C. J. Webb, Gilbert Crispin, Medieval & Renaissance Stud 3 1954; ed B. Blumenkranz, Utrecht and Antwerp 1956.
[Correspondence with Lanfranc and Anselm and Vita Herluini]. In J. A. Robinson, Gilbert Crispin, Abbot of Westminster, Cambridge 1911.
    Hotzmann, W. Zur Geschichte des Investiturstreits: der Traktat des Abtes Gilbert von Westminster. Neues Archiv 50 1933.
    Southern, R. W. St Anselm and Gilbert Crispin, Abbot of Westminster. Medieval & Renaissance Stud 3 1954.

Gilbert, called the 'Universal', Bishop of London
d. 1134

Smalley, B. Gilbertus Universalis, Bishop of London 1128–34, and the problem of the Glossa ordinaria. Recherches de Théologie Ancienne et Médiévale 7–8 1935–6.

Godfrey of Cambrai, Prior of S. Swithun's, Winchester
fl. c. 1100

Epigrammata. Ed T. Wright, Anglo-Latin satirical poets vol 2, 1872 (Rolls ser).
Yunck, J. A. The Carmen de nummo of Godfrey of Cambrai. Annuale Medievale 2 1961.

Goscelin, monk of Canterbury
d. c. 1099

Confortatorius liber ad Evam inclusam. BM ms Sloane 8108. This is the Eve to whom Hilary, below, addressed a poem.
Lives of SS. Augustine of Canterbury, Swithun, Ivo, Wereburga and Eadigitha. In Migne, Patrologia latina vol 155.
Vita S. Vulfridae. Ed M. Esposito, Analecta Bollandiana 21 1913.
Wilmart, A. Ève et Goscelin. Revue Bénédictine 46 1934, 50 1938.

Guy of Amiens
d. 1076

Carmen de Hastingae proelio. Ed F. Michel, Chroniques anglo-normandes vol 3, Rouen 1840; ed and tr C. Morton and H. Muntz, Oxford 1972.

Herbert de Losinga, Bishop of Norwich
d. 1119

Letters and sermons. Ed E. M. Goulburn and H. Symonds, The life, letters and sermons of Bishop Herbert de Losinga, 2 vols 1878. Text and trn of sermons, trn only of letters.
Epistolae. Ed R. Anstruther 1846 (Caxton Soc).

Hilary the Englishman
early 12th century

Versus et ludi. Ed J. J. Champollion-Figeac, Paris 1838; ed J. B. Fuller, New York 1929.
Allen, P. S. Medieval latin lyrics (2). MP 6 1909.
Herkenrath, E. Textkritisches zur Apocalyse des Golias, zu Hilarius und zu Walter von Châtillon. In Studien zur lateinischen Dichtung des Mittelalters, ed W. Stach and H. Walther, Dresden 1931.

Lanfranc
d. 1089

Opera. Ed J. A. Giles 2 vols Oxford 1844; rptd in Migne, Patrologia latina vol 150.
Decreta monachis cantuariensibus remissa. Ed M. D. Knowles 1951; rev in Corpus consuetudinum monasticarum vol 3, Siegburg 1967.
Giles, J. A. (ed). Anecdota Bedae, Lanfranci et aliorum. 1845 (Caxton Soc).
Languemare, E. Lanfranc. Paris 1902.
Macdonald, A. J. Lanfranc: a study of his life, work and writing. Oxford 1926.
Thompson, S. H. Bishop Gundulf of Rochester and the Vulgate. Speculum 6 1931. On Lanfranc as author of the Vulgate corrections attributed to Gundolf.
Southern, R. W. Lanfranc of Bec and Berengar of Tours. In Studies in medieval history presented to F. M. Powicke, Oxford 1948.

Laurence of Durham
d. 1154

Consolatio de morte amici. BM ms Cotton Vesp D 11. Extract in T. Wright, Biographia britannica literaria (Anglo-Norman period), 1842–6.
Dialogorum libri quattuor. Ed J. Raine, Durham 1880 (Surtees Soc).
Hypognosticon. Verse paraphrase of Bible stories; extracts in Surtees Soc edn of his Dialogi, above; in T. Wright, Biographia britannica literaria (Anglo-Norman period), 1842–6; and in J. B. Pitra, Spicilegium Solesmense 2, Paris 1852–8, p. 196.
Vita sanctae Brigidae. Ed Mabillon, Acta sanctorum Feb 1, Paris 1668; ed de Smedt, Acta Sanctorum Hiberniae, 1888.
Hoste, A. A survey of the unedited works of Laurence of Durham with an edition of his letters to Aelred of Rievaulx. Sacris Erudiri 11 1960.

Ordericus Vitalis
d. 1143

Historia ecclesiastica. Ed Le Prévost, Guérard and L. Delisle 5 vols Paris 1838–55; tr T. Forester 1853–6; ed and tr M. Chibnall, The ecclesiastical history of Orderic Vitalis 3 vols Oxford 1969–72.
Société historique et archéologique de l'Orne. Orderic Vital et l'abbaye de Saint-Evroul. Alençon 1912.
Wolter, H. Ordericus Vitalis: ein Beitrag zur kluniazenischen Geschichtsschreibung. Wiesbaden 1955.

Reginald of Canterbury
d. c. 1109

Vita S. Malchi. Ed R. L. Lind, Urbana 1942.
Other poems in Analecta hymnica vol 1, medii aevi, ed G. M. Dreves et al, and in Anglo-Latin satirical poets, ed T. Wright.
Liebermann, F. Reginald von Canterbury. Neues Archiv 13 1888.
Walther, H. Quot-tot: mittelalterliche Liebesgrüsse und Verwandtes. Zeitschrift für Deutsches Altertum 53 1928.
Hammer, J. A. A monastic panegyrist of Horace. PQ 11 1932.
Lind, R. L. Reginald of Canterbury and the rhyming hexameter. Neophilologus 25 1940.
Hunt, R. W. Alberic of Monte Cassino and Reginald of Canterbury. Medieval & Renaissance Stud 1 1941.

Robert Pullen (Pullus) Cardinal
d. c. 1147

Sententiarum theologicarum libri 8. Paris 1655. See Migne, Patrologia latina vol 186.
Poole, R. L. The early lives of Robert Pullen and Nicholas Breakspear. In Essays in medieval history presented to T. F. Tout, Manchester 1925.
Landgraf, A. Some unknown writings of the early scholastic period. New Scholasticism 4 1930.
— Studien zur Theologie des zwölften Jahrhunderts 2: literarhistorische Bemerkungen zu den Sentenzen des Robertus Pullus. Traditio 1 1943.
Courtney, F. Cardinal Robert Pullen. Rome 1954.

Simeon of Durham
fl. 1096–1129

Opera. Ed T. Arnold 1882–5 (Rolls ser); tr J. Stevenson, The Church historians of England vol 3 (2), 1853–6.

William of Malmesbury
d. c. 1142

De antiquitate glastoniensis ecclesiae. Oxford 1727; tr F. Lomax 1908.

Gesta pontificum anglorum. Ed N. E. S. A. Hamilton 1870.

Historia novella. Tr J. Stevenson, The Church historians of England; ed W. Stubbs 1888–9 (Rolls ser); ed and tr K. R. Potter 1955.

Historia regum. Tr J. Stevenson, The Church historians of England vol 3 (1), 1854; ed W. Stubbs 1887 (Rolls ser).

Vita S. Wulfstani. Ed R. R. Darlington 1928; tr J. H. F. Peile, Oxford 1934.

James, M. R. Two ancient English scholars: St Aldhelm and William of Malmesbury. Glasgow 1931.

Farmer, D. William of Malmesbury's life and works. Jnl of Ecclesiastical History 13 1962.

Patterson, R. B. Stephen's Shaftesbury charter: another case against William of Malmesbury. Speculum 43 1968.

(6) THE EARLY PLANTAGENET PERIOD TO 1200

Anonymous

Babio. Ed T. Wright, Early mysteries and other Latin poems of the 12th and 13th centuries, 1854; ed F. Ermini, Rome 1928; ed E. Faral, Bibliothèque de l'Ecole des Hautes Etudes 193 1948; ed and tr M. M. Brennan, Charleston 1968.

Faral, E. Le fabliau latin au Moyen Age. Romania 1 1924.

Baucis et Thraso. Ed H. Hagen, Eine antike Komödie in distischer Nachbildung, Jahrbücher für Klassische Philologie new ser 14 1868.

Faral, E. Le fabliau latin au Moyen Age. Romania 1 1924.

Die lateinische Fortsetzung Wilhelms von Tyrus (for 1185–92). Ed M. Sallock, Leipzig 1934.

Achard of Bridlington (or S. Victor)
d. 1171

De discretione animae et spiritus et mentis. Ed G. Morin, Geisteswelt des Mittelalters, Marburg 1935.

De summa trinitate. Ed E. Martène and V. Durand, Thesaurus novus anecdotorum vol 5, Paris 1717.

Chatillon, J. Théologie, spiritualité et métaphysique dans l'oeuvre oratoire d'Achard de S. Victor. Paris 1969.

Adam du Petit Pont (or de Balsham), Bishop of St Asaph
d. 1181

Ars disserendi. Ed J. Minio-Paluello, 12th-century logic: texts and studies, Rome 1956.

Oratio de ustensilibus ad domum regendam. Ed B. Hauréau, Notices et extraits de quelques manuscrits vol 3, Paris 1890–3 p. 206ff; ed H. von Fallersleben, Neuwied 1853.

Minio-Paluello, L. The Ars disserendi of Adam of Balsham 'Parvipontanus'. Medieval & Renaissance Stud 3 1954.

Adam of Eynsham
d. 1191

Magna vita sancti Hugonis. Ed J. F. Dimock 1864 (Rolls ser).

Aelred of Rievaulx
d. 1167

Opera. Ed Migne, Patrologia latina vol 145.

De anima. Ed C. H. Talbot, Medieval & Renaissance Stud suppl 1 1952 (Warburg Inst).

De Christo puero duodecenni. Ed A. Hoste and J. Dubois, Paris 1958 (with French trn); tr G. Webb and A. Walker 1956.

De institutis inclusarum. Ed C. H. Talbot, Analecta Sacri Ordinis Cisterciensis 7 1951; ed C. Dumont, Paris 1961.

De spirituali amicitia. Ed J. Dubois, L'amitié spirituelle, Bruges 1948 (with French trn).

Oratio pastoralis. Ed C. Dumont, Paris 1961.

Relatio de standardo: on the battle of the Standard. Ed R. Howlett, Chronicles of Stephen, 4 vols 1884–9 (Rolls ser).

Sermones inediti. Ed C. H. Talbot, Series Scriptorum Sacri Ordinis Cisterciensis (Rome) 1 1952.

Sermon on the saints of Hexham. Ed J. Raine, The Priory of Hexham vol 1, 1864 (Surtees Soc).

Speculum caritatis. Tr G. Webb and A. Walker 1962.

Powicke, F. M. Ailred of Rievaulx and his biographer Walter Daniel. Manchester 1922.

Wilmart, A. L'oraison pastorale de l'Abbé Aelred. Revue Bénédictine 37 1925.

—— L'instigateur du Speculum caritatis d'Aelred. Revue d'Ascétique et de Mystique 14 1933.

Egenter, R. Gottesfreundschaft: die Lehre von der Gottesfreundschaft in der Scholastik und Mystik des 12 und 13 Jahrhunderts. Augsburg 1928.

Van Steenberghe, F. Deux théoriticiens de l'amitié au xiie siècle: Pierre de Blois et Aelred de Rievaulx. Revue des Sciences Religieuses 12 1932.

Ducey, L. M. St Ailred and the Speculum caritatis. Catholic Historical Rev 17 1931.

Harvey, T. E. St Aelred of Rievaulx. 1932.

Friedrich, E. Die Oratio pastoralis des hl. Aelred. Cistercienser Chronik (Bregenz) 51 1939.

Sage, C. M. The Manuscripts of St Aelred. Catholic Historical Rev 34 1949.

Dumont, C. L'équilibre humain de la vie cistercienne d'après le bienheureux Aelred de Rievaulx. Collectanea Ordinis Cisterciensium Reformatorum 18 1956.

—— Aspects de la dévotion du bienheureux Aelred à Notre Dame. Ibid 20 1958.

Courcelle, P. Ailred de Rievaulx à l'école des Confessions. Revue des Etudes Augustiniennes 3 1957.

Schilling, R. Aelredus van Rievaulx: Deus amicitia est. Cîteaux Commentarii Cistercienses 8 1957.

Hallier, A. L'expérience spirituelle selon Ailred de Rievaulx. Collectanea Ordinis Cisterciensium Reformatorum 20 1958.

—— Un éducateur monastique, Ailred de Rievaulx. Paris 1959.

Hoste, A. Marginalia bij Aelred's De institutione inclusarum. Cîteaux Commentarii Cistercienses 9 1958.

—— Le traité pseudo-augustinien De amicitia: un résumé d'un ouvrage authentique d'Aelred de Rievaulx. Revue des Etudes Augustiniennes 6 1960.

—— Bibliotheca Aelrediana: a survey of the mss editions and studies concerning Aelred. Steenbrugge 1962.

—— Aelred of Rievaulx and the monastic planctus O munde immunde. Cîteaux Commentarii Cistercienses 18 1967.

—— Aelred of Rievaulx et la dévotion médiévale au Crucifié. Collectanea Ordinis Cisterciensium Reformatorum 29 1967.

Squire, A. Two unpublished sermons of Aelred of Rievaulx: the literary evidence for the preaching of Aelred of Rievaulx. Cîteaux Commentarii Cistercienses 11 1960.

—— Historical factors in the formation of Aelred of Rievaulx. Collectanea Ordinis Cisterciensium Reformatorum 22 1960.

—— Aelred and King David. Ibid.

—— Aelred and the northern saints. Collectanea Ordinis Cisterciensium Reformatorum 23 1961.

—— Aelred of Rievaulx and Hugh of S. Victor. Recherches de Théologie Ancienne et Médiévale 28 1961.

Fisk, A. Aelred of Rievaulx's idea of friendship and love. Cîteaux Commentarii Cistercienses 13 1962.

Pour le 8e centenaire d'Aelred de Rievaulx. Collectanea Ordinis Cisterciensium Reformatorum 29 1967. By P. Miguel et al.

Zeijden, A. van der. Ailred van Rievaulx in het voetspoor van S. Augustinus. Cîteaux Commentarii Cistercienses 18 1967.

Alberic of London
early 13th century

Mythographus tertius. Ed A. Mai, Classici auctores vol 3, Rome 1832; ed G. Bode, Scriptores rerum mythicarum latini tres, Cellis 1834.

Rathbone, E. Master Alberic of London. Medieval & Renaissance Stud 1 1941.

Daniel of Morley
fl. 1175

For bibliography, see C. H. Haskins, Studies in the history of medieval science, *p. 126 note 39*.

Philosophia: or Liber de naturis inferiorum et superiorum. Ed K. Sudhoff, Archiv für Geschichte der Naturwissenschaften 8 1918. See A. Birkenmajer, Eine neue Handschrift des De naturis inferiorum et superiorum des Daniel von Morlai, Archiv für die Geschichte der Naturwissenschaften 9 1920.

Singer, C. Daniel of Morley: an English philosopher of the 12th century. Isis 3 1921.

Muller, M. Die Stellung des Daniel von Morley. Philosophisches Jahrbuch 41 1928.

Silverstein, T. Daniel of Morley: English cosmogonist and student of Arabic science. Medieval Stud 10 1948.

Thorndike, L. Daniel of Morley. EHR 37 1922.

Gervase of Tilbury
fl. 1180

Otia imperialia. Ed G. G. Leibnitz Scriptores rerum Brunswicensium, 2 vols Hanover 1707–10. Extracts in J. Stevenson, Radulphi e Coggeshall Chronicon, 1875 (Rolls ser).

Caldwell, J. R. The autograph manuscript of Gervase of Tilbury. Scriptorium 11 1957.

— The manuscripts of Gervase of Tilbury's Otia imperialia. Scriptorium 16 1962.

— Gervase of Tilbury's addenda to his Otia imperialia. Mediaeval Stud 24 1962.

Richardson, H. G. Gervase of Tilbury. History 46 1961.

Gilbert Foliot
d. 1173

Letters and charters. Ed A. Morey and C. N. L. Brooke, Cambridge 1967.

Morey, A. and C. N. L. Brooke. Gilbert Foliot and his letters. Cambridge 1965.

Henry of Huntingdon
d. 1155

Historia Anglorum. Ed T. Arnold 1879 (Rolls ser).

Satirae et epigrammata (placed at the end of the Historia Anglorum). Ed T. Wright, Anglo-Latin satirical poets, 1872 (Rolls ser).

Schirmer, W. F. Heinrich von Huntingdons Historia Anglorum. Anglia 88 1970.

Hugh the Cantor

History of the Church of York. Ed J. Raine, Historians of the Church of York, 1879–94; ed and tr C. Johnson 1961.

John of Cornwall
fl. 1170

Eulogium ad Alexandrum papam III. Ed Migne, Patrologia latina vol 199.

Pelster, F. Eine ungedruckte Einleitung zu einer zweiter Auflage des Eulogium ad Alexandrum III. Historisches Jahrbuch 54 1934.

Studeny, R. F. Walter of S. Victor and the Apologia de verbo incarnato. Gregorianum 18 1937.

— John of Cornwall, an opponent of nihilianism. Vienna 1939.

Rathbone, E. John of Cornwall: a brief biography. Recherches de Théologie Ancienne et Médiévale 17 1950.

Haring, N. M. The Eulogium ad Alexandrum papam tertium of John of Cornwall. Mediaeval Stud 13 1951.

John de Hanville (Hauteville ?)
fl. 1184

Architrenius. Ed T. Wright, Anglo-Latin satirical poets vol 1.

Gaselee, S. Johannes de Alta villa: notes on the vocabulary of the Architrenius. Speculum 8 1933.

John of Salisbury
d. 1180

Opera. Ed J. A. Giles, Oxford 1848; ed Migne, Patrologia latina vol 199.

Entheticus de dogmate philosophorum. Ed C. Petersen, Hamburg 1843.

Historia pontificalis. Ed R. L. Poole, Oxford 1927; ed and tr M. Chibnall, Edinburgh 1956.

Letters vol 1. Ed W. J. Millor, H. E. Butler and C. L. N. Brooke, Edinburgh 1955.

Metalogicon. Ed C. C. J. Webb, Oxford 1929, tr D. D. McGarry, Berkeley 1955. See Webb, Addenda et corrigenda, Medieval & Renaissance Stud 1 1943.

Policraticus. Ed C. C. J. Webb 2 vols Oxford 1909; political pts tr J. Dickinson as The Statesman's book, New York 1927; tr J. B. Pike as Frivolities of courtiers and footprints of philosophers. Minneapolis 1938.

Schaarschmidt, C. Johannes Saresberiensis. Leipzig 1862.

Dickinson, J. The medieval conception of kingship as developed in the Policraticus of John of Salisbury. Speculum 1 1926.

Waddell, H. John of Salisbury. E & S 13 1928.

Webb, C. C. J. Notes on John of Salisbury. EHR 46 1931.

— John of Salisbury. 1932.

— Note on books bequeathed by John of Salisbury to the Cathedral library of Chartres. Medieval & Renaissance Stud 1 1941.

Daniels, H. Die Wissenschaftslehre des Johannes von Salisbury. Kaldenkirchen 1932.

Poole, R. L. Studies in chronology and history. Oxford 1934.

Kleineck, W. Englische Fürstenspiegel von Policraticus Johanns von Salisbury. Studien zur Englischen Philologie (Halle) 90 1937.

Denis, L. Un humaniste au Moyen Age: Jean de Salisbury. Nova et Vetera 22 1941.

Liebeschütz, J. John of Salisbury and Pseudo-Plutarch. Jnl Warburg & Courtauld Inst 6 1943.

— Medieval humanism in the writings of John of Salisbury. 1950.

— Englische und europäische Elemente in der Erfahrungswelt des Johannes von Salisbury. Welt als Geschichte 11 1951.

— Chartres und Bologna: Naturbegriff und Staatsidee bei Johannes von Salisbury. Archiv für Kulturgeschichte 50 1968.

Ullmann, W. The influence of John of Salisbury on medieval Italian jurists. EHR 59 1944.

Huizinga, J. Ein praegothischer Geist: Johannes von Salisbury. In his Parerga, Basle 1945.

Pratt, R. A. A note on Chaucer and the Policraticus of John of Salisbury. MLN 65 1950.

Dal Pra, M. Giovanni di Salisbury. Milan 1951.

Delahaye, P. Le bien suprême d'après le Policraticus de Jean de Salisbury. Recherches de Théologie Anciennes et Médiévales 20 1953.

Hedbling-Gloor, B. Natur und Aberglaube im Policraticus. Zürich 1956.

Desideri, S. La institutio Trajani. Genoa 1958. On John of Salisbury and the pseudo-Plutarch.

Brown, M. A. John of Salisbury. Franciscan Stud 19 1959.

Macedo de Steffens, D. C. La doctrina del tiranicidio, Juan de Salisbury y Juan de Mariana. Anales de Historia Antigua y Medieval (Buenos Aires) 12 1959.

Misch, G. Studien zur Geschichte der Autobiographie 5: Johann von Salisbury und das Problem des mittelalterlichen Humanismus. Nachrichten der Akademie der Wissenschaften in Göttingen: philologische-historische Klasse 1960.

Barzillay, P. The Entheticus de dogmate philosophorum of Salisbury. Medievalia et Humanistica 16 1964.

Bride, Sr M. John of Salisbury's theory of rhetoric. Studies in Medieval Culture (Univ of Western Michigan) 2 1966.

Rouse, R. and M. John of Salisbury and the doctrine of tyrannicide. Speculum 42 1967.

Joseph of Exeter
fl. 1190

Antiocheis. Fragments in W. Camden, Remaines concerning Britain, 1870 p. 339.

De bello troiano. Ed S. Dresenius 1825.

Jusserand, J. J. De Iosepho Exoniensi. Paris 1887 (with text of De bello troiano bk 1).

Sedgwick, W. B. The Bellum troianum and Joseph of Exeter. Speculum 5 1930.

Riddehough, G. B. A forgotten poet: Joseph of Exeter. JEGP 46 1947.

Nicholas of S. Albans
fl. 1180

De celebranda concepcione beate Marie. Ed C. H. Talbot, Revue Bénédictine 64 1954.

Nigel Wireker (or de Longchamps)
fl. 1190

Tractatus contra curiales et officiales clericos. Ed T. Wright, Anglo-Latin satirical poems vol 1; ed A. Boutemy, Paris 1960.

Speculum stultorum. Ed T. Wright, Anglo-Latin satirical poems vol 1; ed J. H. Mozley and R. R. Raymo, Berkeley 1960.

The Book of Burnel the ass, tr G. W. Regenos, Austin 1959.

Vita S. Pauli primi eremitae. Ed L. M. Kaiser, Classical Folia 14 1960.

Nigel's minor poems are in BM ms Cotton Vespasian D 19; 2 have been ptd in F. J. E. Raby, Secular Latin poetry vol 2.

Mozley, J. H. On the text of the Speculum stultorum. Speculum 4 1929.

— On the text and mss of the Speculum stultorum. Speculum 5 1930.

— The unprinted poems of Nigel Wireker. Speculum 7 1932.

— Nigel Wireker or Wetekere? MLR 27 1932.

— The Latinity of Nigel de Longchamps. Bulletin Ducange 14 1939.

Boutemy, A. Une vie inédite de Paul de Thèbes par Nigellus de Longchamps. Revue Belge 10 1931.

— The manuscript tradition of the Speculum stultorum. Speculum 8 1933.

— A propos d'un ms du Tractatus contra curiales et officiales clericos de Nigellus de Longchamps. Revue Belge 12 1933.

— Sur le 'prologue en prose' et la date du Speculum stultorum. Revue de l'Université de Bruxelles 1 1934.

Raymo, R. R. Gower's Vox clamantis and the Speculum stultorum. MLN 70 1955.

Blaschka, A. Die Gothaer Handschrift 10 des Speculum stultorum verglichen mit der Breslauer Hs 7. Halle-Wittenberg 1959.

Gamer, H. M. Three new versions of the Speculum stultorum. MP 62 1965.

Osbern of Gloucester
fl. 1160

Derivationes. Ed A. Mai, Classici auctores vol 8, Rome 1885.

Loewe, G. and G. Goetz. De glossariorum latinorum origine et fatis. In Corpus glossariorum latinorum vol 7, Leipzig 1923. Text of Osbern's preface on p. 197.

Hunt, R. W. The 'lost' preface to the Liber derivationum of Osbern of Gloucester. Medieval & Renaissance Stud 4 1958.

Osbert of Clare
d. c. 1136

Letters. Ed R. Anstruther 1846; ed E. W. Williamson, Oxford 1929.

Poems in honour of S. Anne. Analecta hymnica vol 15 no 157 1893 and vol 33 no 34 1899.

Vita Eduardi regis. Ed M. Bloch, La vie de S. Edouard le Confesseur par Osbert de Clare. Analecta Bollandiana 41 1923.

Robinson, J. A. Westminster in the 12th century: Osbert of Clare. Church Quart Rev 68 1909.

Wilmart, A. Les compositions d'Osbert de Clare en honneur de S. Anne. Annales de Bretagne 37 1926.

Baugh, A. C. Osbert of Clare, the Sarum breviary and the Middle English Saint Anne. Speculum 7 1932.

Peter of Blois
d. c. 1200

Opera. Ed J. A. Giles 4 vols 1846–7; ed Migne, Patrologia latina vol 207.

For Peter as possible author of nos 29–31 of Carmina burana, see Carmina burana vol 1 pt 1, ed A. Hilka and O. Schumann, Heidelberg 1930, 47–8.

De amicitia christiana et dilectione die et proximi. Ed M. M. Davy, Un traité de l'amour du xiie siècle, Paris 1932.

Dialogus inter regem Henricum secundum et abbatem Bonevallis: un écrit de Pierre de Blois réédité. Ed R. B. C. Huygens, Revue Bénédictine 68 1958.

Some new letters. Ed R. W. Southern, EHR 53 1938.

Cohn, E. S. The manuscript evidence for the letters of Peter of Blois. EHR 41 1926.

Braunholz, E. Die Streitgedichte Peters von Blois und Roberts von Beaufeu über den Wert des Weines und Bieres. Zeitschrift für Romanische Philologie 47 1927.

Van Steenberghe, F. Deux théoriticiens de l'amitié au 12e siècle: Pierre de Blois et Aelred de Rievaulx. Revue des Sciences Religieuses 12 1932.

Ranulf de Glanville
d. 1190

Tractatus de legibus et consuetudinibus Angliae. Ed G. Phillips 2 vols Berlin 1827–8; ed G. E. Woodbine, New Haven 1931; ed and tr G. D. G. Hall, Edinburgh 1965.

Radin, M. Glanvill on the common law: Lex terrae and jus regni. Pennsylvania Univ Law Rev 82 1933.

Southern, R. W. A note on the text of Glanville De legibus et consuetudinibus regni Angliae. EHR 65 1950.

Kaufmann, H. 'Causa debendi' et 'causa petendi' bei Glanvill, sowie im römischen und kanonischen Recht seiner Zeit. Traditio 17 1961.

Richard Fitzneal or Fitznigel
d. 1198

Dialogus de scaccario. Ed A. Hughes, C. G. Crump and C. Johnson, Oxford 1902; ed and tr C. Johnson 1950.

Richard of Devizes
fl. 1191

De rebus gestis regis Richardi primi. Ed R. Howlett, Chronicles of the reigns of Stephen etc vol 3, 1886 (Rolls ser); ed and tr J. T. Appleby 1963.

Richard of S. Victor
b. in Scotland, Prior of the Abbey of S. Victor in Paris
d. c. 1173

Opera. Ed Migne, Patrologia latina vol 196.

Sermons et opuscules inédits. Ed J. Chatillon and W. J. Tulloch, Bruges 1951 (with French trn). Only vol 1 (Exiit edictum) pbd.

De trinitate. Ed J. Ribailler, Paris 1958.

Liber exceptionum. Ed J. Chatillon, Paris 1958.

Opuscules théologiques. Ed J. Ribailler, Paris 1967.

Über die Gewalt der Liebe: ihre vier Stufen. Tr M. Schmidt, Munich 1967.

Ebner, J. Die Erkenntnisslehre Richard von St Victor. Münster 1907.

Andres, F. Die Stufen der Contemplatio in Bonaventuras Itinerarium mentis in Deum und im Beniamin maior des Richard von St Victor. Franziskanische Studien 8 1921.

Ottaviano, C. Riccardo di S. Victore: la vita, le opere, il pensiero. Rome 1933.

—— Riccardo di S. Vittore. Nouvelle Revue Théologique 61 1934.

Moore, P. S. The authorship of the Allegoriae super Vetus et Novum Testamentum. New Scholasticism 9 1935.

Lenglart, M. La théorie de la contemplation mystique dans l'oeuvre de Richard de Saint-Victor. Paris 1935.

Ethier, A. M. Le De trinitate de Richard de Saint-Victor. Institut d'Etudes Médiévales d'Ottawa (Paris) 9 1939.

Guimet, F. Notes en marge d'un texte de Richard de Saint-Victor. Archives d'Histoire Doctrinale et Littéraire du Moyen Age 14 1945.

Chatillon, J. Le contenu, l'authenticité et la date du Liber exceptionum et des Sermones centum de Richard de Saint-Victor. Revue du Moyen Age Latin 4 1948.

—— 'Misit Herodes rex manus': un opuscule de Richard de Saint-Victor égaré parmi les oeuvres de Fulbert de Chartres. Revue du Moyen Age Latin 6 1950.

Dumeige, G. Richard de Saint-Victor et l'idée chrétienne de l'amour. Paris 1952.

—— Ives, Epitre a Séverin et Richard de S. Victor: les quatre degrés de la violente charité. Paris 1955.

Negri, L. Poesia e mistica in Riccardo di San Vittore. Convivium 22 1955.

Walker, G. S. M. Richard of S. Victor, an early Scottish theologian. Scottish Jnl of Theology 2 1958.

Bligh, J. Richard of S. Victor's De trinitate: Augustinian or Abelardian? Heythrop Jnl 1 1960.

Baron, R. Richard de S. Victor a-t-il écrit le De contemplatione? Revue des Sciences Religieuses 36 1962.

Colker, M. L. Richard of S. Victor and the Anonymous of Bridlington. Traditio 18 1962.

Ribailler, J. Richard de S. Victor, de statu interioris hominis. Archives d'Histoire Doctrinale et Littéraire du Moyen Age 34 1967.

Robert of Bridlington
d. c. 1160

Dialogus. Ed and tr a religious of CSMV 1960.

Robert of Cricklade
fl. 1159

Defloratio Pliniana. BM ms Royal 15.

Rück, K. Das Exzerpt der Naturalis historia des Plinius von Robert von Cricklade. Sitzungsberichte der Königlichen Bayerischen Akademie der Wissenschaften 1902.

Orme, M. A reconstruction of Robert of Cricklade's Vita et miracula S. Thomae Cantuariensis. Analecta Bollandiana 84 1966.

For other works attributed to Robert of Cricklade see A. B. Emden, A biographical register of the University of Oxford to 1500 vol 1, Oxford 1957.

Robert of Melun, Bishop of Hereford
d. 1167

Oeuvres. Ed R. M. Martin and R. M. Gallet, Louvain 1932–52.

Martin, R. M. L'oeuvre théologique de Robert de Melun. Revue d'Histoire Ecclésiastique 16 1920.

Pro Petro Abaelardo: un plaidoyer de Robert de Melun contre Saint Bernard. Revue des Sciences Philosophiques et Théologiques 12 1923.

Die Christologie des Robert von Melun. Forschungen zur Christlichen Litteratur- und Dogmengeschichte 15 1927.

Pelster, F. Literaturgeschichtliche Beiträge zu Robert Melun. Zeitschrift für Katholische Theologie 52 1929.

Landgraf, A. Robert de Melun und seine Schule. Biblica 13 1932.

Bliemetzrieder, F. Robert von Melun und die Schule Anselms von Laon. Zeitschrift für Kirchengeschichte 53 1934.

Nash, P. W. The meaning of 'est' in the Sentences 1152–60 of Robert of Melun. Mediaeval Stud 14 1952.

Robert Partes, monk of Reading
fl. c. 1170

Cornog, W. H. The poems of Robert Partes. Speculum 12 1937.

Senatus of Worcester
fl. 1190

Delhaye, P. Deux textes de Senatus de Worcester sur la pénitence. Recherches de Théologie Ancienne et Médiévale 19 1952.

Serlo of Wilton
fl. 1171

Poèmes latins. Ed J. Öberg, Stockholm 1965.

For an account of earlier partial edns, see F. J. E. Raby, Secular Latin poetry vol 2 pp. 111–15.

Hauréau, B. Mémoires sur les récits d'apparitions dans les sermons du Moyen Age. Mémoires de l'Académie des Inscriptions 28, Paris 1894. On Serlo's conversion.

Friend, A. C. Serlo of Wilton: the early years. Bulletin Du Cange 24 1954.

Thomas à Becket
d. 1170

Hymnus de septem gaudiis caelestibus beatae Mariae. Ed Dreves, Analecta hymnica vol 31.

Brown, P. A. The development of the legend of Thomas Becket. Philadelphia 1930.

Walter Daniel
fl. 1167
Vita Aelredi. Ed and tr F. M. Powicke 1950.
Powicke, F. M. Ailred of Rievaulx and his biographer Walter Daniel. Manchester 1922.

Walter of Wimborne
fl. late 12th century
De palpone et assentatore; De mundi cupiditate. Ed T. Wright, Latin poems attributed to Walter Mapes, 1841.
Poems. In Analecta hymnica vol 50, ed G. M. Dreves, Leipzig 1907.

Walter the Englishman
fl. 1177
Fables in verse (Aesop). Ed L. Hervieux, Fabulistes latins vol 2; ed K. McKenzie and W. Oldfather, Illinois Univ Stud 5 1919.

William of Conches
fl. 1154
Philosophia. Basle 1531; Migne, Patrologia latina vol 90 (among works of Bede) and vol 172 (among works of Honorius of Autun).
Dragmaticon. Ed G. Gratarolus, Strasbourg 1567, Frankfurt 1967. Rev version of Philosophia, above.
Glosae super Boetium. Ed J. M. Parent, La doctrine de la Création, Paris 1938.
Glosae super Platonem. Ed J. M. Parent, La doctrine de la création, Paris 1938; ed E. Jeauneau, Paris 1965.
Hauréau, B. Guillaume de Conches. In his Singularités historiques et littéraires, Paris 1894.
Poole, R. L. In his Medieval thought and learning, 1920.
Thorndike, L. History of magic and experimental science. New York 1923. See vol 2 pp. 64–5 for mss of Philosophia and Dragmaticon.
— More mss of the Dragmaticon and the Philosophia. Speculum 20 1945.
Flatten, H. Die Philosophie des Wilhelm von Conches. Coblenz 1929.
Wilmart, A. Préface de Guillaume de Conches pour la dernière part de son dialogue. Analecta Reginensia (Vatican) 1932.
Grabmann, M. Handschriftliche Forschungen und Mitteilungen zum Schriftum des Wilhelm von Conches. Bayerische Akademie der Wissenschaften 1935.
Ottavians, C. Wilhelmi a Cochis philosophia seu Summa philosophiae. Archivio di Storia della Filosofia 2 1933.
— Un brano inedito della Philosophia di Guglielmo di Conches. Naples 1935.
Parent, J. M. La doctrine de la création dans l'école de Chartres. Institut d'Etudes Médiévales d'Ottawa (Paris) 8 1938.
Courcelle, P. Etude critique des commentaires sur la Consolatio philosophiae. Archives d'Histoire Doctrinale et Littéraire 14 1939.
Vernet, A. Un remaniment de la Philosophia. Scriptorium 1 1947.
Jeauneau, E. L'usage de la notion d'integumentum à travers les gloses de Guillaume de Conches. Archives d'Histoire Doctrinale et Littéraire du Moyen Age 24 1957.
— Deux rédactions des gloses de Guillaume de Conches sur Priscien. Recherches de Théologie Ancienne et Médiévale 27 1960.
— Gloses de Guillaume de Conches sur Macrobe: note sur les manuscrits. Archives d'Histoire Doctrinale et Littéraire du Moyen Age 27 1960.
— Gloses sur le Timée du manuscrit Digby 217 de la Bodléienne. Sacris Eruditi 17 1966.
— La lecture des auteurs classiques à l'école de Chartres, un témoin privilégié: les Glosae super Macrobium de Guillaume de Conches. In Classical influences on European culture, ed R. R. Bolgar, Cambridge 1971.

Unauthentic Writings
Moralium dogma philosophorum. Ed Migne, Patrologia latina vol 181; ed J. Holmberg, Das Moralium dogma philosophorum, lateinisch, altfranzösisch und mittelniederfrankisch, Upsala 1929.
Williams, J. R. The authorship of the Moralium dogma philosophorum. Speculum 6 1931.
Glorieux, P. Le Moralium dogma philosophorum et son auteur. Recherches de Théologie Ancienne et Médiévale 15 1948.
Gauthier, R. A. Pour l'attribution à Gauthier de Châtillon du Moralium dogma philosophorum. Revue du Moyen Age Latin 7 1951.
Delhaye, P. Gauthier de Châtillon est-il l'auteur du Moralium dogma? Lille 1953.

(7) THIRTEENTH CENTURY

Anonymous
Dulcis Iesu memoria (poem c. 1200, probably by an English Cistercian). Le Jubilus dit de S. Bernard: étude avec textes. Ed A. Wilmart, Rome 1944.
Thomson, S. H. The Dulcis Jesu memoria in Anglo-Norman and Middle French. MÆ 11 1942.
Raby, F. J. E. The poem Dulcis Iesu memoria. Hymn Soc Bull 33 1945.
Itinerarium peregrinorum et gesta regis Ricardi primi. Ed W. Stubbs, Chronicles of the reign of Richard I, 2 vols 1864–5 (Rolls ser); ed and tr K. Fenwick 1958; ed H. E. Mayer, Stuttgart 1962.
Edward, J. G. In Historical essays in honour of James Tait, Manchester 1933.
Landon, L. The itinerary of King Richard I. 1935.
Liber exemplorum ad usum praedicantium. Ed A. G. Little, Br Soc of Franciscan Stud 1908. Compiled by an English friar in Ireland c. 1275.
Speculum laicorum. Ed J. T. Welter, Paris 1914. See Little, English Franciscan history p. 138. Compiled c. 1280 by an English friar, probably Franciscan.

Adam Marsh (Adam de Marisco) OFM
d. 1257
Epistolae. Ed J. S. Brewer, Monumenta franciscana vol 1, 1858 (Rolls ser). For his other writings see Little, Franciscan school at Oxford, Archivum Franciscanum Historicum 19 1926.
Hunt, R. W. Chapter headings of Augustine's De trinitate ascribed to Adam Marsh. Bodleian Lib Record 5 1956.

Adam of Buckfield (or Bockfeld)
d. c. 1294
Pelster, F. Adam von Bockfeld: ein Oxforder Erklärer des Aristoteles um die Mitte des 13 Jahrhunderts. Scholastik 11 1936.
Callus, D. Two early Oxford masters on the problem of the plurality of forms: Adam of Buckfield and Richard Rufus of Cornwall. Revue Néo-scolastique de Philosophie 42 1939.
Thomson, S. H. A note on the works of Adam de Bocfeld. Medievalia et Humanistica 2 1944.

— A further note on Master Adam de Bocfeld. Medievalia et Humanistica 12 1958.

Bataillon, L. Adam of Bockfield: further mss. Medievalia et Humanistica 13 1960.

Adam of Dryburgh (Adam Scot the Premonstratensian)
d. c. 1212

Opera. Ed Migne, Patrologia latina vol 198.

Ad viros religiosos. Ed F. Patit, Tangerloo 1934. 14 sermons.

De quadripartito exercicio celle. Ed Migne, Patrologia latina vol 153. Ascribed to Guigo II of the Grande Chartreuse; on Adam's claim see E. M. Thompson, The Carthusian order in England pp. 354f.

Birch, W. de G. Sermones fratris Ade Ordinis Praemonstratensis. Edinburgh 1901.

Wilmart, A. Magister Adam Cartusiensis. In Mélanges Mandonnet vol 2, Paris 1930.

— Maître Adam, chanoine prémontré, devenu chartreux à Witham. Analecta Praemonstratensia 9 1933.

Morin, G. Gloriosus Magister Adam. Revue Bénédictine 44 1932.

Thompson, E. M. A fragment of a Witham Charterhouse Chronicle and Adam of Dryburgh. Bull Rylands Lib John 16 1932.

Bullock, J. Adam of Dryburgh. 1958.

Alan of Melsa (Prior of Beverley)
fl. 1212

Tractatus metricus de Sussana. Ed J. H. Mozley, Susanna and the elders: three medieval poems, Studi Medievali new ser 3 1930.

Alan of Tewkesbury
d. 1202

Scripta quae extant. Ed J. A. Giles, Oxford 1846 (Caxton Soc).

Alexander of Hales OFM
d. 1245

Glossa in quattuor libros sententiarum Petri Lombardi. In Bibliotheca franciscana scholastica medii aevi, 2 vols Florence 1951–2.

Quaestio de fato. Ed J. George, Franziskanische Studien 19 1932.

Inauthentic Works

Universae theologiae summa. 4 vols Quarrachi 1924–48. *The Summa fratris Alexandri is a compilation by later Franciscan theologians based on the writings of Alexander, John of la Rochelle, Bonaventure et al: see V. Doucet, The history of the problem of the authenticity of the Summa, Franciscan Stud 7 1947 and F. Henquinet, Fr. Considerans: un des auteurs jumeaux de la Summa fratris Alexandri primitive, Recherches de Théologie Ancienne et Médiévale 15 1948.*

For works on Alexander before 1945 see I. Herscher, A bibliography of Alexander of Hales, Franciscan Stud 5 1945.

Boehner, P. The system of metaphysics of Alexander of Hales. Franciscan Stud 5 1945.

Curtin, M. M. The 'Intellectus agens' in the Summa of Alexander of Hales. Ibid.

Huber, R. M. Alexander of Hales OFM: his life and influence on medieval scholasticism. Ibid.

Mohan, G. E. A manuscript of Alexander of Hales. Ibid.

Prentice, R. The De Fontibus paradisi of Alexander IV on the Summa theologica of Alexander of Hales. Ibid.

Henquinet, F. M. Le commentaire d'Alexandre de Hales sur les Sentences enfin retrouvé. In Miscellanea G. Mercati, Vatican 1946.

Doucet, V. A new source of the Summa fratris Alexandri. Franciscan Stud 6 1946.

— Autour des Prolegomena ad Summam fr. Alexandri. Archivum Franciscanum Historicum 43 1950.

Lottin, O. Le commentaire d'Alexandre de Hales sur les Sentences. Recherches de Théologie Ancienne et Médiévale 14 1947.

Lynch, K. F. A 'terminus ad quem' for the Commentary of Alexander of Hales. Franciscan Stud 10 1950.

— The Quaestio de sacramentis in genere attributed to Alexander of Hales. Franciscan Stud 11 1951.

— The doctrine of Alexander of Hales on sacramental grace. Franciscan Stud 19 1959.

Schneyer, J. B. Eine Sermonsreihe des Mgr Alexander von Hales. Analecta Franciscana Historica 58 1965

Brady, I. The distinctions of Lombard's Book of sentences and Alexander of Hales. Franciscan Stud 25 1965.

Catania, F. J. Knowledge of God in Alexander of Hales and John Duns Scotus. Stud in Medieval Culture (Michigan) 2 1966.

Principe, W. H. Alexander of Hales' theology of the hypostatic union. Toronto 1967.

Alexander Neckham
d. 1217

De naturis rerum et de laudibus divinae sapientae. Ed T. Wright 1863 (Rolls ser). The De vita monachorum, ed Wright, Satirical poets vol 2, is probably not by Neckham.

De nominibus ustensilium. Ed T. Wright, A volume of vocabularies, 1857; ed A. Scheler, Lexicographie latine, Leipzig 1867.

Hymns etc. Analecta hymnica vol 48.

Novus Aesopus. Ed L. Hervieux, Les fabulistes latins vol 2, Paris 1894.

Novus Avianus. Ed L. Hervieux, Les fabulistes latins vol 3, Paris 1894.

Sacerdos ad altare. Ed C. H. Haskins, A list of text books from the close of the 12th century, Harvard Stud 20 1909; rev in his Studies in the history of mediaeval science, Cambridge Mass 1924.

Meyer, P. Notices sur les Corrogationes Promethei d'Alexandre Neckham. Notices et extraits des mss de la Bibliothèque Nationale vol 35 pt 2, 1876.

Mortet, V. Hugue de Fouillou, Pierre le Chantre, Alexandre Neckham, et les critiques dirigées au xiime siècle contre le luxe des constructions. In Mélanges d'histoire offerts à M. Charles Bémont, Paris 1913.

Esposito, M. On some unpublished poems attributed to Alexander Neckham. EHR 30 1915. For a correction see F. M. Powicke, Medieval books of Merton College, Oxford 1931.

Russell, J. C. Alexander Neckham in England. EHR 47 1932.

Gaselee, S. Notes on the vocabulary of A. Neckham. Speculum 14 1939.

Loewe, R. and R. W. Hunt. Alexander Neckham's knowledge of Hebrew. Medieval & Renaissance Stud 4 1958.

Walther, H. Zu den kleineren Gedichten Alexander Neckhams. Mittellateinisches Jahrbuch 2 1965.

Kuttner, S. The tale of the captive bird and the traveller: Nequam, Berechiah and Chaucer. Medievalia et Humanistica new ser 1 1970.

Alfred of Sarashel (Alfridus Anglicus)

De motu cordis. Ed C. Bäumker, Münster 1923.

Quaestiones naturales. Tr H. Gollancz 1920.

Pelzer, A. Une source inconnue de Roger Bacon: Alfred de Sarashel. Archivum Franciscanum Historicum 12 1919.

Lacombe, G. Alfredus Anglicus in Metheora. In Aus der Geisteswelt des Mittelalters: Festgabe M. Grabmann, Münster 1935.

Bartholomew of Glanville (Bartolomaeus Anglicus) OFM
fl. 1230

De proprietatibus rerum. Cologne [1470?], Frankfurt 1601, 1609; tr John Trevisa c. 1495 and J. S. Walsh, Medieval Life 40 1933.
Schneider, A. Metaphysische Begriffe des Bartholomeus Anglicus. In Studien zur Geschichte der Philosophie: Festgabe Clemens Bäumker, Münster 1913.
Plassmann, T. Bartholomeus Anglicus. Archivum Franciscanum Historicum 12 1919.
Boyar, G. E. S. Bartholomeus Anglicus and his encyclopedia. JEGP 19 1920.
P. Michaud-Quantin. Les petites encyclopédies du 13e siècle. Cahiers d'Histoire Mondiale (Neuchâtel) 9 1966.

Edmund Rich, Archbishop of Canterbury
d. 1240

Speculum Sancti Edmundi (Speculum Ecclesiae). Leyden 1677, Paris 1854.
Wallace, W. Life of St Edmund of Canterbury. 1893.
Lacombe, G. La Summa Abendonensis. In Mélanges Mandonnet vol 2, Paris 1930. On Rich and Simon de Henton.

Geoffrey of Aspall
fl. 1286

Macrae, E. Geoffrey of Aspall's Commentaries on Aristotle. Medieval & Renaissance Stud 6 1968.

Geoffrey of Vinsauf
fl. 1210

Comedie. Ed B. Hauréau, Notices et extraits des mss de la Bibliothèque Nationale 29 pt 2. Texts also in G. Cohen, La comédie latine en France au 12e siècle, 2 vols Paris 1931.
Poëtria nova. Ed E. Faral, Les arts poétiques du 12e et 13e siècle, Paris 1924; tr M. F. Nimms, Toronto 1967.
Faral, E. La fabliau latin au Moyen Age. Romania 50 1924.
— Le ms 511 du Hunterian museum de Glasgow. Studi Medievali new ser 9 1936.
Manly, J. M. Chaucer and the rhetoricians. Proc Br Acad 12 1926.
Wilmart, A. L'art poétique de Geoffroi de Vinsauf et les commentaires de Barthélemy de Pise. Revue Bénédictine 41 1929.
Young, K. Chaucer and Geoffrey of Vinsauf. MP 41 1944.
Duncan, E. H. Chaucer's Wife of Bath's prologue and Geoffrey of Vinsauf's Documentum. MP 65 1968.
Kelly, D. The theory of composition in medieval poetry and Geoffrey of Vinsauf's Poëtria nova. Mediaeval Stud 31 1969.

Gervase of Melkey (de Saltu Lacteo)
fl. 1212

Ars versificaria. Summary in E. Faral, Les arts poétiques du 12e et du 13e siècle, Paris 1924; extracts in Faral, Le ms 511 du Hunterian Museum de Glasgow, Studi Medievali new ser 9 1936.

Giraldus Cambrensis (Gerald of Barry, Gerald of Wales)
d. c. 1220

Opera. Ed J. S. Brewer, J. F. Dimock and G. F. Warner 8 vols 1861–91.
De principis instructione. Tr in J. Stevenson, Church historians of England vol 5, 1858.

De rebus a se gestis; Autobiography, tr H. E. Butler 1937.
Invectiones etc. Ed W. S. Davies, Cymmroder 30 1920.
Vita Ethelberti. Ed M. R. James, EHR 32 1917.
Owen, H. Gerald the Welshman. 1904.
Coulter, C. C. and F. P. Magoun. Giraldus Cambrensis and Indo-Germanic philology. Speculum 1 1926.
Powicke, F. M. Gerald of Wales. Bull John Rylands Lib 12 1928; rev in his Christian life in the Middle Ages and other essays, Oxford 1935.
Butler, H. E. Some new pages of Giraldus Cambrensis. MÆ 4 1935.
Holmes, U. T. Gerald the naturalist. Speculum 11 1936.
— Ludos scenicos in Giraldus. MLN 57 1942.
Sanford, E. M. Giraldus Cambrensis' debt to Petrus Cantor. Medievalia et Humanistica 3 1945.
Boutemy, A. Giraud de Barri et Pierre le Chantre: une source de la Gemma ecclesiastica. Revue du Moyen Age Latin 2 1946.
Davies, J. C. Giraldus Cambrensis 1146–1946. Archaeologia Cambrensis 40 1946.
— Giraldus and Powis. Montgomeryshire Collections 1946.
— The Kambriae mappa of Giraldus. Jnl Historical Soc of Church in Wales 2 1950.
Williams, C. H. Giraldus and Wales. Jnl Historical Soc of Church in Wales 1 1947.
Jones, T. Geralt Cymro: Gerald the Welshman. Cardiff 1947.
— Gerald's Itinerary through Wales and description of Wales. Nat Lib of Wales Jnl 6 1950.
Gessler, J. In Giraldum Cambrensem. Latomus 7 1948.
Doney, R. J. Giraldus Cambrensis and the Carthusian order. JEGP 53 1954.
Knowles, D. Some enemies of Gerald of Wales. Studia Monastica 1 1959.
Huygens, R. B. C. Une lettre de Girard le Cambrien à propos de ses ouvrages historiques. Latomus 24 1965.
Reiss, E. The Welsh versions of Geoffrey of Monmouth's Historia. Welsh History Rev 4 1968.
Rowbotham, D. M. The Cambriae descriptio of Gerald the Welshman. Medievalia et Humanistica new ser 1 1970.

Gregory the Englishman
fl. c. 1200

Narracio de mirabilibus Rome. Ed M. R. James, EHR 32 1917; ed F. M. Rushworth, Jnl Roman Stud 9 1921; ed R. Valentini and G. Zucchetti, Codice topografico della Città di Roma vol 3, Rome 1946.

Henry of Avranches (Court poet under Henry III)

Comoda gramatice. Ed J. P. Heironimus and J. C. Russell, Two types of thirteenth-century grammatical poems, Denver 1929.
The shorter Latin poems of Master Henry of Avranches relating to England. Ed J. C. Russell and J. P. Heironimus, Cambridge Mass 1935 (with bibliography).
Winkelmann, E. Drei Gedichte Heinrichs von Avranches am Kaiser Friedrich II. Forschungen zur Deutschen Geschichte 18 1873.
Russell, J. C. Master Henry of Avranches. Speculum 3 1928.
See also Michael of Cornwall, below.

Henry of Bracton
d. 1268

De legibus et consuetudinibus Anglia. Ed T. Twiss 6 vols 1878–83 (Rolls ser); ed G. E. Woodbine 2 vols New Haven 1915.
Bracton's note book. Ed F. W. Maitland 3 vols 1887.
For bibliography see C. Gross, Sources and literature of English history, 1900, 1915 (enlarged).

Schule, F. Bracton on kingship. EHR 60 1945.
Richardson, H. G. Studies in Bracton. Traditio 6 1948.
—— Bracton: the problem of his text. 1965.

Henry of Silgrave
Chronicon. Ed C. Hook 1849.

John Blund
fl. c. 1250
Tractatus de anima. Ed D. A. Callus and R. W. Hunt, Oxford 1970.

John Godard, Cistercian Abbot of Newenham
Epistola ad sororem; Apostropha peccatoris in virginem gloriosam. Ed C. H. Talbot, Analecta sacri Ordinis Cisterciensis 10 1954.

John Holywood (de Sacro Bosco)
fl. 1230
Tractatus de sphaera. Ferrara 1472. A textbook which remained popular till late 16th century.
Harvey, S. W. Chaucer's debt to Sacrobosco. JEGP 34 1935.
Thorndike, L. Robertus Anglicus and the introduction of demons and magic into commentaries upon the Sphere of Sacrobosco. Speculum 21 1946. *See also* his article on Robertus Anglicus, Isis 34 1943.
—— The Sphere of Sacrobosco and its commentators. Chicago 1949.

John of Garland
d. c. 1258
Verse
De mysteriis ecclesiae. Ed B. W. Otto, Commentarii critici in codices bibliothecae Gissensis, Giessen 1842.
De triumphis ecclesiae. Ed T. Wright 1856 (Roxburghe Club).
[Hymns etc]. Analecta hymnica vol 51.
Morale scolarium. Ed L. J. Paetow, Berkeley 1927. Contains list of Garland's works. *See* C. H. Haskins, Manuals for students, in his Studies in mediaeval culture, Oxford 1929.
Stella maris. Ed E. F. Wilson, Cambridge Mass 1946 (Medieval Acad of America).

Prose
Dictionarius. Ed R. Wright, Volume of vocabularies, 1857.
Integumenta Ovidii. Ed F. Ghisalberti, Messina 1933.
Poetria magistri Johannis Anglici de arte prosayca, metrica et rithmica. Ed G. Mari, Romanische Forschungen 13 1902.
Zarncke, F. Zwei mittelalterliche Abhandlungen über den Bau rhythmischer Verse. Leipziger Sitzungsberichte 23 1871.
Habel, E. Die Exempla honestae vitae des Johannes de Garlandia. Romanische Forschungen 29 1911.
Paetow, L. J. The crusading ardour of John of Garland. In The Crusades and other historical essays presented to Dana C. Munro, New York 1928.
Wilmart, A. Commentaire du Distigium de Jean de Garlande. Analecta Reginensia 1933.
Wilson, E. F. The Georgica spiritualia of John of Garland. Speculum 8 1933.
Born, L. K. The mss of the major grammatical works of John of Garland. Trans & Proc Amer Philological Assoc 119 1938.
Vecchi, G. Modi d'arte poetica in Giovanni di Garlandia e il ritmo Aula vernat virginalis. Quadrivium 1 1956.
Saiani, A. Astrologia spiritualis nell' Epithalamium e nella Stella maris. Ibid.
Waite, W. G. Johannes de Garlandia: poet and musician. Speculum 35 1960.
Park, B. A. and E. G. Dallas. Sequentia cum prosa by John of Garland. Medievalia et Humanistica 15 1963.

Lawler, T. F. John of Garland and Horace: a medieval schoolman faces the Ars poetica. Classical Folia 22 1968.

John of Hoveden (or Howden)
d. 1275
Poems. Ed F. J. E. Raby 1939 (Surtees Soc).
Viola. Ed F. J. E. Raby, MLR 30 1935.
Practica chilindri. Ed E. Brock, Essays on Chaucer, 1868 (Chaucer Soc).
Raby, F. J. E. John of Hoveden. Laudate 13 1935.
D'Evelyn C. Meditations on the life and passions of Christ: a note on its literary relationships. In Essays and studies in honor of Carleton Brown, New York 1940. On a ME version of the Philomena.
Stone, L. W. Jean de Howden: poète anglo-normand du xiie siècle. Romania 69 1947.

John of St Giles OP
(physician to Philip Augustus)
fl. 1230
[Sermons]. In M. M. Davy, Les sermons universitaires parisiens de 1230–1, Paris 1931. Bodley ms 786 contains a collection of his medical prescriptions.

John of Wales OFM
d. c. 1283
For a list of his works, see A. G. Little, Grey friars in Oxford, *1892; and of ptd edns,* English Franciscan history, *1917.*
Communiloquium [or Summa Collationum ad omne genus hominum]. Venice 1496; extract ed L. Thorndike, All the world's a chess-board, Speculum 6 1931.
Compendiloquium. Venice 1496.
Breviloquium de philosophia sive sapientia sanctorum. Venice 1496.
Breviloquium de virtutibus antiquorum principum et philosophorum. Venice 1496.
Little, A. G. Studies in English Franciscan history. Manchester 1917.
Welter, J. T. L'exemplum dans la littérature religieuse et didactique du Moyen Age. Paris 1927.
Smalley, B. English friars and antiquity in the early 14th century. Oxford 1960.

John of Wallingford
d. 1258
Chronicle. Ed R. Vaughan 1958.

John Pecham, Archbishop of Canterbury OFM
d. 1292
Verse
Poems [including Philomela praevia]. Analecta hymnica vol 50.
Canticum pauperis pro dilecto. Bibliotheca franciscana ascetica vol 4.
Vier Prosen des Johannes Pecham. Ed E. Peeters, Franziskanische Studien 4 1917.
Pflaum, H. Sortes, Plato, Cicero: satirisches Gedicht des 13 Jahrhunderts. Speculum 6 1931.
Raby, F. J. E. Philomena, praevia temporis amoeni. In Mélanges Joseph de Ghellinck SJ vol 2, Gembloux 1951.
Maximilianus, P. Philomena van John Pecham. Neophilologus 38 1954.
Bruning, E. Nog eens Philomena—me met muzik. Neophilologus 39 1955.

Prose
De perfectione evangelica. Ed A. Wyngaert, Paris 1952 (in part); Quatres chapitres inédits sur la perfection religieuse et autres états de perfection, Collectanea Franciscana 14 1944 (in part).

Jerarchia. Ed M. D. Legge, MÆ 11 1942. Norman-French text.

Questiones tractantes de anima. Ed H. Spettmann, Münster 1918.

Quodlibetum romanum. Ed F. M. Delorme, Rome 1938.

Perspectiva communis. Ed and tr D. C. Lindberg, Madison 1970.

Registrum epistolarum fratris Johannis Peckham. Ed C. T. Martin 3 vols 1882–5 (Rolls ser).

Summa de esse et essentia. Ed F. M. Delorme, Studi Francescani 25 1928.

Tractatus de anima. Ed G. Melani, Biblioteca di Studi Francescani (Florence) 1 1948.

Tractatus tres de paupertate. Ed C. L. Kingsford, A. G. Little and F. Tocco, Br Soc for Franciscan Stud 1910 (with bibliography of Pecham's works).

Ehrle, F. John Peckham, Über den Kampf des Augustinismus und Aristotelismus in der zweiten Hälfte des 13 Jahrhunderts. Zeitschrift für Katholische Theologie 13 1889.

Oliger, L. De pueris oblatis in Ord. Min., cum textu hucusque inedito Fr. Joh. Pecham. Archivum Franciscanum historicum 8 1915.

— Die theologische Question des Joh. Pecham über die vollkommene Armut. Franziskanische Studien 4 1917.

Spettmann, H. Quellencritisches zur Biographie des Johannes Pecham. Franziskanische Studien 2 1915.

— Die Psychologie des Johannes Peckham. Münster 1919.

— Die Ethikkommentar des Johannes Peckham. [Baeumker Festgabe, Münster 1923].

— Der Sentenzenkommentar des Franziskanererzbischofs Johannes Peckham. Divus Thomas (Fribourg) 5 1927.

Callebaut, A. Jean Pecham OFM et l'augustinisme. Archivum Franciscanum Historicum 18 1925.

Doucet, V. Notulae bibliographicae de quibusdam operibus Fr. J. Pecham. Antonianum 8 1933.

Peckham, J. L. Archbishop Peckham as a religious educator. Yale Stud in Religion 7 1934.

Clasen, S. Eine Antwort auf die theologische Quästion des Johannes Pecham über die vollkommene Armut. Franziskanische Studien 25 1938.

Knowles, D. Some aspects of the career of Archbishop Pecham. EHR 57 1942.

Thorndike, L. Duhem's 'disciple of Bacon' identified with John Pecham. Isis 34 1943.

— A John Peckham manuscript. Archivum Franciscanum Historicum 45 1952.

Douie, D. L. Pecham's sermons and collections. In Studies in medieval history presented to F. M. Powicke, Oxford 1948.

— Archbishop Pecham. Oxford 1952.

Crowley, T. John Pecham OFM versus the new Aristotelianism. Bull John Rylands Lib 33 1951.

John Sackville (Johannes de Sicca Villa)
d. after 1292

De principiis naturae. Ed R. M. Giguère OP, Montreal 1956.

Matthew Paris
fl. 1259

Chronica: or historia maior. Ed H. R. Luard 5 vols 1872–80 (Rolls ser).

Flores historiarum [based on Flores historiarum of Roger of Wendover]. Ed H. R. Luard 3 vols 1890 (Rolls ser).

Historia Anglorum: or historia minor. Ed F. H. Madden 3 vols 1866–9 (Rolls ser).

Vitae abbatum. In Thomas Walsingham, Gesta abbatum monasterii S. Albani, ed H. T. Riley 1867–9 (Rolls ser).

Plehn, H. Der politische Charakter von Matheus Parisiensis. Leipzig 1897.

Galbraith, V. H. Roger of Wendover and Matthew Paris. Glasgow 1944.

Powicke, F. M. The compilation of the Chronica maiora of Matthew Paris. Proc Br Acad 30 1944.

Vaughan, R. Matthew Paris. Cambridge 1958.

Michael of Cornwall
fl. 1250

Poem against Master Henry of Avranches. Ed A. Hilka, Mittelalterliche Handschriften: Festgabe zum 60 Geburtstage von H. Degering, Leipzig 1926.

Michael Scot
d. before 1236

Physionomia: or de secretis naturae. Ed R. Foerster, Scriptores physiognomici, Leipzig 1893.

For an account of Michael Scot as a translator and for mss of his work, see C. H. Haskins, Studies in the history of mediaeval science, Cambridge Mass 1924.

Odo of Cheriton
d. 1247

Fabulae et Parabolae. Ed L. Hervieux, Les fabulistes latins vol 4, Paris 1894.

Herbert, J. A. Catalogue of romances in the British sermon. JEGP 53 1954.

Welter, J. T. L'exemplum dans la littérature religieuse et didactique du Moyen Age. Paris 1927.

Friend, A. C. Master Odo of Cheriton. Speculum 23 1948.

— Analogues in Cheriton to the pardoner and his Museum vol 3. 1910.

Ralph or Raoul de Diceto, Dean of S. Paul's
d. 1202

Imagines historiarum. Ed W. Stubbs 2 vols 1876 (Rolls ser).

Ralph Niger
d. 1205

Chronica. Ed R. Anstruther 1851 (Caxton Soc).

Ralph of Coggeshall
d. 1224?

Chronicon anglicanum 1066–1216. Ed J. Stevenson 1875 (Rolls ser).

Richard Clapwell (or Knapwell) OP
fl. 1286

Correctorium corruptorii. Ed P. Glorieux, Les premières polémiques thomistes 1: le Correctorium corruptorii 'Quare'. Kain Belgium 1927.

Chenu, C. D. La première diffusion du Thomisme à Oxford: Klapwell et ses Notes sur les Sentences. Archives d'Histoire Doctrinale et Littéraire du Moyen Age 3 1928.

Pelster, F. Richard von Knapwell OP: seine Quaestiones disputatae und sein Quodlibet. Zeitschrift für Katholische Theologie 52 1928.

— Die Sätze der Londoner Beurteilung von 1286 und die Schriften des Mag. Richard von Knapwell OP. Archivum Fratrum Praedicatorum 16 1946.

Richard Fishacre OP
d. 1248

Quaestio. In A. Daniels, Quellenbeiträge und Untersuchungen zur Geschichte der Gottesbeweise im 13 Jahrhundert, Münster 1908. For another text see F. Stegmuller, Les questions de Robert Kilwardby, Revue de Théologie Ancienne et Médiévale 6 1934.

Martin, R. La Question de l'unité de la Forme substantielle dans le premier collège dominicain à Oxford. Revue Néo-scolastique 22 1920.

Pelster, F. Das Leben und die Schriften des Oxforder Dominikanerlehrers Richard Fishacre. Zeitschrift für Katholische Theologie 54 1930.
— Eine Hs mit Predigten des Richard Fishacre. Zeitschrift für Katholische Theologie 57 1933.
Sharp, D. E. The philosophy of Richard Fishacre (d. 1248). New Scholasticism 7 1933.
Lottin, O. La notion du libre arbitre dans la jeune école dominicaine d'Oxford. Revue des Sciences Philosophiques et Théologiques 24 1935.

Richard Middleton (de Mediavilla) OFM
fl. 1283

In IV libros sententiarum. Venice 1507-9.
Quaestiones quodlibetales. Venice 1509.

Hocedez, E. Richard de Middleton: sa vie, ses oeuvres sa doctrine. Spicilegium Lovaniense 1925.
Durst, B. Die Frage der Armenseelanrufung bei, Richard von Middletown. Franziskanische Studien 10 1923.
Witterbruch, W. Die Gewissenstheorie bei Heinrich von Ghent und Richard von Mediavilla. Eberfeld 1929.
Rucker, P. P. Der Ursprung unserer Begriffe nach Richard von Mediavilla. Münster 1934.
Lampen, W. De manuscriptis Richardi de Mediavilla. Antonianum 16 1941.
Zavalloni, R. Richard de Mediavilla et le controverse sur la pluralité des formes: textes inédits et étude critique. Louvain 1951. With extensive bibliography.
Wlodek, Z. Au sujet des recherches sur la chronologie des oeuvres de Richard de Mediavilla. Medievalia Philosophia Polonorum 3 1959.

Richard Rufus (of Cornwall) OFM
fl. 1250

Fragments of his works in D. A. Callus, Two early Oxford masters, Revue Néo-scolastique de Philosophie 42 1939; in O. Lottin, Psychologie et morale aux xiie et xiiie siècles, 2 vols Louvain 1942-8; and in F. Pelster, Der Oxforder Theologe Richardus Rufus, über die Frage 'utrum Christus in triduo mortis fuerit homo', Recherches de Théologie Ancienne et Medievale 16 1949.
For his sermons see M. M. Davy, Les sermons universitaires parisiens 1230-35, Paris 1931.

Little, A. G. The Franciscan school at Oxford in the 13th century. Archivum Franciscanum Historicum 19 1926.
Pelster, F. Der älteste Sentenzenkommentar aus der Oxforder Franziskanerschule. Scholastik 1 1926.
— Roger Bacons Compendium studii theologiae und der Sentenzenkommentar des Richardus Rufus. Scholastik 4 1929.
— Neue Schriften des englischen Franziskaners Richardus Rufus von Cornwall. Scholastik 8 1933.
— Die älteste Abkürzung und Kritik vom Sentenzkommentar des hl. Bonaventura im Werk des Richardus Rufus. Gregorianum 17 1936.
— Quästionen des Franziskaners Richard Rufus. Scholastik 14 1939.
Henquinet, F. M. Autour des écrits d'Alexandre de Hales et de Richard Rufus. Antonianum 11 1936.

Robert Grosseteste, Bishop of Lincoln
d. 1253

Die philosophische Werken des Robert Grosseteste. Ed L. Baur, Münster 1903.
De veritate, De veritate propositionis and De scientia Dei. Tr R. McKeon, Selections from medieval philosophers vol 1, New York 1929-30.
De luce. Tr C. C. Riedl, Robert Grosseteste on light, Milwaukee 1942.
Epistolae. Ed H. R. Luard 1861 (Ross ser).

Il commento al De mystica theologia del Pseudo-Dionigi Areopagitica. Ed V. Gamba, Milan 1942.
Quaestio de accessu et recessu maris. Ed E. Franceschini, Un inedito di Roberto Grossatesta, Rivista di Filosofia Neoscolastica 44 1952.
Quaestio de calore, de cometis et de operacionibus solis. Ed S. H. Thomson, Medievalia et Humanistica 11 1957.
Quaestio de fluxu et refluxu maris. Ed and tr R. C. Dales, Isis 57 1966.
Visio Philiberti. A dialogue in 'goliardic' verse; it is not improbable that Grosseteste is the author.

For bibliographies see S. H. Thomson, The writings of Grosseteste, Cambridge 1940; and A. C. Crombie, Grosseteste and the origins of experimental science 1100-1700, Oxford 1953.

Baur, L. Die Philosophie des Grosseteste. Münster 1917.
Hocedez, E. La diffusion de la 'Translatio Lincolniensis' du De orthodoxa fide de S. Jean Damascène. Bulletin d'Ancienne Littérature et Archéologie Chrétienne 1913.
Minges, P. Robert Grossetest als Übersetzer der Ethica Nicomachea. Philosophisches Jahrbuch 32 1919.
James, M. R. Robert Grosseteste on the Psalms. Jnl of Theological Stud 23 1922.
Pelster, F. Zwei unbekannte Traktate des Robert Grosseteste. Scholastik 1 1926.
Powicke, F. M. Robert Grosseteste and the Nicomachean ethics. Proc Br Acad 16 1930.
— Robert Grosseteste, Bishop of Lincoln. Bull John Rylands Lib 35 1953.
Franceschini, E. Roberto Grossetesta e le sue traduzioni latine. R. Instituto Veneto di Scienza, Lettere ed Arti 1933-4.
Thomson, S. H. A note on Grosseteste's work of translation. Jnl of Theological Stud 34 1933.
— The text of Grosseteste's De cometis. Isis 19 1933.
— Grosseteste's topical concordance of the Bible and the Fathers. Speculum 9 1934.
— The Summa in 8 Libros Physicorum of Grosseteste. Isis 22 1935.
— The writings of Robert Grosseteste. Cambridge 1940.
— Grosseteste's concordantial signs. Medievalia et Humanistica 9 1955.
— Grosseteste's Quaestio de calore, de cometis et de operacionibus solis. Medievalia et Humanistica 11 1957.
— An unnoticed autograph of Grosseteste. Medievalia et Humanistica 14 1962.
Morgan, M. M. The excommunication of Grosseteste in 1243. EHR 57 1942.
Russell, J. C. Richard of Bardney's account of Robert Grosseteste's early and middle life. Medievalia et Humanistica 2 1944.
— Some notes on the career of Robert Grosseteste. Harvard Theological Rev 48 1955.
Callus, D. A. The Oxford career of Robert Grosseteste. Oxoniensia 10 1945.
— The Summa theologiae of Robert Grosseteste. In Studies in medieval history presented to F. M. Powicke, Oxford 1948.
— (ed). Robert Grosseteste, scholar and bishop: essays in commemoration of the seventh centenary of his death. Oxford 1955.
Muckle, J. T. Robert Grosseteste's use of Greek sources in his Hexameron. Medievalia et Humanistica 3 1945.
Westerman, E. J. A comparison of some of the sermons and the Dicta of Robert Grosseteste. Ibid.
Birkenmayer, A. Robert Grosseteste and Richard Fournival. Medievalia et Humanistica 5 1948.
McKeon, C. K. A study of the Summa philosophiae of the Pseudo-Grosseteste. New York 1948.
Crombie, A. C. Robert Grosseteste and the origins of experimental science 1100-1700. Oxford 1953.

Srawley, J. H. Robert Grosseteste, Bishop of Lincoln. Lincoln 1953.

Hunt, R. W. Mss containing the indexing symbols of Robert Grosseteste. Bodleian Lib Record 4 1953.

— Verses on the life of Robert Grosseteste. Medievalia et Humanistica new ser 1 1970.

Tierney, B. Grosseteste and the theory of papal sovereignty. Jnl of Ecclesiastical History 6 1955.

Dales, R. C. Robert Grosseteste's Commentarius in octo libros physicorum Aristoteles. Medievalia et Humanistica 11 1957.

— Robert Grosseteste's scientific works. Isis 52 1961.

— Robert Grosseteste's treatise: De finitate motus e temporis. Traditio 19 1963.

— A note on Robert Grosseteste's Hexaemeron. Medievalia et Humanistica 15 1963.

— Robert Grosseteste's views on astrology. Medieval Stud 29 1967.

Gieben, S. Traces of God in nature according to Robert Grosseteste. Franciscan Stud 24 1964.

— Robert Grosseteste on preaching (with the edition of the sermon Ex rerum initio. Collectanea Franciscana 37 1967.

— Thomas Gascoigne and Robert Grosseteste. Vivarium 8 1970.

Dales, R. C. and S. Gieben. The proemium to Robert Grosseteste's Hexameron. Speculum 43 1968.

Eastwood, B. S. Medieval empiricism: the case of Grosseteste's Optics. Speculum 43 1968.

Robert Kilwardby OP Archbishop of Canterbury
d. 1279

De natura theologiae. Ed F. Stegmüller, Münster 1935.
De ortu et divisione scientiarum. Extracts in B. Hauréau, Notices et extraits de quelques mss latins vol 5, Paris 1893.

For a provisional list of the commentaries on Aristotle ascribed to Kilwardby, and for a list of questions contained in his commentary on the Sentences, see F. Stegmüller, Les questions du commentaire des sentences de Robert Kilwardby, Recherches de Théologie Ancienne et Médiévale 6 1934. For bibliographies see F. Tocco, Tractatus (Pechami) contra fratrem Robertum Kilwardby, Br Soc of Franciscan Stud 2 1910 and Uberweg-Geyer p. 764.
For extracts from, and summaries of, Kilwardby's other works see the articles below.

Ehrle, F. Der Augustinismus und der Aristotelismus in der Scholastik gegen Ende des 13 Jahrhunderts. Archiv für Literatur und Kirchengeschichte des Mittelalters 5 1889. Pp. 614–32 summarizes articles 1–6 of Kilwardby's letter to Peter of Conflans.

Birkenmajer, A. Der Brief Kilwardbys an Peter von Conflans. In Vermischte Untersuchungen, Münster 1922. On article 7 of the letter.

Chenu, M. D. Le De spiritu imaginativo de Kilwardby. Revue des Sciences Philosophiques et Théologiques 15 1926.

— Le De conscientia de Kilwardby. Revue des Sciences Philosophiques et Théologiques 16 1927.

— Les réponses de S. Thomas et de Kilwardby à la consultation de Jean de Verceil 1271. In Mélanges Mandonnet vol 1, Paris 1930.

— Le traité De tempore de Kilwardby. In Aus der Geisteswelt des Mittelalters: Festgabe M. Grabmann vol 2, Münster 1935.

— Aux origines de la 'science moderne'. Revue des Sciences Philosophiques et Théologiques 29 1940.

Stegmüller, F. Kilwardby über die Möglichkeit der natürlichen Gottesliebe. Divus Thomas (Piacenza) 38 1935.

— Der Traktat des Robert Kilwardby OP, De imagine et vestigio Trinitatis. Archives d'Histoire Doctrinale et Littéraire du Moyen Age 10 1936.

Sommer von Seckendorff, E. Kilwardby und seine philosophische Einleitung De Ortu scientiarum. Historisches Jahrbuch 55 1935.

— Studies in the life of Kilwardby. Rome 1937 (Institutum Historicum Fratrum Predicatorum, Santa Sabina).

Dondaine, H. Le De tempore de Kilwardby. Recherches de Théologie Ancienne et Médiévale 8 1936.

— La question De necessitate incarnationis de Kilwardby. Ibid.

Thomson, S. H. Kilwardby's commentaries In Priscianum and in Barbarismum Donati. New Scholasticism 12 1938.

Callus, D. A. The Tabulae super originalia Patrum of Kilwardby. In Studia medievalia in honorem Raymundi J. Martin OP, Bruges [1948].

— New manuscripts of Kilwardby's Tabulae. Dominican Stud 2 1949.

Thomas, I. Kilwardby on conversion. Dominican Stud 6 1953.

— Maxims in Kilwardby. Dominican Stud 7 1954.

Roger Bacon OFM
d. c. 1292
Commentaries and Text Books

Opera hactenus inedita. 16 vols Oxford 1905–40. Mainly commentaries on Aristotle; vol 6 includes spurious Computus.

The Greek grammar of Roger Bacon and a fragment of his Hebrew grammar. Ed E. Nolan and S. A. Hirsch, Cambridge 1902.

Thomson, S. H. An unnoticed treatise by Roger Bacon on time and motion. Isis 27 1937.

Delorme, F. Le prologue de R. Bacon à son traité De influentiis agentium. Antonianum 18 1943.

Works on Reformation of Theological Thought

Compendium studii theologiae. Ed H. Rashdall, Aberdeen 1911.

Opera quaedam hactenus inedita. Ed J. S. Brewer 1859. 1, Opus tertium; 2, Opus minus; 3, Compendium philosophiae; 4, De secretis operibus artis et de nullitate magiae. Suppls to text of Opus tertium in P. Duhem, Un fragment inédit de l'Opus tertium de Roger Bacon, Quarrachi 1909; and A. G. Little, Part of the Opus tertium of Roger Bacon, including a fragment new printed for the first time, Aberdeen 1912.

Opus maius. Ed J. H. Bridges, 3 vols Oxford 1897–1900. The complete text of pt 7, incompletely pbd by Bridges, is in F. Delorme and E. Massa, Rogeri Baconis moralis philosophia, Turin 1953.

Hoever, H. Roger Bacons Hylomorphismus als Grundlage seiner philosophischen Anschauungen. Limburg 1912.

Baeumker, C. Roger Bacons Natur-philosophie, insbesondere seine Lehre von Materie und Form, Individuation und Universalität. Münster 1916.

Carton, R. L'expérience physique chez Roger Bacon. Paris 1924.

— L'expérience mystique de l'illumination intérieure chez Roger Bacon. Paris 1924.

— La synthèse doctrinale de Roger Bacon. In E. Gilson, Etudes de philosophie médiévale vols 2–3, 5, Paris 1924.

Little, A. G. Roger Bacon. Proc Br Acad 14 1928.

— et al. Roger Bacon: essays. Oxford 1930.

Walle, B. van de. Roger Bacon dans l'histoire de philologie. La France Franciscaine 11–12 1928–9.

Bouyges, M. Roger Bacon a-t-il lu des livres arabes? Archives d'Histoire Doctrinale et Littéraire du Moyen Age 5 1930.

Singer, W. Alchemical writings of Roger Bacon. Speculum 7 1932.

Lutz, E. Roger Bacon's contribution to knowledge. New York 1936.

Sheridan, J. A. Expositio plenior hylomorphismi Fr. Rogeri Baconis Analecta Gregoriana (Philos. 17) Rome 1938.

Woodruff, F. W. Roger Bacon. 1938.

Delorme, F. De auctore compoti sub nomine Rogeri Baconis recenter editi. Antonianum 14 1939.

Crowley, T. Roger Bacon: the problem of the soul in his philosophical commentaries. Louvain and Dublin 1950 (with bibliography).

— Roger Bacon and Avicenna. Philosophical Stud 2 1952.

— Roger Bacon and the problem of universals in his philosophical commentaries. Bull John Rylands Lib 34 1951.

Easton, S. Roger Bacon and his search for a universal science. Oxford 1952 (with bibliography).

Meyer, G. En quel sens peut-on parler de 'méthode scientifique' chez Roger Bacon? Bulletin de Littérature Ecclésiastique 53 1952.

Westacott, E. Roger Bacon in life and legend. 1953.

Macfarlane, L. In Dictionnaire de spiritualité vol 4, Paris 1960 (with bibliography).

Roger Marston OFM
d. c. 1298

Quaestiones disputates; De emanatione aeterna; De statu naturae lapsae; et De anima. Quarrachi 1932. With bibliography.

Pelster, F. Roger Marston OFM. Scholastik 3 1928.

Gilson, E. Marston: un cas d'Augustinisme avicennisant. Archives d'Histoire Doctrinale et Littéraire du Moyen Age 8 1933.

— Sur quelques difficultés de l'illumination augustinienne. Revue Néo-scolastique de Philosophie 36 1934.

Guinagh, K. An unpublished ms of Rogerius Anglicus. Speculum 9 1934.

Belmond, S. La théorie de la connaissance d'après Marston. La France Franciscaine 17 1934.

Prezioso, F. L'attività del soggetto pensante nella gnoseologia di Matteo d'Acquasparta e di Ruggiero Marston. Antonianum 25 1950.

Roger of Hoveden (or Howden)
d. after 1201

Chronica 1192–1201. Ed W. Stubbs 4 vols 1868–71 (Rolls ser).

Gesta Henrici secundi; Gesta Ricardi. Ed W. Stubbs 1867. Stubbs ascribed these to Benedict of Peterborough; see Stenton, below.

Stenton, D. M. Roger of Howden and Benedict. EHR 68 1953.

Roger of Wendover
d. 1236

Chronica sive Flores historiarum. Ed H. O. Coxe 5 vols 1841–4; (Eng Historical Soc); Flores of history, tr J. A. Giles 2 vols 1849; ed H. G. Hewlett 3 vols 1886–9 (Rolls ser).

Jenkins, C. The monastic chronicles and early school of S. Albans. 1923.

Galbraith, V. H. Roger of Wendover and Matthew Paris. Glasgow 1944.

Powicke, F. M. The compilation of the Chronica maiora of Matthew Paris. Proc Br Acad 30 1944.

Kay R. Wendover's last annal. EHR 84 1969.

Stephen of Easton, Abbot of Fountains

Meditationes. Ed A. Wilmart, Revue d'Ascétique et de Mystique 10 1929

Exercitium triplex. Ed A. Wilmart, Revue d'Ascétique et de Mystique 11 1930.

Stephen Langton, Archbishop of Canterbury
d. 1228

Der Sentenzkommentar. Ed A. M. Landgraf, Münster 1952.

Wilmart, A. L'hymne et la séquence du Saint-Esprit. La Vie et les Arts Liturgiques July 1924. On Langton's claim to the authorship of the Veni, sancte Spiritus; see also Raby, Christian-Latin poetry pp. 343f.

Powicke, F. M. Stephen Langton. Oxford 1928.

— In his Christian life in the Middle Ages and other essays, Oxford 1935.

Lacombe, G. The Questions of Cardinal Langton. New Scholasticism 3 1929.

— The authenticity of the Summa of Cardinal Langton. New Scholasticism 4 1930.

Lacombe, G. and B. Smalley. Studies on the commentaries of Cardinal Stephen Langton. Archives d'Histoire Doctrinale et Littéraire du Moyen Age 5–6 1930–1.

Dulong, M. Etienne Langton, versificateur. In Mélanges Mandonnet vol 2, Paris 1930.

Gregory, A. L. The Cambridge ms of the Quaestiones of Stephen Langton. New Scholasticism 4 1930.

— Indices of rubrics and incipits of the principal manuscripts of the Questiones of S. Langton. Archives d'Histoire Doctrinale et Littéraire du Moyen Age 5 1930.

Smalley, B. Langton and the four senses of Scripture. Speculum 6 1931.

— Exempla in the Commentaires of Langton. Bull John Rylands Lib 17 1933.

Major, K. The Familia of Archbishop Langton. EHR 48 1933. With bibliography of Langton by F. M. Powicke.

Roberts, P. B. Stephanus de Lingua-tonate: studies in the sermons of Langton. Toronto 1968.

Thomas de Hibernia OFM
d. 1270

Promptuarium morale. Ed L. Wadding, S. Anthonii de Padua, Concordantiae morales, Rome 1624.

Thomas Docking (also called Thomas Good) OFM
d. c. 1270

In IV libros sententiarum. Paris 1505. For his other works, mainly biblical commentaries, see Little, Grey friars in Oxford pp. 151.

Little, A. G. Docking and his relations to Roger Bacon. In Essays in history presented to R. L. Poole, Oxford 1927. With extracts from Docking's writings.

Catto, J. I. New light on Thomas Docking. Medieval & Renaissance Stud 6 1968.

Thomas of Eccleston OFM
fl. 1250

De adventu fratrum minorum in Angliam. Ed A. G. Little, Collection d'études et de documents sur l'histoire religieuse et littéraire du Moyen Age vol 7, Paris 1904, Manchester 1951 (rev); also ed J. S. Brewer, Monumenta franciscana vol 1, 1858.

Little, A. G. The Lamport fragment of Eccleston and its connexions. EHR 49 1934.

Thomas of York OFM
d. c. 1260

Manus quae contra Omnipotentem tenditur [Treatise against William of S. Amour]. Ed M. Mierbaum, Bettelorden und Weltgeistlichkeit an der Universität Paris, Franziskanische Studien 7 1920.

Sapientiale. Mss: Vatican lat. 4301, 6771; Biblioteca Nazionale, Florence, Conv. Sopp. A. 547. Unpbd; for summaries *see* Grabmann, Longpré, Tressera and Sharp, below.

Grabmann, M. Die Metaphysik des Thomas von York. In Studien zur Geschichte der Philosophie: Festgabe zum 60 Geburtstag C. Baeumker, Münster 1913.

Pelzer, A. Les versions latines des ouvrages de morale conservés sous le nom d'Aristote en usage au xiii⁰ siècle. Revue Néo-scolastique 23 1921. On Sapientale.

Pelster, F. Thomas von York als Verfasser des Traktats Manus quae contra Omnipotentem tenditur. Archivum Franciscanum Historicum 15 1922.

Longpré, E. Fr. Thomas d'York. Archivum Franciscanum Historicum 19 1926.

—— Thomas d'York et Matthieu d'Aquasparta. Archives d'Histoire Doctrinale et Littéraire du Moyen Age 1 1926.

Tressera, F. De doctrinis metaphysicis fr. Thomae de Eboracum OFM. Analecta Sacra Tarraconensia 5 1929.

Sharp, D. E. Franciscan philosophy at Oxford in the thirteenth century. Oxford 1930.

Reilly, J. P. Thomas of York on the efficacy of secondary causes. Mediaeval Stud 15 1953.

Schmitz, K. L. A sermon of Thomas of York on the Passion. Franciscan Stud 24 1964.

Walter Map
d. 1208–10

De nugis curialium. Ed T. Wright 1850 (Camden Soc); ed M. R. James, Oxford 1914; tr M. R. James 1923; tr F. Tupper and M. B. Ogle 1924.

Bradley, H. Notes on Map's De nugis curialium. In his Collected papers, Oxford 1928.

Loomis, R. S. Sir Orfeo and Map's De nugis. MLN 51 1936.

Schullian, D. M. Valerius Maximus and Map. Speculum 12 1937.

Webster, K. G. T. Map's French things. Speculum 15 1940.

Bennett, R. E. Map's Sadius and Galo. Speculum 16 1941.

Boutemy, A. Gautier Map: conteur anglais. Brussels 1945.

Dean, R. J. Unnoticed commentaries on the Dissuasio Valerii of Walter Map. Medieval & Renaissance Stud 2 1950.

Seibt, F. Über den Plan der Schrift De nugis curialium des magisters Map. Archiv für Kulturgeschichte 37 1955.

Peeters, L. Maps De gradone milite strenuissimo. Amsterdam Beiträge zur Älteren Germanistik 1 1972.

Inauthentic Works

The Latin poems commonly attributed to Walter Mapes. Ed T. Wright 1841 (Camden Soc).

The only poems whose attribution to Map may be regarded as certain are those cited in Giraldus Cambrensis, Opera vol 1, *p. 363 and in the* Distinctiones monasticae *(reproduced in* M. Manitius, Geschichte der lateinischen Literatur des Mittelalters *vol 3, p. 269), the* Sigillum Walteri Map, *in* M. R. James, De nugis *p. xxxvii and the* Lancea Longini, *in* Wright, Poems attributed to Mapes *p. xxxv. Manitius vol 3 p. 270 would add the piece on p. 106 of Wright's edn. But if Map's reputation as a poet had not been supported in his own day by a larger body of work, it is difficult to see why so many poems should have come to circulate under his name. Certainly, many of the pieces in Wright's edn are of English origin. See H. Brinkmann,* Die Metamorphosis Goliae und das Streitgedicht Phyllis und Flora, Zeitschrift für Deutsches Altertum *50 1925; K. Strecker,* Walter von Châtillon und seine Schule, Zeitschrift für Deutsches Altertum *52 1927.*

William of La Mare OFM
d. 1298

Correctorium. Ed P. Glorieux, Les premières polémiques thomistes I: Le Correctorium corruptorii Quare, Kain Belgium 1927. Contains text of William of la Mare and the answers of a Thomist, Richard Clapwell or Thomas Sutton.

Questiones disputatae. Vatican ms Borghese lat. 361.

Longpré, E. Guillaume de la Mare. La France Franciscaine 4–5 1921–2.

Pelster, F. Les Declarationes et les Questiones de Guillaume de la Mare. Recherches de Théologie Ancienne et Médiévale 3 1931.

—— Das Ur-Correctorium Wilhelms de la Mare: eine theologische Zensur zu Lehren des hl. Thomas. Gregorianum 28 1947.

Hufnagel, A. Studien zur Entwicklung des Thomistischen Erkenntnisbegriffes im Anschluss an das Correctorium Quare. Münster 1935.

Creytens, R. Autour de la littérature des correctoires. Archivum Fratrum Predicatorum 12 1942.

William of Newburgh
1136–1208

Explanatio sacri epithalamii in matrem sponsi. Ed J. C. Gorman, Fribourg 1960.

Historia rerum anglicarum. Ed R. Howlett, Chronicles of the reigns of Stephen etc, 1884–5; tr J. Stevenson, Church historians of England vol 4, 1853–6.

Jahncke, R. Guilelmus Neubrigensis. Bonn 1912.

William of Sherwood (or Shyreswood)
d. after 1267

Introductiones in logicam. Ed M. Grabmann, Sitzungsberichte der Bayerischen Akademie der Wissenschaften 10 1937; Introduction to logic, tr N. Kretzmann, Minneapolis 1966.

Syncategoremata. Ed J. R. O'Donnell, Mediaeval Stud 3 1941; Treatise on syncategorematic words, tr N. Kretzmann, Minneapolis 1968.

William of Ware OFM
fl. 1290

Quaestiones disputatae, questiones super libros sententiarum. Extracts only ptd: for bibliography *see* E. Gilson, History of Christian philosophy, 1955.

Klug, H. Zur Biographie der Minderbrüder Johannes Duns Scotus und Wilhelm von Ware. Franziskanische Studien 2 1915.

Daniels, A. Zu den Beziehungen zwischen Wilhelm von Ware und Johannes Duns Scotus. Franziskanische Studien 4 1917.

Longpré, E. Guillaume de Ware. La France Franciscaine 5 1922.

Spettman, H. Die philosophiegeschichtliche Stellung des Wilhelms von Ware. Philosophisches Jahrbuch 40 1927.

Lechner, J. Beiträge zum mittelalterlichen Franziskanerschrifttum, vornehmlich der Oxforder Schule des xiii–xiv Jahrhunderts auf Grund einer Florentiner Wilhelm von Ware-Handschrift. Franziskanische Studien 19 1932.

—— Die mehrfachen Fassungen des Sentenzenkommentars des Wilhelm von Ware. Franciscan Stud 31 1949.

Magrini, E. La produzione letteraria di Guglielmo di Ware. Miscellanea Francescana 36 1936.

Emmen, A. Mariologische ideën bij Willem van Ware. Studia Catholica 21 1946.

Pelster, F. Die Kommentare zum vierten Buch der Sentenzen von Wilhelm von Ware zum ersten Buch von einen Unbekannten und von Martin von Alnwick in Cod. 501 Troyes. Scholastik 27 1952.

Gál, G. Gulielmi de Ware, doctrina philosophica. Franciscan Stud 14 1954.

(8) FOURTEENTH CENTURY

Anonymous

Gesta Romanorum. Written c. 1340; probably the work of a Franciscan, largely from English materials, if not actually of English origin. Ed H. Oesterley, Berlin 1872; ed W. Dick, Erlangen 1890 (without the religious application of the stories); tr C. Swan, ed E. A. Baker 1924.

Krepinski, M. Quelques remarques relatives à l'histoire des Gesta Romanorum. Moyen Age 15 1911.

Welter, J. T. L'exemplum dans la littérature religieuse et didactique du Moyen Age. Paris 1927.

Speculum inclusorum. Ed L. Oliger, Rome 1938. Mid 14th-century treatise.

Adam Easton, Cardinal
d. 1397

Pantin, W. A. The Defensorium of Adam Easton. EHR 51 1936.

Adam Murimuth
fl. c. 1350

Continuatio chronicarum. Ed E. M. Thompson 1939 (Rolls ser).

Adam of Woodham (or Godham) OFM
d. 1358

Super quattuor libros sententiarum. Paris Bibliothèque Nationale F.L. 15892, Bibliothèque Mazarine 915. J. Major's edn, Paris 1512, consists of the Abbreviations of Henry d'Oyta.

Ehrle, F. Der Sentenzenkommentar Peters von Candia. Münster 1925.

Leff, G. In his Bradwardine and the Pelagians, Cambridge 1957.

Crathorn OP
fl. c. 1330

Quaestiones de universalibus. Ed J. Kraus, Opuscula et textus: ser scholastica, fasciculus 18–19, Münster 1937.

Kraus, J. Die Stellung des Oxforder Dominikanlehrers Crathorn zu Thomas von Aquin. Zeitschrift für Katholische Theologie 57 1933.

Pelster, F. In Miscellanea Francesco Ehrle vol 1, Rome 1923.

Schmaus, M. Liber propugnatorius des Thomas Anglicus. Münster 1930.

Duns Scotus (Johannes) OFM
1266–1308

For bibliographies see M. Grajewski, Scotistic bibliography of the last decade, Franciscan Stud 1–2 1941–2; U. Smeets, Lineamenta bibliographica, Rome 1942; O. Schafer, Bibliographische Einführungen in das Studium der Philosophie, Berne 1953.

Opera omnia. Ed L. Wadding, Lyons 1639, Paris 1891–5 (with the probably spurious De perfectione statuum). These edns contain several spurious works, in particular the De rerum principio. Ed C. Balić et al, Rome 1950–.

Opus oxoniense in primum librum sententiarum. Venice 1472; tr R. McKeon, Selections from medieval philosophers vol 2, New York 1930. Critical text in Opera omnia, ed Balić above.

Tractatus de primo principio. Ed M. Müller, Freiburg and Baden 1941; ed E. Roche, New York 1949 (with trn); ed A. B. Wolter, Chicago 1966 (rev text, with trn).

Philosophical writings. Ed and tr A. Walter 1962.

Reason and revelation: a question from Duns Scot. Ed and tr. N. Micklem, Edinburgh 1953 (with Latin text).

Minges, P. Duns Scoti doctrina philosophica et theologica. 2 vols Quarracchi 1908, 1930 (rev).

Klein, J. Der Gottesbegriff des Duns Scotus. Paderborn 1913.

Landry, P. La philosophie de Duns Scot. Paris 1922.

Longpré, E. La philosophie du bienheureux Duns Scot. Paris 1924. A criticism of Landry, above.

Harris, C. R. S. Duns Scotus. 2 vols Oxford 1927.

Barth, T. De fundamento univocationis apud Joannem Duns Scotum. Rome 1939.

— De univocationis entis scotisticae intentione principali. Antonianum 28 1953.

— Individualität und Allgemeinheit bei Duns Scotus. Wissenschaft und Weisheit 19 1956.

— Zur univocatio entis bei Duns Scotus. Wissenschaft und Weisheit 21 1958.

Schircel, C. L. The univocity of the concept of being in the philosophy of Duns Scotus. Washington 1942.

Bettoni, E. Duns Scoto. Brescia 1946.

— De argumentationi Doctoris subtilis, quoad existentiam Dei. Antonianum 28 1953.

— Il fondamento della conoscenza umana, secondo Duns Scoto. Franziskanische Studien 47 1965.

Day, S. Intuitive cognition: a key to the significance of the later scholasties. New York 1947. On Duns Scotus and Ockham.

Saint-Maurice, B. de. Jean Duns Scot le docteur du temps nouveau. Paris 1949, 1953 (rev).

Devlin, C. The psychology of Duns Scotus. Oxford 1950.

Gál, G. De Duns Scoti Theorematum authenticitate. Collectanea Franciscana 20 1950.

Holzen, O. Zur Beziehungslehre des Doctor subtilis Duns Scotus. Franziskanische Studien 33 1951.

Vier, P. C. Evidence and its functions according to Duns Scotus. New York 1951 (Franciscan Inst).

Walter, A. Duns Scotus on the necessity of revealed knowledge. Franciscan Stud 11 1951.

Soto, A. The structure of society according to Duns Scotus. Franciscan Stud 11–12 1951–2.

Gilson, E. Jean Duns Scot. Paris 1952.

— Les maîtresses positions de Duns Scot d'après le prologue de L'ordination. Antonianum 28 1953.

— Wille und Sittlichkeit nach Duns Scotus. Wissenschaft und Weisheit 21 1958.

Meier, P. L. Zur Biographie des Duns Scotus. Wissenschaft und Weisheit 15 1952.

— The mss of Duns Scotus in German and Austrian libraries. Medieval & Renaissance Stud 3 1954.

Bérubé, C. La connaissance intellectuelle du singulier matériel chez Duns Scot. Franciscan Stud 13 1953.

Cresswell, J. R. Duns Scotus on the Will. Ibid.

Balić, C. Circa positiones fundamentales Duns Scoti. Antonianum 28 1953.

— Zur kritischer Edition der Werke des Duns Scotus. Scriptorium 8 1954.

Masai, F. L'édition vaticane des oeuvres de Duns Scot. Scriptorium 8 1954.

Pannenberg, W. Die Prädestinations-Lehre des Duns Scotus. Göttingen 1954.

Mühlen, H. Sein und Person nach Duns Scotus. Münster 1954.

Huallachain, C. On recent studies of the opening question in Scotus's Ordinatio. Franciscan Stud 15 1955.

Bonnefoy, J. F. Duns Scot: son milieu, sa doctrine, son influence. Rome 1960.

Hook, B. van. Duns Scotus and the self-evident proposition. New Scholasticism 36 1962.

Dettloff, W. Die Entwicklung der Akzeptions- und Verdienstlehre von Duns Scotus bis Luther. Münster 1963.

Schmitt, C. B. Henry of Ghent, Duns Scotus and Gianfrancesco Pico on Illumination. Mediaeval Stud 25 1963.

Tweedale, M. Scotus and Ockham on the infinity of the most eminent being. Franciscan Stud 23 1963.

O'Brien, A. J. Duns Scotus's teaching on the distinction between essence and existence. New Scholasticism 38 1964.

Brampton, C. K. Duns Scotus at Oxford 1268–1301. Franciscan Stud 24 1964.

Fäh, K. L. J. Duns Scotus: die Erkennbarheit Gottes. Franziskanische Studien 47 1965.

Heeres, W. Wesen und Dasein bei Heinrich von Ghent und Duns Scotus. Ibid.

Ryan, J. K., B. M. Bonansea (ed). John Duns Scotus 1265–1965. Washington 1965.

Schelten, G. Die thomistische Analogielehre und die Universitätslehre des Duns Scotus. Franziskanische Studien 47 1965.

Catania, F. J. Knowledge of God in Alexander of Hales and Duns Scotus. Stud in Medieval Culture (Michigan) 2 1966.

Pusci, L. La nozione della divina omnipotenzia di Giovanni Duns Scotus. Rome 1967.

Wetter, F. Die Trinitätslehre des Duns Scotus. Münster 1967.

Burr, D. Ockham, Scotus and the censure at Avignon. Church History 37 1968.

Prentice, R. Univocity and analogy according to Scotus's Super libros elenchorum Aristotelis. Archives d'Histoire Doctrinale et Littéraire 35 1968.

Veuthey, L. Jean Duns Scot: pensée théologique. Paris 1968.

Pernoud, M. A. The theory of the potentia Dei according to Aquinas, Scotus and Ockham. Antonianum 47 1972.

Henry Knighton (or Cnitthon), Austin Canon
fl. 1371–95

Chronica. Ed J. R. Lumby 2 vols 1889–95 (Rolls ser).
Galbraith, V. H. The chronicle of Henry Knighton. In Studies in honour of Fritz Saxl 1890–1948, 1957.

Henry of Harclay
d. 1317

Pelster, F. Heinrich Harclay, Kanzler von Oxford und seine Quästionen. In Miscellanea Ehrle vol 1, Rome 1924.

— Die Quaestio Heinrichs von Harclay über die zweite Ankunft Christi. Archivio Italiano per la Storia della Pietà 1951.

Kraus, J. Die Universalienlehre des Oxforder Kanzlers Heinrich von Harclay in ihrer Mittelstellung zwischen skotistischem Realismus und ockhamistischem Nominalismus. Divus Thomas (Fribourg) 10–11 1932–3.

Hirsch-Reich, B. Heinrichs von Harclay Polemik gegen die Berechnung der zweiten Ankunft Christi. Recherches de Théologie Ancienne et Médiévale 20 1953.

Maurer, A. Henry of Harclay's question on the univocity of being. Mediaeval Stud 16 1954.

— Henry of Harclay's question on immortality. Mediaeval Stud 19 1957.

— Henry of Harclay's question on the divine ideas. Mediaeval Stud 23 1961.

Hugh of Newcastle (Hugo de Novo Castro) OFM
fl. 1307–17

De victoria Christi contra Anti-Christum. Nuremberg 1471.
Langlois, C. V. Hugo de Novocastro. In Essays in medieval history presented to T. F. Tout, Manchester 1925.

Amoros, L. Hugo von Novo Castro OFM und sein Kommentar zum ersten Buch der Sentenzen. Franziskanische Studien 20 1933.

Auweiler, E. De codice commentarii in IV librum sententiarum Fr. Hugonis de Novo Castro OFM Washingtonii servato. Archivum Franciscanum Historicum 28 1935.

Johannes Beverus (John of London)
d. 1311

Hammer, J. The poetry of Johannes Beverus, with extracts from his Tractatus de Bruto abbreviato. MP 34 1937. An abbreviation in prose and verse of Geoffrey of Monmouth.

John Baconthorp, Carmelite
d. c. 1345

Commentarii in libros I–IV Sententiarum. Paris 1485, Milan 1510, Venice 1527. These edns include only bks 1–3 and the Quaestiones canonicae in bk 4.
Compendium legis Christi. Venice 1527.
Questiones quodlibetales. Cremona 1618.
Textus de immaculata conceptione. Ed L. M. Sagge, Carmelus 2 1955.
Xiberta B. M. De magistro Johanne Baconthorp. Analecta Ordinis Carmelitarum 6 1927, 8 1929.
— Joan Baconthorp Averroista? Criterion 3 1927.
— De scriptoribus scholasticis saeculi xiv ex ordine Carmelitarum. Louvain 1931. With bibliography of Baconthorpe.
Chrysogone du Saint-Sacrement. Maître Jean Baconthorp: les sources, la doctrine, les disciples. Revue Néo-scolastique de Philosophie 34 1932.
Smalley, B. John Baconthorpe's postill on S. Matthew. Medieval & Renaissance Stud 4 1958.

John Canon (or Marbres) OFM
fl. 1320

In libros octo physicorum Aristotelis. Padua 1485.
Questiones de universalibus. Ed J. Kraus, Opera et textus 18, Münster 1937.
Baudry, L. En lisant Jean le Chanoine. Archives d'Histoire Doctrinale et Littéraire 9 1934.

John Daston
fl. 1320

Rosarium secretissimum philosophorum arcanum comprehendens; Visio super artem alchemicam. Ed J. Manget, Bibliotheca chemica curiosa vol 2, Geneva 1702.

John Lutterell
fl. 1324

Hoffman, F. Die erste Kritik des Ockhamismus durch den Oxforder Kanzler J. Lutterell. Breslau 1941.

John of Bromyard
fl. 1390

Summa predicantium. Nuremberg 1485, Venice 1586.
Welter, J. T. L'exemplum dans la littérature religieuse et didactique du Moyen Age. Paris 1927.
Olson, P. A. John Bromyard's response to the Gothic. Medievalia et Humanistica 15 1963.
— John Bromyard and Augustine's Christian doctrine. Eng Lang Notes 3 1966.

John of Mirfield
fl. c. 1370

Florarium Bartholomei. Mss: Cambridge Univ Lib Mm.11.10; BM Royal 7 xi; Gray's Inn Lib 4.
Hartley, P. and H. R. Aldridge. Johannes de Mirfield: his life and works. 1936.

John of Reading OFM
fl. 1320

Longpré, E. Jean de Reading et Jean Duns Scot: l'école franciscaine à Oxford au début du 14e siècle. La France Franciscaine 7 1924.

John of Reading, Benedictine
late 14th century

Chronica 1346–67. Ed J. Tait, Manchester 1914.

John of Rodington OFM
d. c. 1348

Lechner, J. Johannes von Rodington und seine Quodibet de conscientia. In Aus der Geisteswelt des Mittelalters: Studien und Texte M. Grabmann gewidmet vol 2, Münster 1935.
— Die Quästionen der Sentenzenkommentars des Johannes von Rodington. Franziskanische Studien 22 1935.
Nardi, B. Il dubbio iperbolico e Giovanni di Rodinton. In his Soggetto e oggetto del conoscere nella filosofia antica e medievale, Rome 1952 (enlarged).

John of Sheppey
d. 1360

Fabulae. Ed L. Hervieux, Les fabulistes latins vol 4, Paris 1899.

John Ridewall OFM
fl. 1330–40

Commentary on Augustine's De civitate Dei. Mss: Oxford Corpus Christi 186–7; Berlin Theol. lat. fd 581.
Fulgentius metaforalis. Ed H. Liebeschütz, Fulgentius metaforalis, Leipzig 1926.
Smalley, B. John Ridewall's commentary on the De civitate Dei. MÆ 25 1956.
— In her English friars and antiquity in the early 14th century, Oxford 1960.
Kaeppeli, T. Une critique du commentaire de Trevet sur le De civitate Dei. Archivum Fratrum Praedicatorum 29 1959. Commentary attributed to Ridewall.

John of Walsham OFM
fl. 1350

Pelster, F. Die Quästionen des Johannes von Walsham OFM. Franziskanische Studien 34 1952.

John Russel OFM

Smalley, B. John Russel OFM. Recherches Théologiques 23 1956.

John Walwayn (?)

Vita Edwardi II. Ed N. Denholm Young, The life of Edward II by the so-called monk of Malmesbury, Edinburgh 1957.

John Wyclif
c. 1325–84

On Wyclif Canon

Tanner, T. Bibliotheca britannico-hibernica. Ed D. Wilkins 1748.
Shirley, W. W. Catalogue of the original works by Wyclif. Oxford 1865; rev J. Loserth [1924] (Wyclif Soc).
Loserth, J. Das vermeintliche Schreiben Wiclifs an Urban VI und einige verlorene Flugschriften Wiclifs aus seinen letzten Lebenstagen. Historische Zeitschrift 75 1895.
— Wiclifs Sendschreiben, Flugschriften und kleinere Werke kirchenpolitischen Inhalts. Sitzungsberichte der Kaiserlichen Akademie der Wissenschaften, philhist. Klasse 166 1910.

— Zur Kritik der Wyclif-Handschriften. Zeitschrift des Deutschen Vereins für die Geschichte Mährens und Schlesiens 20 1916; rptd as Zur Verbreitung der Wiclifhandschriften in Böhmen in his Huss und Wiclif, Munich 1925 (rev).
Thomson, S. H. Some Latin works erroneously ascribed to Wyclif. Speculum 3 1928.
— Three unprinted opuscula of Wyclif. Speculum 3 1928.
— A 'lost' chapter of Wyclif's Summa de ente. Speculum 4 1929.
— The order of writing of Wyclif's philosophical works. In Ceskou Minulosti (Festschrift to V. Novontný), Prague 1929.
— A Gonville and Caius Wyclif manuscript. Speculum 8 1933.
— Unnoticed mss and works of Wyclif. Jnl of Theological Stud 38 1937.
Breck, A. The mss of Wyclif's De trinitate. Speculum 4 1929.
Stein, I. H. Speculum 5–8 1930–3. Notes.
Smalley, B. Wyclif's Postilla super totam Bibliam. Bodleian Lib Record 4 1953.
Mallard, W. Dating the Sermones quadraginta of Wyclif. Medievalia et Humanistica 17 1966.

Bibliographies

Loserth, J. Neuere Erscheinungen der Wiclif-Literatur. Historische Zeitschrift 53 1885, 62 1889, 95 1905.
— Geschichte des späteren Mittelalters. Munich 1903.
— Wiclif und der Wiclifismus. In Realencyklopädie für protestantische Theologie und Kirche vol 21, ed J. J. Herzog and A. Hauck, Gotha 1908. See also vol 24 (Ergänzungen), 1913.
— Neue Erscheinungen der Wiclif- und Huss-Literatur. Historische Zeitschrift 116 1916.
Workman, H. B. In Encyclopaedia of religion vol 12, ed J. Hastings 1921. A more selective list in his John Wyclif vol i, Oxford 1926.
Whitney, J. P. A note on the work of the Wyclif Society. In Essays in history presented to R. Lane Poole, Oxford 1927.
Manning, B. L. In The Cambridge medieval history vol 7, Cambridge 1932.

Writings

For his English works see col 491, above.
Publications of Wyclif Society (unless otherwise stated).

De ente sive summa intellectualium. Bks 1–2. Pts ptd so far will be found in De ente librorum duorum excerpta, ed M. H. Dziewicki 1909; Summa de ente libri primi tractatus primus et secundus, ed S. H. Thomson, Oxford 1930; and Tractatus de trinitate, ed A. Breck, Boulder 1962.
Thompson, S. H. A 'lost' chapter of Wyclif's Summa de ente. Speculum 4 1929.
Stein, I. H. Another 'lost' chapter of Wyclif's Summa de ente. Speculum 8 1933.
De ente predicamentali. Ed R. Beer 1891. Beer and Thomson consider this to be bk 1 pt 5 of De ente sive summa intellectualium. See S. H. Thomson, A 'lost' chapter, above.
Summa theologiae:
Bks 1–2: Tractatus de mandatis divinis; accedit Tractatus de statu innocencie. Ed J. Loserth and F. D. Matthew 1922.
Bks 3–5: Tractatus de civili dominio: liber primus. Ed R. L. Poole 1885; liber secundus, ed J. Loserth 1900; liber tertius, ed J. Loserth 2 vols 1903–4.
Bk 6: De veritate sacre scripture. Ed R. Buddensieg 3 vols 1905–7.
Thomson, S. H. Unnoticed mss of Wyclif's De veritate sacre scripture. MÆ 12 1943.
Bk 7: Tractatus de ecclesia. Ed J. Loserth 1886.

Bk 8: Tractatus de officio regis. Ed A. W. Pollard and C. Sayle 1887.

Bk 9: Tractatus de potestate pape. Ed J. Loserth 1907.

Bk 10: Tractatus de simonia. Ed Herzberg-Fränkel and M. H. Dziewicki 1898.

Bk 11: Tractatus de apostasia. Ed M. H. Dziewicki 1889.

Bk 12: Tractatus de blasphemia. Ed M. H. Dziewicki 1893.

De compositione hominis. Ed R. Beer 1884.

De dominio divino libri tres. Ed R. L. Poole 1890.

De eucharistia tractatus maior; accedit Tractatus de eucharistia et poenitentia sive de confessione. Ed J. Loserth 1892.

Dialogus sive speculum ecclesie militantis. Ed A. W. Pollard 1886.

Differentia inter peccatum mortale et veniale. Ed J. Loserth and F. D. Matthew, Tractatus de mandatis divinis, 1922.

Opus evangelicum. Bks 1–2: De sermone domini in monte; bks 3–4, De Antichristo, ed J. Loserth 2 vols 1895–6.

Questio ad fratres de sacramento altaris. Ed J. Loserth, De eucharistia tractatus maior, 1892.

Tractatus de benedicta incarnatione. Ed E. Harris 1886.

Tractatus de logica. Ed M. H. Dziewicki 3 vols 1893–9.

Miscellanea philosophica. Ed M. H. Dziewicki 2 vols 1902–5.
1, De actibus animae (in vol 1).
2, De materia et forma (in vol 1).
Of the 9 pieces in these vols these 2 alone appear to be Wyclif's. See Dziewicki introds and S. H. Thomson, above, Some Latin works erroneously ascribed to Wyclif, *Speculum 3 1928.*

— Opera minora. Ed J. Loserth 1913.

— Polemical works. Ed R. Buddensieg 2 vols 1883. Contains 26 tracts, classified as 20 against the sects, 6 against the Pope. Buddensieg doubts the authenticity of De religione privata I only. Loserth expresses no doubts in his revision of Shirley's Catalogue.

Sermones. 4 vols ed J. Loserth 1887–90.

Published otherwise, and unpublished works

For mss of unpbd works see J. Loserth's revision of W. W. Shirley, Catalogue, *1924 (Wyclif Soc).*

Ad parliamentum regis. Ed W. W. Shirley, Fasciculi zizaniorum, 1858 (Rolls ser).

Ad quesita regis et concilii. Ibid.

Bonus et utilis tractatus secundum magistrum Johannem. Ed I. H. Stein, Speculum 7 1932 (as The Latin text of Wyclif's Complaint). *See also* I. H. Stein, The Wyclif manuscript in Florence, Speculum 5 1930.

Contra Killingham Carmelitam. Ed W. W. Shirley, Fasciculi zizaniorum, 1858 (Rolls ser). 2 tracts, one incomplete.

Declarationes. Ed H. T. Riley, Walsingham, Historia anglicana vol 1, 1863 (Rolls ser).

De clavibus ecclesie. Ed S. H. Thomson, Speculum 3 1928.

De condemnatione xix conclusionum. Ed W. W. Shirley, Fasciculi zizaniorum, 1858 (Rolls ser), appendix.

De dotatione ecclesiae sive Supplementum trialogi. Ed G. V. Lechler, Trialogus, Oxford 1869.

De eucharistia conclusiones quindecim. Ed W. W. Shirley, Fasciculi zizaniorum, 1858 (Rolls ser).

De eucharistia confessio. Ed W. W. Shirley, Fasciculi zizaniorum, 1858 (Rolls ser).

De eucharistia confessio. Ed S. H. Thomson, Jnl Theological Stud 33 1932 (as Wyclif's 'lost' De fide sacramentorum). Different from preceding.

De juramento Arnaldi. Ed G. V. Lechler, Johann von Wiclif vol 2, Leipzig 1873.

De officio regis conclusio. Ed S. H. Thomson, Speculum 3 1928.

De versuciis Anti-Christi. Ed I. H. Stein, EHR 47 1932.

Errare in materia fidei quod potuit ecclesia militans. Ed S. H. Thomson, Speculum 3 1928.

Tractatus de officio pastorali. Ed G. V. Lechler, Leipzig 1863.

Trialogus cum Supplemento Trialogi. Ed G. V. Lechler, Oxford 1869.

Unauthentic and Contested Writings

De triplici ecclesia. Ed S. H. Thomson, Speculum 3 1928.

Quaestiones xiii logicae et philosophicae. Ed R. Beer, De ente predicamentali, 1891 (Wyclif Soc). *See* S. H. Thomson, Speculum 3 1928.

Loserth, J. Die ältesten Streitschriften Wiclifs. Sitzungsberichte der Kaiserlichen Akademie der Wissenschaften, phil.-hist. Klasse 160 1909.

Studies

Biographical

Lewis, J. History of the life and sufferings of Wicliffe. 1720, Oxford 1820 (rev).

Lechler, G. V. Johann von Wiclif und die Vorgeschichte der Reformation. 2 vols Leipzig 1873; tr and abridged by P. Lorimer [1884].

Poole, R. L. Wycliffe and movements for reform. 1911.

Wilkins, H. J. Was Wycliffe a negligent pluralist? also John de Trevisa. 1915; appendix, Bristol 1916. Reply by J. H. Dahmus, Speculum 28 1953.

Workman, H. B. Wyclif: a study of the English medieval Church. 2 vols Oxford 1926.

Manning, B. L. Wyclif and the house of Herod. Cambridge Historical Jnl 2 1926.

— Wyclif. In Cambridge medieval history vol 7, Cambridge 1932.

Dahmus, J. H. Further evidence for the spelling Wyclyf. Speculum 16 1941.

Hanrahan, T. J. Wyclif's political activity. Mediaeval Stud 20 1958.

Robson, J. A. Wyclif and the Oxford schools. Cambridge 1961.

Special Aspects

Loserth, J. Hus und Wiclif. Prague 1884, Munich 1925 (rev); tr 1884.

Poole, R. L. Wycliffe's doctrine of dominion. In his Illustrations of the history of medieval thought and learning, 1920.

Odložilík, O. Wycliffe's influence upon central and eastern Europe. Slavonic Rev 7 1929. Bibliographical note at end.

Thomson, S. H. The philosophical basis of Wyclif's theology. Jnl of Religion 11 1931.

— A note on Peter Payne and Wyclif. Medievalia et Humanistica 16 1964.

Peschke, E. Die Bedeutung Wiclefs für die Theologie der Böhmen. Zeitschrift für Kirchengeschichte (Gotha) 54 1935.

Baudry, L. A propos de G. d'Ockham et de Wyclif. Archives d'Histoire Doctrinale et Littéraire 12 1939.

Dahmus, J. H. The prosecution of Wyclyf. New Haven 1952.

— Wyclif and the English government. Speculum 35 1960.

McFarlane, K. B. Wycliffe and the beginnings of English Nonconformity. 1952.

Schlauch, M. A Polish vernacular eulogy of Wyclif [1447]. Jnl of Ecclesiastical History 8 1957.

Vooght, P. de. Les indulgences dans la théologie de Jean Wyclif et de Jean Hus. Recherches de Théologie Religieuse 41 1953.

— Du De consideratione de S. Bernard au De potestate pape de Wyclif. Irenikon 26 1953.

— Wyclif et la scriptura sola. Ephemerides Theologicae Lovanienses 39 1963.

Hurley, M. Scriptura sola: Wyclif and his critics. Traditio 16 1960; New York 1963.

Mallard, W. Wyclif and the tradition of biblical authority. Church History 30 1961.
— Dating the Sermones quadraginta of Wyclif. Medievalia & Humanistica 17 1966.
Kaminsky, H. Wyclifism as the ideology revolution. Church History 32 1963.
Smalley, B. Wyclif's Postilla on the Old Testament and his Principium. In Oxford studies presented to Daniel Callus, Oxford 1964.
— The Bible and eternity: Wyclif's dilemma. Jnl Warburg & Courtauld Inst 27 1964.
Wilks, M. J. Predestination, property and power: Wyclif's theory of dominion and grace. Stud in Church History 2 1965.
Benrath, G. A. Wyclifs Bibelkommentar. Berlin 1966.
Leff, G. Wyclif: the path to dissent. Proc Br Acad 52 1966.
— Wyclif and Hus: a doctrinal comparison. Bull John Rylands Lib 50 1967.
Bainton, R. C. Wyclif and the Augustinian tradition. Medievalia et Humanistica new ser 1 1970.

Kykeley
early 14th century
Quaestio de cooperatione divina. Ed M. Schmaus, Bohoslovia 10 1932.

Malachy OFM
fl. 1310
Libellus septem peccatorum mortalium venena eorumque remedia describens, qui dicitur venenum Malachiae. Paris 1518. *See* J. T. Welter, L'exemplum dans la littérature religieuse et didactique du Moyen Age, Paris 1927.

Martin of Alnwick (Martinus Anglicus) OFM
d. 1336
Lechner, J. Beiträge zum Schrifttum des Martinus Anglicus. Franziskanische Studien 19 1932.

Nicolas Trivet or Trevet
d. c. 1334
Annales sex regum Angliae. Ed T. Hog 1845 (Eng Historical Soc).
Expositio in Leviticum. Merton College Oxford ms 188.
In libros Augustini de civitate Dei. Mss: BM Royal 14 C XIII 8 etc, (often joined with work by Thomas Jorz).
Ehrle, F. Nicolaus Trivet: sein Leben, sein Quolibet und Quaestiones ordinariae. In Festgabe Clemens Bäumker, Münster 1923.
Quaestiones de causalitate scientiae Dei et concursu divino. Ed M. Schmaus, Divus Thomas (Piacenza) 35 1932.
Franceschini, E. Il commento di Nicola Trevet al Tieste de Seneca. In his Studi e note di filologia medievale, Milan 1938. For corrections *see* R. J. Dean, MÆ 10 1941.
Courcelle, P. Etude critique des commentaires sur la Consolatio philosophiae. Archives d'Histoire Doctrinale et Littéraire 14 1939.
Dean, R. J. Ms Bodleian 292 and the Canon of Nicholas Trevet's Works. Speculum 17 1942.
— The earliest known commentary on Livy. Medievalia et Humanistica 3 1945. Correction 4 1946.
— Cultural relations in the Middle Ages, Nicholas Trevet and Nicholas of Prato. SP 45 1948.
— The dedication of Nicholas Trivet's commentary on Boethius. SP 63 1966.
Weiss, R. Notes on the popularity of the writings of Nicholas Trevet in Italy. Dominican Stud 1 1945.
Fabris, V. Il commento di Nicola Trivet al Hercules furens di Seneca. Aevum 28 1954.

Kaeppeli, T. Une critique au commentaire de Nicolas Trevet sur le De civitate Dei. Archivum Fratrum Predicatorum 29 1959.

Nicole Bozon
fl. 1320
Les contes moralisés. Ed L. T. Smith and P. Meyer, Paris 1889 (Société des Anciens Textes Français). Compiled in French by an English Franciscan c. 1320; there is an incomplete Latin version; part of each example is an animal fable; *see* Little, Studies in English Franciscan history, Manchester 1917.

Peter Sutton OFM
fl. 1311
Schmaus, M. Die questio des Petrus Sutton über die Univokation des seins. Collectanea Franciscana 3 1933.
Etzkorn, F. Petrus Sutton (?), Quodlibetum. Franciscan Stud 23 1963.

Ralph de Hengham, Chief Justice
d. 1311
Summa magna and summa parva. Ed W. H. Dunham, Cambridge 1932.

Ranulf Higden
d. 1364
Ars predicandi. Bodley mss 5, 316.
Polychronicon. Ed C. Babington and J. R. Lumby 9 vols 1865–86 (Rolls ser) (with John Trevisa's trn). Vol 8 is by John of Malvern, vol 9 by anon monk of Westminster.
Robinson, J. A. An unrecognised Westminster Chronicle 1381–94. Proc Br Acad 3 1907.
Galbraith, V. H. The autograph ms of Ranulf Higden's Polychronicon. HLQ 22 1959.
Taylor, J. The universal chronicle of Ranulf Higden. Oxford 1966.

Richard of Bury
d. 1345
Philobiblon. Cologne 1473; ed H. Cocheris, Paris 1856; ed E. C. Thomas 1888, 1903 (with trn); ed A. F. West, New York 1889; ed A. Nelson, Stockholm 1922; ed A. Taylor, Berkeley 1948; ed A. Altamura, Naples 1954; ed M. Maclagan, Oxford 1960.
Liber epistolaris. Ed N. Denholm-Young 1950 (Roxburghe Club).
Ghellinck, J. Un évêque bibliophile au 14e siècle. Revue d'Histoire Ecclésiastique 18–19 1922–3.
Denholm-Young, N. Richard de Bury. Trans Royal Historical Soc 4th ser 20 1937.
Weiss, R. The study of Greek in England during the fourteenth century. Rinascimento 2 1951.

Richard of Campsall
d. 1335
Works. Ed E. A. Synan, Toronto 1968.
Synan, E. A. Richard of Campsall: an English theologian of the 14th century. Mediaeval Stud 14 1952.

Richard of Conington OFM
d. 1310
Trctatus de paupertate Fratrum Minorum. Ed A. Heysse, Archivum Franciscanum Historicum 23 1930.
Douie, D. L. Three treatises on evangelical poverty by Fr. Richard Conyngton, Fr. Walter Chatton and an anonymous. Archivum Franciscanum Historicum 24 1931.
Doucet, V. L'oeuvre scolastique de Richard de Conington. Archivum Franciscanum Historicum 29 1936.

Richard Fitzralph, Archbishop of Armagh
d. 1360

Summa de erroribus Armenorum [or] Summa in questionibus Armenorum. Paris 1512. *See* M. Deanesly, Lollard Bible, Cambridge 1920 p. 142 note 1.

De pauperie salvatoris. Bks 1–4 ed R. L. Poole, appendix to Wyclif's De dominio divino, 1890 (Wyclif Soc). Pp. 254f. contain table of contents of remaining 3 books of treatise.

Defensorium curatorum. Ed E. Brown, Fasciculus rerum expetandarum vol 2, 1690.

Gwynn, A. Richard FitzRalph, Archbishop of Armagh. Studies 22 1933, 24–6 1935–7.

— The sermon diary of Richard Fitzralph, Archbishop of Armagh. Proc Royal Irish Acad 44 1937.

— The English Austin friars in the time of Wyclif. Oxford 1940.

— Sermons of Primate Richard Fitzralph. Archivum Historicum 19 1949.

Hammerich, L. L. The beginning of the strife between Richard Fitzralph and the mendicants. Copenhagen 1938.

Leff, G. Richard Fitzralph, commentator of the Sentences. Manchester 1965.

Richard of Ledrede
d. 1360

Peperit virgo. Ed R. L. Greene, Speculum 27 1952. A song.

Richard of Maidstone, Carmelite
d. 1396

Protectorium pauperis. Ed A. Williams, Carmelus 5 1958.

Richard Rolle of Hampole
d. 1349

For Rolle's English writing see col 517, above. A bibliography of his Latin works (mss and ptd edns) will be found in H. E. Allen, Writings ascribed to Rolle, New York 1927.

Early Editions

Explanationes super lectiones beati Job. Oxford 1483.

Speculum spiritualium, additur opusculum Ricardi Hampole de emendatione vitae. Paris 1510.

De emendatione peccatoris. Antwerp 1533 (with 2 extracts from other works), Cologne 1535 (with extracts from other works); ed M. de la Bigne, Magna bibliotheca veterum patrum vol 15, Cologne 1622.

D. Richardi in Psalterium Davidicum atque alia quaedam sacrae scripturae monumenta. Cologne 1536.

D. Richardi enarratio in Threnos. Paris 1542.

Modern Editions

Canticum amoris. Ed A. Wilmart, Revue d'Ascétique et de Mystique 21 1940.

Carmen prosaicum. Ed G. M. Liegey, Mediaeval Stud 19 1957. A prose version by Rolle of extracts from his Melos amoris, below.

Contra amores mundi. Ed P. Theiner, Berkeley 1968.

Incendium amoris. Ed M. Deanesly, Manchester 1915.

Melos amoris [or Melum contemplativorum]. Ed E. J. F. Arnold, Oxford 1957.

Camper, F. M. M. Life of Rolle. 1928.

Whiting, C. E. Rolle of Hampole. Archaeological Jnl 37 1948.

Richard Swineshead (or Suiseth)
fl. 1348

Poorter, A. de. Un recueil peu connu de Questions sur les Sentences. Revue Néo-scolastique de Philosophie 33 1931.

For his scientific works *see* P. Duhem, Etudes sur Léonard de Vinci, Paris 1913.

Robert Cowton OFM
fl. c. 1310

Schwamm, H. Cowton über das göttliche Vorherwissen. Innsbruck 1931.

Schmaus, M. Uno sconosciuto discepolo di Scoto intorno alla prescienza di Dio. Rivista di Filosofia Neo-scolastica (Milan) 24 1932.

Robert Handlo
fl. 1326

Regulae. Ed C. E. H. de Coussemaker, Scriptorum de musica medii aevi nova series vol 1, Paris 1864.

Robert Holcot OP
d. 1349

Liber de moralizationibus. Venice 1505, Basle 1586.

Liber de sapientia Salomonis. Basle 1586.

Super quatuor libros sententiarum quaestiones; Quaedam conferentiae; Determinationes. Lyons 1497.

Welter, J. T. L'exemplum dans la littérature religieuse et didactique du Moyen Age. Paris 1927.

Wey, J. C. The sermo finalis of Holcot. Mediaeval Stud 11 1949.

Smalley, B. Robert Holcot. Archivum Fratrum Praedicatorum 26 1956.

— In her English friars and antiquity in the early 14th century, Oxford 1960.

Muckle, J. T. Utrum theologia sit scientia: a quodlibet question of Holcot. Mediaeval Stud 20 1958.

Baumer, J. Zwang und Freiheit in der Glaubenzustimmung nach Holcot. Scholastik 37 1962.

Moody, E. A. A quodlibetal question of Holkot, on the problem of the objects of knowledge and belief. Speculum 39 1964.

Robert of Reading
fl. c. 1325

Flores historiarum. Ed H. R. Luard 3 vols 1890 (Rolls ser). A continuation 1306–25 of Matthew Paris's Flores.

Roger Conway OFM
fl. 1357

Defensio religionis mendicantium. Lyons 1496; ed M. Goldast, Monarchia vol 2, Frankfurt 1614.

Simon of Faversham
d. 1306

Quaestiones super libro predicamentorum. Ed C. Ottoviano, Memorie della Reale Accademia dei Lincei 6th ser vol 3, fascicule 4 1930.

Quaestiones super tertium de Anima. Ed D. Sharp, Archives d'Histoire Doctrinale et Littéraire du Moyen Age 9 1934.

Powicke, F. M. Master Simon of Faversham. In Mélanges Ferdinand Lot, Paris 1925.

Ottoviano, C. Le opere di Simone di Faversham e la sua posizione nel problema degli universali. Archivio di Filosofia 1 1931.

Grabmann, M. Die Aristoteleskommentare des Simon von Faversham. Sitzungsberichte der Bayerischen Akademie der Wissenschaften 3 1933.

Simon of Henton OP
fl. 1360

Walz, P. A. The Exceptiones from the Summa of Simon of Hinton. Angelicum 13 1936.

Pelster, F. An Oxford collection of sermons of the end of the 13th century. Bodleian Quart Record 6 1930.

Dondaine, H. La Somme de Simon de Hinton. Recherches de Théologie Ancienne et Médiévale 9 1937.

Burch, V. The Excepciones from Simon of Heynton's Summa. Medievalia et Humanistica 3 1945.

Smalley, B. Two biblical commentaries of Simon of Hinton. Recherches de Théologie Ancienne et Médiévale 13 1946.

— Some more exegetical works of Simon of Hinton. Recherches de Théologie Ancienne et Médiévale 15 1948.
— The Quaestiones of Simon of Hinton. In Studies in medieval history presented to F. M. Powicke, Oxford 1948.

Thomas Bradwardine, Archbishop of Canterbury
d. 1349

Ars memorativa. Ed B. Politus, Quaestio de modalibus, Venice 1505.
De arithmetica speculativa. Paris 1516.
De causa Dei. Ed H. Savile 1618.
De geometrica speculativa. Paris 1516.
Tractatus de continuo. Ed E. Stamm, Isis 26 1936.
Tractatus de proportionibus. Ed H. L. Crosby, Madison 1955.
 Werner, K. Die Scholastik des späteren Mittelalters pt 3 (b): der Augustinismus. Vienna 1883.
 Hahn, S. Bradwardinus und seine Lehre von dem menschlichen Willensfreiheit. Münster 1905.
 Laun, J. F. Recherches sur Bradwardine précurseur de Wiclif. Revue d'Histoire et de Philosophie Religieuses 9 1929.
 — Die Prädestinationslehre bei Wyclif und Brad-wardine. In H. Bornkamm, Imago Dei, Giessen 1932.
 Leff, G. Bradwardine's De causa Dei. Jnl of Ecclesias-tical History 7 1956.
 — Bradwardine and the Pelagians. Cambridge 1957.
 Oberman, H. A. Archbishop Bradwardine. Utrecht 1957.
 — Bradwardine: un précurseur de Luther? Revue d'Histoire et de Philosophie Religieuses 40 1960.
 McVaugh, M. Arnald of Villanova and Bradwardine's law. Isis 58 1967.

Thomas Brinton (or Brunton) Bishop of Rochester
d. 1389

Sermons. Ed M. Devlin 2 vols 1954.
 Devlin, M. A. Bishop Thomas Brunton and his sermons. Speculum 14 1939.

Thomas Hopeman OP
fl. 1350

Forte, S. Thomas Hopeman. Archivum Fratrum Praedi-catorum 25 1955.

Thomas of Buckingham OP
d. 1351

Super sententias. Paris 1505.
 Chenu, M. D. Le Questiones de Thomas de Bucking-ham. In Studia medievalia in honorem R. J. Martin, Bruges [1948].

Thomas of Sutton OP
fl. c. 1310

De pluralitate formarum. In Thomae Aquinatis opuscula omnia vol 5, ed P. Mandonnet, Paris 1927.
Quaestiones de reali distinctione inter essentiam et esse. Ed F. Pelster, Münster 1929.
 Schmaus, M. Der liber propugnatorius des Thomas Anglicus. Münster 1930. Perhaps by Thomas of Sutton.
 Ehrle, F. Thomas de Sutton: sein Leben, seine Quod-libet und seine Quaestiones disputatae. Kempten 1913.
 Pelster, F. Thomas von Sutton: ein Oxforder Verteidiger der thomistischen Lehre. Zeitschrift für Katholische Theologie 46 1922.
 — Thomas von Sutton als Verfasser zweier Schriften über die Einheit der Wesensform. Scholastik 3 1928.
 — Thomistische Streitschriften gegen Aegidius Rom-anus und ihre Verfasser: Thomas von Sutton und Robert von Orford. Gregorianum 24 1943.
 — Thomas von Sutton und das Correctorium Quare detraxisti. In Mélanges Auguste Pelzer, Louvain 1947.

Sharp, D. E. Thomas of Sutton. Revue Néo-scholas-tique 37 1934.
Pouillon, H. Les Questions sur la métaphysique de Thomas de Sutton. In Mélanges J. de Ghellinck vol 2, Gembloux 1951.

Thomas Waleys OP
d. c. 1349

Ars predicandi. Ms Bibliothèque Mazarine Latin 569.
De modo componendi sermones. See T. M. Charland, Les artes predicandi, Paris 1938.
Expositio Herculis furentis. Ed V. Ussani, Rome 1959.
Expositio super libros Augustini de civitate Dei. Ms Merton College Oxford 256B.
Expositio super psalmos. 1481.
 Kaeppeli, T. Le procès contre Thomas Waleys. Rome 1936.
 Smalley, B. Thomas Waleys. Archivum Fratrum Praedicatorum 24 1954.
 — In her English friars and antiquity in the early 14th century, Oxford 1960.

Uthred of Boldon
d. 1397

Opera. In Migne, Patrologia latina vol 158.
Meditatio devota. Ed H. Farmer, Studia Anselmiana 43 1958.
 Wilmart, A. In his Auteurs spirituels et textes dévots du Moyen Age, Paris 1932.
 Pantin, W. A. English monks before the suppression of the monasteries. Dublin Rev 201 1937.
 — Two treatises of Uthred of Boldon on the monastic life. In Studies in medieval history presented to F. M. Powicke, Oxford 1948.
 Knowles, D. The censured opinions of Uthred of Boldon. Proc Br Acad 37 1951.

Walter Burley OFM
d. c. 1343

Commentarii in Ethicam Aristotelis. Venice 1500.
Commentarii in libros Posteriorum analyticorum. Oxford 1517.
Commentarii super IX libros physicorum. Venice 1509.
De intentione et remissione formarum. Venice 1519.
De puritate artis logicae. Ed P. Boehner, New York 1951.
De sensibus. Ed H. Shapiro and F. Scott, Munich 1966.
Liber de vitis et moribus philosophorum et poetarum. Ed H. Knust, Stuttgart 1886.
Summa totius logicae. Venice 1508.
 Baudry, L. Les rapports de Guillaume d'Occam et de Burleigh. Archives d'Histoire Doctrinale et Lit-téraire du Moyen Age 9 1934.
 Maier, A. Zu Burleys Politik-Kommentar. Recherches du Théologie Ancienne et Médiévale 14 1947.
 — Handschriftliches zu William Ockham und Burley. Archivum Franciscanum Historicum 48 1955.
 — Burley's Traktat: De intentione et remissione formarum. Franciscan Stud 25 1965.
 Thomson, S. H. Burley's commentary on the politics of Aristotle. In Mélanges Auguste Pelzer, Louvain 1947.
 — An unnoticed Quaestio theologica of Walter of Burley. Medievalia et Humanistica 6 1950.
 — Unnoticed questions of Burley on the Physics. Mitteilungen des Instituts für Oesterreichische Geschichtsforschung 52 1955.
 Stigall, J. O. The ms tradition of the De vitis et moribus philosophorum of Burley. Medievalia et Humanistica 11 1957.
 Hough, J. H. Plautus, student of Cicero, and Burley. Medievalia et Humanistica 11 1957.
 Shapiro, H. Burley and the intension and remission of forms. Speculum 34 1959.
 — A note on Burley's exaggerated Realism. Franciscan Stud 20 1960.

—— Burley's De Deo, natura et arte. Medievalia et Humanistica 15 1963.

Shapiro, H. and M. J. Kitely. Burley's De relativis. Franciscan Stud 22 1962.

Boh, I. Burleigh on conditional-hypothetical propositions. Franciscan Stud 23 1963.

—— An examination of some proofs in Burleigh's propositional logic. Mediaeval Stud 27 1965.

Shapiro, H. and F. Scott. Burley's De toto et parte. Archives d'Histoire Doctrinale et Littéraire 33 1966.

Daly, L. J. The conclusions of Burley's commentary on the Politics 1–5. Manuscripta 12 1968.

Walter of Chatton OFM
d. c. 1330

Douie, D. Three treatises on evangelical poverty by Fr. Richard Conyton, Fr. Walter Chatton and an anonymous. Archivum Franciscanum Historicum 24 1931.

Longpré, E. Gualterio di Catton, un maestro franciscano. Studi Francescani 9 1935.

Baudry, L. Gauthier de Chatton et son commentaire sur les sentences. Archives d'Histoire Doctrinale et Littéraire du Moyen Age 14 1945.

Gál, G. Gualteri de Chatton et Gullielmi de Ockham controversia de natura conceptus universalis. Franciscan Stud 27 1967.

Walter of Evesham
fl. 1320

De speculatione musices. Ed C. E. H. de Coussemaker, Scriptorum de musica medii aevi, new ser vol 1, Paris 1864.

William Flete, Austin Canon
fl. 1360

De remediis contra temptaciones. Ed B. Hackett, William Flete and the De remediis contra temptaciones, Medieval studies presented to Aubrey Gwynn, Dublin 1961. *See col 515, above.*

William Heytesbury
d. 1380

De sensu composito et diviso. Venice 1494.

Consequentiae subtiles. In R. Strode, Consequentiae, Venice 1517.

Duhem, P. La dialectique d'Oxford et la scholastique italienne. Bulletin Italien 12 1912.

Wilson, C. Haytesbury: medieval logic and the rise of mathematical physics. Madison 1966.

Maierù, A. Il problema della verità nelle opere di Guglielmo Heytesbury. Studi Medievali 3rd ser 7 1966.

William of Alnwick OFM
d. 1332

Ledoux, A. Guilelmi Alnisci Questiones disputatae de esse intelligibili et de quolibet. Quaracchi 1937.

Schmaus, M. Guilelmi de Alnwick doctrina de medio quo Deus cognoscit futura contingentia. Bogoslovni Vestnik 1932.

William of Macclesfield OP
d. 1303

For bibliography see F. Pelster, Scholastik 1 1926. William may have been joint-author with Richard of Knapwell of the Correctorium quare; he has also been suggested as author of the unpbd Correctorium questione.

Walz, A. M. Cardinales ordine praedicatorum assumpti. Analecta Ordinis Praedicatorum 33 1922.

Creytens, R. Autour de la littérature des correctoires. Archivum Fratrum Praedicatorum 12 1942.

Pelster, F. Theologisch- und philosophisch-bedeutsame Quästionen des W. von Macclesfield, H. von Harclay

und anonymer Autoren der englischen Hochscholastik in Cod. 501 Troyes. Scholastik 28 1953.

William of Nottingham OFM
d. 1336

Longpré, E. Le commentaire sur les sentences de Guillaume de Nottingham. Archivum Franciscanum Historicum 22 1929.

Balić, C. A propos de quelques ouvrages faussement attribués à J. Duns Scot. Recherches de Théologie Ancienne et Médiévale 2 1930.

Meier, L. In Philosophia perennis: Festgabe Josef Geyser vol i, Regensburg 1930.

Schmaus, M. Guillelmi de Nottingham, doctrina de aeternitate mundi. Antonianum 7 1932.

William of Ockam OFM
d. c. 1350

Opera politica vol 1. Ed J. G. Sykes, Manchester 1940; vol 3, ed H. S. Offler, Manchester 1956; vol 2, Manchester 1963.

Philosophical writings: a selection. Ed and tr P. Boehner, Edinburgh 1957.

De corpore Christi. Strasbourg 1491.

Defensorium (de paupertate Christi) contra Johannem XXII. Venice 1513; ed E. Brown, Fasciculus rerum expetendarum vol 2, 1690.

De sacramento altaris. Strasbourg 1491; ed T. B. Birch, Burlington Iowa 1930.

Dialogus de imperatorum et pontificum potestate. Lyons 1495; ed C. K. Brampton, Oxford 1929 (in part); remainder ed W. Mulder, Archivum Franciscanum Historicum 16–17 1923–4.

Epistola ad fratres minores 1334. Ed L. Baudry, Revue d'Histoire Franciscane 3 1926; ed C. K. Brampton, Oxford 1929.

Expositio aurea super artem veterem. Bologna 1496.

Opus 90 dierum. Louvain 1481; ed M. Goldast, Monarchia vol 2, Frankfurt 1614.

Quaestiones in octo libros physicorum. Venice 1506.

Quaestiones super quattuor libros sententiarum. Lyons 1495; Ordinatio: quaestio prima principalis prologi, ed P. Boehner, Paderborn 1939; Ordinatio d2 q8, ed Boehner, New Scholasticism 16 1942; Ordinatio d36 q1, ed Boehner, Rev of Metaphysics 1 1948.

Quodlibeta septem. Paris 1487; Quodlibeta 2, 7, ed P. Boehner, Rev of Metaphysics 1 1948; The seven Quodlibeta, tr R. McKeon, Selections from medieval philosophers, New York 1928 (selection).

Reportatio qq14–15. Ed P. Boehner, Traditio 1 1943.

Summa totius logicae. Paris 1488; ed P. Boehner, New York 1951–.

Summulae in octo libros phisicorum. Venice 1506.

Tractatus adversus errores Johannis XXII. Louvain 1481; ed M. Goldast, Monarchia vol 2, Frankfurt 1614.

Tractatus de electione Caroli IV. Ed C. von Höfler, Abhandlungen der Königlichen Böhmischen Gesellschaft der Wissenschaften 6 1868.

Tractatus de praedestinatione et de praescientia Dei et de futuris contingentibus. Ed P. Boehner, New York 1945.

Unauthentic and Contested Works

Centiloquium theologicum. Lyons 1495. With Questiones super quattuor libros sententiarum.

De iurisdictione imperatoris in causis matrimonialibus. Heidelberg 1598; ed M. Goldast, Monarchia vol 1, Hanover 1612.

Tractatus de successivis. Ed P. Boehner, New York 1944.

For bibliographies see R. Guelluy, Philosophie et théologie chez Guillaume d'Ockham, Paris 1947; L. Baudry, Guillaume d'Ockham: sa vie, ses oeuvres et ses idées sociales et politiques vol 1, Paris 1949; and on 1919–49 V. Heinck, Franziskanische Studien 32 1950.

Hochstetter, F. Studien zur Metaphysik and Erkenntnislehre Wilhelms von Ockham. Berlin 1927.

Moser, S. Grundbegriffe der Naturphilosophie des Wilhelm von Ockham. Innsbruck 1932.

Moody, E. The logic of William of Ockham. New York 1935.

— Ockham, Buridan and William of Autrecourt. Franciscan Stud 7 1947.

Zuidema, S. U. De philosophie van Occam in zijn Commentar op de Sententien. 2 vols Hilversum 1936.

Tornay, S. C. The nominalism of William of Ockham. New York 1936.

— Ockham: studies and selections. La Salle Ill 1938.

Weinberg, J. Ockham's conceptualism. Philosophical Rev 50 1941.

Giacon, G. Gugliemo di Occam: saggio storico-critico sulla formazione e sulla decadenza della scolastica. 2 vols Milan 1941.

— Occam. Brescia 1943.

Boehner, P. The text tradition of Ockham's Ordinatio. New Scholasticism 16 1942.

— Zu Ockhams Beweis der Existenz Gottes. Franziskanische Studien 32 1950.

— Der Stand der Ockham-Forschung. Franziskanische Studien 34 1952.

— Three sums of logic attributed to William Ockham. Franciscan Stud 11 1951.

— The relative date of Ockham's commentary on the Sentences. Ibid.

— The hypothetical first redaction of Ockham's Expositio aurea. Franciscan Stud 14 1954.

Pegis, A. C. Concerning William of Ockham. Traditio 2 1944.

— Some recent interpretations of Ockham. Speculum 23 1948.

Scholz, R. Wilhelm von Ockham als politischer Denker und sein Breviloquium de principatu tyrannico. Leipzig 1944.

— Wilhelm von Ockham als politischer Denker. Leipzig 1949.

Day, S. Intuitive cognition: a key to the significance of the later scholastics [Duns Scotus and Ockham]. New York 1947.

Bayley, C. C. Pivotal concepts in the political philosophy of Ockham. JHI 10 1949.

Marton, G. Ist Ockhams Relationstheorie Nominalismus? Franziskanische Studien 32 1950.

Salamucha, J. Die Aussagenlogik bei Wilhelm Ockham. Ibid.

Vignaux, P. Sur Luther et Ockham. Franziskanische Studien 32 1950.

Mohan, G. A. The quaestio de relatione attributed to Ockham. Franciscan Stud 11 1951.

Fuchs, O. The psychology of habit according to William Ockham. New York 1952 (Franciscan Inst).

Menges, M. C. The concept of univocity regarding the predication of God and creature according to William of Ockham. New York 1952 (Franciscan Inst).

Vasoli, C. Guglielmo d'Occam. Florence 1953.

Bergmann, G. Some remarks on the ontology of Ockham. Philosophical Rev 63 1954.

Maier, A. Handschriftliches zu William Ockham und Walter Burley. Archivum Franciscanum Historicum 48 1955.

Bettoni, E. Guglielmo Occam nella sua vita e nelle sue opere. Studi Francescani 52 1955.

Kölmel. W. Von Ockham zu Gabriel Biel. Franziskanische Studien 37 1955.

Shapiro, H. Motion, time and place according to William Ockham. Franciscan Stud 16 1956.

Baudry, L. Lexique philosophique de Guillaume d'Ockham. Paris 1958.

Maurer, A. Ockham's conception of the unity of science. Mediaeval Stud 20 1958.

Brampton, C. K. Ockham and his alleged authorship of the tract Quia saepe iuris. Archivum Franciscanum Historicum 53 1960.

— Traditions relating to the death of William Ockham. Ibid.

— The probable date of Ockham's Lectura sententiarum. Archivum Franciscanum Historicum 55 1962.

— The probable order of Ockham's non-polemical works. Traditio 19 1963.

— Ockham and his authorship of the Summulae in libros physicorum. Isis 55 1965.

Turnbull, R. G. Ockham's nominalistic logic. New Scholasticism 36 1962.

Tweedale, M. Scotus and Ockham on the infinity of the most eminent being. Franciscan Stud 23 1963.

Bryhaert, E. M. The Tractatus logicae minor of Ockham. Franciscan Stud 24 1964.

— The Elementarium logicae of Ockham. Franciscan Stud 25 1965.

Matthews, G. B. Ockham's supposition theory and modern logic. Philosophical Rev 73 1964.

Buytaert, E. The Elementarium logicae of Ockham. Franciscan Stud 25 1965.

Henry, D. P. Ockham and the formal distinction. Ibid.

Offler, H. S. The origin of Ockham's octo questiones. EHR 82 1967.

Brown, S. F. Sources for Ockham's Prologue to the Sentences pt 2. Franciscan Stud 27 1967.

Poortman, J. J. Ochêma: de zin van bet hylisch pluralisms, 6 AD. Assen 1967.

Burr, D. Ockham, Scotus and the censure at Avignon. Church History 37 1968.

Miethke, J. Ockhams Weg zur Sozialphilosophie. Berlin 1969.

Bird, O. The tradition of logical topics: Aristotle to Ockham. JHI 23 1962.

Pernoud, M. A. The theory of the potentia Dei according to Aquinas, Scotus and Ockham. Antonianum 47 1972.

William Page (or de Pagula)
d. c. 1332

Boyle, L. E. The oculus sacerdotis and some other works of William of Pagula. Trans Royal Historical Soc 5th ser 5 1955.

Davis, H. W. C. The canon low in England. Zeitschrift der Savigny-Stiftung für Rechtsgeschichte 1913.

William Rymington

O'Brien, R. Two sermons at York synod of William Rymington, 1372 and 1373. Cîteaux Commentarii Cistercienses 19 1968.

(9) FIFTEENTH CENTURY

Entries are in alphabetical order of surnames where known.

John Alcock, Bishop of Ely
1430–1500

Mons perfectionis. 1497.
Gallicantus in sinodo apud Bernwell. [1498].
In die innocentium. nd.
See col 1935, below.

Thomas Bekynton or Beckington
c. 1390–1465

Official correspondence. Ed G. Williams 2 vols 1872 (Rolls ser).

Register. Ed H. C. Maxwell-Lyte and M. C. B. Dawes 2 vols 1934.

Perry, G. G. Bishop Beckington and Henry VI. EHR
9 1894.
Weiss, R. In his Humanism in England during the 15th
century, 1940.
Wilmart, A. Le florilège mixte de Thomas Bekynton.
Medieval & Renaissance Stud 1 1941.
Judd, A. F. The episcopate of Bekynton. Jnl of
Ecclesiastical History 8 1957.

John Blacman
fl. 1457
Memoire of Henry VI. Ed M. R. James, Cambridge 1919.

William Brewyn
fl. 1470
Ms Canterbury Cathedral Z.8.33 ; see A 15th-century guide-
book to the principal churches of Rome, tr C. E. Woodruff 1933.

Alexander Carpenter (Anglicus or Fabricius)
fl. 1429
Destructorium viciorum. Cologne 1480. Numerous edns
to 1521.
Owst, G. R. The Destructorium viciorum. 1952.

Walter Diss
fl. 1404
Carmen de schismate ecclesiae. Ed J. M. Lydius, Nicolai
de Clemangiis opera, Leyden 1613.

Roger Dymokk OP
Liber contra xii errores et haereses Lollardorum. Ed H. S.
Cronin 1922 (Wyclif Soc).
Cronin, H. S. The twelve conclusions of the Lollards.
EHR 22 1907.

Thomas Elham
Liber metricus de Henrico V. In Memorials of Henry V,
1858 (Rolls ser).
Roskell, J. S. and F. Taylor. The authorship and pur-
pose of the Gesta Henrici Quinti. Bull John Rylands
Lib 53-4 1971.

Robert Flemmyng
d. 1483
Lucubriatiunculae tiburtinae (Rome c. 1480); ed V.
Pacifici, Un carme biografico di Sisto IV del 1477,
Tivoli 1923.
Campana, A. Roma di Sisto IV. Strenna dei Romanisti
9 1948.
Weiss, R. New light on humanism in England during
the 15th century. Jnl Warburg & Courtauld Inst 14
1951.

Sir John Fortescue
c. 1394–c. 1476
De laudibus legum Angliae. [1546]; tr F. Gregor 1917;
ed S. B. Chrimes, Cambridge 1942 (with trn).
Works. Ed Lord Clermont 2 vols 1869. Minor writings.
For his English writings see col 666, above.
Skeel, C. A. J. The influence of the writings of Fortescue.
Trans Royal Historical Soc 3rd ser 10 1916.
Jacob, E. F. Fortescue and the law of nature. Bull John
Rylands Lib 16 1934.
Shepherd, M. A. The political and constitutional theory
of Fortescue. In Essays in honor of C. H. McIlwain,
Cambridge Mass 1936.
Mosse, G. L. Fortescue and the problem of papal power.
Medievalia et Humanistica 7 1952.

John Free (or Phreas)
d. 1465
Epistolae. Ed J. E. Spingarn, Unpublished letters of an
English humanist, New York 1903.
Weiss, R. A letter-preface of John Free to John Tiptoft.
Bodleian Quart Record 8 1938.
Mitchell, R. J. John Free. 1955.

Tito Livio Frulovisi
Opera hactenus inedita. Ed C. W. Previté-Orton, Cambridge 1932.
Vita Henrici quinti. Ed T. Hearne, Oxford 1716.
The comedies Eugenius *and* Peregrinatio, *which Frulovisi
produced during his stay in England, can be found in* Opera,
*above. On the importance of his work for English historio-
graphy see* C. L. Kingsford, English historical literature
in the 15th century, *Oxford 1913.*
Sabbadini, R. Tito Livio Frulovisio. Giornale Storico
della Letteratura Italiana 103 1934.
Weiss, R. In Fritz Saxl: a volume of memorial essays,
1957.

Thomas Gascoigne, Chancellor of Oxford
1403–58
Dictionarium theologicum. Mss Lincoln College Oxford
117–18; extracts in J. E. T. Rogers, Loci e libro veri-
tatum, Oxford 1881.
Pronger, W. A. Thomas Gascoigne. EHR 53-4 1938-9.
Gieben, S. Gascoigne and Grosseteste. Vivarium 8 1960.

Geoffrey the Grammarian of Lynn
Promptorium parvulorum. 1499, 1510 etc; ed A. L.
Mayhew 1908 (EETS). A Latin-English dictionary.

John Gower
1330?–1408?
Chronica tripartita and minor poems. Ed H. O. Coxe
1850; ed T. Wright, Political poems vol 1, 1859 (Rolls
ser).
Vox clamantis. Ed H. O. Coxe 1850.
Complete works. Ed G. C. Macaulay 4 vols Oxford
1899–1902. Vol 3 contains all Gower's Latin poems.

John Gunthorpe
d. 1498
Orationes. Ms (B. L.) Bodley 587; extracts in W. F.
Schirmer, Der englische Frühhumanismus, Leipzig
1931.
Schutt, M. Bishop Gunthorpe. MLR 23 1928.
Weiss, R. In his Humanism in England in the 15th
century, 1940.

James Haldenstone, Prior of St Andrews
d. 1443
Epistolae. Ed J. H. Baxter, Copiale prioratus S. Andree,
Oxford 1930.

John Hauboys
fl. 1470
Ed. C. E. H. Coussemaker, Scriptorum de musica medii
aevi, new ser vol 1, Paris 1864.

John Hothby
d. 1487
In Scriptorum de musica medii aevi, new ser vol 3, Paris
1869. De cantu figurato; Regulae supra contrapunc-
tum; Regulae super proportione. Treatises on music.

John Mirk
fl. 1405
Manuale sacerdotum. Mss Cambridge Univ Lib Ff.1.14,
York Cathedral Lib 16.L.8. *For his English works see
cols 488, 497, 687, 692, above.*

Thomas Netter of Walden
d. 1430
Doctrinale fidei ecclesiae. Venice 1571.
In Fasciculi zizaniorum, ed W. W. Shirley 1858 (Rolls ser).

Dominic Mancini
De occupatione regni Angliae per Riccardum III. Ed C. A. J. Armstrong 1936.

Nicolas of Fakenham OFM
d. c. 1407
Determinatio [and other pieces on the schism]. BM ms Harley 3768; ed F. Bliemetzrieder, Traktat des Minoritenprovinzials von England Fr. Nikolaus de Fakenham 1395 über das grosse abendländische Schisma, Archivum Franciscanum Historicum 1–2 1908–9.

Thomas Palmer OP
fl. 1410
De translatione sacrae scripturae in linguam anglicanam. Ed M. Deanesly, The Lollard Bible, Cambridge 1920.

Reginald Pecock, Bishop of Chichester
1395–c. 1460
Collectanea quaedam. Ed J. Foxe, Commentarii rerum in ecclesia gestarum, Strasbourg 1554.
For Pecock's English works see col 665, above.
> Green, V. H. H. Bishop Reginald Pecock. Cambridge 1945.
> Jacob, E. F. Pecock, Bishop of Chichester. Proc Br Acad 39 1953.
> Emerson, E. H. Pecock: Christian rationalist. Speculum 31 1956.

Mauritius a Portu (or O'Fihely) OFM
d. 1513
Expositio in quaestiones dialecticas Iohannis Scoti in Isagogen Porphrii. Ferrara 1499, Venice 1512. For his commentaries on Scotus see Scotus, Opera omnia, Paris 1891–5. A list of his works can be found in A. Wood, Athenae oxonienses vol i, ed P. Bliss 1813.

Thomas of Claxton OP
fl. c. 1400
Quaestiones de distincione inter esse et essentiam. Ed M. Grabmann, Acta Pontificiae Academiae (Rome) 8 1943.

William Sellyng
d. 1494
Orationes. BM ms Cotton Cleopatra E III; the draft of a speech written in 1483 in E. Fueter, Religion und Kirche in England im 15 Jahrhundert, Tübingen 1904; and his 1487 speech before Innocent VIII in U. Balzani, Un ambasciata inglese a Roma, Archivio della Società Romana di Storia Patria 3 1880.

John Shirwood, Bishop of Durham
d. 1494
Liber de ludo arithmomachia. Rome 1482. A game played on boards.
> Allen, P. S. Bishop Shirwood of Durham and his library. EHR 25 1910.

John Strecche
fl. 1407–25
Historia rerum Angliae. BM additional ms 35295; ed F. Taylor, The chronicle of Strecche for the reign of Henry V, Bull John Rylands Lib 16 1932 (in part).

Lorenzo Traversagni da Savona
(lectured at Cambridge 1476–8 and again c. 1482)
Nova rhetorica. 1479 (Caxton). Ptd the St Albans scholemayster 1480. Caxton also ptd a summary 1480.

> Ruysschaert, J. Lorenzo Guglieomo Traversagni di Savone: un humaniste franciscain oublié. Archivum Franciscanum Historicum 46 1953.
> — Les manuscrits autographes de deux oeuvres de Lorenzo Traversagni imprimées chez Caxton. Bull John Rylands Lib 36 1954.

John Trevisa
c. 1330–1402
See col 467, above.
> Fowler, D. C. John Trevisa and the English Bible. MP 58 1960.
For his trn of Higden's Polychronicon see Ranulf Higden, col 794, above.

(Richard) Tryvytlam (or Trevytham)
De laude universitatis Oxoniae. Ed T. Hearne, Historia Ricardi vol 2, Oxford 1729; ed H. Furneaux, Oxford Historical Society Collectanea vol 3, 1896. A poem.

Thomas Walsingham
early 15th century
Annales Ricardi II et Henrici IV. Ed H. T. Riley 1866 (Rolls ser).
Chronicon anglicae 1322–88. Ed E. M. Thompson 1874 (Rolls ser).
Historia anglicana 1272–1422. Ed H. T. Riley 1863–4 (Rolls ser).
Chronica monasterii S. Albani. Ed H. T. Riley 12 vols 1863–76 (Rolls ser).
The St Albans Chronicle 1404–20. Ed V. H. Galbraith, Oxford 1937.
Ypodigma Neustriae. Ed H. T. Riley 1876.
> Galbraith, V. H. Thomas Walsingham and the St Albans Chronicle. EHR 47 1932.

William Wey (or Way)
fl. 1458–62
Itineraria. Ed G. Williams 1857 (Roxburghe Club).

John Whethamstede, Abbot of St Albans
d. 1465
Granarium. Partly in BM mss Arundel 11, 391, and Cotton Nero C.VI. and Tib.D.V; ms Caius College Cambridge 230.
Pabularium. BM ms Egerton 646.
Palearium. In BM ms additional 26,764.
Registrum abbatiae J. Whethamstede. Ed M. T. Riley 2 vols 1872–3 (Rolls ser).
> Schirmer, W. F. In his Der englische Frühhumanismus, Leipzig 1931.
> Jacob, E. F. Florida verborum venustas. Manchester 1933.
> — Englishmen and general councils of the 15th century. History 26 1939.
> Weiss, R. Piero del Monte, John Whethamstede and the library of St Albans abbey. EHR 60 1945.
> — Leonardo Bruni and early English humanism. MLR 36 1941.
> — In his Humanism in England during the fifteenth century, Oxford 1941, 1967 (rev).
> Keller, J. R. The triumph of vice: a formal approach to the medieval complaint against the times. Annuale Medievale 9 1968.

William Worcester
c. 1415–c. 1482
Annales rerum anglicarum. Ed J. Stevenson, Letters and papers illustrative of the wars of the English in France, 1864 (Rolls ser).
Itinerarium. Ed J. Nasmith, Cambridge 1778 (in part); ed and tr J. H. Harvey, Oxford 1969.
> Kendrick, T. D. In his British antiquity, 1950.

R. R. B.

THE RENAISSANCE TO THE
RESTORATION (1500-1660)
1. INTRODUCTION

I. GENERAL WORKS

(1) BIBLIOGRAPHIES

The location of English books to 1640 is incorporated in Pollard and Redgrave, Short-title catalogue, 1926 (Bibl Soc). Earlier bibliographies of independent or historical interest are listed below. See also general bibliographies, col 1, above, and book lists and library catalogues, col 3 f., above. For specialized bibliographies on poetry, drama and prose, see under appropriate sections below. Some early bibliographies serve also as collections of reprints and literary histories.

Leland, J. (1506?–52). Commentarii de scriptoribus britannicis. Ed A. Hall 2 vols Oxford 1709; ed T. Hearne, Collectanea, Oxford 1715, 1770 (enlarged), 1774. Used by Bale for his Summarium and Catalogus, below.

Bale, J. Illustrium majoris Britanniae scriptorum summarium. Ipswich (Wesel?) 1548. Rev and enlarged as Scriptorum illustrium majoris Brytanniae catalogus, 2 pts Basle 1557–9. His notebook, c. 1549–57, used as material for the Catalogus, pbd as Index Britanniae scriptorum, ed R. L. Poole and M. Bateson, Oxford 1902.

Pits, J. Relationum historicarum de rebus anglicis vol 1. Ed W. Bishop, Paris 1619.

Wood, A. Athenae oxonienses: a history of writers educated at Oxford 1500–1695. 2 vols 1691–2; rev and enlarged T. Tanner 1721; ed P. Bliss 4 vols 1813–20 (with addns), New York 1967.

Davies, M. Athenae britannicae: a critical history of Oxford and Cambridge writers and writings, with other authors. 6 vols 1716–19; ed R. G. Thomas, Los Angeles 1962 (selected) (Augustan Reprint Soc).

Tanner, T. Bibliotheca britannico-hibernica. 1748, Tucson 1963.

Ames, J. Typographical antiquities: an historical account of printing in England to 1600. 1749; augmented W. Herbert 3 vols 1785–90; rev T. F. Dibdin 4 vols 1810–19, Detroit 1969. Index to Dibdin's edn, 1899.

Clarke, A. A bibliographical dictionary. 8 vols 1802–6.

Ritson, J. Bibliographia poetica: a catalogue of poets from the 12th to the 16th centuries. 1802.

Brydges, Sir S. E. Censura literaria: containing titles, abstracts and opinions of English books. 10 vols 1805–9, 1815, New York 1966.

— British bibliographer. 4 vols 1810–14, New York 1966.

— Restituta: titles, extracts and characters of old books in English literature. 4 vols 1814–16.

— Res literariae: bibliographical and critical. 3 vols Naples 1821–2.

Beloe, W. Anecdotes of literature and scarce books. 6 vols 1807–12.

Watt, R. and sons. Bibliotheca britannica: or a general index to British and foreign literature. 4 vols Edinburgh 1824 (with subject-index).

Lowndes, W. T. The bibliographer's manual of English literature. 4 vols 1834, 1864 (rev and enlarged H. G. Bohn), 8 vols Detroit 1967.

Halliwell(-Phillipps), J. O. Brief notices of bibliographical rarities in his library. 1855; Supplement, 1862.

Corser, T. Collectanea anglo-poetica: a bibliographical and descriptive catalogue of early English poetry. 11 vols Manchester 1860–83.

Collier, J. P. A bibliographical and critical account of the rarest books in the English language. 2 vols 1865, 4 vols New York 1866, New York 1966.

Hazlitt, W. C. Handbook to the popular, poetical and dramatic literature of Great Britain from the invention of printing to the Restoration. 1867; Supplements, 1876, 1882, 1887–92, 1903; Index (1867–89) by G. J. Gray, 1893; 8 vols New York 1961 (complete).

Arber, E. A transcript of the registers of the Company of Stationers 1554–1640. 4 vols 1875–7; with Index, Birmingham 1894, 5 vols New York 1950. Supplement: Registers 1640–1708, ed G. E. B. Eyre 3 vols 1913–14, New York 1950; The Court records of the Company 1576–1602, ed W. W. Greg and E. Boswell 1930; 1602–40, ed W. A. Jackson 1957. *See also* A companion to Arber: a calendar of documents in Arber's transcript, with text and calendar of supplementary documents, ed W. W. Greg with C. E. Blagden and I. G. Philip, Oxford 1967.

Huth library: catalogue of books. Ed F. S. Ellis 5 vols 1880.

British Museum. Catalogue of English books to 1640. Ed G. Bullen 3 vols 1884.

— Catalogue of the pamphlets, books, newspapers and manuscripts relating to the Civil War, the Commonwealth and Restoration (1640–61). Collected G. Thomason and ed G. K. Fortescue 2 vols 1908.

Sinker, R. Trinity College Library: a catalogue of English books printed before 1601. Cambridge 1885.

Dickson, R. and J. P. Edmond. Annals of Scottish printing 1507–1600. Cambridge 1890.

Grolier Club. Catalogue of early editions of some English writers from Langland to Wither. New York 1893, London 1964.

John Rylands Library. Catalogue of English books to 1640. Ed E. G. Duff, Manchester 1895.

Madan, F. Oxford books: a bibliography of works printed by the Press '1468'–1680. 3 vols Oxford 1895–1931.

Dix, E. R. McC. Catalogue of early Dublin-printed books 1601–1700. 4 vols Dublin 1898–1905; Supplement, 1912; Books prior to 1601, Dublin 1901, 1932.

Cambridge University Library. Early English printed books 1475–1640. Ed C. E. Sayle 4 vols with appendix, Cambridge 1900–7.

Hoe, R. Catalogue of books by English authors before 1700 from his library. Ed J. O. Wright 5 vols New York 1903–5.

Aldis, H. G. A list of books printed in Scotland before 1700. Edinburgh 1904.

Marsh's Library, Dublin. A short catalogue of its books before 1641. Ed N. J. D. White, Oxford 1905.

Pierpont Morgan Library. Catalogue of manuscripts and early printed books. Ed A. W. Pollard et al 4 vols 1906–7.

Palmer, H. R. List of English editions and translations of Greek and Latin classics printed before 1641. 1911.

Esdaile, A. A list of English tales and prose romances printed before 1740. 1912.

Studies in Philology. Recent literature of the English Renaissance: annual bibliography beginning 1916. SP 14 1917–.

Glasgow. A century of books printed in Glasgow 1638–86. Glasgow 1918.

Huntington Library, Henry E. Check-list or brief catalogue: English literature to 1640, compiled by P. S. Goulding under the direction of G. W. Cole. New York 1919; Additions and corrections, 1920. See also the suppl to the record of its books in the Short-title catalogue, ed C. K. Edmonds, Huntington Lib Bull 4 1933.

Clark, W. A., Library. Early English literature 1519–1700. Compiled R. E. Cowan and W. A. Clark 4 vols San Francisco 1920–5.

Childs, J. B. Sixteenth-century books: a bibliography of literature describing books printed between 1501 and 1601. PBSA 17 1923.

Newberry Library, Chicago. Check-list of English books before 1641. Ed M. I. Stearns, Chicago 1923. See also suppl to the record of its books in the Short-title catalogue, ed G. L. Woodward, Chicago 1939.

Clawson, J. L. Catalogue of early English books in his library. Ed S. de Ricci, Philadelphia 1924.

Pollard, A. W. and G. R. Redgrave. A short-title catalogue of books printed in England, Scotland and Ireland, and of English books printed abroad 1475–1640. 2 vols 1926 (Bibl Soc), 1946, 1973 (rev K. Pantzer). Supplemented by STC books in the Huntington Library, ed C. K. Edmonds, Huntington Lib Bull 4 1933; STC books in the Newberry Library Chicago, ed G. L. Woodward, Chicago 1939; STC books at the London Oratory, ed A. F. Allison, Library 5th ser 2 1947. See also W. W. Bishop, A checklist of American copies of STC books, Ann Arbor 1941, 1950 (enlarged); P. G. Morrison, Index of printers, publishers and booksellers in the STC, Charlottesville 1950, 1961; D. Ramage et al, A finding list of English books to 1640 in libraries in the British Isles (excluding Cambridge, Oxford and the national libraries), Durham 1958; F. B. Williams jr, Photo-facsimiles of STC books: a cautionary check list, SB 21 1968. The microfilming of STC books by University Microfilms, Ann Arbor 1938–. For a continuation of the STC, see Wing below.

White, W. A. Catalogue of early English books chiefly of the Elizabethan period, collected by him. Ed H. C. Bartlett, New York 1926.

McAlpin collection of British history and theology in the Union Theological Seminary, New York. Ed C. R. Gillett 5 vols New York 1927–30.

Davies, G. Bibliography of British history: Stuart period 1603–1714. Oxford 1928, 1970 (rev M. F. Keeler); C. Read, Tudor period 1485–1603, Oxford 1933, 1959 (rev).

Bibliographia Aberdonensis. Books printed in the shires of Aberdeen, Banff and Kincardine, and by Aberdonians 1472–1640. Ed J. F. K. Johnstone and A. W. Robertson, Aberdeen 1929.

Cole, G. W. A survey of the bibliography of English literature 1475–1640. PBSA 23 1930.

The Britwell handlist: or short-title catalogue of the principal volumes to 1800, formerly in the library of Britwell Court. 2 vols 1933.

Lathrop, H. B. Translations from the classics into English from Caxton to Chapman 1477–1620. Madison 1933. A survey with a list of trns and suppl to Palmer, above.

Besterman, T. List of bibliographies printed to the end of the 16th century. In The beginnings of systematic bibliography, Oxford 1935, 1936 (rev).

Brown, H. The classical tradition in English literature: a bibliography. Harvard Stud 18 1935.

Case, A. E. A bibliography of English poetical miscellanies 1521–1750. Oxford 1935 (Bibl Soc).

de Ricci, S. and W. J. Wilson. Census of medieval and Renaissance manuscripts in the United States and Canada. 3 vols New York 1935–40, 1961; Supplement, ed W. H. Bond, New York 1962.

Noyes, G. E. Bibliography of courtesy and conduct-books in 17th century England. New Haven 1937.

Spargo, J. W. Some reference books of the 16th and 17th centuries: a finding-list. PBSA 31 1937.

Tannenbaum, S. A. and D. R. Elizabethan bibliographies. Nos 1–40, New York 1937–49; Supplements, London 1967–.

Pinto, V. de S. The English Renaissance 1510–1688. 1938, 1966 (rev with an added ch). Pt 2: bibliography.

Herr, A. F. The Elizabethan sermon: a survey and a bibliography. Philadelphia 1940.

Pforzheimer, Carl H., Library. English literature 1475–1700. Compiled E. V. Unger and W. A. Jackson 3 vols New York 1940.

Taylor, A. Renaissance reference books: a checklist of some bibliographies printed before 1700. Berkeley 1941.

—— Renaissance guides to books: an inventory and some conclusions. Berkeley 1945.

Folger, H. The Folger Shakespeare Memorial Library: a report on progress 1931–41, by J. Q. Adams, Amherst Mass 1942. See also G. E. Dawson, The resources and policies of the Folger Library, Lib Quart 19 1949. For its STC holdings see W. W. Bishop under Pollard and Redgrave, above. Catalogues of manuscripts, 3 vols, and printed books, 28 vols, Boston 1971–.

Seventeenth-century News. 1942–. Since 1950 ed J. M. Patrick. Reviews of current pbns.

Tuve, R. A critical survey of scholarship in the field of English literature of the Renaissance. SP 40 1943.

Utley, F. L. The crooked rib: an analytical index to the argument about women in English and Scots literature to 1568. Columbus 1944.

Craig, H. Recent scholarship of the English Renaissance: a brief survey. SP 42 1945.

Ferguson, F. S. English books before 1640. In The Bibliographical Society 1892–1942: studies in retrospect, 1945. Lists pbns of the Society in the field of English bibliography to 1640.

Wing, D. G. A short-title catalogue of books printed in England, Scotland, Ireland, Wales and British America, and of English books printed in other countries 1641–1700. 3 vols New York 1945–51; Suppls by M. I. Fry and G. Davies, HLQ 16 1953; J. E. Tucker, Wing's STC and translations from the French 1641–1700, PBSA 49 1955; W. G. Hiscock, The Christ Church supplement to Wing, Oxford 1956; J. Alden, Bibliographica hibernica: additions and corrections to Wing, Charlottesville 1955; also his Wing addenda and corrigenda, Charlottesville 1958; E. Wolf, A check-list of the books in the Library Company of Philadelphia supplementary to Wing, Philadelphia 1959; and Wing, A gallery of ghosts: books published between 1641–1700 not found in the STC, New York 1967. See also P. G. Morrison, Index of printers, publishers and booksellers, Charlottesville 1955. The microfilming of STC books by University Microfilms, Ann Arbor 1961–.

Matthews, W. British diaries: an annotated bibliography to 1942. Berkeley 1950.
—— British autobiographies: an annotated bibliography to 1951. Berkeley 1955.
Southern, A. C. Elizabethan recusant prose 1559–82. 1950. An historical and critical account of the books of the Catholic refugees, with annotated bibliography. *See* corrections and addns by A. F. Allison and D. M. Rogers, Library 5th ser 6 1951.
Mish, C. C. English prose fiction 1600–1700: a chronological checklist. Charlottesville 1952, 1967 (rev).
Renaissance News 5– 1952–. Annual list of Renaissance books compiled by R. E. Taylor since 8 1955.
O'Dell, S. A chronological list of prose fiction in English 1475–1640. Cambridge Mass 1954.
Allison, A. F. and D. M. Rogers. A catalogue of Catholic books in English printed abroad or secretly in England 1558–1640. Bognor Regis 1956; Supplement, Recusant History 6 1961.
Allison, A. F. List of books acquired by the British Museum from Chatsworth: part II, English books 1501–1640. Book Collector 8 1959.
Jayne, S. Library catalogues of the English Renaissance. Berkeley 1956.
—— and F. R. Johnson. The Lumley Library: the catalogue of 1609. 1956.
Stamm, R. Englische Literatur. Berne 1957. A critical review of scholarship c. 1935–55 on 1500–1900.
Bibliothèque d'Humanisme et Renaissance 20– 1958–. Bibliographie des articles relatifs à l'histoire de l'humanisme et de la Renaissance.
MacLure, M. The Paul's Cross sermons 1534–1642. Toronto 1958. With register of the sermons.
Jorgensen, P. A. Elizabethan literature today: a review of recent scholarship. Texas Stud in Lit & Lang 1 1960.

Smith, L. B. The 'taste for Tudors' since 1940. Stud in Renaissance 7 1960; rptd in Changing views on British history, ed E. C. Furber, Cambridge Mass 1966; suppl by P. Zagorin, English history 1558–1640, ibid.
Stud in Eng Lit 1500–1900 1– 1961–. Recent studies in the English Renaissance.
Williams, F. B., jr. Index of dedications and commendatory verses in English books before 1641. 1962 (Bibl Soc).
Hamilton, A. C. The modern study of Renaissance English literature: a critical survey. MLQ 26 1965.
Summers, J. H. Notes on recent studies in English literature of the earlier 17th century. Ibid.
Weinberg, B. Scholarship and the southern Renaissance: a victory for history. Ibid.
Bibliographie Internationale de l'Humanisme et de la Renaissance (Geneva) 1– 1966–. Annual bibliography of books and articles on all aspects of the Renaissance.
Adams, H. M. Catalogue of books printed on the Continent of Europe 1501–1600 in Cambridge libraries. 2 vols Cambridge 1967.
Watson, G. The English Petrarchans: a critical bibliography of the Canzoniere. 1967 (Warburg Inst).
Frank, J. Hobbled Pegasus: a descriptive bibliography of minor English poetry 1641–1660. Albuquerque 1968.
Levine, M. Tudor England 1485–1603. Cambridge 1968. A bibliographical handbook.
Lievsay, J. L. Goldentree bibliographies: the sixteenth century, Skelton through Hooker. New York 1968.
Crum, M. First-line index of English poetry 1500–1800 in manuscripts of the Bodleian Library, Oxford. 2 vols Oxford 1969.
A short-title catalogue of foreign books printed up to 1600: books printed or published outside the British Isles now in the National Library of Scotland and the Library of the Faculty of Advocates. Edinburgh 1970.

(2) COLLECTIONS

Collections of poetry, drama and prose may be found in their appropriate sections below. See particularly collections of tracts, col 2023, below.

The Harleian miscellany: a collection of pamphlets and tracts. 8 vols 1744–6; ed W. Oldys 1746 (with catalogue); ed T. Park 10 vols 1808–13; ed J. Malham 12 vols 1808–11 (chronologically arranged).
Somers tracts: a collection of scarce and valuable tracts. 16 vols 1748–52; ed W. Scott 13 vols 1809–15 (rev and enlarged).
Harington, J. Nugae antiquae: a miscellaneous collection of prose and verse written from the reign of Henry VIII to the reign of King James. 2 vols 1769–75, 3 vols 1779 (enlarged); ed T. Park 2 vols 1804, New York 1966.
Capell, E. Notes and various readings to Shakespeare. 3 vols 1779–80, New York 1970. Vol 3, The school of Shakespeare. Extracts from his sources.
Haslewood, J. Ancient critical essays upon English poets and poesy. 2 vols 1811–15.
Brydges, S. E. Excerpta tudoriana: or extracts from Elizabethan literature. 2 vols Lee Priory 1814–18.
—— Archaica: a reprint of scarce old English prose tracts. 2 vols 1815.
Roxburghe Club publications. 1814–, New York 1968–.
Boswell, A. Frondes caducae. 7 vols Auchinleck 1816–18. Reprints of 16th- and 17th-century works.
Triphook, R. Miscellanea antiqua anglicana: a collection of curious tracts. 1816.
Nichols, J. The progresses and public processions of Queen Elizabeth. 3 vols 1823, New York 1964.
—— The progresses, processions and magnificent festivities of King James I. 4 vols 1828, New York 1964.
The British reformers from Wickliff to Jewell. 15 vols [1827]–31.
Camden Society publications. Series 1, 105 vols 1838–72; Descriptive catalogue by J. G. Nichols 1862, 1872;

Catalogue by H. Gough 1881; New series, 62 vols 1871–1901. The Royal Historical Society issued vols 58–62 and series 3, 1900–. List and index to Camden Society pbns 1840–97 and Royal Historical Soc pbns 1871–1924 ed H. Hall 1925. Camden series 4 1964– (Royal Historical Soc).
Percy Society publications. Early English poetry, ballads and popular literature of the Middle Ages. 30 vols 1840–52, New York 1965.
Parker Society publications. 55 vols Cambridge 1841–55; Index by H. Gough, Cambridge 1855. Includes works of the early writers of the Reformed English church.
Library of Anglo-Catholic theology. 88 vols 1841–63.
Wright, T. and J. O. Halliwell(-Phillipps). Reliquiae antiquae: scraps from ancient manuscripts illustrating chiefly early English literature. 2 vols 1841–3, 1845, New York 1966.
Collier, J. P. Shakespeare's library: a collection of the romances, novels, poems and histories used as the foundation of his dramas. 2 vols 1843; rev W. C. Hazlitt 6 vols 1875, New York 1965.
—— Illustrations of early English popular literature. 2 vols 1863, 1864, New York 1966.
—— Illustrations of old English literature. 3 vols 1866, New York 1966.
Ellis, H. Original letters of eminent literary men of the 16th–18th centuries. 1843 (Camden Soc).
Cattermole, R. The literature of the Church of England: selections from the writings of eminent divines. 2 vols 1844.
Hakluyt Society publications. 1st series, 100 vols 1847–99, New York 1963; 2nd series, 1899–; Extra series, Cambridge 1903–.

Halliwell(-Phillipps), J. O. Contributions to early English literature 15th–17th century. 6 pts 1849.
—— Literature of the 16th and 17th centuries illustrated by reprints of tracts. 1851.
Hazlitt, W. C. Shakespeare jest-books. 3 vols 1864, New York 1964.
—— Inedited tracts illustrating the manners, opinions and occupations of Englishmen during the 16th and 17th centuries. 1868, New York 1964.
—— Prefaces, dedications, epistles, selected from early English books 1540–1701. 1874.
—— Fairy tales, legends and romances illustrating Shakespeare and other English writers. 1875.
Spenser Society publications. 55 vols Manchester 1867–95, New York 1966.
Arber, E. English reprints. 30 pts 1868–95.
—— An English garner. 8 vols 1877–97; ed T. Seccombe 12 vols 1903–4 (enlarged); Analytical catalogue, ed H. Guppy, Manchester 1909 (John Rylands Lib).
—— The English scholars library of old and modern works. 5 vols 1878–84, New York 1967.
Ashbee, E. W. Occasional facsimile reprints (of the 16th and 17th centuries). 30 pts 1868–72.
Grosart, A. B. Fuller Worthies' library. 39 vols Edinburgh 1868–76.
—— Miscellanies of the Fuller Worthies' library. 4 vols Blackburn 1871–6, New York 1966.
—— Occasional issues of unique or very rare books. 18 vols 1875–83.
—— Chertsey Worthies' library. 14 vols Blackburn 1876–81.
—— Early English poets. 9 vols 1876–7.
—— The Huth Library of Elizabethan-Jacobean books. 29 vols 1881–6.
Edmonds, C. The Isham reprints. 4 pts 1870–95.
Hindley, C. The old book collector's miscellany. 3 vols 1871–3.
Hunterian Club publications. 68 nos 1872–1902, 16 vols New York [1970?].
Ashton, J. Humour, wit and satire of the 17th century. 1883, New York 1970.
Scottish Text Society publications. 1st series, 65 vols Edinburgh 1884–1918; 2nd series, 26 vols 1911–30; 3rd series, 1931–; 4th series, 1963–.
Tudor translations. Ed W. E. Henley 44 vols 1892–1909; 2nd series ed C. Whibley 12 vols 1924–7. Both rptd, New York 1970.
Pollard, A. F. Tudor tracts 1532–88. 1903, New York 1964. Suppl by C. H. Firth, Stuart tracts 1603–93, 1903, New York 1964.
Smith, G. G. Elizabethan critical essays. 2 vols Oxford 1904.
Magnus, L. Documents illustrating Elizabethan poetry. 1906.
Spingarn, J. E. Critical essays of the 17th century. 3 vols Oxford 1908–9, Bloomington 1957.
Wilson, J. D. Life in Shakespeare's England: a book of Elizabethan prose. Cambridge 1911.
Smith, D. N. Characters from the histories and memoirs of the 17th century. Oxford 1918.

Bodley Head quartos. Ed G. B. Harrison 15 vols 1923–6, Edinburgh 1966.
Hebel, J. W. and H. H. Hudson. Poetry of the English Renaissance 1509–1660. New York 1929; Prose, New York 1952; collected as Tudor poetry and prose, New York 1953.
Judges, A. V. The Elizabethan underworld: a collection of Tudor and early Stuart tracts and ballads of vagabonds. 1930, 1965 (in part).
Gebert, C. An anthology of Elizabethan dedications and prefaces [to 1623]. Philadelphia 1933, New York 1966.
Scholars' facsimiles and reprints. New York 1936–47. Ed H. R. Warfel et al, Gainesville 1951–.
Clements, A. F. Tudor translations: an anthology. Oxford 1940.
Gilbert, A. H. Literary criticism, Plato to Dryden. New York 1940.
Luttrell Society reprints. Oxford 1946–61.
English reprints series. 22 nos Liverpool 1948–67.
Southern, A. C. Elizabethan recusant prose 1559–82. 1950. With annotated bibliography.
Elizabethan Nonconformist texts. 1951–.
Wallerstein, R. C. and R. Quintana. Seventeenth-century verse and prose. 2 vols New York 1951.
McClure, N. E. Sixteenth-century English poetry, New York 1954; Prose, ed K. J. Holzknecht, New York 1954.
Rollins, H. E. and H. Baker. The Renaissance in England: non-dramatic prose and verse of the 16th century. Boston 1954.
Nugent, E. M. The thought and culture of the English Renaissance: an anthology of Tudor prose 1481–1555. Cambridge 1956. Includes brief essays by various scholars.
Pelican book of English prose. Vol 1, Elizabethan and Jacobean prose 1550–1620, ed K. Muir 1956; vol 2, Seventeenth-century prose 1620–1700, ed P. Ure 1956.
Bullough, G. Narrative and dramatic sources of Shakespeare. 1957–.
Clarendon medieval and Tudor series. Ed J. A. W. Bennett et al, Oxford 1958–.
Donno, E. S. Elizabethan minor epics. 1963; suppl by P. S. Miller, Seven minor epics 1596–1624, Gainesville 1967.
Hardison, O. B., jr. English literary criticism: the Renaissance. New York 1963.
Renaissance English Text Society publications. Evanston 1965–.
Renaissance library facsimile editions. Ed A. Shalvi 1966–.
Roberts, J. R. A critical anthology of English recusant devotional prose 1558–1603. Duquesne Stud in Philology ser 7 1966.
Borzoi anthology of 17th-century English literature: poetry. Ed M. K. Starkman 2 vols; prose, ed D. Novarr; literary criticism, ed E. W. Tayler; religious prose, ed A. D. Ferry, New York 1967.
San Fernando Valley State College Renaissance editions. Northridge Cal 1969–.
English recusant prose. Menston 1970–. Facs of 300 vols listed in Allison and Rogers, Catalogue of Catholic books 1558–1640.

(3) LITERARY HISTORY AND CRITICISM

Fuller, T. The history of the Worthies of England. 1662.
Walton, I. The lives of Donne, Wotton, Hooker, Herbert. 1670.
Phillips, E. Theatrum poetarum: or a complete collection of the poets of all ages, particularly those of our own nation. 1675; ed S. E. Brydges, Canterbury 1800, Hildesheim 1970.
Winstanley, W. The lives of the most famous English poets. 1687; ed W. R. Parker, Gainesville 1963 (facs).
Blount, T. P. Censura celebriorum authorum. 1690.
—— De re poetica. 1694.

Warton, T. The history of English poetry from the close of the 11th to the commencement of the 18th century. 3 vols 1774–81; rev W. C. Hazlitt 4 vols 1871, New York 1968. Completed to c. 1600.
Aubrey, J. Lives. 1813.
Hazlitt, W. Lectures on the English poets. 1818.
—— Lectures on the literature of the age of Elizabeth. 1820.
Willmott, R. E. Lives of the English sacred poets. 2 vols 1834–9. With a survey of English sacred poetry.
Coleridge, S. T. Literary remains. Ed H. N. Coleridge 4 vols 1836–9.

—— Coleridge on the seventeenth century. Ed R. F. Brinkley, Durham NC 1955.

Hallam, H. Introduction to the literature of Europe 15th–17th centuries. 4 vols 1837–9.

Gosse, E. W. Seventeenth-century studies: a contribution to the history of English poetry. 1883.

—— From Shakespeare to Pope. Cambridge 1885, New York 1968.

—— The Jacobean poets. 1894.

Saintsbury, G. A history of Elizabethan literature. 1887.

—— A history of criticism and literary taste in Europe. 3 vols Edinburgh 1900–4.

—— The earlier Renaissance. Edinburgh 1901.

—— A history of English criticism: being the English chapters of A history of criticism and literary taste in Europe, revised, adapted and supplemented. Edinburgh 1911.

Schelling, F. E. Poetic and verse criticism of the reign of Elizabeth. Philadelphia 1891, New York 1965.

—— The Queen's progress and other Elizabethan sketches. Boston 1904.

—— English literature during the lifetime of Shakespeare. New York 1910, 1927 (rev).

Jusserand, J. J. Histoire littéraire du peuple anglais. 2 vols Paris 1894–1904; tr 3 vols 1895–1909, 1926 (rev). To the Civil War.

Hannay, D. The later Renaissance. Edinburgh 1898.

Spingarn, J. E. A history of literary criticism in the Renaissance. New York 1899; tr Italian, 1905 (rev and enlarged), tr 1908; ed B. Weinberg, New York 1963.

Smith, G. G. The transition period. Edinburgh 1900.

Lee, S. Great Englishmen of the 16th century. New York 1904.

—— Elizabethan and other essays. Oxford 1929.

Wendell, B. The temper of the 17th century in English literature. New York 1904.

Greg, W. W. Pastoral poetry and pastoral drama. 1906, New York 1959.

Grierson, H. J. C. The first half of the 17th century. Edinburgh 1906.

Swinburne, A. C. The age of Shakespeare. 1908.

Mackail, J. W. The springs of Helicon: the progress of English poetry from Chaucer to Milton. New York 1909, Lincoln Nebraska 1962.

Robertson, J. M. Elizabethan literature. 1914.

Krapp, G. P. The rise of English literary prose. New York 1915.

Berdan, J. M. Early Tudor poetry 1485–1547. New York 1920, Hamden Conn 1961.

Thompson, E. N. S. Literary bypaths of the Renaissance. New Haven 1924.

Legouis, E. The Middle Ages and the Renascence 650–1660. Vol 1 of A history of English literature, with L. Cazamian, 2 vols 1926–7. Tr from French (Paris 1924)

Williamson, G. The Donne tradition: a study in English poetry from Donne to the death of Cowley. Cambridge Mass 1930.

—— Seventeenth-century contexts. 1960, 1969 (rev).

—— The proper wit of poetry. 1961.

—— Milton and others. 1965.

Chambers, R. W. On the continuity of English prose from Alfred to More and his school. In N. Harpsfield, The life and death of Sir Thomas More, ed E. V. Hitchcock 1932 (EETS), 1950 (separately).

Garvin, K. (ed). The great Tudors. 1935.

Dunn, E. C. The literature of Shakespeare's England. New York 1936.

Pinto, V. de S. The English Renaissance 1510–1688. 1938, 1951 (rev), 1966 (rev, with new ch on Literature and music by B. Pattison).

Baldwin, C. S. Renaissance literary theory and practice 1400–1600. New York 1939, Gloucester Mass 1959.

Sharp, R. L. From Donne to Dryden: the revolt against metaphysical poetry. Chapel Hill 1940, Hamden Conn 1965.

Sweeting, E. J. Early Tudor criticism, linguistic and literary. Oxford 1940, New York 1964.

Bush, D. English literature in the earlier seventeenth century 1600–60. Oxford 1945 (OHEL), 1962 (rev). With a comprehensive bibliography.

Hall, V. Renaissance literary criticism: a study of its social content. New York 1945, Gloucester Mass 1959.

Wilson, F. P. Elizabethan and Jacobean. Oxford 1945.

—— Seventeenth-century prose. Cambridge 1960.

Knights, L. C. Explorations: essays in criticism mainly on the literature of the 17th century. 1946.

—— Further explorations. 1965.

Atkins, J. W. H. English literary criticism: the Renascence. 1947.

—— English literary criticism: 17th and 18th centuries. 1951.

Brooke, T. The Renaissance 1500–1660. In A literary history of England, ed A. C. Baugh, New York 1948, 1967 (with bibliographical suppl) (with M. A. Shaaber).

—— Essays on Shakespeare and other Elizabethans. New Haven 1948.

Craig, H. The literature of the English Renaissance. Pt 2 of A history of English literature, ed Craig, New York 1950, 1962 (rev).

Mahood, M. M. Poetry and humanism. 1950.

Wedgwood, C. V. Seventeenth-century English literature. Oxford 1950 (Home Univ Lib), 1970 (rev).

Danby, J. F. Poets on fortune's hill. 1952, 1965 (as Elizabethan and Jacobean poets).

Smith, H. Elizabethan poetry: a study in conventions, meaning and expression. Cambridge Mass 1952, Ann Arbor 1968.

Cruttwell, P. The Shakespearean moment and its place in the poetry of the 17th century. 1954.

Lewis, C. S. English literature in the sixteenth century, excluding drama. Oxford 1954 (OHEL). With a full bibliography.

Evans, M. English poetry in the 16th century. 1955, 1967 (rev).

Ford, B. (ed). A guide to English literature vol 2: The age of Shakespeare; vol 3: From Donne to Marvell. 1955 (Penguin), 1962 (rev).

Walton, G. Metaphysical to Augustan: studies in tone and sensibility in the 17th century. 1955.

Tillyard, E. M. W. The Metaphysicals and Milton. 1956.

Morris, H. Elizabethan literature. Oxford 1958 (Home Univ Lib).

Mason, H. A. Humanism and poetry in the early Tudor period. 1959.

Ellrodt, R. Les poètes métaphysiques anglais. 3 vols Paris 1960.

Alvarez, A. The school of Donne. 1961.

Kawasaki, T. From Southwell to Donne. Stud in Eng Lit (Tokyo) 39 1961.

Levin, H. English literature and the Renaissance. In The Renaissance, ed T. Helton, Madison 1961.

Bradner, L. From Petrarch to Shakespeare. In The Renaissance: a symposium, New York 1953, 1962 (as The Renaissance: six essays by W. K. Ferguson et al).

Keast, W. R. (ed). Seventeenth-century English poetry: modern essays in criticism. New York 1962.

Buxton, J. Elizabethan taste. 1963.

—— A tradition of poetry. 1967.

Barker, A. An apology for the study of Renaissance poetry. In Literary views, ed C. Camden, Chicago 1964.

Checksfield, M. M. Portraits of Renaissance life and thought. 1964.

Schlauch, M. Antecedents of the English novel 1400–1600: from Chaucer to Deloney. Warsaw 1963.

King, J. R. Studies in six 17th-century writers. Athens Ohio 1966.

Poirier, M. Précis d'anglais élisabéthain. Paris 1966.

Muir, K. Introduction to Elizabethan literature. New York 1967.

Adolph, R. The rise of modern prose style. Cambridge Mass 1968.

Grundy, J. The Spenserian poets: a study in Elizabethan and Jacobean poetry. 1969.

Inglis, F. The Elizabethan poets: the making of English poetry from Wyatt to Jonson. 1969.

Dorsten, J. A. van. The radical arts: first decade of an Elizabethan Renaissance. 1970.

Ricks, C. (ed). English poetry and prose 1540–1674. 1970.

Special Studies

Harrison, J. S. Platonism in English poetry of the 16th and 17th centuries. New York 1903, 1965.

Moorman, F. W. The interpretation of nature in English poetry from Beowulf to Shakespeare. Strasbourg 1905.

Robin, P. A. The old physiology in English literature. 1911.

Miller, G. M. The historical point of view in English literary criticism from 1570–1770. Heidelberg 1913, Amsterdam 1967.

Cooper, C. B. Some Elizabethan opinions of the poetry and character of Ovid. Menasha 1914.

Thompson, G. A. Elizabethan criticism of poetry. Menasha 1914.

Tatlock, J. S. P. The siege of Troy in Elizabethan literature. PMLA 30 1915.

Shafer, R. The English ode to 1660. Princeton 1918, New York 1966.

Crane, R. S. The vogue of medieval chivalric romance during the English Renaissance. Menasha 1919.

Thompson, E. N. S. Mysticism in 17th-century literature. SP 18 1921.

— The 17th century English essay. Iowa City 1926, New York 1967.

Clark, D. L. Rhetoric and poetry in the Renaissance. New York 1922, 1963.

— Ancient rhetoric and English Renaissance literature. Shakespeare Quart 2 1951.

Willey, B. Tendencies in Renaissance literary theory. Cambridge 1922.

— The seventeenth-century background: studies in the thought of the age in relation to poetry and religion. 1934, New York 1953.

Schirmer, W. F. Antike, Renaissance und Puritanismus: eine Studie zur englischen Literaturgeschichte des 16 und 17 Jahrhunderts. Munich 1924, 1933 (rev).

Wyld, H. C. Studies in English rhymes from Surrey to Pope. 1923, New York 1965.

— Some aspects of the diction of English poetry. Oxford 1933.

Camp, C. W. The artisan in Elizabethan literature. New York 1923.

Wells, H. W. Poetic imagery illustrated from Elizabethan literature. New York 1924.

Hendrichs, D. Geschichte der englischen Autobiographie von Chaucer bis Milton. Leipzig 1925.

Renwick, W. L. Edmund Spenser: an essay on Renaissance poetry. 1925.

Schoell, F. L. L'Hellénisme français en Angleterre à la fin de la Renaissance. Revue de Littérature Comparée 5 1925.

— Etudes sur l'humanisme continental en Angleterre à la fin de la Renaissance. Paris 1926.

Conley, C. H. The first English translators of the classics. New Haven 1927.

Grierson, H. J. C. Cross currents in English literature of the xviith century. 1929, New York 1958.

Holmes, E. Aspects of Elizabethan imagery. Oxford 1929, New York 1966.

Empson, W. Seven types of ambiguity. 1930, 1947 (rev).

— Some versions of pastoral. 1935.

Schütt, M. Die englische Biographik der Tudor-zeit. Hamburg 1930; suppl for 1603–40, Anglia 81 1963.

Stauffer, D. A. English biography before 1700. Cambridge Mass 1930, New York 1964.

Matthiessen, F. O. Translation: an Elizabethan art. Cambridge Mass 1931.

White, H. C. English devotional literature (prose) 1600–40. Madison 1931.

— Sixteenth-century English devotional literature. In J. Q. Adams memorial studies, Washington 1948.

— Social criticism in popular religious literature of the 16th century. New York 1944, 1965.

Bush, D. Mythology and the Renaissance tradition in English poetry. Minneapolis 1932, New York 1957, 1963 (rev).

— Classical influences in Renaissance literature. Cambridge Mass 1952.

— Themes and variations in English poetry of the Renaissance. Claremont Cal 1957.

— Science and literature. In Seventeenth-century science and arts, ed H. H. Rhys, Princeton 1961.

— The isolation of the Renaissance hero. In Reason and the imagination, ed J. A. Mazzeo, New York 1962.

— Prefaces to Renaissance literature. Cambridge Mass 1965.

— The Renaissance: the literary climate. In The Renaissance image of man and the world, ed B. O'Kelly, Columbus 1966.

— Pagan myth and Christian tradition in English poetry. Philadelphia 1968.

Friederich, W. P. Spiritualismus und Sensualismus in der englischen Barocklyrik. Vienna 1932.

Maynard, K. Science in early English literature 1550–1650. Isis 17 1932.

Knight, G. W. The Christian Renaissance. Toronto 1933.

Mohl, R. The three estates in medieval and Renaissance literature. New York 1933, 1962.

Pearson, L. E. Elizabethan love conventions. Berkeley 1933, New York 1967.

Ball, L. F. The background of the minor English Renaissance epics. ELH 1 1934.

Harrison, C. T. The ancient atomists and English literature of the 17th century. Harvard Stud in Classical Philology 45 1934.

Hornbeak, K. G. The complete letter writer in English 1568–1800. Smith College Stud in Modern Langs 15 1934.

Nowak, L. G. J. Die Alchemie und die Alchemisten in der englischen Literatur. Breslau 1934.

Mason, J. E. Gentlefolk in the making: English courtesy literature 1531–1774. Philadelphia 1935.

White, H. O. Plagiarism and imitation during the English Renaissance. Cambridge Mass 1935, New York 1965.

Allen, D. C. Symbolic color in the literature of the English Renaissance. PQ 15 1936.

— Image and meaning: metaphoric traditions in Renaissance poetry. Baltimore 1960, 1968 (enlarged).

Lewis, C. S. The allegory of love: a study in medieval tradition. Oxford 1936, 1938 (corrected).

— Donne and love poetry in the 17th century. In Seventeenth-century studies presented to Sir Herbert Grierson, Oxford 1938.

— De descriptione temporum. Cambridge 1955.

— The discarded image: an introduction to medieval and Renaissance literature. Cambridge 1964.

— Studies in medieval and Renaissance literature. Cambridge 1966.

Struck, W. Der Einfluss Jakob Boehmes auf die englische Literatur des 17 Jahrhunderts. Berlin 1936.

Clark, E. G. Ralegh and Marlowe: a study in Elizabethan fustian. New York 1937, 1941 (rev).

Crane, W. G. Wit and rhetoric in the Renaissance. New York 1937, Gloucester Mass 1964.

Mills, L. J. One soul in bodies twain: friendship in Tudor literature and Stuart drama. Bloomington 1937.

Hughes, M. Y. The Christ of Paradise regained and the Renaissance heroic tradition. SP 35 1938.

— Spenser's Acrasia and the Circe of the Renaissance. JHI 4 1943.

Sauer, P. von R. English metrical psalms 1600–60: a study in the religious and aesthetic tendencies of that period. Freiburg 1938.

Wright, C. T. The usurer's sin in Elizabethan literature. SP 35 1938.

— The Amazons in Elizabethan literature. SP 37 1940.

Baker, C. D. Certain religious elements in the English doctrine of the inspired poet during the Renaissance. ELH 6 1939.

McEuen, K. A. Classical influence upon the tribe of Ben. Cedar Rapids 1939, New York 1968.

Winters, Y. The 16th-century lyric in England: a critical and historical reinterpretation. Poetry 53–4 1939.

Cawley, R. R. Unpathed waters: studies in the influence of the voyagers on Elizabethan literature. Princeton 1940, New York 1967.

Jonas, L. The divine science: the aesthetic of some representative 17th-century English poets. New York 1940.

Rubel, V. L. Poetic diction in the English Renaissance. New York 1941.

Wilson, H. S. Some meanings of 'nature' in Renaissance literary theory. JHI 2 1941.

Robertson, J. The art of letter writing: an essay on the handbooks published in England during the 16th and 17th centuries. Liverpool 1942.

Daniells, R. Baroque form in English literature. UTQ 14 1945.

— English baroque and deliberate obscurity. Jnl of Aesthetics 5 1947.

— The mannerist element in English literature. UTQ 36 1967.

Funke, O. Probleme des englischen Literaturbarock. In his Wege und Ziele, Berne 1945.

Nearing, H. English historical poetry 1599–1641. Philadelphia 1945.

Doughty, W. L. Studies in religious poetry of the 17th century. 1946, Port Washington NY 1969.

Smith, H. English metrical psalms in the 16th century and their literary significance. HLQ 9 1946.

Perkinson, R. H. The epic in five acts. SP 43 1946.

Boas, F. S. Ovid and the Elizabethans. 1947 (Eng Assoc).

Boyce, B. The Theophrastan character in England to 1642. Cambridge Mass 1947.

— The polemic character 1640–61. Lincoln Nebraska 1955, New York 1969.

Heltzel, V. B. Fair Rosamond: a study of the development of a literary theme. Evanston 1947.

McLennen, J. On the meaning and function of allegory in the English Renaissance. Univ of Michigan Contributions in Modern Philology no 6 1947.

Mincoff, M. Baroque literature in England. Annuaire de l'Université de Sofia, Faculté Historico-philologique 43 1947.

Miriam Joseph, Sr. Shakespeare's use of the arts of language. New York 1947. Pt 1 pbd as Rhetoric in Shakespeare's time: literary theory of Renaissance Europe, New York 1962.

Tuve, R. Elizabethan and metaphysical imagery: Renaissance poetic and 20th-century critics. Chicago 1947.

— Allegorical imagery: some mediaeval books and their posterity. Princeton 1966.

Husain, I. The mystical element in the metaphysical poets of the 17th century. Edinburgh 1948.

Miles, J. The primary language of poetry in the 1640's. Univ of California Pbns in Eng 19 1948; rptd in her Continuity of poetic language, Berkeley 1951.

— Renaissance, 18th-century and modern language in English poetry: a tabular view. Berkeley 1960.

Pattison, B. Music and poetry of the English Renaissance. 1948.

Southern, A. C. Elizabethan recusant prose 1559–82: an historical and critical account of the books of the Catholic refugees. 1950.

Wallerstein, R. C. Studies in 17th-century poetic. Madison 1950.

Zocca, L. R. Elizabethan narrative poetry. New Brunswick NJ 1950.

Allison, A. W. Poetry and rhetoric: in defence of Elizabethan criticism. In English studies in honor of J. S. Wilson, Charlottesville 1951.

Babb, L. The Elizabethan malady: a study of melancholia in English literature 1580–1642. East Lansing 1951.

Bennett, J. W. Genre, milieu and the 'epic-romance'. Eng Inst Essays 1951.

Saunders, J. W. The stigma of print: the social bases of Tudor poetry. EC 1 1951.

— The social situation of 17th-century poetry. In Metaphysical poetry, ed M. Bradbury and D. Palmer 1970.

Williamson, G. The Senecan amble: a study in prose form from Bacon to Collier. Chicago 1951.

Chapman, R. Fortune and mutability in Elizabethan literature. Cambridge Jnl March 1952.

Kermode, F. (ed). English pastoral poetry from the beginnings to Marvell. 1952. With an introd on the Renaissance pastoral.

— The banquet of sense. Bull John Rylands Lib 44 1962; rptd in his Shakespeare, Spenser, Donne, 1971.

Wiley, M. L. The subtle knot: creative scepticism in 17th-century England. 1952.

— Creative sceptics. 1966.

Evans, M. Metaphor and symbol in the 16th century. EC 3 1953. Reply by D. S. Brewer 4 1954.

Higgins, A. I. T. Secular heroic epic poetry of the Caroline period. Berne 1953.

Stevenson, H. A. The major Elizabethan poets and the doctrine of signatures. Florida State Univ Stud no 5 1953.

Baldini, G. Caratteri e personaggi e altri studi sulla poesia e la poetica del Rinascimento inglese. Naples 1954.

Carroll, W. M. Animal conventions in English Renaissance non-religious prose 1550–1600. New York 1954.

Davie, D. Sixteenth-century poetry and the common reader: the case of Thomas Sackville. EC 4 1954. Replies by J. B. Broadbent, Davie and F. W. Bateson, ibid.

Dickson, S. A. Panacea or precious bane: tobacco in 16th-century literature. New York 1954.

Doran, M. Endeavors of art: a study of form in Elizabethan drama. Madison 1954.

Martz, L. L. The poetry of meditation: a study in English religious literature of the 17th century. New Haven 1954, 1962 (rev).

— The paradise within: studies in Vaughan, Traherne and Milton. New Haven 1964.

— The wit of love: Donne, Carew, Crashaw, Marvell. South Bend 1969.

— The action of the self: devotional poetry in the 17th century. In Metaphysical poetry, ed M. Bradbury and D. Palmer 1970.

Røstvig, M.-S. The happy man: studies in the metamorphoses of a classical ideal vol 1 [1600–1700]. Oslo 1954, 1962 (rev).

— et al. The hidden sense and other essays. Oslo 1963. On numerical composition in Milton and other Renaissance poets. Replies by D. Bush, Stud in Eng Lit 1500–1900 6 1966, and by Røstvig 7 1967.

Røstvig, M.-S. Renaissance numerology: acrostics or criticism. EC 16 1966.

Ross, M. M. Poetry and dogma: the transfiguration of eucharistic symbols in 17th-century English poetry. New Brunswick NJ 1954.

Stanford, W. B. The Ulysses theme: a study in the adaptability of a traditional hero. Oxford 1954, 1963 (rev).

Tillyard, E. M. W. The English epic and its background. 1954.

— Reality and fantasy in Elizabethan literature. In Sprache und Literatur Englands und Amerikas, ed C. A. Weber et al, Tübingen 1956.

— Some mythical elements in English literature. 1961.

Wright, H. G. The theme of solitude and retirement in 17th-century literature. Etudes Anglaises 7 1954.
— Boccaccio in England from Chaucer to Tennyson. 1957.
Esch, A. Englische religiöse Lyrik des 17 Jahrhunderts: Studien zu Donne, Herbert, Crashaw, Vaughan. Tübingen 1955.
Groom, B. The diction of poetry from Spenser to Bridges. Toronto 1955.
Sells, A. L. Animal poetry in French and English literature and the Greek tradition. Indiana Univ Pbns, Humanities ser no 35 1955.
— The Italian influence in English poetry from Chaucer to Southwell. 1955.
Starnes, De W. and E. W. Talbert. Classical myth and legend in Renaissance dictionaries. Chapel Hill 1955.
Ashton, J. W. Folklore in the literature of Elizabethan England. Jnl of Amer Folklore 70 1956.
Harrison, T. P. They tell of birds: Chaucer, Spenser, Milton, Drayton. Austin 1956.
Hart, E. F. The answer-poem of the early 17th century. RES new ser 7 1956.
Hibbard, G. R. The country house poem of the 17th century. Jnl Warburg & Courtauld Inst 19 1956.
Lever, J. W. The Elizabethan love sonnet. 1956.
Malloch, A. E. The techniques and function of the Renaissance paradox. SP 53 1956.
Miller, H. K. The paradoxical encomium with special reference to its vogue in England 1600–1800. MP 53 1956.
Milner, R. Music and poetry in the 16th century. Etudes Anglaises 9 1956.
O'Brien, G. W. Renaissance poetics and the problem of power. Chicago 1956.
Peter, J. Complaint and satire in early English literature. Oxford 1956.
Stamm, R. Englischer Literaturbarock? In Die Kunstformen des Barockzeitalters, ed Stamm, Munich 1956.
Enkvist, N. E. The seasons of the year: chapters on a motif from Beowulf to the Shepherd's calendar. Helsinki 1957.
Bottrall, M. Every man a phoenix: studies in 17th-century autobiography. 1958.
Miller, P. W. The Elizabethan minor epic. SP 55 1958. Reply by W. Allen, The non-existent classical epyllion, ibid.
Praz, M. The flaming heart: essays on Crashaw, Machiavelli and other studies in the relations between Italian and English literature from Chaucer to T. S. Eliot. New York 1958, Gloucester Mass 1966.
Staton, W. P. The characters of style in Elizabethan prose. JEGP 57 1958.
Benjamin, E. B. Fame, poetry, and the order of history in the literature of the English Renaissance. Stud in Renaissance 6 1959.
Campbell, L. B. Divine poetry and drama in 16th-century England. Cambridge 1959.
Kurth, B. O. Milton and Christian heroism: biblical epic themes and forms in 17th-century England. Univ of California Pbns in Eng 20 1959.
Lascelles, M. The rider on the winged horse: the poet upon Pegasus as a theme in the Renaissance. In Elizabethan and Jacobean studies presented to F. P. Wilson, Oxford 1959.
Marsh, T. N. Elizabethan ceremony in literature and in the wilderness. Eng Miscellany (Rome) 10 1959.
— Elizabethan wit in metaphor and conceit: Sidney, Shakespeare, Donne. Eng Miscellany (Rome) 13 1962.
Miller, E. H. The professional writer in Elizabethan England: a study of nondramatic literature. Cambridge Mass 1959.
McNamee, M. B. Honor and the epic hero: a study of the shifting concept of magnanimity in philosophy and epic poetry. New York 1960.

Richmond, H. M. Polyphemus in England: a study in comparative literature. Comparative Lit 12 1960.
— 'Rural lyricism': a Renaissance mutation of the pastoral. Comparative Lit 16 1964.
Watson, C. B. Shakespeare and the Renaissance concept of honor. Princeton 1960.
Wedgwood, C. V. Poetry and politics under the Stuarts. Cambridge 1960.
Heninger, S. K. The Renaissance perversion of pastoral. JHI 22 1961.
Janelle, P. English devotional literature in the 16th and 17th centuries. In English studies today: second series, ed G. A. Bonnard, Berne 1961.
Knox, N. The word 'irony' and its context 1500–1755. Durham NC 1961.
Lievsay, J. L. Stefano Guazzo and the English Renaissance 1575–1675. Chapel Hill 1961.
Liljegren, S. B. Studies on the origin and early tradition of English utopian fiction. Upsala 1961.
Sasek, L. A. The literary temper of the English Puritans. Baton Rouge 1961.
Stein, A. On Elizabethan wit. Stud in Eng Lit 1500–1900 1 1961.
Stevens, J. Music and poetry in the early Tudor Court. 1961.
Thompson, J. The founding of English metre. New York 1961.
Bullough, G. Mirror of minds: changing psychological beliefs in English poetry. Toronto 1962.
Hardison, O. B., jr. The enduring monument: a study of the idea of praise in Renaissance literary theory and practice. Chapel Hill 1962.
Steadman, J. M. Felicity and end in Renaissance epic and ethics. JHI 23 1962.
— Achilles and Renaissance epic: moral criticism and literary tradition. In Lebende Antike: Symposion für R. Sühnel, Berlin 1967.
Swardson, H. R. Poetry and the fountain of light: the conflict between Christian and classical traditions in 17th-century poetry. 1962.
Talbert, E. W. The problem of order: Elizabethan political commonplaces and an example of Shakespeare's art. Chapel Hill 1962.
— Mythological allusion and mythological moral. Renaissance Papers 1965.
Waith, E. M. The Herculean hero in Marlowe, Chapman, Shakespeare and Dryden. New York 1962.
Greene, T. M. The descent from heaven: a study in epic continuity. New Haven 1963.
— The flexibility of the self in Renaissance literature. In The disciplines of criticism, ed P. Demetz et al, New Haven 1968.
Hamilton, K. G. The two harmonies: poetry and prose in the 17th century. Oxford 1963.
Kaiser, W. J. Praisers of folly: Erasmus, Rabelais, Shakespeare. Cambridge Mass 1963.
Klein, D. The Elizabethan dramatists as critics. New York 1963.
Petti, A. G. Beasts and politics in Elizabethan literature. E & S new ser 16 1963.
Sowton, I. Hidden persuaders as a means of literary grace: 16th-century poetics and rhetoric in England. UTQ 32 1963.
Broadbent, J. B. Poetic love. 1964.
Dundas, J. Allegory as a form of wit. Stud in Renaissance 11 1964.
Fisch, H. Jerusalem and Albion: the Hebraic factor in 17th-century literature. 1964.
Fletcher, A. Allegory: the theory of a symbolic mode. Ithaca 1964.
Hägin, P. The epic hero and the decline of heroic poetry. Berne 1964.
Hirst, D. Hidden riches: traditional symbolism from the Renaissance to Blake. 1964.

Phillips, J. E. Images of a Queen: Mary Stuart in 16th-century literature. Berkeley 1964.

Schlüter, K. Die englische Ode: Studien zur ihrer Entwicklung unter dem Einfluss der antiken Hymne. Bonn 1964.

Tayler, E. W. Nature and art in Renaissance literature. New York 1964.

Berger, H., jr. The Renaissance imagination: second world and green world. Centennial Rev 9 1965.

Durling, R. M. The figure of the poet in Renaissance epic. Cambridge Mass 1965.

McCoy, D. S. Tradition and convention: a study of periphrasis in English pastoral poetry 1557–1715. Hague 1965, New York 1966.

Mellers, W. Harmonious meeting: a study of the relationship between English music, poetry and theatre c. 1600–1900. 1965.

Scoular, K. W. Natural magic: studies in the presentation of nature in English poetry from Spenser to Marvell. Oxford 1965.

Smith, A. J. Theory and practice in Renaissance poetry: two kinds of imitation. Bull John Rylands Lib 47 1965.

—— The failure of love: love lyrics after Donne. In Metaphysical poetry, ed M. Bradbury and D. Palmer 1970.

Stürzl, E. Der Zeitbegriff in der elisabethanischen Literatur: the lackey of eternity. Vienna 1965.

Woodhouse, A. S. P. The poet and his faith: religion and poetry in England from Spenser to Eliot and Auden. Chicago 1965.

Colie, R. L. Paradoxia epidemica: the Renaissance tradition of paradox. Princeton 1966.

Croll, M. W. Style, rhetoric, and rhythm. Ed J. M. Patrick et al, Princeton 1966. Selections from this collection on Renaissance prose style pbd as 'Attic' and baroque prose style: the anti-Ciceronian movement, Princeton 1966.

Giamatti, A. B. The earthly paradise and the Renaissance epic. Princeton 1966.

—— Proteus unbound: some versions of the sea god in the Renaissance. In The disciplines of criticism, ed P. Demetz et al, New Haven 1968.

LaGuardia, E. Nature redeemed: the imitation of order in three Renaissance poems. Hague 1966.

McNeir, W. Trial by combat in Elizabethan literature. Die Neueren Sprachen 15 1966.

Stewart, S. The enclosed garden: the tradition and the image in 17th-century poetry. Madison 1966.

Clemen, W. Donne and the Elizabethans. In Art, science and history in the Renaissance, ed C. S. Singleton, Baltimore 1967.

Dunlap, R. The allegorical interpretation of Renaissance literature. PMLA 82 1967.

Gottfried, R. Autobiography and art: an Elizabethan borderland. In Literary criticism and historical understanding, ed P. Damon, New York 1967.

Jack, R. D. James VI and Renaissance poetic theory. English 16 1967.

Nuttall, A. D. Two concepts of allegory: a study of Shakespeare's The tempest and the logic of allegorical expression. 1967.

Peterson, D. L. The English lyric from Wyatt to Donne: a history of the plain and eloquent styles. Princeton 1967.

Vinge, L. The Narcissus theme in western European literature up to the early 19th century. Lund 1967.

Webber, J. The eloquent 'I': style and self in 17th-century prose. Madison 1968.

Delany, P. British autobiography in the 17th century. 1969. With list of 17th-century autobiographies.

LaBranche, A. Poetry, history and oratory: the Renaissance historical poem. Stud in Eng Lit 1500–1900 9 1969.

Levin, H. The myth of the golden age in the Renaissance. Bloomington 1969.

Miner, E. The metaphysical mode from Donne to Cowley. Princeton 1969.

Mulder, J. R. The temple of the mind: education and literary taste in 17th-century England. New York 1969.

Murrin, M. The veil of allegory: allegorical rhetoric in the English Renaissance. Chicago 1969.

Fraser, R. The war against poetry. Princeton 1970.

Halewood, W. H. The poetry of grace: Reformation themes and structures in English 17th-century poetry. New Haven 1970.

Hinman, R. B. The apotheosis of Faust: poetry and the new philosophy in the 17th century. In Metaphysical poetry, ed M. Bradbury and D. Palmer 1970.

Vickers, B. Classical rhetoric in English poetry. 1970.

(4) GENERAL BACKGROUND

The following selective list includes studies of the European Renaissance which relate to English.

Burckhardt, J. Die Cultur der Renaissance in Italien. Basle 1860; tr 1878.

Pater, W. Studies in the history of the Renaissance. 1873, 1888 (rev as The Renaissance: studies in art and poetry).

Einstein, L. The Italian Renaissance in England. New York 1902, 1962.

—— Tudor ideals. New York 1921, 1962.

Bayley, H. A new light on the Renaissance displayed in contemporary emblems. 1909, New York 1967.

Sheavyn, P. The literary profession in the Elizabethan age. Manchester 1909, New York 1964; rev J. W. Saunders, Manchester 1967.

Jones, R. M. Spiritual reformers in the 16th and 17th centuries. 1914, Boston 1959.

Heide, A. v. der. Das Naturgefühl in der englischen Dichtung im Zeitalter Miltons. Heidelberg 1915.

Rick, L. Ovids Metamorphosen in der englischen Renaissance. Münster 1915.

Adams, E. N. Old English scholarship in England 1566–1800. New Haven 1917.

Schroeder, C. Platonismus in der englischen Renaissance. Berlin 1920.

Taylor, H. O. Thought and expression in the 16th century. 2 vols New York 1920, 1959 (rev).

Hearnshaw, F. J. C. et al. The social and political ideas of some great thinkers of the Renaissance and the Reformation. 1925, New York 1949, 1926 (with suppl on 16th–17th centuries), 1949.

Anderson, R. L. Elizabethan psychology and Shakespeare's plays. Univ Iowa Humanistic Stud 3 1927.

Cassirer, E. The individual and the cosmos in Renaissance philosophy. New York 1963. Tr from German (Leipzig 1927).

—— The Platonic Renaissance in England. Austin 1953. Tr from German (Leipzig 1932).

Allen, J. W. A history of political thought in the 16th century. 1928, 1957 (with rev bibliography).

—— English political thought 1603–60. Vol 1 (all pbd), 1938.

Kelso, R. The doctrine of the English gentleman in the 16th century. Univ Illinois Stud in Lang & Lit 14 1929.

—— Doctrine for the lady of the Renaissance. Urbana 1956. Both with bibliographies.

Shackford, M. H. Plutarch in Renaissance England. 1929.

Adamson, J. W. The extent of literacy in England in the 15th and 16th centuries. Library 4th ser 10 1930.

Bundy, M. W. 'Invention' and 'imagination' in the Renaissance. JEGP 29 1930.

Latham, M. W. The Elizabethan fairies. New York 1930.

Brinkley, R. F. Arthurian legend in the 17th century. Baltimore 1932, London 1967.

Buckley, G. T. Atheism in the English Renaissance. Chicago 1932, New York 1965.

Dannenberg, F. Das Erbe Platons in England bis zur Bildung Lylys. Berlin 1932.

Jordan, W. K. The development of religious toleration in England from the beginning of the English Reformation to the Restoration. 4 vols 1932–8, Gloucester Mass 1965.

Mitchell, W. F. English pulpit oratory from Andrewes to Tillotson: a study of its literary aspects. 1932, New York 1962. With a select bibliography.

Nelson, N. Individualism as a criterion of the Renaissance. JEGP 32 1933.

Bredvold, L. I. The intellectual milieu of Dryden: studies in some aspects of 17th-century thought. Ann Arbor 1934.

Harrison, G. B. Books and readers 1599–1603. Library 4th ser 14 1933.

More, P. E. and F. L. Cross (ed). Anglicanism: the thought and practice of the Church of England, illustrated from the religious literature of the 17th century. 1935.

Nicolson, M. H. The microscope and the English imagination. Smith College Stud in Modern Langs 16 1935.

—— A world in the moon: a study of the changing attitude toward the moon in the 17th and 18th centuries. Smith College Stud in Modern Langs 17 1936.

—— Voyages to the moon. New York 1948, 1960.

—— The breaking of the circle: studies in the effect of the 'new science' upon 17th-century poetry. Evanston 1950, New York 1960 (rev).

—— Science and imagination. Ithaca 1956. On effect of the telescope and microscope on the literary imagination.

—— The discovery of space. In Medieval and Renaissance studies, ed O. B. Hardison jr, Chapel Hill 1966.

Robb, N. Neoplatonism of the Italian Renaissance. 1935.

Williamson, G. Mutability, decay and 17th-century melancholy. ELH 2 1935.

Wright, L. B. Middle-class culture in Elizabethan England. Chapel Hill 1935, Ithaca 1958.

—— The significance of religious writings in the English Renaissance. JHI 1 1940.

—— and V. A. LaMar (ed). Life and letters in Tudor and Stuart England. Ithaca 1962.

Wright, L. B. (ed). The Elizabethans' America: a collection of early reports by Englishmen on the new world. 1965.

—— The modern relevance of the Renaissance. In Medieval and Renaissance studies, ed O. B. Hardison jr, Chapel Hill 1966.

Bainton, R. H. Changing ideas and ideals in the 16th century. Jnl of Modern History 8 1936.

Bradford, G. Elizabethan women. Ed H. O. White, Cambridge Mass 1936, Freeport NY 1969.

Campbell, L. B. Tudor conceptions of history and tragedy in A mirror for magistrates. Berkeley 1936.

—— The use of historical patterns in the reign of Elizabeth. HLQ 1 1938.

Craig, H. The enchanted glass: the Elizabethan mind in literature. New York 1936, Oxford 1950.

—— New lamps for old: a sequel to the Enchanted glass. Oxford 1960.

Jones, R. F. Ancients and moderns: a study of the background of the Battle of the Books. St Louis 1936, 1961 (rev with subtitle A study of the rise of the scientific movement in 17th-century England).

—— et al. The seventeenth-century: studies in the history of English thought and literature from Bacon to Pope. Stanford 1951.

Jones, R. F. The triumph of the English language: a survey of opinions concerning the vernacular from the introduction of printing to the Restoration. Stanford 1953.

—— The humanistic defence of learning in the mid-17th century. In Reason and the imagination, ed J. A. Mazzeo, New York 1962.

—— The rhetoric of science in England of the mid-17th century. In Restoration and 18th-century literature: essays in honor of A. D. McKillop, Chicago 1963.

Lovejoy, A. O. The great chain of being: a study of the history of an idea. Cambridge Mass 1936.

Pickel, M. B. Charles I as patron of poetry and drama. 1936.

Allen, B. S. Tides in English taste 1619–1800: a background for the study of literature. 2 vols Cambridge Mass 1937, New York 1958.

Chew, S. C. The crescent and the rose: Islam and England during the Renaissance. New York 1937.

—— Time and fortune. ELH 6 1939.

—— The virtues reconciled: an iconographic study. Toronto 1947.

—— The pilgrimage of life. New Haven 1962.

[Tillotson, G.] Elizabethan decoration: patterns in art and passion. TLS July 3 1937; rptd in his Essays in criticism and research, Cambridge 1942.

Johnson, F. R. Astronomical thought in Renaissance England. Baltimore 1937.

—— Elizabethan drama and the Elizabethan science of psychology. In English studies today, ed C. L. Wrenn and G. Bullough, Oxford 1951.

Allen, D. C. The degeneration of man and Renaissance pessimism. SP 35 1938.

—— The star-crossed Renaissance: the quarrel about astrology and its influence in England. Durham NC 1941, New York 1966.

—— The rehabilitation of Epicurus and his theory of pleasure in the early Renaissance. SP 41 1944.

—— The legend of Noah: Renaissance rationalism in art, science and letters. Univ Illinois Stud in Lang & Lit 33 1949; Urbana 1963.

—— Some theories of the growth and origin of language in Milton's age. PQ 28 1949.

—— Doubt's boundless sea: skepticism and faith in the Renaissance. Baltimore 1964.

—— The Renaissance looks at comets. In Wingspread lectures in the humanities I, Racine Wis 1966.

—— Mysteriously meant: the rediscovery of pagan symbolism and allegorical interpretation in the Renaissance. Baltimore 1970.

Bush, D. Tudor humanism and Henry VIII. UTQ 7 1938.

—— The Renaissance and English humanism. Toronto 1939, 1956 (rev).

—— Two roads to truth: science and religion in the early 17th century. ELH 8 1941.

Butt, J. The facilities for antiquarian study in the 17th century. E & S 24 1938.

Haller, W. The rise of Puritanism 1570–1643. New York 1938.

—— and M. Haller. The Puritan art of love. HLQ 5 1942.

Haller, W. Liberty and Reformation in the Puritan Revolution. New York 1955.

Woodhouse, A. S. P. Puritanism and democracy. Canadian Jnl of Economics 4 1938.

—— Religion and some foundations of English democracy. Philosophical Rev 61 1952.

Knappen, M. M. Tudor Puritanism: a chapter in the history of idealism. Chicago 1939, 1965.

Miller, P. The New England mind: the 17th century. New York 1939.

Panofsky, E. Studies in iconology: humanistic themes in the art of the Renaissance. New York 1939.

—— Renaissance and renascences in western art. Stockholm 1960, New York 1969.

Praz, M. Studies in seventeenth-century imagery. 2 vols 1939–47, 1 vol Rome 1964 (enlarged). Tr from Studi sul concettismo, Milan 1934.

—— Baroque in England. MP 61 1964.

Seznec, J. La survivance des dieux antiques: essai sur le rôle de la tradition mythologique dans l'humanisme et dans l'art de la Renaissance. 1939; tr and rev as The survival of the pagan gods, New York 1953.

Tuve, R. Ancients, moderns and Saxons. ELH 6 1939.

Wilson, E. C. England's Eliza. Cambridge Mass 1939, New York 1966.

—— Prince Henry and English literature. Ithaca 1946.

Boyd, M. C. Elizabethan music and musical criticism. Philadelphia 1940.

Collins, J. B. Christian mysticism in the Elizabethan age with its background in mystical methodology. Baltimore 1940.

Ferguson, W. K. The Renaissance. New York 1940, 1963.

—— The Renaissance in historical thought: five centuries of interpretation. Cambridge Mass 1948.

—— The interpretation of the Renaissance: suggestions for a synthesis. JHI 12 1951.

—— The Renaissance, a symposium: essays by Ferguson et al. New York 1953, 1962 (as The Renaissance: six essays).

—— The reinterpretation of the Renaissance. In Facets of the Renaissance, ed W. H. Werkmeister, New York 1959.

—— Renaissance studies. Univ Western Ontario Stud in Humanities 2 1963.

Kristeller, P. O. and J. H. Randall jr. The study of the philosophies of the Renaissance. JHI 2 1941.

Kristeller, P. O. The classics and Renaissance thought. Cambridge Mass 1955, New York 1961 (rev and enlarged as Renaissance thought: the classic, scholastic and humanistic strains).

—— Studies in Renaissance thought and letters. Rome 1956.

—— Renaissance Platonism. In Facets of the Renaissance, ed W. H. Werkmeister, New York 1959.

—— Changing views of the intellectual history of the Renaissance since Burckhardt. In The Renaissance, ed T. Helton, Madison 1961.

—— Renaissance thought II: papers on humanism and the arts. New York 1965.

—— Philosophy and humanism in Renaissance perspective. In The Renaissance image of man and the world, ed B. O'Kelly, Columbus 1966.

Williams, A. The two matters: classical and Christian in the Renaissance. SP 38 1941.

Eccles, M. A bibliographical dictionary of Elizabethan authors. HLQ 5 1942. On supplementing DNB.

Renaissance Conference at the Huntington Library: report of discussions. HLQ 5 1942.

Spencer, T. Shakespeare and the nature of man. New York 1942.

—— The Elizabethan malcontent. In J. Q. Adams memorial studies, Washington 1948.

Tillyard, E. M. W. The Elizabethan world picture. 1943.

—— The English Renaissance: fact or fiction? 1952.

Wallace, K. R. Francis Bacon on communication and rhetoric. Chapel Hill 1943.

Baldwin, T. W. William Shakspere's small Latin and lesse Greeke. 2 vols Urbana 1944.

Blau, J. L. The Christian interpretation of the Cabala in the Renaissance. New York 1944, Port Washington NY 1965.

Kernodle, G. R. From art to theater: form and convention in the Renaissance. Chicago 1944.

Weisinger, H. The self-awareness of the Renaissance as a criterion of the Renaissance. Papers of Michigan Acad 29 1944.

—— Ideas of history during the Renaissance. JHI 6 1945.

—— The Renaissance theory of the reaction against the Middle Ages as a cause of the Renaissance. Speculum 20 1945.

—— The 17th-century reputation of the Elizabethans. MLQ 6 1945.

—— Who began the revival of learning? the Renaissance point of view. Papers of Michigan Acad 30 1945.

—— Renaissance accounts of the revival of learning. SP 45 1948.

—— The English origins of the sociological interpretation of the Renaissance. JHI 11 1950.

—— Another theory of the Renaissance. Bucknell Rev 14 1964.

Baumer, F. le V. The conception of Christendom in Renaissance England. JHI 6 1945.

Benesch, O. The art of the Renaissance in northern Europe: its relation to the contemporary spiritual and intellectual movements. Cambridge Mass 1945.

Fink, Z. S. The classical republicans: an essay in the recovery of a pattern of thought in 17th-century England. Evanston 1945.

Craigie, W. A. The critique of pure English from Caxton to Smollett. Oxford 1946.

Dunn, E. C. The concept of ingratitude in Renaissance English moral philosophy. Washington 1946.

Forest, L. C. T. A caveat for critics against invoking Elizabethan psychology. PMLA 61 1946.

Harding, D. P. Milton and the Renaissance Ovid. Univ Illinois Stud in Lang & Lit 30 1946.

Krapp, R. M. Class analysis of a literary controversy: wit and sense in 17th-century English literature. Science & Soc 10 1946.

Starnes, D. T. and G. E. Noyes. The English dictionary from Cawdrey to Johnson 1604–1755. Chapel Hill 1946.

Baker, H. The dignity of man. Cambridge Mass 1947, New York 1961 (as The image of man: the idea of human dignity in classical antiquity, the Middle Ages and the Renaissance).

—— The wars of truth: studies in the decay of Christian humanism in the earlier 17th century. Cambridge Mass 1952.

—— The race of time: three lectures on Renaissance historiography. Toronto 1967.

Dean, L. F. Tudor theories of history writing. Univ of Michigan Contributions in Modern Philology no 1 1947.

Nelson, N. E. Peter Ramus and the confusion of logic, rhetoric and poetry. Univ of Michigan Contributions in Modern Philology no 2 1947.

Yates, F. A. Queen Elizabeth as Astraea. Jnl Warburg & Courtauld Inst 10 1947.

—— Elizabethan chivalry: the romance of the Accession Day tilts. Jnl Warburg & Courtauld Inst 20 1957.

—— Giordano Bruno and the Hermetic tradition. 1964.

—— The art of memory. 1966.

Battenhouse, R. W. The doctrine of man in Calvin and in Renaissance Platonism. JHI 9 1948.

Farnham, W. The mediaeval comic spirit in the English Renaissance. In J. Q. Adams memorial studies, Washington 1948.

Gombrich, E. H. 'Icones symbolicae': the visual symbol in neoplatonic thought. Jnl Warburg & Courtauld Inst 11 1948.

—— Norm and form: studies in the art of the Renaissance. 1966.

Harrison, T. P. The literary background of Renaissance poisons. SE 27 1948.

Freeman, R. English emblem books. 1948, New York 1966.

Lievsay, J. L. Some Renaissance views of Diogenes the Cynic. In J. Q. Adams memorial studies, Washington 1948.

Wilson, F. P. Authors and patrons in Tudor and Stuart times. Ibid.

Harris, V. All coherence gone. Chicago 1949, London 1966. On the Renaissance controversy over the decay of nature.

—— The arts of discourse in England 1500–1700. PQ 37 1958.

Highet, G. The classical tradition: Greek and Roman influences on Western literature. Oxford 1949.

Strathmann, E. A. The idea of progress: some Elizabethan considerations. Renaissance News 2 1949.

Tuveson, E. L. Millennium and Utopia: a study in the background of the idea of progress. Berkeley 1949.

Haydn, H. The Counter-Renaissance. New York 1950.

Kendrick, T. D. British antiquity. 1950.

Parkes, H. B. Nature's diverse laws: the double vision of the Elizabethans. Sewanee Rev 58 1950.

Rowse, A. L. The England of Elizabeth: the structure of society. 1950.

— The Elizabethans and America. 1959.

Sellery, G. C. The Renaissance: its nature and origins. Madison 1950.

Wilkins, E. H. A general survey of Renaissance Petrarchism. Comparative Lit 2 1950.

Bethell, S. L. The cultural revolution of the 17th century. 1951.

Cruttwell, P. Physiology and psychology in Shakespeare's age. JHI 12 1951.

White, H. C. Tudor books of private devotion. Madison 1951.

— Tudor books of saints and martyrs. Madison 1963.

Bamborough, J. B. The little world of man. 1952. On Elizabethan psychology.

Bennett, H. S. English books and readers 1475 to 1557. Cambridge 1952, 1969 (rev).

— English books and readers 1558 to 1603. Cambridge 1965.

— English books and readers 1603 to 1640. Cambridge 1970.

Bernheimer, R. Wild men in the Middle Ages. Cambridge Mass 1952.

Buford, A. H. History and biography: the Renaissance distinction. In A tribute to G. C. Taylor, Chapel Hill 1952.

Camden, C. The Elizabethan woman. Houston 1952.

Janson, H. W. Apes and ape lore in the Middle Ages and the Renaissance. 1952.

Jayne, S. Ficino and the Platonism of the English Renaissance. Comparative Lit 4 1952.

Kliger, S. The Goths in England: a study in 17th- and 18th-century thought. Cambridge Mass 1952.

Parsons, L. Prince Henry as a patron of literature. MLR 47 1952.

Simonini, R. C. Italian scholarship in Renaissance England. Chapel Hill 1952.

Thomson, P. The literature of patronage 1580-1630. EC 2 1952. Replies by J. W. Saunders and K. Muir 3 1953.

Auerbach, E. Mimesis: the representation of reality in Western literature. Princeton 1953. Tr from German (Berne 1946).

— Scenes from the drama of European literature. New York 1959.

Conklin, G. N. Aspects of Renaissance culture. Middletown Conn 1953.

Curtius, E. R. European literature and the Latin Middle Ages. 1953. Tr from German (Berne 1948).

Kocher, P. H. Science and religion in Elizabethan England. San Marino 1953.

Palmer, R. G. Seneca's De remediis fortuitorum and the Elizabethans. Chicago 1953. An edn with an essay on the influence of Seneca's ethical thought in the 16th century.

Bolgar, R. R. The classical heritage and its beneficiaries. Cambridge 1954, New York 1964. With an appendix on trns from the classics before 1600. Suppl by H. Nørgaard, RES new ser 9 1958.

Caspari, F. Humanism and the social order in Tudor England. Chicago 1954, New York 1968.

Mazzeo, J. A. (ed). Reason and the imagination: studies in the history of ideas 1600-1800. New York 1962.

— Renaissance and seventeenth-century studies. New York 1964.

— Renaissance and revolution: backgrounds to 17th-century English literature. New York 1965.

Crawford, R. M. The Renaissance mirror. Historical Stud (Melbourne) 6 1955.

Ogden, H. V. S. and M. S. English taste in landscape in the 17th century. Ann Arbor 1955.

Ong, W. J. System, space and intellect in Renaissance symbolism. Bibliothèque d'Humanisme et Renaissance 18 1956.

— From allegory to diagram in the Renaissance mind. Jnl of Aesthetics 17 1959.

— The presence of the word: some prolegomena for cultural and religious history. New Haven 1967.

— Tudor writings on rhetoric. Stud in Renaissance 15 1968.

Rosenberg, E. Leicester: patron of letters. New York 1955.

Sarton, G. The appreciation of ancient and medieval science during the Renaissance 1450-1600. Philadelphia 1955.

Saunders, J. L. Justus Lipsius: the philosophy of Renaissance stoicism. New York 1955.

Sells, A. The paradise of travellers: the Italian influence on Englishmen in the 17th century. 1964.

Sypher, W. Four stages of Renaissance style: transformations in art and literature 1400-1700. New York 1955.

Taylor, D. The third Earl of Pembroke as patron of poetry. Tulane Stud in Eng 5 1955.

Bennett, J. W. Britain among the fortunate isles. SP 53 1956.

Howell, W. S. Logic and rhetoric in England 1500-1700. Princeton 1956.

Korninger, S. Die Naturauffassung in der englischen Dichtung des 17 Jahrhunderts. Vienna 1956.

Piggott, S. Antiquarian thought in the 16th and 17th centuries. In English historical scholarship, ed L. Fox, Oxford 1956.

Robertson, J. Rapports du poète et de l'artiste dans la préparation des cortèges du Lord Maire, Londres 1553-1640. In Fêtes de la Renaissance, ed J. Jacquot, Paris 1956.

Smith, A. J. An examination of some claims for Ramism. RES new ser 7 1956. On claims made by R. Tuve, Elizabethan and metaphysical imagery, Chicago 1947. See also G. Watson, Ramus, Miss Tuve and the new Petromachia, MP 55 1958.

Cohn, N. The pursuit of the millennium: revolutionary millenarians and mystical anarchists of the Middle Ages. 1957, 1970 (rev).

Colie, R. L. Light and Enlightenment: the Cambridge Platonists and the Dutch Arminians. Cambridge 1957.

Kantorowicz, E. H. The King's two bodies: a study in mediaeval political theology. Princeton 1957.

— The sovereignty of the artist: a note on the legal maxims and Renaissance theories of art. In his Selected studies, Locust Valley NY 1965.

Tenison, E. M. Elizabethan England: being the history of this country 'in relation to all foreign princes'. 12 vols in 13 Leamington 1933-60.

Winny, J. (ed). The frame of order: an outline of Elizabethan belief taken from treatises of the late 16th century. 1957.

Bowers, R. H. Heraclitus and Democritus in Elizabethan England. South Folklore Quart 22 1958.

Leyden, W. V. Antiquity and authority: a paradox in the Renaissance theory of history. JHI 19 1958.

Macklem, M. The anatomy of the world: relations between natural and moral law from Donne to Pope. Minneapolis 1958.

Nelson, J. C. Renaissance theory of love. New York 1958.

Patrides, C. A. The numerological approach to cosmic order during the English Renaissance. Isis 49 1958.

— Renaissance and modern thought on the last things: a study in changing conceptions. Harvard Theological Rev 51 1958.

— Renaissance thought on the celestial hierarchy: the decline of a tradition. JHI 20 1959.

— The phoenix and the ladder: the rise and decline of the Christian view of history. Univ of California Pbns in Eng 29 1964.

Raggio, O. The myth of Prometheus: its survival and metamorphoses up to the 18th century. Jnl Warburg & Courtauld Inst 21 1958.

Rice, E. F., jr. The Renaissance idea of wisdom. Cambridge Mass 1958.

Rossky, W. Imagination in the English Renaissance: psychology and poetic. Stud in Renaissance 5 1958.

Schoeck, R. J. Early Anglo-Saxon studies and legal scholarship in the Renaissance. Ibid.

Strong, R. C. The popular celebration of the Accession Day of Queen Elizabeth I. Jnl Warburg & Courtauld Inst 21 1958.

Valency, M. In praise of love: an introduction to the love-poetry of the Renaissance. New York 1958.

Westfall, R. S. Science and religion in 17th-century England. New Haven 1958.

Wind, E. Pagan mysteries in the Renaissance. 1958, 1967 (Peregrine) (rev and enlarged).

Baron, H. The Querelle of the ancients and the moderns as a problem for Renaissance scholarship. JHI 20 1959.

— Burckhardt's Civilization of the Renaissance a century after its publication. Renaissance News 13 1960.

— Secularization of wisdom and political humanism in the Renaissance. JHI 21 1960.

Bouwsma, W. J. The interpretation of Renaissance humanism. Washington 1959.

Briggs, K. M. The anatomy of Puck: an examination of fairy beliefs among Shakespeare's contemporaries and successors. 1959.

— Pale Hecate's team: beliefs on witchcraft and magic among Shakespeare's contemporaries. New York 1962.

Clements, R. J. The peregrine Muse: studies in comparative Renaissance literature. Chapel Hill 1959.

— Pictura poesis: literary and humanistic theory in Renaissance emblem books. Rome 1960.

Werkmeister, W. H. (ed). Facets of the Renaissance: essays by W. K. Ferguson et al. Los Angeles 1959.

Brown, H. The Renaissance and historians of science. Stud in Renaissance 7 1960.

de Grève, M. La légende de Gargantua en Angleterre au xvie siècle. Revue Belge 38 1960.

Ferguson, A. B. The Indian summer of English chivalry. Durham NC 1960.

— The articulate citizen and the English Renaissance. Durham NC 1965.

Gilbert, N. W. Renaissance concepts of method. New York 1960.

Heninger, S. K. A handbook of Renaissance meteorology, with particular reference to Elizabethan and Jacobean literature. Durham NC 1960.

— Some Renaissance versions of the Pythagorean tetrad. Stud in Renaissance 8 1961.

— The Tudor myth of Troy-novant. South Atlantic Quart 61 1962.

— Metaphor as cosmic correspondence. In Medieval and Renaissance studies, ed J. M. Headley, Chapel Hill 1968.

— Tudor literature in the physical sciences. HLQ 32 1969.

Huizinga, J. Men and ideas: history, the Middle Ages, the Renaissance. 1960. Tr from his Verzamelde werken 1948–53.

Jacob, E. F. An approach to the Renaissance. In Italian Renaissance studies: a tribute to C. M. Ady, 1960.

— Christian humanism in the late Middle Ages. In Europe in the late Middle Ages, ed J. R. Hale et al, 1965.

Popkin, R. H. The history of scepticism from Erasmus to Descartes. Assen 1960, 1964 (rev).

— (ed). The philosophy of the 16th and 17th centuries. New York 1966.

Helton, T. (ed). The Renaissance: a reconsideration of the theories and interpretations of the age. Madison 1961.

Hibbard, G. R. The early 17th century and the tragic view of life. Renaissance & Modern Stud 5 1961.

Hollander, J. The untuning of the sky: ideas of music in English poetry 1500–1700. Princeton 1961.

Klein, R. The figurative thought of the Renaissance. Diogenes no 32 1961.

Rhys, H. H. (ed). Seventeenth-century science and arts. Princeton 1961.

Sprott, S. E. The English debate on suicide from Donne to Hume. La Salle Ill 1961.

Weinberg, B. A history of literary criticism in the Italian Renaissance. 2 vols Chicago 1961.

Akrigg, G. P. V. Jacobean pageant: or the Court of James I. Cambridge Mass 1962.

Boas, (Hall), M. The scientific Renaissance 1450–1630. New York 1962.

— Scientific thought. Shakespeare Survey 17 1964.

Finney, G. L. Musical backgrounds for English literature 1580–1650. New Brunswick NJ 1962.

Hathaway, B. The age of criticism: the late Renaissance in Italy. Ithaca 1962.

— Marvels and commonplaces: Renaissance literary criticism. New York 1968.

Hoopes, R. Right reason in the English Renaissance. Cambridge Mass 1962.

Lechner, J. M., Sr. Renaissance concepts of the commonplaces. New York 1962.

McLuhan, M. The Gutenberg galaxy: the making of the typographic man. Toronto 1962.

Wightman, W. P. D. Science and the Renaissance. 2 vols Edinburgh 1962.

Lawn, B. The Salernitan questions: an introduction to the history of medieval and Renaissance problem literature. Oxford 1963.

Spitzer, L. Classical and Christian ideas of world harmony. Baltimore 1963.

Van Leeuwen, H. G. The problem of certainty in English thought 1630–90. Hague 1963.

Ziff, L. The literary consequences of Puritanism. ELH 30 1963.

Blench, J. W. Preaching in England in the late 15th and 16th centuries: a study of English sermons 1450–c. 1600. Oxford 1964.

Doran, M. Some Renaissance 'Ovids'. In Literature and society, ed B. Slote, Lincoln Nebraska 1964.

Gabel, L. et al. The Renaissance reconsidered: a symposium. Smith College Stud in History 44 1964.

Greaves, M. The blazon of honour: a study in Renaissance magnanimity. 1964.

Jensen, D. L. The 'Renaissance' in recent thought: 15 years of interpretation. Brigham Young Univ Stud 6 1964.

Raab, F. The English face of Machiavelli: a changing interpretation 1500–1700. 1964.

Romuáldez, A. V. Towards a history of the Renaissance idea of wisdom. Stud in Renaissance 11 1964.

Walker, D. P. The decline of hell: 17th-century discussions of eternal torment. 1964.

Wellington, J. E. Renaissance anti-feminism and the classical tradition. In Sweet smoke of rhetoric: Renaissance essays, ed N. G. Lawrence and J. A. Reynolds, Coral Gables Fla 1964.

Willey, B. The English moralists. 1964.

Eastman, A. M. Prince, people and poet: a note on the English Renaissance. Papers of Michigan Acad 50 1965.

Hauser, A. Mannerism: the crisis of the Renaissance and the origin of modern art. 2 vols 1965. Tr from German.

Hill, C. Intellectual origins of the English Revolution. Oxford 1965.

Rostenberg, L. Literary, political, scientific, religious and legal publishing, printing and bookselling in England 1551–1700. 2 vols New York 1965.

Nauert, C. G. Agrippa and the crisis of Renaissance thought. Urbana 1965.

Artz, F. B. Renaissance humanism 1300–1500. Kent Ohio 1966.

Esler, A. The aspiring mind of the Elizabethan younger generation. Durham NC 1966.

Halio, J. L. The metaphor of conception and Elizabethan theories of the imagination. Neophilologus 50 1966.

O'Kelly, B. (ed). The Renaissance image of man and the world. Columbus 1966.

Scholderer, V. Fifty essays in 15th- and 16th-century bibliography. Ed D. E. Rhodes, Amsterdam 1966.

Spitz, L. W. Occultism and despair of reason in Renaissance thought. JHI 27 1966.

Collinson, P. The Elizabethan Puritan movement. 1967.

Damon, P. History and idea in Renaissance criticism. In Literary criticism and historical understanding, ed Damon, New York 1967.

Dorsten, J. A. van. The arts of memory and poetry. E Studies 48 1967.

Ergang, R. The Renaissance. Princeton 1967.

Levy, F. J. Tudor historical thought. San Marino 1967.

Lewis, A. R. (ed). Aspects of the Renaissance: a symposium. Austin 1967.

Singleton, C. S. (ed). Art, science and history in the Renaissance. Baltimore 1967.

Benson, D. R. 'Ideas' and the problem of knowledge in 17th-century English aesthetics. Eng Miscellany (Rome) 19 1968.

Bercovitch, S. Empedocles in the English Renaissance. SP 65 1968.

Bodemer, C. W. and L. S. King. Medical investigation in 17th-century England. Los Angeles 1968.

Cochrane, K. Orpheus applied: some instances of his importance in the humanist view of language. RES new ser 19 1968.

Hattaway, M. Paradoxes of Solomon: learning in the English Renaissance. JHI 29 1968.

Kirk, R. A seventeenth-century controversy: extremism vs moderation. SE 9 1968.

LaGuardia, E. Aesthetics of analogy. Diogenes no 62 1968.

Roberts, J. D. From Puritanism to Platonism in 17th-century England. Hague 1968.

Seigel, J. E. Rhetoric and philosophy in Renaissance humanism. Princeton 1968.

Warhaft, S. Stoicism, ethics and learning in 17th-century England. Mosaic 1 1968.

Anglo, S. Spectacle, pageantry and early Tudor policy. Oxford 1969.

Bawcutt, N. W. Some Elizabethan allusions to Machiavelli. Eng Miscellany (Rome) 20 1969.

Chastel, A. The myth of the Renaissance 1420–1520. Geneva 1969. Tr from French, 1969.

Close, A. J. Commonplace theories of art and nature in classical antiquity and in the Renaissance. JHI 30 1969.

Coogan, R. M. Petrarch's Trionfi and the English Renaissance. SP 67 1970.

O'Connor, J. J. Amadis de Gaule and its influence on Elizabethan literature. New Brunswick NJ 1970.

Patterson, A. M. Hermogenes and the Elizabethans: seven ideas of style. Princeton 1970.

Pratt, S. M. Jane Shore and the Elizabethans: some facts and speculations. Texas Stud in Lang & Lit 11 1970.

Richmond, H. M. Ronsard and the English Renaissance. Comparative Lit Stud 7 1970.

Weidhorn, M. Dreams in 17th-century English literature. Hague 1970.

Lyons, B. G. Voices of melancholy: studies in literary treatments of melancholy in Renaissance England. 1971.

Hardin, R. F. Ovid in 17th-century England. Comparative Lit 24 1972.

Levy, B. S. (ed). Developments in the early Renaissance. Albany 1972.

Murphy, J. M. The critical elegy of earlier 17th-century England. Genre 5 1972.

O'Malley, C. D. Tudor medicine and biology. HLQ 32 1969.

Trinkaus, C. In our image and likeness: humanity and divinity in Italian humanist thought. 2 vols 1970.

A. C. H.

II. LITERARY RELATIONS WITH THE CONTINENT

This section, which is necessarily selective, begins with 3 introductory sections: General; European Literature in General; and Foreign Influences on English Literature. It is then divided according to languages or groups of languages: International Latin; French; German; Italian; Spanish and Portuguese; Dutch and Flemish; Scandinavian; Russian etc; Hungarian; and others. Material is divided according to topics; individual authors, English and foreign, are entered in alphabetical lists under each topic. Secondary works, which are confined to comparative studies and studies on the impact of an author in a foreign country, are in chronological order. Trns into and from English come within the scope of the section. No distinction is drawn between translators and editors using hack-translators unless positively known; the distinction between trn, adaptation and mere imitation, where given, is offered merely as a guide.

(1) GENERAL

This section gives only a few works useful for general reference. For fuller lists see vol 2 col 69f. and

Baldensperger, F. and W. P. Friedrich. Bibliography of comparative literature. Chapel Hill 1950. Annual suppl: Yearbook of comparative literature, Chapel Hill (later Bloomington) 1952–.

Bibliographie générale de la littérature comparée. Revue de Littérature Comparée 1951–9.

MLA International bibliography. Ed H. T. Meserole, New York 1956–.

Posnett, H. M. Comparative literature. 1886.

Betz, L. P. La littérature comparée: essai bibliographique. Strasbourg 1900, 1904 (enlarged).

Partridge, E. The comparative study of literature. In his A critical medley, Paris 1926.

van Tieghem, P. La littérature comparée. Paris 1931.

Abe, J. Comparative literature. 2 vols Tokyo 1932–3.

Thompson, S. Motif index in folk literature. 6 vols Bloomington 1932–6, Copenhagen 1955–8 (rev).

Chadwick, H. M. and N. K. The growth of literature. 3 vols Cambridge 1932–40.

Jamieson, R. D. A comparison of literatures. 1935.

Holmes, U. T. Comparative literature: past and future. SP 42 1945.

Guyard, M. F. La littérature comparée. Paris 1951.

Spemann, A. Vergleichende Zeittafel der Weltliteratur vom Mittelalter bis zur Neuzeit 1150–1939. Stuttgart 1951.

Friederich, W. P. and D. H. Malone. Outline of comparative literature. Chapel Hill 1954.

Peyre, H. Seventy-five years of comparative literature. Yearbook of Comparative Lit 8 1959.

Aldridge, A. O. et al. The concept of influence in comparative literature: a symposium. Comparative Lit Stud 1963.

— Comparative literature: matter and method. Urbana 1969.

Etiemble, R. Comparaison n'est pas raison: la crise de la littérature comparée. Paris 1963.

Cioranescu, A. Principios de literatura comparada. La Laguna 1964.

Roddier, H. Principes d'une histoire comparée des littératures. Revue de Littérature Comparée 39 1965.

Wellek, R. Comparative literature to-day. Comparative Lit 17 1965.

Nichols, S. G. and R. B. Vowles (ed). Comparatists at work. Blaisdell 1965.

Weinstein, U. Einführung in die vergleichende Literaturwissenschaft. Stuttgart 1968.

Watson, G. Comparative literature. In his Study of literature, 1969.

The following periodicals should also be consulted:

Revue de littérature comparée. Ed F. Baldensperger and P. Hazard, Paris 1921–.

Comparative literature. Eugene 1949–. A quarterly.

Comparative literature studies (Univ of Maryland). College Park 1963–.

(2) EUROPEAN LITERATURE IN GENERAL

Smith, G. G. The transition period. 1900.

Burdach, K. Reformation, Renaissance, Humanismus. Berlin 1918.

Hyma, A. The Christian Renaissance: a history of the devotio moderna. Grand Rapids Iowa 1924.

Allen, P. S. The age of Erasmus. Oxford 1924.

Van Tieghem, P. Précis d'histoire littéraire de l'Europe. Paris 1925.

— Histoire littéraire de l'Europe et de l'Amérique de la Renaissance à nos jours. Paris 1946.

Magnus, L. Dictionary of European literature. 1925.

— A history of European literature. New York 1934.

Toffanin, G. Storia dell' umanesimo. Città di Castello 1933.

Schneider, R. and G. Cohen. La formation du génie moderne. Paris 1936.

Mazzeo, J. A. Renaissance and revolution: the remaking of European thought. 1947.

Babits, M. Geschichte der europäischen Literatur. Vienna 1948.

Ségur, N. Histoire de la littérature européenne. 5 vols Paris 1949–52.

Faure, L. La Renaissance. Paris 1949.

Sellery, G. C. The Renaissance: its nature and origins. Madison 1950.

Haydn, H. The Counter-Renaissance. New York 1950.

Mattingly, G. Renaissance diplomacy. Boston 1955.

Garin, E. L'educazione in Europa 1400–1600. Bari 1957.

Thomas, S. H. Europe in Renaissance and Reformation. 1964.

Artz, F. B. Renaissance humanism 1300–1550. Kent Ohio 1966.

Hay, D. (ed). The age of the Renaissance. 1967.

Koenigsberger, H. G. and G. L. Mosse. Europe in the 16th century. 1968.

Cipolla, C. M. Literacy and development in the West. 1969.

Drama

Creizenach, W. Geschichte des neueren Dramas. 5 vols Halle 1893–1916.

Dubech, L. et al. Histoire générale du théâtre. 5 vols Paris 1931–4.

Mantzius, K. A history of theatrical art. 6 vols New York 1937.

Hewick, M. T. Comic theory in the 16th century. Illinois Stud in Lang & Lit 34 nos 1–2 1950.

— The new drama of the 16th century. JEGP 54 1955.

Baughner, D. C. The braggart in Renaissance comedy. Minneapolis 1954.

Schmidt, L. (ed). Le théâtre populaire européen. Paris 1965.

For Shakespeare see col 1473, below.

Historiography

Fueter, E. Geschichte der neueren Historiographie. Munich and Berlin 1911, 1936 (rev and enlarged); tr French, Paris 1914.

Ferguson, W. F. The Renaissance in historical thought: five centuries of interpretation. Berlin 1948.

Reynolds, B. R. Latin historiography: a survey 1400–1600. Stud in Renaissance 2 1955.

Fussner, F. S. The historical revolution: English historical writing and thought 1580–1640. New York 1962.

Gilmore, M. P. Humanists and jurists. Cambridge Mass 1963.

Levy, F. J. Tudor historical thought. San Marino 1967.

McKisack, M. Medieval history in the Tudor age. 1971.

History of Ideas

Zanta, L. La renaissance du Stoïcisme. Paris 1914.

Taylor, H. O. Thought and expression in the 16th century. New York 1920.

Cassirer, E. Individuum und Cosmos in der Philosophie der Renaissance. Leipzig 1927.

Seznec, J. La survivance des dieux antiques. Paris 1940; tr New York 1953 (Bollingen ser).

Trinkaus, C. E. Adversity's noblemen: the Italian humanists on happiness. New York 1940.

Bray, R. La préciosité et les précieux. Paris 1948.

Dédéyan, C. Le thème de Faust dans la littérature européenne. 2 vols Paris 1954–5.

Axelrad, A. J. Le thème de Sophonisbe dans les principales tragédies de la littérature occidentale. Lille 1956.

Tenenti, A. Il senso della morte e l'amore della vita nel Rinascimento. Turin 1957.

Walker, D. P. Spiritual and demonic magic from Ficino to Campanella. 1958.

Rice, E. F., jr. The Renaissance idea of wisdom. Cambridge Mass 1958.

Hardison, O. B., jr. The enduring monument: the idea of praise in Renaissance literary theory and practice. Chapel Hill 1962.

Branca, V. (ed). Barocco europeo e barocco veneziano. Florence 1963.

Durling, R. M. The figure of the poet in Renaissance epic. 1965.

Yates, F. A. The art of memory. 1968.

Post, R. R. The modern devotion: confrontation with Reformation and Humanism. Leyden 1968.

Literary Criticism and Theory

Clark, D. L. Rhetoric and poetry in the Renaissance. New York 1922.

Spingarn, J. E. History of literary criticism in the Renaissance. New York 1925.

Baldwin, C. S. Renaissance literary theory and practice. New York 1939.

Sweeting, E. Early Tudor criticism, linguistic and literary. Oxford 1940.

Robertson, J. The art of letter writing. Liverpool 1942.

Keller, A. C. Ancients and moderns in the early 17th century. MLQ 11 1950.

Maddison, C. Apollo and the nine: a history of the ode. 1959.

Hall, V. Renaissance literary criticism. Gloucester Mass 1959.

Baron, H. The Querelle des anciens et des modernes as a problem for Renaissance scholarships. JHI 20 1959.

Weinberg, B. A history of literary criticism in the Italian Renaissance. 2 vols Chicago 1961.

Lechner, J. M. Renaissance concepts of the commonplaces. New York 1962.

Smith, A. J. Theory and practice in Renaissance poetry: two kinds of imitation. Bull John Rylands Lib 46 1964.

Taylor, E. W. Nature and art in Renaissance literature. 1964.

Colie, R. Paradoxia epidemica: the Renaissance tradition of paradox. Princeton 1966.

Croll, M. W. Style, rhetoric and rhythm: essays. Princeton 1966.

Silver, I. Creative imitation, originality and literary tradition in the Renaissance. In Renaissance studies in honor of W. L. Wyley, Chapel Hill 1968.

Sonnino, L. A. A handbook of 16th-century rhetoric. 1968.

Social and Political Theory

Hearnshaw, F. J. C. (ed). The social and political ideas of some great thinkers in the 16th and 17th centuries. 1926.

Guerri, D. La corrente popolare nel Rinascimento. Florence 1931.

Gough, J. W. The social contract: a critical study of its development. Oxford 1936.

Sabine, G. H. A history of political theory. 1941.

Martin, H. von. The sociology of the Renaissance. 1944.

White, H. C. Social criticism in popular religious literature of the 16th century. 1944.

d'Entrèves, A. P. Natural law: an introduction to legal philosophy. 1951, 1970 (rev).

Ferguson, A. B. Circumstances and the sense of history in Tudor England. Medieval & Renaissance Stud 1968.

(3) FOREIGN INFLUENCES ON ENGLISH LITERATURE

Bibliographies

Harris, W. J. The first printed translations into English of the great foreign classics. 1909.

Ebisch, W. and I. L. Schücking. A Shakespeare bibliography. Oxford 1931; Supplement 1930–5, Oxford 1937. See G. R. Smith, below.

Noyes, G. E. Bibliography of courtesy and conduct books in 17th-century England. New Haven 1937.

Smith, G. R. A classified Shakespeare bibliography 1936–58. Philadelphia 1963.

The literature of the world in English translation. Vol 2, Slavic literatures, ed R. C. Lewanski and M. Deriugin, New York 1967; vol 3 (2 pts), Romance literatures, ed G. B. Parks and R. Z. Temple, New York 1970.

Studies

Kye, W. B. England as seen by foreigners. 1865.

Jusserand, J. J. The English novel in the time of Shakespeare. 1890.

Lewis, C. M. The foreign sources of modern English versification. New Haven 1898.

Pollard, A. English books printed abroad. Trans Bibl Soc 3 1896.

Koeppel, E. Quellenstudien zu den Dramen Ben Jonsons, John Marstons und Beaumont und Fletchers. Erlangen 1895.

— Quellenstudien zu den Dramen George Chapmans, Philip Massingers und John Fords. Quellen und Forschungen 82 1897.

Brandl, A. Quellen des weltlichen Dramas in England vor Shakespeare. Quellen und Forschungen 83 1898.

Harrison, J. S. Platonism in English poetry of the sixteenth and seventeenth centuries. New York 1903.

Worman, E. J. Alien members of the book trade during the Tudor period. 1906 (Bibl Soc).

Greg, W. W. Pastoral poetry and pastoral drama. 1906.

Tucker, T. G. The foreign debt of English literature. 1907.

Hatcher, O. L. Aims and methods of Elizabethan translators. E Studien 44 1910.

Jones, F. N. Boccaccio and his imitators in German, English, French, Spanish and Italian literature. Chicago 1910.

Bayne, C. G. Anglo-Roman relations 1588–65. 1913.

Finzi, G. Lira italica e lira nordica: saggio sopra le due grande correnti della letteratura europea. Turin 1914.

Scott, M. A. Elizabethan translations from the Italian. New York 1916. Also lists trns from Italian writers of Latin.

Amos, F. R. Early theories of translation. New York 1920.

Schelling, F. E. Foreign influences in Elizabethan plays. New York 1923.

Baker, E. A. The history of the English novel. Vol 1, The age of romance from the beginning to the Renaissance, 1924.

Praz, M. Stanley, Sherburne and Ayres as translators and imitators of Italian, French and Spanish poets. MLR 20 1925.

— Baroque in England. MP 61 1964.

Magnus, L. English literature in its foreign relations. 1927.

— A history of European literature. 1934.

Wolff, M. J. Die Renaissance in der englischen Literatur. Bielefeld 1928.

Aronstein, P. Das englische Renaissance-Drama. Leipzig 1929.

Henderson, C. D. Foreign religious influences in 17th-century Scotland. Edinburgh Rev 249 1929.

Scott, J. G. Les sonnets élizabéthains: les sources et l'apport personnel. Paris 1929.

Matthiessen, F. O. Translation: an Elizabethan art. Cambridge Mass 1931.

Cassirer, E. Die platonische Renaissance in England und die Schule von Cambridge. Leipzig 1932; tr as The Platonic Renaissance in England, Austin 1953.

Bush, D. Mythology and the Renaissance tradition in English poetry. Minneapolis 1932, New York 1965 (rev).

— The Renaissance and English humanism. Toronto 1939.

Pearson, L. E. Elizabethan love conventions. 1933.

Rösler, M. Die Lebensweise der Ausländer in England im späteren Mittelalter und in der Renaissance. E Studien 68 1934.

White, H. O. Plagiarism and imitation during the English Renaissance. 1935.

Mason, J. E. Gentlefolk in the making: studies in the history of English courtesy literature 1531–1774. Philadelphia 1935.

Wright, L. B. Middle class culture in Elizabethan England. Chapel Hill 1935.

Chew, S. C. The crescent and the rose: Islam and England during the Renaissance. Oxford 1937.

Baldwin, C. S. Renaissance literary theory and practice: classicism in the rhetoric and poetic of Italy, France and England 1400–1600. Ed D. L. Clark, New York 1939.

Allen, D. C. The star-crossed Renaissance: the quarrel about astrology and its influence in England. Durham NC 1941.

Dupont, V. L'Utopie et le roman utopique dans la littérature anglaise. Cahors 1941.

Smith, H. Tamburlaine and the Renaissance. In Elizabethan studies in honor of G. F. Reynolds, Boulder 1945.

Charlton, H. B. The Senecan tradition in Renaissance tragedy. 1946.

Wortham, J. Sir Thomas Eliot and the translation of prose. HLQ 11 1948.

— Arthur Golding and the translation of prose. HLQ 12 1949.

Hexter, J. H. More's Utopia: the biography of an idea. Princeton 1952.

Jayne, S. Library catalogues of the English Renaissance. Berkeley 1956.

Miller, H. K. The paradoxical encomium, with special reference to its vogue in England 1000–1800. MP 53 1956.

Brett-James, A. The triple dream: four centuries of English, French and German literature 1531–1930. 1959.

Durkan, J. Cultural background of 16th-century Scotland. Innes Rev 2 1959.

Block, A. The English novel, including translation of foreign fiction. 1961.

Davis, W. R. A map of Arcadia: Sidney's romance in its tradition. 1965.

McConica, J. K. English humanists and Reformation politics under Henry VIII and Edward VI. Oxford 1965.

Jack, R. D. S. James VI and Renaissance poetic theory. English 16 1967.

Johnson, J. W. The formation of English neo-classical thought. Princeton 1967.

Mulder, J. S. The temple of the mind: education and literary taste in 17th-century England. New York 1969.

Blake, N. F. Lord Berners: a survey. Medievalia et Humanistica new ser 2 1971.

Dictionaries and Language Manuals

Polylingual including English; for works on particular languages see below.

Véron, Jean. Dictionariolum puerorum. Paris 1552. English, French, Latin.

Gesner, Conrad. Mithridates: de differentiis linguarum, cum veterum, tum earum quae hodie in usu sunt, observationes. Zürich 1555.

Calepinus, Ambrosius. Dictionarium octolingue. Lyons 1570.

— Dictionarium undecim linguarum. 2 vols Basle 1590.

Baret, John. Alvearie. [1573]. English, French, Latin.

Heyndriex, Heinrich. Colloques ou dialogues avec un dictionnaire en six langues. Antwerp 1576.

Holyband, Claude. The flourie field of foure languages: Latine, French, English, Italian. 1583.

Barlement, Noël van. Familiaria colloquia cum dictionariolo sex linguarum. Antwerp 1584.

— Colloquia et dictionariolum septem linguarum. Liège 1589.

— Colloquia et dictionariolum octo linguarum. Antwerp 1630.

Jonghe, Adrien de (Adrianus Junius). Nomenclator octolinguis. Frankfurt 1602.

Faber, Basilius (Soranus). Le dictionnaire de six langages. Rouen 1611.

Minsheu, John. The guide into tongues. 1617. Covering 11 languages.

Rosier, J. L. The sources and methods of Minsheu's Guide into the tongues. PQ 40 1961.

Howell, J. Lexicon tetraglotton: or an English-French-Spanish-Italian dictionary. 1659–60.

Watson, J. F. The beginnings of the teaching of modern subjects in England. 1909.

— Notes and materials on religious refugees and their relation to education in England before 1685. Huguenot Soc Proc 9 1911.

Starnes, De Witt T. Bilingual dictionaries of Shakespeare's day. PMLA 52 1937.

— Renaissance dictionaries, English-Latin and Latin-English. Austin 1954.

— and E. W. Talbert. Classical myth and legend in Renaissance dictionaries. Chapel Hill 1955.

De Jongh, W. F. J. Western language manuals of the Renaissance. Albuquerque 1949.

Simonini, R. C., jr. The genesis of modern language teaching. Modern Langs Jnl 35 1951.

Sledd, J. A note on the use of Renaissance dictionaries. MP 49 1952.

Collison, R. L. Dictionaries of foreign languages. 1955.

Travel

For travel in particular countries see French etc, below. See also Travel, col 2109, below

Turler, Jerome. De peregrinatione. Strasbourg 1574; tr as The traveiler: bk 1 the maner of travelling over-sea, 1575.

A true report of Sir Anthony Shierlies journey overland to Venice and thence by sea to Antioch etc. 1600. By 2 of his party.

Parry, William. Travels of Sir Anthony Shirley by sea and over land to Persia. 1601.

Palmer, Thomas. An essay of the meanes how to make our travailes into forraine countries the more profitable. 1606.

Coryate, Thomas. Coryats crudities hastily gobled up in 5 moneths travells. 1611.

— Coryats Crambe, the Odcombian banquet: Coriate, traveller for English wits. 1616.

Strachan, M. F. Life and adventures of Coryate. Oxford 1962.

Purchas, Samuel, Purchas his pilgrimage: or relations of the world and the religions observed in all ages and places discovered. 1613.

— Hakluytus postumus: or Purchas his pilgrimes. 1625.

Lithgow, William. A most delectable and true discourse of an admired and painefull peregriniation. 1614.

— The totall discourse. 1632.

Moryson, Fynes. An itinerary first written in the Latin and then translated by him into English. 1617.

Abbot, George. A briefe description of the whole world, with their academies. 1634.

Howell, James. Instructions for foreign travel. 1642.

Herbert of Cherbury, Edward, Lord. His life (including his continental travels 1608–24). Strawberry Hill 1764. Written c. 1643.

Hoby, Thomas. A booke of the travail and life of me, Thomas Hoby. Ed E. Powell, Camden Miscellany 10 1902. Written before 1564.

Mundy, Peter. Travels in Europe and Asia 1608–67: vol 4, Europe 1639–47. Ed R. C. Temple 1907–36.

Smith, E. Foreign visitors in England during the last three centuries. 1889.

Bates, E. S. Touring in 1600. Boston 1911.

Howard, C. English travellers at the Renaissance. 1914.

Coxe, E. G. A reference guide to the literature of travel. 3 vols Seattle 1935.

Letts, M. As the foreigner saw us. 1935.

Penrose, B. Urbane travellers 1591–1635. Philadelphia 1942.

— Travel and discovery in the Renaissance 1420–1620. Cambridge Mass 1952.

—— Tudor and early Stuart voyaging. Washington 1962.
Parks, G. B. Travel as education. In R. F. Jones et al,
The seventeenth century, Stanford 1951.

Stoye, J. W. English travellers abroad 1604–67. 1952.
Parry, J. H. (ed). The European reconnaissance:
selected documents. 1968.

(4) INTERNATIONAL LATIN

*This section includes only such works as can be shown to have exercized an obvious influence on the vernacular literatures;
and in tracing this influence a distinction has been made between writers of continental and those of British origin. For the
former, only English trns and imitations are given; for the latter, trns and imitations in languages other than English have
also been included.*

Bibliographies

Baxter, J. et al. An index of British and Irish Latin writers
AD 400–1520. Archivum Latinitatis Medii Aevi (Paris)
1932.
Allen, D. C. A contribution to the bibliography of
Renaissance Latin quotation books. In his edn of F.
Meres, Treatise of poetry, Urbana 1933.
Bradner, L. A check-list of original neo-Latin dramas by
continental writers printed before 1650. PMLA 58 1943.
Bennett, H. S. List of translations into English 1475–1560.
In his English books and readers 1475 to 1557, Cam-
bridge 1952, 1969 (rev).

Studies

Seebohm, F. The Oxford reformers: Colet, Erasmus,
More. 1867, 1869 (rev).
Green, H. Andrea Alciati and his books of emblems: a
biographical and bibliographical study. 1872.
Arnstädt, F. A. Roger Ascham und seine Geistesver-
wandtschaft mit Johannes Sturm. Plauen 1881.
Boemer, A. Die lateinischen Schülergespräche der
Humanisten. 2 vols Berlin 1897–9.
Spingarn, J. E. A history of literary criticism in the
Renaissance, with special reference to the influence of
Italy in the formation and development of modern
classicism. New York 1899.
Sandys, J. E. A history of classical scholarship volume 2.
Cambridge 1908.
Scott, I. Controversies over the imitation of Cicero and
some phases of their influence on the schools of the
Renaissance. New York 1910.
Watson, F. Religious refugees and English education.
Proc Huguenot Soc of London 1911.
Schoell, F. L. Etudes sur l'humanisme continental en
Angleterre à la fin de la Renaissance. Paris 1926.
Wright, F. A. and T. A. Sinclair. A history of later Latin
literature to the end of the 17th century. 1932.
Ashton, J. W. Peter Martyr on the function and character
of literature. PQ 18 1939.
Mann, W. Lateinische Dichtung in England vom Ausgang
des Frühhumanismus bis zum Regierungsantritt Eliza-
beths. Halle 1939.
Schirmer, W. F. Der englische Frühhumanismus. Leipzig
1939.
Bradner, L. Musae anglicanae: a history of Anglo-Latin
poetry 1500–1925. New York 1940.
Hyma, A. The continental origins of English humanism.
HLQ 4 1941.
Allen, D. C. Latin literature of the Renaissance. MLQ 2
1941.
van Tieghem, P. La littérature latine de la Renaissance.
Paris 1944.
Adams, R. P. Designs by More and Erasmus for a new
social order. SP 42 1945.
Brooke, C. F. T. Latin drama in Renaissance England.
ELH 13 1946.
Campana, A. The origin of the word 'humanist'. Jnl
Warburg & Courtauld Inst 9 1946.
Oppel, H. Der englische Humanismus im Zeitalter
Elizabeths. Mainz 1947.
Hudson, H. H. The epigram in the English Renaissance.
Princeton 1947.

Clark, D. L. John Milton at St Paul's School. New York
1948.
Castelli, A. Note sull' umanesimo in Inghilterra. Milan
1950.
Nadeau, R. Thomas Farnaby: schoolmaster and rhetor-
ician. Quart Jnl of Speech 36 1950.
Kristeller, P. O. Medieval and Renaissance Latin trans-
lations and commentaries. Scriptorium 6 1952.
Curtius, E. R. Europäische Literatur und lateinische
Mittelalter. Berne 1948; tr 1953.
Allen, C. G. The sources of Lily's Latin grammar.
Library 5th ser 9 1954.
Pizzi, C. L'umanista Andrea Ammonio. Florence 1956.
McAvoy, W. C. Falstaff, Erasmus and Ficino. Carroll
Quart 11 1957.
Major, J. M. Sir Thomas Elyot and Renaissance human-
ism. 1957.
Wilson, J. D. Shakespeare's 'small Latin': how much?
Shakespeare Survey 10 1957.
Gaertner, J. A. Latin verse translations of the psalms
1500–1620. Harvard Theological Rev 49 1956.
Grant, W. L. Neo-Latin verse translations of the Bible.
Harvard Theological Rev 52 1959.
—— Neo-Latin literature and the pastoral. Chapel Hill
1965.
Hogrefe, P. The Sir Thomas More circle. Urbana 1959.
Phillips, J. E. and D. C. Allen (ed). Neo-Latin poetry of
the sixteenth and seventeenth centuries. Los Angeles
1965.
Meller, H. and H. J. Zimmermann (ed). Lebende Antike:
Symposion für Rudolf Sühnel. Berlin 1967. Humanist
influence on More, Brathwait, Shakespeare et al.
Dilworth, M. The Latin translator of the Cherrie and the
slae. Stud in Scottish Lit 5 1967.
Seigel, J. E. Rhetoric and philosophy in Renaissance
humanism: the union of eloquence and wisdom.
Princeton 1968.

Dictionaries
(including proper-name dictionaries and language manuals)

Torrentinus, Hermannus. Elucidarius carminum et
historiarum. Deventer 1498.
Calepinus, Ambrosius. Dictionarium. Bergamo 1502,
Basle 1590 (enlarged as Dictionarium undecim linguarum; respondent latinis vocabulis hebraica, graeca,
gallica, italica, germanica, belgica, hispanica, anglica
etc).
Elyot, Thomas. Latin-English dictionary. 1538; enlarged
to include proper names in Bibliotheca Eliotae, 1542,
1548 (rev Thomas Cooper).
Stephanus, Carolus. Dictionarium historicum ac poeticum.
Paris 1553.
Withals, John. A short dictionary (English–Latin) for
yonge beginners. 1553.
Cooper, Thomas. Thesaurus linguae romanae et britannicae. 1565. An enlargement of Elyot's Bibliotheca,
above.
Gyraldus, Lilius Gregorius. De deis gentium. Lyons
1565.
Comes, Natalis (Natali Conti). Mythologiae: sive explica-
tiones fabularum. Venice 1568.
Levins, Peter. Manipulus vocabulorum: a dictionarie of
English and Latine words. 1570.

Thomas, Thomas. Dictionarium linguae latinae et anglicanae. 1587.

Rider, John. Bibliotheca scholastica. 1606.

Paraemologia anglo-latina: or proverbs English-Latin. 1639.

Dugard, William. Vestibulum parvum anglo-latinum [of Comenius], cum dictionario latino-anglico. 1650.

Starnes, D. T. and G. E. Noyes. Renaissance dictionaries, English-Latin and Latin-English. Austin 1954.

Starnes, D. T. and E. W. Talbert. Classical myth and legend in Renaissance dictionaries. Chapel Hill 1955.

Philosophy, Politics, Theology, Learning etc
Continental Writers

Acontius, Jacobus. De methodo. Basle 1558.

Blundevil, T. The true order and method of wryting and reading hystories according to the precepts of F. Patricio and Accontio Tridentino. 1574.

— Strategematum Satanae libri viii. Basle 1565; tr in part as Satan's stratagems, 1645.

Goodwin, John. Theomachia. 1644.

Jacquot, J. Acontius and the progress of tolerance in England. Bibliothèque d'Humanisme et Renaissance 16 1954.

Agricola, Rudolphus. De inventione dialectica libri iii. Louvain 1515. Written c. 1480.

Seton, John. Dialectica. 1545.

Wilson, Thomas. Rule of reason. 1551.

McNally, J. R. Prima pars dialecticae: the influence of Agricolan dialectic upon English accounts of invention. Renaissance Quart 21 1968.

Agrippa, Henricus Cornelius. De incertitudine et vanitate scientiarum. Cologne 1527; Of the vanitie and uncertaintie of artes and sciences, tr James Sanford 1569.

— De nobilitate feminei sexus. Cologne 1532; On the nobility of womankind, tr David Clapham 1542; The glory of women, tr Edward Fleetwood 1652; The glory of women, tr (in verse) H. C. (Henry Care or Hugh Crompton?) 1652.

Barcker, William. The nobility of women. 1559.

— De occulta philosophia. Antwerp 1531; Three books of occult philosophy, tr J. F[reake] 1651; bk 4 to Robert Turner 1655.

Nauert, C. G. Agrippa and the crisis of Renaissance thought. Urbana 1965.

French, P. J. John Dee. 1972.

Alberti, Leon Battista. De amore. Padua 1471; Hecatomphila: the art of love or love discovered in a hundred several kinds, tr (from the French?) 1598.

Albizzi, Bartolomeo. Liber conformitatum S. Francisci cum Christo. Venice [before 1480].

Alberus, Erasmus. Alcoranus Franciscanorum (extracts from Albizzi chosen with satirical intent) Frankfurt 1543; Die Barfüsser Mönche Eulenspiegel und Alcoran, tr Wittenberg 1542; The Alcoran of the barefoot friars, tr 1550.

Andreae, Johann Valentin. Christianopolis. Strasbourg 1619; Modell of a Christian society, tr John Hall, Cambridge 1647.

[Gott, Samuel]. Nova Solyma. 1648.

Dupont, V. L'Utopie et le roman utopique dans la littérature anglaise. Cahors 1941.

Anglerius, Petrus Martyr. De orbe novo decades. Alcala 1516; Decades of the new world, tr bks 1–3 Richard Eden 1555, bks 1–4 M. Lock 1612.

Angles, Johannes. Flores theologicarum quaestionum in secundum librum [of Peter Lombard]. Madrid 1586.

Lodge, Thomas. The Devil conjured. 1596.

Becanus, Martinus. Refutatio torturae Torti. Mainz 1610. Answer to Lancelot Andrewes; see Bellarmino, below.

— De triplici coena. In his Opuscula theologica, 4 vols Mainz 1610–12; tr 1614.

— Dissidium anglicanum de primatu regis. Mainz 1612; The English jarre, [tr J. Wilson], [St Omer] 1612.

Harris, R. The English concord. 1614.

— De radice controversarium. Mainz 1616; tr W.W., [St Omer] 1619.

Bellarmino, Roberto Francesco. Responsio Matthaei Torti ad librum Jacobi regis Magni Britanniae. Rome 1608. An attack on James I's Triplici nodo triplex cuneus: or an apologie for the oath of allegiance, 1607.

— Apologia pro responsione. Rome 1610.

— De ascensio mentis in Deum. Rome 1615; A ladder whereby our minds may ascend to God, tr T.B., Douai 1616.

— De aeterna felicitate sanctorum. Rome 1616; Of the eternal felicity of the saints, tr A.B. (Thomas Everard?), [St Omer] 1638.

— De arte bene moriendi. Cologne 1621; The art of dying well, tr C.E. (Edward Coffin), St Omer 1622.

Whitaker, William. Praelectiones de romano pontifice adversus R. Bellarminum. Cambridge 1599.

Pázmány, Peter. De visibili Christi in terris ecclesia: adversus Gulielmi Whitakeri librum contra Bellarminum. Graz 1605.

Andrewes, Lancelot. Tortura Torti. 1609.

Becanus, Martinus. Refutatio torturae Torti. Mainz 1610.

Thomson, R. Elenchus refutationis torturae Torti. 1611.

Bèze, Théodore de (Beza). Confessio christianae fidei. Geneva 1560; tr R[obert] F[yll] 1565 (from French).

— Summa totius christianismi. In his Tractationes theologicales vol 1, Geneva 1570; Treasure of truth, tr John Stockwood 1576.

— De veris ecclesiae catholicae notis. Geneva 1579; The true and visible marks of the Catholic Church, tr T[homas] W[ilcox] 1582.

Boccaccio, Giovanni. De claris mulieribus. Ulm 1473 (written c. 1360); tr in part 1440–50; Forty-six lives, tr Henry Parker, Lord Morley 1534–47.

Pisan, Christine de. Le livre de la cité des dames [written 1404–5]; The boke of the city of ladies, tr 1521.

The scholehouse of women. 1560.

Painter, William. The palace of pleasure. 2 vols 1566–7.

Massinger, Philip. The maid of honour. 1632.

— De casibus virorum et feminarum illustrium. Strasbourg [1475?] (written c. 1370); The fall of princes: or tragedies of John Bochas, tr John Lydgate (from the French of Laurent de Premierfait c. 1435), 1492.

Cavendish, George. The life and death of Cardinal Wolsey. 1641 (a garbled version), 1853 (first reliable edn).

— Metrical visions. Ed S. W. Singer 1825.

Lyndsay, David. The tragicall death of David Beaton, Bishoppe of St Andrews. [1547].

Sackville, Thomas, George Ferrers and William Baldwin. A mirror for magistrates. 1559.

Hawkins, Thomas. Unhappy prosperity expressed in the histories of Aelius Sejanus and Philippa the Catanian. 1632. 2nd pt after P. Matthieu, Histoire des prosperitez malheureuses d'une femme cathenoise, Paris 1617.

— De genealogia deorum. Reggio 1481.

Hawes, Stephen. The passetyme of pleasure. 1509.

Lodge, Thomas. Honest excuses. [c. 1580].

Sidney, Sir Philip. The defence of poesie. 1595.

Lemmi, C. W. The influence of Boccaccio on Hawes' Pastime of pleasure. RES 5 1929.

Raith, J. Boccaccio in der englischen Literatur von Chaucer bis Painters Palace of pleasure. Munich 1936.

Wright, H. G. Boccaccio in England from Chaucer to Tennyson. 1957.

Bodin, Jean. Methodus ad facilem historiarum cognitionem. Paris 1566.
— Universae naturae theatrum. Lyons 1596; tr French, 1597.
Brown, J. L. The Methodus ad familiarem historiarum cognitionem of J. Bodin. Catholic Univ of America 1939.
— Bodin and Ben Jonson. Revue de Littérature Comparée 20 1940.
Dean, L. F. Bodin's Methodus in England before 1625. SP 39 1942.
Benjamin, E. B. Donne and Bodin's Theatrum. N & Q March 1968.
Bruni, Leonardo (Aretinus). De bello italico adversus Gothos. Fulgineo 1470; tr A[rthur] Golding 1563.
Bucer, Martin. De regno Christi. Basle 1557; A treatise how by the word of God men's almose should be distributed, 1587 (extracts); Judgement concerning divorce, tr J. Milton 1664.
Milton, John. The doctrine and discipline of divorce. 1643, 1644 (rev).
— Gratulatio ad ecclesiam anglicanam. 1584; tr Thomas Hoby 1549.
Harvey, A. E. Bucer in England. Marburg 1906.
Gilbert, A. H. Bucer on education. JEGP 18 1919.
Bullinger, Henricus. Sermonum decades duae. Zürich 1549; tr H. I. 1577.
Calvin, Jean. Christianae religionis institutio. Basle 1536; The institution of Christian religion, tr T[homas] N[orton] 1561; abridged by W. Lawne, tr Christopher Fetherstone, Edinburgh 1585.
Marshall, W. H. Calvin, Spenser and the major sacraments. MLN 74 1959.
Thomas, Helen. Jacob and Esau: 'rigidly Calvinistic'? Stud in Eng Lit 1500–1900 9 1969.
Campanella, Tommaso. De monarchia hispanica. Amsterdam 1640; tr E. Chilmead 1654.
Cardano, Girolamo. De consolatione. Venice 1542; Cardanus's comfort, tr Thomas Bedingfield 1573.
— De subtilitate. Nuremberg 1550.
Browne, Thomas. Pseudodoxia epidemica. 1646.
Comenius, John Amos. Janua linguarum reserata. Leszno 1631; The gate of tongues unlocked, tr T. Horne 1632; tr J. Anchoran 1639.
— Conatuum Comeniarum praeludia. Oxford 1637, 1639 (rev as Pansophia prodromus); tr as A reformation of schools, 1642.
— Orbis sensualium pictus. Nuremberg 1643; tr C. Hoole 1659.
Turnbull, G. H. Samuel Hartlib: life and relation to Comenius. Oxford 1920.
— Hartlib, Dury and Comenius. 1947.
Young, R. F. (ed) Comenius in England. 1932.
Syfret, R. H. The origins of the Royal Society. Notes & Records of Royal Soc 5 1948.
Geissler, H. Comenius und die Sprache. Heidelberg 1959.
Salmon, V. Problems of language teaching: a discussion among Hartlib's friends. MLR 59 1964.
— Language planning in 17th-century England. In In memory of J. R. Firth, 1966.
Pilz, K. Die Ausgaben des Orbis sensualium pictus. Nuremberg 1967.
Trevor-Roper, H. R. Three foreigners: the philosophers of the puritan revolution. In his Religion, the Reformation and social change, 1967. On Comenius, Dury and Hartlib.
Simon, J. The Comenian educational reformers and the Royal Society. Acta Comeniana 26 1970.
Contarini, Gasparo. De magistratibus et republica Venetorum. Venice 1589; The commonwealth and government of Venice, tr L. Lewkenor 1599.
Muir, K. Shakespeare and Lewkenor. RES new ser 7 1956.
Conti, Lotario (Pope Innocent III). De miseria humanae conditionis. [Venice? c. 1470]; The mirror of man's lyfe, tr H[enry] K[erton] 1576; tr G. Gascoigne, The droome of doomesday pt 1, 1576.
Corro, Antonio del. Dialogus theologicus. 1574; A theological dialogue, tr 1575.
— Salmonis concio de summo hominis bono. 1574: Solomon's sermon, tr Thomas Pie 1586.
Crollius, Oswaldus. Basilica chimica: tractatus novus de signaturis rerum internis. Frankfurt 1609; The mysteries of nature, tr H. Pinnell 1657.
Holmes, E. Henry Vaughan and the Hermetic tradition. Oxford 1932.
Curio, Caelius Secundus. Pasquillus ecstaticus. [Basle 1554]; Pasquino in estasi, tr B. Ochino, Rome 1545; Pasquine in a traunce, tr W.P. (from Italian) [1566]; tr German, 1567.
Drexelius, Hieremias. Horologium auxiliaris tutelaris angeli. Munich 1629 (rev); The angel-guardian's clock, tr T.E.H., Rouen 1650.
Erasmus, Desiderius. Adagiorum collectanea. Paris 1500, Venice 1508 (enlarged as Adagiorum chiliades), Proverbes or adagies gathered out of the Chiliades of Erasmus, tr Richard Taverner 1539, 1545 (enlarged); tr Timothy Kendall, Flowers of epigrammes, 1577; tr Bartholomew Robertson (or Robinson) 1621. None of the trns is complete.
— Encheiridion militis christiani. Antwerp 1503–4; Manual of the Christian knight, tr [William Tyndale?] 1533; A godly boke, tr [Thomas Artour?] [1551?].
Coverdale, Miles. A short recapitulation of Erasmus's Encheiridion. [Antwerp?] 1545.
— Moriae encomium. Paris [1511]; The praise of folly, tr Thomas Chaloner 1549.
— De puero Iesu. [Ghent c. 1514]; tr [c. 1536].
— Paraclesis ad christianae philosophiae studium. Basle 1516; An exhortation to the diligent study of scripture, tr [William Roy?] 1529.
— Institutio principis christiani. Basle 1516.
Elyot, Thomas. The boke named the Governour. 1531.
— Querela pacis. Basle 1517; The complaint of peace, tr Thomas Paynell 1559.
Chapman, George. The teares of peace. 1609.
— Declamatio de morte. Basle 1517; A treatise perswadynge a man to suffre patientlye the deth of his frende, [c. 1531].
— Paraphrases in Novum testamentum. Louvain and Basle 1517–24; vol 1 tr Nicholas Udall et al, vol 2 tr Miles Coverdale et al, 1549.
— Encomium artis medicinae. Antwerp 1518; tr [c. 1535].
— Colloquiorum formulae. Basle 1518, Louvain 1519 (authorized), Basle 1524 (enlarged).
Selected colloquies:
Two dyaloges. Tr Edmund Becke, Canterbury [c. 1550]. Cyclops and De rebus et vocabulis.
Amodest meane to marriage. Tr William Leigh 1568.
Seven dialogues. Tr William Burton 1606.
Pleasant dialogues and drammas. Tr Thomas Heywood 1637.
Single colloquies:
A mery dialogue. Tr [John Rastell] [c. 1530]. Coniugium [1557?].
A dialogue called Funus. Tr 1534.
A dialogue entitled pilgrimage of pure devotion. Tr [c. 1536–7]. Peregrinatio religionis ergo.
The epicure. Tr Philip Gerrard 1545. Epicurus.
One dialogue. Tr E[dward] [Hake] 1566. Diversoria.
Conjuration or spirite. Tr Thomas Johnson 1567.
A notable story of two Alchymists. In Reginald Scot, The discoverie of witchcraft, 1584.
Lyly, John. Euphues and his Euphebus. In his Euphues: the anatomy of wit, 1578.
— Encomium matrimonii. Basle 1518; In laude of matrimony, tr Richard Taverner [1530]; tr Thomas Wilson, Arte of rhetorique, 1553.

—— De contemptu mundi. Louvain 1521; tr Thomas Paynell [c. 1531].

Gascoigne, G. The droome of doomes day. 1576.

—— De interdicto esu carnium. Basle 1522; Concernynge the forbedynge of the eatynge of flesshe, tr [c. 1534].

—— Precatio dominica. Basle 1523; A devout treatise on the Pater Noster, tr Margaret Roper 1526.

—— Virginis apud Lauretum cultae liturgia. Basle 1523; A sermon, tr [c. 1533?] (extract).

—— De immensa Dei misericordia. Basle 1524; tr Gentian Hervet [1525].

Gee, J. A. Hervet's English translation with its appended glossary of Erasmus's De immensa Dei misericordia. PQ 15 1936.

Devereux, J. E. An English glossary by Gentian Hervet. Moreana 4 1967.

—— Virginis et martyris comparatio. Basle 1524; tr Thomas Paynell 1537.

—— Exomologesis. Basle 1524; A treatise of confession, tr [c. 1535–6].

—— De pueris liberaliter instituendis. Basle 1529; tr R. Sherry, Treatise of schemes and tropes, [1550–1]; tr Edward Hake, A touchestone for this time present, 1574 (abstract in verse).

—— Epistola ad Balthasarum Mercklinum. Freiburg 1530; Concerning the verity of the sacrament of Christ's body, tr [1534].

—— De civilitate morum puerilium. Basle 1530; Good manners for children, tr Robert Whittington 1532; Civilitie of childhood, tr Thomas Paynell 1560; Directions for writing tr G.D. 1656 (abstract in verse).

—— Apophthegmatum: sive scite dictorum libri 6. Basle 1531; tr Richard Taverner, Garden of wysdome, 1539; tr Nicholas Udall 1542.

—— De amabili ecclesiae concordia. Basle 1533; An introduction to Christian concord, tr Richard Taverner 1545.

—— Explanatio symboli. Basle 1533; Exposition of the common creed, tr [1534].

—— De preparatione ad mortem. Basle 1534; Preparation to death, tr 1538.

—— De puritate ecclesiae christianae. Basle 1536; An exposition of the 15th psalm, tr 1537.

—— Julius exclusus. [Strasbourg 1519?]; Dialogue between Julius II, Genius and S. Peter, tr [1533–4]. Attributed to Erasmus.

Bibliotheca erasmiana: répertoire des oeuvres d'Erasme. 3 vols Ghent 1893.

Allen, P. S. and H. M. Allen. Opus epistolarum D. Erasmi Roterodami. 12 vols Oxford 1906–58. Bibliography of Erasmus's writings in vol 12.

Bang, W. and H. de Vocht. Klassiker und Humanisten: John Lyly und Erasmus. E Studien 36 1906.

Vocht, H. de. De invloed van Erasmus op de engelsche tooneelliteratur der 16e en 17e eeuwen: pt 1, Shakespeare, Jest-books, Lyly. Ghent 1908.

—— The earliest English translations of Erasmus's Colloquia 1536–66. Louvain 1928.

—— and E. Hake. Earliest English translation of Erasmus's Diversoria. Louvain 1928.

Thomson, J. A. K. Erasmus in England. Vorträge der Bibliothek Warburg 1930–1.

Gee, J. A. Tyndale and Erasmus's Encheiridion. PMLA 49 1934.

—— Berthelet's Latin-English publication of the Apophthegmata Graeciae sapientum formerly edited by Erasmus. SP 35 1938.

Hudson Hoyt, H. Current English translations of the Praise of folly. PQ 20 1941. Corrections by C. H. Miller 45 1966.

Phillips, M. M. Erasmus and propaganda: a study of the translations of Erasmus in English and French. MLR 37 1942.

—— (tr). The Adages of Erasmus. Cambridge 1964.

Malloch, A. E. The techniques and functions of the Renaissance paradox. SP 53 1956.

Miller, H. K. The paradoxical encomium with special reference to its vogue in England 1600–1800. MP 53 1956.

Thomson, D. F. S. and H. C. Porter. Erasmus and Cambridge. Oxford 1963.

Margolin, J. C. Douze années de bibliographie érasmienne. Paris 1963.

Reynolds, E. E. Thomas More and Erasmus. New York 1965.

Devereux, E. J. English translators of Erasmus. In Editing sixteenth-century texts, Toronto 1966.

—— Checklist of English translations of Erasmus to 1700. Oxford 1968.

—— Publications of the English Paraphrases of Erasmus under Henry VIII and Edward VI. Bull John Rylands Lib 51 1969.

—— Erasmus and Restoration England. Moreana 6 1969.

Colie, R. L. Some notes on Burton's Erasmus. Renaissance Quart 20 1967.

Starr, G. A. Antedatings from Nicholas Udall's translation of Erasmus's Apophthegmes. N & Q Dec 1967.

Greenfield, J. R. A midsummer night's dream and the Praise of folly. Comparative Lit 20 1968.

Sowards, J. K. Thomas More, Erasmus and Julius II. Ibid.

Stenger, G. The Praise of folly and its parerga. Medievalia et Humanistica new ser 2 1971.

Ficino, Marsiglio. Theologica platonica de immortalitate animae. Florence 1482.

—— Commentaria in Platonem: Symposium. Florence 1483–4.

Spenser, Edmund. Hymnes in honour of love and beautie. 1596.

Harrison, J. S. Platonism in English poetry of the 16th and 17th centuries. New York 1903.

Schroeder, K. Platonismus in der englischen Renaissance vor und bei Thomas Eliot. Berlin 1920.

Schoell, F. L. Les emprunts de G. Chapman à Ficin. Revue de Littérature Comparée 3 1923.

Dannenberg, F. Das Erbe Platons bis zur Bildung Lylys. Berlin 1931.

Jayne, S. Ficino and the Platonism of the English Renaissance. Comparative Lit 4 1952.

—— John Colet and M. Ficino. Oxford 1963.

Hawkes, T. Ficino and Shakespeare. N & Q May 1958.

Arthos, J. Milton, Ficino and the Charmides. Stud in Renaissance 6 1959.

Kristeller, P. O. Die Philosophie des Ficino. Frankfurt 1972.

Gerhard, Johann. Meditationes sacrae. Leyden 1627; tr R. Winterton, Oxford 1633.

Gratalorus, Gulielmus. De memoria reparanda. Zürich 1553; The castel of memory, tr William Fulwood 1563.

Grotius, Hugo. De iure belli et pacis. Paris 1625; Of the law of warre and peace, tr Clement Barksdale 1654.

Filmer, Robert. Observations concerning the originall of government. 1652.

—— De veritate religionis christianae. Paris 1627; tr 1932.

—— Mare liberum. Paris 1633.

Selden, John. Mare clausum. 1635.

—— De imperio summarum potestatum circa sacra. Paris 1647; tr Clement Barksdale 1651.

Hämmerlein, Thomas (Thomas à Kempis). Imitatio Christi. In his Opera, Nuremberg 1494; tr bks 1–3 William Atkynson 1502; tr Richard Whitford [c. 1530]; tr bks 1–3 (from Châteillon's amended French version) Edward Hake 1567 and Thomas Rogers 1580; tr F.B. [Anthony Hoskins] 1633; tr William Page 1639; tr (with papal approval) Rome 1644; tr John Worthington 1654. Copinger, W. A. On the English translations of the Imitatio Christi. Bibliographiana (Manchester) 3 1900.

Heinsius, Daniel. De tragoediae constitutione. Leyden 1611.

Jonson, Ben. Timber: or discoveries made upon man and matter. In his Works vol 3, 1641.

Spingarn, J. E. The sources of Jonson's Discoveries. MP 2 1905.

Sellin, P. R. Daniel Heinsius and Stuart England. Oxford 1967.

— Milton and Heinsius. In Medieval epic to the 'epic theatre' of Brecht, ed R. P. Armato, Los Angeles 1968.

Heresbach, Conrad. Rei rusticae libri 4. Cologne 1570; Four bookes of husbandry, tr Barnaby Googe 1577.

Hozyusz, Stanislaw. De origine heraesium nostri temporis. Louvain 1559; Of the beginning of heresyes, tr R. Shacklock, Antwerp 1565.

Johann Justus. Pharetia divini amoris. Cologne [1533]; An epistle in the person of Christ to faithfull souls, tr P. Howard, Antwerp 1595.

Jovius, Paulus (Paolo Giovio). Descriptio Britanniae, Scotiae, Hyberniae et Orchadum. Venice 1548.

Kirchmeyer, Thomas (Naogeorgos). Agriculturae sacrae libri 5. Basle 1550; The boke of spiritual husbandry, tr B. Googe 1570.

— Regnum papisticum. [Basle] 1553; The popish kingdom, tr B. Googe 1570.

Lindanus, Gulielmus (Willem van der Lindt). Tabulae vigentium haeresion. Antwerp 1558; The betraing of the beastlinesse of heretics, tr Lewis Evans, Antwerp 1565.

Lipsius, Justus. De constantia. Frankfurt 1590; Two books of constancie, tr J. Stradling 1595; tr 1653; tr R.G.M. of A. 1654.

Stradling, J. A direction for travellers taken out of Lipsius. 1592.

Hilberry, C. B. Ben Jonson's ethics in relation to stoic and humanist ethical thought. Chicago 1933.

Saunders, J. L. J. Lipsius: the philosophy of Renaissance Stoicism. New York 1955.

Loarte, Gaspar de. Exercitium vitae christianae. Barcelona 1569; The exercise of a Christian life, [tr Stephen Brinkley], [Rheims] 1579.

— Meditationes de rosario beatae virginis. Venice 1573; Instructions on how to meditate on the mysteries of the rosary, [tr John Fenne], [Rouen 1600].

Luther, Martin. Contra Henricum regem Angliae. Wittenberg 1522.
For other works in this controversy see J. Fisher, Henry VIII and T. More, below.

— In epistolam Pauli ad Galatas commentarius. Basle 1523; A commentary upon Galatians translated for the unlearned, tr 1575.

— Praefatio in epistolam ad Romanos. [Mainz] 1524.

Tyndale, William. Prologue to Romans. 1526.

Lycosthenes, Conradus. Prodigiorum et ostentorum chronicon. Basle 1557.

Batman (Bateman), Stephen. The doome. 1581.

Martyr, Peter. *See Anglerius, above and Vermigli, below.*

Melanchthon, Philipp. Apologia confessionis augustanae. Wittenberg 1531: The apologie of the confession of the Germanyes, tr Richard Taverner [1536?].

— De iustificatione. [Cologne] 1531; The justification of man by faith only, tr Nicholas Lesse 1548.

— De officio principum. Wittenberg 1539; A civile nosegay wherein is contayned not only the office and dewty of all magistrates and judges but of all subjectes. Tr J[ohn] G[oodale] [1550?].

— Defensio coniugii sacerdotum. Strasbourg 1540; Defense defending the mariage of preistes, tr Lewis Beauchame, [Ipswich 1541]; tr G. Joye, [Antwerp 1541.]

Nollius, Henricus. De generatione rerum naturalium. Frankfurt 1615; The chemist's key, tr Henry Vaughan [1656?].

— Naturae sanctuarium: quod est physica hermetica.

Frankfurt 1619; Hermetical physic, tr Henry Vaughan 1655.

Holmes, E. Vaughan and the hermetic philosophy. 1932.

Ochino, Bernardino. A tragoedie: or dialogue of the unjust usurped primacy of the Bishop of Rome. Tr John Ponet 1549. Latin original not extant.

— Dialogi triginta. Basle 1563; A dialogue of polygamy, A dialogue of divorce, tr 1657 (extracts).

Osorio da Fonseca, Hieronimo. De nobilitate civili libri 2; De nobilitate christiana libri 3. Lisbon 1542; The 5 bookes of Hieronimus Osorius contayning a discussion of civile and Christian nobilitie, tr William Blandie 1576.

— Epistola ad Elizabetham Angliae reginam de religione. Paris and Louvain 1563; An epistle to the most excellent Princesse Elizabeth, tr Richard Shacklock, Antwerp 1565.

— In Gualterum Haddonum de vera religione libri 3. Lisbon 1567; tr John Fenne, Louvain 1568. For replies *see* J. Foxe and W. Haddon.

Paracelsus, Aureolus Philippus ('Theophrastes Bombast von Hohenheim). De natura rerum libri vii. Basle 1570; tr F.J. 1650.

— De summis naturae mysteriis libri iii. Basle 1570; Of the supreme mysteries of nature, tr R. Turner 1656. Both influenced Donne.

Patrizi (Petrić), Francesco. De regno et regis institutione. Paris 1518; tr Thomas Elyot, Boke named the Governor, 1531 (in part).

Perondinus, Petrus. Magni Tamerlanis Scytharum imperatoris vita. Florence 1553.

Marlowe, Christopher. Tamburlane. 1587–8.

Petrarch (Francesco Petrarca). De remediis utriusque fortunae. Strasbourg 1468. Written 1366.

Twyne, Thomas. Phisicke against fortune. 1579.

Coogan, R. Petrarch and More's concept of fortune. Italica 46 1969.

— Petrarch and Sir Thomas More. Moreana 22 1969.

Piccolomini, Aeneas Silvius (Pope Pius II). De ortu imperii Romani. Mainz 1535. Written 1446.

Tyndale, William. The obedience of a Christian man. 1528.

Pico della Mirandola, Giovanni. Omnia opera. Bologna 1496.

— Heptaplus. [Florence 1495?].

— Regulae xii partim excitantes, partim dirigentes hominem in pugna spirituali. Bologna 1496; Twelve rules of a Christian lyfe, tr Thomas More [?1510]; The rules of a Christian life, tr Thomas Elyot 1534.

Pico della Mirandola, Giovanni Francesco. Vita Ioannis Pici. Bologna 1496; The life of Jehan Picus, Erle of Myrandule, tr Thomas More [1510?].

W., H. Twelve rules and weapons concerning the spiritual battell. 1589.

Spenser, Edmund. The Fairie Queene. 1590–6, 1609 (with Mutability cantos).

Reynolds, Henry. Mythomystes. 1632.

Caldiero, F. M. The source of Hamlet's What a piece of work is man. N & Q Sept 1951.

Major, J. M. Sir Thomas Elyot and Renaissance Humanism. Lincoln Nebraska 1964.

Gabriele, Vittorio. Giovanni Pico and Thomas More. Moreana 4 1967.

Pistorius, Johann. Artes cabalisticae: hoc est reconditae theologiae et philosophiae scriptorum tomus 1. Basle 1588.

Blau, J. L. Browne's interest in cabalism. PMLA 49 1934.

Porta, Giovanni Battista della. Phytognomonica. Naples 1588.

— Magiae naturalis libri 20. Naples 1589; Natural magick, tr 1658.

Stevenson, H. A. The major Elizabethan poets and the doctrine of signatures. Florida State Univ Stud 5 1952.

Ramus, Petrus (Pierre de la Ramée). Dialecticae institutiones. Paris 1543; The logicke of P. Ramus martyr, tr R. MacIlmaine 1574; The art of logicke, tr Anthony Wotton 1626; Peter Ramus his dialectica, tr R.P[age] 1632.
For the Ramist Rhetorica see Talon, Omer below.
Digby, Everard. Theoria analytica. 1579.
— De duplici methodo libri duo unicam P. Rami methodum refutantes. 1580.
— Admonitioni F. Mildapetti de unica P. Rami methodo retinendo responsio. 1580.
Temple, William (Franciscus Mildapettus). De unica P. Rami methodo retinenda. 1580.
— Pro Mildapetti de unica methodo defensione commentatio. 1581.
— Epistola de dialecticis P. Rami ad Johannem Piscatorem. 1582.
Case, John. Quam vero falsove Ramus in Aristotelem invehatur. 1584.
Fraunce, Abraham. Shepheardes logike c. 1580. BM additional ms 34,361.
— Lawyers logicke. 1588.
Graves, F. P. Ramus and the educational reformation of the 16th century. 1912.
Nelson, N. E. Ramus and the confusion of logic, rhetoric and poetry. Univ of Michigan Contributions in Modern Philology 2 1947.
French, J. M. Milton, Ramus and Edward Phillips. MP 47 1949.
Howell, W. S. Ramus and English rhetoric 1547–1681. Quart Jnl of Speech 37 1951.
— Logic and rhetoric in England 1500–1700. Princeton 1956.
Hooykaas, R. Humanisme, science et réforme: Pierre de la Ramée 1515–72. Leyden 1958.
Ong, W. J. Ramus, method and the decay of dialogue. Cambridge Mass 1958.
— A Ramus and Talon inventory. Cambridge Mass 1958.
Risse, W. Die Entwicklung der Dialektik bei Ramus. Archiv 42 1960.
Gilbert, N. W. Renaissance concepts of method. New York 1960.
Vasoli C. La dialettica e la retorica dell' umanesimo. Milan 1968.
Saumaise, Claude de (Salmasius). Defensio regia pro Carolo I. [no place] 1649; Apologie royale par Charles I, tr Paris 1650. For reply, *see Milton, col 1242, below.*
Scaliger, Julius Caesar. Poetices libri 7. Lyons 1561.
Peacham, Henry. The compleat gentleman. 1622.
— De subtilitate ad Cardanum. Frankfurt 1576.
Browne, Thomas. Pseudodoxia epidemica. 1646.
Sleidanus, Joannes Philippson. Commentarii de statu religionis et reipublicae Carolo Quinto Caesare. Strasbourg 1555: Famous chronicle of our time, tr John Daus 1560; Mock majesty: the siege of Munster, tr 1644 (part of Commentarii).
Hughes, W. Munster and Abingdon. Oxford 1657.
— De quatuor summis imperiis. Helmstadt 1587; A brief chronicle of four principall empires, tr S. Wythers 1563; The key of historie, 1627 (abridged).
See also Froissart, below.
Sprenger, Jacob and Henricus Institoris. Malleus maleficorum. Strasbourg 1486.
Scot, Reginald. Discoveries of witchcraft. 1548.
Wier, Johann. De praestigiis demonum. Basle 1566.
James I, King of England. Demonologie. Edinburgh 1597.
Middleton, Thomas. The witch. [Before 1622].
Heywood, Thomas. The Lancashire witches. 1634.
Sturm, Johanus. De nobilitate anglicana. Strasbourg 1551; Nobilitas liberata: a ritch storehouse for gentlemen, tr T[homas] B[rowne] 1570.

Talon, Omer (Audomerus Talaeus). Rhetorica. Paris 1543. *See Ramus, above.*
Fraunce, Abraham. The Arcadian rhetorike. 1588.
Torsellino, Orazio. De vita Francisci Xaverii. Rome 1594; tr Thomas F., Paris 1632.
— Lauretana historia. Rome 1597; History of Our Lady of Loreto, tr T[homas] P[rice], [Saint Omer] 1608.
Vergilius, Polydorus. Anglica historia. Basle 1534.
Hay, D. Polydore Vergil. Oxford 1952.
Vermigli, Pietro Martire. Defensio doctrinae veteris de eucharistiae sacramento. Zürich 1559; tr Nicholas Udall 1558.
— Loci communes. 1576: tr A. Marten 1583.
Vida, Hieronymus. De arte poetica. Rome 1527.
Fox, R. C. Vida and Samson Agonistes. N & Q Oct 1959.
Jack, R. V. S. James VI and Renaissance poetic theory. English 6 1967.
Vivès, Juan Luis. De institutione feminae christianae. Bruges 1523; The instruction of a Christian woman, tr Richard Hyrde [1540?].
— Introductio ad sapientiam. Bruges 1524; An introduction to wysdome, tr Richard Morison 1540.
— De officio mariti. Bruges 1528; The office and duties of a husband, tr Thomas Paynell [1553?].
— De disciplinis. Antwerp 1531.
Jonson, Ben. Timber. In his Works, 1641.
— Exercitationes animi in deum. Antwerp 1538.
Bradford, J. Private prayers and meditations. 1559.
Day, J. Christian prayers and meditations. 1569.
Bull, H. et al. Christian prayers. 1570.
Vocht, H. de. Vives and his visits to England. Monumenta Humanistica Lovaniensia 4 1934.
Peers, E. A. Vivès in England. In his St John of the Cross and other lectures, 1946.
Zwingli, Ulrich. Quo pacto ingenui adolescentes formandi sunt praeceptiones. Basle 1523; Certeyne precepts, tr Richard Argentine, Ipswich 1548.

British Writers

Bacon, Francis. De sapientia veterum. 1599; The wisdom of the ancients, tr A. Gorges 1619; tr French by J. Baudoin, Paris 1619; Von der alten Weissheit, tr J. W. von Stubenberg, Nuremberg 1659.
Chapelain, Jean. Les sentiments de l'Académie sur le Cid. Paris 1638.
— De dignitate et augmentis scientiarum. 1623 (enlarged version of Advancement of learning 1605); Neuf livres de l'accroissement des sciences, tr Golofer, Paris 1632; tr Gilbert Wats 1640.
— Historia vitae et mortis. 1623; Histoire de la vie et de la mort, tr J. Baudoin, Paris 1647.
— Faber fortunae. 1638; L'artisan de la fortune, tr J. Baudoin, Paris 1640.
Schupp, J. B. Ars ditiscendi. [Marburg] 1648.
— Orator ineptus [1638]. In his Schrifften, Hanau 1663.
Apácai Csere, János. Magyar encyclopédia. Utrecht 1653.
— Oratio de studio sapientiae. Gyula-Fehérvár 1653.
Zschau, W. W. Quellen und Vorbilder in den 'lehrreichen Schriften' Schupps. Halle 1906.
Tavaszy, S. Apácai Csere János személyisége és vilagnézete. Kolozsvár 1925. On his debt to Bacon.
Bale, John. Acta Romanorum pontificum. In his Scriptorum illustrium maioris Brytanniae catalogus, 1557; Bepstliche Geschichte, tr Z. Müntzer 1566, 1571 (rev).
Barclay, William. De potestate papae. Pont à Mousson 1609; Traité de la puissance du pape, tr Pont à Mousson 1611.
Bigges, Walter, Lieutenant Crofts et al. Expeditio F. Draki in Indes occidentales. [1585] Leyden 1588; tr French, Leyden 1588; A summarie and true discourse of Sir Francis Drake's West Indian voyage, tr 1589; tr German, 1589.

Boethius, Hector (Boece). Scotorum historiae. Bks 1–17, Paris 1526; bks 18–pt 19, Paris 1574; tr John Bellenden [1540?]
Holinshed, R. Chronicles. 1577, 1586–7 (rev).
Shakespeare, W. Macbeth. In his Works, 1623. Performed 1605–6.
Bourchier, Thomas. De martyrio fratrum ordinis minorum. Ingolstadt 1583; tr German by Valentinus Friccius, Ingolstadt 1585.
Buchanan, George. De Maria Scotorum regina. 1572; Histoire de Marie, reine d'Ecosse, tr Camus (Buchanan himself?), Edinburgh 1572.
— Rerum scoticarum historia. Edinburgh 1583.
— De iure regni apud Scotos. Frankfurt 1584; Tsamensprieckinghe vant recht der Coninghem, tr B. de Veer, Amsterdam 1598.
Muir, K. Buchanan, Leslie and Macbeth. N & Q Dec 1955.
Camden, William. Britannia. 1586; tr Philemon Holland 1610; tr French by S. de Sorbière, Théâtre du monde pt 4, Amsterdam 1665.
— Annales rerum anglicarum ad annum 1589. 1615, 1625 (rev); tr French, pt 1 P. de Bellegent, Paris 1624, 1627 (complete); tr English by A. Darcie and T. Browne 1625–9, R. Norton 1635.
Campion, Edmund. Oblati certaminis in causa fidei rationes decem. Ingolstadt 1583; Les dix raisons, tr P. Madur, Lyons 1584; Zehen wolgegründete Ursachen, tr Vitus Miletus, Neiss 1589; De thien reden, tr Antwerp 1591; Zehen underschiedeliche Ursachen, tr C. Wetter Ingolstadt 1594; Campianus Edmondnac tiz magiarul irot okai, tr Hungarian by Bálint Balassa, Vienna 1607; Les dix raisons, tr La Brosse, Paris 1612; [tr P. Meynier], Rouen 1654.
Whitaker, W. Ad rationes decem Edmundi Campioni responsio. 1581; tr R. Stocke 1606.
Cockburn, Patrick. De utilitate et excellentia verbi Dei. Paris 1551; De l'utilité et excellence du verbe divin, tr Lyons 1561.
Fisher, John. Assertionis Lutheranae confrontatio. 1523; German trns: 10 articles J. Cochlaeus, Strasbourg 1523; another article Dresden 1525; complete Casparn Meckenlor, Leipzig 1536.
— De veritate corporis et sanguinis Christi. 1527; Fünf Vorrede wider J. Oekolampadium, tr J. Cochlaeus. 1528.
— Defensio regie assertionis. 1525; German trns: pt J. Cochlaeus 1528; another pt G. Witzel, Cologne 1561.
— Psalmi seu precationes. Cologne 1552: Biblisch Betbüchlein, tr Valentinus Winssheim 1554.
Foxe, John. Commentarii rerum in ecclesia gestarum. Strasbourg 1554, Basle 1559 (enlarged); Historia von Thoma Cranmero, tr A. Jonas, Weissenfels 1561 (extract); Actes and monuments, tr and enlarged 1563, 1570 (rev).
— De Christo gratia iustificanti contra Osorium. 1583; tr 1598.
Crespin, Jean. Actes des martyres. Paris 1554. The rev edn of 1564 was the first to draw substantially on Foxe.
Godwin, Francis. Rerum anglicarum annales. 1616; Annales des choses arrivées en Angleterre, tr De Loigny, Paris 1647.
Haddon, Walter. Epistola apologetica ad Hieronimum Osorium. Paris 1563; Sight of the Portugall pearle, tr Abraham Hartwell 1565.
— Contra H. Osorium [completed by J. Foxe]. 1577; Answer apologeticall to Jerome Osorius, tr James Bell 1581.
Henry VIII, King of England. Assertio septem sacramentorum. 1521; German trns: H. Emser 1522; T. Murner, Strasbourg 1522.
For other items in this controversy, see Luther and Fischer above, and More below.
Herbert of Cherbury, Edward. De veritate. Paris 1624; De la vérité, tr 1639.

Hobbes, Thomas. Elementa philosophiae: de cive. 1642; 1647 (enlarged); Eléments philosophiques: du citoyen, tr S. de Sorbière, Amsterdam 1649; Les éléments de la politique [pts 1–2 only] tr Du Verdus, Paris 1660.
— Elementa philosophiae: sectio prima de corpore. 1655; Elements of philosophy: the first section concerning body, tr 1656.
Morize, A. Thomas Hobbes et Sorbière. Revue Germanique 51 1908.
Humfrey, Laurence. Optimates. Basle 1560; tr as The nobles: or of the nobilitye, 1563.
Jewel, John. Apologia ecclesiae anglicanae. 1562; Apology, tr Ann Cooke 1562: German trns: Johann Wolf 1563; A. Colpinger, Neustadt 1589.
Milton, John. Pro populo anglicano defensio contra Claudii Salmasii defensionem. [1651]; tr Dutch, 1651.
— Defensio secunda. 1654.
See Salmasius above.
More, Thomas. Opus Gulielmi Rossei [Thomas More] quo refellit insanas Lutheri calumnias quibus regem Henricum octavum insectatur. 1523.
— Historia Ricardii tertii. 1543 (written 1513–14?); History of Richard III, 1883 (More's own version, incomplete).
Pace, Richard. Laudatio pacis. 1518; Oraison en la louange de la paix, Paris 1518.
Parsons, Robert. De persecutione anglicana. 1582; La persecution meue en Angleterre, tr De Launoy, Paris 1582; Von der tyrannischen Verfolgung der Calvinisten, tr J. C. Hüber, Ingolstadt 1583; Relacion de algunas martyrios en Inglaterra, tr Madrid 1590.
Robinson, John. Ventilatio tranquilla Pseudodoxiae epidemicae. In his Endoxa, 1656; A calm ventilation 1658 [tr by author]. An attack on Sir Thomas Browne.
Sanders, Nicolas. De origine et progressu schismatis anglicanae. Cologne 1585; L'origine et progres du scisme en Angleterre, tr Augsburg 1587; Les trois livres du docteur Nicolas Sanders, tr J.T.A.C. 1587; Warhafte engelländische Historie, tr J. Hiller, Salzburg 1594.
Stapleton, Thomas. Promptuarium catholicum ad instructionem concionatorum contra hereticos. Lyons 1591; Kirchen- und Hauspostill, tr Aegidius Sturzius, Ingolstadt 1595–6.
Travers, Walter. Ecclesiasticae disciplinae explicatio. 1574; A full and plaine declaration, tr Thomas Cartwright, Zürich 1574.
Turner, Robert (Obertus Barnestapolius). Maria Stuarta innocens. Ingolstadt 1588; tr French by G. de Guttery, Paris 1589.
Willis, John. Mnemonica: sive ars reminiscendi. 1618; tr in part as Art of memory, 1621, 1661 (complete).

Drama

Continental Authors

Gnaphaeus, Gulielmus (Gulielmus Fullonius; Willem de Volder). De filio comoedia, Acolasto titula inscripta. Hague 1529; The comedy of Acolastus, tr John Palsgrave 1540.
Nicholson, Samuel. Acolastus his after-wit. 1600.
Jonson, Ben. Cynthia's revels. 1601.
Grotius, Hugo. Christus patiens. Liège 1608; Christ's passion, tr G. Sandys 1640.
— Sophomphaneas. Amsterdam 1635; tr Francis Goldsmith 1652.
Kirchmeyer, Thomas (Naogeorgos). Pammachius. Wittenberg 1538; tr John Bale (lost).
Bale, John. King Johan. [c. 1540].
Foxe, John. Christus triumphans. 1556.
Ravisius Textor, Joannes. Dialogi. Paris 1536. Includes Juvenis, pater, uxor and Thersites.
A new enterlude called Thersytes. [c. 1537].
Ingelend, Thomas. A pretie enterlude called The disobedient child. [1570?].

Stymellius, Christophorus. Studentes. Frankfurt 1549; 22 edns to 1662.

Gascoigne, George. The glasse of government. 1575.

[Richards, Thomas?]. Misogonus. Ed A. Brandl, Quellen und Forschungen 80 1898. Written 1577.

Herford, C. H. In his Literary relations of England and Germany in the 16th century, Cambridge 1886.

Holthausen, F. Studien zum älteren englischen Drama. E Studien 31 1902.

British Authors

Buchanan, George. Jephthes: sive votum, tragoedia. Paris 1554; tr French by C. L. Vesel 1566; Florent Chrestien, Orleans 1567; A. de Fiefmelin, Paris 1601; P. de Brinon, Rouen 1614; tr German by Jonas Bitner 1569; Martin and Silvester Steier, Nuremberg 1571; Johannes Titelius, Stettin 1592; Georg Dedeken, Lübeck 1595; H. Nicephorus, Brunswick 1604; tr Polish by Jan Zawicki 1587.

— Baptistes sive calomnia: tragoedia. Frankfurt 1578 (written c. 1543); tr German by Ambrosius Lobwasser 1583; M. Lingelsheim 1585; French by R. Brisset, Paris 1590; P. de Brinon, Rouen 1613; Dutch by J. de Decker, Amsterdam 1656.

Hume Brown, C. Buchanan: humanist and reformer. Edinburgh 1890.

Robb, T. D. Humanism in Buchanan. 1907.

Gomes dos Santos, D. M. Buchanan e o ambiante Coimbra do seculo 16. Humanitas (Coimbra) 15–16 1963.

Macfarlane, I. D. Buchanan and France. In Studies in French literature presented to H. W. Lawton, Manchester 1964.

— Buchanan and French Humanism. In Humanism in France, ed A. Levi, Manchester 1970.

Foxe, John. Christus triumphans. 1556; Le triomphe de Jésus Christ, tr J. Bienvenu, Geneva 1562; tr John Day 1579.

Miscellaneous Verse

For Latin poets using Petrarchist themes see below.

Continental authors

Angerianus, Hieronymus. Ἐρωτοπαίγνιον. Florence 1512.

Giles Fletcher the elder. Licia. 1593.

Casimir, Matthias (Sarbiewski). Lyricorum libri 4. Epodon liber unus alterque epigrammatum. Antwerp 1632; The odes of Casimire, tr G. Hils 1646.

Sherburne, Edward. Salmacis. 1651.

Røstvig, M. S. The happy man: studies in the metamorphosis of a classical ideal 1600–1700. Oslo and Oxford 1954.

Dedekind, Friedrich. Grobianus. Frankfurt 1549.

S., R. School of sloverie: or Cato turned wrong side outward. 1605.

Dekker, Thomas. The gul's horn-booke. 1609.

Grobiana's Nuptials. [c. 1610].

Bergmeir, F. Dedekind's Grobianus in England. Greifswald 1904.

Rühl, E. Grobianus in England. Berlin 1904.

Fracastoro, Girolamo. Josephus. In his Opera, Venice 1555; The maiden's blush or Joseph, tr J. Sylvester 1620.

Mancinus, Dominicus. De quattuor virtutibus. Paris 1488; The four cardynale virtues, tr a schoolmaster, 1520; The mirror of good manners, tr Alexander Barclay 1523; The plain path to perfect virtue, tr George Turberville 1568.

Palingenius, Marcellus (Pietro Angelo Manzolli). Zodiacus vitae. Venice [1531]: The zodiak of lyfe, tr Barnabe Googe, bks 1–3 1560, bks 4–6 1561, 1565 (complete), 1576 (rev).

Watson, F. The Zodiacus vitae. 1908.

Petrarca, Francesco. Septem psalmi penitentiales. [1491?]; tr George Chapman 1612.

Pico, Giovanni Francesco, Hymnus ad Christum; hymni heroici. Milan 1507.

Feinstein, B. On the hymns of John Milton and Pico. Comparative Lit 20 1968.

Secundus, Joannes. Basia et alia quaedam. Leyden 1539.

Stanley, Thomas. Kisses. 1651.

Crane, D. Johannes secundus; his life, work and influence on English literature. Leipzig 1931.

Schede, Paul (Paulus Melissus). Oda pindarica ad Elizabetham Britanniae reginam. Augsburg 1578.

Spagnuoli, Baptista Mantuanus. Bucolica. Mantua 1495; nos 5–6 tr Alexander Barclay, Eclogues, [c. 1515]; tr George Turberville 1567 (complete); tr T. Harvey 1656.

Bale, John. A lamentable complaynte. [c. 1560?].

Googe, Barnabe. Eclogues, epytaphes and sonettes. 1563.

Spenser, Edmund. The shepheard's calendar. 1579.

Watson, Thomas. Amyntas 1585; The lamentations of Amyntas, tr Abraham Fraunce 1588.

— Amintae gaudia. 1592.

Fraunce, Abraham. The Countess of Pembroke's Ivychurch. 1591.

Kluge, F. Spensers Shepheards calendar und Mantuans Eclogen. Anglia 3 1880.

— Bemerkungen über Spensers Shepheards calendar und die frühere Bukolik. Anglia 9 1886.

Mustard, W. P. The eclogues of Baptista Mantuanus. Baltimore 1911.

Strada, Famiano. Prolusiones et paradigmata eloquentiae. Cologne 1617. Lectures containing verses as stylistic examples.

Ford, John. The lover's melancholy. 1629.

Crashaw, Richard. Delights. In his Steps to the temple, 1646, 1648 (enlarged).

Vegius, Mapheus. Vergilii Aeneidos liber addititius. Paris 1500; tr Gavin Douglas, The 13 bukes of Eneados, 1553.

Brinton, A. C. Mapheus Vegius and his 13th book of the Aeneid. Stanford 1930.

Vida, Marcus. Scacchiae ludus. Cremona 1550; Chesseplay, tr W.B. 1597.

British Authors

Buchanan, George. Franciscanus et fratres [etc]. Geneva 1564; Le cordelier, puis la palinodie, tr Florent Chrestien, Geneva 1567.

— Psalmorum Davidis paraphrasis poetica. Strasbourg 1566.

Kochanowski, Psałterz Dawidowy. 1579.

Owen, John. Epigrammatum libri tres. 1606; Epigrammatum liber singularis, 1607; Epigrammatum libri tres, 2 vols 1612; Epigrams, tr John Vicars 1619 (selection); tr T. Pecke, Parnassi puerperium, 1659; Teutschender Owenus, tr V. Löbern, Hamburg 1651, 1653 (rev as Teutschender Owenus); tr F. von Logau 1653, 1661.

Hayman, Robert. Quodlibets, epigrams and other small parcels. 1628.

Corneille, Pierre. Mélanges poétiques. Paris 1632.

Ancumanus, Bernhardus Nicaeus. Rosarium: das ist Rosegarten. Emden 1641.

Titz, Johann Peter. Florilegii Oweniani centuria. Danzig 1643.

Schultz, Simon. Centuria epigrammatum a Martialis et Oweni libris selectorum. Danzig 1644.

Ekholm, R. Carl Arosell och Owen: ett bidrag till epigrammets historia i Sverige. Samlaren 88 1967.

Wilterdinck, J. B. Huygens als Nachfolger Owens. Tijdschrift voor Nederlandse Taal- en Letterkunde 84 1968.

For other German imitators, see E. Urban, Owenus und die deutschen Epigrammatiker des 17 Jahrhunderts, Berlin 1900, and G. Waterhouse, The literary relations of England and Germany in the 17th century, Cambridge 1914.

Seymour, Lady Anne et al. Annae, Margaritae, Janae, sororum virginum, in mortem Margaritae Valesiae,

Navarrorum reginae, hecatodistichon. Paris 1550; Le tombeau de Marguerite de Valois faict par les trois soeurs princesses en Angleterre. Paris 1551.

Watson, Thomas. Amyntas. 1585; The lamentations of Amyntas, tr Abraham Fraunce 1588.

—— Meliboeus. 1590 (with author's English trn).

—— Amyntae gaudia. 1592.

Prose Fiction, Allegory and Satire

Continental Authors

Bracciolini, Poggio. Facetiarum liber. [Venice 1470]. Merry tales, wittie questions and quicke answers. 1567. The pleasant conceites of old Hobson. 1607.

Colonne, Guido delle. Historia de bello troiano [written 1287]. Cologne 1477; The ancient hystorie and onely chronicle of the warres, tr John Lydgate, 1555; The faythfull and true storye of the destruction of Troye, tr Thomas Paynell 1553.

Piccolomini, Enea Silvio (Pope Pius II). De duobus amantibus. [Rome 1473?]; The goodlee historie of the ladye Lucres of Scene, tr [1550?]; The history of Euryalus and Lucrece, tr W. Braunche 1596; The history of Euryalus and Lucretia, tr C. Aleyn 1639.

—— De curialium miseriis. Milan 1473.

Barclay, Alexander. Egloges, the first thre out of Miserie curialium. [c. 1515].

British Authors

Barclay, John. Euphormionis Lusinini Satyricon. 1603; pt 2, Paris 1607; pt 3 (Apologia Euphormionis pro se), Paris 1610; tr French by I.T.P (Jean Tournet), Paris 1625, M. Nau (pt 1 only), Paris 1626, J. Bérault, Paris 1640.

—— Icon animorum. 1614; The mirror of mindes, tr Thomas May 2 pts 1631–3; Le portrait des esprits, [tr Nanteuil de Bohain], Rheims 1623; Le tableau des esprits, tr Paris 1625; tr German by Johann Seyforten of Ulm, Bremen 1649.

—— Argenis. Paris 1621; 40 edns to 1639; tr Kingsmill Long 1625; Robert le Grys and Thomas May 1629; tr French, Les amours de Poliarque et Argenis by P. de Marcassus, Paris 1622; [N. Guibert], Paris 1623; P. de Marcassus, Paris 1626 (new trn); tr German by Martin Opitz, Breslau 1626; Spanish by Pellicier de Salas, Madrid 1526; by Gabriel de Corral, Madrid 1626; Greek, Leyden 1627; Dutch by Glazemaker, Amsterdam 1643.

Coeffeteau, F. N. Histoire de Poliarque et Argenis [a summary]. Tr German by A. Frideric 1631; tr by Judith Man 1640.

Mouchemberg, M. de. La seconde partie d'Argenis. Paris 1625; tr Latin, 1626; tr Spanish by Pellicier de Salas 1626; tr German by Martin Opitz, Breslau 1631.

Mairet, J. de. Sylvie. Paris 1626.

Du Ryer, P. Argenis et Poliarque. Paris 1630; pt 2, 1631.

Howell, James. Dodona's grove. 1640.

Gott, Samuel. Nova Solyma. 1648.

Braithwait, Richard. Panthalia. 1659.

Mackenzie, George. Aretina. 1660.

Dukas, J. Etude bibliographique et littéraire sur le Satyricon de Barclay. Paris 1880.

Collignon, A. Notes sur l'Euphorion. Nancy 1901.

—— Notes historiques et bibliographiques sur l'Argenis. Nancy 1902.

—— Le portrait des esprits. Paris 1906.

Schmidt, K. F. Johann Barclays Argenis: Ausgaben der Argenis, ihrer Fortsetzungen und Übersetzungen. Berlin 1904.

Bloedau, K. A. von. Grimmelhausens Simplicissimus und seine Vorgänger. Palaestra 51 1908.

Langford, G. Barclay's Argenis: a seminal novel. SE 27 1947.

Colville, K. N. Fame's twilight. 1923.

Fleming, D. A. Barclay: neo-latinist at the Jacobean Court. Renaissance News 19 1966.

—— Barclay's Satyricon: the first satirical roman à clef. MP 65 1967.

Hall, Joseph. Mundus alter et idem. Frankfurt [1605?]; The discovery of a new world, tr J. Healey [1609?]; Utopiae pars ii: die heutige newe alte Welt, tr G. Wintermonat Leipzig 1613.

Petherick, A. E. On the authorship and translations of Mundus alter et idem. GM July 1896.

More, Thomas. Libellus vere aureus de optimo reipublicae statu deque nova insula Utopia. Louvain 1516; Von der wunderbarlichen Innsel Utopia gennant das ander Buch, tr C. Cantiuncula, Basle 1524; La republica nuovamente ritrovata del governo dell'isola Eutopia, tr A. F. Doni, Venice 1548; La description de l'île d'Utopie, tr Jean le Blond, Paris 1550; A fruitful and pleasant worke of the best state of the publyque weal and of the newe yle called Utopia, tr Raphe Robynson 1551; De Utopie: nun erst overghesedt in neder Duytsche, Antwerp 1553; La république d'Utopie, tr C. Chappuys, Paris 1585; Beschreibung der überaus herrlichen Insal Utopia, tr G. Wintermonat, Leipzig 1612; tr Spanish by J. A. Medinilla i Porres, Cordova 1637; L'Utopie, tr S. de Sorbière, Amsterdam 1643.

Rabelais, F. Pantagruel. Lyons [1532?]; Quart livre. Lyons 1546, Paris 1552 (enlarged).

Andreae, J. V. Christianopolis. Strasbourg 1619.

Campanella, T. Civitas solis. 1623.

Bacon, F. The new Atlantis. 1627.

Gott, Samuel. Nova Solyma. 1648.

Glunz, H. Shakespeare und Morus. Kölner Anglistische Arbeiten 32 1938.

Vissner, F. T. Borrowings by Shakespeare from More. Tijdschrift voor Taal en Letteren 27 1939.

Semper, I. J. Shakespeare and More. Catholic Educational Rev 39 1941.

Donner, H. W. Introduction to Utopia. Upsala 1945.

Binder, J. More's Utopia in English: a note on the translation. MLN 62 1947.

Hexter, J. H. More's Utopia: the biography of an idea. Princeton 1952.

Surtz, E. The praise of wisdom: a commentary on the religious and moral problems and backgrounds of More's Utopia. Chicago 1957.

López Estrada, F. La primera versión española de la Utopia de Moro por Jerónimo Antonio de Medinilla (Córdoba 1637). In Collected studies in honour of Américo Castro, Oxford 1965.

Dorsch, T. S. More and Lucian: an interpretation of Utopia. Archiv 203 1967.

Coogan, R. Petrarch and More's concept of fortune. Italica 46 1969.

—— Petrarch and More. Moreana 6 1969.

Schoeck, R. J. More and the Italian heritage of early Tudor humanism. In Arts libéraux et philosophie au Moyen Age, Montreal 1969.

For a fuller bibliography see E. Surtz and J. H. Hexter, Complete works of More vol 4, New Haven 1965.

(5) FRENCH

General studies – Dictionaries and grammars – Travel – History – Philosophy, politics, education etc – Theology – Literary theory and criticism – Drama – Verse – Allegory and satire – Prose fiction.

General Studies

For contemporary accounts see also Travel and History, below.

Desmontiers, Jean. De l'origine, description et merveilles d'Escosse. Paris 1538.

Chambers, David. La recherche des singularitez d'Ecosse. Paris 1579.

Michel, F. Les Ecossais en France et les Français en Ecosse. 2 vols 1862.

Smiles, S. The Huguenots: their settlements, churches and industries in England and Ireland. 1867.

Chatelain, E. Le livre ou cartulaire de la nation d'Angleterre et d'Allemagne de l'Université de Paris. Paris 1891.

Schickler, F. de. Les églises du refuge en Angleterre 1547–1685. Paris 1892.

Haudecoeur, A. Jeanne d'Arc dans la littérature et devant l'opinion en Angleterre. Rheims 1895.

Littleboy, A. L. Relations between French and English literature in the 16th and 17th centuries. 1895.

Plomer, H. R. Robert Copland. Trans Bibl Soc 3 1896. A translator from French.

Jusserand, J. J. French ignorance of English literature in Tudor times. Nineteenth Century April 1898.

—— Shakespeare en France sous l'ancien régime. Paris 1898.

Bastide, C. Huguenot thought in England. Jnl of Comparative Lit 4 1903.

—— Anglais et français du 17e siècle. Paris 1912.

—— The Anglo-French entente in the 17th century. New York 1914.

Teleen, J. M. Milton dans la littérature française. Paris 1904.

Charlanne, L. L'influence française en Angleterre au xviiᵉ siècle. Paris 1906.

Upham, A. H. The French influence in English literature 1558–1660. New York 1908.

Kastner, L. E. The Scottish sonneteers and the French poets. MLR 3 1908.

—— The Elizabethan sonneteers and the French poets. Ibid.

—— Wyatt and the French sonneteers. MLR 4 1909.

Baldensperger, F. Esquisse d'une histoire de Shakespeare en France. In his Etudes d'histoire littéraire, 2 sers Paris 1910.

Lee, S. The French Renaissance in England. Oxford 1910.

Spurgeon, C. F. E. Chaucer devant la critique en Angleterre et en France depuis son temps jusqu'à nos jours. Paris 1911.

Leith, W. F. Pre-reformation scholars in Scotland. Glasgow 1915.

Mathorez, J. Note sur les intellectuels écossais en France au xvie siècle. Bulletin du Bibliophile March 1919.

Lambley, K. The teaching and cultivation of the French language in England during Tudor and Stuart times. Manchester 1920.

Bibliographie de la littérature anglaise traduite en français. Le Navire d'Argent June 1925.

Lawton, H. W. Notes sur Jean Baudoin et ses traductions de l'anglais. Revue de Littérature Comparée 6 1926.

Ascoli, Georges. La Grande-Bretagne devant l'opinion française depuis la guerre de cent ans jusqu'à la fin du 16e siècle. Paris 1927.

—— La Grande-Bretagne devant l'opinion française au 17e siècle. 2 vols Paris 1930. With bibliography.

Koszul, A. Alsace et l'Angleterre au 16e siècle. Revue de Littérature Comparée 9 1929.

Scott, J. G. Les sonnets élizabéthains. Paris 1929.

Smith, J. The French background of Middle Scots literature. 1934.

Brie, F. Französischer Frühhumanismus in England. Anglia 61 1937.

Brown, H. The Mersenne correspondence: a lost letter by Thomas Hobbes. Isis 34 1943.

Tucker, J. E. John Davies of Kidwelly. PBSA 44 1950. With bibliography.

Mourgues, O. de. Metaphysical, baroque and précieuse poetry. Oxford 1953.

Salmon, J. H. M. The French religious wars in English political thought. 1959. With bibliography.

Schoeck, R. J. Law French: status of the scholarship. Kentucky Foreign Lang Quart 6 1959.

Shire, H. M. The thrissil, the rois and the flour-de-lys: a sample-book of state-poems and love-songs showing affinities between Scotland, England and France. Cambridge 1962.

Ross, I. Sonneteering in 16th-century Scotland. SE 44 1964.

Jack, R. D. S. Imitation in the Scottish sonnet. Comparative Lit 20 1968.

Hassell, J. W. Bonaventure des Périers abroad. In Renaissance and other studies in honor of W. L. Wyley, Chapel Hill 1968.

Dictionaries and Grammars

This list is selective. See also A. H. Upham, The French influence in English literature, New York 1908.

French

Barclay, Alexander. Introductorie to write and to pronounce French. 1521.

Caxton, A. Dialogues in French and English. [c. 1483]. Adapted from Livre des métiers (14th century).

Palsgrave, John. L'esclaircissement de la langue française. 1530.

Dewes (or Du Guez), Giles. An introductorie for to learne to rede, to pronounce and to speake French trewly. 1532.

Meurier, Gabriel. Traité pour apprendre à parler anglais et français. Antwerp 1553.

Holyband, Claude. The French Littleton. 1566.

—— The French Schoole-maister. 1573.

—— A treasury of the French tongue, the way to vary all sorts of verbs. 1580.

—— The fluorie field of four languages: Latin, French, English and Italian. 1583.

—— A dictionarie French and English. 1593.

Farrer, L. E. Un devancier de Cotgrave: Claude de Sainliens alias Claude Holyband. Paris 1908.

Bellot, James. The French grammar. 1578.

Baret, John. An alvearie or triple dictionarie in Englishe, Latin and French. [1573].

—— An alvearie or Quadruple dictionarie. 1580. English, Latin, Greek and French.

Eliot, John. Ortho-epia gallica: Eliot's fruits for the French. 1593.

Yates, F. The importance of John Eliot's Ortho-epia gallica. RES 7 1931.

La Mothe le Vayer, G. de. The French alphabet. 1595.

Cotgrave, R. A dictionarie of the French and English tongue. 1611.

Smalley, V. E. The sources of a Dictionarie of the French and English tongues by Randle Cotgrave. Baltimore 1948.

Wodroeph, John. The spared hours of a soldier in his travels or the time marrow of the English tongue. Dort 1623.

Lisle, William. Part of du Bartas, English and French, as may teach an Englishman French, or a Frenchman English. 1625.

De Grave. The pathway to the gate of tongues in Latin, French and English. 1633.

Maupas. Charles. A French grammar and syntaxe. 1634.

Du Gres, G. Dialogi gallico-anglico-latini. Oxford 1639.

English

Mason, Georges. Grammaire anglaise: contenant les règles bien exactes et certaines de la prononciation, orthographie et construction de notre langue. 1622.

Travel

French in Great Britain

Perlin, Etienne. Description des royaumes d'Angleterre et d'Escosse. Paris 1558.

Grévin, Jacques. Sonnets d'Angleterre (written 1567). Ed L. Dorez, Bulletin du Bibliophile 1898.

Rohan, Henri de. Voyage fait en l'an 1600. Amsterdam 1646.

Coulon, L. Le fidèle conducteur pour le voyage d'Angleterre. Paris 1654.

Croker, T. C. (ed). The tour of the French traveller, La Boullaye le Couz, in Ireland 1644. 1837.

Babeau, A. Les voyageurs en France depuis la Renaissance jusqu'à la Révolution. Paris 1885.

Fordham, H. G. The earliest French itineraries. Library 4th ser 1 1921.

Laumonier, P. Ronsard et l'Ecosse. Revue de Littérature Comparée 4 1924.

La Brosse, J. de. Histoire d'un capitaine bourbonnais au 16e siècle, Jacques de la Brosse: ses missions en Ecosse. Paris 1929.

Saint-Amant, M. G. de. Sainte-Marthe en Angleterre. MLN 50 1935.

Legouis, E. Marvell and the two learned brothers Sainte-Marthe. PQ 38 1959.

English and Scots in France

Sir Philip Sidney, 1554–86
   Languet, Herbert. Epistolae politicae et historicae ad Philippum Sydnaeum. Frankfurt 1633.
   Osborn, A. W. Sidney in France. Paris 1932.
   John, L. C. The first edition of the letter of Hubert Languet to Sidney. JEGP 48 1949.

Dallington, Robert. View of France. 1598; rptd as A method for travell, 1604.

Coryate, Thomas. Crudities hastely gobled up in 5 moneths travels in France etc. 1611.

Lithgow, William. A most delectable and true discourse of an admired and painfull peregrination. 1614, 1623 (enlarged).

Moryson, Fynes. An itinerary containing his ten years' travels. 1617.

Heylin, Peter. A full relation of two journeys: the one into the mainland of France, the other of the adjacent islands. 1656

Herbert of Cherbury, Edward, Baron. Life, written by himself. Strawberry Hill 1765. Written 1642–8.

Evelyn, John. Memoirs 1641–1706. Ed W. Bray 2 vols 1818; Diary, ed E. S. de Beer, 6 vols Oxford 1955. Travels in France, Italy and Switzerland 1643–7.

Cameron, J. K. Letters of John Johnston (1565–1611) and Robert Howie (1565–1645). 1963.

History

For contemporary sources used in drama see Drama, below.

French authors (*including Scots writing in French*)

Bouchard, Alain. Les chroniques d'Angleterre et de Bretaigne. Paris 1514.

Chambers, David. Histoire abrégée de tous les roys de France, Angleterre et Escosse. Paris 1579.

Comines, Philippe de. Chronique de Louis XI. Paris 1524; Chronique de Charles VIII, Paris 1528; History, tr Thomas Danett 1596.

Du Bec-Crespin, Jean. Histoire de grand empereur Tamarlanes. Rouen 1595.
   W., H. The history of the great emperor Tamerlane. 1597.

Du Chesne, André. Histoire générale d'Angleterre, d'Escosse et d'Irlande. Paris 1614.

Froissart, Jean. Les chroniques [written c. 1369–1410]. Paris 1495; tr John Bourchier, Lord Berners 1523–5; Latin epitome by Sleidanus (1537), tr P[eter] Golding 1608.

Goulart, Simon. Histoires admirables de notre temps. Paris 1600; Admirable and memorable histories containing the wonders of our time, tr Edward Grimestone 1607.

Mentieth de Salmonet, Robert. Histoire des troubles de la Grande Bretagne. Paris 1649.

Serres, Jean de. Mémoires de la 3e guerre civile de France. 1570; Three parts of commentaries of the civill warres of France, 1574; The fourth part, tr Thomas Timms 1576.
   Golding, Arthur. The lyfe of the most godly Jasper Coligny. 1576.
   — Inventaire général de l'histoire de France. Paris 1597; A general inventory of the history of France, tr Edward Grimestone 1607.

English Authors

Bacon, Francis. The history of the reign of Henry VII. 1622; Histoire du règne de Henri VII, roi d'Angleterre, tr La Tour Hotman, Paris 1627; tr Latin, Leyden 1642.

Philosophy, Politics, Education etc

Balzac, Guez de. Le prince. Paris 1631; tr H.G. 1648.
   — Aristippe ou la cour Paris 1658; Aristippus, tr R.W. 1659.

Bodin, Jean. Les six livres de la république. Paris 1576; The six books of a Commonweal, tr Richard Knolles 1606.
   Brown, John L. Bodin and Ben Jonson. Revue de la Littérature Comparée 20 1940.
   Mosse, G. L. The influence of Bodin's République in English political thought. Medievalia et Humanistica 5 1948.

Charron, Pierre. Traité de la sagesse. Paris 1601; tr S. Lennard 1607–8.

Coignet, Matthieu. Instruction aux princes. Paris 1584; Politique discourse upon truthe and lying, tr Sir Edward Hoby 1586.

Descartes, René. Discours de la méthode. Leyden 1637; A discourse of the method for the well guiding of reason, tr 1649.
   — Le Traité des passions 1649; The passions of the soul, tr 1650.
   Bro[u]ncker, W. Descartes' excellent compendium of music. 1653.
   Davis, John, of Hereford. Treatise against the principles of Descartes. 1654.
   Gilson, E. Descartes et Harvey. Revue Philosophique 90–1 1920.
   Nicolson, M. H. The early stage of Cartesianism in England. SP 26 1929.
   Gregg, J. C. Cudworth and Descartes. Philosophy 8 1933.
   Lamprecht, S. P. The role of Descartes in 17th-century England. Stud in History of Ideas 3 1935.
   Adam, C. Descartes: ses contemporains anglais. Revue de Littérature Comparée 17 1937.
   Anderson, P. R. Descartes's influence in 17th-century England. Etudes Cartésiennes 3 1937.

Frondizi, R. Descartes y la filosofia inglesa del siglo 17. In Escritos en honor de Descartes, La Plata 1938.

Savenson, J. E. Descartes's influence on John Smith. JHI 20 1959.

— Descartes and the Cambridge Platonists. JHI 21 1960.

Sailor, D. B. Cudworth and Descartes. JHI 23 1962.

Sempel, C. The garden: Marvell's Cartesian ecstasy. JHI 28 1967.

Du Vair, Guillaume. De la constance. Paris 1619; tr [1622].

d'Espagne, Jean. Les erreurs populaires qui concernent l'intelligence de la religion. Paris 1643; Popular errors, tr 1648.

Estienne, Henri II. Apologie pour Hérodote. [Geneva] 1566; tr 1599.

— Traité de la conformité des merveilles anciennes avec les modernes. Antwerp and Geneva [1566]; A world of wonders, tr Richard Carew 1607.

Bawcutt, N. W. Possible sources for the Unfortunate traveller. N & Q Feb 1960. On Nashe.

Gentillet, Innocent. Discours sur les moyens de bien gouverner. [Geneva] 1576; A discourse upon the meanes of wel governing a kingdom against Nicolas Machiavel, tr Simon Patricke 1602.

— Apologie pour les Chrestiens de France de la religion évangelique. [Geneva] 1578; tr Jerome Bowes 1579.

Hurault, M. Discours sur l'état de France. 1588; Politicke, moral and martial discourses, tr 1595.

Joubert, Laurent. Erreurs populaires et propos vulgaires. 2 vols Bordeaux 1579–80.

Browne, Thomas. Pseudodoxia epidemica. 1646.

La Mothe le Vayer, G. de. De la liberté et de la servitude. Paris 1643.

Evelyn, John. Of liberty and servitude. 1649.

La Noue, Francois de. Discours politiques et militaires. Basle 1587; The politicke and military discourses, tr E.A[ggas] 1587.

La Primaudaye, Pierre de. Académie française. Paris 1580; The French Academy, tr T.B[owes] 2 pts 1586–94; pt 3 tr R. Dolman 1601; pts 1–4, 1618. Bk 4 tr W.P.

Anderson, R. L. A French source for John Davies of Hereford's system of psychology. PQ 6 1927.

Le Grand, Jacques. Le livre de bonnes moeurs. [Lyons 1487?]; A lytle book called good manners, [c. 1500].

Le Roy, Louis. De la vicissitude ou variété des choses en l'univers. Paris 1575; Of the interchangeable course or varietie of things in the whole world, tr R. Ashley 1594.

Norden, John. Vicissitudo rerum. 1600.

Koller, K. Two Elizabethan expressions of the idea of mutability. SP 35 1938.

Gundershiemer, W. L. Life and works of Louis Le Roy. 1966.

Montaigne, Michel de. Essais. Bordeaux 1580, Paris 1588 (with addns); The essays of morall, politike and millitarie discourses, tr J. Florio 1603.

Bacon, Francis. Essayes. 1597, 1612, 1625 (both enlarged).

Cornwallis, William. Essays. 1600.

Ralegh, Walter. The sceptick. 1651.

Hartlib, Samuel. The true and ready way to learn the Latine tongue. 1654.

Stedefeld, G. F. Hamlet: ein Tendenzdrama Shakespeares gegen die skeptische und kosmopolitische Weltanschauung des Montaigne. Berlin 1871.

Robertson, J. M. Montaigne and Shakespeare. 1897.

Dieckow, F. A. F. John Florios englische Übersetzung der Essais Montaignes und Lord Bacons, Ben Jonsons und Robert Burtons Verhältnis zu Montaigne. Strasbourg 1903.

Routh, H. V. The origins of the essay compared in French and English literatures. MLR 15 1920.

Selby, F. G. Bacon and Montaigne. Criterion 4 1925.

Taylor, G. C. Shakespeare's debt to Montaigne. Cambridge Mass 1925.

Zeitlin, J. The development of Bacon's Essays, with special reference to the question of Montaigne's influence upon them. JEGP 27 1928.

Türck, S. Shakespeare und Montaigne. Berlin 1930.

Nethercot, A. H. Abraham Cowley's Essays. JEGP 29 1930.

Stewart, J. I. M. Montaigne and the Defence of rhyme. RES 9 1933.

Bennett, R. E. Cornwallis's use of Montaigne. PMLA 48 1933.

Deutschbein, M. Shakespeares Kritik an Montaigne in As you like it. Neuphilologische Monatsschrift 5 1934.

— Shakespeares Hamlet und Montaigne. Shakespeare-Jahrbuch 80–1 1944–5.

Franz, W. Shakespeare und Montaigne. Die Neueren Sprachen 40 1934.

Yvon, P. Montaigne chez les Anglo-Saxons. Caen 1935.

Boase, A. The fortunes of Montaigne. 1935.

— The early history of the 'essai' title in France and England. In Studies in French literature presented to H. M. Lawton, Manchester 1968.

Henderson, W. B. Montaigne's Apologie of Raymond Sebond and King Lear. Shakespeare Assoc Bull 14–15 1939–40.

Stapfer. Montaigne et Shakespeare. Bulletin des Amis de Montaigne 2nd ser 6 1939.

Harmon, A. How great was Shakespeare's debt to Montaigne? PMLA 57 1942.

Taylor, G. C. Montaigne-Shakespeare and the deadly parallel. PQ 22 1943.

Dédéyan, C. Montaigne chez ses amis anglo-saxons. 2 vols Paris 1946.

Schmid, E. E. Shakespeare, Montaigne und die schauspielerische Formel. Shakespeare-Jahrbuch 82–3 1946–7.

Faure, E. Montaigne et ses trois premiers-nés: Shakespeare, Cervantes, Pascal. Paris 1948.

Maxwell, J. C. Montaigne and Macbeth. MLR 43 1948.

Legge, D. An English allusion to Montaigne before 1595. RES new ser 1 1950.

Hodgen, M. T. Montaigne and Shakespeare again. HLQ 16 1953.

Cross, G. Marston, Montaigne and morality: the Dutch courtezan reconsidered. ELH 27 1960.

Montano, R. From Montaigne to the Tempest. Umanesimo 1 1967.

Françou, M. Sur la tragédie du mouchoir dans les Essais de Montaigne et dans l'Othello de Shakespeare. Bulletin de la Société des Amis de Montaigne 15 1968.

— Deux notes sur Montaigne: Montaigne et John Evelyn, Montaigne et l'humanisme. Bulletin de la Société des Amis de Montaigne 17 1969.

Pasquier, Etienne. Le monophile. Paris 1555.

Fenton, G. Monophylo: a philosophical discourse and division of love. 1572.

— Recherches de la France. Paris 1560–1621.

Chapman, George and James Shirley. The tragedy of Chabot, admirall of France. 1639.

Philibert de Vienne. Le philosophe de la cour. Lyons 1547; tr G. North 1575.

Scudéry, Georges de. Discours politiques des rois. Paris 1647; Curia politiae: or the apologies of several princes, tr 1654.

Scudéry, Madelaine de. Les femmes illustres. Rouen 1655; Triumphant arch erected and consecrated to the glory of the feminine sex, tr T.B. 1656. First pbd as by Georges de Scudéry.

English Authors

Bacon, Francis. Essayes. 1597, 1612, 1625 (both enlarged); Essais moraux, tr Arthur Gorges 1619; tr J. Baudoin, Paris 1619.
—— The advancement of learning. 1605; Le progrès et avancement aux sciences divines et humaines, tr André Maugars, Paris 1619.
—— Sylva sylvarum: or a natural history. 1627; Histoire naturelle, tr P. Amboise, Paris 1631; tr Latin by J. Gruter, Amsterdam 1653.
—— The new Atlantis. 1627: L'Atlas nouveau, tr P. Amboise, Paris 1631.
Rémusat, C. Bacon: sa vie, son temps, sa philosophie et son influence jusqu'à nos jours. Paris 1857.
Kynaston Snell, H. P. Jean Baudoin et les Essais de Bacon en France jusqu'au 18e siècle. Paris 1939.
Brerewood, Edward. Enquiries touching the diversity of languages and religions. 1614; Recherches curieuses sur la diversité des langues et des religions, tr J. de la Montagne, Paris 1640.
Cecil, William, Lord Burghley. The execution of justice in England. 1583; L'exécution de justice faicte en Angleterre, tr 1584.
Drake, Francis. Second circumnavigation of the world. In Purchas, Purchas his pilgrimes, 1625; Le voyage de Fr. Drach à l'entour du monde, tr F. de Louvencourt, Paris 1637.
Dyke, Daniel. The mystery of self-deceiving. 1615; Le sonde de la conscience, tr Jean Verneuil, Geneva 1634.
Jovy, E. Deux inspirateurs inconnus jusqu'ici des Maximes de la Rochefoucauld: Daniel Dyke et Jean Verneuil. Bulletin du Bibliophile 15 Oct 1909.
[Gauden, John]. Eikôn basiliké: the portraicture of his sacred Majesty. 1648; tr Latin, Hague 1649; Eikôn basiliké: le portrait du roi de la Grande Bretagne, tr J. B. Porrée, Rouen 1649.
Hariot, Thomas. A brief and true report of the Newfoundland of Virginia. Frankfurt 1690; tr French, Frankfurt 1690.
James I. Basilikon doron. 1599; Basilikon doron: ou présent royal, tr Paris 1603; tr J. Hotman, Paris 1604; Présent royal de Jacques 1, tr Pierre Ménard, L'académie des princes, Paris 1646.
Milton, John. Eikonoklastes: in answer to a book entitled Eikôn basilike. 1649; tr French by John Dury 1652.
Settle, John. A true report of the last voyage of Captain Martin Frobisher. 1577; tr French by Nicolas Pithou, Geneva 1578.

Theology and Works of Piety

French Authors

Benedicti, Jean. Somme de péchés. Paris 1589.
Lodge, Thomas. Catharus Diogenes. [1591 ?].
Bèze, Théodore de (Theodorus Beza). Discours de la vie et trespas de M. Jean Calvin. Geneva 1564; On the life and death of Master John Calvin, tr 1578.
—— Response aux actes de la conférence de Mombelliard. Geneva 1587.
Perkins, William. An excellent treatise comforting such as are troubled about their predestination. 1591.
A number of Bèze's sermons were also tr John Hamar.
Calvin, Jean. Petit traicté de la saincte cène. Geneva 1545; Concerning the sacred sacrament, tr M. Coverdale [1549?].
—— Avertissement contre l'astrologie judiciaire. Geneva 1549; An admonition against astrology, tr G[odred] G[ylby] 1561.
—— Traicté des reliques. Geneva 1543; tr Steven Wythers 1561.
A number of Calvin's sermons were also tr John Field, Arthur Golding, Robert Horne et al 1553–79.
Camus, J.-P. Le directeur spirituel désintéressé. Paris 1631; The spiritual director disinterested, tr A. B. Roan, 1633.

Crayon de l'éternité. Douai 1631; Draught of eternity, tr Miles Car 1632.
Caumont, Jean de. Du firmement des catholiques. Paris 1587; The firm foundation of the Catholic religion, tr John Pauncefote, Antwerp 1590.
Caussin, Nicholas. La sainte cour. Paris [1625]; The holy court: or the Christian instruction of men of quality, tr Thomas Hawkins 1626; The unfortunate politique, Oxford 1639 (extract).
Mornay, Philippe de. Excellent discours de la vie et de la mort. La Rochelle 1577; The defense of death, tr E[dward] A[ggas] 1577; A discourse of life and death, tr Countess of Pembroke 1592.
—— Traité de l'église. 1578; A notable treatise on the Church, tr J[ohn] F[ield] 1579.
—— De la vérité de la religion chrestienne. Antwerp 1581; The trewness of the Christian religion, tr Philip Sidney and Arthur Golding 1587.
Buckley, T. T. The indebtedness of John Davies' Nosce teipsum to Philip Mornay's Trewness of the Christian religion. MP 25 1927.
Murphy, C. D. John Davies's versification of Sidney's prose. PQ 21 1942.
Robinson, F. G. A note on the Sidney-Golding translation of Philippe de Mornay's De la vérité de la religion chrestienne. Harvard Lib Bull 17 1969.
Pascal, Blaise. Les provinciales. Cologne 1656–7; Les provinciales: or the mysteries of Jesuitism, tr H[enry] H[ammond] 1657.
Jansen, P. De Pascal à Hammond: les Provinciales en Angleterre. Paris 1954.
Sales, St François de. Introduction à la vie dévote. Paris 1608; tr 1613.
Allison, A. F. Crashaw and S. François de Sales. RES 24 1948.
Rolland, L. C. François de Sales and Jeremy Taylor. Revue de Littérature Comparée 42 1968.
Viret, P. Des principaux points qui sont aujourd'hui en different touchant la sainte cène et la messe. Lyons 1566; The Lordes supper and against the masse, tr 1597.

English Authors

Bayly, Lewis, Practise of pietie. [1612]; La pratique de piété, tr Jean Verneuil, Geneva 1625.
Cooke, Alexander. Pope Joane. 1610; La papesse Jeanne, tr J. de la Montagne, Sedan 1633.
Gouge, William. The whole armour of God. 1616; L'armure complète, tr David Le Clerc, Geneva 1643.
Hall, Joseph. Meditations and vows. 1605; Le Sénèque ressuscité chrétien, tr H. L. de Tourval, Paris pt 1, 1610, 1614 (complete).
—— Heaven upon earth. 1606; Le ciel sur la terre, tr Th. Jacquemot, Geneva [1628].
—— Holy observations pt 1. 1607; pt 2, 1609; Les sainctes observations, tr Geneva 1621.
—— Characters of virtues and vices. 1608; Caractères des vertus et des vices, tr J. L. de Tourval, Paris 1610.
—— Letters. 1608; Épîtres mêlées, tr T. Jacquemot, Geneva 1627.
—— Pharasaism and Christianity compared. 1608; Comparaison du pharasaisme et du christianisme, tr Th. Jacquemot, Geneva 1628.
—— Salomon's divine arts. 1609; Les arts divins de Salomon, tr Th. Jacquemot, Geneva 1632.
—— No peace with Rome. 1609; Nulle paix avec Rome, tr Th. Jacquemot, Geneva 1629.
—— Quo vadis: a just censure of travel. 1617; tr Th. Jacquemot, Geneva 1628.
—— Occasional meditations. 1630; Méditations occasionelles, tr Th. Jacquemot, Geneva 1632.
Chevreau, Urbain. L'Ecole du sage. Paris 1645.
Boissière, Gustave. Urbain Chevreau: sa vie, ses oeuvres. Niort 1909.

Sandys, Edwin. Relation of the state of religion in the western parts of the world. 1605 (garbled edn of Europae speculum); Relation de l'état de la religion, tr C. Diodati, Amsterdam 1641.

Literary Criticism and Letters

Balzac, Guez de. Lettres. Paris 1624; The letters of Mounsier de Balzac, tr W. T[yrwhit] 1634 (pt 1); tr R[ichard] B[aker] 1636-7 (pts 2-3); 1638 (pt 4); 1658 (last letters).

Chapelain, Jean. Préface critique à l'Adone de Marino. Paris 1623.

Davenant, William. Preface to Gondibert. Paris 1650.

Du Bellay, Joachim. Deffense et illustration de la langue françoise. Paris 1549.

Mulcaster, R. The first part of the Elementarie. 1582.

Voiture, V. Recueil de lettres. Paris 1649; Letters of affaires, love and courtship, 2 pts tr John Davies 1655.

Drama

Bèze, Théodore de. Abraham sacrifiant. Geneva 1550; A tragedie of Abraham's sacrifice, tr Arthur Golding 1577.

Corneille, Pierre. Le Cid. Paris 1637; The Cid, tr Joseph Rutter 1637.

— Horace. Paris 1640; Horatius: a Roman tragedy, tr William Lower 1656.

— Polyeucte. Paris 1643; Polyeuctes: or the martyr, tr William Lower 1655.

Canfield, D. F. Corneille and Racine in England. New York 1904.

Kleinschmidt, J. R. Date of the Cid in English. MLN 55 1940.

Lebègue, R. Corneille connaissait-il le théâtre anglais? Revue d'Histoire du Théâtre 1 1950.

Smith, J. H. French sources for six English Comedies 1600-1750. JEGP 47 1948.

Hartnoll, P. Corneille in England. Theatre Research 1958.

Corneille, Thomas. Le berger extravagant. Paris 1652; The extravagant shepherd, tr T.R. 1653.

Desfontaines, Abbé Guyot. La vraye suitte du Cid. Paris 1638.

Rutter, Joseph. The second part of the Cid. 1640.

Dialogue du fol et du sage [c. 1510]. Rouen 1596.

Heywood, John. Witty and Witless [BM ms Harley 1527]. Ed F. W. Fairholt 1846.

Farce de Pernet qui va au vin. Lyons 1548.

Heywood, John. Johan Johan, the husbande, Tyb his wyfe and syr Jhan, the preest. 1533.

Farce nouvelle d'un pardonneur, d'un triacleur et d'une tavernière. Early 16th century. In M. Viollet Leduc, Ancien théâtre français vol 2, Paris 1854.

Heywood, John. The pardoner and the friar. 1533.

Young, K. The influence of French farce upon the plays of John Heywood. MP 2 1904.

Garnier, Robert. Cornélie. Paris 1574.

Kyd, Thomas. Pompey the Great, his faire Cornelia's tragedy. [1594?].

— Marc-Antoine. Paris 1578.

Herbert, Mary, Countess of Pembroke. The tragedie of Antonie. 1590.

Daniel, Samuel. Cleopatra. 1594.

— Philotas. 1595.

Greville, Fulke. Alaham. 1609.

— Mustapha. 1609.

Alexander, William. The monarchicke tragedies. 1607.

Luce, A. H. The Countess of Pembroke's Antonie. Weimar 1897.

Witherspoon, A. M. The influence of Robert Garnier on Elizabethan drama. New Haven 1924.

Grévin, Jacques. César. Paris 1561.

Collischon, G. Jacques Grévins Tragödie Cesar in ihrem Verhältnis zu Muret, Voltaire und Shakespeare. Marburg 1886.

Jodelle, E. Cléopâtre captive. Paris 1553.

Muir, K. Elizabeth I, Jodelle and Cleopatra. Renaissance Drama 1969.

Quinault, Philippe. La généreuse ingratitude. Paris 1656; The noble ingratitude, tr William Lower 1659.

— Le fantosme amoureux. Paris 1658; The amorous phantasm, tr William Lower 1659.

Scudéry, Georges de. Ibrahim ou l'illustre Bassa. 1643.

Settle, E. Ibrahim: the illustrious Bassa. 1677.

English History in French Plays:

La Calprenède, Gautier de Costes de. Jeanne, reine d'Angleterre. Paris 1638.

— Le comte d'Essex. Paris 1639.

— Edouard. Paris 1640.

La Serre, Puget de. Histoire, vie et mort, de Jacques V, roi d'Ecosse ensemble l'histoire de la belle Dunglas. Paris 1621.

— Thomas Morus ou le triomphe de la foi et de la constance. Paris 1642.

Montchrestien, Antoine de. L'Escossaise: ou le désastre. Rouen 1601.

[Belleforest, F. de]. L'innocence de Madame Marie, reine d'Ecosse. 1572.

[Blackwood, Adam]. Le martyre de la reine d'Ecosse. [Edinburgh?] 1587.

Marquigny. Marie Stuart dans l'histoire, dans le drame et dans le roman. Etudes Religieuses 1864.

Lanson, G. Les sources historiques de la reine d'Escosse. Revue Universitaire 1905.

Kipka, K. Maria Stuart im Drama der Welt-literatur vornehmlich des 17 und 18 Jahrhunderts. Leipzig 1907.

Yates, F. A. Some new light on l'Ecossaise de Montchrestien. MLR 22 1927.

Phillips, J. E. Images of a Queen: Mary Stuart in 16th-century literature. 1964.

Griffiths, R. M. The dramatic technique of Montchrestien. Oxford 1970.

Regnault, G. L. Marie Stuard, reine d'Ecosse. Paris 1639. *See Montchrestien, above.*

Lefèore, A. Les sources des tragédies sur le Comte d'Essex (17e siècle) en France et en Angleterre. Revue de Littérature Comparée 40 1966.

French History in English Plays:

Chapman, George. Bussy d'Ambois. 1597.

— The conspiracy and tragedy of Charles, Duke of Byron. 1608.

— The revenge of Bussy d'Ambois. 1613.

[Matthieu, Pierre]. Histoire des troubles en France sous Henri III et Henri IV. Lyons 1594.

Serres, J. de. Inventaire général de l'histoire de la France. Paris 1597; A general inventory of the history of France, tr Edward Grimestone 1607.

Boas, F. S. The sources of Chapman's Conspiracy of Byron and the Revenge of Bussy d'Ambois. Athenaeum 10 Jan 1903.

Gabel, J. B. The original version of Chapman's Tragedy of Byron. JEGP 63 1964.

Chapman, George and James Shirley. The tragedie of Chabot, Admirall of France. 1639.

Pasquier, E. Recherches de la France. Paris 1560-1621.

Koeppel, E. Quellenstudien zu den Dramen Chapmans, Massinger und Fords. Strasbourg 1897.

Ribner, I. The meaning of Chapman's Tragedy of Chabot. MLR 60 1965.

Drayton, Michael and Thomas Dekker. The Civil Wars in France. 1598 (lost).

Fletcher, John and Philip Massinger. The double marriage. 1647. Performed c. 1620.

Comines, P. de. Chroniques et histoire [written 1490-1500]. Paris 1523; tr Thomas Danett 1596.

Waith, E. M. The sources of the Double marriage by Fletcher and Massinger. MLN 64 1949.

Marlowe, Christopher. The massacre at Paris. [1600?].

Massinger, Philip. Believe as you list. 1631.
Cayet, Pierre Victor Palma. Chronologie septennaire. Paris 1605.
— Chronologie novennaire. Paris 1608.
Webster, John. The Guise. 1601 (lost).
Lawrence, W. J. Early French players in England. Anglia 32 1909.
Ristine, F. H. English tragi-comedy: its origin and history. New York 1910.
Lancaster, H. C. French dramatic literature in the 17th century vol. i. Baltimore 1929.

Verse

For the influence of French Petrarchism see Italian Petrarchism, col 891, below.

Billy, Jacques de. Sonnets spirituels. Paris 1573.
Barnes, B. A divine centurie of spiritual sonnets. 1595.
Desportes, Philippe. Roland furieux: imitation d'Arioste. Paris 1572; Rodomonths infernall, tr G[ervase] M[arkham] [1607].
— Les premières oeuvres. Paris 1573.
Lodge, Thomas. Scilla's Metamorphosis. 1589.
— Rosalynde: Euphues' golden legacy. 1590.
— Phillis 1593.
— A Margarite of America. 1596.
Daniel, Samuel. Delia. 1592.
Constable, Henry. Diana. 1592.
Spenser, Edmund. Amoretti. 1595.
E., C. Emaricdulfe. 1595.

Guggenheimer, J. Quellenstudien zu Daniels Delia. Berlin 1898.
Kastner, L. E. Spenser's Amoretti and Desportes. MLR 4 1909.
— Suckling and Desportes. MLR 5–6 1910–11.
Jack, R. D. S. Imitation in the Scottish sonnet. Comparative Lit 20 1968.
Du Bartas, Guillaume de Salluste. La muse chrétienne. Bordeaux 1573; Uranie: or the heavenly muse, tr James VI, King of Scotland, Essays of a prentise, Edinburgh 1584 (extracts); Judith, tr Thomas Hudson 1584.
La semaine ou création du monde. Paris 1578; La seconde semaine, Paris 1584; The furies, tr James VI, King of Scotland, His Majesties poeticall exercises, 1591 (from La seconde semaine); The second day of the first week and third dayes creation, [tr Thomas Winter] 1603, 1604; Bartas his divine weeke and works, tr Joshua Sylvester 1590–1608.
Lisle, William. Four bookes of Dubartas in French and English. 1637.
For a list of trns from Du Bartas see J. Weller, Sylvesters englische Übersetzungen der religiosen Epen des du Bartas, Tübingen 1902; and A. H. Upham, French influence in English literature, New York 1908.
Goulart, Simon. Commentaires sur la sepmaine de la création du monde. Paris 1583; A learned summary upon the famous poem of William of Saluste, Lord of Bartas, tr T[homas] L[odge] 1621.
Drayton, Michael. Moyses in a map of miracles. 1604.
Alexander, William. Dommesday: or the great day of the Lord's judgement. 1614.
Ashton, H. Du Bartas en Angleterre. Paris 1908. On his influence on Breton, Sir John Davies, John Davies of Hereford, Donne, Drayton.
Taylor, G. C. Milton's use of du Bartas. Cambridge Mass 1934.
— The strange case of du Bartas in the Taming of the shrew. PQ 20 1941.
Tilley, M. P. Charles Lamb, Marston and du Bartas. MLN 53 1938.
Baldensperger, F. Un sonnet de William Drummond et son point de départ dans la Semaine de du Bartas. MLN 55 1940.

Creore, A. E. Du Bartas: a reinterpretation. MLQ 1 1940.
Strathmann, E. The 1595 translation of du Bartas' first day. HLQ 8 1945.
Beall, C. B. John Eliot's Ortho-epia gallica and du Bartas-Goulart. SP 43 1946.
Simonsen, V. L. Sylvester's English translation of du Bartas' La première semaine. Orbis Litterarum 8 1952.
Campbell, L. B. Divine poetry and drama in 16th-century England. Cambridge 1959.
Prescott, A. L. An unknown translation of du Bartas (by Robert Barret). Renaissance News 19 1966.
— The reception of Du Bartas in England. Stud in Renaissance 15 1968.
Thomas, D. H. John Eliot's borrowings from Du Bartas in his works. Revue de Littérature Comparée 43 1969.
Du Bellay, Joachim. Les antiquitez du Rome. Paris 1558.
Spenser, Edmund. The visions of Bellay. In J. van der Noodt, Theatre for worldlings, 1569.
— The ruines of Rome. 1591.
Koeppel, E. Visions of Petrarch and visions of Bellay. E Studien 15 1891.
Satterthwaite, A. W. Spenser, Ronsard and du Bellay. Princeton 1960.
Arens, J. C. Du Bellay's 'Face le ciel' adapted by Nicholas Grimald. Papers on Eng Lang & Lit 1 1965.
Jack, R. D. S. Imitation in the Scottish sonnet. Comparative Lit 20 1968.
Durant, Gilles. Le zodiaque amoureux. Paris 1587.
Chapman, George. The amorous zodiache. 1595.
'Labé, Louise' (Louise Charlin, afterwards Perrin). Euvres. Lyons 1555; Débat entre amair et folie, tr Robert Greene 1587 (extract).
Marguerite d'Angoulême, Queen consort of Henry II of Navarre. Le miroir de l'âme pécheresse. Alençon 1531; tr Elizabeth I, Queen of England 1544.
Pemberton, C. Queen Elizabeth's englishings. 1899.
Marot, Clément. L'adolescence clémentine. Paris 1532.
— Oeuvres. Paris 1544.
Spenser, Edmund. The visions of Petrarch. In J. van der Noodt, Theatre for worldlings, 1569; rev in his Complaints, 1591.
— The shepheard's calendar. 1579.
Gifford, Humphrey. A posie of gilliflowers. 1580.
Barnes, Barnabe. First eidillion of Moschus. In his Parthenophil and Parthenope, 1593.
Marlowe, Christopher. Hero and Leander. 1598.
Koeppel, E. Visions of Petrarch and Visions of Bellay. E Studien 15 1891.
Shannon, G. P. Against Marot as a source of Marlowe's Hero and Leander. MLQ 9 1948.
Reamer, O. J. Spenser's debt to Marot re-examined. SE 10 1969.
Pibrac, Guy du Faur de. Quatrains moraux. Lyons 1574; The quadrains of Guy, lord of Pibrac, tr Joshua Sylvester 1605.
Pontoux, Claude de. Les oeuvres. Lyons 1579.
Drayton, Michael. Ideas mirrour. 1594.
Ronsard, Pierre de. Odes et bocage. Paris 1550.
— Amours. Paris 1552, 1553 (rev).
— Hymnes. 2 bks Paris 1555–6.
— Oeuvres. 4 vols Paris 1560.
Spenser, Edmund. The shepheardes calendar. 1579.
Watson, Thomas. Hecatompathia. 1582.
Soothern, John. Pandora. 1589.
Lodge, Thomas. Scilla. 1589.
— Phillis. 1593.
Barnes, Barnabe. Parthenophil and Parthenope. 1593.
— A centurie of spiritual sonnets. 1595.
Montgomerie, Alexander. The cherrie and the slae. 1597.
Drayton, Michael. Poems lyrick and pastorall. 1606.
Drummond of Hawthornden, William. Poems. 1616.

—— Forth festing. 1617.

—— Flowers of Sion. 1623.

Laumonier, P. Ronsard et l'Ecosse. Revue de Littérature Comparée 4 1924.

Grubb, M. Lodge's borrowing from Ronsard. MLN 45 1930.

Baym, M. I. A recurrent poetic theme: Shakespeare and Ronsard. Shakespeare Assoc Bull 12 1937.

Dabney, L. E. John Hays: plagiarist of Ronsard. MLN 61 1946.

Satterthwaite, A. W. Spenser, Ronsard and du Bellay. Princeton 1960.

Smith, M. C. Ronsard and Queen Elizabeth I. Bibliothèque d'Humanisme et de Renaissance 29 1967.

Saint Amant, Marc Antoine Girard de. La solitude. [Before 1620].

Sherburne, Edward. Salmacis, Lyrian and Sylvia. 1651.

Praz, M. Stanley, Sherburne and Ayres as translators and imitators of Italian, Spanish and French poets. MLR 20 1925.

Woledge, G. Saint-Amant, Fairfax and Marvell. MLR 25 1930.

Kastner, L. E. Saint-Amant and the English poets. MLR 26 1931.

Aulsin, R. A. Saint-Amant en Angleterre. MLN 50 1935.

Saint-Gelais, Mellin de. Œuvres. Lyons 1547.

Koeppel, E. Sir Thomas Wyatt und Melin de Saint-Gelais. Anglia 13 1891.

Kastner, L. E. Saint-Amant and the English poets. MLR 26 1931.

Schelandre, Jean de. Les deux premiers livres de la Stuartide. Paris 1611.

Vauquelin de la Fresnaye, Jean. Foresteries. 1555.

Lodge, Thomas. Phillis. 1593.

Studies

Hoffmann, O. Studien zu Alexander Montgomerie. E Studien 20 1895.

Kastner, L. E. Drummond of Hawthornden and the poets of the Pléiade. MLR 4 1909.

—— Drummond of Hawthornden and the French poets of the 16th century. MLR 5 1910.

Borland, L. Montgomerie and the French poets of the early 16th century. MP 11 1913.

Turner, A. French verse in the Oxford and Cambridge poetical miscellanies 1600–60. MLQ 10 1949.

Dilworth, M. New light on Alexander Montgomerie. Bibliotheck 4 1965.

Shire, H. M. Alexander Montgomerie: the opposition of the Court to conscience. Stud in Scottish Lit 3 1966.

—— Song, dance and poetry in the Court of Scotland under King James VI. Cambridge 1969.

Durand, L. G. Sponde and Donne: lens and prism Comparative Lit 21 1969.

Allegory and Satire

Les quinze joies de mariage [written c. 1400]. [c. 1480]; The fyftene joyes of maryage, [tr Robert Copland] 1509. [Tofte, R.?] The batchelors banquet. 1603.

La satyre ménippée. Paris 1594. Attributed to Florent Chrestien, Pierre Pithou, E. Rapin et al.

A pleasant satyre: a satyre menippized. 1595.

Gringore, Pierre. Le Chasteau de labour. Paris 1499.

Barclay, Alexander. The castell of laboure. Paris [1503?].

Lemaire de Belges, Jean. Le temple d'honneur et de vertu. Paris 1504.

Barclay, Alexander. The description of the toure of vertue. 1513.

Meun, Jean Clopinel de. Le dodechedron de fortune [written before 1305]. Paris 1556; The dodechedron of fortune, tr W.B. 1613.

Rabelais, François. Pantagruel. Lyons [1532]; Gargantua. Lyons 1534; The first (second) book of the works of Mr Francis Rabelais, tr Thomas Urquhart 1653.

—— Tiers livre. Lyons 1546.

—— Quart livre. Lyons 1546, Paris 1652 (enlarged).

Supposititious works:

Pantagruéline prognostication. Lyons 1533; Prognostication, tr 'Demetrius Pseudomantis' 1620 (lost).

Cinquiesme livre. Lyons 1562.

Eliot, John. Ortho-epia gallica. 1593.

Nashe, Thomas. Have with you to Saffron Walden. 1596.

—— Lenten stuffe. 1599.

Marston, John, Ben Jonson and George Chapman. Eastward ho. 1605.

Taylor, John. Works. 1630.

Whibley, C. Rabelais en Angleterre. Revue des Etudes Rabelaisiennes 1 1903.

Sainéan, L. Les interprètes de Rabelais en Angleterre et en Allemagne II: Urquhardt. Revue des Etudes Rabelaisiennes 7 1909.

—— L'influence et la réputation de Rabelais: interprètes, lecteurs, imitateurs. Paris 1930.

McKillop, A. D. Some early traces of Rabelais in English literature. MLN 36 1921.

Brown, H. Rabelais in English literature. Cambridge Mass 1933.

Farmer, A. H. Une source de Eastward Ho: Rabelais. Etudes Anglaises 1 1937.

Roe, F. C. Sir Thomas Urquhart and Rabelais. Oxford 1957.

Grève, M. de. Limites de l'influence linguistique de Rabelais en Angleterre au 16e siècle. Comparative Lit Stud (Maryland) 1 1964.

Kidde, C. A. Rabelais in English: Urquhart and Kimes. N & Q March 1968.

See also Sebastian Brant, col 880, below, for the influence of the French trn of his Ship of fools in England.

Prose Fiction

French Authors

Amadis de Gaula

For English trns from the French of N. de Herberay et al see col 912, below.

Artus de Bretaigne. Le preux chevalier Artus de Bretaigne. Paris 1514; The hystorie of Arthur of Lyttell Britayne, tr John Bourchier, Lord Berners [1555?].

Huon de Bordeaux. Les prouesses du noble Huon de Bordeaux [written 1454]. Paris 1513; tr John Bourchier, Lord Berners [1534?].

Hypolyte et Isabelle. Les amours tragiques d'Hypolite et Isabelle. Paris 1610; tr Alexander Hert 1628.

Sydrach. La fontaine de toutes sciences. Paris [1496?]; History of King Boccus and Sydracke, tr Hugh of Caumpenden [1510?].

Valentin et Orson. Valentin et Orson. Lyons 1489; [tr Henry Watson?] [1550], 1637 (rev).

Aneau, Barthélemi. Alector: histoire fabuleuse. Lyons 1560; The cock, tr 1590.

d'Audigier, Vital. Histoire tragi-comique de nos temps sous les noms de Lysandre et de Caliste. Paris 1616; A tragicall history of our times under the borrowed names of Lysander and Callista, tr W.D. 1627; Love and valour celebrated in the person of the author by the name of Adrasto, tr William Barwick 1638 (an episode of the above).

Fletcher, John and Philip Massinger. The lover's progress. 1623.

Boaistuau, P. and F. de Belleforest.

See Bandello, col 898, below.

Boisrobert, François de. Histoire indienne d'Anaxandre et d'Orazie. Paris 1629; The Indian history of Anaxandre and Orazia, [tr William Duncomb] 1639; tr W.G. 1657.

Busche, Alexandre van den (Le Sylvain). Epitomés de cent histoires tragiques. Paris 1581; Certen tragicall cases, tr E.A. 1590; The defence of contraries, tr Anthony Munday 1593.

Camus, Jean Pierre. Elise ou l'innocence coupable. Paris 1621; Elise or innocence guilty, tr J. Jennings 1655.

— L'Iphigénie: rigueur sarmatique. 2 vols Lyons 1625; Nature's paradox: or the innocent impostor, tr Major Wright 1652.

— Diotrephe: histoire valentine. Lyons 1626; Diotrephes: or a historie of valentines, tr Du Verger 1641.

— Petronille. Lyons 1626; Petronilla, tr P.S.P. 1630.

— Les évènements singuliers. 4 vols Lyons 1628; Les relations morales, Paris 1631; Admirable events, selected out of 4 books, together with moral relations, tr Du Verger 1639.

Ceriziers, René de. L'innocence reconnue. Paris 1634; Innocency acknowledged, tr J[ohn] T[asborough], Ghent 1645.

— L'histoire d'Hirlande: ou l'innocence couronnée. In Les trois états de l'innocence, Paris 1646; The crowned innocence, tr 1650; rptd as The innocent lady or the illustrious innocence, 1654.

— Joseph: ou la providence divine. Paris 1642; The innocent lord: or the divine providence, tr William Laver 1665.

Cyrano de Bergerac (Savinien de Cyrano). Les états et empires de la lune. Paris 1657; Selenarchia: or the government of the world in the moon, tr Thomas St Serf 1659.

Atkinson, G. The extraordinary voyage in French literature before 1700. New York 1920.

Desmaretz de Saint-Sorlin, J. de. Ariana. Paris 1632; tr 1636.

Despéreirs, Bonaventure. Récréations et joyeux devis. Paris 1558.

Hassell, J. W. An Elizabethan translation of the tales of Des Périers: the mirror of mirth 1583 and 1592. SP 52 1955.

Gombauld, Jean Ogier de. Endimion. Paris 1624; Endymion, tr Richard Hurst 1639.

Gomberville, Martin Leroy de. Polexandre. Paris 1632 (part), 1637 (complete).

Brown, W. Polexander. 1647.

La Calprenède, Gautier de Costes de. Cassandre. 10 vols Paris 1642–5; Cassandra: the famed romance, [tr George Digby] 1652 (pts 1–3); [tr Charles Cotterell 1644–50] (1653?).

Cléopâtre. 12 vols Paris 1646–57; Hymen's praeludia: being the first part [pts 1–3] of Cleopatra, tr R. Loveday 1652–5; pts 4–7 tr J[ohn] C[oles] 1656–8; pt 8 tr R. Loveday 1652–5; pts 4–7 tr J[ohn] C[oles] 1656–8; pt 8 tr J[ames] W[ebb] 1658; pts 11–12 tr J[ohn] D[avies] 1659.

La Marche, Olivier de la. Le chevalier délibéré. Paris 1493; The resolved gentleman, tr Lewis Lewkenor 1594 (from the Spanish version by Hernando de Acuna).

Maison Neuve, Etienne de (Gallarx). La plaisante histoire de Gerileon d'Angleterre. Paris 1572 (bk 1); tr 1583.

Marguerite d'Angoulême, Queen consort of Henry II, King of Navarre. L'Heptaméron des nouvelles. Paris 1559 (first complete edn); tr 1597; tr R. Codrington 1654.

Painter, William. The palace of pleasure. 1566.

[Middleton, Thomas?]. The revenger's tragaedie. 1607.

Davenant, William. Albovine, King of the Lombards. 1629.

Legouis, P. Réflexions sur la recherche des sources à propos de la Tragédie du vengeur. Etudes Anglaises 1959.

Montreux, Nicolas de (Ollenix du Mont-Sacré). Le premier (second) livre des bergeries de Juliette. 2 vols Lyons 1592; Honour's academy, tr Robert Tofte 1610.

Pisan, Christine de. Le livre de la cité des dames [written 1404–5]. Bibliothèque Nationale Paris ms fr 607; tr B. Anslay 1521.

— Les cent histoires de Troye. Paris [1500?]; tr R.W[yer] [1540?].

Rémy, A. La Galatie, ou les aventures du prince Astiages: histoire de notre temps où sous noms feints sont représentés les amours du roi et de la reine d'Angleterre. Paris 1625.

Saulnier, Gilbert, Sieur du Verdier. Le romant des romants où on verra la suite et la conclusion de Don Bélianis de Grece et des Amadis. Paris 1626–9; The loves and armes of the Greek princes, 3 pts 1640.

Scarron, Paul. Les nouvelles tragicomiques. Paris 1655; Scarron's novels, tr J. Davies of Kidwelly 1657. Includes The fruitless precaution; The hypocrites; The innocent adultery.

Scudéry, Madeleine de. Ibrahim: ou l'illustre bassa. Paris 1641; Ibrahim: or the illustrious Bassa, tr H. Cogan 1652. For tragicomedy under same title by Georges de Scudéry see above.

— Artamène: ou le grand Cyrus. 10 vols Paris 1649–53; The history of Philoxypes and Polyarite, tr 1652 (extract); Artamenes: or the Grand Cyrus, tr F.G. 5 vols 1653–5.

— Clélie. 10 vols Paris 1654–60, tr J. Davies of Kidwelly (pts 1–3) and G. Havers (pts 4–5) 5 vols 1656–61.

Boyle, Robert. Partenissa. 1654.

Sorel, Charles. Le berger extravagant. Paris 1627; The extravagant shepherd: or the history of the shepherd of Lysis, tr John Davies of Kidwelly 1653.

— L'histoire comique de Francion. Paris 1623–33; The history of Francion, tr A person of honour 1655.

d'Urfé, Honoré. L'Astree. Pt 1, Paris 1607; pt 2, Paris 1610; pt 3, Paris 1619; pts 4–5 (by B. Baro), Paris 1627; pt 1 tr John Pyper 1620; tr J.D[avies] 1657–8 (complete).

Fletcher, John. Monsieur Thomas 1639. Performed c. 1613.

— The tragedy of Valentinian. 1647. Performed c. 1614.

Stiefel, A. L. Zur Quellenfrage von Fletchers Monsieur Thomas. E Studien 36 1906.

Yver, Jacques. Le printemps d'Iver. Paris 1572.

Atkinson, D. F. The source of Two gentlemen of Verona. SP 41 1944.

English Authors

Godwin, Francis. Man in the moone. 1638; L'homme dans la lune, tr J.B.D. [Jean Baudoin] Paris 1648.

Cyrano de Bergerac. Les états et empires de la lune. Paris 1657.

Greene, Robert. Pandosto: the triumph of time. 1588; tr G. L. Regnault, Paris 1615.

Du Bail, L. M. Le roman d'Albanie et de Sycile. Paris 1626.

La Serre, Puget de. Pandoste: ou la princesse malheureuse. Paris 1631.

Potez, H. Le premier roman anglais traduit en français. Revue d'Histoire Littéraire 1904.

Sidney, Sir Philip. The Countess of Pembroke's Arcadia. 1590, 1593 (with bks 3–5); L'arcadie de la Comtesse de Pembrok, tr J. Baudoin and G. Chappuis, 1624–5 (complete); tr 'un gentil-homme françois', Paris 1625 (bk 1); tr Geneviève Chappelain, Paris 1625 (bks 2–3).

Galaut, Jean. Phalante: tragédie. Toulouse 1611. Written before 1605.

Mareschal, Antoine. La cour bergère. Paris 1640.

La Calprenède, G. de. Phalante. Paris 1642.

Boisrobert, F. de. La folle gageur: ou les divertissements de la Comtesse de Pembroc. Paris 1653.

Brunhuber, K. Sidneys Arcadia und ihre Nachläufer. Nuremberg 1903.

Lancaster, H. C. Sidney, Galaut, La Calprenède: an early instance of the influence of English literature upon the French. MLN 42 1927.

Studies

Jusserand, J. J. The English novel in the time of Shakespeare. 1890.

Greg, W. W. Pastoral poetry and pastoral drama. 1906.

Haviland, T. P. The roman de longue haleine on English soil. Philadelphia 1931.

Wright, L. B. Middle-class culture in Elizabethan England. Chapel Hill 1935.

(6) GERMAN

General Studies – Travel – Philosophy, politics etc – Theology – Legends – Satires and jestbooks – Verse – Drama – Novels.

General Studies

Howell, James. A discourse of the empire of Germany. 1659.

Elze, Karl. Die englische Sprache und Literatur in Deutschland. Dresden 1864.

Cohn, A. Shakespeare in Germany in the 16th and 17th centuries. 1865.

Schaible, K. H. Geschichte der Deutschen in England von den ersten germanischen Ansiedlungen in Britannien bis zum Ende des 18 Jahrhunderts. Strasbourg 1885.

Herford, C. H. Studies in the literary relations of England and Germany in the sixteenth century. Cambridge 1886.

Jacobs, H. E. The Lutheran movement in England. 1891.

Vetter, T. Englische Flüchtlinge in Zürich während der ersten Hälfte des 16 Jahrhunderts. Zürich 1894.

—— Litterarische Beziehungen zwischen England und der Schweiz im Reformationszeitalter. Zürich 1901.

Herzfeld, G. Zur Geschichte der deutschen Literatur in England. Archiv 105 1900.

Spirgatis, M. L. Englische Literatur auf der Frankfurter Messe von 1561–1620. Leipzig 1902.

Haney, J. L. German literature in England before 1790. Americana Germanica 4 1902.

Bolle, W. Die gedruckten englischen Liederbücher bis 1600. Berlin 1903.

Flügel, E. References to the English language in the German literature of the first half of the 16th century. MP 1 1903.

Koeppel, E. Deutsche Strömungen in der englischen Literatur. Strasbourg 1910.

Waterhouse, G. The literary relations of England and Germany in the 17th century. Cambridge 1914.

Muncker, F. Anschauungen von englischen Staat und Volk in der deutschen Literatur der letzten vier Jahrhunderte: 1, Von Erasmus bis zu Goethe. Sitzungsberichte der Königlichen Bayerischen Akademie der Wissenschaften: philosophisch-philologische Klasse (Munich) 1918.

Morgan, B. Q. A critical bibliography of German literature in English translation 1481–1927. Madison 1922, Stanford 1938 (with suppl 1928–35).

Koszul, A. Les relations entre l'Alsace et l'Angleterre au 16e siècle. Revue de Littérature Comparée 9 1929.

Wölcken, F. Shakespeares Zeitgenossen in der deutschen Dichtung. Neue Forschungen 5 1929.

Radczum W. Das englische Urteil über den Deutschen bis zur Mitte des 17 Jahrhunderts. Berlin 1933.

Blassneck, M. Frankreich als Vermittler englisch-deutscher Einflüsse im 17 und 18 Jahrhundert. Leipzig 1934.

Klein, K. K. Literaturgeschichte des Deutschtums in Ausland. Leipzig 1939.

Wiem, I. Das englische Schrifttum in Deutschland 1518–1600. Leipzig 1940.

Palmer, P. M. The influence of English on the German vocabulary to 1700. Berkeley 1950.

Price, L. M. English literature in Germany 1500–1960. Berkeley 1953.

Sieber, M. Die Universität Basel im 16 Jahrhundert und ihre englische Besucher. Basler Zeitschrift 55 1956.

Welti, M. A. Der Basler Buchdruck und Britannien. Basle 1964.

Davis, G. N. Anglo-German cultural relations and the Thirty Years War. Bull Rocky Mountain Modern Lang Assoc 22 1968.

Burger, H. O. Renaissance – Humanismus – Reformation: deutsche Literatur im europäischen Kontext. Frankfurt 1969.

Kreuder, H.-D. Milton in Deutschland: seine Rezeption in latein- und deutschsprachigen Schrifttum zwischen 1651 und 1732. Berlin 1972.

For a list of incidental writings on events in Germany 1607–38, see G. Waterhouse, above.

Trave

English and Scottish in Germany

Coryate, Thomas. Coryat's crudities, hastely gobbled up in five moneths travell. 1611.

Moryson, Fynes. An itinerary contayning his ten yeares travell through Germany, Bohmerland, Switzerland etc. 1617.

Taylor, John. Three weekes, three daies and three houres travel from London to Hamburgh. 1617.

—— Travels from the city of London in England to the city of Prague in Bohemia. 1620.

Caroe, Thomas. Itinerarium 1630–9. Mainz 1639; Reysebüchlein, tr P.K., Mainz 1640. Irish chaplain in Wallenstein's army.

Germans in England

Rye, W. B. England as seen by foreigners in the days of Elizabeth and James I: comprising translations of the journals of two dukes of Würtemberg in 1592 and 1610. 1865.

Schaibel, K. H. Geschichte der Deutschen in England bis Ende des 18 Jahrhunderts. Strasbourg 1885.

Akrigg, G. P. V. England in 1609. HLQ 14 1951.

Robson-Scott, W. D. German travellers in England 1400–1800. 1953.

Philosophy, Politics, Education, Discovery etc

Bacon, Francis. Essayes. 1597, 1612, 1625 (both enlarged); Getreue Reden, die Sitten-, Regiments- und Hauslehre betreffen, tr J. W. von Stugenberg, Nuremberg 1654.

Drake, Francis. The second circumnavigation of the earth. In S. Purchas, Purchas his pilgrimes, 1625; Erste Schiffart in die Ludsee und folgende umb die ganze Welt, in T. D. Bry, Newe Welt und Amerikanische historien, Frankfurt 1631.

Fish, Simon. A supplicacyon for the beggers. 1529; Klagbrieff der armen, tr Sebastian Franck 1529.

Raleigh, Walter. The discoverie of the large, rich and bewtiful empyre of Guiana. 1596; Wunderbare Beschreibung der goldreichen Königreichs Guianae, tr Levinus Haulsius, Nuremberg 1599.

Settle, John. A true report of the last voyage of Captain Martin Frobisher. 1577; tr German (from French), Nuremberg 1580.

[Wingfield, Anthony]. Discourse written by a gentleman employed in the late voyage of Spain and Portugal. 1589; Relation was der Capitan Drach und Colonel Noriz welche den Don Antonio in das Königreich Portugal einsetzen sollen aussgericht, Munich [1590].

Theology, Works of Piety etc

Boehme, Jakob
32 vols tr 1645–62 by John Sparrow, John Ellistone and Humphrey Blunden. For list see C. J. Barker's edn of Boehme, The high and deep searching out of the three-fold life of man, *tr J. Sparrow 1909.*

Hotham, D. Life of Jacob Boehmen. 1654.

Bailey, M. L. Milton and Boehme. New York 1914.

Jones, R. M. Spiritual reformers in the 16th and 17th centuries. 1914.

Closs, K. Böhmes Aufnahme in England. Archiv 148 1925.

Struck, W. Der Einfluss Boehmes auf die englische Literatur des 17 Jahrhunderts. Berlin 1946.

Buddecke, M. Die Jakob-Böhme Ausgaben. 2 vols Göttingen 1957. With bibliography.

Bucer, Martin. Enarrationes in evangelia Matthei etc. Strasbourg 1527; The mynd and exposition of M. Bucer upon S. Matthew; Woo be to the wordle, Emden 1566.

Hoff, E. Bucer and the English reformation. Oxford 1946.

Bullinger, Heinrich. Der christlich Eestand. Zürich 1540; The Christian state of matrimony, tr Miles Coverdale, [Antwerp] 1541.

— Der alt gloub. Zürich 1539; The old fayth, tr M. Coverdale 1547.

Luther, Martin. Von der Freyheyt eyniss Christen menschen, Wittenberg 1520; A treatise touching the libertie of a Christian, tr James Bell 1579.

— Deutung der grewlichen Figur des Munchkalbs. In Deuttung der czwo grewlichen Figuren Bapstesels czu Rom und Munchkalbsczu Freyberg funden, Wittenberg 1523 (with P. Melanchthon); tr John Brooke, Of two wonderful popish monsters, 1579.

— Geistliche Lieder. Erfurt 1524.

Coverdale, Miles. Goostly psalmes and spiritual songs. [c. 1535].

— Die Heubartikel des christlichen Glaubens. [Wittenberg] 1543; The chief and pryncipall articles of the Christen faythe, tr 1548.

— Tischreden : oder colloquia. Eisleben 1566; Dr Martin Luther's divine discourses at his table, tr Henry Bell 1662.

Tappert, T. G. On the translation of Luther's works. Lutheran Church Quart 19 1947.

Manuel, Niklas. Die Krankheit der Messe. [c. 1527].

Roy, William and Jerome Barlow. Rede me and be not wrothe. 1528.

Melanchthon, Philipp. Der Bapst Esel. In Deuttung der czwo grewlichen Figuren, Wittenberg 1523 (with M. Luther); tr John Brooke, Of two wonderfull popish monsters, 1579.

— Bedencken auffs Interim. [Wittenberg] 1548; A waying and considering of the Interim, tr John Rogers 1548.

Osiander, Andreas. Wie und wohin ein Christ die grausame Plag des Pestilenz fliehen soll. Nuremberg 1533; tr M[iles] C[overdale] 1537.

Sachs, Hans. Disputation zwischen einem Chorherrn und einem Schuhmacher. [Nuremberg] 1524; Goodly dysputacion between a Christen schomaker and a popysshe person, tr Anthony Scoloker 1548.

John Bon and Mast Parson. 1548.

Werdmüller, Otto. Ein Kleinot von Trost und Hilff in allerley Trübsalen. Zürich 1548; A spiritual and most precious pearl, tr Miles Coverdale, Wesel [1555?].

Coverdale, Miles. The hope of the faythful declaring the resurreccion of Iesu Christ past. Wesel [1554?].

— A treatise on death. [Wesel 1555?].

— A godly and learned treatise wherein is proved the true justification of a Christian man. [Wesel 1555?].

— A most fruitful treatise, how a Christian ought to behave himself. [Wesel 1555?].

These 4 treatises stated by Coverdale to be trns from Werdmüller.

Zwingli, Ulrich. Bekentnuss des Glaubens. Zürich [1530]; The rekening and declaration of the faith of Huldrik Zwingly, tr [London?] 1543; tr T. Cottesforde, Geneva 1555.

British Authors

For a fuller list of English theological works in German trn see G. Waterhouse, The literary relations of England and Germany in the 17th century, *Cambridge 1914.*

Dyke, Daniel. The mystery of self-deceiving. 1614; Nosce teipsum: das grosse Geheimnis des Selbstbetrugs, tr D.H.P. (Dietrich Haake Palatinus?), Basle 1638.

— A treatise concerning repentance. 1631; Nützliche Betrachtung der wahren Busse, tr D.H.P. (Dietrich Haake Palatinus?), Frankfurt 1643.

Hall, Joseph. Heaven upon earth. 1606; Himmel auf Erden, tr from Latin by K. Koeler, [Breslau] 1632.

— Characters of the virtues and vices. 1608; Vorbildungen der Tugenden und Laster, tr W.H.N.N., Emden 1628; Kenn-Zeichen der Tugend und Laster, tr G. P. Harsdorfer 1652.

— A treatise concerning repentance. 1631; Nützliche Betrachtung der wahren Busse, Frankfurt 1643.

Parsons, Robert. A true report of the death of Edmund Campion. Rome 1582; Leben und Leyden des Martyrers E. Campiani, 1588.

Perkins, William. A reformed Catholike. Cambridge 1597; Der catolische reformierte Christ, tr Johann Herdelt, Herborn 1602.

Legends

Faust

Historia von D. Johann Fausten, dem weitbeschreyten Zauberer und Schwartzkünstler. Frankfurt 1587.

The historie of the damnable life and deserved death of Doctor John Faustus according to the true copie printed at Franckfort, and translated into English by P.F. 1592. Earlier edn 1588?

Ander Theil D. Johan Faustus Historien. 1593.

The second report of Doctor John Faustus, containing his appearances, and the deedes of Wagner; written by an English gentleman student in Wittenberg. 1594. An imitation of the above.

Marlowe, Christopher. The tragical history of Dr Faustus. 1604. Acted 1592.

Greene, Robert. The honorable historie of frier Bacon and frier Bungay. 1594.

Barnes, Barnabe. The Divil's charter. 1607.

The merry Devill of Edmonton. 1608.

Delius, F. Marlowes Faust und seine Quelle. Göttingen 1881.

Diebler, A. Faust und Wagner-Pantomimen in England. Anglia 7 1884.

Logeman, H. Faustus notes. Recueil de Travaux fascicule 21, Ghent 1898.

Schröder, K. R. Textverhältnisse und Entstehungsgeschichte von Marlowes Faust. Berlin 1909.

Rohde, R. Das englische Faustbuch und Marlowes Tragödie. Halle 1910.

Meeke, G. J. Faust: the man and the myth. Oxford 1930.

Bianquis, G. Faust à travers quatre siècles. Paris 1935.

Palmer, P. M. and R. P. More. The sources of the Faust tradition from Simon Magus to Lessing. New York 1936.

Henel, H. Faust-translations and Faust-mosaics. Monatshefte für Deutschen Unterricht 1938.

Brown, B. D. Marlowe, Faustus and Simon Magus. PMLA 54 1939.

Steiner, A. The Faust legend and the Christian tradition. PMLA 54 1939.

Kocher, P. H. The English Faustus book and the date of Marlowe's Faustus. MLN 55 1940.

— Nashe's authorship of the prose scenes in Faustus. MLQ 3 1942.

—— The early date for Marlowe's Faustus. MLN 58 1943.

Kirschbaum, L. Mephistopheles and the lost 'dragon'. RES 18 1942, 21 1945.

—— Marlowe's Faustus: a reconsideration. RES 19 1943.

Heilman, R. B. The tragedy of knowledge: Marlowe's treatment of Faustus. Quart Rev of Lit 2 1946.

Haile, H. G. The history of Dr Johann Faustus. Urbana 1965.

Homan, S. R. Dr Faustus, Dekker's Old Fortunatus and the morality plays. MLQ 26 1965.

Henning, H. Faust Bibliographie: pt 1, Das Faust-Thema vom 16 Jahrhundert bis 1790. Weimar and Berlin 1970.

Miscellaneous

Wunderbarlicher Bericht von einem Judan, aus Jerusalem bürtig, Ahasuerus genanndt. Schleswig 1564.

Wonderful strange newes out of Germainie of a Jewe that hath lived wanderinge ever since the passion of our Saviour Christ. 1612. A ballad.

Zirus, W. Der ewige Jude in der Dichtung, vornehmlich in der englischen und deutschen. Leipzig 1928.

—— Ahasverus: der ewige Jude, Berlin 1930.

Krappe, A. H. Sur l'origine de la légende du Juif errant. Neophilologus 20 1935.

Boudout, J. Faust et Ahasverus. Revue de Littérature Comparée 16 1936.

Anderson, G. K. The Wandering Jew returns to England. JEGP 45 1946.

—— Popular survivals of the Wandering Jew in England. JEGP 46 1947.

—— The neo-classical chronicle of the Wandering Jew. PMLA 63 1948.

Fortunatus und seine Söhne. Augsburg 1509.

Fortunatus. Frankfurt [1560]; The right pleasant and variable tragical history of Fortunatus, tr Thomas Churchyard 1612.

Dekker, Thomas. The pleasant comedie of old Fortunatus. 1600.

Bolte, J. Zwei Fortunatus-Dramen aus dem Jahre 1643. Euphorion 31 1930.

Muenster, Sebastian. Cosmographia: Beschreibung aller Länder. Basle 1544; Cosmographia universalis, Basle 1550 (Latin version).

Eden, R. A treatise of the new India after Sebastian Munster. 1553.

A briefe collection and compendious extract of strange and memorable thinges, gathered out of the Cosmography of S. Munster. 1572.

The wrathful judgement of God upon Bishop Hatto. 1586. A ballad.

The comical history of the costlie whore. 1633.

Shapiro, I. A. Donne, the Parveolus and Münster's Cosmography. N & Q July 1960.

Satires and Jest-Books

Ein kurtzweilig Lesen von Dyl Eulenspiegel. Strasbourg 1515.

[Andrewe, Lawrence?]. Tyll Howleglas. Antwerp [c. 1510] (fragment).

[Copland, William]. Here beginneth a merye jest of a man called Howleglass. [1528?].

Brie, F. Eulenspiegel in England. Berlin 1903.

Roloff, E. A. Ewiger Eulenspiegel: wie der Schalk war, und was die Welt aus ihm macht. Brunswick 1940.

Der Pfaff vom Kahlenberg. Strasbourg [c. 1500–20].

[Andrewe, Lawrence?]. The parson of Kalenborowe. Antwerp [c. 1520].

Bruder Rausch. [c. 1555] etc.

Freer Rush. 1568.

Dekker, Thomas. If this be not a good play, the Divell is in it. 1612.

Sebastian, Brant. Das Narrenschyff. Basle 1494; tr Latin by Jacob Locher [1497]; French by Pierre Rivière [1497] and Jehan Droyn [1498].

Barclay, Alexander. The shyp of folys of the worlde, translated out of Laten, Frenche and Doche into Englysshe tonge. 1509.

Watson, Henry. The shyppe of fooles, translated out of Frenche. 1509.

Cock Lorell's bote. [c. 1510].

Skelton, John. The bouge of court. [c. 1520].

Copland, Robert. Hye way to the spyttel-house. [c. 1535].

—— Gyl of Braintford's testament. [1560?].

Tarlton, Richard. Jigge of a horse loade of fooles. [c. 1588].

Arnim, Robert. Nest of ninnies. 1608.

Rey, Albert. Skelton's satirical poems in their relation to Lydgate's Order of fools, Cock Lorell's bote and Barclay's Ship of fools. Berne 1890.

Fraustadt, F. Über das Verhältnis von Barclays Ship of fools zur lateinischen, französichen und deutschen Quelle. Breslau 1894.

Pompen, A. The English versions of the Ship of fools. 1925.

Bishop, A. Barclays Ships of fools. Boston Public Lib Quart 3 1951.

Gaier, U. Brant's Narrenschiff and the Humanists. PMLA 83 1968.

Zeydel, E. H. Sebastian Brant and his public. In F. A. Raven, W. K. Legner et al, Germanic studies in honor of E. H. Sehrt, Coral Gables Fla 1968.

Verse

German Authors

Opitz, Martin. Buch von der deutschen Poeterey. Strasbourg 1624.

Loomis, C. G. Opitz in 17th-century England. MLQ 6 1945.

Weckherlin, Georg Rudolf. Triumf bei der Kindtauf zu Stuttgart gehalten. Stuttgart 1616; Triumphal shows, tr the author himself, Stuttgart 1616.

—— Oden und Gesänge. Bk 1, 1618; bk 2, 1619. Imitations of Spenser, Carew, Joshua Sylvester, Daniel, Donne.

—— A panegyric to the Lord Hays. Stuttgart 1619. Written in English.

—— Geistliche und weltliche Gedichte. Amsterdam 1641, 1648 (rev). Imitations of Spenser, Donne, Harington, More, Owen.

Bohm, W. Englands Einfluss auf Weckherlin. Göttingen 1893.

Fischer, H. Weckherlins Gedichte. Tübingen 1893.

Johnson, E. F. Weckherlins Eclogues of the seasons. Tübingen 1922. Influence of Spenser.

Forster, L. G. R. Weckherlin in England. German Life & Letters 3 1939.

—— Weckherlin: zur Kenntnis seines Lebens in England. Basle 1944.

—— Sources for G. R. Weckherlin's life in England. MLR 41 1946.

Greg, W. W. A companion to Arber. Oxford 1967. Weckherlin's patent for printing schoolbooks.

English Authors

Morley, Thomas. Canzonets. 1593; Lustige und artige Liedlein, tr Johann von Steinbach 1624.

Drama

German History in English Plays

The costlie whore. See S. Munster, above.

Chapman, George (?). The tragedy of Alphonsus, Emperor of Germany. 1654.

Elze, K. Chapmans The tragedy of Alphonsus. Leipzig 1867.

Chettle, Henry. The tragedy of Hoffmann: or revenge for a father. 1631.

Ackermann, R. The tragedy of Hoffman von Chettle. Bamberg 1894.

Glapthorne, H. The tragedy of Albertus Wallenstein. 1639.
Bolte, J. Eine englische Wallensteinstragödie in Deutschland. Zeitschrift für Deutsche Philologie 19 1887.
Vetter, T. Wallenstein in der dramatischen Dichtung des Jahrzehnts seines Todes. Frauenfeld 1894.

English History in German Plays

Gryphius, Andreas. Ermorderte Majestät: oder Carolus Stuardus König von Grossbritanien. In his Gedichte: erster Teil, Breslau 1657. Written 1649.

English Authors

Edward III. 1596. Anon.
Ayrer, Jacob. Edouard III. Nuremberg 1608.
Kyd, Thomas. The Spanish tragedy. 1586.
Ayrer, Jacob. Pelimpera. Nuremberg 1608.
Schönwerth, R. Die niederländischen und deutschen Bearbeitungen von Kyds Spanish tragedy. Literarhistorische Forschungen 26 1903.
Machin, Lewis. The dumb knight. 1608.
Ayrer, Jacob. Comedia vom König in Cypern. Nuremberg 1608.
Marlowe, Christopher. *For the influence of Dr Faustus see above.*
Peele, George. The Turkish Mahomet and Hyrin the fair Greek. [1594?] (lost).
Ayrer, Jacob. Eroberung von Konstantinopel. 1608.
Öfterding, M. S. Die Geschichte der schönen Irene in den modernen Literaturen. Würzburg 1897.
Shakespeare, William. Titus Andronicus. 1594.
Heinrich Julius, Duke of Brunswick. Tragoedia von einem ungerathenen Sohn. [1593-4].
— Romeo and Juliet. 1597.
Trautmann, K. Die älteste Nachricht über eine Aufführung von Shakespeares Romeo und Julie in Deutschland (1604). Archiv für Literaturgeschichte 11 1882.
Vogeler, A. Cardenio und Celinde des Andreas Gryphius und Shakespeares Romeo und Julia. Archiv 79 1887.
Wolff, M. J. Die Tragödie von Romio und Julietta. Sh Jb 47 1911.
Sauer, A. Shakespeares Romeo und Julia in den Bearbeitungen und Übersetzungen der deutschen Literatur. Greifswald 1915.
— Hamlet. 1603, 1604.
Der bestrafte Brudermord. Ed H. A. O. Reichard, Olla Podrida 2 1781. Written 1603-10?
Creizenach, W. Die Tragödie Der bestrafte Brudermord oder Prinz Hamlet aus Dänemark und ihre Bedeutung für die Kritik des Shakespearschen Hamlet. Leipzig 1887.
— Der bestrafte Brudermord and its relation to Shakespeare's Hamlet. MP 2 1904.
Evans, M. B. Der bestrafte Brudermord: sein Verhältnis zu Shakespears Hamlet. Bonn 1902; rev in Theatergeschichtliche Forschungen 19 1910.
— Der bestrafte Brudermord and Shakespeare's Hamlet. MP 2 1905.
Weilen, A. von. Hamlet auf der deutschen Bühne bis zur Gegenwart. Schriften der Deutschen Shakespeare-Gesellschaft (Berlin) 3 1908.
Winds, A. Hamlet auf der deutschen Bühne bis zur Gegenwart. Schriften der Gesellschaft für Theatergeschichte (Berlin) 12 1909.
Freudenstein, R. Der bestrafte Brudermord: Shakespeares Hamlet auf der Wanderbühne des 17 Jahrhunderts. Berlin 1958.
— Midsummer night's dream. 1619.
Gryphius, Andreas. Peter Squenz. Written 1657.
Kollewijn, R. A. Über die Quelle des Peter Squenz. Archiv für Literaturgeschichte 9 1880.
Burg, F. Über die Entwicklung des Peter Squenz Stoffes bis Gryphius. Zeitschrift für Deutsches Altertum 25 1881.

Palm, H. (ed). Absurda comica oder Herr Peter Squenz Schimpf-Spiel. Kürschners Deutsche Nationalliteratur 29 1883.

General Studies

For works on the English comedians in Germany before 1930 see bibliographies in Creizenach and Herz, below and L. M. Price, The reception of English literature in Germany, Berkeley 1932.

Englische Comedien und Tragedien. Leipzig 1620, 1624 (enlarged).
Liebeskampff: oder ander Theil der englischen Comödien und Tragödien. Leipzig 1630.
Tittmann, J. (ed). Die Schauspiele der englischen Komödianten in Deutschland. In Deutsche Dichter des 16 Jahrhunderts vol 13, Leipzig 1880.
Bolte, J. Jakob Rosefeldts Moschus: eine Parallele zum Kaufmann von Venedig. Sh Jb 21 1886.
— Deutsche Verwandte von Shakespeares Viel Lärmen um Nichts. Sh Jb 21-2 1886-7.
— Die Singspiele der englischen Komödianten. Berlin 1889.
Creizenach, W. Die Schauspiele der englischen Komödianten. Berlin 1889.
Wysocki, L. G. Andreas Gryphius et la tragédie allemande au 17e siècle. Paris 1893. Ch 3 on Gryphius and Shakespeare.
Herz, E. Englische Schauspieler und englisches Schauspiel zur Zeit Shakespeares in Deutschland. Hamburg 1903.
Schönwerth, R. Die niederländischen und deutschen Bearbeitungen von Thomas Kyds Spanish tragedy. Berlin 1903.
Becker, G. Zur Quellenfrage von Shakespeares Sturm. Sh Jb 43 1907.
Kaulfuss-Diesch, C. Bandellos Novelle Timbreo und Fenecia im deutschen Drama des 17 Jahrhunderts. In Studien zur Literaturgeschichte Albert Köster überreicht, Leipzig 1912. Resemblances between Ayrer's Fenecia and Much ado about nothing.
Fein, N. Die deutschen Nachahmer des Rüpelspiels aus Shakespeares Sommernachtstraum. Brünn 1914.
Heinrich, G. Ayrer und Shakespeare. Magyar Shakespeare Tár 8 1916.
Keppler, E. Gryphius und Shakespeare. Tübingen 1921.
Evans, M. B. Traditions of the Elizabethan stage in Germany. PQ 2 1923.
Flemming, W. Das Schauspiel der Wanderbühne. In Deutsche Literatur in Entwicklungsreihen, ed H. Kindermann, Reihe Barock, Barockdrama 4, Leipzig 1931.
Bäsecke. A. Das Schauspiel der englischen Komödianten in Deutschland. Halle 1935.
ten Hoor, G. J. Ben Jonson's reception in Germany. PQ 14 1935.
Pascal, R. The stage of the Englische Komödianten: three problems. MLR 35 1940.
Korninger, S. Shakespeare und seine deutschen Übersetzer. Sh Jb 92 1956.

Novels

English Authors

Sidney, Sir Philip. The Countesse of Pembroke's Arcadia. 1590, 1593 (with bks 3-5); Arcadia der Gräfin von Pembroke, tr Valentinus Theocritus von Hirschberg, Frankfurt 1629, 1638 (rev M.O.V.B. [Martin Opitz von Boberfeld]).
Brunhuber, K. Sidneys Arcadia und ihre Nachläufer. Nuremberg 1903.
Brie, F. Das Volksbuch vom 'gehörnten Siegfried' und Sidneys Arcadia. Archiv 121 1908.
Bloedau, C. A. von. Grimmelhausens Simplicissimus und seine Vorgänger. Berlin 1908.
Holzinger, W. Der abentheurliche Simplicissimus and Sidneys Arcadia. Colloquia Germanica 1969.

(7) ITALIAN

General Studies – Dictionaries and grammars – Travel – Philosophy – Politics etc – Literary Criticism – Allegory and Satire – Lyric poetry – Epic – Drama – Prose fiction.

General Studies

Thomas, William. The historie of Italie. 1549.

Rossi, S. Un italianista nel cinquecento inglese: Thomas. Aevum 40 1966.

Turler, Jerome. De agro neapolitano. Strasbourg 1574; An excellent description of the delicious realme of Naples, tr 1575.

Mazella, Scipione. Descrittione del regno di Napoli. Naples 1586; Parthenopoeia: or the history of the kingdom of Naples, tr pt 1 Samson Lennard, pt 2 James Howell 1654.

Schottus, Franciscus. Itinerari Italiae rerumque Romanarum libri 3. Antwerp 1600; Italy in its original glory, ruine and revival, tr Edmund Warcupp 1660.

Dallington, Robert. A survey of the Grand Duke's state of Tuscany in 1596. 1605.

Lunadoro, Girolamo and Fioravante Martinelli. Relatione della corte di Roma. Rome 1635; tr H[enry] C[ogan] 1654.

— Roma ricercata nel suo sito. Rome 1644; tr H[enry] C[ogan] 1654.

Howell, James. A survey of the signorie of Venice. 1651.

An English chyrurgion. The character of Italy: or the Italian anatomized. 1660.

Fränkel, L. Romanische, insbesondere italienische Wechselbeziehungen zur englischen Literatur: ein Repertorium auf Grund neuer Veröffentlichungen (1894–6). Erlangen 1900.

Einstein, L. The Italian Renaissance in England. New York 1902.

Allodoli, E. Giovanni Milton e l'Italia. Prato 1907.

Wolff, S. L. Robert Greene and the Italian Renaissance. E Studien 37 1907.

Toynbee, P. Dante in English literature from Chaucer to Cary. 1909.

Scott, M. A. Elizabethan translations from the Italian. New York 1916.

Crane, T. F. Italian social customs of the sixteenth century and their influence on the literature of Europe. New Haven 1920.

Brown, H. Inglesi e Scozzesi all'Università di Padova. 1922.

Schoell, F. L. Les mythologistes italiens de la Renaissance et la poésie élisabéthaine. Revue de Littérature Comparée 4 1924.

Ady, C. M. Italian influences on English history during the period of the Renaissance. History 9 1925.

Praz, M. Secentismo e Marinismo in Inghilterra: Donne, Crashaw. Florence 1925.

— L'Italia di Ben Jonson. Rivista Italiana del Dramma 1937.

— Fortuna della lingua e della cultura italiana in Inghilterra. Romana 3 1939.

— Ricerche anglo-italiane. Rome 1944.

— The flaming heart. 1958.

Jeffrey, V. M. John Lyly and the Italian Renaissance. Paris 1929.

Nicolin, F. Su taluni rapporti di cultura tra l'Italia, l'Olanda e l'Inghilterra al principio del settecento. Naples 1930.

Meozzi, A. Il secentismo e le sue manifestazioni europee in rapporto all'Italia. Pisa 1936.

Rebora, P. Civiltà italiana e civiltà inglese. Florence 1936.

Bonaschi, A. and C. Italian currents and curiosities in English literature from Chaucer to Shakespeare. New York 1937.

Orsini, N. Studi sul Rinascimento italiano in Inghilterra. Florence 1937.

Cantimori, D. Eretici italiani del Cinquecento. Florence 1939.

Fink, Z. S. Venice and English political thought in the 17th century. MP 38 1941.

Bhattacharye, M. M. Italy in Elizabethan pamphlets. Calcutta Rev 83 1943.

Pellegrini, A. M. Giordano Bruno on translation. ELH 10 1943.

Weiss, R. Henry Wotton and Orazio Lombardelli. RES 19 1943.

— Il debito degli umanisti inglesi verso l'Italia. Lettere Italiane 7 1955.

— The spread of Italian humanism. 1964.

Gilbert, A. H. Nevizanus, Ariosto, Florio, Harington and Drummond. MLN 62 1947.

Viglione, F. Italia nel pensiero degli scrittori inglesi. Milan 1947.

Krey, A. C. Padua in the English Renaissance. HLQ 10 1948.

Prezzolini, G. The legacy of Italy. New York 1948.

Corsano, A. Studi sul Rinascimento. Bari 1949.

Simonini, R. C. Italian scholarship in Renaissance England. Chapel Hill 1952.

Friederich, W. P. and D. H. Malone. Italian contributions. In their Outline of comparative literature, Chapel Hill 1954.

Hale, J. R. England and the Italian Renaissance. 1954.

Sells, A. L. The Italian influence in English poetry from Chaucer to Southwell. 1955.

Wilson, E. M. and E. R. Vincent. Thomas Stanley's translations and borrowings from Spanish and Italian poets. Revue de Littérature Comparée 32 1958.

Jacob, E. F. (ed). Italian Renaissance studies: a tribute to the late C. M. Ady. 1960.

Royal Academy of Arts. Italian art and Britain. 1960. On 16th- and 17th-century art collectors.

Hay, D. The Italian Renaissance in its historical background. Cambridge 1961.

Thomson, P. Wyatt and the school of Serafino. Comparative Lit 13 1961.

— Sir Thomas Wyatt and his background. 1964.

Lievsay, J. L. The Elizabethan image of Italy. New York 1964.

Baldi, S. Poesie italiane di Milton. Studi Secenteschi 7 1966.

Bellorini, M. J. Tracce di cultura italiana nella formazione di Thomas North. Aevum 41 1967.

Branca, V. (ed). Rinascimento europeo e rinascimento veneziano. Florence 1967.

Lombardo, L. Shakespeare and Italian criticism. In The disciplines of criticism, ed P. Demetz, T. Greene et al, New Haven 1968.

Parkes, G. B. The decline and fall of the English Renaissance admiration of Italy. HLQ 31 1969.

Schoeck, R. J. Thomas More and the Italian heritage of early Tudor humanism. Actes du 4e Congrès International de Philosophie Médiévale (Montreal) 1969.

McPherson, D. C. Aretino and the Harvey-Nashe quarrel. PMLA 84 1969.

Dictionaries, Grammars and Language Manuals

Thomas, William. Principall rules of the Italian grammar, with a dictionarie for the better understanding of Boccace, Petrarca and Dante. 1550.

Lentulus, Scipio. Italicae grammatices institutio. Venice 1578; tr H.G. 1575.

Florio, John. Florio his first fruites: which yeelde familiar speech, merie proverbs, wittie sentences and golden sayings. 1576.

— Second fruites. 1591.

— A world of wordes. 1598, 1611, 1659 (both rev).

Holyband, Claudius. The flourie field of four languages, for learners of the Latin, French, English, but chieflie the Italian tongues. 1583.

— The Italian schoole-maister. 1597, 1608 (rev F.P.).

Benvenuto Italiano. Il passagiere: the passenger. 1612. Dialogues in English and Italian.

Torriano, Giovanni. The Italian tutor. 1640.

Praz, M. L'Italia di Ben Jonson. In his Machiavelli in Inghilterra ed altri saggi, Florence 1942.

Simonini, R. C. Italian-English language books of the Renaissance. Romanic Rev 42 1951.

— The Italian pedagogy of Claudius Hollyband. SP 49 1952.

Baldi, E. The secretary of the Duke of Norfolk and the first Italian grammar in England. In Studies in English language and literature presented to Karl Brunner, Vienna 1957.

Travel

English and Scottish in Italy

Munday, Anthony. The English Romayne life: discovering the lives of Englishmen in Rome. 1582.

Davies, William. True relation of his travailles and most miserable captivitie under the Duke of Florence. 1614.

Sandys, George. A relation of a journey began in AD 1610 contayning a description (among other places) of the remote parts of Italy. 1615.

Moryson, Fynes. An itinerary contayning his ten yeares' travell. 1617.

Raymond, John. An itinerary contayning a voyage made through Italy [1646–7]. 1648.

Evelyn, John. Memoirs 1641–1706. Ed W. Bray 2 vols 1818; Diary, ed E. S. de Beer 6 vols Oxford 1955 (complete). Travels in France, Italy and Switzerland 1643–7.

Digby, Kenelm. Journal of a voyage into the Mediterranean 1628. Ed J. Bruce 1868.

Penrose, B. Urbane travellers 1591–1635. Philadelphia 1942.

Sells, A. L. Englishmen in Padua from Chaucer to Shelley. Durham Univ Jnl 40 1947.

— The paradise of travellers: the Italian influence on Englishmen in the 17th century. 1966.

Koenigsberger, H. G. English merchants in Naples and Sicily in the 17th century. EHR 12 1947.

McCain, R. English travellers in Italy during the Renaissance. Bull of Bibliography 19 1948.

Liljegren, S. B. Milton at Florence. Neophilologus 43 1959.

Arthos, J. Milton and the Italian cities. 1968.

Italians in England

Chambrun, C. L. de. Giovanni Florio: un apôtre de la Renaissance en Angleterre. Paris 1925.

Koszul, A. L'offrande d'un traducteur: notes sur l'anglais de John Florio. Revue Anglo-américaine 19 1932.

Yates, F. A. John Florio. Cambridge 1934.

— Italian teachers in Elizabethan England. Jnl Warburg Inst 1 1937.

Gargano, G. S. Scapigliatura italiana a Londra sotto Elisabetta e Giacomo I. Florence 1923.

Namer, E. La vita di Vanini in Inghilterra 1614. Lecce 1934.

Fucilla, J. G. De morte et amore [Alciato in England]. PQ 14 1935.

Policardi, S. John Florio e le relazioni culturale fra l'Inghilterra e l'Italia nel 16 secolo. Venice 1947.

Simonini, R. C. John Florio, scholar and humanist. In A tribute to G. C. Taylor, Chapel Hill 1952.

Firpo, L. Francesco Pucci in Inghilterra. Revue Internationale de Philosophie 5 1957.

Bellorini, M. Un medico italiano alla corte di Elisabetta: Giulio Gorgarucci. Eng Miscellany (Rome) 19 1968.

Philosophy, Politics, History, Theology etc

Italian Authors

Balbani, Niccolò. Historia della vita di Galeazzo Caracciolo. Geneva 1587; News from Italy of a second Moses, tr William Carew 1608.

Biondi (Bjundevié), Giovanni Francesco. L'istoria delle guerre civili d'Inghilterra. Venice 1637–44: The history of civil wars in England [Wars of the Roses], tr Henry Carey, Earl of Monmouth 1647.

Botero, Giovanni. Delle cause della grandezza della città. Venice 1589.

Ralegh, W. The prince: or maxims of state. 1642.

— Observations concerning the causes of the magnificence and opulency of cities. 1650.

— Delle relazioni universali. Ferrara 1592.

Fellheimer, J. The section on Italy in the Elizabethan translations of Botero's Relazioni universali. Eng Miscellany (Rome) 8 1957.

Bruno, Giordano. Del'infinito universo et mondi. Venice (for London) 1584.

Godwin, Francis. Man in the moone. 1638.

Wilkins, John. The discovery of a world in the moon. 1638, 1640 (enlarged).

— Lo speccio della bestia trionfante. Venice (for London) 1584.

Carew, Thomas. Coelum britannicum. 1634.

— Degl'heroici furori. Paris (for London) 1585.

König, W. Shakespeare and Giordano Bruno. Sh Jb 11 1876.

Elton, O. Giordano Bruno in England. In his Modern studies, 1907.

Whitebrook, J. C. Fynes Morison, Bruno and William Shakespeare. N & Q 10 Oct 1936.

Yates, F. A. A study of Love's labour lost. 1936.

— The emblematic conceit in Bruno's De gli eroici furori and in the Elizabethan sonnet sequences. Jnl Warburg & Courtauld Inst 6–7 1943–4.

— Bruno and the Hermetic tradition. 1964.

Limentani, L. Bruno a Oxford. Civiltà Moderna 9 1937.

Orsini, N. Giordano ad Oxford nella testimonia di Harvey (June 1583). In his Studi sul rinascimento italiano in Inghilterra, Florence 1937.

Looten, C. Bruno à Londres. Revue de Littérature Comparée 19 1939.

Pellegrini, A. M. Bruno and Oxford. HLQ 5 1942.

— Bruno, Sidney and Spenser. SP 40 1943.

Levinson, R. B. Spenser and Bruno. PMLA 63 1948.

Newman, F. B. Sir Fulke Greville and Bruno. PQ 29 1950.

Singer, D. W. Bruno: his life and thought. New York 1950.

Bruto, Giammichele. La institutione di una fanciulla nata nobilmente. Antwerp 1565; tr W. P. 1598.

Casa, Giovanni della. Il Galateo. Venice 1558; tr Robert Peterson 1576; The rich cabinet, tr 1616 (epitome).

Hawkins, Francis. Youth's behaviour: or decency of conversation among men. 1646 (4th edn).

Castiglione, Baldassare. Il libro del cortegiano. Venice 1528; The courtyer, tr Thomas Hoby 1561.

Ascham, Roger. The scholemaster. 1570.

On civyle and uncivyle life. 1579, 1586 (as the English courtier and countrey gentleman).

Spenser, Edmund. Hymns in honour of love and beautie. In his Four hymnes, 1596.

Cleland, James. HPΩ ΠΑΙΔΕΙΑ: or the institution of a young nobleman. 1607.

Scott, M. A. The book of the courtyer: a possible source of Beatrice and Benedick. PMLA 16 1901.

Lee, R. W. Castiglione's influence on Spenser's early hymns. PQ 7 1928.

Praz, M. Shakespeare, Castiglione e le facezie. In his Machiavelli in Inghilterra, Florence 1942.

Pearce, T. M. Marlowe and Castiglione. MLQ 12 1951.

Vincent, E. R. Il cortegiano in Inghilterra. In Rinascimento europeo e rinascimento veneziano, ed V. Branca, Florence 1967.

Colonna, Francesco. Hypnerotomachia poliphili. Venice 1499; The strife of love in a dream, tr R.D[allington?] 1592.

Cornaro, Ludovico. Discorsi della vita sobria. Padua 1558, Venice 1599 (enlarged); A treatise of temperance and sobriety, tr George Herbert 1634.

Doni, Antonio Francesco. I marmi. Venice 1552.

Rees, D. G. John Florio and Doni. Comparative Lit 15 1963.

Giovio, Paolo (Paulus Jovius). Dialogo dell'imprese militari e amorose. Rome 1555; tr S. Daniel 1585.

Giraldi, Giambattista (Cinthio). Tre dialoghe della vita civile. Monte Regale 1565.

Bryskett, Lodowick. A discourse of civill life. 1606. Written c. 1586.

Guazzo, Stefano. La civil conversatione. Brescia 1574; Civille conversation, bks 1–3 tr G. Pettie from the French of C. Chappuys 1581; bk 4 tr B. Young 1586.

Anderson, M. L. Webster's debt to Guazzo. SP 36 1939.

Lievsay, J. L. Robert Greene, master of arts and Mayster Steeven Guazzo. SP 36 1939.

— Guazzo and the English Renaissance 1575–1675. Chapel Hill 1961.

Guicciardini, Francesco. Istoria d'Italia. Florence 1561; The historie of Guicciardin containing the warres of Italy, tr G. Fenton 1579.

A brief collection of all the notable things in the hystorie of Guicchiardine. 1591.

Dallington, Robert. Amphorismes out of the first quaterne of F. Guicciardine. 1613.

Luciani. V. Guicciardini and his European reputation. New York 1936.

— Bacon and Guicciardini. PMLA 62 1947.

Orsini, N. I ricordi del Guiccardini nell'Inghilterra elisabettiana. In his Studi sul rinascimento italiano in Inghilterra, Florence 1937.

Gottfried, R. B. Geoffrey Fenton's Historie of Guicciardin. Bloomington 1940.

Fellheimer, J. Barnabe Barnes's use of Geoffrey Fenton's Historie of Guicciardin. MLN 57 1942.

— Geoffrey Fenton's Historie of Guicciardin and Holinshed's Chronicles of 1587. MLQ 6 1945.

Guicciardini, P. Le traduzioni inglesi della Storia Guicciardiana nel 16 e 17 secolo. Florence 1951.

Guicciardini, Lodovico. Detti e fatti piacevoli et gravi. Venice 1565, Antwerp 1583 (rev as L'hore di ricreatione); The garden of pleasure, tr John Sandford 1573.

— Descrittione di tutti i Paesi Bassi. Antwerp 1567; Description of the Low Countries gathered into an epitome, [tr Thomas Danett] 1593.

Landi, Ortensio. Paradossi. Lyons 1543.

Cornwallis, William. Essayes: or rather encomiums. 1616.

— Essayes of certain paradoxes. 1616.

Lopes, Duarte and Filippo Pigafetta. Relatione del reame di Congo. Rome 1591; tr A. Hartwell 1597.

Machiavelli, Niccolò. Libro dell'arte della guerra. Florence 1521; The arte of warre, tr Peter Whitehorne 1560.

— Discorsi sopra la prima deca di Tito Livio. [Rome] 1531; tr E[dward] D[acres] 1636.

— Il principe. Rome 1531 (written 1514); Nicholas Machiavel's Prince, tr E[dward] D[acres] 1640; ed H. Craig, Chapel Hill 1944 (from anon ms).

— Istorie florentine. Florence 1532; The Florentine history, tr T[homas] B[edingfield] 1595.

Gentillet, Innocent. Discours sur les moyens de bien gouverner: contre Nicholas Machiavel. [Geneva] 1576; A discourse upon the means of well-governing a kingdom, tr Simon Patericke 1602.

Sidney, Sir Philip. Arcadia. 1590, 1593 (with bks 3–5).

— A discourse to the Queen's Majesty. In Complete works of Sidney vol 3, ed A. Feuillerat, Cambridge 1933.

Scott, Thomas. Vox populi. 1620.

Spenser, Edmund. A view of the present state of Ireland. Dublin 1633. Written 1596.

Ralegh, Walter. The prince: or maxims of state. 1646.

Ellinger, G. Thomas Morus und Machiavelli. Vierteljahrschrift für Kultur und Literatur der Renaissance 1884.

Phillips, W. A. Influence of Machiavelli on the Reformation of England. Nineteenth Century Dec 1896.

Meyer, E. Machiavelli and the Elizabethan drama. Wismar 1897.

Greenlaw, E. A. The influence of Machiavelli on Spenser. MP 7 1909.

Gerber, A. Niccolo Machiavelli: die Handschriften, Ausgaben und Übersetzungen seiner Werke in 16 und 17 Jahrhundert. Gotha 1912.

Kempner, N. Raleghs staatstheoretische Schriften: die Einführung des Machiavellismus in England. Leipzig 1928.

Garfano, G. S. Machiavelli e il Machiavelismo nel teatro Elisabethiano. Marzocco 13 July 1930.

Orsini, N. Bacone e Machiavelli. Genoa 1936.

— Gli studii machiavellici di Milton. In his Studi sul rinascimento italiano in Inghilterra, Florence 1937.

— Le traduzioni elisabettiane inedite di Machiavelli. Ibid.

— Elizabethan ms translations of Machiavelli's Prince. Jnl Warburg & Courtauld Inst 1 1937.

— Nuove ricerche intorno al Machiavellismo nel Rinascimento inglese. Rinascita 1–2 1938–9.

— 'Policy': or the language of Elizabethan Machiavellianism. Jnl Warburg & Courtauld Inst 10 1946.

Sorrentino, A. Storia dell'antimachiavellismo europeo. Naples 1936.

Allen, D. C. An unmentioned Elizabethan opponent of Machiavelli. Italica 14 1937.

Purves, J. The first knowledge of Machiavelli in Scotland. Rinascita 1 1938.

Boughner, D. C. Elizia and Epicene. PQ 19 1940.

— The Devil's disciple: Ben Jonson's debt to Machiavelli. New York 1968.

Jameson, T. H. The Machiavellianism of Gabriel Harvey. PMLA 56 1941.

Praz, M. Machiavelli in Inghilterra ed altri saggi. Rome 1942.

— The flaming heart. New York 1958.

Merchant, W. M. Marlowe and Machiavelli. Comparative Lit Stud 13 1944.

Luciani, V. Bacon and Machiavelli. Italica 24 1947.

— Raleigh's Discourse of war and Machiavelli's Discorsi. MP 46 1948.

Armstrong, W. A. The influence of Seneca and Machiavelli on the Elizabethan tyrant. RES 24 1948.

Ribner, I. Machiavelli and Sidney's Discourse to the Queen's Majesty. Italica 26 1949.

— The significance of Gentillet's Contre-Machiavel. MLQ 10 1949.

— Machiavelli and Sidney: the Arcadia of 1590. SP 47 1950.

— Sidney's Arcadia and the Machiavelli legend. Italica 27 1950.

Nicolini, F. Di alcuni rapporti tra il Vico e il Hobbes con qualche riferamento al Machiavelli. Eng Miscellany (Rome) 1 1950.

Kelley, M. Milton and Machiavelli's Discorsi. SB 4 1952.

Schieder, T. Shakespeare und Machiavelli. Archiv für Kulturgeschichte 33 1951.

Mosse, G. L. The assimilation of Machiavelli in English thought: the casuistry of William Perkins and William Ames. HLQ 17 1954.

Strathmann, E. A. Sir Walter Raleigh: a study in Elizabethan scepticism. New York 1957.

Gasquet, E. S. Machiavelli's Discourses: a forgotten English translation. N & Q April 1958.

Chabod, F. Machiavelli and the Renaissance. 1958.

Mazzeo, J. A. Marvell's Machiavellian Cromwell. JHI 21 1960.

Baron, H. Marvell's A Horatian ode and Machiavelli. JHI 21 1960.

Raab, F. The English face of Machiavelli. 1964.

Angle, S. The reception of Machiavelli in Tudor England: a reassessment. Politica 31 1966.

Paul, L. Machiavelli and More. Moreana 4 1967.

D'Andrea, A. Studies on Machiavelli and his reputation in the 16th century. Medieval & Renaissance Stud 6 1968.

Morris, C. Machiavelli's reputation in Tudor England. Il Pensiero Politico 2 1970.

Mazzoni, Giacomo. Della difesa della Commedia di Dante. Cesena 1573.

Steadman, J. H. Milton and Mazzoni: the genie of the Divina commedia. HLQ 23 1960.

Mercurii, Scipione. Degli errori popolari d'Italia. Venice 1603.

Browne, Thomas. Pseudodoxia epidemica. 1646.

Micanzio, Fulgenzio. Vita del Padre Paolo [Sarpi]. Leyden 1646; tr 1651.

Willis, R. William Harvey: a history of the discovery of the circulation of the blood. 1878. On Harvey's debt to Sarpi.

Minadoi, Giovanni Tommaso. Historia della guerra fra Turchi e Persiani. Venice 1588; tr Abraham Hartwell 1595.

Nannini, Remigio. Considerazioni civili sopra l'historia di F. Guicciardini. Venice 1582: Civil considerations, tr W.T. 1601. From the French version by G. Chappuis.

Ochino, Bernardino. Prediche. 5 vols Geneva 1543. Selections: Certayne sermons, tr 1–6 Richard Argentine; 7–20 Ann Cooke 1548; Sermons of faythe, hope and charitie, tr William Phiston 1580.

Patrizzi, Francesco (Petrić, Patritius). Dieci dialoghi della historia. Venice 1560.

Blundevil, T. The true order and method of wryting and reading histories according to the precepts of Patricio and Accontio Tridentino. 1574.

Pico della Mirandola, Giovanni. Commento sopra una canzona de amore da H. Benivieni. Bologna 1496; A platonicke discourse on love, tr T. Stanley 1651.

Harrison, J. S. Platonism in English poetry of the 16th and 17th centuries. New York 1903.

Collins, J. B. Christian mysticism in the Elizabethan age. Baltimore 1940.

Polo, Marco. Delle meravigliose cose del mondo. Venice 1496; The travels of Marcus Paulus, tr from the Spanish of Rodrigo da Santaella John Frampton 1579.

Rinaldi, Orazio. La dottrina della virtù fuga de' vitii. Padua 1585.

Greene, Robert. Royal exchange. 1590.

Speroni, C. Un' ignota fonte italiana di Robert Greene. Comparative Lit 14 1962.

—— The aphorisms of Orazio Rinaldi, Robert Greene and Lucas Gracián Dantisco. Berkeley 1968.

Rodrigues Girão, João. Lettera annua de Giappone del anno 1624. Milan 1628, Palme of Christian fortitude: the glorious combats of Christians in Japonie, 1630.

Romei, Annibale. Discorsi. Ferrara 1586; The courtier's academy, tr J.K[epers] [1598].

Sansovino, Francesco. Concetti politici. Venice 1578: The quintessence of wit, tr Robert Hitchcock 1590.

Milton, John (ed). The Cabinet-council. 1658. Attributed to Ralegh, but see E. A. Strathmann, TLS 13 April 1956.

Sarpi, Paolo. Historia del concilio tridentino. 1619; tr Nathanael Brent 1620; tr C[hristopher] P[otter] from the French of Giovanni Diodati (1621) 1626 (in part).

Serlio, Sebastiano. Il primo (-quinto) libro d'architettura. Venice 1551; tr from Dutch 1666.

Tasso, Ercole. Dello ammogliarsi: contesa fra i due Tassi, Hercole e Torquato. Bergamo 1596; Of marriage and wiving, tr Robert Tofte 1599.

Tasso, Torquato. Il padre di famiglia. Venice 1583; The householder's philosophie, tr T.K. 1588.

Varchi, Benedetto. Lettura sopra un sonetto della gelosia di Monsignore Della Casa. Mantua 1545; Blazon of jealousy, tr Robert Tofte 1615.

English Authors

Bacon, Francis. Essayes. 1597, 1612, 1625 (both enlarged).

Crinò, A. M. Baconiana: ulteriori documenti sulle versioni italiane 1689 e 1690 dei saggi morali. Eng Miscellany (Rome) 10 1959.

Cecil, William, Lord Burghley. The execution of justice in England. 1583; Atto della giustitia d'Inghilterra, 1584.

Literary Criticism

Bembo, Pietro. Prose della volgare lingua. Venice 1525.

Pope, E. V. The critical background of the Spenserian stanza. MP 23 1926.

Kostić, V. Spenser and Bembian literary theory. Eng Miscellany (Rome) 10 1959.

Fornari, Simone. Spositione sopra Orlando furioso di M. Lodovico Ariosto. Florence 1549.

Harington, John. Preface to his trn of Orlando furioso, 1591.

Tasso, Torquato. Discorsi dell' arte poetica. Venice 1587. For his influence on Spenser see Bembo, above.

Allegory, Satire etc

Alemanni, Luigi. Opera toscane. 2 vols Florence (later Venice) 1532–42.

Wyatt, Thomas. On the courtier's life. 1542.

Bellezza, P. Il primo poeta satirico inglese e le sue imitazioni. Rindiconti Istorici Lombardi 1897.

Ariosto, Ludovico. Le satire. 1534; Satyres, tr 'Gervase Markham' (really Robert Tofte) 1608, 1611 (without translator's name as Ariosto's seven planets).

Boccalini, Trajano. Ragguagli di Parnaso. Venice 1612; Advertisements from Parnassus, tr Henry Carey, Earl of Monmouth 1656.

Suckling, John. A session of the poets. 1637.

[Wither, George?]. Great assises holden in Parnassus. 1645.

Sheppard, Samuel. Socratic session. 1651.

Brotanek, R. Boccalinis Einfluss auf die englische Literatur. Archiv 111 1903.

Gray, P. H. Suckling's A session of the poets as a ballad: Boccalini's influence examined. SP 36 1939.

Marquardt, W. F. The first English translators of Boccalini's Ragguagli di Parnaso. HLQ 15 1951.

Pietro Aretino. Poesie burlesche. In L. Berni et al, Opere burlesche, Florence 1552.

Nashe, Thomas. Apology of Pierce pennilesse. 1592.

McPherson, D. C. Aretino and the Harvey-Nashe quarrel. PMLA 84 1969.

Lyric Poetry

Petrarchism: Italian Sources

Petrarca, Francesco. [Canzoniere]. Venice 1470.

—— The tryumphes of Frances Petrarche. Tr Henry Parker, Baron Morley 1565; The triumphs of love, chastity, death, tr Anna Hume 1644.

Tebaldeo, A. Rime. 1499.

Ciminelli, Serafino de' (Aquilano). Opere. Venice 1502.

Gareth, Benedetto (il Chariteo). Opere volgare. [Naples 1509].
Bembo, Pietro. Rime. Venice 1530.
Ariosto, Lodovico. Rime. Venice 1534.
Rime di diversi eccelenti autori. 2 bks Venice 1545-7.
Firenzuola, Agnolo. Rime. Florence 1549.
Casa, Giovanni della. Rime e prose. Venice 1558.
Rime scelte. 2 bks Venice 1553-63.
Atanagi, Dionigi. De le rime di diversi poeti toscani. 2 vols Venice 1565. Includes Tasso's early sonnets.
Caro, Annibale. Rime. Venice 1569.
Tasso, Torquato. Rime. Venice 1581.
Guarini, Battista. Rime (Madrigali). Venice 1598.

Latin Sources

Tarchaniota Marullus, Michael. Hymni et epigrammata. Florence 1497.
— Neniae. Fani 1515.
Pontanus, Joannes Jovianus. Opera [in verse]. Venice 1505.
Angerianus, Hieronymus. 'Ερωτοπαίγνιον. Florence 1512.
Scaliger, Julius Caesar. Nova epigrammata. Paris 1533.
— Lacrymae. Paris 1534.
— Poemata omnia. [Heidelberg] 1600.
Sannazaro, Jacopo. Opera latine scripta. Venice 1535.
Vulteius, Joannes. Epigrammata. Lyons 1536, 1537 (enlarged).
— Hendecasyllaborum libri 4. Paris 1538.
Secundus, Joannes. Opera. Utrecht 1541.
Bembo, Pietro. Carminum libellus. Venice 1552.
Lotichius, Petrus. Poemata. Leipzig [1563?].
Melissus, Paulus (Paul Schede). Schediasmatum reliquiae. [Heidelberg] 1575.
Buchanan, George. Elegiae. Paris 1579.
Posthius, Joannes. Parerga poetica. Heidelberg 1595.
Blyenburg, Damasus. Veneres Blyenburgicae: sive hortus amorum. Dordrecht 1600.
Gruter, Janus (Ranutius Cherus). Delitiae cc italorum poatarum hujus superioris aevi illustrium. Frankfurt 1608.

French Sources

Du Bellay, Joachim. L'Olive. Paris 1549, 1550 (enlarged).
— Les antiquitez du Rome, plus un songe ou vision. Paris 1558.
— Les regrets. Paris 1558.
Tyard, Pontus de. Erreurs amoureuses. 3 bks Lyons 1549-55.
Ronsard, Pierre de. Les amours. Paris 1552, 1553 (enlarged); Continuation des amours, Paris 1555, 1556, 1560 (both enlarged).
— Sonnets pour Hélène. Paris 1578.
Baïf, Jean Antoine de. Amours de Méline. Paris 1552, 1573 (rev).
— Quatre livres de l'amour de Francine. Paris 1555.
Magny, Olivier de. Les odes. Paris 1559.
Belleau, Rémy. La bergerie. Paris 1565.
Desportes, Philippe. Les premières oeuvres. Paris 1573.

English and Scottish Petrarchists

Songes and sonnettes by Henry Hawarde, late Earle of Surrey, and other. 1557. Tottel's Miscellany.
Turbervile, George. Epitaphs, epigrams, songs and sonnets. 1567.
Howell, Thomas. The arbor of amitie. 1568.
— New sonets and pretie pamphlets. 1568.
— Devises. 1581.
Gascoigne, George. A hundred sundrie flowers. 1573.
Watson, Thomas. Hecatompathia: or passionate centurie of love. 1582.

Sidney, Sir Philip. The Countess of Pembroke's Arcadia. 1590, 1593 (with bks 3-5).
— Astrophel and Stella. 1591.
Daniel, Samuel. Delia. 1592.
— Teares of fancie. 1593.
Constable, Henry. Diana: the praises of his mistres. 1592, 1594 (enlarged).
Barnes, Barnabe. Parthenophil and Parthenope. 1593.
— A divine centurie of spiritual sonnets. [1595].
Lodge, Thomas. Phillis. 1593.
Fletcher, Giles, Senior. Licia: or poems of love. 1593.
'Willobie, Henry'. Willobie his avisa. 1594.
Drayton, Michael. Ideas mirrour. 1594, 1619 (as Idea).
Spenser, Edmund. Complaints. 1591.
— Amoretti and Epithalamion. 1595.
Barnfield, Richard. Cynthia with certain sonnets. 1595.
Shakespeare, William. Sonnets. 1609.
Drummond, William. Poems. 1616.
— Flowers of Sion. 1623.
Donne, John. Poems. 1633.

Studies

Fehse, H. Henry Howard, Earl of Surrey: ein Beitrag zur Geschichte des Petrarchismus in England. Chemnitz 1883.
Koeppel, E. Studien zur Geschichte des englischen Petrarchismus im 16 Jahrhundert. Romanische Forschungen 5 1889.
Vaganay, H. Le sonnet en Italie et an France au 16e siècle: essai de bibliographie comparée. 2 vols Lyons 1903.
Zocco, I. Petrarchismo e Petrarchisti in Inghilterra. Palermo 1906.
Kastner, L. E. Thomas Lodge as an imitator of the Italien poets. MLR 2 1907.
— On the Italian and French sources of Drummond of Hawthornden. MLR 6 1911.
— The Italian and Spanish sources of William Drummond of Hawthornden. In Miscellanea di studi critici in onore di V. Crescini, Cividale 1927.
Hasselkuss, H. K. Petrarkismus in der Sprache der englischen Sonnettdichter der Renaissance. Münster 1927.
Walker, A. The Italian sources of the lyrics of Thomas Lodge. MLR 22 1927.
Scott, J. E. Les sonnets élisabéthains: les sources et l'appel personnel. Paris 1929.
Cecchini, A. Serafino Aquilano e l'influenza della lirica italiana sulla lirica inglese del 1500. Aquila 1934.
Meozzi, A. Il Petrarchismo europeo. Pisa 1934.
— The Italian and Spanish sources of William Drummond of Hawthornden. In Miscellanea di studi critici in onore di Crescini, Cividale 1927.
Chini, A. Il sorgere del Petrarchismo in Inghilterra. Civiltà Moderna 6 1934.
Bizzari, E. L'influenza italiana sugli Amoretti di Spenser. Romana 6 1942.
Fucilla, J. G. Petrarchan translations in British periodicals. Bull of Bibliography 18 1943.
Whitfield, J. H. Petrarch and the Renascence. Oxford 1943.
Gilbert, A. H. Milton quotes from Petrarch. MLN 60 1945.
Zamora, V. Sobre petrarquismo. Santiago de Compostela 1945.
Valente, P. L. Petrarca e Shakespeare. Studi Petrarcheschi 1 1948.
Wilkins, E. H. A general survey of European Petrarchism. Comparative Lit 2 1950.
Russell Brown, T. and B. Harris (ed). Elizabethan poetry. 1950.
Rees, D. G. Petrarch's Trionfo della morte in English. Italian Stud 7 1952.

—— Sir Thomas Wyatt's translations from Petrarch. Comparative Lit 7 1955.

Thomson, P. Petrarch and the Elizabethans. E Studies 10 1955.

—— The first English Petrarchans. HLQ 22 1959.

—— Wyatt and the school of Serafino. Comparative Lit 13 1961.

—— Sonnet 15 of Samuel Daniel's Delia a Petrarchan imitation? Comparative Lit 17 1965.

Kostić, V. Spenser's Amoretti and Tasso's lyrical poetry. Renaissance & Modern Stud 3 1959.

—— Spenser and Bembian literary theory. Eng Miscellany (Rome) 10 1959.

Hietsch, O. Die Petrarca-Übersetzungen Sir Thomas Wyatts. Vienna 1960.

Hughey, R. (ed). The Arundel-Harington ms of Tudor poetry. Columbus 1960. Includes Queen Elizabeth's trn of Petrarch's Trionfo dell' Eternità.

Guss, D. L. Donne's conceit and Petrarchan wit. PMLA 78 1963.

—— Wyatt's Petrarchism. IILQ 29 1965.

—— John Donne, Petrarchist. Detroit 1966.

Mumford, I. L. Petrarchism in early Tudor England. Italian Stud 19 1964.

Baldi, S. Una fonte petrarchesca di Sir Thomas Wyatt. In Friendship's garland: essays presented to Mario Praz, Rome 1966.

Phillips, J. E. Daniel Rogers: a neo-Latin link between the Pléiade and Sidney's Areopagus. In Neo-Latin poetry of the 16th and 17th centuries, Los Angeles 1965.

Righetti, A. Le due versioni Spenseriane della Canzone 323 del Petrarca. Annali di Ca' Foscari (Venice) 5 1966.

Singh, G. S. Il petrarchismo inglese. Osservatore Politico Letterario 13 Jan 1967.

Watson, G. The English Petrarchans: a critical bibliography of the Canzoniere. 1967 (Warburg Inst).

Forster, L. W. The icy fire: five studies in European Petrarchism. Cambridge 1969.

Madrigals etc

Byrd, William. Lyrics, elegiacs, psalms, sonnets and songs of gravity and piety. 1587–8.

Yonge, N. Musica transalpina, altus: madrigales translated out of foure, five and sixe parts, chosen out of divers excellent authors. 1588.

—— The second booke of madrigalles translated out of sundrie Italian authors. 1597.

Watson, Thomas. Superius: the first sett of Italian madrigalls englished. 1590.

Morley, Thomas. The first book of canzonets to two voices. 1595.

—— Canzonets: or short little songs to four voices, collected out of the best and approved Italian authors. 1597.

—— Altus: madrigals to five voices, collected out of the best approved Italian authors. 1598.

Dowland, John. The first book of songs and airs. 1596.

—— A musical banquet. 1610.

Obortello, A. Influssi italiani sulla poesia e la musica elisabettiana. Giornale di Politica e di Letteratura 13 1937.

—— Madrigali italiani in Inghilterra. Milan 1949.

Einstein, A. The Italian madrigal. Princeton 1949.

Kerman, J. Elizabethan anthologies of Italian madrigals. Jnl of Amer Musicological Soc 4 1951.

Elliott, K. Robert Edwards' commonplace-book and Scottish musical history. Scottish Stud 5 1961.

Other Lyric Poets

Alamanni, Luigi. Opere toscane. 2 vols Florence (later Venice) 1532–42.

Wyatt, Thomas. Certain psalms drawn into English meter. 1549.

Michelangelo Buonarotti

Gilbert, C. Michael Angelo's poetry in English verse. Italica 14 1947.

Marino, Giambattisto. Rime. Venice 1602.

Carew, Thomas. Poems. 1640.

Crashaw, Richard. Steps to the temple. 1646, 1648 (enlarged).

Beaumont, Joseph. Psyche: or love's mystery. 1648.

Sherburne, Edward. Salmacis, Lyrian and Sylvia. 1651.

Stanley, Thomas. Poems. 1651.

Petoello, L. A current misconception concerning the influence of Marino's poetry on Crashaw. MLR 52 1957.

Wilson, E. M. and E. R. Vincent. Stanley's translations and borrowings from Spanish and Italian poets. Revue de Littérature Comparée 32 1958.

Tansilli, Luigi. Le lagrime de San Piero. 1560, 1585 (enlarged by another hand).

Southwell, Robert. St Peter's complaint. 1595.

Praz, M. Southwell's St Peter's complaynt and its Italian source. MLR 19 1924.

Janelle, P. Southwell the writer. Clermont-Ferrand 1935.

Valvasone, Erasmo da. Le lagrime della Maddalena. 1587.

Southwell, Robert. Marie Magdalen's funerall teares. 1591.

Drama

Ariosto, Lodovico. Gli suppositi. Rome 1524 (prose), Venice 1542 (verse); Supposes, tr George Gascoigne in his A hundreth sundrie flowers, [1573]. Performed 1566.

Bisaccioni, Hieronimo. I falsi pastori. Verona 1605.

Jeffrey, U. M. Italian influence in Fletcher's Faithful shepherdess. MLR 21 1926.

Bonavelli della Rovere, Guido Ubaldo. Filli di Sciro: favola pastorale. Ferrara 1607; Phillis of Scyros, tr J.S. (James Shirley?) 1655.

Bruno, Giordano. Candelaio. Paris 1582.

Donne, John. The ecstasie. In his Poems, 1633.

Praz, M. John Donne e la poesia del suo tempo. In his Machiavelli in Inghilterra, Rome 1942.

Cucchetti, Giovanni Donato. La Pazzia: favola pastorale. Ferrara, 1581.

Randolph, Thomas. The impossible dowry. 1638.

Dolce, Lodovico. Giocasta. Venice 1549; Jocasta, tr George Gascoigne and Francis Kinaelmarsh 1572 (acted 1566?).

Giraldi, Giambattista [Cinthio]. Epitia. Venice 1583.

Bell, R. H. Cinthio's Epitia and Measure for measure. In Elizabethan studies in honor of G. F. Reynolds, Boulder 1945.

Cavalchini, M. L'Epitia di Giraldi e Measure for measure. Italica 45 1968.

Grazzini, Antonio Francesco. La spiritata. Venice 1582; The bugbears (acted 1561) ed C. Grabau, Archiv 98–9 1897.

Guarini, Gian Battista. Il pastor fido. Venice 1590; The faithful shepherd, tr (Edward?) Dymock 1602; tr Richard Fanshawe 1647.

Daniel, Samuel. The Queen's Arcadia. 1605.

Fletcher, John. The faithful shepherdesse. 1629 (acted c. 1608); La fida pastora, tr Richard Fanshawe 1658.

Brathwait, Richard. Arcadian Princess. 1635. Original work, as trn from 'Mariano Silesio'.

Perella, N. J. Amarilli's dilemma: the Pastor fido and some English authors. Comparative Lit 12 1960.

Neri, N. Il pastor fido in Inghilterra. Turin 1963.

Whitfield, J. H. Sir Richard Fanshawe and the Faithfull shepherd. Italian Stud 19 1964.

Negri, Francesco. Libero arbitrio. [Basle] 1546; Freewyl, tr Henry Cheke (1572–7).

Bradner, L. Henry Cheke's Freewyl. PMLA 49 1934.

Pasqualigo, Luigi. Il fedele. Venice 1759; Fidele and fortune: the deceiptes in love, tr A[nthony] M[unday] 1584.

Paulilli, Anello. Il giuditio di Paride: tragicomedia. Naples 1566.

Peele, George. The araygnement of Paris. 1584.

Pietro Aretino. Il marescalco. Venice 1533.

Chapman, George. May day. 1611.

Campbell, O. J. The relation of Epicoene to Aretino's Il marescalco. PMLA 46 1931.

Porta, Giovanni Battista della. La sorella. Naples 1589.

Gordon, D. J. Middleton's No wit, no help like a woman's and della Porta's La sorella. RES 17 1941.

Secchi, Niccolò. Gl'inganni. Florence 1562.

— L'Interesse. Venice 1581; Self-interest, tr William Reymes 1650.

Kaufman, H. A. Niccolò Secchi as a source for Twelfth night. Shakespeare Quart 6 1955.

Tasso, Torquato, Aminta. Venice 1581; Aminta, [tr Henry Reynolds?] 1628; tr J. Dancer 1660.

Fraunce, Abraham. The lamentations of Amyntas for the death of Phillis. 1587. In part from Thomas Watson's Latin adaptation, Amyntas 1585.

Daniel, Samuel. The Queen's Arcadia. 1605.

Browne, William. Britannia's postorals. 1616.

Rutter, J. Shepherd's holiday. [c. 1620?].

Randolph, Thomas. Amyntas: or the impossible dowry. 1638.

Koeppel, E. Die englische Tasso-Übersetzungen des 16 Jahrhunderts. Anglia 11 1889.

Barzanò, G. Le prime due traduzioni inglese dell' Aminta. Studi Tassiani 5 1955.

Cody, R. The landscape of the mind: pastoralism and platonic theory in Tasso's Aminta and Shakespeare's early comedies. Oxford 1969.

Trissino, Giovanni, Giorgio. Sofonisba. Rome 1524.

Axelrad, A. J. Le thème de Sophonisbe dans les principales tragédies de la littérature occidentale en France, Angleterre, Allemagne. Lille 1965.

General Studies

Schücking, L. Studien über die stofflichen Beziehungen der englischen Komödie zur italienischen bis Lilly. Halle 1901.

Shands, H. A. Massingers The great Duke of Florence und seine Quellen. Halle 1902.

Förster, M. T. W. Gascoigne's Jocasta, a translation from Italian? MP 2 1905.

Gerhardt, E. Massingers Duke of Milan und seine Quellen. Halle 1905.

Greg, W. W. Pastoral poetry and pastoral drama. 1906.

Cunliffe, J. W. The influence of Italian on early Elizabethan drama. MP 4 1907.

Reyher, P. Les masques anglais: étude sur les ballets et la vie de cour en Angleterre 1512–1640. Paris 1909.

Bond, R. W. Early plays from the Italian. Oxford 1911.

Freeburg, V. O. Disguise plots in Elizabethan drama. New York 1915.

Welsford, E. The Italian influence on the English Court masque. MLR 18 1923.

Jeffery, V. M. Italian and English postoral drama of the Renaissance. MLR 19 1924.

Rébora, P. L'Italia nel dramma inglese 1558–1642. Milan 1925.

— Motivi Medicei nel teatro inglese del rinascimento. Rinascita 3 1940.

Smith, W. Italian actors in Elizabethan England. MLN 44 1929.

Lea, K. M. Italian popular comedy: a study of the commedia dell'arte with special reference to the English stage. 2 vols Oxford 1934.

Meozzi, A. La drammatica della rinascita italiana in Europa (sec. 16–17). Pisa 1940.

Orsini, N. La scena italiana in Inghilterra: il trattato di Serlio. Anglia 69 1946.

Gilbert, A. H. The Italian names in Every man out of his humour. SP 44 1947.

Phialas, P. G. Massinger and the commedia dell'arte. MLN 65 1950.

Kaufman, H. The influence of Italian drama on pre-Restoration English comedy. Italica 31 1954.

Miller, M. 16th-century Italian criticism and Milton's theory of catharsis. Stud in Eng Lit 1500–1900 6 1967.

Salingar, L. G. The revenger's tragedy: some possible sources. MLR 60 1965.

Montano, R. From Italian Humanism to Shakespeare: the fight with the angel. Umanesimo 1 1967.

Stäuble, A. La commedia umanistica del Quattrocento. Florence 1968.

Radcliffe-Umstead, D. The birth of modern comedy in Renaissance Italy. Chicago 1969.

Epic

Ariosto, Lodovico. Orlando furioso. Ferrara 1516; Orlando furioso in English heroical verse, tr J. Harington 1591; Two tales, tr R[obert] T[ofte] 1597 (extract).

Spenser, Edmund. The Faerie Queene. 2 vols 1590–6.

Greene, Robert. The history of Orlando furioso. 1594.

Beverley, Peter. Historie of Ariodante and Ieneura. 1600. Acted 1582.

Shakespeare, William. Much ado about nothing. 1600.

— The tempest. 1623.

Drayton, Michael. The barrons war. 1603.

Markham, Gervase. Rodomonth's Infernall. 1607. Trn of P. Desportes, Roland furieux: imitation de l'Arioste, 1572.

Fletcher, Phineas. Sicelides. 1631. Acted King's College, Cambridge 1615.

Kynaston, Francis. Leoline and Sydanis. 1642.

Chamberlayne, William. Pharonnida. 1659.

Warton, T. On Spenser's imitation of Ariosto. 1754.

Dodge, R. E. N. Spenser's imitations from Ariosto. PMLA 12 1897, 35 1920.

Croce, B. Ariosto, Shakespeare e Corneille. Bari 1920; tr 1921.

McMurphy, S. J. Spenser's use of Ariosto for allegory. Univ of Washington Pbns in Lang & Lit 2 1924.

Morrison, M. R. Greene's use of Ariosto in Orlando furioso. MLN 49 1934.

Galimberti, A. Edmondo Spenser: l'Ariosto inglese. Turin 1938.

Rich, T. Harington and Ariosto: study in Elizabethan verse translation. New Haven 1940.

Bottazi, B. Ludovico Ariosto e l'Inghilterra. Reggio Emilia 1941.

Purves, J. The abridgement of Roland furious by John Stewart of Baldynneis and the early knowledge of Ariosto in England. Italian Stud 3 1948.

Townsend, F. L. Sidney and Ariosto. PMLA 61 1946.

Gilbert, A. H. Nevizanus, Ariosto, Florio, Harington and Drummond. MLN 62 1947.

Lea, K. M. Harington's folly. In Elizabethan and Jacobean studies presented to F. P. Wilson, Oxford 1959.

Kostić, V. Ariosto and Spenser. Eng Miscellany (Rome) 17 1966.

— Spenser's sources in Italian poetry. Belgrade 1969.

Alpers, P. J. The poetry of the Fairie Queene. Princeton 1967.

Gabler, H. W. Imitation and parody in Greene's Orlando furioso. Anglia 85 1967.

Gelber, N. Greene's Orlando furioso: a study of thematic ambiguity. MLR 64 1969.

Nelson, T. G. John Stewart of Baldynneis and Orlando furioso. Stud in Scottish Lit 6 1969.

Boiardo, Matteo Maria. Orlando innamorato. Scandiano 1480; Orlando innamorato: the first three books, tr R[obert] T[ofte] 1598. See also 2 16th-century rifaccimenti by F. Berni 1541 and L. Domenichi 1545.

Spenser, Edmund. The Faerie Queene bk 1. 1590.

Blanchard, H. H. Spenser and Boiardo. PMLA 40 1925.

Bond, R. W. Lucian and Boiardo in Timon. In his Studia otiosa, 1938.

Bracciolini, Francesco. La croce racquistata. Venice 1611; The tragedie of Alieste and Eliza, tr Fr. Br. 1638 (in part).

Dante Alighieri. La divina commedia. Foligno 1472.

Lyndsay, David. The dreme. 1528.

Koeppel, E. Dante in der englischen Literatur des 16 Jahrhunderts. Zeitschrift für Vergleichende Literaturgeschichte 3 1890.

Sills, K. C. M. Wyatt and Dante. Jnl of Comparative Lit 4 1903.

Toynbee, P. The earliest reference to Dante in English literature. In Miscellanea di studi in onore di Arturo Graf, Bergamo 1903.

— Dante in English literature from Chaucer to Cary. 1909.

— Britain's tribute to Dante in literature and art: a chronological record of 540 years. Oxford 1921.

Farinelli, Arturo. Dante in Spagna, Francia, Inghilterra, Germania. Turin 1922.

Galimberti, A. Dante nel pensiero inglese. Florence 1922.

Piccoli, V. Dante e Shakespeare. Rassegna Italiana 33 1933.

Vida, A. Reminiscence dantesche in un dramma di Shakespeare. Rassegna Nazionale ser 4 [1939–41].

Friederich, W. P. Dante through the centuries. Comparative Lit 1 1949.

— Dante's fame abroad 1350–1850. Rome 1950.

Arthos, J. Dante, Michelangelo and Milton. 1963.

Obortello, A. Dante e Shakespeare. In Miscellanea di studi danteschi, Genoa 1966.

Morris, H. Macbeth, Dante and the greatest evil. Tennessee Stud in Lit 12 1967.

Marcazano, M. Presenza di Dante nella cultura europea. Atti Montepulciani 1968.

Parker, P. The image of direction in Dante, Shakespeare and Milton. Eng Miscellany (Rome) 19 1968.

Marino, Giambattista. La strage degli innocenti. Venice and Bassano [1610?]; The suspicion of Herod, tr R. Crashaw 1646.

Tasso, Torquato. Gerusalemme liberata. Parma 1581; Godfrey of Bulloigne: or the recoverie of Hierusalem, cantos 1–5 tr R. Carew 1594; Godfrey of Bulloigne, tr Edward Fairfax 1600.

Spenser, Edmund. The Faerie Queene. 2 vols 1590–6.

Browne, William. Britannia's pastorals. 2 bks 1613–16.

Heywood, Thomas. The four prentices of London with the Conquest of Jerusalem. 1615.

Blanchard, H. S. Imitations from Tasso in the Fairie Queene. Berkeley 1925.

Dodge, R. E. N. The text of the Gerusalemme liberata in the versions of Carew and Fairfax. PMLA 44 1929.

Bullock, W. L. Carew's text of the Gerusalemme liberata. PMLA 45 1930.

Castelli, A. La Gerusalemme liberata nella Inghilterra de Spenser. Milan 1936.

Pitou, S. French and English echoes of a descriptive passage in Tasso. MLN 42 1937.

Beall, C. B. A Tasso imitation in Spenser. MLQ 3 1942.

Murphy, J. Elizabethan lyrics from Tasso. MLN 58 1943.

Bell, C. G. A history of Fairfax criticism. PMLA 52 1947.

— Fairfax's Tasso. Comparative Lit 6 1954.

Prince, F. T. The influence of Tasso and Della Casa on Milton's diction. RES 25 1948.

Grundy, J. Tasso, Fairfax and William Browne. RES new ser 3 1952.

Praz, M. Tasso in Inghilterra. In Comitato per le celebrazione de Torquato Tasso, Ferrara 1954, Milan 1957.

Brand, C. P. Tasso: a study of the poet and of his contribution to English literature. Cambridge 1965.

Rasica degli Espositi, G. Una traduzione inedita della Gerusalemme liberata. Studi Tassiani 16 1965.

Gramatti, A. B. Milton and Fairfax's Tasso. Revue de Littérature Comparée 40 1966.

Trissino, Giovanni Giorgio. La Italia liberata da Gotthi. Venice 1547.

Spenser, Edmund. The Faerie Queen bk 2. 1590.

Lemmi, C. W. The influence of Trissino on the Faerie Queene. PQ 7 1928.

Prose Fiction

Assarino, Luca. Stratonica. Venice 1637; La Stratonica: the unfortunate Queen, tr 1651.

Bandello, Matteo. Le novelle. 4 pts Lucca 1554–73. Known in England largely through French trn.

Boaistuau, P. and F. de Belleforest. Histoires tragiques. 2 vols Paris 1559. 18 stories.

— Histoires tragiques. 7 vols Paris and Lyons 1565–95.

Pruvost, R. Les deux premiers tomes de la version française de Bandello. Revue de Littérature Comparée 12 1932.

Hook, F. S. The French Bandello. Univ of Missouri Stud 22 1948.

Collections containing translations or adaptations of several of Bandello's stories:

Painter, William. The palace of pleasure. 2 vols 1566–7.

Fenton, Geoffrey. Certaine tragicall discourses, written out of French and Latin. 1567.

Fortescue, Thomas. The forest. 1571. An adaptation through French and Italian, of Pedro Mexia, Silva de varia lecion, 1554.

Whetstone, George. The rocke of regard. 1576.

— An Heptameron of civill discourses. 1582.

S[mythe], R. Straunge, lamentable and tragical hystories. 1571.

Rich, Barnabe. His farewell to the militarie profession. 1581.

Turbervile, George. Tragicall tales. 1587.

Koeppel, E. George Turbervilles Verhältnis zur italienischen Literatur. Anglia 13 1891.

Translations and adaptations of individual stories:

1.4 Marston, John. The insatiate Countess. 1613.

1.10 Carlell, Lodowick. Osmond the great Turke. 1657. Swinhoe, Gilbert. The unhappy fair Irene. 1658.

1.21 Massinger, Philip. The picture. 1630.

1.22 Shakespeare, William. Much ado about nothing. 1600.

1.26 Beard, Thomas. The theatre of god's judgements. 1597. Webster, John. The Duchess of Malfi. 1623. Acted c. 1614.

1.27 Linche, Richard. The amorous poem of don Diego and Ginevra. 1596. Fellheimer, J. The source of Richard Lynche's amorous poeme of don Diego and Ginevra. PMLA 58 1943.

1.35 Shirley, James. Love's cruelty. 1640.

1.41 Marston, John. The wonder of women: Sophonisba her tragedy. 1606. Murray, David. The tragicall death of Sophonisba. 1611.

1.42 The horrible tyrannie which a Spanish gentlewoman named Violenta executed on her lover Didaco. [Tr Thomas Achelly?] 1576.

1.49 Heywood, T. A woman killed with kindness. 1607.

2.9 The tragicall historye of Rhomeo and Julietta. Tr (from Boaistuau) Arthur Brooke 1562. Shakespeare, William. Romeo and Juliet. 1597.

Fränkel, L. Zur Entwicklungsgeschichte des Stoffes von Romeo und Julia. Zeitschrift für Vergleichende Literaturgeschichte new ser 3–4 1890–1.

Bödtker, A. T. Arthur Brooke and his poem. E Studien 70 1936.

Moore, O. H. Le rôle de Boaistuau dans le développement de la légende de Romeo et Juliette. Revue de Littérature Comparée 9 1929.

2.11 Tourneur, C. The atheist's tragedy. 1611.

2.15 Fletcher, J. and W. Rowley. The maid in the mill. 1647. Written 1623.
Fletcher, J. Four plays in one. 1647.

2.36 Shakespeare, William. Twelfth night. 1623. Acted 1600–1.

2.37 Edward III. 1596. Anon.

2.44 History of John, Lord Mandozze. Tr from Spanish by Thomas Peend 1565.

3.17 A discourse of the great cruelty of a widow, tr Jo Go[bourne] [1570?].
Markham, Gervase and Lewis Machin. The dumb knight. 1608.
The Queen: or the excellency of her sex. 1653. Anon.

3.18 Davenant, William. Albovine. 1629.

4.1 Ford, John. The broken heart. 1633.

Kiesow, K. Die verschiedenen Bearbeitungen der Novelle von der Herzogin von Amalfi des Bandello in der Literatur des 16 und 17 Jahrhunderts. Anglia 17 1894.

Pruvost, R. Matteo Bandello and Elizabethan fiction. Paris 1937.

Gordon, D. J. Much ado about nothing: a possible source of the Hero–Claudio plot. SP 39 1942.

Hoeniger, F. D. Two notes on Cymbeline. Shakespeare Quart 8 1957.

Miglior, G. Bandello e Painter. In Studi e ricerche di letteratura inglese vol 1, ed A. Lombardo, Milan 1967.

Biondi (Bjundević), Giovanni, Francesco. L'Eromena. Venice 1624 (6 bks); Eromena: or love and revenge, tr J. Hayward et al 1632.
La donzella desterrada [a sequel]. 2 vols Venice 1627; The banished virgin, tr J. H[ayward] 1635.
Il Coralbo [a further sequel]. Venice 1635; Coralbo tr 1655 (3 bks).

Boccaccio, Giovanni. Filocolo. Venice 1472 (written c. 1341); A pleasant disport of divers noble personages, tr pt H.G. [Henry Grantham?] (1566?).
Tilney, E. The flower of friendship. 1568.
Melbancke, Brian. Philotimus. 1583.
Lyly, T. Love's metamorphosis. 1607. Written 1588–9?
Wright, H. G. The Elizabethan translation of the Questioni d'amore in the Filocolo. MLR 36 1941.

— L'amorosa Fiametta. Padua 1472 (written c. 1344); Amorous Fiametta, tr Bartholomew Young 1587.
Wright, G. H. The Italian edition of Boccaccio's Fiametta used by Bartholomew Young. MLR 38 1943.

— Ninfale Fiesolano. Venice 1477. Tr from French of A. Guercin (1556) by Jo. Gobourne 1597.

— Il decameron. Venice 1471 (written 1353); tr French by Laurent du Premierfait 1485 (written 1414); tr French by Antoine Le Maçon 1545; [tr John Florio?] 1620.
Wright, H. G. The first English translation of the Decameron 1620. Essays & Stud in Eng Lang & Lit (Upsala) 12 1953.

Collections containing tales from Decameron:
Painter, William. The palace of pleasure. 2 vols 1566–7.
Turbervile, George. Tragicall tales. 1587.
C., H. The forest of fancy. 1579.
Riche, Barnabe. His farewell to the militarie profession. 1581.
Whetstone, George. An heptameron of civill discourses. 1582.

Greene, Robert. Morando: the tritameron of love. 1587.
— Perimedes: the blacke-smith. 1588.
Tarleton's newes out of purgatorie. [1590?].
[Tarleton, R.?]. The cobler of Canterburie. 1590.

Borrowings from individual tales:
2.2 Rinaldo and the widow
Middleton, T. The widow. 1652. Supposedly written with Fletcher and Jonson c. 1610–15.

2.5 Andreuccio
Fraunce, A. Victoria. 1580.
Middleton, T. Blurt, master-constable. 1602.

2.9 Bernabò and Ambruogiolo
Whetstone, G. The rock of regard. 1576.
Westward for smelts. 1620.
Shakespeare, W. Cymbeline. 1623.
Thrall, W. F. Cymbeline, Boccaccio and the wager story in England. SP 28 1931.
Nosworthy, J. M. The sources of the wager plot in Cymbeline. N & Q 1 March 1952.

3.3 The tricked confessor
Marston, J. Parasitaster: or the fawn. 1606.
Jonson, B. The Devil is an ass. 1631. Performed 1616.
Middleton, T. The widow. 1652.

3.5 Ricciardo and the silent woman
H.C. The forest of fancy. 1579.
Jonson, B. The Devil is an ass. 1631.

3.8 Ferondo
Fletcher, J. The night walker. 1633 (rev James Shirley).

3.9 Beltramo and Giletta
Shakespeare, W. All's well that ends well. 1623.

4.1 Guiscardo and Ghismonda
Banester, G. Legenda Sismonde. 1478–86. Based on French trn.
Walter, W. Guystarde and Sygysmonde. 1532.
Wilmot, R. et al. Gismond of Salerne. 1567–8.
Wilmot, R. The tragedie of Tancred and Gismund. 1592.
Orsini, N. La novella boccaccesca di Ghismonda in una tragedia inedita (London 1597). In his Studi sul rinascimento italiano in Inghilterra, Florence 1937.

4.10 Ruggieri and the doctor's wife
Hymenaius. 1578–9.

5.1 Cymon and Iphigenia, tr Latin by P. Beroaldo (c. 1498)
C., T. A pleasant and delightful history of Galesus, Cymon and Iphigenia. [1556–60].

5.7 Theodoro and Violante
Beaumont, F. The triumph of love. 1647.

5.8 Anastasio and Traversaro
T., C. [Christopher Tyne?]. A notable historie of Nastagio and Traversare. 1569.
C., H. The forest of fancy. 1579.
Turberville, G. Tragicall tales. 158.
Shirley, J. A contention for honour and riches. 1633.

6.4 and 6.10 Jests by a cook and a friar
Tarleton, R. Newes out of purgatorie. [Before 1590].

7.6 Isabella, Leonetto and Lambertuccio
Twyne, T. The schoolemaster. 1576.
Sharpham, E. Cupid's whirlgig. 1607.
Rowlande, S. The knave of clubes. 1609.
Tourneur, C. The atheist's tragedy. 1611.
Fletcher, J. Women pleas'd. 1647.

7.7 Lodovico and Beatrice
[Tarleton, R.]. The cobbler of Canterburie. 1630.

8.4 The provost of Fiesole
Fletcher, J. Monsieur Thomas. 1639.

8.7 The scholar and the lady
Massinger, P. The guardian. 1655.

8.8 Spineluccio and Zeppa
Jones, John. Adrasta. 1635.
Fletcher, J. Have a wife and rule a wife. 1640. Licensed 1624.

9.1 Mme Francesca and her two lovers
Cartwright, W. The siege. 1637.
9.2 The abbess and the nun
Twyne, T. The schoolemaster. 1576.
10.1 Coffer of earth, coffer of jewels
Shakespeare, W. The merchant of Venice. 1619.
10.4 Lady rescued from her tomb
Fletcher, J. The knight of Malta. 1647. Performed 1618–19.
10.5 Ansaldo and Dianora
I.C. [John Cumber?]. The two merry milke-maids. 1620.
10.8 Titus and Gisippus, tr Latin by P. Beroaldo, Bologna 1419.
Walter, W. Tytus and Gesyppus. [?].
Elyot, T. The boke called the governour. 1531.
Radcliffe, R. De Titi et Gisippi amicitia. 1547–9.
Lewicke, E. The history of Titus and Gisippus. 1562.
Jenyngis, E. The notable history of two faithful lovers Alphagus and Archelaus. 1574.
Greene, Robert. Philamela. 1592.
Sorieri, L. Boccaccio's story of Tito e Gisippo in European literature. New York 1937.
Smith, J. H. Sempronia, John Lyly and John Foxe's comedy of Titus and Gesippus. PQ 48 1969.
10.10 Griseldis, tr Latin by F. Petrarch (c. 1374); tr 1619.
Chaucer, Geoffrey. The clerk's tale. From French trn of Petrarch's Latin.
Radcliffe, Ralph. De patientia Griseldis. 1547–9.
Philip, John. Patient Grissell. 1566.
Chettle, H., W. Houghton, T. Dekker. Patient Grissell. 1603.
Stevens, J. B. The literary relationships of Chaucer's Clerk's tale. New York 1942.

Koeppel, E. George Turbervills Verhältnis zur italienischen Literatur. Anglia 13 1891.
— Quellen-Studien zu den Dramen Ben Jonsons, John Marstons und Beaumont und Fletchers. Münchener Beiträge 11 1895.
Traversari, G. Bibliografia boccaccesca: scritti intorno al Boccaccio e alla fortuna delle sue opere. Città di Castello 1907.
Loehmann, O. Die Rahmenerzählung des Decameron: ihre Quellen und Nachwirkungen. Halle 1935.
Raith, J. Boccaccio in der englischen Literatur von Chaucer bis Painters Palace of Pleasure. Leipzig 1936.
Rebora, P. Shakespeare e Boccaccio. In his Civiltà italiana e civiltà inglese, Florence 1936.
Raith, J. Boccaccio in der englischen Literatur von Chaucer bis Painters Palace of pleasure: ein Beitrag zur Geschichte der italienischen Novelle in England. Leipzig 1936.
Munsterberg, M. The Decameron in English 1620. More Books 19 1944.
Wright, H. G. The indebtedness of Painter's translations from Boccaccio in the Palace of pleasure to the French version by Le Masson. MLR 46 1951.
— The first English translation of the Decameron 1620. Upsala 1953.
— How did Shakespeare come to know the Decameron? MLR 49 1955.
— Boccaccio in England from Chaucer to Tennyson. 1957.
Nosworthy, J. M. The sources of the wager plot in Cymbeline. N & Q 1 March 1952.
Rodax, Y. R. The real and the ideal in the novella of Italy, France and England: four centuries of change in the Boccaccian tale. Chapel Hill 1968.

Carmeni, Francesco. Novelle amorose de' signori academici incogniti. Cremona 1651; Nisenna (extract) tr an honorable Anti-socordist, 1653.

Doni, Antonio Francesco. La moral filosophia tratta da gli antichi scrittori. Venice 1552; The moral philosophie of Doni, tr Thomas North 1570. An arrangement of Fables of Bidpai.
Gelli, Giovanni Batista. La Circe. Florence 1549; Circes, tr Henry Iden 1557.
— I capricci del bottaio. Florence 1546; The fearful fancies of the Florentine cooper, tr William Barker 1568.
Giovanni Fiorentino (Giovanni Antonio degli Antonii). Il Pecorone. Milan 1554.
1.48 Painter William. Palace of pleasure. 1566–7, 1575 (rev).
2.2 Tarlton, R. Newes out of purgatorie. [Before 1590]. Shakespeare, William. The merry wives of Windsor. 1619.
3.2 [Tarlton, Richard?]. Cobbler of Canterburie. 1590.
4.1 Munday, Anthony. The orator (95th declamation). 1596.
Giraldi, Giambattista (Cinthio). Hecatommithi. Monte Regale 1565.
Painter, William. Palace of pleasure. 1566–7, 1575 (rev).
Rich, Barnabe. His farewell to militarie profession. 1581.
Whetstone, George. Promos and Cassandra 1578. From Cinthio's Decade 8, novel 5.
— A heptameron of civill discourses. 1582.
Middleton, T. and W. Rowley. The fair quarrel. 1617.
Shakespeare, William. Measure for measure. 1623. From Decade 8, novel 5.
— Twelfth night. 1623.
Loredano, Giorgio Francesco. La Dianea. Turin 1627; Dianea: an excellent new romance, tr Aston Cokaine 1654.
— L'Adamo. Venice 1640; The life of Adam, tr J.S. 1659.
Machiavelli, Niccolò. Belfagor. 1549 (written 1515–20); The Divell a married man, tr [1647].
Rich, Barnabe. His farewell to the militarie profession. 1587.
Dekker, Thomas. If it be not good, the Devil is in it. 1612.
Jonson, Ben. The Devil is an ass. 1631. Written 1616.
Hallstein, E. Verhältnis von Jonsons The Devil is an ass und John Wilsons Belphegor or the marriage of the Devil zu Machiavellis Novelle von Belfagor. Halle 1901.
Axon, W. E. A. The story of Belfagor in literature and folklore. Trans Royal Soc of Lit 2nd ser 23 1902.
Johnson, W. S. The Devil is an ass by Ben Jonson. Yale Stud in Eng 24 1905.
Boughner, D. C. Clizia and Epicoene. PQ 19 1940.
Schreiber, W. I. Belphegor. JEGP 44 1945.
Masuccio Salernitano. Il novellino. Milan 1483.
Painter, William. The doctor of laws. In his Palace of pleasure vol 1, 1566.
Marston, John. The Dutch courtesan. 1604.
Brie, F. W. D. Die erste Übersetzung einer italienischen Novelle durch Henry Parker, Lord Morley [Novellino 49]. Archiv 124 1907.
Sannazaro, Giacomo. Arcadia. Venice 1502.
Sidney, Sir Philip. The Countess of Pembroke's Arcadia. 1590, 1593 (with bks 3–5).
Brunhuber, K. Sidneys Arcadia und ihre Nachläufer. Nuremberg 1903.
Genouy, H. L. L'Arcadia de Sidney dans ses rapports avec l'Arcadia de Sannazaro et la Diana de Montemayor. Montpellier 1928.
Kelstone, D. The transformation of Arcadia: Sannazaro and Sidney. Comparative Lit 15 1963.
Hamilton, A. C. Sidney's Arcadia as prose fiction: its relation to its sources. Eng Literary Renaissance 2 1972.
Straparola, Giovanni Francesco. Le piacevoli notti. 2 vols Venice 1550.

Painter, William. The palace of pleasure. 1566–7, 1575 (rev).

C., H. The forest of fancy. 1579. From 1.1.

Shakespeare, William. The merry wives of Windsor. 1619.

Arnim, Robert. The Italian tailor and his boy. 1609. From 8.5.

For the Belfagor story see Machiavelli, above.

Studies

Koeppel, E. Studien zur Geschichte der italienischen Novelle in der englischen Literatur des sechzehnten Jahrhunderts. Strasbourg 1892.

Ott, A. Die italienische Novelle im englischen Drama von 1600 bis zur Restauration. Zürich 1904.

Esdaile, A. J. K. A list of English tales and prose romances printed before 1740. 1912.

Baker, E. A. The history of the English novel. Vols 1–2, 1924–5.

Bush, D. The Petite pallace of Pettie his pleasure. JEGP 27 1928.

Bradner, L. The first English novels: a study of George Gascoigne's Adventures of master F.J. PMLA 45 1930.

Pruvost, R. The source of George Turberville's Tragical tales nos 2, 5 and 8. RES 10 1934.

Italienische Novellen. Tr E. von Bülow et al 3 vols Berlin 1942. Reprints of novelle by Fiorentino, Masuccio, da Porto, Bandello, Straparola, Giraldi et al which directly or indirectly influenced Shakespeare.

Günther, J. von. Italienische Shakespeare-Novellen aus der Renaissance. Meister 1947.

Chickera, E. de. Palace of pleasure: the theme of revenge in Elizabethan translations of the novelle. RES new ser 11 1960.

(8) SPANISH

Bibliographies – Studies – Dictionaries and grammars – Philosophy, politics etc – Theology – Drama – Verse – Prose fiction.

Bibliographies

Knapp, W. A concise bibliography of Spanish grammars and dictionaries 1490–1780. Boston 1884.

Underhill, J. G. Spanish literature in the England of the Tudors, with bibliography of occasional literature relating to Spain published in England. New York 1899.

Holls, E. C. A catalogue of English translations of Spanish plays. Romanic Rev 10 1919.

Bell, A. F. G. Portuguese bibliography. New York 1922.

Alpern, H. English translations of Spanish classics. Hispania 7 1924.

Flores, A. Spanish literature in English translation: a bibliographical syllabus. New York 1926.

Thomas, H. English translations of Portuguese books before 1600. Library 4th ser 7 1926.

Bourland, C. B. The short story in Spain in the 17th century. Northampton Mass 1927.

Sturgis, C. The Spanish world in Elizabethan fiction: a bibliography. Boston 1927.

Ford, J. D. M. and R. Lansing. Cervantes: a tentative bibliography of his works and material concerning him. Cambridge Mass 1931.

Rolfe, F. P. On the bibliography of 17th-century prose fiction. PMLA 49 1934.

Fucilla, J. G. Spanish poetry in English to the year 1850. Hispania 1 1934.

Pane, R. U. English translations from the Spanish 1484–1943: a bibliography. New Brunswick NJ 1944. *See* E. G. Matthews, JEGP 44 1945.

Estorninho, C. Portuguese literature in English translation. In Portugal and Brazil, ed H. V. Livermore and W. J. Entwistle, Oxford 1953.

Sachs, N. P. Hispanic literature in English translation. Hispania 42 1959.

Chandler, F. W. A bibliography of Spanish romances of roguery 1554–68 and their translations. In his Romances of roguery, 1961.

Randall, D. J. B. The golden tapestry: a critical survey of non-chivalric Spanish fiction in English translation 1543–1657. Cambridge 1963.

Stubbing, H. U. Renaissance Spain in its literary relations with England and France: a critical bibliography. Nashville 1968.

General Studies

Avila y Zuñiga, Luis de. Comentario de la guerra de Alemaña. Venice 1548; Commentaries of don Lewis de Avila, tr John Wilkinson 1555.

Beale, Robert. Rerum hispanicarum scriptores. 3 vols Frankfurt 1579. Compiled from the Latin histories of

Juan de Gerona, Rodrigo de Toledo, Rodrigo Sanchez de Arevalo, Alfonso de Santa Maria, L. Marineus Siculus, Antonio de Lebrija, Alvaro Gomez de Castro, Damião de Goes et al.

Browne, John. Marchants avizo. 1589.

Conestaggio, Ieronimo. Dell'unione del regno di Portogallo alla corona di Castiglia. Genoa 1585; tr Edward Blunt 1600.

Campanella, Tommaso. De monarchia hispanica. Amsterdam 1640; tr E. Chilmead 1657.

The character of Spain: or an epitome of their virtues and vices. 1660.

Bahlsen, L. Spanische Quellen der englischen Literatur besonders Englands zu Shakespeares Zeit. Zeitschrift für Vergleichende Literaturgeschichte 6 1893.

Hume, M. A. S. Spanish influence on English literature. 1905.

— Some Spanish influences on Elizabethan literature. Trans Royal Soc of Lit 29 1909.

Fitzmaurice-Kelly, J. The relations between Spanish and English literature. Liverpool 1910.

Schevill, R. On the influence of Spanish literature on English in the early 17th century. Romanische Forschungen 20 1907.

Thomas, H. Spanish and Portuguese romances of chivalry. 1920.

— Shakespeare and Spain. In his Studies in European literature, Oxford 1930.

— Anti-English propaganda in the time of Queen Elizabeth: being the story of the first British printing in the Peninsula. New York 1946.

Madariaga, S. de. English sidelights on Spanish literature. In his Shelley and Calderón, 1920.

— Paralelos anglo-españoles. In his Ensayos anglo-españoles, Madrid 1922.

Moreno–Lacalle, J. Influencias españolas en la literatura inglesa. Bull New England Modern Langs Assoc 12 1922.

Place, E. B. Una nota sobre las fuentes españoles de les Nouvelles de Nicolas Lancelot. Revista de Filologia Española 13 1926.

Schelling, F. E. Foreign influences on Elizabethan plays. 1928.

Saavedra, M. L. Os inglese em Portugal. Biblos (Coimbra) 12 1936.

Ward, H. G. A Spanish legend in English literature. In [Moses] Gaster anniversary volume, 1936.

Pfandl, L. Das England-Erlebnis der Spanier in den Jahren 1554–8. In Gesammelte Aufsätze zur Kulturgeschichte Spaniens, Münster 1938.

Matthews, E. G. Studies in Spanish-English cultural and literary relations. New York 1938.

Ley, C. D. A Inglaterra e os escritores portugeses. Lisbon 1939.

Collins, J. B. Christian mysticism in the Elizabethan age. Baltimore 1940.

Hatzfeld, H. A. El predominio del espiritu español en la literatura europea del siglo 17. Revista de Filologia Hispanica 3 1941.

Russell, P. E. As fontes de F. Lopes: traducão do original inédito ingles de A. Gonçalves Rodrigues. Coimbra 1941.

— A Stuart Hispanist: James Mabbe. Bull Hispanic Stud 30 1953.

— English 17th-century interpretations of Spanish literature. Atlante 1 1953.

Lapp, J. C. The defeat of the Spanish Armada in French poetry on the 16th century. JEGP 43 1944.

Barker, J. W. Influencia de la literatura española en la literatura inglesa. Universidad (Saragossa) 23 1946.

Pastor, A. Breve historia del hispanismo inglés. Arbor (Madrid) 9 1948.

Simpson, E. M. Donne's Spanish authors. MLR 43 1948.

Wilson, E. M. Did John Fletcher read Spanish? PQ 27 1948.

McDiarmid, M. P. The Spanish plunder of William Drummond of Hawthornden. MLR 44 1949.

Turner, P. A. Sobre Pedro Mexia en Inglaterra. Nueva Revista de Filologia Hispánica 3 1949.

Vossler, K. España y Europa. Madrid 1951.

Salazar, Chapela, E. Clásicos españoles en Inglaterra. Cuadernos Americanos 61 1952.

Hesselberg, A. K. A comparative study of the political ideas of Ludovicus Molina and Milton. Washington 1952.

Collmer, R. G. Crashaw's Death more misticall and high. JEGP 55 1956.

Ungerer, G. Anglo-Spanish relations in Tudor literature. Schweizer Anglistische Arbeiten 38 1956.

McCann, E. Oxymora in Spanish mystics and English metaphysical writers. Comparative Lit 13 1961.

Green, O. H. Spain and the western tradition: the Castilian mind in literature from El Cid to Calderon. 4 vols Madison 1963-6.

Loomis, A. J. The Spanish Elizabethans: the English exiles at the Court of Philip II. New York 1963.

Myers, D. T. Encina and Skelton. Hispania 47 1964.

Smieja, F. Lord Herbert [of Cherbury]: a possible Spanish source. N & Q March 1968.

Dictionaries and Grammars

Percyval, Richard. Bibliotheca hispanica: a grammar with a dictionarie in Spanish, English and Latin. 1591.

Stepney, William. The Spanish schoolemaster. 1591.
Bourland, C. B. The Spanish schoole-master and the polyglot derivatives of Noel de Berlaimont's Vocabularium. Revue Hispanique 81 1933.

Corro, Antonio de. Reglas gramaticales. Oxford 1586; The Spanish grammar, tr John Thorius 1590.

Oudin, César. Grammaire et observations de la langue espagnole. Paris 1597; A grammar, Spanish and English, tr James Wadsworth 1622.

Minsheu, John. Spanish grammar: a dictionarie in Spanish and English; dialogues in Spanish. 1599. Based on Percyvall, above.

— Vocabularium hispanico-latinum et anglicum. 1617.

Owen, L. The key of the Spanish tongue. 1605.

Sanford, J. An entrance to the Spanish tongue. 1611.

Bathe, W. Janua linguarum. 1611.

Luna, Juan de. Arte breve para aprender la langue española: a short and compendious art for learning the Spanish tongue. 1623.

Cardim, L. Gramaticas anglo-castelhanas e castelhano-anglicas. Coimbra 1931.

Wright, L. B. Language helps for the Elizabethan tradesman. JEGP 30 1931.

Funke, O. Spanische Sprachbücher im elizabethanischen England. In Studies presented to K. Brunner, Vienna 1957.

Themes
Discoveries and Colonization

Of the new landes and people found by the messengers of the King of Portugale [Emanuel I]. [Antwerp 1520].

Lopes de Castanheda, Fernão. Historia de descobrimento e conquista da India pelos Portugueses. Bk 1, Coimbra 1551; History of the discovery and conquest of the East Indias by the Portigales, tr Nicholas Lichfield 1582.

Las Casas, Bartolome de. Brevissima relacion de la destruycion de las Indias. Seville 1552; The Spanish colonie: or brief chronicle of the acts and gestes of the Spaniards in the West Indies, tr M.S.S. 1583; The tears of the Indians: being an historical and true account of the cruel massacres and slaughters of above 20 millions of innocent people, tr J. Phillips 1656.

Lopez de Gómara, Francisco. Historia de las Indias y conquista de Mexico. Pt 2, 1552; History of the conquest of the West India, tr Thomas Nicholas 1578.

Eden, Richard. Decades of the newe worlde. 1555. Tr and compiled from Peter Martyr Anglerius De orbe novo decades tres, Alcala, 1576; Gonzalo Fernandez de Oviedo y Valdes, La historia general de las Indias, Seville 1535; and Francisco Lopez de Gómara, Historia general de las Indias y conquista de Mexico pt 1, Saragossa 1552.

Zárate, Augustin de. Historia del descubrimiento y conquista del Peru. Antwerp 1555; History of the discovery and conquest of Peru, tr Thomas Nicholas 1581 (from bks 1-4, 6).

Relaçam dos trabalhos que ho governador Fernãdo de Souto e certos fidalgos portugueses passarom no descobrimēto da provincia da Florida. Evora 1557; Virginia richly valued by the description of the maine land of Florida, tr R. Hakluyt 1609.

Cortés, Martin. Breve compendio de la sphera y de la arte de navegar. Seville 1557; tr 1561.

Galvão, Antonio. Tratado de todos os descobrimentos antigos e modernes. Lisbon 1563; The discoveries of the world unto the year 1609, tr 1601.

Monardes, Nicolas. Historia medicinal de las cosas que se traen de nuestras Indias occidentales. Pts 1-2, Seville 1565; Joyful newes out of the newe founde worlde, tr John Frampton 1577 (in part).

Escalante, Bernardino de. Discurso de la navegacion a los reinos del oriente. Seville 1577; A discourse of the navigation which the Portugales doe make, tr John Frampton 1579.

Willes, Richard. History of travayle in the West and East Indies. 1577. Rev from Eden's Decades, above with omissions and addns.

Lopez, Duarte. Relatione del reame di Congo tratta dalli scritti de Oddardo Lopez Portoghese. Rome 1591 (Italian trn); Report of the kingdom of Congo, tr Abraham Hartwell 1597.

Baçan, Alvaro de. Successo de la conquista de la Tercera y de las demas yslas de los Açores. 1583; Discourse of that which happened in the battell at the islands of Azores AD 1582, [1583?].

Nichols, Thomas. Description of the fortunate islandes of Canaria. In R. Hakluyt, Principal navigations, 1598–1600.

Gonsalez de Mendoza, Juan. Historia de las cosas mas notables de la China. Rome 1585; New Mexico: otherwise the voyage of Anthony of Espeio who in the yeare 1583 discovered a lande of 15 provinces, tr 1587; Historie of the great and mightie Kingdom of China, tr Robert Parke 1588 (partly from French of Luc de la Porte).

Hakluyt, Richard. The principal navigations, voyages and discoveries of the English nation. 1589, 1598–1600 (enlarged).

Gage, Thomas. New survey of the West Indies. 1648.

Travel

Langton, R. Pylgrimage to saynt James in Compostell. 1522.

Lithgow, William. Total discourse of the rare adventures and painefull peregrinations of 19 years travayles. 1632.

Foulché-Delbosq, R. Bibliographie des voyages en Espagne et au Portugal. Revue Hispanique 3 1896.

Skillington, V. M. and W. Chapman. The commercial relations of England and Portugal. 1907.

Pfandl, L. Zur Bibliographie der Voyages en Espagne. Archiv 133 1915.

Garcia, Mercadal, J. Viajes de extranjeros por España y Portugal. Madrid 1962.

Philosophy, Politics, Education etc

Felippe, Bartolomé. Tratado del consejo y delos consejeros delos principes. Coimbra 1584; The counsellor, tr John Thorius 1589.

Furio Ceriol, Federico. El consejo i consejeros del principe. Antwerp [1559]; Treatise declaring howe many counsels and what manner of counsellors a prince that will governe well ought to have, tr Thomas Blunderville 1578 (from Italian trn by Alfonso de Ulloa).

Gracián, Baltasar. El héroe. Huesca 1637; The hero, tr J. Skeffington 1652.

   Coster, A. Baltasar Gracián. Revue Hispanique 29 1913.

Gracián Dantisco, Lucas. Galateo Español. 2 pts Barcelona 1593; Galateo Espanol: or the Spanish gallant, tr W.S[tyle] 1640.

   Speroni, C. The aphorisms of Orazio Rinaldi, Robert Greene and Lucas Gracián Dantisco. Berkeley 1968.

Guevara, Antonio de. Libro del emperador Marco Aurelio con relox de principes. Valladolid 1529; The golden book of Marcus Aurelius, tr John Bourchier, Lord Berners 1534 (from the French version of René Bertaut 14 edns by 1600); The diall of princes, tr Thomas North 1557 (from the French of Bertaut).

   Elyot, Thomas. Image of governance: compiled of the actes and sentence of the most noble emperour Alexander Severus. 1540.

   Lyly, John. Euphues, the anatomy of wit. 1578.

   —— Euphues and his England. 1580.

   Landmann, F. Der Euphuismus: sein Wesen, seine Quellen, seine Geschichte. Giessen 1881.

   Ringler, W. The immediate source of Euphuism. PMLA 53 1938.

   Parks, G. B. Before Euphuism. In J. Q. Adams memorial studies, Washington 1948.

—— Aviso de privados y doctrina de cortesanos. Vallodolid 1539; The favoured courtier, tr Thomas North 1568 (from French trn by J. de Rochemare).

—— Epístolas familiares. 2 pts Valladolid 1539–47; Familiar epistles, tr Edward Hellowes 1574 (a selection with other matter); Golden epistles, gathered as well out of the remaynder of Guevara's workes as other authors (supplements Hellowes's selection all but 2 from Guevara), tr Geoffrey Fenton 1575 (from French trn by de Guttery).

   Painter, William. The palace of pleasure [II 12–14]. 1567.

   Breton, Nicolas. Post with a mad packet of letters. 1602.

   Fellheimer, J. Hellowes's and Fenton's translations of Guevara's Epístolas familiares. SP 44 1947.

—— Menosprecio de la corte y alabanza de aldea. Valladolid 1539; A dispraise of the life of a courtier, tr Francis Briant 1548 from French trn by A. Alaigre); A looking-glasse for the courte, 1575 (reprint of Bryan with annotations by T. Tymme); The praise and happiness of country life, tr Henry Vaughan 1651.

Thomas, H. The English translations of Guevara's works. In Estudios eruditos in memoriam de Adolfo Bonilla vol 2, Madrid 1930.

Hidalgo, Gaspar Lucas. Discurso que trata de las excelencias de las bubas. In Dialogos de apacible entretenimiento. Barcelona 1605.

   Cornwallis, William. Praise of the French pox. In Essayes of certain paradoxes, 1616.

Huarte, Juan. Examen de ingenios. Baeza 1575; The examination of men's wits, tr R[ichard] C[arew] 1594 (from Italian trn by Camillo Camilli).

   Iriarte, M. de. Juan de Huarte. Madrid 1939.

Mexia, Pedro. Diálogos. Seville 1547; Pleasaunt dialogue concerning phisicke and phisitians, tr Thomas Newton 1580.

Santa Cruz, Mechier de. Floresta española de apotegmas. 1574; Wits fittes and fancies, tr Anthony Copley 1595.

Valdes, Francisco de. Espejo y deceplina militar. Brussels 1586; The sergeant-major, tr John Thorius 1590.

Mystical Writings, Theology, Sermons etc

Spanish and Portuguese Authors

Alcantara, San Pedro de. De la oración y meditación; A golden treatise of mental prayer, tr G. W[illoughby], Brussels 1632.

Arias, Francisco. Aprovechamiento espiritual. Valencia 1588; A short treatise of exhortation, tr John Sweetman 1617.

—— Libro de la imitación de Christo. Madrid 1599; The judge and A treatise of patience, tr T[oby] M[atthew], St Omer 1621 (extracts), 1630.

Avila, Juan de. Libro espiritual sobre el verso Audi Filia. [c. 1538], 1557 (rev); The audi filia, tr L.T. (Toby Matthew), [St Omer] 1620.

—— Epistolario espiritual. Madrid 1578; Certain selected spiritual epistles, tr Rouen 1631.

Castañiza, Juan de. Combate o lucha espiritual. 1644 (from Italian); The Christian pilgrim in his spiritual conflict, [tr T. Vincent and A. Crowder], Paris 1652; The spiritual combat, tr R.R. [Robert Reade?], Paris 1656.

Daça, Antonio. Vida de sor Juana de la Cruz. Madrid 1613; The historie, life and miracles of sister Joana of the Cross, [tr F. Bell], St Omer 1625.

Estella, Diego de. Tratado de la vanidad del mundo. Salamanca 1574; Contempte of the world and the vanitie thereof, tr G.C., [Douai?] 1584 (probably from an Italian trn).

—— Meditaciones del amor de Dios. Salamanca 1576.

   Janelle, P. Robert Southwell: the writer. Clermont Ferrand 1935.

Fonseca, Cristobal de. Tratado del amor de Dios. Salamanca 1582; A discourse of holy love, tr G. Strode 1652.

—— Discursos para todos los evangelios de la Quaresma. Madrid 1614; Devout contemplations, tr James Masse 1629.

Guevara, Antonio de. Monte calvario. Salamanca 1542; The mount of Calvary, tr 2 bks 1595–7.

Loarte, Gaspar de. Sūma que trata del exercicio espiritual. Alcala 1570. Also attributed to Luis de Granada; The exercise of a Christian life, tr Stephen Brinkley [Rheims 1579?]; tr James Sancer, [Paris 1579; tr F. Meres 1598].

—— Instruiçam e advertencias pera meditar a paixam de Christo. Lisbon 1587; Instructions and advertisements, tr [1600?].

Losa, Francisco de. Vida del siervo de Dios Gregorio López. [Ed Alonso Remon], Madrid 1617; The life of Gregorie Lopes, Paris 1638.

Loyola, Ignatius. Ejercicios espirituales. Rome 1548; A manual of devout meditations drawn out of S Ignatius by T. de Villecastin, tr M. M[ore], [St Omer] 1618.

Luis de Granada. Memorial de la vida christiana. Salamanca 1566; A memorial of a Christian life, [tr Richard Hopkins], Rouen 1586.

—— Libro de la oración y consideración. Salamanca 1567; Of prayer and meditation, [tr Richard Hopkins], Paris 1582; Granadas devotion [pt 2], tr [Francis Meres] 1598 (probably from a French trn).

—— Guia de peccadores. Salamanca 1570; The sinners guyde, tr Francis Meres 1598 (probably from French by Duperron).

—— Suma que trata del exercicio espiritual. Alcala 1570; tr F. Meres 1598 (*see* Loarte, *above*).

Isselt, Michael ab. Flores Lodovici Granatensis eximibus eius opusculis decerpti. Cologne 1598; Flowers of Lodowick of Granado, tr Thomas Lodge 1601.

—— Paradisus precum ex Ludovici Granatensis spiritualibus opusculis aliorumque patrum concinnatus. Cologne 1599; Paradise of prayers, tr Thomas Lodge, 1601.

Hagedorn, M. Reformation und spanische Andachtsliteratur: Luis de Granada in England. Leipzig 1935.

Anthéunis, L. Un refugié anglais, traducteur de Louis de Grenade: Richard Hopkins. Revue d'Histoire Ecclésiastique 35 1939.

Molina, Antonio de. Instrucción de sacerdotes. Lisbon 1610; A treatise of the holy sacrifice of the Masse, tr I.R. [J. Floyd?], [St Omer] 1610.

—— Exercicios espirituales. Burgos 1613; Spirituall exercises, tr E. A. Mechlin 1621.

Nicholas y Sacharles, Juan. El español reformado. 1621; The reformed Spaniard, tr 1621 (from Latin trn).

Nieremberg, Juan Eusebio. De la diferencia entre lo temporal y eterno. Madrid 1640.

—— Partida a la eternidad y preparación a la muerte. 1654.

—— De la constancia en la virtud. 1647.

Vaughan, Henry. Flores solitudinis: certaine rare and elegant pieces viz: two excellent discourses of temperance and patience, life and death by I. E. Nierembergius. 1654.

Perez de Pineda, Juan. Epistola para consolar a los fideles de Jesu Christo. [Geneva] 1560; Comfort against all kinds of calamity, tr John Daniel 1576.

—— Breve tratado de la doctrina antigua de Dios. [Geneva] 1560; Jehovah: a free pardon to all christians, tr John Daniel 1576.

Puente, Luis de la. Meditaciones de los misterios de nuestra santa fe. Valladolid 1605; Meditations upon the mysteries of our faith, tr F. R. Gibbons, St Omer 1610; tr and abridged T. Everard, [St Omer] 1614.

Ribadaneira, Pedro de. Vida del P. Ignacio de Loyola, Madrid 1594; Life of the B. Father Ignatius of Loyola, tr W.M. [M. Walpole], [St Omer] 1616.

Ribera, Francisco de (ed). Vida de la madre Teresa de Jesús. Madrid 1590; The lyf of Mother Teresa of Jesus, tr W.M. [M. Walpole], Antwerp 1611.

Rodriguez, Alonso. Exercicios de perfección y virtudes christianas. Seville 1609.

Trns of individual treatises: A treatise of mental prayer, tr T.B. 1627; The Christian man's guide, tr [T.B.], [St Omer] 1630; A short and sure way to heaven, tr [J.C.], [Douai 1630]; A treatise of humility, tr Rouen 1631; A treatise of modesty and silence, tr [Douai] 1632.

Santa Maria, Juan de. República y policía cristiana. Madrid 1615; Christian policy, tr James M[abbe] 1632.

Soto, Andrés de. Redención del tiempo cautivo. Amberes 1606; The ransom of time being captive, tr J. H[awkins], Douai 1634.

Teresa (de Cepeda) de Jesus, St. Camino de perfección. Salamanca 1587; The flaming heart, tr Tobias Mathew 1623.

Carayon, M. Les trois poèmes de Crashaw sur Sainte Thérèse. In Hommage à Ernest Martineuche: études hispaniques, Paris 1939.

McCann, E. Donne and S. Teresa on the Ecstasy. HLQ 17 1954.

Anderson, J. B. Richard Crashaw, St Teresa and St John of the Cross. Discourse 10 1967.

Petersson, R. T. The art of ecstasy: Saint Theresa, Bernini and Crashaw. 1970.

Valdes, Juan de. Ciento i diez conçideraçiones. [c. 1540]; The hundred and ten considerations, tr Nicholas Ferrar, Oxford 1638 (from an Italian trn with a letter and brief notes by George Herbert).

Valera, Cipriano de. Dos tratados: del papa y de la missa. 1588; Two treatises, tr John Goulborne 1600.

English Authors

Perkins, William. A reformed Catholic. Cambridge 1597; Catolico reformado, tr G. Massan 1599.

Drama

Celestina. Tragi-comedia de Calisto y Melibea. A novel in dialogue containing 16 and, in the expanded version, 21 acts. Its authorship is uncertain, but it appears to have been completed, if not largely written, by Fernando de Rojas c. 1499–1502.

—— A new comedy in the maner of an enterlude: wherein is shewd as well the bewte and good propertes of women as theyr vycys and evyll condicions. [Tr John Rastell?], [c. 1530]. A much truncated version.

—— The Spanish bawd, represented in Celestina. Tr James Mabbe 1631.

Minsheu, John. A Spanish grammar. 1599.

Carayon, M. L'amour et la musique: sur un passage de la Celestina. Revue de Littérature Comparée 3 1923. As an influence on Twelfth Night.

Houck, H. Mabbe's paganisation of the Celestina. PMLA 54 1939.

Russell, P. E. A Stuart Hispanist: James Mabbe, Bull Hispanic Stud 30 1953.

Ugalde, L. The Celestina of 1502. Boston Public Lib Quart 6 1954.

Schoeck, R. J. The influence of La Celestina in England. Boston Public Lib Quart 7 1955. *See* L. Ugalde 7 1955.

Ungerer, G. Anglo-Spanish relations in Tudor literature. Berne 1956.

Quijano Teran, M. La Celestina y Otelo. Mexico City 1957.

Brault, G. J. English translations of the Celestina in the 16th century. Hispanic Rev 28 1960.

'Tirso de Molina' (Gabriel Téllez). El castigo del penseque. Madrid 1627.

Shirley, James. The opportunitie. 1640. Performed 1634.

Bushee, A. H. Three centuries of Tirso de Molina. Philadelphia 1939.

Bowers, R. H. Marlowe's Dr Faustus, Tirso's El condenado por desconfiado and the secret cause. Costerus 4 1972.

Vega Carpio, Lope de. Don Lope de Cardona. Madrid 1618.

Shirley, James. The young admirall. 1637. Performed 1633.

General Studies

Frey, A. R. William Shakespeare and alleged Spanish prototypes. New York 1886.

Stiefel, A. L. Die Nachamung spanischer Komödien in England unter den ersten Stuarts. Romanische Forschungen 5 1890.

—— Die Nachahmung spanischer Komödien in England. Archiv 99 1897.

Koeppel, E. Quellenstudien zu den Dramen Ben Jonsons, John Marstons und Beaumont und Fletchers. Erlangen 1895.

Koch, M. Shakespeare und Lope de Vega. E Studien 20 1895.

Grossman, R. Spanien und das elizabethanische Drama. Hamburg 1920.

Thomas, H. Shakespeare and Spain. Oxford 1922.
—— Shakespeare y España. In Homenaje ofrecido a Menendez Pidal, Madrid 1925.
Birkhead, H. The schism of England: Calderón's play and Shakespeare's. Modern Langs 10 1928.
Schelling, F. E. Foreign influences in Elizabethan plays. 1928.
Bond, R. W. On six plays in Beaumont and Fletcher 1679. RES 11 1935. See E. H. C. Oliphant, Three Beaumont and Fletcher plays, RES 12 1936. On debt of Love's cure to Guillen de Castro's Le Fuerza de la costumbre.
Wilson, E. M. Did John Fletcher read Spanish? PQ 27 1948.
Livermore, A. Gil Vicente e Shakespeare. Revista Universitaria de Lisboa 17 1951.
Crocker, L. G. Hamlet, Don Quijote, La vida es sueño: the quest for values. PMLA 69 1954.
Alexander, J. Parallel tendencies in English and Spanish tragedy in the Renaissance. In Studies in comparative literature, ed W. F. McNeir, Baton Rouge 1962.
Villarejo, O. M. Shakespeare's Romeo and Juliet: its Spanish source. Shakespeare Survey 20 1967.
Salomon, B. Don Diego: infamous Spaniard of English Renaissance drama. Jnl of Popular Culture 1 1968.
Custodio, A. La edad de oro del teatro en España y en Inglaterra. La Torre 1969.

Verse

Boscan-Almogaver, Juan. Las obras de Boscan y algunas de Garcilasso de la Vega. Barcelona 1543.
Googe, Barnabe. Eglogs, epytaphes and sonettes. 1563.
Fraunce, Abraham. Arcadian rhetoric. 1584.
Stanley, Thomas. Poems. 1651.
Drummond, William. Poems. 1656.
Kastner, L. E. (ed). The poetical works of William Drummond of Hawthornden. 2 vols Manchester 1913.
Camõens, Luis de. Os Lusiades. Lisbon 1572; Lusiads, tr Richard Fanshawe 1655.
Thomas, H. Three translators of Gongora and other Spanish poets. Revue Hispanique 48 1920.
Gardim, L. Projeccão de Camões nas letras inglesas. Lisbon 1940.
Ercilla y Zuniga, Alonso de. La Araucana. Pts 1–2, Madrid 1578; pt 3, Madrid 1590; Historie of Araucana, tr George Carew (c. 1600) ed F. Pierce, Manchester 1964.
Pierce, F. Ercilla and England. In Hispanic studies in honour of I. Gonzales Llubera, Valencia 1959.
Garcilaso de la Vega. See Boscan-Almogaver, above.
Gongora y Argote, Luis de. Obras en verso. Madrid 1627; Stanley, Thomas, Poems, 1651.
Thomas, H. Three translators of Gongora and other Spanish poets. Revue Hispanique 48 1920.
Praz, M. Stanley, Sherburne and Ayres as translators and imitators of Italian, Spanish and French poets. MLR 20 1925.
Nethercot, A. H. The reputation of native versus foreign metaphysical poets in England. MLR 25 1930.
Wilson, E. M. and E. R. Vincent. Thomas Stanley's translations and borrowings from Spanish and Italian texts. Revue de Littérature Comparée 32 1958.
Segal, E. Hero and Leander: Gongora and Marlowe. Comparative Lit 15 1963.
Lasso de la Vega, Garcia. See Boscan, above.
Montemayor, Jorge de. See his Diana, below.
Lopez de Mendoza, Iñigo, Marquis de Santillana. Los proverbios, with the gloss by Pedro Diaz de Toledo. Seville 1494; The proverbs of Sir James Lopez de Mendoza, with the paraphrase of D. Peter Diaz of Toledo, tr 1579.
Umphrey, G. W. Spanish ballads in English. MLQ 6–7 1945–6.

Prose Fiction

Abancerraje, O historia de Abindarráez y Jarifa, sometimes attributed to Antonio de Villegas, appeared in later edns of Montemayor's Diana, below; tr Bartholomew Yong 1598 (as part of Diana).
Matulka, B. On the European diffusion of the Last of the Abencerrages story in the 16th century. Hispania 16 1933.
Amadis de Gaula. Bks 1–3, written c. 1300, were rev Garci Gutierrez (or Ordoñez or Rodriguez) de Montalvo who added a 4th bk. The earliest extant edn of these 4 bks, the original Amadis, is Seville 1508. Of the 16 further vols which appeared later: bk 5 was by Gutierrez, bk 6 by Paez de Ribera, bks 7–11 by F. de Silva.
—— The treasurie of Amadis of Fraunce. [Tr from French trn, Thrésor de tous les livres d'Amadis de Gaule, Antwerp 1560 Thomas Paynell], 1568; The first book of Amadis de Gaule, [1590–2?]; The second book, 1595; The ancient and honourable history of Amadis de Gaule, tr Anthony Munday (from French trn of Herberay des Essarts) 1619 (bks 1–4); bk 5, tr 1598 (anon); bk 6 tr Francis Kirkman [1652].
Baret, E. De l'Amadis de Gaule et de son influence sur les moeurs et la littérature au 16e et au 17e siècle, Paris 1873.
Vaganay, H. Amadis en français: essai de bibliographie. Florence 1906.
Byrne, M. St. C. Anthony Munday and his books. Library 4th ser 1 1921.
Hayes, G. R. Anthony Munday's romances of chivalry. Library 4th ser 6–7 1925–6.
Bennett, J. St Bridget, Queen Elizabeth and Amadis de Gaule. ELH 10 1943.
Celestina. See Drama, above.
Los siete libros de la Diana by Jorge de Montemayor. Valencia [1559?]. The intercalated tale Abancerraje was added after Montemayor's death.
—— Segunda parte de la Diana. 1564. By Alonso Perez.
—— Diana enamorada. Valencia 1564. By Gaspar Gil Polo.
—— Diana. Tr Bartholomew Yong 1598 (all 3 pts).
Googe, Barnabe. Eglogs, epytaphes and sonnetes. 1563.
Sidney, Sir Philip. The Countess of Pembroke's Arcadia. 1590, 1953 (with bks 3–5).
Shakespeare, William. The two gentlemen of Verona. 1623.
C., R. The troublesome and hard adventures in love. 1594. Fragmentary copy; complete version 1652.
Spenser, Edmund. The Fairie Queene. 1596 (bks 4–6).
Minsheu, John. Spanish grammar. 1599.
England's Helicon. 1600.
Browne, William. Britannia's pastorals. 2 pts 1613–16.
Harrison, T. P. Googe's Eclogues and Montemayor's Diane. SE 5 1925.
—— Bartholomew Yong, translator. MLR 21 1926.
—— Shakespeare and Montemayor's Diana. SE 6 1926.
—— A probable source of Beaumont and Fletcher's Philaster. PMLA 41 1926.
—— Concerning Two gentlemen of Verona and Montemayor's Diana. MLN 41 1926.
—— A source of Sidney's Arcadia. SE 6 1926.
—— The Fairie Queene and the Diana. PQ 9 1930.
Terrill, T. E. A note of John Donne's early reading. MLN 43 1928.
Cooke, P. J. The Spanish romances in Sidney's Arcadia. Urbana 1939.
Rojas, J. A. M. Apuntes para un estudio de las relaciones literarias de Donne con España. In Ensayos hispano-ingleses: homenaje a Walter Starkie, Barcelona 1948.
Anderson, D. M. Sir Thomas Wilson's translation of Montemayor's Diana. RES new ser 7 1956.
Randall, D. B. J. |The troublesome and hard adventures in love: an English addition to the bibliography of Diana. Bull Hispanic Stud 38 1961.

Espejo de principes y cavalleros. Pt 1 by Iñigo Ortunez de Calahorra, Saragossa 1562; The mirrour of knighthood bk 1, tr Margaret Tiler 1579; bks 2–3 tr R.P. 1599.
Pt 2, probably by Pedro de la Sierra, Valladolid 1585; bks 1–2 tr R.P. 1598.
Pt 3 by Pedro de la Sierra or Marco Martinez, Alcala 1585; bk 1 tr R[obert] P[arke] 1598; bks 2–3, L.A. 1598; bk 4, The ninth part, [tr Robert Parke?] 1601.
Perott, J. D. The probable source of the plot of Shakespeare's Tempest. Pbns of Clark Univ Lib 1 1905.
— The Mirrour of knighthood. Romanic Rev 4 1913.
Atkinson, D. F. Busirano's Castle and Artidan's cave. MLQ 1 1940.
— One R.P. and the authorship of the Mirror of knighthood part nine. MLQ 6 1945.
Evans, D. A. Some notes on Shakespeare and the Mirror of knighthood. Shakespeare Assoc Bull 21–2 1946–7.
La coronica del principe don Florando d'Inglatierra. Lisbon 1545; Palladino of England, tr Anthony Munday 1588 (from French trn by Claude Collet).
La historia de los nobles caualleros de Oliveros de Castilla y Artus dalgarube. Burgos 1498; The hystorye of Olyver of Castille and of the fayre Helayne, 1518.
La vida de Lazarillo de Tormes. Alcala 1554 (possibly by Diego Hurtado de Mendoza); The pleasant history of Lazarillo de Tormes, tr D. Rowland 1576.
— Segunda parte de Lazarillo. Antwerp 1555; The most pleasant and delectable history of Lazarillo de Tormes, tr W. Phiston 1596.
— Segunda parte [by Juan de Luna]. Paris 1620; The pursuit of the historie of Lazarillo de Tormes, tr T. W. Calkley 1622.
Sims, E. R. Four 17th-century translations of Lazarillo de Tormes. Hispanic Rev 5 1937.
Peñuelas, M. C. Algo más sobre la picaresca: Lázaro de Tormes y Jack Wilton de Nashe (1594). Hispania 37 1954.

Palmerin Cycle

Palmerin de Oliva. 2 pts Salamanca 1511; tr Anthony Munday, pt 1 1588, pt 2 1597 (from French trn by Jean Mangin and Italian of Mambrino de Roseo); pt 2 tr William Barley as The delightful history of Celestina the faire, 1596.
Bault, J. G. English translations of the Celestina in the 16th century. Hispanic Rev 28 1960.
Los tres libros de cavallero Primaleón. 1512; The honourable, pleasant and rare conceited history of Palamedos, tr Anthony Munday 1589; Primaleon of Greece pt 1 tr A. Munday and anon 1595; pt 2 tr A. Munday 1596; pt 3 [tr A. Munday?] 1597.
Palmerin d'Inglaterra [pts 1–2 by F. de Moraes]. Toledo 1547–8; Palmerin of England, tr A. Munday [1581–7] (from French trn by J. Vincent); pt 3 (sometimes attributed to Diogo Fernandez Lisboa, but possibly from an Italian original) tr A. Munday 1597 (from a French trn).
Turner, J. C. Munday: an Elizabethan man of letters. Berkeley 1928.
Patchell, M. The Palmerin romances in Elizabethan prose fiction. New York 1947.

Alemán, Mateo. La vida del pícaro Guzmán de Alfarache. Pt 1, Madrid 1599; pt 2, Barcelona 1605; The rogue or the life of Guzmán de Alfarache, tr Diego Puede (James Mabbe) 2 vols 1622–3; The rogue or the life of Guzmán de Alfarache, epitomised by S.S. 1655–6.
Fletcher, John and Philip Massinger. The little French lawyer. 1647. Performed c. 1620.
Cervantes Saavedra, Miguel de. El ingenioso hidalgo don Quixote de la Mancha. Madrid 2 pts 1605–15; 1615; The history of the valorous and wittie knight errant,

Don Quixote of the Mancha, [tr Thomas Shelton] 2 pts 1612–20.
Beaumont, Francis and John Fletcher. The knight of the burning pestle. 1613.
— The coxcombe. 1647. Performed 1610.
Gayton, E. Pleasant notes upon Don Quixote. 1654.
Davenport, Robert. The city nightcap. 1661. Licensed 1624.
George, J. Thomas Shelton, translator. Bull of Hispanic Stud 35 1958.
Knowles, E. B. Thomas Shelton, translator of Don Quixote. Stud in Renaissance 5 1958.
Verbitsky, B. Hamlet y Don Quijote. Bueños Aires 1964.
— Novelas exemplares. Madrid 1613; Exemplarie novells in 6 bks, tr J. Mabbe 1640. Trn contains Las dos doncellas, La señora Cornelia, El amante liberal, La fuerza de la sangre, La española inglesa, El celoso extremeno.
Heywood, Thomas. The fair maid of the west. 2 pts [c. 1610–30]. From El amante liberal.
Massinger, Philip et al. The fair maid of the inn. 1626. From La ilustre fregona.
Fletcher, John. Rule a wife and have a wife. 1640. Licensed 1624. From El casamiento engañoso.
— The chances. 1647. From La señora Cornelia.
— Love's pilgrimage. 1647. From Las dos doncellas.
Middleton, Thomas and William Rowley. The Spanish gypsie. 1653. Performed 1623. From La fuerza de la sangre and La gitanilla.
Most of these writers used the French trn by Rosset and d'Audiguier 1618.
Pierce, F. James Mabbe and la española inglesa. Revue de Littérature Comparée 23 1949.
— Los trabajos de Persiles y Sigismunda. Madrid 1617; The travels of Persiles and Sigismunda, tr 1619 (dedication signed M.L.).
Fletcher, John and Philip Massinger. The custome of the country. 1647. Performed 1619.

Rosenbach, A. S. W. The curious-impertinent in English dramatic literature before Shelton's translation of Don Quixote. MLN 17 1902.
Fitzmaurice-Kelly, J. Cervantes in England. Proc Br Acad 1 1905.
Armas y Cadernas, José de. Cervantes en la literatura inglesa. Madrid 1916.
Ford, J. D. M. and R. Lansing. Cervantes: a tentative bibliography. Cambridge Mass 1931.
Hazard, P. Don Quichotte au cours des siècles. In his Don Quichotte de Cervantes, Paris 1931.
— La fortuna de don Quijote en la literatura europea. Boletin de Instituto de las Españas 1934.
Turgenev, Ivan. Hamlet and Don Quixote. In The Anatomy of Don Quixote, ed M. J. Bernadete and A. Flores, New York 1932.
Sacoto Arias, A. Hamlet y don Quijote: o la dialéctica de la locura. América (Quito) 1939.
Knowles, E. B. Four articles on Don Quixote in England. New York 1939.
— Don Quixote through English eyes. Hispania 23 1940.
— Allusions to Don Quixote before 1660. PQ 20 1941.
— The first and second editions of Shelton's Don Quixote [1612, 1620]. Hispanic Rev 9 1941.
— Cervantes and English literature. In Cervantes across the centuries, ed A. Flores and M. J. Bernadete, New York 1947.
Meier, H. Zur Entwicklung des europäischen Quijote-Deutung. Romanische Forschungen 54 1940.
Grant, R. P. Cervantes' El casamiento engañoso and Fletcher's Rule a wife and have a wife. Hispanic Rev 12 1944.
Maxwell, B. The source of the principal plot of the Fair maid of the inn. MLN 59 1944.
Peery, W. The curious-impertinent in Amends for ladies [Nathaniel Field]. Hispanic Rev 14 1946.

Grismer, R. L. Cervantes: a bibliography. New York 1946.

Flores, A. and M. J. Bernadete (ed). Cervantes across the centuries. New York 1947.

Hilton, R. Four centuries of Cervantes: the historical anatomy of a best-selling masterpiece. Hispania 30 1947.

Peers, E. A. Cervantes in England. Bull Spanish Stud 24 1947.

— Cervantes en Inglaterra. In Homenaje a Cervantes, Valencia 1950.

Singer, A. E. The literary progeny of Cervantes' El licenciado Vidriera. West Virginia Univ Bull 5 1947.

Bruton, J. G. Cervantes en Inglaterra. In his Cervantes, Montevideo 1948.

FitzGerald, T. A. Cervantes' popularity abroad. Modern Lang Jnl 32 1948.

Wilson, E. M. Cervantes and the English literature of the 17th century. Bulletin Hispanique 50 1948.

Starkie, W. Cervantes y la novela inglesa. In Homenaje a Cervantes, Valencia 1950.

Palau y Dulcet, A. Bibliografia de Cervantes. Barcelona 1950.

Goult, P. Cervantes et les écrivains anglais du 17e siècle. Lettres Romanes 5 1951.

Martin, W. Shakespeare und Cervantes. Sh Jb 103 1957.

Howard, W. D. Cervantes and Fletcher. MLR 56 1961.

Reese, I. G. Cervantes and Shakespeare: a comparative study. Proc Pacific NW Conference on Foreign Langs 1964.

Palacin Inglesias, G. B. El Quijote en la literatura universal. Madrid 1965.

Burton, A. P. Cervantes seen through English eyes in the 17th and 18th centuries. Bull of Hispanic Stud 45 1968.

Cespedes y Meneses, Gonzalo. Poema tragico del Español Gerardo. Madrid 1615; Gerardo the unfortunate Spaniard, tr Leonard Digges 1622.

Fletcher, John. The Spanish curate. 1647. Performed 1622.

— and William Rowley. The maid in the mill. 1647. Written 1623.

Fitzmaurice-Kelly, J. Un hispanófilo inglés del siglo 17. In Homenaje a Menendez y Pelayo, Madrid 1899.

Fernandez (Lisboa), Diogo. See Palmerin cycle, above.

Fernandez, Jeronimo. Don Belianis de Grecia. Madrid 1547; The honour of chivalrie, set downe in the historie of don Bellianis, tr L.A. 1598.

Flores, Juan de. Los amores de Grisel y Mirabella. Seville 1495.

— Histoire de Aurelio et Isabelle. Antwerp 1556 (with parallel trns in French, Italian, Spanish and English), London 1586 (with Spanish omitted).

— A pair of turtle doves: or the tragicall history of Bellora and Fidelio. Tr 1606. Sometimes attributed to Robert Greene.

Fletcher, John. Women pleas'd. 1647. Written c. 1620.

Matulka, B. The novels of Juan de Flores and their European diffusion. New York 1931.

Garcia, Carlos. La desordenada codicia de los bienos ajenos. Paris 1619; The sonne of the rogue, tr William Melvin 1638. Also appeared as Lavernae 1650 and Guzman, Hinde and Hamman outstript 1657.

Gil Polo. See Diana, above.

Gracián Dantisco, Lucas. Galateo español. 2 pts Barcelona 1595; Galateo espagnol, tr William Style 1640 (with novella, Axa and the Prince).

Randall, D. B. J. Axa and the prince: a rediscovered novela and its English translator. JEGP 60 1961.

Mexia, Pedro. Silva de varia lección. Seville 1542; The forest: or collection of historyes, tr Thomas Fortescue 1571 (from French trn by Claude Gruget).

Painter, W. Palace of pleasure. 1566-7.

Marlowe, C. Tamburlaine. 1587-8.

Milles, Thomas. The treasurie of ancient and modern times. 2 pts 1613-19.

Baildon, John. Rarities of the world. 1651.

Allen, D. C. Jacques' Seven ages and Pedro Mexia. MLN 56 1941.

Izard, T. C. The principal source for Marlowe's Tamburlaine. MLN 58 1943.

Maxwell, J. C. William Painter's use of Mexía. N & Q Jan 1954.

Montalvo, Garci Gutierrez de. See Amadis de Gaule, above.

Moraes, F. de. See Palmerin cycle, above.

Ortiz de Melgarejo, Antonio. Casa de locos de amor. 1627 (with Sueños by Quevedo y Villegas, below; tr with them in Richard Crashaw, Visions, 1640.

Ortunez de Calahorra, Diego. See Espejo de principes, above.

Paez de Ribera, Ruy. See Amadis de Gaule, above.

Pérez, Alonso. See Diana, above.

Pérez de Montalvan, Juan. Sucesos y prodigios de amor. Madrid 1624; Aurora (from La hermosa Aurora) and Ismenia and the Prince (from La prodigiosa), tr Thomas Stanley 1647; The illustrious shepherdess (from La villana del Pinto) and the imperious brother (from El envidioso castigado), tr E[dward] P[hillips] 1656.

Quevedo Villegas, Gómez de. Cartas del caballero della tenaza. Saragossa 1625; The provident knight, tr John Davies of Kidwelly 1657 (from French trn by La Geneste) (bound with La vida de Buscan below).

— Historia de la vida del Buscan. Saragossa 1626; The life and adventures of Buscan, tr John Davies of Kidwelly 1657 (from French trn by La Geneste).

— Sueños. Barcelona 1627; Visions or hels kingdom, tr Richard Crashaw 1640 (from French trn by La Geneste) (including trn of the Casa de locos de amor by Ortiz de Melgarejo, above).

— Infierno enmendado. Barcelona 1628; Hell reformed or a glasse for favorits, tr Edward Messervy 1641 (from French trn by La Geneste).

Thomas, H. The English translations of Quevedo's La vida del Buscon. Revue Hispanique 81 1933.

Tucker, J. E. John Davies of Kidwelly; translator from the French. PBSA 44 1950.

Quintana, Francisco de. Experiencias de amor y fortuna. 1626; The history of don Fenise, tr from French 1651.

Salas Barbadillo, Alonso Jerónimo. La hya de Celestina. Saragossa 1612; The hypocrites, tr John Davies of Kidwelly [c. 1660] (after French trn by Scarron).

Wilson, E. M. Take a wife and have a wife and El sagaz estacion. RES 24 1948.

San Pedro, Diego de. Tratado de amores de Arnalte y Lucenda. Burgos 1491; A certayn treatye moste wittely divised, tr John Clerc 1543 (from French trn by Herberay des Essarts); The prettie and wittie historie of Arnalte and Lucenda, tr Claudius Hollyband 1575 (from Italian trn by B. Maraffi); The evill-intreated lover, tr Leonard Lawrence 1639; Arnaldo or the injur'd lover, tr T.S. 1660 (from modified Italian trn by G. Brusoni).

— Cárcel de amor. Seville 1492, Saragossa 1523 (with sequel by N. Nunez); The Castell of love, tr John Bourchier, Lord Berners [c. 1548] (from the French of R. Bertaut) (with Nunez's sequel).

Crane, W. G. Lord Berners' translation of Diego de San Pedro's Cárcel de amor. PMLA 49 1934.

Koszul, A. La première traduction d'Arnalte et Lucenda et les débuts de la nouvelle sentimentale en Angleterre. Publications de la Faculté des Lettres de l'Université de Strasbourg fascicule 105 1946.

Sierra, Pedro de la. See Espejo de principes, above.

Silva, F. de. See Amadis de Gaula, above.

Torquemada, Antonio de. Jardín de flores curiosas. Salamanca 1570; The Spanish Mandeville of miracles, tr Lewis Lewkenor 1600.

Vega, Carpio, Lope de. El peregrino en su patria. Barcelona 1604; The pilgrime of Casteele, tr [William Dutton?] 1621 (from French trn by Vital d'Audiguier).

Fletcher, J. The Pilgrim. 1652. Acted 1621–2.
Maxwell, B. The date of the Pilgrim. PQ 13 1934.
Villegas, Antonio de. *See Abencerraje, above.*
Zayas y Sotomayor, María de. Novelas ejemplares y amorosas. Saragossa 1637; The innocent adultery (from El juez de su causa) and The fruitless precaution (from El prevenido engañado), tr [c. 1660] John Davies of Kidwelly [c. 1660] (from French trn by Scarron).

Studies

Chandler, F. W. Romances of roguery. New York 1899.
—— The literature of roguery. 2 vols Boston 1907.
Rennert, H. Spanish pastoral romances. Philadelphia 1912.
Thomas, H. Spanish and Portuguese romances of chivalry. Cambridge 1920.

Entwistle, W. J. The Arthurian legend in the literature of the Spanish peninsula. 1925.
Habel, U. Die Nachwirkung des pikaresken Romans in England. Breslau 1930.
Bataillon, M. Le roman picaresque. Paris 1931.
Bourne, J. A. Some English translations of 17th-century Spanish novels. MLR 31 1936.
Cooke, P. J. The Spanish romances in Sir Philip Sidney's Arcadia. Urbana 1939.
Bowers, T. Thomas Nashe and the picaresque novel. In Humanistic studies in honor of J. C. Metcalf, New York 1941.
Hughes, L. and A. H. Scouten. Some theatrical adaptations of a picaresque tale. SE 25 1946.
Alter, R. Rogue's progress: studies in the picaresque novel. Cambridge Mass 1964.

(9) DUTCH ETC

Dictionaries etc – Studies – Travel – Individual authors.

Dictionaries, Grammars, Linguistic Influences

The English, Latin, French and Dutch scholemaster. [1639].
Hexham, H. A large Netherdutch and English dictionarie. Rotterdam 1568.
Llewellyn, E. C. The influence of the Low Dutch element in the English vocabulary. Oxford 1936.
Bense, J. F. Dictionary of the Low Dutch element in the English vocabulary. Hague 1939.
Zandvoort, R. W. De invloed van de engelse letterkunde. In De letterkunde van de Renaissance ed G. S. Overdien, 's Hertogenbosch 1947.
Alston, R. C. English grammars in Dutch and Dutch grammars in English. E Studies 45 1964.

Studies

Guicciardini, Ludovico. Descrittione di tutti i Paesi Bassi. Antwerp 1565; The description of the Low Countries, tr Thomas Danett 1593.
Le Petit, J. F. La grande chronique ancienne et moderne de Hollande. Dordrecht 1601; The Low Country commonwealth, tr Ed Grimestone 1609.
Grotius, Hugo. De antiquitate reipublicae Batavicae. 1610; tr Thomas Woods 1649.
Lupton, Donald. An exact and compendious description of that fair, great and fat country of Flanders. 1658.
Peacock, E. Index to English-speaking students graduated at Leiden University. 1882.
Edmundson, G. Milton and Vondel. Academy 31 Oct, 21 Nov 1885.
Pollard, A. English books printed abroad. Trans Bibl Soc 3 1896.
Worman, E. J. Alien members of the book trade during the Tudor period. 1906.
Van Schelven, A. A. De nederduitsche vluchtelingen-kerken der 16 eeuw in Engeland en Duitschland. Hague 1906.
Wilson, J. D. Richard Schilders and the English puritans. Trans Bibl Soc 11 1911.
Guilday, P. English Catholic refugees on the Continent 1558–1795 vol i: colleges in the Low Countries. 1914.
Vries, J. D. de. Holland's influence on English language and literature. Chicago 1916.
Bense, J. F. Anglo-Dutch relations from the earliest times to the death of William III. Hague 1926.
Nicolin, F. Su taluni rapporti di cultura tra l'Italia, l'Olanda e l'Inghilterra el principio del settecento. Naples 1930.
Smith, R. W. English-speaking students of medicine at Leiden. Leyden 1932.
Singleton, R. H. Milton's Comus and the Comus of Erycius Puteanus. PMLA 57 1943.

Lefèvre, J. L'Angleterre et la Belgique à travers les cinq derniers siècles. Paris 1946.
Londeboom, J. Austin Friars: history of the Dutch reformed church in London 1550–1950. Hague 1950.
Arents, P. De vlaamse schrijvers in het Engels vertaald 1481–1949. Ghent 1950.
Holaday, A. Thomas Heywood and the Low Countries. MLN 66 1951.
Bachrach, A. G. H. The foundation of the Bodleian library and 17th-century Holland. Neophilologus 36 1952.
—— A note on Huygens: visitor to mid-17th century England and Wales. E Studies 40 1959.
—— Sir Constantine Huygens and Britain 1596–1687. Oxford 1962.
Colie, R. Some thankfulnesse to Constantine: a study of English influence upon the early works of Constantine Huygens. Hague 1956.
—— Light and enlightenment. Cambridge 1957.
—— Constantine Huygens and the metaphysical mode. Germanic Rev 1959.
Weevers, T. The poetry of the Netherlands in its European context. 1960.
Riewald, J. G. New light on the English actors in the Netherlands c. 1590–1660. E Studies 41 1960.
Van Dorsten, J. A. Thomas Basson. Leyden 1961.
—— Poets, patrons and professors: Sir Philip Sidney, Daniel Rogers and the Leiden humanists. Leyden 1962.
Bullough, G. Milton and cats. In Essays in English literature presented to A. S. P. Woodhouse, Toronto 1964.
Davies, D. W. Dutch influences on English culture 1558–1625. Ithaca 1965.
Forster, L. W. Janus Grunter's English years. Oxford 1967.
Nauwelaerts, M. A. Un ami anversois de More et d'Erasme: Petrus Aegidius. Moreana 4 1967.
Bromley, J. S. and E. Kossman (ed). Britain and the Netherlands. Groningen 1968.
Sellin, P. R. Caesar Calandrini, the London Dutch and Milton's quarrels in Holland. HLQ 31 1968.
—— Daniel Heinsius and Stuart England. 1968.
—— Puritan and Anglican: a Dutch perspective. SP 65 1968.
Downs, B. W. Three 17th-century Hamlets. In European context: studies in the history and literature of the Netherlands, ed P. K. King and P. F. Vincent 1972.

Travel

Gascoigne, George. The fruits of war. Voyage into Holland. In his A hundred sundrie flowers, [1573].
—— The spoil of Antwerp. [1576?].
Churchyard, Thomas. The first part of Churchyards Chips. 1575.

—— A lamentable description of the woeful wars in Flanders. 1578.
—— A pleasant labyrinth. 1579.
—— The taking of Mechlin. 1580.
Coryate, Thomas. Crudities. 1611.
Moryson, Fynes. An itinerary containing his ten yeares travell. 1617.
Overbury, Thomas. Observations upon the state of the 17 provinces in 1609. 1626.
Sandys, Edwin. Europae speculum. 1629.
Howell, James. Epistolae Ho-elianae. 1645.
[Feltham, Owen]. Brief character of the Low Countries (1648). 1652.
Evelyn, John. Memoirs 1641–1706. Ed W. Bray 2 vols 1818; Diary, ed E. S. de Beer 6 vols Oxford 1955 (with account of his travels in the Low Countries 1641).
Nevison, J. L. Emanuel van Meteren 1535–1612. Proc Huguenot Soc of London 1952–8.

Individual Authors

See also Erasmus, Fullonius (Gnaphaeus), Grotius and Heinsius, under International Literature, above.

Dutch Authors

Marnix, Philips van. Biënkorf der h. Roomsche kerche. 1576; The beehive of the Romish church, tr George Gilpin 1579.
Matelief, Cornelis. Historiale vande reyse des Admiraels C. Matelief naer de Oost-Indien. Rotterdam 1608; A voyage into the East Indies, tr 1608.
Niclas, Hendrik. Mirabilia opera Dei: etlicke wunderwercken Godes. [no place] 1550; Certain wonderful works of God, tr C. Vitell 1575.
Numerous theological works by Niclas setting out the doctrines of the Family of Love were tr C. Vitell 1574–5.
Noot, Jan Baptista van der. Het theatre oft tooneel. Antwerp 1568; Theatre [for] voluptuous wordlings, tr Theodore Roest 1569.
Pienaar, W. J. B. Edmund Spenser and Jonker van der Noot. E Studies 8 1926.

Forster, L. W. The translator of the Theatre for worldlings. E Studies 48 1967.
Vondel, Joost van den. Maria Stuart of gemartelde Majestät. Amsterdam 1646.

English Authors

Cecil, William, Lord Burghley. The execution of justice in England. 1583; D'executie van iustitie in Engelandt, tr 1584.
Fletcher, J. and P. Massinger. Sir John van Olden Barnevelt. 1883. Performed 1619.
Hall, Joseph. Contemplations upon the holy storie. 8 vols 1612–26; Contemplationes Sionis, tr F. Schottenius, Amsterdam 1642.
Shakespeare, William. Titus Andronicus. 1594; Aran en Titus, tr J. Vos 1641.
—— Romeo and Juliet. 1597.
Struys J. Romeo en Juliette. Amsterdam 1634.
—— Much ado about nothing. 1600.
Starter, J. J. Timbre de Cardone ende Fenecie van Messina. Leeuwarden 1618.
—— Hamlet. 1603.
Brandt, Geeraert the elder. De veinzende Torquatus. Amsterdam 1645.
—— Midsummer night's dream. 1619.
Gramsbergen, M. Kluchtige tragoedie of de Hertog van Pierlepon. 1650.
—— The taming of the shrew. 1623; Dolle Bruiloft, tr Sybant 1654.
Cohn, A. Shakespeare in Germany in the 16th and 17th centuries. 1865.
Moltzer, H. E. Shakespeare's invloed op het nederlandsch toneel der zeventiende eeuw. Groningen 1874.
Peenink, R. Nederland en Shakespeare. Hague 1936.
Arens, J. C. Shakespeare's Venus and Adonis: a Dutch translation printed in 1621. Neophilologus 52 1968.
Sidney, Sir Philip. Defence of poesie. 1595.
Rodenburgh, T. Eglantiers poëtens borstweringh. Amsterdam 1619.

(10) SCANDINAVIAN

Bibliographies – Studies – Travel – Antiquarianism – Individual Authors

Bibliographies

Solberg, T. A bibliography of the important books in English relating to the Scandinavian countries. In F. W. Horn, History of the literature in the Scandinavian north, Chicago 1884.
Bay, J. C. Denmark in English and American literature: a bibliography. Chicago 1915.
Pettersen, H. Bibliotheca norvegica vol 2. Oslo 1918.
Seaton, E. Literary relations of England and Scandinavia in the 17th century. Oxford 1935. Extensive bibliograhy.
Afzelius, N. A bibliographical list of books in English on Sweden and literary works translated into English from Swedish. Stockholm 1936.
—— Books in English on Sweden: a bibliographical list. Stockholm 1951.

Studies

Muenster, Sebastian. Cosmographia Bk 4: De regnis septentrionalibus. Basle 1544.
North, George. The description of Swedland, Gotland and Finland collected chiefly out of S. Muenster. 1561.
Krantzius, Albertus. Chronica regnorum aquilonarium Daniae, Sueciae et Norvagiae. Strasbourg 1546.
Boorde, Andrew. The fyrst boke of the introduction of knowledge. [1547?].
Magnus, Olaus. Historia de gentibus septentrionalibus. Rome 1555; A compendious history of the Goths, Swedes and Vandals, 1568 (epitome).

Arngrim, Jonsson. Brevis commentarius de Islandia. Copenhagen 1593; with English trn in Hakluyt, The principal navigations etc, 1598.
—— Rerum islandicarum libri tres. Extracts tr in Purchas, Pilgrimes pt 3, 1625.
Boty, Ivan. A treatise of Iver Boty a Gronlander translated out of the North language into High Dutch in the yeere 1560 and after out of High Dutch into Low Dutch and this was out of Low Dutch by Master William Steer (in 1608). In Purchas, Pilgrimes pt 13, 1625.
Blefken, Dithmar. Islandia. Liège 1607; tr in Purchas, Pilgrimes pt 3, 1625.
Hiltebrandus, Andreas. Genealogia regum Sueciae. Stettin 1631; Genealogy of the Kings in Sweden, tr S.L. (Sir Samuel Luke?) 1632.
Bolte, J. Englische Komödianten in Dänemark und Schweden. Sh Jb 21 1886.
Nordby, C. H. Influence of old Norse literature upon English literature. Columbia Univ Germanic Stud 1 1903.
Wright, H. G. Studies in Anglo-Scandinavian literary relations. Bangor 1919.
Allen, R. Old Icelandic sources in the English novel. Philadelphia 1933.
Craigie, W. A. The northern element in English literature. Toronto 1933.
Seaton, E. Literary relations of England and Scandinavia in the 17th century. Oxford 1935.
Dietz, H. Nordischer Mythus in der englischen Literatur. Neuphilologische Monatsschrift 10 1939.

Travel

English and Scots in Scandinavia

Moryson, Fynes. An itinerary containing his ten yeares travell. 1617.

Monro, Robert. His expedition with the worthy Scots regiment levied in 1626 for his Majesties service of Denmark. 1637.

Whitelocke, Bulstrode. Journal of the Swedish embassy 1653–4. Ed C. Morton 1772.

Munday, Peter. Travels in Europe and Asia 1608–67. Ed R. C. Temple 1907–36. Vol 4, Europe 1639–47.

Scandinavians in England

Olafsson, Jon. Aefisaga Jons Olafssonar India fara. Ed S. Blöndal, Copenhagen 1908–9.

Antiquarianism

Writers on British antiquities interested in Scandinavian origins were the first to provide details about Scandinavian history.

Camden, William. Britannia. 1586; Britain, tr Philemon Holland 1610.

Verstegan, Richard. A restitution of decayed intelligence in antiquities concerning the English nation. Antwerp 1605.

Spehman, Henry. Archeologus: in modum glossarii ad rem antiquam posteriorem. 1626.

Scandinavian Writers

Pedersen, Christiern. Den rette wey till hiemmerigis rige. 1531; The right way to the kingdome of hevine, tr John Gau 1533.

Saxo Grammaticus. Danorum historiae libri 16. Paris 1514. Written in 12th century.

Belleforest, F. de. Histoires tragiques. Paris 1571–98.

Nashe, Thomas. Pierce pennilesse 1592 (The tale of Asuitas and Asmundus derived from Saxo through Georgius Pictorius, De daemonum ortu. 1563.

Shakespeare, William. Hamlet. 1603.

Schröder, F. R. Der Ursprung der Hamletsage. Germanisch-romanische Monatsschrift 26 1938.

Sperber, H. The Conundrums in Saxo's Hamlet episode. PMLA 64 1949.

Boberg, I. M. Saxo's Hamlet. American-Scandinavian Rev 44 1956.

Burton, William. Anatomy of melancholy. Oxford 1621.

Heywood, Thomas. Gunaikeion: or nine books of various history concerning women. 1657.

Burton and Heywood, who use similar material, derive it from Saxo through Krantzius and Olaus Magnus; see Studies, above.

More, Henry. Preexistency of the soul. 1647.

Latham, D. Two dissertations on the Hamlet of Saxo Grammaticus and of Shakespeare. 1872.

Gericke, R. Shakespeare Hamlet-Quellen: Saxo Grammaticus Belleforest and the Hystorie of Hamblett. Leipzig 1881.

English Writers

James, I. Basilikon doron. 1599; Regium donum: eller konungzlich föräringh, tr E. Schrodero, Stockholm 1606.

(11) RUSSIAN

Webbe, Edward. Rare and wonderful thinges borne in Russia (and other countries). [1590?].

Fletcher, Giles, the elder. The Russe commonwealth. 1591.

Smith, Thomas. Voiage and entertainment in Rushia. 1605.

Milton, John. A brief history of Moscovia. 1682. Written c. 1650?

Hamel, J. England and Russia. Tr J. S. Leigh 1854.

— Anglichane v Rossii v 16 i 17 stoletiyakh. St Petersburg 1865.

Horsey, Jerome. Travels [in Russia 1573–91]. In E. Bond, Russia at the close of the 16th century, 1856.

Tolstoi, I. Pervyya sorok let snoshenii mezhdu Rossieiu i Anglieiu 1553–93. St Petersburg 1875.

Mikulin, G. I. Donesenie Mikulina. In Sbornik Imperatorskogo Russkogo istoricheskogo obshchestva vol 38, St Petersburg 1875.

Morozov, P. Ocherki iz istorii russkoi dramy 17–18 stoletii. St Petersburg 1888.

Simoni, P. K. Velikorusskie pesni zapisannyye v 1619–20 dlya Richarda Jamesa. Sbornik Otdeleniya Russkogo Yazyka i Slovesnosti 82 1907.

Psalmon, F. Un russisant anglais au 16e–17e siècles: Richard James 1592–1638. Bulletin de Géographie Historique et Descriptive 8 1911.

Gerson, A. The organisation and the early history of the Muscovy company. New York 1912.

Meyendorff, A. Anglichane 17 i 18 stoletiya o russkikh i o Rossii. In Sbornik statey posvyashchonnyk P. V. Struve, Prague 1925.

Simmons, E. J. English literature and culture in Russia 1553–1840. Cambridge Mass 1935.

Kamenetsy, B. Materialy o politicheskikh i kul'turnykh otnoscheniyakh Rossii i Anglii v 16–19 vv. v russkikh izdaniyakh. Istoricheskiy Zhurnal 11 1942.

Alekseyev, M. P. Angliyskiy yazyk v Rossii i russkiy yazyk v Anglii. Uchonyye Zapiski Leningradskogo Universiteta, no 72 seriya filologicheskikh nauk, vypusk 9 1944.

— Angliya i anglichane v pamyatnikakh moskovskoy pis'mennosti 16–17 vv. Uchonyye Zapiski Leningradskogo Universiteta, seriya istoricheskikh nauk, vypusk 15 1947.

— Slovari inostrannykh yazykov v russkom azbukovnike 17 veka. Leningrad 1968.

Konovalov, S. Anglo-Russian relations 1617–18. Oxford Slavonic Papers 1 1951.

— Anglo-Russian relations 1620–4. Oxford Slavonic Papers 4 1953.

— Thomas Chamberlayne's description of Russia 1631. Oxford Slavonic Papers 5 1954.

Simmons, J. S. G. and B. O. Unbegaun. Slavonic vocabularies in the Bodleian Library. Oxford Slavonic Papers 2 1951.

Barnicot, J. D. A. and J. S. G. Simmons. Some unrecorded early-printed Slavonic books in English libraries. Ibid.

Ruffman, K.-H. Das Russlandbild in Shakespeares England. Göttingen 1952.

Anderson, M. S. English views of Russia in the 17th century. Slavonic & East European Rev 33 1954.

— Britain's discovery of Russia 1553–1815. 1958.

Draper, J. W. Shakespeare and Muscovy. Slavonic & East European Rev 33 1954.

Radovskiy, M. I. Iz istorii anglo-russkikh nauchnykh svyazey. Moscow and Leningrad 1961.

Ryan, W. F. Rathborne's Surveyor 1616–25: the first translation from English? Oxford Slavonic Papers 11 1964.

Pennington, A. E. A 16th-century English slavist. MLR 62 1967. On William Stephen in Russia.

Berry, E. Richard Hakluyt and Turberville's poems on Russia. PBSA 61 1967.

Evans, N. Dr Timothy Willes and his mission to Russia 1599. Oxford Slavonic Papers new ser 2 1969.

Other Slavonic Countries

Middleton, Thomas. Sir Robert Sherley, sent ambassadour in the name of the King of Persia to Sigismond III, King of Poland, his royal entertainment into Cracovia. 1609.

Taylor, John. His travels from the citty of London in England to the citty of Prague in Bohemia. 1620.

Blount, Henry, A voyage into the Levant 1634–6 into Dalmatia, Sclavonia, Bosnia etc. 1636.

Mathesius, V. English literature and the Czecho-Slovaks. 1921.

Stojanović, D. Anglo-Yugoslav cultural relations. Contemporary Rev Feb 1940.

Kleiner, K. Sedm set lat angloceských vztaku. 1942.

Wellek, R. Bohemia in early English literature. Amer Slavonic & East European Rev 2 1943.

Jasnowski, J. England and Poland in the 16th and 17th centuries. 1948.

Grabowski, T. Les relations entre la Pologne et l'Angelterre à l'époque de la réforme et au 18e siècle. Comptes-Rendus de la Société des Amis des Sciences (Poznan) 1948.

Bejblik, A. L'influence de Beaumont et Fletcher sur Julius Zeyer. Časopis pro Moderni Filologii 1949. In Czech.

Leo, M. La Bulgarie et son peuple sous la domination Ottomane, tels que les ont vus les voyageurs anglo-saxons 1586–1878. Sofia 1949.

Polšensky, J. England and Bohemia in Shakespeare's day. Philologica Pragensia 1964.

Świderska, H. Jan Dantyszek, a Polish diplomat in England. Oxford Slavonic Papers 10 1962.

Crowell, T. Y. (ed). The reader's encyclopedia of Shakespeare. New York 1966. For Shakespeare's influence in Poland from 1605.

Krzyżanowski, J. Historia literatury polskiej. Warsaw 1966 (3rd edn rev). On influence of George Buchanan and John Barclay and for Polish visitors to England.

For South Slavs writing Italian see Patricius and Biondi, above.

(12) HUNGARIAN

Campion, Edmund. Rationes decem. Ingolstadt 1583; Campianus Edmondnac tiz magiarul irot okai, tr Bálint Balassa, Vienna 1607.

Pázmany, Peter. De visibili Christi in terris ecclesia: adversus Gulielmi Whitakeri librum contra Bellarminum. Graz 1605. An attack on Whitaker, Praelectiones de romano pontifice, Cambridge 1599.

Apácai Csere, János. Magyar encyclopedia. Utrecht 1653.

— Oratio de studio sapientiae. Gyula-Fehérvár 1653.
Both works indebted to Francis Bacon.

Brett, Samuel. A narrative of the proceedings of a great councel of Jews assembled in the plain of Ageda in Hungaria. 1655.

Blount, Henry. A voyage into the Levant: a breife relation of a journey lately performed 1634–6 into Hungary (and other countries). 1687.

Dezsi, L. Szenczi Molnár Albert 1574–1633. Budapest 1897. Visited England 1624.

Fest, S. Angol irodalmi hatások hazánkban Széchényi István fellépéséig. Budapest 1917.

Tavassy, S. Apácai Csere János személyisége és vilagnézete. Kolozsvár 1925.

Tronchon, H. En guise d'introduction à une bibliographie critique de l'influence anglaise en Hongrie. Revue des Etudes Hongroises 1928.

Szentkirályi, J. and A. Lászlo. Hungaro-britannica bibliographia. Angol Filológia Tanulmányok 1–6 1936–8, 1941.

Kerekgyartó, E. English in Hungary: a 17th-century grammar. Hungarian Quart 5 1939.

Gál, I. Early travellers from Upper Hungary in England. Danubian Rev 7 1939.

— Hungary and the Anglo-Saxon world. Budapest 1947.

— Sir Philip Sidney's guidebook to Hungary [Pietro Bizarri's Pannonicum bellum]. Hungarian Stud in Eng 1969.

Berg, P. Angol hatások 17ik századi irodalmunkban. Budapest 1946.

Moholi, J. English-Hungarian connections in the humanist circle of Erasmus of Rotterdam. History 32 1947.

Tezla, A. An introductory bibliography to the study of Hungarian literature. Cambridge Mass 1964. With bibliography of foreign influences and trns.

— Hungarian authors: a bibliographical handbook. Cambridge Mass 1970.

Leader, N. A. M. Hungarian classical ballads and their folklore. Cambridge 1967. Discusses Scottish parallels.

(13) OTHER COUNTRIES

Cambini, Andrea. Libro della origine de Turchi. Florence 1529; Two notable commentaries, tr John Shute, Venice 1560–1 (with addns from Francesco Sansovino, Dell'origine e imperio de Turchi).

Giovio, Paolo. Commentarii delle cose de Turchi. Florence 1531; tr Peter Ashton 1546.

Ramberti, Benedetto. Libri tre delle cose de Turchi. Venice 1539; The order of the Great Turke's court, tr 1542.

Georgevic, Bartlomaeus. De origine imperii Turcorum. Wittenberg 1562 (with De moribus condicionibus et nequitia Turcorum), tr Hugh Gough [1570?].

Nicolay, N. de. Les quatre premiers livres des navigations et peregrinations orientales. Lyons 1568; Navigations and voyages made into Turkie, tr T. Washington the younger 1585.

Newton, T. A notable history of the Saracens drawn out of T. Curio. 1575.

Lonicenus, Philippus. Chronica turchica. Frankfurt 1678; The state and summe of the Turkish religion, tr 1597.

Soranzo, Lazaro. L'Ottomano. Ferrara 1594; tr Abraham Hartwell 1603.

Sandys, George. A relation of a journey begun AD 1610: containing a description of the Turkish empire. 1615.

[Osborne, Francis]. Political reflections upon the government of the Turks. Oxford 1656.

Moore, Andrew. A compendious history of the Turks. 1660.

Dallam, Thomas. Diary of a voyage to Constantinople. 1599–1600. Ed J. T. Bent 1893.

Iorga, N. La Pénétration des idées de l'occident dans le sud-est de l'Europe au 17e et au 18e siècles. Revue Historique du Sud-est Européen Jan–Sept 1924.

Rice, W. G. Early English travellers to Greece and the Levant. Univ of Michigan Pbns 10 1933.

Chew, S. C. The crescent and the rose. New York 1937.

Eichholz, D. E. A Greek traveller in Tudor England: N. Nuncius. Greece & Rome 16 1947.

Spencer, T. J. B. Fair Greece sad relic: literary philhellenism from Shakespeare to Byron. 1954.

R. R. B.

III. BOOK PRODUCTION AND DISTRIBUTION

I. Bibliography

A. GENERAL BIBLIOGRAPHY

B. EVIDENCE AND METHODS

II. The Accessory Crafts

C. PARCHMENT AND PAPER: THE MAKING AND IMPORTATION OF PAPER

D. WRITING AND THE MANUSCRIPT BOOK: (1) *The manuscript book*; (2) *Handwriting*; (3) *Penmanship*; (4) *Autographs: the authenticity of individual hands.*

E. BOOKBINDING: (1) *Bibliographies and dictionaries*; (2) *History and practice*; (3) *Exhibitions, individual collections and catalogues.*

F. THE ILLUSTRATION OF BOOKS: (1) *Catalogues and dictionaries*; (2) *History and practice.*

III. Printing and Bookselling

G. THE HISTORY AND PRACTICE OF PRINTING: (1) *Bibliographies*; (2) *General studies*; (3) *Typefounding and typography: types and ornaments*; (4) *Printing practice*, (a) *General; printer's copy*; (b) *Composition*; (c) *Proofing*; (d) *Correction and cancellation*; (e) *Imposition*; (f) *Press-work*; (g) *Format: miscellaneous.*

H. PUBLICATION, DISTRIBUTION AND BOOKSELLING: (1) *Bibliographies*; (2) *General history*; (3) *Special forms of publication*; (a) *Privately printed books*; (b) *Children's books*; (c) *Newspapers*; (d) *Music and ballads*; (e) *Maps*; (f) *Exotic languages*; (g) *Miscellaneous.*

I. PRINTERS AND BOOKSELLERS: (1) *Dictionaries, lists and accounts of printers and booksellers*; (2) *The Stationers' Company*; (3) *Labour relations*; (4) *Patentees.*

J. LONDON PRINTERS AND BOOKSELLERS

K. PRINTING AND BOOKSELLING IN THE PROVINCES

L. SCOTTISH PRINTING AND BOOKSELLING

M. IRISH PRINTING AND BOOKSELLING

N. WELSH PRINTING AND BOOKSELLING

O. ENGLISH PRINTING ABROAD

P. THE OVERSEAS BOOK TRADE

Q. THE REGULATION OF THE TRADE: (1) *General primary authorities*; (2) *Contemporary material*; (3) *Historical accounts*; (4) *Piracy and secret printing.*

R. AUTHORSHIP AND COPYRIGHT

S. LISTS OF BOOKS AND TRADE CATALOGUES: GENERAL: (1) *Contemporary*; (a) *Bibliographies*; (b) *The Stationers' Company registers*; (c) *Trade catalogues*; (2) *Modern*; (a) *Subject and period lists*; (b) *Catalogues of libraries and exhibitions.*

T. OTHER LISTS: (1) *Contemporary*; (a) *Authors*; (b) *Publishers*; (c) *Divinity*; (d) *Plays*; (e) *History*; (f) *Miscellaneous*; (2) *Modern.*

IV. Libraries and Book Collectors

U. LIBRARIES: (1) *General*; (2) *Individual libraries and catalogues.*

V. BOOK COLLECTORS AND COLLECTING: (1) *Choice of books*; (2) *General works on collectors and collecting*; (3) *Individual collectors and catalogues.*

I. BIBLIOGRAPHY

A. GENERAL BIBLIOGRAPHY

Dibdin, T. F. Bibliographical decameron: or ten days pleasant discourse upon illuminated mss and subjects connected with early engraving typography and bibliography. 3 vols 1817, 1969.

Lowndes, W. T. The bibliographer's manual of English literature. 5 vols 1834; rev H. G. Bohn 5 vols 1857–64, 1883–6, 1967.

Bohn, H. G. Appendix to the Bibliographer's manual of English literature: containing an account of books issued by literary and scientific societies and printing clubs; books printed at private presses; privately printed series; and the principal literary and scientific serials. 1865 (as vol 6 of Bibliographer's manual, above; thereafter ptd with it).

Cole, G. W. Do you know your Lowndes? a bibliographical essay on William Thomas Lowndes and incidentally on Robert Watt and Henry G. Bohn. PBSA 33 1939.

Catalogue of an exhibition of books etc illustrative of the history and progress of printing and bookselling in England 1477–1800 held at Stationers' Hall 1912. 1912.

Catalogus der bibliotheek van de vereeniging ter bevordering van de belangen des boekhandels te Amsterdam. 4 vols Hague 1920–34. Supplements: 1927–39, 1940; 1940–9, 1949; 1949–64, 1965.

Handbuch der Leipzig Bibliothekswissenschaft. Ed F. Milkau and G. Leyh 3 vols Leipzig 1931–40; rev G. Leyh 3 vols Wiesbaden 1950–65.

Cole, G. W. Index to bibliographical papers. 1933.

Wroth, L. C. (ed). A history of the printed book. Dolphin 3 1938 (priv ptd).

Ulrich, C. F. and K. Küp. Books and printing: a selected list of periodicals 1880–1942. New York 1943. For a list of more recent periodicals see Bibliography in Britain, below.

Selective check list of bibliographical scholarship for 1949: pt 2, later Renaissance to the present. SB 3 1951– (annually). 1949 list by L. Clark and F. T. Bowers, lists since 1950 by H. J. Heaney. Lists for 1949–55 with single index pbd separately SB 10 1957. Lists (ser B) 1956–62, 1968 (Bibl Soc of Univ of Virginia).

Carter, J. The ABC of book collecting. 1952, 1972 (rev).

Binns, N. Introduction to historical bibliography. 1953, 1962 (enlarged).

Ramage, D. A finding-list of English books to 1640 in libraries in the British Isles. Durham 1958.

Glaister, G. A. Glossary of the book. 1960.

Bibliography in Britain: a classified list of books and articles published in the United Kingdom 1962. Ed J. S. G. Simmons, Oxford 1963– (annually).

Harvard University Library. Widener Library shelflist no 7, bibliography and bibliographical periodicals: classified listing by call numbers, alphabetical listing by author or title, chronological listing. Cambridge Mass 1966.

Taubert, S. Bibliopola: pictures and texts about the book trade. 2 vols 1966. Primarily pictures.

Mullins, E. L. C. A guide to the historical and archaeological publications of societies in England and Wales 1901–33.

B. EVIDENCE AND METHODS

Pollard, A. W. Some points in bibliographical description. Trans of Bibl Soc 9 1908.

Madan, F. Memorandum. Ibid.

'The degressive principle': impressions of Burke. TLS 7 July 1966 (a review of W. B. Todd, A bibliography of Edmund Burke). Letter by J. W. Carter with reviewer's reply 4 Aug 1966. Further letters by Carter, 11 Aug, by W. B. Todd, 1 Sept and G. T. Tanselle, 22 Sept 1966.

— Some experiences of a bibliographer. Library 4th ser 1 1920.

McKerrow, R. B. An introduction to bibliography for literary students. Oxford 1927, 1928 (corrected).

Esdaile, A. A student's manual of bibliography. 1931; ed R. Stokes 1967 (4th edn). Primarily for students of librarianship.

Greg, W. W. What is bibliography? Trans of Bibl Soc 12 1914.

— The present position of bibliography. Library 4th ser 11 1930.

— Bibliography: an apologia. Library 4th ser 13 1932.

— A formulary of collation. Library 4th ser 14 1934.

— The rationale of copy-text. SB 3 1951; rptd in G. Watson, The literary thesis: a guide to research, 1970. *All rptd in Greg*, Collected papers, *ed J. C. Maxwell*, *Oxford 1966*.

— The Shakespeare First Folio. Oxford 1955.

Bowers, F. T. Notes on running-titles as bibliographical evidence. Library 4th ser 18 1938.

— The headline in early books. Eng Inst Annual 1941.

— Criteria for classifying hand-printed books as issues and variant states. PBSA 41 1947.

— Principles of bibliographical description. Princeton 1949.

— Purposes of descriptive bibliography with some remarks on methods. Library 5th ser 8 1953.

— Shakespeare's text and the bibliographical method. SB 6 1954.

— Textual and literary criticism. Cambridge 1959.

— Bibliography and textual criticism. Oxford 1964. *See* Of text and type, TLS 24 March 1966.

— Bibliography and Restoration drama: Clark Memorial lecture. Los Angeles 1966.

— Bibliography revisited. Library 5th ser 24 1969.

Hinman, C. New uses for headlines as bibliographical evidence. Eng Inst Annual 1941.

— Shakespeare's texts—then, now and tomorrow. SB 18 1965.

Bald, R. C. Editorial problems: a preliminary survey. SB 3 1951.

— Evidence and inference in bibliography. In A mirror for modern scholars, ed L. A. Beaurline, Charlottesville 1966.

Todd, W. B. On the use of advertisements in bibliographical studies. Library 5th ser 8 1953.

Foxon, D. The technique of bibliography. Cambridge [1955].

Williams, P. New approaches to textual problems in Shakespeare. SB 8 1956.

Maas, P. Textual criticism. Oxford 1958. Tr from German.

Dearing, V. A. A manual of textual analysis. Oxford 1959.

Neill, D. G. Printed books 1640–1800. Lib Trends 7 1959.

Bateson, F. W. Modern bibliography and the literary artifact. In English studies today: 2nd series, Berne 1961.

Jackson, W. A. Bibliography and literary studies: a Zeitlin lecture. Los Angeles 1962.

Hill, T. H. Spelling and the bibliographer. Library 5th ser 18 1963.

Turner, R. K. Analytical bibliography and Shakespeare's text. MP 62 1964.

Gaskell, P. The bibliographical press movement. Jnl of Printing Historical Soc 1 1965.

— A new introduction to bibliography. Oxford 1972.

McKenzie, D. F. An early printing house at work: some notes for bibliographers. Wellington 1965 (priv ptd).

— Printers of the mind: some notes on bibliographical theories and printing-house practices. SB 22 1969.

Turner, R. K. Reappearing types as bibliographical evidence. SB 19 1966.

Tanselle, G. T. Tolerances in bibliographical description. Library 5th ser 23 1968.

— The use of type-damage as evidence in bibliographical description. Ibid.

II. THE ACCESSORY CRAFTS
C. PARCHMENT AND PAPER: THE MAKING AND IMPORTATION OF PAPER

Sotheby, S. L. The typography of the xvth century: being specimens with their watermarks. 1845.

— Principia typographica; to which is added an attempt to elucidate the character of the papermarks of the period. 3 vols and suppl 1858.

Hunter, J. Specimens of marks used by the early manufacturers of paper as exhibited in documents in the public archives of England. Archaeologia 38 1857.

Patent Office. Abridgements of specifications relating to the manufacture of paper pasteboard and papier mâché. 1858.

— Abridgements of specification relating to cutting, folding and ornamenting paper etc. Pt 2 1636–1866, 1879 (2nd edn).

Jenkins, R. Paper making in England 1588–1788. Library Assoc Record 2–4 1900–2; rptd in Collected papers 1936 (Newcomen Soc).

Duff, E. G. English printing on vellum to the end of 1600. 1902 (Lancashire Bibl Soc).

Briquet, C. L. Les filigranes. 4 vols Paris 1907, Berlin 1929. Although the only English watermark here recorded is that of John Tate (*see* colophon to Wynkyn de Worde, Bartholomaeus de proprietatibus rerum, 1496) it is indispensable for identifying the sources of English paper supply before 1600.

Aitken, P. H. Some notes on the history of paper. Trans Bibl Soc 13 1914.

Le Clert, L. Le papier: recherches et notes pour servir à l'Histoire du papier, principalement à Troyes et aux environs depuis le xive siècle. 2 vols Paris 1926.

Heawood, E. The position on the sheet of early watermarks. Library 4th ser 9 1929.

— Sources of English paper supply. Library 4th ser 10–11 1929–31.

— Papers used in England after 1600. Library 4th ser 11 1931; further notes, 5th ser 11 1947.

— Watermarks mainly of the seventeenth and eighteenth centuries. Hilversum 1950. *See A. H. Stevenson, below.*

Hunter, D. Papermaking through eighteen centuries. New York 1930, 1947 (rev).

— Papermaking: the history and technique of an ancient craft. 1943, 1947 (enlarged).

Clapperton, R. H. Paper: an historical account of its making by hand from earliest times down to the present day. Oxford 1934.

— The history of papermaking in England. Paper Maker 22 1953.

Churchill, W. A. Watermarks in paper in Holland, England, France etc in the seventeenth and eighteenth centuries. Amsterdam 1935.

Thompson, D. V. Medieval parchment-making. Library 4th ser 16 1935.

— The materials of medieval painting. 1936.

Degaast, G. Les vieux moulins à papier d'Auvergne. Gutenberg-Jahrbuch 1936.

Schulte, A. Papiermühlen- und Wasserzeicherforschung. Ibid.

Labarre, E. J. Dictionary and encyclopaedia of paper and papermaking. Oxford 1937, 1952 (rev and enlarged).

— The sizes of paper: their names, origin and history. In Buch und Papier, Leipzig 1949.

— The study of watermarks in Great Britain: English index to Briquet's Watermarks. In A miscellany on watermarks supplementing Dr Briquet's Les filigranes, Hilversum 1952.

— A short guide to books on watermarks. Hilversum 1955. Anon.

Lloyd, L. C. Paper-making in Shropshire 1656–1912. Trans of Shropshire Archaeological Soc 44 1938; suppl 53 1950.

Saxl, H. Histology of parchment. In Technical studies in the field of fine arts, William Hayes Fogg Art Museum, Cambridge Mass 1939.

Pollard, H. G. Notes on the size of the sheet. Library 4th ser 25 1945.

Oldman, C. B. Watermark dates in English paper. Ibid.

Waterston, R. Early paper making near Edinburgh. Book of Old Edinburgh Club 25 1945. Further notes 27 1949.

Stevenson, A. H. New uses of watermarks as bibliographical evidence. SB 1 1949.

— A critical study of Heawood's Watermarks. PBSA 45 1951.

— Chain-indentations in paper as evidence. Library 5th ser 6 1951; SB 6 1954.

— Shakespearean dated watermarks. SB 4 1952.

— Watermarks are twins. Ibid.

— Observations on paper as evidence. Univ of Kansas Pbns: Lib ser 2 1961.

— Paper as bibliographical evidence. Library 5th ser 17 1962.

— Tudor rose from John Tate. SB 20 1967.

Povey, K. and I. J. C. Foster. Turned chain-lines. Library 5th ser 5 1950.

Povey, K. Variant formes in Elizabethan printing. Library 5th ser 10 1955.

Papiergeschichte. Darmstadt 1951–.

Shorter, A. H. Early paper-mills in Kent 1588–1738. N & Q 21 July 1951.

Janot, J. M. Les moulins à papier de la région vosgienne. Nancy 1952.

Sullivan, F. Little pitchers in the big years: being a study of the water pitcher watermark in Elizabethan England. Paper Maker 20 1953.

Bühler, C. F. Watermarks and the dates of 15th-century books. SB 9 1957.

Carter, H. Wolvercote mill: a study in paper-making at Oxford. Oxford 1957.

Finerty, E. T. History of paper mills in Hertfordshire. Paper Maker & British Trade Jnl May–June 1957.

Shorter, A. H. Paper mills and paper makers in England 1495–1800. Hilversum 1957.

Coleman, D. C. The early British paper industry and the Huguenots. Proc Huguenot Soc of London 19 1958.

— The British paper industry 1495–1860: a study in industrial growth. Oxford 1958.

Simmons, J. S. G. The Leningrad method of watermark reproduction. Book Collector 10 1961.

Jamieson, H. D. Watermark by an x-ray method. Book Collector 14 1965.

Thomas, J. H. Paper-making and local history: a guide to sources. Local Historian 8 1968.

Papermaking: art and craft. Washington 1968 (Lib of Congress).

D. WRITING AND THE MANUSCRIPT BOOK

Brown, T. J. Latin palaeography since Traube. Trans Cambridge Bibl Soc 3 1959–63.

University of London Library. The palaeography collection. Ed J. Gibbs 2 vols Boston 1968.
See also col 9, above.

(1) THE MANUSCRIPT BOOK

Scriveners' Company. The case of the free scriveners of London, set forth in a report from a Committee of the Court of Assistants of the Company of Scriveners, London, to the Masters, Wardens and Assistants of the Company, at their Court, holden the 23d day of June 1748. 1748.

Kirchoff, A. Handscriftshändler des Mittelalters. Leipzig 1853.

Wattenbach, W. Das Schriftswesen im Mittelalter. Leipzig 1871, 1896 (rev).

Coxe, H. O. The apocalypse of St John. 1876 (Roxburghe Club).

Bradley, J. W. Dictionary of miniaturists, illuminators, calligraphers and copyists. 3 vols 1887–9.

James, M. R. On fine art as applied to the illustration of the Bible, sec ix–xiv, exemplified chiefly by Cambridge mss. Proc Cambridge Antiquarian Soc 7 1893.

— A descriptive catalogue of the manuscripts in the Fitzwilliam Museum. Cambridge 1895.

— Catalogue of manuscripts and early printed books from the libraries of William Morris, Richard Bennett, Bertram fourth Earl of Ashburnham and other sources, now forming part of the library of J. Pierpont Morgan: manuscripts. 1906.

— The Trinity College apocalypse. 1909 (Roxburghe Club).

— The Chaundler manuscripts. 1916 (Roxburghe Club).

—— La estoire de Seint Ædward le Rei. 1920 (Roxburghe Club).

—— A descriptive catalogue of Latin manuscripts in the John Rylands Library Manchester. 2 vols Manchester 1921.

—— A Peterborough psalter and bestiary of the xivth century. 1921 (Roxburghe Club).

—— The apocalypse in Latin and French. 1922 (Roxburghe Club).

—— An English Bible-picture book of the 14th century. Walpole Soc 11 1923.

—— Drawings of Matthew Paris. Walpole Soc 14 1926.

—— The bestiary. 1928 (Roxburghe Club).

—— Marvels of the East. 1929 (Roxburghe Club).

—— and E. G. Millar. The Bohun manuscripts. 1936 (Roxburghe Club).

Madan, F. Books in manuscript. 1893.

Pollard, A. W. Some pictorial and heraldic initials. Bibliographica 3 1897. Reproduces contemporary illustrations of scribes at work.

Putnam, G. H. Books and their makers during the Middle Ages: a study of the conditions of the production and distribution of literature from the fall of the Roman Empire to the close of the xviith century. 2 vols New York 1897.

Thompson, E. M. Calligraphy in the Middle Ages. Bibliographica 3 1897.

Dziatzko, K. Untersuchungen über ausgewählte Kapitel des antiken Buchwesens. Leipzig 1900.

Traube, L. Vorlesungen und Abhandlungen: I, zur Paläographic und Handschriftenkunde, Munich 1909; III, Kleine Schriften, Munich 1920.

Warner, G. F. and H. A. Wilson. The Benedictional of St Æthelwold. 1910 (Roxburghe Club).

Homburger, O. Die Anfänger der Malschule von Winchester in x Jahrhundert. Leipzig 1912.

Herbert, J. A. The Sherborne Missal. 1920 (Roxburghe Club).

Cockerell, S. C. and M. R. James. Two East Anglian psalters at the Bodleian Library, Oxford. 1926 (Roxburghe Club).

—— The work of W. de Brailes. 1930 (Roxburghe Club).

Horman, W. Vulgaria. Ed M. R. James 1926 (Roxburghe Club). The English–Latin dialogues vividly reflect current practice and opinion on paper, writing, printing and bookselling.

Millar, E. G. English illuminated manuscripts of the xivth and xvth centuries. Paris 1928.

—— An illuminated manuscript of La somme le Roy attributed to the Parisian miniaturist Honoré. 1953 (Roxburghe Club). Reproduces and discusses contemporary instructions to the illuminator.

Saunders, O. E. English illumination. 2 vols Florence and Paris 1928.

Steele, R. The pecia. Library 4th ser 11 1931.

Lowe, E. A. Codices latinae antiquiores. 11 vols Oxford 1934–6. Includes all insular mss before 800, listed by current location; see especially vol 2 (Great Britain and Ireland) and preface to vol 6 (France).

Wormald, F. English kalendars before AD 1100. 1934.

—— The survival of Anglo-Saxon illumination after the Norman Conquest. Proc Br Acad 30 1944.

—— Decorated initials in English manuscripts from AD 900–1100. Archaeologia 91 1945.

—— and P. M. Giles. A handlist of the additional manuscripts in the Fitzwilliam Museum. Trans Cambridge Bibl Soc 1 1949–53.

Wormald, F. A medieval description of two illuminated psalters. Scriptorium 6 1952.

—— English drawings of the tenth and eleventh centuries. 1952.

—— The miniatures in the Gospels of St Augustine. 1954.

—— The Benedictional of St Ethelwold. 1959.

—— An English eleventh-century psalter with pictures: British Museum Cotton ms Tiberius C. vi. Walpole Soc 38 1962.

—— Anglo-Saxon initials in a Paris Boethius ms. Gazette des Beaux-Arts 6th ser 62 1963.

—— and P. M. Giles. Illuminated manuscripts in the Fitzwilliam Museum. Cambridge 1966.

Destrez, J. La pecia dans les manuscrits universitaires du xiiie et du xive siècle. Paris 1935.

Lesne, E. Les livres, 'scriptoria' et bibliothèques du commencement du viiie à la fin du xie siècle. In Histoire de la propriété écclésiastique en France, iv, Mémoires et travaux publiés par des professeurs des Facultés Catholiques de Lille, fasc. xlvi, Lille 1938.

Mynors, R. A. B. Durham Cathedral manuscripts to the end of the twelfth century. Oxford 1939.

—— Catalogue of the manuscripts of Balliol College, Oxford. Oxford 1963.

Manly, J. M. and E. Rickert. The text of the Canterbury Tales. Chicago 1940. The many surviving mss provide a useful paradigm of the manufacture and distribution of vernacular mss.

Goldschmidt, E. P. Medieval texts and their first appearance in print. 1943 (Bibl Soc).

Chaytor, H. J. From script to print. Cambridge 1945.

Bennett, H. S. The production and dissemination of vernacular manuscripts in the 15th century. Library 5th ser 1 1946.

Jones, L. W. Pricking manuscripts: the instruments and their significance. Speculum 21 1946.

Masai, F. Essai sur l'origine de la miniature dite irlandaise. Brussels 1947.

—— Paléographie et codicologie. Scriptorium 4 1950.

Lehman, J. J. G. Mittelalterliche Büchertitel. 2 vols Munich 1949–53.

Levison, W. England and the Continent in the eighth century. Oxford 1949.

Goldschmidt, E. P. Preserved for posterity. New Colophon 7 1950.

Oakeshott, W. The sequence of English medieval art. 1950.

Pächt, O. 'Hugo Pictor'. Bodleian Lib Rec 3 1950.

—— The rise of pictorial narrative in 12th-century England. Oxford 1962.

——, C. R. Dodwell and F. Wormald. The St Alban's Psalter. 1960.

Santifaller, L. Beiträge zur Geschichte der Beschreibstoffe in Mittelalter. Graz 1953.

Ivy, F. S. The bibliography of the manuscript book. In The English library before 1700, ed F. Wormald and C. E. Wright 1958.

Early English manuscripts in facsimile. Ed B. Colgrave and P. A. M. Clemoes, Copenhagen 1951–.

Delaissé, L. M. J. Edition et codicologie. Scriptorium 7 1953.

—— La miniature flamande: le mécénat de Philippe le Bon. Brussels, Paris and Amsterdam 1959.

—— Towards a history of the mediaeval book. Divinitas 11 1967.

Dodwell, C. R. The Canterbury school of illumination. 1954.

Rickert, M. Painting in Britain: the Middle Ages. 1954, 1965 (rev).

Vaughan, R. Matthew Paris. Cambridge 1958.

Funke, F. Buchkunde: ein Überblick über die Geschichte des Buch- und Schriftwesens. Leipzig 1959.

Bühler, C. F. The fifteenth-century book: the scribes, the printers, the decorators. Philadelphia 1960.

Ker, N. R. From 'above top line' to 'below top line': a change in scribal practice. Celtica 5 1960.

—— English manuscripts in the century after the Norman conquest. Oxford 1960.

—— Medieval manuscripts in British libraries: 1, London. Oxford 1969.

Black, M. H. The evolution of a book-form: the octavo bible from manuscript to the Geneva version. Library 5th ser 16 1961.

— The evolution of a book-form: II, the folio Bible to 1560. Library 5th ser 18 1963.

Crum, M. Notes on the physical characteristics of some manuscripts of the poems of Donne and of Henry King. Library 5th ser 16 1961.

Watson, A. G. A sixteenth-century collector: Thomas Dackomb 1496–c. 1572. Library 5th ser 18 1963.

Roth, C. Pledging a book in medieval England. Library 5th ser 19 1964.

Pollard, H. G. The medieval town clerks of Oxford. Oxoniensia 31 1966.

— The oldest statute book of the University. Bodleian Lib Record 8 1968. This and the preceding examine the structure of two Oxford books, the City Liber Albus and the University Registrum A.

Scott, J. L. A mid-15th-century English illuminating shop and its customers. Jnl Warburg & Courtauld Inst 31 1968.

Lucas, P. J. John Capgrave OSA (1393–1464): scribe and 'publisher'. Trans Cambridge Bibl Soc 5 1969.

[Hunt, R. W. and A. C. de la Mare]. Duke Humfrey and English humanism in the fifteenth century: catalogue of an exhibition held in the Bodleian Library, Oxford. Oxford [1970].

De la Mare, A. C. Catalogue of the collection of medieval mss bequeathed to the Bodleian Library Oxford by J. P. R. Lyell. Oxford 1971.

Patterson, S. A comparison of minor initial decoration in 13th-century mss. Library 5th ser 26 1971.

(2) HANDWRITING

Wright, Andrew. Court-hand restored. 1776 etc, 1912.

Skeat, W. W. Twelve facsimiles of old English manuscripts. Oxford 1892.

Kenyon, F. G. Facsimiles of biblical mss in the British Museum. 1900.

Steffens, F. Lateinische Palaeographie. 4 pts Fribourg 1903–10; tr French, 1910.

Johnson, C. and H. Jenkinson. English court hand AD 1066 to 1500. 2 vols Oxford 1912.

Greg, W. W. Facsimiles of twelve early English manuscripts in the library of Trinity College Cambridge. Oxford 1913.

Jenkinson, H. English current writing and early printing. Trans of Bibl Soc 13 1915.

— Elizabethan handwritings: a preliminary sketch. Library 4th ser 3 1923.

— The later courthands in England. 2 vols Cambridge 1926.

Thompson, E. M. Handwriting. In Shakespeare's England vol 1, Oxford 1916.

Byrne, M. St C. Elizabethan handwriting for beginners. RES 1 1925.

McKerrow, R. B. The capital letters in Elizabethan handwriting. RES 3 1927.

Tannenbaum, S. A. Problems in Shakespeare's penmanship. New York 1927.

— The handwriting of the Renaissance. New York 1930.

Crous, E. and J. Kirchner. Die gotischen Schriftarten. Leipzig 1928.

Katterbach, B., A. Pelzer and C. Silva-Tarouca. Codices latini saeculi xiii. 1930 (Exempla scripturarum).

Katterbach, B. and C. Silva-Tarouca. Epistolae et instrumenta saeculi xiii. 1930 (Exempla scripturarum).

Lowe, E. A. Codices latinae antiquiores. 11 vols Oxford 1934–66. Includes all insular mss before 800, listed by current location; see especially vol 2 (Great Britain and Ireland) and preface to vol 6 (France).

— English uncial. Oxford 1961.

Judge, C. B. Specimens of sixteenth-century handwriting. Cambridge Mass 1936.

Ker, N. R. The date of the 'tremulous' Worcester hand. Leeds Stud in Eng 6 1937.

— William of Malmesbury's handwriting. EHR 59 1944.

Schulz H. C. Thomas Hoccleve, scribe. Speculum 12 1937.

Pollard, H. G. The Company of Stationers before 1557. Library 4th ser 18 1938.

Mallon, J., R. Marichal and C. Perrat. L'écriture latine de la capitale romaine à la minuscule. Paris 1939

Grieve, H. E. P. Some examples of English handwriting, twelfth to seventeenth century. Chelmsford 1949.

— More examples of English handwriting, thirteenth to eighteenth century. Chelmsford 1950.

— Examples of English handwriting. Chelmsford 1954.

Mynors, R. A. B. A fifteenth-century scribe: 'T'. Werken. Trans Cambridge Bibl Soc 1 1949–53.

Vaughan, R. The handwriting of Matthew Paris. Ibid.

Bishop, T. A. M. Notes on Cambridge manuscripts. Trans Cambridge Bibl Soc 1– 1950– (in progress).

— Canterbury scribes' work. Durham Philobiblon 2 pt 1 1955.

— Scriptores Regis. Cambridge 1961.

— English Caroline minuscule. Oxford 1971.

Boussard, J. Influences insulaires dans la formation de l'écriture gothique. Scriptorium 5 1951.

Hajnal, I. Universities and the development of writing. Scriptorium 6 1952, 11 1957.

— L'enseignement de l'écriture aux universités médiévales. Budapest 1959 (2nd edn).

Denholm-Young, N. Handwriting in England and Wales. Cardiff 1954.

Bischoff, Bernhard. Paläographie der abendländischen Buchschriften vom v bis zum xii Jahrhundert. In Relazioni del x congresso internazionale di scienze storiche, Rome 1955.

Burgoyne, P. A. Cursive handwriting. Leicester [1955].

Kirchner, J. Scriptura latina libraria. Munich 1955.

— Scriptura gothica libraria. Munich and Vienna 1966.

Doyle, A. I. The work of a late 15th-century English scribe, William Ebesham. Bull John Rylands Lib 39 1957.

— More light on John Shirley. MÆ 30 1961.

Hector, L. C. The handwriting of English documents. 1958, 1966 (rev).

Catalogues des mss en écriture latine portant des indications de date, de lieu ou de copiste. Ed C. M. D. Samaran and R. Marichal. Pts 1–2, 5–6, 8 vols Paris 1959–68 (in progress).

— Mss datés conservés dans les Pays-Bas: catalogue paléographique. Ed G. I. Lieftinck 2 vols Amsterdam 1964– (in progress).

— Katalog der datierten Handschriften in lateinischer Schrift in Österreich. Ed F. Unterkircher 2 vols Vienna 1969– (in progress).

— Mss datés conservés en Belgique. Ed F. Masai and M. Wittek. Pt 1, Ghent 1970– (in progress).

Casamassima, E. Literae gothicae: note per la storia della riforma grafica umanistica. La Bibliofilia 62 1960.

— Per una storia delle dottrine paleografiche dall' umanesimo a Jean Mabillon. Studi Medievali 3rd ser 5 1964.

Fairbank, A. and B. Wolpe. Renaissance handwriting: an anthology of italic scripts. 1960.

— and B. Dickins. The italic hand in Tudor Cambridge. Cambridge 1963.

Wright, C. E. English vernacular hands from the 12th to the 15th centuries. Oxford 1960.

Wright, D. H. Some notes on English uncial. Traditio 17 1961.

Dawson, G. E. and L. Kennedy-Skipton. Elizabethan handwriting 1500–1650. New York 1966.

Vezin, J. Mss des xe et xie siècles copiés en Angleterre en minuscule caroline et conservés à la Bibliothèque Nationale de Paris. In Humanisme actif: mélanges offerts à Julien Cain, Paris 1968.

Thomson, S. H. Latin book hands of the later Middle Ages. Cambridge 1969.

Parkes, M. English cursive book-hands 1250–1500. Oxford 1969.

[Hunt, R. W. and A. C. de la Mare]. Duke Humfrey and English humanism in the fifteenth century: catalogue of an exhibition held in the Bodleian Library Oxford. Oxford [1970].

(3) PENMANSHIP

Baildon, John and John de Beauchesne. A booke containing divers sortes of hands, as well the English as the French secretarie. 1570, 1571, 1590, 1591, 1602, 1615.

Clement, Francis. The Petie schole, with an English orthographie, wherein by rules lately prescribed is taught a method to enable both a child to read perfectly within one moneth, and also the unperfect to write English aright. 1587.

Coote, Edmund. The English schoole-master. 1596, 1636, 1704 (25th edn) etc.

Gething, Richard. A coppie-booke. 1616, 1619 (enlarged as Calligraphotechnia: or the art of faire writing), 1642, 1652.

— Chirographia. 1645, [1648], 1664 (as Gething's Redivivus).

Billingsley, Martin. The Pen's excellencie, or the secretarie's delighte. [1618].

Browne, David. The new invention intituled Calligraphia: or the art of fair writing. St Andrews 1622.

Davies, John. [The anatomie of fair writing]. [c. 1620], 1636 (as The writing schoole-master or the anatomie of fair writing).

Cocker, Edward. Art's glory: or the penman's treasure. 1657.

— The pen's transcendencie: or faire writing's labyrinth. 1657.

— Pen's triumph. 1658.

No copies of Pen's experience [*before 1657*], Pen's gallantry [*1657*] *or* Copy of fair writing [*1657*] *are known to survive.*

Gery, Peter. Gerii viri in arte scriptoria quondam celeberrimi opera. 1659.

Massey, William. The origin and progress of letters. 1763. The 2nd pt consists of biographies of English writing masters, arranged alphabetically.

Strange, E. F. The early English writing masters. Bibliographica 3 1897.

Day, L. F. Penmanship of the 16th, 17th and 18th centuries. 1911.

Heal, A. The English writing masters and their copy-books: a biographical dictionary and a bibliography. Cambridge 1931.

Clair, C. Clement Perret, calligrapher, Library 5th ser 2 1956.

Van Dijk, S. J. An advertisement sheet of an early 14th-century writing master at Oxford. Scriptorium 10 1956.

Wolpe, B. A newe booke of copies 1574. Oxford 1962.

— Florilegium alphabeticum: alphabets in medieval manuscripts. In Calligraphy and palaeography: essays presented to Alfred Fairbank on his seventieth birthday, 1965.

Pepper, R. D. Francis Clement's Petie schole at the Vautrollier Press 1587. Library 5th ser 22 1967.

(4) AUTOGRAPHS: THE AUTHENTICITY OF INDIVIDUAL HANDS

Nichols, J. G. Autographs of royal, noble and remarkable personages from the reign of Richard II to Charles II. 1829.

[Turner, D.] Guide to the historian towards the verification of mss, by reference to engraved facsimiles of handwriting. Yarmouth 1848.

Sotheby, S. L. Ramblings in the elucidation of the autograph of Milton. 1861.

Hardy, W. J. The handwriting of the Kings and Queens of England. 1893.

Thompson, Sir E. M. Autograph mss of Anthony Munday. Trans of Bibl Soc 14 1917.

— Shakespeare's handwriting. Oxford 1916.

English literary autographs 1550–1660. Pt 1, dramatists; pt 2, poets; pt 3, prose writers. Ed W. W. Greg with J. P. Gilson, Hilary Jenkinson, R. B. McKerrow and A. W. Pollard, Oxford 1925–32.

Flower, D. J. N. and A. N. L. Munby. English poetical autographs from Sir Thomas Wyat to Rupert Brooke. 1938.

Brown, T. J. English literary autographs 1–50. Book Collector 1–13 1952–64.

— The detection of faked literary manuscripts. Book Collector 2 1953.

E. BOOKBINDING

(1) BIBLIOGRAPHIES AND DICTIONARIES

Prideaux, S. T. Bibliography of works on bookbinding. 1892 (priv ptd); rptd in her Historical sketch of bookbinding, 1893.

Mejer, W. Bibliographie der Buchbinderei-Literatur. Leipzig 1925; suppl 1924–32 by H. Herbst, Leipzig 1933.

Hobson, G. D. Books on bookbinding. Book Collector's Quart 7 1932.

Howe, E. A list of London bookbinders 1648–1815. 1950 (Bibl Soc).

Hobson, A. R. A. The literature of bookbinding. Cambridge 1954.

London School of Printing and Graphic Arts etc. Library book lists, bookbinding and warehouse work: a guide to the literature to 1957. 1959.

(2) HISTORY AND PRACTICE

A generall note of the prises for binding all sorts of bookes. 1619. Broadside; Soc of Antiquaries, Catalogue by Lemon, below, no 17 1.

To the most Honorable Assembly of the Commons House of Parliament: the binders of bookes in London doe most humblie shew, complaining of the Company of the

Goldbeaters and of their monopoly of the importation and sale of gold foliat. [1621]. Broadside; Soc of Antiquaries, Lemon, no 186.

To the most Honorable Assembly of the Commons House of Parliament: the binders of bookes in London doe most humblie shew, the George Withers gent hath lately composed a book which he calleth the songs and hymns of the Church; and complaining of the grievance that, according to his privilege, no psalm book, Bible, Testament or other service book should be bound and sold, unless the said Songs and Hymns were bound up with them. [1624]. Soc of Antiquaries, Lemon no 225.

A generall note of the prises of binding all sorts of bookes. [18 June 1646]. BM (Thomason Tracts) 669, folio 10 (60).

A general note of the prices of binding all sorts of books. 1669; ed W. A. Jackson, Cambridge Mass 1951.

The bookbinders case unfolded (c. 1690). Ed B. C. Middleton, Library 5th ser 17 1962. A contemporary glossary of 17th-century binders' terms.

A general note of the prices of binding all sorts of books in calves-leather; agreed on by the bookbinders, Freemen of the City of London. 1695. Broadside; copy in BM Harley mss 5910 pt 1, folio 115.

Bagford, J. [Notes on bookbinding]. [c. 1700]; ed J. Davenport, Trans of Bibl Soc 7 1904.

Dibdin, T. G. Of bookbinding, ancient and modern. In The bibliographical decameron vol 2, 1817.

[Hannett, J.] Bibliopegia: or the art of bookbinding in all its branches, by J. A. Arnett. 1835, 1865 (6th edn); as part 1 of An inquiry into the nature and form of the books of the ancients, with a history of the art of bookbinding, by J. A. Arnett, 1837, 1843, 2 pts 1865.

Woolnough, C. W. The art of marbling as applied to book edges and paper. 1853, 1881.

Patent Office. Abridgements of specifications relating to skins, hides and leather 1627–1866. 1872.

— Abridgements of specifications relating to cutting, folding and ornamenting paper etc 1636–1866. 1879.

Prideaux, S. T. An historical sketch of bookbinding, with a chapter on early stamped bindings by E. G. Duff. 1893.

Horne, H. P. The binding of books: an essay in the history of gold-tooled bindings. 1894, 1915, 1927.

Davenport, C. J. Royal English bookbindings. 1896.

— Little Gidding bindings. Bibliographia 11 1896.

— English embroidered bookbindings. 1899.

— Thomas Berthelet, Royal printer and bookbinder to Henry VIII. Chicago 1901 (Caxton Club).

— English heraldic book-stamps. 1909. A copy with much necessary annotation and correction by E. G. Duff is in Cambridge Univ Lib; another, similarly annotated by W. A. Jackson, is in the Houghton Lib, Harvard.

Gibson, Strickland. Some notable Bodleian bindings, 12th to 18th centuries. Oxford 1901–4.

— Early Oxford bindings. 1903 (Bibl Soc).

Gray, G. J. The earlier Cambridge stationers and bookbinders and the first Cambridge printer. 1904 (Bibl Soc).

— Queen Elizabeth and bookbinding. Library ser 7 1916.

Skipton, H. P. K. The life and times of Nicholas Ferrar [of Little Gidding]. 1907.

Duff, E. G. The bindings of Thomas Wotton. Library 3rd ser 1 1910.

— Scottish bookbinding, armorial and artistic. Trans of Bibl Soc 17 1919.

Weale, W. H. J. and L. Taylor. Early stamped bookbindings in the British Museum. 1922.

Goldschmidt, E. P. Gothic and Renaissance bookbindings. 2 vols 1928.

Hobson, G. D. English bookbinding before 1500. Cambridge 1929.

— Bindings in Cambridge libraries. Cambridge 1929.

— English bindings 1490–1940 in the library of J. R. Abbey. 1940.

— Blind-stamped panels in the English book-trade c. 1485–1555. 1944 (Bibl Soc).

Menzies, W. B. Some early bookbindings in the Aberdeen University Library. Aberdeen Univ Rev 25 1938.

Loring, R. B. Decorated book papers. Cambridge Mass 1942; ed P. Hofer, Cambridge Mass 1952.

Jackson, W. A. Notes on English Publishers' bindings of the sixteenth and seventeenth centuries. In Bookmen's holiday: notes and studies in tribute to H. M. Lydenberg, New York 1943.

— English title-labels to the end of the seventeenth century. Harvard Lib Bull 2 1948.

— Printed wrappers of the fifteenth to eighteenth centuries. Harvard Lib Bull 6 1952.

Oldham, J. B. Shrewsbury School library bindings: catalogue raisonné. Oxford 1943 (priv ptd).

— Notes on some tools used by the 'Unicorn Binder'. Library 5th ser 2 1947.

— An unrecorded Cambridge panel (c. 1524). Trans Cambridge Bibl Soc 1 1949–53.

— English blind-stamped bindings. Cambridge 1952.

— Blind panels of English binders. Cambridge 1958.

Bühler, C. F. The bindings of books printed by William Caxton. PBSA 38 1944.

Diehl, E. Bookbinding: its background and technique. 2 vols New York 1946.

Van Regemorter, B. Evolution de la technique de la reliure du viie au xiie siècle. Scriptorium 2 1948.

— Le codex relié depuis son origine jusqu'au haut Moyen Age. Le Moyen Age 61 1965.

Howe, E. A list of London bookbinders 1648–1815. 1950 (Bibl Soc).

Carter, J. W. Early trade bindings. Book Collector 1 1952. Answers and further notes by A. N. L. Munby and J. P. Harthan, ibid, and A. R. A. Hobson 2 1953.

Nixon, H. M. English bookbindings. Book Collector 1 1952– (in progress).

— Twelve books in fine bindings from the library of J. W. Hely-Hutchinson. Oxford 1953.

— Broxbourne Library: styles and designs of bookbinding. 1956.

— Roger Bartlett's bookbindings. Library 5th ser 17 1962.

— English Elizabethan bookbindings. In Essays in honour of Victor Scholderer, Mainz 1970.

Craig, M. J. Irish bookbindings 1600–1800. 1954.

Ker, N. R. Fragments of medieval manuscripts used as pastedowns in Oxford bindings, with a survey of Oxford binding c. 1515–1620. Oxford 1954.

— The chaining, labelling and inventory numbers of manuscripts belonging to the old University Library. Bodleian Lib Record 5 1954–6.

— The Virgin and Child Binder, LVL and William Horman. Library 5th ser 17 1962.

Mitchell, W. S. A history of Scottish bookbinding 1432–1650. 1955. With bibliography.

Philip, I. G. Roger Bartlett, bookbinder. Library 5th ser 10 1955.

Pollard, H. G. Changes in the style of bookbindings 1550–1830. Library 5th ser 11 1956.

— The construction of English twelfth-century bindings. Library 5th ser 17 1962.

— The names of some English fifteenth-century binders. Library 5th ser 25 1970.

Lowther, A. W. G. Titling slips in 17th-century books. Book Collector 9 1960. Reply by H. G. Pollard, ibid.

Powell, R. A lecture on the repair and rebinding for Trinity College, Dublin, of the Book of Kells, the Book of Durrow and the Book of Armagh and Dimma. Dublin 1961.

— The Lichfield St Chad's Gospels: repair and rebinding 1961–2. Library 5th ser 20 1965.

Barber, Giles. Notes on some English centre- and corner-piece bindings c. 1600. Ibid.

Middleton, B. C. A history of English craft bookbinding technique. 1963.

Painter, G. D. Caxton through the looking glass: an enquiry into the offsets on a fragment of Caxton's 15 Oes; with a census of Caxton bindings. Gutenberg Jahrbuch 1963.

Weber, C. J. One thousand and one fore-edge paintings. Waterville Maine 1949; Irvington-on-Hudson NY 1966 (rev as Fore-edge painting; a historical survey of a curious art in book decoration). *See* TLS 29 June 1967.

Herbrüggen, H. S. Unbekannte Einbände aus William Caxtons Werkstatt. In Festschrift für Edgar Mertner, Munich 1969.

(3) EXHIBITIONS, INDIVIDUAL COLLECTIONS AND CATALOGUES

Burlington Fine Arts Club. Catalogue of the exhibition of bookbindings. 1891.

Holmes, R. R. Specimens of royal, fine and historical bookbinding selected from the Royal Library, Windsor Castle. 1893.

Weale, W. H. J. Bookbindings and rubbings of bookbindings in the National Art Library, South Kensington. 2 vols 1894-8.

Fletcher, W. Y. English bookbindings in the British Museum. 1895.

Quaritch, B. A catalogue of English and foreign bookbindings offered for sale. 1921.

Hobson, G. D. Thirty bindings described by G. D. Hobson. 1926 (First Edns Club).

— Bindings in Cambridge libraries. Cambridge 1929.

— (ed). English bindings 1490-1940 in the library of J. R. Abbey. 1940 (priv ptd).

De Ricci, S. British and miscellaneous signed bindings in the Mortimer L. Schiff collection. New York 1935.

Rye, R. A. and M. S. Quinn. Historical and armorial bookbindings exhibited in the University Library. 1937 (Univ of London).

Oldham, J. B. Shrewsbury School Library bindings. 1943 (priv ptd). Includes Christopher Chapman, Thomas Elliott.

Nixon, H. M. Broxbourne library: styles and designs of bookbindings from the 12th to the 20th century. 1956.

Miner, D. (ed). The history of bookbinding 525-1950: an exhibition at the Walters Art Gallery, Baltimore. Baltimore 1957.

Sommerlad, M. J. Scottish 'wheel' and 'herring-bone' bindings in the Bodleian Library: an illustrated handlist. Oxford 1967 (Bibl Soc).

Fine bindings 1500-1700 from Oxford libraries: catalogue of an exhibition. Oxford 1968 (Bodley).

F. THE ILLUSTRATION OF BOOKS

For medieval book painting, see the bibliographies in the Oxford history of British art, *ed T. S. R. Boase, below.*

Hind, A. M. A short history of engraving and etching. 1908, 1923 (rev). With large bibliography.

Bland, D. A bibliography of book illustration. 1951, 1954 (rev).

(1) CATALOGUES AND DICTIONARIES

Stent, P. A catalogue of plates and pictures. [c. 1649-53], 1662, 1673 (after transfer of Stent's business to John Overton as A catalogue of books, pictures and maps). Broadsides.

Walpole, H. A catalogue of the engravers who have been born or resided in England. Strawberry Hill 1763; ed J. Dallaway 1828 (with Anecdotes of painting); ed R. P. Wornum 1849.

'Bromley, Henry' (A. Wilson). A catalogue of engraved British portraits. 1793.

Stephens, F. G. Catalogue of political and personal satires in the British Museum 1320-1770. 4 vols 1870-83.

Bradley, J. W. Dictionary of miniaturists, illuminators, calligraphers and copyists. 3 vols 1887-9.

O'Donoghue, F. M. and H. M. Hake. Catalogue of engraved British portraits in the British Museum. 6 vols 1908-25. With suppl.

Johnson, A. F. A catalogue of engraved and etched English titlepages to 1691. 1934 (Bibl Soc).

Bushnell, G. E. Scottish engravers: a biographical dictionary of Scottish engravers and of engravers who worked in Scotland to the beginning of the 19th century. 1949.

Hind, A. M. Engraving in England in the sixteenth and seventeenth centuries: a descriptive catalogue with introductions, 1, The Tudor period, Cambridge 1952; 2, The reign of James I, Cambridge 1955; 3, The reign of Charles I, by M. Corbett and M. Norton, Cambridge 1964.

(2) HISTORY AND PRACTICE

Evelyn, J. Sculptura: or the history and art of chalcography and engraving in copper; with an ample enumeration of the most renowned masters and their works; to which is annexed a new manner of engraving or mezzo tinto. 1662, 1755; ed F. C. Bell 1906 (with unptd pt 2).

Edwards, E. Anecdotes of painters. 1808.

Chatto, W. A. A treatise on wood engraving, historical and practical; with illustrations engraved by J. Jackson. 1839; ed H. G. Bohn 1861, [c. 1900].

Wright, T. A history of caricature and grotesque in literature and art, with illustrations by F. W. Fairholt. 1865.

Coxe, H. O. The apocalypse of St John. 1876 (Roxburghe Club).

Pollard, A. W. Early illustrated books. 1893.

— Woodcuts in English plays printed before 1660. Library 1st ser 1 1900.

— Some notes on English illustrated books. Trans of Bibl Soc 6 1901.

Fagan, L. A. History of engraving in England. 3 pts 1893.

James, M. R. On fine art as applied to the illustration of the Bible, sec. ix-xiv, exemplified chiefly by Cambridge mss. Proc of Cambridge Antiquarian Soc 7 1893.

— The apocalypse in Latin and French. 1922 (Roxburghe Club).

— An English Bible-picture book of the 14th century. Walpole Soc 11 1923.

— Drawings of Matthew Paris. Walpole Soc 14 1926.

—— The bestiary. 1928 (Roxburghe Club).

Colvin, S. Early engravings and engravers in England 1545–1695. 1905.

Salaman, M. C. The old engravers of England 1540–1800. [1906].

Austin, S. History of engraving to the time of Bewick. [1908].

Hind, A. M. A short history of engraving and etching. 1908, 1923 (rev).

—— Introduction to a history of woodcuts. 1936.

—— Engraving in England in the sixteenth and seventeenth centuries: a descriptive catalogue with introductions, 1, The Tudor period, Cambridge 1952; 2, The reign of James I, Cambridge 1955; 3, The reign of Charles I, by M. Corbett and M. Norton, Cambridge 1964.

Chubb, Thomas. The printed maps in the atlases of Great Britain and Ireland 1579–1870. 1927.

Hodnett, E. English woodcuts 1480–1535. 1935 (Bibl Soc).

Poortenaar, J. The art of the book and its illustration. 1935.

Gray, B. The English print. 1937.

Weitenkampf, F. The illustrated book. Cambridge Mass 1938.

Wormald, F. The development of English illumination in the twelfth century. Jnl of Br Archaeological Assoc 3rd ser 8 1943.

—— The survival of Anglo-Saxon illuminations after the Norman Conquest. Proc Br Acad 30 1944.

—— English drawings of the tenth and eleventh centuries. 1952.

—— The miniatures in the gospels of St Augustine (Corpus Christi College ms 286). Cambridge 1954.

—— The benedictional of St Ethelwold. 1959.

—— An English eleventh-century psalter with pictures: British Museum Cotton ms. Tiberius c. vi. Walpole Soc 38 1962.

Benesch, O. Artistic and intellectual trends from Rubens to Daumier as shown in book illustration. Cambridge Mass 1943.

Boase, T. S. R. Illustrations of Shakespeare's plays in the 17th and 18th centuries. Jnl Warburg & Courtauld Inst 10 1947.

—— English art 1100–1216. Oxford 1953.

Saxl, F. and R. Wittkower. British art and the Mediterranean. Oxford 1948.

Evans, J. English art 1307–1461. Oxford 1949.

Pächt, O. Hugo Pictor. Bodleian Lib Record 3 1950.

—— The rise of pictorial narrative in twelfth-century England. Oxford 1962.

—— The pre-carolingian roots of early romanesque art. Studies in Western art vol i, ed M. Meiss, Princeton 1963.

Letts, M. The source of the woodcuts in Wynkyn de Worde's edition of Mandeville's travels 1499 (STC 17,247). Library 5th ser 6 1951.

Swarzenski, H. Der Stil der Bibel Carilefs von Durham: Form und Inhalt. In Kunstgeschichtliche Studien für Otto Schmitt, Stuttgart 1951.

Bland, D. The illustration of books. 1951, 1962 (enlarged).

—— A history of book illustration. 1958, 1969 (enlarged).

Hofer, P. Baroque book illustration: a short survey from the collection in the Department of Graphic Arts, Harvard College Library. Cambridge Mass 1952.

Rice, D. Talbot. English art 871–1100. Oxford 1952.

Millar, E. G. An illuminated manuscript of 'La somme le Roy' attributed to the Parisian miniaturist Honoré. 1953 (Roxburghe Club). On contemporary instructions to the illuminator.

Brieger, P. English art 1216–1307. Oxford 1957.

Whinney, M. and O. Millar. English art 1625–1714. Oxford 1957.

Merchant, W. M. Shakespeare and the artist. Oxford 1959.

Cleaver, J. A history of graphic art. 1963.

Rostenberg, L. English publishers in the graphic arts 1599–1700: a study of the printsellers and publishers of engravings, art and architectural manuals, maps and copy books. New York 1963. See J. Horden, Library 5th ser 19 1964.

Bliss, D. P. A history of wood-engraving. 1964.

British Museum. English book illustration 966–1946. 1965.

III. PRINTING AND BOOKSELLING

G. THE HISTORY AND PRACTICE OF PRINTING

(1) BIBLIOGRAPHIES

Bullen, G. (ed). Catalogue of the loan collection of antiquities, curiosities and appliances concerned with the art of printing. 1877.

Bigmore, E. C. and C. A. Wyman. A bibliography of printing. 3 vols 1880–6.

St Bride Foundation. Catalogue of the technical reference library of works on printing and the allied arts [by R. A. Peddie]. 1919.

Hart, H. Bibliotheca typographica. Rochester NY 1933.

Catalogue of the periodicals relating to printing and allied subjects in the technical library of the St Bride Institute, with an introduction by Ellic Howe. [1952].

Newberry Library, Chicago. Dictionary catalogue of the history of printing from the John M. Wing Foundation. 6 vols Boston 1961.

(2) GENERAL STUDIES

A brief discourse concerning printing and printers. 1663. See C. Blagden, The 'Company' of Printers, SB 13 1960.

Atkins, R. The original and growth of printing, collected out of the history and records of this kingdome. 1664.

Verwey, H. de la F. Frederik Corcellis: knech van Laurens Jansz Coster of de gevolgen van een drukfout. De Gulden Passer 28 1950.

Ames, Joseph. Typographical antiquities: being an historical account of printing in England; with some memoirs of our ancient printers and a register of the books printed by them from the year 1471 to 1600. 1749; rev William Herbert 3 vols 1785–90; rev T. F. Dibdin 4 vols 1810–19.

See An index to Dibdin's edition of the typographical antiquities first compiled by Joseph Ames, with some references to the intermediate edition by William Herbert, *1899 (Bibl Soc)*.

Hansard, T. C. Typographia: an historical sketch of the origin and progress of the art of printing. 1825, 1966.

Patent Office. Abridgement of specifications relating to printing 1617–1857. 1859, 1969 (Printing Historical Soc).

Bradshaw, Henry. Collected papers. Cambridge 1889.

Putnam, G. H. Books and their makers during the Middle Ages: a study of the conditions of the production and distribution of literature from the fall of the Roman Empire to the close of the 17th century. 2 vols New York 1897.

Plomer, H. R. A short history of English printing 1476–1898. 1900, [1920] (rev).

—— The King's printing house under the Stuarts. Library 1st ser 1 1901.

Aldis, H. G. The book trade 1557–1625. CHEL vol 4 1909.

—— Book production and distribution 1625–1800. CHEL vol 11 1915.

—— The printed book. Cambridge 1916.

Peddie, R. A. An outline of the history of printing; to which is added the history of printing in colours. 1917.

Sellers, H. Italian books printed in England before 1640. Library 4th ser 5 1925.

Wiborg, F. B. Printing ink: a history with a treatise on modern methods of manufacture and use. New York 1926.

Der Buchdruck der Niederlande, Englands und der nordischen Länder. Berlin 1930 (Buchdruck des 15 Jahrhunderts pts 3–5).

Flower, D. On music printing 1473–1701. Book Collector's Quart 5 1931.

Wroth, L. C. The colonial printer. New York 1931 (priv ptd), Portland Maine 1938 (rev and enlarged). Illuminates London practice.

Muir, P. H. English imprints after 1640. Library 4th ser 14 1934.

Poortenaar, J. The art of the book and its illustration. 1935.

McMurtrie, D. C. The book: the story of printing and bookmaking. New York 1937, 1943 (rev).

Wroth, L. C. (ed). A history of the printed book. New York 1938.

—— Typographic heritage: selected essays. New York 1949.

Plant, M. The English book trade: an economic history of the making and sale of books. 1939, 1965 (rev).

Barge, H. Geschichte der Buchdruckerkunst von ihren Anfängen bis zur Gegenwart. Leipzig 1940.

Howe, E. 'The trade': passages from the literature of the printing craft 1550–1935. 1943 (priv ptd).

Meynell, F. English printed books. 1945.

Johnson, J. and S. Gibson. Print and privilege at Oxford to 1700. Oxford 1946.

Munby, A. N. L. The gifts of Elizabethan printers to the library of King's College, Cambridge. Library 5th ser 2 1947. On John and Richard Day, Richard Jugge and Thomas James.

Lehmann-Haupt, H. One hundred books about bookmaking: a guide to the study and appreciation of printing. New York 1949.

Goldschmidt, E. P. The printed book of the Renaissance. Cambridge 1950.

Steinberg, S. H. Five hundred years of printing. 1955 (Pelican), 1959 (rev).

De Roover, R. The business organisation of the Plantin press in the setting of sixteenth-century Antwerp. De Gulden Passer 34 1956.

Bühler, C. F. The fifteenth-century book: the scribes, the printers, the decorators. Philadelphia 1960.

Clair, C. Christopher Plantin. 1960.

—— A history of printing in Britain. 1965.

Handover, P. Printing in London from 1476 to modern times: competitive practice and technical invention. 1960.

McKenzie, D. F. Two bills for printing. Library 5th ser 15 1960.

—— Printers' perks: paper windows and copy money. Ibid.

Printing and the mind of man: catalogue of an exhibition at Earl's Court. 1963; ed J. Carter and P. H. Muir 1967 (enlarged).

King, A. Four hundred years of music and printing. 1964.

Rostenberg, L. Literary, political, scientific, religious and legal publishing, printing and bookselling in England 1551–1700. New York 1965. See J. Hordern, Library 5th ser 21 1966.

Ungerer, G. The printing of Spanish books in Elizabethan England. Library 5th ser 20 1965.

Voet, L. The making of books in the Renaissance as told by the archives of the Plantin-Moretus Museum. Printing & Graphic Arts 10 1965.

Berry, W. T. and J. E. Poole. Annals of printing: a chronological encyclopedia. Oxford 1966.

Greg, W. W. Collected papers. Ed J. C. Maxwell, Oxford 1966.

—— A companion to Arber. Oxford 1967. Gives a large number of original documents, ms and ptd, on the organization of the book trade up to 1640, either calendared, if in Arber's Transcripts of the Registers of the Stationers' Company, or in full.

Bloy, C. H. A history of printing ink 1440–1850. 1967.

Horman, W. Vulgaria. Ed M. R. James 1926 (Roxburghe Club).

(3) TYPEFOUNDING AND TYPOGRAPHY: TYPES AND ORNAMENTS

The types from which books were ptd in England before 1660 were generally imported from abroad or cast from matrices similarly imported. Many of the works given below refer to the continental sources of typographic material used in England.

Bigmore, E. C. and C. W. Wyman. A bibliography of printing. 3 vols 1880–6.

Howe, E. Bibliotheca typographica: printing-types and typography. Signature new ser 10 1950.

Mores, E. R. A dissertation on English typographical founders and foundries. 1778 (priv ptd), 1779 (with appendix by John Nichols); ed D. B. Updike, New York 1924 (Grolier Club); ed H. G. Carter and C. B. Ricks, Oxford 1961, below.

Hansard, T. C. Typographia: an historical sketch of the origin and progress of the art of printing. 1825, 1966.

—— Treatises on printing and type-founding, from the 7th edn of the Encyclopedia britannica. Edinburgh 1841.

Patent Office. Abridgement of specifications relating to printing 1617–1857. 1859, 1969 (Printing Historical Soc).

Reed, T. B. A history of the old English letter foundries. 1887. *See A. F. Johnson, 1952 below.*

Duff, E. Early English printing: a series of facsimiles of all the types used in England during the 15th century. 1896.

Sayle, C. E. Initial letters in early English printed books. Trans of Bibl Soc 7 1904.

Proctor, Robert. The French Royal Greek types and the Eton Chrysostom. Ibid.

Steele, Robert. The earliest English music printing: a description and bibliography of English printed music to the close of the sixteenth century. 1903 (Bibl Soc).

Greg, W. W. Notes on the types, borders etc used by Thomas Berthelet. Trans of Bibl Soc 8 1906.

Dix, E. R. McC. The ornaments used by John Franckton, printer at Dublin. Ibid.

—— The initial letters and factotums used by John Franckton, printer in Dublin. Library 2 1922.

Squire, W. B. Catalogue of the printed music published between 1487 and 1800. 2 vols 1912 (BM).

McKerrow, R. B. Printers' and publishers' devices in England and Scotland 1485–1640. 1913 (Bibl Soc).

—— and F. S. Ferguson. Title page borders used in England and Scotland 1485–1640. 1932 (Bibl Soc). Addns, Library 4th ser 17 1936.

Updike, D. B. Printing types: their history, forms and use. 2 vols Cambridge Mass 1922, 1937 (with addns), 1951 (rev), 1963 (rev).

Lynam, E. W. The Irish character in print 1571–1923. Library 4th ser 4 1924.

Morison, S. Four centuries of fine printing: 272 examples 1465–1924. 1924, 1949 (abridged), 1960 (rev).

— L'inventaire de la fonderie Le Bé selon la transcription de Jean-Pierre Fournier. Paris 1957.

— The typographic book 1450–1935: a study of fine typography in 350 title and text pages, with supplementary material by Kenneth Day. 1963.

— and H. Carter. John Fell the University Press and the 'Fell' types bequeathed in 1686 to Oxford by Fell. 1967.

John Fell 1625–86: Bishop, printer and typefounder. Catalogue of an exhibition at the office of the Oxford University Press, Ely House, Dover Street, London W1. Oxford 1967.

Johnson, A. F. Gothic script types in England. Book Collector's Quart 6 1932.

— A catalogue of engraved and etched English title-page to 1691. 1934 (Bibl Soc).

— Type designs: their history and development. 1934, 1959 (rev). With bibliography.

— Sources of Roman and Italic types used by English printers in the 16th century. Library 4th ser 7 1936.

— The supply of types in the 16th century. Library 4th ser 24 1944.

— (ed). T. B. Reed, A history of the old English letter. 1952 (rev and enlarged).

— The type-specimens of Claude Lamesle: a facsimile of the first edition printed at Paris in 1742. Amsterdam 1965.

All collected in his Selected essays on books and printing, *ed P. H. Muir, Amsterdam 1969.*

Berry, W. T. and A. F. Johnson. Catalogue of specimens of printing types by English and Scottish printers and founders 1650–1830. Oxford 1934.

— A note on the literature of British type specimens, with a supplement to the catalogue of specimens 1665–1830. Signature new ser 16 1952.

Plomer, H. R. English printers' ornaments. 1924.

Osborne, L. E. The Whitchurch compartment in London and Mexico. Library 4th ser 8 1928.

Isaac, F. English and Scottish printing types, 1501–35 and 1508–41 (1535–58; 1552–8). 2 vols 1930–2 (Bibl Soc). A ser of facs showing all the types used during this period.

— Elizabethan Roman and Italic types. Library 4th ser 14 1934.

— English printers' types of the sixteenth century. 1936.

Davies, H. W. Devices of the early printers 1457–1560. 1935.

Harmon, M. Classical elements in early printers' marks. In Classical studies in honor of W. A. Oldfather, Urbana 1943.

Heal, A. Seventeenth-century trade cards. Alphabet & Image 8 1948.

Dickins, B. The Irish broadside of 1571 and Queen Elizabeth's types. Trans Cambridge Bibl Soc 1 1949–53.

— John Heaz: Elizabethan letter-founder to the printers. Ibid.

— Printing with Anglo-Saxon types 1566–1715: catalogue of a small exhibition at Corpus Christi College, Cambridge. Cambridge 1952.

Miller, C. W. A London ornament stock 1598–1683. SB 7 1955.

Carter, H. The types of Christopher Plantin. Library 5th ser 11 1956.

— and H. D. L. Vervliet. Civilité types. Oxford 1966.

— The type specimen of Delacolonge: les caractères et les vignettes de la fonderie du sieur Delacolonge [Lyons 1773]. Amsterdam 1969.

Fern, A. M. Typographical specimen books in the Broxbourne Library. Book Collector 5 1956.

Veyrin-Forrer, Jeanne. Antoine Augereau, graveur de lettres et imprimeur parisien. Mémoires de la Fédération des Sociétés Historiques et Archéologiques de Paris et de l'Ile de France 8 1956.

— and A. Jammes. Les premiers caractères de l'imprimerie royale: étude sur un spécimen inconnu de 1643. Paris 1958.

Moxon, J. Mechanick exercises on the whole art of printing. Ed H. Davis and H. Carter, Oxford 1958, 1962 (rev).

Ferguson, W. C. Some addition to McKerrow's Printers' and publishers' devices. Library 5th ser 13 1958.

Simmons, J. S. G. Specimens of printing types before 1850 in the typographical library at the University Press, Oxford. Book Collector 8 1959.

Desgraves, L. Les Haultin 1571–1623. Geneva 1960.

Parker, M., K. Melis and H. D. L. Vervliet. Typographica Plantiniana II: early inventories of punches, matrices and moulds, in the Plantin-Moretus archives. Antwerp 1960.

Mores, Edward Rowe. A dissertation upon English typographical founders and foundries (1778); with a catalogue and specimen of the type foundry of John James (1782). Ed H. Carter and C. Ricks, Oxford 1961.

Abercrombie, D. Augmenting the Roman alphabet: some orthographic experiments of the last four centuries. Monotype Recorder 42 1962.

Bromwich, J. The first book printed in Anglo-Saxon types. Trans Cambridge Bibl Soc 3 1962.

Dowding, G. An introduction to the history of printing types: an illustrated summary of the main stages in the development of type design from 1440 up to the present time. [1962].

Lewis, J. N. C. Printed ephemera: the changing use of types and letterforms in England and American printing. Ipswich 1962.

Dreyfus, J. (ed). Type specimen facsimiles; reproductions of 15 type specimen sheets issued between the 16th and 18th centuries. 1963. With introductory essay by S. Morison, On the classification of typographical variations.

— Type specimen fascimiles 16–18. 1972.

Evans, D. D. The Grovers, letter-founders. Library 5th ser 18 1963.

Vervliet, H. D. L. The Garamond types of Christopher Plantin. Jnl of Printing Historical Soc 1 1965.

— The type specimen of the Vatican Press 1628. Amsterdam 1967.

— Sixteenth-century printing types of the Low Countries. Amsterdam 1968.

Hellinga, W. and L. The fifteenth-century printing types of the Netherlands. Amsterdam 1966.

McKenzie, D. F. The Cambridge University Press 1696–1712. Cambridge 1966. An unequalled source on contemporary printing practice, much of it applicable to earlier years.

Lavin, J. A. Three 'owl' blocks 1590–1640. Library 5th ser 22 1967.

— Additions to McKerrow's Devices. Library 5th ser 23 1968.

Tanselle, G. T. The identification of type faces in bibliographical description. PBSA 60 1966; Jnl of Typographic Research 1 1967.

Wakeman, Geoffrey. The design of Day's saxon. Library 5th ser 22 1967.

(4) PRINTING PRACTICE

(a) General; Printer's Copy

Gaskell, P., G. Barber and G. Warrilow. An annotated list of printers' manuals to 1850. Jnl of Printing Historical Soc 4 1968.

Hornschuch, Jerome. Ὀρθοτυπογεαφία: instructio operas typographicas correcturis. Leipzig 1608.

Moxon, Joseph. Mechanick exercises. 1677–[83]; ed T. L. De Vinne 2 vols New York 1896. The section on printing occupies the 2nd pt. *See* H. Davis, below.

Smith, T. The printer's grammar. 1755.

[Luckombe, P.] A concise history of the origin and progress of printing; with practical instructions to the trade in general. 1770, 1771 (pt 2 with the author's name), 1965.

The printer's grammar. 1787. The text is based on Smith, The printer's grammar, 1755, enlarged and considerably adapted by an anon writer close to the Fry typefoundry.

Stower, C. The printer's grammar. 1808, 1965. Based on the text of the 1755 and 1787 grammars, but substantially rewritten with 4 new chs (on overseers' work, the readers, the warehouseman, and wages and costing) and 10 appendices.

Johnson, J. Typographia: or the printers' instructor. 2 vols 1824, 1 vol 1967.

Hansard, T. C. Typographia: an historical sketch of the origin and progress of the art of printing; with practical directions for conducting every department in an office; with a description of stereotype and lithography. 1825, 1966.

Savage, W. On the preparation of printing ink. 1832.

— Dictionary of the art of printing. 1841, 1967.

Greg, W. W. The printing of the Beaumont and Fletcher Folio of 1647. Library 4th ser 2 1922.

— An Elizabethan printer and his copy. Library 4th ser 4 1925.

— From manuscript to print. RES 13 1937.

— The variants in the first quarto of King Lear. 1940 (Bibl Soc).

McKerrow, R. B. The Elizabethan printer and dramatic manuscripts. Library 4th ser 12 1931.

Rushforth, M. Two John Taylor manuscripts at Leonard Lichfield's press. Library 4th ser 11 1931.

Bone, G. Extant mss printed from by Wynkyn de Worde. Library 4th ser 12 1931.

Willoughby, E. E. The printing of the first folio. 1933 (Bibl Soc).

Allen, D. C. Some contemporary accounts of Renaissance printing methods. Library 4th ser 16 1936.

Pershing, J. H. Storage of printed sheets in the seventeenth century. Library 4th ser 17 1937.

Bald, R. C. Bibliographical studies in the Beaumont and Fletcher folio of 1647. 1938.

Schulz, H. C. Manuscript printer's copy for a lost early English book. Library 4th ser 22 1942.

Bühler, C. F. Variants in English incunabula. In Bookmen's holiday: notes and studies written and gathered in tribute to H. M. Lydenberg, New York 1943.

Bowers, F. T. Notes on standing type in Elizabethan printing. PBSA 40 1946.

— The printing of Hamlet Q2. SB 7 1955.

Bond, W. H. Casting off copy by Elizabethan printers: a theory. PBSA 42 1948.

Gerritsen, J. The printing of the Beaumont and Fletcher folio of 1647. Library 5th ser 3 1948.

Crow, J. Thomas Goad and the dolefull euen-song: an editorial experiment. Trans Cambridge Bibl Soc 1 1949–53.

Willoughby, E. E. A long use of a setting of standing type. SB 2 1950. Speed's Genealogie c. 1631–40.

Hunter, G. K. The marking of sententiae in Elizabethan printed plays, poems and romances. Library 5th ser 6 1951.

Morgan, M. M. A specimen of early printer's copy, Rylands Eng ms 2 (Lydgate's Fall of Princes). John Rylands Lib Bull 33 1951.

— Pynson's manuscript of Dives and pauper. Library 5th ser 8 1953.

Mitchner, R. W. Wynkyn de Worde's use of the Plimpton manuscript of De proprietate rerum. Library 5th ser 6 1951.

Hinman, C. Cast-off copy for the First Folio of Shakespeare. SB 6 1953.

— The printing and proof-reading of the Shakespeare First Folio. Oxford 1963.

Brown, J. R. The printing of John Webster's Plays. SB 6 1954, 8 1956, 15 1962.

Ruysschaert, J. Les manuscrits autographes de deux oeuvres de Lorenzo Guglielmo Traversagni imprimées chez Caxton. Bull John Rylands Lib 36 1954.

Cairncross, A. S. Quarto copy for the folio Henry V. SB 8 1956.

Cantrell, P. L. and G. W. Williams. The printing of the second quarto of Romeo and Juliet 1599. SB 9 1957.

Hosley, R. Quarto copy for Q2 Romeo and Juliet. Ibid.

Stevenson, A. Thomas Thomas makes a dictionary. Library 5th ser 13 1958.

Davis, H. and H. Carter (ed). Joseph Moxon, Mechanick exercises on the whole art of printing. Oxford 1958, 1962 (rev).

Carter, H. and B. Wolpe. Pepys's copy of Moxon's Mechanick exercises. Library 5th ser 14 1959.

Turner, Robert K. Standing type in Tomkis's Albumazar. Library 5th ser 13 1958.

— The printing of Philaster Q1 and Q2. Library 5th ser 15 1960.

— The printing of Beaumont and Fletcher's The Maid's tragedy, Q1 1619. SB 13 1960.

— Printing methods and textual problems in A midsummer night's dream, Q1. SB 15 1962.

Waller, F. O. Printer's copy for the Two noble kinsmen. SB 11 1958.

Mackenzie, D. F. Notes on printing at Cambridge c. 1590. Trans Cambridge Bibl Soc 3 1959.

Price, H. T. Author, compositor and metre: copy-spelling in Titus Andronicus and other Elizabethan printings. PBSA 53 1959.

Evans, F. B. The printing of Spenser's Faerie Queene in 1596. SB 18 1965.

Price, G. R. Dividing the copy for Michaelmas Term. PBSA 60 1966.

Turner, R. K. The Beaumont and Fletcher folio of 1647. In Dramatic works in the Beaumont and Fletcher canon vol 1, ed F. T. Bowers, Cambridge 1966.

— The printers and the Beaumont and Fletcher folio of 1647, section 2. SB 20 1967.

Brown, M. N. The printer's copy of Halifax's Observations on a late libel. Library 5th ser 26 1971.

Fehrenbach, R. J. The printing of James Shirley's The politician (1655). SB 24 1971.

Lavin, J. A. The first and second printers of Sidney's Astrophil and Stella. Library 5th ser 26 1971.

(b) Composition

Carleton, G. M. The Elizabethan compositor. Columbia Univ Graduate Record pt 2 Jan–Feb 1906.

Simpson, P. Shakespearian punctuation. Oxford 1911.

McKerrow, R. B. Elizabethan printers and the composition of reprints. Library 4th ser 5 1925.

Hinman, C. Principles governing the use of variant spellings as evidence of alternate setting by two compositors. Library 4th ser 21 1941.

— The prentice hand in the tragedies of the Shakespeare First Folio, compositor E. SB 9 1957.

Ong, W. J. Historical background of Elizabethan and Jacobean punctuation theory. PMLA 59 1944.

Bowers, F. T. Bibliographical evidence from the printer's measure. SB 2 1950.

Price, G. R. Compositors' method with two quartos reprinted by Augustine Mathewes. PBSA 44 1950.

Walker, Alice. The folio text of 1 Henry IV. SB 6 1954.

— Compositor determination and other problems in Shakespearian texts. SB 7 1955.

— Some editorial principles, with special reference to Henry V. SB 8 1956.

Brown, J. R. The compositors of Hamlet Q2 and The merchant of Venice. SB 7 1955.

Hook, F. S. The two compositors in the first quarto of Peele's Edward 1. SB 7 1955.

Cantrell, P. L. and G. W. Williams. Roberts's compositors in Titus Andronicus Q2. SB 8 1956.

Williams, P. New approaches to textual problems in Shakespeare. SB 8 1956.

Williams, G. W. Setting by formes in quarto printing. SB 11 1958.

McKenzie, D. F. Compositor B's role in The merchant of Venice, Q2. 1619. SB 12 1959.

Ferguson, W. C. The composition of Henry IV part 2, Much ado about nothing, the Shoemaker's holiday and the First part of the contention. SB 13 1960.

— A note on printers' measures. SB 15 1962.

Turner, R. K. The printing of A King and no King Q1. SB 18 1965.

Sayce, R. A. Compositorial practices and the localisation of printed books 1530–1800. Library 5th ser 21 1966.

Kable, W. S. The influence of justification on spelling in Jaggard's compositor B. SB 20 1967.

— Compositor B, the Pavier Quartos, and copy spellings. SB 21 1968.

Gaskell, P. The lay of the case. SB 22 1969.

Gabler, H. W. Cupid's revenge (Q1) and its compositors: part 1, composition and printing. SB 24 1971.

— John Beale's compositors in A king and no king Q1 (1619). Ibid.

(c) Proofing

McKerrow, R. B. The use of the galley in Elizabethan printing. Library ser 2 1922.

Brooke, C. F. T. Elizabethan proof corrections in the first part of the Contention (1600), with facsimiles. Huntington Lib Bull no 2 1931.

Jackson, W. A. Proof-reading in the sixteenth and seventeenth centuries. Colophon 1 1935.

Simpson, P. Proof-reading in the sixteenth, seventeenth and eighteenth centuries. 1935, 1970 (with foreword by H. Carter).

Greg, W. W. A proof sheet of 1606. Library 4th ser 17 1937.

Hinman, C. A proof-sheet in the first folio of Shakespeare. Library 4th ser 23 1943.

— New light on the proof reading for the first folio of Shakespeare. SB 3 1951.

— The proof-reading of the first folio text of Romeo and Juliet. SB 6 1954.

Bowers, F. T. Elizabethan proofing. In J. Q. Adams memorial studies, Washington 1948.

McIlwraith, A. K. Marginalia on press-corrections in books of the early seventeenth century. Library 5th ser 4 1949.

Munby, A. N. L. A Cambridge proof-sheet of 1617. Book Collector 3 1954.

Brown, A. A proof-sheet in Thomas Heywood's The Iron Age. Library 5th ser 10 1955.

Brown, J. R. A proof-sheet from Nicholas Oke's printing-shop. SB 11 1958.

Yamada, A. A proof-sheet in An humerous days mirth 1599, printed by Valentine Simms. Library 5th ser 21 1966.

Foxon, D. F. The varieties of early proof: Cartwright's Royal slave 1639, 1640. Library 5th ser 25 1970.

Hargreaves, G. D. 'Correcting in the slip': the development of galley proofs. Library 5th ser 26 1971.

(d) Correction and Cancellation

Chapman, R. W. Cancels. 1930.

Tillotson, G. and A. Pen and ink corrections in mid-xviith-century books. Library 4th ser 14 1933.

Wolf, E. Press-corrections in sixteenth and seventeenth-century quartos. PBSA 36 1942.

Bowers, F. T. An examination of the method of proof correction in Lear. Library 5th ser 2 1947.

Peery, W. Pen and ink corrections in seventeenth-century books. Ibid.

Bühler, C. F. Corrections in Caxton's Cordiale. PBSA 48 1954.

Wood, E. R. Cancels and corrections in A discovery of errors 1622. Library 5th ser 13 1958.

(e) Imposition

Bowers, F. T. Notes on running-titles as bibliographical evidence. Library 4th ser 18 1938.

— The headline in early books. Eng Inst Annual 1941.

— Running-title evidence for determining half-sheet imposition. SB 1 1949.

Bond, W. H. Imposition by half-sheets. Library 4th ser 22 1941.

— New examples of imposition by half-sheets. Harvard Lib Bull 2 1948.

Hinman, C. New uses for headlines as bibliographical evidence. English Inst Annual 1941.

Norwood, L. F. Imposition of a half sheet in duodecimo. Library 5th ser 1 1946.

Oliver, L. M. Single-page imposition in Foxe's Acts and monuments 1570. Ibid.

Dunkin, P. S. Foxe's Acts and monuments 1570 and single-page imposition. Library 5th ser 2 1947.

— The ghost of the turned sheet. PBSA 45 1951.

Povey, K. Variant formes in Elizabethan printing. Library 5th ser 10 1955.

— On the diagnosis of half-sheet impositions. Library 5th ser 11 1956.

— Variant forms in Elizabethan printing. Ibid.

— Twenty-fours with three signatures. SB 9 1957.

— The optical identification of first formes. SB 13 1960.

Cook, D. F. Inverted imposition. Library 5th ser 12 1957.

Dawson, G. E. Guide-lines in small formats [about 1600]. SB 14 1961.

(f) Press-work

Hart, H. On the red printing in the 1611 Bible. Library 2nd ser 2 1911. Addn by R. B. McKerrow, ibid.

Johnson, F. R. Press corrections and press-work in the Elizabethan printing shop. PBSA 40 1946.

Foxon, D. F. On printing 'at one pull', and distinguishing impressions by point-holes. Library 5th ser 11 1956.

Povey, K. Working to rule 1600–1800: a study of press-men's practice. Library 5th ser 20 1965.

(g) Format etc

Povey, K. and I. J. C. Foster. Turned chain-lines. Library 5th ser 5 1950.

Foxon, D. F. Some notes on agenda format. Library 5th ser 8 1953.

Mish, C. C. Black letter as a social discrimination in the 17th century. PMLA 68 1953.

Jackson, W. A. Printed quire and sheet numbers. Harvard Lib Bull 8 1954.

— An English printed sheet-number of 1579. Library 5th ser 16 1961.

Lowther, A. W. G. Titling slips in 17th-century books. Book Collector 9 1960. Reply by H. G. Pollard, ibid.

Black, M. H. The evolution of a book-form: the octavo Bible from manuscript to the Geneva version. Library 5th ser 16 1961.

— The evolution of a book form II: the folio Bible to 1560. Library 5th ser 18 1963.

Dawson, G. E. Guidelines in small formats. SB 14 1961.

H. PUBLICATION, DISTRIBUTION AND BOOKSELLING

(1) BIBLIOGRAPHIES

Katalog der Bibliothek des Börsenvereins der deutschen Buchhändler. 2 vols in 3 Leipzig 1885–1902.

Growell, A. Three centuries of English booktrade bibliography. 1903.

Peet, W. H. Bibliography. In F. A. Mumby, The romance of bookselling, 1910, 1969 (rewritten as Publishing and bookselling).

London School of Economics. Classified catalogue of a collection of works on publishing and bookselling in the British Library of Political and Economic Science. 1936, 1962.

(2) GENERAL HISTORY

Ellis, H. Copies of original papers illustrative of the management of literature by printers and stationers in the middle of the reign of Queen Elizabeth. Archaeologia 25 1834.

Knight, C. Shadows of the old booksellers. 1865; ed S. Unwin 1927.

Rogers, J. E. T. A history of agriculture and prices in England. 7 vols Oxford 1866–1902. See vol 4 ch 20, vol 5 ch 22, for prices of books, paper etc.

Curwen, H. A history of booksellers. [1873].

Arber, E. A transcript of the register of the Company of Stationers of London. 5 vols 1875–90 (priv ptd).

Roberts, William. The earlier history of English bookselling. 1889, 1892, Detroit 1967 (rptd from 1889).

Two references to the English book trade circa 1525. Bibliographica 1 1895.

Putnam, G. H. Books and their makers during the Middle Ages: a study of the conditions of the production and distribution of literature from the fall of the Roman Empire to the close of the 17th century. 2 vols New York 1897.

Wheatley, H. B. The prices of books: an inquiry into the changes in the prices of books which have occurred in England at different periods. 1898.

Welch, C. St Paul's Cathedral and its early literary associations. Trans London & Middlesex Archaeological Soc 1 1905.

Steele, R. L. Printers and books in Chancery. Library 2nd ser 10 1909.

Aldis, H. G. The book trade 1557–1625. CHEL vol 4 1909.

— Book production and distribution 1625–1800. CHEL 11 1915.

Mumby, F. A. The romance of bookselling: a history from the earliest times to the 20th century. 1910, 1930 (re-written as Publishing and bookselling: a history), 1969 (rev). With bibliography by W. H. Peet.

Pollard, A. W. Records of the English Bible. 1911.

Shaylor, J. The fascination of books. 1912.

Homer, H. R. Bibliographical notes from the Privy Purse expenses of Henry VII. Library 3rd ser 4 1913.

— Some Elizabethan book sales. Library 3rd ser 7 1916.

Sellers, H. Italian books printed in England before 1640. Library 4th ser 5 1925.

Bosanquet, E. F. English seventeenth-century almanacks. Library 4th ser 10 1930.

— Notes on further addenda to English printed almanacks and prognostications. Library 4th ser 18 1938.

Schramm, W. L. The cost of books in Chaucer's time. MLN 48 1938.

Harrison, G. B. Books and readers 1559–1603. Library 4th ser 14 1934.

Löffler, K. and J. Kirchner. Lexikon des gesamten Buchwesens. 3 vols Leipzig 1934–7.

Bell, H. E. The price of books in medieval England. Library 4th ser 17 1936.

Klotz, E. L. A subject analysis of English imprints for every tenth year from 1480 to 1640. HLQ 1 1938.

Plant, M. The English book trade: an economic history of the making and sale of books. 1939.

Bühler, C. F. Sir John Paston's Grete boke: a 15th-century bestseller. MLN 56 1941.

Loomies, L. H. The Auchinleck manuscripts and a possible London bookshop of 1330–40. PMLA 67 1942.

Goldschmidt, E. P. Medieval texts and their first appearance in print. 1943 (Bibl Soc).

Bennett, H. S. Printers, authors and readers 1475–1557. Library 5th ser 4 1949.

— Notes on English retail book prices 1480–1560. Library 5th ser 5 1950.

— English books and readers 1475–1557. Cambridge 1952, 1969 (rev); 1558–1603, Cambridge 1965; 1603–40, Cambridge 1970.

Widman, H. Geschichte des Buchhandels. Stuttgart 1952.

Johnson, F. R. Notes on English retail book-prices 1550–1640. Library 5th ser 5 1950. Addns by G. B. Evans, ibid.

Kirchner, J. Lexikon des Buchwesens. 2 vols Stuttgart 1952.

Oates, J. C. T. Booksellers' guarantees. Library 5th ser 10 1955.

Greg, W. W. Some aspects and problems of London publishing between 1550 and 1650. Oxford 1956.

— A companion to Arber. Oxford 1967.

Printing and the mind of man: catalogue of an exhibition at Earl's Court. 1963; ed J. Carter and P. H. Muir 1967 (enlarged).

Vocabulary in French and English: a facsimile of Caxton's edition c. 1480. Ed J. C. T. Oates and L. C. Harmer, Cambridge 1964. The conversational phrases include information on 'George the bookseller' and other aspects of the trade.

Rostenberg, L. Literary, political, scientific, religious and legal publishing, printing and bookselling in England 1551–1700. New York 1965.

Pollard, H. G. and A. Ehrman. The distribution of books by catalogue. 1965 (Roxburghe Club).

Ungerer, G. The printing of Spanish books in Elizabethan England. Library 5th ser 20. 1965.

Simmons, J. Publications of 1623. Library 5th ser 21 1966.

Humphreys, K. W. The distribution of books in the later Middle Ages. Libri 17 1967.

Horman, W. Vulgaria. Ed M. R. James 1926 (Roxburghe Club).

Hobson, A. R. A. A sale by candle in 1608. Library 5th ser 26 1971.

(3) SPECIAL FORMS OF PUBLICATION

(a) Privately Printed Books

Martin, J. Bibliographical catalogue of privately printed books. 1834, 1854, 1968.

Bohn, H. G. Appendix to Bibliographer's manual of English literature: containing an account of books issued by literary and scientific societies and printing clubs; books printed at private presses; privately printed series; and the principal literary and scientific serials vol 6, 1865, 1886, 1967.

Cave, R. The private press. 1971.

(b) Children's Books

Field, E. M. The child and his book: some account of children's literature in England. [1891], [1895].

Tuer, A. W. History of the horn-book. 1897.

— Pages and pictures from forgotten children's books. 1898-9.

Darton, F. J. H. Children's books in England. Cambridge 1932; ed K. Lines, Cambridge 1958. With bibliography.

Bernard Quaritch Ltd. Early school books. 1932 (Catalogue no 464).

Meigs, C. (ed). A critical history of children's literature in English from earliest times to the present. New York 1953.

Muir, P. H. English children's books 1600-1900. 1954.

Sloane, W. Children's book in England and America in the 17th century: a history and checklist. New York 1955.

Targ, W. (ed). Bibliophile in the nursery. Cleveland 1957.

St John, J. The Osborne collection of early children's books 1566-1910. Toronto 1958. With list of publishers, booksellers and printers.

Thwaite, M. F. From primer to pleasure: an introduction to the history of children's books in England from the invention of printing to 1900. 1963. With annotated bibliography.

Good, D. A catalogue of the Spencer collection of early children's books and chapbooks presented to the Harris Public Library. Preston 1967.

(c) Newspapers

Bond, R. P. Studies of British newspapers and periodicals from their beginnings to 1800: a bibliography. Chapel Hill 1946.

Morison, S. The bibliography of newspapers and the writing of history. Library 5th ser 9 1954.

Bourne, H. R. Fox. English newspapers. 2 vols 1887.

Muddiman, J. G. (J. B. Williams). A history of English journalism to the founding of the Gazette. 1908.

Crane, R. S. and F. B. Kaye. A census of British newspapers and periodicals. Chapel Hill 1927.

Shaaber, M. A. Some forerunners of the newspaper in England 1476-1622. Philadelphia 1929.

Morison, S. The English newspaper. Cambridge 1932.

Dahl, F. A bibliography of English corantos and periodical newsbooks. 1952 (Bibl Soc).

Bond, R. P. (ed). Studies in the early English periodical. Chapel Hill 1957.

(d) Music and Ballads

Kidson, F. British music publishers, printers and engravers, with bibliographical lists of musical works published. 1900.

Humphries, C. W. and W. C. Smith. Music publishing in the British Isles from the earliest times to the middle of the 19th century: a dictionary. 1954.

Blagden, C. Notes on the ballad market in the second half of the 17th century. SB 6 1954.

Walker, A. D. Music printing and publishing: a bibliography. Lib Assoc Record 65 1963.

Playford, John. A catalogue of all the musick-bookes that have been printed in England, either for voyce or instruments. [1653].

Catalogue of the English song books: part of the library of Sir John Stainer. 1891 (priv ptd). Sold at Hodgson's, June 1932. See W. N. H. Harding, Book Collector 11 1962.

Squire, W. B. Catalogue of the printed music published between 1487 and 1800 now in the British Museum. 2 vols 1912; suppls 1912; ed W. C. Smith 1940.

Day, C. L. and E. B. Murrie. English song-books 1651-1702 and their publishers. Library 4th ser 16 1936.

— English song-books 1651-1702. 1940 (Bibl Soc). With index of printers.

Schnapper, E. B. (ed). The British Union-Catalogue of early music printed before 1801. 2 vols 1957.

Flower, D. On music printing 1473-1701. Book Collector's Quart 4 1931.

Murrie, E. B. Hand list of printers and publishers of English song-books 1651-1702. Trans Edinburgh Bibl Soc 1 1938.

Pattison, B. Notes on early music printing. Library 4th ser 19 1939.

Deutsch, O. E. Music bibliography and catalogues. Library 4th ser 23 1943.

King, A. H. Recent work in music bibliography. Library 4th ser 26 1946.

— Some British collectors of music c. 1600-1960. Cambridge 1963.

— Four hundred years of music printing. 1964, 1968 (rev).

— The significance of John Rastell in early music printing. Library 5th ser 26 1971.

(e) Maps

British Museum. Catalogue of printed maps, charts and plans. 2 vols 1885, 15 vols 1967 (to 1964). The London entry is issued separately.

Phillips, P. L. A list of geographical atlases in the Library of Congress. 4 vols 1909-20; vol 5 by C. E. Le Gear, 1958.

Chubb, T. The printed maps in the atlases of Great Britain and Ireland 1579-1870. 1927.

Stent, P. A catalogue of plates and pictures. [c. 1649-53], 1662, 1673 (after transfer of Stent's business to John Overton as A catalogue of books, pictures and maps). Broadsides.

Cox, E. G. A reference guide to the literature of travel, including voyages, geographical descriptions, adventures, shipwrecks and expeditions. 3 vols Seattle 1935-49.

Crone, G. R. and R. A. Skelton. English collections of voyages and travels 1625-1826. In Richard Hakluyt and his successors, ed E. Lynam 1946.

Crone, G. R. Maps and their makers. 1953, 1968 (rev).

Tooley, R. V. Maps and map-makers. 1952.

— A dictionary of mapmakers: including cartographers, geographers, publishers, engravers etc from the earliest times to 1900. Map Collector's Ser 28 1966 (Map Collectors' Circle).

Robinson, A. H. W. Marine cartography in Britain: history of the sea chart to 1855. Leicester 1962.

Darlington, I. and J. L. Howgego. Printed maps of London c. 1553-1850. 1964. See Jnl of Soc of Archivists 3 1966.

Skelton, R. A. County atlases of the British Isles 1579-1850. 1964 (priv ptd).

— The early map printer and his problems. Penrose Annual 57 1964.

Lister, R. How to identify old maps and globes; with a list of cartographers, engravers, publishers and printers concerned with printed maps and globes from c. 1500 to c. 1850. Hamden Conn 1965.

(f) Exotic Languages

Abrahams, I. and C. E. Sayle. The purchase of Hebrew books by the English Parliament in 1647. Trans Jewish Historical Soc of England 8 1917.

Roth, C. Magna bibliotheca anglo-judaica. 1937.

—— The Hebrew press in London (in Hebrew). Kirjath Sepher (Jerusalem) 14 1937.

—— The origins of Hebrew typography in England. Jnl of Jewish Bibliography (New York) 1 1938.

—— Jews in Oxford after 1290. Oxoniensia 15 1950.

—— The Marrano typography in England. Library 5th ser 15 1960.

Weiss, R. England and the decree of the Council of Vienne on the teaching of Greek, Arabic, Hebrew and Syriac. Bibliothèque d'Humanisme et Renaissance 14 1952.

Lieftinck, G. I. The Psalterium Hebraycum from St Augustines Canterbury rediscovered in the Scaliger bequest at Leyden. Trans Cambridge Bibl Soc 2 1954–8.

Carter, H. The longevity of a type-face. Library 5th ser 17 1962.

(g) Miscellaneous

Muir, K. Elizabeth remainders. Library 5th ser 13 1958.

Turner, R. K. Standing type in Tomkis's Albumazar. Library 5th ser 13 1958.

I. PRINTERS AND BOOKSELLERS

(1) DICTIONARIES, LISTS AND ACCOUNTS OF PRINTERS AND BOOKSELLERS

Timperley, C. H. A dictionary of printers. 1839, 1842 (as An encyclopaedia of literary and typographical anecdote).

Duff, E. G. Hand-lists of English printers 1501–56. Pt 1, Wynkyn de Worde, Julian Notary, R. and W. Faques, John Skot. 1895 (Bib. Soc).

—— H. R. Plomer and R. Proctor. Hand-lists of English printers 1501–56. Pt 2, R. Pynson, R. Copland. J. Rastell, P. Treveris, R. Bankes, L. Andrewe, W. Rastell, T. Godfray, J. Byddell. 1896 (Bibl Soc).

—— W. W. Greg, R. B. McKerrow, and A. W. Pollard. Hand-lists of English printers 1501–56. Pt 3, T. Berthelet, J. Butler, J. Herford, T. Gibson, J. Nicholson, R. Grafton, J. Mayler, T. Raynalde, W. Middleton, R. Kele, R. Lant, R. Wolfe. 1905 (Bib. Soc).

—— H. R. Plomer and A. W. Pollard. Hand-lists of English printers 1501–56. Pt 4, H. Pepwell, R. Redman, R. Wyer, T. Petyt, E. Whitchurch, J. Cawood, N. Hyll, J. Day, R. Jugge, W. Powell, W. Copland. R. Tottel, 1913 (Bibl Soc).

—— The stationers at the sign of the Trinity. Bibliographica 1 1895.

—— A century of the English book trade: short notices of all printers, stationers, bookbinders, 1457 to 1557. 1905 (Bibl Soc).

—— The printers, stationers and booksellers of London from 1476 to 1535. Cambridge 1906.

—— Early chancery proceedings concerning members of the book trade. Library 2nd ser 8 1907.

—— Notes on stationers from the Lay subsidy rolls of 1523–4. Library 2nd ser 9 1908.

—— The fifth edition of Burton's Anatomy of melancholy. Library 4th ser 4 1924.

Plomer, H. R. Notices of printers and printing in the state papers. Bibliographica 2 1896.

—— The Long Shop in the Poultry. Ibid.

—— New documents relating to English printers and publishers of the 16th century. Trans Bibl Soc 4 1898.

—— Notices of English stationers in the archives of the City of London. Trans Bibl Soc 6 1901.

—— St Paul's Cathedral and its bookselling tenants. Library 2nd ser 3 1902.

—— Abstracts from the wills of English printers and stationers from 1492 to 1650. 1903 (Bibl Soc).

—— The booksellers of London Bridge. Library 2nd ser 4 1903.

—— Westminster Hall and its booksellers. Library 2nd ser 6 1905.

—— A dictionary of the booksellers and printers who were at work in England, Scotland and Ireland from 1641 to 1667. 1907 (Bibl Soc).

—— Some notices of men connected with the English book trade from the Plea Rolls of Henry VIII. Library 3rd ser 1 1910.

—— The Church of St Magnus and the booksellers of London Bridge. Library 3rd ser 2 1911.

—— Some early booksellers and their customers. Library 3rd ser 3 1912.

—— Wynkyn de Worde and his contemporaries. 1925.

McKerrow, R. B. A dictionary of the printers and booksellers in England, Scotland and Ireland, and of foreign printers of English books, 1557–1640. 1910 (Bibl Soc).

—— Booksellers, printers and stationers. In Shakespeare's England vol 2, Oxford 1916.

Morrison, P. G. Index of printers, publishers and booksellers in STC. Charlottesville 1950.

Index of printers, publishers and booksellers in Donald Wing's STC 1641–1700. Charlottesville 1955.

Smyth, Richard. The obituary of Richard Smyth, secondary of the poultry compter, London: being a catalogue of all such persons as he knew in their life extending from 1627 to 1674. Ed H. Ellis 1849 (Camden Soc).

Worman, E. J. Alien members of the book trade during the Tudor period: being an index to those whose names occur in the returns of aliens, letters of denization, and other documents published by the Huguenot Society. 1906 (Bibl Soc).

Wheatley, H. B. Signs of booksellers in St Paul's Churchyard. Trans Bibl Soc 9 1908.

Welch, C. The City Printers. Trans Bibl Soc 14 1917.

Lathrop, H. B. The first English printers and their patrons. Library 4th ser 3 1923.

Steele, R. The King's printers. Library 4th ser 7 1927.

Ferguson, F. S. Relations between London and Edinburgh printers and stationers (–1640). Library 4th ser 8 1928.

Byron, H. J. Some exchequer cases involving members of the book trade 1534–58. Library 4th ser 16 1936.

Murrie, E. B. Hand list of printers and publishers of English song-books 1651–1702. Trans Edinburgh Bibl Soc 1 1938.

Jenkins, G. The Archpriest controversy and the printers 1601–3. Library 5th ser 2 1947.

Mortimer, R. S. The first century of Quaker printers. Jnl of Friends Historical Soc 40 1948.

Humphries, C. W. and W. C. Smith. Music publishing in the British Isles: a dictionary of engravers, printers, publishers and music sellers. 1954.

Hamill, F. Some unconventional women before 1800: printers, booksellers and collectors. PBSA 49 1955.

Juchoff, R. Kölnischer und niederrheinischer Drucker. Cologne 1960. On the German part of the careers of Caxton, Rood and Siberch.

Rostenberg, L. English publishers in the graphic arts 1599–1700. New York 1963.

— Literary, political, scientific, religious and legal publishing, printing and bookselling in England 1551–1700: 12 studies. 2 vols New York 1965. On Thomas Wight, Thomas Thorpe, Nathaniel Butler and Nicholas Bourne, John Bellamy, William Dugard, Michael Sparke and Livewell Chapman.

Bald, R. C. Dr Donne and the booksellers. SB 18 1965.

Miller, W. E. Printers and stationers in the parish of St Giles Cripplegate 1561–1640. SB 19 1966.

Redlich, F. Some English stationers of the 17th and 18th centuries in the light of their autobiographies. Business History 8 1966.

(2) THE STATIONERS' COMPANY

Many original documents on the formation and early history of the Company and the trade generally were ptd in a usually reliable transcript in Arber's Transcript of the Stationers' registers, below. These documents were inserted by Arber where he thought appropriate, and are not easy to find. All these documents are calendared (with Arber's transcript corrected), and other documents ptd for the first time in Greg, Companion to Arber, below.

The Orders, Rules and Ordinances made by the Mystery of Stationers of London. 1678, 1692 (with addns), [c. 1860] (facs).

The Charters and Grants of the Company now in force. 1741, 1825.

Nichols, John. The Stationers' Company. In Literary anecdotes of the xviiith century vol 3, 1812.

— Historical notices of the Worshipful Company of Stationers of London. 1864.

A sketch of the history and privileges of the Company. 1871.

Arber, E. (ed). Transcript of the registers of the Company of Stationers of London 1554–1640. 5 vols 1875–94.

Rivington, C. R. The records of the Worshipful Company of Stationers of London. 1883; rptd in Trans of Middlesex Archaeological Soc 6 1885; and by E. Arber, Transcript of the registers vol 5, 1894.

— A short account of the Worshipful Company of Stationers. 1903 (priv ptd). Mainly rptd from notes on the Stationers' Company, Library 2nd ser 4 1903.

— A brief account of the Worshipful Company of Stationers. [1910].

A concise account of the origin and present position of the English stock of the Stationers' Company; also the charter of the Company, and the grants of the English Stock, and the byelaws regulating the Stock. 1893 (priv ptd).

Index to Liber A of the records of the Company of Stationers. 1902 (priv ptd).

Plomer, H. R. Some notes on the Latin and Irish stocks of the Company of Stationers. Library 8 1907.

— Catalogue of records at Stationers' Hall, with an introductory note by A. W. Pollard. Library 4th ser 6 1926.

Eyre, G. E. B. (ed). Transcript of the registers of the Worshipful Company of Stationers 1640–1708 [1709]. 3 vols 1913–14 (Roxburghe Club).

Records of the Court of the Stationers' Company, 1576 to 1602 from Register B. Ed W. W. Greg and E. Boswell 1930 (Bibl Soc).

Siebert, F. S. Regulation of the press in the seventeenth century: excerpts from the records of the court of the Stationers' Company. Journalism Quart 13 1936.

Pollard, H. G. The Company of Stationers before 1557. Library 4th ser 18 1937.

— The early constitution of the Stationers' Company. Ibid.

Hodgson, S. Papers and documents recently found at Stationers' Hall. Library 4th ser 25 1945.

Johnson, J. and S. Gibson. Print and privilege at Oxford to 1700. 1946.

Thomas, S. Richard Smith: 'foreign to the Company'. Library 5th ser 3 1948.

Howe, E. The London compositor. 1947.

— A list of London bookbinders 1648–1815. 1950 (Bibl Soc). For the operation of the Company *see* introd.

Dickins, B. Stationers made free of the City in 1551/2 and 1552. Trans Cambridge Bibl Soc 1 1950.

Blagden, C. The English stock of the Stationers' Company. Library 5th ser 10 1955.

— The English Stock of the Stationers' Company in the time of the Stuarts. Library 5th ser 12 1957.

— Charter trouble: written on the occasion of the quater-centenary of the granting of a charter to the Stationers' Company. Book Collector 6 1957.

— Early Cambridge Printers and the Stationers' Company. Trans Cambridge Bibl Soc 2 1957.

— The Stationers' Company in the Civil War Period. Library 5th ser 13 1958.

— The Stationers' Company: a history 1403–1959. 1960.

— The 'Company' of printers. SB 13 1960.

Greg, W. W. Richard Robinson and the Stationers' Register. MLR 50 1955; rptd in his Collected papers, Oxford 1966.

— The English stock of the Stationers' Company. Library 5th ser 11 1956.

— A companion to Arber. Oxford 1967.

Kirschbaum, L. Shakespeare and the Stationers. Columbus 1955.

Jackson, W. A. Records of the Court of the Stationers' Company 1602–40. 1957 (Bibl Soc).

— Variant entry fees of the Stationers' Company. PBSA 51 1957.

Kahl, W. F. A checklist of books, pamphlets and broadsides in the London Livery companies. Guildhall Miscellany 2 1962.

Bond, R. P. John Partridge and the Company of Stationers. SB 16 1963.

Pritchard, A. George Withers' quarrel with the stationers. SB 16 1963.

Colson, N. E. Wither and the stationers. SB 19 1966.

Morris, J. Restrictive practices in the Elizabethan book trade: the Stationers' Company v. Thomas Thomas 1583–8. Trans Cambridge Bibl Soc 4 1967.

(3) LABOUR RELATIONS

Furniss, E. S. The position of the laborer in a system of nationalism. Boston 1920.

Plant, M. The English book trade: an economic history of the making and sale of books. 1939.

Howe, E. 'The trade': passages from the literature of the printing craft 1550–1935. 1943 (priv ptd).

— The London compositor. 1947.

Coleman, D. C. Labour in the English economy of the 17th century. Economic History Rev 2nd ser 8 1956.

McKenzie, D. F. Apprenticeship in the Stationers' Company, 1555–1640. Library 5th ser 13 1958.

— A list of printers' apprentices 1605–40. SB 13 1960.

— Stationers' Company apprentices 1605–40. Charlottesville 1961.

Voet, L. The printers' chapel in the Plantinian house. Library 5th ser 16 1961.

Avis, F. C. Chapel rules of the early printers. Gutenberg Jahrbuch 1969.

(4) PATENTEES

Price, W. H. The English patents of monopoly. 1906.

Steele, R. Catalogue of royal proclamations. 1910. Introd on patents.

The University Patents

Johnson, J. and S. Gibson. Print and privilege at Oxford to 1700. Oxford 1946.

The King's Printer

Plomer, H. R. The King's Printing House under the Stuarts. Library 2nd ser 2 1901.

Steele, R. The King's Printers. Library 4th ser 7 1927.

The Bible Patent

Pollard, A. W. Records of the English Bible. 1911.

The English Stock of the Stationers' Company

The orders, rules and ordinances made by the Mystery of Stationers of London. 1678; suppls 1681, 1683; 1692; [c. 1860] (facs of 1692).

The charters and grants of the Company now in force. 1741, 1825.

Nichols, J. G. Literary anecdotes of the 18th century vol 3. 1812.

—— Historical notices of the Worshipful Company of Stationers of London. Trans of London & Middlesex Archaeological Soc 2 1861.

A concise account of the origin and present position of the English Stock of the Stationers' Company; also the charter of the Company, and the grants of the English Stock, and the byelaws regulating the Stock. 1893 (priv ptd).

The Law Patent

Atkins, R. The original and growth of printing, collected out of history and the records of this kingdome, wherein is also demonstrated that printing appertaineth to the prerogative royal; and is a flower of the crown of England. 1664.

The case of the booksellers and printers stated; with answers to the objections of the patentee [Colonel Atkins]. [1666].

The case of the booksellers and printers, relating to the patentees for the sole printing all books of the common-law. [1669?].

The King's grant of privilege for the sole printing common-law-books defended and the legality thereof asserted. 1669.

Spencer, L. The printing of Sir George Croke's reports. SB 11 1958.

Salmon, V. An ambitious printing project of the early seventeenth century. Library 5th ser 16 1961. The exploitation of Joseph Webbe's textbook patent.

J. LONDON PRINTERS AND BOOKSELLERS

For lists and accounts of London printers and booksellers, see above.

Edward Allde

McKerrow, R. B. Allde as a typical trade printer. Library 4th ser 10 1930.

John Awdelay

Jones, E. J. Tra vo lleuad. Nat Lib of Wales Jnl 5 1947. First Welsh prayer book and psalter ptd in 1567 by Awdelay.

William Barley

Lievsay, J. L. Barley: Elizabethan printer and bookseller. SB 8 1956.

Thomas Basson

Van Dorsten, J. A. Basson 1555–1613: English printer at Leiden. Leyden 1961.

John Bellamy

Rostenberg, L. Literary, political, scientific, religious and legal publishing, printing and bookselling in England 1551–1700. New York 1965.

Thomas Berthelet

Davenport, C. J. Berthelet: printer and bookbinder to Henry VIII. Chicago 1901 (Caxton Club).

Rose-Troup, F. Two book bills of Catherine Parr. Library 3rd ser 2 1911.

Clair, C. Thomas Berthelet. Gutenberg Jahrbuch 1966.

John Biddel and James Gaver, successors to Wynkyn de Worde

Jackson, W. A. A London booksellers' ledger of 1535. Colophon 1936.

Pollard, H. G. and A. Ehrman. The distribution of books by catalogue. 1965 (Roxburghe Club).

Edward Blount

Lee, S. An Elizabethan bookseller. Bibliographica 1 1895.

R. Blower

Sturman, B. A date and a printer for A looking glasse for London and England Q4. SB 21 1968.

Samuel Browne

Weil, E. Browne: printer to the University of Heidelberg 1655–62. Library 5th ser 5 1950.

Thomas Brudenell

Plomer, H. R. A printer's bill in the xviith century. Library 1st ser 7 1906.

John Busby

Greg, W. W. The two John Busby's. Library 4th ser 24 1944.

Nathaniel Butter and Nicholas Bourne

Rostenberg, L. Literary, political, scientific, religious and legal publishing, printing and bookselling in England 1551–1700. New York 1965.

Henry Bynneman

Plomer, H. R. Bynneman: printer 1566–83. Library 1st ser 9 1908.

Giacopo Castelvetro

Rosenberg, E. Castelvetro: Italian publisher in Elizabethan London and his patrons. HLQ 6 1943.

William Caxton

Middleton, C. The origin of printing in England. Cambridge 1735.

Lewis, J. The life of Caxton. 1737.

Blades, W. The life and typography of Caxton. 2 vols 1861–3, 1877 (as The biography), 1882 (rev), 1897.

Duff, E. William Caxton. Chicago 1905 (Caxton Club).

de Ricci, S. A census of Caxtons. 1909 (Bibl Soc).

Plomer, H. R. William Caxton. 1925.

Aurner, N. S. Caxton. 1926.

Caxton's prologues and epilogues. Ed W. J. B. Crotch 1928 (EETS). With preliminary summary of recently discovered material.

Pollard, A. W. The New Caxton indulgence. Library 4th ser 9 1929.

Crotch, W. J. B. Caxton's son-in-law. Ibid.

Hittmair, R. Caxton: Englands erster Drucker und Verleger. Innsbruck 1931.

Bühler, C. F. The dictes and sayings of the Philosophers. Library 4th ser 15 1935.

—— Caxton variants. Library 4th ser 17 1937.

—— Three notes on Caxton. Ibid.

—— Caxton's history of Jason. PBSA 34 1940.

—— Two Caxton problems. Library 4th ser 20 1940.

—— The bindings of books printed by Caxton. PBSA 38 1944.

—— Caxton's Blanchardin and Eglantine. PBSA 39 1945.

—— Some observations on the dictes and sayings of the philosophers. Library 5th ser 8 1953.

—— Corrections in Caxton's Cordiale. PBSA 48 1954.

—— A Caxton ghost made and laid. PBSA 59 1965.

Oakeshott, W. F. Caxton and Malory's Morte D'Arthur. Gutenberg Jahrbuch 1935.

Bennett, H. S. Caxton and his public. RES 19 1943.

Legman, G. A word on Caxton's dictes. Library 5th ser 3 1948.

Jeremy, Sr M. Caxton's original additions to the Legenda aurea. MLN 64 1949.

Mortimer, J. E. An unrecorded Caxton at Ripon Cathedral. Library 5th ser 8 1953.

Ruysschaert, J. Les manuscrits autographes de deux oeuvres de Lorenzo Guglielmo Traversagni imprimées chez Caxton. Bull John Rylands Lib 36 1954.

Kerling, N. J. M. Caxton and the trade in printed books. Book Collector 4 1955.

Morgan, P. and G. D. Painter. The Caxton Legenda at St Mary's. Warwick. Library 5th ser 12 1957.

Tanner, L. C. Caxton's houses at Westminster. Library 5th ser 12 1957.

Sands, D. B. Caxton as a literary critic. PBSA 50 1957.

Lenaghan, R. T. The variants in Caxton's Esope. PBSA 55 1961.

Painter, G. D. Caxton through the looking glass: an enquiry into the offsets on a fragment of Caxton bindings. Gutenberg Jahrbuch 1963.

Pollard, M. and A. N. L. Munby. Did Mr Cavendish burn his Caxtons? Book Collector 12 1963.

Vocabulary in French and English: a facsimile of Caxton's edition c. 1480. Ed J. C. T. Oates and L. C. Harmer, Cambridge 1964.

Blake, N. F. Caxton and the Mercers' Company. Book Collector 15 1966.

—— William Caxton. 1969.

Herbrüggen, H. S. Unbekannte Einbände aus Caxtons Werkstatt. In Festschrift für Edgar Mertner, Munich 1969.

Livewell Chapman

Rostenberg, L. Literary, political, scientific, religious and legal publishing, printing and bookselling in England 1551–1770. New York 1965.

Thomas Chard

Jahn, R. Letters and book-lists of Thomas Chard 1583–4. Library 4th ser 4 1924.

Paige, D. An additional letter and booklist of Chard, stationer of London 1588/90. Library 4th ser 21 1941.

Berry, L. E. Charde: printer and bookseller. Library 5th ser 15 1960.

John Charlewood

Lavin, J. A. The first two printers of Sidney's Astrophil and Stella. Library 5th ser 26 1971.

Philip Chetwind

Farr, H. Chetwind and the Allott Copyrights. Library 4th ser 15 1935.

Thomas Colwell

Hale, D. G. Colwell: Elizabethan printer. Library 5th ser 19 1964.

Robert Copland

Plomer, H. R. Copland: printer and translator. Trans Bibl Soc 3 1896.

Andrew Crooke

Stevenson, A. H. Shirley's publishers: the partnership of Crooke and Cooke. Library 4th ser 25 1945.

John Danter

Lavin, J. A. *See Charlewood, above.*

John Day

Nichols, J. G. Day the printer. GM Nov and suppl 1832.

Munby, A. N. L. The gifts of Elizabethan printers to the library of King's College, Cambridge. Library 5th ser 2 1947.

Bromwich, J. The first book printed in Anglo-Saxon types. Trans Cambridge Bibl Soc 3 1962.

Wakeman, G. The design of Day's saxon. Library 5th ser 22 1967.

Henry Denham

Plomer, H. R. Henry Denham, printer. Library 2nd ser 10 1909.

Gregory Dexter

Wan, P. F. Dexter of London and New England, 1610–1700. Rochester NY 1949.

Robert Dexter

Greg, W. W. The English schoolmaster: Dexter v. Burby 1602. Library 4th ser 23 1943.

William Dugard

Rostenberg, L. Literary, political, scientific, religious and legal publishing, printing and bookselling in England 1551–1700. New York 1965.

Thomas East

Plomer, H. R. Thomas East, printer. Library 2nd ser 2 1901.

Eliot's Court Printing House

Plomer, H. R. The Eliot's Court Printing House 1584–1674. Library 4th ser 2 1922.

—— The Eliot's Court Press: decorative blocks and initials. Library 4th ser 3 1923.

Richard Field

Kirwood, A. E. M. Richard Field, printer. Library 4th ser 12 1931.

William Fitzer

Weil, E. Fitzer: the publisher of Harvey's De motu cordis 1628. Library 4th ser 24 1944.

Thomas Godfrey

Butterworth, C. C. The Godfrey edition of Proverbs and Ecclesiastes. Friends of Pennsylvania Univ Lib Chron 15 1948.

Richard Grafton

Kingdon, J. A. Incidents in the lives of Thomas Poyntz and Richard Grafton. 1895 (priv ptd).

—— Richard Grafton, citizen and grocer of London: a sequel to Poyntz and Grafton. 1901 (priv ptd).

Sisson, C. J. Grafton and the London Grey Friars. Library 4th ser 11 1931.

William Jaggard

Jaggard, W. Shakespeare's publishers: notes on the Tudor-Stuart period of the Jaggard Press. Liverpool 1907.

Willoughby, E. E. A printer of Shakespeare: the books and times of Jaggard.

William Jones

Curtis, M. H. Jones: Puritan printer and propagandist. Library 5th ser 19 1964.

Richard Jugge

Munby, A. N. L. The gifts of Elizabethan printers to the library of King's College, Cambridge. Library 5th ser 2 1947.

Francis Kirkham

Head, R. and F. Kirkman. The English rogue. 1665, 1672, 1680, 1679, [1700?], 1723, 1759, 1776 etc (abridged). Pt 2 chs 22–4 is a first-hand if fictitious account of the contemporary bookseller's life.

Bald, R. C. Kirkman: bookseller and author. MP 41 1944.

Francis Kirkman

Gibson, S. A bibliography of Kirkman. Pbns Oxford Bibl Soc new ser 1 1949.

Gerritsen, J. The dramatic piracies of 1661: a comparative analysis. SB 2 1958.

William Leybourn

Kenney, C. E. William Leybourn 1662–1716. Library 5th ser 5 1950.

Nicholas Ling

Hebel, J. W. Ling and England's Helicon. Library 4th ser 5 1925.

William de Machlinia

Smith, G. William de Machlinia: the Primer on Vellum printed by him in London about 1484. 1929.

Dialogus de libertate ecclesiastica 1483. Berlin 1932 (facs).

Stephen Mierdman

Hoppe, H. R. The birthplace of Stephen Mierdman, Flemish printer in London c. 1549–52. Library 5th ser 3 1948.

Clair, C. On the printing of certain Reformation Books. Library 5th ser 18 1963. Books with London imprints actually printed by Crom, Mierdman etc.

Wijnman, H. F. The mysterious sixteenth-century printer Nicolaes von Oldenborch: Antwerp or Emden? In Studia bibliographica in honorem Herman de la Fontaine Verwey, Amsterdam 1966.

Vervliet, H. D. L. Sixteenth-century printing types of the Low countries. Amsterdam 1968.

Humphrey Moseley

Reed, J. C. Humphrey Moseley, publisher. Proc Oxford Bibl Soc 2 1928.

Joseph Moxon

Davis, H. and H. Carter (ed). Joseph Moxon, Mechanick exercises on the whole art of printing. Oxford 1958, 1962 (rev).

Carter, H. and B. Wolpe. Pepys's copy of Moxon's Mechanick exercises. Library 5th ser 14 1959.

Bliss, C. S. Some aspects of 17th-century English publishing with special reference to Joseph Moxon. Los Angeles 1965.

Julian Notary and Andrew Rowe

Welch, C. E. Julian Notary and Andrew Rowe: two contemporary records. Library 5th ser 11 1956.

John Playford

Day, C. L. and E. B. Murrie. Playford v. Pearson. Library 4th ser 18 1938.

William Pickering

Gray, G. J. Pickering: the earliest bookseller on London Bridge 1556–71. Trans of Bibl Soc 4 1898.

Richard Pynson

Plomer, H. R. Pynson v. Henry Squyer. Trans Bibl Soc 6 1904.

—— Two law-suits of Pynson. Library 2nd ser 10 1909.

—— Pynson: glover and printer. Library 4th ser 3 1923.

Pynson's dealings with John Russhe. Library 3rd ser 9 1918.

Morgan, M. M. Pynson's manuscript of Dives and Pauper. Library 5th ser 8 1953.

Oates, J. C. T. Pynson and the Holy Blood of Hayles. Library 5th ser 13 1958.

Rhodes, D. E. Some documents printed by Pynson for St Botolph's, Boston, Lincs. Library 5th ser 15 1960.

John Rastell

Plomer, H. R. Rastell and his contemporaries. Bibliographica 2 1896.

Reed, A. W. Rastell, printer, lawyer, venturer, dramatist and controversialist. Trans of Bibl Soc 17 1919.

Nash, R. Rastell fragments at Dartmouth. Library 4th ser 24 1944.

King, A. H. The significance of Rastell in early music printing. Library 5th ser 26 1971.

William Rastell

Reed, A. W. The editor of Sir Thomas More's English Works: Rastell. Library 4th ser 4 1924.

—— Early Tudor drama: Medwall, the Rastells, Heywood and the More circle. 1926.

Vervliet, H. D. L. Sixteenth-century printing types of the Low Countries. Amsterdam 1968.

Robert Redman

Butterworth, C. C. Redman's Prayers of the Byble 1535. Library 5th ser 3 1948.

Robert Robinson

Welsh, R. F. The printer of the 1594 octavo of Marlowe's Edward II. SB 17 1964. Robert Robinson, not Richard Bradock.

John Rothwell

Parker, W. R. Milton, Rothwell and Simmons. Library 4th ser 18 1938.

John Shirley

Brusendorff, A. The Chaucer tradition. Copenhagen 1925.

Hammond, E. P. English verse between Chaucer and Surrey. 1927.

Bennett, H. S. Chaucer and the fifteenth century. Oxford 1947 (OHEL).

Peter Short

Thompson, S. P. Peter Short, printer and his marks. Trans Bibl Soc 4 1898.

Hugh Singleton

Byron, H. J. Spenser's first printer: Hugh Singleton. Library 4th ser 14 1933.

Richard Smith

Thomas, S. Richard Smith: foreign to the Company. Library 5th ser 3 1948.

Michael Sparke

Rostenberg, L. Literary, political, scientific, religious and legal publishing, printing and bookselling in England 1551–1700. New York 1965.

William Stansby

Davis R. B. George Sandys v. Stansby: the 1632 edition of Ovid's Metamorphosis. Library 5th ser 3 1948.

George Thomason

The will of George Thomason. Library 2nd ser 10 1909.

See also G. K. Fortescue, Introduction to the catalogue of the Thomasson tracts in the British Museum.

Spencer, L. The professional and literary connexions of Thomason. Library 5th ser 13 1958.

Thomas Thorpe

Rostenberg, L. Literary, political, scientific, religious and legal publishing, printing and bookselling in England 1551–1700. New York 1965.

Richard Tottel

Plomer, H. R. Richard Tottel. Bibliographica 3 1897.

Byrom, H. J. Tottel his life and work. Library 4th ser 8 1928.

Thomas Vautrollier

Lefanu, W. R. Thomas Vautrollier, printer and bookseller. Proc Huguenot Soc of London 20 1958–64.

—— André Wechel (with a checklist of his publications 1553–81). Proc Huguenot Soc of London 21 1966.

Kirschbaum, L. The copyright of Elizabethan plays. Library 5th ser 14 1959.

Clair, C. Christopher Plantin's trade connections with England. Library 5th ser 15 1960.

—— Thomas Vautrollier. Gutenberg Jahrbuch 1960.

Pepper, Robert D. Francis Clement's Petie schole at the Vautrollier Press 1587. Library 5th ser 22 1967.

Thomas Walkley

Simpson, P. Walkley's piracy of Wither's Poems in 1620. Library 4th ser 6 1926.

Henry Walley

Finkelpearl, P. J. Walley of the Stationers' Company and John Marston. PBSA 56 1962.

John Wayland

Byrom, H. J. John Wayland: printer, scrivener and litigant. Library 4th ser 11 1931.

Jackson, W. A. Wayland's edition of the Mirror for magistrates. Library 4th ser 13 1933.

Richard Whitaker

Bohannon, M. E. A London bookseller's bill 1635–9. Library 4th ser 18 1938.

Thomas Wight

Rostenberg, L. Literary, political, scientific, religious and legal publishing, printing and bookselling in England 1551–1700. New York 1965.

Edward Winslow

Wolkins, G. G. Winslow (OV 1606–11), King's scholar and printer. Proc Amer Antiquarian Soc 60 1951.

John Wolfe

Hoppe, H. R. Wolfe: printer and publisher 1579–1601. Library 4th ser 14 1933.

Benger, F. B. Wolfe and a Spanish book. Library 5th ser 3 1948. Tractado 1559 with Turin imprint, ptd in London.
Reyner Wolfe
Sayle, C. E. Reyner Wolfe. Trans of Bibl Soc 13 1915.
Wynkyn de Worde
Plomer, H. R. Wynkyn de Worde and his contemporaries. 1925.
Bone, G. Extant mss printed from by Wynkyn de Worde. Library 4th ser 12 1931.
Bowers, F. T. Printing evidence in Wynkyn de Worde's

edition of the Life of Johan Picus by St Thomas More. PBSA 43 1949.
Mitchner, R. W. Wynkyn de Worde's use of the Plumpton manuscript of De proprietatibus rerum. Library 5th ser 6 1951.
Mead, H. R. A new title from de Worde's press. Library 5th ser 9 1954.
Robert Wyer
Plomer, H. R. Wyer: printer and bookseller. 1897 (Bibl Soc).
Lathrop, H. B. Some rogueries of Wyer. Library 3rd ser 5 1914.

K. PRINTING AND BOOKSELLING IN THE PROVINCES

Cotton, H. Typographical gazetteer. 2 sers Oxford 1831 (2nd edn), Oxford 1866.
Allnutt, W. H. Notes of printers and printing in the provincial towns of England and Wales. 1879. With an alphabetical list of towns, specifying date, printer, book and reference.
— English provincial presses. Bibliographica 2 1896.
Plomer, H. R. and R. A. Peddie. Stephen Bulkley, printer. Library 8 1907.
Duff, E. G. The English provincial printers, stationers and bookbinders to 1557. Cambridge 1912.
Humphreys, A. L. A handbook to county bibliography. 1917.
Bloom, J. H. English tracts, pamphlets and printed sheets, issued in Suffolk, Leicester, Stafford, Warwick and Worcester 1473–1650. 2 vols 1922–3.
Hawkes, A. J. The Birchley Hall Secret Press. Library 4th ser 7 1927. Reply by C. A. Newdigate, below.
Cole, G. W. Index to bibliographical papers. 1933.
Morgan, P. English provincial printing. Birmingham 1958 (priv ptd).
— English provincial imprints. Library 5th ser 22 1967.
Historical Manuscripts Commission. Record repositories in Great Britain. 1964.
Isaac, P. C. G. The history of the book trade in the North: a preliminary report on a group research project. Library 5th ser 23 1968.
Bristol
Hyett, F. A. Notes on the first Bristol and Gloucestershire printers. Trans Bristol & Gloucestershire Archaeological Soc 20 1896.
Cambridge
Bowes, R. Biographical notes on the University printers. Cambridge Antiquarian Soc Communications 26 1886; Cambridge 1886 (separately).
— A catalogue of books printed at or relating to Cambridge 1521–1893. Cambridge 1894. Index by E. J. Worman, Cambridge 1894.
— and G. J. Gray. John Siberch: bibliographical notes 1886–1905. Cambridge 1906.
Bradshaw, H. On the books printed by John Siberch at Cambridge in 1521–2. Introd, facs. Henry Bullock's Oratorio, Cambridge 1886.
Jenkinson, F. J. H. On a letter from P. Kaetz to J. Siberch. Proc Cambridge Antiquarian Soc 7 1893.
Gray, G. J. The earlier Cambridge stationers and bookbinders and the first Cambridge printer. 1904 (Bibl Soc).
— and W. M. Palmer. Abstracts from the wills and testamentary documents of printers, binders and stationers of Cambridge 1504–1699. 1915.
Gray, G. J. John Siberch, the first Cambridge printer 1521–2. Cambridge 1921.
— The Cambridge University Press and John Siberch. Library 4th ser 8 1928.
Bartholomew, A. T. Catalogue of books bequeathed to the University by John Willis Clark. 1912.
Roberts, S. C. A history of the Cambridge University Press 1521–1921. Cambridge 1921.

Barnes, G. R. A list of books printed in Cambridge at the University Press 1521–1800. Cambridge 1935.
Munby, A. N. L. The gifts of Elizabethan printers to the library of King's College, Cambridge. Library 5th ser 2 1947. Includes Thomas Thomas.
Ferguson, F. S. John Siberch of Cambridge: an unrecorded book from his press and new light on his material. Trans Cambridge Bibl Soc 1 1949–53.
Blagden, C. Early Cambridge printers and the Stationers' Company. Trans Cambridge Bibl Soc 2 1957.
Stevenson, A. Thomas Thomas makes a dictionary. Library 5th ser 13 1958.
Morris, J. Restrictive practices in the Elizabethan book trade: the Stationers' Company v. Thomas Thomas 1583–8. Trans Cambridge Bibl Soc 4 1967.
— Thomas Thomas, printer to the University of Cambridge 1583–8. Trans Cambridge Bibl Soc 4 1968.
Corsten, S. 'Primus utriusque linguae in Anglia impressor': Johann Lair von Siegburg und seine Typen. In Heimatbuch der Stadt Siegburg vol 2, Siegburg 1967.
Treptow, O. Johann Lair von Sieburg—John Siberch—der erste Buchdrucker der Universität Cambridge. Ibid; tr Cambridge 1971.
Canterbury
Plomer, H. R. James Abree: printer and bookseller of Canterbury. 1913.
Chester
Stewart-Brown, R. A Chester bookseller's lawsuit of 1653. Library 4th ser 9 1929.
— The stationers, booksellers and printers of Chester. Trans Historical Soc of Lancs & Cheshire 83 1934.
Devonshire
Dredge, J. I. Devon booksellers and printers in the 17th and 18th centuries, with three supplements. Plymouth 1885–91 (priv ptd).
Attwood, J. S. Booksellers and printers in Devon and Cornwall in the 17th and 18th centuries. Plymouth 1917 (priv ptd). Suppl to Dredge, above.
Exeter
Plomer, H. R. An Exeter bookseller [John Gropall], his friends and contemporaries. Library 3rd ser 8 1917.
Baldwin, T. W. Loves labours won. Carbondale 1957. Fragments of Christopher Hunt's daybook, below.
Ipswich
Beck, F. G. M. A new Ipswich book of 1548. Library 2nd ser 10 1909.
Watson, S. F. Some materials for a history of printing and publishing in Ipswich. Proc Suffolk Inst of Archaeology 24 1949.
Manchester
Earwaker, J. P. Notes on the booksellers of Manchester prior to 1700. Trans Lancashire & Cheshire Antiquarian Soc 6 1888.
Newcastle
Welford, R. Early Newcastle typography 1639–1800. Newcastle 1907. Rptd from Archaeologia Aeliana 3rd ser 3 1907.

Newcastle-upon-Tyne Public Libraries Commission. Local catalogue of material concerning Newcastle and Northumberland. Newcastle 1932. With index of printers 1639–1850.

Oxford

The day-book of John Dorne 1520. Ed F. Madan, Oxford Historical Society Collectanea vol 1, 1885. An earlier day-book, c. 1519, is recorded by Madan in vol 2.

Madan, F. The early Oxford press '1468'–1640. Oxford 1895.

—— A chart of Oxford printing '1468'–1900. 1904 (Bibl Soc).

—— Oxford literature 1450–1640 and 1641–50. Oxford 1912. Really vol 2 of the Early Oxford press, above.

—— Oxford literature 1651–80. Oxford 1931.

—— The Oxford Press: the struggle for a place in the sun 1650–75. Library 4th ser 6 1926.

—— Oxford books: vol 3 1650–1800. Oxford 1931.

Duff, E. G. A bookseller's accounts circa 1510. Library 1st ser 8 1907.

Gibson, S. Abstracts from the wills and testamentary documents of binders, printers and stationers of Oxford, from 1493 to 1638. 1907 (Bib. Soc).

Lindsay, T. M. An Oxford bookseller [John Dorne] in 1520. Glasgow 1907.

Gibson, S. and D. M. Rogers. The Earl of Leicester and printing at Oxford. Bodleian Lib Record 2 1949.

Gibson, S. and J. Johnson. Print and privilege at Oxford to the year 1700. Oxford 1946.

Morison, S. and H. Carter. John Fell, the University Press and the 'Fell' types bequeathed in 1686 to Oxford by Fell. Oxford 1967.

Cordeaux, E. H. and D. H. Merry. A bibliography of printed works relating to the University of Oxford. Oxford 1968.

St Albans

Blades, W. Some account of the typography of St Albans in the xvth century. 1860 (priv ptd).

Shrewsbury

Allnutt, W. H. The King's printer at Shrewsbury. Library 1st ser 1 1900.

Lloyd, L. C. The book trade in Shropshire. Trans Shropshire Archaeological & Natural History Soc 48 1936.

Rodger, A. Roger Ward's Shrewsbury stock: an inventory of 1585. Library 5th ser 13 1958.

Shropshire

Lloyd, L. C. The book trade in Shropshire: some account of the stationers, booksellers and printers at work in the county to about 1800. Trans Shropshire Archaeological & Natural History Soc 48 1936.

Somerset

Green, E. Bibliotheca somersetiensis. 3 vols Taunton 1902.

Staffordshire

Simms, R. Bibliotheca staffordiensis. Lichfield 1894.

Stratford-upon-Avon

Morgan, P. Early booksellers, printers and publishers in Stratford. Trans Birmingham Archaeological Soc 67 1948.

Warrington

Rylands, W. H. Booksellers in Warrington 1639 to 1657; with the full list of the contents of a stationer's shop there in 1647. Proc Historical Soc of Lancs & Cheshire 37 1888.

Winchester

Piper, A. C. The book trade in Winchester 1549–1789. Library 2nd ser 7 1916.

Worcestershire

Burton, J. R. Early Worcestershire printers and books. Associated Architectural Soc Reports (Lincoln) 24 1897.

York

Davies, R. A memoir of the York Press in the 16th, 17th and 18th centuries. Westminster 1868.

L. SCOTTISH PRINTING AND BOOKSELLING

Aldis, H. G. A list of books printed in Scotland before 1700. 1904 (Edinburgh Bibl Soc), 1972 (enlarged).

Reid, J. Bibliotheca scoto-gadelica. Glasgow 1832.

Dickson, R. and J. P. Edmond. Annals of Scottish printing from the introduction of the art in 1507 to the beginning of the xviith century. Cambridge 1890.

Edmond, J. P. Bibliographical gleanings 1890–3: being additions and corrections to the annals of Scottish printing. Papers of Edinburgh Bibl Soc 1 1896.

Mackay, S. A short note of the local presses of Scotland; with a list of books relating to Fife. Papers of Edinburgh Bibl Soc 3 1899.

Maclean, D. Typographia scoto-gadelica: or books printed in the Gaelic of Scotland [1567–1914]. Edinburgh 1915.

Duff, E. G. The fifth edition of Burton's Anatomy of melancholy. Library 4th ser 4 1924.

Bald, M. A. Vernacular books imported into Scotland 1500 to 1625. Scottish Historical Rev 23 1926.

Ferguson, F. S. Relations between London and Edinburgh printers and stationers to 1640. Library 4th ser 8 1928.

Couper, W. J. Copyright in Scotland before 1709. Trans Glasgow Bibl Soc 1931.

Johnson, A. F. Type-designs and type founding in Scotland. Trans Edinburgh Bibl Soc 2 1944.

Avis, F. C. The first hundred years of Scottish printing. Gutenberg Jahrbuch 1955.

Aberdeen

Edmond, J. P. The Aberdeen printers: Edward Raban to James Nicol 1620–1736. Aberdeen 1886.

—— Last notes on the Aberdeen printers. Aberdeen 1888.

Duff, E. G. The early career of Edward Raban, afterwards first printer at Aberdeen. Library 3rd ser 2 1922.

Johnstone, J. F. K. and A. W. Robertson. Bibliographia Aberdonensis: being an account of books relating to or printed in the shires of Aberdeen, Banff, Kincardine, or written by natives or residents, or by officers, graduates or alumni of the Universities of Aberdeen. Vol 1 (–1640), vol 2 (1641–1700). Aberdeen 1929–30 (Third Spalding Club).

Edinburgh

Inventory of work done for the State by his Majesty's Printer in Scotland (Evan Tyler) 1642–7. Edinburgh 1815.

Lee, J. Memorial for the Bible Societies of Scotland: containing remarks on the complaint of His Majesty's printer against the Marquess of Huntly and others, with an appendix of original papers. Edinburgh 1824. Also Additional memorial, Edinburgh 1826; and W. J. Couper, An index to Principal Lee's Memorial for the Bible Societies of Scotland, Glasgow 1918.

Collection of the wills of printers and stationers in Edinburgh between the years 1577 and 1687. Bannatyne Miscellany 2 1836.

Dobson, W. T. The history of the Bassandyne Bible. Edinburgh 1887.

Edmond, J. P. Notes on the inventories of Edinburgh printers 1577–1603. Papers Edinburgh Bibl Soc 1 1896.

Cowan, W. Andro Hart and his press 1601–39; with a hand-list of books. Ibid.

Aldis, H. G. Thomas Finlason and his press 1604–7, with a hand-list of books. Ibid.

Beattie, W. A hand-list of works from the press of John Wreittoun at Edinburgh 1624–c. 1639. Trans Edinburgh Bibl Soc 2 1941.

Nine tracts from the first Scottish press. Ed W. Beattie, Edinburgh 1950. Chepman and Myllar Prints.

Jackson, W. A. Robert Waldegrave and the books he printed or published in 1603. Library 5th ser 13 1958.

Glasgow

Graham, M. The early Glasgow press. Glasgow 1906.

Couper, W. J. The origins of Glasgow printing. Edinburgh 1911.

Murray, D. Printing in Glasgow 1638–1742. Records Glasgow Bibl Soc 2 1913.

A century of books printed in Glasgow 1638–86, shown in the Kelvingrove Galleries, Glasgow, June 1918. Records Glasgow Bibl Soc 5 1920.

Maclehose, J. The Glasgow University Press 1638–1931. Glasgow 1931.

Perth

Carnie, R. H. Perth booksellers and bookbinders in the records of the wright calling 1538–1864. Bibliotheck 1 1958.

—— Publishing in Perth before 1807. Dundee 1960 (Abertay Historical Soc).

St Andrews

Bushnell, G. H. Catalogue of the productions of the early presses at St Andrews. St Andrews 1926.

—— The life and work of Edward Raban, St Andrews' most famous printer. St Andrews 1928.

Carnie, R. H. Stationers and bookbinders in the records of the Hammermen of St Andrews. Bibliotheck 3 1962.

M. IRISH PRINTING AND BOOKSELLING

Dix, E. R. McC. Irish provincial printing prior to 1701. Library 1st ser 2 1901.

—— List of books, pamphlets etc printed wholly or partly in Irish. Dublin 1905.

—— A list of Irish towns and the dates of the earliest printing in each. Dublin 1909 (2nd edn).

Dottin, G. Les livres irlandais imprimés de 1571 à 1820. Paris 1910.

Lynam, E. W. The Irish character in print 1571–1923. Library 4th ser 4 1924.

Dickins, B. The Irish broadside of 1571 and Queen Elizabeth types. Trans Cambridge Bibl Soc 1 1949–53.

Alden, J. E. Deception in Dublin: problems in 17th-century Irish printing. SB 6 1954.

—— Deception compounded: further problems in 17th-century Irish printing. SB 11 1958.

Walsh, M. O'N. Irish books printed abroad 1475–1700: an interim checklist. Irish Book 2 1963.

Eager, A. R. A guide to Irish bibliographical material: being a bibliography of Irish bibliographies and some sources of information. 1964.

Cork

Dix, E. R. McC. List of books etc printed in the city of Cork in the 17th and 18th centuries. 13 pts Cork

1904–12. Rptd from Jnl Cork Historical & Archaeological Soc. See Proc Royal Irish Acad 30 1913.

Dublin

Dix, E. R. McC. The earliest Dublin printing 1551–1600. Dublin 1901, 1932 (rev as Printing in Dublin prior to 1601).

—— List of books etc printed in Dublin 1601–1700. 4 pts and suppl, Dublin 1898–1912.

—— The earliest Dublin printers and the Company of Stationers of London. Trans Bibl Soc 7 1904.

—— The ornaments used by John Francton, printer at Dublin. Trans Bibl Soc 8 1906.

—— Humfrey Powell: the first Dublin printer. Proc Royal Irish Acad 27 1908.

—— William Kearney: the second Dublin printer. Proc Royal Irish Acad 28 1910.

—— An old Dublin stationer's will and inventory. Library 2nd ser 2 1911. Isaac Gower.

—— The initial letters and factotums used by John Franckton, printer in Dublin. Library 3rd ser 2 1922.

Wall, T. The sign of Dr Hay's head: some account of the hazards and fortunes of Catholic printers and publishers in Dublin from the later penal times to the present. Dublin 1958.

N. WELSH PRINTING AND BOOKSELLING

There was no printing in Wales until 1718, but there are several works of importance dealing with printing in Welsh prior to 1660.

Williams, Moses. Cofrestr o'r holl Lyfrau Printjedig gan mwyaf a gyfansoddwyd yn y Jaith Gymraeg, neu a gyfjeithwyd iddi hyd y Flwyddyn 1717. 1717; rptd Welsh Bibl Soc Carmarthen 1912.

Rowlands, William. Cambrian bibliography 1546–1800 edited and enlarged by D. Silvan Evans. Llanidloes 1869.

Davies, W. Ll. Welsh books entered in the Stationers' Registers, 1554–1708. Jnl Welsh Bibl Soc Carmarthen 2 1921.

Short-title list of Welsh books 1546–1700. Ibid.

O. ENGLISH PRINTING ABROAD

Duthilloeuil, H. R. Bibliographie Douaisienne. Douai 1842 (rev).

Frere, E. Des livres de liturgie des églises d'Angleterre imprimés à Rouen dans les xvme et xvime siècles. Rouen 1867.

Dexter, H. C. Congregationalism of 300 years. 1879.

Theux de Montjardin, X. de. Bibliographie Liégoise. Bruges 1885 (rev).

Gillow, J. A literary and biographical history: or biographical dictionary of English Catholics 1534–1900. 5 vols 1885–1902.

Proctor, R. Jan Van Doesborgh, printer at Antwerp: an essay in bibliography. 1894 (Bibl Soc).

Pollard, A. W. English books printed abroad. Trans Bibl Soc 3 1896.

Bled, O. Les Jésuites anglais à Saint Omer. St Omer 1897.

Haudecoeur, W. G. La conservation providentielle du Catholicisme en Angleterre: ou histoire du Collège Anglais. Rheims 1898.

Wilson, J. D. Richard Schilders and the English Puritans. Trans Bibl Soc 11 1911.

Steele, R. Notes on English books printed abroad 1525–48. Ibid.

—— Hans Lufft of Marburg. Library 3rd ser 2 1911.

Plomer, H. R. The Protestant Press in the reign of Queen Mary. Library 3rd ser 1 1910.

Newdigate, C. A. Notes on the xviith-century printing press of the English College of St Omer. Library 3rd ser 10 1919.

— Birchley—or St Omers. Library 4th ser 7 1927. A rejoinder to A. J. Hawkes, col 965, above.

Harris, R. and S. K. Jones. The Pilgrim Press: a bibliographical and historical memorial of the books printed at Leyden by the Pilgrim Fathers. Cambridge 1922.

Kronenberg, M. E. Notes on English printing in the Low Countries 1491–1540. Library 4th ser 9 1929.

Isaac, F. Egidius van der Erve and his English printed books. Library 4th ser 12 1931.

Johnson, A. F. English books printed abroad. Library 5th ser 4 1949.

Clair, C. On the printing of certain Reformation Books. Library 5th ser 18 1963. Books with London imprints ptd by Crom, Mierdman etc.

Wijnman, H. F. The mysterious sixteenth-century printer Nicolaes van Oldenborch: Antwerp or Emden? In Studia bibliographica in honorem Herman de la Fontaine Verwey. Amsterdam 1966. A comprehensive account, proving that 'Nicolaes van Oldenborch' was a pseudonym used by both Crom and Mierdmans.

P. THE OVERSEAS BOOK TRADE

For the Catalogues of Frankfort Fair books, probably imported by John Bill 1617–27, see col 978, below.

Fetherstone, Henry. Catalogus librorum in diversis locis Italiae emptorum. 1628.

Martine, Robert. Catalogus librorum ex Italia. 1633.

— Catalogus librorum ex Roma, Venetiis aliisque Italiae locis. 1635.

Plomer, H. R. The importation of books into England in the xvth and xvith centuries. Library 4th ser 4 1924.

— The importation of Low Country and French books into England 1480 and 1502–3. Library 4th ser 9 1929.

Baxter, J. H. and C. J. Fordyce. Books published abroad by Scotsmen before 1700. Glasgow Bibl Soc 1933.

Sheppard, L. A. The printers of the Coverdale Bible 1535. Library 4th ser 16 1936.

Hoppé, H. R. The birth-year of Gillis van Diest I, Antwerp printer of English books. Library 5th ser 3 1948.

Johnson, A. F. English books printed abroad. Library 5th ser 4 1949.

— The exiled English Church at Amsterdam and its press. Library 5th ser 5 1950.

Skelton, R. A. Pieter van der Keere. Ibid.

Clair, Colin. Christopher Plantin's trade-connexions with England and Scotland. Library 5th ser 14 1959.

Carter, H. Archbishop Laud and scandalous books from Holland. In Studia bibliographica in honorem Herman de la Fontaine Verwey, Amsterdam 1966.

Lefanu, W. R. André Wechel (with a checklist of his publications 1553–81). Proc Huguenot Soc of London 21 1966.

Van de Woude, S. Sir Henry Savile's Chrysostomus edi-

tion in the Netherlands. In Studia bibliographica in honorem Herman de la Fontaine Verwey, Amsterdam 1966. On Sir Dudley Carleton's vain attempts to use his diplomatic connections to sell his father-in-law's book.

[Thomason, George]. Catalogus librorum in diversis Italiae locis emptorum, anno 1636, qui Londini in caemeterio Sancti Pauli ad insigne rosae prostant venales. 1637. This catalogue has now been definitely attributed to Thomason: see H. G. Pollard and A. Ehrman, The distribution of books by catalogue, 1965.

— Catalogus librorum diversis Italiae locis emptorum. 1647.

Martine, Robert. Catalogus librorum ex praecipuis Italiae emptoriis selectorum. 1639.

— Catalogus librorum e diversis Europae regionibus congestorum. 1640.

— Catalogue des diverses livres Françoises, recueillés dans la France. 1640.

— Catalogus libb. ex Italiae emporiis selectorum. 1650.

Whitaker, Richard. Catalogus librorum quos de Nundinis Francofurtensibus autumnalibus anni 1645, ac alibi comparavit Rich. Whitakerus, bibliopola Londinensis: apud quem jam prostant venales. 1645.

Martin, John and James Allestrye. The library of Joannes Riolan. 1655.

Pulleyn, Octavian. Catalogus librorum in omne genere insignium. 1657.

Bald, M. A. Vernacular books imported into Scotland: 1500 to 1625. Scottish Historical Rev 23 1926.

Q. THE REGULATION OF THE BOOK TRADE

Many of the original documents are ptd in calendared form, if in Arber, Transcript of the registers of the Stationers' Company, or in full in W. W. Greg, A companion to Arber.

(1) GENERAL PRIMARY AUTHORITIES

The original documents from which many of the compilations listed below are abridged are still preserved in the Public Record Office, London. The most useful introd to the various types of document there preserved is the official Guide to the contents of the Public Record Office, 3 vols 1963–8.

Nicolas, Sir Harris. Proceedings and Ordinances of the Privy Council of England. Vol 7 (1540–2), 1837.

Acts of the Privy Council of England. New ser (1542–1621), ed J. R. Dasent et al 37 vols 1890–1930.

Redgrave, G. R. The Privy Council in its relation to literature and printing. Trans Bibl Soc 7 1904.

Calendar of letters and papers, foreign and domestic, of the reign of Henry VIII 1509–47. Ed J. S. Brewer and J. R. Gairdner 21 vols in 34 1862–1910; vol 1 3 pts 1920 (new edn).

Calendar of State papers, domestic series, of the reigns of Edward VI, Mary, Elizabeth and James I preserved in the Public Record Office 1547–1625. Ed R. Lemon and M. A. E. Green 12 vols 1856–72.

Calendar of State papers, domestic series, of the reign of

Charles I (1625–49). Ed J. Bruce, W. D. Hamilton and S. C. Lomas 23 vols 1858–97.

Calendar of State papers, domestic series, of the Commonwealth 1649–60. Ed M. A. E. Green 13 vols 1875–86.

Star Chamber. Many important cases concerning the regulation of printing were heard in the Star Chamber. Those ptd are cited below, but most remain in ms. The best list of these is in C. Schofield, A study of the Court of Star Chamber, Chicago 1900. See also Public Record Office, List of proceedings in the Court of Star Chamber vol 1 (1485–1558), 1901.

BM: Department of mss. Additional ms 326, no 7; see also Harley ms 6265, no 19. These contain the proceedings against Stephen Vallenger in 1582, for distributing seditious books. Star Chamber.

For the control of the book-trade by the University, see Munimenta academica oxon, ed. J Anstey and S. Gibson 1868 (Rolls ser); Statuta antiqua universitatis oxoniensis, Oxford 1931.

Rushworth, John. Historical collections of private passages of state, weightly matters in law, remarkable proceedings in five Parliaments 1618–48. 8 vols 1659–1701, 1721 (best edn). Star Chamber.

Reports of cases in the Star Chamber and Court of High Commission. Ed S. R. Gardiner 1886 (Camden Soc). This covers for the Star Chamber, Easter Term 1631 to Trinity Term 1632; for the Court of High Commission, Oct 1631–June 1632.

Steele, Robert. A bibliography of royal proclamations 1485–1714, with an historical essay. Bibliotheca Lindesiana: catalogue of the printed books (of James Lindsay, Earl of Crawford), vols 5–6, Aberdeen 1910.

Halliwell(-Phillipps), J. O. A collection of ancient documents respecting the office of the Master of the Revels. 1870.

Herbert, Sir Henry. Dramatic records of Sir Henry Herbert, Master of the Revels 1623–73. Ed J. Q. Adams, New Haven 1917.

Marcham, Frank. The King's Office of Revels 1610–22. 1925.

(2) CONTEMPORARY MATERIAL

For various documents see BM Harley ms 5910 (e.g. folios 86, 105–9, 123).

Proclamation for resisting and withstanding the most damnable heresies. 1529. Contains list of prohibited books.

Ordinances decreed [in Star Chamber] for reformation of divers disorders in printing and uttering of Bookes. 1566 (Soc of Antiquaries, Lemon no 57).

Barker, Christopher. A note on the state of the company of printers, booksellers and bookebinders, December 1582. Ms among the Burghley Papers, BM Lansdowne mss vol 48 no 82 (folio 189), ptd in Archaeologia 25 1834, and in Arber I. 114–16, 144.

To the Right Reverend and Right Honourable the Lords Spirituall and Temporal assembled in Parliament, An abstract of the general grievances of the poore freemen and journeymen printers oppressed, and kept in servile bondage all their lives by the unlawful ordinances of the Master and Wardens of the Company which they fortifie only by a warrant dormant. [March 1614?] Broadside: Bagford collection; also Soc of Antiquaries, Lemon no 214; Arber, Transcript of the Stationers' Register vol 4 p. 525.

An abstract of his Majestie's letters patents granted unto Roger Wood and Thomas Symcocke for the sole printing of paper and parchment on the one side. 1620. Broadside.

Wither, George. The schollers purgatory, discovered in the Stationers' Commonwealth, imprinted for the honest stationers. [1625?]; rptd in Miscellaneous works of George Wither, 1st collection, 1872 (Spenser Soc).

The humble petition of the stationers, printers and booksellers of the citie of London, on the introduction of a bill reducing the printers to a certain number, and for the avoiding of unskilful printers. [13 Feb 1631?] (Soc of Antiquaries, Lemon no 312).

A decree of the Starre-Chamber concerning printing, made July 11 1637. 1637; rptd in Memoirs of Thomas Hollis, 2 vols 1780.

An order made by the House of Commons, 29 Jan that the printers doe neither print nor reprint anything without the name and consent of the author. [1641]. Broadside: BM Thomason Tracts E 207 (2).

[Sparke, Michael]. Scintilla: or a light broken into darke warehouses, with observations on the monopolies of seaven severall patents and two charters, practised and performed by a mistery of some printers, sleeping stationers and combining booksellers. 1641; rptd in Arber's transcript vol 4, and in T. H. Darlow and H. F. Moule, Historical catalogue of the printed editions of Holy Scripture in the Library of the British and Foreign Bible Society vol 1, 1903.

A new discovery of the prelate's tyranny in their late prosecutions of Mr William Pryn, Dr John Bastwick and Mr Henry Burton. 1641.

The petition of the printers of London. [March 1642]. BM Thomason tracts 669, folio 4 (79).

The London printer's lamentation. 1642.

An ordinance of the Lords and Commons for prohibiting the printing of any lying pamphlet. 1642.

A briefe relation of certain passages at the censure of Dr Bastwick, Mr Burton and Mr Prynne. 1643; rptd in Harleian miscellany vol 4, 1809.

A particular of the names of the Licensers appointed by the House of Commons for printing. [14 June 1643].

An order of the Lords and Commons for regulating of printing and suppressing the great abuses in printing libels; also authorising the Master and Wardens of the Stationers' Company to make diligent search, seize and carry away all such books etc. 1643.

Milton, John. Areopagitica: or a plea for the liberty of unlicensed printing. 1644.

To the High Court of Parliament: the petition of the masters and workmen printers of London. [1645?]. Broadside: Bagford collection.

An ordinance of the Lords and Commons against unlicensed or scandalous pamphlets, and for better regulating of printing. 1647.

An order of the Commons prohibiting the printing of laying pamphlets. 1647.

To the Commons: the petition of firm friends to the Parliament [in favour of 'the unrestricted freedom of printing']. [18 Jan 1649].

Ball, W. A brief treatise concerning the regulating of printing, humbly presented to the Parliament of England. 1651.

The beacon set on fire: or the humble information of certain stationers. 1652.

[Sparke, Michael]. A second beacon fired by Scintilla. 1652.

The beacons quenched. 1652.

[Cheynell, Francis]. The beacon flameing. 1652.

A second beacon fired. 1654.

Goodwin, John. A fresh discovery of the High-Presbyterian Spirit: or the quenching of the second beacon fired. 1654.

Orders of the Lord Protector for putting into execution the Laws made against printing unlicensed books. 1655.

To Parliament: the petition of the workmen-printers, freemen of the City of London. [14 April 1659]. Against the monopoly of printing Bibles, possessed by Henry Hills and John Field.

The London printer his lamentation: or the press oppressed or overpressed. 1660; rptd in Harleian miscellany vol 3, 1809.

Greg, W. W. A companion to Arber. Oxford 1967.

(3) HISTORICAL ACCOUNTS

Strype, John. The life and acts of John Whitgift. 2 vols 1717–18, 3 vols Oxford 1822 (rev).

[Hart, W. H.] Index expurgatorius anglicanus. 5 pts 1872–8.

Masson, D. The life of John Milton. 6 vols 1859–80, 1881 (vol 1 rev).

Gardiner, S. R. Documents relating to the proceedings against William Prynne in 1634 and 1736, with a biographical fragment by the late John Bruce. 1877 (Camden Soc).

Farber, J. A. Books condemned to be burnt. 1892.

Axon, W. E. A. The licensing of Montagu's Miscellanea spiritualia [1648]. Library 1st ser 2 1901.

Plomer, H. R. Some dealings of the Long Parliament with the press. Library 2nd ser 10 1909.

Fowell, F. and F. Palmer. Censorship in England. 1913.

Pollard, A. W. The regulation of the book trade in the xvith century. Library 3rd ser 7 1916.

Klein, A. J. Intolerance in the reign of Queen Elizabeth. Boston 1917.

Reed, A. W. The regulation of the book trade before the proclamation of 1538. Trans of Bibl Soc 15 1919.

Feasey, E. I. The licensing of the mirror for magistrates. Library 4th ser 3 1923.

Kuhl, E. The Stationers' Company and censorship 1599–1601. Library 4th ser 9 1929.

Dowling, M. Sir John Hayward's troubles over his life of Henry IV. Library 4th ser 11 1931.

McKerrow, R. B. Richard Robinson's Eupolemia and the licensers. Library 4th ser 11 1931.

Clyde, W. M. The struggle for the freedom of the press from Caxton to Cromwell. 1934.

— Parliament and the press 2. Library 4th ser 14 1934.

Siebert, F. S. Regulation of the press in the seventeenth century; excerpts from the records of the court of the Stationers' Company. Journalism Quart 13 1936.

— Freedom of the press in England 1476–1776: the rise and decline of Government controls. Urbana 1952.

Bald, R. C. Early copyright legislation and its bibliographical interest. PBSA 36 1942.

Greg, W. W. Entrance, licence and publication. Library 4th ser 25 1945.

— Entrance and copyright. Library 4th ser 26 1946.

— Ad imprimendum solum. Library 5th ser 9 1954; rptd in his Collected papers, Oxford 1966.

— Samuel Harsnett and Hayward's Henry IV. Library 5th ser 11 1956; rptd in Collected papers, Oxford 1966.

— Licensers for the press etc to 1640. Oxford 1962.

Johnson, J. and S. Gibson. Print and privilege at Oxford to 1700. Oxford 1946.

Kirschbaum, L. Author's copyright in England before 1640. PBSA 40 1946.

Simpson P. Literary piracy in the Elizabethan Age. Pbns Oxford Bibl Soc new ser 1 1947. Developed in his Studies in Elizabethan drama, Oxford 1955, as The official control of Tudor and Stuart printing.

Blagden, C. Book trade control in 1566. Library 5th ser 13 1957.

Spencer, L. The printing of Sir George Croke's reports. SB 11 1958.

Williams, F. B. The Laudian imprimatur. Library 5th ser 15 1960.

McManaway, J. G. Privilege to print. SB 16 1963.

Loades, D. M. The Press under the early Tudors: a study in censorship and sedition. Trans Cambridge Bibl Soc 4 1964.

Carter, H. Archbishop Laud and scandalous books from Holland. In Studia bibliographica in honorem Herman de la Fontaine Verwey, Amsterdam 1966.

Thomas, D. Long time burning: a history of literary censorship in England. 1969.

(4) PIRACY AND SECRET PRINTING

Plomer, H. R. A secret press at Stepney in 1596. Library 1st ser 4 1903.

— Secret printing during the Civil War. Library 2nd ser 5 1904.

— Bishop Bancroft and a Catholic Press. Library 2nd ser 8 1907.

Pierce, W. An historical introduction to the Marprelate tracts. 1908.

— The Marprelate tracts 1588, 1589. 1911.

— John Penry: his life, times and writings. 1923.

Wilson, J. D. A new tract from the Marprelate Press. Library 2nd ser 10 1909.

Pollard, A. W. Shakespeare's fight with the pirates. 1917, Cambridge 1920 (rev).

Duff, E. G. The fifth edition of Burton's Anatomy of melancholy. Library 4th ser 4 1924. Pirated in Scotland.

Gillett, C. R. Burned books: neglected chapters in British history and literature. 2 vols New York 1932.

Jackson, W. A. Counterfeit printing in Jacobean times. Library 4th ser 15 1934.

Judge, C. B. Elizabethan book-pirates. Cambridge Mass 1934.

Johnson, F. R. Printers' 'copy books' and the black market in the Elizabethan book trade. Library 5th ser 1 1946.

Greg, W. W. Was the first edition of Pierce Penniless a piracy? Library 5th ser 7 1952; rptd in his Collected papers, Oxford 1966.

Allison, A. F. and D. M. Rogers. A catalogue of Catholic books in English printed abroad or secretly in England 1558–1640. 2 pts Bognor Regis, 1956.

Freeman, A. The fatal vesper and the doleful evensong: claim-jumping in 1623. Library 5th ser 22 1967.

R. AUTHORSHIP AND COPYRIGHT

Robinson, Richard. Eupolemia. 1603; ed G. M. Vogt, SP 21 1924. See also R. B. McKerrow, GM April 1906. An account of Robinson's literary earnings.

Furnivall, F. J. Pynson's contracts with Horman and Palsgrave. Trans of Philological Soc 1867.

Copinger, W. A. The law of copyright in works of literature and art. 1870; ed F. E. and E. P. Skone James 1965 (rev).

Hazlitt, W. C. Prefaces, dedications and epistles from early English books 1540–1701. 1874 (priv ptd).

Scrutton, T. E. The law of copyright. 1883, 1903 (rev).

Bowker, R. R. Copyright: its law and its literature. 1886. With bibliography by T. Solberg.

— Copyright: its history and its law. New York 1912.

Wheatley, H. B. The dedication of books to patron and friend. 1887.

Birrell, A. The law and history of copyright in books. 1889.

Brown, W. F. W. The origin and growth of copyright. Law Mag & Rev 34 1908.

Sheavyn, P. The literary profession in the Elizabethan age. Manchester 1909, 1967 (rev J. W. Saunders).

Smith, D. N. Authors and patrons. In Shakespeare's England vol 2, Oxford 1916.

Albright, E. M. Notes on the status of literary property 1500–45. MP 17 1919.

— Dramatic publication in England 1580–1640. New York 1927.

Holzknecht, K. J. Literary patronage in the Middle Ages. Philadelphia 1924.

Couper, W. J. Copyright in Scotland before 1709. Records of Glasgow Bibl Soc 9 1931.

Partridge, R. C. B. The history of the legal deposit of books throughout the British Empire. 1938.

Pforzheimer, W. Copyright and scholarship. Eng Inst Annual 1940.

Bald, R. C. Early copyright litigation and its bibliographical interest. PBSA 36 1942.

Shaaber, M. A. The meaning of the imprint in early printed books. Library 4th ser 24 1944.

Dawson, G. E. The copyright of Shakespeare's dramatic works. Missouri Univ Stud 21 1946.

Bush, D. Seventeenth-century authorship. Mint 2 1948.

Hazen, A. T. One meaning of the imprint. Library 5th ser 6 1951.

Hoppe, H. R. The copyright-holder of the second edition of the Rheims New Testament (Antwerp 1600), Richard Gibbons SJ. Ibid.

Saunders, J. W. The stigma of print: a note on the social bases of Tudor poetry. EC 1 1951.

— The profession of English letters. 1964.

Williams, F. B. Special presentation epistles before 1641: a preliminary check-list. Library 5th ser 7 1952.

Shapiro, I. A. Publication dates before 1640. TLS 6 Feb 1953.

Greg, W. W. Copyright in unauthorised texts. In Elizabethan and Jacobean studies presented to F. P. Wilson, Oxford 1959.

Kirschbaum, L. The copyright of Elizabethan plays. Library 5th ser 14 1959.

Miller, E. H. The professional writer in Elizabethan England. Cambridge Mass 1959.

Sisson, C. J. The laws of Elizabethan copyright: the stationers' view. Library 5th ser 15 1960.

Hepburn, J. The author's empty purse and the rise of the literary agent. Oxford 1968. With extensive bibliography on the author-publisher relationship.

S. LISTS OF BOOKS AND TRADE CATALOGUES: GENERAL

(1) CONTEMPORARY

Arber, E. Contemporary lists of books produced in England. Bibliographies 3 1897.

Growell, A. Three centuries of English book trade bibliography. New York 1903 (Dibdin Club). With important bibliography of general publishing trade catalogues by W. Eames.

Cole, G. W. A survey of the bibliography of English literature 1475–1640. PBSA 23 1930.

Besterman, T. The beginnings of systematic bibliography. Oxford 1935.

Pollard, H. G. General lists of books printed in England. Bull Inst of Historical Research 12 1935.

— and A. Ehrman. The distribution of books by catalogue from the invention of printing to 1800, based on materials in the Broxbourne Library. 1965 (Roxburghe Club). The fullest account of the subject, with chronological lists of trade catalogues and other documents, ms and ptd.

Taylor, A. Renaissance guides to books. 1945.

(a) Bibliographies

Leland, John. Commentarii de scriptoribus britannicis. Ed Anthony Hall, Oxford 1709. A better edn is that of Thomas Hearne in vol 5 of his edn of Leland's Collectanea, Oxford 1715, 1770, 1774.

Bale, John. Illustrium Majoris Britanniae scriptorum summarium in quinque centurias divisum. 'Ipswich' (Wesel) 1548.

— Scriptorum illustrium Maioris Britanniae catalogus. 2 pts Basle 1557–9.

— Index Britanniae scriptorum quos collegit J. Baleus. Ed R. L. Poole and M. Bateson, Oxford 1902.

(b) The Stationers' Company Registers

Arber, E. A transcript of the Register of the Company of Stationers of London 1554–1640. 5 vols 1875–94 (priv ptd).

Eyre, G. E. B. A transcript of the registers of the Worshipful Company of Stationers of London from 1640 to 1709. 3 vols 1913 (Roxburghe Club).

Rollins, H. E. An analytical index to the ballad entries 1557–1709 in the registers of the Company of Stationers of London. Chapel Hill 1924.

(c) Trade Catalogues

Maunsell, Andrew. The first [second] part of the catalogue of English printed bookes; which concerneth such matters of diuinities, as have bin either written in our owne tongue or translated out of anie other language: and have bin published to the glory of God and edification of the Church of Christ in England; gathered into alphabet, and such method as it is, by Andrew Maunsell bookseller. 1595. Pt 2 deals with technical books; no more was pbd.

Jaggard, William. A catalogue of such English bookes as lately have bene, and now are in printing for publication, from the ninth day of October 1618 untill Easter Terme. Only known copy in Bodley.

Catalogus universalis pro Nundinis Francofurtensibus Vernalibus, de anno M.DC.XVII. 1617. There are, for some years at least, 3 different issues of this catalogue. Ser 'Ex officina Nortoniana apud J. Billium' was continued twice yearly, from spring 1617 to autumn 1620. Ser 2, for the Latin Stock of the Stationers' Company, consisted of 3 issues, autumn 1619, and spring and autumn 1620. Ser 3, 'Francofurti' (London: for John Bill or others) ran from spring 1621 to autumn 1628; copies of autumn 1625, spring 1626 and autumn 1627 issues do not appear to have survived; the last may not have been issued. It was continued to the autumn of 1628. It is probably only an abbreviated reprint of the official Fair catalogue; but from autumn 1622 to autumn 1626 there was added a suppl called Books printed in English since the last Vernal Mart.

A catalogue of certaine books, which have been published and (by authoritie) printed in England both in Latin and English, since the yeare 1626, untill November this present yeare 1631; now published for supply since the intermission of the English catalogue, with intention hereafter to publish it exactly every yeare. 1631. No continuation has been found.

[London, William]. A catalogue of the most vendible books in England, orderly and alphabetically digested; under heads of divinity, history, physick and chirurgery, law, arithmetick, geometry, astrologie, dialling, measuring land and timber, gageing, navigation, merchandize, limning, military discipline, heraldry, fortification and fireworks, husbandry, gardening, romances, poems, playes etc, with Hebrew, Greek and Latin books for schools and scholars. 1658. This is the 2nd issue. It was first issued in the previous year. To this 1658 issue was added A supplement of new books, come forth since August 1st, 1657 till June 1st, 1658, where this ends.

But all that appeared was A catalogue of new books by way of supplement to the former: being such as have been printed from that time, till Easter Term 1660, London 1660.

(2) MODERN

(a) Subject and Period Lists

Wanley, Humfrey. Antiquae literaturae septentrionalis liber alter: linguarum veterum septentrionalium thesaurus. Ed George Hickes, Oxford 1705.

Tanner, Thomas. Bibliotheca britannico-hibernica. 1748.

Clarke, A. A bibliographical dictionary: containing a chronological account, alphabeticcaly arranged, of the most curious, scarce, useful and important books, which have been published from the infancy of printing to the beginning of the 19th century, which biographical anecdotes of authors, printers and publishers. 6 vols (with suppl 2 vols) 1802–6.

Watt, R. Bibliotheca britannica: or a general index to British and foreign literature. 4 vols Edinburgh 1824, 1967.

Lowndes, W. T. The bibliographer's manual of English literature. 4 vols 1834; rev H. G. Bohn 6 vols 1857–64, 1883–6, 1967.

Collier, J. P. A bibliographical and critical account of the rarest books in the English language. 2 vols 1865.

Arber, E. (ed). Transcript of the registers of the Company of Stationers of London 1554–1640. 5 vols 1875–94.

Eyre, G. E. B. (ed). Transcript of the registers of the Worshipful Company of Stationers 1640–1708 (1709). 3 vols 1913–14 (Roxburghe Club).

Hazlitt, W. C. Handbook to the popular, poetical and dramatic literature of Great Britain, from the invention of printing to the Restoration. 1876.
— Collections and notes 1867–76. 1876; 2nd series, 1882; 3rd and final series, 1887; supplement to 3rd series, 1889; 2nd supplement to 3rd series, 1892; Collections and notes: 4th series, 1903.

Gray, G. J. General index to Hazlitt's Handbook and Collections 1867–89. 1893.

Hoskins, E. Horae Beatae Mariae Virginis: or Sarum and York primers, with kindred books, and primers of the reformed Roman use. 1901.

Duff, E. G. XVth-century English books: a bibliography of books and documents printed in England and of books for the English market printed abroad. 1917 (Bibl Soc).

Pollard, A. W., G. R. Redgrave et al. A short-title catalogue of books printed in England, Scotland and Ireland, and of English books printed abroad 1475–1640. 2 vols 1926 (Bibl Soc). See also:

Edmonds, C. K. Huntington supplement to the record of its books in STC Huntington Lib Bull 4 1933.

Bishop, W. W. Check-list of American copies of STC books. Ann Arbor 1944, 1950 (enlarged).

Alison, A. F. Early English books at the London Oratory: a supplement to STC. Library 5th ser 2 1947.

Wing, D. G. Short-title catalogue of books printed in England, Scotland, Ireland, Wales and British America, and of English books printed in other countries 1641–1700. 3 vols New York 1945–51.

Wing, D. G. A gallery of ghosts: books published between 1641 and 1700 not found in the Short-title catalogue. New York 1967.

Fry, M. I. and G. Davies. Supplements to the STC 1641–1700. HLQ 16 1953.

Alden, J. Bibliographica hibernica: additions and corrections to Wing. Charlottesville 1955 (Bibl Soc of Univ of Virginia).

Morrison, P. G. Index of printers, publishers and book-sellers in Donald Wing's STC 1641–1700. Charlottesville 1955 (Bibl Soc of Univ of Virginia).

Tucker, J. E. Wing's STC and translations from the French 1641–1700. PBSA 49 1955.

Hiscock, W. G. The Christ Church supplement to Wing's STC 1641–1700. Oxford 1956.

Wolf, E. Check-list of the books in the Library Company of Philadelphia in and supplementary to Wing's STC 1641–1700. Philadelphia 1959.

Ker, N. R. Catalogue of manuscripts containing Anglo-Saxon. Oxford 1957.

A list of books printed in the British Isles and of English books printed abroad before 1701 in the Guildhall Library. 2 vols 1966–7.

(b) Catalogues of Libraries and Exhibitions

Steevens, George. A catalogue of the curious and valuable library which will be sold by auction by Mr King. 1800.

Reed, Isaac. A catalogue of the curious and extensive library which will be sold by auction by Messrs King and Lochee. 1807.

[Griffith, A. F.] Bibliotheca anglo-poetica. 1815.

Heber, Richard. Bibliotheca heberiana. 13 pts 10 April 1834–22 Feb 1837.

Malone, Edmond. Catalogue of the early English poetry and other works, illustrative of the British drama, collected by Edmond Malone, and now preserved in the Bodleian Library. Oxford 1836.

Douce, Francis. Catalogue of the books and manuscripts bequeathed to the Bodleian Library. Oxford 1840.

Corser, T. Collectanea anglo-poetica. 11 vols Manchester 1860–83. The later vols ed J. Crossley.

Dyce, A. A catalogue of the printed books and manuscripts bequeathed to the South Kensington Museum. 2 vols 1875.

Bullen, G. (ed). Caxton celebration 1877. Catalogue of the loan collection of antiquities, curiosities and appliances connected with the art of printing. [1877].

[Ellis, F. S.] The Huth library. A catalogue of the printed books [etc]. 5 vols 1880. Sale catalogue, Sotheby's 12 pts 12 June 1911–27 Feb 1922.

British Museum. Catalogue of books printed in England, Scotland and Ireland, and of books in English printed abroad, to the year 1640. Ed G. Bullen 3 vols 1884. The subject indexes are still valuable; and the cross-references are useful in using the Short-title catalogue, above.

Katalog der Bibliothek des Börsenvereins der deutschen Buchhändler. 2 vols in 3 Leipzig 1885–1902.

Society of Antiquaries. Catalogue of a collection of printed broadsides in the possession of the Society of Antiquaries, compiled by Robert Lemon. 1886.

Grolier Club. Catalogue of original and early editions of some of the poetical and prose works of English writers from Langland to Wither. New York 1894; From Wither to Prior, 3 vols New York 1905.

Duff, E. G. Catalogue of books in the John Rylands Library, Manchester, printed in England, Scotland and Ireland, and of books in English printed abroad to the end of the year 1640. Manchester 1895.

Cambridge University Library. Early English printed books in the University Library, Cambridge 1475–1640. Ed C. E. Sayle 4 vols Cambridge 1900–7. This is the fullest catalogue extant which arranges English books to 1640 under their printers.

Cole, G. W. A catalogue of books consisting of English literature and miscellanea including many original editions of Shakespeare forming part of the library of E. D. Church. 2 vols New York 1909.

Lindsay, J. L. (Earl of Crawford). Bibliotheca Lindesiana. Vols 1–4, Printed books, Aberdeen 1910.

Catalogue of an exhibition of books etc illustrative of the history and progress of printing and bookselling in England 1477–1800, held at Stationers' Hall 25–29 June 1912, by the International Association of Antiquarian Booksellers. 1912.

Christie-Miller, W. H. Auction catalogues of the Britwell Court Library. 21 parts Sotheby's 15 Aug 1916–25 July 1927.

English incunabula in the John Rylands Library. Manchester 1930.

Catalogue of the collection of broadsides in the University Library, London. 1930.

Britwell handlist: or short-title catalogue of the principal volumes from Caxton to 1800 formerly in the library of Britwell Court, Buckinghamshire. 1933.

Foxcroft, A. B. Catalogue of English books and fragments 1477–1535 in the Public Library of Victoria. Melbourne 1933.

Carl H. Pforzheimer library: English literature 1475–1700. 3 vols New York 1940.

Catalogue of books printed in the fifteenth century now in the British Museum, part 8: France. 1949.

A catalogue of books in the Bristol reference library printed in England and Ireland up to 1640 and of English books printed abroad during the same period. Bristol 1954.

Wilkinson, C. H. A small collection at Oxford. Book Collector 5 1956.

T. OTHER LISTS
(1) CONTEMPORARY

(a) Authors
(in alphabetical order)

Francis Bacon
in Resuscitatio, ed W. Rawley, William Lee 1657.

Thomas Becon
in The sycke man's salve, John Day 1561.

Hugh Broughton
An advertisement to the reader, George Thomason 1649. A broadside announcing a collected edn, listing 78 books known to the publisher and asking for the loan of mss of any not included.

Henry Hammond
in Jeremy Taylor, The golden grove, Richard Royston 1655 (9 titles); Jeremy Taylor, An answer to a letter touching original sin, Royston 1655 (7 titles); Jeremy Taylor, Σνμβόλον Ἠθικοπολεμικόν 1657 (8 titles).

James Howell
in Scipio Mazella, Parthenopeia, Humphrey Moseley 1654.

Edward Leigh
in A system or Body of Divinity, William Lee 1654.

John Ley
in A debate concerning the English liturgy, Edward Brewster 1656.

Joseph Mede
in The key of the revelation and Παεαλειπόμενα, both Philemon Stephens 1649, 1650. Also contains books by Mede pbd by Samuel Man and John Clarke.

Simon Miller
Courteous Reader, these books following are printed for Simon Miller, [c. 1660].

John Owen
in Of the mortification of sinne, Thomas Robinson, Oxford 1656; also in God's presence, Philemon Stephens 1656.

James Prideaux
in Fasciculus controversiarum, Thomas Robinson, Oxford 1652.

William Prynne
A catalogue of printed books written by William Prynne, Michael Sparke 1643; and Edward Thomas 1660.

James Shirley
in The maide's revenge and The humorous courtier, both William Cooke 1639, 1640. An enlarged version in Six new plays. Humphrey Robinson and Humphrey Moseley 1653.

Jeremy Taylor.
in Holy Living, 2nd edn, Richard Royston 1651 (5 titles, 1 p.); Holy dying, Royston 1651 (3 titles, 2 pp.); The golden grove, Royston 1655 (11 titles, 1 p.); Answer to a letter touching original sin, Royston 1656 (9 titles); Σνμβόλον Ἠθικοπολεμικόν, [Royston 1657 (5 titles).

John Taylor
in A common whore and an arrant thief, both Henry Gasson 1635.

Thomas Usher
in Chronologia sacra, ed T. Barlow, Richard Davis and E. and J. Forrest, Oxford 1660.

T. White
in A contemplation of heaven, 'Paris' 1654.

(b) Publishers
(in alphabetical order)

Peter Actors
Invoice in Bodley, F. Madan, Collectanea vol 1, 1885 (Oxford Historical Soc).

Robert Allot
Invoice of 1635. F. S. Ferguson, Relations between London and Edinburgh printers and stationers, Library 4th ser 8 1928. Gives contemporary stationers' lists; see below.

Anonymous
Daybook, BM Egerton ms 2974.
Dibdin, T. F. Bibliomania 1842.
Daybook, in Jesus College Oxford.
Duff, E. G. Library 2nd ser 8 1907.
Munby, A. N. L. Fragment of a bookseller's day-book of 1622. Book Collector 3 1954.

Robert Barker and John Bill
A note of the severall sortes of bookes in the warehouses of the Kings Majesties Printing House [i.e. of Robert Barker and John Bill]. [1620]. Broadside; Soc of Antiquaries, Lemin, no 174.

Thomas Bassandyne
Books left in will. In F. S. Ferguson, Relations, above.

G. Bedel and T. Collins, in T. Goffe, Three excellent tragedies, 1656. See William Lee, below.

Jane Bell
in R. Green, Friar Bacon and Friar Bungay, 1655; W. Shakespeare, King Lear, 1655; P. Sidney, Ourania, 1655.

John Biddel and James Gaver, successors to Wynkyn de Worde
Jackson, W. A. A London bookseller's ledger of 1535. Colophon new ser 1 1936.
Pollard, H. G. and A. Ehrman. The distribution of books by catalogue. 1965 (Roxburghe Club). Attributes and dates 1537 or 1539.

Robert Booth
Inventory of stock post mortem.
In W. H. Rylands, Booksellers in Warrington, above.

Nicholas Bourne
in Robert Wittie, Popular errors, 1651.

Edward Brewster
in S. Birckbeck, Treatise of the four last things, 1655.

James Cathkin (?)
Daybooks 1621, 1623–4. F. S. Ferguson, Relations, above.

Thomas Chard
Jahn, R. Letters and book-lists of Chard 1583–4. Library 3rd ser 4 1924.
Paige, D. An addition letter and booklist of Chard, stationer of London. [1588/90]. Library 4th ser 11 1941.

Henry Charteris
Books left in will. F. S. Ferguson, Relations, above.

Robert Charteris
in Philotus, Edinburgh 1603.

Peter Coles
in F. Glisson, Treatise of the ricketts, 1651.

Andrew Crooke
in T. Browne, Religio medici, 1656. (4th edn).

Richard Davis, Oxford
in Z. Bogan, Meditation of mirth, 1653.

John Dorne, Oxford
The day-book of Dorne 1520. Ed F. Madan, Oxford Historical Soc Collectanea vol 1, 1885. An earlier day-book, c. 1519, is recorded by Madan in vol 2.

Francis Eglesfield and James Boler
in David Dickson, Short explanation of the epistle to the Hebrews, 1649.

Edward Forrest, Oxford
in W. Lyford, Three sermons, 1654.

Samuel Gellibrand
in John Wilkins, Ecclesiastes 1651 (3rd edn), 1653 (4th edn).

Joseph Godwin, Oxford
in Hugh Lloyd, Phrases elegantiores, 1654.

Robert Gourlaw
Books left in will. F. S. Ferguson, Relations, above.

John Holden
in L. Lessius, Sir Walter Rawley's ghost, 1651.

William Hope
in J.H., The holy lives of God's prophets, 1653.

Christopher Hunt, Exeter
in T. W. Baldwin, Loves labours won, Carbondale 1957. Gives the text of fragments of Christopher Hunt's daybook at Blandford Fair in Dorset 1603–7, including record of the sale of a copy of Shakespeare's lost comedy.

William Leake
in J[ohn] H[art], The Fort-Royall of Holy Scriptures, 1649; W. Shakespeare, Merchant of Venice, 1652; Beaumont and Fletcher, Philaster, 1652.

William Lee, M. Walbank, D. Pakeman and G. Bedell
in E. Leigh, A system or body of divinity 1654; E. Pagitt, Heresiography, 1654 (5th edn).

John Martin
A catalogue of books printed for John Martin, Jam. Allestry and Thom. Dicas; and are to be sold at the Bell in St Paul's Church-yard. [1660].

M. Meighen, G. Bedell and T. Collins in Cabala, 1653.

William Morden, Cambridge
in J. Smith, Selected discourses, 1660.

Humphrey Moseley
Courteous reader, these books following are printed for Humphrey Moseley.
1650, [1650], [1651], [1653], [1654], [1656], 1660. See W. W. Greg, Bibliography of the English printed drama vol 3, 1170–81.
Also in The Cid, 1650 (2nd edn); The Academy of Compliments, 1650; F. Strada, De bello belgico, 1651; Procopius, 1651; Middleton and Rowley, The changeling, 1653; Shirley, The Court secret, 1653.

Richard Pynson
Invoice, in Public Record Office. H. R. Plomer, Library 1st ser 10 1909.

Thomas Robinson, Oxford
in Henry Jeanes, The want of church government, 1653.

Richard Royston
in Jeremy Taylor, Holy dying, 1651; Taylor, Great exemplar, 1653 (2nd edn, 1 p. folio); Taylor, Holy living, 1654 (4th edn, 4 pp. octavo); Taylor, The golden grove, 1655 (before 25 March); John Spotswood, History of the Church in Scotland, 1655; W. Lyford, Plain man's senses, 1655; R. Sherlock, The Quaker's wilde questions, 1655 (6 Nov); William Langley, The persecuted minister, 1655 (20 Nov); Taylor, Answer to a letter touching original sin, 1656 (1 p., books newly pbd), Taylor, Συμβόλον Ἠθικοπολεμικόν, 1657 (2 pp. folio).

William Raybould
in F. Fullwood, The churches and ministry of England, 1652.

Ralph Smith
in David Dickson, A brief explication of the first fifty psalms, 1653; W. Spinstowe, The Wels of salvation opened, 1655.

Philemon Stephens
in R. Abbott, The Christian family builded by God, 1653; J. Trapp, A commentary on the twelve minor prophets, 1654.

Richard Tomlins
in C. Sydenham, Hypocrisie discovered, 1654.

William Weekly, Ipswich and J. Rothwell in C. Beck, The universal character. 1657.

(c) Divinity

A catalogue of the most approved divinity books, which have been printed or re-printed about twenty years past, and continued down to this present year. 1655, 1655 (John Rothwell), 1657 (2nd edn); Supplement, Aug 1660.

[Crowe, W.] The present state of An exact collection or catalogue of our English writers on the Old and New Testament. 1663.

—— Catalogue of our English writers on the Old and New Testaments. 1668. First pbd under another title in 1663; really an enlarged edn of Verneuil's work (see under Bodley, below).

—— Elenchus scriptorum in sacram scripturam. 1672.

(d) Plays

All the following lists are rptd and discussed in W. W. Greg, Bibliography of the English printed drama vol 3, pp. 1320–62.

Edward Archer
in Thomas Massinger and others, The old law, 1656.

Richard Rogers and William Ley
in Thomas Goffe, The careless shepherdess, 1656.

Francis Kirkman
in Tom Tyler and his wife, 1661 (690 plays), Pierre Corneille, Nicomède, tr John Dancer 1671 (806 plays).

Langbaine, G. Momus triumphans. 1688, 1688 (as A new catalogue of English plays).

—— An account of the English dramatic poets. Oxford 1691.

—— The lives and characters of the English dramatic poets. [1698]. This shorter edn has addns by Charles Gildon et al.

(e) History

Pits, John. Relationum historicarum de rebus anglicis. Vol 1, Paris 1619. No more was pbd; usually cited as De illustribus Angliae scriptoribus.

Ware, Sir James. De scriptoribus Hiberniae. Dublin 1639; tr Walter Harris in his edn of Ware's Works, 1746.

(f) Miscellaneous

James, Thomas. Index generalis librorum prohibitorum a pontificiis. Oxford 1627.

A catalogue of plates and pictures. Pbd Peter Stent c. 1649–53.

Playford, John. A catalogue of all the musick-bookes that have been printed in England, either for voyce or instruments. [1653].

Gore, Thomas. Catalogus plerumque omnium authorum qui de re heraldica scripserunt. Oxford 1668, 1674 (enlarged).

Cooper, William. A catalogue of chymicall books. At end of The philosophical epitaph of W.C. seq, 1673.

Tooker, C. (bookseller). The famous collection of papers and pamphlets of all sorts from the year 1600 down to this day, commonly known by the name of William Miller's Collection. [c. 1695], [c. 1696], [c. 1705].

(2) MODERN

British Museum: Thomason collection. Catalogue of the pamphlets, books, newspapers and manuscripts relating to the Civil War, the Commonwealth and Restoration 1640–61. Ed G. K. Fortescue 2 vols 1908.

Madan, F. Notes on the Thomason collection of Civil War tracts. Bibliographica 3 1897.

Hiscock, W. G. The Thomason tracts. TLS 11 Jun 1942.

Spencer, L. The professional and literary connexions of George Thomason. Library 5th ser 13 1958.

Greg, W. W. A list of masques, pageants etc. 1902 (Bibl Soc). Appendixes 1–2.

— A catalogue of the books presented by Edward Capell to the library of Trinity College Cambridge. Cambridge 1903. Shakespeariana.

— A bibliography of the English printed drama to the Restoration. 4 vols 1939–59 (Bibl Soc).

Linton, M. National Library of Scotland and Edinburgh University Library copies of plays in Greg's Bibliography of the English printed drama. SB 15 1962.

Bosanquet, E. F. English printed almanacks and prognostications: a bibliographical history to the year 1600. 1917 (Bibl Soc). Addns, Library 4th ser 1928, 18 1937.

Smith, W. M. A list of bibliographies of theological and biblical literature published in Great Britain and America 1595–1931. Coatesville 1931.

Spargo, J. W. Some reference books of the 16th and 17th centuries: a finding-list. PBSA 31 1937.

Allison, A. F. and D. M. Rogers. A catalogue of Catholic books in English printed abroad or secretly in England 1558–1640. 2 pts Bognor Regis 1956.

U. LIBRARIES

Cannons, H. G. T. Bibliography of library economy: a classified index to the professional periodical literature relating to library economy, printing, methods of publishing, copyright, bibliography etc 1876–1920. Chicago 1927; Library literature 1921–32, 1934 (suppl). Suppls 1933–5, 1936–9, 1940–2 and triennially.

Burton, M. and M. E. Vosburgh. A bibliography of librarianship: classified and annotated guide to the library literature of the world. 1934.

Read, E. A. A checklist of books, catalogues and periodical articles relating to the cathedral libraries of England. Oxford Bibl Soc Occasional Pbns no 6 1970.

(1) GENERAL

'John Boston of Bury'. Catalogus scriptorum ecclesiae. Part printed by D. Wilkins in T. Tanner, Bibliotheca britannico-hibernica, 1748, pp. xviii–xliii. See also M. R. James, On the Abbey of St Edmund at Bury, Cambridge 1895 (Cambridge Antiquarian Soc); The list of libraries prefixed to the catalogue of John Boston and kindred documents, Collectanea franciscana vol 2, Manchester 1922; R. A. B. Mynors, The Latin classics known to Boston of Bury, in Fritz Saxl 1890–1948: a volume of memorial essays from his friends in England, ed D. J. Gordon, Edinburgh 1957; and R. H. Rouse, Bostonus Buriensis and the author of the Catalogus scriptorum ecclesiae, Speculum 41 1966.

Leland, John. The laboryouse journey and serche of J. Leylande for Englandes antiquities, geuen of hym as a newe yeares gyfte to Kynge Henry the VIII, with declaracyons enlarged by J. Bale. 1549.

— Collectanea. Ed Thomas Hearne 6 vols Oxford 1715.

— Itinerary. Ed L. T. Smith 5 vols 1907–8.

Clarke, A. L. John Leland and Henry VIII. Library 3rd ser 2 1912.

James, Thomas. Ecloga oxonio-cantabrigiensis tributa in libros duos. 1600. A catalogue of mss in college libraries.

Jacob, Louys. Traicté des plus belles bibliothèques publiques & particulières qui ont esté & qui sont à présent dans le monde. 2 pts Paris 1644. On England, pp. 242–307.

Bernard, E. Catalogi manuscriptorum Angliae et Hiberniae. Oxford 1697.

Beloe, W. Anecdotes of literature and scarce books. 6 vols 1807–14.

[Clarke, W. and W. Beckford]. Repertorium bibliographicum: or some account of the most celebrated English libraries. 1819.

Botfield, B. Notes on English Cathedral libraries. 1849.

Merryweather, F. S. Bibliomania in the Middle Ages. 1849, New York 1900 (with introd by C. Orr).

Report from the Select Committee on Public libraries. 1849.

First report of the Royal Commission on the state and condition of the cathedral and collegiate churches of England and Wales 1852. 1854.

Edwards, E. Memoirs of libraries. 2 vols 1859. Part of vol 1 2nd edn, Newport (Isle of Wight) 1885, 1901 (priv ptd).

— Libraries and founders of libraries. 1864.

— Free town libraries. 1869.

— The lives of the founders of the British Museum 1570–1870. 1870.

Reynolds, H. E. Our cathedral libraries. Trans & Proc of First Annual Meeting of the Library Association 1878.

Becker, G. Catalogi bibliothecarum antiqui, Bonn 1885. All catalogues then known up to 1300, with references 1300–1500 to where they may be found.

Gottlieb, T. Ueber mittelalterliche Bibliotheken. Leipzig 1890. Addns to Edwards, Memoirs, above.

Plomer, H. R. References to books in the reports of the Historical Mss Commissioners. Bibliographica 3 1897.

Garnett, R. Librarianship in the xviith century. In Essays in librarianship and bibliography, 1899.

Clark, J. W. The care of books: as essay on the development of libraries and their fittings to the end of the 18th century. 1901.

Morgan, A. Monastic libraries. Library Assoc Record 6 1904.

Richardson, E. C. The medieval library. Harper's Monthly Mag April 1905.

The literature of libraries in the xviith and xviiith centuries. Ed J. C. Dana and H. W. Kent 6 pts Chicago 1906. Reprints Naude, Durie etc.

Gasquet, F. A. Some notes on medieval monastic libraries. In his Old English Bible and other essays, 1908.

Savage, E. A. The story of libraries and book collecting. 1908.

— The care of books in early Irish monasteries. Library 2nd ser 10 1909.

— Old English libraries. 1911. Contains a useful list of library catalogues before 1525.

— Notes on the early monastic libraries of Scotland. Papers of Edinburgh Bibl Soc 14 1926–30.

Abrahams, I. and C. E. Sayle. The purchase of Hebrew books by the English Parliament in 1647. Trans Jewish Historical Soc of England 8 1914.

Garrod, H. W. The library regulations of a medieval college. Library 4th ser 8 1928.

Streeter, B. H. The chained library: a survey of four centuries in the evolution of the English library. 1931.

Lesne, E. Les livres, 'scriptoria' et bibliothèques du commencement du viiie à la fin du xie siècle. In Histoire de la propriété ecclesiastique en France IV: mémoires et travaux publiés par des professeurs des Facultés Catholiques de Lille, fasc 46, Lille 1938.

Thompson, J. W. The medieval library. Chicago 1939, 1957 (rev B. B. Boyer).

Ker, N. R. Medieval libraries of Great Britain: a list of surviving books. 1941, 1964 (rev) (Royal Historical Soc).

— The migration of mss from the English medieval libraries. Library 4th ser 23 1947.

— Oxford college libraries in the sixteenth century. Bodleian Lib Record 6 1959.

— Cathedral libraries. Lib History 1 1967.

— Medieval manuscripts in British libraries 1: London. Oxford 1969.

Weiss, R. Humanism in England during the fifteenth century. 1941, 1957, Oxford 1967 (rev).

— New light on humanism in England during the fifteenth century. Jnl Warburg & Courtauld Inst 14 1951.

— The study of Greek in England during the fourteenth century. Rinascimento 2 1951.

Hands, M. S. G. and M. S. Smith. The cathedral libraries catalogue. Library 5th ser 2 1947. Ptd catalogues of cathedral libraries in England and Wales listed in appendix.

Thornton, J. L. A mirror for librarians: selected readings in the history of librarianship. 1948; Classics of librarianship, 1957. Combined as Selected readings in the history of librarianship, 1966.

Wright, C. E. The dispersal of the monastic libraries and the beginnings of Anglo-Saxon studies. Trans Cambridge Bibl Soc 1 1949–53.

Knowles, D. The religious orders in England vol 2. Cambridge 1955. Ch 26 on monastic libraries.

Jayne, S. Library catalogues of the English Renaissance. Berkeley 1956.

The English library before 1700. Ed F. Wormald and C. E. Wright 1958.

Irwin, R. The origins of the English library. 1958, 1966 (rev as The English library: sources and history).

— The heritage of the English library. 1964.

Central Council for the care of churches: the parochial libraries of the Church of England; with an historical introduction [by N. R. Ker], notes on early printed books and their care and an alphabetical list of parochial libraries past and present. 1959.

Durkan, J. and A. Ross. Early Scottish libraries. Glasgow 1961.

Gneuss, H. Englands Bibliotheken im Mittelalter und ihr Untergang. In Festschrift für Walter Hübner, Berlin 1964.

Humphreys, K. W. The book provisions of the medieval friars 1215–1400. Amsterdam 1964.

Kelly, T. Early public libraries: a history of public libraries in Great Britain before 1850. 1966. Primarily on the precursors of the public library; with list of early endowed libraries.

(2) INDIVIDUAL LIBRARIES AND CATALOGUES

Aberdeen

Catalogue of books belonging to the theological library of Marischal College. Aberdeen 1790, 1811.

Mitchell, W. S. The common library of New Aberdeen. Libri 4 1954.

Arbroath Abbey

Durkan, J. An Arbroath book inventory of 1473. Bibliotheck 3 1962. On books left to Arbroath Abbey by Richard Guthrie.

Barking Abbey

Doyle, A. I. Books connected with the Vere family and Barking Abbey. Trans of Essex Archaeological Soc new ser 25 1955–60.

Barnwell Priory, Cambridgeshire

The observances in use at the Augustinian Priory at Barnwell, Cambridgeshire. Ed J. W. Clark, Cambridge 1897.

Bermondsey Priory

Denholm-Young, N. Edward of Windsor and Bermondsey Priory. EHR 48 1957.

Bristol City Library

Tovey, C. The Bristol City Library. Bristol 1853. For Bishop Carpenter's library see Worcester, below.

Matthews, E. R. N. History of the Public Library in Bristol. Bristol 1906.

Bury St Edmunds

James, M. R. On the Abbey of St Edmund at Bury. 1895 (Cambridge Antiquarian Soc).

Bartholomew, A. T. and C. Gordon. On the library at King Edward VI School, Bury St Edmunds. Library 3rd ser 1 1910.

Cambridge

Hartshorne, C. H. Book rarities of the University of Cambridge. 1829.

Sayle, C. E. Annals of the Cambridge University Library 1278–1900. Cambridge 1916.

Oates, J. C. T. The libraries at Cambridge 1570–1700. In English libraries before 1700, ed F. Wormald and C. E. Wright 1958.

Munby, A. N. L. Cambridge college libraries: aids for research students. Cambridge 1960, 1962 (rev).

Cambridge, Caius College

James, M. R. Descriptive catalogue of the manuscripts in the library of Gonville and Caius College. 2 vols and suppl 1907–14.

Cambridge, Christ's College

James, M. R. A descriptive catalogue of the Western manuscripts in the library of Christ's College. Cambridge 1905.

Cambridge, Clare College

James, M. R. A descriptive catalogue of the Western manuscripts in the library of Clare College. Cambridge 1905.

Hunt, R. W. Medieval inventories of Clare College. Trans Cambridge Bibl Soc 1 1950.

Cambridge, Corpus Christi College

James, M. R. Descriptive catalogue of the manuscripts in the library of Corpus Christi College. 2 vols Cambridge 1909–12.

Gaselee, S. Early printed books in the library of Corpus Christi College. With addenda. Cambridge 1921–2

Fletcher, J. M. and J. K. McConica. A sixteenth-century inventory of Corpus Christi College, Cambridge. Trans Cambridge Bibl Soc 3 1961.

Cambridge, Emmanuel College
Worsley Wood, P. A hand-list of English books in the library of Emmanuel College printed before 1641. 1915 (Bibl Soc).
James, M. R. Western manuscripts in the library of Emmanuel College: a descriptive catalogue. Cambridge 1904.

Cambridge, Jesus College
James, M. R. A descriptive catalogue of manuscripts in the library of Jesus College. Cambridge 1895.

Cambridge, King's College
James, M. R. A descriptive catalogue of manuscripts in the library of King's College, Cambridge. Cambridge 1895.
Munby, A. N. L. The gifts of Elizabethan printers to the library of King's College, Cambridge. Library 5th ser 2 1947. John and Richard Day, Richard Jugge and Thomas Thomas.
— Notes on King's College Library in the fifteenth century. Trans Cambridge Bibl Soc 1 1949–53.
Thompson, W. D. J. Notes on King's College library 1500–70. Trans Cambridge Bibl Soc 2 1954.

Cambridge, Magdalene College
James, M. R. A descriptive catalogue of manuscripts in the library of Magdalene College. Cambridge 1909.

Cambridge, Pembroke College
James, M. R. A descriptive catalogue of the manuscripts in the library of Pembroke College; with a handlist of the printed book to 1500 by E. H. Minns. Cambridge 1905.

Cambridge, Peterhouse
James, M. R. A descriptive catalogue of the manuscripts in the library of Peterhouse, with an essay on the history of the library by J. W. Clark. Cambridge 1899.

Cambridge, Queens' College
James, M. R. A descriptive catalogue of Western manuscripts in the library of Queens' College. Cambridge 1905.
Plaistowe, F. G. Early printed books to 1500 in the library of Queens' College. Cambridge 1910.

Cambridge, St Catharine's College
Bilderbeck, J. B. Early printed books in the library of St Catharine's College. Cambridge 1911.
James, M. R. A descriptive catalogue of manuscripts in the library of St Catharine's College. Cambridge 1925.

Cambridge, St John's College
James, M. R. A descriptive catalogue of manuscripts in the library of St John's College. Cambridge 1913.

Cambridge, Sidney Sussex College
James, M. R. The Western manuscripts in the library of Sidney Sussex College. Cambridge 1895.

Cambridge, Trinity College
James, M. R. The Western manuscripts in the library of Trinity College. Cambridge 4 vols 1900–4.

Cambridge, Trinity Hall
James, M. R. A descriptive catalogue of the manuscripts in the library of Trinity Hall. Cambridge 1907.

Cambridge, University Library
Sayle, C. E. Annals of Cambridge University Library. Library 3rd ser 6 1915.
Oates, J. C. T. and H. L. Pink. Three sixteenth-century catalogues of the University Library, Cambridge. Trans Cambridge Bibl Soc 1 1949–53.

Canterbury
James, M. R. The ancient libraries of Canterbury and Dover. Cambridge 1903.
Beazeley, M. History of the Chapter Library of Canterbury Cathedral. Trans Bibl Soc 8 1906.
Lieftinck, G. I. The Psalterium hebraycum from St Augustine's Canterbury rediscovered in the Scaliger Bequest at Leyden. Trans Cambridge Bibl Soc 2 1954–8.
Bishop, T. A. M. Notes on Cambridge mss. Ibid.
Ker, N. R. English manuscripts in the century after the Conquest. Oxford 1960.

Carlisle
Holtby, R. T. Carlisle library and records. Trans Cumberland & Westmorland Antiquarian Soc new ser 66 1966.

Cashel
Alderson, F. Cashel Cathedral library. Book Collector 17 1968.

Chirbury, Shropshire
Wilding, W. On a library of chained books at Chirbury. Trans of Shropshire Archaeological & Natural History Soc 8 1885; rptd from Jnl of Br Archaeological Assoc 1883.

Coventry
The Accessions Book (c. 1600–10) of the Coventry Grammar School library is in the Cambridge University Library.

Dorset
Fletcher, J. M. J. Chained books in Dorset and elsewhere. Proc Dorset Natural History & Antiquarian Field Club 35 1914.

Dover
Haines, C. R. The library of Dover Priory; its catalogue and extant volumes. Library 4th ser 8 1928. See also under Canterbury, above.

Dublin
Abbott, T. K. The book of Trinity College, Dublin 1591–1891. Dublin 1892.
White, N. J. D. An account of Archbishop Marsh's Library, Dublin. Dublin 1926.
The library of Trinity College, Dublin. TLS 16 March 1956.

Dulwich
Warner, G. F. Catalogue of the manuscripts and muniments of Alleyn's College of God's Gift at Dulwich. 1881.

Durham
Catalogi veteres librorum ecclesiae cathedralis Dunelm: catalogues of the library of Durham Cathedral, at various periods from the Conquest to the Dissolution, including catalogues of the Abbey of Hulne, and of the mss preserved in the library of Bp Cosin. Ed J. Raine and B. Botfield 1838 (Surtees Soc).

Durham Cathedral
Hughes, H. D. A history of Durham Cathedral library. Durham 1925.
Mynors, R. A. B. Durham Cathedral manuscripts to the end of the twelfth century. Oxford 1939.
Greenslade, S. L. The contents of the library of Durham Cathedral. Durham & Northumberland Architectural & Archaeological Soc Trans 11 1965.

Edinburgh, Town Library
Will of Clement Little (d. 1580) and list of 76 books bequeathed to town. In Maitland Club Miscellany vol 1, 1833–4.

Edinburgh, University Library
[Finlayson, C. P.] Benefactors of the library in five centuries: exhibition catalogue no 3. Edinburgh 1963.
— and S. M. Simpson. The library of the University of Edinburgh: the early period 1580–1710. Lib History 1 1967.

Eton College
James, M. R. A descriptive catalogue of the manuscripts of Eton College. Cambridge 1895.
Birley, R. Some unrecorded Cambridge books in the library of Eton College. Trans Cambridge Bibl Soc 1 1949–53.
— The history of Eton College Library. Library 5th ser 2 1956.
— The Storer collection in Eton College library. Book Collector 5 1956.

—— Eton College library: one hundred books selected and annotated. Eton 1969 (priv ptd), 1970.
—— The history of Eton College Library. Eton 1970.

Exeter
Förster, M. The Exeter book. 1933.
Lloyd, L. J. The library of Exeter Cathedral. Exeter 1954.

Fife
Anderson, A. The old libraries of Fife. Fife 1953.

Finchale Priory
Raine, J. The priory of Finchale. Surtees Soc 6 1837.

Glasgow University Library
Arthur, A. Catalogue librorum impressorum in bibliotheca. 2 vols Glasgow 1791; suppls 1825, 1835.
Dickson, W. P. Notes on the history of Glasgow University Library. Glasgow 1888.
Black, H. M. and P. Gaskell. Special collections in Glasgow University Library. Book Collector 16 1967.

Gloucestershire
Williams, T. W. Gloucester medieval libraries. Trans of Bristol & Gloucestershire Archaeological Soc 31 1908.

Grantham
Carlyle, E. I. Francis Trigge. In Dictionary of national biography vol 57, 1899. See T. Kelly, Early public libraries, 1966, p. 73.

Halifax
Hanson, T. W. Halifax parish church under the Commonwealth. Trans Halifax Antiquarian Soc 1909.
—— Halifax Parish church library. Trans Halifax Antiquarian Soc 1951.

Hereford
James, M. R. The library of the Grey Friars of Hereford. In Collectanea franciscana vol 1, Aberdeen 1914.
Morgan, F. C. Hereford Cathedral library: its history and contents, with an appendix of early printed books. Hereford 1952.
Tallon, M. Hereford Cathedral library. 1963.

Ipswich
An ancient public library. TLS 18 Aug 1950.

Isleworth, Syon Monastery
Bateson, M. Catalogue of the library of Syon Monastery, Isleworth. Cambridge 1898.

King's Lynn
Mair, T. E. The church libraries of King's Lynn. Antiquary 40 1904.

Kings Norton
Brassington, W. S. Thomas Hall and the old library founded by him at King's Norton. Library Chron 5 1888.

Kinloss, Perthshire
Durkan, J. The beginnings of humanism in Scotland. Innes Rev 1953.

Lambeth, Palace of the Archbishop of Canterbury
Maitland, S. R. List of early printed books in the archiepiscopal library at Lambeth. 1843.
—— Index of English books, printed before 1600, in the archiepiscopal library at Lambeth. 1845.
James, M. R. A descriptive catalogue of the manuscripts of Lambeth Palace. Cambridge 1932.
—— The history of Lambeth Palace Library. Trans Cambridge Bibl Soc 3 1959.
Cox-Johnson, A. Lambeth Palace Library 1610–64. Trans Cambridge Bibl Soc 2 1958.
Bill, G. Lambeth Palace Library. Library 5th ser 21 1966.

Lancashire
Christie, R. C. The old church and school libraries of Lancashire. Chetham Soc new ser 7 1885.

Leicester Abbey
James, M. R. and A. H. Thompson. Catalogue of the library of Leicester Abbey. Trans of Leicestershire Archaeological Soc 19–21 1935–40.

Leicester Town Library
Herne, F. S. The Town Library, Leicester. Trans Leicester Literary & Philosophical Soc new ser 3 1891–5.
Deedes, C., J. E. and J. L. Stocks. The Old Town Hall library of Leicester. Oxford 1919.

Lewisham
Black, W. H. (ed). Bibliothecae Colfanae catalogus. 1831. Introd describes Abraham Colfe and the Leathersellers' endowed library.

Lichfield Cathedral
Savage, H. E. Lichfield Cathedral: a cathedral library. Lichfield 1934.
Ker, N. R. Patrick Young's catalogue of the manuscripts of Lichfield Cathedral. Medieval & Renaissance Stud 2 1950.

Lincolnshire
Liddel, J. R. Leland's Lists of manuscripts in Lincolnshire monasteries. EHR 54 1939.

Lincoln Cathedral
Jackson, W. A. The Lincolne nosegay books. Antiquarian Booksellers' Association Annual 1953.
Griffiths, D. N. Lincoln Cathedral library. Book Collector 19 1970.

London
[Bagford, J.] An account of London libraries. Monthly Miscellany or Memoirs for the Curious June 1708.
Rye, R. A. Students' guide to the libraries of London. 1908, 1910, 1927 (rev and enlarged).
Irwin, R. (ed). The libraries of London. 1949; ed R. Irwin and R. Staveley 1961 (rev).
Bland, D. S. A bibliography of the Inns of Court and Chancery. 1965 (Seldon Soc, suppl ser 3). Section L deals with libraries.

London, College of Arms
Black, W. H. Catalogue of the Arundel manuscripts in the library of the College of Arms. 1839 (not pbd). Lists 55 other mss as well as those given to the College by Henry, Duke of Norfolk in 1678.

London, Dutch Church, Austin Friars
A catalogue of books, manuscripts, letters, etc belonging to the Dutch Church, Austin Friars, London. 1879.

London, Gray's Inn
Horwood, A. J. A catalogue of the ancient manuscripts belonging to the Honourable Society of Gray's Inn. 1869.

London, Guildhall
Brewer, T. Memoir of the life and times of John Carpenter. 1836, 1856 (rev).
Prie, J. E. A descriptive account of the Guildhall of the City of London. 1886.
Welsh, C. The Guildhall library and its work. Library 1st ser 1 1889.
Borrajo, E. M. The Guildhall library. Lib Assoc Record 10 1908.
Smith, R. The library at Guildhall in the 15th and 16th centuries. Guildhall Miscellany 1 1952–6.

London, Huguenot Churches at Threadneedle Street & Soho Square
Turner, W. The archives and library of the French Protestant church, Soho Square, formerly Threadneedle Street. Proc Huguenot Soc of London 14 1929–33.
—— An early Huguenot library in Threadneedle Street. Proc Huguenot Soc of London 18 1947–52.

London, Lincoln's Inn
Hunter, J. Three catalogues. 1838.

London, Merchant Taylors' School
Sayle, R. T. D. Annals of Merchant Taylors' School Library. Library 4th ser 15 1935.

London, Middle Temple
Catalogue. Ed B. Shower 1700; [ed C. Worsley?] 1754.

London, Royal College of Physicians
Merrett, Christopher. Museum Harveianum. 1660.

London, St Paul's Cathedral

Atkins, W. M. St Paul's Cathedral: a short history of the library and its archives. In A record of the Friends of St Paul's, 1954.

London, Sion College

Spenser, John. Catalogus universalis librorum omnium in Bibliotheca Collegii Sionii apud Londinensis. 1650.

Reading, William. The history of the ancient and present state of Sion College, and of the London Clergy's Library there. 1724.

London, Royal Library

Warner, G. F. and J. P. Gilson. Catalogue of western manuscripts in the old Royal and King's collections in the British Museum. 4 vols 1921.

Milman, W. H. Some account of Sion College in the city of London and its library. [1880].

Pearce, E. H. Sion College and Library. Cambridge 1913.

Edmonston, E. Sion College. Book Collector 14 1965.

London, Westminster Abbey

Robinson, J. A. and M. R. James. The manuscripts of Westminster Abbey. Cambridge 1909.

Manchester, Chetham's Library

Radcliffe, J. Bibliotheca Chethamiensis: sive bibliothecae publicae mancuniensis catalogus. 2 vols Manchester 1791; vol 3 ed W. P. Greswell, Manchester 1826; vol 4 ed T. Jones, Manchester 1862; index by T. Jones, Manchester 1863.

Raines, F. R. and C. W. Sutton. Life of Humphrey Chetham. 2 vols Manchester 1903 (Chetham Soc new ser 49–50).

Maclure, A. F. The minute books of Chetham's hospital and library, Manchester. Trans Lancashire & Cheshire Antiquarian Soc 40 1923.

Lofthouse, H. Unfamiliar libraries: Chetham's Library. Book Collector 5 1956.

Smith, H. S. A. Readers and books in a 17th-century library. Lib Assoc Record 65 1963.

Chetham also founded libraries in the parish churches of Manchester and Bolton, and the chapels of Turton and Gorton.

Marlborough

Kempson, E. G. H. The vicar's library, St Mary's, Marlborough. Wiltshire Archaeological & Natural History Mag 51 1945–7.

Monk Bretton, Yorkshire

Hunter, J. English monastic libraries: a catalogue of the library of the priory of Bretton in Yorkshire; notices of the libraries belonging to other religious houses. 1831.

Newcastle-on-Tyne

Mackenzie, E. A descriptive and historical account of Newcastle-upon-Tyne. 2 vols Newcastle 1827.

Hicks, E. B. and G. E. Richmond (ed). A catalogue of the Newcastle chapter library and of the churchwardens' or old parish library. Newcastle 1890.

Norwich, Cathedral

Beeching, H. C. and M. R. James. The library of the cathedral church of Norwich. Norfolk Archaeology 19 1917.

Ker, N. R. Medieval manuscripts from Norwich Cathedral priory. Trans Cambridge Bibl Soc 1 1949–53.

Norwich, City Library

Stephen, G. A. Three centuries of a city library: an historical and descriptive account of the Norwich Public Library, established 1608. Norwich 1917.

Hepworth, P. and M. Alexander. City of Norwich Libraries: history and treasures. Norwich 1957.

— Norwich public libraries: Norfolk and Norwich Record Office. Norwich 1965.

Keeling, D. F. Norwich Public Library: a select bibliography. 1966.

Oxford

Myres, J. N. L. Oxford libraries in the 17th and 18th centuries. In The English library before 1700: studies in its history, ed F. Wormald and C. E. Wright 1958.

Ker, N. R. Oxford college libraries in the sixteenth century. Bodleian Lib Record 5 1959.

Oxford, All Souls College

Catalogue of manuscripts in the library of All Souls College. Oxford 1842. *See also* BM additional ms 4608 folios 100, 100b.

Oxford, Balliol College

Mynors, R. A. B. Catalogue of the manuscripts of Balliol College, Oxford. Oxford 1963.

Oxford, Bodleian Library

Catalogues: (under faculties) ed Thomas James 1605; (alphabetical) ed Thomas James 1620; (Appendix to 1620) ed John Rous 1635; (of biblical commentaries) ed John Verneuil 1635; [2nd edn of Verneuil (in English)] ed John Verneuil 1642.

Bodley, Sir Thomas. Life, written by himself [in 1609], Oxford 1647; rptd with addns as Trecantale Bodleianum, Oxford 1913.

Bodley, Sir Thomas. Reliquiae Bodleianae. Ed T. Hearne 1703.

— Letters to Thomas James. Ed G. W. Wheeler, Oxford 1926.

Macray, W. D. The annals of the Bodleian Library. 1868, Oxford 1890 (with addns).

Wheeler, G. W. The earliest catalogues of the Bodleian Library. Oxford 1928 (priv ptd).

The Bodleian in the 17th century: guide to an exhibition 1951. Oxford 1951.

Ker, N. R. The chaining, labelling and inventory numbers of manuscripts belonging to the Old University Library. Bodleian Lib Record 5 1954–6.

Oxford, Christ Church

Kitchin, G. W. Catalogus codicum manuscriptorum qui in bibliotheca Aedis Christi apud Oxon. ad servantur. Oxford 1867.

Oxford, Corpus Christi College

Liddell, J. R. The library of Corpus Christi College, Oxford in the sixteenth century. Library 4th ser 18 1938.

Oxford, Jesus College

Fordyce, C. J. and T. M. Knox. The library of Jesus College, Oxford, with an appendix on the books bequeathed thereto by Lord Herbert of Cherbury. Proc Oxford Bibl Soc 5 1937.

Oxford, Lincoln College

Weiss, R. The earliest catalogues of the library of Lincoln College. Bodleian Quart Record 8 1935–8.

See under Robert Flemmyng, below.

Oxford, Magdalen College

Driver, G. R. Magdalen College library: a list of books printed before 1641 not in the Bodleian Library Oxford. 1930 (Oxford Bibl Soc).

Magdalen Hall (now Hertford College)

Catalogus librorum in bibliotheca aulae magdalensis. Ed H. Wilkinson, Oxford 1661.

Oxford, Merton College

Allen, P. S. Early documents connected with the Library of Merton College, Oxford. Library 4th ser 4 1924.

Garrod, H. W. The library regulations of a medieval college. Library 4th ser 8 1928.

Powicke, F. M. The mediaeval books of Merton College. Oxford 1931.

Oxford, New College

Coxe, H. O. Catalogus codicum manuscriptorum Collegii Novi. Oxford 1852.

Oxford, Oriel College

Fletcher, C. R. L. A catalogue of the library of Oriel College in the year 1375. Oxford Historical Soc Collectanea 5 1885.

Peterborough
    James, M. R. Lists of mss formerly in Peterborough Abbey Library, with preface and identifications by M. R. James. Trans Bibl Soc 1926 (suppl 5).
Pott Shrigley, Cheshire
    Dodgson, J. M. A library at Pott Chapel c. 1493. Library 5th ser 15 1960.
Repton, Derbyshire
    Bigsby, R. A historical and topographical description of Repton. 1854. Original list of books ptd in J. C. Cox, Churchwardens' Accounts, 1913, p. 121.
Rochester
    Ker, N. R. English manuscripts in the century after the Norman Conquest. Oxford 1960.
St Alban's Abbey
    Walsingham, T. Gesta abbatum monasterii sancti Albani, ed H. T. Riley 1867 (Rolls ser).
    Richard de Bury's books from the Abbey of St Alban's. Bodleian Lib Record 3 1951.
    Weiss, R. Piero de Monte, John Whethamstede and the library of St Alban's Abbey. EHR 60 1945.
St Andrews
    Inventories of Buikis in the Colleges of Sanct Androis [1588–1612]. Maitland Club Miscellany (Edinburgh) vol 1 pt 2 1833.
    Bushnell, G. H. Unfamiliar libraries 3: St Andrews University Library. Book Collector 7 1958.
Salisbury Cathedral
    Ker, N. R. Salisbury Cathedral manuscripts and Patrick Young's catalogue. Wiltshire Archaeological & Natural History Mag 53 1950.
Shrewsbury
    Oldham, J. B. Shrewsbury School library: its earlier history and organization. Library 4th ser 16 1935.
    — Shrewsbury School library. Trans Shropshire Archaeological Soc 51 1943.
    — Shrewsbury School library. Library 5th ser 14 1959.
Somerset
    Williams, T. W. Somerset medieval libraries. Somerset Archaeological & Natural History Soc (Bristol) 1897.
Suffolk
    Fitch, J. A. Some ancient Suffolk parochial libraries. Proc Suffolk Inst of Archaeology 30 1964.

Titchfield Abbey, Yorkshire
    Wilson, R. M. The medieval library of Titchfield Abbey. Proc Leeds Philosophical & Literary Soc 5 1940.
Wales
    Phillips, D. R. The romantic history of the monastic libraries of Wales. Swansea 1912.
Warwick, St Mary's Church
    Morgan, P. and G. D. Painter. The Caxton Legenda at St Mary's Warwick. Library 5th ser 12 1957.
Wells, Cathedral
    Clark, J. W. On the chained libraries at Cesena, Wells and Guildford. Proc Cambridge Antiquarian Soc 8 1895.
Winchester College
    Oakeshott, W. F. Winchester College library before 1750. Library 5th ser 9 1954.
    Blakiston, J. M. G. Unfamiliar libraries 11: Winchester College. Book Collector 16 1967.
Worcester, Cathedral
    Floyer, J. K. A thousand years of a Cathedral library. Reliquary Jan 1901.
    Hamilton, S. G. Catalogue of manuscripts preserved in the chapter library of Worcester Cathedral. Oxford 1906.
    Wilson, J. M. The library of printed books in Worcester Cathedral. Library 3rd ser 2 1912.
    Bannister, H. M. Bishop Roger of Worcester. EHR 32 1917.
    Catalogus librorum manuscriptorum bibliothecae Wigorn., made in 1622–3 by Patrick Young. Ed I. Atkins and N. R. Ker, Cambridge 1944.
Worcester, Bishop Carpenter's Library
    Clark, J. W. The care of books. Cambridge 1901, 1902, pp. 121–3.
York, Augustinian Friars
    James, M. R. The catalogue of the library of the Augustinian Friars at York, now first edited from the ms at Trinity College, Dublin. In Fasciculus Ioanni Willis Clark dictatus, Cambridge 1909.
York, Cathedral
    Raine, J. A catalogue of the printed books in the library of the Dean and Chapter of York. York 1896.
    Harrison, F. The Dean and Chapter library. In York Minster Cathedral tracts, ed A. H. Thompson, York 1927.

V. BOOK COLLECTORS AND COLLECTING

(1) CHOICE OF BOOKS

Bury, Richard d'Aungergille de (Bishop of Durham). Philobiblon: Tractatus pulcherrimus de amore librorum. Cologne 1473; ed Thomas James, Oxford 1599; ed A. F. West 3 vols New York 1889 (Grolier Club); tr J. B. Inglis 1832 and E. C. Thomas 1888; ed M. Maclagan Oxford 1960 (Thomas's trn).
Durie, John. The reformed librarie keeper; whereunto is added the description of one of the chiefest libraries in Germanie [i.e. Wolfenbüttel]. 1650.
Naudé, G. Instructions concerning erecting of a library now interpreted by Jo Evelyn. 1661. First pbd in French, Paris 1628.

Crawford and Balcarres, Earl of. Gabriel Naudé and John Evelyn. Library 4th ser 12 1932.
Dibdin, T. F. The library companion: or the young man's guide and the old man's comfort in the choice of a library. 1824.
Plomer, H. R. Books mentioned in wills. Trans Bibl Soc 7 1904.
The literature of libraries in the xviith and xviiith centuries. Ed J. C. Dana and H. W. Kent 6 pts Chicago 1906; N. J. Methuen 1967. Reprints of Naudé, Durie etc.
Taylor, A. Renaissance guides to books. 1945.

(2) GENERAL WORKS ON COLLECTORS AND COLLECTING

Jacob, Louys. Traicté des plus belles bibliothèques publiques & particulières qui ont esté & qui sont à présent dans le monde. 2 pts Paris 1644. On England pp. 242–307.
[Oldys, W.] The British librarian. 1738.
Beloe, W. Anecdotes of literature and scarce books. 6 vols 1806–10.

Dibdin, T. F. Bibliomania. 1809, 1811 (enlarged), 1842 (further enlarged), 1876, 1903, 1969.
— The bibliographical Decameron. 3 vols 1817.
[Beresford, J.] Bibliosophia, or book-wisdom: containing some account of the pride, pleasure and privileges of that glorious vocation, book-collecting. 1810.

Merryweather, F. S. Bibliomania in the Middle Ages. 1849; ed H. B. Copinger 1933.

Burton, J. H. The bookhunter. Edinburgh 1860, 1882 (enlarged).

Edwards, E. Libraries and founders of libraries. 1865.

— Free town libraries in Britain, France, Germany and America; together with brief notices of book-collectors, and of the respective places of deposit of their surviving collections. 1869.

— Lives of the founders of the British Museum 1570–1870. 1870.

Quaritch, B. (ed). Contributions towards a dictionary of English book collectors. 14 pts 1892–1921.

Bisticci, Vespasiano da. Vite di huomini illustri del secolo 15. Ed L. Frati 2 vols Bologna 1892–3; tr 1926.

Elton, C. I. and M. A. The great book-collectors. 1893.

Roberts, W. The bookhunter in London. 1895.

Fletcher, W. Y. English book collectors. 1902.

Hazlitt, W. C. The book collector. 1904.

Davenport, C. English heraldic book stamps. 1909. A copy with much necessary annotation by W. A. Jackson in the Houghton Library, Harvard.

de Ricci, S. English collectors of books and mss and their marks of ownership 1530–1900. Cambridge 1930, 1960. W. A. Jackson's much annotated copy is in the Houghton Library, Harvard.

Schirmer, W. F. Der englische Früh-humanismus. Leipzig 1931, Tübingen 1963 (rev).

Carter, J. Taste and technique in book collecting. Cambridge 1948, 1970 (rev and enlarged).

King, A. H. Some British collectors of music c. 1600–1960. Cambridge 1963.

Munby, A. N. L. The libraries of English men of letters. 1964.

Harrison, J. and P. Laslett. The library of John Locke. Oxford 1965 (Oxford Bibl Soc).

(3) INDIVIDUAL COLLECTORS AND CATALOGUES

Arthur Agarde (1540–1615)
Lee, S. L. In Dictionary of national biography vol 1.
Wright, C. E. The Elizabethan Society of Antiquaries and the formation of the Cottonian Library. In The English library before 1700, ed F. Wormald and C. E. Wright 1958.

Thomas Allen (1542–1632)
Ker, N. R. Allen's manuscripts. Bodleian Lib Record 2 1941–9.

John Argentine (c. 1442–1508)
Rhodes, D. E. Provost Argentine of King's and his books. Trans Cambridge Bibl Soc 2 1954–8.
— John Argentine, Provost of King's. Amsterdam 1967.

Elias Ashmole (1617–92)
Black, W. H. A descriptive, analytical and critical catalogue of the manuscripts bequeathed unto the University of Oxford. Oxford 1845.
Josten, C. H. (ed). Elias Ashmole 1617–92. 5 vols Oxford 1966.

John Bale (1495–1563)
McCusker, H. Books and mss formerly in the possession of John Bale. Library 4th ser 16 1935.

Robert Beale (1541–1601)
Rigg, J. M. In Dictionary of national biography vol 4.

John, Duke of Bedford (1389–1435)
Barber, M. J. The books and patronage of learning of a 15th-century prince. Book Collector 12 1963.

Thomas Bekynton (c. 1390–1465)
James, M. R. The Chaundler manuscripts. 1916 (Roxburghe Club).
Hay, D. Flavio Biondo and the Middle Ages. Proc Br Acad 45 1959.
[Hunt, R. W. and A. C. de la Mare]. Duke Humfrey and English humanism in the fifteenth century: catalogue of an exhibition held in the Bodleian Library, Oxford. Oxford [1970].

Sir Thomas Bludder (c. 1590–1655)
Leivsay, J. L. and R. B. Davis. A Cavalier library 1643. SB 6 1954.

Richard Bole
See under William Gray.

William Brygon (d. 1469)
[Hunt, R. W. and A. C. de la Mare]. Duke Humfrey and English humanism in the fifteenth century: catalogue of an exhibition held in the Bodleian Library, Oxford. Oxford [1970].

Simon Burley (1336–88)
Scattergood, V. J. Two medieval booklists. Library 5th ser 23 1968.

Richard de Bury (1281–1345)
Thomas, E. Was Richard de Bury an imposter? Library 1st ser 1 1888.

Vogel, E. G. Erinnerungen an einige verdienstvolle Bibliophilen des 14ten und 15ten Jahrhunderts. Serapeum 4.

Richard d'Aungerville of Bury: fragments of his register and other documents. Surtees Soc 119 1910.

Ghellinck, J. de. Un évêque bibliophile au xive siècle. Revue d'Histoire Ecclésiastique 18 1922.

Denholm-Young, N. Collected papers on medieval subjects. Oxford 1946.

Richard de Bury's books from the abbey of St Alban's. Bodleian Lib Record 3 1951.

Christopher and William Carye
Watson, A. G. Christopher and William Carye, collector of monastic manuscripts, and 'John Carye'. Library 5th ser 20 1965.

William Cecil, Baron Burghley (1520–98) and the Cecil family
Bibliotheca illustris: sive catalogus variorum librorum auctio habebitur Londini Nov 21, 1687, per T. Bentley & B. Walford. This sale catalogue contains Burghley's library in the main, though some later books have been added.
Salisbury, Marquess of. The library at Hatfield House, Hertfordshire. Library 5th ser 18 1963.

Charles I (1600–49)
Murdock, W. G. B. King Charles I as a book lover. Book Lover's Mag 6 1907.

Thomas Chaundler (c. 1418–90)
James, M. R. The Chaundler manuscripts. 1916 (Roxburghe Club).

Archbishop Henry Chichele (c. 1362–1443)
Jacob, E. F. Two lives of Archbishop Chichele. Bull John Rylands Lib 16 1932.

John Clement (d. 1572)
Reed, A. W. Clement and his books. Library 6 1926.

Sir Edward Coke (1552–1634)
Hassall, W. O. A catalogue of the library of Coke. New Haven 1950 (Yale Law Lib).

Edward Conway, 2nd Viscount Conway
Plomer, H. R. A Cavalier's library. Library 2nd ser 5 1904.

Sir Robert Cotton (1571–1633)
Smith, T. Catalogus librorum manuscriptorum bibliothecae Cottonianae. Oxford 1696. Life of Cotton, pp. vii–ix.
Planta, J. A catalogue of manuscripts in the Cottonian library. 1802.
Wright, C. E. The Elizabethan Society of Antiquaries and the formation of the Cottonian Library. In The English library before 1700, ed F. Wormald and C. E. Wright 1958.

Robert Grosseteste (d. 1253)
Thomas, S. The writings of Grosseteste. Cambridge 1940.
Hunt, R. W. Manuscripts containing the indexing symbols of Grosseteste. Bodleian Lib Record 4 1953.
Callus, D. A. (ed). Grosseteste: scholar and Bishop. Oxford 1955.
Barbour, R. A manuscript of Pseudo-Dionysius Areopagiticus copied for Grosseteste. Bodleian Lib Record 6 1958.

John Gunthorpe (d. 1498)
Munby, A. N. L. Notes on King's College library in the fifteenth century. Trans Cambridge Bibl Soc 1 1949–53.
Mynors, R. A. B. A fifteenth-century scribe: T. Werken. Ibid.
[Hunt, R. W. and A. C. de la Mare]. Duke Humfrey and English humanism in the fifteenth century: catalogue of an exhibition held in the Bodleian Library, Oxford. Oxford [1970].

Edward Gwynn (d. 1645?)
Jackson, W. A. Edward Gwynn. Library 4th ser 15 1934.

Robert Hare (d. 1611)
Cooper, T. In Dictionary of national biography vol 24.
James, M. R. Catalogue of the manuscripts at Trinity Hall, Cambridge. Cambridge 1907, pp. 1–4.

Gabriel Harvey (1545–1630?)
Hazlitt, W. C. In B. Quaritch, Dictionary of English book-collectors pt 13, 1899.

Sir Christopher Hatton (1540–91)
James, C. W. Some notes on the library of printed books at Holkham. Library 4th ser 11 1931.
Hassall, W. O. The books of Hatton at Holkham. Library 5th ser 5 1951.

Anthony Higgin
The library catalogue of Anthony Higgin, Dean of Ripon (1608–24). Ed J. E. Mortimer, Leeds 1962. See A. G. Watson, The manuscripts of Henry Savile of Banke, 1969 (Bibl Soc) p. 8.

Andrew Holes (fl. 1414–44)
Da Bisticci, Vespasiano da. Vite di huomini illustri, del secolo 15. Ed L. Frati 2 vols Bologna 1892–3; tr 1926.
Bennett, J. W. Andrew Holes. Speculum 19 1944.
Hunt, R. W. Humanistic script in Florence in the early fifteenth century. In Calligraphy and palaeography: essays presented to Alfred Fairbank, 1965.
[Hunt, R. W. and A. C. de la Mare]. Duke Humfrey and English humanism in the fifteenth century: catalogue of an exhibition held in the Bodleian Library, Oxford. Oxford [1970].

Thomas Howard, 2nd Earl of Arundel (1586–1646)
Bibliotheca Norfolciana. 1681.
Black, W. H. Catalogue of the Arundel mss in the library of the College of Arms. 1829.
Catalogue of manuscripts in the British Museum new ser 1 pt 1, 1834.
Harvey, M. F. S. The life, correspondence and collections of Thomas Howard, Earl of Arundel. 1921.

Lord William Howard (1563–1640)
Ornsby, G. Selections from the household books of the Lord William Howard. Surtees Soc 68 1878.
Mathew, D. The library at Naworth. In For Hilaire Belloc: essays in honor of his 72nd birthday, ed D. Woodruff 1942. Mainly based on preceding.

Edward Hyde, Earl of Clarendon (1609–74)
Hardacre, P. H. Portrait of a bibliophile 1: Clarendon. Book Collector 7 1958.

The Isham family
Edmonds, C. The Lamport Garland. 1882 (Roxburghe Club).
Graves, R. E. The Isham books. Bibliographica 3 1897.
Jackson, W. A. The Lamport Hall–Britwell Court books. In Joseph Quincy Adams memorial studies, Washington 1948.

Hallam, H. A. N. Lamport Hall revisited. Book Collector 16 1967.

James I (1566–1625)
The library of James VI 1578–83, from a manuscript in the hand of Peter Young, his tutor. Ed G. F. Warner, Edinburgh 1893 (Scottish Historical Soc).

John of Basingstoke
Weiss, R. The study of Greek in England during the fourteenth century. Rinascimento 2 1951.

Ben Jonson (1573?–1637)
Herford, C. H. and P. Simpson. Ben Jonson vol 1. Oxford 1925 pp. 250–71.

Thomas Knyvett, 1st Baron Knyvett (d. 1622)
The Knyvett Letters. Ed B. Schofield 1949.

Archbishop Simon Langham (d. 1376)
Robinson, J. A. and M. R. James. The manuscripts of Westminster Abbey. Cambridge 1909.

William Lambarde (1536–1601)
Nichols, J. Bibliotheca typographica Britannica vol 1, 1780–90, pp. 493–532.

William Laud (1573–1645)
Fletcher, W. Y. English book-collectors. 1902.

Geoffrey de Lawath
James, M. R. Catalogue of the manuscripts of Pembroke College, Cambridge. Cambridge 1905.

Thomas Linacre (c. 1460–1524)
Weiss, R. Notes on Thomas Linacre. In Miscellanea Giovanni Mercati vol 4, Vatican 1946.

Clemens Little (d. 1580)
Catalogus librorum (left to the City of Edinburgh to start the University Library). Maitland Club Miscellany vol 1 pt 2, Edinburgh 1833.

Lumley, John, 1st Baron Lumley (c. 1534–1609)
Jayne, S. and F. R. Johnson. The Lumley library: the catalogue of 1609. 1956.

Sir William More (1520–after 1576)
Evans, J. Extracts from the private account-book of Sir William More. Archeologia 36 1855.

James Morice
Oates, J. C. T. 'English bokes concernyng to James Morice'. Trans Cambridge Bibl Soc 3 1960.

Archbishop George Neville (c. 1433–76)
Tait, J. Letters of John Tiptoft, Earl of Worcester and Archbishop Neville to the University of Oxford. EHR 25 1920.
James, M. R. Greek manuscripts in England before the Renaissance. Library 4th ser 7 1927.
Weiss, R. The Library of John Tiptoft, Earl of Worcester. Bodleian Quart Record 8 1935–8.
[Hunt, R. W. and A. C. de la Mare]. Duke Humfrey and English humanism in the fifteenth century: catalogue of an exhibition held in the Bodleian Library, Oxford. Oxford [1970].

Matthew Parker (1504–75)
Strype, John. The life and acts of Matthew Parker. 1711, 3 vols Oxford 1921.
Correspondence. Ed J. Bruce 1853 (Parker Soc).
James, M. R. The sources of Archbishop Parker's collection of mss at Corpus Christi College, Cambridge, with a reprint of the catalogue of Thomas Markaunt's Library. Cambridge Antiquarian Soc 1899.
Pearce, E. C. Matthew Parker. Library 4th ser 6 1926.
Greg, W. W. Books and bookmen in the correspondence of Archbishop Parker. Library 4th ser 16 1936.
Wright, C. E. The dispersal of the monastic libraries and the beginnings of Anglo-Saxon studies, Matthew Parker and his circle: a preliminary study. Trans Cambridge Bibl Soc 1 1949–53.
—— The dispersal of the libraries in the sixteenth century. In The English library before 1700, ed F. Wormald and C. E. Wright 1958.

Henry Percy, 9th Earl of Northumberland (1564–1632)
Batho, G. R. The library of the 'Wizard' Earl: Henry Percy, ninth Earl of Northumberland (1564–1632). Library 5th ser 15 1960.

Sir William Pickering (1516–75)
Philip, I. G. Pickering and his books. Book Collector 5 1956.

Sir John Prise
Ker, N. R. Sir John Prise. Library 5th ser 10 1955.

Bryan Rowe (d. 1521)
Norton, F. J. The library of Bryan Rowe, Vice-Provost of King's College. Trans Cambridge Bibl Soc 2 1954–8.

Royal Library
Warner, G. F. and J. P. Gilson (ed). Catalogue of Western manuscripts in the Old Royal and King's Collections in the British Museum. 4 vols 1921.
King, A. H. The royal music library. TLS 25 April 1958; Book Collector 7 1958.

Francis Russell, Earl of Bedford (1527?–85)
Byrne, M. St C. and G. S. Thomson. 'My Lord's books' (1584). RES 7 1931.

John Russell (c. 1420–94)
[Hunt, R. W. and A. C. de la Mare]. Duke Humfrey and English humanism in the fifteenth century: catalogue of an exhibition held in the Bodleian Library, Oxford. Oxford [1970].

William of St Carilef (d. 1096)
Raine, J. (ed). Catalogi veteres ecclesiae cathedralis Dunelmensis. 1838 (Surtees Soc) pp. 117–18.

Sir Henry Savile (1549–1622)

Sir Thomas Savile (1545–1607)
Carr, W. In Dictionary of national biography vol 50.
Munby, A. N. L. Phillipps Studies no 4: the formation of the Phillipps Library between 1841 and 1872. Cambridge 1956.
Birley, R. The Eton College collections: I, The history of Eton College Library. Eton 1970.

Henry Savile of Banke (1568–1617)
Gilson, J. P. The Library of Henry Savile of Banke. Trans Bibl Soc 9 1908.
Watson, A. G. The manuscripts of Henry Savile of Banke. 1969 (Bibl Soc).

Nicholas Saxton
See under William Gray, above.

William Say (c. 1400–68)
[Hunt, R. W. and A. C. de la Mare]. Duke Humfrey and English humanism in the fifteenth century: catalogue of an exhibition held in the Bodleian Library, Oxford. Oxford [1970].

John Selden (1584–1654)
Barratt, D. M. The library of Selden and its later history. Bodleian Lib Rec 3 1951.

John Shirwood (d. 1494)
Allen, P. S. Bishop Shirwood of Durham and his library. EHR 25 1910.
[Hunt, R. W. and A. C. de la Mare]. Duke Humfrey and English humanism in the fifteenth century: catalogue of an exhibition held in the Bodleian Library, Oxford. Oxford [1970].

Richard Smyth (1590–1675)
Bibliotheca Smithiana: sive catalogus librorum horum auctio habebitur Londini, May 15 1682 per R. Chiswell. A sale catalogue; the collection was started by Humfrey Dyson, above.
Duff, E. G. The library of Richard Smith. Library 2nd ser 8 1907.

Charles Somerset (c. 1585–1667)
Nixon, H. M. The Broxbourne library: styles and designs of bookbindings. 1956 (priv ptd).
Birley, R. The Eton College collections: I, The history of Eton College Library. Eton 1970.

Sir Henry Spelman (1564?–1641)
[The library of Sir Henry Spelman]. Sold for J. Harding, 28 November 1709; [2nd pt], E. Curll [1710?].
Carr, W. In Dictionary of national biography vol 53.

Henry Stafford, 1st Baron Stafford (1501–63)
Anderson, A. M. The books and interests of Henry, Lord Stafford. Library 5th ser 21 1966.

George Thomason (c. 1602–66)
British Museum: Thomason collection. Catalogue of the pamphlets, books, newspapers and manuscripts relating to the Civil War, the Commonwealth and Restoration 1640–61. Ed G. K. Fortescue 2 vols 1908.
Madan, F. Notes on the Thomason Collection of Civil War tracts. Bibliographica 3 1897.
Hiscock, W. G. The Thomas tracts. TLS 11 June 1942.
Spencer, L. The professional and literary connexions of Thomason. Library 5th ser 13 1958.

William Thynne (d. 1546)
[Guido delle Colonne]. The ancient historie and onely trewe cronicle of the warres betwixte the Grecians and Troyans translated by John Lydgate. 1555. Preface by R. Braham.
Manly, J. M. and E. Rickert. The text of the Canterbury tales. 8 vols Chicago 1940.

John Tiptoft, Earl of Worcester (1427–70)
Bisticci, Vespasiano da. Vite di huomini illustri. Ed L. Frati 2 vols Bologna 1892–3; tr 1926.
Tait, J. Letters of Tiptoft and Archbishop Neville to the University of Oxford. EHR 25 1920.
Weiss, R. The library of Tiptoft. Bodleian Quart Record 8 1936.
— Another Tiptoft manuscript. Ibid.
— Tiptoft and Ludovico Carbone. Rinascimento 8 1957.
— Uno scolare inglese dello studio padovano: Tiptoft. Quaderni dell'Università di Padova 1 1968.
Mitchell, R. J. A Renaissance library: the collection of Tiptoft. Library 4th ser 18 1937.
Delz, J. John Free und die Bibliothek Tiptofts. Italia Mediovale e Humanistica 11 1968.

James Ussher, Archbishop of Armagh (1581–1656)
Works. Ed C. R. Elrington and J. H. Todd 17 vols Dublin 1847–64. Particularly the life of Ussher by Elrington in vol 1.
O'Sullivan, W. Ussher as a collector of manuscripts. Hermathena 88 1956.

Stephen Vallenger (d. 1581)
Plomer, H. R. Stephen Vallenger. Library 2nd ser 2 1901.

William de Walcote
Scattergood, V. J. Two medieval book-lists. Library 5th ser 23 1968.

Sir James Ware (1594–1666)
Librorum manuscriptorum in bibliotheca Jacobi Waraei equitis: catalogus. Dublin 1648.
G[ibson], E. Librorum manuscriptorum in duabus insignibus bibliothecis; altera Tenisoniana, Londini; altera Dugdaliana, Oxonii; catalogus. Oxford 1692. Ware's mss, bought by Clarendon, were then on loan to Tenison's library.

Abbot John Whethamstede (c. 1392–1465)
Weiss, R. Piero del Monte, John Whethamstede and the library of St Alban's Abbey. EHR 60 1945.

John Williams, Archbishop of York (1582–1650)
Hacket, John (Bishop of Lichfield). Scrinia reserata: a memorial offer'd to the great deservings of John Williams. 1693.

Frances Wolfreston (fl. 1603–25)
Sotheby & Co. Catalogue of the remains of a library partly collected during the reign of King James I, 24 May 1856.

William Worcester (c. 1415–c. 1482)
Gasquet, F. N. In his An Old English Bible and other essays, 1897.
Weiss, R. Humanism in England. Oxford 1941, 1967 (rev).
[Hunt, R. W. and A. C. de la Mare]. Duke Humfrey and English humanism in the fifteenth century: catalogue of an exhibition held in the Bodleian Library, Oxford. Oxford [1970].

Thomas Wotton (1521–87)

    Moss, W. E. The English Grolier: a catalogue of books in gold-tooled bindings from the library of Thomas Wotton. Worth 1942 (priv ptd).

    Nixon, H. M. Twelve books in fine bindings from the library of J. W. Hely-Hutchinson. Oxford 1953 (Roxburghe Club).

    —— The Broxbourne library: styles and designs of book-bindings from the twelfth to the twentieth century. 1956 (priv ptd).

Henry Wriothesley, 3rd Earl of Southampton (1573–1624)

    Baker, T. In his A history of the College of St John, Cambridge, 2 vols Cambridge 1869.

    Wallis, P. J. The library of William Crashawe. Trans Cambridge Bibl Soc 2 1958.

William of Wykeham (1324–1404)

    Leach, A. F. Wykeham's books at New College. Oxford Historical Soc Collectanea 3 1896.

N. J. B.

2. POETRY

I. INTRODUCTION

(1) BIBLIOGRAPHIES

Collier, J. P. Extracts from the register of the Stationers' Company. 2 vols 1848–9 (Shakespeare Soc).
—— A bibliographical and critical account of the rarest books in the English language. 2 vols 1865.
Halliwell(-Phillipps), J. O. A catalogue of ballads and poems presented to the Chetham Library. 1851.
—— A catalogue of an unique collection of ancient English broadside ballads. 1856.
Corser, T. Collectanea anglo-poetica. 5 vols in 11 1860–83 (Chetham Soc).
Lemon, R. Catalogue of a collection of broadsides in the possession of the Society of Antiquaries. 1866.
Furnivall, F. J. Captain Cox: his ballads and books. 1871 (Ballad Soc).
Arber, E. A transcript of the registers of the Company of Stationers of London 1554–1640. 5 vols 1875–94 (priv ptd).

Newton, T. W. Catalogue of old ballads in the possession of Frederic Ouvry. 1877 (priv ptd).
Bibliotheca Lindesiana. Catalogue of a collection of English ballads of the 17th and 18th centuries. 1890 (priv ptd).
Eyre, G. E. B. A transcript of the registers of the worshipful Company of Stationers 1640–1708. 3 vols 1913–14 (Roxburghe Club).
Rollins, H. E. An analytical index to the ballad-entries in the Stationers' Registers. Chapel Hill 1924.
Case, A. E. A bibliography of English poetical miscellanies 1521–1750. 1935 (Bibl Soc).
White, E. A. and M. Dean-Smith. An index of English songs. 1951 (English Folk-Dance & Song Soc).

(2) MISCELLANIES AND REPRESENTATIVE BALLAD-COLLECTIONS

For miscellanies in languages other than English, largely university productions, see Case, above.

The Court of Venus. [1538] (fragment in Bodley), [1548] (as A boke of balettes) (fragment in Univ of Texas), [1562] (as The Courte of Venus) (fragment in Folger Lib); ed R. A. Fraser, Durham NC 1955.
Stopes, C. C. The metrical psalms and the Courte of Venus. Athenaeum 24 June 1899.
—— The authorship of the Newe Courte of Venus. Athenaeum 1 July 1899.
—— In her Shakespeare's industry, 1916.
Foxwell, A. K. In her Poems of Wiat vol 2, 1913.
Griffith, R. H. A lost boke of balettes. TLS 5 July 1928. Reply by E. M. W. Tillyard 12 July 1928.
—— The boke of balettes again. TLS 4 Sept 1930.
—— and R. A. Law. A boke of balettes and the Courte of Venus. SE 10 1930.
Law, R. A. More about the Boke of balettes. TLS 26 Dec 1929.
Huttar, C. A. Wyatt and the several editions of the Court of Venus. SB 19 1966.
Certayne chapters of the proverbes of Salomon. [1550] (fragment).
Huttar, C. A. Poems by Surrey and others in a printed miscellany circa 1550. Eng Miscellany (Rome) 16 1965.
—— Amer Philosophical Soc Year Book 1968.
Christmas carolles newely imprinted. [1550]; ed E. B. Reed, Cambridge Mass 1932 (with fragments of other edns as Christmas carols ptd in the sixteenth century).
Songes and sonettes. 5 June 1557, 31 July 1557 (rev with addns), 31 July 1557, 1559, 1559, 1565, 1567, 1574, 1585, 1587; ed G. Sewell 1717; ed T. Percy [1767] (not pbd); ed G. F. Nott [1814] (not pbd); ed J. P. Collier, Seven English poetical miscellanies, 1867; ed E. Arber 1870 (as Tottel's miscellany); ed H. E. Rollins 2 vols Cambridge Mass 1928–9 (as Tottel's miscellany), 1965 (with addns).
Warton, T. In his History of English poetry vol 3, 1781. Section 21.
Plomer, H. R. Richard Tottell. Bibliographica 3 1897.

Greg, W. W. Tottel's miscellany. Library 1st ser 5 1904.
Padelford, F. M. The relation of the 1812 and 1815–16 editions of Surrey and Wyatt. Anglia 29 1906.
Byrom, H. J. Tottel's miscellany 1717–1817. RES 3 1927.
—— The case for Nicholas Grimald as editor of Tottell's miscellany. MLR 27 1932.
Sherburn, G. Songes and sonettes. TLS 24 July 1930.
Parker, W. R. The sonnets in Tottel's miscellany. PMLA 54 1939.
Brooks, C. The history of Percy's edition of Surrey (Tottel's miscellany). In his Correspondence of Thomas Percy and Richard Farmer, Baton Rouge 1946.
A handefull of pleasant delites, by Clement Robinson and divers others. [1566] (fragment in Huntington Lib), 1584, [1600] (fragment); ed T. Park, Heliconia vol 2, 1815; ed E. Arber 1878; ed J. Crossley, Manchester 1871 (Spenser Soc); ed H. E. Rollins, Cambridge Mass 1924; ed A. Kershaw 1926.
Rollins, H. E. The date, authors and contents of A handfull. JEGP 18 1919; MLN 41 1926.
—— In J. Q. Adams memorial studies, Washington 1948.
The paradyse of daynty devises. 1576, 1578 (rev), 1580 (rev), 1585 (rev), [1590], 1596, [1596], 1600, 1606; ed S. E. Brydges 1810; ed J. P. Collier, Seven English poetical miscellanies, 1867; ed H. E. Rollins, Cambridge Mass 1927.
Lithgow, R. A. D. The paradise of dainty devises. Trans Royal Soc of Lit 17 1895.
Stopes, C. C. In her Shakespeare's industry, 1916.
Starnes, D. T. Sources of poems 48 and 49 in the Paradise of dainty devices. PQ 6 1927.
A gorgious gallery of gallant inventions. 1578; ed T. Park, Heliconia vol 1, 1815; ed H. Ellis, Three collections of English poetry, 1845 (Roxburghe Club); ed J. P. Collier, Seven English poetical miscellanies, 1867; ed H. E. Rollins, Cambridge Mass 1926.
A booke of epitaphes made upon the death of Sir William Buttes. [1584].

Verses of prayse and joye, written upon her Majesties preservation. 1586; ed F. S. Boas, Works of Thomas Kyd, Oxford 1901.

Brittons bowre of delights. 1591, 1597; ed H. E. Rollins, Cambridge Mass 1933.

Syr P. S. his Astrophel and Stella. 1591, [1591].

The phoenix nest. 1593; ed T. Park, Heliconia vol 2, 1815; ed J. P. Collier, Seven English poetical miscellanies, 1867; ed H. Macdonald 1926; ed H. E. Rollins, Cambridge Mass 1931.

Gosse, E. Sunday Times 24 April 1927.

McNeal, T. H. Shakespeare Assoc Bull 13 1938.

Sandison, H. E. PMLA 61 1946.

Certayne worthye manuscript poems of great antiquity. 1597; ed J. Ballantyne, Edinburgh 1812.

The arbor of amorous devises by Nicholas Breton et al. 1597; ed A. B. Grosart in his edn of Breton vol 1, 1879; ed H. E. Rollins, Cambridge Mass 1936.

Politeuphia: wits commonwealth, by John Bodenham. 1597, 1598, [1608], [1610], [1620], [1626], [1630], [1640], [1641], 1647, 1650, 1653, 1655 (17th edn), 1661, 1663, 1667, 1669, 1671, 1674, 1678, 1684, 1687, 1688, 1698, 1699, 1706.

The passionate pilgrime, by W. Shakespeare. 1599, 1612 (3rd edn).

Bel-vedere: or the garden of the Muses. 1600, 1610 (as The garden of the Muses), 1875 (Spenser Soc).

Crawford, C. Belvedere: or the garden of the Muses. E Studien 43 1911.

Starnes, D. T. Some sources of Wits theatre of the little world 1599 and Bodenham's Belvedere 1600. PQ 30 1951.

Englands Helicon. 1600, 1614 (with addns); ed S. E. Brydges, Br Bibliographer 3 1812; ed J. O. Halliwell(-Phillipps) 1865 (selection); ed J. P. Collier, Seven English poetical miscellanies, 1867; ed A. H. Bullen 1887; ed H. Macdonald 1925, 1950 (ML); ed H. E. Rollins 2 vols Cambridge Mass 1935.

Hebel, J. W. Nicholas Ling and England's Helicon. Library 2nd ser 5 1924.

Macdonald, H. England's Helicon. TSL 23 April 1925. Replies by M. St C. Byrne 7 May, G. Murphy, H. C. Bartlett and Macdonald 14 May, Macdonald 21 May 1925.

Lewis, C. S. TLS 9 May 1952.

Englands Parnassus. 1600; ed T. Park, Heliconia vol 3, 1815; ed J. P. Collier, Seven English poetical miscellanies, 1867; ed C. Crawford, Oxford 1913.

Crawford, C. Englands Parnassus. N & Q May 1908–28 June 1909.

Williams, F. B. Notes on Englands Parnassus. MLN 52 1937.

Strange histories of kings, princes, dukes etc by Thomas Deloney et al. 1600, 1602, 1607, 1612 (rev), 1631 (rev), 1674 (rev as The royal garland of love and delight); ed J. P. Collier 1841 (Percy Soc); ed F. O. Mann in his edn of Deloney, Oxford 1912.

Loves martyr: or Rosalins complaint by Robert Chester. 1601, 1611 (as The annals of Great Brittaine).

A poetical rhapsody. 1602, 1608 (rev), 1611 (rev), 1621 (rev); ed S. E. Brydges 3 vols 1814–17; ed N. H. Nicolas 2 vols 1826; ed J. P. Collier, Seven English poetical miscellanies, 1867; ed A. H. Bullen 2 vols 1890–1; ed H. E. Rollins 2 vols Cambridge Mass 1931–2.

Rollins, H. E. A.W. and A poetical rhapsody. SP 29 1932.

Adams, J. Q. A new song by Robert Jones. MLQ 1 1940.

A crowne-garland of goulden roses, by Richard Johnson. 1612, 1631, 1659, 1662, 1680, 1683, 1692; ed W. Chappell 1842 (Percy Soc), 1845.

Mausoleum: or the choisest floures of the epitaphs, written on the death of Prince Henrie. 1613.

Three elegies on the most lamented death of Prince Henrie. 1613.

Certain elegies done by sundrie excellent wits with satyres and epigrames. 1618, 1620; ed E. V. Utterson, Ryde 1843 (priv ptd).

The Muses welcome to the high and mightie Prince James at his Majesties happie return. Edinburgh 1618.

A description of love. 1620 (2nd edn), 1625 (5th edn), 1629, 1636 (8th edn), 1638.

The golden garland of princely pleasures and delicate delights, by Richard Johnson. 1620 (3rd edn), 1690 (13th edn, with addns).

Funerall elegies upon the most untimely death of the honourable and most hopefull Mr John Stanhope. 1624.

Loves garland: or posies for rings, handkerchers and gloves. 1624; ed J. O. Halliwell(-Phillipps), Literature of the sixteenth and seventeenth centuries 1851; ed E. Arber, English garner vol 1, 1877; ed J. R. Brown 1883.

The garland of good will by Thomas Deloney. 1628, 1631, 1659, 1678, 1685, 1688, [1690], [1696], [1700], 1709, 1760; ed J. H. Dixon 1851 (Percy Soc).

Annalia Dubrensia: upon the yeerely celebration of Mr Robert Dovers Olympick games upon Cotswold-hills. 1636; ed A. B. Grosart, Manchester 1877; ed E. R. Vyvyan, Cheltenham 1878.

Death repealed by a thankfull memoriall. 1638.

Jonsonus virbius: or the memorie of Ben Johnson revived by the friends of the Muses. 1638.

Justa Edouardo King naufrago. Cambridge 1638.

Festum voluptatis: or the banquet of pleasure, by Samuel Pick.

Rollins, H. E. Samuel Pick's borrowings. RES 7 1931.

The academy of complements: or the lover's secretary [by John Gough]. 1640, 1650, 1654, 1658, 1663, 1664, 1670, 1684, 1685 ('5th edn'), 1705, 1727, 1750, 1760, 1790, 1795.

Good and true, fresh and new Christmas carols. 1642.

Verses on the death of the right valiant Sir Beirll Grenvil. Oxford 1643, 1644, 1684.

Wits recreations by Sir J[ohn] M[ennis] and J[ames] S[mall]. 1640, 1641, 1645 (as Recreation for ingenious head-pieces), 1650, 1654, [1663], 1667, 1683; ed T. Park, Musarum deliciae vol 1, 1817; ed J. C. Hotten 1874.

Lachrymae Musarum: the tears of the Muses. 1649, 1650.

The loves of Hero and Leander with choice peices of drollery. 1651, 1653, 1662 (as Ovid de arte amandi), [1667], 1672, 1677, 1682, 1684, 1689, 1705.

Newes from the dead [by Richard Watkins]. Oxford 1651.

Certain verses written by severall of the authors friends to be reprinted with the second edition of Gondibert. 1653 (3 edns).

The harmony of the Muses: or the gentlemans and ladies choisest recreation, by C.R. 1654.

Songs and poems of love and drollery, by T[homas] W[eaver]. 1654.

The English treasury of wit and language, by John Cotgrave. 1655.

The marrow of complements. 1655.

Musarum deliciae: or the Muses recreation, by Sir J[ohn] M[ennis] and J[ames] S[mith]. 1655, 1656.

Wits interpreter: the English Parnassus, by J[ohn] C[otgrave]. 1655, 1662 (with addns), 1671 (with addns).

Choyce drollery: songs and sonnets. 1656; ed J. W. Ebsworth, Boston Lincs 1876.

Cupid's master-piece: or the free-school of witty and delightful complements. [1656], 1685.

Parnassus biceps: or severall choice pieces of poetry, by Abraham Wright. 1656; ed G. Thorn-Drury 1927.

Sportive wit: the Muses merriment [by John Phillips]. 1656.

Wit and drollery, jovial poems. 1656, 1661, 1682 (rev).

The English Parnassus: or a helpe to English poesie, by Joshua Poole. 1657, 1677.

The mysteries of love and eloquence: or the arts of wooing and complementing, by E[dward] P[hillips]. 1658, 1685 (3rd edn), 1699 (as The beau's academy).

Naps upon Parnassus: a sleepy Muse nipt and pincht, though not awakened [by Samuel Austen the younger]. 1658.

Wit restor'd in severall select poems, not formerly publish't. 1658; ed T. Park, Musarum deliciae, 1817.

J. Cleaveland revived. 1659, 1660 (with addns), 1662, 1668, 1687 (as Works of Mr John Cleveland, with addns), 1699, 1742.

Three poems upon the death of his late Highnesse Oliver Lord Protector. 1659, 1682 (as Three poems upon the death of the late usurper Oliver Cromwell), 1709 (as A panegyrick on Oliver Cromwell).

Le prince d'amour: or the prince of love. 1660, 1669.

Ratts rhimed to death: or the Rump-Parliament hang'd up in the shambles. 1660, 1660 (as The rump: or a collection of songs and ballads), 1662 (as Rump: or an exact collection of the choycest songs relating to the late times), 2 vols 1731 (as A collection of loyal songs).

Park, T. Heliconia. 3 vols 1815.

Ballads and other fugitive pieces poetical from the collections of Sir James Balfour. Edinburgh 1834.

U[tterson], E. V. A little book of ballads. Newport 1836 (priv ptd).

Collier, J. P. Old ballads from early printed copies. 1840 (Percy Soc).
— Eight ballads, from the original black-letter copies. 1846 (priv ptd).
— A book of Roxburghe ballads. 1847.
— Broadside black-letter ballads. 1868 (priv ptd).
— Twenty-five old ballads and songs from mss. 1869 (priv ptd).

Wright, T. Political ballads published in England during the Commonwealth. 1841 (Percy Soc).
— Songs and ballads chiefly of the reign of Philip and Mary. 1860 (Roxburghe Club). See H. E. Rollins, MLN 34 1919.

Ellis, H. Three collections of English poetry of the latter part of the sixteenth century. 1845 (Roxburghe Club).

Farr, E. Select poetry chiefly devotional of the reign of Queen Elizabeth. 2 vols 1845 (Parker Soc).

Hannah, J. The courtly poets from Raleigh to Montrose. 1870.
— Poems of Raleigh, Wotton and other courtly poets 1540–1650. 1875.

Rimbault, E. F. A little book of songs and ballads. 1851.

Bell, R. Early ballads. 1856.

Child, F. J. English and Scottish ballads. 8 vols Boston 1857–8, 5 vols 1882–98 (rev as The English and Scottish popular ballads).

Wilkins, W. W. Political ballads of the seventeenth and eighteenth centuries. 2 vols 1860.

[Halliwell-Phillipps, J. O.] Ancient ballads and broadsides published in the sixteenth century. 1867 (Philobiblon Soc), 1867 (as A collection of 79 black-letter ballads).

Furnivall, F. J. and W. R. Morfill. Ballads from mss. 2 vols 1868–73 (Ballad Soc).

Furnivall, F. J. Love-poems and humourous ones. 1874 (Ballad Soc).

Chappell, W. and J. W. Ebsworth. Roxburghe ballads. 9 vols 1869–97 (Ballad Soc).

Hazlitt, W. C. Inedited poetical miscellanies 1584–1700. 1870.

Boedderer, K. Englische Lieder und Balladen aus dem 16 Jahrhundert. Jahrbuch für Romanische und Englische Sprache 14–15 1875–6.

Ebsworth, J. W. Bagford ballads. 2 vols 1878 (Ballad Soc).

Linton, W. J. Rare poems of the sixteenth and seventeenth centuries. New Haven 1882.

Ashton, J. Humor, wit and satire of the seventeenth century. 1883.
— A century of ballads. 1888.

Goldsmid, E. Quaint gleanings from ancient poetry. Edinburgh 1884.

Bullen, A. H. Poems, chiefly lyrical, from romances and prose-tracts of the Elizabethan age. 1890.

Schelling, F. E. A book of Elizabethan lyrics. Boston 1895.
— A book of seventeenth-century lyrics. Boston 1899.

Carpenter, F. I. English lyric poetry 1500–1700. 1897.

Farmer, J. S. Merry songs and ballads prior to 1800. 5 vols 1897.

Arber, E. The Surrey and Wyatt anthology 1509–47. 1900.
— The Spenser anthology 1548–91. 1899.
— The Shakespeare anthology 1592–1616. 1899.
— The Jonson anthology 1617–37. 1899.
— The Milton anthology 1638–74. 1899.

Bolle, W. Das Liederbuch Ms Rawlinson poet. 185. Archiv 114 1905. Reply by A. E. H. Swaen 116 1906.

Symons, A. A sixteenth-century anthology. 1905.

Clark, A. Shirburn ballads 1585–1616. 1907.

Padelford, F. M. Early sixteenth-century lyrics. Boston 1907.
— The songs in ms Rawlinson C.813. Anglia 31 1908. Reply by W. Bolle 34 1911.

Firth, C. H. Naval songs and ballads. 1908 (Navy Records Soc).

Collmann, H. L. Ballads and broadsides chiefly of the Elizabethan period. 1912 (Roxburghe Club).

Brougham, E. M. V. Corn from olde fieldes. 1918.
— News out of Scotland: being a miscellaneous collection of verse and prose. 1926.

Massingham, H. J. A treasury of seventeenth-century English verse. 1919.

Rollins, H. E. Old English ballads 1553–1625. Cambridge 1920.
— A Pepysian garland 1595–1639. Cambridge 1922.
— Cavalier and Puritan: ballads of the Great Rebellion. New York 1923.
— The pack of Autolycus. Cambridge Mass 1927.
— The Pepys ballads. 8 vols Cambridge Mass 1929–32.

Rohde, E. S. The old-world-pleasaunce. 1925.

Ault, N. Elizabethan lyrics. 1925, 1949 (rev).
— Seventeenth-century lyrics. 1928, 1950 (rev).
— A treasury of unfamiliar lyrics. 1938.

Duncan, E. Lyrics from the old song books. 1927.

Hammond, E. P. English verse between Chaucer and Surrey. Durham NC 1927.

Judson, A. C. Seventeenth-century lyrics. Chicago 1927.

Draper, J. W. A century of broadside elegies of the seventeenth century. 1928.

Peacock, W. English verse vol 1. 1928.

Campbell, K. W. Anthology of English poetry: 16th and 17th centuries. 1929.

Hebel, J. W. and H. H. Hudson. Poetry of the English Renaissance 1509–1660. New York 1929.

Howarth, R. G. Minor poets of seventeenth century. 1931 (EL), 1953 (rev).

Chambers, E. K. The Oxford book of sixteenth-century verse. Oxford 1932.

Greenhood, D. Tom of Bedlam's Song. San Francisco 1933.

Grierson, H. J. C. and G. Bullough. The Oxford book of seventeenth-century verse. Oxford 1934.

Nichols, J. B. A book of old ballads. 1934.

Green, R. L. The early English carols. Oxford 1935.

Auden, W. H. and J. Garrett. The poet's tongue. 1935.

Auden, W. H. and N. H. Pearson. Poets of the English language vols 1–2. New York 1951.

Harvey, A. S. Ballads, songs and rhymes of East Anglia. 1935.

Brinkley, R. F. English poetry of the seventeenth century. New York 1936.

Marshall, L. B. Rare poems of the seventeenth century. Cambridge 1936.

Goss, J. Ballads of Britain. 1937.

Black, W. M. Elizabethan and seventeenth-century lyrics. Philadelphia 1938.
Whimster, D. C. A century of lyrics 1550–1650. 1938.
Guiney, L. I. Recusant poets. 1938.
Simpson, C. and R. Lamson. Elizabethan and Shakespearean musicke for the recorder. Boston 1941.
Boas, F. S. Songs and lyrics from the English play books. 1945.
— Songs and lyrics from English masques and light operas. 1949.
Bullett, G. Silver poets of the sixteenth century. 1947 (EL).

Delattre, F. and C. Chemin. Les chansons élisabéthaines. Paris 1948.
Hayward, J. Seventeenth-century poetry. 1948.
Jagger, J. H. The poet's progress. 1949.
Muir, K. Elizabethan lyrics: a critical anthology. 1952.
Rollins, H. E. and H. C. Baker. The Renaissance in England. Boston 1954.
Hughey, R. The Arundel Harington manuscript of Tudor poetry. 2 vols Columbus 1960.
Lucie-Smith, E. The penguin book of Elizabethan verse. 1965 (Penguin).

(3) GENERAL STUDIES

Warton, T. The history of English poetry vol 3. 1781.
Brydges, S. E. Censura literaria. 10 vols 1805–9, 1815.
— The British bibliographer. 4 vols 1810–14.
— Restitua. 4 vols 1815–16.
[Fry, J.] Pieces of ancient poetry. Bristol 1814.
E., B. Ballads. GM Dec 1850. BM additional ms 15225.
Chappell, W. Popular music of the olden time. 2 vols 1855–9; ed H. E. Woolridge 2 vols 1893.
— Some account of an unpublished collection of songs and ballads by King Henry VIII and his contemporaries. Archaeologia 41 1867.
Langton, R. The black-letter ballads in the Free Reference Library, Manchester. Trans Lancs & Cheshire Antiquarian Soc 2 1884.
Bullen, A. H. Carols and poems. 1886.
Koeppel, E. Studien zur Geschichte des englischen Petrarchismus im sechzehnten Jahrhundert. Romanische Forschungen 5 1889.
Flügel, E. Liedersammlungen des XVI Jahrhunderts, besonders aus der Zeit Heinrichs VIII. Anglia 12 1889, 26 1903.
Marchi, L. de L'influenza della lirica italiana sulla lirica inglese nel secolo xvi. Nouva Antologia 58 1895.
The Elizabethan lyric. Quart Rev 196 1902.
Erskine, J. The Elizabethan lyric. New York 1903.
Sievers, R. Thomas Deloney: eine Studie über Balladenliteratur der Shakspere-Zeit. Berlin 1904.
Zocco, I. Petrarchismo e Petrarchisti in Inghilterra. Palermo 1906.
Swaen, A. E. H. Notes on some old songs. Archiv 121 1908.
— Notes on ballads and tunes in W. Sampson's Vowbreaker. Neophilologus 3 1918.
— Ballads, tunes and dances in Nash's works. Neophilologus 5 1920.
Firth, C. H. The ballad history of the reigns of the later Tudors. Trans Royal Historical Soc 3 1909.
— The ballad history of the reign of James I. Trans Royal Historical Soc 5 1911.
— The reign of Charles I. Trans Royal Historical Soc 6 1912. Ballad history.
— Ballads and broadsides. In Shakespeare's England vol 2, Oxford 1916.
Reed, E. B. English lyrical poetry. New Haven 1912.
Hustvedt, S. B. Ballad criticism in Scandinavia and Great Britain. New York 1916.
Scott, M. A. Elizabethan translations from the Italian. Boston 1916.
Rollins, H. E. The black-letter broadside ballad. PMLA 34 1919.
Berdan, J. M. Early Tudor poetry. New York 1920.
Wells, H. W. Poetic imagery illustrated from Elizabethan literature. New York 1924.
Whipple, T. K. Martial and the English epigram from Sir Thomas Wyatt to Ben Jonson. Berkeley 1925.
von Schaubert, E. Zur Geschichte der black-letter broadside ballad. Anglia 50 1926.
Baskervil, C. R. The Elizabethan jig. Chicago 1929.

Genouy, H. L'élément pastoral dans la poésie narrative et le drame en Angleterre de 1579 à 1640. Paris 1929.
Shaaber, M. A. Some forerunners of the newspaper in England 1476–1622. Philadelphia 1929.
Tannenbaum, S. A. Unfamiliar versions of some Elizabethan poems. PMLA 45 1930.
Bush, D. Mythology and the Renaissance tradition in English poetry. Minneapolis 1933.
Quennell, P. C. Aspects of seventeenth-century verse. 1933, 1947 (rev).
Tonelli, L. L'amore nella poesia e nel pensiero del Rinascimento. Florence 1933.
Ball, L. F. The background of the minor English Renaissance epics. ELH 1 1934.
Willcock, G. D. Passing pitifull hexameters: a study of quantity and accent in English Renaissance verse. MLR 29 1934.
Campbell, L. B. The Christian Muse. Huntington Lib Bull no 8 1935.
— Richard Tarlton and the earthquake of 1580. HLQ 4 1941.
Thompson, W. M. Der Tod in der englischen Lyrik des siebzehnten Jahrhunderts. Breslau 1935.
Wagner, B. M. New songs of the reign of Henry VIII. MLN 50 1935.
Weitzmann, F. W. Notes on the Elizabethan 'elegie'. PMLA 50 1935.
Bontoux, G. La chanson en Angleterre au temps d'Elisabeth. Oxford 1936.
Elizabeth decoration: patterns in art and passion. TLS 3 July 1937.
Smart, G. K. English non-dramatic blank verse in the sixteenth century. Anglia 61 1937.
Williams, F. B. Richard Johnson s borrowed tears. SP 34 1937.
Bernard, J. E. The prosody of the Tudor interlude. New Haven 1939.
Wilson, E. C. England's Eliza. Cambridge Mass 1939.
Winters, Y. The sixteenth-century lyric in England: a critical and historical interpretation. Poetry 53–4 1939.
Jonas, L. The divine science: the aesthetic of some representative seventeenth-century English poets. New York 1940.
Sensabaugh, G. F. Platonic love and the Puritan rebellion. SP 37 1940.
Wasserman, E. R. Elizabethan poetry 'improved'. MP 37 1940.
— Elizabethan poetry in the eighteenth century. Urbana 1947.
Pottle, F. A. The idiom of poetry. Ithaca 1941.
Rubel, V. L. Poetic diction in the English Renaissance from Skelton through Spenser. New York 1941.
Utley, F. L. The crooked rib. Columbus 1941.
Tate, A. The language of poetry. Princeton 1942.
Mizener, A. Some notes on the nature of English poetry. Sewanee Rev 51 1943.
Murphy, J. Elizabethan lyrics from Tasso. MLN 58 1943.
Policardi, S. Lyrical poetry in Renaissance England. Milan 1943.

Simpson, P. The rhyming of stressed and unstressed syllables in Elizabethan verse. MLR 38 1943.

Bradner, L. Poems on the defeat of the Spanish Armada. JEGP 43 1944.

Nearing, H. English historical poetry 1599–1641. Philadelphia 1945.

Church, M. The first English pattern poems. PMLA 61 1946.

Dunn, E. C. The concept of ingratitude in Renaissance English moral poetry. Washington 1946.

Miles, J. Major adjectives in English poetry from Wyatt to Auden. Berkeley 1946.

— The primary language of poetry in the 1640's. Berkeley 1948.

— The continuity of poetic language. Berkeley 1951.

Starnes, D. T. The poetic dictionary and the poet. Texas Univ Lib Chron 2 1946.

Austin, W. B. William Withie's notebook. RES 23 1947.

Day Lewis, C. The colloquial element in English poetry. Newcastle 1947.

Schueller, H. M. The Renaissance forerunners of the neo-classical lyric. MLN 62 1947.

Tuve, R. Elizabethan and metaphysical imagery. Chicago 1947.

Bond, W. H. The Cornwallis-Lysons manuscript. In J. Q. Adams memorial studies, Washington 1948.

Bühler, C. F. Four Elizabethan poems. Ibid.

Pattison, B. Music and poetry of the English Renaissance. 1948.

Scholl, E. H. English metre once more. PMLA 63 1948.

Hendrickson, G. L. Elizabethan quantitative hexameters. PQ 28 1949.

Turner, A. French verse in the Oxford and Cambridge poetical miscellanies. MLQ 10 1949.

Mahood, M. M. Poetry and humanism. 1950.

Nicolson, M. H. The breaking of the circle: studies in the effect of the 'New Science' upon seventeenth-century poetry. Evanston 1950.

Taylor, A. P. The sick tune. MLN 65 1950.

Wallerstein, R. Studies in seventeenth-century poetic. Madison 1950.

Zocca, L. R. Elizabethan narrative poetry. New Brunswick NJ 1950.

Bateson, F. W. 'Dissociation of sensibility'. EC 1 1951. Replies by E. Thompson and Bateson 2 1952.

Ing, C. M. Elizabethan lyrics: a study of the development of English metres. 1951.

Saunders, J. W. The stigma of print: a note on the social bases of Tudor poetry. EC 1 1951.

Thomson, J. A. K. Classical influences on English poetry. 1951.

Smith, H. Elizabethan poetry: a study in conventions, meaning and expression. Cambridge Mass 1952, 1968 (rev).

Danby, J. F. Poets on Fortune's Hill: studies in Sidney, Shakespeare, Beaumont and Fletcher. 1952, 1964 (rev as Elizabethan and Jacobean poets).

Hunter, G. K. The Elizabethan hexameter and the Elizabethan madrigal. PQ 32 1953.

Cruttwell, P. The Shakespearean moment and its place in the poetry of the seventeenth century. 1954.

Cunningham, J. V. Logic and lyric. MP 51 1954.

Evans, M. English poetry in the sixteenth century. 1955.

Lever, J. W. The Elizabethan love sonnet. 1956.

Milner, R. Music and poetry in the sixteenth century. Etudes Anglaises 9 1956.

Telheim, M. The Elizabethan lyric. Papers of Michigan Acad 43 1957.

Valency, M. J. In praise of love: an introduction to love-poetry of the Renaissance. 1958.

Davis, H. and H. Gardner (ed). Elizabethan and Jacobean studies presented to F. P. Wilson. Oxford 1959.

Mason, H. A. Humanism and poetry in the early Tudor period. 1959.

Allen, D. C. Image and meaning: metaphoric traditions in Renaissance poetry. Baltimore 1960, 1968 (rev).

Sternfeld, F. W. Tudor poems. TLS 14 July 1961.

Stevens, J. E. Music and poetry in the early Tudor court 1480–1530. 1961.

Donno, E. S. Elizabethan minor epics. 1963.

Southall, R. The Devonshire manuscript collection of early Tudor poetry 1532–41. RES new ser 15 1964.

Goldstein, L. M. The Pepys ballads. Library 5th ser 21 1966.

Simpson, C. The British broadside ballad and its music. New Brunswick NJ 1966.

Thomson, P. Elizabethan lyrical poets. 1967.

Long, J. H. The ballad medley and the fool. SP 67 1970.

T. Y.

II. TUDOR POETRY

JOHN SKELTON
1460?–1529

Bibliographies

Kinsman, R. S. and T. Yonge. Skelton: canon and census. [Darien Conn 1968].

Collections

Certayne bokes. [1545], [1554], [1560].

Pithy pleasaunt and profitable workes. Ed J. Stow 1568, 1736.

Poetical works. Ed A. Dyce 2 vols 1843, 3 vols Boston 1856 (with addns [by F. J. Child]).

A selection from the poetical works. Ed W. H. Williams, Isbister 1902.

Poems. Ed R. Hughes 1924.

Skelton (laureate). Ed R. Graves 1927.

Complete poems. Ed P. Henderson 1931, 1948 (rev), 1959 (rev), 1964 (rev).

Poems. Ed R. Gant [1949].

Skelton: a selection from his poems. Ed V. de S. Pinto 1950.

Poems. Ed R. S. Kinsman, Oxford 1969.

§1

The bowge of Courte. [1499], [1510]. Anon.

A ballade of the Scottysshe Kynge. [1513] (anon); ed J. Ashton 1882.

The tunnyng of Elynour Rummyng. [1521] (fragment), 1624, 1718; ed H. Stearns 1928; ed anon 1930; Worcester Mass 1953.

A goodly garlande or chapelet of laurell. 1523; ed E. P. Hammond, English verse between Chaucer and Surrey, Durham NC 1927.

Dyvers balettys and dyties solacyous. [1527].

Agaynste a comely coystrowne. [1527].

A replycacion agaynst certayne yong scolers. [1528].

Magnyfycence. [1533], 1821 (Roxburghe Club); ed R. L. Ramsay 1905, 1908 (EETS); ed J. Farmer 1910.

Collyn Clout. [1530], [1545], [1554], [1560].

Phyllyp Sparowe. [1545], [1554], [1560].
Why come ye nat to Courte. [1545], [1554], [1560]; ed J. Zupitza, Archiv 85 1890 (ms fragment).
Speculum principis. Ed F. M. Salter, Speculum 9 1934.
The bibliotheca historica of Diodorus Siculus. Ed F. M. Salter and H. L. R. Edwards 2 vols 1956-7 (EETS).

§ 2

Merie tales of Skelton. [1567]; ed W. C. Hazlitt 1866.
Warton, T. In his History of English poetry vol 2, 1778. Section 15.
Some account of the life of Skelton. [1800].
Southern, H. Skelton's poetical works. Retrospective Rev 6 1822.
GM Sept 1844.
Quart Rev 73 1844.
Browning, E. B. In her Greek Christian poets and the English poets, 1863.
A satirical laureate of the sixteenth century. Dublin Univ Mag Dec 1866.
Skelton. Amer Church Rev 25 1873.
'The Lancashire Witch'. Buried poets: Skelton. Dublin Univ Mag May 1877.
Krumpholz, H. von Skelton und sein Morality play Magnyfycence. Prosnitz 1881.
Schoneberg, G. Die Sprache Skeltons in seinen kleineren Werken. Marburg 1888.
Zupitza, J. Handschriftliche Bruchstücke von Skeltons Why come ye nat to Courte? Archiv 85 1890.
Bradley, H. Two puzzles in Skelton. Academy 1 Aug 1896.
Hooper, J. Skelton, laureate. GM Sept 1897.
Rey, A. Skelton's satirical poems in their relation to Lydgate's Order of fools, Cocke Lorell's bote and Barclay's Ship of fools. Berne 1899.
Koelbing, A. Zur Characteristik Skeltons. Stuttgart 1904.
Hooper, E. S. Skelton's Magnyfycence and Cardinal Wolsey. MLN 16 1901.
Manning, C. U. Skelton, laureate, parson of Disse 1504. Antiquary 41 1905.
Thümmel, A. Studien über Skelton. Leipzig 1905.
Brie, F. Skelton-Studien. E Studien 37 1907.
— Zwei verlorene Dichtungen von Skelton. Archiv 138 1919.
Dodds, M. H. Early political plays. Library 2nd ser 4 1913.
SeBoyar, G. E. Skelton's Replycacion. MLN 28 1913.
Berdan, J. M. On the dating of Skelton's satires. PMLA 29 1914.
— The poetry of Skelton: a Renaissance survival of medieval Latin influence. Romance Rev 6 1915.
— Speke parrot: an interpretation. MLN 30 1915.
— In his Early Tudor poetry, New York 1920.
Bischoffberger, E. Der Einfluss Skeltons auf die englische Literatur. Freiburg 1914.
Cook, A. S. Skelton's Garland of laurel and Chaucer's House of fame. MLR 11 1916.
Dunbabin, R. L. Notes on Skelton. MLR 12 1917.
Westlake, H. F. Skelton in Westminster. TLS 27 Oct 1921.
Golding, L. Merie Skelton. Saturday Rev 14 Jan 1922.
Lloyd, L. J. Skelton: a forgotten poet. Eng Rev May 1925.
— A note on Skelton. RES 5 1929.
— Skelton and the new learning. MLR 24 1929.
— Skelton: a sketch of his life and writings. Oxford 1938.
Stearns [Sale], H. The date of the Garlande of laurell. MLN 43 1928.
— Skelton and Christopher Garnesche. MLN 43 1928.
— The date of Skelton's Bowge of Court. MLN 52 1937.
[Blunden, E.] Skelton. TLS 20 June 1929.
Edwards, H. L. R. Syr Capten of Catywade. TLS 9 Aug 1934. Replies by B. Redstone 16 Aug, H. L. R. Edwards 30 Aug 1934.
— Pereles pomegarnet. TLS 27 Dec 1934.
— Skelton: a genealogical study. RES 11 1935.

— 'Pleris cum musco'. TLS 12 Sept 1936. Replies by G. P. C. Sutton, E. A. Bunyard 19 Sept, P. Abrahams 3 Oct 1936.
— Hermoniake. TLS 24 Oct 1936.
— A Skelton emendation. TLS 19 Dec 1936.
— Robert Gaguin and the English poets 1489-90. MLR 32 1937.
— Skelton at Diss. TLS 22 May 1937.
— and W. Nelson. The dating of Skelton's later poems. PMLA 53 1938.
— Learning and Skelton. Life & Letters 23 1939.
— Skelton: the life and times of an early Tudor poet. 1949.
Hall, W. C. Skelton. Papers of Manchester Literary Club 59 1933.
Gordon, I. A. Skelton's Philip Sparrow and the Roman service-book. MLR 29 1934.
— Skelton's Speke parrot. TLS 1 Feb 1934.
— New light on Skelton. TLS 20 Sept 1934. Replies by J. Lloyd, H. L. R. Edwards, E. Ellam 27 Sept 1934, F. M. Salter 17 June 1935.
— A Skelton query. TLS 15 Nov 1934.
— Skelton: poet laureate. Melbourne 1943.
Auden, W. H. In The great Tudors, ed K. Garvin 1935.
Nelson, W. Skelton's Speke parrot. PMLA 51 1936.
— Skelton laureate. New York 1939.
Fraser, G. S. Skelton and the dignity of poetry. Adelphi 13 1936.
Pyle, F. The origins of the Skeltonic. N & Q 21 Nov 1936.
'Hibernicus'. Skelton's reputation. N & Q 29 July 1939.
Workman, S. K. Versions by Skelton, Caxton and Berners of a prologue by Diodorus Siculus. MLN 56 1941.
Andrews, H. C. Baldock, Herts and Skelton. N & Q 25 April 1942.
Atkins, J. W. H. In his English literary criticism: the medieval phase, Cambridge 1943.
Frost, G. L. and R. Nash. Good order: a morality fragment. SP 41 1944.
Tilney-Bassett, J. G. Skelton and the Tilneys. TLS 11 Nov 1944.
Fisher, A. S. T. Birds of paradise. N & Q 10 March 1945. Reply by W. W. Skeat 19 May 1945.
Salter, F. M. Skelton's contribution to the English language. Trans Royal Soc of Canada 5 1945.
Tillemans, T. Skelton: a conservative. E Studies 27 1946.
Harvey, J. H. Eleanor Rumming. TLS 26 Oct 1946.
Howarth, R. G. Notes on Skelton. N & Q 1 May 1948.
Kinsman, R. S. Phyllyp sparowe: titulus. SP 47 1950.
— Skelton's Colyn Clout: the mask of Vox populi. In Essays critical and historical dedicated to Lily B. Campbell, Berkeley 1950.
— The 'Buck' and the 'Fox' in Skelton's Why come ye nat to Courte? PQ 29 1952.
— The printer and date of publication of Skelton's Agaynste a comely coystrowne and Dyvers balettys. HLQ 16 1953.
— Skelton's Uppon a deedman's hed: new light on the origin of the Skeltonic. SP 50 1953.
— Eleanora rediviva: fragments of an edition of Skelton's Elynour Rummyng, ca 1521. HLQ 18 1955.
— A Skelton reference c. 1510. N & Q June 1960.
— The voices of dissonance: pattern in Skelton's Colyn Clout. HLQ 26 1963.
— A lamentable of Kyng Edward the IIII. HLQ 29 1966.
— Skelton's Magnyfycence: the strategy of the 'olde sayde sawe'. SP 63 1966.
— Skelton mocks the Muse: reference to Roman matters in his poetry and to the 'Epic Theatre' of Brecht. Univ of California Stud in Comparative Lit 1 1968.
Huxley, H. H. Philip Sparrow. N & Q 6 Jan 1951.
Forster, E. M. In his Two cheers for democracy, 1951.
McManaway, J. G. An uncollected poem of Skelton (?). N & Q 31 March 1951.

Swallow, A. The pentameter lines in Skelton and Wyatt. MP 48 1951.
—— Skelton: the structure of the poem. PQ 32 1953.
Pollet, M. Skelton et le Yorkshire. Etudes Anglaises 5 1952.
—— Skelton: contribution à l'histoire de la prérenaissance anglaise. Paris 1962; tr 1971.
Carpenter, N. C. Skelton and music: roty bully joys. RES new ser 6 1955.
—— Skelton. New York [1968].
—— Skelton's hand in William Cornish's musical parable. Comparative Lit 22 1970.
Ringler, W. John Stow's editions of Skelton's Workes and of Certaine worthye manuscript poems. SB 8 1956.
Holloway, J. Skelton. Proc Br Acad 44 1959; rptd in his Charted mirror, 1960.
Chalker, J. The literary seriousness of Skelton's Speke parrot. Neophilologus 44 1960.
Green, P. John Skelton. 1960 (Br Council pamphlet).
Harris, W. O. Wolsey and Skelton's Magnyfycence: a re-evaluation. SP 57 1960.
—— Skelton's Magnyfycence and the cardinal virtue tradition. Chapel Hill 1965.
Heisermann, A. R. Skelton and satire. Chicago 1961.
—— The thematic importance of Skelton's allusion to Horace in Magnyfycence. Stud in Eng Lit 1500–1900 3 1963.
Schulte, E. Skelton nella tradizione poetica inglese. Annali dell' Instituto Universitario 4 1961.
—— Skelton, Petrarcha e l'amore della gloria nel The garland of laurel. Annali dell' Instituto Universitario 5 1962.
—— La poesia di Skelton. Naples 1963.
Fish, S. E. Aspects of rhetorical analysis: Skelton's Philip Sparrow. Studia Neophilologica 34 1962.
—— Skelton's poetry. New Haven 1965.
Larson, S. J. What is the Bouge of Court? JEGP 61 1962.
Myers, O. T. Encina and Skelton. Hispania 47 1964.
Swart, J. Skelton's Philip sparrow. In English studies presented to R. W. Zandwoort, Amsterdam 1964.
Tucker, M. J. California ms AC 523, formerly Phillipps ms 3841. N & Q Oct 1964.
—— Skelton and Sheriff Hutton. Eng Lang Notes 4 1967.
—— The ladies in Skelton's Garland of laurel. Renaissance Quart 22 1969.
—— Setting in Skelton's Bowge of Courte: a speculation. Eng Lang Notes 7 1970.
Phillips, N. Observations on the derivative method of Skelton's realism. JEGP 65 1966.
Harrington, D. V. Skelton's Manerly Margery Mylk and Ale. Explicator 25 1967.
Spina, E. Skeltonic meter in Elynour Rummyng. SP 64 1967.
Brownlow, F. W. Speke parrot: Skelton's allegorical denunciation of Cardinal Wolsey. SP 65 1968.
Hawkins, R. Structure through irony in the Tunning of Elinor Rumming. Univ Rev 34 1968.
Gingerich, O. and M. J. Tucker. The astronomical dating of Skelton's Garland of laurel. HLQ 32 1969.
McGrath, L. F. Speke parrot and Plautus. N & Q Dec 1969.

ALEXANDER BARCLAY
1475?–1552
Bibliographies
Jamieson, T. H. A bibliographical catalogue. In his edn of Ship of fools, 1874.

Collections
The ship of fools. 1570.
Certayne egloges. Manchester 1885 (Spenser Soc).
Eclogues. Ed B. White 1928 (EETS).

§1
The castell of laboure. Paris [1503], London [1505], 1506, 1506; ed A. W. Pollard 1905 (Roxburghe Club).
The shyp of folys. 1509; ed T. H. Jamieson 2 vols Edinburgh 1874.
[Eglog 1]. [1510] (fragment), [Cambridge 1523] (fragment).
The lyf of saynt George. 1515; ed W. Nelson 1955 (EETS).
The famous cronycle of the warre agaynst Jugurth. [1520], [1525], 1557 (rev T. Paynell).
The lyfe of the blessed martyr Saynte Thomas. [1520]. Anon.
The fyfth egloge. [1518].
The fourth egloge. [1521].
The myrrour of good maners. [1523], Manchester 1885 (Spenser Soc).
A lytell cronycle. 1525. Anon.
The eglogs. [1530], [1548], [1560]. Eclogues 1–3.

§2
Jamieson, T. H. Notice of the life and writings of Barclay. 1874 (priv ptd).
Herford, C. H. In his Studies in the literary relations of England and Germany in the sixteenth century, 1886.
Reissert, O. Die Eklogen des Barclay. Neuphilologische Beiträge (Hanover) 1886.
Sommer, H. O. In his Erster Versuch über die englische Hirtendichtung, Marburg 1888.
Fraustadt, F. Über das Verhältnis von Barclays Ship of fools zur lateinischen, französischen und deutschen Quelle. Breslau 1894.
Mustard, W. P. Notes on the Egloges of Barclay. MLN 24 1909.
Berdan, J. M. Barclay: poet and preacher. MLR 8 1913.
—— In his Early Tudor poetry, New York 1920.
Schultz, J. R. The life of Barclay. JEGP 18 1919.
—— Barclay and the later eclogue writers. MLN 35 1920.
—— The method of Barclay's eclogues. JEGP 32 1933.
Pompen, A. The English versions of the Ship of fools. 1925.
Pyle, F. The barbarous metre of Barclay. MLR 32 1937.
Cochester, L. S. Barclay. MLR 37 1942.
Nelson, W. New light on Barclay. RES 19 1943.
Guttman, S. Barclay: a product of his age. Papers of Michigan Acad 35 1951.
Lyall, R. J. Barclay and the Edwardian reformation. RES new ser 20 1969.

SIR THOMAS WYATT
1503?–42

Ms: BM Egerton 2711 has 12 autograph poems and 6 others with autograph corrections.

Bibliographies etc
Hangen, E. C. A concordance to the complete poetical works of Wyatt. Chicago 1941.

Collections
Works. Ed G. F. Nott 1816.
Poetical works. [Ed N. H. Nicolas] 1831.
Poetical works. Ed C. C. Clarke, Edinburgh 1868.
Poetical works. Ed J. Yeowell 1898.
Poetry. Ed E. M. W. Tillyard 1929. A selection.
Collected poems. Ed K. Muir 1949 (ML).
Some poems. Ed A. Swallow, New York 1949.
Collected poems. Ed K. Muir and P. Thomson, Liverpool 1969. First complete edn.

§ 1

Plutarckes boke of the quyete of mynde. [1528]; ed C. R. Baskervill, Cambridge Mass 1931 (facs).

Certayne psalmes chosen out of the psalter of David. 1549.

Songes and sonnettes. 5 June 1557. Tottel includes 97 poems by Wyatt. *For edns see col 1007, above.*

Unpublished poems. Ed K. Muir, Liverpool 1961.

§ 2

[Howard, H.] An excellent epitaffe of Wyat. [1542].

Leland, J. Naeniae in mortem Viati. 1542.

Warton, T. In his History of English poetry vol 3, 1781. Section 20.

Bruce, J. Recovery of the lost accusation of Wyatt by Bishop Bonner. GM June 1850.

— Unpublished anecdotes of Wyatt. GM Sept 1850.

Simonds, W. E. Wyatt and his poems. Boston 1889.

Alscher, R. Wyatt und seine Stellung in der Entwickelungs-geschichte der englischen Literatur und Verkunst. Vienna 1886.

Koeppel, E. Wyatt und Melin de Saint-Gelais. Anglia 13 1890. Replies by J. M. Berdan, MLN 23 1908, MLR 4 1909; L. E. Kastner, ibid.

Flügel, E. Die handschriftliche Überlieferung der Gedichte von Wyatt. Anglia 18–19 1896–7.

Segre, C. In his Studi petrarcheschi, Florence 1903.

Lathrop, B. The sonnet forms of Wyatt and Surrey. MP 2 1905.

Foxwell, A. K. A study of Wyatt's poems. 1911.

Stopes, C. C. In her Shakespeare's industry, 1916.

Berdan, J. M. In his Early Tudor poetry, New York 1920.

Hammond, E. P. Poems 'signed' by Wyatt. MLN 37 1922.

Padelford, F. M. The scansion of Wyatt's early sonnets. SP 20 1923.

Chambers, E. K. In his Wyatt and some collected studies, 1933.

Chini, E. Il sorgere del petrarchismo in Inghilterra e la poesia di Wyatt. Civiltà Moderna 6 1934.

Hayes, A. McH. Wyatt's letters to his son. MLN 49 1934.

Cecchini, A. Serafino Aquilano e la lirica inglese del '500. Aquila 1935.

Utley, F. L. Wyatt as a Scottish poet. MLN 60 1945.

Harding, D. W. The rhythmical intention in Wyatt's poetry. Scrutiny 14 1946.

Miles, J. In her Major adjectives in English poetry, Berkeley 1946.

Smith, H. The art of Wyatt. HLQ 9 1946.

Johnson, S. F. and W. R. Orwen. Wyatt's The lover compareth his state. Explicator 5 1947.

Mackerness, E. D. The transitional nature of Wyatt's poetry. English 7 1948.

Swallow, A. The pentameter lines in Skelton and Wyatt. MP 48 1951. Reply by R. O. Evans, JEGP 53 1954.

Moore, A. K. The design of Wyatt's They fle from me. Anglia 71 1952.

Baldi, S. La poesia di Wyatt. Florence 1953.

— Sir Thomas Wyatt. 1961 (Br Council pamphlet).

Harrier, R. C. Notes on the text and interpretation of Wyatt's poetry. N & Q June 1953. Replies by K. Muir, June 1953; J. C. Maxwell, Aug 1953.

— Notes on Wyatt and Anne Boleyn. JEGP 53 1954.

Johnson, S. F. Wyatt's They flee from me. Explicator 11 1953. Replies by E. E. Duncan-Jones 12 1953, F. M. Combellack 17 1959; A. Stein, Sewanee Rev 67 1959; G. W. Whiting, EC 10 1960, H. Morris, ibid.

Mason, H. A. Wyatt and the Psalms. TLS 27 Feb, 6 March 1953.

— In his Humanism and poetry in the early Tudor period, 1959.

Maxwell, J. C. Surrey's lines on Wyatt. N & Q March 1953.

Watson, M. R. Wyatt, Chaucer and 'terza rima'. MLN 68 1953.

Evans, R. O. Some aspects of Wyatt's metrical technique. JEGP 53 1954.

— Some autobiographical aspects of Wyatt's verse. N & Q Feb 1958. Reply by R. C. Harrier, May 1959.

Long, J. H. Blame not Wyatt's lute. Renaissance News 7 1954.

Rees, D. G. Wyatt's translations from Petrarch. Contemporary Lit 7 1955.

— Wyatt and Petrarch. MLR 52 1957.

Fucilla, J. G. The direct source of Wyatt's epigram In dowtful brest. Renaissance News 9 1956.

Lever, J. W. In his Elizabethan love sonnet, 1956.

Mumford, I. L. Musical settings to the poems of Wyatt. Music & Letters 37 1956.

— Wyatt's songs: a trio of problems in manuscript sources. Music & Letters 38 1957.

— The canzone in sixteenth-century English verse. Eng Miscellany (Rome) 11 1960.

Hainsworth, J. D. Wyatt's use of the love convention. EC 7 1957. Reply by A. S. Gerard 9 1959.

Hoeniger, F. D. A Wyatt manuscript. N & Q March 1957.

Newman, J. An Italian source for Wyatt's Madame, withouten many wordes. Renaissance News 10 1957.

Wiatt, W. H. A source for Wyatt's What menythe thys? Renaissance News 11 1958.

— On the date of Wyatt's knighthood. JEGP 60 1961.

— Wyatt's astrologer. Eng Lang Notes 4 1966.

— Wyatt and Anne Boleyn. Eng Lang Notes 6 1968.

Hietsch, O. Die Petrarcaübersetzungen Wyatts. Vienna 1959.

Muir, K. An unrecorded Wyatt manuscript. TLS 20 May 1960. Replies by R. Southall 27 May, K. Muir 3 June, R. Southall 10 June 1960.

— Life and letters of Wyatt. Liverpool 1963.

— The texts of Wyatt's penitential psalms. N & Q Dec 1967.

Thompson, J. In his Founding of English metre, 1960.

— Wyatt's wordplay. Annuale Medievale 1 1960.

Wyatt, S. The Wyatts and the Cheneys. 1960.

Hughey, R. In her Arundel Harington manuscript of Tudor poetry, Columbus 1960.

Stevens, J. In his Music and poetry in the early Tudor Court, 1961.

Berthoff, A. The falconer's dream of trust: Wyatt's They fle from me. Sewanee Rev 71 1963.

Nelson, C. E. A note on Wyatt and Ovid. MLR 58 1963.

Schwartz, E. The meter of some poems of Wyatt. SP 60 1963.

Tydeman, W. M. Wyatt's poems and the Blage manuscript: verbal resemblances. N & Q Aug 1963.

Endicott, A. M. A note on Wyatt and Serafino D'Aquilano. Renaissance News 17 1964.

Greene, R. L. Wyatt's 'They fle from me' and the busily seeking critics. Bucknell Rev 12 1964.

Southall, R. The courtly maker. 1964.

— Wyatt's Ye old mule. Eng Lang Notes 5 1967.

Thomson, P. Wyatt and his background. 1964.

Weiss, W. In his Der Refrain in der elisabethanischen Lyrik, Munich 1964.

Guss, D. L. Wyatt's Petrarchism: an instance of creative imitation in the Renaissance. HLQ 29 1965.

Huttar, C. A. Forsake me never for no new: a note on Wyatt's poetic diction. N & Q May 1965.

— Wyatt and the several editions of the Court of Venus. SB 19 1966.

Kökeritz, H. Dialectical traits in Wyatt's poetry. In Franciplegius: medieval and linguistic studies in honor of F. P. Magoun jr, New York 1965.

Maynard, W. The lyrics of Wyatt: poems or songs? RES new ser 16 1965.

— To Smithe of Camden. RES new ser 18 1967.

Nathan, L. E. Tradition and newfangleness in Wyatt's They fle from me. ELH 32 1965.

Wentersdorf, K. P. The imagery of Wyatt. Studia Neophilologica 37 1965.

Friedman, D. M. The 'thing' in Wyatt's mind. EC 16 1966.

— Wyatt's amoris personae. MLQ 27 1966.

— The mind in the poem: Wyatt's They fle from me. Stud in Eng Lit 1500–1900 7 1967.

— Wyatt and the ambiguities of fancy. JEGP 67 1968.

Lindsay, D. W. Wyatt's They fle from me: a prosodic note. Forum for Modern Lang Stud 3 1967.

Plasberg, E. Covert drama in Wyatt's They fle from me. California Eng Jnl 3 1967.

McCanles, M. Love and power in the poetry of Wyatt. MLQ 29 1968.

Ormerod, D. Wyatt and the execution of Mark Smeaton. Papers on Lang & Lit 4 1968.

Daalder, J. Rhetoric and revision in Wyatt's poems. Jnl of Australasian Univ Lang & Lit Assoc 31 1969.

Twombly, R. G. Beauty and the (subverted) beast: Wyatt's They fle from me. Texas Stud in Lang & Lit 10 1969.

HENRY HOWARD, EARL OF SURREY
1517?–47

Collections

Songes and sonettes. Ed E. Curll 1717.

Works. Ed G. F. Nott 1815.

Poetical works. [Ed N. H. Nicolas] 1831.

Poetical works. Ed R. Bell 1854.

Poetical works. Ed C. C. Clarke, Edinburgh 1868. With Shakespeare's poems.

Poems. Ed F. M. Padelford, Seattle 1920, 1928 (rev).

Original poems. 1929.

[Poems]. Ed G. Bullett 1947 (in Silver poets of the sixteenth century) (EL).

To a lady. Ed D. Geary 1957.

Poems. Ed E. Jones, Oxford 1964.

§ 1

An excellent epitaffe of Syr Thomas Wyat. [1542].

The fourth boke of Virgill. [1554]; ed H. Hartman, Purchase NY 1935 (with facs).

Certain bokes of Virgiles Aeneais. 1557, 1814 (Roxburghe Club); ed F. H. Ridley, Berkeley 1963.

Songes and sonettes. 1557. For other edns see col 1007, above. Tottel includes 40 poems by Surrey.

§ 2

Schröer, A. Ueber die Anfaenge des Blankverses in England. Anglia 4 1881.

Fehse, H. Surrey: ein Beitrag zur Geschichte des Petrarchismus in England. Chemnitz 1883.

Emerson, O. F. The development of blank verse: a study of Surrey. MLN 4 1889.

Bapst, E. Deux gentilshommes-poètes de la cour de Henry VIII. Paris 1891.

Dittes, R. Zu Surreys Aeneisübertragung. Beiträge zur Neueren Philologie 1902.

Fest, O. Über Surreys Virgilübersetzung, nebst Neuausgabe des vierten Buches nach Tottels Originaldruck und der bisher ungedruckten [BM] Ms Hargrave 205. Berlin 1903.

Imelmann, R. Zu den Anfängen des Blankverses: Surreys Aeneis in ursprünglicher Gestalt. Sh Jb 41 1905.

Lathrop, B. The sonnet forms of Wyatt and Surrey. MP 2 1905.

Padelford, F. M. The manuscript poems of Surrey. Anglia 29 1906.

Willcock, G. D. A hitherto uncollated version of Surrey's translation of the fourth book of the Aeneid. MLR 14–15 1919–20, 17 1922.

Berdan, J. M. In his Early Tudor poetry, New York 1920.

Hudson, H. H. Surrey and Martial. MLN 38 1923.

Casady, E. A reinterpretation of Surrey's character and actions. PMLA 51 1936.

— Henry Howard, Earl of Surrey. New York 1938.

Gray, M. M. Surrey's vocabulary. TLS 3 Oct 1936. Replies by E. Bannister 24 Oct, M. M. Gray 31 Oct, L. F. Casson 7 Nov 1936.

Camp, T. W. Another version of the Thinges that cause a quiet life. MLN 52 1937.

Putt, S. G. A suppressed hendiadys in a poem by Surrey. MLR 34 1939.

Surrey's triumphs. TLS 18 Jan 1947.

Oras, A. Surrey's technique of phonetic echoes. JEGP 50 1951.

Towne, F. Surrey's Certain books of Virgil's Aeneis 2. 272. Explicator 8 1949.

Chapman, R. Surrey in France. TLS 7 March 1952.

Mason, H. A. Wyatt and the Psalms. TLS 6 March 1953.

— In his Humanism and poetry in the early Tudor period, 1959.

Evans, M. In his English poetry in the sixteenth century, 1955.

Lever, J. W. In his Elizabethan love sonnet, 1956.

Mumford, I. L. Musical settings to the poems of Surrey. Eng Miscellany (Rome) 8 1957.

— Italian aspects of Surrey's lyrics. Eng Miscellany (Rome) 16 1965.

Chapman, H. W. In her Two Tudor portraits, 1960.

Davies, M. B. Surrey at Boulogne. HLQ 23 1960.

Hughey, R. In her Arundel Harington manuscript of Tudor poetry, Columbus 1960.

Muir, K. Surrey poems in the Blage manuscript. N & Q Oct 1960.

Ridley, F. H. Surrey's debt to Gawin Douglas. PMLA 76 1961.

Tucker, M. J. California ms AC 523, formerly Phillipps ms 3841. N & Q Oct 1964.

Huttar, C. A. Poems by Surrey and others in a printed miscellany circa 1550. Eng Miscellany (Rome) 16 1965.

Thomson, P. Firenzuola, Surrey and Watson. Renaissance News 18 1965.

Matthew, T. C. Surrey's Prisoned in Windsor, he recounteth his pleasure there passed. Explicator 27 1968.

Harris, W. O. 'Love that doth raine': Surrey's creative imitation. MP 66 1969.

A MIRROR FOR MAGISTRATES

Thomas Sackville's Induction was first ptd in 1563 edn. The ms of his Buckingham is at St John's College, Cambridge.

Bibliographies

Case, A. E. In his A bibliography of English poetical miscellanies, 1935 (Bibl Soc).

Jackson, W. A. In his Carl H. Pforzheimer library: English literature 1475–1700 vol 2, New York 1940 (priv ptd).

Collections

The mirrour for magistrates. Ed J. Higgins 1587. First and last pts.

A mirrour for magistrates. Ed R. Niccols 1610, 1619 (as The falles of unfortunate princes), 1620. 3 pts.

Mirror for magistrates. Ed J. Haslewood 3 vols 1815. 3 pts.

Parts added to the mirror for magistrates. Ed L. B. Campbell, Cambridge 1946. First and 2nd pts.

§1

A memorial of suche princes as have been unfortunate in the realme of England. [1555]. Fragments of a suppressed edn.
A myrroure for magistrates. Ed W. Baldwin 1559, 1563 (with addns), 1571, 1574 (as The last part), 1575, 1578 (with addns); ed L. B. Campbell, Cambridge 1938.
The first parte of the mirror for magistrates. Ed J. Higgins 1574, 1575 (with addns); ed J. Haslewood, Br Bibliographer 4 1814.
The seconde part of the mirroure for magistrates, by T. Blenerhasset. 1578.
The complaint of Henry Duke of Buckingham. Ed M. Hearsey, New Haven 1936.

§2

Warton, T. In his History of English poetry vol 3, 1781. Sections 30-3.
Trench, W. F. A mirror for magistrates: its origin and influence. 1898 (priv ptd).
— William Baldwin. MLQ 1 1899.
Davies, J. A mirror for magistrates, considered with special reference to the sources of Sackville's contributions. Leipzig 1906.
Laemmerhirt, C. R. Thomas Blenerhassets Second part of the Mirror for magistrates: eine Quellenstudie. Weimar 1909.
Bartlett, H. C. Library 3rd ser 3 1912. On Baldwin's authorship.
Feasey, E. I. The licensing of the Mirror for magistrates. Library 4th ser 3 1922.
— William Baldwin. MLR 20 1925.
Bush, D. Classical lives in the Mirror for magistrates. SP 22 1925.
Farnham, W. John Higgins' Mirror and Locrine. MP 23 1926.
— The Mirror for magistrates and Elizabethan tragedy. JEGP 25 1926.
— The progeny of A mirror for magistrates. MP 29 1932.
Hearsey, M. Thomas Sackville. TLS 18 April 1929.
— The ms of Sackville's contribution to the Mirror for magistrates. RES 8 1932.
Davies, G. Mirror for magistrates. TLS 23 July 1931.
Jackson, W. A. Wayland's edition of the Mirror for magistrates. Library 4th ser 13 1932.
Taylor, M. A. Lord Cobham and the Mirror for magistrates. Shakespeare Assoc Bull 8 1933.
Pyle, F. A mirror for magistrates. TLS 28 Dec 1935.
Rowse, A. L. Mirror for magistrates. TLS 15 April 1939.
Bühler, C. F. A survival from the Middle Ages: William Baldwin's use of the dictes and sayings. Speculum 23 1948.
Peery, W. Tragic retribution in the 1559 Mirror for magistrates. SP 46 1949.
— A metrical puzzle in the Mirror for magistrates. MLN 56 1941.
Thaler, A. Literary criticism in A mirror for magistrates. JEGP 49 1950.
Davie, D. Sixteenth-century poetry and the common reader: the case of Thomas Sackville. EC 4 1954.
Campbell, L. B. In her Collected papers, New York 1968.

GEORGE GASCOIGNE
1542?-77
Bibliographies

Tannenbaum, S. A. Gascoigne: a concise bibliography. New York 1942.
Johnson, R. C. In his Minor Elizabethans, 1968 (Elizabethan Bibliographies suppls).

Price, J. E. A secondary bibliography of Gascoigne. Bull of Bibliography 25 1968.

Collections
The pleasauntest workes. 1587. Another issue as The whole woorkes.
Complete poems. Ed W. C. Hazlitt 2 vols 1869-70.
Complete works. Ed J. W. Cunliffe 2 vols Cambridge 1907-10.

§1

A hundreth sundrie flowres. [1573]; ed B. M. Ward 1926; ed C. T. Prouty, Columbia Missouri 1942.
The glasse of gouernement. 1575; ed J. S. Farmer, Amersham 1914 (facs).
The posies. 1575.
The whole arte of venerie or hunting. [1575], 1611, 1908.
A delicate diet, for daintiemouthde droonkardes. 1576; ed F. G. Waldron 1789.
The droomme of doomes day. 1576, 1586.
The princelye pleasures at the Courte at Kenelwoorth. 1576 (no known copy), 1821.
The spoyle of Antwerpe. 1576.
The steele glas. 1576; ed E. Arber 1868.
The tale of Hemetes the heremite. In Synesius, A paradoxe, 1579; in The Queenes Majesties entertainment at Woodstocke, 1585.

§2

Whetstone, G. A remembrance of the wel imployed life and godly end of Gascoigne. 1577.
Herford, C. H. Gascoigne's Glass of government. E Studien 9 1886.
— In his Studies in the literary relations of England and Germany in the sixteenth century, Cambridge 1886.
Schelling, F. E. The life and writings of Gascoigne. Boston 1893.
Cunliffe, J. W. Authorship of the Queen's Majesty's entertainment at Woodstock. PMLA 26 1911.
Ward, B. M. Gascoigne and his circle. RES 2 1926. Reply by F. E. Teager 7 1931.
— The death of Gascoigne. RES 2 1926.
— The will of John Bacon. RES 3 1927.
— Further research on A hundreth sundrie flowres. RES 4 1928.
Ambrose (Oldfield), G. Gascoigne. RES 2 1926.
— New light on the life of Gascoigne. RES 13 1937.
Cawley, R. R. Gascoigne and the siege of Famagusta. MLN 43 1928.
Bradner, L. The first English novel: a study of Gascoigne's Adventures of Master F.J. PMLA 45 1930.
— Point of view in Gascoigne's fiction. Stud in Short Fiction 3 1965.
Hankins, J. E. A note on Gascoigne's biography. MP 30 1932.
Bowers, F. T. Notes on Gascoigne's A hundreth sundrie flowres and The posies. Harvard Stud 16 1934.
— Gascoigne and the Oxford cipher. MLN 52 1937.
Prouty, C. T. Gascoigne in the low countries. RES 12 1936.
— Gascoigne and Elizabeth Bacon Breton Boyes Gascoigne. RES 16 1940.
— Gascoigne: Elizabethan courtier, soldier and poet. New York 1942.
— and R. Prouty. Gascoigne, The noble art of venerie, and Queen Elizabeth at Kenilworth. In J. Q. Adams memorial studies, Washington 1948.
Brooks, E. St J. Gascoigne and Hatton. TLS 16 Jan 1937.
— The burial place of Gascoigne. RES new ser 5 1954.
Flournoy, F. William Breton, Nicholas Breton and Gascoigne. RES 16 1940.
Robertson, J. Gascoigne and the Noble arte of venerie and hunting. MLR 37 1942.
Mabbott, T. O. Gascoigne on Marcus Aurelius and 'Boemia'. N & Q 24 Aug 1946.

Starnes, D. T. The complaint of Philomene: a rejoinder. SE 26 1947.

Furniss, W. T. Gascoigne and Chaucer's 'pesen'. MLN 68 1953.

Going, W. T. Gascoigne and the term 'sonnet sequence'. N & Q May 1954. Reply by L. A. Sasek, April 1956.

Adams, P. Gascoigne's Master F. J. as original fiction. PMLA 73 1958.

Modic, J. L. Gascoigne and Ariosto again. Comparative Lit 14 1962.

Maveety, S. R. Versification in the Steele glas. SP 60 1963.

Anderau, A. Gascoignes The adventures of Master F. J. Berne 1966.

Lanham, R. A. Narrative structure in Gascoigne's F. J. Stud in Short Fiction 4 1966.

Smith, C. W. Structural and thematic unity in Gascoigne's The adventures of Master F. J. Papers on Lang & Lit 2 1966.

Maxwell, J. C. The shrew and a shrew: the suitors and the sisters. N & Q April 1968.

Rohr, M. R. Gascoigne and 'my master Chaucer'. JEGP 67 1968.

Jordan, S. M. The Captive and Gascoigne's Supposes. Classical Bull 45 1969.

NICHOLAS BRETON
1545?–1626?

Bibliographies

Tannenbaum, S. A. and D. R. Tannenbaum. Breton: a concise bibliography. New York 1947.

Robertson, J. In her edn of Breton's Poems not hitherto reprinted, Liverpool 1952.

Collections

The works in verse and prose. Ed A. B. Grosart 2 vols 1879 (priv ptd).

A mad world my masters and other prose works. Ed U. Kentish-Wright 2 vols 1929.

Poems not hitherto reprinted. Ed J. Robertson, Liverpool 1952.

§1

A smale handfull of fragrant flowers. 1575; ed T. Park, Heliconia vol 1, 1815.

A floorish upon fancie. 1577, 1582 (with addns), [1585] (fragment); ed T. Park, Heliconia vol 1, 1815.

The workes of a young wyt. 1577.

A discourse in commendation of maister Frauncis Drake. 1581.

The historie of the life and fortune of don Federigo di Terra Nuova. 1590.

Brittons bowre of delights. 1591, 1597 (with omissions); ed H. E. Rollins, Cambridge Mass 1933.

Marie Magdalens love; A solemne passion. 1595, 1598 (A solemne passion, alone), 1622, 1623, [1625].

Auspicante Jehova. 1597.

The wil of wit, wits wil or wils wit. 1597, 1599, 1606 (5th edn); ed J. O. Halliwell-Phillipps 1860.

Wits trenchmour. 1597.

The passions of the spirit. 1599; ed J. O. Halliwell-Phillipps, A brief description of manuscripts in the Public Library at Plymouth, 1853 (as The Countesse of Penbrooke's passion); ed N.B.G. 1862 (as A poem on our Saviour's passion by Mary Sidney Countess of Pembroke).

Pasquils mad-cap and mad-cappes message. 1600, 1626.

The second part of Pasquil's mad-cap, intituled the fooles-cap. 1600, 1600 (as Pasquils fooles-cap).

Pasquils mistresse. 1600.

Pasquils passe, and passeth not. 1600.

Melancholike humours. 1600; ed S. E. Brydges 1815; ed G. B. Harrison 1929.

No whippinge nor trippinge. 1601; ed C. Edmonds 1895.

The strange fortunes of two excellent princes. 1600.

A divine poeme. 1601; ed S. E. Brydges, Excerpta tudoriana vol 2, 1817.

An excellent poeme. 1601; ed S. E. Brydges 1814.

The soules heavenly exercise. 1601.

The mothers blessing. 1602, 1621 (with addns).

Olde mad-cappes new gally-mawfrey. 1602.

The passion of a discontented minde. 1602.

A poste with a madde packet of letters. 1602, 1603 (with addns), 1605, 1605 (2nd pt), 1606, 1607 (with addns), 1609, 1613, 1620, 1623, 1630, 1633, 1634, 1637, 1650, 1660, 1669, 1678, 1685.

The soules harmony. 1602, 1622 (6th edn), 1630, 1635 (9th edn), 1676 (11th edn).

Wonders worth the hearing. 1602.

A true description of unthankfulnesse. 1602.

A dialogue full of pithe and pleasure. 1603.

A merrie dialogue betwixt the taker and the mistaker. 1603, 1635 (as A mad world my masters).

Grimellos fortunes. 1604; ed E. G. Morice, Two pamphlets, Bristol 1936.

The passionate shepheard. 1604; ed F. Ouvry 1877 (priv ptd).

A piece of Friar Bacons brazen-heads prophesie. 1604.

An olde mans lesson 1605; ed E. G. Morice, Two pamphlets, Bristol 1936.

Honest counsaile. 1605.

The honour of valour. 1605.

I pray you be not angrie. 1605, 1624, 1632.

The soules immortall crowne. 1605.

Choice, chance and change. 1606; ed A. B. Grosart, Manchester 1881.

A murmurer. 1607.

Wits private wealth. 1607, 1611, 1612, 1613, 1615, 1625, 1629, 1639, 1643, 1664, 1670 (7th edn).

Divine considerations of the soule. 1608.

The uncasing of Machivils instructions to his sonne. 1613, 1613, 1615, 1635 (abridged), 1681 (as Machiavil's advice).

I would and would not. 1614.

Characters upon essaies. 1615; ed S. E. Brydges, Archaica vol 1, 1815.

The good and the badde. 1616, 1643 (as Englands selected characters).

Crossing of proverbs. 1616, 1631.

Crossing of proverbs: the second part. [1616], 1632, 1668, [1670] (as The last part).

The hate of treason. 1616.

Machiavells dogge. 1617.

The Court and country. 1618; ed W. C. Hazlitt, Inedited tracts, 1868; ed S. Pargellis and W. H. Dunham jr, Complaint and reform in England 1436–1714, New York 1938.

Conceyted letters newly layde open. 1618, 1632, 1638.

Strange newes out of divers countries. 1622.

Soothing of proverbs. 1626.

Fantasticks. 1626; ed J. O. Halliwell-Phillipps, Books of character, 1857 (extracts); ed B. Rhys, The twelve moneths, Waltham St Lawrence 1927 (extracts).

The figure of foure. 1631, 1636.

The figure of foure: the second part. 1626, 1636, 1653 (as The last part), 1654.

Character of Queen Elizabeth. Ed J. Nichols, The progresses and public procession of Queen Elizabeth vol 2, 1788.

§2

Nicholson, B. The religion of Breton. N & Q 27 June 1874.

—— Thomas Watson and Breton. Athenaeum 13 Oct 1877.

—— Breton and the Countess of Pembroke's passion. Athenaeum 9 March 1878.

—— The authorship of No whipping etc 1601. Athenaeum 30 Aug 1879.

Tappan, E. M. Breton and George Gascoigne. MLN 11 1896.

— The poetry of Breton. PMLA 13 1898.

Kuskop, T. F. C. Breton und seine Prosaschriften. Leipzig 1902.

Greenough, C. N. Breton: character-writer and quadrumaniac. In G. L. Kittredge anniversary papers, Boston 1913.

Bullen, A. H. In his Elizabethans, 1924.

Macdonald, D. Breton. Aberdeen Univ Rev Nov 1928.

Crawford, C. Greenes funeralls 1594 and Breton. SP extra ser 1 1929.

Monroe, N. E. Breton as a pamphleteer. Philadelphia 1929.

Whiting, M. B. Breton, gentleman. Fortnightly Rev May 1929.

Bowers, F. T. An addition to the Breton canon. MLN 45 1930.

Blunden, E. Breton's prose. In his Votive tablets, 1931.

Rollins, H. E. A small handful of fragrant flowers. Huntington Lib Bull no 9 1936.

— Breton's The works of a young wit 1577. SP 33 1936.

Williams, F. B. An unrecognized edition of Breton. MLR 32 1937.

Heltzel, V. B. Breton, Elyot and the Court of honour. MLN 53 1938.

Kentish-Wright, U. Shakespeare and Breton. Cornhill Mag June 1939.

Flournoy, F. William Breton, Breton and George Gascoigne. RES 16 1940.

Davenport, A. A quarrel of the satirists. MLR 37 1942.

Sullivan, F. Breton: a poste with a packet of madde letters. PBSA 37 1943.

Carlton, W. J. Breton, N. & Q 4 Oct 1947.

Heidrich, O. Breton: sein Leben und seine Gedichte. Leipzig 1901.

Crudell, H. W. A note on Breton. N & Q Oct 1962.

Doughtie, E. Breton and two songs by Dowland. Renaissance News 17 1964.

Shakeshaft, M. Breton's The passion of a discontented mind: some new problems. Stud in Eng Lit 1500–1900 5 1965.

Crupi, C. The date of Breton's Mavillia. N & Q Jan 1969.
T. Y.

EDMUND SPENSER
1552?–99

Bibliographies etc

Osgood, C. G. A concordance to the poems of Spenser. Washington 1915, Gloucester Mass 1963.

Whitman, C. H. A subject-index to the poems of Spenser. New Haven 1918, New York 1966.

Carpenter, F. I. A reference guide to Spenser. Chicago 1923, New York 1950; A bibliographical supplement by D. F. Atkinson, Baltimore 1937, New York 1967; Annotated bibliography 1937–60 by W. F. McNeir and F. Provost, Pittsburgh 1962 (Duquesne Stud).

Johnson, F. R. A critical bibliography of the works of Spenser printed before 1700. Baltimore 1933, London 1966.

Wurtsbaugh, J. Two centuries of Spenserian scholarship, 1609–1805. Baltimore 1936, New York 1969.

Williams, K. The present state of Spenser studies. Texas Stud in Lit & Lang 7 1966.

Hamilton, A. C. The Faerie Queene. In Critical approaches to six major English works, ed R. M. Lumiansky and H. Baker, Philadelphia 1968.

Spenser newsletter. 1– 1970–.

Collections

The Faerie Queen; The shepheards calendar; together with the other works of England's arch-poet Edm. Spenser, collected into one volume. 1611[–12, –13] (first folio), 1617.

The works of that famous English poet, Mr Edmond Spenser. 1679. With An account of his life [brief]; with other new additions, Brittain's Ida [by Phineas Fletcher], Bathurst's Latin trn of Shepheardes calender and A view.

Works. Ed J. Hughes 5 [and 6] vols 1715, 6 vols 1750 (rev).

Poetical works. Ed J. Aikin 6 vols 1802 (with glosses and notes), 1810 etc.

Works. Ed H. J. Todd 8 vols 1805 (with selection of notes from various commentators), 1 vol 1845, 1850 etc.

Poetical works. Ed G. S. Hillard 5 vols Boston 1839.

Poetical works. Ed F. J. Child 5 vols Boston 1855, 1864 (rev) (with glosses and notes).

Poetical works. Ed G. Gilfillan 5 vols Edinburgh 1859, 1865 etc.

Poetical works. Ed J. P. Collier 5 vols 1862 etc (with notes).

Complete works. Ed R. Morris with memoir by J. W. Hales 1869, 1897 (rev) etc (Globe edn).

Complete works. Ed A. B. Grosart 9 vols 1882–4 (priv ptd).

Complete poetical works. Ed R. E. N. Dodge, Boston 1908 etc (Cambridge edn, with few notes).

Poetical works. Ed J. C. Smith and E. de Selincourt 3 vols Oxford 1909–10 (with bibliographical and textual notes), 1 vol Oxford 1912 (OSA) (with Spenser-Harvey correspondence, abridged textual notes and essay by de Selincourt).

Works. Ed W. L. Renwick 4 vols 1928–34. With notes; omits Faerie Queene but includes all the other poems and A view).

Works. Ed W. L. Renwick 8 vols Oxford 1930–2.

The shepherds calendar and other poems. Ed P. Henderson 1932 (EL).

Works: a variorum edition. Ed E. Greenlaw, C. G. Osgood, F. M. Padelford and R. Heffner 10 vols Baltimore 1932–49, 1958. Faerie Queene bk 1 ed Padelford 1932; bk 2 ed Greenlaw 1933; bk 3 ed Padelford 1934; bk 4 ed Heffner 1935; bk 5 ed Heffner 1936; bks 6–7 ed general editors 1938; Minor poems ed Osgood and H. G. Lotspeich vol 1 1943, vol 2 1947; Prose works ed R. Gottfried 1949; Life of Spenser by A. C. Judson 1945; Index by Osgood, Baltimore 1957. Issued 11 vols 1966.

Selected poetry (with introductory essay and notes). Ed W. B. Yeats, Edinburgh 1906; ed W. L. Renwick, Oxford 1923 (with essays by Hazlitt, Coleridge and Leigh Hunt); ed C. S. Lewis in Major British writers; ed G. B. Harrison, New York 1954; ed L. Kirschbaum, New York 1956; ed D. C. Allen in Masters of British literature, ed R. A. Pratt, New York 1958; ed W. Nelson 1964; ed R. Kellogg and O. Steele, New York 1965; ed F. Kermode, Oxford 1965; ed A. C. Hamilton, New York 1966; ed H. MacLean, New York 1968 (with criticism); ed I. C. Sowton, Toronto 1968; ed E. Honig, New York 1968; ed A. K. and C. Hieatt, New York 1970; ed S. K. Heninger jr, Boston 1970; tr Italian, 1966.

§ I

A theatre [for] voluptuous worldlings, devised by S. John van-der Noodt. 1569, New York 1936 (facs). Contains Epigrams and Sonets tr Spenser, rev in Complaints, 1591, below.

The shepheardes calender: conteyning twelve æglogues proportionable to the twelve moneths. 1579 (anon), 1581, 1586, 1591, 1597, 1653 (with Bathurst's Latin trn); ed H. O. Sommer 1890 (facs), New York 1967; ed C. H. Herford 1895 (with introd and notes); San Marino 1926 (facs of 1597); San Marino 1927 (facs of 1579); Menston 1968 (facs); tr Italian, 1950.

The Faerie Queene, disposed into twelve books, fashioning xii morall vertues. 1590 (bks 1–3). For later edns see below.

Complaints: containing sundrie small poemes of the worlds vanitie. 1591. Contains The ruines of time; The teares of the Muses; Virgils gnat; Prosopopoia: or Mother

Hubberds tale; Ruines of Rome, by Bellay; Muiopotmos: or the fate of the butterflie (dated 1590); Visions of the worlds vanitie; The visions of Bellay; The visions of Petrarch.

Daphnaida: an elegie upon the death of the noble and vertuous Douglas Howard. 1591, 1596 (with Fowre hymnes), San Marino 1927 (facs).

Sonnet to M. Gabriell Harvey. Appended to Harvey's Foure letters, 1592; dated 1586.

Axiochus: a most excellent dialogue, written in Greeke by Plato, translated by Edw. Spenser. 1592; ed F. M. Padelford, Baltimore 1934. On the question of authorship see Variorum prose works, above, appendix 2.

Amoretti and Epithalamion. 1595; ed S. Lee, Elizabethan sonnets, 1904, New York 1964; ed C. Van Winkle, New York 1926 (Epithalamion only), London and New York 1927 (facs); tr Italian, 1954; Menston 1968 (facs); Epithalamion, ed E. Welsford, New York 1969 (with Fowre hymnes); New York 1969 (facs). Amoretti tr French, 1914.

Colin Clouts come home againe 1595. Includes Astrophel: a pastorall elegie upon the death of Sidney, together with other poems on Sidney's death by other hands (The dolefull lay of Clorinda has been attributed to Spenser); tr Italian, 1956.

Commendatory sonnet prefixed to Nennio: or a treatise of nobility, written by Sir John Baptiste Nenna of Bari; done into English by William Jones 1595.

The Faerie Queene, disposed into twelue bookes, fashioning xii morall vertues. 2 vols 1596. Bks 1–3, first pbd 1590, with The second part containing books 4–6; *for later edns see below.*

Fowre hymnes. 1596 (with 2nd edn of Daphnaida); ed L. Winstanley, Cambridge 1907 (Hymnes only); San Marino 1927 (facs of 1596); ed E. Welsford, New York 1969 (with Epithalamion, essay and notes).

Prothalamion: or a spousall verse in honour of the double marriage of Ladie Elizabeth and Ladie Katherine Somerset. 1596, San Marino 1927 (facs).

Commendatory sonnet prefixed to the Historie of George Castriot surnamed Scanderbeg, newly translated out of French by Z.I. 1596.

Commendatory sonnet prefixed to the Commonwealth and government of Venice, written by the Cardinall Gasper Contareno and translated by Lewis Lewkenor. 1599.

The Faerie Queene. 1609 (containing first edn of fragment of bk vii or the Mutabilitie cantos); ed T. Birch 3 vols 1751 (with life); ed R. Church 4 vols 1758–9 (with notes); ed J. Upton 2 vols 1758 (with detailed notes); ed T. J. Wise 6 vols 1895–7; ed J. W. Hales 2 vols 1897 (EL); ed K. M. Warren 6 vols 1879–1900 (with notes); ed J. C. Smith, Oxford 1909 (see Works, above); tr French, 1933; tr Japanese, 1969.

Book 1. Ed G. W. Kitchin, Oxford 1867, 1872, 1897 (rev); ed H. M. Percival 1893; ed L. Winstanley, Cambridge 1915; ed P. C. Bayley, Oxford 1966; tr Italian, 1829, 1954.

Book 2. Ed Kitchin, Oxford 1872; ed Winstanley, Cambridge 1914; ed Bayley, Oxford 1965.

Book 5. Ed A. B. Gough, Oxford 1918.

Book 6. Ed T. A. Wolff 1959.

Mutability cantos. Ed S. P. Zitner 1968; tr Italian, 1827. *All these edns have introds, notes and glosses.*

A view of the present state of Ireland. In The historie of Ireland, ed J. Ware, Dublin 1633, 1763 etc, New York 1970; in Works, 1679, above; ed H. Morley 1890; ed W. L. Renwick, Works, 1928–34, above (modernized with notes); Oxford 1970 (with notes). Written 1596.

A briefe discourse of Ireland by Spencer *was ptd in Grosart's edn of Spenser's* Works, *above, and in the Variorum edn of the* Prose works, *above.*

Letters

Three proper, and wittie, familiar letters. 1580; Two other, very commendable letters, 1580 (by Spenser and Gabriel Harvey); portions ed G. G. Smith, Elizabethan critical essays vol 1, Oxford 1904; Poetical works, Oxford 1912 (OSA), above.

§2

Critical studies extracted in the Variorum edn are not listed below unless they retain an independent interest.

Webbe, W. In his A discourse of English poetry, 1586.

Digby, K. A discourse concerning Spenser. BM additional ms 41, 846, transcribed in E. W. Bligh, Sir Kenelm Digby and his Venetia, 1932.

— Observations on the 22nd stanza in the 9th canto of the 2nd book of Spenser's Faery Queen. 1644.

Hughes, J. Remarks on the Faerie Queene. In his Works, 1715.

Jortin, J. Remarks on Spenser's poems. 1734, 1790 (expanded in his Tracts).

Spence, J. In his Polymetis, 1747.

Warton, T. Observations on the Faerie Queene. 1752, 1762 (enlarged), New York 1969.

Upton, J. Preface to the Faerie Queene. 1758.

Hurd, R. In his Letters on chivalry and romance, 1762.

Hazlitt, W. In his Lectures on the English poets, 1818.

Coleridge, S. T. In his Literary remains vol 1, 1836. Lecture 3 delivered 1818. See T. M. Raysor, Coleridge's miscellaneous criticism, Cambridge Mass 1936.

Hunt, L. In his Imagination and fancy, 1844.

Craik, G. L. Spenser and his poetry. 3 vols 1845.

Ruskin, J. In his Stones of Venice vol 3, 1853.

Courthope, W. J. The genius of Spenser. 1868.

Lowell, J. R. Essay on Spenser. North Amer Rev 120 1875; rptd in his Writings, Boston 1890–2.

Church, R. W. Spenser. 1879 (EML).

Dowden, E. Spenser, the poet and teacher. In his Transcripts and studies, 1887.

Randall, A. E. S. The sources of Spenser's classical mythology. Boston 1896.

Mackail, J. W. In his Springs of Helicon, 1909.

Harper, C. A. The sources of the British chronicle history in Spenser's Faerie Queene. Philadelphia 1910, New York 1964.

Boehme, T. Spensers literarisches Nachleben bis zu Shelley. Berlin 1911.

Cory, H. E. The critics of Spenser. Berkeley 1911, New York 1964.

— Spenser: a critical study. Berkeley 1917, New York 1965.

Langdon, I. Materials for a study of Spenser's theory of fine art. Ithaca 1911 (priv ptd), Darby Pa 1969.

Padelford, F. M. The political and ecclesiastical allegory of Faerie Queene 1. Boston 1911.

— Spenser and the Puritan propaganda. MP 11 1914.

— The political, economic and social views of Spenser. JEGP 14 1915.

— The spiritual allegory of the Faerie Queene 1. JEGP 22 1923.

— The allegory of chastity in the Faerie Queene. SP 21 1924.

— Aspects of Spenser's vocabulary. PQ 20 1941.

Winbolt, S. E. Spenser and his poetry. 1912.

Jones, H. S. V. Spenser's defense of Lord Grey. Univ of Illinois Stud in Lang & Lit 5 1919.

— A Spenser handbook. New York 1930.

Jack, A. A. A commentary on the poetry of Chaucer and Spenser. Glasgow 1920.

DeMoss, W. F. The influence of Aristotle's Politics and Ethics on Spenser. Chicago 1920.

Renwick, W. L. The critical origins of Spenser's diction. MLR 17 1922.

— Spenser: an essay on Renaissance poetry. 1925, 1964.

— In The great Tudors, ed K. Garvin 1935.
— The Faerie Queene. Proc Br Acad 33 1947.
— Edmund Spenser. 1952.
Hughes, M. Y. Spenser and the Greek pastoral triad. SP 20 1923.
— Virgil and Spenser. Berkeley 1929.
— Spenser's Palmer. ELH 2 1935.
— Spenser's Acrasia and the Circe of the Renaissance. JHI 4 1943.
— England's Eliza and Spenser's Medina. JEGP 43 1944.
— The Arthurs of the Faerie Queene. Etudes Anglaises 6 1953.
— Spenser 1552–1952. Trans of Wisconsin Acad 42 1953.
Legouis, E. Edmund Spenser. Paris 1923, 1956 (rev). In French.
— Edmund Spenser. 1926. Partly tr from preceding.
McMurphy, S. J. Spenser's use of Ariosto for allegory. Univ of Washington Pbns in Lang & Lit 2 1924, Folcroft Pa 1969.
Plomer, H. R. Spenser's handwriting. MP 21 1924.
Taylor, A. E. Spenser's knowledge of Plato. MLR 19 1924.
Blanchard, H. H. Spenser and Boiardo. PMLA 40 1925.
Landrum, G. W. Spenser's use of the Bible and his alleged Puritanism. PMLA 41 1926.
— Spenser's 'clouded heaven'. Shakespeare Assoc Bull 11 1936. On sky-imagery.
— Imagery of water in the Faerie Queene. ELH 8 1941. On imagery see also Shakespeare Assoc Bull 16 1941 (flora and fauna); 17 1942 (domestic and occupational life); 18 1943 (fire).
— St George redivivus. PQ 29 1950.
Notcutt, H. C. The Faerie Queene and its critics. E & S 12 1926.
Pope, E. F. Renaissance criticism and the diction of the Faerie Queene. PMLA 41 1926.
Henley, P. Spenser in Ireland. Cork 1928, Folcroft Pa 1969.
Lemmi, C. W. Symbolism of the classical episodes in the Faerie Queene. PQ 8 1929.
Saurat, D. In his La littérature et l'occultisme, Paris 1929; tr 1930.
Wyld, H. C. Spenser's diction and style in relation to those of later English poetry. In A grammatical miscellany offered to Otto Jespersen, Copenhagen 1930.
Bush, D. Mythology and the Renaissance tradition in English poetry. Minneapolis 1932, 1963 (rev).
Draper, J. W. Classical coinage in the Faerie Queene. PMLA 47 1932.
Greenlaw, E. Studies in Spenser's historical allegory. Baltimore 1932.
Lotspeich, H. G. Classical mythology in the poetry of Spenser. Princeton 1932.
McElderry, B. R., jr. Archaism and innovation in Spenser's poetic diction. PMLA 47 1932.
Millican, C. B. Spenser and the Table Round. Cambridge Mass 1932.
— Spenser's and Drant's poetic names for Elizabeth: Tanaquil, Gloria and Una. HLQ 2 1939.
Davis, B. E. C. Spenser: a critical study. Cambridge 1933.
Judson, A. C. Spenser in southern Ireland. Bloomington 1933.
— The life of Spenser. Baltimore 1945 (in Variorum).
— The 17th-century lives of Spenser. HLQ 10 1947.
— Spenser and the Munster officials. SP 44 1947.
— The 18th-century lives of Spenser. HLQ 16 1953.
Byrom, H. J. Spenser's first printer: Hugh Singleton. Library 4th ser 14 1934.
Hard, F. 'Princelie pallaces': Spenser and Elizabethan architecture. Sewanee Rev 42 1934.
Spens, J. Spenser's Faerie Queene: an interpretation. 1934, New York 1967.
Fowler, E. B. Spenser and the system of courtly love. Louisville 1935.

Green, Z. E. Observations on the epic similes in the Faerie Queene. PQ 14 1935.
— Swooning in the Faerie Queene. SP 34 1937.
Hintz, H. W. The Elizabethan entertainment and the Faerie Queene. PQ 14 1935.
Jenkins, R. Newes out of Munster: a document in Spenser's hand. SP 32 1935.
Smith, C. G. Spenser's theory of friendship. Baltimore 1935.
— Spenser's proverb lore. Cambridge Mass 1970.
Smith, R. M. Una and Duessa. PMLA 50 1935. See also 61 1946.
— Spenser's tale of the two sons of Milesio [5.4]. MLQ 3 1942.
— Origines Arthurianae: the two crosses of the Red Cross Knight. JEGP 54 1955.
— Spenser's scholarly script and 'right writing'. In Studies in honor of T. W. Baldwin, Urbana 1958.
Bradford, G. In his Elizabethan women, New York 1936.
Buyssens, E. Aristotelianism and anti-Puritanism in Spenser's allegory of the three sisters [2.2]. E Studies 18 1936.
Castelli, A. La Gerusalemme liberata nella Inghilterra di Spenser. Milan 1936.
Lewis, C. S. In his Allegory of love, Oxford 1936.
— Studies in medieval and Renaissance literature. Ed W. Hooper, Cambridge 1966. Includes Edmund Spenser (1954); On reading the Faerie Queene (1941); Neoplatonism in the poetry of Spenser (1961); Spenser's cruel Cupid (previously unpbd); Genius and genius (1936).
— Spenser's images of life. Ed A. Fowler, Cambridge 1967.
Rathborne, I. E. A new source for Spenser's Faerie Queene I. SP 33 1936. On sermon Against disobedience and wilful rebellion.
— The meaning of Spenser's fairyland. New York 1937.
— The political allegory of the Florimell-Marinell story. ELH 12 1945.
Sugden, H. W. The grammar of the Faerie Queene. Philadelphia 1936.
Allen, D. C. Arthur's diamond shield in the Faerie Queene. JEGP 36 1937.
— On the closing lines of the Faerie Queene. MLN 64 1949.
Bennett, J. W. Did Spenser starve? MLN 52 1937.
— Spenser's garden of Adonis revisited. JEGP 41 1942. Replies by B. Stirling and Bennett, ibid.
— The evolution of the Faerie Queene. Chicago 1942.
— Genre, milieu and the epic-romance. Eng Inst Essays 1951.
— Britain among the Fortunate Isles. SP 53 1956.
Gottfried, R. B. Spenser and the Italian myth of locality. SP 34 1937.
— The pictorial element in Spenser's poetry. ELH 19 1952.
— Spenser and the Historie of Cambria. MLN 72 1957.
— Spenser expands his text. Renaissance News 16 1963.
— 'Our new poet': archetypal criticism and the Faerie Queene. PMLA 83 1968.
Jenkins, R. Spenser with Lord Grey in Ireland. PMLA 52 1937.
— Spenser: the uncertain years 1584–9. PMLA 53 1938.
— Spenser and Ireland. ELH 19 1952.
Neill, K. Spenser on the regiment of women: a note on the Faerie Queene V.v.25. SP 34 1937.
— Spenser's Acrasia and Mary Queen of Scots. PMLA 60 1945.
— The degradation of the Red Cross Knight. ELH 19 1952.
Viglione, F. La poesia lirica di Spenser. Genoa 1937.
Webb, W. S. Vergil in Spenser's epic theory. ELH 4 1937.
Fletcher, J. B. The legend of Cambel and Triamond in the Faerie Queene. SP 35 1938.
— The Puritan argument in Spenser. PMLA 58 1943.

Galimberti, A. Spenser: 'l'Ariosto inglese'. Turin 1938.

Schulze, I. L. Reflections of Elizabethan tournaments in the Faerie Queene IV.iv and V.iii. ELH 5 1938.

Thornton, F. C. The French element in Spenser's poetical works. Toulouse 1938.

Baldwin, C. S. The Faerie Queene as romance. In Renaissance literary theory and practice, ed D. L. Clark, New York 1939.

Harrison, T. P., jr. Divinity in Spenser's Garden of Adonis. SE 19 1939.

— Aspects of primitivism in Shakespeare and Spenser. SE 1940.

— Jonson's The sad shepherd and Spenser. MLN 58 1943.

— They tell of birds: Chaucer, Spenser, Milton, Drayton. Austin 1956.

Heffner, R. Spenser's family. HLQ 2 1939.

Hulbert, V. B. The Belge episode in the Faerie Queene [5.10–11]. SP 36 1939.

Knight, G. W. In his Burning oracle, Oxford 1939. Essay on the Spenserian fluidity; rptd in his Poets of action, 1967.

Michie, S. The Faerie Queene and Arthur of little Britain. SP 36 1939.

Mounts, C. E. Spenser's seven bead-men and the corporal works of mercy. PMLA 54 1939.

— Virtuous duplicity in the Faerie Queene. MLQ 7 1946.

— Spenser and the Countess of Leicester. ELH 19 1952.

— Spenser and the Earl of Essex. Renaissance Papers 1958–60.

Atkinson, D. F. Busirane's castle and Artidon's cave. MLQ 1 1940. On Mirrour of knighthood as a source.

— The Pastorella episode in the Faerie Queene. PMLA 59 1944.

— 'The wandering knight', the Red Cross Knight and 'Miles Dei'. HLQ 7 1944.

Collins, J. B. In his Christian mysticism in the Elizabethan age with its background in mystical methodology, Baltimore 1940.

Hopper, V. F. Spenser's house of temperance. PMLA 55 1940.

Koller, K. Abraham Fraunce and Spenser. ELH 7 1940.

— The Travayled pylgrime by Stephen Batman and Faerie Queene ii. MLQ 3 1942.

— Art, rhetoric and holy dying in the Faerie Queene with special reference to the Despair canto. SP 61 1964.

McNeir, W. F. Canto unity in the Faerie Queene. PQ 19 1940.

— Ariosto's Sospetto, Gascoigne's Suspicion and Spenser's Malbecco. In Festschrift für Walther Fischer, Heidelberg 1959.

— The sacrifice of Serena: Faerie Queene VI.viii.31–51. In Festschrift für Edgar Mertner, Munich 1969.

Nelson, H. B. Amidas v. Bracidas [5.4]. MLQ 1 1940.

Rix, H. D. Rhetoric in Spenser's poetry. State College Pa 1940.

Shanley, J. L. A study of Spenser's gentleman. Evanston 1940.

— Spenser's temperance and Aristotle. MP 43 1946.

Blair, S. M. The succession of lives in Spenser's three sons of Agape [4.3]. MLQ 2 1941.

Gilbert, A. H. The ladder of lechery: Faerie Queene III. i. 45. MLN 56 1941. Reply by J. Hutton 57 1942.

— Spenserian armor. PMLA 57 1942.

— Belphoebe's misdeeming of Timias. PMLA 62 1947.

— Those two brethren giants: Faerie Queene II. xi. 15. MLN 70 1955.

— Spenserian comedy. Tennessee Stud in Lit 2 1957.

Kahin, H. A. Spenser and the school of Alanus. ELH 8 1941.

Lievsay, J. L. Braggadocchio: Spenser's legacy to the character-writers. MLQ 2 1941.

Osgood, C. G. In his Poetry as a means of grace, Princeton 1941.

Rubel, V. L. Poetic diction in the English Renaissance from Skelton through Spenser. New York 1941.

Walter, J. H. The Faerie Queene: alterations and structure. MLR 36 1941. See also 38 1943.

Baldwin, T. W. The genesis of some passages which Spenser borrowed from Marlowe. ELH 9 1942. Replies by W. B. C. Watkins 11 1944; Baldwin 12 1945.

Hutton, J. Spenser and the Cinq points en amours. MLN 57 1942.

Phillips, J. E. The background of Spenser's attitude toward women rulers. HLQ 5 1942.

— The woman ruler in the Faerie Queene. Ibid.

— Spenser's syncretistic religious imagery. ELH 36 1969.

— Renaissance concepts of justice and the structure of Faerie Queene v. HLQ 33 1970.

Starnes, D. T. Spenser and the Graces. PQ 21 1942.

— Spenser and the Muses. SE 22 1942.

— and E. W. Talbert. In their Classical myth and legend in Renaissance dictionaries, Chapel Hill 1955.

Stoll, E. E. Criticism criticized: Spenser and Milton. JEGP 41 1942.

Camden, C. The architecture of Spenser's house of Alma. MLN 58 1943.

Hankins, J. E. The sources of Spenser's Britomartis. MLN 58 1943.

— Spenser and the Revelation of St John. PMLA 60 1945.

Pellegrini, A. M. Bruno, Sidney and Spenser. SP 40 1943.

Buchan, A. M. The political allegory of the Faerie Queene IV. ELH 11 1944.

Siegel, P. N. Spenser and the Calvinist view of life. SP 41 1944.

Stein, A. Stanza continuity in the Faerie Queene. MLN 59 1944.

Woodworth, M. K. The Mutability cantos and the succession. PMLA 59 1944.

Boegholm, N. On the Spenserian style. Etudes Linguistiques 1944, Travaux du Cercle Linguistique de Copenhagen 1 1945.

Bowers, F. T. Evidences of revision in the Faerie Queene III. i, ii. MLN 60 1945.

— The Faerie Queene II: Mordant, Ruddymane and the nymph's well. In English studies in honor of James Southall Wilson, Charlottesville 1951.

Bradner, L. Spenser's connections with Hampshire. MLN 60 1945.

— Spenser and the Faerie Queene. Chicago 1948.

Pearce, R. H. Primitivistic ideas in the Faerie Queene. JEGP 44 1945.

Van Doren, M. In his Noble voice: a study of ten great poems, New York 1946.

Vallese, T. Spenser. Naples 1947. A study and Italian trn of Faerie Queene I. i.

Brooke, T. In Essays on Shakespeare and other Elizabethans, ed L. Bradner, New Haven 1948.

Gray, H. D. Shakespeare's rival poet. JEGP 47 1948.

Honig, E. Hobgoblin on Apollo. Kenyon Rev 10 1948.

Kendrick, T. D. The elfin chronicle. TLS 7 Feb, 15 May 1948. Replies by I. E. Rathborne 24 April, K. M. Buck 19 June, K. T. Duffield 26 June, F. A. Yates 3 July 1948.

Owen, W. J. B. A Spenser note. MLR 43 1948. On Letter to Raleigh. Reply by J. Spens 44 1949; rejoinder 45 1950.

— 'In these XII books severally handled and discoursed'. ELH 19 1952.

— Orlando Furioso and stanza-connection in the Faerie Queene. MLN 67 1952.

— The structure of the Faerie Queene. PMLA 68 1953.

— Narrative logic and imitation in the Faerie Queene. Comparative Lit 7 1955.

Woolf, V. In her Moment and other essays, 1948.

Brooke, N. S. C. S. Lewis and Spenser: nature, art and the Bower of Bliss. Cambridge Jnl April 1949.

Mayhall, J. Shakespeare and Spenser: a commentary on differences. MLQ 10 1949.

Schoeck, R. J. Alliteration as a means of stanza connection in the Faerie Queene. MLN 64 1949.

Woodhouse, A. S. P. Nature and grace in the Faerie Queene. ELH 16 1949.

— The poet and his faith: religion and poetry in England from Spenser to Eliot and Auden. Chicago 1965.

Glazier, L. The struggle between good and evil in Faerie Queene I. College Eng April 1950.

— The nature of Spenser's imagery. MLQ 16 1955.

Sirluck, E. A note on the rhetoric of Spenser's Despair. MP 47 1950.

— Milton revises the Faerie Queene. MP 48 1951.

— The Faerie Queene book II and the Nicomachean ethics. MP 49 1952.

Wagner, G. Talus. ELH 17 1950.

Watkins, W. B. C. Shakespeare and Spenser. Princeton 1950.

Whitaker, V. K. The religious basis of Spenser's thought. Stanford 1950.

— The theological structure of the Faerie Queene I. ELH 19 1952.

Edwards, J. M. Spenser and his philosophy. Cambridge Jnl 4 1951.

Miller, M. Nature in the Faerie Queene. ELH 18 1951.

Weld, J. S. The complaint of Britomart [3.4.8–10]: wordplay and symbolism. PMLA 66 1951.

Green, C. H. Sir John Salisbury as Spenser's Timias. SE 31 1952.

Holloway, J. The seven deadly sins in the Faerie Queene II. RES new ser 3 1952.

Maxwell, J. C. The truancy of Calidore. ELH 19 1952.

— Guyon, Phaedria and the Palmer. RES new ser 5 1954.

Mueller, W. R. and D. C. Allen (ed). That soueraine light: essays in honor of Spenser. Baltimore 1952. 9 essays rptd from ELH 19 1952; listed separately.

— Spenser's critics: changing currents in literary taste. Syracuse 1959.

— Spenser and recent scholarship. Texas Stud in Lit & Lang 3 1961.

Saunders, J. W. The façade of morality. ELH 19 1952.

Stampfer, J. L. The Cantos of mutability: Spenser's last testament of faith. UTQ 21 1952.

Williams, K. 'Eterne in mutabilitie': the unified world of the Faerie Queene. ELH 19 1952.

— Venus and Diana: some uses of myth in the Faerie Queene. ELH 28 1961.

— Romance tradition in the Faerie Queene. Research Stud of Washington State Univ 32 1964.

— Spenser's Faerie Queene: the world of glass. 1966.

— Vision and rhetoric: the poet's voice in the Faerie Queene. ELH 36 1969.

Butler, P. R. Rivers of Milton and Spenser. Quart Rev 291 1953.

Falls, M. R. Spenser's Kirkrapine and the Elizabethans. SP 50 1953.

Moloney, M. F. St Thomas and Spenser's virtue of magnificence. JEGP 52 1953.

Nelson, W. A source for Spenser's Malbecco. MLN 68 1953. Argues for Gascoigne, Adventures of Master F. J.

— (ed). Form and convention in the poetry of Spenser. New York 1961 (Eng Inst Essays).

— The poetry of Spenser: a study. New York 1963.

— Queen Elizabeth, Spenser's Mercilla and a rusty sword. Renaissance News 18 1965.

Ricks, B. Catholic sacramentals and symbolism in the Faerie Queene. JEGP 52 1953.

Caspari, F. In his Humanism and the social order in Tudor England, Chicago 1954.

Chew, S. C. Spenser's pageant of the seven deadly sins. In Studies in art and literature for Belle da Costa Greene, Princeton 1954.

Durling, R. M. The Bower of Bliss and Armida's palace. Comparative Lit 6 1954.

— The figure of the poet in Renaissance epic. Cambridge Mass 1965.

Emry, H. T. Two houses of Pride: Spenser's and Hawthorne's. PQ 33 1954.

Harder, K. B. Nashe and Spenser. In Essays in honor of W. C. Curry, Nashville 1954.

Hoopes, R. 'God guide thee, Guyon': nature and grace reconciled in the Faerie Queene II. RES new ser 5 1954. Reply by A. S. P. Woodhouse 6 1955; by E. Sirluck, ibid.

Tillyard, E. M. W. In his English epic and its background, 1954.

Chang, H. Allegory and courtesy in Spenser: a Chinese view. Edinburgh 1955.

Groom, B. The diction of poetry from Spenser to Bridges. Toronto 1955.

Huckabay, C. The structure of Faerie Queene IV. Studia Neophilologica 27 1955.

Oras, A. Intensified rhyme links in the Faerie Queene: an aspect of Elizabethan rhymecraft. JEGP 54 1955.

— Spenser and Milton: some parallels and contrasts in the handling of sound. Eng Inst Essays 1956.

Arthos, J. On the poetry of Spenser and the form of romances. 1956.

Evans, R. O. Spenser's role in the controversy over quantitative verse. Neuphilologische Mitteilungen 57 1956.

— Spenserian humor: Faerie Queene III and IV. Neuphilologische Mitteilungen 60 1959.

Friedland, L. S. Spenser's 'Sabaoth's rest'. MLQ 17 1956. On the concluding lines of Faerie Queene.

Guth, H. P. Unity and multiplicity in the Faerie Queene. Anglia 74 1956.

— Allegorical implications of artifice in Spenser's Faerie Queene. PMLA 76 1961.

Berger, H., jr. The allegorical temper: vision and reality in the Faerie Queene II. New Haven 1957.

— The prospect of imagination: Spenser and the limits of poetry. Stud in Eng Lit 1500–1900 I 1961.

— A secret discipline: Faerie Queene VI. Eng Inst Essays 1961.

— Spenser's Gardens of Adonis: force and form in the Renaissance imagination. UTQ 30 1961.

— Spenser's Faerie Queene I: prelude to interpretation. Southern Rev 2 1966.

— The Spenserian dynamics. Stud in Eng Lit 1500–1900 8 1968.

— (ed). Spenser: a collection of critical essays. Englewood Cliffs NJ 1968.

— Archaism, immortality and the Muse in Spenser's poetry. Yale Rev 58 1969.

— Two Spenserian retrospects: the antique Temple of Venus and the primitive marriage of rivers. Texas Stud in Lit & Lang 10 1969.

— The discarding of Malbecco: conspicuous allusion and cultural exhaustion in the Faerie Queene III. ix–x. SP 66 1969.

— Faerie Queene III: a general description. Criticism 11 1969.

— The structure of Merlin's chronicle in the Faerie Queene III.iii. Stud in Eng Lit 1500–1900 9 1969.

Freeman, R. Edmund Spenser. 1957 (Br Council pamphlet), 1962 (rev).

Hamilton, A. C. Spenser and Tourneur's Transformed metamorphosis. RES new ser 8 1957.

— Spenser's Letter to Ralegh. MLN 73 1958. Replies by W. J. B. Owen 75 1960; D. Baker 76 1961.

— Spenser and Langland. SP 55 1958; rev and expanded in The visions of Piers Plowman and the Faerie Queene, Eng Inst Essays 1961.

— The structure of allegory in the Faerie Queene. Oxford 1961.

— Spenser's pastoral. ELH 33 1966.

— Spenser and the common reader. ELH 35 1968.

Blayney, M. S. and G. H. The Faerie Queene and an English version of Chartier's Traité de l'espérance. SP 55 1958.

Hotson, L. The Blatant Beast. In Studies in honor of T. W. Baldwin, Urbana 1958.

Orange, L. E. Spenser's word-play. N & Q Sept 1958.

— Spenser's Old Dragon [1.11]. MLN 74 1959.

— Sensual beauty in Faerie Queene I. JEGP 61 1962.

Potts, A. F. Shakespeare and the Faerie Queene. Ithaca 1958.

Steadman, J. M. Una and the clergy: the ass symbol in the Faerie Queene. Jnl Warburg & Courtauld Inst 21 1958.

— Spenser's House of Care: a reinterpretation. Stud in Renaissance 7 1960.

— Spenser's Errour and the Renaissance allegorical tradition. Neuphilologische Mitteilungen 62 1961.

— The 'inharmonious blacksmith': Spenser and the Pythagoras legend. PMLA 79 1964.

Wind, E. In his Pagan mysteries in the Renaissance, 1958, 1967 (rev).

Cope, J. I. Jonson's reading of Spenser: the genesis of a poem. Eng Miscellany (Rome) 10 1959.

Fowler, A. D. S. Six knights at Castle Joyous. SP 56 1959.

— Emblems of temperance in the Faerie Queene II. RES new ser 11 1960.

— The river Guyon. MLN 75 1960.

— The image of mortality: Faerie Queene II.i–ii. HLQ 24 1961.

— Oxford and London marginalia to the Faerie Queene. N & Q Nov 1961.

— Spenser and the numbers of time. 1964.

Gang, T. M. Nature and grace in the Faerie Queene: the problem reviewed. ELH 26 1959. Reply by A. S. P. Woodhouse 27 1960.

Heninger, S. K., jr. The Orgoglio episode in the Faerie Queene. ELH 26 1959.

Kostić, V. Spenser and the Bembian linguistic theory. Eng Miscellany (Rome) 10 1959.

— Ariosto and Spenser. Eng Miscellany (Rome) 17 1966.

Marshall, W. H. Calvin, Spenser and the major sacraments. MLN 74 1959.

Sonn, C. R. Spenser's imagery. ELH 26 1959.

— Sir Guyon in the Cave of Mammon. Stud in Eng Lit 1500–1900 1 1961.

Berry, H. and E. K. Timings. Spenser's pension. RES new ser 11 1960.

Bradbrook, M. C. No room at the top: Spenser's pursuit of fame. In Elizabethan poetry, ed J. R. Brown and B. Harris 1960.

Dallett, J. B. Ideas of sight in the Faerie Queene. ELH 27 1960.

— The Faerie Queene IV.i–v: a synopsis of discord. MLN 75 1960.

Ellrodt, R. Neoplatonism in the poetry of Spenser. Geneva 1960.

English, H. M., jr. Spenser's accommodation of allegory to history in the story of Timias and Belphoebe. JEGP 59 1960.

Kermode, J. F. The cave of Mammon. In Elizabethan poetry, ed J. R. Brown and B. Harris 1960.

— Spenser and the allegorists. Proc Br Acad 48 1962.

— The Faerie Queene, I and V. Bull John Rylands Lib 47 1965.

Parker, M. P. The allegory of the Faerie Queene. Oxford 1960.

— The image of direction in Dante, Spenser and Milton. Eng Miscellany (Rome) 19 1968.

Satterthwaite, A. W. Spenser, Ronsard and Du Bellay: a Renaissance comparison. Princeton 1960.

Foltinek, H. Die wilden Männer in Spensers Faerie Queene. Die Neueren Sprachen 10 1961.

Fox, R. C. Temperance and the seven deadly sins in the Faerie Queene II. RES new ser 12 1961.

Frye, N. The structure of imagery in the Faerie Queene. UTQ 30 1961.

Hawkins, S. Mutabilitie and the cycle of the months. Eng Inst Essays 1961.

Hough, G. Spenser and Renaissance iconography. EC 11 1961. Replies by A. Fowler and J. R. Browning, ibid.

— A preface to the Faerie Queene. 1962.

— First commentary on the Faerie Queene: annotations in Lord Bessborough's copy of the first edition of the Faerie Queene. 1964 (priv ptd).

Knowles, A. S., jr. Spenser's natural man. Renaissance Papers 1958–60.

MacLure, M. Nature and art in the Faerie Queene. ELH 28 1961.

— Spenser: an introductory essay. Queen's Quart 73 1966.

Manzalaoui, M. A. The struggle for the house of the soul: Augustine and Spenser. N & Q Nov 1961.

Snyder, S. Guyon the wrestler. Renaissance News 14 1961.

Torczon, V. J. Spenser's Orgoglio and Despaire. Texas Stud in Lit & Lang 3 1961.

Walton, C. E. 'To maske in myrthe': Spenser's theatrical practices in the Faerie Queene. Emporia State Research Stud 9 1961.

Nevo, R. Spenser's Bower of Bliss and a key metaphor from Renaissance poetic. In Studies in Western literature vol 10, ed D. A. Fineman, Jerusalem 1962.

Hieatt, A. K. Scudamour's practice of 'maistrye' upon Amoret. PMLA 77 1962.

— Milton's Comus and Spenser's false genius. UTQ 38 1969.

Hill, R. F. Colin Clout's courtesy. MLR 57 1962.

Holleran, J. V. Spenser's Braggadocchio. In Studies in English Renaissance literature, ed W. F. McNeir, Baton Rouge 1962.

— Spenser's irony in Faerie Queene II. McNeese Rev (Louisiana) 15 1964.

Nestrick, W. V. 'The virtuous and gentle discipline of gentlemen and poets'. ELH 29 1962.

Shroeder, J. W. Spenser's erotic drama: the Orgoglio episode. ELH 29 1962.

Beum, R. Some observations on Spenser's verse forms. Neuphilologische Mitteilungen 64 1963.

Cosman, M. P. Spenser's ark of animals: animal imagery in the Faerie Queene. Stud in Eng Lit 1500–1900 3 1963.

Fish, S. Nature as concept and character in the Mutabilitie cantos. College Lang Assoc Jnl (Baltimore) 6 1963.

Greene, T. In his Descent from Heaven: a study in epic continuity. New Haven 1963.

Major, J. W., jr. The education of a young knight. Univ Kansas City Rev 29 1963.

McAuley, J. Spenser and George Eliot: a critical excursion. Hobart 1963.

Nellist, B. The allegory of Guyon's voyage: an interpretation. ELH 30 1963.

Osgood, C. G. In his Creed of a humanist, Seattle 1963.

Paolina, M. Spenser and Dante. Eng Miscellany (Rome) 14 1963.

Ringler, R. N. Spenser and the Achilleid. SP 60 1963.

— The Faunus episode. MP 63 1966.

— Dryden at the House of Busirane. E Studies 49 1968.

Blissett, W. Spenser's Mutabilitie. In Essays in English literature presented to A. S. P. Woodhouse, Toronto 1964.

— Florimell and Marinell. Stud in Eng Lit 1500–1900 5 1965.

Dundas, J. Allegory as a form of wit. Stud in Renaissance 11 1964.

— Elizabethan architecture and the Faerie Queene: some structural analogies. Dalhousie Rev 45 1966.

— The rhetorical basis of Spenser's imagery. Stud in Eng Lit 1500–1900 8 1968.

Fletcher, A. Allegory: the theory of a symbolic mode. Ithaca 1964.

Graziani, R. Elizabeth at Isis Church. PMLA 79 1964.

— Philip II's impresa and Spenser's Souldan. Jnl Warburg & Courtauld Inst 27 1964.

Miller, L. H., jr. Phaedria, Mammon and Sir Guyon's education by error. JEGP 63 1964.

— A secular reading of the Faerie Queene II. ELH 33 1966.

— Arthur, Maleger and history in the allegorical context. UTQ 35 1966.

Roche, T. P., jr. The kindly flame: a study of the Faerie Queene III and IV. Princeton 1964.

Tayler, E. W. In his Nature and art in Renaissance literature, New York 1964.

Ashley, L. R. N. Spenser and the ideal of the gentleman. Bibliothèque d'Humanisme et Renaissance 27 1965.

Evans, F. B. The printing of the Faerie Queene in 1596. SB 18 1965.

MacNeice, L. In his Varieties of parable, 1965.

Marotti, A. F. Animal symbolism in the Faerie Queene: tradition and the poetic context. Stud in Eng Lit 1500–1900 5 1965.

Scott, W. O. Proteus in Spenser and Shakespeare: the lover's identity. Shakespeare Stud 1 1965.

Staton, W. F., jr. Ralegh and the Amyas-Aemylia episode [4.7–9]. Stud in Eng Lit 1500–1900 5 1965.

— Italian pastorals and the conclusion of the Serena story. Stud in Eng Lit 1500–1900 6 1966.

Stock, A. G. Yeats on Spenser. In In excited reverie: a centenary tribute to Yeats, ed A. N. Jeffares and K. G. W. Cross 1965.

Bahr, H. W. The misery of Florimell: the ladder of temptation. Southern Quart 4 1966.

Bayley, P. C. Order, grace and courtesy in Spenser's world. In Patterns of love and courtesy: essays in memory of C. S. Lewis, 1966.

Cheney, D. Spenser's image of nature: wild man and shepherd in the Faerie Queene. New Haven 1966.

Colie, R. L. In her Paradoxia epidemica, Princeton 1966.

Friedmann, A. E. The Diana-Acteon episode in Ovid's Metamorphoses and the Faerie Queene. Comparative Lit 18 1966.

Fromm, H. Spenserian jazz and the aphrodisiac of virtue. Eng Miscellany (Rome) 17 1966.

Giamatti, A. B. In his Earthly paradise and the Renaissance epic, Princeton 1966.

Hutton, J. Spenser's 'adamantine chains': a cosmological metaphor. In The classical tradition: studies in honor of Harry Caplan, Ithaca 1966.

Iredale, R. O. Giants and tyrants in Faerie Queene v. RES new ser 17 1966.

LaGuardia, E. In his Nature redeemed: the imitation of order in three Renaissance poems, Hague 1966. On Epithalamion, Faerie Queene III–IV.

MacIntyre, J. Spenser's herculean heroes. Humanities Assoc Bull 17 1966.

— Artegall's sword and the Mutabilitie cantos. ELH 33 1966.

Ramsay, J. C. The garden of Adonis and the garden of forms. UTQ 35 1966.

Tuve, R. Allegorical imagery: some mediaeval books and their posterity. Princeton 1966.

— Essays: Spenser, Herbert, Milton. Ed T. P. Roche jr, Princeton 1970. Includes The Red Crosse Knight and mediaeval demon stories (1929); A mediaeval commonplace in Spenser's cosmology (1933); Spenser and the Zodiake of life (1935); Spenser's reading: the De claris mulieribus (1936); Spenser and mediaeval mazers (1937); Spenser and some pictorial conventions (1940); 'Spenserus' (1964).

Zitner, S. P. Spenser's diction and classical precedent. PQ 45 1966.

Alpers, P. J. The poetry of the Faerie Queene. Princeton 1967.

— How to read the Faerie Queene. EC 18 1968.

— (ed). Spenser: a critical anthology. 1969 (Penguin).

Alworth, E. P. Spenser's concept of nature. In His firm estate: essays in honor of F. J. Eikenberry, Tulsa 1967.

Clark, J. P. 'His earnest unto game': Spenser's humor in the Faerie Queene. Emporia State Research Stud 15 1967.

Craig, M. The secret wit of Spenser's language. In Elizabethan poetry: modern essays in criticism, ed P. J. Alpers, New York 1967.

Cummings, R. M. A note on the arithmological stanza: Faerie Queene II. ix. 22. Jnl Warburg & Courtauld Inst 30 1967.

Lanham, R. A. The literal Britomart. MLQ 28 1967.

Major, J. M. Paradise regained and Spenser's legend of holiness. Renaissance Quart 20 1967.

Moorman, C. In his A knyght there was: the evolution of the knight in literature, Lexington Kentucky 1967.

Oruch, J. B. Spenser, Camden and the poetic marriages of rivers. SP 64 1967.

Rusche, H. Pride, humility, and grace in the Faerie Queene I. Stud in Eng Lit 1500–1900 7 1967.

South, M. H. A note on Spenser and Sir Thomas Browne. MLR 62 1967.

Watson, E. A. F. Spenser. 1967.

Williams, A. Flower on a lowly stalk: Faerie Queen VI. East Lansing 1967.

Bell, B. W. The comic realism of Una's dwarf. Massachussetts Stud in Eng 1 1968.

Bieman, E. Britomart in Faerie Queen v. UTQ 37 1968.

Bryan, R. A. Apostasy and the fourth bead-man in the Faerie Queene. Eng Lang Notes 5 1968.

Carscallen, J. 'The goodly frame of temperance': the metaphor of cosmos in the Faerie Queene II. UTQ 37 1968.

Cirillo, A. R. Spenser's 'faire hermaphrodite'. PQ 47 1968.

— The fair hermaphrodite: love-union in the poetry of Donne and Spenser. Stud in Eng Lit 1500–1900 9 1969.

Cutts, J. P. Spenser's mermaids. Eng Lang Notes 5 1968.

Dunseath, T. K. Spenser's allegory of justice in Faerie Queene v. Princeton 1968.

Elliott, J. R., jr (ed). The Prince of poets: essays on Spenser. New York 1968.

Feinstein, B. The Faerie Queene and cosmogonies of the Near East. JHI 29 1968.

Grellner, M. A. Britomart's quest for maturity. Stud in Eng Lit 1500–1900 8 1968.

Holland, J. F. The cantos of Mutabilitie and the form of the Faerie Queene. ELH 35 1968.

Neuse, R. Book VI as conclusion to the Faerie Queene. ELH 35 1968.

Rose, M. Heroic love: studies in Sidney and Spenser. Cambridge Mass 1968.

Sale, R. Reading Spenser: an introduction to the Faerie Queene. New York 1968.

Sehrt, E. T. Der Wald des Irrtums: zur allegorischen Funktion von Faerie Queene I.vii–ix. Anglia 86 1968.

Anderson, J. H. Redcrosse and the descent into hell. ELH 36 1969.

— The July eclogue and the house of Holiness: perspective in Spenser. Stud in Eng Lit 1500–1900 10 1970.

— 'Nor man it is': the knight of justice in the Faerie Queene v. PMLA 85 1970.

— The Knight and the Palmer in the Faerie Queene II. MLQ 31 1970.

— Whatever happened to Amoret? Criticism 13 1971.

Aptekar, J. Icons of justice: iconography and thematic imagery in Faerie Queene v. New York 1969.

Baybak, M., P. Delany and A. K. Hieatt. Placement 'in the middest' in the Faerie Queene. Papers on Lang & Lit (Illinois) 5 1969.

Davidson, C. The idol of Isis Church. SP 66 1969.

Gransden, K. W. A critical commentary on the Faerie Queene. 1969.

Grundy, J. In her Spenserian poets, 1969.

Huston, J. D. The function of the mock hero in the Faerie Queene. MP 66 1969.

Kaske, C. V. The dragon's spark and sting and the structure of Red Cross's dragon-fight: Faerie Queene I.xi-xii. SP 66 1969.

Kostic, V. Spenser's sources in comparative literature. Belgrade 1969.

Murrin, M. In his Veil of allegory: allegorical rhetoric in the English Renaissance, Chicago 1969.

Northrop, D. A. Spenser's defence of Elizabeth. UTQ 38 1969.

Pecheux, M. C. Spenser's Red Cross and Milton's Adam. Eng Lang Notes 6 1969.

Reamer, O. J. Spenser's debt to Marot. Texas Stud in Lit & Lang 10 1969.

Rosinger, L. Spenser's Una and Queen Elizabeth. Eng Lang Notes 6 1969.

Spurgeon, P. O. Spenser's Muses. Renaissance Papers 1969.

Uhlig, C. Ouroboros-symbolik bei Spenser. Germanisch-romanische Monatsschrift 19 1969.

Blitch, A. F. The Mutability cantos 'in meet order ranged'. Eng Lang Notes 7 1970.

Cullen, P. Guyon microchristus: the cave of Mammon re-examined. ELH 37 1970.

Cummings, R. M. An iconographical puzzle: Spenser's Cupid at the Faerie Queene II.viii. Jnl Warburg & Courtauld Inst 33 1970.

— (ed). Spenser: the critical heritage. 1971.

Evans, M. Spenser's anatomy of heroism: a commentary on the Faerie Queene. Cambridge 1970.

Freeman, R. The Faerie Queene: a companion for readers. 1970.

Gransden, K. W. Allegory and personality in Spenser's heroes. EC 20 1970.

Hill, J. M. Braggadocchio and Spenser's golden world concept. ELH 37 1970.

Hill, R. F. Spenser's allegorical 'houses'. MLR 65 1970.

Holleran, J. V. A view of comedy in the Faerie Queene. In Essays in honor of E. L. Marilla, Baton Rouge 1970.

Knight, W. N. The narrative unity of the Faerie Queene v. RES new ser 21 1970.

MacIntyre, J. The Faerie Queene I: toward making it more teachable. College Eng Feb 1970.

Magill, A. J. Spenser's Guyon and the mediocrity of the Elizabethan settlement. SP 67 1970.

Waters, D. D. Duessa as theological satire. Columbia Missouri 1970.

Bayley, P. Spenser: prince of poets. 1971.

Berger, H. Busirane and the war between the sexes: an interpretation of the Faerie Queene III.xi-xii. Eng Literary Renaissance 1 1971.

Brill, L. W. Chastity as ideal sexuality in the Faerie Queene III. Stud in Eng Lit 1500-1900 11 1971.

Culp, D. W. Courtesy and fortune's chance in the Faerie Queene VI. MP 68 1971.

– Courtesy and moral virtue. Stud in Eng Lit 1500-1900 11 1971.

Dees, J. S. The narrator of the Faerie Queene: patterns of response. Texas Stud in Lang & Lit 12 1971.

Gilde, H. C. 'The sweet lodge of love and deare delight': the problem of Amoret. PQ 50 1971.

— Spenser's Hellenore and some Ovidian associations. Comparative Lit 23 1971.

Fletcher, A. The prophetic moment: an essay on Spenser. Chicago 1971.

Giamatti, A. B. Spenser: from magic to miracle. In Four essays on romance, ed H. Baker, Cambridge Mass 1971.

Hankins, J. E. Source and meaning in Spenser's allegory: a study of the Faerie Queene. Oxford 1971.

Hill, I. T. Britomart and 'Be bold, be not too bold'. ELH 38 1971.

Hollander, J. Spenser and the mingled measure. Eng Literary Renaissance 1 1971.

Kirkpatrick, R. Appearances of the Red Cross Knight in the Faerie Queene II. Jnl Warburg & Courtauld Inst 34 1971.

MacDonald, K. I. Allegorical landscape in the Faerie Queene I-III. Durham Univ Jnl 63 1971.

Miller, L. H., jr. The ironic mode in the Faerie Queene I & II. Papers on Lang & Lit (Illinois) 7 1971.

Oakeshott, W. Carew Ralegh's copy of Spenser. Library 5th ser 26 1971.

Snare, G. Spenser's fourth grace. Jnl Warburg & Courtauld Inst 34 1971.

Wells, W. (ed). Spenser allusions in the 16th and 17th centuries: part I, 1580-1625. Chapel Hill 1971.

Cain, T. H. Spenser and the Renaissance Orpheus. UTQ 41 1972.

Cheney, D. Spenser's Hermaphrodite and the 1590 Faerie Queene. PMLA 87 1972.

Hamilton, A. C. (ed). Essential articles on Spenser. Hamden Conn 1972.

Thompson, C. A. Spenser's 'Many faire pourtraicts, and many a faire feate'. Stud in Eng Lit 1500-1900 12 1972. On III i, xi.

Tonkin, H. Spenser's courteous pastoral: the Faerie Queene VI. Oxford 1972.

Wilson, R. R. The deformation of narrative time in the Faerie Queene. UTQ 41 1972.

Kennedy, J. M. and J. A. Reither (ed). A theatre for Spenserians. Toronto 1973.

The Minor Poems and Prose

Greg, W. W. In his Pastoral poetry and pastoral drama, 1906.

Higginson, J. J. Spenser's Shepherd's calender in relation to contemporary affairs. New York 1912.

Stein, H. Studies in Spenser's Complaints. New York 1934.

Parmenter, M. Spenser's Twelve aeglogues proportionable to the twelve monethes. ELH 3 1936.

Hard, F. E.K.'s reference to painting: some 17th-century adaptations. ELH 7 1940.

Hulbert, V. B. Diggon Davie. JEGP 41 1942. See P. E. McLane 46 1947.

Starnes, D. T. E.K.'s classical allusions reconsidered. SP 39 1942.

— Spenser and E.K. SP 41 1944. Replies by R. W. Mitchner 42 1945 and R. Jenkins 45 1948.

Bennett, J. W. St Bridget, Queen Elizabeth and Amadis of Gaul. ELH 10 1943. On Shepheardes calender, July.

Friedland, L. S. Spenser's 'Wrenock'. Shakespeare Assoc Bull 18 1943.

— A source of Spenser's The oak and the briar. PQ 33 1954. Suggests Gascoigne, The princely pleasure at Kenilworth Castle.

— The illustrations in the Theatre for worldlings. HLQ 19 1956.

Wrenn, C. L. On re-reading the Shepheardes calender. E & S 29 1943.

Jenkins, R. Who is E.K.? Shakespeare Assoc Bull 19-20 1944-5. Suggests Spenser.

Wells, W. 'To make a milde construction': the significance of the opening stanzas of Muiopotmos. SP 42 1945.

Austin, W. B. Spenser's sonnet to Harvey. MLN 62 1947.

Judson, A. C. Mother Hubberd's Ape. MLN 63 1948.

Mohl, R. Studies in Spenser, Milton and the theory of monarchy. New York 1949.

Bullitt, J. M. The use of rhyme link in the sonnets of Sidney, Drayton and Spenser. JEGP 49 1950.

Kliger, S. Spenser's Irish tract and tribal democracy. South Atlantic Quart 49 1950.

Mounts, C. E. The Ralegh-Essex rivalry and Mother Hubberds tale. MLN 65 1950.

— Colin Clout: priest of Cupid and Venus. High Point College Stud 3 1963.

— The evolution of Spenser's attitude toward Cupid and Venus. High Point College Stud 4 1964.

Spitzer, L. Spenser, Shepheardes Calender March 61-114, and the Variorum edition. SP 47 1950.

Norton, D. S. The tradition of prothalamia. In English studies in honor of James Southall Wilson, Charlottesville 1951.

Jenkins, R. Rosalind in Colin Clouts come home againe. MLN 67 1952.

Adams, M. Ronsard and Spenser: the commentary. Renaissance Papers 1954.

Bludau, D. Humanismus und Allegorie in Spensers Sonetten. Anglia 74 1956.

Carpenter, N. C. Spenser and Timotheus: a musical gloss on E.K.'s gloss. PMLA 71 1956. On October eclogue.

Hamilton, A. C. The argument of Spenser's Shepheardes calender. ELH 23 1956.

Lever, J. W. In his Elizabethan love sonnet, 1956. On Amoretti.

McNeir, W. F. Spenser's 'pleasing Alcon'. Etudes Anglaises 9 1956.

— An apology for Spenser's Amoretti. Die Neueren Sprachen 14 1965.

Stephenson, E. A. Some stylistic links between Spenser and E.K. Renaissance Papers 1956.

Durr, R. A. Spenser's calendar of Christian time. ELH 24 1957.

Enqvist, N. E. The seasons of the year: chapters on a motif from Beowulf to the Shepheardes calender. Helsinki 1957.

Greene, T. M. Spenser and the epithalamic convention. Comparative Lit 9 1957.

Stewart, J. T. Renaissance psychology and the ladder of love in Castiglione and Spenser. JEGP 56 1957. Influence on the Fowre hymnes.

Hyman, L. W. Structure and meaning in Spenser's Epithalamion. Tennessee Stud in Lit 3 1958.

Kostić, V. Spenser's Amoretti and Tasso's lyrical poetry. Renaissance & Modern Stud 3 1959.

Satterthwaite, A. W. A re-examination of Spenser's translations of the 'sonets' from A theatre for worldlings. PQ 38 1959.

Smith, J. N. Spenser's Prothalamion: a new genre. RES new ser 10 1959.

Allen, D. C. Image and meaning. Baltimore 1960, 1968 (rev). Includes essays on Shepheardes calender (March) and Muiopotmos.

Hieatt, A. K. Short time's endless monument: the symbolism of the numbers in Spenser's Epithalamion. New York 1960.

— The daughters of Horus: order in the stanzas of Epithalamion. Eng Inst Essays 1961.

Sasek, L. A. William Smith and the Shepheardes calender. PQ 39 1960.

Martz, L. L. The Amoretti: 'most goodly temperature'. Eng Inst Essays 1961.

McLane, P. E. Spenser's Shepheardes calender: a study in Elizabethan allegory. Notre Dame 1961.

— Spenser and the primitive church. Eng Lang Notes 1 1964.

Osgood, C. G. Epithalamion and Prothalamion: 'and theyr eccho ring'. MLN 76 1961.

Smith, H. The use of conventions in Spenser's minor poems. Eng Inst Essays 1961.

Stillinger, J. A note on the printing of E. K.'s glosses. SB 14 1961.

Thompson, J. In his Founding of English metre, New York 1961. On Shepheardes calender.

Wright, C. T. Anthony Mundy, 'Edward' Spenser and E.K. PMLA 76 1961.

Yuasa, N. A study of metaphor in Spenser's Amoretti. Stud in Eng Lit (Tokyo) 38 1961.

Heninger, S. K., jr. The implications of form for the Shepheardes calender. Stud in Renaissance 9 1962.

Staton, W. F., jr. Spenser's 'April' lay as a dramatic chorus. SP 59 1962.

Wine, M. L. Spenser's 'Sweete Themmes': of time and the river. Stud in Eng Lit 1500–1900 2 1962.

Woodward, D. H. Some themes in Spenser's Prothalamion. ELH 29 1962.

Clemen, W. Spenser's Epithalamion. Munich 1964. With text of poem.

Cummings, L. Spenser's Amoretti 8: new manuscript versions. Stud in Eng Lit 1500–1900 4 1964.

Howarth, H. Wyatt, Spenser and the canzone. Italica 41 1964.

Maclean, H. Fulke Greville and E.K. Eng Lang Notes 1 1964. Denies any connection.

Markland, M. F. A note on Spenser and the Scottish sonneteers. Stud in Scottish Lit 1 1964.

Moreau, J. Introduction à la lecture des hymnes de Spenser. Revue de Théologie et de Philosophie 97 1964.

Stevenson, W. H. The spaciousness of Spenser's Epithalamion. REL 5 1964.

Berger, H. Spenser's Prothalamion: an interpretation. EC 15 1965.

— Mode and diction in the Shepheardes calender. MP 67 1970.

Heyen, W. Narration in Spenser's Epithalamion. Ball State Univ Forum 6 1965.

Kellogg, R. Thought's astonishment and the dark conceits of Spenser's Amoretti. Renaissance Papers 1965.

Taylor, E. F. The Knight's tale: a new source for Spenser's Muiopotmos. Ibid.

Ahrends, G. Liebe, Schönheit und Tugend als Strukturelemente in Sidneys Astrophel and Stella und in Spensers Amoretti. Bonn 1966.

Berlin, N. Chaucer's Book of the Duchess and Spenser's Daphnaïda: a contrast. Studia Neophilologica 38 1966.

Hill, E. M. Flattery in Spenser's Fowre hymnes. West Virginia Univ Bull, Philological Papers 15 1966.

Neuse, R. The triumph over hasty accidents: a note on the symbolic mode of the Epithalamion. MLR 61 1966.

Wiersma, S. M. Spenser's statement of the Christian hope: a reading of the Prothalamion. Universitas (Wayne State Univ) 4 1966.

Ricks, D. M. Convention and structure in Spenser's Amoretti. Proc Utah Acad of Science, Arts & Letters 44 1967.

Welsford, E. Spenser's Fowre hymnes and Epithalamion: a study of Spenser's doctrine of love. New York 1967. With introd, text and notes.

Cain, T. H. The strategy of praise in Spenser's 'Aprill'. Stud in Eng Lit 1500–1900 8 1968.

Cirillo, A. R. Spenser's Epithalamion: the harmonious universe of love. Ibid.

Clemen, W. The uniqueness of Spenser's Epithalamion. In The poetic tradition: essays on Greek, Latin and English poetry, ed D. C. Allen and H. T. Rowell, Baltimore 1968.

Fujii, H. Spenser's Astrophel and Renaissance ways of idealization. Stud in Eng Lit (Tokyo) Eng no 1968.

Wickert, M. A. Structure and ceremony in Spenser's Epithalamion. ELH 35 1968.

Williams, F. B., jr. Spenser, Shakespeare and Zachary Jones. SQ 19 1968.

Cullen, P. Imitation and metamorphosis: the golden-age eclogue in Spenser, Milton and Marvell. PMLA 84 1969.

— Spenser, Marvell and Renaissance pastoral. Cambridge Mass 1970.

Hume, A. Spenser, Puritanism and the Maye eclogue. RES new ser 20 1969.

MacCaffrey, I. G. Allegory and pastoral in the Shepheardes calender. ELH 36 1969.

Meyer, S. An interpretation of Spenser's Colin Clout. Cork 1969.

Quitslund, J. A. Spenser's image of sapience. Stud in Renaissance 16 1969.

Røstvig, M.-S. The Shepheardes calender: a structural analysis. Renaissance & Modern Stud 13 1969.

Snare, G. The Muses on poetry: Spenser's Teares of the Muses. Tulane Stud in Eng 17 1969.

Bristol, M. D. Structural patterns in two Elizabethan pastorals. Stud in Eng Lit 1500–1900 10 1970. Shepheardes calender and Drayton's Shepheardes garland.

Court, F. E. The theme and structure of Spenser's Muiopotmos. Stud in Eng Lit 1500–1900 10 1970.

Dunlop, A. The unity of Spenser's Amoretti. In Silent poetry: essays in numerological analysis, ed A. D. S. Fowler 1970.

Johnson, W. C. Rhyme and repetition in Spenser's Amoretti. Xavier Univ Stud 9 1970.

—— Spenser's sonnet diction. Neuphilologische Mitteilungen 71 1970.

Anderson, J. H. 'Nat worthe a boterflye': Muiopotmos and the Nun's Priest's tale. Jnl Medieval & Renaissance Stud 1 1971.

Bondanella, P. E. and J. Conaway. Two kinds of Renaissance love: Spenser's Astrophel and Ronsard's Adonis. E Studies 52 1971.

Cummings, P. M. Spenser's Amoretti as an allegory of love. Texas Stud in Lang & Lit 12 1971.

Ingham, P. Spenser's use of dialect. Eng Lang Notes 8 1971.

O'Connell, M. Astrophel: Spenser's double elegy. Stud in Eng Lit 1500–1900 11 1971.

Rollinson, P. B. A generic view of Spenser's Four hymns. SP 68 1971.

A. C. H.

SIR PHILIP SIDNEY
1554–86

Bibliographies etc

Juel-Jensen, B. Some uncollected authors. Book Collector 11–12 1962–3. Early edns of Arcadia etc.

Tannenbaum, S. A. Sidney: a concise bibliography. New York 1941; G. R. Guffey, Supplement 1941–65, 1967.

Donow, H. S. A concordance to the sonnet sequences of Daniel, Drayton, Shakespeare, Sidney and Spenser. Carbondale 1969.

Godshalk, W. L. Recent studies in Sidney. Eng Literary Renaissance 2 1972.

For mss and early edns see Poems, *ed Ringler, 1962 below.*

Collections

The Countesse of Pembrokes Arcadia: the third time published with new additions. 1598 (with Certaine sonets, Defence of poesie, Astrophel and Stella, Her most excellent Majestie [or Lady of May]), Edinburgh 1599, London 1605, 1613 (as 4th edn, with A dialogue betweene two shepherds), Dublin 1621 (with suppl by Sir W. A[lexander]—*see* Mitchell 1969 below; reissued London 1622, 1623), London 1627 (with Sixth booke by R. B[ellings] dated 1628, separately ptd Dublin 1624), reissued as 7th edn London 1629, 1633, 1638 (with 2nd suppl by Ja. Johnstoun), 1655 (with portrait, life, spurious Remedie for love), 1662 (11th edn), 1674 (as 13th edn), 3 vols 1724–5 (as Works, 14th edn, [ed J. Henley], with new life), Dublin 1739.

Englands Helicon. 1600, 1614. 14 poems.

Bibliographical miscellanies. [Ed P. Bliss], Oxford 1813. 5 poems from Bodley ms Rawlinson poetry 85.

Miscellaneous works. Ed W. Gray, Oxford 1829, Boston 1860, London 1893, New York 1966. Life, Defence of poesy, Astrophel and Stella, Miscellaneous poems (including Certain sonnets), Lady of May, Valour anatomized [by Donne], Letter to Queen, Defence of Leicester, 20 letters.

Complete poems. Ed A. B. Grosart 2 vols 1873, 3 vols 1877.

Astrophel and Stella und Defense of poesie. Ed E. Flügel, Halle 1889.

Defence of poesie; Letter to Queen; Defence of Leicester. Ed G. E. Woodberry, Boston 1908.

Complete works. Ed A. Feuillerat 4 vols Cambridge 1912–26; vol 1 rptd 1922; 4 vols (vol 2 without poems) 1962 etc. Vol 1 Arcadia 1590; vol 2 last pt of Arcadia 1593, other Arcadia poems, Astrophel and Stella 1591, Certaine sonets, Dialogue betweene two shepherds, Two pastorals, Lady of May, attributed poems; vol 3 Defence of poesie, Irish affairs, Letter to Queen, Defence of Leicester, Correspondence (114 letters), Psalms (1–43), Trewnesse of Christian religion (chs 1–6), Valour anatomized (by Donne), Will; vol 4 Old Arcadia (from Folger Clifford ms).

Poems. Ed W. A. Ringler jr, Oxford 1962. Critical text, commentary, bibliography of textual sources.

Five courtier poets of the English Renaissance. Ed R. M. Bender, New York 1967. Certain sonnets, Astrophel, Psalms 1–43, 13 other poems.

Selected prose and poetry. Ed R. Kimbrough, New York 1969. Defence, Astrophel, 1580 letter to Robert, selections from Old and New Arcadia, 26 poems.

Selected poetry and prose. Ed D. Kalstone, New York 1970. Lady of May, Astrophel, Apology, selected poems.

§ 1

Goldwel, H. A briefe declaration of the shews in Whitson weeke last. 1581; rptd R. Holinshed, Chronicles, 1587; ed J. Nichols, Progresses of Queen Elizabeth vol 2, 1788, 1823. Contains 2 poems probably by Sidney; *see* Fogel 1960 below.

A woorke concerning the trewnesse of the Christian religion by Philip of Mornay Lord of Plessie Marlie, begunne to be translated by Sir P. Sidney and finished by A. Golding. 1587, 1592, 1604, 1617, 1646. Probably entirely the work of Golding; *see* Tenison, vol 7 under 1933, and Ringler, SP 1950 below.

The Countesse of Pembrokes Arcadia. 1590 (3 bks, New Arcadia); ed H. O. Sommer 1891 (facs with bibliographical introd, rptd C. Dennis, Kent Ohio 1970); ed A. Feuillerat, Cambridge 1912 (with variants from 1593–1674 edns). The Arcadia augmented and ended 1593 (5 bks, last 3 from ms of Old Arcadia); ed A. Feuillerat 1922 (last 3 bks, with variants from 1598–1674 edns); 13 edns 1598–1739; The famous history of heroick acts: an abstract of Pembroke's Arcadia, ed J.N. 1701; Moderniz'd by Mrs [D.] Stanley 1725 (in 4 bks); ed H. Friswell 1867 (abbreviated from 1655), 1893; ed E. A. Baker 1907 (modernized from 1739 with Alexander's suppl and Bellings' 6th bk), 1921; The original version now for the first time printed, ed A. Feuillerat, Cambridge 1926 (from Folger Clifford ms of Old Arcadia); Selections, ed R. Syfret 1966; Old Arcadia, ed J. Robertson, Oxford 1973 (critical text with commentary).

Tr French: ms fragment by J. L. de Tourval c. 1607–10 (in A. W. Osborn, Sidney en France, 1932); J. Baudouin, 3 pts Paris 1624–5, *see* H. W. Lawton, Revue de Littérature Comparée 6 1926; G. Chappelain, 3 pts Paris 1625. Tr German: V. Theocritus, Frankfurt 1630 (for 1629, from French); gebessert von M.O[pitz] 1638 (with 6th bk), 2 vols Leyden 1642, Frankfurt 1643, Leyden 1646, Amsterdam 1659 (for 1658), *see* A. Wurmb, Die deutsche Uebersetzung von Sidneys Arcadia, Hanover 1911. Tr Dutch: Felix van Sambix de Jonghe, Delft 1639, 1641, Amsterdam 1659. Tr Italian: L. Alessandri, Venice 1659.

Syr P. S. his Astrophel and Stella; sundry other rare sonnets [by Daniel, Campion, Greville and anon]. 1591 (Newman; corrupt text); ed E. Flügel 1889; A. Feuillerat 1922 (with variants from Newman's 2nd quarto, BM ms additional 15,232, Arcadia 1598–1674), Menston 1970 (facs); [1597–1600] (Lownes; omits Newman's dedication and Nashe's preface); Sir P.S. his Astrophel and Stella, 1591 (Newman; partly corrected through sonnet 95, without prose preliminaries and Other sonnets). In Arcadia 1598 (from an authoritative ms);

12 edns 1599–1739; ed E. Arber, An English garner vol 1, 1877, rptd S. Lee, Elizabethan sonnets vol 1, 1904; ed A. W. Pollard 1888; ed M. Wilson 1931; ed M. Poirier, Paris [1957] (with French trn); ed K. Hart 1959; ed V. Gentili, Bari 1965 (with elaborate notes in Italian); ed M. Putzel, New York 1967.
Tr French: C. M. Garnier, Paris 1943 (without songs); M. Poirier, above.

The defence of poesie. 1595 (Ponsonby); rptd in 13 edns of Arcadia 1598–1739; Glasgow 1752; [ed J. Warton] 1787 (with Jonson's Discoveries); ed A. Feuillerat 1923 (with variants from Olney, De L'Isle and Dudley ms, 1598–1674 Arcadia); 1928 (facs); Menston 1968 (facs); An apologie for poetrie, 1595 (Olney); ed E. Arber 1868; ed G. Gregory Smith, Elizabethan critical essays vol 1, Oxford 1904 (with valuable notes). Mss: Viscount De L'Isle and Dudley 1226; Norwich Public Lib, ptd M. R. Mahl, Northridge Cal 1969; substantive quotations in W. Temple's ms Analysis. More than 10 19th-century and 20 20th-century edns, many often rptd, of which the most useful are: ed A. S. Cook, Boston 1890; ed E. S. Shuckburgh, Cambridge 1891; ed G. Shepherd 1965 (with elaborate notes); ed J. A. Van Dorsten, Oxford 1966 (modernized critical text without apparatus).
Tr Spanish: J. de Bustamente?, Bibliotéca Nacional Madrid ms 3908 (early 17th century), see K. Newels, Anglia 72 1954; ed D. O. Chambers, [no place] 1968. Tr Dutch: T. Rodenburgh, Eglentiers poetens borst-weringh, Amsterdam 1619 (selections), see W. Zuidema, Tijdschrift voor Nederlandsche taal-en Letterkunde 22 1903; J. de Haes, Rotterdam 1712, 1720, Delft 1724, see J. F. Vanderheyden, Verslagen en mededelingen van de koninklijke vlaamse academie voor taal- en letterkunde 1964; A. Verwey, Amsterdam 1891. Tr Polish: J. Swierzowicz, Lwow 1912. Tr Italian: S. Policardi, Padua 1947; E. Buonpane, Florence 1954. Tr French: M. Lebel, Quebec 1965.

Certaine sonets. In 13 edns of Arcadia 1598–1739; Cleveland 1890, Boston 1904, London 1906 (with Defence of poesie), 1909 (with Defence of poesie).

[The lady of May]. In 13 edns of Arcadia 1598–1739; rptd J. Nichols, Progresses of Queen Elizabeth vol 1, 1788, 1823; ed E. W. Parks and R. C. Beatty, The English drama, New York 1935. Arthur A. Houghton jr (Helmingham Hall) ms, ed R. Kimbrough and P. Murphy, Renaissance Drama new ser 1 1968.

Defence of the Earl of Leicester. Pierpont Morgan Lib ms MA 1475 (holograph), ptd A. Collins, Letters and memorials of state vol 1, 1746.

Psalms (1–43 by Sidney, rest by the Countess of Pembroke). For 14 mss see Poems, ed Ringler, 1962, and Huntington Lib ms Ellesmere 11,636 (see Seronsy 1966 below); Sotheby & Co 24 Nov 1969, lot 135. The Psalmes of David, [ed S. W. Singer] 1823; J. Ruskin, Rock honey-comb, 1877 (selections with comment); ed J. C. A. Rathmell, Garden City NY 1963. See col 1906, below.

Letters from and to Sidney

Holinshed, R. Chronicles. 1587. Last letter, to Wier p. 1555 (Feuillerat no 114).
A very godly letter by Sir H. Sidney unto P. Sidney [c. 1566]. Ed W. Gruffith 1591; partly rptd Oxford 1929.
Profitable instructions. 1633. To R. Sidney [c. Feb 1579] (no 38).
H. Langueti epistolae ad P. Sydnaeum. Frankfurt 1633 (see John 1949 below), Leyden 1646; ed D. Dalrymple (Lord Hailes), Edinburgh 1776. 96 letters to Sidney.
Cabala. 1663. To the Queen, p. 201.
Collins, A. Letters and memorials of state. 1746. 10 letters.
Gray, W. Miscellaneous works of Sidney. Oxford 1829. 16 new letters.
Pears, S. A. The correspondence of Sidney and Languet. 1845; rptd W. A. Bradley, Boston 1912. 17 Latin and 3 English by Sidney, selections from Languet, with trns.

Feuillerat, A. Works of Sidney vols 3–4. Cambridge 1923–6. 115 letters.
Sotheby & Co 26 June 1967. Lot 741 (65 letters from foreign correspondents, now in Marie-Louise and J. M. Osborn Collection, Yale Univ Lib), Lot 742 (11 from R. Dorset, now in Christ Church Oxford). See J. M. Osborn, TLS 30 April 1970.
Levy, C. S. A supplementary inventory of Sidney's correspondence. MP 67 1969. Lists 10 new by Sidney, 73 to him (not including Languet and 76 in Sotheby sale).
See Bühler 1936, McMahon 1947, Bond 1954 and 1955, Levy 1966, Buxton and Osborn 1972, below.

Dedications to Sidney

F. B. Williams jr, Index of dedications, Oxford 1962, lists 30 to Sidney in English books ptd 1578–1605; to these add Novum testamentum graece, ed H. Stephanus, Paris 1576; P. Rami commentariorum de religione christiana libra IV, ed T. Banosius, Frankfurt 1577; L. Danaeus, Geographiae poeticae, Geneva 1580; A. Fraunce, Victoria [c. 1580–3], Viscount De L'Isle and Dudley ms (ed G. C. Moore Smith, Louvain 1906, Bang); Herodiani historiae libri VIII, ed H. Stephanus, Paris 1581; A. Fraunce, A comparison of Ramus his logike with that of Aristotle [c. 1581–3], BM ms additional 34,361; A. Fraunce, De usu dialectices [c. 1581–3], Bodley ms Rawlinson D 345; N. Monardes, Simplicium medicamentorum historiae liber tertius, tr C. Clusius, Antwerp 1582; Sir H. Finch, Nomotechnia: or the common law of England, [c. 1582], Bodley ms Rawlinson C 43; W. Temple, Analysis tractationis de poesi, [c. 1584], De L'Isle and Dudley ms 1095; J. Dousa the elder, Odarum britannicarum liber I, Leyden 1586; J. Lipsius, De recta pronuntiatione latinae linguae dialogus, Antwerp 1586.

§2

For more complete lists see bibliographies of Tannenbaum and Guffey, above.

Sidney, Sir P. [Autobiography as Philisides in 4th eclogues of Old Arcadia, written c. 1580].
Temple, W. Analysis tractationis de poesi, c. 1584. De L'Isle and Dudley ms 1095. See J. P. Thorne, A Ramistical commentary on Sidney's Apologie, MP 54 1957.
[Gifford, G.] The manner of Sidneyes death (c. 1586). BM ms Cotton Vitellius C.xvii, extracts in Zouch 1808; B. Juel-Jensen ms, ptd Oxford 1959, see A. B. Grosart, Works of Greville vol 4, 1870 p. vii; J. Robertson 1964 below.
Eickius, A. Elogium Roberti Comitis Leycestrii cum elogio P. Sidnei. Utrecht 1586.
D[ay], A. Upon the life and death of Sidney. [1586?].
Molineux, E. In Holinshed's Chronicles, 1587, p. 1554–5.
Churchyard, T. The epitaph of Sidney. [1587]; rptd S. Butler, Sidneiana, 1837.
Academiae cantabrigiensis lachrymae. Ed A. Neville 1587.
Philip, J. The life and death of Sidney. 1587; rptd S. Butler, Sidneiana, 1837.
Whetstone, G. Sidney. [1587]; rptd A. Boswell, Frondes caducae, 1816.
Peplus. Ed J. Lloyd, Oxford 1587.
Exequiae. Ed W. Gager, Oxford 1587.
Epitaphia in mortem Sidneii. Ed G. Benedictus, Leyden 1587.
Lant, T. Sequitur celebritas et pompa funeris. 1588. 30 engravings of funeral.
Fraunce, A. The Arcadian rhetorike: made plaine by examples out of Homer, Virgil, Sydnei, Tasso, Salust, Boscan and Garcilasso. [1588]; ed E. Seaton, Oxford 1950 (Luttrell Soc).
Moffet, T. Nobilis [1589]; Lessus lugubris 1593. Ms ed and tr V. B. Heltzel and H. H. Hudson, San Marino 1940.

Breton, N. Amoris lachrimae. In Brittons bowre of delights, 1591; ed H. E. Rollins, Cambridge Mass 1933.

Stow, J. In his Annales of England, 1592. On Netherlands campaign.

Spenser, E. Colin Clouts come home again; Astrophel: a pastorall elegie upon the death of Sidney (with other elegies by L. B[ryskett, M. Roydon, Sir W. Ralegh] and anon [last 3 rptd from Phoenix nest 1593]). 1595.

Meres, F. In his Palladis tamia, 1598; ed D. C. Allen, Urbana 1933.

Hoskyns, J. Directions for speech and style exemplified out of Arcadia [written 1599]; ed H. H. Hudson, Princeton 1935 (from ms).

Baudius, D. Poematum nova editio. Leyden 1607. On meeting with Sidney in 1585.

Holland, H. In his Heroologia anglica, [Arnheim 1620]. Portrait and biography.

Naunton, Sir R. In his Fragmenta regalia, 1641; ed E. Arber 1870.

Greville, F. The life of Sidney. 1652; ed N. Smith, Oxford 1907. Written 1610–12.

Aubrey, J. In his Lives, 1813. Written c. 1687.

Winstanley, W. In his Lives of the most famous English poets, 1687.

Wood, A. In his Athenae oxonienses vol 1, 1691; with addns by P. Bliss 1813.

Cooper, E. In his Muses library, 1737.

Collins, A. In his Letters and memorials of state vol 1, 1746.

Lennox, C. In her Shakespear illustrated vol 2, 1754. Arcadia as source of Lear.

Walpole, H. In his Catalogue of the royal and noble authors of England vol 1, 1758. Comment on Sidney in account of Greville.

Zouch, T. Memoirs of the life and writings of Sidney. York 1808, 1809.

Cotton, H. Christian Remembrancer June 1821. On Psalms.

Lamb, C. Defence of Sidney's sonnets. London Mag Sept 1823; rptd in his Last essays of Elia, 1833.

Butler, S. Sidneiana. 1837 (Roxburghe Club). Biographical documents.

Peltz, G. F. Memorials of Sidney. Archaeologia 28 1840.

Holland, J. In his Psalmists of Britain vol 1, 1843.

Craik, G. L. In his Romance of the peerage vol 1, 1848.

Collier, J. P. Sidney and his works. GM April 1850.

D[avis], S. M. The life and times of Sidney. Boston 1859, New York 1875.

Bourne, H. R. Fox. A memoir of Sidney. 1862. Inferior popular revision as Sidney: type of English chivalry, 1891.

Macdonald, G. In his England's antiphon, Philadelphia 1868. On Psalms.

Koeppel, E. Studien zur Geschichte des englischen Petrarchismus. Romanische Forschungen 5 1890.

Scott, F. N. Boccaccio's De genealogia deorum and Sidney's Apologie. MLN 6 1891.

Plomer, H. R. The Edinburgh edition of Sidney's Arcadia. Library 2nd ser 1 1900.

Greg, W. W. In his Pastoral poetry and pastoral drama, 1906.

Dobell, B. New light on Sidney's Arcadia. Quart Rev 211 1909. On discovery of Old Arcadia mss.

Baskervill, C. R. Sidney's Arcadia and the Tryall of Chevalry. MP 10 1912.

Wolff, S. L. In his Greek romances in Elizabethan fiction, New York 1912.

Greenlaw, E. Sidney's Arcadia as an example of Elizabethan allegory. In G. L. Kittredge anniversary papers, Boston 1913.

— The captivity episode in Sidney's Arcadia. In J. M. Manly anniversary studies, Chicago 1923.

Wallace, M. W. The life of Sidney. Cambridge 1915. The standard biography.

Brie, F. Sidneys Arcadia. Strasbourg 1918. On classical sources; in German.

Behler, M. Die Beziehungen zwischen Sidney und Spenser. Archiv 146 1923.

Whitney, L. Concerning nature in Arcadia. SP 24 1927.

Scott, J. G. In her Les sonnets élisabéthains, Paris 1929. Ch 2.

Zandvoort, R. W. Sidney's Arcadia: a comparison between the two versions. Amsterdam 1929.

Empson, W. In his Seven types of ambiguity, 1930. On Old Arcadia no 71.

Briggs, W. D. Political ideas in Sidney's Arcadia. SP 28–9 1931–2.

Wilson, M. Sidney. 1931.

Osborn, A. W. Sidney en France. Paris 1932.

Tenison, E. M. In her Elizabethan England vols 1–9, Leamington Spa 1933–50.

Zeeveld, W. G. The uprising of the commons in Sidney's Arcadia. MLN 48 1933.

Goldman, M. S. Sidney and the Arcadia. Urbana 1934. Chivalric background.

— Sidney and Harington as opponents of superstition. JEGP 54 1955.

Hanford, J. H. and S. R. Watson. Personal allegory in the Arcadia. MP 30 1934.

Syford, C. The direct source of the Pamela-Cecropia episodes. PMLA 49 1934.

Willcock, G. D. Passing pitefull hexameters. MLR 29 1934.

Yates, F. A. In her John Florio, 1934. On quarrel with Sanford.

— The emblematic conceit in Bruno's De gli eroici furori and the Elizabethan sonnet sequences. Jnl Warburg & Courtauld Inst 6 1943.

— The romance of the accession day tilts. Jnl Warburg & Courtauld Inst 20 1957.

Banks, T. H. Astrophel and Stella reconsidered. PMLA 50 1935.

Hudson, H. H. Penelope Devereux as Sidney's Stella. Huntington Lib Bull no 7 1935.

— An Oxford epigram book. HLQ 2 1939. On Greville's editorship of 1590 Arcadia.

Hughey, R. The Harington ms and related documents. Library 4th ser 15 1935.

— (ed). The Arundel Harington ms. 2 vols Columbus 1960.

Myrick, K. O. Sidney as a literary craftsman. Cambridge Mass 1935, Lincoln Nebraska 1965 (with rev bibliography by W. L. Godshalk).

Sargent, R. M. In his Life and lyrics of Sir Edward Dyer, Oxford 1935.

Bühler, C. F. On the date of the letter by Sidney to C. Plantin. RES 12 1936.

Riese, T. In his Die englische Psalmdichtung im sechzehnten Jahrhundert, Münster 1937.

Baughan, D. E. Sidney and the matchmakers. MLR 33 1938.

— Sidney's Defence of Leicester and the Revised Arcadia. JEGP 51 1952.

John, L. C. In her Elizabethan sonnet sequences, New York 1938.

— The first edition of the letters of Languet. JEGP 48 1949.

— Sir Stephen Le Sieur and Sidney. MLQ 17 1956.

Koszul, A. Les Sidney à Strasbourg. Bulletin de la Faculté des Lettres de Strasbourg 16 1938.

Wagner, B. M. New poems by Sidney. PMLA 53 1938.

Watson, S. R. Sidney at Bartholomew Fair. PMLA 53 1938.

McPeek, J. A. S. In his Catullus in Britain, Cambridge Mass 1939.

Pratt, W. S. In his Music of the French Psalter of 1572, New York 1939.

Siebeck, B. Das Bild Sidneys. Weimar 1939. On reputation.

Samuel, I. The influence of Plato on Sidney's Defense. MLQ 1 1940.

Craigie, J. Sidney's King James of Scotland. TLS 20 Dec 1941. On date of Defence.

Rubel, V. L. In her Poetic diction in the English Renaissance, New York 1942.

Wiles, A. G. D. Parallel analyses of the two versions of Sidney's Arcadia. SP 39 1942.

—— Sir William Alexander's continuation of Sidney's Arcadia. Stud in Scottish Lit 3 1966.

Bond, W. H. The epitaph of Sidney. MLN 58 1943.

—— Two ghosts: Herbert's Baripenthes and the Vaughan-Holland portrait of Sidney. Library 4th ser 24 1944.

—— Casting off copy by Elizabethan printers. PBSA 42 1948.

—— A letter from Sidney to C. Plantin. Harvard Lib Bull 8 1954.

—— A letter of Languet about Sidney. Harvard Lib Bull 9 1955.

Pellegrini, A. M. Bruno, Sidney and Spenser. SP 40 1943.

Campbell, L. B. Sidney as the learned soldier. HLQ 7 1944.

—— In her Divine poetry and drama in 16th-century England, Cambridge 1959.

Dowlin, C. M. Sidney and other men's thought. RES 20 1944.

Spencer, T. The poetry of Sidney. ELH 12 1945; rptd in his Selected essays, New Brunswick NJ 1966.

Smith, H. English metrical psalms in the 16th century. HLQ 9 1946.

—— In his Elizabethan poetry, Cambridge Mass 1952.

Townsend, F. L. Sidney and Ariosto. PMLA 61 1946.

McMahon, A. P. Sidney's letter to the Camerarii. PMLA 62 1947.

Rowe, K. T. Romantic love and parental authority in Sidney's Arcadia. Ann Arbor 1947.

Thaler, A. Shakespeare and Sidney: the influence of the Defense. Cambridge Mass 1947.

Tuve, R. In her Elizabethan and metaphysical imagery, Chicago 1947.

Duhamel, P. A. Sidney's Arcadia and Elizabethan rhetoric. SP 45 1948.

Phillips, J. E. Buchanan and the Sidney circle. HLQ 12 1948.

—— Daniel Rogers. In Neo-Latin poetry of the 16th and 17th centuries, Los Angeles 1965 (Clark Lib).

Poirier, M. Sidney: le chevalier poète élizabéthain. Lille 1948.

—— Quelques sources des poèmes de Sidney. Etudes Anglaises 11 1958.

Eagle, R. L. The Arcadia 1593 title-page border. Library 5th ser 4 1949.

Hendrickson, G. L. Elizabethan quantitative hexameters. PQ 28 1949.

Ribner, I. Machiavelli and Sidney's Discourse to the Queen. Italica 26 1949.

—— Machiavelli and Sidney: the Arcadia of 1590. SP 47 1950.

—— Sidney's Arcadia and the structure of King Lear. Studia Neophilologica 24 1952.

—— Sidney on civil insurrection. JHI 13 1952.

Muir, K. and J. F. Danby. Arcadia and King Lear. N & Q 4 Feb 1950.

Muir, K. Astrophel and Stella 31. N & Q Feb 1960.

—— Sidney. 1960 (Br Council pamphlet).

Ringler, W. A., jr. Master Drant's rules. PQ 29 1950.

—— Poems attributed to Sidney. SP 47 1950.

Danby, J. F. In his Poets on fortune's hill, 1952.

Hughes, M. Y. New evidence on the charge that Milton forged the Pamela prayer in Eikon basilike. RES new ser 3 1952.

Lyles, A. M. A note on Sidney's use of Chaucer. N & Q March 1953.

Buxton, J. Sidney and the English Renaissance. 1954, 1964.

—— On the date of Lownes' Astrophel and Stella. Bodleian Lib Rev 6 1960.

—— In his Elizabethan taste, 1963.

—— and B. Juel-Jensen. Sidney's first passport rediscovered. Library 5th ser 25 1970.

Buxton, J. An unpublished letter. TLS 24–31 March, 14 April 1972. See R. L. Davids 7–28 April 1972.

—— Sidney and Theophrastus. Eng Literary Renaissance 2 1972.

Ewing, S. B. A new manuscript of Greville's Life of Sidney. MLR 49 1954. In Shrewsbury Public Library; another is owned by B. Juel-Jensen.

Murphy, K. M. The 109th and 110th sonnets of Astrophel and Stella. PQ 34 1955.

Walker, D. P. A background to Pamela's refutation of Cecropia. Bibliothèque d'Humanisme et Renaissance 17 1955.

Anderson, D. M. The Dido incident in Sidney's Arcadia. N & Q Oct 1956.

—— The trial of the princes in the Arcadia. RES new ser 8 1957.

Hamilton, A. C. Sidney and Agrippa. RES new ser 7 1956.

—— Sidney's idea of the right poet. Comparative Lit 9 1957.

—— The modern study of Renaissance English literature. MLQ 25 1965.

—— Et in Arcadia ego. MLQ 27 1966.

—— Sidney's Astrophel and Stella as a sonnet sequence. ELH 36 1969.

—— Sidney's Arcadia as prose fiction: its relation to its sources. Eng Literary Renaissance 2 1972.

Lever, J. W. In his Elizabethan love sonnet, 1956.

Coulman, D. Spotted to be known. Jnl Warburg & Courtauld Inst 20 1957.

Williams, G. W. The printer of the first folio of Sidney's Arcadia. Library 5th ser 12 1957.

Biagi, A. L'areopago e la Difesa della poesia. Naples 1958.

Bryant, D. C. A peece of a logician. In his Rhetorical idiom, Ithaca 1958.

Judson, A. C. Sidney's appearance: a study in Elizabethan portraiture. Bloomington 1958.

Young, R. B. English Petrarke: a study of Sidney's Astrophel and Stella. New Haven 1958.

Dent, R. W. In his John Webster's borrowing, Berkeley 1960.

Ferguson, A. B. In his Indian summer of English chivalry, Durham NC 1960.

Fogel, E. G. A possible addition to the Sidney canon. MLN 75 1960.

—— The mythical sorrows of Astrophel. In Studies in honour of M. Schlauch, Warsaw 1966.

Gohn, E. S. Primitivistic motifs in Sidney's Arcadia. Papers of Michigan Acad 45 1960.

Robertson, J. Sidney and his poetry. In Elizabethan poetry, ed J. R. Brown and B. Harris 1960.

—— Sidney and Lady Rich. RES new ser 15 1964.

—— Sidney and Bandello. Library 5th ser 21 1966.

—— Macbeth on sleep and Sidney's Astrophil and Stella 39. N & Q April 1967.

Süllinger, J. The biographical problem of Astrophel and Stella. JEGP 59 1960.

Williamson, G. The convention of the extasie. In his Seventeenth-century contexts, 1960. On Astrophil song 8.

Alonso, D. Poesia correlativa inglesa. Filologia Moderna 1 1961.

Montgomery, R. L., jr. Symmetry and sense: the poetry of Sidney. Austin 1961.

Thompson, J. In his Founding of English meter, 1961.

Van Dorsten, J. A. Poets, patrons and professors: Sidney, D. Rogers and the Leiden humanists. Oxford 1962.

—— Gruterus and Sidney's Arcadia. RES new ser 16 1965.

—— Sidney and Languet. HLQ 29 1966.

—— The arts of memory and poetry. E Studies 48 1967.

Hallam, G. W. Sidney's supposed Ramism. Renaissance Papers 1963.

Schlauch, M. In her Antecedents of the English novel, Oxford 1963.

Howe, A. R. Astrophel and Stella: why and how. SP 61 1964.

Levy, F. J. Sidney and the idea of history. Bibliothèque d'Humanisme et Renaissance 26 1964.

— Sidney reconsidered. Eng Literary Renaissance 2 1972.

Challis, L. The use of oratory in Sidney's Arcadia. SP 62 1965.

Crompton, N. J. R. Sidney and symbolic heraldry. Coat of Arms 8 1965.

Davis, W. R. and R. A. Lanham. Sidney's Arcadia. New Haven 1965. Monographs by Davis on the New and by Lanham on the Old Arcadia.

Davis, W. R. In his Idea and act in Elizabethan fiction, Princeton 1969.

Doughtie, E. Sidney, Tessier, Batchelar and A musicall banquet. Renaissance News 18 1965.

Kalstone, D. Sidney's poetry: contexts and interpretations. Cambridge Mass 1965.

Orgel, S. In his Jonsonian masque, Cambridge Mass 1965.

Ahrends, G. Liebe, Schönheit und Tugend als Strukturelemente in Sidneys Astrophel and Stella. Bonn 1966.

Duncan-Jones, K. Sidney's Urania. RES new ser 17 1966.

— Nashe and Sidney: the tournament in the Unfortunate traveller. MLR 63 1968.

— A note on Irish poets and the Sidneys. E Studies 49 1968.

Elton, W. R. In his King Lear and the gods, San Marino 1966.

Jakobson, R. The grammatical texture of a sonnet from Sidney's Arcadia. In Studies in honour of M. Schlauch, Warsaw 1966. On Old Arcadia 20.

Levy, C. S. An unpublished letter of Sidney. N & Q July 1966.

Marenco, F. Sidney e l'Arcadia nella critica letteraria. Filologia e Letteratura 12 1966.

— Per una nuova interpretazione dell' Arcadia. Eng Miscellany (Rome) 17 1966.

— Arcadia puritana: l'use della tradizione. Bari 1966.

— Astrophil and Stella. Filologia e Letteratura 13 1967.

— Sidney studi 1965-6. Ibid.

— Double plot in Sidney's Old Arcadia. MLR 64 1969.

Rees, J. Greville and the revision of Arcadia. RES new ser 17 1966.

— Greville's epitaph on Sidney. RES new ser 19 1968.

Roberts, M. Sidney and the neo-classical tradition. EC 16 1966.

Rota, F. L'Arcadia di Sidney e il teatro. Bari 1966.

Seronsy, C. C. Another Huntington ms of the Sidney Psalms. HLQ 29 1966.

Stanford, A. Anne Bradstreet's portrait of Sidney. Early Amer Lit Newsletter 1 1966.

Blackburn, T. H. E. Bolton's Cabanet royal: a reply to Sidney's Apology. Stud in Renaissance 14 1967.

Delasanta, R. The epic voice: Arcadia. Hague 1967.

Dempsey, P. K. Sidney's And have I heard her say. Explicator 25 1967.

Dipple, E. The fore conceit of Sidney's eclogues. In Literary monographs, ed E. Rothstein and T. K. Dunseath, Madison 1967.

— Harmony and pastoral in the Old Arcadia. ELH 35 1968.

— Unjust justice in the Old Arcadia. Stud in Eng Lit 1500–1900 10 1970.

— Metamorphosis in Sidney's Arcadias. PQ 50 1971.

— The captivity episode in the New Arcadia. JEGP 70 1971.

Endicott, A. Pip, Philip and Astrophel: Dickens's debt to Sidney? Dickensian 63 1967.

Fraser, R. A. Sidney the humanist. South Atlantic Quart 66 1967.

Gottfried, R. Autobiography and art. In Selected papers from the English Institute, ed P. Damon, New York 1967.

Hogan, P. G., jr. Sidney and Titian. South Central Bull 27 1967.

— Sidney Spenser: a courtesy-friendship formulation. Forum 9 1971.

Juel-Jensen, B. Sidney's Arcadia 1638: an unrecorded issue. Library 5th ser 22 1967.

— Sidney's Arcadia London 1599 a ghost. Book Collector 16 1967.

— The Tixall ms of Sidney's paraphrase of the Psalms. Book Collector 18 1969.

Lindheim, N. R. Sidney's Arcadia book II: retrospective narrative. SP 64 1967.

— Vision, revision and the 1593 text of the Arcadia. Eng Literary Renaissance 2 1972.

Mahl, M. R. A treatise of horsman shipp. TLS 21 Dec 1967. On discovery of Norwich ms of Defence.

Ogden, J. Hazlitt, Lamb and Astrophel and Stella. Trivium 2 1967.

Pontedera, C. Poetica e poesia nell'Apology for poetry. Annali di Ca' Foscari (Venice) 6 1967.

Rudenstine, N. L. Sidney's poetic development. Cambridge Mass 1967.

Ryken, L. Sidney's Leave me O love. Explicator 26 1967.

Andrews M. C. The sources of Andromana. RES new ser 19 1968.

Beaty, F. L. Lodge's Forbonius and Prisceria and Sidney's Arcadia. E Studies 49 1968.

Cohen, E. I. The Old Arcadia: a treatise in moderation. Revue Belge 46 1968.

Cooper, S. M. The sonnets of Astrophel and Stella: a stylistic study. Hague 1968.

Howell, R. Sidney: the shepherd knight. 1968. A biography.

Isler, A. D. The allegory of the hero and Sidney's two Arcadias. SP 65 1968.

— Heroic poetry and Sidney's two Arcadias. PMLA 83 1968.

— Moral philosophy and the family in Sidney's Arcadia. HLQ 31 1968.

— Sidney, Shakespeare and the slain-not-slain. UTQ 37 1968.

Kennedy, J. M. In her edn of Yong's trn of Montemayor's Diana, Oxford 1968.

Lanham, R. A. Sidney: the ornament of his age. Southern Rev (Adelaide) 2 1968.

— Astrophil and Stella: pure and impure persuasion. Eng Literary Renaissance 2 1972.

McPherson, D. C. A possible origin for Mopsa. Stud in Renaissance 21 1968.

Rose, M. Heroic love: studies in Sidney and Spenser. Cambridge Mass 1968.

Woodward, D. H. T. Fuller, W. Dugard and the pseudonymous life of Sidney 1655. PBSA 62 1968. Reply by B. Juel-Jensen 63 1969.

Brodwin, L. L. The structure of Astrophel and Stella. MP 67 1969.

Cohen, E. Z. Sidney as ambassador. Historical Mag of Protestant Episcopal Church 38 1969.

Cotter, J. F. Sidney's Astrophil and Stella 40, 75. Explicator 27 1969.

— The songs in Astrophil and Stella. SP 67 1970.

— The 'baiser' group in Astrophil and Stella. Texas Stud in Lit & Lang 12 1970.

Evans, F. B. The concept of the fall in Sidney's Apologie. Renaissance Papers 1969.

Farmer, N. K., jr. Greville and the poetic of plain style. Texas Stud in Lit & Lang 11 1969.

— Greville and Coke: verses on Sidney. HLQ 33 1970.

Freer, C. The style of Sidney's Psalms. Lang & Style 2 1969.

Gal, I. Sidney's guidebook to Hungary. Hungarian Stud in Eng 4 1969.

Harfst, B. P. Astrophel and Stella: precept and example. Papers on Lang & Lit 5 1969.

Holzinger, W. Simplicissimus and Sidney's Arcadia. Colloquia Germanica 2 1969.

Knowlton, E. C. Sidney on Italian rhymes. N & Q Dec 1969.

Leimberg, I. Shakespeares Komödien und Sidneys Goldene Welt. Jahrbuch der Deutschen Shakespeare-Gesellschaft West 1969.

Mitchell, A. and K. Foster. Sir W. Alexander's supplement to Arcadia. Library 5th ser 24 1969.

Robinson, F. G. A note on the Sidney-Golding translation of Mornay. Harvard Lib Bull 17 1969.

Ryken, L. The drama of choice in Astrophel and Stella. JEGP 68 1969.

Taylor, A. B. A note on Ovid in Arcadia. N & Q Dec 1969.

Davidson, C. Nature and judgment in the Old Arcadia. Papers on Lang & Lit 6 1970.

Fabry, F. J. Sidney's verse adaptations to Italian art songs. Renaissance Quart 23 1970.

Fowler, A. In his Triumphal forms, 1970.

Gregory, E. R., jr. Du Bartas, Sidney and Spenser. Comparative Lit Stud 7 1970.

Hyman, V. R. Sidney's definition of poetry. Stud in Eng Lit 1500–1900 10 1970.

Jenkins, A. A second Astrophel and Stella cycle. Renaissance Papers 1970.

Kimbrough, R. Sidney. New York 1970.

O'Connor, J. J. In his Amadis de Gaule and its influence on Elizabethan literature, New Brunswick NJ 1970.

Partee, M. H. Sidney and the Renaissance knowledge of Plato. E Studies 51 1970.

Turner, M. The heroic ideal in Sidney's Revised Arcadia. Stud in Eng Lit 1500–1900 10 1970.

—— Image and metaphor in the Revised Arcadia. Eng Literary Renaissance 2 1972.

Barnes, C. The complex speaking voice of Sidney's Defence. PMLA 86 1971.

Beach, D. M. The poetry of idea: Sidney and the theory of allegory. Texas Stud in Lit & Lang 13 1971.

Cutts, J. P. More manuscript versions of poems by Sidney. Eng Lang Notes 9 1971.

Koppenfels, W. von. Two notes on imprese. Renaissance Quart 29 1971.

Lavin, J. A. The first two printers of Sidney's Astrophil and Stella. Library 5th ser 26 1971. John Charlewood Q1, John Danter Q2.

Lindenbaum, P. Sidney's Arcadia: the endings of the three versions. HLQ 34 1971.

Osborn, J. M. Sidney's horoscope. TLS 1 Jan 1971. See J. M. Addey 15 Jan 1971.

—— Sidney and Pietro Bizari. Renaissance Quart 24 1971.

—— Young Philip Sidney. New Haven 1972. A biography with trns of letters from Languet et al.

Hardison, O. B., jr. The two voices of Sidney's Apology for poetry. Eng Literary Renaissance 2 1972.

Kinney, A. F. Parody and its implications in Sidney's Defense of poesie. Stud in Eng Lit 1500–1900 12 1972.

Parker, R. W. Terentian structure and Sidney's Original Arcadia. Eng Literary Renaissance 2 1972.

FULKE GREVILLE, BARON BROOKE
1554–1628

Collections

Certaine learned and elegant workes written in his youth and familiar exercise with Sir Philip Sidney. 1633. Humane learning, Fame and honour, Warres, Alaham, Mustapha, Caelica, 2 prose letters to a lady and G. Varney.

The remains: poems of monarchy and religion. 1670; ed G. A. Wilkes, Oxford 1965 (from ms).

Cooper, E. In her Muses library, 1737. Selections.

The works in verse and prose complete. Ed A. B. Grosart 4 vols Blackburn 1870 (Fuller Worthies' Lib).

Selections from the works. Ed A. B. Grosart 1894. Extracts under topical headings.

Poems and dramas. Ed G. Bullough 2 vols Edinburgh [1939], New York 1945. Contents of 1633 Workes, above, except prose, from mss.

Five courtier poets. Ed R. M. Bender, New York 1967.

Selected poems. Ed T. Gunn, Chicago 1968. Caelica and 5 choruses.

§ 1

The tragedy of Mustapha. 1609; rptd R. Dodsley, A collection of old plays vol 2, 1744.

Caelica. In Workes, 1633; ed M. F. Crow, Elizabethan sonnet cycles vol 4, 1898; ed U. M. Ellis-Fermor, Newtown 1936. No 29 attributed to E.O. in Other sonnets appended to Syr P.S. his Astrophel and Stella, 1591, [1597–1600]; no 52 in J. Dowland, The first booke of songes or ayres, 1597; no 1 in M. Cavendish, Ayres in tabletorie, 1598; no 52 anon in Englands Helicon, 1600, 1614 (with 2 other poems, nos 77 and 79 in H. E. Rollins edn 1935, attributed to M.F.G. but cancelled as Ignoto); no 29 in J. Dowland, The second booke of songes or ayres, 1600; 13 Caelica poems and another on death of Greville in M. Peerson, Mottects, 1630.

The life of the renowned Sir Philip Sidney. 1652; ed S. E. Brydges 2 vols Lee Priory 1816; ed N. Smith, Oxford 1907.

The Arundel Harington ms. Ed R. Hughey 2 vols Columbus 1960. Contains poem attributed to Greville.

The five yeares of King James, by Sr Foulk Grevill. 1643. Not his; see N & Q 21 Nov 1868.

§ 2

Naunton, R. In his Fragmenta regalia, 1641.

Winstanley, W. In his Lives of the most famous English poets, 1687.

Walpole, H. In his Catalogue of the royal and noble authors of England vol 1, 1758.

Collier, J. P. Sidney and his works. GM April 1850.

Croll, M. The works of Greville. Philadelphia 1903.

Schelling, F. E. In his Queen's progress, Boston 1904.

Cushman, R. N. Concerning Greville's tragedies. MLN 24 1909.

Bullen, A. H. In his Elizabethans, 1924.

Greg, W. W. Notes on old books. Library 4th ser 7 1926; suppl by G. Bullough, TLS 15 Oct 1931. On 1633 Workes.

Kuhl, E. P. Contemporary politics in Elizabethan drama. PQ 7 1928.

Scott, J. G. In her Les sonnets élisabéthains, Paris 1929. Ch 3.

Rice, W. G. The sources of Greville's Alaham. JEGP 30 1931.

Bullough, G. Fulke Greville. MLR 28 1933. A biography.

—— Sénèque, Greville et le jeune Shakespeare. In Les tragédies de Sénèque et le théâtre de la Renaissance, ed J. Jacquot, Paris 1964.

Purcell, J. M. Astrophel and Stella and Greville's Caelica. PMLA 50 1935.

Ellis-Fermor, U. M. In her Jacobean drama, 1936.

Yates, F. A. Greville. TLS 7 Aug 1937.

Hudson, H. H. An Oxford epigram book. HLQ 2 1939. On editorship of Arcadia.

Orsini, N. Greville: tra il mondo e Dio. Milan 1941.

Thaler, A. Franklin and Greville. PMLA 56 1941.

Frost, W. Greville's Caelica: an evaluation. New York 1942.

Morgan, M. McC. Greville's birth. TLS 4 Nov 1944.

Utz, H. W. Die Anschauungen über Wissenschaft und Religion im Werke Grevilles. Berne 1948.

Newman, F. B. Greville and Bruno: a possible echo. PQ 29 1950.

Ure, P. Greville's dramatic characters. RES new ser 1 1950.
— A note on opinion in Daniel, Greville and Chapman. MLR 46 1951.
Jacquot, J. Religion et raison d'état dans l'oeuvre de Greville. Etudes Anglaises 5 1952.
Maclean, H. N. Greville: kingship and sovereignty. HLQ 16 1953.
— Bacon, Greville, history and biography. N & Q March 1956.
— Greville on war. HLQ 21 1958.
— Reliquiae Bodleianae letter 232. Bodleian Lib Record 6 1960. Letter to Bacon.
— Greville's poetic. SP 61 1964.
Ewing, S. B. A new ms of Greville's Life of Sidney. MLR 49 1954. In Shrewsbury Public Library; other mss in Trinity College Cambridge and in possession of B. Juel-Jensen.
Strider, R. E. L. Robert Greville, Lord Brooke. Cambridge Mass 1958. On adopted son of Greville.
Wilkes, G. A. The sources of Mustapha. N & Q Aug 1958.
— The sequence of the writings of Greville. SP 56 1959.
Rossky, W. Imagination in the English Renaissance. Stud in Renaissance 5 1959.
Oras, A. Mustapha and R. Wilmot's Tancred and Gismund. N & Q Jan 1960.
Snow, V. F. Bacon's advice to Greville on research techniques. HLQ 23 1960.
Williamson, G. The convention of the Extasie. In his Seventeenth-century contexts, 1960.
McLane, P. E. Spenser's Shepheardes calender. South Bend 1961. Identifies E.K. as Greville; opposed by H. N. Maclean, Eng Lang Notes 1 1963.
Morris, I. The tragic vision of Greville. Shakespeare Survey 14 1961.
Mahoney, J. L. Donne and Greville: attitudes toward mutability. College Lang Assoc Jnl (Baltimore) 5 1962.
Inglis, F. Metaphysical poetry and the greatness of Greville. Melbourne Critical Rev 8 1965.
Rees, J. Greville and the revision of [Sidney's] Arcadia. RES new ser 17 1966.
— Greville's epitaph on Sidney. RES new ser 19 1968.
— Greville: a critical biography. Berkeley 1971.
Heidtmann, P. The lyrics of Greville. Ohio Univ Rev 10 1968.
Farmer, N., jr. Greville and the poetic of plain style. Texas Stud in Lit & Lang 11 1969.
— Greville's letter to a cousin in France and the problem of authorship in cases of formula writing. Renaissance Quart 22 1969.
— Greville and Sir John Coke: letters on a history lecture and verses on Sidney. HLQ 33 1970.
Kelliher, W. H. Byron and Brooke. TLS 29 May 1969.
Rebholz, R. A. Life of Greville. Oxford 1971.

ROBERT SOUTHWELL SJ
c. 1561–95

Bibliographies

McDonald, J. H. The poems and prose writings of Southwell: a bibliographical study. Oxford 1937 (Roxburghe Club). See also introd to Poems, ed McDonald and Brown, 1967 below; for prose, col 1933 below.

Collections

S. Peters complaint; Saint Mary Magdalens funerall teares [prose]; sundry other poems, by R. S. [St Omer] 1616, 1620.
St Peters complaint; Mary Magdal[ens] teares [prose]; with other workes by R.S. 1620 (set up from 1615 Saint Peters complaint and 1595 Moeniae, adds prose Mary Magdalens teares, Triumphs over death, and Short rules of good life), 1630, 1636 (for 1634);

ed W. B. Turnbull 1856 (as Poetical works, from 1636 poems and ms, with memoir), [1886] (as Complete works, without Turnbull's name).
Prose works. Ed W. J. Walter 1828.
Complete poems. Ed A. B. Grosart 1872 (with memoir).
Complete works. 1876. Omits Epistle of comfort.
Selected poems (with poems of Constable and Drummond). Ed W. Jerrold, Hull 1906.
Spiritual exercises and devotions. Ed J. M. de Buck, tr P. E. Hallett 1931. Prose.
The book of Southwell. Ed C. M. Hood, Oxford 1926. Shorter poems.
Poems. Ed J. H. McDonald and N. P. Brown, Oxford 1967. Standard edn.

§1

Marie Magdalens funerall teares. 1591, 1592, 1594, 1602, 1609; ed W. Tooke 1772; rptd 1823 (from 1636, above), 1827. Prose.
Saint Peters complaint; other poemes. 1595, 1595 (rev with 8 new poems), 1595, 1597, 1599, Edinburgh [1599], 1634, London 1602 ('newlie augmented' with 7 new poems), [1607–9], 1615 (all anon); ed W. J. Walter 1817 (from 1595 and ms, with memoir).
Moeniae: or certaine excellent poems omitted in the last impression of Peters complaint, all composed by R.S. 1595 (3 edns).
The triumphs over death. 1595, 1596, 1596; rptd S. E. Brydges in Archaica vol 1, 1815; ed J. W. Trotman 1914 (from ms). Prose.
A short rule of good life; Advice of a sonne. [1597?], [1598?], [1602–5], Douai [1603–10] (2 issues), St Omer 1622. Advice of a sonne rptd 1632 (4 edns), 1633, 1636. Anon; prose. See col 1933, below.
An epistle of comfort. Paris [1604?], [no place] 1605, [St Omer] 1616; ed M. Waugh 1965. Anon; prose.
An humble supplication to her Majestie. [English secret press] 1595 (for 1601?) (anon); ed R. C. Bald, Cambridge 1953. Prose, written 1591.
A hundred meditations on the love of God. Ed J. Morris 1873 (from ms). Prose trn of Diego de Estella. See col 1933 below.
[A foure-fold meditation, by R.S. 1606; ed C. Edmonds 1895, who attributes it to Southwell, is probably by Philip Howard Earl of Arundel.]

§2

[Waldron, F. G.] In appendix to his edn of Jonson's Sad shepheard, 1783.
P[ark], T. Memoirs of Southwell. GM Nov 1798.
Southwell's works. Retrospective Rev 4 1821.
Possoz, A. Vie du père Southwell. Paris 1866.
Backer, A. de, et al. Bibliothèque des écrivains de la Compagnie de Jésus. Liege 1869–76, Brussels 1890–1909.
M[acLeod], J. G. Southwell: scholar, poet and martyr. Month 12 1877.
T[hurston], H. Southwell the Euphuist. Month 83 1895.
— Philip Earl of Arundel. Month 86 1896. On authorship of Foure-fold meditation.
— Southwell and his Peter's plaint. Month 96 1905.
— An autograph ms of Southwell. Month 143 1924. McDonald no 5.
Pollen, J. H. A rare Catholic tract. Month 99 1902. On Humble supplication.
Praz, M. Southwell's St Peter's complaint and its Italian source. MLR 19 1924.
Newdigate, C. A. The authorship of Southwell's Hundred meditations. Month 146 1925.
— Birchley or St Omers? Library 4th ser 7 1926. On printing of 1616 St Peters complaint.
— A new chapter in the life of Southwell. Month 157 1931.
Beatificationis et declarationis martyrii G. Haydock, J. Roberts, A. Bell, R. Southwell, P. Howard et sociorum. 4 vols Rome 1928–9.

Morton, Sr R. A. An appreciation of Southwell. Philadelphia 1929.

Robbie, H. J. L. The authorship of A foure-fould meditation. RES 5 1929.

Mascaró, J. Diégo de Estella and Southwell. TLS 20–7 Nov 1930.

Janelle, P. Southwell the writer. Clermont-Ferrand 1935.

Mangam, C. R. Southwell and the Council of Trent. Revue Anglo-américaine 12 1935.

Guiney, L. I. In her Recusant poets, 1939.

Collins, J. B. In his Christian mysticism in the Elizabethan age, 1940.

Moseley, D. H. Southwell in London. Commonweal 34 1941.

— Blessed Robert Southwell. New York 1957.

Devlin, C. Southwell and the Marprelates. Month 175 1948.

— Southwell and contemporary poets. Month 4 1950.

— The patriotism of Southwell. Month 10 1953.

— The life of Southwell, poet and martyr. 1956.

Martz, L. L. In his Poetry of meditation, New Haven 1954, 1962 (rev).

Sells, A. L. In his Italian influence in English poetry from Chaucer to Southwell, Bloomington 1955.

Dwyer, J. J. Southwell. Month 16 1956.

Campbell, L. B. In her Divine poetry and drama in sixteenth-century England, Cambridge 1959.

Roberts, J. R. The influence of the Spiritual exercises of St Ignatius on the nativity poems of Southwell. JEGP 59 1960.

Dickinson, J. W. Southwell's Burning babe and W. Alabaster. N & Q Nov 1961.

Morris, H. In articulo mortis. SE 11 1961.

Eleanor, Mother M. Hopkins' Windhover and Southwell's Hawk. Renascence 15 1962.

Kawasaki, T. From Southwell to Donne. Stud in Eng Lit (Tokyo) 39 1963.

Maurer, W. R. Spee, Southwell and the poetry of meditation. Comparative Lit 15 1963.

Loomis, R. The Barrett version of Southwell's Short rule of good life. Recusant History 7 1964.

White, H. C. Southwell: metaphysical and baroque. MP 61 1964.

Brown, N. P. The structure of Southwell's St Peter's complaint. MLR 61 1966.

Robinson, R. In her Five Catholic poets, 1966.

Cavanaugh, Sr J. C. The library of Lady Southwell and Capt Sibthorpe. SB 20 1967.

Daly, P. M. Southwell's Burning babe and the emblematic practice. Wascana Rev 3 1968.

McKay, F. M. Southwell's The visitation 11–12. Explicator 27 1968.

Schten, C. Southwell's Christ's bloody sweat: a meditation on the Mass. Eng Miscellany (Rome) 20 1969.

O'Connor, D. Southwell's and Cosin's versions of Lauda Sion Salvatorem. N & Q Nov 1970.

SAMUEL DANIEL
1563–1619

Bibliographies etc

Sellers, H. A bibliography of the works of Daniel 1585–1623. Proc Oxford Bibl Soc 2 1928; Supplementary note, 2 1930. Lists works, commendatory poems, mss; prints 4 letters and will.

Tannenbaum, S. A. Daniel: a concise bibliography. New York 1942; G. R. Guffey, Supplement 1942–65, 1967.

Donow, H. S. A concordance to the sonnet sequences of Daniel, Drayton, Shakespeare, Sidney and Spenser. Carbondale 1969.

Collections

Delia; An ode; the Complaint of Rosamond. 1592, 1592, Menston 1969 (facs); ed J. P. Collier 1870.

Delia and Rosamond augmented; Cleopatra. 1594, 1595, 1598.

Poeticall essayes. 1599. Sheets of 1595 Civile wars (5 bks), Musophilus, Letter from Octavia, Cleopatra, Rosamond.

Works. 1601, 1602. Contents of 1599, above, and 6th bk of Civil wars, Delia (57 sonnets), An ode, A pastorall.

A panegyrike congratulatorie to the Kings Majestie; certaine epistles (to Sir Tho. Egerton, Lord Henry Howard, Margaret Countesse of Cumberland, Lucie Countesse of Bedford, Lady Anne Clifford, Henry Earle of Southampton); A defence of ryme. [1603], 1603, Menston 1969 (facs).

Certaine small poems; the Tragedie of Philotas. 1605. Letter from Octavia, Cleopatra, Rosamond, An ode, A pastorall, Ulisses and the Syren, Philotas.

Certaine small workes. 1607 (contents of 1605, above, except Philotas, with Musophilus, Queenes Arcadia, Funerall poeme upon the Earle of Devonshire), 1611 (with Delia, Philotas).

The tragedie of Philotas. 1607. Philotas, A panegyrike congratulatorie, Certaine epistles, The passion of a distressed man, A defence of ryme.

The whole workes in poetrie. 1623 (sheets of 1609 Civile wares; contents of 1607 Philotas, except Defence of ryme, and 1611 Workes; with A description of beauty, To the angell spirit of Sʳ Phillip Sidney [by Mary Herbert Countess of Pembroke], Letter to a worthy Countesse, To James Montague Bishop of Winchester, Hymens triumph, Vision of the twelve goddesses— edited by Daniel's brother John), 1635 (sheets Aa–Tt8 reissued as Drammaticke poems).

The poetical works of Mr S. Daniel. 2 vols 1718 (from 1623, above); rptd in [R. Anderson], Poets of Great Britain vol 4, Edinburgh 1793; A. Chalmers, English poets vol 3, 1810.

Complete works in verse and prose. Ed A. B. Grosart 5 vols 1885–96, New York 1963. Prints preface and short extract only from Paulus Jovius; for poems omitted see H. Sellers, Additions to the text, MLR 11 1916.

A selection from the poetry of Daniel and Drayton. Ed H. C. Beeching 1899.

Poems and A defence of ryme. Ed A. C. Sprague, Cambridge Mass 1930.

§ I

The worthy tract of Paulus Jovius contayning a discourse of imprese. 1585. Prose trn of Dialogo dell' imprese militari e amorose, 1555.

Syr P. S. his Astrophel and Stella; other sonnets of divers gentlemen. 1591, [1597–1600], Menston 1970 (facs). Other sonnets, which include 28 by Daniel, rptd E. Arber, An English garner vol 1, 1877; S. Lee, Elizabethan sonnets vol 1, 1904.

Delia. In collections, above, 1592 (50 sonnets), 1592 (54 sonnets), 1594 (55 sonnets), 1595, 1598, 1601 (57 sonnets), 1611, 1623; ed E. Arber, An English garner vol 3, 1880; ed M. F. Crow, Elizabethan sonnet cycles vol 2, 1896; ed S. Lee, Elizabethan sonnets vol 2, 1904; ed A. Esdaile 1908 (with Drayton's Idea).

Rosamond. In collections, above, 1592, 1592, 1594, 1595, 1601, 1611, 1623; ed N. Alexander, Elizabethan narrative verse, 1967.

The tragedie of Cleopatra. In collections, above, 1594, 1595, 1599, 1601, 1605, 1607, 1611, 1623; rptd Glasgow 1751; ed M. Lederer, Louvain 1911 (from 1611); ed G. Bullough, Narrative and dramatic sources of Shakespeare vol 5, 1964 (from 1599).

The first fowre bookes of the civile warrs; the fift booke. 1595; rptd in Poeticall essayes, 1599; Works, 1601 (with 6th bk); The civile wares corrected and continued, 1609 (8 bks); ed L. Michel, New Haven 1958.

Musophilus. In collections, above, 1599, 1601, 1607, 1611, 1623; ed R. Himelick, West Lafayette Ind [1965].

Letter from Octavia. In collections, above, 1599, 1601, 1605, 1607, 1611, 1623.

A panegyrike congratulatorie. [1603]; in collections, above, [1603], 1603, 1607, 1623; rptd J. Nichols, Progresses of James I vol 1, 1828.

A defence of ryme. In collections, above, [1603], 1603, 1607, 1623; ed J. Haslewood, Ancient critical essays vol 2, 1815; ed E. Rhys, Literary pamphlets vol 1, 1897; ed G. G. Smith, Elizabethan critical essays vol 2, Oxford 1904; ed E. D. Jones, English critical essays, Oxford 1922; ed G. B. Harrison 1925 (with Campion's Observations), Edinburgh 1966.

The true description of a royal masque. 1604 (surreptitious edn); The vision of the 12 goddesses, 1604; rptd in Workes, 1623; ed J. Nichols, Progresses of James I vol 1, 1828; ed E. Law 1880; ed H. A. Evans, English masques, 1897; ed J. Rees, A book of masques in honour of A. Nicoll, Cambridge 1967.

The tragedie of Philotas. In collections, above, 1605, 1607, 1611, 1623; ed L. Michel, New Haven 1949.

The Queenes Arcadia: a pastorall trage-comedie. 1606; rptd in Workes, 1607, 1611, 1623.

A funerall poeme uppon the Earle of Devonshyre. [1606]; rptd in Workes, 1607, 1611, 1623.

Danyel, J. Songs for the lute, viol and voice. 1606. Music for 2 poems.

Tethys festival [a masque]. In The order of the creation of Prince Henrie, Prince of Wales, 1610; rptd Somers tracts vol 1, 1750, vol 2, 1809; J. Nichols, Progresses of James I vol 2, 1828.

The first part of the historie of England. 1612 (to Stephen), 1613; The collection of the historie of England, [1618] (to Edward III), 1621, 1621, 1626, 1626, 1634, 1650 (with J. Trussell's continuation), 1685; in A complete history of England vol 1, 1706, 1719. Prose.

Hymens triumph: a pastorall tragicomaedie. 1615; rptd in Workes, 1623; partly rptd J. Nichols, Progresses of James I vol 2, 1828.

An introduction to a breviary of the history of England. 1693. Prose; attributed to Sir W. Ralegh, but see Gottfried 1956 and Godshalk 1963, below.

The prayse of private life. Ed N. E. McClure, Letters and epigrams of Sir John Harington, Philadelphia 1930. Prose paraphrase of Petrarch, De vita solitaria. Attributed to Daniel by Sellers; see Supplementary note 1930 to his Bibliography, above.

§2

For more complete lists see bibliographies of Tannenbaum and Guffey, above.

Fuller, T. In his History of the worthies of England, 1662.

Wood, A. In his Athenae oxonienses, 1691.

Oldmixon, J. Reply to the Bp of Rochester's vindication: an account of the alterations in Daniel's History. 1732.

Cooper, E. In her Muses library, 1737. With biography by W. Oldys.

Cunningham, P. Will of Daniel. Shakespeare Soc Papers 4 1849.

Guggenheim, J. Quellenstudien zu Daniels Delia. Berlin 1898.

Lee, S. In his Elizabethan sonnets vol 1, 1904. Introd on sources.

Moorman, F. W. Shakespeare's history plays and Daniel's Civile wars. Sh Jb 40 1904.

Greg, W. W. In his Pastoral poetry and pastoral drama, 1906.

Kastner, L. E. The Elizabethan sonneteers and the French poets. MLR 3 1908.

— The Italian sources of Daniel's Delia. MLR 7 1912.

Brady, G. P. Daniel: a critical study. Urbana 1923.

Jeffery, V. M. Sources of Daniel's Queen's Arcadia. MLR 19 1924.

Daniel, M. S. An Elizabethan Wordsworth. Dublin Rev 176 1925.

Brettle, R. E. Daniel and the Children of the Queen's revels. RES 3 1927.

Sellers, H. Two new letters of Daniel. TLS 24 March 1927.

Scott, J. G. In her Les sonnets élisabéthains, Paris 1929. Ch 8.

Stewart, J. I. M. Montaigne and the Defence of rhyme. RES 9 1933.

Schütze, J. Daniels Cleopatra und Shakespeare. E Studien 71 1936. See Norman, 1959 below.

Eccles, M. Daniel in France and Italy. SP 34 1937.

Hotson, L. The marigold of poets. Trans Royal Soc of Lit new ser 17 1938.

Stirling, B. Daniel's Philotas and the Essex case. MLQ 3 1942. See G. A. Wilkes, A reconsideration 23 1962.

Rollins, H. E. In his New variorum edition of Shakespeare's Sonnets, 2 vols Philadelphia 1944.

Tillyard, E. M. W. In his Shakespeare's history plays, 1946.

— In his English epic and its background, 1954.

Heltzel, V. B. In his Fair Rosamond: the development of a literary theme, Evanston 1947.

McKisack, M. Daniel as historian. RES 23 1947.

Shackford, M. H. Daniel's poetical epistles, especially to the Countess of Cumberland. SP 45 1948.

McManaway, J. G. Bibliographical notes on Daniel's Civil wars. SB 4 1951.

Rees, J. Daniel's Cleopatra and two French plays. MLR 47 1952.

— Daniel: a critical and biographical study. Liverpool 1964.

Seronsy, C. C. Daniel's ms Civil wars with some unpublished stanzas. JEGP 52 1953.

— Well-languaged Daniel: a reconsideration. MLR 52 1957.

— The doctrine of cyclical recurrence and some related ideas in Daniel. SP 54 1957.

— Daniel and Wordsworth. SP 56 1959.

— Daniel's Complaint of Rosamond: origins and influence. Lock Haven Bull 2 1960.

— Samuel Daniel. New York 1967.

— and R. Krueger. A ms of Daniel's Civil wars bk 3. SP 63 1966.

Cutts, J. P. Original music. N & Q May 1954. Ms settings of songs from Hymen's triumph and Delia 6.

Miller, E. H. Daniel's revisions in Delia. JEGP 53 1954.

Michel, L. and C. C. Seronsy. Shakespeare's history plays and Daniel. SP 52 1955.

Gottfried, R. B. The authorship of A breviary of the history of England. SP 53 1956.

— Daniel's method of writing history. Stud in Renaissance 3 1956.

Blissett, W. Daniel's sense of the past. E Studies 38 1957.

Himelick, R. A fig for Momus and Daniel's Musophilus. MLQ 18 1957.

Schanzer, E. Daniel's revision of his Cleopatra. RES new ser 8 1957. See J. Rees 9 1958.

Bludau, D. Sonnettstruktur bei Daniel. Sh Jb 94 1958.

Norman, A. M. Z. Daniel's Cleopatra and Antony and Cleopatra. Shakespeare Quart 9 1958.

— Cleopatra and the date of Antony and Cleopatra. MLR 54 1959.

The Arundel Harington ms. Ed R. Hughey 2 vols Columbus 1960. Letter from Octavia.

Schaar, C. Shakespeare's Sonnets, Daniel's Delia and their literary background. Lund 1960.

Leishman, J. B. In his Themes and variations in Shakespeare's sonnets, 1961.

Hentz, A. L. A Senecan source for Daniel's epistle to Southampton. N & Q June 1962.

Talbert, E. W. In his Problem of order, Chapel Hill 1962.

Buxton, J. In his Elizabethan taste, 1963.

Godshalk, W. L. Daniel's History. JEGP 63 1964.

Thomson, P. Daniel's Delia 15: a Petrarchan imitation. Comparative Lit 17 1965.

Chang, J. S. Machiavellianism in Daniel's Civil wars. Tulane Stud in Eng 14 1965.

Harlow, C. G. Shakespeare, Nashe and the ostrich crux in 1 Henry IV. Shakespeare Quart 17 1966.

Spencer, T. Two classic Elizabethans: Daniel and Sir J. Davies. In his Selected essays, New Brunswick NJ 1966.

Hebert, C. A. Belinda and Rosamond. College Eng Assoc Critic 30 1967.

Lambrechts, G. Sur deux prétendues sources de Richard II. Etudes Anglaises 20 1967.

Maxwell, J. C. Rebel powers: Shakespeare and Daniel. N & Q April 1967.

Goldman, L. Daniel's Delia and the emblem tradition. JEGP 67 1968.

Howarth, R. G. The model-source of John Webster's Monumental column. Eng Stud in Africa 11 1968.

Spriet, P. Daniel: sa vie, son oeuvre. Bordeaux 1968.

Williamson, C. F. The design of Delia. RES new ser 19 1968.

La Branche, A. Poetry, history and oratory: the Renaissance historical poem. Stud in Eng Lit 1500–1900 9 1969.

Freeman, A. An epistle for two. Library 5th ser 25 1970. Ms of Epistle to Lady Margaret.

Kau, J. Daniel and the Renaissance impresa-makers. Harvard Lit Bull 18 1970.

Logan, G. M. Daniel's Civil wars and Lucan's Pharsalia. Stud in Eng Lit 1500–1900 11 1971.

MICHAEL DRAYTON
1563–1631

Bibliographies etc

Juel-Jensen, B. Bibliography of the early editions of Drayton. In Works of Drayton vol 5, ed Hebel, Tillotson and Newdigate, Oxford 1961.

Tannenbaum, S. A. Drayton: a concise bibliography. New York 1941; G. R. Guffey, Supplement 1941–65, 1967.

Donow, H. S. A concordance to the sonnet sequences of Daniel, Drayton, Shakespeare, Sidney and Spenser. Carbondale 1969.

Collections

The tragicall legend of Robert Duke of Normandy; The legend of Matilda; The legend of Peirs Gaveston, the latter two newly corrected and augmented. 1596.

Englands heroicall epistles newly corrected; Idea. 1600, 1602.

The barrons wars [revised text of Mortimeriados]; Englands heroicall epistles [reissue of 1602, above]. 1603.

Poems. 1605 (Barrons warres; Englands heroicall epistles; Idea (63 sonnets); legends of Robert, Matilda and Gaveston, 1888 (Spenser Soc), 1608 (newly corrected), 1610, 1613, [c. 1616], 1619 (2 issues; with Cromwell and rev contents of 1606? Poemes lyrick and pastorall), 1630, 1637, Menston 1969 (facs of 1619).

Poemes lyrick and pastorall: Odes; Eglogs; The man in the moone. [1606?], 1891 (Spenser Soc).

The battaile of Agincourt [different from the Ballad]; The miseries of Queene Margarite; Nimphidia; The quest of Cinthia; The shepheards Sirena; The moone-calfe; Elegies upon sundry occasions. 1627, 1631, Menston 1970 (facs of 1627).

The Muses Elizium: ten nymphalls; Noahs floud; Moses his birth and miracles [revision of 1604 Moyses]; David and Golia. 1630, 1892 (Spenser Soc).

Works. [Ed C. Coffey] 1748 (Agincourt from 1627 or 1631, Polyolbion, Poems from 1630 or 1637); Appendix, [c. 1752] (Owl, Man in the moon, Odes and Eclogues from 1619, Muses elysium from 1630), 4 vols 1753 (reprint of 1748 and Appendix).

Works. In Poets of Great Britain vol 3, [ed R. Anderson], Edinburgh 1793; in English poets vol 4, ed A. Chalmers 1810.

Poems. Ed J. P. Collier 1856 (Roxburghe Club).

Complete works. Ed R. Hooper 3 vols 1876. Polyolbion and Harmony of the Church only.

Selections from the poems. Ed A. H. Bullen 1883.

A selection from the poetry of Daniel and Drayton. Ed H. C. Beeching 1899.

Minor poems. Ed C. Brett 1907.

Complete works. Ed J. W. Hebel 4 vols Oxford 1931–3; vol 5, 1941 (variant readings by J. W. Hebel, introds and notes by K. Tillotson and B. H. Newdigate, bibliography by G. Tillotson), 5 vols 1961 (with new bibliography by B. Juel-Jensen). The standard edn.

Poems. Ed J. Buxton 2 vols 1953 (ML).

§1

The harmonie of the Church: spirituall songes and holy hymnes. 1591, 1610 (as A heavenly harmonie); ed A. Dyce 1843 (Percy Soc).

Idea: the shepheards garland in nine eglogs. 1593; ed J. P. C[ollier] [1870] (facs).

Peirs Gaveston. [1593–4], [1595?]; rptd in collections, above, 1596, 1605, 1608, 1610, 1613, [c. 1616], 1619, 1630, 1637.

Ideas mirrour: amours in quaterzains. 1594 (51 sonnets); rptd in collections, above (as Idea, rev and expanded), 1599, 1600, 1602, 1605, 1608, 1610, 1613, [c. 1616], 1619, 1630, 1637; ed E. Arber, An English garner vol 6, 1883; ed M. F. Crow, Elizabethan sonnet cycles vol 3, 1897; ed S. Lee, Elizabethan sonnets vol 2, 1904; ed A. Esdaile 1908 (with Daniel's Delia). A total of 103 sonnets with 4 other poems.

Matilda, the daughter of Lord Fitzwater. 1594, 1594; rptd in collections above, 1596, 1605, 1608, 1610, 1613, [c. 1616], 1619, 1630, 1637.

Endimion and Phoebe: Ideas Latmus. 1595; ed J. P. C[ollier] [1870] (facs); ed J. W. Hebel, Oxford 1925; ed E. S. Donno, Elizabethan minor epics, New York 1963.

Mortimeriados: the civell warres of Edward the Second and the barrons. 1596, [1596?]; rev as The barrons wars in collections, above, 1603, 1605, 1608, 1610, 1613, [c. 1616], 1619, 1630, 1637.

Englands heroicall epistles. 1597, 1598 (enlarged), 1599; rptd in collections, above, 1605, 1608, 1610, 1613, [c. 1616], 1619, 1630, 1637; separately rptd nd, 1697 (same setting of type), 1737, 1788; epistles of Rosamond and Henry tr Latin by N. Hookes in Amanda, 1653.

The first part of the historie of Sir John Oldcastle. 1600, 1600 (for 1619); in W. Shakespear's Comedies, histories and tragedies, 1664 (2nd issue of 3rd folio), 1685 (4th folio); ed C. F. T. Brooke, The Shakespeare apocrypha, Oxford 1908; ed P. Simpson, Oxford 1908 (Malone Soc). A play written with A. Munday, R. Hathway and R. Wilson.

Englands Helicon. 1600, 1614; ed H. E. Rollins, Cambridge Mass 1935. 5 poems: nos 7, 14, 56, 74, 126.

To the Majestie of King James: a gratulatorie poem. 1603, 1603, Amsterdam 1969 (facs).

Moyses in a map of his miracles. 1604; rptd in The Muses elizium, 1630 (as Moses his birth and miracles).

The owle. 1604 (4 edns); rptd in collections, above, 1619, 1630, 1637.

A paean triumphall for the societie of goldsmiths congratulating his Highnes entring the citie. 1604; rptd J. Nichols, Progresses of King James vol 1, 1828.

The legend of great Cromwell. 1607, 1609 (as The historie of the life and death of the Lord Cromwell); rptd in A mirour for magistrates, 1610; in collections, above, 1619, 1630, 1637.

Poly-Olbion [pt 1]. [1612], 1613, 1622 (18 songs with notes by J. Selden); pt 2, 1622 (songs 19–30); [c. 1630] (both pts reissued as The faerie land), 1889–90 (Spenser Soc).

Ward, J. The first set of English madrigals. 1613. 3 songs, with music by Ward.

Certain elegies done by sundrie excellent wits; satyres and epigrams [by H. Fitzgeffrey]. 1618, 1620 (on Lady P. Clifton and sons of Lord Sheffield); rptd in collections, above, 1627, 1631.

The ballad of Agincourt. In 1606? collection, above; rptd B.H.N[ewdigate], Oxford 1926 (with Ode to the Virginian voyage); [ed B. Juel-Jensen] Oxford 1951 (from 1619 with new holograph stanza from R. Butcher's copy).

The battaile of Agincourt. In 1627 collection, above; ed R. Garnett 1893.

Epistle to H. Reynolds. In 1627 collection, above; ed J. E. Spingarn, Seventeenth-century critical essays, Oxford 1908; tr Greek by H. Stubbe in Deliciae poetarum anglicanorum in graecum verse, Oxford 1658.

Nymphidia. In 1627 collection, above; rptd as The history of Queen Mab: the story upon which the entertainment now exhibiting at Drury-lane is founded, 1751, 1751; ed S. E. Brydges, Lee Priory 1814; ed J. Gray 1896 (with the Muses elizium); ed H. F. B. Brett-Smith, Oxford 1921; ed J. C. Squire, Oxford 1924; tr German, 1873; Sh Jb 9 1874.

The quest of Cynthia. In 1627 collection, above; rptd [1923] (Medici Soc).

§2

For more complete lists see bibliographies of Tannenbaum and Guffey, above. Early studies are noted in K. Tillotson and B. H. Newdigate's notes to vol 5 of Works, 1941.

[Oldys, W.] In Biographia britannica vol 3, 1750.

Elton, O. An introduction to Drayton. 1895 (Spenser Soc).

— Drayton: a critical study. 1905, New York 1966.

Probst, A. Daniels Civil wars und Draytons Barons wars: eine Quellenstudie. Strasbourg 1902.

Whittaker, L. Drayton as a dramatist. PMLA 18 1903.

— The sonnets of Drayton. MP 1 1904.

Greg, W. W. In his Pastoral poetry and pastoral drama, 1906.

Child, H. H. CHEL vol 4 1909.

Claassen, W. Draytons Englands heroicall epistles: eine Quellenstudie. Leipzig 1913.

Numeratzky, W. Draytons Belesenheit und literarische Kritik. Berlin 1915.

Long, E. Drayton's Eighth nymphal. SP 13 1916.

Adams, J. Q. Drayton's To the Virginia voyage. MLN 33 1918.

[Blunden, E.] Happy island. TLS 17 Aug 1922; rptd in his Votive tablets, 1931.

Cawley, R. R. Drayton and the voyagers. PMLA 38 1923.

— Drayton's use of Welsh history. SP 22 1925.

Jenkins, R. Drayton's relations to the school of Donne in the Shepheards Sirena. PMLA 38 1923. Replies by J. W. Hebel 39 1924, Jenkins 42 1927.

— The source of Drayton's Battle of Agincourt. PMLA 41 1926.

Hebel, J. W. Drayton and Shakespeare. MLN 41 1926.

Keller, W. Draytons angebliche Mitarbeit an Heinrich VI. E Studien 57 1923.

Bullen, A. H. In his Elizabethans, 1924.

Gourvitch, I. The Welsh element in the Poly-Olbion. RES 4 1928.

— Drayton's debt to Geoffrey of Monmouth. Ibid.

— A note on Drayton and Philemon Holland. MLR 25 1930. Reply by K. M. Constable (later Tillotson), MLR 26 1931.

Scott, J. G. In her Les sonnets élisabéthains, Paris 1929. Ch 10.

Noyes, R. Drayton's literary vogue since 1631. Indiana Univ Stud 22 1935.

Haskell, G. P. Drayton's secondary modes. Urbana 1936.

Tillotson, K. The language of Drayton's Shepheards garland. RES 13 1937.

— Drayton as historian in the Legend of Cromwell. MLR 34 1939.

— Drayton and Richard III. RES 15 1939.

Williams, F. B., jr. A sonnet by Drayton? TLS 11 Dec 1937.

John, L. C. In her Elizabethan sonnet sequences, New York 1938.

St Clair, F. Y. Drayton's first revision of his sonnets. SP 36 1939.

Tillotson, G. Contemporary praise of Poly-Olbion. RES 16 1940.

Newdigate, B. H. Drayton and his circle. Oxford 1941.

Harrison, T. P. Drayton's herbals. SE 22 1943.

— In his They tell of birds, Austin 1956.

Le Comte, E. S. In his Endymion in England, New York 1944.

Nearing, H., jr. In his English historical poetry 1599–1641, Philadelphia 1945.

Heltzel, V. B. In his Fair Rosamond, Evanston 1947.

Praz, M. Drayton. E Studies 28 1947.

Allen, D. C. In his Legend of Noah, Urbana 1949.

Shapiro, I. A. Drayton at Polesworth. N & Q 12 Nov 1949.

Zocca, L. R. In his Elizabethan narrative poetry, New Brunswick NJ 1950.

Taylor, D., jr. Drayton and the Countess of Bedford. SP 49 1952.

Juel-Jensen, B. Polyolbion and other books by Drayton. Library 5th ser 8 1953.

— Three lost Drayton items. Book Collector 9 1960.

— Fine and large-paper copies. Library 5th ser 19 1964, 23 1968.

— Drayton and Drummond: a lost autograph letter rediscovered. Library 5th ser 21 1966.

Duclos, P.-Ch. Drayton. Revue des Langues Vivantes 20 1954.

Lever, J. W. In his Elizabethan love sonnet, 1956.

Friedrich, G. The genesis of Drayton's ode To the Virginian voyage. MLN 72 1957.

Heffner, R. L., jr. Drayton's Lady I.S. N & Q Sept 1958.

Ackerman, C. A. Drayton's revision of the Shepheards garland. College Langs Assoc Jnl (Baltimore) 3 1959.

Briggs, K. M. In her Anatomy of Puck, 1959.

Miller, E. H. In his Professional writer in Elizabethan England, Cambridge Mass 1959.

Buxton, J. In his Elizabethan taste, 1963.

LaBranche, A. Drayton's Barons warres and the rhetoric of historical poetry. JEGP 62 1963.

— The twofold vitality of Drayton's Odes. Comparative Lit 15 1963.

— Poetry, history and oratory: the Renaissance historical poem. Stud in Eng Lit 1500–1900 9 1969.

Buchloh, P. G. Drayton: Barde und Historiker, Politiker und Prophet. Neumünster 1964.

Grundy, J. Brave translunary things. MLR 59 1964.

Robertson, J. Drayton and the Countess of Pembroke. RES new ser 16 1965.

Whitfield, C. Clifford chambers: the Muses quiet port. N & Q Oct 1965.

Berthelot, J. A. Drayton. New York 1967.

Schönert, J. Draytons Sonett-Revisionen. Anglia 85 1967.

Benson, D. R. Idea and the problem of knowledge in 17th-century aesthetics. Eng Miscellany (Rome) 19 1968.

Hardin, R. F. Convention and design in Drayton's Heroical epistles. PMLA 83 1968.

— The composition of Poly-Olbion and the Muses elizium. Anglia 86 1968.

Moore, W. H. Sources of Drayton's conception of Poly-Olbion. SP 65 1968.

Nagy, N. C. de. Drayton's England's heroical epistles: a study in themes and compositional devices. Berne 1968.

Davis, W. R. Drayton's Idea of 1619. SP 66 1969.

Friedman, S. Antony and Cleopatra and Drayton's Mortimeriades. Shakespeare Quart 20 1969.

Parsons, D. S. J. The odes of Drayton and Jonson. Queen's Quart 75 1969.

Bristol, M. D. Structural patterns in two Elizabethan pastorals. Stud in Eng Lit 1500–1900 10 1970.

Hiller, G. G. Drayton's Muses Elizium. RES new ser 21 1970.

THOMAS CAMPION
1567–1620

Collections

Works. Ed A. H. Bullen 1889.

Lyric poems. Ed E. Rhys [1896].

Songs and masques; observations. Ed A. H. Bullen 1903.

Poetical works in English. Ed P. S. Vivian [1907] (ML).

Works. Ed P. S. Vivian, Oxford 1909. Complete, with biography.

Works: complete songs, masques and treatises, selection of Latin verse. Ed W. R. Davis, Garden City NY 1967. With trns of Latin verse.

§1

Syr P.S. his Astrophel and Stella; other sonnets of divers gentlemen. 1591, [1597–1600], Menston 1970 (facs). Includes 5 songs signed Content, identified as Campion's by G. C. Moore Smith in his edn of A. Fraunce, Victoria, 1906.

Poemata: Ad Thamesin; Fragmentum umbrae; Liber elegiarum; Liber epigrammatum. 1595.

A booke of ayres to be song to the lute, orpherian and base violl by P. Rosseter. 1601; music ed E. H. Fellowes, English school of lutenist song writers, 1st ser 4, 13, 1922; words ed E. H. Fellowes, English madrigal verse, Oxford 1920, rev F. W. Sternfeld and D. Greer, Oxford 1967. Words and music of pt 1 by Campion; see Berringer 1943, below.

Observations in the art of English poesie. 1602; ed J. Haslewood, Ancient critical essays vol 2, 1815; ed E. Rhys, Literary pamphlets vol 1, 1897; ed G. Gregory Smith, Elizabethan critical essays vol 2, Oxford 1904; ed E. D. Jones, English critical essays, Oxford 1922 (WC); ed G. B. Harrison 1925, Edinburgh 1966 (with Daniel's Defence of ryme); Menston 1968 (facs of 1602).

The discription of a maske at White-Hall in honour of the Lord Hayes and his bride; other small poemes. 1607; rptd J. Nichols, Progresses of James I vol 2, 1828; ed K. Talbot 1924 (for a production at Hatfield); Amsterdam 1969 (facs of 1607).

The first booke of ayres. [1613?].

Two bookes of ayres. [c. 1613]; music ed E. H. Fellowes, English school of lutenist song writers, 2nd ser 1–2, 1925; words ed E. H. Fellowes, English madrigal verse, Oxford 1920, rev F. W. Sternfeld and D. Greer, Oxford 1967.

A relation of the entertainment given by Lord Knowles; the lords maske on the marriage night of the Count Palatine and the Ladie Elizabeth. 1613; rptd J. Nichols, Progresses of James I vol 2, 1828; Lords maske ed H. A. Evans, English masques, 1897; ed I. A. Shapiro, A book of masques in honour of A. Nicoll, Cambridge 1967.

Songs of mourning bewailing the death of Prince Henry. 1613.

A new way of making fowre parts in counterpoint. [c. 1614]; rptd J. Playford, Brief introduction to the skill of musick, 1660, 1661, 1667, 1671.

The description of a maske at the mariage of the Earle of Somerset; ayres by severall authors sung in the maske. 1614; rptd J. Nichols, Progresses of James I vol 2, 1828.

The third and fourth booke of ayres. [1617?]; music ed E. H. Fellowes, English school of lutenist song writers, 2nd ser 10–1, 1926; words ed E. H. Fellowes, in his

English madrigal verse, Oxford 1920, rev F. W. Sternfeld and D. Greer, Oxford 1967.

Ayres that were sung and played at Brougham Castle. 1618; words rptd E. H. Fellowes, English madrigal verse, Oxford 1920, rev F. W. Sternfeld and D. Greer, Oxford 1967. 10 songs with music by G. Mason and J. Earsden, words possibly by Campion.

Epigrammatum libri II; Umbra; Elegiarum liber unus. 1619, [1628–9].

A friends advice in [a] ditty concerning the variable changes in this world. [c. 1625?], [after 1640].

The man of life upright, illustrated by R. Graham. Leicester 1962. From R. Alison, An howres recreation in musicke, 1606.

§2

Daniel, S. A defence of ryme. [1603]. Reply to Observations.

Vivian, P. S. CHEL 4 1909.

MacDonagh, T. Campion and the art of English poetry. Dublin 1913.

Lynd, R. Campion. Athenaeum 26 Sept 1919.

Flood, W. H. G. Campion: his Irish ancestry. Music Student Aug 1920.

Gosse, E. Campion. Music Student April 1920.

Savage, H. Campion and his dark lady. Bookman's Jnl 16–23 April 1920.

Bullen, A. H. In his Elizabethans, 1924.

Heseltine, P. Two unpublished poems by Campion. London Mercury Feb 1926.

Welsford, E. In her Court masque, Cambridge 1927.

Lovett, D. Variant readings. MLN 46 1931.

Benham, A. R. Campion and Horace. PQ 12 1933.

Schramm, W. L. Campion, Horace and Catullus. PQ 12–13 1933–4.

Bradner, L. References to Chaucer in Campion's Poemata. RES 12 1936.

—— In his Musae anglicanae, New York 1940.

Kastendieck, M. M. England's musical poet. New York 1938.

Berringer, R. W. Campion's share in A booke of ayres. PMLA 58 1943.

Short, R. W. The metrical theory and practice of Campion. PMLA 59 1944.

Schueller, H. M. Renaissance forerunners of the neoclassic lyric. MLN 62 1947.

Bühler, C. F. Four Elizabethan poems. In J. Q. Adams memorial studies, Washington 1948.

Pattison, B. In his Music and poetry of the English Renaissance 1948, 1970 (rev).

Pelz, C. W. Campion: an Elizabethan neo-classicist. MLQ 11 1950.

Ing, C. In her Elizabethan lyrics, 1951.

Cunningham, J. V. Campion and Propertius. PQ 31 1952.

McElwee, W. The murder of Sir Thomas Overbury. New York 1952. Background of Somerset masque.

Shapiro, I. A. Campion's medical degree. N & Q 8 Nov 1952.

Cutts, J. P. Original music. N & Q May 1954. St Michael's College ms 1018.

—— Jacobean masque and stage music. Music & Letters 35 1954. For Lord Hayes' and Lords' masques.

Sabol, A. J. In his Songs and dances for the Stuart masque, Providence 1957.

Sternfeld, F. W. A song from Campion's Lord's masque. Jnl Warburg & Courtauld Inst 20 1957.

Candelaria, F. H. Cummings and Campion. N & Q April 1959.

Davis, W. R. A note on accent and quantity in A booke of ayres. MLQ 22 1961.

—— Melodic and poetic structure: the examples of Campion and Dowland. Criticism 4 1962.

Greer, D. What if a day: an examination of the words and the music. Music & Letters 43 1962.

—— T. Heywood's parody of a lyric by Campion. N & Q Sept 1965.

—— Campion the musician. Lute Soc Jnl 9 1967.

Samson, P. Words for music. Southern Rev (Adelaide) 1 1963.

Wilkinson, L. P. Propertius and Campion. London Mag April 1967.

Spink, I. Campion's entertainment at Brougham Castle 1616. In Music in English Renaissance drama, ed J. H. Long, Lexington Kentucky 1968.

Weiss, W. Die Airs im Stilwandel. Anglia 87 1969.

Irwin, J. T. Campion and the musical emblem. Stud in Eng Lit 1500–1900 10 1970.

Lowbury, E., T. Salter and A. Young. Campion: poet, composer, physician. 1970.

SIR JOHN DAVIES
1569–1626
Collections

Nosce teipsum; Hymnes of Astraea. 1619.

Nosce teipsum; Hymnes of Astraea; Orchestra. 1622.

On the immortality of the soul [Nosce teipsum, from Tate's edn] with an essay by Dr T. Sheridan; A discovery of the causes why Ireland was never entirely subdued [prose]. Dublin 1733.

Poetical works. Ed T. Davies 1773 (Nosce teipsum from Tate's edn, Astraea, Orchestra); rptd [R. Anderson], Poets of Great Britain vol 2, Edinburgh 1793; A. Chalmers, English poets vol 5, 1810.

Works in prose and verse. Ed A. B. Grosart 3 vols Blackburn 1869–76.

Complete poems. Ed A. B. Grosart 2 vols 1876.

Orchestra; Nosce teipsum; Astraea. Ed E. Arber, English garner vol 5, Birmingham 1882; rptd A. H. Bullen, Longer Elizabethan poems, Westminster 1903.

Poems. Ed C. Howard, New York 1941. Facs of Orchestra, Nosce teipsum, Astraea, Epigrames, and reprint of Gulling sonnets.

Silver poets of the 16th century. Ed G. Bullett 1947 (EL). Includes Orchestra, Nosce teipsum, selected poems.

§1

Orchestra: a poeme of dauncing. 1596; ed R. S. Lambert, Wembley Hill 1922; ed E. M. W. Tillyard 1945.

Epigrammes and elegies by J. D[avies] and C.M[arlowe]. Middleburg [Edinburgh?] 1598?], [1599?], Menston 1970 (facs of first edn); Ovids elegies: three bookes by C.M.; Epigrames by J.D., 'Middleburg' [i.e. London c. 1600] (2 edns), [c. 1630], [c. 1640]; ed G. Robinson, Works of Marlowe vol 3, 1826; ed A. Dyce, Works of Marlowe, 1850, 1865; ed C. Edmonds 1870 (with Shakespeare's Venus and Adonis and Passionate pilgrime); ed C. F. T. Brooke, Works of Marlowe, Oxford 1910; 1925 (Haslewood Books).

Hymns of Astraea in acrosticke verse. 1599.

Nosce teipsum in two elegies: of humane knowledge, of the soule of man. 1599 (2 edns; see Eberle 1948, below), 1602, 1608; ed T. Jenner 1653 (pt 2 only, as A work for none but angels and men), 1682; ed W.R[avenhill] 1688; ed N. Tate 1697, 1714, 1715, Glasgow 1749; ed E. Capell, Prolusions, 1760.

A poetical rapsody. Ed F. Davison 1602 (contains A hymne in prayse of musicke, ten sonnets to Philomel), 1608 (with Yet other 12 wonders of the world, A lotterie 1601, A contention betwixt a wife a widdowe and a maide), 1611, 1621. The xii wonders of the world rptd with music by J. Maynard 1611; and E. V. Utterson, Ryde 1842 (without music). A lotterie rptd with music by R. Jones, Ultimum vale, 1608; Conway ms version, Shakespeare Soc Papers 2 1845.

Gullinge sonnets. Chetham ms 8012; ed A. B. Grosart, Dr Farmer Chetham ms vol 1, Manchester 1873.

Epithalamion: 10 sonnets on marriage of Elizabeth Vere to William Stanley Earl of Derby 1595. Ed R. Krueger, RES new ser 13 1962 (from ms).

Sir Martin Mar-people his coller of esses, *1590, is by another John Davies*; A new post; with soveraigne salve to cure the worlds madnes by Sir I.D., *1620, [1625?], is a reissue of R. Mason*, Reasons academie, *1605, 1609. For Davies' historical and legal writings see col 2237, below*.

§2

Jenner, T. A work for none but angels and men: a book shewing what the soule is. 1658. Prose paraphrase of Nosce teipsum.

R[avenhill], W. Nosce teipsum: a leading-step to the knowledge of our selves. 1689. Prose commentary inspired by Nosce teipsum.

Cooper, E. In her Muses' library, 1737.

Biographia britannica 3 1750.

Woolrych, H. W. In his Lives of eminent serjeants-at-law vol 1, 1869.

Nicholson, B. Sir John Davies. Athenæum 29 Jan 1876.

Sneath, E. H. Philosophy in poetry: a study of Nosce teipsum. New York 1903. With text of poem.

Seemann, M. Sir John Davies: sein Leben und seine Werke. Vienna 1913.

Holmes, M. D. The poet as philosopher: a study of Nosce teipsum. 1921.

Bredvold, L. I. The sources used by Davies in Nosce teipsum. PMLA 38 1923.

Ramsay, M. P. In his Les doctrines médiévales chez Donne, 1917, 1924 (rev).

Whipple, T. K. In his Martial and the English epigram, Berkeley 1925.

Buckley, T. T. The indebtedness of Davies' Nosce teipsum to P. Mornay's Trewnesse of the Christian religion. MP 25 1927.

Tilley, M. P. The comedy Lingua and Davies's Nosce teipsum. MLN 44 1929.

Bensly, E. An epigram in Grosart's edition of Davies. N & Q 27 Feb 1937. Addns by D. G. Redding, Nov 1961, and B. Harris, Jan 1962. Not by Davies.

Kruuse, J. Nosce teipsum. In his Digtere og traditioner, Copenhagen 1939.

Perkinson, R. H. The polemical use of Nosce teipsum. SP 36 1939.

Tannenbaum, S. A. Editorial notes. Shakespeare Assoc Bull 16 1941.

Sparrow, J. Some later editions of Nosce teipsum. Library 5th ser 1 1946. Addns by R. H. Perkinson 2 1947, G. A. Wilkes, TLS 20 Oct 1961. On edns of 1688, 1697, 1773.

Peery, W. The three souls again. PQ 27 1948.

Tillyard, E. M. W. Orchestra. In his Five poems, 1948. Text and comment.

Eberle, G. J. Nosce teipsum 1599: a bibliographical puzzle. SB 1 1949.

McNeir, W. F. Marston vs Davies and Terpsichore. PQ 29 1950.

Simpson, P. Unprinted epigrams of Davies. RES new ser 3 1952.

Smith, H. In his Elizabethan poetry, Cambridge Mass 1952.

Nosworthy, J. M. The publication of Marlowe's Elegies and Davies's Epigrams. RES new ser 4 1953. Postscript 15 1964.

Rogers, P. B. Davies' Gulling sonnets. Bucknell Rev 4 1953.

Schoeck, R. J. Nosce teipsum and the two John Davies. MLR 50 1955.

Eliot, T. S. In his On poetry and poets, 1957.

Kennedy, R. F. Unprinted epigrams by Davies. TLS 7 Aug 1959.

—— Another Davies ms. RES new ser 15 1964.

Bowers, R. H. An Elizabethan ms continuation of Nosce teipsum. MP 58 1960.

Sanderson, J. L. Unpublished epigrams of Davies. RES new ser 12 1961.

Krueger, R. Orchestra complete, epigrams, unpublished poems. RES new ser 13 1962.

Wilkes, G. A. The poetry of Davies. HLQ 25 1962.

Finkelpearl, P. J. Davies and [Rudyerd's] Prince d'amour. N & Q Aug 1963.

Colie, R. L. The rhetoric of transcendence. PQ 43 1964.

Spencer, T. Two classic Elizabethans: Daniel and Davies. In his Selected essays, New Brunswick NJ 1966.

Baldwin, J. C. John Heywood and Davies: a change in the tradition of the 16th-century satiric epigram. Satire News Letter 5 1967.

van Dorsten, J. A. The arts of memory and poetry. E Studies 48 1967.

Gill, R. and R. Krueger. The early editions of Marlowe's Elegies and Davies's Epigrams. Library 5th ser 26 1971.

W. A. R.

III. THE ELIZABETHAN SONNET

See also under Poetry: Introduction, above.

(1) MODERN ANTHOLOGIES

Dyce, A. Specimens of English sonnets. 1833.

Main, D. M. A treasury of English sonnets. 1880.

—— Three hundred English sonnets. Edinburgh 1884.

Crow, M. F. Elizabethan sonnet cycles. 4 vols 1896–8. Reprints Lodge's Phillis, Fletcher's Licia, Daniel's Delia, Constable's Diana, Drayton's Idea, Griffin's Fidessa, Smith's Chloris, Greville's Caelica.

Quiller-Couch, A. T. English sonnets. 1897.

Nichols, J. B. B. A little book of English sonnets. 1899.

Lee, S. Elizabethan sonnets. 2 vols Westminster 1904. Introd; reprints Sidney's Astrophel and Stella, T.W.'s Tears of fancie, Barnes's Parthenophil and Parthenophe, Lodge's Phillis, Fletcher's Licia, Constable's Diana, Daniel's Delia, Percy's Coelia, Zepheria, Drayton's Idea, Spenser's Amoretti, Griffin's Fidessa, R.L.'s Diella, Smith's Chloris, Tofte's Laura (not sonnets).

Robertson, W. The golden book of English sonnets. 1913.

Crosland, T. W. H. The English sonnet. [1917].

B., B. A garland of Elizabethan sonnets. 1923.

(2) GENERAL STUDIES

Gascoigne, G. Certayne notes of instruction concerning the making of verse. In his Posies, 1575.

Sidney, Sir P. The defence of poesie. 1595. Written c. 1582.

James VI. The essayes of a prentise in the divine art of poesie. Edinburgh 1584.

[Puttenham, G.] The arte of English poesie. 1589.

Warton, T. A history of English poetry: an unpublished continuation. Ed R. M. Baine, Los Angeles 1953 (Augustan Reprint Soc). Written before 1790.

Lentzner, C. A. Ueber das Sonett und seine Gestaltung in der englischen Dichtung bis Milton. Halle 1886.

Koeppel, E. Studien zur Geschichte des englischen Petrarchismus. Romanische Forschungen 5 1890.

Kastner, L. E. Elizabethan sonneteers and the French poets. MLR 3 1903.

Lee, S. Elizabethan sonnets vol 1. 1904. Introd.

—— In his French Renaissance in England, Oxford 1910.

Zocco, I. Petrarchismo e Petrarchisti in Inghilterra. Palermo 1906.

Scott, M. A. In her Elizabethan translations from the Italian, Boston 1916.

Bullock, W. L. The genesis of the English sonnet form. PMLA 38 1923.

Schirmer, W. F. Das Sonett in der englischen Literatur. Anglia 37 1925.

Scott, J. G. The names of the heroines of Elizabethan sonnet-sequences. RES 2 1926.

—— Minor Elizabethan sonneteers and their greater predecessors. Ibid.

—— Les sonnets élisabéthains. Paris 1929.

Hasselkuss, H. K. Der Petrarkismus in der Sprache der englischen Sonnettdichter der Renaissance. Münster 1927.

[Fries, C. C.] The early modern English dictionary: sonnet. PMLA 47 1932.

Pearson, L. E. Elizabethan love conventions. Berkeley 1933.

Vaganay, H. Les sonnets élisabéthains. Revue de Littérature Comparée 14 1934.

Brewer, W. Sonnets and sestinas. Boston 1937.

John, L. C. The Elizabethan sonnet sequences: studies in conventional conceits. New York 1938.

Parker, W. R. The sonnets in Tottel's Miscellany. PMLA 54 1939.

Rollins, H. E. In his New variorum edition of Shakespeare's sonnets, 2 vols Philadelphia 1944.

Siegel, P. N. The Petrarchan sonneteers and Neo-Platonic love. SP 42 1946.

Bullitt, J. M. The use of rhyme link in the sonnets of Sidney, Drayton and Spenser. JEGP 49 1950.

Smith, H. In his Elizabethan poetry, Cambridge Mass 1952. Ch 3.

Mönch, W. Das Sonett: Gestalt und Geschichte. Heidelberg 1955.

Lever, J. W. The Elizabethan love sonnet. 1956.

Prince, F. T. The sonnet from Wyatt to Shakespeare. In Elizabethan poetry, ed J. R. Brown and B. Harris 1960.

Schaar, C. An Elizabethan sonnet problem: Shakespeare's Sonnets, Daniel's Delia and their literary background. Lund 1960.

—— Elizabethan sonnet themes and the dating of Shakespeare's sonnets. Lund 1962.

Leishman, J. B. Themes and variations in Shakespeare's sonnets. 1961.

Hayes, L. A. The sonnets. Pittsburgh 1966.

Watson, G. The English Petrarchans: a critical bibliography of the Canzoniere. 1967 (Warburg Inst).

(3) INDIVIDUAL SONNETEERS

The Earliest English Sonnets to 1590

This list attempts to be complete. J. Bale (Index, ed Poole p. 66) said that Edmund first Baron Sheffield (d. 1549) wrote 'Sonettos Italico more', but no trace of these remains. Thomas Warton, History of English poetry vol 3, 1781, p. 58, said on the authority of Oldys that 'Henry Lord Berners translated some of Petrarch's sonnets'; there was no Henry Lord Berners, and John Bourchier Lord Berners (d. 1533) is not known to have written verse. Warton's mention (p. 58) of a ms owned by Lord Eglinton containing sonnets by Henry VIII refers to BM ms additional 31,922 which contains no quatorzains. The anon sonnet ptd from a ms of G. Bowes by Wright and Halliwell, Reliquiae antiquae vol 2, 1843, is by Gascoigne.

Wyatt, Sir Thomas (d. 1542): 29 (24 in BM ms Egerton 2711, 5 more in R. Tottel, Songes and sonettes, 1557, in Rollins' edn nos 75, 84, 101 (double), 102, plus 3 rondeaux rewritten as sonnets, nos 69–70, 103); all ptd G. F. Nott, Works of Surrey and Wyatt vol 2, 1816.

BM ms additional 17,492 (Devonshire ms): 4 (3 anon, folios 75, 77, 81, ptd as Wyatt's by Nott pp. 143–5; one by E.K. [Sir Edmund Knyvet d. 1546], ptd K. Muir, Proc Leeds Philosophical Soc 6 1947).

Surrey, Earl of, Henry Howard (d. 1547): 15 (14 in Tottel; Tottel no 9 is not Surrey's; one in W. Camden, Remaines, 1605); rptd G. F. Nott, Works of Surrey and Wyatt vol 1, 1815.

Lambeth ms 265, folio 106: one in Surreyan form by 'TER' in early 16th-century hand?; ptd C. F. Bühler, MLN 72 1957.

Baldwin, William (d. 1563): one in C. Langton, Treatise of phisick, 1547; rptd T. W. Camp, MLN 52 1937.

Morley, Lord, Henry Parker (d. 1556): one in BM ms Royal A xv, probably before 1547, ptd E. Flügel, Anglia 13 1891; cf his Epitaph on Lord Delaware (d. 1554) in G. Legh, Accedens of armory, 1562 (15 lines), rptd J. Loveday, 1887 (Roxburghe Club).

Hall, John (d. 1566?): one in his The proverbes of Salomon, [1549] A5; rptd as anon in Tottel, no 285; see H. E. Rollins, TLS 14 Jan 1932.

Cambridge University Library ms Mm.3.12 p. 287: one anon on Bp W. Rugg, c. 1549.

BM ms additional 36,529, folios 44ᵛ–8 and 66ᵛ: 14 anon mid 16th-century; 12 ptd K. Muir, Proc Leeds Philosophical Soc 6 1950.

Bieston, Roger: one in his The bayte and snare of fortune, [1550?] B4ᵛ.

Trinity College Dublin ms D.2.7 (Blage ms): 3 anon before 1551; ptd K. Muir, Unpublished poems from the Blage ms, Liverpool 1960, pp. 6, 9, 17.

Whythorne, Thomas (d. 1596): one in Bodley ms English Miscellaneous c. 33, written c. 1555; ptd J. M. Osborn, The autobiography of Whythorne, Oxford 1961, p. 70.

Vaux?, Baron, Thomas (d. 1556): one in Tottel, no 9 (attributed to 'L Vawse' in BM ms additional 28,635 folio 139ᵛ).

Grimald, Nicholas (d. 1562): 3 in Tottel, nos 137, 146, 156.

Tottel, R. Songes and sonnettes 1557: 9 anon (nos 173, 179, 186, 218–19, 232–3, 241, 300).

Harington? John, the elder (d. 1582): 2 written after 1558 ptd in Nugae antiquae, ed H. Chalmers 1769 pp. 87, 198.

Anon: 26 in A meditation of a penitent sinner in maner of a paraphrase upon the 51 psalme, appended to A.L., Sermon of Calvin upon Ezechias, 1560.

Dorset, Earl of, Thomas Sackville (d. 1608): one in T. Hoby's trn of Castiglione's Courtyer, 1561; rptd E. Flügel, Anglia 13 1891.

Blundeville, Thomas: one written 1561 in his Three morall treatises 1580 B5ᵛ.

Broke, Arthur (d. 1563): 5 (3 in his Tragicall historye of Romeus and Juliet, 1562; rptd P. A. Daniel 1875 (New Shakespeare Soc); 2 in L. Humphrey, The nobles, 1563; ed V. B. Heltzel, Shakespeare Quart 22 1971).

Googe, Barnabe (d. 1594): 3 in his Eglogs, epytaphes and sonettes, 1563 (2 by Googe and one tailed by L. Blundeston); ed E. Arber 1871 pp. 95, 98, 105; cf 91. See H. H. Hudson, Poetry of the English Renaissance, New York 1929 p. 952, and P. N. U. Hartung, E Studies 11 1929.

Garter, Bernard (fl. 1563–78): 3 in his Tragicall historie between two English lovers 1563, 1565.

Gascoigne, George (d. 1577): 37 (one in his Jocasta 1566, ptd 1575, 31 in his A hundreth sundrie flowres 1573, one more in his Posies 1575, one in his Hemetes the heremyte [BM ms Royal 18A.xlviii 1576], one in 2nd edn of [T. Bedingfield's] trn of Cardanus comforte 1576, one in Sir Humphrey Gilbert, A discourse of a new passage to Cataia 1576, one in C. Holyband, Frenche Littleton [1576]); all rptd in Works of Gascoigne, ed J. W. Cunliffe 2 vols Cambridge 1907–10.

Fulwood, W.: one in his Enimie of idlenesse, 1568 A5.

Fyldinge, Ferdinand: one in T. Jeney, Discours of the present troobles in France, 1568 D4ᵛ; ed J. A. van Dorsten, The radical arts, Leyden 1970.

Spenser, Edmund (d. 1599): 87 (2 in J. van der Noodt, A theatre [of] worldlings 1569 (with 14 unrhymed quatorzains), one written c. 1580 in ms (Cambridge Univ Dd.5.75 folio 37ᵛ, Bodley Rawlinson Poetry 85 folio 7ᵛ, BM Harley 1392 (2) folio 28, later ptd as Amoretti no 8; see L. Cummings, Stud in Eng Lit 1500–1900 4 1964), one dated 1586 in G. Harvey, Foure letters 1592, 17 in his Faerie Queene 1590, 66 in his Complaints 1591 (entered 1590, with 2 ptd 1569]). Written later: 87 more in his Amoretti 1595, 3 commendatory 1595, 1596, 1599; all rptd in Poetical works, ed Smith and de Selincourt 3 vols Oxford 1909–10.

Arundel Harington ms: 4 anon written in 1560's?; ed R. Hughey, Columbus 1960, nos 146, 150, 256, 258.

Goodyer, Sir Henry (d. 1595) and Thomas Norton (d. 1584); 6 written 1572 (3 each in Bodley ms Gough Norfolk 43 folio 53ᵛ (ed J. P. Collier, Camden Miscellany 3 1855), Arundel Harington ms ed Hughey nos 147–8, and Goodyer's 3 only in Marsh's Library Dublin ms Z.3.5.21 folios 2–3).

Tusser, Thomas (d. 1580): 2 in his Five hundreth points of good husbandry 1573; ed W. Payne and S. J. Herrtage 1878 (English Dialect Soc) pp. 150–1.

M.C. and R.S.: 2 (one each in Gascoigne's Posies 1575); rptd Cunliffe vol 1, 1907.

Bowyer, Nicholas: one in Gascoigne's Steele glas 1576; rptd Cunliffe vol 2, 1910.

E.S.: one in Paradyse of daynty devises 1576; ed H. E. Rollins, Cambridge Mass 1927, no 38.

Sidney, Sir Philip (d. 1586): 139+3? (18 in his Old Arcadia 1577–80, 13 in his Certain sonnets 1577–81, 108 in his Astrophel and Stella c. 1582, 2 possibly his in H. Goldwel, A briefe declaration [1581]; see E. G. Fogel, MLN 75 1960; one possibly his in Bodley ms Rawlinson Poetry 85); all rptd in Poems, ed Ringler, Oxford 1962.

Whetstone, George (d. 1587?): 2 (one in his A remembraunce of G. Gaskoigne [1577?], rptd A. Chalmers, English poets vol 2, 1810; one in his A mirror of Fraucis Earle of Bedford 1575, rptd T. Park, Heliconia vol 2, 1815).

P[roctor], T[homas], A gorgious gallery of gallant inventions 1578: 5 anon F4ᵛ, H1ᵛ, I3, O2ᵛ, O4; ed H. E. Rollins, Cambridge Mass 1926.

W.A., A speciall remedie against the furious force of lawlesse love 1578: 2 e4ᵛ; rptd H. Ellis 1844 (Roxburghe Club).

J.C., A poor knight his pallace of private pleasures 1579:
3 I1v–2; rptd H. Ellis 1844 (Roxburghe Club).

Churchyard, Thomas (d. 1604): 2 (one in his Chance
1580 [entered 1578] K2, one in his Charge 1580 D2v).

Dyer, Sir Edward (d. 1607): one written c. 1581 ptd with
Sidney's Certain sonnets 1598; rptd R. M. Sargent,
Life and lyrics of Dyer, Oxford 1935.

Howell, Thomas H. his devises 1581: 14 (12 by Howell,
one by E.L., one by J[ohn] K[eeper]); ed W. Raleigh,
Oxford 1906 (facs).

Watson, Thomas (d. 1593): 3 (one in his Hecatompathia
[1582], ed E. Arber 1870; 2 in his Italian madrigalls
englished 1590, rptd F. I. Carpenter JEGP 2 1899).
One later probably his in Phoenix nest 1593 O1v, ed
H. E. Rollins, Cambridge Mass 1931.

Bucke, G[eorge] (d. 1623): one in Watson's Hecatompathia [1582], ed E. Arber 1870.

Yates, James: 2 in his The castell of courtesie 1582 Q1v.

Brooke, Baron, Fulke Greville (d. 1628): 41 in his Caelica,
written after 1582; ptd in Workes written in his youth
with Sir P. Sidney 1633; ed G. Bullough, Poems and
dramas of Greville vol 1, 1939.

BM ms additional 15,232 fols 9v–11v: 5 anon after 1582.

Harvard ms f MS English 1015 folio 17: 2 anon before 1583.

Young, Bartholomew: 29 tr 1583 in his Diana of George
of Montemayor 1598; pts 1 and 3 ed J. M. Kennedy,
Oxford 1968.

Soowthern, John, Pandora 1584: 25; ed G. B. Parks, New
York 1938 (facs).

BM ms additional 41,499A folio 6: one anon 1584; ptd
E. K. Chambers, Sir Henry Lee, Oxford 1936, p. 271.

Gorges, Sir Arthur (d. 1625): 27 in BM ms Egerton 3165
written 1584–9 (with 4 written after 1599); ed H. E
Sandison, Poems of Gorges, Oxford 1953.

Dymoke, [Sir] Edward (d. 1625): 3 in Univ of Edinburgh
ms De.5.96 folios 2–3, on Sir Philip Sidney after 1586.

Byrd, W. Psalmes sonets and songs 1588: 2 anon (nos
18, 20); rptd E. H. Fellowes, English madrigal verse,
Oxford 1920.

Yonge, N. Musica transalpina 1588: 6 anon; rptd A. H.
Bullen, Some shorter Elizabethan poems [1903].

Bodley ms Rawlinson Poetry 85: 6 anon after 1588, folios
9, 16v, 18v(2), 25v, 108v.

Byrd, W. Songs of sundrie natures 1589: 6 anon (nos 10,
12, 15, 17, 26, 36); rptd Fellowes 1920.

Lodge, Thomas (d. 1625): 4 (2 in his Scillaes metamor-
phosis 1589, 2 in his Rosalynde 1590). Later 40 in his
Phillis 1593, one in Phoenix nest 1593, one in his
Margarite of America 1596; all ed E. Gosse, Works of
Lodge, 4 vols Glasgow 1883.

Breton, Nicholas (d. 1626?): 3 in his Historie of Don
Frederigo 1590; rptd J. Robertson, Poems by Breton,
Liverpool 1952 pp. xlix–l. Others later.

Constable, Henry (d. 1613): 66 (63 in South Kensington
Museum ms Dyce 44, 2 more in Marsh's Library
Dublin ms Z.3.5.21, one more in his Diana 1592 A3;
all written by 1590). Probably his written later: 17
'Spirituall sonnettes by H:C:' in BM ms Harley 7553
folios 32–40, one in Edmund Bolton, Elements of
armories 1160 A1v; all ed J. Grundy, Poems of Constable,
Liverpool 1960.

Greene, Robert (d. 1592): one in his Never too late 1590;
one later in his Groatsworth of wit 1592; ed J. C. Collins,
Plays and poems of Greene vol 2, Oxford 1905 pp. 295,
315.

Ralegh, Sir Walter (d. 1618): one in Spenser, Faerie
Queene 1590; 2 written later; ed A. M. C. Latham,
Poems of Ralegh 1951, nos 13 and 11, 12, 23.

Sylvester, Joshua (d. 1618): one in his trn of du Bartas, A
canticle of the victorie obteined by Henrie the Fourth
at Ivry, 1590. Others later.

Collections of Sonnets Printed after 1590

*For Scottish sonneteers (William Fowler, King James VI and
I, Alexander Montgomery, John Stewart of Baldynneis),
see cols 2423f., below.*

Sidney, Sir Philip. Astrophel and Stella; other sonnets of
divers gentlemen. 1591, [1597–1600] (107 by Sidney,
28 by Daniel), 1591 (corrected text, without Other
sonnets), 1598 (in Arcadia) (108, best text); rptd in 12
folio edns 1599–1674.

Spenser, Edmund. Complaints. 1591 (entered 1590)
(Ruines of Rome 33, Visions of the worlds vanitie 12,
Visions of Bellay 15, Visions of Petrarch 7).

— Amoretti. 1595 (88).

Constable, Henry. Diana by H.C. 1592 (23); Diana of
H.C. augmented, [1594–7] (2 edns) (77: 27 by Constable,
8 by Sidney, one by R. Smyth, 41 anon).

Daniel, Samuel. Delia. 1592 (50), 1592 (54), 1595 (55),
1598, 1601 (in Works) (57), 1602 (another issue), 1611,
1623.

Harvey, Gabriel. Foure letters and certaine sonnets. 1592,
1592 (19, with 4 in blank verse).

Barnes, Barnabe. Parthenophil and Parthenophe. 1593
(112).

— A divine centurie of spiritual sonnets. 1595 (100).

Fletcher, Giles, the elder. Licia. 1593 (54).

Lodge, Thomas. Phillis. 1593 (40).

T.W. The tears of fancie. 1593 (53, with 8 lost).

Lok, Henry. Sundry Christian passions. 1593 (200).

— Ecclesiasticus; sundrie sonets of Christian passions
augmented; other sonets of a feeling conscience. 1597
(88 new).

Drayton, Michael. Ideas mirrour. 1594 (51); rev and
enlarged in collections as Idea, 1599, 1600, 1602, 1605,
1608, 1610, 1613, [c. 1616], 1619, 1630, 1637 (total 107,
of which 4 not sonnets).

Percy, William. Sonnets to the fairest Coelia. 1594 (20).

Zepheria. 1594 (35). Anon.

Barnfield, Richard. Cynthia; certaine sonnets [20];
Cassandra. 1595.

E.C. Emaricdulfe. 1595 (40).

Chapman, George. Ovids banquet of sence; a coronet for
his mistresse philosophie [10]; amorous zodiacke. 1595.

Griffin, Bartholomew. Fidessa. 1596 (62).

R.L. Diella: certain sonnets [38]; Don Diego and
Gynevra. 1596.

Smith, William. Chloris. 1596 (50).

Salusbury, Sir John. The patrone his pathetical posies,
appended to Robert Parry, Sinetes passions, 1597
(32).

Rogers, Thomas. Celestiall elegies. 1598 (41).

Davies, Sir John. Hymnes of Astraea in acrosticke verse.
1599 (26).

— Gulling sonnets (9), written 1596–1604; ptd from ms
1873.

— Epithalamion on the marriage of Elizabeth Vere and
the Earl of Derby (10), written 1595; ptd from ms
1962.

Newton, Thomas. Atropoion Delion: the death of Delia
[Queen Elizabeth]. 1603 (26).

Stirling, Earl of, Sir William Alexander. Aurora: the
first fancies of the authors youth. 1604 (106), probably
written before 1592.

Shakespeare, William. Sonnets. 1609 (154), written in
1590's?

C[onstable], H[enry]. Spiritual sonnettes (17), written in
1590's; ptd from ms 1815.

Alabaster, William. Divine meditations (77), written
1597–8; ptd from ms 1959.

W. A. R.

IV. MINOR TUDOR POETRY

Authors are listed here who pbd long poems or collections of verse of more than pamphlet length ; cross-references are given for major and minor poets whose main entries appear in other sections. Authors of only dispersed shorter poems are not listed. A card file listing first lines and authors of all ptd and ms verse of the Tudor period is being compiled at the University of Chicago.

Ritson, J. Bibliographia poetica. 1802. Lists works by 569 16th-century poets.

British Museum Department of Manuscripts. English poetry: first and last lines. 17 vols, ms in Students' Room; microfilm copies at Shakespeare Institute, Stratford; Washington Univ Library, St Louis; Univ of Chicago Library. Includes acquisitions to c. 1900; no author-index.

Lee, S. Elizabethan sonnets. 2 vols 1904. Texts and first-line index of 15 collections.

English madrigal verse 1588–1632. Ed E. H. Fellowes, Oxford 1920; rev F. W. Sternfeld and D. Greer, Oxford 1967. Texts, with first-line and author-indexes, of contents of all the song books.

Rollins, H. E. Edns of ptd Tudor anthologies 1920–37. *See col 1007f., above.*

— Index to ballad entries in the Stationers' Registers. SP 21 1924.

Brown, C. and R. H. Robbins. Index of Middle English verse. New York 1943. Supplement by R. H. Robbins and J. L. Cutler, Lexington Kentucky 1965. Includes many 16th-century items.

Zocca, L. Elizabethan narrative verse. New Brunswick NJ 1950. Author-index.

Williams, F. B., jr. Index of dedications and commendatory verses in English books before 1641. Oxford 1962 (Bibl Soc).

Crum, M. First-line index of English poetry 1500–1800 in mss of the Bodleian Library. 2 vols Oxford 1968. Contains author-index, and identifies many anon items.

T.A.

The massacre of money. 1602. An allegory, 'the first fruites of my labours'. Wrongly attributed to T. Achelley and T. Aylworth.

W.A. artificer

A speciall remedie against the furious force of lawlesse love. 1579; ed H. Ellis 1844 (Roxburghe Club). 10 didactic poems. Wrongly attributed to W. Averell.

THOMAS ACHELLEY
fl. 1568–95

Ms: Cupidinis et Psychis nuptiae heroico carmine donata, *Harvard ms English 1277 (dated 1573).*

§1

The key of knowledge: prayers and meditations. [1572]. Prose.

A most lamentable historie conteyning the tyrannie which Violenta executed upon her lover Didaco. 1576.

Commendatory poem. In T. Watson, Hekatompathia, [1582].

Englands Parnassus. 1600. Contains 13 unidentified verse quotations attributed to Achelly.

§2

Ritson, J. In his Bibliographia poetica, 1802. Violenta and Didaco from tale 42 of W. Painter, Palace of pleasure, 1566.

Jones, C. E. The English Boccaccio. Neuphilologische Mitteilungen 57 1956.

Freeman, A. The writings of Achelley. Library 5th ser 35 1970.

ADAM BELL

Adambel, Clym of the Cloughe, and Wyllyam of Cloudesle. [1510?] (fragment), 1536 (fragment), [c. 1565], 1605, [c. 1605], 1610, 1628, [c. 1630], 1632, [c. 1640], 1648, 1668, 1683, 1698, [1700?]; rptd in Percy's Reliques 1765, [Ritson's] Ancient popular poetry 1791, Hazlitt's Remains vol 2, 1866, Child's Ballads 1888 no 116.

WILLIAM ALABASTER
1568–1640

Manuscripts

Elisaeis: apotheosis poetica principis Elizabethae, liber primus. Mss Bodley Rawlinson D 293, Emmanuel College Cambridge 68, Newberry Library 210,756.

The conversion of Alabaster. Ms English College Rome. Prose autobiography written 1598.

Epigrammata. Bodley mss Rawlinson D 283, 293.

§1

Roxana tragædia. 1632 (anon), 1632 (a plagiarii unguibus vindicata, aucta et agnita). *See col 1763, below.*

Sonnets. Ed G. M. Story and H. Gardner, Oxford 1959. 77 sonnets written 1597–8, from mss.

See DNB and Story's introd to Sonnets, *above, for Latin theological treatises.*

§2

Hallam, H. In his Introduction to the literature of Europe vol 3, 1854.

Dobell, B. The sonnets of Alabaster. Athenaeum 26 Dec 1903.

Pollen, J. H. Alabaster: a newly discovered Catholic poet. Month April 1904.

Boas, F. S. In his University drama in the Tudor age, Oxford 1914.

Guiney, L. I. In her Recusant poets, 1938.

Bradner, L. In his Musae anglicanae, New York 1940.

Rope, H. E. G. The conversion of Alabaster. Venerabile (Rome) Dec 1948.

Dickinson, J. Southwell's Burning babe and Alabaster. N & Q Nov 1961.

— V. Colonna, Desportes and Alabaster. Revue de Littérature Comparée 25 1961.

Kawasaki, T. From Southwell to Donne. Stud in Eng Lit (Tokyo) 39 1963.

Sakamoto, Y. Alabaster's Sonnets and the Counter-Reformation. Domisha Univ Stud in Humanities 108 1968.

SIR WILLIAM ALEXANDER,
EARL OF STIRLING
1567?–1640

Collections

The monarchick tragedies. 1604 (Croesus and Darius only; probably part of Woorkes with 1604 Aurora and 1604 Paraenesis), 1607 (reissue of Croesus and Darius with cancel title, adding Alexandræan tragedy and Julius Caesar), 1616.

Recreations with the Muses. 1637. Foure monarchicke tragedies, Doomes-day, A paraenesis to Prince Henry, Jonathan an heroicke poeme.

Poems. Ed A. Chalmers, English poets vol 5, 1810. Omits tragedies.

Selected poems. Ed E. Sanford, Works of the British poets vol 4, Philadelphia 1819. 13 poems from Aurora.

Poetical works. Ed R. Alison 3 vols Glasgow 1870–2.

Poetical works. Ed L. E. Kastner and H. B. Charlton 2 vols 1921–9 (STS). With bibliography and essay on Senecanism.

§1

A short discourse of the late attemptat against his Majesties person. [Edinburgh] 1600, [London] 1600 (piracy). Anon prose, on Gowrie conspiracy.

The tragedie of Darius. Edinburgh 1603, London 1604 (probably part of Monarchick tragedies).

Aurora: containing the first fancies of the authors youth. 1604. 106 sonnets and 20 other poems, probably written before 1592.

A paraenesis to the Prince [Henry]. 1604.

An elegie on the death of Prince Henrie. Edinburgh 1612, 1613 (variant issue).

Doomes-day. [Edinburgh] 1614, London 1720.

Supplement by Sir W. A[lexander], to bk 3 of Sir Philip Sidney's Arcadia. 1616–18 (2 settings), bound in 1613, Dublin 1621, London 1622–3 (Arcadia; see Mitchell 1969, below); rptd in 8 edns of Arcadia 1627–1739, and in edn by E. A. Baker 1907, 1921. Prose.

An encouragement to colonies. 1624, 1625 (variant issue), 1630 (another issue as The mapp of New-England); rptd 1867 (Bannatyne Club); ed E. F. Slafter, Alexander and American colonization, Boston 1873 (Prince Soc). Prose.

The psalmes of King David translated by King James. Oxford 1631 etc; Edinburgh 1712 (as part of The book of common prayer for the use of the Church of Scotland). Partly the work of Alexander; see Holland 1843, below and col 1909, below.

Anacrisis: a censure of some poets ancient and modern. In Works of William Drummond of Hawthornden, Edinburgh 1711; ed J. E. Spingarn, Critical essays of the 17th century vol 1, Oxford 1908. Prose; written c. 1634.

§2

Reasons against the reception of King James' metaphrase of the Psalms. Bannatyne Miscellany 1 1827.

[James I]. The complaint of the Muses upon Sir W. Alexander. Ms sonnet ptd in Miscellany of the Abbotsford Club vol 1, Edinburgh 1837.

Holland, J. In his Psalmists of Britain vol 1, 1843.

Rogers, C. In his Memorials of the Earl of Stirling, 2 vols 1877.

Beumelburg, H. Alexander als dramatischer Dichter. Halle 1880.

Fergusson, R. M. In his Alexander Hume and his intimates, Paisley 1899.

Kastner, L. E. The Scottish sonneteers and the French poets. MLR 3 1907.

Rohr-Sauer, P. von. In his English metrical psalms from 1600 to 1660, Freiburg 1938.

MacGrail, T. H. Sir W. Alexander. Edinburgh 1940.

A., E. L. A plea for new Scotland. More Books 16 1941.

Dent, R. W. John Webster's debt to Alexander. MLN 65 1950.

—— In his John Webster's borrowing, Berkeley 1960.

Wiles, A. G. D. The date of publication and composition of Alexander's Supplement to Sidney's Arcadia. PBSA 50 1956.

—— Alexander's continuation of Sidney's Arcadia. Stud in Scottish Lit 3 1966.

McDiarmid, M. P. Scots versions of poems by Sir Robert Aytoun and Alexander. N & Q Jan 1957.

Gordon, T. C. In his Four notable Scots, Stirling 1960.

Juel-Jensen, B. Some uncollected authors. Book Collector 11 1962.

Ure, P. The Duchess of Malfi: another debt to Alexander. N & Q Aug 1966.

Revard, S. P. Milton's Eve and the Evah of Alexander's Dommes-day. Papers on Lang & Lit 3 1967.

Mitchell, A. and K. Foster. Alexander's Supplement to Sidney's Arcadia. Library 5th ser 24 1969.

THOMAS ALSOPPE

The brevyate tragycall hystorie of the fayre Custance. [c. 1525] (fragment). Based on Chaucer's Man of Law's tale.

ROBERT ARMIN
1565?–1610

Quips upon questions: a clownes conceite, by C. de C. Snuffe. 1600; ed F. Ouvry 1875 (attributed to John Singer; but see T. W. Baldwin, MLN 39 1924).

The Italian taylor and his boy. 1609; rptd 1810; ed A. B. Grosart, Works of Armin, Manchester 1880. Tr from Straparola 8.5.

For plays and jest book, see cols 1729, 2027, below.

HENRY ARTHINGTON
fl. 1592–1607

§1

The seduction of Arthington by Hacket. [1592]. Prose and 5 poems.

The exhortation of Salomon. 1594. Prose sermon.

Provision for the poore explaned. 1597. Prose sermon.

Principall points of holy profession. 1607.

§2

[Cosin, R.] Conspiracie for pretended reformation. 1592.

JAMES ASKE

Elizabetha triumphans: the practizes the Popes have used by moving her subjects to rebellion, how her Excellency was entertained at Tilbery, and the overthrow had against the Spanish fleete. 1588; rptd J. Nichols, Progresses of Queen Elizabeth vol 2, 1823.

LEMEKE AVALE

A commemoration or dirige of bastarde Edmonde Boner. 1569.

WILLIAM AVERELL, schoolmaster

§1

An excellent historic of Charles and Julia, two Welshe lovers. 1581.

A dyall for dainty darlings. 1584, 1590 (as Foure notable histories, whereunto is added a dialogue expressing the corruptions of this age). Prose fiction.

A mervailous combat of contrarieties. 1588. Prose dialogue.

§2

Hale, D. G. The fable of the belly. Comparative Lit Stud 5 1968.

R.B.

Orpheus his journey to Hell and his music to the ghosts. [1595].

SIR NICHOLAS BACON
1509–79

§1

The recreations of his age. Ed [C.H.O.] Daniel, Oxford 1919. 36 poems written before 1558 edited from ms of M. H. Marsden (another ms Huntington Library HM 1340).
[Latin verse inscriptions in his house at Gorhambury]. In J. Weever, Ancient funerall monuments, 1631.

§2

Hudson, H. H. In his Epigram in the English Renaissance, Princeton 1947.
Sandeen, E. R. The origin of Bacon's book-plate. Trans of Cambridge Bibl Soc 2 1958.
Simpson, A. In his Wealth of the gentry, Cambridge 1961. Ch 2.

ROBERT BAKER
fl. 1563

The first voyage to Guinie with the Minion 1562; the second voyage to Guinie in 1563. In R. Hakluyt, Principall navigations, 1589 (L5ᵛ–M5ᵛ); ed D. B. Quinn and R. A. Skelton, Cambridge 1965 (facs). See B. Penrose, Baker: an ancient mariner of 1565, Boston 1942 (Club of Odd Volumes).

WILLIAM BALDWIN
c. 1515–63

Collections

The mirror for magistrates. Ed L. B. Campbell, Cambridge 1938. Item nos below refer to this edn.
Beware the cat; Funerals of Edward VI. Ed W. P. Holden, New London Conn 1963.

§1

Sonnet before C. Langton, Treatise of phisick, 1547; ed T. W. Camp, MLN 52 1936; Holden p. 86.
A treatise of morall phylosophie. 1547 (for 1548) (4 bks, prose and 62 verse tags), 1550 (for 1551), [1551 ?], [1552 ?], [c. 1555], [c. 1555] (enlarged T. Paulfreyman; 7 bks, 104 verse tags), 1557 (for 1558 ?), 1564 ('again enlarged by the first aucthor'; 10 bks, 151 verse tags), 1567 (3rd time enlarged T. Paulfreyman), 1571, 1575, 1579 (4th time enlarged), 1584, 1587, 1591, 1596, 1600, 1605, 1610, [c. 1620] ('sixt time enlarged'), [c. 1620], [c. 1620], [c. 1637], [c. 1640], 1651; ed E. Arber 1908 (from 4-bk c. 1555]; ed R. H. Bowers, Gainesville 1967 (facs of c. 1620).
The canticles or balades of Salomon in Englysh metres. 1549.
A memorial of suche princes as have been unfortunate in England. [1554?]. Fragment of suppressed edn of Mirror; probably contained 21 tragedies: the 19 ptd 1559, with Ferrer's Duke Humfrey and Elianor Cobham ptd 1578.
A myrroure for magistrates. [1559]. Contains 19 tragedies: dedication, to the reader, prose links and nos 4, 8, 13, 18 by Baldwin; 2, 7, 9–12, 14–17 probably by Baldwin; 1, 3 by G. Ferrers; 5 by T. Chaloner; 6 by T. Phaer; 19 doubtfully attributed to J. Skelton; see R. S. Kinsman, HLQ 29 1966.
A myrrour for magistrates. 1563. Adds Induction and 8 tragedies: prose links and probably nos 20 and 23 by

Baldwin, 21 by J. Dolman, Induction and 22 by Sackville, 24 by F. Seager, 25 by T. Churchyard, 26 by G. Ferrers, 27 by Cavyl. For later edns and comment see col 000, above.
Beware the cat. 1570 (J. Alde, preserved only in transcript in BM additional ms 24,628, ptd J. O. Halliwell[-Phillipps] 1864), 1570 (W. Gryffith, fragment), 1584; preliminaries ed W. C. Hazlitt, Prefaces dedications epistles, 1874; ed Holden 1963 (from 1584). Satirical prose fiction, one poem, written c. 1553.
The funeralles of King Edward the Sixt. 1560 (for 1561?), 1610 (wrongly attributed to Sir J. Cheke), 1817 (Roxburghe Club, from 1560); ed W. Trollope, History of Christ's Hospital, 1834 (from 1610). 2 poems written 1553.

§2

A shorte answere to the boke called Beware the cat. [1570]; ed H. Huth, Fugitive tracts in verse: first series, 1875; Holden 1963.
Collier, J. P. In his History of English dramatic poetry vol 1, 1831.
H[ore], H. F. Old Irish tales. N & Q 3 April 1852.
—— Beware the cat. Jnl Kilkenny Archaeological Soc 5 1859.
Malcomson, R. Beware the cat. Jnl of Historical & Archaeological Assoc of Ireland 3rd ser 1 1868.
Trench, W. F. Baldwin. Modern Quart of Lang & Lit 1 1899.
Brie, F. Beware the cat. Anglia 37 1913.
—— Baldwin als Dramatiker. Anglia 38 1914.
Feuillerat, A. Documents relating to the revels at Court in the time of King Edward VI and Queen Mary. Louvain 1914.
Feasey, E. I. Baldwin. MLR 20 1925.
Starnes, D. T. Sir T. Elyot and the Sayings of the philosophers. SE 13 1933.
Campbell, L. B. The lost play of Aesop's crow. MLN 49 1934.
Camp, T. W. Another version of [Surrey's] The thinges that cause a quiet lyffe. MLN 52 1937.
Bühler, C. F. Baldwin's use of the Dictes and sayings. Speculum 23 1948.
Freeman, A. Baldwin: the last years. N & Q Aug 1961.
But see M. Maclure, Paul's cross sermons, Toronto 1958.

JOHN BALE
1495–1563

An answere to a papystycall exhortacyon pretendyng to avoyde false doctryne. [Antwerp c. 1548] (anon); ed H. Huth, Fugitive tracts in verse: first series, 1875.
For his plays see col 1403, below and for his bibliographical collections which list many poets, col 807, above. See also Hugh Hilarie, below.

THE BANQUET OF DAINTIES
The banquet of dainties. [1566?].

WILLIAM BARLOW, Bishop of Chichester
d. 1568

Rede me and be not wrothe. [Strasbourg 1528], [Antwerp] 1546. Anon; also attributed to William Roy.
A propre dyaloge betwene a gentillman and an husband man. [Antwerp 1529?], 1530 (with prose Treatyse that we ought to have the scripture in Englysshe). Anon; also attributed to Roy. This and Rede me ed F. Fry 1863 and ed E. Arber 1871; see A. Koszul, Was Bp Barlowe Friar Jerome Barlowe?, RES 4 1928.

BARNABE BARNES
1571–1609

Collections
Poems. Ed A. B. Grosart, [Blackburn] 1875.

§1

Parthenophil and Parthenophe: sonnettes, madrigals, elegies and odes. [1593] (anon); ed E. Arber, English garner vol 5, 1882; ed S. Lee, Elizabethan sonnets vol 1, 1904; ed M. H. Dodds, Ten poems, Tynemouth 1929 (selection); ed V. A. Doyno, Carbondale 1971.

A divine centurie of spirituall sonnets. 1595; ed T. Park, Heliconia vol 2, 1815.

Foure bookes of offices enabling privat persons for the service of princes. 1606. Prose.

The Divils charter: a tragaedie of Pope Alexander the Sixt. 1607; ed R. B. McKerrow 1904 (Bang's Materialien vol 6); ed [J. H. Farmer] 1913 (facs). *See col 1730, below.*

§2

Dowden, E. Barnes. Academy 2 Sept 1876.

Herford, C. H. In his Literary relations of England and Germany, Cambridge 1886.

Knight, J. Barnes. Athenaeum 20 Aug 1904.

Swaen, A. E. H. et al. Notes on the Devil's charter. MLR 1–2 1906–7.

Kastner, L. E. Elizabethan sonneteers and the French poets. MLR 3 1908.

Bayley, A. R. Barnes. N & Q 12 April 1924.

Smith, G. C. M. Barnes and Harington. TLS 10 March 1927.

Scott, J. G. In her Les sonnets élisabéthains, Paris 1929.

Eccles, M. In Thomas Lodge and other Elizabethans, ed C. J. Sisson, Cambridge Mass 1933.

Fellheimer, J. Barnes' use of G. Fenton's Historie of Guicciardin. MLN 57 1942.

Dickey, F. Forgeries in the Stationers' Register. Shakespeare Quart 11 1960.

Scharr, C. In his Elizabethan sonnet themes, Lund 1962.

Davidson, C. Barnes' Divine centurie. Lock Haven Rev 11 1969.

Jackson, M. P. Shakespeare's sonnets, Parthenophil and Parthenope and a Lover's complaint. N & Q April 1972.

RICHARD BARNFIELD
1574–1627

Ms of Shepherdes confession *etc, Folger Lib 300.2.*

Collections
Complete poems. Ed A. B. Grosart 1876 (Roxburghe Club). Wrongly attributes My flocks feed not and Isham ms items.

Poems. Ed E. Arber, Birmingham 1882.

In Some longer Elizabethan poems, ed A. H. Bullen, Westminster 1903.

Poems. Ed M. Summers [1936]. Text from Arber, above.

§1

The affectionate shepheard. 1594; ed J. O. Halliwell(–Phillipps) 1847 (Percy Soc). Anon, but claimed in Cynthia, below.

Cynthia; certaine sonnets; the legend of Cassandra. 1595, 1595; ed E. V. Utterson, Ryde 1841.

The encomion of Lady Pecunia; the complaint of poetrie for the death of liberalitie; the combat betweene conscience and covetousnesse; poems in divers humors. 1598 (separate title-pages, but continuous signatures for last 3 items), 1605 (Pecunia expanded, only 2 Poems in

divers humors); ed A. Boswell 1816 (Roxburghe Club); ed J. P. Collier, Illustrations of Old English literature vol 1, 1866.

The passionate pilgrim by W. Shakespeare. 1599. Contains 2 of Barnfield's poems.

A lovers newest curranto. [c. 1620]. Anon broadside.

[Greenes funeralls, by R.B. gent. 1594; ed R. B. McKerrow 1911, Stratford 1922. Attributed to Barnfield on slender evidence by McKerrow and H. Morris].

§2

The phonetic writings of Robert Robinson. Ed E. J. Dobson 1957 (EETS). Phonetic transcript of Lady Pecunia from 17th-century ms.

Crawford, C. Barnfield, Marlowe and Shakespeare. N & Q 14 Sept, 5 Oct 1901; rptd in Collectanea vol 1, Stratford 1906.

Henneman, J. B. Barnfield's ode As it fell upon a day. In An English miscellany for Dr [F. J.] Furnivall, Oxford 1901.

McNeir, W. F. Barnfield's borrowings from Spenser. N & Q Dec 1955.

Morris, H. Barnfield, Amyntas and the Sidney circle. PMLA 74 1959. Reply by W. F. Staton jr and Morris 76 1961.

—— Barnfield the affectionate shepheard. Tulane Stud in Eng 10 1960.

—— Barnfield: Colin's child. [Tallahassee] 1963.

WILLIAM BASSE
1580?–1654

Sword and buckler. 1602; Three pastoral elegies, 1602. *See col 1298, below.*

THOMAS BASTARD
1566–1618

§1

Chrestoleros: seven bookes of epigrames. 1598; ed A. B. Grosart, Manchester 1880; ed G. B. Harrison 1932.

Serenissimo monarchae Iacobo magnae Brittanniae. 1605. Latin verse.

Twelve sermons. 1615. Prose.

§2

Sanderson, J. L. Bastard's disclaimer of An Oxford libel. Library 5th ser 17 1962.

STEPHEN BATMAN
d. 1584

The travayled pylgrime. 1569. Allegorical narrative; trn of Olivier de la March, Le chevalier delibere, 1483. *See* S. C. Chew, Pilgrimage of life, New Haven 1962.

For prose writings see DNB.

NATHANIEL BAXTER
fl. 1569–1611

The lectures of J. Calvine upon Jonas; an exposition of the two last epistles of John by A. Marlorate. 1578 (prose tr of Latin and one poem, Baxters complaint), 1580 (without poem).

Sir Philip Sydneys Ouránia: Endimions song and tragedie containing all philosophie. 1606, 1653. *See* M. Eccles, A biographical dictionary of Elizabethan authors, HLQ 5 1942.

SIR JOHN BEAUMONT
1583–1627

The metamorphosis of tabacco. 1602. Anon.
See col 1098, below.

THOMAS BECON
1512–67
Collections

Worckes. 3 vols 1560–4. Contains Newe dialog, Invective and 15 shorter poems.
Writings. Ed J. Ayre 3 vols Cambridge 1843–4 (Parker Soc). Longer poems omitted.

§ 1

A newe dialog betwene thangell of God and the shepherdes in the felde concernynge the nativite of Jesus Christ. [1547?]; rptd in his Worckes vol 2, 1560.
An invective against whoredome. In his Worckes vol 2, 1560.
For religious prose see DNB and col 1922, below; also Hugh Hilarie, below.

§ 2

Bailey, D. S. Becon and the reformation of the Church in England. Edinburgh 1952.

LADY BESSY

The most pleasant song of Lady Bessy and how she married Henry VII. Ms of W. Bateman (late 17th century), ed T. Heywood 1829; ed J. O. Halliwell(-Phillipps) 1847 (Percy Soc) (from Bateman ms and BM ms Harley 367 c. 1600); ed F. J. Furnivall, Percy folio vol 3, 1868 (from ms c. 1650). Written after 1495.

PETER BEVERLEY

The history of Ariodanto and Jenevra. [c. 1570] (fragment), [c. 1575]. Trn of Ariosto, entered 1565–6; ed C. T. Prouty, Sources of Much ado about nothing, New Haven 1950.

ROGER BIESTON

The bayte and snare of fortune. [1554?] (2 edns). Dialogue between money and man, probably tr from C. Platin, Le débat de l'homme et de l'argent.

RALPH BIRCHENSHA

A discourse upon the late defeat given to the arch-rebels Tyrone and Odonnell. 1602.

THOMAS BLENERHASSET
1550?–1624(5?)

The seconde part of the mirrour for magistrates from the conquest of Caesar to Williame the Conquerour. 1578 (12 tragedies), 1610 (in A mirour for magistrates, newly enlarged, ed R. Niccols, 10 tragedies), 1619, 1620, 1621; ed J. Haslewood, Mirror for magistrates in five parts pt 2, 1815 (from 1578); ed L. B. Campbell, Parts added to the Mirror for magistrates, Cambridge 1946 (from 1578, with biography). *See* R. Lammerhirt, Blenerhasset's Second part of the Mirror: eine Quellenstudie, Weimar 1909.

A revelation of the true Minerva [Queen Elizabeth]. 1582; ed J. W. Bennett, New York 1941 (facs).
A direction for the plantation in Ulster. 1610. Prose.

THOMAS BLUNDEVILLE
fl. 1558–61

Three morall treatises: the learned Prince; the fruites of foes; the porte of rest [prose]. 1580 (Fruites of foes, entered 1558–9, Learned Prince 1561). Adapted from Plutarch, the first 2 in verse. *See* K. Muir, Blundeville, Wyatt and Shakespeare, N & Q Aug 1961.
For prose writings on horsemanship and science see DNB.

JOHN BON

See Luke Shepherd, below.

BOOK OF A GHOSTLY FATHER

A boke of a ghoostly fader that confesseth his ghoostly chylde. [1522?]. By 'Higgis'.

ANDREW BORDE
1490?–1549

The fyrst boke of the introduction of knowledge. [1555?], [1562?]; ed F. J. Furnivall 1870 (EETS). Prose with 41 poems on national types, written before 1548; *see* E. Cooper, Muses' library, 1737.
The merry tales of the mad-men of Gottam, by A.B. of physicke doctor. [c. 1565], 1630; ed J. O. Halliwell (-Phillipps) 1840; ed W. C. Hazlitt, Shakespeare jest-books vol 3, 1864; ed S. J. Kahrl, Evanston 1965. Prose.
For other prose writings see DNB and cols 2023, 2026, 2131, 2136, 2357, 2366, below.

HENRY BRADSHAW
d. 1513

§ 1

The holy lyfe and history of Saynt Werburge. 1521; ed E. Hawkins 1848 (Chetham Soc); ed C. Horstmann 1887 (EETS).
The lyfe of Saynt Radegunde. [1521?] (anon); ed F. Brittain, Cambridge 1926.

§ 2

Winstanley, W. In his Lives of the most famous poets, 1687.
Gerould, G. H. In his Saints' legends, Boston 1916.
Salter, F. M. An un-noticed acrostic. MLN 49 1934.
See col 649, above.

THOMAS BRICE
d. 1570

A compendious regester in metre conteining the names of the membres of Jesus Christ burned since the death of Edwarde the sixte to the beginnyng of the raign of Elizabeth. 1559, 1599 (with omissions as A briefe register); ed E. Arber, English garner vol 4, 1882.
Against filthy writing and such like delighting. [1562].

ARTHUR BROKE
d. 1563

§ 1

The tragicall historye of Romeus and Juliet, written first in Italian by Bandell. 1562, 1567, 1587; ed E. Malone, Supplement to Shakespeare, 1780; ed Boswell-Malone, Variorum Shakespeare vol 6, 1821; ed J. P. Collier,

School of Shakespeare, 1843; ed W. C. Hazlitt, Shakespeare's library vol 1, 1875; ed P. A. Daniel 1875 (Shakespeare Soc); ed J. J. Munro 1908 (modernized); ed G. Bullough, Narrative and dramatic sources of Shakespeare vol 1, 1957; Adapted from P. Boaistua and F. de Belleforest, Histoires tragiques extraictes de Bandel, Paris 1559.

The agreement of sondry places of Scripture, translated out of French. 1563 (entered 1560). Prose.

§ 2

Reddig, E. Die epische Technik Brookes. Göttingen 1927.
Bödker, A. T. Broke and his poem. E Studien 70 1935.
Crundell, H. W. Brooke and Romeo and Juliet. N & Q June 1962. On play produced at Inner Temple 1561.
Bland, D. S. Broke, G. Legh and the Inner Temple. N & Q Jan 1969.
Heltzel, V. B. A poem by Broke. Shakespeare Quart 22 1971.

THOMAS BROKE the younger

An epitaphe declaring the life and end of D. Edm. Boner; an answere [to An epitaphe made by a papist]; a reply to a slaunderous libell. [1570].

PAUL BUSHE, Bishop of Bristol
1490-1558

The extripacion of ignorancy. [1526].

E.C.

Emaricdulfe: sonnets written by E.C. esquier. 1595; ed C. Edmonds, A Lamport garland, 1881 (Roxburghe Club).

H.C.

The forrest of fancy: pleasaunte histories in meeter and prose. 1579. Prose with 51 poems.

J.C. gent.

A poor knight his pallace of private pleasures, written by a student in Cambridge and published by J.C. gent. 1579; ed H. Ellis 1844 (Roxburghe Club).

J.C.

Alcilia: Philoparthens loving folly. 1595, 1613 ('whereunto is added Pigmalions image [by J. Marston], The love of Amos and Laura [by S. Page], and also Epigrammes by Sir J. H[arington] and others'), 1619 (without Epigrammes), 1628 (contents of 1613); Alcilia rptd W. Wagner, Sh Jb 10 1875; ed A. B. Grosart, Manchester 1879; ed E. Arber, English garner vol 4, 1882; ed A. H. Bullen, Some longer Elizabethan poems, Westminster 1904.

J.C.

Saint Marie Magdalens conversion. 1603.

T.C. gent.

A pleasant and delightful history of Galesus, Cymon and Iphigenia, translated out of Italian by T.C. gent.

[c. 1565]. From Boccaccio's Decameron 5.1; see H. G. Wright, Boccaccio in England, 1957. T.C. probably identical with C.T., below.

A notable historye of Nastagio and Traversari, translated by C.T. 1569. From Boccaccio, Decameron 1.8. See Wright, above, and J. Raith, Boccaccio in der englischen Literatur, Munich 1936.

THE CALENDAR OF SHEPHERDS

The kalendayr of the shyppars. Paris 1503 (verse of the original trn in prose).

The kalender of shepherdes. 1506 (prose with 15 poems, tr for R. Pynson from Compost et kalendrier des bergers), 1508 (21 poems, rev R. Copland), [c. 1510], 1511, [1514], 15[18?] (25 poems), 1528, 1556, 1559, [1570?], [1580?], [c. 1585], [1595?], [c. 1600], 1604, 1611, 1618, 1631, 1656; ed H. O. Sommer 1892 (facs of 1503 and 1506).

CAPISTRANUS

See John of Capistrano, below.

RICHARD CAREW of Anthony
1555-1620

§ 1

Godfrey of Bulloigne: the recoverie of Hierusalem, by T. Tasso, the first part containing five cantos imprinted in both languages. [1594]; ed A. B. Grosart, Manchester 1881.

A herrings tayle: a poeticall fiction of divers matters. 1598; abridged in The survey of Cornwall, ed F. E. Halliday 1953.

For prose writings see col 2211, below.

§ 2

Nash, R. On the indebtedness of Fairfax's Tasso to Carew. Italica 34 1957.

THE CASTLE OF LABOUR

The castle of labour. [Paris c. 1503] (fragment), [London 1505?] (fragment), London 1506, [1510?], [1510?] (fragment), [1525?] (fragment); ed A. W. Pollard, Edinburgh 1905 (Roxburghe Club, facs of 1506). Anon trn of P. Gringore, Le chasteau de labour; attributed to A. Barclay by Bale; J. M. Berdan, Early Tudor poetry, 1920, against.

GEORGE CAVENDISH
1500-61?

Metrical visions. In his Life of Cardinal Wolsey, ed S. W. Singer vol 2, 1825 (from ms); extracts in English verse between Chaucer and Surrey, ed E. P. Hammond, Durham NC 1927.

See col 2205, below.

MASTER CAVYL (HUMPHREY CAVELL?)

The wilfull fall of Blacke Smyth [Michael Joseph]. In A myrrour for magistrates, 1563 etc; ed L. B. Campbell, Cambridge 1938, no 27.

JOHN CHALKHILL
fl. 1600

See col 1303, below.

SIR THOMAS CHALONER the elder
1521–65

§1

Kyng Richarde the Seconde. In A myrroure for magistrates, 1559 etc; ed L. B. Campbell, Cambridge 1938,
no 5.

In laudem Henrici Octavi. 1560. Anon but rptd 1579
below; Latin verse.

De templi divi Pauli incendio. 1561; rptd in 1579 below.
Latin verse.

De republica Anglorum instauranda libri decem [and other
shorter poems]. Ed W.Malim 1579. Latin verse written
1560–4.

Helen to Paris. In Nugae antiquae vol 2, ed T. Park 1804
(from BM additional ms 36,529).

For prose trns see DNB.

§2

Bradner, L. In his Musae anglicanae, New York 1940.

GEORGE CHAPMAN
1559?–1634

The shadow of night [etc]. 1594; Ovids banquet of sence
[etc], 1595; continuation of Marlowe's Hero and
Leander, 1598 etc; Seaven bookes of the Iliades of
Homere, 1598 (bks 1–2, 7–11); Achilles shield, 1598
(from Iliad bk 18). *See col 1637, below.*

BARTHOLOMEW CHAPPELL

The garden of prudence: a pathetical discourse touching
the vanities of the world, the calamities of hell and the
felicite of heaven. 1595.

SIR ROBERT CHESTER
fl. 1587–1601

§1

Loves martyr: or Rosalins complaint, allegorically shadowing the truth of love in the constant fate of the phoenix
and turtle, a poeme translated out of the Italian; some
new compositions of severall moderne writers [Shakes-
peare, Jonson, Chapman et al]. 1601, 1611 (as The
anuals of Great Brittaine); ed A. B. Grosart, Manchester
1878 (New Shakspere Soc). On Marriage of Sir John
Salusbury and birth of his daughter 1586–7.

Poems by Sir J. Salusbury and Chester. Ed C. Brown,
Bryn Mawr 1913, London 1914 (EETS). From Christ
Church Oxford ms 184; contains about 8 poems by
Chester.

See col 1304, below.

§2

Watson, E. Natural history in Love's martyr. Renaissance
& Modern Stud 8 1964.

THOMAS CHURCHYARD
c. 1530–1604

*Unique ms poems in BM Cotton Caligula B.v (variant of
Siege of Lieth in Chippes 1575; Egerton 2877 (The welcome*

home of the Earle of Essex from Cales 1596); *Egerton
3165 (ed H. E. Sandison, Poems of Sir Arthur Gorges,
Oxford 1953); Royal 17.B.vii (A rebuke to rebellion,
ptd Nichols vols 2–3, 1788–1823); Bodley Rawlinson Poetry
172 (ptd Goldwyn 1967); Harvard Typographical 19 (ptd
Goldwyn 1967).*

*Ms poems also in print: Arundel Harington (ed R. Hughey
1960); BM additional 15,225, 26,737, Cotton Vespasian
A.25 (ed K. Boedekker, Jahrbuch für Romanische und
Englische Sprache 14–15 1875–6), Harley 7392; Cambridge
Univ Lib Dd 5.75; Bodley Rawlinson Poetry 85; Folger
1232.3; Pepys Lib Maitland folio (ed W. A. Craigie 1919–
27 STS), Reidpeth (Cambridge Univ Lib Ll.5.10).*

Bibliographies

Ritson, J. In his Bibliographia poetica, 1802. *See* Churchyard's Challenge, 1593, for his own list of his writings;
and Chalmers, ed Chippes 1817, Adnitt 1880, and
Chester 1937, below.

Collections

The contention bettwyxte Churchyeard and Camell upon
David Dycers dreame. 1560.

The first parte of Churchyardes chippes. 1575, 1578; rptd
G. Chalmers 1817 (with memoir and bibliography);
ed J. P. Collier, Illustrations of early English poetry,
[1870]. 13 poems and prose.

A generall rehearsall of warres [prose]; some tragedies and
epitaphes. [1579] (2 issues).

A pleasaunte laborinth called Churchyardes chance. 1580.
70 poems.

A light bondell of livly discourses called Churchyardes
charge. 1580; ed J. P. Collier, Illustrations of early
English poetry, [1870]. 10 poems.

A revvying of the deade. 1591. 5 epitaphs.

A feast full of sad cheere. 1592. 8 poems.

Churchyards challenge. 1593. 18 poems, 5 prose discourses.

Nichols, J. In his Progresses of Queen Elizabeth, 3 vols
1788–1805, 1823. Pageants and verses to the Queen.

Collman, H. L. Ballads and broadsides. 1912 (Roxburghe Club). 9 broadsides.

§1

[Churchyard–Camel flyting c. 1552: see R. Lemon, Catalogue of printed broadsides in Soc of Antiquaries
London, 1866]. Davy Dycars dreame, rptd in Westerne
Wyll upon the debate betwyxte Churchyard and Camell,
c. 1552, in Chance, 1580; ed H. E. Rollins and H. Baker,
The Renaissance in England, Boston 1954; A replication
to Camels objection; The surrejoindre unto Camels
rejoindre; A playn and fynall confutacion of cammells
corlyke oblatracion; all 4 rptd in Contention, 1560, and
Collman nos 19, 21 ,23, 25.

A myrour for man. [1552], 1594 (rev in The mirror of
man).

Shores wife. In A myrrour for magistrates, 1563 etc,
1593 (rev in Challenge); ed E. Cooper, Muses' library,
1737; ed S. E. Brydges, Censura literaria vol 2, 1806;
ed Rollins and Baker, The Renaissance in England,
Boston 1954.

A farewell cauld Churcheyeards rounde. [1566]; ed J. P.
Collier, Old ballads, 1840 (Percy Soc); Collman no 26.

A greatter thanks for Churchyardes welcome home. [1566];
Collman no 28.

Churchyardes lamentacion of freyndshyp. [1566]; ed J. P.
Collier, Roxburghe ballads, 1847; Collman no 29.

Churchyardes farewell. [1566]; Collman no 30; Arundel
Harington ms, ed R. Hughey 1960, no 321.

Commendatory poem in Pithy workes of maister Skelton,
collected by J. S[tow]. 1568.

The epitaphe of the Earle of Penbroke. 1570; Collman
no 31.

Come bring in Maye with me: a discourse of rebellion. 1570.

The thre first bookes of Ovids De tristibus translated. [1572], 1578, 1580, 1816 (Roxburghe Club).

Commendatory verse to Huloets dictionarie. Ed J. Higgins 1572; ed L. B. Campbell, Parts added to the Mirror for magistrates, Cambridge 1946.

Commendatory verse to L. Lloyd, Pilgrimage of princes, [1573].

He perswadeth his freend. In Paradise of dainty devices, 1576 etc (no 23).

A prayse of maister M. Forboishers voyage to Meta Incognita. 1578. Prose, with one poem.

A discourse of the Queenes Majesties entertainement in Suffolk and Norffolk [prose and verse]; a welcome home to M. Frobusher; a commendation of Sir H. Gilberts ventrous journey. [1578]; ed Nichols vol 2, 1788, 1823; 1851.

A lamentable description of the wofull warres in Flaunders. 1578. Prose, with 2 poems.

The miserie of Flaunders, calamitie of Fraunce, misfortune of Portugall. [1579], 1876.

The moste true reporte of James Fitz Morrice death. [1579?]. Prose.

A warning for the wise of the late earthquake. 1580. Prose, with one poem.

A plaine report of the takyng of Macklin. [1580]. Prose.

A scourge for rebels. 1584. Prose.

The epitaph of Sir Phillip Sidney. [1587]; ed S. Butler, Sidneiana, 1837 (Roxburghe Club).

Thomas Wolsey. In Mirour for magistrates, 1587 etc; ed H. Morley, Cavendish's Wolsey, 1885.

The worthines of Wales. 1587; ed T. Evans 1776; ed C. E. Simms 1876 (Spenser Soc). Verse and prose.

A sparke of friendship [prose]; a description of a paper-mill built by M. Spilman. 1588; rptd in Harleian miscellany vol 3, 1774, vol 2, 1809; Nichols vol 2, 1788, 1823.

A handeful of gladsome verses given to the Queenes Majesty at Woodstocke. 1592.

A pleasant conceite presented to the Queenes Majestie. [1593]; Nichols vol 2, 1788, vol 3, 1823.

Giacomo di Grassi his true arte of defence englished by I.G. 1594. Ed Churchyard, who wrote prose dedication and To the reader.

The mirror of man [rev from 1552, above]; and manners of men. 1594; ed A. Boswell, Frondes caducae, 1816.

A musicall consort called Churchyards charitie; a praise of poetrie out of Sir Phillip Sidney. 1595; ed A. Boswell, with above.

The honor of the lawe. 1596.

A sad funerall of Sir F. Knowles. 1596; ed A. Boswell, with above.

A pleasant discourse of Court and wars called his cherrishing: a commendation of those that serve prince and countrie. 1596; ed A. Boswell, with above.

The welcome home of the Earle of Essex. 1598 (fragment). On 1596 Cadiz expedition; full text in BM Egerton ms 2877.

A wished reformation of wicked rebellion. 1598.

The fortunate farewel to the Earle of Essex. 1599; ed Nichols vols 2–3, 1788–1823.

The wonders of the ayre, the trembling of the earth. 1602.

A true discourse of the Governours in the Netherlands and the civill warres there. 1602. Prose, tr with R. Robinson from E. van Meteren; autobiographical passages added.

Sorrowful verses on [the] death of Queene Elizabeth. [1604]; Collman no 32; Rollins and Baker, The Renaissance in England, Boston 1954.

Churchyards good will: an epitaph for the Abp of Canterbury. 1604; T. Park, Heliconia vol 3, 1815; H. Huth, Fugitive tracts vol 2, 1875.

[The history of Fortunatus, abstracted in English by T.C., 1676 etc, has been attributed to Churchyard]. Prose.

§2

Winstanley, W. In his Lives of the most famous English poets, 1687.

Cooper, E. In her Muses library, 1737.

[Bliss, P.] In his Bibliographical miscellanies, Oxford 1813. Memoir and 2 autobiographical poems.

Collier, J. P. In his Poetical decameron vol 2, 1820.

Cole, R. Churchyard the poet. N & Q 9 July 1864. Transcript of will.

Jackson, J. E. Churchyard's letter to the Earl of Hertford. N & Q 27 Oct 1877.

Adnitt, H. W. Churchyard. Trans Shropshire Archaeological & Natural History Soc 3 1880, rptd Shrewsbury [1884]. Biography and bibliography.

Thaler, A. Churchyard and Marlowe. MLN 38 1923.

Byrne, M. S. Churchyard's spelling. Library 4th ser 5 1925.

Smith, G. C. M. Taking lodgings in 1591. RES 8 1932.

Gamzue, B. B. Elizabeth and literary patronage. PMLA 49 1934.

Chester, A. G. Churchyard's pension. PMLA 50 1935.

— Notes on the bibliography of Churchyard. MLN 52 1937.

Bennett, J. W. Churchyard's description of the Queen's entertainment at Woodstock in 1592. MLN 55 1940.

Zocca, L. R. In his Elizabethan narrative poetry, New Brunswick NJ 1950.

Langsam, G. G. In his Martial books and Tudor verse, New York 1951.

Lewis, C. S. The sheepheard's slumber. TLS 9 May 1952.

Rahter, C. A. Some notes on the career and personality of Churchyard. N & Q June 1960. Corrected by W. H. Challen, Aug 1961.

Goldwyn, M. H. Notes on the biography of Churchyard. RES new ser 17 1966.

— Some unpublished mss of Churchyard. SP 64 1967.

— Churchyard's marriages. N & Q Dec 1967.

Geimer, R. A. A note on the birthdate of Churchyard. N & Q Dec 1967.

— Evidence of Churchyard's first pension. RES new ser 20 1969.

Morgan, P. Fragments of lost works found in bindings: The welcome home of the Earle of Essex 1598. Bodleian Lib Record 7 1967.

Pratt, S. M. Jane Shore and the Elizabethans. Texas Stud in Lit & Lang 11 1969.

Brown, B. Churchyard and the Worthines of Wales. Anglo-Welsh Rev 18 1970.

ANTHONY CHUTE
d. 1595

Beawtie dishonoured written under the title of Shores wife. 1593.

Remonstrance to the Duke de Mayne. 1593. Prose trn.

Tabaco: the opinions of the late and best phisitions that have written of the qualities thereof. 1595; ed F. P. Wilson, Oxford 1961 (Luttrell Soc). Prose: see R. J. Kane, Chute, T. Nashe and the first English work on tobacco, RES 7 1931.

HENOCH CLAPHAM
d. 1614

A briefe of the Bible drawn into English poesy and illustrated by apt annotations. Edinburgh 1596, London 1603, 1608, 1639.

Ælohim-triune displayed by his workes physical and metaphysical in a poeme of diverse forme: the first part. 1601. On Genesis 1.

COCK LORREL'S BOAT

Cocke Lorelles bote. [1510?], [1519?] (fragment); ed H. Drury 1817 (Roxburghe Club); J. Maidment, Edinburgh 1841; E. F. Rimbault 1845 (Percy Soc); J. P. Edmond, Aberdeen 1884. *See* P. R. Baumgartner, From medieval fool to Renaissance rogue, Annuale Medievale (Duquesne) 4 1963.

GEORGE COLCLOUGH

The spectacle to repentance. 1571.

COLIN BLOWBOLS TESTAMENT

Colin Blowbols testament. Bodley ms Rawlinson C 86; ptd J. O. Halliwell(-Phillipps), Nugae poeticae, 1844; W. C. Hazlitt, Remains of Early English popular poetry vol 1, 1864.

PETER COLSE

Penelopes complaint: a mirrour for wanton minions taken out of Homers Odissea. 1596; ed A. B. Grosart, Manchester 1880.

THOMAS COMBE
fl. 1593

§1

The theatre of fine devices. 1614. Entered 1593; an emblem book tr from French of G. de la Perrière.

§2

Freeman, R. In her English emblem books, 1948.
Donno, E. S. In her edn of Sir John Harington, Metamorphosis of Ajax, 1962.

LA CONNAISSANCE D'AMOURS

A lyttell treatyse cleped la conusaunce damours. [1528?].

HENRY CONSTABLE
1562–1613

Collections
Sonnets and other poems. Ed W. C. Hazlitt 1859.
Poems and sonnets. Ed J. Gray 1897.
Poems. Ed J. Grundy, Liverpool 1960. Standard edn.

§1

Commendatory sonnet to James VI, Poeticall exercises, 1591.
Examen pacifique de la doctrine des Huguenots. 'Paris' (for London) 1589, 'Caen' (for London) 1590; tr W.W. as The Catholike moderator, 1623 (4 edns), 1624. Anon; prose.
Diana. 1592. 23 sonnets.
Diana: augmented with divers quatorzains of honorable and lerned personages. [1594], [1595]; ed J. Littledale 1818 (Roxburghe Club); [ed S. W. Singer] 1818; ed E. Arber, English garner vol 2, 1879; ed M. F. Crow, Elizabethan sonnet cycles vol 2, 1896; ed S. Lee, Elizabethan sonnets vol 2, 1904. Reprints 27 of Constable's sonnets, adds 41 by unknown authors, 8 by Sidney, one by R. Smith.

Four commendatory sonnets to Sir P. Sidney, Apologie for poetry, 1595.
A poetical rapsody. 1602. Includes 2 poems by Constable.
Harleian miscellany vol 9, ed T. Park 1812. Sonnets from the Todd ms, now Victoria & Albert Museum ms Dyce 44.
Spirituall sonnettes [from BM Harley ms 7553]. In Heliconia vol 2, ed T. Park 1815.

§2

Todd, H. J. In his Poetical works of Milton vol 5, 1801. Ms poems (now Dyce 44).
Dowden, E. An Elizabethan ms collection. Modern Quart of Lang & Lit 1 1898. Marsh's Library Dublin ms Z.3.5.21.
Kastner, L. E. Elizabethan sonneteers and the French poets. MLR 3 1908.
— The Italian sources of Daniel's Delia. MLR 7 1912.
Westcott, A. F. In his New poems by James I, New York 1911.
Scott, J. G. A Latin version of a sonnet of Constable's. MLR 20 1925.
— In her Les sonnets élisabéthains, Paris 1929. Ch 9.
Rollins, H. E. Chettle. TLS 1 Oct 1931. Poems signed H.C. in Englands Helicon not by Constable.
Guiney, L. I. In her Recusant poets, 1938.
John, L. C. In her Elizabethan sonnet sequences, New York 1938.
Muir, K. The order of Constable's sonnets. N & Q Oct 1954.
Wickes, G. In his Biographical studies vol 2, Bognor Regis 1954.
— Constable: courtier poet. Renaissance Papers 1956.
— Constable's Spiritual sonnets. Month 18 1957.
Bossy, J. A propos of Constable. Recusant History 6 1962.
Kawasaki, T. From Southwell to Donne. Stud in Eng Lit (Tokyo) 39 1963.
Sledd, H. B. The '1584' publication of Constable's Diana. SB 23 1970.

ROBERT COPLAND
fl. 1508–47

§1

The complaynte of them that ben to late maryed. [1505?] (fragment), [1518]; rptd Somers tracts vol 2, 1753, vol 8, 1815; ed J. P. Collier, Illustrations of early English popular literature vol 1, 1863. Trn of P. Gringore, La complainte de trop tard marié, 1505.
The seven sorowes that women have when theyr husbandes be deade. [1565?]. Written 1526.
A complaynt of them that be to soone maryed. 1535. Trn of P. Gringore, La complainte du trop tôt mariée.
The hye way to the spyttell hous. [1536?]; ed E. V. U[tterson], Early popular poetry vol 2, 1817; ed W. C. Hazlitt, Remains of the early popular poetry of England vol 4, 1866; ed A. V. Judges, Elizabethan underworld, 1930. Written ab. 1530.
Gyl of Braintfords testament. [1560?], [1561?]; ed F. J. Furnivall 1871 (priv ptd).
Copland wrote verse prologues or envoys for W. Nevill, The castell of pleasure, [1518]; W. Walter, The spectacle of lovers, 1520; St Austin of Abingdon, The myrrour of the chyrche, 1521; A. Barclay, The introductory to write French, 1521 (French verses); A. Chertsey, The passyon of Our Lorde, 1521; The taverne of goostly helthe, 1522; The life of Ipomydon, [c. 1522]; The syege of Rodes, 1524; The secretes of Arystotle, 1528; The doctrynall of mekenesse, 1529; Chaucer, The assemble of foules, 1530; The rosarye of Our Lady, 1531; W. Walter, Guystarde and Sygysmonde, 1532.

Translated verse in The kalender of shepherdes, *1508, 15[18?], 1528 etc ;* [The life of Christ, *c. 1520). For prose writings see col 690, above and DNB and Francis 1961, below.*

§ 2

Dibdin, T. F. In his Typographical antiquities vol 3, 1815.
Plomer, H. R. Copland: printer and translator. Trans Bibl Soc 3 1896.
—— In his Wynkyn de Worde and his contemporaries, 1925.
Hammond, E. P. In her English verse between Chaucer and Surrey, Durham NC 1927. Introd and extracts.
White, B. Two tracts on marriage by Copland. Huntington Lib Bull no 1 1931.
Simpson, P. In his Proof-reading in the 16th, 17th and 18th centuries, Oxford 1935.
Wright, L. B. In his Middle-class culture in Elizabethan England, Chapel Hill 1935.
Utley, F. L. In his Crooked rib, Columbus 1944.
Bennett, H. S. In his English books and readers 1475 to 1557, Cambridge 1952, 1969 (rev).
Francis, F. C. Copland: sixteenth-century printer and translator. Glasgow 1961.

ANTHONY COPLEY
1567–1607?

§ 1

Wits fittes and fancies [prose]; Loves owle: An idle conceited dialogue betwene love and an olde man. 1595, 1596, 1614 (2 edns, without Loves owle). From R. Cotta, Dialogo entre el amor y un caballero viejo.
A fig for fortune. 1596, 1883 (Spenser Soc). Allegorical narrative.
An answere to a letter of a Jesuited gentleman. 1601. Prose.
Another letter to his disjesuited kinseman. 1602. Prose.

§ 2

Guiney, L. I. In her Recusant poets, 1938.

ROGER COTTON, draper
fl. 1590–6

A direction of the waters of lyfe. 1590, [1592], 1592, 1610 (as A direct way to the waters of life). Prose.
An armor of proofe brought from the tower of David to fight against Spannyardes. 1596 (2 issues). Repeats in verse the points of Direction, above.
A spirituall song: containing an historicall discourse from the infancie of the world. 1596.

MILES COVERDALE
1488–1568

§ 1

Goostly psalmes and spirituall songes drawne out of the Holy Scripture. [1539?]; ed G. Pearson, Remains of Bp Coverdale, Cambridge 1846 (Parker Soc); selections in E. Clapton and G. C. Richards, Our prayer book psalter, 1934. 42 trns from Lutheran hymn books.
For trns of Bible and other prose see cols 1814, 1832, below.

§ 2

Mitchell, A. F. In his Wedderburns and their work, Edinburgh 1867.
—— and C. H. Herford. Academy 31 May, 21 June 1884.

—— In his A compendious book of godly and spiritual songs, 1897 (STS).
Herford, C. H. In his Studies on the literary relations of England and Germany, Cambridge 1886.

ROBERT CROWLEY
1518?–88

The confutation of the mishapen aunswer. [1548]. Includes M. Hogarde, The abuse of the sacrament of the aultare.
The psalter of David newely translated. 1549.
The voyce of the laste trumpet blowen bi the seventh angel: xii lessons to twelve several estates of menne. 1549, 1550; ed J. M. Cowper, Select works of Crowley, 1872 (EETS).
One and thyrtye epigrammes. 1550, 1550, 1573; ed Cowper, above.
The vision of Pierce Plowman. 1550 (3 cdns). Ed Crowley.
Philargyrie of greate Britayne. 1551; ed W. A. Marsden 1931. Anon; ptd for Crowley.
Pleasure and payne, Heaven and Hell. 1551; ed Cowper, above.
Certaine praiers and graces. In F. Segar, The schoole of vertue, 1582 etc.
For prose writings see DNB and col 1333, below.

THOMAS CUTWODE

See Tailboys Dymoke, below.

T.D.

Canaans calamitie: the destruction of Jerusalem by Tytus the sonne of Vaspasian. 1598, 1618, 1640, 1677; ed A. B. Grosart, Non-dramatic works of Dekker vol 1, 1884; ed F. O. Mann, Works of Thomas Deloney, Oxford 1912. Based on Josephus.

JOHN DAVIES of Hereford
1565–1618
Collections

Complete works. Ed A. B. Grosart 2 vols Edinburgh 1878. Reprints all items below except Verses for Queen Elizabeth, Wits bedlam, Writing schoolemaster, A divine psalme.

§ 1

Mirum in modum: a glimpse of Gods glorie and the soules shape. 1602.
Microcosmos: the discovery of the little world. Oxford 1603, 1605, 1611.
Wittes pilgrimage through a world of amorous sonnets and other passages. [1605?].
Bien venu: Greate Britaines welcome to the Danes. 1606; ed P. Birkelund, Copenhagen 1957 (with German trn of H. Roberts, Relatio wie Christianus Quartus zu Dennemarck im Königreich Engellandt angelanget).
Summa totalis: an addition to mirum in modum. 1607.
The holy roode: Christ crucified described in speaking-picture. 1609.
Humours heav'n on earth; the civile warres of death; the triumph of death: the picture of the plague in 1603. 1609.
The scourge of folly: satyricall epigrammes; a descant upon English proverbs; to worthy persons; papers complaint. [1611?]. Papers complaint rptd as A scourge for paper-persecutors, preceded by A continu'd inquisition by A. H[olland], 1624.

The Muses sacrifice: divine meditations; rights of the living and dead. 1612.
[Verses below engraved portrait of Princess Elizabeth. c. 1611.]
The Muses-teares for the losse of Henry Prince of Wales. 1613.
An eclogue between Willy and Wernocke. In W. Browne, The sheapherdes pipe, 1614; rptd in George Withers, Workes, 1620.
A select second husband for Sir Thomas Overburies wife. 1616.
Wits bedlam. 1617. Epigrams and epitaphs.
[Verses for portrait of Queen Elizabeth. Before 1625.]
The writing schoolemaster. [c. 1625] (fragment), 1631 (6th edn), 1636 (16th edn). Handwriting manual with engraved plates.
A divine psalme; an elogie upon the patron [i.e. pattern] of Scripture; divine epigrams. 1652.

§ 2

Fuller, T. In his Worthies of England, 1662.
Wood, A. In his Athenae oxonienses vol 1, 1691.
Heidrich, H. Davies und sein Bild von Shakespeares Umgebung. Berlin 1924. Corrections by R. B. McKerrow, RES 1 1925.
Whipple, T. K. In his Martial and the English epigram, 1925.
Anderson, R. L. A French source for Davies' system of psychology. PQ 6 1927.
Ennis, L. Wit's bedlam. Huntington Lib Bull 11 1937.
Murphy, C. D. Davies' versification of Sidney's prose. PQ 21 1942.
Wilkes, G. A. The humours heav'n on earth and a suppressed poem. N & Q June 1959.
Rope, H. E. G. Davies: Catholic and rhymer. Anglo-Welsh Rev 11 1961.
Thompson, H. H. A new poem. N & Q June 1962.
— A new poem. Ball State Univ Forum 8 1968.

ANGEL DAY
fl. 1575–95

The English secretorie. 1587, 1592, 1595, 1599, 1607, 1614, 1621, 1625, [1626?]. Prose model letters; see J. K. Robertson, Art of letter writing, 1942.
Daphnis and Chloe, finished in a pastorall termed the Shepheards holidaie. 1587; ed J. Jacobs 1890. Trn of Longus from French of J. Amyot; prose with interspersed poems. Shepheards holidaie is a poem in praise of Queen Elizabeth.
Upon the life and death of Sir Phillip Sidney, by A.D. [1587].

THOMAS DELONEY
1543?–1607?

13 ballads. Deloney edited Garland of good will, 1631 (entered 1593); Strange histories, 1602. See col 2054, below.

For Edward de Vere, Earl of Oxford, see col 1154 below.

ROBERT DEVEREUX, EARL OF ESSEX
1566–1601

Poems. Ed A. B. Grosart 1872.

JOHN DICKENSON
fl. 1594–8

Collections

Prose and verse. Ed A. B. Grosart, Manchester 1878.

§ 1

Deorum consessus: sive Apolonis ac Minervae querela. 1591. Latin verse.
Arisbas: Euphues amidst his slumbers, or Cupids journey to Hell. 1594. Prose, with 10 poems.
The shepheardes complaint in English hexameters; other conceits. [1596]. 9 poems with short prose links.
Greene in conceipt: the tragique historie of faire Valeria of London. 1598. Prose, with 4 poems.

DOCTOR DOUBLE ALE
See Luke Shepherd, below.

JOHN DOLMAN
1540–c. 1598

Lord Hastynges. In A myrrour for magistrates, 1563 etc; ed L. B. Campbell, Cambridge 1938, no 21. See ELH 4 1937.
Those fyve questions which Cicero disputed in his manor of Tusculanum. 1561. Prose trn.

JOHN DONNE
1572–1631

See col 1169, below.

ANNE DOWRICH
fl. 1589–96

The French historie: a discourse of three bloodie broiles that have happened in France for the Gospell. 1589.
Commendatory verse in Hugh Dowriche, The jaylors conversion, 1596.

THOMAS DRANT
d. 1578

§ 1

Impii cuiusdam epigrammatis quod edidit R. Shaklockus in mortem C. Scoti. 1565. Latin and English verse.
A medicinable morall: two bookes of Horace his satyres englyshed; waylyngs of Hieremiah; epigrammes [Latin and English]. 1566. see col 1333, below
Horace his arte of poetrie, pistles and satyrs englished. 1567.
Epigrams and sentences spirituall in vers of Gregori Nazanzen englished. 1568.
In Selomonis Ecclesiasten paraphrasis poetica. 1572. Latin verse.
Praesul; sylva. [1576]. Latin verse.
Commendatory verses in J. Sadler, Four books of Vegetius, 1572; L. Lloyd, A pilgrimage of princes, 1573; A. Neville, Kettus, 1582.

§ 2

Spenser, E. and G. Harvey. Three letters; two letters. 1580.
Jiriczek, O. L. Der elisabethanische Horaz. Sh Jb 48 1911.
Brooks, H. Donne and Drant. TLS 16–30 Aug 1934.
Bradner, L. In his Musae anglicanae, New York 1940.
Ringler, W. A., jr. Master Drant's rules. PQ 29 1950.
Buxton, J. In his Sir Philip Sidney and the English Renaissance, 1954.

JOHN DROUT
fl. 1570

The pityfull historie of two loving Italians, Gaulfrido and
 Barnardo le vayne, translated out of Italian. 1570; [ed
 J. P. Collier 1844].

TRANSLATOR OF DU BARTAS

The first day of the worldes creation: the first weeke of
 W. Salustius Lord of Bartas. 1595. Tr by a 'nameless
 countriman' of Anthony Bacon.

SIR EDWARD DYER
d. 1607
Collections

Hannah, J. In his Poems of Raleigh and other courtly
 poets, 1870. 4 poems, with discussion of canon.
Writings in verse and prose. Ed A. B. Grosart 1872.
 12 poems.
Sargent, R. M. At the Court of Queen Elizabeth: the life
 and lyrics of Dyer. Oxford 1935. Adds 3 poems.

§1

[The prayse of nothing by E.D., 1585; ed J. P. C[ollier
 1840?], prose, ascription to Dyer based on a forgery;
 see Sargent, above and Dickey, below.]
A sweet sonet: my minde to me a kingdome is. [1624?].
 Anon, ascribed to Edward de Vere Earl of Oxford
 by Harvard fMS 1015 folio 14ᵛ.

§2

Wagner, B. M. New poems by Dyer. RES 11 1935.
Sandison, H. E. But this and then no more: a note on the
 suggested ascriptions to Dyer and to Gorges. RES 14
 1938.
—— (ed). Poems of Sir Arthur Gorges. Oxford 1953.
Dickey, F. Forgeries in the Stationers' Register. Shakespeare Quart 11 1960.

TAILBOYS DYMOKE
fl. 1584–1602

§1

Caltha poetarum: or the bumble bee, by T. Cutwode
 [pseudonym]. 1599, 1815 (Roxburghe Club).

§2

O'Conor, N. J. In his Godes peace and the Queenes, 1934.
Hotson, L. Marigold of the poets. Trans Royal Soc of Lit
 17 1938.

J.G.E. (JOHN EGERTON?)

Englands hope against Irish hate. 1600.

RICHARD EDWARDS
1523?–66

§1

The paradyse of daynty devises. 1576, 1578, 1580, 1585,
 [1590?], 1596, 1596, 1600, 1606; ed H. E. Rollins,

Cambridge Mass 1927. Anthology by Edwards et al;
 see col 1008 above.
Life and poems. Ed L. Bradner, New Haven 1927.
 For plays see col 1415, below.

§2

Starnes, D. T. Sources of poems. PQ 6 1927.
Rollins, H. E. A note on Edwards. RES 4 1928. Fragment of Palamon and Arcite and another poem from mss.

THOMAS EDWARDS

§1

Cephalus and Procris; Narcissus. 1595; ed W. E. Buckley
 1882 (Roxburghe Club); ed E. S. Donno, Elizabethan
 minor epics, New York 1963 (Cephalus and Procris
 only).
Romanus. A. Parvum theatrum urbium. 1595. Contains
 Latin verse by Edwards.

§2

Stopes, C. C. Edwards. MLR 16 1921.

WILLIAM ELDERTON
d. 1592?

16 ballads. See col 2044, below.

QUEEN ELIZABETH I
1533–1603

Queen Elizabeth's englishings of Boethius, Plutarch and
 Horace. Ed E. C. Pemberton 1889 (EETS).
Flügel, E. Poems by Queen Elizabeth. Anglia 14 1892.
Phillips, J. E. Elizabeth I as a Latin poet. Renaissance
 News 16 1963.
Poems. Ed L. Bradner, Providence 1964.
Black, L. G. A lost poem by Queen Elizabeth. TLS 23
 May 1968.

EDMUND ELVIDEN

The closet of counsells: the advice of divers philosophers
 translated in to Englishe verse; a discription of the
 abuses and vanities of the worlde. 1569, 1573.
The metaphoricall historie of Pesistratus and Catanea.
 [1570?].
A neweyeres gift to the rebellious persons in the north
 partes of England. 1570; rptd H. Huth, Fugitive tracts
 vol 1, 1875.

MAID EMLYN

The boke of mayde Emlyn that had v husbandes and all
 kockoldes. [c. 1520] (fragment), [c. 1525]; ed G. Isted
 1820 (Roxburghe Club); ed E. F. Rimbault 1842 (Percy
 Soc); ed W. C. Hazlitt, Remains of the popular poetry
 of England vol 4, 1866. See F. L. Utley, Crooked rib,
 Columbus 1944.

THOMAS ESTE

See Passions of the spirit, below.

WILLIAM EVANS

Pietatis lachrymae: teares of devotion. 1602.

ROBERT FABYAN
d. 1513

Prima pars cronecarum. 1516, 1533 (as Fabyans cronycle), 1542 (2 issues, expurgated), 1559 (continued to 8 Jan 1559), 1559 (continued to 8 May); ed H. Ellis, The new chronicles of England and France, 1811. Written 1504, prose and 71 poems. Mss of pt 2: BM Cotton C.xi; Harvard fMS 766 (printer's copy for 1516 edn). *See* W. Winstanley, Lives of the most famous English poets, 1687.

EDWARD FAIRFAX
d. 1635

§1

Godfrey of Bulloigne done into English heroicall verse. 1600, 1624, 1687, Dublin 1726, London 1749, 1817, 1817, 1844, 1853; ed H. Morley 1890, 1901; ed R. Weiss, Carbondale 1962. Trn of Tasso, Gerusalemme liberata.
Eclogue the fourth: Egon and Alexis. Ed E. Cooper, Muses' library, 1737; ed W. Grainge, Harrogate 1882 (with A discourse of witchcraft).
Eclogue: Hermes and Lycaon; ed W. Grainge, Harrogate 1882 (from ms).
For prose Discourse of witchcraft *see col 2379, below.*

§2

Castelli, A. La Gerusalemme liberata nella vita intellectuale del popolo inglese. Florence 1914.
Bell, C. G. A history of Fairfax criticism. PMLA 62 1947.
— Fairfax's Tasso. Comparative Lit 6 1954.
Nash, R. On the indebtedness of Fairfax's Tasso to Carew. Italica 34 1957.

THOMAS FENNE
fl. 1590

Fennes frutes: a dialogue betweene fame and the scholler; the lamentable ruines which attend on warre; that it is not requisite to derive our pedigree from the unfaithfull Trojans [prose]; Hecubaes mishaps discoursed by way of apparition [long verse narrative]. 1590.

GEORGE FERRERS
1500?–79

§1

Robert Tresilian and Thomas of Wudstocke. In A myrrour for magistrates, 1559, nos 1, 3; Edmund Duke of Somerset 1563, no 26; Elianor Cobham and Humfrey Duke of Glocester 1578, nos 28–9; ed L. B. Campbell, Cambridge 1938 (with biography).
Poem. In The princelye pleasures at the Courte at Kenelwoorth, 1576 (unique copy destroyed, rptd in Kenilworth illustrated, 1821); in Works of Gascoigne vol 2, ed J. W. Cunliffe, Cambridge 1910.

§2

Taylor, M. A. Lord Cobham and the Mirror. Shakespeare Assoc Bull 8 1933.
Campbell, L. B. Humphrey Duke of Gloucester and Elianor Cobham in the Mirror. Huntington Lib Bull no 5 1934.

THOMAS FEYLDE

§1

The contraverse bytwene a lover and a jaye. [1529?], [1532?]; ed T. F. Dibdin 1818 (Roxburghe Club); ed E. Arber, Dunbar anthology, 1901 (modernized).

§2

Berdan, J. M. In his Early Tudor poetry, New York 1920.
Utley, F. L. In his Crooked rib, Columbus 1944. No 313.

FIFTEEN JOYS OF MARRIAGE

§1

The fyftene joyes of maryage. [c. 1507] (fragment), 1509. Tr from Antoine de La Sale?, Les quinze joyes de mariage.

§2

Wilson, F. P. In his Batchelars banquet, Oxford 1929.
Utley, F. L. In his Crooked rib, Columbus 1944. No 274.

JOHN FISHER, student in Oxford

[Three dialogues between Spudeus and Gelasimus, Eda and Agna, and Wisdome and Wylle]. 1558.

CHARLES FITZGEFFREY
1575?–1638

Sir Francis Drake. 1596; Affaniae sive epigrammatum libri tres, Cenotaphia, Oxford 1601; The blessed birthday, Oxford 1634.
See col 1308, below.

ABRAHAM FLEMING
1552?–1607

§1

The Bucolikes drawne into English. 1575. Trn of Virgil.
An epitaph upon W. Lambe. [1580].
The Bucoliks, Georgiks, newly translated. 1589.
Also prose trns.

§2

Dodson, S. C. Fleming: writer and editor. SE 34 1955.

GILES FLETCHER the elder
1546–1611

Bibliographies

Berry, L. E. Fletcher the Elder: a bibliography. Trans Cambridge Bibl Soc 3 1961.

Collections

English works. Ed L. E. Berry, Madison 1964. Licia, Russe commonwealth, Tartars, letters.

§1

Of the Russe commonwealth. 1591, 1643, 1657; epitomized in R. Hakluyt, Voyages vol 1, 1598; S. Purchas, Pilgrimes vol 3, 1625; J. Harris, Compleat collection of voyages vol 1, 1705; ed E. A. Bond 1856 (Hakluyt Soc); ed R. Pipes and J. V. A. Fine jr, Cambridge Mass 1966;

A. J. Schmidt, Ithaca 1968; tr French, 1864; Russian, 1848, 1867, 1905. Prose.

Licia: poems of love; the rising to the crowne of Richard the Third. [1593?](anon); ed A. B. Grosart, Manchester 1871; ed E. Arber, English garner vol 8, 1896; Licia, ed M. F. Crow, Elizabethan sonnet cycles vol 1, 1896; ed S. Lee, Elizabethan sonnets vol 2, 1904. 54 sonnets adapted from Angerianus et al with 7 other poems.

De literis antiquae Britanniae. 1633. Latin verse.

The Tartars or Ten Tribes. In S. Lee, Israel Redux, 1677; in Memoirs of the life and writings of W. Whiston, 1749, 1753. Prose.

For Latin occasional poems see DNB and Berry's bibliography and introd, above.

§2

Churchill, R. B. Richard the Third up to Shakespeare. Berlin 1900.

Kastner, L. E. The Elizabethan sonneteers and the French poets. MLR 3 1908.

Scott, J. G. The sources of Fletcher's Licia. MLR 20 1925.

—— In her Les sonnets élisabéthains, Paris 1929. Ch 7.

John, L. C. In her Elizabethan sonnet sequences, New York 1938.

Bradner, L. In his Musae anglicanae, New York 1940.

Austin, W. B. Milton's Lycidas and two Latin elegies by Fletcher. SP 44 1947.

Raymo, R. R. Three new Latin poems of Fletcher. MLN 71 1956.

Berry, L. E. Three poems by Fletcher in Poemata varii argumenti, 1678. N & Q April 1959.

—— Fletcher's Licia. Library 5th ser 15 1960.

—— Fletcher and the Earl of Essex. N & Q Feb 1960.

—— Fletcher and Milton's History of Moscovia. RES new ser 11 1960.

—— Five Latin poems by Fletcher. Anglia 79 1961.

—— Phineas Fletcher's account of his father. JEGP 60 1961.

Lindsay, R. O. Hakluyt and Of the Russe common wealth. PBSA 57 1963.

FLODDEN FIELD

Flowden feilde. BM mss Harley 293,367, ed H. Weber, Flodden field, 1808; BM ms additional 27,879, ed J. W. Hales and F. J. Furnivall, Bishop Percy's folio ms vol 1, 1867. For another poem on the battle *see* Scottish field col 1143, below.

WILLIAM FORREST
fl. 1530–81

§1

A newe ballade of the marigolde. [1553?]; ed T. Park, Harleian miscellany vol 10, 1813; ed H. E. Rollins, Old English ballads, Cambridge 1920.

Pater noster and Te dcum. In J. Foxe, Actes and monuments, 1563.

The history of Grisild the second. Ed W. D. Macray 1875 (Roxburghe Club) (from ms). On divorce of Katherine of Aragon, written 1558.

Theophilus. Ed F. Ludorff, Anglia 7 1884 (from ms). Written 1572.

For other poems in ms see DNB and Macray's introd, above: History of Joseph the chaiste *1545*, The pleasant poesie of princelie practice *1548* (*extract in Starkey's* Life and letters, *EETS 1878*), Metaphrase of the Psalms *1551*, Life of the Blessed Virgin *1572–81*.

§2

Gerould, G. H. In his Saints' legends, Boston 1916.

Guiney, L. I. In her Recusant poets, 1938.

ABRAHAM FRAUNCE
fl. 1582–1633

§1

The Arcadian rhetorike. [1588]; ed E. Seaton, Oxford 1950 (Luttrell Soc); Menston 1969 (facs of 1588). Prose with verse quotations.

The lamentations of Amyntas for the death of Phillis. 1587, 1588, 1589, 1591 (in Yvychurch), 1596; ed F. Dickey, Chicago 1967. Trn in English hexameters of T. Watson's Latin Amyntas.

Insignium, armorum, emblematum, hieroglyphicorum et symbolorum explicatio. 1588. Latin prose.

The lawiers logike. 1588, Menston 1969 (facs). Prose.

The Countesse of Pembrokes Yvychurch. 1591. Trns in English hexameters: Amyntas pastorall [Tasso's Amintas], Phillis funerall [Watson's Amyntas], Lamentation of Corydon for Alexis [Virgil's Eclogue 2], The beginning of Heliodorus his Æthiopical history.

The Countesse of Pembrokes Emanuel: the nativity, passion, buriall and resurrection of Christ, with certaine psalmes of David, all in English hexameters. 1591; ed A. B. Grosart, Manchester 1872.

The third part of the Countesse of Pembrokes Yvychurch: Amintas dale, wherein are conceited tales of the pagan gods in English hexameters. 1592. Verse with prose comment explaining allegory.

Victoria. Ed G. C. M. Smith, Louvain 1906 (Bang's Materialien 14) (from ms). Latin verse play tr from L. Pasqualigo, Il Fidele; biographical introd.

The shepheardes logike. Menston 1969 (facs of BM additional ms 34,361).

§2

Winstanley, W. In his Lives of the most famous English poets, 1687.

Koller, K. Fraunce and Spenser. ELH 7 1940.

Staton, W. F., jr. Thomas Watson and Fraunce. PMLA 76 1961. Reply to H. Morris, Barnfield, Amyntas and the Sidney circle 74 1959.

ULPIAN FULWELL
fl. 1568–86

The flower of fame: the bright renowne of Henry the VIII. 1575; ed T. Park, Harleian miscellany vol 9, 1808. Verse with interspersed prose.

The first part of the eight liberall science: ars adulandi, the art of flattery, with the confutation thereof. 1576, 1579, [1580?]. 7 prose dialogues, one in verse.

For his play Like wil to like *see col 1407, below.*

C. G. gent.

The minte of deformities. 1600. Satire.

DUNSTAN GALE
fl. 1596

Pyramus and Thisbe. 1617, 1626; ed P. W. Miller, Seven minor epics, Gainesville 1967 (facs). Dedication dated 1596; based on Ovid's Metamorphoses.

BERNARD GARTER
fl. 1563–78

The tragicall and true historie which happened betwene two English lovers 1563. 1565, 1568.

A dittie in the worthie praise of an high and mightie prince. [1566]. On Thomas Howard, 4th Duke of Norfolk.

Of trust and triall; A strife betwene Appelles and Pigmalion. 1566 (with J. Canand, The fantasies of a troubled mannes head, and Of evyll tounges).

The joyfull receyving of the Queenes Majestie into Norwich. [1578] (2 edns); rptd J. Nichols, in his Progresses of Queen Elizabeth vol 2, 1823. Ed Garter with verses by him, with Maske by H. Goldingham.

A newyeares gift dedicated to the Popes Holinesse. 1579. Verse and prose, with reprint of C. Tunstall and J. Stokesley, A letter unto R. Pole Cardinall 1560.

THE JEASTE OF SYR GAWAYNE

[The jest of Sir Gawaine]. [c. 1530?] (fragments), [c. 1540?] (last leaf only). Bodley ms Douce 261 (1564 transcript of last 541 lines of a lost print); ed F. Madden, Syr Gawayne, 1839 (Bannatyne Club). *See col 408, above.*

A PROPRE DYALOGE BETWENE A GENTILLMAN AND AN HUSBAND MAN

See William Barlowe, above.

HUMFREY GIFFORD

A posie of gilloflowers. 1580; Poems, ed A. B. Grosart, Blackburn 1870; Complete poems and translations in prose, ed A. B. Grosart, Manchester 1875; ed F. J. H. Darton 1933. Verse and prose.

JOHN GOD

A discourse of the great crueltie of a widowe towards a yong gentleman and by what meanes he requited the same. [1570].

ARTHUR GOLDING
1536?–1606

§1

The fyrst fower bookes of P. Ovidius Nasos Metamorphosis translated into Englishe meter. 1565.

The xv bookes of P. Ovidius Naso entytuled Metamorphosis translated into English meeter. 1567, 1575, 1584, 1587, 1593, 1603, 1612, 1675; ed W. H. D. Rouse 1904 (as Shakespeare's Ovid); ed J. M. Cohen, Carbondale 1961 (from Rouse).

A briefe discourse on the late murther of George Saunders. 1573, 1577; ed R. Simpson, School of Shakespeare vol 2, 1878; ed L. T. Golding 1937. Prose.

A tragedie of Abrahams sacrifice, written in French by T. Beza and translated into Inglish. 1577; ed M. W. Wallace, Toronto 1906.

A discourse upon the earthquake. 1580; ed L. T. Golding with above. Prose.

Commendatory poem to Barrets Alvearie, 1580; ed L. T. Golding with above.

See also col 2390, below.

§2

Witz, E. In his Die englischen Ovidübersetzungen des 16 Jahrhunderts, Leipzig 1915.

Golding, L. T. An Elizabethan Puritan. New York 1937.

Robinson, F. G. A note on the Sidney-Golding translation of Mornay. Harvard Lib Bull 17 1969.

Taylor, A. B. Peend and Golding. N & Q Jan 1969.

— George Peele and Golding's Metamorphoses. N & Q Aug 1969.

Wilson, R. F. Golding's Metamorphoses and Shakespeare's Midsummer night's dream. Eng Lang Notes 7 1969.

CHRISTOPHER GOODWYN

A lytell prosses called the chaunce of the dolorous lover, newely compyled 1520. [1520?].

The maydens dreme compyled 1442. [1542?]. Tr from Le songe doré de la pucelle.

BARNABE GOOGE
1540–94

§1

The first thre bokes of the zodyake of lyfe. 1560; The firste syxe bokes, 1561; The zodiake of life by Marcellus Palingenius, 1565 (12 bks), 1576, 1588; ed R. Tuve, New York 1947 (facs of 1576 edn).

Eglogs, epytaphes and sonettes. 1563; ed E. Arber 1871; Selected poems, ed A. Stephens, Denver 1961.

A newe booke called the shippe of safegarde. 1569.

The popish kingdome or reigne of Antichrist, written in Latin verse by T. Naogeorgus [Kirchmeyer] and englyshed. 1570; ed R. C. Hofe 1880.

Foure bookes of husbandry collected by C. Heresbachius. 1577, 1578, 1586, 1596, 1601, 1614 (enlarged), 1631 (enlarged G. Markham). Prose trn.

The overthrow of the gout written in Latin verse by C. Balista. 1577. Verse trn.

The proverbes of Sir J. Lopez de Mendoza with the paraphrase of P. Diaz of Toledo, translated out of Spanishe. 1579. Verse proverbs with prose commentary.

The vertues of a new terra sigillata lately found out in Germany, by A. Bertholdus. 1587. Prose trn from Latin.

A prophecie lately transcribed from an old manuscript of Doctor Barnaby Googe predicting the rising and falling of the United Provinces. 1672.

§2

Greg, W. W. In his Pastoral poetry and pastoral drama, 1906.

Harrison, T. P. Googe's Eglogs and Montemayor's Diana. SE 5 1925.

Mustard, W. P. In his Eclogues of B. Mantuanus, Baltimore 1921.

Hartung, P. N. U. Sonettes of Googe. E Studies 11 1929.

Hudson, H. H. Sonnets by Googe. PMLA 48 1933.

SIR ARTHUR GORGES
1557?–1625

Collections

Poems. Ed H. E. Sandison, Oxford 1953.

§1

Lucans Pharsalia. 1614.

The wisedome of the Ancients. 1619, 1622. Prose trn of F. Bacon, De sapientia veterum liber, 1609.

Essays moraux. 1619. French prose trn of F. Bacon, Essayes.

The Olympian catastrophe. Ed R. Davies 1925 (from ms).

Observations concerning the Royall Navy. 1650. Attributed to Gorges by Sandison, 1928 below; also attributed to Sir W. Ralegh.

§2

Sandison, H. E. Gorges, Spenser's Alcyon and Ralegh's friend. PMLA 43 1928.
—— The Vanytyes of Gorges' youth. PMLA 61 1946.
Gorges, R. In his Story of a family through eleven centuries, Boston 1944.

EDWARD GOSYNHYLL
fl. 1542

§1

The prayse of all women, called Mulierum Pean. [1542?], [1560?]. Answer to The scholehouse of women, col 1143 below.

§2

White, B. Three rare books about women. Huntington Lib Bull no 2 1931.
Utley, F. L. In his Crooked rib, Columbus 1944. No 347.

JOHN GRANGE
fl. 1577

The golden Aphroditis. 1577. Prose fiction with 36 poems. *See col 2052, below.*

WILLIAM GRAY of Reading
d. 1557

Dormer, E. W. Gray of Reading: a 16th-century controversialist and ballad writer. Reading 1923. Biography and collected poems.

ROBERT GREENE
1558–92

See col 1437, below.

THOMAS GREEPE
d. 1634

The true newes of the exploytes performed by Syr Frauncis Drake at Santo Domingo and Carthagena but also nowe at Cales. 1587; ed D. W. Waters, Hartford Conn 1955 (facs). *See* J. P. Collier, Poetical decameron vol 1, 1820.

THE LIFE OF ST GREGORY'S MOTHER

The lyfe of saynt Gregoryes mother. [1500?] (fragment), 1515 (fragment), [1548?]; ed W. A. Ringler jr, Studies in honor of D. T. Starnes, Austin 1967. A late quatrain version of the ME Trental of St Gregory.

BARTHOLOMEW GRIFFIN
d. 1602

§1

Fidessa more chaste then kind. 1596; ed [P. Bliss], Chiswick 1815; ed A. B. Grosart, Manchester 1876;

ed E. Arber, English garner vol 5, 1882; ed M. F. Crow, Elizabethan sonnet cycles vol 3, 1896; ed S. Lee, Elizabethan sonnets vol 2, 1904. 62 sonnets; no 3 attributed to Shakespeare in Passionate pilgrime 1599.

§2

Kastner, L. E. The Elizabethan sonneteers and the French poets. MLR 3 1908.
Scott, J. G. Minor Elizabethan sonneteers. RES 2 1926.
—— In her Les sonnets élisabéthains, Paris 1929.
Izon, J. Griffin and Sir Thomas Lucy. TLS 19 April 1957.

NICHOLAS GRIMALD
1519?–62?
Collections

Life and poems. Ed L. R. Merrill, New Haven 1925.

§1

Christus redivivus: comoedia tragica. Cologne 1543; ed J. M. Hart, PMLA 14 1899. Latin verse.
Archipropheta: tragoedia. Cologne 1548. Latin verse.
Latin and English commendatory verse. In W. Turner, A preservative agaynst the poyson of Pelagius, 1551.
M.T. Ciceroes thre bokes of duties. 1556, 1558, 1568, 1574, 1583, 1596, [1600?]. Prose trn.
Songes and sonettes by the Earle of Surrey and other. 1557 (40 poems by Grimald); 8 edns 1557–87 (10 poems). *See col 1007, above.*
Oratio ad pontifices in aede Paulina 1553. 1583. Latin prose.
In P. V. Maronis quatuor libros Georgicorum in oratione soluta paraphrasis. 1591. Virgil's text with Latin prose paraphrase, written 1549.

§2

Herford, C. H. In his Studies in the literary relations of England and Germany, Cambridge 1886. On Archipropheta.
Grimaldi, S. The descent of the family of Grimaldi. 1895.
Hudson, H. H. Grimald's translations from Beza. MLN 39 1924.
Taylor, G. C. Christus redivivus and the Hegge resurrection play. PMLA 41 1926.
Shannon, G. P. Grimald's heroic couplet and the Latin elegiac distich. PMLA 45 1930.
—— Grimald's list of the Muses. MLQ 8 1947.
Byrom, H. J. The case for Grimald as editor of Tottel's Miscellany. MLR 27 1932.
Guiney, L. I. In her Recusant poets, 1938.

MATTHEW GROVE

The tragicall historie of Pelops and Hippodamia; epigrams, songes and sonnettes. 1587; ed A. B. Grosart, Manchester 1878. Narrative and 87 short poems, no quatorzains.

ELIZABETH GRYMESTON
d. 1603

Miscellanea; meditations; memoratives. 1604, [1606?] (augmented), [1608?], [1618?]. Prose, scattered verse, Odes in imitation of the seven poenitentiall psalmes. *See* F. M. McKay, A note on R. Verstegan's poetry, N & Q Oct 1968.

TRANSLATOR OF GUARINI

Il pastor fido: or the faithfull shepheard, translated out of Italian. 1602, 1633. Tr by a kinsman and countryman of Sir E. Dymock.

EDWARD GUILPIN
fl. 1598–1601

§1

Skialetheia: or a shadowe of truth in certain epigrams and satyres. 1598 (anon); ed E. V. Utterson, Ryde 1843; ed J. P. C[ollier 1870]; ed A. B. Grosart, Manchester 1878; ed G. B. Harrison 1931.
The whipper of the satyre his pennance in a white sheete: or the beadles confutation. 1601 (anon); ed A. Davenport, Whipper pamphlets pt 2, Liverpool 1951.

§2

Bennett, R. E. Donne and Gilpin. RES 15 1939.

T.H.

The fable of Ovid treting of Narcissus, translated out of Latin, with a moral ther unto. 1560; ed W. E. Buckley in his edn of T. Edwards, Cephalus and Procris, 1882 (Roxburghe Club); ed N. Alexander, Elizabethan narrative verse, 1967 (without the moral).

T.H.

Oenone and Paris. [1594]; ed J. Q. Adams, Washington 1943; ed E. S. Donno, Elizabethan minor epics, New York 1963. Based on Ovid's Heroides 5; Adams attributes to T. Heywood. See J. D. Parsons, Earliest critical notice of Shakespeare, N & Q 20 July 1929.

EDWARD HAKE
fl. 1566–1604

One dialogue or colloquy entitled Diversoria. 1566. Prose trn of Erasmus.
The imitation on following of Christ. 1567, 1568 (with The perpetuall rejoyce of the godly), 1568 (for 1571?). Prose trn of Thomas à Kempis.
A touchestone for this time present [prose]; a compendious forme of education. 1574.
A commemoration of the raigne of our soveraigne Lady Elizabeth, newly set foorth. [1576?], [1579?] (as A joyfull continuance of the commemoration); ed T. Park, Harleian miscellany vol 9, 1809. Verse and prose.
Newes out of Powles churchyarde now newly renued and amplified: otherwise entituled syr Nummus, written in English satyrs. [1579]; ed C. Edmonds 1872. 8 satires.
An oration conteyning an expostulation. [1587]. Prose; speech delivered as Mayor of Windsor to Queen, 10 Aug 1586.
Of golds kingdome and this unhelping age described in sundry poems. 1604.

ARTHUR HALL
fl. 1563–1604

§1

A letter sent by F.A. touching a quarell between A. Hall and M. Mallorie. [1579]. Prose.

Ten bookes of Homers Iliades translated out of French. 1581.

§2

Wright, H. G. The life and works of Arthur Hall of Grantham. 1919.

JOHN HALL
1529?–66?

§1

Certayne chapters taken out of the proverbes of Salomon, wythe other chapters of the holye Scrypture and certayne psalmes of David. [1548–9] (Certayne lessons, Proverbes, Ecclesiastes, Sapientia 6, Ecclesiasticus 9, Psalms 34, 54, 112, 114–15, Against nigardie (a printer's filler not by Hall), [1549] (imperfect), 1550 (title adds: Whych proverbes of late were set forth, imprinted and untruely entituled to be thee doynges of Mayster Thomas Sternhold; omits Certayne lessons, Psalms 34, 54, 115, Against nigardie; adds Thessalonians and Psalms 25, 64, 113, 145). Certayne lessons, Proverbes, and Against nigardie rptd in Certayne chapters of the proverbes of Salomon drawen into metre by Thomas Sterneholde, [1549–50]; Psalm 112 rptd F. Seager in his Certayne psalmes, 1553; Sapientia 6, Ecclesiasticus 9, and Psalms 34, 54, 115 rptd by Hall in his Courte of Vertu, 1565.
Commendatory poem. In T. Gale, Certaine workes of chirurgerie, 1563.
A poesie in forme of a vision agaynst wytche crafte. 1563.
The Courte of Vertu: contaynynge many holy songes, sonettes, psalmes and ballettes. 1565 (all extant copies lack title-page); ed R. A. Fraser 1961.
For medical writings see DNB

§2

Rollins, H. E. Tottel's Miscellany and Hall. TLS 14 Jan 1932.
Huttar, C. A. Poems by Surrey and others in a printed miscellany. Eng Miscellany (Rome) 16 1965.

JOSEPH HALL
Bishop of Norwich
1574–1656
Collections

Complete poems. Ed A. B. Grosart, Manchester 1879.
Collected poems. Ed A. Davenport, Liverpool 1949.

§1

Virgidemiarum: first three bookes of tooth-lesse satyrs. 1597, 1598, 1602.
Virgidemiarum: the three last bookes of byting satyres. 1598, 1599. All 6 bks rptd W. Thompson, Oxford 1753, and 13 other edns (see Davenport, above); ed S. W. Singer, Chiswick 1824 (with notes by T. Warton); Works of J. Hall, vol 12, ed P. Hall, Oxford 1839; ed K. Schulze, Berlin 1910 (with commentary).
The Kings prophecie. 1603; rptd W. E. Buckley 1882 (Roxburghe Club).
Some fewe of Davids psalms metaphrased. In Holy observations, 1607; rptd with other works 8 times to 1639; see Davenport, above and col 1907, below.
For prose works see col 1977, below.

§2

Alden, R. M. In his Rise of formal satire in England, Philadelphia 1899.
Allen, M. S. In his Satire of John Marston, Columbus 1920.

Beckwith, E. A. On the Hall-Marston controversy. JEGP 25 1926.

Salyer, S. M. Hall's satires and the Harvey-Nashe controversy. SP 25 1928.

Davenport, A. Weever's Epigrammes and the Hall-Marston quarrel. RES 11 1935.

— The quarrel of the satirists. MLR 37 1942.

Stein, A. The second English satirist. MLR 38 1943.

— Hall's imitation of Juvenal. MLR 43 1948.

MacKinnon, M. H. M. Harington and Bishop Hall. PQ 37 1958.

Kernan, A. In his Cankered Muse, New Haven 1959.

McNeir, W. F. Hall's Fortunio and Raymundus once more. N & Q July–Aug 1959.

Jensen, E. J. Hall and Marston: the role of the satirist. Satire News Letter 4 1967.

JOHN HARINGTON the elder
d. 1582

Hughey, R. Harington of Stepney. Middletown Ohio 1971.

SIR JOHN HARINGTON
1560–1612

Collections

Letters and epigrams. Ed N. E. McClure, Philadelphia 1930.

§1

Orlando furioso in English heroical verse. 1591, 1607, 1634; ed G. Hough 1962; ed R. Gottfried, Bloomington 1963 (selection); A preface or apologie of poetrie [prose], ed G. G. Smith, Elizabethan critical essays vol 2, Oxford 1904. Verse trn of Ariosto.

A new discourse of a stale subject called the Metamorphosis of Ajax; an anatomie [by T. Combe]; an apologie. 1596 (4 edns); ed S. W. Singer, Chiswick 1814; ed P. Warlock and J. Lindsay 1927; ed E. S. Donno 1962. Prose.

Epigrammes by Sir J.H. and others. In J.C., Alcilia, 1613, 1628 (20 epigrams); Epigrams both pleasant and serious, 1615, 1615 (116 epigrams);

The most elegant and witty epigrams digested into foure bookes, 1618 (ed N. E. McClure, Philadelphia 1926, with 80 additional), 1625, 1633 (appended to 1634 Orlando furioso, above). 346 epigrams.

The Englishmans docter: or the school of Salerne. 1607, 1608, 1609, Edinburgh 1613, London 1617, 1624; ed F. R. Packard and F. H. Garrison, New York 1920; Salerno 1953 (with Latin). Verse trn of J. de Mediolano.

Nugae antiquae. Ed H. Harington 2 vols 1769–75, 3 vols 1779, 1792; ed T. Park 2 vols 1804 (with addns). Poems and prose from family papers.

A briefe view of the state of the Church of England. Ed J. Chetwind 1653; ed T. Park, Nugae antiquae vol 2, 1804 (with corrections from autograph ms BM Royal 17 B xxii). Prose.

A tract on the succession to the crown. Ed C. R. Markham 1880 (from York ms) (Roxburghe Club). Prose.

The Arundel Harington ms of Tudor poetry. Ed R. Hughey 2 vols Columbus 1960. Ms anthology of 324 poems compiled by John the elder and his son, including some of their own composition.

The prayse of private life. BM ms additional 30,161; in McClure, above. Prose; also attributed to Samuel Daniel.

§2

Winstanley, W. In his Lives of the most famous English poets, 1687.

Cooper, E. In her Muses' library, 1737.

Rehfeld, G. Harington: ein Nachahmer Rabelais. Halle 1914.

Raleigh, W. In his Some authors, Oxford 1923.

Greg, W. W. An Elizabethan printer and his copy. Library 4th ser 4 1924.

McMurphy, S. J. In her Spenser's use of Ariosto, Seattle 1924.

Smith, G. C. M., N. E. McClure and V. T. Harlow. TLS 10 March, 19 May, 14 July, 27 Oct 1927.

Kirwood, A. E. The Metamorphosis of Ajax and its sequels. Library 4th ser 12 1931.

Hughey, R. The Harington ms and related documents. Library 4th ser 15 1935.

Rich, T. Harington and Ariosto. New Haven 1940.

Trotter, M. G. Harington's sources. TLS 30 Dec 1944.

Goldman, M. S. Sidney and Harington as opponents of superstition. JEGP 54 1955.

Meadows, D. In his Elizabethan quintet, 1956.

MacKinnon, M. H. M. Harington and Bishop Hall. PQ 37 1958.

Lea, K. M. Harington's folly. In Elizabethan and Jacobean studies presented to F. P. Wilson, Oxford 1959.

Schmutler, K. E. Harington's metrical paraphrases of the penitential psalms: three ms versions. PBSA 53 1959.

Cutts, J. P. Harington's epigrammatic lyric. N & Q Feb 1960.

Nelson, T. G. A. Harington and Dante. N & Q Dec 1969.

— Harington: a mistaken attribution. Ibid.

— Harington as a critic of Sidney. SP 67 1970.

Taylor, A. B. Peend and Golding. N & Q Jan 1969.

EDMUND HATFELD

See St Ursula, below.

STEPHEN HAWES
fl. 1503–11

§1

The example of vertu. [1509?], [c. 1520?] (fragment), 1530; modernized E. Arber, in his Dunbar anthology, 1901. Written 1503.

The pastyme of pleasure. [1509] (fragments), 1517, 1554 (as The histories of graunde amoure), 1555; ed R. Southey, Select works of the British poets, 1831; ed T. Wright 1845 (Percy Soc); ed W. E. Mead 1928 (EETS).

A joyfull medytacyon of the coronacyon of Henry the eyght. [1509]; ed D. Laing 1865 (Abbotsford Club).

The convercyon of swerers. 1509, [1509?], [c. 1530], 1551 (fragment); rptd in Laing, above.

The comforte of lovers. [1515?]. Written 1511.

§2

Bale, J. In his Scriptorum illustrium, 1557.

Warton, T. In his History of English poetry vol 2, 1777.

Fuhr, K. Lautuntersuchungen zu Hawes Pastime. Marburg 1891.

Schick, J. In his edn of Temple of glass, 1891 (EETS).

Burkart, E. A. The pastime of pleasure: critical introduction to a proposed new edition. 1899.

Zander, F. Hawes Passetyme verglichen mit Spensers Faerie Queene. Rostock 1903.

Natter, H. Untersuchung der Quellen von Hawes Pastime. Passau 1911.

Berdan, J. M. In his Early Tudor poetry, New York 1920.

Lemmi, C. W. The influence of Boccaccio on Hawes's Pastime. RES 5 1929.

Wells, W. Hawes and the Court of Sapience. RES 6 1930.

Bühler, C. F. Kynge Melyzyus and the Pastime. RES 10 1934.

Atkins, J. W. H. In his English literary criticism: medieval, Cambridge 1943.

Sellers, H. Two poems by Hawes and an early medical tract. BM Quart 13 1939.

Church, M. The first English pattern poems. PMLA 61 1946.

Morgan, A. The convercyon of swerers: another edition. Library 5th ser 24 1969.

See also col 650, above.

WILLIAM HENDRED

A boke in Frenche called Le pelerynage de lhomme and in oure tunge the Pylgrymage of mankynd, in prose compounded by William Hendred and now at the commaundemente of the same compyled in metre. 1508 (fragment), [1520?].

PRESERVATION OF HENRY VII

The first booke of the preservation of King Henry VII when he was but Earle of Richmond, compiled in English rythmicall hexameters; the second booke of the tyranny of King Richard. 1599.

HENRY VIII
1491–1547

BM ms additional 31,922. Words and music of 109 songs, 17 subscribed Henry VIII. *See* W. Chappell, Some account of an unpublished collection of songs and ballads of King Henry VIII and his contemporaries, Archaeologia 67 1867. Words ptd E. Flügel, Anglia 12 1889; F. Macnamara, Miscellaneous writings of Henry VIII, Waltham St Lawrence 1924 (10 songs); J. Stevens, Music and poetry in the early Tudor Court, 1961; Words and music ed Lady Mary Trefusis, Songs, ballads and instrumental pieces composed by King Henry the Eighth, Oxford 1912 (Roxburghe Club); J. Stevens, Music at the Court of Henry VIII, 1962 (Musica Britannica 18).

HERACLITUS AND DEMOCRITUS

The riddles of Heraclitus and Democritus. 1598. 51 in verse.

MARY HERBERT, COUNTESS OF PEMBROKE
1561–1621

§1

A dicourse of life and death written in French by Ph. Mornay [prose]; Antonius: a tragoedie written also in French by Ro. Garnier. 1592, 1600, 1606, 1607; 1595 (Antonie alone); ed A. Luce, Weimar 1897; ed G. Bullough, Narrative and dramatic sources of Shakespeare vol 5, 1964.

Sir P. Sidney, The Countesse of Pembrokes Arcadia augmented and ended. 1593, 1598 (with new addns) etc. Ed Lady Mary with H. S[tanford]; *see col 1048, above.*

[The doleful lay of Clorinda. In E. Spenser, Astrophel, 1595. Written by Spenser; *see* Osgood and Rix, below.]

A dialogue between two shepheards, Thenot and Piers, in praise of Astrea. In A poetical rapsody, ed F. Davison 1602 etc; rptd J. Nichols, Progresses of Queen Elizabeth vol 3, 1823.

To the angell spirit of Sir P. Sidney. In S. Daniel, Whole workes in poetrie, 1623. Shorter version, wrongly

attributed to Daniel. Longer version ed W. A. Ringler jr, Poems of Sidney, Oxford 1962 (from B. Juel-Jensen ms of Psalms, which also contains an unpbd dedicatory poem by Lady Mary to Queen Elizabeth).

The psalmes of David translated into divers and sundry kindes of verse. [Ed S. W. Singer], Chiswick 1823; ed J. C. A. Rathmell, Garden City NY 1963 (both from De L'Isle and Dudley ms). Lady Mary translated psalms 43–150; for account of mss and revision *see* Ringler, above.

The triumphe of death translated out of Italian [of Petrarch]. Inner Temple Petyt ms 538.43.1; ed F. B. Young, PMLA 27 1912; rptd in her Mary Sidney, 1912.

[The Countess of Pembrooks passion. Not by Lady Mary; *see* The passions of the spirit, below.]

§2

Donne, John. Upon the translation of the psalmes by Sir P. Sydney and his sister. In his Poems, 1635.

Walpole, H. In his Catalogue of royal and noble authors vol 2, 1758.

Holland, J. In his Psalmists of Britain vol 1, 1843.

Sidney, P. The subject of all verse: an account of a famous epitaph. Oxford 1907.

Young, F. B. Mary Sidney Countess of Pembroke. 1912.

Long, P. W. The lay of Clorinda. MLN 31 1916.

Osgood, C. G. The doleful lay of Clorinda. MLN 35 1920.

Riese, T. In his Die englische Psalmdichtung im sechzehnten Jahrhundert, Münster 1937.

Rix, H. D. Spenser's rhetoric and the Doleful lay. MLN 53 1938.

Beauchamp, V. W. Sidney's sister as translator of Garnier. Renaissance News 10 1957.

Robertson, J. Drayton and the Countess of Pembroke. RES new ser 16 1965.

JASPER HEYWOOD
1535–98

§1

The sixt tragedie of L.A. Seneca entituled Troas. 1559 (2 issues), [1560?]; rptd in Seneca his tenne tragedies, 1581; ed J. Jeligh 1887 (Spenser Soc); ed H. de Vocht, Louvain 1913 (Bang's Materialien 41); ed T. S. Eliot 1927.

The seconde tragedie of Seneca: Thyestes. 1560; rptd as above.

L.A. Senecae tragedia prima: Hercules furens. 1561 (Latin and English); rptd as above.

8 poems. In Paradise of dainty devices, 1576 (nos 10, 12, 95–6), 1578 (with no 100), 1585 (with nos 124, 126–7); ed H. E. Rollins, Cambridge Mass 1927.

§2

Greg, W. W. Seneca's Troas translated by J. Heywood. Library 4th ser 11 1930.

Guiney, L. I. In her Recusant poets, 1938.

JOHN HEYWOOD
1497?–1580?

A dialogue of proverbes concernyng two maner of mariages. 1546 (10 edns to 1598); An hundred epigrammes, 1550 (9 edns to 1598 expanded to 600 epigrams); A balade specifieinge the mariage betwene our soveraigne lord and lady, [1554]; The spider and the flie, 1556; A balet touching the takynge of Scarborow Castell, [1557]; A ballad against sklander and detraccion, [1562]; Of a number of rattes, [c. 1562]. *See col 1413, below.*

JOHN HIGGINS
fl. 1569–90

§1

Commendatory verse to J. Sadler's translation of Vegetius' Foure bookes of martiall policye, [1572]; rptd Campbell, below.

The first parte of the Mirour for magistrates from the comming of Brute to the incarnation of Jesu Christe. 1574 (first issue Induction and 16 tragedies; 2nd issue adds Irenglas), 1575, 1587 (40 tragedies), 1620 (rev R. Niccols); rptd J. Haslewood vol 1, 1815 (from 1587); ed L. B. Campbell, Parts added to the Mirror for magistrates, Cambridge 1946 (with biography). *See col 1024, above.*

For prose works see DNB and Campbell's introd.

§2

Winstanley, W. In his Lives of the most famous English poets, 1682.
Cooper, E. In her Muses' library, 1737.
Zimmermann, H. Quellenuntersuchungen zum ersten Teil von Higgins Mirror. Munich 1902.
Bush, D. Classical lives in the Mirror. SP 22 1925.
Farnham, W. Higgins' Mirror and Locrine. MP 23 1926.

HUGH HILARIE

The resurreccion of the masse with the wonderful vertues of the same. 'Strasburgh' (for London or Wesel) 1554. Also attributed to J. Bale and T. Becon.

MILES HOGARDE (or HUGGARDE)
fl. 1548–57

§1

The abuse of the blessed sacrament of the aultare. In R. Crowley, The confutation of the mishapen aunswer, [1548].
The assault of the sacrament of the alter. 1554. Written 1549.
A new treatyse in maner of a dialoge whiche sheweth the excellency of mannes nature. [1550?].
A treatise declaring howe Christ by perverse preachyng was banished out of this realme. 1554.
A treatise entitled the pathwaye to the towre of perfection. 1554.
A mirrour of love. 1555.
A newe ABC paraphrasticallye applied. 1557.
A myrroure of myserie. Huntington Lib ms HM 121, dated 1557.
Poems attributed in BM ms additional 15,233, ed J. O. Halliwell(-Phillipps), Redford's Wyt and scyence, 1848 (Shakespeare Soc), and Harley 3444.
For prose and lost poems see Ritson, below, and DNB.

§2

Ritson, J. In his Bibliographia poetica, 1802.
W., B. In S. E. Brydges, British bibliographer vol 4, 1814.
Guiney, L. I. In her Recusant poets, 1938.

HUGH HOLLAND
1563?–1633

§1

Pancharis: the love between Owen Tudyr and the Queen. 1603; ed J. P. Collier, Illustrations of Old English literature vol 2, 1866.
A cypres garland for our late soveraigne King James. 1625.
For commendatory poems to Shakespeare and others see F. B. Williams jr, Index of dedications, Oxford 1962 (Bibl Soc).

§2

Guiney, L. I. In her Recusant poets, 1938.
Thomas, A. S. V. In D. Williams, Eisteddfod Genedlaethol vol 2, 1943.

ROBERT HOLLAND
1557–1622?

The holie historie of our lord Jesus Christs nativitie, life, actes, miracles, doctrine, death, passion, resurrection and ascension. 1594.

WILFRID HOLME

The fall and evill successe of rebellion in old Englishe verse. 1572 (2 issues, one nd). Written 1538, on the Northern Rebellion. *See* A. G. Dickins, Yorkshire Archaeological Jnl. 39 1956.

JOHN HOPKINS
d. 1570

See col 1899f., below.

PHILIP HOWARD, 1st EARL OF ARUNDEL
1557–95

§1

Callophisus. [1581]. Prose challenge for tournament.
An epistle in the person of Christ to the faithfull soule, written first by that learned Lanspergius, and after translated into English by one of no small fame. Antwerp 1595, [St Omer] 1610 (by Philip late Earle of Arundell, ed J.W. priest); ed J. Philp 1867, 1871; ed a monk of Parkminster 1926. Prose trn from Latin of J. Justus, Landsberger.
A foure-fould meditation of the foure last things, composed in a divine poeme by R. S[outhwell] the author of S. Peters complaint [error for P. Howard]. 1606 (fragment); ed H. Thurston, Month Oct 1894; ed C. Edmonds 1895 (complete text from Bodley ms Rawlinson poetry 219). Also in Folger ms 1232.3, Harvard ms English 749, Bodley ms Tanner 118, Oscott College ms Peter Mowle's book.
Verses: O Christ my lord. Sydenham ms prayer book, ptd Catholic Record Soc 7 1909; L. I. Guiney below (from Bodley ms Tanner 118).
Verses: In the wrackes of Walsingham. Bodley ms Rawlinson poetry 219; ed J. W. Hales, Bishop Percy's folio ms vol 3, 1868; ed C. H. Firth, Trans Royal Historical Soc 3rd ser 2 1908. Anon. Guiney, below, denies Howard's authorship.

§2

[Howard, H. G. F.] Duke of Norfolk. The lives of P. Howard Earl of Arundel and of Anne Dacres his wife, edited from original mss. 1857.

Scott, E. J. L. In his Letter-book of Gabriel Harvey, 1884 (Camden Soc).

T[hurston], H. Philip Earl of Arundel. Month Jan 1896. Rejects attribution of A foure-fold meditation to Southwell.

Pollen, J. H. and W. MacMahon. The Venerable P. Howard Earl of Arundel. Catholic Record Soc 21 1919.

Beatificationis et declarationis martyrii G. Haydock, P. Howard et sociorum. 4 vols Rome 1928–9.

Robbie, H. J. L. The authorship of A foure-fold meditation. RES 5 1929.

Guiney, L. I. In her Recusant poets, 1938.

THOMAS HOWELL
fl. 1568

Collections
Poems. Ed A. B. Grosart 1879.

§1

The arbor of amitie: pleasant poems and pretie poesies. 1568.

Newe sonets and pretie pamphlets newly augmented. [1570?] (imperfect), [1575?] (fragment).

Howell his devises. 1581; ed W. Raleigh, Oxford 1906.

THOMAS HUDSON
fl. 1584–1610

The historie of Judith. Edinburgh 1584; in J. Sylvester, Bartas his devine weekes and workes, 1608, 1611, 1613, 1621, 1633, 1641; ed J. Craigie, Edinburgh 1941 (STS). Tr from French of du Bartas.

HUGH of LEICESTER

A merry jest of Dane Hew, munk of Leicestre. [1560?]; ed S. E. Brydges, British bibliographer vol 2, 1812; ed C. H. Hartshorne, Ancient metrical tales, 1829; ed W. C. Hazlitt, Remains of the early popular poetry of England vol 3, 1866.

WILLIAM HUNNIS
fl. 1550–97

§1

Certayne psalmes drawen into English meter. 1550.

The paradise of dainty devices. 1576–1606; ed H. E. Rollins, Cambridge Mass 1927. 20 poems by Hunnis.

The princelye pleasures at Kenilworth. 1576 (no known copy); rptd in Kenilworth illustrated, 1821. Verses by Hunnis.

A hyve full of hunnye: the firste booke of Moses called Genesis. 1578.

Seven sobs of a sorrowfull soule of sinn; handfull of honisuckles etc. 1583, 1585, 1587, 1589, 1592, 1597, 1600, 1602, 1604, 1609, 1615, 1618, Edinburgh 1621, London 1629, 1636. Entered 1581.

Hunnies recreations: foure godlie discourses. 1588, 1595 (with Two notable treatises).

For play Jacob and Esau attributed to him see col 1420, below.

§2

Stopes, C. C. Jacob and Esau. Athenaeum 28 April 1900.
—— Hunnis and the revels of the Chapel Royal. Louvain 1910 (Bang's Materialien 29).

Allen, D. C. In his Legend of Noah, Urbana 1949.

HUNTING OF THE CHEVIOT

§1

Hunttis of Chevet. Bodley ms Ashmole 48 (transcript from repertory of R. Sheale c. 1559); ed T. Hearne, G. Neubrigensis historia vol 1, Oxford 1719; ed T. Percy, Reliques vol 1, 1765; ed T. Wright, Songs and ballads of the reign of Philip and Mary, 1860 (Roxburghe Club); ed W. W. Skeat, Specimens of English literature, 1880; ed F. J. Child, English and Scottish popular ballads vol 3, Boston 1889 (no 162A); ed D. Hamer, Towards restoring the Hunting of the Cheviot, RES new ser 20 1969 (reconstructed text). English version of earlier lost Scottish narrative of battle of Otterburn (1388); for other redactions see Child no 161A, and Chevy Chase (17th century) Child 162B.

§2

Sidney, P. In his Defence of poesie, 1595.
Addison, J. Spectator nos 70, 74, 1711.
May, S. W. Sheale and the ballad of Chevy Chase. Amer N & Q 9 1971.

W. I.

See John Weever, below.

THE IMAGE OF HYPOCRISY

The image of hypocrisy. BM ms Lansdowne 794; ed A. Dyce, Works of Skelton vol 2, 1843. Written c. 1534.

JACOB

Thystory of Jacoby and his twelve sones. [1510?], [c. 1520] (fragment), [1522–3], [c. 1525] (fragments), [1570?], [1575?]; ed J. P. Collier, Illustrations of early English popular literature vol 1, 1863.

WELCOME TO JAMES I

Englands welcome to James King of England. 1603.

THOMAS JENNY
fl. 1566–84

Maister Randolphes phantasey. 1566; ed R. Cranstoun, Satirical poems vol 1, 1891 (STS). Attack on Mary Queen of Scots.

A discours of the present troobles in Fraunce. Antwerp (for Paris) 1568; ed J. A. van Dorsten, The radical arts, Leyden 1970. Tr from Ronsard.

EDWARD JENYNGES
fl. 1565–74

§1

The famous history of the vertuous and godly woman Judyth translated into Englysh meter. 1565 (only title-page extant).

The notable hystory of two faithfull lovers named Alfagus anb [sic] Archelaus translated into English meeter. 1574. Entered 1566–7; based on story of Titus and Gisippus in Sir Thomas Elyot, Boke named the governour, 1531.

§2

Parks, G. B. Still another Titus and Gysippus. N & Q Oct 1956.
Wright, H. G. In his Boccaccio in England, 1957.

JEST

See Wife lapped in morel's skin, below.

JOHN BON AND MASTER PARSON

See Luke Shepherd, below.

JOHN OF CAPISTRANO

Capystranus. [c. 1515] (incomplete), [1527?] (fragment), [1530?] (fragment). Narrative of siege of Belgrade in 1456; *see* E. Rona, Hungary in a medieval poem, in Studies in honour of M. Schlauch, Warsaw 1966.

RICHARD JOHNSON
1573–1659?

Musarum plangores: upon the death of Sir Christopher Hatton. [1591]; Nine worthies of London, 1592 (verse and prose); The pleasant walkes of Moore-fields, 1607 (verse and prose); Crowne garland, 1612; Golden garland, 1620 (3rd edn). *See cols 2025, 2027, 2053 below.*

JOSEPH OF ARMATHIA

The lyfe of Joseph of Armathia. 1520; ed W. W. Skeat 1871 (EETS). *See also col 413, above.*

THE JOUSTS OF MAY AND JUNE

The justes of the moneth of Maye parfurnysshed and done by Charles Brandon, Thomas Knyvet, Gyles Capell and Wyllyam Hussy; the justes and tourney of the moneth of June parfurnysshed and done by Rychard Graye Erle of Kent, by Charles Brandon with there two aydes agaynst all comers. [1507]; ed C. H. Hartshorne, Ancient metrical tales, 1829 (Maye only); ed W. C. Hazlitt, Remains of the early popular poetry of England vol 2, 1866 (Maye and June).

ARTHUR KELTON
fl. 1546

§1

A commendacion of Welshmen. 1546.
A chronycle with a genealogie declaring that the Brittons and Welshmen are dyscended from Brute. 1547.

§2

Millican, C. B. In his Spenser and the table round, Cambridge Mass 1932.

TIMOTHY KENDALL
fl. 1577

§1

Flowers of epigrammes out of sundrie the moste singular authours. 1577, Manchester 1874 (Spenser Soc).

§2

Lathrop, H. B. J. Cornarius and the early English epigrammatists. MLN 43 1928.

Rollins, H. E. In his Tottel's Miscellany vol 2, Cambridge Mass 1929.
Hudson, H. H. In his Epigram in the English Renaissance, Princeton 1947.

WILLIAM KETHE
d. 1608?

A ballet declaringe the fal of the whore of Babylone in tytuled Tye thy mare Tom boye: an exortacion to the Papists. [1548?].
Of misrule contending with Gods word by name. [1553?].
[W. Keth his seeing glasse] unto the nobilitie and jentlemen of England: the prayer of Daniel in meeter. [1555?].
Commendatory poem to C. Goodman, How superior powers oght to be obeyd, 1558.
94th psalm. In The appelation of J. Knox, 1558.
[25 psalms]. In The forme of prayers used in the Englishe congregation at Geneva, 1561 etc. *See col 1903, below.*
A sermon made at Blanford Forum. [1571?]. Prose.

THOMAS KNELL junior
fl. 1570

An epitaph upon the life and death of D. Boner sometimes unworthy Bishop of London. 1569; rptd Harleian miscellany vol 1, 1744, 1808.
An answer to a papisticall byll cast in the streetes of Northampton. 1570 (anon), [1570] (longer answer signed T. Knell jun); rptd Northampton tracts: 2nd series, 1881. Includes text of the 'byll'.
A piththy note to Papists all and some that joy in Feltons martirdome. [1570]; ed J. P. Collier, Illustrations of early English popular literature vol 1, 1863.
A declaration of such tempestious fluddes as hath been in divers places in England. 1571. *See* G. J. Gray, Trans Bibl Soc 4 1898.
An historical discourse of the life and death of Doctor Story. [1571].

THE KNIGHT OF COURTESY

The knight of curtesy and the lady of Faguell. [1568?]. *See col 450, above.*

G. KYTTES

The unluckie firmentie. [c. 1572] (imperfect). Comic narrative.

E.L.

Romes monarchie: [from] the first foundation by Romulus to Nero, translated out of the French and Italian histories. 1596.

F.L.

Ovidius Naso his remedie of love. 1600. Trn.

R.L. gent

§1

Diella: certain sonnets; the amorous poem of Dom Diego and Gynevra. 1596; ed E. Arber, English garner vol 7, 1883; ed A. B. Grosart, Manchester 1877; ed E. V. Utterson, Ryde 1841 (sonnets only); ed E. Goldsmid, Bookworms garner, 1888; ed S. Lee, Elizabethan sonnets vol 2, 1904; Dom Diego only ed P. W. Miller, Seven minor epics of the English Renaissance, Gainesville 1967 (facs). Has been attributed to Richard Linche and Richard Lylesse.

§2

Scott, J. G. Minor Elizabethan sonneteers. RES 2 1926.
—— In her Les sonnets élisabéthains, Paris 1929.
Fellheimer, J. The source of Lynche's Don Diego and Ginevra. PMLA 58 1943.
Zocca, L. R. In his Elizabethan narrative poetry, New Brunswick NJ 1950.

V.L. or U.L.

The pleasaunt pathewaye leadynge to a vertues and honest lyfe, by V.L. [1552?]. Also attributed to Urban Lynyng.

W.L.

Nothing for a new-yeares gift. 1603. See William Lisle, below.

LADY BESSY

See Bessy, above.

THE LAMENTATION OF TROY

See Sir John Ogle, below.

JOHN LANE
fl. 1600–30

§1

Tom Tel-Troths message and his pens complaint. 1600; ed F. J. Furnivall 1876 (New Shakspere Soc).
An elegie upon the death of our late soveraigne Elizabeth. 1603.
Alarm to the poets. 1648. Written before 1615.
Chaucers Squiers tale brought to light by J. Lane. 1888 (Chaucer Soc) (from ms). Written 1615.
For mss of The corrected historie of Sir Gwy Earle of Warwick, written 1617, and Tritons trumpet to the twelve monethes, written 1621, see DNB.

§2

Phillips, E. In his Theatrum poetarum, 1675.
Corser, T. In his Collectanea anglo-poetica, 1870 (Chetham Soc).

LEICESTER

See Hugh of Leicester, above.

EDWARD LEWICKE
fl. 1562

§1

The history of Titus and Gisippus. 1562; ed H. G. Wright, Early English versions of Guiscardo and Ghismonda and Titus and Gisippus, 1937 (EETS). Versified from Sir Thomas Elyot, Boke named the governour, 1531.

§2

Collier, J. P. In his Poetical decameron vol 2, 1820.
Zocca, L. R. In his Elizabethan narrative poetry, New Brunswick NJ 1950.
Wright, H. G. In his Boccaccio in England, 1957.

WILLIAM LISLE
1569?–1637

Babilon: a part of the seconde weeke of Du Bartas. 1595, 1596 (another issue).
The colonies of Bartas. 1598.
A Saxon treatise by Ælfricus. 1623. Prose and 2 poems.
Part of Du Bartas English and French. 1625, 1637 (as Foure bookes of Dubartas).
The faire Æthiopian. 1631, 1638 (as The famous historie of Heliodorus).
See also W.L., above.

LODOWICK LLOYD
fl. 1573–1610

The pilgrimage of princes. [1573], 1586, 1607, 1653 (as The marrow of history), 1659. Prose and 2 poems.
An epitaph upon Syr Edward Saunders. [1576]; rptd in The paradyse of daynty devises 1578, ed H. E. Rollins, Cambridge Mass 1927 (no 103); ed H. L. Collman, Ballads and broadsides, 1912.
A dittie to the Queens Majestie. 1579; ed S. E. Brydges, British bibliographer vol 1, 1810.
Certaine Englishe verses presented unto the Queens Majesty by L.L. 1586; ed H. Huth, Fugitive tracts: 1st series, 1875 (no 27).
The choyce of jewels. 1607. Prose and verse acrostics to Queen Anne.
Hilaria: the triumphant feast for the fift of August. 1607.

RICHARD LLOYD

A briefe discourse of the actes and conquests of the Nine Worthies. 1584.

THOMAS LODGE
1558–1625

Complaint of truth. In An alarum against usurers, 1584; Scillaes metamorphosis, 1589. 16 poems in Phoenix nest, 1593. Phillis; Elstred, 1593; A fig for Momus, 1595. Scattered poems in prose works. See col 1434, below.

HENRY LOK
1553?–1608?

§1

Sundry Christian passions contained in two hundred sonnets. 1593.
Ecclesiasticus; sundry psalms of David; sundrie sonets of Christian passions augmented; other affectionate sonets. 1597; ed A. B. Grosart 1871. 215 sonnets and other poems.

§2

Westcott, A. F. In his New poems by James I, New York 1911.
Scott, J. G. In her Les sonnets élisabéthains, Paris 1929.

THE LORD OF LORN

Lord of Learne. BM ms additional 27,879; J. W. Hales and F. J. Furnivall, Bishop Percy's folio ms vol 1, 1867. English version, entered 1580, of the Scottish Roswall and Lillian.
See col 448, above.

LORD'S PRAYER

A metricall declaration of the vij petitions of the pater noster. [c. 1530].

THOMAS LOVELL
1553–98

A dialogue between custom and veritie concerning dauncing and minstrelsie. [1581].

JOHN LYLY
1554?–1606

Six court comedies. 1632 (adds songs). *See col 1423, below.*

C.M.

See Christopher Middleton, col 1127, below.

T.M. gent

See Thomas Middleton, col 1127, below.

JOHN MARBECK
fl. 1541–85?

The holie historie of King David drawne into English meetre. 1579.

JOHN MARDELEY
fl. 1548–58

§1

A declaration of thee power of Gods worde concerning the holy supper of the Lord. [1548]. Prose, and verse Complaynt agaynst the styffenecked.
A necessarie instruction for all covetous ryche men. [1548?]. Prose, one poem.
A shorte resytal of certayne holy doctours whych proveth that the naturall body of Christ is not conteyned in the Sacrament of the Lordes supper but fyguratyvely. [1548?].
The instetucione off the Lordes Supper [and other poems]. BM ms Royal 17 B 37, dated 1558.

§2

Bale, J. In his Catalogus 1557, Index 1902.

ST MARGARET OF SCOTLAND

[Life of St Margaret of Scotland. c. 1530 (fragment).]

GERVASE MARKHAM
1568?–1637

The tragedie of Sir Richard Grinvile. 1595; The poem of poems: the song of King Salomon devided into eight eclogues, [1596]; Devoreux: teares for the losse of King Henry Third of Fraunce and the death of Walter Devoreaux, written in French by Madam G. Petau Maulette and paraphrastically translated, 1597; The teares of the beloved: the lamentation of St John concerning the death and passion of Christ, 1600; The newe metamorphosis, BM ms additional 14,824-6 (narrative poem in 24 bks written 1600–14); Marie Magdalens lamentations for the losse of her master Jesus, 1601, 1604; Rodomonths infernall: Ariastos conclusions of the marriage of Rogero with Bradamanth, written in French by P. de Portes and paraphrastically translated, 1607; The famous whore: the complaint of Paulina mistres unto Cardinall Hypolito of Est, 1609. *See col 2011, below.*

CHRISTOPHER MARLOWE
1564–93

Hero and Leander. [Lost edn 1593?], 1598; finished by G. Chapman, 1598 etc; Certaine of Ovids elegies, Middleburgh (for Edinburgh? 1598?), [1599?] (10 only with Davies' Epigrammes); All Ovids elegies: 3 bookes, Middleburg (for London c. 1600) (with Davies' Epigrames) etc; Lucans first booke, 1600 etc; The passionate sheepheard to his love, in Passionate pilgrime, 1599 (4 stanzas attributed to Shakespeare); in Englands Helicon, 1600 (6 stanzas attributed to Marlowe). Lines by G. Markham attributed to Marlowe in Englands Parnassus, 1600; *see* J. Crow, TLS 4 Jan 1947. *See col 1444, below.*

GEORGE MARSHALL

A treatise declaring the firste originall of sacrifice and of the firste receavinge of the Christen fayth here in Englande. 1554; ed H. Huth, Fugitive tracts: 1st series, 1875; ed L. I. Guiney, Recusant poets, 1939 (extracts).

JOHN MARSTON
1576–1634

The metamorphosis of Pigmalions image and certaine satyres. 1598; The scourge of villanie: three bookes of satyres, 1598, 1599, 1599. *See col 1690, below.*

MARY THE BLESSED VIRGIN

The song of Mary the mother of Christ: containing his life and passion; the teares of Christ in the garden; a prayer in contempt of the world; the description of the heavenly Jerusalem; another on the same subject; a sinners supplication. 1601; ed L. I. Guiney, Recusant poets, 1939 (extracts, attributed to Henry Walpole).

ST MARY MAGDALENE

Complaynte of the lover of Cryst saynt Mary Magdaleyn. [1520?]; as The lamentatyon of Mary Magdaleyne in edns of Chaucer 1526 etc; ed G. Chalmers, English poets vol 1, 1810; ed C. Tame, English religious literature, 1871; ed B. M. Skeat, Zürich 1897.
Marie Magdalens lamentations. 1601. *See G. Markham, above.*

THE UPCHERINGE OF THE MASS

See Luke Shepherd, below.

CHRISTOPHER MIDDLETON
1560?–1628

The historie of heaven containing the poetical fictions of all the starres in the firmament. 1596.
The legend of Humphrey Duke of Glocester. 1600; rptd Harleian miscellany vol 10, 1813.
See also col 2054 below.

THOMAS MIDDLETON
1580–1627

The wisdome of Solomon paraphrased. 1597; Micro-cynicon: sixe snarling satyres by T.M. gent, 1599; The ghost of Lucrece by T.M. gent, 1600.
See col 1646, below.

THE MILLER OF ABINGTON

A mery jest of the mylner of Abyngton. [c. 1532], [c. 1575]; ed T. Wright, Anecdota literaria, 1844; ed W. C. Hazlitt, Remains of the early popular poetry of England vol 3, 1866; ed H. Varnhagen, E Studien 9 1886; ed J. Raith, Die Geschichte von der vertauschten Wiege, Leipzig 1936. Based on Chaucer's Reeve's tale.

A MIRROR FOR MAGISTRATES

See col 1024, above.

THOMAS MOFFET
1553–1604

Nobilis: in laudem equitis P. Sydnii [Latin prose, written 1593–4]; Lessus lugubris: ob desiderium P. Sydnii [Latin verse, written 1589]. BM ms Sloane 4014, ed and tr V. B. Heltzel and H. H. Hudson, San Marino 1940.
The silkewormes and their flies described in verse by T.M. 1599.
For medical and entomological writings see DNB and Heltzel and Hudson, above.

PETER MOONE
fl. 1548

§1

A short treatyse of certayne thinges abused in the popysh church. Ipswich [1548].
[Verse sermon against Papists. Ipswich 1548 (anon fragment)].

§2

Wheat, C. H. P. Moone and J. Ramsey: verse satirists of the English Reformation. SP 46 1949.
Dickens, A. G. P. Moone the Ipswich gospeller and poet. N & Q Dec 1954.

EDWARD MORE
1537?–1620

§1

A lytle treatyse called the defence of women made agaynst the schole howse of women. 1560 (entered and preface dated 1557); ed E. V. U[tterson], Select pieces of early popular poetry vol 2, 1817.

§2

Stein, H. Six tracts about women. Library 2nd ser 15 1934.
Utley, F. L. In his Crooked rib, Columbus 1944.

SIR THOMAS MORE
1478–1535

The lyfe of Johan Picus Erle of Myrandula. [1510?], [c. 1525] (prose and 4 poems); A mery gest how a sergeaunt wolde lerne to be a frere, [1516?], [c. 1565]; Epigrammata, Basle 1518, 1520 (Latin verse); The boke of the fayre gentylwoman Lady Fortune, [c. 1540]; Workes, 1557 (contains poems: Sergeant, nyne pageauntes, of the deth of Quene Elisabeth, Boke of Fortune, Mirandula). *See col 1792, below.*

WILLIAM MUGGINS

Londons mourning garment for the death of her wealthy cittizens and other her inhabitants. 1603. An account of the 1603 plague.

RICHARD MULCASTER
1530?–1611

Cato christianus. [1600]. Latin verse.
In mortem serenissimae reginae Elizabethae. 1603. Latin and English verse.
The translation of certaine Latine verses upon her Majesties death. 1603. Separate edn of the blank verse portion of the preceding.
For his educational treatises, Positions 1581 and Elementarie 1582, see col 2276 above.

ANTHONY MUNDAY
1560–1633

The mirrour of mutabilitie. 1579; The paine of pleasure, 1580; [Ballad in praise of the navy, c. 1584] (fragment); A banquet of daintie conceits, 1588 (entered 1584); Englands Helicon, 1600 (contains 7 poems signed Shepherd Tony, some probably from the lost Sweet sobs and amorous complaints of shepherds and nymphs, entered 1583). Scattered verses in prose works; *see col 1464, below.*

A.N.

A warning to all trayterous Papistes. 1586.

THOMAS NASHE
1567–1601?

The choice of valentines (written before 1593, 3 mss); Dido Queene of Carthage, by C. Marlowe and T. Nash, 1594 (play); Summers last will and testament, 1600 (play). Scattered verses in prose works; *see col 1456 below.*

WILLIAM NEVILL
1497–c. 1545

§ 1

The castell of pleasure. 1518, [1530?]; ed R. D. Cornelius 1930 (EETS).

§ 2

Lewis, C. S. In his Allegory of love, Oxford 1936.

ALEXANDER NEVILLE
1544–1614

The lamentable tragedie of Œdipus out of Seneca. 1563; rptd in Seneca his tenne tragedies, ed T. Newton 1581, 1927 (with introd by T. S. Eliot). Written 1560. *See col 1421 below.*

B. Googe, Eglogs epytaphes and sonettes, 1563. 4 poems by Neville.

De furoribus Norfolcensium Ketto duce; Norvicus. 1575 (3 issues); Kettus rptd in C. Ockland, Anglorum praelia, 1582. Latin verse on Kett's rebellion and description of Norwich; tr R. Woods, Norfolkes furies with a description of Norwich, 1615, 1623.

Academiae cantabrigiensis lacrymae tumulo D. P. Sidneij sacratae. 1587. Ed Neville, who contributed prose funeral oration and 3 Latin poems.

THOMAS NEWBERY
fl. 1563

A booke called Dives Pragmaticus. 1563; ed H. Huth, Fugitive tracts: 1st series, 1875; ed P. E. Newbery and H. C. Wyld, Manchester 1910 (facs). A vocabulary manual in verse.

HUMFREY NEWTON
1466–1536

Robbins, R. H. The poems of Newton. PMLA 65 1950. Prints 17 poems by Newton and 6 by others from Bodley ms Latin miscellany c. 66.

THOMAS NEWTON of Cheshire
1542?–1607

Seneca his tenne tragedies. 1581; ed J. Leigh 1887 (Spenser Soc); ed T. S. Eliot 2 vols 1927. Ed Newton, who translated Thebais.

Aliquot heroum hodie viventium a T. Newtono exarata. In J. Leland, Principum ac illustrium aliquot et eruditorum in Anglia virorum encomia, trophaea, genethliaca et epithalamia, 1589; rptd T. Hearne, Itinerary of J. Leland vol 5, 1770. Latin verse.

For trns and other prose see DNB; for Latin and English commendatory verses see F. B. Williams jr, Index of dedications, 1962 (Bibl Soc).

THOMAS NEWTON gent.

Atropoion Delion: the death of Delia our late Eliza. 1603; ed J. Nichols, Progresses of Queen Elizabeth vol 3, 1805.

SAMUEL NICHOLSON
fl. 1600

Acolastus his after-witte: stultorum tragi-comedia. 1600; ed J. O. Halliwell(-Phillipps) 1866; ed A. B. Grosart, Manchester 1876.

Translator of HENDRIK NICLAS
(CHRISTOPHER VITELL?)
fl. 1555–79

Comoedia: a worke in ryme contayning an enterlude of myndes witnessing the mans fall from God. [Cologne 1574?]. Closet drama.

A new balade or songe of the Lambs feaste. 1574; ed L. Haberly, Long Crendon Bucks [1930].

All the letters of the ABC in ryme. [Cologne] 1575.

Terra pacis: a true testification of the spirituall lande of peace. [Cologne 1575?]. Prose, with 2 chs in verse.

ANTHONY NIXON
fl. 1602–16

The Christian navy. 1602.

Elizaes memoriall; King James his arrivall; Romes downefall. 1603.

Great Brittaines generall joyes: the mariage of the princes Fredericke and Elizabeth. 1613.

JOHN NORDEN
1548–1625?

§ 1

A sinful mans solace. 1585. Prose and verse.

Vicissitudo rerum: an elegiacall poem. 1600, 1601 (another issue as The store house of varieties); ed D. C. Collins 1931 (Shakespeare Assoc Facs).

A pensive soules delight. 1603, 1615.

The labyrinth of mans life. 1614.

§ 2

Gerrish, W. B. John Norden. 1903.

Pollard, A. W. The unity of Norden. Library 3rd ser 7 1926.

Koller, K. The source of Vicissitudo rerum. SP 35 1938.

THOMAS NORTON
1532–84

Commendatory poems. In W. Turner, A preservative agaynst the poyson of Pelagius, 1551.

R. Tottel, Songes and sonettes, 1557 (2 poems); ed H. E. Rollins, Cambridge Mass 1928, nos 257, 289. Anon, attributed to Norton in BM ms Cotton Titus A.xxiv.

Norton translated 25 psalms in The whole booke of psalmes collected into Englysh by T. Starnhold, J. Hopkins and others, *1562 etc. See col 1899, below.*

[3 sonnets in answer to Sir Henry Goodyere, 1572], Arundel Harington ms; ed Hughey no 148; Bodley ms Gough Norfolk 93 ptd J. P. Collier, Camden miscellany 3 1855; Marsh's Library Dublin ms Z.3.5.21.

For Gorboduc see col 1772, below.

THOMAS NUCE
d. 1617

The ninth tragedie of Seneca called Octavia, translated by T.N. [1566]; rptd in Seneca his tenne tragedies, 1581, 1887, 1927.

Latin and English commendatory verses. In J. Studley's trn of Seneca's Agamemnon, 1566.

THE NUTBROWN MAID

A ballade of the notte browne mayde. In R. Arnold, Chronicle, [Antwerp 1503?], [Southwark 1525?]; rptd in Muses Mercury vol 1, 1707; ed E. Capell, Prolusions 1760; T. Percy, Reliques, 1765; W. C. Hazlitt in his Remains vol 2, 1866; W. W. Skeat, Specimens of English literature, 1871; ed W. A. Ringler jr, English literary Renaissance vol 1, 1971 (critical text); tr French by E. Legouis, La fille brune, Paris 1926.

The new notborune mayd upon the passion of Cryste. [c. 1535]; ed I. Isted 1820 (Roxburghe Club); ed W. C. Hazlitt, Remains vol 3, 1866. A religious parody of above.

I.O.

See Sir John Ogle, below.

CHRISTOPHER OCLAND
fl. 1572–90

§1

Anglorum praelia, ab 1327 usque ad 1558. 1580, 1582 (4 edns with Εἰρηναρχία and A. Neville's Kettus), 1582 (2 edns, with Εἰρηναρχία); tr J. Sharrock, The valiant actes of the English nation, 1585 (verse). Latin verse.

Εἰρηναρχία: sive Elizabetha: de pacatissimo Angliae statu imperante Elisabetha; illustrissimorum virorum qui sunt Elisabethae Reginae a consiliis catalogus. 1582, 1582 (5 edns, with Anglorum praelia as above); tr J. Sharrock, Elizabeth Queene, 1585 (verse). Latin verse.

Elizabetheis: de pacatissimo Angliae statu liber secundus, in quo hispanicae classis profligatio explicantur. 1589. Latin verse.

The fountaine and welspring of all variance: wherein is declared that Rome is signified by the name of Babylon in the Revelation of S. John. 1589. Prose.

The Pope's farwel written originally in Latine verse by C. Ocland and ptd in 1582, with some remarques upon the late plot. [1680?].

§2

Acts of the Privy Council. Ed A. Dasent new ser 13 1896. Prescribes Anglorum praelia as school text.

Bradner, L. In his Musae anglicanae, New York 1940.

SIR JOHN OGLE
1569–1640

The lamentation of Troy for the death of Hector: an olde womans tale, by I.O. 1594; ed E. C. Wilson, Chicago 1959, who identifies I.O. as Ogle.

SIR THOMAS OVERBURY
1581–1613

See cols 2043, 2139, below.

JOHN OWEN
1560–1622

See col 1336, above.

HENRY PARKER, 8th Baron Morley
1476–1556

§1

The exposition of the psalme [94] Deus ultionem. 1539. Prose, tr 1534.

Forty-six lives translated from Boccaccio's De claris mulieribus. In F. G. Waldron, Literary museum, 1792 (extracts); ed H. G. Wright 1943 (EETS). Prose, tr 1534-7.

Masuccio novella 49. BM ms Royal 18 A.lxii; ed F. Brie, Archiv 124 1920. Prose, tr 1543-7.

The tryumphes of F. Petrarcke. [1555?]; ed J. E. T. Loveday 1887 (Roxburghe Club); in E. P. Hammond, English verse between Chaucer and Surrey, Durham NC 1927 (extracts); ed D. D. Carnicelli, Cambridge Mass 1971. Tr before 1547.

An Italion ryme called soneto. BM ms Royal A. xv; ed E. Flügel, Verschollene Sonette, Anglia 13 1891; in his Neuenglisches Lesebuch, Halle 1895; Hammond as above. Tr before 1547.

Epitaph on Sir T. West Lord Delaware. In G. Legh, The accedens of armory, 1562; ed T. Park in his edn of H. Walpole, A catalogue of the royal and noble authors of England vol 1, 1806; ed S. E. Brydges in his edn of A. Collins, The peerage of England vol 5, 1812; ed Loveday as above; ed L. I. Guiney, Recusant poets, 1939. Written 1554.

2 poems in Bodley ms Ashmole 48; 2nd ed P. Bliss in his edn of A. Wood, Athenae oxonienses vol 1, 1810; both ed T. Park in S. E. Brydges, The British bibliographer vol 4, 1814; ed Flügel Lesebuch above; E. Arber, in his Surrey and Wyatt anthology, 1900; ed Guiney as above (first poem only with notes).

§2

For biography see DNB and introds of Loveday, Hammond, Guiney and especially Wright, above.

Wright, H. G. Lord Morley and A. Dürer. MLR 40 1945.
—— In his Boccaccio in England, 1957.
Parks, G. B. The genesis of Tudor interest in Italian. PMLA 77 1962.

MATTHEW PARKER, Archbishop of Canterbury
1504–75

The whole psalter translated into English metre. [1567?]. *See* Theron, Warton's account of Abp Parker's Psalms, GM Dec 1781.

ROBERT PARRY
fl. 1588–97

Moderatus: the historie of the blacke knight. 1595. Prose with 22 poems.

Sinetes passions upon his fortunes. 1597. 'The patrone his pathetical poesies' at end, by Sir John Salusbury, rptd C. Brown 1914 (EETS), with biography of Parry.

JOHN PARTRIDGE
fl. 1566–73

An admonition or warning to England. In The great wonders that are chaunced in the realme of Naples, translated by J.A., 1566.

The notable hystorie of two famous princes Astianax and Polixana. 1566.

The hystorie of the valiaunt knight Plasidas, [o]therwise called Eustas. [1566]; ed J. P. Collier, Illustrations of old English literature vol 3, 1866; H. H. Gibbs 1873 (Roxburghe Club).

The historie of the worthy lady Pandavola, daughter to the great Turke. 1566; ed Gibbs above.

The end and confession of J. Felton. [1570].

The treasurie of commodious conceits. 1573, [1580 lost 2nd edn], 1584 (4th edn), 1584 (amplified), 1586, 1591, 1596, 1600, 1608, 1627, 1633, 1637. Prose.

The widowes treasure. 1585, [1586?], 1588, 1595, 1599, [c. 1610], 1627, 1631, 1639. Prose.

THE PASSIONS OF THE SPIRIT

§1

The passions of the spirit. 1599 (entered and dedication dated 1594); ed J. O. Halliwell(-Phillipps), A briefe description of the mss in the public library at Plymouth, 1853 (as Unpublished poem by Breton); ed N.G.B., A poem on Our Saviour's passion by Mary Sidney Countess of Pembroke, 1862 (from BM ms Sloane 1303); ed A. B. Grosart, Poems of Nicholas Breton vol 2, 1879. Ptd by and dedication signed by Thomas Este, who could be the author.

§2

H. N & Q 22 May 1852. On ms in private hands.

Nicholson, B. T. Watson and N. Breton. Athenaeum 13 Oct 1877, 9 March 1878. Attributes to Nicholas Breton.

Robertson, J. In her Poems by Nicholas Breton not hitherto reprinted, Liverpool 1952. No 12, accepts as by Breton, notes anon ms Bodley Tanner 221.

GEORGE PEELE
1556–96

Pareus. 1585 (Latin verse); An eglogue gratulatorie to Robert Earl of Essex, 1589; A farewell to Sir J. Norris and Syr F. Drake: a tale of Troy, 1589, 1604 (Tale of Troy only); Polyhymnia, 1590; The honour of the garter, [1593?]. *See col 1431, below.*

THOMAS PEEND
fl. 1565

The historie of John Lord Mandozze. 1565. Tr from Boaistuau, Histoires tragiques, tale 6.

The pleasant fable of Hermaphroditus and Salmacis, with a morall. 1565. Tr from Ovid, Metamorphoses bk 4. *See* A. B. Taylor, Peend and A. Golding, N & Q Jan 1969; A note on Marlowe, ibid.

WILLIAM PEERIS (PYERS)
fl. 1520

The discente of the lorde Percis. BM ms Royal 18.D.ii; ed J. Besley 1845 (from Bodley transcript).

The proverbis at likingfelde. BM ms Royal 18.D.ii; Antiquarian repertory 3–4 1780–4; ed E. Flügel, Anglia 14 1892.

WILLIAM PERCY
1575–1648

§1

Sonnets to the fairest Coelia. 1594; ed S. E. Brydges, Lee Priory 1818; ed A. B. Grosart, Manchester 1877; ed

E. Arber, English garner vol 6, 1883; ed S. Lee, Elizabethan sonnets vol 2, 1904.

A poor madrigall. In B. Barnes, Foure bookes of offices, 1606.

Comaedyes and Pastoralls with their songs; one booke of epigrammes, exscriptum 1647. Duke of Northumberland ms. Contains 6 plays, the first 2 ed J. Haslewood 1824 (Roxburghe Club): The cuck-queanes and cuckolds errants or the bearing down the inne: a comaedye (prose); The faery pastorall or forrest of elves; Arabia sitiens or a dream of a dry year, 1601; The aphrodysial or a sea feast, 1602; A country's tragedy in vacuniam or Cupids' sacrifice, 1602; Necromantes or the two supposed heads, 1602.

§2

Grabau, C. Zur englischen Bühne um 1600. Sh Jb 38 1902.

Albright, V. E. Percy's plays as proof of the Elizabethan stage. MP 11 1913.

Reynolds, G. F. Percy and his plays. MP 12 1914.

Scott, J. G. In her Les sonnets élisabéthains, Paris 1929.

Dodds, M. H. Percy and Charles Fitzjeffrey. N & Q 13 June, 4 and 25 July, 3–10 Oct 1931.

—— A dreame of a drye yeare. JEGP 32 1933.

—— A forrest tragaedye in vacunium. MLR 40 1945.

Hillebrand, H. N. W. Percy as an Elizabethan amateur. HLQ 1 1938.

Hughes, L. and A. H. Scouten. Some theatrical adaptations of a picaresque tale. SE 25 1946.

Race, S. J. P. Collier. N & Q 7, 21 Jan, 5 Aug 1950.

Wright, H. G. In his Boccaccio in England, 1957.

HENRY PETOWE
fl. 1598–1635

§1

The second part of Hero and Leander: conteyning their further fortunes. 1598; ed L. Chabalier, Hero et Leandre, Paris 1911.

Philochasander and Elanira the faire lady of Britaine. 1599.

Elizabetha quasi vivens: Elizas funerall. 1603, 1603; ed T. Park, Harleian miscellany vol 10, 1813; ed J. Nichols, Progresses of Queen Elizabeth vol 3, 1823; ed S. E. Brydges, Restituta vol 3, 1814–16 (verse only). Verse and prose.

Englands Caesar: his Majesties most royall coronation. 1603; rptd in Harleian miscellany vol 10, 1813; ed J. Nichols, Progresses of James I vol 1, 1828.

An honorable president for great men to the memory of J. Bancks, citizen and mercer of London. 1630.

The artillery garden London. 1635.

§2

Shannon, G. P. Petowe's continuation of Hero and Leander. MLN 44 1929.

Crathern, A. T. A romanticized version of Hero and Leander. MLN 46 1931.

Joseph, B. L. Correspondence. English 8 1950.

Zocca, L. R. In his Elizabethan narrative poetry, New Brunswick NJ 1950.

PETER PETT

Times journey to seeke his daughter truth; truths letter to fame of Englands excellencie. 1599.

THOMAS PHAER
1510?–60

Commendatory poem to J. de Porcia's The preceptes of warre, tr P. Betham 1544.
Owen Glendour. In A myrrour for Magistrates. [1555 fragment], 1559 etc; ed L. B. Campbell, Cambridge 1938, no 6.
The seven first bookes of the Eneidos of Virgill. 1558; The nyne fyrst bookes with so much of the tenthe as coulde be founde, 1562; The whole xii bookes the residue supplied by Thomas Twyne, 1573; The thirteene bookes (Maphaeus Vegius' 13th bk tr Twyne), 1584, 1596, 1600, 1607, 1620. BM ms additional 36,529 (bks 1–3).
For legal and medical works see DNB.

JOHN PHILLIP(S)
fl. 1566–94

Bibliographies
Greg, W. W. Phillip: notes for a bibliography. Library 3rd ser 1 1910.

§1
The examination and confession of certaine wytches at Chensforde [Chelmsford]. 3 pts 1566. Prose, with verses by Phillip; rptd Philobiblon miscellanies 8, 1863–4.
Balad intituled a cold pye for the papists. [1570?].
An epitaph on the death of the Ladie Maioresse Avenet [i.e. Avenon]. 1570; ed J. Lilly, Collection of black-letter ballads, 1867.
A frendly alarum to the true-harted subjectes of England. [1570].
An epytaphe of Sir W. Garrat. 1571.
The history of Cleomines and Juliet. [1577?] (fragment).
An epitaph on the death of Lady Margarit Douglasis. [1578].
A commemoration of the Ladye Margrit Duglasis good grace. [1578].
An epitaph on the death of Lord Henry Wrisley, Earle of Southampton. 1581; ed J. Lilly, Collection of black-letter ballads, 1867.
The life and death of Sir Phillip Sidney. 1587; ed S. Butler, Sidneiana, 1837 (Roxburghe Club).
A commemoration of Sir C. Hatton. 1591; ed C. Edmonds, Lamport garland, 1881 (Roxburghe Club).
A commemoration of Dame Helen Branch. 1594.
For his Commodye of pacient and meeke Grissill, [1566?], *see col 1417, below.*

PHILOGAMUS

See Luke Shepherd, below.

THE PILGRIMAGE OF MANKIND

See William Hendred, above.

THE PILGRIM'S TALE

The pylgrymse tale. In The Court of Venus, [1539]; ed F. J. Furnivall, Thynne's Animadversions, 1876 (Chaucer Soc); ed R. A. Fraser, The Court of Venus, Durham NC 1955. *See* R. A. Fraser, Political prophecy in the Pilgrim's tale, South Atlantic Quart 56 1957.

THE PLOWMAN'S TALE
§1
The plowmans tale. [c. 1535] (lacks title-page), [1545?] (lacks title-page); rptd as next to last Canterbury tale in Workes of Chaucer, 1542; ed W. W. Skeat, Works of Chaucer vol 7, Oxford 1897. Skeat dates composition c. 1395, Bradley early 16th century. *See col 545, above.*

§2
Thynne, F. In his Animadversions, 1599; ed F. J. Furnivall 1876 (Chaucer Soc).
Dart, J. In his Westmonasterium vol 1, 1723.
Bradley, H. The plowman's tale. Athenaeum 12 July 1902.
Irvine, A. S. A ms copy of the Plowman's tale. SE 12 1932.

A PORE HELPE
See Luke Shepherd, below.

THOMAS POWELL
1572?–1635?

Loves leprosie. 1598; ed E. F. Rimbault 1842 (Percy Soc) (from a transcript).
The passionate poet: a description of the Thracian Ismarus. 1601.
Vertues due: the life of Katherine Howard late Countess of Nottingham (by T.P. gent). 1603; ed C. Edmonds, A Lamport garland, 1881 (Roxburghe Club).
For prose see DNB and col 1136, below.

ROBERT PRICKET
fl. 1603–45

The souldiers wish unto his sovereigne lord King James; poem to the Lord Maior of London. 1603.
Honors fame in triumph riding: the life and death of the Earle of Essex. 1604.
Times anotomie. 1606.
The Jesuits miracles: or new popish wonders. 1607.

THOMAS PROCTER
fl. 1578–84

A gorgeous gallery of gallant inventions, 1578.
The triumph of truth. [1585?]; ed J. P. Collier, Illustrations of old English literature vol 2, 1866.
Commendatory poems to A. Mundy's Mirrour of mutabilitie, 1579, and T.F.'s Newes from the north, 1579.

THE PROUD WIFE'S PATERNOSTER
§1
The proude wyves pater noster. 1560; ed E. V. U[tterson], Select pieces of early popular poetry vol 2, 1816; ed W. C. Hazlitt, Remains of the early popular poetry of England vol 4, 1866.

§2
Stein, H. Six tracts about women. Library 4th ser 15 1935.
Utley, F. L. In his Crooked rib, Columbus 1944. No 240.

C. PYRRYE

The praise and dispraise of women: a dialogue uppon know before thou knitte. [1569]. Entered 1563-4. *See* F. L. Utley, The crooked rib, Columbus 1944, no 210.

ST RADEGUNDE

See Henry Bradshaw, above.

SIR WALTER RALEGH
1554-1618

See col 2214, below.

LAURENCE RAMSEY
fl. 1550-88

The practice of the Divell against the true professors of Gods holy worde. [1577?].
A short discourse of Syr Nicholas Bacon. [1579].

WILLIAM RANKINS
fl. 1587-1601

A mirrour of monsters: the manifold vices caused by the infectious sight of playes. 1587. Prose.
The English ape: the Italian imitation by W.R. 1588. Prose.
Seaven satyres applyed to the weeke [and other poems]. 1598; ed A. Davenport, Liverpool 1948.
Commendatory poem to J. Bodenham's Belvedere, 1600.

REDE ME AND BE NOT WROTH

See William Barlow, above.

THE REMEDY OF LOVE

The remedy of love. In Workes of Geffray Chaucer, 1532, ed W. W. Skeat 1905 (facs), Menston 1970 (facs), 1542, [1545?], 1561, 1598, 1602, 1687, 1721; [ed R. Anderson], Poets of Great Britain vol 1, Edinburgh 1795; ed A. Chalmers, English poets vol 1, 1810. *See* F. L. Utley, The crooked rib, no 255.

HUGH RHODES
fl. 1540

Stans puer ad mensam: otherwyse called the boke of norture, newly imprinted. [before 1540], [1545?], [1560?], [1560?], 1568, [c. 1570], 1577 (as The boke of nurture newly corrected); ed F. J. Furnivall, The babees book, 1868 (EETS).

JOHN RHODES, Minister of Enborne
fl. 1588-1606

The countrie mans comfort: religious recreations printed 1588 and since enlarged. 1637. Entered 1588.
An answere to a Romish rime lately printed and entituled A proper new ballad wherein are contayned Catholike questions to the Protestant, by I.R. 1602.

An epitaph on the death of John [Whitgift] Archbishop of Canterburie. 1604. By Rhodes?
A briefe summe of the treason intended against the King and state November 5 1605 [and other poems]. 1606, 1606.

ROBERT THE DEVIL

Roberte the Devyll. [1510?] (fragment); ms copy of c. 1564 print (BM ms Egerton 3132) ed I. Herbert 1798; ed W. C. Hazlitt, Remains of the early popular poetry of England vol 1, 1864. Metrical version of prose trn ptd 1502? *See* R. Flower, The manuscript of the poem of Roberte the Deuyll, BM Quart 9 1934.

HENRY ROBERTS
fl. 1585-1606

§1

Fames trumpet soundinge: commemorations of the lives and deathes of Sir Walter Mildmay and Sir Martin Calthrop. 1589; ed H. Huth, Fugitive tracts: 1st series, 1875.
The trumpet of fame: Sir F. Drakes and Sir J. Hawkins farewell. 1595; ed T. Park, Lee Priory 1818.
Lancaster his allarums in Brasill. [1595]. Prose account of Capt James Lancaster, prefatory poem.
For romances see col 2053, below.

§2

Wright, L. B. H. Robarts: patriotic propagandist and novelist. SP 29 1932.
—— In his Middle-class culture in Elizabethan England, Chapel Hill 1935.

ROBIN CONSCIENCE

The booke in meeter of Robin Conscience. [1560?] (fragment), [after 1584] (imperfect); ed W. C. Hazlitt, Remains of the early popular poetry of England vol 3, 1866. Dialogue.

ROBIN HOOD

§1

[A lytell geste of Robyn hode]. [1500] (de Worde) (fragment), [1500?] (Pynson) (fragments), [1506?] (de Worde), [Antwerp 1510-15?] (van Doesborch), [London 1516?] (Notary) (fragment), [1560?] (W. Copland) (with the Playe of Robin Hoode), [1590?]; 1506? ed J. Ritson, Robin Hood vol 1, 1795; ed J. M. Gutch, Robin Hode vol 1, 1847; ed E. Flügel, Neuenglisches Lesebuch, Halle 1895; 1510-15? ed D. Laing, Golagros and Gawane, Edinburgh 1827; ed F. J. Child, English and Scottish ballads vol 5, Boston 1878, 1886, vol 3 1888 (as English and Scottish popular ballads, no 117 with elaborate introd), 1 vol 1904; ed G. Stevenson, Pieces from the Chepman and Myllar prints, Edinburgh 1918 (STS); ed W. Beattie, Chepman and Myllar prints, Edinburgh 1950 (facs).
[Robin Hood and the Potter]. Cambridge Univ ms Ee.4.35 (before 1525); ed J. Ritson, Robin Hood vol 1, 1795 etc; ed J. M. Gutch, Robin Hode vol 2, 1847; ed F. J. Child, English and Scottish ballads vol 5, Boston 1878 etc (no 121 in 1888 edn).
For plays see col 1418, Peele col 1431, Munday col 1464, below.

§2

Ritson, J. Robin Hood. 2 vols 1795, 1832 (rev); 7 edns to 1885.
Gutch, J. M. A lytell gest of Robin Hode. 2 vols 1847.
Child, F. J. English and Scottish popular ballads vol 3. Boston 1888 (introd to nos 117–54).
Clawson, W. H. The gest of Robin Hood. Toronto 1909.
Haworth, P. English hymns and ballads. Oxford 1927.
Gable, J. H. A bibliography of Robin Hood. Lincoln Nebraska 1939.
Moreland, C. C. Ritson's life of Robin Hood. PMLA 50 1935.
Harris, P. V. The truth about Robin Hood. 1951.
Hilton, R. H. The origins of Robin Hood. Past & Present 14 1958. See J. C. Holt 18 1960, M. Keen 19 1961.
Keen, M. In his Outlaws of medieval legend, Toronto 1961.
Oates, J. C. T. A note on the Pynson and Lettersnijder editions. SB 16 1963.
Bessinger, J. B., jr. Robin Hood: folklore and historiography. Tennessee Stud in Lit 11 1966.
Fowler, D. C. In his Literary history of the popular ballad, Durham NC 1968.

CLEMENT ROBINSON
fl. 1566–84

A handefull of pleasant delites. [c. 1575] (fragment), 1584, [1595?] (fragment). See col 1008, above.

RICHARD ROBINSON of Alton
fl. 1569–89

The rewarde of wickednesse discoursing the sundrye monstrous abuses of wicked ungodlye worldelinges. [1574].
A golden mirrour: pithie and figurative visions prognosticating good fortune to England; poems on the names of sundrie both noble and worshipfull. 1589; ed T. Corser, Manchester 1851 (Chetham Soc).

RICHARD ROBINSON of London
fl. 1576–1600

§1

Certain selected histories for Christian recreations with their severall moralizations. [1577].
A dyall of dayly contemplacion. 1578. Revision of de Worde's 1499 print of William of Touris' Contemplacyon of synners, prose and verse.
A learned assertion of the life of Prince Arthure. 1582; ed W. E. Mead 1925 (EETS). Prose trn of John Leland, Assertio Arturii, 1544.
The auncient order, societie and unitie laudable of Prince Arthure and his knightly armory of the round table: a three fold assertion in favour of English archery. 1583.
For other prose trns, see DNB and Short-title catalogue.

§2

Vogt, G. M. R. Robinson's Eupolemia. SP 21 1924. Reprints BM ms Royal 18 A.lxvi.
McKerrow, R. B. Robinson's Eupolemia and the licensers. Trans Bibl Soc new ser 11 1930.

ROBERT ROCHE
1576–1629

Eustathia: the constancie of Susanna. Oxford 1599.

THOMAS ROGERS of Bryanston
1574?–1609?

§1

Celestiall elegies dedeploring [sic] the death of the Ladie Fraunces Countesse of Hertford: funerall verses touching the death of Mathew Ewens. 1598; ed C. Edmonds, A Lamport garland, 1881 (Roxburghe Club). 41 sonnets.
Leicesters ghost. In Leicester's commonwealth, 1641, 1641; ed F. B. Williams jr, Chicago 1971 (from mss).

§2

Williams, F. B., jr. Rogers of Bryanston. Harvard Stud 16 1934.
— Leicester's Ghost. Harvard Stud 18 1935.
— R. Johnson's borrowed tears. SP 34 1937.
— Rogers on Raleigh's atheism. N & Q Oct 1968.
Sisson, C. J. A topical reference in the Alchemist. In J. Q. Adams memorial studies, Washington 1948.

JOHN ROSSE

Lacies nobilitie. In Sir John Ferne, Blazon of gentrie, 1586.
The authors tears upon the death of Sir William Sackvile. Bodley ms Douce 277, dated 1592.

FRANCIS ROUS the elder
1579–1659

Thule or vertues historie. 1598; ed J. Crossley, Manchester 1878 (Spenser Soc).
The psalmes of David in English meeter, ordered by the Committee of the House of Commons [to] be published for the generall use. 1643, 1646. See col. 1911, below.
For devotional writings in prose, see DNB.

RICHARD ROWLANDS
fl. 1565–1620

§1

Odes in imitation of the seaven penitential psalmes; other poemes. [Antwerp] 1601.
For prose works see DNB.

§2

Sermon, H. Richardus Versteganus. Ghent 1893.
Rombauts, E. Richard Verstegen. Koninklijke Vlaamse Academie voor Taal- en Letterkunde 6 1933.
Guiney, L. I. In her Recusant poets, 1939.
McKay, F. M. A note on R. Verstegan's poetry. N & Q Oct 1968.

SAMUEL ROWLANDS
1570?–1630?

The betraying of Christ; other poems, 1598; The letting of humours blood in the head-vaine, 1600; Tis merrie when gossips meete, 1602; Ave Caesar, 1603. Many later poems; see col 1335, below.

WILLIAM ROY

See William Barlow, above.

R.S. esquire

§1

The amorous contention of Phillis and Flora, translated out of a Latine coppie. In George Chapman, Ovids banquet of sence, 1595, 1598 (separately as Phillis and Flora by R.S. esquire); ed P. B. Bartlett, Poems of Chapman, New York 1941. Possibly by Richard Stapleton, who may also have translated from French of Gilles Durant the preceding poem in Chapman's Banquet, The amorous zodiack.

§2

Lee, S. Chapman's Amorous zodiacke. MP 3 1905.
Rollins, H. E. In his edn of Phoenix nest, Cambridge Mass 1931.

FRANCIS SABIE
fl. 1587–96
§1

The fisher-mans tale: the life and love of Cassander a Grecian knight. 1595. Entered 1594; details from Greene's Pandosto, 1588.
Flora's fortune: the second part of the Fisher-mans tale. 1595; [ed J. O. Halliwell (-Phillipps)] 1867 (both pts, from Bodley ms Douce 280).
Pans pipe: three pastorall eglogues in English hexameter. 1595.
Adams complaint; the olde worldes tragedie; David and Bathsheba. 1596.

§2

Collier, J. P. In his Poetical decameron vol 1, 1820.
Allen, D. C. In his Legend of Noah, Urbana 1949.
Stanford, A. Sabie: a biographical sketch. HLQ 25 1962.
— Shakespeare and Sabie. Shakespeare Quart 15 1964.

THOMAS SACKVILLE, 1st EARL OF DORSET
1536–1608

Collections
Works. Ed R. W. Sackville-West 1859. Gorboduc, Induction and Buckingham, letters, biography.

§1
Sonnet before T. Hoby's translation of Castiglione's Courtyer. 1561, 1577, 1588; ed W. Raleigh 1900; ed W. B. D. Henderson, nd (EL).
The tragedie of Gorboduc: three actes wrytten by Thomas Norton and the two last by T. Sackville, shewed before the Quenes Majestie [at] Whitehall, 18 Jan 1561 (for 1562). 1565, [1570], 1590 (with Lydgate's Serpent of devision). *See col 1772, below.*
Induction and Complaynt of Henrye Duke of Buckingham.

In A myrrour for magistrates, 1563 etc; ed L. B. Campbell, Cambridge 1938 (Induction and no 22). St John's College Cambridge ms 364, ed M. Hearsey, New Haven 1936; Induction rptd E. Cooper, Muses library, 1737 (selection); Works of Surrey and Sackville, ed R. Bell 1854; Sackville-West 1859.
Poem on Sir Philip and Sir Thomas Hobby, asserted to be in Sackville's hand by J. P. Collier, Shakspere Soc Papers 4 1849.

§2
Koeppel, E. Chaucers Romaunt of the rose und Sackvilles Induction. Archiv 101 1898.
Davies, J. A myrroure for magistrates considered with reference to the sources of Sackville's contributions. Leipzig 1906.
Clark, A. M. Sackville's personification of old age. TLS 23 Jan 1920.
Sackville-West, V. Knole and the Sackvilles. 1922.
Stenberg, T. Sackville's Buckingham and Milton's Satan. N & Q 11 Feb 1928. Reply by L. R. M. Strachan 25 Feb 1928.
Bush, D. In his Mythology and the Renaissance tradition in English poetry, Minneapolis 1932.
Anon. A poet turned statesman. TLS 25 Jan 1936.
Pyle, F. Sackville and A mirror for magistrates. RES 14 1938.
Rubel, V. L. In her Poetic diction in the English Renaissance, New York 1941.
Swart, J. Sackville: a study in 16th-century poetry. Groningen 1949.
Davie, D. A. Sixteenth-century poetry and the common reader: the case of Sackville. EC 4 1954.
Orrick, A. H. Sackville's sonnets. N & Q Jan 1956.
Griffin, R. J. Notes on musical devices in Sackville's verse. Neuphilologische Mitteilungen 63 1962.
Howarth, R. G. Sackville and A mirror for magistrates. Eng Stud in Africa 6 1963.
Bacquet, P. Le Moyen Age anglais et les idées morales de Sackville. Bulletin de la Faculté des Lettres de Strasbourg 42 1964.
— Contribution à l'étude de Sackville. Die Neueren Sprachen 13 1964.
— Un contemporain d'Elisabeth I: Sackville. Geneva 1966.
Hogue, L. L. Sackville's Buckingham 58. Explicator 28 1969.
See Mirror for magistrates, col 1024, above.

SALMACIS AND HERMAPHRODITUS

§1
Salmacis and Hermaphroditus. 1602; rptd in Poems by Francis Beaumont, 1640, 1653, ed A. Chalmers, Works of the English poets vol 6, 1810; 1660 (as Poems: the golden remains of F. Beaumont and J. Fletcher); ed Dramaticus, Shakespeare Soc Papers 3 1847; ed G. Jones 1951; ed E. S. Donno, Elizabethan minor epics, 1963; ed N. Alexander, Elizabethan narrative verse, 1967. Ms copies of 1602 in Bodley Rawlinson poetry 120D and Cambridge Univ Mm.4.13. Probably not by Beaumont.

§2
Macaulay, G. C. In his Francis Beaumont: a critical study, 1883.
Gayley, C. M. In his Francis Beaumont: dramatist, 1914.
Finkelpearl, P. J. The authorship of Salmacis and Hermaphroditus. N & Q Oct 1969. Attributes to Beaumont.
Sell, R. The authorship of the Metamorphosis of tabacco and Salmacis and Hermaphroditus. N & Q Jan 1972.

ROBERT SALTWOOD
fl. 1530–48

A comparyson bytwene iiij byrdes, the larke, the nyghtin-
gale, the thrusshe and the cucko. [Canterbury 1548?].

SIR JOHN SALUSBURY
1567–1612
Collections

Poems by Salusbury and Robert Chester. Ed C. Brown
1914 (EETS).

§1

The patrone his pathetical posies. In R. Parry, Sinetes
passions, 1597; ed Brown, above.

WILLIAM SAMUEL
fl. 1550–69

The practice practiced by the Pope and his prelates.
[1550?].
A warnyng for the cittie of London. [1550?].
The abridgement of goddes statutes [the Pentateuch] in
myter. 1551.
The love of God. [1559?].
An abridgement of all the canonical books of the olde
Testament in Sternholds meter. 1569.

THE SCHOOLHOUSE OF WOMEN
§1

A lytle boke named the schole house of women wherin
every man may rede a goodly prayse of the condicyons of
women. 1541, 1560, 1572; ed E. V. U[tterson], Select
pieces of early popular poetry vol 2, 1817; ed W. C.
Hazlitt, Remains of the early popular poetry of England
vol 4, 1866.

§2

White, B. Three rare books about women. Huntington
Lib Bull no 2 1931.
Stein, H. Six tracts about women. Library 4th ser 15 1935.
Utley, F. L. In his Crooked rib, Columbus 1944 (no 292).

GREGORY SCOT
1553–76

A briefe treatise agaynst certayne errors of the Romish
Church. 1574. Written 1570.

THOMAS SCOTT
fl. 1602

Four paradoxes: of arte, of lawe, of warre, of service. 1602,
1611.

SCOTTISH FIELD

Scotish feilde. Lyme ms, ed J. Robson, Chetham Soc
miscellany vol 2, 1855; BM ms additional 27,879, ed
J. W. Hales and F. J. Furnivall, Bishop Percy's folio
ms vol 1, 1867; ed J. P. Oakden, Chetham Soc miscellany
vol 6, 1935. Alliterative, written after 1515. On Flodden
field; for another poem see col 1105, above.

FRANCIS SEAGER
fl. 1549?–63

A brefe declaration of the great myseries in courtes ryall
by Alayn Charatre [Chartier], newly augmented by
F. Segar. 1549 (fragment). An edn of Caxton's prose
trn with a prefatory poem by Seager.
The schoole of vertue and booke of good nourture for
chyldren; the duties of eche degree. [c. 1550] (fragment),
1557, 1582 (with Certaine praiers and graces by R.
C[rowley]), 1593, 1620, 1621, [1626], [c. 1630], [c. 1635],
[c. 1640], 1817; ed F. J. Furnivall, The babees book,
1868 (EETS) (from 1557); abridged in Richard West,
School of vertue, 1619.
Certayne psalmes drawen into Englyshe metre wyth notes
to synge; a discription of the lyfe of man. 1553.
Richard [III] Duke of Glocester. In A myrrour for
magistrates 1563 etc; ed L. B. Campbell, Cambridge
1938, no 24. See Shakespeare, Richard III, col 1486,
below.

WILLIAM SHAKESPEARE
1564–1616

Venus and Adonis. 1593; Lucrece, 1594; The passionate
pilgrim, 1599 (wrongly attributed); The Phoenix and
turtle, in R. Chester, Loves martyr, 1601; Sonnets; A
lovers complaint, 1609; To the Queen by the players,
159[9] (possibly by Shakespeare; see S. W. May and
W. A. Ringler jr, MP 70 1972). See col 1557, below.

JOHN SHARROCK
fl. 1585

Elizabeth Queene: a declaration of the peaceable state of
England; a catalogue of the noble men of her Majesties
counsaile. 1585. Tr from Latin of C. Ocland; see col
1131, above.

LUKE SHEPHERD
fl. 1548–54
Bibliographies

Bale, J. In his Index Britanniae scriptorum, ed R. L.
Poole and M. Bateson, Oxford 1902.

Collections

Germann, F. Shepherd: ein Satirendichter der englischen
Reformationszeit. Augsburg 1911.

§1

Antipus. [1548?]; in The comparison betwene the antipus
and the antigraphe, [1548?]. Anon, attributed by Bale.
Doctour doubble ale. [1548?]; ed C. H. Hartshorne,
Ancient metrical tales, 1829; ed W. C. Hazlitt, Remains
of the early popular poetry of England vol 3, 1866.
Anon, attributed by Bale.
John Bon and Mast person. [1548?]; ed J. Smeeton 1807
(facs); ed W. H. Black 1852 (Percy Soc); ed W. C.
Hazlitt, Remains of the early popular poetry of England
vol 4, 1866. Anon, attributed by Bale.
Pathose: or an inward passion of the pope for the losse of
hys daughter the masse. [1548?] (imperfect). Anon,
attributed by Germann on basis of style.
Phylogamus. [1548?]. Anon, attributed by Bale.
A godlye and holesome preservatyve against desperation.
[1548?]. Anon, prose, attributed by Bale.
A pore helpe: the buklar and defence of mother holy kyrke.
[1549] (2 edns); ed J. Strype, Ecclesiastical memorials

vol 2, 1721, 1733, Oxford 1812; ed W. C. Hazlitt, Remains of the early popular poetry of England vol 3, 1866. Anon, attributed by Bale.
The upcheringe of the messe. [1548?]. Anon, attributed by Bale.

SHEPHERDS

See Calendar of Shepherds, above.

A SKELTONICAL SALUTATION

A Skeltonicall salutation of the Spanish nation in setting forth an Armado. Oxford 1589, London 1589; ed A. Dyce, Poetical works of John Skelton vol 1, 1843 (extracts).

THE SMITH AND HIS DAME

See col 459, above.

SIR THOMAS SMITH
1513–77

§1

Certaigne psalmes translated in the Tower with other prayers and songues. BM ms Royal 17 A xvii, dated 1549; ed B. Danielsson, Stockholm Stud in Eng 12 1963. [The hollie commaundmentes tenne, in Arundel Harington ms, no 323 (ed R. Hughey, Columbus 1960) is not his]. *For prose works see DNB and 1898 below.*

§2

Strype, J. Life of Sir Thomas Smith. 1698, Oxford 1820.
Dewar, M. Smith: a Tudor intellectual in office. 1964.

WALTER SMITH
d. 1538

Twelve mery gestys of one called Edyth. 1525, 1573; ed W. C. Hazlitt, Shakespeare jest books vol 3, 1864. *See* A. W. Reed, The wydow Edyth, Library 3rd ser 9 1918, rptd in his Early Tudor drama, 1926.

WILLIAM SMITH
fl. 1596

Collections
Poems. Ed L. A. Sasek, Baton Rouge 1970.

§1

Chloris: the complaint of the passionate despised shepheard. 1596; ed A. B. Grosart, Manchester 1877; ed E. Arber, English garner vol 8, 1896; ed M. F. Crow, Elizabethan sonnet cycles vol 3, 1896; ed S. Lee, Elizabethan sonnets vol 2, 1904. 49 sonnets and 3 other poems.
A new yeares guift: a posie upon certen flowers presented to the Countesse of Pembrooke by the author of Chloris. BM ms additional 35,186.

§2

Scott, J. G. Minor Elizabethan sonneteers. RES 2 1926.
—— In her Les sonnets élisabéthains, Paris 1929.
Sasek, L. A. W. Smith and the Shepheardes calendar. PQ 39 1960.

SOLOMON AND MARCOLPHUS

The sayinges or proverbes of King Salomon with the answers of Marcolphus, translated out of Frenche. [1529?].

JOHN SOOWTHERN
fl. 1584

§1

Pandora: the musyque of the beautie of his mistresse Diana. 1584; ed G. B. Parks, New York 1938 (facs). 25 sonnets, other poems.

§2

[Puttenham, G.] In his Arte of English poesie, 1589 (bk 3 ch 22, on sources in Ronsard).
Lee, S. In his Elizabethan sonnets vol 1, 1904 (introd).
Shafer, R. In his English ode to 1600, Princeton 1918.
Scott, J. G. In her Les sonnets élisabéthains, Paris 1929.
Bradner, L. In his Poems of Queen Elizabeth I, Providence 1964, p. 76.

THE SQUIRE OF LOW DEGREE

See col 446, above.

THOMAS STANLEY, Bishop of Sodor and Man
d. 1570

[An historicall poem touching the family of Stanley]. BM ms Harley 541, John Rylands Lib ms 202; ed J. O. Halliwell (-Phillipps), Palatine anthology, 1850.

RICHARD STANYHURST
1547–1618

§1

Thee first foure bookes of Virgil his Aeneis; oother poetical devises. Leyden 1582, London 1583; ed J. Maidment, Edinburgh 1836; ed E. Arber, English scholars' library 1880, 1895; ed D. van der Haar, Amsterdam 1933; ed G. Gregory Smith, Elizabethan critical essays vol 1, Oxford 1904 (extracts from prose dedication and preface); 2 Oother devises rptd in R.B.'s Greenes funeralls, 1594. *For prose works see DNB and col 2132, below, and A. C. Southern, English recusant prose, 1950.*

§2

Schmidt, H. Stanyhursts Uebersetzung von Vergils Aeneide. Breslau 1887.
Bernigau, C. Orthographie und Aussprache in Stanyhursts englischer Übersetzung den Aeneide. Marburger Studien zur Englischen Philologie 8 1904.
Guiney, L. I. In her Recusant poets, 1939.

RICHARD STAPLETON

See R.S. esquire, above.

THOMAS STERNHOLD
d. 1549

Certayne psalmes chosen out of the psalter of David. [1549?] (19 psalms), [1549?]; Al suche psalmes as T. Sternehold didde in his life time draw into metre, 1549

(37, and 7 by J. Hopkins), 1551 (3 edns), 1553 (6 edns); in The forme of prayers used in the Englishe congregation at Geneva, Geneva 1556, 1558, 1561, 1561, 1562; Psalmes 1560; Foure score and seven psalmes 1561; The whole booke of psalmes, 1562 (40 by Sternhold); more than 285 edns to 1640. *See col 1899, below.*

[Certayne chapters of the proverbes of Salomon drawn into metre by T. Sterneholde, [1549–50], contains nothing by Sternhold; *see* John Hall, above].

THOMAS STORER
1571–1604

The life and death of Thomas Wolsey. 1599; ed T. Park, Heliconia vol 2, 1815, Oxford 1826. *See* W. Winstanley, Lives of the most famous English poets, 1687.

SIR JOHN STRADLING
1563–1637

See col 1319, below.

JOHN STUDLEY
1545?–90?

The seventh tragedie of Seneca: Medea. 1566; in Seneca his tenne tragedies, 1581; ed E. M. Spearing, Louvain 1913 (Bang's Materialien 38).

The eyght tragedie of Seneca: Agamemnon. 1566; rptd with above.

Seneca his tenne tragedies. Ed T. Newton 1581 (with Hippolytus and Hercules OEteus by Studley); ed J. Jeligh 1887 (Spenser Soc); ed H. de Vocht, Louvain 1913 (Bang's Materialien 41); ed T. S. Eliot 2 vols 1927.

For Latin verse and prose see DNB.

JOSHUA SYLVESTER
1563–1618

§ I

A canticle of the victorie obteined by Henrie the Fourth at Ivry, written in French by William Salustius lord of Bartas. 1590; reissued with following item.

The triumph of faith; the sacrifice of Isaac; the ship-wreck of Jonas; a song of the victorie obtained by the French King at Yvry, written in French by W. Salustius lord of Bartas. 1592.

The profit of imprisonment: a paradox, written in French by Odet de la Noue lord of Teligni. 1594.

Monodia: an elegie in commemoration of Dame Hellen Branch widowe. [1594] (with Triumph of faith, above, appended).

The second weeke or childhood of the world. 1598. Trn of du Bartas.

Bartas his devine weekes and workes. 1605 (includes Τετράστιχα: the quadrains of G. de Faur [French and English, another edn 1614]), 1605, 1608 (with T. Hudson's trn of The historie of Judith), 1611, 1613, 1621 (with a collection of all the other workes translated and written by J. Sylvester), 1633, 1641; ed F. C. Haber, Gainesville 1965 (facs).

Posthumous Bartas: the third day of his second week. 1606.

Posthumus Bartas: the fore-noone of the fourth day of his second week. 1607.

Automachia: the self-conflict of a Christian. 1607. Trn from Latin of George Goodwin.

The heroyk life of Henry the Fourth, translated by E. Grimeston; a panegyre of Henry the Fourth, translated J. Sylvester. 1612. Tr from Pierre Matthieu.

Lachrimae lachrimarum. 1612, [1612?], 1613 (with Other elegies).

The parliament of vertues royal. 1614. 5 pts, tr from Jean Bertaut et al.

The second session of the parliament of vertues reall. 2 pts 1615.

Tobacco battered and the pipes shattered. [1617–20]. Also issued as part of Second session, above.

The sacred workes of that famous poet Silvester. 1620.

The maidens blush: or Joseph. 1620. Trn of Girolamo Fracastoro.

The wood-mans bear: a poeme. 1620.

Panthea: or divine wishes and meditations. 1630.

Nebuchadnezzars fierie furnace, nach dem Ms Harley 7576. Ed M. Rösler, Louvain 1936 (Bang's Materialien 12). Anon play, attributed to Sylvester by Rösler.

§ 2

Dunster, C. Considerations on Milton's early reading 1800.

Ashton, H. Du Bartas en Angleterre. Paris 1908.

Upham, A. H. In his French influence in English literature, New York 1909.

Taylor, G. C. Milton's use of Du Bartas. Cambridge Mass 1934.

Campbell, L. B. In her Divine poetry and drama in 16th-century England, Cambridge 1959.

Williams, F. B., jr. The bear facts about Sylvester, the woodman. Eng Lang Notes 9 1971.

See also col 1320, below.

C.T.

See T.C., above.

F.T.

The debate between pride and lowliness. [1570]; ed J. P. Collier 1851 (Shakespeare Soc), who attributes to Francis Thynne.

J.T.

An ould facioned love. 1594. Trn of T. Watson, Amintae gaudia 1592.

TERENCE IN ENGLISH

Terens in Englysh: the translacyon of the furst comedy callyd Andria. [Paris c. 1520].

TRANSLATOR OF THEOCRITUS

Six idillia chosen out of Theocritus. Oxford 1588; ed E. Arber, English garner vol 8, 1896; ed A. H. Bullen, Some longer Elizabethan poems, Westminster 1903.

ST THOMAS à BECKET

[Verse life of St Thomas. c. 1520 (fragment)].

FRANCIS THYNNE
1545?–1608

Emblemes and epigrams. Ellesmere ms dated 1600; ed F. J. Furnivall 1876 (EETS).

A discourse upon the Lord Burghley his creste; a discourse upon the philosophers armes. Bodley ms Ashmole 766.

For prose works see DNB.

EMERY TILNEY

A song of the Lordes supper. [1550].

ROBERT TOFTE
1562-1620

§1

Laura: the toyes of a traveller, by R.T. gent. 1597; ed E. Arber, English garner vol 8, 1896; ed S. Lee, Elizabethan sonnets vol 2, 1904. 124 short poems, 30 said not to be by R.T.

Two tales translated out of Ariosto, the one in dispraise of men the other in disgrace of women, by R.T. gent. 1597. K-N4, probably continuation of Orlando inamorato below.

Alba: the months minde of a melancholy lover; certaine divine poems by R.T. gent. 1598; ed A. B. Grosart, Manchester 1880.

Orlando inamorato: the three first bookes of Boiardo done into English heroicall verse, by R.T. 1598. Entered 1592.

A controversy between the two Tassi [Ercole and Torquato] of marriage and wiving, done into English by R.T. gent. 1599. Prose.

The batchelars banquet. 1603, 1604, 1630, 1631 (all anon); ed F. P. Wilson, Oxford 1929, who attributes to Tofte; also attributed to T. Dekker. Based on Les quinze joyes de mariage attributed to Antoine de la Sale. Prose.

Ariostos satyres by Garvis Markham. 1608, 1609, 1611 (as Ariostos seven planets, with a new addition of three Elegies, anon). Claimed by Tofte in Blazon of jealousie, below.

Honours academie: the famous pastorall of the faire shepherdesse Julietta; divers histories, englished by R.T. 1610. Entered 1607; tr from French of N. de Montreaux.

The blazon of jealousie, translated by R.T. 1615. From Italian of B. Varchi.

§2

Halliwell (-Phillipps), J. O. Some account of Tofte's Alba. 1865.

Scott, J. G. In her Les sonnets élisabéthains, Paris 1929.

Kahrl, G. M. Tofte's annotations in the Blazon of jealousie. Harvard Stud 18 1935.

Williams, F. B. Robert Tofte. RES 13 1937.

Fox, C. A. O. Notes on Shakespeare and Tofte. Swansea 1957.

Hardin, R. F. Tofte's translation of Ariosto's satires. Satire Newsletter 7 1970.

CYRIL TOURNEUR
1575?-1626

The transformed metamorphosis. 1600; A funerall poeme upon Sir Francis Vere, 1609; A griefe on the death of Prince Henrie, 1613. *See col 1695, below.*

TREATISE

See Beauty of women, Knight of courtesy, above, and Wife lapped in morel's skin, below.

THREE TREATISES

See Thomas Blundeville, above.

JOHN TRUSSEL

Raptus I Helenae: the first rape of faire Hellen. 1595; ed M. A. Shaaber, Shakespeare Quart 8 1957. *See* TLS 9-16 July 1931.

Trussel wrote 3 prefatory poems for and edited R. Southwell, The triumphs over death, ed J. W. Trotman 1914 (from mss).

See J.T., above.

GEORGE TURBERVILE
c. 1544-c. 1597

§1

The eclogs of B. Mantuan [Spagnuoli] turned into English. 1567, 1572, 1594; ed D. Bush, New York 1937 (facs). Entered 1566-7.

The heroycall epistles of Ovidius, with Aulus [Angelus] Sabinus aunsweres. 1567 (3 edns), 1569, [1570?], [c. 1584], 1600; ed F. S. Boas 1928. Entered 1566-7.

Epitaphes, epigrams, songs and sonets, with a discourse of the affections of Tymetes to Pyndara. 1567 (newly corrected with addns), 1570; ed A. Chalmers, English poets vol 2, 1810; ed J. P. Collier [1867]. Entered 1566-7.

A plaine path to perfect vertue devised by [D.] Mancinus. 1568. Entered 1567-8.

The author being in Muscovia [1568-9] wrytes to certaine his frendes in England of the state of the place. In his Tragical tales, 1587; in R. Hakluyt, The principall navigations of the English nation, 1589.

The booke of faulconrie or hauking collected out of the best aucthors. 1575, 1611 (corrected, 2 issues). Prose.

The noble arte of venerie or hunting, translated out of the best authors. [1575] (anon), 1611; rptd in Tudor and Stuart library, 1908. Prose, 15 poems; by George Gascoigne; *see* Prouty, below.

Tragical tales translated out of sundrie Italians. 1587, Edinburgh 1837.

Commendatory verses to G. Fenton, Certaine tragicall discourses, 1567; D. Roulands's trn of Lazarillo de Tormes, 1586 (entered 1568-9).

§2

Wood, A. In his Athenae oxonienses vol 1, 1691.

Cooper, E. In her Muses' library, 1737.

Koeppel, E. Turberviles Verhältniss zur itahinischen litteratur. Anglia 13 1891.

Rollins, H. E. New facts about Turbervile. MP 15 1918.

Whipple, T. K. In his Martial and the English epigram, Berkeley 1925.

Lathrop, H. B. J. Cornarius's Selecta epigrammata graeca. MLN 43 1928.

Pruvost, R. The source of Turbervile's Tragical tales nos 2, 5 and 8. RES 10 1934.

—— In his Bandello and Elizabethan fiction, Paris 1937.

Hodgson, N. H. George Turbervile. TLS 15 May 1937.

Hankins, J. E. The life and works of Turbervile. Lawrence Kansas 1940.

M., M. The booke of falconrie, Tragical tales. More Books 18 1943.

Prouty, C. T. and R. George Gascoigne, The noble arte of venerie. In J. Q. Adams memorial studies, Washington 1948.

Zocca, L. R. In his Elizabethan narrative poetry, New Brunswick NJ 1950.

Wright, H. G. In his Boccaccio in England, 1957.

Berry, L. E. R. Hakluyt and Turberville's poems on Russia. PBSA 61 1967.

Sheidley, W. E. Turbervile and the problem of passion. JEGP 69 1970.

—— Lycidas: an early analogue by Turberville. MP 69 1972.
—— Turbervile's epigrams from the Greek anthology. Stud in Eng Lit 1500-1900 12 1972.

THOMAS TUSSER
1524?-80

§ 1

A hundreth good pointes of husbandrie. 1557, rptd S. E. Brydges, British bibliographer vol 3 1810; rptd C. Clark, Great Totham 1834; 1570 (enlarged with A hundreth good poynts of huswifery), 1571; ed D. Hartley 1931.
Five hundreth points of good husbandry united to as many of good huswiferie. 1573 (3 edns), 1574, 1576, 1577, 1580 (newly augmented to a fourth part more), 1585, 1586, 1590, 1593, 1597, 1599, Edinburgh 1599, London 1604, 1610, 1614, 1620, 1630, 1638, 1672, 1692; ed Sir W. Scott, Somers tracts vol 3, 1810 (from 1599); rptd 1931 with Foreword by E. V. Lucas and Benediction by Rudyard Kipling; ed W. Mavor 1812 (from 1573); ed W. Payne and S. J. Herrtage 1878 (English Dialect Soc); ed D. Hartley 1931 (from 1571); selections in Tusser redivivus, 1710 (with comment by D. Hillman), 1744; ed W. Southey, Select works of the British poets, 1831; Selections, Ipswich 1954 (National Federation of Women's Inst).

§ 2

Fuller, T. In his Worthies of England, 1662.
Winstanley, W. In his lives of the most famous English poets, 1687.
Warton, T. In his History of English poetry vol 3, 1781.
Clark, C. The last will of Tusser: his metrical autobiography. Great Totham 1846.
McDonald, D. In his Agricultural writers 1200-1800, 1908.
Hewlett, M. The English Hesiod. Cornhill Mag Jan 1920.
Fussell, G. E. Farmers' calendars from Tusser to Arthur Young. Economic History 2 1933.
Tarleton, J. Tusser in Essex and Suffolk. Essex Rev 47 1938.

THOMAS TWYNE
1543-1613

Tr bks 11-13 of Aeneid, 1573 etc. See Thomas Phaer, above.

CHRISTOPHER TYE
1497?-1572

The actes of the apostles translated into Englyshe metre with notes to synge and to play upon the lute. 1553. *See* W. Winstanley, Lives of the most famous English poets, 1687.

T. TYRO

Tyros Roring Megge. 1598.

NICHOLAS UDALL
1505-56

Verses for coronation of Queen Anne (Boleyn), written 1533. Scattered verses in prose trns. See col 1415, below.

THOMAS UNDERDOWNE
fl. 1566-87

The excellent historye of Theseus and Ariadne. 1566.
Ovid his invective against Ibis translated into English meeter. 1569, 1577. Verse with prose versions of stories told.
For his prose trn of Heliodorus see col 2169, below.

UNDO YOUR DOOR

See Squire of Low Degree, above.

ST URSULA

The lyf of Saynt Ursula after the cronycles of Englonde, translated e sermone Latino. [1509?], 1818 (Roxburghe Club).

WILLIAM VALLANS
fl. 1578-90

§ 1

Commendatory verse to John Wharton, Dreame, 1578.
A tale of two swannes: the original and increase of the river Lee. 1590; ed T. Hearne, Leland's Itinerary vol 5, Oxford 1711.
Poem on poverty of John Stowe in BM ms Harley 367, folio 129.

§ 2

Gottfried, R. B. Spenser and the myths of locality. SP 34 1937.

ROBERT VAUGHAN
fl. 1542

§ 1

A dyalogue defensyve for women agaynst malycyous detractoures. 1542.

§ 2

White, B. Three rare books about women. Huntington Lib Bull no 2 1931. Attributes to Robert Burdet.
Utley, F. L. In his Crooked rib, Columbus 1944.

SIR WILLIAM VAUGHAN
c. 1575-1641

§ 1

Ἐρωτοπαίγνιον pium: continens Canticum canticorum Salomonis et psalmos aliquot selectiores. 1597. Latin verse.
Poematum libellus. 1598. Latin verse.
The golden grove moralized in three books. 1600, 1608 (enlarged); ed G. G. Smith, Elizabethan critical essays vol 2, Oxford 1904 (extracts). Prose.
Naturall and artificiall directions for health. 1600, 1602, 1607, 1612, 1617, 1626, 1633. Prose.
Cambrensium Caroleia, by Orpheus Junior. 1625, 1630. Latin verse on marriage of Charles I.
The golden fleece transported from Cambrioll Colchios, by Orpheus Junior. 1626. 3 pts, prose and verse, on Newfoundland.
The Church Militant from the yeare 33 untill 1640. 1640.
For other prose works see DNB.

§2

Yates, F. A. In her John Florio, Cambridge 1934.
Bradner, L. In his Musae anglicanae, New York 1940.
Eccles, M. A biographical dictionary of Elizabethan authors. HLQ 5 1942.

THOMAS VAUX, 2nd BARON VAUX OF HARROWDEN
1510–56
Collections

Poems. Ed A. B. Grosart 1872.
Poems. Ed L. P. Vonalt, Denver 1960.

§1

Songes and sonettes. 1557 etc; ed H. E. Rollins, Cambridge Mass 1928, nos 9 (attributed to Surrey), 211–12, 217. 4 anon poems.
The paradyse of daynty devises. 1576 etc; ed H. E. Rollins, Cambridge Mass 1927, nos 8, 16–17, 37, 48, 71, 80–1, 87–92, 113. 15 poems.

§2

Hannah, J. In his Courtly poets from Raleigh to Montrose, 1870. Prints 4 poems and attributes 14 others.
Guiney, L. I. In her Recusant poets, 1939.
Anstruther, G. Vaux of Harrowden: a recusant family. 1953.
Hughey, R. In her Arundel Harington ms, Columbus 1960. 4 poems, one (no 173) unique.

RICHARD VENNAR(D)
d. 1615?

Englands joy. [1601?]. On Lord Mountjoy's defeat of Tyrone.
The right way to heaven, and the true testimonie of a faithfull and loyall subject. 1601, 1602 (another issue with addns and omissions, rptd J. Nichols, Progresses of Queen Elizabeth vol 3, 1823), [1605] (extract with new verses). Prose, with verses praising the Queen.
The plot of the play called Englands joy. [1602]; ed T. Park, Harleian miscellany vol 10, 1813; ed S. Lee, Trans New Shakespeare Soc 1 1887. Prose advertisement; see E. K. Chambers, Elizabethan stage vol 3, 1923.
An apology. 1614; ed J. P. Collier, Illustrations of old English literature vol 3, 1866. Prose autobiography.

VENUS

See Court of Venus, above.

EDWARD DE VERE, 17th EARL OF OXFORD
1550–1604
Bibiography

Ritson, J. In his Bibliographia poetica, 1802.

Collections

Poems. Ed A. B. Grosart 1872. 22 poems.
Poems. Ed J. T. Looney 1921. Adds songs from Lyly's plays and poems in England's Helicon; thinks Oxford is Shakespeare.
For Oxford Shakespeare controversy, see col 1575, below.

§1

Commendatory poem in T. Bedingfield's trn Cardanus comforte, 1573.
The paradyse of daynty devises. 1576 etc; ed H. E. Rollins, Cambridge Mass 1927, nos 30, 76–7, 82–6. 8 poems.
Brittons bowre of delights. 1591; ed H. E. Rollins, Cambridge Mass 1933, no 40. One poem. Another is wrongly attributed in Syr P. S[idney] his Astrophel and Stella, 1591 (Faction that ever dwelles, by F. Greville).
The Phoenix nest. 1593 (one poem: What cunning can expresse); rptd in Englands Helicon, 1600.
T.W., The tears of fancie. 1593 (one poem: Who taught thee first to sigh, attributed to Oxford in Bodley ms Rawlinson poetry 85 folio 16^v).
A sweet sonet: my minde to me a kingdome is. [1624?]. Anon, but tentatively attributed to Oxford in Harvard fMS 1015 folio 14^v.
Other poems in mss: Bodley Rawlinson poetry 85; BM Harley 7392, Tanner 306; Marsh's Lib Dublin Z 3.5.21; Folger 1.112; etc.

§2

[Puttenham, G.] In his Arte of English poesie, 1589.
Walpole, H. In his Royal and noble authors vol 1, 1758; ed T. Park 1806 (with addns).
Hannah, J. In his Courtly poets from Raleigh to Montrose, 1870. Prints 5 poems and attributes 16 others.
Greg, W. W. A hundreth sundry flowers. Library 4th ser 7–8 1927–8.
Ward, B. M. The seventeenth Earl of Oxford. 1928.
Smith, G. C. M. Taking lodging in 1591. RES 8 1932.
Eggar, K. E. Oxford as musician. Proc of Music Assoc 1935.
Bennett, J. W. Oxford and Endimion. PMLA 55 1942.
Lewis, C. S. The sheepheard's slumber. TLS 9 May 1942.
Clark, R. B. The Earl of Oxford and the Queen's English. N & Q July 1957.

RICHARD VERSTEGEN

See Richard Rowlands, above.

CHRISTOPHER VITELL(S)

See Hendrik Niclas, above.

VOX POPULI VOX DEI

Vox populi, vox Dei. BM ms Harley 367 (anon), Cambridge Univ ms Nn.4.5 (Skelton); ed J. Littledale 1843 (Roxburghe Club); ed A. Dyce, Poetical works of John Skelton vol 2, 1843; ed W. C. Hazlitt, Remains of the early popular poetry of England vol 3, 1866; ed F. J. Furnivall, Ballads from mss vol 1, 1868–72. Against enclosures, written c. 1547.

D.W., Archdeacon

Certaine godly instructions verie necessarie to be learned of the younger sort. 1580, [1586?]; also appended to Richard Rice, An invective against vices taken for vertue, 1581. Entered 1578.

R.W.

A recantation of famous Pasquin of Rome. 1570. Attack on Bishop Edmund Bonner.

T.W.

§1

The tears of fancie: or love disdained. 1593; ed E. Arber, Thomas Watson, Poems, 1870; modernized S. Lee, Elizabethan sonnets vol 1, 1904.
The lamentation of Melpomene for the death of Belpheebe our late Queene. 1603.

§2

Collier, J. P. Registers of the Stationers' Company. N & Q 24 May 1862.
Nicholson, B. Thomas Watson and Nicholas Breton. Athenaeum 13 Oct 1877.
Beach, J. W. A sonnet of Watson and a stanza of Spenser. MLN 18 1903.
Scott, J. G. The sources of Watson's Tears of fancie. MLR 21 1926.
—— In her Les sonnets élisabéthains, Paris 1929.
Wilson, E. C. In his England's Eliza, Cambridge Mass 1939.
Dickey, F. Forgeries in the Stationers' Register. Shakespeare Quart 11 1960. 'By T. Watson' under Tears of fancie a Collier forgery.

WILLIAM WALTER
fl. 1520

§1

The spectacle of lovers: a dyalogue bytwene love and councell of good women and bad. [1510?] (fragment), [1533?]. With verse envoy by R. Copland.
Tytus and Gesyppus. [c. 1525]; ed H. G. Wright, Early English versions of tales from the Decameron, 1937 (EETS). Trn of Boccaccio's Decameron 10.8 through Latin of P. Beroaldo.
Guystarde and Sygysmonde. 1532, 1818 (Roxburghe Club); ed H. G. Wright, 1937, above. Trn of Boccaccio's Decameron 4.1 through Latin of L. Bruni, with interpolated verses by R. Copland.

§2

Utley, F. L. In his Crooked rib, Columbus 1944.
Wright, H. G. In his Boccaccio in England, 1957.

WILLIAM WARNER
1558–?1609

§1

Pan his syrinx or pipe. [1584], 1597 (as Syrinx or a seavenfold historie newly perused); ed W. A. Bacon, Evanston 1950 (with biography). Prose fiction.
Albions England. 1586 (4 bks from Noah to Norman Conquest), 1589 (rev and continued, 6 bks to Henry VII), 1592 (3rd time corrected and augmented, 9 bks to Elizabeth), 1596 (rev and newly enlarged, 12 bks with prose epitome), 1597 (another issue), 1602 (13 bks), 1612; ed A. Chalmers, English poets vol 4, 1810 (from 1596, without epitome).
A continuance of Albions England. 1606 (bks 14–16 to James I).

Menaecmi out of Plautus by W.W. 1595; ed J. Nichols, Six old plays vol 1, 1779; ed W. C. Hazlitt, Shakespeare's library vol 1, 1875; 1905 (with Comedy of Errors); ed W. H. D. Rouse 1912 (with Latin text); ed G. Bullough, Narrative and dramatic sources of Shakespeare vol 1, 1957. Prose trn. *See* Shakespeare, A comedy of errors, *col 1488, below.*

§2

Winstanley, W. In his Lives of the most famous English poets, 1687.
Wood, A. In his Athenae oxonienses vol 1, 1721.
Cooper, E. In her Muses library, 1737.
Scott, A. In his Amwell: a descriptive poem, 1776. Date of Warner's death.
Collier, J. P. In his Poetical decameron vol 1, 1820.
Madden, F. In his Havelok the Dane, 1828 (Roxburghe Club). Source of Argentile and Curan.
Brie, F. Zu Warners Albions England. Archiv 137 1912.
Huf, H. Albion's England: Quellenuntersuchungen zu den ersten Büchern. Munich 1912.
Cawley, R. R. Warner and the voyagers. MP 20 1922.
Birley, R. In his Sunk without trace, 1962. Albion's England.

ARTHUR WARREN

The poore mans passions; poverties patience. 1605.

WILLIAM WARREN

A pleasant new fancie: the nurcerie of names. 1581.

THOMAS WATSON
1557?–92

Collections

Poems. Ed E. Arber 1870, Westminster 1895, 1910. Hekatompathia, Meliboeus, An eglogue, T.W.'s Tears of fancie (not by Watson), commendatory poems and dedications.

§1

Sophoclis Antigone interprete T. Watsono; huic adduntur pompae quaedam. 1581. Latin verse.
The Εκατομπαθία: or passionate centurie of love. [1582], 1869 (Spenser Soc); ed S. K. Henninger jr, Gainesville 1964 (facs).
Amyntas. 1585 (Latin verse); tr Abraham Fraunce, The lamentations of Amyntas translated into English hexameters, 1587, 1588, 1589, 1591 (in The Countesse of Pembrokes Yvychurch), 1596; both ed W. F. Staton jr and F. M. Dickey, Chicago 1967.
Compendium memoriae localis. [1585?]. Latin prose.
Coluthi Thebani Helenae raptus Latinus paraphraste. 1586. Latin verse.
A gratification unto John Case for his booke in praise of musicke. [1586?] (anon, music by W. Byrd); ed M. C. Boyd, Elizabethan music and musical criticism, Philadelphia 1940 (facs); attributed to Watson in Bodley ms Rawlinson poetry 148, ed J. Haslewood, British bibliographer vol 2, 1812.
Meliboeus: sive ecloga in obitum D. Francisci Walsinghami. 1590. Latin verse.
An eglogue upon the death of Sir Francis Walsingham. 1590. Watson's own trn of his Meliboeus.
The first sett of Italian madrigalls englished. 1590 (music by W. Byrd); ed F. I. Carpenter, JEGP 2 1899 (with sources); ed W. Bolle, Palaestra 29 1903; English madrigal verse, ed E. H. Fellowes, Oxford 1967 (3rd edn rev F. W. Sternfeld and D. Greer).

A dialogue of Bernard Palcssy concerning waters and fountains translated out of French. Harvard ms English 707. Prose, written c. 1590.

Amintae gaudia. 1592 (Latin verse); tr I.T. as An ould facioned love, 1594.

The Phoenix nest. 1593. 3 poems; *see Staton, 1963 below.*

Poems in BM mss additional 10,309, Egerton 2230, Harley 3277, Sloane 1867, 3731. For Tears of fancie, see T. W., above.

It is unlikely that the play Thorny Abbey, *by T.W., in* Gratiae theatrales, *1662, is by Watson.*

§2

Winstanley, W. In his Lives of the most famous English poets, 1687.

P[ark], T. Farther notices of Watson. GM Aug 1798.

Mitford, J. Watson's Ekatompathia. GM May 1846. On G. Steevens' copy, now at Harvard.

Hall, H. Watson and his relations. Athenaeum 23 Aug 1890.

Greg, W. W. English versions of Watson's Latin poems. MLQ 6 1903.

Oliphant, E. H. C. Problems of authorship in Elizabethan dramatic literature. MP 8 1911. Attributes Thorny Abbey to Watson; *see* S. Schoenbaum, Internal evidence and Elizabethan dramatic authorship, 1966.

Scott, J. G. In her Les sonnets élisabéthains, Paris 1929.

Eccles, M. In his Christopher Marlowe in London, Cambridge Mass 1934. A biography.

Bradner, L. In his Musae anglicanae, New York 1940.

Smith, H. In his Elizabethan poetry, Cambridge Mass 1952.

Ringler, W. A., jr. Spenser and Watson. MLN 69 1954.

Murphy, W. M. Watson's Hecatompathia and the Elizabethan sonnet sequence. JEGP 56 1957.

Morris, B. R. Watson and Troilus and Cressida. N & Q May 1958.

Morris, H. Barnfield, Amyntas and the Sidney circle. PMLA 74 1959. Replies by Staton and Morris 76 1961.

Staton, W. F., jr. The influence of Watson on Elizabethan Ovidian poetry. Stud in Renaissance 6 1959.

— A Lodge borrowing from Watson. Renaissance News 14 1961.

— Watson's authorship of Aurora now. N & Q Aug 1963.

Austin, W. B. Watson's adaptation of an epigram by Martial. Renaissance News 13 1960. Reply by Staton in his edn of Amyntas, 1967 above.

Dickey, F. Forgeries in the Stationers' Register. Shakespeare Quart 11 1960. Tears of fancie not by Watson.

Cecioni, C. G. Appunti per una biografia di Watson. Siculorum Gymnasium 16 1963.

— Introduzione all' Ekatompathia. Siculorum Gymnasium 17 1964.

— Primi studi su Watson. Catania 1964.

— Frances Walsingham ispiratrice del l'Hecatompathia. Rivista di Letterature Moderne e Comparate 20 1967.

— Watson e la tradizione petrarchista. Milan 1969.

Schücking, L.L. Zur Verfasserschaft der Spanish tragedy. Baycrische Akademie der Wissenschaften 4 1963. Suggests Watson.

Clubb, L. G. Gabriel Harvey and the two Thomas Watsons. Renaissance News 19 1966.

JOHN WEEVER
1576–1632

§1

Epigrammes in the oldest cut and newest fashion. 1599; ed R. B. McKerrow, Oxford 1911.

Faunus and Melliflora: or the original of our English satyres. 1600; ed A. Davenport, Liverpool 1948; ed E. S. Donno, Elizabethan minor epics, New York 1963.

An agnus Dei. 1601, 1603, 1606, 1610. Verse life of Christ.

The mirror of martyrs: the life and death of Sir John Oldcastle. 1601, 1873 (Roxburghe Club); ed W. B. Rye, Archaeologica Cantiana 6 1887 (extract).

The whipping of the satyre. 1601 (Ad lectorem signed W.I.); ed A. Davenport, The whipper pamphlets, Liverpool 1951.

Ancient funerall monuments. 1631, 1661, 1767 (with addns by W. Tooke); Society of Antiquaries ms 127–8. Prose, with 251 verse epitaphs by various authors.

§2

Davenport, A. Weever's Epigrammes and the Hall-Marston quarrel. RES 11 1935.

— The quarrel of the satirists. MLR 28 1942.

— Weever, Ovid and Shakespeare. N & Q 26 Nov 1949.

GEORGE WHETSTONE
c. 1551–87

§1

Commendatory poems to G. Gascoigne, Posies, 1575; T. Kendall, Floweres of epigrammes, 1577.

The rocke of regard. 1576; ed J. P. Collier [1870]. Verse and prose fiction.

A remembraunce of George Gaskoigne. [1577]; ed A. Chalmers, Works of the English poets vol 2, 1810; Bristol 1815, London 1821 (with Gascoigne, Princely pleasures); ed E. Arber 1868 (with Gascoigne, Notes of instruction etc); Edinburgh 1885.

The right excellent historye of Promos and Cassandra devided into two commicall discourses. 1578; [ed J. Nichols], Six old plays vol 1, 1779; ed W. C. Hazlitt, Shakespeare's library vol 6, 1875; ed I. Gollancz, Oxford 1909; ed J. S. Farmer, Tudor facsimile texts, 1910; ed G. Bullough, Narrative and dramatic sources of Shakespeare vol 2, 1958; ed G. G. Smith, Elizabethan critical essays vol 1, Oxford 1904 (epistle only). 2-pt verse play, unacted. *See* Shakespeare's Measure for measure, *col 1527, below.*

Verses of 20 good precepts. In The paradyse of daynty devises, 1578 etc.

A remembrance of Sir Nicholas Bacon. [1579]; ed A. Boswell, Auchinleck 1816.

An heptameron of civill discourses. 1582, 1593 (as Aurelia the paragon of pleasure). Prose fiction, some verse.

A remembraunce of Sir James Dier. [1582–3?]; ed A. Boswell, Auchinleck 1816.

A remembraunce of Thomas [Radcliffe], late Earle of Sussex. 1583; ed A. Boswell, Auchinleck 1816.

A mirour for magestrates of cyties; a touchstone for the time. 1584, 1586 (as The enemie to unthryftinesse). Prose.

A mirror of the life of Frauncis [Russell] Earle of Bedford. 1585; ed T. Park, Heliconia vol 2, 1815.

The honorable reputation of a souldier. 1585, Leyden 1586 (with Dutch trn). Prose.

The English myrror. 1586. Prose.

The censure of a loyall subject. 1587 (2 issues); ed J. P. Collier, Illustrations of early English popular literature vol 1, 1863. Prose dialogue on Babington conspiracy.

Sir Philip Sidney his honorable life. [1587]; ed A. Boswell, Auchinleck 1816.

§2

Rawlidge, R. A monster late found out. Amsterdam 1628. Contains synopsis of Whetstone, Mirour for magestrates of cyties.

Budd, F. W. Rouillet's Philamira and Whetstone's Promos and Cassandra. RES 6 1930.

Eccles, M. Whetstone's death. TLS 16 July, 27 Aug 1931.
—— Emendations in Promos and Cassandra. N & Q Jan 1971.
Prouty, C. T. Whetstone, Peter Beverly and the sources of Much ado about nothing. SP 38 1941.
—— Whetstone's Rinaldo and Giletta and Grange's The golden aphroditis. In Studies in honor of A. H. R. Fairchild, Columbia Missouri 1946.
—— Whetstone and the sources of Measure for measure. Shakespeare Quart 15 1964.
Izard, T. C. Whetstone: mid-Elizabethan gentleman of letters. New York 1942.
Miller, E. H. Whetstone: professional epitapher. N & Q June 1958.
Purcell, H. D. Whetstone's Englysh myrror and Marlowe's Jew of Malta. N & Q Aug 1966.

GEOFFREY WHITNEY
1548?–1601
§1

A choice of emblemes and other devises. Leyden 1586; ed H. Green 1866; Menston 1969 (facs of 1586). Ms dedication copy to Earl of Leicester at Harvard.
Commendatory poems to G. Whetstone, The honorable reputation of a souldier, Leyden 1586; James Dousa the elder, Odarum britannicarum liber 1, Leyden 1586; Spenser, Amoretti and Epithalamion, 1595 (signed G.W. I[unior]).

§2

Praz, M. In his Studi sul concettismo, Milan 1934; tr with addns as Studies in 17th-century imagery, 2 vols 1939–47.
Gordon, D. J. Veritas filia temporis: Hadrianus Junius and Whitney. Jnl Warburg & Courtauld Inst 3 1940.
Gottfried, R. The G.W. Senior and G.W.I. of Spenser's Amoretti. MLQ 3 1942.
Muir, P. H. Whitney's Choice of emblems. TLS 9 Jan 1943.
Freeman, R. In her English emblem books, 1948.
Rusche, H. G. Two proverbial images in Whitney's A choice of emblemes and Marlowe's The Jew of Malta. N & Q July 1964.

ISABELLA WHITNEY
fl. 1567–75

The copy of a letter by a yonge gentilwoman to her unconstant lover, by Is.W.; a loveletter sent to a yonge mayden, by W.G. [1567].
A sweet nosgay: or pleasant posye contayning a hundred and ten phylosophicall flowers. [1575].

WILLIAM WHITTINGHAM
1524?–79

The forme of prayers used in the Englishe congregation at Geneva. 1556 (includes trns of 7 psalms and Ten Commandments), 1558 (8 more psalms and Song of Simeon); numerous later edns as part of Whole booke of psalmes, 1562 etc.
See col 1899, below.

THOMAS WHYTHORNE
1528–96
§1

Songes for three, fower, and five voyces. 1571; ed R.

Immelmann, Sh Jb 39 1903 (words of 76 songs, music of 3rd pt only).
A book of songs and sonetts, with discoorses of the chylds, yoong mans and entring old mans lyfe. Bodley ms English Miscellaneous c.33, written c. 1576; ed J. M. Osborn, Autobiography of Thomas Whythorne, Oxford 1961 (old spelling), 1962 (modernized). Prose with 197 poems.
Duos or songs for two voices. 1590; ed W. Bergmann, Fifteen duos in canon for divers recorders, 1955 (last pt only). Words and music of 51 songs.

§2

'Warlock, Peter' (P. Heseltine). Whythorne: an unknown Elizabethan composer. Oxford 1925.
Osborn, J. M. The beginnings of autobiography in England. Los Angeles 1959.

A WIFE LAPPED IN MOREL'S SKIN

A merry jeste of a shrewde and curste wyfe lapped in morelles skin. [1580?]; ed E. V. U[tterson], Select pieces of early popular poetry vol 2, 1817, 1825; ed T. Amyot, The old Taming of the shrew, 1844 (Shakespeare Soc); ed W. C. Hazlitt, Remains of the early popular poetry of England vol 4, 1866; Shakespeare's library vol 4, 1875; See Shakespeare's Taming of the shrew, col 1491, below.

EDWARD WILKINSON
fl. 1600

E.W. his Thameseidos, devided into three bookes or cantos. 1600.
Isahacs inheritance. 1603.

ANDREW WILLET
1562–1621
§1

Sacrarum emblematum centuria una. Cambridge [1596?]. Latin and English verse.
For prose works see DNB.

§2

Barksdale, C. In his A remembrancer of excellent men, 1670. A biography.
Tramer, I. In her Studien zu den Anfängen der puritanischen Emblemliteratur, Berlin 1934.
Freeman, R. In her English emblem books, 1948.

HENRY WILLOBY
1574?–96?
§1

Willobie his Avisa: or the true picture of a modest maid and of a chast and constant wife. 1594, 1605 (4th time corrected), 1609, 1635 (5th time corrected); ed A. B. Grosart, Manchester 1880; ed C. Hughes 1904; ed G. B. Harrison 1926; ed N. B. de Luna, Oxford 1969; ed N. Alexander, Elizabethan narrative verse, 1967 (selection).

§2

Acheson, A. Shakespeare's sonnet story. 1922.
Chambers, E. K. In his William Shakespeare, 2 vols Oxford 1930.

Brooke, C. F. T. In his Essays on Shakespeare and other Elizabethans, New Haven 1948.

de Luna, N. B. The Queen declined: Willobie his Avisa, an interpretation with the text of the original edition. Oxford 1969.

THOMAS WINTER
b. 1579

The second day of the first weeke of Lord Bartas. 1603. The third dayes creation, done out of French [of du Bartas]. 1604.

WIVES

See Proud wife's paternoster, col 1136, above.

HENRY WOTTON
fl. 1578

§1

A courtlie controversie of Cupids cautels: conteyning five tragicall histories entermedled with sonets and rithmes, translated out of French [of J. Yver]. 1578. Prose fiction containing 36 poems.

§2

Boas, F. S. In his Works of Thomas Kyd, Oxford 1901. Wotton as source of Soliman and Perseda.

Atkinson, D. F. The source of Two gentlemen of Verona. SP 41 1944.

Schlauch, M. In her Antecedents of the English novel, Oxford 1963.

Pogue, J. C. The two gentlemen of Verona and Wotton's Courtlie controversie. Emporia State Research Stud 10 1962.

Myers, K. W. A neglected Hamlet source. Emporia State Research Stud 15 1966.

Tufte, V. England's first epithalamium. Eng Miscellany (Rome) 20 1969.

SIR HENRY WOTTON
1568–1639

See col 1325, below.

WILLIAM WYRLEY
1565–1618?

The true use of armorie [prose]; the life and death of Sir John Chandos; the life and death of Sir John de Gralhy. 1592.

JAMES YATES servingman
fl. 1582

The castell of courtesie; the holde of humilitie; the chariot of chastitie; a dialogue between age and youth; and other matters. 1582. See T. Corser, Collectanea anglo-poetica, 1883 (Chetham Soc).

BARTHOLOMEW YOUNG
fl. 1577–1600

Diana of George of Montemayor translated out of Spanish 1598 (with continuations: The second part by Alonso Perez, Enamoured Diana by Gaspar Gil Polo); pt 3 (Spanish text and Young's trn) ed R.L. and M. B. Grismer, Minneapolis 1959; pts 1 and 3 ed J. M. Kennedy, Oxford 1968. Written 1583; prose fiction containing 156 poems, 25 rptd in Englands Helicon, 1600.

ZEPHERIA

Zepheria. 1594; ed T. Corser, Manchester 1869 (Spenser Soc); ed E. Arber, English garner vol 5, 1882; ed S. Lee, Elizabethan sonnets vol 2, 1904. 35 sonnets and 6 other poems See J. G. Scott, Les sonnets élisabéthains, Paris 1929.

W. A. R.

V. JACOBEAN AND CAROLINE POETRY

See also introductory sections to Poetry 1500–1660, col 1007, above.

(1) COLLECTIONS AND ANTHOLOGIES

Saintsbury, G. Minor poets of the Caroline period. 3 vols Oxford 1905–21.

Fellowes, E. H. English madrigal verse 1588–1632. Oxford 1920, 1929 (rev), 1967 (rev and enlarged by F. W. Sternfeld and D. Greer).

Grierson, H. J. C. Metaphysical lyrics and poems. Oxford 1921.

— and G. Bullough. The Oxford book of seventeenth-century verse. Oxford 1934.

Ault, N. Seventeenth-century lyrics from the original texts. 1928, 1950 (rev).

Howarth, R. G. Minor poets of the seventeenth century. 1931 (EL), 1953 (rev).

Brinkley, R. F. English poetry of the seventeenth century. New York 1936.

Marshall, L. B. Rare poems of the seventeenth century. Cambridge 1936.

Scott, W. C. The fantasticks. 1945.

White, H. C., R. C. Wallerstein and R. Quintana. Seventeenth-century verse and prose: vol i, 1600–60. New York 1951.

Kermode, F. English pastoral poetry. 1952.

Angel, J. W. Selections from seventeenth-century songbooks. Los Angeles 1954 (Augustan Reprint Soc).

Cutts, J. P. and F. Kermode. Seventeenth-century songs, now first printed from the Bodleian ms. Reading 1956. For identifications see E. E. Duncan-Jones, N & Q Jan 1961.

Cutts, J. P. Seventeenth-century songs and lyrics, from the original music manuscripts. Columbia Missouri 1959.

Lamson, R. and H. Smith. Renaissance England: poetry and prose from the Reformation to the Restoration. New York 1956.

Gardner, H. The metaphysical poets. 1957 (Penguin), Oxford 1961 (rev), London 1967 (Penguin), 1972 (rev).

Bald, R. C. Seventeenth-century English poetry. New York 1959.

Sabol, A. J. Songs and dances for the Stuart masque. Providence 1959.

Dalglish, J. Eight metaphysical poets. 1961.

Hamilton, K. G. The poetry of wit and reason: a selection of poetry from Drayton to Cowper. Brisbane 1961.

Souris, A. Poèmes de Donne, Herbert et Crashaw mis en musique par leurs contemporains Coperario, Ferrabosco, John Wilson, Corkine, John Hilton. Introd by J. Jacquot, Paris 1961 (Centre National de la Recherche Scientifique).

Warnke, F. J. European metaphysical poetry. New Haven 1961.

Pagnini, M. Lirici carolini e repubblicani. Naples 1962.

Priest, H. M. Renaissance and baroque lyrics. Evanston 1962.

Bell, C. A. and G. H. Fell. From the seventeenth century. Melbourne 1963.

Blunden, E. and B. Mellor. Wayside poems of the seventeenth century: an anthology. Hong Kong 1963.

Furnivall, F. J. Loose and humorous songs from Bishop Percy's folio manuscript. 1963 (facs).

Martz, L. L. The meditative poem: an anthology of seventeenth-century verse. New York 1963.

—— The Anchor anthology of seventeenth-century verse vol 1. New York 1969.

Witherspoon, A. M. and F. J. Warnke. Seventeenth-century prose and poetry. New York 1963.

Hussey, M. Jonson and the Cavaliers. 1964.

Kenner, H. Seventeenth-century poetry: the schools of Donne and Jonson. New York 1964.

Inglis, F. English poetry 1550–1660. 1965.

Partridge, A. C. The tribe of Ben: pre-Augustan classical verse in English. 1966.

Smith, E. H. American poems 1793. Ed W. K. Bottorff, Gainesville 1966.

Danielsson, B. and D. M. Vieth. The Gyldenstolpe manuscript: miscellany of poems by John Wilmot, Earl of Rochester and other Restoration authors; Royal Library, Stockholm, ms Vu69. Stockholm 1967 (facs).

Davis, B. and E. Davis. Poets of the early seventeenth century. 1967.

Eade, C. Some English Iliads: Chapman to Dryden. Arion 6 1967.

French, D. P. Minor English poets 1660–1780: a selection from Alexander Chalmers' The English poets. New York 1967.

Miller, P. S. Seven minor epics of the English Renaissance 1598–1624. Gainesville 1967 (facs).

Starkman, M. K. Seventeenth-century English poetry. 2 vols New York 1967.

Meserole, H. T. Seventeenth-century American poetry. Garden City NY 1968.

Honig, E. and O. Williams. The major metaphysical poets of the seventeenth century: John Donne, George Herbert, Richard Crashaw and Andrew Marvell. New York 1969.

Poems from a manuscript miscellany in the Robert White collection, Newcastle University Library. Newcastle 1969.

Skelton, R. The Cavalier poets. 1970.

Sylvester, R. S. The Anchor anthology of seventeenth-century verse vol 2. New York 1969.

Wardroper, J. Love and drollery: a selection of amatory, merry and satirical verse of the seventeenth century. 1969.

Willy, M. The metaphysical poets. 1971.

(2) GENERAL STUDIES

See L. E. Berry, A bibliography of studies in metaphysical poetry 1939–60, Madison 1964. Suppl to T. Spencer, 1939 below.

Gosse, E. From Shakespeare to Pope. 1885.

—— The Jacobean poets. 1894.

Abbey, C. J. Religious thought in old English verse. 1892.

Dowden, E. Puritan and Anglican: studies in literature. 1900.

Harrison, J. S. Platonism in English poetry of the 16th and 17th centuries. New York 1903.

Clutton-Brock, A. The fantastic school of English poetry. In Cambridge modern history vol 4, Cambridge 1906.

Hutchinson, F. E. The sacred poets. CHEL vol 7 1911.

Moorman, F. W. Cavalier lyrists. Ibid.

Saintsbury, G. Lesser Caroline poets. Ibid.

Inge, W. R. English religious poetry. Trans Royal Soc of Lit 33 1915.

Quiller-Couch, A. T. In his Studies in literature: first series, Cambridge 1918.

Shafer, R. The English ode to 1660. Princeton 1918.

Alden, R. M. The lyrical conceits of the metaphysical poets. SP 17 1920.

Eliot, T. S. The metaphysical poets. TLS 20 Oct 1921; rptd in his Homage to John Dryden, 1924 and Selected essays, 1932. A review of Grierson's anthology, above. The unpbd ms of his 1926 Clark lectures on the Metaphysicals is in the library of King's College Cambridge.

Nethercot, A. H. The reputation of the metaphysical poets during the seventeenth century. JEGP 23 1924.

—— The reputation of the metaphysical poets during the age of Pope. PQ 4 1925.

—— The reputation of the metaphysical poets during the age of Johnson. SP 22 1925.

Lea, K. M. Conceits. MLR 20 1925.

Read, H. The nature of metaphysical poetry. In Reason and romanticism, 1926.

—— In his Phases of poetry, 1929.

Grierson, H. J. C. In his Cross-currents in seventeenth-century literature, 1929.

Schelling, F. E. Devotional poetry in the reign of Charles I. In Shakespeare and 'demi-science', Philadelphia 1927.

Williamson, G. The Donne tradition: English poetry from Donne to Cowley. Cambridge Mass 1930.

—— Strong lines. E Studies 18 1936; rptd in his Seventeenth-century contexts, 1960.

—— Seventeenth-century contexts. 1960.

—— The proper wit of poetry. 1961.

—— Six metaphysical poets: a reader's guide. New York 1967, London 1968 (as A reader's guide to the metaphysical poets).

Friederich, W. P. Spiritualismus und Sensualismus in der englischen Barocklyrik. Vienna 1932.

Bennett, J. Four metaphysical poets. Cambridge 1934, 1953 (rev), 1964 (enlarged as Five metaphysical poets). On Donne, Herbert, Vaughan, Crashaw; later Marvell.

Leishman, J. B. The metaphysical poets: Donne, Herbert, Vaughan, Traherne. Oxford 1934.

Praz, M. Studi sul concettismo. Milan 1934; tr with addns and new bibliography as Studies in seventeenth-century imagery, 2 vols 1939–47 (Warburg Inst), 1 vol Rome 1964 (rev).

—— The flaming heart: essays on Crashaw, Machiavelli and other studies of the relations between Italian and English literature from Chaucer to T. S. Eliot. Garden City NY 1958.

—— Literary resurrections. E Studies 42 1961.

—— Baroque in England. MP 61 1964.

Sharp, R. L. Some light on metaphysical obscurity and roughness. SP 31 1934.

—— Observations on metaphysical imagery. Sewanee Rev 43 1935.

—— From Donne to Dryden: the revolt against metaphysical poetry. Chapel Hill 1940, Hamden Conn 1965 (rev).

Smith, J. On metaphysical poetry. In Determinations, ed F. R. Leavis 1934.

Wallerstein, R. C. The development of the rhetoric and metre of the heroic couplet, especially in 1625–45. PMLA 50 1935.

—— Studies in seventeenth-century poetics. Madison 1950.

Wild, F. Zum Problem des Barocks in der englischen Dichtung. Anglia 59 1935.

Leavis, F. R. The line of wit. In his Revaluation, 1936; rptd in Seventeenth-century English poetry, ed W. R. Keast, New York 1962.

Meissner, P. Die geistesgeschichtlichen Grundlagen des englischen Literaturbarocks. Munich 1934.

Rohr-Sauer, P. von. English metrical psalms from 1600 to 1660. Freiburg 1938.

McEuen, K. A. Classical influence upon the Tribe of Ben. Cedar Rapids Iowa 1939.

Spencer, T. and M. Van Doren. Studies in metaphysical poetry: two essays and a bibliography. New York 1939.

Potter, G. R. A protest against the term 'conceit'. PQ 20 1941.

Brandenburg, A. S. The dynamic image in metaphysical poetry. PMLA 57 1942.

Knights, L. C. On the social background of metaphysical poetry. Scrutiny 13 1945; rptd in his Further explorations, 1965.

Daniells, R. English baroque and deliberate obscurity. Jnl of Aesthetics 5 1946.

Starnes, D. T. The poetic dictionary and the poet. Texas Univ Lib Chron 2 1946.

Schueller, H. M. The Renaissance forerunners of the neo-classical lyric. MLN 62 1947.

Doughty, W. L. Studies in the religious poetry of the seventeenth century. 1947.

Tuve, R. Elizabethan and metaphysical imagery: Renaissance poetic and twentieth-century critics. Chicago 1947.

Miles, J. The primary language of poetry in the 1640s. Berkeley 1948.

Bredvold, L. I. The rise of English classicism: a study in methodology. Comparative Lit 2 1950.

Keast, W. R. Johnson's criticism of the metaphysical poets. ELH 17 1950.

—— (ed). Seventeenth-century poetry: modern essays in criticism. New York 1962, 1971 (with addns).

Mahood, M. M. In her Poetry and humanism, 1950.

Nicolson, M. H. The breaking of the circle. Evanston 1950.

Bateson, F. W. Dissociation of sensibility. EC 1 1951. With replies.

Jones, R. F. et al. The seventeenth century. Stanford 1951.

Smith, H. W. The dissociation of sensibility. Scrutiny 18 1952.

Mazzeo, J. A. Critique of some modern theories of metaphysical poetry. MP 49 1952.

Vallette, J. Fortunes d'un apophtegme. Mercure de France 314 1952. On 'dissociation of sensibility'.

Wiley, M. L. The subtle knot: creative scepticism in seventeenth-century England. Cambridge Mass 1952.

Bethell, S. L. Gracián, Tesauro and the nature of metaphysical wit. Northern Miscellany 1 1953.

Ross, M. M. A note on the Metaphysicals. Hudson Rev 6 1953.

—— Poetry and dogma: the transfiguration of eucharistic symbols in seventeenth-century poetry. New Brunswick NJ 1954.

Watkin, E. I. Poets and mystics. 1953.

Cruttwell, P. The Shakespearean moment and its place in the poetry of the seventeenth century. 1954.

—— Makers and persons. Hudson Rev 12 1959.

Korninger, S. Mensch und Natur in der englischen Dichtung des frühen 17 Jahrhunderts. In Festschrift für Leo von Hibler, Wiener Beiträge zur Englischen Philologie 62 1954.

—— Die Naturauffassung in der englischen Dichtung des 17 Jahrhunderts. Vienna 1956.

Martz, L. L. The poetry of meditation: a study in English religious literature of the seventeenth century. New Haven 1954, 1962 (with addns).

—— The paradise within: studies in Vaughan, Traherne and Milton. New Haven 1964.

—— The wit of love: Donne, Carew, Crashaw, Marvell. Notre Dame Ind 1969.

Phillips, J. E. Poetry and music in the seventeenth century. In Music and literature in England in the seventeenth and eighteenth centuries. Los Angeles 1954.

Røstvig, M.-S. Casimire Sarbiewski and the English ode. SP 51 1954.

—— The happy man: studies in the metamorphosis of a classical idea 1600–1700. 2 vols Oslo and Oxford 1954–8, 1962 (rev).

Wright, H. G. The theme of solitude and retirement in seventeenth-century literature. Etudes Anglaises 7 1954.

Blunden, E. Some seventeenth-century Latin poems by English writers. UTQ 25 1955.

Brinkley, R. F. (ed). Coleridge on the seventeenth century. Durham NC 1955.

Bush, D. Seventeenth-century poets and the twentieth century. MHRA Annual Bull 27 1955.

—— Themes and variations in English poetry of the Renaissance. Claremont Cal 1957.

—— et al. Seventeenth-century science and the arts. Princeton 1962.

Cutts, J. P. Some Jacobean and Caroline dramatic lyrics. N & Q March 1955.

—— Early seventeenth-century lyrics at St Michael's College. Music & Letters 37 1956.

—— Mris Elizabeth Davenant 1624: Christ Church ms mus. 87. RES new ser 10 1959.

Esch, A. Englische religiöse Lyrik des 17 Jahrhunderts: Studien zu Donne, Herbert, Crashaw, Vaughan. Tübingen 1955.

—— Structure and style in some minor religious epics of the seventeenth century. Anglia 78 1960.

Walton, G. Metaphysical to Augustan: studies in tone and sensibility in the seventeenth century. Cambridge 1955.

Warnke, F. J. Marino and the English Metaphysicals. Stud in Renaissance 2 1955.

Willy, M. The nature of poetry. English 10 1955.

—— Three metaphysical poets: Crashaw, Traherne, Vaughan. 1961 (Br Council pamphlet).

Watson, G. Hobbes and the metaphysical conceit. JHI 16 1955. Reply by T. M. Gang 17 1956.

—— The language of the Metaphysicals. In Literary English since Shakespeare, ed Watson, New York 1970.

Denonain, J.-J. Thèmes et formes de la poésie 'métaphysique'. Paris 1956.

Ford, B. (ed). From Donne to Marvell. 1956 (Pelican), 1968 (rev).

Hart, E. F. The answer-poem of the early seventeenth century. RES new ser 7 1956.

Hibbard, G. R. The country house poem of the seventeenth century. Jnl Warburg & Courtauld Inst 19 1956.

—— The early seventeenth century and the tragic view of life. Renaissance & Modern Stud (Nottingham) 5 1961.

Jayakant, M. The metaphysical style in xvii-century literature. Allahabad Univ Stud 1956.

Miller, H. K. The paradoxical encomium with special reference to its vogue in England 1600–1800. MP 53 1956.

Notestein, W. Four worthies. 1956. John Chamberlain, Anne Clifford, John Taylor, Oliver Heywood.

O'Brien, G. W. Renaissance poetics and the problem of power. Chicago 1956.

Peltola, N. The compound epithet and its use in American poetry from Bradstreet through Whitman. Helsinki 1956.

Tillyard, E. M. W. The Metaphysicals and Milton. 1956.

—— In his Some mythical elements in English literature, 1961.

Kermode, F. Dissociation of sensibility. Kenyon Rev 19 1957.

—— (ed). The metaphysical poets: key essays on metaphysical poetry and the major metaphysical poets. Greenwich Conn 1969.

Macklem, M. The anatomy of the world: relations between natural and moral law from Donne to Pope. Minneapolis 1958.

McManaway, M. R. Poets in the Parish of St Giles, Cripplegate. Shakespeare Quart 9 1958.

Muraoka, I. Imagery of English poems of the 17th century. Tokyo 1958.

—— The historical background of metaphysical poetry. Stud in Eng Lit (Tokyo) 1960.

Prasad, S. K. The metaphysical poets: a revaluation. Sri Aurobindo Circle (Bombay) 14 1958.

Press, J. The chequer'd shade: reflections on obscurity in poetry. Oxford 1958.

Smith, A. J. The metaphysic of love. RES new ser 9 1958.

—— Theory and practice in Renaissance poetry: two kinds of imitation. Bull John Rylands Lib 47 1965.

—— Anglicanism and the poets. TLS 3 March 1959.

Attal, J.-P. Qu'est-ce que la poésie métaphysique? Critique Aug–Sept 1959.

Duncan, J. E. The revival of metaphysical poetry. Minneapolis 1959.

Gamberini, S. Poeti metafisici e cavalieri in Inghilterra. Florence 1959.

Richmond, H. M. The intangible mistress. MP 56 1959.

—— The school of love: the evolution of the Stuart love lyric. Princeton 1964.

Bigelow, G. E. Rhetoric and American poetry of the early national period. Gainesville 1960.

Ellrodt, R. Les poètes métaphysiques anglais. 3 vols Paris 1960.

—— La vogue de l'image scientifique dans la poésie anglaise du dix-septième siècle. Etudes Anglaises 14 1961.

—— Scientific curiosity and metaphysical poetry in the seventeenth century. MP 61 1964.

Patrides, C. A. The microcosm of man: some references to a commonplace. N & Q Feb 1960.

Skelton, R. Cavalier poets. 1960 (Br Council pamphlet).

Wedgwood, C. V. Poetry and politics under the Stuarts. Cambridge 1960.

—— Truth and opinion. 1960.

Ackerman, C. A. John Lyly and fashionable Platonism in Caroline poetry. Lock Haven Bull 3 1961.

Alouse, D. Poesia correlativa inglesa en los siglos xvi y xvii. Filologia Moderna (Madrid) 1 1961.

Alvarez, A. The school of Donne. 1961.

Collmer, R. G. The meditation on death and its appearance in metaphysical poetry. Neophilologus 45 1961.

—— The function of death in certain metaphysical poems. McNeese Rev 16 1965.

Heninger, S. K., jr. The Renaissance perversion of pastoral. JHI 22 1961.

Hollander, J. The untuning of the sky: ideas of music in English poetry 1500–1700. Princeton 1961.

Knowles, D. In his English mystical tradition, 1961.

McCann, E. Oxymora in Spanish mystics and English metaphysical writers. Comparative Lit 13 1961.

Nelson, L., jr. Baroque lyric poetry. New Haven 1961.

Osgood, C. G. Epithalamion and prothalamion: 'and theyr eccho ring'. MLN 76 1961.

Beaurline, L. A. Dudley North's criticism of metaphysical poetry. HLQ 25 1962.

Bullough, G. Mirror of minds: changing psychological beliefs in English poetry. Toronto 1962.

Grigson, G. Poets in their pride. 1962.

Levin, H. The American voice in English poetry. Langue et Littérature 6 1962.

Swardson, H. R. Poetry and the foundation of light: observations on the conflict between Christian and classical traditions in seventeenth-century poetry. 1962.

Brodbar, H. Late Renaissance astronomy and the 'new philosophy'. Forum (Houston) 3 1963.

Cohen, J. M. The baroque lyric. 1963.

Gray, D. Two songs of death. NM 64 1963.

Halewood, W. H. Mannerism in English poetry. Bucknell Rev 11 1963.

—— Poetry of grace: Reformation themes and structures in seventeenth-century English verse. New Haven 1971.

Hamilton, K. G. The two harmonies: poetry and prose in the seventeenth century. Oxford 1963.

Leach, E. Some commercial terms in seventeenth-century poetry. N & Q Nov 1963.

Nevo, R. The dial of virtue: a study of poems on affairs of state in the seventeenth century. Princeton 1963.

Sparrow, J. Hymns and poetry. TLS 11 Jan 1963. Reply by F. W. Sternfeld 1 Feb 1963.

Broadbent, J. B. In his Poetic love, 1964.

Doughtie, E. George Hanford's Ayres: unpublished Jacobean song verse. Anglia 82 1964.

Fisch, H. Jerusalem and Albion: the hebraic factor in seventeenth-century literature. 1964.

Melchiori, G. Poeti metafisici inglesi del seicento. Milan 1964.

Prasad, V. Metaphysical poetry and poetic maturity. Jammu & Kashmir Univ Rev 7 1964.

Waggoner, H. H. Puritan poetry. Criticism 6 1964.

Dewey, T. B. Some 'careless' seventeenth-century rhymes. BNYPL March 1965.

Hunter, J. The metaphysical poets. 1965.

La Hood, M. J. 'Carpe diem' in the Renaissance. Eng Record 15 1965.

Peel, D. F. Syncretistic elements in seventeenth-century metaphysical poetry. North West Missouri State College Stud 29 1965.

Scoular, K. W. Natural magic: studies in the presentation of nature in English poetry from Spenser to Marvell. Oxford 1965.

Seturaman, V. S. Skelton and the Metaphysicals. In Critical essays on English literature, Madras 1965.

Summers, J. H. Notes on recent studies in English literature of the earlier seventeenth century. MLQ 26 1965.

—— The heirs of Donne and Jonson. 1970.

Kawasaki, T. Metaphysical poetry and alchemy. Stud in Eng Lit (Tokyo) 43 1966.

King, J. R. Studies in six seventeenth-century writers. Athens Ohio 1966.

Loiseau, J. The baroque element in English and French poetry of the late sixteenth and early seventeenth century. In English studies today: fourth series, ed J. Cellini and G. Melchiori, Rome 1966.

McCoy, D. S. Tradition and convention: a study of periphrasis in English pastoral elegy from 1557–1715. Hague 1966.

Sanderson, J. L. Poems on an affair of state: the marriage of Somerset and Lady Essex. RES new ser 17 1966.

Stewart, S. N. The enclosed garden: the tradition and the image in seventeenth-century poetry. Madison 1966.

Williams, F. B., jr. Commendatory verses: the rise of the art of puffing. SB 19 1966.

Buxton, J. A tradition of poetry. 1967.

Hasan, M. English epithalamic verse of the earlier seventeenth century. Indian Jnl of Eng Stud 8 1967.

Jack, R. D. James VI and Renaissance poetic theory. English 16 1967.

Peterson, D. L. The English lyric from Wyatt to Donne: a history of the plain and eloquent styles. Princeton 1967.

Taylor, E. Literary criticism of 17th-century England. New York 1967.

Gross, T. L. The roots of American poetry. Yale Rev 57 1968.

Lacey, V. Poems of sixteenth and seventeenth century. N & Q Feb 1968.

Murrin, M. Poetry as literary criticism. MP 65 1968.

Waggoner, H. American poets from the Puritans to the present. Boston 1968.

Williams, R. Pastoral and counter-pastoral. Critical Quart 10 1968.

Armstrong, J. The paradise myth. 1969.

Bradbury, M. and D. Palmer (ed). Metaphysical poetry. 1969.

De Nagg, N. C. Tendenzen in der frühen amerikanischen Lyrik. In Festschrift Rudolf Stamm, zu seinem sechzigsten Geburtstag, Berne 1969.

Hawkins, A. L. A strain of trivia in minor metaphysical poetry. College Lang Assoc Jnl (Baltimore) 12 1969.

Hearnshaw, F. J. C. English history in contemporary poetry no 4: Court and Parliament 1588–1688. 1969.

Miner, E. The metaphysical mode from Donne to Cowley. Princeton 1969.

— The Cavalier mode from Jonson to Cotton. Princeton 1971.

Ruthven, K. K. The conceit. 1969.

Tokson, E. H. The image of the negro in four seventeenth-century love poems. MLQ 30 1969.

McKay, F. M. A seventeenth-century collection of religious poetry: Bodleian ms Eng poet b. 5. Bodleian Lib Record 8 1970.

Söderholm, T. End-rhymes of Marvell, Cowley, Crashaw, Lovelace and Vaughan. Acta Academiae Aboensis 39 1970.

Stanwood, P. G. Poetry manuscripts of the seventeenth century in the Durham Cathedral Library. Durham Univ Jnl new ser 31 1970.

Stein, A. Metaphysical poets. Yale Rev 59 1970.

Donne, Sandys, Phineas Fletcher, Drummond, Giles Fletcher, Wither, Browne, Herrick, King, Quarles, Herbert, Carew, Habington, Davenant, Waller, Suckling, Crashaw, Denham, Cowley, Lovelace, Marvell, Vaughan, Traherne

JOHN DONNE
1572–1631

Bibliographies etc

Keynes, G. L. A bibliography of Donne. Cambridge 1914, 1932, 1958, Oxford 1973 (rev and enlarged).

White, W. Donne since 1900: a bibliography of periodical articles. Bull of Bibliography 16 1937; rptd separately, Boston 1942.

— Sir Geoffrey Keynes' bibliography of Donne: a review with addenda. Bull of Bibliography 22 1959.

Combs, H. C. and Z. R. Sullens. Concordance to the English poems of Donne. Chicago 1940.

Main, C. F. New texts of Donne. SB 9 1957.

Manuscripts

De Havilland, M. Two unpublished manuscripts of Donne. London Mercury Dec 1925.

Robbie, H. J. L. RES 3–4 1927–8. Undescribed Donne mss.

Simpson, E. M. Two manuscripts of paradoxes and problems. RES 3 1927.

— More manuscripts of Donne's paradoxes and problems. RES 10 1934.

Wood, H. H. A seventeenth-century manuscript of poems by Donne and others. E & S 17 1931.

Potter, G. R. Manuscript versions of three sermons by Donne. JEGP 44 1945.

Gardner, H. L. Donne mss for the Bodleian. TLS 11 March 1960.

Crum, M. Notes on the physical characteristics of some manuscripts of the poems of Donne and Henry King. Library 5th ser 16 1961.

Whitlock, B. W. Note on two Donne manuscripts. Renaissance News 18 1965.

Gordan, J. D. The Westmorland manuscript of Donne's poems: anniversary exhibition catalogue of the Berg collection 1940–65. BNYPL Oct 1965.

MacColl, A. A new manuscript of Donne's poems. RES new ser 19 1968.

Armitage, C. M. Donne's poems in the Huntington manuscript 198: new light on the Funerall. SP 63 1966.

Collections and Selections

Poems. 1633, 1635, 1639, 1649, 1650, 1654, 1669, 1719, Edinburgh 1779 (Bell's poets); ed R. Anderson [1793] (Poets of Great Britain vol 4); ed A. Chalmers 1810 (Johnson's lives of poets vol 5); ed J. R. Lowell, Boston 1855, 1855 (with poetical works of Skelton); ed A. B. Grosart 1872 (complete works in 2 vols); ed J. R. Lowell 2 vols New York 1895 (from 1633 text); ed E. K. Chambers, introd by G. Saintsbury 1896 (ML); ed H. J. C. Grierson 2 vols Oxford 1912, 1 vol Oxford 1929 (OSA) (without notes); ed J. Hayward, Complete poetry and selected prose, 1929 (Nonesuch Lib), 1930; ed R. S. Hillyer, New York [1941] (with Blake's poems); ed R. E. Bennett, Chicago [1942]; ed C. M. Coffin, New York [1952] (Modern Lib); ed H. I'A. Fausset 1958 (EL); ed J. T. Shawcross 1967; ed F. Kermode, [New York] 1968.

LXXX sermons. 1640. With Walton's life.

Fifty sermons. 1649.

XXVI sermons. 1660, 1661 (2 issues).

Works. Ed H. Alford 6 vols 1839.

Selections from the works of Donne. Ed D. A. Talboys, Oxford 1840.

Selected passages from the sermons. Ed L. P. Smith, Oxford 1919.

Ten sermons. Ed G. L. Keynes 1923 (Nonesuch Press).

Selected shorter poems. Ed G.D.H. and M. I. Cole 1928.

Complete poetry and selected prose. Ed J. Hayward 1929 (Nonesuch Lib), 1936 (rev).

Selected poems 1633. Ed F. Delattre 1946.

Poetry and prose, with Walton's life. Ed H. W. Garrod, Oxford 1946.

Poems. Ed J. Hayward 1950 (Penguin). A selection.

Selected poems. Ed J. Reeves 1952.

Divine poems. Ed H. Gardner, Oxford 1952; Elegies, and Songs and sonnets, ed Gardner, Oxford 1965; Satires, epigrams and verse letters, ed W. Milgate, Oxford 1967. The standard edn.

Complete sermons. Ed G. R. Potter and E. M. Simpson
10 vols Berkeley and Los Angeles 1953-62.
Songs and sonets. Ed T. Redpath 1956.
Sermons. Ed T. A. Gill, New York 1958.
Sermons on the Psalms and Gospels, with a selection of
prayers and meditations. Ed E. M. Simpson, Berkeley
1963.
The showing forth of Christ: sermons of Donne. Ed E.
Fuller, New York 1964.
Selected poetry. Ed M. M. Bewley, New York 1966.
Donne's poetry. Ed A. L. Clements, New York 1966.
Complete English poems. Ed A. J. Smith 1971 (Penguin).
Donne's prebend sermons. Ed J. M. Mueller, Cambridge
Mass 1971.
*Some love poems tr French, Revue de Littérature Comparée
16 1936; see also* Poèmes choisis, *ed P. Legouis, Paris
[1955];* Poèmes, *tr J. Fuzier and Y. Denis, Paris 1962;
and selected poems tr Italian by G. Melchiori, Bari 1962.*

§ I

Pseudo-martyr. 1610. A Protestant prose text for English
Catholics.
Conclave Ignati. [1611], [1611]; Ignatius his conclave,
1611 (3 edns), 1626, 1634, 1635, 1653, 1680; ed C. M.
Coffin, New York 1941 (facs of first English edn); ed
T. S. Healy, Oxford 1969 (both versions, Latin and
English).
An anatomy of the world. 1611, ed G. L. Keynes, Cam-
bridge 1951 (Roxburghe Club) (facs); The second
anniversary: of the progress of the soule, 1612 (with
First anniversary), 1621, 1625; ed J. Sparrow, New York
1927 (facs); Shaftesbury 1929; The anniversaries, ed
F. Manley, Baltimore 1963. In Second anniversary,
only Of the progress of the soul is by Donne.
[Sermon of valediction at his going into Germany preached
at Lincoln's Inn April 18 1619. Ed E. M. Simpson
1932; ed G. R. Potter, Stanford 1946.]
Sermon on Acts i, 8. 1622, 1624.
Sermon on Judges xx. 15 [i.e. v. 20]. 1622 (3 issues).
Encaenia: the feast of Dedication celebrated at Lincoln's
Inn in a sermon on Ascension day. 1623.
Three sermons. 1623, 1624.
Devotions upon emergent occasions. 1624, 1624, 1624,
1626, 1627, 1634, 1638, Oxford 1841; ed J. Sparrow,
Cambridge 1923 (with bibliographical note by G. L.
Keynes); ed W. H. Draper [1925].
First sermon preached to King Charles. 1625.
Four sermons. 1625.
Sermon preached at Whitehall. 1626.
Five sermons. 1626, Menston 1970 (facs).
Sermon of Commemoration. 1627.
Death's duell. 1632, 1633, 1633.
Juvenilia: or certaine paradoxes and problemes. 1633,
1633, 1652 (with addns as Paradoxes, problems, essayes,
characters; usually bound with Essayes in divinity,
below), 1652 (slightly rev); ed R. E. Bennett, New York
1936 (facs).
Sermon on John viii. 15. 1634. Part of Six sermons, below.
Six sermons. 1634.
Two sermons. 1634.
Sermon upon Ecclesiastes xii. 1. In Sapientia clamitaus,
1638, 1639.
Biathanatos. 1646, 1648, 1700; ed J. W. Hebel, New York
[1930] (facs).
Essayes in divinity. 1651 (usually bound with Juvenilia
1652, above); ed A. Jessopp 1855; ed E. M. Simpson,
Oxford 1952.
To Mr E[verard] G[uilpin]. In E. Gosse, Life and letters
of Donne, 1899.
Sermon on Psalm xxxviii. 9. 1921 (facs of Dowden ms).
Catalogus librorum. Ed E. M. Simpson 1930 (with trn).
Rptd from Poems 1650, 1654, 1669, 1719.
An elegy. Ed E. K. Chambers, RES 7 1931. From Hol-
gate ms, Pierpont Morgan Lib, New York.

Letters, Diaries etc

Poems. 1633, 1635, 1639, 1649, 1650, 1654, 1669, 1719.
Each contains same 11 letters. 1635-1719 add 4.
LXXX sermons. 1640. Letter in Walton's Life.
Letters to severall persons of honour. 1651, 1654; ed
E. E. Merrill jr, New York 1910.
Cabala. 1654, 1663, 1691. 2 letters.
Walton, I. Life of Donne. 1658. 5 letters.
— Life of Herbert. 1670. 4 letters.
— Lives of Donne, Wootton, Hooker, Herbert. 1670.
9 letters.
Collection of letters made by Sir Tobie Matthew. 1660,
1692. 38 letters to and from Donne.
The Loseley manuscripts. Ed A. J. Kempe 1835. 10
letters.
Works of Donne vol 6. Ed H. Alford 1839.
Camden Society. Letters and documents illustrating
relations between England and Germany at the com-
mencement of the Thirty Years' War. Ed S. R. Gardiner
1868. Letter to Carleton.
— Fortescue papers. Ed S. R. Gardiner 1871. Letter to
Buckingham.
Collection of autograph letters formed by A. Morrison
vol 3. 1896. Letter to Carew 23 July 1624.
Gosse, E. Life and letters of Donne. 2 vols 1899. Includes
19 unpbd letters.
Simpson, E. M. A study of the prose works of Donne.
Oxford 1924. 32 unpbd letters.
London Mercury Dec 1925. One letter from Loseley
mss.
Hayward, J. (ed). Donne's complete poetry and selected
prose. 1929. 3 unpbd letters.
Letter to Sir Nicholas Carey (Carew, 21 June 1625). Ed
T. Spencer, Cambridge Mass 1929.
Catalogue of books from Bridgewater Library sold at
Sotheby's 19 March 1951. Lot 109: Pseudo-martyr,
1610, with attached letter to Lord Ellesmere. Catalogue
has transcript and some copies include collotype.

§ 2

Walton, I. The life of Donne. 1640 (in LXXX sermons),
1658 (enlarged).
Dowden, E. In his New studies in literature, 1895.
Jessop, A. John Donne. 1897.
Gosse, E. The life and letters of Donne. 2 vols 1899.
Ashton, H. Du Bartas en Angleterre. Paris 1908.
Chambers, E. K. Donne: diplomatist and soldier. MLR 5
1910.
Simpson, E. M. Donne's sermons and their relation to
his poetry. MLR 7 1912.
— A chronological arrangement of Donne's sermons.
MLR 8 1913.
— Donne and Overbury's characters. MLR 18 1923.
— A study of the prose works of Donne. Oxford 1924,
1948 (rev).
— A note on Donne's punctuation. RES 4 1928.
— Jonson and Donne: a problem of authorship. RES 15
1939.
— Notes on Donne. RES 20 1944.
— The date of Donne's Hymne to God my God, in my
sicknesse. MLR 41 1946.
— Donne's Spanish authors. MLR 43 1948.
— Biographical value of Donne's sermons. RES new ser
2 1951.
— Donne and the Church. TLS 25 May 1956.
— Two notes on Donne. RES new ser 16 1965.
Moore Smith, G. C. Donniana. MLR 8 1913.
Picavet, F. Medieval doctrines in the works of Donne and
Locke. Mind 16 1917.
Ramsay, M. Les doctrines médiévales chez Donne. 1917,
1924 (rev).
Sampson, J. A contemporary light upon Donne. E & S
7 1921.

Bredvold, L. I. The naturalism of Donne in relation to some Renaissance traditions. JEGP 22 1923.
— In his Studies in Shakespeare, Milton and Donne vol 1, Ann Arbor 1925.
Fausset, H. I'A. John Donne. 1924.
Sparrow, J. On the date of Donne's Hymne to God my God. MLR 19 1924.
— Donne's table-talk. London Mercury May 1928.
— Donne and contemporary preachers. E & S 16 1930.
— A motto of Donne. TLS 30 March 1946.
— Errata slip in Donne's Anniversaries. TLS 29 June 1946. Reply H. J. C. Grierson 20 July 1946.
— Two epitaphs by Donne. TLS 26 March 1949.
— More Donne. TLS 13 March 1953.
— Donne's books in the Middle Temple. TLS 29 July–5 Aug 1955.
— The text of Donne. TLS 21 Dec 1956.
— Dr Donne and Scaliger. TLS 28 Feb 1958.
— Hymns and poetry. TLS 11 Jan 1963.
— George Herbert and Donne among the Moravians. BNYPL Dec 1964.
— Donne's books in Oxford. TLS 25 Nov 1965. Replies by L. Forster 9 Dec; J. Callard and R. S. Pirie 23 Dec; C. Dobb 30 Dec 1965.
— Donne's books. TLS 6 Jan 1966. Replies by G. L. Keynes 13 Jan 1966; I. A. Shapiro 20 Jan 1966; L. Forster and D. L. Graham 27 Jan 1966.
[Sparrow, J.] Ill Donne, well Donne: scholarship and para-scholarship. TLS 6 April 1967. Replies by John Holloway 13 April, E. Le Comte 11 May, L. P. Curtis 18 May 1967.
— Manuscript corrections in the two issues of Donne's Biathanatos. Book Collector 21 1972.
Praz, M. Secentismo e Marinismo in Inghilterra. Florence 1925.
— La poesia metafisica inglese del Seicento: Donne. Rome 1945.
— Donne and Dickens. TLS 20 Feb 1959.
Wilder, M. L. Did Jonson write the Expostulation attributed to Donne? MLR 21 1926.
Wilson, F. P. The early life of Donne. RES 3 1927.
Legouis, P. Donne the craftsman. Paris 1928.
— Some lexicographical notes and queries on Donne's satires. Studia Neophilologica 14 1942.
— Le thème du rêve dans le Clitandre de Pierre Corneille et The dreame de Donne. Revue d'Histoire du Théâtre 2 1951, 4 1952.
— L'état présent des controverses sur la poésie de Donne. Etudes Anglaises 5 1952.
— Donne, l'amour et les critiques. Etudes Anglaises 10 1957.
— Donne and William Cowper. Anglia 76 1958.
Williamson, G. The Donne tradition. Cambridge Mass 1930.
— The libertine Donne. PQ 13 1934; rptd in his Seventeenth-century contexts, 1960.
— Donne's Farewell to love. MP 36 1939.
— Textual difficulties in the interpretation of Donne's poetry. MP 38 1940; rptd in his Seventeenth-century contexts, 1960.
— In his Proper wit of poetry, 1961.
— In his Milton and others, 1965.
— Donne's satirical Progresse of the soule. ELH 36 1969.
Shapiro, I. A. The text of Donne's letters. RES 7 1931.
— Donne the astronomer: date of eighth problem. TLS 3 July 1937. Replies by W. F. Mitchell 10 July 1937; J. Lindsay 24 July 1937; P. Legouis 31 July 1936.
— The date of Donne's poem To Mr George Herbert. N & Q 29 Oct 1949.
— Donne's birthdate. N & Q 19 July 1952.
— Walton and the occasion of Donne's Devotions. RES new ser 9 1958.
— Donne, the Parvishes, and Munster's 'cosmographey'. N & Q July 1966.
— Donne in 1605-6. TLS 26 Jan 1967.

Bald, R. C. Donne's influence in English literature. Morpeth 1932.
— William Milbourne, Donne and Thos Jackson. RES 24 1948.
— Donne's activities. TLS 13 May 1949.
— Donne's early verse letters. HLQ 15 1952.
— Donne's letters. TLS 24 Oct 1952.
— Donne and the Drurys. Cambridge 1959.
— Historical doubts respecting Walton's Life of Donne. In Essays in English literature presented to A. S. P. Woodhouse, Toronto 1964.
— Dr Donne and the booksellers. SB 18 1965.
— Donne: a life. Ed W. Milgate, Oxford 1970.
Hughes, M. Y. The lineage of the Extasie. MLR 27 1932.
— Kidnapping Donne. In California essays in criticism: series 2, Berkeley 1934, which includes G. R. Potter, Donne's discovery of himself.
— Milton's celestial battle and the theogonies. In Studies in honor of T. W. Baldwin, Urbana 1958.
— Some of Donne's Ecstasies. PMLA 75 1960.
Spencer, T., T. S. Eliot et al. A garland for Donne 1631–1931. Cambridge Mass 1931.
Doggett, F. A. Donne's Platonism. Sewanee Rev 42 1934.
Alexander, H. Donne, poet and divine. Queen's Quart 42 1935.
Bennett, R. E. Donne and Sir Thos Roe. TLS 31 Jan 1935. Reply by I. A. Shapiro 7 Feb 1935.
— Donne and the Queen. TLS 29 Aug 1936.
— Tracts from Donne's library. RES 13 1937.
— Walton's use of Donne's letters. PQ 16 1937.
— Donne and Everard Gilpin. RES 15 1939.
— Donne's letters from the Continent in 1611-12. PQ 19 1940.
— Donne's Letters to severall persons of honour. PMLA 56 1941.
Maxwell, I. R. Donne's library. TLS 11 July 1935.
Simpson, P. A book from Donne's library. Oriel Record (Oxford) 1935.
Wasilifky, A. M. Donne the rhetor: a study of the tropes and figures of the St Paul's sermons. Ithaca 1935.
Gretton, G. H. Donne: the spiritual background. Hamburg 1936.
— Donne: seine Beziehung zu seiner Zeit und sein Einfluss auf seine 'nichtmetaphysischen' Nachfolger. Düsseldorf 1938.
— Donne on conversion. Theology 32 1936.
Husain, I. The dogmatic and mystical theology of Donne. 1938.
Gros, L.-G. Présentation de Donne. Cahiers du Sud Nov 1936.
— Donne: étude et traduction. Paris 1964.
Lindsay, J. Donne and Giordano Bruno. TLS 20 June 1936. Replies by R. Ince 27 June 1936; F. A. Yates 4 July 1936; and J. Lindsay 11 July 1936.
More, J. F. Scholasticism, Donne and the metaphysical conceit. Revue Anglo-américaine 13 1936.
Potter, G. R. Donne's Extasie: contra Legouis. PQ 15 1936.
— and J. Butt. Editing Donne and Pope. Los Angeles 1953.
Potter, G. R. Donne: poet to priest. In Five Gayley lectures 1947-54, Berkeley 1954.
Teager, F. S. Patronage of Joseph Hall and Donne. PQ 15 1936.
Tredegar, Viscount. Donne: lover and priest. Essays by Divers Hands 15 1936.
Langston, B. A Donne poem overlooked. TLS 18 Jan 1936. Replies by B. H. Newdigate and J. Hayward 25 Jan 1936; I. A. Shapiro and E. K. Chambers 1 Feb 1936; B. H. Newdigate 8 Feb 1936; and R. B. Botting 14 March 1936.
Atkins, S. H. Donne's satires. TLS 22 May 1937. See subsequent correspondence on date of satires.
Coffin, C. M. Donne and the new philosophy. New York 1937.

—— Donne's divinity. Kenyon Rev 16 1954.

Douds, J. B. Donne's technique of dissonance. PMLA 52 1937.

Umbach, H. H. The rhetoric of Donne's sermons. Ibid.

—— The merit of metaphysical style in Donne's Easter sermons. ELH 12 1945.

—— When a poet prays. Cresset 17 1954. On Donne's prayers.

Heuer, H. Browning and Donne. E Studien 72 1938.

Keynes, G. L. Death's duell. TLS 24 Sept 1938. With correspondence.

—— Books from Donne's library. Trans Cambridge Bibl Soc 1 1949–53.

—— Donne's sermons. TLS 28 May 1954.

—— Dr Donne and Scaliger. TLS 21 Feb 1958. See J. Sparrow 28 Feb 1958.

—— Donne's books. TLS 13 Jan 1966. See I. A. Shapiro 20 Jan, L. Forster 27 Jan, J. Sparrow 6 Jan 1966.

Lewis, C. S. Donne and love poetry. In Seventeenth-century studies presented to Sir Herbert Grierson, Oxford 1938. Reply by J. Bennett, ibid. Both rptd in Seventeenth-century English poetry, ed W. R. Keast, New York 1962.

Lewis, E. G. The question of toleration in the works of Donne. MLR 33 1938.

Bowers, F. T. The interpretation of Donne's tenth elegy. MLN 54 1939.

Rugoff, M. A. Donne's imagery: a study in creative sources. New York 1939.

Nicolson, M. H. Kepler, the 'Somnium' and Donne. JHI 1 1940.

Allen, D. C. Donne's suicides. MLN 56 1941.

—— Donne and the bezoar. Ibid.

—— Dean Donne sets his text. ELH 10 1943.

—— Donne's knowledge of Renaissance medicine. JEGP 42 1943.

—— Donne and Pierio Valeriano. MLN 58 1943, 60 1945.

—— Donne and the tower of Babel. MLN 64 1949.

—— Three notes on Donne's poetry with a side glance at Othello. MLN 65 1950. Annotations on Triple fool; Satyre 3; A feaver.

—— The double journey of Donne. In A tribute to George Coffin Taylor, Chapel Hill 1952.

—— A note on Donne's Elegy viii. MLN 68 1953.

—— Donne's The will. MLN 69 1954.

—— Donne's compass figure. MLN 71 1956.

—— Donne on the mandrake. MLN 74 1959.

—— Love in a grave. Ibid.

—— The genesis of Donne's dreams. MLN 75 1960.

—— Donne and ship metaphor. MLN 76 1961.

—— Milton and the love of angels (related to Donne's Extasie). Ibid.

—— Donne's Sapho to Philaenis. Eng Lang Notes 1 1964.

—— Doubts boundless sea: skepticism and faith in the Renaissance. Baltimore 1964.

Benham, A. R. The myth of Donne the rake. In Renaissance studies in honor of Hardin Craig, Stanford 1941.

Munoz Rojas, J. A. Un libro español en la biblioteca de Donne. Revista de Filologia Española 25 1941.

Battenhouse, R. W. The grounds of religious toleration in the thought of Donne. Church History 11 1942.

Cooper, H. Donne and Virginia in 1610. MLN 57 1942.

Duncan, E. H. Donne's alchemical figures. ELH 9 1942.

Milgate, W. Donne the lawyer. TLS 1 Aug 1942.

—— The date of Donne's birth. N & Q 16 Nov 1946.

—— Donne's art gallery. N & Q 23 July 1949.

—— Early references to Donne. N & Q 27 May, 10 June, 8 July, 2 Sept 1950.

—— References to Donne. N & Q Oct 1953.

—— A difficult allusion in Donne and Spenser. N & Q Jan 1966.

—— The date of Donne's marriage: a reply. Etudes Anglaises 22 1969.

Stein, A. Donne and the couplet. PMLA 57 1942.

—— Donne and the satiric spirit. ELH 11 1944.

—— Donne's harshness and Elizabethan tradition. SP 41 1944.

—— Donne's prosody. PMLA 59 1944.

—— Donne's obscurity and the Elizabethan tradition. ELH 13 1946.

—— Structures of sound in Donne's verse. Kenyon Rev 13 1951.

—— Donne and the 1920's: a problem in historical consciousness. ELH 27 1960.

—— Donne's lyrics: the eloquence of action. Minneapolis 1962.

—— Donne's prosody. In G. Hemphill, Discussions of poetry: rhythm and sound, Boston 1964.

Hardy, E. Donne: a spirit in conflict. 1942.

Svendsen, K. Donne's Hymne to God the Father. Explicator June 1944.

Gardner, H. Donne: a note on Elegy 5. MLR 39 1944.

—— Notes on Donne's verse letters. MLR 41 1946.

—— and J. B. Leishman. Poetic tradition in Donne. TLS 11 May 1956.

Gardner, H. Donne and the Church. TLS 25 May 1956.

—— Another note on Donne: Since she whome I lov'd. MLR 52 1957.

—— The argument about the Ecstasy. In Elizabethan and Jacobean studies presented to F. P. Wilson, Oxford 1959.

—— (ed). Donne: a collection of critical essays. Englewood Cliffs NJ 1962.

—— Donne's platan tree. TLS 26 Aug 1965.

—— and W. P. H. Merchant. John Donne. CQ 8 1966.

Gardner, H. On editing Donne. TLS 24 Aug 1967.

Garrod, H. W. The date of Donne's birth. TLS 30 Dec 1944.

—— Donne and Mrs Herbert. RES 21 1945.

—— The Latin poem addressed by Donne to Dr Andrews. RES 21 1945.

Moloney, M. F. Donne: his flight from medievalism. Urbana 1944.

—— Donne's metrical practice. PMLA 65 1950.

Wiggins, E. L. Logic in the poetry of Donne. SP 42 1945.

Lederer, J. Donne and emblematic practice. RES 22 1946.

Brooks, C. In his Well wrought urn, New York 1947.

Hickey, R. L. Donne and Virginia. PQ 26 1947.

—— Donne's art of memory. Tennessee Stud in Lit 3 1958.

—— Donne's art of preaching. Nashville 1956.

Martz, L. L. Donne in meditation: the Anniversaries. ELH 14 1947.

—— Donne and meditative tradition. Thought 34 1959.

—— Donne: the meditative voice. Massachusetts Rev 1 1960.

—— In his Wit of love, Notre Dame Ind 1969.

Roberts, D. R. The death wish of Donne. PMLA 62 1947.

Cleveland, E. D. Donne's The primrose. Explicator Oct 1949.

Grierson, H. J. C. Donne and the via media. MLR 43 1948.

—— The metaphysics of Donne and Milton. In his Criticism and creation, 1949.

Empson, W. Donne and the rhetorical tradition. Kenyon Rev 11 1949; rptd in Seventeenth-century poetry: modern essays in criticism, ed W. R. Keast, New York 1962.

—— Donne the space man. Kenyon Rev 19 1957.

—— Donne in the new edition. CQ 8 1966.

Henderson, H. Donne's The will. Explicator June 1949.

Hotson, L. A crux in Donne. TLS 16 April 1949 f.

Murray, W. A. Donne and Paracelsus. RES 25 1949.

—— Donne's gold-leaf and his compasses. MLN 73 1958.

—— What was the soul of the apple? RES new ser 10 1959.

Pafford, J. H. P. Donne's library. TLS 2 Sept 1949 f.

—— Donne: an early nineteenth-century estimate. N & Q April 1959.

—— An early Donne reference. N & Q Oct 1966.

Potts, L. J. Ben Jonson and the seventeenth century. E Studies 1949. On Jonson and Donne.

Siegel, P. N. Donne's 'paradoxes and problems'. PQ 28 1949.

Sporri-Sigel, E. Liebe und Tod in Donnes Dichtung. Siebnen 1949.

Thomson, P. Donne and the Countess of Bedford. MLR 44 1949.

Ball, L., jr. Donne's The computation. Explicator April 1950.

Gierasch, W. Donne's Negative love. Explicator Nov 1950.

Gleckner, R. F. and G. Smith. Donne's Loves usury: an analysis of the puns and innuendoes in this poem. Explicator 8 1950.

Keister, D. A. Donne's The will. Explicator May 1950.

Mabbott, T. O. Donne's The will. Ibid.

—— Donne's Satyre II. 71–2. Explicator Dec 1957.

Matsuura, K. A study of Donne's imagery. Eibungaku-kenkyu 26 1950.

—— A study of the imagery of Donne. Tokyo 1953.

Sprott, S. E. The legend of Donne the libertine. UTQ 19 1950.

Symes, G. The paradoxes of poetry. English 8 1950. On Donne, Vaughan and Herbert.

Unger, L. H. Donne's poetry and modern criticism. Chicago 1950.

—— The man in the name-essays on the experience of poetry. Minneapolis 1956.

Wiley, M. L. Donne and the poetry of scepticism. Hibbert Jnl 48 1950.

Atkinson, A. D. Donne quotations in Johnson's dictionary. N & Q Sept 1951.

Harding, D. W. Coherence of theme in Donne's poetry. Kenyon Rev 13 1951.

Jack, I. Pope and 'the weighty bullion of Dr Donne's satires'. PMLA 66 1951.

Leishman, J. B. Donne: the monarchy of wit. 1951, 1962 (rev).

Louthan, D. The poetry of Donne: a study in explication. New York 1951.

Main, W. W. Donne's Elegie xix, Going to bed. Explicator Nov 1951.

Maxwell, J. C. Donne and the 'new philosophy'. Durham Univ Jnl 7 1951.

Miles, J. The language of the Donne tradition. Kenyon Rev 13 1951.

Ochojski, P. M. Did Donne repent his apostasy? Amer Benedictine Rev 1 1951.

White, H. C. Donne and the psychology of spiritual effort. In The seventeenth century: studies by R. F. Jones et al, Stanford 1951.

—— Donne and the psychology of spiritual effort. TLS 22 Feb 1952.

Baruch, F. R. Donne and Herbert. TLS 30 May 1952. Reply by J. B. Leishman 13 June 1952.

Bewley, M. Religious cynicism in Donne's poetry. Kenyon Rev 14 1952.

Eldredge, F. Further allusions and debts to Donne. ELH 19 1952.

Frye, R. M. John Donne junior on Biathanatos: a presentation letter. N & Q 8 Nov 1952.

Jacobsen, E. The fable is inverted: or Donne's Aesop. Classica et Mediaevalia 7 1952.

Novarr, D. Donne's letters. TLS 24 Oct 1952.

—— Donne's Epithalamion made at Lincoln's Inn: context and date. RES new ser 7 1956.

—— The dating of Donne's La Corona. PQ 36 1957.

—— The making of Walton's Lives. Ed M. H. Abrams, F. E. Mineka and W. M. Sale jr, Ithaca 1958.

—— The two hands of Donne. MP 62 1964.

Skinner, M. Donne not in Germany 1602. N & Q 29 March 1952.

Smith, H. W. The dissociation of sensibility. Scrutiny 18 1952.

Simon, I. Some problems of Donne criticism. Langues Vivantes 40 1952.

Turnell, M. Donne's quest for unity. Commonweal 19 Oct 1952.

Whitlock, B. W. Donne's 'first letter'. TLS 22 Aug 1952. Replies by I. A. Shapiro 12 Sept; D. Novarr 19 Sept; R. C. Bald 26 Sept 1952 f.

—— 'Cabal' in Donne's sermons. N & Q April 1953.

—— The Dean and the yeoman. N & Q Sept 1954.

—— John Syminges: a poet's step-father. N & Q Oct–Nov 1954.

—— Donne at St Dunstan's. TLS 16–23 Sept 1955.

—— Ye curioust schooler in Cristendom. RES new ser 6 1955.

—— Edward Alleyn's draft letter to Donne. RES new ser 8 1957.

—— The heredity and childhood of Donne. N & Q July–Aug, Oct 1959.

—— The family of Donne 1588 91. N & Q Oct 1960.

—— Donne's university years. E Studies 43 1962.

Baker, L. M. The letters of Elizabeth, Queen of Bohemia. 1953. Includes a letter to Donne.

Brown, N. P. A note on the imagery of Donne's Loves growth. MLR 48 1953.

Collins, C. Donne's The canonization. Explicator Oct 1953.

Duncan, J. E. The intellectual kinship of Donne and Browning. SP 50 1953.

—— The revival of metaphysical poetry: the history of a style, 1800 to the present. Minneapolis 1959.

Emslie, M. A Donne setting. N & Q Nov 1953.

—— Barclay Squire and Grierson's Donne. N & Q Jan 1955.

Herman, G. Donne's Holy sonnets xiv. Explicator Dec 1953.

—— Donne's Goodfriday 1613: riding westward. Explicator June 1956.

Hynes, S. L. A note on Donne and Aquinas. MLR 8 1953.

Johnson, S. F. Donne's Satires I. Explicator June 1953.

Levenson, J. C. Donne's Holy sonnets xiv. Explicator March 1953.

Lorca, J. G. Un aspecto de Donne: su originalidad. Insula (Madrid) 86 (suppl) 1953.

Lowe, R. L. Browning and Donne. N & Q Nov 1953.

Moran, B. Some notes on Donne's attitude to the problem of body and soul. Ingiliz Filolokisi Dergisi (Istanbul) 3 1953.

—— Donne's poem The dream. Litera 6 1959.

Morris, D. The poetry of Gerard Manley Hopkins and T. S. Eliot in the light of the Donne tradition. Swiss Stud in Eng 33 1953.

Saunders, J. W. Donne and Daniel. EC 3 1953.

Tate, A. The point of dying: Donne's virtuous men. Sewanee Rev 59 1953.

Wright, H. G. Some sixteenth- and seventeenth-century writers on the plague. E & S new ser 6 1953.

Adams, R. M. Donne and Eliot: Metaphysicals. Kenyon Rev 16 1954.

Bennett, J. A. W. A note on Donne's Crosse. RES new ser 5 1954.

—— Donne, Elegy 16, [line] 31. N & Q July 1966.

Drinkwater, D. J. More references to Donne. N & Q Dec 1954.

Gransden, K. W. John Donne. 1954.

Hunt, C. Donne's poetry: essays in literary analysis. New Haven 1954.

Kermode, F. Donne allusions in Howell's familiar letters. N & Q Aug 1954.

—— John Donne. 1957 (Br Council pamphlet).

—— (ed). Discussions of Donne. Boston 1963.

—— In his Shakespeare, Spenser, Donne: Renaissance essays, 1971.

Kuhlmann, H. Donne: Betrachtungen über Elend und Grösse der Menschen. Die Neueren Sprachen new ser 1954.

Levenson, P. C. Donne's Holy sonnets xiv. Explicator April 1954.

McCann, E. Donne and Saint Teresa on the ecstasy. HLQ 17 1954.

Sawin, L. The earliest use of 'autumnal'. MLN 69 1954.

—— Donne's The canonization 7. Explicator March 1955.

Sharp, R. L. Donne's Good-morrow and cordiform maps. MLN 69 1954.

—— In his From Donne to Dryden, 1955.

—— Donne's Autumnall and the barren plane tree. N & Q June 1962.

Warren, A. The very reverend Dr Donne. Kenyon Rev 16 1954.

—— Donne's Extasie. SP 55 1958.

Willy, M. The poetry of Donne: its interest and influence today. E & S new ser 7 1954.

Davenport, A. An early reference to Donne. N & Q Jan 1955.

Elmon, P. Donne's dark lantern. PBSA 49 1955.

Esch, A. In his Englische religiöse Lyrik des 17 Jahrhunderts, Tübingen 1955.

—— Paradise and Calvary: zu Donnes Hymne to God, my God, in my sicknesse, vers. 21–2. Anglica 78 1960.

Evans, M. English poetry in the sixteenth century. 1955.

Francis, W. N. Donne's Goodfriday 1613: riding westward. Explicator Feb 1955.

Grenander, M. E. Donne's Holy sonnets 12. Explicator 13 1955.

—— Holy sonnets vii and xvii: Donne. Boston 1960.

Malloch, A. E. Donne's Pseudo-Martyr and Catalogus librorum aulicorum. MLN 70 1955.

—— The definition of sin in Donne's Biathanatos. MLN 72 1957.

—— Donne and the casuists. Stud in Eng Lit 1500–1900 2 1962.

Novak, M. An unrecorded reference in a poem by Donne. N & Q Nov 1955.

Poetic tradition in Donne. TLS 16 March 1956.

Cobb, L. S. Donne's Satyre II. 71–2. Explicator March 1956.

—— Donne's Satyre II. 49–57. Explicator Nov 1956.

Cox, R. G. The poems of Donne. In From Donne to Dryden, ed B. Ford 1956 (Pelican).

Cross, K. G. Balm in Donne and Shakespeare: ironic intention in the Extasie. MLN 71 1956.

Gale, R. L. Donne's The sunne rising 27–30. Explicator Dec 1956.

Goldberg, M. A. Donne's A lecture upon the shadow. Explicator May 1956.

Knox, G. Donne's Holy sonnets 14. Explicator Oct 1956.

Maud, R. N. Donne's First anniversary. Buffalo Univ Stud in Eng 2 1956.

Ornstein, R. Donne, Montaigne and natural law. JEGP 55 1956.

Phelps, G. The prose of Donne and Browne. In From Donne to Dryden, ed B. Ford 1956 (Pelican).

Rooney, W. J. The Canonisation: the language of paradox reconsidered. ELH 23 1956.

—— Donne's Second prebend sermon: a stylistic analysis. Texas Stud in Lit & Lang 4 1962.

Sleight, R. Donne: A nocturnall upon St Lucie's day, being the shortest day. Interpretation 10 1956.

Smith, A. J. Two notes on Donne. MLR 51 1956.

—— Donne in his time: a reading of the Extasie. Rivista di Letteratura Moderne e Comparate 10 1957.

—— Sources of difficulty and of value in the poetry of Donne. Letterature Moderne 7 1957.

—— The metaphysic of love. RES new ser 9 1958.

—— New bearings in Donne: Aire and angels. English 13 1960.

—— Donne, Songs and sonets. 1964.

—— The phoenix and the urn. TLS 13 May 1965.

—— A Donne poem in holograph. TLS 7 Jan 1972. Replies by H. Gardner 21 Jan, P. L. Heyworth 24 March 1972.

Alvarez, A. Donne and his circle. Listener 23 May 1957.

—— In his School of Donne, 1961.

Bradbrook, F. W. Donne and Ben Jonson. N & Q April 1957.

Coanda, R. Hopkins and Donne: 'mystic' and metaphysical. Renascence 9 1957.

Emerson, K. T. Two problems in Donne's Farewell to love. MLN 72 1957.

Hagopian, J. V. Some cruxes in Donne's poetry. N & Q Nov 1957.

—— A difficult crux in Donne's Satyre II. MLN 73 1958.

—— Donne's Love's diet 20–4. Explicator Oct 1958.

Hall, V., jr. Donne's Satyre II. 71–2. Explicator Jan 1957.

Hilberry, C. The first stanza of Donne's Hymne to God my God, in my sicknesse. N & Q Aug 1957.

Madison, A. L. Explication of Donne's The flea. N & Q Feb 1957.

Main, C. F. New texts of Donne. SB 9 1957.

Mazzeo, J. A. Notes on Donne's alchemical imagery. Isis 48 1957.

—— In his Renaissance and seventeenth-century studies, New York 1964.

Nathanson, L. Dryden, Donne and Cowley. N & Q May 1957.

—— The context of Dryden's criticism of Donne's and Cowley's love poetry. N & Q Feb 1957.

Parish, J. E. Donne as a Petrarchan. N & Q Sept 1957.

—— The parley in the Extasie. Xavier Univ Stud 4 1965.

Warnke, F. J. Donne's The anniversarie. Explicator Nov 1957.

Combellack, F. M. Jonson's To John Donne. Explicator Oct 1958.

Cross, G. Another Donne allusion. N & Q Dec 1958.

Falk, R. E. Donne's Resurrection, imperfect. Explicator Dec 1958.

Hasan, M. ul. Donne's imagery. Aligarh 1958.

Joseph, Brother F. S. C. Donne's A valediction forbidding mourning 1–18. Explicator April 1958.

Macklem, M. In his Anatomy of the world: relations between natural and moral law from Donne to Pope, Minneapolis 1958.

Marshall, W. H. A possible interpretation of Donne's The second anniversary (lines 33–6). N & Q Dec 1958.

—— Elizabeth Drury and the heathens. N & Q Dec 1958.

Powers, D. Donne's compass. RES new ser 9 1958.

Press, J. In his Chequer'd shade: reflections on obscurity in poetry, Oxford 1958.

Richmond, H. M. Donne and Ronsard. N & Q Dec 1958.

Russell, J. D. Donne's A lecture upon the shadow. Explicator Nov 1958.

Seng, P. J. Donne's compass image. N & Q May 1958.

Soens, A. L. Casaubon and Donne. TLS 2 May 1958.

Stapleton, L. The theme of virtue in Donne's verse epistles. SP 55 1958.

Ulrey, P. The 'One' in Donne's poetry. Renaissance Papers 1958–60.

Attal, J.-P. Qu'est-ce que la poésie métaphysique? Critique Aug–Sept 1959.

Bollier, E. P. T. S. Eliot and Donne: a problem in criticism. Tulane Stud in Eng 9 1959.

Carey, J. Clement Paman (Paman and Donne). TLS 27 March 1959.

C., S. Donne's The legacie. Explicator Nov 1959.

Dorsten, J. A. van. Juygens en de engelse metaphysical poets. Tijdschrift voor Nederlandse Taalen Letterkunde (Leyden) 76 1959.

Duncan-Jones, E. E. Marvell, Jonson and the first sunset. TLS 3 April 1959.

—— The barren plane-tree in Donne's The autumnall. N & Q Feb 1960.

—— Donne's praise of autumnal beauty: Greek sources. MLR 56 1961.

Manley, F. Chaucer's rosary and Donne's bracelet: ambiguous coral. MLN 74 1959.

Newton, W. A study of Donne's sonnet 14. Anglican Theological Rev 41 1959.

Peterson, D. L. Donne's Holy sonnets and the Anglican doctrine of contrition. SP 56 1959.

—— In his English lyric from Wyatt to Donne, Princeton 1967.

Richmond, H. M. The intangible mistress. MP 56 1959.

Scott, R. I. Donne and Kepler. N & Q June 1959.

Stephenson, A. A. G. M. Hopkins and Donne. Downside Rev 77 1959.

Tillotson, K. Donne's poetry in the nineteenth century 1800–72. In Elizabethan and Jacobean studies presented to F. P. Wilson, Oxford 1959.

Bauerle, R. F. Donne redone and undone. N & Q Oct 1960.

Chambers, A. B. The meaning of the Temple in Donne's La Corona. JEGP 59 1960.

Combecher, H. Donnes Annunciation: eine Interpretation. Die Neueren Sprachen 9 1960.

Crossett, J. Bacon and Donne. N & Q Oct 1960.

Durr, R. A. Donne's The primrose. JEGP 59 1960.

Ellrodt, R. Chronologie des poèmes de Donne. Etudes Anglaises 13 1960.

—— L'inspiration personelle et l'esprit du temps chez les poètes métaphysiques anglais: première partie. Paris 1960. Vol 1, Donne et les poètes de la tradition chrétienne.

—— Etudes critiques: nouvelle édition de Donne. Etudes Anglaises 20 1967.

Kawasaki, T. Donne's Microcosm: some queries to Prof Empson. Stud in Eng Lit (Tokyo) 36 1960.

—— From Southwell to Donne. Stud in Eng Lit (Tokyo) 39 1963.

—— The world of Donne. Tokyo 1967.

Lerner, L. The truest poetry: an essay on the question What is literature? 1960.

Morgan, B. Q. Compulsory patterns in poetry. PMLA 75 1960.

Perella, N. J. Amarilli's dilemma: the Pastor Fido and some English authors. Comparative Lit 12 1960.

Poynter, F. N. L. Donne and William Harvey. Jnl of History of Medicine 15 1960.

Quinn, D. B. Donne and Tyr. MLN 75 1960.

—— Donne's principles of biblical exegesis. JEGP 61 1962.

—— Donne's Anniversaries as celebration. Stud in Eng Lit 1500–1900 9 1969.

Sowton, I. Religious opinion in the prose letters of Donne. Canadian Jnl of Theology 6 1960.

Banzer, J. 'Compound manner': Emily Dickinson and the metaphysical poets. Amer Lit 32 1961.

Chambers, A. B. Goodfriday 1613: riding westward. ELH 28 1961.

Clements, A. L. Donne's Holy sonnet 14. MLN 76 1961.

Collmer, R. G. The background of Donne's reception in Holland. Mississippi Quart 14 1961.

—— Donne and Charron. E Studies 46 1965.

—— Donne's poetry in Dutch letters. Comparative Lit Stud 2 1965.

—— Donne and Borges. Revue de Littérature Comparée 43 1969.

Cowan, S. A. Donne's The legacy. Explicator May 1961.

Fleissner, R. F. Donne and Dante: the compass figure reinterpreted. MLN 76 1961.

George, C. H. and K. In their Protestant mind of the English Reformation, Princeton 1961.

Gérard, A. Mannerism and the scholastic structure of Donne's Extasie. Publications de l'Université de l'Etat à Elisabethville 1 1961.

Levine, J. A. The Dissolution: Donne's twofold elegy. ELH 28 1961.

Lowe, I. Donne, the middle way: the reason-faith equation in Donne's sermons. JHI 22 1961.

Manley, F. Walton's Angler and Donne: a probable allusion. MLN 76 1961.

Morris, H. In articulo mortis. Tulane Stud in Eng 9 1961.

Mueller, W. R. Donne's adulterous female town. MLN 76 1961.

—— Donne: preacher. Princeton 1962.

Schwartz, E. Donne's Elegie X (the Dreame). Explicator June 1961.

Webber, J. The prose styles of Donne's Devotions upon emergent occasions. Anglia 79 1961.

—— Contrary music: the prose style of Donne. Madison 1963.

Bryan, R. A. Donne's use of the anathema. JEGP 61 1962.

—— Translatio: concepts in Donne's The progress of the soul. In All these to teach: essays in honor of C. A. Robertson, Gainesville 1965.

Evans, G. B. Two notes on Donne: the Undertaking; A valediction: of my name, in the window. MLR 57 1962.

Hardison, O. B., jr. The enduring monument: a study of the idea of praise in Renaissance literary theory and practice. Durham NC 1962.

Harris, V. Donne and the theatre. PQ 41 1962.

Henry, N. and P. R. Moody. Donne's A lecture upon the shadow. Explicator March 1962.

Highet, G. In his Anatomy of satire, Princeton 1962.

Jones, R. F. The humanistic defence of learning in the mid-seventeenth century. In Reason and imagination: studies in the history of ideas 1600–1800, ed J. A. Mazzeo, New York 1962.

Linneman, Sr M. Rose Ann. Donne as catalyst in the poetry of Elinor Wylie, Wallace Stevens, Herbert Read and William Empson. Xavier Univ Stud 1 1962.

Mahoney, J. L. Donne and Greville: two Christian attitudes toward the Renaissance idea of mutability and decay. College Langs Assoc Jnl (Baltimore) 5 1962.

Marsh, T. N. Elizabethan wit in metaphor and conceit: Sidney, Shakespeare, Donne. Eng Miscellany (Rome) 13 1962.

Molella, L. Donne's A lecture upon the shadow. Thoth 3 1962.

Munoz Rojas, J. A. Encuentro con Donne. Papeles de Son Armadans (Majorca) 27 1962.

Silhol, R. Réflexions sur les sources et la structure de A litanie de Donne. Etudes Anglaises 15 1962.

Sloan, T. A. A rhetorical analysis of Donne's The prohibition. Quart Jnl of Speech 48 1962.

—— The persona as rhetor: an interpretation of Donne's Satyr 3. Quart Jnl of Speech 51 1965.

Spitzer, L. In his Essays on English and American literature, Princeton 1962.

Zimmerman, H.-J. Ein Autograph-Fragment von Popes The second satire of Dr John Donne, versified. Archiv 199 1962.

Carey, J. Time & Tide 10 April 1963.

—— Notes on two of Donne's Songs and sonnets. RES new ser 16 1965.

Chitanand, T. P. Donne's The progress of the soul. Indian Jnl of Eng Stud 4 1963.

Höltgen, K. J. Einc Emblemfolge in Donnes Holy sonnet xiv. Archiv 200 1963.

—— Unpublished early verses On Dr Donne's Anatomy. RES new ser 22 1971.

Kuna, F. M. T. S. Eliot's dissociation of sensibility and the critics of metaphysical poetry. EC 13 1963.

Ringler, R. N. Two sources for Dryden's The Indian Emperour, Donne's First anniversarie and the Faerie Queene I and II. PQ 42 1963.

—— Donne's specular stone. MLR 60 1965.

Samson, P. Words for music. Southern Rev (Adelaide) 1 1963.

Vining, E. G. Take heed of loving me. Philadelphia 1963.

Brilli, A. Gli 'Amores' Ovidiani e la poesia de Donne. Studi Urbinati di Storia, Filosofia e Letteratura 38 1964.

Geraldine, Sr M. Erasmus and the tradition of paradox. SP 61 1964.
— Donne and the mindes indeavours. Stud in Eng Lit 1500–1900 5 1965.
— Donne's Notitia: the evidence of the satires. UTQ 36 1966.
Halio, J. L. The term 'perfection' as used by various poets including Donne. Eng Lang Notes 1 1964.
McCullen, J. T., jr. and L. E. Bowling. Literary corruptions of an ancient myth. Southern Folklore Quart 28 1964.
Nellist, B. F. Donne's Storm and calm and the descriptive tradition. MLR 59 1964.
Rickey, M. E. Donne's The relique 27–8. Explicator March 1964.
Rowe, F. A. I launch at paradise: a consideration of Donne, poet and teacher. 1964.
Rowland, D. B. Mannerism-style and mood: an anatomy of four works in three art forms. New Haven 1964.
Shawcross, J. T. Donne's A lecture upon the shadow. Eng Lang Notes 1 1964.
— Donne's A nocturnal upon S. Lucies Day. Explicator March 1965.
— Donne and Drummond's manuscripts. Amer N & Q 5 1967.
— An early nineteenth-century life of Donne: an edition with notes and commentary. Jnl of Rutgers Univ Lib 32 1968.
Sinha, V. N. Donne and the romantic theory of imagination. Criticism & Research (Banaras Hindu Univ) 1964.
Sullens, Z. R. Neologisms in Donne's English poems. Annali dell' Istituto Universitario Orientale, Sezione Germanica (Naples) 7 1964.
Weiss, W. Der Refrain in der elisabethanischen Lyrik. Munich 1964.
Yoklavich, J. Donne and the Countess of Huntingdon. PQ 43 1964.
Andreasen, N. J. C. Donne's Devotions and the psychology of assent. MP 62 1965.
— Donne: conservative revolutionary. Princeton 1967.
Bender, T. K. The platan tree in Donne, Horace and Theocritus. TLS 12 Aug 1965.
Buckley, V. Donne's passion. Melbourne Critical Rev 8 1965.
Chari, V. K. The dramatic in Donne. Indian Jnl of Eng Stud 6 1965.
Clair, J. A. Donne's The canonization. PMLA 80 1965.
Cornelius, D. K. Donne's Holy sonnet 14. Explicator Nov 1965.
Daniels, E. F. and W. J. Dean. Donne's Elegy 7. 22. Explicator Dec 1965.
Daniels, E. F. Donne's Satire 3. 52. Explicator Feb 1970.
Davies, H. S. Text or context? REL 6 1965. Replies by H. Gardner, W. J. M. Bronzwaer and D. W. Lindsay, ibid. On Air and angels.
Demaray, J. G. Donne's three steps to death. Personalist 46 1965.
Forster, L. Donne's books. TLS 9 Dec 1965.
Gorlier, C. Il poeta e la nuova alchimia. Paragone 16 1965.
Guss, D. L. Donne's Petrarchism. JEGP 44 1965.
— Donne, Petrarchist: Italianate conceits and love theory in the Songs and sonets. Detroit 1966.
Herbold, A. Seeking secrets of poetiquenesse? Donne's dialects in the divine poems. Moderna Språk 59 1965.
Howarth, R. G. In his A pot of gillyflowers, Cape Town 1965.
Hughes, R. E. Donne's Nocturnall upon S. Lucies day: a suggested resolution. Cithara 4 1965.
— The woman in Donne's Anniversaries. ELH 34 1967.
— The progress of the soul: the interior career of Donne. New York 1969.
Le Comte, E. Grace to a witty sinner: a life of Donne. New York 1965.

Low, D. A. An eighteenth-century imitation of Donne's first satire. RES new ser 26 1965.
Meller, H. S. The phoenix and the well-wrought urn. TLS 22 April 1965.
Morris, W. E. Donne's The sunne rising 30. Explicator Feb 1965.
Pirie, R. S. Fine paper copies of Donne's Biathanatos. Book Collector 14 1965.
Raspa, A. Theology and poetry in Donne's Conclave. ELH 32 1965.
Wagner, L. W. Donne's secular and religious poetry. Lock Haven Rev 7 1965.
Wright, L. B. (ed). In The Elizabethans' America, Cambridge Mass 1965.
Zuberi, I.-H. Donne's concept of toleration in Church and State. Univ of Windsor Rev (Ontario) 1 1965.
Boorman, S. C. Some Elizabethan notes 2: a possible allusion in Donne's A tale of a citizen and his wife. Trivium 1 1966.
Bross, A. C. Alexander Pope's revisions of Donne's satyres. Xavier Univ Stud 5 1966.
Chambers, A. B. The fly in Donne's Canonization. JEGP 65 1966.
Clive, M. Jack and the doctor. 1966.
England, M. W. and J. Sparrow. Hymns unbidden. New York 1966 (New York Public Lib). Rptd from BNYPL 1964–6.
Gifford, W. A Donne allusion. N & Q Jan 1966.
— Donne's sermons on the 'grand days'. HLQ 29 1966.
— Time and place in Donne's sermons. PMLA 82 1967.
— Donne on candlemas at St Paul's? N & Q Oct 1969.
Harrington, D. V. Donne's The relique. Explicator Nov 1966.
Harrison, R. Donne's To the Countess of Huntingdon (man to God's image . . .). Explicator Dec 1966.
Johnson, C. H. Reason's double agents. Chapel Hill 1966.
LaBranche, A. Blanda elegeia: the background to Donne's Elegies. MLR 61 1966.
Love, H. The argument of Donne's First anniversary. MP 64 1966.
— Donne's To his mistress going to bed 45. Explicator Dec 1967.
McCanles, M. Paradox in Donne. Stud in Renaissance 13 1966.
Menasce, E. Donne: ultimo poeta del Medio Evo. Studi Revel 75 1966.
Miller, C. H. Donne's A nocturnall upon S. Lucies day and the nocturn of matins. Stud in Eng Lit 1500–1900 6 1966.
Morillo, M. Donne's compasses: circles and right lines. Eng Lang Notes 3 1966.
Potter, M. A note on Donne. N & Q Oct 1966.
Raizis, M. B. The epithalamion tradition and Donne. Wichita State Univ Bull 42 1966.
Roberts, M. If it were Donne when 'tis done. EC 16 1966.
Ruotolo, L. P. The trinitarian framework of Donne's Holy sonnet 14. JHI 27 1966.
Woolf, V. In her Collected essays vol 1, 1966.
Zivley, S. Imagery in Donne's Satyres. Stud in Eng Lit 1500–1900 6 1966.
Alphonse, Sr M. Donne's Love's growth. Explicator Jan 1967.
Block, H. M. The alleged parallel of metaphysical and symbolist poetry. Comparative Lit Stud (Maryland) 4 1967.
Broich, U. Form und Bedeutung der Paradoxie im Werk Donnes. Germanisch-romanische Monatsschrift 48 1967.
Dicker, H. The bell of Donne. Centennial Rev 2 1967.
Doebler, B. A. Donne's debt to the great tradition: old and new in his treatment of death. Anglia 85 1967.
French, A. L. Dr Gardner's dating of the Songs and sonets. EC 17 1967.

—— The psychopathology of Donne's Holy sonnets. Critical Rev 13 1970.

Gamberini, S. Saggio su Donne. La Spezia 1967.

Gibbs, A. M. A Davenant imitation of Donne? RES new ser 18 1967.

Heatherington, M. E. 'Decency' and 'zeal' in the sermons of Donne. Texas Stud in Lit & Lang 9 1967.

MacColl, A. The new edition of Donne's love poems. EC 17 1967.

Matchett, W. H. Donne's Peece of chronicle. RES new ser 18 1967.

Mueller, J. M. A borrowing of Donne's Christmas sermon of 1621. HLQ 30 1967.

Pagnini, M. Sulle funzioni semilogiche della poesia di Donne. Lingua et Stile (Bologna) 2 1967.

Sackton, A. Donne and the privacy of verse. Stud in Eng Lit (Tokyo) 7 1967.

Schwartz, E. Donne's Holy sonnets 14. Explicator Nov 1967.

Stanwood, P. G. A Donne discovery. TLS 19 Oct 1967.

—— 'Essentiall joy' in Donne's Anniversaries. Texas Stud in Lit & Lang 13 1971.

Vizioli, P. A poesia latina de Donne. O Estado de São Paulo: Supplemento Literario 4 1967.

Wolfe, R. H. and E. F. Daniels. Rime and idea in Donne's Holy sonnet 10. Amer N & Q 5 1967.

Baker-Smith, D. Donne and the mysterium crucis. Eng Miscellany (Rome) 19 1968.

Beck, R. A precedent for Donne's imagery in Goodfriday 1613: riding westward. RES new ser 19 1968.

Benjamin, E. B. Donne and Bodin's Theatrum. N & Q March 1968.

Cameron, A. B. Donne and Dryden: their achievement in the verse epistle. Discourse 11 1968.

Corin, F. A note on Donne's Canonization. E Studies 50 1968.

Graziani, R. Donne's The extasie and ecstasy. RES new ser 19 1968.

Gregory, E. R., jr. The balance of parts: imagistic unity in Donne's Elegy 19. Univ Rev (Kansas City) 35 1968.

Heist, W. W. Donne on divine grace: Holy sonnet no 14. Papers of Michigan Acad 53 1968.

Jackson, R. S. 'Dount wisely': Donne's Christian skepticism. Cithara 8 1968.

Murrin, M. Poetry as literary criticism. MP 65 1968.

Pomeroy, E. Donne's The sunne rising. Explicator Sept 1968.

Prosky, M. Donne's Aire and angels. Explicator Dec 1968.

Roberts, J. R. Donne's Satyre III reconsidered. CLA Jnl 12 1968.

Thumboo, E. Donne's The bracelet (Elegy XI). Explicator Oct 1968.

Traci, P. The supposed new rhetoric of Donne's Songs and Sonets. Discourse 11 1968.

Bell, A. H. Donne's atonement conceit in the Holy sonnets. Cresset 32 1969.

Cirillo, A. R. The fair Hermaphrodite: love-union in the poetry of Donne and Spenser. Stud in Eng Lit 1500–1900 9 1969.

Durand, L. G. Sponde and Donne: lens and prism. Comparative Lit 21 1969.

Haefner, G. Donne, the Canonization: eine Interpretation. Die Neueren Sprachen 18 1969.

Koppenfels, W. von. Donnes Liebesdichtung und die Tradition von Tottels Miscellany. Anglia 87 1969.

Lawniczak, D. A. Donne's sainted lovers again. Serif 6 1969.

Mahony, P. The Anniversaries: Donne's rhetorical approach to evil. JEGP 68 1969.

Moore, T. V. Donne's use of uncertainty as a vital force in Satyre III. MP 67 1969.

Murphy, J. The young Donne and the Senecan amble. Bull Rocky Mountain Modern Lang Assoc 23 1969.

Nelly, U. The poet Donne: a study in his dialectic method. Cork 1969.

Selden, R. Donne's The dampe, lines 22–4. MLR 64 1969.

Sicherman, C. M. The mocking voices of Donne and Marvell. Bucknell Rev 17 1969.

—— Donne's timeless Anniversaries. UTQ 39 1970.

Simpson, A. L., jr. Donne's Holy sonnets XII. Explicator May 1969.

Stewart, J. F. Image and idea in Donne's The good-morrow. Discourse 12 1969.

—— Irony in Donne's The funeral. Ibid.

Voss, A. E. The structure of Donne's Anniversaries. Eng Stud in Africa (Johannesburg) 12 1969.

Wanninger, M. T. Donne's Holy sonnets XIV. Explicator Dec 1969.

Wilson, G. R., jr. The interplay of perception and reflection: mirror imagery in Donne's poetry. Stud in Eng Lit 1500–1900 9 1969.

Day, W. B. Sterne, Josephus and Donne. N & Q March 1970.

Delany, P. Donne's Holy sonnet 5, lines 13–14. Amer N & Q 9 1970.

Gleason, J. B. Dr Donne in the courts of kings: a glimpse from marginalia. JEGP 69 1970.

Kelly, T. J. Donne's 'firme substantiall love'. Critical Rev 13 1970.

Khanna, U. Donne's A valediction forbidding mourning: some possible alchemical allusions. N & Q Nov 1970.

Mahoney, P. J. The heroic couplet in Donne's Anniversaries. Style 4 1970.

Mann, L. A. A note on the text of Donne's sermon preached at St Paul's Cross 24 March 1616/7. N & Q Nov 1970.

Martin, P. Donne in Twicknam Garden. Critical Survey 4 1970.

McLaughlin, E. The extasie: deceptive or authentic? Bucknell Rev 18 1970.

Meurs, J. C. Donne in the twentieth century. Levende Talen 1970.

Rauber, D. F. Donne's Farewell to love: a crux revisited. Concerning Poetry 3 1970.

Sayama, E. Donne: the middle phase. Tokyo 1970.

Schleiner, W. The imagery of Donne's sermons. Providence 1970.

Stampfer, J. Donne and the metaphysical gesture. New York 1970.

Summers, J. H. The heritage of Donne and Jonson. UTQ 39 1970.

Thornburg, T. R. Donne's The extasie: a definition of love. Ball State Univ Forum 11 1970.

Tomlinson, T. B. Donne and his critics. Critical Rev 13 1970.

Winny, J. A preface to Donne. 1970.

Deubel, V. Tradierte Bauformen und lyrische Struktur: die Veränderung elisabethanischer Gedichtschemata bei Donne. Stuttgart 1971.

Fox, R. A. Donne's Anniversaries and the art of living. ELH 38 1971.

Grant, P. Augustinian spirituality and the Holy sonnets of Donne. ELH 38 1971.

Sanders, J. W. Donne's poetry. Cambridge 1971.

Lebans, W. M. The influence of the classics in Donne's Epicedes and obsequies. RES new ser 23 1972.

Slights, C. 'To stand inquiring right': the casuistry of Donne's Satyre III. Stud in Eng Lit 1500–1900 12 1972.

GEORGE SANDYS
1578–1644

Bibliographies

Bowers, F. T. and R. B. Davis. Sandys: a bibliographical catalogue of printed editions in England to 1700. BNYPL April–June 1950.

Collections

Selections from the paraphrases, with memoir [by H. J. Todd]. 1839.
Poetical works. Ed R. Hooper 2 vols 1872.

§1

A relation of a journey. 1615, 1621, 1627, 1632, 1637, 1652 (as Sandys travailes), 1658, 1670, 1673, 1864.
The first five books of Ovid's Metamorphosis. 1621 (3 issues). No copy of first issue is known; for copies of 2nd issue see Bowers and Davis, above; for 3rd, see McManaway, below.
Ovid's Metamorphosis englished by G.S. 1626, 1628 (unauthorized), Oxford 1632 (rev and with An essay to the translation of Virgil's Aeneis), 1638, 1640, 1656, 1664, 1669, 1678, 1690.
A paraphrase upon the Psalmes, by G.S. 1636. See col 1911, below.
A paraphrase upon the divine poems. 1638, 1648, 1676. An enlarged edn of preceding.
Christ's passion: a tragedie. 1640, 1640, 1687, 1693. Tr from Hugo Grotius.
A paraphrase upon the song of Solomon, by G.S. 1641, 1642.

§2

Brodribb, C. W. Ovid, Sandys and Milton. N & Q 2–16 Aug 1924. See also TLS 14 Aug 1924.
—— Lore from Sandys's Ovid. N & Q 28 May 1927.
Barker, R. H. Sandys's Relation. Trans Wisconsin Acad 30 1937.
de Beer, E. S. Sandys's account of Campania. Library 4th ser 17 1937.
Chew, S. C. In his Crescent and the rose, New York 1937.
Davis, R. B. Sandys: poet-adventurer. Americana 33 1939.
—— Early editions of Sandys's Ovid. PBSA 35 1941.
—— Two new manuscript items for a Sandys bibliography. PBSA 37 1943.
—— America in Sandys's Ovid. William & Mary Quart 4 1947.
—— Sandys v. William Stansby: the 1632 edition of Ovid's Metamorphosis. Library 5th ser 3 1948.
—— Sandys and two 'uncollected' poems. HLQ 12 1948.
—— Sandys: poet-adventurer. New York 1955.
—— In re Sandys's Ovid. SB 8 1956.
—— Sandys's Song of Solomon: its manuscript versions and their circulation. PBSA 50 1956.
—— Volumes from Sandys's library now in America. Virginia Mag of History & Biography 65 1957.
Cawley, R. R. Burton, Bacon and Sandys. MLN 56 1941.
Bowers, F. T. Two notes on running titles as bibliographical evidence: 1, Sandys, Ovid's Metamorphosis 1632; 2, Sandys, Christ's passion 1640. PBSA 42 1948.
McManaway, J. G. The first five books of Ovid's Metamorphosis, 1621, englished by Sandys. SB 1 1948.
Grundy, J. Keats and Sandys. N & Q Feb 1955.
Schmutzler, K. E. Another manuscript version of Sandys's Song of Solomon. PBSA 53 1959.
Kranidas, T. Milton and the author of Christ's suffering. N & Q March 1968.

PHINEAS FLETCHER
1582–1650

Collections

Poems. Ed A. B. Grosart 4 vols 1869 (Fuller Worthies' Lib).
Spenser of his age. Ed W. Jerrold 1905. Selected poems.
Poetical works of Giles and Phineas Fletcher. Ed F. S. Boas 2 vols Cambridge 1908–9.

§1

Locustae: vel pietas Jesuitica. 2 pts [Cambridge] 1627. The locusts or apollyonists.
Brittain's Ida written by that renowned poët Edmond Spencer. 1628. Really by Fletcher.
Sicelides a piscatory. 1631. Anon. Variant texts in BM additional ms 4453 and Bodley Rawlinson poetry ms 214.
Joy in tribulation: or consolations for afflicted spirits. 1632.
The way to blessedness: or a treatise on the first psalme. 1632.
Sylva poetica. Cambridge 1633. Part of Giles Fletcher, De literis antiquae Britanniae.
The purple island. Cambridge 1633, 1633. Includes Piscatorie eclogs, Poetical miscellanies, and Elisa or an elegie upon the unripe decease of Antonie Irby. The Piscatorie eclogs and Elisa have separate title-pages, each with imprint Cambridge 1633. Purple island rptd 1783, ed H. Headley 1816. Piscatorie eclogs and Poetical miscellanies rptd Edinburgh 1771, Amsterdam 1971 (facs of 1633).
A father's testament. 1670.
Venus and Anchises—Britain's Ida—and other poems. Ed E. Seaton 1926 (Royal Soc of Lit) (from ms).

§2

Cory, H. E. Spenser, the school of the Fletchers and Milton. Berkeley 1912.
Waibel, K. Fletcher's Purple island. E Studien 58 1924.
Baldwin, E. C. Milton and Fletcher. JEGP 33 1934.
Langdale, A. B. Fletcher. New York 1937.
—— Fletcher's marriage: a parallel to the Shakespeare marriage records. N & Q 4 Nov 1939.
Stewart, B. T. A borrowing from Spenser by Fletcher. MLN 56 1941.
—— A note on Spenser and Fletcher. PQ 26 1947.
Wasserman, E. R. Moses Browne and the 1783 edition of Giles and Phineas Fletcher. MLN 56 1941.
Watson, S. R. Milton's use of Fletcher's Purple island. N & Q 12 April 1941.
Sheldon, D. C. Note on a Latin poem by either Giles Fletcher or his brother Phineas. MLR 46 1951.
Patrick, J. M. Milton, Fletcher, Spenser and Ovid: sin at Hell's gate. N & Q Sept 1956.
Berry, L. E. Fletcher: additions and corrections. N & Q Feb 1960.
—— Phineas Fletcher's account of his father. JEGP 60 1961.
Stroup, T. B. Milton's two-handed engine and Fletcher's two-edged sword. N & Q Oct 1959.
Baldwin, R. G. Fletcher: his modern readers and his Renaissance ideals. PQ 40 1961.
—— Dubious claims for the anatomy in the Purple island. N & Q Oct 1962.

WILLIAM DRUMMOND OF HAWTHORNDEN
1585–1649

For a bibliography see Poetical works vol i, ed L. E. Kastner 1913.

Collections

The history of Scotland 1423–1542. 1655, 1680, 1681, 1682. Virtually a collected edn of Drummond's prose; includes Cypresse grove, various political tracts and selected letters. Preface by 'Mr Hall of Grayes Inn'.
Poems. 1656, 1659. Preface by Edward Phillips. Contains most pbd poems and 35 new poems, 2 probably not Drummond's.

Works. [Ed J. Sage and T. Ruddiman], Edinburgh 1711. Adds about 40 poetical pieces and hymns, many of doubtful authenticity, various tracts and papers, a selection of Drummond's correspondence, and a memoir by Bishop Sage.

Poems. 1790, 1791.

Poems. [Ed T. Maitland and D. Irving] 1832 (Maitland Club).

Poems. Ed P. Cunningham 1833, Edinburgh 1852.

Poetical works. Ed W. B. Turnbull 1856, 1890.

Poems. Ed W. C. Ward 2 vols 1894 (ML), [1905].

Poetical works, with A cypress grove. Ed L. E. Kastner, Manchester 1913, Edinburgh 1913 (STS).

§1

Tears on the death of Meliades. Edinburgh 1613, 1614 (3rd edn), 1614.

Mausoleum: or the choisest flowres of the epitaphs. Edinburgh 1613; rptd D. Laing, Fugitive Scottish poetry of the seventeenth century ser 1, Edinburgh 1853. 3 poems by Drummond.

Poems. [Edinburgh? 1614?] (priv ptd for distribution to Drummond's friends?), Edinburgh 1616 (expanded and rev as Poems: amorous, funerall, divine, pastorall, in sonnets, songs, sextains, madrigals); rptd [by T. Maitland], Edinburgh 1832. Edn of 1616 includes, with separate undated title-page, Madrigals and epigrams by W.D., Menston 1969 (facs of 1614?), Amsterdam 1969 (facs of 1616).

In memory of Euphemia Kyninghame. [Edinburgh 1616].

Forth feasting: a panegyricke to the King's most excellent Majestie. Edinburgh 1617, 1618 (in The Muses welcome [to King James]); ed J. Adamson with a new sonnet by Drummond prefixed 1656.

A midnight's trance. 1619, 1630 (as A cypresse grove, with Flowers of Sion), 1905, 1907 (with note by A. H. Bullen); ed S. Clegg 1919; ed R. Ellrodt, Oxford 1951 (from 1619).

Flowres of Sion; to which is adjoyned his Cypresse grove. [Edinburgh] 1623 (3 issues), Edinburgh 1630 (adds 4 poems).

Auctarium bibliothecae Edinburgenae. 1627.

The entertainment of the high and mighty monarch Charles King of Great Britaine. Edinburgh 1633.

To the exequies of the honourable Sr Antonye Alexander, knight: a pastorall elegie. Edinburgh 1638.

Polemo-Medinia inter Vitarvam et Nebernam. [Edinburgh? 1645?], [Aberdeen? 1670?], Oxford 1691 (as Accedit Jacobi id nominis quinti regis Scotorum cantilena rustica etc), Edinburgh 1742, Glasgow 1748, 1768, 1813 (in Carminum variorum macaronicorum of the Conventus gymnasticus of Edinburgh). Macaronic verse.

The drunkards character. 1646.

The drunkard forewarn'd. 1680.

Muckomachy: or the midden-fecht. Edinburgh 1846. Poem in 3 cantos, with addns by later hands.

The diary. Miscellany of Scottish Soc 5 1942.

§2

Conversations of Ben Jonson with Drummond. Ed D. Laing 1842 (Shakespeare Soc); ed R. F. Patterson 1923; ed C. H. Herford and P. Simpson, Ben Jonson vol 1, Oxford 1925.

Laing, D. A brief account of the Hawthornden manuscripts in the possession of the Society of Antiquaries of Scotland; with extracts, containing unpublished letters and poems of Drummond. Trans Soc Antiquaries of Scotland 4 1831.

Masson, D. Drummond. 1873.

Maclean, C. M. Alexander Scott, Montgomerie and Drummond as lyric poets. 1915.

Simpson, P. The genuineness of the Drummond conversations. RES 2 1926.

Greene, G. S. Drummond's borrowings from Donne. PQ 11 1932.

Wallerstein, R. C. The style of Drummond in its relation to his translations. PMLA 48 1933.

Joly, A. Drummond. Lille 1935.

Rugoll, M. A. Drummond's debt to Donne. PQ 16 1937.

Baldensperger, F. Un sonnet de Drummond et son point de départ dans la Semaine de Du Bartas. MLN 55 1940.

Gilbert, A. H. Johnson and Drummond or Gil on the King's senses. MLN 62 1947.

—— Nevizanus, Ariosto, Florio, Harington and Drummond. Ibid.

Smith, G. The influence of Sir John Hayward and Joshua Sylvester upon Drummond's Cypresse grove. PQ 26 1947.

Hydaspies in Midlothian. TLS 9 Dec 1949.

McDiarmid, M. P. The Spanish plunder of Drummond. MLR 44 1949.

Praz, M. Drummond and Crashaw. TLS 21 Oct 1949.

Ellrodt, R. An earlier version (1619) of Drummond's Cypresse grove. English 7 1949.

—— Drummond's revision of A cypresse grove. MLR 47 1952.

—— More Drummond borrowings. HLQ 16 1953.

—— Drummond's Cypresse grove and the Somnium Scipionis. N & Q Oct 1962.

Fogle, F. R. A critical study of Drummond. Oxford 1952.

Maclaine, A. H. Drummond's Polemo-Medinia as a source for the Blythsome bridal. N & Q Sept 1954.

Cutts, J. P. Drummond. N & Q April 1957.

Main, C. F. Ben Jonson and an unknown poet on the King's senses. MLN 74 1959.

Kastner, L. E. The Italian and Spanish sources of Drummond. In Miscellanea di studi critici in onore di V. Crescini, Turin 1960.

Arens, J. C. Twee sonnetten bij Revius en Drummond. Neophilologus 47 1963.

Seronsy, C. C. An autograph letter on Daniel and Drummond by Swinburne. N & Q Aug 1965.

Barker, J. R. A pendant to Drummond's conversations. RES new ser 16 1965.

Macdonald, R. H. Drummond, Miss Euphemia Kyninghame and the Poems. MLR 60 1965.

—— The library of Drummond of Hawthornden. Edinburgh 1971.

—— Drummond at Hawthornden: the season at Bourges 1706. Comparative Drama 4 1970.

Juel-Jensen, B. Drayton and Drummond: a lost autograph letter rediscovered. Library 5th ser 21 1966.

Shawcross, J. T. Donne and Drummond's ms. Amer N & Q March 1967.

Fritz, H. Drummond's authentic voice. Lock Haven Rev 9 1967.

Paganelli, E. Lettere e note inedite di Drummond. Eng Miscellany (Rome) 19 1968.

Jack, R. Drummond: the major Scottish sources. Stud in Scottish Lit 6 1968.

GILES FLETCHER the younger, 1588?–1623

Collections

Poems. Ed A. B. Grosart 1868 (Fuller's Worthies' Lib).

Complete poems. Ed A. B. Grosart 1876.

Poetical works of Giles and Phineas Fletcher. Ed F. S. Boas 2 vols Cambridge 1908–9.

Complete poems. Ed D. C. Sheldon, Madison 1938.

§1

Sorrowes joy: or a lamentation for our late deceased soveraigne Elizabeth, with a triumph for the prosperous succession of our gratious King James. Cambridge 1603. Attributed to Fletcher.

Christs victorie and triumph in heaven and earth, over and after death. Cambridge 1610, 1610, 1632, 1640, London 1640; 1783 (with The purple island), 1824 (with life and extracts from George Herbert); ed R. Cattermole and H. Stebbing 1834; ed W. T. Brooke [1888]; ed N. Alexander, Elizabethan narrative verse, 1967.
The reward of the faithfull. 1623, 1923. Prose.

§2

Cory, H. E. Spenser, the school of the Fletchers and Milton. Berkeley 1912.
Sheldon, D. C. A note on a Latin poem by either Giles Fletcher the younger or his brother Phineas. MLR 46 1951.
Holaday, A. Giles Fletcher and the Puritans. JEGP 54 1955.

GEORGE WITHER
1588–1667

Bibliographies
Axon, E. The Spenser Society and its work. Library 1st ser 7 1895.
Sidgwick, F. In Poetry of Wither vol 1, 1902.
Grolier Club. Contributions to English bibliography vol 3. New York 1905. Items 1013–76.

Collections
Workes: containing satyrs, epigrams, eclogues, sonnets and poems. 1620. Pirated.
Juvenilia. 1622, 1626, 1633, 3 pts 1871 (Spenser Soc). Abuses stript and whipt, The scourge, Epigrams, Prince Henries obsequies, A satyre, Epithalamia, Shepheards hunting; Menston 1970 (facs of 1622). 1633 and some copies of 1622 add Wither's Motto, Faire-virtue and some minor verse.
Ecchoes from the sixth trumpet. [1666], 1668 (as Nil ultra: or the last works of Captain George Wither), 1669 (as Fragmenta prophetica: or the remains of George Wither). Excerpts from Wither's prophetic poems connected by short prose paragraphs, and some new verse.
Extracts from Juvenilia. Ed 'Aretephil' [A. Dalrymple] 1785. With running commentary.
Select lyrical passages, written about 1622. Ed S. E. Brydges [1815].
Juvenilia. [Ed J. M. Gutch] 4 vols [Bristol 1820]. Includes several of the other early pieces besides Juvenilia.
Miscellaneous works. 6 vols 1872–3 (Spenser Soc). These, together with the other Spenser Soc reprints, form an almost complete edn of Wither.
Poems. Ed H. Morley 1891.
Poetry. Ed F. Sidgwick 2 vols 1902. With important biographical introd.
Four scarce poems of Wither. Ed J. M. French, Huntington Lib Bull no 2 1931. Includes The tired petitioner; Carmenternarium semicynicum; A timelie caution; Predictions of the overthrow of popery.

§1

Prince Henries obsequies or mournefull elegies upon his death. 1612, 1622, 1633.
Epithalamia: or nuptiall poems. 1612, 1633.
Abuses stript and whipt; also the Scourge, Epigrams. 1613 (at least 4 edns), 1614, 1615, 1617, 1622.
[W. Browne], Shepheard's pipe. 1614. Contains Wither's Thirsis and Alexis and Another eclogue, rptd as Eclogues 5–6 of Shepheard's hunting, below, as well as To his Melissa, which may be Wither's.
A satyre: dedicated to his most excellent Majestie. 1614, 1615 (at least 2 edns), 1616.

Fidelia. 1615, 1617, 1619, 1622; ed S. E. Brydges 1815 (text of 1619 collated with 1633); ed E. Arber, English garner vol 6, 1883 (from 1615).
The shepheards hunting. 1615 (3 edns); ed S. E. Brydges 1814 (text of 1633 collated with 1615 and 1622); ed R. Southey, Select works of the British poets, 1831.
A preparation to the Psalter. 1619, 1884 (Spenser Soc).
Exercises upon the first psalme. 1620, 1892 (Spenser Soc).
The songs of the Old testament, translated into English measures. 1621.
Wither's motto: Nec habeo, nec careo, nec curo. [London] 1621, nd (with engraved title-page), 1621 (engraved title-page), 1623 (with postscript, at least 2 edns); ed S. E. Brydges, Restituta vol 1, 1814.
Faire-virtue, the mistresse of Phil'arete. 1622, 1622, 1622 (both with new title-pages, once perhaps as part of Juvenilia), 1626, 1633; ed S. E. Brydges 1818 (text of 1622); ed E. Arber, English garner vol 4, 1882.
The hymnes and songs of the Church, translated and composed by G.W. 1623, 1623, [1624?]; ed S. E. Brydges 1815; ed H. E. Havergall 1846; ed E. Farr 1856; 1881 (Spenser Soc).
The schollers purgatory, discovered in the stationers commonwealth, and described in a discorse apologeticall. [1625?].
Britain's remembrancer. 1628, 2 pts 1880 (Spenser Soc). Extracts rptd 1642, 1643, both as Mr Wither his prophesie and as Wither's remembrancer; 1691 (in A collection of many wonderful prophecies), 1734 (in A warning to the inhabitants of Europe).
The psalmes of David translated into lyrick verse. Netherlands 1632, 2 pts 1881 (Spenser Soc).
A collection of emblemes, ancient and moderne. 4 bks 1635 (bks 2–4 dated 1634, various issues same year); ed J. Horden, Menston 1968 (facs); Zug [1969] (facs).
The nature of man written in Greek by Nemesius, englished. 1636, 1657.
A new song of a young mans opinion of the difference between good and bad women. Broadside, before 1640.
Heleluiah: or Britans second remembrancer. 1641; ed E. Farr 1856, 3 pts 1879 (Spenser Soc). Extracts as Wither's remembrancer, 1643.
A prophesie written long since. 1641.
Read and wonder: a warre between two entire friends, the Pope and the Divell. 1641.
Campo-Musae: or the field-musings of Captain George Wither. 1643, 1643, 1644, 1661.
Se defendendo: a shield, and shaft, against detraction. [1643].
Mercurius rusticus: or a countrey messenger. [1643]. Anon.
Letters of advice: touching the choice of knights and burgesses for the Parliament. [1644], 1645.
The speech without doore. [1644].
[?] The two incomparable Generalissimo's of the world briefly described. [1644?]. Signed G.W.
Wither's prophesie of the downfal of Antichrist. 1644.
The Great Assises holden in Parnassus by Apollo. 1645.
Vox pacifica: a voice tending to the pacification of God's wrath. 1645.
To the most honourable the Lords and Commons: petition. [1646].
Justitiarius justificatus: justice justified. [1646].
Opobalsamum anglicanum: an English balme, lately pressed out of a shrub and spread upon these papers. 1646.
What peace to the wicked? 1646. Anon. Attributed by Thomason.
Amygdala britannica, almonds for parrets. 1647. Anon. Attributed by Thomason.
Carmen expostulatorium. 1647.
Major Wither's disclaimer. 1647.
Articles presented against this Parliament, by Terrae-Filius. 1648.

A si quis, or queries. 1648. Excerpts in Ecchoes, 1666, 1840 (priv ptd).

Carmen-ternarium semi-cynicum. [1648?].

Prosopopoeia britannica: Britans genius, or good-angel, personated. 1648.

The tired petitioner. [1648]. Excerpts in Ecchoes, 1666.

A thankful retribution. 1649. Excerpts in Ecchoes, 1666.

An allarum from Heaven: or a memento to the great councell, by G.W. 1649.

Vaticinium votivum: or Palaemon's prophetick prayer. [1649] (2 edns, one with cancel). Anon.

Carmen eucharisticon: a private thank-oblation. 1649.

Respublica anglicana: or the historie of Parliament in their late proceedings. 1650, 1883 (Spenser Soc).

The true state of the case of. 1650.

Three grains of spirituall frankincense. 1651.

British appeals, with Gods mercifull replies. 1651, 1651.

A timely caution. 1652.

The dark lantern: containing a dim discoverie. 1653 (with A perpetuall Parliament).

Westrow revived. 1653.

The modern states-man. 1654.

To the Parliament of the Common-wealth: the humble petition of GW. [1654].

The protector. 1655.

Vaticinium causuale. 1655.

Boni ominis votum: a good omen to the next Parliament. [1656].

A cause allegorically stated. 1657. Excerpts in Ecchoes, 1666.

A suddain flash timely discovering some reason wherefore the stile of Protector should not be deserted by these nations. 1657.

The petition and narrative of Geo. Wither esq. [1659].

Epistolium-vagum-prosa-metricum: or an epistle at random. 1659.

A cordial confection, to strengthen their hearts whose courage begins to fail. 1659.

Salt upon salt: made out of certain ingenious verses upon the late storm and the death of his Highness ensuing. 1659.

Speculum speculativum, or a considering-glass: being an inspection into the present and late sad condition of these nations. 1660 (3 edns).

Furor-poeticus propheticus. 1660.

Fides-anglicana: or a plea for the publick-faith of these nations. 1660. Concludes with a list by Wither of his works—including many never ptd and some lost in ms.

Predictions of the overthrow of Popery. 1660, 1688.

The prisoners plea. 1661.

An improvement of imprisonment, disgrace, poverty, into real freedom; honest reputation; perdurable riches. 1661.

Joco-serio, Strange news, of a discourse between two dead giants. 1661. A retort to A dialogue between Colbrant and Brandamore.

A triple paradox: affixed to a counter-mure raised against the world, the flesh and the Devil. 1661.

Paralellogrammaton, An epistle to the three nations of England, Scotland and Ireland. 1662, 1882 (Spenser Soc).

A proclamation in the name of the King of Kings, to all the inhabitants of the Isles of Great Brittain. 1662. Re-issued same year with Sig. A re-set.

Verses intended to the King's Majesty. 1662, 1662.

Tuba-pacifica, Seasonable precautions, whereby is sounded forth a retreat from the war intended between England and the United-Provinces. 1664.

A memorandum to London, occasioned by the pestilence. 1665. Includes Warning-piece to London, and Single sacrifice offered to almighty God.

Meditations upon the Lords Prayer. 1665.

Three private meditations. 1665, 1666.

Sigh for the Pitchers [upon the engagement expected 31 May 1666 with the Dutch]. 1666, 1666 (title corrected to Sighs).

Majesty in misery. 1681.

Mr Geo Withers revived. 1683. An extract from Britains remembrancer.

Divine poems (by way of paraphrase) on the Ten Commandments. 1688, 1728.

The grateful acknowledgement of a late trimming regulator. 1688.

The strange and wonderful prophecy. 1689. 1646 edn apparently not extant.

Withers redevivus. 1689.

A paraphrase of the Ten Commandments. 1697.

Vox vulgi: a poem in censure of the Parliament of 1661. Ed W. D. Macray 1880 (from ms).

The history of the pestilence 1625. Ed J. M. French, Cambridge Mass 1932 (from Magdalene College Cambridge ms, perhaps autograph).

[To the King when he was Prince of Wales]. Ed A. Pritchard, An unpublished poem by Wither, MP 61 1963.

§2

Aubrey, J. In his Brief lives, ed A. Clark 2 vols Oxford 1898.

Simpson, P. Walkley's piracy of Wither's poems in 1620. Library 3rd ser 6 1925.

Firth, C. H. Wither. RES 2 1926.

French, J. M. Wither in prison. PMLA 45 1930.

—— Notes on two puritan poets: Marvell and Wither. N & Q 16 April 1938.

—— Wither's verses to Dr John Raven. PMLA 63 1948.

—— Two notes on Milton and Wither. N & Q Nov 1954.

—— Thorn-Drury's notes on Wither. HLQ 23 1960.

Anderson, P. B. Wither and the Regalia. PQ 14 1935.

Borowski, B. Die Anspielung auf Avians Fabel De cupido ct invido in Withers Abuses stript and whipt. Anglia 59 1935.

Kirschbaum, L. Walkley's supposed piracy of Wither's Workes in 1620. Library 4th ser 19 1938.

Templeman, W. D. Some commendatory verses by Wither. N & Q 19 Dec 1942.

Kendall, L. H., jr. Wither's authorship of the Great Assises. N & Q March 1953.

—— A letter from Milton to Wither? N & Q Nov 1953.

—— Notes on some works attributed to Wither. RES new ser 5 1954.

—— Wither's What peace to the wicked? N & Q July 1955.

—— Wither in prison. N & Q Sept 1955.

—— An unrecorded prose pamphlet by Wither. HLQ 20 1957.

—— Wither's Three private meditations. Book Collector 6 1957.

Wright, H. G. Some sixteenth- and seventeenth-century writers on the plague. E & S new ser 6 1953.

Clark, E. M. Milton and Wither. SP 56 1959.

Freeman, A. A note on Wither. N & Q Nov 1960.

Pritchard, A. Wither's Motto and Browne's Religio medici. PQ 40 1961.

—— Wither and the Somers Islands. N & Q Nov 1961.

—— Wither: the poet as prophet. SP 59 1962.

—— A manuscript of Wither's psalms. HLQ 27 1963.

—— Abuses stript and whipt and Wither's imprisonment. RES new ser 14 1963.

—— Wither's quarrel with the stationers: an anonymous reply to the Schollers purgatory. SB 16 1963.

Manzalaoui, M. Wither and Chaucer's Troilus and Criseyde 1. 813ff. N & Q March, Aug 1964.

Carlson, N. E. Wither and the stationers. SB 19 1966.

—— Wither and his creditors. N & Q Sept 1967.

—— Wither and the statute office. N & Q March 1969.

—— Wither—dead at last! Michigan Academician 1 1969.

Hensley, C. S. The later career of Wither. Hague 1969.

WILLIAM BROWNE OF TAVISTOCK
1590?–1645?

Collections

Works: containing Britannia's pastorals, The shepherd's pipe, The Inner Temple masque and other poems. Ed W. Thompson [and T. Davies] 3 vols 1772.

Whole works. Ed W. C. Hazlitt 2 vols 1868–9 (Roxburghe Lib).

Poetical works. Ed G. Goodwin, with introd by A. H. Bullen 2 vols 1894 (ML).

§1

An elegie on the never inough bewailed death [of Henry Prince of Wales]. 1613. With another by Fulke Greville.

Britannia's pastorals. Bk 1, 1613; bks 1 (rev)–2, 1616, 1623; ed R. Southey, Select works of the British poets, 1831; ed W. Thompson 1845; bk 3 (incomplete), ed T. C. Croker 1852 (Percy Soc) (from ms); Menston 1969 (facs of bks 1–2).

[An elegy, signed WB]. In Thomas Overbury (elder), Sir Thomas Overbury his wife, 1616.

The Inner Temple masque. (Acted 13 Jan 1614). In Works, 1772; ed G. Jones 1954 (with essay on Browne and the English masque); ed R. F. Hill, A book of masques in honour of Allardyce Nicoll, Cambridge 1967.

The shepherd's pipe. 1614, 1620 (as part of Wither's works).

[Commendatory poem, signed WB]. In Massinger, The Duke of Millaine, 1623.

[Commendatory poem, signed WB]. In Massinger, The bondman, 1624.

The history of Polexander [by Marin Le Roy] done into English by William Browne. 1647 (with 2nd title-page dated 1648).

Original poems never before published. Ed S. E. Brydges, Ickham 1815 (for 1816). From BM ms Lansdowne 777.

An uncollected poem by Browne. G. Tillotson, N & Q 20 Jan 1940.

§2

Moorman, F. W. Browne, his Britannia's pastorals. Quellen und Forschungen 81 1897.

Sidney, P. 'The subject of all verse': being an enquiry into the authorship of a famous epitaph. 1907.

Candy, H. C. On the first two editions of Book 1 of Britannia's pastorals. Library 2nd ser 9 1918.

Loane, G. Britannia's pastorals. TLS 14 Sept, 12 Oct 1922. Textual notes.

Tillotson, G. A manuscript of Browne. RES 6–7 1930–1.

— Towards a text of Browne's Britannia's pastorals. Library 2nd ser 11 1930.

Mabbot, T. O. Notes by Milton. TLS 17 Nov 1932.

Tillotson, K. Drayton, Browne and Wither. TLS 27 Oct 1937.

Holaday, A. Browne's Epitaph on the Countess of Pembroke. PQ 28 1949. A version ptd in Heywood's Life and death of Queen Elizabeth.

McClennan, J. Browne as satirist. Papers of Michigan Acad 33 1949.

Grundy, J. A note on Browne of Tavistock. N & Q 29 Sept 1951.

— Tasso, Fairfax and Browne. RES new ser 3 1952.

— Browne and the Italian pastoral. RES new ser 4 1953.

— Keats and Browne. RES new ser 6 1955.

— A new manuscript of the Countess of Pembroke's epitaph. N & Q Feb 1960.

Cutts, J. P. Original music to Browne's Inner Temple masque and other Jacobean music. N & Q May 1954.

ROBERT HERRICK
1591–1674

Bibliographies etc

Cox, E. M. Notes on the bibliography of Herrick. Library 3rd ser 8 1917.

Kerr, M. M. A bibliography of Herrick. Oxford 1936.

MacLeod, M. L. A concordance to the poems of Herrick. Oxford 1936.

Some editions of Herrick. Book Handbook 1948.

Tannenbaum, S. A. and D. R. Herrick: a concise bibliography. New York 1949.

Guffey, G. R. Robert Herrick 1949–65. 1968 (Elizabethan Bibliographies suppl).

Collections

Witts recreations. 1650 (4th edn). Many of Herrick's poems are included.

Select poems from the Hesperides. Ed J. N[ott], Bristol [1810].

Works. [Ed T. Maitland] 2 vols Edinburgh 1823 (with life), 2 vols 1825 (as Poetical works).

Hesperides. Ed H. G. Clarke 2 vols 1844, 1846 (with memoir by S. W. S[inger]), Boston 1856.

Hesperides. Ed G.T.F. 1852.

Poetical works. Ed E. Walford 1859.

Hesperides. Ed W. C. Hazlitt 2 vols 1869, 1890.

Complete poems. Ed A. B. Grosart 3 vols 1876.

Chrysomela: a selection from the lyrical poems. Ed F. T. Palgrave 1877.

Selections. Ed A. Dobson [1883].

Herrick his flowers. Oxford 1891.

Hesperides and Noble numbers. Ed A. W. Pollard, with preface by A. C. Swinburne 2 vols 1891 (ML).

Poetical works. Ed G. Saintsbury 2 vols 1893.

Selections. Ed E. E. Hale, Boston 1895.

Poetical works. Ed F. W. Moorman, Oxford 1915, 1921 (text only), 2 vols 1935.

Poetical works. Ed H. Wolfe 4 vols 1928.

Herrick. Ed H. Newbolt 1923.

Poems. 1932 (Augustan Books).

Poems. Oxford 1935 (WC).

Some poems. Norfolk Va 1942.

The love poems of Herrick and Donne. Ed L. Untermeyer, New Brunswick NJ 1948.

Poetical works. Ed L. C. Martin, Oxford 1956, 1965.

Selected poems. Ed J. Hayward 1961.

Complete poetry. Ed J. M. Patrick, New York 1963, 1968 (with introd and new foreword).

§1

Hesperides: or, the works both humane and divine. 1648. Includes, with a separate title and pagination, His noble numbers, 1647, Menston 1969 (facs).

Poor Robin's visions. 1677. Sometimes attributed to Herrick.

A song for two voices. 1700 [?].

§2

Hale, E. E. Die chronologische Anordnung der Dichtungen Herricks. Halle 1892.

Briscoe, J. P. Herrick's women, love and flowers. In Bibelots 1899.

Thomson, J. Indexes to the first lines and subjects of the poems of Herrick. Philadelphia 1901.

Moorman, F. W. Herrick: a biographical and critical study. 1910, [1924].

Delattre, F. Herrick: contribution à l'étude de la poésie lyrique en Angleterre au dix-septième siècle. Bruges 1912.

Judson, A. C. Herrick's Pillar of fame. Texas Rev 5 1920.

— Herrick's grave. N & Q 3 June 1922.

Wayne, F. A study of Herrick. Harvard College Bull 83 1925.

Mandel, L. Herrick: the last Elizabethan. Chicago 1927.

Blunden, E. In his Votive tablets, 1931.

Roeckerath, N. Der Nachruhm Herricks und Wallers. Leipzig 1931.

Aiken, P. The influence of the Latin elegists on English lyric poetry 1600–50. Univ of Maine Stud 22 1932.

Macaulay, R. They were defeated. 1932. A novel.

Hooker, E. N. Herrick and the song-books. TLS 2 Feb 1933.

Ault, N. Herrick and song-books. TLS 20 April 1933.

Lossing, M. L. Herrick: his epigrams and lyrics. UTQ 2 1933.

Powys, L. Herrick's Fairies. Spectator 21 July 1933.

— Herrick: minister of grace. Saturday Rev of Lit 8 Feb 1936.

Easton, E. I. Youth immortal: a life of Herrick. Boston 1934.

Arvin, N. Homage to Herrick. Nat Rev 82 1935.

Leavis, F. R. English poetry in the seventeenth century. Scrutiny 4 1935; rptd in his Revaluation, 1936.

Ruggles, M. Horace and Herrick. Classical Jnl 31 1936.

Howarth, R. G. A song of Herrick's altered by Burns. N & Q 27 Aug 1938.

— Verses in Herrick's Church. N & Q April 1954.

— Herrick's epitaph on his niece Elizabeth. N & Q Aug 1955.

— Two poems by Herrick? N & Q Sept 1955. Reply by J. C. Maxwell, Nov 1955.

— An early elevation of Herrick. N & Q Aug 1955.

— Attributions to Herrick. N & Q June 1958.

Loane, G. G. Herrick's sources. N & Q 30 March 1940.

Herrick's To the virgins. Explicator Oct 1942.

Daniels, E. Herrick's Upon Julia's clothes. Explicator March 1943.

Hirsch, E. L. Herrick's The argument of his book. Explicator Nov 1943.

Gilbert, A. H. Herrick on death. MLQ 5 1944.

Mill, A. J. Herrick's Another grace for a child. Explicator June 1945.

Hess, M. W. Nature and spirit in Herrick's poetry. Personalist 27 1946.

— Herrick's golden apples: the Hesperides. Catholic World 167 1948.

Regenos, G. W. The influence of Horace on Herrick. PQ 26 1947.

Kirby, T. A. The triple tun. MLN 62 1947.

Henry, N. Herrick's Upon Julia's clothes. Explicator April 1947.

Cronin, J. E. The hag in the Cloud. N & Q 5 Aug 1950. On Shelley's debt.

Musgrove, S. The universe of Herrick. Auckland Univ Bull 38 1950.

Archibald, R. C. There is a lady sweet and kind. N & Q Aug 1953.

Whitaker, T. R. Herrick and the fruits of the garden. ELH 12 1955.

Smyth, C. A Herrick epitaph. TLS 13 May 1955.

Rau, F. Herrick. Die Neueren Sprachen 1955.

Schneider, E. Herrick's Upon Julia's clothes. Explicator March 1955. Reply by N. Henry, Dec 1955.

Taylor, W. F. The humanism of Herrick. Amer Lit 28 1956.

Staudt, V. P. Horace and Herrick on carpe diem. Classical Bull 33 1957.

Leiter, L. H. Herrick's Upon Julia's clothes. MLN 73 1958.

— Herrick's Upon Julia's clothes. Explicator Jan 1967.

Candelaria, F. H. Ronsard and Herrick. N & Q July 1958.

Fletcher, G. B. Herrick and Latin authors. N & Q June 1959.

Chute, M. Two gentle men: the lives of Herbert and Herrick. New York 1959.

Cohen, H. Herrick's To Electra. Explicator March 1959.

Crum, M. An unpublished fragment of verse by Herrick. RES new ser 11 1960.

Spitzer, L. Herrick's Delight in disorder. MLN 76 1961.

Press, J. Herrick. 1961 (Br Council pamphlet).

Swardson, H. R. Poetry and the fountain of light. 1962.

Starkman, K. Noble numbers and the poetry of devotion. In Reason and imagination, ed J. A. Mazzeo, New York 1962.

Harris, W. O. Herrick's Upon Julia's clothes. Explicator Dec 1962.

Weeks, L. E. Julia unveiled. CEA Critic 25 1963.

Song, K.-J. Herrick as a love-poet. Eng Lang & Lit (Korea) 14 1963.

Wentersdorf, K. P. Herrick's floral imagery. Studia Neophilologica 36 1964.

Sanders, C. Herrick's The carkanet. Explicator Nov 1964. Reply by C. A. Huttar, Dec 1965.

Lougy, R. Herrick's The hock cart: or harvest home 51–55. Explicator Oct 1964.

Woodward, D. H. Herrick's Oberon poems. JEGP 64 1965.

Tyner, R. Herrick's Crisped yew. N & Q Oct 1965.

— Herrick's To Denham on his prospective poem 3. Explicator May 1965.

Ross, R. J. Herrick's Julia in silks. EC 15 1965.

Reed, M. L. Herrick among the maypoles: Dean Prior and the Hesperides. Stud in Eng Lit 1500–1900 5 1965.

Rea, J. Persephone in Corinna's going a-Maying. College Eng April 1965.

Höltgen, K. J. Herrick, the Wheeler family and Quarles. RES new ser 16 1965.

— Herrick and Mrs Wheeler. TLS 17 March 1966.

D'Avanzo, H. L. Herrick's The mad maid's song. Amer N & Q 4 1965.

Toback, P. B. Herrick's Corinna's going a-Maying and the epithalamian tradition. Seventeenth-century News 24 1966.

Schucter, J. D. Herrick's Upon Julia's clothes. Explicator Nov 1966.

Rollin, R. B. Missing the hock cart: an explication re-explicated. Seventeenth-century News 24 1966.

— Herrick. New York 1966.

— A thief in Herrick's Hesperides. N & Q Sept 1967.

Hughes, R. E. Herrick's Hock cart: companion piece to Corinna's going a-Maying. College Eng 1966.

Clark, P. O. Herrick's The hock cart or harvest home. Explicator April 1966.

Goldshalk, W. L. Art and nature: Herrick and history. EC 17 1967.

Deming, R. H. Herrick's classical ceremony. ELH 34 1967.

— The use of the past: Herrick and Hawthorne. Jnl of Pop Culture 2 1968.

Allen, D. C. Herrick's Rex tragicus. In Studies in honor of D. T. Starnes, Austin 1967.

Cowan, S. A. A note on the Hock-cart. Seventeenth-century News 25 1968.

Ishii, S. A study of Herrick. Tokyo 1968.

— Essays on Herrick; with a selection from his Hesperides done into Japanese. Tokyo 1968.

Weinberg, G. S. Herrick's Upon Julia's clothes. Explicator Oct 1968.

DeNeef, A. L. Herrick and the ceremony of death. Renaissance Papers 1970.

Ditsky, J. M. A case of insufficient evidence: L. C. Martin's 'R.H.' poems and Herrick. Ball State Univ Forum 11 1970.

Kimmey, J. L. Herrick's persona. SP 67 1970.

— Herrick's satirical epigrams. E Studies 51 1970.

Farmer, N. K., jr. Herrick's commonplace book? some observations and questions. PBSA 66 1972.

HENRY KING
Bishop of Chichester
1592-1669

Collections

Sacred poems. Ed J. Hannah, Oxford 1843.
English poems. Ed L. Mason, New Haven 1914.
Minor Caroline poets vol 3. Ed G. Saintsbury, Oxford 1921. King's English poems and critical introd.
Poems. Ed J. Sparrow 1925. With bibliography by G. L. Keynes.
Poems. Ed J. R. Baker, Denver 1960.
Poems. Ed M. Crum, Oxford 1965.
The tribe of Ben: pre-Augustan classical verse in English. Ed A. C. Partridge 1966.

§ 1

Elegy upon Charles I. 1648. Anon.
A groane at the funerall of Charles the first. 1649, 1649 (as A deepe groane).
Psalmes of David turned into meeter. 1651, 1654, 1671. *See col 1913, below.*
Poems, elegies, paradoxes and sonnets. 1657 (unauthorized), 1664 (with addns), 1700 (as Ben Johnson's poems, elegies, paradoxes and sonnets).

§ 2

Mason, L. The life and works of King. Trans Connecticut Acad 18 1913.
Simpson, P. The Bodleian manuscripts of King. Bodleian Quart Record 5 1929.
— John and Henry King. Bodleian Lib Record 4 1953. Corrections to the above.
Gardiner, D. King and Robert Berkeley. TLS 19 Feb 1944.
Gleckner, R. F. King's The exequy. Explicator May 1954.
— King: a poet of his age. Trans Wisconsin Acad of Science, Arts & Letters 45 1956.
Crum, M. Notes on the physical characterics of some manuscripts of poems of Donne and King. Library 5th ser 16 1961.
Berman, R. King and the seventeenth century. 1964.
Mohanty, H. P. King's The exequy. Indian Jnl of Eng Stud 7 1966.
Low, A. A metrical device in the Exequy. MLR 63 1968.

FRANCIS QUARLES
1592-1644

Bibliographies

Horden, J. Quarles: a bibliography of his works to the year 1800. Oxford 1953 (Oxford Bibl Soc).

Collections

Divine poems [A feast for wormes, Hadassa, Job militant, Sions elegies, Sions sonets, Alphabet of elegies (on Dr Ailmer)]. 1630, 1633, 1634 (with The historie of Samson, Elegy on Dr Wilson, and Mildreiados (on Lady Luckyn)), 1638, 1642.
The loyall convert, with the New distemper. 1645.
The profest royalist [Loyall convert, New distemper, Whipper whipt]. 1645.
Solomons recantation with Enchiridion. 1649.
Enchiridion with Solomons recantation. 1860.
Complete works in prose and verse. Ed A. B. Grosart 3 vols Edinburgh 1880-1.
Hosanna and Threnodes. Ed J. Horden, Liverpool 1960.

§ 1

A feast for wormes: a poeme of the history of Jonah. 1620, 1626.

Hadassa: or the history of Queene Ester. 1621.
Job militant. 1624.
Sions elegies, wept by Jeremie the prophet. 1624, 1625.
Sions sonets, sung by Solomon. 1625, 1905.
Argalus and Parthenia. 1629, 1630, 1632, 1632, [c. 1632] (3 edns), 1647 etc.
Historie of Samson. 1631.
Divine fancies. 1632, 1633, 1636, 1638, 1641.
Quarlëis [Lusus poeticus poetis]. 1634.
Emblemes. 1635, 1635 (some copies with Quarlëis, above), 1639, 1643. From 1639 usually pbd with Hieroglyphikes; many edns and reissues before 1900.
An elegie upon Sir Julius Caesar. 1636, 1875.
An elegie upon Mr John Wheeler. 1637.
Hieroglyphikes of the life of man. 1638 (from 1639 usually pbd with Emblemes, above); ed J. Horden, Leeds 1969 (facs).
Memorials upon the death of Sir Robert Quarles. 1639.
Enchiridion. 1640 (enlarged), 1641, 1644 etc, 1695 (as Institutions, essays and maxims, political, moral and divine), 1698, 1698 (as Wisdom's better than money).
Sighes at the contemporary deaths of the Countess of Cleaveland and Mistrisse Cicily Killegrue with An elegie upon the death of Sir John Wolstenholme. 1640.
Threnodes on Lady Masham and William Cheyne. 1641.
Observations concerning princes and states upon peace and warre. 1642.
The loyall convert. 1644 (5 edns, one counterfeit dated 1643), 1645.
The whipper whipt. 1644.
The new distemper. 1645.
Solomons recantation, entituled Ecclesiastes, paraphrased. 1645, 1648, 1649, 1680 (with Enchiridion).
Barnabas and Boanerges. 1644 (2nd pt of completed work), 1646 (as Judgement and Mercie); Judgement and Mercy, 1646 (first pt of completed work); Boanerges and Barnabas: or judgement and mercie, 1646 (complete work) etc.
The shepheards oracle. 1644 (one Eclogue); The Shepheards oracles, 1646 (10 Eclogues); 1646 (with The shepheards oracle added as Eclogue XI), 1646.
Hosanna: or divine poems on the passion of Christ. 1647.
The virgin widow. 1649.

§ 2

Lohnes, A. Der Einfluss der Bibel auf die Dichtungen des Quarles. Heidelberg 1909.
Haight, G. S. The publication of Quarles's Emblems. Library 4th ser 15 1934.
— The sources of Quarles's Emblems. Library 4th ser 16 1935.
— The author of the Address in Quarles's Shepheards oracles. MLN 59 1944.
Horden, J. Edmund Marmion's illustrations for Quarles' Argalus and Parthenia. Trans Cambridge Bibl Soc 2 1954.
— Kipling and Quarles. TLS 26 Feb 1960.
Hone, J. Quarles and Hugh of St Victor. TLS 6 May 1955. Reply by J. Horden 27 May 1955.
Howell, A. C. Augustus Toplady and Quarles' Emblems. SP 57 1960.
Broughton, S. R. First-line index to poems in Grosart's edition of Quarles. [Oxford] 1961.
Hasan, M. The date of Solomons recantation. N & Q April 1965.
— Quarles: a study of his life and poetry. Aligarh 1966.
Höltgen, K. J. The date of Solomons recantation. N & Q Oct 1965.
— Herrick, the Wheeler family and Quarles. RES new ser 16 1965.
— Quarles: Emblem V. 11, As the hart panteth after the water-brooks. In Die englische Lyrik, ed K. H. Göller, Düsseldorf 1968.

—— Arbor, scala und fons vitae: Vorformen devotionaler Embleme in einer mittelenglischen Handschrift (BM additional ms 37,049). In Symposium für W. F. Schirmer, Tübingen 1968.

Davies, H. N. Quarles' hybrid strain. Eng Lang Notes 4 1967.

GEORGE HERBERT
1593–1633

Bibliographies etc

Palmer, G. H. A Herbert bibliography. Cambridge Mass 1911. Mainly a description of books collected by compiler.

Mann, C. A concordance to the English poems of Herbert. Boston 1927.

Tannenbaum, S. A. and D. R. A concise bibliography of Herbert. New York 1946.

Caldwell, H. B., E. E. Samaha jr and D. G. Fricke. A recent bibliography 1960–7. Seventeenth-century News 26 1968; H. Tonkin, Addenda, 27 1969.

Collections

Herbert's remains. 1652. Ed Barnabas Oley 3 pts, with separate title-page. Includes: A priest to the temple; Jacula prudentum; Apothegmes); 1836 (as The remains of that sweet singer of the Temple, George Herbert), 1841 (with lives by Izaak Walton and Oley), 1848; Menston 1970 (facs of 1652).

Works. Preface by W. Pickering, annotations of S. T. Coleridge 2 vols 1835–6, 1846, 1859. Includes A paradox, from Rawlinson mss in Bodley, 17 Latin letters from the Orator's book at Cambridge, Latin poems, Oley's and Walton's lives.

Works. Ed R. A. Willmott 1854 etc.

Complete works. Ed A. B. Grosart 3 vols 1874 (Fuller Worthies' Lib). Uses for first time Williams ms, and prints from it 6 English poems and 2 sets of Latin poems; and from Playford's psalms and hymns 1671 some psalms attributed to Herbert.

English works newly arranged and annotated by G. H. Palmer. 3 vols 1905.

Works. Ed F. E. Hutchinson, Oxford 1941, 1945 (corrected).

Selected poems. Ed D. Brown 1960.

Poems. Ed H. Gardner, Oxford 1961 (WC).

Select hymns taken out of Herbert's Temple 1697. Ed W. E. Stephenson, Los Angeles 1962 (Augustan Reprint Soc).

The Latin poetry: a bilingual edition. Ed and tr M. McCloskey and P. R. Murphy, Athens Ohio 1965.

A choice of Herbert's verse. Ed R. S. Thomas 1967.

Selected poems. Ed G. Reeves 1971.

§1

Epicedium cantabrigiense. Cambridge 1612. 2 Latin poems by Herbert.

Lacrymae cantabrigienses. Cambridge 1619. One Latin poem by Herbert.

Ecclesiastes Solomonis, by J[ames] D[uport]. 1622. Contains Musae responsoriae, ad Andreae Melvini anti-tami-cami-categoriam.

Oratio habita coram dominus legatis. 1623.

Oratio quâ Principis Caroli reditum ex Hispaniis celebravit Georgius Herbert. Cambridge 1623.

Memoriae Francisci, Baronis de Verulamio, sacrum. 1626. One Latin poem by Herbert.

A sermon of commemoration of the Lady Danvers by John Donne. 1627. Contains Herbert's Parentalia.

The temple: sacred poems and private ejaculations. Cambridge 1633, 1633, 1634, 1635, 1638, 1641, 1660, 1667, 1674 (with Walton's life, and portrait by R. White), 1678 (some copies dated 1679), 1695, Bristol 1799, Lowell Mass 1834 (first American edn); ed G. Gilfillan 1853; ed C. C. Clarke 1863; ed A. B. Grosart 1876 (from

undated Huth copy of first edn), 1882 (with essay by J. H. Shorthouse); ed R. A. Willmott 1880; ed E. Rhys 1885; ed E. C. S. Gibson 1899; ed A. R. Waller 1902 (with A priest to the temple); ed W. Alexander [1904]; ed A. Waugh 1907; ed F. Meynell 1927 (from Bodley ms); Menston 1968 (facs of 1633). See col 1910, below.

Hygiasticon by L. Lessius. 1634, 1634, 1636, 1678 (as The temperate man), Oxford 1935 (as How to live for 100 yrs). A treatise of temperance and sobrietie, by Luigi Cornaro (1475–1566), tr Herbert from Lessius' Latin version 1613.

Prefatory epistle [and 'briefe notes'] in The hundred and ten considerations of Signior John Valdesso. Oxford 1638, 1646 (a garbled edn); ed F. Chapman 1905.

Outlandish proverbs selected by Mr G.H. In Witts recreation, 1640, 1651 (separately as Jacula prudentum); ed T. Park, Facetiae, 2 vols 1817.

A priest to the temple: or the countrey parson his character, and rule of holy life. 1652, 1671 (with a new preface by B[arnabas] O[ley], 1675, 1701 etc; ed H. C. Beeching 1898, 1916; ed G. M. Forbes 1949 (selected passages).

Letters

Epistolary curiosities. Ed R[ebecca] W[est] 2 pts 1818. Includes unpbd letters; all collected in Works, ed Hutchinson 1941.

§2

Walton, Izaak. The life of Herbert. 1670, 1674 (with Temple), 1675 etc.

Addison, J. False wit. Spectator 7 May 1711.

Herbert, Edward (Baron Herbert of Cherbury). [Autobiography]. Strawberry Hill 1764; ed S. Lee 1886, [1906] (rev). By George's elder brother.

—— Poems English and Latin. Ed G. C. Moore Smith, Oxford 1923.

Coleridge, S. T. Biographia literaria vol 2. 1817. Chs 19–20.

Herbert's poems. Retrospective Rev 3 1821.

Ferrar, N. Two lives. Ed J. E. B. Mayor, Cambridge 1855.

Smith, I. G. Herbert. Christian Remembrancer July 1862.

Daniell, J. J. Life of Herbert. 1893 (anon), 1898 (with author's name), 1902. Contains ecclesiastical documents overlooked by previous biographers.

Herbert. TLS 22 Dec 1905.

Hyde, A. G. Herbert and his times. 1906.

More, P. E. In his Shelburne essays, Princeton 1906.

Buchanan, E. S. George Herbert, melodist. 1910.

Herbert. TLS 1 April 1920.

Clutton-Brock, A. In his More essays on books, 1921.

Moore Smith, G. C. Wordsworth and Herbert. N & Q 13 Jan 1923.

Lucas, F. L. Herbert. Life & Letters Dec 1928.

Fletcher, J. M. J. George Herbert. [1929].

—— Herbert of Bemerton: poet and saint. [1933].

Beachcroft, T. O. Nicholas Ferrar and Herbert. Criterion 12 1932.

Eliot, T. S. Herbert. Spectator 12 March 1932.

—— George Herbert. 1962 (Br Council pamphlet).

Anderton, H. I. Herbert. TLS 9 March 1933.

Hutchinson, F. E. Herbert: a tercentenary. Nineteenth Century March 1933.

—— John Wesley and Herbert. London Quart 161 1936.

—— Herbert. In Seventeenth-century studies presented to Sir Herbert Grierson, Oxford 1938.

—— Missing Herbert mss. TLS 15 July 1939.

—— The first edition of Herbert's Temple. Oxford Bibl Soc Pbns 5 1939.

Bennett, J. In her Four metaphysical poets, Cambridge 1934, 1953 (rev).

Leishman, J. B. In his Metaphysical poets, Oxford 1934.

Sharp, R. L. Some light on metaphysical obscurity and roughness. SP 31 1934.

Herbert. TLS 2 March 1933.

Parson Herbert. Times 3 March 1933.

Sparrow, J. The text of Herbert. TLS 14 Dec 1933.
— Hymns and poetry. TLS 11 Jan 1963. *See also* F. W. Sternfeld 1 Feb 1963.
— Herbert and Donne among the Moravians. BNYPL Dec 1964.
Blunden, E. Herbert's Latin poems. E & S 19 1934. For corrections, *see* A. Brulé, Revue Anglo-américaine Oct 1934.
Wright, H. G. Was Herbert the author of Jacula prudentum? RES 11 1935.
Blackstone, B. A paper by Herbert. TLS 15 Aug 1936. Comment by F. E. Hutchinson 22 Aug 1936.
Warren, A. Herbert. Amer Rev 7 1936; rptd in his Rage for order, Chicago 1948.
Luke, S. An old handbook on the pastoral office. London Quart 162 1937.
Hayes, A. M. Counterpoint in Herbert. SP 35 1938.
May, G. L. George Herbert. 1938.
Meyer, G. P. The blackamoor and her love. PQ 17 1938. Reply by C. C. Coulter 18 1939.
Thompson, E. N. The Temple and the Christian year. PMLA 54 1939.
de Selincourt, E. Herbert. Hibbert Jnl 39 1941.
Freeman, R. Herbert and the emblem books. RES 17 1941.
— Parody as a literary form: Herbert and Wilfred Owen. EC 13 1963.
Bradbrook, M. C. The liturgical tradition in English verse: Herbert and Eliot. Theology 44 1942.
Wilson, F. P. A note on Herbert's The quidditie. RES 19 1943.
McLuhan, H. M. Herbert's Virtue. Explicator Oct 1943.
Allen, D. C. Herbert's Sycamore. MLN 59 1944.
D., G. H. Herbert and Dante. N & Q 12 Aug 1944.
Douds, J. B. Herbert's use of the transferred verb. MLQ 5 1944.
Howarth, R. G. Herbert. N & Q 9 Sept 1944.
Knights, L. C. Herbert. Scrutiny 12 1944; rptd in his Explorations, 1946.
Norton, D. S. Herbert's The collar. Explicator April 1944. Reply by T. O. Mabbott, Nov 1944.
Mead, D. S. Herbert's The pulley. Explicator Dec 1945.
Oliver, P. Herbert. Action 1945.
Ross, M. M. Herbert and the humanist tradition. UTQ 16 1947.
Itrat-Husain. The mystical element in the metaphysical poets. Edinburgh 1948.
Cropper, M. B. Flame touches flame. 1949. Studies of Herbert et al.
Gibbs, J. An unknown poem of Herbert. TLS 30 Dec 1949.
Benjamin, E. B. Herbert's Vertue. Explicator Nov 1950.
Tuve, R. On Herbert's Sacrifice. Kenyon Rev 12 1950. Reply by W. Empson, ibid.
— A reading of Herbert. Chicago 1952.
— Herbert and Caritas. Jnl Warburg & Courtauld Inst 22 1959.
— Sacred 'parody' of love poetry, and Herbert. Stud in Renaissance 8 1961.
Zitner, S. P. Herbert's Jordan poems. Explicator Nov 1950.
Bickham, J. M. Herbert's The collar. Explicator Dec 1951.
Blackburn, W. Lady Magdalen Herbert and her son George. South Atlantic Quart 50 1951.
Silver, L. H. The first edition of Walton's Life of Herbert. Harvard Lib Bull 5 1951.
Summers, J. H. Herbert's form. PMLA 66 1951.
— The angels. Quart Rev of Lit 6 1951. Trns of Latin poems Lucus 1–2, 29 and Memoriae matris sacrum 5.
— Herbert's Trinitie Sunday. Explicator Feb 1952.
— Herbert: his religion and art. Cambridge Mass 1954.
Barruch, F. R. Donne and Herbert. TLS 30 May 1952. *See* J. B. Leishman 13 June 1952.

Bottrall, M. Herbert and the Country parson. Listener 3 April 1952.
— Herbert. 1954.
D., A. Five notes on Herbert. N & Q 27 Sept 1952. Corrections and addns to Hutchinson's edn.
Eldredge, F. Herbert's Jordan. Explicator Oct 1952.
Burke, K. On covery, re- and dis-. Accent 13 1953.
Knieger, B. Herbert's Redemption. Explicator Feb 1953.
— The religious verse of Herbert. College Langs Assoc Jnl 4 1960.
— The purchase-sale: patterns of business imagery in the poetry of Herbert. Stud in Eng Lit 1500–1900 6 1966.
Leach, E. A. John Wesley's use of Herbert. HLQ 16 1953.
— More seventeenth-century admirers of Herbert. N & Q Feb 1960.
— Lydgate's The dolerous pyte of Crystes passioun and Herbert's The sacrifice. N & Q Nov 1960.
— Yeats's A friend's illness and Herbert's Vertue. N & Q June 1962.
Thornton, R. D. Polyphiloprogenitive: the sapient stulers. Anglican Theological Rev 35 1953.
Akrigg, G. P. Herbert's 'caller'. N & Q Jan 1954.
Emslie, M. Herbert's Jordan 1. Explicator April 1954.
Martz, L. L. In his Poetry of meditation, New Haven 1954.
Moloney, M. F. A suggested gloss for Herbert's Box where sweets … N & Q Feb 1954.
— A note on Herbert's Season'd timber. N & Q Oct 1957.
Esch, A. In his Englische religiöse Lyrik des 17 Jahrhunderts, Tübingen 1955.
Davenport, A. Herbert and Ovid. N & Q March 1955.
Duncan-Jones, E. E. Benlowes's borrowings from Herbert RES new ser 6 1955.
Wickes, G. Herbert's views on poetry. Revue des Langues Vivantes 4 1955.
Hilberry, C. Two cruxes in Herbert's Redemption. N & Q Dec 1956.
— Herbert's Doomsday. Explicator Jan 1958.
Koretz, G. H. The rhyme scheme in Herbert's Man. N & Q April 1956.
Manning, S. Herbert's The pearl 38. Explicator Jan 1956.
Collmer, R. G. Herbert's Businesse 15–30. Explicator Nov 1957.
Levang, D. Herbert's The church militant and the chances of history. PQ 36 1957.
Taylor, I. A. Cavalier sophistication in the poetry of Herbert. Anglican Theological Rev 39 1957.
Adler, J. H. Form and meaning in Herbert's Discipline. N & Q June 1958.
Evans, G. B. Herbert's Jordan. N & Q May 1958.
Joselyn, Sr M. Herbert and Hopkins: two lyrics. Renascence 10 1958.
— Herbert and Muir: pilgrims of their age. Renascence 15 1963.
Novarr, D. The making of Walton's Lives. Ed M. H. Abrams, F. E. Mineka and W. M. Sale jr, Ithaca 1958.
Rickey, M. E. Rhymecraft in Edward and George Herbert. JEGP 57 1958.
— Herbert's technical development. JEGP 62 1963.
— Utmost art: complexity in the verse of Herbert. Lexington Kentucky 1966.
Chute, M. G. Two gentle men: the lives of Herbert and Herrick. New York 1959.
Montgomery, R. L., jr. The province of allegory in Herbert's verse. Texas Stud in Lit & Lang 1 1960.
Hughes, R. E. Herbert's rhetorical world. Criticism 3 1961.
— Herbert and the incarnation. Cithara 4 1964.
Gaskell, R. Herbert's Vanitie. CQ 3 1961.
Hart, J. Herbert's The collar re-read. Boston Univ Stud in Eng 5 1961.
Sanders, W. Herbert and the scholars. Melbourne Critical Rev 4 1961.

— 'Childhood is health': the divine poetry of Herbert. Melbourne Critical Rev 5 1962.

Souris, A. *See col 1163, above.*

Allen, W. S. A note on Herbert's The pearl: Matth 13.45. N & Q June 1962.

Blackie, J., E. P. Smith and R. Gaskell. Herbert's Vanitie. CQ 4 1962.

Bowers, F. T. Herbert's sequential imagery: the Temper. MP 59 1962.

Bradner, L. New poems by Herbert: the Cambridge Latin gratulatory anthology of 1613. Renaissance News 15 1962.

Duckles, V. John Jenkins's settings of lyrics by Herbert. Musical Quart 48 1962.

Grieder, T. Philip Pain's daily meditations and the poetry of Herbert. N & Q June 1962.

Kranz, G. Herbert: ein Dichter des Anglikanertums. Hochland 55 1962.

Lott, B. ME 'drinken' and 'drink' in Herbert. Indian Jnl of Eng Stud 3 1962.

Rauter, H. Eine Anleihe Sternes bei Herbert. Anglia 80 1962.

Sloane, W. Herbert's reputation 1650–1710: good reading for the young. N & Q June 1962.

Story, G. M. Herbert's Inventa bellica: a new ms. MP 59 1962.

Swardson, H. R. Poetry and the fountain of light. 1962.

Walker, J. D. The architectonics of Herbert's The temple. ELH 29 1962.

Williamson, K. Herbert's reputation in the eighteenth century. PQ 41 1962.

Wolfe, J. E. Herbert's Assurance. College Langs Assoc Jnl 5 1962.

Colie, R. L. Logos in the Temple: Herbert and the shape of content. Jnl Warburg & Courtauld Inst 26 1963.

Daniels, E. F. Herbert's balm and bay: synonyms? Seventeenth-century News 20 1963.

— Herbert's The quip, line 23: Say, I am thine. Eng Lang Notes 2 1964.

— Herbert's The quip. Explicator Sept 1964.

— Herbert's The quip, line 15: a 'de-explication', Amer N & Q 3 1965.

Fryxell, L. D. Herbert: anti-metaphysical poet? Discourse 6 1963.

Pérez, Gallego C. La Iglesia Anglicana como estructura y símbolo en Herbert. Revista de Literatura 23 1963.

Swanston, H. The second temple. Durham Univ Jnl 25 1963.

Watson, G. The fabric of Herbert's Temple. Jnl Warburg & Courtauld Inst 26 1963.

Blanchard, M. M. The leap into darkness: Donne, Herbert and God. Renascence 17 1964.

Endicott, A. M. The structure of Herbert's The temple: a reconsideration. UTQ 34 1965.

— The soul in paraphrase: Herbert's library. Renaissance News 19 1966.

Greenwood, E. B. Herbert's sonnet Prayer: a stylistic study. EC 15 1965.

Kirkwood, J. J. and G. W. Williams. 'Anneal'd' as baptism in Herbert's Love-joy. Amer N & Q 4 1965.

Leiter, L. H. Herbert's Anagram. College Eng April 1965.

Mohanty, H. P. Herbert's The collar. Indian Jnl of Eng Stud 6 1965.

Ostriker, A. Song and speech in the metrics of Herbert. PMLA 80 1965.

Pacey, D. Easter homage to Herbert. Atlantic Advocate 55 1965.

Scheuerle, W. H. A reading of Herbert's Content. USF Lang Quart 4 1965.

Thorpe, J. Herbert's Love iii. Explicator Oct 1965.

Tillotson, G. Herbert's Rope of sands. TLS 22 April 1965. Replies 29 April, 6 May 1965.

Whiting, P. R. Two notes on Herbert. N & Q April 1965.

England, M. W. and J. Sparrow. Hymns unbidden: Donne, Herbert, Blake, Emily Dickinson and the hymnographers. New York 1966.

Hanley, Sr S. W. Herbert's Frailtie. Explicator Oct 1966.

— Herbert's Ana-Mary/Army-gram. Eng Lang Notes 4 1966.

— Temples in the Temple: Herbert's study of the Church. Stud in Eng Lit 1500–1900 8 1968.

Knepprath, H. E. Herbert: university orator and country parson. Southern Speech Jnl 32 1966.

McGill, W. J., jr. Herbert's view of the Eucharist. Lock Haven Rev 8 1966.

Mollenkott, V. R. The many and the one in Herbert's Providence. College Langs Assoc Jnl 10 1966.

Pennel, C. A. and W. P. Williams. The unity of the Temple. Xavier Univ Stud 5 1966.

Stewart, S. Time and the Temple Stud in Eng Lit 1500–1900 6 1966.

Brown, W. J. Herbert's The collar and Shakespeare's 1 Henry 4. Amer N & Q 6 1967.

Champion, L. S. Body vs soul in Herbert's The collar. Style 1 1967.

French, R. W. Herbert's Vertue. Explicator Sept 1967.

Poggi, V. Herbert. Bologna 1967.

Weiss, W. A note on Herbert's The collar. N & Q March 1967.

Ziegelmaier, G. Liturgical symbol and reality in Herbert's poetry. Amer Benedictine Rev 18 1967.

Carnes, V. The unity of Herbert's The temple: a reconsideration. ELH 35 1968.

Davies, H. N. Sweet music in Herbert's Easter. N & Q March 1968.

Harbinson, M. J. A crux in Herbert's The sacrifice. N & Q March 1968.

Howard, T. T. Herbert and Crashaw: notes on meditative focus. Gordon Rev 11 1968.

Levitt, P. M. and K. G. Johnston. Herbert's The collar and the story of Job. Papers on Lang & Lit 4 1968.

Murrin, M. Poetry as literary criticism. MP 65 1968.

Stein, A. Herbert's prosody. Lang & Style 1 1968.

— Herbert's lyrics. Baltimore 1968.

Unrau, J. 3 notes on Herbert. N & Q March 1968.

Whitlock, B. W. The baroque characteristics of the poetry of Herbert. Cithara 7 1968.

McGuire, P. C. Herbert's Jordan II and the plain style. Michigan Academician 1 1969.

Carpenter, M. From Herbert to Marvell: poetics in A wreath and the Coronet. JEGP 69 1970.

El-Gabalawy, S. Herbert's affinities with the homiletical mode. Humanities Assoc Bull 21 1970.

— The pilgrimage: Herbert's favourite allegorical technique. College Langs Assoc Jnl 13 1970.

Fish, S. E. Letting go: the reader in Herbert's poetry. ELH 37 1970.

Gallagher, M. P. Rhetoric, style and Herbert. Ibid.

Handscombe, R. J. Herbert's The collar: a study in frustration. Lang & Style 3 1970.

Huntley, F. L. A crux in Herbert's The temple. Eng Lang Notes 8 1970.

Reiter, R. E. Herbert and his biographers. Cithara 9 1970.

Vendler, H. H. Herbert's 'vertue'. Ariel 1 1970.

Williams, R. D. Two baroque game poems on 'grace': Herbert's Paradise and Milton's On time. Criticism 12 1970.

Brown, C. C. and W. P. Ingoldsby. Herbert's Easter-wings. HLQ 35 1972.

Ende, F. von. Herbert's The sonne: in defense of the English language. Stud in Eng Lit 1500–1900 12 1972.

THOMAS CAREW
1595?–1640
Collections

Poems, songs and sonnets; together with a masque. [Ed T. Davies?] 1772.
A selection from the poetical works. Ed J. Fry 1810.
Works. Ed T. Maitland, Edinburgh 1824.
Poems. 1845.
Poems. Ed W. C. Hazlitt 1870.
Poems and masque. Ed J. W. Epsworth 1893.
Poems. Ed A. Vincent 1898 (ML).
Ed R. G. Howarth, Minor poets of the seventeenth century, 1931 (EL), 1953 (rev).
Poems, with his masque Coelum britannicum. Ed R. Dunlap, Oxford 1949.

§1

The heire [by Thomas May]. 1622, 1633. Includes To Thomas May.
The just Italian [by William Davenport]. 1630. Includes To M. D'avenant.
Madrigals and ayres [by Walter Porter]. 1632. 2 songs by Carew.
Poems [by John Donne]. 1633. Includes An elegie upon Donne.
Coelum britannicum: a masque at Whitehall. 1634 (anon), 1640.
The witts [by William Davenant]. 1636. Includes a commendatory poem.
A paraphrase upon the divine poems [by George Sandys]. 1636. Includes a commendatory poem.
Romulus and Tarquin [by M. V. Malvezzi, tr H. Cary of Lepington]. 1637. Includes a commendatory poem.
Madagascar [by Davenant]. 1638. Includes a commendatory poem.
Poems. [Ed Aurelian Townshend?] 1640 (includes, with separate title but continuous pagination, Coelum britannicum), 1642 ('revised and enlarged', adds 8 poems, one by Waller), 1651 (as Poems, with a maske; adds 3 poems), 1670 (as Poems, songs and sonnets, together with a masque), 1671; Menston 1969 (facs, including Wyburd ms). See also cols 1908–9, below.

§2

Quiller-Couch, A. T. In his Adventures in criticism, 1896.
Powell, C. L. New material on Carew. MLR 11 1916.
Dunlap, R. Carew, Thomas Carey and the Sovereign of the seas. MLN 56 1941.
Herrick, A. Carew. TLS 12 April 1947.
Duncan-Jones, E. E. Carew and Guez de Balzac. MLR 46 1951.
— Carew's Upon the King's sickness. Explicator Dec 1954.
Shapiro, I. A. Carew's Obsequies to the Lady Anne Hay. N & Q Jan 1951.
Howarth, R. G. A poem by Carew? N & Q Nov 1952.
Emslie, M. Carew's Disdaine returned. Explicator Oct 1953.
Blanshard, R. A. Carew and the Cavalier poets. Trans Wisconsin Acad 43 1954.
— Carew and Jonson. SP 52 1955.
— Carew's master figures. Boston Univ Stud in Eng 3 1957.
Briggs, A. S. Carew and Shakespeare. N & Q May 1956.
Ruoff, J. E. Carew's early reputation. N & Q Feb 1957.
Selig, E. I. The flourishing wreath: a study of Carew's poetry. New Haven 1958.
Davison, D. Carew's poetry: a query. Melbourne Critical Rev 4 1961.
McKeen, D. B. The Carew family and its connexions. N & Q Feb 1963.
Pederson, L. A. Thoreau's rhetoric and Carew's lines. Thoreau Soc Bull 82 1963.

Pellegrini, G. Coelum britannicum. Rivista di Letterature Moderne e Comparate 15 1963.
Palmer, P. Carew: an unnoticed allusion to Davenant's illegitimacy. N & Q Feb 1963.
— Carew: an allusion to Venus and Adonis. N & Q July 1966.
— Carew's reference to the Shepherd's paradise. N & Q Aug 1966.
— Lovelace: some unnoticed allusions to Carew. N & Q March 1967.
King, B. The strategy of Carew's wit. REL 5 1964.
— Green ice and a breast of proof. College Eng April 1965.
Halliday, F. E. A Cornish chronicle: the Carews of Antony from Armada to Civil War. Newton Abbot 1967.
Delany, P. Attacks on Carew in William Habington's poems. Seventeenth-century News 26 1968.
Murrin, M. Poetry as literary criticism. MP 65 1968.
Parfitt, G. A. The poetry of Carew. Renaissance & Modern Stud 12 1968.

WILLIAM HABINGTON
1605–54
Collections

Castara: a collation of the editions of 1634, 1635 and 1640. Ed H. C. Combs, Evanston 1939.
Poems. Ed K. Allott, Liverpool 1948.

§1

Castara. 2 pts 1634 (anon), 1 vol 1635 (corrected and augmented; adds 3 prose characters and 26 poems), 1636 (a variant of 1635), 1640 (adds 3rd pt: character A holy man and 22 poems); ed C. A. Elton, Bristol [1812]; ed R. Southey, Select works of the British poets, 1831; ed E. Arber 1870, 1895 (with collation of 3 original edns).
The Queen of Arragon. 1640 (anon); rptd Dodsley's Old plays vol 10, 1744; ed R. Thyer 1759; ed W. C. Hazlitt vol 13, 1875. See Samuel Butler's Remains vol 1, ed Thyer. A tragi-comedy.
The historie of Edward the Fourth. 1640; rptd and attributed to Habington, W. Kennett, Complete history of England vol 1, 1706.
Observations upon historie. 1641.
Several books contain commendatory verses by Habington, e.g. the 1647 folio of Beaumont and Fletcher, Jonsonus virbius 1638 (name given as W. Abington). There is a poem addressed to the author of Castara in Witts recreation 1640, and another in Bodley ms Malone 18 folio 68.

§2

Nosworthy, J. M. William Habington. TLS 5 June 1937.
Combs, H. C. Habington's Castara and the date of his marriage. MLN 43 1948.
Delany, P. Attacks on Carew in Habington's poems. Seventeenth-century News 26 1968.

SIR WILLIAM DAVENANT
1606–68

For bibliographies see A. Harbage, Sir William Davenant, Philadelphia 1935; Gondibert, ed D. F. Gladish, Oxford 1971.

Collections

Madagascar, with other poems. 1638, 1648.
Works. 1673.
Select works of the British poets. Ed R. Southey 1831. Gondibert and selections from the non-dramatic poems.

Dramatic works. Ed J. Maidment and W. H. Logan 5 vols Edinburgh 1872–4, 1964.
Selected poems. Ed D. Bush, Cambridge Mass 1943.
Shorter poems and songs from the plays and masques. Ed A. M. Gibbs, Oxford 1972. Adds 6 poems to the canon.

§1

The tragedy of Albovine. 1629.
The cruel brother. 1630. A tragedy.
The just Italian. 1630.
The temple of love. 1634 (for 1635). A masque.
The platonick lovers. 1636, 1665 (with The witts). A tragi-comedy.
The witts. 1636, 1665 (with The platonick lovers, as Two excellent plays); ed I. Reed, Dodsley's Old plays vol 8, 1780; ed W. Scott, Ancient British drama vol 1, 1810; ed J. P. Collier, Dodsley's Old plays vol 8, 1825–7. A comedy.
The triumphs of the Prince d'Amour. 1635. A masque.
Britannia triumphans. 1637 (for 1638). A masque.
Luminalia or the festivall of light. 1637 (anon); ed A. B. Grosart [1876]. A masque, attributed to Davenant.
Salmacida spolia. 1639; ed W. R. Chetwood, Select collection of old plays, Dublin 1750; ed H. A. Evans, English masques, 1879. A masque.
To the honourable knights, citizens etc. 1641 (at least 2 edns, one undated).
The unfortunate lovers. 1643, 1649. A tragedy.
London, King Charles his Augusta. 1648. Although ascribed to Davenant in the printer's epistle, T. H. Banks states it is not his.
Love and honour. 1649; ed J. W. Tupper, Boston 1909.
A discourse upon Gondibert. Paris 1650. Also issued as The preface to Gondibert. Ed J. E. Spingarn, Seventeenth-century critical essays vol 2, Oxford 1908.
Gondibert: an heroick poem. 1651 (8° and 4°), Menston 1970 (facs); ed D. F. Gladish, Oxford 1971.
The siege of Rhodes. 1656, 1659, 1663 (rev and expanded as The siege of Rhodes: the first and second part), 1670.
The first days entertainment at Rutland House. 1657.
The cruelty of the Spaniards in Peru. 1658.
The history of Sr Francis Drake. Pt 1 (all ptd), 1659.
Panegyrick to his Excellency the Lord Generall Monck. 1659. Folio sheet.
Prologue to his Majesty at the first play presented. 1660. Single folio.
Poem upon his sacred Majesties return. 1660.
Poem to the King's most sacred Majesty. 1663.
The rivals. 1668, 1669. A comedy.
The man's the master. 1669, 1775. A comedy.
The tempest. 1670, 1695 (with Works of John Dryden); ed M. Summers, Shakespearian adaptations, 1922. With John Dryden. A comedy, adapted from Shakespeare.
The law against lovers. 1673, 1970.
Macbeth, with all the alterations, amendments, additions and new songs. 1674, 1674, 1687, 1695, 1697, 1710; ed C. Spencer, New Haven 1961 (from Yale ms). Adapted from Shakespeare.
The seventh and last canto of the third book of Gondibert. 1685; ed J. G. McManaway, MLQ 1 1940 (from 2 known copies).
[Shakespeare's] Julius Caesar [with alterations by Davenant and John Dryden]. In A collection of plays by eminent hands, 1719.

§2

Certain verses written by several of the authors friends. 1653.
Hurd, R. Q. Horatii Flacci epistola ad Augustum. 1751.
Aiken, J. and A. L. In their Miscellaneous pieces in prose, 1773. On Gondibert.
Elze, K. Davenant. Sh Jb 4 1869.
Campbell, K. The source of the Siege of Rhodes. MLN 13 1898.

— The source of Davenant's Albovine. JEGP 4 1902.
— Notes on Davenant's life. MLN 18 1903.
Firth, C. H. Davenant and the revival of drama during the Protectorate. EHR 18 1903.
Gronauer, G. Davenant's Gondibert. Munich 1911.
Hooper, E. S. The authorship of Luminalia and notes on some other poems of Davenant. MLR 8 1913.
Thaler, A. Thomas Heywood, Davenant and the Siege of Rhodes. PMLA 39 1924.
Spencer, H. Davenant's Macbeth and Shakespeare's. PMLA 40 1925.
Richardson, W. R. Davenant as American colonizer. ELH 1 1934.
Dowlin, C. M. Davenant's Gondibert, its preface and Hobbes' answer: a study in English neo-classicism. Philadelphia 1934.
— The first edition of Gondibert: quarto or octavo? Library 4th ser 20 1940.
Harbage, A. Davenant. Philadelphia 1935.
Marchant, E. C. Davenant. Oxford 1936 (Davenant Soc).
Swedenborg, H. T., jr. Rules and English critics of the epic 1650–1800. SP 35 1938.
Nethercot, A. H. Davenant: poet laureate and playwright-manager. Chicago 1938, New York 1967 (with additional notes).
— Scribblings in a copy of D'Avenant's Gondibert. N & Q July 1970.
McManaway, J. G. The 'lost' canto of Gondibert. MLQ 1 1940.
Stamm, R. Davenant and Shakespeare's imagery. E Studies 24 1942.
Southern, R. Davenant: father of English scenery. Life & Letters 32 1942.
Perkinson, R. H. The epic in five acts. SP 43 1946.
Marilla, E. L. Vaughan to Davenant. PQ 27 1948.
Turner, W. A. Milton's aid to Davenant. MLN 63 1948.
Rundle, J. U. Davenant's The man's the master and the Spanish source. MLN 65 1950.
de Mandach, A. The first translator of Molière: Davenant or Colonel Henry Howard. MLN 66 1951.
Berry, H. Three new poems by Davenant. PQ 31 1952.
Duncan-Jones, E. E. Milton's late court-poet. N & Q Nov 1954.
Haywood, C. The songs and masque in the New Tempest: an incident in the battle of the two theatres. HLQ 19 1955.
Riewald, J. G. Laureates in Elysium: Davenant and Southey. E Studies 37 1956.
Cope, J. I. Rhetorical genres in Davenant's First day's entertainment at Rutland House. Quart Jnl of Speech 45 1959.
Kaufmann, R. J. Suckling and Davenant satirised by Brome. MLR 55 1960.
Dust, A. I. The seventh and last canto of Gondibert and two dedicatory poems. JEGP 60 1961.
Spencer, C. Davenant's Macbeth from the Yale ms. New Haven 1961.
Palmer, P. Carew: an unnoticed allusion to Davenant's illegitimacy. N & Q Feb 1963.
Feil, J. P. Davenant exonerated. MLR 58 1963.
Hönnighausen, L. Der Stilwandel im dramatischen Werk Davenants. Anglistische Studien 3 1965.
Squier, C. Davenant's comic assault on préciosité: The platonic lovers. Univ of Colorado Stud, Ser in Lang & Lit 10 1966.
Collins, H. S. The comedy of Davenant. Hague 1967.
Gibbs, A. M. A Davenant imitation of Donne? RES new ser 18 1967.
Freehafer, J. Brome, Suckling, and Davenant's theatre project of 1639. Texas Stud in Lit & Lang 10 1968.

EDMUND WALLER
1606–87

Bibliographies

Osborne, M. T. Advice-to-a-painter 1633–1856. Austin 1949. An annotated list.

Collections

Poems. 1645 (3 edns), 1664, 1668, 1682, 1686 (2 issues), 1693, etc, Menston 1971 (facs).

Divine poems. 1685.

The second part of Mr Waller's poems. 1690, 1690, 1705, 1711, 1712, 1722. The anon preface is generally attributed to Francis Atterbury.

Works in verse and prose. Ed E. Fenton 1729, 1730, 1742, 1752, 1758 etc, 1772 (with a life by P. Stockdale) etc.

Poems. Ed S. Johnson, Works of English poets vol 8, 1779 etc.

The poetical works of Waller and Denham. Ed G. Gilfillan, Edinburgh 1857.

Poems. Ed G. Thorn-Drury 1893, 2 vols [1905] (ML).

§1

Rex redux. Cambridge 1633. Contains Waller's To the King on his return.

[Commendatory poem to George Sandys]. In Sandys, A paraphrase upon the divine poems, 1638.

[Commendatory poem upon Ben Jonson]. In Jonsonus virbius, 1638.

An honourable and learned speech against prelates' innovations. 1641.

Mr Waller's speech in the Painted Chamber 6 July 1641. 1641.

A worthy speech. 1641. That parliaments are only way for advancing the King's affairs; and that the restoring of goods and freedom is a chief means to maintain religion and obedience.

[To my Lord Admiral]. In Thomas Carew, Poems, 1642 (2nd edn).

To the Kings most excellent Majesty. 1642.

Speech 4 July 1643. 1643. In defence of himself before the House of Commons.

The works of Waller in this Parliament. 1645. Some copies dated 1644.

The life and death of William Laud. 1645.

Witts recreations. 1645 (3rd edn). Contains the following poems of Waller, some under different titles indicated in brackets: To Amoret, 'Amoret! the milky way'; To Phylis, 'Phylis! why should we delay' (The cunning courtezan); The fall (The reply); Of the marriage of the dwarfs (On the two dwarfs that married); The bud; On the discovery of a lady's painting (On a patch'd up madam); Of loving at first sight (The reply to the contrary); The self-banished (The melancholy lover); To a friend of their loves (The variable lover); To Zelinda (The ladyes slave); To the mutable fair (The reply); On a brede of divers colours; Chloris and Hylas (On the approaching spring); Go, lovely rose! (On the rose); Under a lady's picture (To be ingraven under the Queen's picture); To one married to an old man (To the wife being marryed to that old man).

A discourse upon Gondibert. Paris 1650. Contains Waller's To Davenant. Rptd with Gondibert 1651.

[Commendatory poem To Davenant]. In A discourse upon Gondibert, Paris 1650; rptd with Gondibert, 1651 etc.

Ayres and dialogues. 1653. Contains the following poems of Waller, some under different titles indicated in brackets: The bud; To a lady singing (To the same lady singing); While I listen to thy voice. Vol 2, 1655, contains Waller's To Chloris 'Chloris! since first' (To a lady, more affable); Go, lovely rose!

Poems by Francis Beaumont gent. 1653. Includes 4 poems: Say, lovely dream (from Poems, 1645), Of loving at first sight, To the mutable fair, song Behold the brand of beauty tossed.

[Commendatory poem to Mr Wase] in Grati Falisci Cynegeticon by Christopher Wase, 1654.

[Ad comitem Monumetensem]. In History of the wars of Flanders, by H. Carey, 1654.

A panegyrick to my Lord Protector. 1655 (folio), 1655 (4°).

[Commendatory poem to John Evelyn]. In An essay on Lucretius, by J. Evelyn, 1656.

[Commendatory poem to Sir Thomas Higgins]. In A prospective of the naval triumph by Busenello, 1658.

Upon the late storme, and the death of his Highnesse. [1658], 1659 (in Three poems upon the death of his late Highnesse).

The passion of Dido. 1658, 1679. By Waller and Sidney Godolphin.

To the King, upon his Majesties happy return. [1660].

To my Lady Morton. 1661. Signed E.W.

A poem on St James's Park. 1661.

To the Queen, upon her Majesty's birthday. [1663].

Pompey the great: a tragedy, translated out of the French by certain persons of honour. 1664. Act 1 by Waller.

Upon her Majesty's new buildings at Somerset House. 1665. Sometimes attributed to Denham.

[Pandoras not being approved]. In Three plays by Sir William Killigrew, 1665. Commendatory poem to Killigrew.

Instructions to a painter for the drawing of the posture and progress of his Majesties forces at sea. 1666. See also John Denham, below.

[To a friend of the author]. In Historical applications by George, first Earl of Berkeley. 1666.

Of the Lady Mary. 1677.

A poem on the present assembling. [1679].

[Upon the Earl of Roscommon's translation]. In Horace's Art of poetry made English, by the Earl of Roscommon, 1680.

[Commendatory poem to Dr George Rogers]. In Oratio anniversaria, 1682 (some copies without date).

The new masque for [F. Beaumont's and J. Fletcher's] The maids' tragedy. [1683?].

A poem upon the present assembly of Parliament. 1685.

The maid's tragedy, altered. 1690.

[Poem upon the death of Oliver Cromwell]. In The life of Oliver Cromwell [by Isaac Kimber], 1724, 1725, 1731 etc.

[Neve, P.] Cursory remarks on some of the ancient English poets. 1789. Contains Waller's When he was at sea, and In answer to one who writ against a fair lady.

English poets. Ed A. Chalmers 1810. Contains Waller's To the Prince of Orange, and On Mrs Higgons.

On the marriage of Mrs Frances Cromwell and Mr Rich. First ptd by B. Chew, Essays and verses about books, New York 1926 (priv ptd).

§2

Stockdale, P. Life of Waller. 1772.

Johnson, S. In his Lives of the poets vol 1, 1781.

Thorn-Drury, G. Poems. 1901. Introd.

Aldington, R. Notes on Waller's poems. Living Age 312 1922.

Grierson, H. J. C. Poems by Waller. TLS 29 Dec 1927.

Lloyd, C. Waller as a member of the Royal Society. PMLA 43 1928.

Roeckerath, N. Der Nachruhm Herricks und Wallers. Leipzig 1931.

de Beer, E. S. An uncollected poem by Waller. RES 8 1932.

Riske, E. T. Waller in exile. TLS 13 Oct 1932.

Hardacre, P. H. A letter from Waller to Thomas Hobbes. HLQ 11 1948.

Midgley, E. G. Pope, Suckling and Waller. N & Q 2 Sept 1950. Reply by J. C. Maxwell 14 Oct 1950.

Richmond, H. M. The intangible mistress. MP 61 1959.

—— The fate of Waller. South Atlantic Quart 60 1961.

Allison, A. A. Towards an Augustan poetic: Waller's 'reform' of English poetry. Lexington Kentucky 1962.

Chernaik, W. L. Waller's Panegyric to my Lord Protector and the poetry of praise. Stud in Eng Lit 1500–1900 4 1964.

—— The poetry of limitation: a study of Waller. New Haven 1968.

Erskine-Hill, H. H. Waller and Samuel Butler: two poetic debts to Hall's Occasional meditations. N & Q April 1965.

Atterbury, F. Exhumations III: Atterbury's preface to Waller. EC 15 1965.

O Hehir, B. The early acquaintance of Denham and Waller. N & Q Jan 1966.

Miner, E. The poetic picture, painted poetry of the Last instructions to a painter. MP 63 1966.

Means, J. A. Three notes on Pope. N & Q Nov 1967.

Korshin, P. J. The evolution of neoclassical poetics. Eighteenth-century Stud 2 1968.

Hayman, J. An image of the sultan in Waller's Of love and A very heroical epistle in answer to Ephelia. N & Q Oct 1968.

Wikelund, P. R. Thus I passe my time in this place: an unpublished letter of Thomas Hobbes. Eng Lang Notes 6 1969.

—— Waller's fit of versifying: deductions from a holograph fragment, Folger ms x.d.309. PQ 49 1970.

SIR JOHN SUCKLING
1609–42

Bibliographies

Yeo, C. M. Suckling: a bibliography. 1948.
For mss, edns and dubia, see Clayton-Beaurline, below.

Collections

Works. 1676, 1696 (contains the 4 plays, each dated 1694), 1709, 1719, Dublin 1766, 2 vols 1770.

Selections. Ed A. Suckling 1836.

Poems, plays and other remains. Ed W. C. Hazlitt 2 vols 1874, 1892 (rev).

Works. Ed A. H. Thompson 1910, New York 1964.

Suckling's poems and letters from manuscript. Ed H. Berry, Univ of Western Ontario Stud in Humanities 1 1960.

Works. Ed T. Clayton and L. A. Beaurline 2 vols Oxford 1971. Vol 1, Non-dramatic works; vol 2, Plays.

§ 1

[To Lord Lepington]. In Romulus and Tarquin, 1638. H. Cary's trn from Malvezzi's Italian.

[To William Davenant]. In Davenant's Madagascar, 1638.

Aglaura. 1638 (anon), 1646, Menston 1970 (facs).

The copy of a letter written to the Lower Houses of Parliament. 1641.

A letter by . . . from France. 1641.

Copy of a letter found in the privy lodgeings. 1641.

The discontented colonel. [1642] (unauthorized); rptd in Fragmenta aurea, below, as Brennoralt.

Fragmenta aurea. 1646. Contains, each with separate title and pagination: Poems, Aglaura, Goblins, Brennoralt, An account of religion by reason, and Letters to divers eminent personages, all dated 1646; 1648 (in 4 pts, each dated 1648), 1658 (in Last remains of Suckling, 1659 (includes, each with separate title-page dated 1659 and separate pagination: Letters to several persons of honor, and The sad one). For reprints and surreptitious edns see Clayton's edn of Works vol 1, 1971.

A letter from Sir J.S. to Mr H. German. [1660?]. Written 1640.

§ 2

Llewelyn, P. Suckling. Freeman 7 1923.

Lynch, K. M. The social mode of Restoration comedy. New York 1927.

Williamson, G. An attribution to Suckling. MLN 1 1935.

Henderson, F. C. Traditions of 'précieux' and 'libertin' in Suckling's poetry. ELH 4 1937.

Sensabaugh, G. F. An answer to Suckling's Why so pale and wan, fond lover? MLN 52 1938.

Krzyzanowski, J. The sources of Suckling's Brennoralt. TLS 9 April 1938. Reply by F. Henderson 4 Feb 1939.

Gray, P. H. Suckling's A session of the poets as a ballad: Boccalini's influence examined. SP 36 1939.

Niemeyer, C. A misdating of A ballade upon a wedding. MLN 56 1941.

The singing cavalier: Suckling's Muse. TLS 9 May 1942.

Bald, R. C. A note on Suckling's A session of the poets. MLN 58 1943.

Wallerstein, R. C. Suckling's imitation of Shakespeare: a Caroline view of his art. RES 19 1943.

Benham, A. R. Suckling's A session of the poets. MLQ 6 1945.

Horne, C. J. A letter sent to Suckling from France. N & Q 11 Aug 1945.

The cheerful poet. TLS 4 Sept 1946.

Midgley, E. G. Pope, Suckling and Waller. N & Q 2 Sept 1950.

Price, G. R. A reply to Suckling's Why so pale and wan. N & Q 22 Dec 1951.

Wyllie, J. C. The printer of a 1641 Suckling pamphlet. PBSA 47 1953.

Clayton, T. S. Thorn-Drury's marginalia on Suckling. N & Q April 1959.

—— Suckling and the Cranfields. TLS 29 Jan 1960.

—— An historical study of the portraits of Suckling. Jnl Warburg & Courtauld Inst 23 1960.

Candelaris, F. H. Ovid and the indifferent lovers. Renaissance News 13 1960.

Beaurline, L. A. The canon of Suckling's poems. SP 57 1960.

—— New poems by Suckling. SP 59 1962.

—— Why so pale and wan: an essay in critical method. Texas Stud in Lit & Lang 4 1962.

—— An editorial experiment: Suckling's A session of the poets. SB 16 1963.

Beaurline, L. A. and T. Clayton. Notes on early editions of Fragmenta aurea. SB 23 1970.

Kaufmann, R. J. Suckling and Davenant satirised by Brome. MLR 55 1960.

Broadbent, J. B. In his Poetic love, 1964.

Armitage, C. M. Identification of the New York Public Library manuscript Suckling collection, and of the Huntington manuscript 198. SB 19 1966.

Freehafer, J. Brome, Suckling and Davenant's theatre project of 1639. Texas Stud in Lit & Lang 10 1968.

—— The Italian night piece and Suckling's Aglaura. JEGP 67 1968.

RICHARD CRASHAW
1612 or 1613–49

For mss see L. C. Martin's edn of Works, pp. liv–lxxxi; this edn also records the first appearance of all occasional pieces. See also Samaha, col 1235 below.

Collections

Epigrammata sacra selecta, cum anglica versione: sacred epigrams englished. 1682. Crashaw is not named, but all the Latin epigrams are his. The anon trns are by Clement Barksdale.

Poetry, with some account of the author by P[eregrine] P[hillips]. 1785.

Select beauties of ancient English poetry vol 1. Ed H. Headly 1787. Prints all Sospetto d'Herode, except Argomento and the first 4 stanzas.

The suspicion of Herod. Kensington 1834.

Poetical works. Ed G. Gilfillan, Edinburgh 1857. Based on 1670, below.

Complete works. Ed W. B. Turnbull 1858.

Complete works. Ed A. B. Grosart 2 vols 1872–3; suppl 1887–8.

Poems. Ed C. C. Clarke [1881].

Delights of the Muses. Ed J. R. Tutin, Great Fencote 1900. Secular poems.

English poems. Ed E. Hutton 1901.

Poems. Ed A. R. Waller, Cambridge 1904.

Poems. Ed J. R. Tutin, with introd by H. C. Beeching [1905] (ML).

Religious poems. Ed R. A. E. Shepherd 1914.

Poems English, Latin and Greek. Ed L. C. Martin, Oxford 1927, 1957. With some unpbd poems and new biographical matter.

Verse in English. New York 1949.

Complete poetry. Ed G. W. Williams, Garden City NY 1970.

§ 1

Epigrammatum sacrorum liber. Cambridge 1634. Dedication signed R.C.

Steps to the temple: sacred poems, with other delights of the Muses. 1646, 1648 ('second edition wherein are added divers pieces not before extant'), 1670 (2nd edn, with Carmen deo nostro); Menston 1970 (facs of 1646). Grosart vol 2 p. viii records an undated reissue of this with 'the third edn' on the title-page, but it has not been traced. *See col 1913, below.*

Carmen deo nostro, te decet hymnus, sacred poems. Paris 1652 (ed Thomas Car, alias Miles Pinkney, the poet's friend; 3 engravings probably by Crashaw); ed J. R. Tutin [1897].

A letter from Crashaw to the Countess of Denbigh, against irresolution and delay in matters of religion. [1653]. No printer's name or date. A contemporary hand has 1653, and G. Thomason has added 'Sept 23' above the year. It differs widely from the version in Carmen, 1652, above; *see* Martin, pp. 236, 348, 446.

Poemata et epigrammata: editio secunda, auctior et emendatior. Cambridge 1670, 1674 (with new title-leaf).

Musicks duell [from Steps to the temple 1646]. 1935.

Caritas nimia. Worcester [1964].

§ 2

Sharland, E. C. Crashaw and Mary Collet. Church Quart Rev 73 1912.

Minor poems of Joseph Beaumont. Ed E. Robinson 1914. On parallels between Beaumont and Crashaw.

Martin, L. C. A Crashaw and Shelley parallel. MLR 11 1916.

— A hitherto unpublished poem of Crashaw. London Mercury June 1923. Epithalamium.

— An unedited Crashaw manuscript. TLS 18 April 1952.

Comfrey, B. A note on Crashaw. MLN 36 1921.

Williams, I. A. Epitaphs on a husband and wife. London Mercury Feb 1923.

Chalmers, Lord. Crashaw: poet and saint. In In memoriam Adolphus W. Ward, Cambridge 1924.

Praz, M. In his Secentismo e Marinismo in Inghilterra, Florence 1925.

— Richard Crashaw. Brescia 1946.

— Drummond and Crashaw. TLS 21 Oct 1949.

— The flaming heart: Crashaw and the baroque. Garden City NY 1958.

Crashaw's poetical works. TLS 17 Dec 1927.

Hutchinson, F. E. Crashaw. Church Quart Rev 106 1928.

Eliot, T. S. In his For Lancelot Andrewes, 1928.

Tholen, W. Crashaw: ein englischer Dichter und Mystiker der Barockzeit. Das Neue Ufer 48 1928.

Warren, A. Crashaw and Peterhouse. TLS 13 Aug 1931, 3 Nov 1932.

— Crashaw and St Teresa. TLS 25 Aug 1932.

— The mysticism of Crashaw. Church Quart Rev 116 1933.

— Crashaw's Epigrammata sacra. JEGP 33 1934.

— The reputation of Crashaw in the seventeenth and eighteenth centuries. SP 31 1934.

— Crashaw. MP 32 1935.

— Crashaw's reputation in the nineteenth century. PMLA 51 1936.

— Crashaw: a study in baroque sensibility. Ann Arbor 1939.

Foy, T. Richard Crashaw, 'poet and saint'? Dublin 1933.

Beachcroft, T. O. Crashaw and the baroque style. Criterion 13 1934.

Wallerstein, R. C. Crashaw: a study in style and poetic development. Madison 1935, 1959.

Barker, F. G. Crashaw and Andrewes. TLS 21 Aug 1937.

Bernard, M. More than a woman. Catholic World 160 1944.

Scott, W. S. In his Fantasticks, 1945.

Poet and saint. TLS 1 June 1946.

Allison, A. F. Some influences on Crashaw's poem On a prayer book sent to Mrs M.R. RES 23 1947.

— Crashaw and St Francis de Sales. RES 24 1948.

A poet of delights. TLS 19 Aug 1949.

Turnell, M. Crashaw after 300 years. Nineteenth Century Aug 1949.

Willey, B. Richard Crashaw. 1949. A memorial lecture.

Williams, G. W. Textual revision in Crashaw's Upon the bleeding Crucifix. SB 1 1949.

— Crashaw and the Little Gidding bookbinders. N & Q Jan 1956.

— Image and symbol in the sacred poetry of Crashaw. Columbia SC 1963.

Meath, C. The tumbling images of Crashaw. Listener 1 Sept 1949.

Moloney, M. F. Crashaw 1649–1949. Catholic World 169 1949.

Cammell, C. R. The divine poet: Crashaw. Nat & Eng Rev 135 1950.

Maxwell, J. C. Steps to the temple: 1646 and 1648. PQ 29 1950.

Jacquot, J. Le duel musical de Crashaw et sa source italienne. Revue de Littérature Comparée 25 1951.

Peter, J. Crashaw and the Weeper. Scrutiny 19 1953.

Wallis, P. J. Crashaw: puritan divine, poet and bibliophile. N & Q March 1954.

Watkin, E. I. In his Poets and mystics, 1954.

Adams, R. M. Taste and bad taste in metaphysical poetry: Crashaw and Dylan Thomas. Hudson Rev 8 1955.

Esch, A. Englische religiöse Lyrik des 17 Jahrhunderts. Tübingen 1955.

Manning, S. The meaning of the Weeper. ELH 22 1955.

Rickey, M. E. Crashaw and Vaughan. N & Q June 1955.

— Chapman and Crashaw. N & Q Nov 1956.

— Rhyme and meaning in Crashaw. Lexington Kentucky 1961.

Collmer, R. G. Crashaw's Death more mysticall and high. JEGP 55 1956.

Petoello, L. A current misconception concerning the influence of Marino's poetry on Crashaw's. MLR 52 1957.

Madsen, W. G. A reading of Musicks duell. In Studies in honor of John Wilcox, Detroit 1958.

Saveson, J. E. Crashaw. TLS 28 Feb 1958.

Goldfarb, R. M. Crashaw's Suppose he had been tabled at thy teats. Explicator March 1961.

Souris, A. (ed). Poèmes de Donne, Herbert et Crashaw mis en musique par leurs contemporains G. Coperario, A. Ferrabosco, J. Wilson, W. Corkine, J. Hilton. Paris 1961.

Willy, M. In her Three metaphysical poets: Crashaw, Traherne, Vaughan, 1961 (Br Council pamphlet).

Bawcutt, N. W. A seventeenth-century allusion to Crashaw. N & Q June 1962.

Leach, E. Some commercial terms in seventeenth-century poetry. N & Q Nov 1963.

Swanston, H. The second Temple. Durham Univ Jnl 25 1963.

Gilman, H. Crashaw's reflexive recoil. Seventeenth-century News 22 1964.

Miller, C. H. The order of stanzas in Cowley and Crashaw's On hope. SP 61 1964.

Pritchard, A. Puritan charges against Crashaw and Beaumont. TLS 2 July 1964.

Yoklavich, J. Not by Crashaw, but Cornwallis. On 5 poems from Bodley ms Tanner 465. MLR 59 1964.

—— A manuscript of Crashaw's poems from Loseley. Eng Lang Notes 2 1964.

Jauernick, S. Crashaw's Hymne auf Santa Teresa. Die Neueren Sprachen 14 1965.

Geha, R , jr. Crashaw, the ego's soft fall. Amer Imago 23 1966.

Raspa, A. Crashaw and the Jesuit poetic. UTQ 36 1966.

Stanwood, P. G. Crashaw at Rome. N & Q July 1966.

Anderson, J. B. Crashaw, St Teresa and St John of the Cross. Discourse 10 1967.

Chambers, L. In defense of the Weeper. Papers in Lang & Lit 3 1967.

Harrison, R. Erotic imagery in Crashaw's Musicks duell. Seventeenth-century News 25 1967.

Bertenasco, M. F. A new look at Crashaw and The weeper. Texas Stud in Lit & Lang 10 1968.

—— Crashaw and the emblem. E Studies 49 1968.

Kelliher, W. H. Crashaw's contemporary reputation. N & Q Oct 1968.

—— Crashaw at Cambridge and Rome. N & Q Jan 1972.

Cirillo, A. R. Crashaw's Epiphany hymn: the Dawn of Christian time. SP 67 1970.

Jacobus, L. A. Crashaw as mannerist. Bucknell Rev 18 1970.

Petersson, R. T. The art of ecstasy: St Teresa, Bernini and Crashaw. New York 1970.

Singh, B. Crashaw in the eighteenth century. N & Q July 1970.

Söderholm, T. *See col 1170, above.*

SIR JOHN DENHAM
1615–69

Bibliographies

Osborne, M. T. Advice-to-a-painter 1633–1856. Austin 1949. An annotated list.

Collections

Poems and translations. 1668, 1671, 1684, 1703, 1709 (for 1710), 1719; ed S. Johnson 1779, 1790 etc.

Poetical works of Waller and Denham. Ed G. Gilfillan, Edinburgh 1857.

Poetical works. Ed T. H. Banks, New Haven 1928 (with a bibliography).

§ 1

A letter sent to William Laud. 1641. Attributed to Denham.

The Sophy. 1642, 1667 (separate title-page but ptd with Poems and translations 1668), 1671, 1684.

Coopers Hill. 1642, 1643, 1650, 1655, 1709 (in A collection of the best English poetry vol 1) etc; ed B. O Hehir, Expans'd hieroglyphics, Berkeley 1969; Latine redditum, 1675 (a Latin trn by Moses Pengry).

Mr Hampdens speech. [1643, 2 edns]. Anon; rptd in Rump: or an exact collection etc, 1662, [1874].

[On Mr John Fletcher's works]. In Comedies and tragedies by Beaumont and Fletcher, 1647 etc.

[Commendatory poem to Richard Fanshaw]. In Fanshawe's trn of Guarini, Il pastor fido, 1648 etc, rptd with Coopers hill 1650 etc.

[Elegie upon Lord Hastings]. In R.B., Lachrymae musarum, 1649, 1650.

[To five principal members of the honourable House of Commons]. In The Rump, 1662.

Second advice to the painter. 1667, 1667 (enlarged as The second and third advice to a painter), 1667, 1667 (as Directions to a painter). Sometimes attributed to Marvell.

The anatomy of play. 1651. Anon.

Certain verses to be reprinted with Gondibert. 1653. Contains poems by Denham.

The destruction of Troy. 1656. Anon.

Panegyrick on Monck. 1659. Anon.

A relation of a Quaker. [1659] (anon); ptd as News from Colchester in The Rump 1660 etc.

Prologue to his Majesty at the first play at the Cock-pit. 1660. Anon.

The true Presbyterian without disguise. 1661, 1680. Authorship uncertain.

[On Mr Abraham Cowley]. In Several copies of verses on the death of Cowley, 1667. Also issued separately.

The famous battel of the catts. 1668. Authorship uncertain.

Cato Major, of old age. 1669, 1717 (in A collection of the best English poetry vol 2).

[Commendatory poem to Edward Howard]. In Howard, The Brittish princes, 1669.

Horace, by Corneille. 1678. 5th act tr Denham.

To his mistress. In C. Gildon, Chorus poetarum, [1694].

A version of the psalms. 1714.

Fifth part of miscellany poems. 1716. Contains a portion of The sophy, entitled Verses.

Further advice to a painter. 1673.

His M———y's speech. In Bibliotheca curiosa, ed E. Goldsmid, Edinburgh 1885.

The laurel and the ax.

Madam Semphronia's farewel.

The last 5 attributions are doubtful.

§ 2

Wood, A. In his Athenae oxonienses, 2 vols Oxford 1691–2; ed P. Bliss 6 vols 1813–20.

Aubrey, J. In his Brief lives, ed A. Clark 2 vols Oxford 1898.

Johnson, S. In his Lives of the poets, 1779–81.

Aubin, R. A. Materials for a study of the influence of Cooper's Hill. ELH 1 1934.

Wasserman, E. R. In his Subtler language, Baltimore 1959.

Putney, R. The view from Coopers Hill. Univ of Colorado Stud in Lang & Lit 6 1961.

O Hehir, B. Vergil's first Georgic and Denham's Cooper's Hill. PQ 42 1963.

—— Lost, authorized and pirated editions of Denham's Coopers Hill. PMLA 79 1964.

—— Denham's Coopers Hill and Poole's English Parnassus. MP 61 1964.

—— The early acquaintance of Denham and Waller. N & Q Jan 1966.

—— Harmony from discords: a life of Denham. Berkeley 1968.

Osborn, J. M. New poems by Denham. TLS 1 Sept 1966.

Hamilton, H. L. Lines by Denham. TLS 22 Sept 1966.

Means, J. A. Three notes on Pope. N & Q Nov 1967.

Korshin, P. J. The evolution of neoclassical poetics. Eighteenth-century Stud 2 1968.

ABRAHAM COWLEY
1618–67

Bibliographies

Loiseau, J. In his Cowley: sa vie, son oeuvre, Paris 1931.

Collections

Works. 1668 (also re-issued with corrections), 1669, 1672, 1674, 1678, 1680, 1680 etc.

The second part of the works. 1681, 1681, 1682, 1684.

The second and third part of the works. 1689, 1700, 1708, 1711, 1721.

Poems of Cowley and others composed into song by William King. Oxford 1668. 16 poems by Cowley, 15 from Mistress.

Songs set by Pietro Reggio. [1680]. Contains 33 songs from Anacreontiques and Mistress.

Select works in verse and prose. [Ed R. Hurd] 2 vols 1772, Dublin 1772, London 1777 (enlarged).

Complete works in verse and prose. Ed A. B. Grosart 2 vols Edinburgh 1881.

English writings. Ed A. R. Waller 2 vols Cambridge 1905–6.

Prose works. Ed J. R. Lumby, Cambridge 1887, 1923 (rev A. Tilley).

Essays and other prose writings. Ed A. B. Gough, Oxford 1915.

The mistress, with other select poems. Ed J. Sparrow 1926 (Nonesuch Press).

Poetry and prose, with Thomas Sprat's life and observations by Dryden, Addison, Johnson and others. Ed L. C. Martin, Oxford 1949.

§1

Poeticall blossomes. 1633 ('by A.C.'), 1636 ('enlarged', adds Sylva: or divers copies of verses), 1637.

Loves riddle: a pastorall comaedie. 1638.

Naufragium joculare: comedia. 1638. Tr C. Johnson as Fortune in her wits, 1705.

Prologue and epilogue [from Guardian]. 1642, 1650.

A satyre against separatists. 1642 ('by A.C.', 2 edns), 1660, 1675. Not by Cowley?

A satyre: the puritan and the papist. 1643 (anon); rptd as Cowley's in Wit and loyalty reviv'd, 1682; rptd Somers tracts vol 5, 1811.

The mistress: or several copies of love-verses. 1647.

The foure ages of England. 1648, 1675, 1705. Ascribed to Cowley on title-page, but disowned by him in preface to Poems 1656.

The guardian: a comedie. 1650. Performed 12 March 1641.

Poems. 1656, Menston 1971 (facs). Contains Preface, Miscellanies, Mistress, Pindarique odes, Davideis. Extracts pbd separately; see col 1913, below.

Ode, upon the blessed restoration and returne of his sacred Majestie Charles the Second. 1660.

A proposition for the advancement of experimental philosophy. 1661, Menston 1969 (facs).

Visions and prophecies. 1661 (for 1660), 1688 (as Definition of a tyrant), 1745 (as A vision concerning Cromwell; in Harleian miscellany vol 5), 1808, 1810.

A. Couleii plantarum libri duo. 1662, 1668 (enlarged to 6 bks as Abrahami Couleii Angli poemata latina), 1678; partly tr as A translation of the sixth book of Mr Cowley's Plantarum, 1680, 1683 (as An heroick poem); tr Nahum Tate as Cowley's History of plants, 1795.

Verses lately written upon several occasions. 1663. Publisher's note refers to unauthorized edn, Dublin 1663, of which no copy is known.

Cutter of Coleman street: a comedy. 1663; ed C. M. Gayley, Representative English comedies vol 4, 1903.

The garden, by A.C. In Poems upon divers occasions, with a character of a London scrivener, by J. Wells,

1667, 1679 (in John Evelyn, Sylvae); rptd in Evelyn, Kalendarium hortense, 1691 etc; ed A. A. Hyatt 1911.

[To the Royal Society]. In Thomas Sprat, History of the Royal Society, 1667 etc.

A poem on the late civil war. 1679; in John Dryden (ed), The third part of Miscellany poems, 1716, 1727. An extensive fragment.

Verses to Mr Hobbes. In Thomae Hobbes vita, 1681.

Drinking song [by Cowley], scolding wife and the jolly sailor. Boston and Middelburg [1840?].

§2

Johnson, S. In his Lives of the poets, 1779–81.

Gosse, E. In his Seventeenth-century studies, 1883.

Firth, C. H. Cowley at the Restoration. Academy 7 Oct 1893.

Macbride, J. M. A study of Cowley's Davideis. JEGP 2 1901.

Shafer, R. In his English ode, Princeton 1918.

Moore Smith, G. C. Cowley and Lord Falkland. N & Q 15 Oct 1921.

Nethercot, A. H. The relation of Cowley's Pindarics to Pindar's odes. MP 19 1921.

—— The reputation of Cowley. PMLA 38 1923.

—— Cowley's Discourse concerning style. RES 2 1926.

—— Cowley as dramatist. RES 4 1928.

—— The letters of Cowley. MLN 43 1928.

—— The essays of Cowley. JEGP 29 1930.

—— Cowley: the Muse's Hannibal. Oxford 1931.

Sparrow, J. The text of Cowley's Mistress. RES 3 1927.

—— The text of Cowley's satire The puritan and the papist. Anglia 58 1934.

Loiseau, J. Cowley: sa vie, son oeuvre. Paris 1931.

—— Cowley's reputation in England. Paris 1931.

—— Un livre récent sur Cowley. Etudes Anglaises 41 1963.

Wiley, A. N. The prologue and epilogue to the Guardian. RES 10 1934.

Krempien, H. H. Der Stil der Davideis im Kreise ihrer Vorläufer. Hamburg 1936.

Walton, G. A poem by Cowley. TLS 5 Dec 1936.

Vincent, H. P. Three unpublished letters of Cowley. MLN 54 1939.

Das, P. K. Cowley and Wordsworth's Skylark. MLR 35 1940.

Simmons, J. An unpublished letter from Cowley. MLN 57 1942.

Hussey, R. A question by Byron. N & Q 4 Feb 1945. Reply by W. Thorpe 7 April 1945.

Allen, D. C. Cowley's Pindar. MLN 63 1948.

Elledge, S. Cowley's ode Of wit and Longinus on the sublime: a study of one definition of the word 'wit'. MLQ 9 1948.

Miller, C. W. Cowley and Evelyn's Kalendarium hortense. MLN 63 1948.

Kermode, F. The date of Cowley's Davideis. RES 25 1949.

Turner, A. The University miscellanies: some neglected early texts of Cleveland and Cowley. MLN 64 1949.

Mead, H. R. Two issues of Cowley's Vision. PBSA 45 1951.

Korn, A. L. MacFlecknoe and Davideis. HLQ 14 1951.

Vieth, D. M. Rochester and Cowley. TLS 12 Oct 1951.

Ghosh, J. C. Cowley. Sewanee Rev 61 1953.

Brooks, H. F. Dryden and Cowley. TLS 19 April 1957. Replies by A. Arber 7 June, and W. K. Scudamore 14 June 1957.

Cohane, J. J. Cowley and Yeats. TLS 10 May 1957.

Nathanson, L. The context of Dryden's criticism of Donne's and Cowley's love poetry. N & Q Feb, May 1957.

Williamson, G. In his A reader's guide to the metaphysical poets, 1957.

—— The context of Marvell's Hortus and Garden. MLN 76 1961.

Suerbaum, U. Die Lyrik der Korrespondenzen. Pöpinghaus 1958.

Duncan, M. Cowley's elegy on John Littleton. N & Q Nov 1960.

Hinman, R. B. Cowley's world of order. Oxford 1960.

Rawlinson, D. Cowley and the current status of metaphysical poetry. EC 13 1963.

Miller, C. H. The order of stanzas in Cowley and Crashaw's On hope. SP 61 1964.

Walton, G. Cowley. EC 14 1964. Reply by D. Rawlinson, ibid.

Goldstein, H. D. Anglorum Pindarus: model and milieu. Comparative Lit 17 1965.

Barnum, P. H. The two angels in Cowley's Mistress. Thoth 7 1966.

Calderhead, J. C. The cherry and the laurel: a note on the sources of lines in stanza 10 of the Garden by Cowley. N & Q Sept 1967.

Pritchard, A. Six letters by Cowley. RES new ser 18 1967.

Spencer, L. M. Johnson and Cowley. New Rambler June 1967.

Söderholm, T. *See col 1170, above.*

RICHARD LOVELACE
1618–57?

Bibliographies

Ker, C. S. A bibliography of Lovelace. 1949.

Collections

Lucasta. Ed S. W. S[inger], 1817–18. Originally issued as vols 1 and 4 of Select Early English poets.

Lucasta. Ed W. C. Hazlitt 1864, 1897.

Lucasta: I, Epodes, odes, sonnets, songs etc; II, Posthume poems. Ed H. Child 1904.

Lucasta. Ed W. L. Phelps 2 vols Chicago 1921.

Poems. Ed C. H. Wilkinson 2 vols Oxford 1925, 1 vol Oxford 1930.

§1

Lucasta: epodes, odes, sonnets, songs etc; to which is added Amarantha: a pastorall. 1649 (3 issues).

Lucasta; posthume poems. Ed D. P. Lovelace 2 pts 1659–60. Includes Elegies sacred to the memory of the author, 1660.

§2

Hartmann, C. The Cavalier spirit and its influence on the life and work of Lovelace. 1925.

Judson, A. C. Who was Lucasta? MP 23 1925.

Wilkinson, C. H. Poems vol 1. Introd.

— Lovelace. TLS 14 Aug 1937.

Evans, W. M. Lawes and Lovelace's Loose saraband. PMLA 54 1939.

— To Amathea. PQ 23 1944.

— An early Lovelace text. PMLA 60 1945.

— Lovelace's Mock song. PQ 24 1945.

— The rose: a song by Wilson and Lovelace. MLQ 7 1946.

— Lovelace's concept of prison life in the Vintage to the dungeon. PQ 26 1947.

— Tormenting fires. MLQ 9 1948.

Lindsay, P. For King or Parliament. 1949.

Pearson, N. H. Lovelace's To Lucasta, going to the warres. Explicator June 1949.

Hulme, E. W. Lovelace's Song to Althea. N & Q 4 March 1950.

Cutts, J. P. John Wilson and Lovelace's The rose. N & Q April 1953.

Berry, H. and E. K. Timings. Lovelace at court and a version of his The scrutinie. MLN 69 1954.

Nathan, N. Lovelace's Flie. N & Q Oct 1955.

Duncan-Jones, E. E. Two allusions in Lovelace's poems. MLR 51 1956.

— Lovelace and the great eclipse of 1652. N & Q Nov 1957.

Allen, D. C. An explication of Lovelace's The grassehopper. MLQ 18 1957.

Williamson, C. F. Two notes on the poems of Lovelace. MLR 52 1957.

Jones, G. F. Lov'd I not honour more: the durability of a literary motif. Comparative Lit 11 1959.

O'Regan, M. J. The fair beggar: decline of a baroque theme. MLR 55 1960.

Arens, J. C. Sarbiewski's Ode against tears imitated by Lovelace, Yalden and Watts. Neophilologus 47 1963.

Holland, N. N. Literary value: a psychoanalytic approach. Lit & Psychology 14 1964. *See* comment by R. Rogers, reply by Holland, and note by H. M. Richmond, ibid.

King, B. Green ice and a breast of proof. College Eng April 1965.

— The grasse-hopper and allegory. Ariel 1 1970.

Palmer, P. Lovelace: some unnoticed allusions to Carew. N & Q March 1967.

Söderholm, T. *See col 1170, above.*

Weidhorn, M. Richard Lovelace. New York 1970.

Wadsworth, R. L., jr. On the Snayl by Lovelace. MLR 65 1970.

Anselment, R. A. 'Griefe triumphant' and 'victorious sorrow': a reading of Lovelace's The falcon. JEGP 70 1971.

ANDREW MARVELL
1621–78

Bibliographies

Marvell tercentenary celebration: descriptive catalogue of exhibits. Hull 1921.

Spencer, T. and M. Van Doren. In Marvell: two essays and a bibliography, New York 1939.

Osborne, M. T. Advice-to-a-painter 1633–1856. Austin 1949. An annotated list.

Kuntz, J. M. In Poetry explication: a checklist of interpretations since 1925, Denver 1962.

Berry, L. E. Marvell: a bibliography of studies in metaphysical poetry 1939–60. Madison 1964.

Donovan, D. G. Marvell 1927–67: a checklist. 1969 (Elizabethan Bibliographies suppl).

The best bibliographies will be found in H. M. Margoliouth, Marvell's poems and letters vol 1, Oxford 1927, 1952, 1971 (both rev); and in P. Legouis, Marvell: poet, puritan, patriot, Paris 1928, Oxford 1965 (rev).

Collections

For anthologies, in which Marvell's poems have had an important place, see Legouis pp. 473–5. For Poems on affairs of state, in which Marvell's satires were included, see Margoliouth pp. 209–12; Poems on affairs of state, New Haven 1963–.

Miscellaneous poems by Andrew Marvell esq. 1681, Menston 1969 (facs). In all but 2 known copies the 3 Cromwell poems have been cancelled.

Works. Ed T. Cooke 2 vols 1726, 1772. Poems, satires and a few letters.

Works. Ed E. Thompson 3 vols 1776. Poems, satires, prose works and letters and a life by the editor.

Poetical works. Boston 1857, 1870, 1878 (in Poetical works of Milton and Marvell), [1880 or 1881].

Complete works in verse and prose. Ed A. B. Grosart 4 vols 1872–5.

Poems and satires. Ed G. A. Aitken 2 vols 1892, 1901 (ML).

Poems and some satires. Ed E. Wright 1904.

Miscellaneous poems. 1923.

Poems and letters. Ed H. M. Margoliouth 2 vols Oxford 1927 (complete except for prose), 1952 (corrected with addns), 1971 (rev P. Legouis and E. E. Duncan-Jones).

Poems printed from the unique copy in the British Museum with some other poems. Ed H. Macdonald 1952 (ML).

Selected poetry and prose. Ed D. Davison 1952.
Some poems. Ed J. Winny 1962.
Poems. Ed C. V. Wedgwood 1964 (Folio Soc).
The Latin poetry of Marvell. Ed W. A. McQueen and K. A. Rockwell, Univ of North Carolina Stud in Comparative Lit 34 1964 (with English trn).
Selected poetry. Ed F. Kermode 1967.
Selected poems. Ed P. G. Pugliatti, Bari 1967.
Complete poetry. Ed G. de F. Lord, New York 1968.
Poems. Ed M. Seymour-Smith 1969.

§1

An elegy upon the death of my Lord Francis Villiers. [1648]. Only known copy at Worcester College Oxford; anon; attribution not conclusively proved.
The first anniversary of the government under his Highness the Lord Protector. 1655.
The character of Holland. 1665, 1672.
Advice to a painter. [1679?]; rptd in State poems, 1689, 1697 etc. *See also John Denham, above.*
The rehearsal transpros'd. 1672, 1672, 1672 (pirated), 1672 (censored edn with addns and amendments), 1673.
The rehearsal transpros'd: the second part. 1673, 1674; ed D. I. B. Smith, Oxford 1971 (both pts).
Mr Smirke. 1676, 1681.
An account of the growth of Popery. Amsterdam 1677, [1678]; rptd in State tracts 1689, 1693.
Remarks upon a late disingenuous discourse by T.D. 1678; ed J. Brown, Theological tracts vol 3, Edinburgh 1853–4.
A short historical essay. 1680, 1687, 1703.

§2

Miège, G. A relation of three embassies from his sacred Majestie Charles II to the Great Duke of Muscovie, the King of Sweden and the King of Denmark; written by an attendant on the embassies. 1669.
Wood, A. In his Athenae oxonienses, 2 vols Oxford 1691–2; ed P. Bliss 6 vols 1813–20.
Cooke, T. Life. Prefixed to his edn, 1726 above.
Biographia britannica vol 5. 1760.
Thompson, E. Life. Prefixed to his edn, 1776, above.
Landor, W. S. In his Lingering conversations, 5 vols 1824–9.
Dove, J. The life of Marvell, the celebrated patriot; with extracts and selections from his prose and poetical works. 1832.
Coleridge, H. The life of Marvell. Hull 1835. The Dove-Coleridge life also appeared, with considerable variations, in Biographia borealis, 1833, and Lives of illustrious worthies of Yorkshire, 1835.
Aubrey, J. In his Brief lives, ed A. Clark 2 vols Oxford 1898; ed E. G. McGehee, Oxford 1973.
Beeching, H. C. The lyrical poems of Marvell. Nat Rev July 1901.
Birrell, A. Marvell. 1905 (EML).
Poscher, R. Marvells poetische Werke. Vienna 1908.
Marvell tercentenary tributes. 1922.
Margoliouth, H. M. Marvell: some biographical points. MLR 17 1922.
— Marvell in Rome. TLS 5 June 1924.
— Marvell's Thyrsis and Dorinda. TLS 19 May 1950.
Legouis, P. Marvell: further biographical points. MLR 18 1923.
— Marvell's Maniban. RES 2 1926.
— Marvell: poète, puritain, patriote. Paris 1928; tr Oxford 1965 (abridged), 1968 (rev).
— Marvell and Addison. RES 10 1934.
— Marvell and Massinger: a source of the Definition of love. RES 23 1947.
— La purge de Gargantua ou Marvell et Tallemant des Reaux. Etudes Anglaises 6 1953.
— Notes on Marvell. N & Q May 1953.

— Marvell and the new critics. RES new ser 8 1957.
— Marvell's grasshoppers. N & Q March 1958.
— Marvell and 'the two learned brothers of St Marthe'. PQ 38 1959.
— Marvell's Nymph complaining for the death of her faun: a *mise au point.* MLQ 21 1960.
Eliot, T. S. Andrew Marvell. TLS 31 March 1921; rptd in his Homage to John Dryden, 1924 and in his Selected essays, 1932.
Sackville-West, V. Marvell. 1929.
Empson, W. Marvell's Garden. In his Some versions of pastoral, 1935.
Robbins, C. A note on an otherwise unprinted speech by Marvell. MLR 31 1936.
— Documents: Carlisle and Marvell in Russia, Sweden and Denmark 1663–4. History of Ideas Newsletter 3 1957.
— A Marvell letter. TLS 19 Dec 1958.
— Marvell to Sir Henry Thompson. TLS 20 March 1959.
— Marvell's religion: was he a new Methodist? JHI 23 1962.
— Six letters by Marvell. Etudes Anglaises 17 1964.
Wattie, M. The death of Marvell. TLS 2 May 1936. Reply by C. Robbins 9 May 1936.
Hennecke, H. Marvell. Europäische Revue 13 1937.
French, J. M. Notes on two puritan poets, Marvell and Wither. N & Q 16 April 1938.
King, A. H. Some notes on Marvell's Garden. E Studies 20 1938.
Tupper, F. S. Mary Palmer, alias Mrs Marvell. PMLA 53 1938.
Ward, C. E. Marvell's widow. TLS 14 May 1938.
Brooks, H. F. Authorship of Britannia and Rawleigh: additional evidence against ascription to Marvell. N & Q 31 Aug 1940.
Putt, S. G. Mosaiques of the air: a note on Marvell. English 2 1939.
Bradbrook, M. C. and M. G. Lloyd Thomas. Andrew Marvell. Cambridge 1940.
Daniel, R. To his coy mistress. Explicator March 1943.
Rainbow, M. F. Marvell and nature. Durham Univ Jnl 37 1945.
Sedgwick, A. Marvell. TLS 27 Oct 1945.
Davies, G. The date of Britannia and Rawleigh. HLQ 9 1946.
Hill, C. Society and Marvell. Modern Quart 4 1946.
— Marvell and the 'good old cause'. Mainstream 12 1959.
Orwen, W. R. Marvell's The garden. N & Q 14 Dec 1946.
— Marvell and Buckingham. N & Q 6 Jan 1951.
— Marvell's 'narrow case'. N & Q May 1955.
— Marvell's 'bergamot'. N & Q Aug 1955.
Walton, G. The poetry of Marvell: a summing up. Politics & Letters no 4 1948.
Duncan-Jones, E. E. Marvell in 1656. TLS 2 Dec 1949.
— Notes on Marvell's poems. N & Q March, Oct 1953. Reply by H. M. Margoliouth, May 1953.
— Milton and Marvell. TLS 31 July 1953.
— T.C. of A prospect of flowers. TLS 30 Oct 1953.
— Marvell and the Cinque Ports. TLS 11 Nov 1955.
— Marvell his own critic. N & Q Sept 1956.
— Benlowes, Marvell and the divine Casimire: a note. HLQ 20 1957.
— Marvell's Inscribenda luparae. TLS 26 April 1957. *See also* M. Toynbee, Verses on the Louvre, 17 May, and P. Legouis 4 Oct 1957.
— Marvell's 'friend in Persia'. N & Q Nov 1957.
— New allusions to Marvell. TLS 20 June 1958.
— Marvell, Johnson and the first sunset. TLS 3 April 1959.
— Marvell and the song In guilty night. TLS 9 Sept 1960.
— The erect sword in Marvell's Horatian ode. Etudes Anglaises 15 1962.
— Marvell's letter to John Trott. N & Q Jan 1966.

—— Smart and Marvell. N & Q May 1967.

—— 'J.W.' and a lost portrait of Marvell by Lely. N & Q Nov 1968.

—— Marvell's quotation from Rochester. N & Q May 1972. *See also Phare, 1963 below.*

Osborne, M. T. Advice-to-a-painter poems. Austin 1949.

Turner, W. A. Milton, Marvell and 'Dradon' at Cromwell's funeral. PQ 28 1949.

Garvin, K. Marvell the anchorite. TLS 11 Aug 1950.

Klonsky, M. A guide through the garden. Sewanee Rev 58 1950.

Wallerstein, R. C. In her Studies in seventeenth-century poetic, Madison 1950.

Muir, K. A Virgilian echo in Marvell. N & Q 17 March 1951.

—— Marvell. Univ of Leeds Rev 3 1952.

Macdonald, H. Marvell's Miscellaneous poems 1681. TLS 13 July, 24 Aug 1951.

Martin, L. C. Marvell, Massinger and Sidney. RES new ser 2 1951.

McChesney, J. Marvell's The garden. Explicator Oct 1951. Reply by D. A. Keister, ibid.

Proudfoot, L. Marvell: Sallust and the Horatian ode. N & Q 19 July 1951.

Blakiston, N. Marvell at Eton. TLS 8 Feb 1952.

Bühler, C. F. A letter by Marvell. N & Q 11 Oct 1952.

Bush, D. Marvell and Sidney. RES new ser 3 1952.

—— Marvell's Horatian ode. Sewanee Rev 60 1952. Reply by C. Brooks 61 1953.

Cutts, J. P. Marvell's Thyrsis and Dorinda. TLS 8 Aug 1952.

Kermode, F. Two notes on M. N & Q 29 March, 10 May 1952.

—— The argument of Marvell's The garden. EC 2 1952.

—— Definitions of love. RES new ser 7 1956.

—— Marvell transprosed. Encounter Nov 1966.

Le Comte, E. S. Marvell's The nymph complaining for the death of her faun. MP 50 1952. Reply by K. Williamson 51 1954.

Simeone, W. A probable antecedent of Marvell's Horatian ode. N & Q 19 July 1952.

Day, R. A. Marvell's 'glew'. PQ 32 1953.

Gwynn, F. L. Marvell's To his coy mistress. Explicator May 1953.

Howarth, R. G. Marvell: an emendation. N & Q Aug 1953.

Summers, J. H. Marvell's 'nature'. ELH 20 1953.

—— Marvell's political poetry. Seventeenth-century News 21 1963.

Winny, J. A Marvell emendation. TLS 2 Oct 1953.

Withington, E. Marvell and Montague: another source for the Definition of love. RES new ser 4 1953.

Røstvig, M.-S. Benlowes, Marvell and the divine Casimire. HLQ 18 1954.

—— Marvell's The garden: a hermetic poem. E Studies 40 1959.

—— Upon Appleton House and the universal history of man. E Studies 42 1961.

Davison, D. Marvell and politics. N & Q May 1955.

—— Marvell's The definition of love. RES new ser 6 1955.

—— A Marvell allusion in Ward's diary. N & Q Jan 1955.

—— Notes on Marvell's To his coy mistress. N & Q Dec 1958.

—— Marvell's poems. 1964.

—— Notes on Marvell's The garden. N & Q Jan 1966.

Emerson, E. H. Marvell's The nymph complaining on the death of her faun. Etudes Anglaises 8 1955. Reply by P. Legouis, ibid.

Foster, R. E. A tonal study: Marvell. Univ of Kansas City Rev 22 1955.

Lerner, L. D. Marvell: an Horatian ode. In Interpretations, ed J. Wain 1955.

Senn, G. T. The text of Marvell's poems. N & Q July 1955.

Allen, D. C. Marvell's Nymph. ELH 23 1956.

—— Love in a grave. MLN 74 1959.

Bradbrook, F. W. The poetry of Marvell. In The Pelican guide to English literature vol 3, ed B. Ford 1956.

Farnham, A. E. Saint Teresa and the coy mistress. Boston Univ Stud in Eng 2 1956.

Hibbard, G. R. The country house poem of the seventeenth century. Jnl Warburg & Courtauld Inst 19 1956.

Hyman, L. W. Ideas in Marvell's poetry. History of Ideas Newsletter 2 1956.

—— Marvell's Garden. ELH 25 1958.

—— Politics and poetry in Marvell. PMLA 73 1958.

—— Marvell's Coy mistress and desperate lover. MLN 75 1960.

—— Marvell. New York 1964.

—— Marvell's Coy mistress as fact or poem. MLQ 26 1965.

—— Andrew Marvell. 1968.

Sasek, L. A. Marvell's To his coy mistress. Explicator April 1956.

Sedelow, W. A., jr. Marvell's To his coy mistress. MLN 71 1956.

Carens, J. F. Marvell's Cromwell poems. Bucknell Rev 7 1957.

Colie, R. L. Marvell's Bermudas and the puritan paradise. Renaissance News 10 1957.

—— My ecchoing song: Marvell's poetry of criticism. Princeton 1970.

Grundy, J. Marvell's grasshoppers. N & Q April 1957.

Iser, W. To his coy mistress. Die Neueren Sprachen Dec 1957.

Isham, G. Abram van den Bempde. N & Q Nov 1957.

Wall, L. N. Marvell and the third Dutch war. N & Q July 1957.

—— Some notes on Marvell's sources. N & Q April 1957.

—— A note on Marvell's letters. N & Q March 1958.

—— Marvell of Meldreth. N & Q Sept 1958.

—— Marvell's friends in the city. N & Q June 1959.

—— Marvell and Seneca. N & Q May 1961.

—— Marvell and the Skinners. N & Q June 1962.

—— Thomas Randolph and Marvell's Coy mistress. N & Q March 1968.

Wheatcroft, J. Marvell and the winged chariot. Bucknell Rev 6 1957.

Brant, R. L. Hawthorne and Marvell. Amer Lit 30 1958.

Lord, G. de F. Two new poems by Marvell? BNYPL Nov 1958.

—— From contemplation to action: Marvell's poetical career. PQ 46 1967.

—— (ed). Marvell: a collection of critical essays. Englewood Cliffs NJ 1968.

Putney, R. Our vegetable love: Marvell and Burton. In Studies in honor of T. W. Baldwin, Urbana 1958.

Press, J. Andrew Marvell. 1958 (Br Council pamphlet).

Saveson, J. E. Marvell's On a drop of dew. N & Q July 1958.

Sharrock, R. The date of Marvell's To his coy mistress. TLS 31 Oct 1958. Replies by E. E. Duncan-Jones 5 Dec 1958, Sharrock 16 Jan 1959.

Skelton, R. Rowland Watkins and Marvell. N & Q Dec 1958. Reply by M. H. Dodds, June 1959.

Spitzer, L. Marvell's Nymph complaining for the death of her faun: sources versus meaning. MLQ 19 1958.

Allentuck, M. E. Marvell's 'pool of air'. MLN 74 1959.

Bain, C. E. The Latin poetry of Marvell. PQ 38 1959.

Carroll, J. J. The sun and the lovers in To his coy mistress. MLN 74 1959.

Coolidge, J. S. Martin Marprelate, Marvell, and 'decorum personae' as a satirical theme. PMLA 74 1959.

—— Marvell and Horace. MP 63 1965.

Corder, J. Marvell and nature. N & Q Feb 1959.

Fogel, E. G. The case for internal evidence. BNYPL June 1959. Replies by G. de F. Lord and A. Sherbo, July 1959.

Schmitter, D. M. Marvell's 'treasurer'. N & Q July–Aug 1959.

—— The occasion for Marvell's Growth of Popery. JHI 31 1960.

—— and P. Legouis. The cartography of the Definition of love. RES new ser 12 1961.

Alvarez, A. Marvell and the poetry of judgment. Hudson Rev 13 1960.

Colaiacomo, P. Alcuni aspetti della poesia di Marvell. Eng Miscellany (Rome) 11 1960.

Mazzeo, J. A. Cromwell as Machiavellian Prince in Marvell's An Horatian ode. JHI 21 1960. Reply by H. Baron, ibid.

—— Cromwell as Davidic King. In Reason and the imagination, ed Mazzeo, New York 1962.

—— In his Renaissance and seventeenth-century studies, New York 1964.

Millgate, M. The two voices of Marvell. Listener 21 April 1960.

Mitchell, C. Marvell's The mower to the glo-worms. Explicator May 1960.

Rosenberg, J. D. Marvell and the Christian idiom. Boston Univ Stud in Eng 4 1960.

Salerno, N. A. Marvell's The unfortunate lover. Explicator April 1960.

—— Marvell and the 'furor hortensis'. Stud in Eng Lit 1500–1900 8 1968.

Chambers, A. B. 'I was but an inverted tree': notes towards the history of an idea. Stud in Renaissance 8 1961.

Gérard, A. S. Marvell's An Horatian ode upon Cromwell's return from Ireland 118. Explicator Nov 1961.

Leishman, J. B. Some themes and variations in the poetry of Marvell. Proc Br Acad 47 1961.

—— The art of Marvell's poetry. Ed J. Butt 1966, 1968 (rev).

Maxwell, J. C. Marvell. N & Q Aug 1961.

—— Two notes on Marvell's language. N & Q Oct 1968.

—— Marvell and logic. N & Q July 1970.

Syfret, R. H. Marvell's Horatian ode. RES new ser 12 1961.

Vortriede, W. Ein Gedicht von Marvell. Neue Rundschau 72 1961.

Wallace, J. M. Marvell's 'lusty mate' and the ship of the commonwealth. MLN 76 1961.

—— Marvell's Horatian ode. PMLA 77 1962.

—— Marvell and Cromwell's kingship: the first anniversary. ELH 30 1963.

—— Destiny his choice: the loyalism of Marvell. Cambridge 1968.

Williamson, G. The context of Marvell's Hortus and Garden. MLN 76 1961.

—— Bias in Marvell's Horatian ode. In his Milton and others, 1965.

Cinquemani, A. M. Marvell's The mower against gardens. Explicator May 1962.

Everett, B. Marvell's The mower's song. CQ 4 1962.

Hecht, A. Shades of Keats and Marvell. Hudson Rev 15 1962.

Miller, B. E. Logic in Marvell's To his coy mistress. North Dakota Quart 30 1962.

Patrick, J. M. Marvell's The unfortunate lover. Explicator April 1962.

Pitman, M. R. Marvell and Sir Henry Wotton. RES new ser 13 1962.

Swardson, H. R. Poetry and the fountain of light. 1962.

Toliver, H. E. Marvell's Definition of love and poetry of self-exploration. Bucknell Rev 10 1962.

—— Pastoral form and idea in some poems of Marvell. SE 5 1963.

—— The strategy of Marvell's Resolve against created pleasure. Stud in Eng Lit 1500–1900 4 1964.

—— Marvell's ironic vision. 1965.

Brett, R. L. Marvell. Time & Tide 21 March 1963.

Brooks, C. Literary criticism: Marvell's Horatian ode. In Explication as criticism, ed W. K. Wimsatt jr, New York 1963.

Goldberg, J. P. Two Tennysonian allusions to a poem of Marvell. N & Q July 1963.

Hogan, P. G., jr. Marvell's 'vegetable love'. SP 60 1963.

Phare, E. E. Marvell's Switzer tulips. TLS 12 April 1963.

Stewart, S. N. Marvell and the garden enclosed. Seventeenth-century News 21 1963.

Hartman, G. H. Marvell, St Paul and the body of hope. ELH 31 1964.

—— The nymph complaining for the death of her faun: a brief allegory. EC 18 1968.

Hartwig, J. The principle of measure in To his coy mistress. College Eng May 1964.

Holditch, K. Marvell's The garden. Explicator Sept 1964.

MacCaffrey, I. G. Some notes on Marvell's poetry, suggested by a reading of his prose. MP 61 1964.

Simmons, J. L. Marvell's The picture of little T.C. in a prospect of flowers. Explicator 22 1964.

Zwicky, L. Marvell's The definition of love. Explicator March 1964.

Calderwood, J. L. Marvell's The coronet. Eng Record 15 1965.

Goldberg, S. L. Marvell: self and art. Melbourne Critical Rev 8 1965.

McQueen, W. A. The missing stanzas in Marvell's Hortus. PQ 44 1965.

Nevo, R. Marvell's Songs of innocence and experience. Stud in Eng Lit 1500–1900 5 1965.

Reese, J. E. Marvell's Nymph in a new light. Etudes Anglaises 18 1965. Reply by P. Legouis, ibid.

Schulze, E. J. The reach of wit: Marvell's The definition of love. Papers of Michigan Acad 50 1965.

Warnke, F. J. Play and metamorphosis in Marvell's poetry. Stud in Eng Lit 1500–1900 5 1965.

Berthoff, A. E. The voice of allegory: Marvell's The unfortunate lover. MLQ 27 1966.

—— The allegorical metaphor: Marvell's The definition of love. RES new ser 17 1966.

Datta, K. Marvell's prose and poetry: more notes. MP 63 1966.

—— Marvell and Wotton: a reconsideration. RES new ser 19 1968.

Godshalk, W. L. Marvell's The mower to the glo-worms. Explicator Oct 1966.

Miner, E. The 'poetic picture, painted poetry' of the Last instructions to a painter. MP 63 1966.

—— The death of innocence in Marvell's Nymph complaining for the death of her faun. MP 65 1967.

Smith, D. The political beliefs of Marvell. UTQ 36 1966.

Sutherland, J. R. A note on the satirical poetry of Marvell. PQ 45 1966.

Tysdahl, B. J. Marvell's The garden. N & Q May 1966.

Walcutt, C. C. Marvell's The garden. Explicator Jan 1966.

Benjamin, E. B. Marvell's Bermudas. CEA Critic 29 1967.

Berger, H., jr. Marvell's Garden: still another interpretation. MLQ 28 1967.

—— Marvell: The poem as green world. Forum for Modern Lang Stud 3 1967.

Calderhead, J. C. The cherry and the laurel: a note on the source of lines in stanza 10 of the Garden by Abraham Cowley. N & Q Sept 1967.

Field, P. J. Marvell and the Rape of the lock. N & Q Nov 1967.

Hofmann, K. Das Bild in Marvells lyrischen Gedichten. Heidelberg 1967.

King, B. In search of Marvell. REL 8 1967.

—— 'The mower against gardens' and the Levellers. HLQ 33 1970.

Parish, J. Back to the Bermudas. CEA Critic 30 1967.

Stempel, D. The Garden: Marvell's Cartesian extasy. JHI 28 1967.

Stewart, S. The enclosed garden: the tradition and image in seventeenth-century poetry. 1966.

Wood, W. J. Marvell's An Horatian ode upon Cromwell's return from Ireland. Theoria 28 1967.

Guild, N. Marvell's The nymph complaining for the death of her faun. MLQ 29 1968.

French, A. L. Dryden, Marvell and political poetry. Stud in Eng Lit 1500–1900 8 1968.

Jones, E. Marvell's The nymph complaining for the death of her faun. Explicator May 1968.

Moldenhaur, J. J. The voices of seduction in To his coy mistress: a rhetorical analysis. SE 10 1968.

Solomon, J. A reading of Marvell's Garden. Eng Stud in Africa 11 1968.

Wilcher, R. Details from the natural histories in Marvell's poetry. N & Q March 1968.

— Marvell's cherry: a reply to Mr Salerno. Etudes Anglaises 23 1970.

Wilding, M. Marvell and the Rape of the lock. N & Q Oct 1968.

— Marvell's reputation for patriotism and probity. N & Q July 1970.

Wilding, M. (ed). Marvell: modern judgements. 1969.

Winterton, J. B. Some notes on Marvell's Bermudas. N & Q March 1968.

Carey, J. (ed). Marvell: a critical anthology. 1969 (Pelican).

Wilson, A. J. N. Marvell, An Horatian ode upon Cromwel's return from Ireland: the thread of the poem and its use of classical allusion. CQ 11 1969.

Anselment, R. A. Satiric strategy in Marvell's The rehearsal transpros'd. MP 68 1970.

— 'Betwixt jest and earnest': ironic reversal in Marvell's The rehearsal transpros'd. MLR 66 1971.

Berthoff, A. E. The resolved soul: a study of Marvell's major poems. Princeton 1970.

Carpenter, M. From Herbert to Marvell: poetics in A wreath and the Coronet. JEGP 69 1970.

— Marvell's Garden. Stud in Eng Lit 1500–1900 10 1970.

Carscallen, J. Marvell's infinite parallels. UTQ 39 1970.

Creaser, J. Marvell's effortless superiority. EC 20 1970.

Cummings, R. M. The difficulty of Marvell's Bermudas. MP 67 1970.

Evett, D. 'Paradice's only map': the 'topos' of the 'locus amoenus' and the structure of Marvell's Upon Appleton House. PMLA 85 1970.

Friedman, D. M. Marvell's pastoral art. 1970.

Kelliher, W. H. A new text of Marvell's To his coy mistress. N & Q July 1970.

Gearin-Tosh, M. Marvell's Last instructions: textual errors and their poetic significance. Studia Neophilologica 42 1970.

— Marvell's Sad tortoise. N & Q July 1970.

— Marvell's steward. Ibid.

Gransden, K. W. Time, guilt and pleasure: a note on Marvell's nostalgia. Ariel 1 1970.

Rollin, R. B. Images of libertinism in Every man in his humor and To his coy mistress. Papers on Lang & Lit 6 1970.

Serio, J. N. Marvell's The garden: an anagogic reading. Ohio Univ Rev 12 1970.

Söderholm, T. See col 1170, above.

Summers, C. J. The frightened architects of Marvell's Horatian ode. Seventeenth-century News 28 1970.

Dorenkamp, A. G. Marvell's geometry of love. Eng Lang Notes 9 1971.

Wilson, R. Marvell's Denton. TLS 26 Nov 1971. Replies by J. Newman 28 Jan 1972, A. A. Tait 11 Feb, J. Turner 31 March 1972.

Burdon, P. H. Marvell and Richard Flecknoe in Rome. N & Q Jan 1972.

HENRY VAUGHAN
'Silurist'
1622–95

Bibliographies etc

Marilla, E. L. A comprehensive bibliography of Vaughan. Tuscaloosa 1948.

— and J. D. Simmonds. Vaughan: a bibliographical supplement 1946–60. Tuscaloosa 1963.

Berry, L. E. In his A bibliography of studies in metaphysical poetry 1939–60, Madison 1964.

Tuttle, I. Concordance to Vaughan's Silex scintillans. University Park Pa 1969.

Collections

Complete works. Ed A. B. Grosart 4 vols 1870–1. With poems of Thomas Vaughan.

Secular poems. Ed J. R. Tutin, Hull 1893.

Poems. Ed E. K. Chambers, introd by H. C. Beeching 2 vols 1896 (ML).

Sacred poems: being a selection. 1897.

Poems. Ed I. Gollancz 1900.

Golden thoughts from Vaughan selected by W. R. Nicoll. Glasgow [1902].

Heavens way, selected from works of Vaughan by A. L. J. Gosset. 1903 (for 1902).

Poems. Ed E. Hutton 1904.

Works. Ed L. C. Martin 2 vols Oxford 1914, 1 vol Oxford 1957 (rev). With bibliography.

Vaughan and Marvell: a choice from their poems by F. Meynell. 1918.

Poems, and essays and two letters. Ed F[rancis] M[eynell] 1924.

Poems. Gregynog 1924. Selected by E. Rhys.

Henry Vaughan, Silurist. Ed F[rancis] M[eynell] 1924. (Nonesuch Press). Selection.

The fantasticks: Donne, Herbert, Crashaw, Vaughan. Ed W. S. Scott 1946.

Secular poems. Ed E. L. Marilla, Upsala, Cambridge Mass and Copenhagen 1958.

Selected prose and verse. Ed L. C. Martin, Oxford 1963 (OSA).

Complete poetry. Ed F. Fogle, New York 1965.

Selection from Vaughan. Ed C. Dixon 1967.

§ I

Poems, with the tenth satyre of Juvenal englished. 1646.

Silex scintillans: or sacred poems and private ejaculations. 1650, 1655 ('second edition in two books', i.e. an augmented reissue), 1847 (with memoir by H. F. Lyte), Boston 1856, 1858, 1883; ed W. Clare 1885 (facs); ed I. Gollancz 1900; ed W. A. Lewis Bettany [1905]; Leeds 1968 (facs). See col 1913, below.

Olor iscanus: a collection of some select poems, and translations, published by a friend. 1651, 1679. Prose trn from Plutarch, Maximus Tyrius and Guevara.

The Mount of Olives: or solitary devotions. 1652; ed L. I. Guiney 1902; ed B. H. Wall 1904.

Flores solitudinis: certaine rare and elegant pieces, viz two excellent discourses of 1, temperance and patience; 2, life and death, by I[ohannes] E[usebius] Nierembergius; The world contemned, by Eucherius, Bp of Lyons, and the life of Paulinus, Bp of Nola, collected in his sickness and retirement by Vaughan. 1654. Each of the 3 sections has separate title-page; all are trns from Jesuit works.

Hermetical physick, by Henry Nollius, englished. 1655.

The chymists key to open and to shut: or the true doctrine of corruption and generation, written by Hen. Nollius, published by Eugenius Philalethes. 1657 (for 1655?). Trn of Nollius, De generatione, 1615. Attributed by L. C. Martin, below.

Thalia rediviva: the pass-times and diversions of a country-muse, in choice poems on several occasions; with some learned remains of the eminent Eugenius Philalethes [Thomas Vaughan]. 1678.

§2

Vaughan's Olor Iscanus. Retrospective Rev 3 1821.

Brown, J. In his Horae subsecivae ser 1, 1858.

Shairp, J. C. In his Sketches in history and poetry, 1887.

Guiney, L. I. In her A little English gallery, New York 1894.

Palgrave, F. T. In his Landscape in poetry, 1897.

Letters of Oxford Welshmen. Ed R. Ellis, Oxford 1903 (facs).

Sichel, E. Vaughan, Silurist. Monthly Rev April 1903.

Spens, J. Two periods of disillusion. 1909.

Johnson, L. In his Post liminium: essays and critical papers, 1911.

Hodgeson, G. E. A study in illumination. [1914].

Heide, Anna von der. Das Naturgefühl in der englischen Dichtung im Zeitalter Miltons. Heidelberg 1915.

Vaughan and Herrick. Athenæum 12 June 1915.

The poetry of Vaughan. TLS 15 July 1915.

Brett-Smith, H. F. B. Vaughan and D'Avenant. MLR 11 1916.

Bensly, E. Notes on Vaughan. MLR 14 1919.

Clutton-Brock, A. In his More essays on books, 1921.

Loudon, K. M. Two mystic poets. 1922. Crashaw and Vaughan.

Henry Vaughan. TLS 20 April 1922.

Merrill, L. R. Vaughan's influence upon Wordsworth's poetry. MLN 37 1922.

Wells, H. W. Tercentenary of Vaughan. 1922.

Sencourt, R. Out-flying philosophy. 1925.

Lucas, F. L. In his Authors dead and living, 1926.

Judson, A. C. Cornelius Agrippa and Henry Vaughan. MLN 41 1926.

—— Vaughan as a nature poet. PMLA 42 1927.

—— The source of Vaughan's ideas concerning God in nature. SP 24 1927.

Blunden, E. On the poems of Vaughan, with his principal Latin poems translated into English verse. 1927.

Eliot, T. S. The Silurist. Dial Sept 1927.

Martin, L. C. Vaughan and Cowper. MLR 22 1927.

More, P. E. In his New Shelburne essays vol 5, Princeton 1928.

Holmes, E. Vaughan and the Hermetic philosophy. Oxford 1932.

Morgan, G. E. F. Henry Vaughan, Silurist. TLS 3 Nov 1932.

Clough, W. O. Vaughan and the Hermetic philosophy. PMLA 48 1933.

Smith, A. J. Some relations between Henry Vaughan and Thomas Vaughan. Papers of Michigan Acad 18 1933. See R. M. Wardle, PMLA 2 1936.

Bennett, J. In her Four metaphysical poets, Cambridge 1934, 1953 (rev as Five metaphysical poets).

Leishman, J. B. In his Metaphysical poets: Donne, Herbert, Vaughan, Traherne, Oxford 1934.

McMaster, H. N. Vaughan and Wordsworth. RES 11 1935.

Galland, R. Poèmes de Vaughan. Hermes 2 1936. French trn of Night and Cock-crowing, with commentary.

Howarth, R. G. Vaughan and Boethius. N & Q 25 July 1936.

—— Notes on Vaughan. N & Q Feb 1960, May 1961, Oct 1962.

Edwards, J. G. Vaughan and Jesus College. Jesus College Mag (Oxford) 1937.

Martin, L. C. Vaughan and the theme of infancy. In Seventeenth-century studies presented to Sir Herbert Grierson, Oxford 1938.

—— Vaughan and Hermes Trismegistus. RES 18 1942.

—— Vaughan and the Chymists key. TLS 11 Dec 1953.

Wagner, H. Das Weltbild Vaughans. Heidelberg 1939.

Parker, W. R. Vaughan and his publishers. Library 4th ser 20 1940.

Hughes, M. Y. The theme of pre-existence and infancy in the Retreate. PQ 20 1941.

Attwater, D. Vaughan, the Silurist: a Christian poet. Catholic World 153 1941.

Marilla, E. L. Vaughan and the Civil War. JEGP 41 1942.

—— Henry and Thomas Vaughan. MLR 39 1944.

—— The significance of Vaughan's literary reputation. MLQ 5 1944.

—— The religious conversion of Vaughan. RES 21 1945.

—— Vaughan's conversion: a recent view. MLN 63 1948.

—— Vaughan to Sir William Davenant. PQ 27 1948.

—— 'The publisher to the reader' of Olor Iscanus. RES 24 1948.

—— The secular and religious poetry of Vaughan. MLQ 9 1948.

—— Vaughan. JEGP 57 1958.

—— Vagaries of modern literary criticism. In Studies in English Renaissance literature, ed W. F. McNeir, Baton Rouge 1962.

—— The mysticism of Vaughan: some observations. RES new ser 18 1967.

Walley, H. R. The strange case of Olor Iscanus. RES 18 1942. Reply by F. E. Hutchinson, ibid.

Allen, D. C. Vaughan's The ass. MLN 58 1943.

—— Vaughan's Salome on ice. PQ 23 1944.

—— Vaughan's Cock-crowing and the tradition. ELH 21 1954.

Vaughan's Peace. Explicator April 1943.

Simpson, P. Vaughan's epitaph. N & Q 28 Aug 1943. Reply by F. E. Hutchinson 20 May 1944.

Stewart, B. T. The meaning of Silex Scintillans. PQ 22 1943.

—— Hermetic symbolism in Vaughan's The night. PQ 29 1950.

Robertson, J. The use made of Owen Felltham's Resolves: a study in plagiarism. MLR 39 1944. Influence on Vaughan et al.

Svendsen, K. Vaughan's Man. Explicator June 1944.

Lehmann, R. P. Vaughan and Welsh poetry. PQ 24 1945.

Childe, W. R. Vaughan. Essays by Divers Hands 22 1946.

Reynolds, L. Vaughan. Dublin Mag 21 1946.

Cheek, P. M. The Latin element in Vaughan. SP 44 1947.

Hutchinson, F. E. Vaughan: a life and interpretation. Oxford 1947.

Marsh, E. Vaughan. TLS 19 July 1947.

Walters, R. H. Vaughan and the alchemists. RES 23 1947.

Cropper, M. B. In her Flame touches flame, 1949.

Margoliouth, H. M. A Vaughan emendation. N & Q 14 May 1949.

Kermode, J. F. The private imagery of Vaughan. RES new ser 1 1950.

Bethell, S. L. The poetry of Vaughan. In his Cultural revolution of the seventeenth century, 1951.

—— The theology of Henry and Thomas Vaughan. Theology 56 1953.

Erede, A. Un delicato poeta del Seicento inglese: Vaughan. Studium 48 1951.

Stead, W. F. Some unknown verses by Vaughan. TLS 8 Feb 1952.

Craig, G. A. and F. Gilbert. Vaughan and the Chymists key. TLS 11 Dec 1953.

de la Mare, W. In his Private view, 1953.

Williamson, E. W. Henry Vaughan. 1953.

Oliver, H. J. The mysticism of Vaughan: a reply. JEGP 53 1954.

Martz, L. L. In his Poetry of meditation, New Haven 1954, 1962 (rev).

—— Vaughan: the man within. PMLA 78 1963.

—— In his Paradise within, New Haven 1964.

Barksdale, R. K. The nature of Vaughan. Western Humanities Rev 9 1955.

Esch, A. In his Englische religiöse Lyrik des 17 Jahr-hunderts, Tübingen 1955.

Gesner, C. A note on Vaughan. MLR 50 1955.

Perrine, L., M. Emslie and C. Turner Wright. Vaughan's The queer. Explicator May 1955.

Rickey, M. E. Crashaw and Vaughan. N & Q June 1955.

Francis, W. N. Vaughan's The waterfall. Explicator June 1956.

Hilberry, C. Vaughan's The morning-watch. Explicator April 1956.

Pettet, E. C. A simile in Vaughan. TLS 27 Jan 1956.

— Of paradise and light: a study of Vaughan's Silex Scintillans. Cambridge 1960.

Durr, R. A. Vaughan's theme and its pattern: Regenera-tion. SP 54 1957.

— Vaughan's The night. JEGP 51 1960.

— Vaughan's pilgrim and the birds of night: the Proffer. MLQ 21 1961.

— Vaughan's spring on the hill. MLN 76 1961.

— On the mystical poetry of Vaughan. Cambridge Mass 1962.

Madsen, W. G. A reading of Musicks duell. In Studies in honor of J. Wilcox, Detroit 1958.

Raby, F. J. E. Vaughan's glittering flint. TLS 28 Feb 1958. See G. Midgley 7 March 1958.

Farnham, F. The imagery of Vaughan's The night. PQ 38 1959.

Garner, R. Vaughan. Chicago 1959.

— The unprofitable servant in Vaughan. Lincoln Nebraska 1963.

Røstvig, M.-S. The happy man: studies in the metamor-phosis of a classical ideal 1600–1700. Oslo and Oxford 2 vols 1954–9, 1962 (rev).

— Syncretistic imagery and the unity of Vaughan's The world. Papers on Lang & Lit 5 1969.

Ellrodt, R. In his L'inspiration personelle et l'esprit du temps chez les poètes métaphysiques anglais, Paris 1960.

Simmonds, J. D. The date of Vaughan's Silex Scintillans. N & Q Feb 1960.

— The problem of Vaughan's illness. Anglia 78 1960.

— The dedication of Vaughan's Silex Scintillans. E Studies 41 1960.

— Vaughan: imprisonment, Boethius and Owen Fell-tham. N & Q May 1961.

— The publication of Olor Iscanus. MLN 76 1961.

— Vaughan's 'To his friends . . .' N & Q Nov 1961.

— The identity of Vaughan's suppressed poems. MLQ 22 1961.

— Vaughan's masterpiece and its critics: the World revaluated. Stud in Eng Lit 1500–1900 2 1962.

— Some traditional oxymora in Vaughan's secular verse. Die Neueren Sprachen 11 1962.

— Vaughan and the great chain of being. In Studies in English Renaissance literature, ed W. F. McNeir, Baton Rouge 1962.

— Vaughan's The book: hermetic or meditative? Neophilologus 47 1963.

— Vaughan's Amoret and Etesia. PQ 42 1963.

— Vaughan's Fellow-prisoner. E Studies 45 1964.

Banzer, J. 'Compound manner': Emily Dickinson and the metaphysical poets. Amer Lit 32 1961.

Jennings, E. In her Every changing shape, 1961.

Olsen, P. A. Vaughan's The world: the pattern of meaning and the tradition. Comparative Lit 13 1961.

Praz, M. In his Literary resurrections, 1961.

Willy, M. In her Three metaphysical poets, 1961 (Br Council pamphlet).

Bowers, F. T. The star symbol in Vaughan's poetry. Renaissance Papers 1961.

— Vaughan's multiple time scheme. MLQ 23 1962.

Rudrum, A. W. Vaughan's The book: a hermetic poem. Jnl of Australian Universities Lang & Lit Assoc 1961.

— Vaughan and the theme of transfiguration. Southern Rev 1 1963.

— Vaughan's The night: some hermetic notes. MLR 64 1969.

— The influence of alchemy in the poems of Vaughan. PQ 49 1970.

— Vaughan's 'Welshness': the verb 'trample'. Eng Lang Notes 9 1971.

— Vaughan's The tempest: a source in Cornelius Agrippa. N & Q Jan 1972.

Lee, K.-S. The poetry of Vaughan. Eng Lang & Lit (Korea) 1962.

Rickey, M. E. Vaughan, the Temple and poetic form. SP 59 1962.

Daniels, E. F. Vaughan's The world 38–9. Explicator May 1964.

— Vaughan's 'regeneration': an emendation. Amer N & Q 9 1970.

Wiehe, R. E. Two images in Vaughan. E Studies 45 1964.

MacCaffrey, I. G. The meditative paradigm. ELH 32 1965.

Stein, A. The paradise within and the paradise without. MLQ 26 1965.

Williams, J. Abergavenny: historical notes. Abergavenny 1965.

Williamson, G. In his Milton and others, 1965.

— In his Six metaphysical poets, New York 1967.

Chambers, L. H. Vaughan's allusive technique: biblical allusions in the Night. MLQ 27 1966.

Datow, W. The water-fall von Vaughan. Die Neueren Sprachen 15 1966.

Jack, R. D. Scottish sonneteer and Welsh metaphysical: a study of the religious poetry of Sir William Mure and Vaughan. Stud in Scottish Lit 3 1966.

King, J. R. In his Studies in six 17th-century writers, Athens Ohio 1966.

Morris, B. R. Cleveland and Vaughan: some borrowings. N & Q July 1966.

Stewart, S. N. In his Enclosed garden: the tradition and the image in seventeenth-century poetry, Madison 1966.

Thorpe, M. Siegfried Sassoon. Leyden and Oxford 1966. On affinities of mood with Vaughan.

Harrold, W. Blake's Tyger and Vaughan's Cock-crowing. N & Q Jan 1967.

Leardi, M. La poesia di Vaughan. Florence 1967.

Low, A. Vaughan's The morning-watch. Explicator Oct 1967.

Pebworth, T.-L. The problem of Restagnates in Vaughan's The water-fall. Papers in Lang & Lit 3 1967.

Sandbank, S. Vaughan's Apology for darkness. Stud in Eng Lit 1500–1900 7 1967.

Wiese, G. A new source for Vaughan's Man in darkness. N & Q March 1967.

Bradford, M. E. A. Vaughan's The night: a consideration of metaphor and meditation. Arlington Quart 1 1968.

Chambers, L. H. Vaughan's The world: the limits of extrinsic criticism. Stud in Eng Lit 1500–1900 8 1968.

Goldknopf, D. The disintegration of symbol in a meditative poet. College Eng 30 1968.

Grant, P. Hermetic philosophy and the nature of man in Vaughan's Silex Scintillans. JEGP 67 1968.

Spitz, L. Process and stasis: aspects of nature in Vaughan and Marvell. HLQ 32 1969.

Stephens, J. Hermetic symbols and the Christian context in Vaughan's poetry. Eng Notes 3 1969.

Dale, J. Biblical allusion in Vaughan's The world. E Studies 51 1970.

Söderholm, T. See col 1170, above.

Wilson, G. E. A characteristic of Vaughan's style and two meditative poems, Corruption and Day of Judgement. Style 4 1970.

THOMAS TRAHERNE
1637–74

Bibliographies

Samaha, E. E., jr. Crashaw and Traherne: a bibliography 1938–66. Seventeenth-century News 27 1969.

Guffey, G. R. Traherne and the 17th-century Platonists 1900–66. 1969 (Elizabethan Bibliographies suppl).

Collections

Poetical works, now first published from the original manuscripts. Ed B. Dobell 1903.

Poetical works. Ed G. I. Wade 1932. The poems ptd in 1903, above, but in ms spelling, with poems from the Burney ms.

Centuries, poems and thanksgivings. Ed H. M. Margoliouth 2 vols Oxford 1958.

Poems, centuries and three thanksgivings. Ed A. Ridler, Oxford 1966 (OSA).

§ 1

Roman forgeries. 1673.

Christian ethicks: or divine morality opening the way to blessedness. 1675 (8 poems); ed M. Bottrall 1962 (modernized); ed G. R. Guffey and C. L. Marks, Ithaca 1968.

A serious and patheticall contemplation of the mercies of God. 1699 (anon, but identified by Dobell); ed R. Daniells, Toronto 1941.

Hexameron: or meditations on the six days of creation. 1717 (pt i of A collection of meditations and devotions by S. Hupton); ed G. R. Guffey, Los Angeles 1966 (Augustan Reprint Soc).

Centuries of meditations, now first printed from the author's manuscripts. Ed B. Dobell 1908, 1960 (as Centuries, with note by H. M. Margoliouth); ed J. Farrar, New York 1960.

Traherne's poems of felicity. Ed H. I. Bell 1910 (from ms). The ms (BM Burney 392) was prepared for the press, probably by the poet's brother Philip; it contains 39 poems not in Dobell's edn. There are considerable variations in the 23 poems which appear in both ms collections.

Felicities. Ed A. T. Quiller-Couch 1935.

Of magnanimity and charity. Ed J. R. Slater, New York 1942.

There is a French trn of poems with commentary by J. Wahl, Mesures April 1936.

§ 2

Dobell, B. An unknown seventeenth-century poet. Athenæum 1900.

Thompson, E. N. The philosophy of Traherne. PQ 8 1929.

Beachcroft, T. O. Traherne and the Cambridge Platonists. Dublin Rev April 1930.

— Traherne and the doctrine of felicity. Criterion 9 1930.

Wade, G. I. The manuscripts of the poems of Traherne. MLR 26 1931.

— Traherne as divine philosopher. Hibbert Jnl 32 1934.

— Traherne and the spiritual value of nature study. London Quart Rev 159 1934.

— Traherne, with a selected bibliography by R. A. Parker. Princeton 1944, 1946 (rev).

Iredale, Q. Traherne. Oxford 1935.

Wahl, J. Traherne. Etudes Anglaises 14 1961.

Grandvoinet, R. Traherne and the doctrine of felicity. Etudes de Lettres (Lausanne) 13 1939.

Wilson, G. H. Traherne and Wordsworth. London Quart 164 1939.

Bennett, J. A. Traherne and Brasenose. N & Q 25 Aug 1945.

— The manuscripts of Traherne. Bodleian Lib Record 3 1951.

Bury, R. G. A passage in Traherne. TLS 8 June 1940. Reply by P. J. Dobell 15 June 1940.

Gilbert, A. H. Traherne as artist. MLQ 8 1947.

Colby, F. L. Traherne and Henry More. MLN 62 1947.

Howarth, R. G. Felicity in Traherne. N & Q 12 June 1948.

Willy, M. In her Life was their cry, 1950.

— Traherne: felicity's perfect lover. English 12 1959.

— In her Three metaphysical poets, 1961 (Br Council pamphlet).

Hepburn, R. W. Traherne: the nature and dignity of imagination. Cambridge Jnl Sept 1953.

Salter, K. W. The date of Traherne's ordination. N & Q July 1954. Reply by H. M. Margoliouth, Sept 1954.

— Traherne and a romantic heresy. N & Q Aug 1955.

— Traherne: mystic and poet. 1964.

Russell, A. The life of Traherne. RES new ser 6 1955.

Colie, R. L. Traherne and the infinite: the ethical compromise. HLQ 21 1957.

Wallace, J. M. Traherne and the structure of meditation. ELH 25 1958.

Marshall, W. H. Traherne and the doctrine of original sin. MLN 73 1958.

Bottrall, M. Traherne's praise of the creation. CQ 1 1959.

Jennings, E. The accessible art: a study of Traherne's Centuries. Twentieth Century Feb 1960.

Owen, C. A. The authorship of Meditations on the six days of creation and Meditations and devotions on the life of Christ. MLR 56 1961.

Williams, M. G. Traherne: centre of God's wealth. Cithara 3 1963.

Cappuzzo, M. Traherne. Rendiconti 98 1964.

Martz, L. L. In his Paradise within, New Haven 1964.

Webb, W. Traherne's Silence. N & Q March 1964.

Staley, T. F. The theocentric vision of Traherne. Cithara 4 1964.

Ridlon, H. G. The function of the Infant-Ey in Traherne's poetry. SP 61 1964.

Osborn, J. M. A new Traherne manuscript. TLS 8 Oct 1964.

Marks, C. L. Traherne's commonplace book. PBSA 58 1964.

— Traherne's Church's year-book. PBSA 60 1966.

— Traherne and Hermes Trismegistus. Renaissance News 19 1966.

— Traherne and Cambridge Platonism. PMLA 81 1966.

— Traherne's early studies. PBSA 62 1968.

Clements, A. L. On the mode and meaning of Traherne's mystical poetry: the preparative. SP 61 1964.

— The mystical poetry of Traherne. Cambridge Mass 1969.

MacCaffrey, I. G. The meditative paradigm. ELH 32 1965.

Korte, D. M. Traherne's The estate. Thoth 6 1965.

Webber, J. I and thou in the prose of Traherne. Papers on Lang & Lit 2 1966.

Sandbank, S. Traherne on the place of man in the universe. Stud in Eng Lang & Lit (Jerusalem) 53 1966.

Ridler, A. Traherne: some wrong attributions. RES new ser 18 1967.

Harrison, T. P. Senecca and Traherne. Arion 6 1967.

Guffey, G. R. Traherne on original sin. N & Q March 1967.

— Margoliouth's emendation of a line in Traherne's For a man to act. Amer N & Q June 1967.

— and R. Uphaus. Traherne: perception as process. Univ of Windsor Rev (Ontario) 3 1968.

Goldknopf, D. The disintegration of symbol in a meditative poet. College Eng Oct 1968.

Day, M. M. Traherne and the doctrine of pre-existence. SP 65 1968.

Rizzardi, A. La poesia di Traherne. Urbino 1969.

Sauls, L. The careless compositor for Christian ethicks. PBSA 63 1969.

—— Traherne's hand in the Creden-hill records. Library 5th ser 24 1969.

Sickerman, C. M. Traherne's Ficino notebook. PBSA 63 1969.

Drake, B. Traherne's songs of innocence. MLQ 31 1970.

Sherrington, A. T. Mystical symbolism in the poetry of Traherne. St Lucia 1970.

Stewart, S. The expanded voice: the art of Traherne. San Marino 1970.

Cox, G. H. Traherne's Centuries: a Platonic devotion of 'divine philosophy'. MP 69 1971.

R. D. D. and J. H.

VI. JOHN MILTON
1608–74

For mss and their locations see W. R. Parker, Milton, *1968; H. Darbishire*, The ms of Paradise lost bk i, *1931; M. Treip*, Milton's punctuation, *1970*.

(1) BIBLIOGRAPHIES ETC

A verbal index to Milton's Paradise lost, adapted to every edition but the first. 1741.

Cleveland, C. D. A complete concordance to the poetical works of Milton. 1867.

Bradshaw, J. A concordance to the poetical works of Milton. 1894.

Almack, E. A bibliography of the King's book or Eikon basilike. 1896.

Osgood, C. G. The classical mythology of Milton's English poems. New York 1900.

Lockwood, L. E. Lexicon to the English poetical works of Milton. New York 1907.

Milton tercentenary. The portraits, prints and writings of Milton, exhibited at Christ's College Cambridge 1908. Cambridge 1908.

Milton: facsimile of the autographs and documents in the British Museum. 1908.

Pollard, A. W. The bibliography of Milton. Library 1st ser 10 1909.

Thompson, E. N. S. Milton: a topical bibliography. New Haven 1916.

Gilbert, A. H. A geographical dictionary of Milton. New Haven 1919.

Cooper, L. A concordance of the Latin, Greek and Italian poems of Milton. Halle 1923.

Granniss, R. S. The Beverly Chew collection of Milton portraits. BNYPL Jan 1926.

Stevens, D. H. A reference guide to Milton from 1800 to the present day. Chicago 1930.

Fletcher, H. F. Contributions to a Milton bibliography 1800–1930. Urbana 1931.

—— The first edition of Milton's History of Britain. JEGP 35 1936.

—— Collections of first editions of Milton's works, University of Illinois Library. Urbana 1953.

—— The 17th-century separate printings of Milton's Epitaphium Damonis. JEGP 61 1962.

Henry E. Huntington Library and Art Gallery. An exhibition of William Blake's watercolor drawings of Milton's Paradise lost. San Marino 1936.

Patterson, F. A. and F. R. Fogle. An index to the Columbia edition of the works of Milton. 2 vols New York 1940.

Baker, C. H. C. Some illustrators of Milton's Paradise lost 1688–1850. Library 5th ser 3 1949.

Hanford, J. H. In his A Milton handbook, New York 1946, 1970 (rev).

—— with C. W. Crupi. Milton. New York 1966.

Whitechapel Art Gallery. An exhibition of paintings and drawings by John Martin 1789–1854. 1953.

Hughes, M. Y. The 17th-century. In Contemporary literary scholarship, ed L. Leary, New York 1958.

Huckaby, C. Milton: a bibliographical supplement 1929–57. Pittsburgh 1960, 1969 (rev).

Huntley, F. L. Milton studies in Japan. Comparative Lit 13 1961.

Le Comte, E. S. A Milton dictionary. New York 1961.

Patrides, C. A. Annotated reading list. In Milton's Lycidas, New York 1961.

—— Annotated reading list. In Milton's epic poetry, 1967 (Pelican).

Stratman, C. J. Milton's Samson Agonistes: a checklist of criticism. Restoration & 18th-century Theatre Research 4 1965.

Flannagan, R. C. (ed). Milton newsletter. Athens Ohio 1967–70; continued as Milton quarterly, 1970–.

Parker, W. R. In his Milton: a biography, Oxford 1968. Milton's pbns, surviving copies of their 17th-century edns etc.

Samuel, I. Paradise lost. In Critical approaches to six major English works, ed R. M. Lumiansky and H. Baker, Philadelphia 1968.

Hudson, G. W. Paradise lost: a concordance. Detroit 1970.

Pointon, M. R. Milton and English art. Manchester 1970. On Milton's illustrators; with bibliography.

Wittreich, J. A. Illustrators of Paradise regained and their subjects. In his Calm of mind, Cleveland 1971. Includes essay on Blake's illustrations, with catalogue.

Bush, D. In English poetry: select bibliographical guides, ed A. E. Dyson 1971.

Ingram, W. and K. Swaim. A concordance to Milton's English poetry. 1972.

(2) COLLECTIONS

Verse and Prose

Works in verse and prose. Ed J. Mitford 8 vols 1841.

Poetry and prose, with essays by Johnson, Hazlitt and Macaulay. Ed B. G. Madan, Oxford 1920.

The student's Milton. Ed F. A. Patterson, New York 1930, 1933 (rev).

Works. Ed F. A. Patterson et al 18 vols New York 1931–8. The Columbia edn. Suppl by T. O. Mabbott, J. M.

French and M. Kelley, N & Q, 4 Nov 1939, 17 July 1940, 12 July 1941, 10 June 1950, 30 Aug 1952.

Complete poetry and selected prose. Ed E. H. Visiak, New York 1938.

Complete poetry and selected prose. New York 1942, 1950 (introd by C. Brooks).

Selected poetry and prose. Ed C. R. Bull, Melbourne 1948.

Paradise lost and selected poetry and prose. Ed N. Frye, New York 1951.

Complete poems and major prose. Ed M. Y. Hughes, New York 1957.

Poems and selected prose. Ed M. H. Nicolson, New York 1962.

Verse

Poems of Mr John Milton, both English and Latin, compos'd at several times. 1645.

Poems etc upon several occasions. 1673.

Poetical works. Ed Patrick Hume 1695.

Poetical works. 2 vols 1705.

Poetical works. 2 vols 1707, 1720 (with Addison's essays), 1725, 1727, 1730, 1731, 3 vols 1746–7; ed J. Hawkey 2 vols Dublin 1747–52; ed T. Newton 3 vols 1749–53; 2 vols 1753, 1758, Edinburgh 1762, 4 vols 1770, 1773, 1776.

L'Allegro and Il Penseroso. Glasgow 1751.

Milton's Italian poems. Tr J. Langhorne 1776.

Poems. Ed S. Johnson 3 vols 1779.

Poems upon several occasions. Ed T. Warton 1785.

Poetical works. 2 vols 1790; ed W. Hayley 3 vols 1794–7; 2 vols 1795–6; ed J. H. Todd 6 vols 1801, 7 vols 1809 (rev); ed J. Aikin 3 vols 1805.

Latin and Italian poems. Tr W. Cowper, ed W. Hayley 1908.

Life and poetical works with notes by William Cowper. Ed W. Hayley 4 vols Chichester 1810. With trn of Andreini's Adamo.

Latin and Italian poems. Tr J. G. Strutt 1814.

Poetical works. Ed E. Hawkins 4 vols 1824.

Poetical works, with Cowper's translations. 3 vols 1826.

Poetical works. Ed J. Mitford 3 vols 1832 (Aldine); ed E. Brydges 6 vols 1835; ed H. Stebbing 1839.

Poetical works of Milton, Thomson and Young. Ed H. F. Cary 1841.

Poetical works, with a memoir by J. Montgomery. 2 vols 1843.

Poetical works. Ed C. D. Cleveland, Philadelphia 1853; ed G. Gilfillan 2 vols Edinburgh 1853.

Poems. Ed T. Keightley 2 vols 1859.

English poems. Ed R. C. Browne 2 vols 1866.

Poetical works. Ed D. Masson 3 vols 1874, 1890 (rev); ed J. Bradshaw 3 vols 1878.

Sonnets. Ed M. Pattison 1883; ed A. Sampson, New York 1886.

Minor poems. Ed W. J. Rolfe, New York 1887; ed O. Elton 5 vols Oxford 1893–1900.

The Cambridge Milton for schools. Ed A. W. Verity 10 vols Cambridge 1891–6.

Complete poetical works. Ed W. V. Moody, Boston [1899], 1924 (rev E. K. Rand), 1941 (rev H. F. Fletcher).

Facsimile of the ms of Milton's minor poems preserved in the library of Trinity College. Ed W. A. Wright, Cambridge 1899.

Poetical works. Ed H. C. Beeching, Oxford 1900, 1940 (WC) (adapted).

Lyric and dramatic poems. Ed M. W. Sampson, New York 1901.

Minor English poems. Ed H. C. Beeching 1903.

Poetical works. Ed W. A. Wright, Cambridge 1903; ed W. Raleigh 1905; ed H. Newbolt [1924].

Sonnets. Ed J. S. Smart, Glasgow 1921.

Poems. Ed H. J. C. Grierson 2 vols 1925.

Poems in English, with illustrations by William Blake. 2 vols 1926.

Complete poems. Ed F. A. Patterson, New York 1930.

Latin poems. Ed W. Mackellar, New Haven 1930.

The Cambridge ms of Milton: Lycidas and some of the other poems. Ed F. A. Patterson, New York 1933 (facs).

Poems. Ed J. H. Hanford, New York 1936, 1953 (rev).

Paradise regained, the minor poems and Samson Agonistes. Ed M. Y. Hughes, New York 1937.

Samson Agonistes and the English sonnets. Ed A. M. Percival, New York 1931.

Minor poems: facsimile of the 1645 edition. New York 1934.

Milton's Lament for Damon and his other Latin poems. Tr W. W. Skeat, ed E. H. Visiak, Oxford 1935.

Minor poems. Ed T. P. Cross, Cambridge Mass 1936.

Complete poetical works. Ed H. F. Fletcher, Boston 1941.

Complete poetical works reproduced in photographic facsimile. Ed H. F. Fletcher 4 vols Urbana 1943–8.

Paradise lost and other poems. Ed M. Kelley, New York 1943.

The portable Milton. Ed D. Bush, New York 1949, 1969 (as The essential Milton).

Poems of Mr John Milton: the 1645 edition. Ed C. Brooks and J. E. Hardy, New York 1951.

Comus and the shorter poems. Ed E. M. W. and P. B. Tillyard 1952.

Poetical works. Ed H. Darbishire 2 vols Oxford 1952–5.

Complete English poems. Ed 'John Gawsworth' 1953.

Selected English poems. Ed L. Lerner 1953 (Penguin).

Poems. Ed B. A. Wright 1956.

Dramatic poems. Ed G. and M. Bullough 1958.

Paradise lost and other poems. Ed L. S. LeComte, New York 1961.

Paradise lost, Paradise regained, Samson Agonistes. Ed H. Bloom, New York 1962.

Complete English poetry. Ed J. T. Shawcross, New York 1963.

Complete English poems. Ed J. Jump, New York 1964.

Milton. Ed W. G. Madsen, New York 1964.

Complete poetical works. Ed D. Bush, Boston 1965, Oxford 1966.

Sonnets. Ed E. A. J. Honigmann 1966.

Samson Agonistes and the shorter poems. Ed I. G. MacCaffrey, New York 1966.

Paradise lost and Paradise regained. Ed C. Ricks, New York 1968.

Poems. Ed J. Carey and A. Fowler 1969, 2 vols 1971 (corrected).

Variorum commentary. Ed M. Y. Hughes et al 1970–.

The Cambridge Milton. Ed J. B. Broadbent et al, Cambridge 1972–.

The Macmillan Milton. Ed C. A. Patrides et al 1972–.

Prose

A complete collection of the historical, political and miscellaneous works. Ed J. Toland 3 vols 1694–8.

Works. 1697. Prose.

A complete collection of the historical, political and miscellaneous works of Milton, containing several original papers of his never before published. Ed T. Birch 2 vols 1738, 1753 (enlarged).

Prose works. Ed C. Symmons 7 vols 1806.

Prose works, with new translations and an introduction by G. Burnett. 2 vols 1809.

Prose works. Ed R. Fletcher 1833, 1838 (with index); ed R. W. Griswold 2 vols Philadelphia 1845; ed J. A. St John 5 vols 1848–53 (Bohn's Lib).

Autobiography of Milton: or Milton's life in his own words. Ed J. G. Graham 1872.

An introduction to the prose and poetical works of Milton, comprising all the autobiographical passages of his works. Ed H. Corson 1899.

Prose. Ed M. W. Wallace, Oxford 1925 (WC).

Areopagitica and other prose writings. Ed W. Haller, New York 1927.

Private correspondence and academic exercises. Ed and tr P. B. and E. M. W. Tillyard, Cambridge 1932.

Milton on himself. Ed J. S. Diekhoff, New York 1939.

Prose selections. Ed M. Y. Hughes, New York 1947.

Areopagitica and Of education, with autobiographical passages from other prose works. Ed G. H. Sabine, New York 1951.

Complete prose works. Ed D. M. Wolfe et al 8 vols New Haven 1953–. The Yale edn.

Areopagitica and other prose works. Ed K. M. Burton 1955.
Prose. Ed J. M. Patrick, New York 1967.
Prose works 1641–50. Menston 3 vols 1967–8 (facs).

§ I

An epitaph on the admirable dramaticke poet W. Shakespeare. In Shakespeare's second folio, 1632; also in folios of 1664, 1685, and in Shakespeare, Poems, 1640.

['Comus']. A maske presented at Ludlow Castle 1634 on Michaelmas night, before the Right Honorable John Earle of Bridgewater. 1637; ed H. J. Todd, Canterbury 1798, 1799; ed H. B. Sprague, New York 1876; ed W. Bell 1890; A. W. Verity, Cambridge 1891; ed O. Elton, Oxford 1893; ed L. S. Livingston, New York 1903 (facs); ed Lady Alix Egerton 1910; ed D. Figgis 1926; ed E. H. Visiak 1937; ed A. S. Collins 1938; ed J. M. Evans 1939; ed E. M. W. Tillyard 1952; ed F. T. Prince 1968 etc. Stage adaptations listed in bibliographies, above. Tr Latin, 1698; Italian, 1802, 1948; Hungarian, 1960; Japanese, 1929, 1960; French, 1964 etc.

Lycidas. In Justa Edovardo King naufrago, ab amicis mœrentibus, amoris et μνείας χάριν, Cambridge 1638; ed C. S. Jerram 1874; ed O. Elton 1893; ed W. Bell 1938; ed C. A. Patrides, New York 1961 etc. Entire volume: Dublin 1835, London 1939 (facs) etc. Tr Latin, 1694 (paraphrase), 1874; Greek, 1797; Italian, 1930, 1941, 1948; Japanese, 1939; Hungarian, 1960; Dutch, 1963 etc.

Epitaphium Damonis. [1640?]; tr W. W. Skeat 1933; H. Waddell 1943, UTQ 16 1947 and in Milton's Lycidas, ed C. A. Patrides, New York 1961.

[Sonnet to Henry Lawes. In Choice psalmes, put into musick by Henry and William Lawes. 1648].

Of reformation touching Church discipline in England, and the causes that hitherto have hindered it. 1641 (May); ed W. T. Hale, New Haven 1916.

Of prelatical episcopacy, and whether it may be deduc'd from the Apostolical times. 1641 (June?), 1654.

Animadversions upon the remonstrant's defence, against Smectymnuus. 1641 (Aug), 1954.

The reason of Church-government urg'd against prelaty. 1641 (Dec?), 1654.

An apology against a pamphlet call'd A modest confutation of the animadversions upon the remonstrant against Smectymnuus. 1642, 1654; ed M. C. Jochums, Urbana 1950.

The doctrine and discipline of divorce, restor'd to the good of both sexes from the bondage of canon law and other mistakes to Christian freedom, guided by the rule of charity. 1643 (Aug), 1644 (Feb) (rev).

Of education, to Master Samuel Hartlib. 1644 (June), 1673; ed O. Browning, Cambridge 1883 (facs); ed E. E. Morris 1895; ed O. M. Ainsworth, New Haven 1928; ed F. Schlupp, Würzburg 1935; ed G. H. Sabine, New York 1951; cd M. Davis 1963 etc.

The judgement of Martin Bucer concerning divorce now englisht. 1644 (Aug).

Areopagitica: a speech of Mr John Milton for the liberty of unlicenc'd printing, to the Parliament of England. 1644 (Nov); ed J. W. Hales, Oxford 1866; ed E. Arber 1868; ed H. Morley 1886; ed J. R. Lowell 1890; ed H. B. Cotterill 1904; ed R. C. Jebb 1918; ed W. Haller 1927; 1934 (facs); ed F. B. Pinion 1956; ed M. Davis 1963 etc; tr Greek, 1932; Italian, 1933; French, 1956; German, 1944; Spanish, 1941; Danish, 1936; Japanese, 1948, 1955; Bengali, 1963; Hindi, 1965 etc.

Colasterion: a reply to a nameless answer against the Doctrine and discipline of divorce. 1645 (March).

Tetrachordon: expositions upon the foure chiefe places in Scripture which treat of mariage, or nullities in mariage. 1645 (March).

Poems of Mr John Milton, both English and Latin, compos'd at several times. 1645, 1673; 1926 (facs of 1645); ed C. Brooks and J. E. Hardy, New York 1951. Numerous edns of separate poems listed in Bibliographies, above.

The Trinity ms. Ed W. A. Wright, Cambridge 1899; 1933; Menston 1970. 3 facs of autograph ms in Trinity College, Cambridge, written c. 1633–48, including Arcades, Comus, Lycidas, 17 sonnets etc.

The tenure of kings and magistrates. 1649 (Feb), 1650 (Feb); ed W. T. Allison, New York 1911.

Observations upon the articles of peace with the Irish rebels, on the letter of Ormond to Col Jones. 1649.

ΕΙΚΟΝΟΚΛΑΣΤΗΣ, in answer to a book intitl'd ΕΙΚΩΝ ΒΑΣΙΛΙΚΗ, the portrature of his sacred Majesty in his solitudes and sufferings. 1649 (Oct), 1650 (rev), 1690.

Pro populo anglicano defensio, contra Claudii anonymi, alias Salmasii, defensionem regiam. 1651 (Feb), 1651, 1658; tr J. Washington 1692.

Pro populo anglicano defensio secunda, contra infamen libellum anonymum cui titulus, Regii sanguinis clamor ad cœlum adversus parricidas anglicanos. 1654 (May); ed G. Crantzius, Hague 1654; tr R. Fellowes 1806; F. Wrangham 1816.

Pro se defensio contra Alexandrum Morum ecclesiasten libelli famosi, cui titulus, Regii sanguinis clamor ad cœlum adversus parricidas anglicanos. 1655 (Aug); tr G. Burnett 1809.

The Cabinet-Council. 1658. Attributed to Sir Walter Ralegh.

A treatise of civil power in ecclesiastical causes, shewing that it is not lawfull for any power on earth to compell in matters of religion. 1659 (Feb).

Considerations touching the likeliest means to remove hirelings out of the church. 1659 (Aug), 1839.

The readie and easie way to establish a free commonwealth, and the excellence thereof compar'd with the inconveniences and dangers of readmitting kingship in this nation. 1660 (March), 1660 (April); ed E. M. Clark, New Haven 1915.

Brief notes upon a late sermon titl'd the Fear of God and the King; preach'd and sinc publish'd by Matthew Griffith DD and chaplain to the late King. 1660 (April).

Paradise lost: a poem written in ten books. 1667, 1674 (rev as A poem in twelve books), 1678, 1688, 1691–2, 1693; ed P. Hume 1695, 1705, 1720 (with Addison's essays); ed R. Bentley 1732, 1738; ed T. Newton 1749; ed Capel Lofft, Bury St Edmunds 1792; ed J. B. Williams 1824; ed J. Prendeville 1840; ed H. Stebbing 1848; ed R. H. Shepherd 1873; ed D. Masson 1877 (facs); ed R. Vaughan 1882; ed A. W. Verity 1910; ed G. H. Cowling and H. F. Hallett 1926; ed G. M. Davis 1931; 1931 (Cresset Press); ed M. Y. Hughes, New York 1935, 1962 (facs); ed J. H. Hanford, New York 1936; 1937 (Golden Cockerel Press); illustr William Blake, New York 1941 (Heritage Press); ed M. Kelley, New York 1943; ed C. Ricks 1968; Menston 1968 (facs) etc. Also in Collections, above. For edns of individual books see Bibliographies, above. Trns include: Latin, 1690 (paraphrase), 1702 (bk 1), 1741, 1750; French, 1729, 1754, 1787, 1805, 1836, 1838, 1951; Swedish, 1815, 1961; Dutch, 1728, 1798–1811, 1875; German, 1682, 1732, 1792, 1807–13, 1828, 1865, 1948; Italian, 1735, 1796, 1801, 1811, 1820, 1933, 1938, 1950; Spanish, 1812, 1914, 1946, 1950, 1955, 1965; Portuguese, 1823, 1956, 1962; Hebrew, 1871; Modern Greek, 1887; Japanese, 1929, 1929, 1938–41; Finnish, 1933; Russian, 1956; Czech, 1960; Albanian, 1960; Korean, 1961, 1963.

The manuscript of Milton's Paradise lost book 1. Ed H. Darbishire, Oxford 1931.

Accedence commenc't grammar, supply'd with sufficient rules for the use of such as, younger or elder, are desirous, without more trouble than needs, to attain the Latin tongue. 1669.

The history of Britain, that part especially now call'd England. 1670; ed F. Maseres 1818.

Paradise regain'd: a poem, in iv books; to which is added Samson Agonistes. 1671, 1680, 1688; ed T. Newton 1752; ed C. Dunster 1795; ed C. S. Jerram 1877; ed W. H. D. Rouse 1897; ed L. C. Martin, Oxford 1925; 1931 (Cresset Press); ed E. H. Blakeney 1932; ed M. Y. Hughes, New York 1937; ed E. M. Pope, Baltimore 1947; Menston 1968 (facs); tr Italian, 1948; French, 1955; etc.

Samson Agonistes. 1681, 1688; ed J. C. Collins, Oxford 1883; ed C. S. Jerram 1890; ed A. M. Percival 1890; ed A. W. Verity, Cambridge 1892; ed E. K. Chambers 1897; ed C. T. Onions 1905; ed V. Hammer, Florence 1931; 1931 (Raven Press); ed A. J. Wyatt and A. J. F. Collins 1932; ed M. Y. Hughes, New York 1937; ed J. E. Bradshaw 1949; ed A. E. Barker, New York 1950; ed F. T. Prince, Oxford 1957; ed R. E. Hone, San Francisco 1966; ed I. G. MacCaffrey, New York 1966; Menston 1968 (facs); ed M. Davis 1668; tr French, 1937; Italian, 1941, 1948; German, 1947; Danish, 1930; Spanish, 1949; Japanese, 1934; Hebrew, 1950; Hungarian, 1955; etc.

Artis logicae plenior institutio, ad Petri Rami methodum concinnata; adjecta est praxis analytica et Petri Rami vita. 1672.

Of true religion, hæresy, schism, toleration, and what best means may be urg'd against the growth of Popery. 1673.

A declaration: or letters patents of the election of this present King of Poland, John the Third, now faithfully translated from the Latin copy. 1674.

Epistolarum familiarum liber unus: quibus accescerunt, ejusdem, jam olim in collegio adolescentis, prolusiones quaedam oratoriae. 1674; tr J. Hall, Philadelphia 1829; Private correspondence and academic exercises, tr P. Tillyard, Cambridge 1932.

Literae pseudo-senatus anglicani, Cromwelli reliquorumque perduellium nomine ac jussu conscriptae a Joanne Miltono. 1676, 1690.

Character of the Long Parliament and Assembly of Divines, in MDCXLI. 1681; rptd Harleian miscellany vol 5, 1810.

A brief history of Moscovia and of other less known countries lying eastward of Russia as far as Cathay. 1682; ed D. S. Mirsky 1929; ed R. R. Cawley, Princeton 1941.

Milton's republican letters: or a collection of such as were written by command of the late Commonwealth of England. 1682.

Letters of State from the year 1649 till the year 1659. 1694; ed H. Fernow, Hamburg 1903.

Examen poeticum duplex. 1698. Contains 4 of the early Latin poems.

Original letters and papers of State addressed to Oliver Cromwell concerning the affairs of Great Britain from the year 1649 to 1658. Ed J. Nickolls 1743.

De doctrina christiana libri duo posthumi, quos ex schedis manuscriptis deprompsit et typis mandari primus curavit C. R. Sumner. 1825; tr C. R. Sumner 1825.

Original papers, illustrative of the life and writings of John Milton, including 16 letters of State written by him, now first published. Ed W. D. Hamilton 1859.

A common-place book. Ed A. J. Horwood 1876, 1877 (rev).

§2

For 17th-century comments on Milton, see W. R. Parker, Milton's contemporary reputation, Columbus 1940; for early biographies, The early lives of Milton, ed H. Darbishire 1932; for illustr edns, M. R. Pointon, Milton and English art, Manchester 1970.

Hall, John. A humble remonstrance. 1641.

Smectymnuus. A modest confutation of a slanderous and scurrilous libel, entituled Animadversions. 1642.

Du Moulin, P. Regii sanguinis clamor ad cœlum adversus parricidas anglicanos. Hague 1652, 1653.

Filmer, Robert. Observations concerning the originall of government upon Mr Hobs Leviathan, Mr Milton against Salmasius etc. 1652.

Harrington, James. The censure of the Rota upon Mr Milton's book entitled the Ready and easie way. 1660.

Salmasius, C. de. Claudii Salmasii ad Johannem Miltonum responsio. Dijon 1660.

A proclamation for calling in and suppressing of two books written by John Milton; the one intituled Johannis Miltoni Angli, pro populo anglicano defensio, and the other Εἰκονοκλάστης. 1660 (13 Aug).

L'Estrange, Roger. No blind guides, in answer to a seditious pamphlet of J. Milton's intituled Brief notes upon a late sermon titl'd the Fear of God and the King. 1660.

Phillips, Edward. Theatrum poetarum anglicanorum. 1675.

Toland, John. The life of Milton. 1699, 1761.

— Amyntor: or a defence of Milton's life. 1699, 1761.

Addison, Joseph. [Notes upon the twelve books of Paradise lost]. Spectator 5 Jan–3 May 1712; 1719. See vol 2 col 1102.

Ellwood, T. The history of the life of. 1714.

Voltaire. The epick poetry of the European nations from Homer down to Milton. 1727.

The essay On Milton, ed D. Flower, Cambridge 1954.

Clarke, S. Some reflections on that part of a book called Amyntor: or the defence of Milton's life, which relates to the writings of the primitive Fathers. 1731.

[Routh, B.] Lettres critiques sur le Paradis perdu, et reconquis de Milton. Paris 1731.

Meadowcourt, R. A critique on Milton's Paradise regained. 1732.

— A critical dissertation with notes on Paradise regained. 1748.

Pearce, Z. A review of the text of Milton's Paradise lost. 1732, 1733. On Bentley's edn.

Bentley, R. Dr Bentley's emendations on the twelve books of Paradise lost. 1734.

Richardson, J. (father and son). Explanatory notes and remarks on Milton's Paradise lost. 1734.

Bodmer, J. J. Critische Abhandlung von dem Wunderbaren in der Poesie in einer Vertheidigung des Gedichtes J. Miltons von dem Verlohrnen Paradiese. Zürich 1740.

Peck, F. New memoirs of the life and poetical works of Mr John Milton. 1740.

Richardson, R. Zoilomastix: or a vindication of Milton from the charges of W. Lauder. 1747.

Lauder, W. An essay on Milton's use and imitation of the moderns in his Paradise lost. 1750.

— A letter to the Rev Mr Douglas, occasioned by his vindication of Milton. 1751.

— Delectus auctorum sacrorum Miltono facem praelucentium. 1752.

Douglas, J. Milton vindicated from the charge of plagiarism brought against him by Mr Lauder. 1751.

Racine, L. Le Paradis perdu, avec la vie de l'auteur et discours sur le poëme. Paris 1754; tr K. John, Life of Milton together with observations on Paradise lost, 1930.

Neve, P. A note on the disinterment of Milton's coffin. 1770.

Johnson, S. In his Lives of the poets, 1779–81.

Darby, S. A letter to T. Warton, on his late edition of Milton's juvenile poems. 1785.

Burney, C. Remarks on the Greek verses of Milton. 1790.

Disraeli, I. In his Curiosities of literature, 7 vols 1791–1834.

Dunster, C. Considerations on Milton's early reading and the prima stamina of his Paradise lost. 1800.

Mosneron, J. Vie de Milton. Paris 1804.

Mortimer, C. E. An historical memoir of the poetical life of Milton. 1805.

Todd, H. J. Some account of the life and writings of Milton. In Poetical works vol 1, 1809.

Aubrey, J. In his Brief lives, 2 vols 1813.

Wood, A. In his Fasti oxonienses vol i, ed P. Bliss 1815.

Godwin, W. Lives of Edward and John Phillips, to which are added 1, Collections, for the life of Milton by John Aubrey; 2, The life of Milton by Edward Phillips. 1815.

Hazlitt, W. On Shakespeare and Milton. In his Lectures on the English poets, 1818.

Scolari, F. Saggio di critica sul Paradiso perduto. Venice 1818.

Landor, W. S. In his Imaginary conversations, 5 vols 1824-9.

— Last fruit off an old tree. 1853.

Macaulay, T. B. Milton. Edinburgh Rev 83 1825.

— In his Miscellaneous writings, 1860. An imaginary conversation of Cowley and Milton.

Channing, W. E. Remarks on the character and writings of Milton. Boston 1826.

Cann, C. A scriptural and allegorical glossary to Milton's Paradise lost. 1828.

Ivimey, J. Milton: his life and times, religious and political opinions. 1833.

Brydges, S. E. Milton. 1835.

Coleridge, S. T. In his Literary remains, 2 vols 1836.

— Seven lectures on Shakespeare and Milton, ed J. P. Collier 1856.

— In Coleridge on the 17th century, ed R. F. Brinkley, Durham NC 1955.

Emerson, R. W. Milton. North Amer Rev 47 1838; rptd in Essays from North American Review, New York 1879.

De Quincey, T. Life of Milton. Blackwood's Mag Dec 1839.

— In his Collected works, 16 vols 1853-60. Vol 6 pp. 31-52, vol 10 pp. 79-98; based on pbns in Blackwood's Mag 1842.

Masson, D. The three devils: Luther's, Milton's and Goethe's. Fraser's Mag Dec 1844.

— In his Essays biographical and critical, Cambridge 1856.

— The life of Milton: narrated in connexion with the political, ecclesiastical and literary history of his time. 7 vols 1859-94, 1881 (vol i rev).

Geoffroy, A. Etude sur les pamphlets politiques et religieux de Milton. Paris 1848.

Hunter, J. Milton: a sheaf of gleanings after his biographers and annotators. 1850.

Marsh, J. F. Papers connected with the affairs of Milton and his family. Chetham Soc Miscellany 1851.

— Notice of the inventory of the effects of Mrs Milton, widow of the poet. Liverpool 1855.

— On the engraved portraits and pretended portraits of Milton. Liverpool 1860.

des Essarts, E. De veterum poetarum tum Graeciae, tum Romae apud Miltonem imitatione. Paris 1858.

Hamilton, W. D. Original papers illustrative of the life and writings of Milton. 1859 (Camden Soc).

Keightley, T. Life, opinions and writings of Milton. 1859.

Liebert, G. Milton. In his Studien zur Geschichte des englischen Geistes, Hamburg 1860.

Lotheissen, F. Studien über Miltons poetische Werke. Budingen 1860.

Sotheby, S. L. Ramblings in the elucidation of the autograph of Milton. 1861.

Scherer, E. In his Etudes critiques sur la littérature contemporaine, Paris 1863-5; tr 1891.

Wiese, L. Miltons Verlorenes Paradies. Berlin 1863.

von Treitschke, H. In his Historische und politische Aufsätze, Leipzig 1865.

de Guerle, E. Milton: sa vie et ses œuvres. Paris 1868.

Owen, R. Milton and Galileo. Fraser's Mag May 1869.

Pauli, R. In his Aufsätze zur englischen Geschichte, Leipzig 1869.

Jebb, R. C. Milton's Areopagitica: a commentary. [1872].

Bayne, P. John Milton. Contemporary Rev Aug 1873.

Münch, W. Die Entstehung des Verlorenen Paradieses. Cleve 1874.

Symonds, J. A. The blank verse of Milton. Fortnightly Rev Dec 1874.

Lowell, J. R. In his Among my books: series 2, Boston 1876.

Stern, A. Milton und seine Zeit. 2 vols Leipzig 1877-9.

Arnold, M. In his Mixed essays, 1879.

— In his Essays in criticism series 2, 1888.

Bagehot, W. In his Literary studies, 2 vols 1879.

Brooke, S. A. Milton. 1879.

Gosse, E. Studies in the literature of Northern Europe. 1879. On Vondel and Milton.

— The Milton manuscripts at Trinity. Atlantic Monthly May 1900.

Pattison, M. Milton. 1879 (EML).

Hodgson, S. H. In his Outcast essays, 1881.

Wülcker, R. Caedmon and Milton. Anglia 4 1881.

Axon, W. E. A. Milton's Comus and Fletcher's Faithful shepherdess. Manchester 1882.

Ademello, A. La Leonora di Milton e di Clemente IX. Milan [1885].

Edmundson, G. Milton and Vondel. 1885.

Birrell, A. In his Obiter dicta: series 2, 1887.

Dowden, E. In his Transcripts and studies, 1888.

— In his Puritan and Anglican: studies in literature, 1900.

Garnett, R. Life of Milton. 1890.

Jenny, G. Miltons Verlorenes Paradies in der deutschen Literatur des 18 Jahrhunderts. St Gallen 1890.

Meyer, J. B. Miltons pädagogische Schriften und Aüsserungen. Langensalza 1890.

Rost, W. Die Orthographie der ersten Quartoausgabe von Miltons Paradise lost. Leipzig 1892.

Schlesinger, A. Der Natursinn bei Milton. Leipzig 1892.

Bridges, R. Milton's prosody. Oxford 1893, 1901 (rev), 1921 (with A chapter on accentual verse and notes).

Hales, J. W. In his Folia literaria, 1893.

Harris, H. Was Paradise lost suggested by the Mystery Plays? MLN 10 1895.

Vodoz, J. An essay on the prose of Milton. Zürich 1895.

Gurteen, S. H. The epic of the Fall of Man: a comparative study of Caedmon, Dante and Milton. New York 1896.

Orchard, T. N. The astronomy of Paradise lost. 1896, 1913 (rev).

Masterman, J. H. The age of Milton. 1897.

Kuhns, O. Dante's influence on Milton. MLN 13 1898.

Trent, W. P. Milton: a short study of his life and works. New York 1899.

Osgood, C. G. The classical mythology of Milton's English poems. New York 1900.

— In his Voice of England, New York 1935.

— In his Poetry as a means of grace, Princeton 1941.

— Paradise lost for beginners; Areopagitica. Both in his Creed of a humanist, Seattle 1963.

Raleigh, W. Milton. 1900.

Scott, A. M. Über das Verhältnis von Drydens State of innocence zu Miltons Paradise lost. Halle 1900.

Brown, G. D. Syllabification and accent in the Paradise lost. Baltimore 1901.

Bywater, I. Milton and the Aristotelian definition of tragedy. Jnl of Philology 27 1901.

Scheifers, B. On the sentiment for nature in Milton's poetical works. Eisleben 1901.

Stephen, L. New lights on Milton. Quart Rev 194 1901.

Thomas, W. De epico apud Joannem Miltonium versu. Paris 1901.

Parsons, E. S. The earliest life of Milton. EHR 17 1902.

Scrocca, A. Studio critico sul Paradiso perduto del Milton. Naples [1902].

Neilson, W. A. Nova Solyma: a romance attributed to Milton. MP 1 1904. On W. Begley's edn 1902.

Buff, F. Miltons Paradise lost in seinem Verhältnisse zur Aeneide, Ilias und Odyssee. Munich 1904.

Telleen, J. M. Milton dans la littérature française. Paris 1904.

Wendel, B. The temper of the seventeenth century in English literature. 1904.

Collins, J. C. Miltonic myths and their authors. In his Studies in poetry and criticism, 1905.

Williamson, G. C. Milton. 1905.

Cooper, L. The Abyssinian Paradise in Coleridge and Milton. MP 3 1906.

Greg, W. W. In his Pastoral poetry and pastoral drama, 1906.

Tatlock, J. S. P. Milton's Sin and Death. MLN 21 1906.

Allodoli, E. Giovanni Milton e l'Italia. Prato 1907.

More, P. E. The true theme of Paradise lost. In his Shelburne essays: series 4, 1907.

— How to read Lycidas. In his On being human, Princeton 1936.

Woodhull, M. The epic of Paradise lost. New York 1907.

Papers read at the Milton tercentenary 1908. Proc Br Acad 3 1908.

Thomas, W. Milton's heroic line viewed from an historical standpoint. MLR 2–3 1907–8.

— Le sentiment de la nature dans Milton. Revue Germanique 7 1911.

Ashton, H. L'Influence sur Milton. In his Du Bartas en Angleterre, Paris 1908.

Chesterton, G. K. Taste for Milton (1908). In his A handful of authors, ed D. Collins 1953.

— Milton: man and poet. Catholic World Jan 1917.

— Milton the aesthete. In G. K. Chesterton, ed W. H. Auden 1970.

Milton tercentenary number. Christ's College Mag 23 1908. Articles and notes.

Chauvet, P. La religion de Milton. Paris 1909.

Cook, A. S. Notes on Milton's Ode on the morning of Christ's nativity. Trans Connecticut Acad of Arts & Sciences 15 1909.

Hamilton, H. F. The sources of Milton's Lycidas. Sewanee Rev 17 1909.

Havens, R. D. The early reputation of Paradise lost. E Studien 40 1909.

— The influence of Milton on English poetry. Cambridge Mass 1922.

Hudson, W. H. Milton and his poetry. 1909.

Milton memorial lectures 1908. Ed P. W. Ames 1909.

Mustard, W. P. Later echoes of the Greek bucolic poets. Amer Jnl of Philology 30 1909.

Hanford, J. H. The pastoral elegy and Milton's Lycidas. PMLA 25 1910.

— Milton and the return to humanism. SP 16 1919.

— A Milton handbook. New York 1926, 1946 (rev); rev J. G. Taaffe, New York 1970.

— The marriage of Edward Phillips and Anne Milton. RES 9 1933.

— Milton's poem on the death of a fair infant. Ibid.

— That shepherd who first taught the chosen seed: a note on Milton's Mosaic inspiration. UTQ 8 1939.

— Milton forswears physic. Bull Medical Lib Assoc 32 1944.

— John Milton, Englishman. New York 1949.

— Paradise lost annotated by Thomas Edwards. Princeton Univ Lib Chron 23 1962.

— Milton in Italy. Annuale Medievale 5 1964.

— Milton: poet and humanist. Cleveland 1966. Reprints 8 essays.

Jones, S. K. The authorship of Nova Solyma. Library ser 1 1910.

Kittredge, G. L. Milton and Roger Williams. MLN 25 1910.

Lockwood, L. E. Milton's corrections to the minor poems. Ibid.

Morton, E. P. The technique of English non-dramatic blank verse. Chicago 1910.

Roberts, W. W. Chateaubriand and Milton. MLR 5 1910.

Gajšek, S. Milton und Caedmon. Leipzig 1911.

Norlin, G. The conventions of the pastoral elegy. Amer Jnl of Philology 32 1911.

Saintsbury, G. Milton. CHEL 7 1911.

— Milton and the grand style. In his Collected essays and papers, 1923.

Visser, M. Miltons Prosawerken. Rotterdam 1911.

Cory, H. E. Spenser, the school of the Fletchers and Milton. Berkeley 1912.

Friedland, L. S. Milton's Lycidas and Spenser's Ruines of time. MLN 27 1912.

Robbins, F. E. The hexaemeral literature: a study of the Greek and Latin commentaries on Genesis. Chicago 1912.

Woodberry, G. E. In his Great writers, New York 1912.

Hübener, G. Die stilistische Spannung in Miltons Paradise lost. Halle 1913.

Sampson, A. Studies in Milton. New York 1913.

Spaeth, S. G. Milton's knowledge of music. Weimar 1913.

Bailey, M. L. Milton and Jakob Boehme: a study of German mysticism in 17th-century England. New York 1914.

Pizzo, E. Miltons Verlorenes Paradies im deutschen Urteilen des 18 Jahrhunderts. Berlin 1914.

Sandys, J. E. The literary sources of Milton's Lycidas. Trans Royal Soc of Lit 2nd ser 32 1914.

Thompson, E. N. S. Essays on Milton. New Haven 1914.

— Milton's Of education. SP 15 1918.

— Milton's knowledge of geography. SP 16 1919.

— Milton's prose style. PQ 14 1935.

— For Paradise lost xi–xii. PQ 22 1943.

Bailey, J. Milton. Oxford 1915.

Good, J. W. Studies in the Milton tradition. Urbana 1915.

Erskine, J. The theme of death in Paradise lost. PMLA 32 1917.

Greenlaw, E. A better teacher than Aquinas. SP 14 1917.

— Spenser's influence on Paradise lost. SP 17 1920.

Powell, C. L. English domestic relations 1487–1653. New York 1917.

Liljegren, S. B. Studies in Milton. Lund 1918.

— Milton at Florence. Neophilologus 43 1959.

Moore, O. H. The infernal council. MP 16 1918.

Ramsay, R. L. Morality themes in Milton's poetry. SP 15 1918.

Rusk, R. R. In his Doctrines of the great educators, 1918, 1965 (rev).

Baker, A. T. Milton and Chateaubriand. Manchester 1919.

Gilbert, A. H. Pierre Davity: his Geography and its use by Milton. Geographical Rev 7 1919.

— The Cambridge manuscript and Milton's plans for an epic. SP 16 1919.

— Milton and the mysteries. SP 17 1920.

— The problem of evil in Paradise lost. JEGP 22 1923.

— Some critical opinions on Milton. SP 33 1936.

— The theological basis of Satan's rebellion and the function of Abdiel in Paradise lost. MP 40 1942.

— On the composition of Paradise lost. Chapel Hill 1947.

— Critics of Mr C. S. Lewis on Milton's Satan. Shakespeare Assoc Quart 47 1948.

— Is Samson Agonistes unfinished? PQ 28 1949.

— Milton's defense of bawdry. In SAMLA studies in Milton, ed J. M. Patrick, Gainesville 1953.

— Form and matter in Paradise lost book iii. JEGP 60 1961.

Stevens, D. H. The order of Milton's sonnets. MP 17 1919.

— Milton papers. Chicago 1927.

Sherburn, G. W. The early popularity of Milton's minor poems. MP 17 1920.

Glicksman, H. Lowell on Milton's Areopagitica. MLN 35 1920.

— The sources of Milton's History of Britain. Madison 1920.

Lindelöf, U. Milton. Helsinki 1920.

Mutschmann, H. Der andere Milton. Bonn 1920.

— The secret of Milton. Dorpat 1925.

— Milton's projected epic of the rise and future greatness of the Britannic nation. Tartu 1936.

Saurat, D. Blake and Milton. Bordeaux 1920, 1935 (rev).
—— La pensée de Milton. Paris 1920.
—— Milton, man and thinker. 1924, 1944 (rev).
—— Milton and the King's prayer. RES 1 1925.
—— Milton et le matérialisme chrétien en Angleterre. Paris 1928.
Fischer, W. Der alte und der neue Milton. Germanisch-romanische Monatsschrift 10 1922.
Rand, E. K. Milton in rustication. SP 19 1922.
Douady, J. La Création et le fruit défendu selon Milton. Paris 1923.
Visiak, E. H. Milton Agonistes: a metaphysical criticism. 1923.
—— The animus against Milton. Derby 1945.
—— The portent of Milton: some aspects of his genius. 1958.
Bredvold, L. I. Milton and Bodin's Heptaplomeres. SP 21 1924.
Candy, H. C. H. Some newly discovered stanzas written by Milton on engraved scenes illustrating Ovid's Metamorphoses. 1924.
—— Milton's early reading of Sylvester. N & Q 8 Feb 1930.
—— Milton's autographs established. Library 4th ser 13 1932.
Curry, W. C. Samson Agonistes yet again. Sewanee Rev 32 1924.
—— Milton's dual concept of God as related to creation. SP 47 1950.
—— Some travels of Milton's Satan and the road to Hell. PQ 29 1950.
—— The genesis of Milton's world. Anglia 70 1951.
—— Milton's ontology, cosmogony and physics. Lexington 1957. Mostly reprints.
Herford, C. H. Dante and Milton. Manchester 1924, Oxford 1927 (as The post-war mind of Germany and other European essays).
Langdon, I. Milton's theory of poetry and fine art. New Haven 1924.
Larson, M. A. The influence of Milton's divorce tracts on Farquhar's Beaux strategem. PMLA 39 1924.
—— The modernity of Milton. Chicago 1927.
—— Milton and Puritanism clarified. PQ 9 1930. Reply by E. N. S. Thompson, ibid.
Nicolson, M. H. The spirit world of Milton and More. SP 22 1925.
—— Milton and Hobbes. SP 23 1926.
—— Milton and the Conjectura Cabbalistica. PQ 6 1927.
—— Milton and the Bible. In The Bible and its literary associations, ed M. B. Crook, New York 1937.
—— Milton's Hell and the Phlegraean fields. UTQ 7 1938.
—— In her Breaking of the circle: studies in the effect of the new science upon seventeenth-century poetry, Evanston 1950, New York 1960 (rev).
—— Milton and the telescope. In her Science and imagination, Ithaca 1956.
—— Milton: a reader's guide to his poetry. New York 1963.
—— The discovery of space. In Medieval and Renaissance studies, ed O. B. Hardison, Chapel Hill 1966.
Schirmer, W. F. Antike, Renaissance und Puritanismus. Munich 1924.
Grannis, R. S. The Beverley Chew collection of Milton portraits. BNYPL Jan 1926.
Fletcher, H. F. Milton's Semitic studies and some manifestations of them in his poetry. Chicago 1926.
—— The use of the Bible in Milton's prose. Urbana 1929.
—— Milton's rabbinical readings. Urbana 1930.
—— Milton's Homer. JEGP 38 1939.
—— Milton's private library: an additional title. PQ 28 1949.
—— A possible origin of Milton's counterpoint or double rhythm. JEGP 54 1955.
—— The intellectual development of Milton. 2 vols Urbana 1956–61.
—— Milton's Demogorgon. JEGP 57 1958.
—— Milton's old Damoetas. JEGP 60 1961.

Garrod, H. W. Milton's lines on Shakespeare. E & S 12 1926.
Kreipe, C. E. Milton's Samson Agonistes. Halle 1926.
Peers, E. A. Milton in Spain. SP 23 1926.
Haller, W. Before Areopagitica. PMLA 42 1927.
—— (ed). Tracts on liberty in the Puritan revolution. 3 vols New York 1935.
—— In his Rise of Puritanism, New York 1938.
—— Milton and the Levellers. HLQ 5 1942.
—— For the liberty of unlicenc'd printing. Amer Scholar 14 1945.
—— Hail wedded love. ELH 13 1946.
—— What needs my Shakespeare? Shakspeare Quart 3 1952.
—— In his Liberty and reformation in the Puritan revolution, New York 1955.
—— Milton and the Protestant ethic. Jnl of Br Stud 1 1961.
—— The tragedy of God's Englishman. In Reason and imagination, ed J. A. Mazzeo, New York 1962.
—— and M. Haller. The Puritan art of love. HLQ 5 1942.
Magoun, F. P. The Chaucer of Spenser and Milton. MP 25 1927.
Sheppard, J. T. In his Aeschylus and Sophocles, 1927.
Welsford, E. The Court masque: a study in the relationship between poetry and the revels. 1927.
Albrecht, W. Über das Theatrum poetarum von Miltons Neffen Edward Phillips. Leipzig 1928.
Agar, H. Milton and Plato. Princeton 1928.
Grierson, H. J. C. John Milton. Criterion 7 1928.
—— Milton: the man and the poet. In his Cross currents in English literature of the seventeenth century, 1929.
—— Milton and Wordsworth: poets and prophets: a study of their reactions to political events. Cambridge 1937.
—— Milton's theology. RES 14 1938.
—— A note upon the Samson Agonistes of Milton and Sampson of Heilige Wraeck by Joost van den Vondel. In his Essays and addresses, 1940.
—— Criticism and creation: their interactions. E & S 29 1943.
—— Milton and liberty. MLR 39 1944.
—— The metaphysics of Donne and Milton; Milton and political liberty. Both in his Criticism and creation, 1949.
Martin, B. The date of Milton's first marriage. SP 25 1928.
Ullrich, H. Deutsche Milton-Übersetzungen vom 18 Jahrhundert bis zum Gegenwart. Stuttgart 1928.
Baldwin, E. C. Some extra-biblical Semitic influences upon Milton's story of the Fall of Man. JEGP 28 1929.
—— Milton and Phineas Fletcher. JEGP 33 1934.
—— Shook the arsenal: a note on Paradise regained. PQ 18 1939.
Elliott, G. R. Milton and the present state of poetry. In his Cycle of modern poetry, Princeton 1929.
Hartwell, K. Lactantius and Milton. Cambridge Mass 1929.
Helsztyński, S. Milton in Poland. SP 26 1929.
Keith, A. L. Personification in Milton's Paradise lost. Eng Jnl 17 1929.
Noyes, A. A French view of Milton. In his Opalescent parrot, 1929.
Riley, E. H. Milton's tribute to Virgil. SP 26 1929.
Schücking, L. L. Die Spiegelung der puritanischen Ehe in Miltons Verlorenem Paradies. In his Die Familie im Puritanismus, Leipzig 1929, Berne 1964 (rev); tr as The Puritan family, 1969.
Thaler, A. The Shaksperian element in Milton; Milton in the theatre. Both in his Shakspere's silences, Cambridge Mass 1929.
—— Shakespeare and Milton once more. In SAMLA studies in Milton, ed J. M. Patrick, Gainesville 1953.
—— Shakespearean recollection in Milton: a summing-up. In his Shakespeare and our world, Knoxville 1966.
Blunden, E. Milton and the new consciousness. Nation (London) 26 April 1930.
Dustoor, P. E. Legends of Lucifer in early English and in Milton. Anglia 54 1930.

Howe, M. L. Anapestic feet in Paradise lost. MLN 45 1930.

Kelly, F. J. Milton and Dante: a few points of contrast. Catholic World Nov 1930.

Quintana, R. Notes on English educational opinion during the 17th century. SP 27 1930.

Read, A. W. The disinterment of Milton's remains. PMLA 45 1930.

Siebert, T. Untersuchungen über Milton Kunst vom psychologischen Standpunkt aus. Anglia 42 1930.

— Egozentrisches in Miltons Schreibweise, mit besonderer Berücksichtigung des Satan in Paradise lost. Anglia 43 1931.

Sorsby, A. On the nature of Milton's blindness. Br Jnl of Ophthalmology 14 1930.

Stoll, E. E. Was paradise well lost?; Milton in the hands of the learned; Milton, Puritan of the 17th century. All in his Poets and playwrights, Minneapolis 1930.

— Belial as an example; Milton a Romantic; Time and space in Milton; From the superhuman to the human in Paradise lost. All in his From Shakespeare to Joyce, New York 1944.

Tillyard, E. M. W. Milton. 1930, 1966 (rev).

— The Miltonic setting. Cambridge 1938.

— Milton and the English epic tradition. In Seventeenth-century studies presented to Sir Herbert Grierson, Oxford 1938.

— Milton and the classics. Proc Classical Assoc 35 1938.

— The causeway from Hell to the world in the tenth book of Paradise lost. SP 38 1941.

— Studies in Milton. 1951.

— Milton. 1952 (Br Council pamphlet).

— In his English epic and its background, 1954.

— The metaphysicals and Milton. 1956.

— On annotating Paradise lost books ix and x. JEGP 60 1961.

— The literary kinds and Milton. In his Essays literary and educational, 1962.

Farnell, L. R. Milton and Pindar. TLS 1 Oct 1931. Comment by R. Shafer 3 Dec 1931.

Herbster, S. I. Paradise lost: a study for the modern preacher. Lutheran Church Quart 4 1931.

Looten, C. C. J. Milton et la musique. Revue Anglo-américaine 9 1931.

— Milton et l'idée du poète. Ibid.

— Les débuts de Milton pamphlétaire. Etudes Anglaises 1 1937.

— Milton: quelques aspects de son génie. Paris 1938.

Oras, A. Milton's editors and commentators from Patrick Hume to Henry John Todd 1695–1801. Oxford 1931, New York 1967 (rev).

— Notes on some Miltonic usages. Tartu 1938.

— Echoing verse endings in Paradise lost. In South Atlantic studies for S. E. Leavitt, Washington 1953.

— Milton's blank verse and the chronology of his major poems. In SAMLA studies in Milton, ed J. M. Patrick, Gainesville 1953.

— Milton's early rhyme schemes and the structure of Lycidas. MP 52 1954.

— The multitudinous orb: some Miltonic elements in Shelley. MLQ 16 1955.

— Spenser and Milton: some parallels and contrasts in the handling of sound. Eng Inst Essays 1956 (Sound and poetry).

— Darkness visible: notes on Milton's descriptive procedures in Paradise lost. In All these to teach: essays in honor of C. A. Robertson, Gainesville 1965.

— Blank verse and chronology in Milton. Gainesville 1966.

Pettigrew, R. C. Emerson and Milton. Amer Lit 3 1931.

Ransom, J. C. In his God without thunder: an unorthodox defence of orthodoxy, 1931.

— A poem nearly anonymous [Lycidas]. Amer Rev 4 1933; rptd in his World's body, New York 1938.

— The idea of a literary anthropologist and what he might say of the Paradise lost of Milton. Kenyon Rev 21 1959.

Reck, J. Das Prinzip der Freiheit bei Milton. Erlangen 1931.

Taylor, G. C. Some patristic conventions common to Shakespeare and Milton. SP 28 1931.

— Milton's use of Du Bartas. Cambridge Mass 1934.

— Milton's English. N & Q 27 Jan 1940.

— Why read Milton now? In Twentieth-century English, ed W. S. Knickerbocker, New York 1946.

Thibaut de Maisières, M. In his Les poèmes inspirés du début de la genèse à l'époque de la Renaissance, Louvain 1931.

Vince, C. A. Milton in Italy. In his Lectures and diversions, 1931.

Whaler, J. Compounding and distribution of similes in Paradise lost. MP 28 1931.

— Grammatical nexus of the Miltonic simile. JEGP 30 1931.

— The Miltonic simile. PMLA 46 1931.

— Animal simile in Paradise lost. PMLA 47 1932.

— Counterpoint and symbol: an inquiry into the rhythm of Milton's epic style. Copenhagen 1956.

Willoughby, E. E. Milton's taxes 1641–2. MLR 26–7 1931–2.

Wright, B. A. Milton's first marriage. MLR 26–7 1931–2.

— The alleged falsehoods in Milton's account of his continental tour. MLR 28 1933.

— Milton's Paradise lost. 1962.

— A note on Milton's diction. In Th' upright heart and pure, ed A. P. Fiore, Pittsburgh 1967.

Bøgholm, N. Milton and Paradise lost. Copenhagen 1932.

Brinkley, R. F. Milton and the Arthurian story. In her Arthurian legend in the seventeenth century, Baltimore 1932.

— Milton in French literature of the nineteenth century. UTQ 27 1958.

Bush, D. In his Mythology and the Renaissance tradition in English poetry, Minneapolis 1932, New York 1963 (rev).

— In his Renaissance and English humanism, Toronto 1939.

— Paradise lost in our time. Ithaca 1945.

— The critical significance of biographical evidence: Milton. Eng Inst Essays 1946.

— Virgil and Milton. Classical Jnl 47 1952.

— Ironic and ambiguous allusion in Paradise lost. JEGP 60 1961.

— In Explication and criticism, ed W. K. Wimsatt, New York 1963.

— John Milton. New York 1964.

— The date of Milton's Ad patrem. MP 61 1964.

— The isolation of the Renaissance hero. In his Prefaces to Renaissance literature, Cambridge Mass 1965.

— Calculus racked him. In his Engaged and disengaged, Cambridge Mass 1966. Against numerological interpretation.

Darbishire, H. (ed). The early lives of Milton. 1932. Contains 6 biographies.

— The chronology of Milton's handwriting. Library 14th ser 1933.

— Milton's Paradise lost. Oxford 1951. A lecture.

— Milton's poetic language. E & S new ser 10 1957.

Lewis, C. S. A note on Comus. E & S 8 1932; rptd in his Studies in medieval and Renaissance literature, Cambridge 1966.

— A preface to Paradise lost. Oxford 1942.

McColley, G. The theory of a plurality of worlds as a factor in Milton's attitude toward the Copernican hypothesis. MLN 47 1932.

— Milton's dialogue on astronomy: the principal immediate sources. PMLA 52 1937.

— The astronomy of Paradise lost. SP 34 1937.

— The epic catalogue of Paradise lost. ELH 4 1937.

— Milton's techniques of source adaptation. SP 35 1938.
— The Book of Enoch and Paradise lost. Harvard Theological Rev 31 1938.
— Milton's lost tragedy. PQ 18 1939.
— Paradise lost. Harvard Theological Rev 32 1939.
— Paradise lost: an account of its growth and major origins. Chicago 1940.
— Milton and Moses Bar-Cepha. SP 38 1941.
Mackellar, W. Milton and Grotius. TLS 15 Dec 1932.
Raymond, D. B. Oliver's secretary: Milton in the era of revolt. New York 1932.
Shigeno, T. A study of Paradise lost. Tokyo 1932. In Japanese.
Smith R. W. The source of Milton's Pandemonium. MP 29 1832.
Whiting, G. W. Milton's crystalline sphere and Ben Gerson's heavens. RES 8 1932.
— The sources of Eikonoklastes: a resurvey. SP 32 1935.
— A pseudonymous reply to Milton's Of prelatical episcopacy. PMLA 51 1936.
— Milton and comets. ELH 4 1937.
— Milton's literary milieu. Chapel Hill 1939.
— The Father to the Son. MLN 65 1950.
— Christ's miraculous fast. MLN 66 1951.
— Samson Agonistes and the Geneva Bible. Rice Inst Pamphlet 38 1951.
— Pareus, the Stuarts, Laud and Milton. SP 50 1953.
— Milton and this pendant world. Austin 1958.
— Abdiel and the prophet Abdias. SP 60 1963.
— and A. Gossman. Siloa's brook, the pool of Siloam and Milton's Muse. SP 58 1961.
Williams, C. In his English poetic mind, Oxford 1932.
— The deification of reason. In Reason and beauty in the poetic mind, Oxford 1933.
— The new Milton. London Mercury July 1937.
— Introduction to English poems of Milton, Oxford 1940 (WC); rptd in his Image of the city, ed A. Ridler 1958.
Dorian, D. C. The question of autobiographical significance in L'Allegro and Il Penseroso. MP 31 1933.
— The English Diodatis: a history of Charles Diodati's family and his friendship with Milton. New Brunswick NJ 1950.
Farrison, W. E. The classical allusions in Paradise lost Books i and ii. Eng Jnl 22 1933.
Ferrau, A. Milton revoluzionarie. Rassegna Italiana 34 1933.
Hammond, M. Concilia deorum from Homer through Milton. SP 30 1933.
Iwahashi, T. The poetic metaphysics of Paradise lost. Tokyo 1933. In Japanese.
Kemble, J. Milton and his blindness. In his Idols and invalids, 1933.
Leavis, F. R. Milton's verse. Scrutiny 2 1933; rptd in his Revaluation, 1936.
— Mr Eliot and Milton; In defence of Milton. Both in his Common pursuit, 1952.
Post, M. M. Milton's twin lyrics at 300. Eng Jnl 22 1933. On L'Allegro and Il Penseroso.
Praz, M. The metamorphoses of Satan. In his Romantic agony, Oxford 1933.
— Milton and Poussin. In Seventeenth-century studies presented to Sir Herbert Grierson, Oxford 1938; in his Gusto neoclassico, Florence 1940 (in Italian); in Le paradis perdu 1667–1967, ed J. Blondel, Paris 1967 (in French).
— Baroque in England. MP 61 1964.
Saito, T. Milton. Tokyo 1933. In Japanese.
Scherpbier, H. Milton in Holland: a study in the literary relations of England and Holland before 1730. Amsterdam 1933.
Stevens, A. K. Milton and chartism. PQ 12 1933.
Vogt, K. F. Milton als Publizist. Würzburg 1933.
Wilde, H.-O. Miltons geistesgeschichtliche Bedeutung. Heidelberg 1933.

— Miltons persönliche und ideale Welt in ihrer Beziehung zum Aristokratismus. Bonn 1933.
Wilmer, W. H. The blindness of Milton. JEGP 32 1933.
Bodkin, M. Archetypal patterns in poetry: psychological studies of imagination. Oxford 1934.
Brown, E. G. Milton's blindness. New York 1934.
Clyde, W. M. In his Struggle for the freedom of the press from Caxton to Cromwell, Oxford 1934.
Diekhoff, J. S. Rhyme in Paradise lost. PMLA 49 1934. Addns by J. M. Purcell, MLN 59 1944.
— Terminal pause in Milton's verse. SP 32 1935.
— The punctuation of Comus. PMLA 51 1936.
— The milder shades of Purgatory. MLN 52 1937.
— (ed). Milton on himself: Milton's utterances upon himself and his works. New York 1939.
— Milton's prosody in the poems of the Trinity manuscript. PMLA 54 1939.
— Critical activity of the poetic mind: Milton. PMLA 55 1940.
— The function of the prologues in Paradise lost. PMLA 57 1942.
— Eve, the Devil and Areopagitica. MLQ 5 1944.
— Milton's Paradise lost: a commentary on the argument. New York 1946.
— The Trinity manuscript and the dictation of Paradise lost. PQ 28 1949.
— The general education of a poet: Milton. Jnl of General Education 14 1962.
— (ed). A maske at Ludlow: essays on Milton's Comus. Cleveland 1968. With 11 essays.
— Eve's dream and the paradox of fallible perfection. Milton Quart 4 1970.
Godolphin, F. R. B. Milton, Lycidas and Propertius. MLN 49 1934.
— Notes on the techniques of Milton's Latin elegies. MP 37 1940.
Kelley, M. Milton, Ibn Ezra and Wollebius. MLN 49 1934.
— Milton and the third Person of the Trinity. SP 32 1935.
— Milton's library. TLS 19 Dec 1936.
— Milton autographs. TLS 2 Oct 1937.
— The theological dogma of Paradise lost iii 173–202. PMLA 52 1937.
— Milton and miracles. MLN 53 1938.
— Milton's use of begot in Paradise lost v 603. SP 38 1941.
— This great argument: a study of Milton's De doctrina christiana as a gloss upon Paradise lost. Princeton 1941. See Hunter, Bright essence, col 1263 below.
— The annotations in Milton's family Bible. MLN 63 1948.
— Daniel Skinner, Lord Preston and Milton's commonplace book. MLN 64 1949.
— Milton and Machiavelli's Discorsi. SB 4 1952.
— Additional texts of Milton's State papers. MLN 67 1952.
— Milton's later sonnets and the Cambridge manuscript. MP 54 1956.
— Milton's Arianism again considered. Harvard Theological Rev 54 1961.
— The composition of Milton's De doctrina christiana: the first stage. In Th'upright heart and pure, ed A. P. Fiore, Pittsburgh 1967.
— The recovery, printing and reception of Milton's Christian doctrine. HLQ 31 1967.
— Milton and the Trinity. HLQ 33 1970.
— and S. D. Atkins. Milton's annotations of Aratus. PMLA 70 1955.
— Milton's annotations of Euripides. JEGP 60 1961.
— Milton and the Harvard Pindar. SB 17 1964.
Macaulay, R. Milton. 1934.
Martin, L. C. Thomas Warton and the early poems of Milton. Proc Br Acad 20 1934.

Nethercot, A. H. Milton, Jonson and the young Cowley. MLN 49 1934.

Parsons, E. S. Milton's seasonal inspiration. MLN 49 1934.

Pilato, S. de. Un inspiratore del Paradiso perduto: P. Serafino della Salandra. Potenza 1934.

Richter, W. Der Hiatus im englischen Klassizismus (Milton, Dryden, Pope). Freiburg 1934.

Schork, W. Die Dramenpläne Miltons. Freiburg in Quakenbrück 1934.

Tihany, L. C. Milton's Brief history of Muscovia. PQ 13 1934.

Wolfe, D. M. Milton and Mirabeau. PMLA 49 1934.

— Milton, Lilburne and the people. MP 31 1934. See MLN 56 1941.

— Milton's conception of the ruler. SP 33 1936.

— Milton in the Puritan revolution. New York 1941.

— The role of Milton's Christ. Sewanee Rev 51 1943.

— Milton and Hobbes: a contrast in social temper. SP 41 1944.

— Limits of Miltonic tolerations. JEGP 60 1961.

— Milton and Cromwell: April 1653. In English studies today: 4th series, ed I. Cellini and G. Melchiori, Rome 1966.

— Milton and his England. Princeton 1971.

Belloc, H. Milton. 1935.

Campbell, L. B. The Christian Muse. Huntington Lib Bull 8 1935.

Clark, W. S. Milton and the Villa Diodati. RES 11 1935.

Clements, T. The angels in Paradise lost. Quart Rev 164 1935.

Dworsky, B. R. Milton and the rabbinical Bible. TLS 25 April 1935. Reply by T. Gaster 9 May 1935.

Eliot, T. S. A note on the verse of Milton. E & S 21 1935.

— Milton. Proc Br Acad 33 1947; rptd in his On poetry and poets, 1957 (shortened).

Empson, W. Milton and Bentley: the pastoral and the innocence of man and nature. In his Some versions of pastoral, 1935.

— 'All' in Paradise lost. In his Structure of complex words, 1951.

— The loss of Paradise. In The Northern miscellany of literary criticism, 1953.

— Adam and Eve. Listener 14 July 1960.

— Heaven's awful monarch. Listener 21 July 1960.

— Satan argues his case. Listener 7 July 1960.

— Milton's God. 1961, 1965 (rev with addns).

French, J. M. Milton as a historian. PMLA 50 1935.

— The date of Milton's blindness. PQ 15 1936.

— Milton and the politicians. Ibid.

— Milton as a satirist. PMLA 51 1936.

— Milton, Needham and Mercurius Politicus. SP 33 1936.

— The autographs of Milton. ELH 4 1937.

— Milton's annotated copy of Gildas. Harvard Stud in Philology 20 1938.

— The Powell-Milton bond. Ibid

— Milton's family Bible. PMLA 53 1938.

— Milton in chancery: new chapters in the lives of the poet and his father. New York 1939.

— Mute inglorious Miltons. MLN 1 1940.

— That late villain Milton. PMLA 55 1940.

— The burning of Milton's Defensio in France. MLN 56 1941.

— Milton's supplicats. HLQ 5 1942.

— Chips from Milton's workshop. ELH 10 1943.

— The baptism of Milton's daughter Mary. MLN 63 1948.

— The date of Milton's First Defense. Library 5th ser 3 1948.

— Milton, Ramus and Edward Phillips. MP 47 1949.

— (ed). The life records of Milton. 5 vols New Brunswick NJ 1949–58.

— The digressions in Lycidas. SP 50 1953.

— Mr Secretary Milton at work. South Atlantic Quart 55 1956.

— Light and work in L'Allegro and Il Penseroso. South Atlantic Quart 58 1959.

— The reliability of Anthony Wood and Milton's Oxford MA. PMLA 75 1960.

— Some notes on Milton's Accedence commenc't grammar. JEGP 60 1961.

— Milton and the barbarous dissonance. Texas Stud in Lang & Lit 4 1962.

— Moseley's advertisements of Milton's poems 1650–60. HLQ 25 1962.

— Some notes on Milton from Nouvelles ordinaires de Londres. N & Q Feb 1962.

Gray, F. C. Milton's counterpoint: classicism and romanticism in the poetry of Milton. Sewanee Rev 43 1935.

Harrison, T. P., jr. The Latin pastorals of Milton and Castiglione. PMLA 50 1935.

— (ed). The pastoral elegy: an anthology. Austin 1939.

— The haemony passage in Comus again. PQ 20 1943.

— They tell of birds: Chaucer, Spenser, Milton, Drayton. Austin 1956.

Havens, P. S. Dryden's tagged version of Paradise lost. In Essays in dramatic literature: the [T. M.] Parrott presentation volume, Princeton 1935.

Howard, L. Early American copies of Milton. Huntington Lib Bull no 7 1935.

— The influence of Milton on colonial American poetry. Huntington Lib Bull no 9 1936.

— The invention of Milton's great argument. HLQ 9 1946.

Parker, W. R. On Milton's early literary program. MP 33 1935.

— The Trinity ms and Milton's plans for a tragedy. JEGP 34 1935.

— Milton's Hobson poems: some neglected texts. MLR 31 1936.

— Milton's debt to Greek tragedy in Samson Agonistes. Baltimore 1937.

— Milton, Rothwell and Simmons. Library 4th ser 18 1938.

— Milton and Thomas Young 1602–28. MLN 53 1938.

— Milton's contemporary reputation. Columbus 1940.

— Above all liberties: Milton's relations with his earliest publishers. Princeton Univ Lib Chron 2 1941.

— Milton and Edward Phillips. TLS 28 Feb 1942.

— Milton on King James II. MLQ 3 1942.

— John Milton, scrivener 1590–1632. MLN 59 1944.

— Milton's last sonnet. RES 21 1945. Comment by F. Pyle 25 1949; Parker and Pyle, new ser 2 1951.

— Notes on the chronology of Milton's Latin poems. In A tribute to G. C. Taylor, Chapel Hill 1952.

— The anonymous life of Milton. TLS 3 Sept 1957. By Cyriack Skinner? Comments by R. W. Hunt 11 Oct, M. Kelley 27 Dec 1957.

— Wood's life of Milton: its sources and significance. PBSA 52 1958.

— Education: Milton's ideas and ours. College Eng Oct 1962.

— Notes on the text of Samson Agonistes. JEGP 60 1961.

— The date of Samson Agonistes. PQ 28 1949. Reply by E. Sirluck, JEGP 60 1661.

— Milton: a biography. 2 vols Oxford 1968.

— Milton's Commonplace Book: an index and notes. Milton Newsletter 3 1969.

— The date of Samson Agonistes. In Calm of mind, ed J. A. Wittreich, Cleveland 1971.

— Problems in Milton biography. Milton Quart 5 1971.

Parsons, E. S. The authorship of the anonymous life of Milton. PMLA 50 1935.

Seaton, E. Literary relations of England and Scandinavia in the 17th century. Oxford 1935. On Milton and Salmasius, pp. 107–9.

— Comus and Shakespeare. E & S 31 1945.

Sewell, A. Milton and the Mosaic law. MLR 30 1935.

—— A study in Milton's Christian doctrine. Oxford 1939.

Timberlake, P. Milton and Euripides. In Essays in dramatic literature: the [T. M.] Parrott presentation volume, Princeton 1935.

Williamson, G. Milton and the mortalist heresy. SP 32 1935; rptd in following.

—— The obsequies for Edward King. In his Seventeenth-century contexts, 1960.

—— Milton and others. 1965. Reprints 6 essays on Milton.

Woodhouse, A. S. P. Milton, Puritanism and liberty. UTQ 4 1935.

—— Milton and his age. UTQ 5 1935.

—— The argument of Milton's Comus. UTQ 11 1941. Addn 19 1950.

—— Notes on Milton's early development. UTQ 13 1943.

—— The approach to Milton: a note on practical criticism. Trans Royal Soc of Canada 38 1944.

—— Notes on Milton's views on the creation: the initial phase. PQ 28 1949.

—— Samson Agonistes and Milton's experience. Trans Royal Soc of Canada 43 1949.

—— The historical criticism of Milton. PMLA 66 1951.

—— Milton's pastoral monodies. In Studies in honor of G. Norwood, Toronto 1952.

—— Pattern in Paradise lost. UTQ 22 1953.

—— Milton the poet. Toronto 1955. A lecture.

—— Theme and pattern in Paradise regained. UTQ 25 1956.

—— Tragic effect in Samson Agonistes. UTQ 28 1959.

—— The heavenly Muse. Toronto 1972.

Wyld, H. C. The significance of -'n and -en in Milton's spelling. E Studien 70 1935.

Baker, C. H. C. William Blake, painter. Huntington Lib Bull 10 1936. On Blake's illustrations of Paradise lost.

—— Some illustrators of Milton's Paradise lost 1688–1850. Library 5th ser 3 1948–9. Addn by T. Balston 4 1950.

Cameron, K. W. Milton's library. TLS 24 Oct 1936.

Coffman, G. R. The parable of the Good Shepherd, De contemptu mundi and Lycidas. ELH 3 1936.

Cowling, G. Milton's Paradise lost. In his Shelley and other essays, Melbourne 1936.

de Filippis, M. Milton and Manso: cups or books? PMLA 51 1936.

Dobrée, B. Milton and Dryden: a comparison and contrast in poetic ideas and poetic method. ELH 3 1936.

Galland, R. Milton et Buchanan. Revue Anglo-américaine 13 1936.

Runtz-Rees, C. Flower garlands of the poets: Milton, Shakespeare, Spenser, Marot, Sannazaro. In Mélanges offerts à M. Abel LeFranc, Paris 1936.

Schneider, R. Milton zwischen Politik und Geschichte. Die Literatur 38 1936.

Trowbridge, H. Joseph Warton's classification of English poets. MLN 51 1936.

Barker, A. E. Milton's schoolmasters. MLR 32 1937.

—— Christian liberty in Milton's divorce pamphlets. MLR 35 1940.

—— The pattern of Milton's Nativity Ode. UTQ 10 1941.

—— Milton and the Puritan dilemma. Toronto 1942.

—— And on his crest sat horror: 18th-century interpretations of Milton's sublimity and his Satan. UTQ 11 1942.

—— Structural pattern in Paradise lost. PQ 28 1949.

—— Seven types of Milton criticism. UTQ 25 1956.

—— Structural and doctrinal pattern in Milton's later poems. In Essays presented to A. S. P. Woodhouse, Toronto 1964.

—— (ed). Milton: modern essays in criticism. New York 1965. With 33 essays (abridged).

—— The relevance of regeneration. In Paradise lost: a tercentenary tribute, ed B. Rajan, Toronto 1969.

Dubbel, S. E. Leisure at Horton. South Atlantic Quart 36 1937.

Finley, J. H. Milton and Horace: a study of Milton's sonnets. Harvard Stud in Classical Philology 48 1937.

Johnson, F. R. In his Astronomical thought in Renaissance England, Baltimore 1937.

Lovejoy, A. O. Milton and the paradox of the fortunate Fall. ELH 4 1937; rptd in his Essays in the history of ideas, Baltimore 1948.

—— Milton's dialogue on astronomy. In Reason and the imagination, ed J. A. Mazzeo, New York 1962.

Oman, C. Of poor Mr King, Milton and certain friends. Cornhill Mag Nov 1937.

Orsini, N. Gli studii machiavellici del Milton. In his Studii sul Rinascimento italiano in Inghilterra, Florence 1937.

Pritchard, J. P. The Fathers of the Church in the works of Milton. Classical Jnl 33 1937.

Rice, W. G. Paradise regained. Papers of Michigan Acad 22 1937.

—— A note on Areopagitica. JEGP 40 1941.

—— Fate in Paradise lost. Papers of Michigan Acad 31 1945.

Schirmer, W. F. Die epische Dichtung und Milton. In his Geschichte der englischen Literatur, Halle 1937.

Spadala, E. Tre principi dei diavoli: Lucifer di Dante, Plutone di Tasso, Satana di Milton. Ragusa 1937.

Allen, J. W. Milton's writings of 1641–2. In his English political thought 1603–44, 1938.

Binyon, L. A note on Milton's imagery and rhythm. In Seventeenth-century studies presented to Sir Herbert Grierson, Oxford 1938.

Brennecke, E., jr. John Milton the elder and his music. New York 1938.

Chaffurin, L. Milton. Les Langues Modernes 36 1938.

Eastman, F. In his Men of power, Nashville 1938.

Firth, C. H. Milton as an historian. In his Essays historical and literary, Oxford 1938.

Gehman, H. S. Milton's use of Hebrew in the De doctrina christiana. Jewish Quart Rev 24 1938.

Green, C. C. The paradox of the Fall in Paradise lost. MLN 53 1938.

Hammerle, K. To save appearances (Paradise lost viii 82): ein Problem der Scholastik. Anglia 62 1938.

Hughes, M. Y. The Christ of Paradise regained and the Renaissance heroic tradition. SP 35 1938.

—— The historical setting of Milton's Observations on the articles of peace, 1649. PMLA 64 1949.

—— New evidence on the charge that Milton forged the Pamela prayer in the Eikon basilike. RES new ser 3 1952.

—— Milton's celestial battle and the theogonies. In Studies in honor of T. W. Baldwin, Urbana 1958.

—— Some illustrators of Milton: the expulsion from Paradise. JEGP 60 1961.

—— Ten perspectives on Milton. New Haven 1965.

—— Devils to adore for deities. In Studies in honor of D. T. Starnes, Austin 1967.

—— Merit in Paradise lost. HLQ 31 1967.

—— Milton's limbo of vanity. In Th' upright heart and pure, ed A. P. Fiore, Pittsburgh 1967.

—— Satan now dragon grown (Paradise lost x 529). Etudes Anglaises 20 1967.

—— Beyond disobedience. In Approaches to Paradise lost, ed C. A. Patrides 1968.

—— Earth felt the wound. ELH 36 1969.

—— Milton's Eikon basilike. In Calm of mind, ed J. A. Wittreich, Cleveland 1971.

—— The Miltonic future. MLR 66 1971.

Kreter, E. Bildungs- und Erziehungsideale bei Milton. Halle 1938.

Mackail, J. W. Bentley's Milton. In his Studies in humanism, 1938.

Maxey, C. C. Voices of freedom. In his Political philosophies, New York 1938.

Murry, J. M. Milton. In his Heaven – and earth, 1938, New York 1938 (as Heroes of thought).

—— Milton's prosody. In his Poets, critics, mystics, ed R. Rees, Carbondale 1970.

Powys, J. C. In his Enjoyment of literature, New York 1938.

Sanderlin, G. The influence of Milton and Wordsworth on the early Victorian sonnet. ELH 5 1938.

Menzies, W. Milton: the last poems. E & S 24 1938.

Aldridge, A. O. Milton's and Pope's conception of God and man. Bibliotheca Sacra 96 1939.

Banks, T. H. The meaning of gods in Paradise lost. MLN 54 1939.

— The banquet scene in Paradise regained. PMLA 55 1940.

— A source for Lycidas 154–8. MLN 62 1947.

— Milton's imagery. New York 1950.

Benham, A. R. The so-called anonymous or earliest life of Milton. ELH 6 1939. Reply by E. S. Parsons 9 1942.

— Things unattempted yet in prose or rime. MLQ 14 1953.

Bennett, J. W. Milton's use of the vision of Er. MP 36 1939.

Fink, Z. S. Wine, poetry and Milton's Elegia sexta. E Studies 21 1939.

— Milton's retirement to Horton and Renaissance literary theory. E Studies 22 1940.

— Venice and English political thought in the 17th century. MP 38 1940.

— The political implications of Paradise regained. JEGP 40 1941.

— Milton and the theory of climatic influence. MLQ 2 1941.

— Immortal government: the free commonwealth. In his Classical republicans, Evanston 1945.

Gilman, W. E. Milton's rhetoric: studies in his defense of liberty. Columbia Missouri 1939.

Haviland, T. P. Milton: religious liberal. Christian Register 118 1939.

— How well did Poe know Milton? PMLA 69 1954.

Knight, G. W. The frozen labyrinth: an essay on Milton. In his Burning oracle, Oxford 1939.

— Chariot of wrath: the message of Milton to democracy at war. 1942.

— In his Golden labyrinth: a study of British drama, 1962.

Morand, P. P. De Comus à Satan: l'œuvre poétique de Milton expliquée par sa vie. Paris 1939.

Stillman, D. G. Milton as proof reader. MLN 54 1939.

Babb, L. The background of Il Penseroso. SP 27 1940.

— The moral cosmos of Paradise lost. East Lansing 1970.

Bradner, L. In his Musae anglicanae: a history of Anglo-Latin poetry 1500–1925, New York 1940.

Carver, P. L. The angels in Paradise lost. RES 16 1940.

Dennis, L. The puzzle of Paradise lost. California Univ Chron 24 1940.

Fletcher, G. B. A. Milton's Latin poems. MP 37 1940.

Guidi, A. John Milton. Brescia 1940.

— Milton e Hopkins. Eng Miscellany (Rome) 6 1955.

Jonas, L. In his Divine science: the aesthetic of some representative 17th-century English poets, New York 1940.

Lumiansky, R. M. Milton's English again. MLN 55 1940.

Montgomery, W. A. The Epitaphium Damonis in the stream of the classical lament. In Studies for W. A. Read, Baton Rouge 1940.

Rickword, E. Milton: the revolutionary intellectual. In his English revolution 1640, 1940.

Shuster, G. N. Milton and the metaphysical poets. In his English ode from Milton to Keats, New York 1940.

Smith, L. P. Milton and his modern critics. Oxford 1940.

Visser, M. Het leven van Milton. Amsterdam 1940.

Williams, A. Milton and the Book of Enoch. Harvard Theological Rev 33 1940.

— Milton and the Renaissance commentaries on Genesis. MP 37 1940.

— Conservative critics of Milton. Sewanee Rev 49 1941.

— Renaissance commentaries on Genesis and some elements of the theology of Paradise lost. PMLA 56 1941.

— Areopagitica revisited. UTQ 14 1944.

— The motivation of Satan's rebellion in Paradise lost. SP 42 1945.

— In his Common expositor: an account of the commentaries on Genesis 1527–1633, Chapel Hill 1948.

Scott-Craig, T. S. K. Milton's use of Wolleb and Ames. MLN 55 1940.

— Concerning Milton's Samson. Renaissance News 5 1952.

— The craftsmanship and theological significance of Milton's Art of logic. HLQ 17 1953.

— Miltonic tragedy and Christian vision. In The tragic vision and the Christian faith, ed N. A. Scott, New York 1957.

Adams, J. R. The theism of Paradise lost. Personalist 22 1941.

Cawley, R. R. Milton's literary craftsmanship: a study of A brief history of Muscovia, with an edition of the text. Princeton 1941.

— Milton and the literature of travel. Princeton 1951.

Chambers, R. W. Poets and their critics: Langland and Milton. Proc Br Acad 27 1941.

Evans, W. M. In his Henry Lawes: musician and friend of poets, New York 1941.

— Hobson appears in comic song. PQ 26 1947.

Hendrickson, G. L. Milton, Salmasius – and synizesis. PQ 20 1941.

McLachlan, H. The religious opinions of Milton, Locke and Newton. Manchester 1941.

Siegel, P. N. A paradise within thee in Milton, Byron and Shelley. MLN 56 1941.

— Milton and the humanist attitude toward women. JHI 11 1950.

Watson, S. R. Milton's use of Phineas Fletcher's Purple island. N & Q 12 April 1941.

— Milton's ideal day. PMLA 57 1942.

Wolff, S. L. Milton's Advocatum nescio quem: Milton, Salmasius and John Cook. MLQ 2 1941.

Beller, E. A. Milton and Mercurius Politicus. HLQ 5 1942.

Bundy, M. W. Eve's dream and the temptation in Paradise lost. Washington State College Research Stud 10 1942.

— Milton's prelapsarian Adam. Washington State College Research Stud 13 1945.

— Milton's exalted man. In Essays presented to B. R. McElderry, Athens Ohio 1967.

Evans, G. B. Two new ms versions of Milton's Hobson poems. MLN 57 1942.

— Milton and the Hobson poems. MLQ 4 1943. See also 9 1948.

Horrell, J. Milton, limbo and suicide. RES 18 1942.

Jahanger, R. P. M. Vondel and Milton. Bombay 1942.

Le Comte, E. S. New light on the haemony passage in Comus. PQ 21 1942.

— Milton's attitude toward women in the History of Britain. PMLA 62 1947.

— That two-handed engine and Savonarola. SP 47 1950. Addn 49 1952.

— Yet once more: verbal and psychological pattern in Milton. New York 1953.

— Milton's infernal council and Mantuan. PMLA 69 1954.

— Samson Agonistes and Aureng-Zebe. Etudes Anglaises 2 1958.

— A Milton dictionary. New York 1961.

— Milton as satirist and wit. In Th' upright heart and pure, ed A. P. Fiore, Pittsburgh 1967.

Pershing, J. H. The different states of the first edition of Paradise lost. Library 4th ser 22 1942.

Daube, D. Three notes on Paradise regained. RES 19 1943.

Eisenstein, S. In his Film sense, 1943.

Elledge, S. Milton, Sappho (?) and Demetrius. MLN 58 1943.

— (ed). Milton's Lycidas edited to serve as an introduction to criticism. New York 1966. With several critiques, abridged.

Farrell, A. Joshua Poole and Milton's minor poems. MLN 58 1943.

Graves, R. Wife to Mr Milton. 1943. Fiction.
— The ghost of Milton. In his Common asphodel, 1949.
— Milton muddles through. New Republic 27 May 1957. On L'Allegro.

Haug, R. Milton and Sir John Harington. MLQ 4 1943.

McKenzie, K. Echoes of Dante in Milton's Lycidas. Italica 20 1943.

Mineka, F. E. The critical reception of Milton's De doctrina christiana. SE 22 1943.

Parks, G. B. The occasion of Milton's Moscovia. SP 40 1943.
— Milton's Moscovia not history. PQ 31 1952.

Quiller-Couch, A. T. In his Cambridge lectures, 1943.

Ross, M. M. Milton's royalism: a study of the conflict of symbol and idea in the poems. Ithaca 1943.
— Milton and Sir John Stradling. HLQ 14 1951.
— Milton and the Protestant aesthetic. In his Poetry and dogma, New Brunswick NJ 1954.

Singleton, R. H. Milton's Comus and the Comus of Erycius Puteanus. PMLA 58 1943.

Stroup, T. B. Implications of the theory of climatic influence in Milton. MLQ 4 1943.
— Gay's mohocks and Milton. JEGP 46 1947.
— Lycidas and the Marinell story. In SAMLA studies in Milton, ed J. M. Patrick, Gainesville 1953.
— Parallel entrances and exits in Paradise lost. Tennessee Stud in Lit 6 1961.
— The Cestus: manuscript of an anonymous 18th-century imitation of Comus. Stud in Eng Lit 1500–1900 2 1962.
— Religious rite and ceremony in Milton's poetry. Lexington Kentucky 1968.
— Dido, the phoenix and Milton's sonnet xviii. Milton Quart 6 1970.

Wright, N. Milton's use of Latin formularies. SP 40 1943.

Yule, G. U. The word muing in Milton's Areopagitica. RES 19 1943. Comment by L. C. Martin 21 1945.

Hillway, T. Milton's theory of education. College Eng April 1944.

Boughner, D. C. Milton's Harapha and Renaissance comedy. ELH 11 1944.

Fuller, E. John Milton. New York 1944.

Hamilton, G. R. Hero or fool? a study of Milton's Satan. 1944.

Jones, J. Areopagitica 1644–1944. Lib Chron 1 1944.

Keeton, G. W. The tercentenary of the Areopagitica. Contemporary Rev Nov 1944.

Lynskey, W. A critic in action: Mr Ransom. College Eng Feb 1944. On Lycidas.

Purcell, J. M. Rime in Paradise lost. MLN 59 1944.
— Milton y los siete tipos de ambigüedad. Estudios 1 1953.

St Clair, F. Y. The rhythm of Milton's Nativity ode. College Eng May 1944.

Sensabaugh, G. F. The milieu of Comus. SP 41 1944.
— Areopagitica adapted. MLN 61 1946. See also HLQ 13 1950.
— Milton in the Revolution settlement. HLQ 9 1946.
— Milton on learning. SP 43 1946. Comment by I. Samuel, PMLA 64 1949.
— Milton and the doctrine of passive obedience. HLQ 13 1949.
— That grand Whig Milton. Stanford 1952.
— Milton in early America. Princeton 1964.

Wright, C. T. Something more about Eve. SP 41 1944.

Anand, M. R. The example of Milton. In Freedom of expression, ed H. Ould 1945.

Bowra, C. M. Milton and the destiny of man. In his From Virgil to Milton, 1945.

— Samson Agonistes. In his Inspiration and poetry, 1955.

Buxton, C. R. Prophets of Heaven and Hell: Virgil, Dante, Milton, Goethe. Cambridge 1945.

Corcoran, M. I. Milton's Paradise with reference to the hexameral background. Washington 1945.
— Milton: Paradise lost. In The great books: a Christian appraisal, ed H. C. Gardiner vol 3, New York 1951.

Ellis-Fermor, U. Samson Agonistes and religious drama. In her Frontiers of drama, 1945.

Evans, B. I. Milton and the modern press. In Freedom of expression, ed H. Ould 1945.

Hardy, J. E. Lycidas. Kenyon Rev 7 1945.

Laski, H. J. The Areopagitica after 300 years. In Freedom of expression, ed H. Ould 1945.

Musgrove, S. Is the devil an ass? RES 21 1945.

Neumann, J. H. Milton's prose vocabulary. PMLA 60 1945.

Rajan, B. Simple, sensuous and passionate. RES 21 1945.
— Paradise lost and the 17th-century reader. 1947.
— Paradise lost: the critic and the historian. Univ of Windsor Rev 1 1965.
— Lycidas: the shattering of the leaves. SP 64 1967.
— Paradise lost: the hill of history. HLQ 31 1967.
— Jerusalem and Athens: the temptation of learning in Paradise regained. In Th' upright heart and pure, ed A. Fiore, Pittsburgh 1967.
— In order serviceable. MLR 63 1968.
— Comus: the inglorious likeness. UTQ 63 1968.
— (ed). Paradise lost: a tercentenary tribute. Toronto 1969.
— Paradise lost: the providence of style. Milton Stud 1 1969.
— The lofty rhyme: a study of Milton's major poetry. 1970. Reprints 9 essays.

Read, H. Milton; The Areopagitica. Both in his A coat of many colours, 1945.

Spaeth, J. D. Epic conventions in Paradise lost. In Elizabethan studies in honor of G. F. Reynolds, Boulder 1945.

Svendsen, K. Milton and Malleus maleficarum. MLN 60 1945.
— Milton's sonnet on the massacre in Piedmont. Shakespeare Assoc Bull 20 1945.
— Adam's soliloquy in Book x of Paradise lost. College Eng April 1949.
— Epic address and reference and the principle of decorum in Paradise lost. PQ 28 1949.
— Milton's aerie microscope. MLN 64 1949.
— Science and structure in Milton's Doctrine of divorce. PMLA 67 1952.
— Milton and Science. Cambridge Mass 1956.
— Milton's Pro se defensio and Alexander More. Texas Stud in Lang & Lit 1 1959.
— Satan and science. Bucknell Rev 9 1960.
— John Martin and the expulsion scene of Paradise lost. Stud in Eng Lit 1500–1900 1 1961.
— Milton and Alexander More: new documents. JEGP 60 1961.
— Milton and the hundred articles against Alexander More. In Th' upright heart and pure, ed A. P. Fiore, Pittsburgh 1967.
— Paradise lost as an alternative. Humanities Assoc Bull 18 1967.

Allen, D. C. Milton and the sons of God. MLN 61 1946.
— Milton's Comus as a failure in artistic compromise. ELH 16 1949.
— A note on Comus. MLN 64 1949.
— Some theories of the growth and origin of language in Milton's age. PQ 28 1949.
— Two notes on Paradise lost. MLN 68 1953.
— The harmonious vision: studies in Milton's poetry. Baltimore 1954.
— Milton and the name of Eve. MLN 74 1959.
— Milton and the descent to light. JEGP 60 1961.

—— Milton, Elegy five: In adventum veris. In his Image and meaning, Baltimore 1968 (enlarged).

Clark, D. L. Milton's schoolmasters. HLQ 9 1946.

—— Milton at St Paul's school. New York 1948.

—— Milton and William Chappell. HLQ 18 1955.

—— Milton's rhetorical exercises. Quart Jnl of Speech 46 1960.

Clark, E. M. Milton and the warfare of peace. South Atlantic Quart 45 1946.

—— Milton's Abyssinian Paradise. SE 29 1950.

—— Milton's English poetical vocabulary. SP 53 1956.

—— Milton and Wither. SP 56 1959.

Eastland, E. W. Milton's ethics. Nashville 1946.

Eisenring, A. J. T. Milton's De doctrina christiana. Fribourg 1946.

Ekfelt, F. E. The graphic diction of Milton's English prose. PQ 25 1946.

—— Latinate diction in Milton's English prose. PQ 28 1949.

Harding, D. P. Milton and the Renaissance Ovid. Urbana 1946.

—— The club of Hercules: studies in the classical background of Paradise lost. Urbana 1962.

Hunter, W. B., jr. Milton and thrice great Hermes. JEGP 45 1946.

—— Milton's materialistic life principle. JEGP 45 1946.

—— Eve's demonic dream. ELH 13 1946.

—— Prophetic dreams and visions in Paradise lost. MLQ 9 1948.

—— The sources of Milton's prosody. PQ 28 1949.

—— Milton's power of matter. JHI 13 1952.

—— New words in Milton's English poems. In Essays in honor of W. C. Curry, Nashville 1954.

—— Milton's Arianism reconsidered. Harvard Theological Rev 52 1959.

—— The meaning of Holy Light in Paradise lost iii. MLN 74 1959.

—— Holy Light in Paradise lost. Rice Inst Pamphlet 46 1960.

—— Milton on the Incarnation: some more heresies. JHI 21 1960.

—— Milton translates the psalms. PQ 40 1961.

—— Some speculations on the nature of Milton's blindness. Jnl History of Medicine 17 1962.

—— Milton's Urania. Stud in Eng Lit 1500–1900 4 1964.

—— Some problems in Milton's theological vocabulary. Harvard Theological Rev 57 1964.

—— Milton and Richard Cromwell. Eng Lang Notes 3 1966.

—— The heresies of Satan. In Th' upright heart and pure, ed A. P. Fiore, Pittsburgh 1967.

—— The center of Paradise lost. Eng Lang Notes 7 1969.

—— Milton on the exaltation of the Son: the war in heaven in Paradise lost. ELH 36 1969.

—— Milton and the Waldensians. Stud in Eng Lit 1500–1900 11 1971.

—— The obedience of Christ in Paradise regained. In Calm of mind, ed J. A. Wittreich, Cleveland 1971.

—— (ed). Bright essence: studies in Milton's theology. Salt Lake City 1971.

Hutchinson, F. E. Milton and the English mind. 1946.

Kliger, S. The urbs aeterna in Paradise regained. PMLA 61 1946.

—— In his Goths in England, Cambridge Mass 1952.

—— Milton in Italy and the lost Malatesti ms. SP 51 1954.

MacKenzie, P. Milton's visual imagination: an answer to T. S. Eliot. UTQ 16 1946.

Owen, E. Milton and Selden on divorce. SP 43 1946.

Schaus, H. The relationship of Comus to Hero and Leander and Venus and Adonis. SE 25 1946.

Van Doren, M. Paradise lost. In his Noble voice, New York 1946.

Wagenknecht, R. Milton in Lycidas. College Eng April 1946.

Wilson, E. C. In his Prince Henry and English literature, Ithaca 1946. On Lycidas.

Atkins, J. W. H. The last phase: Jonson and Milton. In his English literary criticism: the Renascence, 1947.

Austin, W. B. Milton's Lycidas and two Latin elegies by Giles Fletcher the elder. SP 44 1947.

Battenhouse, H. M. In his Poets of Christian thought, New York 1947.

Brooks, C. The light symbolism in L'Allegro–Il Penseroso. In his Well wrought urn, New York 1947.

—— Milton and critical re-estimates. PMLA 66 1951.

—— Eve's awakening. In Essays in honor of W. C. Curry, Nashville 1954.

—— Milton and the New Criticism. In his A shaping joy, 1971.

—— and J. E. Hardy. Essays in analysis. In their Poems of Mr John Milton, New York 1951.

Bruser, F. Comus and the rose song. SP 44 1947.

Day, M. Milton and Lydgate. RES 23 1947.

de Beer, E. S. St Peter in Lycidas. Ibid.

Gordon, R. K. Keats and Milton. MLR 42 1947.

Jones, C. W. Milton's brief epic. SP 44 1947.

Lever, J. W. Paradise lost and the Anglo-Saxon tradition. RES 23 1947.

Lumpkin, B. W. Fate in Paradise lost. SP 44 1947.

McNulty, J. B. Milton's influence on Wordsworth's early sonnets. PMLA 62 1947. Comment by R. D. Havens 63 1948.

Pope, E. M. Paradise regained: the tradition and the poem. Baltimore 1947.

Roberts, D. R. The music of Milton. PQ 26 1947.

Samuel, I. Plato and Milton. Ithaca 1947.

—— Milton on learning and wisdom. PMLA 64 1949.

—— The dialogue in Heaven: a reconsideration of Paradise lost iii 1–417. PMLA 72 1957.

—— Dante and Milton: the Commedia and Paradise lost. Ithaca 1966.

—— Paradise lost. In Critical approaches to six major English works, ed R. M. Lumiansky and H. Baker, Philadelphia 1968.

—— Paradise lost as mimesis. In Approaches to Paradise lost, ed C. A. Patrides 1968.

—— Milton on style. Cornell Lib Jnl 9 1969.

—— Milton and the ancients on the writing of history. Milton Stud 2 1970.

—— Samson Agonistes as tragedy. In Calm of mind, ed J. A. Wittreich, Cleveland 1971.

—— Milton on comedy and satire. HLQ 35 1972.

Turner, W. A. Milton and Spenser's grandson. N & Q 13 Dec 1947.

—— Milton's aid to Davenant. MLN 63 1948.

—— Milton's aid to the Polyglot Bible. MLN 64 1949.

—— Milton, Marvell and Dryden at Cromwell's funeral. PQ 28 1949.

Waldock, A. J. A. Paradise lost and its critics. Cambridge 1947.

Burke, K. The imagery of killing. Hudson Rev 1 1948. On Samson Agonistes.

—— Words anent logology. In Perspectives in literary symbolism, ed J. Strelka, University Park Pa 1968. Largely on De doctrina christiana.

Cairns, E. E. The theology of Paradise lost. Bibliotheca Sacra 105–6 1948–9.

Daiches, D. Lycidas. In his A study of literature for readers and critics, Ithaca 1948.

—— Religion, poetry and the dilemma of the modern writer. In his Literary essays, Edinburgh 1956.

—— Milton. 1957.

—— The opening of Paradise lost. In The living Milton, ed F. Kermode 1960.

—— Some aspects of Milton's pastoral imagery. In his More literary essays, Edinburgh 1968.

Douglas, N. On Paradise lost. Life & Letters Aug 1948.

Flatter, R. Samson Agonistes and Milton. TLS 7 Aug 1948. Comments by F. F. Farnham-Flower and M. Kelley 21 Aug, Flatter 4 Sept 1948.

Gardner, H. Milton's Satan and the theme of damnation in Elizabethan tragedy. E & S ('English Studies') new ser 1 1948; rptd below.

— A reading of Paradise lost. Oxford 1965.

Gullette, G. A. Some inadequacies of method in the study of Milton's sources. Papers of Michigan Acad 32 1948. Reply by A. Williams, ibid.

Jones, P. F. Satan and the narrative structure of Paradise lost. In If by your art, ed A. L. Starrett, Pittsburgh 1948.

Maxwell, J. C. Gods in Paradise lost. N & Q 29 May 1948.

— Plato and Milton. MLR 43 1948.

— The pseudo-problem of Comus. Cambridge Jnl March 1948.

— Milton's knowledge of Aeschylus: the argument from parallel passages. RES new ser 3 1952.

— Milton's Samson and Sophocles' Heracles. PQ 33 1954.

Miller, M. Milton's imagination and the idyllic solution. Western Rev 13 1948.

— Paradise lost: the double standard. UTQ 20 1951

Mims, E. Milton: dissenter and heretic. In his Christ of the poets, New York 1948.

Pyle, F. And old Damoetas lov'd to hear our song. Hermathena 71 1948.

— Milton's sonnet on his late espoused saint. RES 25 1949. Comment by W. R. Parker and Pyle, RES new ser 1 1951.

— Milton's first sonnet on his blindness. RES new ser 9 1958. Reply by A. Gossman, G. W. Whiting and Pyle 12 1961.

Schultz, H. Satan's serenade. PQ 27 1948.

— Christ and Antichrist in Paradise regained. PMLA 67 1952.

— A book was writ of late. MLN 69 1954.

— Milton and forbidden knowledge. New York 1955.

Thomson, J. A. K. In his Classical background of English literature, 1948.

— The epic tradition in modern times: Milton. In his Classical influences on English poetry, 1951.

Turner, P. Woman and the fall of man. E Studies 29 1948.

Worden, W. S. Milton's approach to the story of the fall. ELH 15 1948.

Adams, R. P. The archetypal pattern of death and rebirth in Milton's Lycidas. PMLA 64 1949.

Blenner-Hassett, R. Geoffrey of Monmouth and Milton's Comus. Studia Neophilologica 21 1949, MLN 64 1949.

Blondel, J. Le thème de la tentation dans le Comus de Milton. Revue d'Histoire et de Philosophie Religieuses 28–9 1949.

— Milton poète de la Bible dans le Paradis perdu. Archives des Lettres Modernes nos 21–2 1959.

— Sur dix années de critique Miltonienne. Etudes Anglaises 16 1963.

— Le Comus de Milton: masque neptunien. Paris 1964.

— The function of mythology in Comus. Durham Univ Jnl 58 1966.

— Milton's Eden. In English studies today: 4th series, ed I. Cellini and G. Melchiori, Rome 1966. French version in following.

— (ed). Le paradis perdu 1667–1967. Paris 1967. With 11 essays.

— Le merveilleux dans le paradis Miltonien: chant iv. Etudes Anglaises 20 1967.

Condee, R. W. Milton's theories concerning epic poetry: their sources and influence on Paradise lost. Urbana 1949.

— The formalized openings of Milton's epic poems. JEGP 50 1951.

— Ovid's exile and Milton's rustication. PQ 37 1958.

— The structure of Milton's Epitaphium Damonis. SP 62 1965.

— Mansus and the panegyric tradition. Stud in Renaissance 15 1968.

— No local wounds of head or heel: the dynamic structure of Paradise lost. Jnl of General Education 21 1969.

— Milton's dialogue with the epic: Paradise regained and the tradition. Yale Rev 59 1970.

Conklin, G. N. Biblical criticism and heresy in Milton. New York 1949.

Grace, W. J. Orthodoxy and aesthetic method in Paradise lost and the Divine Comedy. Comparative Lit 1 1949.

— Notes on Robert Burton and Milton. SP 52 1955.

— Milton, Salmasius and the natural law. JHI 24 1963.

— Ideas in Milton. Notre Dame Ind 1968.

Henry, N. H. Milton and Overton. TLS 14 Oct 1949. Comment by E. A. Payne 25 Oct 1949.

— Milton and Hobbes: mortalism and the intermediate state. SP 48 1951.

— Who meant licence when they cried liberty? MLN 56 1951.

— Milton's last pamphlet: theocracy and intolerance. In A tribute to G. C. Taylor, Chapel Hill 1952.

— The mystery of Milton's Muse. Renaissance Papers 1967.

— Milton: Anglican. Renaissance Papers 1969.

Krouse, F. M. Milton's Samson and the Christian tradition. Princeton 1949.

Macklem, M. Love, nature and grace in Milton. Queen's Quart 56 1949.

Mayerson, C. W. The Orpheus image in Lycidas. PMLA 64 1949.

Mohl, R. The theme of Paradise lost; Milton and the idea of perfection. Both in her Studies in Spenser, Milton and the theory of monarchy, New York 1949.

— Milton on some of the writing of his day. In Studies in language and literature in honour of M. Schlauch, Warsaw 1966.

— Milton and his commonplace book. New York 1969.

Neiman, F. Milton's sonnet 20. PMLA 64 1949.

Ogden, H. V. S. The principles of variety and contrast in 17th-century aesthetics, and Milton's poetry. JHI 10 1949.

— The crisis of Paradise lost reconsidered. PQ 36 1957.

Prince, F. T. The influence of Tasso and Della Casa on Milton's diction. RES 25 1949.

— The Italian element in Milton's verse. Oxford 1954.

— On the last two books of Paradise lost. E & S new ser 11 1958.

— Milton e Tasso. Rivista di Letterature Moderne e Comparate 13 1960.

— Milton and the theatrical sublime. In Approaches to Paradise lost, ed C. A. Patrides 1968.

Rogers, L. Milton's blindness: a suggested diagnosis. Jnl of History of Medicine 4 1949.

Stein, A. Milton and metaphysical art: an exploration. ELH 16 1949.

— Satan: the dramatic role of evil. PMLA 65 1950.

— Answerable style: essays on Paradise lost. Minneapolis 1953.

— Structures of sound in Milton's verse. Kenyon Rev 15 1953.

— Heroic knowledge: an interpretation of Paradise regained and Samson Agonistes. Minneapolis 1957.

— Satan's metamorphoses: the internal speech. Milton Stud 1 1969.

— (ed). On Milton's poetry. New York 1970. 20 essays, with introd.

Taylor, I. E. Milton's views on the teaching of foreign languages. Modern Lang Jnl 33 1949.

Trevelyan, G. M. Milton's Areopagitica. In his An autobiography and other essays, 1949.

Vallese, T. Un presunto plagio di Milton. Naples 1949.

Wallerstein, R. C. Rhetoric in the English Renaissance: two elegies. Eng Inst Essays 1948. On Lycidas.

—— Iusta Edouardo King. In her Studies in 17th-century poetic, Madison 1950.

Warner, R. John Milton. 1949.

Adams, H. H. The development of the flower passage in Lycidas. MLN 65 1950.

Bateson, F. W. Milton. New Statesman 19 Aug 1950.

—— The money-lender's son: L'Allegro and Il Penseroso. In his English poetry: a critical introduction, 1950.

—— Paradise regained: a dissentient appendix. In The living Milton, ed F. Kermode 1960.

Bertschinger, M. Man's part in the fall of woman. E Studies 31 1950.

Bongiorno, A. Tendencies in Milton's Of education. Jnl of General Education 4 1950.

Bottrall, M. The baroque element in Milton. Eng Miscellany (Rome) 1 1950.

Bryant, J. A. A note on Milton's use of Machiavelli's Discorsi. MP 47 1950.

—— Milton and the art of history: a study of two influences on A brief history of Moscovia. PQ 29 1950. Replies by G. B. Parks and Bryant 31 1952.

—— Milton's view on universal and civil decay. In SAMLA studies in Milton, ed J. M. Patrick, Gainesville 1953.

Chew, A. Joseph Hall and Milton. ELH 17 1950.

Frye, R. M. Milton and the modern man. Quart Rev 288 1950.

—— The teachings of classical Puritanism on conjugal love. Stud in Renaissance 2 1955.

—— Milton's first marriage. N & Q 1956.

—— God, man and Satan: patterns of Christian thought and life in Paradise lost, Pilgrim's progress and the great theologians. Princeton 1960.

—— In his Perspective on man: literature and the Christian tradition, Philadelphia 1961.

—— Theological and non-theological structures in tragedy. Shakespeare Stud 4 1968.

—— Reason and grace: Christian epistemology in Dante, Langland and Milton. In Action and conviction in early modern Europe, ed T. K. Rabb and J. E. Seigel, Princeton 1969.

—— and C. R. Dahlberg. Milton's sonnet 23 on his late espoused saint. N & Q 23 July 1949.

Gilliam, J. F. Scylla and Sin. PQ 29 1950.

Gordon, G. S. The youth of Milton. In his Lives of authors, 1950.

Hellings, P. A note on the sonnets of Milton. Life & Letters March 1950.

Howarth, R. G. Milton and Camões. Southerly (Sydney) 11 1950.

Jackson, E. Milton's sonnet 20. PMLA 65 1950.

Little, M. Milton's Ad patrem and the younger Gill's In natalem mei parentis. JEGP 49 1950.

Mahood, M. M. The baroque artist; Milton's heroes. Both in her Poetry and humanism, 1950.

Mertner, E. Die Bedeutung der kosmischen Konzeption in Miltons Dichtung. Anglia 69 1950.

Patrick, J. M. The date of Milton's Of prelatical episcopacy. HLQ 13 1950.

—— (ed). SAMLA studies in Milton: essays on Milton and his works by members of the South Atlantic Modern Language Association. Gainesville 1953.

—— The influence of Thomas Ellwood upon Milton's epics. In Essays in history and literature, ed H. Bluhm, Chicago 1965.

—— Milton and Thomas Ellwood: a reconsideration. Milton Newsletter 2 1968.

—— Significant aspects of the Miltonic state papers. HLQ 33 1970.

Peckham, M. Blake, Milton and Edward Burney. Princeton Univ Lib Chron 40 1950.

Pommer, H. F. Milton and Melville. Pittsburgh 1950.

Rice, E. The supreme freedom. In Great expressions of human rights, ed R. M. MacIver, New York 1950.

Stedmont, J. M. English prose of the 17th century. Dalhousie Rev 30 1950.

Thorpe, J. (ed). Milton criticism: selections from four centuries. New York 1950. With 16 essays and several extracts.

—— On the pronunciation of names in Samson Agonistes. HLQ 31 1967.

Tinker, C. B. Blake: dreams of Milton. Art News 1950.

—— Samson Agonistes. In Tragic themes in western literature, ed C. Brooks, New Haven 1955.

Vivante, L. In his English poetry and its contribution to the knowledge of a creative principle, 1950.

Wedgwood, C. V. In her Seventeenth-century English literature, Oxford 1950 (Home Univ Lib), 1970 (rev).

—— Milton and his world. 1969.

Zagaria, R. Serafino de Salandra: inspiratore di Milton. Bari 1950.

Bainton, R. H. The bard of speech unbound: Milton. In his Travail of religious liberty, Philadelphia 1951.

Birrell, T. A. The figure of Satan in Milton and Blake. In Satan, ed B. de Jésus-Marie 1951.

Brown, J. R. Some notes on the native elements in the diction of Paradise lost. N & Q 29 Sept 1951.

Duncan, E. H. Satan-Lucifer: lightning and thunderbolt. PQ 30 1951.

—— The natural history of metals and minerals in the universe of Milton's Paradise lost. Osiris 11 1954.

Forster, E. M. The tercentenary of the Areopagitica. In his Two cheers for democracy, 1951.

Hutcherson, D. R. Milton's epithets for Eve. Virginia Univ Stud new ser 4 1951.

—— Milton's Adam as a lover. Univ of Mississippi Stud in Eng 2 1961.

—— Milton's Eve and the other Eves. Ibid.

Miller, S. Two references in Milton's Tenure of Kings. JEGP 50 1951.

—— The text of the 2nd edition of Milton's Eikonoklastes. JEGP 52 1953.

Moore, J. R. Milton among the Augustans: the infernal council. SP 48 1951.

Nazari, E. Problemi Miltoniani. Palermo 1951.

Nicholas, C. Milton's medieval British readings. Urbana 1951.

—— The editions of the early Church historians used by Milton. JEGP 51 1952.

—— Introduction and notes to Milton's History of Britain. Urbana 1957.

Ralli, A. In his Poetry and faith, 1951.

Robins, H. F. The key to a problem in Milton's Comus. MLQ 12 1951.

—— The crystalline sphere and the waters above in Paradise lost. PMLA 69 1954.

—— Milton's first sonnet on his blindness. RES new ser 7 1956. Replies by F. Pyle 9 1958, A. Gossman, G. W. Whiting, Pyle 12 1961.

—— That unnecessary shell of Milton's world. In Studies in honor of T. W. Baldwin, Urbana 1958.

—— Satan's journey: direction in Paradise lost. JEGP 60 1961.

—— If this be heresy: a study of Milton and Origen. Urbana 1963.

Sherwin, O. Milton for the masses: John Wesley's edition of Paradise lost. MLQ 12 1951.

Shumaker, W. Flowerets and sounding seas: a study in the affective structure of Lycidas. PMLA 66 1951.

—— Paradise lost and the Italian epic tradition. In Th' upright heart and pure, ed A. P. Fiore, Pittsburgh 1967.

—— Unpremeditated verse: feeling and perception in Paradise lost. Princeton 1967.

Sirluck, E. Milton revises the Faerie Queene. MP 48 1951.

—— Milton's critical use of historical sources: an illustration. MP 50 1952.

—— Eikon basilike, Eikon Alethini and Eikonoklastes. MLN 69 1954.

—— Areopagitica and a forgotten licensing controversy. RES new ser 11 1960.

— Milton's idle right hand. JEGP 60 1961. On the poetry of 1641–60.

— Some recent suggested changes in the chronology of Milton's poems. Ibid.

— Milton's political thought: the first cycle. MP 61 1964.

— Paradise lost: a deliberate epic. Cambridge 1967. A lecture.

Spitzer, L. Understanding Milton. Hopkins Rev 4 1951. Reply by G. Boas, ibid. On sonnet 23.

Yoffie, L. R. C. Chaucer's white paternoster, Milton's angels and a Hebrew night prayer. Southern Folklore Quart 15 1951.

Baker, H. In his Wars of truth: studies in the decay of Christian humanism in the earlier 17th century, 1952.

— Where liberty lies: freedom of conscience in Milton's day and in ours. Southwest Rev 41 1956.

Boltwood, R. M. Turnus and Satan as epic villains. Classical Jnl 47 1952.

Christensen, P. A. On liberty in our time: Milton and Mill. Western Humanities Rev 6 1952.

Cooper, L. Abyssinian paradise in Coleridge and Milton. In his Late harvest, Ithaca 1952.

Dickson, D. W. D. Milton's Son of God: a study in imagery and orthodoxy. Papers of Michigan Acad 36 1952.

Duhamel, P. A. Milton's alleged Ramism. PMLA 67 1952.

Ferry, A. D. The authority of the narrative verse in Paradise lost. In In defense of reading, ed R. A. Brower and R. Poirier, New York 1952.

— The bird, the blind bard and the fortunate Fall. In Reason and the imagination, ed J. A. Mazzeo, New York 1962.

— Milton's epic voice: the narrator in Paradise lost. Cambridge Mass 1963.

— Milton and the Miltonic Dryden. Cambridge Mass 1968.

Fogle, F. R. Milton lost and regained. HLQ 15 1952.

— Milton as historian. In Milton and Clarendon by Fogle and H. R. Trevor-Roper, Los Angeles 1965 (Clark Lib).

— The action of Samson Agonistes. In Essays presented to B. R. McElderry, Athens Ohio 1967.

Hesselberg, A. K. A comparative study of the political theories of Ludovicus Molina SJ and Milton. Washington 1952.

Jamison, M. T. The 20th-century critics of Milton and the problem of Satan in Paradise lost. Washington 1952.

Jones, F. L. Shelley and Milton. SP 49 1952.

Joseph, M. Orthodoxy in Paradise lost. Laval Théologique et Philosophique 8 1952.

Kemp, L. On a sonnet by Milton. Hopkins Rev 6 1952. On What I consider.

Kirkconnell, W. The celestial cycle: the theme of Paradise lost in world literature with translations of the major analogues. Toronto 1952.

— That invincible Samson: the theme of Samson Agonistes in world literature with translations of the major analogues. Toronto 1964.

Peter, J. Reflections on the Milton controversy. Scrutiny 19 1952.

— A critique of Paradise lost. 1960.

Price, A. F. Incidental imagery in Areopagitica. MLN 49 1952.

Smith, H. No middle flight. HLQ 15 1952.

Spencer, T. J. B. Milton: the first English philhellene. MLR 47 1952.

— Longinus in English criticism: influences before Milton. RES new ser 8 1957.

— Milton: the great rival. Listener 25 July 1963.

— Paradise lost: the anti-epic. In Approaches to Paradise lost, ed C. A. Patrides 1968.

Starnes, D. T. Proper names in Milton: new annotations. In A tribute to G. C. Taylor, Chapel Hill 1952.

— The Hesperian gardens in Milton. SE 31 1952.

— and E. W. Talbert. Milton and the dictionaries. In their Classical myth and legend in Renaissance dictionaries, Chapel Hill 1955.

Taylor, D., jr. The battle in Heaven in Paradise lost. Tulane Stud in Eng 3 1952.

— Grace as a means of poetry: Milton's pattern for salvation. Tulane Stud in Eng 4 1954.

— The storm scene in Paradise regained: a reinterpretation. UTQ 24 1955.

— Milton and the paradox of the fortunate fall once more. Tulane Stud in Eng 9 1959.

— Milton's treatment of the judgment and the expulsion in Paradise lost. Tulane Stud in Eng 10 1960.

Thompson, W. L. The source of the flower passage in Lycidas. N & Q 1 March 1952.

Werblowsky, R. J. Z. Lucifer and Prometheus: a study of Milton's Satan. 1952. Introd by C. G. Jung.

— Milton and the Conjectura cabbalistica. Jnl Warburg & Courtauld Inst 18 1955.

Wilcox, S. C. and J. M. Raines. Lycidas and Adonais. MLN 67 1952.

Abrams, M. H. In his Mirror and the lamp: romantic theory and the critical tradition, New York 1953.

— Five types of Lycidas. In Milton's Lycidas, ed C. A. Patrides, New York 1961.

Beerbohm, M. Agonising Samson. In his Around theatres, 1953. Review of a 1908 performance.

Bell, M. The fallacy of the fall in Paradise lost. PMLA 68 1953. Comment by W. Shumaker et al 70 1955.

Boggs, E. R. Selected precepts of freedom to choose in Paradise lost. Peabody Jnl of Education 30 1953.

Boone, L. P. The language of Book vi Paradise lost. In SAMLA studies in Milton, ed J. M. Patrick, Gainesville 1953.

Bottkol, J. M. The holograph of Milton's letter to Holstenius. PMLA 68 1953.

Bowers, R. H. The accent on youth in Comus. In SAMLA studies in Milton, ed J. M. Patrick, Gainesville 1953.

Carpenter, N. C. The place of music in L'Allegro and Il Penseroso. UTQ 22 1953.

— Spenser's Epithalamion as inspiration for Milton's L'Allegro and Il Penseroso. N & Q July 1956.

Chester, A. G. Milton, Latimer and the Lord Admiral. MLQ 14 1953.

Craig, H. An ethical distinction by Milton. In his Written word and other essays, Chapel Hill 1953.

Daniells, R. Humour in Paradise lost. Dalhousie Rev 33 1953.

— Milton, mannerism and baroque. Toronto 1963.

— A happy rural seat of various view. In Paradise lost: a tercentenary tribute, ed B. Rajan, Toronto 1969.

Enkvis, N. E. The functions of magic in Milton's Comus. Neuphilologische Mitteilungen 54 1953.

Fell, K. From myth to martyrdom: towards a view of Milton's Samson Agonistes. E Studies 34 1953.

Fricker, R. Eigenart und Grenzen von Miltons Bildersprache. Anglia 71 1953.

Healey, M. A. Milton and Hopkins. UTQ 22 1953.

Kane, R. J. Blind mouths in Lycidas. MLN 68 1953.

Kellog, G. A. Bridge's Milton's prosody and Renaissance metrical theory. PMLA 68 1953.

Kermode, F. Milton's hero. RES new ser 4 1953.

— Samson Agonistes and Hebrew prosody. Durham Univ Jnl new ser 14 1953.

— Adam unparadised. In Living Milton, below; rptd in his Shakespeare, Spenser, Donne, 1971.

— (ed). The living Milton. 1960. 10 essays.

Nott, K. Old Puritan writ large. In her Emperor's clothes, 1953.

Ochi, F. Milton studies. Kyoto 1953. Partly in English.

Orel, H. The Dynasts and Paradise lost. South Atlantic Quart 52 1953.

Parish, J. E. Pre-Miltonic representations of Adam as a Christian. Rice Inst Pamphlet 40 1953.

—— Milton and an anthropomorphic God. SP 56 1959.

—— Milton and God's curse on the serpent. JEGP 58 1959.

—— Standing prostrate: the paradox in Paradise lost x.1099 and xi.1. Eng Miscellany (Rome) 15 1964.

—— Milton and the rape of Proserpina. E Studies 48 1967.

—— Milton and the well-fed angel. Eng Miscellany (Rome) 18 1967.

Rebora, P. Milton a Firenze. Nuova Antologia 459 1953.

Rinehart, K. A note on the first 14 lines of Milton's Lycidas. N & Q March 1953.

Sprott, S. E. Milton's art of prosody. Oxford 1953.

Weathers, W. Paradise lost as archetypal myth. College Eng Feb 1953.

Weaver, R. M. Milton's heroic prose. In his Ethics of rhetoric, Chicago 1953.

West, R. H. The substance of Milton's angels. In SAMLA studies in Milton, ed J. M. Patrick, Gainesville 1953.

—— The terms of angelic rank in Paradise lost. In Essays in honor of W. C. Curry, Nashville 1954.

—— Milton and the angels. Athens Georgia 1955.

—— Milton as a philosophical poet. In Th' upright heart and pure, ed A. P. Fiore, Pittsburgh 1967.

Zanco, A. La concezione della donna in Milton. Letteratura Moderne 4 1953.

Adams, R. M. The text of Paradise lost: emphatic and unemphatic spellings. MP 52 1954.

—— Empson and Bentley: something about Milton too. Partisan Rev 21 1954.

—— Ikon: Milton and the modern critics. Ithaca 1955, 1966 (as Milton and the modern critics).

—— Bounding Lycidas. Hudson Rev 23 1970.

—— Contra Hartman: possible and impossible structures of Miltonic imagery. In Seventeenth-century imagery, ed E. Miner, Berkeley 1971.

Arthos, J. On A mask presented at Ludlow-Castle. Ann Arbor 1954.

—— Milton, Ficino and the Charmides. Stud in Renaissance 6 1959.

—— Milton's Sabrina, Virgil and Porphyry. Anglia 79 1961.

—— The realms of being in the epilogue of Comus. MLN 76 1961.

—— Dante, Michelangelo and Milton. 1963.

—— Milton, Andreini and Galileo. In Approaches to Paradise lost, ed C. A. Patrides 1968.

—— Milton and the Italian cities. 1968.

—— Milton on the passions: a study of Samson Agonistes. MP 69 1972.

Block, E. A. Milton's gout. Bull History of Medicine 28 1954.

Butler, A. Z. The pathetic fallacy in Paradise lost. In Essays in honor of W. C. Curry, Nashville 1954.

Carlisle, A. I. Milton and Ludwig Lavater. RES new ser 5 1954.

Emerson, E. H. Milton's war in Heaven: some problems. MLN 69 1954.

—— The new criticism of Paradise lost. South Atlantic Quart 54 1955.

—— English Puritanism from John Hooper to Milton. Durham NC 1968.

—— A note on Milton's early Puritanism. In Essays in honor of E. L. Marilla, Baton Rouge 1970.

Goodman, P. Milton's On his blindness. In his Structure of literature, Chicago 1954.

Haun, E. An inquiry into the genre of Comus. In Essays in honor of W. C. Curry, Nashville 1954.

Howard, D. R. Milton's Satan and the Augustinian tradition. Renaissance Papers 1954.

Huntley, F. L. Milton, Mendoza and the Chinese landship. MLN 69 1954. On Paradise lost iii. 431–42.

—— A justification of Milton's paradise of fools. ELH 21 1954.

—— Milton studies in Japan. Comparative Lit 13 1961.

—— A background in folklore for the blind mouths passage in Lycidas. Milton Newsletter 1 1967.

—— Before and after the Fall: some Miltonic patterns of systasis. In Approaches to Paradise lost, ed C. A. Patrides 1968.

Jeffrey, L. N. Virgil and Milton. Classical Outlook 31 1954.

Lerner, L. D. The Miltonic simile. EC 4 1954.

—— Farewell rewards and fairies: an essay on Comus. JEGP 70 1971.

Madan, F. F. A revised bibliography of Salmasius's Defensio regia and Milton's Pro populo anglicano defensio. Library 5th ser 9 1954. Supersedes article in 4th ser 4 1923.

Nelson, L., jr. Góngora and Milton: toward a definition of the baroque. Comparative Lit 6 1954.

—— In his Baroque lyric poetry, New Haven 1961.

Stapleton, L. Milton and the new music. UTQ 23 1954. On Nativity ode.

—— Milton's conception of time in the Christian doctrine. Harvard Theological Rev 57 1964.

—— Perspectives of time in Paradise lost. PQ 45 1966.

Zagorin, P. In his A history of political thought in the English revolution, 1954.

Chinol, E. La caduta dal paradiso terrestre. Eng Miscellany (Rome) 6 1955.

—— Il dramma divino e il dramma umano nel Paradiso perduto. Naples 1958.

Cleveland, E. On the identity motive in Paradise regained. MLQ 16 1955.

Davies, G. Milton in 1660. HLQ 18 1955.

Durr, R. A. Dramatic pattern in Paradise lost. Jnl of Aesthetics 13 1955.

Dyson, A. E. The interpretation of Comus. E & S new ser 8 1955.

—— The meaning of Paradise regained. Texas Stud in Lang & Lit 3 1961.

—— Virtue unwavering: Milton's Comus. In his Between two worlds, 1971.

Evans, R. O. Proofreading of Paradise lost. N & Q Sept 1955.

—— Milton's elisions. Gainesville 1966.

Fiore, A. P. The problem of 17th-century soteriology in reference to Milton. Franciscan Stud 15 1955.

—— The paradox of the angelic fall in Paradise lost. Duquesne Rev 46 1 1966.

—— (ed). Th' upright heart and pure: essays on Milton commemorating the tercentenary of the publication of Paradise lost. Pittsburgh 1967. 11 papers.

—— Freedom, liability and the state of perfection in Paradise lost. Milton Quart 5 1971.

Fixler, M. The unclean meats of the Mosaic law and the banquet scene in Paradise regained. MLN 70 1955.

—— Milton and the kingdoms of God. Evanston 1964.

—— Milton's passionate epic. Milton Stud 1 1969.

—— The Apocalypse within Paradise lost. In New essays on Paradise lost, ed T. Kranidas, Berkeley 1969.

—— The Orphic technique of L'Allegro and Il Penseroso. Eng Literary Renaissance 1 1971.

Freedman, M. Dryden's memorable visit to Milton. HLQ 18 1955.

—— All for love and Samson Agonistes. N & Q Dec 1956.

—— Dryden's reported reaction to Paradise lost. N & Q Jan 1958.

—— Satan and Shaftesbury. PMLA 74 1959.

—— Milton and Dryden on rhyme. HLQ 24 1961.

—— Milton's On Shakespeare and Henry Lawes. Shakespeare Quart 14 1963.

—— The tagging of Paradise lost: rhyme in Dryden's The state of innocence. Milton Quart 5 1971.

Grenander, M. E. Samson's middle: Aristotle and Dr Johnson. UTQ 24 1955.

Groom, B. In his Diction of poetry from Spenser to Bridges, Toronto 1955.

Muir, K. John Milton. 1955.

Saunders, J. W. Milton, Diomede and Amaryllis. ELH 22 1955.

Schanzer, E. Milton's Hell revisited. UTQ 24 1955.

Stavrou, C. N. Milton, Byron and the Devil. Univ of Kansas City Rev 21 1955.

Sypher, W. Four stages of Renaissance style: transformations in art and literature 1400–1700. New York 1955. On Milton and baroque.

Watkins, W. B. C. An anatomy of Milton's verse. Baton Rouge 1955.

Wickert, M. Miltons Entwürfe zu einem Drama vom Sündenfall. Anglia 73 1955.

Battestin, M. C. John Crowe Ransom and Lycidas: a reappraisal. College Eng Jan 1956.

Broadbent, J. B. Links between poetry and prose in Milton. E Studies 37 1956.

— Milton and Arnold. EC 6 1956.

— Milton's rhetoric. MP 56 1959.

— The Nativity ode. In The living Milton, ed F. Kermode 1960.

— Some graver subject: an essay on Paradise lost. 1960.

— Milton: Comus and Samson Agonistes. 1961.

— Milton's mortal voice and his omnific word. In Approaches to Paradise lost, ed C. A. Patrides 1968.

— The private mythology of Paradise regained. In Calm of mind, ed J. A. Wittreich, Cleveland 1971.

Cheek, M. Of two sonnets of Milton. Renaissance Papers 1956.

— Milton's In quintum Novembris: an epic foreshadowing. SP 54 1957.

Cormican, L. A. Milton's religious verse. In Pelican guide to English literature vol 3: from Donne to Marvell, ed B. Ford 1956.

Fisher, P. F. Milton's theodicy. JHI 17 1956.

— Milton's logic. JHI 23 1962.

Foerster, D. M. Homer, Milton and the American revolt against epic poetry 1812–60. SP 53 1956.

Grün, R. H. Das Menschenbild Miltons in Paradise lost. Heidelberg 1956.

Hankins, J. E. The pains of the afterworld: fire, wind and ice in Milton and Shakespeare. PMLA 71 1956.

— Milton and Olaus Magnus. In Studies in honor of T. W. Baldwin, Urbana 1958.

Herbert, C. Comic elements in the scenes of Hell in Paradise lost. Renaissance Papers 1956.

Hill, D. M. Satan on the burning lake. N & Q April 1956.

Howell, W. S. In his Logic and rhetoric in England 1500–1700, Princeton 1956.

Kenrick, E. F. Paradise lost and the Index of prohibited books. SP 53 1956.

Lodge, A. Satan's symbolic syndrome: a psychological interpretation of Milton's Satan. Psychoanalytic Rev 43 1956.

Loewenson, L. E. G. von Berge: translator of Milton and Russian interpreter (1649–1722). Slavonic & East European Rev 34 1956.

Lutter, T. John Milton. Budapest 1956. In Hungarian.

— Miltons Verlorenes Paradies: ein Interpretationsversuch. Zeitschrift für Anglistik und Amerikanistik 5 1957.

Magon, L. Die drei ersten deutschen Versuche einer Übersetzung von Miltons Paradise lost. In Gedenkschrift für F. J. Schneider, Weimar 1956.

Myers, R. M. Handel, Dryden and Milton: being a series of observations on the poems of Dryden and Milton, as alter'd and adapted by various hands, and set to musick by Mr Handel. Cambridge 1956.

O'Brien, G. W. In his Renaissance poetics and the problem of power, Chicago 1956.

Sasek, L. A. Milton's patriotic epic. HLQ 20 1956.

— The drama of Paradise lost books xi and xii. In Studies in English Renaissance literature, ed W. F. McNeir, Baton Rouge 1962.

— Plato and his equal Xenophon. Eng Lang Notes 7 1970. On allusion in Milton's Apology.

— Milton's criticism of Greek literature in Paradise regained. In Essays in honor of E. L. Marilla, Baton Rouge 1970.

Sayers, D. L. Dante and Milton. In her Further papers on Dante, 1957.

Blisset, W. Caesar and Satan. JHI 18 1957.

Damon, S. F. Blake and Milton. In The divine vision, ed V. de S. Pinto 1957.

Duncan, J. E. Milton's four-in-one Hell. HLQ 20 1957.

Ethel, G. Hell's marching music. MLQ 18 1957.

Holloway, J. Milton and Arnold. EC 7 1957.

— Paradise lost and the quest for reality. Forum (St Andrews) 3 1967.

Kerslake, J. F. The Richardsons and the cult of Milton. Burlington Mag Jan 1957.

Maclean, H. N. Milton's fair infant. ELH 24 1957.

Mayoux, J.-J. Un classique de la liberté. Critique 118 1957. On Areopagitica.

— Aspects de l'imagination de Milton. Etudes Anglaises 20 1967.

Moloney, M. F. The prosody of Milton's Epitaph, L'Allegro and Il Penseroso. MLN 72 1957.

— Plato and Plotinus in Milton's cosmogony. PQ 40 1961.

Patrides, C. A. Paradise lost and the mortalist heresy. N & Q June 1957.

— Renaissance and modern thought on the last things. Harvard Theological Rev 51 1958.

— Renaissance ideas on man's upright form. JHI 19 1958.

— Milton and the Protestant theory of the Atonement. PMLA 74 1959.

— Renaissance thought on the celestial hierarchy. JHI 20 1959; tr Italian, Sophia 33 1965.

— (ed). Milton's Lycidas: the tradition and the poem. New York 1961. With 14 essays and bibliography.

— As relações de Milton com Portugal. Revista da Faculdade de Letras de Universidade de Lisboa 6 1962.

— Renaissance interpretations of Jacob's Ladder. Theologische Zeitschrift 18 1962.

— The tree of knowledge in the Christian tradition. Studia Neophilologica 34 1962.

— Adam's happy fault and 17th-century apologetics. Franciscan Stud 23 1963.

— Paradise lost and the theory of accommodation. Texas Stud in Lit & Lang 5 1963.

— Psychopannychism in Renaissance Europe. SP 60 1963.

— The bloody and cruell Turke: the background of a Renaissance commonplace. Studies in Renaissance 10 1963.

— The protevangelium in Renaissance theology and Paradise lost. Stud in Eng Lit 1500–1900 3 1963.

— Milton and Arianism. JHI 25 1964.

— Renaissance and modern views on Hell. Harvard Theological Rev 57 1964.

— In his Phoenix and the ladder: the rise and decline of the Christian view of history, Berkeley 1964; rev in his Grand design of God: the literary form of the Christian view of history, 1972.

— The beast with many heads: Renaissance views on the multitude. Shakespeare Quart 16 1965.

— The cessation of the oracles: the history of a legend. MLR 60 1965.

— The Godhead in Paradise lost: dogma or drama? JEGP 64 1965.

— Milton and the Christian tradition. Oxford 1966.

— John Milton. Observer 13 Aug 1967. On iconography of Paradise lost.

— (ed). Milton's epic poetry: essays on Paradise lost and Paradise regained. 1967 (Peregrine). With 16 essays and bibliography.

— Paradise lost and the language of theology. In Language and style in Milton, ed R. D. Emma and J. T. Shawcross, New York 1967.

— (ed). Approaches to Paradise lost: the York tercentenary lectures. 1968. With 13 papers.

—, W. B. Hunter and J. H. Adamson. Bright essence: studies in Milton's theology. Salt Lake City 1971.

Reesing, J. The materiality of God in Milton's De doctrina christiana. Harvard Theological Rev 50 1957.

— Milton's poetic art: a mask, Lycidas and Paradise lost. Cambridge Mass 1968.

Reiss, E. An instance of Milton's use of time. MLN 72 1957.

Rupp, E. G. Milton and Paradise lost. In his Six makers of English religion, 1957.

Steadman, J. M. Sin and the serpent of Genesis 3 (Paradise lost ii.650–3). MP 54 1957.

— Milton and patristic tradition: the quality of hell-fire. Anglia 76 1958.

— Recognition in the fable of Paradise lost. Studia Neophilologica 31 1959.

— The God of Paradise lost and the Divina Commedia. Archiv 195 1959.

— Milton and Mazzoni: the genre of the Divina Commedia. HLQ 23 1960.

— Paradise lost and the tragic illustrious. Anglia 78 1960.

— Tradition and innovation in Milton's Sin: the problem of literary indebtedness. PQ 39 1960.

— Busiris, the Exodus and Renaissance chronography. Revue Belge 39 1961.

— Miracle and the epic marvellous in Paradise lost. Archiv 198 1961.

— Sin, Errour, Echidna and the viper's blood. MLR 56 1961.

— Chaste Muse and Casta Juventus: Milton, Minturno and Scaliger on inspiration and the poet's character. Italica 40 1963.

— Dalila, the Ulysses myth and Renaissance allegorical tradition. MLR 57 1962.

— Milton's haemony: etymology and allegory. PMLA 77 1962.

— Allegory and verisimilitude in Paradise lost. PMLA 78 1963.

— Eyelids of the morn: a biblical metaphor. Harvard Theological Rev 56 1963.

— Meaning and name: some Renaissance interpretations of Urania. Neuphilologische Mitteilungen 64 1963.

— Peripeteia in Milton's epic fable. Anglia 81 1963.

— Spirit and Muse: a reconsideration of Milton's Urania. Archiv 200 1963.

— Urania, wisdom and scriptural exegesis. Neophilologus 47 1963.

— Eve's dream and the conventions of witchcraft. JHI 26 1965.

— Verse without rime: 16th-century Italian defences of versi sciolti. Italica 41 1964.

— Demetrius, Tasso and stylistic variation in Paradise lost. E Studies 47 1966.

— Ethos and dianoia: character and rhetoric in Paradise lost. In Language and style in Milton, ed R. D. Emma and J. T. Shawcross, New York 1967.

— Milton and the Renaissance hero. Oxford 1967.

— The tragic glass: Milton, Minturno and the Condition humaine. In Th' upright heart and pure, ed A. P. Fiore, Pittsburgh 1967.

— Milton and Renaissance epic theory. In Medieval epic to the epic theatre of Brecht, Univ of Southern California Stud in Comparative Lit 1 1968.

— Milton's epic characters: image and idol. Chapel Hill 1968.

— Milton's rhetoric: Satan and the unjust discourse. Milton Stud 1 1969.

— Paradise lost. In English poetry and prose 1540–1674, ed C. Ricks 1970.

— Passions well imitated: rhetoric and poetics in the preface to Samson Agonistes. In Calm of mind, ed J. A. Wittreich, Cleveland 1971.

Summers, J. H. Milton and the cult of conformity. Yale Rev 46 1957.

— The Muse's method: an introduction to Paradise lost. Cambridge Mass 1962.

— (ed). The lyric and dramatic Milton. New York 1965. With 6 essays.

— The movement of the drama. Ibid. On Samson Agonistes.

— The embarrassments of Paradise lost. In Approaches to Paradise lost, ed C. A. Patrides 1968.

— Milton and celebration. Milton Quart 5 1971.

Tuve, R. Images and themes in five poems by Milton Cambridge Mass 1957.

— A name to resound for ages. Listener 28 Aug 1958.

— New approaches to Milton; Baroque and mannerist Milton. Both in her Essays, Princeton 1970.

Vahid, S. A. Iqbal and Milton. Pakistan Quart 8 1957.

Withim, P. M. A prosodic analysis of Milton's 7th sonnet. Bucknell Rev 6 1957.

Wrenn, C. T. The language of Milton. In Studies in English language and literature, ed S. Korninger, Vienna 1957.

Adamson, J. H. The war in Heaven: Milton's version of the Merkabah. JEGP 57 1958.

— Kepler and Milton. MLN 74 1959.

— Milton's Arianism. Harvard Theological Rev 53 1960.

— Milton and the creation. JEGP 61 1962.

—, W. B. Hunter and C. A. Patrides. Bright essence: studies in Milton's theology. Salt Lake City 1971.

Berkeley, D. S. The revision of the Orpheus passage in Milton. N & Q Aug 1958.

— Thematic implications of Milton's paradise of fools. In Papers on Milton, ed P. H. Griffith and L. F. Zimmerman, Tulsa 1969.

Bollier, E. P. T. S. Eliot and Milton: a problem in criticism. Tulane Stud in Eng 8 1958.

Cope, J. I. Satan's disguises. MLN 73 1958.

— The metaphoric structure of Paradise lost. Baltimore 1962.

— Fortunate falls as form in Milton's fair infant. JEGP 63 1964.

— Paradise regained: inner ritual. Milton Stud 1 1969.

Hartman, G. Milton's counterplot. ELH 25 1958.

— Adam on the grass with balsamum. ELH 36 1969.

Hirai, M. Milton. Tokyo 1958. In Japanese.

Hone, R. E. New light on the Milton-Phillips family relationship. HLQ 22 1958.

— The pilot of the Galilean lake. SP 56 1959. On Lycidas.

— (ed). Milton's Samson Agonistes: the poem and materials for analysis. San Francisco 1966. 9 essays.

Hunter, G. K. The structure of Milton's Areopagitica. E Studies 39 1958.

Koehler, G. S. Milton on numbers, quantity and rime. SP 55 1958.

Lloyd, M. Justa Edouardo King. N & Q Oct 1958.

— The fatal bark. MLN 75 1960. On Lycidas.

— The two worlds of Lycidas. EC 11 1961.

Madsen, W. G. The idea of nature in Milton's poetry. In Three studies in the Renaissance, by R. B. Young et al, New Haven 1958.

— The fortunate Fall in Paradise lost. MLN 74 1959.

— The voice of Michael in Lycidas. Stud in Eng Lit 1500–1900 3 1963.

— From shadowy types to truth: studies in Milton's symbolism. New Haven 1968.

Morris, H. Some uses of angel iconography in English literature. Comparative Lit 10 1958.

Nash, R. Chivalric themes in Samson Agonistes. In Studies in honor of J. Wilcox, Detroit 1958.

Rigter, G. H. Milton's treatment of Satan in Paradise lost. Neophilologus 42 1958.

Ullanaess, S. P. N. John Milton. Kirke og Kultur 63 1958.

Whiteley, M. Verse and its feet. RES new ser 9 1958.

Widmer, K. The iconography of renunciation: the Miltonic simile. ELH 25 1958.

Lievsay, J. L. Milton among the nightingales. Renaissance Papers 1958–60.

Briggs, K. M. In her Anatomy of Puck, 1959. On Comus.

Combecher, H. Drei Sonette—drei Epochen: eine vergleichende Interpretation. Die Neueren Sprachen 8 1959.

Frye, N. Literature as context: Milton's Lycidas. In Comparative literature: proceedings of the 2nd Congress of International Comparative Literature Association, ed W. P. Friederich, Chapel Hill 1959; rptd in his Fables of identity, New York 1963.

— The return of Eden. Toronto 1965, London 1966 (as Five essays on Milton's epics).

— The revelation to Eve. In Paradise lost: a tercentenary tribute, ed B. Rajan, Toronto 1969.

Herman, W. R. Heroism and Paradise lost. College Eng Oct 1959.

Hunt, H. M. Hail wedded love. In his Natural history of love, New York 1959.

Irwin, D. Fuseli's Milton gallery. Burlington Mag Dec 1959.

Jayne, S. The subject of Milton's Ludlow mask. PMLA 74 1959.

Kurth, B. O. Milton and Christian heroism: biblical epic themes and forms in 17th-century England. Berkeley 1959.

Lewalski, B. K. Milton: political beliefs and polemical methods 1659–60. PMLA 74 1959.

— Theme and structure in Paradise regained. SP 57 1960.

— Milton on learning and the learned-ministry controversy. HLQ 24 1961.

— Structure and the symbolism of vision in Michael's prophecy, Paradise lost books xi–xii. PQ 42 1963.

— Milton's brief epic: the genre, meaning and art of Paradise regained. Providence 1966.

— Innocence and experience in Milton's Eden. In New essays on Paradise lost, ed T. Kranidas, Berkeley 1969.

— Samson Agonistes and the tragedy of the Apocalypse. PMLA 85 1970.

— Milton: revaluation of romance. In Four essays on romance, ed H. Baker, Cambridge Mass 1971.

MacCaffrey, I. G. Paradise lost as myth. Cambridge Mass 1959.

— Lycidas: the poet in a landscape. In The lyric and dramatic Milton, ed J. H. Summers, New York 1965.

— The theme of Paradise lost book iii. In New essays on Paradise lost, ed T. Kranidas, Berkeley 1969.

Major, J. M. Comus and the Tempest. Shakespeare Quart 10 1959.

— Milton's view of rhetoric. SP 64 1967.

— Paradise regained and Spenser's legend of holiness. Renaissance Quart 20 1967.

Petit, H. H. The second Eve in Paradise regained. Papers of Michigan Acad 44 1959.

Sabol, A. J. In his Songs and dances for the Stuart masque, Providence 1959. On Comus.

Samarin, R. Milton and Russian culture. Soviet Lit 1 1959.

Schlingloff, M. Milton Bildersprache im Paradise lost. Die Neueren Sprachen 8 1959.

Shawcross, J. T. Notes on Milton's amanuenses. JEGP 58 1959.

— The manuscript of Arcades. N & Q Oct 1959.

— Certain relationships of the manuscripts of Comus. PBSA 54 1960.

— Speculations on the dating of the Trinity ms of Milton's poems. MLN 75 1960.

— Division of labor in Justa Edovardo King naufrago. Lib Chron 27 1961.

— The chronology of Milton's major poems. PMLA 76 1961.

— Establishment of a text of Milton's poems through a study of Lycidas. PBSA 56 1962.

— What we can learn from Milton's spelling. HLQ 26 1963.

— Henry Lawes's setting of songs for Milton's Comus. Jnl of Rutgers Univ Lib 28 1964.

— The balanced structure of Paradise lost. SP 62 1965.

— Milton's Tenure of Kings and magistrates: date of composition, editions and issues. PBSA 60 1966.

— The Son in his ascendance. MLQ 27 1966.

— A metaphoric approach to reading Milton. Ball State Univ Forum 8 1967.

— The metaphor of inspiration in Paradise lost. In Th' upright heart and pure, ed A. P. Fiore, Pittsburgh 1967.

— Milton's Italian sonnets: an interpretation. Univ of Windsor Rev 3 1967.

— Orthography and the text of Paradise lost. In Language and style in Milton, ed R. D. Emma and J. T. Shawcross, New York 1967.

— The prosody of Milton's translation of Horace's 5th ode. Tennessee Stud in Lit 13 1968.

— The style and genre of Paradise lost. In New essays on Paradise lost, ed T. Kranidas, Berkeley 1969.

— (ed). Milton: the critical heritage. 1970.

— Paradise lost and the theme of exodus. Milton Stud 2 1970.

— Form and content in Milton's Latin elegies. HLQ 33 1970.

— Irony as tragic effect: Samson Agonistes and the tragedy of hope. In Calm of mind, ed J. A. Wittreich, Cleveland 1971.

Stanton, R. Typee and Milton: paradise well lost. MLN 74 1959.

Starkman, M. K. The militant Miltonist: or the retreat from humanism. ELH 26 1959.

Untermeyer, L. Blind visionary: Milton. In his Lives of the poets, New York 1959.

Wallace, J. M. Milton's Arcades. JEGP 58 1959.

Watkins, J. W. N. Milton's vision of a reformed England. Listener 22 Jan 1959.

Bekker, H. The religio-philosophical orientation of Vondel's Lucifer, Milton's Paradise lost and Grotius' Adamus Exul. Neophilologus 44 1960.

Bergonzi, B. Criticism and the Milton controversy. In The living Milton, ed F. Kermode 1960.

Berry, L. E. Giles Fletcher the elder and Milton's A brief history of Moscovia. RES new ser 11 1960.

Brett, R. L. Milton's Lycidas. In his Reason and the imagination, Oxford 1960.

Clavering, R., and J. T. Shawcross. Anne Milton and the Milton residences. JEGP 59 1960.

— Milton's European itinerary and his return home. Stud in Eng Lit 1500–1900 5 1965.

Colie, R. Time and eternity: paradox and structure in Paradise lost. Jnl Warburg & Courtauld Inst 23 1960; rptd in her Paradoxia epidemica, Princeton 1966.

Cook, A. Milton's abstract music. UTQ 29 1960.

Daniels, E. F. Milton's fallen angels: self-corrupted or seduced? N & Q Dec 1960.

— Samson in Areopagitica. N & Q March 1964.

— Climactic rhythms in Lycidas. Amer N & Q 1968.

Davie, D. Syntax and music in Paradise lost. In The living Milton, ed F. Kermode 1960.

Fox, R. C. Satan's triad of vices. Texas Stud in Lang & Lit 2 1960.

— Moseley's advertisements of Milton's poems 1650–60. HLQ 25 1962.

— The character of Moloc in Paradise lost. Die Neueren Sprachen 9 1962.

— The character of Mammon in Paradise lost. RES new ser 13 1962.

— The allegory of Sin and Death in Paradise lost. MLQ 24 1963.

Fraser, G. S. Approaches to Lycidas. In The living Milton, ed F. Kermode 1960.

Gossman, A. Ransom in Samson Agonistes. Renaissance News 13 1960.
— Milton's Samson as the tragic hero purified by trial. JEGP 61 1962.
— Samson, Job and the exercise of saints. E Studies 45 1964.
— The use of the tree of life in Paradise lost. JEGP 65 1966.
Guthke, K. S. Goethe, Milton und der humoristische Gott. Goethe 22 1960.
Hamburger, M. The sublime art: notes on Milton and Hölderlin. In The living Milton, ed F. Kermode 1960.
Jarrett-Kerr, M. Milton: poet and paraphrast. EC 10 1960.
Kendall, W. How to read Milton's Areopagitica. Jnl of Politics 22 1960.
Klammer, E. The fallacy of the felix culpa in Milton's Paradise lost. Cresset 23 1960.
McNamee, M. B. Magnanimity in Milton. In his Honor and the epic hero, New York 1960.
Maddison, C. In her Apollo and the nine: a history of the ode, 1960.
Martz, L. L. Paradise regained: the meditative combat. ELH 27 1960; rptd as Paradise regained: the interior teacher, in his Paradise within, New Haven 1964.
— Paradise lost: the journey of the mind. Ibid.
— The rising poet 1945. In The lyric and dramatic Milton, ed J. H. Summers, New York 1965.
— (ed). Milton: a collection of critical essays. Englewood Cliffs NJ 1966. 12 essays.
— Chorus and character in Samson Agonistes. Milton Stud 1 1969.
— Paradise lost: princes of exile. ELH 36 1969.
— Paradise lost: the power of choice. Ventures 10 1970.
— Paradise lost: the realms of light. Eng Literary Renaissance 1 1971.
Morgan, C. S. Samson: the tragic hero. Nota Bene 3 1960.
Patrick, J. M. Milton's conception of sin as developed in Paradise lost. Logan Utah 1960.
Pecheux, M. C. The concept of the second Eve in Paradise lost. PMLA 75 1960.
— The conclusion of Book vi of Paradise lost. Stud in Eng Lit 1500–1900 3 1963.
— Abraham, Adam and the theme of exile in Paradise lost. PMLA 80 1965.
— O foul descent!: Satan and the serpent form. SP 62 1965.
— The second Adam and the Church in Paradise lost. ELH 34 1967.
— Spenser's Red Cross and Milton's Adam. Eng Lang Notes 6 1969.
— Sin in Paradise regained: the biblical background. In Calm of mind, ed J. A. Wittreich, Cleveland 1971.
Redman, H. Albert Joseph Ulpien Hennet: early French Miltonist. Romance Notes 1 1960.
Robson, W. W. The better fortitude. In The living Milton, ed F. Kermode 1960.
Samuels, C. T. Tragic vision in Paradise lost. Univ of Kansas City Rev 27 1960.
— Milton's Samson and rational Christianity. Dalhousie Rev 43 1963.
Straumann, H. Miltons Epos von den Abtrünnigen: Stufen einer Sinndeutung. Zürich 1960. A lecture.
Waggoner, G. R. The challenge to single combat in Samson Agonistes. PQ 39 1960.
Wain, J. Strength and isolation: pessimistic notes of a Miltonolater. In The living Milton, ed F. Kermode 1960.
Wilkinson, D. The escape from pollution: a comment on Comus. EC 10 1960. Replies by G. Rons, ibid; W. Leahy 11 1961.
Wilson, H. Milton's reaction to his blindness. Medical History 4 1960.
Ayers, R. W. A suppressed edition of Milton's Defensio secunda 1654. PBSA 55 1961.

— The John Phillips—John Milton Angli responsio: editions and relations. PBSA 56 1962. Also on its date, PQ 38 1959.
— Milton's Letter to a friend and the anarchy of 1659. Jnl of Historical Stud 1 1967.
Beck, R. J. Milton and the spirit of his age. E Studies 42 1961.
Beum, R. The pastoral realism of Lycidas. Western Humanities Rev 15 1961.
— The rhyme in Samson Agonistes. Texas Stud in Lang & Lit 4 1962.
— So much gravity and ease. In Language and style in Milton, ed R. D. Emma and J. T. Shawcross, New York 1967.
Borinski, L. von. Miltons Paradise regained. Die Neueren Sprachen 6 1961.
Cox, L. S. Food-word imagery in Paradise regained. ELH 28 1961.
— The ev'ning dragon in Samson Agonistes: a reappraisal. MLN 76 1961.
— Natural science and figurative design in Samson Agonistes. ELH 35 1968.
Das Gupta, R. K. Milton on Shakespeare. Shakespeare Survey 14 1961.
Day, D. Adam and Eve in Paradise lost iv. Texas Stud in Lang & Lit 3 1961.
Ebbs, J. D. Milton's treatment of poetic justice in Samson Agonistes. MLQ 22 1961.
Frank, J. Milton's movement toward Deism. Jnl of Br Stud 1 1961.
— The unharmonious vision: Milton as a baroque artist. Comparative Lit Stud 3 1966.
Garvin, K. Snakes in the grass (with particular attention to Satan, Lamia, Christabel). RES new ser 2 1961.
Hardison, O. B., jr. Milton's On time and its scholastic background. Texas Stud in Lang & Lit 3 1961.
— In his Enduring moment: a study of the idea of praise in Renaissance literary theory and practice, Chapel Hill 1962.
— Written records and truths of spirit in Paradise lost. Milton Stud 1 1969.
Hollander, J. In his Untuning of the sky: ideas of music in English poetry 1500–1700, Princeton 1961.
Howarth, H. Eliot and Milton: the American aspect. UTQ 30 1961.
Huckaby, C. Satan and the narrative structure of Paradise lost. Studia Neophilologica 33 1961.
— The Satanist controversy of the 19th century. In Studies in English Renaissance literature, ed W. F. McNeir, Baton Rouge 1962.
— The benificent God of Paradise lost. In Essays in honor of E. L. Marilla, Baton Rouge 1970.
McFadden, G. Dryden's most barren period and Milton. HLQ 24 1961.
Manley, F. Milton and the beasts of the field. MLN 76 1961.
— Moloch on demonic motion. Ibid.
Maresca, T. E. The Latona myth in Milton's sonnet 12. MLN 76 1961.
Marshall, W. H. Paradise lost: felix culpa and the problem of structure. MLN 76 1961.
Merrill, H. G. Political drama of the Salmasian controversy: an essay in perspective. In Studies in honor of J. C. Hodges and A. Thaler, Knoxville 1961.
Miles, J. The primary language of Lycidas. In Milton's Lycidas, ed C. A. Patrides, New York 1961.
Ricks, C. Over-emphasis in Paradise regained. MLN 76 1961.
— Milton's grand style. Oxford 1963.
— Milton, Poems 1645; Paradise regained and Samson Agonistes. In English poetry and prose 1540–1674, ed Ricks 1970.
Rooney, W. J. J. Discrimination among values. Jnl of General Education 13 1961.

Roth, L. Hebraists and non-Hebraists of the 17th century. Jnl of Semitic Stud 6 1961.

Sellin, P. R. Sources of Milton's catharsis: a reconsideration. JEGP 60 1961. *See also* his Daniel Heinsius and Stuart England, Leyden 1968.

— Milton's epithet agonistes. Stud in Eng Lit 1500–1900 4 1964.

— Caesar Calandrini, the London Dutch and Milton's quarrels in Holland. HLQ 31 1968.

Shattuck, C. H. Macready's Comus: a prompt-book study. JEGP 60 1961.

Slakey, R. L. Milton's sonnet On his blindness. ELH 28 1961.

Tate, E. Milton's L'Allegro and Il Penseroso: balance, progression or dichotomy? MLN 76 1961.

Varandyan, E. P. Milton's Paradise lost and Zoroaster's Zenda Vesta. Comparative Lit 13 1961.

Wheeler, T. Magic and morality in Comus. In Studies in honor of J. C. Hodges and A. Thaler, Knoxville 1961.

— Milton's 23rd sonnet. SP 58 1961.

— Milton's blank verse couplets. JEGP 66 1967.

Wilkes, G. A. The thesis of Paradise lost. Melbourne 1961.

— Paradise regained and the conventions of the sacred epic. E Studies 44 1963.

— The interpretation of Samson Agonistes. HLQ 26 1963.

Barnett, P. R. Theodore Haak FRS 1605–90: the first German translator of Paradise lost. Hague 1962. With Haak's trn of bks i–iii.

Cirillo, A. R. Noon-midnight and the temporal structure of Paradise lost. ELH 29 1962.

— Hail holy light and divine time in Paradise lost. JEGP 68 1969.

— The design of Samson Agonistes: time, light and the phoenix. In Calm of mind, ed J. A. Wittreich, Cleveland 1971.

Coffin, C. M. Creation and the self in Paradise lost. ELH 39 1962; rptd with prefatory note by J. C. Ransom in Kenyon Alumni Bull 20 1962.

Douglas, J. W. Milton's dance of life. Downside Rev 80 1962.

Finney, G. L. Milton and music. In her Musical backgrounds for English literature 1580–1650, New Brunswick NJ 1962.

Fleischauer, W. Johnson, Lycidas and the norms of criticism. In Johnsonian studies, ed M. Wahba, Cairo 1962.

Gohn, E. S. The Christian ethic of Paradise lost and Samson Agonistes. Studia Neophilologica 34 1962.

Hoopes, R. Milton: prime wisdom. In his Right reason in the English Renaissance, Cambridge Mass 1962.

Howell, A. C. Anibal Galindo's Spanish translation of Milton's Paradise lost. Revue de Littérature Comparée 36 1962.

Hunt, W. On even ground: a note on the extramundane location of Hell in Paradise lost. MLQ 23 1962.

Jones, K. A note on Milton's Lycidas. Amer Imago 19 1962.

Lawry, J. S. Eager thought: dialectic in Lycidas. PMLA 77 1962.

— Reading Paradise lost: the grand masterpiece to observe. College Eng May 1964.

— Euphrasy and rue: books xi and xii, Paradise lost. Ball State Univ Forum 8 1967.

— The shadow of Heaven: matter and stance in Milton's poetry. Ithaca 1968.

— Travellers in Pandemonium. Ball State Univ Forum 11 1970.

McAlister, F. L. Milton and the anti-academics. JEGP 61 1962.

MacCallum, H. R. Milton and figurative interpretation of the Bible. UTQ 31 1962.

— Milton and sacred history: books xi and xii of Paradise lost. In Essays presented to A. S. P. Woodhouse, Toronto 1964.

— Most perfect hero: the role of the Son in Milton's theodicy. In Paradise lost: a tercentenary tribute, ed B. Rajan, Toronto 1969.

Manuel, M. The 17th-century critics and biographers of Milton. Trivandrum 1962.

Mehl, D. Zur Interpretation des Paradise regained. Deutsche Vierteljahrsschrift für Literaturwissenschaft 36 1962.

Miller, D. D. Eve. JEGP 61 1962.

Moritz-Siebeck, B. Der Limbus-Passus in Miltons Paradise lost (III. 440–97). Anglia 79 1962.

— Untersuchungen zu Miltons Paradise lost: Interpretation der beiden Schlussbücher. Berlin 1963.

Newmeyer, E. Beza and Milton: new light on the temptation of learning. BNYPL Oct 1962.

Noah, J. E. Oliver Cromwell, Protector, and the English press. Journalism Quart 39 1962.

Radzinowicz, M. A. Eve and Dalila: renovation and the hardening of the heart. In Reason and the imagination, ed J. A. Mazzeo, New York 1962.

— Samson Agonistes and Milton the politician in defeat. PQ 44 1965.

— Man as a probationer of immortality: Paradise lost xi–xii. In Approaches to Paradise lost, ed C. A. Patrides 1968.

Ramsey, P. Lycidas: a proper poem. In his Lively and the just, University Ala 1962.

Richardson, J. Virgil and Milton once again. Comparative Lit 14 1962.

Sankey, B. T. Coleridge on Milton's Satan. PQ 41 1962.

Scheuerle, W. Satan the cormorant. Thoth 3 1962.

Sharrock, R. Godwin on Milton's Satan. N & Q Dec 1962.

Sims, J. H. The Bible in Milton's epics. Gainesville 1962.

— Paradise lost: Arian document or Christian poem? Etudes Anglaises 20 1967.

— Camoëns' Lusiads and Milton's Paradise lost: Satan's voyage to Eden. In Papers on Milton, ed P. H. Griffith and L. F. Zimmerman, Tulsa 1969.

— Perdita's flowers o' th' spring and vernal flowers in Lycidas. Shakespeare Quart 22 1971.

Smith, C. I. Some ideas on education before Locke. JHI 23 1962.

Sperry, S. M. Keats, Milton and the Fall of Hyperion. PMLA 77 1962.

Swardson, H. R. In his Poetry and the fountain of light: observations on the conflict between Christian and classical tradition in 17th-century poetry, 1962.

Thompson, C. A. That two-handed engine will smite: time will have a stop. SP 59 1962.

Thorsler, P. L. In his Byronic hero, Minneapolis 1962.

Unger, L. Yeats and Milton. South Atlantic Quart 61 1962.

Waddington, R. B. Appearance and reality in Satan's disguises. Texas Stud in Lang & Lit 4 1962.

— Melancholy against melancholy: Samson Agonistes as Renaissance tragedy. In Calm of mind, ed J. A. Wittreich, Cleveland 1971.

Allison, A. W. A heterodox note on Milton's orthodoxy. Papers of Michigan Acad 48 1963.

Baumgartner, P. R. Milton and patience. SP 60 1963.

Berman, R. The order of Lycidas. Kenyon Alumni Bull 21 1963.

Buylla, J. B. A. La traducción de Jovellanos del libro primero del Paraíso perdido de Milton. Filología Moderna 4 1963. With text.

Carey, J. The date of Milton's Italian poems. RES new ser 14 1963.

— Milton's Ad patrem 35–7. RES new ser 15 1964.

— Sea, snake, flower and flame in Samson Agonistes. MLR 62 1967.

— Milton. 1969.

Chambers, A. B. Chaos in Paradise lost. JHI 24 1963.

— Milton's Proteus and Satan's visit to the sun. JEGP 62 1963.

— Wisdom and fortitude in Samson Agonistes. PMLA 78 1963.

—— Three notes on Eve's dream in Paradise lost. PQ 46 1967.

—— The falls of Adam and Eve in Paradise lost. In New essays on Paradise lost, ed T. Kranidas, Berkeley 1969.

Cobb, C. W. Milton and blank verse in Spain. PQ 42 1963.

Coolidge, J. S. Boethius and that last infirmity of noble mind. PQ 42 1963.

—— Great things and small: the Virgilian progression. Comparative Lit 17 1965.

Cutts, J. P. The miserific vision: a study of some of the basic structural imagery of Paradise lost. Eng Miscellany (Rome) 14 1963.

Goldberg, S. L. The world, the flesh and Comus. Melbourne Critical Rev 6 1963.

Greene, T. M. In his Descent from Heaven: a study in epic continuity, New Haven 1963.

Harris, W. O. Despair and patience as the truest fortitude in Samson Agonistes. ELH 30 1963.

Hill, C. The politics of Milton. Listener 12 Sept 1963.

Jones, W. M. Immortality in two of Milton's elegies. In Myth and symbol, ed B. Slote, Lincoln 1963.

Laskowsky, H. J. Miltonic dialogue and the principle of antithesis in Book iii of Paradise regained. Thoth 4 1963.

Martin, J. R. The portrait of Milton at Princeton and its place in Milton iconography. Princeton 1961. Addns in Princeton Univ Lib Chron 24 1963.

Murphy, J. L. A choice subject and a curious form: L'Allegro and Il Penseroso. Univ of Colorado Stud 9 1963.

Nelson, J. G. The sublime Puritan: Milton and the Victorians. Madison 1963.

Pearce, D. R. The style of Milton's epic. Yale Rev 52 1963.

Pole, D. Milton and critical method. Br Jnl of Aesthetics 3 1963.

Pursell, W. v. L. Love's place in the orderly system of marriage in Paradise lost. In her Love and marriage in three English authors, Stanford Honors Essays in Humanities 7 1963.

Røstvig, M.-S. The hidden sense: Milton and the Neoplatonic method of numerical composition. In her Hidden sense and other essays, Oslo 1963.

—— In her Happy man: studies in the metamorphoses of a classical idea vol I (1600–1700), Oslo 1964.

—— Milton and the science of numbers. In English studies today: 4th series, ed I. Cellini and G. Melchiori, Rome 1966.

—— Renaissance numerology: acrostics or criticism? EC 16 1966.

Schiff, G. Johann Heinrich Füsslis Milton-Galerie. Zürich 1963.

Scott, W. O. Ramism and Milton's conception of poetic fancy. PQ 42 1963.

Semple, W. H. The Latin poems of Milton. Bull John Rylands Lib 46 1963.

Simon, I. The thesis of Paradise lost. Revue des Langues Vivantes 29 1963.

Spevack-Husmann, H. The mighty Pan: Miltons mythologische Vergleiche. Münster 1963.

Thorsler, P. L. The romantic mind is its own place. Comparative Lit 15 1963.

Young, A. Milton vs Paradise lost. Listener 13 June 1963.

Beer, J. Milton, lost and regained. Proc Br Acad 50 1964.

Bullough, G. Milton and [Jacob] Cats. In Essays presented to A. S. P. Woodhouse, Toronto 1964.

—— Polygamy among the Reformers. In Renaissance and modern essays, ed G. R. Hibbard 1966.

Clair, J. A. A note on Milton's Arianism. In Essays and studies in language and literature, ed H. H. Petit, Pittsburgh 1964.

Clare, M. Samson Agonistes: a study in contrast. New York 1964.

Emma, R. D. Milton's grammar. Hague 1964.

—— Grammar and Milton's English style. In Language and style in Milton, ed R. D. Emma and J. T. Shawcross, New York 1967.

Fisch, H. In his Jerusalem and Albion: the Hebraic factor in 17th-century literature, 1964.

—— Hebraic style and motifs in Paradise lost. In Language and style in Milton, ed R. D. Emma and J. T. Shawcross, New York 1967.

—— Blake's Miltonic moment. In William Blake, ed A. H. Rosenfeld, Providence 1969.

Fraser, J. Paradise lost book ix: a minority opinion. Melbourne Critical Rev 7 1964.

Gleason, J. B. The nature of Milton's Moscovia. SP 61 1964.

Greaves, M. Magnanimous to correspond with Heaven. In her Blazon of honour, 1964.

Greene, D. The sin of pride. New Mexico Quart 34 1964. On Samson Agonistes.

Hägin, P. F. The epic hero and the decline of heroic poetry: a study of the neo-classical English epic with special reference to Milton's Paradise lost. Berne 1964.

Hart, J. Paradise lost and order. College Eng May 1964.

Hays, H. R. The bosom snake. In his Dangerous sex: the myth of feminine evil, New York 1964.

Hobsbaum, P. The criticism of Milton's epic similes. Studia Neophilologica 36 1964.

Honan, P. Belial upon Setebos. Tennessee Stud in Lit 9 1964. Milton's influence on Browning.

Huntley, J. F. Proairesis, synteresis and the ethical orientation of Milton's Of education. PQ 43 1964.

—— A revaluation of the chorus' role in Milton's Samson Agonistes. MP 64 1966.

—— The ecology and anatomy of criticism: Milton's sonnet 19 and the bee simile in Paradise lost i. 768–76. Jnl of Aesthetics 24 1966.

—— Milton's 23rd sonnet. ELH 34 1967.

—— Gourmet cooking and the vision of paradise in Paradise lost. Xavier Univ Stud 8 1969.

Jochums, M. C. The legend of the voice from Heaven. N & Q Feb 1964.

Klein, J. L. Some Spenserian influences on Milton's Comus. Annuale Medievale 5 1964.

Knight, D. The dramatic center of Paradise lost. South Atlantic Quart 63 1964.

Knightley, W. J. The perfidy of the devils' council. Univ of Missouri Stud in Eng 5 1964.

Kranidas, T. Adam and Eve in the Garden: a study of Paradise lost book v. Stud in Eng Lit 1500–1900 4 1964.

—— Satan's first disguise. Eng Lang Notes 2 1964.

—— Decorum and the style of Milton's antiprelatical tracts. SP 62 1965.

—— Milton and the rhetoric of zeal. Texas Stud in Lang & Lit 6 1965.

—— The fierce equation: a study of Milton's decorum. Hague 1965.

—— Dalila's role in Samson Agonistes. Stud in Eng Lit 1500–1900 6 1966.

—— A view of Milton and the traditional. Milton Stud 1 1969.

—— (ed). New essays on Paradise lost. Berkeley 1969. 7 essays.

Lever, K. Milton and Homer: the monarchs of the mount. Bucknell Rev 12 1964.

McLaughlin, E. T. Coleridge and Milton. SP 61 1964.

—— Milton and Thomas Ellwood. Milton Newsletter 1 1967.

Morris, J. M. Paradise lost now. Amer Scholar 33 1964.

—— Milton and the imagination of time. South Atlantic Quart 67 1968.

Mueller, M. E. Pathos and katharsis in Samson Agonistes. ELH 31 1964.

—— The theme and imagery of Milton's last sonnet. Archiv 201 1964.

—— 16th-century Italian criticism and Milton's theory of catharsis. Stud in Eng Lit 1500–1900 6 1966.

—— Paradise lost and the Iliad. Comparative Lit Stud 6 1969.

Orange, L. E. The role of the deadly sins in Paradise regained. Southern Quart 2 1964.

Paolucci, A. Dante's Satan and Milton's Byronic hero. Italica 41 1964.

Riese, T. A. Die Theatralik der Tugend in Miltons Comus. In Festschrift für W. Hübner, Berlin 1964.

Saillens, E. Milton: poète combattant. Paris 1959; tr Milton: man, poet, polemist, Oxford 1964.

— Une hypothèse à propos de Comus. Etudes Anglaises 12 1959.

— Coup d'œil sur les débuts de Milton en France. Etudes Anglaises 20 1967.

Sewell, E. Individual life as myth. In her Human metaphor, Notre Dame Ind 1964. On the last poems.

Spitz, D. Milton's Areopagitica. In his Essays in the liberal idea of freedom, Tucson 1964.

Stoehr, T. Syntax and poetic form in Milton's sonnets. E Studies 45 1964.

Toliver, H. E. Complicity of voice in Paradise lost. MLQ 25 1964.

— The splinter coalition. In New essays on Paradise lost, ed T. Kranidas, Berkeley 1969.

— Milton: Platonic levels and Christian transformation. In his Pastoral forms and attitudes, Berkeley 1971.

Watson, J. R. Divine Providence and the structure of Paradise lost. EC 14 1964.

Watson, T. G. Johnson and Hazlitt on the imagination in Milton. Southern Quart 2 1964.

Zwicky, L. Kairos in Paradise regained: the divine plan. ELH 31 1964.

Ades, J. I. The pattern of temptation in Comus. Papers on Eng Lang & Lit 1 1965.

Barber, C. L. A Mask presented at Ludlow Castle: the masque as a masque. In The lyric and dramatic Milton, ed J. H. Summers, New York 1965.

Bercovitch, S. Three perspectives on reality in Paradise lost. Univ of Windsor Rev 1 1965.

— Milton's haemony: knowledge and belief. HLQ 33 1970. On Comus.

Brand, C. P. In his Torquato Tasso: a study of the poet and of his contribution to English literature, Cambridge 1965.

Bryan, R. A. Adam's tragic vision in Paradise lost. SP 62 1965.

Dawson, S. W. and A. J. Smith. Two points of view: Samson Agonistes. Anglo-Welsh Rev 14 1965.

Dorfman, A. El Lycidas de Milton: poema barroco. Anales de la Universidad de Chile 123 1965.

Dorris, G. E. Paolo Rossi and the first Italian translation of Paradise lost. Italica 42 1965.

Ehrstine, J. The faces of an ironic God. Universitas 3 1965.

Frazier, H. Time as structure in Milton's Nativity ode. Ibid.

Hardy, J. P. Johnson and Raphael's counsel to Adam. In Johnson, Boswell and their circle: essays presented to L. F. Powell, Oxford 1965.

Hyman, L. W. Milton's On the late massacre in Piedmont. Eng Lang Notes 3 1965.

— Paradise lost: the argument and the rhythmic pattern. Minnesota Rev 5 1965.

— Milton's Samson and the modern reader. College Eng Oct 1966.

— The publication of Paradise lost 1667-74. Jnl of Historical Stud 1 1967.

— Poetry and dogma in Paradise lost book viii. College Eng April 1968.

— The unwilling martyrdom in Samson Agonistes. Tennessee Stud in Lit 13 1968.

— Christ's Nativity and the pagan deities. Milton Stud 2 1970.

— The reader's attitude in Paradise regained. PMLA 85 1970.

— Belief and disbelief in Lycidas. College Eng Feb 1972.

Illo, J. The misreading of Milton. Columbia Univ Forum 8 1965. On Areopagitica.

Landon, M. Milton's History of Britain: its place in English historiography. Univ of Missouri Stud in Eng 6 1965.

Landy, M. Character portrayal in Samson Agonistes. Texas Stud in Lang & Lit 7 1965.

— Language and the seal of silence in Samson Agonistes. Milton Stud 2 1970.

Law, D. G. Milton and Chalfont St Giles. [1965?] (priv ptd). A pamphlet.

Mellers, W. The genesis of masque. In his Harmonious meeting: a study of the relationship between English music, poetry and theatre c. 1600-1900, 1965.

Mitchell, C. Dalila's return: the importance of pardon. College Eng May 1965.

Mollenkott, V. R. The Bible, the classics and Milton. Christianity Today 9 1965.

— The cycle of sins in Paradise lost book xi. MLQ 27 1966.

— Milton's mortalism: treatise vs poetry. Seventeenth-Century News 26 1968.

— Relativism in Samson Agonistes. SP 67 1970.

Moss, L. The rhetorical style of Samson Agonistes. MP 62 1965.

Oruch, J. B. Milton as adjutant-general? Stud in Eng Lit 1500-1900 5 1965.

Pelletier, R. R. The Revolt of Islam and Paradise lost. Keats-Shelley Jnl 14 1965.

Sambrook, A. J. Milton's creation heresy paralleled. E Studies 46 1965.

San Juan, E., jr. The natural context of spiritual renewal in Samson Agonistes. Ball State Univ Forum 6 1965.

— On the motif of incongruence in Samson Agonistes. Orbis Litterarum 23 1968.

Tung, M. The Abdiel episode: a contextual reading. SP 62 1965.

— Samson impatiens: a reinterpretation of Milton's Samson Agonistes. Texas Stud in Lang & Lit 9 1968.

Weidhorn, M. Dreams and guilt. Harvard Theological Rev 58 1965.

— Eve's dream and the literary tradition. Tennessee Stud in Lit 12 1967.

— The anxiety dream in literature from Homer to Milton. SP 64 1967.

— In his Dreams in 17th-century English literature, Hague 1970.

Weismiller, E. The dry and rugged verse. In The lyric and dramatic Milton, ed J. H. Summers, New York 1965. On Samson Agonistes.

— Materials dark and crude: a partial genealogy for Milton's Satan. HLQ 31 1967.

Wilkenfeld, R. B. Act and emblem: the conclusion of Samson Agonistes. ELH 32 1965.

— The seat at the center: an interpretation of Comus. ELH 33 1966.

— Theoretics or polemics? Milton criticism and the dramatic axiom. PMLA 82 1967.

Ziegelmaier, G. The comedy of Paradise lost. College Eng April 1965.

Allain, M. The humanist's dilemma: Milton, God and reason. College Eng Feb 1966.

Anthony, H. S. Mercurius Politicus under Milton. JHI 27 1966.

Baldi, S. Poesie italiane di Milton. Studi Secenteschi 7 1966.

Blau, S. D. Milton's salvational aesthetic. Jnl of Religion 46 1966.

Carrithers, G. H., jr. Milton's Ludlow Mask: from chaos to community. ELH 33 1966.

Champion, L. S. The conclusion of Paradise lost: a reconsideration. College Eng Feb 1966.

Evans, J. X. Imagery as argument in Milton's Areopagitica. Texas Stud in Lang & Lit 8 1966.

Fabian, D. R. Milton's sonnet 23 and Lev. 18-19. Xavier Univ Stud 5 1966.

Fenderson, L. H. The onomato-musical element in Paradise lost. College Lang Assoc Jnl 9 1966.

Fido, M. Milton on love. Oxford Rev 3 1966.

Fogle, R. H. Johnson and Coleridge on Milton. Bucknell Rev 14 1966.

Foxell, N. On his blindness. In his Ten poems analysed, 1966.

Fraser, R. On Milton's poetry. Yale Rev 56 1966.

Giamatti, A. B. Milton. In his Earthly paradise and the Renaissance epic, Princeton 1966.

Harrington, D. V. Feeling and form in Milton's sonnets. Western Humanities Rev 20 1966.

Heyworth, P. L. The composition of Milton's At a solemn musick. BNYPL Sept 1966.

King, J. R. Psyche's tasks: Milton's sense of self. In his Studies in six 17th-century writers, Athens Ohio 1966.

Laguardia, E. Milton's Comus. In his Nature redeemed: the imitation of order in three Renaissance poems, Hague 1966.

Levin, H. Paradises heavenly and earthly. HLQ 29 1966.

Mackin, C. R. Aural imagery as Miltonic metaphor: the temptation scenes of Paradise lost and Paradise regained. In Explorations of literature, ed R. D. Reck, Baton Rouge 1966.

Murray, P. Paradise lost: a Christian poem in a post-Christian age. Studies 60 1966.

— Milton, the modern phase: a study of 20th-century criticism. 1967.

Phillips, N. Milton's limbo of vanity and Dante's vestibule. Eng Lang Notes 3 1966.

Riffe, N. L. Milton on Paradise regained. N & Q Jan 1966.

Rogers, K. M. In his Troublesome helpmate: a history of misogyny in literature, Seattle 1966.

Rudrum, A. A critical commentary on Milton's Paradise lost. 1966.

— A critical commentary on Milton's Comus and shorter poems. 1967.

— (ed). Milton: modern judgements. 1968. 14 essays.

— A critical commentary on Milton's Samson Agonistes. 1969.

— Polygamy in Paradise lost. EC 20 1970.

St George, P. P. Psychomachia in Books v and vi of Paradise lost. MLQ 27 1966.

Tschumi, R. The evolution of myths from Dante to Milton. In English studies today, ed I. Cellini and G. Melchiori, Rome 1966; tr French in Le paradis perdu 1667–1967, ed J. Blondel, Paris 1967.

Tuveson, E. The pilot of the Galilean lake. JHI 27 1966. On Lycidas.

Wilding, M. Paradise lost and linguistic precision. Balcony 5 1966.

— Milton's Paradise lost. Sydney 1969.

Williams, H. and P. Milton and music: or the pandaemonic organ. Musical Times 107 1966.

Wynkoop, W. M. Three children of the universe: Emerson's view of Shakespeare, Bacon, Milton. Hague 1966.

Aryanpur, M. Paradise lost and the Odyssey. Texas Stud in Lang & Lit 9 1967.

Bender, W. Johann Jacob Bodmer und Johann Miltons Verlorenes Paradies. Jahrbuch der Deutschen Schiller-Gesellschaft 11 1967.

Berger, H., jr. Archaism, vision and revision: studies in Virgil, Plato and Milton. Centennial Rev 11 1967.

Boddy, M. Milton's translation of Psalms 80–8. MP 64 1967.

Boswell, J. C. Milton and prevenient grace. Stud in Eng Lit 1500–1900 7 1967.

Boyette, P. E. Milton's Eve and the Neoplatonic graces. Renaissance Quart 20 1967.

— Sexual metaphor in Milton's cosmology, physics and ontology. Renaissance Papers 1967.

— Something more about the erotic motive in Paradise lost. Tulane Stud in Eng 15 1967.

— Milton's divorce tracts and the law of marriage. Tulane Stud in Eng 17 1969.

— Milton's abstracted sublimities: the structure of meaning in A mask. Tulane Stud in Eng 18 1970.

Brooke-Rose, C. Metaphor in Paradise lost: a grammatical analysis. In Language and style in Milton, ed R. D. Emma and J. T. Shawcross, New York 1967.

Brunel, P. L'Enfer dans le Paradis perdu: du mythe au symbole. In Le paradis perdu 1667–1967, ed J. Blondel, Paris 1967.

Burden, D. H. The logical epic: a study of the argument of Paradise lost. 1967.

Camoin, F. Milton's Satan. Massachusetts Stud in Eng 1 1967.

Couffignal, R. Le Paradis perdu de Victor Hugo à Pierre-Jean Jouve. In Le paradis perdu 1667–1967, ed J. Blondel, Paris 1967.

Davidson, C. The dialectic of temptation. Ball State Univ Forum 8 1967. On Paradise regained.

— Sceptre and keys and visual images in Paradise lost. Dalhousie Rev 48 1968.

Demaray, J. G. The thrones of Satan and God: backgrounds to divine opposition in Paradise lost. HLQ 31 1967.

— Milton and the masque tradition. Cambridge Mass 1968.

— Arcades as a literary entertainment. Papers on Lang & Lit 8 1972.

Deutsch, A. Milton after Vatican Council II. Amer Benedictine Rev 18 1967.

Di Cesare, M. A. Advent'rous song: the texture of Milton's epic. In Language and style in Milton, ed R. D. Emma and J. T. Shawcross, New York 1967.

— Paradise lost and epic tradition. Milton Stud 1 1969.

Dobson, E. J. Milton's pronunciation. In Language and style in Milton, ed R. D. Emma and J. T. Shawcross, New York 1967.

Duvall, R. F. Time, place, persons: the background of Milton's Of Reformation. Stud in Eng Lit 1500–1900 7 1967.

Fasel, I. Whitman and Milton. Walt Whitman Rev 8 1967.

Fish, S. E. Surprised by sin: the reader in Paradise lost. 1967.

— Discovery as form in Paradise lost. In New essays on Paradise lost, ed T. Kranidas, Berkeley 1969.

— Question and answer in Samson Agonistes. CQ 11 1969.

— Inaction and silence in Paradise regained. In Calm of mind, ed J. A. Wittreich, Cleveland 1971.

— Reasons that imply themselves: imagery, argument and the reader in Reason of Church government. In Seventeenth-century imagery, ed E. Miner, Berkeley 1971.

Flory, A. M. Free movement and baroque perspective in Milton's Areopagitica. Xavier Univ Stud 6 1967.

Fluchère, H. Milton: poète vivant? Etudes Anglaises 20 1967.

Gabrieli, V. Milton agonista. Cultura 5 1967.

Gillet, J. Remarques sur un concours entre traducteurs de Milton sous l'Empire. In Le paradis perdu 1667–1967, ed J. Blondel, Paris 1967.

Gransden, K. W. Paradise lost and the Aeneid. EC 17 1967.

Gross, B. E. Free love and free will in Paradise lost. Stud in Eng Lit 1500–1900 7 1967.

Hagenbüchle, R. Sündenfall und Wahrheit in Miltons Paradise lost. Berne 1967.

Hamilton, K. G. The structure of Milton's prose. In Language and style in Milton, ed R. D. Emma and J. T. Shawcross, New York 1967.

Hulme, H. M. On the language of Paradise lost. Ibid.

— Milton's use of colloquial language in Paradise lost. MLR 64 1969.

Jones-Davies, M. T. Note sur la légende de Sabrina dans le Comus de Milton. Etudes Anglaises 20 1967.

Kaufmann, R. J. Bruising the serpent: Milton as a tragic poet. Centennial Rev 11 1967.

Knoepflmacher, U. C. The post-romantic imagination: Adam Bede, Wordsworth and Milton. ELH 3 1967.

Langford, T. The temptations in Paradise regained. Texas Stud in Lit & Lang 9 1967.

Legouis, P. Dryden plus Miltonien que Milton? Etudes Anglaises 20 1967.

Lejosne, R. Satan républicain. In Le paradis perdu 1667–1967, ed J. Blondel, Paris 1967.

McQueen, W. A. Point of view in Paradise lost: books i–ii. Renaissance Papers 1967.

—— The hateful siege of contraries: Satan's interior monologues in Paradise lost. Milton Quart 4 1970.

Meier, H. H. Xanaduvian residues. E Studies 48 1967.

Milner, M. Le Satan de Milton et l'épopée romantique française. In Le paradis perdu 1667–1967, ed J. Blondel, Paris 1967.

Muldrow, G. M. An irony in Paradise regained. Papers on Lang & Lit 3 1967.

—— The beginning of Adam's repentance. PQ 46 1967. Milton and the drama of the soul. Hague 1970.

Neumann, H. Milton's Adam and Dostoyevsky's Grand Inquisitor on the problem of freedom before God. Personalist 48 1967.

Neuse, R. Metamorphosis and symbolic action in Comus. ELH 34 1967.

Nieman, L. J. The nature of the temptations in Paradise regained books i–ii. Kansas City Univ Rev 34 1967.

Ong, W. J. Idea titles in Milton's milieu. In Studies in honor of D. T. Starnes, Austin 1967.

Osborne, L. J. Ecclesiastical satire in Milton's Lycidas. Stockton Cal 1967. A lecture.

Pequigney, J. Milton's sonnet 19 reconsidered. Texas Stud in Lang & Lit 8 1967.

Pujals, E. El paraíso perdido de Milton en su tercecentenario. Cuadernos Hispanoamericanos 72 1967.

—— Estructura y concepto de El paraíso perdido de Milton. Atlántida 5 1967.

Qvarnström, G. The enchanted palace: some structural aspects of Paradise lost. Stockholm 1967.

Revard, S. P. The dramatic function of the Son in Paradise lost: a commentary on Milton's trinitarianism. JEGP 66 1967.

—— Milton's critique of heroic warfare in Paradise lost v and vi. Stud in Eng Lit 1500–1900 7 1967.

Roscelli, W. J. The metaphysical Milton 1625–31. Texas Stud in Lang & Lit 8 1967.

Rozenberg, P. Don, amour et sujétion dans le Paradis perdu. In Le paradis perdu 1667–1967, ed J. Blondel, Paris 1967.

Seaman, J. E. Homeric parody at the gates of Hell. MLR 62 1967.

—— The chivalric cast of Milton's epic hero. E Studies 49 1968.

—— The moral paradox of Paradise lost. Hague 1971.

Seebacher, J. Comment peut-on être Milton? In Le paradis perdu 1667–1967, ed J. Blondell, Paris 1967.

Sendry, J. In Memoriam and Lycidas. PMLA 82 1967.

Sigworth, O. F. Johnson's Lycidas: the end of Renaissance criticism. Eighteenth-Century Stud 1 1967.

Baker, S. A. Sannazaro and Milton's brief epic. Comparative Lit 20 1968.

—— Milton's uncouth swain. Milton Stud 3 1971.

Beer, G. Richardson, Milton and the status of evil. RES new ser 19 1968.

Bell, V. M. Johnson's Milton criticism in context. E Studies 49 1968.

Bonham, M. H. The anthropomorphic God of Paradise lost. Papers of Michigan Acad 53 1968.

Brockbank, P. The measure of Comus. E & S new ser 21 1968.

—— Within the visible diurnal sphere: the moving world of Paradise lost. In Approaches to Paradise lost, ed C. A. Patrides 1968.

Burgess, A. The Milton revolution. In his Urgent copy, 1968.

Carson, B. H. Milton's Samson as parvus sol. Eng Lang Notes 5 1968.

Chatman, S. Milton's participial style. PMLA 83 1968.

Crump, G. M. (ed). 20th-century interpretations of Samson Agonistes. Englewood Cliffs NJ 1968. With 7 essays and some extracts.

Davidson, A. Milton on the music of Henry Lawes. Milton Newsletter 2 1968.

Doyno, V. Parallel structure and verbal artifice in Milton's Comus. Milton Newsletter 2 1968.

Emslie, M. Milton on Lawes: the Trinity ms revisions. In Music in English Renaissance drama, ed J. H. Long, Lexington Kentucky 1968.

Evans, J. M. Paradise lost and the Genesis tradition. Oxford 1968.

Feinstein, B. On the hymns of John Milton and Gian Francesco Pico. Comparative Lit 20 1968.

Fields, A. W. Milton and self-knowledge. PMLA 83 1968.

French, D. P. Pope, Milton and the Essay on man. Bucknell Rev 16 1968.

Geckle, G. L. Miltonic idealism: L'Allegro and Il Penseroso. Texas Stud in Lit & Lang 9 1968.

Goldsmith, R. H. Triumph and tragedy in Samson Agonistes. Renaissance Papers 1968.

Grose, C. Some uses of sensuous immediacy in Paradise lost. HLQ 31 1968.

—— Milton on Ramist similitude. In Seventeenth-century imagery, ed E. Miner, Berkeley 1971.

—— Lucky words: process of speech in Lycidas. JEGP 70 1971.

Harris, B. That soft seducer, love: Dryden's The state of innocence and fall of man. In Approaches to Paradise lost, ed C. A. Patrides 1968.

Herron, D. Poetic vision in two sonnets of Milton. Milton Newsletter 2 1968.

Hinnant, C. H. Freedom and form in Milton's Lycidas. Papers of Michigan Acad of 53 1968.

Hobbs, M. The young Milton. New York 1968. A children's book.

Julian, J. A mediaeval interpretation of Milton's Garden of Eden. Kentucky Rev 2 1968.

Kastor, F. S. In his own shape: the stature of Satan in Paradise lost. Eng Lang Notes 5 1968.

—— Miltonic narration: Christ's Nativity. Anglia 86 1968.

—— Milton's tempter: a genesis of a subportrait in Paradise lost. HLQ 33 1970.

—— By force or guile eternal war. JEGP 70 1971. On Paradise lost iv. 776–1015.

Kelly, L. G. Contaminatio in Lycidas: an example of Vergilian poetics. Revue de l'Université d'Ottawa 38 1968.

Knott, J. R., jr. The pastoral day in Paradise lost. MLQ 29 1968.

—— The visit of Raphael: Paradise lost book v. PQ 47 1968.

—— Milton's Heaven. PMLA 85 1970.

—— Symbolic landscape in Paradise lost. Milton Stud 2 1970.

—— Milton's pastoral vision: an approach to Paradise lost. Chicago 1971.

Low, A. The parting in the garden in Paradise lost. PQ 47 1968.

—— Action and suffering: Samson Agonistes and the irony of alternatives. PMLA 84 1968.

—— Angels and food in Paradise lost. Milton Stud 1 1969.

—— Tragic pattern in Samson Agonistes. Texas Stud in Lang & Lit 11 1969.

—— The image of the tower in Paradise lost. Stud in Eng Lit 1500–1900 10 1970.

—— No power but of God: vengeance and justice in Samson Agonistes. HLQ 34 1971.

Marilla, E. L. Milton and modern man: selected essays. University Ala 1968.

—— Milton on the Crucifixion. Etudes Anglaises 22 1969.

Miner, E. Felix culpa in the redemptive order of Paradise lost. PQ 47 1968.

Morris, B. Not without song: Milton and the composers. In Approaches to Paradise lost, ed C. A. Patrides 1968.

Nemser, R. A reinterpretation of the unexpressive nuptial song. Milton Newsletter 2 1968. On Lycidas.

Parker, P. The image of direction in Dante, Spenser and Milton. Eng Miscellany (Rome) 19 1968.

Parsons, C. O. The classical and humanist context of Paradise lost ii. 495–505. JHI 29 1968.

Peniche Vallado, L. Milton: el homero englés. Cuadernos Americanos 156 1968.

Prescott, A. L. The reception of Du Bartas in England. Stud in Renaissance 15 1968.

Raleigh, J. H. Lycidas: yet once more. Prairie Schooner 42 1968.

Roston, M. Drama without a stage. In his Biblical drama in England, 1968. Largely on Samson Agonistes.

Rusche, H. Biblical allusion and imagery in a passage of Paradise lost. E Studies 49 1968.

Smith, R. E. Adam's fall. ELH 35 1968.

Stone, C. F. Milton's self-concerns and ms revisions in Lycidas. MLN 83 1968.

Trapp, J. B. The iconography of the fall of man. In Approaches to Paradise lost, ed C. A. Patrides 1968.

Webber, J. Milton: the prose style of God's English poet. In her Eloquent I: style and self in 17th-century prose. Madison 1968.

— The Son of God and power of life in three poems by Milton. ELH 37 1970.

Wilson, J. Milton's use of the image relationship in Paradise lost. Discourse 15 1968.

Winter, K. A comprehensive approach to Lycidas. Washington State Univ Research Stud 36 1968.

Wittreich, J. A. Milton, man and thinker: apotheosis in romantic criticism. Bucknell Rev 16 1968.

— The Satanism of Blake and Shelley reconsidered. SP 65 1968.

— Milton's destin'd urn: the art of Lycidas. PMLA 84 1969.

— (ed). The Romantics on Milton: formal essays and critical studies. Cleveland 1970.

— (ed). Calm of mind: tercentenary essays on Paradise regained and Samson Agonistes. Cleveland 1971. 14 essays.

— Milton's idea of the orator. Milton Quart 6 1972.

Zweig, P. Paradise lost. In his Heresy of self-love, New York 1968.

Andreach, R. J. Paradise lost and the Christian configuration of the Waste land. Papers on Lang & Lit 5 1969.

Armstrong, J. Paradise lost. In his Paradise myth, Oxford 1969.

Auffret, J. Pagano-Christian symbolism in Lycidas. Anglia 87 1969.

Baruch, F. R. Time, body and spirit at the close of Samson Agonistes. ELH 36 1969.

Bowers, F. Adam, Eve and the Fall in Paradise lost. PMLA 84 1969.

Brodwin, L. L. Miltonic allusion in Absalom and Achitophel. JEGP 68 1969.

Butler, F. The Holy Spirit and odors in Paradise lost. Milton Newsletter 3 1969.

Clark, I. Milton and the image of God. JEGP 68 1969.

Critical essays on Milton from ELH. Baltimore 1969. 15 essays.

Cullen, P. Imitation and metamorphosis: the golden-age eclogue in Spenser, Milton and Marvell. PMLA 84 1969.

Demaray, H. D. The literary gardens of Andrew Marvell and Milton. In her edn of Gardens and culture, Beirut 1969.

Dempsey, I. To attain something like prophetic strain. In Papers on Milton, ed P. M. Griffith and L. F. Zimmerman, Tulsa 1969.

Duncan, I. L. John Wesley edits Paradise lost. In Essays in memory of Christine Burleson, Johnson City Tennessee 1969.

Forrest, J. F. The Fathers in Milton: evil thought in blameless mind. Canadian Jnl of Theology 15 1969. On Paradise lost v. 117–19.

Friedman, D. M. Harmony and the poet's voice in some of Milton's early poems. MLQ 30 1969.

— Lycidas: the swain's paideia. Milton Stud 3 1971.

Gillham, D. G. Milton's Gods. In The sole function, ed J. A. Berthoud and C. O. Gardner, 1969.

Gregory, E. R. The road not taken: Milton's literary career and L'Allegro–Il Penseroso. Discourse 12 1969.

Griffith, P. M. A short view of Wharton's criticism of Milton. In Papers on Milton, ed P. M. Griffith and L. F. Zimmerman, Tulsa 1969.

Grundy, J. The Spenserians and Milton. In Spenserian poets, 1969.

Hieatt, A. K. Milton's Comus and Spenser's False Genius. UTQ 38 1969.

Hill, A. A. Imagery and meaning: a passage from Milton and from Blake. Texas Stud in Eng Lit & Lang 11 1969.

Hinz, E. J. New light On his blindness. Massachusetts Stud in Eng 2 1969.

Hunt, B. C. Wordsworth's marginalia on Paradise lost. BNYPL March 1969.

Jefferson, D. W. Milton's austerity and moral disdain. In The morality of art, ed Jefferson 1969.

Koehler, G. S. Milton's milky stream. Jnl of Amer Folklore 82 1969. On folk sources.

— Satan's journey in Paradise lost. Fabula 10 1969.

— Milton's use of color and light. Milton Stud 3 1971.

Lacy, L. B. Samuel Johnson and William Lauder: malevolence in the criticism of Milton. New Rambler 7 1969.

Leishman, J. B. Milton's minor poems. Ed G. Tillotson 1969.

Lieb, M. Paradise lost and the 20th-century reader. Cithara 9 1969.

— The dialectics of creation: patterns of birth and regeneration in Paradise lost. Amherst Mass 1970.

— Milton and the kenotic Christology. ELH 37 1970.

Mulder, J. R. In his Temple of the mind: education and literary taste in 17th-century England, New York 1969.

Newton, J. M. A speculation about landscape. Cambridge Quart 4 1969.

Perry, R. L. Billy Budd: Melville's Paradise lost. Midwest Quart 10 1969.

Robertson, D. Metaphor in Samson Agonistes. UTQ 38 1969.

Rosenberg, D. M. Theme and structure in Milton's auto-biographies. Genre 2 1969.

— Parody of style in Milton's polemics. Milton Stud 2 1970.

— Milton's Masque: a social occasion for philosophic laughter. SP 67 1970.

Rosenblatt, J. P. Celestial entertainment in Eden: book v of Paradise lost. Harvard Theological Rev 62 1969.

— Structural unity and temporal concordance: the war in heaven in Paradise lost. PMLA 87 1972.

— Adam's Pisgah vision. ELH 39 1972.

Ruddick, W. Paradise lost i and ii. Oxford 1969.

Samaha, E. E. Light and dark in the setting of Paradise regained. Eng Lang Notes 6 1969.

Schaar, C. The Sospetto d'Herode and Paradise lost. E Studies 50 1969.

Taaffe, J. G. Michaelmas, the lawless hour and the occasion of Milton's Comus. Eng Lang Notes 6 1969.

— (ed). J. H. Hanford, A Milton handbook. New York 1970.

Treip, M. Milton's punctuation and changing English usage 1582–1676. 1969.

Turlington, B. Milton's Lycidas and Horace's Odes i. 7. Tennessee Philological Bull 6 1969.

Tyson, J. P. The Satan tragedy of Paradise lost. In Papers on Milton, ed P. M. Griffith and L. F. Zimmerman, Tulsa 1969.

Via, J. A. The rhythm of regenerate experience: L'Allegro and Il Penseroso. Renaissance Papers 1969.
— Milton's The passion: a successful failure. Milton Quart 5 1971.
Zimmerman, L. F. And justify the ways: a suggested context. In Papers on Milton, ed P. M. Griffith and L. F. Zimmerman, Tulsa 1969.
Avery, C. Paradise lost and the power of language. English 19 1970.
Berek, P. Plain and ornate styles and the structure of Paradise lost. PMLA 85 1970.
Brisman, L. Serpent error: Paradise lost x. 216–18. Milton Stud 2 1970.
Carnes, V. Time and language in Milton's Paradise lost. ELH 37 1970.
Chang, Y. Z. Why did Milton err on two Chinas? MLR 65 1970. On Paradise lost xii. 376–96.
Christopher, G. Homeopathic physic and natural renovation in Samson Agonistes. ELH 37 1970.
Collett, J. H. Milton's use of classical mythology in Paradise lost. PMLA 85 1970.
Flower, A. C. The critical context of the preface to Samson Agonistes. Stud in Eng Lit 1500–1900 10 1970.
Foley, J. Sin, not time: Satan's first speech in Paradise lost. ELH 37 1970.
Fowler, A. To shepherd's ear: the form of Milton's Lycidas. In Silent poetry: essays in numerological analysis, 1970.
French, R. W. Voice and structure in Lycidas. Texas Stud in Lit & Lang 12 1970.
Gleason, M. What surmounts the reach of human sense. In Essays in honor of E. L. Marilla, Baton Rouge 1970.
Goldman, J. Insight into Milton's Abdiel. PQ 49 1970.
Halewood, W. H. Paradise lost. In his Poetry of grace, New Haven 1970.
Halkett, J. G. Milton and the idea of matrimony: a study of the divorce tracts and Paradise lost. New Haven 1970.
Hawkins, S. Samson's catharsis. Milton Stud 2 1970.
Higgs, E. D. The thunder of God in Paradise lost. Milton Quart 4 1970.
Hill, J. S. Vocation and spiritual renovation in Samson Agonistes. Milton Stud 2 1970.
Hoffman, N. Y. Samson's other father: the character of Manoa in Samson Agonistes. Ibid.
Jacobus, L. A. Thaumaturgike in Paradise lost. HLQ 33 1970.
— Self-knowledge in Paradise lost: conscience and contemplation. Milton Stud 3 1971.
Leitch, V. B. The landscape of hell in Paradise lost. Canadian Jnl of Theology 16 1970.
Meier, T. K. Milton's Nativity ode: sectarian ode. MLR 65 1970.
Otten, C. Homer's moly and Milton's rue. HLQ 33 1970. On Paradise lost xi. 411–22.
Pointon, M. R. Milton and English art. Manchester 1970.
Plotkin, F. Milton's inward Jerusalem: Paradise lost and the ways of knowing. Hague 1970.
Riggs, W. G. The poet and Satan in Paradise lost. Milton Stud 2 1970.
Rollinson, P. B. The central debate in Comus. PQ 49 1970.
Ryken, L. The apocalyptic vision in Paradise lost. Ithaca 1970.
Sadler, L. V. Typological imagery in Samson Agonistes: noon and the dragon. ELH 37 1970.
— Renegeration and typology: Samson Agonistes in its relation to De doctrina christiana, Paradise lost and Paradise regained. Stud in Eng Lit 1500–1900 7 1972.
Safer, E. B. and T. L. Erskine (ed). L'Allegro and Il Penseroso. Columbus 1970. 15 essays and extracts.
Stein, R. A. The sources and implications of the Jobean analogies in Paradise regained. Anglia 86 1970.
Stollman, S. S. Samson as dragon and a scriptural tradition. Eng Lang Notes 6 1969.
— Milton's Samson and the Jewish tradition. Milton Stud 3 1971.

— Analogues and sources for Milton's great task-master. Milton Quart 6 1972. On sonnet 7.
Stringer, G. The unity of L'Allegro and Il Penseroso. Texas Stud in Lit & Lang 12 1970.
Sundell, R. H. The narrator as interpreter in Paradise regained. Milton Stud 2 1970.
Swaim, K. M. Retributive justice in Lycidas: the two-handed engine. Ibid.
— Mighty Pan: tradition and an image in Milton's Nativity hymn. SP 68 1971.
— The art of the maze in book ix of Paradise lost. Stud in Eng Lit 1500–1900 7 1972.
Turner, A. L. Milton and Janssen's sea atlas. Milton Quart 3 1970.
Wagenknecht, E. C. The personality of Milton. Norman Oklahoma 1970.
Wasser, H. John Quincy Adams on the opening lines of Paradise lost. Amer Lit 42 1970.
Blackburn, T. H. Uncloister'd virtue: Adam and Eve in Milton's paradise. Milton Quart 3 1970.
Blamires, H. Milton's creation: a guide through Paradise lost. 1971.
Breasted, B. Comus and the Castlehaven scandal. Milton Stud 3 1971.
Cavanagh, M. A meeting of epic and history: books xi and xii of Paradise lost. ELH 39 1971.
Cohen, K. O. Milton's God in council and in war. Milton Stud 3 1971.
Curran, S. Paradise regained and the Romantic four-book epic. In Calm of mind, ed J. A. Wittreich, Cleveland 1971.
Durkin, M. B. Iterative figures and images in Paradise lost xi and xii. Ibid.
Edwards, T. R. The hero as subversive: Satan. In his Imagination and power, 1971.
Fletcher, A. The transcendental masque: an essay on Milton's Comus. Ithaca 1971.
Grant, J. E. and J. Rhodes. Blake's designs for L'Allegro and Il Penseroso. Blake Newsletter 4 1971.
Guss, D. L. A brief epic: Paradise regained. SP 68 1971.
Hamilton, G. D. Creating the garden anew: the dynamics of Paradise regained. PQ 50 1971.
— Milton's defensive God: a reappraisal. SP 69 1972.
Harada, J. The mechanism of human reconciliation in Paradise lost. PQ 50 1971.
Hardy, J. P. L'Allegro and Il Penseroso; Lycidas. Both in his Reinterpretations, 1971.
Haskin, D. Divorce as a path to union with God in Samson Agonistes. ELH 38 1971.
Helms, R. His dearest meditation: the dialogue in heaven in book III of Paradise lost. Milton Quart 5 1971.
Johnson, J. T. The covenant idea and the Puritan view of marriage. JHI 32 1971.
Knights, L. C. Hooker and Milton: a contrast in styles. In his Public voices, 1971.
Labriola, A. C. Divine urgency as a motive for conduct in Samson Agonistes. PQ 50 1971.
Lyons, B. G. Milton's Il Penseroso and the idea of time. In her Voices of melancholy, 1971.
McCaffrey, P. Paradise regained: the style of Satan's Athens. Milton Quart 5 1971.
Miller, L. The Italian imprimaturs in Milton's Areopagitica. PBSA 65 1971.
Moore, F. H. Astraea, the Scorpion and the heavenly scales. ELH 38 1971.
Morris, D. B. Drama and stasis in Milton's Ode on the Nativity. SP 68 1971.
Olsen, V. N. The New Testament logia on divorce: a study of their interpretation from Erasmus to Milton. Tübingen 1971.
Partridge, A. C. Milton; Paradise lost and Samson Agonistes. Both in his Language of Renaissance poetry, 1971.
Potter, L. A preface to Milton. 1971.

Rama Sarma, M. V. The heroic argument: a study of Milton's heroic poetry. Madras 1971.

Shaw, C. M. The unity of Comus. Xavier Univ Stud 10 1971.

Tisch, J. H. Between the idyllic and the sublime: some aspects of the reception of Milton in Switzerland. In Affinities, ed R. W. Last 1971.

Ulreich, J. C. Sufficient to have stood: Adam's responsibility in book IX. Milton Quart 5 1971.

—— Milton on the fortunate Fall. JHI 32 1971.

Weber, B. J. The construction of Paradise lost. Carbondale 1971.

—— The schematic structure of Paradise regained: a hypothesis. PQ 50 1971.

West, M. The consolatio in Milton's funeral elegies. HLQ 34 1971.

McColley, D. K. Free will and obedience in the separation scene of Paradise lost. Stud in Eng Lit 1500–1900 7 1972.

Mortimer, A. The Italian influence on Comus. Milton Quart 6 1972.

Pittion, J.-P. Milton, La Place and Socinianism. RES new ser 23 1972.

Quinones, R. J. In his Renaissance discovery of time, Cambridge Mass 1972.

Sheidley, W. E. Lycidas: an early Elizabethan analogue. MP 69 1972. On George Turberville's Epitaph on Arthur Brooke.

Winston, A. Milton: poet as politician. History Today April 1972.

C. A. P.

VII. MINOR JACOBEAN AND CAROLINE POETRY (1603–60)

See also Miscellanies, col 1007, above; Epigrams and Formal Satire, col 1333, below; Song Books, col 1337, below; and Scottish Poetry, col 2421, below. For dramatic and other writings by the following poets see Index.

Saintsbury   Minor poets of the Caroline period, ed G. Saintsbury 3 vols Oxford 1905–21.

JOHN ABBOT, alias JOHN RIVERS
1588?–1650

§ 1

Jesus præfigured, or a poeme of the holy name of Jesus in five bookes: the first and second bookes. [Antwerp?] 1623 (anon); ed D. M. Rogers, Menston 1970 (facs).

The sad condition of a distracted kingdome. 1645. Anon poem on Civil War, based on 'A fable of Philo the Jew'.

Devout rhapsodies. [1647] (some with title-page dated 1648). Signed J. A. Rivers.

§ 2

Rogers, D. M. In his Biographical studies 1534–1829 vols 1–2, Bognor Regis 1951–2. With bibliography.

WILLIAM ALABASTER
1568–1640

§ 1

Sonnets. Ed G. M. Story and H. Gardner, Oxford 1959.

§ 2

Dobell, B. The sonnets of Alabaster. Athenaeum 26 Dec 1903.

Dickinson, J. W. Southwell's Burning babe and Alabaster. N & Q Nov 1961.

—— An image of the passion: Vittoria Colonna, Philippe Desportes and Alabaster. Revue de Littérature Comparée 25 1961.

McKay, F. M. The compiler of Oscott College ms E.3.11. N & Q Dec 1967.

See also col 1080, above.

CHARLES ALEYN
d. 1640

§ 1

The battailes of Crescey and Poictiers. 1631, 1633.
The historie of that wise prince Henrie the Seventh. 1638;

ed J. Nichols, Bibliotheca topographica britannica vol 7, 1780.

§ 2

Lievsay, J. L. Bacon versified. HLQ 14 1951.

Burnham, L. G. Aleyn's The historie of Henrie the Seventh. Book Collector 6 1957.

JOHN ANDREWES
b. 1583

The anatomie of baseness. 1615; ed A. B. Grosart 1871.

A subpaena from the high imperiall court of heaven. 1617, 1620, 1623. Attributed to Andrews by Halkett and Laing.

JOHN AUSTIN
1613–69

§ 1

Devotions in the antient way of offices. Paris 1668, Roan 1672 (as Devotions: first part in the ancient way of offices), 1675 (Second part), Roan 1684 (First and second parts) etc, 1700 (as Devotions in the ancient way of offices, reformed by a person of quality [S. Hopton]; ed R. F. Littledale 1889. Includes hymns.

ROBERT AYLETT
1583–1655?

Collections

Divine and moral speculations in metrical numbers. 1654. Contains (some with separate title-leaf): The song of songs, The brides ornament, Five moral meditations, Five divine and moral meditations, Susanna, Joseph, Urania, A wife not ready made but bespoken (with title-leaf dated 1653).

§ 1

Peace with her foure gardens: viz morall meditations. 1622.

Susanna: or the arraignment of the two unjust elders. 1622.

Thrifts equipage: viz five divine and morall meditations. 1622.
Joseph: or Pharoah's favorite. 1623.
The brides ornaments: viz five meditations morall and divine. 1625.
A wife not ready made but bespoken. 1653 (also with separate title-leaf, in Divine and moral speculations), Great Totham 1847 (priv ptd).
Devotions. 1655. Includes A good woman, The humble mans prayer.

§2

Huntington Lib Bull no 10 1936.
Padelford, F. M. Aylet: a supplement. HLQ 2 1939.
Lewalski, B. K. David's troubles remembred: an analogue to Absalom and Achitophel. N & Q Sept 1964.

SIR ROBERT AYTON (or AYTOUN)
1570–1638
Collections

[Latin poems]. In Arthur Johnston, Delitiae poetarum scotorum pt 1, 1637.
Poems. Ed C. Rogers 1844, 1871 (with memoir and Latin poems). See W. Roberts, The Rogers editions of Ayton, PBSA 58 1964.
A choice of poems and songs. Ed H. M. Shire, Cambridge 1961.
The English and Latin poems. Ed C. B. Gullans, Edinburgh 1963.

§1

De foelici et semper augusto Jacobi. Paris 1603. Latin panegyric on James I.
Basia: sive strena Cal. Jan. ad Jacobum Hayum. 1605.
In obitum Thomae Rhaedi, epicidium. 1624. Signed R.A.
Lesus in funere R. Thorii. 1626. Latin elegy.
Poems. 1827 (Bannatyne Miscellany vol 1).
New poems by Ayton. Ed C. B. Gullans, MLR 55 1960.

§2

McDiarmid, M. P. Scots versions of poems by Ayton and Sir William Alexander. N & Q Jan 1957. Ms in Nat Lib of Scotland.
Roberts, W. Saint-Amant, Ayton and the tobacco sonnet. MLR 54 1959.
Gullans, C. B. Ralegh and Ayton: the disputed authorship of Wrong not sweete empress of my heart. SB 13 1960.

THOMAS BANCROFT
fl. 1633–58
§1

The gluttons feaver. 1633.
Two bookes of epigrammes and epitaphs. 1639.
[To the never-dying memory of the noble Lord Hastings] in Richard Brome, Lachrymae musarum, 1649.
The heroical lover or Antheon and Fidelta. 1658, 1658.

§2

Charvat, W. Thomas Bancroft. PMLA 47 1932.

WILLIAM BARKSTED
fl. 1611
Collections

Poems. Ed A. B. Grosart 1876.

Seven minor epics of the English Renaissance. Ed P. W. Miller, Gainesville 1967 (facs).

§1

Mirrha the mother of Adonis. 1607.
Hiren: or the faire Greeke. 1611.
That which seems best is worst. 1617. Verse paraphrase of Juvenal's tenth satire, sometimes attributed to Barksted or William Basse.
See also col 1691, below.

§2

O'Connor, J. J. A Jacobean allusion to the Turkish Mahomet and Hiren the fair Greek. PQ 35 1956.

ROBERT BARON
1630–58
§1

ʾΕΡΩΤΟΠΑΙΓΝΙΟΝ: or the Cyprian academy. 1647, 1648. A romance; prose and verse.
Pocula castalia. 1650.
See also col 1731, below.

§2

Slagle, K. C. Baron: Cavalier poet. N & Q 12 Oct 1935.
Forker, C. R. Baron's use of Webster, Shakespeare and other Elizabethans. Anglia 83 1965.

ROBERT BARRET
fl. 1600

The sacred warr. Ms in Bodley, written 1603–6.
Also Theorike and practike of moderne warres, 1598.

WILLIAM BASSE
1580?–1654
Collections

The pastorals and other workes. Ed J. P. Collier [1870]. From ms prepared for pbn 1653, but not ptd.
Works. Ed R. W. Bond 1893.

§1

Sword and buckler. 1602.
Three pastoral elegies. 1602.
Great Brittaines sunnes-set bewailed. Oxford 1613, Oxford 1872 (facs).
Maister Basse his careere. [c. 1625]. A ballad.

§2

Ault, N. A memento for mortalitie. TLS 12 Jan 1933.
Humphrey, E. V. Study of Basse. New York 1953.

SIR JOHN BEAUMONT
1583–1627
Collections

Poems. Ed A. Chalmers, Works of English poets vol 6, 1810.
Select poems, with a life. Ed E. Sanford, Works of British poets vol 5, 1819.
Poems. Ed A. B. Grosart 1869.

§ 1

The metamorphosis of tobacco. 1602; ed J. P. Collier, Illustrations of early English popular literature vol 1, 1863. A mock-heroic poem.

Bosworth Field, with a taste of the variety of other poems. 1629, 1710.

The theatre of Apollo: an entertainment written by Sir John Beaumont in 1625. Ed W. W. Greg 1926.

§ 2

Williams, G. The pattern of neo-classical wit. MP 33 1935.

Newdigate, B. H. Beaumont's The crowne of thornes. RES 17 1942.

Wallerstein, R. C. Beaumont's The crowne of thornes: a report. JEGP 53 1954.

Schulz, H. C. A hitherto unrecorded autograph. HLQ 33 1970.

Sell, R. D. The handwriting of Beaumont and the editing of his poems. Ibid.

—— The authorship of the Metamorphosis of tobacco and Salmacis and Hermaphroditus. N & Q Jan 1972.

JOSEPH BEAUMONT
1616–99

Collections

Original poems in English and Latin. Ed J.G. [John Gee?], Cambridge 1749.

Poems. Ed A. Chalmers, English poets vol 6, 1810.

Poetical works. Ed A. Grosart 2 vols 1877–80.

Minor poems. Ed E. Robinson 1914. From autograph ms.

§ 1

Psyche: or love's mysterie, displaying the intercourse betwixt Christ and the soule. 1648, 1651; ed C. Beaumont, Cambridge 1702 (with corrections and 4 new cantos).

§ 2

Stanwood, P. G. St Teresa and Joseph Beaumont's Psyche. JEGP 57 1963.

—— A portrait of Stuart orthodoxy. Church Quart Rev 165 1964.

Pritchard, A. Puritan charges against Crashaw and Beaumont. TLS 2 July 1964.

THOMAS BEEDOME
d. 1641?

Collections

Select poems. Ed F. Meynell 1928.

Poems divine and humane. Pisa 1954. Text in English, introd and notes in Italian.

§ 1

Poems divine and humane. Ed H. Glapthorne 1641.

§ 2

Shaver, C. L. Thomas Beedome. MLN 53 1938.

Pagnini, M. Thomas Beedome. Pisa 1954.

EDWARD BENLOWES
1603?–76

§ 1

Sphinx theologica: sive musica templi. Cambridge [1636]. Includes Latin poems.

Papa perstriclus, (Echo) ictus. 1645. Verse attacks on Pope Innocent X.

A poetic descant upon a private musick-making. [1649]. Signed E. Benevolus.

Theophila, or loves sacrifice: a divine poem by E.B. 1652; Saintsbury.

The summary of wisedome. 1657; Saintsbury.

A glance at the glories of sacred friendship. 1657.

Oxonii encomium. Oxford 1672. One English poem, the rest in Latin.

Magia coelestis. Oxford 1673. Latin couplets; broadsheet.

Oxonia elogia. [Oxford 1673]. Latin poems.

§ 2

Saintsbury, G. Benlowes' Theophila. Bibliographer 2 1903.

Robbie, J. H. L. Benlowes: a seventeenth-century plagiarist. MLR 23 1928.

Niemeyer, C. New light on Benlowes. RES 12 1936.

Jenkins, H. A poet in Chancery. MLR 32 1937.

—— Benlowes and Milton. MLR 43 1948.

—— Benlowes: biography of a minor poet. 1952.

Roditi, E. The wisdom and folly of Benlowes. Comparative Lit 2 1950.

Hill, C. Benlowes and his times. EC 3 1953.

Røstvig, M.-S. Benlowes, Marvell and the divine Casimire. HLQ 18 1954.

Duncan-Jones, E. E. Benlowes' borrowings from George Herbert. RES new ser 6 1955.

—— Benlowes and Alexander Brome. N & Q Nov 1956. Reply by C. F. Main, June 1957.

—— Benlowes, Marvell and the divine Casimire: a note. HLQ 20 1957.

WILLIAM BOSWORTH
1607–50

The chast and lost lovers, Arcadius and Sepha. 1651, 1653; Saintsbury.

ANNE BRADSTREET
1612–72

Bibliographies

Wegelin, O. A list of editions of the poems of Anne Bradstreet, with several additional books relating to her. Amer Book Collector 4 1933.

Stanford, A. Anne Bradstreet: an annotated checklist. Early Amer Lit 3 1968.

Collections

Works. Ed J. H. Ellis, Charlestown 1867, New York 1932.

Poems. Ed F. E. Hopkins, New York 1897.

Poems and prose remains. Ed C. E. Norton, New York 1897.

Works. Ed J. Hensley, Cambridge Mass 1967.

Poems. Ed R. Hutchinson, New York 1969.

§ 1

The tenth muse lately sprung up in America. 1650, Boston 1678 (as Several poems), 1758; ed J. K. Piercy, Gainesville 1965 (facs). Contains letters and occasional pieces.

§ 2

Campbell, H. S. Anne Bradstreet and her time. Boston 1891.

Bradstreet, M. Anne Bradstreet: her life and works. Historical Collections, Topsfield (Mass) Historical Soc 1 1895.

Vancura, Z. Baroque poetry in America. Stud in Eng, Charles Univ Prague 4 1933.

Svensen, J. K. Anne Bradstreet in England: a bibliographical note. Amer Lit 13 1941.

Whicher, G. F. Alas all's vanity: or a leaf from the first American edition of Several poems by Anne Bradstreet. New York 1942.

Crowder, R. 'Phoenix Spenser': a note on Anne Bradstreet. New England Quart 17 1944.

Wade-White, E. The tenth muse: a tercentenary appraisal of Anne Bradstreet. William & Mary Quart 8 1951.

Crowder, R. Anne Bradstreet and Keats. N & Q Sept 1956.

Berryman, J. Homage to Mistress Bradstreet. New York 1956. Poems.

Tedeshini, L. B. Anne Bradstreet. Studi Americani (Rome) 3 1957.

Galinsky, H. Anne Bradstreet, Du Bartas und Shakespeare. In Festschrift für Walter Fischer, Heidelberg 1959.

Johnson, C. John Berryman and Mistress Bradstreet: a relation of reason. EC 14 1964.

Hensley, J. The editor of Anne Bradstreet's Several poems. Amer Lit 35 1964.

Piercy, J. K. Anne Bradstreet. New York 1965.

Stanford, A. Anne Bradstreet's portrait of Philip Sidney. Early Amer Lit Newsletter 1 1966.

—— Anne Bradstreet as a meditative writer. California Eng Jnl 2 1966.

—— Anne Bradstreet: dogmatist and rebel. New Eng Quart 39 1966.

Richardson, R. D., jr. The puritan poetry of Anne Bradstreet. Texas Stud in Lit & Lang 9 1967.

Hamblen, A. A. Anne Bradstreet: portrait of a puritan lady. Cresset 32 1968.

Johnston, T. E., jr. A note on the voices of Anne Bradstreet, Edward Taylor, Roger Williams and Philip Pain. Early Amer Lit 3 1968.

McMahon, H. Anne Bradstreet, Bertault and Dr Crooke. Ibid.

Holder, A. Anne Bradstreet resurrected. Concerning Poetry 2 1969.

Kehler, D. Anne Bradstreet and Spencer. Amer N & Q 8 1970.

Laughlin, R. M. Anne Bradstreet: poet in search of form. Amer Lit 42 1970.

Rosenfeld, A. H. Anne Bradstreet's Contemplations: patterns of form and meaning. New England Quart 43 1970.

White, E. W. Anne Bradstreet: the tenth muse. New York 1972.

RICHARD BRATHWAIT
1588?-1673

See col 1336, below.

ALEXANDER BROME
1620-66

Collections

Select poems with a life. Ed E. Sanford, Works of British poets vol 5, 1819.

§1

A Canterbury tale translated out of Chaucers Old English. 1641. Attributed to Brome.

Cromwell's panegyrick. 1647. Verse satire; signed Charolophilos.

A copie of verses, said to be composed by his Majestie. [1648]. Attributed to Brome.

The cunning lovers: a comedy as it was acted at the private house in Drury Lane. 1654.

A record in rithme. [1659?]. Verse satire.

Arsy versy: or the second martyrdom of the Rump. [1660]. A ballad.

Bumm-foder: or waste-paper proper to wipe the nations rump with. [1660?]. A ballad.

A congratulatory poem [on] the return of King Charls [sic]. 1660.

Poems upon several occasions. 1660.

Songs and other poems. 1661, 1664, 1668; rptd A. Chalmers, English poets vol 6, 1810.

Rump: or an exact collection of the choycest poems and songs. 1662; rptd as A collection of loyal songs written against the Rump Parliament, 1731.

For trns of Horace, 1666, see vol 2 col 1497.

§2

Brooks, H. F. Contributors to Brome's Horace. N & Q 19 March 1938. Reply by W. J. Cameron, Feb 1957.

McCusker, H. A royalist ballad writer. More Books 13 1938.

Hanson, L. Points in the bibliography of Cleveland and Brome. RES 18 1942.

EDWARD BUCKLER
1610-1706

§1

A buckler against the fear of death. 1640, 1646 (as Midnights meditations of death), 1649 (as Death dissected). Formerly attributed to Edward Benlowes.

§2

Buckler, W. H. Buckler, poet and preacher. 1936.

Mead, H. R. Three issues of A buckler against the fear of death. Library 4th ser 21 1940.

WILLIAM CARTWRIGHT
1611-43

See col 1765, below.

Plays and poems. Ed G. B. Evans, Madison 1951.

PATRICK CARY (or CAREY)
1624-56

§1

Poems, from a ms written in the time of Oliver Cromwell. 1771. Ms dated 1651.

Trivial poems and triolets. Ed Sir Walter Scott 1819, 1820; Saintsbury. The whole, of which 1771 above gave only a part.

§2

Weber, K. Lucius Cary. New York 1940.

MARGARET CAVENDISH, DUCHESS OF NEWCASTLE
1623–73

Collections

[Select poems]. In G. Colman and B. Thornton, Poems by eminent ladies, 1755.
The Cavalier and his lady: selections from the works of the first Duke and Duchess of Newcastle. Ed E. Jenkins 1872.
Select poems. Ed E. Brydges 1813.

§1

Philosophicall fancies. 1653. Prose and verse.
Poems and fancies. 1653, 1664, 1668 (as Poems: or several fancies in verse).
The worlds olio. 1655, 1671. Contains 2 poems: But I would have this monarchy I make and Of all my works this work which I have writ.
Natures pictures. 1656, 1671. Stories in prose and verse, part-author with William Cavendish, below.
Philosophical letters. 1664. Contains one poem: Eternal God, infinite deity.
For her plays see col 1736 below.

§2

Whibley, C. In his Essays in biography, 1913.
Perry, H. T. E. The first Duchess of Newcastle and her husband as figures in literary history. Boston 1918.
Woolf, V. In her Common reader, 1925.
Turberville, A. S. History of Welbeck Abbey and its owners vol 1. 1938.
Meyer, G. D. The scientific lady in England 1650–1760. Berkeley 1955.
Grant, D. Margaret the First. 1957.
Gagen, J. Honor and fame in the works of the Duchess of Newcastle. SP 56 1959.

WILLIAM CAVENDISH, 1st DUKE OF NEWCASTLE
1592–1676

Collections

The Cavalier and his lady: selections from the works of the first Duke and Duchess of Newcastle. Ed E. Jenkins 1872.

§1

Natures pictures. 1656, 1671. Joint author with his wife Margaret.
Margaret Cavendish, Philosophical letters. 1664. One dedicatory poem.
The charms of liberty: a poem. 1709, 1709. With poems by various hands.
Phanseys. Ed D. Grant 1965. Written c. 1645.
For his plays see col 1736, below.

JOHN CHALKHILL
fl. 1600

§1

Alcilia: Philoparthens loving folly. 1613. Signed I.C. Sometimes ascribed to Chalkhill.
Thealma and Clearchus. 1683; ed S. W. Singer 1820; Saintsbury. Preface by Izaak Walton.

§2

Oliver, H. J. Izaak Walton as author of Love and truth and Thealma and Clearchus. RES 25 1949.

Croft, P. J. Izaak Walton's Chalkhill. TLS 27 June 1958. Comment by J. Grundy 15 Aug 1958.

ROBERT CHAMBERLAIN
1607–60

Nocturnall lucubrations. 1638, 1652.
Conceits, clinches, flashes and whimsies. 1639, 1640 (enlarged as Jocabella); ed J. O. Halliwell (-Phillipps) 1860; ed W. C. Hazlitt 1866.
Balaams ass cudgeld. 1661. Verse reply to nonconformist poem Balaam's ass.

WILLIAM CHAMBERLAYNE
1619–89

§1

Pharonnida: an heroic poem. 1659; ed S. W. Singer 1820; Saintsbury.
England's jubilee. 1660; Saintsbury.

§2

Johnson, R. B. The birth of romance. 1928.
Perkinson, R. H. The epic in five acts. SP 43 1946.
Parsons, A. E. A forgotten poet. MLR 45 1950.

SIR ROBERT CHESTER
1566?–1640?

Collections

Poems by John Salusbury and Chester. Ed C. Brown, Bryn Mawr 1913, London 1914 (EETS).

§1

Love's martyr. 1601, 1611 (as The anuals [sic] of Great Brittaine); ed A. B. Grosart, Occasional Issues 7 1878 (and New Shakespeare Soc).

§2

Halliwell-Phillipps, J. O. Some account of Chester's Love's martyr. 1875.
White, I. R. Love's martyr. TLS 21 July 1932.
Harrison, T. P. Love's martyr: a new interpretation. SE 30 1951.
Matchett, W. H. The phoenix and the turtle: Shakespeare's poem and Chester's Loves martyr. Hague 1965.
Watson, E. Natural history in Love's martyr. Renaissance & Modern Stud 8 1964.

JOHN CLEVELAND
1613–58

Bibliographies

Morris, B. R. Cleveland: a bibliography of his poems. 1967 (Bibl Soc).

Collections

Works. [Ed J. Lake and S. Drake] 1687, 1699.
Poems. Ed J. M. Berdan, New York 1903, New Haven 1911. Saintsbury.
Poems. Ed B. R. Morris and E. Withington, Oxford 1967.

§1

The character of a London-diurnal; with several select poems by the same author. 1644. Not all by Cleveland.

The character of a moderate intelligencer, with some select poems. [1647].

The Kings disguise. [1647].

The hue and cry after Sir John Presbyter. 1649. Verse satire.

Poems by J.C. with additions. 1651, 1653, 1654, 1656, 1657, 1658, 1659, 1661 etc.

The idol of the clownes, or the Insurrection of Wat the Tyler. 1654, 1654, 1658 (as The rustick rampant), [1658] (as The rebellion of the rude multitude).

J. Cleaveland revived. 1659, 1660, 1662, 1668.

Clievelandi vindiciae: or Clieveland's genuine poems, orations, epistles etc. 1677.

For his characters see col 2045, below ; and for his news-books, cols 2089, 2091, below.

§ 2

Williamson, G. In his Donne tradition, Cambridge Mass 1930.

Gapp, S. V. Notes on Cleveland. PMLA 46 1931.

Mathieson, J. F. Cleveland on 'tyranny'. N & Q 19 Aug 1939.

Hanson, L. Points in the bibliography of Cleveland and Brome. RES 18 1942.

Turner, A. The university miscellanies: some neglected early texts of Cleveland and Cowley. MLN 64 1949.

Woolf, H. B. Cleveland's 'West Saxon poet'. PQ 30 1951.

Kimmey, J. L. Cleveland and the satiric couplet in the Restoration. PQ 37 1958.

Wedgwood, C. V. A metaphysical satirist. Listener 8 May 1958.

Cowley, W. The dialect poetry of Cleveland. Trans Yorkshire Dialect Soc 1 1961.

Withington, E. The canon of Cleveland's poetry. BNYPL May–June 1963.

Nevo, R. In her Dial of virtue, Princeton 1963.

Holland, J. B. An eighteenth-century lute ms in New York Public Library. BNYPL Sept 1964.

Woodward, D. H. Notes on the canon of Cleveland's poetry. BNYPL Oct 1964.

Morris, B. R. A reconsideration of Cleveland's authorship of Epitaphium Thomae Comitis Straffordi. Neophilologus 49 1965.

— Cleveland and Vaughan: some borrowings. N & Q July 1966.

Dewey, T. B. Some 'careless' seventeenth-century rhymes. BNYPL March 1965.

Korshin, P. J. The evolution of neoclassical poetics. Eighteenth-century Stud 2 1968.

Kelliher, H. Anecdotes of Jonson and Cleveland. N & Q May 1972.

SIR ASTON COCKAYNE
1608–84

See col 1737, below.

ANNE COLLINS

Divine songs and meditacions. 1653; ed S. N. Stewart, Los Angeles 1961 (Augustan Reprint Soc) (selected).

THOMAS COLLINS

The penitent publican. 1610.

The teares of love. 1615.

JOHN COLLOP
fl. 1660

Collections

Poems. Ed C. Hilberry, Madison 1962.

§ 1

Poesis rediviva: or poesie reviv'd. 1656.

Itur satyricum, in loyal stanzas. 1660.

§ 2

Drinkwater, J. An unknown poet. Yale Rev new ser 10 1921.

— In his A book for bookmen, 1926.

Steadman, J. M. Collop and the flames without light. N & Q Sept 1955.

Hilberry, C. Medical poems from Collop's Poesis rediviva. Jnl History of Medicine 11 1956.

Dust, A. I. Charles Cotton's comments on Collop's poetry. N & Q March 1967.

RICHARD CORBETT
1582–1635

Collections

Chalmers' English poets vol 5 1810.

Three poems. Cambridge 1951.

Poems. Ed J. A. W. Bennett and H. R. Trevor-Roper, Oxford 1955. With account of mss, early edns and dubia.

§ 1

Certain elegant poems. 1647 etc. Amplified in later edns.

Poetica stromata, by R.C. [Holland or France?] 1648.

The time's whistle: or a new daunce of seven satires, and other poems. Ed J. M. Cowper 1871 (from ms). Signed R.C.

§ 2

Crofts, J. E. V. A life of Bishop Corbett. E & S 10 1924.

Laski, M. Corbet's Rewards. TLS 13 Nov 1959. Replies by J. A. W. Bennett 20 Nov; R. L. Green 27 Nov; H. E. Melville 4 Dec; K. Henderson 18 Dec 1959.

RALPH CRANE
fl. 1625

§ 1

The works of mercy, both corporeall and spirituall. 1621, [1625?] (as The pilgrimes New-Yeares-gift).

§ 2

Wilson, F. P. Crane: scrivener to the King's players. Library 3rd ser 7 1926.

— Jonson and Crane. TLS 8 Nov 1941.

Greg, W. W. Some notes on Crane's ms of the Witch. Library 3rd ser 22 1942.

Howard-Hill, T. H. Crane's parentheses. N & Q Sept 1965.

THOMAS CRANLEY
fl. 1635

Amanda: or the reformed whore. 1635, 1639 (as The converted courtezan), 1889 (priv ptd F. Ouvry).

HUGH CROMPTON
fl. 1657

The glory of women. 1652. Verse trn of H. C. Agrippa, De nobilitate fœminei sexus.

Poems: being a fardle of fancies. 1657.

Pierides: or the Muse's mount. [1658?].

SAMUEL CROSSMAN
1624?–84

The young mans meditation: or some few sacred poems [pt 2 of The young mans monitor]. 1664, 1678 (in The young mans calling), [1695] etc, 1863 (facs of 1664).

GEORGE DANIEL
1616–57

§ 1

Poems. Ed A. B. Grosart, Boston Lincs 1878.
Selected poems. Ed T. B. Stroup, Lexington Kentucky 1959.

§ 2

Nearing, H., jr. 'Yorke in choller' and other unrecorded allusions to Richard II. N & Q 10 Aug 1946.
Stroup, T. B. Daniel: Cavalier poet. Renaissance Papers 1958.
Davies, H. N. Daniel's 'heightened peggs'. N & Q Oct 1969.

JAMES DAY

§ 1

A new spring of divine poetrie. 1637.

§ 2

Pinsent, P. A. Plagiarism by Thomas Jordan. N & Q Sept 1967.

E[DMUND] E[LYS]
1634?–1707?

The Bishop's downfall, or the prelat's snare: a poeme by E.E. 1642. Attributed by Wing.
Dia poemata. 1655, 1655.
An alphabet of elegiack groans. 1656. Signed E.E.
Divine poems. 1658, 1659.
Miscellanea. [Oxford] 1658, Oxford 1662.
Anglia rediviva. 1660, nd.

MILDMAY FANE, EARL OF WESTMORLAND
1602–66

See col 1740, below.

SIR RICHARD FANSHAWE
1608–66

See col 1741, below.

ROBERT FARLEY (or FARLIE)

R. Fairlaei Neanica. Edinburgh 1628. Latin poems and epigrams.
Naulogia: sive inventa navis. [c. 1630?].
Kalendarium humanae vitae: the kalendar of man's life. 1638.
For his emblems, see col 1327, below.

OWEN FELLTHAM
1602?–68

§ 1

Poems annent the keeping of Yule. [1650?]. Taken from Resolves.
Lusoria: or occasional pieces. Appended to Resolves, 1661 (8th edn) and later edns. *See also col 2048, below.*

§ 2

Robertson, J. Felltham of Great Billing. N & Q 27 Nov 1937.
— The poems of Felltham. MLN 58 1943.
— The use made of Felltham's Resolves: a study in plagiarism. MLR 39 1944.
McCrea, H. 'New form and various composition': development in the form of Felltham's Resolves. MP 51 1953.
Patrides, C. A. Bacon and Feltham: victims of literary piracy. N & Q Feb 1958.
See also J. D. Simmonds, col 1233 above.

CHARLES FITZGEFFREY
1575?–1638

Collections
Complete poems. Ed A. B. Grosart 1881.

§ 1

Sir Francis Drake. 1596, 1596; ed S. E. Brydges, Lee Priory 1819.
C. Fitzgeofridi affaniae. 1601. Latin poems and epigrams.
The blessed birthday celebrated; also holy raptures. Oxford 1634, 1636, London 1654.

§ 2

Moore Smith, G. C. Fitzgeffrey: poet and divine. MLR 15 1919.

HENRY FITZGEFFREY
fl. 1617

Satyres and satyricall epigrams. 1617, 1618 (as Certain elegies, done by sundrie excellent wits, with satyres and epigrammes), 1620, [1843].

JOSEPH FLETCHER
1582?–1637

Collections
Poems. Ed A. B. Grosart 1869.

§ 1

Christes bloodie sweat. 1613, 1616. Signed I.F.
The historie of the perfect-cursed-blessed man. 1628, 1629. Contains emblems by Thomas Cecil.

R. FLETCHER

Ex otio negotium: or Martial his epigrams translated; with sundry poems and fancies. 1656. Of the 46 poems, 27 are ptd as addns to Poems of John Cleveland, 1661, 1665.
Radius heliconicus: or the revolution of a free state. nd.

THOMAS FORDE
fl. 1647–61

See col 2050, below.

THOMAS FULLER
1608–61

See col 2233, below.

SIDNEY GODOLPHIN
1610–43
Collections

Saintsbury.
Poems. Ed W. Dighton, Oxford 1931.

§ 1

The passion of Dido for Aeneas. 1658, 1679. Completed by Waller. Verse trn of Virgil, Aeneid bk iv.

§ 2

Teresa, Sr M. Godolphin and the Muses fairest light. MLN 61 1946.

ROBERT GOMERSALL
1602?–44?

The Levite's revenge. 1628, 1633 (in Poems, below).
The tragedie of Lodovick Sforza Duke of Milan. 1628, 1633 (in Poems, with separate title-leaf); ed B. R. Pearn, Louvain 1933 (Bang's Materialien vol 8). Verse drama, with poems.
Poems. 1633.

JOHN HAGTHORPE

Divine meditations and elegies. 1622; ed S. E. Brydges 1816 (selection, as Hagthorpe revived).
Visiones rerum. 1623.
Hagthorpe revived: or select specimens of a forgotten poet. Ed S. E. Brydges, Lee Priory 1817.

JOHN HALL
1627–56
Collections

Poems. Ed S. E. Brydges 1816; Saintsbury.

§ 1

Poems. Cambridge 1646. Includes: The second booke of divine poems by J.H. (with separate title-leaf dated 1647).
Hierocles upon the golden verses of Pythagoras englished. 1657. Includes An account of the author, by John Davies, of Kidwelly.
For Hall's essays see col 2049; for his version of Longinus col 2172; for his Emblems with elegant figures, col 1329, below. See also col 1112, above.

§ 2

Quintana, R. Hall and Samuel Butler: a note. MLN 44 1929.
Haller, W. Two early allusions to Milton's Areopagitica. HLQ 12 1949.

Turnbull, G. H. Hall's letters to Samuel Hartlib. RES new ser 4 1953.

WILLIAM HAMMOND
b. 1614
Collections

Poems. Ed S. E. Brydges 1816; Saintsbury.

§ 1

Poems by W.H. 1655.

§ 2

Volume II of Hammond's poems, hymns, psalms and spiritual songs. BM Quart 11 1937.

PATRICK HANNAY
Collections

Poetical works. [Glasgow] 1875 (Hunterian Club).

§ 1

The nightingale. Sheretine and Mariana. 1622; ed E. V. Utterson 1841; ed D. Laing 1875 (Hunterian Club); Saintsbury.
A happy husband. 1619 (with bastard title-leaf dated 1618) (with R. Brathwait, Good wife).
Two elegies on the late death of Queen Anne. 1619.

§ 2

Ting, N. T. The historical sources of Hannay's Sheretine and Mariana. JEGP 43 1944.

WILLIAM HARBERT of Glamorgan
fl. 1604
Collections

Poems. Ed A. B. Grosart 1870.

§ 1

A prophecie of Cadwallader, last King of the Brittaines. 1604. Verse history of English kings.
Englands sorrowe: or a farewell to Essex. 1606. Colophon dated 1605.
[Commendatory verses]. In Peter Erondelle, French garden, 1608.
[Commendatory verses]. In William Browne, Britannia's pastorals, 1625.

CHRISTOPHER HARVEY
1597–1663
Collections

Complete poems. Ed A. B. Grosart 1874.

§ 1

The synagogue. 1640, 1647, 1651, 1657, 1661, 1667, 1673, 1679, 1703, 1709, 1799, 1836. Often rptd with Herbert's Temple from 1641, though with separate title-page and pagination.
The school of the heart. 1647, 1664, 1675, 1723, 1777 (with Quarles), 1778, 1808 (with Quarles), 1812, 1816, 1823, 1838, 1844, 1845, 1853, 1857, 1859, 1863, 1866

(with Quarles). Trn of Benedict van Haeften's *Scholar cordis*; often rptd with Quarles's *Emblemes* and *Hieroglyphikes*.

§2

Howell, A. C. John Wykes: the printer of the first edn of the Synagogue. N & Q 29 March 1952.
— Harvey's The synagogue. SP 49 1952.

MATTHEW HAVILAND

A monument of God's most gracious preservation of England. [1635?].

ROBERT HEATH
fl. 1650

§1

Clarastella. 1650; Selections, [ed W. G. Hutchison], Hull 1905; Gainesville 1970 (facs).
See also col 1336, below.

§2

Howarth, R. G. Attributions to Herrick. N & Q June 1958.
Candelaria, F. H. Heath and an ambiguity in Wing's STC. N & Q Feb 1960.
Crosland, G. N. Note on an unpublished ms by Heath. N & Q Jan 1972.

EDWARD HERBERT, 1st BARON HERBERT OF CHERBURY
1583–1648

Bibliographies
There are bibliographies in G. H. Palmer, A Herbert bibliography, *Cambridge Mass 1911;* M. M. Rossi, La vita, le opere, i tempi di Edoardo Herbert, *Florence 1947, and in* F. E. Hutcheson's edn of De religione laici, *New Haven 1944.*

Collections
Poems. Ed J. C. Collins 1881.
Poems. Ed G. C. Moore Smith, Oxford 1923.
Minor poets of the seventeenth century. Ed R. G. Howarth 1931 (EL), 1953 (rev).

§1

Occasional verses. 1665, Menston 1969 (facs); Poems, ed G. C. Moore Smith, Oxford 1923.
The life of Lord Herbert written by himself. Ed Horace Walpole, Strawberry Hill 1765 (from ms); ed S. Lee 1886, 1906 (rev); ed C. H. Herford, New Town 1928.
For Herbert's prose see cols 2129, 2333, below.

Letters
The Herbert correspondence. Ed W. J. Smith, Cardiff 1963.

§2

Pilley, J. G. Mersenne and Herbert. TLS 15 Feb 1934.
Chapman, R. W. Herbert and the Bodleian. Bodleian Quart Record 8 1938.
Willey, B. Herbert: a spiritual Quixote of the seventeenth century. E & S 27 1941.
Hanford, J. H. Herbert and his son. HLQ 5 1942.
Keister, D. A. Lady Kent and the two Sir Edwards. MLN 61 1946.
— Donne and Herbert: an exchange of verses. MLQ 8 1947.

— The birth date of Herbert. MLN 62 1947. Reply by H. C. Lancaster 63 1948.
Rossi, M. M. La vita, le opere, i tempi di Herbert. 3 vols Florence 1947.
Harrison, J. L. Herbert's two sonnets on black. N & Q Aug 1953.
Warnke, F. J. Two previously unnoted mss of poems by Herbert. N & Q April 1954.
Dart, T. Herbert's lute-book. Music & Letters 38 1957.
Rickey, M. E. Rhymecraft in Edward and George Herbert. JEGP 57 1958.
Patrides, C. A. Milton and his contemporaries on the Chains of Satan. MLN 73 1958.
Smieja, F. Herbert: a possible Spanish source. N & Q March 1968.
Hébert, C. A. The platonic love poetry of Herbert. Ball State Univ Forum 11 1970.

THOMAS HEYWOOD
1574?–1641

See col 1682, below.

BARTEN HOLYDAY
1593–1661

See col 1769, below.

NICHOLAS HOOKES
1628–1712

Amanda. 1653, 1923.
Miscellanea poetica. 1653. Usually bound with Amanda, above. Includes Latin elegies and a poem to Dr Busby.

ROBERT HOWARD (alias Louis of Nazareth OFM)
d. c. 1676

§1

A sacred poem describing the life and death of S. Marie of Aegipt. 1640; ed D. M. Rogers, Menston 1970 (facs).

§2

Allison, A. F. Howard, Franciscan. Library 5th ser 3 1949. With bibliography.

JAMES HOWELL
1594?–1666

See col 2225, below.

SIR FRANCIS HUBERT
d. 1629

Collections
Poems. Ed B. Mellor, Hong Kong 1961.

§1

The deplorable life and death of Edward the Second. 1628, 1628, 1629 (enlarged), 1631 (with cancel title).
Egypts favorite: the historie of Joseph. 1631.

PATHERICKE JENKYN (or JENKYNS)

Amorea: the lost lover. 1661.

THOMAS JORDAN
c. 1620–85?

See col 1746, below.

RALPH KNEVET
1600–71

Collections
Shorter poems. Ed A. M. Charles, [Columbus 1966.]

§1

Στρατιωτικον: or a discourse of militarie discipline. 1628.
Rhodon and Isis: a pastorall. 1631. Verse drama.
Funerall elegies. 1637. To Lady Katherine Paston.
A gallery to the temple; lyrical poems upon sacred occasions. Ed G. Pellegrini, Pisa 1954.
See also col 1748, below.

§2

Millican, C. B. Knevet: author of the supplement to Spenser's Faerie Queen. RES 14 1938; rptd separately 1938.
Charles, A. M. The manuscript of Knevet's Gallery to the temple (BM additional ms 27,447). N & Q May 1959.
Merchant, W. M. Knevet of Norfolk: poet of Civill warre. E & S new ser 13 1960.
Höltgen, K. J. Knevet's ordination. N & Q Aug 1967.
— Knevet under the Commonwealth. N & Q Aug 1967.

SIR FRANCIS KYNASTON
1587–1642

§1

Musae querulae de regis in Scotiam profectione. 1633. Latin poems by A. Johnstone with Kynaston's verse trns.
Amorum Troili et Creseidae: libri duo priores anglico-latini. Oxford 1635. Chaucer in rimed Latin.
Corona Minervae: or a masque. 1635. Anon. In verse.
Leoline and Sydonis: Cynthiades. 1642; Saintsbury. A romance.

§2

Seccombe, H. G. Notes on Kynaston. RES 8 1932.
Turnbull, G. H. Samuel Hartlib's connection with Kynaston's Musaeum Minervae. N & Q 19 Jan 1952.

WILLIAM LATHUM

§1

Phyala lachrymarum. 1634.

§2

Marshall, L. B. Lathum: a seventeenth-century poet. RES 8 1932.
— Five minor poets. TLS 29 Sept 1932.

LEONARD LAWRENCE

A small treatise betwixt Arnalte and Lucenda. 1639. Signed L.L. Verse trn from Spanish of D. Hernandez de San Pedro, who claimed falsely to be translating from Greek.
Epithalamium. 1650. Attributed by Wing.

SIR WILLIAM LEIGHTON

Vertue triumphant. 1603.
The teares or lamentations of a sorrowful soule. 1613 (words only), 1614 (composed with musicall ayres). Only first 8 pieces are by Leighton.
See also col 1355, below

CHRISTOPHER LEVER

A crucifixe. 1607.
Queene Elizabeths teares. 1607; ed A. B. Grosart, Fuller worthies miscellany, 1870 (with A crucifixe).

MARTIN LLUELYN
1618–82

§1

An elegie on William [Laud], Archbishop of Canterbury. 1644.
A satyr occasioned by the author's survey of a scandalous pamphlet intituled The King's cabanet opened. Oxford 1645. Anon.
Men-miracles, with other poemes. 1646, 1656, 1661 (as The marrow of the Muses), 1679.
William Harvey, Exercitationes de generatione animalium. 1653. One poem.
An elegie [on the death of Henry Duke of Gloucester]. Oxford 1660.
To the Kings most excellent Majesty. [1660]. Includes poems to Dukes of York and Gloucester.
Wickham wakened: or the Quaker's madrigall in rime dogerell [sic]. [Oxford] 1672. Perhaps by Lluelyn.

§2

Wallerstein, R. C. Lluelyn: Cavalier and 'metaphysical'. JEGP 35 1936.
Cutts, J. P. Dramatic writing of Llewellyn. PQ 47 1968.

WILLIAM LOE
d. 1645

An hymne orsong [sic] of seaven straines [with other poems]. [Hamburg] 1620, Hamburg 1620; ed A. B. Grosart, Fuller worthies miscellany I, 1870 (as Songs of Sion).

SHAKERLEY MARMION
1603–39

§1

A moral poem intituled the legend of Cupid and Psyche. 1637 (some copies with variant title-page dated 1638), 1666 (as Cupid's courtship: or the celebration of a marriage between the god of love and Psiche; signed SM); ed S. W. Singer, Chiswick 1820 (as Cupid and Psyche: a legend); Saintsbury; ed A. J. Nearing, Philadelphia 1944.
See also col 1750, below.

§2

Hoffmann, A. Das Psyche-Märchen des Apuleius in der englischen Literatur. Strasbourg 1908.

HUMPHREY MILL

Poems occasioned by a melancholy vision. 1639.
A nights search. Pt 1, 1640; pt 2, 1646 (some copies with title-page dated 1652), 1652 (a duplicate of 1646 but with a frontispiece, a new title-page and some explanatory verses).

HENRY MORE
1614–87

See col 2334, below.

THOMAS NABBES
1605–41?

See col 1752, below.

RICHARD NICCOLS
1584–1616

Expicedium: a funeral oration [on Elizabeth I]. 1603 (anon), Amsterdam 1969 (facs).
The cuckow. 1607.
['A winter nights vision' and 'Englands Eliza']. In A mirrour for magistrates, newly enlarged with a last part, 1610. Niccols edited the whole.
Three precious tears of blood in memory of Henry the Great [by Henry IV, King of France]. 1611. A verse trn by Niccols.
The three sisters teares. 1613.
The furies, with vertue's encomium: or the image of honour, in two bookes of epigrammes. 1614 (signed R.N.); rptd Harleian miscellany vol 10, 1808 (with Monodia, below).
Monodia or Walthams complaint, upon the death of the Lady Honor Hay. 1615; rptd with Furies, above, in Harleian miscellany vol 10, 1808.
Londons artillery. 1616.
Sir Thomas Overburies vision. 1616 (signed R.N.); rptd Harleian miscellany vol 7, 1744 etc; ed J. Maidment 1873 (Hunterian Club); ed A. S. Reid, Gainesville 1957 (facs), 1966 (priv ptd).
The beggars ape. 1627 (anon), New York [1936] (facs).

SAMUEL PAGE
1574–1630

The love of Amos and Laura. In I.C.'s Alcilia, 1613, 1619, 1628; ed A. B. Grosart 1879.

CLEMENT PAMAN
fl. 1660

Short poems often found in 17th-century mss but never collected; see BM and Bodley ms catalogues. One piece in N. Ault, Seventeenth-century lyrics, 1928. See J. Carey, Clement Paman, TLS 27 March 1959.

HENRY PEACHAM the younger
1578?–1642?

§1

The more the merrier. 1608. Epigrams.
Thomas Coryate, Odcombian banquet. 1611. 4 burlesque poems.
Arthur Standish, Commons complaint. 1611, 1611, 1612. With poems by Peacham.
The period of mourning disposed into six visions [on death of Henry, Prince of Wales], together with nuptiall hymnes [on marriage of Frederick and Princess Elizabeth]. 1613, 1613 (with variant), 1789, 1792.
Prince Henry revived. 1615.

Thalias banquet. 1620. Epigrams, signed H.P.
An Aprill shower shed in abundance of teares. 1624. Elegy on Richard Sackville, Earl of Dorset.
Thestylis atrata. 1634. Elegy on Frances, Countess of Warwick.
See also col 1330, below.

§2

Pitman, M. C. The epigrams of Peacham and Henry Parrot. MLR 29 1934.
—— Studies in the works of Henry Peacham. Bull Inst of Historical Research 11 1934.
Cawley, R. R. Peacham: his contributions to English poetry. University Park Pa 1971.

THOMAS PESTEL
1584?–1659?

Collections
Poems. Ed H. Buchan, Oxford 1940.

§1

Sermons and devotions. 1659.
See H. A. Buchan, Pestel's poems in ms Malone 14, Bodleian Quart Record 7 1933.

'PHILANDER'

Tarquin and Lucretia. 1669.

THOMAS PHILIPOT
d. 1682

Collections
Poems. 1646; ed L. C. Martin, Liverpool 1950.

§1

A congratulatory elegie offered up to the Earle of Essex upon his investiture [as] Lord Chamberlaine. 1641.
Elegies offer'd up to the memory of W. Glover. 1641.
An elegie [on] Robert Earle of Essex. 1646.
England's sorrow. 1646. An elegy on Robert, Earl of Essex.
Capellus viribus. 1662. Elegies to Arthur Lord Capell.
Aesop's fables, with his life. 3 pts 1666, 1687 (with addns), 1703. A polyglot edn in English, French and Latin; the English only by Philipot.

SAMUEL PICK

§1

Festum voluptatis: or the banquet of pleasure, containing divers choyce love-poesies, songs etc. 1639.

§2

Rollins, H. E. Pick's borrowings. RES 7 1931.

EDMUND PRESTWICH

Hippolytus, translated out of Seneca; together with divers other poems. 1651.

JOHN QUARLES
1624–65

A direfull anathema against peace-haters. [1647]. Wrongly attributed to Francis Quarles.
Fons lachrymarum: or a fountain of teares. 1648 (some copies dated 1649), 1655, 1677. Includes verse paraphrase of Lamentations of Jeremiah, Divine meditations, An elegy upon Sir Charles Lucas. The Discourse between the soul and the world and the elegy on Sir Charles Lucas were omitted in 1655 edn.
Regale lectum miseriae: or a kingly bed of misery. 1649, 1649 (with Englands sonets), 1649, 1659, 1660, 1679.
God's love and mans unworthiness. 1651, 1655 (with Divine meditations) etc.
Tyranny of the Dutch. 1653.
The banishment of Tarquin: or the reward of lust. 1655. With Shakespeare, Rape of Lucrece.
Divine meditations upon several subjects. 1655, 1671, 2 pts 1679.
An elegie on James Ussher. 1656.
The history of the most vile Dimagorus. 1658. A continuation of Francis Quarles, Argalus and Parthenia.
Rebellions downfall. 1662. Broadsheet verses on the Restoration.
Londons disease and cure: being a soveraigne receipt against the plague. 1665. A broadsheet.
Citizens flight. 1665.
Self-conflict: or the powerful motions between the flesh and the spirit. 1680, 1684 (as Triumphant chastity). A trn from Jacob Cats, Selbststreit [1647].

THOMAS RANDOLPH
1605–36

See col 1773, below.

NATHANIEL RICHARDS
1612?–54?

The celestiall publican: a sacred poem. 1630, 1631 (as Seven poems: divine, morall and satyricall), 1632 (as Poems divine, morall, satyricall), 1641 (enlarged as Poems sacred and satyricall).
The tragedy of Messallina the Roman emperesse, as it hath beene acted by the company of his Majesties revells. 1640; ed A. R. Skemp, Louvain 1910 (Bang's Materialien vol 30).
Truth's acrostick: an elegie [on Sir Paul Pindar]. [London 1650].
Upon the declaration of his Majesty King Charles of England the Second. 1660.

THOMAS ROBINSON
§ 1

The life and death of Mary Magdalene. Ed H. O. Sommer 1899 (EETS). Written c. 1620.

§ 2

Elton, W. Two Milton notes. N & Q 4 Oct 1947.

ALEXANDER ROSS
1591–1654
§ 1

Rerum judaicarum memorabiliorum. 3 pts 1617 (bastard title dated 1619), 1632 (with 4th bk). Latin verse.

Three decades of divine meditations. [1630].
[Poemata]. In A. Johnston (ed), Delitiae poetarum scotorum pt 2, Amsterdam 1637.
Mel heliconium. 1642.
A centurie of divine meditations upon predestination [and] sixteen meditations upon Gods justice and mercy. 1646.
[Praelibatio ad Theophilae amoris]. In Edward Benlowes, Theophila, 1652. Ross's trn into Latin verse of the first canto.
For Ross's prose see col 2337, below.

§ 2

McColley, G. Milton's technique of source adaptation. SP 35 1938.

JOHN RUSSELL of Magdalene College
Cambridge

An elegie upon the death of Gustavus Adolphus. [Cambridge 1633?], 1634 (with The two famous pitcht battels).
The two famous pitcht battels of Lypsich and Lutzen. Cambridge 1634, 1634 (variant).

JOHN SALTMARSH
c. 1610–47

See col 1999, below.

SAMUEL SHEPPARD
§ 1

The times displayed. 1646.
God and Mammon: or no fellowship betwixt light and darkness. 1646 (signed S.S.); in Fugitive tracts 2nd ser, 1875 (priv ptd) (facs).
[An hymne to God]. In The year of jubile, 1646.
The faerie King. In Bodley ms Rawlinson poetry 28.
The loves of Amandus and Sophronia. 1650.
Epigrams theological, philosophical and romantick. 1651.
Fortunes tennis-ball: or the most excellent history of Dorastus and Fawnia rendered into verse. 1688. Signed S.S. From Robert Greene's Pandosto.

§ 2

Rollins, H. E. Sheppard and his Praise of poets. SP 24 1927.

JAMES SHIRLEY
1596–1666

See col 1725, below.

JAMES SMITH
1605–67

Verses in collections by Smith and Sir J. Mennis: Witts recreations, *1640, 1817;* Musarum deliciae, *1655, 1656, 1817;* Wit and drollery, *1656, 1661;* Wit restor'd, *2 pts 1658 (contains* The innovation of Penelope and Ulysses *by J.S.), 1817.*

THOMAS STANLEY the elder
1625–78

Bibliographies
Flower, M. Stanley: a bibliography of his writings in prose and verse. Trans Cambridge Bibl Soc 1 1950.

Collections
Poems and translations. Ed G. M. Crump, Oxford 1962.

§1

Poems and translations. 1647 (priv ptd), 1651 (as Poems), 1652, 1657 (in John Gamble, Ayres and dialogues); ed S. E. Brydges 1814 (from 1651); ed L. I. Guiney, Hull 1907, 1923 (only trns from Joannes Secundus); Saintsbury.
For his The history of philosophy, *1655–62, see col 2338, below, and for his trns from Anacreon, Bion, Moschus, Secundus, Ausonius etc col 2165–6, below.*

§2

Praz, M. Stanley, Sherburne and Ayres as translators and imitators of Italian, Spanish and French poets. MLR 20 1925.
M., M. Stanley, scholar and poet. More Books 13 1938.
Bentley, G. E. James Shirley and a group of unnoted poems on the wedding of Stanley. HLQ 2 1939.
Crump, G. M. A Stanley manuscript. TLS 26 July 1957.
— Thorn-Drury's notes on Stanley. N & Q March 1958.
— Stanley's manuscript of his poems and translations. Trans Cambridge Bibl Soc 2 1958.
Osborn, J. M. Stanley's 'lost' register of friends. Yale Univ Lib Gazette 32 1958.
Roberts, H. A. Stanley of Cumberlow Green. N & Q Sept 1958. Reply by G. Isham, Dec 1958.
O'Regan, M. J. The French sources of Stanley's paraphrases of Psalms 139 and 148. MLR 59 1964.
Wilson, E. M. and E. R. Vincent. Stanley's translations and borrowings from Spanish and Italian poems. Revue de Littérature Comparée 32 1958.

MATTHEW STEVENSON

Occasion's offspring. 1645, 1654.
The twelve moneths. 1661, 1928. Prose.
Bellum presbyteriale. 1661.
Florus britannicus. 1662. Brief prose biographies of English kings, each ending with a commendatory poem.
Poems. 1665, 1673 (as Poems: or a miscellany). There are 2 known variant title-pages of 1673: 1673 (as Norfolk drollery) and 1685 (as The wits: or poems and songs on various occasions).
The Quaker's wedding, October 24 1671. 1671.
The low estate of the Countess of Holland on her deathbed. 1672.
The wits paraphras'd. 1680.

SIR JOHN STRADLING
1563–1637

Two bookes of constancie, written in Latine, by J. Lipsius, containing principallie a comfortable conference in common calamities, englished by J. Stradling. 1594, 1595; ed R. Kirk, New Brunswick NJ 1939.
Joannis Stradlingi epigrammatum libri quatuor. 1607.
Beati pacifici: a divine poem. 1623.
Divine poems. 1625; ed A. B. Grosart 1883.

WILLIAM STRODE
1602–45

For bibliography see J. I. Dredge, A few sheaves of Devon bibliography, *5 pts Plymouth 1889–96 (6th sheaf).*

Collections
Poetical works. Ed B. Dobell 1907.
Four poems. Flansham 1934.
See also col 1774, below.

§2

Babb, L. The background of Il Penseroso. SP 37 1940.
Crum, M. C. William Fulman and an autograph ms of the poet Strode. Bodleian Lib Record 4 1953.
Main, C. F. Notes on some poems attributed to Strode. PQ 34 1955.
Morris, H. The poetry of Strode. Tulane Stud in Eng 7 1957.
— Strode's longer elegy. Renaissance News 12 1959.

JOSHUA SYLVESTER
1563–1618

Collections
Collected works and trns pbd as pt of G. de Saluste du Bartas, Bartas his devine weekes and workes, *1620–1.*

Sacred workes gathered in one volume. 2 pts 1620, 1620 (variant edn as All the small workes).
Works. Ed A. B. Grosart 2 vols 1880.

§1

Monodia. [1594]. Elegy on Dame Helen Branch.
[Dedicatory verses, signed J.S.]. In George Goodwin, Automachia, 1607, [1615?], 1621 (in Bartas his devine weekes).
Lachrimae lachrimarum. 1612, [1612], 1613, 1613, Amsterdam 1969 (facs).
The Parliament of vertues royal. 2 vols 1614–15. Contains poems and trns by Sylvester.
Tobacco battered and the pipes shattered. [1617–20]. Verse satire.
The wood-man's bear: a poeme. 1620.
[The mysterie of mysteries]. In Bartas his devine weekes, 1620–1.
Panthea: or divine wishes and meditations. 1630. With poems by various hands.

§2

Weller, P. Sylvesters englische Übersetzungen der religiösen Epen des Du Bartas. Tübingen 1902.
Taylor, G. C. Milton's use of Du Bartas. Cambridge Mass 1934.
Campbell, L. B. The Christian Muse. Huntington Lib Bull no 8 1935.
Smith, J. The influence of John Hayward and of Sylvester on Drummond's Cypresse grove. PQ 26 1947.
Hunter, W. B. The sources of Milton's prosody. PQ 28 1949.
Simonsen, V. L. Sylvester's translation of Du Bartas' La première semaine. Orbis Litterarum 8 1950.
Ure, P. Two passages in Sylvester's Du Bartas and their bearing on Shakespeare's Richard II. N & Q Sept 1953.
Williams, F. B., jr. Robert Nicholson: a minor Maecenas. N & Q 1 Jan 1954. On Sylvester's patron.
— The bear facts about Sylvester, The woodman. Eng Lang Notes 9 1971.
Potter, J. L. Sylvester's shaped sonnets. N & Q Sept 1957.
Illo, J. Animal sources for Milton's Sin and Death. N & Q Nov 1960.
— Dryden, Sylvester and the correspondence of melancholy winter and cold age. Eng Lang Notes 1 1963.

JOHN TATHAM

See col 1756, below.

EDWARD TAYLOR
1645?–1729

Bibliographies

Hoffman, C. A. Taylor: a selected bibliography. Bull of Bibliography 23 1961. *See* G. Russell, Addenda, 27 1970.

Etulain, R. W. Taylor: a checklist. Early Amer Lit 4 1969.

Leary, L. Articles on American literature 1950–67. Durham NC 1970.

Collections

Poetical works. Ed T. H. Johnson, New York 1939, Princeton 1939.

Poems. Ed B. D. Samison, Yale Univ Lib Gazette 28 1954.

Stanford, D. E. Sacramental meditations by Taylor. Yale Univ Lib Gazette 31 1956.

—— Nineteen unpublished poems by Taylor. Amer Lit 29 1957.

Poems. Ed D. E. Stanford, New Haven 1960, 1963 (abridged).

Seventeenth-century American poetry. Ed H. T. Meserole, New York 1968.

§1

Taylor requested that none of his poems be pbd and the mss were deposited in Yale Univ Lib by his grandson.

A meditation upon the glory of God. Ed M. A. Neufield, Yale Univ Lit Gazette 25 1951. Written 13 Feb 1687.

A transcript of Taylor's Metrical history of Christianity. Ed D. E. Stanford, Cleveland 1962.

Mignon, C. W. Another Taylor manuscript at Yale. Yale Univ Lib Gazette 41 1966.

Kaiser, L. M. and D. E. Stanford. The Latin poems of Taylor. Yale Univ Lib Gazette 40 1965.

§2

Weathers, W. T. Taylor: hellenistic Puritan. Amer Lit 18 1946.

——Taylor and the Cambridge Platonists. Amer Lit 26 1954.

Wright, N. The morality tradition in the poetry of Taylor. Ibid.

Lind, S. E. Taylor: a revaluation. New England Quart 21 1948.

Laurentia, Sr M. Taylor's Meditation forty-two. Explicator Dec 1949.

Pearce, H. R. Taylor: the poet as Puritan. New England Quart 26 1950.

Blau, H. Heaven's sugar cake: theology and imagery in the poetry of Taylor. New England Quart 26 1953.

Goodman, W. B. Taylor writes his love. New England Quart 27 1954.

Stanford, D. E. Taylor and the Lord's Supper. Amer Lit 27 1955.

—— The giant bones of Claverack, New York 1705. New York History 40 1959.

—— The earliest poems of Taylor. Amer Lit 32 1960.

—— The puritan poet as preacher: an Edward Taylor sermon. Stud in Amer Lit 26 1961.

—— The parentage of Taylor. Amer Lit 33 1961.

Black, M. Taylor: Heaven's sugar cake. New England Quart 29 1956.

Tedeschini, L. B. Edward Taylor. Studi Americani 2 1956.

McNamara, A. M. Taylor's Sacramental meditation six. Explicator Oct 1958.

Hodges, R. R. Taylor's Artificial man. Amer Lit 21 1959.

Murphy, F. E. X. An Edward Taylor manuscript book. Ibid.

—— Taylor's attitude toward publication. Amer Lit 34 1962.

—— Taylor's metrical history of Christianity. Ibid.

—— Edward Taylor. Minneapolis 1965. A pamphlet.

Grabo, N. S. Catholic tradition, puritan literature and Taylor. Papers of Michigan Acad 45 1959.

—— Taylor on the Lord's Supper. Boston Public Lib Quart 12 1960.

—— The poet to the Pope: Taylor to Solomon Stoddard. Amer Lit 32 1960.

—— The veiled vision: the role of aesthetics in early American intellectual history. William & Mary Quart 19 1962.

—— The appeale tried: another Taylor manuscript. Amer Lit 24 1962.

—— Edward Taylor. New York 1962.

—— (ed). Christographia. New Haven 1962.

—— Taylor's Spiritual huswifery. PMLA 79 1964.

—— Taylor's treatise concerning the Lord's Supper. East Lansing 1966.

—— 'God's determinations': touching Taylor's critics. Seventeenth-century News 28 1970.

Hedberg, Johannes. Meditations, linguistic and literary, on Meditation twenty-nine by Taylor. Moderna Språk 54 1960.

Jordan, R. J. Taylor's The ebb and flow. Explicator April 1962.

Manierre, W. R. Verbal patterns in the poetry of Taylor. College Eng Jan 1962.

Medlicott, A. Notes on Taylor from the diaries of Stephen Williams. Amer Lit 34 1962.

Shepherd, E. Taylor's injunction against publication. Amer Lit 33 1962.

Poet in a wilderness. TLS 3 Feb 1962.

Woodward, R. H. Automata in Hawthorne's Artist of the beautiful and Taylor's Meditation 56. Emerson Soc Quart 31 1963.

Clendenning, J. Piety and imagery in Taylor's The reflexion. Amer Quart 16 1964.

Fender, S. Taylor and the Application of redemption. MLR 59 1964.

Ballinger, M. The metaphysical echo. Eng Stud in Africa 8 1965.

Junkins, D. Taylor's revisions. Amer Lit 37 1965.

—— Should stars wooe lobster claws?: a study of Taylor's poetic practice and theory. Early Amer Lit 3 1968.

Mignon, C. W. Some notes on the history of the Taylor manuscripts. Yale Univ Lib Gazette 39 1965.

—— Taylor's Preparatory meditations: a decorum imperfection. PMLA 83 1968.

Thomas, J. L. Drama and doctrine in Gods determinations. Amer Lit 36 1965.

Bhattacharya, S. C. Taylor: the American metaphysical poet. Modern Rev 121 1966.

Thorpe, P. Taylor as poet. New England Quart 39 1966.

Griffith, C. Taylor and the momentum of metaphor. Eng Lang Notes 33 1966.

Halbert, C. L. Tree of life imagery in the poetry of Taylor. Amer Lit 38 1966.

Benton, R. M. Taylor's use of his text. Amer Lit 39 1967.

Prosser, E. Taylor's poetry. New England Quart 40 1967.

Brumm, U. The tree of life in Taylor's Meditations. Early Amer Lit 3 1968.

Carlisle, E. F. The puritan structure of Taylor's poetry. Amer Quart 1 1968.

Griffith, E. M. The structure and language of Taylor's Meditation 2. 112. Early Amer Lit 3 1968.

Johnston, T. E., jr. Taylor: an American emblematist. Ibid.

—— A note on the voices of Anne Bradstreet, Taylor, Roger Williams and Philip Pain. Ibid.

Rowe, K. E. A biblical illumination of Taylorian art. Amer Lit 40 1968.

Werge, T. The tree of life in Taylor's poetry: the sources of the puritan image. Early Amer Lit 3 1968.
Allen, J. B. Taylor's catholic wasp: exegetical convention in Upon a spider catching a fly. Eng Lang Notes 7 1970.
Keller, K. Taylor's bawdry. New England Quart 43 1970.
Davis, T. M. and V. L. Davis. Taylor on the day of judgement. Amer Lit 43 1972.

JEREMY TAYLOR
1613–67

See col 1984, below.

AURELIAN TOWNSHEND (or TOWNSEND)
1583?–1643?
Collections
Poems and masks. Ed E. K. Chambers, Oxford 1912.

§1
Townshend's poems are scattered through ms miscellanies. For poems in mss of Bodley see M. Crum, First-line index, 2 vols Oxford 1969. A few were ptd before Chambers's collected edn.
[Commendatory verses]. In Henry Lawes, Choice psalmes set to music, 1648.
[Commendatory verses]. In Henry Lawes, Ayres and dialogues, 1655.
[2 poems set to music]. In Lawes, Second book of ayres, 1655.
[Upon his constant mistress]. In Choice drollery, 1656 (anon); ed J. W. Ebsworth 1876.
[Upon kind and true love]. In Wit's interpreter, 1655 (anon); in Choice drollery, 1656 etc.
[Youth and beauty, Thou shepheard whose intentive eye]. In W. Beloe, Anecdotes of literature vol 6, 1812.
[To the lady May, Upon kind and true love]. In A. H. Bullen, Speculum amantis, 1889.
[His mistress found]. In Richard Carew, Poems and a masque, ed J. W. Ebsworth 1893.
For plays and masques, see col 1757, below.

§2
Moore Smith, G. C. Aurelian Townshend. MLR 12 1917.
—— Townsend. TLS 23 Oct 1924.
Veevers, E. Albion's triumph: a further corrected state of the text. Library 5th ser 16 1961.
—— Official accounts for two masques by Townshend. N & Q April 1962.
—— A masque fragment by Townsend. N & Q Sept 1965. Reply by P. Palmer, Aug 1966.

HENRY TUBBE
1618–55

Meditations divine and morall by H.T. 1659.
Henry Tubbe. Ed G. C. Moore Smith, Oxford 1915. A selection from ms.

THOMAS WASHBOURNE
1606–87
Collections
Poems. Ed A. B. Grosart 1868.

§1
Divine poems. 1654.

§2
Leach, E. More seventeenth-century admirers of Herbert. N & Q Feb 1960.

ROWLAND WATKYNS

§1
Flamma sine fumo: or poems without fictions. 1662; ed P. C. Davies, Cardiff 1968.

§2
Marshall, L. B. TLS 29 Sept 1932.
Skelton, R. Watkins and Andrew Marvell. N & Q Dec 1958. Reply by M. H. Dodds, June 1959.
Davies, P. Watkyns: a Breconshire poet of the seventeenth century. Anglo-Welsh Rev 16 1967.

JOHN WEEVER
1576–1632

Epigrammes in the oldest cut. 1599; ed R. B. McKerrow, Oxford 1911.
Faunus and Melliflora. 1600; ed A. Davenport, Liverpool 1948. Includes A prophesie of this present yeare 1600.
Agnus dei. 1601, 1603, 1606, 1610.
The mirror of martyrs. 1601, 1873 (Roxburghe Club).
Rochester bridge: a poem written in AD 1601. Ed W. B. Rye, Archaeologia cantiana, 1887.
See col 1158, above.

NATHANIEL WHITING
fl. 1629–63

§1
Le hore di recreatione: or the pleasant historie of Albino and Bellama, by N.W. 1637, 1638, 1639 (as The most pleasant historie of Albino and Bellama); Saintsbury.

§2
Shirren, A. J. The Whitings of Etton and Aldwincle. N & Q April–May 1953.
Higgins, A. I. T. Secular heroic epic poetry. Swiss Stud in Eng 31 1953.
Whiting, J. R. S. Whiting family. N & Q Feb 1969.

MICHAEL WIGGLESWORTH
1631–1705
Collections
Seventeenth-century American poetry. Ed H. T. Meserole, New York 1968.

§1
The day of doom. [Cambridge Mass 1662 ?] (no known copy), [1666], London 1666, 1673, [Cambridge Mass 1683] etc, New York 1867

(with autobiography etc); ed K. B. Murdock, New York 1929.

Meat out of the eater. Cambridge 1670, 1689 (4th edn) (with Riddles unriddled).

[Letters to Increase Mather]. Collections Mass Historical Soc 4th ser 8 1868.

God's controversy with New England (1662). Proc Mass Historical Soc 1st ser 12 1873.

Diary 1653-7: the conscience of a Puritan. Ed E. S. Morgan, Trans Colonial Soc of Mass 35 1951, New York 1965.

§2

Dean, J. W. Memoir of Wigglesworth. Albany 1871.

Matthiessen, F. O. Wigglesworth: a puritan artist. New England Quart 1 1928.

Jones, M. B. Notes for a bibliography of Wigglesworth's Day of Doom and Meat out of the eater. Proc Amer Antiquarian Soc new ser 39 1930.

—— Wigglesworth's Meat out of the eater. Yale Univ Lib Gazette 5 1931.

Crowder, R. Meat out of the eater. Boston Public Lib Quart 11 1959.

—— No featherbed to Heaven: a biography of Wigglesworth. East Lansing 1962.

Strange, A. Wigglesworth reads the poets. Amer Lit 31 1959.

Goff, F. R. Rare books: Americana. Quart Jnl of Current Acquisitions 16 1960.

Gummere, R. M. Wigglesworth: from kill-joy to comforter. Classical Jnl 62 1966.

—— Seven wise men of colonial America. Cambridge Mass 1967.

Alexis, G. T. Wigglesworth's 'easiest room'. New England Quart 42 1969.

Brack, O. M., jr. Wigglesworth and the attribution of I walk'd and did a little molehill view. Seventeenth-century News 28 1970.

SIR HENRY WOTTON (or WOOTTON)
1568-1639

Collections

Reliquiae Wottonianae: or a collection of lives, letters, poems, with characters of sundry personages and other pieces. Ed Izaak Walton 1651 (with life), 1654 (with addns), 1672, 1685 (with letters to Lord Zouch). Prose with 14 poems. *See col 1911, below.*

Poems. Ed A. Dyce 1843 (Percy Soc).

Poems by Wooton and others. Ed J. Hannah 1845, 1870 (as The courtly poets from Raleigh to Montrose), 1875 (as Poems of Raleigh, Wotton and other courtly poets), 1892.

§1

[You meaner beauties of the night]. In Michael East, Sixt set of bookes, 1624.

The elements of architecture. 1624; ed S. T. Prideaux 1903; ed F. Hard 1968. Prose.

Ad regem e Scotia reducem HW plausus et vota. 1633. Latin prose.

A parallel betweene Robert late Earle of Essex and George late Duke of Buckingham. 1641; ed S. E. Brydges 1814. Prose.

A short view of the life and death of George Villiers Duke of Buckingham. 1642; rptd in Harleian miscellany vol 8, 1744. Prose.

A panegyrick of King Charles. 1649. Prose.

The state of Christendom: or a discovery of many hidden mysteries of the times. 1657. Prose.

Letters

Letters to Sir Edmund Bacon. 1661.

Letters and dispatches from Wotton 1617-20. Ed G. Tomline 1850 (Roxburghe Club).

Smith, L. P. The life and letters of Wotton. 2 vols Oxford 1907. With list of mss etc.

Crinò, A. M. Fatti e figure del Seicento anglo-toscano. Florence 1957. With unpbd letters.

§2

Walton, I. The life of Wotton. In his Reliquiae Wottonianae, 1651 etc, above.

Ward, A. W. Wotton: a biographical sketch. 1898.

Fox, A. W. In his A book of bachelors, 1899.

More, P. E. In his Shelburne essays: 5th series, New York 1908.

Asquith, H. H. Wotton; with some general reflections on style in English poetry. Oxford 1919 (Eng Assoc).

Hamer, D. You meaner beauties of the night. N & Q 16 July 1932.

Atkinson, D. F. Wotton and the new astronomy. SP 32 1935.

—— The source of Two gentlemen of Verona. SP 41 1944.

Hard, F. Ideas from Bacon and Wotton in William Sanderson's Graphice. SP 36 1939.

—— Wotton: Renaissance Englishman. Pacific Spectator 7 1953.

Weiss, R. Wotton and Orazzio Lombardelli. RES 19 1943.

Leishman, J. B. You meaner beauties of the night. Library 4th ser 26 1945.

Weld, J. S. Some problems of euphuistic narrative. Robert Greene and Wotton. SP 45 1948.

Main, C. F. Wotton's The character of a happy life. Library 5th ser 10 1955.

Novarr, D. The making of Walton's Lives. Ithaca 1958.

Fitzgerald, H. Emendations to Wotton. TLS 23 Dec 1960. Reply by C. O. Fox 10 Feb 1961.

Pitman, M. R. Marvell and Wotton. RES new ser 13 1962.

Pogue, J. C. The two gentlemen of Verona and Wotton's A courtlie controversie of Cupid's cautels. Emporia State Research Stud 10 1962.

Stuart, G. W., jr. Two more anonymous printings by John Dawson. PBSA 57 1963. Includes Wotton's Life of Buckingham.

Datta, K. Marvell and Wotton: a reconsideration. RES new ser 19 1968.

LADY MARY WROTH
c. 1586-1640

§1

The Countesse of Mountgomeries Urania. 1621. Prose romance, with a collection of sonnets and poems as Pamphilia to Amphilanthus.

§2

O'Connor, J. J. James Hay and Urania. N & Q April 1955.

SIR CHRISTOPHER WYVILL
1614-72?

Certain serious thoughts. 1647.

R. D. D. and J. H.

VIII. EMBLEM BOOKS

(1) BIBLIOGRAPHIES

Renard, J. Catalogue des oeuvres imprimées de C. F. Menestrier de la compagnie de Jésus. Paris 1883.

Backer, A. de and A. and C. Sommervogel. Bibliothèque de la compagnie de Jésus. 11 vols Brussels and Paris 1890–1932.

Vries, A. G. C. de. De Nederlandsche emblemata. Amsterdam 1899.

Rümann, A. Die illustrierten deutschen Bücher des 18 Jahrhunderts. Stuttgart 1927.

Praz, M. Studi sul concettismo. Milan 1934; tr 2 vols 1939–47 (enlarged as Studies in seventeenth-century imagery) (Warburg Inst) (vol 2: A bibliography of emblem books), 1 vol Rome 1964 (enlarged). See H. L. Gumbert, Emblem books not listed by Praz, Folium 1 1951; K.-L. Selig, Addenda to Praz, MLN 70 1955.

Freeman, R. English emblem books. 1948. With bibliography of English emblem books.

Rice, H. C., jr. More emblem books. Princeton Univ Lib Chron 18 1957.

Vinken, P. J. H. L. Spiegel's Antrum platonicum: a contribution to the iconology of the heart. Oud-Holland 75 1960.

Landwehr, J. Dutch emblem books. Utrecht 1962.

— Fable-books printed in the Low Countries until 1800. Nieuwkoop 1963.

Schuman, S. Emblems and the Renaissance drama: a checklist. Research Opportunities in Renaissance Drama 12 1969.

(2) COLLECTIONS

Ripa, C. Iconologia. Rome 1593, Milan 1602, Rome 1603 (first illustr edn), Padua 1611, Siena 1613, Padua 1618, 3 vols Parma 1620, Padua 1625, 1630, 1 vol Venice 1645, 1669, 5 vols Perugia 1764–6. Many trns; see Praz, above, 1964. First English trn 1709.

Picinelli, F. Mondo simbolico. Milan 1653, Cologne 1681.

Brune, J. de. Emblemata of zinne-werck. 1661, Soest 1970.

Verrien, N. Livre curieux pour les sçavans et artistes. Paris [1685?], 1696 (as Recueil d'emblèmes, devises et figures hiéroglyphiques), 1724.

Elger, W. den. Zinne-beelden der liefde. Leyden 1703.

Spinniker, A. Leerzaame zinnebeelden. Haarlem 1714.

— Vervolg der leerzaame zinnebeelden. Haarlem 1758.

Delafosse, J. C. Nouvelle iconologie historique. Paris 1768.

Silvestre, L.-C. Marques typographiques: ou recueil des monogrammes, chiffres, enseignes, emblèmes, devises, rébus et fleurons des libraires et imprimeurs. 2 vols Paris 1853–67.

Pigot, R. (ed). Moral emblems from Cats and Farlie. 1860.

Chassant, A. and H. Tausin. Dictionnaire des devises historiques et héraldiques. 5 vols Paris 1878; suppl 1895. Mottoes.

Demmin, A. Encyclopädie der Schriften-, Bilder- und Wappenkunde. Leipzig 1879.

Meyer, F. S. Handbook of ornament. Karlsruhe 1888, 1892, New York 1957.

Verneuil, P. Dictionnaire des symbols, emblèmes et attributs. Paris [1897].

Künstle, K. Ikonographie der christlichen Kunst. 2 vols Freiburg 1926–8.

Koch, R. The book signs. 1930.

Marle, V. R. S. van. Iconographie de l'art profane au Moyen-Age et à la Renaissance. 2 vols Hague 1931–2.

Knipping, B. De iconografie van de Contra-Reformatie in de Nederlanden. 2 vols Hilversum 1939–40.

Droulers, E. Dictionnaire des attributs, allégories, emblèmes et symboles. Turnhout 1949.

Helm, A. Symbole, profane Sinnbilder, Embleme und Allegorien. Munich 1952.

Santi, A. Bibliografia della enigmistica. Florence 1952.

Ferguson, G. Signs and symbols in Christian art. New York and Oxford 1954.

Réau, L. Iconographie de l'art chrétien. 5 vols Paris 1955–9.

Pigler, A. Barockthemen: eine Auswahl von Verzeichnissen zur Ikonographie des 17 und 18 Jahrhunderts. 2 vols Budapest 1956.

Tervarent, G. de. Attributs et symboles dans l'art profane 1450–1600. 2 vols Geneva 1958; suppl 1964.

Aurenhammer, H. Lexikon der christlichen Ikonographie. Vienna 1959–.

Cirlot, J. E. A dictionary of symbols. 1962. Tr J. Sage from Diccionario de simboles tradicionales. Includes list of sources and critical studies.

Moralia horatiana: Einführung und Bildkommentar von Walter Brauer. Wiesbaden 1963.

Lurker, M. Bibliographie zur Symbolkunde. 3 vols Baden-Baden 1964–.

Spegel, Hagvin (1645–1714). Emblemata: inledning och kommentar av Bernt Olsson. Stockholm 1966.

Henkel, A. and H. Schöne. Emblemata: Handbuch zur Sinnbildkunst des xvi und xvii Jahrhunderts. Stuttgart 1967. With list of sources and critical studies.

Horden, J. (ed). English and continental emblem books. 57 vols Menston 1969– (facs).

(3) EARLY TREATISES

Ruscelli, G. Discorso. Venice 1556. With P. Giovio, Ragionamento.

— Le imprese. Venice 1566, 2 pts 1572–80 (corrected and enlarged by F. Patritio), 1 vol 1580, 2 pts 1583–4.

Simeoni, G. Le imprese heroiche et morali. Lyons 1559; tr French as Les devises ou emblèmes héroïques et morales, Lyons 1559, 1561.

— Le sentenziose imprese et dialogo del Symeoni. Lyons 1560. Some copies dated 1562, with different title-page and ascribed to P. Giovio and Simeoni.

Farra, A. Settenario dell' humana riduttione. Venice 1571, 1594. Pt 7 contains Filosofia simbolica: overo delle imprese.

Taegio, B. Il Liceo. Milan 1571. Bk 2.

Contile, L. Ragionamento sopra le proprietà delle imprese. Pavia 1574.

Palazzi. G. A. I discorsi sopra l'imprese. Bologna 1575.

Bargagli, S. Dell'imprese. Siena 1578, Venice 1589, 1594 (with pts 2–3).

Caburacci, F. Trattato dove si dimostra il vero, et novo modo di fare le imprese. Bologna 1580.

Daniel, S. The worthy tracts of Paulus Iovius. 1585. Trn and enlargement of P. Giovio, Dialogo dell'imprese militari et amorose.

Fraunce, A. Insignium, armorum, emblematum, hieroglyphicorum et symbolorum, quae ab Italie imprese nominantur, explicatio. 1588.

Capaccio, G. C. Delle imprese. 3 pts Naples 1592.

Tasso, T. Dialogo dell'imprese. Naples 1594, Florence 1859.

Tasso, E. Della realtà et perfettione delle imprese. Bergamo 1612.

d'Amboise, A. (ed). Discours ou traicté des devises. Paris 1620. By François d'Amboise, compiled by his son.

Estienne, H. L'art de faire les devises. Paris 1645; tr T. Blount as The art of making devises, 1646, 1648 (some copies dated 1650).

Le Moyne, P. Devises héroiques et morales. Paris 1649. Emblems with text.

—— De l'art des devises. Paris 1666.

Tesauro, E. Il cannocchiale Aristotelico. Venice 1655, 1663 (enlarged), 1678, Turin 1670, Bologna 1675 (with addns), Venice 1682; tr Latin as Idea argutae et ingeniosae dictionis, Cologne 1714.

Menestrier, C. F. L'art des emblèmes. Lyons 1662.

—— La philosophie des images. 2 vols Paris 1682–3, Lyons 1694.

—— L'art des emblèmes où s'enseigne la morale par les figures de la fable, de l'histoire et de la nature. Paris 1684. Different from 1662, above.

—— La science et l'art des devises. Paris 1686.

Bouhours, D. Les entretiens d'Ariste et d'Eugène. Paris 1671, 1682, Amsterdam 1708; ed R. Radouent, Paris 1920.

(4) EMBLEM BOOKS IN ENGLISH

(in alphabetical order)

§1

A., H. (Henry Hawkins, 1577–1646). Partheneia sacra. Rouen 1633; ed I. Fletcher, Aldington 1950 (facs); ed J. Horden, introd by K. J. Höltgen, Menston 1971 (facs).

—— The devout hart. 1634. Tr from Latin version of Estienne Luzvic, Le coeur dévot, 1627.

Anon. Emblems divine, moral, natural and historical. 1673.

—— Protestants' vade-mecum. 1680.

Arwaker, Edmund, the younger. Pia desideria. 1686, 1690, 1702, 1712. Tr from Herman Hugo, Pia desideria, 1624.

Astry, Sir James. The royal politician. 2 vols 1700, 1725. Tr from Diego Saavedra Fajardo, Idea de un principle politico cristiano, 1640.

'Abricht, Johann' (Jonathan Birch). Divine emblems after the fashion of Master Francis Quarles. 1838, 1839.

Ayres, Philip (1638–1712). Emblemata amatoria. 1683, 1714, [1725?], [1750?]; Saintsbury; ed J. Horden, Menston 1969 (facs). Polyglot work in Latin, English, Italian and French.

Bunyan, John (1628–88). A book for boys and girls: or country rhimes for children. 1686, 1701 (as A book for boys and girls: or temporal things spiritualised) (both edns without plates), 1724 (9th edn) etc (as Divine emblems: or temporal things spiritualised).

B., R, 'Robert or Richard Burton' (Nathaniel Crouch). Delights for the ingenious. 1684, 1721, 1732 (6th edn). A shortened, unauthorized version of Wither, A collection of emblemes, 1635.

Combe, Thomas. The theatre of fine devices. 1614. Tr from Guillaume de la Perrière, Le théâtre des bons engins, 1539.

de Montenay, Georgette. A booke of armes or remembrance, wherin ar one hundred godly emblemata. Frankfurt 1619. Polyglot work in Latin, Spanish, Italian, High Dutch, English and Low Dutch, tr from Emblèmes: ou devises chrestiennes, 1571.

Farley, Robert. Lychnocausia sive moralia facum emblemata: lights moral emblems. 1638, 1860 (as More emblems with aphorisms. In Latin and English.

G., H. [Sir Henry Goodere?]. The mirrour of majestie: or the badges of honour conceitedly emblazoned, with emblems annexed, poetically unfolded. 1618; ed H. Green and J. Croston, Manchester and London 1870 (Holbein Soc) (facs).

H., J. (John Hall, 1627–56). Emblems with elegant figures. Cambridge and London 1658 (probably ptd 1648 as Sparkles of divine love); ed J. Horden, Menston 1970 (facs).

Harvey, Christopher (1597–1663). Schola cordis: or the heart of it selfe, gone away from God; brought back to him and instructed to him in 47 emblems. 1647, 1664, 1674, 1675, 1723, 1777, 1778, 1808, 1812, 1816, 1823, 1845, 1866, 1874; ed A. B. Grosart, Complete poems, 1874. From Benedict van Haeften, Schola cordis, 1629; frequently attributed to Quarles and several times ptd with his Emblemes and hieroglyphikes.

Jenner, Thomas (fl. 1631–56). The soules solace: or thirty and one spiritual emblems. 1626, 1631, 1639, 1651 (as Divine mysteries that cannot be seene, made plain by that which may be seene).

M., E. (Edward Manning?). Ashrea: or the grove of beatitude, represented in emblems and by the art of memory. 1665; ed J. Horden, Menston 1970 (facs).

Peacham, Henry (1578?–1642?). Minerva Britanna: or a garden of heroical devises. 1612, Menston 1966 (facs); ed J. Horden, Menston 1969 (facs). There are also 3 emblem books by Peacham in ms, all earlier than Minerva Britanna, each from the Basilikon doron of James I: BM (Harley ms 6855 art. 13, Royal ms 12.A.lxvi), Bodley (Rawlinson ms Poetry 146).

Quarles, Francis. See col 1199, above.

S., P. The heroicall devises of M. Claudius Paradin; whereunto are added the Lord Gabriel Symeons and others, translated out of Latin by P.S. 1591. From 1557 edn of Paradin, Devises héroiques, 1551.

Vaenius, Otho (Otto van Veen). Amorum emblemata. Antwerp 1608. Polyglot work in Latin, English and Italian; 3 other issues of the same date with different languages.

Whitney, Geoffrey (1548–1601?). A choice of emblemes and other devises. Leyden 1586; ed H. Green 1866 (facs); ed J. Horden, Menston 1969 (facs).

Willet, Andrew (1562–1621). Sacrorum emblematum centuria una. Cambridge [between Feb 1591 and Aug 1592]. No plates; verses in Latin and English.

Wither, George (1588–1667). A collection of emblemes, ancient and modern. 1635; ed J. Horden, Menston 1968 (facs).

§2

Green, H. Shakespeare and the emblem writers. 1870.

—— Alciati and his books of emblems. 1872, New York nd.

Thomas, H. The Emblemata amatoria of Philip Ayres. 1910.

Bayley, H. The lost language of symbolism. 1912.

Haig, E. The floral symbolism of the great masters. 1913.

Gielhow, K. Die Hieroglyphenkunde des Humanismus in der Allegorie der Renaissance. Jahrbuch der Kunsthistorischen Sammlungen des allerh. Kaiserhauses 32 1915.

Volkmann, L. Bilderschriften der Renaissance. Leipzig 1923, Nieuwkoop 1962, 1969.

Funk, M. Le livre belge à gravures. Paris and Brussels 1925.

Bennett, M. R. The legend of the green tree and the dry. Archaeological Jnl 83 1929.

Spamer, A. Das kleine Andachtsbild. Munich 1930.

Haight, G. S. See Quarles, col 1200, above.

Praz, M. See Bibliographies, above.

Tramer, I. Studien zu den Anfängen der puritanischen Emblemliteratur in England: Willet–Wither. Berlin 1934.

Bulard, M. Le scorpion symbole du peuple juif. Paris 1935.

Blunt, A. The Hypnerotomachia Poliphili in 17th-century France. Jnl of Warburg Inst 1 1938.

— Blake's pictorial imagination. Jnl Warburg & Courtauld Inst 6 1943.

— Blake's Brazen serpent. Ibid.

Janson, H. W. The Putto with the Death's head. Art Bull 19 1937.

— Monkeys and monkey lore in mediaeval art. Art News 46 1947.

— Apes and ape lore in the Middle Ages and the Renaissance. 1952 (Warburg Inst).

Wittkower, R. Patience and chance: the story of an emblem for Ercole II of Ferrara. Jnl of Warburg Inst 1 1938.

— Chance, time and virtue. Ibid.

— Transformations of Minerva in Renaissance imagery. Jnl of Warburg Inst 2 1939.

— Eagle and serpent: a study in the migration symbols. Ibid.

Ameisenowa, Z. The tree of life in Jewish iconography. Ibid.

Rudolph, H. 'Vanitas': die Bedeutung mittelalterlicher und humanistischer Bildinhalte in der niederländischen Malerei des 17 Jahrhunderts. In Festschrift Wilhelm Pinder zum 60 Geburtstage, Leipzig 1938.

Callisen, S. A. The iconography of the cock on the column. Art Bull 21 1939. Reply by A. K. Coomaraswamy, ibid.

Chew, S. C. Time and Fortune. ELH 6 1939.

— Verstegen and the Amorum emblemata of van Veen. HLQ 8 1945.

— The pilgrimage of life. New Haven 1962.

Charbonneau-Lassay, L. La mystérieuse emblématique de Jésus-Christ: le bestiaire du Christ. Bruges 1940.

Rahner, H. Antenna crucis I: Odysseus Mastbaum. Zeitschrift für Katholische Theologie 65 1941.

— Antenna Crucis II: das Meer der Welt. Zeitschrift für Katholische Theologie 66 1942.

— Antenna Crucis III: das Schiff aus Holz. Ibid.

Stuhlfauth, G. Das Schiff als Symbol der altchristlichen Kunst. Rivista di Archeologia Cristiana 19 1942.

Yates, F. A. The emblematic conceit in Bruno's De gli eroici furori and in the Elizabethan sonnet sequences. Jnl Warburg & Courtauld Inst 6 1943.

Clements, R. J. The cult of the poet in Renaissance emblem literature. PMLA 59 1944.

— Pen and sword in Renaissance emblem literature. MLQ 5 1944.

— Condemnation of the poetic profession in Renaissance emblem literature. SP 43 1946.

— Iconography on the nature and inspiration of poetry in Renaissance literature. PMLA 70 1955.

— Emblem books on literature's role in the revival of learning. SP 54 1957.

— Ars emblematica. Romanistisches Jahrbuch 8 1957.

— Picta poesis: literary and humanistic theory in Renaissance emblem books. Rome 1960.

Sharrock, R. Bunyan and the English emblem writers. RES 21 1945.

Stegemeier, H. Problems in emblem literature. JEGP 45 1946.

— Sub verbo 'Sinnbild'. In Humaniora: essays honoring Archer Taylor, Locust Valley NY 1960.

Friedmann, H. The symbolic goldfinch: its history and significance in European devotional art. Washington 1946 (Bollingen ser).

Heckscher, W. S. Bernini's elephant and obelisk. Art Bull 29 1947.

— Aphrodite as a nun. Phoenix 7 1953.

— Renaissance emblems. Princeton Univ Lib Chron 15 1954.

Read, J. The alchemist in life, literature and art. 1947.

Freeman, R. English emblem books. 1948.

Freyhan, R. The evolution of the Caritas figure in the thirteenth and fourteenth centuries. Jnl Warburg & Courtauld Inst 2 1948.

Gombrich, E. H. Icones symbolicae: the visual image in Neo-Platonic thought. Ibid.

Ettinghausen, R. The unicorn. Washington 1950.

Lehner, E. Symbols, signs and signets. Cleveland 1950.

Gumbert, H. L. Buch und Druckpresse in der emblematischen Literatur. Das Antiquariat 7 1951.

Navanutty, P. Blake and emblem literature. Jnl Warburg & Courtauld Inst 15 1952.

Deonna, W. The crab and the butterfly: a study in animal symbolism. Ibid.

Huhn, V. Löwe und Hind als Symbole des Rechts. Mainfränkisches Jahrbuch für Geschichte und Kunst 7 1955.

Vanuxem, J. Emblèmes baroques dans l'art et dans les fêtes au temps de Louis XIV. Kunstchronik 8 1955.

Panofsky, E. and D. Pandora's box: the changing aspects of a mythical symbol. New York 1956.

Lawall, D. B. Notes on a newly acquired ms devise book. Princeton Univ Lib Chron 18 1957.

Behling, L. Die Pflanze in der mittelalterlichen Tafelmalerei. Weimar 1957.

— Die Pflanzenwelt der mittelalterlichen Kathedralen. Cologne and Graz 1964.

Bruyn, J. and J. A. Emmens. The sunflower again. Burlington Mag 99 1957.

Ross, T. W. Five fifteenth-century 'emblem' verses from BM add ms 37,049. Speculum 32 1957.

Demetz, P. The elm and the vine: notes toward the history of a marriage topos. PMLA 73 1958.

Iversen, E. Hieroglyphic studies in the Renaissance. Burlington Mag 100 1958.

— The myth of Egypt and its hieroglyphs in European tradition. Copenhagen 1961.

Ong, W. J. From allegory to the diagram in the Renaissance mind. Jnl of Aesthetics 17 1959.

Watkins, R. Alberti's emblem 'the winged eye' and his name Leo. Mitteilungen des Kunsthistorischen Instituts in Florenz 9 1960.

Jongh, E. de and P. J. Vinken. Frans Hals als voortzetter van een emblematische traditie. Oud-Holland 76 1961.

Timm, W. Der gestrandete Wal eine motivkundliche Studie. Staatliche Museen zu Berlin, Forschungen und Berichte 3–4 1961.

McDonald, W. B. Christliche Sonnensymbolik. Graphis 18 1962.

Selig, K.-L. Emblem literature: directions in recent scholarship. Yearbook of Comparative & General Lit 12 1963.

Fletcher, A. Allegory: the theory of a symbolic mode. Ithaca 1964.

Schöne, A. Emblematik und Drama im Zeitalter des Barock. Munich 1964, 1968 (rev).

Vodosek, P. Das Emblem in der deutschen Literatur der Renaissance und des Barock. Jahrbuch des Wiener Goethevereins 68 1964.

Monroy, E. F. von. Embleme und Emblembücher in den Niederlanden 1560–1630: eine Geschichte der Wandlungen ihres Illustrationsstils. Utrecht 1964.

Jöns, D. W. Das 'Sinnen-Bild': Studien zur allegorischen Bildlichkeit bei A. Gryphius. Stuttgart 1966.

de Groot, H. B. The Ouroboros and the Romantic poets: Renaissance emblem in Blake, Coleridge and Shelley. E Studies 50 1969.

Hoefnagel, D. A seventeenth-century emblem book. Dartmouth College Lib Bull 11 1970.

Kirchner, G. Fortuna in Dichtung und Emblematik des Barock: Tradition und Bedeutungswandel eines Motivs. Stuttgart [1970].

Owen, J. H. The stricken deer and the emblem tradition. BNYPL Feb 1971.

Schumann, S. Two notes upon emblems and the English Renaissance drama. N & Q Jan 1971.

Sellin, P. R. The first collection of Dutch love emblems: the identity of Theocritus à Ganda. MLR 66 1971.

R. D. D. and J. H.

IX. EPIGRAMS AND FORMAL SATIRE

For popular verse satire see col 2023 f., below.

Crowley, Robert (1518?–88). One and thyrtye epigrammes. 1550; ed J. M. Cowper 1872 (EETS).

Heywood, John (1497?–1580?). Two hundred epigrammes. 1555.

—— An hundred epigrammes. 1556.

—— A fourth hundred of epygrams. 1560.

—— John Heywoodes woorkes, with one hundred of epigrammes; and three hundred of epigrammes; and a fifth hundred of epigrams; whereunto are now newly added a syxt hundred of epigrams. 1562. *See* J. C. Baldwin, Heywood and Sir John Davies, Satire Newsletter 5 1967. *See also col 1116, below.*

Songes and sonettes. 1557. Tottel; includes Wyatt's satires.

Drant, Thomas (d. 1578). A medicinable morall: that is, the two bookes of Horace his satyres englyshed; also epigrammes. 1566. *See* O. L. Jiriczek, Der elisabethanische Horaz, Sh Jb 47 1911; Zu Drants Horaz, Sh Jb 55 1919; M. C. Randolph, Drant's definition of satire, N & Q 14 June 1941.

Turbervile, George (c. 1544–97). Epitaphes, epigrams, songs and sonets. 1567. *See also col 1150, above.*

Gascoigne, George (1542?–77). The stele glas: satyre. 1576. *See also col 1025, above.*

Kendall, Timothy. Flowres of epigrammes out of sundrie the moste singular authors. 1577; rptd 1874 (Spenser Soc).

Epigrammes and elegies by J.D[avies] and C.M[arlowe]. 2 pts Middleburg [1598?]. *See under Sir John Davies, col 1071, above;* P. Simpson, Unprinted epigrams of Davies, RES new ser 3 1952; J. M. Nosworthy, The publication of Marlowe's Elegies and Davies's Epigrams, RES new ser 4 1953.

Donne, John (1572–1631). Satires. In his Poems, 1633. *See col 1169, above.*

Lodge, Thomas (c. 1557–1625). A fig for Momus: containing satyres, eclogues and epistles. 1595; ed A. Boswell, Frondes caducae vol 3, Auchinleck 1817. *See* S. H. Atkins, A fig for Momus, TLS 7 Feb 1935; Dyer at Woodstock, TLS 3 Feb 1945; and col 1434, below.

Hall, Joseph (1574–1656). Virgidemiarum: sixe bookes; first three bookes of tooth-lesse satyrs. 1597, 1598, 1602.

—— Virgidemiarum: sixe bookes; three last bookes of byting satyres. 1598, 1599.
Both rptd in edns of Hall's Works, ed J. Pratt 1808; ed P. Hall, Oxford 1837–9; ed P. Winter, Oxford 1863; Complete poems, ed A. B. Grosart, Manchester 1879; ed A. Davenport, Liverpool 1949. For Hall's religious writings see col 1977, below.

Salyer, S. M. Hall's satires and the Harvey-Nashe controversy. SP 25 1928.

Atkins, S. H. Fortunio and Raymundus. TLS 3 Oct 1935. Replies by W. F. McNeir 30 May 1936, 4 Dec 1937; A. Davenport 1 Jan 1938.

—— Naenius and Furius. TLS 30 May 1936.

—— Who was Labeo? TLS 4 July 1936. *See also* J. D. Parsons 11 July 1936; A. G. H. Dent 18 July 1936; S. H. Atkins 25 July 1936.

Kane, R. J. Hall and Work for chimny-sweepers. PMLA 51 1936. *See also* A. Davenport, TLS 27 March 1937; S. H. Atkins 3 April, 26 June 1937; R. J. Kane 12 June 1937.

Davenport, A. Three uncollected poems by Hall. N & Q 31 Jan 1942.

—— Interfused sources in Hall's satires. RES 18 1942.

—— Dekker's Westward hoe and Hall's Virgidemiae. N & Q 5 April 1947.

'Olybrius'. Verses attributed to Hall. N & Q 29 Aug 1942.

Stein, A. The second English satirist. MLR 38 1943.

—— Hall's imitation of Juvenal. MLR 43 1948.

Chew, A. Hall and neo-stoicism. PMLA 65 1950.

—— Hall and Milton. ELH 17 1950.

Kinloch, T. F. The life and works of Hall. 1951.

Maxwell, J. C. Hall: Virgidemiarum IV. i. 171–2. N & Q Jan 1954.

Caputi, A. Certain satires and the Hall-Marston quarrel. N & Q June 1954.

McNeir, W. F. Hall's Fortunio and Raymundus once more. N & Q July–Aug 1959.

Guilpin, Everard. Skialetheia: or shadow of truth in certain epigrams and satyres. 1598; rptd by A. B. Grosart 1878; ed G. B. Harrison 1931 (Shakespeare Assoc Facs).

—— The whipper of the satyre his pennance. 1601; ed A. Davenport, Liverpool 1951. With Breton.
See R. E. Bennett, Donne and Gilpin, RES 15 1939; P. J. Finkelpearl, Donne and Gilpin, RES new ser 14 1963; R. E. Brettle, Guilpin and Marston, RES new ser 16 1965.

Marston, John (1576–1634). The metamorphosis of Pigmalions image, and certaine satyres. 1598 (by W.K.).

—— The scourge of villanie: three bookes of satyres. 1598 (by W. Kinsayder).
For other edns of both works see col 1689, below. See also M. S. Allen, The satire of Marston, Columbus 1920; A. Caputi, Marston: satirist, Ithaca 1961, P. J. Finkelpearl, Marston of the Middle Temple, Cambridge Mass 1969.

Rankins, William (fl. 1587–1601). Seaven satyres applyed to the weeke. 1598; ed A. Davenport, Liverpool 1948. *See* J. George, A note on Rankins, N & Q 1 Oct 1949.

Tyro, T. Tyros Roring Megge. 1598.

Bastard, Thomas (1566–1618). Chrestoleros: seven bookes of epigrames. 1598. *See* S. H. Atkins, Thomas Bastard, TLS 26 Sept 1936; A. G. Chester, Bastard's lost satire, N & Q 9 Dec 1950. *See also col 1086, above.*

Barnfield, Richard (1574–1627). Encomion of Lady Pecunia. 1598. *See also col 1085, above.*

Weever, John (1576–1632). Epigrammes in the oldest cut and newest fashion. 1599; ed R. B. McKerrow 1911.

—— Faunus and Melliflora. 1600; ed A. Davenport, Liverpool 1948.

—— The whipping of the satyre. 1601 (by 'W.I.'); ed A. Davenport, Liverpool 1951.

See A. Davenport, Weever's Epigrammes and the Hall-Marston quarrel, *RES 11 1935 and col. 1158, above.*

M., T. Micro-cynicon: six snarling satyres. 1599. Attributed Thomas Middleton and rptd in edns of his Works, ed Dyce 1840 and Bullen 1885–6. *See col 1646, below.*

Goddard, William. A mastif whelp, with other ruff-island-like currs. [Dort? 1599].

—— A neaste of waspes latelie found out in the Law Countreys. 1615; ed C. H. Wilkinson, Oxford 1921.

—— A satyricall dialogue betweene Alexander the Great and Diogynes. [Dort? 1616?].

Rowlands, Samuel (1570?–1630?). The letting of humors blood in the head-vaine. 1600.

—— Humors looking-glasse. 1608 (anon); ed J. P. Collier 1870. Sometimes attributed to Rowlands. *See col 2013, below.*

Tourneur, Cyril (1575?–1626). The transformed metamorphosis. 1600. *See col 1695, below.*

Thynne, Francis (1545?–1608). Emblemes and epigrames. Ed F. J. Furnivall 1876 (EETS). Written 1600.

Breton, Nicholas (1545?–1626?). Pasquils mad-cap and mad-cappes message. 1600.

—— The second part of Pasquils mad-cap, intituled the fooles-cap. 1600.

—— Pasquils mistresse. 1600.

—— Pasquils passe and passeth not. 1600.

—— No whipping nor tripping: but a kinde friendly snipping. 1601; ed A. Davenport, Liverpool 1951. *See also col 1027, above.*

Cooke, John. Epigrames, served out in 52 severall dishes. [c. 1604] (by 'I.C. Gent').

Woodhouse, Peter. Democritus his dream. 1605; ed A. B. Grosart 1877.

P[arrot], H[enry]. The mous-trap. 1606.

—— Epigrams. 1608.

—— Laquei ridiculosi: or springes for woodcocks. 1613.

—— The mastive, or young-whelpe of the old-dogge: epigrams and satyrs. 1615.

—— Cures for the itch: characters, epigrams, epitaphs. 1626.

See M. C. Pitman, Epigrams of Henry Peacham and Parrot, *MLR 29 1934; F. B. Williams,* The epigrams of Parrot, *Harvard Stud 20 1938;* Parrot's stolen feathers, *PMLA 52 1937.*

West, Richard. The court of conscience: or Dick Whippers sessions. 1607.

—— Wits ABC: or a centurie of epigrams. [1608].

Middleton, Richard, of York. Epigrams and satyres. [1608]; rptd [Edinburgh 1840].

Peacham, Henry (1576?–1643?). The more the merrier. 1608.

—— Thalia's banquet furnished with newly devised epigrammes. 1620.

See under Parrot, above, for criticism.

[Tofte, Robert (1562–1620)]. Ariostos satyres. 1608, 1609, 1611. Erroneously ascribed on title-page to G. Markham; *see col 1149, above.*

Heath, John. Two centuries of epigrammes. 1610.

—— The house of correction: or certayn satiricall epigrams. [1619].

Sharpe, Roger. More fooles yet. 1610. Epigrams.

Scot, Thomas. Philomythie or philomythologie, wherein

outlandish birds, beasts and fishes are taught to speake true English verse. 2 pts 1616, 1616 (enlarged), 1622.

—— The second part of Philomythie. 1625.

Davies, John, of Hereford (1565–1618). The scourge of folly. [1611?].

—— Wits Bedlam. 1617. *See L. Ennis,* Wits Bedlam of John Davies, *Huntington Lib Bull 11 1937 and col 1098, above.*

Taylor, John (1580–1653). The sculler: or gallimawfry of sonnets, satyres and epigrams. 1612.

—— Epigrammes: being ninety in number; besides two new made satyres. 1651. *See also col 2014, below.*

Gamage, William. Linsi woolsie: or two centuries of epigrammes. Oxford 1613.

Wither, George (1588–1667). Abuses stript and whipt. 1613. *See also col 1191, above.*

Freeman, Thomas. Rubbe and a great cast: epigrams. 2 pts 1614.

N[iccols], R[ichard] (1584–1616). The furies, with vertues encomium, in two bookes of epigrammes. 1614.

C., R. The times whistle: or a new daunce of seven satires and other poems. [1614?]; ed J. M. Cowper 1871 (EETS).

Brathwait, Richard (1588?–1673). A strappado for the Divell: epigrams and satyres. 1615; ed J. W. Ebsworth, Boston 1878.

—— Natures embassie: or the wilde-mans measures, danced naked by twelve satyres. 1621. *See also col 2020, below.*

Anton, Robert. The philosophers satyrs. 1616, 1617 (as Vices anotimie).

Fitzgeffrey, Henry. Satyres and satiricall epigrams. 1617.

—— Certain elegies done by sundrie excellent wits, with satyres and epigrammes. 1618.

Harington, Sir John (1560–1612). Epigrams both pleasant and serious. 1615.

—— The most elegant and witty epigrams. 1618; ed N. E. McClure, Philadelphia 1930. *See also col 1113, above.*

Jonson, Ben (1572–1637). Epigrams. In his Workes, 1616. *See col 1655, below.*

Hutton, Henry. Follie's anatomie: or satyres and satiricall epigrams. 1619; rptd E. F. Rimbault 1842 (Percy Soc).

Owen, John (1560–1622). Epigrams of that most wittie and worthy epigrammatist Mr John Owen. Tr John Vicars 1619.

—— Certaine epigrams out of his first foure bookes. Tr Robert Hayman, Quodlibets, 1628, below.

[Wroth, Sir Thomas (1584–1672)]. The abortive of an idle hour: or a century of epigrams. 1620.

Ashmore, John. Certain selected odes of Horace englished, with epigrammes. 1621.

Martyn, Joseph. Newe epigrams, having in their company a mad satyre. 1621.

Hayman, Robert. Quodlibets lately come over from New Britaniola. 3 pts 1628.

Epigrammes. [Rouen before 1634]. Anti-Protestant; ms in Bodley.

Randolph, Thomas (1605–36). Aristippus: or the joviall philosopher. 1630. *See col 1773, below.*

Epigrammes, mirrour of new reformation. 1634.

Chamberlain, Robert (1607?–60). Nocturnall lucubrations; whereunto are added epigrams and epitaphs. 1638.

—— Conceits, clinches, flashes and whimsies. 1639, 1640 (rev as Jocabella); ed J. O. Halliwell (-Phillipps) 1860; ed W. C. Hazlitt 1864 (in Old English jest-books no 3).

Bancroft, Thomas. Two bookes of epigrammes and epitaphs. 1639. *See col 1297, above.*

Carew, Thomas (1595?–1640). In his Poems, 1640.

Urquhart, Sir Thomas (1611–60). Epigrams: divine and moral. 1641. *See col 2236, below.*

Herrick, Robert (1591–1674). In his Hesperides, 1648 (with epigrams).

Heath, Robert. Clarastella; together with poems occasional, elegies, epigrams, satyrs. 1650. *See col 1311, above.*

Sheppard, Samuel. Epigrams, theological, philosophical and romantick. 1651. *See col 1318, above.*

Eliot, John. Poems: consisting of epistles and epigrams, satyrs, epitaphs and elegies, songs and sonnets. 1658, 1661.

Pecke, Thomas. Parnassi puerperium: epigrams. 1659.

Studies

Collier, J. P. In his Poetical decameron, 2 vols Edinburgh 1820.

Shade, O. Satiren und Pasquille aus der Reformationszeit. Hanover 1856.

Dodd, H. P. The epigrammatists. 1870, 1875, Detroit 1969.

Alden, R. M. The rise of formal satire in England. Philadelphia 1899.

Walker, H. In his English satire and satirists, 1925.

Whipple, T. K. Martial and the English epigram from Wyatt to Jonson. Berkeley 1925.

Lathrop, H. B. Janus Cornarius's Selecta epigrammata graeca and the early English epigrammatists. MLN 43 1928.

Campbell, O. J. In his Comicall satyre and Shakespeare's Troilus and Cressida, San Marino 1938.

Randolph, M. C. The medical concept in English Renaissance satiric theory. SP 38 1941.

Hudson, H. H. The epigram in the English Renaissance. Princeton 1947.

Brooks, H. F. The imitation in English poetry, especially in formal satire, before the age of Pope. RES 25 1949.

Wilcox, J. Informal publication of late sixteenth-century verse satire. HLQ 13 1950.

John Rainolds, epigrammatist. Bodleian Lib Record 3 1950.

Smith, H. In his Elizabethan poetry, Cambridge Mass 1952.

Peter, J. Complaint and satire in early English literature. Oxford 1956.

Sutherland, J. In his English satire, Cambridge 1958.

Kernan, A. In his Cankered Muse, New Haven 1959.

Harris, B. 'Men like satyrs'. In Elizabethan poetry, ed J. R. Brown and Harris 1960.

Paulson, R. In his Fictions of satire, Baltimore 1967.

Lecocq, L. La satire en Angleterre de 1588 à 1603. Paris 1969.

Gransden, K. W. Tudor verse satire. 1970.

J. S. W.

X. SONG BOOKS

(1) MANUSCRIPTS

This section summarizes only the more important mss. References to collections are abbreviated in col 1343, below.

Early Tudor Songs

Selections in A collection of songs and madrigals of the 15th century, *and* Madrigals by English composers of the close of the 15th century, *1891 and 1893 (Plainsong and Medieval Music Soc). The fullest account of the repertory is J. Stevens, Music and poetry, 1961.*

BM additional 5465, c. 1500 (*14 songs ed J. S. Smith in* A collection of English songs [*1779*]; *words in B. Fehr, Archiv 106 1901, and Stevens*). BM additional 5665, c. 1470–c. 1520 (*words in B. Fehr, Archiv 106 1901, and Stevens*). BM additional 31,922, c. 1515 (*words in Flügel, Liedersammlungen, and Stevens; pieces by Henry 8 ed Lady Mary Trefusis in* Songs, ballads and instrumental pieces, *Oxford 1912; ed J. Stevens, Music at the Court of Henry 8, Musica britannica 18 1962 (complete). See also W. Chappell, Archaeologia 41 1867; J. Stevens, Rounds and canons, Music & Letters 32 1951).*

BM Royal appendix 58 (*words in Flügel, Liedersammlungen; see also J. Ward, The lute music of ms Royal appendix 58, Jnl of Amer Musicological Soc 13 1960 and Stevens, Music and poetry, ch 7*).

Mid-century Part-songs

BM additional 30,513 (Mulliner bk). *Ed D. Stevens, Musica britannica 1 1951 (complete), 1954 (rev); part-songs by R. Johnson, J. Shepherd, R. Edwards and anon ed D. Stevens in* The Oriana series nos 113–18 1955 (*separately*); *2 part-songs T. Tallis and anon ed D. Stevens, Choral library no 346 1952. See also D. Stevens, The Mulliner book: a commentary, [1952] and articles by the same in Musique et poésie au xvie siècle, ed J. Jacquot, Paris 1954, and Musical Times July 1955. Other part-songs ed Elliott and Shire, Music of Scotland. See also W. H. Rubsamen, Scottish and English music of the Renaissance [in Taitt ms, Clark Memorial Lib, Univ of California, Los Angeles], in Festschrift Heinrich Besseler, Leipzig 1961.*

Consort Songs (c. 1550–early 17th century)

Selections: Warlock, The first [second, third] book of Elizabethan songs; Brett, Consort songs.

BM additional 17,786–91, 17,792–7, 18,936–9, 30,480–4; London, Royal College of Music, 684, 2049; Oxford, Christ Church 984–8; New York Public Lib, Drexel 4180–5.

17th-century Songs

Selections: Smith, Musica antiqua; Dolmetsch, Select English songs; Warlock and Wilson, English ayres (enlarged); E. H. Fellowes, Songs and lyrics from the plays of Beaumont and Fletcher, 1928; Cutts, La musique de scène; Cutts, Seventeenth-century songs and lyrics (words only); Sabol, Songs and dances; Souris and Jacquot, Poèmes de Donne, Herbert et Crashaw; I. Spink, Robert Johnson: ayres, songs and dialogues, ELS ser 2 17 1961; Spink, English songs. See also under Cooper and Ferrabosco, below.

Cambridge, Fitzwilliam Museum 52.D; King's College, Rowe ms 2 (*P. Oboussier, Music & Letters 34 1953); Trinity College R.16.29 (songs by George Handford) (poems ed E. Doughtie, Anglia 82 1964; poems ed Stern-feld and Greer in Fellowes, English madrigal verse (3rd edn); poems ed Doughtie in Lyrics from English airs; ed Greer, els no 23 1970 (facs)).* Carlisle, Cathedral pt-books (*J. W. Brown, An Elizabethan song-cycle, and Some Elizabethan lyrics, Cornhill 48–9 1920–1, rev in his Round Carlisle Cross ser 2, Carlisle 1922, ser 6, 1926; G. D. Spearitt, Richard Nicholson and the 'Joane, quoth John' songs, Stud in Music 2 1968 (with edn of 11 songs);* Dublin, Trinity College, F.5.13; Edinburgh, Nat Lib of Scotland 5.2.14, 5.2.17; Univ Lib, Dc.1.69 (*J. P. Cutts, Musica Disciplina 13 1959); Glasgow, Univ Lib R.d. 58–61; BM additional 4900 (late 16th century), 10,337, 10,338 (George Jeffries's autograph), 11,608, 14,399, 15,117 (M. Joiner, RMA Research Chron 7 1969), 15,118, 24,665 (poems ed 'Peter Warlock', Giles Earle his booke, 1932), 29,396, 29,481, 31,432 (William Lawes's auto-graph) (Cutts, Library 5th ser 7 1952; M. C. Crum, Library 5th ser 9 1954), 53,723 (P. J. Willetts, The Henry Lawes autograph, 1969), 32,339, Eg 2013, 2971

(M. Cyr, *RMA Research Chron 9 1971*); Lambeth Palace 1041; New York Public Lib, Drexel 4041 (*Cutts, Musica Disciplina 18 1964*), 4175 (*Cutts, Musica Disciplina 16 1962*), 4257 (*Gamble ms*) (*C. W. Hughes, Music & Letters 26 1945*; *V. Duckles, Jnl of Amer Musicological Soc 1 1948*); Bodley Mus sch.f.575, Mus.b.1 (*John Wilson's autograph*) (*J. P. Cutts, Musica Disciplina 10 1956*; *19 poems ed Cutts and F. Kermode, Seventeenth-*century songs from a Bodleian ms, *Reading 1956*), don.c.57 (*Cutts, Music & Letters 34 1953*); Oxford, Christ Church 87 (*Cutts, RES new ser 10 1959*), 439, 736–8; Paris, Conservatoire, Rés. 2489 (*Cutts, Musica Disciplina 23 1969*); Tenbury, St Michael's College 1018 and 1019 (*Cutts, Music & Letters 37 1956*). *For other mss see Elliott and Shire*, Music of Scotland.

(2) BIBLIOGRAPHIES ETC

Rimbault, E. F. Bibliotheca madrigaliana. 1847. Lists pbns of madrigalists and lutenists, with contents.

Steele, R. R. The earliest English music printing. 1903. To 1600.

Kidson, F. John Playford and 17th-century music publishing. Musical Quart 4 1918.

Pattison, B. Notes on early music printing. Library 4th ser 19 1939.

Day, C. L. and E. B. Murrie. English song-books 1651–1702 and their publishers. Library 4th ser 16 1936.

— English song-books 1651–1702: a bibliography with a first-line index of songs. 1940 (Bibl Soc).

Schnapper, E. B. The British union-catalogue of early music printed before the year 1801. 2 vols 1957.

Répertoire international des sources musicales: recueils imprimés xvie–xviie siècles. Munich 1960.

Spink, I. Sources of English song 1620–60. Miscellanea Musicologia: Adelaide Stud in Musicology 1 1966.

Doe, P. M. Register of [British] theses on music. RMA Research Chron 3 1963; Suppls 4 1964, 6 1966, 8 1970 etc.

Adkins, C. Doctoral dissertations [American] in musicology. Philadelphia 1971 (5th edn). Annual suppls in Jnl of Amer Musicological Soc.

Ford, W. K. Music in England before 1800: a select bibliography. 1967.

(3) DICTIONARIES

Pulver, J. A dictionary of old English music and musical instruments. 1923.

— A biographical dictionary of old English music. 1927.

Die Musik in Geschichte und Gegenwart. Ed F. Blume 14 vols and suppl Cassel 1949–68.

Grove's dictionary of music and musicians: 5th edition. Ed E. Blom 9 vols 1954; suppl, 1961.

(4) GENERAL HISTORIES

Burney, C. A general history of music. 4 vols 1776–89, 1789 (vol 1 only); ed F. Mercer 2 vols New York 1935.

Hawkins, Sir John. General history of music. 5 vols 1776, 2 vols (and suppl of illustrations) 1853, 3 vols 1875, 2 vols New York 1963 (rptd from 1853).

Walker, E. A history of music in England. 1907, 1924; rev J. A. Westrup 1952.

Boyd, M. C. Elizabethan music and musical criticism. Philadelphia 1940, 1962 (rev).

Reese, G. Music in the Renaissance. New York 1954, 1959 (rev).

A history of song. Ed D. Stevens 1960.

The new Oxford history of music 4: the age of humanism 1540–1630. Ed G. Abraham 1968.

(5) STUDIES OF SONG, PART-SONG AND MADRIGAL

[Arkwright, G. E. P.] Early Elizabethan stage music. Musical Antiquary 1 1910, 4 1913; 1968.

Arkwright, G. E. P. Elizabethan choirboy plays and their music. Proc Royal Musical Assoc 40 1914.

Bridge, J. F. The old cryes of London. 1921.

Fellowes, E. H. The English madrigal composers. 1921, 1948 (rev).

'Warlock, Peter' (P. Heseltine). The English ayre. 1926.

Dent, E. J. Foundations of English opera. 1928.

— The musical form of the madrigal. Music & Letters 11 1930.

Baskervill, C. R. The Elizabethan jig and related song drama. Chicago 1929.

Evans, W. McC. Ben Jonson and Elizabethan music. Lancaster Pa 1929.

Gibbon, J. M. Melody and the lyric from Chaucer to the Cavaliers. 1930.

Ainsworth, E. G. Stanzas of the Orlando Furioso in English collections of madrigals. RES 7 1931.

Pattison, B. Sir Philip Sidney and music. Music & Letters 15 1934.

— Music and poetry of the English Renaissance. 1948.

Greene, R. L. The early English carol. 1935.

Bontoux, G. La chanson en Angleterre au temps d'Elisabeth. Oxford 1936.

Walker, D. P. Musical humanism in the 16th and early 17th centuries. Music Rev 2–3 1941–2.

Westrup, J. A. Domestic music under the Stuarts. Proc Royal Musical Assoc 68 1942.

— L'influence de la musique italienne sur le madrigal anglais. In Musique et poésie au xvie siècle, ed J. Jacquot, Paris 1954.

Helm, E. B. Italian traits in the English madrigal. Music Rev 7 1946.

Einstein, A. The Italian madrigal. 3 vols Princeton 1949.

Obertello, A. Madrigali italiani in Inghilterra. Milan 1949.

Jones, D. The Elizabethan lyric. Score 2 1950.

Ing, C. M. Elizabethan lyrics: a study in the development of English metres. 1951.

Ward, J. The 'dolfull domps'. Jnl of Amer Musicological Soc 4 1951.

— Music for A handefull of pleasant delites. Jnl of Amer Musicological Soc 10 1957.

— Joan qd John and other fragments at Western Reserve University. In Aspects of medieval and Renaissance music: a birthday offering to Gustave Reese, New York [1966].

Smith, H. Elizabethan poetry. Cambridge Mass 1952.

Stevens, J. Carols and Court songs of the early Tudor period. Proc Royal Musical Assoc 77 1952.

— The Elizabethan madrigal: 'perfect marriage' or 'uneasy flirtation'. E & S new ser 11 1958.

— Music and poetry in the early Tudor court. 1961.

Hart, E. F. Caroline lyrics and contemporary song-books. Library 5th ser 8 1953.

— The Restoration catch. Music & Letters 34 1953.

Woodfill, W. L. Musicians in English society from Elizabeth to Charles I. Princeton 1953.

Arnold, D. Croce and the English madrigal. Music & Letters 35 1954.

Dart, T. Rôle de la danse dans l'ayre anglais. In Musique et poésie au xvie siècle, ed J. Jacquot, Paris 1954.

La luth et sa musique. Ed J. Jacquot, Paris 1958.

Mellers, W. La mélancholie au début du xviie siècle et le madrigal anglais. In Musique et poésie au xvie siècle, ed J. Jacquot, Paris 1954.

— Words and music in Elizabethan England. In The age of Shakespeare, ed B. Ford 1955 (Pelican).

— Harmonious meeting. 1963.

Carpenter, N. C. Skelton and music: roty bully joye. RES new ser 6 1955.

Long, J. H. Blame not Wyatt's lute. Renaissance News 7 1954. On setting of Blame not my lute in Folger ms 448.16; replies by M. Bukofzer and O. Gombosi 8 1955.

Cutts, J. P. Robert Johnson: King's musician in his Majesty's public entertainment. Music & Letters 36 1955.

— Two hitherto unpublished settings of sonnets from the Passionate pilgrim. Shakespeare Quart 9 1958. Prints settings of Venus and young Adonis and Fair Cytherea from Bodley ms Mus.b.1.

— Henry Shirley's The martyred soldier. Renaissance News 12 1959. A setting of Victory, victory, hell is beaten down in Bodley ms Don.c.57.

— Robert Johnson and the Court masque. Music & Letters 41 1960.

— Music and [Fletcher's] The mad lover. Stud in Renaissance 8 1961.

— William Lawes's writing for the theater and the Court. Jnl of Amer Musicological Soc 16 1963.

— Every woman in her humor. Renaissance News 18 1965.

Mumford, I. L. Musical settings to the poems of Sir Thomas Wyatt. Music & Letters 37 1956, 39 1958.

— Musical settings to the poems of Henry Howard, Earl of Surrey. Eng Miscellany (Rome) 8 1957.

— Sir Thomas Wyatt's verse and Italian musical sources. Eng Miscellany (Rome) 12 1963.

Duckles, V. Florid embellishment in English song of the late 16th and 17th centuries. Annales Musicologiques 5 1957.

— The lyrics of John Donne as set by his contemporaries. In Bericht über den Siebenten Internationalen Musikwissenschaftlichen Kongress Köln 1958, Cassel 1959.

— John Jenkins' settings of lyrics by George Herbert. Musical Quart 48 1962.

— The English musical elegy of the late Renaissance. In Aspects of medieval and Renaissance music: a birthday offering to Gustave Reese, New York [1966].

— and F. B. Zimmerman. Words to Music. Los Angeles 1967.

Mishkin, H. G. Irrational dissonance in the English madrigal. In Essays on music in honor of Archibald Thompson Davison, Cambridge Mass 1957.

Spink, I. English seventeenth-century dialogues. Music & Letters 38 1957.

— English Cavalier songs 1620–60. Proc Royal Musical Assoc 86 1960.

Raynor, H. Words for music. Monthly Musical Record Sept–Oct 1958.

— Framed to the life of the words. Music Rev 19 1958.

Sabol, A. J. Two songs with accompaniment for an Elizabethan choirboy play. Stud in Renaissance 5 1958. What meat eats the Spaniard and Love for such a cherry lip in Blurt, Master Constable.

Finney, G. L. Music: a book of knowledge in Renaissance England. Stud in Renaissance 6 1959.

— Musical backgrounds for English literature 1580–1650. New Brunswick NJ [1962].

Emslie, McD. Nicholas Lanier's innovations in English song. Music & Letters 41 1960.

Ingram, R. W. Words and music. In Elizabethan poetry, ed J. R. Brown and B. Harris 1960.

Lefkowitz, M. William Lawes. 1960.

Seng, P. J. Two unpublished stage songs for the aery of children. Renaissance News 13 1960. O the joys that soon should waste in Cynthia's revels, and The dark is my delight in The Dutch courtesan.

— The vocal songs in the plays of Shakespeare: a critical history. Cambridge Mass 1967.

Hollander, J. The untuning of the sky: ideas of music in English poetry 1500–1700. Princeton 1961.

Brett, P. The English consort song 1570–1625. Proc Royal Musical Assoc 88 1962.

Greer, D. What if a day: an examination of the words and music. Music & Letters 43 1962.

— An early setting of lines from Venus and Adonis. Music & Letters 45 1964.

— The part-songs of the English lutenists. Proc Royal Musical Assoc 94 1968.

— Music for Shakespeare's Samingo. Shakespeare Quart 23 1972.

Kerman, J. The Elizabethan madrigal: a comparative study. New York 1962.

Olshausen, U. Das lautenbegleitete Sololied in England um 1600. Frankfurt 1963.

Sternfeld, F. W. Music in Shakespearean tragedy. 1963, 1967 (rev).

— and M. J. Chan. Come live with me and be my love. Comparative Lit 22 1970.

Doughtie, E. Words for music: simplicity and complexity in the Elizabethan air. Rice Univ Stud 51 1965.

Maynard, W. The lyrics of Wyatt: poems or songs? RES new ser 16 1965.

Smallman, B. Endor revisited: English biblical dialogues of the seventeenth century. Music & Letters 46 1965.

Spearitt, G. D. The consort songs and madrigals of Richard Nicholson. Musicology 2 1967.

Music in English Renaissance drama. Ed J. H. Long, Lexington Kentucky 1968.

Shire, H. M. Song, dance and poetry of the Court of Scotland under King James 6. Cambridge 1969.

Ruff, L. M. and A. Wilson. Allusion to the Essex downfall in lute song lyrics. Lute Soc Jnl 12 1970.

Fabry, F. J. Sidney's verse adaptations of two 16th-century Italian art-songs. Renaissance Quart 23 1970. Musical settings for Certain sonnets 3–4 and 26.

Boorman, S. Notari, Porter and the lute. Lute Soc Jnl 13 1971.

Coxon, C. Handlist of the sources of John Jenkins' vocal and instrumental music. RMA Research Chron 9 1971.

(6) COLLECTIONS (FROM 1800)

Smith, J. S. Musica antiqua. 2 vols 1812. A selection of music from 12th to 18th centuries.

Oliphant, T. La musa madrigalesca. 1837. A selection of poems from the ptd songbooks.

Musical Antiquarian Society. Publications 19 vols 1841–8. Includes edns of madrigalists and lutenists.

Chappell, W. Popular music of the olden time. 2 vols 1859; rev H. E. Wooldridge as Old English popular music 1893, New York 1961; ed F. W. Sternfeld, New York 1965 (from 1859).

Arkwright, G. E. P. The old English edition. 25 vols 1889–1902.

Flügel, E. Liedersammlungen des 16 Jahrhunderts. Anglia 12 1889. Prints the poems from xx songes 1530 and BM mss additional 31,922 and Royal App 58.

Dolmetsch, A. Select English songs and dialogues of the 16th and 17th centuries. 2 vols 1898–1912.

Cox, F. A. English madrigals in the time of Shakespeare. 1899. A selection of song book poetry with first-line index to ptd songbooks 1588–1638.

Bolle, W. Die gedruckten englischen Liederbücher bis 1600. Berlin 1903. Reprints poems from song books to 1600.

Benson, L. The Oriana collection of early madrigals British and foreign. 100 pts [1905–15].

Fellowes, E. H. The English madrigal school. 36 vols 1913–24; rev R. T. Dart et al as The English madrigalists, 1956–.

— The English school of lutenist song writers. Ser 1, 16 vols 1920–32; ser 2, 16 vols 1925–7; rev R. T. Dart et al as The English lute-songs, 1959–. Under this new title the following additional vols have been pbd: ser 1, 17 1959; ser 2, 17–21 1961–9.

— Elizabethan and Jacobean part songs. 45 pts 1920–40. A selection of part-songs by Dowland, Bartlet, Campion, Cavendish, Ford, Pilkington, Jones.

— English madrigal verse. Oxford 1920, 1929 (rev); rev and enlarged F. W. Sternfeld and D. Greer, Oxford 1967.

Potter, F. H. Reliquary of English song. 2 vols New York 1915–16, 1943–4.

'Warlock, Peter' (P. Heseltine) and P. Wilson. English ayres. 4 vols 1922–5, 6 vols 1927–31 (enlarged), [1964].

'Warlock, Peter'. The first [second, third] book of Elizabethan songs. 3 vols 1926. Consort songs for voice and viols from mss.

Warlock also edited single sheet-music edns of part-songs by the lutenists in the Curwen edn as English madrigals and part songs.

Scott, C. K. Euterpe: a collection of madrigals and other music of the 16th and 17th centuries. 70 pts 1928–36. Includes selected part-songs by lutenists.

Obertello, A. Madrigali italiani in Inghilterra. Milan 1949.

Greenberg, N., W. H. Auden and C. Kallman. An Elizabethan song book. Garden City NY 1955.

Elliott, K. and H. M. Shire. Music of Scotland 1500–1700. Musica britannica 15 1957.

Cutts, J. P. Seventeenth-century songs and lyrics. Columbia Missouri 1959. Poems selected from music mss.

— La musique de scène de la troupe de Shakespeare. Paris 1959.

Sabol, A. J. Songs and dances for the Stuart masque. Providence 1959. Mainly from mss.

Dart, R. T. Invitation to madrigals. Vols 1–, 1961–.

Souris, A. and J. Jacquot. Poèmes de Donne, Herbert et Crashaw mis en musique par leur contemporains. Paris 1961.

Stevens, J. Music and poetry in the early Tudor Court. 1961. Prints the poems set to music in BM mss additional 5465, 5665, 31,922.

Elliott, K. Musa jocosa mihi. 1966. 12 songs by Lawes, Wilson et al to poems by Sir Robert Ayton.

Simpson, C. The British broadside ballad and its music. New Brunswick NJ 1966. *See also* J. M. Ward, Apropos the British broadside ballad and its music, Jnl of Amer Musicological Soc 20 1967.

Brett, P. Consort songs. Musica britannica 22 1967.

Stevens, D. The Penguin book of English madrigals for four voices. 1967 (Penguin).

— The second Penguin book of English madrigals [for 5 voices]. 1970 (Penguin).

English lute songs 1597–1632: a collection of facsimile reprints. Ed D. Greer, I. Harwood, D. Poulton and F. Traficante 36 pts Menston 1967–71 (facs). Separate pts and in 9 bound vols: vol 1, pts 1–3; vol 2, pts 4–7; vol 3, pts 9–13; vol 4, pts 14–19; vol 5, pts 20–3; vol 6, pts 24–5; vol 7, pts 26–30; vol 8, pts 8, 31–4; vol 9 pts 35–6.

Doughtie, E. Lyrics from English airs 1596–1622. Cambridge Mass 1970. Contains all the lute-song lyrics except those by Campion.

Spink, I. English songs 1625–60. Musica britannica 33 1971. Songs by N. Lanier, R. Ramsey, A. [?]. Bales, S. Mace, J. Jenkins, J. Wilson, H. Lawes, J. Hilton, C. Coleman, S. Ives, W. Lawes, W. Webb, W. Caesar ('Smegergill'), G. Jeffreys, J. Atkins, T. Brewer, T. Blagrave, J. Taylor, T. Charles, J. Savile, E. Coleman, J. Goodgroome, Lady Mary Dering, R. Smith, J. Cave, J. Gamble, R. Hill, A. Marsh, anon.

English madrigals 1588–1630: a collection of facsimile reprints. Ed F. W. Sternfeld and D. Greer, Menston 1972–.

(7) SEPARATE SONG BOOKS ETC 1500–1660

References to collections above are generally abbreviated to the surname of the editor and the opening words of the title, e.g. Spink, English songs. *The following special references are used:*

EM   E. H. Fellowes, The English madrigalists (formerly The English madrigal school)
ELS   E. H. Fellowes et al, The English lute-songs (formerly The English school of lutenist song writers)
els   English lute songs: a collection of facsimile reprints

XX SONGES

§ 1

xx songes, ix of iiii partes and xi of thre partes. 1530. Poems rptd in Flügel, Liedersammlungen. Songs by T. Ashwell, W. Cornysh, R. Cowper (Cooper), R. Fayrfax, R. Jones, R. Pygott, J. Qwynneth, T. Stretton, J. Taverner. Only the bassus pt-book survives complete (BM).

§ 2

Greene, R. L. The early English carols. 1935.
Nixon, H. M. The book of xx songs. BM Quart 16 1951.
Stevens, J. Music and poetry in the early Tudor Court. 1961.

JOHN HALL
1529?–66?

§ 1

[The Court of Vertue. 1565]. Title-page lacking: title from Stationers' register. Ed R. A. Fraser 1961.

§ 2

Fraser, R. A. An amateur Elizabethan composer. Music & Letters 33 1952.
— Early Elizabethan songs. Musica Disciplina 7 1953.
Stevens, J. Music and poetry in the early Tudor Court. 1961.
Huttar, C. A. Wyatt and the several editions of the Court of Venus. SB 19 1966.

THOMAS WHYTHORNE
1528-96

§ 1

Songes for three, fower and five voyces. 1571. Tenor pt
rptd R. Imelmann, Sh Jb 39 1903; 11 songs ed 'Peter
Warlock' (P. Heseltine), Oxford choral songs nos
354-64, 1927; 3 songs ed M. Bukofzer, New York 1947.
Duos: or songs for two voices. 1590.
Autobiography. Ed J. M. Osborn, Oxford 1961 (original
phonetic spelling), 1962 (modernized).

§ 2

'Warlock, Peter' (P. Heseltine). Whythorne: an unknown
Elizabethan composer. 1927.

WILLIAM BYRD
1543-1623

Collections

Ed Fellowes, EM 14-16 1920, 1962-5 (rev).
Collected vocal works. Ed E. H. Fellowes, vols 12-16,
1948-9, 1962- (rev). Includes ms works not listed below.

§ 1

A gratification unto Master John Case. [c. 1586-8]. A
6-pt motet; only Cantus II survives (Cambridge Univ
Lib).
Psalmes, sonets and songs of sadnes and pietie. 1588,
[c. 1599].
Songs of sundrie natures, some of gravitie and others of
myrth. 1589, 1610; ed Arkwright, Old English edition
6-9, 1892-3.
Psalmes, songs and sonnets: some solemne, others joyfull,
framed to the life of the words. 1611.
See also Yonge, Musica transalpina, 1588, Watson, Italian
madrigalls englished, 1590, and Leighton, Teares or
lamentacions, 1614.

§ 2

Fellowes, E. H. Byrd: a short account of his life and work.
Oxford 1923, 1928 (rev).
— William Byrd. Oxford 1936, 1948 (rev).
Howes, F. William Byrd. 1928.
Dent, E. J. Byrd and the madrigal. In Musikwissen-
schaftliche Beiträge: Festschrift für J. Wolf, Berlin
1929.
Westrup, J. A. William Byrd. Music & Letters 24
1943.
Brown, D. Byrd's 1588 volume. Music & Letters 38 1957.
Zimmerman, F. B. Advanced tonal design in the part-
songs of Byrd. In Bericht über den Siebenten Inter-
nationalen Musikwissenschaftlichen Kongress Köln
1958, Cassel 1959.
Brett, P. and R. T. Dart. Songs by Byrd in manuscripts
at Harvard. Harvard Lib Bull 14 1960.
Andrews, H. K. Printed sources of Byrd's Psalmes,
sonets and songs. Music & Letters 44 1963.
— The technique of Byrd's vocal polyphony. 1966.

NICHOLAS YONGE
d. 1619

Selections

Ferrabosco: madrigals from Musica transalpina. Ed
Arkwright, Old English edition 11-12, 1894.
Marenzio: 10 madrigals from Musica transalpina. Ed
R. A. Harman 1955.

§ 1

Musica transalpina: madrigales translated of foure, five
and sixe parts, chosen out of divers excellent authors,
with the first and second part of La verginella made by
Maister Byrd. 1588; poems rptd in Fellowes, English
madrigal verse (3rd edn); ed D. Stevens 1972 (facs).
An anthology of Italian madrigals compiled by Yonge.
Musica transalpina: the second booke of madrigalles to 5
and 6 voyces, translated out of sundrie Italian authors.
1597; ed D. Stevens 1972 (facs). Compiled by Yonge.

§ 2

Einstein, A. The Elizabethan madrigal and Musica
transalpina. Music & Letters 25 1944.
Obertello, A. Madrigali italiani in Inghilterra. Milan 1949.
Includes the Italian and English texts of both collections.
Kerman, J. The Elizabethan madrigal. New York 1962.
Ch 2.

THOMAS WATSON
1557?-92

§ 1

The first sett, of Italian madrigalls englished. 1590.
Poems rptd in Fellowes, English madrigal verse (3rd
edn). Italian madrigals, mostly by Marenzio, tr Watson;
also 2 by Byrd.
For Watson's other works see col 1156, above.

§ 2

Carpenter, F. I. Watson's Italian madrigals englished
1590. JEGP 2 1899. With Italian and English texts.
Obertello, A. Madrigali italiani in Inghilterra. Milan
1949. With Italian and English texts.
Kerman, J. The Elizabethan madrigal. New York 1962.
Ch 2.

THOMAS MORLEY
1557-1602?

Collections

Ed Fellowes, EM 1-4, 1913, 1956- (rev), 32, 1923, 1962
(rev).

§ 1

Canzonets: or little short songs to three voyces. 1593,
1602 (enlarged), 1606, 1631; tr German, 1612 (lost),
1624; text of 1624 rptd Bolle, Die gedruckten englischen
Liederbücher; ed J. E. Uhler, Baton Rouge 1957 (facs
of 1624).
Madrigalls to foure voyces. 1594, 1600 (enlarged).
The first booke of canzonets to two voyces. 1595, 1619;
ed D. H. Boalch, Oxford 1950; tr Italian, c. 1595 (lost);
ed J. E. Uhler, Baton Rouge 1954 (facs of 1595).
The first book of balletts to five voyces. 1595, 1600; tr
Italian, 1595; German, 1609; ed E. F. Rimbault,
Musical Antiquarian Soc [5 1842]; rptd Bolle, Die
gedruckten englischen Liederbücher (text of 1609);
rptd Obertello, Madrigali italiani (English and Italian
texts).
Canzonets or little short songs to foure voyces: celected
out of the best and approv'd Italian authors. 1597.
Compiled by Morley, with English texts; 2 pieces by
Morley himself. Italian and English texts rptd Obertello,
Madrigali italiani; ed C. A. Murphy in ¡Morley's
editions of Italian canzonets and madrigals, Tallahassee
1964.
Canzonets or little short aers to five and six voices. 1597.

A plaine and easie introduction to practicall musicke. 1597, 1608, 1771; ed E. H. Fellowes 1937 (facs), 1970 (facs); ed R. A. Harman 1952.

Madrigals to five voyces celected out of the best approved Italian authors. 1598. Compiled by Morley, with English texts. Italian and English texts rptd Obertello, Madrigali italiani; ed C. A. Murphy in Morley's editions of Italian canzonets and madrigals, Tallahassee 1964.

The first booke of ayres. 1600; ed Fellowes ELS 1st ser 16 1932, 1958, 1966 (both rev); ed Greer, els no 33 1970 (facs). Unique copy (incomplete) in Folger Shakespeare Lib, Washington.

The triumphes of Oriana, to 5 and 6 voices: composed by divers severall aucthors. 1601, 1601; ed W. Hawes [1814]; ed Benson, Oriana collection [1905]. Compiled by Morley, and containing madrigals by M. East, D. Norcome, J. Mundy, E. Gibbons, J. Bennet, J. Hilton the elder, G. Marson, R. Carlton, J. Holmes, R. Nicholson, T. Tomkins, M. Cavendish, W. Cobbold, J. Farmer, J. Wilbye, T. Hunt, T. Weelkes, J. Milton the elder, G. Kirbye, R. Jones, J. Lisley, E. Johnson and Morley himself.

§2

Brennecke, E. Shakespeare's collaboration with Morley. PMLA 54 1939.

Deutsch, O. E. The editions of Morley's Introduction. Library 4th ser 23 1943.

Gordon, P. The Morley-Shakespeare myth. Music & Letters 28 1947.

Obertello, A. Madrigali italiani in Inghilterra. Milan 1949.

Beck, S. The case of O mistress mine. Renaissance News 6 1953. Reply by V. Duckles 7 1954.

—— Morley: the first book of consort lessons. New York 1959.

Uhler, J. E. Morley's madrigals for four voices. Music & Letters 36 1955.

Arnold, D. Gastoldi and the English ballett. Monthly Musical Record March–April 1956.

Strong, R. C. Queen Elizabeth I as Oriana. Stud in Renaissance 6 1959.

Zimmerman, F. B. Italian and English traits in the music of Morley. Anuario Musical 14 1959.

Kerman, J. The Elizabethan madrigal. New York 1962. Ch 5.

Doughtie, E. Robert Southwell and Morley's First book of ayres. Lute Soc Jnl 4 1962.

Dart, R. T. A suppressed dedication [to Sir John Puckering] for Morley's four-part madrigals of 1594. Trans Cambridge Bibl Soc 3 1963.

Greer, D. The lute songs of Morley. Lute Soc Jnl 8 1966.

JOHN MUNDY
d. 1630

Songs and psalmes composed into 3, 4 and 5 parts. 1594; ed Fellowes, EM 35 1924, 1961 (rev).
See also Morley, Triumphes of Oriana, 1601.

NEW BOOKE OF TABLITURE
§1

A new booke of tabliture. 1596; ed W. W. Newcomb as Lute music of Shakespeare's time, University Park Pa 1966; poems rptd in Fellowes, English madrigal verse; songs ed Greer, ELS 2nd ser 21 1969. An anon instruction book in playing the lute etc, with some songs and poems. Ptd by William Barley.

§2

Ward, J. M. Barley's songs without words. Lute Soc Jnl 12 1970.

JOHN DOWLAND
1563–1623
Collections

Ed Fellowes, ELS 1st ser 1–2 1920–1, 1965 (rev), 5–6 1922, 1969 (rev), 10–11 1923, 1961 (rev), 12 1924, 1969 (rev), 14 1925, 1969 (rev).

Fifty songs. Ed E. H. Fellowes 2 vols 1925, 1971 (rev).

Ayres for four voices, transcribed E. H. Fellowes. Ed R. T. Dart and N. Fortune, Musica britannica 6 1953, 1963 (rev).

Ed Poulton, els nos 14–18 1968–70.

§1

The first booke of songes or ayres of fowre partes with tableture for the lute. 1597, 1600, 1603, 1606, 1613; ed W. Chappell, Musical Antiquarian Soc [12 1844].

The second booke of songs or ayres. 1600.
The third and last booke of songs or aires. 1603.
A pilgrimes solace. 1612.
See also Robert Dowland A musicall banquet, 1610, and Leighton, Teares or lamentacions, 1614.

§2

Fellowes, E. H. The songs of Dowland. Proc Royal Musical Assoc 56 1930.

Dowling, M. The printing of Dowland's Second booke of songs or ayres. Library 4th ser 12 1932.

Manning, R. M. Lachrymae: a study of Dowland. Music & Letters 25 1944.

Mies, O. H. Dowland's Lachrymae tune. Musica Disciplina 4 1950.

Poulton, D. Dowland's songs and their instrumental forms. Monthly Musical Record Sept 1951.

—— Dowland, Doctor of Musick. Consort 20 1963.

—— Dowland's patrons and friends. Lute Soc Jnl 5 1963.

—— Was Dowland a singer? Lute Soc Jnl 7 1965.

—— John Dowland. 1972.

Dart, R. T. Rôle de la danse dans l'ayre anglais. In Musique et poésie au xvie siècle, ed J. Jacquot, Paris 1954.

Richardson, B. New light on Dowland's continental movements. Monthly Musical Record Jan–Feb 1960.

Davis, W. R. Melodic and poetic structure: the examples of Campion and Dowland. Criticism 4 1962.

Hill, C. Dowland: some new facts and a quatercentenary tribute. Musical Times Nov 1963. Reply by D. Poulton, Jan 1964, with correspondence March–April 1964.

GEORGE KIRBYE
1565?–1634

The first set of English madrigalls. 1597; ed Fellowes, EM 24 1922, 1961 (rev).
See also Morley, The triumphes of Oriana, 1601. For the location of ms madrigals see Die Musik in Geschichte und Gegenwart.

ANTONY HOLBORNE
d. 1602?

The cittharn schoole. 1597. Contains 6 vocal pieces by William Holborne, ed Fellowes, EM 36 1924, 1961 (rev).

THOMAS WEELKES
1575?–1632
Collections

Ed Fellowes, EM 9–12 1916, 1967–8 (rev), 13 1916, 1965 (rev).

§1

Madrigals to 3, 4, 5 and 6 voyces. 1597; ed E. J. Hopkins, Musical Antiquarian Soc [8 1843].
Balletts and madrigals to five voyces. 1598, 1608; ed Arkwright, Old English edition 13–15 1895.
Madrigals of 5 and 6 parts. 1600.
Ayres or phantasticke spirites for three voices. 1608; ed Arkwright, Old English edition 16–17 1895–6.
The cries of London. Ed Brett, Consort songs (ms).
See also Morley, Triumphes of Oriana, *1601, and Leighton*, Teares or lamentacions, *1614*.

§2

Fellowes, E. H. Thomas Weelkes. Proc [Royal] Musical Assoc 42 1916.
Arnold, D. M. Weelkes and the madrigal. Music & Letters 31 1950.
Kerman, J. The Elizabethan madrigal. New York 1962. Ch 6.
Brown, D. Weelkes: a biographical and critical study. 1969.
Monson, C. Weelkes: a new fa-la. Musical Times Feb 1972.

JOHN WILBYE
1574–1638
Collections

Ed Fellowes, EM 6–7 1914, 1966 (rev).

§1

The first set of English madrigals. 1598; ed J. Turle, Musical Antiquarian Soc [2 1841], Menston 1972 (facs).
The second set of madrigales. 1609; ed G. W. Budd, Musical Antiquarian Soc [16 1846].
See also Morley, Triumphes of Oriana, *1601, and Leighton*, Teares or lamentacions, *1614*.

§2

Fellowes, E. H. John Wilbye. Proc [Royal] Musical Assoc 41 1915.
Heurich, H. Wilbye in seinem Madrigalen. Augsburg 1931.
Collet, R. Wilbye: some aspects of his music. Score 4 1951.
Kerman, J. The Elizabethan madrigal. New York 1962. Ch 6.

MICHAEL CAVENDISH
1565?–1628

[Madrigals and airs: the main title is missing from the unique BM copy]. 1598; the madrigals ed Fellowes, EM 36 1924, 1961 (rev); the airs ed Fellowes, ELS 2nd ser 7 1926; ed Greer, els no 8 1971 (facs).
See also Morley, Triumphes of Oriana, *1601*.

GILES FARNABY
c. 1565–1640

Canzonets to fowre voyces, with a song of eight parts. 1598; ed Fellowes, EM 20 1922, 1963 (rev).

JOHN BENNET

Madrigalls to foure voyces. 1599; ed E. J. Hopkins, Musical Antiquarian Soc [15 1845]; ed Fellowes, EM 23 1922.
There are 2 ms pieces in Brett, Consort songs. *See also Morley*, Triumphes of Oriana, *1601 and Ravenscroft*, Briefe discourse, *1614*.

JOHN FARMER

The first set of English madrigals. 1599; ed Fellowes, EM 8 1914.
See also Morley, Triumphes of Oriana, *1601*.

ROBERT JONES the younger
b. c. 1577
Collections

Ed Fellowes, ELS 2nd ser 4 1925, 1959 (rev), 5–6 1926, 14–15 1927.
Ed Greer, els nos 26–30 1967–71 (facs).

§1

The first booke of songes and ayres. 1600.
The second booke of songs and ayres. 1601.
Ultimum vale, with a triplicity of musicke. 1605.
The first set of madrigals. 1607; ed Fellowes, EM 35 1924, 1961 (rev).
A musicall dreame: or the fourth booke of ayres. 1609.
The Muses gardin for delights: or the fift booke of ayres. 1610; poems rptd W. B. Squire, Oxford 1901; 12 songs ed 'Peter Warlock' (P. Heseltine) and P. Wilson 1923 (vol 2 of English ayres).
See also Morley, Triumphes of Oriana, *1601, and Leighton*, Teares or lamentacions, *1614*.

§2

Fellowes, E. H. The text of the song-books of Jones. Music & Letters 8 1927.
Adams, J. Q. A new song by Jones. MLQ 1 1940. With facs of the song in Folger ms V.b.278.

RICHARD CARLTON
c. 1558–c. 1638

Madrigals to five voyces. 1601; ed Fellowes, EM 27 1923, 1960 (rev).
See also Morley, Triumphes of Oriana, *1601*.

PHILIP ROSSETER
1568–1623

§1

A booke of ayres. 1601; poems ed A. H. Bullen, The works of Dr Thomas Campion, 1889; poems ed P. Vivian, Campion's works, Oxford 1909, 1966; words and music ed Fellowes, ELS 1st ser 4 and 13 1922–4, 1960, 1969 (both rev) (Campion's songs), 8–9 1923, 1966 (rev) (Rosseter's songs); poems ed W. R. Davis, Works of Campion, Garden City NY 1967, London 1969; ed Greer, els no 36 1970 (facs). This book contains 21 songs by Campion and 21 by Rosseter.

§2

Pattison, B. Rosseter: poet and musician. Musical Times Nov 1931.

Kastendieck, M. M. England's musical poet Thomas Campion. New York 1938. Ch 4.

Berringer, R. W. Campion's share in A booke of ayres. PMLA 58 1943.

Vlam, C. and R. T. Dart. Rosseters in Holland. Galpin Soc Jnl 11 1958.

Fortune, N. Rosseter and his songs. Lute Soc Jnl 7 1965.

Lowbury, E., T. Salter and A. Young. Thomas Campion. 1970. Ch 4.

THOMAS CAMPION

See col 1069, above.

THOMAS BATESON
c. 1570–1630
Collections

Ed Fellowes, EM 21–2 1922, 1958–60 (rev).

§1

The first set of English madrigales. 1604; ed E. F. Rimbault, Musical Antiquarian Soc [16 1846].

The second set of madrigales. 1618.

MICHAEL EAST or ESTE
c. 1580–1648
Collections

Ed Fellowes, EM 29–31 1923, 1960–2 (rev).

§1

Madrigales to 3, 4 and 5 parts. 1604.

The second set of madrigales. 1606.

The third set of bookes. 1610.

The fourth set of bookes. 1618, 1619.

The sixt set of bookes. 1624. Contains mostly sacred compositions.

The fifth, 1618 and seventh, 1638 books contain pieces without words.

See also Morley, Triumphes of Oriana, *1601.*

THOMAS GREAVES

Songes of sundrie kindes. 1604; madrigals and consort songs ed Fellowes, EM 36 1924, 1961 (rev); lute airs ed I. Spink, ELS 2nd ser 18 1962; ed Greer, els no 22 1971 (facs).

TOBIAS HUME
d. 1645
Collections

Ed Traficante, els nos 24–5 1969 (facs).

The first part of ayres. 1605; 4 songs ed Greer, ELS 2nd ser 21 1969. Mostly instrumental pieces.

Captaine Hume's poeticall musicke. 1607; one song ed Greer, ELS 2nd ser 21 1969. Mostly instrumental pieces.

FRANCIS PILKINGTON
c. 1562–1638
Collections

Ed Fellowes, EM 25 1923, 1959 (rev), 26 1923, 1958 (rev).

§1

The first booke of songs or ayres of 4 parts. 1605; ed Arkwright, Old English edition 18–20 1897–8; ed Fellowes, ELS 1st ser 7 1922, 1970 (rev), 15 1925, 1970 (rev); ed Greer, els no 34 1969 (facs).

The first set of madrigals and pastorals. 1613.

The second set of madrigals, and pastorals. 1624.

See also Leighton, Teares of lamentacions, *1614.*

RICHARD ALISON

An howres recreation in musicke, apt for instrumentes and voyces. 1606; ed Fellowes, EM 33 1924, 1961 (rev).

JOHN BARTLET

A booke of ayres with a triplicitie of musicke. 1606; ed Fellowes, ELS 2nd ser 3 1925; ed Greer, els no 3 1967, (facs).

JOHN COOPER (COPRARIO)
c. 1575–1626
Collections

Ed G. Hendrie and R. T. Dart, ELS 1st ser 17 1959.

Ed Greer, els nos 9–10 1970 (facs).

§1

Funeral teares for the death of the Right Honorable the Earle of Devonshire. 1606.

Songs of mourning: bewailing the untimely death of Prince Henry. 1613. Words by Thomas Campion; *see col 1069, above.*

There are also 3 songs from Campion's Masque for the Earl of Somerset (1614) and one ms song in ELS 17. BM ms Eg 3665 contains 21 villanellas by Cooper. See also Leighton, Teares or lamentacions, *1614.*

See also Rules how to compose, ed M. Bukofzer, Los Angeles 1952 (ms facs).

JOHN DANYEL
d. 1630

§1

Songs for the lute viol and voice. 1606; ed Fellowes, ELS 2nd ser 8 1926, 1970 (rev); ed Greer, els no 13 1970 (facs).

§2

Judd, P. The songs of Danyel. Music & Letters 17 1936.

Scott, D. Danyel: his life and songs. Lute Soc Jnl 13 1971.

THOMAS FORD
c. 1580–1648

Musicke of sundrie kindes, set forth in two bookes. 1607; the songs ed Fellowes, ELS 1st ser 3 1921, 1966 (rev); ed Greer, els no 21 1971 (facs).

See also Leighton, Teares or lamentacions, *1614 and Hilton* Catch that catch can, *1652. For mss see* Die Musik in Geschichte und Gegenwart.

HENRY YOULL

Canzonets to three voyces. 1608; ed Fellowes, EM 28 1923, 1968 (rev).

ALFONSO FERRABOSCO
the younger
c. 1575–1628

§ 1

Ayres. 1609; ed Fellowes, ELS 2nd ser 16 1927; ed Greer, els no 20 1970 (facs).
See also Leighton, Teares or lamentacions, *1614. There are also some ms songs by Ferrabosco, ed I. Spink, ELS 2nd ser 19 1966.*

§ 2

Cutts, J. P. Le rôle de la musique dans les masques de Ben Jonson. In Les fêtes de la Renaissance, Paris 1956.
Sternfeld, F. W. Song in Jonson's comedy. In Studies in the English Renaissance drama, ed J. W. Bennett et al, New York 1959. On Come my Celia.
Doughtie, E. Ferrabosco and Jonson's The houre-glasse. Renaissance Quart 22 1969.

THOMAS ROBINSON

§ 1

New citharen lessons. 1609. Contains 2 songs, one ed D. Greer, ELS 2nd ser 21 1969.

§ 2

Dart, R. T. The cittern and its English music. Galpin Soc Jnl 1 1948.

THOMAS RAVENSCROFT
c. 1592–c. 1633
Collections

Fellowes, English madrigal verse (3rd edn). Reprints words only.
'Warlock, Peter' (P. Heseltine). Pammelia and other rounds and catches. 1928. Contains all Ravenscroft's rounds and catches.

§ 1

Pammelia: musicks miscellanie, or mixed varietie of pleasant roundelayes and delightful catches. 1609, 1618; ed M. Leach, Pbns Amer Folklore Soc, bibl & special ser 12 Philadelphia 1961 (facs). Collected by Ravenscroft.
Deuteromelia: or the second part of musicks melodie. 1609. Collected by Ravenscroft.
Melismata: musicall phansies. 1611. Collected by Ravenscroft.
A briefe discourse. 1614. Compositions by Ravenscroft, John Bennet and Edward Peirs (Pearce).

§ 2

Mark, J. Thomas Ravenscroft. Musical Times Oct 1924.
Lawrence, W. J. Ravenscroft's theatrical associations. MLR 19 1924.

Cutts, J. P. Dametas' song in Sidney's Arcadia. Renaissance News 11 1958. Musical setting in Pammelia.
Sabol, A. J. Ravenscroft's Melismata and the children of Paul's. Renaissance News 12 1959.
For similar ms collections of rounds and catches see G. Bantock and H. O. Anderton, The Melvill book of roundels, *1916 and J. Vlasto*, An Elizabethan anthology of rounds, *Musical Quart 40 1954.*

WILLIAM CORKINE
Collections

Ed Fellowes, ELS 2nd ser 12–13 1926–7.
Ed Greer, els nos 11–12 1970 (facs).

§ 1

Ayres, to sing and play to the lute and basse viol. 1610.
The second book of ayres. 1612.

ROBERT DOWLAND
c. 1586–1641

§ 1

A musicall banquet. 1610; ed P. Stroud, ELS 2nd ser 20 1968; ed D. Poulton, els no 19 1969 (facs). Compiled by Robert Dowland and containing songs by J. Dowland, D. Batchelar, R. Martin, R. Hales, [G.] Tessier, P. Guédron, D. Megli, G. Caccini and anon.

§ 2

[Arkwright, G. E. P.]. Robert Douland's Musicall banquet 1610. Musical Antiquary 1 1910.

JOHN MAYNARD
1577–1633?

§ 1

The XII wonders of the world. 1611; ed I. Harwood, els no 32 1970 (facs). Words by Sir John Davies; *see col 1071, above.*

§ 2

Harwood, I. Maynard and the XII wonders of the world. Lute Soc Jnl 4 1962.

ORLANDO GIBBONS
1583–1625

§ 1

The first set of madrigals and mottets of 5 parts. 1612; ed G. Smart, Musical Antiquarian Soc [3 1841]; ed Fellowes, EM 5 1914, 1964 (rev).
See also Leighton, Teares or lamentacions, *1614; The Cries of London ed Brett*, Consort songs (ms).

§ 2

Fellowes, E. H. Gibbons and his family. 1925, 1951 (rev).
Jacquot, J. Lyrisme et sentiment tragique dans les madrigaux d'Orlando Gibbons. In Musique et poésie au xvie siècle, ed Jacquot, Paris 1954.
Kerman, J. The Elizabethan madrigal. New York 1962. Ch 4.

HENRY LICHFILD

The first set of madrigals of 5 parts. 1613; ed Fellowes, EM 17 1922, 1970 (rev).

JOHN WARD
1571–1638

The first set of English madrigals. 1613; ed Fellowes, EM 19 1922, 1968 (rev).
See also Leighton, Teares or lamentacions, *1614*.

SIR WILLIAM LEIGHTON
d. 1616

§1

The teares or lamentacions of a sorrowfull soule. 1613 (words only), 1614 (with musical settings by Leighton, J. Dowland, J. Milton the elder, R. Johnson, T. Ford, E. Hooper, R. Kindersley, N. Giles, J. Coprario (Cooper), J. Bull, W. Byrd, F. Pilkington, T. Lupo, R. Jones, M. Peerson, O. Gibbons, T. Weelkes, J. Ward, J. Wilbye, A. Ferrabosco the younger, T. Thopull); selections ed J. F. Bridge, Sacred motets or anthems for four and five voices by W. Byrde and his contemporaries, [1922]; ed C. Hill 1970 (complete).

§2

Moore, V. L. Psalmes, teares and broken music. Bull John Rylands Lib 46 1964.

JOHN AMNER
d. 1641

Sacred hymnes, of 3, 4, 5 and 6 parts. 1615.

ROBERT TAILOUR

Sacred hymns. 1615. Settings by Tailour of psalm paraphrases by Sir Edwin Sandys.

GEORGE MASON and JOHN EARSDEN

§1

The ayres that were sung and played, at Brougham Castle in Westmerland, in the Kings entertainment. 1618; ed I. Spink, ELS 2nd ser 18 1963; ed Greer, els no 31 1970 (facs). The poems are generally attributed to Campion: *see col 1069, above.*

§2

Spink, I. Campion's entertainment at Brougham Castle 1617. In Music in English Renaissance drama, ed J. H. Long, Lexington Kentucky 1968.

THOMAS VAUTOR

The first set: beeing songs of divers ayres and natures. 1619; ed Fellowes, EM 34 1924, 1958 (rev).

MARTIN PEERSON
1571?–1650

Collections

Fellowes, English madrigal verse. Words only.
Complete works. Ed M. Wailes 1953–. Only a few pieces have so far appeared, pbd in separate sheet edns.

§1

Private musicke: or the first booke of ayres and dialogues. 1620; 4 songs ed Warlock and Wilson, English ayres (enlarged edn) vols 4 and 6.
Mottects or grave chamber musique. 1630.
See also Leighton, Teares or lamentacions, *1614*.

§2

Wailes, M. Martin Peerson. Monthly Musical Record Nov 1952.
—— Martin Peerson. Proc Royal Musical Assoc 80 1954.
Jones, A. Peerson: some new facts. Monthly Musical Record Sept 1955.

JOHN ATTEY

The first booke of ayres of foure parts. 1622; ed Fellowes, ELS 2nd ser 9 1926; ed Greer, els no 2 1967 (facs).

THOMAS TOMKINS
1572–1656

§1

Songes of 3, 4, 5 and 6 parts. 1622; ed Fellowes, EM 18 1922, 1960 (rev).
See also Morley, Triumphes of Oriana, *1601*.

§2

Rose, B. Thomas Tomkins. Proc Royal Musical Assoc 82 1956.
Stevens, D. Thomas Tomkins. 1957, New York 1967 (rev).

JOHN HILTON the younger
1599–1657

§1

Ayres: or fa las for three voyces. 1627; ed J. Warren, Musical Antiquarian Soc [13 1844]; ed Fellowes, English madrigal verse (words only); ed A. Goodchild 1955–60 (selection).
Catch that catch can: or a choice collection of catches, rounds and canons for 3 or 4 voyces. 1652 (collected by Hilton); rev and enlarged J. Playford 1658, 1663, 1667, [1669] (as The musical companion), 1672, 1673; ed Scott, Euterpe no 56 (selection); New York 1970 (facs of 1652).
For mss see Die Musik in Geschichte und Gegenwart.

§2

Brennecke, E. What shall we have that killed the deer? Musical Times Aug 1952.
Hart, E. F. The Restoration catch. Music & Letters 24 1953.

WALTER PORTER
c. 1590?–1659

§1

Madrigales and ayres of two, three, foure and five voyces. 1632; ed Fellowes, English madrigal verse (words only); ed Greer, els 35 1969 (facs).
Mottets for two voyces. 1657.
For a few works in later pbns see Die Musik in Geschichte und Gegenwart.

§2

Arkwright, G. E. P. An English pupil of Monteverdi. Musical Antiquary 4 1913.
Hughes, C. W. Porter, pupil of Monteverdi. Musical Quart 20 1934.
Spink, I. Porter and the last book of English madrigals. Acta Musicologica 26 1954. *See also* 27 1955.

MUSICALL BANQUET

A musicall banquet. 1651. Pbd by J. Benson and J. Playford. Pt 3, as Musick and mirth, contains catches and rounds by W. Crawford, W. Ellis, J. Hilton, T. Holmes, W. Howes, W. Lawes, E. Nelham, W. Smegergill and anon.

MUSICKS RECREATION

Musicks recreation: on the lyra viol. 1652, 1661, 1669, 1682. Pbd by J. Playford. Contains 2 anon songs.

SELECT MUSICALL AYRES AND DIALOGUES

Select musicall ayres and dialogues, for one and two voyces. 1652. Pbd by J. Playford. Pt 2 as The second booke of ayres. Songs by C. Colman, R. Johnson, N. Lanier, H. Lawes, W. Lawes, W. Smegergill, R. Smith, J. Taylor, W. Webb, J. Wilson, anon. *See below.*
Select musicall ayres and dialogues, in three bookes. 1653. Pbd by J. Playford. Contains most of the songs ptd in the preceding work with addn of a 3rd bk of 15 songs by N. Lanier, W. Lawes, W. Tompkins, W. Webb and J. Wilson; 1659 (enlarged as Select ayres and dialogues for one, two and three voyces), 1669 (as bk 1 of The treasury of musick); The treasury of musick, Ridgewood NJ 1966 (facs); ed Spink, English songs (selection).

HENRY LAWES
1595–1662

Selections

Dolmetsch, Select English songs: 9 songs by Lawes.
Potter, Reliquary 1: 9 songs by Lawes.
Lewis, A. One song in Samuel Pepys, three songs of his choice. Paris 1936.
—— Lawes: three songs from the Treasury of music. Paris 1938.
5 songs ed H. J. Foss in The mask of Comus, ed E. H. Visiak 1937.
Dart, R. T. Ten ayres by Lawes. 1956.
Sabol, Songs and dances: 6 songs by Lawes.
Jesson, R. William and Henry Lawes: [4] dialogues for two voices and continuo [from Treasury of musick]. University Park Pa 1964.
Spink, English songs. 28 songs by Lawes.

§1

Ayres and dialogues: the first booke. [Pbd by J. Playford] 1653; Select ayres and dialogues (bk 2 of Treasury of musick), 1669 (selection); The treasury, Ridgewood NJ 1966 (facs).
The second book of ayres, and dialogues. [Pbd by J. Playford] 1655; Select ayres and dialogues (bk 2 of Treasury of musick), 1669 (selection); The treasury, Ridgewood NJ 1966 (facs).
Ayres and dialogues: the third book. [Pbd by J. Playford] 1658, 1669 (as bk 3 of Treasury of musick); The treasury, Ridgewood NJ 1966 (facs).
See also Hilton, Catch that catch can, *1652 ;* Select musicall ayres, *1652 ;* Select musical ayres, *1653 ;* A brief introduction to the skill of music, *1660 ;* The musical companion, *1673 ;* New ayres and dialogues, *1678 ;* Synopsis of vocal musick, 1680. *For mss see* Die Musik in Geschichte und Gegenwart.

§2

Bridge, J. F. Twelve good musicians from John Bull to Henry Purcell. 1920. Ch 8.
Evans, W. McC. Lawes: musician and friend of poets. New York 1941.
—— To Amathea. PQ 23 1944.
Hart, E. F. Introduction to Lawes. Music & Letters 32 1951.
Maynard, W. Henry Hughes: a forgotten poet. Music & Letters 33 1952.
McGrady, R. J. Lawes and the concept of 'just note and accent'. Music & Letters 50 1969.
Willetts, P. J. The Lawes manuscript [BM additional 53,723, formerly Loan 35]. 1969.

JOHN PLAYFORD
1623–86

§1

A breefe introduction to the skill of musick. 1654 (no songs), 1655 (8 anon songs), 1658 (no songs), 1660 (33 songs by T. Brewer, T. Campion, J. Dowland, H. Lawes, W. Lawes, J. Savile, W. Webb, J. Wilson, anon); over 20 edns to 1730; 1966 (facs of 1674).

§2

Kidson, F. Playford and 17th-century music publishing. Musical Quart 4 1918.
Pulver, J. Playford's Introduction to the skill of music. Monthly Musical Record July 1922.
Hayes, G. R. Playford's Skill of musick. Musical Opinion Feb 1926.
Day, C. L. and E. B. Murrie. English song-books 1651–1702 and their publishers. Library 4th ser 16 1936.
—— English song-books 1651–1702: a bibliography. 1940 (Bibl Soc).

JOHN GAMBLE
1615?–87

Selections

Spink, English songs.

§1

Ayres and dialogues. 1656, 1657.
Ayres and dialogues: the second book. 1659.

§2

Hughes, C. W. Gamble's commonplace book. Music & Letters 26 1945.

Duckles, V. The Gamble manuscript [New York Public Lib, Drexel 4257] as a source of continuo song in England. Jnl of Amer Musicological Soc 1 1948.

JOHN WILSON
1595–1674
Selections

Cutts, Musique de la troupe de Shakespeare: 12 songs.

Holst, I. Ten songs from Wilson's Cheerful ayres or ballads. 1959.

Spink, English songs: 13 songs.

§1

Cheerfull ayres or ballads. 1660. Songs by R. Johnson, N. Lanier, J. Wilson and anon originally composed for one voice, arranged for 3 voices by Wilson.

See also Hilton, Catch that catch can, *1652 etc;* Select musicall ayres and dialogues, *1652, 1653;* Select ayres and dialogues, *1659; Playford*, A breefe introduction, *1660;* The treasury of music, *1669.*

§2

Cutts, J. P. Wilson and Lovelace's The rose. N & Q April 1953.

—— Seventeenth-century lyrics: Oxford, Bodleian ms Mus.b.1. Musica Disciplina 10 1956.

—— Seventeenth-century songs and lyrics from Edinburgh University Library music ms DC 1.69. Musica Disciplina 13 1959.

—— Thomas Heywood's The gentry to the King's Head and John Wilson's setting. N & Q Oct 1961. With list of Wilson's music for Court and theatrical entertainments.

Duckles, V. The 'curious' art of Wilson: an introduction to his songs and lute music. Jnl of Amer Musicological Soc 7 1954.

D. C. G.

3. DRAMA

I. INTRODUCTION

(1) BIBLIOGRAPHIES AND DICTIONARIES OF PLAYS AND DRAMATISTS

See W. W. Greg, A list of masques etc, 1902, and Malone Soc Collections vol 1 pts 4–5, Oxford 1911, vol 2 pt 3, Oxford 1931, for accounts of the earliest bibliographers' lists.

Phillips, E. Theatrum poetarum. 1675; rev S. E. Bridges 1800.

Winstanley, W. Lives of the most famous English poets. 1687.

Langbaine, G. Momus triumphans. 1688.

— An account of the English dramatick poets. Oxford 1691, 1698 (rev), 1699.

Jacob, G. The poetical register. 1719, 1723.

Mottley, J. A complete list of all the English dramatic poets. In T. Whincop, Scanderbeg: or love and liberty: a tragedy written by the late Thomas Whincop esq; to which are added A list of all the dramatic authors and some account of their lives, and of all the dramatic pieces ever published in the English language, to the year 1747, 1747.

Baker, D. E. The companion to the playhouse. 2 vols 1764; rev I. Reed 2 vols 1782; rev S. Jones 3 vols 1812.

Capell, E. Notitia dramatica: or tables of ancient plays. Rptd in his Notes and various readings vol 3, 1783.

Halliwell-Phillipps, J. O. A dictionary of old English plays. 1860.

Lowe, R. W. A bibliographical account of English theatrical literature. 1888.

Arnott, J. F. and J. W. Robinson. English theatrical literature 1559–1900: a bibliography incorporating R. W. Lowe's A bibliographical account of English theatrical literature 1888. 1970.

Hazlitt, W. C. A manual for the collector and amateur of old English plays. 1892.

Greg, W. W. A list of English plays written before 1643 and printed before 1700. 1892.

— A list of masques, pageants etc, supplementary to A list of English plays. 1902.

— A bibliography of the English printed drama to the Restoration. 4 vols 1939–59 (Bibl Soc).

— Authorship attribution in the early play-lists 1656–71. Trans Edinburgh Bibl Soc 2 1946.

— The date of the earliest play-catalogues. Library 5th ser 21 1947.

Chambers, E. K. The medieval stage. 2 vols Oxford 1903.

— The Elizabethan stage. 4 vols (and index vol) Oxford 1923.

Schelling, F. E. Elizabethan drama. 2 vols Boston 1908.

Reyher, P. Bibliographie des ballets de 1603 à 1640. In his Les masques anglais, Paris 1909.

Creizenach, W. Verlorengegangene englische Dramen aus dem Zeitalter Shakespeares. Sh Jb 54 1918.

Sibley, G. M. The lost plays and masques 1500–1642. Ithaca 1933.

Barrett, W. P. Chart of plays 1584–1623. 1934.

Harbage, A. Elizabethan and seventeenth-century play manuscripts. PMLA 50 1935. Addns 52 1937.

— Notes on manuscript plays. TLS 20 June 1936.

— Annals of English drama 975–1700. Philadelphia 1940; rev S. Schoenbaum 1964.

— A choice ternary: belated issues of Elizabethan plays. N & Q July 1942.

Dawson, G. E. An early list of Elizabethan plays. Library 4th ser 15 1935.

Kirschbaum, L. A census of bad quartos. RES 14 1938.

McCabe, W. H. The play-list of the English college of St Omers 1592–1762. Revue de Littérature Comparée 17 1938.

Adams, J. Q. Hill's list of early plays in ms. Library 4th ser 20 1940.

Wells, H. W. A chronological list of extant plays produced in or about London 1581–1642. New York 1940, Oxford 1940.

Woodward, G. L. and J. G. McManaway. A check-list of English plays 1641–1700. Chicago 1945; F. T. Bowers, Supplement, Charlottesville 1949.

Taylor, A. Renaissance guides to books: an inventory and some conclusions. Berkeley 1945.

Stratman, C. J. A survey of the Bodleian library's holdings in the field of English printed tragedy. Bodleian Lib Record 7 1964.

— Dramatic play-lists 1591–1963. BNYPL Feb–March 1966.

— Bibliography of English printed tragedy 1565–1900. Carbondale 1966.

Ribner, I. Tudor and Stuart drama. New York 1966.

Young, S. C. A check-list of Tudor and Stuart induction plays. PQ 48 1969.

Berquist, G. W. Three centuries of English and American plays: a checklist; England 1500–1800, United States 1714–1830. New York 1963.

Lennam, T. N. S. Sir Edward Dering's collection of play-books 1619–24. Shakespeare Quart 16 1965.

Bentley, G. E. The Jacobean and Caroline stage. 7 vols Oxford 1941–68. Vols 3–5 on plays and playwrights.

Hunter, G. K. In F. P. Wilson, The English drama 1485–1585, Oxford 1969 (OHEL).

(2) COLLECTIONS OF PLAYS

Collections on Shakespeare have been omitted. For the content of earlier collections see W. C. Hazlitt, A manual for the collector of old English plays, 1892; for later, E. K. Chambers, The Elizabethan stage vol 3, Oxford 1923. The contents of 3 major collections are given here under Bang, Farmer and Greg.

Dodsley, R. A select collection of old plays. 12 vols 1744; enlarged by I. Reed 12 vols 1780; ed O. Gilchrist and J. P. Collier 12 vols 1825-7; ed W. C. Hazlitt 15 vols 1874-6 (83 plays). *See T. Amyot, below.*

Chetwood, W. R. A select collection of old plays. Dublin 1750.

Hawkins, T. The origin of the English drama. 3 vols Oxford 1773.

Lamb, C. Specimens of the English dramatic poets. 1808; ed I. Gollancz 2 vols 1893.

Scott, W. Ancient British drama. 3 vols 1810.

Dilke, C. W. Old English plays. 6 vols 1814-15.

Baldwyn, C. The old English drama. 2 vols 1825.

Collier, J. P. Five old plays. 1828, 1833.

— Five old plays 1851. A different selection.

White, T. The old English drama. 3 vols 1830.

Child, F. J. Four old plays. Cambridge Mass 1848.

Amyot, T. et al. A supplement to Dodsley's Old English plays. 4 vols 1853.

Keltie, J. S. The works of the British dramatists. 1870.

Hazlitt, W. C. Shakespeare's library. Pt 1, 4 vols; pt 2, 2 vols 1875.

Simpson, R. The school of Shakspere. 2 vols 1878.

Bullen, A. H. A collection of old English plays. 4 vols 1882-5.

— Old English plays. New ser 3 vols 1887-90.

The Mermaid series. 1887-1909. Selected plays separately edited.

Pollard, A. W. English miracle plays, moralities and interludes. Oxford 1890, 1927 (rev). Selected scenes.

The Temple dramatists. 1896-1906; new ser 1933. Selected single plays, separately edited.

Manly, J. M. Specimens of the pre-Shaksperean drama. 2 vols Boston 1897-8.

Jahrbuch der deutschen Shakespeare-Gesellschaft. 1897-1964. Earlier vols sometimes contain texts of plays.

Brandl, A. Quellen des weltlichen Dramas in England vor Shakespeare: ein Ergänzungsband zu Dodsleys Old English plays. Quellen und Forschungen 80 1898.

Baker, G. P. et al. The belles-lettres series: section 3, The English drama. Boston 1902-15. Selected plays, separately edited.

Bang, W. Materialien zur Kunde des älteren englischen Dramas. Louvain 1902-14. Continued by H. de Vocht as Materials for the study of old English drama, Louvain 1927-58. 69 vols in all. From this series only facs of plays are listed, in order of pbn:

H. Chettle and J. Day, The blind beggar of Bednall Green 1659; The King and Queen's entertainment at Richmond 1656; T. Heywood, Pleasant dialogues and dramas 1637; Everyman; Godly Queen Hester 1561; B. Barnes, The Devil's charter 1607; B. Jonson, Dramas 1616; Pedantius; Jonson, Everyman in his humour 1601; Jonson, The sad shepherd 1640; The interlude of Youth, with fragments of the play of Lucres and of Nature; The Queen 1653; A. Fraunce, Victoria ms; Jonson, Every man out of his humour 1600 (Holmes); Jonson, Every man out of his humour 1600 (Ling); A. Brewer, The love-sick King 1655; T. Dekker, Satiro-mastix 1602; Jonson, The fountain of self-love 1601 (Cynthia's revels); J. Ford, Dramatic works pt 1; Everyman (Skot's edn); J. Bale, King Johan (ms); (G. Chapman), Sir Gyles Goosecappe 1606; Everyman (Pynson fragments); T. Richards, Tragedy of Messalina 1640; S. Daniel, The tragedy of Cleopatra 1611; A new interlude of Impatient Poverty 1560; How a man may choose a good wife from a bad 1608; E. Sharpham, The fleire 1607;

J. Mason, The turk 1610 and 1632; J. Studley, Seneca's Agamemnon and Medea (trn) 1566; Jonson, A tale of a tub 1640; W. Heming, The Jew's tragedy 1662; Jasper Heywood, Seneca's Troas, Thyestes, Hercules Furens (trn) 1559, 1560, 1561; W. Sampson, Vow-breaker 1636; T. May, Tragedy of Julius Agrippina; J. Ford, Dramatic works pt 2; S. Baylie, The wizard (ms); Lust's dominion 1657; R. Gomersall, The tragedy of Lodovick Sforsa 1628; Jonson, Poetaster 1602, Sejanus 1605; Nebuchadnezzars fierie furness (ms); Jonson, Volpone 1607; M. Fane, Raguaillo d'Oceano, Candy restored (mss); N. Udall, Roister Doister 1566?; J. Rickets, Byrsa basilica (ms) and trn by R. H. Bowers; T. Middleton, The witch (ms); Jonson, The alchemist 1612; L. Barry, Ramalley 1611.

Gayley, C. M. et al. Representative English comedies. 3 vols New York 1904-14. Contains 19 plays from John Heywood to Shirley, with critical introds.

Farmer, J. S. Early English dramatists. 12 vols 1905-8.

— The museum dramatists. 1906.

— Tudor facsimile texts. 143 vols 1907-14. *TFT.* Some texts rptd in the Student's facs edn; plays are listed in alphabetical order by title:

T. Lupton, All for money 1578; R.B., Apius and Virginia 1575; Arden of Feversham 1592; P. Massinger, Believe as ye list (ms); The birth of Merlin 1662; J. Day, The blind beggar of Bednal Green 1659; T.D., The bloody banquet 1620; Caesar and Pompey 1607; Calisto and Melebea 1527?; T. Preston, Cambyses 1569?; The castle of perseverance (ms); J. Bale, The chief promises of God 1538; Clyomon and Clamydes 1599; R. Wilson, The cobbler's prophecie 1594; N. Woodes, The conflict of conscience 1581; The contention between liberality and prodigality 1602; The contention betwixt York and Lancaster 1594; R. Edwards, Damon and Pithias 1571; A. Munday, The death of Robert, Earl of Huntingdon 1601; B. Barnes, The Devil's charter 1607; C. Marlowe and T. Nashe, Dido, Queene of Carthage 1594; T. Ingelend, The disobedient child 1570?; Marlowe, Doctor Faustus 1604; Munday, The downfall of Robert, Earl of Huntingdon 1601; G. Chapman et al, Eastward hoe 1605; W. Haughton, Englishmen for my money 1616; Everyman 1500-6?; Every woman in her humour 1609; Fair Em 1631; The fair maid of Bristow 1605; The famous victories of Henry the fifth 1598; T. Sackville and T. Norton, Ferrex and Porrex 1565; R. Greene, Friar Bacon and Friar Bungay 1594; W.S. (William Stevenson?), Gammer Gurton's needle 1575; Gentleness and nobility 1527-9?; George a Greene 1599; R. Wilmot et al, Gismond of Salerne (ms); G. Gascoigne, The glass of government 1575; J. Cooke, Greene's tuquoque 1614; Grim the collier of Croydon 1662; Histrio-mastix 1610; H. Chettle, Hoffman 1631; S.S., The honest lawyer 1616; J. Pickering, Horestes 1567; How a man may choose a good wife from a bad 1602; Impatient poverty 1560; Jack Drum's entertainment 1601; Jack Juggler 1563; Jacob and Esau 1568; Johan the evangelist 1550?; Munday, John-a-Kent and John-a-Cymber (ms); J. Heywood, John John the husband 1546?; King Darius 1565; King Edward the Third 1596; King Leir 1605; W. Shakespeare, King Richard the Third 1597; A knack to know an honest man 1596; A knack to know a knave 1594; A larum for London 1602; U. Fulwell, Like will to like 1587; The life and death of Jack Straw 1593; The life and death of Captain Thomas Stukeley 1605; L. Wager, The life and repentance of Mary Magdalene 1567; Locrine 1595; The London prodigal 1605; W. Wager, The longer thou livest, the more foole thou art 1569?; Look about you and be not wroth 1600; T. Lodge and R. Greene, A looking glass for London 1598; R. Wever, Lusty Juventus 1560?; J. Skelton, Magnyfycence 1530?; Mankind (ms); The marriage of wit and science 1569?; J. Lyly, The maid's metamorphosis 1600; The merry Devil of Edmonton 1608; Mind, will and understanding (Wisdom) (ms); G. Wilkins, The miseries of enforced marriage 1607; T. Hughes, The misfortunes of Arthur 1587; Mucedorus, 1598; H. Medwall, Nature 1516–20?; (J. Rastell), The nature of the four elements 1517–27; Nero 1607; New custom 1573; Nice wanton 1560; S.R., The noble soldier 1634; T. Dekker and J. Webster, Northward hoe 1607; J. Heywood, The pardoner and the frere 1533; H. Chettle et al, Patient Grissil 1603; The pedler's prophecy 1595; The pilgrimage to Parnassus (ms); J. Heywood, The play of love 1534; J. Heywood, The play of the weather 1533; G. Whetstone, Promos and Cassandra 1578; W.S., The puritan 1607; L. Barry, Ram alley 1611; Respublica (ms); The return from Parnassus 2 pts (ms and 1606); Richard Duke of York 1600; T. Middleton and T. Dekker, The roaring girl 1611; (Chapman) Sir Gyles Goosecappe 1606; M. Drayton et al, Sir John Oldcastle 1600; Munday et al, Sir Thomas More (ms); Dekker and J. Webster, Sir Thomas Wyat 1607; Solimon and Perseda 1599 (doubtful); Swetnam the woman-hater 1620; The taming of a shrew 1594; R. Wilmot et al, Tancred and Gismund 1591; J. Bale, The temptation of Our Lord 1538; Thersites 1562?; Thomas Lord Cromwell 1602; R. Wilson, The three ladies of London 1584; J. Bale, The three laws 1538; Wilson, The three lords and three ladies of London 1590; G. Wapull, The tide tarrieth no man 1576; Tom Tyler and his wife 1661; The trial of treasure 1567; The troublesome reign of King John 1591; The trial of chivalry 1605; H. Porter, The two angry women of Abington 1599; R. Yarington, Two lamentable tragedies 1601; R. Armin, Two maids of Moreclacke 1609; The two merry milkmaids 1620; J. Fletcher and Shakespeare, The two noble kinsmen 1634; Two wise men 1619; R.A., The valiant welshman 1615; S. Brandon, The virtuous Octavia 1598; A warning for fair women 1599; The wars of Cyrus 1594; The weakest goeth to the wall 1600; Wealth and health 1557?; Dekker and Webster, Westward hoe 1607; S. Rawley, When you see me you know me 1613; Wily beguiled 1606; The wisdom of Doctor Dodypoll 1600; J. Redford, Wit and science (ms); The wit of a woman 1604; J. Heywood, Witty and witless (ms); The world and the child 1522; A Yorkshire tragedy 1608; Youth 1530?, 1557?, 1562?.

Greg, W. W., F. P. Wilson and A. Brown. The Malone Society reprints. Oxford 1907–. Facs with introds usually on textual matters; listed here in order of pbn:
G. Peele, The battle of Alcazar 1594; R. Greene, The history of Orlando Furioso 1594; The interlude of Johan the evangelist 1550?; The interlude of wealth and health 1557?; The history of king Leir 1605; J. Rastell?, The interlude of Calisto and Melebea 1527?; W.S., The tragedy of Locrine 1595; A. Munday, The life of Sir John Oldcastle 1600; R. Greene, The tragical reign of Selimus 1594; Peele, The old wives tale 1595; J. Philip, The play of patient Grissell 1569?; Iphigenia ct Aulis tr Lady Lumley (ms); S. Brandon, The virtuous Octavia 1598; A. Munday?, Fidele and Fortunio: the two Italian gentlemen 1585 (imperfect); the second maiden's tragedy (ms); Peele, The arraignment of Paris 1584; Tom Tyler and his wife 1661; T. Lodge, The wounds of civil war 1594; A knack to know an honest man

1596; The birth of Hercules (ms); R.B., Apius and Virginia 1575; Peele, King Edward the first 1593; The comedy of George a greene 1599; The tragedy of Caesar's revenge 1606?; The book of Sir Thomas More (ms); Peele, The love of King David and fair Bethsabe 1599; H. Porter, The two angry women of Abington 1599; The weakest goeth to the wall 1600; Wily beguiled 1606; W. Haughton, Englishmen for my money 1616; The resurrection of Our Lord (ms imperfect); Clyomon and Clamydes 1599; Look about you 1600; A larum for London 1602; The contention between liberality and prodigality 1602; The wit of a woman 1604; Lady Elizabeth Cary: the tragedy of Mariam 1616; R. Wilson, The cobler's prophecy 1594; The pedlar's prophecy 1595; R. Wilmot et al, The tragedy of Tancred and Gismund 1591; The tragedy of Tiberius 1607; The Welsh embassador (ms); Jonson, Every man out of his humour 1600 (Holme); Greene, The Scottish history of James the Fourth 1598; J. Marston, Antonio and Mellida, and Antonio's revenge 1602; The Christian Prince (ms); Munday, John a Kent and John a Cumber (ms); T. Kyd, The Spanish tragedy, with additions 1602; Marlowe, Edward 2nd 1594; Greene, Alphonsus King of Aragon 1599; Greene, Friar Bacon and friar Bungay 1594; P. Massinger, Believe as you list (ms); Fair Em 1593?; Edmund Ironside (ms); Chapman, The blind beggar of Alexandria 1598; P. Massinger, The parliament of love (ms); Marlowe, The massacre at Paris (1594?); The true tragedy of Richard 3rd 1594; The first part of the reign of king Richard 2nd: or Thomas of Woodstock (ms); The two noble ladies (ms); The rare triumphs of love and fortune 1589; J. Bale, King Johan (ms); T. Lodge and Greene, A looking glass for London and England 1594; W. Mountfort, The launching of the Mary (ms); Jack Juggler 1563?; J. Lyly, Alexander and Campaspe 1584; N. Udall, Ralph Roister Doister 1566?; T. Heywood, If you know not me you know nobody 2 pts 1605; John of Bordeaux (ms); J. Clavell, The soddered citizen (ms); T. Garter, The most virtuous and godly Susanna 1578; Jack Juggler 1565–70? (3rd edn); Charlemagne: or the distracted Emperor (ms); Chapman, An humorous day's mirth 1597; Lyly, Mother Bombie 1594; Arden of Feversham 1592; T. Middleton, The witch (ms); Kyd, The Spanish tragedy 1592; J. Rastell?, Gentleness and nobility 1527–9?; J. Day, Law tricks 1608; J. Fletcher, Demetrius and Evanthe: or the humorous lieutenant (ms); H. Chettle, The tragedy of Hoffman 1631; J. Fletcher, Bonduca (ms); J. Redford, Wit and science (ms); N. Woodes, The conflict of conscience 1581; S. Rowley, When you see me you know me 1613; Middleton, Honourable entertainments 1621; T. Heywood, The captives (ms); R. Daborne, Poor man's comfort (ms); Dick of Devonshire (ms); July and Julian (ms); The life and death of Jack Straw 1594; Jacob and Essau 1568; R. Edwards, Damon and Pythias 1571; The fatal marriage (ms); H. Glapthorne, The lady mother (ms); The telltale (ms); The marriage of wit and science 1569–70; The knave in grain 1640; T.D., The bloody banquet 1639; J. Pickering, Horestes 1567; The fair maid of the Exchange 1607; G. Wilkins, The miseries of enforced marriage 1607; A knack to know a knave 1594; The wisdom of Doctor Doddypoll 1600; A. Munday, The downfall of Robert Earl of Huntingdon 1601; Munday, The death of Robert Earl of Huntingdon 1601.

The Malone Society collections. Oxford 1907–. The earlier vols contain fragmentary plays:
Vol 1 pt 1, Love feigned and unfeigned: a fragmentary morality; The prodigal son: a fragmentary interlude c. 1530; pt 2, Robin Hood and the sheriff of Nottingham c. 1475; A play of Robin Hood for May-games;

The play of Lucrece: a fragmentary interlude; pt 3, Albion knight: an imperfect morality; Temperance and humility: a fragmentary morality; pts 4–5, The cruel debtor: a fragmentary morality; vol 2 pt 2, The cruel debtor: a further fragment; pt 3, Somebody and others, or the spoiling of Lady Verity: a fragment.

Brooke, C. F. T. The Shakespeare apocrypha. Oxford 1908.

— and N. B. Paradise. English drama 1580–1642. Boston 1933.

Thorndike, A. H. The minor Elizabethan drama. 2 vols 1910 (EL).

Bond, R. W. Early plays from the Italian. Oxford 1911.

Neilson, W. A. The chief Elizabethan dramatists. Boston 1911.

Cunliffe, J. W. Early English classical tragedies. Oxford 1912.

Schelling, F. E. et al. Masterpieces of the English drama. New York 1912.

— Typical Elizabethan plays. New York 1926, 1931 (enlarged).

Wheeler, C. B. Six plays by contemporaries of Shakespeare. Oxford 1915 (WC).

Tatlock, J. S. P. and R. G. Martin. Representative English plays. New York 1916.

Adams, J. Q. Chief pre-Shakespearean dramas. Boston 1924.

Oliphant, E. H. C. Shakespeare and his fellow dramatists. 2 vols New York 1929.

Rylands, G. Six Elizabethan tragedies. 1931.

Spencer, H. Elizabethan plays. Boston 1933.

Baskervill, C. R., V. B. Heltzel and A. H. Nethercot. Elizabethan and Stuart plays. New York 1934.

Boas, F. S. Five pre-Shakespearean comedies. Oxford 1934 (WC).

McIlwraith, A. K. Five Elizabethan comedies. Oxford 1934 (WC).

— Five Elizabethan tragedies. Oxford 1938 (WC).

— Five Stuart tragedies. Oxford 1953 (WC).

Dunn, E. C. Eight famous Elizabethan plays. New York 1932.

Howard, E. J. Ten Elizabethan plays. 1935.

Cellini, B. Drammi pre-Shakespeariani. Naples 1958.

Bald, R. C. Six Elizabethan plays. Boston 1963.

Franklin, A. Seven miracle plays. Oxford 1963.

Harrier, R. C. An anthology of Jacobean and Stuart drama. 2 vols New York 1963.

Lawrence, R. G. Early seventeenth-century drama. 1963 (EL).

Regents Renaissance drama series. Lincoln Nebraska 1963–. Modernized texts of individual plays, separately edited.

New Mermaids series. 1964–. Modernized texts of individual plays, separately edited.

Armstrong, W. A. Elizabethan history plays. Oxford 1965 (WC).

Fountainwell drama texts. Edinburgh 1968–. Old-spelling texts of individual plays, separately edited.

Gomme, A. H. Jacobean tragedies. Oxford 1969.

Masques

Nichols, J. The progresses and public processions of Queen Elizabeth. 4 vols 1788–1821, 3 vols 1823.

— The progresses, processions and magnificent festivities of King James I. 4 vols 1828.

Cunningham, P. and J. P. Collier. Inigo Jones: a life; and five Court masques. 1848.

Evans, H. A. English masques. 1897.

Sabol, A. J. Songs and dances for the Stuart masque. New York 1959.

Spencer, T. J. B. and S. W. Wells (ed). A book of masques in honour of Allardyce Nicoll. Cambridge 1967.

Lefkowitz, M. Trois masques à la cour de Charles d'Angleterre. Paris 1970. Texts and music of Shirley, The triumph of peace; The triumphs of the Prince d'amour; Davenant, Britannia triumphans.

(3) HISTORY, CRITICISM AND SPECIAL STUDIES

Dryden, J. Essays [1663–1700]. Ed W. P. Ker 2 vols Oxford 1900; Of dramatic poesy and other essays, ed G. Watson 2 vols 1962 (EL).

Rymer, T. The tragedies of the last age considered and examined. 1678.

— A short view of tragedy. 1693.

Langbaine, G. An account of the English dramatick poets. Oxford 1691.

Baker, D. E. The companion to the playhouse. 2 vols 1764, 1782 (rev as Biographia dramatica), 3 vols in 4 1812.

Warton, T. The history of English poetry. 4 vols 1774–81; ed W. C. Hazlitt 4 vols 1871.

Lamb, C. Specimens of the English dramatic poets. 1808; ed I. Gollancz 2 vols 1893.

Schlegel, A. W. Vorlesungen über dramatische Kunst. Heidelberg 1809–11; tr 1846.

Hazlitt, W. Lectures on the dramatic literature of the age of Elizabeth. 1818.

Collier, J. P. The history of English dramatic poetry to the time of Shakespeare, and annals of the stage to the Restoration. 3 vols 1831, 1879 (rev).

Coleridge, S. T. Literary remains. Vols 1–2, 1836.

— Notes and lectures upon Shakespeare and some of the old poets and dramatists. Ed Sara Coleridge 2 vols 1849.

Mézières, A. J. F. Prédécesseurs et contemporains de Shakspeare. Paris 1863.

— Contemporains et successeurs de Shakspeare. Paris 1864.

Klein, J. L. Geschichte des Dramas. Vols 12–13, Leipzig 1865–86.

Hazlitt, W. C. Handbook to the popular and dramatic literature of Great Britain. 1867.

— The English drama and stage 1543–1664. 1869.

Ward, A. W. A history of English dramatic literature to the death of Queen Anne. 2 vols 1875, 3 vols 1899 (rev).

Jusserand, J. J. Le théâtre en Angleterre jusqu'aux prédécesseurs immédiats de Shakespeare. Paris 1878.

Proelss, R. Geschichte des neuren Dramas. 3 vols Leipzig 1880–3.

Symonds, J. A. Shakspere's predecessors in the English drama. 1884, 1900 (rev), 1906.

Fleay, F. G. A chronicle history of the London stage 1559–1642. 1890.

— A biographical chronicle of the English drama 1559–1642. 2 vols 1891.

Lowell, J. R. The old English dramatists. Boston 1892.

Creizenach, W. Geschichte des neueren Dramas. 5 vols Halle 1893–1916; partly tr as The English drama in the age of Shakespeare, 1916.

Boas, F. S. Shakspere and his predecessors. 1896.

— An introduction to Tudor drama. Oxford 1933.

— An introduction to Stuart drama. Oxford 1946.

Seccombe, T. and J. W. Allen. The age of Shakespeare 1579–1631. 2 vols 1903.

Matthews, B. The development of the drama. New York 1904.

Crawford, C. Collectanea. 2 vols Stratford 1906–7.

Swinburne, A. C. The age of Shakespeare. 1908.

— Contemporaries of Shakespeare. 1919.

Thorndike, A. H. Tragedy. Boston 1908.

— English comedy. New York 1929.

Schelling, F. E. Elizabethan drama 1558–1642. 2 vols Boston 1908.

— Elizabethan playwrights: a short history of the English drama to 1642. 1925.

CHEL vols 5–6. Cambridge 1910.
Brooke, G. F. T. The Tudor drama. 1912.
Wallace, C. W. The evolution of the English drama up to Shakespeare. Berlin 1912.
Symons, A. Studies in the Elizabethan drama. 1920.
Eliot, T. S. The sacred wood. 1920.
— Elizabethan essays. 1934.
Spens, Janet. Elizabethan drama. 1922.
Archer, W. The old drama and the new. 1923.
Harrison, G. B. Shakespeare's fellows. 1923.
— The story of Elizabethan drama. Cambridge 1924.
Nicoll, A. British drama: an historical survey. 1925.
Reed, A. W. Early Tudor drama. 1926.
Mackenzie, A. M. The playgoer's handbook to the English Renaissance drama. 1927.
Eckhardt, E. Das englische Drama im Zeitalter der Reformation und der Hochrenaissance. Berlin 1928.
— Das englische Drama der Spätrenaissance: Shakespeares Nachfolger. Berlin 1929.
Sisson, C. J. The Elizabethan dramatists, except Shakespeare. 1928.
— Lost plays of Shakespeare's age. Cambridge 1936.
Aronstein, P. Das englische Renaissance-Drama. Leipzig 1929.
Le théâtre élisabéthain. Cahiers du Sud 10 1933.
Ellis-Fermor, U. M. The Jacobean drama: an interpretation. 1936, 1958 (rev).
— The frontiers of drama. 1945.

Knights, L. C. Drama and society in the age of Jonson. 1937.
Wells, H. W. Elizabethan and Jacobean playwrights. New York 1939.
Parrott, T. M. and R. H. Ball. A short view of Elizabethan drama. New York 1943.
Maugeri, A. Il dramma elisabettiano. 3 vols Ferrara 1944–6.
Wilson, F. P. Elizabethan and Jacobean. Oxford 1945.
— The English drama 1485–1585. Oxford 1969 (OHEL).
Messiaen, P. Théâtre anglais: Moyen Age et 16e siècle. Paris 1949.
Stamm, R. Geschichte des englischen Theaters. Berne 1951.
Foligno, C. Note sul dramma inglese. Naples 1951.
Simpson, P. Studies in Elizabethan drama. Oxford 1955.
Sanvic, R. Le théâtre élisabéthain. Brussels 1955.
Brown, J. R. and B. Harris (ed). Jacobean theatre. 1960.
— (ed). Elizabethan theatre. 1966.
Kaufmann, R. (ed). Elizabethan drama. New York 1961.
Blanchart, P. Le théâtre contemporain et les élisabéthains. Etudes Anglaises 13 1961.
Clunes, A. The British theatre. 1965.
Anikst, A. Teatr epokhi Shekspira. Moscow 1965.
Cunningham, J. E. Elizabethan and early Stuart drama. 1966.
Barish, J. A. The new theater and the old: reversions and rejuvenations. In Reinterpretations of Elizabethan drama, ed N. Rabkin, New York 1969.

SPECIAL STUDIES

Tragedy

Singer, H. W. Das bürgerliche Trauerspiel in England. Leipzig 1892.
Fischer, R. Zur Kunstentwicklung der englischen Tragödie bis zu Shakespeare. Strasbourg 1893.
Simpson, P. The theme of revenge in Elizabethan tragedy. Proc Br Acad 21 1935; rptd in his Studies in Elizabethan drama, Oxford 1955.
Bradbrook, M. C. Themes and conventions of Elizabethan tragedy. Cambridge 1935.
Bowers, F. T. The audience and the revenger of Elizabethan tragedy. SP 31 1934.
— The audience and the poisoners of Elizabethan tragedy. JEGP 36 1937.
— Elizabethan revenge tragedy 1587–1642. Princeton 1940.
Spencer, T. Death and Elizabethan tragedy. Cambridge Mass 1936.
Craig, H. The shackling of accidents: a study of Elizabethan tragedy. PQ 19 1940.
Adams, H. H. English domestic or homiletic tragedy 1575–1642. New York 1943.
Prior, M. E. The language of tragedy. New York 1947.
Leech, C. The implications of tragedy. English 6 1947; rptd in his Shakespeare's tragedies and other studies in seventeenth-century drama, 1950.
Clemen, W. Die Tragödie vor Shakespeare: ihre Entwicklung im Spiegel der dramatischen Rede. Heidelberg 1955; tr as English tragedy before Shakespeare: the development of dramatic speech, 1961.
Sewell, R. B. The vision of tragedy. New Haven 1959.
Johnson, S. F. The tragic hero in early Elizabethan drama. In Studies in English Renaissance drama, ed J. W. Bennett et al, New York 1959.
Ornstein, R. The moral vision of Jacobean tragedy. Madison 1960.
Ribner, I. Jacobean tragedy: the quest for moral order. 1962.
Hathorn, R. I. Tragedy, myth and mystery. Bloomington 1962.
Harbage, A. Intrigue in Elizabethan tragedy. In Essays

on Shakespeare and Elizabethan drama in honor of Hardin Craig, New York 1962.
Turner, R. Y. Pathos and the Gorboduc tradition 1560–90. HLQ 25 1962.
Stroup, T. B. The testing pattern in Elizabethan tragedy. Stud in Eng Lit 1500–1900 3 1963; rptd in his Microcosmos, Lexington Kentucky 1965.
Utz, H. Das Bedentungsfeld 'Leid' in der englischen Tragödie vor Shakespeare. Berne 1963.
Tomlinson, T. B. A study of Elizabethan and Jacobean tragedy. Cambridge 1964.
Bohm, R. Wesen und Funktion der Sterberede im elizabethanischen Drama. Hamburg 1964.
Palmer, D. J. Elizabethan tragic heroes. In Elizabethan theatre, ed J. R. Brown and B. Harris 1966.
McDonald, C. O. The rhetoric of tragedy: form in Stuart drama. Amherst 1966.
Cole, D. The comic accomplice in Elizabethan revenge tragedy. Renaissance Drama 9 1966.
Sibly, J. The duty of revenge in Tudor and Stuart drama. REL 8 1967.
Aggeler, G. Irony and honour in Jacobean tragedy. Humanist Assoc Bull 18 1968.

Pastoral

Winscheid, K. Die englische Hirtendichtung von 1597–1675. 1895.
Chambers, E. K. English pastorals: introduction. 1895.
Thorndike, A. H. The pastoral element in the English drama before 1605. MLN 14 1900.
Laidler, J. History of pastoral drama in English until 1700. E Studien 35 1905.
Greg, W. W. Pastoral poetry and pastoral drama. 1906.
Bayne, R. Masque and pastoral. CHEL 6 1910.
Genouy, H. L'élément pastoral dans la poésie narrative et le drame en Angleterre de 1579 à 1640. Paris 1929.

Masque

Evans, H. A. English masques. 1897. Introd.
Brotanek, R. Die englischen Maskenspiele. Vienna 1902.
Reyher, P. Les masques anglais 1512–1640. Paris 1909, New York 1964.

Simpson, P. The masque. In Shakespeare's England vol 2, Oxford 1916.

Welsford, E. The Court masque. Cambridge 1927.

Bentley, G. E. In A book of masques in honour of Allardyce Nicoll, Cambridge 1967.

Ewbank, I. 'These pretty devices': a study of masques in plays. Ibid.

—— The eloquence of masques. Renaissance Drama new ser 1 1968.

Comedy

Palmer, J. Comedy. 1914.

Bradbrook, M. C. The growth and structure of Elizabethan comedy. 1955.

Curry, J. V. Deception in Elizabethan comedy. Chicago 1955.

Chubb, L. G. Pictures for the reader: a series of illustrations to comedy 1591–2. Renaissance Drama 9 1966.

Gibbons, B. Jacobean city comedy. 1967.

History

Schelling, F. E. The English chronicle play. New York 1902.

Smith, R. M. Froissart and the English chronicle play. 1915.

Schirmer, W. Über das Historiendrama in der englischen Renaissance. Archiv 179 1941.

Ribner, I. Morality roots of the Tudor history play. Tulane Stud in Eng 3 1954.

—— The English history play in the age of Shakespeare. Princeton 1957.

Wilson, F. P. The English history play. In his Shakespearian and other studies, Oxford 1969.

Academic and School Drama

Churchill, G. B. and W. Keller. Die lateinischen Universitätsdramen Englands in der Zeit der Königin Elisabeth. Sh Jb 34 1898. Suppl by L. B. Morgan 47 1911.

Boas, F. S. University plays. CHEL 6 1910.

—— University drama in the Tudor age. Oxford 1914.

McConaughty, J. L. The school drama. 1913.

Moore Smith, G. C. College plays performed in the University of Cambridge. Cambridge 1923.

Motter, T. H. V. The school drama in England. 1929.

Tucker Brooke, C. F. Latin drama in Renaissance England. ELH 12 1946.

Bowers, R. H. Some Folger academic drama manuscripts. SB 12 1959.

Schuster, L. A. Pioneering in neo-Latin drama. Renaissance Drama 6 1963.

Bradner, L. Desiderata for the study of neo-Latin drama. Ibid.

Stříbrný, Z. Anglicke školské drama v dodobí humanismu. Philologica Pragensia 3 1964. English academic drama in the age of humanism.

Other Types

See also Structure and Composition, below.

Chase, L. N. The English heroic play. New York 1903.

Child, C. G. The rise of the heroic play. MLN 19 1904.

Thompson, E. N. S. The English moral plays. New Haven 1910.

Baskervill, C. R. Some evidence for early romantic plays in England. MP 14 1916.

—— The Elizabethan jig and related song drama. Chicago 1929, New York 1965.

Ellison, L. M. The early romantic drama at the English Court. Chicago 1917.

Reed, A. W. The beginnings of the English secular and romantic drama. 1922 (Shakespeare Assoc lecture).

Craig, H. Morality plays and Elizabethan drama. Shakespeare Quart 1 1950.

Craik, T. W. The Tudor interlude. Leicester 1958.

Campbell, L. B. Divine poetry and drama in sixteenth-century England. Cambridge 1961.

Russell, P. Romantic narrative plays 1570–90. In Elizabethan theatre, ed J. R. Brown and B. Harris 1966.

Helm, A. The mummers' play. Theatre Notebook 18 1964.

Roston, M. Biblical drama in England. 1968.

Origins and Influences

Native Influences

Farnham, W. The medieval heritage of Elizabethan tragedy. Berkeley 1936.

Rossiter, A. P. English drama from early times to the Elizabethans. 1950.

Doran, M. Endeavors of art: a study of form in Elizabethan drama. Madison 1954.

Weimann, R. Zur Entstehungsgeschichte des elisabethanischen Dramas. Zeitschrift für Anglistik und Amerikanistik 1956.

Bevington, D. M. From Mankind to Marlowe: the growth of structure in the popular drama of Tudor England. Cambridge Mass 1962.

Bradbrook, M. C. English dramatic form: a history of its development. 1965.

Stroup, T. B. Microcosmos: the shape of the Elizabethan play. Lexington Kentucky 1965.

Margeson, J. M. R. The origins of English tragedy. Oxford 1967.

Classical and Foreign Influences (in order of period)

See also Literary Relations with the Continent, below.

Watt, L. M. Attic and Elizabethan tragedy. 1908.

Palmer, H. R. List of English editions and translations of Greek and Latin classics before 1641. 1911.

Barrill, E. W. Heredity as fate in Greek and Elizabethan drama. JEGP 19 1920.

Lathrop, H. B. Translations from the classics into English. 1933.

Bowers, F. T. Classical antecedents of Elizabethan drama. Tennessee Stud in Lit 7 1962.

Ballweg, O. Das klassizistische Drama zur Zeit Shakespeares. Heidelberg 1909.

Blissett, W. Lucan's Caesar and the Elizabethan villain. SP 53 1956.

Cunliffe, J. W. The influence of Seneca on Elizabethan tragedy. 1893.

Manly, J. M. The influence of the tragedies of Seneca upon early English drama. In F. J. Miller, Tragedies of Seneca translated into English verse, Chicago 1907.

Charlton, H. B. The Senecan tradition in Renaissance tragedy. In Poetical works of Sir William Alexander vol i, ed Charlton and L. E. Kastner 1921 (Scottish Text Soc).

Lucas, F. L. Seneca and Elizabethan tragedy. Cambridge 1922.

Gilbert, A. H. Seneca and the criticism of Elizabethan tragedy. PQ 13 1934.

Beckingham, C. F. Seneca's fatalism and Elizabethan tragedy. MLR 32 1936.

Wells, H. W. Senecan influence on Elizabethan tragedy: a re-estimation. Shakespeare Assoc Bull 19 1944.

Ure, P. On some differences between Senecan and Elizabethan tragedy. Durham Univ Jnl new ser 10 1949.

Jacquot, J. Les tragédies de Sénèque et le théâtre élisabéthain. Etudes Anglaises 14 1961.

—— (ed). Les tragédies de Sénèque et le théâtre de la Renaissance. Paris 1964.

Soellner, R. The madness of Hercules and the Elizabethans. Comparative Lit 10 1958.

Hunter, G. K. Seneca and the Elizabethans: a case-study in influence. Shakespeare Survey 20 1967.

Armstrong, W. A. The influence of Seneca and Machiavelli on the Elizabethan tyrant. RES 24 1948.

Meyer, E. Machiavelli and the Elizabethan drama. Berlin 1897.

Gargano, G. S. Scapigliatura italiano a Londra. Florence 1923.

— Machiavelli e il machiavelismo nel teatro elisabethiano. Marzocco 13 July 1930.

Praz, M. Machiavelli and the Elizabethans. Proc Br Acad 14 1928; rptd in his Machiavelli in Inghilterra ed altri saggi, Rome 1942.

'Lee, Vernon'. The Italy of the Elizabethan dramatists. Euphorion 1884.

Rebora, P. L'Italia nel dramma inglese 1558–1642. Milan 1925.

— Temi medici nel dramma inglese del Rinascimento. In his Momenti di cultura italiana e inglesa, Mazara 1952.

Scott, M. A. Elizabethan translations from the Italian. Boston 1916.

Cunliffe, J. W. Italian prototypes of masque and dumbshow. PMLA 22 1907.

— The influence of Italian on early Elizabethan drama. MP 4 1907.

Smith, H. Pastoral influence in English drama. 1897.

Jeffrey, V. M. Italian and English pastoral drama of the Renaissance. MLR 19 1924.

Lievsay, J. L. Italian favole boscarecce and Jacobean stage pastoralism. In Essays on Shakespeare and Elizabethan drama in honor of Hardin Craig, New York 1962.

— Continental antecedents of Elizabethan drama. Tennessee Stud in Lit 7 1962.

Ott, A. Die italienische Novelle im englischen Drama von 1600 bis zur Restauration. Zürich 1904.

Schücking, L. L. Studien über die stofflichen Beziehungen der englischen Komödie zur Italienischen bis Lilly. Halle 1901.

Smith, W. Italian and Elizabethan comedy. MP 5 1908.

— The commedia dell'arte. New York 1912.

Lea, K. M. Italian popular comedy: a study in the commedia dell' arte 1560–1620, with special reference to the English stage. 2 vols Oxford 1934.

Felver, C. S. The commedia dell'arte and English drama in the sixteenth and early seventeenth centuries. Renaissance Drama 6 1963.

Welsford, E. The Italian influence on the English Court masque. MLR 18 1923.

Upham, A. H. The French influence in English literature from the accession of Elizabeth to the Restoration. New York 1908.

Villey, P. Montaigne et les poètes dramatiques anglais du temps de Shakespeare. Revue d'Histoire Littéraire 24 1917.

Witherspoon, A. M. The influence of Robert Garnier on Elizabethan drama. New Haven 1924.

McDiarmid, M. P. The influence of Robert Garnier on some Elizabethan tragedies. Etudes Anglaises 11 1958.

Jondorf, G. Robert Garnier and the themes of political tragedy in the sixteenth century. Cambridge 1969.

Herford, C. H. Studies in the literary relation of England and Germany in the sixteenth century. Cambridge 1886.

Schelling, F. E. Foreign influences in Elizabethan plays. New York 1923.

Stiefel, A. L. Die Nachahmung spanischer Komödien in England unter den ersten Stuarts. Romanische Forschungen 5 1890.

Bahlsen, L. Spanische Quellen der dramatischen Litteratur besonders Englands zu Shakespeares Zeit. Zeitschrift für Vergleichende Litteraturgeschichte 6 1893.

Underhill, J. G. Spanish literature in the England of the Tudors. New York 1899.

Fitzmaurice-Kelly, J. Cervantes in England. Proc Br Acad 2 1905.

Grossman, R. Spanien und das elisabethanische Drama. Hamburg 1920.

Feldman, A. B. Dutch humanism and the Tudor dramatic tradition. N & Q 16 Aug 1952.

Wright, L. B. The scriptures and the Elizabethan stage. MP 26 1928.

Herrick, M. T. Susanna and the elders in sixteenth-century drama. In Studies in honor of T. W. Baldwin, Urbana 1958.

Ewbank, I. The house of David in Renaissance drama. Renaissance Drama 8 1965.

Structure and Composition

Carpenter, F. I. Metaphor and simile in the minor Elizabethan drama. Chicago 1895.

Hubbard, F. G. Repetition and parallelism in the earlier Elizabethan drama. PMLA 20 1905.

— A type of blank verse line found in the earlier Elizabethan drama. PMLA 32 1917.

Muncaster, M. The use of prose in Elizabethan drama. MLR 14 1919.

Macdonald, J. F. The use of prose in English drama before Shakespeare. UTQ 2 1933.

Vollmann, E. Ursprung und Entwicklung des Monologs bis zu seiner Entfaltung bei Shakespeare. Bonn 1934.

Eichorn, T. Prosa und Vers im vorshakespeareschen Drama. Sh Jb 84–6 1948–50.

Oras, A. Pause patterns in Elizabethan and Jacobean drama: an experiment in prosody. Gainesville 1960.

Koskenniemi, I. Studies in the vocabulary of English drama 1550–1600, excluding Shakespeare and Ben Jonson. Turku 1962.

— Figurative negation in Renaissance drama. Neuphilologische Mitteilungen 67 1967.

Friedland, L. S. Dramatic unities in England. JEGP 10 1911.

Buland, M. The presentation of time in the Elizabethan drama. New York 1912.

Fenton, D. The extra-dramatic moment in Elizabethan plays before 1616. Philadelphia 1930.

Alden, R. M. The use of comic material in the tragedy of Shakespeare and his contemporaries. JEGP 13 1914.

Winslow, O. E. Low comedy as a structural element in English drama to 1642. Chicago 1926 (priv ptd).

Forsythe, R. S. Comic effects in Elizabethan drama. Univ of North Dakota Quart Jnl 17 1927.

Whiting, B. J. Proverbs in the earlier English drama. Cambridge Mass 1938.

Sackton, A. H. The paradoxical encomium in Elizabethan drama. SE 28 1949.

Eckhardt, E. Die metrische Unterscheidung von Ernst und Komik in den englischen Moralitäten. E Studien 1927.

Bernard, J. E. Prosody of the Tudor interlude. New Haven 1939.

Hanford, J. H. The debate element in Elizabethan drama. In Anniversary papers by colleagues and pupils of G. L. Kittredge, Boston 1913.

Waith, E. Controversia in the English drama. PMLA 68 1953.

Templeman, W. D. The place of the lyric in Elizabethan drama before 1600. Western Reserve Bull 30 1927.

Bowden, W. R. The English dramatic lyric 1603–42. New Haven 1951.

Arkwright, G. E. P. Early Elizabethan stage music. Musical Antiquary 1909–13.

Stevens, J. Music and poetry in the early Tudor Court. Cambridge 1961.

Schwab, H. Das Schauspiel im Schauspiel zur Zeit Shakespeares. Vienna 1896.

Boas, F. S. The play within the play. 1927 (Shakespeare Assoc lecture).

Brown, A. The play within a play: an Elizabethan dramatic device. E & S new ser 13 1960.

Foster, F. A. Dumb show in Elizabethan drama before 1620. E Studien 44 1911.

Pearn, R. B. Dumb-show in Elizabethan drama. RES 11 1935.

Mehl, D. The Elizabethan dumb show. 1965.

— Emblematik im englischen Drama der Shakespearezeit. Anglia 87 1969.

Fansler, H. E. The evolution of technic in Elizabethan tragedy. Chicago 1914.

Freeburg, V. O. Disguise plots in Elizabethan drama. New York 1915.

Bradbrook, M. C. Shakespeare and the use of disguise in Elizabethan drama. EC 2 1952.

Empson, W. Double plots. In his Some versions of pastoral, 1935.

Rabkin, N. The double plot: notes on the history of a convention. Renaissance Drama 7 1964.

Hay, C. Renaissance and Restoration dramatic plotting. Renaissance Drama 9 1966.

Levin, R. The Elizabethan 'three-level' play. Renaissance Drama 11 1968.

— The unity of Elizabethan multiple-plot drama. ELH 34 1967.

— Sexual equations in the Elizabethan double plot. Lit & Psychology 16 1966.

Muir, K. The dramatic function of anachronism. Proc Leeds Philosophical & Literary Soc 6 1951.

Nicoll, A. 'Tragical-comical-historical-pastoral': Elizabethan dramatic nomenclature. Bull John Rylands Lib 43 1961.

Stewart, B. T. Characterization through dreams in the drama of Shakespeare's day. Tennessee Stud in Lit 1 1916.

Hoffmann, F. Die typischen Situationen im elisabethanischen Drama und ihr Pattern. Sh Jb 94 1958.

Devi, S. The preliminaries of drama. Indian Rev 1959.

Sehrt, E. Der dramatische Auftakt in der elizabethanischen Tragödie. Göttingen 1960.

Turner, R. Y. The causal induction in some Elizabethan plays. SP 60 1963.

Greenfield, T. N. The induction in Elizabethan drama. Eugene 1969.

Jewkes, W. T. Act division in Elizabethan and Jacobean plays 1583–1616. 1958.

Miles, T. Place-realism in a group of Caroline plays. RES 18 1942.

Hyde, Mary. Playwriting for Elizabethans 1600–5. New York 1946.

Foakes, R. A. The profession of playwright. In Early Shakespeare, ed J. R. Brown and B. Harris 1961.

Character Types and Characteristic Scenes

Graf, H. Der Miles gloriosus im englischen Drama bis zur Zeit des Bürgerkrieges. Schwerin 1891.

Boughner, D. C. The braggart in Renaissance comedy. 1954.

Cushman, L. The Devil and the Vice in the English dramatic literature before Shakespeare. Halle 1900.

Withington, R. 'Vice' and 'parasite': a note on the evolution of the Elizabethan villain. PMLA 49 1934; rptd in his Excursions in English drama, 1937.

Mares, F. H. The origin of the figure called the Vice in Tudor drama. HLQ 22 1958.

Spivack, B. Shakespeare and the allegory of evil: the history of a metaphor in relation to his villains. New York 1958.

Weimann, R. Redekonventionen des Vice. Zeitschrift für Anglistik und Amerikanistik 1967.

Eckhardt, E. Die lustige Person im älteren englischen Drama. Berlin 1902.

Peers, E. A. Elizabethan drama and its mad folk. Cambridge 1914.

McCullen, J. T. Madness and isolation of character in Elizabethan and early Stuart drama. SP 48 1951.

— The function of songs aroused by madness in Elizabethan drama. In A tribute to G. C. Taylor, Chapel Hill 1952.

Reed, R. R. Bedlam on the Jacobean stage. Cambridge Mass 1952.

Goldsmith, R. H. The wild man on the English stage. MLR 53 1958.

Boyer, C. The villain as hero in Elizabethan tragedy. 1914.

McIntyre, C. F. The later career of the Elizabethan villain-hero. PMLA 40 1925.

Schücking, L. L. The baroque character of the Elizabethan tragic hero. Proc Br Acad 24 1938.

Stonex, A. B. The usurer in the Elizabethan drama. PMLA 31 1916.

Zandvoort, R. W. The messenger in the early English drama. E Studies 3 1921.

Camp, C. W. The artisan in Elizabethan literature. New York 1924.

Cardozo, L. J. The contemporary Jew in the Elizabethan drama. Amsterdam 1925.

Van der Spek, C. The Church and the churchman in English dramatic literature before 1642. Amsterdam 1930.

Myers, A. M. Representation and misrepresentation of the Puritan in Elizabethan drama. Philadelphia 1931.

Jones, E. Othello's countrymen: the African in English Renaissance drama. Oxford 1965.

Feldman, A. B. Dutch exiles and Elizabethan playwrights. N & Q 8 Dec 1951.

— The Flemings in Shakespeare's theatre. N & Q 21 June 1952.

— Netherlanders on the London stage. N & Q 4 Aug 1951.

Scott, F. R. Teg: the stage Irishman. MLR 42 1947.

Bartley, J. O. Teague, Shenkin and Sawney: an historical study of the earliest Irish, Welsh and Scottish characters in English plays. Cork 1954.

Eckhardt, E. Die Dialekt- und Ausländertypen des älteren englischen Dramas. Bang's Materialien vols 27, 30, 1910–1.

Clough, W. P. The broken English of foreign characters of the Elizabethan stage. PQ 12 1933.

Yearsley, M. Doctors in Elizabethan drama. 1934.

Silvette, H. The doctor on the stage. Annals of Medical History new ser 8–9 1936–7; rptd as The doctor on the stage, Knoxville 1967.

Rosenbach, A. S. W. The curious impertinent in English dramatic literature. MLN 17 1902.

Vandiver, E. P. The Elizabethan dramatic parasite. SP 32 1935.

Milligan, B. The roaring boy in Tudor and Stuart literature. Shakespeare Assoc Bull 15 1940.

Snuggs, H. L. The comic humours: a new interpretation. PMLA 62 1947.

Busby, O. M. Studies in the development of the fool in the Elizabethan drama. 1923.

Welsford, E. The fool: his social and literary history. 1935.

Empson, W. The praise of folly. In his Structure of complex words, 1951. On the clown.

Collaboration, Authorship and Textual Studies

Fleay, F. G. On metrical tests as applied to dramatic poetry. Trans New Shakespeare Soc 1 1874.

Thompson, E. N. S. Elizabethan dramatic collaboration. E Studien 40 1909.

Oliphant, E. H. C. Problems of authorship in Elizabethan dramatic literature. MP 8 1911.

— Collaboration in Elizabethan drama: Mr W. J. Lawrence's theory. PQ 8 1929.

— How not to play the game of parallels. JEGP 28 1929.

Greg, W. W. 'Bad' quartos outside Shakespeare: Battle of Alcazar and Orlando Furioso. Library 3rd ser 10 1919.

— Some aspects and problems of London publishing between 1550 and 1650. Oxford 1956.

Pollard, A. W. Elizabethan spelling as a literary and bibliographical clue. Library 4th ser 4 1923.

Sykes, H. D. Sidelights on Elizabethan drama. Stratford 1924.

Bald, R. C. 'Assembled' texts. Library 4th ser 12 1931.

Byrne, M. St Clare. Bibliographical clues in collaborative plays. Library 4th ser 13 1932.

Tiegs, A. Zur Zusammenarbeit englischer Berufsdramatiker unmittelbar vor, neben und nach Shakespeare. Breslau 1933.

Price, H. T. Towards a scientific method of textual criticism for the Elizabethan drama. JEGP 36 1937.

Harbage, A. Elizabethan-Restoration palimpsest. MLR 35 1940.

Bentley, G. E. Authenticity and attribution in Jacobean and Caroline drama. Eng Inst Annual 1942.

Reinhold, H. Die metrische Versahnung als Kriterium für Fragen der Chronologie und Authentizität. Archiv 181 1942.

Kirschbaum, L. An hypothesis concerning the origin of bad quartos. PMLA 60 1945.

Lyman, D. B. Apocryphal plays of university wits. In English studies in honor of J. S. Wilson, Charlottesville 1951.

Ashe, D. J. The non-Shakespearian bad quartos as provincial acting versions. Renaissance Paper 1954.

Prior, M. E. Imagery as a test of authorship. Shakespeare Quart 6 1955.

Maxwell, B. Studies in the Shakespeare apocrypha. New York 1956.

Bowers, F. T. Old-spelling editions of dramatic texts. In Studies in honor of T. W. Baldwin, Urbana 1958.

Craig, H. The criticism of Elizabethan dramatic texts. In Studies in honor of J. S. Wilson, Charlottesville 1951.

— Textual degeneration of Elizabethan Stuart plays. Rice Inst Pamphlets 1 1960.

Brown, J. R. The rationale of old-spelling editions of the plays of Shakespeare and his contemporaries. SB 13 1960. Reply by A. Brown, ibid.

Foxon, D. F. and W. B. Todd. Thomas J. Wise and the pre-Restoration drama: a supplement. Library 5th ser 16 1961.

Fogel, E. G. Electronic computers and Elizabethan texts. SB 15 1962.

Partridge, A. C. Orthography in Shakespeare and Elizabethan drama. 1964.

Schoenbaum, S. Internal evidence and Elizabethan dramatic authorship: an essay in literary history and method. 1966.

Miscellaneous Studies

For Music see under Theatre, below.

Sugden, E. H. A topographical dictionary to the works of Shakespeare and his fellow dramatists. Manchester 1925.

Lindabury, R. V. A study of patriotism in the Elizabethan drama. Princeton 1931.

Paletta, G. Fürstengeschick und innerstaatlicher Machtkampf im englischen Renaissancedrama. Breslau 1934.

Grosse, F. Das englische Renaissancedrama im Spiegel zeitgenössischer Staatstheorien. Breslau 1935.

Wolff, M. J. Die soziale Stellung der englischen Renaissancedramatiker. E Studien 71 1936.

Reese, G. C. The question of the succession in Elizabethan drama. SE 22 1942.

Anderson, R. L. Kingship in Renaissance drama. SP 41 1944.

Armstrong, W. A. The Elizabethan conception of the tyrant. RES 22 1946.

Boas, F. S. Queen Elizabeth in drama and related studies. 1950.

Bevington, D. M. Tudor drama and politics: a critical approach to topical meaning. Cambridge Mass 1968.

— Drama and polemics under Queen Mary. Renaissance Drama 9 1966.

Russell, H. K. Elizabethan dramatic poetry in the light of natural and moral philosophy. PQ 12 1933.

Gilbert, A. H. Logic in the Elizabethan drama. SP 32 1935.

Ransom, H. Some legal elements in Elizabethan plays. SE 16 1936.

Clarkson, P. S. and C. T. Warren. The law of property in Shakespeare and the Elizabethan drama. Baltimore 1942.

Blayney, G. H. Wardship in English drama 1600–50. SP 53 1956.

Peter, J. Complaint and satire in early English literature. Oxford 1956.

Mason, E. C. Satire on women and sex in Elizabethan tragedy. E Studies 31 1950.

Gagen, J. The new woman: her emergence in English drama 1600–1730. New York 1954.

Blayney, G. H. The enforcement of marriage in English drama 1600–50. PQ 38 1959.

Wilson, E. M. Family honour in the plays of Shakespeare's predecessors and contemporaries. E & S new ser 6 1953.

Barber, C. L. The idea of honour in the English drama 1591–1700. Stockholm 1957.

Sensabaugh, G. F. Love ethics in Platonic Court drama 1625–42. HLQ 1 1938.

Leech, C. Pacifism in Caroline drama. Durham Univ Jnl 31 1939.

— Love and escape in Caroline plays. Durham Univ Jnl new ser 1 1940.

— Catholic and Protestant drama. Durham Univ Jnl new ser 2 1941; rptd in his Shakespeare's tragedies, 1950.

Babb, L. The physiological conception of love in the Elizabethan and early Stuart drama. PMLA 56 1941.

— Love melancholy in the Elizabethan and early Stuart drama. Bull History of Medicine 13 1943.

— Scientific theories of grief in some Elizabethan plays. SP 40 1943.

— Melancholic villainy in the Elizabethan drama. Papers of Michigan Acad 29 1943.

— The Elizabethan malady. East Lansing 1951.

Anderson, D. K. The banquet of love in English drama 1595–1642. JEGP 63 1964.

Gerard, A. S. The loving killers: the rationale of righteousness in baroque tragedy. Stud in Comparative Lit 2 1965.

Johnson, J. J. The spoils of love and vengeance: a study of the Jacobean revenge tragedy motivated by lust. Xavier Univ Stud 7 1968.

Koldewey, E. Über die Willensfreiheit im älteren englischen Drama. Würzburg 1937.

Praz, M. La fortuna del dramma elisabettiano. In his Studi e svaghi inglesi, Florence 1937.

Gardner, H. Milton's Satan and the theme of damnation in Elizabethan tragedy. E & S ('English Studies') new ser 1 1948.

West, R. H. The invisible world: a study of pneumatology in Elizabethan drama. Athens Georgia 1939.

Saleski, R. E. Supernatural agents in Christian imagery: world studies in Elizabethan dramatists. JEGP 38 1939.

Reed, R. R. The occult on the Tudor and Stuart stage. Boston 1965.

Hoffmann, G. Wandlungen des Gebets im elisabethanischen Drama. Deutsche Shakespeare-Gesellschaft West Jahrbuch 1966.

Korninger, S. Die Geisterszene im elisabethanischen Drama. Ibid.

Lawrence, W. J. The dedication of early English plays. Life & Letters July 1929.

Wright, L. B. The reading of plays during the Puritan revolution. Huntington Lib Bull no 6 1934.

Cawley, R. R. The voyagers and Elizabethan drama. Boston 1938.

Matthiessen, F. O. Towards our understanding of Elizabethan drama. Southern Rev 4 1938.

Williams, R. D. Antiquarian interest in Elizabethan drama before Lamb. PMLA 53 1938.

Bentley, G. E. John Cotgrave's English treasury of wit and language and the Elizabethan drama. SP 40 1943.

Mish, C. C. Comparative popularity of early fiction and drama. N & Q 21 June 1952.

Pellegrini, G. Barocco inglese. Florence 1953.

Klein, D. The Elizabethan dramatists as critics. New York 1963.

Ross, L. J. Art and the study of early English drama. Renaissance Drama 6 1963.

Berlin, N. The base string: the underworld in Elizabethan drama. Rutherford 1968.

Fraser, R. Elizabethan drama and the art of abstraction. Comparative Drama 2 1968.

Putt, S. G. The relevance of Jacobean drama. E & S new ser 23 1970.

II. THEATRES AND ACTORS

(1) DOCUMENTARY SOURCES: *Public records, playhouse and private records*

(2) BIBLIOGRAPHIES AND GENERAL HISTORIES OF THE STAGE

(3) CENSORSHIP AND GOVERNMENT REGULATION OF THE STAGE

(4) COURT, PUBLIC AND PRIVATE THEATRES

(5) COMPANIES, ACTORS AND PRODUCTION

(6) THEATRE MANAGEMENT AND STAGE MANAGEMENT

The material of this section is covered comprehensively in the following: E. K. Chambers, The Elizabethan stage, 4 vols Oxford 1923 (with index by B. White 1934); G. E. Bentley, The Jacobean and Caroline stage, 7 vols Oxford 1941–68; J. T. Murray, English dramatic companies 1558–1642, 2 vols 1910; L. Hotson, The Commonwealth and Restoration stage, Cambridge Mass 1928; G. Wickham, Early English stages 1300–1660, vol 1 1300–1576, vol 2 pt 1 1576–1597–8, 1959, 1963– (in progress). The following sections usually exclude general works already listed under Introduction, above, and those mentioned in this note.

(1) DOCUMENTARY SOURCES

Public Records

Mss preserved in the muniment room at Loseley House. Ed A. J. Kempe 1835.

Extracts from the accounts of the revels at Court in the reigns of Queen Elizabeth and King James I. Ed P. Cunningham 1842 (Shakespeare Soc). *See* S. A. Tannenbaum, Shakespeare forgeries in the revels accounts, New York 1928.

Calendar of state papers: domestic ser Edward 6, Mary, Elizabeth and James 1. Ed R. Lemon and M. A. Everett Green 12 vols 1856–72; Charles 1, ed J. Bruce and W. D. Hamilton 18 vols 1858–78; Commonwealth and Protectorate, ed Green 15 vols 1875–86.

Notices illustrative of the drama extracted from the Chamberlain's accounts and other mss of the borough of Leicester. Ed W. Kelly 1865.

A collection of ancient documents respecting the office of Master of the revels. Ed J. O. Halliwell-Phillipps 1870.

Transcripts of the registers of the Company of Stationers 1554–1640. Ed E. Arber 5 vols 1875–94.

Overall, W. H. and H. C. Analytical index to the series of records known as the Remembrancia: Archives of the City of London 1579–1664. 1878.

Middlesex county records. Ed J. C. Jeaffreson 4 vols 1887–1902; ed W. J. Hardy 1905.

Acts of the Privy Council of England. New ser, ed J. R. Dasent 32 vols 1890–1907.

Calendar of the patent rolls. 1891–1908.

Malone Society collections. Vol 1, Dramatic records of the City of London: the Remembrancia, Records from the Lansdowne mss, Dramatic records from the patent rolls: company licences, Dramatic records from the Privy Council register 1603–42. Ed E. K. Chambers and W. W. Greg, Oxford 1907, 1908, 1909, 1911; vol 2, Dramatic records of the City of London: the repertories, journals and letter books, ed E. J. Mill and E. K. Chambers; Dramatic records of the Lord Chamberlain's office, ed E. Boswell and E. K. Chambers, Oxford 1931; vol 3, A calendar of dramatic records in the books of the livery companies of London 1485–1640, ed J. Robertson and D. J. Gordon, Oxford 1954; vol 4, More records from the Remembrancia, ed F. P. Wilson, Oxford 1956; vol 5, A calendar of dramatic records in the books of the London cloth-workers' company (addenda to Collections 3), ed J. Robertson. Companies of players entertained by the Earl of Cumberland and Lord Clifford 1607–39, ed L. Stone; The academic drama in Oxford: extracts from the records of four colleges, ed R. E. Alton, Oxford 1959; vol 6, Dramatic records in the declared accounts of the treasury of the chamber 1558–1642, ed D. Cook, Oxford 1961; vol 7, Records of plays and players in Kent 1450–1642, ed G. E. Dawson, Oxford 1965.

Documents relating to the office of the revels in the time of Queen Elizabeth. Ed A. Feuillerat. In Materialen vol 21, ed W. Bang, Louvain 1908.

Documents relating to the revels at Court in the time of King Edward 6 and Queen Mary. Ed A. Feuillerat, Materialien vol 44, ed W. Bang, Louvain 1914.

Dramatic records from the Privy Council register, James 1 and Charles 1. Ed C. C. Stopes, Sh Jb 48 1912.

Playhouse and Private Records
(listed in groups)

Stow, J. A survey of London. 1598, 1603 (rev); rev J. Strype 2 vols 1720; ed C. H. Kingsford 3 vols Oxford 1908–27.

Wilkinson, R. Londina illustrata. 2 vols 1819.

Hentzner, P. Itinerarium Germaniae, Galliae, Angliae, Italiae. Nuremberg 1612; tr H. Walpole 1797.

Moryson, F. An itinerary. 1617; 4 vols Glasgow 1907–8.

Rye, W. B. England as seen by foreigners in the days of Elizabeth and James the first: comprising translations of the journals of the two Dukes of Wurtemberg in 1592 and 1610; with extracts from the travels of foreign princes and others. 1865.

Diary of the journey of Philip Junius Duke of Stettin-Pomerania through England in the year 1602. Ed G. von Bulow and W. Powell, Trans Royal Historical Soc new ser 6 1892.

Platter, T. Thomas Platters des Jüngeren Englandfahrt im Jahre 1599. Ed H. Hecht, Halle 1929.

Schanzer, E. Thomas Platter's observations on the Elizabethan stage. N & Q Nov 1956.

Machyn, H. The diary of Henry Machyn, citizen and merchant taylor of London 1550–63. Ed J. G. Nichols 1848 (Camden Soc).

Forman, S. The autobiography and personal diary of Dr Simon Forman 1552–1602. Ed J. O. Halliwell(-Phillipps) 1849.

Wilson, J. D. and R. W. Hunt. The authenticity of Simon Forman's Bocke of plaies. RES 23 1947.

Pafford, J. H. Simon Forman's Bocke of plaies. RES 35 1959.

Race, S. Simon Forman's Bocke of plaies examined. N & Q Jan 1958.

Alleyn, E. A collection of original documents illustrative of the life and times of Edward Alleyn. Ed J. P. Collier 1843 (Shakespeare Soc).

Warner, G. F. A catalogue of the manuscripts and muniments of Alleyn's college of God's gifts at Dulwich. 1881.

Briley, J. Edward Alleyn and Henslowe's will. Shakespeare Quart 9 1958.

Wright, W. S. Edward Alleyn, actor and benefactor. Theatre Notebook 20 1966.

Henslowe, P. The diary of Philip Henslowe from 1591–1609. Ed J. P. Collier 1845 (Shakespeare Soc).

Greg, W. W. (ed). Henslowe's diary. 2 pts 1904–8.

— (ed). Henslowe's papers: being documents supplementary to Henslowe's diary. 1907. See also T. W. Baldwin, Posting Henslowe's accounts. JEGP 26 1927.

— A fragment from Henslowe's diary. Library 4th ser 19 1939. Addn by J. Q. Adams 20 1940.

— Dramatic documents from the Elizabethan playhouse: stage plots, actor's part, prompt books. 2 vols Oxford 1931.

— Collected papers. Ed J. C. Maxwell, Oxford 1966.

Foakes, R. A. and R. T. Rickert (ed). Henslowe's diary. Cambridge 1961.

— An Elizabethan stage drawing? Shakespeare Survey 13 1961. From Henslowe's diary.

Foakes, R. A. The significance of Henslowe's diary. Philologica Pragensia 1960.

— Henslowe and the theatre of the 1590's. Renaissance Drama 6 1963.

Manningham, J. The diary of John Manningham of the Middle Temple 1602–3. Ed J. Bruce 1868 (Camden Soc).

Chambers, E. K. (ed). Four letters on theatrical affairs. In Malone Society collections vol 2, Oxford 1923.

Feil, J. P. Dramatic references from the Scudamore papers [1610–38]. Shakespeare Survey 11 1958.

Boas, F. S. Crosfield's diary and the Caroline stage. Fortnightly Rev 1 April 1925.

Bentley, G. E. The diary of a Caroline theatregoer. MP 35 1938. Sir Humphrey Mildmay 1592–1666?

Semper, I. J. The Jacobean theatre through the eyes of Catholic clerics. Shakespeare Quart 3 1952.

— Jacobean playhouses and Catholic clerics. Month July 1952.

(2) BIBLIOGRAPHIES AND GENERAL HISTORIES OF THE STAGE

Arnott, J. F. and J. W. Robinson. English theatrical literature 1559–1900: a bibliography incorporating R. W. Lowe's A bibliographical account of English theatrical literature 1888. 1970.

Nungezer, E. A dictionary of actors and of other persons associated with the public representation of plays in England before 1642. New Haven 1929.

Flecknoe, R. A short discourse of the English stage. Appended to Love's kingdom, 1664; rptd W. C. Hazlitt, English drama and stage, 1869; ed J. E. Spingarn, Critical essays of the seventeenth century vol 2, Oxford 1928.

Wright, J. Historia histrionica: an historical account of the English stage. In A dialogue of plays and players, 1699; rptd in R. Dodsley, A select collection of old plays, ed W. C. Hazlitt 1874–6; ed W. Ashbee 1872 (facs); ed A. Lang 1903.

Downes, J. Roscius anglicanus: or an historical review of the stage 1708. Ed J. Knight 1886; ed M. Summers 1928.

Malone, E. An historical account of the rise and progress of the English stage, and of the economy and usages of our ancient theatres. In his Plays and poems of William Shakespeare vol 1 pt 2, 1790; and in Boswell's Malone vol 3, 1821.

Chalmers, G. An account of the rise and progress of the English stage. In his An apology for the believers in the

Shakespeare papers, 1797. See also A supplemental apology for the believers in the Sheakespear papers, 1799.

Lawrence, W. J. The Elizabethan playhouse and other studies. Stratford 1912.

— The Elizabethan playhouse: 2nd series. Stratford 1913.

Archer, W. and W. J. Lawrence. The Playhouse. In Shakespeare's England vol 2, Oxford 1916.

Thorndike, A. H. Shakespeare's theater. New York 1916.

Adams, J. Q. Shakespearean playhouses. Boston 1917.

Rollins, H. E. A contribution to the history of the English Commonwealth drama. SP 18 1921.

— The Commonwealth drama: miscellaneous notes. SP 20 1923.

Kernodle, G. R. From art to theatre: form and convention in the Renaissance. Chicago 1943.

Nicoll, A. Studies in the Elizabethan stage since 1900. Shakespeare Survey 1 1948.

— (ed). Shakespeare Survey 12. Cambridge 1959.

Southern, R. The seven ages of the theatre. 1962.

Jacquot, J. (ed). Les fêtes de la Renaissance. Paris 1956.

— (ed). Dramaturgie et société: xvie et xviie siècles. 2 vols Paris 1968.

Bentley, G. E. (ed). The seventeenth-century stage: a collection of critical essays. Chicago 1968.

Galloway, D. (ed). The Elizabethan theatre. 2 vols 1969–70.

Prouty, C. T. (ed). Studies in the Elizabethan theatre. Hamden Conn 1961.

(3) CENSORSHIP AND GOVERNMENT REGULATION OF THE STAGE

See particularly E. K. Chambers, The Elizabethan stage vol 1: the Revels office; the control of the stage; *and G. Wickham,* Early English stages *vol 2 pt 1.*

Simpson, R. The political use of the stage in Shakespeare's time. Trans New Shakspere Soc pt 2 1874.

Lee, S. The topical side of the Elizabethan drama. Trans New Shakspere Soc 1887–92.

Dasent, J. R. (ed). Acts of the Privy Council of England. New ser, 32 vols 1890–1907.

Chambers, E. K. Notes on the history of the revels office under the Tudors. 1906.

— The Elizabethan Lords Chamberlain. In Malone Society collections vol 1, Oxford 1907.

— and W. W. Greg (ed). Dramatic records from the Privy Council Register, James I and Charles I. In Malone Society collections vol 1, Oxford 1911.

Percy, E. The Privy Council under the Tudors. 1907.

Gildersleeve, V. C. Government regulation of the Elizabethan drama. New York 1908.

Feuillerat, A. Le bureau des menusplaisirs et la mise en scène à la cour d'Elizabeth. Louvain 1910.

— (ed). Documents relating to the office of the revels in the time of Queen Elizabeth. In Materialien vol 21, ed W. Bang, Louvain 1908.

— (ed). Documents relating to the revels at Court in the time of King Edward 6 and Queen Mary. In Materialien vol 44, ed W. Bang, Louvain 1914.

Graves, T. S. Some allusions to religious and political plays. MP 9 1912.

— The Court and the London theatres during the reign of Queen Elizabeth. Menasha 1913.

— The political use of the stage during the reign of James I. Anglia 38 1914.

Hornemann, C. Das Privy Council von England zur Zeit der Königin Elisabeth. Hanover 1912.

Stopes, C. C. (ed). Dramatic records from the Privy Council register, James I and Charles I. Sh Jb 48 1912.

— The seventeenth-century accounts of the Master of the Revels. 1922 (Shakespeare Assoc).

Adams, J. Q. The dramatic records of Sir Henry Herbert, Master of the Revels 1623–73. New Haven 1917.

Adair, E. R. The sources for the history of the [Privy] Council in the sixteenth and seventeenth centuries. 1924.

Marcham, F. The King's Office of the Revels. RES 2 1926.

— and J. P. Gilson (ed). The King's Office of the Revels 1610–22: fragments of mss. 1925.

Eccles, M. Sir George Buc, Master of the Revels. In Thomas Lodge and other Elizabethans, ed C. J. Sisson, Cambridge Mass 1933.

Griffin, W. J. Notes on early Tudor control of the stage. MLN 58 1943.

Dawson, G. E. Copyright of plays in the early seventeenth century. Eng Inst Essays 1947.

Edinborough, A. The early Tudor revels office. Shakespeare Quart 2 1951.

Challen, W. H. Sir George Buck Kt, Master of the Revels. N & Q July–Aug 1957.

Greg, W. W. Copyright in unauthorized texts. In Elizabethan and Jacobean studies presented to F. P. Wilson, Oxford 1959.

Kirschbaum, L. The copyright of Elizabethan plays. Library 5th ser 14 1959.

Sisson, C. J. The laws of Elizabethan copyright: the stationers' view. Library 5th ser 15 1960.

(4) COURT, PUBLIC AND PRIVATE THEATRES

See E. K. Chambers, G. E. Bentley and G. Wickham, above. Related forms of theatrical presentation, such as civic pageantry and academic entertainments, are listed below, as well as studies of individuals associated with royal, private and public arts of theatre.

Court and Civic Entertainment

Nichols, J. The progresses and public processions of Queen Elizabeth. 4 vols 1788–1821, 3 vols 1823.

— The progresses, processions and magnificent festivities of King James I. 4 vols 1828.

Nichols, J. G. London pageants. 1837.

Fairholt, F. W. History of Lord Mayors' pageants. 1843–4 (Percy Soc).

— The civic garland. 1845.

Cunningham, P. and J. P. Collier. Inigo Jones: a life; and five Court masques. 1848 (Shakespeare Soc).

Kelly, W. Royal progresses and visits to Leicester. 1884.

Stopes, C. C. William Hunnis. Sh Jb 27 1892.

— William Hunnis and the revels of the Chapel Royal. In Materialien vol 29, ed W. Bang, Louvain 1910.

Brotanek, R. Die englischen Maskenspiele. Vienna 1902.

Chambers, E. K. Court performances before Queen Elizabeth. MLR 2 1906.

— Court performances under James I. MLR 4 1909.

Reyher, P. Les masques anglais. Paris 1909.

Helmholtz-Phelan, A. A. The staging of the Court drama to 1595. PMLA 24 1909.

Cunliffe, J. W. (ed). The Queen's Majesty's entertainment at Woodstock. PMLA 26 1911.

Lawrence, W. J. The mounting of the Carolan masques. In his The Elizabethan playhouse, Stratford 1912.

Boas, F. S. University drama in the Tudor age. Oxford 1914.

Withington, R. English pageantry: an historical outline. 2 vols Cambridge Mass 1918–20.

Thaler, A. The players at Court. JEGP 19 1920.

Steele, M. S. Plays and masques at Court during the reigns of Elizabeth, James and Charles. New Haven 1926.

Leech, C. Sir Henry Lee's entertainment at Woodstock. PMLA 26 1911.

Nicoll, A. Royal divertisements. Theatre Arts Monthly Feb 1935.

— Stuart masques and the Renaissance stage. 1937.

Renwick, W. L. Alfonso Ferrabosco. RES 11 1935.

Hotson, L. (ed). Queen Elizabeth's entertainment at Mitcham: poet, painter and musician. New Haven 1953. On John Lyly.

Bland, D. S. The barriers. Guildhall Miscellany 1956. On Guildhall Lib ms 4160 1616.

Palme, P. The triumph of peace: a study of the Whitehall banqueting house. Stockholm 1956.

Taylor, R. The masque and the lance: the third Earl of Pembroke in Jacobean Court entertainments. 1958.

Bradbrook, M. C. Drama as offering: the 'princely pleasures at Kenelworth'. Rice Inst Pamphlets 1 1960.

Anglo, S. The evolution of the early Tudor disguising, pageant and mask. Renaissance Drama new ser 1 1968.

Bergeron, D. M. The emblematic nature of English civic pageantry. ELH 35 1968.

Wickham, G. The Stuart mask. In his Shakespeare's dramatic heritage, 1969.

Public and Private Theatres

Older studies which retain factual or speculative interest are listed first, followed by modern studies grouped under specific theatres where possible.

Ellis, H. The history and antiquities of the parish of St Leonard Shoreditch and liberty of Norton Folgate. 1798.

'Hood, Eu.' (Joseph Haslewood). Of the London theatres. GM Aug 1813–July 1814.

Tomlins, T. E. Origin of the Curtain theatre and mistakes regarding it. Shakespeare Soc Papers 1 1844.

Cunningham, P. The Whitefriars, the Salisbury Court and the Duke's theatres. Shakespeare Soc Papers 4 1849.

Rendle, W. The Bankside, Southwark and the Globe. 1877. Appended to Harrison's Description of England pt 2, ed F. J. Furnivall 1878 (New Shakspere Soc).

— Old Southwark and its people. 1878.

— The playhouses at Bankside in the time of Shakespeare. Walford's Antiquarian 7–8 1885.

— and P. Newman. The inns of old Southwark and their associations. 1888.

Gaedertz, K. T. Zur Kenntnis der altenglischen Bühne. Bremen 1888. Includes de Witt's description and plan of the Swan theatre.

Greenstreet, J. The Whitefriars theatre in the time of Shakespeare. Trans New Shakspere Soc 1 1888.

— The Blackfriars playhouse: its antecedents. Athenaeum 17 July 1886, 7 Jan 1888.

— The Blackfriars theatre in the time of Shakespeare. Athenaeum 7–12 April 1888.

Ordish, T. F. Early London theatres. 1894.

Wallace, C. W. Old Blackfriars theatre: fresh discovery of documents. Times 11 Sept 1906.

— Three London theatres of Shakespeare's time. Nebraska Univ Stud 8 1908. On Red Bull, Fortune and Bear garden.

— The first London theatre. Nebraska Univ Stud 13 1913.

Archer, W. The Fortune theatre. Tribune 12 Oct 1907; Sh Jb 44 1908.

— The Swan drawing. Tribune 11 Jan 1908.

Feuillerat, A. The origins of Shakespeare's Blackfriars theatre. Sh Jb 48 1912.

— Blackfriars records. In Malone Society collections vol 2, Oxford 1913.

Graves, T. S. A note on the Swan theatre. MP 9 1912.

— Notes on the Elizabethan theatres. SP 17 1920.

— Richard Rawlidge on London playhouses. MP 18 1920.

— Some references to Elizabethan theatres. SP 19 1922.

Braines, W. W. Holywell priory and the site of the Theatre Shoreditch. 1915 (LCC).

— The site of the Theatre Shoreditch. London Topographical Records 11 1917.

— The site of the Globe playhouse Southwark. 1921, 1924 (enlarged).

Theatre Construction, Sites, Appearance and Reconstruction, including Models

See also Production, below.

Wheatley, H. B. On a contemporary drawing of the interior of the Swan theatre. Trans New Shakspere Soc 1888.

Logeman, H. Johannes de Witt's visit to the Swan theatre. Anglia 19 1897.

Chambers, E. K. The stage of the Globe. In his Works of Shakespeare vol 10, Stratford 1907.

— Illustrations of the interiors of playhouses: (a) Arend van Buchell's copy of a drawing by Johannes de Witt of the Swan theatre c. 1596; (b) a small engraving from the title-page of W. Alabaster's Roxana 1632; (c) a similar engraving from the title-page of N. Richards's Messalina 1640; (d) an engraved frontispiece to The Wits, Francis Kirkman's editions 1672, 1673. 1914.

Godfrey, W. H. An Elizabethan playhouse. Architectural Rev 23 1908.

— A scale model of the Fortune theatre. Architectural Rev 31 1912.

Adams, J. Q. The four pictorial representations of the Elizabethan stage. JEGP 10 1911.

Forestier, A. The Fortune theatre reconstructed. Illustr London News 12 Aug 1911.

Bell, H. Contributions to the history of the English playhouse. Architectural Rev 1913.

Brereton, J. le G. De Witt at the Swan. In his A book of homage, 1916.

— The Elizabethan playhouse. In his Writings on Elizabethan drama, Melbourne 1948.

The site of the Globe playhouse. In London County Council survey of London, 1921.

Hubbard, G. On the site of the Globe playhouse of Shakespeare. 1923.

Sisson, C. J. The theatres and companies. In A companion to Shakespeare studies, ed H. Granville-Barker and G. B. Harrison, Cambridge 1934.

— Mr and Mrs Browne of the Boar's Head. Life & Letters 16 1936.

Adams, J. C. The Globe playhouse: its design and equipment. Cambridge Mass 1942.

— 'That virtuous fabric'. Shakespeare Quart 2 1951. On the Globe.

Nicoll, A. A note on the Swan theatre drawing. Shakespeare Survey 1 1948.

Shapiro, I. A. The Bankside theatres: early engravings. Shakespeare Survey 1 1948.

— An original drawing of the Globe theatre. Shakespeare Survey 2 1949.

Barker, R. The structure of the first Globe theatre. Shakespeare Assoc Bull 24 1949.

Hotson, L. The projected amphitheatre. Shakespeare Survey 2 1949.

— Shakespeare's arena. Sewanee Rev 61 1953.

— Shakespeare's wooden O. 1959.

Roberts, J. R. H. and W. H. Godfrey (ed). Bankside. In London County Council survey of London vol 22, 1950.

Smith, I. Notes on the construction of the Globe model. Shakespeare Quart 2 1951.

— Theatre into Globe. Shakespeare Quart 3 1952.

— Shakespeare's Blackfriars playhouse: its history and its design. New York 1964.

Feldman, A. B. Dutch theatrical architecture in Elizabethan London. N & Q 11 Oct 1952.

Hodges, G. W. Unworthy scaffolds. Shakespeare Survey 3 1950.

— The Globe restored. 1953.

— The lantern of taste. Shakespeare Survey 12 1959. On design of the Elizabethan theatre.

Prouty, C. T. An early Elizabethan play-house. Shakespeare Survey 6 1953. On Trinity Hall.

Clark, W. S. The early Irish stage: the beginnings to 1720. Oxford 1955.

Wilson, F. P. The Elizabethan theatre. Neophilologus 39 1955.

— Lambarde, the Bel Savage and the theatre. N & Q March 1963.

Bordinat, P. A new site for the Salisbury Court theatre. N & Q Feb 1956.

Armstrong, W. A. The Elizabethan private theatres: facts and problems. Soc for Theatre Research 1958.

— The audience of the Elizabethan private theatres. RES new ser 10 1959.

— The enigmatic Elizabethan stage. English 13 1961.

Rothwell, W. F. Was there a typical Elizabethan stage? Shakespeare Survey 12 1959.

Southern, R. On reconstructing a practicable Elizabethan public playhouse. Shakespeare Survey 12 1959.

Kernodle, G. R. The open stage: Elizabethan or existentialist? Shakespeare Survey 12 1959.

Harris, A. J. William Poel's Elizabethan stage: the first experiment. Theatre Notebook 17 1962.

Reynolds. G. F. The return of the open stage. In Essays on Shakespeare and Elizabethan drama in honor of Hardin Craig, 1962.

Hosley, R. An approach to the Elizabethan stage. Renaissance Drama 6 1963.

— A reconstruction of the second Blackfriars. In The Elizabethan theatre, ed D. Galloway 1969.

— Elizabethan theatres and audiences. Research Opportunities in Renaissance Drama 10 1967.

Dawson, G. E. London's bull-baiting and bear-baiting arena in 1562. Shakespeare Quart 15 1964.

Langhams, E. A. A picture of the Salisbury Court theatre. Theatre Notebook 19 1965.

Whalley, J. The Swan theatre in the sixteenth century. Theatre Notebook 20 1965.

Somerset, J. A. B. William Poel's first full platform stage. Theatre Notebook 21 1966.

Mullin, D. C. An observation on the origin of the Elizabethan theatre. Educational Theatre Jnl 19 1967.

Wren, R. M. The five-entry stage at Blackfriars. Theatre Research 81 1967.

— Salisbury and the Blackfriars theatre. Theatre Notebook 23 1969.

Berry, H. The playhouse in the Boar's Head inn. In The Elizabethan theatre, ed D. Galloway 1969.

Rowan, D. F. A neglected Jones-Webb theatre project: Barber-surgeons' hall writ large. New Theatre Mag 9 1969.

— The cockpit-in-court. In The Elizabethan theatre, ed D. Galloway 1969.

Yates, F. A. The theatre of the world. 1969.

Gurr, A. The Shakespearean stage 1574–1642. Cambridge 1970.

Shapiro, M. Three notes on the theatre at Paul's c. 1569–c. 1607. Theatre Notebook 24 1970.

(5) COMPANIES, ACTORS AND PRODUCTION

Boy Actors

Davies, W. R. Shakespeare's boy actors. 1939.

Jamieson, M. Shakespeare's celibate stage. In Papers mainly Shakespearian collected by G. I. Duthie, 1964; rptd in The seventeenth-century stage, ed G. E. Bentley, Chicago 1968.

The Boy Companies

Albrecht, A. Das englische Kindertheater. Halle 1883.

Maas, H. Die Kindertruppen. Göttingen 1901.

— Äussere Geschichte der englischen Theatertruppen in dem Zeitraum von 1559 bis 1642. In Materialien vol 19, ed W. Bang, Louvain 1907.

Nairn, J. A. Boy actors under the Tudors and Stuarts. Trans Royal Soc of Lit 33 1913.

Hillebrand, H. N. The child actors. Urbana 1926.

Bradbrook, M. C. 'Silk? satin? kersey? rags?': the choristers' theatre under Elizabeth and James. Stud in Eng Lit 1500–1900 1 1961.

The Children of Paul's

Simpson, W. S. Gleanings from old Saint Paul's. 1889.

Bumpus, J. S. The organists and composers of St Paul's Cathedral. 1891.

McDonnell, M. F. J. A history of St Paul's school. 1909.

Leach, A. F. St Paul's school. Jnl of Education 31 1909.

— St Paul's school before Colet. Archaeologia 62 1910.

Flood, W. H. G. Master Sebastian. Musical Antiquary 3–4 1911–13.

Hillebrand, H. N. Sebastian Westcote, dramatist and master of the children of Paul's. JEGP 14 1915.

Brown, A. A note on Sebastian Westcott and the play presented by the children of St Paul's. MLQ 12 1951.

Gair, W. R. La compagnie des enfants de St Paul Londres 1559–1606. In Dramaturgie et société vol 2, ed J. Jacquot, Paris 1968.

Jacquot, J. Le répertoire des compagnies d'enfants à Londres 1600–10. Ibid. On the children of Paul's and the children of the Chapel, later of the Queen's revels.

Lennam, T. The children of Paul's 1551–82. In The Elizabethan theatre vol 2, ed D. Galloway 1970.

Rimbault, E. F. The old cheque book of the Chapel Royal. 1872 (Camden Soc).

Stopes, C. C. W. Hunnis. Sh Jb 27 1892.

— W. Hunnis, the dramatist. Athenaeum 31 March 1900.

— Mary's Chapel Royal and her coronation play. Athenaeum 9 Sept 1905.

— W. Hunnis and the revels of the Chapel Royal. In Materialien vol 29, ed W. Bang, Louvain 1910.

Durand, W. Y. Notes on Richard Edwards. JEGP 4 1902.

— Some errors concerning Richard Edwards. MLN 23 1908.

Wallace, C. W. The children of the Chapel at Blackfriars 1597–1603. Nebraska Univ Stud 8 1908.

Manly, J. M. The children of the Chapel Royal and their masters. CHEL vol 6 1910.

Feuillerat, A. The origin of Shakespeare's Blackfriars theatre. Sh Jb 48 1912.

Flood, W. H. G. Queen Mary's Chapel Royal. EHR 33 1918.

Hillebrand, H. N. The early history of the Chapel Royal. MP 18 1920.

Lecocq, L. Le théâtre de Blackfriars de 1596 à 1606. In Dramaturgie et société vol 2, ed J. Jacquot, Paris 1968.

The Children of the King's Revels

Greenstreet, J. The Whitefriars theatre in the time of Shakespeare. Trans New Shakspere Soc pt 3 1889.

Hillebrand, H. N. The children of the King's revels at Whitefriars. JEGP 21 1922.

The Adult Companies

Greenstreet, J. Documents relating to the players at the Red Bull, Clerkenwell and the Cockpit in Drury Lane in the time of James I. Trans New Shakspere Soc 1880–5.

Maas, H. Äussere Geschichte der englischen Theatertruppen in dem Zeitraum von 1559 bis 1642. In Materialien vol 19, ed W. Bang, Louvain 1907.

Murray, J. T. English dramatic companies 1558–1642: vol 1, London companies; vol 2, provincial companies. 1910.

Wallace, C. W. The Swan theatre and the Earl of Pembroke's servants. E Studien 43 1911.

Chambers, E. K. Plays of the King's men in 1641. In Malone Society collections vol 1, Oxford 1911.

— Elizabethan stage gleanings. RES 1 1925.

Thaler, A. The Elizabethan dramatic companies. PMLA 35 1920.

Baldwin, T. W. The organisation and personnel of the Shakespearean company. Princeton 1927.

Sisson, C. J. Notes on early Stuart stage history. MLR 37 1942.

— The Red Bull company and the importunate widow. Shakespeare Survey 7 1954.

Harbage, A. Shakespeare and the rival traditions. New York 1952.

Court Performances and Provincial Tours

Cunningham, P. Extracts from the accounts of the revels at Court. 1842 (Shakespeare Soc).

Halliwell-Phillipps, J. O. The visits of Shakespeare's company of actors to the provincial cities and towns of England. Brighton 1887.

Murray, J. T. English dramatic companies in the towns outside of London 1550–1600. MP 2 1905.

Chambers, E. K. Court performances before Queen Elizabeth. MLR 2 1906.

— Court performances under James I. MLR 4 1909.

— Players at Ipswich. In Malone Society collections vol 2 pt 3, Oxford 1931.

Thaler, A. The players at Court 1564–1642. JEGP 19 1920.

— The travelling players in Shakespeare's England. MP 17 1920.

— Strolling players and provincial drama after Shakespeare. PMLA 37 1922.

— Faire Em (and Shakespeare's company?) in Lancashire. PMLA 46 1931.

Tillotson, G. Othello and the Alchemist at Oxford in 1610. TLS 20 July 1933.

Crundell, H. W. Visits of dramatic companies to Bristol 1587–1600. N & Q 11 June 1936.

Brown, A. Sebastian Westcott at York. MLR 47 1952.

Greenslade, S. L. The Elizabethan theatre. TLS 25 April 1952. On performances in Durham.

Rosenfeld, S. Dramatic companies in the provinces in the sixteenth and seventeenth centuries. Theatre Notebook 8 1954.

Stone, L. Companies of players entertained by the Earl of Cumberland and Lord Clifford, 1607–39. In Malone Society collections vol 5, Oxford 1959.

Dawson, G. E. Records, plays and players in Kent 1450–1642. In Malone Society collections vol 7, Oxford 1965.

Salingar, L. G., G. Harrison and B. Cochrane. Les comédiens et leur public en Angleterre de 1520 à 1640. In Dramaturgie et société vol 2, ed J. Jacquot, Paris 1968.

English Actors Abroad

See E. K. Chambers, The Elizabethan stage vol 2: the international companies.

Tittman, J. Die Schauspiele der englischen Komödianten in Deutschland. Leipzig 1880.

Cohn, A. Englische Komödianten in Köln 1592–1656. Sh Jb 21 1886.

Meissner, J. Die englischen Komödianten in Österreich. Sh Jb 19 1884.

Trautmann, K. Englische Komödianten in Nürnberg bis zum Schluss des 30jährigen Krieges 1593–1648: englische Komödianten in Ulm 1602. Archiv für Literaturgeschichte 14–15 1886–7.

Bolte, J. Englische Komödianten in Dänemark und Schweden. Sh Jb 23 1888.

— Die Singspiele der englischen Komödianten und ihrer Nachfolger in Deutschland, Holland und Skandinavien. Hamburg 1893.

— Das Danziger Theater im 16 und 17 Jahrhundert. Hamburg 1895.

— Englische Komödianten in Münster und Ulm. Sh Jb 36 1900.

Creizenach, W. Die Schauspiele der englischen Komödianten. Berlin 1889.

Meyer, C. F. Englische Komödianten am Hofe des Herzogs Philipp Julius von Pommern-Wolgast. Sh Jb 38 1902.

Herz, E. Englische Schauspieler und englisches Schauspiel zur Zeit Shakespeares in Deutschland. Hamburg 1903.

Brandl, A. Englische Komödianten in Frankfurt. Sh Jb 40 1904.

Harris, C. The English comedians in Germany before the Thirty Years War: the financial side. PMLA 22 1907.

Yates, F. A. English actors in Paris during the lifetime of Shakespeare. RES 1 1925.

Freden, G. A propos du théâtre anglais en Allemagne: l'auteur inconnu des Comédies et tragédies anglaises de 1620. Revue de Littérature Comparée 8 1928.

— Friedrich Menius und das Repertoire der englischen Komödianten in Deutschland. Stockholm 1937.

Baesecke, A. Das Schauspiel der englischen Komödianten in Deutschland. Halle 1935.

Pascal, R. The stage of the 'Englische Komödianten': three problems. MLR 35 1940.

Lea, K. M. English players at the Swedish Court. MLR 26 1931.

Gray, M. M. Queen Elizabeth's players. TLS 14 Jan 1939. In Scotland 1589.

Wikland, E. Elizabethan players in Sweden 1591–2: facts and problems. Stockholm 1962.

Hoppe, H. R. English actors at Ghent in the seventeenth century. RES 25 1949.

— George Jolly at Bruges 1648. RES new ser 5 1954.

— English acting companies at the Court of Brussels in the seventeenth century. RES new ser 6 1955.

Feldman, A. B. Playwrights and pike-trailers in the Low Countries. N & Q May 1953.

Riewald, J. G. New light on the English actors in the Netherlands. E Studies 41 1960.

Foreign Actors in England

Smith, W. Italian and Elizabethan comedy. MP 5 1908.

— The commedia dell'arte. New York 1912.

— Italian actors in Elizabethan England. MLN 44 1929.

Lawrence, W. J. Early French players in England. In The Elizabethan playhouse, Stratford 1912.

Chambers, E. K. Italian players in England. TLS 12 May 1921.

Fletcher, I. K. Italian comedians in England in the seventeenth century. Theatre Notebook 8 1954.

Rosenfeld, S. Foreign theatrical companies in Great Britain in the seventeenth and eighteenth centuries. Soc for Theatre Research pamphlet ser no 4 1954.

Actors and Acting

Halliwell(-Phillipps), J. O. Tarlton's Jests and news out of purgatory; with notes and some account of the life of Tarlton. 1844 (Shakespeare Soc).

Collier, J. P. Memoirs of the principal actors in the plays of Shakespeare. 1846 (Shakespeare Soc).

— Memoirs of Edward Alleyn. 1841.

— A collection of original documents illustrative of the life and times of Edward Alleyn. 2 vols 1843 (Shakespeare Soc).

Fleay, F. G. On the actor lists 1578–1642. Trans Royal Historical Soc 9 1881.

Young, W. The history of Dulwich College; with a life of Edward Alleyn. 2 vols Edinburgh 1889.

Wallace, C. W. Gervase Markham, dramatist. Sh Jb 46 1910.

Chambers, E. K. Two early player-lists. In Malone Society collections vol 1, Oxford 1911.

Stopes, C. C. Burbage and Shakespeare's stage. 1913.

Simpson, P. Actors and acting. In Shakespeare's England vol 2, Oxford 1916.

Gaw, A. Actors' names in the register of St Botolph Aldgate. PMLA 40 1925.

— John Sincklo as one of Shakespeare's actors. Anglia 49 1926.

Graves, T. S. Women on the pre-Restoration stage. SP 22 1925.

Denkinger, E. M. Actors' names in the register of St Botolph Aldgate. PMLA 41 1926.

Gray, A. K. Robert Armine, the foole. PMLA 42 1927.

Greg, W. W. Edward Alleyn. 1927 (Shakespeare Soc).

Harrison, G. B. Shakespeare's actors. 1927 (Shakespeare Assoc).

Bentley, G. E. New actors of the Elizabethan period. MLN 44 1929.

Boswell, E. Young Mr Cartwright. MLR 24 1929.

Nungezer, E. A dictionary of actors and of other persons associated with the public representation of plays in England before 1642. New Haven 1929.

Harbage, A. Elizabethan acting. Oxford 1951, 1964 (rev).

Campbell, L. B. Richard Tarlton and the earthquake of 1580. HLQ 4 1941.

McNeir, W. F. Gayton on Elizabethan acting. Folklore Quart 12 1948.

Bowers, R. H. Gesticulation in Elizabethan acting. Folklore Quart 12 1948.

Bachrach, A. G. H. The great chain of acting. Neophilologus 33 1949.

Bethell, S. L. Shakespeare's actors. RES new ser 1 1950.

Brook, D. A pageant of English actors. 1950.

Joseph, B. L. Elizabethan acting. Oxford 1951, 1964 (rev).

Hosking, G. L. The life and times of Edward Alleyn. 1952.

Brown, J. R. On the acting of Shakespeare's plays. Quart Jnl of Speech 34 1953; rptd in The seventeenth-century stage, ed G. E. Bentley, Chicago 1968.

Foakes, R. A. The player's passion: some notes on Elizabethan psychology and acting. E & S new ser 7 1954.

Rosenberg, M. Elizabethan actors: men or marionettes? PMLA 69 1954.

Klein, D. Elizabethan acting. PMLA 71 1956.

Mithal, H. S. D. 'Will, my Lord of Leicester's jesting player'. N & Q Oct 1958. Reply by R. C. Bald, March 1959.

—— Mr Kemp, called Don Gulielmo. N & Q Jan 1960.

Mills, L. J. The acting in university comedy of early seventeenth-century England. In Studies in English Renaissance drama, ed J. W. Bennett et al, New York 1959.

Riewald, J. G. Some later Elizabethan and early Stuart actors and musicians. E Studies 40 1959.

David, R. Shakespeare and the players. Proc Br Acad 47 1961.

Bradbrook, M. C. The rise of the common player: a study of actor and society in Shakespeare's England. 1962.

—— The status seekers: society and the common player in the reign of Elizabeth I. HLQ 24 1961; rptd in The seventeenth-century stage, ed G. E. Bentley, Chicago 1968.

Gurr, A. J. Who strutted and bellowed? Shakespeare Survey 16 1963.

Armstrong, W. A. Actors and theatres. Shakespeare Survey 17 1964.

Wright, W. S. Edward Alleyn: actor and benefactor. Theatre Notebook 20 1966.

Madker, L. The theory of Elizabethan acting. In The Elizabethan theatre vol 2, ed D. Galloway 1970.

Production and Staging

Creizenach, W. Geschichte des neueren Dramas. 5 vols Halle 1893–1916.

Mantzius, K. Skuespilkunstens historie. 5 vols Copenhagen 1897–1907; tr 6 vols 1903–21.

Brodmeier, C. Die Shakespeare-Bühne nach den alten Bühnenweisungen. Jena 1902.

Moenkemeyer, P. Prolegomena zu einer Darstellung der englischen Volksbühne zur Elisabeth- und Stuart-Zeit nach den alten Bühnenweisungen. Göttingen 1905.

Reynolds, G. F. Some principles of Elizabethan staging. 2 pts Chicago 1905; MP 2 1905.

—— What we know of the Elizabethan stage. MP 9 1912.

—— William Percy and his plays. MP 12 1914.

—— The staging of Elizabethan plays at the Red Bull theater 1605–25. New York 1940.

—— Some problems of Elizabethan staging. Colorado Univ Stud general ser A 26 1941.

—— Staging Elizabethan plays. Shakespeare Assoc Bull 24 1949.

—— Was there a 'tarras' in Shakespeare's Globe? Shakespeare Survey 4 1951.

Wegener, R. Die Bühneneinrichtung des Shakespeareschen Theaters nach den zeitgenössischen Dramen. Halle 1907.

Child, H. H. The Elizabethan theatre. CHEL vol 6 1910.

Pilch, L. Shakespeare als Regisseur. Zeitschrift für Französischen und englischen Unterricht 10 1911.

Reese, G. H. Studien und Beiträge zur Geschichte der englischen Schauspielkunst im Zeitalter Shakespeares. Jena 1911.

Lawrence, W. J. The Elizabethan playhouse and other studies. 2 sers Stratford 1912–13.

—— Pre-Restoration stage studies. Cambridge Mass 1927.

—— The physical conditions of the Elizabethan public playhouse. Cambridge Mass 1927.

—— Those nut-cracking Elizabethans. 1935.

—— Some characteristics of the Elizabethan-Stuart stage. E Studien 32 1902.

—— Night performances in the Elizabethan theatres. E Studien 48 1915.

—— New light on the Elizabethan theatre. Fortnightly Rev May 1916.

—— A forgotten playhouse custom of Shakespeare's day. In A book of homage to Shakespeare, 1916.

Albright, V. E. Percy's plays as proof of the Elizabethan stage. MP 11 1913.

Thorndike, A. H. From outdoors to indoors on the Elizabethan stage. In Anniversary papers by colleagues and pupils of G. L. Kittredge, Boston 1913.

Poel, W. Shakespeare in the theatre. 1915.

—— Some notes on Shakespeare's stage and plays. 1916.

Dickinson, T. H. Some principles of Shakespeare staging. In Wisconsin Shakespeare studies, Madison 1916.

Rhodes, R. C. The stagery of Shakespeare. Birmingham 1922.

Bradbrook, M. C. Elizabethan stage conditions. Cambridge 1932.

Isaacs, J. Production and stage-management at the Blackfriars theatre. 1933 (Shakespeare Assoc).

Kernodle, G. R. From art to theatre: form and convention in the Renaissance. Chicago 1943.

McDowell, J. H. Conventions of medieval art in Shakespearian staging. JEGP 47 1948.

Triebel, L. A. Sixteenth-century stagecraft in European drama: a survey. MLQ 11 1950.

Saunders, J. W. Vaulting the rails. Shakespeare Survey 7 1954.

Armstrong, W. A. 'Canopy' in Elizabethan theatrical terminology. N & Q Oct 1957.

Hosley, R. The gallery over the stage in the public playhouse of Shakespeare's time. Shakespeare Quart 8 1957.

Nicoll, A. Passing over the stage. Shakespeare Survey 12 1959.

Stamm, R. Elizabethan stage-practice and the transmutation of source material by the dramatists. Shakespeare Survey 12 1959.

Weiner, A. B. Elizabethan interior and aloft scenes: a speculative essay. Theatre Survey 1961.

Jones, E. D. The physical representation of African characters on the English stage during the 16th and 17th centuries. Theatre Notebook 17 1962.

Southern R. The contribution of the interludes to Elizabethan staging. In Essays on Shakespeare and Elizabethan drama in honour of Hardin Craig, 1963.

King, T. J. The staging of plays at the Phoenix in Drury Lane 1617–42. Theatre Notebook 19 1965.

Scenery, Costume and Properties

Reynolds, G. F. Trees on the stage of Shakespeare. MP 4 1907.

Stopes, C. C. Elizabethan stage scenery. Fortnightly Rev June 1907.

Boas, F. S. and W. W. Greg. James I at Oxford in 1605: property lists from the university archives. In Malone Society collections vol 1, Oxford 1909.

Wallace, C. W. Globe theatre apparel. 1909.

Keith, W. G. The designs for the first movable scenery on the English stage. Burlington Mag 25 1914.

Lawrence, W. J. The Elizabethan stage throne. Texas Rev Jan 1918.

—— Bells on the Elizabethan stage. Fortnightly Rev July 1924.

Graves, T. S. The Devil in the playhouse. South Atlantic Quart 19 1920.

Campbell, L. B. Scenes and machines on the English stage during the Renaissance. Cambridge 1923.

Simpson, P. and C. F. Bell. Designs by Inigo Jones for masques and plays at Court. Oxford 1924 (Malone Soc and Walpole Soc).

Bradner, L. Stages and stage scenery in Court drama before 1558. RES 1 1925.

Wright, L. B. Elizabethan sea drama and its staging. Anglia 51 1927.

Winninghof, E. Das Theaterkostüm bei Shakespeare. Münster 1928.

Hunt, T. B. The scenes as Shakespeare saw them. In T. M. Parrott presentation volume, Princeton 1935.

Linthicum, M. C. Costume in the drama of Shakespeare and his contemporaries. Oxford 1936.

Nicoll, A. Scenery between Shakespeare and Dryden. TLS 15 Aug 1936.

Kelly, F. M. Shakespearian costume for stage and screen. 1938.

McDowell, J. H. Tudor Court staging: a study in perspective. JEGP 44 1945.

Feldman, A. B. Hans Ewouts: artist of the Tudor Court theatre. N & Q 10 June 1950.

Southern, R. Changeable scenery: its origin and development in the British theatre. 1952.

—— and C. W. Hodges. Colour in the Elizabethan theatre. Theatre Notebook 6 1952.

Miller, W. E. Periaktoi in the old Blackfriars. MLN 74 1959.

—— Periaktoi: around again. Shakespeare Quart 15 1964. On stage machines in the old Blackfriars.

Smith, H. H. Some principles of Elizabethan stage costume. Jnl Warburg & Courtauld Inst 25 1962.

Tatarkiewicz, W. Theatrica: the science of entertainment from the 12th to the 17th century. JHI 26 1965.

Music in the Theatre

Arkwright, G. E. P. Early Elizabethan stage music. Musical Antiquary 1–4 1909–13.

—— Elizabethan choirboys and their music. Proc Musical Assoc 1914.

Cowling, G. H. Music on the Shakespearian stage. 1913.

Lawrence, W. J. Music in the Elizabethan theatre. Musical Quart 6 1920.

Flood, G. Early Tudor composers. 1925.

Moore, J. H. The songs of the public theaters in the time of Shakespeare. JEGP 28 1929.

Woodfill, W. F. Musicians in English society from Elizabeth to Charles I. Princeton 1953.

Cutts, J. P. Jacobean masque and stage music. Music & Letters 35 1954.

—— Some Jacobean and Caroline dramatic lyrics. N & Q March 1955.

—— Musique de scène de la troupe de Shakespeare. Paris 1959.

Manifold, J. S. The music in English drama from Shakespeare to Purcell. 1956.

Hosley, R. Was there a music-room in Shakespeare's Globe? Shakespeare Survey 13 1960.

Stevens, J. Music and poetry in the early Tudor Court. Cambridge 1961.

Long, J. H. (ed). Music in Renaissance drama. Lexington Kentucky 1968.

Jigs, Variety Entertainments, Extemporal Acting

Graves, T. S. The ass as actor. South Atlantic Quart 15 1916.

—— The Elizabethan trained ape. MLN 35 1920.

—— Some aspects of extemporal acting. SP 19 1922.

Strunk, W. The Elizabethan showman's ape. MLN 32 1917.

Lawrence, W. J. He's for a jig or —. TLS 3 July 1919.

—— Horses on the Elizabethan stage. TLS 5 June 1919.

—— Shakespeare and the Italian comedians. TLS 11 Nov 1920.

Wright, L. B. Will Kemp and the commedia dell'arte. MLN 41 1926.

—— Animal actors on the English stage before 1642. PMLA 42 1927.

—— Juggling tricks and conjuring on the English stage before 1642. MP 24 1927.

—— Stage duelling in the Elizabethan theater. MLR 22 1927; rptd in The seventeenth-century stage, ed G. E. Bentley, Chicago 1968.

—— Variety entertainments by Elizabethan strolling players. JEGP 26 1927.

—— Variety-show clownery on the pre-Restoration stage. Anglia 52 1928.

—— Vaudeville dancing and acrobatics in Elizabethan plays. E Studien 63 1928.

—— Madmen as vaudeville performers on the Elizabethan stage. JEGP 30 1931.

Marschall, W. Das Sir Thomas Moore-Manuskript und die englische Commedia dell'arte. Anglia 52 1928.

Baskervill, C. R. The Elizabethan jig and related song drama. Chicago 1929.

Lea, K. M. Italian popular comedy. 2 vols Oxford 1934.

(6) THEATRE MANAGEMENT AND STAGE MANAGEMENT

See E. K. Chambers, The Elizabethan stage vol 1, The actors' economies.

Maas, H. Äussere Geschichte der englischen Theatertruppen in dem Zeitraum von 1559 bis 1642. In Materialien vol 19, ed W. Bang, Louvain 1907.

Wallace, C. W. The Globe and Blackfriars systems of finance. TLS 2–9 Oct 1909.

—— Shakespeare and the Blackfriars. Century Mag Sept 1910.

Aronstein, P. Die Organisation des englischen Schauspiels im Zeitalter Shakespeares. Germanisch-romanische Monatsschrift 2 1910.

Baskervill, C. R. The custom of sitting on the Elizabethan stage. MP 8 1911.

Graves, T. S. The origin of the custom of sitting on the stage. JEGP 13 1914.

—— Night scenes in the Elizabethan theatres. E Studien 47 1914.

—— Organized applause. South Atlantic Quart 19 1920.

Thaler, A. Shakespeare's income. SP 15 1918.

—— Playwright's benefits and interior gathering in the Elizabethan theatre. SP 16 1919.

—— The 'Free-list' and theatre tickets in Shakespeare's time and after. MLR 15 1920.

—— Shakespeare to Sheridan: a book about the theatre of yesterday and today. Cambridge Mass 1922.

—— Minor actors and employees in the Elizabethan theatre. MP 20 1922.

Adams, J. Q. The housekeepers of the Globe. MP 17 1919.

Rhodes, R. C. Shakespeare's prompt books: 1, Stage directions; 2, The curtains. TLS 21–8 July 1921.

Holzknecht, K. J. Theatrical billposting in the age of Elizabeth. PQ 1 1923.

Engelen, J. Die Schauspieler-Ökonomie in Shakespeares Dramen. Münster 1926.

Wilson, F. P. Ralph Crane, scrivener to the King's players. Library 4th ser 7 1926; rptd in The seventeenth-century stage, ed G. E. Bentley, Chicago 1968.

Baldwin, T. W. The organisation and personnel of the Shakespearian company. Princeton 1927.

Bald, R. C. The entrance to the Elizabethan theatre. Shakespeare Quart 3 1952.

Main, W. W. Dramaturgical norms in Elizabethan repertory. SP 54 1957.

Demadre, A. Un témoin: Thomas Nashe. In Dramaturgie et société vol 2, ed J. Jacquot, Paris 1968. Nashe as witness of playhouse practice.

Ringler, W. A. The number of actors in Shakespeare's early plays. In The seventeenth-century stage, ed G. E. Bentley, Chicago 1968.

Audiences

Sisson, C. J. Le goût public et le théâtre élisabéthain. Dijon 1921.

Harbage, A. Shakespeare's audience. New York 1941.

Armstrong, W. A. The audience of the Elizabethan private theatres. RES new ser 10 1959; rptd in The seventeenth-century stage, ed G. E. Bentley, Chicago 1968.

Leech, C. The Caroline audience. MLR 36 1942; rptd in his Shakespeare's tragedies and other studies in seventeenth-century drama, 1950.

Hosley, R. Elizabethan theatres and audiences. Research Opportunities in Renaissance Drama 10 1967.

Johnson, R. C. Audience involvement in the Tudor interludes. Theatre Notebook 24 1970.

Miscellaneous

Graves, T. S. The 'act-time' in Elizabethan theatres. SP 12 1915.

Hunter, M. Act- and scene-division in the plays of Shakespeare. RES 2 1926.

Greg, W. W. The evidence of theatrical plots for the history of the Elizabethan stage. RES 1 1925.

— Two Elizabethan stage-abridgements: the Battle of Alcazar and Orlando Furioso. Oxford 1928.

— Act-divisions in Shakespeare. RES 4 1928.

— Dramatic documents from the Elizabethan playhouse: stage plots, actors' plots, prompt books. 2 vols Oxford 1931.

Lawrence, W. J. Act-intervals in early Shakespearian performances. RES 4 1928.

Sack, M. Darstellerzahl und Rollenverteilung bei Shakespeare. Leipzig 1928.

Hart, A. Play abridgement: length of plays, time allotted for representation, acting versions. RES 8 1932, 10 1934; rptd in Shakespeare and the homilies, Melbourne 1935.

Adams, J. Q. The author-plot of an early seventeenth-century play. Library 4th ser 26 1946.

Bromberg, M. Theatrical wagers: a sidelight on the Elizabethan drama. N & Q Dec 1951.

McCullen, J. T. The use of parlor and tavern games in Elizabethan and early Tudor drama. MLQ 14 1953.

Jewkes, W. T. Act division in Elizabethan and Jacobean plays 1583–1616. Hamden Conn 1958.

Oras, A. Pause patterns in Elizabethan and Jacobean drama: an experiment in prosody. Gainesville 1960.

III. THE PURITAN ATTACK ON THE STAGE

(1) BIBLIOGRAPHIES

Gardiner, S. R. Documents relating to William Prynne. 1877 (Camden Soc).

Lowe, R. W. A bibliographical account of English theatrical literature. 1888; rev in J. F. Arnott and J. W. Robinson, English theatrical literature 1559–1900: a bibliography, 1970.

Symmes, N. S. Les débuts de la critique dramatique. Paris 1903.

Thompson, E. N. S. The controversy between the Puritans and the stage. New York 1903.

Chambers, E. K. The Elizabethan stage vol 4. Oxford 1923. Documentary material.

Wickham, G. Early English stages vol 2 pt 1. 1963.

(2) CONTEMPORARY ACCOUNTS

Manuscripts

Field, Nathaniel. Feild the players letter to Mr Sutton preacher att St Mary Overs 1616; Calendar of state papers, domestic, James I 89 no 105; rptd J. O. Halliwell-(Phillipps), The remonstrance of Nathan Field, 1865; and in his Illustrations of the life of Shakespeare vol 1 appendix 23, 1874.

Gager, William. See Corpus Christi College library Oxford ms 352, 6; and University College library Oxford ms J 18; and under F. S. Boas and K. Young, below.

Remembrancia: a series of records preserved in the office of the town clerk of the City of London. Documents rptd in Malone Society collections vol 1 pt 1, Oxford 1907. See the City's letter books, the journals of the Common Council, and the repertories of the Court of Aldermen.

Printed works
(in alphabetical order)

Agrippa. Henrie Cornelius Agrippa, of the vanitie and uncertaintie of artes and sciences, englished by Ja. San. gent. 1569, 1575.

Alley, William. ΠΤΩΧΟΜΥΣΕΙΟΝ: the poore mans librarie. 2 vols 1565, 1570.

Ascham, Roger. The scholemaster. 1570.

Babington, Gervase. A very fruitfull exposition of the commaundments by way of questions and answeres for greater plainnesse. 1583; partly rptd in F. J. Furnivall, Stubbes's Anatomy of abuses pt 1, 1879 (New Shakespeare Soc).

Beard, Thomas. The theatre of God's judgments translated out of the French and augmented. 1597, 1612.

Bodin, Jean. Les six livres de la république. Paris 1576; tr R. Knolles 1606.

Brome, Alexander. Rump: or an exact collection of the choycest poems and songs relating to the late times. 1662.

Bucer, Marton. Scripta anglicana. Basle 1577.

Case, John. Speculum moralium quaestionum in universam ethicen Aristotelis. Oxford 1585, 1589.

Chettle, Henry. Kind-harts dreame: conteining five appritions, with their invectives against abuses raigning. 1593; rptd in Elizabethan and Jacobean quartos, ed G. B. Harrison 1923.

Coke, Sir Edward. The Lord Coke his speech and charge; with a discoverie of the abuses and corruption of officers. 1607.

Crashawe, William. The sermon preached at the crosse Feb 14 1607. 1607.

Elyot, Sir Thomas. The boke named the governour. 1531; ed H. H. S. Croft 2 vols 1880.

Fenton, Sir Geoffrey. Certain tragicall discourses written out of Frenche and Latin. 1567.

— A forme of Christian pollicie gathered out of French. 1574.

Ferrarius. A woorke of Johannes Ferrarius Montanus, touchynge the good orderynge of a common weale, englished by William Bavande. 1559.

Field, John. A godly exhortation, by occasion of the late judgement of God shewed at Parris-garden, the thirteenth day of Januarie. 1583.

Gainsford, Thomas. The rich cabnit furnished with a varietie of exquisite discriptions, exquisite characters, witty discourses and delightful histories. 1616.

Gosson, Stephen. The schoole of abuse: conteining a pleasaunt invective against poets, pipers, plaiers, jesters and such like caterpillers of a commonwealth. 1579, 1587; ed Walter Scott, Somers tracts vol 3, 1809–15 (2nd edn); rptd J. P. Collier 1841 (Shakespeare Soc); ed E. Arber 1895.

— The Ephemerides of Phialo, devided into three bookes. 1579, 1586.

— Playes confuted in five actions. 1582; rptd in W. C. Hazlitt, English drama and stage, 1869.

— Pleasant quippes for upstart newfangled gentlewomen. 1596 (anon); ed E. F. Rimbault 1841; ed E. J. Howard, Oxford Ohio 1942.

— The trumpet of warre: a sermon preached at Paules crosse the seventh of Maie 1598. [1598].

Greene, John. A refutation of the apology for actors. 1615. See T. Heywood, below.

Greene, Robert. Greenes never too late: or a powder of experience sent to all youthfull gentlewomen. 1590.

Harvey, Gabriel. Three proper and wittie, familiar letters, touching the earthquake in April last, lately passed between two universitie men. 1580; ed A. B. Grosart, Harvey's works, 3 vols 1884.

Heywood, Thomas. An apology for actors. 1612, 1625 (as The actors vindication); ed Walter Scott, Somers tracts vol 3, 1809–15 (2nd edn); ed J. P. Collier 1841 (Shakespeare Soc).

Lake, Osmund. A probe theologicall: or the first part of the Christian pastors proofe of his learned parishioners faith. 1612.

Laneham, Robert. A letter: wherein part of the entertainment untoo the Queenz Majesty at Killingwoorth castl, in Warwik sheer in this soomerz progress 1575 iz signified. 1575; ed F. J. Furnivall, Captain Cox, his ballads and books, 1871 (Ballad Soc).

Lodge, Thomas. Honest excuses: a reply to Stephen Gosson's Schoole of abuse in defence of poetry musick and stage plays. 1579; ed D. Lang, A defence of poetry, 1853 (Shakespeare Soc); ed E. Gosse, Complete works of Lodge, 1883; ed G. Saintsbury, Elizabethan and Jacobean pamphlets, 1892.

— An alarum against usurers: containing tryed experiences against wordly abuses. 1584; ed D. Lang 1853 (Shakespeare Soc); ed E. Gosse, Complete works of Lodge, 1883.

Lupton, Donald. London and the countrey carbonadoed and quartred into severall characters. 1632; rptd Harleian miscellany vol 9, 1808; ed J. O. Halliwell-(Phillipps), Books of characters, 1857.

Mariana, Juan de. Tratado contra los juegos publicos; rptd in Obras, biblioteca de autores espanoles, 2 vols Madrid 1854.

— De rege et regis institutione. Toledo 1599.

Nashe, Thomas. The anatomie of absurditie: contayning a breefe confutation of the slender imputed prayses to feminine perfection, with a short description of the severall practises of youth, and sundry follies of our licentious times. 1589; ed R. B. McKerrow, Nashe's Works vol 1, 1904.

— Pierce penilesse his supplication to the Divell. 1592; ed R. B. McKerrow, Nashe's Works vol 1, 1904.

Newes from the north: otherwise called the conference between Simon certain and Pierce plowman, faithfully collected and gathered by T. F. Student. 1585.

Newton, Thomas. A treatise, touching dyce-play and prophane gaming, written in Latine by Lambertus Danaeus. 1586.

North, Thomas. The diall of princes, compiled by the reverende father in God, Don Anthony of Guevera, Bysshop of Guadix, preacher and cronicler to Charles the Fyft Emperour of Rome; englysshed oute of the Frenche. 1557.

Northbrooke, John. Spiritus est vicarius Christi in terra: a treatise wherein dicing, dauncing, vaine playes or enterlude with other idle pastimes &c commonly used on the sabboth day, are reproved by the authoritie of the word of God and auntient writers: made dialoguewise. 1577, 1579; ed J. P. Collier 1843 (Shakespeare Soc).

Overbury, Sir Thomas. A wife now the widdow of Sir Thomas Overburye: being a most exquisite and singular poem of the choice of a wife. 1614; ed E. F. Rimbault, Miscellaneous works of Overbury, 1856.

Prynne, William. Histriomastix: the players scourge, or actors tragoedie, divided into two parts; where it is largely evidenced, by divers arguments, by the concurring authorities and resolutions of sundry texts of scripture, of the whole primitive church, both under the law and gospell, of 55 synodes and councels, of 71 fathers and Christian writers before the yeare of our Lord 1200, of above 150 foraigne and domestique Protestant and Popish authors since, of 40 heathen philosophers, historians, poets, of many heathen, many Christian nations, republiques, emperors, princes, magistrates, of sundry apostolicall, canonicall, imperial constitutions, and of our owne English statutes, magistrates, universities, writers, preachers, that popular stage-plays (the very pompes of the Divell which we renounce in baptisme, if we beleeve the fathers) are sinfull, lewde, ungodly spectacles, and most pernicious corruptions, condemned in all ages, as intolerable mischiefes to churches, to republickes, to the manners, mindes, and soules of men; and that the profession of play-poets, of stage-players, together with the penning, acting, and frequenting of stage playes, are unlawfull, infamous and misbeseeming Christians. 1633.

— Mr William Prynn his defence of stage-plays: or a retraction of a former book of his called Histriomastix. 1549. A forgery; rptd in W. C. Hazlitt, English drama and stage, 1869.

— The vindication of William Prynne esquire from some scandalous papers and imputations newly printed and published to traduce and defame him in his reputation from the King's head in the Strand, Jan 10 1648. A broadside; ed J. P. Collier, Poetical Decameron, 2 vols 1820; ed W. C. Hazlitt, English drama and stage, 1869.

Rainolds, John. Th'overthrow of stage-playes, by the way of controversie betwixt D. Gager and D. Rainoldes, wherein all the reasons that can be made for them are notably refuted, th'objections aunswered and the case so cleared and resolved, as that the judgement of any man, that is not froward and perverse, may easily be satisfied; whereunto are added also and annexed in th'end certain latine letters betwixt the sayed Maister Rainoldes and D. Gentiles, reader of the civill law in Oxford, concerning the same matter. 1599, Oxford 1629.

Rankins, William. A mirrour of monsters: wherein is plainely described the manifold vices and spotted enormities that are caused by the infectious sight of playes, with the description of the subtile slights of Sathan, making them his instruments. 1587.

Rawlidge, Richard. A monster lately found out and discovered: or the scourging of tipplers. 1627.

A second and third blast of retrait from plaies and theatres: the one whereof was sounded by a reverend Byshop dead long since; the other by a worshipful and zealous gentleman now alive; one showing the filthiness of plaies in times past, the other the abhomination of theatres in the time present; both expresly proving that the commonweale is nigh unto the curse of God, wherein either plaiers be made of, or theatres maintined; set forth by Anglo-phile Eutheo. 1580; ed W. C. Hazlitt, English drama and stage, 1869.

A short treatise against stage-plays. Middelburgh 1625; ed W. C. Hazlitt, English drama and stage, 1869.

Sidney, Sir Philip. An apologie for poetrie. 1595; ed G. Shepherd 1965.

Stephens, John. Satyrical essayes, characters and others: or accurate and quick descriptions fitted to the life of their subjects. 1615; ed J. O. Halliwell(-Phillipps), Books of characters, 1857.

Stockwood, John. A sermon preached at Paules crosse on Barthelmew day, being the 24th of August. 1578.

Stubbes, Philip. A fearefull and terrible example of Gods juste judgement, executed upon a lewde fellow, who usually accustomed to sweare by Gods blood, which may be a caveat to all the whole world, that they blaspheme not the name of their God by swearing. 1581; ed J. P. Collier, Broadside blackletter ballads printed in the 16th and 17th centuries, 1868.

— Two wunderfull and rare examples of the undeffered and present approching judgement of the Lord our God: the one upon a wicked and pernitious blasphemer of the name of God and servant to one Maister Frauncis Pennell, gentleman, dwelling at Boothbie in Lincolnshire, three myles from Granthan; the other upon a woman named Joane Bowser, dwelling at Donnington, in Leicester, to whome the Divell verie straungely appeared as in the discourse following you may reade in June last 1581. Ed J. P. Collier, Shakespeare Soc papers vol 4, 1848.

— The anatomie of abuses: containing a discoverie, or brief summarie, of such notable vices and imperfections as now raigne in many Christian countreyes of the worlde, but (especiallie) in a verie famous ilande called Ailgna; together with most fearfull examples of Gods judgementes, executed upon the wicked for the same, as well in Ailgna of late, as in other places elsewhere; verie Godly, to be read of all true Christians, everie where, but most needfull to be regarded in Englande; made dialogue-wise. 1583, 1595 (5th edn); ed F. J. Furnivall 1877–9 (New Shakspere Soc).

— The second part of the Anatomie of abuses: conteining the display of corruptions, with a perfect description of such imperfections, blemishes and abuses as now reigning in everie degree, require reformation for fears of Gods vengeance to be powred upon the people and countrie, without speedie repentance and conversion unto God: made dialoguewise. 1583; ed F. J. Furnivall 1882 (New Shakspere Soc).

— The intended treason of Doctor Parrie and his complices against the Queenes moste excellent Majestie; with a letter sent from the Pope to the same effect. 1585; ed J. P. Reardon, Shakespeare Soc papers vol 3, 1847.

— A christal glasse for Christian women: contayning An excellent discourse of the godly life and Christian death of Mistresse Katherine Stubbes who departed this life in Burton uppon Trent, in Staffordshire, the 14 day of December 1590. 1591, 1647; partly ed F. J. Furnivall 1879 (New Shakspere Soc).

— A perfect pathway to felicitie: conteining godly meditations and praiers fit for all times, and necessarie to be practized of all good Christians. 1592; partly ed F. J. Furnivall 1879 (New Shakspere Soc).

— A motive to good workes: or rather, to true Christianitie indeede; wherein by the waie is shewed how farre wee are behinde not onely our fore-fathers in good workes, but also many other creatures in the endes of our creation, with the difference betwixt the pretenced good workes of the anti-Christian Papist and the good workes of the Christian Protestant. 1593.

A treatise of daunses: wherein it is showed that they are as it were accessories and dependants (or things annexed) to whoredom; where also by the way is touched and proved that plays are joyned and knit together in a ranck or rowe with them. 1581.

A true reporte of the death and martyrdome of M. Campion Jesuite and priest observid and written by a Catholicke priest, which was present thereat. Douay 1582.

Twyne, Thomas. Phisicke against fortune, as well prosperous as adverse, conteyned in two bookes: whereby men are instructed with lyke indifferencie to remedie theyr affections, as well in tyme of prosperitie, as also of the foule lowryng stormes of adversitie; written in Latine by Frauncis Petrarch, a most famous poet and oratour, and now first englished. 1579.

Wager, Lewis. A new enterlude, never before this tyme imprinted, entreating of the life and repentaunce of Marie Magdalene; not only godly, learned and fruitfull, but also well furnished with pleasant myrth and pastime, very delectable for those which shall heare or reade the same. 1566, 1567; ed F. I. Carpenter, Chicago 1902.

Whetstone, George. A mirour for magestrates of cyties: representing the ordinaunces, policies and diligence of the noble Emperour Alexander (surnamed) Severus, to suppresse and chastise the notorious vices noorished in Rome, by the superfluous nomber of dicing-houses, tavarns and common stewes: suffred and cherished by his beastly predecessour Heluogabalys, with sundrie grave orations by the said noble Emperor concerning reformation; and hereunto is added A touchstone for the time: containyng many perillous mischiefes, bred in the bowels of the citie of London by the infection of some of these sanctuaries of iniquitie. 1584.

White, Thomas. A sermon preached at Pawles crosse on Sunday the thirde of November 1577, in the time of the plague. 1578.

Wither, George. Abuses stript and whipt: or satirical essayes. 1613 (4 edns).

The stage-players complaint, in a pleasant dialogue between Cane of the Fortune, and Reed of the Friers, deploring their sad and solitary conditions for want of imployment, in this heavie and contagious time of the plague in London. 1641.

Certaine propositions offered to the consideration of the honourable houses of parliament. 1642; rptd in Antiquarian repertory vol 3, 1808.

The actors remonstrance, or complaint: for the silencing of their profession and banishment from their severall play-houses; in which is fully set downe their grievances for their restraint; especially since stage-playes, only of all publike recreations are prohibited; the exercise at the beares colledge and the motions of puppets being still in force and vigour. 1643; ed W. C. Hazlitt, The English drama and stage 1543–1664, 1869; ed C. Hindley, Miscellanea antiqua anglicana vol 3, 1873.

An ordinance of the Lords and Commons assembled in Parliament for the utter suppression and abolishing of all stage-playes and interludes, with the penalties to be inflicted on the actors and spectators herein exprest, Die Veneris 11 Februarii 1647; ordered by the Lords assembled in Parliament that this ordinance for the suppression of stage-playes shall be forthwith printed and published. 1647.

Modern Studies

Selden, John. Opera omnia. Ed D. Wilkins 3 vols in 6 1726.

— Table talk. Ed S. H. Reynolds, Oxford 1892.

Harington, Sir John. Nugae antiquac. Ed H. Harington, with illustrative notes by T. Park 2 vols 1804.
—— Letters and epigrams. Ed N. E. McClure, Philadelphia 1926.
Howell, T. B. (ed). A complete collection of state trials. 34 vols 1809. Vol 3 contains Proceedings against William Prynne.
Wright, T. Queen Elizabeth and her times. 2 vols 1838.
Grindal, E. The remains of Edmund Grindal, Archbishop of Canterbury. 1843 (Parker Soc).
Halliwell-(Phillipps), J. O. (ed). Tarlton's Jests and News out of Purgatory. 1844 (Shakespeare Soc).
—— Illustrations of the life of Shakespeare pt 1. 1874.
—— Outlines of the life of Shakespeare. 2 vols 1882.
Parker, M. The correspondence of Matthew Parker. Ed J. Bruce and T. T. Perowne 1852 (Perowne Soc).
Calendar of state papers. Domestic series: reigns of Edward 6, Mary, Elizabeth, 1547–89. Ed R. Lemon 1856.
Hazlitt, W. C. The English drama and stage. 1869.
Furnivall, F. J. Captain Cox, his ballads, and books, or Robert Laneham's letter. 1871 (Ballad Soc); 1907 (Shakespeare Lib).
—— Shakespeare's England: William Harrison's Description of England. 1876 (New Shakspere Soc).
—— Philip Stubbes's Anatomy of abuses in Shakspere's youth. 1877 (New Shakspere Soc).
Kingsley, C. Plays and Puritans. 1873.
Lodge, Thomas. Complete works. Ed E. Gosse 12 vols Glasgow 1873–9, 4 vols Glasgow 1883, New York 1963.
Simpson, R. The political use of the stage in Shakespere's time. Trans New Shakspere Soc pt 2 1874.
Harrison, W. Harrison's Description of England: being books 2 and 3 of his Description of Britaine and England. Ed F. J. Furnivall 3 pts and suppl 1877–1908 (New Shakspere Soc) with addns by C. C. Stopes, pt 4 suppl; ed L. Withington 1902 (selected, with Furnivall's introd).
Analytical index to the series of records known as the Remembrancia, preserved among the archives of the City of London 1579–1664. 1878.
Fleay, F. G. Shakespeare and Puritanism. Anglia 7 1884.
Firth, C. H. The suppression of the drama during the Protectorate and Commonwealth. N & Q 18 Aug 1888.
Symmes, H. S. Les débuts de la critique dramatique en Angleterre jusqu'à la mort de Shakespeare. Paris 1903.
Thompson, E. N. S. The controversy between the Puritans and the stage. New York 1903.

Hutchinson, J. Memoirs by his wife, Lucy. Ed C. H. Firth 1906.
Boas, F. S. A 'Defence of Oxford plays and players'. Fortnightly Rev Aug 1907.
—— University drama in the Tudor age. Oxford 1914. See ch 10 on Gager, Rainoldes and the Oxford plays.
Gildersleeve, V. C. Government regulation of the Elizabethan drama. New York 1908.
Wilson, J. D. The title of Lodge's reply to Gosson's School of abuse. MLR 3 1908.
Nashe, T. Works. Ed R. B. McKerrow 5 vols 1910, 1958 (with F. P. Wilson, A supplement).
Cullen, C. Puritanism and the stage. Proc Royal Philosophical Soc of Glasgow 43 1912.
Young, K. Rainoldes, Letter to Thomas Thornton. In Shakespeare studies by members of the Department of English of the University of Wisconsin, Madison 1916.
—— William Gager's Defence of the academic stage. Trans Wisconsin Acad of Sciences, Arts & Letters 18 1916. Contains Gager's Momus, correspondence of Gager and Rainoldes, Gager's letter of 31 July 1592.
Graves, T. S. Notes on Puritanism and the stage. SP 18 1921.
Lounsbury, T. R. A Puritan censor of the stage. Yale Rev 12 1923. On Prynne.
Turner, C. Anthony Mundy. Berkeley 1928.
Grierson, H. J. C. In his Cross currents in English literature of the seventeenth century, 1929.
Taylor, G. C. Another Renaissance attack on the stage. PQ 9 1930.
Paradise, N. B. Thomas Lodge: the history of an Elizabethan. New Haven 1931.
Sisson, C. J. Thomas Lodge and his family. In Thomas Lodge and other Elizabethans, ed C. J. Sisson, Cambridge Mass 1933.
Walker, A. The life of Thomas Lodge. RES 9–10 1933–4.
Ringler, W. Stephen Gosson. Princeton 1942.
—— The first phase of the Elizabethan attack on the stage 1558–79. HLQ 5 1942.
Davis, J. L. The case for comedy in Caroline theatrical apologetics. PMLA 58 1943.
Meadley, T. D. Attack on the theatre c. 1580–1680. London Quart 1953.
Lamont, W. M. Marginal Prynne 1600–69. 1963.
Morgan, E. S. Puritan hostility to the theatre. Proc of Amer Philosophical Soc 110 1966.

B. H.

IV. MORALITIES

In this and the following sections an attempt has been made to record the whole dramatic output of the period now in print. Undramatic dialogues, and trns not intended for the stage, have generally been omitted. Abbreviations (Adams, Brandl, Malone Soc, TFT etc) refer to collections of plays, col 1363, above.

(1) GENERAL STUDIES

Seifert, J. Die Wit- und Science-Moralitäten des 16 Jahrhunderts. Karolinenthal 1892.
Bolte, J. Der Teufel in der Kirche. Zeitschrift für Vergleichende Litteraturgeschichte 11 1897.
Cushman, L. W. The Devil and Vice in English dramatic literature before Shakespeare. Halle 1900.
Eckhardt, E. Die lustige Person im älteren englischen Drama. Berlin 1902.
—— Die metrische Unterscheidung von Ernst und Komik in den englischen Moralitäten. E Studien 62 1927.
Thompson, E. N. S. The English moral play. Trans of Connecticut Acad of Arts & Sciences 14 1910.

Haslinghuis, E. J. De duivel in het drama der Middeleeuwen. Leyden 1912.
Mackenzie, W. R. The English moralities from the point of view of allegory. Boston 1914.
Moore, J. R. Ancestors of Autolycus in the English moralities and interludes. Washington Univ Stud 9 1922.
Allison, T. E. The Paternoster play and the origin of the Vice. PMLA 39 1924.
Withington, R. The development of the 'Vice'. In Essays in memory of Barrett Wendell, Cambridge Mass 1926.
—— 'Vice' and 'Parasite': a note on the evolution of the Elizabethan villain. PMLA 49 1934.

—— The Vice: ancestry, development; morality play and melodrama. In his Excursions in English drama, New York 1937.

Wright, L. B. Social aspects of some belated moralities. Anglia 54 1930.

Brooks, N. C. Latin morality dialogue of the fifteenth century. JEGP 42 1934.

Whiting, B. J. Proverbs in the earlier English drama. Cambridge Mass 1938.

Bernard, J. E. The prosody of the Tudor interlude. New Haven 1939.

Wright, N. Morality play tradition in the poetry of Edward Taylor. Amer Lit 28 1946.

Craig, H. Morality plays and Elizabethan drama. Shakespeare Quart 1 1950.

—— Miracles and moralities. In his English religious drama of the Middle Ages, Oxford 1955.

Rossiter, A. P. English drama from early times to the Elizabethans. 1950.

Edinborough, A. The early Tudor Revels Office. Shakespeare Quart 2 1951.

Feldman, A. B. Dutch humanism and the Tudor dramatic tradition. N & Q 16 Aug 1952.

Lombardo, A. 'Morality' e 'interlude'. Eng Miscellany (Rome) 5 1954.

Ribner, I. Morality roots of the Tudor history play. Tulane Stud in Eng 4 1954.

Craik, T. W. The Tudor interlude. Leicester 1958.

—— The Tudor interlude and later Elizabethan drama. In Elizabethan theatre, ed J. R. Brown and B. Harris 1966.

McCutchan, J. W. Justice and equity in the English morality play. JHI 19 1958.

Mares, F. H. The origin of 'the Vice' in Tudor drama. HLQ 22 1958.

Bevington, D. M. From Mankind to Marlowe. Cambridge Mass 1962.

Pineas, R. The English morality play as a weapon of religious controversy. Stud in Eng Lit 1500–1900 2 1962.

—— Tudor drama and politics. Oxford 1968.

Happé, P. Tragic themes in three Tudor moralities. Stud in Eng Lit 1500–1900 5 1965.

Weimann, R. Redekonventionen des Vice. Zeitschrift für Anglistik und Amerikanistik 1967.

Wickham, G. Dramatic qualities of the English morality play and moral interlude. In his Shakespeare's dramatic heritage, 1969.

Wilson, F. P. The early Tudor morality and interlude; the late Tudor morality play. In his English drama 1485–1585, Oxford 1969 (OHEL).

See also the general works of Brandl, Chambers, Collier, Creizenach, Ward and Warton, col 1367f., above.

(2) PRE-TUDOR MORALITIES

The Macro plays (Mankind; Wisdom, who is Christ; the Castell of Perseverance). Ed F. J. Furnivall and A. W. Pollard 1904 (EETS); TFT 1907.

The Castell of Perseverance. Ed A. W. Pollard, English miracle plays, 1890 (in part).

Lombardo, A. Morality play. Rivista di Letterature Moderne 4 1953.

Willis, J. Stage directions in the Castell of Perseverance. MLR 51 1956.

Southern, R. W. Medieval theatre in the round. 1957.

Henry, A. K. The Castle of Perseverance: the stage direction at line 1767. N & Q Dec 1965.

Schell, E. T. On the imitation of life's pilgrimage in the Castle of Perseverance. JEGP 67 1968.

The four cardinall virtues. Ed W. W. Greg, Malone Society collections vol 4, 1957. A fragment.

Wisdom, who is Christ. Ed W. B. D. Turnbull 1837 (Abbotsford Club) (as Mind, will and understanding); ed F. J. Furnivall, Digby plays, 1882 (New Shakspere Soc).

Smart, W. K. Some English and Latin sources and parallels. Madison 1912.

Molloy, J. J. A theological interpretation of the moral play Wisdom who is Christ. Washington 1952.

Bevington, D. M. Political satire in the morality Wisdom who is Christ. Renaissance Papers 1963.

Mankind. Ed A. W. Pollard, English miracle plays, 1890 (in part); Manly vol 1; Brandl; ed J. S. Farmer, 'Lost' Tudor plays, 1907; Adams.

Keiller, M. M. The influence of Piers Plowman in Mankind. PMLA 26 1911.

Mackenzie, W. R. A new source of Mankind. PMLA 27 1912.

Smart, W. K. Some notes on Mankind. MP 14 1917.

—— Mankind and the mumming plays. MLN 32 1917.

Baker, D. C. The date of Mankind. PQ 42 1963.

The pride of life. Ed J. Mills, Proc Royal Soc Antiquaries of Ireland 1891; Brandl. A fragment.

Holthausen, F. Pride of life. Archiv 108 1901.

(3) EARLY TUDOR MORALITIES

JOHN BALE
1495–1563

Bibliographies

Davies, W. T. A bibliography of Bale. Proc Oxford Bibl Soc 4 1939, new ser 1 1947.

Mozley, J. F. Bale. N & Q 29 Dec 1945.

Collections

Dramatic writings. Ed J. S. Farmer 1907.

§1

[God's promises]. A tragedye or enterlude manyfestyng the chefe promyses of God unto man, compyled 1538. [1547?], 1577, 1578; rptd Dodsley vol 1; Hazlitt's Dodsley vol 1; TFT 1908; ed W. Marriott, Collection of English miracle plays, Basle 1838; ed E. Jones, Erlangen 1909; ed E. Rhys, Everyman with other interludes, 1909 (EL).

[John Baptist]. A briefe comedy or enterlude of Johan Baptystes, compyled 1538; rptd Harleian miscellany vol 1, 1744, 1808.

[Temptation]. A brefe comedy or enterlude concernynge the temptacyon of our Lorde, compyled 1538. [1548?]; rptd A. B. Grosart, Miscellanies of Fuller worthies' library vol 1, 1870; TFT 1909; ed P. Schwemmer, Nuremburg 1919.

[Three laws]. A comedy concernynge thre lawes, of nature, Moses and Christ, compyled 1538. [1548?], 1562; ed A. Schroeer, Anglia 5 1882; TFT 1908.

King Johan. 1538 (first version), 1558–62 (2nd) (Huntington Lib ms); ed J. P. Collier 1838 (Camden Soc); Manly vol 1; Bang vol 25; ed J. H. P. Pafford 1931 (Malone Soc); ed W. A. Armstrong, English history plays, 1965; extracts in A. W. Pollard, English miracle plays, 1927.

For Bale's Summarium, see col 807 above. For his numerous controversial works, see selection by H. Christmas 1849 (Parker Soc), and C. H. and T. Cooper, Athenae cantabrigienses, 1858–61. See also H. McCusker, Books and manuscripts formerly in the possession of Bale, *Library* *4th ser 16 1935.*

§2

Cason, C. E. Additional lines to Bale's Kynge Johan. JEGP 27 1928. Correction by J. H. P. Pafford 30 1931.

Barke, H. Bales Kynge John und sein Verhältnis zur zeitgenössischen Geschichtsschreibung. Würzburg 1937.

Garret, C. The resurrection of the masse by Hugh Hilarie – or John Bale? Library 4th ser 21 1940.

Harris, J. W. Bale: a study in the minor literature of the Reformation. Urbana 1940.

McCusker, H. Bale: dramatist and antiquary. Bryn Mawr 1942.

Miller, E. S. The Roman rite in Bale's King John. PMLA 64 1949.

Wheat, C. H. A poor helpe, Ralph Roister-Doister and Three laws. PQ 28 1949.

Adams, B. B. Doubling in Bale's King Johan. SP 62 1965.

Blatt, T. B. The plays of Bale. Copenhagen 1969.

SIR DAVID LINDSAY
1490?–1555

Ane satire of the thrie estaitis. Edinburgh 1602. *See col 2427, below.*

HENRY MEDWALL
b. c. 1462

§1

Nature [1516–20?]. Ptd W. Rastell [1530?]; Brandl; Bang vol 12 1905; TFT 1908; ed J. S. Farmer, 'Lost' Tudor plays, 1907 (facs of fragment).

§2

Mackenzie, W. R. A source for Medwell's Nature. PMLA 22 1914.

For Medwall's Fulgens and Lucrece, see col 1412, below.

JOHN RASTELL
1475?–1536

§1

[Four elements]. A new interlude of the nature of the four elements. [1517–27?]; rptd J. O. Halliwell(-Phillipps) 1848 (Percy Soc); Hazlitt's Dodsley vol 1; ed J. Fischer, Marburger Studien 1903; ed J. S. Farmer, Six anonymous plays, 1905; TFT 1908; ed A. W. Pollard, English miracle plays, 1927. *See also col 1412, below.*

§2

Parks, G. B. The geography of the Interlude of the four elements. PQ 17 1938.

—— Rastell and Waldseemüller's map. PMLA 58 1943.

Nugent, E. M. Sources of Rastell's The nature of the four elements. PMLA 57 1942.

Parr, J. More sources of Rastell's Interlude of the four elements. PMLA 60 1945.

—— Rastell's geographical knowledge of America. PQ 27 1948.

JOHN REDFORD
c. 1486–1547

§1

Wyt and scyence. [1530?]; ed J. O. Halliwell(-Phillipps) 1848 (Shakespeare Soc); Manley vol 1; ed J. S. Farmer,

'Lost' Tudor plays, 1907; TFT 1908; Adams; ed A. Brown 1952 (Malone Soc). Ms BM additional 15,233, probably autograph.

§2

Seifert, J. Wit-und-Science Moralitäten. Prague 1892.

Hauke, H. Redfords The play of wit and science und seine spätere Bearbeitung. 1904.

Baskervill, C. R. Mummers' wooing plays in England. MLR 21 1923.

Pfatteicher, C. John Redford. Cassel 1934.

Tannenbaum, S. A. Editorial notes on Wyt and Science. PQ 14 1935.

Withington, R. Experience, the mother of science. PMLA 57 1942.

Brown, A. Two notes on Redford. MLR 43 1948.

—— The play of Wit and science. PQ 28 1949.

Habicht, W. The wit-interludes and the form of pre-Shakespearean comedy. Renaissance Drama 1965.

Velz, J. W. and C. P. Daw. Tradition and originality in Wyt and science. SP 65 1968.

For biographical details see W. H. G. Flood, Early Tudor composers, 1925; J. Pulver, Biographical dictionary of old English music, 1927; Grove's Dictionary of music and musicians, 1954.

JOHN SKELTON
1460?–1529

Magnyfycence. [1533]. *See col 1016, above.*

RICHARD WEVER
fl. c. 1549–53

[Lusty juventus]. An enterlude called lusty Juventus. [1550?; entered Stationers' Register 1560], [1565?]; ed T. Hawkins, Origins of the English drama vol 1, 1773; Hazlitt's Dodsley vol 2; ed J. S. Farmer 1905 (Early Eng Drama Soc); TFT 1907.

ANONYMOUS PLAYS

[Albyon Knight]. [1537–65? entered Stationers' Register 1565], [1566?]; ed J. P. Collier, Shakespeare Soc Papers vol 1, 1844 (fragment); ed J. S. Farmer, Anonymous plays, 1906; ed W. W. Greg, Malone Society collections vol 1, 1909.

Dodds, M. H. The date of Albion Knight. Library 2nd ser 4 1913.

[The summoning of Everyman]. [1509–19]. Ptd Pynson, nd (2 edns), J. Skot, nd (2 edns); ed T. Hawkins, Origins of English drama vol 1, 1773; ed K. Goedeke, Hanover 1865; Hazlitt's Dodsley vol 1; H. Logemann, Ghent 1892 (with Dutch text); ed K. H. de Raaf, Groningen 1897; ed F. Sidgwick 1902; ed A. W. Pollard, Fifteenth-century prose and verse, 1903; ed M. J. Moses, New York 1903; ed J. S. Farmer 1905 (Early English Drama Soc); Bang vol 4, 1904 (Skot's edn), vol 24 1909 (Skot's other edn), vol 28 1910 (2 Pynson fragments); TFT 1912; ed J. S. Tatlock and R. G. Martin, Representative English plays, 1915; Adams; ed J. Allen, Three medieval plays, 1953; ed A. C. Cawley, Everyman and medieval miracle plays, 1959 (EL); ed Cawley, Everyman, Manchester 1961; Wellington 1968 (modernized text based on Skot).

Holthausen, F. and E. Koelbing. Brief notes. E Studien 21 1895.

Sidgwick, F. Everyman. N & Q 7 Feb 1903.

Roersch, A. Elckerlijk-Everyman. Archiv 113 1904.

Bang, W. Zu Everyman. E Studien 35 1905.

Manly, J. M. Elckerlijk-Everyman: a question of priority. MP 8 1910. *See* F. Wood, ibid.

Bates, E. P. Everyman and the Talmud. Athenaeum 29 Nov 1913. *See* M. J. Landa 6 Dec 1913.

Tigg, E. R. Elckerlijc prior to Everyman? JEGP 38 1939.

Van Mierlo, J. De prioriteit van Elckerlijk tegenover Everyman gebandhaafd. Antwerp 1948.

de Vocht, H. Everyman: a comparative study of texts and sources. Bang new ser vol 5 1949.

Takahashi, G. A study of Everyman. Tokyo 1952.

Lombardo, A. Morality play. Rivista di Letterature Moderne 4 1953.

Zandvoort, R. W. Everyman-Elckerlijc. Etudes Anglaises 6 1953.

Ryan, L. V. Doctrine and dramatic structure in Everyman. Speculum 32 1957.

Kaula, D. Time and the timeless in Everyman and Doctor Faustus. College Eng 2 1960.

Thomas, H. S. The meaning of the character Knowledge in Everyman. Mississippi Quart 14 1961.

— Some analogies of Everyman. Mississippi Quart 16 1963.

Van Laan, T. F. Everyman: a structural analysis. PMLA 78 1963.

Kossmann, H. Fellowship his fer: a note on Everyman's false friend. In English studies presented to R. W. Zandvoort, Amsterdam 1964.

Johnson, W. H. The double desertion of Everyman. Amer N & Q 6 1968.

[Godly Queene Hester] [1527] (entered Stationers' Register 1561); ed J. P. Collier, Early English popular literature vol 1, 1863; ed A. B. Grosart, Miscellanies of Fuller worthies' library, 1879; Bang vol 5, 1904; ed J. S. Farmer, Anonymous plays, 1906.

[Good Order]. 1533 (fragment).

Frost, G. L. and R. Nash. Good order: a morality fragment. SP 41 1944.

Hyckescorner. [1512?] [1516?] (de Worde), [1526?] (J. Waley) (fragment), [1560?]; ed T. Hawkins, Origins of the English drama vol 1, 1773; Hazlitt's Dodsley vol 1; Manly vol 1; ed J. S. Farmer, Anonymous plays, 1906; TFT 1908.

Schell, E. T. Youth and Hyckescorner: which came first? PQ 45 1966.

[Impacyente poverte] [1560; entered Stationers' Register 1560]. 1560; ed J. S. Farmer, 'Lost' Tudor plays, 1907; Bang vol 33, 1911.

[Johan the Evangelyst] [1520?]. [1550?]; 1907 (Malone Soc); TFT 1907.

Bradley, H. Textual notes on the Enterlude of Johan the Evangelist. MLR 2 1906. Reply by W. H. Williams 3 1907.

Dahlstrom, C. E. W. L. The name Indecision in John the Evangelist. MLN 58 1943.

[Nice wanton] [1560? entered Stationers' Register 1560]. 1560, [1565?]; ed Hazlitt's Dodsley vol 2; Manly vol 1; ed J. S. Farmer, Anonymous plays, 1905; TFT 1908 (from undated edn), 1909 (from 1560 edn).

[Respublica 1553]. *See col 1365, above.*

[Resurrection of our Lord] [1530–60?] (fragmentary ms in Folger Lib). Ed J. D. Wilson and B. Dobell 1912 (Malone Soc). *See col 740, above.*

[Somebody, Avarice and Minister]. Fragment, tr c. 1550 from French Protestant morality, La vérité cachée. Ed S. R. Maitland, A list of some of the early printed books at Lambeth, 1843; ed W. W. Greg, Malone Society collections vol 2, 1931 (as Somebody and others) (facs).

[Temperance and humility] [1535?] (fragment). [1537?]. Ed W. W. Greg, Malone Soc collections vol 1, 1901.

[Welth and Helth] [1554? entered Stationers' Register 1557]. [1557?]; TFT 1907; ed J. S. Farmer, 'Lost' Tudor plays, 1907; ed W. W. Greg and P. Simpson 1907 (Malone Soc) (corrected Malone Soc collections vol 1, 1908); ed F. Holthausen, Kiel 1908, 1922 (rev).

Hunter, M. Notes on the interlude of Wealth and Health. MLR 3 1907.

Craik, T. W. The political interpretation of two Tudor interludes: Temperance and Humility and Wealth and Health. RES new ser 4 1953.

[The worlde and the chylde]. 1522, 1817 (Roxburghe Club); ed J. P. Collier, Dodsley's old plays vol 12, 1827; Hazlitt's Dodsley vol 1; Manly vol 1; ed J. S. Farmer, Anonymous plays, 1905; TFT 1909; ed J. Hampden 1935.

MacCracken, H. N. A source of Mundus et infans. PMLA 23 1908.

[Youth] [1520?; entered Stationers' Register 1557]. [1530?] (fragment), [1557?], [1562?] (J. Waley, nd (Copland); ed J. O. Halliwell (-Phillipps) 1849; Hazlitt's Dodsley vol 2; Bang vol 12, 1905; TFT 1908, 1909 (first 2 edns). Fragment ed S. R. Maitland, A list of some of the early printed books at Lambeth, 1843.

Schell, E. T. Youth and Hyckescorner: which came first? PQ 45 1966.

(4) ELIZABETHAN MORALITIES

ULPIAN FULWELL
d. 1586

Like will to like. 1568 (entered Stationers' Register 1568), [1570?], 1587; ed Hazlitt's Dodsley vol 3; ed J. S. Farmer 1906 (Early Eng Drama Soc); TFT 1909 (edn of 1587).

Ribner, I. A 1576 allusion to Chaucer. N & Q 21 Jan 1950.

— Fulwell and his family. N & Q 14 Oct 1950.

— Fulwell and the Court of High Commission. N & Q 23 June 1951.

THOMAS GARTER
fl. 1569

Susanna. 1578 (entered Stationers' Register 1563, 1569); ed B. I. Evans and W. W. Greg 1937 (Malone Soc).

Pilger, R. Die Dramatisierungen der Susanna im 16 Jahrhundert. Zeitschrift für Deutsche Philologie 1880.

Evans, B. I. TLS 2 May 1936.

Herrick, M. T. Susanna and the elders in sixteenth-century drama. In Studies in honor of T. W. Baldwin, Urbana 1958.

THOMAS LUPTON
fl. 1583

All for money. 1578 (entered Stationers' Register 1577); ed J. O. Halliwell(-Phillipps), Literature of the sixteenth and seventeenth centuries, 1851; ed E. Vogel, Sh Jb 1904; TFT 1910.

Craik, T. W. Some notes on Thomas Lupton's All for money. N & Q June 1954.

LEWIS WAGER
fl. 1566

Mary Magdalene. 1567 (entered Stationers' Register 1566); ed F. I. Carpenter, Chicago 1902, 1904 (rev); TFT 1908 (edn of 1567). *See* R. Imelmann, Archiv 3 1903.

WILLIAM WAGER
fl. 1565–9

§1

The longer thou livest the more fool thou art [1564?].
[1569?] (entered Stationers' Register 1569); ed A.
Brandl, Sh Jb 1910; TFT 1910.
Inough is as good as a feast. [1565?]; ed S. de Ricci, New
York 1920 (facs).
[The cruel debtor]. 1566. Fragments ed F. J. Furnivall,
Trans New Shakspere Soc 1878; ed W. W. Greg, Malone
Soc collections vols 1–2 1911–23.

§2

Imelmann, R. Archiv 111 1903. Cruel debtor by Wager.
Olive, L. M. Wager and the Trial of treasure. HLQ 9 1946.
McCutchan, J. W. 'Noseted' and 'snotty-nose'. MLN
65 1950.

GEORGE WAPULL
fl. 1576

The tyde taryeth no man [1576?]. 1576 (entered
Stationers' Register 1576); ed J. P. Collier, Illustrations
of early English popular literature, 1863; ed E. Rüht,
Sh Jb 1907; TFT 1910.

ROBERT WILSON
fl. 1572–1600

§1

The three ladies of London. 1584, 1592 (variant text); ed
J. P. Collier, Five old plays, 1851; Hazlitt's Dodsley;
TFT 1911.
The three lords and three ladies of London. 1590; ed
J. P. Collier, Five old plays, 1851; Hazlitt's Dodsley
vol 6; TFT 1912.
The cobler's prophesie. 1594; ed W. Dibelius, Sh Jb 33
1897; TFT 1911; ed A. C. Wood 1914 (Malone Soc).

§2

Gourritch, I. Robert Wilson 'the elder' and 'the younger'.
N & Q 2 Jan 1926.
Golding, S. R. Wilson and 'Sir Thomas More'. N & Q
7–14 April 1928.
Mann, I. A political cancel in the Coblers prophesie.
Library 3rd ser 23 1928.
— Copy for the 1592 quarto of the Three ladies of London.
PQ 33 1944.
— A lost version of the Three ladies of London. PMLA
59 1944.
— More Wilson parallels. N & Q 17 June 1944.
— The Dibelius edition of the Coblers prophesie. N & Q
11 Aug 1945.
— Notes on the Malone Society reprint of the Coblers
prophesie. Library 3rd ser 26 1946.
Bowers, F. T. Dekker, Wilson and the Shoemakers'
holiday. MLN 64 1949.
Nathanson, L. 'Copertinent' and 'Copurtenance'. MLN
71 1956.
— Variants in Wilson's The three lords. Library 5th
ser 13 1958.
Mithal, H. S. D. The two-Wilsons controversy. N & Q
March 1959.
— Variants in Wilson's The three lords of London.
Library 5th ser 18 1963.
Lavin, J. A. Two notes on the Cobler's prophecy. N & Q
April 1962.

NATHANIEL WOODES
fl. 1550–94

§1

The conflict of conscience. 1581 (2 states: one has name
of Francis Spera on title-page and a tragic ending; the
other calls the author Philogus and has a happy ending);
ed J. P. Collier, Five old plays, 1851; Hazlitt's Dodsley;
TFT 1911; 1952 (Malone Soc).

§2

Wine, C. Nathaniel Wood's Conflict of conscience. PMLA
50 1935.
— Woodes: author of the morality play The conflict of
conscience. RES 15 1939.
Oliver, L. M. John Foxe and the Conflict of conscience.
HLQ 10 1947.
Campbell, L. B. Dr Faustus: a case of conscience. PMLA
67 1952.

ANONYMOUS PLAYS

Liberalitie and prodigalitie. 1602; rptd Hazlitt's Dodsley;
TFT 1912; 1913 (Malone Soc).
Hillebrand, H. N. Sebastian Westcote and Liberalitie
and prodigalitie. JEGP 14 1915.
The story of King Daryus. 1577 (entered Stationers'
Register 1565); ed J. O. Halliwell (-Phillipps) 1860;
Brandl; ed J. S. Farmer, Anonymous plays, 1906; TFT
1907 (from 1577 edn); 1909 (from 1565 edn).
[Love feigned and unfeigned]. 1540–60; ed A. Esdaile,
Malone Society collections vol 1, 1908. Ms BM (frag-
ment).
Daw, E. B. Love fayned and unfayned and the English
Anabaptists. PMLA 32 1917.
Scragg, L. L. Love feigned and unfeigned: a note on
the rise of allegory on the Tudor stage. Eng Lang
Notes 3 1966.
The mariage of witte and science. [1569?] (entered
Stationers' Register 1569); rptd Hazlitt's Dodsley vol 2;
TFT 1909; 1961 (Malone Soc).
Withington, R. Experience: the mother of Science.
PMLA 57 1942.
Race, S. J. The moral play of Wit and science. N & Q
March 1953.
Varma, R. S. Act and scene divisions in Wit and science.
N & Q March 1963.
— Philosophical and moral ideas in Wit and science.
PQ 44 1965.
The marriage of wit and wisdom [1570 or 1579 in ms].
Ed J. O. Halliwell (-Phillipps) 1846; ed J. S. Farmer,
Anonymous plays, 1908; TFT 1909.
Tannenbaum, S. A. Comments on the Marriage of wit
and wisdom. PQ 9 1930.
Tilley, M. P. Notes on the Marriage of wit and wisdom.
Shakespeare Assoc Bull 10 1935.
Race, S. J. The marriage of wit and wisdom. N & Q
Jan 1953.
New custome. 1573; Dodsley vol 1; Hazlitt's Dodsley
vol 3; ed J. S. Farmer, Anonymous plays, 1906; TFT
1908.
Oliver, L. M. John Foxe and the drama New custom.
HLQ 10 1947.
The pedler's prophecie. 1595 (entered Stationers'
Register 1594); rptd TFT 1911; 1914 (Malone Soc).
Sometimes attributed to Robert Wilson, above on
analogy with the Cobler's prophecie. For date see G. L.
Kittredge, Harvard Stud & Notes in Philology 16
1934.
Pineas, R. Polemical technique in the Pedlar's prophecie.
Eng Lang Notes 6 1969.
Philotus. *See col 2429, below.*

The triall of treasure. 1567; ed J. O. Halliwell (-Phillipps) 1842 (Percy Soc); Hazlitt's Dodsley; ed J. S. Farmer, Anonymous plays, 1906; TFT 1908.

Daw, E. B. Two notes on the Trial of treasure. MP 15 1918.

Wright, L. B. Social aspects of some belated moralities. Anglia 54 1930.

Oliver, L. M. William Wager and the Trial of treasure. HLQ 9 1946.

V. THE EARLY COMEDIES

Medwall, Rastell, Heywood, Udall and their contemporaries

Abbreviations used in this section (Adams, Bang, Gayley, TFT etc) refer to collections of plays, col 1363, above.

(1) GENERAL STUDIES

Bale, John. Illustrium Majoris Britanniae scriptorum summarium. Ipswich 1584; Index, ed R. L. Poole and M. Bateson, Oxford 1902.

Cunningham, P. Extracts from the accounts of revels at Court in the reigns of Queen Elizabeth and King James. 1842 (Shakespeare Soc).

Symonds, J. A. Shakespeare's predecessors. 1884, 1900 (rev).

Gayley. Introd to vol 1.

Chambers, E. K. The medieval stage. 2 vols Oxford 1903.
— Court performances before Queen Elizabeth. MLR 2 1906.
— Notes on the history of the Revels Office under the Tudors. 1906.

Feuillerat, A. Documents relating to the Office of the Revels in the time of Queen Elizabeth. Bang vol 21, 1908.
— Documents relating to the Office of the Revels in the time of King Edward IV and Queen Mary. Bang vol 44, 1914.

Bond, R. W. Early plays from the Italian. Oxford 1911. Introd.

Wallace, C. W. The evolution of the English drama up to Shakespeare. Berlin 1912.

Brooke, C. F. T. The Tudor drama. 1912.

Boas, F. S. University drama in the Tudor age. Oxford 1914.
— An introduction to Tudor drama. 1933.

Moore Smith, G. C. The academic drama at Cambridge. Malone Society collections vol 2, 1923.

Reed, A. W. Early Tudor drama. 1926.

Greg, W. W. Notes on some early plays. Library 3rd ser 11 1930.

Whiting, B. J. Proverbs in the earlier English drama. Cambridge Mass 1938.

Bernard, J. E. The prosody of the Tudor interlude. New Haven 1939.

Griffin, W. J. Notes on early Tudor control of the stage. MLN 58 1943.

McDowell, J. H. Tudor Court staging. JEGP 44 1945.

Benger, F. B. Calendar of references to Sir Thomas Benger (Master of the Revels 1560–72). 1946.

Rossiter, A. P. English drama from early times to the Elizabethans. 1950.

Edinborough, A. The early Tudor Revels Office. Shakespeare Quart 2 1951.

Feldman, A. B. Dutch humanism and the Tudor dramatic tradition. N & Q 51 Aug 1952.

Bradbrook, M. C. The growth and structure of Elizabethan comedy. 1955.

Hogrefe, P. The Sir Thomas More circle. Urbana 1959.

Habicht, W. The wit-interludes and the form of pre-Shakespearean 'romance comedy'. Renaissance Drama 8 1966.

Wilson, F. P. The English drama 1485–1585. Oxford 1969 (OHEL).

HENRY MEDWALL
b. c. 1462

§ 1

Fulgens and Lucres. [c. 1515]; Bang 1905 (fragment); Malone Society collections 1909; ed S. de Ricci, New York 1920 (facs); ed F. S. Boas and A. W. Reed, Oxford 1926; ed F. S. Boas, Five pre-Shakespearean comedies, Oxford 1934.

For Medwall's morality Nature see col 1405, above.

§ 2

Reed, A. W. Sixt Birck and Henry Medwall. RES 2 1926.

Wright, L. B. Notes on Fulgens and Lucres. MLN 41 1926.

Baskervill, C. R. Conventional features of Medwall's Fulgens and Lucres. MP 24 1927.

Jones, C. E. Notes on Fulgens and Lucres. MLN 50 1935.

Lowers, J. K. High comedy elements in Medwall's Fulgens and Lucres. ELH 8 1941.

JOHN RASTELL
1475?–1536

§ 1

[Calisto and Melebea]. [c. 1527]; rptd Hazlitt's Dodsley; ed J. S. Farmer, Anonymous plays, 1905; 1908 (Malone Soc); H. W. Allen 1908; TFT 1909.

Gentylnes and Nobylyte. [1527?], [1535?]; ed S. E. Brydges and J. Haslewood, British bibliographer vol 4, 1814; ed J. H. Burn 1829; ed J. S. Farmer 1908; TFT 1908; K. W. Cameron, Raleigh NC 1941; 1950 (Malone Soc).

Both plays attributed to Rastell, but also to Heywood. For Rastell's Nature of the four elements see col 1405, above.

§ 2

Rosenbach, A. W. S. Influence of the Celestina in the early English drama. Sh Jb 39 1903. On Calisto.

Brooke, C. F. T. Gentleness and Nobility: authorship and source. MLR 6 1911. Attribution to Heywood.

Reed, A. W. John Rastell. Trans Bibl Soc 15 1920.

Dunn, E. C. Rastell and Gentleness and Nobility. MLR 12 1917. Attribution to Rastell.

Cameron, K. W. Authorship and sources of Gentylnes and Nobylyte. Raleigh NC 1941.

Nash, R. Rastell fragments at Dartmouth. Library 4th ser 24 1944.

JOHN HEYWOOD
1497?–1580?

Bibliographies

Cameron, K. W. The background of Heywood's Witty and witless. Raleigh NC 1941.
Tannenbaum, S. A. and D. R. Heywood: a concise bibliography. New York 1947.

Collections

Woorkes. 1562, 1566, 1576, 1587, 1598; rptd 1867 (Spenser Soc); ed J. Sharman 1874; ed J. S. Farmer 1906 (with 3 ballads and 1534 birthday poem to Princess Mary).
Dramatic writings. Ed J. S. Farmer 1905 (Early Eng Drama).
Works and miscellaneous short poems. Ed B. A. Milligan, Urbana 1956.

§1
Dramatic Writings

Johan Johan. 1522, [1819] (Chiswick Press); Brandl; ed Gayley; ed J. S. Farmer, Two Tudor shrew plays, 1908; TFT 1909; Adams.
The pardoner and the frere. 1533; ed F. J. Child, Four old plays, 1848; Hazlitt's Dodsley; ed J. S. Farmer 1906; ed A. W. Pollard, English miracle plays, 1927 (in part).
A play of love. 1533; ptd Waley?; rptd Brandl; TFT 1909 (Waley); ed K. W. Cameron, Raleigh NC 1944.
The play of the wether. 1533; ptd Rastell?; Awdeley?; Kytson?; rptd Brandl; ed Gayley; TFT 1908–9 (1533 and Awdeley); Adams; ed K. W. Cameron, Raleigh NC 1941.
The foure PP. [1543–7?]; Myddylton; Copland?; 1569; rptd R. Dodsley, Collection of old plays vol 1; Ancient British Drama; Hazlitt's Dodsley; Manly; TFT 1908 (Myddylton); Adams; ed F. S. Boas, Five pre-Shakespearean comedies, Oxford 1934.
Wytty and wytless. Ed F. W. Fairholt 1846 (Percy Soc) (abridged); TFT 1909; K. W. Cameron, Raleigh NC 1941. Ms: BM Harley 367.

Non-dramatic Writings

[A dialogue conteining the number in effect of all the proverbes in the English tongue. [1549?] (signed J.H.; unique copy in BM lacks all before signature c), 1561 ('newly overseen and somewhat augmented').
An hundred epigrammes. 1550.
Two hundred epigrammes, upon the hundred proverbes, with a thyrde hundred newly added. 1555.
A fourth hundred of epygrams, newly invented. 1560.
The spider and the flie. 1556; rptd 1894 (Spenser Soc).

§2
Dramatic Writings

Swoboda, W. Heywood als Dramatiker. Vienna 1888.
Greg, W. W. An unknown edition of Heywood's Play of love. Archiv 106 1901.
Young, K. The influence of French farce upon the plays of Heywood. MP 2 1904.
Holthausen, F. Zu Heywoods Wetterspiel. Archiv 116 1906.
Bang, W. Heywood und sein Kreis. E Studien 38 1907.
Hillebrand, H. N. On the authorship of the interludes attributed to Heywood. MP 13 1915.
Reed, A. W. The canon of Heywood's plays. Library 2nd ser 9 1918.
Bolwell, R. S. Life and works of Heywood. New York 1921.
de la Bere, R. Heywood: entertainer. 1937. With text of Wytty and wyttles, Pardoner and the frere, the Four PP, Johan Johan.
McCain, J. W. Heywood's The foure PP: a debt to Skelton. N & Q 19 March 1938.

Withington, R. Paranomasia in Heywood's plays. Smith College Stud in Modern Langs 21 1939.
Phy, W. The chronology of Heywood's plays. E Studien 74 1940.
Maxwell, I. R. French farce and Heywood. Melbourne 1946.
Craik, T. W. The true source of Heywood's Johan Johan. MLR 45 1950.
— Experiment and variety in Heywood's plays. Renaissance Drama 7 1964.
Elton, W. Heywood's Johan Johan. TLS 24 Feb 1950.
Schoeck, R. J. Satire of Wolsey in Heywood's Play of love. N & Q 17 March 1951. Replies by D. S. Bland 24 Nov 1951, Schoeck 24 May 1952.
Sultan, S. The audience-participation episode in Johan Johan. JEGP 52 1953.
— Johan Johan and its debt to French farce. JEGP 53 1954.
Bevington, D. M. Is Heywood's Play of the weather really about the weather? Renaissance Drama 7 1964.
Canzler, D. G. Quarto editions of the play of the weather. PBSA 62 1968.

Non-dramatic Writings

Graves, T. S. The Heywood circle and the Reformation. MP 10 1913.
— On the reputation of Heywood. MP 21 1923.
Hillebrand, H. N. John Heywood. MP 13 1916.
Baskervill, C. R. John Heywood. Ibid.
Reed, A. W. Heywood and his friends. Library 2nd ser 8 1917.
McCain, J. W. Heywood and classical mythology. N & Q 19 March 1938.
— Oratory, rhetoric and logic in the writings of Heywood. Quart Jnl of Speech 26 1940.
Cameron, K. W. Heywood and Richard Stonely. Shakespeare Assoc Bull 14 1939.
Long, R. A. Heywood, Chaucer and Lydgate. MLN 64 1949.
Miller, E. S. Guilt and penalty in Heywood's Pardoner's lie. MLQ 10 1949.
Shoeck, R. J. A source for Heywood's Spider and the flie. N & Q 2 July 1951.
Hauser, D. R. Date of Heywood's Spider and the flie. MLN 70 1955.
Habenicht, R. E. (ed). Heywood's A dialogue of proverbs. Berkeley 1963.
Baldwin, J. C. Heywood and Sir John Davies: a change in the tradition of the sixteenth-century satiric epigram. Satire Newsletter 5 1967.

NICHOLAS UDALL
c. 1505–56

§1
Dramatic Works

Ralph Roister Doister [written 1545–53. Entered Stationers' Register 1566]. [1566?]; ed T. Briggs 1818; ed F. Marshall 1821; ed T. White, Old English drama vol 1, 1830; ed W. D. Cooper 1847 (Shakespeare Soc); ed E. Arber 1869; Hazlitt's Dodsley vol 3; Manly vol 2; Gayley vol 1; Adams; ed J. S. Farmer 1906 (Early Eng Drama Soc), and Museum dramatists, 1907; ed C. G. Child 1913; ed F. S. Boas, Five pre-Shakespearian comedies, 1934; W. W. Greg 1935 (Malone Soc); Bang vol 14, 1939.
Respublica [written 1553]. Ed J. P. Collier, Illustrations of English literature vol 1, 1866; Brandl; ed J. S. Farmer, 'Lost' Tudor plays, 1907; TFT 1908; ed W. W. Greg 1952 (EETS) (superseding L. A. Magnus edn, 1905).

Ezechias. Lost play performed before Queen Elizabeth at King's College Cambridge, 3 Aug 1654. *See* A. R. Moon, TLS 19 April 1928.

Jacke Jugeler, Jacob and Esau, *and* Thersites *have also been attributed to Udall.*

Other Writings

Floures for Latine spekynge. 1533 (preface dated 1535), 1538, 1544, 1560; rev John Higgins 1575, 1581.

Apopthegmes compiled in Latin by Erasmus. 1542, 1564.

The first tome of the paraphrase of Erasmus upon the Newe testament. 1548, 1551.

A discourse concerning the Lordes Supper. [1550?]. From P. M. Vermigh.

Compendiosa totius anatomie delineatio. [1553], 1557, 1559 (enlarged). An English version from Thomas Geminus. *See col. 2371, below.*

Verses made at the Coronation of Queen Anne. Ed J. Nichols, Progresses of Elizabeth vol 1, 1788; ed F. J. Furnivall, Ballads from manuscript, 1870 (Ballad Soc); ed E. Arber, English garner vol 2, 1879 (English only).

An answer to the articles of the comoners of Devonsheir and Cornwall. Ed N. Pocock, Troubles connected with the Prayer Book of 1549, 1844 (Camden Soc).

§2

Kempe, A. J. (ed). The Loseley manuscripts. 1886.

Walter, M. Beiträge zu Ralph Royster Doyster. E Studien 5 1882.

Graf, H. Der Miles gloriosus im englischen Drama bis zur Zeit des Bürgerkrieges. Schwerin 1891.

Hales, J. W. The date of the first English comedy. E Studien 18 1893.

Flügel, E. Udall's dialogues and interludes. In [F. J.] Furnivall miscellany, Oxford 1901.

Williams, W. H. Ralph Roister Doister. E Studien 36–7 1906–7.

— Ralph Roister Doister and the Wasps. MLR 7 1912.

Maulsby, D. L. The relation between Udall's Roister Doister and the comedies of Plautus and Terence. E Studien 38 1907.

Hinton, J. The source of Ralph Roister Doister. MP 11 1913.

Chislett, W. Ralph Roister Doister. MLN 29 1914.

Dudok, G. Ralph Roister Doister: did its author write Jacke Juggler? Neophilologus 1 1915.

Reed, A. W. Udall and Thomas Wilson. RES 1 1925.

Baldwin, T. W. and M. C. Linthicum. The date of Roister Doister. PQ 6 1927.

Chitty, M. Nicholas Udall. TLS 22 July 1939.

Sullivan, F. Ralph Roister Doister: an immaculate copy. N & Q 13 April 1940.

Gaselee, S. The date of Ralph Roister Doister. Etoniana 28 Dec 1943.

Miller, E. S. Roister Doister's Funeralls. SP 43 1946.

Perry, W. The prayer for the Queen in Roister Doister. SE 27 1948.

— Udall as timer-server. N & Q 19 March–2 April 1949.

Wheat, C. H. A poore helpe, Ralph Roister Doister and Three laws. PQ 28 1949.

Edgerton, W. L. The apostasy of Udall. N & Q 27 May 1950.

— The date of Roister Doister. PQ 44 1965.

— Nicholas Udall. New York 1966.

Webster, H. L. Ralph Roister Doister and the little eyases. N & Q 31 March 1951.

Craik, T. W. The text of Respublica: a conjecture. N & Q July 1953.

Carpenter, N. C. Ralph Roister Doister: miles versus clericus. N & Q May 1960.

Plumstead, A. W. Satirical parody in Ralph Roister Doister: a reinterpretation. SP 60 1963.

— Who pointed Roister's letter? N & Q Sept 1963.

See also:

Byrom, H. J. Some lawsuits of Udall. RES 11 1935.

Edgerton, W. L. Udall in the index of prohibited books. JEGP 55 1956.

(2) OTHER COMEDIES

RICHARD EDWARDS
1523?–66

§1

Damon and Pithias [performed before Queen Elizabeth, probably Christmas 1564, by Children of Chapel Royal. Entered Stationers' Register 1567]. 1571, 1582; rptd Dodsley's Collection of old plays vol 1, 1744; ed S. E. Brydges 1810; Hazlitt's Dodsley vol 4; ed J. S. Farmer 1906; TFT 1908 (from 1571 edn).

Palamon and Arcite. Lost play: summary of the plot and occasion in J. Bereblock, Commentarii, rptd C. Plummer, Elizabethan Oxford, Oxford 1887 (Oxford Historical Soc).

For The paradyse of daynty devises, *1576, see col 1008, above, and for the fragmentary collection of stories attributed to him, see col 1101, above.*

§2

Durand, W. Y. Notes on Edwards. JEGP 4 1902.

— Some errors concerning Edwards. MLN 23 1908.

— Palaemon and Arcyte, Progne, Marcus Geminus, and the theatre in which they were acted. PMLA 20 1905.

Wallace, C. W. The children of the Chapel at Blackfriars 1597–1603. Lincoln Nebraska 1908.

Cunliffe, J. W. In his Early English classical tragedies, Oxford 1912. Preface.

Boas, F. S. In his University drama in the Tudor age, Oxford 1914.

Hillebrand, H. N. The child actors. Univ of Illinois Stud in Lang & Lit 11 1926.

Bradner, L. Life and poems of Edwards. New Haven 1927.

Mills, L. J. Some aspects of Damon and Pithias. Indiana Univ Stud 75 1927.

Steinberg, T. Damon and Pithias and the Tempest. N & Q 26 Feb 1927.

Rollins, H. E. (ed). The paradise of dainty devices. Cambridge Mass 1927. Corrections by Rollinas in J. Q. Adams memorial studies, Washington 1948.

— A note on Edwards. RES 4 1928.

Newlin, C. M. Some sources of Edwards's Damon and Pithias. MLN 47 1932.

Jackson, J. L. Three notes on Edwards's Damon and Pithias. PQ 29 1950.

— A use of special rhetoric in an Elizabethan play. Quart Jnl of Speech 34 1950.

Armstrong, W. A. Damon and Pithias and Renaissance theories of tragedy. E Studies 39 1958.

Holaday, A. Shakespeare, Edwards and the Virtues reconciled. JEGP 66 1967.

THOMAS INGELEND
fl. 1560

§1

The disobedient child. [1570?]; ed J. O. Halliwell (-Phillipps) 1848 (Percy Soc); Hazlitt's Dodsley vol 2;

ed J. S. Farmer, Dramatic writings of Richard Wever and Ingelend, 1905; TFT 1908.

§2

Holthausen, F. Studien zum älteren englischen Drama. E Studien 31 1902.

JOHN PHILLIP(S)
fl. 1566–94

§1

Commodye of pacient Grissill. [1569?]; rptd 1909 (Malone Soc). Written 1566? Entered Stationers' Register 1566, 1569.

§2

Swaen, A. E. H. Some notes on Pacient Grissill. E Studien 22 1896.
Greg, W. W. Phillip: notes for a bibliography. Library 2nd ser 1 1910.
Wright, L. B. A political reflection in Phillip's Patient Grissell. RES 4 1928.
Krzyzanowski, J. Conjectural remarks on Elizabethan dramatists. N & Q 16 Sept 1950.

WILLIAM STEVENSON?
fl. 1553

§1

Gammer Gurton's nedle. 1575, 1661; ed R. Dodsley, Collection of old plays vol 1, 1744; ed T. Hawkins, Origin of English drama vol 1, 1773; Ancient British drama vol 1; Manly vol 2; ed Gayley vol 1; ed J. S. Farmer, Anonymous plays, 1906; TFT 1910; ed H. F. B. Brett-Smith, Oxford 1920; ed F. S. Boas, Five pre-Shakespearean comedies, Oxford 1934.

§2

Bradley, H. Athenaeum 6 Aug 1898. Identifies 'Mr S. Mr of Art' as William Stevenson.
Ross, C. H. The authorship of Gammer Gurton's needle. Anglia 19 1897.
Boas, F. S. In his University drama in the Tudor age, 1914. Fullest account of authorship controversy.
Roberts, C. W. The authorship of Gammer Gurton's nedle. PQ 19 1939.
Watt, H. A. The staging of Gammer Gurton's nedle. In Elizabethan studies in honor of G. F. Reynolds, Boulder 1945.
Whiting, B. J. Diccon's French cousin. SP 42 1945.
Ingram, R. W. Gammer Gurton's needle: comedy not quite of the lowest order? Stud in Eng Lit 1500–1900 8 1968.

GEORGE WHETSTONE
1544?–87?

§1

Promos and Cassandra. 1578; ed J. Nichols, Six old plays vol 1, 1779; ed W. C. Hazlitt, Shakespeare's library vol 6, 1875; ed G. Bullough, Narrative and dramatic sources

of Shakespeare vol 2, 1958; ed I. Gollancz, Shakespeare classics, Oxford 1909; TFT 1910.
For Whetstone's other writings, see col 1158, above.

§2

Budd, F. E. Rouillet's Philanira and Whetstone's Promos and Cassandra. RES 6 1930.
—— Material for a study of the sources of Measure for measure. Revue de Littérature Comparée 11 1931.
Prouty, C. T. Whetstone, Peter Beverley and the sources of Much ado about nothing. SP 38 1941.
—— Whetstone and the sources of Measure for measure. Shakespeare Quart 15 1964.
Izard, T. C. Whetstone: mid-Elizabethan gentleman of letters. New York 1942.
Miller, E. H. Whetstone: profession epitapher. N & Q June 1952.
Purcell, H. D. Whetstone's English myrror and Marlowe's Jew of Malta. N & Q Aug 1966.

ANONYMOUS PLAYS

The bugbears. Ed C. Grabau, Archer 98–9 1897; ed R. W. Bond, Early plays from the Italian, Oxford 1911. Ms: BM Lansdowne 807. Tr by John Jeffere? from A. F. Grazzini, La spiritata, 1561.
Clyomon and Clamydes. 1599; ed A. Dyce, Peele's dramatic works, 1839, 1861; ed A. H. Bullen, Peele's works, 1882; ed W. W. Greg 1913 (Malone Soc); TFT 1913; B. J. Littleton, Hague 1968. Written c. 1570–83.
Kellner, L. Sir Clyomon and Sir Clamydes. E Studien 13 1889.
Morley, H. In his English writers vol 9, 1895.
Kittredge, G. L. Notes on Elizabethan plays. JEGP 2 1898. Attributes to Thomas Preston.
Ellison, L. M. The early romantic drama at the English Court. 1917. On source.
Common condicions. [1576?] (2 edns); ed Brandl (2nd edn); ed J. S. Farmer, Five anonymous plays, 1908 (2nd edn); ed C. F. T. Brooke, New Haven 1915 (facs of first edn). Fragment written c. 1576.
Love and fortune. 1589; ed J. P. Collier, Five old plays, 1851 (Roxburghe Club); Hazlitt's Dodsley vol 6; ed W. W. Greg 1930 (Malone Soc).
Robin Hood. [1560?] ('with a newe play for to be played in Maye games'); ed J. Ritson, Robin Hood vol 1, 1795; ed F. J. Child, English and Scottish popular ballads vol 5, 1878; Manly vol 2 (Robin Hood and the Sheriff of Nottingham in Manly vol 1); ed W. W. Greg, Malone Society collections vol 1, 1908; TFT 1914.
Thersytes. [1562?]; ed J. Haslewood, Two interludes, 1820 (Roxburghe Club); ed F. J. Child, Four old plays, 1848; Hazlitt's Dodsley vol 1; ed E. W. Ashbee 1876 (facs); ed A. W. Pollard, English miracle plays, Oxford 1890, 1927 (abridged); ed J. S. Farmer, Six anonymous plays, 1905; TFT 1912. Written 1537.
Holthausen, F. Studien zum älteren englischen Drama. E Studien 31 1902.
Moon, A. R. Was Nicholas Udall the author of Thersites? Library 3rd ser 7 1927.
Tom Tyler and his wife. 1661; ed F. E. Schelling, PMLA 15 1900; ed J. S. Farmer, Two Tudor shrew plays, 1906, Six anonymous plays, 1906; ed G. C. Moore Smith, and W. W. Greg 1910 (Malone Soc); TFT 1912. Written 1560?
Krzyzanowski, J. Conjectural remarks on Elizabethan dramatists. N & Q 16 Sept 1950.

(3) SCHOOL AND PRODIGAL SON PLAYS

General Studies

Wilson, H. B. The history of Merchant-Taylors' School. 2 vols 1814.

Herford, C. H. Studies in the literary relationships of England and Germany in the sixteenth century. Cambridge 1886.

Cloetta, W. Beiträge zur Literaturgeschicht edes Mittelalters und der Renaissance. 2 vols Halle 1890–2.

Bolte, J. Lateinische Literaturdenkmäler des xv und xvi Jahrhunderts. Berlin 1891.

Bahlmann, P. Die lateinischen Dramen von Wimphelings Stylpho bis zur Mitte des sechzehnten Jahrhunderts 1480–1550. Münster 1893.

— Die Erneurer des antiken Dramas und ihre ersten dramatischen Versuche 1314–1478. Münster 1896.

Sergeaunt, J. Annals of Westminster School. 1898.

Watson, F. The English grammar schools. 1898.

Fisher, G. W. Annals of Shrewsbury School. 1899.

Maxwell-Lyte, H. C. History of Eton College 1440–1898. 1899 (3rd edn).

Leach, A. F. Some English plays and players. In [F. J.] Furnivall miscellany, Oxford 1901.

Scott, E. J. L. Accounts of the Westminster play 1564 and 1616. Athenaeum 14 Feb 1903. On Heautontimoroumenos and Miles gloriosus.

Roeder, A. Menechmi und Amphitruo im englischen Drama. Leipzig 1904.

Maulsby, D. L. The relation between Udall's Roister Doister and the comedies of Plautus and Terence. E Studien 38 1907.

Woodruff, C. E. and H. J. Cape. Schola regis cantuariensis. 1908.

Wilson, J. D. Euphuism and the prodigal son. Library 1st ser 10 1909.

Motter, T. V. H. The school drama in England. 1929.

GEORGE GASCOIGNE
1542?–77

The glasse of government. 1575. *See col 1025, above.*

THOMAS INGELEND

The disobedient child. [1570?]. *See col 1416, above.*

JOHN PALSGRAVE
d. 1554

§ I

Johannis Palsgravi londoniensis exphrasis anglica in comoediam Acolasti: the comedye of Acolastus translated into our Englysshe tongue. 1540; ed P. L. Carver 1937 (EETS).

§ 2

Carver, P. L. Palsgrave's translation of Acolastus. Library 3rd ser 14 1934.

NICHOLAS UDALL
1505–56

Ralph Roister Doister. [1566?]. *See col 1414, above.*

ANONYMOUS PLAYS

The birthe of Hercules. Ed M. M. Wallace 1903. Ms trn of Amphitruo 1610?

Jacke Jugeler. 1563, [1565?], 3rd edn?; ed J. Haslewood, Two interludes, 1820 (Roxburghe Club); ed E. W. Ashbee 1876 (facs); ed F. J. Child, Four old plays, 1848; ed A. B. Grosart, Fullers worthies' miscellanies vol 4, 1873; Hazlitt's Dodsley 2; ed J. S. Farmer, Anonymous plays, 1907, TFT 1912; ed W. H. Williams, Cambridge 1914; ed E. L. Smart and W. W. Greg 1937 (Malone Soc).

Williams, W. H. The date and authorship of Jacke Jugeler. MLR 7 1912.

Moore Smith, C. G. Jacke Jugeler ll. 256–259. MLR 10 1915.

Dudok, G. Has Jack Juggler been written by the same author as Ralph Roister Doister? Neophilologus 1 1916.

Marienstras, R. Jack Juggler: aspects de la conscience individuelle dans une farce du 16e siècle. Etudes Anglaises 16 1963.

Voisine, J. and R. Marienstras. A propos de Jack Juggler. Etudes Anglaises 18 1965.

Jacob and Esau. 1568; Hazlitt's Dodsley 2; ed J. S. Farmer, Six anonymous plays, 1906; TFT 1908; ed J. Crow and F. P. Wilson 1956 (Malone Soc).

Stopes, C. C. The interlude of Jacob and Esau. Athenaeum 28 April 1900. Attributes to William Hunnis.

Misogonus. 1577?; Brandl; ed J. S. Farmer, Six anonymous plays, 1906; ed R. W. Bond, Early plays from the Italian, 1911. Mutilated ms at Chatsworth, dated 1577.

Kittredge, G. L. Misogonus and Laurence Johnson. JEGP 3 1901.

Bang, W. Ralph Roister Doister. Literaturblatt für Germanische und Romanische Philologie 23 1902.

Tannenbaum, S. A. Shakesperian scraps. New York 1933.

Miller, E. S. 'Magnificat nunc dimittis' in Misogonus. MLN 60 1945.

Bevington, D. M. Misogonus and 'Laurentius Bariowna'. Eng Lang Notes 2 1964.

Nice wanton. 1560. *See col 1408 above.*

[The prodigal son]. [c. 1530]. Black-letter fragment ptd Malone Society collections vol 1, 1907.

Terens in Englysh. [1520?].

Thersytes. [1562?]. *See col 1418, above.*

VI. THE EARLY TRAGEDIES

The section on University Plays, col 1761, below, should be consulted for Latin and academic tragedies. Abbreviations (Manly, TFT etc) refer to collections of plays, col 1363, above.

(1) GENERAL STUDIES

Cunliffe, J. W. The influence of Seneca on Elizabethan tragedy. 1893.
— The influence of Italian on early Elizabethan drama. MP 4 1907.
— Early English classical tragedies. Oxford 1912. Introd.
Churchill, G. B. Richard the Third up to Shakespeare. Berlin 1900.
Schelling, F. E. The English chronicle play. New York 1902. List of plays, pp. 276–86.
Reynolds, G. F. Some principles of Elizabethan staging. MP 2–3 1905.
Hubbard, F. G. Repetition and parallelism in the earlier Elizabethan drama. PMLA 20 1905.
Moorman, F. W. The pre-Shakespearean ghost. MLR 1 1906.
Chambers, E. K. Court performances before Queen Elizabeth. MLR 2 1907.
Manly, J. M. The influence of the tragedies of Seneca upon early English drama. In F. J. Miller's trn of Seneca's tragedies, Chicago 1907.
Durand, W. Y. Palaemon and Arcyte, Progne, Marcus Geminus and the theatre in which they were acted, as described by John Bereblock 1566. PMLA 20 1909.
Jockers, E. Die englischen Seneca: Uebersetzer des 16 Jahrhunderts. Strasbourg 1909.
Ristine, F. H. English tragicomedy. New York 1910.
Brooke, C. F. T. The Tudor drama. 1912.
Spearing, E. M. The Elizabethan translations of Seneca's tragedies. Cambridge 1912.
Boas, F. S. University drama in the Tudor age. Oxford 1914.
Ellison, L. M. The early romantic drama of the English Court. Chicago 1917.
Lucas, F. L. Seneca and Elizabethan tragedy. Cambridge 1922.
Witherspoon, A. M. The influence of Robert Garnier on Elizabethan tragedy. PQ 14 1934.

Eliot, T. S. Shakespeare and the stoicism of Seneca. In Selected essays, 1932.
Gilbert, A. H. Seneca and the criticism of Elizabethan tragedy. PQ 14 1934.
Spencer, T. Death and Elizabethan tragedy. 1936.
Beckingham, C. F. Seneca's fatalism and Elizabethan tragedy. 1937.
Whiting, B. J. Proverbs in the earlier English drama. Cambridge Mass 1938.
Baker, H. Induction to tragedy. 1939.
Mendell, C. W. Our Seneca. New Haven 1941.
Wells, H. W. Senecan influence on Elizabethan dramatists: a re-estimation. Shakespeare Assoc Bull 19 1944.
Swan, M. W. Seneca: texts and translations. More Books 20 1945.
Charlton, H. B. The Senecan tradition in Renaissance tragedy. 1946.
Armstrong, W. B. The influence of Seneca and Machiavelli on the Elizabethan tyrant. RES 24 1948.
Ure, P. On some differences between Senecan and Elizabethan tragedy. Durham Univ Jnl new ser 10 1948.
Palmer, R. G. Seneca's De remediis fortuitorum and the Elizabethans. Chicago 1953.
Clemen, W. Tragödie vor Shakespeare. Heidelberg 1955; tr 1961.
Dahinten, G. Die Geisterszene in der Tragödie vor Shakespeare. Göttingen 1958.
Jacquot, J. and M. Oddon. Les tragédies de Sénèque et le théâtre de la Renaissance. Paris 1964.
Mehl, D. Der Pantomime im der Drama der Shakespearezeit. Heidelberg 1964; tr as The Elizabethan dumb show, 1965.
Evans, G. L. Shakespeare, Seneca and the kingdom of violence. In Roman drama, ed T. A. Dorey and D. R. Dudley 1965.
Hunter, G. K. Seneca and the Elizabethans: a case-study in influence. Shakespeare Survey 20 1967.

(2) TRANSLATIONS FROM SENECA

Seneca his tenne tragedies. 1581; ed J. Leigh 1887 (Spenser Soc); ed T. S. Eliot 1927.

JASPER HEYWOOD
1535–98

The sixt tragedie of Seneca entituled Troas. 1559, 1559, [1560?]; ed H. de Vocht, Bang 41 1913. Comment by W. W. Greg, Library 3rd ser 11 1931.
The seconde tragedie of Seneca, entituled Thyestes. 1560; ed H. de Vocht, Bang 41 1913; ed A. K. McIlwraith, Five Elizabethan tragedies, Oxford 1938 (WC).
The first tragedie of Seneca, entituled Hercules Furens. 1561; ed H. de Vocht, Bang 41 1913.
See col 1116, above.

ALEXANDER NEVYLE
1544–1614

The lamentable tragedie of Oedipus. 1563; rev in Tenne tragedies, 1581. *See* E. M. Spearing, Alexander Nevile's translation of Seneca's Oedipus MLR 15 1920.

T[HOMAS] N[UCE]
d. 1617

The ninth tragedie of Seneca, called Octavia. [1566].

JOHN STUDLEY
b. c. 1547

The seventh tragedie of Seneca, entituled Medea. 1566; ed E. M. Spearing, Bang 38 1913.
The eyght tragedie of Seneca, entituled Agamemnon. 1566; ed E. M. Spearing, Bang 38 1913.
See also col 1147, above.

(3) OTHER TRAGEDIES

JANE, LADY LUMLEY

Iphigenia in Aulis. [1555?] (ms BM Reg. 15 A. ix); ed H. H. Child 1909 (Malone Soc); ed G. Becker, Sh Jb 44 1910.

HENRY CHEKE

[Free will]. A certayne tragedie wrytten fyrst in Italian, by F. N. B[assano]. [1561?].

THOMAS NORTON
1532–84
and
THOMAS SACKVILLE
1536–1608

Gorboduc. 1565, [1570?] (as The tragidie of Ferrex and Porrex), 1590; Dodsley; Manly; TFT 1908.

JOHN PICKERING

§1

A new enterlude of vice conteyninge the histoye of Horestes. 1567; ed J. P. Collier, Illustrations of old English literature vol 2, 1866; Brandl; TFT 1910.

§2

Happé, P. Tragic themes in three Tudor moralities. Stud in Eng Lit 1500–1900 5 1965.
Johnson, R. C. Press variants in Cambises; The third quarto of Cambises. N & Q July 1968.

RICHARD EDWARDS
1524–66

Damon and Pithias. 1571. See col 1415, above.

GEORGE GASCOIGNE
1542?–77
and
FRANCIS KINWELMERSHE
d. 1580?

Jocasta. Ed F. J. Child, Four old plays, Cambridge Mass 1848; ed J. W. Cunliffe, Boston 1906.

R.B.

§1

Apius and Virginia. 1575; ed C. W. Dilke, Old English plays vol 5, 1815; ed J. P. Collier, Dodsley's old plays vol 8, 1826; Hazlitt's Dodsley 4; ed J. S. Farmer 1908 (Early Eng Drama Soc); TFT 1908; ed R. B. McKerrow 1911 (Malone Soc).

§2

Happé, P. Tragic themes in three Tudor moralities. Stud in Eng Lit 1500–1900 5 1965.

GEORGE WHETSTONE
1544?–87?

Promos and Cassandra. 1578. See col 1417, above.

THOMAS HUGHES

The misfortunes of Arthur. 1587. See col 1770, below.

ROBERT WILMOT et al

Tancred and Gismund. See col 1776, below.

D. S. B.

VII. LATER ELIZABETHAN DRAMA

Lyly, Kyd, Peele, Lodge, Greene, Marlowe, Nashe

See I. Ribner, Tudor and Stuart drama, New York 1966; C. J. Stratman, Bibliography of English printed tragedy 1565–1900, Carbondale 1966.
For collections listed below as abbreviations (Bang, Gayley, TFT etc) see col 1363, above.

JOHN LYLY
1554–1606

Bibliographies

Tannenbaum, S. A. Lyly: a concise bibliography. New York 1940.
Johnson, R. C. Lyly 1935–65. 1968.

Collections

Complete works. Ed R. W. Bond 3 vols Oxford 1902, 1967.
Sixe Court comedies. Ed E. Blount 1632. Includes Endimion; Alexander and Campaspe; Sapho and Phao; Gallathea; Midas; Mother Bombie.
Dramatic works. Ed F. W. Fairholt 2 vols 1858, 1892.

§1

Euphues: the anatomy of wit. [1578], [1579], 1579 ('corrected and augmented'), 1580, 1581, 1585, 1587, 1595, 1597, 1601, 1605, 1606, 1607, 1613; ed F. Landmann, Englische Sprach- und Literaturdenkmale, ed K. Vollmöller, Heilbronn 1887; ed R. Ashley and E. M. Moseley, Elizabethan fiction, New York 1953; ed J. Winny, The descent of Euphues, Cambridge 1957.
Euphues and his England. 1580 (3 edns), 1581, 1582, 1584, 1586, 1588, 1592, 1597, 1601, 1605, 1606, 1609, 1613.
Euphues [both pts]. 1617, 1623, 1630, 1631, 1636; ed E. Arber 1868, 1895; ed M. W. Croll and H. Clemons 1916.

A moste excellent comedie of Alexander, Campaspe and Diogenes, played before the Queenes Majestie on New Yeares Day at night by her Majesties children and the children of Poules. 1584 (3 edns, all anon, 2nd–3rd as Campaspe; headlines in all edns, A tragicall comedie of Alexander and Campaspe), 1591; rptd in Dodsley's old plays vol 2, 1744; in Ancient British drama vol 1, 1810; ed J. M. Manly, Specimens vol 2, 1897; ed G. P. Baker, Gayley vol 1, 1903; ed W. W. Greg 1933 (Malone Soc); ed A. K. McIlwraith, Five Elizabethan comedies, Oxford 1935 (WC).

Sapho and Phao, played before the Queenes Majestie on Shrove-tewsday by her Majesties children and the boyes of Paules. 1584, 1591.

Endimion, the man in the moone, playd before the Queenes Majestie at Greenewich on Candlemas day at night by the chyldren of Paules. 1591 (anon); rptd [C. W. Dilke], Old English plays vol 2, 1814; ed G. P. Baker 1894; Brooke and Paradise; Baskervill et al.

Gallathea, as it was playde before the Queenes Majestie at Greenewich on Newyeeres day at night by the chyldren of Paules. 1592 (anon); ed A. B. Lancashire 1969 (RRDS) (with Midas).

Midas, plaied before the Queenes Majestie upon Twelfe day at night by the children of Paules. 1592 (anon); rptd [C. W. Dilke], Old English plays vol 1, 1814; ed J. Winny, Three Elizabethan plays, 1959; ed A. B. Lancashire 1969 (RRDS) (with Gallathea).

Mother Bombie, as it was sundrie times plaied by the children of Powles. 1594 (anon), 1598; rptd [C. W. Dilke], Old English plays vol 1, 1814; ed K. M. Lea and D. N. Smith 1948 (Malone Soc).

The woman in the moone, as it was presented before her Highnesse. 1597.

Loves metamorphosis: a wittie and courtly pastorall, first playd by the children of Paules, and now by the children of the Chappell. 1601.

Pappe with an hatchett, alias a figge for my godsonne, or crack me this nut, or a countrie cuffe, that is, a sound boxe of the eare, for the idiot Martin. [1589] (anon); rptd J. Petheram 1844; ed G. Saintsbury, Elizabethan and Jacobean pamphlets, 1892. Probably by Lyly.

A whip for an ape: or Martin displaied. [1589], [1589] (as Rhythmes against Martin Marre-Prelate) (anon); rptd I. D'Israeli, Quarrels of authors vol 3, 1814. Possibly by Lyly.

Queen Elizabeth's entertainment at Mitcham: poet, painter and musician. Ed L. Hotson 1953. Attribution to Lyly uncertain.

The maydes metamorphosis, *1600, and several anon entertainments and fragments of entertainments have also been assigned to Lyly, but without much plausibility.*

§2

Morley, H. Euphuism. Quart Rev 109 1861.
Weymouth, R. F. Analysis of Euphuism and its elements. Trans Philological Soc 1870–2.
Landmann, F. Shakespeare and Euphuism. Trans New Shakspere Soc 1880–5.
—— Der Euphuismus: sein Wesen, seine Quelle, seine Geschichte. Giessen 1881.
—— Euphues: Lyly. Heilbronn 1887.
Lauchert, F. Der Einfluss der Physiologus auf Euphuismus. E Studien 14 1890.
Child, C. G. Lyly and Euphuism. Erlangen 1894.
Bond, R. W. Lyly: novelist and dramatist. Quart Rev 183 1896.
—— Introd to his edn of the Complete works, 1902, 1967.
—— Lyly's doubtful poems. Athenaeum 9 May 1903.
—— Lyly's songs. RES 6–7 1930–1.
Baker, G. P. In Gayley vol 1, 1903.
Greg, W. W. On the authorship of the songs in Lyly's plays. MLR 1 1905. *See also* W. J. Lawrence, TLS 20 Dec 1923; W. W. Greg 3 Jan 1924; J. R. Moore, PMLA

42 1927; R. W. Bond, RES 6–7 1930–1; G. K. Hunter, Appendix to his Lyly, 1962.
—— In his Pastoral poetry and pastoral drama, 1906. Ch 4.
Wilson, J. D. Lyly. Cambridge 1905, New York 1970.
—— Lyly's relations by marriage. MLR 5 1910.
—— Euphues and the prodigal son. Library 2nd ser 10 1909.
Bang, W. and H. de Vocht. Klassiker und Humanisten: Lyly und Erasmus. E Studien 36 1906.
Long, P. W. The purport of Lyly's Endimion. PMLA 24 1909; Addendum, MP 8 1911.
—— From Troilus to Euphues. In Anniversary papers by colleagues and pupils of G. L. Kittredge, Boston 1913.
Brie, F. Lyly und Greene. E Studien 42 1910.
Feuillerat, A. Lyly: contribution à l'histoire de la Renaissance en Angleterre. Cambridge 1910.
Woolf, S. L. A source of Euphues. MP 7 1910.
Croll, M. W. The sources of the Euphuistic rhetoric. In Euphues, ed Croll and Clemons, 1916; rptd in his Style, rhetoric and rhythm, Princeton 1966.
Whipple, T. K. Isocrates and Euphuism. MLR 11 1916.
Wilson, F. P. An ironicall letter. MLR 15 1920.
Lawrence, W. J. The problem of Lyly's songs. TLS 20 Dec 1923.
Golding, S. R. The authorship of the Maid's metamorphosis. RES 2 1926.
Tilley, M. P. Elizabethan proverb lore in Lyly's Euphues, and in Pettie's Petite pallace. New York 1926.
—— Euphues and Ovid's Heroical epistles. MLN 45 1930.
Moore, J. R. The songs in Lyly's plays. PMLA 42 1927.
Jeffery, V. M. Lyly and the Italian Renaissance. Paris 1928, New York 1969.
Pruvost, R. Réflexions sur l'Euphuisme. Revue Anglo-américaine 8 1931.
Jones, D. Lyly at St Bartholomew's: or much ado about washing. In Lodge and other Elizabethans, ed C. J. Sisson, Cambridge Mass 1933, 1966.
Allen, D. C. Neptune's Agar in Lyly's Gallathea. MLN 49 1934.
—— A note on Lyly's Midas. MLN 60–1 1945–6.
Torretta, L. L'Italofobia di Lyly e i rapporti dell' Euphues col Rinascimento italiano. Giornale Storico della Letteratura Italiana 103 1934.
Howarth, R. G. Dipsas in Lyly and Marston. N & Q 9 July 1938.
Ringler, W. The immediate source of Euphuism. PMLA 53 1938.
Willcox, A. Medical references in the dramas of Lyly. Annals of Medical History 10 1938.
Austin, W. B. Lyly and Queen Elizabeth. N & Q 4 March 1939.
—— William Withie's notebooks: lampoons on Lyly and Gabriel Harvey. RES 23 1947.
Boughner, D. C. The background of Lyly's Tophas. PMLA 54 1939.
Knight, G. W. Lyly. RES 15 1939.
Dodds, M. H. Songs in Lyly's plays. TLS 28 June 1941.
Matthews, E. G. Gil Polo, Desportes and Lyly's Cupid and my Campaspe. MLN 56 1941.
Swart, G. Lyly and Pettie. E Studies 23 1941.
Bennett, J. W. Oxford and Endimion. PMLA 57 1942.
Tillotson, G. The prose of Lyly's comedies. In his Essays in criticism and research, 1942.
Perkinson, R. H. The epic in five acts. SP 43 1946.
Huppé, B. F. Allegory of love in Lyly's Court comedies. ELH 14 1947.
Kahin, H. A. Jane Anger and Lyly. MLQ 8 1948.
Parks, G. B. Before Euphues. In J. Q. Adams memorial studies, Washington 1948.
Parr, J. Astrology motivates a comedy. In his Tamburlaine's malady and other essays, Tuscaloosa 1953. On Woman in the moone.
Davenport, A. Notes on Lyly's Campaspe and Shakespeare. N & Q Jan 1954.
King, W. N. Lyly and Elizabethan rhetoric. SP 52 1955.

Parnell, P. E. Moral allegory in Lyly's Love's metamorphosis. SP 52 1955.

Barish, J. The prose-style of Lyly. ELH 23 1956.

Bryant, J. A., jr. The nature of the allegory in Lyly's Endymion. Renaissance Papers 1956.

Brown, J. R. and M. Cottier. A note on the date of Lyly's Galathea. MLR 51 1956.

Borinski, L. The origin of the euphuistic novel. In Studies in honor of T. W. Baldwin, Urbana 1958.

Mincoff, M. Shakespeare and Lyly. Shakespeare Survey 14 1961.

Hornát, J. Mamilia: Robert Greene's controversy with Euphues. Philologica Pragensia 5 1962.

Hunter, G. K. Lyly: the humanist as courtier. 1962.

— Lyly and Peele. 1968 (Br Council pamphlet).

Turner, R. Y. Some dialogues of love in Lyly's comedies. ELH 29 1962.

Zandvoort, R. W. What is Euphuism? In Mélanges Fernand Mossé in memoriam, Paris 1962.

Teets, B. E. Two faces of style in Renaissance prose fiction. In Sweet smoke of rhetoric, ed N. G. Lawrence and J. A. Reynolds, Coral Gables Miami 1964.

Best, M. R. A note on the songs in Lyly's plays. N & Q March 1965.

— A theory of the literary genesis of Lyly's Midas. RES new ser 17 1966.

— The staging and production of the plays of Lyly. Theatre Research 9 1968.

— Lyly's static drama. Renaissance Drama new ser 1 1968.

— Nashe, Lyly and Summers last will and testament. PQ 48 1969.

Powell, J. Lyly and the language of play. In Elizabethan theatre, ed J. R. Brown and B. Harris 1966.

Bevington, D. M. Lyly and Queen Elizabeth: royal flattery in Campaspe and Sapho and Phao. Renaissance Papers 1967.

Sarieva, L. Lyly's dramatic technique. Godišnik na Sofijskija Universitet, Fakultet pro Zapadni Filologii 61 1967.

Davis, W. R. In his Idea and act in Elizabethan fiction, Princeton 1969. Ch 4.

Dent, R. W. Lyly in 1588. Eng Lang Notes 7 1969.

Lancashire, A. C. Lyly and Shakespeare on the ropes. JEGP 68 1969. On a passage in Midas.

Saccio, P. The Court comedies of Lyly: a study in allegorical dramaturgy. Princeton 1969.

Smith, J. H. Sempronia, Lyly and John Foxe's comedy of Titus and Gesippus. PQ 48 1969.

Kolin, P. C. A possible source for Lyly's Eubulus. Amer N & Q 10 1972.

THOMAS KYD
1558–94

Bibliographies etc

Crawford, C. A concordance to the works of Kyd. 3 pts Louvain 1906–10 (Bang).

Tannenbaum, S. A. Kyd: a concise bibliography. New York 1951.

Johnson, R. C. Kyd 1940–66. 1968.

Collections

Works. Ed F. S. Boas, Oxford 1901, 1955 (with suppl). With biographical and critical introd.

§1

The householders philosophie [by Torquato Tasso] now translated by T.K. 1588.

The Spanish tragedie, newly corrected and amended of such grosse faults as passed in the first impression. [1592] (anon), 1594, 1599, 1602 ('newly corrected,

amended and enlarged with new additions of the Painters part, and others, as it hath of late been divers times acted'), 1603, 1610, 1615, 1618, 1623, 1633; rptd R. Dodsley, Collection of old plays vol 2, 1744; ed T. Hawkins, Origin of the English drama vol 2, 1773; ed I. Reed, Dodsley's Old plays vol 3, 1780; Ancient British drama 1; ed J. P. Collier, Dodsley's Old plays vol 3, 1825; Hazlitt's Dodsley 5; Manly 2; ed J. Schick 1898; ed J. Schick, Berlin 1901; ed W. W. Greg 1925 (1602 edn) (Malone Soc); Brooke and Paradise; Baskervill et al; ed A. K. McIlwraith, Five Elizabethan tragedies, Oxford 1938 (WC); ed W. W. Greg and D. N. Smith 1949 (1592 edn) (Malone Soc); ed C. T. Prouty, New York 1951; ed P. Edwards 1959 (RP); ed B. L. Joseph 1964 (New Mermaids); Leeds 1966 (facs of 1592); ed A. S. Cairncross 1967 (RRDS) (with the First part of Hieronimo; ed T. W. Ross 1968; ed J. R. Mulryne 1970; tr Italian, Teatro elisabettiano, ed M. Praz, Florence 1948; tr German, Das Theater der Shakespearezeit, Leipzig 1964.

The trueth of the most wicked and secret murthering of John Brewen. 1592; ed J. P. Collier, Illustrations of early English popular literature vol 1, 1863, New York 1966; ed A. F. Hopkinson, Play sources, 1913.

Cornelia. 1594, 1595 (as Pompey the Great his faire Corneliaes tragedie, effected by her father and husbandes downe-cast, death and fortune, written in French by that excellent poet Ro. Garnier, and translated into English by Thomas Kid); rptd R. Dodsley, Collection of old plays vol 11, 1744; Hazlitt's Dodsley 5; ed H. Gassner, Munich 1894.

Fragments. In England's Parnassus, 1600.

The following anon plays (see cols 1552 f., below) have also been assigned to Kyd: Arden of Feversham, The contention of York and Lancaster, Edward III, The first part of Jeronimo, King Leir, The rare triumphs of love and fortune, Soliman and Perseda, The taming of a shrew, The true tragedy of Richard III, *as well as a lost* Hamlet *and Shakespeare's* Titus Andronicus.

§2

Sarrazin, G. Die Entstehung der Hamlet-Tragödie. Anglia 12–13 1890–1.

— Der Verfasser von Soliman and Perseda. E Studien 15 1891.

— Kyd und sein Kreis. Berlin 1892.

Cunliffe, J. W. In his Influence of Seneca on Elizabethan tragedy, 1893.

Schoenwerth, R. Die niederländischen und deutschen Bearbeitungen von Kyds Spanish tragedy. Berlin 1903.

Michael, A. O. Der Stil in Kyds Originaldramen. Berlin 1905.

Routh, J. E. Kyd's rime schemes and the authorship of Soliman and Perseda and the First part of Jeronimo. MLN 20 1905.

Crawford, C. In his Collectanea, 2 vols Stratford 1906–7.

Moorman, F. W. The pre-Shakespearean ghost. MLR 1 1906.

Brereton, J. le G. Notes on the text of Kyd. E Studien 37 1907.

Wiehl, K. Kyd und sein Vers. Kempten 1911.

— Kyd und Soliman and Perseda. E Studien 44 1912.

Lawrence, W. J. Soliman and Perseda. MLR 9 1914.

Gray, H. D. The first quarto Hamlet. MLR 10 1915; PMLA 42 1927.

— Reconstruction of a lost play. PQ 7 1928.

Brandl, A. Kyd an den Privy Council über Marlowe. Archiv 92 1921.

Brown, F. K. Marlowe and Kyd. TLS 2 June 1921. Reply by F. S. Boas 30 June 1921.

Witherspoon, A. M. In his Influence of Robert Garnier on Elizabethan drama, New Haven 1924.

Baldwin, T. W. On the chronology of Kyd's plays. MLN 40 1925.

— Kyd's early company connections. PQ 6 1927.
— Parallels between Soliman and Perseda and Garnier's Bradamante. MLN 51 1936.
Greg, W. W. The Spanish tragedy: a leading case. Library 4th ser 6 1925.
Smit, J. de. Kyd: l'homme, l'oeuvre, le milieu, suivi de la Tragédie espagnole. Brussels 1925.
Forsythe, R. S. Notes on the Spanish tragedy. PQ 5 1926.
Mustard, W. P. Notes on Kyd's works. Ibid.
Bowers, F. T. Kyd's Pedringano: sources and parallels. Harvard Stud 13 1931.
— A note on the Spanish tragedy. MLN 53 1938.
— In his Elizabethan revenge tragedy, Princeton 1940.
Crundell, H. W. The 1602 additions to the Spanish tragedy. N & Q 4 March 1933, 4 Aug 1934. Reply by R. G. Howarth 7 April 1934.
— The authorship of the Spanish tragedy additions. N & Q 4 Jan 1941.
Buckley, G. T. Who was 'the late Arrian'? MLN 49 1934.
Baker, H. Ghosts and guides: Kyd's Spanish tragedy and the mediaeval tragedy. MP 33 1935.
— In his Induction to tragedy, Baton Rouge 1939.
Bradbrook, M. C. In her Themes and conventions of Elizabethan tragedy, Cambridge 1935.
Grubb, M. Kyd's borrowings from Garnier's Bradamante. MLN 50 1935.
Biesterfeldt, P. W. Die dramatische Technik Kyds. Halle 1936.
Farnham, W. In his Medieval heritage of Elizabethan tragedy, Berkeley 1936.
Schücking, L. L. The Spanish tragedy additions. TLS 12–19 June, 17 July 1937. Reply by F. S. Boas 26 June 1937.
— Die Zusätze zur Spanish tragedy. Leipzig 1938.
— Zur Verfasserschaft der Spanish tragedy. Munich 1963.
Stoll, E. E. Hamlet and the Spanish tragedy: quartos 1 and 2. MP 35 1937, 37 1939.
Wells, W. The authorship of King Leir. N & Q 16 Dec 1939.
— Kyd and the Chronicle history. N & Q 30 March, 6 April 1940.
— Alphonsus, Emperor of Germany. N & Q 28 Sept–5 Oct 1940.
Gorrell, R. M. John Payne Collier and the Murder of John Brewen. MLN 57 1942.
Østerberg, V. (paraphrased by J. D. Wilson). Nashe's 'Kid in Aesop': a Danish interpretation. RES 18 1942.
Hazen, A. T. Type facsimiles. MP 44 1947. On Smeeton facs of Solyman and Perseda.
Rubow, P. V. Shakespeare og hans samtidige. Copenhagen 1948.
Levin, H. An echo from the Spanish tragedy. MLN 64 1949.
Carrère, F. Le théâtre de Kyd. Toulouse 1951.
— La tragédie espagnole de Kyd et le Coeur brisé de John Ford. Etudes Anglaises 8 1955.
Clemen, W. In his Die Tragödie vor Shakespeare, Heidelberg 1955; tr 1961.
Empson, W. The Spanish tragedy. Nimbus 3 1956; rptd in Elizabethan drama; modern essays in criticism, ed R. J. Kaufmann, New York 1961.
McDiarmid, M. P. A reconsidered parallel between Shakespeare's King John and Kyd's Cornelia. N & Q Dec 1956.
Wittig, K. Gedanken zu Kyds Spanish tragedy. In Strena anglica: Festschrift für Otto Ritter, Halle 1956.
Cleeve, B. T. The 'lost' Hamlet. Studies 46 1957.
Ratliff, J. D. Hieronimo explains himself. SP 54 1957.
Wiatt, W. H. The dramatic function of the Alexandro-Villuppo episode in the Spanish tragedy. N & Q Aug 1958.
Reiman, D. H. Marston, Jonson and the Spanish tragedy additions. N & Q Sept 1960.

Heyningen, C. van. The additions to Kyd's Spanish tragedy. Theoria 17 1961.
Cannon, C. K. The relation of the additions of the Spanish tragedy to the original play. Stud in Eng Lit 1500–1900 2 1962.
Chickera, E. de. Divine justice and private revenge in the Spanish tragedy. MLR 57 1962.
Johnson, S. F. The Spanish tragedy: or Babylon revisited. In Essays on Shakespeare and Elizabethan drama in honor of Hardin Craig, Columbia Missouri 1962.
Price, H. T. Titus Andronicus and the additions to the Spanish tragedy. N & Q Sept 1962.
Turner, R. Y. Pathos and the Gorboduc tradition 1560–90. HLQ 25 1962.
Freeman, A. Shakespeare and Solyman and Perseda. MLR 58 1963.
— New records of Kyd and his family. N & Q Sept 1965.
— Kyd: facts and problems. Oxford 1967.
— The printing of the Spanish tragedy. Library 5th ser 24 1969.
Lambrechts, G. Edward III: œuvre de Kyd. Etudes Anglaises 16 1963.
Pal, R. M. Kyd, the Spanish tragedy: the establishment of a tradition in Elizabethan tragedy. Agra Univ Jnl of Research 11 1963.
Hunter, G. K. The spoken dirge in Kyd, Marston and Shakespeare: a background to Cymbeline. N & Q April 1964.
— Ironies of justice in the Spanish tragedy. Renaissance Drama 8 1966.
Kallapur, S. T. Two studies in Kyd. Jnl Karnatak Univ (Dharwar) 8 1964.
Levin, M. H. Vindicta mihi: meaning, morality and motivation in the Spanish tragedy. Stud in Eng Lit 1500–1900 4 1964.
Tomlinson, T. B. In his A study of Elizabethan and Jacobean tragedy, Cambridge 1964. Ch 4.
Fuzier, J. Kyd et l'éthique du spectacle populaire. Les Langues Modernes 59 1965.
— Carrière et popularité de la Tragédie espagnole en Angleterre. In Dramaturgie et société, ed J. Jacquot, Paris 1968.
Jensen, E. J. Kyd's Spanish tragedy: the play explains itself. JEGP 64 1965.
Joseph, B. L. The Spanish tragedy and Hamlet: two exercises in English Seneca. In Classical drama and its influence, ed M. J. Anderson 1965.
Laird, D. Hieronimo's dilemma. SP 62 1965.
Barish, J. A. The Spanish tragedy: or the pleasures and perils of rhetoric. In Elizabethan theatre, ed J. R. Brown and B. Harris 1966.
Edwards, P. Kyd and early Elizabethan tragedy. 1966.
Goodstein, P. Hieronimo's destruction of Babylon. Eng Lang Notes 3 1966.
Hapgood, R. The judge in the firie tower: another Virgilian passage in the Spanish tragedy. N & Q Aug 1966.
Schaar, C. 'They hang him in the arbour'. E Studies 47 1966. Replies by J. L. Smith and Schaar, ibid.
Stamm, R. The theatrical physiognomy of the Spanish tragedy and Hamlet. In English studies today: 4th series, ed I. Cellini and G. Melchiori, Rome 1966.
Hidekatsu, N. Revenge and ghost: a study of the Spanish tragedy. Stud in Eng Lit (Tokyo) 44 1967.
Cairncross, A. S. Kyd and the Myrmidons. Arlington Quart 1 1968.
Coursen, H. R., jr. The unity of the Spanish tragedy. SP 65 1968.
Dudrap, C. La tragédie espagnole face à la critique élisabéthaine et jacobéenne. In Dramaturgie et société, ed J. Jacquot, Paris 1968.
Plard, H. Adaptations de The Spanish tragedy dans les Pays-Bas et en Allemagne 1595–1640. Ibid.
Ross, T. W. Kyd's The Spanish tragedy: a bibliographical hypothesis. Bull Rocky Mt Modern Lang Assoc 22 1968.

Stevenson, W. Shakespeare's hand in the Spanish tragedy. Stud in Eng Lit 1500–1900 8 1968.

Adams, B. B. The audiences of the Spanish tragedy. JEGP 68 1969.

Bercovitch, S. Love and strife in Kyd's Spanish tragedy. Stud in Eng Lit 1500–1900 9 1969.

Burrows, K. C. The dramatic and structural significance of the Portuguese sub-plot in the Spanish tragedy. Renaissance Papers 1969.

Murray, P. B. Thomas Kyd. New York 1969.

Faber, M. D. and C. Skinner. The Spanish tragedy: act IV. PQ 49 1970.

Broude, R. Time, truth and right in the Spanish tragedy. SP 68 1971.

GEORGE PEELE
1556–96

Bibliographies

Larsen, T. A bibliography of the writings of Peele. MP 32 1934.

Tannenbaum, S. A. Peele: a concise bibliography. New York 1940.

Horne, D. H. In his Life and minor works of Peele, New Haven 1952. With list of unptd ms materials.

Johnson, R. C. Peele 1939–65. 1968.

Collections

Works. Ed A. Dyce 2 vols 1828, 3 vols 1829–39.

Dramatic and poetical works of Robert Greene and Peele. Ed A. Dyce 1861, 1879.

Plays and poems. Ed H. Morley 1887.

Works. Ed A. H. Bullen 2 vols 1888, 1969 (with introd by H. W. Wells).

Poetry: a selection. Ed E. Tandy 1927.

Life and works. Ed C. T. Prouty et al.

Vol 1, Life and minor works, ed D. H. Horne, New Haven 1952. Includes Tale of Troy; Hunting of Cupid; Device of the pageant borne before Wolstan Dixi; Descensus Astreae; A farewell: Eclogue gratulatory; Polyhymnia; Honour of the Garter; Praise of chastity; Anglorum feriae etc.

Vol 2, ed F. S. Hook and J. Yoklavich, New Haven 1960. Includes Edward I, ed Hook; Battle of Alcazar, ed Yoklavich (with special bibliography).

Vol 3, ed R. M. Benbow, E. M. Blistein and Hook, New Haven 1970. Includes Araygnment of Paris, ed Benbow; David and Bethsabe, ed Blistein; Old wives tale, ed Hook.

§1

The araygnment of Paris: a pastoral presented before the Queenes Majestie by the children of her Chappell. 1584 (anon); ed O. Smeaton 1905; ed H. H. Child 1910 (Malone Soc); Brooke and Paradise; Baskervill et al.

The device of the pageant borne before Woolstone Dixi Lord Maior of the Citie of London. 1585; rptd Harleian miscellany vol 10, 1813; ed J. Nichols, Progresses of Elizabeth vol 2, 1823; ed F. W. Fairholt, Lord Mayors' pageants, 1843 (Percy Soc). Unique copy in Bodley.

A farewell entituled to the famous and fortunate generalls of our English forces, Sir John Norris and Syr Frauncis Drake knights, and all theyr brave and resolute followers; whereunto is annexed A tale of Troy. 1859. The Tale of Troy was rptd 1604 (rev); no copy is now extant, but the text is given in Dyce and Bullen, above.

An eglogue gratulatorie entituled to the Right Honorable and renowned shepheard of Albions Arcadia, Robert Earle of Essex and Ewe, for his welcome into England from Portugall. 1589. Unique copy in Bodley.

Polyhymnia: describing the honourable triumph at tylt before her Majestie on the 17 of November last past, being the three and thirtith yeare of her Highnesse raigne. 1590.

Descensus Astreae: the device of a pageant borne before M. William Webb, Lord Maior of the Citie of London. [1591]; rptd Harleian miscellany vol 10, 1813; ed F. W. Fairholt, Lord Mayors' pageants, 1843 (Percy Soc). Unique copy in London Guildhall.

The honour of the Garter, displaied in a poem gratulatorie, entituled to the worthie and renowned Earle of Northumberland. [1593]; Englands Parnassus, 1600 (excerpts).

The famous chronicle of King Edward the First, sirnamed Edward Longshankes, with his returne from the Holy Land; also the life of Lleuellen rebell in Wales; lastly, the sinking of Queene Elinor, who sunck at Charingcrosse and rose again at Pottershith, now named Queenehithe. 1593, 1599; ed J. P. Collier, Dodsley's Old plays vol 11, 1827; ed W. W. Greg 1911 (Malone Soc).

The battell of Alcazar, fought in Barbarie betweene Sebastian King of Portugall and Abdelmelec King of Marocco, with the death of Captaine Stukeley, as it was sundrie times plaid by the Lord High Admirall his servants. 1594 (anon); ed W. W. Greg 1907 (Malone Soc).

The old wives tale: a pleasant conceited comedie played by the Queenes Majesties players. 1595 ('by G.P.'); ed F. B. Gummere, Gayley 1; ed W. W. Greg 1908 (Malone Soc); Brooke and Paradise; Baskervill et al; ed A. K. McIlwraith, Five Elizabethan comedies, Oxford 1934 (WC); Menston 1969 (facs).

The love of King David and fair Bethsabe, with the tragedie of Absalon, as it hath ben divers times plaied on the stage. 1599; ed T. Hawkins, Origin of English drama vol 2, 1773; Manly 2; ed W. W. Greg 1912 (Malone Soc).

The hunting of Cupid. Ed W. W. Greg, Malone Society collections vol 1, 1911 (from fragmentary excerpts in the commonplace book of William Drummond of Hawthornden). The original edn (Stationers' Register 26 July 1591) is lost.

Two Elizabethan stage abridgements: the Battle of Alcazar and Orlando Furioso. Ed W. W. Greg 1922 (Malone Soc).

Anglorum feriae: Englandes hollydayes, beginninge happyly the 38 yeare of the raigne of our soveraigne Ladie. Ed R. (or W. S.) Fitch, Ipswich [c. 1830] (from autograph ms BM additional 21,432).

Merrie conceited jests of George Peele. 1607, [1620?], 1627, 1657, 1671; ed W. C. Hazlitt, Shakespeare's jestbooks vol 2, 1864; ed C. Hindley, Old book collector's miscellany vol 1, 1871. Though Bullen included this work in his edn, it is no longer accepted as Peele's.

The following plays have also been partially or wholly assigned to Peele: Alphonsus Emperor of Germany, Captain Thomas Stukeley, Clyomon and Clamydes, Contention of York and Lancaster, George a Greene, Histriomastix, Jack Straw, Troublesome reign of King John, Knack to know a knave, Leir, Locrine, Mucedorus, Soliman and Perseda, Taming of a shrew, True tragedy of Richard III, Wily beguiled, Wisdom of Dr Dodipoll, and Shakespeare's Henry VI and Titus Andronicus.

§2

Gummere, F. B. In Gayley 1.

Greg, W. W. In his Pastoral poetry and pastoral drama, 1906. Ch 4.

—— Bad quartos outside Shakespeare: Alcazar and Orlando. Library 3rd ser 10 1919.

—— The evidence of theatrical plots for the history of the Elizabethan stage. RES 1 1925.

—— A Collier mystification. Ibid.

Schulz, E. In his Die englischen Schwankbücher bis herab zu Dobsons Drie Bobs, Berlin 1912. Pt 1, ch 5.

Cheffaud, P. H. Peele. Paris 1913.

Tatlock, J. S. P. The siege of Troy in Elizabethan literature, especially in Shakespeare and Heywood. PMLA 30 1915.

Sykes, H. D. In his Sidelights on Shakespeare, Stratford 1919.
— The authorship of a Knack to know a knave. N & Q 31 May–7 June 1924.
— Peele's borrowing from Du Bartas. N & Q 15–22 Nov 1924.
— In his Sidelights on Elizabethan drama, 1924.
Jeffery, V. M. Italian and English pastoral drama 2: source of Peele's Arraignment of Paris. MLR 19 1924.
Bates, K. L. The date of Peele's death. MLN 35 1920.
Jones, G. The intention of Peele's Old wives' tale. Aberystwyth Stud 7 1925.
Clapp, S. L. C. Peele's use of folklore in the Old wives' tale. SE 6 1926.
Gilbert, A. H. The source of Peele's Arraignment of Paris. MLN 41 1926.
Larsen, T. The canon of Peele's works. MP 26 1928.
— The early years of Peele, dramatist 1558–88. Trans Royal Soc of Canada 22 1928.
— The father of Peele. MP 26 1928.
— The growth of the Peele canon. Library 4th ser 11 1930.
— Peele in the Chancellor's court. MP 28 1930.
— The date of Peele's Old wives' tale. MP 30 1932.
— The Old wives' tale by Peele. Trans Royal Soc of Canada 29 1935.
— The historical and legendary background of Peele's Battle of Alcazar. Trans Royal Soc of Canada 33 1939.
Sampley, A. M. The text of Peele's David and Bethsabe. PMLA 46 1931.
— Verbal tests for Peele's plays. SP 30 1933.
— Peele's Descensus Astreae and Marlowe's Edward II. MLN 50 1935.
— Plot structure in Peele's plays as a test of authorship. PMLA 51 1936.
Dowling, H. M. The date and order of Peele's plays. N & Q 11–18 March 1933.
Christian, M. G. Middleton's acquaintance with the Merrie conceited jests of Peele. PMLA 50 1935.
Brinkman, H. Die dramatische Kunst in Peeles Arraignment of Paris. Münster 1938.
Jenkins, H. Peele's Old wives' tale. MLR 34 1939; rptd in Shakespeare's contemporaries, ed M. Bluestone and N. Rabkin, Englewood Cliffs NJ 1961.
Brooke, C. F. T. A Latin poem by Peele? HLQ 3 1940.
Wilson, R. H. Reed and Warton on the Old wives' tale. PMLA 55 1940.
Parks, G. B. Peele and his friends as ghost-poets. JEGP 41 1942; rptd Shakespeare Assoc Bull 22 1947.
Rice, W. G. A principal source of the Battle of Alcazar. MLN 58 1943.
Brereton, J. le G. Stage arrangement in Peele's David and Bethsabe I.i. In his Writings on Elizabethan drama, Melbourne 1948.
Wilson, J. D. In his edn of Shakespeare's Titus Andronicus, Cambridge 1948. Introd.
— In his edns of Shakespeare's Henry VI pts 1–2, Cambridge 1952. Introds.
Maxwell, J. C. Peele and Shakespeare: a stylometric test. JEGP 49 1950.
Ribner, I. Shakespeare and Peele: the death of Cleopatra. N & Q 7 June 1952. Replies by J. D. Reeves and H. Nørgaard 11 Oct 1952.
Robertson, J. and D. J. Gordon (ed). Malone Society collections vol 3. Oxford 1954. On Lord Mayors' shows etc.
— et al (ed). Malone Society collections vol 5. Oxford 1959.
Reeves, J. D. The judgment of Paris as a device of Tudor flattery. N & Q Jan 1954.
— The cause of the Trojan War, according to Peele. N & Q Aug 1955.
— Perseus and the flying horse in Peele and Heywood. RES new ser 6 1955.

— Two perplexities in Peele's Edward I. N & Q Aug 1956.
— Peele's Arraignment again. N & Q Oct 1956.
Ashe, D. J. The text of Peele's Edward I. SB 7 1955.
Clemen, W. In his Die Tragödie vor Shakespeare, Heidelberg 1955; tr 1961. Ch 11.
Hook, F. S. The two compositors in the first quarto of Peele's Edward I. SB 7 1955.
— The ballad sources of Edward I. N & Q Jan 1956.
Ewbank (Ekeblad), I.-S. The background of Peele's Araygnement of Paris. N & Q June 1956.
— The love of King David and fair Bethsabe: a note on Peele's biblical drama. E Studies 39 1958.
— The house of David in Renaissance drama: a comparative study. Renaissance Drama 8 1966.
Cutts, J. P. Peele's Hunting of Cupid. Stud in Renaissance 5 1958.
Campbell, L. B. In her Divine poetry and drama in sixteenth-century England, Cambridge 1959. Ch 9.
Ferrara, F. In his Jests e merry tales, Rome 1960.
Goldstone, H. Interplay in Peele's Old wives' tale. Boston Univ Stud in Eng 4 1960.
Lyons-Render, S. Folk motifs in Peele's Old wives' tale. Tennessee Folklore Soc Bull 26 1960.
Mazzaro, J. L. Peele and A farewell to arms: a thematic tie? MLN 75 1960. Reply by C. A. Keeler 76 1961.
Blair, C. On the question of unity in Peele's David and Bethsabe. In Studies in honor of John C. Hodges and Alwin Thaler, Knoxville 1962.
Bradbrook, M. C. Peele's Old wives' tale: a play of enchantment. E Studies 43 1962.
Ross, A. Severed heads in wells: an aspect of the well cult. Scottish Stud 6 1962.
Adams, C. A. The tales in Peele's Old wives' tale. Midwest Folklore 13 1963.
Nørgaard, H. Peele's Edward I and two Queen Elinor ballads. In English studies presented to R. W. Zandvoort: a supplement to E Studies 45 1964.
Stasio, C. de. Il linguaggio drammatico di Peele. Eng Miscellany (Rome) 15 1964.
Jones, E. In his Othello's countrymen, Oxford 1965. Ch 3. On Battle of Alcazar.
Musgrove, S. Peele's Old wives' tale: an afterpiece? Jnl of Australasian Univs Lang & Lit Assoc 23 1965.
Ashley, L. R. N. Authorship and evidence: a study of attribution and the Renaissance drama, illustrated by the case of Peele 1556–96. Geneva 1968.
Ball, B. W. Peele's Huanebango: a caricature of Gabriel Harvey. Renaissance Papers 1968.
Burckhardt, S. Shakespeare, Peele and the King of Scots. In his Shakespearian meanings, Princeton 1968.
Hendy, A. von. The triumph of chastity: form and meaning in the Arraignment of Paris. Renaissance Drama new ser 1 1968.
Hunter, G. K. Lyly and Peele. 1968 (Br Council pamphlet).
Lesnick, H. G. The structural significance of myth and flattery in Peele's Arraignment of Paris. SP 65 1968.
Taylor, A. B. Peele and Golding's Metamorphoses. N & Q Aug 1969.
Bergeron, D. M. The Elizabethan Lord Mayor's show. Stud in Eng Lit 1500–1900 10 1970.

THOMAS LODGE
1558–1625

Bibliographies

Paradise, N. B. In his Lodge, New Haven 1931.
Tannenbaum, S. A. Lodge: a concise bibliography. New York 1940.
Johnson, R. C. Lodge 1939–65. 1968.

Collections

Complete works. Ed E. Gosse 4 vols Glasgow 1883 (Hunterian Club), New York 1963. Omits trns.

§1

[A defence of poetry, music and stage plays. Original title may have been Honest excuses; *see* J. D. Wilson, MLR 3 1908]. [1579?]; ed D. Laing 1853 (Shakespeare Soc); extracts rptd in Elizabethan critical essays vol 1, ed G. G. Smith, Oxford 1904. A reply to S. Gosson, The schoole of abuse, 1579.

An alarum against usurers, [with] the delectable historie of Forbonius and Prisceria [and] the lamentable complaint of Truth over England. 1584; ed D. Laing 1853 (Shakespeare Soc).

Scillaes metamorphosis, enterlaced with the unfortunate love of Glaucus, with sundrie other poems and sonnets. 1589, 1610 (as A most pleasant historie of Glaucus and Scilla); rptd S. W. S[inger], Chiswick 1819; ed E. S. Donno, Elizabethan minor epics, 1963; ed N. Alexander, Elizabethan narrative verse, 1967.

Rosalynde: Euphues golden legacie. 1590, 1592, 1596, 1598, 1604, 1609, 1612 (as Euphues golden legacie), 1614, 1623, 1634, 1642; ed F. G. Waldron, A Shakespeare miscellany, 1802; ed J. P. Collier, Shakespeare's library vol 1, 1843; ed W. C. Hazlitt, Shakespeare's library vol 2, 1875; ed H. Morley 1887; ed H. H. Furness, New variorum edn of Shakespeare's As you like it, 1890; ed W. W. Greg 1907, 1931; ed E. C. Baldwin, Boston and New York 1923; ed G. Bullough, Narrative and dramatic sources of Shakespeare vol 2, 1958.

Catharos: Diogenes in his singularitie. 1591 ('by T.L. gent').

The famous, true and historicall life of Robert second Duke of Normandy. 1591 ('by T.L.G.').

Euphues shadow, the battaile of the sences [with] the Deafe mans dialogue. 1592 ('by T.L. gent').

The life and death of William Long beard, with manye other histories. 1593 ('by T.L. gent'); ed J. P. Collier, Illustrations of old English literature vol 2, 1866, New York 1966.

Phillis: honoured with pastorall sonnets, elegies and amorous delights, [with] the Tragicall complaynt of Elstred. 1593; ed M. F. Crow, Elizabethan sonnetcycles vol 1, Chicago 1896; ed S. Lee, Elizabethan sonnets vol 2, 1904 (selections).

The wounds of civill war, lively set forth in the true tragedies of Marius and Scilla, as it hath beene publiquely plaide in London by the Lord high Admirall his servants. 1594; ed J. P. Collier, Dodsley's Old plays vol 8, 1825; Hazlitt's Dodsley 7; ed J. D. Wilson 1910 (Malone Soc); ed J. W. Houppert 1969 (RRDS).

A looking glasse for London and England, made by Thomas Lodge, gentleman, and Robert Greene, in artibus magister. 1594, 1598, 1602, [1605?], 1617; rptd 1914 (TFT); ed W. W. Greg 1932 (Malone Soc); ed T. Hayashi, Metuchen NJ and Folkestone 1970. *See also under Greene, below.*

A fig for Momus: containing satyres, eclogues and epistles. 1595 ('by T.L. gent'); ed A. Boswell, Frondes caducae no 3, Auchinleck 1817.

The Divel conjured. 1596 (signed T.L.).

A margarite of America. 1596; ed J. O. Halliwell (-Phillipps) 1859; ed G. B. Harrison 1927 (with R. Greene's Menaphon).

Wits miserie and the worlds madnesse. 1596 (signed T.L.), Amsterdam and New York 1969 (facs).

Prosopopeia: containing the teares of the mother of God. 1596 (dedication signed T.L.). Attribution doubtful.

The flowers of Lodowicke of Granado. 1601 ('by T.L.'). Trn of Michael ab Isselt, Flores Lodovici Granatensis.

The famous and memorable workes of Josephus. 1602, 1609, 1620, 1632, 1640, 1655, 1670, 1683, 1693.

A treatise of the plague. 1603. Trn of F. Valleriole, Traicté de la peste, Lyons 1566. *See* E. Cuvelier, Etudes Anglaises 21 1968.

The workes of Lucius Annaeus Seneca. 1614, 1620, 1632. Selections: ed W. Clode 1888; ed W. H. D. Rouse 1899 (Temple Classics).

A learned summary upon the famous poem of William of Saluste Lord of Bartas, translated out of French. 1621 ('by T.L.'), 1637, 1638.

The poore mans talentt. Ed E. Gosse, Complete works vol 4, 1883 (from Norfolk-Collier ms). Another ms BM additional 34,212.

§2

Gosse, E. In his Seventeenth-century studies, 1885. Rptd from introd to his edn of Complete works.

Carl, R. Über Lodges Leben und Werke. Anglia 10 1887.

Arkle, A. H. The flowers of Lodowicke of Granada. N & Q 31 March 1906.

Wilson, J. D. The missing title of Lodge's reply to Gosson's School of abuse. MLR 3 1908.

Lee, S. In his French Renaissance in England, 1910.

Walker, A. Italian sources of lyrics of Lodge. MLR 22 1927.

— Some sources of the prose pamphlets of Lodge. RES 8 1932.

— The life of Lodge. RES 9–10 1933–4.

Scott, J. G. In her Les sonnets élisabéthains, Paris 1929. Ch 6.

Paradise, N. B. Thomas Lodge. New Haven 1931. With bibliography.

Sisson, C. J. Lodge and his family. In his Lodge and other Elizabethans, Cambridge Mass 1933, 1966.

Tenney, E. A. Thomas Lodge. Ithaca 1935, New York 1969.

Swaen, A. E. H. A looking-glass for London and England: nutmegs and ginger. MLR 33 1938.

Law, R. A. A looking glasse and the scriptures. SE 19 1939.

Ringler, W. The sources of Lodge's Reply to Gosson. RES 15 1939.

Davenport, A. Samuel Rowlands and Lodge. N & Q 2 Jan 1943.

N., M. The first English edition of Josephus. More Books 18 1943.

Atkins, S. H. Dyer at Woodstock. TLS 3 Feb 1945.

Condee, R. W. Lodge and a Lucan passage from Mirandula. MLN 63 1948.

Duncan, E. H. Lodge's use of Agrippa's chapter on alchemy. Nashville 1951.

McNeir, W. P. The date of a Looking glass for London. N & Q July 1955.

Armstrong, W. A. Tamburlaine and the Wounds of civil war. N & Q Sept 1958.

Himelick, R. A fig for Momus and Daniel's Musophilus. MLQ 18 1957.

Ryan, P. M. Thomas Lodge, gentleman. 1958.

Mincoff, M. What Shakespeare did to Rosalynde. Sh Jb 96 1960.

Sørensen, K. Lodge's translation of Seneca's De beneficiis compared with Arthur Golding's version: a textual analysis with special reference to Latinisms. Copenhagen 1960.

— Lodge's Seneca. Archiv 149 1962.

Hornát, J. Spisovatelské počátky Lodge [The literary beginnings of Lodge]. Časopis pro Moderní Filologii 43 1961. With English summary

Staton, W. F., jr. A Lodge borrowing from Watson. Renaissance News 14 1961.

McAleer, J. J. Lodge's verse interludes. College Langs Assoc Jnl (Baltimore) 6 1962.

Kaul, R. K. Lodge, Shakespeare and the olde daunce. Lit Criterion (Mysore) 6 1963.

George, J. Additional materials on the life of Lodge between 1604 and 1613. In Papers mainly Shakespearian, ed G. I. Duthie, Edinburgh 1964.

Davis, W. R. Masking in Arden: the histrionics of Lodge's Rosalynde. Stud in Eng Lit 1500–1900 5 1965.

— In his Idea and act in Elizabethan fiction, Princeton 1969. Ch 3.

Houppert, J. W. Lodge's letters to William Trumbull. Renaissance News 18 1965.

Homan, S. R. A looking-glass for London and England: the source for Dekker's If it be not a good play, the Devil is in it. N & Q Aug 1966.

Rae, W. D. Thomas Lodge. New York 1967.

Beaty, F. L. Lodge's Forbonius and Prisceria and Sidney's Arcadia. E Studies 49 1968.

Cuvelier, E. A treatise of the plague de Lodge 1603: traduction d'un ouvrage médical français. Etudes Anglaises 21 1968.

Sturman, B. A date and a printer for a Looking glasse for London and England, Q4. SB 21 1968.

Pierce, R. B. The moral languages of Rosalynde and As you like it. SP 68 1971.

ROBERT GREENE
1558–92

Bibliographies

Tannenbaum, S. A. Greene: a concise bibliography. New York 1939; Supplement, New York 1945.

Johnson, R. C. Robert Greene 1945–65. 1968.

Hayashi, T. Greene criticism: a comprehensive bibliography. Metuchen NJ and Folkestone 1971.

Collections

Dramatic works, to which are added his poems. Ed A. Dyce 2 vols 1831.

Poems of Greene and Christopher Marlowe. Ed R. Bell 1856, 1876.

Dramatic and poetical works of Greene and George Peele. Ed A. Dyce 1861, 1879.

Life and complete works in prose and verse. Ed A. B. Grosart 15 vols 1881–6 (Huth Lib), New York 1964.

Plays and poems. Ed J. C. Collins 2 vols Oxford 1905, New York 1970. See W. W. Greg, MLR 1 1906; R. A. Law, MLN 22 1907.

Complete plays. Ed T. H. Dickinson 1909 (Mermaid ser).

§1

Mamillia: a mirrour or looking-glasse for the ladies of England. 1583, 1593.

Arbasto: the anatomie of fortune. 1584, 1589, 1594, 1617 (as The historie of Arbasto), 1626.

Gwydonius: the carde of fancie. 1584, 1587, 1593, 1608 (as Greenes carde of fancie); ed G. Saintsbury, Shorter novels vol 1, 1929 (EL); ed F. Ferrara, Due romanzi, Naples 1950 (with Greenes mourning garment).

The debate between Follie and Love, translated out of French by Robert Greene. 1584, 1587, 1593. From Louise Labé, Débat de Folie et d'Amour, Lyons 1555.

Morando: the tritameron of love. Pt 1, 1584; pts 1–2, 1587.

The myrrour of modestie. 1584; ed J. P. Collier, Illustrations of old English literature vol 3, 1866, New York 1966.

An oration or funerall sermon uttered at Roome, at the buriall of Gregorie the 13. 1585. Tr by Greene from the French. Not in Grosart, above.

Planetomachia. 1585.

Euphues his censure to Philautus. 1587, 1634.

Penelopes web. 1587, 1601.

Alcida: Greenes metamorphosis. 1588, 1617.

Pandosto: the triumph of time. 1588 (running title, The historie of Dorastus and Fawnia), 1592, 1595, 1607, 1609, 1614, 1619, 1621, 1629, 1632 etc; ed W. C. Hazlitt, Shakespeare's library vol 4, 1875; ed H. Morley 1887 (with Shakespeare's Winter's tale), 1905; ed P. G. Thomas 1907; ed J. Winny, The descent of Euphues, Cambridge 1957.

Perimedes the blacke-smith. 1588.

Ciceronis amor: Tullies love. 1589, 1592, 1597, 1601, 1605, 1609, 1611, 1616, 1628, 1639; ed E. H. Miller, Gainesville 1954 (with A quip for an upstart courtier) (facs of 1589).

Menaphon: Camillas alarum to slumbering Euphues (with an epistle by Thomas Nashe). 1589, 1599, 1605, 1610 (as Greenes Arcadia, or Menaphon), 1616, 1632; rptd S. E. Brydges, Archaica vol 2, 1815; ed E. Arber 1880; ed G. B. Harrison 1927 (with Lodge's Margarite of America).

The Spanish masquerado. 1589, 1589.

Greenes never too late [in two pts; the second entitled Francescos fortunes]. 1590, 1600, 1607, 1611, 1616, [1620?], 1621, [1630?], 1631.

Greenes mourning garment. 1590, 1597, 1616; ed F. Ferrara, Due romanzi, Naples 1960 (with Gwydonius).

The Royal Exchange, fyrst written in Italian, and dedicated to the Signorie of Venice, now translated into Englishe and offered to the Cittie of London. 1590. An adaptation of Orazio Rinaldi, Dottrina della virtù et fuga de' vitii; see C. Speroni, Comparative Lit 14 1962.

Greenes farewell to folly. 1591, 1617.

A maydens dream; upon the death of Sir Christopher Hatton. 1591.

A notable discovery of coosnage. 1591 (running title, The art of conny-catching), 1592; ed J. O. Halliwell (-Phillipps) 1859; ed G. B. Harrison 1923; ed A. V. Judges, Elizabethan underworld, 1930.

The second part of conny-catching. 1591, 1592; ed G. B. Harrison 1923 (with A notable discovery); ed A. V. Judges, Elizabethan underworld, 1930.

The thirde and last part of conny-catching. 1592; ed G. B. Harrison 1923; ed A. V. Judges, Elizabethan underworld, 1930; ed G. R. Hibbard, Three Elizabethan pamphlets, 1951.

A disputation betweene a hee conny-catcher and a shee conny-catcher. 1592, 1615 (as Theeves falling out, true men come by their goods), 1617, 1621, 1637; ed G. B. Harrison 1923 (with The thirde part of conny-catching); ed A. V. Judges, Elizabethan underworld, 1930.

The blacke bookes messenger. 1592; ed G. B. Harrison 1924 (with The defence of conny catching); ed A. V. Judges, Elizabethan underworld, 1930.

Philomela: the Lady Fitzwaters nightingale. 1592, 1615, 1631; rptd S. E. Brydges, Archaica vol 1, 1815.

A quip for an upstart courtier. 1592 (3 edns), 1606, 1620, 1622, 1635; rptd in Harleian miscellany vol 5, 1745; ed J. P. Collier, Miscellaneous tracts, 1870; ed C. Hindley, Old book collectors' miscellany vol 3, 1873; ed E. H. Miller, Gainesville 1955 (with Ciceronis amor) (facs of the unique copy of first edn, now in the Huntington Lib, containing the attack on the Harvey brothers cancelled in later issues); tr Dutch, 1601.

Greenes groats-worth of witte, bought with a million of repentance. 1592, 1596, 1600, 1616, 1617, 1621, 1629, 1637 etc; ed S. E. Brydges, Lee Priory 1813; ed C. Hindley, Old book collectors' miscellany vol 1, 1871; ed C. M. Ingleby, Shakspere allusion-books pt 1, 1874 (New Shakspere Soc); ed G. B. Harrison 1923 (with The repentance of Robert Greene); ed A. C. Ward, A miscellany of tracts and pamphlets, Oxford 1927 (WC); Menston 1969 (facs of 1592).

The repentance of Robert Greene Maister of Artes. 1592; ed G. B. Harrison 1923 (with Greenes groats-worth).

Mamillia: the second part of the triumph of Paris. 1593.

The historie of Orlando Furioso, one of the twelve pieres of France, as it was plaid before the Queenes Majestie. 1594, 1599; ed W. W. Greg and R. B. McKerrow 1907 (Malone Soc).

The honorable historie of Frier Bacon and Frier Bongay, as it was plaid by her Majesties servants. 1594, 1630, 1655; ed J. P. Collier, Dodsley's Old plays vol 8, 1826; ed A. W. Ward, Old English drama, 1878; Gayley 1; rptd 1914 (TFT); ed W. W. Greg 1926 (Malone Soc);

Brooke and Paradise; Baskervill et al; ed B. Cellini, Florence 1953 (with John of Bordeaux); ed D. Seltzer 1963 (RRDS); ed J. A. Lavin 1969 (New Mermaids ser).

The Scottish historie of James the Fourth, slaine at Flodden, entermixed with a pleasant comedie presented by Oboram King of Fayeries, as it hath bene sundrie times publikely plaide. 1598; Manly 2; ed A. E. H. Swaen and W. W. Greg 1921 (Malone Soc); ed J. A. Lavin 1967 (New Mermaids ser); ed N. Sanders 1970 (RP).

The comicall historie of Alphonsus King of Aragon, as it hath bene sundrie times acted, made by R.G. 1599; ed W. W. Greg 1926 (Malone Soc).

Greenes Orpharion, wherein is discovered a musicall concorde of pleasant histories. 1599.

A paire of turtle doves: or the tragicall history of Bellora and Fidelio. 1606. Trn of Juan de Flores, La historia de Grisel y Mirabella, 1529.

A looking glasse for London and England, made by Thomas Lodge, gentleman, and Robert Greene, in artibus magister. 1594, 1598, 1602, [1605?], 1617; rptd 1914 (TFT); ed W. W. Greg 1932 (Malone Soc); ed T. Hayashi, Metuchen NJ and Folkestone 1970.

Two Elizabethan stage abridgments: the Battle of Alcazar and Orlando Furioso. Ed W. W. Greg 1922 (Malone Soc).

A pleasant conceyted comedie of George a Greene, the pinner of Wakefield, as it was sundry times acted by the servants of the Right Honourable the Earle of Sussex. 1599; rptd Dodsley's Old plays vol 1, 1744; vol 3, 1780, vol 3, 1825; Ancient British drama vol 1, 1810; ed F. W. Clark 1911 (Malone Soc); rptd 1913 (TFT); Baskervill et al; ed E. A. Horsman, Liverpool 1956. Probably by Greene.

The defence of conny catching by Cuthbert Cunny-catcher. 1592; ed J. E. Adlard 1859; ed G. B. Harrison 1924 (with Blacke bookes messenger). Possibly by Greene.

Greenes vision, written at the instant of his death. [1592]. Possibly by Greene, though disavowed by him.

The first part of the tragicall raigne of Selimus, as it was playd by the Queenes Majesties players. 1594 (anon), 1638 ('written by T.G.'); ed A. B. Grosart 1898 (Temple Dramatists); ed W. Bang 1908 (Malone Soc). Doubtfully attributed to Greene; 6 passages assigned to him in R. Allot, Englands Parnassus, 1600.

John of Bordeaux, or the second part of Friar Bacon. Ed W. L. Renwick 1936 (from ms in Duke of Northumberland's Lib at Alnwick) (Malone Soc); ed B. Cellini, Florence 1953 (with Friar Bacon). Possibly by Greene rev Chettle.

The following anon plays (see cols 1469 f., below) have also been wholly or partially assigned to Greene: The contention of York and Lancaster, Edward III, Fair Em, The troublesome reign of King John, A knack to know a knave, The Thracian wonder, Leir, Locrine, Mucedorus, The taming of a shrew, Thomas Lord Cromwell, as well as Shakespeare's Titus Andronicus and Henry VI.

§2

Storojenko, N. Life of Greene. In Works vol i, ed A. B. Grosart 1881.

Creizenach, W. Zu Greenes James the Fourth. Anglia 8 1885.

Herford, C. H. Greene's romances and Shakespeare. Trans New Shakspere Soc 1888.

Gayley, C. M. Greene: his life and the order of his plays. In Gayley 1.

Woodberry, G. E. Greene's place in comedy. In Gayley 1.

Koeppel, E. Locrine and Selimus. Sh Jb 41 1905.

Wolff, S. L. Greene and the Italian Renaissance. E Studien 37 1907.

— In his Greek romances in Elizabethan prose fiction, New York 1912.

Chandler, F. W. In his Literature of roguery vol 1, Boston 1907. Ch 3.

Brie, F. Lyly und Greene. E Studien 42 1910.

Aydelotte, F. In his Elizabethan rogues and vagabonds, Oxford 1913.

Jordan, J. C. Robert Greene. New York 1915. With bibliography.

Cole, G. W. Bibliography: a forecast. Trans Bibl Soc of America 14 1920. On the Heber copy of A quip for an upstart courtier and the 1595 edn of Pandosto.

McCallum, J. D. Greene's Friar Bacon and Friar Bungay. MLN 35 1920.

Harrison, G. B. In his Shakespeare's fellows, 1923. Ch 2.

McKerrow, R. B. Greene and Gabriel Harvey. TLS 8 March 1923.

Goree, R. G. Concerning repetitions in Greene's romances. PQ 3 1924.

Round, P. Z. Greene's materials for Friar Bacon and Friar Bungay. MLR 21 1926.

South, H. P. The upstart crow. MP 25 1927.

van Dam, B. A. P. Alleyn's player's part of Greene's Orlando Furioso and the text of the Q of 1594. E Studies 11 1929.

— Greene's Alphonsus. E Studies 13 1931.

— Greene's James IV. E Studies 14 1932.

Camden, C. Chaucer and Greene. RES 6 1930.

Sykes, H. D. Greene and George a Greene. RES 7 1931, 9 1933.

Baskervill, C. R. A prompt copy of A looking glass for London and England. MP 30 1932.

Hudson, R. Greene's James IV and contemporary allusions to Scotland. PMLA 47 1932.

McNeal, T. H. The Clerk's tale as a possible source for Pandosto. PMLA 47 1932.

— Who is Sylvia? and other problems in the Greene-Shakespeare relationship. Shakespeare Assoc Bull 13 1938.

— The tyger's heart wrapt in a player's hide. Ibid.

— The literary origins of Greene. Shakespeare Assoc Bull 14 1939.

— Studies in the Greene-Shakespeare relationship. Shakespeare Assoc Bull 15 1940.

Sanders, C. Greene and the Harveys. Bloomington 1932.

— Greene and his 'editors'. PMLA 48 1933.

— and W. A. Jackson. A note on Greene's Planetomachia 1585. Library 4th ser 16 1936.

Bald, R. C. The Locrine and George-a-Greene title-page inscriptions. Library 4th ser 15 1935.

Jenkins, H. On the authenticity of Greene's Groatsworth of wit and the Repentance of Robert Greene. RES 11 1935.

Renwick, W. L. Greene's 'Ridstall man'. MLR 29 1934. Reply by H. G. Wright 30 1935.

Simpson, E. A Greene quarto. TLS 21 Nov 1936. On a perfect copy of Friar Bacon 1594.

Wentworth, C. L. A probable source for George a Greene. TLS 4 July 1936.

Allen, D. C. Science and invention in Greene's prose. PMLA 53 1938.

Pruvost, R. Greene et ses romans. Paris 1938.

— Greene a-t-il accusé Shakespeare de plagiat? Etudes Anglaises 12 1959.

Swaen, A. E. H. A looking-glass for London and England: nutmegs and ginger. MLR 33 1938.

Law, R. A. A looking glasse and the scriptures. SE 19 1939.

Lievsay, K. L. Greene, Master of Arts, and 'Mayster Guazzo'. SP 36 1939.

— Greene's panther. PQ 20 1941; rptd in Renaissance studies in honor of Hardin Craig, Stanford 1941.

— Newgate penitents: further aspects of Elizabethan pamphlet sensationalism. HLQ 7 1944.

Vincent, C. J. Further repetitions in the works of Greene. PQ 18 1939.

— Pettie and Greene. MLN 54 1939.

Boas, F. S. Greene, Marlowe and Machiavelli. TLS 3 Aug 1940.

McNeir, W. F. Greene's Tomliuclin: Tamburlaine or Tom a Lincoln? MLN 58 1943.

— The origin of Ateukin in Greene's James IV. MLN 62 1947.

— The traditional element in the character of Greene's Friar Bacon. SP 45 1948.

— Greene and John of Bordeaux. PMLA 64 1949.

— The date of Greene's Vision. N & Q 1 April 1950.

— Reconstructing the conclusion of John of Bordeaux. PMLA 66 1951.

— A proverb of Greene's emended. N & Q 15 March 1952.

— The date of A looking glass for London. N & Q July 1955.

— Greene's medievalization of Ariosto. Revue de Littérature Comparée 29 1955.

Muir, K. Locrine and Selimus. TLS 12 Aug 1944.

— Greene and Troilus and Cressida. N & Q April 1955.

— Greene as dramatist. In Essays on Shakespeare and Elizabethan drama in honor of Hardin Craig, Columbia Missouri 1962.

Hoppe, H. R. John of Bordeaux: a bad quarto that never reached print. In Studies in honor of A. H. R. Fairchild, Columbia Missouri 1946.

D., A. A quotation from Greene in Dekker's Shoemaker's holiday. N & Q 28 June 1947.

Joseph, B. 'Theefe of Thessaly'. TLS 22 March 1947, 21 June 1947. Replies by H. K. Barton 5 April, E. Seaton 19 April 1947. On a phrase in Orlando Furioso.

Maxwell, J. C. An emendation in Greene. N & Q 4 Oct 1947. On A Looking glass for London l. 148.

— Greene's 'Ridstall man'. MLR 44 1949.

Oliver, L. M. The Spanish masquerado: a problem in double edition. Library 5th ser 2 1947.

Weld, S. J. Some problems of Euphuistic narrative: Greene and Wotton. SP 45 1948.

Parr, J. Sources of the astrological prefaces in Greene's Planetomachia. SP 46 1949.

— Ateukin the astrologer in James the Fourth. In his Tamburlaine's malady and other essays, Tuscaloosa 1953.

— Greene and his classmates at Cambridge. PMLA 77 1962.

MacLaine, A. H. Greene's borrowing from his own prose fiction in Friar Bacon and James IV. PQ 30 1951.

Mildenberger, K. Greene at Cambridge. MLN 66 1951.

Miller, E. H. The defence of cony-catching 1592: the argument of H. C. Hart. N & Q 24 Nov 1951.

— Deletions in Greene's A quip for an upstart courtier. HLQ 15 1952.

— Further notes on the authorship of the Defence of cony-catching. N & Q 11 Oct 1952.

— The sources of Greene's A quip for an upstart courtier. N & Q April–May 1953.

— The editions of Greene's A quip for an upstart courtier. SB 6 1954.

— The relationship of Greene and Thomas Nashe 1588–92. PQ 33 1954.

— Robert Parson's Resolution and the Repentance of Robert Greene. N & Q March 1954.

— Samuel Rid's borrowings from Greene. N & Q June 1954.

— A best-seller brought up to date: later printings of Greene's A disputation. PBSA 52 1958.

— In his Professional writer in Elizabethan England, Cambridge Mass 1959.

Thomas, S. The meaning of Greene's attack on Shakespeare. MLN 66 1951.

— The printing of Greene's Groatsworth of witte and Kind-Harts dreame. SB 19 1966.

Walker, R. The upstart crow. TLS 10 Aug 1951.

Wilson, J. D. Malone and the upstart crow. Shakespeare Survey 4 1951.

— In his edn of Shakespeare's 2 Henry VI, Cambridge 1952. Introd.

Towne, F. White magic in Friar Bacon? MLN 57 1952.

Jacquot, J. Ralegh's 'hellish verses' and the Tragicall raigne of Selimus. MLR 48 1953.

— The tragicall raigne of Selimus et la conception élisabéthaine de l'athée. Etudes Anglaises 7 1954.

— A propos du Tragicall raigne of Selimus: le problème des emprunts aux classiques à la Renaissance. Etudes Anglaises 16 1963.

Johnson, F. R. The editions of Greene's three parts of conny-catching: a bibliographical analysis. Library 5th ser 9 1954.

Clemen, W. In his Die Tragödie vor Shakespeare, Heidelberg 1955; tr 1961. Ch 12.

Ribner, I. Greene's attack on Marlowe: some light on Alphonsus and Selimus. SP 52 1955.

Nathanson, L. A quip for an upstart courtier and the Three ladies of London. N & Q Sept 1956.

Schrickx, W. Nashe, Greene and Shakespeare in 1592. Revue des Langues Vivantes 22 1956.

Ewbank (Ekeblad), I.-S. King Lear and Selimus. N & Q May 1957.

Ellis-Fermor, U. M. Marlowe and Greene: a note on their relations as dramatic artists. In Studies in honor of T. W. Baldwin, Urbana 1958; rptd in her Shakespeare the dramatist and other papers, ed K. Muir 1961.

Pearson, J. P. The defence of cony catching. N & Q April 1959.

Ferrara, F. L'opera narrativa di Greene. Naples 1960.

Parker, R. B. Alterations in the first edition of Greene's A quip for an upstart courtier. HLQ 23 1960.

— A Dutch edition of Greene's A quip for an upstart courtier 1601. N & Q April 1960.

Dent, R. W. Greene's Gwydonius: a study in Elizabethan plagiarism. HLQ 24 1961.

Sanders, N. The comedy of Greene and Shakespeare. In Early Shakespeare, ed J. R. Brown and B. Harris 1961.

— Greene's 'Tomliuclin'. N & Q June 1962.

— Greene's way with a source. N & Q March 1967. On Greene's Farewell to folly and la Primaudaye's French academy.

Shapiro, I. A. The first edition of Greene's Quip for an upstart courtier. SB 14 1961.

— An unexpected earlier edition of the Defence of conny-catching. Library 5th ser 18 1963. Correction, ibid.

Wells, S. Greene and Pliny. N & Q Nov 1961.

— Some words in 1588. N & Q June 1962. On Perymedes and Pandosto.

Bradbrook, M. C. Beasts and gods: Greene's Groatsworth and the social purpose of Venus and Adonis. Shakespeare Survey 15 1962.

Hornát, J. Mamilia: Greene's controversy with Euphues. Philologica Pragensia 5 1962.

— Two Euphuistic stories of Greene: the Carde of fancie and Pandosto. Philologica Pragensia 6 1963.

Kettner, E. J. Love's labour's lost and the Harvey-Nashe-Greene quarrel. Emporia State Research Stud 10 1962.

Lawlor, J. Pandosto and the nature of dramatic romance. PQ 41 1962.

Speroni, C. Un' ignota fonte italiana di Greene. Comparative Lit 14 1962. On the source of the Royal Exchange.

— The aphorisms of Orazio Rinaldi, Greene and Lucas Gracian Dantisco. Berkeley 1968.

— Did Greene have Shakespeare in mind? MLN 87 1972. On the 'upstart crow'.

Nelson, M. A. The sources of George a Greene, the pinner of Wakefield. PQ 42 1963.

Quaintance, R. E., jr. The French source of Greene's What thing is love. N & Q Aug 1963.

Teets, B. E. Two faces of style in Renaissance prose fiction. In Sweet smoke of rhetoric, ed N. G. Lawrence and J. A. Reynolds, Coral Gables Miami 1964.

Esler, A. Greene and the Spanish Armada. ELH 32 1965. On Spanish masquerado.

Freeman, A. An unacknowledged work of Greene. N & Q Oct 1965. On An oration or funeral sermon at the buriall of Gregorie 13 1585 as a trn by Greene.

— Notes on the text of 2 Henry VI and the upstart crow. N & Q April 1968.

Mukherjee, S. K. The text of Greene's Orlando Furioso. Indian Jnl of Eng Stud 6 1965.

Pennell, C. A. The authenticity of the George a Greene title-page inscriptions. JEGP 64 1965.

— Greene and 'King or Kaisar'. Eng Lang Notes 3 1965.

Velz, J. W. Greene and Philip of Macedon. N & Q May 1965.

Applegate, J. The classical learning of Greene. Bibliothèque d'Humanisme et Renaissance 28 1966.

Austin, W. B. The posthumous Greene pamphlets: a computerized study. Shakespeare News Letter Nov–Dec 1966.

Bass, E. Swinburne, Greene and the Triumph of time. Victorian Poetry 4 1966.

Dean, J. S., jr. Borrowings from Greene's Philomela in Davenport's the City-night-cap. N & Q Aug 1966.

— Antedatings from Greene. N & Q April 1969.

Homan, S. R. A looking-glass for London and England: the source of Dekker's If it be not a good play. N & Q Aug 1966.

Marder, L. Greene's attack on Shakespeare: a posthumous hoax? Shakespeare News Letter Sept 1966.

Drew, P. Was Greene's young Juvenal Nashe or Lodge? Stud in Eng Lit 1500–1900 7 1967.

Gabler, H. W. Imitation und Parodie in Greenes Orlando Furioso. Anglia 85 1967.

Biller, J. E. A link between Greene and Tarlton. Amer N & Q 6 1968.

Sturman, B. A date and a printer for A looking glass for London and England, Q4. SB 21 1968.

Davis, W. R. In his Idea and act in Elizabethan fiction, Princeton 1969. Ch 5.

Gelber, N. Greene's Orlando Furioso: a study of thematic ambiguity. MLR 64 1969.

CHRISTOPHER MARLOWE
1564–93

Bibliographies etc

Crawford, C. Marlowe concordance. Bang 34, new ser 2–3, 6–7 1911–32.

Brooke, C. F. T. The Marlowe canon. PMLA 37 1922.

Tannenbaum, S. A. Marlowe: a concise bibliography. New York 1937; Supplement, New York 1947.

Bakeless, J. In his Tragicall history of Marlowe vol 2, Cambridge Mass 1942, Hamden 1964.

British Museum. William Shakespeare 1564–1616 and Marlowe 1564–93: an exhibition of books, manuscripts etc. 1964.

Johnson, R. C. Marlowe 1946–65. 1967.

Collections

Works. Ed W. Oxberry [1818–20]; [ed G. Robinson] 3 vols 1826.

Works, with notes and some account of life and writings. Ed A. Dyce 3 vols 1850, 1 vol 1858 etc.

Poems of Robert Greene and Marlowe. Ed R. Bell 1856, 1876.

Works. Ed F. Cunningham 1870; ed A. H. Bullen 3 vols 1885, New York 1970.

Plays. Ed H. Ellis 1887 etc (Mermaid ser).

Works. Ed C. F. T. Brooke, Oxford 1910.

Works and life. Ed R. H. Case et al 6 vols 1930–3, New York 1966. Includes Life and Dido, ed C. F. T. Brooke 1930; Tamburlaine, ed U. M. Ellis-Fermor 1930; Jew of Malta and Massacre at Paris, ed H. S. Bennett 1931;

Edward II, ed H. B. Charlton and R. D. Waller 1933, 1955 (rev F. N. Lees); Doctor Faustus, ed F. S. Boas 1932; Poems, ed L. C. Martin 1931.

Three plays. Ed J. Hampden 1940. Includes Tamburlaine; Dr Faustus; Edward II.

Plays and poems. Ed M. R. Ridley 1955 (EL).

Plays. Ed L. Kirschbaum, New York 1962; ed I. Ribner, New York 1963; ed J. B. Steane 1969 (Penguin).

Poems. Ed M. MacLure 1968 (RP); ed S. Orgel 1971 (Penguin); ed R. Gill 1971.

§1

Tamburlaine the Great, divided into two tragicall discourses, as they were sundrie times shewed upon stages in the Citie of London by the Lord Admyrall his servantes. 1590, 1593, 1597, 1605–6; ed A. Wagner, Heilbronn 1885, Englische Sprach- und Literaturdenkmale (ed K. Vollmöller et al); Brooke and Paradise (pt 1 only); Baskervill et al; ed T. A. Wolff 1964; ed J. D. Jump 1967 (RRDS); ed J. W. Harper 1971 (New Mermaids ser).

The troublesome raigne and lamentable death of Edward the Second, King of England, as it was sundrie times publiquely acted in the Citie of London, by the Earle of Pembrooke his servants. 1594, 1598, 1612, 1622; rptd Dodsley's Old plays vol 2, 1744; Ancient British drama vol 1, 1810; ed [C. W. Dilke], Old English plays, 1814; ed W. Wagner, Hamburg 1871; ed F. G. Fleay 1873, 1877; ed O. W. Tancock, Oxford 1879, 1899; ed A. W. Verity 1896 (Temple Dramatists); ed W. D. Briggs 1914; ed W. W. Greg 1925 (Malone Soc); ed E. E. Reynolds, Cambridge 1930; Brooke and Paradise; Baskervill et al; ed R. G. Lunt 1940; ed R. S. Knox 1965; ed R. Gill 1967; ed W. M. Merchant 1967 (New Mermaids ser); ed I. Ribner, New York 1970; tr German, 1964; tr French, 1966.

The tragedie of Dido Queene of Carthage, played by the Children of her Majesties Chappell, written by Christopher Marlowe and Thomas Nash gent. 1594; rptd in Old English drama vol 2, 1825; ed A. B. Grosart, Works of Nashe vol 6, 1885; ed R. B. McKerrow, Works of Nashe vol 2, 1904, 1958; rptd 1914 (TFT); ed H. J. Oliver 1968 (RP) (with the Massacre at Paris).

The massacre at Paris, with the death of the Duke of Guise, as it was plaide by the Lord High Admirall his servants. [1594?]; ed W. W. Greg 1928 (Malone Soc; ed H. J. Oliver 1968 (RP) (with Dido); Amsterdam and New York 1971 (facs). Ms fragment in Folger Lib.

Epigrammes and Elegies [of Ovid], by J[ohn] D[avies] and C[hristopher] M[arlowe]. Middleburg [1595?] (2 edns); rptd [1830?]; rptd 1925.

All Ovids Elegies: 3 bookes, by C[hristopher] M[arlowe]; epigrams by J[ohn] D[avies]. Middleburg [1595–1600?] (2 edns), [c. 1640] (2 edns); ed C. Edmonds 1870, 1925.

Hero and Leander. 1598 (unique copy in Folger Lib), 1598 (with Chapman's continuation), 1600, 1606, 1609, 1613, 1617, 1622, 1629, 1637; ed S. E. Brydges, Restituta vol 2, 1815; rptd 1820; ed S. W. Singer, Select early English poets vol 8, 1821; ed P. B. Bartlett, Poems of George Chapman, New York 1941, 1962; ed G. Baldini, Parma 1952 (with Shakespeare's Venus and Adonis); ed E. S. Donno, Elizabethan minor epics, 1963; Menston 1968 (facs of 1598, Marlowe and Chapman); ed L. L. Martz, Washington 1972 (facs of 1598 Marlowe) (Folger Lib).

Lucans first booke translated line for line. 1600; ed T. Percy and G. Steevens, Poems in blank verse, 1807.

The passionate shepherd to his love. In Englands Helicon, 1600.

The tragicall history of D. Faustus, as it hath been acted by the Earle of Nottingham his servants, written by Ch. Marl. 1604, 1609, 1611, 1616 (with addns), 1619, 1620, 1624, 1628, 1631, 1663; [ed C. W. Dilke], Old English plays vol 1, 1814; ed W. Wagner 1877; ed A. W. Ward

1878 etc; ed H. Morley 1883; ed H. Breymann, Englische Sprach- und Literaturdenkmale, Heilbronn 1885; ed I. Gollancz 1897 (Temple Dramatists); rptd 1914 (TFT); ed H. Osborne 1932; Brooke and Paradise; Baskervill et al; ed M. Etherington 1937; ed B. Ashmore 1948; ed R. H. Robbins, New York 1948; Parallel texts (1604 and 1616), ed W. W. Greg, Oxford 1950; A conjectural reconstruction by Greg, Oxford 1950; ed P. H. Kocher, New York 1950; ed J. D. Jump 1962 (RP); ed R. Gill 1965 (New Mermaids ser); ed I. Ribner, New York 1966; Menston 1970 (facs of 1604, 1616); tr Dutch, 1960; tr German, 1964. *See cols 878–9, above.*

The famous tragedy of the rich Jew of Malta, as it was played before the King and Queene, in his Majesties Theatre at White-Hall, by her Majesties servants. 1633; ed I. Reed, Dodsley's Old plays vol 8, 1780; Ancient British drama vol 1, 1810; ed J. P. Collier, Dodsley's Old plays vol 8, 1827; ed A. Wagner, Englische Sprach- und Literaturdenkmale, Heilbronn 1889; Brooke and Paradise; ed R. Van Fossen 1964 (RRDS); ed T. W. Craik 1966 (New Mermaids ser); Menston 1970 (facs of 1633); ed I. Ribner, New York 1970; Amsterdam and New York 1971 (facs).

The following anon plays have also been wholly or partially ascribed to Marlowe: Alarum for London, Arden of Feversham, The contention of York and Lancaster, Edward III, Locrine, Lust's dominion, Selimus, The taming of a shrew, The troublesome reign of King John, *and Shakespeare's* Titus Andronicus, Henry VI *and* Richard III.

§2

Beard, T. The theatre of Gods judgements. 1597.

Vaughan, W. The golden grove. 1600.

Broughton, J. Of the dramatic writers who preceded Shakespeare. GM Jan–April and suppl 1830.

Herford, C. H. and A. Wagner. The sources of Tamburlaine. Academy 24 1883.

Symonds, J. A. In his Shakspere's predecessors, 1884.

Boas, F. S. In his edn of Works of Thomas Kyd, Oxford 1901, 1955. Introductory and supplementary documents.

—— Marlowe and Kyd. TLS 30 June 1921.

—— Marlowe and his circle. Oxford 1929, 1931.

—— and E. V. Hall, Richard Baines, informer: a new sidelight on Marlowe. Nineteenth Century Dec 1932.

—— Marlowe: a biographical and critical study. Oxford 1940, 1953 (rev).

—— Informer against Marlowe. TLS 16 Sept 1949. Reply by A. C. Southern 21 Oct 1949.

Ingram, J. H. Marlowe and his associates. 1904, New York 1970.

Brereton, J. le G. Notes on the text of Marlowe. Anglia Beiblatt 16 1905.

—— Marlowe: some textual notes. MLR 6 1911.

—— Marlowe's dramatic art studied in Tamburlaine. In his Writings on Elizabethan drama, Melbourne 1948.

Brooke, C. F. T. On the date of the first edition of Marlowe's Edward II. MLN 24 1909.

—— A prototype of Marlowe's Jew of Malta. TLS 8 June 1921.

—— Marlowe's versification and style. SP 19 1922.

—— The reputation of Marlowe. Trans Connecticut Acad of Arts & Sciences 25 1922.

—— Notes on Marlowe's Doctor Faustus. PQ 12 1933.

Smith, G. C. M. Marlowe at Cambridge. MLR 4 1909.

Danchin, F. C. En marge de la seconde partie de Tamburlaine. Revue Germanique 1912.

—— Quelques documents concernant les dramaturges Thomas Kyd et Marlowe. Revue Germanique 9 1914.

Baker, G. P. Dramatic technique in Marlowe. E & S 4 1913.

Eliot, T. S. Notes on the blank verse of Marlowe. In his Sacred wood, 1920; rptd as Marlowe in his Selected essays, 1932, 1951, and in his Elizabethan essays, 1934.

Brandl, A. Kyd an den Privy Council über Marlowe. Archiv 142 1921.

Brown, F. K. Marlowe and Kyd. TLS 2 June 1921.

Seaton, E. Marlowe and his authorities. TLS 16 June 1921.

—— Marlowe's map. E & S 10 1924.

—— Fresh sources for Marlowe. RES 5 1929.

—— Marlowe, Robert Poley and the Tippings. Ibid.

—— Robert Poley's ciphers. RES 7 1931.

—— Marlowe's light reading. In Elizabethan and Jacobean studies presented to F. P. Wilson, Oxford 1959.

Simpson, P. The 1604 text of Marlowe's Dr Faustus. E & S 7 1921.

—— Marlowe's Faustus. E & S 14 1929; rptd in his Studies in Elizabethan drama, Oxford 1955.

Briggs, W. D. On a document concerning Marlowe. SP 20 1923.

—— Marlowe's Faustus. MLN 38 1923.

Holthausen, F. Zur vergleichenden Märchen- und Sagenkunde. Anglia Beiblatt 34 1923.

Symons, A. A note on the genius of Marlowe. Eng Rev 36 1923.

Thaler, A. Churchyard and Marlowe. MLN 38 1923.

Berdan, J. M. Marlowe's Edward II. PQ 3 1924.

Hotson, J. L. The death of Marlowe. 1925.

Rosenberg, W. L. Marlowes Faustus und Goethes Faust. Neue Zeitung 7 1925.

Herrington, H. W. Marlowe: rationalist. In Essays in memory of Barrett Wendell, Cambridge Mass 1926.

Moore, H. Gabriel Harvey's references to Marlowe. SP 23 1926.

Spence, L. The influence of Marlowe's sources on Tamburlaine. MP 24 1926; PMLA 42 1927.

Bush, D. The influence of Marlowe's Hero and Leander on early mythological poems. MLN 42 1927.

—— Notes on Marlowe's Hero and Leander. PMLA 44 1929.

Ellis-Fermor, U. M. Christopher Marlowe. 1927.

—— In her Jacobean drama, 1936.

—— In her Frontiers of drama, 1945.

—— Marlowe and Greene: a note on their relations as dramatic artists. In Studies in honor of T. W. Baldwin, Urbana 1958; rptd in her Shakespeare the dramatist and other papers, ed K. Muir 1961.

Gray, A. K. Some observations on Marlowe, government agent. PMLA 43 1928.

Camden, C. Marlowe and Elizabethan psychology. PQ 8 1929.

—— Tamburlaine: the choleric man. MLN 44 1929.

Flasdieck, H. M. Zur Datierung von Marlowes Faust. E Studien 64–5 1929–30.

Lawrence, C. E. Marlowe the man. Quart Rev 255 1930.

Thorp, W. The ethical problem in Marlowe's Tamburlaine. JEGP 29 1930.

Heller, O. Faust and Faustus: a study of Goethe's relation to Marlowe. St Louis 1931.

Praz, M. Marlowe. E Studies 13 1931.

Robertson, J. M. Marlowe: a conspectus. 1931.

Bradbrook, M. C. Hero and Leander. Scrutiny 2 1933.

—— In her Themes and conventions of Elizabethan tragedy, Cambridge 1935. Ch 6.

—— In her School of night, 1936.

—— Marlowe's Dr Faustus and the eldritch tradition. In Essays on Shakespeare and Elizabethan drama in honor of Hardin Craig, Columbia Missouri 1962.

—— The inheritance of Marlowe. Theology 67 1964.

De Kalb, E. Robert Poley's movements as a messenger of the Court 1588–1601. RES 9 1933.

Adams, J. Q. The massacre at Paris leaf. Library 4th ser 14 1934.

Eccles, M. Marlowe in London. Cambridge Mass 1934.

—— Marlowe in Kentish tradition. N & Q 13–27 July 1935.

Mills, L. J. The meaning of Edward II. MP 32 1934.

van Dam, B. A. P. The Collier leaf [of Massacre at Paris].
E Studies 16 1934.
— Marlowe's Tamburlaine. Ibid.
Tilley, M. P. and J. K. Roy. Proverbs and proverbial
allusions in Marlowe. MLN 50 1935.
Henderson, P. And morning in his eyes: a book about
Marlowe. 1936.
— Christopher Marlowe. 1952.
— Christopher Marlowe. 1956, 1962 (rev).
Searle, J. Marlowe and Chrysostom. TLS 15 Feb 1936.
Taylor, R. A. A tentative chronology of Marlowe and some
other Elizabethan plays. PMLA 51 1936.
Bakeless, J. E. Marlowe and his father. TLS 2 Jan 1937.
Reply by E. Seaton 5 June 1937.
— Marlowe and the newsbooks. Journalism Quart 14
1937.
— Marlowe: the man in his time. New York 1937.
— The tragicall history of Marlowe. 2 vols Cambridge
Mass 1942. With bibliography.
Brooks, E. St. J. Marlowe in 1589–92? TLS 27 Feb 1937.
Reply by F. S. Boas 6 March 1937.
Cellini, B. La vita e il carattere di Marlowe. Rome
1937.
— Echi di Greene nel Dr Faustus di Marlowe. Rivista
di Letteratura Moderne 3 1952.
Clark, E. G. Elizabethan fustian: a study in the social
and political background of the drama with particular
reference to Marlowe. New York 1937.
— Ralegh and Marlowe: a study in Elizabethan fustian.
New York 1941.
Hall, E. V. Testamentary papers 3: Marlowe's death at
Deptford Strand 1593 – wills of jurors at inquest. 1937.
Wills, M. M. Marlowe's role in borrowed lines. PMLA
52 1937.
Zanoco, A. Marlowe: saggio critico. Florence 1937.
Kocher, P. H. The development of Marlowe's character.
PQ 17 1938.
— The witchcraft basis in Marlowe's Faustus. MP 38
1940.
— The English Faustus book and the date of Marlowe's
Faustus. MLN 55 1940.
— Marlowe's atheist lecture. JEGP 39 1940.
— François Hotman and Marlowe's the Massacre at
Paris. PMLA 56 1941.
— Backgrounds for Marlowe's atheist lecture. In Renaiss-
ance studies in honor of Hardin Craig, Stanford 1941;
PQ 20 1941.
— Marlowe's Art of war. SP 39 1942.
— Nashe's authorship of the prose scenes in Faustus.
MLQ 3 1942.
— Some Nashe marginalia concerning Marlowe. MLN
57 1942.
— The early date for Marlowe's Faustus. MLN 58 1943.
— A Marlowe sonnet. PQ 24 1945.
— Marlowe: a study of his thought, learning and charac-
ter. Chapel Hill 1946.
— Contemporary pamphlet backgrounds for Marlowe's
Massacre at Paris. MLQ 8 1947.
— Marlowe, individualist. UTQ 17 1948.
— English legal history in Marlowe's Jew of Malta.
HLQ 26 1963.
Brown, B. D. Marlowe, Faustus and Simon Magus.
PMLA 54 1939.
Norman, C. Marlowe's London. Theatre Arts Monthly
April 1939.
— The Muses' darling: the life of Marlowe. New York
1946.
Smith, J. Marlowe's Dr Faustus. Scrutiny 8 1939.
Hankins, J. E. Biblical echoes in the final scene of Dr
Faustus. In Studies in English in honor of R. D.
O'Leary and S. L. Whitcomb, Lawrence Kansas 1940.
Smith, M. B. Marlowe's imagery and the Marlowe canon.
Philadelphia 1940.
Wolthuis, G. W. The Rector in Marlowe's Dr Faustus.
Neophilologus 25 1940.

Allen, D. C. Renaissance remedies for fortune: Marlowe
and the Fortunati. SP 38 1941.
— Marlowe's Dido and the tradition. In Essays on
Shakespeare and Elizabethan drama in honor of Hardin
Craig, Columbia Missouri 1962.
Battenhouse, R. W. Marlowe's Tamburlaine. Nashville
1941, 1964 (rev).
— Tamburlaine: the scourge of God. PMLA 56 1941.
— Marlowe reconsidered: some reflections on Levin's
Overreacher. JEGP 52 1953.
Pitcher, S. M. Some observations on the 1663 edition of
Faustus. MLN 56 1941.
Baldwin, T. W. The genesis of some passages which
Spenser borrowed from Marlowe. ELH 9 1942. Replies
by W. B. C. Watkins and Baldwin 11–12 1944–5.
— Marlowe's Musaeus. JEGP 54 1955.
Gardner, H. The Second Part of Tamburlaine the Great.
MLR 37 1942.
— Milton's Satan and the theme of damnation in
Elizabethan tragedy. E & S ('English Studies') new
ser 1 1948; rptd in Elizabethan drama: modern essays
in criticism, ed R. J. Kaufmann, New York 1961.
Horrell, J. Peter Fabell and Dr Faustus. N & Q 18 July
1942.
Kirschbaum, L. Mephistopheles and the lost 'dragon'. RES
18 1942, 21 1945.
— Marlowe's Faustus: a reconsideration. RES 19 1943.
— The good and bad quartos of Dr Faustus. Library
4th ser 26 1946.
— Some light on the Jew of Malta. MLQ 7 1946.
McCloskey, J. C. The theme of despair in Marlowe's
Faustus. College Eng Nov 1942.
Walley, H. R. Shakespeare's debt to Marlowe in Romeo
and Juliet. PQ 21 1942.
Allodoli, E. La morte di Ramus secondo Marlowe.
Rinascita 6 1943.
Izard, T. C. The principal source for Marlowe's Tambur-
laine. MLN 58 1943.
Mizener, A. The tragedy of Marlowe's Dr Faustus.
College Eng Nov 1943; rptd in Shakespeare's contem-
poraries, ed M. Bluestone and N. Rabkin, Englewood
Cliffs NJ 1961.
Greg, W. W. The copyright of Hero and Leander.
Library 4th ser 24 1944.
— The damnation of Faustus. MLR 41 1946; rptd in
Shakespeare's contemporaries, ed M. Bluestone and
N. Rabkin, Englewood Cliffs NJ 1961.
Parr, J. Tamburlaine's malady. PMLA 59 1944; rptd in
his Tamburlaine's malady and other essays, Tuscaloosa
1953.
— The horoscope of Mycetes! in Tamburlaine 1. PQ 25
1946; rptd ibid.
— Astrological 'characters' in Dr Faustus' 'magic circle'.
Ibid.
Churchill, R. C. Keats and Marlowe. Contemporary Rev
March 1945.
Hillier, R. L. The imagery of colour, light and darkness
in the poetry of Marlowe. In Elizabethan studies and
other essays in honor of G. F. Reynolds, Boulder 1945.
Johnson, F. R. Marlowe's 'imperial heaven'. ELH 12
1945.
— Marlowe's astronomy and Renaissance scepticism.
ELH 13 1946.
Greene, C. Dr Faustus's tragedy of individualism. Science
& Soc 10 1946.
Oliver, L. M. Rowley, Foxe and the Faustus additions.
MLN 60 1945.
Smith, H. Tamburlaine and the Renaissance. In Eliza-
bethan studies and other essays in honor of G. F.
Reynolds, Boulder 1945.
Taylor, G. C. Marlowe's 'now'. Ibid.
Heilman, R. B. The tragedy of knowledge: Marlowe's
treatment of Faustus. Quart Rev of Lit 2 1946.
Nosworthy, J. M. The Marlowe manuscript. Library 4th
ser 26 1946.

—— Some textual anomalies in the 1604 Dr Faustus. MLR 41 1946.

—— The publication of Marlowe's Elegies and Davies's Epigrams. RES new ser 4 1953; Postscript 15 1964.

—— Coleridge on a distinct prospect of Faust. E & S new ser 10 1957.

Crow, J. Marlowe yields to Jervis Markham. TLS 4, 18 Jan 1947. Replies by P. Davies 11 Jan 1947; F. S. Boas 18 Jan 1947; E. P. Kuhl 21 June 1947; R. G. Howarth 5 July 1947. On the authorship of I walked along a stream.

D'Agostino, N. Ideologia del Marlowe. Rivista di Letterature Moderne 2 1948.

—— Christopher Marlowe. Rome 1950.

Houk, R. A. Dr Faustus and A shrew. PMLA 62 1947.

Kleinstück, J. Untersuchungen zu Marlowes Faust. Darstellung und Deutung 5 1947.

Maxwell, J. C. The sin of Faustus. Wind & Rain 4 1947.

—— The assignment of speeches in the Jew of Malta. MLR 43 1948.

—— Two notes on Marlowe's Faustus. N & Q 6 Aug 1949.

—— Hero and Leander and Love's labour's lost. N & Q 2 Aug 1952.

—— Tamburlaine part I, IV. iv. 77–9. N & Q 11 Oct 1952.

—— How bad is the text of the Jew of Malta? MLR 48 1953.

—— The plays of Marlowe. In Pelican guide to English literature vol 2, ed B. Ford 1955.

—— Notes on Dr Faustus. N & Q July 1964.

Neville, E. H. Tamburlaine. TLS 12 July 1947.

Duthie, G. I. The dramatic structure of Marlowe's Tamburlaine the Great, parts I and II. E & S ('English Studies') new ser 1 1948.

—— Some observations on Marlowe's Doctor Faustus. Archiv 203 1966.

Harrison, T. P. Further background for the Jew of Malta and the Massacre at Paris. PQ 27 1948.

—— Shakespeare and Marlowe's Dido Queen of Carthage. SE 35 1956.

Hussey, M. Marlowe's quotations. N & Q 11 Dec 1948.

Martin, L. C. Lucan—Marlowe—?Chapman. RES 24 1948.

Shannon, G. P. Against Marot as a source of Marlowe's Hero and Leander. MLQ 9 1948.

Atkinson, A. D. Marlowe and the voyagers. N & Q 11–25 June 1949.

—— A possible schoolfellow of Marlowe. N & Q 3 Sept 1949.

Dick, H. G. Tamburlaine's sources once more. SP 46 1949.

Eagle, R. L. The mystery of Marlowe's death. Adelphi 25 1949.

—— The mystery of Marlowe's death. N & Q 13 Sept 1952.

Feasey, L. and E. The validity of the Baines document. N & Q 26 Nov 1949.

—— Marlowe and the Homilies. N & Q 7 Jan 1950.

—— Marlowe and the commination service. N & Q 15 April 1950.

—— Marlowe and the prophetic dooms. N & Q 19 Aug, 16 Sept 1950. On connexions between Tamburlaine and Isaiah and Revelation.

—— Marlowe and the Christian humanists. N & Q 23 June 1951.

Lees, F. N. A Faustus ballad. N & Q 10 Dec 1949.

—— Dido Queen of Carthage and the Tempest. N & Q April 1964.

Barrington, M. Marlowe's alleged atheism. N & Q 10 June 1950. Reply by L. and E. Feasey 2 Sept 1950.

Carpenter, N. C. Music in Dr Faustus: two notes. N & Q 29 April 1950.

—— Infinite riches: a note on Marlovian unity. N & Q 3 Feb 1951.

—— 'Miles' versus 'Clericus' in Marlowe's Faustus. N & Q 1 March 1952.

—— A reference to Marlowe in Charles Butler's Principles of musik 1636. N & Q Jan 1953.

George, J. An allusion to Marlowe? N & Q 1 April 1950.

Liu, J. Y. The name of an Arabian king in Marlowe's Tamburlaine. N & Q 7 Jan 1950.

—— The interpretation of three lines in Marlowe's Tamburlaine, part I. N & Q 1 April 1950.

—— A Marlo-Shakespearian image cluster. N & Q 4 Aug 1951.

Mahood, M. M. Marlowe's heroes. In her Poetry and humanism, 1950; rptd in Elizabethan drama: modern essays in criticism, ed R. J. Kaufmann, New York 1961.

Martin, B. C. Shore's wife as a source of the epilogue to Dr Faustus. N & Q 29 April 1950.

Gilbert, A. H. 'A thousand ships'. MLN 66 1951.

—— Tamburlaine's 'pampered jades'. Rivista di Letterature Moderne 4 1953.

Pearce, T. M. Marlowe and Castiglione. MLQ 12 1951.

—— Marlowe's the Jew of Malta. Explicator 9 1951.

—— Jasper Heywood and Marlowe's Dr Faustus. N & Q 10 May 1952.

—— Tamburlaine's 'discipline to his three sons': an interpretation of Tamburlaine, part II. MLQ 15 1954.

—— Evidence for dating Marlowe's Tragedy of Dido. In Studies in the English Renaissance drama, ed J. W. Bennett et al, New York 1959.

Poirier, M. Christopher Marlowe. 1951.

Bowers, F. T. The text of Marlowe's Dr Faustus. MP 49 1952.

Brooke, N. The moral tragedy of Dr Faustus. Cambridge Jnl Aug 1952.

—— Marlowe as a provocative agent in Shakespeare's early plays. Shakespeare Survey 14 1961.

—— Marlowe the dramatist. In Elizabethan theatre, ed J. R. Brown and B. Harris 1966.

Campbell, L. B. Dr Faustus: a case of conscience. PMLA 67 1952.

Jantz, H. An Elizabethan statement on the origin of the German Faust book with a note on Marlowe's sources. JEGP 51 1952.

Johnson, S. F. Marlowe's King Edward II. Explicator 10 1952.

Langston, B. Marlowe's Faustus and the Ars moriendi tradition. In A tribute to G. C. Taylor, Chapel Hill 1952.

Levin, H. The overreacher: a study of Marlowe. Cambridge Mass 1952.

—— Marlowe today. Tulane Drama Rev 8 1964.

Lewis, C. S. Hero and Leander. Proc Br Acad 38 1952; rptd in his Selected literary essays, Cambridge 1969; and in Elizabethan poetry: modern essays in criticism, ed P. J. Alpers, New York 1967.

Maugeri, A. Greene, Marlowe e Shakespeare: tre studi biografici. Messina 1952.

—— Edward II, Richard III e Richard II: note critiche. Messina 1952.

Röhrman, H. The way of life: a thematic exposition of some plays of Marlowe and Shakespeare. Arnhem 1952.

Fricker, R. The dramatic structure of Edward II. E Studies 34 1953.

Galloway, D. The Ramus scenes in Marlowe's the Massacre at Paris. N & Q April 1953.

Jacquot, J. La pensée de Marlowe dans Tamburlaine. Etudes Anglaises 6 1953.

Miller, P. W. A function of myth in Marlowe's Hero and Leander. SP 50 1953.

—— The problem of justice in Marlowe's Hero and Leander. N & Q April 1957.

Ribner, I. The idea of history in Marlowe's Tamburlaine. ELH 20 1953.

—— Marlowe and Machiavelli. Comparative Lit 6 1954.

—— Tamburlaine and the Wars of Cyrus. JEGP 53 1954.

—— Marlowe's Edward II and the Tudor history play. ELH 22 1955.

—— Greene's attack on Marlowe: some light on Alphonsus and Selimus. SP 52 1955.

—— In his English history play in the age of Shakespeare, 1957. Ch 3.

—— Marlowe's 'tragicke glasse'. In Essays on Shakespeare and Elizabethan drama in honor of Hardin Craig, Columbia Missouri 1962.

—— Marlowe and the critics. Tulane Drama Rev 8 1964.

—— Marlowe and Shakespeare. Shakespeare Quart 15 1964; rptd in Shakespeare 400, ed J. G. McManaway 1964.

Wilson, F. P. Marlowe and the early Shakespeare. Oxford 1953.

Brown, P. W. F. St Clement and Dr Foster. N & Q April 1954.

Mundy, P. W. The ancestry of Marlowe. N & Q Aug 1954.

Rickey, M. E. Astronomical imagery in Tamburlaine. Renaissance Papers 1954.

Sunesen, B. Marlowe and the dumb show. E Studies 35 1954.

Clemen, W. In his Die Tragödie vor Shakespeare, Heidelberg 1955; tr 1961. Chs 8, 10.

Defosse, M. Christopher Marlowe. Paris 1955.

Ornstein, R. The comic synthesis in Dr Faustus. ELH 22 1955.

—— Marlowe and God: the tragic theology of Dr Faustus. PMLA 83 1968.

Williams, M. T. The temptations in Marlowe's Hero and Leander. MLQ 16 1955.

Fabian, B. Marlowe's Dr Faustus. N & Q Feb 1956.

—— A note on Marlowe's Faustus. E Studies 41 1960.

Frye, R. M. Marlowe's Dr Faustus: the repudiation of humanity. South Atlantic Quart 55 1956.

Hart, J. P. Prospero and Faustus. Boston Univ Stud in Eng 2 1956.

Lever, K. The image of man in Tamburlaine, part 1. PQ 35 1956.

McCullen, J. T. Dr Faustus and Renaissance learning. MLR 51 1956.

Mezzadri, P. Nota su Tamburlaine. Letterature Moderne 6 1956.

Michel, L. The possibility of a Christian tragedy. Thought 31 1956; rptd in Tragedy: modern essays in criticism, ed L. Michel and R. B. Sewall, Englewood Cliffs NJ 1961.

Perry, W. Marlowe's irreverent humor: some open questions. Tulane Stud in Eng 6 1956.

Steadman, J. M. Faustus and Averroes. N & Q Oct 1956.

—— Averroes and Dr Faustus: some additional parallels. N & Q Sept 1962.

Aden, J. M. Hero and Belinda. N & Q Jan 1957.

Babb, H. S. Policy in Marlowe's The Jew of Malta. ELH 24 1957.

Brooks, C. Tamburlaine and attitudes towards women. ELH 24 1957.

—— The unity of Marlowe's Dr Faustus. In To Nevill Coghill from friends, 1966.

Cameron, K. W. Transcendantal hell in Emerson and Marlowe. Emerson Soc Quart 1 1957.

Hook, F. S. Marlowe, Massinger and Webster quartos. N & Q Feb 1957.

Shield, H. A. The death of Marlowe. N & Q March 1957.

Taylor, R. T. Maximinus and Tamburlaine. N & Q Oct 1957.

Wild, F. Studien zu Marlowes Tamburlaine. In Brunner Festschrift: Wiener Beiträge zur Englischen Philologie 65 1957.

Armstrong, W. A. Tamburlaine and the Wounds of civil war. N & Q Sept 1958.

—— Marlowe's Tamburlaine: the image and the stage. Hull 1966.

Bradbrook, F. W. Marlowe and Keats. N & Q March 1958.

Butrym, A. A Marlowe echo in Kyd. N & Q March 1958.

Cutts, J. P. The ultimate source of Tamburlaine's white, red, black and death? N & Q April 1958.

—— Dido, Queen of Carthage. N & Q Sept 1958.

—— The Marlowe canon. N & Q Feb 1959.

—— Tamburlaine 'as fierce Achilles was'. Comparative Drama 1 1967.

Fraser, R. A. The art of Hero and Leander. JEGP 57 1958.

Jacobsen, E. Translation a traditional craft: an introductory sketch with a study of Marlowe's Elegies. Copenhagen 1958.

Leech, C. The two-part play: Marlowe and the early Shakespeare. Sh Jb 94 1958.

—— Marlowe's Edward II: power and suffering. CQ 1 1959.

—— Marlowe's humor. In Essays on Shakespeare and Elizabethan drama in honor of Hardin Craig, Columbia Missouri 1962.

—— The acting of Marlowe and Shakespeare. Colorado Quart 13 1964.

—— The structure of Tamburlaine. Tulane Drama Rev 8 1964.

—— (ed). Marlowe: a collection of critical essays. Englewood Cliffs NJ 1964.

—— Venus and her nun: portraits of women in love by Shakespeare and Marlowe. Stud in Eng Lit 1500–1900 5 1965.

—— The hesitation of Pyrrhus. In The morality of art, ed D. W. Jefferson 1969.

Nathanson, L. Tamburlaine's pampered jades and Gascoigne. N & Q Feb 1958.

Versfeld, M. Some remarks on Marlowe's Faustus. Eng Stud in Africa 1 1958.

Wehling, M. M. Marlowe's mnemonic nominology, with especial reference to Tamburlaine. MLN 73 1958.

Baker, D. C. Ovid and Faustus: the 'noctis equi'. Classical Jnl 55 1959.

Cooper, B. An Ur-Faustus? N & Q Feb 1959.

Hookham, H. Tamburlaine, the Great Emir. History Today March 1959.

—— Tamburlaine the Conqueror. 1962. On the historical Tamburlaine.

Laboulle, L. J. A note on Bertolt Brecht's adaptation of Marlowe's Edward II. MLR 54 1959.

Peet, D. R. The rhetoric of Tamburlaine. ELH 26 1959.

Reed, R. R., jr. Nick Bottom, Dr Faustus and the ass's head. N & Q July–Aug 1959.

Schuster, E. and H. Oppel. Die Bankett-Szene in Marlowe's Tamburlaine. Anglia 77 1959.

Flosdorf, J. W. The 'odi et amo' theme in the Jew of Malta. N & Q Jan 1960.

Hoy, C. Ignorance in knowledge: Marlowe's Faustus and Ford's Giovanni. MP 57 1960.

Kaula, D. Time and the timeless in Everyman and Dr Faustus. College Eng Oct 1960.

Quinn, M. The freedom of Tamburlaine. MLQ 21 1960.

Crabtree, J. H., jr. The comedy in Marlowe's Dr Faustus. Furman Stud 9 1961.

Hunter, G. K. The wars of Cyrus and Tamburlaine. N & Q Oct 1961.

—— The theology of Marlowe's the Jew of Malta. Jnl Warburg & Courtauld Inst 27 1964.

—— Five-act structure in Dr Faustus. Tulane Drama Rev 8 1964.

Muir, K. The chronology of Marlowe's plays. Proc Leeds Philosophical & Literary Soc 5 1961.

—— Marlowe's Dr Faustus. Philologia Pragensia 9 1966.

Stříbrný, Z. Marlowe. Časopis pro Moderni Filologii 43 1961. With English summary.

Beall, C. N. Definition of theme by unconsecutive event: structure as induction in Marlowe's Dr Faustus. Renaissance Papers 1962.

Bevington, D. In his From Mankind to Marlowe, Cambridge Mass 1962. Chs 14–17.

Brockbank, J. P. Marlowe's Dr Faustus. 1962.

Cole, D. Suffering and evil in the plays of Marlowe. 1962.

—— Marlowe 1564–1964: a survey. Shakespeare News Letter 14 1964.

Crundell, H. W. Nashe and Dr Faustus. N & Q Sept 1962.

Davidson, C. Dr Faustus of Wittenberg. SP 59 1962.

—— Dr Faustus at Rome. Stud in Eng Lit 1500–1900 9 1969.

Fieler, F. B. Tamburlaine part 1 and its audience. Gainesville 1962.

Freeman, A. A source for the Jew of Malta. N & Q April 1962.

Heller, E. Faustus's damnation: the morality of knowledge. Listener 11 Jan 1962.

Heninger, S. K., jr. The passionate shepherd and the philosophical nymph. Renaissance Papers 1962.

Marsh, T. N. Marlowe's Hero and Leander. Explicator 21 1962.

Ransom, M., R. Cook and T. M. Pearce. German Valdes and Cornelius in Marlowe's Dr Faustus. N & Q Sept 1962.

Waith, E. M. In his Herculean hero in Marlowe, Chapman, Shakespeare and Dryden, 1962.

—— Edward II: the shadow of action. Tulane Drama Rev 8 1964.

—— Marlowe and the jades of Asia. Stud in Eng Lit 1500–1900 5 1965.

Zimansky, C. A. Marlowe's Faustus: the date again. PQ 41 1962.

Cantelupe, E. B. Hero and Leander: Marlowe's tragicomedy of love. College Eng Jan 1963.

Dameron, J. L. Marlowe's 'ships of war'. Amer N & Q 2 1963.

Dent, R. W. Ovid, Marlowe and the Insatiate Countess. N & Q Sept 1963.

—— Marlowe, Spenser, Donne, Shakespeare and Joseph Wybarne. Renaissance Quart 22 1969.

Deyermond, A. D. Skelton and the epilogue to Marlowe's Dr Faustus. N & Q Nov 1963.

Frey, L. H. Antithetical balance in the opening and close of Dr Faustus. MLQ 24 1963.

Rogers, D. M. Love and honor in Marlowe's Dido Queen of Carthage. Greyfriar 6 1963.

Segal, E. Hero and Leander: Gongora and Marlowe. Comparative Lit 15 1963.

Welsh, R. F. Evidence of Heywood's spellings in the Jew of Malta. Renaissance Papers 1963.

—— The printer of the 1594 octavo of Marlowe's Edward II. SB 17 1964.

Westlund, J. The orthodox Christian framework of Marlowe's Faustus. Stud in Eng Lit 1500–1900 3 1963.

Alexander, P. Shakespeare, Marlowe's tutor. TLS 2 April 1964. Reply by T. W. Baldwin 23 April 1964.

Barber, C. L. 'The form of Faustus' fortunes good or bad'. Tulane Drama Rev 8 1964.

—— The death of Zenocrate: 'conceiving and subduing both' in Marlowe's Tamburlaine. Lit & Psychology 16 1966. Reply by N. N. Holland, ibid.

Brodwin, L. L. Edward II: Marlowe's culminating treatment of love. ELH 31 1964.

—— In her Elizabethan love tragedy, New York 1971. On Dido.

Brown, J. R. Marlowe and the actors. Tulane Drama Rev 8 1964.

D'Andrea, A. Studies on Machiavelli and his reputation in the sixteenth century 1: Marlowe's prologue to the Jew of Malta. Mediaeval & Renaissance Stud 5 1964.

Denonain, J.-J. Un nommé Christopher Marlowe, gentleman. Caliban 1 1964.

Goldman, A. 'The fruitful plot of scholarism graced'. N & Q July 1964.

Grigson, G. The toplesse towres. TLS 23 April 1964.

Grotowski, J. Dr Faustus in Poland. Tulane Drama Rev 8 1964.

Harbage, A. Innocent Barabas. Ibid.

Jump, J. D. Spenser and Marlowe. N & Q July 1964.

—— (ed). Dr Faustus: a casebook. 1969.

Kimbrough, R. Tamburlaine: a speaking picture in a tragic glass. Renaissance Drama 7 1964.

Kitagawa, T. A study of Marlowe. Tokyo 1964.

Klein, J. W. Marlowe. TLS 8 Oct 1964. Replies by E. Fisher 15 Oct, and Klein 22 Oct 1964.

Miller, J. M. Marlowe, 1964. Claremont Quart 11 1964.

Morris, H. Marlowe's poetry. Tulane Drama Rev 8 1964.

Palmer, D. J. Magic and poetry in Dr Faustus. CQ 6 1964.

—— Marlowe's naturalism. In Christopher Marlowe, ed B. Morris 1968.

Parfenov, A. Marlowe 1564–93. Moscow 1964.

Peschmann, H. Marlowe 1564–93: 'infinite riches in a little room'. English 15 1964.

Powell, J. Marlowe's spectacle. Tulane Drama Rev 8 1964.

Robertson, T. Directing Edward II. Ibid.

Rowse, A. L. Marlowe: a critical biography. 1964.

Rusche, H. G. Two proverbial images in Whitney's A choice of emblemes and Marlowe's The Jew of Malta. N & Q July 1964.

Sachs, A. The religious despair of Dr Faustus. JEGP 63 1964.

Sanders, W. Marlowe's Dr Faustus. Melbourne Critical Rev 7 1964.

—— In his Dramatist and the received idea, Cambridge 1968.

Steane, J. B. Marlowe: a critical study. 1964.

Tomlinson, T. B. In his Study of Elizabethan and Jacobean tragedy, Cambridge 1964. Chs 3–4.

Urry, W. Marlowe and Canterbury. TLS 13 Feb 1964.

Wada, Y. Edward II as tragic hero. Stud in Eng Lit (Tokyo) 41 1964.

Wickham, G. 'Exeunt to the cave': notes on the staging of Marlowe's plays. Tulane Drama Rev 8 1964; rptd in his Shakespeare's dramatic heritage, 1969.

—— Shakespeare's Richard II and Marlowe's Edward II. In his Shakespeare's dramatic heritage, 1969.

Bohm, R. Die Marlowe-Forschung der letzten beiden Jahrzehnte. Anglia 83 1965.

Cubeta, P. M. Marlowe's poet in Hero and Leander. College Eng April 1965.

Haile, H. G. The history of Dr Johann Faustus: recovered from the German. Urbana 1965.

Homan, S. R., jr. Dr Faustus, Dekker's Old Fortunatus and the morality plays. MLQ 26 1965.

—— Chapman and Marlowe: the paradoxical hero and the divided response. JEGP 68 1969.

Knights, L. C. The strange case of Marlowe. In his Further explorations, 1965.

LePage, P. V. The search for godhead in Marlowe's Tamburlaine. College Eng May 1965.

Oliver, H. J. Marlowe's Massacre at Paris. TLS 11 Nov 1965.

—— Oxberry's Marlowe. N & Q Aug 1969.

Richards, S. Marlowe's Tamburlaine II: a drama of death. MLQ 26 1965.

Schaubert, E. von. Shelleys Tragödie The Cenci und Marlowes Doppeldrama Tamburlaine. Paderborn 1965.

Smith, W. D. The nature of evil in Dr Faustus. MLR 60 1965.

—— The substance of meaning in Tamburlaine part 1. SP 67 1970.

Wraight, A. D. and V. F. Stern. In search of Marlowe: a pictorial biography. 1965.

Wyler, S. Der Begriff der Macht in Marlowes Tamburlaine 1. Zürich 1965.

—— Marlowe's technique of communication with his audience. E Studies 48 1967.

Banarjee, C. Dr Faustus: a Christian reinterpretation. Quest 48 1966.

Brooks, C. The unity of Marlowe's Dr Faustus. In To Nevill Coghill from friends, 1966.

Friedman, A. W. The shackling of accidents in Marlowe's Jew of Malta. Texas Stud in Lit & Lang 8 1966.

Garcus, J. C. La double aliénation d'Edouard II. Les Langues Modernes 60 1966.

Grobler, P. du P. Raptures of air and fire: Marlowe en die ontwikkeling van die Elizabethaanse blank vers. Standpunte 19 1966.

Hawkins, S. The education of Faustus. Stud in Eng Lit 1500–1900 6 1966.

Kostié, Marlowe's Hero and Leander and Chapman's continuation. In Renaissance and modern essays presented to Vivian de Sola Pinto, 1966.

Lambin, G. Marlowe et la France. Etudes Anglaises 19 1966.

Leiter, L. H. Marlowe's Passionate shepherd to his love. College Eng March 1966.

McAlindon, T. Classical mythology and Christian tradition in Marlowe's Dr Faustus. PMLA 81 1966.

Ostrowski, W. The interplay of the subjective and the objective in Marlowe's Dr Faustus. In Studies in language and literature in honour of Margaret Schlauch, Warsaw, 1966.

Perret, M. Edward III: Marlowe's dramatic technique. REL 7 1966. On the Prince in Edward II.

Purcell, H. D. Whetstone's English Myrror and Marlowe's Jew of Malta. N & Q Aug 1966.

Roddick, L. Ornament or essence? imagery in Marlowe's verse. Words (Wellington) 2 1966.

Rothstein, E. Structure as meaning in the Jew of Malta. JEGP 65 1966.

Sims, J. H. In his Dramatic uses of Biblical allusions in Marlowe and Shakespeare, Gainesville 1966.

Snyder, S. Marlowe's Dr Faustus as an inverted saint's life. SP 63 1966.

Speaight, R. Marlowe: the forerunner. REL 7 1966.

Sternlicht, S. Tamburlaine and iterative sun-image. Eng Record 16 1966, 18 1967.

Walton, C. E. Una M. Ellis-Fermor to W. W. Greg on the damnation of Faustus: an unpublished letter. Emporia State Research Stud 15 1966.

Henning, H. Zum 100 Geburtstag eines seltenen Buches: Marlowes Faust in der Übersetzung von Wilhelm Müller 1818. Marginalien 21 1967.

Kahler, E. Dr Faustus from Adam to Sartre. Comparative Drama 1 1967.

Morgan, G. Harlequin Faustus: Marlowe's comedy of hell. Humanities Assoc Bull 18 1967.

Ovchinnikova, F. G. Marlo i Shekspir. Uchenye Zapiski: Leningradskii Pedagogicheskii Institut 306 1967.

Traci, P. J. Marlowe's Faustus as artist: a suggestion about a theme in the play. Renaissance Papers 1967.

Bawcutt, N. W. Marlowe's Jew of Malta and Foxe's Acts and monuments. N & Q July 1968.

—— Machiavelli and Marlowe's Jew of Malta. Renaissance Drama new ser 3 1970.

—— James Broughton's edition of Marlowe's plays. N & Q Dec 1971.

Brooks, H. F. Marlowe and early Shakespeare. In Christopher Marlowe, ed B. Morris 1968.

Cockcroft, R. Emblematic irony: some possible significances of Tamburlaine's chariot. Renaissance & Modern Stud 12 1968.

Egan, R. A Muse of fire: Henry V in the light of Tamburlaine. MLQ 29 1968.

Gibbons, B. Unstable Proteus: the tragedy of Dido Queen of Carthage. In Christopher Marlowe, ed B. Morris 1968.

Gill, R. 'Snakes leape by verse'. Ibid. On trn of Ovid's Elegies.

Hattaway, M. Marlowe and Brecht. Ibid.

—— The theology of Marlowe's Dr Faustus. Renaissance Drama new ser 3 1970.

Knoll, R. E. Christopher Marlowe. New York 1968.

Merchant, W. M. Marlowe the orthodox. In Christopher Marlowe, ed B. Morris 1968.

Morris, B. Comic method in Hero and Leander. Ibid.

Mulryne, J. B. and S. Fender. Marlowe and the comic distance. Ibid.

Rousseau, G. S. Marlowe's Dido and a rhetoric of love. Eng Miscellany (Rome) 19 1968.

Smith, J. L. The Jew of Malta in the theatre. In Christopher Marlowe, ed B. Morris 1968.

Ahrends, G. Die Bildersprache in Marlowes Edward II. Germanisch-romanische Monatsschrift new ser 19 1969.

Bates, P. A. Faust: sources, works, criticism. New York 1969.

Bluestone, M. Libido speculandi: doctrine and dramaturgy in contemporary interpretations of Marlowe's Dr Faustus. In Reinterpretations of Elizabethan drama, ed N. Rabkin, New York 1969 (Eng Inst).

Burwick, F. Marlowe's Dr Faustus: two manners, the argumentative and the passionate. Neuphilologische Mitteilungen 70 1969.

Craik, T. W. Faustus's damnation reconsidered. Renaissance Drama new ser 2 1969.

Farnham, W. (ed). Twentieth-century interpretations of Dr Faustus. Englewood Cliffs NJ 1969.

Gruninger, H. W. Brecht und Marlowe. Comparative Lit 21 1969.

Jensen, E. J. Marlowe our contemporary? some questions of relevance. College Eng May 1969.

Lambrechts, G. Nashe et la Didon de Marlowe. Bulletin de la Faculté des Lettres de Strasbourg 47 1969.

Manley, F. The nature of Faustus. MP 66 1969.

Masington, C. G. Marlowe's artists: the failure of imagination. Ohio Univ Rev 11 1969.

O'Neill, J. (ed). Critics on Marlowe. 1969.

Smidt, K. Two aspects of ambition in Elizabethan tragedy: Dr Faustus and Macbeth. E Studies 50 1969.

Taylor, A. B. A note on Marlowe's Hero and Leander. N & Q Jan 1969. On Marlowe's debt to T. Peend, Hermaphroditus and Salmacis.

Fanta, C. C. Marlowe's Agonists. Cambridge Mass 1970.

French, A. L. The philosophy of Dr Faustus. EC 20 1970. Replies by S. Nagarajan, ibid, and J. Jensen 21 1971.

Lancashire, A. B. Timon of Athens: Shakespeare's Dr Faustus. Shakespeare Quart 21 1970.

Neuse, R. Atheism and some functions of myth in Marlowe's Hero and Leander. MLQ 31 1970.

O'Brien, M. A. Christian belief in Dr Faustus. ELH 37 1970.

Weisstein, U. The first version of Brecht/Feuchtwanger's Leben Eduards des Zweiten von England and its relation to the standard text. JEGP 69 1970.

Broich, U. Machiavelli and das Drama der Shakespeare-Zeit. Anglia 89 1971. On Tamburlaine and Jew of Malta.

Brown, W. J. Marlowe's debasement of Bajazet: Foxe's Acts and monuments and Tamburlaine part 1. Renaissance Quart 24 1971.

Godshalk, W. L. Marlowe's Dido Queen of Carthage. ELH 38 1971.

Stroup, T. B. Doctor Faustus and Hamlet: contrasting kinds of Christian tragedy. Comparative Drama 5 1971.

Woods, S. The passionate shepherd and the Nimph's reply: a study of transmission. HLQ 34 1971.

Summers, C. J. and T.-L. Pebworth. Marlowe's Faustus and the Earl of Pembroke's motto. Eng Lang Notes 9 1972.

Walsh, W. P. Sexual discovery and Renaissance morality in Marlowe's Hero and Leander. Stud in Eng Lit 1500–1900 12 1972.

THOMAS NASHE

1567–1601?

Bibliographies

Tannenbaum, S. A. Nashe: a concise bibliography. New York 1941.

Johnson, R. C. Nashe 1941–65. 1968.

Collections

Complete works. Ed A. B. Grosart 6 vols 1881–5 (Huth Lib).

Works. Ed R. B. McKerrow 5 vols 1904–10, Oxford 1958 (with corrections and supplementary notes by F. P. Wilson).

Selected works. Ed S. Wells 1964. Includes Pierce Penniless; Summer's last will and testament; Terrors of the night; Unfortunate traveller etc.

§1

The anatomie of absurditie. 1589; ed J. P. Collier, Illustrations of old English literature vol 3, 1866, New York 1966.

Pierce Penilesse his supplication to the Divell. 1592 (3 edns), 1593, 1595; ed J. P. Collier 1842 (Shakespeare Soc), Miscellaneous tracts, 1870; ed G. R. Hibbard, Three Elizabethan pamphlets, 1951; Menston 1969 (facs of 1592).

Strange newes, of the intercepting certaine letters. 1592, 1593, 1593 (as The apologie of Pierce Pennilesse); ed J. P. Collier, Miscellaneous tracts, 1870; Menston 1969 (facs of 1592).

Christs teares over Jerusalem. 1593, 1594 (with new preliminary matter), 1613; ed S. E. Brydges, Archaica vol 1, 1815; Menston 1970 (facs of 1593 with appendix of 1594 revisions).

The terrors of the night. 1594.

The unfortunate traveller: or the life of Jacke Wilton. 1594, 1594 ('newly corrected and augmented'); ed E. Gosse 1892; ed S. C. Chew, New York 1926; ed H. F. B. Brett-Smith, Oxford 1927; ed G. Saintsbury, Shorter novels vol 1, 1929 (EL); illustr M. Ayrton 1948; ed R. Ashley and E. M. Moseley, Elizabethan fiction, New York 1953; ed J. Berryman, New York 1960; Menston 1971 (facs of 1594, 'newly corrected and augmented'); tr French, 1954.

Have with you to Saffron-Walden. 1596; ed J. P. Collier, Miscellaneous tracts, 1870.

Nashes lenten stuffe: the praise of red herring. 1599; rptd Harleian miscellany vol 6, 1745, vol 2, 1809, vol 6, 1810; rptd C. Hindley, Old book collector's miscellany vol 1, 1871.

A pleasant comedie called Summers last will and testament. 1600; ed J. P. Collier, Dodsley's Old plays vol 9, 1826; Hazlitt's Dodsley 8.

The choise of valentines. Ed J. S. Farmer 1899. Not in Grosart; in subscribers' copies only of McKerrow 1904–10; in McKerrow 1958. Folger Lib has ms copy, giving name of the dedicatee, Lord Strainge, in full.

To the gentlemen students of both universities. Preface to R. Greene, Menaphon, 1589, col 1438 above; ed G. G. Smith, Elizabethan critical essays vol 1, Oxford 1904.

Somewhat to reade for them that list. Preface to Sir P. Sidney, Astrophel and Stella, 1591, col 1048 above.

An almond for a parrat. 1590; ed J. Petheram, Puritan discipline tracts, 1846. Included among the doubtful works by McKerrow, this pamphlet is now widely accepted as Nashe's. See D. J. McGinn, PMLA 59 1944.

For the Marprelate tracts conjecturally ascribed to Nashe see col 1961, below. For The tragedie of Dido Queene of Carthage, *written by Christopher Marlowe and Thomas Nash gent, 1594, see under Marlowe, above. It has also been suggested that Nashe had a hand in the anon* A knack to know a knave, *1594, in Marlowe's* Dr Faustus, *and in Shakespeare's* 1 Henry VI. *Doubtfully attributed to Nashe is* A wonderfull strange and miraculous astrologicall prognostication, *1591, rptd in Elizabethan and Jacobean pamphlets, ed G. Saintsbury 1892.*

§2

Cunliffe, J. W. Nashe and the earlier Hamlet. PMLA 21 1906.

McKillop, A. D. Some early traces of Rabelais in English literature. MLN 36 1921.

Mustard, W. P. Notes on Nash's works. MLN 40 1925.

Salyer, S. M. Hall's satires and the Harvey-Nashe controversy. SP 25 1928.

Kane, R. J. Anthony Chute, Nashe and the first English work on tobacco. RES 7 1931.

Brown, H. In his Rabelais in English literature, Cambridge Mass 1933.

Allen, D. C. The anatomie of absurditie. SP 32 1935.

—— A text from Nashe on the Latin literature of the sixteenth century. Washington State College Research Stud 5 1937.

Johnson, F. R. The first edition of Gabriel Harvey's Foure letters. Library 4th ser 15 1935.

—— Gabriel Harvey's Three letters: a first issue of his Foure letters. Library 5th ser 1 1946.

Bradbrook, M. C. In her School of night, 1936.

Wilson, F. P. Some English mock-prognostications. Library 4th ser 19 1939; rptd in his Shakespearian and other studies, Oxford 1969.

—— Another allusion to Nashe. N & Q Feb 1960.

Bowers, F. T. Nashe and the picaresque novel. In Humanistic studies in honor of John Calvin Metcalf, Charlottesville 1941.

Davenport, A. An Elizabethan controversy: Harvey and Nashe. N & Q 28 Feb 1942.

—— Shakespeare and Nashe's Pierce Penilesse. N & Q Sept 1953.

—— In his edn of Poems of Joseph Hall, Liverpool 1949. Introd.

—— In his edn of Poems of John Marston, Liverpool 1961. Introd.

Kocher, P. H. Nashe's authorship of the prose scenes in Faustus. MLQ 3 1942.

—— Some Nashe marginalia concerning Marlowe. MLN 57 1942.

Østerberg, V. (paraphrased by J. D. Wilson). Nashe's 'Kid in Aesop'. RES 18 1942.

de Beer, E. S. Nashe: the notices of Rome in the Unfortunate traveller. N & Q 31 July 1943.

McGinn, D. J. Nashe's share in the Marprelate controversy. PMLA 59 1944.

—— The allegory of the beare and the foxe in Pierce Penilesse. PMLA 61 1946.

—— A quip from Tom Nashe. In Studies in the English Renaissance drama, ed J. W. Bennett, O. Cargill and V. Hall jr, 1959.

Q., D. Bacon, Nashe and Dante. N & Q 23 Feb 1946.

Wilson, J. D. In his edn of Shakespeare's 1 Henry IV, Cambridge 1946. Cites parallels from Nashe.

Mackerness, E. D. A note on Nashe and style. English 6 1947.

—— Nashe and William Cotton. RES 25 1949.

—— Christs teares and the literature of warning. E Studies 33 1952.

Sackton, A. H. Nashe as an Elizabethan critic. SE 26 1947.

Feasey, L. The unfortunate traveller. TLS 2 Oct 1948.

—— and E. Nashe's The unfortunate traveller: some Marlovian echoes. English 7 1948.

Croston, A. K. The use of imagery in the Unfortunate traveller. RES 24 1948.

Latham, A. M. C. Satire on literary themes and modes in the Unfortunate traveller. E & S ('English Studies') new ser 1 1948.

Thomas, S. New light on the Nashe-Harvey quarrel. MLN 63 1948.

Leishman, J. B. In his edn of Three Parnassus plays 1598–1601, 1949. Introd.

Ebbs, J. D. A note on Nashe and Shakespeare. MLN 66 1951.

Hunter, J. B. The unfortunate traveller as a sidelight on Elizabethan security. N & Q 17 Feb 1951.

Summersgill, T. L. The influence of the Marprelate controversy upon the style of Nashe. SP 48 1951. Replies by D. J. McGinn and Summersgill, ibid.

— Harvey, Nashe and the Three Parnassus plays. PQ 31 1952.

Greg, W. W. Was the first edition of Pierce Penilesse a piracy? Library 5th ser 7 1952.

Evans, G. B. Nashe and the dram of eale. N & Q Sept 1953. Note by R. L. Eagle, Dec 1953.

— Shakespeare's 1 Henry IV and Nashe. N & Q July–Aug 1959.

Harder, K. B. Nashe's rebuke of Spenser. N & Q April 1953.

— Nashe and Spenser. In Essays in honor of Walter Clyde Curry, Nashville 1954.

York, E. C. Shakespeare and Nashe. N & Q Sept 1953.

— Nashe and Mandeville. N & Q April 1957.

Bradbrook, F. W. Nashe and Shakespeare. N & Q Nov 1954.

Miller, E. H. The relationship of Robert Greene and Nashe 1588–92. PQ 33 1954.

— In his Professional writer in Elizabethan England, Cambridge Mass 1959.

Marcus, H. Nash über Deutschland. Archiv 192 1955.

Howarth, R. G. Two Elizabethan writers of fiction: Nashe and Thomas Deloney. Cape Town 1956.

Schrickx, W. Shakespeare's early contemporaries: the background of the Harvey-Nashe polemic and Love's labour's lost. Antwerp 1956.

— Nashe, Greene and Shakespeare in 1592. Revue des Langues Vivantes 22 1956.

— Onion: a sobriquet relevant to Nashe. Revue des Langues Vivantes 27 1961.

— Titus Andronicus and Nashe. E Studies 50 1969.

Austin, W. B. Concerning a woodcut. Shakespeare Quart 8 1957.

Snortum, N. K. The title of Nashe's Pierce pennilesse. MLN 72 1957.

Staton, W. F., jr. The characters of style in Elizabethan prose. JEGP 57 1958.

Barber, C. L. In his Shakespeare's festive comedy, Princeton 1959. Ch 4. On Summer's last will and testament.

Bawcutt, N. W. Possible sources for the Unfortunate traveller. N & Q Feb 1960.

— Nashe and Bodin. N & Q March 1967.

Kinsman, R. S. Priscilla's grote: an emendation in Nashe's Unfortunate traveller. N & Q Feb 1960.

Drew, P. Nashe's authorship of An almond for a parrat. N & Q June 1960.

— Nashe, Sebastian Münster and An almond for a parrat. N & Q Oct 1960.

— Edward Daunce and the Unfortunate traveller. RES new ser 11 1960.

— Was Greene's young Juvenal Nashe or Lodge? Stud in Eng Lit 1500–1900 7 1967.

Perkins, D. Issues and motivations in the Nashe-Harvey quarrel. PQ 39 1960.

Harlow, C. G. Nashe, Robert Cotton the antiquary and the Terrors of the night. RES new ser 12 1961.

— Nashe and William Cotton MP. N & Q Nov 1961.

— Nashe's visit to the Isle of Wight and his publications of 1592–4. RES new ser 14 1963.

— Nashe and the council-table ass. N & Q Nov 1963.

— A source for Nashe's Terrors of the night and the authorship of 1 Henry VI. Stud in Eng Lit 1500–1900 5 1965.

— Shakespeare, Nashe and the ostrich crux in 1 Henry IV. Shakespeare Quart 17 1966.

— Did Gabriel Harvey read Nashe's Christ's tears? N & Q Dec 1969.

Petti, A. G. Political satire in Pierce Penilesse. Neophilologus 45 1961.

— Beasts and politics in Elizabethan literature. E & S new ser 16 1963.

Crundell, H. W. Nashe and Dr Faustus. N & Q Sept 1962.

Freeman, A. Two notes on A knack to know a knave. N & Q Sept 1962.

Hibbard, G. R. Nashe: a critical introduction. 1962.

Kettner, E. J. Love's labour's lost and the Harvey-Nashe-Greene quarrel. Emporia State Research Stud 10 1962.

Miller, W. E. The hospitall of incurable fooles. SB 16 1963.

Pratt, S. M. Antwerp and the Elizabethan mind. MLQ 24 1963.

Gibbons, Sr M. Polemic, the rhetorical tradition and the Unfortunate traveller. JEGP 63 1964.

Sanderson, J. L. An unnoted text of Nashe's The choice of valentines. Eng Lang Notes 1 1964.

Teets, B. E. Two faces of style in Renaissance prose fiction. In Sweet smoke of rhetoric, ed N. G. Lawrence and J. A. Reynolds, Coral Gables Miami 1964.

Kaula, D. The low style in Nashe's The unfortunate traveller. Stud in Eng Lit 1500–1900 6 1966.

Bateson, F. W. Editorial commentary. EC 17 1967. Replies by J. C. Maxwell and Bateson, ibid. On editorial principles of McKerrow's Nashe.

Lanham, R. A. Tom Nashe and Jack Wilton: personality as structure in the Unfortunate traveller. Stud in Short Fiction 4 1967.

Trimpi, W. The practice of historical interpretation and Nashe's Brightness falls from the ayre. JEGP 66 1967.

Demadre, A. Un témoin: Nashe. In Dramaturgie et société, ed J. Jacquot, Paris 1968.

Duncan-Jones, K. Nashe and Sidney: the tournament in the Unfortunate traveller. MLR 63 1968.

Scoufos, A. L. Nashe, Johnson and the Oldcastle problem. MP 65 1968.

Best, M. R. Nashe, Lyly and Summers last will and testament. PQ 48 1969.

Davis, W. R. In his Idea and act in Elizabethan fiction, Princeton 1969. Ch 6.

Lambrechts, G. Nashe et la Didon de Marlowe. Bulletin de la Faculté des Lettres de Strasbourg 47 1969.

McPherson, D. C. Aretino and the Harvey-Nashe quarrel. PMLA 84 1969.

Koppenfels, W. von. Nashe und Rabelais. Archiv 207 1970.

— Two notes on imprese in Elizabethan literature: Sidney's Arcadia and the tournament scene in the Unfortunate traveller. Renaissance Quart 24 1971.

Jones, D. An example of anti-Petrarchan satire in Nashe's Unfortunate traveller. Yearbook of Eng Stud 1 1971.

Little, J. Nashe's song Adieu, farewell earth's bliss. Explicator 30 1971.

G. R. H.

VIII. MINOR ELIZABETHAN DRAMA (1560–1603)

See also University Plays, cols 1761–80, below and Minor Jacobean and Caroline Drama, cols 1729–62, below. The latter includes several plays possibly written in the Elizabethan period though pbd later. The abbreviations (Hazlitt's Dodsley, TFT etc) refer to collections of plays listed col 1363, above.

SIR WILLIAM ALEXANDER, EARL OF STIRLING
1567?–1640

See col 1080, above.

SAMUEL BRANDON

The tragicomoedie of the vertuous Octavia. 1598; ed R. B. McKerrow 1909 (Malone Soc); rptd 1912 (TFT).

HENRY CHETTLE
1560?–1607?

§ 1

Kind harts dreame. [1593]; ed E. F. Rimbault 1842 (Percy Soc); ed C. M. Ingleby, Shakspere allusion-books pt 1, 1874 (New Shakspere Soc); ed G. B. Harrison 1923.
Piers Plainnes seaven yeres prentiship. 1595; ed H. Varnhagen, Erlangen 1900; ed J. Winny, Descent of Euphues, Cambridge 1957.
The downfall of Robert, Earle of Huntington, acted by the Earle of Notingham, Lord High Admirall of England his servants. 1601; ed J. P. Collier, Five old plays, 1828, 1833; Hazlitt's Dodsley 8; rptd 1913 (TFT); ed J. C. Meagher 1965 (Malone Soc). With Anthony Munday.
The death of Robert, Earle of Huntington, acted by the Earle of Notingham, Lord High Admirall of England his servants. 1601; ed J. P. Collier, Five old plays, 1828, 1833; Hazlitt's Dodsley 8; rptd 1913 (TFT); ed J. C. Meagher 1967 (Malone Soc). With Munday.
The pleasant comodie of Patient Grissil, as it hath beene sundrie times lately plaid by the Earle of Nottingham (Lord High Admirall) his servants. 1603; ed J. P. Collier 1841 (Shakespeare Soc); ed A. B. Grosart, Works of Dekker vol 5, 1886; ed G. Hübsch, Erlangen 1893; rptd 1911 (TFT); ed F. T. Bowers, Dramatic works of Dekker vol 1, 1953. With William Haughton and Thomas Dekker.
Englandes mourning garment. [1603]; rptd in Harleian miscellany vol 3, 1809; ed C. M. Ingleby, Shakspere allusion-books pt 1, 1874 (New Shakspere Soc).
The tragedy of Hoffman or a revenge for a father, as it hath bin divers times acted with great applause at the Phenix in Druery-lane. 1631; ed H. B. L[eonard] 1852; ed R. Ackermann 1894; rptd 1913 (TFT); ed H. Jenkins and C. J. Sisson 1951 (Malone Soc).
The blind-beggar of Bednal-Green. 1659. *See under* Day, *below.*
Most of Chettle's plays and collaborations, as recorded in Henslowe's diary, have been lost. The Trial of chivalry, The weakest goeth to the wall, *Hand A in* Sir Thomas More *and Yarrington's* Two lamentable tragedies *have been ascribed to him.*

§ 2

Delius, N. Chettles Hoffman und Shakespeares Hamlet. Sh Jb 9 1874.
Thorndike, A. H. The relations of Hamlet to contemporary revenge plays. PMLA 17 1902.

Sykes, H. D. The dramatic works of Chettle. N & Q 7 April–19 May 1923.
Jones, F. L. The trial of chivalry: a Chettle play. PMLA 41 1926.
Byrne, M. St C. Bibliographical clues in collaborate plays. Library 4th ser 13 1933.
Jenkins, H. The life and work of Chettle. 1934.
— Chettle and Dekker. TLS 25 Oct 1941.
— The 1631 quarto of Hoffman. Library 5th ser 6 1951.
Bowers, F. T. In his Elizabethan revenge tragedy, Princeton 1940.
Hummel, R. O. Chettle, England's mourning garment 1603. Library 5th ser 1 1946.
Schlochauer, E. J. A note on the variants in the dedication of Chettle's Tragedy of Hoffman. PBSA 42 1948.
Feldman, A. Shakespeare and the scholars. N & Q 24 Dec 1949, 23 Dec 1950. Replies by H. Parsons 24 June 1950, J. C. Maxwell 5 Aug 1950.
Thomas, S. Chettle and the first quarto of Romeo and Juliet. RES new ser 1 1950.
— The printing of Greene's Groatsworth of witte and Kind-harts dreame. SB 19 1966.
Wright, C. T. Mundy and Chettle in Grub Street. Boston Univ Stud in Eng 5 1961.
Davis, W. R. In his Idea and act in Elizabethan fiction, Princeton 1969. Ch 6.

SAMUEL DANIEL
1563–1619

For Daniel's tragedies (Cleopatra, Philotas), pastorals (The Queenes Arcadia, Hymens triumph) and masks (The vision of the 12 goddesses, Tethys festival), see col 1062, above. The Maydes metamorphosis, 1600 (anon), has also been ascribed to him without much plausibility.

JOHN DAY
c. 1574–c. 1640

Collections

Works. Ed A. H. Bullen 2 vols 1881, West Orange NJ 1963 (with additional introd by R. Jeffs).

§ 1

The Ile of Guls, as it hath been often playd in the blacke Fryars, by the Children of the Revels. 1606, 1606, 1633; ed G. B. Harrison 1936 (Malone Soc).
The travailes of the three English brothers, Sir Thomas, Sir Anthony, Mr Robert Shirley, as it is now play'd by her Majesties servants. 1607 (Dedication signed John Day, William Rowley and George Wilkins).
Humour out of breath: a comedie divers times latelie acted, by the Children of the Kings Revells. 1608; ed J. O. Halliwell (-Phillipps) 1860; ed A. Symons in Nero and other plays, 1888 (Mermaid ser).
Law-trickes or, who would have thought it, as it hath bene divers times acted by the Children of the Revels. 1608; ed J. Crow and W. W. Greg 1950 (Malone Soc).
The Parliament of Bees, with their proper characters. 1641; ed A. Symons, Nero and other plays, 1888 (Mermaid ser). BM Lansdowne ms 725 is a variant text.

The blind-beggar of Bednal-Green, with the merry humor of Tom Strowd the Norfolk yeoman, as it was divers times publickly acted by the Princes servants. 1659; ed W. Bang, Bang 1, 1902; rptd 1914 (TFT). With Chettle.

Peregrinatio scholastica. In Bullen, where the text is based on BM ms Sloane 3150. There is another ms in Huntington Lib with a different dedication. *See* M. E. Borish, MLN 55 1940.

The following anon plays have also been ascribed to Day: Edward IV, The fair maid of Bristol, The maid's metamorphosis, The noble soldier, Three Parnassus plays, Lust's dominion *and Yarington's* Two lamentable tragedies.

§2

Swinburne, A. C. In his Contemporaries of Shakespeare, 1919.

Sykes, H. D. The dramatic works of Chettle. N & Q 7 April–19 May 1923.

Golding, S. R. The Parliament of Bees. RES 3 1927.

Borish, M. E. Day's Humour out of breath. Harvard Stud 16 1934.

—— Day's Law tricks and George Wilkins. MP 34 1937.

—— A second version of Day's Peregrinatio scholastica. MLN 55 1940.

Peery, W. Notes on Bang's edition of the Blind beggar of Bednal-Green. E Studies 27 1946.

—— Corrections at press in the Blind beggar of Bednal-Green. PBSA 41 1947.

—— The noble soldier and the Parliament of bees. SP 48 1951.

Bromberg, E. The reputation of Philip Henslowe. Shakespeare Quart 1 1950. On Parliament of Bees.

Schoenbaum, S. Day and Elizabethan drama. Boston Public Lib Quart 5 1953.

Bradbrook, M. C. In her Growth and structure of Elizabethan comedy, Cambridge 1955. Ch 10.

Hoeniger, F. D. In his edn of Shakespeare's Pericles, 1963 (New Arden). Introd and Appendix B.

MICHAEL DRAYTON
1563–1631

The first part of the true and honorable historie of the life of Sir John Oldcastle, the good Lord Cobham, as it hath been lately acted by the Earle of Notingham, Lord High Admirall of England his servants. 1600. With Anthony Munday, Richard Hathway and Robert Wilson.

For general bibliography of Drayton's works, see col 1065, above. Edward IV, The London prodigal, The merry devil of Edmonton, Sir Thomas More, and Thomas Lord Cromwell *have also been partially or wholly ascribed to him.*

FULKE GREVILLE, 1st BARON BROOKE
1554–1628

See col 1057, above.

WILLIAM HAUGHTON
c. 1575–1605

§1

English-men for my money: or a pleasant comedy called A woman will have her will. 1616, 1626, 1631; rptd C. Baldwyn, Old English drama vol 1, 1825; Hazlitt's Dodsley 10; rptd 1911 (TFT); ed W. W. Greg 1912 (Malone Soc); ed A. C. Baugh 1917.

Grim the collier of Croyden: or the Devil and his dame, with the Devil and Saint Dunston. 1662 (in Gratiae theatrales, where it is ascribed to 'I.T.', who probably revised it for the press); rptd in Ancient British drama vol 3, 1810; Hazlitt's Dodsley 7; rptd 1912 (TFT).

The pleasant comodie of Patient Grissill. 1603. *See under Chettle, above.*

Haughton may also have collaborated in Lust's dominion *and Yarington's* Two lamentable tragedies.

§2

Farmer, J. S. In his Hand list, 1914. Ascribes Grim the collier of Croyden to John Tatham.

Lawrence, W. J. Englishmen for my money. RES 1 1925.

Sykes, H. D. The authorship of Grim the collier of Croydon. MLR 14 1919.

Thompson, D. W. Belphegor in Grim the collier and Riche's Farewell. MLN 50 1935.

Harbage, A. A choice ternary: belated issues of Elizabethan plays. N & Q 18 July 1942.

ANTHONY MUNDAY
1560–1633

Bibliographies

Turner, C. In her Munday: an Elizabethan man of letters, Berkeley 1928.

Tannenbaum, S. A. Munday, including the Play of Sir Thomas More: a concise bibliography. New York 1942.

Johnson, R. C. Munday 1941–66. 1968.

§1

The mirrour of mutabilitie: or principall part of the Mirrour for magistrates, selected out of the sacred scriptures by A.M. 1579.

The paine of pleasure. 1580.

A view of sundry examples, reporting many straunge murthers. [1580?].

Zelauto: the fountaine of fame. 1580; ed J. Stillinger, Carbondale 1963.

An advertisement and defence for trueth against her backbiters. 1581. Anon.

The true reporte of the prosperous successe which God gave unto our English soldiours in Ireland, gathered out of letters of most credit and circumstance and more at large than in the former printed copie. [1581] (signed A.M.).

A breefe discourse of the taking of Edmund Campion. 1581.

A courtly controversie betweene Loove and Learning betweene a ladie and a gentleman of Scienna. 1581.

A discoverie of Edmund Campion and his confederates, published by A.M. 1582.

A breefe aunswer made unto two seditious pamphlets. 1582.

A breefe and true reporte of the execution of certaine traytours at Tiborne, gathered by A.M. 1582.

The English Romayne life. 1582, 1590; rptd in Harleian miscellany vol 7, 1744, 1808; ed G. B. Harrison 1925.

A watch-woord to Englande, to beware of traytours. 1584 (2 edns, signed A.M.).

Fedele and Fortunio: the deceites in love, excellently discoursed in a very pleasaunt and fine conceited comoedie of two Italian gentlemen; translated out of Italian, and set downe according as it hath beene presented before the Queenes most excellent Majestie. 1585 (anon); ed P. Simpson 1909 (Malone Soc); ed F. Flügge, Archiv 123 1909. An adaptation of L. Pasqualigo, Il Fedele. Chapman and Gosson have also been suggested as translator.

A banquet of daintie conceits, written by A.M. 1588; rptd in Harleian miscellany vol 9, 1746, 1812.

Palmerin D'Oliva, written in the Spanish, Italian and French, and from them turned into English by A.M. 1588, 1597, 1597 (The second part of Palmerin D'Oliva), 1615 (pt 1), 1616 (2 pts), 1637 (2 pts).

The famous, pleasant and variable historie of Palladine of England, translated out of French by A.M. 1588.

The declaration of the Lord de la Noue, upon his taking armes, truely translated according to the French copie by A.M. 1589.

The honorable, pleasant and rare conceited historie of Palmendos, translated out of French by A.M. 1589, 1633, 1653.

[The first book of Amadis of Gaule]. [1590] (title-page and dedication missing in only extant copy), 1595 (The second booke of Amadis de Gaule, translated by L. Pyott [A. Munday?]), 1618 (The ancient and honourable history of Amadis de Gaule, pts 3 and 4, translated by A.M.), 1619 (pts 1–2 as The ancient, famous and honourable history of Amadis de Gaule, written in French by the Lord of Essars, Nicholas de Herberay).

The copple of the Anti-Spaniard, translated out of French. 1590.

The masque of the League and the Spanyard discovered, faythfully translated out of the French coppie. 1592 (signed A.M.), 1605 (as Falshood in friendship). Trn of A., L.T., Le masque de la Ligue et de l'Hespagnol découvert.

Archaioplutos: or the riches of elder ages, written in French by Guil. Thelin, Lord of Gutmont and Morillonuilliers. 1592.

Gerileon of England: the second part of his historie, written in French by Estienne de Maisonneufve and translated into English by A.M. 1592.

The defence of contraries: paradoxes against common opinion, translated out of French by A.M. 1593, 1602 (anon as Paradoxes against common opinion). From Charles Estienne.

The first booke of Primaleon of Greece. 1595 (first 4 sheets only by Munday), 1596 (The second booke of Primaleon of Greece, translated out of French by A.M.), 1619 (The famous historie of Primaleon of Greece [bks 1–3] translated out of French and Italian into English by A.M.).

[The first part of Palmerin of England]. [1596] (title-page missing in only extant copy), 1596 (The second part of the no less rare then excellent and stately historie of Palmerin of England, translated out of French by A.M.), 1602 (The third and last part of Palmerin of England, translated into English by A.M.), 1609 (pt 1), 1616 (pt 2), 1639 (2 pts).

A breefe treatise of the vertue of the crosse, translated out of French. 1599.

The first part of the true and honorable historie of the life of Sir John Oldcastle. 1600; ed C. F. T. Brooke, Shakespeare apocrypha, Oxford 1908; ed P. Simpson 1908 (Malone Soc); rptd 1911 (TFT). With Drayton, Hathway and Wilson.

The downfall of Robert, Earle of Huntington, acted by the Earle of Notingham, Lord High Admirall of England his servants. 1601; ed J. P. Collier, Five old plays, 1828, 1833; Hazlitt's Dodsley 8; rptd 1913 (TFT); ed J. C. Meagher 1965 (Malone Soc). With Chettle.

The death of Robert, Earle of Huntington, acted by the Earle of Notingham, Lord High Admirall of England his servants. 1601; ed J. P. Collier, Five old plays, 1828, 1833; Hazlitt's Dodsley 8; rptd 1913 (TFT); ed J. C. Meagher 1967 (Malone Soc). With Chettle.

The strangest adventure that ever happened: containing a discourse concerning the King of Portugall Don Sebastian, all first done in Spanish [by J. Teixera], then in French. 1601 (signed A.M.); rptd in Harleian miscellany vol 4, 1809.

The true knowledge of a mans owne selfe, written in French by Monsieur du Plessis, Lord of Plessie Marly [Philippe de Mornay], translated by A.M. 1602.

A true and admirable historic of a mayden of Consolens in Poictiers. 1603 (signed A.M.), 1604.

The dumbe divine speaker, written in Italian by Fra. Giacomo Affinati d'Acuto Romano and truelie translated by A.M. 1605.

The triumphes of re-united Britannia, performed in honor of Sir Leonard Holliday Lord Mayor. 1605; rptd J. Nichols, Progresses of James I vol 2, 1828.

The admirable deliverance of 266 Christians by J. Reynard [J. Fox], Englishman, from the Turkes. 1608. Anon.

The conversion of a most noble lady of Fraunce, truely translated out of French. 1608.

Camp-bell: or the Ironmongers faire feild. [1609]. Pageant at the installation of Sir T. Campbell as Lord Mayor.

Londons love to the royal Prince Henrie, meeting him on the river of Thames. 1610 (anon); rptd J. Nichols, Progresses of James I vol 2, 1828.

A briefe chronicle of the successe of times from the creation of the world to this instant. 1611.

Chruso-Thriambos: the triumphes of gold, at the inauguration of Sir James Pemberton in the dignity of Lord Maior, devised and written by A.M. 1611; ed J. H. P. Pafford 1962 (priv ptd).

Himatia-Poleos: the triumphes of olde draperie, at the entertainment of Sr. Thomas Hayes Lord Maior, devised and written by A.M. 1614.

Metropolis Coronata, the triumphes of ancient drapery in a second yeeres performance, in honour of Sir John Jolles Lord Maior, devised and written by A.M. 1615; rptd J. Nichols, Progresses of James I vol 3, 1828.

Chrysanaleia: the golden fishing, applauding the advancement of Mr John Leman to the dignitie of Lord Maior. 1616; rptd J. Nichols, Progresses of James I vol 3, 1828; ed J. G. Nichols 1884 (as The Fishmongers' pageant, 1616).

Sidero-Thriambos: or steele and iron triumphing, applauding the advancement of Sir Sebastian Harvey to the dignitie of Lord Maior, devised and written by A.M. 1618.

The triumphs of the golden fleece, performed at the enstaulment of Mr Martin Lumley in the Maioraltie. 1623.

John a Kent and John a Cumber: a comedy printed from the original manuscript. Ed J. P. Collier 1851 (Shakespeare Soc); rptd 1912 (TFT); ed M. St C. Byrne 1923 (Malone Soc). Autograph ms in Huntington Lib (HM 500).

Sir Thomas More: a play now first printed. Ed A. Dyce 1844 (Shakespeare Soc); ed A. F. Hopkinson 1902 (priv ptd); ed C. F. T. Brooke, Shakespeare apocrypha, Oxford 1908; 1910 (TFT); ed W. W. Greg 1911 (Malone Soc), 1961 (with minor corrections and suppl by H. Jenkins). BM Harley ms 7368. See also under Shakespeare, col 1551, below.

§2

Wilson, J. D. Munday, pamphleteer and pursuivant. MLR 4 1909.

Greg, W. W. Autograph plays by Munday. MLR 8 1913.

Thomas, H. The Palmerin romances. Trans Bibl Soc 13 1915.

—— The romance of Amadis of Gaul. Sociedade Portugesa de Estudas Historicos (Porto) 1916.

—— Spanish and Portuguese romances of chivalry. 1920.

Parrott, T. M. The authorship of Two Italian gentlemen. MP 13 1916.

Byrne, M. St C. The date of Munday's journey to Rome. Library 3rd ser 9 1919.

—— The shepherd Tony: a recapitulation. MLR 15 1920. On Munday as author of Two Italian gentlemen.

—— Munday and his books. Library 4th ser 1 1921.

—— Munday's spelling as a literary clue. Library 4th ser 4 1924.

—— Bibliographical clues in collaborate plays. Library 4th ser 13 1933.

Crane, R. S. In his Vogue of medieval chivalric romance during the English Renaissance, Menasha 1919.

Thompson, E. M. The autograph manuscripts of Mundy. Trans Bibl Soc 14 1919.

Hayes, G. Munday's romances of chivalry. Library 4th ser 6 1926; Postscript 7 1927.

Aronstein, P. Ein dramatischer Kunsthandwerker. Archiv 149–50 1926–7.

Lloyd, B. Mundy, dramatist. N & Q 5 Feb 1927.

Turner (Wright), C. Mundy: an Elizabethan man of letters. Berkeley 1928. With bibliography.

—— Young Mundy again. SP 56 1959.

—— Mundy, 'Edward' Spenser and E.K. PMLA 76 1961.

—— Mundy and the Bodenham miscellanies. PQ 40 1961.

—— Mundy and Chettle in Grub Street. Boston Univ Stud in Eng 5 1961.

—— Lazarus Pyott and other inventions of Mundy. PQ 42 1963.

Ashton, J. W. John a Kent and John a Cumber. PQ 8 1929; MLN 48 1933; PMLA 49 1934.

Crundell, H. W. Munday and King Leir. N & Q 5 May 1934.

Sellers, H. English verse of the sixteenth century. BM Quart 12 1938.

Thompson, B. H. Munday's journey to Rome 1578–9. Durham Univ Jnl 24 1941.

Patchell, M. The Palmerin romances in Elizabethan prose fiction. 1947.

Robertson, J. and D. J. Gordon (ed). In Malone Society Collections 3, 1954. On Munday's pageants.

Eccles, M. In Studies in the English Renaissance drama, ed J. W. Bennett et al, 1959.

Hotson, L. Mundy's birth-date. N & Q Jan 1959.

Hosley, R. Munday, John Heardson and the authorship of Fedele and Fortunio. MLR 55 1960.

—— The date of Fedele and Fortunio. MLR 57 1962.

—— The authorship of Fedele and Fortunio. HLQ 30 1967.

Shapiro, I. A. Shakespeare and Mundy. Shakespeare Survey 14 1961.

Huntley, F. L. Ben Jonson and Mundy: or the Case is altered altered again. PQ 41 1962.

Kenny, A. Munday in Rome. Recusant History 6 1962.

Jackson, M. P. Mundy and Sir Thomas More. N & Q March 1963.

Galigani, G. La English Romayne life di Mundy. Rivista di Letterature Moderne e Comparate 18 1965.

Meagher, J. C. Hack-writing and the Huntingdon plays. In Elizabethan theatre, ed J. R. Brown and B. Harris 1966.

Bergeron, D. M. Munday: pageant poet to the City of London. HLQ 30 1967.

—— Prince Henry and English civic pageantry. Tennessee Stud in Lit 13 1968.

—— Munday's son Richard. Amer N & Q 7 1969.

—— The emblematic nature of English civic pageantry. Renaissance Drama new ser 1 1968.

—— In his English civic pageantry 1558–1642, 1971. Ch 5.

Creigh, G. Zelauto and Italian comedy: a study in sources. MLQ 29 1968.

Forker, C. R. Two notes on John Webster and Munday: unpublished entries in the records of the Merchant Taylors. Eng Lang Notes 6 1968.

O'Connor, J. J. Amadis de Gaul and its influence on Elizabethan literature. New Brunswick NJ 1970.

WILLIAM PERCY
1575–1648

See col 1133, above.

HENRY PORTER
d. 1599

§1

The pleasant historie of the two angrie women of Abington, as it was lately playde by the Right Honorable the Earle of Nottingham, Lord High Admirall, his servants. 1599, 1599; Hazlitt's Dodsley 7; ed H. Ellis, Nero and other plays, 1888 (Mermaid ser); Gayley 1; rptd 1911 (TFT); ed W. W. Greg 1912 (Malone Soc).

§2

Shear, R. E. New facts about Porter. PMLA 42 1927. Reply by E. H. C. Oliphant 43 1928.

Hotson, L. The adventure of the single rapier. Atlantic Monthly July 1931; rptd in his Shakespeare's Sonnets dated, 1949. On Porter's death.

Nosworthy, J. M. Notes on Porter. MLR 35 1940.

—— Porter. English 6 1946.

—— The case is altered. JEGP 51 1952.

—— The two angry families of Verona. Shakespeare Quart 3 1952.

—— In his Shakespeare's occasional plays, 1965.

Baldwin, M. The two angry women and Wily beguiled. PQ 20 1941; rptd in Renaissance studies in honor of Hardin Craig, Stanford 1941.

Bowers, F. T. Notes on the Two angry women. N & Q 24 June 1948.

Morris, A. C. Proverbial lore in the Two angry women of Abington. In Folklore studies in honor of A. I. Hudson, North Carolina Folklore 13 1967.

SAMUEL ROWLEY
d. 1624

§1

When you see me you know me, or the famous chronicle historie of King Henry the Eight, with the birth and vertuous life of Edward Prince of Wales, as it was playd by the high and mightie Prince of Wales his servants. 1605, 1613, 1621, 1632; ed K. Elze, Dessau 1874; rptd 1912 (TFT); ed F. P. Wilson 1952 (Malone Soc).

H. D. Sykes, Sidelights on Elizabethan drama, *1924*, ascribes to Rowley the Famous victories of Henry V, *the prose scenes in the* Taming of a shrew, *the clowning passages in Greene's* Orlando, *and the prose scenes of* Wily beguiled. *Rowley was also responsible, with William Bird, for the addns to Marlowe's* Faustus.

§2

Bullen, A. H. In his edn of Works of John Day vol 1, 1881, 1963.

Golding, S. R. The Parliament of Bees. RES 3 1927.

Oliver, L. M. Rowley, Foxe and the Faustus additions. MLN 60 1945.

Houk, R. A. Dr Faustus and A Shrew. PMLA 62 1947.

Greg, W. W. In his edn of Dr Faustus 1604–16: parallel texts, Oxford 1950.

Somerset, J. A. B. New facts concerning Rowley. RES new ser 17 1966.

MARY HERBERT (née SIDNEY), COUNTESS OF PEMBROKE
1561–1621

§1

A discourse of life and death, written in French by Ph. Mornay; Antonius: a tragedie, written also in French by Ro. Garnier; both done in English by the Countess of Pembroke. 1592.

The tragedie of Anthonie. 1595; ed A. Luce, Weimar 1897; ed G. Bullough, Narrative and dramatic sources of Shakespeare vol 5, 1964.

A dialogue betweene two shepheards, Thenot and Piers, in praise of Astraea, made by the excellent lady the Lady Mary Countesse of Pembrook. In Davison's Poetical rapsody, 1602.

§2

Young, F. B. Mary Sidney, Countess of Pembroke. 1912.

Witherspoon, A. M. In his Influence of Robert Garnier on Elizabethan drama, 1924.

ROBERT YARINGTON
fl. 1594-1601

§1

Two lamentable tragedies: the one of the murther of Maister Beech, a chaundler in Thames-streete, and his boye, done by Thomas Merry; the other of a young childe murthered in a wood by two ruffins, with the consent of his unckle, by Rob Yarington. 1601; ed A. H. Bullen, Old English plays vol 4, 1885; rptd 1913 (TFT).

§2

Law, R. A. Yarington's Two lamentable tragedies. MLR 5 1910.

Wagner, B. M. Yarington. MLN 45 1930.

ANONYMOUS PLAYS 1580-1603
Collections

The school of Shakespeare. Ed R. Simpson 2 vols 1878. Includes Captain Thomas Stukeley; Jack Drum's entertainment; Warning for fair women; Fair Em; with A larum for London, separately ptd 1872.

Three Elizabethan plays. Ed J. Winny, Cambridge 1959. Includes Edward III; Mucedorus.

Six early plays related to the Shakespeare canon. Ed E. B. Everitt and R. L. Armstrong, Copenhagen 1965. Includes King Leir; The weakest goeth to the wall; Edmund Ironside; The troublesome reign of King John; Edward III; Woodstock.

Individual Plays

Fedele and Fortunio. See under Munday, above.

The troublesome raigne of King John of England, as it was sundry times publikely acted by the Queenes Majesties players in the honourable Citie of London. 1591.

The second part of the troublesome raigne of King John. 1591.

The first and second part of the troublesome raigne of John, King of England, written by W. Sh. 1611, 1622; rptd J. Nichols, Six old plays vol 2, 1779; ed W. C. Hazlitt, Shakespeare's library vol 5, 1875; ed F. J. Furnivall 1888 (facs); ed C. Praetorius 1888 (facs); rptd 1911 (TFT); ed F. J. Furnivall and J. Munro 1913; ed H. H. Furness, New Variorum edn of Shakespeare's King John, 1919; ed G. Bullough, Narrative and dramatic sources of Shakespeare vol 4, 1962.

Smith, G. C. M. Shakespeare's King John and the Troublesome reign. In English miscellany presented to F. J. Furnivall, Oxford 1901.

Sykes, H. D. In his Sidelights on Shakespeare, 1911. Assigns play to Peele.

Elson, J. Studies in the King John plays. In J. Q. Adams memorial studies, Washington 1948.

Simmons, J. L. Shakespeare's King John and its source: coherence, pattern and vision. Tulane Stud in Eng 17 1969.

See also under Shakespeare, col 1501, below.

The tragedye of Solyman and Perseda. [1592?], 1599, [1815] (facs, with date 1599 and, in some copies, 'J. Smeeton, printer, St Martin's Lane' on verso of titlepage); rptd T. Hawkins, Origin of the English drama vol 2, 1773; Hazlitt's Dodsley 5; ed F. S. Boas, Works of Kyd, Oxford 1901, 1955; rptd 1912 (TFT) (from 1815 reprint). See under Kyd, col 1427, above.

The lamentable and true tragedie of M. Arden of Feversham in Kent. 1592, 1599, 1633. See under Shakespeare, col 1555, below.

The life and death of Jacke Straw, a notable rebell in England, who was kild in Smithfield by the Lord Maior of London. 1593 (colophon 1594), 1604; Hazlitt's Dodsley 5; ed H. Schütt, Heidelberg 1901; rptd 1911 (TFT); ed K. Muir and F. P. Wilson 1957 (Malone Soc).

Adkins, M. G. M. A theory about Jack Straw. SE 28 1949. Relates play to social situation in England 1585-93.

Bergeron, D. M. Jack Straw in drama and pageant. Guildhall Miscellany 2 1968.

A pleasant commodie of Faire Em, the Millers daughter of Manchester, as it was sundrie times publiquely acted by the Lord Strange his servants. [1593?], 1631. See under Shakespeare, col 1555, below.

The first part of the contention betwixt the two famous houses of Yorke and Lancaster. 1594. See under Shakespeare, col 1484, below.

A most pleasant and merie new comedie, intituled A knacke to knowe a knave, newlie set forth as it hath sundrie tymes bene played by Ed. Allen and his companie; with Kemps applauded merrimentes of the men of Goteham in receiving the King into Goteham. 1594; ed J. P. Collier, Five old plays, 1851; Hazlitt's Dodsley 6; rptd 1911 (TFT); ed G. R. Proudfoot 1964 (Malone Soc).

Adkins, M. G. M. The genesis of dramatic satire against the Puritans. RES 22 1946.

Bennett, P. E. The Oswald fragment and A knacke to knowe a knave. N & Q 7 July 1951.

— An apparent allusion to Titus Andronicus. N & Q Oct 1955.

— The word 'Goths' in A knacke to knowe a knave. N & Q Nov 1955.

Freeman, A. Two notes on A knack to know a knave. N & Q Sept 1962.

The first part of the tragicall raigne of Selimus, as it was playd by the Queenes Majesties players. 1594, 1638. See under Greene, col 1439, above.

A pleasant conceited historie, called the Taming of a shrew, as it was sundry times acted by the Right Honorable the Earle of Pembrook his servants. 1594, 1596, 1607. See under Shakespeare, col 1491, below.

The true tragedie of Richard the Third, as it was played by the Queenes Majesties players. 1594; ed B. Field 1844 (Shakespeare Soc); ed W. C. Hazlitt, Shakespeare's library vol 6, 1875; ed H. H. Furness, New variorum edn of Shakespeare's Richard III, 1909; ed W. W. Greg 1929 (Malone Soc); ed G. Bullough, Narrative and dramatic sources of Shakespeare vol 3, 1960 (selection).

Churchill, G. B. In his Richard III up to Shakespeare. Berlin 1900.

Mott, L. F. Foreign politics in an old play. MP 19 1921.

Wilson, J. D. Shakespeare's Richard III and the True tragedy of Richard III. Shakespeare Quart 3 1952.

Ribner, I. In his English history play in the age of Shakespeare, 1957, 1965. Ch 3.

Bullough, G. In his Narrative and dramatic sources of Shakespeare vol 3, 1960.

The warres of Cyrus, King of Persia, played by the children of her Majesties Chappell. 1594; ed W. Keller, Sh Jb 37

1901; rptd 1911 (TFT); ed J. P. Brawner, Urbana 1942. Based on a play by Richard Farrant (fl. 1564-80)?

Lawrence, W. J. The earliest private theatre play. TLS 11 Aug 1921.

Ribner, I. Tamburlaine and the Wars of Cyrus. JEGP 53 1954.

Hunter, G. K. The Wars of Cyrus and Tamburlaine. N & Q Oct 1961.

The lamentable tragedie of Locrine, newly set forth, overseene and corrected, by W.S. 1595. *See under Shakespeare, col 1555, below.*

The true tragedie of Richard Duke of Yorke and the death of good King Henrie the Sixt, with the whole contention betweene the two houses Lancaster and Yorke, as it was sundrie times acted by the Earle of Pembroke his servants. 1595. *See under Shakespeare, col 1484, below.*

The raigne of King Edward the Third, as it hath bin sundrie times plaied about the Citie of London. 1596, 1599. *See under Shakespeare, col 1552, below.*

A pleasant conceited comedie, called A knacke to know an honest man, as it hath beene sundrie times plaied about the Citie of London. 1596; ed H. de Vocht 1910 (Malone Soc); rptd 1912 (TFT).

The famous victories of Henry the Fifth: containing the honourable Battell of Agincourt, as it was plaide by the Queenes Majesties players. 1598, 1617; rptd J. Nichols, Six old plays vol 2, 1779; ed W. C. Hazlitt, Shakespeare's library vol 5, 1875; ed P. A. Daniel 1887 (facs); rptd 1912 (TFT); ed G. Bullough, Narrative and dramatic sources of Shakespeare vol 4, 1962 (selection).

Ward, B. M. The famous victories of Henry V: its place in Elizabethan dramatic literature. RES 4 1928.

See also under Shakespeare, col 1509, below.

A most pleasant comedie of Mucedorus, newly set foorth, as it hath bin sundrie times plaide in the honorable Cittie of London. 1598, 1606 etc. *See under Shakespeare, col 1556, below.*

A pleasant conceyted comedie of George a Greene, the Pinner of Wakefield, as it was sundry times acted by the servants of the Right Honorable the Earle of Sussex. 1599. *See under Greene, col 1439, above.*

The first and second parts of King Edward the Fourth, as it hath divers times beene publikely played by the Earle of Derby his servants. 1599, 1600, 1605, 1613, 1619, 1626; ed B. Field 1842 (Shakespeare Soc); ed R. H. Shepherd, Dramatic works of Thomas Heywood. *See under Heywood, col 1682, below.*

A warning for faire women: containing the most tragicall and lamentable murther of Master George Sanders of London, merchant, as it hath beene lately diverse times acted by the Lord Chamberlaine his servants. 1599; rptd R. Simpson, School of Shakespeare vol 2, 1878; rptd 1912 (TFT).

Adams, J. Q. The authorship of a Warning for fair women. PMLA 28 1913.

Adams, H. H. In his English domestic or homiletic tragedy 1575-1642, New York 1943.

Marshburn, J. H. A cruell murder donne in Kent and its literary manifestations. SP 46 1949.

A pleasant commodie called Look about you, as it was lately played by the Lord High Admirall his servantes. 1600; Hazlitt's Dodsley 7; rptd 1912 (TFT); ed W. W. Greg 1913 (Malone Soc). May be the same play as Dekker's lost Bear a brain.

Jones, F. L. Look about you and the Disguises. PMLA 44 1929.

Nelson, M. A. Look about you and the Robin Hood tradition. N & Q April 1962.

Lancashire, A. B. Look about you as a history play. Stud in Eng Lit 1500-1900 9 1969.

The maydes metamorphosis, as it hath beene sundrie times acted by the children of Powles. 1600; ed A. H. Bullen, Old English plays vol 1, 1882; ed R. W. Bond, Works of Lyly vol 3, Oxford 1902; rptd 1912 (TFT).

Cutts, J. P. A note on the Maydes metamorphosis. N & Q July 1957.

See also under Lyly, col 1425, above.

The weakest goeth to the wall, as it hath bene sundry times plaide by the Earle of Oxenforde, Lord Great Chamberlaine of England his servants. 1600, 1618; rptd 1911 (TFT); ed W. W. Greg 1912 (Malone Soc).

Cranfill, T. M. Barnabe Rich's Sappho and the Weakest goeth to the wall. SE 25 1946.

The wisdome of Doctor Dodypoll, as it hath bene sundrie times acted by the children of Powles. 1600; ed A. H. Bullen, Old English plays vol 3, 1884; rptd 1912 (TFT); ed M. N. Matson 1964 (Malone Soc).

Koeppel, E. Shakespeares Julius Caesar und die Entstehungszeit des anonymen Dramas the Wisdom of Doctor Dodypoll. Sh Jb 43 1907.

A larum for London: or the siedge of Antwerpe, as it hath been playde by the Lord Chamberlaine his servants. 1602; ed R. Simpson 1872; rptd 1912 (TFT); ed W. W. Greg 1913 (Malone Soc).

Feldman, A. B. The rape of Antwerp in a Tudor play. N & Q June 1958.

A pleasant conceited comedie wherein is shewed how a man may chuse a good wife from a bad. 1602. *See under Thomas Heywood, col 1682, below.*

Il pastor fido: or the faithfull shepheard, translated out of Italian into English. 1602, 1633. By John Dymocke?

The true chronicle historie of the whole life and death of Thomas Lord Cromwell, written by W.S. 1602. *See under Shakespeare, col 1556, below.*

The first part of Jeronimo, with the warres of Portugall and the life and death of Don Andraea. 1605; Dodsley's Old plays vol 3, 1780, 1825; Ancient British drama vol 1; Hazlitt's Dodsley 4; ed F. S. Boas, Works of Kyd, Oxford 1901, 1955; ed A. S. Cairncross 1967 (with the Spanish tragedy) (RRDS). *See under Kyd, col 1428, above.*

The famous historye of the life and death of Captaine Thomas Stukeley, as it hath beene acted. 1605; rptd R. Simpson, School of Shakespeare vol 1, 1878; rptd 1911 (TFT).

Schelling, F. E. Stucley, gentleman adventurer. In his Queen's progress, [1904].

Brooke, Z. N. The expedition of Thomas Stukeley in 1578. EHR 28 1913.

Adams, J. Q. Captain Thomas Stukeley. JEGP 15 1916.

Yoklavich, J. M. Captain Thomas Stukeley. N & Q March 1963. On source.

Levinson, J. C. The sources of Captain Thomas Stukeley. Eng Lang Notes 9 1971.

The true chronicle history of King Leir and his three daughters, Gonorill, Ragan and Cordella, as it hath beene divers and sundry times lately acted. 1605; rptd J. Nichols, Six old plays vol 2, 1779; ed W. C. Hazlitt, Shakespeare's library vol 6, 1875; ed W. W. Greg 1907 (Malone Soc); ed S. Lee 1909; ed R. Fischer, Quellen zu König Lear, Bonn 1914. *See also under Shakespeare, col 1534, below.*

Sir Thomas More (BM ms Harley 7368). *See under Shakespeare, col 1551, below.*

Edmund Ironside, the English King: a trew chronicle history called War hath made all friends (BM ms Egerton 1994, fols 97-118). Ed E. Boswell 1927 (Malone Soc).

Boas, F. S. In his Shakespeare and the universities, 1923.

Jackson, M. P. Shakespeare and Edmund Ironside. N & Q Sept 1963.

The tragedy of Thomas of Woodstock (BM ms Egerton 1994, fols 161-185b). Ed J. O. Halliwell (-Phillipps) 1870 (as A tragedy of King Richard the Second); ed W. Keller, Sh Jb 35 1899 (as Richard II part 1); ed W. P. Frijlinck 1929 (Malone Soc) (as The first part of the reign of King Richard the Second, or Thomas of Woodstock); ed A. P. Rossiter 1946 (as Woodstock);

ed W. A. Armstrong, Elizabethan history plays, Oxford 1965 (WC) (as Woodstock).

Boas, F. S. In his Shakespeare and the universities, 1923.

Lloyd, B. Jonson and Thomas of Woodstock. TLS 17 July 1924.

Rossiter, A. P. Prolegomenon to the anonymous Woodstock. Durham Univ Jnl 37 1944.

Brereton, J. le G. In his Writings on Elizabethan drama, Melbourne 1948.

Elson, J. J. The non-Shakespearian Richard II and Shakespeare's Henry IV part I. SP 32 1935.

Ribner, I. In his English history play in the age of Shakespeare, Princeton 1957, London 1965 (rev).

John of Bordeaux: or the second part of Friar Bacon. *See under Greene, col 1439, above.*

G. R. H.

IX. WILLIAM SHAKESPEARE
1564–1616

(1) BIBLIOGRAPHIES;

(2) CONCORDANCES, GLOSSARIES, DICTIONARIES ETC;

(3) SHAKESPEARE SOCIETIES AND PERIODICALS;

(4) COLLECTIONS;

(5) PLAYS;

(6) POEMS;

(7) LIFE AND PERSONALITY OF SHAKESPEARE: *Shakespeare's life; Shakespeare's personality and interests; Controversies about authorship;*

(8) CRITICISM: *Technical criticism; Aesthetic criticism; Shakespeare's influence.*

This section is designed to include only items of substantial scholarly interest and the most important trns in major languages. For more detailed lists see Bibliographies, below, notably the annual bibliography in Sh Quart.

Sh   *Shakespeare*

Sh Jb   *Shakespeare-Jahrbuch. This abbreviation includes Deutsche Shakespeare-Gesellschaft West Jahrbuch (1965–), annuals of east and west being distinguished since that year by 'Weimar' or 'Heidelberg'.*

(1) BIBLIOGRAPHIES

General Bibliographies

Current literature is listed in Sh Quart (jnl of Sh Assoc of America), Annual Bibliography of Eng Lang & Lit (Modern Humanities Research Assoc), Year's Work in Eng Stud (Eng Assoc), Sh Survey, Sh Jb, PMLA and, for periodicals, Abstracts of Eng Stud.

[Wilson, J.] Catalogue of all the books, pamphlets etc relating to Shakespeare. 1827.

Halliwell (-Phillipps), J. O. Shakespeariana: a catalogue of the early edns of Shakespeare's plays and of the commentaries and other publications illustrative of his works. 1841.

Trimm, F. Shakespeariana from 1564 to 1864: an account of the Shakespearian literature of England, Germany, France and other European countries with bibliographical introductions. 1865, 1872 (rev).

Jahrbuch der Deutschen Shakespeare-Gesellschaft. Berlin (later Weimar) 1865–.

Hubbard, J. M. Catalogue of the works of Shakespeare and Shakespeariana in the Barton collection of the Boston Public Library. 2 vols Boston 1878–80.

British Museum. Catalogue of printed books: Shakespeare. 1897–.

Lee, S. A catalogue of Shakespeariana. 1899.

— A Shakespeare reference library. 1910 (Eng Assoc); rev E. K. Chambers 1925, S. W. Wells 1969.

Greg, W. W. In his A list of English plays written before 1643 and printed before 1700, 1900 (Bibl Soc).

— In his Catalogue of the books presented by Edward Capell to the library of Trinity College in Cambridge, Cambridge 1903.

— A descriptive catalogue of the early editions of the works of Shakespeare preserved in the library of Eton College. Oxford [1909].

Shaw, A. C. Birmingham free libraries: index to the Shakespeare memorial library. 3 pts Birmingham 1900–3.

Scherzer, J. American editions of Shakespeare 1753–1866. PMLA 22 1907.

Pollard, A. W. Shakespeare folios and quartos 1594–1685. 1909.

Katalog der Bibliothek der deutschen Shakespeare-Gesellschaft. Weimar 1909.

Aldis, H. G., F. W. Moorman, E. Walder and J. G. Robertson. Shakespeare. CHEL vol 5 1910.

Jaggard, W. Shakespeare bibliography: a dictionary of every known issue of the writings of our national poet and of recorded opinion thereon in the English language. Stratford 1911, New York 1959.

Bartlett, H. C. Shakespeare: original and early editions of his quartos and folios, his source books and those containing contemporary notices. New Haven 1922.

Herford, C. H. A sketch of recent Shakespearean investigation 1893–1923. 1923.

Gollancz, I. In commemoration of the first folio tercentenary: a resetting of the preliminary matter of the first folio, with a catalogue of Shakespeareana exhibited in the hall of the Company of Stationers. 1923.

Chambers, E. K. Shakespeare: a study of facts and problems. 2 vols Oxford 1930. Each ch preceded by critical bibliographical note.

Ebisch, W. and L. L. Schücking. A Shakespeare bibliography. Oxford 1931; Supplement 1930–5, Oxford 1937.

A companion to Shakespeare studies. Ed H. Granville-Barker and G. B. Harrison, Cambridge 1934.

Ford, H. L. Shakespeare 1700–40: a collation of the editions and separate plays. Lavorrick 1935 (priv ptd).

Wilson, F. P. Shakespeare and the new bibliography. In The Bibliographical Society 1892–1942: studies in retrospect, ed F. C. Francis 1945; ed H. Gardner, Oxford 1970.

Lüdeke, H. Shakespeare-Bibliographie für die Kriegsjahre 1939–46: pt I. Archiv 187 1950.

British Museum. Shakespeare: an excerpt from the general catalogue of printed books. 1964.

A new companion to Shakespeare studies. Ed K. Muir and S. Schoenbaum, Cambridge 1971.

(2) CONCORDANCES, GLOSSARIES, DICTIONARIES ETC

Nares, R. A glossary: or collection of words, phrases, names and allusions to customs, proverbs etc [in] Shakespeare and his contemporaries. 1822, 2 vols 1859 (rev J. O. Halliwell (-Phillipps) and T. Wright). *See* TLS 1 June 1922.

Clarke, M. C. The complete concordance to Shakspere. 1845, 1870 (rev).

Schmidt, A. Shakespeare-Lexicon: vollständiger englischer Sprachschatz mit allen Wörtern, Wendungen und Satzbildungen in den Werken des Dichters. 2 vols Berlin 1874-5, 1902 (rev G. Sarrazin).

Bellamy, G. S. The new Shaksperian dictionary of quotations. 1875.

Bartlett, J. A new and complete concordance to Shakespeare. 1894.

Dyce, A. A glossary to the works of Shakespeare. Rev H. Littledale 1902.

Foster, J. A Shakespeare word-book. [1908].

Edwardes, M. A pocket lexicon and concordance to Shakespeare. 1909.

Cunliffe, R. J. A new Shakespearian dictionary. 1910.

Onions, C. T. A Shakespeare glossary. Oxford 1911, 1953 (rev).

Skeat, W. W. A glossary of Tudor and Stuart words, especially from the dramatists. Rev A. L. Mayhew, Oxford 1914.

Kellner, L. Shakespeare-Wörterbuch. Leipzig 1922.

Stokes, F. G. A dictionary of the characters and proper names in Shakespeare. 1924.

Schultz, J. H. A glossary of Shakespeare's hawking language. SE 1938.

Partridge, E. Shakespeare's bawdy: a literary and psychological essay and a comprehensive glossary. 1947, 1969 (rev).

Tilley, M. P. A dictionary of the proverbs in England in the sixteenth and seventeenth centuries. Ann Arbor 1950. With a Shakespeare index.

Thomson, W. H. Shakespeare's characters: a historical dictionary. Altrincham 1951.

Halliday, F. E. A Shakespeare companion 1550-1950. 1952, 1964 (rev as A Shakespeare companion 1564-1964), 1969 (Pelican).

Browning, D. C. A dictionary of Shakespeare quotations. 1953, 1961 (rev).

Stevenson, B. The standard book of Shakespeare quotations. 1953.

Kökeritz, H. Shakespeare's names: a pronouncing dictionary. New Haven 1959.

Falconer, A. F. A glossary of Shakespeare's sea and naval terms, including gunnery. 1965.

Campbell, O. J. and E. G. Quinn. The reader's encyclopedia of Shakespeare. New York 1966.

Spevack, M. A complete and systematic concordance to the works of Shakespeare. 6 vols Hildesheim 1968-70.

Howard-Hill, T. H. The Oxford old-spelling Shakespeare concordances. SB 22 1969.

— Oxford Shakespeare concordances. Oxford 1969-.

(3) SHAKESPEARE SOCIETIES AND PERIODICALS

See F. S. Boas, Shakespeare Societies, past and present, *Sh Rev 1 1928*.

Shakespeare Society. 1841-52. 48 pbns 1841-53. For titles *see* Jaggard above, pp. 606-7.

Deutsche Shakespeare-Gesellschaft 1864-. Sh Jb, Berlin (later Weimar) 1865-. From 1964 also Deutsche Shakespeare-Gesellschaft West, Sh Jb (Heidelberg) 1965-.

New Shakspere Society. 1874-86. 27 pbns. For titles and contents *see* Jaggard above, pp. 228-31.

New York Shakespeare Society. 1885-1903. 13 pbns New York 1885-1903. For titles *see* Jaggard above, p. 232.

Shakespeare Association. 1917-[55]. 18 pamphlets.

Oxford 1917-35. For titles *see* Ebisch and Schücking above, p. 171. Also texts, facs and studies.

Shakespeare Association of America Inc. 1926-. Sh Assoc Bull 1926-49.

Shakespeare review. Stratford May-Oct 1928.

Shakespeare survey. Cambridge 1948-. Includes annual survey of scholarship.

Shakespeare quarterly. New York 1950-. Replaces Sh Assoc Bull as jnl of Sh Assoc of America, above. Includes annual bibliography.

Shakespeare newsletter. New York 1950-.

Shakespeare studies. Ed J. L. Barroll, Cincinnati 1965-.

Shakespearean research opportunities. Ed W. R. Elton, Riverside Cal 1969-.

(4) COLLECTIONS

(1) The Four Folios

Bartlett pp. 50-4; Ebisch and Schücking pp. 50-2; Chambers vol 1, pp. 126-7.

(a) The First Folio

Mr William Shakespeares comedies, histories and tragedies, published according to the true originall copies [with Droeshout portrait]; London, printed by Isaac Jaggard and Ed. Blount. 1623. Colophon: Printed at the charges of W. Jaggard, Ed. Blount, J. Smethweeke and W. Aspley, 1623. The arrangement of the preliminary leaves varies in different copies. There are also textual variations, due to corrections in the press. Ed John Heming and Henry Condell, and contains: Tempest; Two gentlemen of Verona; Merry wives of Windsor; Measure for measure; Comedy of errours; Much adoo about nothing; Loves labour lost; Midsommer nights dreame; Merchant of Venice; As you like it; Taming of

the shrew; Alls well that ends well; Twelfe-night; Winters tale; King John; Richard the Second; First part of Henry the Fourth; Second part of Henry the Fourth; Henry the Fift; First part of Henry the Sixt; Second part of Henry the Sixt; Third part of Henry the Sixt; Richard the Third; King Henry the Eight; [Troylus and Cressida]; Coriolanus; Titus Andronicus; Romeo and Juliet; Timon of Athens; Julius Caesar; Macbeth; Hamlet; King Lear; Othello, the Moore of Venice; Anthony and Cleopater; Cymbeline.

Reprints

E. and J. Wright 1807-8; L. Booth 3 vols 1864; H. Staunton 1866 (photolithographic facs); J. O. Halliwell (-Phillipps) 1876 (reduced facs); S. Lee, Oxford 1902 (facs); 1910 (Methuen); H. Kökeritz and C. T. Prouty, New Haven 1954 (reduced facs); C. Hinman, New York 1968 (facs).

Studies

Lee, S. Census of extant copies of the First Folio. Oxford 1902; also in his facs edn, Oxford 1902.

— Notes and additions to the census. Oxford 1906; also in Library 1st ser 7 1906.

Greg, W. W. The bibliographical history of the First Folio. Library 1st ser 4 1903.

Cole, G. W. The First Folio: a further word regarding the correct arrangement of its preliminary leaves. New York 1909.

Keller, W. Shakespeares literarisches Testament. E Studien 50 1916.

— Die Anordnung von Shakespeares Dramen in der ersten Folio-Ausgabe. Sh Jb 56 1920.

— Shakespeare, Ben Jonson und die Folio. Sh Jb 60 1924.

Hecht, H. Shakespeares Testament und die Vorrede der Schauspieler zur ersten Folio. Germanisch-romanische Monatsschrift 10 1922.

Rhodes, R. C. Shakespeare's First Folio. Oxford 1923.

Pollard, A. W. The foundations of Shakespeare's text. Proc Br Acad 10 1923.

Studies in the First Folio. Ed I. Gollancz 1924. Includes J. D. Wilson, The task of Heminge and Condell; S. Lee, A survey of First Folios; W. W. Greg, The First Folio and its publishers.

Förster, M. Zum Jubiläum der Shakespeare-Folio. Zeitschrift für Bücherfreunde 16 1924.

Stoll, E. E. On the anniversary of the Folio. In Shakespeare studies, New York 1927.

Casson, F. F. Notes on a Shakespeare First Folio in Padua. MLN 51 1936.

Rendall, G. H. Ben Jonson and the First Folio edition of Shakespeare's plays. Colchester 1939.

Smith, R. M. Why a First Folio remained in England. RES 15 1939.

Dawson, G. E. A bibliographical problem in the First Folio of Shakespeare. Library 4th ser 23 1942.

Hinman, C. A proof sheet in the First Folio of Shakespeare. Ibid.

— Mark III: new light on the proof-reading for the First Folio of Shakespeare. SB 3 1951.

— Variant readings in the First Folio of Shakespeare. Sh Quart 4 1953.

— Cast-off copy for the First Folio of Shakespeare. Sh Quart 6 1955.

— The prentice hand in the tragedies of the Shakespeare First Folio: compositor E. SB 9 1957.

— Six variant readings in the First Folio of Shakespeare. Lawrence Kansas 1961.

— The printing and proof-reading of the First Folio of Shakespeare. 2 vols Oxford 1963.

Greg, W. W. The Shakespeare First Folio: its bibliographical and textual history. Oxford 1955.

Shroeder, J. W. The great folio of 1623: Shakespeare's plays in the printing house. Hamden Conn 1956.

Bowers, F. T. What Shakespeare wrote. Sh Jb 98 1962.

(b) The Second, Third and Fourth Folios

Mr William Shakespeares comedies, histories and tragedies, published according to the true originall coppies: the second impression [with Droeshout portrait], London, printed by Tho. Cotes, for Robert Allot, and are to be sold at his shop at the signe of the Blacke Beare in Pauls Church-yard. 1632. Some copies have one 'p' in 'copies'; others have John Smethwick, Richard Hawkins, William Aspley or Richard Meighen for Allot.

Reprint

1909 (Methuen facs).

Studies

Smith, C. A. The chief differences between the First and Second Folios. E Studien 30 1902.

Smith R. M. The variant issues of Shakespeare's Second Folio and Milton's first published English poem. Bethlehem Pa 1928.

Mr William Shakespeares comedies, histories and tragedies, published according to the true original copies: the third impression; [with Droeshout portrait], London, printed for Philip Chetwinde. 1663. First issue of Third Folio. Some copies are without portrait.

Mr William Shakespear's comedies, histories and tragedies, published according to the true original copies: the third impression; and unto this impression is added seven plays, never before printed in folio, viz Pericles Prince of Tyre; The London prodigall; The history of Thomas Ld Cromwell; Sir John Oldcastle Lord Cobham; The Puritan widow; A Yorkshire tragedy; The tragedy of Locrine; London, printed for P.C. 1664. Second issue of Third Folio with the 7 additional plays.

Reprints

1905 (Methuen facs).

Studies

McManaway, J. G. A miscalculation in the printing of the Third Folio. Library 5th ser 9 1954.

Mr William Shakespear's comedies, histories and tragedies, published according to the true original copies; unto which is added seven plays, never before printed in folio, viz Pericles Prince of Tyre; The London prodigal; The history of Thomas Lord Cromwel; Sir John Oldcastle Lord Cobham; The Puritan widow; A Yorkshire tragedy; The tragedy of Locrine: the fourth edition. London, printed for H. Herringman, E. Brewster and R. Bentley, at the Anchor in the New Exchange, the Crane in St Paul's Church-Yard and in Russel-Street Covent-Garden. 1685. Also found with 2 other imprints.

Reprints

1904 (Methuen facs).

Studies

Bowers, F. T. Robert Roberts: a printer of Shakespeare's Fourth Folio. Sh Quart 2 1951.

Dawson, G. E. Some bibliographical irregularities in the Shakespeare Fourth Folio. SB 4 1952.

(2) Principal Later Collections

See W. S. Brassington, Handlist of collective editions of Shakespeare's works published before 1800, Stratford 1898; H. B. Wheatley, Shakespeare's editors from 1623 to the 20th century, Trans Bibl Soc 14–15 1915–17; A. Nicoll, The editors of Shakespeare from First Folio to Malone, in Studies in the First Folio, 1924 (Sh Assoc); H. L. Ford, Shakespeare 1700–40: a collation of the editions and separate plays, Luborick 1935 (priv ptd). Also Jaggard, pp. 498–558; Ebisch and Schücking, pp. 53–8; Chambers vol I, ch ix.

Rowe, N. The works of Shakespeare, revis'd and corrected, with an account of the life and writings of the author. 6 vols 1709. A 7th vol, including the poems and critical essays by Charles Gildon, followed in 1710, probably without authority. It was, however, rptd in the 3rd issue of Rowe's 2nd edn, 9 vols 1714. See A. Jackson, Rowe's edition of Shakespeare, Library 2nd ser 10 1930.

Pope, A. The works of Shakespeare, collated and corrected. 6 vols 1723–5 (separate title-leaves to vols dated 1723). A supplementary 7th vol of the poems, ed George Sewell, followed in 1725. Rptd 8 vols Dublin 1725–6, 10 vols 1728, 10 vols 1728 (corrected and adding Pericles and the spurious plays), 9 vols 1731 (plays only), 8 vols 1734–6 (plays only), 9 vols 1635 (for 1735; plays only), 16 vols Glasgow 1752–7, 8 vols Glasgow 1766, 9 vols Birmingham 1768. *See* T. R. Lounsbury, The first editors of Shakespeare (Pope and Theobald), 1906; H. Schmidt, Die Shakespeare-Ausgabe von Pope, Giessen 1912.

Theobald, L. The works of Shakespeare, collated with the oldest copies, and corrected; with notes, explanatory and critical. 7 vols 1733, Dublin 1739, 8 vols 1740, 1752, 1757, 1762, 1767, 12 vols 1772, 8 vols 1773, 12 vols [1777?]. Plays only. *See* J. C. Collins, The Porson of Shakespearean critics, in his Essays and studies, 1895; T. R. Lounsbury, The first editors of Shakespeare (Pope and Theobald), 1906; R. F. Jones, Lewis Theobald, New York 1919; W. Mertz, Die Shakespeare-Ausgabe von Theobald, Giessen 1925.

Hanmer, T. The works of Shakespeare, carefully revised and corrected. 6 vols Oxford 1743–4, 1744–6, 1745, 9 vols 1747, 1748, 1750–1. 1760, 6 vols Oxford 1770–1, 1771. Adds Theobald's and Capell's variant readings, Pope's preface, Rowe's life, new notes by Percy, Warton and John Hawkins, and Collins's verses epistle. Plays only.

Warburton, W. The works of Shakespeare: the genuine text, collated with all the former editions and then corrected and emended, is here settled; being restored from the blunders of the first editors, and the inter-polations of the two last; with a comment and notes, critical and explanatory, by Mr Pope and Mr Warburton. 8 vols 1747, Dublin 1747. Plays only.

[Blair, H.] The works of Shakespeare: in which the beauties observed by Pope, Warburton and Dodd are pointed out. 8 vols Edinburgh 1753, London 1753, Edinburgh 1761, 1769, 1769, 1771, London [1771?]. Plays only.

Johnson, S. The plays of Shakespeare, with the corrections and illustrations of various commentators, to which are added notes. 8 vols 1765, 10 vols Dublin 1766, 8 vols 1768. *See* R. E. Scholes, Dr Johnson and the biblio-graphical criticism of Shakespeare, Sh Quart 11 1960; D. D. Eddy, Samuel Johnson's editions of Shakespeare, PBSA 56 1962; A. Sherbo, Johnson as editor of Shake-speare, in Samuel Johnson: a collection of critical essays, ed D. J. Greene, Englewood Cliffs NJ 1965.

Steevens, G. Twenty of the plays of Shakespeare: being the whole number printed in quarto during his life-time, or before the Restoration; collated where there were different copies and publish'd from the originals. 4 vols 1766. Midsummer night's dream, 1600; Merry wives, 1619, 1630, 1602; Much ado, 1600; Merchant of Venice, 1600; Love's labour's lost, 1631; Taming of the shrew, 1631; King Lear, 1608; King John, 1611; King Richard the Second, 1615; King Henry the Fourth, 1613; King Henry the Fourth: second part, 1600; King Henry the Fifth, 1608; King Henry the Sixth, nd; King Richard the Third, 1612; Titus Andronicus, 1611; Troilus and Cressida, 1609; Romeo and Juliet, 1597 and 1609; Hamlet, 1611; Othello, 1622; Sonnets, 1609; King Lear [Leir], 1605.

[Capell, E.] Shakespeare: his comedies, histories and tragedies, set out by himself in quarto or by the players his fellows in folio and now faithfully republish'd with an introduction; whereunto will be added, in some other volumes, notes critical and explanatory and a body of various readings. 10 vols 1767–8. The promised notes and various readings did not appear until 1779–83 (3 vols), though a first pt was pbd [1774]. *See* A. Walker, Edward Capell and his editions of Shakespeare, Proc Br Acad 46 1961.

Johnson, S. and G. Steevens. The plays of Shakespeare, with the corrections and illustrations of various commentators; to which are added notes by Samuel Johnson and George Steevens, with an appendix [by Richard Farmer]. 10 vols 1773. Based on Johnson's edn, above.

[Steevens, G.] The plays of Shakespeare, with the correc-tions and illustrations of various commentators; to which are added notes by Samuel Johnson and George Steevens: the second edition, revised and augmented. 10 vols 1778. Includes Malone's Attempt to ascertain the order in which the plays attributed to Shakespeare were written. Malone also added a supplement, 2 vols 1780, with notes, the first draft of his History of the stage, and the poems and doubtful plays. He added a further appendix in 1783.

[Reed, I.] The plays of Shakespeare, with the corrections and illustrations of various commentators; to which are added notes by Samuel Johnson and George Steevens: third edition revised and augmented by the editor of Dodsley's Collection of old plays. 10 vols, 1785. Includes notes by Malone.

Malone, E. The plays and poems of Shakespeare, collated verbatim with the most authentick copies; with the corrections and illustrations of various commentators, to which are added, an essay on the chronological order of his plays; an essay relative to Shakespeare and Jonson; a dissertation on the three parts of King Henry VI; an historical account of the English stage; and notes by E. Malone. 10 vols 1790.

[Steevens, G.] The plays of Shakespeare, with the correc-tions and illustrations of various commentators; to which are added notes by Samuel Johnson and George Steevens: the fourth edition, revised and augmented with a glossarial index. 15 vols 1793.

The plays and poems of Shakespeare, corrected from the latest and best London editions, with notes, by Samuel Johnson; to which are added a glossary and the life of the author. 8 vols Philadelphia 1795–6. First Amer edn.

Wagner, C. The dramatic works of Shakespeare. 8 vols Brunswick 1797–1801. First continental edn.

Reed, I. The plays of Shakespeare, with the corrections and illustrations of various commentators; to which are added notes by Samuel Johnson and George Steevens: fifth edition, revised and augmented by Isaac Reed, with a glossarial index. 21 vols 1803. First variorum edn. Embodies Steevens's last corrections.

[Bowdler, T.] The family Shakespeare. 4 vols Bath 1807. 20 plays.

Reed, I. The plays of Shakespeare, with the corrections and illustrations of various commentators; to which are added notes by Samuel Johnson and George Steevens, revised and augmented by Isaac Reed: sixth edition. 21 vols 1813. 2nd variorum edn.

[Boswell, J.] The plays and poems of Shakespeare, with the corrections and illustrations of various commen-tators, comprehending a life of the poet, and an enlarged history of the stage. 21 vols 1821. 3rd variorum edn. Based on Malone's edn, above, and on his ms collections.

Harness, W. Dramatic works. 8 vols 1825.

Singer, S. W. Dramatic works. 10 vols 1826. Includes life by C. Symmons.

Campbell, T. Dramatic works. 1838. With life and remarks.

Knight, C. The pictorial edition of the works. 8 vols 1838–43, 1864–7. Introductory notices, notes, variant readings, glossary, biography, music to the songs, and many wood engravings. Knight was also responsible for several later edns.

Collier, J. P. The works: the text formed from an entirely new collation of the old editions, with the various readings, notes, a life of the poet, and a history of the early English stage. 8 vols 1842–4, 1844–53, 6 vols 1858 (as Comedies, histories, tragedies and poems), 8 vols 1878 (as Plays and poems). The forged notes and emen-dations from early ms corrections in a copy of the folio, 1632, were issued as a supplemental vol in 1853.

Verplanck, G. C. Shakespeare's plays, with his life, critical introductions and notes, original and selected. 3 vols New York [1844]–7.

Hudson, H. N. Works. 11 vols Boston 1851–6.

— Complete works. 20 vols Boston 1880–1. Harvard edn.

Halliwell (-Phillipps), J. O. The works: the text formed from a new collation of the early editions; to which are added all the original novels and tales on which the plays are founded; copious archaeological annotations; an essay on the formation of the text; and a life of the poet. 16 vols 1853–65.

Delius, N. Shakespeares Werke. 2 vols Elberfeld 1854, 7 vols Elberfeld 1882.

Lloyd, W. W. Dramatic works. 10 vols 1855–6. Based on Singer's edn, with new life and critical essays.

Dyce, A. Works: the text revised. 6 vols 1857, 9 vols 1864–7 (adds glossary), 10 vols 1895–1901. Life, notices of early edns, account of the plays.

White, R. G. Works. 12 vols Boston 1857–66.

— The Riverside Shakespeare. 3 vols Boston 1883.

Staunton, H. Plays. 3 vols 1858–60, 6 vols 1860, 1894.

Cowden Clarke, M. Shakespeare's works. 2 vols New York 1860, 4 vols 1864 (with C. Cowden Clarke's assistance).

Clark, W. G., J. Glover and W. A. Wright. Works. 9 vols Cambridge 1863–6, 1891–3 (rev). The 'Cambridge' Shakespeare; the 'Globe' edn, based on it, 1 vol 1864 etc.

Marsh, J. B. The reference Shakespeare. 1864. Plays only.

Clark, W. G. and W. A. Wright. Shakespeare's select plays. 10 vols Oxford 1868–83. Clarendon Press edn.

Furness, H. H. and H. H. Furness jr. A new variorum edition of the works of Shakespeare. Philadelphia 1871–. The fullest of all edns of the plays. The following vols have appeared: Romeo and Juliet; Macbeth; Hamlet, 2 vols; Lear; Othello; Merchant of Venice; As you like it; Tempest; Midsummer night's dream; Winter's tale; Much ado; Twelfth night; Love's labour's lost; Richard III; Antony and Cleopatra; Julius Caesar; King John; Cymbeline; Coriolanus; Henry IV; Sonnets, 2 vols; Poems, 2 vols; Troilus and Cressida; Richard II. New Variorum.

Rolfe, W. J. Works. 40 vols New York 1871–96.

Furnivall, F. J. The Leopold Shakespeare. 1877.

Furnivall, F. J. et al. Plays and poems in quarto. 43 vols 1880–91 (facs).

Dowden, E. Works. 12 vols 1882–3 (Parchment Lib).

Plays. 13 vols 1886–91. Falcon edn. Separate plays by various editors including H. C. Beeching, A. C. Bradley, E. K. Chambers, O. Elton. Falcon.

Irving, H. and F. A. Marshall. The Henry Irving Shakespeare. 8 vols 1888–90, 1906. With stage history of each play.

Morgan, A., et al. The comedies, histories and tragedies. 22 vols New York 1888–1906 (New York Shakespeare Soc). Parallel texts of the plays from the quartos and folio. Bankside.

Verity, A. W. The Pitt Press Shakespeare. 13 vols Cambridge 1890–1905. Incomplete. Much ado, ed G. Sampson 1923.

Craig, W. J. The Oxford Shakespeare. [1891] etc. Also in 3 vols, with general introd by A. C. Swinburne and separate introds to plays and poems by E. Dowden.

The Warwick Shakespeare. 13 vols 1893–1938. Incomplete. Separate plays by various editors, including F. S. Boas, E. K. Chambers, C. H. Herford, G. C. Moore Smith etc. Warwick.

Gollancz, I. The Temple Shakespeare. 40 vols 1894–6 etc.

Craig, W. J., R. H. Case et al. The Arden Shakespeare. 37 vols 1899–1924. W. O. Brigstocke, All's well; J. W. Holme, As you like it; Henry Cuningham, Comedy of errors, Macbeth, Midsummer night's dream; W. J. Craig and R. H. Case, Coriolanus; E. Dowden, Cymbeline, Hamlet, Romeo and Juliet; M. Macmillan, Julius Caesar; R. P. Cowl and A. E. Morgan, 1 Henry IV; R. P. Cowl, 2 Henry IV; H. A. Evans, Henry V; H. C. Hart and C. K. Pooler, 1, 2, 3 Henry VI; C. K. Pooler, Henry VIII, Merchant of Venice, Sonnets, Poems;

I. B. John, King John, Richard II; A. H. Thompson, Richard III; H. C. Hart, Love's labour's lost, Merry wives, Measure for measure, Othello; W. J. Craig, King Lear; G. R. Trenery, Much ado; K. Deighton, Pericles, Timon of Athens, Troilus and Cressida; R. W. Bond, Taming of the shrew, Two gentlemen; Morton Luce, Tempest, Twelfth night; H. B. Baildon, Titus Andronicus; F. W. Moorman, Winter's tale. Arden.

Herford, C. H. Works. 10 vols 1899–1900. Eversley edn.

Henley, W. E. and W. Raleigh. Works. 10 vols 1901–4. Edinburgh Folio edn.

Porter, C. and H. A. Clarke. Complete works. 13 vols New York 1903–8. Pembroke edn. Introd by J. C. Collins.

— First Folio edition. 40 vols New York 1903–12. Amer First Folio edn; plays only.

Neilson, W. A. Complete dramatic and poetic works. Boston 1906. Cambridge edn.

Bullen, A. H. Works. 10 vols Stratford 1907. Stratford Town edn. Includes H. Davey, Memoir of Shakespeare; J. J. Jusserand, Ben Jonson's views on Shakespeare's art; R. Bridges, On the influence of the audience; H. C. Beeching, On the religion of Shakespeare, and On the sonnets; E. K. Chambers, The stage of the Globe; M. H. Spielmann, Portraits of Shakespeare.

Furnivall, F. J. and W. G. Boswell-Stone. The old spelling Shakespeare. 17 vols 1907–12. Incomplete.

Gordon, G. S. Nine plays: Merchant of Venice, Midsummer night's dream, As you like it, the Tempest, King Richard II, King Henry V, Julius Caesar, Hamlet and Macbeth. Oxford 1908.

Lee, S. Works. 20 vols 1910. Caxton edn.

Neilson, W. A., A. H. Thorndike et al. The Tudor Shakespeare. 40 vols New York 1911–13.

Herford, C. H. et al. Heath's Shakespeare. [1915]–. Heath.

Cross, W. L., C. F. T. Brooke et al. The Yale Shakespeare. 40 vols New Haven 1918–28. C. B. Tinker, Tempest; K. Young, Two gentlemen; G. V. Santvoord, Merry wives; C. F. T. Brooke, Much ado, 1, 2, 3 Henry VI; Coriolanus; W. L. Cross and C. F. T. Brooke, Love's labour's lost; W. H. Durham, Midsummer night's dream, Romeo and Juliet, Measure for measure; W. L. Phelps, Merchant of Venice, King Lear; J. R. Crawford, As you like it, Hamlet, Richard III; H. T. E. Perry, Taming of the shrew; G. H. Nettleton, Twelfth night; F. E. Pierce, Winter's tale; L. M. Buell, Richard II; S. B. Hemingway, 1, 2 Henry IV, Cymbeline; R. D. French, Henry V, Comedy of errors; S. T. Williams, Timon of Athens, King John; L. Mason, Julius Caesar, Othello; C. M. Lewis, Macbeth; H. S. Canby, Antony and Cleopatra; E. B. Reed, Sonnets; A. M. Witherspoon, Titus Andronicus; J. M. Berdan and C. F. T. Brooke, Henry VIII; A. E. Case, All's well; A. R. Bellinger, Pericles; N. B. Paradise, Troilus and Cressida; A. Feuillerat, Venus and Adonis and the other poems.

Quiller-Couch, A. T., J. D. Wilson et al. Works. Cambridge 1921–66. New Cambridge.

Granville-Barker, H. The players' Shakespeare. 1923–.

Farjeon, H. The works of Shakespeare. 7 vols 1929–34 (Nonesuch Press), 4 vols 1953 (with new introd by I. Brown). Nonesuch.

Ridley, M. R. The new Temple Shakespeare. 39 vols 1934–6.

Holznecht, K. J. and N. E. McClure. Selected plays of Shakespeare. 3 vols New York 1936–7.

Kittredge, G. L. Works. Boston 1936, Chicago 1958.

Harrison, G. B. The Penguin Shakespeare. 1937–64.

The New Clarendon Shakespeare. Oxford 1938–. Incomplete.

Neilson, W. A. and C. J. Hill. Complete plays and poems. Boston 1942.

Crofts Classics. New York 1946–.

Kittredge, G. L. Sixteen plays. New York 1946.

Harrison, G. B. Twenty-three plays and the sonnets. New York 1948.

Alexander, P. Complete works. 1951.

Craig, H. Complete works. Chicago 1951.

Ellis-Fermor, U., H. F. Brooks and H. Jenkins. The Arden Shakespeare. 1951–. Intended as rev edn of the Craig-Case Arden edn of 1899–1924, above, but in practice entirely new.

Sisson, C. J. Complete works. [1954].

Classics Club College Shakespeare: complete works. Princeton 1956. Based on Johnson-Steevens-Reed, 1803 above.

Munro, J. The London Shakespeare. 6 vols 1957.

Complete works, with the Temple notes, the history of Shakespeare's life, his will, an introduction to each play, and an index to characters. Cleveland 1958.

Harrison, G. B. The narrative poems. 1959 (Penguin).

Hubler, E. L. Shakespeare's songs and poems. New York 1959.

Prince, F. T. Poems. 1960 (New Arden).

Osborn, J. M., L. L. Martz and E. M. Waith. Shakespeare's poems. New Haven 1964. Facs of earliest edns.

Maxwell, J. C. Poems. Cambridge 1966 (New Cambridge).

Wilbur, R. and A. Harbage. Poems. Baltimore 1966 (Pelican).

Pitt, D. G. Complete sonnets and poems. New York 1966.

Campbell, O. J. The sonnets, songs and poems. New York 1967.

Burto, W. Poems. New York 1968 (Signet).

Harbage, A. The complete Pelican Shakespeare. Baltimore 1969.

Other important edns in progress are named under individual plays and poems, below.

§1

(5) PLAYS

Arranged in the chronological order of composition adopted in Chambers.

A. Quartos

Chambers has a Table of Quartos, vol 2 pp. 394–6.

Collection of lithographic facsimiles of the early quarto editions of the separate works of Shakespeare by E. W. Ashbee. Ed J. O. Halliwell (-Phillipps) 48 vols 1862–76.

Shakspere quarto facsimiles: issued under the superintendence of F. J. Furnivall. 43 vols 1880–9. Photolithographic facs by William Griggs with introds by various editors.

Shakespeare's quartos in collotype facs. Oxford 1939–. The following have already appeared: King Lear (Pied Bull quarto 1608), Merchant of Venice (Hayes quarto 1600), Merry wives of Windsor (1602), Hamlet (second quarto 1604–5), Pericles (1609), Romeo and Juliet (second quarto 1599), Hamlet (first quarto 1603), Troilus and Cressida (1609), Love's labour's lost (1598), Richard II (1597), Richard III (1597), 1 Henry IV (1598), Henry V (1600), The true tragedy (1595), Much ado about nothing (1600).

Other facsimile editions: Titus Andronicus (1594), New York 1937; Hamlet (second quarto, 1604), San Marino 1938; Hamlet (first quarto, 1603), Great Neck NY 1962, Frankfurt 1967.

Studies

Fleay, F. G. Tabular view of the quarto editions of Shakespeare's works, 1593–1630. Trans New Sh Soc 1 1874.

Greg, W. W. On certain false dates in Shakespearian quartos. Library 1st ser 9 1908.

Jaggard, W. False dates in Shakespearian quartos. Library 1st ser 10 1909.

Neidig, W. J. The Shakespeare quartos of 1619. MP 8 1910.

—— False dates on Shakespeare quartos. Century Mag 80 1910.

Huth, A. H. and A. W. Pollard. On the supposed false dates in certain Shakespeare quartos. Library 2nd ser 1 1910.

Wheatley, H. B. Post-Restoration quartos of Shakespeare's plays. Library 2nd ser 4 1913.

Bartlett, H. and A. W. Pollard. A census of Shakespeare's plays in quarto 1594–1709. New Haven 1916, 1939.

Bartlett, H. First edns of Shakespeare's quartos. Library 3rd ser 16 1935.

Kirschbaum, L. A census of bad quartos. RES 14 1938.

—— An hypothesis concerning the origin of the bad quartos. PMLA 60 1945.

Sisson, C. J. Shakespeare's quartos as prompt-copies, with some account of Cholmeley's plays and a new Shakespeare allusion. RES 18 1942.

Hart, A. Stolne and surreptitious copies: a comparative study of Shakespeare's bad quartos. Melbourne 1943.

Hodgson and Co. The remarkable story of the Shakespearian quartos of 1619: being a brief record of the unravelling of the puzzle in Shakespearian bibliography and an account of the unlooked-for discovery of a 'set' of the quartos in 1619. 1946.

Craig, H. A new look at Shakespeare's quartos. Stanford 1961.

For other articles on the quartos and related problems, see under individual plays, and the sections on transmission of the text, below.

B. Plays in 1623 Folio

1, 2, 3 Henry VI; Richard III; Comedy of errors; Titus Andronicus; Taming of the shrew; Two gentlemen of Verona; Love's labour's lost; Romeo and Juliet; Richard II; A midsummer night's dream; King John; Merchant of Venice; 1, 2 Henry IV; Much ado about nothing; Henry V; Julius Caesar; As you like it; Twelfth night; Hamlet; Merry wives of Windsor; Troilus and Cressida; All's well that ends well; Measure for measure; Othello; King Lear; Macbeth; Antony and Cleopatra; Coriolanus; Timon of Athens; Cymbeline; Winter's tale; Tempest; Henry VIII.

For sources of the plays, in addn to works mentioned under individual plays, see G. Bullough, Shakespeare's narrative and dramatic sources, 6 vols 1957–66; T. J. B. Spencer, Shakespeare's Plutarch, 1964 (Peregrine).

1, 2, 3 Henry VI

The first part of the contention betwixt the two famous houses of Yorke and Lancaster, with the death of the good Duke Humphrey, and the banishment and death of the Duke of Suffolke, and the tragicall end of the proud Cardinall of Winchester, with the notable rebellion of Jacke Cade; and the Duke of Yorkes first claime unto the Crowne; London, printed by Thomas Creed, for Thomas Millington, and are to be sold at his shop under Saint Peters Church in Cornwall. 1594; ed F. J. Furnivall 1891 (facs).

The first part of the contention betwixt the two famous houses of Yorke and Lancaster. 1600.

The true tragedie of Richard Duke of Yorke and the death of good King Henrie the Sixt, with the whole contention betweene the two houses of Lancaster and Yorke, as it was sundrie times acted by the Right Honourable the Earle of Pembroke his servants; printed at London by P[eter] S[hort] for Thomas Millington, and are to be sold at his shoppe under Saint Peters Church in Cornwall. 1595; ed T. Tyler 1891 (facs); ed W. W. Greg, Oxford 1958 (facs).

The true tragedie of Richarde Duke of Yorke, and the death of good King Henrie the Sixt. 1600.

The whole contention betweene the two famous houses, Lancaster and Yorke, with the tragicall ends of the good Duke Humfrey, Richard Duke of Yorke and King Henrie the Sixt, divided into two parts and newly corrected and enlarged; written by William Shakespeare gent; printed at London for T[homas] P[avier]. [1619]; ed F. J. Furnivall 2 pts 1886 (facs).

Modern Editions

C. W. Thomas, pt 2, New York 1892 (Bankside: parallel texts of Contention and Folio 1); A. Morgan, pt 3, New York 1892 (Bankside: parallel texts of True tragedie and Folio 1); II. C. Hart, 3 pts 1909–10 (Arden); C. F. T. Brooke, 3 pts New Haven 1918–23 (Yale); J. D. Wilson, 3 pts Cambridge 1952 (New Cambridge); A. S. Cairncross, 3 pts 1957–64 (New Arden); W. W. Greg, Oxford 1958 (facs of True tragedy); F. Fergusson and C. J. Sisson, 3 pts New York 1963 (Laurel); L. B. Wright and V. A. LaMar, 3 pts New York 1967 (Folger); M. Crane, pt 3, New York 1968 (Signet); G. L. Kittredge, rev I. Ribner, 3 pts Waltham Mass 1969.

Studies

Shakspere's Holinshed. Ed W. G. Boswell-Stone 1896.

Malone, E. A dissertation on the three parts of King Henry VI, tending to show that these plays were not originally written by Shakespeare. 1787, 1792 (expanded); rptd in Third variorum Shakespeare vol 18, ed J. Boswell 1821.

Knight, C. An essay on the three parts of King Henry VI and King Richard III. In Pictorial Shakespeare vol 7, 1843.

Delius, N. Zur Kritik der Doppeltexte des Shakespeareschen King Henry VI (pt 2–3). Sh Jb 15 1880.

Schmidt, K. Margareta von Anjou vor und bei Shakespeare. Berlin 1906.

Brooke, C. F. T. The authorship of the 2nd and 3rd pts of King Henry VI. Trans Connecticut Acad 17 1912.

Seyferth, P. In welchem Verhältnis steht H6B zur The contention und H6C zu The true tragedie? Anglia 40 1916.

Gray, H. D. The purport of Shakespeare's contribution to 1 Henry VI. PMLA 32 1917.

Pollard, A. W. The York and Lancaster plays in the Shakespeare Folio. TLS 26 Sept 1918.

Alexander, P. 2 Henry VI and the copy for the Contention 1594. TLS 9 Oct 1924.

—— 3 Henry VI and Richard Duke of York. TLS 13 Nov 1924.

—— Shakespeare's Henry VI and Richard III. Cambridge 1929.

Kingsford, C. L. Fifteenth-century history in Shakespeare's plays. In his Prejudice and promise in xvth-century England, Oxford 1925.

Gourvitch, J. Drayton and Henry VI. N & Q 18 Sept–9 Oct 1926.

Gaw, A. The origin and development of 1 Henry VI in relation to Shakespeare, Marlowe, Peele and Greene. Los Angeles 1926.

Chambers, E. K. The relation of the Contention to 2 and 3 Henry VI. Proc Oxford Bibl Soc 2 1926.

van Jan, E. Das literarische Bild der Jeanne d'Arc 1429–1926. Halle 1928.

Doran, M. Henry VI pts 2 and 3: their relation to the Contention and the True tragedy. Iowa City 1928.

Greer, C. A. The York and Lancaster quarto-folio sequence. PMLA 48 1933.

—— The place of 1 Henry VI in the York–Lancaster tetralogy. PMLA 53 1938.

—— Revision and adaptation in 1 Henry VI. SE 1942.

McKerrow, R. B. A note on 2 Henry VI and the Contention of York and Lancaster. RES 9 1933.

—— A note on the bad quartos of 2 and 3 Henry VI and the Folio text. RES 13 1937.

King, L. The use of Hall's Chronicles in the Folio and quarto texts of Henry VI. PQ 13 1934.

—— 2 and 3 Henry VI: which Holinshed? PMLA 50 1935.

—— Text sources of the Folio and quarto Henry VI. PMLA 51 1936.

Denny, C. F. The sources of 1 Henry VI as an indication of revision. PQ 16 1937.

Knickerbocker, W. S. Shakespearean alarum. Sewanee Rev 45 1937.

—— Shakespearean excursion: who wrote 2 and 3 Henry VI? Ibid.

Jordan, J. E. The reporter of 2 Henry VI. PMLA 64 1949.

Kirschbaum, L. The authorship of 1 Henry VI. PMLA 67 1952.

Jackson, B. On producing Henry VI. Sh Survey 6 1953.

Prouty, C. T. The contention and Shakespeare's 2 Henry VI. New Haven 1954.

Law, R. A. The chronicles and the three parts of Henry VI. SE 33 1955.

McManaway, J. G. The contention and 2 Henry VI. Wiener Beiträge zur Englischen Philologie 65 1957.

McNeal, T. H. Margaret of Anjou: romantic princess and troubled Queen. Sh Quart 9 1958.

Brockbank, J. P. The frame of disorder: Henry VI. In Early Shakespeare, ed J. R. Brown and B. Harris 1961.

Dickinson, H. Shakespeare's Henry yea-and-nay. Drama Critique 4 1961.

Mincoff, M. Henry VI pt 3 and the True tragedy. E Studies 42 1961.

—— The composition of 1 Henry VI. Sh Quart 16 1965.

Oppel, H. Der Tod Beauforts. In Festschrift zum 75 Geburtstag von Theodor Spira, Heidelberg 1961.

Berman, R. S. Fathers and sons in the Henry VI plays. Sh Quart 13 1962.

Turner, R. Y. Significant doubling of roles in Henry VI pt 2. Lib Chron 30 1964.

Harlow, C. G. A source for Nashe's Terrors of the night and the authorship of 1 Henry VI. Stud in Eng Lit 1500–1900 5 1965.

Ricks, D. M. Shakespeare's emergent form: a study of the structure of the Henry VI plays. Logan 1968.

Müller, H. Die Gestaltung des Volkes in Shakespeares Historiendramen, untersucht am Beispiel Heinrichs VI. Sh Jb (Weimar) 106 1970.

Riggs, D. Shakespeare's heroical histories: Henry VI and its literary tradition. Cambridge Mass 1971.

Weiss, T. In his Breath of clowns and kings: Shakespeare's early comedies and histories, 1971.

Richard III

The tragedy of King Richard the Third: containing his treacherous plots against his brother Clarence, the pittiefull murther of his iunocent [sic] nephewes, his tyrannicall usurpation; with the whole course of his detested life, and most deserved death, as it hath beene lately acted by the Right Honourable the Lord Chamberlaine his servants; at London printed by Valentine Sims, for Andrew Wise, dwelling in Paules Chuch-yard [sic], at the signe of the Angell. 1597 (anon); ed J. O. Halliwell (-Phillips) 1863 (facs); ed P. A. Daniel 1886 (facs); ed W. W. Greg, Oxford 1959 (facs).

The tragedie of King Richard the Third, by William Shake-speare. 1598, ed J. O. Halliwell (-Phillips) 1867 (facs); 1602 ('newly augmented' but in fact identical with earlier edns), ed J. O. Halliwell (-Phillips) 1865 (facs); ed P. A. Daniel 1888; 1605, ed Halliwell 1863 (facs); 1612, ed Halliwell 1871 (facs); 1622, ed P. A. Daniel 1889 (facs); 1629, 1634.

Modern Editions

W. A. Wright, Oxford 1880; E. A. Calkins, New York 1891 (Bankside: parallel 4° 1 and Folio 1); G. Macdonald 1896 (Warwick); A. H. Thompson 1907 (Arden); H. H. Furness jr, Philadelphia 1908 (New Variorum); J. R. Crawford, New Haven 1927 (Yale); J. D. Wilson, Cambridge 1954 (New Cambridge); F. Fergusson and C. J. Sisson, New York 1958 (Laurel); G. B. Evans, Baltimore 1959 (Pelican); A. S. Downer 1959 (Oxberry's 1822 edn with Hackett's notes on Kean's performance); W. W. Greg, Oxford 1959 (facs of 4° 1); L. B. Wright and V. A. LaMar, New York 1960 (Folger); M. Eccles, New York 1964 (Signet); E. A. J. Honigmann 1968 (New Penguin).

Studies

Shakspere's Holinshed. Ed W. G. Boswell-Stone 1896.

Churchill, G. B. Richard III up to Shakespeare. Berlin 1900.

Hammond, E. P. The tent scene in Richard III. MLN 17 1902.

Schmidt, K. Margareta von Anjou vor und bei Shakespeare. Berlin 1906.

Wood, A. I. P. The stage history of Shakespeare's King Richard III. New York 1909.

Koeppel, E. Shakespeares Richard III und Senecas Troades. Sh Jb 47 1911.

Wilhelm, F. Zu Seneca und Shakespeare. Archiv 129 1912.

Law, R. A. Richard III, act 1, scene 4. PMLA 27 1912.

—— Richard III: a study in Shakespeare's composition. PMLA 60 1945.

Moriarty, W. D. The bearing on dramatic sequence of the varia in Richard III and King Lear. MP 10 1913.

Campbell, O. J. A Dutch analogue of Richard III 1651. In Shakespeare studies by members of the University of Wisconsin, Madison 1916.

—— The position of the Roode en witte roos in the saga of King Richard III. Madison 1919.

Goetze, G. Die Richard-Anna-Szene in Shakespeares Richard III. Anglia 41 1917.

Pollard, A. W. The York and Lancaster plays in the First Folio. TLS 26 Sept 1918.

Babcock, R. W. An introduction to the study of the text of Richard III. SP 24 1927.

Alexander, P. Shakespeare's Henry VI and Richard III. Cambridge 1929.

Greer, C. A. The relation of Richard III to the True tragedy of Richard Duke of York and 3 Henry VI. SP 29 1932.

Patrick, D. L. The textual history of Richard III. Stanford 1936.

Mutz, W. Der Charakter Richards III in der Darstellung des Chronisten Holinshed und des Dramatikers Shakespeare, mit einem Beitrag zu seiner Charakterpsyche. Berlin 1936.

Griffin, W. J. An omission in the Folio text of Richard III. RES 13 1937.

Rossiter, A. P. The structure of Richard III. Durham Univ Jnl 31 1938.

Thomas, S. The antic Hamlet and Richard III. New York 1943.

Smith, F. M. The relation of Macbeth to Richard III. PMLA 60 1945.

Williams, P. Richard III: the battle orations. In English studies in honor of J. S. Wilson, Charlottesville 1951.

Wilson, J. D. Shakespeare's Richard III and the True tragedy of Richard the Third 1594. Sh Quart 3 1952.

—— The composition of the Clarence scenes in Richard III. MLR 53 1958.

Walton, J. K. The copy for the folio text of Richard III, with a note on the copy for the folio text of King Lear. Auckland 1955. See F. T. Bowers, below.

Clemen, W. Clarences Traum und Ermordung. Munich 1955.

—— Kommentar zu Shakespeares Richard III. Göttingen 1957; tr 1968.

Arnold, A. The recapitulation dream in Richard III and Macbeth. Sh Quart 6 1955.

Kendall, P. M. Richard III. New York 1956.

Cairncross, A. S. Coincidental variants in Richard III. Library 5th ser 12 1957.

—— The quartos and Folio text of Richard III. RES new ser 8 1957.

Bowers, F. T. The copy for the Folio Richard III. Sh Quart 10 1959. On J. K. Walton, above.

Krieger, M. The dark generations of Richard III. Criticism 1 1959.

Dollarhide, L. E. Two unassimilated movements of Richard III: an interpretation. Mississippi Quart 14 1961.

Lordi, R. J. The relationship of Richardus tertius to the main Richard III plays. Boston Univ Stud in Eng 5 1961.

Smidt, K. Iniurious imposters and Richard III. Oslo 1964.

—— Memorial transmission and quarto copy in Richard III. Oslo 1970.

Heilman, R. B. Satiety and conscience: aspects of Richard III. Antioch Rev 24 1964.

Brooke, N. Reflecting gems and dead bones: tragedy versus history in Richard III. CQ 7 1965.

Honigmann, E. A. J. The text of Richard III. Theatre Research 7 1965.

Berman, R. Anarchy and order in Richard III and King John. Sh Survey 20 1967.

Gaudy, R. Une interprétation de Richard III. La Nouvelle Critique 182 1967.

Dean, L. F. Shakespeare's Richard III. In Studies in language, literature and culture of the Middle Ages, ed E. B. Atwood and A. A. Hill, Austin 1969.

French, A. L. The world of Richard III. Sh Stud 4 1969.

Faure, F. Langage religieux et langage pétrarquiste dans Richard III de Shakespeare. Etudes Anglaises 23 1970.

McNeir, W. F. The masks of Richard III. Stud in Eng Lit 1500–1900 11 1971.

Weiss, T. In his Breath of clowns and kings: Shakespeare's early comedies and histories, 1971.

Comedy of Errors

In First Folio, 1623.

Modern Editions

A. Morgan, New York 1894 (Bankside); H. Cuningham 1906 (Arden); A. T. Quiller-Couch and J. D. Wilson, Cambridge 1922 (New Cambridge); R. D. French, New Haven 1926 (Yale); R. A. Foakes 1962 (New Arden); P. A. Jorgensen, Baltimore 1964 (Pelican); H. Levin, New York 1965 (Signet); G. L. Kittredge, rev I. Ribner, Waltham Mass 1966.

For a concordance see T. H. Howard-Hill, Oxford 1969.

Studies

Rouse, W. H. D. The Menaechmi: the original of Shakespeare's Comedy of errors. 1912. Latin text and Elizabethan trn.

Roeder, K. Menechmi und Amphitruo im englischen Drama bis zur 1661. Leipzig 1904.

Lang, F. Shakespeares Comedy of errors in englischer Bühnenbearbeitung. Rostock 1909.

Gill, E. M. A comparison of the characters in the Comedy of errors with those in the Menaechmi. SE 5 1925.

Gaw, A. The evolution of the Comedy of errors. PMLA 41 1926.

Baldwin, T. W. Shakespeare adapts a hanging. Princeton 1931.

— Three homilies in the Comedy of errors. In Essays on Shakespeare and Elizabethan drama in honor of Hardin Craig, Columbia Missouri 1962.
— On the compositional genetics of the Comedy of errors. Urbana 1965.
— Errors and Marprelate. In Studies in honor of De Witt Starnes, Austin 1967.
Charlton, H. B. Shakespeare's recoil from romanticism. Bull John Rylands Lib 15 1931.
Elliott, G. R. Weirdness in the Comedy of errors. UTQ 9 1939.
Parks, G. B. Shakespeare's map for the Comedy of errors. JEGP 39 1940.
Thomas, S. The date of the Comedy of errors. Sh Quart 7 1956.
Brooks, H. Themes and structure in the Comedy of errors. In Early Shakespeare, ed J. R. Brown and B. Harris 1961.
Barber, C. L. Shakespearian comedy in the Comedy of errors. College Eng April 1964.
Williams, G. The comedy of errors rescued from tragedy. REL 5 1964.
Schlösser, A. Das Motiv der Entfremdung in der Komödie der Irrungen. Sh Jb (Weimar) 101 1965.
Clubb, L. G. Italian comedy and the Comedy of errors. Comparative Lit 19 1967.
Henze, R. The comedy of errors: a freely binding chain. Sh Quart 22 1971.
Weiss, T. In his Breath of clowns and kings: Shakespeare's early comedies and histories, 1971.

Titus Andronicus

The most lamentable Romaine tragedie of Titus Andronicus, as it was plaide by the Right Honourable the Earle of Darbie, Earle of Pembrooke and Earle of Sussex their servants; London, printed by John Danter, and are to be sold by Edward White and Thomas Millington, at the little north doore of Paules at the signe of the Gunne. 1594. Anon. The only copy known, now in Folger Lib, was discovered in Sweden in 1905.
The most lamentable Romaine tragedie of Titus Andronicus. 1600, ed J. O. Halliwell (-Phillipps) 1867; ed A. Symons 1885 (facs); 1611 (as The most lamentable tragedie).
Tr German, Eine sehr klägliche Tragoedia von Tito Andronico und der hoffertigen Kayserin, in Engelische Comedien und Tragedien, 1620; rptd W. Creizenach in Die Schauspiele der englischen Komödianten, Berlin 1889.
Tr Dutch, Jan Vos, Aran en Titus, af Wraak en Weerwraak, 1641.

Modern Editions

A. Morgan, New York 1890 (Bankside: parallel texts of 4° and Folio 1); H. B. Baildon 1904 (Arden); A. M. Witherspoon, New Haven 1926 (Yale); J. Q. Adams, New York 1937 (facs of unique copy of 4° (1594) in Folger Lib); J. D. Wilson, Cambridge 1948 (New Cambridge); J. C. Maxwell 1953 (New Arden); S. Barnet, New York 1964 (Signet); L. B. Wright and V. A. LaMar, New York 1965 (Folger); G. L. Kittredge, rev I. Ribner, Waltham Mass 1969.

Studies

Sarrazin, G. Germanische Heldensage in Shakespeares Titus Andronicus. Archiv 97 1896.
Crawford, C. The date and authenticity of Titus Andronicus. Sh Jb 36 1900.
Baker, G. P. 'Titus and Vespacia' and 'Titus and Ondronicus' in Henslowe's Diary. PMLA 16 1901.
Keller, W. Die neuaufgefundene Quarto des Titus Andronicus von 1594. Sh Jb 41 1905.
— Titus Andronicus: ein Vortrag. Sh Jb 89 1938.
Greg, W. W. In Henslowe's Diary vol 2, 1908. P. 159.
— Titus Andronicus. MLR 14 1919.

Dibelius, W. Zur Stoffgeschichte des Titus Andronicus. Sh Jb 48 1912.
Gray, H. D. The authorship of Titus Andronicus. In [Ewald] Flügel memorial volume, Stanford 1916.
— Titus Andronicus once more. MLN 34 1919.
— The Titus Andronicus problem. SP 17 1920.
— Shakespeare's share in Titus Andronicus. PQ 5 1926.
Brooke, C. F. T. Titus Andronicus and Shakespeare. MLN 34 1919.
Parrott, T. M. Shakespeare's revision of Titus Andronicus. MLR 14 1919.
— Further observations on Titus Andronicus. Sh Quart 1 1950.
Granger, F. Shakespeare and the legend of Andronicus. TLS 1 April 1920. See later correspondence.
Symons, A. Titus Andronicus and the tragedy of blood. In his Studies in the Elizabethan drama, 1920.
Rhodes, R. C. Titus and Vespasian. TLS 17 April 1924. See later correspondence.
Chambers, E. K. The first illustration to Shakespeare. Library 3rd ser 5 1925.
Clark, E. G. Titus and Vespasian. MLN 41 1926.
Gray, A. K. Shakespeare and Titus Andronicus. SP 25 1928.
Bolton, J. S. G. The authentic text of Titus Andronicus. PMLA 44 1929.
— Titus Andronicus: Shakespeare at thirty. SP 30 1933.
McKerrow, R. B. A note on Titus Andronicus. Library 3rd ser 15 1934.
Price, H. T. The language of Titus Andronicus. Papers of Michigan Acad 21 1935.
— The authorship of Titus Andronicus. JEGP 42 1943.
— The first quarto of Titus Andronicus. Eng Inst Essays 1947.
— Author, compositor and metre: copy-selling in Titus Andronicus and other Elizabethan printings. PBSA 53 1961.
Baker, H. Induction to tragedy. Baton Rouge 1939.
Hastings, W. T. The hardboiled Shakespeare. Sh Assoc Bull 17 1942.
Law, R. A. The Roman background of Titus Andronicus. SP 40 1943.
Wilson, J. D. Titus Andronicus on the stage in 1595. Sh Survey 1 1948.
Sargent, R. M. The source of Titus Andronicus. SP 46 1949.
Maxwell, J. C. Peele and Shakespeare: a stylometric test. JEGP 49 1950.
Cantrell, P. L. and G. W. Williams. Roberts' compositors in Titus Andronicus Q2. SB 8 1956.
Hill, R. F. The composition of Titus Andronicus. Sh Survey 10 1957.
Waith, E. M. The metamorphosis of violence in Titus Andronicus. Ibid.
Oppel, H. Titus Andronicus. Heidelberg 1960.
Ungerer, G. An unrecorded Elizabethan performance of Titus Andronicus. Sh Survey 14 1961.
Hamilton, A. C. Titus Andronicus: the form of Shakespearian tragedy. Sh Quart 14 1963.
Korninger, S. Shakespeares Titus Andronicus. Moderne Sprachen 7 1963.
Adams, J. C. Shakespeare's revisions in Titus Andronicus. In Shakespeare 400, ed J. G. McManaway, New York 1964.
Harrison, T. P. Titus Andronicus and King Lear: a study in continuity. In Shakespearean essays, ed A. Thaler and N. Sanders, Knoxville 1964.
Brooke, N. The tragic spectacle in Titus Andronicus and Romeo and Juliet. In Shakespeare: the tragedies, ed C. Leech 1966.
Cutts, J. P. Shadow and substance: structural unity in Titus Andronicus. Comparative Drama 2 1968.
Schlösser, A. Titus Andronicus. Sh Jb (Weimar) 104 1968.
Ettin, A. V. Shakespeare's first Roman tragedy. ELH 37 1970.

Kramer, J. E. Titus Andronicus: the 'fly-killing' incident. Sh Stud 5 1970.

Reese, J. E. The formalization of horror in Titus Andronicus. Sh Quart 21 1970.

Shadoian, J. Titus Andronicus. Discourse 13 1970.

Stamm, R. Der Gebrauch der Spiegeltechnik in Titus Andronicus: ein Blick in das Regiebuch Shakespeares. Sprachkunst 1 1970.

Weiss, R. In his Breath of clowns and kings: Shakespeare's early comedies and histories, 1971.

Taming of the Shrew

A pleasant conceited historie called the taming of a shrew, as it was sundry times acted by the Right Honorable the Earle of Pembrook his servants; printed at London by Peter Short and are to be sold by Cuthbert Burbie, at his shop at the Royall Exchange. 1594, ed J. O. Halliwell (-Phillipps) 1876 (facs); ed F. J. Furnivall 1886; TFT 1912; rptd T. Amyot 1844; ed F. S. Boas 1908; 1596, 1607. Alternatively held to be the source or a 'bad quarto' of the Folio I play.

A wittie and pleasant comedie called the taming of the shrew, as it was acted by his Majesties servants at the Blacke Friers and the Globe; written by Will. Shakespeare, printed by W.S. for John Smethwicke, and are to be sold at his shop in Saint Dunstones Churchyard under the Diall. 1631. Rptd from Folio I.

Modern Editions

A. R. Frey, New York 1888 (Bankside: parallel texts of A shrew and Folio I); R. W. Bond 1904 (Arden), 1929; H. T. E. Perry, New Haven 1921 (Yale); A. T. Quiller-Couch and J. D. Wilson, Cambridge 1928 (New Cambridge); F. Fergusson and C. J. Sisson, New York 1958 (Laurel); L. B. Wright and V. A. LaMar, New York 1963 (Folger); R. Hosley, Baltimore 1964 (Pelican); R. B. Heilman, New York 1966 (Signet); G. L. Kittredge, rev I. Ribner, Waltham Mass 1967; G. R. Hibbard 1968 (New Penguin).

Studies

Delius, N. Shakespeares Taming of the shrew. Elberfeld 1864.

Bolte, J. Eine Parallele zu Shakespeares The taming of the shrew. Sh Jb 27 1892.

Tolman, A. H. What has become of Shakespeare's play Love's labour's won? Chicago 1902.

Schomburg, E. H. The taming of the shrew. Halle 1904.

Kuhl, E. P. Shakespeare's purpose in dropping Sly. MLN 36 1921.

—— The authorship of the Taming of the shrew. PMLA 40 1925.

Sykes, H. D. The authorship of the Taming of a shrew, the Famous victories of Henry V and the additions to Marlowe's Faustus. 1919 (Sh Assoc Pamphlet); rptd in his Sidelights on Elizabethan drama, 1924.

Alexander, P. The taming of a shrew. TLS 16 Sept 1926.

—— The original ending of the Taming of the shrew. Sh Quart 20 1969.

Ashton, F. H. The revision of the Folio text of the Taming of the shrew. PQ 6 1927.

van Dam, B. A. P. The taming of a shrew. E Studies 10 1928.

Charlton, H. B. The taming of the shrew. Bull John Rylands Lib 16 1932.

Whiting, B. J. Old maids lead apes in hell. E Studien 70 1936.

Houk, R. A. The integrity of Shakespeare's The taming of the shrew. JEGP 39 1940.

—— The evolution of the Taming of the shrew. PMLA 57 1942.

—— Strata in the Taming of the shrew. SP 39 1942.

—— Shakespeare's heroic shrew. Sh Assoc Bull 18 1943.

—— Shakespeare's shrew and Greene's Orlando. PMLA 62 1947.

Gray, H. D. The taming of a shrew. PQ 20 1941.

Duthie, G. I. The taming of a shrew and the Taming of the shrew. RES 19 1943.

Craig, H. The shrew and A shrew: possible settlement of an old debate. In Elizabethan studies in honor of G. F. Reynolds, Boulder 1945.

Parrott, T. M. The taming of the shrew: a new study of an old play. Ibid.

Greenfield, T. N. The transformation of Christopher Sly. PQ 33 1954.

Bradbrook, M. C. Dramatic role as social image: a study of the Taming of the shrew. Sh Jb 94 1958.

Shroeder, J. W. The taming of a shrew and the Taming of the shrew: a case reopened. JEGP 57 1958.

—— A new analogue and possible source for the Taming of a shrew. Sh Quart 10 1959. Caxton's tale of Queen Vastis in the Book of the knight of La Tour Landry.

Waldo, T. R. and T. W. Herbert. Musical terms in the Taming of the shrew: evidence of single authorship. Ibid.

Tillyard, E. M. W. Some consequences of a lacuna in the Taming of the shrew. E Studies 43 1962.

—— The fairy-tale element in the Taming of the shrew. In Shakespeare 1564–1964, ed E. A. Bloom, Providence 1964.

Seronsy, C. C. Supposes as the unifying theme in the Taming of the shrew. Sh Quart 14 1963.

Hosley, R. Sources and analogues of the Taming of the shrew. HLQ 27 1964.

Hibbard, G. R. The taming of the shrew: a social comedy. In Shakespearean essays, ed A. Thaler and N. Sanders, Knoxville 1964.

Sanders, N. Themes and imagery in the Taming of the shrew. Renaissance Papers 1963.

Orange, L. E. The punning of the shrew. Southern Quart 3 1965.

Brunvand, J. H. The folk-tale origin of the Taming of the shrew. Sh Quart 17 1966.

Jayne, S. The dreaming of the shrew. Ibid.

Heilman, R. B. The taming untamed: or the return of the shrew. MLQ 27 1966.

Ribner, I. The morality of farce: the Taming of the shrew. In Essays in American and English literature presented to Bruce Robert McElderry jr, Columbus 1968.

Thorne, W. B. Folk elements in the Taming of the shrew. Queen's Quart 75 1968.

Harrold, W. E. Shakespeare's use of Mostellaria in the Taming of the shrew. Sh Jb (Heidelberg) 1970.

Henze, R. Role playing in the Taming of the shrew. Southern Humanities Rev 4 1970.

Weiss, T. In his Breath of clowns and kings: Shakespeare's early comedies and histories, 1971.

Two Gentlemen of Verona

In First Folio, 1623.

Modern Editions

R. W. Bond 1906 (Arden); A. T. Quiller-Couch and J. D. Wilson, Cambridge 1921 (New Cambridge); K. Young, New Haven 1924 (Yale); B. Evans, New York 1964 (Signet); F. Fergusson and C. J. Sisson, New York 1964 (Laurel); B. A. W. Jackson, Baltimore 1964 (Pelican); L. B. Wright and V. A. LaMar, New York 1964 (Folger); N. Sanders 1968 (New Penguin); G. L. Kittredge, rev I. Ribner, Waltham Mass 1969; C. Leech, 1969 (New Arden).

For a concordance see T. H. Howard-Hill, Oxford 1970.

Studies

Fleay, F. G. On the date and composition of the Two gentlemen of Verona. Trans New Sh Soc 1874. With comment by F. J. Furnivall.

Norpoth, H. Metrisch-chronologische Untersuchung von Shakespeares Two gentlemen of Verona. Bonn 1916.

Campbell, O. J. The two gentlemen of Verona and Italian comedy. In Michigan studies in Shakespeare, Milton and Donne, New York 1925.

Harrison, T. P. Concerning the Two gentlemen of Verona and Montemayor's Diana. MLN 41 1926.

Charlton, H. B. Romanticism in Shakespearian comedy. Bull John Rylands Lib 14 1930.

Wales J. G. Shakespeare's use of English and foreign elements in the setting of the Two gentlemen of Verona. Trans Wisconsin Acad 27 1932.

Small, S. A. The ending of the Two gentlemen of Verona. PMLA 48 1933.

Parks, G. B. The development of Two gentlemen of Verona. Huntington Lib Bull 2 1937.

Allen, M. S. Brooke's Romeus and Iuliet as a source for the Valentine-Sylvia plot in Two gentlemen of Verona. SE 18 1938.

Atkinson, D. F. The source of Two gentlemen of Verona. SP 41 1944.

Sargent, R. M. Sir Thomas Elyot and the integrity of the Two gentlemen of Verona. PMLA 65 1950.

Pruvost, R. The two gentlemen of Verona, Twelfth night et Gl' ingannati. Etudes Anglaises 13 1960.

Danby, J. F. Shakespeare criticism and the Two gentlemen of Verona. CQ 2 1960.

Brooks, H. F. Two clowns in a comedy (to say nothing of the dog): the Two gentlemen of Verona. E & S new ser 16 1963.

Wells, S. The failure of the Two gentlemen of Verona. Sh Jb 99 1963.

Stephenson, W. E. The adolescent dream-world of the Two gentlemen of Verona. Sh Quart 17 1966.

Schlösser, A. Betrachtungen über Die beiden Veroneser. Sh Jb (Weimar) 103 1967.

Godshalk, W. L. The structural unity of Two gentlemen of Verona. SP 66 1969.

Weimann, R. Laughing with the audience: the Two gentlemen and the popular tradition of comedy. Sh Survey 22 1969; rptd in German in Sh Jb (Weimar) 106 1970.

Weiss, T. In his Breath of clowns and kings: Shakespeare's early comedies and histories, 1971.

Love's Labour's Lost

A pleasant conceited comedie called Loves labors lost, as it was presented before her Highnes this last Christmas, newly corrected and augmented by W. Shakespere; imprinted at London by W[illiam] W[hite] for Cutbert Burby. 1598; ed J. O. Halliwell (-Phillipps) 1869 (facs); ed F. J. Furnivall 1880 (facs); ed W. W. Greg, Oxford 1957 (facs).

Loves labours lost: a wittie and pleasant comedie, as it was acted by his Majesties servants at the Blacke-Friers and the Globe, written by William Shakespeare. 1631.

Modern Editions

H. H. Furness, Philadelphia 1904 (New Variorum); I. H Platt, New York 1906 (Bankside: parallel texts of 4⁰ 1 and Folio 1); H. C. Hart 1906 (Arden); H. B. Charlton 1917 (Heath); A. T. Quiller-Couch and J. D. Wilson, Cambridge 1923 (New Cambridge); W. L. Cross and C. F. T. Brooke, New Haven 1925 (Yale); R. W. David 1951 (New Arden); L. B. Wright and V. A. LaMar, New York 1962 (Folger); A. Harbage, Baltimore 1963 (Pelican); J. L. Calderwood, Dubuque Iowa 1970 (Blackfriars).

Studies

Halliwell(-Phillipps), J. O. Memoranda on Love's labour's lost. 1879.

Lee, S. A new study of Love's labour's lost. GM Oct 1880.

Fleay, F. G. Shakespeare and Puritanism. Anglia 7 1884.

Pater, W. Love's labour's lost. In his Appreciations, 1889.

McClumpha, C. F. Parallels between Shakespeare's sonnets and Love's labour's lost. MLN 15 1900.

de Perott, J. Eine spanische Parallele zu Love's labour's lost. Sh Jb 44 1908.

Phelps, J. Father Parsons in Shakespeare. Archiv 133 1915.

— The source of Love's labour's lost. Sh Assoc Bull 17 1942.

Charlton, H. B. A textual note on Love's labour's lost. Library 2nd ser 8 1917.

— A disputed passage in Love's labour's lost. MLR 12 1917.

— The date of Love's labour's lost. MLR 13 1918.

Gray, H. D. The original version of Love's labour's lost. Stanford 1918.

Roberts, J. H. The nine worthies. MP 19 1922.

Gray, A. K. The secret of Love's labour's lost. PMLA 39 1924.

Campbell, O. J. Love's labour's lost restudied. In Michigan studies in Shakespeare, Milton and Donne, New York 1925.

Granville-Barker, H. In his Prefaces to Shakespeare series 1, 1927.

Eichler, A. Love's labour's lost und As you like it als Hofaufführungen. E Studien 64 1929.

Taylor, R. The date of Love's labour's lost. New York 1932.

Clark, E. L. The satirical comedy Love's labour's lost: a study. New York 1933.

Boughner, D. C. Don Armado as a gallant. Revue Anglo-américaine 12 1935.

— Don Armado and the commedia dell'arte. SP 37 1940.

Yates, F. A. A study of Love's labour's lost. Cambridge 1936.

Kirschbaum, L. Is the Spanish tragedy a leading case? Did a bad quarto of Love's labour's lost ever exist? JEGP 37 1938.

Draper, J. W. Tempo in Love's labour's lost. E Studies 29 1948.

Babcock, W. Fools, fowls and pertaunt-like in Love's labour's lost. Sh Quart 2 1951.

Roesen, B. Love's labour's lost. Sh Quart 4 1953.

Brown, R. B. The satiric use of 'popular' music in Love's labour's lost. Southern Folklore Quart 23 1959.

Harbage, A. Love's labour's lost and the early Shakespeare. PQ 41 1962.

Hoy, C. Love's labour's lost and the nature of comedy. Sh Quart 13 1962.

Nevinson, J. L. A show of nine worthies. Sh Quart 14 1963.

Lambrechts, G. 'The brief and the tedious of it': note sur le texte de Love's labour's lost. Etudes Anglaises 17 1964.

Lawrence, N. G. A study of taffeta phrases . . . and honest kersey noes. In Sweet smoke of rhetoric, ed N. G. Lawrence and J. A. Reynolds, Coral Gables 1964.

Matthews, W. Language in Love's labour's lost. E & S new ser 17 1964.

Calderwood, J. L. Love's labour's lost: a wantoning with words. Stud in Eng Lit 1500–1900 5 1965.

Cunningham, J. V. With that facility: false starts and revisions in Love's labour's lost. In Essays on Shakespeare, ed G. W. Chapman, Princeton 1965.

Schlösser, A. Love's labour's lost: Shakespeares Jahrmarkt der Eitelkeit. Zeitschrift für Anglistik und Amerikanistik 13 1965.

Memmo, P. E. The poetry of the Stilnovisti and Love's labour's lost. Comparative Lit 18 1966.

McLay, C. M. The dialogues of spring and winter. Sh Quart 18 1967.

Westlund, J. E. Fancy and achievement in Love's labour's lost. Ibid.

Godshalk, W. L. Pattern in Love's labour's lost. Renaissance Papers 1968.

Agnew, G. K. Berowne and the progress of Love's labour's lost. Sh Stud 4 1969.

Berry, R. The words of Mercury. Sh Survey 22 1969.

Lord, G. Die Figur des Pedanten bei Shakespeare. Sh Jb (Heidelberg) 1969.

Hassel, R. C. Shakespeare's comic epilogues: invitations to festive communion. Sh Jb (Heidelberg) 1970.

Romeo and Juliet

An excellent conceited tragedie of Romeo and Juliet, as it hath been often (with great applause) plaid publiquely, by the right Honourable the L. of Hunsdon his servants; London, printed by John Danter. 1597; ed H. A. Evans 1886 (facs); rptd P. A. Daniel 1874 (New Shakespeare Soc); W. A. Wright, Cambridge Shakespeare vol 9, 1893; ed F. G. Hubbard, Madison 1924. The 'bad' 4⁰.

The most excellent and lamentable tragedie of Romeo and Juliet, newly corrected, augmented and amended, as it hath bene sundry times publiquely acted, by the Right Honourable the Lord Chamberlaine his servants; London, printed by Thomas Creede for Cuthbert Burby, and are to be sold at his shop neare the Exchange. 1599; ed H. A. Evans 1886 (facs); rptd P. A. Daniel 1874 (New Shakespeare Soc); ed P. A. Daniel 1875 (New Shakespeare Soc). The 'good' 4⁰.

The most excellent and lamentable tragedie of Romeo and Juliet. 1609, nd (2 issues, 2nd adding 'written by W. Shakespeare', ed H. A. Evans 1887 (facs)), 1637.

Tr German, Romio und Julietta, ptd A. Cohn 1865, from Vienna Hofbibliothek ms 13,107.

Modern Editions

T. Mommsen, Oldenburg 1859 (parallel texts of 4⁰1 and 4⁰2); H. H. Furness, Philadelphia 1871 (New Variorum), 1909; P. A. Daniel 1874 (parallel texts of 4⁰1 and 4⁰2); B. R. Field, New York 1889 (Bankside; parallel texts); E. Dowden 1900 (Arden); W. H. Durham, New Haven 1917 (Yale); G. Sampson, Cambridge 1936; W. W. Greg, Oxford 1949 (William Drummond's copy of 4⁰2 1599); R. Hosley, New Haven 1954 (Yale); G. I. Duthie and J. D. Wilson, Cambridge 1955 (New Cambridge); F. Fergusson and C. J. Sisson, New York 1958 (Laurel); L. B. Wright and V. L. Freund, New York 1959 (Folger); J. E. Hankins, Baltimore 1960 (Pelican); G. W. Williams, Durham NC 1964; G. L. Kittredge, rev I. Ribner, Waltham Mass 1967; T. J. B. Spencer 1967 (New Penguin); M. Spevack, Dubuque Iowa 1970 (Blackfriars).

Studies

Brooke's Romeus and Juliet. Ed J. J. Munro 1908 (Sh Classics).

Daniel, P. A. Brooke's Romeus and Juliet and Painter's Rhomeo and Julietta. 1875.

Spalding, T. A. On the first quarto of Romeo and Juliet. Trans New Sh Soc 1878.

Delius, N. Brookes episches und Shakespeares dramatisches Gedicht von Romeo und Juliet. Sh Jb 16 1881.

McClumpha, C. F. Shakespeare's sonnets and Romeo and Juliet. Sh Jb 40 1904.

Fuller, H. de W. Romeo and Juliette. MP 4 1906.

Smith, W. A comic version of Romeo and Juliette. MP 7 1909.

Hemingway, S. B. The relation of A midsummer night's dream to Romeo and Juliet. MLN 26 1911.

Gray, H. D. Romeo, Rosaline and Juliet. MLN 29 1914.

Wilson, J. D. and A. W. Pollard. The 'stolne and surreptitious' Shakespearian texts: Romeo and Juliet 1597. TLS 14 Aug 1919.

Tilley, M. P. A parody of Euphues in Romeo and Juliet. MLN 41 1926.

Hjort, G. The good and bad quartos of Romeo and Juliet and Love's labour's lost. MLR 21 1926.

van Dam, B. A. P. Did Shakespeare revise Romeo and Juliet? Anglia 51 1927.

Law, R. A. On Shakespeare's changes of his source material in Romeo and Juliet. Texas Univ Stud 9 1929.

Moore, O. H. Le rôle de Boaistuau dans le développement de la légende de Roméo et Juliette. Revue de Littérature Comparée 9 1929.

— Shakespeare's deviations from Romeus and Juliet. PMLA 52 1937.

Granville-Barker, H. In his Prefaces to Shakespeare: series 2, 1930.

Hauvette, H. La morte vivante. Paris 1933.

Cain, H. E. Crabbed age and youth in Romeo and Juliet. Sh Assoc Bull 9 1934.

— A technique of motivation in Romeo and Juliet. Sh Assoc Bull 22 1947.

— Romeo and Juliet: a reinterpretation. Sh Assoc Bull 22 1947.

— Parting and justice in Romeo and Juliet. Tennessee Stud in Lit 7 1962.

Gaw, A. The impromptu mask in Shakespeare, with special reference to the staging of Romeo and Juliet. Sh Assoc Bull 11 1936.

Hoppe, H. R. The first quarto version of Romeo and Juliet II. vi and IV. v. 43 ff. RES 14 1938.

— The bad quarto of Romeo and Juliet. Ithaca 1948.

Draper, J. W. Shakespeare's star-crossed lovers. RES 15 1939.

— Contrast of tempo in the balcony scene. Sh Assoc Bull 22 1947.

— Patterns of style in Romeo and Juliet. Studia Neophilologica 21 1949.

Walley, H. R. Shakespeare's debt to Marlowe in Romeo and Juliet. PQ 21 1942.

Guide, A. The humour of Juliet's nurse. Bull History of Medicine 17 1946.

Smith R. M. Three interpretations of Romeo and Juliet. Sh Assoc Bull 23 1948.

Bowling, L. E. The thematic framework of Romeo and Juliet. PMLA 64 1949.

Evans B. The brevity of Friar Lawrence. PMLA 65 1950.

Olive, W. J. 'Twenty good nights': the Knight of the burning pestle, the Family of love, and Romeo and Juliet. SP 47 1950.

Pettet, E. C. The imagery of Romeo and Juliet. English 8 1950.

Thomas, S. Henry Chettle and the first quarto of Romeo and Juliet. RES new ser 1 1950.

Bonnard, G. A. Romeo and Juliet: a possible significance? RES new ser 2 1951.

Duthie, G. I. The text of Romeo and Juliet. SB 4 1952.

Nosworthy, J. M. The two angry families of Verona. Sh Quart 3 1952.

Hosley, R. The corrupting influence of the bad quarto on the received text of Romeo and Juliet. Sh Quart 4 1953.

— Quarto copy for Q2 Romeo and Juliet. SB 9 1957.

Lewis, A. Shakespeare y el rinacimiento: Romeo y Julieta. Cuadernos Americanos 72 1953.

Hinman, C. The proof-reading of the first folio text of Romeo and Juliet. SB 6 1954.

Durrant, G. H. What's in a name? a discussion of Romeo and Juliet. Theoria 8 1956.

Cantrell, P. L. and G. W. Williams. The printing of the second quarto of Romeo and Juliet. SB 9 1957.

McArthur, H. Romeo's loquacious friend. Sh Quart 10 1959.

Ribner, I. Then I denie you starres: a reading of Romeo and Juliet. In Studies in the English Renaissance drama, ed J. W. Bennett, O. Cargill and V. Hall, New York 1959.

Levin, H. Form and formality in Romeo and Juliet. Sh Quart 11 1960.

Lawlor, J. Romeo and Juliet. In Early Shakespeare, ed J. R. Brown and B. Harris 1961.

Siegel, P. N. Christianity and the religion of love in Romeo and Juliet. Sh Quart 12 1961.

Sjögren, G. 'Sirrah, go hire me twenty cunning cooks'. Ibid.

Driver, T. F. The Shakespearian clock: time and the vision of reality in Romeo and Juliet and the Tempest. Sh Quart 15 1964.

Tanselle, G. T. Time in Romeo and Juliet. Ibid.

Laird, D. The generation of style in Romeo and Juliet. JEGP 63 1964.

Evans, R. O. The osier cage: rhetorical devices in Romeo and Juliet. Lexington Kentucky 1966.

Peterson, D. L. Romeo and Juliet and the art of moral navigation. In Pacific Coast studies in Shakespeare, ed W. F. McNeir and T. N. Greenfield, Portland 1966.

Stewart, S. Romeo and necessity. Ibid.

Adams, B. B. The prudence of Prince Escalus. ELH 35 1968.

Goldberg, M. A. The multiple masks of Romeo: towards a new Shakespearean production. Antioch Rev 28 1968.

Gray, J. C. Romeo and Juliet and some Renaissance notions of love, time and death. Dalhousie Rev 48 1968.

Leunberg, I. Shakespeares Romeo und Julia. Munich 1968.

Muir, K. The imagery of Romeo and Juliet. Literary Half-Yearly (Mysore) 9 1968.

Parker, D. H. Light and dark imagery in Romeo and Juliet. Queen's Quart 75 1968.

Johnson, R. C. Four young men: Romeo and Juliet. Univ Rev 36 1969.

Nevo, R. Tragic form in Romeo and Juliet. Stud in Eng Lit 1500–1900 9 1969.

Pearce, T. M. Romeo and Juliet as situation ethics. In Shakespeare in the Southwest, ed T. J. Stafford, Austin 1969.

Berman, R. The two orders of Romeo and Juliet. Moderna Språk 64 1970.

Mason, H. A. In his Shakespeare's tragedies of love, 1970.

Snyder, S. Romeo and Juliet: comedy into tragedy. EC 20 1970.

Richard II

The tragedie of King Richard the Second, as it hath beene publikely acted by the Right Honourable the Lorde Chamberlaine his servants; London, printed by Valentine Simmes for Androw Wise, and are to be sold at his shop in Paules Church yard at the signe of the Angel. 1597 (anon); ed J. O. Halliwell (-Phillips) 1862 (facs); ed W. A. Harrison 1888 (facs); ed W. W. Greg, rev C. Hinman, Oxford 1966 (facs).

The tragedie of King Richard the Second, by William Shakespeare. 1598, ed J. O. Halliwell (-Phillipps) 1869 (facs); 1598, ed A. W. Pollard 1916 (facs); 1608, 1608 (as 'with new additions of the Parliament Sceane, and the deposing of King Richard', though the earlier issue also contains the new scene); ed J. O. Halliwell (-Phillipps) 1858 (facs); ed W. A. Harrison 1888; 1615, ed J. O. Halliwell (-Phillipps) 1870 (facs); 1634, ed P. A. Daniel 1887 (facs).

Modern Editions

E. K. Chambers 1891 (Falcon); A. Waites, New York 1892 (Bankside; parallel texts of 4° 1 and Folio 1); C. H. Herford 1893 (Warwick); I. B. John 1912 (Arden); L. M. Buell, New Haven 1921 (Yale); J. D. Wilson, Cambridge 1939 (New Cambridge); T. Spencer, New York 1949 (Crofts); M. W. Black, Philadelphia 1955 (New Variorum); P. Ure 1956 (New Arden); R. P. Petersson, New Haven 1957 (Yale); M. W. Black, Baltimore 1957 (Pelican); F. Fergusson and C. J. Sisson, New York 1961 (Laurel); L. B. Wright and V. A. LaMar, New York 1962 (Folger); K. Muir, New York 1963 (Signet); W. W. Greg, rev C. Hinman, Oxford 1966 (1597 4°); G. L. Kittredge, rev I. Ribner, Waltham Mass 1966; S. Wells 1969 (New Penguin).

Studies

Shakspere's Holinshed. Ed W. G. Boswell-Stone 1896.

Plomer, H. R. An examination of some existing copies of Hayward's King Henrie IV. Library 1st ser 3 1902.

Moorman, F. W. Shakespeare's history-plays and Daniel's Civile wars. Sh Jb 40 1904.

Swinburne, A. C. In Three plays of Shakespeare, 1909.

Pollard, A. W. The tragedy of King Richard II. 1916. Introd to facs of 4°3.

Kohler, J. Die Staatsidee Shakespeares in Richard II. Sh Jb 53 1917.

Chambers, E. K. The date of Richard II. RES 1 1925.

Albright, E. M. Shakespeare's Richard II and the Essex conspiracy. PMLA 42 1927.

—— Shakespeare's Richard II, Hayward's history of Henry IV and the Essex conspiracy. PMLA 46 1931.

Kuhl, E. P. Shakespeare and Hayward. SP 25 1928.

Heffner, R. Shakespeare, Hayward and Essex. PMLA 45 1930.

Dodson, S. C. The Northumberland of Shakespeare and Holinshed. SE 1939.

Tillotson, K. Drayton and Richard II 1597–1600. RES 15 1939.

Doran, M. Imagery in Richard II and Henry IV. MLR 37 1942.

Draper, J. W. The character of Richard II. PQ 21 1942.

Altick, R. D. Symphonic imagery in Richard II. PMLA 62 1947.

Brereton, J. le G. Shakespeare's Richard II. In his Writings on Elizabethan drama, Melbourne 1948.

—— Some notes on Richard II. Ibid.

Black, M. W. The sources of Shakespeare's Richard II. In J. Q. Adams memorial studies, Washington 1948.

Jorgensen, P. A. Vertical patterns in Richard II. Sh Assoc Bull 23 1948.

Kliger, S. The sun imagery in Richard II. SP 45 1948.

Ribner, I. Bolingbroke: a true Machiavellian. MLQ 9 1948.

Law, R. A. Deviations from Holinshed in Richard II. SE 29 1950.

Leon, H. J. Classical sources for the garden scene in Richard II. PQ 29 1950.

Stirling, B. Bolingbroke's 'decision'. Sh Quart 2 1951.

Bonnard, G. A. The actor in Richard II. Sh Jb 87–8 1952.

Dean, L. F. Richard II: the state and the image of the theater. PMLA 67 1952.

Hasker, R. E. The copy for the First Folio Richard II. SB 5 1953.

Ure, P. Two passages in Sylvester's Du Bartas and their bearing on Shakespeare's Richard II. N & Q Sept 1953.

—— Shakespeare's play and the French sources of Holinshed's and Stow's account of Richard II. N & Q Oct 1953.

Bogard, T. Shakespeare's second Richard. PMLA 70 1955.

Suzman, A. Imagery and symbolism in Richard II. Sh Quart 7 1956.

Thompson, K. F. Richard II: martyr. Sh Quart 8 1957.

McPeek, J. A. S. Richard and his shadow world. Amer Imago 15 1958.

Quinn, M. The King is not himself: the personal tragedy of Richard II. SP 56 1959.

Hill, R. F. Dramatic techniques and interpretations in Richard II. In Early Shakespeare, ed J. R. Brown and B. Harris 1961.

Provost, F. On justice and the music in Richard II and King Lear. Annuale Mediaevale 2 1961.

—— The sorrows of Shakespeare's Richard II. In Studies in English Renaissance literature, ed W. F. McNeir, Baton Rouge 1962.

Anderson, D. K. Richard II and Perkin Warbeck. Sh Quart 13 1962. Shakespeare's influence on Ford.

Berman, R. Richard II: the shaping of love. Moderna Språk 58 1964.

Cutts, J. P. Christian and classical imagery in Richard II. Universitas (Detroit) 2 1964.

Halstead, W. L. Artifice and artistry in Richard II and Othello. In Sweet smoke of rhetoric, ed N. Grimes and J. A. Reynolds, Coral Gables 1964.

Hockey, D. C. A world of rhetoric in Richard II. Sh Quart 15 1964.

Reiman, D. H. Appearance, reality and moral order in Richard II. MLQ 25 1964.

Yamamoto, T. The verbal structure of Richard II. Zeitschrift für Anglistik und Amerikanistik 12 1964.

Elliott, J. R. Richard II and the medieval. Renaissance Papers 1965.

— History and tragedy in Richard II. Stud in Eng Lit 1500–1900 8 1968.

Speaight, R. Shakespeare and the political spectrum, as illustrated by Richard II. In Stratford papers on Shakespeare 1964, ed B. W. Jackson, Toronto 1965.

Traversi, D. Richard II. Ibid.

Humphreys, A. R. Richard II. 1967.

Grabes, H. The tragedie of King Richard II. Poetica (Munich) 2 1968.

Hawkes, T. The word against the word: the role of language in Richard II. Lang & Style (Carbondale) 2 1969.

Jeffares, A. N. In one person many people: King Richard II. In The morality of art: essays presented to G. Wilson Knight, 1969.

Montgomery, R. L. The dimensions of time in Richard II. Sh Stud 4 1969.

Grivelet, M. Shakespeare's 'war with time': the sonnets and Richard II. Sh Survey 23 1970.

Harris, K. M. Sun and water imagery in Richard II. Sh Quart 21 1970.

MacIsaac, W. J. The three cousins in Richard II. Sh Quart 22 1971.

A Midsummer Night's Dream

A midsommer nights dreame, as it hath beene sundry times publickely acted by the Right Honourable the Lord Chamberlaine his servants; written by William Shakespeare; imprinted at London, for Thomas Fisher, and are to be soulde at his shoppe, at the signe of the White Hart in Fleete-streete. 1600; ed J. O. Halliwell (-Phillipps) 1864 (facs); ed J. W. Ebsworth 1880 (facs).

A midsommer nights dreame, as it hath beene sundry times publikely acted by the Right Honourable the Lord Chamberlaine his servants; written by William Shakespeare; printed by James Roberts. 1600 (for 1619); ed J. O. Halliwell (-Phillipps) 1865 (facs); ed J. W. Ebsworth 1880 (facs).

Modern Editions

W. Reynolds, New York 1890 (Bankside; parallel texts of 4° and Folio 1); H. H. Furness, Philadelphia 1895 (New Variorum); E. K. Chambers 1897 (Warwick); H. Cuningham 1905 (Arden); W. H. Durham, New Haven 1918 (Yale); A. T. Quiller-Couch and J. D. Wilson, Cambridge 1924 (New Cambridge); G. L. Kittredge, Boston 1939; F. W. Robinson, Melbourne 1940; L. B. Wright and V. A. LaMar, New York 1958 (Folger); M. Doran, Baltimore 1959 (Pelican); F. Fergusson and C. J. Sisson, New York 1960 (Laurel); W. Clemen, New York 1963 (Signet); G. L. Kittredge, rev I. Ribner, Waltham Mass 1967; S. Wells 1967 (New Penguin).

Studies

Sidgwick, F. The sources and analogues of A midsummer night's dream. 1908 (Sh Classics).

Halliwell (-Phillipps), J. O. An introduction to Shakespeare's Midsummer night's dream. 1841.

— Illustrations of the fairy mythology of Shakespeare's Midsummer night's dream. 1845 (Sh Soc).

— Memoranda on Shakespeare's Midsummer night's dream. 1879.

Halpin, N. J. Oberon's vision in the Midsummer night's dream illustrated by a comparison with Lyly's Endymion. 1843 (Sh Soc).

Flügel, E. Pyramys and Tysbe. Anglia 12 1889.

Hart, G. Die Pyramus-und-Thisbe Saga. Passau 1889.

Tobler, R. Shakespeares Sommernachtstraum und Montemayors Dramen. Sh Jb 34 1898.

Vollhardt, W. Die Beziehungen des Sommernachtstraums zum italienischen Schäferdrama. Leipzig 1899.

Reich, H. Der Mann mit dem Eselkopf: ein Mimodrama vom klassischen Altertum verfolgt bis auf Shakespeare. Sh Jb 40 1904.

Greg, W. W. On certain false dates in Shakespearian quartos. Library 1st ser 9 1908.

Hemingway, S. B. The relation of Midsummer night's dream to Romeo and Juliet. MLN 26 1911.

Chambers, E. K. The occasion of A midsummer night's dream. In A book of homage to Shakespeare, 1916.

Lefranc, A. La réalité dans A midsummer night's dream. In Mélanges Bernard Bouvier, Paris 1920.

Rickert, E. Political propaganda and satire in A midsummer night's dream. MP 21 1923.

Priestley, J. B. Bully Bottom. In his English comic characters, 1925.

Spencer, H. A nice derangement. MLR 25 1930.

van Kranendonk, A. G. Spenserian echoes in A midsummer night's dream. E Studies 14 1932.

Charlton, H. B. A midsummer night's dream. Bull John Rylands Lib 17 1933.

Cambillard, C. Le songe d'une nuit d'été: thème astrologique. Etudes Anglaises 3 1939.

Legouis, E. La psychologie dans Le songe d'une nuit d'été. Ibid.

Miller, D. C. Titania and the changeling. E Studies 22 1939.

Law, R. A. The 'preconceived pattern' of A midsummer night's dream. SE 23 1943.

Bethurum, D. Shakespeare's comment on medieval romance in A midsummer night's dream. MLN 60 1945.

Generosa, Sr M. Apuleius and A midsummer night's dream: analogue or source, which? SP 42 1945.

Poirier, M. Sidney's influence upon A midsummer night's dream. SP 44 1947.

Schanzer, E. The central theme of A midsummer night's dream. UTQ 20 1951.

— The moon and the fairies in A midsummer night's dream. UTQ 24 1955.

Siegel, P. N. A midsummer night's dream and the wedding guests. Sh Quart 4 1953.

Bonnard, G. A. Shakespeare's purpose in Midsummer-night's dream. Sh Jb 92 1956.

Dillingham, W. B. Bottom: the third ingredient. Emory Univ Quart 12 1956.

Fisher, P. F. The argument of A midsummer night's dream. Sh Quart 8 1957.

Olson, P. A. A midsummer night's dream and the meaning of Court marriage. ELH 24 1957.

Briggs, K. M. In her Anatomy of Puck, 1959.

Zitner, S. P. The worlds of A midsummer night's dream. South Atlantic Quart 59 1960.

Doran, M. A midsummer night's dream: a metamorphosis. Rice Inst Pamphlet 46 1961.

Kersten, D. Shakespeares Puck. Sh Jb 98 1962.

Staton, W. F. Ovidian elements in A midsummer night's dream. HLQ 26 1963.

Dent, R. W. Imagination in A midsummer night's dream. In Shakespeare 400, ed J. G. McManaway, New York 1964.

Herbert, T. W. Invitations to cosmic laughter in A midsummer night's dream. In Shakespearean essays, ed A. Thaler and N. Sanders, Knoxville 1964.

Robinson, J. W. Palpable hot ice: dramatic burlesque in A midsummer night's dream. SP 61 1964.

Calderwood, J. L. A midsummer night's dream: the illusion of drama. MLQ 26 1965.

Young, D. P. Something of great constancy: the art of A midsummer night's dream. New Haven 1966.

Allen, J. A. Bottom and Titania. Sh Quart 18 1967.

Fender, S. Shakespeare: A midsummer night's dream. 1968.

Greenfield, T. N. A midsummer night's dream and the Praise of folly. Comparative Lit 20 1968.

Robinson, J. E. The ritual and rhetoric of A midsummer night's dream. PMLA 83 1968.

Homan, S. R. The single world of A midsummer night's dream. Bucknell Rev 17 1969.

Taylor, M. The darker purpose of A midsummer night's dream. Stud in Eng Lit 1500–1900 9 1969.

Willson, R. F. Golding's Metamorphoses and Shakespeare's burlesque method in A midsummer night's dream. Eng Lang Notes 7 1969.

Cody, R. In his Landscape of the mind, Oxford, 1970.

Hassel, R. C. Shakespeare's comic epilogues: invitations to festive communion. Sh Jb (Heidelberg) 1970.

Weiss, T. In his Breath of clowns and kings: Shakespeare's early comedies and histories, 1971.

King John

In First Folio, 1623.

Modern Editions

F. G. Fleay 1878; A. Morgan, New York 1892 (Bankside; parallel texts); G. C. Moore Smith 1900 (Warwick); I. B. John 1907 (Arden); H. H. Furness jr, Philadelphia 1919 (New Variorum); S. T. Williams, New Haven 1927 (Yale); J. D. Wilson, Cambridge 1936 (New Cambridge); E. A. J. Honigmann 1954 (New Arden); F. Fergusson and C. J. Sisson, New York 1963 (Laurel); W. H. Matchett, New York 1963 (Signet); G. L. Kittredge, rev I. Ribner, Waltham Mass 1967.

Studies

The troublesome raigne of John King of England. 1591; The second part of the Troublesome raigne of King John, 1591, ed F. J. Furnivall 2 pts 1888 (facs); ed J. S. Farmer, TFT 1911, rptd F. J. Furnivall and J. Munro 1913; 1611 (as First and second part), 1622.

Smith, G. C. Moore. Shakespeare's King John and the Troublesome raigne. In An English miscellany presented to Dr [F. J.] Furnivall, Oxford 1901.

Liebermann, F. Shakespeare als Bearbeiter des King John. Archiv 142–3 1921–2.

Harrison, G. B. Shakespeare's topical significances 1: King John. TLS 13 Nov 1930.

Greenewald, G. M. Shakespeare's attitude towards the Catholic Church in King John. Washington 1938.

Ash, D. F. Anglo-French relations in King John. Etudes Anglaises 3 1939.

Petit-Dutaillis, C. Un héros shakespearien: le Bâtard de Falconbridge. Académie des Inscriptions: comptes rendus. 1943.

— Le roi Jean et Shakespeare. Paris 1945.

Elson, J. Studies in the King John plays. In J. Q. Adams memorial studies, Washington 1948.

Salter, F. M. The problem of King John. Trans Royal Soc of Canada 3rd ser 43 1949.

Bonjour, A. The road to Swinstead Abbey: a study of the sense and structure of King John. ELH 18 1951.

— Bastinado for the Bastard? E Studies 45 1964.

Pettet, E. C. Hot irons and fever: a note on some of the imagery of King John. EC 4 1954.

Law, R. A. On the date of King John. SP 54 1957.

— King John and King Leir. Texas Stud in Lit & Lang 1 1960.

Calderwood, J. L. Commodity and honour in King John. UTQ 29 1960.

Sisson, C. J. King John: a history play for Elizabethans. In Stratford papers on Shakespeare, ed B. W. Jackson, Toronto 1961.

Matchett, W. H. Richard's divided heritage in King John. EC 12 1962.

Shattuck, C. H. (ed). William Charles Macready's King John: a facsimile prompt-book. Urbana 1962.

Elliott, J. R. Shakespeare and the double image of King John. Sh Stud 1 1965.

Burckhardt, S. King John: the ordering of the present time. ELH 33 1966.

Schlösser, A. Shakespeares King John als geschichtliche Lektion. Zeitschrift für Anglistik und Amerikanistik 14 1966.

Boklund, G. The troublesome ending of King John. Studia Neophilologica 40 1968.

Simmons, J. L. Shakespeare's King John and its source: coherence, pattern and vision. Tulane Stud in Eng 17 1969.

Price, J. R. King John and the problematic art. Sh Quart 21 1970.

Weiss, T. In his Breath of clowns and kings: Shakespeare's early comedies and histories, 1971.

The Merchant of Venice

The most excellent historie of the merchant of Venice, with the extreme crueltie of Shylocke the Jewe towards the sayd merchant, in cutting a just pound of his flesh, and the obtayning of Portia by the choyse of three chests; as it hath beene divers times acted by the Lord Chamberlaine his servants; written by William Shakespeare; at London, printed by J[ames] R[oberts] for Thomas Heyes, and are to be sold in Paules Churchyard, at the signe of the Greene Dragon. 1600; ed J. O. Halliwell (-Phillipps) 1870 (facs); ed F. J. Furnivall 1887 (facs); ed W. W. Greg, Oxford 1939 (facs).

The excellent history of the merchant of Venice, with the extreme cruelty of Shylocke the Jew towards the saide merchant in cutting a just pound of his flesh, and the obtaining of Portia, by the choyse of three caskets; written by W. Shakespeare; printed by J. Roberts. 1600 (for 1619), ed J. O. Halliwell (-Phillipps) 1865 (facs); ed F. J. Furnivall 1880 (facs); 1637, 1652.

Modern Editions

W. Reynolds, New York 1888 (Bankside; parallel texts of 4° and Folio I); H. H. Furness, Philadelphia 1888 (New Variorum); C. K. Pooler 1905 (Arden); W. L. Phelps, New Haven 1923 (Yale); A. T. Quiller-Couch and J. D. Wilson, Cambridge 1926 (New Cambridge); G. C. Taylor and R. Smith, Boston 1936 (interlinear); W. W. Greg, Oxford 1939 (Hayes 4°I); J. R. Brown 1955 (New Arden); L. B. Wright and V. L. Freund, New York 1957 (Folger); F. Fergusson and C. J. Sisson, New York 1958 (Laurel); B. Stirling, Baltimore 1959 (Pelican); A. D. Richardson, New Haven 1960 (Yale); K. Myrick, York 1965 (Signet); G. L. Kittredge, rev I. Ribner, Waltham Mass 1966; W. M. Merchant 1967 (New Penguin).

For a concordance see T. H. Howard-Hill, Oxford 1970.

Studies

Lee, S. The original of Shylock. GM Feb 1880.

— Elizabethan England and the Jews. Trans New Sh Soc 1888.

Clouston, W. A. Shylock and his predecessors. Academy 18 June, 6 Aug 1887.

Hales, J. W. Shakespeare and the Jews. EHR 9 1894.

Dimock, A. The conspiracy of Dr Lopez. Ibid.

Stoll, E. E. Shylock. JEGP 10 1911; expanded in his Shakespeare studies, New York 1927.

— Shakespeare's Jew. UTQ 8 1939.

Creizenach, W. Betrachtungen über den Kaufmann von Venedig. Sh Jb 51 1915.

Baskervill, C. R. Bassanio as an ideal lover. In [J. M.] Manly anniversary studies, Chicago 1923.

van Dam, B. A. P. The text of the Merchant of Venice. Neophilologus 13 1927.

Small, S. A. Shaksperean character interpretation: the Merchant of Venice. Göttingen 1927.

— The Jew. MLR 26 1931.

Brown, B. D. Medieval prototypes of Lorenzo and Jessica. MLN 44 1929.

Tretiak, A. The merchant of Venice and the alien question. RES 5 1929.

Granville-Barker, H. In his Prefaces to Shakespeare: series 2, 1930.

Schlauch, M. The pound of flesh story in the north. JEGP 30 1931.

Cardozo, J. L. The background of Shakespeare's Merchant of Venice. E Studies 14 1932.

Roth, C. The background of Shylock. RES 9 1933.

Wood, F. T. The merchant of Venice in the eighteenth century. E Studies 15 1933.

Charlton, H. B. Shakespeare's Jew. Bull John Rylands Lib 18 1934.

Wilson, J. H. Granville's 'stock-jobbing Jew'. PQ 13 1934.

Digeon, A. Le jeu de l'amour et de l'amitié dans le Marchand de Venise. Revue Anglo-américaine 13 1936.

Martin, B. Shakespeare's Shylock. Dalhousie Rev 17 1937.

Pettigrew, H. P. Bassanio: the Elizabethan lover. PQ 16 1937.

Weigelin, E. Die gerichtliche Entscheidung in Shakespeares Kaufmann von Venedig. Die Neueren Sprachen 45 1937.

Flasdieck, H. M. Jüdisches im und zum Merchant of Venice. Neuphilologische Monatsschrift 9 1938.

Traver, H. I will try confusions with him. Sh Assoc Bull 13 1938.

Hannigan, J. E. Shylock and Portia. Sh Assoc Bull 14 1939.

Draper, J. W. The psychology of Shylock. Bull History of Medicine 8 1940.

— The tempo of Shylock's speech. JEGP 44 1945.

Ariail, J. M. In defence of Bassanio. Sh Assoc Bull 16 1941.

Murry, J. M. The significance of Shylock. Adelphi 22 1945.

Pettet, E. C. The merchant of Venice and the problem of usury. E & S 31 1945.

West, E. J. The use of contrast in the Merchant of Venice. Sh Assoc Bull 21 1946.

Sinsheimer, H. Shylock: the history of a character or the myth of the Jew. 1947.

Bishop, D. H. Shylock's humour. Sh Assoc Bull 23 1948.

Natan, N. Three notes on the Merchant of Venice. Ibid.

— Shylock, Jacob and God's judgment. Sh Quart 1 1950.

Graham, C. B. Standards of value in the Merchant of Venice. Sh Quart 4 1953.

Brown, J. R. The compositors of Hamlet Q 2 and the Merchant of Venice. SB 7 1955.

McKenzie, D. F. Compositor B's role in the Merchant of Venice Q 2 1619. SB 12 1959.

Bloom, A. Shakespeare on Jew and Christian: an interpretation of the Merchant of Venice. Social Research 30 1960.

Midgley, G. The merchant of Venice: a reconsideration. EC 10 1960.

Hurrell, J. D. Love and friendship in the Merchant of Venice. Texas Stud in Lit & Lang 3 1961.

Lelyveld, T. Shylock on the stage. Cleveland 1961.

Smith, J. H. Shylock: 'devil incarnation' or 'poor man ... wronged'? JEGP 60 1961.

Burckhardt, S. The merchant of Venice: the gentle bond. ELH 29 1962.

Grebanier, B. The truth about Shylock. New York 1962.

Whitfield, C. Sir Lewis Lewkenor and the Merchant of Venice: a suggested connexion. N & Q April 1964.

Mitchell, C. The conscience of Venice: Shakespeare's merchant. JEGP 63 1964.

Smith, W. D. Shakespeare's Shylock. Sh Quart 15 1964.

Fujimara, T. H. Mode and structure in the Merchant of Venice. PMLA 81 1966.

Hapgood, R. Portia and the Merchant of Venice: the gentle bond. MLQ 28 1967.

Bronstein, H. Shakespeare, the Jews and the Merchant of Venice. Sh Quart 20 1969.

Donow, H. S. Shakespeare's caskets: unity in the Merchant of Venice. Sh Stud 4 1969.

Felheim, M. The merchant of Venice. Ibid.

Cooper, J. R. Shylock's humanity. Sh Quart 21 1970.

Hyman, L. W. The rival lovers in the Merchant of Venice. Ibid.

Echeruo, M. J. C. Shylock and the 'conditioned imagination'. Sh Quart 22 1971.

1, 2 Henry IV
Part 1

There are 4 leaves in the Folger collection which J. O. Halliwell (-Phillipps) showed to be a portion of the first and hitherto unknown edn of the First Part, pbd by Wise early in the year 1598.

The history of Henrie the Fourth; with the battell at Shrewsburie betweene the King and Lord Henry Percy, surnamed Henrie Hotspur of the North; with the humorous conceits of Sir John Falstalffe; at London, printed by P. S[hort] for Andrew Wise, dwelling in Paules churchyard, at the signe of the Angell. 1598; ed J. O. Halliwell (-Phillipps) 1866 (facs); ed H. A. Evans 1881 (facs); ed W. W. Greg, rev C. Hinman, Oxford 1966 (facs).

The history of Henrie the Fourth, with the battell at Shrewsburie betweene the King and Lord Henry Percy, surnamed Henry Hotspur of the North; with the humorous conceits of Sir John Falstalffe; newly corrected by W. Shake-speare. 1599, ed J. O. Halliwell (-Phillipps) 1861 (facs); 1604, ed Halliwell 1871 (facs); 1608, ed Halliwell 1867 (facs); 1613, ed Halliwell 1867 (facs); 1622, 1632, 1639, 1700.

Modern Editions

W. H. Fleming, New York 1890 (Bankside; parallel texts of 4° 1 and Folio 1); R. P. Cowl and A. E. Morgan 1914 (Arden); S. B. Hemingway, New Haven 1917 (Yale), Philadelphia 1936 (New Variorum); G. L. Kittredge, Boston 1940; R. C. Bald, New York 1946 (Crofts); J. D. Wilson, Cambridge 1946 (New Cambridge); M. A. Shaaber, Baltimore 1957 (Pelican); F. Fergusson and C. J. Sisson, New York 1959 (Laurel); A. R. Humphreys 1960 (New Arden); L. B. Wright and V. A. LaMar, New York 1961 (Folger); M. Mack, New York 1965 (Signet); W. W. Greg, rev C. Hinman, Oxford 1966 (facs of 4° 1); G. L. Kittredge, rev I. Ribner, Waltham Mass 1966; P. H. Davison 1968 (New Penguin).

Part 2

The second part of Henrie the Fourth, continuing to his death, and coronation of Henrie the Fift, with the humours of Sir John Falstaffe and swaggering Pistoll; as it hath been sundrie times publikely acted by the Right Honourable the Lord Chamberlaine his servants written by William Shakespeare; London, printed by V[alentine] S[immes] for Andrew Wise and William Aspley. 1600 (III. i, originally omitted, is found in some copies in cancel sheet of 6 leaves); ed J. O. Halliwell (-Phillipps) 1866 (facs); ed H. A. Evans 1882 (facs).

Modern Editions

W. H. Fleming, New York 1890 (Bankside; parallel texts of 4° and Folio 1); S. B. Hemingway, New Haven 1921 (Yale); R. P. Cowl 1923 (Arden); M. A. Shaaber, Philadelphia 1940 (New Variorum); J. D. Wilson, Cambridge 1946 (New Cambridge); A. Chester, Baltimore 1957 (Pelican); L. B. Wright and V. A. LaMar, New York 1962 (Laurel); A. R. Humphreys 1966 (New Arden); G. L. Kittredge, rev I. Ribner, Waltham Mass 1966.

Parts 1 and 2

King Henry the Fourth; printed from a contemporary ms circa 1610. Ed J. O. Halliwell (-Phillipps) 1845 (Shakespeare Soc); The Dering ms, 'a compilation in a 17th-century hand of scenes from Q 5 of Part 1 and Q of Part 2, probably for private performance, with alterations in the hand of Sir Edward Dering (1598-1644) of Surrenden, Kent' (Chambers).

Studies

The famous victories of Henry the Fifth: containing the honourable battell of Agincourt. 1598; ed P. A. Daniel 1887 (facs).

Shakspere's Holinshed. Ed W. G. Boswell-Stone 1896.

Halliwell (-Phillipps), J. O. On the character of Sir John Falstaff, as originally exhibited by Shakespeare in the two parts of King Henry IV. 1841.

Solly-Flood, F. The story of Prince Henry of Monmouth and Chief-Justice Gascoign. Trans Royal Historical Soc 3 1886.

Moorman, F. W. Shakespeare's history-plays and Daniel's Civile wars. Sh Jb 40 1904.

Baeske, W. Oldcastle-Falstaff in der englischen Literatur bis zu Shakespeare. Berlin 1905.

Ainger, A. Sir John Falstaff. In his Lectures and essays, 1905.

Bradley, A. C. The rejection of Falstaff. In his Oxford lectures on poetry, 1909.

Harcourt, L. W. The two Sir John Falstaffs. Trans Royal Historical Soc 4 1910.

Kingsford, C. L. The first English life of Henry V. 1911.

Ax, H. The relation of Shakespeare's Henry IV to Holinshed. Freiburg 1912.

Stoll, E. E. Falstaff. MP 12 1914.

Cunliffe, J. W. The character of Henry V as Prince and King. In Columbia Shakespearian studies, New York 1916.

Baker, H. T. The two Falstaffs. MLN 34 1919.

Tolman, A. H. Why did Shakespeare create Falstaff? PMLA 34 1919.

Pollard, A. W. The variant settings in 2 Henry IV and their spellings. TLS 21 Oct 1920.

Monaghan, J. Falstaff and his forebears. SP 18 1921.

Spargo, J. W. An interpretation of Falstaff. Washington Univ Stud 9 1922.

Morgan, A. E. Some problems of Shakespeare's Henry IV. Sh Assoc Pamphlets 1924.

Cowl, R. P. Some literary allusions in Henry IV. TLS 26 March 1925.

— Echoes of Henry IV in Elizabethan drama. TLS 22 Oct 1925.

— Some 'echoes' in Elizabethan drama of Shakespeare's King Henry IV, pts 1 and 2, considered in relation to the text of those plays. Helsinki 1926.

— King Henry IV and other plays: an experiment with 'echoes'. 1927.

— Notes on the text of King Henry IV. 1927.

— Sources of the text of King Henry IV. 1929.

Priestley, J. B. Falstaff and his circle. In his English comic characters, 1925.

Morris, J. E. The date of Henry IV. TLS 28 Jan 1926.

Bowling, W. G. The wild Prince Hal in legend and literature. Washington Univ Stud 13 1926.

Knowlton, E. C. Falstaff redux. JEGP 25 1926.

Law, R. A. Structural unity in the two parts of Henry IV. SP 24 1927.

— The composition of Shakespeare's Lancastrian trilogy. Texas Stud in Lit & Lang 3 1961.

Newdigate, B. H. Falstaff, Shallow and the Stratford musters. London Mercury Feb 1927.

Schücking, L. L. The quarto of King Henry IV pt 2. TLS 25 Sept 1930.

Taylor, M. A. Shakespeare and Gloucestershire. RES 7 1931.

Hartmann, H. Prince Hal's 'shew of zeale'. PMLA 46 1931.

Cazamian, L. The humor of Falstaff. Johns Hopkins Alumni Mag 23 1933.

Knights, L. C. Notes on comedy. Scrutiny 2 1933.

Charlton, H. B. Falstaff. Bull John Rylands Lib 19 1935.

Elson, J. J. The non-Shakespearean Richard II and Henry IV pt 1. SP 32 1935.

Hart, A. Was the second part of King Henry IV censored? In Shakespeare and the homilies, Melbourne 1935.

Purcell, J. M. N & Q 1 June 1935. On dating.

Boughner, D. C. Pistol and the roaring boys. Sh Assoc Bull 11 1936.

— Traditional elements in Falstaff. JEGP 43 1944.

— Vice, braggart and Falstaff. Anglia 72 1954.

Starnes, D. T. More about the Prince Hal legend. PQ 15 1936.

Petsch, R. Shakespeares König Heinrich IV und das Geschichtsdrama in England. Sh Jb 73 1937.

Draper, J. W. Falstaff and the Plautine parasite. Classical Jnl 33 1938.

— 'A fool and jester'. MLQ 7 1946.

Shirley, J. W. Falstaff: an Elizabethan glutton. PQ 17 1938.

Dodson, S. C. The Northumberland of Shakespeare and Holinshed. SE 19 1939.

O'Connor, W. V. When Elizabethans laughed. Sh Assoc Bull 14 1939.

Small, S. A. The reflective element in Falstaff. Ibid.

— Hotspur and Falstaff. Sh Assoc Bull 16 1941.

Doran, M. Imagery in Richard II and Henry IV. MLR 37 1942.

King, A. H. Some notes on ambiguity in 1 Henry IV. Studia Neophilologica 14 1942.

Sims, R. E. The green old age of Falstaff. Bull History of Medicine 13 1943.

Wilson, J. D. The fortunes of Falstaff. Cambridge 1943.

Dean, L. F. Shakespeare's treatment of conventional ideas. Sewanee Rev 52 1944.

Spencer, B. T. 2 Henry IV and the theme of time. UTQ 13 1944.

— The stasis of Henry IV, pt 2. Tennessee Stud in Lit 6 1961.

Koller, K. Falstaff and the art of dying. MLN 60 1945.

Brooks, C. and R. B. Heilman. Understanding drama. New York 1945. Text of pt 1 with critical discussion.

Levin, H. Falstaff uncolted. MLN 61 1946.

McManaway, J. G. The cancel in the quarto of 2 Henry IV. In Studies in honor of A. H. R. Fairchild, Columbia Missouri 1946.

Oliver, L. M. Sir John Oldcastle: legend or literature? Library 5th ser 1 1946.

Salter, F. M. The play within the play of 1 Henry IV. Trans Royal Soc of Canada 3rd ser 40 1946.

Waldock, A. J. A. The men in buckram. RES 23 1947.

Hotson, L. Ancient Pistol. Yale Rev 38 1948; rptd in his Shakespeare's sonnets dated, 1949.

Shaaber, M. A. The unity of Henry IV. In J. Q. Adams memorial studies, Washington 1948.

Traversi, D. A. 1 Henry IV; 2 Henry IV. Scrutiny 15 1948.

Brennecke, E. Shakespeare's 'singing man of Windsor'. PMLA 66 1951.

Walker, A. Quarto copy and the 1623 folio: 2 Henry IV. RES new ser 2 1951.

— The folio text of 1 Henry IV. SB 6 1954.

Hunter, W. B. Falstaff. South Atlantic Quart 50 1951.

Cain, H. E. Further light on the relation of 1 and 2 Henry IV. Sh Quart 3 1952.

Zeeveld, W. G. 'Food for powder'; 'food for worms'. Ibid.

Empson, W. Falstaff and Mr Dover Wilson. Kenyon Rev 15 1953.

Leech, C. The unity of 2 Henry IV. Sh Survey 6 1953.

Sprague, A. C. Gadshill revisited. Sh Quart 4 1953.

Hunter, G. K. Henry IV and the Elizabethan two-part play. RES new ser 5 1954.

— Shakespeare's politics and the rejection of Falstaff. CQ 1 1959.

Fiehler, R. How Oldcastle became Falstaff. MLQ 16 1955.

Shaaber, M. A. The folio text of 2 Henry IV. Sh Quart 6 1955.

Evans, G. B. The Dering ms of Shakespeare's Henry IV and Sir Edward Dering. JEGP 54 1955.

—— (ed). Supplement to Henry IV pt 1. Sh Quart 7 1956. Suppl to 1936 New Variorum.

Jenkins, H. The structural problem in Shakespeare's Henry IV. 1956.

Spivack, B. Falstaff and the Psychomachia. Sh Quart 8 1957.

Auden, W. H. The fallen city: some reflections on Shakespeare's Henry IV. Encounter Nov 1959.

McNamara, A. M. Henry IV: the King as protagonist. Sh Quart 10 1959.

Bradbrook, M. C. The old lad of the castle. Sh Quart 11 1960.

Dorius, R. J. A little more than a little. Ibid.

Jorgensen, P. A. 'Redeeming time' in Shakespeare's Henry IV. Tennessee Stud in Lit 5 1960.

—— The 'dastardly treachery' of Prince John of Lancaster. PMLA 76 1961.

Dickinson, H. The reformation of Prince Hal. Sh Quart 12 1961.

Evans, G. L. The comical-tragical-historical method: Henry IV. In Early Shakespeare, ed J. R. Brown and B. Harris 1961.

Reno, R. H. Hotspur: the integration of character and theme. Renaissance Papers 1962.

Tomlinson, M. Henry IV. Melbourne Critical Rev 6 1963.

Fish, C. Henry IV: Shakespeare and Holinshed. SP 61 1964.

Schlösser, A. Legende, Wunschbild und Wirklichkeit in Heinrich IV. Zeitschrift für Anglistik und Amerikanistik 12 1964.

Barish, J. A. The turning away of Prince Hal. Sh Stud 1 1965.

Berman, R. The nature of guilt in the Henry IV plays. Ibid.

Hapgood, R. Falstaff's vocation. Sh Quart 16 1965.

Toliver, H. E. Falstaff, the Prince and the history play. Ibid.

Knowles, R. Unquiet and the double plot of 2 Henry IV. Sh Stud 2 1966.

Newman, F. B. The rejection of Falstaff and the rigorous charity of the King. Ibid.

Scoufos, A. L. The 'martyrdom' of Falstaff. Ibid.

—— Gads Hill and the structure of comic satire. Sh Stud 5 1970.

La Branche, A. If thou wert sensible of courtesy: private and public virtue in 1 Henry IV. Sh Quart 17 1966.

Landt, D. B. The ancestry of Sir John Falstaff. Ibid.

McNeir, W. F. Structure and theme in the first tavern scene of 1 Henry IV. In Pacific Coast studies in Shakespeare, ed W. F. McNeir and T. N. Greenfield, Portland 1966.

McGuire, R. L. The play-within-the-play in 1 Henry IV. Sh Quart 18 1967.

Mitchell, C. The education of the true Prince. Tennessee Stud in Lit 12 1967.

Shaw, J. The staging of parody and parallels in 1 Henry IV. Sh Survey 20 1967.

Schuchter, J. D. Prince Hal and Francis: the imitation of an action. Sh Stud 3 1967.

Berkeley, D. and D. Eidson. The theme of Henry IV pt 1. Sh Quart 19 1968.

Goss, A. G. The justification of Prince Hal. Texas Stud in Lit & Lang 10 1968.

Nahm, M. Falstaff, incongruity and the comic: an essay in aesthetic criticism. Personalist 49 1968.

Barber, C. Prince Hal, Henry V and the Tudor monarchy. In The morality of art: essays presented to G. Wilson Knight, 1969.

Bradbrook, M. C. King Henry IV. In Stratford papers 1965–7, ed B. A. W. Jackson, Hamilton Ont 1970.

Palmer, D. Casting off the old man: history and St Paul in Henry IV. CQ 12 1970.

Pettigrew, J. The mood of Henry IV part 2. In Stratford papers 1965–7, ed B. A. W. Jackson, Hamilton Ont 1970.

Schell, E. T. Prince Hal's second reformation. Sh Quart 21 1970.

Sorelino, G. The Smock Alley prompt books of 1 and 2 Henry IV. Sh Quart 22 1971.

Much Ado about Nothing

Much adoe about nothing, as it hath been sundrie times publikely acted by the Right Honourable the Lord Chamberlaine his servants; written by William Shakespeare; London, printed by V. S[immes] for Andrew Wise and William Aspley. 1600; ed J. O. Halliwell (-Phillipps) 1865 (facs); ed P. A. Daniel 1886 (facs).

Modern Editions

W. H. Fleming, New York 1889 (Bankside; parallel texts); H. H. Furness, Philadelphia 1899 (New Variorum); F. S. Boas 1916; C. F. T. Brooke, New Haven 1917 (Yale); A. T. Quiller-Couch and J. D. Wilson, Cambridge 1923 (New Cambridge); G. R. Trenery 1924 (Arden); A. G. Newcomer 1929; C. T. Prouty, New York 1948 (Crofts); J. W. Bennett, Baltimore 1958 (Pelican); F. Fergusson and C. J. Sisson, New York 1960 (Laurel); L. B. Wright and V. A. LaMar, New York 1964 (Folger); G. L. Kittredge, rev I. Ribner, Waltham Mass 1967; R. A. Foakes 1968 (New Penguin).

Studies

Scott, M. A. The book of the courtyer: a possible source of Benedick and Beatrice. PMLA 16 1901.

Law, R. A. Notes on Shakespeare's Much ado. SE 12 1932.

Wales, J. G. Shakespeare's use of English and foreign elements in the setting of Much ado. Trans Wisconsin Acad 28 1933.

Gaw, A. Is Shakespeare's Much ado a revised earlier play? PMLA 50 1935.

Page, N. The public reputation of Hero. Ibid.

Danchin, F. C. Une source de Much ado about nothing. Revue Anglo-américaine 13 1936. A pleasant comedie of two Italian gentlemen 1585.

Bennett, M. L. Shakespeare's Much ado about nothing and its possible Italian sources. SE 17 1937.

Draper, J. W. Benedick and Beatrice. JEGP 41 1942.

—— Dogberry's due process of law. JEGP 42 1943.

Gordon, D. J. Much ado about nothing: a possible source for the Hero-Claudio plot. SP 39 1942.

Smith, J. Much ado about nothing. Scrutiny 13 1946.

Prouty, C. T. The sources of Much ado about nothing. New Haven 1951.

Neill, K. More ado about Claudio: an acquittal for the slandered groom. Sh Quart 3 1952.

Craik, T. W. Much ado about nothing. Scrutiny 19 1953.

Hockey, D. C. Notes notes, forsooth. Sh Quart 8 1957.

Wey, J. J. 'To grace harmony': musical design in Much ado about nothing. Boston Univ Stud in Eng 4 1960.

Carrington, N. T. Shakespeare: Much ado about nothing. 1961.

Everett, B. Much ado about nothing. CQ 3 1961.

Owen, C. A. Comic awareness, style and dramatic technique in Much ado about nothing. Boston Univ Stud in Eng 5 1961.

Gilbert, A. Two Margarets: the composition of Much ado about nothing. PQ 41 1962.

Smith, J. H. The composition of the quarto of Much ado about nothing. SB 16 1963.

Felheim, M. Comic realism in Much ado about nothing. Philologica Pragensia 7 1964.

Hartley, L. Claudio and the unmerry war. College Eng May 1965.

Mulryne, J. R. Shakespeare: Much ado about nothing. 1965.

Mueschke, P. and M. Illusion and metamorphosis in Much ado about nothing. Sh Quart 18 1967.

Wain, J. The Shakespearean lie-detector: thoughts on Much ado about nothing. CQ 9 1967.

Lewalski, B. K. Love, appearance and reality: much ado about something. Stud in Eng Lit 1500–1900 8 1968.

McCollom, W. G. The role of wit in Much ado about nothing. Sh Quart 19 1968.

Rose, S. Love and self love in Much ado about nothing. EC 20 1970.

Berry, R. Much ado about nothing: structure and texture. E Studies 52 1971.

Henze, R. Deception in Much ado about nothing. Stud in Eng Lit 1500–1900 11 1971.

Henry V

The cronicle history of Henry the Fift, with his battell fought at Agin Court in France, togither with Auntient Pistoll, as it hath bene sundry times playd by the Right Honorable the Lord Chamberlaine his servants; London, printed by Thomas Creede for Tho. Millington and John Busby, and arc to be sold at his house in Carter Lane, next the Powle head. 1600; ed J. O. Halliwell (-Phillipps) 1867 (facs); ed A. Symons 1886 (facs); ed W. W. Greg, Oxford 1956 (facs); rptd B. Nicholson 1875 (New Sh Soc), W. A. Wright 1893 (Cambridge Shakespeare vol 9).

The chronicle history of Henry the Fift, with his battell fought at Agin Court in France; together with Auntient Pistoll, as it hath been sundry times playd by the Right Honorable the Lord Chamberlaine his servants. 1602, ed J. O. Halliwell (-Phillipps) 1867 (facs); 1608 (for 1619), ed Halliwell 1870 (facs), ed A. Symons 1886.

Modern Editions

B. Nicholson and P. A. Daniel 1877 (New Sh Soc) (parallel texts of 4° 1 and Folio 1); W. G. Boswell-Stone 1880 (New Sh Soc); H. P. Stokes, New York 1892 (Bankside); parallel texts); G. C. Moore Smith 1896 (Warwick); H. A. Evans 1903 (Arden); E. Roman, Marburg 1908 (parallel texts of 4° 1, 4° 3 and Folio 1); R. D. French, New Haven 1918 (Yale); K. Schrey, Frankfurt 1938; G. L. Kittredge, New York 1945; J. D. Wilson, Cambridge 1947 (New Cambridge); J. H. Walter 1954 (New Arden); W. W. Greg, Oxford 1956 (facs of 4° 1); R. J. Dorius, New Haven 1956 (Yale); L. B. Wright and V. Freund, Baltimore 1957 (Pelican); L. B. Wright and V. A. LaMar, New York 1960 (Folger); F. Fergusson and C. J. Sisson, New York 1962 (Laurel); J. R. Brown, New York 1965 (Signet); G. L. Kittredge, rev I. Ribner, Waltham Mass 1967; A. R. Humphreys 1968 (New Penguin).

Studies

The famous victories of Henry the Fifth: containing the honourable battell of Agincourt. 1598.

Shakspere's Holinshed. Ed W. G. Boswell-Stone 1896.

Kabel, P. Die Sage von Heinrich V bis zu Shakespeare. Berlin 1908.

Wilson, J. D. Martin Marprelate and Shakespeare's Fluellen. Library 2nd ser 3 1912.

Pollard, A. W. and J. D. Wilson. The 'stolne and surreptitious' Shakespearian texts: Henry V 1600. TLS 13 March 1919.

Gould, G. A new reading of Henry V. Eng Rev 29 1919.

Price, H. T. The text of Henry V. Newcastle-under-Lyme 1920.

— The quarto and folio texts of Henry V. PQ 12 1933.

Wallis, N. H. Some aspects of Shakespeare's Richard II and Henry V. In his Ethics of criticism, 1924.

Craig, H. The relation of the first quarto version to the First Folio version of Shakespeare's Henry V. PQ 6 1927.

Poel, W. The five act divisions in Henry V. TLS 6 Oct 1927.

Ward B. M. The famous victories of Henry V: its place in Elizabethan dramatic literature. RES 4 1928.

Albright, E. M. The Folio version of Henry V in relation to Shakespeare's times. PMLA 43 1928.

Simison, B. D. A source for the first quarto of Henry V. MLN 46 1931.

— Stage-directions: a test for the playhouse origin of the first quarto Henry V. PQ 11 1932.

Radoff, M. L. The influence of the French farce in Henry V and the Merry wives. MLN 48 1933.

Law, R. A. Holinshed as source for Henry V and King Lear. SE 14 1934.

— The choruses in Henry V. SE 35 1956.

Okerlund, G. The quarto version of Henry V as a stage adaptation. PMLA 49 1934.

Grether, E. Das Verhältnis von Shakespeares Heinrich V zu Sir Thomas Elyots Governour. Marburg 1938.

Smith, W. D. The Henry V choruses in the First Folio. JEGP 53 1954.

Cairncross, A. S. Quarto copy for Folio Henry V. SB 8 1956.

Braddy, H. Shakespeare's Henry V and the French nobility. Texas Stud in Lit & Lang 3 1961.

Fleissner, R. F. Falstaff's green sickness unto death. Sh Quart 12 1961.

Price, G. R. Henry V and Germanicus. Ibid.

Battenhouse, R. W. Henry V as heroic comedy. In Essays on Shakespeare and Elizabethan drama in honor of Hardin Craig, Columbia Missouri 1962.

Berman, R. S. Shakespeare's Alexander: Henry V. College Eng April 1962.

Duthie, G. I. The quarto of Shakespeare's Henry V. In Papers mainly Shakespearian, ed G. I. Duthie, Edinburgh 1964.

Mitchell, C. Henry V: the essential King. In Shakespearean essays, ed A. Thaler and N. Sanders, Knoxville 1964.

Zimbardo, R. A. The formalism of Henry V. In Shakespeare encomium, ed A. Paolucci, New York 1964.

Phialas, P. G. Shakespeare's Henry V and the second tetralogy. SP 62 1965.

Hutchison, H. F. Shakespeare and Henry V. History Today April 1967.

Hobday, C. H. Imagery and irony in Henry V. Sh Survey 21 1968.

Petit, J. B. 'This wooden O': théâtre et signe dans les choeurs de Henry V. Etudes Anglaises 21 1968.

Kelly, R. L. Shakespeare's Scroop and the spirit of Cain. Sh Quart 20 1969.

Williamson, M. L. The episode with Williams in Henry V. Stud in Eng Lit 1500–1900 9 1969.

Akrigg, G. P. V. Henry V: the epic hero as dramatic protagonist. In Stratford papers 1965–7, ed B. A. W. Jackson, Hamilton Ont 1970.

Julius Caesar

In First Folio, 1623; ed J. D. Wilson [1929] (facs).

Julius Caesar: a tragedy. 1684, nd, nd, nd, nd, 1619. See H. Bartlett, Library 2nd ser 4 1913.

Modern Editions

A. D. Innes 1893 (Warwick); M. Hunter 1900; M. Macmillan 1902 (Arden); F. H. Sykes 1909; H. H. Furness jr, Philadelphia 1913 (New Variorum); L. Mason, New Haven 1919 (Yale); G. C. Taylor and R. Smith, Boston 1936 (interlinear); P. Schultz, Münster 1936; K. Schrey, Frankfurt 1938; G. Skillan 1938; G. L. Kittredge, Boston 1939; J. D. Wilson, Cambridge 1949 (New Cambridge); H. T. Price, New York 1949 (Crofts); T. S. Dorsch 1955 (New Arden); F. Fergusson and C. J. Sisson, New York 1958 (Laurel); A. Kernan, New Haven 1959 (Yale), L. B. Wright and V. L. Freund, New York 1959 (Folger), S. F. Johnson, Baltimore 1960 (Pelican); W. and B. Rosen, New York 1963 (Signet); G. L. Kittredge, rev I. Ribner, Waltham Mass 1966; N. Sanders 1967 (New Penguin).

Studies

Shakespeare's Plutarch vol 1. Ed C. F. T. Brooke 1909 (Sh Classics).

Craik, G. L. The English of Shakespeare, illustrated in a philological commentary on his Julius Caesar. 1857.

Koeppel, E. Shakespeares Julius Caesar und die Entstehungszeit des anonymen Dramas The wisdom of Dr Dodypoll. Sh Jb 43 1907.

MacCallum, M. W. Shakespeare's Roman plays and their background. 1910.

Ayres, H. M. Shakespeare's Julius Caesar in the light of some other versions. PMLA 25 1910.

Sarrazin, G. Shakespeare und Orlando Pescetti. E Studien 46 1913.

Boecker, A. A probable Italian source of Shakespeare's Julius Caesar. New York 1913.

Faggi, A. Il Giulio Cesare di Shakespeare. Rome 1916.

Tassin, A. de V. Julius Caesar. In Columbia Shakespearian studies, New York 1916.

Robertson, J. M. The origination of Julius Caesar. 1923.

Wells, W. The authorship of Julius Caesar. 1923.

Shackford, M. H. Julius Caesar and Ovid. MLN 41 1926.

Woelcken, F. Shakespeares Julius Caesar und Marlowes Massacre at Paris. Sh Jb 63 1927.

Granville-Barker, H. In his Prefaces to Shakespeare: series 1, 1927.

Shestov, L. The ethical problem in Julius Caesar. New Adelphi June 1928.

Hunter, M. Politics and character in Shakespeare's Julius Caesar. Essays by Divers Hands 10 1931.

Morsbach, L. Shakespeares Cäsarbild. Heidelberg 1935.

Deutschbein, M. Die Tragik in Shakespeares Julius Caesar. Anglia 62 1938.

Klein, D. Has Cassius been misinterpreted? Sh Assoc Bull 14 1939.

Spiegelberger, W. Shakespeares Caesarbild. Neuphilologische Monatsschrift 10 1939.

Staedler, E. Die klassischen Quellen der Antoniusrede in Shakespeares Julius Caesar. Ibid.

Azzalino, W. Stilkundliche Betrachtung der Reden des Brutus und des Antonius in Julius Caesar (III. ii). Neuphilologische Monatsschrift 11 1940.

Coles, B. Shakespeare studies: Julius Caesar. New York 1940.

Musgrove, S. Julius Caesar. Sydney 1941.

Evans, G. B. Julius Caesar: a seventeenth-century ms. JEGP 41 1942.

—— The problem of Brutus: an eighteenth-century solution. In Studies in honor of T. W. Baldwin, Urbana 1958.

Draper, J. W. Cassius and Brutus. Bull History of Medicine 13 1943.

Wickert, M. Antikes Gedankengut in Shakespeares Julius Caesar. Sh Jb 82–3 1946–7.

Wilson, J. D. Ben Jonson and Julius Caesar. HLQ 13 1950.

Felheim, M. The problem of time in Julius Caesar. Quart Jnl of Speech 37 1951.

Stirling, B. 'Or else this were a savage spectacle'. PMLA 66 1951.

—— Brutus and the death of Portia. Sh Quart 10 1959.

—— Julius Caesar in revision. Sh Quart 13 1962.

Smith, W. D. Duplicate revelations of Portia's death. Sh Quart 4 1953.

Rees, J. Julius Caesar: an earlier play and an interpretation. MLR 50 1955.

Schanzer, E. The problem of Julius Caesar. Sh Quart 6 1955.

—— The tragedy of Shakespeare's Brutus. ELH 22 1955.

Breyer, B. R. A new look at Julius Caesar. In Essays in honor of W. C. Curry, Nashville 1956.

Bennett, P. E. The statistical measurement of a stylistic trait in Julius Caesar and As you like it. Sh Quart 8 1957.

Ribner, I. Political issues in Julius Caesar. JEGP 56 1957.

Barroll, J. L. Shakespeare and Roman history. MLR 53 1958.

Bonjour, A. The structure of Julius Caesar. Liverpool 1958.

Ornstein, R. Seneca and the political drama of Julius Caesar. JEGP 57 1958.

Charney, M. Shakespeare's style in Julius Caesar and Antony and Cleopatra. ELH 26 1959.

—— Shakespeare's Roman plays. Cambridge Mass 1961.

Hall, V. Julius Caesar: a play without political bias. In Studies in the English Renaissance drama, ed J. W. Bennett, O. Cargill and V. Hall, New York 1959.

Smith G. R. Brutus, virtue and will. Sh Quart 10 1959.

Sisson, C. J. The Roman plays. In The living Shakespeare, ed R. Gittings 1960.

Coursen, H. R. The fall and decline of Julius Caesar. Texas Stud in Lit & Lang 4 1962.

Spencer, T. J. B. Shakespeare: the Roman plays. 1963 (Br Council pamphlet).

Traversi, D. A. Shakespeare: the Roman plays. 1963.

Knights, L. C. Personality and politics in Julius Caesar. Anglica 19 1964.

Rabkin, N. Structure, convention and meaning in Julius Caesar. JEGP 63 1964.

Sanders, N. The shift of power in Julius Caesar. REL 5 1964.

Peterson, D. L. Wisdom consumed in confidence: an examination of Shakespeare's Julius Caesar. Sh Quart 16 1965.

Anson, J. S. Julius Caesar: the politics of the hardened heart. Sh Stud 2 1966.

Bowden, W. R. The mind of Brutus. Sh Quart 17 1966.

Hapgood, R. Speak hands for me: gesture as language in Julius Caesar. Drama Survey 5 1966.

Hartsock, M. E. The complexity of Julius Caesar. PMLA 81 1966.

Rackin, P. The pride of Shakespeare's Brutus. Lib Chron 32 1966.

Simmons, J. L. Shakespeare's Julius Caesar: the Roman actor and the man. Tulane Stud in Eng 16 1968.

Prior, M. E. The search for a hero in Julius Caesar. Renaissance Drama new ser 2 1969.

Velz, J. W. Clemency, will and just cause in Julius Caesar. Sh Survey 22 1969.

—— 'If I were Brutus now': role-playing in Julius Caesar. Sh Stud 4 1969.

—— 'Pirate Hills' and the quartos of Julius Caesar. PBSA 63 1969.

—— The text of Julius Caesar in the Second Folio. Sh Quart 20 1969.

—— Undular structure in Julius Caesar. MLR 66 1970.

Bellringer, A. W. Julius Caesar: room enough. CQ 12 1970.

Chang, J. S. M. J. Julius Caesar in the light of Renaissance historiography. JEGP 69 1970.

Edinborough, A. Julius Caesar. In Stratford papers 1965–7, ed B. A. W. Jackson, Hamilton Ont 1970.

Henze, R. Power and spirit in Julius Caesar. Univ Rev 37 1970.

Kaufmann, R. J. and C. J. Ronan. Shakespeare's Julius Caesar: an Apollonian and comparative reading. Comparative Drama 4 1970.

Palmer, D. J. Tragic error in Julius Caesar. Sh Quart 21 1970.

As You Like It

In First Folio, 1623; ed J. D. Wilson [1929] (facs).

Modern Editions

H. H. Furness, Philadelphia 1890 (New Variorum); J. W. Holme 1914 (Arden); J. R. Crawford, New Haven 1919 (Yale); A. T. Quiller-Couch and J. D. Wilson, Cambridge 1926 (New Cambridge); G. L. Kittredge, Boston 1939; S. C. Burchell, New Haven 1954 (Yale); F. Fergusson and C. J. Sisson, New York 1959 (Laurel);

R. M. Sargent, Baltimore 1959 (Pelican); L. B. Wright and V. L. Freund, New York 1959 (Folger); A. Gilman, New York 1963 (Signet); G. L. Kittredge, rev I. Ribner, Waltham Mass 1967; H. J. Oliver 1968 (New Penguin).
For a concordance see T. H. Howard-Hill, Oxford 1970.

Studies

Lodge's Rosalynde: being the original of Shakespeare's As you like it. Ed W. W. Greg 1907 (Sh Classics).

Herford, C. H. Shakespeare's masters and As you like it. 1890.

Thorndike, A. H. The relation of As you like it to Robin Hood plays. JEGP 4 1901.

Stoll, E. E. Shakespeare, Marston and the malcontent type. MP 3 1906.

— Jaques and the antiquaries. MLN 54 1939.

Conrad, H. Die Erzählung von Gamelyn als Quelle zu Shakespeares As you like it. Sh Jb 46 1910.

Rea, J. D. Jaques in praise of folly. MP 17 1919.

Landau, L. Some parallels to Shakespeare's 'seven ages'. JEGP 19 1920.

Tolman, A. H. Shakespeare's manipulation of his sources in As you like it. MLN 37 1922.

Priestley, J. B. Touchstone. In his English comic characters, 1925.

Eichler, A. Love's labour's lost und As you like it als Hofaufführungen. E Studien 64 1929.

Newdigate, B. H. Harington, Jaques and Touchstone. TLS 3–10 Jan 1929.

Clark, C. A. A study of As you like it. 1932.

Deutschbein, M. Shakespeares Kritik an Montaigne in As you like it. Neuphilologische Monatsschrift 5 1934.

Draper, J. W. Orlando and the younger brother. PQ 13 1934.

— As you like it and 'Belted Will' Howard. RES 12 1936.

— Jaques' 'seven ages' and Bartholomaeus Anglicus. MLN 54 1939.

— Shakespeare's Orlando innamorato. MLQ 2 1941.

Fink, Z. S. PQ 14 1935. On Jaques.

Smith, J. As you like it. Scrutiny 9 1941.

Wilcox, J. Putting Jaques into As you like it. MLR 36 1941.

Barber, C. L. The use of comedy in As you like it. PQ 21 1942.

Bennett, J. W. Jaques' seven ages. Sh Assoc Bull 18 1943.

Chew, S. C. 'This strange eventful history'. In J. Q. Adams memorial studies, Washington 1948.

Staebler, W. Shakespeare's play of atonement. Sh Assoc Bull 24 1949.

Goldsmith, R. H. Touchstone: critic in motley. PMLA 68 1953.

Baird, R. C. As you like it and its source. In Essays in honor of W. C. Curry, Nashville 1954.

Jenkins, H. As you like it. Sh Survey 8 1955.

Bernard, M. A. Paradox of Shakespeare's golden world. Philippine Stud 4 1956.

Draper, R. P. Shakespeare's pastoral comedy. Etudes Anglaises 11 1958.

Schäfer, D. Die Bedeutung des Rollenspiels in Shakespeares Wie es Euch gefällt. Sh Jb 94 1958.

Gardner, H. As you like it. In More talking of Shakespeare, ed J. Garrett 1959.

Lascelles, M. Shakespeare's pastoral comedy. Ibid.

Mincoff, M. What Shakespeare did to Rosalynde. Sh Jb 96 1960.

Shattuck, C. H. (ed). Mr Macready produces As you like it: a prompt-book study. Urbana 1962.

Doran, M. 'Yet am I inland bred'. In Shakespeare 400, ed J. G. McManaway, New York 1964.

Jamieson, M. S. Shakespeare: As you like it. 1965.

Knowles, R. Myth and type in As you like it. ELH 33 1966.

Schutte, W. M. The worlds of As you like it. Wisconsin Stud in Lit 1 1969.

Barnet, S. 'Strange events': improbability in As you like it. Sh Stud 4 1969.

Berry, R. No exit from Arden. MLR 66 1970.

Cody, R. In his Landscape of the mind, Oxford 1970.

Hassel, R. C. Shakespeare's comic epilogues: invitations to festive communion. Sh Jb (Heidelberg) 1970.

Palmer, D. J. Art and nature in As you like it. PQ 49 1970.

Twelfth Night

In First Folio, 1623; ed J. D. Wilson [1928] (facs).

Modern Editions

A. D. Innes 1895 (Warwick); H. H. Furness, Philadelphia 1901 (New Variorum); M. Luce 1906 (Arden); G. H. Nettleton, New Haven 1922 (Yale); A. T. Quiller-Couch and J. D. Wilson, Cambridge 1930 (New Cambridge); M. Eccles, New York 1948 (Crofts); W. P. Holden, New Haven 1954 (Yale); C. T. Prouty, Baltimore 1958 (Pelican); F. Fergusson and C. J. Sisson, New York 1959 (Laurel); L. B. Wright and V. A. LaMar, New York 1960 (Folger), H. Baker, New York 1965 (Signet); G. L. Kittredge, rev I. Ribner, Waltham Mass 1966; M. M. Mahood 1968 (New Penguin).
For a concordance see T. H. Howard-Hill, Oxford 1970.

Studies

Rich's Apolonius and Silla: an original of Shakespeare's Twelfth night. 1912 (Sh Classics).

Logeman, H. Johannes de Witt's visit to the Swan theatre. Anglia 19 1897.

de Perott, J. Noch eine eventuelle Quelle zum Heiligen Dreikönigsabend. Sh Jb 46 1910.

Tilley, M. P. The organic unity of Twelfth night. PMLA 29 1914.

Gollancz, I. Malvolio. In A book of homage to Shakespeare, 1916.

Archer, W. The two Twelfth nights. Fortnightly Rev Dec 1918.

Symons, A. Twelfth night. In his Studies in the Elizabethan drama, 1920.

Priestley, J. B. The Illyrians. In his English comic characters, 1925.

Bradley, A. C. Feste the jester. In his A miscellany, 1929.

Wilson, J. D. Twelfth night and the gunpowder plot. TLS 13 June 1929.

Thaler, A. The original Malvolio. Sh Assoc Bull 7 1932.

Mueschke, P. and J. Fleisher. Jonsonian elements in the comic underplot of Twelfth night. PMLA 48 1933.

Draper, J. W. Olivia's household. PMLA 49 1934.

— The Twelfth night of Shakespeare's audience. Stanford 1950.

Wright, L. B. A conduct book for Malvolio. SP 31 1934.

Gordon, D. J. Twelfth night and Gli ingannati. Bolletino degli Studi Inglesi 7 1939.

Pyle, F. Twelfth night, King Lear and Arcadia. MLR 43 1948.

West, E. J. Bradleyan reprise: on the fool in Twelfth night. Sh Assoc Bull 24 1949.

Hotson, L. The first night of Twelfth night. 1954.

Crane, M. Twelfth night and Shakespearian comedy. Sh Quart 6 1955.

Hollander, J. Musica mundana and Twelfth night: sound and poetry. Eng Inst Essays 1956.

Holland, N. N. Cuckold or counsellor in Twelfth night. Sh Quart 8 1957.

Salingar, L. G. On the design of Twelfth night. Sh Quart 9 1958.

Jenkins, H. Twelfth night. Rice Inst Pamphlet 45 1959.

Williams, P. Mistakes in Twelfth night and their resolution. PMLA 76 1961.

Doran, M. Pyramus and Thisbe once more. In Essays on Shakespeare and Elizabethan drama in honor of Hardin Craig, Columbia Missouri 1962.

Forbes, L. What you will? Sh Quart 13 1962.

Gérard, A. Shipload of fools: a note on Twelfth night. E Studies 45 1964.

Markels, J. Shakespeare's confluence of tragedy and comedy: Twelfth night and King Lear. In Shakespeare 400, ed J. G. McManaway, New York 1964.

Mincoff, M. Twelfth night: an end and a beginning. Philoloski Pregled 1 1964.

Leech, C. Twelfth night and Shakespearean comedy. Toronto 1965.

Lewalski, B. K. Thematic patterns in Twelfth night. Sh Stud 1 1965.

Eagleton, T. Language and reality in Twelfth night. CQ 9 1967.

Palmer, D. J. Art and nature in Twelfth night. Ibid.

Schwartz, E. Twelfth night and the meaning of Shakespearean comedy. College Eng April 1967.

Preston, D. R. The minor characters in Twelfth night. Sh Quart 21 1970.

Prouty, C. T. In Stratford papers 1965–7, ed B. A. W. Jackson, Hamilton Ont 1970.

Hamlet

The tragical historie of Hamlet Prince of Denmarke by William Shake-speare, as it hath beene diverse times acted by his Highnesse servants in the Cittie of London; as also in the two universities of Cambridge and Oxford, and elsewhere; at London printed for N[icholas L[ing] and John Trundell. 1603; ed J. O. Halliwell (-Phillipps) 1866 (facs); ed F. J. Furnivall 1880 (facs); A. B. Weiner, Great Neck NY 1962 (facs); ed L. Berger, Frankfurt 1967 (facs); rptd W. A. Wright 1893 (Cambridge Shakespeare, vol 9); ed F. G. Hubbard, Madison 1920; ed G. B. Harrison 1924; Cambridge Mass 1931; ed W. W. Greg, Oxford 1951.

The tragicall historie of Hamlet, Prince of Denmarke, by William Shakespeare, newly printed and enlarged to almost as much againe as it was, according to the true and perfect coppie; at London, printed by J[ames] R[oberts] for N[icholas] L[ing] and are to be sold at his shoppe under Saint Dunstons Church in Fleet-street. 1604 (in some copies 1605); ed J. O. Halliwell (-Phillipps) 1867 (facs); ed F. J. Furnivall 1880 (facs); ed W. W. Greg, Oxford 1940 (facs).

The tragedy of Hamlet Prince of Denmarke, by William Shakespeare. 1611, [1630?], 1637, 1676, 1676, 1683, 1695, 1695, 1703, 1703.

Tr German, Tragoedia: der bestrafte Bruder-mord oder Prinz Hamlet aus Dännemark, ed H. A. O. Reichard, Olla podrida vol 2, 1781; ed A. Cohn with Eng trn in Shakespeare in Germany, 1865; ed W. Creizenach, Schauspiele der englischen Komödianten, 1889. Ms in Library of Gotha, dated 1710.

Modern Editions

S. Timmins 1860 (parallel texts of 4° 1 and 4° 2); H. H. Furness, Philadelphia 1877 (New Variorum); E. P. Vining, New York 1890 (Bankside; parallel texts of 4° 1 and Folio 1); W. Viëtor, Marburg 1891, 1913 (parallel texts of 4° 1, 4° 2, Folio 1); E. K. Chambers 1894 (Warwick); E. Dowden 1899 (Arden); J. D. Wilson, Cambridge 1934 (New Cambridge); G. C. Taylor and R. Smith, Boston 1936 (interlinear); Second quarto, 1604: facsimile of Huntington Library copy, ed O. J. Campbell, San Marino 1938; A critical edition of the second quarto 1604, ed T. M. Parrott and H. Craig, Princeton 1938; G. L. Kittredge, Boston 1939; Second quarto 1604–5, 1940 (Shakespeare Quarto Facs); R. C. Bald, New York 1946 (Crofts); G. Rylands, Oxford 1947 (New Clarendon); E. Jones 1947 (with a psychoanalytical study); H. Oldendorf and H. Arguile, Cape Town 1948; First quarto 1603, 1951 (Shakespeare Quarto Facs); F. Fergusson and C. J. Sisson, New York 1958 (Laurel); L. B. Wright and V. L. Freund, New York 1959 (Folger); A. B. Weiner, Great Neck NY 1962 (facs 4° 1); E. Hubler, New York 1963 (Signet); L.

Berger, Frankfurt 1967 (facs 4° 1); G. L. Kittredge, rev I. Ribner, Waltham Mass 1967.

Sources

Shakespeares Hamlet-Quellen: Saxo Grammaticus, Belleforest und die Hystorie of Hamblet. Ed R. Gericke and M. Moltke, Leipzig 1881.

Hamlet in Iceland. Ed I. Gollancz 1898.

Corpus Hamleticum: Hamlet in Sage und Dichtung, Kunst und Musik. Ed J. Schick 3 vols Berlin 1912–Leipzig 1933.

The sources of Hamlet. Ed I. Gollancz 1926 (Sh Classics).

Studies

Nicholson, B. Kemp and the play of Hamlet: Yorick and Tarlton. Trans New Sh Soc 1880.

Creizenach, W. Die Tragödie Der bestrafte Brudermord und ihre Bedeutung für die Kritik des Shakespeareschen Hamlet. Leipzig 1887.

—— Der bestrafte Brudermord and its relation to Shakespeare's Hamlet. MP 2 1904.

Sarrazin, G. Der Name Ophelia. E Studien 21 1895.

Elton, O. Shakespeare's Hamlet. 1894. With trn of Saxo Grammaticus.

Thorndike, A. H. The relation of Hamlet to contemporary revenge plays. PMLA 17 1902.

Bradley, A. C. Hamlet. In his Shakespearean tragedy, 1904.

Jack, A. E. Thomas Kyd and the Ur-Hamlet. PMLA 20 1905.

Stoll, E. E. Shakespeare, Marston and the malcontent type. MP 3 1906.

—— Hamlet: an historical and comparative study. Minneapolis 1919.

—— Hamlet the man. 1935 (Eng Assoc lecture).

—— Hamlet and the Spanish tragedy, quartos 1 and 2: a protest. MP 35 1938.

—— Hamlet and the Spanish tragedy again. MP 37 1940.

—— Mainly controversy: Hamlet, Othello. PQ 24 1946.

Cunliffe, J. W. Nash and the earlier Hamlet. PMLA 21 1906.

Allen, J. L. The lost Hamlet of Kyd. Westminster Rev 170 1908.

Huizinga, J. Rosenkranz und Güldenstern. Sh Jb 46 1910.

Greg, W. W. The Hamlet quartos. MLR 5 1910.

—— Hamlet's hallucination. MLR 12 1917.

—— The Hamlet texts and recent work in Shakespeare bibliography. MLR 14 1919.

—— Principles of emendation in Shakespeare. Proc Br Acad 14 1928.

—— What happens in Hamlet. MLR 31 1936.

Jones, E. The Oedipus-complex as an explanation of Hamlet's mystery. Amer Jnl of Psychology 21 1910.

—— A psycho-analytic study of Hamlet. 1922.

—— Hamlet and Oedipus. 1949.

Gollancz, I. The name Polonius. Archiv 132 1914.

—— Polonius. In A book of homage to Shakespeare, 1916.

Murray, G. Hamlet and Orestes. Oxford 1914.

Gray, H. D. The first quarto of Hamlet. MLR 10 1915.

—— Did Shakespeare write a tragedy of Dido? MLR 15 1920.

—— Thomas Kyd and the first quarto of Hamlet. PMLA 42 1927.

—— Reconstruction of a lost play. PQ 7 1928.

—— The date of Hamlet. JEGP 31 1932.

—— Some methods of approach to the study of Hamlet. SP 45 1948.

van Dam, B. A. P. Are there interpolations in the text of Hamlet? In A book of homage to Shakespeare, 1916.

—— The text of Shakespeare's Hamlet. 1924.

Wilson, J. D. The copy for Hamlet 1603. Library 2nd ser 9 1918.

—— The Hamlet transcript 1593. Ibid. Pbd together in book form, 1918.

—— The parallel plots in Hamlet. MLR 13 1918.

— The play scene in Hamlet restored. Athenaeum July–Aug, Oct–Nov 1918.
— Spellings and misprints in the second quarto of Hamlet. E & S 10 1924.
— The manuscripts of Shakespeare's Hamlet, and the problems of its transmission. 2 vols Cambridge 1934.
— What happens in Hamlet. Cambridge 1935.
— Nashe's 'Kyd in Aesop'. RES 18 1942.
Hubbard, F. G. The 'Marcellus' theory of the first quarto of Hamlet. MLN 33 1918.
— The readings of the first quarto of Hamlet. PMLA 38 1928.
Robertson, J. M. The problem of Hamlet. 1919; Hamlet once more, 1923.
Lawrence, W. W. The play-scene in Hamlet. JEGP 14 1919.
— Hamlet and the mouse-trap. PMLA 54 1939.
— Hamlet's sea voyage. PMLA 59 1944.
— Hamlet and Fortinbras. PMLA 61 1946.
Ferguson, E. L. The play-scene in Hamlet. MLR 14 1919.
Eliot, T. S. In his Sacred wood, 1920.
Østerberg, V. Studier over Hamlet-texterne. Copenhagen 1920.
— Prince Hamlet's age. Copenhagen 1924.
Jones, H. M. The King in Hamlet. Austin 1921.
Winstanley, L. Hamlet and the Scottish succession. 1921.
— Hamlet and the Essex conspiracy. Aberystwyth Stud 6–7 1924–5.
Clutton-Brock, A. Shakespeare's Hamlet. 1922.
Spencer, H. Hamlet under the Restoration. PMLA 38 1923.
— Seventeenth-century cuts in Hamlet's soliloquies. RES 9 1933.
Fox, W. S. Lucian in the grave scene of Hamlet. PQ 2 1923.
Malone, K. The literary history of Hamlet. Heidelberg 1923.
— On the etymology of Hamlet. PQ 4 1925, RES 3–4 1927–8.
de Groot, H. Hamlet: its textual history. Amsterdam 1923.
Lawrence, W. J. The ghost in Hamlet. Nineteenth Century 1924; rptd in his Shakespeare's workshop, Oxford 1928.
— The date of Hamlet. TLS 8 April 1926; rptd ibid.
— Hamlet as Shakespeare staged it. Johns Hopkins Alumni Mag 14 1926; rptd in his Pre-Restoration stage studies, Cambridge Mass 1927.
— The mystery of the Hamlet first quarto. Criterion 5 1927; rptd in his Shakespeare's workshop, Oxford 1928.
— The pirates of Hamlet. Criterion 8 1929.
— The dumb show in Hamlet. Life & Letters Nov 1930.
Diamond, W. Wilhelm Meister's interpretation of Hamlet. MP 23 1925.
Clark, C. A study of Hamlet. Stratford 1926.
Conrad, B. R. Hamlet's delay. PMLA 41 1926.
O'Sullivan, M. I. Hamlet and Dr Timothy Bright. Ibid.
Bradby, G. F. The problems of Hamlet. 1928; rptd in Short studies in Shakespeare, 1929.
Santayana, G. Hamlet. Life & Letters June 1928.
Ramelli, G. Studi sugli apocriphi shakespeariani: The tragicall historie of Hamlet. Turin 1930.
Schücking, L. L. Zum Problem der Überlieferung des Hamlet-Textes. Leipzig 1931.
— The churchyard-scene an afterthought? RES 11 1935.
— Der Sinn des Hamlet. Leipzig 1935; tr Oxford 1937 (enlarged).
Waldock, A. J. A. Hamlet: a study in critical method. Cambridge 1931.
Widmann, W. Hamlets Bühnenlaufbahn 1601–1877. Leipzig 1931 (Shakespeare-Gesellschaft).
Chapman. J. A. Hamlet. 1932.
Bowers, F. T. Alphonsus Emperor of Germany and the Ur-Hamlet. MLN 48 1933.
— The printing of Hamlet Q2. SB 7 1955.

— Hamlet as minister and scourge. PMLA 70 1955.
— The textual relation of Q2 to Q1 Hamlet. SB 8 1956.
— Hamlet's fifth soliloquy. In Essays on Shakespeare and Elizabethan drama in honor of Hardin Craig, Columbia Missouri 1962.
— Dramatic structure and criticism: plot in Hamlet. In Shakespeare 400, ed J. G. McManaway, New York 1964.
— The moment of final suspense in Hamlet: 'we defy augury'. In Shakespeare 1564–1964, ed E. A. Bloom, Providence 1964.
Childs, R. de S. Influence of the Court tragedy on the play scene in Hamlet. JEGP 32 1933.
Richards, I. T. The meaning of Hamlet's soliloquy. PMLA 48 1933.
Walley, H. R. The dates of Hamlet and Marston's The malcontent. RES 9 1933.
— Shakespeare's conception of Hamlet. PMLA 48 1933.
Draper, J. W. The elder Hamlet and the ghost. Sh Assoc Bull 9 1934.
— Revue Anglo-américaine 11 1934, PQ 14 1935, Sh Jb 71 1935, E Studien 69 1935, Revue de Littérature Comparée 15 1935. Character-studies.
— The Hamlet of Shakespeare's audience. Durham NC 1938.
Stone, G. W. Garrick's long lost alteration of Hamlet. PMLA 49 1934.
Weigelin, E. Hamlet-Studien. Stuttgart 1934.
Bullough, G. The murder of Gonzago. MLR 30 1935.
Brock, J. H. E. The dramatic purpose of Hamlet. Cambridge 1935.
Hart, A. The vocabulary of the first quarto of Hamlet. RES 12 1936.
Alexander, P. The text of Hamlet. Ibid.
— Hamlet: father and son. Oxford 1955.
Beatty, J. M. The King in Hamlet. Sh Assoc Bull 11 1936.
Cairncross, A. S. The problem of Hamlet: a solution. 1936.
Cameron, K. W. Hamlet's fourth soliloquy and Samuel Ward. Sh Assoc Bull 11 1936.
Flatter, R. Hamlets Flucht in den Tod. Vienna 1936.
— Hamlet's father. 1949.
— Shakespeare: Hamlet. Frankfurt 1959.
Frassati. La volontia in Amleto. Bologna 1936.
Granville-Barker, H. The casting of Hamlet: a fragment. London Mercury Nov 1936.
— In his Prefaces to Shakespeare: series 3, 1936.
Morgan, M. Hamlet the Dane. Philadelphia 1936.
Smith, R. M. Hamlet and Gertrude: or the conscience of the Queen. Sh Assoc Bull 11 1936.
Spriggs, C. O. Hamlet on the eighteenth-century stage. Quart Jnl of Speech 22 1936.
Cazamian, L. Humor in Hamlet. Rice Inst Pamphlets 24 1937.
Gray, A. A. The fencing match in Hamlet. RES 13 1937.
Kirschbaum, L. The date of Shakespeare's Hamlet. SP 34 1937.
— The sequence of scenes in Hamlet. MLN 55 1940.
— Hamlet and Ophelia. PQ 35 1956.
Pyles, T. Rejected Q2 readings in the New Shakespeare Hamlet. ELH 4 1937.
Coles, B. Shakespeare studies: Hamlet. New York 1938.
Gardner, H. L. Lawful espials. MLR 33 1938. On Ophelia.
Groom, B. The varieties of style in Hamlet. E & S 24 1938.
Kunstler, G. Der dramatische Aufbau von Hamlet. Zeitschrift für Ästhetik 1 1938.
Plowman, M. Some values in Hamlet. Adelphi 14 1938.
Spencer, T. Hamlet and the nature of reality. ELH 5 1938.
Bonjour, A. On artistic unity in Hamlet. E Studies 21 1939.
— Hamlet and the phantom clue. E Studies 35 1954.
— The question of Hamlet's grief. E Studies 43 1962.
Guttman, S. The fencing bout in Hamlet. Sh Assoc Bull 14 1939.

Sen, T. Hamlet's treatment of Ophelia in the nunnery scene. MLR 35 1940.

Sisson, C. J. The mouse-trap again. RES 16 1940.

Doran, M. That undiscovered country. PQ 20 1941.

—— The language of Hamlet. HLQ 27 1964.

Duthie, G. I. The 'bad' quarto of Hamlet. Cambridge 1941.

Morgan, R. Some stoic lines in Hamlet and the problem of interpretation. PQ 20 1941.

Hankins, J. E. The character of Hamlet and other essays. Chapel Hill 1941.

Campbell, O. J. What is the matter with Hamlet? Yale Rev 32 1942.

Hudson, A. P. Romantic apologiae for Hamlet's treatment of Ophelia. ELH 9 1942.

Jackson, J. L. The exchange of weapons in Hamlet. MLN 57 1942.

Lewis, C. S. Hamlet: the Prince or the poem? Proc Br Acad 28 1942; rptd in his Selected literary essays, Cambridge 1969.

Mackenzie, W. R. Rosencrantz and Guildenstern. In Studies in honor of F. W. Shipley, Washington 1942.

Prior, M. E. The play scene in Hamlet. ELH 9 1942.

—— The thought of Hamlet and the modern temper. ELH 15 1948.

Sampley, A. M. Hamlet among the mechanists. Sh Assoc Bull 17 1942.

Wales, J. G. Horatio's commentary: a study in the warp and woof of Hamlet. Ibid.

Montgomerie, W. Mirror for magistrates: the solution of the mouse-trap in Hamlet. Life & Letters Jan 1943.

Shoemaker, F. Aesthetic experience and the humanities. New York 1943.

Thomas, S. The antic Hamlet and Richard III. New York 1943.

Babb, L. Hamlet, melancholy and the Devil. MLN 59 1944.

Barfield, O. The form of Hamlet. In his Romanticism comes of age, 1944.

Deutschbein, M. Der Hamletmonolog 'To be or not to be'. Sh Jb 80–1 1944–5.

—— Shakespeare's Hamlet and Montaigne. Ibid.

Castelain, M. L'énigme d'Hamlet. Paris 1946.

Feibleman, J. The theory of Hamlet. JHI 7 1946.

Nosworthy, J. M. The structural experiment in Hamlet. RES 22 1946.

—— Hamlet and the player who could not keep counsel. Sh Survey 3 1950.

Semper, I. Hamlet without tears. Iowa City 1946.

Venable, E. The Hamlet problem and its solution: an interpretative study. Cincinnati 1946.

Berry, F. Young Fortinbras. Life & Letters Feb 1947.

Conklin, P. S. A history of Hamlet criticism 1601–1821. New York 1947.

Verkoren, L. Lets over vorm en inhoud van Shakespeares Hamlet. Neophilologus 31 1947.

Campbell, L. B. Polonius: the tyrant's ears. In J. Q. Adams memorial studies, Washington 1948.

Law, R. A. Belleforest, Shakespeare and Kyd. Ibid.

Madariaga, S. de. On Hamlet. 1948, 1964 (rev).

Salter, F. M. Shakespeare's interpretation of Hamlet. Trans Royal Soc of Canada 3rd ser 42 1948.

Walker, R. The time is out of joint: a study of Hamlet. 1948.

Detmold, G. Hamlet's 'all but blunted purpose'. Sh Assoc Bull 24 1949.

Houston, P. H. There's nothing either good or bad but thinking makes it so. Ibid.

Spaeth, J. D. Horatio's Hamlet. Ibid.

Hogrefe, P. Artistic unity in Hamlet. SP 46 1949.

Godfrey, D. R. The player's speech in Hamlet: a new approach. Neophilologus 34 1950.

Jack, A. A. Young Hamlet: a conjectural resolution of some of the difficulties in the plotting of Shakespeare's play. Aberdeen 1950.

Lawlor, J. J. The tragic conflict in Hamlet. RES new ser 1 1950; rev in his Tragic sense in Shakespeare, 1960.

Le Comte, E. S. The ending of Hamlet as a farewell to Essex. ELH 17 1950.

Levin, H. An explication of the player's speech. Kenyon Rev 12 1950.

—— The antic disposition. Sh Jb 94 1958.

—— The question of Hamlet. New York 1959.

Savage, D. S. Hamlet and the pirates: an exercise in literary detection. 1950.

Smidt, K. Notes on Hamlet. E Studies 31 1950.

Battenhouse, R. W. The ghost in Hamlet: a Catholic 'lynch-pin'? SP 48 1951.

—— Hamlet's apostrophe on man: clue to the tragedy. PMLA 66 1951.

Caldiero, F. M. The source of Hamlet's 'What a piece of work is a man'. N & Q 29 Sept 1951.

Eliot, T. S. Poetry and drama. Cambridge Mass 1951; rptd in his On poetry and poets, 1957.

Elliott, G. R. Scourge and minister: a study of Hamlet as a tragedy of revengefulness and justice. Durham NC 1951.

Paterson, J. The word in Hamlet. Sh Quart 2 1951.

Trehern, E. M. More about Hamlet. Cairo 1951.

Rubow, P. V. Shakespeare's Hamlet. Copenhagen 1951.

Walker, A. The textual problem of Hamlet: a reconsideration. RES new ser 2 1951.

—— Collateral substantive texts (with special reference to Hamlet). SB 7 1955.

Williamson, C. C. H. (ed). Readings on the character of Hamlet 1661–1947. 1951.

Mack, M. The world of Hamlet. Yale Rev 41 1952.

Stirling, B. Theme and character in Hamlet. MLQ 13 1952.

Joseph, B. L. Conscience and the King: a study of Hamlet. 1953.

Bennett, J. W. Characterization in Polonius' advice to Laertes. Sh Quart 4 1953.

Green, A. J. The cunning of the scene. Ibid.

Empson, W. Hamlet when new. Sewanee Rev 61 1953.

Stevenson, D. L. An objective correlative to T. S. Eliot's Hamlet. Jnl of Aesthetics 13 1954.

Brown, J. R. The compositors of Hamlet Q2 and the Merchant of Venice. SB 7 1955.

—— and B. Harris (ed). Hamlet. 1963. Essays by various hands.

Jenkins, H. The relation between the second quarto and the folio text of Hamlet. SB 7 1955.

—— Hamlet and Ophelia. Proc Br Acad 49 1964.

Diekmann, E. Shakespeares Hamlet: Grundzüge einer Deutung. Die Neueren Sprachen 10 1955.

Emslie, M. Pepys' Shakespeare song. Sh Quart 6 1955. Morelli's setting for To be or not to be.

Lambin, G. Une première ébauche d'Hamlet (mars 1587). Les Langues Modernes 49 1955.

West, R. H. King Hamlet's ambiguous ghost. PMLA 70 1955.

Leech, C. Studies in Hamlet 1901–55. Sh Survey 9 1956.

—— The hestitation of Pyrrhus. In The morality of art: essays presented to G. Wilson Knight, 1969.

Foakes, R. A. Hamlet and the Court of Elsinore. Sh Survey 9 1956.

Honigmann, E. A. J. The date of Hamlet. Ibid.

Heilbrun, C. The character of Hamlet's mother. Sh Quart 8 1957.

Hunter, G. K. Isocrates' precepts and Polonius' character. Ibid.

Isaacs, J. William Poel's prompt-book of Fratricide punished. 1957.

Freudenstein, R. Der bestrafte Brudermord: Shakespeares Hamlet auf der Wanderbühne des 17 Jahrhunderts. Hamburg 1958.

Major, J. M. The 'letters seal'd' in Hamlet and the character of Claudius. JEGP 57 1958.

Reed, R. R. Hamlet: the pseudo-procrastinator. Sh Quart 9 1958.

Smith, J. H., L. D. Pizer and E. K. Kaufman. Hamlet, Antonio's revenge and the Ur-Hamlet. Ibid.

Deming, B. The world of Hamlet. Tulane Drama Rev 1959.

Howard, D. R. Hamlet and the contempt of the world. South Atlantic Quart 58 1959. The de contemptu mundi theme.

Grebanier, B. The heart of Hamlet. New York 1960.

Knights, L. C. An approach to Hamlet. 1960.

Montgomerie, W. More an antique Roman than a Dane. Hibbert Jnl 58 1960.

Babcock, W. Hamlet: a tragedy of errors. Lafayette Ind 1961.

Foster, R. Hamlet and the word. UTQ 30 1961.

Joseph, Sr Miriam. Discerning the ghost in Hamlet. PMLA 76 1961.

McElroy, D. Rhetorical patterns in Hamlet. N & Q April 1961.

Reno, R. H. Hamlet's quintessence of dust. Sh Quart 12 1961.

Swart, J. I know not 'seems': a study of Hamlet. REL 2 1961.

Calhoun, J. S. Hamlet and the circumference of action. Renaissance News 15 1962.

Johnston, A. The player's speech in Hamlet. Sh Quart 13 1962.

Levine, R. A. The tragedy of Hamlet's world view. College Eng April 1962.

McDonald, C. O. Decorum, ethos and pathos in the heroes of Elizabethan tragedy, with particular reference to Hamlet. JEGP 61 1962.

Ringler, W. A. Hamlet's defense of the players. In Essays on Shakespeare and Elizabethan drama in honor of Hardin Craig, Columbia Missouri 1962.

Muir, K. The imagery of Hamlet. Literary Half-Yearly (Bangalore) 3 1962.

— Shakespeare: Hamlet. 1963.

— Imagery and symbol in Hamlet. Etudes Anglaises 17 1964.

Coursen, H. R. That within: Hamlet and revenge. Bucknell Rev 11 1963.

Forker, C. R. Shakespeare's theatrical symbolism and its function in Hamlet. Sh Quart 14 1963.

Wagner, L. W. Ophelia: Shakespeare's pathetic plot device. Ibid.

Warhaft, S. The mystery of Hamlet. ELH 30 1963.

Bailey, H. P. Hamlet in France: from Voltaire to Laforgue. Geneva 1964.

Braddy, H. Hamlet's wounded name. El Paso 1964.

Camden, C. On Ophelia's madness. In Shakespeare 400, ed J. G. McManaway, New York 1964.

Craig, H. Hamlet as a man of action. HLQ 27 1964.

Hastings, W. T. Is Hamlet a hoax? In Shakespeare 1564–1964, ed E. A. Bloom, Providence 1964.

Holmes, M. The guns of Elsinore. 1964.

Jorgensen, P. A. Hamlet and the restless Renaissance. In Shakespearean essays, ed A. Thaler and N. Sanders, Knoxville 1964.

— Hamlet's therapy. HLQ 27 1964.

Manfull, L. L. The histrionic Hamlet. Educational Theatre Jnl 16 1964.

Maxwell, B. Hamlet's mother. In Shakespeare 400, ed J. G. McManaway, New York 1964.

Phialas, P. G. Hamlet and the grave-maker. JEGP 63 1964.

Reid, B. L. The last act and the action of Hamlet. Yale Rev 54 1964.

Sanders, N. Metamorphoses of the Prince: some critical and theatrical interpretations of Hamlet 1864–1964. In Shakespearean essays, ed A. Thaler and N. Sanders, Knoxville 1964.

Seng, P. J. Ophelia's songs in Hamlet. Durham Univ Jnl 25 1964.

Stabler, A. P. The sources of Hamlet: some corrections of the record. Research Stud (Pullman) 32 1964.

— Elective monarchy in the sources of Hamlet. SP 62 1965.

Boklund, G. Judgement in Hamlet. In Essays on Shakespeare, ed G. W. Chapman, Princeton 1965.

Bradbrook, M. C. An interpretation of Hamlet. Hiroshima Stud in Eng Lang & Lit 11 1965.

Charney, M. Hamlet without words. ELH 32 1965.

— Style in Hamlet. Princeton 1969.

Cooperman, S. Shakespeare's anti-hero: Hamlet and the underground man. Sh Stud 1 1965.

Fluchère, H. Hamlet et la conscience moderne. Bulletin de la Faculté des Lettres et Sciences Humaines 43 1965.

Grivelet, M. Hamlet et le nuage. Ibid.

Hapgood, R. Hamlet nearly mad: the dramaturgy of delay. Tulane Drama Rev 9 1965.

Levitsky, R. M. Rightly to be great. Sh Stud 1 1965.

Newell, A. The dramatic context and meaning of Hamlet's To be or not to be soliloquy. PMLA 80 1965.

Orange, L. E. Hamlet's mad soliloquy. South Atlantic Quart 64 1965.

Pollin, B. R. Hamlet: a successful suicide. Sh Stud 1 1965.

Randall, D. B. J. Ecce signum! Hamlet's handsaw again. Renaissance Papers 1965.

Rupp, R. H. Hamlet and the politics of providence. Xavier Univ Stud 4 1965.

Sjögren, G. A contribution to the geography of Hamlet. Sh Jb (Weimar) 101 1965.

— Hamlet and the coronation of Christian IV. Sh Quart 16 1965.

Cox, R. L. Hamlet's hamartia: Aristotle or St Paul? Yale Rev 55 1966.

Farrell, J. P. Hamlet's final role: symbolism in the duel scene. Bucknell Rev 14 1966.

Halio, J. L. Hamlet's alternative. Texas Stud in Lit & Lang 8 1966. Suicide or Christian forbearance.

Sehrt, E. T. Zur Umstimmungsszene bei Shakespeare: Hamlet III.iv. Sh Jb (Heidelberg) 1966.

Strandberg, V. H. The revenger's tragedy: Hamlet's costly code. South Atlantic Quart 65 1966.

Van Laan, T. F. Ironic reversal in Hamlet. Stud in Eng Lit 1500–1900 6 1966.

Walcutt, C. C. Hamlet: the plot's the thing. Michigan Quart Rev 5 1966.

Prosser, E. Hamlet and revenge. Stanford 1967.

Viebrock, H. Shakespeares Hamlet: die Tragödie des Gewissens. Frankfurt 1967.

Falk, D. V. Proverbs and the Polonius destiny. Sh Quart 18 1967.

French, A. L. Hamlet and the moralists. Oxford Rev 6 1967.

Lewis, C. The genesis of Hamlet. Port Washington NY 1967.

Taylor, M. A. A new look at the old sources of Hamlet. Hague 1968.

Piper, W. B. Of Hamlet's transformation. Southern Humanities Rev 2 1968.

Taylor, M. Tragic justice and the house of Polonius. Stud in Eng Lit 1500–1900 8 1968.

Booth, H. On the value of Hamlet. In Reinterpretations of Elizabethan drama, ed N. Rabkin, New York 1969.

Olsson, Y. B. In search of Yorick's skull: notes on the background of Hamlet. Sh Stud 4 1969.

Replogle, C. Not bawdy, not burlesque: the play within the play in Hamlet. MP 67 1969.

Davidson, C. The triumph of time. Dalhousie Rev 50 1970.

Gellert, B. The iconography of melancholy in the graveyard scene in Hamlet. SP 67 1970.

Hutton, V. Hamlet's fear of death. Univ Rev 37 1970.

McAlindon, T. Indecorum in Hamlet. Sh Stud 5 1970.

Cannon, C. J. 'As in a theater': Hamlet in the light of Calvin's doctrine of predestination. Stud in Eng Lit 1500–1900 11 1971.

Horwich, R. Hamlet and Eastward ho. Ibid.

Taylor, M. The conflict in Hamlet. Sh Quart 22 1971.

Merry Wives of Windsor

A most pleasant and excellent conceited comedie of Syr John Falstaffe and the merrie wives of Windsor, enter-mixed with sundrie variable and pleasing humors of Syr Hugh the Welch Knight, Justice Shallow and his wise cousin M. Slender, with the swaggering vaine of Auncient Pistoll and Corporall Nym; by William Shakespeare, as it hath bene divers times acted by the Right Honor-able my Lord Chamberlaines servants, both before her Majestie and elsewhere; London, printed by T. C[reede] for Arthur Johnson, and are to be sold at his shop in Powles churchyard, at the signe of the Flower de Leuse and the Crowne. 1602; ed J. O. Halliwell (-Phillipps) 1866 (facs); ed P. A. Daniel 1881 (facs); ed W. W. Greg, Oxford 1910 (facs); rptd Halliwell 1842 (Shake-speare Soc); W. A. Wright 1893 (Cambridge Shakespeare vol 9).

A most pleasant and excellent conceited comedy of Sir John Falstaffe and the merry wives of Windsor; with the swaggering vaine of Ancient Pistoll and Corporal Nym; written by W. Shakespeare. 1619, ed J. O. Halliwell (-Phillipps) 1866 (facs); 1630, 1664.

Modern Editions

A. Morgan, New York 1888 (Bankside; parallel texts); H. C. Hart 1904 (Arden); W. W. Greg, Oxford 1910 (facs of 4° 1); A. T. Quiller-Couch and J. D. Wilson, Cambridge 1921 (New Cambridge); G. van Santvoord, New Haven 1922 (Yale); F. T. Bowers, Baltimore 1963 (Pelican); L. B. Wright and V. A. LaMar, New York 1964 (Folger); W. Green, New York 1965 (Signet); H. J. Oliver 1971 (New Arden).

For a concordance see T. H. Howard-Hill, Oxford 1969.

Studies

Halliwell (-Phillipps), J. O. An account of the only known manuscript of Shakespeare's plays. 1843.

Bruce, J. D. Two notes on the Merry wives. MLR 7 1912.

Friedrich, P. Studien zur englischen Stenographie im Zeitalter Shakespeares. Leipzig 1914.

Robertson, J. M. The problem of the Merry wives of Windsor. 1917 (Sh Assoc).

Pollard, A. W. and J. D. Wilson. The 'stolne and surrep-titious' Shakespearian texts: the Merry wives of Windsor. TLS 7 Aug 1919.

Forsythe, R. S. A Plautine source of the Merry wives of Windsor. MP 18 1920.

—— The merry wives of Windsor: two new analogues. PQ 7 1928.

Schücking, L. L. The fairy scene in the Merry wives in folio and quarto. MLR 19 1924.

Campbell, O. J. The Italianate background of the Merry wives of Windsor. In Michigan essays and studies, Ann Arbor 1932.

Radoff, M. L. MLN 48 1933. On influences of French farces.

Crofts, J. E. V. Shakespeare and the post-horses. Bristol 1937.

Sewell, S. The relation between the Merry wives of Windsor and Jonson's Every man in his humour. Sh Assoc Bull 16 1941.

Bruce, D. H. The merry wives and Two brethren. SP 39 1942. On Shakespeare's debt to Barnabe Riche.

Ogburn, V. H. The merry wives quarto: a farce interlude. PMLA 57 1942.

Bracy, W. The merry wives of Windsor: the history and transmission of Shakespeare's text. Columbia Missouri 1952.

Long, J. H. Another masque for the Merry wives of Windsor. Sh Quart 3 1952.

Green, W. Shakespeare's Merry wives of Windsor. Princeton 1962.

Steadman, J. M. Falstaff as Actaeon: a dramatic emblem. Sh Quart 14 1963.

Goldstein, L. Some aspects of marriage and inheritance in Shakespeare's Merry wives of Windsor and Chap-man's All fools. Zeitschrift für Anglistik und Amerikan-istik 12 1964.

Bennett, A. L. The sources of Shakespeare's Merry wives. Renaissance Quart 23 1970.

Troilus and Cressida

See S. A. Tannenbaum, Troilus and Cressida: a concise bibliography, New York 1943.

The historie of Troylus and Cresseida, as it was acted by the Kings Majesties servants at the Globe; written by William Shakespeare; London, imprinted by G. Eld for R. Bonian and H. Walley, and are to be sold at the Spred Eagle in Paules churchyeard, over against the great north doore. 1609; ed J. O. Halliwell (-Phillipps) 1871 (facs); ed W. W. Greg, Oxford 1952 (facs).

The famous historie of Troylus and Cresseid, excellently expressing the beginning of their loves, with the con-ceited wooing of Pandarus Prince of Licia; written by William Shakespeare; London, imprinted by G. Eld for R. Bonian and H. Walley, and are to be sold at the Spred Eagle in Paules church-yeard, over against the great north doore. 1609 (2nd issue with new title and epistle inserted); ed J. O. Halliwell (-Phillipps) 1863 (facs); ed H. P. Stokes 1886 (facs).

Modern Editions

A. Morgan, New York 1889 (Bankside; parallel texts); K. Deighton 1906 (Arden); J. S. P. Tatlock, New York 1912 (Tudor); N. B. Paradise, New Haven 1927 (Yale); B. Dobrée 1938 (Warwick); W. W. Greg, Oxford 1952 (facs of 4° 1); H. N. Hillebrand and T. W. Baldwin, Philadelphia 1953 (New Variorum); A. J. Campbell, New Haven 1956 (Yale); J. D. Wilson and A. Walker, Cambridge 1958 (New Cambridge); V. K. Whitaker, Baltimore 1958 (Pelican); D. Seltzer, New York 1963 (Signet); L. B. Wright and V. A. LaMar, New York 1966 (Folger); G. L. Kittredge, rev I. Ribner, Waltham Mass 1967.

Studies

Ulrici, H. Ist Troilus und Cressida 'comedy' oder 'tragedy' oder 'history'? Sh Jb 9 1874.

Herford, C. H. Troilus and Cressida and Euphues, his censure to Philautus. Trans New Sh Soc 1888.

Small, R. A. In his Stage-quarrel between Ben Jonson and the so-called poetasters, Breslau 1899.

Adams, J. Q. Timon of Athens and the irregularities in the First Folio. JEGP 7 1908.

Tatlock, J. S. P. The siege of Troy in Elizabethan litera-ture, especially in Shakespeare and Heywood. PMLA 30 1915.

—— The Welsh Troilus and Cressida and its relation to the Elizabethan drama. MLR 10 1915.

—— The chief problem in Shakespeare. Sewanee Rev 24 1916.

Lawrence, W. W. The love-story in Troilus and Cressida. In Columbia University Shakespearian studies, ed B. Matthews and A. H. Thorndike, New York 1916.

—— Troilus, Cressida and Thersites. MLR 37 1942.

Rollins, H. E. The Troilus-Cressida story from Chaucer to Shakespeare. PMLA 32 1917.

Robertson, J. M. In his Shakespeare and Chapman, 1917.

Campbell, O. W. Troilus and Cressida: a justification. London Mercury Nov 1921.

Alexander, P. Troilus and Cressida 1609. Library 3rd ser 9 1928.

Keller, W. Shakespeares Troilus and Cressida. Sh Jb 66 1930.

Taylor, G. C. Shakespeare's attitude towards love and honor in Troilus and Cressida. PMLA 45 1930.

Tannenbaum, S. A. A critique of the text of Troilus and Cressida. Sh Assoc Bull 9 1934.

Spencer, T. A commentary on Shakespeare's Troilus and Cressida. Stud in Eng (Tokyo) 16 1936.

Kenny, H. Shakespeare's Cressida. Anglia 61 1937.

Campbell, O. J. Comicall satyre and Shakespeare's Troilus and Cressida. San Marino 1938.

Traversi, D. A. Troilus and Cressida. Scrutiny 7 1939.

Sewell, A. Notes on the integrity of Troilus and Cressida. RES 19 1943.

Elton, W. Shakespeare's portrait of Ajax in Troilus and Cressida. PMLA 63 1948.

Legouis, P. Troilus devant le mariage. Les Langues Modernes 42 1948.

Reynolds, G. F. Troilus and Cressida on the Elizabethan stage. In J. Q. Adams memorial studies, Washington 1948.

Williams, P. The second issue of Troilus and Cressida 1609. SB 2 1950.

— Shakespeare's Troilus and Cressida: the relationship of quarto and Folio. SB 3 1951.

Baldwin, T. W. Structural analysis of Troilus and Cressida. In Shakespeare-Studien: Festschrift für H. Mutschmann, Marburg 1951.

Dunkel, W. D. Shakespeare's Troilus. Sh Quart 2 1951.

Greg, W. W. The printing of Shakespeare's Troilus and Cressida in the first quarto. PBSA 45 1951.

Knights, L. C. Troilus and Cressida again. Scrutiny 18 1952.

Kendall, P. M. Inaction and ambivalence in Troilus and Cressida. In English studies in honor of J. S. Wilson, Charlottesville 1952.

Heuer, H. Troilus and Cressida in neuerer Sicht. Sh Jb 89 1953.

Presson, R. K. Shakespeare's Troilus and Cressida and the legends of Troy. Madison 1953.

Arnold, A. The Hector-Andromache scene in Shakespeare's Troilus and Cressida. MLQ 14 1953.

Nowottny, W. M. T. 'Opinion' and 'value' in Troilus and Cressida. EC 4 1954.

Muir, K. Troilus and Cressida. Sh Survey 8 1955.

Bowden, W. R. The human Shakespeare and Troilus and Cressida. Sh Quart 8 1957.

Goldberg, S. L. Art and freedom: the aesthetic of Ulysses. ELH 24 1957.

Bradbrook, M. C. What Shakespeare did to Chaucer's Troilus and Cressida. Sh Quart 9 1958.

Swanston, H. F. G. The baroque elements in Troilus and Cressida. Durham Univ Jnl new ser 4 1957.

Gérard, A. Meaning and structure in Troilus and Cressida. E Studies 40 1959.

Harrier, R. C. Troilus divided. In Studies in the English Renaissance drama, ed J. W. Bennett, O. Cargill and V. Hall jr, New York 1959.

Kleinstück, J. Ulysses' speech on degree as related to the play of Troilus and Cressida. Neophilologus 43 1959.

Knowland, A. S. Troilus and Cressida. Sh Quart 10 1959.

Morris, B. The tragic structure of Troilus and Cressida. Ibid.

Schmidt di Simoni, K. Shakespeares Troilus und Cressida. Heidelberg 1960.

Daniels, F. Q. Order and confusion in Troilus and Cressida. Sh Quart 12 1961.

Kaula, D. Will and reason in Troilus and Cressida. Ibid.

Main, W. W. Character amalgams in Shakespeare's Troilus and Cressida. SP 58 1961.

Enck, J. J. The peace of the Poetomachia. PMLA 77 1962.

Kimbrough, R. The origins of Troilus and Cressida: stage, quarto and Folio. Ibid.

— Shakespeare's Troilus and Cressida and its setting. Cambridge Mass 1964.

— The problem of Thersites. MLR 59 1964.

— The Troilus log: Shakespeare and 'box-office'. Sh Quart 15 1964.

Spencer, T. J. B. 'Greeks' and 'merrygreeks': a background to Timon of Athens and Troilus and Cressida. In Essays on Shakespeare and Elizabethan drama in honor of Hardin Craig, Columbia Missouri 1962.

Foakes, R. A. Troilus and Cressida reconsidered. UTQ 32 1963.

Almeida, B. H. C. de M. F. de. Troilus and Cressida: romantic love revisited. Sh Quart 15 1964.

Bayley, J. Shakespeare's only play. In Stratford papers on Shakespeare 1963, ed B. W. Jackson, Toronto 1964.

Bonjour, A. Hector and the 'one in sumptuous armour'. E Studies 45 1964.

Dyer, F. B. The destruction of Pandare. In Shakespeare encomium, ed A. Paolucci, New York 1964.

Farnham, W. Troilus in shapes of infinite desire. In Shakespeare 400, ed J. G. McManaway, New York 1964.

Lyons, C. P. The trysting scenes in Troilus and Cressida. In Shakespearean essays, ed A. Thaler and N. Sanders, Knoxville 1964.

Rickey, M. E. 'Twixt the dangerous shores: Troilus and Cressida again. Sh Quart 15 1964.

Savage, J. E. Troilus and Cressida and Elizabethan Court factions. Univ of Mississippi Stud in Eng 5 1964.

Stamm, R. The glass of Pandar's praise: the word-scenery, mirror passages and reported scenes in Shakespeare's Troilus and Cressida. E & S new ser 17 1964.

Coghill, N. A prologue and an epilogue, and Morte Hector: a map of honour. In his Shakespeare's professional skills, Cambridge 1965.

Kaufmann, R. J. Ceremonies for chaos: the status of Troilus and Cressida. ELH 32 1965.

Marsh, D. R. C. Interpretation and misinterpretation: the problem of Troilus and Cressida. Sh Stud 1 1965.

Rabkin, N. Troilus and Cressida: the uses of the double plot. Ibid.

Shalvi, A. 'Honor' in Troilus and Cressida. Stud in Eng Lit 1500–1900 5 1965.

Elton, W. R. Shakespeare's Ulysses and the problem of value. Sh Stud 2 1966.

Oates, J. C. The ambiguity of Troilus and Cressida. Sh Quart 17 1966.

Thompson, K. F. Troilus and Cressida: the incomplete Achilles. Sh Quart 19 1968.

Hargreaves, H. A. An essentially tragic Troilus and Cressida. Humanities Assoc Bull 18 1967.

Smith, J. O. Essence and existence in Shakespeare's Troilus and Cressida. PQ 46 1967.

Binney, J. The heroic warriors. Discourse 11 1968.

Gagen, J. Hector's honor. Sh Quart 19 1968.

Newlin, J. T. The modernity of Troilus and Cressida: the case for theatrical criticism. Harvard Lib Bull 17 1969.

Soellner, R. Prudence and the price of Helen. Sh Quart 20 1969.

Stein, A. Troilus and Cressida: the disjunctive imagination. ELH 36 1969.

Thomson, P. Rant and cant in Troilus and Cressida. E & S new ser 20 1969.

Ramsey, J. W. The provenance of Troilus and Cressida. Sh Quart 21 1970.

All's Well That Ends Well

In First Folio, 1623.

Modern Editions

W. O. Brigstocke 1904 (Arden); A. E. Case, New Haven 1926 (Yale); A. T. Quiller-Couch and J. D. Wilson, Cambridge 1929 (New Cambridge); G. K. Hunter 1959 (New Arden); F. Fergusson and C. J. Sisson, New York 1961 (Laurel); J. A. Barish, Baltimore 1964 (Pelican); S. Barnet, New York 1965 (Signet); L. B. Wright and V. A. LaMar, New York 1965 (Folger); B. Everett 1970 (New Penguin).

For a concordance see T. H. Howard-Hill, Oxford 1970.

Studies

Delius, N. Shakespeare's All's well that ends well and Paynter's Giletta of Narbonne. Sh Jb 22 1887.

Boyle, R. All's well that ends well and Love's labour's won. E Studien 14 1890.

Westenholz, F. P. von. Shakespeares Gewonnene Liebesmüh. Allgemeine Zeitung 1 1902.

Tolman, A. H. What has become of Shakespeare's play Love's labour's won? Chicago 1902.

Lawrence, W. W. The meaning of All's well that ends well. PMLA 37 1922.

—— In his Shakespeare's problem comedies, New York 1931.

Hastings, W. T. Sh Assoc Bull 10 1935. Notes.

Legouis, E. La comtesse de Roussillon. English 1 1937.

Bradbrook, M. C. Virtue is the true nobility: a study of the structure of All's well that ends well. RES new ser 1 1950.

Wilson, H. S. Dramatic emphasis in All's well that ends well. HLQ 13 1950.

Leech, C. The theme of ambition in All's well that ends well. ELH 21 1954.

Arthos, J. The comedy of generation. EC 5 1955.

Carter, A. H. In defense of Bertram. Sh Quart 8 1957.

Adams, J. F. All's well that ends well: the paradox of procreation. Sh Quart 13 1962.

Nagarajan, S. The structure of All's well that ends well. EC 10 1960.

Turner, R. Y. Dramatic conventions in All's well that ends well. PMLA 75 1960.

Price, J. G. From farce to romance: All's well that ends well 1756–1811. Sh Jb 99 1963.

—— The unfortunate comedy: a study of All's well that ends well and its critics. Toronto 1968.

Ranald, M. L. The betrothals of All's well that ends well. HLQ 26 1963.

Calderwood, J. L. Styles of knowing in All's well. MLQ 25 1964.

Halio, J. L. All's well that ends well. Sh Quart 15 1964.

Hethmon, R. H. The case for All's well: what is wrong with the King? Drama Critique 7 1964.

Hapgood, R. The life of shame: Parolles and All's well. EC 15 1965.

Coghill, N. All's well revalued. In Studies in English language and literature in honour of Margaret Schlauch, Warsaw 1966.

Bennett, J. W. New techniques of comedy in All's well that ends well. Sh Quart 18 1967.

Warren, R. Why does it end well? Helena, Bertram and the sonnets. Sh Survey 22 1969.

Dennis, C. All's well that ends well and the meaning of 'agape'. PQ 50 1971.

Leggatt, A. All's well that ends well: the testing of romance. MLQ 32 1971.

Measure for Measure

In First Folio, 1623.

Modern Editions

H. C. Hart 1905 (Arden); A. T. Quiller-Couch and J. D. Wilson, Cambridge 1922 (New Cambridge); W. H. Durham, New Haven 1926 (Yale); D. Harding, New Haven 1954 (Yale); R. C. Bald, Baltimore 1956 (Pelican); F. Fergusson and C. J. Sisson, New York 1962 (Laurel); E. Leisi, Heidelberg 1964 (old spelling); S. Nagarajan, New York 1964 (Signet); J. W. Lever 1965 (New Arden); G. L. Kittredge, rev I. Ribner, Waltham Mass 1967; J. M. Nosworthy 1969 (New Penguin).

For a concordance see T. H. Howard-Hill, Oxford 1969.

Studies

Whetstone's Historie of Promos and Cassandra. Ed I. Gollancz 1909 (Sh Classics).

Pater, W. Measure for measure. In his Appreciations, 1889.

Legouis, E. Shakespeare: Mesure pour mesure. Revue des Cours et Conférences 18 1910.

Suddard, M. Measure for measure as a clue to Shakespeare's attitude towards Puritanism. In his Studies and essays, Cambridge 1912.

Crawford, J. P. W. A sixteenth-century Spanish analogue of Measure for measure. MLN 35 1920.

Symonds, A. Measure for measure. In his Studies in the Elizabethan drama, 1920.

Gould, G. A new reading of Measure for measure. Eng Rev 36 1923.

Koszul, A. La technique dramatique de Shakespeare étudiée dans le premier acte de Measure for measure. Revue de l'Enseignement des Langues Vivantes 44 1927.

Falconer, J. A. Shakespeare's lost chance. Neophilologus 14 1928.

Durham, W. H. Measure for measure as measure for critics. In California essays in criticism, ed W. H. Durham, Berkeley 1929.

Wilson, R. H. The Mariana plot of Measure for measure. PQ 9 1930.

Lawrence, W. W. In his Shakespeare's problem comedies, New York 1931.

—— Measure for measure and Lucio. Sh Quart 9 1958.

Lawson, R. Lucio in Measure for measure. E Studies 19 1937.

Reimer, C. J. Der Begriff der Gnade in Shakespeares Measure for measure. Marburg 1937.

Chambers, R. W. The Jacobean Shakespeare and Measure for measure. Proc Br Acad 33 1937; rptd in his Man's unconquerable mind, 1939.

Bradbrook, M. C. Authority, truth and justice in Measure for measure. RES 17 1941.

Knights, L. C. The ambiguity of Measure for measure. Scrutiny 10 1942.

Leavis, F. R. The greatness of Measure for measure. Ibid; rptd in his Common pursuit, 1952.

Traversi, D. A. Measure for measure. Ibid.

Ball, R. H. Cinthio's Epitia and Measure for measure. In Elizabethan studies in honor of G. F. Reynolds, Boulder 1945.

Battenhouse, R. W. Measure for measure and Christian doctrine of the atonement. PMLA 61 1946.

Dodds, W. M. T. The character of Angelo in Measure for measure. MLR 41 1946.

Maxwell, J. C. Measure for measure: a footnote to recent criticism. Downside Rev 65 1947.

—— Creon and Angelo: a parallel study. Greece & Rome 18 1949.

West, E. J. Dramatist at the crossroads. Sh Assoc Bull 22 1947.

McGinn, D. J. The precise Angelo. In J. Q. Adams memorial studies, Washington 1948.

Pope, E. M. The Renaissance background of Measure for measure. Sh Survey 2 1949.

Harding, D. P. Elizabethan betrothals and Measure for measure. JEGP 49 1950.

Leech, C. The meaning of Measure for measure. Sh Survey 3 1950.

Smith, R. M. Interpretations of Measure for measure. Sh Quart 1 1950.

Sypher, W. Shakespeare as casuist. Sewanee Rev 58 1950.

Krieger, M. Measure for measure and Elizabethan comedy. PMLA 66 1951.

Fergusson, F. Philosophy and theatre in Measure for measure. Kenyon Rev 14 1952.

Lascelles, M. Shakespeare's Measure for measure. 1953.

Wilson, H. S. Action and symbol in Measure for measure and the Tempest. Sh Quart 4 1953.

Coghill, N. Comic form in Measure for measure. Sh Survey 8 1955.

Millet, S. The structure of Measure for measure. Boston Univ Stud in Eng 2 1956.

Ornstein, R. The human comedy: Measure for measure. Univ of Kansas City Rev 24 1957.

Mikkelson, R. S. To catch a saint: Angelo in Measure for measure. Western Humanities Rev 13 1958.

Lever, J. W. The date of Measure for measure. Sh Quart 10 1959.

Mainusch, H. Gnade und Gerechtigkeit in Shakespeares Measure for measure. Die Neueren Sprachen new ser 8 1959.

Stevenson, D. L. The role of James I in Shakespeare's Measure for measure. ELH 26 1959.

Sjögren, G. The setting of Measure for measure. Revue de Littérature Comparée 35 1961.

Southall, R. Measure for measure and the Protestant ethic. EC 11 1961.

Dickinson, J. Renaissance equity and Measure for measure. Sh Quart 13 1962.

Dunkel, W. Law and equity in Measure for measure. Ibid.

McCord, H. Law and equity in Measure for measure. Washington Research Stud 30 1962.

Smith, W. D. More light on Measure for measure. MLQ 23 1962.

Marsh, D. R. C. The mood of Measure for measure. Sh Quart 14 1963.

Nagarajan, S. Measure for measure and Elizabethan betrothals. Ibid.

Prouty, C. T. George Whetstone and the sources of Measure for measure. In Shakespeare 400, ed J. G. McManaway, New York 1964.

Musgrove, S. Some composite scenes in Measure for measure. Sh Quart 15 1964.

Hall, L. S. Isabella's angry ape. Ibid.

Hapgood, R. The Provost and equity in Measure for measure. Ibid.

Freedman, W. A. The Duke in Measure for measure. Tennessee Stud in Lit 9 1964.

Gilbert, A. H. The more Shakespeare he: Measure for measure. In Shakespearean essays, ed A. Thaler and N. Sanders, Knoxville 1964.

Hyman, L. Mariana and Shakespeare's theme in Measure for measure. Univ Rev 31 1964.

Skulsky, H. Pain, law and conscience in Measure for measure. JHI 25 1964.

Cole, H. C. The 'Christian' context of Measure for measure. JEGP 64 1965.

Howarth, H. Shakespeare's flattery in Measure for measure. Sh Quart 16 1965.

Bennett, J. W. Measure for measure as royal entertainment. New York 1966.

Callahan, R. D. The theme of government in Measure for measure. Paunch (Buffalo) 25 1966.

Mansell, D. 'Seemers' in Measure for measure. MLQ 27 1966.

Mincoff, M. Measure for measure: a question of approach. Sh Stud 2 1966.

Stevenson, D. The achievement of Shakespeare's Measure for measure. Ithaca 1966.

Kaufmann, R. J. Bond slaves and counterfeits: Shakespeare's Measure for measure. Sh Stud 3 1967.

Sale, R. The comic mode of Measure for measure. Sh Quart 19 1968.

Bache, W. B. Measure for measure as dialectical art. Lafayette Ind 1969.

Hamburger, M. P. Besonderheiten der Herzogsfigur in Measure for measure. Sh Jb (Weimar) 105 1969.

Nuttall, A. D. Measure for measure: quid pro quo? Sh Stud 4 1969.

Beckerman, B. A Shakespearean experiment: the dramaturgy of Measure for measure. In The Elizabethan theatre II, ed D. Galloway, Hamden Conn 1970.

Gechle, G. L. Shakespeare's Isabella, CQ 12 1970.

Schlösser, A. Implizierte Satire in Masz für Masz. Sh Jb (Weimar) 106 1970.

Wasson, J. Measure for measure: a text for Court performance? Sh Quart 21 1970.

Weil, H. Form and contexts in Measure for measure. CQ 12 1970.

Gelb, H. Duke Vincentio and the illusion of comedy: or All's not well that ends well. Sh Quart 22 1971.

Othello

See S. A. Tannenbaum, Othello: a concise bibliography, New York 1943.

The tragoedy of Othello, the Moore of Venice, as it hath beene diverse times acted at the Globe, and at the Black-Friers, by his Majesties servants; written by William Shakespeare; London, printed by N[icholas] O[kes] for Thomas Walkley, and are to be sold at his shop, at the Eagle and Child, in Brittans Bursse. 1622; ed J. O. Halliwell (-Phillipps) 1864 (facs); ed H. A. Evans 1855 (facs).

The tragoedy of Othello, the Moore of Venice. 1630, ed H. A. Evans 1885 (facs); 1655, 1681, 1687, 1695, 1705.

Modern Editions

H. H. Furness, Philadelphia 1886 (New Variorum); T. R. Price, New York 1890 (Bankside; parallel texts); H. C. Hart 1903 (Arden); L. Mason, New Haven 1918 (Yale); C. H. Herford 1920 (Warwick); M. Eccles, New York 1946 (Crofts); M. M. A. Schroer, Heidelberg 1949 (parallel texts of 4° 1 and Folio 1, with 4° 2 variants); J. D. Wilson and A. Walker, Cambridge 1955 (New Cambridge); L. B. Wright and V. L. Freund, New York 1957 (Folger); M. R. Ridley, 1958 (New Arden); G. E. Bentley, Baltimore 1958 (Pelican); F. Fergusson and C. J. Sisson, New York 1959 (Laurel).

Studies

Moulton, R. G. Othello as a type of plot. Trans New Sh Soc 1887–92.

Bradley, A. C. In his Shakespearean tragedy, 1904.

Swinburne, A. C. In his Three plays of Shakespeare, 1909.

de Fonblanque, E. M. The Italian sources of Othello. Fortnightly Rev June 1911.

Stoll, E. E. Othello: an historical and comparative study. Minneapolis 1915.

—— Othello the man. Sh Assoc Bull 9 1934.

—— Source and motive in Macbeth and Othello. RES 19 1943.

—— Mainly controversy: Hamlet, Othello. PQ 24 1946.

—— An Othello all too modern. ELH 13 1946.

—— Another Othello all too modern. In J. Q. Adams memorial studies, Washington 1948.

—— Slander in drama. Sh Quart 4 1953.

Brooke, C. F. T. The romantic Iago. Yale Rev 7 1918.

Whitney, L. Did Shakespeare know 'Leo Africanus'? PMLA 37 1922.

Krappe, A. H. A Byzantine source of Shakespeare's Othello. MLN 39 1924.

Winstanley, L. Othello as the tragedy of Italy. 1924.

Gilbert, A. H. Scenes of discovery in Othello. PQ 5 1926.

Tesch, A. Zum Namen Desdemona. Germanisch-romanische Monatsschrift 17 1929.

Knight, G. W. The style of Othello. Fortnightly Rev April 1929.

Draper, J. W. 'Honest Iago'. PMLA 46 1931.

—— 'This poor trash of Venice'. JEGP 30 1931.

—— Captain general Othello. Anglia 55 1931.

—— Othello and Elizabethan army life. Revue Anglo-américaine 9 1932.

—— Desdemona: a compound of two cultures. Revue de Littérature Comparée 13 1933.

—— The jealousy of Iago. Neophilologus 25 1939.

—— Changes in the tempo of Desdemona's speech. Anglica 1 1946.

—— Patterns of tempo and humor in Othello. E Studies 28 1947.

Cameron, K. W. Othello, quarto 1, reconsidered. PMLA 47 1932.
— The text of Othello: an analysis. PMLA 49 1934.
Kelcy, A. Notes on Othello. PQ 12 1933.
Brock, J. H. E. Iago and some Shakespearean villains. Cambridge 1937.
Tannenbaum, S. A. The wronged Iago. Sh Assoc Bull 12 1937.
Baldensperger, F. Was Othello an Ethiopian? Harvard Stud 20 1938.
Leavis, F. R. Diabolic intellect and the noble hero. Scrutiny 6 1938; rptd in his Common pursuit, 1952.
Stroup, T. B. Shakespeare's use of a travelbook commonplace. PQ 17 1938.
Mandin, L. Etude Shakespearienne: le mystère de la perle et du judéen. Mercure de France Oct 1939.
Miller, D. C. Iago and the problem of time. E Studies 22 1940.
Kirschbaum, L. The modern Othello. ELH 11 1944.
Stirling, B. Psychology in Othello. Sh Assoc Bull 19 1944.
Withington, R. Shakespeare and race-prejudice. In Elizabethan studies in honor of G. F. Reynolds, Boulder 1945.
Poirier, M. Le double temps dans Othello. Etudes Anglaises 5 1952.
Granville-Barker, H. Othello. In his Prefaces to Shakespeare: series 4, 1946.
Moore, J. R. The character of Iago. In Studies in honor of A. H. R. Fairchild, Columbia Missouri 1946.
Bowman, T. D. In defense of Emilia. Sh Assoc Bull 22 1947.
Maugeri, A. Otello e la storia del capitano moro. Messina 1947.
Prior, M. E. Character in relation to action in Othello. MP 44 1947.
Raymond, W. O. Motivation and character portrayal in Othello. UTQ 17 1947.
Sedgewick, G. G. Of irony, especially in drama. Toronto 1948.
Bonnard, G. Are Othello and Desdemona innocent or guilty? E Studies 30 1949.
Camden, C. Iago on women. JEGP 48 1949.
Wilcox, J. Othello's crucial moment. Sh Assoc Bull 24 1949.
Flatter, R. The Moor of Venice. 1950.
Jordan, H. H. Dramatic illusion in Othello. Sh Quart 1 1950.
Jorgensen, P. A. Honesty in Othello. SP 47 1950.
Rand, F. P. The over-garrulous Iago. Sh Quart 1 1950.
Traversi, D. A. Othello. Wind & Rain 6 1950.
Burke, K. Othello: an essay to illustrate a method. Hudson Rev 4 1951.
Heilman, R. B. More fair than black: light and dark in Othello. EC 1 1951.
— The economics of Iago and others. PMLA 68 1953.
— An approach to Othello. Sewanee Rev 64 1956.
— Magic in the web: action and language in Othello. Lexington Kentucky 1956.
— Wit and witchcraft: thematic form in Othello. Arizona Quart 12 1956.
Kliger, S. Othello: the man of judgement. MP 48 1951.
Muir, K. The jealousy of Iago. Eng Miscellany (Rome) 2 1951.
Webb, H. J. The military background in Othello. PQ 30 1951. See J. R. Moore 31 1952.
— Rude am I in my speech. E Studies 39 1958.
Nowottny, W. M. T. Justice and love in Othello. UTQ 21 1952.
Bethell, S. L. Shakespeare's imagery: the diabolical images in Othello. Sh Survey 5 1952.
Siegel, P. N. The damnation of Othello. PMLA 68 1953.
Elliott, G. R. Flaming minister: a study of Othello as tragedy of love and hate. Durham NC 1953.
Money, J. Othello's It is the cause . . . : an analysis. Sh Survey 6 1953.

Weisinger, H. Iago's Iago. Kansas City Univ Rev 20 1954.
Rosenberg, M. The refinement of Othello in the eighteenth-century British theatre. SP 51 1954.
— A sceptical look at sceptical criticism. PQ 33 1954.
— In defense of Iago. Sh Quart 6 1955.
— The masks of Othello. Berkeley 1961.
Gardner, H. The noble Moor. Proc Br Acad 41 1955.
— Othello: a retrospect. Sh Survey 21 1968.
Ribner, I. Othello and the pattern of Shakespearian tragedy. Tulane Stud in Eng 5 1955.
Sproule, A. F. A time scheme for Othello. Sh Quart 7 1956.
Gérard, A. Egregiously an ass: the dark side of the Moor. Sh Survey 10 1957.
— Alack, poor Iago! intellect and action in Othello. Sh Jb 94 1958.
Arnold, A. The function of Brabantio in Othello. Sh Quart 8 1957.
Arthos, J. The fall of Othello. Sh Quart 9 1958.
Hubler, E. The damnation of Othello: some limitations on the Christian view of the play. Ibid.
Spivack, B. Shakespeare and the allegory of evil. New York 1958.
Alexander, P. Under which king, Bezonian? In Elizabethan and Jacobean studies presented to F. P. Wilson, Oxford 1959. On the death of Othello.
Lerner, L. The Machiavel and the Moor. EC 9 1959.
Bayley, J. In his Characters of love, 1961.
Hawkes, T. Iago's use of reason. SP 58 1961.
Ross, L. J. The use of a 'fit-up' booth in Othello. Sh Quart 12 1961.
— Shakespeare's 'dull clown' and symbolic music. Sh Quart 17 1966.
— 'A fellow almost damn'd in a fair wife'. Eng Lang Notes 5 1968.
Ranald, M. L. The indiscretions of Desdemona. Sh Quart 14 1963.
Williamson, K. 'Honest' and 'false' in Othello. Studia Neophilologica 35 1963.
Adams, M. S. 'Ocular proof' in Othello and its source. PMLA 79 1964.
Jorgensen, P. A. 'Perplexed in the extreme': the role of thought in Othello. In Shakespeare 400, ed J. G. McManaway, New York 1964.
Matthews, G. M. Othello and the dignity of man. In Shakespeare in a changing world, ed A. Kettle 1964.
McCullen, J. T. Iago's use of proverbs. Stud in Eng Lit 1500–1900 4 1964.
McGee, A. Othello's motive for murder. Sh Quart 15 1964.
Warnken, H. L. Iago as a projection of Othello. In Shakespeare encomium, ed A. Paolucci, New York 1964.
Watson, T. L. The detractor-backbiter: Iago and the tradition. Texas Stud in Lit & Lang 5 1964.
West, R. H. The Christianness of Othello. Sh Quart 15 1964.
Babcock, W. Iago: an extraordinary honest man. Sh Quart 16 1965.
Muir, K. The text of Othello. Sh Stud 1 1965.
Wentersdorf, K. P. Structure and characterization in Othello and King Lear. College Eng May 1965.
Hapgood, R. The trials of Othello. In Pacific Coast studies in Shakespeare, ed W. F. McNeir and T. N. Greenfield, Portland Oregon 1966.
Richmond, H. Love and justice: Othello's Shakespearean context. Ibid.
Kaula, D. Othello possessed: notes on Shakespeare's use of magic and witchcraft. Sh Stud 2 1966.
Shaw, J. 'What is the matter?' in Othello. Sh Quart 17 1966.
Doran, M. Good name in Othello. Stud in Eng Lit 1500–1900 7 1967.
Echeruo, M. J. C. The context of Othello's tragedy. Southern Rev (Adelaide) 2 1967.

Stewart, D. J. Othello: Roman comedy as nightmare. Emory Univ Quart 22 1967.

Alexander, N. Thomas Rymer and Othello. Sh Survey 21 1968.

Allen, N. B. The two parts of Othello. Ibid.

Almeida, B. H. C. de M. F. de. Othello: a tragedy built on a comic structure. Ibid.

Hibbard, G. R. Othello and the pattern of Shakespearian tragedy. Ibid.

Scragg, L. Iago: vice or devil? Ibid.

Hallstead, R. N. Idolatrous love: a new approach to Othello. Sh Quart 19 1968.

Shaffer, E. S. Iago's malignity motivated: Coleridge's unpublished opus magnum. Ibid.

Watts, R. A. The comic scenes in Othello. Ibid.

Davidson, C. Structure and theme in Othello. Discourse 12 1969.

Johnson, R. C. Roderigo, that 'poor trash of Venice'. Univ Rev 35 1969.

Mercer, P. Othello and the form of heroic tragedy. CQ 11 1969.

Morris, H. No amount of prayer can possibly matter. Sewanee Rev 77 1969.

Stempel, D. The silence of Iago. PMLA 84 1969.

Doran, M. Iago's 'if': an essay on the syntax of Othello. In The drama of the Renaissance, ed E. M. Blistein, Providence 1970.

Evans, K. W. The racial factor in Othello. Sh Stud 5 1970.

Homan, S. R. Iago's aesthetics: Othello and Shakespeare's portrait of an artist. Ibid.

Hyman, S. E. Iago: some approaches to the illusion of his motivation. 1970.

— Portraits of the artist: Iago and Prospero. Shenandoah 21 1970.

Mason, H. A. In his Shakespeare's tragedies of love, 1970.

Schwartz, E. Stylistic 'impurity' and the meaning of Othello. Stud in Eng Lit 1500–1900 10 1970.

Zacha, R. B. Iago and the commedia dell'arte. Arlington Quart 1971.

King Lear

M. William Shak-speare his true chronicle historie of the life and death of King Lear and his three daughters, with the unfortunate life of Edgar, sonne and heire to the Earle of Gloster, and his sullen and assumed humor of Tom of Bedlam, as it was played before the Kings Majestie at Whitehall upon S. Stephans night in Christmas hollidayes, by his Majesties servants playing usually at the Gloabe on the Bancke-side; London, printed for Nathaniel Butter, and are to be sold at his shop in Pauls Church-yard at the signe of the Pide Bull neere St Austins Gate. 1608 (sheets D–G, K found in corrected and uncorrected forms; see W. W. Greg, RES 1 1925 p. 469); ed J. O. Halliwell (-Phillipps) 1868 (facs); ed P. A. Daniel 1885 (facs); ed W. W. Greg, Oxford 1939 (facs).

Mr William Shake-speare his true chronicle history of the life and death of King Lear and his three daughters, with the unfortunate life of Edgar, sonne and heire to the Earle of Glocester, and his sullen and assumed humour of Tom of Bedlam. 1608 (for 1619), ed J. O. Halliwell (-Phillipps) 1867 (facs), ed P. A. Daniel 1885 (facs); 1655.

Modern Editions

H. H. Furness, Philadelphia 1880 (New Variorum); A. A. Adee, New York 1890 (Bankside; parallel texts); W. Viëtor, Marburg 1892 (parallel texts); W. J. Craig 1901 (Arden); D. N. Smith 1902 (Warwick); W. L. Phelps, New Haven 1917 (Yale); W. W. Greg, Oxford 1939 (facs of 4° 1); G. I. Duthie, Oxford 1949; K. Muir 1952 (New Arden); L. B. Wright and V. L. Freund, New York 1957 (Folger); A. Harbage, Baltimore 1958 (Pelican); G. I. Duthie and J. D. Wilson, Cambridge 1960 (New Cambridge); F. Fergusson and C. J. Sisson, New York 1962 (Signet); G. L. Kittredge, rev I. Ribner, Waltham Mass 1967.

Studies

The true chronicle history of King Leir, and his three daughters, Gonorill, Ragan and Cordella. 1605; rptd 1907 (Malone Soc facs); TFT 1910; ed S. Lee 1909 (Sh Classics).

Shakspere's Holinshed. Ed W. G. Boswell-Stone 1896.

Sampson, M. W. On the date of King Lear. MLQ 5 1902.

Bradley, A. C. In his Shakespearean tragedy, 1904.

Perrett, W. The story of King Lear from Geoffrey of Monmouth to Shakespeare. Berlin 1904.

Law, R. A. On the date of King Lear. PMLA 21 1906.

— Holinshed as source for Henry V and King Lear. SE 14 1934.

— Holinshed's Leir story and Shakespeare's. SP 47 1950.

— King Leir and King Lear: an examination of the two plays. In Studies in honor of T. W. Baldwin, Urbana 1958.

Greg, W. W. On certain false dates in Shakespearian quartos. Library 1st ser 9 1908.

— The staging of King Lear. RES 16 1940. Postscript 22 1946.

— The date of King Lear and Shakespeare's use of earlier versions of the story. Library 4th ser 20 1940.

— Time, place and politics in King Lear. MLR 35 1940.

— The function of bibliography in literary criticism illustrated in a study of the text of King Lear. Neophilologus 18 1933.

Swinburne, A. C. In his Three plays of Shakespeare, 1909.

Cunnington, R. H. The revision of King Lear. MLR 5 1910.

Moriarty, W. D. The bearing on dramatic sequence of the varia in Richard III and King Lear. MP 10 1913.

Schücking, L. L. Eine Anleihe Shakespeares bei Tourneur. E Studien 50 1916.

Radebrecht, F. Shakespeares Abhängigkeit von John Marston. Cöthen 1918.

Winstanley, L. Macbeth, King Lear and contemporary history. Cambridge 1922.

Craig, H. The ethics of King Lear. PQ 4 1925.

— The composition of King Lear. Renaissance Papers 1961.

Granville-Barker, H. In his Prefaces to Shakespeare: series 1, 1927.

Blunden, E. Shakespeare's significances. 1929 (Sh Assoc lecture).

Doran, M. The text of King Lear. Stanford 1931.

— Elements in the composition of King Lear. SP 30 1933.

— The quarto of King Lear and Bright's shorthand. MP 33 1935.

Ashton, J. W. The wrath of King Lear. JEGP 31 1932.

Kelcy, A. Notes on King Lear. PQ 11 1932.

Adams, J. Q. The quarto of King Lear and shorthand. MP 31 1933.

Kreider, P. V. Gloucester's eyes. Sh Assoc Bull 8 1933.

Bransom, J. S. H. The tragedy of King Lear. Oxford 1934.

Stoll, E. E. Kent and Gloster. Life & Letters March 1934.

Harrison, G. B. The background to King Lear. TLS 28 Dec 1935.

Atkinson, D. F. King Lear: another contemporary account. ELH 3 1936. Gerard Legh, Accedens of armory, 1562.

Fijn van Draat, P. King Lear. Anglia 61 1937.

— If Cordelia . . . Anglia 63 1939.

Draper, J. W. The occasion of King Lear. SP 34 1937.

— The old age of King Lear. JEGP 39 1940.

— Patterns of tempo and humor in King Lear. Bull History of Medicine 21 1947.

Darby, R. H. Astrology in Shakespeare's King Lear. E Studies 20 1938.

Gurland, I. Das Gestaltungsgesetz von Shakespeares König Lear. Würzburg 1938.

Henderson, W. B. D. Montaigne's Apologie of Raymond Sebond and King Lear. Shakespeare Assoc Bull 14–15 1939–40.

Nosworthy, J. M. King Lear: the moral aspect. E Studies 21 1939.

Perkinson, R. H. Is this the promised end? E Studien 83 1939.

—— Shakespeare's revision of the Lear story and the structure of King Lear. PQ 22 1943.

Watkins, W. B. C. The two techniques in King Lear. RES 18 1942; rptd in his Shakespeare and Spenser, Princeton 1950.

Kernodle, G. F. The symphonic form of King Lear. In Elizabethan studies in honor of G. F. Reynolds, Boulder 1945.

Kirschbaum, L. The true text of King Lear. Baltimore 1945.

—— Banquo and Edgar: character or function. EC 7 1957.

Hobday, C. H. The social background of King Lear. Modern Quart Miscellany 1 1946.

Small, S. A. The King Lear quarto. Sh Assoc Bull 21 1946.

Smith, R. M. King Lear and the Merlin tradition. MLQ 7 1946.

Bickersteth, G. L. The golden world of King Lear. Proc Br Acad 34 1947.

Heilman, R. B. The two natures in King Lear. Accent 8 1947.

—— This great stage: image and structure in King Lear. Baton Rouge 1948.

—— The unity of King Lear. Sewanee Rev 56 1948.

—— The Lear world. Eng Inst Essays 1948.

Muir, E. The politics of King Lear. Glasgow 1947; rptd in his Essays on literature and society, 1949.

Parr, J. Edmund's nativity in King Lear. Sh Assoc Bull 21 1946; rptd, with The 'late eclipses' in King Lear, in his Tamburlaine's malady and other essays, Tuscaloosa 1953.

Adams, J. C. The original staging of King Lear. In J. Q. Adams memorial studies, Washington 1948.

Bald, R. C. Thou, nature, art my goddess: Edmund and Renaissance free thought. Ibid.

Campbell, O. J. The salvation of King Lear. ELH 15 1948.

Fort, J. B. La signification de King Lear. Les Langues Modernes 42 1948.

Pyle, F. Twelfth night, King Lear and Arcadia. MLR 43 1948.

Williams, P. The compositor of the Pied Bull Lear. SB 1 1949.

—— Two problems in the Folio text of King Lear. Sh Quart 4 1953.

Danby, J. F. Shakespeare's doctrine of nature: a study of King Lear. 1949.

Keast, W. R. Imagery and meaning in the interpretation of King Lear. MP 47 1950; rptd in Critics and criticism, ed R. S. Crane, Chicago 1952.

Lothian, J. M. King Lear: a tragic reading of life. 1950.

Maxwell, J. C. The technique of invocation in King Lear. MLR 45 1950.

Muir, K. and J. F. Danby. Arcadia and King Lear. N & Q 4 Feb 1950.

'Orwell, George' (E. Blair). Lear, Tolstoy and the Fool. In his Shooting an elephant, 1950.

Isenberg, A. Cordelia absent. Sh Quart 2 1951.

Muir, K. Samuel Harsnett and King Lear. RES new ser 2 1951.

Williams, G. W. The poetry of the storm in King Lear. Sh Quart 2 1951.

Ribner, I. Sidney's Arcadia and the structure of King Lear. Studia Neophilologica 24 1952.

—— Shakespeare and legendary history: Lear and Cymbeline. Sh Quart 7 1956.

—— The gods are just: a reading of King Lear. Tulane Drama Rev 2 1958.

Maclean, N. Episode, scene, speech and word: the madness of Lear. In Critics and criticism, ed R. S. Crane, Chicago 1952.

Cauthen, I. B. Compositor determination in the First Folio King Lear. SB 5 1953.

Traversi, D. A. King Lear. Scrutiny 19 1953.

—— King Lear. In Stratford papers on Shakespeare 1964, ed B. W. Jackson, Toronto 1965.

Rosier, J. L. The lex aeterna and King Lear. JEGP 53 1954.

Cairncross, A. S. The quartos and the Folio text of King Lear. RES new ser 6 1955.

Siegel, P. N. Adversity and the miracle of love in King Lear. Sh Quart 6 1955.

Craik, T. W. Cordelia as 'last and least' of Lear's daughters. N & Q Nov 1956.

Musgrove, S. The nomenclature of King Lear. RES new ser 7 1956.

Kahn, S. J. Enter Lear mad. Sh Quart 8 1957.

Morris, I. Cordelia and Lear. Ibid.

Barish, J. A. and M. Waingrow. 'Service' in King Lear. Sh Quart 9 1958.

Frost, W. Shakespeare's rituals and the opening of King Lear. Hudson Rev 10 1958.

Block, E. A. King Lear: a study in balanced and shifting sympathies. Sh Quart 10 1959.

French, C. S. Shakespeare's 'folly': King Lear. Ibid.

Hockey, D. C. The trial pattern in King Lear. Ibid.

Elliott, G. R. The initial contrast in Lear. JEGP 58 1959.

Burckhardt, S. King Lear: the quality of nothing. Minnesota Rev 2 1961.

Stroup, T. B. Cordelia and the Fool. Sh Quart 12 1961.

Alpers, P. J. King Lear and the theory of the sight pattern. In In defense of reading, ed R. A. Brower and R. Poirier, New York 1962.

Baker, J. V. An existential examination of King Lear. College Eng April 1962.

Bennett, J. W. The storm within: the madness of Lear. Sh Quart 13 1962.

Fleissner, R. F. The 'nothing' element in King Lear. Ibid.

McCloskey, J. C. The emotive use of animal imagery in King Lear. Ibid.

Schoff, F. G. King Lear: moral example or tragic protagonist. Ibid.

Fraser, R. A. Shakespeare's poetics in relation to King Lear. 1962.

Hogan, J. J. Cutting his text according to his measure: a note on the Folio King Lear. PQ 41 1962.

Brooke, N. Shakespeare: King Lear. 1963.

—— The ending of King Lear. In Shakespeare 1564–1964, ed E. A. Bloom, Providence 1964.

Cutts, J. P. Lear's 'learned Theban'. Sh Quart 14 1963.

Jenkins, R. The Socratic imperative and King Lear. Renaissance Papers 1963.

Knights, L. C. King Lear as metaphor. In Myth and symbol, ed B. Slote, Lincoln Nebraska 1963.

Spencer, C. A word for Tate's King Lear. Stud in Eng Lit 1500–1900 3 1963.

Anshutz, H. L. Cordelia and the Fool. Washington Research Stud 32 1964.

Berman, R. Sense and substance in King Lear. Neuphilologische Mitteilungen 65 1964.

Eastman, A. M. King Lear's 'poor fool'. Papers of Michigan Acad 49 1964.

Hillier, R. L. The dramatic structure of King Lear. Univ of Wyoming Pbns 29 1964.

Jayne, S. Charity in King Lear. In Shakespeare 400, ed J. G. McManaway, New York 1964.

Jones, J. L. King Lear and the metaphysics of thunder. Xavier Univ Stud 3 1964.

Myrick, K. Christian pessimism in King Lear. In Shakespeare 1564–1964, ed E. A. Bloom, Providence 1964.

Smidt, K. The quarto and the Folio Lear: another look at the theories of textual derivation. E Studies 45 1964.

Frye, D. The context of Lear's unbuttoning. ELH 32 1965.

Honigmann, E. A. J. Spelling tests and the first quarto of King Lear. Library 5th ser 20 1965.

London, P. W. The stature of Lear. Univ of Windsor Rev 1 1965.

Mack, M. King Lear in our time. Berkeley 1965.

—— 'We came crying hither': an essay on some characteristics of King Lear. In Essays on Shakespeare, ed G. W. Chapman, Princeton 1965.

Mortenson, P. The role of Albany. Sh Quart 16 1965.

Presson, R. K. Boethius, King Lear and 'Maystresse Philosophie'. JEGP 64 1965.

Šimko, J. King Lear and Timon of Athens. Philologica Pragensia 8 1965.

Stevenson, W. Albany as archetype in King Lear. MLQ 26 1965.

Velz, J. W. Division, confinement and the moral structure of King Lear. Rice Univ Stud 51 1965.

Wentersdorf, K. P. Structure and characterization in Othello and King Lear. College Eng May 1965.

Elton, W. R. King Lear and the gods. San Marino 1966.

Jackson, E. M. King Lear: the grammar of tragedy. Sh Quart 17 1966.

Rosenberg, J. D. King Lear and his comforters. EC 16 1966.

Skulsky, H. King Lear and the meaning of chaos. Sh Quart 17 1966.

Black, J. An Augustan stage-history: Nahum Tate's King Lear. Restoration & 18th-century Theatre Research 6 1967.

Gardner, H. L. King Lear. 1967.

Ingham, P. A note on the aural errors in the first quarto of King Lear. Sh Stud 3 1967.

Jorgensen, P. A. Lear's self-discipline. Los Angeles 1967.

Mason, H. A. King Lear. Cambridge Quart 2 1967.

Peck, R. A. Edgar's pilgrimage: high comedy in King Lear. Stud in Eng Lit 1500–1900 7 1967.

Stuart, B. K. Truth and tragedy in King Lear. Sh Quart 18 1967.

Hole, S. The background of divine action in King Lear. Stud in Eng Lit 1500–1900 8 1968.

Lyons, C. R. The folly of love in King Lear. Revue des Langues Vivantes 34 1968.

Marks, C. L. Speak what we feel: the end of King Lear. Eng Lang Notes 5 1968.

McNeir, W. F. The role of Edmund in King Lear. Stud in Eng Lit 1500–1900 8 1968.

Oppel, H. Die Gerichtsszene in King Lear. Mainz 1968.

Rosinger, L. Gloucester and Lear: men who act like gods. ELH 35 1968.

Stockholder, K. The multiple genres of King Lear: breaking the archetypes. Bucknell Rev 16 1968.

Vickers, B. King Lear and the Renaissance paradoxes. MLR 63 1968.

Riemer, A. P. Darker purpose: an approach to Shakespeare's King Lear. Sydney 1968.

Donner, H. W. 'Is this the promised end?': reflections on the tragic ending of King Lear. E Studies 50 1969.

McCullen, J. T. Edgar: the wise bedlam. In Shakespeare in the Southwest, ed T. J. Stafford, Austin 1969.

Rackin, P. Delusion as resolution in King Lear. Sh Quart 21 1970.

Barron, F. King Lear and his fool. Educational Theatre Jnl 22 1970.

Enright, D. J. Shakespeare and the students. 1970.

Hargreave, H. A. A visual contradiction in King Lear. Sh Quart 21 1970.

Leider, E. W. Plainness of style in King Lear. Ibid.

Weitz, M. The coinage of man: King Lear and Camus's L'étranger. MLR 66 1970.

Macbeth

In First Folio, 1623; ed J. D. Wilson [1928] (facs).

Modern Editions

W. G. Clark and W. A. Wright, Oxford 1869; H. H. Furness, Philadelphia 1873, rev H. H. Furness jr 1903 (New Variorum); E. K. Chambers 1893 (Warwick); J. M. Manly 1896; M. H. Liddell 1903; H. Conrad 1907; H. Cuningham 1912 (Arden); C. M. Lewis, New Haven 1918 (Yale); G. C. Taylor and R. Smith, Boston 1939; J. D. Wilson, Cambridge 1947 (New Cambridge); K. Muir 1951 (New Arden); E. M. Waith, New Haven 1954 (Yale); A. Harbage, Baltimore 1956 (Pelican); F. Fergusson and C. J. Sisson, New York 1959 (Laurel); L. B. Wright and V. A. LaMar, New York 1960 (Folger); S. Barnet, New York 1963 (Signet); G. L. Kittredge, rev I. Ribner, Waltham Mass 1966; G. K. Hunter 1967 (New Penguin).

Studies

Shakspere's Holinshed. Ed W. G. Boswell-Stone 1896.

Sarrazin, G. Shakespeares Macbeth und Kyds Spanish tragedy. E Studien 21 1895.

Bradley, A. C. In his Shakespearean tragedy, 1904.

Lawrence, W. J. The mystery of Macbeth. Fortnightly Rev Nov 1920; rptd in his Shakespeare's workshop, Oxford 1928.

Symons, A. In his Studies in the Elizabethan drama, 1920.

Winstanley, L. Macbeth, King Lear and contemporary history. Cambridge 1922.

Bald, R. C. Macbeth and the 'short' plays. RES 4 1928.

Kittredge, G. L. Witchcraft in old and new England. Cambridge Mass 1929.

Knight, G. W. Macbeth and the nature of evil. Hibbert Jnl 28 1930.

Curry, W. C. 'Tumbling nature's germens'. SP 29 1932.

—— The demonic metaphysics of Macbeth. SP 30 1933.

—— Macbeth's changing character. JEGP 34 1935.

Tonge, M. Black magic and miracles in Macbeth. JEGP 31 1932.

Thaler, A. The lost scenes of Macbeth. PMLA 49 1934.

Robertson, J. M. Literary detection: a symposium on Macbeth. 1931.

Sargeaunt, W. D. Macbeth: a new interpretation of the text of Shakespeare's play. 1936.

Hunter, E. R. Macbeth as a morality. Sh Assoc Bull 12 1937.

Coles, B. Shakespeare studies: Macbeth. New York 1938.

Draper, J. W. Historic local colour in Macbeth. Revue Belge 17 1938.

—— Macbeth as a compliment to James I. E Studien 62 1938.

—— The gracious Duncan. MLR 36 1941.

—— Macbeth, 'infirme of purpose'. Bull History of Medicine 10 1941.

—— Patterns of humor and tempo in Macbeth. Neophilologus 31 1947.

Buch-Marchand, E. Macbeth: eine Charakteranalyse. Sh Jb 77 1941.

Doran, M. That undiscovered country. PQ 20 1941.

Franz, W. Zu der Sprache von Shakespeares Macbeth (Akt IV). Anglia 65 1941.

Calhoun, H. V. James I and the witch scenes in Macbeth. Sh Assoc Bull 17 1942.

Stunz, A. N. The date of Macbeth. ELH 9 1942.

Stoll, E. E. Source and motive in Macbeth and Othello. RES 19 1943.

Smith, F. M. The relation of Macbeth to Richard III. PMLA 60 1945.

Arthos, J. The naive imagination and the destruction of Macbeth. ELH 14 1947.

Brooks, C. The naked babe and the cloak of manliness. In his Well wrought urn, New York 1947.

Nosworthy, J. M. Macbeth at the Globe. Library 5th ser 2 1947.

Schmetz, L. Die Charakterisierung der Personen durch die Sprache in Macbeth. Sh Jb 74–6 1948–50.

Spargo, J. W. The knocking at the gate in Macbeth: an essay in interpretation. In J. Q. Adams memorial studies, Washington 1948.

Walker, R. The time is free: a study of Macbeth. 1949.

Muir, K. The uncomic pun. Cambridge Jnl May 1950.

— Image and symbol in Macbeth. Sh Survey 19 1966.

Paul, H. N. The royal play of Macbeth. New York 1950.

Bradbrook, M. C. The sources of Macbeth. Sh Survey 4 1951.

Campbell, L. B. Political ideas in Macbeth iv. iii. Sh Quart 2 1951.

Stein, A. Macbeth and word-magic. Sewanee Rev 59 1951.

Zandvoort, R. W. Dramatic motivation in Macbeth. Les Langues Modernes 45 1951; rptd in his Collected papers, Groningen 1954.

Fergusson, F. Macbeth as the imitation of an action. Eng Inst Essays 1951.

Empson, W. Dover Wilson on Macbeth. Kenyon Rev 14 1952.

Law, R. A. The composition of Macbeth with reference to Holinshed. SE 31 1952.

Frye, R. M. Macbeth and the powers of darkness. Emory Univ Quart 8 1952.

Stirling, B. The unity of Macbeth. Sh Quart 4 1953.

Arnold, A. The recapitulation dream in Richard III and Macbeth. Sh Quart 6 1955.

Jack, J. H. Macbeth, King James and the Bible. ELH 22 1955.

Speaight, R. Nature and grace in Macbeth. Essays by Divers Hands new ser 27 1955.

Adam, R. J. The real Macbeth: King of Scots. History Today 7 1957.

Flatter, R. Who wrote the Hecate-scene? Sh Jb 93 1957.

— Macbeth. Frankfurt 1958.

Kirschbaum, L. Banquo and Edgar: character or function? EC 7 1957.

Tomlinson, T. B. Action and soliloquy in Macbeth. EC 8 1958.

Hagemann, G. Shakespeares Macbeth: Gestalt und Gehalt. Frankfurt 1958.

Blissett, W. The secret'st man of blood: a study of dramatic irony in Macbeth. Sh Quart 10 1959.

Clarke, C. C. Darkened reason in Macbeth. Durham Univ Jnl 53 1960.

Amnéus, D. A. A missing scene in Macbeth. JEGP 60 1961.

— The Cawdor episode in Macbeth. JEGP 63 1964.

Duthie, G. I. Shakespeare's Macbeth: a study in tragic absurdity. In English studies today, ed G. Bonnard, Berne 1961.

— Antithesis in Macbeth. Sh Survey 19 1966.

Harcourt, J. B. I pray you, remember the porter. Sh Quart 12 1961.

Markels, J. The spectacle of deterioration: Macbeth and the 'manner' of tragic imitation. Ibid.

Bernad, M. A. The five tragedies in Macbeth. Sh Quart 13 1962.

Brown, J. R. Shakespeare: the tragedy of Macbeth. 1963.

Cunningham, D. G. Macbeth: the tragedy of the hardened heart. Sh Quart 14 1963.

Dyson, J. P. The structural function of the banquet scene in Macbeth. Ibid.

Kantak, V. Y. An approach to Shakespearian tragedy: the 'actor' image in Macbeth. Sh Survey 16 1963.

Knights, L. C. Poetry and philosophy in Macbeth. Literary Criterion (Mysore) 6 1963.

Huntley, F. L. Macbeth and the background of Jesuitical equivocation. PMLA 79 1964.

Rogers, H. L. 'Double profit' in Macbeth. Melbourne 1964.

Walton, J. K. Macbeth. In Shakespeare in a changing world, ed A. Kettle 1964.

Biggins, D. Scorpions, serpents and treachery in Macbeth. Sh Stud 1 1965.

Reid, B. L. Macbeth and the play of absolutes. Sewanee Rev 73 1965.

Ewbank, I.-S. The fiend-like Queen: a note on Macbeth and Seneca's Medea. Sh Survey 19 1966.

McGee, A. R. Macbeth and the furies. Ibid.

Merchant, W. M. His fiend-like queen. Ibid.

Debax, J. P. Macbeth et la tradition de la moralité, avec référence particulière aux images vestimentaires. Caliban (Toulouse) new ser 5 1968.

Taylor, M. Ideals of manhood in Macbeth. Etudes Anglaises 21 1968.

Bartholomeusz, D. Macbeth and the players. Cambridge 1969. Productions from Globe to Mermaid.

Lombardo, A. Lettura del Macbeth. Vicenza 1969.

Rissanen, M. Nature's copy, great bond and lease of nature in Macbeth. Neuphilologische Mitteilungen 70 1969.

Parker, B. L. Macbeth: the great illusion. Sewanee Rev 78 1970.

Davidson, C. The primrose way: a study of Shakespeare's Macbeth. Conesville Iowa 1970.

Enright, D. J. In his Shakespeare and the students, 1970.

Bauduin, J. Les éléments baroques dans Macbeth et leur utilisation. Etudes Anglaises 24 1971.

Jorgensen, P. A. Our naked frailties. Berkeley 1971.

Antony and Cleopatra

In First Folio, 1623; ed J. D. Wilson [1929] (facs).

Modern Editions

R. H. Case, 1906 (Arden); H. H. Furness jr, Philadelphia 1907 (New Variorum); H. S. Canby, New Haven 1921 (Yale); T. Spencer, New York 1948 (Crofts); J. D. Wilson, Cambridge 1950 (New Cambridge); M. R. Ridley 1954 (New Arden); P. G. Phialas, New Haven 1956 (Yale); M. Mack, Baltimore 1960 (Pelican); F. Fergusson and C. J. Sisson, New York 1961 (Laurel); L. B. Wright and V. A. LaMar, New York 1961 (Folger); B. Everett, New York 1964 (Signet); G. L. Kittredge, rev I. Ribner, Waltham Mass 1967.

Studies

Shakespeare's Plutarch vol 2. Ed C. F. T. Brooke 1909 (Sh Classics).

Bradley, A. C. Shakespeare's Antony and Cleopatra. In his Oxford lectures on poetry, 1909.

MacCallum, M. W. In his Shakespeare's Roman plays and their background, 1910.

Bayfield, M. A. A study of Shakespeare's versification. Cambridge 1920.

Symonds, A. Antony and Cleopatra. In his Studies in the Elizabethan drama, 1920.

Gundolf, F. Antonius und Cleopatra. Sh Jb 62 1926.

Schücking, L. L. In his Die Charakterprobleme bei Shakespeare, Leipzig 1927.

Simpson, L. Shakespeare's Cleopatra. Fortnightly Rev May 1928.

Stoll, E. E. Cleopatra. MLR 23 1928; rptd in his Poets and playwrights, Minneapolis 1930.

Granville-Barker, H. In his Prefaces to Shakespeare: series 2, 1930.

Schütze, J. Daniels Cleopatra und Shakespeare. E Studien 71 1936.

Leavis, F. R. Antony and Cleopatra and All for love: a critical exercise. Scrutiny 5 1937.

Buck, E. Cleopatra, eine Charakterdeutung: zur Interpretation von Shakespeares Antony and Cleopatra. Sh Jb 74 1938.

Binder, R. Der dramatische Rhythmus in Shakespeares Antonius und Cleopatra. Würzburg 1939.

Lyman, D. B. Janus in Alexandria: a discussion of Antony and Cleopatra. Sewanee Rev 48 1940.

Cecil, D. Antony and Cleopatra. Glasgow 1944; rptd in his Poets and storytellers, 1949.

Kirschbaum, L. Shakespeare's Cleopatra. Sh Assoc Bull 19 1944.

Jenkin, B. Antony and Cleopatra: some suggestions on the monument scenes. RES 21 1945.

Griffiths, G. S. Antony and Cleopatra. E & S 31 1945.

Draper, J. W. Speech-tempo and humor in Shakespeare's Antony. Bull History of Medicine 20 1946.

Seaton, E. Antony and Cleopatra and the Book of Revelation. RES 22 1946.

Westbrook, P. D. Horace's influence on Shakespeare's Antony and Cleopatra. PMLA 62 1947.

Wilson, E. C. Shakespeare's Enobarbus. In J. Q. Adams memorial studies, Washington 1948.

Bacon, W. A. The suicide of Antony. Sh Assoc Bull 24 1949.

Knights, L. C. On the tragedy of Antony and Cleopatra. Scrutiny 16 1949.

Jorgensen, P. A. Enobarbus' broken heart and the estate of English fugitives. PQ 30 1951.

Berkeley, D. S. The crux of Antony and Cleopatra. Bull Oklahoma Agricultural & Mechanical College 50 1953.

Cunningham, D. G. The characterization of Shakespeare's Cleopatra. Sh Quart 6 1955.

Stempel, D. The transmigration of the crocodile. Sh Quart 7 1956.

Barnet, S. Recognition and reversal in Antony and Cleopatra. Sh Quart 8 1957.

Charney, M. Shakespeare's Antony: a study of image themes. SP 54 1957.

Barroll, J. L. Antony and pleasure. JEGP 57 1958.
— Scarrus and the scarred soldier. HLQ 22 1958.
— Enobarbus' description of Cleopatra. SE 37 1959.

Norman, A. M. Z. Daniel's The tragedie of Cleopatra and Antony and Cleopatra. Sh Quart 9 1958.
— The tragedie of Cleopatra and the date of Antony and Cleopatra. MLR 54 1959.

Spencer, B. T. Antony and Cleopatra and the paradoxical metaphor. Sh Quart 9 1958.

Stein, A. The image of Antony: lyric and tragic imagination. Kenyon Rev 21 1959.

Couchman, G. W. Antony and Cleopatra and the subjective convention. PMLA 76 1961.

Goldberg, S. L. The tragedy of the imagination: a reading of Antony and Cleopatra. Melbourne Critical Rev 4 1961.

Muir, K. The imagery of Antony and Cleopatra. Kwartalnik Neofilologeczny 8 1961.

Bonjour, A. From Shakespeare's Venus to Cleopatra's Cupids. Sh Survey 15 1962.

Lever, J. W. Venus and the second chance. Ibid.

Daiches, D. Imagery and meaning in Antony and Cleopatra. E Studies 43 1962.

Lloyd, M. Antony and the game of chance. JEGP 61 1962.

Hawkes, T. and M. Quinn. Two points of view on Antony and Cleopatra. Anglo-Welsh Rev 13 1963.

MacMullen, K. V. Death imagery in Antony and Cleopatra. Sh Quart 14 1963.

Thomas, M. O. Cleopatra and the 'mortal wretch'. Sh Jb 99 1963.

Bowling, L. E. Antony's internal disunity. Stud in Eng Lit 1500–1900 4 1964.

Foakes, R. A. Vision and reality in Antony and Cleopatra. Durham Univ Jnl 25 1964.

Frost, D. L. Antony and Cleopatra—all for love: or the world ill lost? Topic 7 1964.

Kaula, D. The time sense of Antony and Cleopatra. Sh Quart 15 1964.

Nandy, D. The realism of Antony and Cleopatra. In Shakespeare in a changing world, ed A. Kettle 1964.

Smith, J. O. The alchemy of Antony and Cleopatra. Bucknell Rev 1964.

Smith, S. M. 'This great solemnity': a study of the presentation of death in Antony and Cleopatra. E Studies 45 1964.

Stirling, B. Cleopatra's scene with Seleucus: Plutarch, Daniel and Shakespeare. In Shakespeare 400, ed J. G. McManaway, New York 1964.

Stroup, T. B. The structure of Antony and Cleopatra. Ibid.

Caputi, A. Shakespeare's Antony and Cleopatra: tragedy without terror. Sh Quart 16 1965.

Doran, M. 'High events as these': the language of hyperbole in Antony and Cleopatra. Queen's Quart 72 1965.

Mills, L. J. The tragedies of Shakespeare's Antony and Cleopatra. Bloomington 1965.

Ornstein, R. The ethic of the imagination: love and art in Antony and Cleopatra. In Later Shakespeare, ed J. R. Brown and B. Harris 1966.

Perret, M. Shakespeare's use of messengers in Antony and Cleopatra. Drama Survey 5 1966.

Shapiro, S. A. The varying shore of the world: ambivalence in Antony and Cleopatra. MLQ 27 1966.

Shaw, J. Cleopatra and Seleucus. REL 7 1966.

Waddington, R. B. Antony and Cleopatra: what Venus did with Mars. Sh Stud 2 1966.

Blissett, W. Dramatic irony in Antony and Cleopatra. Sh Quart 18 1967.

Krook, D. Tragic and heroic in Shakespeare's Antony and Cleopatra. In Studies in the drama, ed A. Sachs, Jerusalem 1967.

Nevo, R. The masque of greatness. Sh Stud 3 1967.

Fitch, R. E. No greater crack. Sh Quart 19 1968.

Lyons, C. R. The serpent, the sun and 'Nilus' slime': a focal point for the ambiguity of Shakespeare's Antony and Cleopatra. Rivista di Letterature Moderne e Comparate (Florence) 21 1968.

Markels, J. The pillar of the world: Antony and Cleopatra. In his Shakespeare's development, Columbus 1968.

Morgan, M. M. Your crown's awry: Antony and Cleopatra in the comic tradition. Komos (Melbourne) 1 1968.

Riemer, A. P. A reading of Shakespeare's Antony and Cleopatra. Sydney 1968.

Williamson, M. L. Fortune in Antony and Cleopatra. JEGP 67 1968.
— Patterns of development in Antony and Cleopatra. Tennessee Stud in Lit 14 1969.

Moore, J. R. The enemies of love: the example of Antony and Cleopatra. Kenyon Rev 31 1969.

Rose, P. L. The politics of Antony and Cleopatra. Sh Quart 20 1969.

Simmons, J. L. The comic pattern and vision in Antony and Cleopatra. ELH 36 1969.

Barroll, J. L. Shakespeare and the art of character: a study of Antony. Sh Stud 5 1970.

Fisch, H. Antony and Cleopatra: the limits of mythology. Sh Survey 23 1970.

Homan, S. R. Divided response and the imagination in Antony and Cleopatra. PQ 49 1970.

Mason, H. A. In his Shakespeare's tragedies of love, 1970.

Traci, P. J. The love play of Antony and Cleopatra. Hague 1970.

Williamson, M. The political context of Antony and Cleopatra. Sh Quart 21 1970.

Coriolanus

In First Folio, 1623; ed J. D. Wilson [1928] (facs).

Modern Editions

E. K. Chambers 1898 (Warwick); G. S. Gordon, Oxford 1912; W. J. Craig and R. H. Case 1922 (Arden); C. F. T. Brooke, New Haven 1924 (Yale); H. H. Furness jr, Philadelphia 1928 (New Variorum); H. Levin, Baltimore 1956 (Pelican); J. D. Wilson, Cambridge 1960 (New Cambridge); F. Fergusson and C. J. Sisson, New York 1962 (Laurel); L. B. Wright and V. A. LaMar, New York 1962 (Folger); G. L. Kittredge, rev I. Ribner, Waltham Mass 1967; G. R. Hibbard, 1967 (New Penguin).

Studies

Shakespeare's Plutarch vol 2. Ed C. F. T. Brooke 1909 (Sh Classics).

MacCallum, M. W. In his Shakespeare's Roman plays and their background, 1910.

Bradley, A. C. Coriolanus. Proc Br Acad 3 1912; rptd in his A miscellany, 1929.

Murry, J. M. A neglected heroine of Shakespeare. London Mercury 1922; rptd in his Countries of the mind, 1922.

Tolman, A. H. The structure of Shakespeare's tragedies, with special reference to Coriolanus. MLN 37 1922.

Hayhurst, C. H. A history of the text of Coriolanus. Chicago 1924.

Baumgarten, E. Gemeinschaft und Gewissen in Shakespeares Coriolan. Die Neueren Sprachen 43 1935.

King, A. H. Notes on Coriolanus. E Studies 19–20 1937–8.

Traversi, D. A. Coriolanus. Scrutiny 6 1938.

Heuer, H. Shakespeare und Plutarch: Studien zu Wertwelt und Lebensgefühl im Coriolanus. Anglia 62 1938.

—— From Plutarch to Shakespeare: a study of Coriolanus. Sh Survey 10 1957.

Draper, J. W. Shakespeare's Coriolanus: a study in Renaissance psychology. West Virginia Univ Bull 3 1939.

Burns, W. The character of Marcius Coriolanus. Poet-Lore 52 1946.

Granville-Barker, H. Coriolanus. In his Prefaces to Shakespeare: series 5, 1947.

Maxwell, J. C. Animal imagery in Coriolanus. MLR 42 1947.

Harrison, G. B. A note on Coriolanus. In J. Q. Adams memorial studies, Washington 1948.

Jorgensen, P. A. Shakespeare's Coriolanus: Elizabethan soldier. PMLA 64 1949.

Lees, F. N. Coriolanus, Aristotle and Bacon. RES new ser 1 1950.

Pettet, E. C. Coriolanus and the midlands insurrection of 1607. Sh Survey 3 1950.

Honig, E. Sejanus and Coriolanus: a study in alienation. MLQ 12 1951.

Ribner, I. The tragedy of Coriolanus. E Studies 34 1953.

Enright, D. J. Coriolanus: tragedy or debate? EC 4 1954. Reply by I. R. Browning 5 1955.

Dean, L. F. Voice and deed in Coriolanus. Univ of Kansas City Rev 21 1955.

Charney, M. The dramatic use of imagery in Shakespeare's Coriolanus. ELH 23 1956.

—— The imagery of food and eating in Coriolanus. In Essays in literary history presented to J. Milton French, New Brunswick NJ 1960.

Hofling, C. An interpretation of Shakespeare's Coriolanus. Amer Imago 14 1957.

Sen, S. K. What happens in Coriolanus. Sh Quart 9 1958.

Muir, K. The background of Coriolanus. Sh Quart 10 1959.

Oliver, H. J. Coriolanus as tragic hero. Ibid.

Smith, G. R. Authoritarian patterns in Shakespeare's Coriolanus. Lit & Psychology 9 1959.

Rouda, F. H. Coriolanus: a tragedy of youth. Sh Quart 12 1961.

Chappell, F. Shakespeare's Coriolanus and Plutarch's life of Cato. Renaissance Papers 1962.

Proser, M. Coriolanus: the constant warrior and the state. College Eng April 1963.

Schlösser, A. Reflections upon Shakespeare's Coriolanus. Philologica Pragensia 6 1963.

Sheldon, E. K. Sheridan's Coriolanus: an eighteenth-century compromise. Sh Quart 14 1963.

Gordon, D. J. Name and fame: Shakespeare's Coriolanus. In Papers mainly Shakespearian, ed G. I. Duthie, Edinburgh 1964.

Grass, G. Le Coriolan de Shakespeare et Brecht. Preuves Oct 1964.

—— Vor- und Nachgeschichte der Tragödie des Coriolanus von Livius und Plutarch über Shakespeare bis zu Brecht und mir. Moderna Språk 58 1964.

Hill, R. F. Coriolanus: violentest contrariety. E & S new ser 17 1964.

Neumeyer, P. F. Ingratitude is monstrous: an approach to Coriolanus. College Eng Dec 1964.

Carr, W. T. 'Gracious silence': a selective reading. E Studies 46 1965.

Frye, D. Commentary in Shakespeare: the case of Coriolanus. Sh Stud 1 1965.

Mitchell, C. Coriolanus: power as honor. Ibid.

Calderwood, J. L. Coriolanus: wordless meanings and meaningless words. Stud in Eng Lit 1500–1900 6 1966.

Craig, H. Coriolanus: interpretation. In Pacific Coast studies in Shakespeare, ed W. F. McNeir and T. N. Greenfield, Portland Oregon 1966.

Poisson, R. Coriolanus as Aristotle's magnanimous man. Ibid.

Rabkin, N. Coriolanus: the tragedy of politics. Sh Quart 17 1966.

Wickham, G. Coriolanus: Shakespeare's tragedy in rehearsal and performance. In Later Shakespeare, ed J. R. Brown and B. Harris 1966.

Colman, E. A. The end of Coriolanus. ELH 34 1967.

McCanles, M. The dialectic of transcendence in Shakespeare's Coriolanus. PMLA 82 1967.

Littlewood, J. C. F. Coriolanus. Cambridge Quart 2–3 1967–8.

Davidson, C. Coriolanus: a study in political dislocation. Sh Stud 4 1969.

Langman, F. H. 'Atmosphere' and repeated action in Coriolanus. Southern Rev 3 1969.

Stockholder, K. The other Coriolanus. PMLA 85 1970.

Hale, D. C. Coriolanus: the death of a political metaphor. Sh Quart 22 1971.

Timon of Athens

In First Folio, 1623.

Modern Editions

K. Deighton 1905 (Arden); J. C. Maxwell, Cambridge 1957 (New Cambridge); H. J. Oliver 1959 (New Arden); F. Fergusson and C. J. Sisson, New York 1963 (Laurel); C. Hinman, Baltimore 1964 (Pelican); M. Charney, New York 1965 (Signet); G. L. Kittredge, rev I. Ribner, Waltham Mass 1967; L. B. Wright and V. A. LaMar, New York 1968 (Folger); G. R. Hibbard 1970 (New Penguin).

Studies

Bradley, A. C. King Lear and Timon. In his Shakespearean tragedy, 1904.

Clemons, W. H. The sources of Timon. Princeton Univ Bull 15 1904.

Adams, J. Q. Timon of Athens and the irregularities of the First Folio. JEGP 7 1908.

—— The Timon plays. JEGP 9 1910.

Wright, E. H. The authorship of Timon of Athens. New York 1910.

Parrott, T. M. The problem of Timon of Athens. 1923 (Shakespeare Assoc Pamphlet).

Sykes, H. D. The problem of Timon. N & Q 4 Aug–15 Sept 1923; rptd in his Sidelights on Elizabethan drama, 1924.

Wecter, D. Shakespeare's purpose in Timon of Athens. PMLA 43 1928.

Bond, R. W. Lucian and Boiardo in Timon of Athens. MLR 25 1930.

Draper, J. W. The theme of Timon of Athens. MLR 29 1934.

—— The psychology of Shakespeare's Timon. MLR 35 1940.

—— Patterns of tempo in Shakespeare's Timon of Athens. Sh Assoc Bull 23 1948.

Haug, R. A. The authorship of Timon of Athens. Sh Assoc Bull 15 1940.

Ellis-Fermor, U. Timon of Athens: an unfinished play. RES 18 1942.

Collins, A. S. Timon of Athens: a reconsideration. RES 22 1946.

Muir, K. Timon of Athens and the cash-nexus. Modern Quart Miscellany 1 1946.

Pettet, E. C. Timon of Athens: the disruption of feudal morality. RES 23 1947.

Maxwell, J. C. Timon of Athens. Scrutiny 15 1948.

Empson, W. Timon's dog. In his Structure of complex words, 1951.

Spencer, T. Shakespeare learns the value of money: the dramatist at work on Timon of Athens. Sh Survey 6 1953.

Bonnard, G. A. Note sur les sources de Timon of Athens. Etudes Anglaises 7 1954.

Merchant, W. M. Timon and the conceit of art. Sh Quart 6 1955.

Draper, R. P. Timon of Athens. Sh Quart 8 1957.

Goldsmith, R. A. Did Shakespeare use the old Timon comedy? Sh Quart 9 1958.

Honigmann, E. A. J. Timon of Athens. Sh Quart 12 1961.

Spencer, T. J. B. 'Greeks' and 'merrygreeks': a background to Timon of Athens and Troilus and Cressida. In Essays on Shakespeare and Elizabethan drama in honor of Hardin Craig, Columbia Missouri 1962.

Cook, D. Timon of Athens. Sh Survey 16 1963.

Paulin, B. La mort de Timon d'Athènes. Etudes Anglaises 17 1964.

Bacquet, P. Réflexions sur la technique dramatique de Shakespeare dans Timon d'Athènes. Bulletin de la Faculté des Lettres et Sciences Humaines de Strasbourg 43 1965.

Kuckhoff, A.-G. Timon von Athen: Konzeption und Aufführungspraxis. Sh Jb (Weimar) 101 1965.

Waggoner, G. K. Timon of Athens and the Jacobean duel. Sh Quart 16 1965.

Bradbrook, M. C. The comedy of Timon: a reveling play of the Inner Temple. Renaissance Drama 9 1965. Anon ms in Victoria and Albert Museum.

— The tragic pageant of Timon of Athens. Cambridge 1966.

Butler, F. The strange critical fortunes of Shakespeare's Timon of Athens. Ames Iowa 1966.

Ramsey, J. W. Timon's imitation of Christ. Sh Stud 2 1966.

Goldstein, L. Alcibiades' revolt in Timon of Athens. Zeitschrift für Anglistik und Amerikanistik 15 1967.

Swigg, R. Timon of Athens and the growth of discrimination. MLR 62 1967.

Knights, L. C. Timon of Athens. In The morality of art: essays presented to G. Wilson Knight, 1969.

Morsberger, R. E. Timon of Athens: tragedy or satire? In Shakespeare in the southwest, ed T. J. Stafford, Austin 1969.

Lancashire, A. Timon of Athens: Shakespeare's Dr Faustus. Sh Quart 21 1970.

Cymbeline

In First Folio, 1623.

Modern Editions

C. M. Ingleby 1886; A. J. Wyatt 1897 (Warwick); E. Dowden 1903 (Arden); H. H. Furness jr, Philadelphia 1913 (New Variorum); S. B. Hemingway, New Haven 1924 (Yale); J. M. Nosworthy 1955 (New Arden); J. C. Maxwell, Cambridge 1960 (New Cambridge); F. Fergusson and C. J. Sisson, New York 1964 (Laurel); R. B. Heilman, Baltimore 1964 (Pelican); L. B. Wright and V. A. LaMar, New York 1965 (Folger); R. Hosley, New York 1968 (Signet); G. L. Kittredge, rev I. Ribner, Waltham Mass 1969.

For a concordance see T. H. Howard-Hill, Oxford 1970.

Studies

Shakspere's Holinshed. Ed W. G. Boswell-Stone 1896.

Robertson, J. M. The interlude in Cymbeline. In his Shakespeare and Chapman, 1917.

Lawrence, W. W. The wager in Cymbeline. PMLA 35 1920.

Granville-Barker, H. In his Prefaces to Shakespeare: series 2, 1930.

Thrall, W. F. Cymbeline, Boccaccio and the wager story in England. SP 28 1931.

Raith, J. Die Historie von den vier Kaufleuten (Frederyke of Jennen). Leipzig 1936.

Tinkler, F. C. Cymbeline. Scrutiny 7 1939.

Stephenson, A. A. The significance of Cymbeline. Scrutiny 10 1942.

Evans, W. M. Shakespeare's Hark, harke ye larke. PMLA 60 1945.

Koenig, V. F. A new perspective on the wager cycle. MP 44 1947.

Camden, C. The Elizabethan Imogen. Rice Inst Pamphlet 38 1951.

Wilson, H. S. Philaster and Cymbeline. Eng Inst Essays 1951.

Smith, W. D. Cloten with Caius Lucius. SP 49 1952.

Fischer, W. Shakespeares späte Romanzen. Sh Jb 91 1955.

Brockbank, P. History and histrionics in Cymbeline. Sh Survey 11 1958.

Stoltzenberg, G. von. Shakespeares Cymbeline: Versuch zur Deutung. Germanisch-romanische Monatsschrift 39 1958.

Jones, E. Stuart Cymbeline. EC 11 1961.

Gesner, C. Cymbeline and the Greek romance: a study in genre. In Studies in English Renaissance literature, ed W. F. McNeir, Baton Rouge 1962.

Hoeniger, F. D. Irony and romance in Cymbeline. Stud in Eng Lit 1500–1900 2 1962.

Marsh, D. R. C. The recurring miracle: Cymbeline and the last plays. Pietermaritzburg 1962.

Moffet, R. Cymbeline and the nativity. Sh Quart 13 1962.

Swander, H. Cymbeline and the blameless hero. ELH 31 1964.

— Cymbeline: religious idea and dramatic design. In Pacific Coast studies in Shakespeare, ed W. F. McNeir and T. N. Greenfield, Portland Oregon 1966.

Harris, B. 'What's past is prologue': Cymbeline and Henry VIII. In Later Shakespeare, ed J. R. Brown and B. Harris 1966.

Mowat, B. A. Cymbeline: crude dramaturgy and aesthetic distance. Renaissance Papers 1966.

Kirsch, A. C. Cymbeline and coterie dramaturgy. ELH 34 1967.

Hill, G. 'The true conduct of human judgment': some observations on Cymbeline. In The morality of art: essays presented to G. Wilson Knight, 1969.

Shaheen, N. The use of Scripture in Cymbeline. Sh Stud 4 1969.

Thorne, W. B. Cymbeline: 'lopp'd branches' and the concept of regeneration. Sh Quart 20 1969.

Winter's Tale

In First Folio, 1623; ed J. D. Wilson [1929] (facs).

Modern Editions

H. H. Furness, Philadelphia 1898 (New Variorum); F. W. Moorman 1912 (Arden); F. E. Pierce, New Haven 1918 (Yale); A. T. Quiller-Couch and J. D. Wilson, Cambridge 1931 (New Cambridge); J. H. P. Pafford 1956 (New Arden); B. Maxwell, Baltimore 1956 (Pelican); F. Fergusson and C. J. Sisson, New York 1959 (Laurel); F. Kermode, New York 1963 (Signet); L. B. Wright and V. A. LaMar, New York 1966 (Folger); G. L. Kittredge, rev I. Ribner, Waltham Mass 1967; E. Schanzer 1969 (New Penguin).

Studies

Greene's Pandosto, or Dorastus and Fawnia: being the original of Shakespeare's Winter's tale. Ed P. G. Thomas 1907 (Sh Classics).

Mount, C. D. Sir Philip Sidney and Shakespeare. N & Q 22 April 1893.

Jusserand, J. J. The winter's tale. 1907; rptd in his School for ambassadors, 1924.

Symons, A. The winter's tale. In his Studies in the Elizabethan drama, 1920.

Tannenbaum, S. A. Textual and other notes on the Winter's tale. PQ 7 1928.

Lancaster, H. C. Hermione's statue. SP 29 1932.

Tinkler, F. C. The winter's tale. Scrutiny 5 1937.

Taylor, G. C. Hermione's statue again. Sh Assoc Bull 13 1938. Shakespeare's return to Bandello.

White, C. A biography of Autolycus. Sh Assoc Bull 14 1939.

Hastings, W. T. The ancestry of Autolycus. Sh Assoc Bull 15 1940.

Hughes, M. Y. A classical versus a social approach to Shakespeare's Autolycus. Ibid.

Wilson, H. S. 'Nature and art' in Winter's tale (IV. iv. 86 ff). Sh Assoc Bull 18 1943.

Bethell, S. L. The winter's tale: a study. 1947.

Hoeniger, F. D. The meaning of the Winter's tale. UTQ 20 1950.

Siegel, P. N. Leontes a jealous tyrant. RES new ser 1 1950.

Bonjour, A. The final scene of the Winter's tale. E Studies 33 1952.

—— La jalousie de Léontes: une quintessence de l'art Shakespearien. In Mélanges offerts à M. Georges Bonnard, Geneva 1966.

—— Polixenes and the winter of his discontent. E Studies 50 1969.

Trienens, R. J. The inception of Leontes' jealousy in the Winter's tale. Sh Quart 4 1953.

Bryant, J. A. Shakespeare's allegory: the Winter's tale. Sewanee Rev 63 1955.

Fischer, W. Shakespeares späte Romanzen. Sh Jb 91 1955.

Arnold, P. Das Wintermärchen und die Geschichte von Dorastus und Fawnia. Das Neue Forum 8 1958.

Lascelles, M. Shakespeare's pastoral comedy. In More talking of Shakespeare, ed J. Garrett 1959.

Pafford, J. H. P. Music and the songs in the Winter's tale. Sh Quart 10 1959.

Biggins, D. 'Exit pursued by a beare': a problem in the Winter's tale. Sh Quart 13 1962.

Frye, N. Recognition in the Winter's tale. In Essays on Shakespeare and Elizabethan drama in honor of Hardin Craig, Columbia Missouri 1962.

Lawlor, J. Pandosto and the nature of dramatic romance. PQ 41 1962.

Bryant, J. H. The winter's tale and the pastoral tradition. Sh Quart 14 1963.

Scott, W. O. Seasons and flowers in the Winter's tale. Ibid.

Smith, H. Leontes' 'affectio'. Ibid.

Cottrell, B. W. The winter's tale. In Lovers meeting, ed A. Wright, Pittsburgh 1964.

Ewbank, I.-S. The triumph of time in the Winter's tale. REL 5 1964.

Milward, P. A theology of grace in the Winter's tale. Eng Lit & Lang (Tokyo) 2 1964.

Schanzer, E. The structural pattern in the Winter's tale. REL 5 1964.

Maveety, S. R. What Shakespeare did with Pandosto: an interpretation of the Winter's tale. In Pacific Coast studies in Shakespeare, ed W. F. McNeir and T. N. Greenfield, Portland Oregon 1966.

Pyle, F. The winter's tale: a commentary on the structure. 1968.

Meldrum, R. M. Dramatic intention in the Winter's tale. Humanities Assoc Bull 19 1968.

Nathan, N. Leontes' provocation. Ibid.

Smith, J. The language of Leontes. Ibid.

Thorne, W. B. 'Things newborn': a study of the rebirth motive in the Winter's tale. Ibid.

Cox, L. S. The role of Autolycus in the Winter's tale. Stud in Eng Lit 1500–1900 9 1969.

Livingston, M. L. The natural art of the Winter's tale. MLQ 30 1969.

Matchett, W. H. Some dramatic techniques in the Winter's tale. Sh Survey 22 1969.

Mowat, B. A. A tale of sprights and goblins. Sh Quart 20 1969.

Muir, K. The conclusion of the Winter's tale. In The morality of art: essays presented to G. Wilson Knight, 1969.

Hartwig, J. The tragicomic perspective of the Winter's tale. ELH 37 1970.

Weinstein, P. M. An interpretation of pastoral in the Winter's tale. Sh Quart 22 1971.

Tempest

In First Folio, 1623; ed J. D. Wilson [1928] (facs).

Modern Editions

H. H. Furness, Philadelphia 1892 (New Variorum); F. S. Boas 1897 (Warwick); M. Luce 1902 (Arden); W. Vickery 1911 (Rowfant Club); C. B. Tinker, New Haven 1918 (Yale); A. T. Quiller-Couch and J. D. Wilson, Cambridge 1921 (New Cambridge); G. L. Kittredge, Boston 1939; A. Harbage, New York 1946 (Crofts); F. Kermode 1954 (New Arden); D. Horne, New Haven 1955 (Yale); N. Frye, Baltimore 1959 (Pelican); F. Fergusson and C. J. Sisson, New York 1961 (Laurel); L. B. Wright and V. A. LaMar, New York 1961 (Folger); R. Langbaum, New York 1965 (Signet); G. L. Kittredge, rev I. Ribner, Waltham Mass 1967; A. Righter 1968 (New Penguin).

For a concordance see T. H. Howard-Hill, Oxford 1969.

Studies

Jakob Ayrer: Dramen. Ed A. von Keller, Stuttgart 1865.

Lee, S. The American Indian in Elizabethan England. Scribner's Mag 1907.

—— Caliban's visits to England. Cornhill Mag May 1913.

Gilbert, A. H. The tempest: parallelism in characters and situations. JEGP 14 1915.

Gayley, C. M. Shakespeare and the founders of liberty in America. New York 1917.

Robertson, J. M. The masque in the Tempest. In his Shakespeare and Chapman, 1917.

—— The masque in the Tempest. TLS 31 March 1921.

Bell, R. The topography of the Tempest. Contemporary Rev Dec 1917.

Rea, J. D. A source for the storm of the Tempest. MP 17 1919.

—— A note on the Tempest. MLN 35 1920.

Ward, A. W. Shakespeare and the makers of Virginia. Proc Br Acad 8 1919.

Gray, H. D. The sources of the Tempest. MLN 35 1920.

—— Some indications that the Tempest was revised. SP 18 1921.

Lawrence, W. J. The masque in the Tempest. Fortnightly Rev June 1920.

—— Shakespeare avrebbe tratto il soggetto di la Tempesta da scenari italiani? Le Lettere 2 1923.

Law, E. Shakespeare's Tempest as originally produced at Court. [1921] (Sh Assoc Pamphlet).

Still, C. Shakespeare's mystery play. 1921.

—— The timeless theme. 1936.

Lefranc, A. L'origine d'Ariel. In Cinquantenaire de l'Ecole Pratique des Hautes Etudes, Paris 1921.

Chambers, E. K. The integrity of the Tempest. RES 1 1925.

Longworth-Chambrun, C. Revue de Littérature Comparée 5 1925. On French influences.

Eichler, A. Shakespeares The tempest als Hofaufführung. In Festgabe für Karl Luick, Marburg 1925.

Cawley, R. R. Shakespeare's use of the voyagers in the Tempest. PMLA 31 1926.

Fouquet, K. Jakob Ayrers Sidea, Shakespeares Tempest und das Märchen. Marburg 1929.

Bushnell, N. S. Natural supernaturalism in the Tempest. PMLA 47 1932.

Knight, G. W. The Shakespearian Tempest. Oxford 1932, London 1953, 1963 (rev).

Stoll, E. E. The tempest. PMLA 47 1932.

Curry, W. C. Sacerdotal science in Shakespeare's The tempest. Archiv 168 1935.

Wilson, J. D. The meaning of the Tempest. Newcastle 1936.

Howarth, R. G. Shakespeare's Tempest. Sydney 1936.

Grégoire, H. The Bulgarian origin of the Tempest. SP 37 1940.

McCloskey, J. C. Caliban, savage clown. College Eng May 1940.

Auden, W. H. The sea and the mirror. In his For the time being, 1945.

McPeek, J. A. S. The genesis of Caliban. PQ 25 1946.

Hankins, J. E. Caliban, the bestial man. PMLA 62 1947.

Mason, R. The unresolved Antonio. Modern Reading 14 1947.

Nosworthy, J. M. The narrative sources of the Tempest. RES 24 1948.

Johnson, W. S. The genesis of Ariel. Sh Quart 2 1951.

Dobrée, B. The tempest. E & S new ser 5 1952.

Wilson, H. S. Action and symbol in Measure for measure and the Tempest. Sh Quart 4 1953.

Oppel, H. Die Gonzalo-Utopie in Shakespeares Sturm. Deutsche Vierteljahrsschrift für Literaturwissenschaft 38 1954.

Knox, B. The tempest and the ancient comic tradition. Eng Inst Essays 1954.

Fischer, W. Shakespeares späte Romanzen. Sh Jb 91 1955.

Cutts, J. P. Music and the supernatural in the Tempest. Music & Letters 39 1958.

Goldsmith, R. H. The wild man on the English stage. MLR 53 1958. Partly on Caliban.

Gesner, C. The tempest as pastoral romance. Sh Quart 10 1959. On influence of Daphnis and Chloe.

Kuhl, E. P. Shakespeare and the founders of America: the Tempest. PQ 41 1962.

Reed, R. R. The probable origin of Ariel. Sh Quart 11 1960. Munday's John a Kent?

Hilberry, C. The tempest, act 4. College Eng April 1962.

Davidson, F. The tempest: an interpretation. JEGP 62 1963.

Zimbardo, R. A. Form and disorder in the Tempest. Sh Quart 14 1963.

Driver, T. F. The Shakespearian clock: time and the vision of reality in Romeo and Juliet and the Tempest. Sh Quart 15 1964.

Gohn, E. The tempest: theme and structure. E Studies 45 1964.

Phillips, J. E. The tempest and the Renaissance idea of man. In Shakespeare 400, ed J. G. McManaway, New York 1964.

Robinson, J. E. Time and the Tempest. JEGP 63 1964.

West, R. H. Ariel and the outer mystery. In Shakespeare 1564–1964, ed E. A. Bloom, Providence 1964.

— Ceremonial magic in the Tempest. In Shakespearean essays, ed A. Thaler and N. Sanders, Knoxville 1964.

Ebner, D. The tempest: rebellion and the ideal state. Sh Quart 16 1965.

Brockbank, P. The tempest: conventions of art and empire. In Later Shakespeare, ed J. R. Brown and B. Harris 1966.

Draper, J. W. Monster Caliban. Revue de Littérature Comparée 40 1966.

Carnes, V. Renaissance conceptions of mind, imagination and art in Shakespeare's The tempest. North Dakota Quart 35 1968.

Craig, H. Magic in the Tempest. PQ 47 1968.

Devereux, E. J. Sacramental imagery in the Tempest. Humanities Assoc Bull 19 1968.

Brown, J. R. Shakespeare: the Tempest. 1969.

Coursen, H. R. Prospero and the drama of the soul. Sh Stud 4 1969.

Ryken, L. The temptation theme in the Tempest and the question of dramatic suspense. Tennessee Stud in Lit 14 1969.

Bartenschlager, K. Shakespeares The tempest: der ideale Traum und Prosperos Magic. Sh Jb (Heidelberg) 1970.

Berger, H. 'Miraculous harp': a reading of the Tempest. Sh Stud 5 1970.

Boughner, D. C. Jonsonian structure in the Tempest. Sh Quart 21 1970.

McNeir, W. F. The tempest: space-time and spectacle-theme. Arlington Quart 1970.

Seiden, M. Utopianism in the Tempest. MLQ 31 1970.

Smith, I. Ariel and the masque in the Tempest. Sh Quart 21 1970.

Uphouse, R. W. Virtue in Vengeance: Prospero's rarer action. Bucknell Rev 18 1970.

Henry VIII

In First Folio, 1623.

Modern Editions

D. N. Smith 1899 (Warwick); C. K. Pooler 1915 (Arden); J. M. Berdan and C. F. T. Brooke, New Haven 1925 (Yale); R. A. Foakes 1957 (New Arden), J. C. Maxwell, Cambridge 1962 (New Cambridge); F. D. Hoeniger, Baltimore 1966 (Pelican); G. L. Kittredge, rev I. Ribner, Waltham Mass 1968; S. Schoenbaum, New York 1968 (Signet); L. B. Wright and V. A. LaMar, New York 1968 (Folger).

Studies

Shakspere's Holinshed. Ed W. G. Boswell-Stone 1896.

S[pedding], J. On the several shares of Shakespeare and Fletcher in the play of Henry VIII. GM Oct 1850; Trans New Sh Soc 1874.

Sykes, H. D. King Henry VIII. In his Sidelights on Shakespeare, Stratford 1919.

Symonds, A. The question of Henry VIII. In his Studies in the Elizabethan drama, 1920.

Ege, K. Shakespeares Anteil an Heinrich VIII. Sh Jb 58 1922.

Nicolson, M. H. The authorship of Henry VIII. PMLA 37 1922.

Maxwell, B. Fletcher and Henry VIII. In [J. M.] Manly anniversary studies, Chicago 1923. See also his review of Sykes, above, MP 23 1926.

Lawrence, W. J. The stage directions in King Henry VIII. TLS 18 Dec 1930.

Alexander, P. Conjectural history: or Shakespeare's Henry VIII. E & S 16 1931.

Clark, C. A study of Shakespeare's Henry VIII. 1931.

Kermode, F. What is Shakespeare's Henry VIII about? Durham Univ Jnl new ser 9 1948.

Parker, A. A. Henry VIII in Shakespeare and Calderón. MLR 44 1948.

Partridge, A. C. The problem of Henry VIII reopened: some linguistic criteria for the two styles apparent in the play. Cambridge 1949.

Oras, A. 'Extra monosyllables' in Henry VIII and the problem of authorship. JEGP 52 1953.

Law, R. A. Holinshed and Henry VIII. SE 36 1957.

— The double authorship of Henry VIII. SP 56 1959.

Foakes, R. A. On the First Folio text of Henry VIII. SB 10 1958.

Bertram, P. Henry VIII: the conscience of the King. In In defense of reading, ed R. A. Brower and R. Poirier, New York 1962.

Mincoff, M. Henry VIII and Fletcher. Sh Quart 12 1961.

Tillyard, E. M. W. Why did Shakespeare write Henry VIII? CQ 3 1961.

Cutts, J. P. Shakespeare's song and masque hand in Henry VIII. Sh Jb 99 1963.

Schlösser, A. Konturen unter der Oberfläche in Heinrich VIII. Zeitschrift für Anglistik und Amerikanistik 12 1964.

Wasson, J. In defense of Henry VIII. Research Stud (Pullman) 32 1964.

Felperin, H. Shakespeare's Henry VIII: history as myth. Stud in Eng Lit 1500–1900 6 1966.

Berman, R. King Henry VIII: history and romance. E Studies 48 1967.

Richmond, H. M. Shakespeare's Henry VIII: romance redeemed by history. Sh Stud 4 1969.

C. Plays Excluded from the Folio

Sir Thomas More, Edward III, Pericles, Two noble kinsmen, other ascribed plays.

Collections

For a fuller list see E. K. Chambers, Elizabethan stage vol 3, 1923, p. 204.

Pseudo–Shakspere'sche Dramen. Ed N. Delius 5 pts Elberfeld 1854–74.

Pseudo–Shakespearian plays. Ed K. Warnke and L. Proescholdt 5 pts Halle 1883–8.

Shakespeare's doubtful plays. Ed A. F. Hopkinson 3 vols 1891–5.

The Shakespeare apocrypha. Ed C. F. T. Brooke, Oxford 1908. 14 plays in old spelling; detailed introd.

Six early plays related to the Shakespeare canon. Ed E. B. Everitt and R. L. Armstrong, Copenhagen 1965. Leir, Weakest goeth to the wall, Edmund Ironside, Troublesome reign, Edward III, Woodstock.

General Studies

Elze, K. Notes on Elizabethan dramatists. Halle 1880.

Sachs, R. Die Shakespeare zugeschriebenen zweifelhaften Stücke. Sh Jb 27 1892.

Hopkinson, A. F. Essays on Shakespeare's doubtful plays. 1900. Rptd from his edn of the plays 1891–5.

Moorman, F. W. Plays of uncertain authorship attributed to Shakespeare. CHEL vol 5 1910.

Petersen, O. Pseudoshakespearesche Dramen. Anglia 37 1913.

Sykes, H. D. In his Sidelights on Shakespeare, Stratford 1919.

Maxwell, B. Studies in the Shakespeare apocrypha. New York 1956.

Sir Thomas More

The book of Sir Thomas Moore. Ed J. S. Farmer 1908 (facs); ed A. Dyce 1844 (Sh Soc); ed A. F. Hopkinson 1902; ed C. F. T. Brooke, Shakespeare apocrypha, Oxford 1908; ed W. W. Greg 1911 (Malone Soc); ed J. Shirley, Canterbury 1938; ed H. Jenkins, Complete works of Shakespeare, ed C. J. Sisson 1954. BM ms Harley 7368.

Studies

Hall, A. Shakespeare's handwriting. 1899.

Greg, W. W. Autograph plays by Anthony Munday. MLR 8 1913.

—— Shakespeare's hand once more. TLS 24 Nov–1 Dec 1927.

—— T. Goodal in Sir Thomas More. PMLA 44 1929.

Schücking, L. L. Das Datum des pseudo-shakespeareschen Thomas More. E Studien 46 1913.

—— Shakespeare and Sir Thomas More. RES 1 1925.

Thompson, E. M. Shakespeare's handwriting. Oxford 1916.

Simpson, P. The play of Sir Thomas More and Shakespeare's hand in it. Library 2nd ser 8 1917.

Green, A. The apocryphal Sir Thomas More and the Shakespeare holograph. Amer Jnl of Philology 39 1918.

Oliphant, E. H. C. Sir Thomas More. JEGP 18 1919.

Lawrence, W. J. Was Sir Thomas More ever acted? TLS 1 July 1920.

Stevenson, W. H. Shakespeare's schoolmaster and handwriting. TLS 8 Jan 1920.

Byrne, M. St C. Anthony Munday and his books. Library 3rd ser 1 1921.

Shakespeare's hand in the play of Sir Thomas More. Cambridge 1923. Studies by A. W. Pollard, W. W. Greg, E. M. Thompson, J. D. Wilson and R. W. Chambers.

Greenwood, G. The Shakespeare signatures and Sir Thomas More. 1924.

Harrison, G. B. The date of Sir Thomas More. RES 1 1925.

Pollard, A. W. Verse tests and the date of Sir Thomas More. Ibid.

Tannenbaum, S. A. Shakespeare's unquestioned autographs and the addition to Sir Thomas Moore. SP 22 1925.

—— The booke of Sir Thomas Moore. New York 1927.

—— Problems in Shakespeare's penmanship. New York 1927.

—— More about the Booke of Sir Thomas Moore. PMLA 43 1928.

Acheson, A. Shakespeare, Chapman et Sir Thomas More. Revue Anglo-américaine 3 1926.

—— Shakespeare, Chapman and Sir Thomas More. 1931.

Spurgeon, C. Imagery in the Sir Thomas More fragment. RES 6 1930.

Chambers, R. W. Some sequences of thought in Shakespeare and in the 147 lines of Sir Thomas More. MLR 26 1931.

Schütt, M. Die Quellen des Book of Sir Thomas More. E Studien 68 1933.

Collins, D. C. On the date of Sir Thomas More. RES 10 1934.

Deutschberger, P. Shakespeare and Sir Thomas More. Sh Assoc Bull 18 1943.

Bald, R. C. The booke of Sir Thomas More and its problems. Sh Survey 2 1949.

—— The booke of Sir Thomas More and its problems. In Evidence for authorship: essays on problems of attribution, ed D. V. Erdman and E. G. Fogel, Ithaca 1966.

Nosworthy, J. M. Shakespeare and Sir Thomas More. RES new ser 6 1955.

—— Hand B in Sir Thomas More. Library 5th ser 11 1956.

Jenkins, H. A supplement to Greg's edition of Sir Thomas More. In Collections vol 6, 1962 (Malone Soc).

Wentersdorff, K. P. The date of the additions in the Booke of Sir Thomas More. Sh Jb (Heidelberg) 101 1965.

Clayton, T. The 'Shakespearean' additions in the Book of Sir Thomas Moore: some aids to scholarly and critical Shakespearean studies. Nashville 1969.

McMillin, S. The book of Sir Thomas More: a theatrical view. MP 68 1970.

Edward III

The raigne of King Edward the Third, as it hath bin sundrie times plaied about the Citie of London. 1596; ed J. S. Farmer, TFT 1910 (facs).

The raigne of King Edward the Third. 1599.

Modern Editions

E. Capell, Prolusions, 1760; N. Delius, Pseudo-Shakspere'-sche Dramen pt 1, Elberfeld 1854; K. Warnke and L. Proescholdt, Halle 1886; G. C. Moore Smith 1897 (Temple Dramatists); C. F. T. Brooke, Shakespeare apocrypha, Oxford 1908; E. B. Everitt and R. L. Armstrong, Six early plays related to the Shakespeare canon, Copenhagen 1965.

Studies

Swinburne, A. C. Note on the historical play of King Edward III. GM Aug–Sept 1879.

Smith, R. M. Edward III: a study of the authorship. JEGP 10 1911.

Platt, A. Edward III and Shakespeare's sonnets. MLR 6 1911.

Golding, S. R. The authorship of Edward 3. N & Q 5 May 1928.

Østerberg, V. The 'Countess-scenes' of Edward III. Sh Jb 65 1929.

Hart, A. The vocabulary of Edward III. In his Shakespeare and the homilies, Melbourne 1935.

Muir, K. A reconsideration of Edward III. Sh Survey 6 1953.

—— Shakespeare as collaborator. 1960.

Koskenniemi, I. Themes and imagery in Edward III. Neuphilologische Mitteilungen 65 1964.

Wentersdorff, K. P. The date of Edward III. Sh Quart 16 1965.

Pericles

The late and much admired play called Pericles, Prince of Tyre, with the true relation of the whole historie, adventures and fortunes of the said Prince; as also the no lesse strange and worthy accidents in the birth and life of his daughter Mariana, as it hath been divers and sundry times acted by his Majesties servants at the Globe on the Banck-side; by William Shakespeare; imprinted at London for Henry Gosson, and are to be sold at the signe of the Sunne in Pater-noster row etc. 1609; ed J. O. Halliwell (-Phillipps) 1862 (facs); ed P. Z. Round 1886 (facs); ed S. Lee, Oxford 1905 (facs).

The late and much admired play called Pericles, Prince of Tyre. 1609 (title identical with 4° 1, above, differentiated by 'Eneer Gower' for 'Enter Gower' on signature A 2), ed J. O. Halliwell (-Phillipps) 1871 (facs); 1619, 1630, 1630, 1635.

Modern Editions

A. Morgan, New York 1891 (Bankside; parallel texts); K. Deighton 1907 (Arden); A. R. Bellinger, New Haven 1925 (Yale); W. W. Greg, Oxford 1940 (facs of 4° 1); J. C. Maxwell, Cambridge 1956 (New Cambridge); F. D. Hoeniger 1963 (New Arden); E. Schanzer, New York 1965 (Signet); J. G. McManaway, Baltimore 1967 (Pelican); L. B. Wright and V. A. LaMar, New York 1968 (Folger).

Studies

Wilkins, George. The painfull adventures of Pericles Prince of Tyre: being the true history of the play of Pericles, as it was lately presented by the worthy and ancient poet John Gower. 1608; ed T. Mommsen, Oldenburg 1857; ed K. Muir, Liverpool 1953.

Baker, H. T. The authorship of Pericles V. i. 1–101. MLN 22 1907.

—— The relation of Shakespeare's Pericles to George Wilkins's novel. PMLA 23 1908.

Thomas, D. L. On the play Pericles. E Studien 39 1908.

Garrett, R. M. Gower in Pericles. Sh Jb 48 1912.

Graves, T. S. On the date and significance of Pericles. MP 13 1916.

Steinhäuser, K. Die neueren Anschauungen über die Echtheit von Shakespeares Pericles. Heidelberg 1918.

Sykes, H. D. Wilkins and Shakespeare's Pericles, Prince of Tyre. In his Sidelights on Shakespeare, Stratford 1919.

Crosse, G. Pericles on the stage. N & Q 7 May 1921.

Gray, H. D. Heywood's Pericles revised by Shakespeare. PMLA 40 1925.

Østerberg, V. Grevinden af Salisbury af Marina af Shakespeare. Copenhagen 1926.

Cowl, R. P. The authorship of Pericles and the date of the Life and death of Lord Cromwell. 1927.

Allen, P. Shakespeare, Jonson and Wilkins as borrowers. 1928.

Spiker, S. George Wilkins and the authorship of Pericles. SP 30 1933.

Hastings, W. T. Exit George Wilkins? Sh Assoc Bull 11 1936.

—— Shakespeare's part in Pericles. Sh Assoc Bull 14 1939.

Craig, H. Pericles and the Painfull adventures. SP 45 1948.

Parrott, T. M. Pericles: the play and the novel. Sh Assoc Bull 23 1948.

Muir, K. The problem of Pericles. E Studies 25 1949.

—— Shakespeare as collaborator. 1960.

Edwards, P. An approach to the problem of Pericles. Sh Survey 5 1952.

Tompkins, J. M. S. Why Pericles? RES new ser 3 1952.

Arthos, J. Pericles, Prince of Tyre: a study in the dramatic use of romantic narrative. Sh Quart 4 1953.

Evans, B. The poem of Pericles. In The image of the work: essays in criticism by B. H. Lehman et al, Berkeley 1955.

Goolden, P. Antiochus's riddle in Gower and Shakespeare. RES new ser 6 1955.

Melchiori, G. Note sul problema di Pericles. Eng Miscellany (Rome) 10 1959.

Hoeniger, F. D. How significant are textual parallels? a new author for Pericles? Sh Quart 11 1960.

Barker, G. A. Themes and variations in Shakespeare's Pericles. E Studies 44 1963.

Bullough, G. Pericles and the verse in Wilkins's Painfull adventures. Bulletin de la Faculté des Lettres et Sciences de Strasbourg 43 1965.

Felperin, H. Shakespeare's miracle play. Sh Quart 18 1967.

Greenfield, T. N. A reexamination of the 'patient' Pericles. Sh Stud 3 1967.

Schiffhorst, G. J. The imagery of Pericles and what it tells us. Ball State Univ Forum 8 1967.

Cutts, J. P. Pericles' 'downright violence'. Sh Stud 4 1969.

Lake, D. J. The Pericles candidates: Heywood, Rowley, Wilkins. N & Q April 1970. On Wilkins as likely author of 'non-Shakespearean' sections.

Wood, J. O. The running image in Pericles. Sh Stud 5 1970.

Thorne, W. B. Pericles and the incest-fertility opposition. Sh Quart 22 1971.

Two Noble Kinsmen

The two noble kinsmen: presented at the Blackfriers by the Kings Majesties servants, with great applause; written by the memorable worthies of their time, Mr John Fletcher and Mr William Shakspeare gent; printed at London by Tho. Cotes for John Waterson, and are to be sold at the signe of the Crowne in Pauls churchyard. 1634; ed J. S. Farmer, TFT 1920 (facs); rptd H. Littledale 1876 (New Shakspere Soc).

Fifty comedies and tragedies written by Francis Beaumont and John Fletcher gentlemen. 1679.

Modern Editions

W. W. Skeat 1875; H. Littledale 1885 (New Sh Soc); W. J. Rolfe, New York 1891; C. H. Herford 1897 (Temple); C. F. T. Brooke, Shakespeare apocrypha, Oxford 1908; F. O. Walker, Chicago 1957 (old spelling); C. Leech, New York 1966 (Signet); G. R. Proudfoot 1970 (Regents Renaissance Drama).

Studies

Oliphant, E. H. C. The works of Beaumont and Fletcher. E Studien 15 1891.

—— The plays of Beaumont and Fletcher. New Haven 1927.

Thorndike, A. H. The influence of Beaumont and Fletcher on Shakespeare. Worcester Mass 1901.

Durand, W. Y. Notes on Richard Edwardes. JEGP 4 1902.

Petersen, O. The two noble kinsmen. Anglia 38 1914.

Sykes, H. D. The authorship of the Two noble kinsmen. MLR 11 1916; rptd in his Sidelights on Shakespeare, Stratford 1919.

Lawrence, W. J. New light on the Two noble kinsmen. TLS 14 July 1921. *See* later correspondence.

Cruikshank, A. H. Massinger and the Two noble kinsmen. Oxford 1922.

Gray, H. D. Beaumont and the Two noble kinsmen. PQ 2 1923.

Ege, K. Der Anteil Shakespeares an The two noble kinsmen. Sh Jb 59 1924.

Bradley, A. C. Scene-endings in Shakespeare and in the Two noble kinsmen. In his A miscellany, 1929.

Hart, A. Shakespeare and the vocabulary of the Two noble kinsmen. In his Shakespeare and the homilies, Melbourne 1935.

Spencer, T. The two noble kinsmen. MP 36 1939.

Mincoff, M. The authorship of the Two noble kinsmen. E Studies 33 1952.

Muir, K. Shakespeare's hand in the Two noble kinsmen. Sh Survey 11 1958.

— Shakespeare as collaborator. 1960.

Waller, F. O. Printer's copy for the Two noble kinsmen. SB 10 1958.

Bertram, P. The date of the Two noble kinsmen. Sh Quart 13 1962.

Edwards, P. On the design of the Two noble kinsmen. REL 5 1964.

Cutts, J. P. Shakespeare's song and masque hand in the Two noble kinsmen. Eng Miscellany (Rome) 18 1967.

Other Plays Ascribed to Shakespeare

See B. Maxwell, Studies in the Shakespeare apocrypha, New York 1956.

The lamentable and true tragedie of M. Arden of Feversham in Kent. 1592, 1599, 1633; ed E. Jacob, Faversham 1770 (ascribed to Shakespeare); ed A. H. Bullen 1887; ed R. Bayne 1897 (Temple); ed C. F. T. Brooke, Shakespeare apocrypha, Oxford 1908; ed H. Macdonald 1947 (Malone Soc).
See C. Crawford, Sh Jb 39 1903; H. D. Sykes, Sidelights on Shakespeare, Stratford 1919; W. W. Greg, Shakespeare and Arden of Feversham, RES 21 1945; J. M. Nosworthy, The Southouse text of Arden of Feversham, Library 5th ser 5 1950.

The birth of Merlin: or the childe hath found his father; written by William Shakespear and William Rowley. 1662; ed N. Delius, Pseudo-Shakspere'sche Dramen pt 3, Elberfeld 1856; ed K. Warnke and L. Proescholdt, Pseudo-Shakespearian plays pt 4, Halle 1887; ed A. F. Hopkinson, Shakespeare's doubtful plays vol 2, 1892; ed C. F. T. Brooke, Shakespeare apocrypha, Oxford 1908.
See F. A. Howe, MP 4 1906; W. Wells, MLR 16 1921.

A pleasant commodie of faire Em, the millers daughter of Manchester, with the love of William the Conqueror. [1605?], 1631; ed N. Delius, Pseudo-Shakspere'sche Dramen pt 5, Elberfeld 1874; ed K. Warnke and L. Proescholdt, Pseudo-Shakespearian plays pt 1, Halle 1883; ed A. F. Hopkinson, Shakespeare's doubtful plays vol 3, 1895; ed C. F. T. Brooke, Shakespeare apocrypha, Oxford 1908; ed W. W. Greg 1927 (Malone Soc).
See K. Elze, Sh Jb 15 1880; G. Steinschneider, Das pseudo-Shakespeare'sche Drama Fair Em, Prowsnitz 1892; P. Lohr, Le printemps d'yver und die Quelle zu Fair Em, Munich 1912.

The lamentable tragedie of Locrine, the eldest sonne of King Brutus, newly set foorth, overseene and corrected,

by W.S. 1595; ed A. F. Hopkinson, Shakespeare's doubtful plays vol 2, 1892; ed C. F. T. Brooke, Shakespeare apocrypha, Oxford 1908; ed R. B. McKerrow, 1908 (Malone Soc).
See C. Crawford, N & Q 26 Jan–18 May 1901; W. S. Gaud, MP 1 1904; E. Koeppel, Sh Jb 41 1905; T. Erbe, Die Locrinesage, Halle 1904; A. Neubner, König Lokrin, Berlin 1908.

The London prodigall, by William Shakespeare. 1605; Ancient British drama vol 1, 1810; ed A. F. Hopkinson, Shakespeare's doubtful plays vol 2, 1893; C. F. T. Brooke, Shakespeare apocrypha, Oxford 1908.

A most pleasant comedie of Mucedorus, the Kings sonne of Valentia. 1598, 1610, 1611, 1613, 1615 ('amplified with new additions'), 1618, 1619, 1621, [1626?], 1629, 1631, 1634, 1639; ed J. P. Collier 1824; ed N. Delius, Pseudo-Shakspere'sche Dramen pt 4, Elberfeld 1874; Hazlitt's Dodsley vol 7; ed K. Warnke and L. Proescholdt, Halle 1887; ed A. F. Hopkinson, Shakespeare's doubtful plays vol 2, 1893; ed C. F. T. Brooke, Shakespeare apocrypha, Oxford 1908.
See W. Wagner, Sh Jb 11 1876, 14 1879; K. Elze, Sh Jb 15 1880, E Studien 6 1883; E. Soffé, Ist Mucedorus ein Schauspiel Shakespeares?, Brunn 1887; W. W. Greg, Sh Jb 40 1904; L. Kirschbaum, Texts of Mucedorus, MLR 50 1955, reply by W. W. Greg, ibid.

The Puritaine: or the widdow of Watling-streete, written by W.S. 1607; Ancient British drama vol 1, 1810; ed A. F. Hopkinson, Shakespeare's doubtful plays vol 3, 1895; ed C. F. T. Brooke, Shakespeare apocrypha, Oxford 1908; ed S. Heaven [1955].
See A. H. Bullen, Works of Thomas Middleton, 1885 (introd).

The first part of the true and honorable historie of the life of Sir John Old-castle, the good Lord Cobham. 1600, 1600 (for 1619, 'written by William Shakespeare'); Ancient British drama vol 1, 1810; ed A. F. Hopkinson, Shakespeare's doubtful plays vol 3, 1894; ed C. F. T. Brooke, Shakespeare apocrypha, Oxford 1908; ed P. Simpson 1908 (Malone Soc).
See W. Baeske, Oldcastle-Falstaff bis zu Shakespeare, Berlin 1905.

The true chronicle historie of the whole life and death of Thomas Lord Cromwell, written by W.S. 1602; Ancient British drama vol 1, 1810; ed A. F. Hopkinson, Shakespeare's doubtful plays vol 1, 1891; ed C. F. T. Brooke, Shakespeare apocrypha, Oxford 1908.
See W. Streit, Jena 1904.

A Yorkshire tragedy, written by W. Shakespeare. 1608, 1619; Ancient British drama vol 1, 1810; ed A. F. Hopkinson, Shakespeare's doubtful plays vol 1, 1891; ed C. F. T. Brooke, Shakespeare apocrypha, Oxford 1908.
See H. D. Sykes, JEGP 16 1917, Sidelights on Shakespeare, Stratford 1919; M. Friedländer, Some problems of A Yorkshire tragedy, SP 35 1938; G. H. Blayney, Dramatic pointing in the Yorkshire tragedy, N & Q May 1957.

Cardenio. *See* E. K. Chambers, Shakespeare: a study of facts and problems vol 1 pp. 538–42, vol 2 p. 343.

On 20 May 1613 Heminge was paid for Court performances of 'sixe severall plays…one other Cardenno', and 2 months later for the performance at Greenwich of a play 'called Cardenna'. In 1653 Humphrey Moseley registered 'The history of Cardennio, by Mr Fletcher and Shakespeare'. In 1727 was produced, and in 1728 pbd, Double falsehood, or the distrest lovers: a play, as it is acted at the Theatre Royal in Drury Lane; written originally by W. Shakespeare and now revised and adapted to the stage by Mr Theobald, the author of Shakespeare restor'd.
See J. Cadwalader, Theobald's alleged Shakespeare manuscript, MLN 56 1941; K. Muir, Cardenio, Etudes Anglaises 11 1958, Shakespeare as collaborator, 1960; C. A. Zimansky, Cardenio, PQ 38 1959; H. C.

Frazier, Theobald's The double falsehood: a revision of Shakespeare's Cardenio?, Comparative Drama 1 1967, The rifling of beauty's stores: Theobald and Shakespeare, Ncuphilologische Mitteilungen 69 1968; J. Freehafer, Cardenio: by Shakespeare or Fletcher?, PMLA 84 1969.

(6) POEMS

Modern Editions

Poems. Ed G. Wyndham 1898; Poems and sonnets, ed E. Dowden 1903; Poems and Pericles, ed S. Lee 5 vols Oxford 1905 (facs of earliest edns); Poems, ed C. K. Pooler 1911 (Arden); Poems, ed H. E. Rollins, Philadelphia 1938 (New Variorum); Sonnets, with A lover's complaint and the Phoenix and the turtle, ed W. Thomson, Oxford 1938; Sonnets, songs and poems, ed H. W. Simon, New York 1951, 1960; Narrative poems, ed G. B. Harrison 1959 (Penguin); Songs and poems, ed E. L. Hubler, New York 1959; Poems, ed F. T. Prince 1960 (New Arden); Poems: facsimile of earliest editions, ed J. M. Osborn, L. L. Martz and E. M. Waith, New Haven 1964; Sonnets, songs and poems, ed O. J. Campbell, New York 1967; Poems, ed W. Burto, New York 1968 (Signet); Poems, ed J. C. Maxwell, Cambridge 1969 (New Cambridge); Minor poems, ed G. L. Kittredge, rev I. Ribner, Waltham Mass 1970.

Studies

Reimer, H. Der Vers in Shakespeares nichtdramatischen Werken. Bonn 1908.

Groos, K. and I. Netto. Psychologisch-statistische Untersuchungen über die visuellen Sinneseindrücke in Shakespeares lyrischen und epischen Dichtungen. E Studien 43 1910.

Saintsbury, G. Shakespeare: Poems. CHEL vol 5 1910.

Farr, H. Notes on Shakespeare's printers and publishers. Library 3rd ser 3 1923.

Baldwin, T. W. On the literary genetics of Shakespeare's poems and sonnets. Urbana 1950.

Ewbank, I.-S. Shakespeare's poetry. In A new companion to Shakespeare studies, ed K. Muir and S. Schoenbaum, Cambridge 1971.

Lever, J. W. Shakespeare's narrative poems. Ibid.

See H. H. Furness, A concordance to Shakespeare's poems, Philadelphia 1874.

See also General Criticism, below, and introds to edns of the poems.

Venus and Adonis

Venus and Adonis; vilia miretur vulgus: mihi flavus Apollo Pocula Castalia plena ministret aqua; London, imprinted by Richard Field, and are to be sold at the sign of the white Greyhound in Paules church-yard. 1593; ed J. O. Halliwell (-Phillipps) 1867 (facs); ed A. Symons 1886 (facs); ed S. Lee, Oxford 1905 (facs, with bibliography); Menston 1969 (facs).

Venus and Adonis. 1594 (rev), [1594-6?] (only extant copy in Folger Lib lacks title), 1596, 1599 (facs 1870), 1599, 1602, 1617, 1620, Edinburgh 1627, London 1630 [1630-6?] (only extant copy in Bodley lacks title), 1636.

For modern edns see above.

Studies

Dürnhöfer, M. Shakespeares Venus und Adonis im Verhältnis zu Ovids Metamorphosen und Constables Schäfergesang. Halle 1890.

Brown, C. Shakespeare and the horse. Library 2nd ser 3 1912.

Marschall, W. Shakespeares Orthographie. Anglia 51 1927.

Spencer, H. Shakespeare's use of Golding in Venus and Adonis. MLN 44 1929.

Putney, R. Venus and Adonis: amour with humor. PQ 20 1941.

— Venus Agonistes. Univ Colorado Stud in Lang & Lit 4 1953.

Price, H. T. The function of imagery in Venus and Adonis. Papers of Michigan Acad 31 1945.

Hatto, A. T. Venus and Adonis and the boar. MLR 41 1946.

Miller, R. P. Venus, Adonis and the horses. ELH 19 1952.

— The myth of Mars's hot minion in Venus and Adonis. ELH 26 1959.

Jackson, R. S. Narrative and imagery in Shakespeare's Venus and Adonis. Papers of Michigan Acad 43 1958.

Allen, D. C. On Venus and Adonis. In Elizabethan and Jacobean studies presented to F. P. Wilson, Oxford 1959.

Hamilton, A. C. Venus and Adonis. Stud in Eng Lit 1500–1900 1 1961.

Palmatier, M. A. A suggested new source in Ovid's Metamorphoses for Shakespeare's Venus and Adonis. HLQ 24 1961.

Bonjour, A. From Shakespeare's Venus to Cleopatra's Cupids. Sh Survey 15 1962.

Bradbrook, M. C. Beasts and gods: Greene's Groatsworth of Witte and the social purpose of Venus and Adonis. Ibid.

Lever, J. W. Venus and the second chance. Ibid.

Bowers, R. H. Anagnorisis, or the shock of recognition, in Shakespeare's Venus and Adonis. Renaissance Papers 1962.

Cantelupe, E. B. An iconographical interpretation of Venus and Adonis: Shakespeare's Ovidian comedy. Sh Quart 14 1963.

Griffin, R. J. 'These contrarieties such unity do hold': patterned imagery in Shakespeare's narrative poems. Stud in Eng Lit 1500–1900 4 1964.

Muir, K. Venus and Adonis: comedy or tragedy? In Shakespearean essays, ed A. Thaler and N. Sanders, Knoxville 1964.

Rabkin, N. Venus and Adonis and the myth of love. In Pacific Coast studies in Shakespeare, ed W. F. McNeir and T. N. Greenfield, Portland Oregon 1966.

Lucrece

Lucrece; London, printed by Richard Field, for John Harrison, and are to be sold at the signe of the white Greyhound in Paules churhyard [sic]. 1594 (running-title as The rape of Lucrece); ed J. O. Halliwell (-Phillipps) 1867 (facs); ed F. J. Furnivall 1886 (facs); ed S. Lee, Oxford 1905 (facs with bibliography).

Lucrece. 1598, 1600, 1607, 1616 (as The rape of Lucrece), 1624, 1632, 1655 (adds J. Quarles, The banishment of Tarquin).

For modern edns see above.

Studies

Ewig, W. Shakespeares Lucrece: eine literarhistorische Untersuchung. Anglia 22 1899; Kiel 1899.

Marschall, W. Shakespeares Orthographie. Anglia 51 1927.

— Das 'Argument' zu Shakespeares Lucrece. Anglia 53 1929.

Kuhl, E. P. Shakespeare's Rape of Lucrece. PQ 20 1941.

Tolbert, J. M. The argument of Shakespeare's Lucrece: its sources and authorship. SE 29 1950.

Oppel, H. Das Bild der brennenden Troja in Shakespeares Rape of Lucrece. Sh Jb 87–8 1951–2.

Walley, H. R. The rape of Lucrece and Shakespearean tragedy. PMLA 76 1961.

Allen, D. C. Some observations on the Rape of Lucrece. Sh Survey 15 1962.

Muir, K. The rape of Lucrece. Anglica 19 1964.
Frye, R. M. Shakespeare's composition of Lucrece: new evidence. Sh Quart 16 1965.
Montgomery, R. L. Shakespeare's gaudy: the method of the Rape of Lucrece. In Studies in honor of De Witt T. Starnes, Austin 1967.

Passionate Pilgrim

The passionate pilgrime, by W. Shakespeare; at London printed for W. Jaggard, and are to be sold by W. Leake at the Greyhound in Paules churchyard. 1599 (2nd title on C3, Sonnets to sundry notes of musicke); ed C. Edmonds 1870 (facs); E. Dowden 1883 (facs); ed S. Lee, Oxford 1905 (facs).
The passionate pilgrime: or certaine amorous sonnets, betweene Venus and Adonis, newly corrected and augmented, by W. Shakespeare; the third edition, whereunto is newly added two love-epistles, the first from Paris to Hellen, and Hellens answere backe againe to Paris. 1612. 2nd edn not known. The Epistles are by Thomas Heywood. Some copies are found without Shakespeare's name, possibly owing to Heywood's protest against piracy in his Apology for actors 1612.
For modern edns see above. Also ed J. Q. Adams, New York 1939 (facs of 1599 from Folger Lib); ed H. E. Rollins, New York 1940 (facs of 1612 from Folger Lib).

Studies

Höhnen, A. Shakespeares Passionate pilgrim. Jena 1867.
Halliwell-Phillipps, J. O. In his Outlines vol 1, 1890.
Kuhl, E. P. Shakespeare and the Passionate pilgrim. MLN 34 1919.

Phoenix and Turtle

Loves martyr: or Rosalins complaint, allegorically shadowing the truth of love, in the constant fate of the phoenix and turtle; a poeme translated out of the Italian by Robert Chester; to these are added some new compositions of severall moderne writers whose names are subscribed to their severall workes, upon the first subject: viz the phoenix and turtle; London, imprinted for E[dward] B[lount]. 1601, 1611 (as The anuals of Great Brittaine); ed A. B. Grosart 1878 (New Sh Soc).
For modern edns see above. Also ed B. H. Newdigate, Oxford 1937; G. Bullett 1938; W. H. Matchett, New York 1965 (with Chester's Love's martyr).

Studies

Fairchild, A. H. R. The phoenix and turtle: a critical and historical interpretation. E Studien 33 1904.
Brown, C. Poems by Sir John Salusbury and Robert Chester. 1914 (EETS).
Bonnard, G. Shakespeare's contribution to R. Chester's Love's martyr: the phoenix and the turtle. E Studies 19 1937.
Benham, G. The phoenix and the turtle. TLS 19-26 July 1941.
Sitwell, O. The sole Arabian tree. TLS 26 April 1941. On a possible source. See also 3 May-16 Aug 1941.
Cunningham, J. V. 'Essence' and the Phoenix and turtle. ELH 19 1952.
Straumann, H. Phönix und Taube. Zürich 1953. With German trn.
Bates, R. Shakespeare's The phoenix and turtle. Sh Quart 6 1955.
Ong, W. J. Metaphor and the twinned vision. Sewanee Rev 63 1955.
Richards, I. A. The sense of poetry: Shakespeare's The phoenix and the turtle. Daedalus 87 1959.
Seltzer, D. 'Their tragic scene': the Phoenix and turtle and Shakespeare's love tragedies. Sh Quart 12 1961.
Ellrodt, R. An anatomy of the Phoenix and the turtle. Sh Survey 15 1962.
Copland, M. The dead phoenix. EC 15 1965.

Matchett, W. H. The phoenix and the turtle: Shakespeare's poem and Chester's Love's martyr. Hague 1965.
Empson, W. The phoenix and the turtle. EC 16 1966.
Dronke, P. The phoenix and the turtle. Orbis Litterarum 23 1968.
Campbell, K. T. S. The phoenix and the turtle as a signpost of Shakespeare's development. Br Jnl of Aethetics 10 1970.

Sonnets

Shake-speares sonnets, never before imprinted; at London by G. Eld for T. T[horpe] and are to be solde by John Wright, dwelling at Christ Church gate. 1609 (some copies have William Aspley instead of John Wright; appended is A lovers complaint, by William Shakespeare); ed T. Tyler 1886(facs); ed S. Lee, Oxford 1905 (facs); 1925 (J. Cape); 1926 (N. Douglas).
Poems, written by Wil. Shake-speare gent. 1640. Includes sonnets and A lover's complaint, and interspersed among them the full contents of Passionate pilgrim 1612, together with some other poems, most not attributed to Shakespeare. Rptd 1885 (A. R. Smith).

Modern Editions

E. Dowden 1881; T. Tyler 1890; G. Wyndham 1898 (with Poems); S. Butler 1899; C. C. Stopes 1904; H. C. Beeching 1904; A. H. Bullen 1905; W. H. Hadow, Oxford 1907; C. M. Walsh 1908; R. M. Alden, Boston 1916 (variorum); C. K. Pooler 1918 (Arden); E. B. Reed, New Haven 1923 (Yale); T. G. Tucker, Cambridge 1924; C. F. T. Brooke, New York 1936; T. Brooke, Oxford 1936; New York 1936 (facs); H. E. Rollins 2 vols Philadelphia 1944 (New Variorum); Thorpe's edition of Shakespeare's sonnets 1609, ed C. L. de Chambrun, Aldington 1950; F. Fergusson and C. J. Sisson, New York 1960 (Laurel); D. Bush and A. Harbage, Baltimore 1961 (Pelican); M. Seymour-Smith 1963; W. Burto, New York 1964; W. G. Ingram and T. Redpath 1964; A. L. Rowse 1964; J. D. Wilson, Cambridge 1966 (New Cambridge); L. B. Wright and V. A. LaMar, New York 1967 (Folger); Menston 1968 (facs of 1609); J. Fuzier, Paris 1970 (text, some trns, sources and bibliography).
For a concordance see H. S. Donow, A concordance to the sonnet sequences of Daniel, Drayton, Shakespeare, Sidney and Spenser, Carbondale 1970.

Studies

Stopes, C. C. Shakespeare's sonnets. Sh Jb 25 1890.
—— The date of Shakespeare's sonnets. Athenaeum 19-26 March 1898.
Archer, W. Shakespeare's sonnets. Fortnightly Rev Dec 1897.
Lee, S. Shakespeare and the Earl of Pembroke. Fortnightly Rev Feb 1898.
—— In his A life of Shakespeare, 1898, 1925 (rev).
—— Ovid and Shakespeare's sonnets. Quart Rev 210 1909.
Tyler, T. The Herbert-Fitton theory of Shakespeare's sonnets. 1898.
McClumpha, C. F. Shakespeare's sonnets and Love's labour's lost. MLN 15 1900.
—— Shakespeare's sonnets and A midsummer night's dream. MLN 16 1901.
—— Shakespeare's sonnets and Romeo and Juliet. Sh Jb 40 1904.
Filon, A. Les sonnets de Shakespeare. Revue des Deux Mondes April 1901.
Acheson, A. Shakespeare and the rival poet. 1903.
—— Mistress Davenant: the dark lady of Shakespeare's sonnets. 1913.
—— Shakespeare's sonnet story 1592-8. 1922.
Hughes, C. Willobie his Avisa. 1904.
Bates, E. S. The sincerity of Shakespeare's sonnets. MP 8 1911.

Mackail, J. W. Shakespeare's sonnets. In his Lectures on poetry, 1911.

de Montmorency, J. E. G. The 'other poet' of Shakespeare's sonnets. Contemporary Rev June 1912.

Alden, R. M. The quarto arrangement of Shakespeare's sonnets. In Anniversary papers by colleagues and pupils of G. L. Kittredge, Boston 1913.

— The 1640 text of Shakespeare's sonnets. MP 14 1917.

Gray, H. D. The arrangement and the date of Shakespeare's sonnets. PMLA 30 1915.

— Shakespeare's rival poet. JEGP 47 1948. Spenser.

Wolff, M. J. Petrarkismus und Antipetrarkismus in Shakespeares Sonetten. E Studien 40 1916.

— Shakespeare und der Petrarkismus. Die Neueren Sprachen 28 1921.

Ord, H. Chaucer and the rival poet in Shakespeare's sonnets. 1921.

Poel, W. et al. Shakespeare and the Davenants. TLS 2 June–4 Aug 1921.

Redin, M. The friend in Shakespeare's sonnets. E Studien 56 1922.

Forrest, H. T. S. The five authors of 'Shake-speares sonnets'. 1923.

Emerson, O. F. Shakespeare's sonnetteering. SP 20 1923.

Fort, J. A. The two date sonnets of Shakespeare. Oxford 1924.

— The time-scheme of Shakespeare's sonnets. Nineteenth Century 1926.

— Thorpe's text of Shakespeare's sonnets. RES 2 1926.

— The story contained in the second series of Shakespeare's sonnets. RES 3 1927.

— Further notes on Shakespeare's sonnets. Library 3rd ser 9 1928.

— A time-scheme for Shakespeare's sonnets. 1929.

— The order and chronology of Shakespeare's sonnets. RES 9 1933.

Bray, D. The original order of Shakespeare's sonnets. 1925.

— The art-form of the Elizabethan sonnet sequence and Shakespeare's sonnets. Sh Jb 63 1927.

— Shakespeare's sonnet sequence. 1938.

Fischer, R. Shakespeares Sonette (Gruppierung, Kunstform). Ed K. Brunner, Vienna 1925.

Harrison, G. B. Willobie his Avisa. 1926. Introd.

— The mortal moon. TLS 29 Nov 1928.

Robertson, J. M. The problems of the Shakespeare sonnets. 1926.

Marschall, W. Aus Shakespeares poetischen Briefwechsel. Heidelberg 1926.

— Das Zentralproblem der Shakespeare Sonette. Anglia 51 1927.

Beckwith, E. On the chronology of Shakespeare's sonnets. JEGP 25 1926.

Spira, T. Shakespeares Sonette in Zusammenhang seines Werkes. Königsberg 1929.

Scott, J. G. Les sonnets élisabéthains: les sources et l'apport personnel. Paris 1929.

Murry, J. M. Concerning sonnet 107. New Adelphi March 1929.

Douglas, A. The true history of Shakespeare's sonnets. 1933.

Kellner, L. Shakespeares Sonette. E Studien 68 1933.

Mattingly, G. The date of Shakespeare's sonnet 107. PMLA 48 1933.

Dannenberg, F. Shakespeares Sonette: Herkunft, Wesen, Deutung. Sh Jb 70 1934.

Knights, L. C. Shakespeare's sonnets. Scrutiny 3 1934; rptd in his Explorations, 1946.

Empson, W. They that have power. In his Some versions of pastoral, 1935.

Archer, C. 'Thou' and 'you' in the sonnets. TLS 27 June 1936.

Nisbet, U. The onlie begetter. 1936.

Evans, W. McC. Lawes' version of Shakespeare's sonnet 116. PMLA 51 1936.

Young, H. M. C. The sonnets of Shakespeare: a psycho-sexual analysis. Madison 1936.

Angell, P. K. Light on the dark lady: a study of some Elizabethan libels. PMLA 52 1937. Elizabeth Trentham, wife of Edward de Vere, Earle of Oxford.

Wells, H. W. A new preface to Shakespeare's sonnets. Sh Assoc Bull 12 1937.

Schmidt, W. Sinnesänderung und Bildvertiefung in Shakespeares Sonetten. Anglia 62 1938.

Deutschbein, M. Shakespeares persönliche und literarische Sonette. Sh Jb 77 1941.

Hutton, J. Analogues of Shakespeare's sonnets 153–4: contributions to the history of a theme. MP 38 1941.

Cellini, B. Vita e arte nei Sonetti di Shakespeare. Rome 1943.

Anspacher, L. K. Shakespeare as poet and lover and the enigma of the sonnets. New York 1944.

Spain, M. M. Who wrote Shakespeare's sonnets? Baltimore 1945.

Mackenzie, B. A. Shakespeare's sonnets: their relations to his life. Cape Town 1946.

Rubow, P. V. Shakespeare's sonnets. Orbis Litterarum 4 1946.

Clarkson, P. S. and C. T. Warren. Pleading and practice in Shakespeare's sonnet 46. MLN 62 1947.

Hotson, L. Shakespeare's sonnets dated and other essays. 1949. Replies by F. W. Bateson and I. A. Shapiro, EC 1 1951.

— More light on Shakespeare's sonnets. Sh Quart 2 1951.

— Mr W.H. 1964.

Goldsmith, V. K. Words out of a hat? alliteration and assonance in Shakespeare's sonnets. JEGP 49 1950.

Smith, H. No cloudy stuffe to puzzle intellect: a testimonial misapplied to Shakespeare. Sh Quart 1 1950.

Hubler, E. The sense of Shakespeare's sonnets. Princeton 1952.

Nowottny, W. M. T. Formal elements in Shakespeare's sonnets: sonnets 1–6. EC 2 1952.

Nosworthy, J. M. All too short a date: internal evidence in Shakespeare's sonnets. Ibid.

Hunter, G. K. The dramatic technique of Shakespeare's sonnets. EC 3 1953.

Stone, W. B. Shakespeare and the sad augurs. JEGP 52 1953.

Masson, D. I. Free patterns in Shakespeare's sonnets. Neophilologus 38 1954.

Jouve, P. J. Sonnets de Shakespeare. Mercure de France May 1955.

— Sur les sonnets de W.S. Revue de Paris April 1955.

Knight, G. W. In his Mutual flame, 1955.

Michel, L. Shakespeare's sonnet 107. JEGP 54 1955.

Lever, J. W. In his Elizabethan love sonnet, 1956.

Schaar, C. Shakespeare's sonnets 50–51 and Tebaldeo's sonnet 107. E Studies 38 1957.

— An Elizabethan sonnet problem. 1960.

— Elizabethan sonnet themes and the dating of Shakespeare's sonnets. Lund 1962.

— Conventional and unconventional in the descriptions of scenery in Shakespeare's sonnets. E Studies 45 1964.

Berry, F. 'Thou' and 'you' in Shakespeare's sonnets. EC 8 1958.

Herbert, T. W. Sound and sense in two Shakespeare sonnets. Tennessee Stud in Lit 3 1958.

Davis, J. M. and J. E. Grant. A critical dialogue on Shakespeare's sonnet 71. Texas Stud in Lit & Lang 1959.

Leishman, J. B. Variations on a theme in Shakespeare's sonnets. In Elizabethan and Jacobean studies presented to F. P. Wilson, Oxford 1959. The immortality conferred by poetry.

— Themes and variations in Shakespeare's sonnets. 1961.

Prince, F. T. The sonnet from Wyatt to Shakespeare. In Elizabethan poetry, ed J. R. Brown and B. Harris 1960.

Gérard, A. S. Iconic organisation in Shakespeare's sonnet 146. E Studies 42 1961.

Grundy, J. Shakespeare's sonnets and the Elizabethan sonneteers. Sh Survey 15 1962.

Hubler, E. et al. The riddle of Shakespeare's sonnets. New York 1962.

Mahood, M. M. Love's confined doom. Sh Survey 15 1962.

Schroeter, J. Shakespeare's not 'to-be-pitied lover'. College Eng Jan 1962. Reply by R. L. White, Sonnet 73 again, CLA Jnl 6 1962.

Stirling, B. More Shakespeare sonnet groups. In Essays on Shakespeare and Elizabethan drama in honor of Hardin Craig, Columbia Missouri 1962.
— Sonnets 127–154. In Shakespeare 1564–1964, ed E. A. Bloom, Providence 1964.
— Sonnets 109–126. Centennial Rev 8 1964.
— The Shakespeare sonnet order: poems and groups. Berkeley 1968.

Braddy, H. Shakespeare's sonnet plan and the effect of folk belief. Midwest Folklore 12 1963.

Kaula, D. 'In war with time': temporal perspective in Shakespeare's sonnets. Stud in Eng Lit 1500–1900 3 1963.

Landry, H. Interpretations in Shakespeare's sonnets. Berkeley 1963.
— The marriage of true minds: truth and error in sonnet 116. Sh Stud 3 1967.

Pirkhofer, A. M. A pretty pleasing pricket: on the use of alliteration in Shakespeare's sonnets. Sh Quart 14 1963.

Wilson, J. D. An introduction to the sonnets of Shakespeare for the use of historians and others. Cambridge 1963.

Bradbrook, M. C. A new reading of sonnets 85 and 86. Filološki Pregled 1 1964.

Krieger, M. A window to criticism: Shakespeare's sonnets and modern poetics. Princeton 1964.

Otten, K. Gedankenentwicklung und Gruppenaufbau in Shakespeares Sonetten der Freundesliebe. Die Neueren Sprachen new ser 13 1964.

Akrigg, G. P. V. The Shakespeare of the sonnets. Queen's Quart 72 1965.

Levin, H. Sonnet 129 as a dramatic poem. Sh Quart 16 1965.

Baldi, S. Shakespeare's sonnets as literature. In Shakespeare celebrated, ed L. B. Wright, Ithaca 1966.

Leisi, E. A possible emendation of Shakespeare's sonnet 146. E Studies 47 1966.

Bates, P. A. Shakespeare's sonnets and pastoral poetry. Sh Jb (Wiemar) 103 1967.

Eckhoff, L. Shakespeare's sonnets in a new light. Studia Neophilologica 39 1967.

Peterson, D. L. Shakespeare's sonnets. In his English lyric from Wyatt to Donne, Princeton 1967.

Winny, J. M. The master-mistress: a study of Shakespeare's sonnets. 1968.

Cook, I. R. W. William Harvey and Shakespeare's sonnets. Sh Survey 21 1968.

Huttar, C. A. The Christian basis of Shakespeare's sonnet 146. Sh Quart 19 1968.

Booth, S. An essay on Shakespeare's sonnets. New Haven 1969.

Parker, D. Verbal moods in Shakespeare's sonnets. MLQ 30 1969.

Grivelet, M. Shakespeare's 'war with time': the sonnets and Richard II. Sh Survey 23 1970.

Russ, J. R. Time's attributes in Shakespeare's sonnets. E Studies 52 1971.

A Lover's Complaint

Editions: *see Sonnets, above.*

Studies

Mackail, J. W. A lover's complaint. E & S 3 1912.

Robertson, J. M. Shakespeare and Chapman: a thesis of Chapman's authorship of A lover's complaint and his origination of Timon of Athens. 1917.

Muir, K. A lover's complaint: a reconsideration. In Shakespeare 1564–1964, ed E. A. Bloom, Providence 1964.

Jackson, M. P. Shakespeare's A lover's complaint: its date and authenticity. Auckland 1965.

Miscellaneous

Esdaile, K. A. Shakespeare's verses in Tong Church. Shrewsbury 1939.

(7) LIFE AND PERSONALITY OF SHAKESPEARE

A. SHAKESPEARE'S LIFE

(1) Documents

See *E. K. Chambers*, Shakespeare: a study of the facts and problems, *vol 2, appendix A, Oxford 1930; S. Schoenbaum*, Shakespeare's lives, *Oxford 1970.*

Lambert, D. H. Cartae Shakespeareanae, Shakespeare documents: a chronological catalogue of extant evidence. 1904.

Neilson, W. A. and A. H. Thorndike. The facts about Shakespeare. New York 1913, 1931 (rev).

Brooke, C. F. T. Shakespeare of Stratford: a handbook for students. New Haven 1926.

Butler, P. Materials for the life of Shakespeare. Chapel Hill 1930.

Hotson, L. I, Shakespeare, do appoint Thomas Russell esquire . . . 1937.

de Chambrun, C. L. Shakespeare rediscovered by means of public records, secret reports and private correspondence newly set forth as evidence on his life and work. Ed G. B. Harrison, New York 1938.

Lewis, B. R. The Shakespeare documents: facsimiles, transliterations, translations and commentary. Stanford 1940.

The principal forgeries are listed in Chambers, vol 2, appendix F. For the literature provoked by the forgeries of Ireland

and Collier, and the alleged forgeries of Cunningham, see Ebisch and Schücking, pp. 24–6, and the following:

Stamp, A. E. The disputed Revels accounts. 1930 (Sh Assoc).

Klein, D. The case of Forman's Booke of plaies. PQ 11 1932.

Tannenbaum, S. A. More about the forged Revels accounts. New York 1932.
— Shaksperian scraps and other Elizabethan fragments. New York 1933. Collier forgeries.
— Shakespeare forgeries in the Revels accounts. Port Washington NY 1966.

Wilson, J. D. and R. W. Hunt. The authenticity of Simon Forman's Boke of plaies. RES 23 1947.

Grebanier, B. D. N. The great Shakespeare forgery. New York 1965.

(2) Principal Biographies

Rowe, N. Some account of the life etc of Shakespeare. In his edn of Works, 1709.

Drake, N. Shakespeare and his times. 2 vols 1817.

Malone, E. Life of Shakespeare. In 3rd variorum edn vol 2, 1821.

Collier, J. P. New facts regarding the life of Shakespeare 1835.
— New particulars regarding the works of Shakespeare. 1836.

—— Traditionary anecdotes of Shakespeare. 1838.
—— Further particulars regarding Shakespeare and his works. 1839.
—— Life of Shakespeare. 1844.
Knight, C. Shakespeare. 1843.
Halliwell (-Phillipps), J. O. The life of Shakespeare. 1848.
—— Illustrations of the life of Shakespeare. 1874.
—— Outlines of the life of Shakespeare. Brighton 1881, 1887 (rev).
Elze, K. Shakespeare. Halle 1876; tr 1888.
Ingleby, C. M. Shakespeare; the man and the book. 2 vols 1877–81.
Fleay, F. G. A chronicle history of the life and work of Shakespeare. 1886.
Brandes, G. Shakespeare. 2 vols Copenhagen 1896; tr 2 vols 1898.
Sarrazin, G. Shakespeares Lehrjahre. Weimar 1897.
Lee, S. A life of Shakespeare. 1898, 1925 (rev). The DNB article is also by Lee.
Rolfe, W. J. A life of Shakespeare. Boston 1904.
Raleigh, W. Shakespeare. 1907 (EML).
Saintsbury, G. Shakespeare: life and plays. CHEL vol 5 1910; ed H. Waddell, Cambridge 1934.
Smeaton, O. Shakespeare: his life and work. [1912] (EL).
Brandl, A. Shakespeares Leben-Umwelt-Kunst. Berlin 1922.
Alden, R. M. Shakespeare. New York 1922, 1932 (rev O. J. Campbell).
Adams, J. Q. A life of Shakespeare. Boston 1923.
Lamborn, E. A. G. and G. B. Harrison. Shakespeare: the man and his stage. 1925.
Chambrun, C. L. de. Shakespeare: acteur-poète. Paris 1926; tr New York 1927.
—— Shakespeare retrouvé: sa vie, son oeuvre. Paris 1947; tr 1956.
Smart, J. S. Shakespeare: truth and tradition. 1928.
Chambers, E. K. Shakespeare: a study of facts and problems. 2 vols Oxford 1930; abridged C. Williams 1933. Index by B. White, 1934 (Sh Assoc).
Wilson, J. D. The essential Shakespeare. Cambridge 1932.
Parrott, T. M. Shakespeare: a handbook. New York 1934.
Fripp, E. I. Shakespeare: man and artist. Ed F. C. Wellstood 2 vols Oxford 1938.
Alexander, P. Shakespeare's life and art. 1939.
Spencer, H. The art and life of Shakespeare. New York 1940.
Baldensperger, F. La vie et l'oeuvre de Shakespeare. Montreal 1945.
Reese, M. M. Shakespeare: his world and his work. 1953.
Chute, M. Shakespeare of London. New York 1957.
Rebora, P. Shakespeare: la vita, l'opera, il messaggio. Milan 1958.
Bentley, G. E. Shakespeare: a biographical handbook. New Haven 1961.
Quennell, P. C. Shakespeare: the poet and his background. 1963.
Rowse, A. L. Shakespeare: a biography. 1963.
Rosignoli, M. P. The life and times of Shakespeare. 1968. Tr from Italian.
Ribner, I. Shakespeare: an introduction to his life, time and theatre. Waltham Mass 1969.
Burgess, A. Shakespeare. 1970.
Schoenbaum, S. Shakespeare's lives. Oxford 1970.
—— The life of Shakespeare. In A new companion to Shakespeare studies, ed K. Muir and Schoenbaum, Cambridge 1971.

(3) Special Studies

Hunter, J. New illustrations of Shakespeare. 1845.
French, G. R. Shakespeareana genealogica. 1869.
Dowden, E. Shakespeare: a critical study of his mind and art. 1874.
Blacker, C. Stratford-on-Avon and Shakespeare. Sh Jb 32 1896.

Stopes, C. C. Shakespeare's Warwickshire contemporaries. Stratford 1897, 1907 (expanded).
—— Shakespeare's family: being a record of the ancestors and descendants of Shakespeare, with some account of the Ardens. 1901.
—— Shakespeare's fellows and followers: a special set of facts collected from the Lord Chamberlain's papers. Sh Jb 46 1910.
—— Burbage and Shakespeare's stage. 1913.
—— Shakespeare's environment. 1914, 1918 (expanded).
—— The life of Henry, third Earl of Southampton. Cambridge 1922.
—— Early records illustrating the personal life of Shakespeare. In Shakespeare and the theatre, 1927 (Sh Assoc).
Elton, C. I. Shakespeare: his family and friends. Ed A. H. Thompson 1904.
Gray, J. W. Shakespeare's marriage. 1905.
Haney, J. L. The name of Shakespeare: a study in orthography. Philadelphia 1906.
Spielmann, M. H. On the portraits of Shakespeare. In Stratford town Shakespeare vol 10, 1907.
—— Shakespeare's portraiture. In Studies in the First Folio, 1924 (Sh Assoc).
Tannenbaum, S. A. The Shakespeare coat-of-arms. New York 1908.
—— A new study of Shakespeare's will. SP 23 1926.
Kingsley, R. G. Shakespeare in Warwickshire. Nineteenth Century May 1910.
Law, E. Shakespeare as groom of the chamber. 1910.
Wallace, C. W. Shakespeare and his London associates. Nebraska Univ Stud 10 1910.
—— Shakespeare's money interest in the Globe theater. Century Mag Sept 1910.
—— Shakespeare and the Blackfriars. Ibid.
Thaler, A. Shakespeare's income. SP 15 1918.
Savage, R. and E. I. Fripp. Minutes and accounts of the corporation of Stratford-upon-Avon 1553–1620. 1921 (Dugdale Soc).
Fripp, E. I. Master Richard Quyny. Oxford 1924.
—— Shakespeare's Stratford. Oxford 1928.
—— Shakespeare's haunts near Stratford. Oxford 1929.
—— Shakespeare studies. 1930.
Brooke, C. F. T. Shakespeare's moiety of the Stratford tithes. MLN 40 1925.
Gray, A. A chapter in the early life of Shakespeare. Cambridge 1926.
Salzmann, L. F. Shakespeare and the quarter sessions. London Mercury Nov 1926.
Addy, S. O. Shakespeare's will: the stigma removed. N & Q 16 Jan–6 Feb 1926.
—— Shakespeare's marriage. N & Q 23–30 Oct 1926.
—— The proving of Shakespeare's will. N & Q 22 Oct 1927.
—— Shakespeare's Puritan relations. N & Q 21 April 1928.
Barnard, E. A. B. New links with Shakespeare. Cambridge 1930.
Farnham, H. W. Shakespeare's economics. New Haven 1931.
Hotson, L. Shakespeare versus Shallow. 1931.
Harrison, G. B. Shakespeare at work 1592–1603. 1933.
Baker, O. In Shakespeare's Warwickshire and the unknown years. 1937.
Brooks, A. Will Shakespeare: factotum and agent. 1937.
Herrmann, B. War Shakespeare ein Schauspieler? Würzburg 1937.
McNeal, T. H. The tyger's heart wrapt in a player's hide. Sh Assoc Bull 13 1938.
Cartier, G. Quelques précisions au sujet de l'acteur Shakespeare. Mercure de France April 1939.
Everett, A. L. Shakespeare in 1596. Sh Assoc Bull 14 1939.
Castle, E. Shakespeare und seine Truppe. Sh Jb 76 1940.
Rose, W. The story of Anne Whately and Shakespeare. 1940.

Hoops, J. Shakespeares Name und Herkunft. Heidelberg 1941.

McManaway, J. G. The licence for Shakespeare's marriage. MLN 57 1942.

— A new Shakespeare document. Sh Quart 2 1951. Folger mss 2068.7–8.

Knight, G. W. The olive and the sword: a study of Shakespeare's England. Oxford 1944.

Taylor, R. Shakespeare's cousin, Thomas Greene and his kin: possible light on the Shakespeare family background. PMLA 60 1945.

Swinyard, L. Shakespeare's Stratford-upon-Avon. 1946.

Günther, A. Der junge Shakespeare: sieben unbekannte Jahre. Stuttgart 1947.

Mitchell, C. M. The Shakespeare circle: a life of Dr John Hall, Shakespeare's son-in-law. Birmingham 1947.

Lambin, G. Shakespeare était-il essexien? Les Langues Modernes 42 1948.

Taylor, G. C. Did Shakespeare, actor, improvise in Every man in his humour? In J. Q. Adams memorial studies, Washington 1948.

Wentersdorff, K. Shakespeares erste Truppe: ein Beitrag zur Aufklärung des Problems der sogenannten 'verlorenen Jahre'. Sh Jb 84–6 1948–50.

Duff Cooper, A. Sergeant Shakespeare. 1949.

Brennecke, E. All kinds of Shakespeares: factual, fantastical, fictional. Sh Quart 1 1950.

Schrickx, W. Shakespeare and the school of night: an estimate and further interpretation. Neophilologus 35 1950.

Sisson, C. J. Studies in the life and environment of Shakespeare since 1900. Sh Survey 3 1950.

Fox, L. An early copy of Shakespeare's will. Sh Survey 4 1951.

Stevenson, R. Shakespeare's interest in Harsnet's Declaration. PMLA 67 1952.

Esdaile, K. Some fellow-citizens of Shakespeare in Southwark. E & S new ser 5 1952.

Berryman, J. Shakespeare at thirty. Hudson Rev 6 1953.

Isaacs, J. Shakespeare's earliest years in the theatre. Proc Br Acad 39 1953.

Keen, A. and M. Lubbock. The annotator. 1954. On the 'lost years'.

Eccles, M. Shakespeare in Warwickshire. Madison 1961.

Joseph, H. Shakespeare's son-in-law: John Hall, man and physician; with a facsimile of the second edition of Hall's Select observations on English bodies. Hamden Conn 1964.

Rowse, A. L. Shakespeare's Southampton. 1965.

Akrigg, G. P. V. Shakespeare and the Earl of Southampton. Cambridge Mass 1968.

B. SHAKESPEARE'S PERSONALITY AND INTERESTS

(1) General Studies

Bagehot, W. Shakespeare the man. In his Literary studies vol 1, 1879.

Smith, G. Shakespeare the man. Toronto 1899.

Stephen, L. Shakespeare the man. In his Studies of a biographer, 4 vols 1898–1902.

Bradley, A. C. Shakespeare the man. In his Oxford lectures on poetry, 1909.

Harris, F. The man Shakespeare. New York 1909.

Lee, S. The impersonal aspect of Shakespeare's art. 1909 (Eng Assoc lecture).

Dowden, E. Is Shakespeare self-revealed? In his Essays modern and Elizabethan, 1910.

Masson, D. Shakespeare personally. Ed R. Masson 1914.

Beeching, H. C. The benefit of the doubt. In A book of homage to Shakespeare, Oxford 1916.

— The character of Shakespeare. Proc Br Acad 8 1917.

Brewster, W. T. The restoration of Shakespeare's personality. In Columbia University Shakespearean studies, ed B. Matthews and A. H. Thorndike, New York 1916.

Mackail, J. W. Shakespeare after three hundred years. Proc Br Acad 7 1916.

Richter, H. Shakespeare der Mensch. Leipzig 1923.

Harman, E. G. The 'impersonality' of Shakespeare. 1925.

Gregor, J. Shakespeare: der Aufbau eines Zeitalters. Vienna 1935.

Kittredge, G. L. The man Shakespeare. Sh Assoc Bull 11 1936.

Clark, E. T. The man who was Shakespeare. New York 1937.

Haemmerling, K. Der Mann, der Shakespeare heisst. Berlin 1938.

Eckhardt, E. Shakespeares Anschauungen über Religion und Sittlichkeit, Staat und Volk. Weimar 1940.

Wolff, E. Gedanken über das Shakespeare-Problem. Hamburg 1946.

Bliss, W. The real Shakespeare: a counterblast to commentators. 1947.

Norman, C. So worthy a friend: Shakespeare. New York 1947.

— The playmaker of Avon. Philadelphia 1949.

Holm, H. Der Schwan von Avon. Vienna 1948.

Thorndike, R. In the steps of Shakespeare. 1948.

Brown, I. Shakespeare: a biography and an interpretation. 1949.

— Shakespeare and his world. 1964.

Hill, F. E. To meet Will Shakespeare. Toronto 1949.

Dobbs, L. Shakespeare revealed. 1951.

Smith, H. In search of the real Shakespeare. Yale Rev 40 1951.

Craig, H. Man successful. In Shakespeare 400, ed J. G. McManaway, New York 1964.

(2) Education

Baynes, T. S. What Shakespeare learnt at school. In his Shakespeare studies, 1894.

Leach, A. F. English schools at the Reformation. 1896.

Watson, F. The curriculum and text-books of English schools in the seventeenth century. Trans Bibl Soc 6 1902

Bayley, A. R. Shakespeare's school. N & Q 26 Oct 1907, 22 April 1916.

Blach, S. Shakespeares Lateingrammatik: Lilys Grammatica latina. Sh Jb 44–5 1908–9.

Stowe, A. M. English grammar schools in the reign of Queen Elizabeth. New York 1908.

Watson, F. The English grammar schools to 1660. Cambridge 1908.

— The old English grammar schools. Cambridge 1916.

Sandys, J. E. Education. In Shakespeare's England vol 1, Oxford 1916.

Stevenson, W. H. Shakespeare's schoolmaster and handwriting. TLS 8 Jan 1920.

Plimpton, G. The education of Shakespeare, illustrated from the schoolbooks in use at his time. 1933.

Brown, D. What Shakespeare learned at school. Bucknell Univ Stud 1 1941.

Baldwin, T. W. Shakespeare's petty school. Urbana 1943.

— Shakespeare's small Latine and lesse Greeke. Urbana 1944.

Wilson, F. P. Shakespeare's reading. Sh Survey 3 1950; rptd in his Shakespearian and other studies, Oxford 1969.

Simonini, R. C. Language lesson dialogues in Shakespeare. Sh Quart 2 1951.

Whitaker, V. K. Shakespeare's use of learning: an inquiry into the growth of his mind and art. San Marino 1953.

Thompson, C. R. Schools in Tudor England. In Life and letters in Tudor and Stuart England, ed L. B. Wright and V. A. LaMar, Ithaca 1962.

Hunter, G. K. Shakespeare's reading. In A new companion to Shakespeare studies, ed K. Muir and S. Schoenbaum, Cambridge 1971.

(3) Religion, Philosophy and Psychology

Carter, T. Shakespeare: Puritan and recusant. Edinburgh 1897.

Bowden, H. S. and R. Simpson. The religion of Shakespeare. 1899.

Moulton, R. G. The moral system of Shakespeare. New York 1903.

Beeching, H. C. On the religion of Shakespeare. In Stratford Town edn of Works vol 10, 1907.

Lee, S. Aspects of Shakespeare's philosophy. In Shakespeare and the modern stage, 1907.

Dowden, E. Elizabethan psychology. In his Essays modern and Elizabethan, 1910.

Bundy, M. W. Shakespeare and Elizabethan psychology. JEGP 23 1924.

Jones, H. The ethical idea in Shakespeare. In Essays on literature and education, ed H. J. W. Hetherington 1924.

Craig, H. Shakespeare's depiction of passions. PQ 4 1925.

— Shakespeare and formal logic. In Studies in English philology: a miscellany in honor of F. Klaeber, Minneapolis 1929.

— Shakespeare and Elizabethan psychology. In Shakespeare-Studien: Festschrift für H. Mutschmann, Marburg 1951.

— Shakespeare and the here and now. PMLA 67 1952.

Schücking, L. L. Shakespeares Persönlichkeitsideal. Neue Jahrbücher für Wissenschaft und Jugendbildung 3 1927.

Fripp, E. I. The religion of Shakespeare's father. Hibbert Jnl 26 1928.

Anderson, R. L. Elizabethan psychology and Shakespeare's plays. Iowa City 1928.

Campbell, L. B. Shakespeare's tragic heroes. Cambridge 1930.

Baton, A. M. The philosophy of Shakespeare. Kingsport Tenn 1937.

Curry, W. C. Shakespeare's philosophical patterns. Baton Rouge 1937.

Klein, T. Die religiöse Wirklichkeit bei Shakespeare. Zeitwende 13 1937.

Daniels, R. B. Shakespeare and Puritans. Sh Assoc Bull 13 1938.

Schindler, P. Den religiøse baggrund for Shakespeare. Edda 25 1938.

Allen, D. C. Shakespeare and the doctrine of cosmic identities. Sh Assoc Bull 14 1939.

Schümmer, T. Shakespeare: nordischer Mythus und christliche Metaphysik. Hochland 36 1939.

Law, R. A. Shakespeare in the Garden of Eden. SE 1941.

Deutschberger, P. Shakespeare on degree: a study of backgrounds. Sh Assoc Bull 17 1942.

Spencer, T. Shakespeare and the nature of man. New York 1942.

Semper, I. J. Shakespeare's religion once more. Catholic World May 1943.

Wilson, J. D. Shakespeare's universe. Edinburgh Univ Jnl 11 1942.

Yates, F. A. Shakespeare and the Platonic tradition. Edinburgh Univ Jnl 12 1943.

Armstrong, E. A. Shakespeare's imagination: a study of the psychology of association and inspiration. Lincoln Nebraska 1946, 1963 (rev and expanded).

de Groot, J. H. The Shakespeares and 'the old faith'. New York 1946.

Horne, H. H. Shakespeare's philosophy of love. Bradenton Beach Florida 1946.

Thies, F. Shakespeare und die Idee der Unsterblichkeit. Dortmund 1947.

Heuer, H. Der Geist und seine Ordnung bei Shakespeare. Sh Jb 84–6 1948–50.

Mutschmann, H. and K. Wentersdorf. Shakespeare und der Katholizismus. Speyer 1950; tr New York 1952.

McCurdy, H. G. The personality of Shakespeare. New Haven 1953.

Sehrt, E. T. Vergebung und Gnade bei Shakespeare. Stuttgart 1953.

Schilling, K. Shakespeare: die Idee des Menschseins in seinen Werken. Munich 1953.

Spalding, K. J. The philosophy of Shakespeare. 1953.

Coleman, H. Shakespeare and the Bible. New York 1955.

Parker, M. H. The slave of life. 1955.

Speaight, R. Nature in Shakespearian tragedy. 1955.

Bush, G. D. Shakespeare and the natural condition. Cambridge Mass 1956.

Emery, L. La vision shakespearienne du monde et de l'homme. Lyons 1957.

Soellner, R. The four primary passions: a Renaissance theory reflected in the works of Shakespeare. SP 55 1958.

Vyvyan, J. The Shakespearean ethic. 1959.

— Shakespeare and Platonic beauty. 1961.

Bryant, J. A. Hippolyta's view: some Christian aspects of Shakespeare's plays. Lexington Kentucky 1961.

Matthews, H. M. V. Character and symbol in Shakespeare's plays. Cambridge 1962. On Christian elements.

Frye, R. M. Shakespeare and Christian doctrine. Princeton 1962.

Battenhouse, R. W. Shakespearian tragedy as Christian. Centennial Rev 7 1964.

Mendle, R. W. S. Revelation in Shakespeare: a study of the supernatural, religious and spiritual elements in his art. 1964.

Merchant, W. M. Shakespeare's theology. REL 5 1964.

Howse, E. M. Spiritual values in Shakespeare, Toronto 1965.

Knight, G. W. Shakespeare and religion. New York 1967.

Turner, F. Shakespeare and the nature of time: moral and philosophical themes in some poems and plays by Shakespeare. Oxford 1970.

Wilson, E. M. Shakespeare and Christian doctrine: some qualifications. Sh Survey 23 1970.

Elton, W. R. Shakespeare and the thought of his age. In A new companion to Shakespeare studies, ed K. Muir and S. Schoenbaum, Cambridge 1971.

(4) The Supernatural

See also Religion, Philosophy and Psychology, above. For a bibliography see Jaggard, below.

Lavater, L. Of ghostes and spirites walking by nyght. 1572; ed J. D. Wilson and M. Yardley 1929 (Sh Assoc).

Scot, R. The discoverie of witchcraft. 1584; ed M. Summers 1930.

Spalding, T. A. Elizabethan demonology. 1880.

Dyer, T. F. T. Folk-lore of Shakespeare. 1883.

Jaggard, W. Folklore, superstition and witchcraft in Shakespeare: a bibliography. 1896.

Nutt, A. The fairy mythology in Shakespeare. 1900.

Wilson, W. Shakespeare and astrology. Boston 1903.

Gibson, J. P. Shakespeare's use of the supernatural. Cambridge 1908.

Lucy, M. Shakespeare and the supernatural. Liverpool 1908.

Stewart, H. H. The supernatural in Shakespeare. 1908.

Notestein, W. A history of witchcraft in England 1558–1718. Washington 1911.

Clark, C. Shakespeare and science. Birmingham 1929.

— Shakespeare and the supernatural. 1932.

Kittredge, G. L. Witchcraft in old and new England. Cambridge Mass 1929.

Latham, M. W. Elizabethan fairies. New York 1930.

Sondheim, M. Shakespeare and the astrology of his time. Jnl of Warburg Inst 2 1939.

Parr, J. Shakespeare's artistic use of astrology. In his Tamburlaine's malady and other essays, Tuscaloosa 1953.

Smith, W. D. The Elizabethan rejection of judicial astrology and Shakespeare's practice. Sh Quart 9 1958.

Briggs, K. M. In her Anatomy of Puck, 1959.

Green, R. L. Shakespeare and the fairies. Folk Lore 73 1962.

Strathmann, E. A. The Devil can cite Scripture. In Shakespeare 400, ed J. G. McManaway, New York 1964.

(5) The State, Society and Politics

Hofmannsthal, H. von. Shakespeares Könige und grosse Herren. Sh Jb 41 1905.

Tolstoi, L. N. Shakespeare. Hanover 1906; tr 1907.

Lee, S. Shakespeare and patriotism. In his Shakespeare and the modern stage, 1907.

— Shakespeare and public affairs. Contemporary Rev Aug–Sept 1913.

Tupper, F. The Shakespearean mob. PMLA 27 1912.

Tolman, A. H. Is Shakespeare aristocratic? PMLA 29 1914.

Gayley, C. M. Shakespeare and the founders of liberty in America. New York 1917.

Raleigh, W. Shakespeare and England. Proc Br Acad 8 1918.

Chambers, R. W. The expression of ideas—particularly political ideas—in the three pages and in Shakespeare. In Shakespeare's hand in the Play of Sir Thomas More, Cambridge 1923.

Marriott, J. A. R. Shakespeare and politics. Cornhill Mag Dec 1927.

Schelling, F. E. The common folk of Shakespeare. In Shakespeare and 'demi-science', Philadelphia 1927.

Charlton, H. B. Shakespeare, politics and politicians. 1929 (Eng Assoc lecture).

Ward, B. M. Shakespeare and the Anglo-Spanish war 1585–1604. Revue Anglo-américaine 7 1930.

Harrison, G. B. Shakespeare's topical significances. TLS 13–20 Nov 1930.

Glunz, H. H. Shakespeares Staat. Frankfurt 1940.

Stirling, B. Anti-democracy in Shakespeare. MLQ 2 1941.

Thaler, A. Shakespeare and democracy. Knoxville 1941.

Craig, H. Shakespeare and the normal world. Rice Inst Pamphlet 31 1944.

Prym von Becherer, G. Der Makrokosmos im Weltbild der Shakespearezeit. Sh Jb 82–3 1946–7.

Speaight, R. Shakespeare and politics. 1946 (Wedmore memorial lecture).

Fischer, W. Zur Frage der Staatsauffassung in Shakespeares Königsdramen. In Shakespeare-Studien: Festschrift für H. Mutschmann, Marburg 1951.

Knights, L. C. Shakespeare and political wisdom: a note on the personalism of Julius Caesar and Coriolanus. Sewanee Rev 61 1953.

— Shakespeare's politics, with some reflections on the nature of tradition. Proc Br Acad 43 1957; rptd in his Further explorations, 1965.

Eckhoff, L. Shakespeare: spokesman of the third estate. Oslo 1954.

Borinski, L. 'Soldat' und 'Politiker' bei Shakespeare. Sh Jb 91 1955.

Brooks, H. F. Shakespeare and the Governour. Sh Quart 14 1963.

Schneider, R. Das Bild der Herrschaft in Shakespeares Drama. Sh Jb 93 1957.

Bloom, A. D. and H. V. Jaffa. Shakespeare's politics. New York 1964.

Keeton, G. W. Shakespeare's legal and political background. 1967.

Hurstfield, J. The historical and social background. In A new companion to Shakespeare studies, ed K. Muir and S. Schoenbaum, Cambridge 1971.

(6) The Law

Rushton, W. L. Shakespeare a lawyer. 1858.

— Shakespeare's legal maxims. 1859.

— Shakespeare's testamentary language. 1869.

— Shakespeare illustrated by the lex scripta. 1870.

Campbell, J. Shakespeare's legal acquirements. 1859.

Devecmon, W. C. In re Shakespeare's legal acquirements. 1899 (New York Sh Soc).

Allen, C. Notes on the Bacon-Shakespeare question. Boston 1900.

Collins, J. C. Was Shakespeare a lawyer? In his Studies in Shakespeare, 1904.

White, E. J. Commentaries on the law in Shakespeare. St Louis 1911.

Greenwood, G. G. Shakespeare's law and Latin. 1916.

— Shakespeare's law. 1920.

Underhill, A. Law. In Shakespeare's England vol 1, Oxford 1916.

Barton, D. P. Links between Shakespeare and the law. 1929.

Keeton, G. W. Shakespeare and his legal problems. 1930.

— Shakespeare's legal and political background. 1967.

Clarkson, P. S. and C. T. Warren. The law of property in Shakespeare and the Elizabethan drama. Baltimore 1942.

Young, G. M. Shakespeare and the termers. Proc Br Acad 33 1947; rptd in his Today and yesterday, 1948.

(7) Natural History and Medicine

Patterson, R. The natural history of the insects mentioned in Shakespeare's plays. 1838.

Bucknill, J. C. The medical knowledge of Shakespeare. 1860.

— The mad folk of Shakespeare. 1867.

Beisley, S. Shakespeare's garden. 1864.

Harting, J. E. The ornithology of Shakespeare. 1871.

Ellacombe, H. N. The plant-lore and garden craft of Shakespeare. Exeter [1878].

Phipson, E. The animal-lore of Shakespeare's time. 1883.

Moyes, J. Medicine and kindred arts in the plays of Shakespeare. Glasgow 1896.

Seager, H. W. Natural history in Shakespeare's time. 1896.

Dowden, E. Shakespeare as a man of science. In his Essays modern and Elizabethan, 1910.

Cartaz, A. La toxicologie dans les drames de Shakespeare. Paris 1911.

Robin, P. A. In his Old physiology in English literature, 1911.

Geikie, A. The birds of Shakespeare. 1916.

Savage, F. G. The flora and folk-lore of Shakespeare. Cheltenham 1923.

Singleton, E. The Shakespeare garden. 1923.

Somerville, H. Madness in Shakespearian tragedy. 1929.

Luce, M. Shakespeare and botany. In Man and nature, 1935.

Rohde, E. S. Shakespeare's wild flowers, fairy lore, gardens, herbs, gatherers of simples and bee lore. 1935.

Knowlton, E. C. Nature and Shakespeare. PMLA 51 1936.

Watson, E. M. Medical lore in Shakespeare. Annals of Medical History 8 1936.

Anderson, R. L. 'As heart can think'. Sh Assoc Bull 12 1937.

Woolenberg, R. Shakespeare, Persönliches aus Welt und Werk: Abhandlungen zur Geschichte der Medizin und der Naturwissenschaften. Berlin 1939.

Cook, P. Shakespeare, botanist. Sh Assoc Bull 15 1940.

Draper, J. W. The humors and Shakespeare's characters. Durham NC 1945.

Simpson, R. R. Shakespeare and medicine. Edinburgh 1959.

Edgar, I. I. Shakespeare, medicine and psychiatry. New York 1970.

(8) Geography, Travel, the Army and the Sea
(including alleged travels)

Sugden, E. H. A topographical dictionary to the works of Shakespeare and his fellow dramatists. Manchester 1925.

Thoms, W. J. Was Shakespeare ever a soldier? In his Three notelets on Shakespeare, 1865.

Elze, K. Shakespeares mutmassliche Reisen. Sh Jb 8 1873

Elze, T. Italienische Skizzen zu Shakespeare. Sh Jb 13–15 1878–80.

— Venezianische Skizzen zu Shakespeare. Munich 1899.

Sarrazin, G. Shakespeare in Mantua? Sh Jb 29 1894.

— Neue italienische Skizzen zu Shakespeare. Sh Jb 36 1900.

— Shakespeare in Mailand? Sh Jb 46 1910.

Stefansson, J. Shakespeare at Elsinore. Contemporary Rev Jan 1896.

Bristol, F. M. Shakespeare and America. Chicago 1898.

Keller, W. Zu Shakespeares italienische Reise. Sh Jb 35 1899.

Koeppel, E. War Shakespeare in Italien? Ibid.

Logeman, H. Shakespeare et Helsingör. In Mélanges Paul Fredericy, Brussels 1904.

Lawrence, W. J. Was Shakespeare ever in Ireland? Sh Jb 42 1906.

Sullivan, E. Shakespeare and the waterways of North Italy. Nineteenth Century Aug 1908.

— Shakespeare and Italy. Nineteenth Century Jan–Feb 1918.

Collison-Morley, L. Shakespeare in Italy. Stratford 1916.

Smart, J. S. Shakespeare's Italian names. MLR 11 1916.

Tilley, M. P. Shakespeare and Italian geography. JEGP 16 1917.

Nulli, A. Shakespeare in Italia. Milan 1918.

Eagle, R. A. Shakespeare and Italy. Nineteenth Century June 1923.

Taylor, E. G. R. Tudor geography 1485–1583. 1930.

— Late Tudor and early Stuart geography 1583–1650. 1934.

Jeffery, V. M. Shakespeare's Venice. MLR 27 1932.

Farinelli, A. Shakespeares Italien. Sh Jb 75 1939.

Nutt, S. M. The arctic voyages of William Barents in probable relation to certain of Shakespeare's plays. SP 39 1942.

Duff Cooper, A. Sergeant Shakespeare. 1949.

Grillo, E. Shakespeare and Italy. Glasgow 1949.

Lambin, G. Sur la trace d'un Shakespeare inconnu. Les Langues Modernes 45–6 1951–2.

Penrose, B. Travel and discovery in the Renaissance 1420–1620. Cambridge Mass 1952.

— Tudor and early Stuart voyaging. Washington 1962.

Borinski, L. 'Soldat' und 'Politiker' bei Shakespeare. Sh Jb 91 1955.

Rowse, A. L. In his Expansion of Elizabethan England, 1955.

Jorgensen, P. A. Divided command in Shakespeare. PMLA 70 1955. On historical battles in Shakespeare.

— Shakespeare's military world. Los Angeles 1956.

Waters, D. W. In his Art of navigation in England in Elizabethan and early Stuart times, 1958.

Falconer, A. F. Shakespeare and the sea. 1964.

— A glossary of Shakespeare's sea and naval terms, including gunnery. 1965.

Holmes, M. The guns of Elsinore. 1964.

(9) Music, Art and Other Interests

Ellacombe, H. N. Shakespeare as an angler. 1883.

Naylor, E. W. Shakespeare and music; with illustrations from the music of the 16th and 17th centuries. 1896.

Rushton, W. L. Shakespeare an archer. 1897.

Madden, D. H. The diary of Master William Silence: a study of Shakespeare and Elizabethan sport. 1897.

Mauntz, A. von. Heraldik im Diensten der Shakespeare-Forschung. Berlin 1903.

Loewe, H. Shakespeare und die Waldmannskunst. Sh Jb 40 1904.

Brown, C. Shakespeare and the horse. Library 2nd ser 3 1912.

Matthews, B. Shakespeare as an actor. North Amer Rev 1912.

Herford, C. H. Shakespeare and the arts. Bull John Rylands Lib 11 1927.

Rothery, G. C. The heraldry of Shakespeare. 1930.

Thorp, M. F. Shakespeare and the fine arts. PMLA 46 1931.

Dent, E. J. Shakespeare and music. In A companion to Shakespeare studies, ed H. Granville-Barker and G. B. Harrison, Cambridge 1934.

Fairchild, A. H. R. Shakespeare and the arts of design (architecture, sculpture and painting). Columbia Missouri 1937.

Brennecke, E. Shakespeare's musical collaboration with Morley. PMLA 54 1939.

Fatout, P. With horn and hound. Sh Assoc Bull 20 1945.

Scott-Giles, C. W. Shakespeare's heraldry. 1950.

Prange, G. Shakespeares Äusserungen über die Tänze seiner Zeit. Sh Jb 89 1953.

Long, J. H. Shakespeare's use of music. Gainesville 1955.

— Shakespeare's use of music: the final comedies. Gainesville 1962.

Sternfeld, F. W. The dramatic and allegorical function of music in Shakespeare's tragedies. Annales Musicologiques 3 1955.

— Shakespeare's use of popular song. In Elizabethan and Jacobean studies presented to F. P. Wilson, Oxford 1959.

— Music in Shakespearean tragedy. 1963.

— Shakespeare and music. In A new companion to Shakespeare studies, ed K. Muir and S. Schoenbaum, Cambridge 1971.

Manifold, J. S. In his Music in English drama from Shakespeare to Purcell, 1956.

Auden, W. H. Music in Shakespeare. Encounter Dec 1957.

Chambers, H. A. A Shakespeare song book. 1957. 3 centuries of musical settings.

Merchant, W. M. Shakespeare and the artist. Oxford 1959.

Ruppel, K. H. Shakespeare und die Oper. Sh Jb 95 1959.

Bousted, A. Music to Shakespeare. Oxford 1964.

Dickinson, A. E. F. Shakespeare in music. Durham Univ Jnl 25 1964.

Hartnoll, P. (ed). Shakespeare in music. 1964. See especially J. Stevens, Shakespeare and the music of the Elizabethan stage.

Ingram, R. H. Hamlet, Othello and King Lear: music and tragedy. Sh Jb 100 1964.

Clemen, W. H. Shakespeare and music. Sh Jb (Heidelberg) 1966.

Seng, P. J. The vocal songs in the plays of Shakespeare: a critical history. Cambridge Mass 1967.

Edwards, P. Shakespeare and the confines of art. 1968.

Dunn, C. M. The function of music in Shakespeare's romances. Sh Quart 20 1969.

C. CONTROVERSIES ABOUT AUTHORSHIP

Early literature on the Shakespeare-Bacon controversy and on similar 'anti-Stratfordian' theories is listed in Ebisch and Schücking, pp. 182–6. For more recent pbns see annual bibliography in Sh Quart. See also col 1154, above.

Friedman, W. and E. The Shakespearean ciphers examined. Cambridge 1957.

Churchill, R. C. Shakespeare and his betters. 1958.

Gibson, H. N. The Shakespeare claimants. 1962.

McManaway, J. G. The authorship of Shakespeare. Washington 1962.

McMichael, G. and E. M. Glenn (ed). Shakespeare and his rivals: a casebook on the authorship controversy. New York 1962.

(8) CRITICISM

A. TECHNICAL CRITICISM

A companion to Shakespeare studies. Ed H. Granville-Barker and G. B. Harrison, Cambridge 1934. C. J. Sisson, The theatres and companies; H. Granville-Barker, Shakespeare's dramatic art; G. Rylands, Shakespeare the poet; G. D. Willcock, Shakespeare and Elizabethan English; E. J. Dent, Shakespeare and music; A. L. Attwater, Shakespeare's sources; B. Dobrée, Shakespeare and the drama of his time; A. W. Pollard, Shakespeare's text; T. S. Eliot and J. Isaacs, Shakespearian criticism; J. Isaacs, Shakespearian scholarship; H. Child, Shakespeare in the theatre to the present time.

A new companion to Shakespeare studies. Ed K. Muir and S. Schoenbaum, Cambridge 1971. S. Schoenbaum, The life of Shakespeare; R. Hosley, The playhouses and the stage; D. Seltzer, The actors and acting; G. K. Hunter, Shakespeare's reading; R. Quirk, Shakespeare and the English language; B. Vickers, Shakespeare's use of rhetoric; I.-S. Ewbank, Shakespeare's poetry; J. W. Lever, Shakespeare's narrative poems; D. Bevington, Shakespeare the Elizabethan dramatist; M. C. Bradbrook, Shakespeare the Jacobean dramatist; F. W. Sternfeld, Shakespeare and music; J. Hurstfield, The historical and social background; W. R. Elton, Shakespeare and the thought of his age; A. C. Sprague, Shakespeare's plays on the English stage; P. Ure, Shakespeare and the drama of his time; G. B. Evans, Shakespeare's text: approaches and problems; M. A. Shaaber, Shakespeare criticism: Dryden to Bradley; S. Wells, Shakespeare criticism since Bradley.

(1) Sources and Influences

Collections of Sources

[Lennox, C.] Shakespeare illustrated: or the novels and histories on which the plays of Shakespeare are founded. 3 vols 1753–4, 1756.

[Nichols, J.] Six old plays on which Shakespeare founded his Measure for measure, Comedy of errors, the Taming of the shrew, King John, King Henry IV and King Henry V, King Lear. 2 vols 1779.

Capell, E. The school of Shakespeare. In his Notes and various readings to Shakespeare vol 3, 1783.

Echtermayer, T., L. Henschel and K. Simrock. Quellen des Shakespeare in Novellen, Märchen und Sagen. 3 pts Berlin 1831, 2 pts Bonn 1870.

Collier, J. P. Shakespeare's library: a collection of the romances, novels, poems and histories, used by Shakespeare as the foundation of his dramas. 2 vols [1843] 1850; rev W. C. Hazlitt 6 vols 1875 (adding the plays).

Halliwell (-Phillipps), J. O. The works of Shakespeare. 16 vols 1853–65. Includes 'all the original novels and tales on which the plays are founded'.

Hazlitt, W. C. Shakespeare's jest-books. 3 vols 1864.

— Fairy tales, legends and romances illustrating Shakespeare and other early English writers. 1875.

Furness, H. H. and H. H., jr. A new variorum edition of the works of Shakespeare. Philadelphia 1871–. Reprints with each play its source or sources.

Skeat, W. W. Shakespeare's Plutarch. 1875.

Leo, F. A. Four chapters of North's Plutarch. 1878.

Boswell-Stone, W. G. Shakspere's Holinshed. 1896, 1907.

Gollancz, I. et al. The Shakespeare classics. 11 vols 1907–13. For individual titles *see* under separate plays, above.

Schubring, P. Shakespeares italienische Novellen. Berlin 1920.

Nicoll, A. and J. Holinshed's Chronicles as used in Shakespeare's plays. 1927 (EL).

Schanzer, E. Shakespeare's Appian. Liverpool 1956.

Bullough, G. Narrative and dramatic sources of Shakespeare. 7 vols 1957–. The most complete collection.

Rouse, W. H. D. Shakespeare's Ovid: being Golding's translation of the Metamorphoses. 1961.

Spencer, T. J. B. Shakespeare's Plutarch. 1964 (Peregrine).

— Elizabethan love stories. 1968 (Pelican).

Hosley, R. Shakespeare's Holinshed. New York 1968.

Modern Studies

General Studies

Farmer, R. Essay on the learning of Shakespeare. Cambridge 1767, 1767 (expanded); rptd in Eighteenth-century essays on Shakespeare, ed D. N. Smith, Glasgow 1903.

Anders, H. R. D. Shakespeare's books. Berlin 1904.

Stopes, C. C. Shakespeare's industry. 1916.

Thorndike, A. H. Shakespeare as a debtor. New York 1916.

Wheatley, H. B. Shakespeare as a man of letters. Trans Bibl Soc 14 1919.

Bartlett, H. C. Shakespeare: original and early editions of his quartos and folios, his source books and those containing contemporary notices. New Haven 1922. A bibliography.

Kellett, E. E. Shakespeare as a borrower. In his Suggestions, Cambridge 1923.

Schelling, F. E. In his Foreign influences in Elizabethan plays, New York 1923.

Whitaker, V. K. Shakespeare's use of his sources. PQ 20 1941.

— Shakespeare's use of learning: an inquiry into the growth of his mind and art. San Marino 1953.

Guttman, S. The foreign sources of Shakespeare's works: an annotated bibliography of the commentary on this subject between 1904 and 1940, together with lists of certain translations available to Shakespeare. New York 1947.

Krzyzanowski, J. Shakespearian modifications (methodical prolegomena). Wroclaw 1948. Analysis of sources to demonstrate motives for alterations.

Muir, K. Shakespeare's sources 1: comedies and tragedies. 1957.

Prouty, C. T. Some observations on Shakespeare's sources. Sh Jb 96 1960.

Satin, J. H. Shakespeare and his sources. Boston 1966.

Classical Influences

Stapfer, P. Shakespeare et l'antiquité. 2 vols Paris 1879–80; tr 1880.

Delius, N. Klassische Reminiszenzen in Shakespeares Dramen. Sh Jb 18 1883.

Cruikshank, A. H. The classical attainments Shakespeare. In his Noctes shakespearianae, 1887.

Cunliffe, J. W. In his Influence of Seneca on Elizabethan tragedy, 1893.

Root, R. K. Classical mythology in Shakespeare. New York 1903.

Collins, J. C. Shakespeare as a classical scholar. In his Studies in Shakespeare, 1904.

Watt, L. M. In his Attic and Elizabethan tragedy, 1908.

Theobald, W. The classical element in the Shakespeare plays. Ed R. M. Theobald 1909.

Bush, D. Notes on Shakespeare's classical mythology. PQ 6 1927.

— Classical myth in Shakespeare's plays. In Elizabethan and Jacobean studies presented to F. P. Wilson, Oxford 1959.

Rick, L. Shakespeare und Ovid. Sh Jb 55 1919.

Coulter, C. C. The Plautine tradition in Shakespeare. JEGP 19 1920.

Lucas, F. L. In his Seneca and Elizabethan tragedy, Cambridge 1922.

Heuer, H. Lebensgefühl und Wertwelt in Shakespeares Römerdramen. Zeitschrift für Neusprachlichen Unterricht 37 1938.

Kranz, W. Shakespeare und die Antike. E Studien 73 1938.

Stoll, E. E. Shakespeare's forbears. MLN 54 1939. On relation to classical art.

Baldwin, T. W. Shakespeare's small Latine and lesse Greeke. 2 vols Urbana 1944.

Boas, F. S. Aspects of classical legend and history in Shakespeare. Proc Br Acad 29 1944.

Wolff, E. Shakespeare und die Antike. Die Antike 20 1944; rptd in Antike und Abendland 1 1945.

Martin, L. C. Shakespeare, Lucretius and the commonplaces. RES 21 1945.

Starnes, D. T. Shakespeare and Apuleius. PMLA 60 1945.

Johnson, F. R. Shakespearian imagery and Senecan imitation. In J. Q. Adams memorial studies, Washington 1948.

Boyce, B. The Stoic consolatio and Shakespeare. PMLA 64 1949.

Law, R. A. On certain proper names in Shakespeare. SE 30 1951. On Plutarch as source.

Thomson, J. A. K. Shakespeare and the classics. 1952.

Simpson, P. Shakespeare's use of Latin authors. In his Studies in Elizabethan drama, Oxford 1955.

Spencer, T. J. B. Shakespeare and the Elizabethan Romans. Sh Survey 10 1959.

Wilson, J. D. Shakespeare's 'small Latin'—how much? Ibid.

Honigmann, E. A. J. Shakespeare's Plutarch. Sh Quart 10 1959. On neglect of 'comparison' chs.

Evans, G. L. Shakespeare, Seneca and the kingdom of violence. In Roman drama, ed T. A. Dorey and D. R. Dudley 1965.

Livermore, A. Shakespeare and St Augustine. Quart Rev 303 1965.

Lothian, J. M. Shakespeare's charactery. Oxford 1966. On Shakespeare's kinship with authors of Theophrastian 'characters'.

Kaufmann, R. J. The Senecan perspective and the Shakespearean poetic. Comparative Drama 1 1967.

Velz, J. W. Shakespeare and the classical tradition: a critical guide to commentary. Minneapolis 1968.

Brower, R. A. Hero and saint: Shakespeare and the Graeco-Roman heroic tradition. Oxford 1971.

Continental Influences

König, W. Shakespeare und Dante. Sh Jb 7 1872.

— Über die Entlehnungen Shakespeares, insbesondere aus Rabelais und einigen italienischen Dramatikern. Sh Jb 9 1874.

Feis, J. Shakespeare and Montaigne. 1884.

Murray, J. R. In his Influence of Italian upon English literature during the sixteenth and seventeenth centuries, Cambridge 1886.

Beyersdorff, R. Giordano Bruno und Shakespeare. Sh Jb 26 1891.

Meyer, E. In his Machiavelli and the Elizabethan drama, Heidelberg 1897.

Robertson, J. M. Montaigne and Shakespeare. 1897.

Underhill, J. G. Spanish literature in the England of the Tudors. New York 1899.

Hooker, E. R. The relation of Shakespeare to Montaigne. PMLA 17 1902.

Collins, J. C. Shakespeare and Montaigne. In his Studies in Shakespeare, 1904.

Upham, A. H. The French influence in English literature from the accession of Elizabeth to the Restoration. New York 1908.

Sarrazin, G. Shakespeare und Orlando Pescetti. E Studien 46 1913.

Lee, S. Shakespeare and the Italian Renaissance. Proc Br Acad 6 1915.

Villey, P. Montaigne and Shakespeare. 1916.

Thomas, H. Shakespeare and Spain. 1922.

Rébora, P. L'Italia nel dramma inglese 1558–1642. Milan 1925.

Taylor, G. C. Shakespeare's debt to Montaigne. Oxford 1925.

— Montaigne-Shakespeare and the deadly parallel. PQ 22 1943.

Harrison, T. P. Shakespeare and Montemayor's Diana. Austin 1926.

Lothian, J. M. Shakespeare's knowledge of Aretino's plays. MLR 25 1930.

Best, G. P. Le Montaigne de Shakespeare. Bulletin des Amis de Montaigne 2nd ser 8 1940.

Harmon, A. How great was Shakespeare's debt to Montaigne? PMLA 57 1942.

Schmid, E. E. Shakespeare, Montaigne und die schauspielerische Formel. Sh Jb 82–3 1946–7.

Faure, E. Montaigne et ses trois premiers-nés: Shakespeare, Cervantes, Pascal. Paris 1948.

Capocci, V. Genio e mestiere: Shakespeare e la commedia dell'arte. Bari 1950.

Hodgen, M. T. Montaigne and Shakespeare again. HLQ 16 1952.

Smith, C. G. Shakespeare's proverb lore: his use of the Sententiae of Leonard Culman and Publilius Syrus. Cambridge Mass 1963.

Hunter, G. K. Shakespeare's reading. In A new companion to Shakespeare studies, ed K. Muir and S. Schoenbaum, Cambridge 1971.

English Influences

Hense, C. C. John Lilly und Shakespeare. Sh Jb 7–8 1872–3.

Hermann, E. Shakespeare und Spenser. In his Drei Shakespeare-Studien, Erlangen 1879.

Goodlet, J. Shakespeare's debt to John Lilly. E Studien 5 1882.

Verity, A. W. The influence of Marlowe on Shakespeare's earlier style. Cambridge 1886.

Thorndike, A. H. The influence of Beaumont and Fletcher on Shakespeare. Worcester Mass 1901.

Aronstein, P. Shakespeare und Ben Jonson. E Studien 34 1904.

Rushton, W. L. Shakespeare and the Arte of English poesie. Liverpool 1909.

Tynan, J. L. The influence of Greene on Shakespeare's early romance. PMLA 27 1912.

Schücking, L. L. Eine Anleihe Shakespeares bei Tourneur. E Studien 50 1916.

Robertson, J. M. Shakespeare and Chapman. 1917.

Radebrecht, F. Shakespeares Abhängigkeit von John Marston. Cöthen 1918.

Starnes, D. T. Shakespeare and Elyot's Governour. Austin 1927.

Gatch, K. H. Shakespeare's allusions to the older drama. PQ 7 1928.

Stern, A. Shakespeare und Marlowe. Archiv 156 1929.

Craig, H. Shakespeare and Wilson's Arte of rhetorique. SP 28 1931.

Hart, A. Shakespeare and the homilies. In his Shakespeare and the homilies and other pieces, Melbourne 1934.

Luce, M. Spenser and Shakespeare. In his Man and nature, 1935.

Zeeveld, W. G. The influence of Hall on Shakespeare's English historical plays. ELH 3 1936.

Thaler, A. Shakespeare and Spenser. Sh Assoc Bull 10–11 1935–6.

— Shakespeare and Sir Philip Sidney: the influence of the Defense of poesy. Cambridge Mass 1947.

Stalker, A. Shakespeare, Marlowe and Nashe. Stirling 1936.

Keller, W. Ben Jonson and Shakespeare. Sh Jb 73 1937.

McNeal, T. H. Who is Silvia? and other problems in the Greene-Shakespeare relationship. Sh Assoc Bull 13 1938. See also 15 1940.

Glunz, H. H. Shakespeare und Morus. Bochum 1938.

Gray, H. D. Shakespeare, Southampton and Avisa. Stanford 1941.

Evans, D. A. Some notes on Shakespeare and the Mirror of knighthood. Sh Assoc Bull 21–2 1946–7.

Law, R. A. Daniel's Rosamund and Shakespeare. SE 26 1947.

Mayhall, J. Shakespeare and Spenser: a commentary on differences. MLQ 10 1949.

Pettet, E. C. Shakespeare and the romance tradition. 1950.

Watkins, W. B. C. Shakespeare and Spenser. Princeton 1950.

Bradbrook, M. C. Shakespeare and Elizabethan poetry. 1951.

— Shakespeare the craftsman. Cambridge 1968. On medieval background.

Cruttwell, P. Physiology and psychology in Shakespeare's age. JHI 12 1951.

Wilson, F. P. Marlowe and the early Shakespeare. Oxford 1953.

Michel, L. and C. C. Seronsy. Shakespeare's history plays and Daniel: an assessment. SP 52 1955.

Potts, A. F. Shakespeare and the Faerie Queene. Ithaca 1958.

Coghill, N. Shakespeare's reading in Chaucer. In Elizabethan and Jacobean studies presented to F. P. Wilson, Oxford 1959.

MacNalty, A. S. Shakespeare and Sir Thomas More. E & S new ser 12 1959.

Muir, K. Shakespeare among the commonplaces. RES new ser 10 1959. On minor source material.

— Blundeville, Wyatt and Shakespeare. N & Q Aug 1961.

Rees, J. Shakespeare's use of Daniel. MLR 55 1960.

Lascelles, M. Sir Dagonet in Arthur's show. Sh Jb 96 1960. Malory's influence seen in Falstaff and Shallow.

Brooke, N. Marlowe as provocative agent in Shakespeare's early plays. Sh Survey 14 1961.

Mincoff, M. Shakespeare and Lyly. Ibid.

Shapiro, I. A. Shakespeare and Mundy. Ibid.

Sanders, N. The comedy of Greene and Shakespeare. In Early Shakespeare, ed J. R. Brown and B. Harris 1961.

Brooks, H. F. Shakespeare and the Governour. Sh Quart 14 1963.

Freeman, A. Shakespeare and Solyman and Perseda. MLR 58 1963.

Hunter, G. K. Shakespeare's reading. In A new companion to Shakespeare studies, ed K. Muir and S. Schoenbaum, Cambridge 1971.

Biblical Influences

Wordsworth, C. On Shakespeare's knowledge and use of the Bible. 1864, 1892.

Carter, T. Shakespeare and Holy Scripture. 1905.

Burgess, W. The Bible in Shakespeare. New York 1918.

Noble, R. Shakespeare's biblical knowledge. 1935.

Abend, M. Some biblical influences in Shakespeare's plays. N & Q 23 Dec 1950.

Coleman, H. Shakespeare and the Bible. New York 1955.

Miscellaneous Influences

Green, H. Shakespeare and the emblem writers. 1870.

Brie, F. Shakespeare und die Impresa-Kunst seiner Zeit. Sh Jb 50 1914.

Jente, R. The proverbs of Shakespeare. Washington Univ Stud 13 1926.

Lever, K. Proverbs and sententiae in the plays of Shakespeare. Sh Assoc Bull 13 1938.

Hankins, J. E. Shakespeare's derived imagery. Lawrence Kansas 1953.

Wilson, F. P. The proverbial wisdom of Shakespeare. Cambridge 1961; rptd in his Shakespearian and other studies, Oxford 1969.

(2) Transmission of the Text, Chronology etc

See Ebisch and Schücking pp. 44–8, and E. K. Chambers vol 1, chs 4–6.

Printing and Publishing

Blades, W. Common typographical errors, with especial reference to the text of Shakespeare. Athenaeum 27 Jan 1872.

— Shakespeare and typography. 1872.

van Dam, B. A. P. and C. Stoffel. Shakespeare: prosody and text. Leyden 1900.

Plomer, H. R. The printers of Shakespeare's plays and poems. Library 1st ser 7 1906.

Pollard, A. W. Shakespeare folios and quartos. 1909.

— King Richard II: a new quarto. 1916.

— The manuscripts of Shakespeare's plays. Library 2nd ser 7 1916.

— Shakespeare's fight with the pirates. Cambridge 1920.

— The foundations of Shakespeare's text. Proc Br Acad 10 1923.

Pollard, A. W. and H. C. Bartlett. A census of Shakespeare's plays in quarto. 1916.

Pollard, A. W. and J. D. Wilson. The 'stolne and surreptitious' Shakespearian texts. TLS 9–16 Jan 1919.

— What follows if some of the good quarto editions of Shakespeare's plays were printed from his autograph manuscripts? Trans Bibl Soc 15 1920.

Wilson, J. D. The copy for Hamlet 1603. 1918.

— The tempest. Cambridge 1921. With general introd to New Cambridge edn.

— Spellings and misprints in the second quarto of Hamlet. E & S 10 1924.

Rhodes, R. C. Shakespeare's prompt books. TLS 21–8 July 1921.

Lawrence, W. J. The theory of assembled texts. TLS 11 Jan 1923.

— The secret of 'the bad quartos'. Criterion 10 1931.

Simpson, P. The bibliographical study of Shakespeare. Proc Oxford Bibl Soc 1 1923.

Farr, H. Notes on Shakespeare's printers and publishers. Library 3rd ser 3 1923.

van Dam, B. A. P. Textual criticism of Shakespeare's plays. E Studies 6 1925.

Kellner, L. Restoring Shakespeare: a critical analysis of the misreadings in Shakespeare's works. Leipzig 1925.

Albright, E. M. Dramatic publication in England 1580–1640. New York 1927. With bibliography.

Greg, W. W. Principles of emendation in Shakespeare. Proc Br Acad 14 1928.
—— The editorial problem in Shakespeare: a survey of the foundations of the text. Oxford 1942, 1951, 1954 (both rev).
—— The Shakespeare First Folio: its bibliographical and textual history. Oxford 1955.
Kirwood, A. E. M. Richard Field, printer 1589–1604. Library 3rd ser 12 1931.
Willoughby, E. E. The printing of the first folio. 1933 (Bibl Soc).
Ford, H. L. Shakespeare 1700–40: a collation of the editions and separate plays, with some account of T. Johnson and R. Walker. Oxford 1935.
McKerrow, R. B. A suggestion regarding Shakespeare's manuscripts. RES 11 1935.
Black, M. W. and M. A. Shaaber. Shakespeare's seventeenth-century editors 1632–85. New York 1937.
Summers, M. The first illustrated Shakespeare. Connoisseur 102 1938. On Rowe 1709.
Swan, M. W. S. Shakespeare's poems: the first three Boston editions. PBSA 36 1941.
Dawson, G. E. The copyright of Shakespeare's dramatic work. In Studies in honor of A. H. R. Fairchild, Columbia Missouri 1946.
—— Three Shakespearian piracies 1723–9. SB 1 1949.
—— Warburton, Hanmer and the 1745 edition of Shakespeare. SB 2 1950.
Boase, T. S. R. Illustrations of Shakespeare's plays in the seventeenth and eighteenth centuries. Jnl Warburg & Courtauld Inst 10 1947.
Bowers, F. T. An examination of the method of proof correction in Lear. Library 5th ser 2 1947.
—— Shakespeare's text and the bibliographical method. SB 6 1954.
—— On editing Shakespeare and the Elizabethan dramatists. Philadelphia 1955.
—— McKerrow's editorial principles for Shakespeare reconsidered. Sh Quart 6 1955.
—— What Shakespeare wrote. Sh Jb 98 1962.
Carter, A. H. On the use of details of spelling, punctuation and typography to determine the dependence of the editions. SP 44 1947. Especially in Love's labour's lost 4°1 1598, and Passionate pilgrim, O, O2, 1599.
Kirschbaum, L. How Jane Bell came to print the third quarto of Shakespeare's King Lear. PQ 17 1948. On 4°3 1655.
—— Shakespeare and the stationers. Columbus 1955.
Eastman, A. M. Johnson's Shakespearian labours in 1765. MLN 63 1948.
—— Johnson's Shakespeare and the laity: a textual study. PMLA 65 1950.
—— The texts from which Johnson printed his Shakespeare. JEGP 49 1950.
McManaway, J. G. The two earliest prompt books of Hamlet. PBSA 43 1949.
Sherbo, A. Warburton and the 1745 Shakespeare. JEGP 51 1952.
—— Johnson as editor of Shakespeare. In Samuel Johnson: a collection of critical essays, ed D. J. Greene, Englewood Cliffs NJ 1965.
Nowottny, W. M. T. The canon and the text; Editors, editions and critics. Both in Works, ed C. J. Sisson 1954.
Walker, A. Compositor determination and other problems in Shakespearian texts. SB 7 1955.
—— Some editorial principles (with special reference to Henry V). SB 8 1956.
—— Principles of annotation: some suggestions for editors of Shakespeare. SB 9 1957.
—— Edward Capell and his edition of Shakespeare. Proc Br Acad 46 1961.
Brown, A. Editorial problems in Shakespeare: semi-popular editions. SB 8 1956.
—— The great variety of readers. Sh Survey 18 1965. Historical survey of pbn of plays.

Shroeder, W. H. The great Folio of 1623: Shakespeare's plays in the printing house. Hamden Conn 1956.
Hinman, C. The prentice hand in the tragedies of the Shakespeare First Folio: compositor E. SB 9 1957.
—— Six variant readings in the First Folio of Shakespeare. Lawrence Kansas 1961.
—— The printing and proof-reading of the First Folio of Shakespeare. 2 vols Oxford 1963.
—— Shakespeare's text—then, now and tomorrow. Sh Survey 18 1965.
Price, H. T. Author, compositor and metre: copy-spelling in Titus Andronicus and other Elizabethan printings. PBSA 53 1959.
Brown, J. R. The rationale of old-spelling editions of the plays of Shakespeare and his contemporaries. SB 13 1960. Reply by A. Brown, ibid.
Ferguson, W. C. The compositors of 2 Henry IV, Much ado about nothing, the Shoemakers' holiday and the first part of the Contention. Ibid.
Scholes, R. E. Dr Johnson and the bibliographical criticism of Shakespeare. Sh Quart 11 1960.
Eddy, D. D. Samuel Johnson's editions of Shakespeare. PBSA 56 1962.
Honigmann, E. A. J. The stability of Shakespeare's text. 1965.
Waller, F. O. The use of linguistic criteria in determining the copy and dates for Shakespeare's plays. In Pacific Coast studies in Shakespeare, ed W. F. McNeir and T. N. Greenfield, Portland Oregon 1966.
Kable, W. S. Compositor B, the Pavier quartos and copy spellings. SB 21 1968.
Wilson, F. P. Shakespeare and the new bibliography. Ed H. L. Gardner, Oxford 1970.
Evans, G. B. Shakespeare's text. In A new companion to Shakespeare studies, ed K. Muir and S. Schoenbaum, Cambridge 1971.

Shorthand and Shakespeare's Text

Levy, M. Shakespeare and shorthand. 1884.
—— Shakespeare and Timothy Bright. 1910.
Dewischeit, C. Shakespeare und die Stenographie. Sh Jb 34 1898.
Friedrich, P. Studien zur englischen Stenographie im Zeitalter Shakespeares. Leipzig 1914.
Price, H. T. The text of Henry V. Newcastle-under-Lyme 1920.
Pollard, A. W. Shakespeare's fight with the pirates. Cambridge 1920.
van Dam, B. A. P. The text of Shakespeare's Hamlet. 1924.
Kraner, W. Zur englischen Kurzschrift im Zeitalter Shakespeares: das Jane-Seager-Manuskript. Sh Jb 67 1931.
Matthews, W. Shorthand and the bad Shakespeare quartos. MLR 27–8 1932–3.
—— Peter Bales, Timothy Bright and Shakespeare. JEGP 34 1935.
—— Shakespeare and the reporters. Library 3rd ser 15 1935, 17 1937.
Greg, W. W. King Lear: mislineation and stenography. Library 3rd ser 17 1937.
Förster, M. Shakespeare and shorthand. PQ 16 1937.
Duthie, G. I. Elizabethan shorthand and the first quarto of King Lear. Oxford 1950.

Shakespeare's Handwriting

See E. K. Chambers vol 1, pp. 499–515.

Simpson, R. Are there any extant manuscripts in Shakespeare's handwriting? N & Q 1 July 1871.
Spedding, J. Shakespeare's handwriting. N & Q 21 Sept 1872.
Thompson, E. M. Shakespeare's handwriting. Oxford 1916.
—— Shakespeare's handwriting. In Shakespeare's England vol 1, Oxford 1916.

—— Two pretended autographs of Shakespeare. Library 2nd ser 8 1917.

Tannenbaum, S. A. Shakespeare's unquestioned autographs and the additions to Sir Thomas More. SP 22 1925.

—— Problems in Shakespeare's penmanship. New York 1927.

—— New Shakespeare signatures. Sh Assoc Bull 13 1938.

Chambrun, C. L. de. The book Shakespeare used. New York 1935. On annotated copy of Holinshed.

Cadwalader, J. Theobald's alleged Shakespeare manuscript. MLN 56 1941.

Rossiter, A. P. Prognosis on a Shakespeare problem. Durham Univ Jnl new ser 2 1941. On annotated copy of Hall's Chronicles.

Adams, J. Q. A new signature of Shakespeare? Bull John Rylands Lib 27 1943. In Lambard's Archaionomia 1568.

McLaren, M. By me: a report upon the apparent discovery of some working notes of Shakespeare in a sixteenth-century book. 1949. On annotated copy of Hall.

Everitt, E. B. The young Shakespeare. Copenhagen 1954. Claims Edmund Ironside as a Shakespeare holograph.

Keen, A. and R. Lubbock. The annotator: the pursuit of an Elizabethan reader of Hall's Chronicle, involving some surmises about the early life of Shakespeare. 1954.

Chronology of the Plays

See Ebisch and Schücking pp. 187–8, and E. K. Chambers vol 1, pp. 243–74; also under Style and Prosody, below.

Malone, E. An attempt to ascertain the order in which the plays attributed to Shakespeare were written. In Steevens's edn of Works, 1778; rev in Malone's edn, 1790, and again in 3rd variorum edn, 1821.

Hurdis, J. Cursory remarks upon the arrangement of the plays of Shakespeare. 1792.

Chalmers, G. The chronology of Shakespeare's dramas. In his A supplemental apology, 1799.

Furnivall, F. J. The succession of Shakespeare's works and the use of metrical tests in settling it. 1874.

Ingram, J. K. On the 'weak endings' of Shakespeare. Trans New Sh Soc 1874.

Fleay, F. G. Metrical tests as applied to dramatic poetry. Ibid.

—— Metrical tests applied to Shakespeare. In C. M. Ingleby, Shakespeare: the man and the book vol 2, 1881.

Stokes, H. P. An attempt to determine the chronological order of Shakespeare's plays. 1878.

Pulling, F. S. The 'speech-ending' test applied to twenty of Shakespeare's plays. Trans New Sh Soc 1879.

Schipper, J. Shakespeares Blankvers. In his Englische Metrik pt 2, Bonn 1888.

Sarrazin, G. Zur Chronologie von Shakespeares Jugenddramen. Sh Jb 30 1894.

—— Chronologie von Shakespeares Dichtungen. Sh Jb 32 1896.

—— Shakespeares Lehrjahre. Weimar 1897.

Conrad, H. Metrische Untersuchungen zur Feststellung der Abfassungszeit von Shakespeares Dramen. Sh Jb 31 1895.

—— Kennen wir Shakespeares Entwicklungsgang? Preussische Jahrbücher 122 1905.

—— Eine neue Methode der chronologischen Shakespeare-Forschung. Germanisch-romanische Monatsschrift 1 1909.

Ward, A. W. Chronological order of Shakespeare's plays. In his History of English dramatic literature vol 2, 1899.

Ekwall, E. Die Shakespeare-Chronologie. Germanisch-romanische Monatsschrift 3 1911.

Gray, H. D. The chronology of Shakespeare's plays. MLN 46 1931.

Law, R. A. On the dating of Shakespeare's plays. Sh Assoc Bull 11 1936.

McManaway, J. G. Recent studies in Shakespeare's chronology. Sh Survey 3 1950.

Wentersdorf, K. Shakespearian chronology and the metrical tests. In Shakespeare-Studien: Festschrift für H. Mutschmann, Marburg 1951.

Honigmann, E. A. J. Shakespeare's 'lost source plays'. MLR 49 1954.

Mincoff, M. The chronology of Shakespeare's early works. Zeitschrift für Anglistik und Amerikanistik 12 1964; Sh Jb (Weimar) 101 1965.

Authenticity

See E. K. Chambers vol 1, pp. 205–42.

Hoffmann, F. H. Über die Beteuerungen in Shakespeares Dramen. Halle 1894.

Thompson, E. N. S. Elizabethan dramatic collaboration. E Studien 40 1908.

Oliphant, E. H. C. Shakespeare's plays: an examination. MLR 3–4 1908–9.

—— Collaboration in Elizabethan drama. PQ 8 1929.

—— The Shakespeare canon. Quart Rev 259 1932.

Manly, J. M. Cuts and insertions in Shakespeare's plays. SP 14 1917.

Robertson, J. M. Shakespeare and Chapman. 1917.

—— The Shakespeare canon. 4 pts 1922–32.

—— An introduction to the study of the Shakespeare canon. 1924.

—— The genuine in Shakespeare. 1930.

Keller, W. Shakespeare als Überarbeiter fremder Dramen. Sh Jb 58 1922.

Chambers, E. K. The disintegration of Shakespeare. Proc Br Acad 11 1924.

—— The unrest in Shakespearean studies. Nineteenth Century Feb 1927.

Gaw, A. Actors' names in basic Shakespearean texts. PMLA 40 1925.

Lawrence, W. J. Early dramatic collaboration: a theory. In his Pre-Restoration stage studies, Cambridge Mass 1927.

—— Shakespeare's workshop. Oxford 1928. Includes Shakespeare's lost characters; A new Shakespearean test.

Bald, R. C. Macbeth and the 'short' plays. RES 4 1928.

Hart, A. The number of lines in Shakespeare's plays. RES 8 1932.

Mair, J. The fourth forger: William Ireland and the Shakespeare papers. 1938.

Hastings, W. T. The fourth forger. Sh Assoc Bull 14 1939.

—— 'Shakespeare' Ireland's first folio. Colophon new ser 1 1940.

—— Shakespeare was Shakespeare. Amer Scholar 28 1959.

Wilson, J. D. Malone and the upstart crow. Sh Survey 4 1951.

Feuillerat, A. The composition of Shakespeare's plays: authorship, chronology. New Haven 1953. See F. T. Bowers, MP 51 1954.

Friedman, W. and E. The Shakespearean ciphers examined. Cambridge 1957.

Churchill, R. C. Shakespeare and his betters. 1958.

Gibson, H. N. The Shakespeare claimants. 1962.

McManaway, J. G. The authorship of Shakespeare. Washington 1962.

McMichael, G. and E. M. Glenn (ed). Shakespeare and his rivals: a casebook on the authorship controversy. New York 1962.

Grebanier, B. D. N. The great Shakespeare forgery. New York 1965.

(3) Textual Criticism

The Year's Work in Eng Stud and Sh Survey present annual summaries of significant work on the text, and studies are listed in the Sh Quart annual bibliography. Many textual articles are listed above under individual plays; see also preceding section.

Works. Ed W. G. Clark, J. Glover and W. A. Wright 9 vols Cambridge 1863–8 etc. Preface provides succinct account of previous textual criticism.

Walder, E. Shakespearean criticism, textual and literary, from Dryden to the end of the 18th century. Bradford 1895.

— The text of Shakespeare. CHEL vol 5 1910.

Lounsbury, T. R. The first editors of Shakespeare (Pope and Theobald). 1906, New York 1906 (as The text of Shakespeare: its history from the quartos to Theobald).

Theobald, L. Shakespeare restored: or a specimen of the many errors as well committed as unemended by Mr Pope in his late edition of this poet; designed to restore the true reading of Shakespeare in all the editions ever yet printed. 1726, 1740.

Upton, J. Critical observations on Shakespeare. 1746, Dublin 1747, London 1748 (rev with preface on Warburton's edn).

Grey, Z. A word or two of advice to William Warburton, a dealer in many words. 1746.

— A free and familiar letter to William Warburton. 1750.

— Remarks upon a late edition of Shakespeare [Warburton's], with a defence of Sir Thomas Hanmer. [1751], 1752 (as Examination of a late edition).

— Critical, historical and explanatory notes on Shakespeare with emendations of the text and metre. 2 vols 1754.

Edwards, T. A supplement to Mr Warburton's edition of Shakespeare: being the canons of criticism and glossary collected from the notes in that celebrated work. 1748, 1748, 1753 (rev Edwards and Richard Roderick as Canons of criticism), 1753, 1758, 1765 (with Roderick's Remarks on Shakespeare).

Holt, J. An attempte to rescue that aunciente English poet Maister Williaume Shakespere from the maney errours faulsely charged on him by certaine newfangled wittes. 1749, 1750 (as Remarks on the Tempest).

[Nichols, P.] The castrated letter of Sir Thomas Hanmer in the sixth volume of Biographia britannica. 1763. Exposes Warburton's treatment of Hanmer.

Heath, B. A revisal of Shakespeare's text, where the alterations introduced into it by the more modern editors and critics are particularly considered. 1765.

Kenrick, W. A review of Doctor Johnson's new edition of Shakespeare, in which the ignorance, or inattention, of that editor is exposed. 1765.

— A defence of Mr Kenrick's Review. 1766.

Tyrwhitt, T. Observations and conjectures upon some passages of Shakespeare. Oxford 1766.

Capell, E. Notes and various readings to Shakespeare. [1774] (pt 1), 3 vols 1779–83 (extended, with addns by J. Collins).

Ritson, J. Remarks, critical and illustrative, on the text and notes of the last edition of Shakespeare. 1783. On the Johnson-Steevens-Reed-Malone edn of 1778.

— The quip modest: a few words by way of supplement to Remarks, occasioned by the republication of that edition. 1788, 1788 (with rev preface, toning down abuse of Steevens).

— Cursory criticisms on the edition of Shakespeare published by Edmond Malone. 1792.

Mason, J. M. Comments on the last edition of Shakespeare's plays. 1785. On the Johnson-Steevens-Reed-Malone edn of 1778.

— Comments on the plays of Beaumont and Fletcher, with an appendix containing some further observations on Shakespeare, extended to the late editions of Malone and Steevens. 2 pts 1797–8.

— Comments on the several editions of Shakespeare's plays, extended to those of Malone and Steevens. Dublin 1807.

Malone, E. A letter to Richard Farmer relative to the edition of Shakespeare published in 1790, and some late criticisms of that work. 1792, 1792. Replies to Ritson's Cursory criticisms.

Seymour, E. H. Remarks, critical, conjectural and explanatory, upon the plays of Shakespeare, resulting from a collation of the early copies with that of Johnson and Steevens, edited by Isaac Reed. 2 vols 1805.

Pye, H. J. Comments on the commentators on Shakespeare. 1807.

Douce, F. Illustrations of Shakespeare and of ancient manners. 2 vols 1807, 1 vol 1839.

Nichols, F. Illustrations of the literary history of the eighteenth century. 8 vols 1817–58. Vol 2 includes correspondence of Theobald, Thirlby and Warburton on Shakespeare.

Collier, J. P. Reasons for a new edition of Shakespeare's works. 1841.

— Notes and emendations to the text of Shakespeare's plays, from early manuscript corrections in a copy of the folio of 1632. 1852.

Dyce, A. Remarks on Mr Collier's and Mr Knight's editions. 1844.

[Spalding, W.] Recent editions of Shakespeare. Edinburgh Rev 81 1845. On Knight's edns.

Badham, C. Criticism applied to Shakespeare. 1846.

— The text of Shakespeare. In his Cambridge essays, 1856.

Knight, C. Old lamps, or new?: a plea for the original editions of the text of Shakespeare. 1853.

Walker, W. S. A critical examination of the text of Shakespeare. Ed W. H. Lettsom 3 vols 1860.

Ingleby, C. M. The still lion: an essay towards the restoration of Shakespeare's text. 1867, 1875 (enlarged as Shakespeare hermeneutics).

Daniel, P. A. Notes and conjectural emendations of certain doubtful passages in Shakespeare's plays. 1870.

Bulloch, J. Studies on the text of Shakespeare. 1878.

Vaughan, H. H. New readings and new renderings of Shakespeare's tragedies. 3 vols 1878–86. Henry VIII, Richard III, Cymbeline.

Gould, G. Corrigenda and emendations of the text of Shakespeare. 1881, 1884.

Morgan, J. A. Some Shakespearean commentators. Cincinnati 1882.

van Dam, B. A. P. and C. Stoffel. Shakespeare: prosody and text. Leyden 1900.

Elton, O. Recent Shakespearian criticism. In his Modern studies, 1907.

Stewart, C. D. Some textual difficulties in Shakespeare. New Haven 1914.

Pollard, A. W. See Printing and Publishing, above.

Kellner, L. Restoring Shakespeare: a critical analysis of the misreadings in Shakespeare's works. Leipzig 1925.

— Erläuterungen und Textverbesserungen zu vierzehn Dramen Shakespeares. Leipzig 1931.

Greg, W. W. Principles of emendation in Shakespeare. Proc Br Acad 14 1928.

— The editorial problem in Shakespeare: a survey of the foundations of the text. Oxford 1942, 1951, 1954 (both rev).

— The Shakespeare First Folio: its bibliographical and textual history. Oxford 1955.

Adams, J. Q. Elizabethan playhouse manuscripts and their significance for the text of Shakespeare. Johns Hopkins Alumni Mag 21 1932.

McKerrow, R. B. The treatment of Shakespeare's text by his earlier editors. Proc Br Acad 19 1933.

— Prolegomena for the Oxford Shakespeare: a study in editorial method. Oxford 1939.

Hastings, W. T. To the next editor of Shakespeare: notes for his prospectus. Colophon 2 1937.

Doran, M. An evaluation of evidence in Shakespearean textual criticism. Eng Inst Annual 1941.

Black, M. W. Problems in the editing of Shakespeare: interpretation. Eng Inst Essays 1947.

Shaaber, M. A. Problems in the editing of Shakespeare: text. Ibid.

Muir, K. A test for Shakespearian variants. N & Q 25 Nov 1950.

Alexander, P. Restoring Shakespeare: the modern editor's task. Sh Survey 5 1952.

Flatter, R. 'The true originall copies' of Shakespeare's plays. Proc Leeds Philosophical & Literary Soc 7 1952.

Walker, A. Textual problems of the First Folio: Richard III, King Lear, Troilus and Cressida, 2 Henry IV, Othello. Cambridge 1953.

— Collateral substantive texts (with special reference to Hamlet). SB 7 1955.

— Compositor determination and other problems in Shakespearean texts. Ibid.

— Some editorial principles (with special reference to Henry V). SB 8 1956.

— Principles of annotation: some suggestions for editors of Shakespeare. SB 9 1957.

Bowers, F. T. The printing of Hamlet Q2. SB 7 1955.

— On editing Shakespeare and the Elizabethan dramatists. Philadelphia 1955.

Brown, A. Editorial problems in Shakespeare: semi-popular editions. SB 8 1956.

Sisson, C. J. New readings in Shakespeare. Cambridge 1956.

Williams, P. New approaches to textual problems in Shakespeare. SB 8 1956.

Brown, J. R. The rationale of old-spelling editions of the plays of Shakespeare and his contemporaries. SB 13 1960. Reply by A. Brown, ibid.

Honigmann, E. A. J. The stability of Shakespeare's text. 1965.

— On the indifferent and one-way variants in Shakespeare. Library 5th ser 22 1967.

Waller, F. O. The use of linguistic criteria in determining the copy and dates for Shakespeare's plays. In Pacific Coast studies in Shakespeare, ed W. F. McNeir and T. N. Greenfield, Portland Oregon 1966.

Dobrée, B. How to edit Shakespeare. In The morality of art: essays presented to G. Wilson Knight, 1969.

Wilson, F. P. Shakespeare and the new bibliography. Ed H. L. Gardner, Oxford 1970.

Evans, G. B. Shakespeare's text: approaches and problems. In A new companion to Shakespeare studies, ed K. Muir and S. Schoenbaum, Cambridge 1971.

Walton, J. K. The quarto copy for the First Folio of Shakespeare. Dublin 1971.

(4) Language, Vocabulary, Style and Prosody
Language

See also A. G. Kennedy, A bibliography of writings on the English language, *New Haven 1927*.

Walker, W. S. A critical examination of the text of Shakespeare, with remarks on his language. 3 vols 1860.

Abbott, E. A. A Shakespearian grammar. 1869 etc.

Franz, W. Shakespeare-Grammatik. 2 vols Halle 1898–1900, Heidelberg 1924.

— Orthographie, Lautgebung und Wortbildung in den Werken Shakespeares mit Ausspracheproben. Heidelberg 1905.

Jespersen, O. Shakespeare and the language of poetry. In his Growth and structure of the English language, Leipzig 1905, 1938 (rev); rptd in Literary English since Shakespeare, ed G. Watson, New York 1970.

Tilley, M. P. Some evidence in Shakespeare of contemporary effort to refine the language of the day. PMLA 31 1916.

Bradley, H. Shakespeare's English. In Shakespeare's England vol 2, Oxford 1916.

Langworthy, C. A. A verse-sentence analysis of Shakespeare's plays. PMLA 46 1931.

Willcock, G. D. Shakespeare as a critic of language. 1934 (Eng Assoc Pamphlet).

— Shakespeare and rhetoric. E & S 29 1943.

— Shakespeare and Elizabethan English. Sh Survey 7 1954.

Mackie, W. S. Shakespeare's English. MLR 31 1936.

Wilson, F. P. Shakespeare and the diction of common life. Proc Br Acad 27 1941; rptd in his Shakespearian and other studies, Oxford 1969.

Eccles, M. Shakespeare's use of 'look how' and similar idioms. JEGP 42 1943.

Joseph, Sr M. Shakespeare's use of the arts of language. New York 1947. On rhetoric.

Prior, M. E. In his Language of tragedy, New York 1947.

Ransom, J. C. On Shakespeare's language. Sewanee Rev 55 1947.

Briese, Y. M. Notes on the compound participle in the works of Shakespeare and his contemporaries. Suomalaisen Tiedeakatemian Toimituksia B 63 1950.

Bland, D. S. Shakespeare and the 'ordinary word'. Sh Survey 4 1951.

Mahood, M. M. The fatal Cleopatra: Shakespeare and the pun. EC 1 1951.

Empson, W. In his Structure of complex words, 1951. Fool in Lear, Timon's dog, Honest in Othello, Sense in Measure for measure.

Evans, B. I. The language of Shakespeare's plays. 1952.

Hulme, H. M. Shakespeare's language. In Works, ed C. J. Sisson 1954.

— Shakespeare and the Oxford English Dictionary. RES new ser 6 1955.

— On the interpretation of Shakespeare's text. E Studies 38 1957.

— Shakespeare's text: some notes on linguistic procedure and its relevance to textual criticism. E Studies 39 1958.

— The spoken language and the dramatic text: some notes on the interpretation of Shakespeare's language. Sh Quart 9 1958.

— Explorations in Shakespeare's language. 1962.

— Shakespeare's language. In Shakespeare's world, ed J. R. Sutherland and J. Hurstfield 1964.

Muir, K. Shakespeare and rhetoric. Sh Jb 90 1954.

Sutherland, J. R. The language of Shakespeare's last plays. In More talking of Shakespeare, ed J. Garrett 1959.

Salmon, V. Sentence structures in colloquial Shakespearian English. Trans of Philological Soc 1965.

— Some functions of Shakespearian word-formation. Sh Survey 23 1970.

Smithers, G. V. Guide-lines for interpreting the uses of the suffix -ed in Shakespeare's English. Ibid.

Vickers, B. Shakespeare's use of rhetoric. In A new companion to Shakespeare studies, ed K. Muir and S. Schoenbaum, Cambridge 1971.

Quirk, R. Shakespeare and the English language. Ibid.

Pronunciation and Orthography

Ellis, A. J. On early English pronunciation with especial reference to Shakespeare and Chaucer. 5 vols 1867–89 (EETS).

Viëtor, W. Shakespeare's pronunciation. 2 vols Marburg 1906.

Zachrisson, R. E. Shakespeares uttal. Upsala 1914.

Pollard, A. W. Elizabethan spelling as a literary and bibliographical clue. Library 3rd ser 4 1923.

Wilson, J. D. Bibliographical links between the three pages and the good quartos. In Shakespeare's hand in the play of Sir Thomas More, Cambridge 1923.

Sievers, E. Shakespeares Anteil am King Lear. In Anglica vol 2, Leipzig 1925.

Marschall, W. Shakespeares Orthographie. Anglia 51 1927.

Price, H. T. The first quarto of Titus Andronicus. Eng Inst Essays 1947. On spelling forms.

Kökeritz, H. Shakespeare's pronunciation. New Haven 1953.

Partridge, A. C. Shakespeare's orthography in Venus and Adonis and some early quartos. Sh Survey 7 1954.

— Orthography in Shakespeare and Elizabethan drama. 1964.

Cusack, B. Shakespeare and the tune of the time. Sh Survey 23 1970.

Punctuation

Simpson, P. Shakespearian punctuation. Oxford 1911, 1969.
— The bibliographical study of Shakespeare. Proc Oxford Bibl Soc 1 1923.
Pollard, A. W. Shakespeare's fight with the pirates. Cambridge 1917.
Sullivan, E. Punctuation in Shakespeare. Nineteenth Century Dec 1921.
Works. Ed A. T. Quiller-Couch and J. D. Wilson, Cambridge 1921–66. *See* Wilson's note in Tempest.
Alden, R. M. The punctuation of Shakespeare's printers. PMLA 39 1924.
Fries, C. C. Shakespearian punctuation. In Studies in Shakespeare, Milton and Donne, New York 1925.
Jenkinson, H. Notes on the study of English punctuation of the sixteenth century. RES 2 1926.
Isaacs, J. A note on Shakespeare's dramatic punctuation. Ibid.
Alexander, P. Shakespeare's punctuation. TLS 17 March 1932.
— Shakespeare's punctuation. Proc Br Acad 31 1945.
Thorndike, A. H. Parentheses in Shakespeare. Sh Assoc Bull 9 1934.
Carter, A. H. The punctuation of Shakespeare's Sonnets of 1609. In J. Q. Adams memorial studies, Washington 1948.
Flatter, R. Shakespeare's producing hand: a study of his marks of expression to be found in the First Folio. 1948. Mainly on Macbeth.

Vocabulary

General Works

Ekwall, E. Shakespeare's vocabulary: its etymological elements. Upsala 1903.
Franz, W. Die Wortbildung bei Shakespeare. E Studien 35 1905.
Whall, W. B. Shakespeare's sea terms explained. Bristol 1910.
Bastide, C. La France et les Français dans le théâtre de Shakespeare. Edda 6 1916.
Gordon, G. S. Shakespeare's English. Leeds 1928.
Mackie, W. S. Shakespeare's English, with the help of the NED. MLR 31 1936.
Craig, H. S. Duelling scenes and terms in Shakespeare's plays. Univ of California Pbns in Eng 9 1940.
Hart, A. The growth of Shakespeare's vocabulary. RES 19 1943.
— Vocabularies of Shakespeare's plays. Ibid.
Partridge, E. Shakespeare's bawdy: a literary and psychological essay and a comprehensive glossary. 1947, 1969 (rev).
Becker, D. Shakespeares Englisch und seine Erforschbarkeit mit Hilfe des NED. Sh Jb 84–6 1948–50.
Pafford, J. H. P. Words used only once in Shakespeare. N & Q 1958.
Falconer, A. F. A glossary of Shakespeare's sea and naval terms, including gunnery. 1965.
Salmon, V. Elizabethan colloquial English in the Falstaff plays. Leeds Stud in Eng new ser 1 1967.
Hudson, K. Shakespeare's use of colloquial language. Sh Survey 23 1970.
Jorgensen, P. A. Shakespeare's dark vocabulary. In The drama of the Renaissance, ed E. M. Blistein, Providence 1970.
Quirk, R. Shakespeare and the English language. In A new companion to Shakespeare studies, ed K. Muir and S. Schoenbaum, Cambridge 1971.

Dialects

Huntley, R. W. A glossary of the Cotswold Gloucestershire dialect. 1869.
Northall, G. F. A Warwickshire word-book. 1896 (Eng Dialect Soc).

Morgan, A. A study in Warwickshire dialect. 1900 (New York Sh Soc).
Förster, M. Die kymrischen Einlagen bei Shakespeare. Germanisch-romanische Monatsschrift 12 1924.
Hulme, H. A Warwickshire word-list. MLR 46 1951.
— Explorations in Shakespeare's language. 1962.

Style

Spalding, W. A letter on Shakespeare's authorship of the Two noble kinsmen and on the characteristics of Shakespeare's style and the secret of his supremacy. Edinburgh 1833, London 1876 (New Sh Soc).
Rushton, W. L. Shakespeare's euphuisms. 1871.
— Shakespeare and the Arte of English poesie. Liverpool 1909.
Clarke, C. C. and M. C. The Shakespeare key, unlocking the treasures of his style. 1879.
Sharpe, H. The prose in Shakespeare's plays. Trans New Sh Soc 1885.
Sarrazin, G. Wortechos bei Shakespeare. Sh Jb 33–4 1897–8.
— Aus Shakespeares Meisterwerkstatt: stilgeschichtliche Studien. Berlin 1906.
Kellett, E. E. Some notes on a feature in Shakespeare's style. In his Suggestions, Cambridge 1923.
Michels, W. Barockstil bei Shakespeare und Calderón. Frankfurt 1928; rptd in Revue Hispanique 1929.
Rylands, G. Notes and quotations preparatory to a study of Shakespeare's diction and style. In his Words and poetry, 1928.
— Shakespeare's poetic energy. Proc Br Acad 37 1951.
— The poet and the player. Sh Survey 5 1952.
Kolbe, F. C. Shakespeare's way. 1930.
Spurgeon, C. F. E. Leading motives in the imagery of Shakespeare's tragedies. 1930 (Sh Assoc lecture).
— Shakespeare's iterative imagery: 1 as undersong, 2 as touchstone. Proc Br Acad 17 1931.
— Shakespeare's imagery and what it tells us. Cambridge 1935.
Clemen, W. H. Shakespeares Bilder: ihre Entwicklung und ihre Funktionen im dramatischen Werk. Bonn 1935; tr and enlarged as The development of Shakespeare's imagery, 1951.
— Shakespeares Monologe. Göttingen 1964.
— Shakespeare's soliloquies. Cambridge 1964.
Elton, O. Style in Shakespeare. Proc Br Acad 22 1936.
Franz, W. Zur Sprachkunst Shakespeares. Anglia 72 1938.
Wells, H. W. The continuity of Shakespearian prose. Sh Assoc Bull 15 1940.
Buell, L. M. A prose period in Shakespeare's career? MLN 56 1941.
Ness, F. W. The use of rhyme in Shakespeare's plays. New Haven 1941.
Armstrong, E. A. Shakespeare's imagination: a study of the psychology of association and inspiration. 1946, Lincoln Nebraska 1963 (rev and expanded).
Orsini, N. La lingua poetica di Shakespeare. Anglica 1 1946.
Huchon, R. Le style de Shakespeare. Les Langues Modernes 41 1947.
Craig, H. Shakespeare's bad poetry. Sh Survey 1 1948.
Jackson, J. L. Shakespeare's dog-and-sugar imagery and the friendship tradition. Sh Quart 1 1950.
Crane, M. Shakespeare's prose. Chicago 1951.
Schrickx, W. Solar symbolism and related imagery in Shakespeare. Revue Belge 29 1951.
Foakes, R. A. Suggestions for a new approach to Shakespeare's imagery. Sh Survey 5 1952.
Baldini, G. Mellifluous Shakespeare. Eng Miscellany (Rome) 4 1953.

Halliday, F. E. The poetry of Shakespeare's plays. 1954.

Willcock, G. D. Language and poetry in Shakespeare's early plays. 1955.

Mahood, M. M. Shakespeare's word play. 1956.

Ehrl, C. Sprachstil und Charakter bei Shakespeare. Heidelberg 1957.

Lawlor, J. Mind and hand: some reflections on Shakespeare's imagery. Sh Quart 8 1957.

Schanzer, E. Atavism and anticipation in Shakespeare's style. EC 7 1957.

Bonjour, A. Résonances shakespeariennes. Neuchâtel 1958.

Daiches, D. Shakespeare's poetry. In The living Shakespeare, ed R. Gittings 1960.

Knights, L. C. Shakespeare's imagery. Ibid.

Muir, K. Shakespeare's soliloquies. Occidente (Lisbon) Aug 1964.

Sutherland, J. R. How the characters talk. In Shakespeare's world, ed J. R. Sutherland and J. Hurstfield 1964. On verse style.

— The moving pattern of Shakespeare's thought. In Papers mainly Shakespearian, ed G. I. Duthie, Edinburgh 1964.

Hobday, C. H. Why the sweets melted: a study in Shakespeare's imagery. Sh Quart 16 1965.

Vickers, B. The artistry of Shakespeare's prose. 1968.

— Shakespeare's use of rhetoric. In A new companion to Shakespeare studies, ed K. Muir and S. Schoenbaum, Cambridge 1971.

Borinski, L. Konstante Stilformen in Shakespeares Prosa. Sh Jb (Heidelberg) 1969.

Hibbard, G. R. Words, action and artistic economy. Sh Survey 23 1970.

Prosody

Walker, W. S. On Shakespeare's versification. 1854.

Bathurst, C. Remarks on the difference in Shakespeare's versification in different periods of his life. 1857.

Fleay, F. G. On metrical tests as applied to dramatic poetry. Trans New Sh Soc 1 1874.

Pulling, F. S. The speech-ending test applied to twenty of Shakespeare's plays. Trans New Sh Soc 6 1879.

van Dam, B. A. P. and C. Stoffel. Shakespeare: prosody and text. Leyden 1900.

van Dam, B. A. P. In his Text of Shakespeare's Hamlet, 1924. Chs 6–7.

Bayfield, M. A. Shakespeare's versification and the early texts. TLS 13 June 1918.

— A study of Shakespeare's versification. Cambridge 1920.

Young, G. Shakespeare as a metrist. In his English prosody on inductive lines, Cambridge 1928.

Franz, W. Shakespeares Blankvers, mit Nachträgen zu des Verfassers Shakespeare-Grammatik. Tübingen 1932, 1935 (rev).

West, E. J. GBS, music and Shakespearean blank verse. In Elizabethan studies and other essays in honor of G. F. Reynolds, Boulder 1945.

Draper, J. W. The tempo of Shakespeare's speech. E Studies 27 1946.

le Page, R. P. The dramatic delivery of Shakespeare's verse. E Studies 32 1951.

Simpson, P. Shakespeare's versification: a study of development. In his Studies in Elizabethan drama, Oxford 1955.

Sipe, D. L. Shakespeare's metrics. New Haven 1968.

B. AESTHETIC CRITICISM

See Ebisch and Schücking pp. 139–47; R. W. Babcock, A preliminary bibliography of eighteenth-century criticism of Shakespeare, SP extra ser 1 1929; and Bartlett, below.

(1) Anthologies of Criticism
(including allusion books)

Blount, T. P. De re poetica: or remarks upon poetry. 1694.

Garrick, D. Testimonies to the genius and merits of Shakespeare. Appended to Garrick's Ode on Shakespeare, 1769.

Steevens, G. Detached pieces of criticism. Appended to Johnson-Steevens edns of Works, 1778, 1785, 1793.

Ingleby, C. M. Shakespeare's centurie of prayse. 1874 (New Sh Soc); rev L. T. Smith 1879 (New Sh Soc).

Furnivall, F. J. Allusions to Shakespeare AD 1592–1693: supplement to Shakespeare's centurie of prayse. 1880 (New Sh Soc).

— Some three hundred fresh allusions to Shakespeare from 1594 to 1694. 1886 (New Sh Soc).

Smith, D. N. Eighteenth-century essays on Shakespeare. Glasgow 1903, Oxford 1963. With detailed introd.

— Shakespeare criticism. Oxford 1916 (WC).

Hughes, C. E. The praise of Shakespeare: an English anthology. 1904.

Warner, B. Famous introductions to Shakespeare's plays. New York 1906. Rowe to Malone.

Munro, J. The Shakespeare allusion-book: a collection of allusions from 1591 to 1700, originally compiled by C. M. Ingleby, L. Toulmin Smith and F. J. Furnivall, and now re-edited. 2 vols 1909, Oxford 1932 (rev E. K. Chambers).

— More Shakespeare allusions. MP 13 1916.

[Thorn-Drury, G.] Some seventeenth-century allusions to Shakespeare. 1920; More seventeenth-century allusions to Shakespeare, 1924.

Bartlett, H. C. Shakespeare: original and early editions, source books and those containing contemporary notices. New Haven 1922. A bibliography.

Black, A. B. and R. M. Smith. Shakespeare allusions and parallels. Bethlehem Pa 1931.

Bradby, A. (ed). Shakespeare criticism 1919–35. Oxford 1936 (WC).

Halliday, F. E. Shakespeare and his critics. 1949.

Wagner, B. The appreciation of Shakespeare: a collection of criticism—philosophic, literary and aesthetic—by great writers and scholar-critics of the eighteenth, nineteenth and twentieth centuries. Georgetown 1949.

Ridler, A. (ed). Shakespeare criticism 1935–60. Oxford 1963 (WC).

Lerner, L. (ed). Shakespeare's tragedies. 1963 (Pelican).

Charney, M. (ed). Shakespeare's Roman plays. Boston 1964.

Dorius, R. J. (ed). Shakespeare's histories. Boston 1964.

Herrnstein, B. (ed). Shakespeare's sonnets. Boston 1964.

Leech, C. (ed). Shakespeare, the tragedies: a collection of critical essays. Chicago 1965.

— Shakespeare's comedies. 1967 (Pelican).

Palmer, D. J. (ed). Shakespeare's later comedies: an anthology of modern criticism. 1971 (Pelican).

(2) The History of Criticism

Knight, C. A history of opinion on the writings of Shakespeare. In Cabinet edn of Shakespeare, suppl 1847.

Hallam, G. Contributions to a history of Shakespearean criticism. In Shakespeariana, 1892 (New York Sh Soc).

Henderson, W. A. et al. Addison's knowledge of Shakespeare. N & Q 19 Aug, 9 Sept 1893.

Walder, E. Shakespearean criticism, textual and literary, from Dryden to the end of the eighteenth century. Bradford 1895.

Hamelius, P. Die Kritik in der englischen Literatur des 17 und 18 Jahrhunderts. Leipzig 1897.

Morton, E. P. Shakespeare in the seventeenth century. JEGP 1 1897.

Lounsbury, T. R. Shakespeare as a dramatic artist, with an account of his reputation at various periods. New York 1901.

— Shakespeare and Voltaire. New York 1902.

— The text of Shakespeare: its history from the quartos to Theobald. New York 1906.

Gloede, O. Shakespeare in der englischen Literatur des 17 und 18 Jahrhunderts. Doberan 1902.

Brandl, A. Edward Young: ein Beitrag zur Geschichte der Shakespeare-Kritik des 18 Jahrhunderts. Sh Jb 39 1903.

Bradley, A. C. Eighteenth-century estimates of Shakespeare. Scottish Historical Rev 1 1904.

Child, M. Mr Spectator and Shakespeare. Library 1st ser 6 1905.

Evans, H. A. A Shakespearian controversy of the eighteenth century. Anglia 28 1905.

Adler, J. Zur Shakespeare-Kritik des 18 Jahrhunderts: die Shakespeare-Kritik im Gentleman's Magazine. Königsberg 1906.

Johnson, C. F. Shakespeare and his critics. Boston 1909.

Dowden, E. Some Old Shakespearians. In Essays modern and Elizabethan, 1910.

Gundolf, F. Shakespeare und der deutsche Geist. Berlin 1911.

Götz, H. J. Die komischen Bestandteile von Shakespeares Tragödien in der Kritik Englands. Giessen 1917.

Neumann, J. H. Shakespearean criticism in the Tatler and Spectator. PMLA 39 1924.

Tolman, A. H. The early history of Shakespeare's reputation. In his Falstaff and other Shakespearean topics, New York 1925.

Raysor, T. M. The study of Shakespeare's characters in the 18th century. MLN 42 1927.

Looten, C. La première controverse internationale sur Shakespeare entre l'abbé Le Blanc et W. Guthrie. Lille 1927.

Smith, D. N. Shakespeare in the eighteenth century. Oxford 1928.

Babcock, R. W. A preliminary bibliography of eighteenth-century criticism of Shakespeare. SP extra ser 1 1929.

— The genesis of Shakespeare idolatry 1766–99. Chapel Hill 1931.

Ralli, A. A history of Shakespearian criticism. 2 vols Oxford 1932.

Pillai, V. K. A. Shakespeare criticism from the beginnings to 1765. 1933.

Lovett, D. Shakespeare as a poet of realism in the eighteenth century. ELH 2 1935.

— Shakespeare's characters in eighteenth-century criticism. Baltimore 1935.

Rothe, H. Der Kampf um Shakespeare: ein Bericht. Leipzig 1936.

Sanderlin, G. The reputation of Shakespeare's sonnets in the early nineteenth century. MLN 54 1939.

Westfall, A. V. R. American Shakesperian criticism 1607–1865. New York 1939.

Marder, L. His exits and his entrances: the story of Shakespeare's reputation. Philadelphia 1963.

Spencer, T. J. B. The course of Shakespeare criticism. In Shakespeare's world, ed J. R. Sutherland and J. Hurstfield 1964.

Kermode, F. (cd). Four centuries of Shakespearean criticism. New York 1965.

Eastman, A. M. A short history of Shakespearean criticism. Ann Arbor 1968.

Stavisky, A. Y. Shakespeare and the Victorians: roots of modern criticism. Norman Oklahoma 1969. Survey of Victorian criticism.

Shaaber, M. A. Shakespeare criticism: Dryden to Bradley. In A new companion to Shakespeare studies, ed K. Muir and S. Schoenbaum, Cambridge 1971.

Wells, S. Shakespeare criticism since Bradley. Ibid.

(3) Principal Critics to 1800

This list includes the more important early allusions and some of the prefaces to edns of Shakespeare. It should, however, be supplemented by the Collections above, many of which contain critical prefaces and notes, and by Textual Criticism above. Most of the earlier items, or selections from them, are rptd in Anthologies, above. E. K. Chambers, vol 2 appendixes A–B, reprints contemporary allusions and later biographical scraps.

Greene, R. Greenes Groats-worth of witte, bought with a million of repentance. 1592.

Chettle, H. Kind-Harts dreame. 1593.

— Englandes mourning garment. 1603. Verse.

T., H. Oenone and Paris. 1594. Verse. *See* J. D. Parsons, Earliest critical notice of Shakespeare, N & Q 20 July 1929.

Willobie, H. Willobie his Avisa. 1594; ed C. Hughes 1904; ed G. B. Harrison 1926. Verse.

C[ovell], W. Polimanteia. 1595.

Edwards, T. Cephalus and Procris. 1595. Verse.

Meres, F. Palladis tamia: wits treasury, being the second parts of Wits commonwealth. 1598.

Barnefield, R. A remembrance of some English poets. In The encomion of Lady Pecunia, 1598. Verse.

Weever, J. Ad Gulielmum Shakespeare. In Epigrammes in the oldest cut, and newest fashion, 1599. Verse.

Davies, J. To our English Terence, Mr Will Shakespeare. In The scourge of folly: consisting of satyricall epigramms, and others, 1611. Verse.

Freeman, T. To Master W. Shakespeare. In Rubbe and a great cast, 1614. Verse.

Jonson, B. To the memory of my beloved, the author Mr W. Shakespeare: and what he hath left us. Prefixed to First Folio, 1623. Verse.

— De Shakespeare nostrati. In his Timber: or discoveries, 1641.

Holland, H. Upon the lines and life of the famous scenick poet, Master W. Shakespeare. Prefixed to First Folio, 1623. Verse.

Heminge, J. and H. Condell. To the great variety of readers. Ibid.

Digges, L. To the memorie of the deceased author, Maister W. Shakespeare. Ibid. Verse.

Milton, J. An epitaph on the admirable dramatic poet W. Shakespeare. Ibid. Verse. *See* H. W. Garrod, E & S 12 1926.

S., I. M. On worthy Master Shakespeare and his poems. Ibid. Verse.

Basse, W. On Mr W. Shakespeare. In Donne's Poems, 1633. Verse.

An elegie on the death of that famous writer and actor Mr W. Shakespeare. Appended to Poems, 1640. Verse.

Winstanley, W. In his English worthies, 1660, 1684.

— In his Lives of the most famous English poets, 1687.

Baker, R. In his Theatrum redivivum, 1662.

Fuller, T. In his History of the worthies of England, 1662. Under Warwickshire.

Newcastle, Margaret Cavendish, Duchess of. In her CCXI sociable letters, 1664. Letter 123.

Evelyn, J. In his Diary 1641–1706, ed W. Bray 2 vols 1818.

Pepys, S. In his Diary 1659–69, cd Lord Braybrooke 2 vols 1825.

Dryden, J. In his Of dramatick poesie: an essay, 1668.

— Troilus and Cressida. 1679. Preface.

Phillips, E. In his Theatrum poetarum, 1675.

Rymer, T. In his Tragedies of the last age considered, 1678.

— In his A short view of tragedy, 1693.

Aubrey, J. In his Brief lives, ed A. Clark 2 vols Oxford 1898. Written c. 1681.

Lee, N. Lucius Junius Brutus. 1681. Preface.

Langbaine, G. In his Momus triumphans, 1688.

— In his An account of the English dramatic poets, 1691, 1699 (rev C. Gildon).

Dennis, J. In his Impartial critic, 1692, 1697.
— The comical gallant. 1702. Preface.
— An essay on the genius and writings of Shakespeare. 1711, 1712.
Some reflections on Mr Rymer's Short view of tragedy, and an attempt at a vindication of Shakespeare. In Miscellaneous letters and essays, ed C. Gildon 1694.
Drake, J. In his Historia anglo-scotica, 1703.
Douglas, Hypolitus, Earl of. Secret history of Mackbeth. 1708.
Rowe, N. Some account of the life etc of Mr W. Shakespeare. Prefixed to his edn of Works, 1709.
Steele, R. and J. Addison. The tatler. 1709–11.
— The spectator. 1711–12, 1714; ed D. F. Bond 5 vols Oxford 1964.
Gildon, C. An essay on the art, rise and progress of the stage. In Poems, 1710.
— Remarks on the plays of Shakespeare. Ibid.
Pope, A. The works of Shakespeare vol 1. 1725. Preface.
Theobald, L. Shakespeare restored. 1726.
Roberts, J. An answer to Mr Pope's preface. 1729.
Some account of the present state of the British Islands, with a notice of Shakespeare. 1734.
Some remarks on the tragedy of Hamlet. 1736. Perhaps by Sir T. Hanmer. See however C. D. Thorpe, MLN 49 1934.
Peck, F. Explanatory and critical notes on divers passages of Shakespeare's plays. Appended to New memoirs of Milton, 1740.
Morris, C. An essay towards fixing the true standards of wit and humour. 1744. On Falstaff.
Johnson, S. Miscellaneous observations on Macbeth. 1745.
— Proposals for printing Shakespeare. 1756.
— The plays of Shakespeare vol 1. 1765. Preface.
Upton, J. Critical observations on Shakespeare. 1746, 1748.
Guthrie, W. Essay on English tragedy, with remarks on the Abbé Le Blanc's observations on the English stage. 1747, 1749, 1757.
Edwards, T. A supplement to Mr Warburton's edition: being the canons of criticism. 1747, 1748, 1750, 1753, 1757, 1758, 1765.
Whalley, P. Enquiry into the learning of Shakespeare. 1748.
Holt, J. An attempte to rescue that aunciente English poet. 1749, 1750.
— Proposals for publishing an edition of Shakespeare. 1750.
Miscellaneous observations on the tragedy of Hamlet. 1752.
Lennox, C. Shakespeare illustrated: or the novels and histories on which the plays of Shakespeare are founded. 3 vols 1753–4, 1756.
Hume, D. History of England. 1754. Appendix to the Reign of James I.
— In his Four dissertations, 1757.
Roderick, R. Remarks on Shakespeare. In T. Edwards, Canons of criticism, 1758 (6th edn).
Heath, B. A revisal of Shakespeare's text. 1765.
Steevens, G. Proposals for an edition of Shakespeare. 1766.
Tyrwhitt, T. Observations and conjectures upon some passages of Shakespeare. 1766.
Farmer, R. Essay on the learning of Shakespeare. Cambridge 1767, 1767 (enlarged), 1799.
— Shakespeariana. 1798.
[Warner, R.] A letter to David Garrick esq concerning a glossary to the plays of Shakespeare, to which is annexed a specimen. 1768.
Montagu, E. An essay on the genius and writings of Shakespeare. 1769, 1770, 1772, 1773, 1778, 1785, 1810.
Hall, J. Illustrations of Shakespeare. 1773.
Capell, E. Notes and various readings to Shakespeare. 3 vols [1774]–83.
P[rescot], K. Shakespeare: an essay. 1774.

Richardson, W. A philosophical analysis and illustration of some of Shakespeare's remarkable characters. 1774, 1774, 1775, 1780, 1784, 1786, 1797, 1798, 1812.
— Essays on Shakespeare's dramatic characters of Richard III, King Lear and Timon of Athens. 1784, 1785, 1786, 1797, 1798, 1812.
— Essays on Shakespeare's dramatic character of Sir John Falstaff and on his female characters. 1789, 1797, 1798, 1812.
[Gentleman, F.] Introduction to Shakespeare's plays. In Bell's edn, 1774.
Griffith, E. The morality of Shakespeare's drama. 1775, 1777.
Mortimer, J. H. Shakespeare's characters. 1775.
Pilon, F. An essay on the character of Hamlet. 1777. As performed by Henderson.
Morgann, M. An essay on the dramatic character of Falstaff. 1777, 1820, 1825; ed W. A. Gill 1912.
Jordan, J. Original collections on Shakespeare and Stratford. [1780], 1864.
— The families of Shakespeare and Hart. [1790], 1865.
Felton, S. Imperfect hints toward a new edition of Shakespeare. 1782, 1787.
[Jackson, W.] Thirty letters on various subjects. 2 vols 1783. 2 letters on Shakespeare.
Davies, T. Dramatic miscellanies. 3 vols 1783–4, 1 vol 1785.
Whately, T. Remarks on some of the characters of Shakespeare. 1785, 1808, 1839.
Kemble, J. P. Macbeth reconsidered. 1786.
Becket, A. A concordance to Shakespeare. 1787.
Robertson, T. Hamlet. Trans Edinburgh Soc 11 1788.
Stack, R. Falstaff. Trans Irish Acad 2 1788.
Ayscough, S. Index to the remarkable passages and words of Shakespeare. 1790.
Mason, G. Collection of English words used by Shakespeare. 1790.
Hurdis, J. Cursory remarks upon the arrangement of the plays of Shakespeare. 1792.
Whiter, W. Specimen of a commentary on Shakespeare. 1794; ed A. Over and M. Bell 1966.
Plumptre, J. Observations on Hamlet: being an attempt to prove it indirect censure on Mary Queen of Scots. 1796.
— Appendix to observations on Hamlet. 1797.
Essays by a society of gentlemen at Exeter. 1796. Includes On literary fame and the historical characters of Shakespeare; An apology for the character and conduct of Iago; An apology for the character and conduct of Shylock. By R. Hole?
Lee, S. Pepys and Shakespeare. Fortnightly Rev Jan 1906; rptd in his Shakespeare and the modern stage, 1907.
Jusserand, J. J. Ben Jonson's views on Shakespeare's art. In Stratford Town Shakespeare vol 10, 1907.
Raleigh, W. (ed). Johnson on Shakespeare. Oxford 1908, 1925 (corrected). An edn of 1765 Preface, notes etc.
Babcock, R. W. William Richardson's criticism of Shakespeare. JEGP 28 1929.
Carver, P. L. The influence of Maurice Morgann. RES 6 1930.
Thorpe, C. D. Thomas Hanmer and the anonymous essay on Hamlet. MLN 49 1934.
Lovett, D. Shakespeare's characters in eighteenth-century criticism. Baltimore 1935.
Butt, J. Pope's taste in Shakespeare. Oxford 1936 (Sh Assoc).
Eidson, J. O. Dryden's criticism of Shakespeare. SP 33 1936.
Rothe, H. Der Kampf um Shakespeare: ein Bericht. Leipzig 1936.
Strout, A. L. John Wilson (Christopher North) as a Shakespeare critic. Sh Jb 72 1936.
Hart, C. W. Dr Johnson's 1745 Shakespearian proposals. MLN 53 1938.

Sanderlin, G. The repute of Shakespeare's sonnets in the early nineteenth century. MLN 54 1939.

Westfall, A. V. R. American Shakespearian criticism 1607–1865. New York 1939.

Kilby, C. S. Horace Walpole on Shakespeare. SP 38 1941.

Schmitz, R. M. Scottish Shakespeare. Sh Assoc Bull 16 1941. On Hugh Blair's Shakespeare criticism.

Wallerstein, R. C. Dryden and the analysis of Shakespeare's techniques. RES 19 1943.

Evans, G. B. A seventeenth-century reader of Shakespeare. RES 21 1945. An anon diary in Bodley.

Ribner, I. Dryden's Shakespearian criticism and the neo-classical paradox. Sh Assoc Bull 21 1946.

Wilson, R. H. 'Brave new world' as Shakespeare criticism. Sh Assoc Bull 21 1946.

Stone, G. W. David Garrick's significance in the history of Shakespearian criticism. PMLA 65 1950.

— Shakespeare in the periodicals 1700–40. Sh Quart 2–3 1951–2.

Sherbo, A. Dr Johnson on Macbeth 1745 and 1765. RES new ser 2 1951.

— Samuel Johnson, editor of Shakespeare. Urbana 1956.

— (ed). Johnson's notes to Shakespeare. 3 vols Los Angeles 1956–8.

— (ed). Johnson on Shakespeare. In Yale edn of works of Johnson vols 7–8, New Haven 1966.

Stafford, J. Henry Norman Hudson and the Whig use of Shakespeare. PMLA 66 1951.

Sutherland, W. O. S. Polonius, Hamlet and Lear in Aaron Hill's Prompter. SP 49 1952.

Tave, S. M. Corbyn Morris: Falstaff, humor and comic theory in the eighteenth century. MP 50 1953.

Hardy, B. Walter Whiter and Shakespeare. N & Q Feb 1953.

Carlisle, C. J. The nineteenth-century actors versus the closet critics. SP 51 1954.

Zimansky, C. A. (ed). The critical works of Thomas Rymer. New Haven 1956.

Barnet, S. George Steevens: editor. Sh News Letter 7 1957.

Fraser, R. A. Pope and Shakespeare. South Atlantic Quart 59 1960.

Wimsatt, W. K. (ed). Samuel Johnson on Shakespeare. New York 1960, London 1969 (Pelican).

Gardner, H. Johnson on Shakespeare. New Rambler 17 1965.

Griffith, P. M. Joseph Warton's criticism of Shakespeare. Tulane Stud in Eng 14 1965.

Over, A. and M. Bell (ed). Walter Whiter, A specimen of a commentary on Shakespeare. 1966.

Shaaber, M. A. Shakespeare criticism: Dryden to Bradley. In A new companion to Shakespeare studies, ed K. Muir and S. Schoenbaum, Cambridge 1971.

(4) The Nineteenth and Twentieth Centuries

Elton, O. Recent Shakespeare criticism. In his Modern studies, 1907.

Stoll, E. E. Anachronism in Shakespeare criticism. MP 7 1910.

— Modern sceptical criticism of Shakespeare. Sewanee Rev 35 1928.

— Recent Shakespeare criticism. Sh Jb 74 1938.

Herford, C. H. The German contribution to Shakespeare. In A book of homage to Shakespeare, ed I. Gollancz, Oxford 1916.

Chambers, E. K. The disintegration of Shakespeare. Proc Br Acad 11 1924.

— The unrest in Shakespearean studies. Nineteenth Century Feb 1927.

Haines, C. M. Shakespeare in France: criticism, Voltaire to Victor Hugo. Oxford 1927.

Small, S. A. The return to Shakespeare: the historical realists. Baltimore 1927.

Greenlaw, E. Recent trends in Shakespeare criticism. Sh Assoc of Amer Bull 2 1927.

Legouis, E. La réaction contre la critique romantique de Shakespeare. E & S 13 1928.

Robertson, J. M. Shakespearean idolatry. Criterion 9 1930. Reply by J. D. Wilson, ibid.

— The state of Shakespeare study: a critical conspectus. 1931.

Wilson J. D. Thirteen vols of Shakespeare: a retrospect. MLR 25 1930.

Alexander, P. Conjectural history: or Shakespeare's Henry VIII. E & S 16 1931.

Connes, G. Etat présent des études shakespeariennes. Paris 1932.

Reul, P. de. La 'désintégration' de Shakespeare. Brussels 1932.

Knights, L. C. How many children had Lady Macbeth? Cambridge 1932; rptd in his Explorations, 1946.

Sisson, C. J. The mythical sorrows of Shakespeare. Proc Br Acad 20 1934.

Shakespeare scholars at work. TLS 1 May 1937. Survey of scholarship 1837–1937.

Ellis-Fermor, U. Some recent research in Shakespeare's imagery. 1937 (Sh Assoc).

— English and American Shakespeare studies 1937–52. Anglia 71 1952.

Knox, R. S. Shakespeare: a diversity of doctrine. UTQ 7 1938.

Gillet, L. Nouvelles recherches sur Shakespeare. Revue des Deux Mondes Sept 1938.

Ribner, I. Lear's madness in the nineteenth century. Sh Assoc Bull 22 1947.

Wilson, F. P. Shakespeare today. Britain Today March 1947.

Campbell, O. J. Shakespeare and the 'new' critics. In J. Q. Adams memorial studies, Washington 1948.

— A review of recent scholarship. Sh Quart 2 1951.

Craig, H. Trend of Shakespearian scholarship. Sh Survey 2 1949.

Hastings, W. T. The new critics of Shakespeare. Sh Quart 1 1950.

Muir, K. Fifty years of Shakespearian criticism 1900–50. Sh Survey 4 1951.

— Some Freudian interpretations of Shakespeare. Proc Leeds Philosophical & Literary Soc 7 1952.

A. C. Bradley. TLS 30 March 1951.

Schücking, L. L. Über einige Probleme der neueren und neuesten Shakespeare-Forschung. Germanisch-romanische Monatsschrift new ser 2 1952.

Babcock, R. W. Historical criticism of Shakespeare. MLQ 13 1952.

Nicoll, A. Co-operation in Shakespearian scholarship. Proc Br Acad 38 1952.

Jenkins, H. Shakespeare's history plays 1900–51. Sh Survey 6 1953.

Schirmer, W. F. Alte und neue Wege der Shakespeare-Kritik. Bonn 1953.

Bradbrook, M. C. Fifty years of the criticism of Shakespeare's style: a retrospect. Sh Survey 7 1954.

Maxwell, J. C. Simple or complex? some problems in the interpretation of Shakespeare. Durham Univ Jnl new ser 15 1954. On Henry V and Julius Caesar.

Krabbe, H. Bernard Shaw on Shakespeare. Aarhus 1955.

Brown, J. R. The interpretation of Shakespeare's comedies 1900–53. Sh Survey 8 1955.

Collins, P. A. W. Shaw on Shakespeare. Sh Quart 8 1957.

Halliday, F. E. The cult of Shakespeare. 1957.

Barnet, S. Coleridge on puns: a note to his Shakespeare criticism. JEGP 56 1957.

— Coleridge's marginalia in Stockdale's Shakespeare of 1784. Harvard Lib Bull 12 1958.

Maxwell, J. C. Shakespeare's Roman plays 1900–56. Sh Survey 10 1957.

Edwards, P. Shakespeare's romances 1900–57. Sh Survey 11 1958.

Hardy, B. 'I have a smack of Hamlet': Coleridge and Shakespeare's characters. EC 8 1958.

Stamm, R. Shaw und Shakespeare. Sh Jb 94 1958.

Hawkes, T. (ed). Coleridge's writings on Shakespeare. New York 1959.

—— Coleridge on Shakespeare: a selection of the essays, notes and lectures. 1969 (Pelican).

Badawi, M. M. Coleridge's formal criticism of Shakespeare. EC 10 1960.

Wilson, E. (ed). Shaw on Shakespeare. New York 1961, London 1969 (Pelican).

Sternfeld, F. W., A. Nejgebauer and J. W. Lever. Twentieth-century studies in Shakespeare's songs, sonnets and poems. Sh Survey 15 1962.

Nicoll, A. Shakespeare in his own age. Sh Survey 17 1964.

Falk, R. Shakespeare in America: a survey to 1900. Sh Survey 18 1965.

Hoffman, D. S. Some Shakespearian music 1660–1900. Ibid.

Jackson, J. R. de J. Coleridge on Shakespeare's preparation. REL 7 1965.

Foakes, R. A. The text of Coleridge's 1811–12 Shakespeare lectures. Sh Survey 23 1970.

—— (ed). Coleridge on Shakespeare: the text of the lectures of 1811–12. 1971.

Wells, S. Shakespeare criticism since Bradley. In A new companion to Shakespeare studies, ed K. Muir and S. Schoenbaum, Cambridge 1971.

(5) General Criticism

Douce, F. Illustrations of Shakespeare. 2 vols 1807, 1839.

Schlegel, A. W. Vorlesungen über dramatische Kunst und Literatur. 2 vols Heidelberg 1809–11; tr 1815.

Hazlitt, W. Characters of Shakespeare's plays. 1817 etc; ed W. C. Hazlitt 1873.

Drake, N. Shakespeare and his times. 2 vols 1817.

—— Memorials of Shakespeare by various writers. 1828.

Tieck, L. Das Buch über Shakespeare. Ed H. Lüdeke, Halle 1920.

Guizot, F. De Shakespeare et de la poésie dramatique. Paris 1822.

—— Shakespeare et son temps. Paris 1852; tr 1852.

Jameson, A. Shakespeare's heroines. 2 vols 1832 etc.

Ulrici, H. Über Shakespeares dramatische Kunst. Halle 1839 etc; tr 1846, 2 vols 1876.

Coleridge, S. T. Notes and lectures upon Shakespeare and some of the old poets and dramatists. Ed Sara Coleridge 2 vols 1849; Shakespearean criticism, ed T. M. Raysor 2 vols Cambridge Mass 1930, London 1960 (EL); Coleridge on Shakespeare: the text of the lectures of 1811–12, ed R. A. Foakes 1971.

Gervinus, G. G. Shakespeare. 4 vols Leipzig 1849–50 etc; tr 2 vols 1862.

Knight, C. Studies of Shakespeare. 1851.

Maginn, W. Shakespeare papers: pictures grave and gay. 1859, 1860 (enlarged).

Mézières, A. Shakespeare: ses oeuvres et ses critiques. Paris 1860.

De Quincey, T. Shakespeare: a biography. Edinburgh 1864. Reprints On the knocking at the gate in Macbeth (first ptd 1823) and article on Shakespeare in Encyclopaedia britannica 1838 (7th edn).

Hugo, V. Shakespeare. Paris 1864; tr 1864.

Dowden, E. Shakspere: a critical study of his mind and art. 1875 etc; ed W. D. Howe, New York 1918.

—— A Shakspere primer. 1877.

—— Introduction to Shakspere. 1893.

Fleay, F. G. Shakespeare manual. 1876, 1878.

—— Introduction to Shakespearian study. 1877.

—— Chronicle history of the life and work of Shakespeare. 1886.

Elze, K. Abhandlungen zu Shakespeare. Halle 1877; tr 1888.

Swinburne, A. C. A study of Shakespeare. 1880.

—— Three plays of Shakespeare. 1909. On Lear, Othello, Richard II.

Hales, J. W. Notes and essays on Shakespeare. 1884.

Moulton, R. G. Shakespeare as a dramatic artist. Oxford 1885 etc.

—— The moral system of Shakespeare. 1903.

White, R. G. Studies in Shakespeare. Boston 1885.

Delius, N. Abhandlungen zu Shakespeare. 2 vols Berlin 1889.

ten Brink, B. Shakespeare: fünf Vorlesungen. Strasbourg 1893, 1894; tr 1895.

Boas, F. S. Shakespeare and his predecessors. 1896.

Brandes, G. Shakespeare. Copenhagen 1896 etc; tr 2 vols 1896.

Fleming, W. H. Shakespeare's plots: a study in dramatic construction. New York 1902.

Bradley, A. C. Shakespearean tragedy: lectures on Hamlet, Othello, King Lear, Macbeth. 1904.

Collins, J. C. Studies in Shakespeare. 1904.

Brooke, S. A. On ten plays of Shakespeare. 1905, 1920.

—— Ten more plays of Shakespeare. 1913, 1920.

Luce, M. A handbook to the works of Shakespeare. 1906.

Tolstoy, L. N. Shakespeare. New York 1906 etc.

Baker, G. P. The development of Shakespeare as a dramatist. New York 1907.

Raleigh, W. Shakespeare. 1907 (EML).

Figgis, D. Shakespeare: a study. 1911.

Masefield, J. William Shakespeare. [1911] (Home Univ Lib)., 1933 (rev), 1954 (rev).

—— Shakespeare and spiritual life. Oxford 1924 (Romanes lecture).

Matthews, B. Shakespeare as a playwright. New York 1913.

Shakespearean studies. Ed B. Matthews and A. H. Thorndike, New York 1916.

A book of homage to Shakespeare. Ed I. Gollancz, Oxford 1916.

Kittredge, G. L. Shakespeare: an address. Cambridge Mass 1916.

Stopes, C. C. Shakespeare's industry. 1916.

Quiller-Couch, A. T. Shakespeare's workmanship. 1918.

Croce, B. Ariosto, Shakespeare e Corneille. Bari 1920; tr 1921.

Dyboski, R. Rise and fall in Shakespeare's dramatic art. 1923 (Sh Assoc lecture).

Chambers, E. K. Shakespeare: a survey. 1925.

Granville-Barker, H. From Henry V to Hamlet. Proc Br Acad 11 1925.

—— Prefaces to Shakespeare. 5 sers 1927–47, 4 vols 1963.

—— Associating with Shakespeare. 1932 (Sh Assoc lecture).

Tolman, A. H. Falstaff and other Shakespearean topics. New York 1925.

Eliot, T. S. Shakespeare and the stoicism of Seneca. 1927 (Sh Assoc lecture); rptd in his Elizabethan essays, 1934.

Haines, C. M. The development of Shakespeare's stagecraft. 1927 (Sh Assoc lecture).

Lewis, W. The lion and the fox: the rôle of the hero in the plays of Shakespeare. 1927.

Schelling, F. E. Shakespeare and the 'demi-science'. Philadelphia 1927.

Stoll, E. E. Shakespeare studies. New York 1927.

—— Poets and playwrights. Minneapolis 1930.

—— Art and artifice in Shakespeare. New York 1933.

—— Shakespeare and other masters. Cambridge Mass 1940.

—— Symbolism in Shakespeare. MLR 42 1947. Against the 'New Criticism'.

Nicoll, A. Studies in Shakespeare. 1928. On Hamlet, Othello, Lear, Macbeth.

—— Shakespeare. 1952.

Gundolf, F. Shakespeare: sein Wesen und Werk. 2 vols Berlin 1928–9.

Bailey, J. Shakespeare. 1929.

Bradby, G. F. Short studies in Shakespeare. 1929.

Knight, G. W. Myth and miracle: an essay on the symbolism of Shakespeare. [1929].
— The wheel of fire: essays in interpretation of Shakespeare's sombre tragedies. Oxford 1930, 1949 (with addns).
— The imperial theme: further interpretations of Shakespeare's tragedies. Oxford 1932, 1951 (rev).
— The crown of life: Shakespeare's final plays. Oxford 1947.
Wilson, J. D. The Elizabethan Shakespeare. Proc Br Acad 15 1929.
— The essential Shakespeare. Cambridge 1932.
— New ideas and discoveries about Shakespeare. Virginia Quart Rev 23 1947.
Abercrombie, L. A plea for the liberty of interpreting Shakespeare. Proc Br Acad 16 1930.
Mackail, J. W. The approach to Shakespeare. Oxford 1930.
Aspects of Shakespeare: being British Academy lectures by L. Abercrombie [et al]. Oxford 1933.
Drinkwater, J. Shakespeare. 1933.
Smith, L. P. On reading Shakespeare. 1933.
Squire, J. C. Shakespeare as a dramatist. 1935.
Ellis-Fermor, U. M. In her Jacobean drama, 1936.
— The study of Shakespeare. 1948.
— Shakespeare the dramatist and other papers. Ed K. Muir 1961.
Murry, J. M. Shakespeare. 1936.
Smirnov, A. A. Shakespeare: a Marxist interpretation. New York 1936.
Empson, W. and G. Garrett. Shakespeare survey. 1937. On Othello, Timon, Tempest.
Gillet, L. Shakespeare. Paris 1937.
Muir, K. and S. O'Loughlin. The voyage to Illyria: a new study of Shakespeare. 1937.
Schneider, F. R. Der wahre Kampf um Shakespeare. Würzburg 1937.
Cadoux, A. T. Shakespearian shelves: an essay in ethics. 1938.
Feely, J. M. Shakespeare's maze further deciphered. New York 1938.
Jacob, G. Shakespeare-Studien. Hamburg 1938.
Menon, C. N. Shakespeare criticism: an essay in synthesis. Oxford 1938.
Traversi, D. A. Approach to Shakespeare. 1938, New York 1956 (enlarged).
Kranendonk, A. G. van. Shakespeare en zijn tijd. Amsterdam 1938.
Alexander, P. Shakespeare's life and art. 1939.
— A Shakespeare primer. 1951.
— Shakespeare. Oxford 1964.
Hardman, D. R. What about Shakespeare? 1939.
Harrison, G. B. Introducing Shakespeare. 1939 (Pelican).
Van Doren, M. Shakespeare. New York 1939.
Meissner, P. On reading Shakespeare. Proc Br Acad 26 1940.
Hotson, L. 'Not of an age': Shakespeare. Sewanee Rev 49 1941.
— Shakespeare's sonnets dated and other essays. 1949.
— Shakespeare's motley. 1952.
Spencer, B. T. This Elizabethan Shakespeare. Sewanee Rev 49 1941.
Lemonnier, L. Shakespeare. Paris 1943.
Bethell, S. L. Shakespeare and the popular dramatic tradition. 1944.
Chambers, E. K. Shakespearean gleanings. Oxford 1944.
Pinto, V. de S. Shakespeare and the dictators. Essays by Divers Hands 21 1944.
Forest, L. C. T. A caveat for critics against invoking Elizabethan psychology. PMLA 61 1946.
Knights, L. C. In his Explorations, 1946. Includes essays on Macbeth, Hamlet, sonnets etc.
— Some Shakespearean themes. 1959.
— In his Further explorations, 1965. Includes essays on Julius Caesar, Lear, Shakespeare's politics etc.

Muir, K. The future of Shakespeare. Penguin New Writing 25 1946.
Orsini, N. La critica shakespeariana: sguardo d'insieme. Anglica 1 1946.
— La pregiudiziale storistica nella critica di Shakespeare. Ibid.
— Stato attuale della filologia shakespeareana. Paideia 8 1953.
Harbage, A. As they liked it: an essay on Shakespeare and morality. New York 1947.
— Shakespeare and the rival traditions. New York 1952.
Rebora, P. Shakespeare. Milan 1947.
Reyher, P. Essai sur les idées dans l'oeuvre de Shakespeare. Paris 1947.
Delius, R. von. Shakespeare: eine Neudeutung seines Geistes. Hamburg 1947.
Quadri, G. Shakespeare e la maturità della coscienza tragica. Florence 1947.
Brooke, C. F. T. Essays on Shakespeare and other Elizabethans. New Haven 1948.
Croce, B. Shakespeare. Ed N. Orsini, Bari 1948.
Craig, H. An interpretation of Shakespeare. New York 1948.
Fluchère, H. Shakespeare: dramaturge élisabéthain. Marseilles 1948; tr 1953.
O'Connor, F. The road to Stratford: a critical study of Shakespeare. 1948.
Sitwell, E. A notebook on Shakespeare. 1948.
Chute, M. Shakespeare of London. New York 1949.
Stauffer, D. A. Shakespeare's world of images: the development of his moral ideas. New York 1949.
Holznecht, K. J. The background of Shakespeare's plays. New York 1950.
Duthie, G. I. Shakespeare. 1951.
Goddard, H. C. The meaning of Shakespeare. Chicago 1951.
Ruegg, A. Shakespeare: eine Einführung in seine Dramen. Berne 1951.
Sewell, A. Character and society in Shakespeare. Oxford 1951.
Danby, J. F. In his Poets on fortune's hill, 1952, 1964 (as Elizabethan and Jacobean poets). Includes essays on Sidney and the late Shakespearian romance, King Lear and Christian patience, Antony and Cleopatra.
Hubner, M. Shakespearean studies and other essays. Princeton 1952.
Leavis, F. R. In his Common pursuit, 1952. Includes essays on Othello, Measure for measure, the last plays.
Schmitt, S. Shakespeare: Drama und Bühne. Sh Jb 89 1953.
Cruttwell, P. The Shakespearean moment and its place in the poetry of the seventeenth century. 1954.
Garrett, J. (ed). Talking of Shakespeare. 1954; More talking of Shakespeare, 1959.
Laqueur, R. Shakespeares dramatische Konzeption. Tübingen 1955.
Lüthi, M. Shakespeares Dramen. Berlin 1956.
Webster, M. Shakespeare today. 1956.
Brunner, K. Shakespeare. Tübingen 1957.
Biancotti, A. Shakespeare. Turin 1957.
Crow, J. Deadly sins of criticism: or seven ways to get Shakespeare wrong. Sh Quart 9 1958.
Fredén, G. Shakespeare. Stockholm 1958.
Schlüter, K. Shakespeares dramatische Erzählkunst. Heidelberg 1958.
Rossiter, A. P. Angel with horns and other Shakespeare lectures. Ed G. Storey 1961.
Ludowyk, E. F. Understanding Shakespeare. Cambridge 1962.
Oppel, H. Shakespeare: Studien zum Werk und zur Welt des Dichters. Heidelberg 1963.
Arthos, J. The art of Shakespeare. New York 1964.
Coghill, N. Shakespeare's professional skills. Cambridge 1964.

Kott, J. Szkice o Szekspirze. Warsaw 1964; tr as Shakespeare our contemporary 1964.

Wright, L. B. Shakespeare for everyman. New York 1964.

Milward, P. An introduction to Shakespeare's plays. Tokyo 1967.

Siegel, P. N. Shakespeare in his time and ours. Notre Dame 1968.

Holland, N. N. The Shakespearean imagination: a critical introduction. Bloomington 1968.

Bradbrook, M. C. Shakespeare the craftsman. 1969.

Evans, G. L. Shakespeare. 2 vols 1969.

McManaway, J. G. Studies in Shakespeare, bibliography and theatre. Ed R. Hosley, A. C. Kirsch and J. W. Velz, New York 1969.

Frye, R. M. Shakespeare: the art of the dramatist. Boston 1970.

SPECIAL STUDIES
(6) Characterization and Character-Types

Wright, E. H. Reality and inconsistency in Shakespeare's characters. New York 1916.

Schücking, L. L. Die Charakterprobleme bei Shakespeare. Leipzig 1919, 1927; tr New York 1922.

Wales, J. G. Character and action in Shakespeare. Wisconsin Univ Stud 17 1923.

Young, K. Samuel Johnson on Shakespeare: one aspect. Wisconsin Univ Stud 18 1924.

Stoll, E. E. In his Shakespeare studies, New York 1927.

Campbell, L. B. Shakespeare's tragic heroes: slaves of passion. Cambridge 1930.

Byrne, Sr St G. Shakespeare's use of the pronoun of address: its significance in characterization and motivation. Washington 1936.

Berkelman, R. G. Shakespeare, ventriloquist. Sewanee Rev 46 1938. On variety in the language of characters.

Hunter, E. R. Shakespeare's mouthpieces: manner of speech as a mark of personality in a few Shakespeare characters. Sewanee Rev 47 1939.

Spencer, T. The isolation of the Shakespearean hero. Sewanee Rev 52 1944.

Kirschbaum, L. Shakespeare's 'good' and 'bad'. RES 21 1945.

—— Character and characterisation in Shakespeare. Wayne Nebraska 1962.

Yoder, A. Animal analogy in Shakespeare's character-portrayal. New York 1947.

Morozov, M. M. The individualization of Shakespeare's characters through imagery. Sh Survey 2 1949.

Stewart, J. I. M. Character and motive in Shakespeare: some recent appraisals examined. 1949.

Simpson, L. The secondary heroes of Shakespeare and other essays. 1950.

Fricker, R. Kontrast und Polarität in den Charakterbildern Shakespeares. Berne 1951.

Wiese, B. von. Gestaltungen des Bösen in Shakespeares dramatischen Werk. Sh Jb 89 1953.

Coe, C. N. Shakespeare's villains. New York 1957.

—— Demi-devils: the character of Shakespeare's villains. New York 1963.

Langbaum, R. Character versus action in Shakespeare. Sh Quart 8 1957.

Draper, J. W. Chacterization in Shakespeare's plays. West Virginia Univ Bull 1958.

Ridley, M. R. Plot and character in the plays. In The living Shakespeare, ed R. Gittings 1960.

Ure, P. Shakespeare and the inward self of the tragic hero. Durham 1961.

Individual Character-Types

Jameson, A. B. Shakespeare's heroines. 1832.

Heine, H. Shakespeares Mädchen und Frauen. In Sämtliche Werke vol 5, Leipzig 1839.

Ruskin, J. In his Sesame and lilies, 1865. On Shakespeare's heroines.

Martin, H. F. On some of Shakespeare's female characters. 1885.

Johnson, L. The fools of Shakespeare. In Noctes Shakesperianae, 1887 (Winchester College Sh Soc); rptd in his Post liminium, 1911.

Pater, W. Shakespeare's English kings. In his Appreciations, 1889.

Davey, S. Fools, jesters and comic characters in Shakespeare. Trans Royal Soc of Lit 23 1902.

Hofmannsthal, H. von. Shakespeares Könige und grosse Herren. Sh Jb 41 1905.

Moorman, F. W. Shakespeare's ghosts. MLR 1 1906.

Stoll, E. E. The objectivity of the ghosts in Shakespeare. PMLA 22 1907.

—— Criminals in Shakespeare and in science. MP 10 1912.

—— The criminals. In his Shakespeare studies, New York 1927.

—— The ghosts. Ibid.

—— Shakespeare's young lovers. Oxford 1937.

—— Heroes and villains: Shakespeare, Middleton, Byron, Dickens. RES 18 1942.

Harris, F. The women of Shakespeare. New York 1912.

Tupper, F. The Shakespearean mob. PMLA 27 1912.

Gray, H. D. The evolution of Shakespeare's heroine. JEGP 12 1913.

Bastide, C. La France et les Français dans le théâtre de Shakespeare. Edda 6 1916.

Hughes, A. E. Shakespeare and his Welsh characters. 1918 (Sh Assoc).

Harries, F. J. Shakespeare and the Welsh. 1919.

Friedlander, G. Shakespeare and the Jew. 1921.

Kellett, E. E. Shakespeare's Amazons. In his Suggestions, Cambridge 1923.

—— Shakespeare's children. Ibid.

Mackenzie, A. M. The women in Shakespeare's plays. 1924.

Stobart, J. C. Shakespeare's monarchs. 1926.

Henneke, A. Shakespeares englische Könige. Sh Jb 66 1930.

Wilson, J. D. The schoolmaster in Shakespeare's plays. Essays by Divers Hands 9 1930.

McPeck, J. A. S. Shakespeare and the fraternity of unthrifts. Harvard Stud 14 1932.

Quiller-Couch, A. T. Paternity in Shakespeare. Proc Br Acad 18 1932.

Small, S. A. Shakespeare's coxcomb characters. Sh Assoc Bull 8 1933.

—— Shakespeare's ghosts. Sh Assoc Bull 11 1936.

Wood, F. T. Shakespeare and the plebs. E & S 18 1933.

Frasure, L. D. Shakespeare's constables. Anglia 58 1934.

Toole, M. M. Shakespeare's courtiers. Sh Assoc Bull 9 1934.

Blos, H. Die Auffassung der Frauengestalten in dem Werke der Mrs Cowden Clarke The girlhood of Shakespeare's heroines. Erlangen 1936.

Brock, J. H. E. Iago and some Shakespearean villains. Cambridge 1937.

Günther, H. F. K. Shakespeares Mädchen und Frauen. Sh Jb 73 1937.

Vallese, T. Donne shakespeariane. Milan 1937.

Draper, J. W. Bastardy in Shakespeare's plays. Sh Jb 74 1938.

—— Falstaff's Robin and other pages. SP 36 1939.

Keller, W. Die Franzosen in Shakespeares Dramen. Sh Jb 76 1940.

Sampley, A. M. A warning piece against Shakespeare's women. Sh Assoc Bull 15 1940.

Schell, J. S. Shakespeare's gulls. Ibid.

Smith, M. E. The lunatic, the lover and the poet. Sh Assoc Bull 16 1941.

Watson, C. B. Shakespeare's dukes. Ibid.

Gates, W. B. The reality of Shakespeare's 'supers'. Sh Assoc Bull 20 1945.

Holbrook, S. C. Husbands in Shakespeare. Ibid.

Palmer, J. Political characters of Shakespeare. 1945.

— Comic characters of Shakespeare. 1946; rptd together with Political characters of Shakespeare, above, 1962.

Harbage, A. Shakespeare's ideal man. In J. Q. Adams memorial studies, Washington 1948.

Sitwell, E. On the clowns and fools of Shakespeare. Life & Letters May 1948.

Stirling, B. The populace in Shakespeare. New York 1949.

Jorgensen, P. A. Military rank in Shakespeare. HLQ 14 1950.

Stevenson, R. Shakespeare's cardinals and bishops. Crozer Quart 27 1950.

Stroedel, W. Die Gestalt des Usurpators in Shakespeares Dramen. Sh Jb 87–8 1951–2.

Goldsmith, R. H. Wise fools in Shakespeare. East Lansing 1956.

McNeal, T. H. Shakespeare's cruel queens. HLQ 22 1958.

Brooks, C. Shakespeare's romantic shrews. Sh Quart 11 1960.

Felver, C. S. Robert Armin: Shakespeare's fool. Kent Ohio 1961.

Scott, W. I. D. Shakespeare's melancholics. 1962.

Leech, C. Shakespeare's Greeks. In Stratford papers on Shakespeare, ed B. W. Jackson, Toronto 1964.

— Shakespeare's comic dukes. REL 5 1964.

— Venus and her nun: portraits of women in love by Shakespeare and Marlowe. Stud in Eng Lit 1500–1900 5 1965.

Jones, E. D. Othello's countrymen: the African in English Renaissance drama. 1965.

Ellis, R. The fool in Shakespeare: a study in alienation. CQ 10 1968.

Evans, H. C. Comic constables: fictional and historical. Sh Quart 20 1969.

Muir, K. Shakespeare's poets. Sh Survey 23 1970.

(7) Influence of Theatrical Conditions

Hale, E. E. The influence of theatrical conditions on Shakespeare. MP 1 1904.

Bradley, A. C. Shakespeare's theatre and audience. In his Oxford lectures on poetry, 1909.

Schmidt, J. E. Shakespeares Dramen und sein Schauspielerberuf. Berlin 1914.

Sisson, C. J. Le goût public et le théâtre élisabéthain jusqu'à la mort de Shakespeare. Dijon [1921].

Granville-Barker, H. The stagecraft of Shakespeare. Fortnightly Rev July 1926.

Cowling, G. H. Shakespeare and the Elizabethan stage. 1927 (Sh Assoc lecture).

Isaacs, J. Shakespeare as a man of the theatre. 1927 (Sh Assoc lecture).

Harrison, G. B. Shakespeare's actors. 1927 (Sh Assoc lecture).

Bridges, R. The influence of the audience on Shakespeare's drama. In his Collected essays vol 1, Oxford 1927.

Bradbrook, M. C. Elizabethan stage conditions: a study of their place in the interpretation of Shakespeare's plays. Cambridge 1932.

Spencer, H. How Shakespeare staged his plays: some notes on the dubiety of non-textual evidence. Johns Hopkins Alumni Mag 20 1932.

Sprague, A. C. Shakespeare and the audience. Cambridge Mass 1935.

— Shakespeare's plays on the English stage. In A new companion to Shakespeare studies, ed K. Muir and S. Schoenbaum, Cambridge 1971.

Adams, J. C. Shakespeare's stage: new facts and figures. Theatre Arts Monthly May 1936.

— The Globe playhouse: its design and equipment. Cambridge Mass 1942, New York 1961 (rev).

Knickerbocker, W. S. The pragmatic Shakespeare. Sewanee Rev 44 1936.

Linthicum, M. C. Costume in the drama of Shakespeare and his contemporaries. Oxford 1936.

Lawrence, W. J. Speeding up Shakespeare: studies of the bygone theatre and drama. 1937.

Davies, W. R. Shakespeare's boy actors. 1939.

Harbage, A. Shakespeare's audience. New York 1941.

Hart, A. Did Shakespeare produce his own plays? MLR 36 1941.

Jackson, J. L. The fencing actor-lines in Shakespeare's plays. MLN 57 1942.

Small, S. A. Shakespeare's stage business. Sh Assoc Bull 18 1943.

Bennett, H. S. Shakespeare's audience. Proc Br Acad 30 1944.

— Shakespeare's stage and audience. Neophilologus 33 1949.

Bentley, G. E. Shakespeare and the Blackfriars. Sh Survey 1 1948.

— Shakespeare and his theatre. Lincoln Nebraska 1964.

Hodges, C. W. Shakespeare and the players. 1948.

— The Globe restored. 1953, 1968 (rev and expanded).

— Will Shakespeare and the Globe Theatre. New York 1955.

Lüdeke, H. Shakespeares Globus-Theater nach den neuesten Ergebnissen der Forschung. Sh Jb 74–6 1948–50.

McDowell, J. H. Conventions of medieval art in Shakespearian staging. JEGP 47 1948.

Nicoll, A. Studies in the Elizabethan stage since 1900. Sh Survey 1 1948.

Bethell, S. L. Shakespeare's actors. RES new ser 1 1950.

Smith, W. New light on stage directions in Shakespeare. SP 47 1950.

— Evidence of scaffolding on Shakespeare's stage. RES new ser 2 1951.

— Stage settings in Shakespeare's dialogue. MP 50 1953.

— The Elizabethan stage and Shakespeare's entrance announcements. Sh Quart 4 1953.

— Stage business in Shakespeare's dialogue. Ibid.

Venezky, A. S. Pageantry on the Shakespearian stage. New York 1951.

Prior, M. E. The Elizabethan audience and the plays of Shakespeare. MP 49 1952.

de Banke, C. Shakespearean stage production: then and now. New York 1953.

Flatter, R. Shakespeare der Schauspieler. Sh Jb 89 1953.

Stamm, R. Shakespeare's word scenery, with some remarks on stage-history and the interpretation of his plays. Zürich 1954.

Harbage, A. The role of the Shakespearean producer. Sh Jb 91 1955.

Joseph, B. L. The Elizabethan stage and the art of Elizabethan drama. Ibid.

— Acting Shakespeare. 1960.

Smith, I. Shakespeare's Globe playhouse. New York 1956.

— Shakespeare's Blackfriars playhouse. New York 1964.

Hosley, R. The gallery over the stage in the public playhouse of Shakespeare's time. Sh Quart 8 1957.

— Shakespeare's use of a gallery over the stage. Sh Survey 10 1957.

— The discovery-space in Shakespeare's Globe. Sh Survey 12 1959.

— A reconstruction of the second Blackfriars. In The Elizabethan theatre, ed D. Galloway, Toronto 1969.

— The playhouses and the stage. In A new companion to Shakespeare studies, ed K. Muir and S. Schoenbaum, Cambridge 1971.

Hotson, L. Shakespeare's 'wooden O'. 1959.

Brooks, C. Shakespeare's heroine actresses. Sh Jb 96 1960.

Holmes, M. Shakespeare's public. 1960.

Righter, A. Shakespeare and the idea of the play. 1960. On actor-audience relations in Elizabethan theatre.

Saunders, J. W. Staging at the Globe 1599–1613. Sh Quart 11 1960.

David, R. Shakespeare and the players. Oxford 1962.

Beckerman, B. Shakespeare at the Globe 1599–1609. New York 1962.

Hook, L. The Curtain. Sh Quart 13 1962.

Bradbrook, M. C. Shakespeare and the Elizabethan theatre. Eng Lang & Lit (Seoul) 15 1964.

Angus, W. Acting Shakespeare. Queen's Quart 72 1965. Historical survey.

Brown, J. R. The study and practice of Shakespeare production. Sh Survey 18 1965.
— Shakespeare's plays in performance. 1967.
— Shakespeare's dramatic style. 1970.

Berry, H. The stages and boxes at Blackfriars. SP 63 1966.

Shapiro, I. A. Robert Fludd's stage-illustration. Sh Stud 2 1966.

Yates, F. A. New light on the Globe theatre. New York Rev of Books 26 May 1966.
— The stage in Robert Fludd's memory system. Sh Stud 3 1967.

Styan, J. L. Shakespeare's stagecraft. Cambridge 1967.

Dodd, K. M. Another Elizabethan theater in the round. Sh Quart 21 1970. Open-air theatre at Walsham-le-Willows, Suffolk.

Gurr, A. The Shakespearean stage 1574–1642. Cambridge 1970.

Seltzer, D. The actors and acting. In A new companion to Shakespeare studies, ed K. Muir and S. Schoenbaum, Cambridge 1971.

Ure, P. Shakespeare and the drama of his time. Ibid.

(8) Special Aspects of Dramatic Technique

Daniel, P. A. Time analysis of the plots of Shakespeare's plays. Trans New Sh Soc 1877–9.

Spedding, J. On the division of the acts in Lear, Much ado and Twelfth night. Ibid.

Arnold, M. le R. The soliloquies of Shakespeare. New York 1911.

Stoll, E. E. Hamlet and Iago. In [G. L.] Kittredge anniversary papers, Boston 1913.
— The comic method. In his Shakespeare studies, New York 1927.
— 'Multi-consciousness' in the theatre. PQ 29 1950.

Alden, R. M. The use of comic material in the tragedy of Shakespeare and his contemporaries. JEGP 13 1914.

Scholes, P. A. The purpose behind Shakespeare's use of music. Proc Musical Assoc 1917.

Koppel, R. Das Primitiv in Shakespeares Dramatik. Berlin 1918.

Schücking, L. L. Die Handlungsbegründung. In his Die Charakterprobleme bei Shakespeare, Leipzig 1919.

Hunter, M. Act and scene division in the plays of Shakespeare. RES 2 1926.

Wilson, J. D. Act- and scene-divisions in the plays of Shakespeare. RES 3 1927.

Thaler, A. Shakespeare and the unhappy happy ending. PMLA 42 1927; rptd in his Shakespeare's silences, below.
— Shakespeare's silences. Cambridge Mass 1929.
— Delayed exposition in Shakespeare. Sh Quart 1 1950.

Greg, W. W. Act-divisions in Shakespeare. RES 4 1928.

Willoughby, E. E. The heading Actus Primus, Scaena Prima, in the First Folio. Ibid.

Matheson, B. S. The invented personages in Shakespeare's plays. Philadelphia 1933.

Draper, J. W. Court vs. country in Shakespeare's plays. JEGP 33 1934.
— Mistaken identity in Shakespeare's comedies. Revue Anglo-américaine 11 1934.
— The tempo-patterns of Shakespeare's plays. Heidelberg 1957.
— Dramatic irony in Shakespeare's earlier plays. West Virginia Univ Philological Papers 12 1959.

Kreider, P. V. The mechanics of disguise in Shakespeare's plays. Sh Assoc Bull 9 1934.
— Repetition in Shakespeare's plays. Princeton 1941.

David, R. The Janus of poets: being an essay on the dramatic value of Shakespeare's poetry, both good and bad. Cambridge 1935.

Raysor, T. M. The aesthetic significance of Shakespeare's handling of time. SP 32 1935.

Deaton, M. Something Shakespeare left out. Sh Assoc Bull 11 1936.

Lawrence, W. J. Something new about Shakespeare. London Mercury July 1936.

Morsbach, L. Shakespeares dramatische Kunst und ihre Voraussetzungen, mit einem Ausblick auf die Hamlet-Tragödie. Göttingen 1940.

Mincoff, M. K. Plot-construction in Shakespeare. Sofia Univ Annual 37 1941.

Craig, H. Shakespeare's development as a dramatist in the light of his experience. SP 39 1942.

Kennedy, M. B. The oration in Shakespeare. Chapel Hill 1942.

Sewell, A. Place and time in Shakespeare's plays. SP 42 1945.

McCloskey, J. C. The plot device of false report. Sh Assoc Bull 21 1946.

Baldwin, T. W. Shakespeare's five-act structure. Urbana 1947.
— On act and scene division in the Shakespeare First Folio. Carbondale 1965.

Ellis-Fermor, U. Shakespeare the dramatist. Proc Br Acad 34 1948.
— Shakespeare and the dramatic mode. Neophilologus 37 1953.

Price, H. T. Mirror scenes in Shakespeare. In J. Q. Adams memorial studies, Washington 1948.
— Construction in Shakespeare. Ann Arbor 1951.

Wiles, R. M. 'In my mind's eye, Oratio.' UTQ 18 1948. On use of words instead of actions in crises.

Salter, F. M. Shakespeare's use of silence. Trans Royal Soc of Canada 3rd ser 45 1951.

Burris, Q. G. 'Soft! Here follows prose.' Sh Quart 2 1951.

Bradbrook, M. C. Shakespeare and the use of disguise in Elizabethan drama. EC 2 1952.

Clemen, W. Wandlung des Botenberichts bei Shakespeare. Munich 1952.
— Schein und Sein bei Shakespeare. Munich 1959.
— Shakespeares Monologe. Göttingen 1964.
— Shakespeare's soliloquies. Cambridge 1964 (rev trn).

Holloway, J. Dramatic irony in Shakespeare. Northern Miscellany 1 1953.

Harbage, A. The role of the Shakespearean producer. Sh Jb 91 1955.

Joseph, B. L. The Elizabethan stage and the art of Elizabethan drama. Ibid.
— Acting Shakespeare. 1960.

Long, J. H. Shakespeare's use of music. Gainesville 1955.

Mattingly, A. S. The playing time and manner of delivery of Shakespeare's plays in the Elizabethan theatre. Speech Monographs 21 1955.

Müller-Bellinghausen, A. Die Wortkulisse bei Shakespeare. Sh Jb 91 1955. On acting technique.

Parker, M. H. D. The slave of life: Shakespeare and the idea of justice. 1955.

Manifold, J. S. The music in English drama: from Shakespeare to Purcell. 1956.

Auden, W. H. Music in Shakespeare. Encounter Dec 1957.

Chambers, H. A. A Shakespeare song book. 1957. 3 centuries of musical settings.

Leech, C. Shakespeare's use of a five-act structure. Die Neueren Sprachen 6 1957.
— Shakespeare's prologues and epilogues. In Studies in honor of T. W. Baldwin, Urbana 1958.
— The two-part play: Marlowe and the early Shakespeare. Sh Jb 95 1959.
— Ephesus, Troy, Athens: Shakespeare's use of locality. In Stratford papers on Shakespeare 1963, ed B. W. Jackson, Toronto 1964.

Oppel, H. Shakespeare und das Leid. Sh Jb 93 1957.

Schlüter, K. Shakespeares dramatische Erzählkunst. Heidelberg 1958.

Driver, T. F. The sense of history in Greek and Shakespearean tragedy. New York 1960.

Snuggs, H. L. Shakespeare and five acts. New York 1960.

Watson, C. B. Shakespeare and the Renaissance concept of honor. Princeton 1960.

Boustead, A. Music to Shakespeare. Oxford 1964.

Dickinson, A. E. F. Shakespeare in music. Durham Univ Jnl 25 1964.

Muir, K. Shakespeare's soliloquies. Occidente (Lisbon) Aug 1964.

Dunn, C. M. The function of music in Shakespeare's romances. Sh Quart 20 1969.

Wickham, G. Shakespeare's dramatic heritage: collected studies in mediaeval, Tudor and Shakespearean drama. 1969.

Brown, J. R. Shakespeare's dramatic style. 1970.

Bevington, D. Shakespeare the Elizabethan dramatist. In A new companion to Shakespeare studies, ed K. Muir and S. Schoenbaum, Cambridge 1971.

Bradbrook, M. C. Shakespeare the Jacobean dramatist. Ibid.

Dramatic Types

Tragedy

Bradley, A. C. Shakespearean tragedy: lectures on Hamlet, Othello, King Lear, Macbeth. 1904.

MacCallum, M. W. Shakespeare's Roman plays and their background. 1910.

Klein, M. Forum and Aufbau der Tragödien Macbeth, Othello, Lear, Hamlet. Anglia 56 1932.

Draper, J. W. The realism of Shakespeare's Roman plays. SP 30 1933.

Knight, G. W. The wheel of fire. 1930, 1949 (with 3 new essays).

—— The imperial theme. Oxford 1931, 1951 (with new preface).

Raysor, T. M. Intervals of time and their effect upon dramatic values in Shakespeare's tragedies. JEGP 37 1938.

Schmidt, W. Shakespeares Leben und der Sinn der Tragödien. Die Neueren Sprachen 46 1938.

Myrick, K. O. The theme of damnation in Shakespearian tragedy. SP 38 1941.

Grace, W. J. The cosmic sense in Shakespearian tragedy. Sewanee Rev 50 1942.

Anderson, R. L. Excessive goodness a tragic fault. Sh Assoc Bull 19 1944.

Fairchild, A. H. R. Shakespeare and the tragic theme. Columbia Missouri 1944.

Meissner, P. Gestaltung und Deutung des Tragischen bei Shakespeare. Sh Jb 80-1 1944-5.

Cady, F. W. Motivation of the inciting force in Shakespeare's tragedies. In Elizabethan studies in honor of G. F. Reynolds, Boulder 1945.

Campbell, L. B. Bradley revisited: forty years after. SP 44 1947.

Schücking, L. L. Shakespeare und der Tragödienstil seiner Zeit. Berne 1947.

Schneider, R. Macht und Gewissen in Shakespeares Tragödie. Berlin 1947.

Charlton, H. B. Shakespearian tragedy. Cambridge 1948.

Connolly, T. F. Shakespeare and the double man. Sh Quart 1 1950.

Cunningham, J. V. Tragedy in Shakespeare. ELH 17 1950.

—— Woe or wonder: the emotional effect of Shakespearian tragedy. Denver 1951.

Dyson, H. V. D. The emergence of Shakespeare's tragedy. Proc Br Acad 36 1950.

Farnham, W. Shakespeare's tragic frontier: the world of his final tragedies. Berkeley 1950. See R. Roth, MP 49 1952.

Leech, C. Shakespeare's tragedies and other studies in seventeenth-century drama. 1950.

Mincoff, M. The structural pattern of Shakespeare's tragedies. Sh Survey 3 1950.

Waith, E. M. Manhood and valour in two Shakespearian tragedies. ELH 17 1950. Macbeth, Antony and Cleopatra.

Harrison, G. B. Shakespeare's tragedies. 1951.

James, D. G. The dream of learning. Oxford 1951. On Hamlet and Lear.

Brown, H. Enter the Shakespearean tragic hero. EC 3 1953.

Oppel, H. Shakespeares Tragödien und Romanzen: Kontinuität oder Umbruch? Wiesbaden 1954.

Speaight, R. Nature in Shakespearian tragedy. 1955.

Siegel, P. N. Shakespearian tragedy and the Elizabethan compromise. New York 1956.

Stirling, B. Unity in Shakespearian tragedy: the interplay of theme and character. New York 1956.

Dickey, F. M. Not wisely but too well: Shakespeare's love tragedies. San Marino 1957.

Wilson, H. S. On the design of Shakespearian tragedy. Toronto 1957.

Barroll, J. L. Shakespeare and Roman history. MLR 53 1958.

Dunkel, W. D. The meek shall inherit the earth: a study in Shakespearean tragedy. Theology Today 195 1958.

Hill, R. F. Shakespeare's early tragic mode. Sh Quart 9 1958.

Danby, J. F. The tragedies. In The living Shakespeare, ed R. Gittings 1960.

Lawlor, J. The tragic sense in Shakespeare. 1960.

Muir, K. Shakespeare and the tragic pattern. Oxford 1960.

—— Shakespeare: the great tragedies. 1961.

Ribner, I. Patterns in Shakespearian tragedy. 1960.

Rosen, W. Shakespeare and the craft of tragedy. Cambridge Mass 1960.

Sisson, C. J. The Roman plays. In The living Shakespeare, ed R. Gittings 1960.

—— Shakespeare's tragic justice. 1962.

Charney, M. Shakespeare's Roman plays. Cambridge Mass 1961.

Holloway, J. The story of the night: studies in Shakespeare's major tragedies. 1961.

Jenkins, H. The tragedy of revenge in Shakespeare and Webster. Sh Survey 14 1961.

—— The catastrophe in Shakespearean tragedy. Edinburgh 1969.

Michel, L. Shakespearean tragedy: critique of humanism from the inside. Massachusetts Rev 2 1961.

Spencer, T. J. B. Shakespeare: the Roman plays. 1963 (Br Council pamphlet).

Traversi, D. A. Shakespeare: the Roman plays. 1963.

Foakes, R. A. Shakespeare's later tragedies. In Shakespeare 1564-1964, ed E. A. Bloom, Providence 1964.

Hawkes, T. Shakespeare and the reason. 1964. On tragedies and problem plays.

Heilman, R. B. To know himself: an aspect of tragic structure. REL 5 1964.

—— 'Twere best not know myself: Othello, Lear, Macbeth. In Shakespeare 400, ed J. G. McManaway, New York 1964.

Nowottny, W. Shakespeare's tragedies. In Shakespeare's world, ed J. R. Sutherland and J. Hurstfield 1964.

Whitaker, V. K. The mirror up to nature: the technique of Shakespeare's tragedies. San Marino 1965.

McFarland, T. Tragic meanings in Shakespeare. New York 1966.

Frye, N. Fools of time: studies in Shakespearian tragedy. Toronto 1967.

Bowers, F. T. Death in victory: Shakespeare's tragic reconciliations. In Studies in honor of De Witt T. Starnes, Austin 1967.

Brooke, N. Shakespeare's early tragedies. 1968.

Stampfer, J. L. The tragic engagement: a study of Shakespeare's classical tragedies. New York 1968.

Battenhouse, R. W. Shakespearean tragedy: its art and its Christian premises. Bloomington 1969.

Carlisle, C. T. Shakespeare from the greenroom: actors' criticisms of four major tragedies. Chapel Hill 1969. On Hamlet, Othello, Lear, Macbeth.

Frye, R. M. Theological and non-theological structures in tragedies. Sh Stud 4 1969.

Mason, H. A. Shakespeare's tragedies of love. 1970.

Historical Plays

Courtenay, T. P. Commentaries on the historical plays of Shakespeare. 2 vols 1840, 1861.

Simpson, R. The politics of Shakespeare's historical plays. Trans New Sh Soc 1874.

— On the political use of the stage in Shakespeare's time. Ibid.

Warner, B. E. English history in Shakespeare's plays. New York 1894, 1903.

Davey, S. The relation of poetry to history, with special reference to Shakespeare's historical plays. Trans Royal Soc of Lit 24 1903.

Moorman, F. W. Shakespeare's history-plays and Daniel's Civile Wars. Sh Jb 40 1904.

Marriott, J. A. R. English history in Shakespeare. 1918. Rptd from Fortnightly Rev June 1916–17.

Pollard, A. W. The York and Lancaster plays. TLS 20–7 Sept 1918.

Steinitzer, A. Shakespeares Königsdramen. Munich 1922.

Hearnshaw, F. J. C. Shakespeare as historian. Contemporary Rev Dec 1923.

Stobart, J. C. Shakespeare's monarchs. 1926.

Henneke, A. Shakespeares englische Könige. Sh Jb 66 1930.

Messiaen, P. Les drames historiques de Shakespeare. Revue des Cours et Conférences 39–40 1938–9, Revue Universitaire 48 1939.

Mroz, M. B. Divine vengeance: a study in the philosophical backgrounds of the revenge motif as it appears in Shakespeare's chronicle history plays. Washington 1941.

Tillyard, E. M. W. Shakespeare's history plays. 1944.

Laird, J. Shakespeare on the wars of England. In his Philosophical excursions into English literature, Cambridge 1946.

Campbell, L. B. Shakespeare's 'histories': mirrors of Elizabethan policy. San Marino 1947.

Holzknecht, K. J. An outline of Shakespeare's English history plays. Sh Assoc Bull 22 1947.

Craig, H. Shakespeare and the history plays. In J. Q. Adams memorial studies, Washington 1948.

Chapman, R. The wheel of fortune in Shakespeare's historical plays. RES new ser 1 1950.

Bethell, S. L. The comic element in Shakespeare's histories. Anglia 71 1952.

Ribner, I. The political problem in Shakespeare's Lancastrian tetralogy. SP 49 1952.

— The English history play in the age of Shakespeare. Princeton 1957.

Clemen, W. H. Anticipation and foreboding in Shakespeare's early histories. Sh Survey 6 1953.

Brunner, K. Middle-class attitudes in Shakespeare's histories. Ibid.

David, R. Shakespeare's history plays: epic or drama? Ibid.

Law, R. A. Links between Shakespeare's history plays. SP 50 1953.

— Shakespeare's historical cycle: organism or compilation? SP 51 1954. Reply by E. M. W. Tillyard, ibid.

Schirmer, W. F. Glück und Ende der Könige in Shakespeares Historien. Cologne 1954.

Kleinstück, J. The problem of order in Shakespeare's histories. Neophilologus 38 1954.

Traversi, D. A. Shakespeare: from Richard II to Henry V. 1957.

Lawlor, J. Shakespeare: the chronicles. 1960.

Morris, H. The histories. In The living Shakespeare, ed R. Gittings 1960.

Muir, K. Source problems in the histories. Sh Jb 96 1960.

— Image and symbol in Shakespeare's histories. Bull John Rylands Lib 50 1967.

Reese, M. M. The cease of majesty. 1961.

Knights, L. C. Shakespeare: the histories. 1962.

Webber, J. The renewal of the King's symbolic role: from Richard II to Henry V. Texas Stud in Lit & Lang 4 1962.

Bullough, G. The uses of history. In Shakespeare's world, ed J. R. Sutherland and J. Hurstfield 1964.

Morton, A. L. Shakespeare's historical outlook. Zeitschrift für Anglistik und Amerikanistik 12 1964.

Sprague, A. C. Shakespeare's histories: plays for the stage. 1964.

Turner, R. Y. Characterization in Shakespeare's early history plays. ELH 31 1964.

— Shakespeare and the public confrontation scene in early history plays. MP 62 1964.

Humphreys, A. R. Shakespeare and the Tudor perception of history. In Shakespeare celebrated, ed L. B. Wright, New York 1966.

La Guardia, E. Ceremony and history: the problem of symbol from Richard II to Henry V. In Pacific Coast studies in Shakespeare, ed W. F. McNeir and T. N. Greenfield, Portland Oregon 1966.

Winny, J. M. The player king: a theme of Shakespeare's histories. 1968.

Wilson, F. P. The English history play. In his Shakespearian and other essays, ed H. L. Gardner, Oxford 1969.

Kernan, A. The Henriad: Shakespeare's major history plays. Yale Rev 59 1969.

Kelly, H. A. Divine providence in the England of Shakespeare's histories. Cambridge Mass 1970.

Pierce, R. B. Shakespeare's history plays: the family and the state. Columbus 1971.

Weiss, T. The breath of clowns and kings: Shakespeare's early comedies and histories. 1971.

Comedy

Dowden, E. Shakespeare as a comic dramatist. In Gayley vol 1, 1903.

Ker, W. P. A note on the form of Shakespeare's comedies. Edda 6 1916.

Charlton, H. B. A note on Shakespeare's romantic comedies. In Anglica: A. Brandl überreicht, Leipzig 1925.

— Shakespearian comedy. 1938.

Quiller-Couch, A. T. Shakespeare's comedies. In his Studies in literature: series 3, Cambridge 1929.

Lawrence, W. W. Shakespeare's problem comedies. New York 1931.

Jacobi, W. Form und Struktur der Shakespeareschen Komödien. Berlin 1937.

Messiaen, P. Les comédies de Shakespeare. Revue des Cours et Conférences 38 1937.

Durham, W. H. What art thou, Angelo? California Univ Pbns in Eng 8 1941.

Gordon, G. S. Shakespearian comedy and other studies. Oxford 1944.

Closson, H. Shakespeare et la comédie de l'aventure. Brussels 1945.

Stevenson, D. L. The love-game comedy. New York 1946.

Frye, N. The argument of comedy. Eng Inst Essays 1948.

— Comic myth in Shakespeare. Trans Royal Soc of Canada 3rd ser 46 1952.

— Characterization in Shakespeare's comedy. Sh Quart 4 1953.

— A natural perspective: the development of Shakespearean comedy and romance. New York 1965.

Parrott, T. M. Shakespearean comedy. Oxford 1949.

Coghill, N. The basis of Shakespearian comedy: a study in medieval affinities. E & S new ser 3 1950.

Barber, C. L. The saturnalian pattern in Shakespeare's comedy. Sewanee Rev 59 1951.

— Shakespeare's festive comedy. Princeton 1959.

Sen Gupta, S. C. Shakespearian comedy. Calcutta 1951.

Whitaker, V. K. Philosophy and romance in Shakespeare's 'problem comedies'. In The seventeenth century: studies by R. F. Jones et al, Stanford 1951.

Thompson, K. F. Shakespeare's romantic comedies. PMLA 67 1952.

Desai, C. N. Shakespearian comedy. Indore City 1953.

Borinski, L. Shakespeare's comic prose. Sh Survey 8 1955.

Brown, J. R. Shakespeare and his comedies. 1957, 1962 (rev).

Tillyard, E. M. W. The nature of comedy and Shakespeare. 1958.

— Shakespeare's early comedies. 1965.

Blistein, E. M. The object of scorn: an aspect of the comic antagonist. Western Humanities Rev 14 1960. On unsympathetic comic types.

David, R. The comedies. In The living Shakespeare, ed R. Gittings 1960.

Evans, B. Shakespeare's comedies. Oxford 1960.

Traversi, D. A. Shakespeare: the early comedies. 1960 (Br Council pamphlet), 1964 (rev).

Sehrt, E. T. Wandlungen der Shakespeareschen Komödie. Sh Jb 95 1959; rptd Göttingen 1961.

Ure, P. Shakespeare: the problem plays. 1961 (Br Council pamphlet).

Hunter, G. K. Shakespeare: the late comedies. 1962 (Br Council pamphlet).

Berman, R. Shakespearean comedy and the uses of reason. South Atlantic Quart 63 1964.

Brown, A. Shakespeare's treatment of comedy. In Shakespeare's world, ed J. Sutherland and J. Hurstfield 1964.

Hubler, E. The range of Shakespeare's comedy. In Shakespeare 400, ed J. G. McManaway, New York 1964.

Baxter, J. S. Present mirth: Shakespeare's romantic comedies. Queen's Quart 72 1965.

Bonazza, B. O. Shakespeare's early comedies: a structural analysis. Hague 1965.

Phialas, P. G. Shakespeare's romantic comedies: the development of their form and meaning. Chapel Hill 1966.

Toole, W. B. Shakespeare's problem plays. Hague 1966.

Wilson, F. P. Shakespeare's comedies. In his Shakespearian and other studies, ed H. L. Gardner, Oxford 1969.

Kantak, V. Y. An approach to Shakespearian comedy. Sh Survey 22 1969.

Champion, L. S. The evolution of Shakespeare's comedy. Cambridge Mass 1970.

Cody, R. The landscape of the mind: pastoralism and Platonic theory in Tasso's Aminta and Shakespeare's early comedies. Oxford 1970.

Hassel, R. C. Shakespeare's comic epilogues: invitations to festive communion. Sh Jb (Heidelberg) 1970.

Martz, W. J. Shakespeare's universe of comedy. 1970.

Weiss, T. The breath of clowns and kings: Shakespeare's early comedies and histories. 1970.

Other Dramatic Types

Cunliffe, J. W. The masque in Shakespeare's plays. Archiv 125 1910.

Greenlaw, E. Shakespeare's pastorals. SP 13 1916.

Morsbach, L. Shakespeares Prologe, Epiloge und Chorus-Reden. Berlin 1929.

Pongs, H. Shakespeare und das politische Drama. Dichtung und Volkstum 37 1936.

James, D. G. In his Scepticism and poetry, 1937. Includes a study of the last plays.

Tillyard, E. M. W. Shakespeare's last plays. 1938.

— Shakespeare's problem plays. 1949.

Phillips, J. E. The state in Shakespeare's Greek and Roman plays. New York 1940.

Spencer, T. Appearance and reality in Shakespeare's last plays. MP 39 1942.

Knight, G. W. The crown of life: essays in interpretation of Shakespeare's final plays. Oxford 1947.

Oppel, H. Der späte Shakespeare. Hamburg 1949.

— Shakespeares Tragödien und Romanzen: Kontinuität oder Umbruch? Wiesbaden 1954.

Wincor, R. Shakespeare's festival plays. Sh Quart 1 1950. On the last plays.

Leavis, F. R. The criticism of Shakespeare's last plays. In his Common pursuit, 1952.

Bland, D. S. The heroine and the sea: an aspect of Shakespeare's last plays. EC 3 1953.

Traversi, D. A. Shakespeare: the last phase. 1954.

Fischer, W. Shakespeares späte Romanzen. Sh Jb 91 1955.

Guidi, A. L'ultimo Shakespeare. Milan 1957.

Edwards, P. Shakespeare's romances 1900–57. Sh Survey 11 1958.

Leech, C. The structure of the last plays. Ibid.

Nicoll, A. Shakespeare and the Court masque. Sh Jb 94 1958.

Nosworthy, J. M. Music and its function in the romances of Shakespeare. Sh Survey 11 1958.

— Shakespeare's occasional plays: their origin and transmission. 1965.

Dobrée, B. The last plays. In The living Shakespeare, ed R. Gittings 1960.

Hoy, C. Comedy, tragedy and tragicomedy. Virginia Quart Rev 36 1960.

Kermode, F. Shakespeare: the final plays. 1963 (Br Council pamphlet).

Schanzer, E. The problem plays of Shakespeare: a study of Julius Caesar, Measure for measure, Antony and Cleopatra. 1963.

Talbert, E. W. Elizabethan drama and Shakespeare's early plays. Chapel Hill 1963.

Hawkes, T. Shakespeare and the reason. 1964. On tragedies and problem plays.

Bowers, J. L. The romances. In Shakespeare at 400, ed R. G. Howarth, Cape Town 1965.

Brown, J. R. Laughter in the last plays. In Later Shakespeare, ed J. R. Brown and B. Harris 1966.

Salingar, L. G. Time and art in Shakespeare's romances. Renaissance Drama 9 1966.

Seltzer, D. The staging of the last plays. In Later Shakespeare, ed J. R. Brown and B. Harris 1966.

Wells, S. W. Shakespeare and romance. Ibid.

Hamilton, A. C. The early Shakespeare. San Marino 1967.

Cutts, J. P. Rich and strange: a study of Shakespeare's last plays. Pullman Washington 1968.

— The shattered glass: a dramatic pattern in Shakespeare's early plays. Detroit 1968.

Miscellaneous Elements

Moorman, F. W. The interpretation of nature in English poetry from Beowulf to Shakespeare. Strasbourg 1905.

Hanford, J. H. Suicide in the plays of Shakespeare. PMLA 27 1912.

Sullivan, E. What Shakespeare saw in nature. Nineteenth Century July 1913.

Pyre, J. F. A. Shakespeare's pathos. In Shakespeare studies by members of the Department of English of the University of Wisconsin, Madison 1916.

Herford, C. H. The normality of Shakespeare, illustrated in his treatment of love and marriage. 1920 (Eng Assoc lecture); rptd in his Shakespeare's treatment of love and marriage and other essays, 1921.

Grierson, H. Friendship in Shakespeare's plays. Contemporary Rev Nov 1921.

Luce, M. Nature in Shakespeare. Nineteenth Century Sept 1922.

— Love in Shakespeare. Nineteenth Century Sept 1924.

Kellett, E. E. Some medievalisms in Shakespeare. In his Suggestions, Cambridge 1923.

— Shakespeare and marriage. Ibid.

Noble, R. Shakespeare's use of song. Oxford 1923.

— Shakespeare's songs and stage. 1927 (Sh Assoc lecture).

Legouis, E. The Bacchic element in Shakespeare's plays. Proc Br Acad 12 1926.

Rannie, D. W. Scenery in Shakespeare's plays and other studies. Oxford 1926.

Schücking, L. L. Die Familie bei Shakespeare. E Studien 62 1927.

Stoll, E. E. 'Reconciliation' in tragedy: Shakespeare and Sophocles. UTQ 4 1934.

Draper, J. W. Political themes in Shakespeare's later plays. JEGP 35 1936.

—— Flattery: a Shakespearian tragic theme. PQ 17 1938.

Taylor, G. C. The medieval element in Shakespeare. Sh Assoc Bull 12 1937.

—— Shakespeare's use of the idea of the beast in man. SP 52 1945.

Burre, H. Das Freundschaftsmotiv und seine Abwandlung in den Dramen Shakespeares. Marburg 1938.

Cox, E. H. Another medieval convention in Shakespeare. Sh Assoc Bull 13 1938.

—— Shakespeare and some conventions of old age. SP 39 1942.

Eckhoff, L. Heroismus und politische Führertum bei Shakespeare. Zeitschrift für Neusprachlichen Unterricht 37 1938.

Walker, A. L. Convention in Shakespeare's description of emotion. PQ 18 1938.

Gronauer, G. Die Frage der Realität der Geisterscheinungen in Shakespeares Dramen. Erlangen 1939.

Bhattacherje, M. M. 'Courtesy' in Shakespeare. Calcutta 1940.

Harrison, T. P. Aspects of primitivism in Shakespeare and Spenser. SE 1940.

Price, H. T. Shakespeare as a critic. PQ 20 1941.

McCloskey, J. C. Fear of the people as a minor motive in Shakespeare. Sh Assoc Bull 17 1942.

Campbell, O. J. Shakespeare's satire. Oxford 1943.

Morozov, M. M. Humanism in Shakespeare's works. Sh Assoc Bull 18 1943.

Brooks, C. Shakespeare as a symbolist poet. Yale Rev 34 1945.

Cazamian, L. L'humour de Shakespeare. Paris 1945.

Lengefeld, K. von. Shakespeare und die Kunstepochen des Barock und des Manierismus. Sh Jb 82–3 1946–7.

Partridge, E. Shakespeare's bawdy: a literary and psychological essay and a comprehensive glossary. 1947.

Fiedler, L. A. The defense of the illusion and the creation of myth: device and symbol in the plays of Shakespeare. Eng Inst Essays 1948.

Hubler, E. Three Shakespearean myths: mutability, plenitude and reputation. Ibid.

Kirschbaum, L. Shakespeare's stage blood and its critical significance. PMLA 64 1949.

Pettet, E. C. Shakespeare's conception of poetry. E & S new ser 3 1950.

Cormican, L. A. Medieval idiom in Shakespeare. Scrutiny 17 1951.

Craig, H. Motivation in Shakespeare's choice of materials. Sh Survey 4 1951.

Williams, G. C. Shakespeare's basic plot situation. Sh Quart 2 1951.

Hotson, L. Shakespeare's motley. 1952.

Röhrman, H. Marlowe and Shakespeare: a thematic exposition of some of their plays. Arnhem 1952.

Wickert, M. Das Schattenmotiv bei Shakespeare. Anglia 71 1953.

Holloway, J. Dramatic irony in Shakespeare. Northern Miscellany 1 1953.

Oppel, H. Zur Problematik des Willenkampfes bei Shakespeare. Sh Jb 89 1953.

—— Shakespeare und das Leid. Sh Jb 93 1957.

Hammerle, K. Das Laubenmotiv bei Shakespeare und Spenser. Anglia 71 1953.

Jorgensen, P. A. Shakespeare's use of war and peace. HLQ 16 1953.

—— Divided command in Shakespeare. PMLA 70 1955. On treatment of historical battles.

Clemen, W. H. Schein und Sein bei Shakespeare. Munich 1959.

Driver, T. F. The sense of history in Greek and Shakespearean tragedy. New York 1960.

Melchiori, B. 'Still harping on my daughter'. Eng Miscellany (Rome) 11 1960. On incest.

Watson, C. B. Shakespeare and the Renaissance concept of honor. Princeton 1960.

Lüthi, M. Ironie in Shakespeares Spielen. Neue Zürcher Zeitung 19 April 1964.

Spencer, T. J. B. The great rival: Shakespeare and the classical dramatists. In Shakespeare 1564–1964, ed E. A. Bloom, Providence 1964.

Klose, D. Shakespeare und Ovid. Sh Jb (Heidelberg) 1968.

Wickham, G. Shakespeare's dramatic heritage: collected studies in medieval, Tudor and Shakespearean drama. 1969.

C. SHAKESPEARE'S INFLUENCE

Adaptations

The principal adaptations are listed in Bartlett, pp. 71–82. They have been collected in the Bankside Restoration Shakespeare, ed J. A. Morgan 1898–1908 (New York Sh Soc). For treatises on particular adaptations see Ebisch and Schücking under separate plays, above, and, more recently, the Sh Quart bibliographies. See also general histories of the stage, col 1367, above.

Genest, J. Some account of the English stage 1660 to 1830. 10 vols Bath 1832.

Stage adaptations of Shakespeare. Cornhill Mag July 1863.

Delius, N. Dryden und Shakespeare. Sh Jb 4 1869.

Vincke, G. von. Bearbeitungen und Aufführungen Shakespearescher Stücke vom Tode des Dichters bis zum Tod Garricks. Sh Jb 9 1874.

—— Shakespeare auf der englischen Bühne seit Garrick. Sh Jb 22 1887.

Hudson, W. H. Early mutilators of Shakespeare. Poet Lore 4 1892.

Kilbourne, F. W. Stage versions of Shakespeare before 1800. Poet Lore 15 1904.

—— Alterations and adaptations of Shakespeare. Boston 1906.

Williams, J. D. E. Sir Wm Davenant's relation to Shakespeare. Strasbourg 1905.

Egan, M. E. Imitators of Shakespeare. In his Ghost in Hamlet, Chicago 1906.

Finck, H. F. Shakespearean operas. Nation (New York) 23 March 1916.

Squire, W. B. Shakespearean operas. In A book of homage to Shakespeare, ed I. Gollancz, Oxford 1916.

Pollard, A. W. The improvers of Shakespeare. Library 1st ser 14 1916.

Odell, G. C. D. Shakespeare from Betterton to Irving. 2 vols New York 1920, London 1963.

Sharp, R. F. Travesties of Shakespeare's plays. Library 3rd ser 1 1920.

Nicoll, A. Dryden as an adapter of Shakespeare. 1922 (Sh Assoc lecture).

Summers, M. Shakespeare adaptations. Boston 1922. Introd.

Spencer, H. Davenant's Macbeth and Shakespeare's. PMLA 40 1925.
—— Improving Shakespeare. PMLA 41 1926.
—— Shakespeare improved. Cambridge Mass 1927.
—— Shakespearean cuts in Restoration Dublin. PMLA 57 1942.
Child, H. The Shakespearian productions of John Philip Kemble. 1935 (Sh Assoc pamphlet).
Brandl, A. Eine neue Art, Shakespeare zu spielen. In his Forschungen und Charakteristiken, Berlin 1936.
Knight, G. W. Principles of Shakespearian production. 1936, 1949 (Pelican) (with new appendix), 1964 (rev as Shakespearian production).
Myers, A. M. British-American staging of Shakespeare. Sh Assoc Bull 12 1937.
Stone, G. W. Garrick's presentation of Antony and Cleopatra. RES 13 1937.
—— Garrick and an unknown operatic version of Love's labour's lost. RES 15 1939.
—— A midsummer night's dream in the hands of Garrick and Colman. PMLA 54 1939.
—— Garrick's handling of Macbeth. SP 38 1941.
—— Garrick's production of King Lear. SP 45 1948.
—— The god of his idolatry: Garrick's theory of acting and dramatic composition with especial reference to Shakespeare. In J. Q. Adams memorial studies, Washington 1948.
Stahl, E. L. Shakespeare-Gestaltung auf dem englischen Theater im 19 Jahrhundert. Sh Jb 74 1939.
Bald, R. C. Shakespeare on the stage in Restoration Dublin. PMLA 56 1941.
Webster, M. Shakespeare without tears. New York 1942.
Scouten, A. H. Shakespeare's plays in the theatre repertory when Garrick came to London. SE 1944.
—— and L. Hughes. A calendar of performances of 1 and 2 Henry IV during the first half of the eighteenth century. JEGP 43 1944.
Sprague, A. C. Shakespeare and the actors: the stage business in his plays 1660–1905. Cambridge Mass 1944.
—— Shakespeare and William Poel. UTQ 17 1947.
—— Shakespearian players and performances. Cambridge Mass 1953.
—— The stage business in Shakespeare's plays: a postscript. 1954.
Downer, A. S. Mr Dangle's defence: acting and stage history. Eng Inst Essays 1946.
Byrne, M. St C. A history of Shakespearian production in England, part 1: 1700–1800. 1948.
—— Fifty years of Shakespearian production 1898–1948. Sh Survey 2 1949.
Farjeon, H. The Shakespearian scene: dramatic criticisms. 1949. On 20th-century productions.
Mann, I. R. The first recorded production of a Shakespearian play in Stratford. Sh Assoc Bull 24 1949.
Purdom, C. B. Producing Shakespeare. 1950.
Watkins, R. On producing Shakespeare. 1950.
David, R. Shakespeare's comedies and the modern stage. Sh Survey 4 1951.
Gielgud, J. Tradition, style and the theatre today. Ibid.
Hogan, C. B. Shakespeare in the theatre 1701–1800. 2 vols Oxford 1952–7.
Mander, R. and J. Mitchenson. Hamlet through the ages. 1952.
Wilson, J. D. and T. C. Worsley. Shakespeare's histories at Stratford 1951. 1952.
Hook, L. Shakespeare improv'd: or a case for the affirmative. Sh Quart 4 1953.
Armstrong, W. A. Shakespeare and the acting of Edward Alleyn. Sh Survey 7 1954.
Bryant, J. A. Shakespeare's Falstaff and the mantle of Dick Tarlton. SP 51 1954.
Speaight, R. William Poel and the Elizabethan revival. 1954.
Branam, G. C. Eighteenth-century adaptations of Shakespearean tragedy. Berkeley 1956.

Ruppel, K. H. Shakespeare und die Oper. Sh Jb 95 1959.
Evans, G. B. Shakespearean prompt-books of the seventeenth century. 4 vols Charlottesville 1961–6. Vol 1, The Padua Macbeth, 1961; vol 2, The Padua Measure for measure and the Winter's tale, 1963; vol 3, The 'Nursery' Comedy of errors and Midsummer night's dream; vol 4, The Smock Alley Hamlet, 1966.
Spencer, C. (ed). Davenant's Macbeth. New Haven 1961.
—— Five Restoration adaptations of Shakespeare. Urbana 1965. Macbeth, 1674; Tempest, 1674; History of King Lear, 1681; Tragical history of King Richard III, 1700; Jew of Venice, 1701.
Shattuck, C. H. William Charles Macready's King John: a facsimile prompt-book. Urbana 1962.
—— Mr Macready produces As you like it: a prompt-book study. Urbana 1962.
—— The Shakespeare promptbooks: a descriptive catalogue. Urbana 1965.
—— Shakespeare promptbooks of the 17th and 18th centuries. Restoration & 18th-century Theatre Research 3 1965.
—— Edwin Booth's Hamlet. Harvard Lib Bull 15 1967.
—— The Hamlet of Edwin Booth. Urbana 1969.
Deelman, C. The great Shakespeare jubilee. 1964.
England, M. W. Garrick's jubilee. Columbus 1964.
Stockholm, J. M. Garrick's folly. 1964.
Trewin, J. C. Shakespeare on the English stage 1900–64: a survey of productions. 1964.
Wells, S. W. Shakespearian burlesques. Sh Quart 16 1965. 19th-century burlesques.
Bernhardt, W. W. Troilus and Cressida and Dryden's Truth found too late. Sh Quart 20 1969.

Literary Influence in England

Only books and articles recording fairly substantial influence are listed. For notes recording traces of influence and echoes and allusions, see annual bibliographies in Sh Quart.

Elliott, G. R. Shakespeare's significance for Browning. Anglia 32 1909.
Dibelius, W. Dickens und Shakespeare. Sh Jb 52 1916.
Rothbarth, M. Pope and Shakespeare. Anglia 39 1916.
Brewer, J. W. Shakespeare's influence on Sir Walter Scott. Boston 1925.
Cowl, R. P. Echoes of Henry IV in Elizabethan drama. TLS 22 Oct 1925.
—— Some echoes in Elizabethan drama of Shakespeare's King Henry IV. 1927.
Murry, J. M. Keats and Shakespeare. Oxford 1925.
Thaler, A. The Shakespearean element in Milton. PMLA 40 1925; expanded in his Shakespeare's silences, Cambridge Mass 1929.
—— Shakespeare and Sir Thomas Browne. In his Shakespeare's silences, Cambridge Mass 1929.
—— Shakespeare and our world. Tennessee Stud in Lit 2 1957.
—— Shakespeare and our world. Knoxville 1966.
Garrod, H. W. Milton's lines on Shakespeare. E & S 12 1926.
Taylor, G. C. Shakespeare and Milton again. SP 23 1926.
Spurgeon, C. F. E. Keats's Shakespeare. Oxford 1928.
Jones, F. L. Echoes of Shakespeare in later Elizabethan drama. PMLA 45 1930.
Sutherland, J. R. Shakespeare's imitators in the eighteenth century. MLR 28 1933.
Du Bois, A. E. Shakespeare and 19th-century drama. ELH 1 1934.
Probst, E. Der Einfluss Shakespeares auf die Stuart-Trilogie Swinburnes. Munich 1934.
Price, H. T. Allusions to Shakespeare. Sh Assoc Bull 11 1936. On 17th century. See also W. Sloane 13 1938.
McGinn, D. J. Shakespeare's influence on the drama of his age studied in Hamlet. New Brunswick NJ 1938.
McKeithan, D. M. The debt to Shakespeare in the Beaumont-and-Fletcher plays. Austin 1938.

Vandiver, E. P. Sh Assoc Bull 12–14 1937–9, 21 1946, Forman Stud 34 1951. Notes on influence in Victorian period.

Brown, I. and G. Fearon. Amazing monument: a short history of the Shakespeare industry. 1939.

Mooney, E. A. Tennyson's earliest Shakespeare parallels. Sh Assoc Bull 15 1940.

Gordon, R. K. Shakespeare's Henry IV and the Waverley novels. MLR 37 1942.

Bentley, G. E. Shakespeare and Jonson: their reputations in the seventeenth century compared. 2 vols Chicago 1945.

Haber, T. B. What fools these mortals be! Housman's poetry and the lyrics of Shakespeare. MLQ 6 1945.

Moore, J. R. The tempest and Robinson Crusoe. RES 21 1945.

Weber, C. J. Tragedy and the good life. Dalhousie Rev 25 1945. Shakespeare and Hardy.

Seaton, E. Comus and Shakespeare. E & S 31 1945.

Heilman, R. B. Falstaff and Smollett's Micklewhimmen. RES 22 1946.

Heine, A. Shakespeare in James Joyce. Sh Assoc Bull 24 1949.

Langston, B. Shelley's use of Shakespeare. HLQ 12 1949.

Peery, W. Shakhisbeard at Finnegans Wake. SE 30 1951.
— The Hamlet of Stephen Dedalus. SE 31 1952.

Noyes, R. G. The Thespian mirrors: Shakespeare in the eighteenth-century novel. Providence 1953.

Hodgart, M. J. C. Shakespeare and Finnegans Wake. Cambridge Jnl Sept 1953.

Smith, C. J. The effect of Shakespeare's influence on Wordsworth's The borderers. SP 50 1953.

Musgrove, S. Shakespeare and Jonson. Auckland 1957.

Schutte, W. M. Joyce and Shakespeare: a study in the meaning of Ulysses. New Haven 1957.

Davril, R. Shakespeare and Ford. Sh Jb 94 1958.

Adler, J. H. Shakespeare and Christopher Fry. Educational Theatre Jnl 11 1959.

Fricker, R. Shakespeare und das englische romantische Drama. Sh Jb 95 1959.

Gerstner-Hirzel, A. Die Bedeutung Shakespeares für T. S. Eliot. Ibid.

Knight, G. W. Shakespeare and Byron's plays. Ibid.

Major, J. M. Comus and the Tempest. Sh Quart 10 1959.

James, D. G. Keats and King Lear. Sh Survey 13 1960.

Schanzer, E. Heywood's Ages and Shakespeare. RES new ser 11 1960.

Biggins, D. Measure for measure and the Heart of Midlothian. Etudes Anglaises 14 1961.

Viebrock, H. Shakespeare und die englische Romantik. Sh Jb 97 1961. Influence on Coleridge and Keats.

Bemrose, J. M. A critical examination of the borrowings from Venus and Adonis and Lucrece in Samuel Nicholson's Acolastus. Sh Quart 15 1964.

Proudfoot, R. Shakespeare and the new dramatists of the King's men 1606–13. In Later Shakespeare, ed J. R. Brown and B. Harris 1966.

Frost, D. L. The school of Shakespeare: the influence of Shakespeare on English drama 1600–42. Cambridge 1968.

Shakespeare Abroad

Only the principal trns of the complete works, or of substantial portions of the works, are listed here. For trns of individual plays see annual bibliographies.

General Studies

Robertson, J. G. The knowledge of Shakespeare on the Continent at the beginning of the eighteenth century. MLR 1 1906.
— Shakespeare on the Continent. CHEL vol 5 1910.

Herford, C. H. A sketch of the history of Shakespeare's influence on the Continent. Bull John Rylands Lib 9 1925.

Witmann, W. Hamlets Bühnenlaufbahn 1601–1877. Leipzig 1931.

Ralli, A. A history of Shakespearian criticism. 2 vols Oxford 1932.

Conklin, P. S. A history of Hamlet criticism 1601–1821. New York 1947.

FRENCH

Histories and Studies

Michiels, A. Histoire des idées littéraires en France. Brussels 1842.

Lacroix, A. De l'influence de Shakespeare sur le théâtre français. Brussels 1856.

Pellissier, G. Le drame Shakespearien en France. In his Essais de littérature contemporaine, Paris 1893.

Engel, J. Shakespeare in Frankreich. Sh Jb 34 1898.

Jusserand, J. J. Shakespeare en France. Paris 1898; tr 1899.

Baldensperger, F. Esquisse d'une histoire de Shakespeare en France. In Etudes d'histoire littéraire: série 2, Paris 1910.

Haines, C. Shakespeare in France. 1925 (Sh Assoc).

Rudwin, M. Shakespeare en France. Sh Assoc Bull 20 1945.

Chambrun, C. L. de. Shakespeare across the Channel. In J. Q. Adams memorial studies, Washington 1948.

Smet, R. de. Othello in Paris and Brussels. Sh Survey 3 1950.

Horn-Monval, M. Les traductions françaises de Shakespeare. Paris 1964.

Seventeenth Century

Jusserand, J. J. Allusions to Shakespeare. Revue Critique d'Histoire et de Littérature 14 Nov 1887.

Texte, J. Sur la première mention du nom de Shakespeare dans un ouvrage imprimé en français. Revue d'Histoire Littéraire 15 Oct 1894.

Lancaster, H. C. The alleged first foreign estimate of Shakespeare. MLN 63 1948.

Eighteenth Century

Lotheissen, F. Literatur und Gesellschaft in Frankreich zur Zeit der Revolution. Weimar 1872.

Blaze de Bury, H. Shakespeare et Voltaire. Revue des Deux Mondes 15 Aug 1873; rptd in his Tableaux romantiques de littérature et d'art, Paris 1878.

König, W. Voltaire und Shakespeare. Sh Jb 10 1875.

Kühn, C. Ueber Ducis in seiner Beziehung zu Shakespeare. Jena 1875.

Morandi, L. Voltaire contro Shakespeare, Baretti contro Voltaire. Rome 1882, Città di Castello 1884 (rev and enlarged).

Rosières, R. La littérature en France de 1750 à 1800. Revue Politique et Littéraire 19 Aug 1882; rptd in his Recherches sur la poésie contemporaine, Paris 1896.

Penning, G. E. Ducis als Nachahmer Shakespeares. Bremen 1884.

Humbert, C. Voltaire ein Bewunderer Shakespeares. Neue Jahrbücher für Philologie und Pädagogik (Leipzig) 133–4 1886.

Ballantyne, A. Voltaire's visit to England. 1893.

Lion, H. Les tragédies et les théories dramatiques de Voltaire. Paris 1896.

Faguet, E. Voltaire critique de Shakespeare. Revue des Cours et Conférences 15 Nov 1900.

Lounsbury, T. R. Shakespeare and Voltaire. New York 1902.

Dubedout, E. J. Shakespeare and Voltaire. MP 3 1905.

Robertson, J. G. The knowledge of Shakespeare on the Continent at the beginning of the eighteenth century. MLR 1 1906.

Cushing, M. G. P. le Tourneur. New York 1909.

Dargan, E. P. Shakespeare and Ducis. MP 10 1906.

Briese, W. Shakespeares Julius Caesar und La mort de César von Voltaire. Zeitschrift für Französischen und Englischen Unterricht 15 1916.

Van Tieghem, P. L'année littéraire (1754–90) comme intermédiaire en France des littératures étrangères. Paris 1917.

Finch, M. B. and E. A. Peers. Walpole's relations with Voltaire. MP 18 1920.

Hunter, A. C. Un introducteur de la littérature anglaise en France: J. B. Suard. Paris 1925.

Sonet, E. Voltaire et l'influence anglaise. Rennes 1926.

Chase, C. B. The young Voltaire. New York 1926.

Looten, C. La première controverse internationale sur Shakespeare entre l'abbé Le Blanc et W. Guthrie. Lille 1927.

Dargan, E. P. The question of Voltaire's primacy in establishing the English vogue. In Mélanges Baldensperger, Paris 1930.

Downs, B. W. Ducis's two Hamlets. MLR 30 1936.

Monaco, M. Shakespeare on the French stage in the eighteenth century. Bryn Mawr 1939.

Shackleton, R. Shakespeare in French translation. Modern Languages 23 1941. On 18th-century trns of La Place, Le Tourneur, Ducis.

Havens, G. R. Voltaire and English critics of Shakespeare. Franco-Amer pamphlets 2 1944.

Vanderhoof, M. B. (ed). Hamlet, a tragedy adapted from Shakespeare (1770) by Jean François Ducis: a critical edition. Proc Amer Philosophical Soc 97 1953.

Desné, R. Diderot et Shakespeare. Revue de Littérature Comparée 41 1967.

Besterman, T. Voltaire on Shakespeare. Stud on Voltaire & Eighteenth Century 54 1967.

Nineteenth and Twentieth Centuries

Gautier, T. Histoire de l'art dramatique en France. 2 vols Paris 1858–9.

Reymond, W. Corneille, Shakespeare et Goethe: étude sur l'influence anglo-germanique en France au xixe siècle. Berlin 1864.

Renard, G. L'influence de l'Angleterre sur la France depuis 1830. Nouvelle Revue 15 Aug 1885.

Wattendorff, L. Essai sur l'influence que Shakespeare a exercée sur la tragédie romantique française. Pt 1, Coblenz 1888.

—— Essay on the influence which Shakespeare exercised on the French romantic tragedy. Pt 2, Coblenz 1889.

Fricke, E. Der Einfluss Shakespeares auf Mussets Dramen. Basle 1901.

Latreille, C. G. Sand et Shakespeare. In Annales Internationales d'Histoire, Congrès de Paris: section vi, Histoire comparée des littératures, Paris 1901.

Le Roy, A. L'aube du théâtre romantique. Paris 1904.

Gunnell, D. Stendhal et l'Angleterre. Paris 1908.

Borgerhoff, J. L. Le théâtre anglais à Paris sous la Restauration. Paris 1913.

Latreille, C. Un épisode de l'histoire de Shakespeare en France. Revue d'Histoire Littéraire de la France 23 1916.

Girard, H. Emile Deschamps. Paris 1921.

Draper, F. M. W. The rise and fall of the French romantic drama, with special reference to the influence of Shakespeare, Scott and Byron. 1923.

Larat, J. La tradition et l'exotisme dans l'oeuvres de Ch. Nodier. Paris 1923.

Carré, J. M. Maeterlinck et les littératures étrangères. Revue de Littérature Comparée 6 1929.

Reynaud, L. Le romantisme: ses origines anglo-germaniques. Paris 1926.

Sessely, A. Influence de Shakespeare sur A. de Vigny. Berne 1928.

Estève, E. Banville et Shakespeare. In Mélanges Baldensperger, Paris 1930.

Rickey, H. W. Musset Shakespearien. Bordeaux 1932.

Keys, A. C. Les adaptations musicales de Shakespeare en France jusqu'en 1870. Paris 1933.

Baym, M. Baudelaire and Shakespeare. Sh Assoc Bull 15 1940.

Whitridge, A. Shakespeare and Delacroix. Sh Assoc Bull 17 1942.

Guille, F. V. François-Victor Hugo et son oeuvre. Paris 1950.

Legouis, E. La terre de Zola et le Roi Lear. Revue de Littérature Comparée 27 1953.

Berton, J. C. Shakespeare et Claudel. Geneva 1958.

Merian-Genast, E. Der Einfluss Shakespeares auf das französische romantische Drama. Sh Jb 95 1959.

Fort, J. B. François-Victor Hugo, traducteur de Shakespeare. Etudes Anglaises 13 1960.

Alter, J. V. Apollinaire and two Shakespeare sonnets. Comparative Lit 14 1962.

Bailey, H. P. Hamlet in France from Voltaire to Laforgue. Geneva 1964.

Translations

Complete Works

Shakespeare, traduit de l'Anglois par P. Le Tourneur, le Comte de Catuelan et J. Fontaine-Malherbe. 20 vols Paris 1776–82; rev F. Guizot, F. de Barante and A. P[ichot] 13 vols Paris 1821.

Oeuvres complètes. Tr M. F. Michel 3 vols Paris 1839.

Oeuvres complètes. Tr B. Laroche 2 vols Paris 1839–40, 7 vols Paris 1842–3.

Oeuvres complètes. Tr F.-V. Hugo 18 vols Paris 1859–66.

Oeuvres complètes. Tr E. Montégut 10 vols Paris 1867–73.

Oeuvres dramatiques. Tr G. Duval 8 vols Paris 1908–9.

Les comédies; les tragédies; les drames historiques; et les poèmes lyriques: nouvelle traduction française par P. Messiaen. 3 vols Paris 1939–44.

Oeuvres complètes. Ed P. Leyris and H. Evans, Paris 1957.

Selections

Le théâtre anglois. [Tr P. A. de la Place] 8 vols Paris 1745.

Chefs d'oeuvre de Shakespeare. Tr A. Bruguière de Sorsum, rev M. de Chênedollé 2 vols Paris 1826.

Chefs-d'oeuvre de Shakespeare traduits par les plus célèbres littérateurs sous la direction de D. O'Sullivan. 3 vols Paris 1836–9.

Legouis, E. Pages choisies des grands écrivains: Shakespeare. Paris 1899.

Oeuvres choisies: traduction et notice par G. Roth. 3 vols Paris 1918.

Oeuvres choisies: traduction nouvelle par A. Feuillerat (Les cent chefs-d'oeuvre étrangers). 2 vols Paris 1922.

Les tragédies de Shakespeare. Tr S. Bing and J. Capeau 5 vols Paris 1939.

The Poems

Poèmes et sonnets, traduits en ver français par E. Lafond. Paris 1856.

Sonnets, traduits en vers français par A. Copin. Paris 1888. Partly pbd in Revue d'Art Dramatique 1887–8.

Sonnets, traduits en sonnets français par F. Henry. Paris 1900.

Sonnets: essai d'une interprétation en vers français par Ch. M. Garnier. Cahiers de la Quinzaine 23 Dec 1906, 31 March 1907; rev in Collection Shakespeare, 1922.

Les poèmes intimes et le Pèlerin passionné. Tr A. Doysié, Paris 1919.

Vénus et Adonis. Tr E. Godefroy, Paris 1921. First ptd in Vers et Prose 11–12 1907–8.

Sonnets. Tr E. Le Brun, Paris [1927].

Vénus et Adonis, suivi du Pèlerin passionné. Tr M. Chastelain, Paris 1939.

Le viol de Lucrèce. Tr M. Chastelain, Paris 1944.

Les sonnets de Shakespeare, traduits en vers français et accompagnés d'un commentaire continu par F. Baldensperger. Berkeley 1943.

Poèmes. Tr J. Fuzier, ed H. Fluchère, Paris 1960.

Poèmes et sonnets. Tr P. Rafroidi et J.-P. Hulin, Paris 1965.

Criticism

Boyer, A. The compleat French master. [1700?], [1705?], 1710.

Le spectateur ou le Socrate moderne, traduit de l'anglois. Amsterdam 1714, 1716–18, 1722–30. Translator's note.

Dissertation sur la poésie anglaise. Journal Littéraire (Hague) 1717.

Prévost, A. F. Mémoires d'un homme de qualité. Paris 1728.

—— Le pour et le contre. Paris 1733 etc. Articles on Shakespeare, 1738 etc.

Voltaire, F. A. de. Essai sur la poésie épique. Paris 1728.

—— Oedipe. Paris 1730. Préface.

—— Brutus. Paris 1731. Préface: Discours sur la tragédie à Mylord Bolingbroke.

—— Zaïre. Paris 1733. Epitre dédicatoire.

—— Letters concerning the English nation. 1733 (a trn); Lettres sur les Anglois, 'Basle' (for London) 1734.

—— La mort de César. Paris 1936. Préface.

—— Sémiramis. Paris 1749. Dissertation sur la tragédie.

—— Appel à toutes les nations de l'Europe. Paris 1761; rptd as Du théâtre anglais par Jerôme Carré in Contes de Guillaume Vadé, Paris 1764.

—— Observations sur le J. César de Shakespeare. Preface to Commentaires sur Médée et le Cid, in Théâtre de P. Corneille, Paris 1764.

—— Questions sur L'Encyclopédie (Art dramatique, Goût etc). 1770–1. Included in Dictionnaire philosophique, ed Kehl, Paris 1784–90.

—— Lettre à l'Académie française. Paris 1776.

—— Irène. Paris 1778. Lettre à L'Académie.

Riccoboni, L. Réflexions historiques et critiques sur les différents théâtres de l'Europe. Paris 1738.

Le Blanc, Abbé. Lettres d'un François. 3 vols Hague 1745, Amsterdam 1751.

La Place, P. A. de. Discours sur le théâtre anglois. In Théâtre anglois, Paris 1745.

Hénault, Président. Nouveau théâtre françois: François II. Paris 1747. Préface.

Chauffepié, J. G. de. Nouveau dictionnaire historique. Vol 4, Amsterdam 1750 etc.

Diderot, D., J. d'Alembert et al. Encyclopédie. Paris 1750 etc.

Fiquet du Bocage. Lettres sur le théâtre anglois. 2 vols Paris 1752.

L'Année Littéraire. Paris 1754–90.

Journal Etranger Dec 1755.

d'Arnaud, F. T. de Baculard. Supplément à la 1ère édition du Comte de Comminges: second discours préliminaire. Hague 1765.

Suard, J. B. A. Essai historique sur l'origine et le progrès du drame anglais: observations sur Shakespeare. In his Variétés littéraires, 4 vols Paris 1768.

Marmontel, J. F. Chefs-d'oeuvre dramatiques: discours sur la tragédie. Paris 1773.

Journal Anglais 1 1775.

Mercier, S. De la littérature et des littérateurs. Paris 1778.

Rivarol, A. De l'universalité de la langue française. Paris 1785; rptd in his Oeuvres vol 2, Paris 1808.

Chénier, M. J. Lettre sur Jules César [1788]. In A. Chénier, Oeuvres posthumes, Paris 1826.

La Harpe, F. J. Cours de littérature. Paris 1799.

—— Correspondance littéraire avec le Grand Duc de Russie. Paris 1801.

Staël, Mme de. De la littérature. Paris 1800.

Chateaubriand, F. R. de. Shakespeare. Mercure de France 1801. In Oeuvres complètes vol 8, Paris 1836–9; incorporated in Essai sur la littérature anglaise (1836) vol 33, 1836–9.

—— Essai sur la littérature anglaise. Paris 1836; Oeuvres complètes vol 33, Paris 1836–9. Partly pbd in Revue des Deux Mondes 1 Jan 1836.

Grimm, F. M. and D. Diderot. Correspondance littéraire. Paris 1812; ed Tourneux 1877.

[Dupin, C.] Lettre à Milady Morgan sur Racine et sur Shakespeare. Paris 1818.

Geoffroy, J. L. Cours de littérature dramatique. Paris 1819–20.

Buchon, J. A. Biographie de Shakespeare et coup d'oeil général sur le caractère distinctif de son génie. Revue Encyclopédique 11 1821.

Guizot, F. P. G. Sur la vie et les oeuvres de Shakespeare. In Oeuvres complètes, Paris 1821.

—— Shakespeare et son temps. Paris 1852; tr 1852.

'Stendhal' (Henri Beyle). Racine et Shakespeare. 2 vols Paris 1823–5.

Hugo, V. Cromwell. Paris 1827. Préface.

Le Globe. 1824–30. Especially the 28 articles by C. Magnin 1827–8 rptd in his Causeries et méditations, Paris 1843.

Villemain, A. F. Essai littéraire sur Shakespeare. In Nouveaux mélanges historiques et littéraires, Paris 1827; rev in his Etudes de littérature ancienne et étrangère, Paris 1846.

Deschamps, E. Etudes françaises et étrangères. Paris 1828.

Duport, P. Essais littéraires sur Shakespeare. 2 vols Paris 1828; tr 1834.

Vigny, A. de. Othello. Paris 1830. Préface (1829).

—— Seconde préface d'Othello. Paris 1839.

'Morlaix, A.' (L. de Wailly). Sonnets de Shakespeare. Revue des Deux Mondes 15 Dec 1834.

Chasles, P. Caractères et paysages. Paris 1833.

—— Cervantès et Shakespeare. Revue de Paris new ser 13 1835.

—— Etudes sur Shakespeare, Marie Stuart et l'Arétin. Paris 1851; rptd in his L'Angleterre au xvie siècle, Paris 1879.

—— Etudes contemporaines. Paris 1867.

—— Shakespeare's sonnets. Athenaeum 25 Jan 1862, Feb–May 1867.

Dumas, A. Sur le génie de Shakespeare. Preface to B. Laroche's trn. Paris 1839.

Girardin, Saint-Marc. In his Cours de littérature dramatique, Paris 1843.

Sainte-Beuve, A. de. Causeries du lundi. 15 vols Paris 1851–62.

Lemoinne, J. Etudes critiques et biographiques. Paris 1853.

Janin, J. Histoire de la littérature dramatique. Paris 1853.

Lucas, H. Curiosités dramatiques et littéraires. Paris 1855.

Montégut, E. Types modernes en littérature: Hamlet. Revue des Deux Mondes 1 April 1856; rptd in his Types littéraires et fantaisies esthétiques, Paris 1882.

—— Une hypothèse sur la Tempête. Revue des Deux Mondes 1 Aug 1865; rptd in his Essais sur la littérature anglaise, Paris 1883.

Mézières, A. Shakespeare: ses oeuvres et ses critiques. Paris 1860.

Rio, A. F. Shakespeare. Paris 1864; rptd as Shakespeare Catholique, Paris 1875.

Hugo, V. W. Shakespeare. Paris 1864; tr 1864.

Lamartine, A. de. Shakespeare et son oeuvre. Paris 1864; tr in his Biography and portraits of some celebrated people, 1866.

Taine, H. In his Histoire de la littérature anglaise, Paris 1864.

Büchner, A. Les comédies de Shakespeare. Paris 1865.

—— Hamlet le Danois. Paris 1878.

Schérer, E. Etudes critiques sur la littérature contemporaine vol 3. Paris 1866; tr G. Saintsbury 1891.

Blaze de Bury, H. Shakespeare et ses musiciens. Revue des Deux Mondes 15 May 1867; rptd in Tableaux romantiques de littérature et d'art, Paris 1878.

—— Hamlet et ses commentateurs depuis Goethe. Revue des Deux Mondes 15 March 1868; rptd ibid.

Courdaveaux, V. Caractères et talents. Paris 1867.

—— Etudes sur la littérature ancienne et moderne. Paris 1867.

Jullien, B. Shakespeare considéré comme poète dramatique. Paris 1867.

Brierre de Boismont, A. Shakespeare. In his Etudes médico-psychologiques sur les hommes célèbres. Paris 1869.

Gomont, H. Le César de Shakespeare: étude historique et littéraire. Paris 1874.

Onimus, E. La psychologie médicale dans les drames de Shakespeare. Revue des Deux Mondes 1 April 1876.

Lichtenberger, E. De carminibus Shakesperiensibus cum nova Thorpianae inscriptionis interpretatione. Paris 1877.

Reinach, T. Hamlet. Nouvelle Revue 1 1879.

Stapfer, P. Shakespeare et l'antiquité; Molière, Shakespeare et la critique allemande. 2 vols Paris 1879–80; tr 1880.

Copin, A. Les sonnets de Shakespeare. Revue d'Art Dramatique Nov–Dec 1887.

Bourget, P. In his Etudes et portraits vol 1, Paris 1889.

Darmesteter, J. Shakespeare. Paris 1889.

Pinloche, A. De Shakesperii Hamleto et germanica tragoedia quae inscribitur: Der bestrafte Brudermord. Paris 1890.

Bouchor, M. Shakespeare au théâtre. Revue de Paris 1 Sept 1895.

Pilon, E. Les fêtes athéniennes: les sites Shakespeariens. Revue d'Art Dramatique 5 Feb 1898.

Legouis, E. Introd to his Pages choisies, Paris 1900.

—— The Bacchic element in Shakespeare's plays. Proc Br Acad 12 1926; tr French, Revue Anglo-américaine 3 1926.

—— La réaction contre la critique romantique de Shakespeare. E & S 13 1928.

Coquelin, C. Molière et Shakespeare. Grande Revue 1 Jan 1901.

Filon, A. Les sonnets de Shakespeare. Revue des Deux Mondes 15 April 1901.

Delacour, A. La religion de Shakespeare. Mercure de France Feb 1902.

Brémond, H. La légende de Shakespeare. Etudes July–Sept 1902.

—— Les généraux de Shakespeare. Correspondant 25 April 1916.

Bellaigue, C. Shakespeare et la musique. Revue des Deux Mondes 15 May 1903.

Jusserand, J. J. In his Histoire littéraire du peuple anglais vol 2, Paris 1904; tr 1906.

—— In his School for ambassadors, 1924.

Castelain, M. Shakespeare et Ben Jonson. Revue Germanique 3 1907.

Pellissier, G. Shakespeare et la superstition Shakespearienne. Paris 1914.

Richepin, J. A. A travers Shakespeare. Paris 1914.

Chevrillon, A. Shakespeare et l'âme anglaise. Revue de Paris 15 May 1916; rptd in his Trois études de littérature anglaise, Paris 1921; tr 1923.

Vigouroux, A. La pathologie mentale dans les drames de Shakespeare. Annales Médico-psychologiques 10th ser 10 1918.

Longworth-Chambrun, C. G. Florio: un apôtre de la Renaissance. 1921.

—— Shakespeare acteur-poète. Paris 1926; tr 1927.

—— Shakespeare, Southampton et la conjuration d'Essex. Revue Anglo-américaine 3 1925.

Feuillerat, A. Shakespeare, Oeuvres choisies. Paris 1922. Introd.

Bastide, C. Shakespeare et les idées politiques de son temps. Revue des Sciences Politiques 46 1923.

'Fagus' (G. Faillet). Essai sur Shakespeare. Amiens 1923.

Looten, C. Shakespeare et la religion. Paris 1924.

Marie, A. A la recherche de Shakespeare. Paris 1924.

Pourtalès, G. de. De Hamlet à Swann. Paris 1924.

Berthelot, R. La sagesse Shakespearienne. Revue de Métaphysique et de Morale 23 April 1926; rptd in La sagesse de Shakespeare et de Goethe, Paris 1930.

Fréjaville, G. Les travestis de Shakespeare. Paris 1930.

Gillet, L. Shakespeare. Paris 1931.

GERMAN

Histories and Studies

Koberstein, A. Shakespeare in Deutschland. Sh Jb 1 1865.

Genée, R. Geschichte der Shakespeareschen Dramen in Deutschland. Leipzig 1870.

Oehlmann, W. Shakespeares Wert für unsere nationale Literatur. Sh Jb 5 1870.

Richter, K. A. Beiträge zum Bekanntwerden Shakespeares in Deutschland. 3 pts Breslau 1909–12.

Brandl, A. Shakespeare and Germany. Proc Br Acad 6 1913.

Price, L. M. English-German literary influences: bibliography and survey. Berkeley 1920.

Förster, M. Shakespeare und Deutschland. Sh Jb 57 1921.

Kahn, L. W. Shakespeares Sonette in Deutschland. Berne 1935.

Kindermann, H. Shakespeare und das deutsche Volkstheater. Sh Jb 72 1936.

Ritter, E. Die Dramaturgie der Zyklenaufführungen von Shakespeares Königsdramen in Deutschland. Emsdetten 1937.

Petsch, R. Die dramatischen Figuren bei Shakespeare, Goethe, Kleist und anderen Dramatikern. Archiv 173 1938.

Schlosser, R. Der deutsche Shakespeare. Sh Jb 74 1938.

Müller, J. Shakespeare im Deutschunterricht. Zeitschrift für Deutschkunde 52 1939.

Stahl, E. L. Shakespeare und das deutsche Theater. Stuttgart 1947.

Special Periods

Cohn, A. Shakespeare in Germany in the 16th and 17th centuries. 1865.

Hense, C. C. Deutsche Dichter in ihrem Verhältnis zu Shakespeare. Sh Jb 5–6 1870–1. The Sturm und Drang period and Goethe, Schiller, Kleist, Tieck.

Suphan, B. Shakespeare im Anbruch der klassischen Zeit unserer Literatur. Sh Jb 25 1890.

Walther, E. Der Einfluss Shakespeares auf die Sturm und Drangperiode unserer Literatur. Chemnitz 1890.

Joachimi-Dege, M. Deutsche Shakespeare-Probleme im 18 Jahrhundert und im Zeitalter der Romantik. Leipzig 1907.

Böhtlingk, A. Shakespeare und unsere Klassiker 1: Lessing und Shakespeare; 11: Goethe und Shakespeare; 111: Schiller und Shakespeare. 3 vols Leipzig 1909–10.

Gundolf, F. Shakespeare und der deutsche Geist vor dem Auftreten Lessings. Heidelberg 1911, Berlin 1911 (enlarged as Shakespeare und der deutsche Geist).

Richter, K. A. Shakespeare in Deutschland 1739–70. Oppeln 1912.

Brüggemann, F. (ed). Die Aufnahme Shakespeares auf der Bühne der Aufklärung in den sechziger und siebziger Jahren. Leipzig 1937. German trns of 4 plays.

Pascal, R. Shakespeare in Germany 1740–1815. Cambridge 1937.

Kluckhohn, P. Die Dramatiker der deutschen Romantik als Shakespeare-Jünger. Sh Jb 74 1938.

Schweinshaupt, G. Shakespeares Dramatik in ihrer gehaltlichen und formalen Umwandlung auf dem österreichischen Theater des 18 Jahrhunderts. Königsberg 1938.

Sehrt, E. T. Shakespeareforschung 1937–52 in Deutschland und der Schweiz. Anglia 71 1952.

Brennecke, E. and H. Shakespeare in Germany 1590–1700, with translations of five early plays. Chicago 1964. Titus Andronicus, Midsummer night's dream, Merchant of Venice, Twelfth Night, Hamlet.

Individual Authors

Götzinger, E. Das Shakespeare-Büchlein des Armen Mannes im Toggenburg [Ulrich Bräker] vom Jahre 1780. Sh Jb 12 1877.

Leo, F. A. Shakespeare und Goethe. Sh Jb 24 1889.

Wagner, C. B. Shakespeares Einfluss auf Goethe. Halle 1890.

Jacobowski, L. Klinger und Shakespeare. Freiburg 1891.

Rauch, H. Lenz und Shakespeare. Freiburg 1891.

Huther, A. Goethes Götz von Berlichingen und Shakespeares historische Dramen. Cottbus 1893.

Bartmann, H. Grabbes Verhältnis zu Shakespeare. Münster 1898.

Engel, F. Spuren Shakespeares in Schillers dramatischen Werken. Magdeburg 1901.

Zelak, D. Tieck und Shakespeare. Leipzig 1902.

Meisnest, F. W. Lessing und Shakespeare. PMLA 19 1904.

Schalles, E. A. Heines Verhältnis zu Shakespeare. Berlin 1904.

Kettner, G. Lessing und Shakespeare. Neue Jahrbücher für das Klassische Altertum 19 1907.

Alberts, W. Hebbels Stellung zu Shakespeare. Berlin 1908.

Gebhard, R. Shakespeare und Schopenhauer. Sh Jb 47 1911.

Hüttmann, W. C. F. Weisse und seine Zeit im ihrem Verhältnis zu Shakespeare. Bonn 1912.

Zinkernagel, F. Herders Shakespeare-Aufsatz. Bonn 1912.

Bolin, W. Grillparzers Shakespeare-Studien. Sh Jb 51 1915.

Gross, E. Grillparzers Verhältnis zu Shakespeare. Ibid.

Braun, H. Grillparzers Verhältnis zu Shakespeare. Munich 1916.

Fischer, B. Otto Ludwigs Trauerspielplan Der Sandwirt von Passeier und sein Verhältnis zu den Shakespeare-Studien. Greifswald 1916.

Friedrich, E. Gottsched—Shakespeare—Tolstoi. Die Neueren Sprachen 24 1917.

Lüdeke, H. Ludwig Tiecks Shakespeare-Studien. Frankfurt 1917.

— Ludwig Tieck und das alte englische Theater. Frankfurt 1922.

Nussberger, M. Schiller als politischer Dichter; Shakespeare und das deutsche Drama. Zürich 1917.

Eckert, H. Goethes Urteile über Shakespeare. Göttingen 1918.

Leitzmann, A. Dodds Beauties of Shakespeare als Quelle für Goethe und Herder. Sh Jb 55 1919.

Ludwig, A. Nietzsche und Shakespeare. Sh Jb 56 1920.

Corssen, M. Kleists und Shakespeares dramatische Gestalten. Sh Jb 58 1922.

— Kleist und Shakespeare. Weimar 1930.

Schneider, K. H. W. von Gerstenberg als Verkünder Shakespeares. Sh Jb 58 1922.

Deetjen, W. Goethe und Tiecks elisabethanische Studien. Sh Jb 65 1929.

Stern, A. Moses Mendelssohn und Shakespeare. Neue Schweizer Rundschau 1929.

Walzel, O. Der Kritiker Lessing und Shakespeare. Sh Jb 65 1929.

Deye, E. Shakespeare und Schiller. Munich 1931.

Petersen, J. Schiller und Shakespeare. Euphorion 32 1931.

Bartels, A. Hebbel und Shakespeare. Heide Holstein 1932.

Richter, H. Goethe und Shakespeare. Die Neueren Sprachen 40 1932.

Wahr, G. B. Goethe's Shakespeare. PQ 11 1932.

— The Hauptmann Hamlet. PQ 16 1937.

Dünninger, J. Raabe und Shakespeare. Germanisch-romanische Monatsschrift 22 1934.

Pfeiffer, E. Shakespeares und Tiecks Märchendramen. Bonn 1934.

Richter, F. Otto Ludwigs Trauerspielplan Tiberius Gracchus und sein Zusammenhang mit den Shakespeare-Studien. Breslau 1935.

Steck, P. Schiller und Shakespeare: eine statistische Untersuchung. Sh Jb 71 1935.

Fries, C. Shakespeare bei Kleist. Archiv 168 1936.

Jacob, G. Shakespeares Naturverbundenheit im Vergleich mit Schillers und Goethes Verhältnis zur Natur. Hamburg 1937.

Friese, H. Zu Goethes Hamleterklärung. Zeitschrift für Neusprachlichen Unterricht 37 1938.

Glücksmann, H. Grillparzer und Shakespeare. Jahrbuch der Grillparzer-Gesellschaft 34 1938.

Voigt, F. A. and A. Reichart. Hauptmann und Shakespeare: ein Beitrag zur Geschichte des Fortlebens Shakespeares in Deutschland. Breslau 1938.

Graham, P. G. Hebbel's study of King Lear. In Essays contributed in honor of President William Allan Neilson, Northampton Mass 1939.

Salinger, H. Shakespeare's tyranny over Grillparzer. Monatshefte für Deutschen Unterricht 31 1939.

Hering, G. F. Grabbe und Shakespeare. Sh Jb 76 1940.

Schöffler, H. Shakespeare und der junge Goethe. Ibid.

Lanz, M. Friedrich Maximilian Klinger und Shakespeare. Zürich 1941.

Verschaeve, C. Goethe und Shakespeare. Bruges 1941.

Wadepuhl, W. Heine und Shakespeare. Sh Assoc Bull 21 1946.

Kayser, R. Georg Herweghs Shakespeare-Auffassung. German Quart 20 1947.

Rehder, H. Novalis and Shakespeare. PMLA 63 1948.

Schröder, R. A. Goethe und Shakespeare. Sh Jb 84–6 1948–50.

Oppel, H. Das Shakespeare-Bild Goethes. Mainz 1949.

Schwartz, A. Otto Ludwig's Shakespearian criticism. In Perspectives of criticism, ed H. Levin, Cambridge Mass 1950.

Flatter, R. The veil of beauty: some aspects of verse and prose in Shakespeare and Goethe. JEGP 50 1951.

Krumpelmann, J. T. Kleist's Krug and Shakespeare's Measure for measure. Germanic Rev 26 1951.

— Shakespeare's Falstaff dramas and Kleist's Zerbrochener Krug. MLQ 12 1951.

Dobbek, W. Herder und Shakespeare. Sh Jb 91 1955.

Leuca, G. Wieland and the introduction of Shakespeare into Germany. German Quart 28 1955.

Meyen, F. Johann Joachim Eschenburg 1743–1820. Brunswick NJ 1957.

Steck, P. Der Einfluss Shakespeares auf die Technik der Meisterdramen Schillers. Sh Jb 96 1960.

Boyd, J. Goethe und Shakespeare. Cologne 1962.

The Translations
Modern Studies

Assman, C. Shakespeare und seine deutschen Übersetzer. Liegnitz 1843.

Genée, R. Geschichte der Shakespeareschen Dramen in Deutschland. Leipzig 1870.

Vincke, G. von. Zur Geschichte der deutschen Shakespeare-Übersetzungen. Sh Jb 16–17 1881–2.

Schroeer, A. Über Shakespeare-Übersetzungen. Die Neueren Sprachen 16 1909.

Drews, W. König Lear auf der deutschen Bühne im 17 und 18 Jahrhundert. Berlin 1932.

Mensel, E. H. (ed). Die erste deutsche Romeo-Übersetzung. Northampton Mass 1933.

Bergmann, A. Probe einer vergessenen Lear-Übersetzung. Sh Jb 72 1936. By A. von Sieten, 1914.

Ackermann, E. Shakespeare-deutsch: eine Einführung in das Übersetzungswerk von W. Josten. Hamburg 1937.

Gillies, A. Ludwig Tieck's English studies at the University of Göttingen 1792–4. JEGP 36 1937.

Ehrenreich, A. Ein deutscher Shakespeare von Walter Josten. Neuphilologische Monatsschrift 9 1938.

Voigt, F. A. and W. A. Reichart. Hauptmann und Shakespeare, mit einem Aufsatz und dramatischen Szenen von G. Hauptmann. Breslau 1938.

Winter, J.-W. Dorothea Tiecks Macbeth-Übersetzung. Berlin 1938.

Schücking, L. L. Shakespeares Stil als Übersetzungsproblem. Sh Jb 84–6 1948–50.

Stricker, K. Deutsche Shakespeare-Übersetzung im letzten Jahrhundert. Sh Jb 92 1956.

Heun, H. G. Shakespeare in deutschen Übersetzungen. Berlin 1957.

Atkinson, M. E. August Wilhelm Schlegel as translator of Shakespeare. Oxford 1959. Hamlet, Twelfth night, Julius Caesar.

Principal Translations

For early trns of individual plays see L. Unflad, Die Shakespeare-Literatur in Deutschland, Munich 1880. More recent trns are listed in annual bibliographies, such as those in Sh Jb and Sh Quart.

Wieland, C. M. Shakespeares theatralische Werke. 8 vols Zürich 1762–6. Prose. See M. Simpson, Eine Vergleichung der Wielandschen Shakespeare-Übersetzung mit dem Originale, Munich 1898; E. Stadler, Wielands Shakespeare, Strasbourg 1910; F. W. Meinsnest, Wieland's translation of Shakespeare, MLR 9 1914.

Eschenburg, J. J. Shakespeares Schauspiele. 13 vols Zürich 1775–82. Prose.

—— Shakespeares Schauspiele. 22 vols Strasbourg 1778–Mannheim 1783. See H. Uhde-Bernays, Der Mannheimer Shakespeare, Berlin 1902; H. Schrader, Eschenburg und Shakespeare, Marburg 1911.

Schlegel, A. W. Shakespeares dramatische Werke. 8 vols Berlin 1797–1801. Vol 9 added 1810. Only 17 plays. See M. Bernays, Zur Entstehungsgeschichte des Schlegel'schen Shakespeare, Leipzig 1872; R. Genée, A. W. Schlegel und Shakespeare, Berlin 1903; B. Assmann, Studien zur A. W. Schlegelschen Shakespeare-Übersetzung, Die Wortspiele, Dresden 1906.

—— Shakespeares dramatische Werke. Rev L. Tieck 9 vols Berlin 1825–33.

—— and L. Tieck. Shakespeares dramatische Werke. 12 vols Berlin 1839–40. See M. Bernays, Der Schlegel-Tiecksche Shakespeare, Sh Jb 1 1865; W. Wetz, Zur Beurteilung der Schlegel-Tieckschen Shakespeare-Übersetzung, E Studien 28 1900; A. Brandl, L. Fulda, P. Heyse und A. Wilbrandt über die Schlegel-Tiecksche Shakespeare-Übersetzung, Sh Jb 37 1901; F. Deibel, Dorothea Schlegel, Greifswald 1904; H. Lüdeke, Zur Tieckschen Shakespeare-Übersetzung, Sh Jb 55 1919; Ludwig Tiecks erste Shakespeare-Übersetzung 1794, Sh Jb 57 1921; Ludwig Tieck und das alte englische Theater, Frankfurt 1922; W. Fischer, Ludwig Tiecks Shakespeare, Die Neueren Sprachen 34 1926.

—— Shakespeares dramatische Werke. Rev H. Ulrici 12 vols Berlin 1867–71 (Deutsche Shakespeare-Gesellschaft); ed R. Gosche and R. Tschischwitz 8 vols Berlin 1877; rev M. Bernays 12 vols Berlin 1891; ed A. Brandl 10

vols Leipzig 1897–9; rev H. Conrad 5 vols Stuttgart 1905; ed W. Keller 5 vols Berlin 1912; ed J. Bab 9 vols Stuttgart 1923; ed L. L. Schücking and E. von Schaubert 10 vols Munich 1925–9 etc.

Voss, J. H., H. and A. Shakespeares Schauspiele. 9 vols Leipzig 1818–29.

Benda, J. W. O. Shakespeares dramatische Werke. Rev L. Tieck 9 vols Berlin 1825–33.

Ortlepp, Ernst. Shakespeares dramatische Werke. 16 vols Stuttgart 1838–9.

Böttger, A. et al. Shakespeares sämtliche dramatische Werke. 12 vols Leipzig 1839.

Keller, A. and M. Rapp. Shakespeares dramatische Werke. 37 vols Stuttgart 1843–7.

Dingelstedt, F. et al. Shakespeare in deutscher Übersetzung. 10 vols Hildburghausen 1867.

Bodenstedt, F. et al. Shakespeares dramatische Werke. 9 vols Leipzig 1867–71.

——, F. Freiligrath et al. Poetische Werke. Frankfurt 1957.

Gundolf, F. Shakespeare in deutscher Sprache. 10 vols Berlin 1908–23.

Rothe, H. Shakespeare in neuer Übersetzung. 3 vols Leipzig 1935, 9 vols Baden-Baden 1956–8, Munich 1963 (Der elisabethanische Shakespeare).

Mantey, K. G. Shakespeare-Volkslieder: Lieder aus Shakespeares dramatischen Werken. Leipzig 1939.

Krämer, I. Sonette. Basle 1945.

Rühle, O. Ausgewählte Werke. Stuttgart 1950.

Flatter, R. Shakespeare neu übersetzt. Vienna and Munich 1952–6.

Baudissin, W. Gesammelte Werke. 16 vols Munich 1964–5.

Criticism of Shakespeare

Morhof, D. G. Unterricht von der teutschen Sprache und Poesie. Kiel 1682.

Cramer, J. F. Vindiciae nominis germanici, contra quosdam obtrectatores gallos. Amsterdam 1694.

Acta eruditorum. Leipzig 1695.

Feind, B. Gedanken von der Opera, Gedichte 1. Stade 1708.

Allgemeines historisches Lexicon vol 4. Ed J. F. Buddens, Leipzig 1709.

Der Vernünfftler. Hamburg 1713. No 85.

Compendiöses Gelehrten-Lexicon. Ed J. B. Mencke, Leipzig 1715.

Bentheim, H. L. Engelländischer Kirch- und Schulen-Staat. Leipzig 1732 (2nd edn).

Bodmer, J. J. Miltons Verlust des Paradieses. Zürich 1732. Preface.

—— Critische Abhandlung von dem Wunderbaren in der Poesie. Zürich 1740.

—— Critische Betrachtungen der poetischen Gemählde der Dichter. Zürich 1741.

Borck, K. W. von. Versuch einer gebundenen Übersetzung des Trauerspiels vom Tode des Julius Caesar. Berlin 1741.

Gottsched, J. C. Beyträge zur kritischen Historie der deutschen Sprache vol 7. Leipzig 1741.

Schlegel, J. E. Vergleichung Shakespeares und Andreas Gryphs. In Gottsched's Beyträge vol 7, Leipzig 1741.

Neuer Büchersaal der schönen Wissenschaften und freyen Künste. Leipzig 1744–9.

Lessing, G. E. Beiträge zur Historie und Aufnahme des Theaters. 1750.

—— Theatralische Bibliothek. 1758.

—— Briefe, die neueste Literatur betreffend. No 17, 16 Feb 1759.

—— Hamburgische Dramaturgie. Nos 12, 15, 73, 1767–8.

Neue Erweiterungen der Erkenntnis und des Vergnügens. Frankfurt 1753 (life of Shakespeare), 1756 (trn of scenes from Richard III).

Neue Probestücke der englischen Schaubühne. Basle 1758. Trn of Romeo and Juliet.

Gerstenberg, H. W. von. Briefe über Merkwürdigkeiten der Literatur. Nos 14–18, Schleswig 1766–7.

Goethe, J. W. von. Zum Shakespeares Tag. 1771.

— Götz von Berlichingen. 1773.

— Wilhelm Meisters Lehrjahre. 1795–6.

— Romeo und Julia für das Theater bearbeitet. 1812.

— Shakespeare und kein Ende. 1815.

Herder, J. G. In his Von deutscher Art und Kunst, Hamburg 1773.

Lenz, J. M. R. Anmerkungen übers Theater nebst angehängtem übersetztem Stück Shakespeares, Amor vincit omnia [Love's labour's lost]. Leipzig 1774.

Eschenburg, J. J. Über Shakespeare. Zürich 1787.

Schlegel, A. W. Etwas über Shakespeare bei Gelegenheit Wilhelm Meisters. Die Hoven 4 1796.

— Über Shakespeares Romeo und Julia. Die Hoven 10 1797.

— Über dramatische Kunst und Literatur. Heidelberg 1809–11. Lectures 22–7.

Tieck, J. L. Der Sturm; nebst einer Abhandlung über Shakespeares Behandlung des Wunderbaren. Berlin 1796.

— Kritische Schriften vol 4. Leipzig 1852.

— Das Buch über Shakespeare. Ed H. Lüdeke, Halle 1920.

Schlegel, F. Die Griechen und Römer. Neustrelitz 1797.

— Geschichte der alten und neuen Literatur. Vienna 1815.

Schiller, J. F. von. Macbeth. 1801.

— Othello. 1805. Based on H. Voss's trn, above.

Ulrici, H. Über Shakespeares dramatische Kunst und sein Verhältnis zu Calderon und Goethe. Halle 1829.

Heine, H. Shakespeares Mädchen und Frauen. In his Sämtliche Werke vol 5, Leipzig 1839.

Hegel, G. W. F. Vorlesungen über Ästhetik. 3 vols Berlin 1842–3; ed F. Bassenge, Berlin 1955.

Gervinus, G. G. Shakespeare. 4 vols Leipzig 1849–50.

— Händel und Shakespeare. Leipzig 1868.

Delius, N. Der Mythus von Shakespeare. Bonn 1851.

— Über das englische Theaterwesen zu Shakespeares Zeit. Bonn 1853.

— Abhandlungen zu Shakespeare. 2 sers Elberfeld 1878–88.

Immermann, K. Theaterbriefe. Berlin 1851.

Mommsen, T. Marlowe und Shakespeare. Eisenach 1854.

— Romeo und Juliet. Oldenburg 1859.

Kreyssig, F. Vorlesungen über Shakespeare. 3 vols Berlin 1858.

Vischer, F. T. Kritische Gänge: neue Folge. Stuttgart 1861.

— Shakespeare-Vorträge. 6 vols Berlin 1899–1905.

Friesen, H. von. Shakespearestudien 3 vols Vienna 1864–76.

— Briefe über Shakespeares Hamlet. Leipzig 1864.

Tschischwitz, B. Shakespeare-Forschungen. Halle 1868.

Ludwig, O. Shakespeare-Studien. Leipzig 1871.

Bodenstedt, F. Shakespeares Frauencharaktere. Leipzig 1875.

Werder, K. Vorlesungen über Shakespeares Hamlet. Berlin 1875.

— Vorlesungen über Shakespeares Macbeth. Berlin 1885.

Elze, K. Shakespeare. Halle 1876.

— Abhandlungen zu Shakespeare. Halle 1877.

ten Brink, B. Shakespeare: fünf Vorlesungen. Strasbourg 1893.

Sarrazin, G. Shakespeares Lehrjahre. Weimar 1897.

Schücking, L. L. Shakespeare im literarischen Urteil seiner Zeit. Heidelberg 1898.

— Die Charakterprobleme bei Shakespeare. Leipzig 1919.

Wolff, M. J. Shakespeare: Studien und Aufsätze. Leipzig 1903.

— Shakespeare: der Dichter und sein Werk. 2 vols Munich 1908.

Wetz, W. Die Lebensnachrichten über Shakespeare. Heidelberg 1912.

Brandl, A. Shakespeares Leben—Umwelt—Kunst. Berlin 1922.

Richter, H. Shakespeare der Mensch. Leipzig 1923.

Gundolf, F. Shakespeare: sein Wesen und Werk. 2 vols Berlin 1928–9.

More recent German critical works are listed in earlier sections.

OTHER COUNTRIES

Major trns since 1955 are recorded; for earlier trns see national bibliographies or annual Shakespeare bibliographies.

Africa

Clark, J. P. The example of Shakespeare. 1970.

Belgium

Decrux, J. Forces constructives dans Hamlet et dans La Princesse Maleine de Maurice Maeterlinck. Comparative Lit Stud 11 1943.

China

Complete works. Tr Liang Schich'iu 37 vols Taipei 1967.

Czechoslovakia

Complete works. Tr V. J. Sládek, J. Vrchlický and A. Klášterny, Prague 1959–64.

Plays. Tr E. A. Saudek, Prague 1963.

Babler, O. F. Shakespeare's King Lear in Czech translations. N & Q 3 Feb 1951.

Simko, J. Shakespeare in Slovakia. Sh Survey 4 1951.

Pokorny, J. Shakespeare in Czechoslovakia. Prague 1955.

Greece

Boltz, A. Shakespeare in Griechenland. Sh Jb 11 1876.

Wagner, W. Shakespeare in Griechenland. Sh Jb 12 1877.

Holland

Loffelt, A. Nederlandsche navolgingen van Shakespeare en van de oude engelsche dramatici in de 17 eeuw. Nederlandsch Spectator 1868.

Moltzer, H. E. Shakespeare's invloed op het nederlandsch tooneel der zeventiende eeuw. Groningen 1874.

Arnold, T. J. I. Shakespeare in de nederlandsche letterkunde en op het nederlandsch tooneel. Bibliographische Adversaria 4 1879; Hague 1879.

— Shakespeare-bibliography in the Netherlands. Bibliographische Adversaria 4 1879; Hague 1879.

Pennink, B. Nederland en Shakespeare. Hague 1936.

Decroos, J. Deutschlands Einfluss auf die Shakespeare-Pflege im niederländischen Sprachgebiet. Sh Jb 87–8 1951–2.

Hungary

Complete plays. Budapest 1955.

Complete works. Tr J. Arany, L. Áprily et al 2 vols Budapest 1965.

Greguss, A. Shakespeare in Ungarn. Budapest 1879.

Berzeviczy, A. Shakespeares és a Magyar Nemzetlélek. Magyar Sh-Tár 8 1896.

Bayer, J. Shakespeare drámai hazánkban. 2 vols Budapest 1909. A full Shakespeare bibliography.

Riedl, F. Shakespeare és a Magyar irodalom. Budapest 1916.

Császár, E. Shakespeare és a Magyar költészet. Budapest 1917.

Haraszti, Z. Shakespeare in Hungary. Boston 1929.
Marle, T. B. Shakespeare in Budapest. Hungarian Quart 4 1939.
Yolland, A. Shakespeare in Hungary. Ibid.
Mark, T. R. The first Hungarian translation of Shakespeare. Sh Quart 9 1958. Kazinczy's prose Hamlet, 1790.

India

Legouis, E. La révolte de l'Inde contre Shakespeare. Revue Anglo-américaine 2 1925.
Sisson, C. J. Shakespeare in India. 1926 (Sh Assoc).
Shahani, R. G. Shakespeare through eastern eyes. 1932.
Menon, C. N. Shakespeare's tragedies through Indian eyes. Madras 1934.

Italy

Sonnetti. Tr A. Rossi, Turin 1952.
Il teatro di Shakespeare. Tr C. V. Lodovici 3 vols Turin 1960.
Il teatro di Shakespeare. Tr C. Rusconi 3 vols Rome 1961.
Opere complete. Tr G. Baldini 3 vols Milan 1963.
Tutte le opere. Introd by M. Praz, Florence 1964.

Reforgiato, V. Shakespeare e Manzoni. Catania 1908.
Bellezza, P. Shakespeare e Manzoni. Milan 1927.
Ferrando, G. Shakespeare in Italy. Sh Assoc Bull 5 1930.
Crinò, A. M. La prima traduzione italiana di un dramma di Shakespeare. Rassegna Nazionale 1932.
— Le traduzioni di Shakespeare in Italia nel Settecento. Rome 1950.
d'Amico, S. Shakespeare e Goldoni: il primo festival teatrale di Venezia. Rassegna dell'Istruzione Artistica 5 1934.
Rebora, P. Shakespeare tradotto in italiano. Leonardo 5 1934.
— Comprensione e fortuna di Shakespeare in Italia. Comparative Lit 1 1949.
Wolff, M. J. Antonio Conti in seinem Verhältnis zu Shakespeare. JEGP 37 1938.
Ortolano, G. Goldoni e Shakespeare. Rivista Italiana del Dramma 4 1940.
Fucilla, J. G. Shakespeare in Italian criticism. PQ 20 1941.
Draper, J. W. Shakespeare and the conversazione. Italica 23 1946.
Pastore, A. (ed). Shakespeare degli Italiani. Turin 1950.
Orsini, N. Shakespeare in Italy. Comparative Lit 3 1951.

Japan

Complete works. Tr Y. Nakano et al 8 vols Tokyo 1967.

Walter, E. Shakespeare in Japan. Sh Jb 51 1915.

Korea

Complete works. Tr Suk-Kee Yoh et al 4 vols Seoul 1964.

Poland

Plays. Tr J. Pazskowski 6 vols Warsaw 1927.

Calina, J. Shakespeare in Poland. 1923 (Sh Assoc).
— Shakespeare in Poland. Polish Rev 6 1946.
Helsztyński, S. Polish translations of Shakespeare in the past and today. Zeitschrift für Anglistik und Amerikanistik 12 1964; Sh Jb 101 1965.

Portugal

Obras completas. Tr C. A. Nunes, Rio de Janeiro 1966.

Michaëlis de Vasconcellos, C. Shakespeare in Portugal. Sh Jb 15 1880.
Condamin, J. Un royal traducteur de Shakespeare: Louis, Roi de Portugal. In his Etudes et souvenirs, Paris 1883.
Figueiredo, F. de. Shakespeare e Garrett. Sao Paulo 1950.

Rumania

Beza, M. Shakespeare in Roumania. 1931 (Sh Assoc).
Radulescu, I. H. Les intermédiaires français de Shakespeare en Roumanie. Revue de Littérature Comparée 18 1938.
Duţu, A. Shakespeare in Rumania. Bucharest 1964.

Russia

Complete works. Ed A. Smirnov and A. Anikst 8 vols Moscow 1957–60.

Pokrowskij, M. Puschkin und Shakespeare. Sh Jb 43 1907.
Lirondelle, A. Catherine II, élève de Shakespeare. Revue Germanique 4 1908.
— Shakespeare en Russie 1748–1840. Paris 1912.
Gebhard, R. Ivan Turgenjew in seinen Beziehungen zu Shakespeare. Sh Jb 45 1909.
Friedrichs, E. Shakespeare in Russland. E Studien 50 1916.
Simmons, E. J. Catherine the Great and Shakespeare. PMLA 47 1932.
— In his English literature and culture in Russia, Cambridge Mass 1935.
Knight, G. W. Shakespeare and Tolstoy. Oxford 1934; rptd in his Wheel of fire, 1949 (4th edn).
Lerner, N. O. Pushkin's relations to Shakespeare. Zven'ia 5 1935.
Smirnov, A. A. Shakespeare: a Marxist interpretation. Tr S. Volochova et al, New York 1936.
Zagorsky, M. Shakespeare in Russia. TLS 12 Aug 1944.
Blum, E. Shakespeare in the USSR. Sh Assoc Bull 20 1945.
Morozov, M. M. Shakespeare on the stages of Erevan, Tbilisi, Baku. Ibid.
— Boris Pasternak's translation of Othello. Ibid.
— Shakespeare on the Soviet stage. Tr D. Magarschak 1947.
— The study of Shakespeare in the Soviet Union. Amer Rev of Soviet Union 8 1947.
Zanco, A. Shakespeare in Russia e altri saggi. Turin 1945.
Gifford, H. Shakespearian elements in Boris Godunov. Slavonic & East European Rev 24 1947.
Lang, D. M. Sumarkov's Hamlet: a misjudged Russian tragedy of the eighteenth century. MLR 43 1948.
Luther, A. Shakespeare in Russland. Sh Jb 84–6 1948–50.
Gibian, G. Pushkin's parody on the Rape of Lucrece. Sh Quart 1 1950.
— Measure for measure and Pushkin's Angelo. PMLA 66 1951.
— Shakespeare in Soviet Russia. Russian Rev 12 1952.
— Tolstoi and Shakespeare. Hague 1957.
Wolff, T. A. Shakespeare's influence on Pushkin's dramatic work. Sh Survey 5 1952.
Pasternak, B. Comment j'ai traduit Shakespeare en russe. Lettres Françaises 647 1956; Twentieth Century Sept 1958.
Stroud, T. A. Hamlet and the Seagull. Sh Quart 9 1958.
Adling, W. Gorki und Shakespeare. Sh Jb (Weimar) 105 1969.

Scandinavia

Dramatiske vaerker. Tr Danish by V. Osterberg, Copenhagen 1958.

Bolin, W. Zur Shakespeare-Literatur Schwedens. Sh Jb 15 1880.
Palmblad, H. V. E. Shakespeaere and Strindberg. Germanic Rev 3 1928.
Tonstad, T. Wergeland og Shakespeare. Edda 28 1928.
Molin, N. Shakespeare og Sverige intill 1800. Gothenburg 1931.
Rubow, P. Shakespeare paa Dansk. Copenhagen 1932.
— Studien over danske Shakespeare-Oversaettelser. Acta Philologica Scandinavica 8 1933.

Bulman, J. Strindberg and Shakespeare. 1933.
Börge, V. Strindberg und Shakespeare. Sh Jb 73 1937.
Einarsson, S. Shakespeare á 'Íslandi. Winnipeg. 1939.
Henriques, A. Shakespeare i Danmark og i Sverige. Nordisk Tidskrift 16 1940.
— Shakespeare and Denmark. Sh Survey 3 1950.
Willey, N. L. Oehlenschlaeger's Amleth. Scandinavian Stud 17 1942.
Koht, H. Shakespeare and Ibsen. JEGP 44 1945.
Arestad, S. Ibsen and Shakespeare: a study in influence. Scandinavian Stud 19 1946.
Magon, L. Deutschland, Shakespeare und der Norden. Sh Jb 82–3 1946–7.
Donner, H. W. Svenska översättningar av Shakespeare's Macbeth. Åbo 1950. Geijer's trn.
Andersson, H. Strindberg's Master Olof and Shakespeare. Upsala 1952.
Rougemont, D. de. Kierkegaard and Hamlet: two Danish princes. Anchor Rev 1 1955.
Bull, F. The influence of Shakespeare on Wergeland, Ibsen and Björnson. Tr from Norwegian, Norseman 15 1957.
Andreasson, A. Strindberg and Shakespeare. Länstidningen Östersund June 1962.
Jensen, N. L. Shakespeare in Denmark. Durham Univ Jnl 25 1964.

Spain
Obras completas. Tr L. A. Marin, Barcelona 1960.

Ruppert y Ujaravi, R. Shakespeare en España. Madrid 1920.
Schütt, M. Hat Calderón Shakespeare gekannt? die Quellen von Calderóns La Cisma de Inglaterra. Sh Jb 61 1925.
Par, A. Contribución a la Bibliografía española de Shakespeare. Barcelona 1930.
— Shakespeare en la literatura española. 2 vols Madrid 1935.
— Representaciones Shakespearianas en España. 2 vols Madrid 1936–40.
Esquerra, R. Shakespeare a Catalunya. Barcelona 1937.
Stoll, E. E. A Spanish Hamlet. MP 47 1950.
Moore, J. R. A Spanish Hamlet. MLR 45 1950.
Thomas, H. Shakespeare in Spain. Proc Br Acad 36 1950.
Fitzgerald, T. A. Shakespeare in Spain and Spanish America. Modern Lang Jnl 35 1951.
Ley, C. D. Shakespeare para Españoles. Madrid 1951.

Switzerland
Vetter, T. Shakespeare und die deutsche Schweiz. Sh Jb 48 1912.
Kuery, H. Simon Grynaeus von Basel 1725–99: der erste deutsche Übersetzer von Shakespeares Romeo und Julia. Zürich 1935.
Engel, C. E. Shakespeare in Switzerland in the eighteenth century. Comparative Lit Stud 17–18 1945.

Bircher, M. and H. Straumann. Shakespeare und die deutsche Schweiz bis zum Beginn des 19 Jahrhunderts: eine Bibliographie raisonnée. Berne 1971.

United States of America
Churchill, G. B. Shakespeare in America. Sh Jb 42 1906.
Cairns, W. B. Shakespeare in America. Edda 6 1916.
Thorndike, A. H. Shakespeare in America. Proc Br Acad 13 1927.
Harrison, R. C. Walt Whitman and Shakespeare. PMLA 44 1929.
Furness, C. J. Walt Whitman's estimate of Shakespeare. Harvard Stud 14 1932.
Paul, H. N. Shakespeare in Philadelphia. Proc Amer Philosophical Soc 76 1937.
Shurter, J. W. Shakespearian performances in pre-revolutionary America. South Atlantic Quart 36 1937.
Willoughby, E. E. The reading of Shakespeare in colonial America. PBSA 31 1937.
Dunn, E. C. Shakespeare in America. New York 1939.
Shockley, M. S. Shakespeare's plays in the Richmond theatre 1819–38. Sh Assoc Bull 15 1940.
Vandiver, E. P. James Fenimore Cooper and Shakespeare. Ibid.
Fale, R. P. Emerson and Shakespeare. PMLA 56 1941.
— Shakespeare's place in Walt Whitman's America. Sh Assoc Bull 17 1942.
Gates, W. B. O. Henry and Shakespeare. Sh Assoc Bull 19 1944.
Sprague, A. C. The first American performance of Richard II. Ibid.
Peery, T. A. Emerson, the historical frame and Shakespeare. MLQ 9 1948.
Berkelman, R. Lincoln's interest in Shakespeare. Sh Quart 2 1951.
Olson, C. Melville et Shakespeare. Temps Modernes 7 1951.
Stovall, F. Whitman, Shakespeare and the Baconians. PQ 31 1952.
— Whitman's knowledge of Shakespeare. SP 49 1952.
Gates, W. B. Shakespearean elements in Irving's Sketch book. Amer Lit 30 1959.

Yugoslavia
The works, translated into Serbo Croatian. Ed M. Vitorović and L. Lazic, Belgrade 1963.

Bryner, C. Shakespeare among the Slavs. ELH 8 1941.
Popovic, V. Shakespeare in post-war Yugoslavia. Sh Survey 4 1951.
Torbarina, J. On translating Shakespeare. In English studies today, ed G. A. Bonnard, Berne 1961.
Filipović, R. Shakespeare in Croatia: an annotated bibliography. Studia Romanica et Anglica (Zagreb) 1964.

T. S. D

X. JACOBEAN AND CAROLINE DRAMA

Chapman, Middleton, Jonson, Dekker, Heywood, Marston, Tourneur, Webster, Massinger, Beaumont and Fletcher, Rowley, Ford, Shirley

See I. Ribner, Tudor and Stuart drama, New York 1966.
For collections listed below as abbreviations (Bang, Gayley, TFT etc) see col 1363, above.

GEORGE CHAPMAN
1559?–1634

Bibliographies

Tannenbaum, S. A. Chapman: a concise bibliography. New York 1938; Supplement, New York 1946.

Yamada, A. Chapman: a checklist of editions, biography and criticism 1946–65. Research Opportunities in Renaissance Drama 10 1967; addns by G. Ray 11 1968.

Collections

Comedies and tragedies. [Ed R. H. Shepherd] 3 vols 1873. Includes Alphonsus and Revenge for honour with plays listed below, omitting Eastward hoe and Sir Giles Goosecap.

Works. Ed R. H. Shepherd 3 vols 1874–5. Includes Second maiden's tragedy, Two wise men and all the rest fools, Alphonsus, Ball and Revenge for honour with plays listed below, omitting Sir Giles Goosecap. Vols 2–3 include the trns and poems; vol 2 with introd by A. C. Swinburne, later issued separately.

George Chapman. Ed W. L. Phelps 1895 (Mermaid ser). Contains All fools, Bussy D'Ambois, The revenge of Bussy D'Ambois, Conspiracy and tragedy of Charles Duke of Byron.

Plays. Ed T. M. Parrott 2 vols 1910–14. Includes Alphonsus, Ball and Revenge for honour with plays listed below.

Plays: the comedies. Ed A. Holaday et al, Urbana 1970. Contains Blind beggar of Alexandria, An humorous day's mirth, Gentleman usher, All fools, May day, Monsieur D'Olive, Widow's tears, Memorable masque.

Poems. Ed P. B. Bartlett, New York 1941.

Chapman's Homer: the Iliad, the Odyssey and the lesser Homerica. Ed A. Nicoll 2 vols New York 1956.

§1

Σκία νυκτός: the shadow of night, containing two poeticall hymnes, devised by G.C. gent. 1594; rptd A. Acheson, Shakespeare and the rival poet, 1903.

Ovids banquet of sence, A coronet for his mistresse Philo-sophie, and his amorous zodiacke, with a translation of a Latin coppie written by a fryer. 1595, 1639; rptd A. Acheson, Shakespeare and the rival poet, 1903; ed E. S. Donno, Elizabethan minor epics, 1963; ed N. Alexander, Elizabethan narrative verse, 1968; Menston 1970 (facs). The trn The amorous contention of Phillis and Flora was rptd 1598 as by R.S. (Richard Stapleton?) who may be the author.

Achilles shield, translated as the other seven bookes of Homer out of his eighteenth booke of Iliades. 1598, Oxford 1931.

The blinde begger of Alexandria, most pleasantly dis-coursing his variable humours in disguised shapes full of conceite and pleasure, as it hath beene sundry times publickly acted in London by the Right Honorable the Earle of Nottingham, Lord High Admirall his servantes. 1598; ed W. W. Greg 1928 (Malone Soc).

Seaven bookes of the Iliades of Homere, prince of poets, translated according to the Greeke in judgement of his best commentaries. 1598. Bks 1–2, 7–11.

A pleasant comedy entituled An humerous dayes myrth,

as it hath beene sundrie times publikely acted by the Right Honourable the Earle of Nottingham, Lord High Admirall his servants, by G.C. 1599; ed D. N. Smith 1938 (Malone Soc).

Peristeros: or the male turtle. In R. Chester, Love's martyr, 1601; ed A. B. Grosart 1878 (New Shakspere Soc); ed B. H. Newdigate, The phoenix and the turtle, Oxford 1937.

Al fooles, a comedy, presented at the Black fryers, and lately before his Majestie. 1605; ed I. Reed, Dodsley vol 4, 1780; Ancient British drama vol 2, 1810; ed J. P. Collier, Dodsley vol 4, 1825; ed T. M. Parrott 1907; ed F. Manley 1968 (Regents ser).

Eastward hoe, as it was playd in the Black-friers by the children of her Majesties revels, made by Geo. Chap-man, Ben Jonson, Joh. Marston. 1605 (first edn reissued and 2 further edns ptd in this year); ed R. Dodsley, A select collection of old plays vol 4, 1744; ed W. R. Chetwood, Memoirs of Jonson, 1756; ed I. Reed, Dodsley vol 4, 1780; Ancient British drama vol 2, 1810; ed J. P. Collier, Dodsley vol 4, 1825; ed F. E. Schelling 1904; ed J. W. Cunliffe, Gayley vol 2, 1913; TFT 1914; ed J. H. Harris, New Haven 1926; ed C. F. T. Brooke and N. B. Paradise, English drama, 1933; ed H. Spencer, Elizabethan plays, 1933. Also included in collections of Marston, below, and in Herford–Simpson edn of Jonson, below.

The gentleman usher. 1606; ed T. M. Parrott 1907; ed J. H. Smith 1970 (Regents ser).

Monsieur D'Olive: a comedie, as it was sundrie times acted by her Majesties children at the Blacke-friers. 1606; ed C. W. Dilke, Old English plays vol 3, 1814.

Sir Gyles Goosecap knight: a comedie presented by the chil. of the chappell. 1606, 1636 (both edns anon, but Chapman's authorship accepted; see G. L. Kittredge, Notes on Elizabethan plays, JEGP 2 1899; T. M. Parrott, The authorship of Sir Giles Goosecap, MP 4 1906); ed A. H. Bullen, Old English plays vol 3, 1884; ed W. Bang and R. Brotanek, Bang vol 26, 1909; TFT 1912.

Bussy D'Ambois: a tragedie, as it hath been often presented at Paules. 1607 (some copies dated 1608) (anon), 1641 ('being much corrected and amended by the author before his death'; re-issued 1641, 1646, 1657); ed C. W. Dilke, Old English plays vol 3, 1814; ed F. S. Boas 1905; ed W. A. Neilson, Chief Elizabethan drama-tists, 1911; ed C. F. T. Brooke and N. B. Paradise, English drama 1933; ed H. Spenser, Elizabethan plays, 1933; ed C. R. Baskervill, Elizabethan and Stuart plays, 1934; ed A. K. McIlwraith, Five Stuart tragedies, Oxford 1953 (WC); ed J. Jacquot, Paris 1960; ed N. Brooke 1964 (Revels ser); ed R. Lordi 1964 (Regents ser); ed M. Evans 1965 (New Mermaid ser).

The conspiracie and tragedie of Charles Duke of Byron, Marshall of France, acted lately in two playes at the Black-friers. 1608, 1625.

Euthymiæ raptus: or the teares of peace, with interlocu-tions. 1609; rptd A. Acheson, Shakespeare and the rival poet, 1903.

Homer, prince of poets, translated according to the Greeke in twelve bookes of his Iliads. [1609?], 1611. Reprints the 7 bks of 1598 and adds 3–6 and 12.

The Iliads of Homer, prince of poets, never before in any language truely translated, with a comment uppon some of his chiefe places. [1611]; ed R. Hooper 2 vols 1857;

ed H. Morley 1883. Adds bks 13–24 and substitutes new versions of 1–2.

May-day: a witty comedie, divers times acted at the Blacke fryers. 1611; ed C. W. Dilke, Old English plays vol 4, 1814.

An epicede or funerall song on the death of Henry Prince of Wales. 1612; ed S. E. Brydges 1818.

Petrarchs seven penitentiall psalmes, paraphrastically translated with other philosophicall poems and a Hymne to Christ upon the crosse. 1612.

The widdowes teares: a comedie, as it was often presented in the Black and White friers. 1612; ed R. Dodsley, A select collection of old plays vol 4, 1744; ed I. Reed, Dodsley vol 6, 1780; ed J. P. Collier, Dodsley vol 6, 1825; ed E. Smeak 1966 (Regents ser).

The memorable maske of the two honorable houses or Inns of Courte, the Middle Temple and Lyncolns Inne, as it was performed before the King at White-hall on Shrove Munday at night, being the 15 of February 1613, at the princely celebration of the most royall nuptials of the Palsgrave and his thrice gratious Princesse Elizabeth, with a description of their whole show, invented and fashioned by our kingdomes most artfull and ingenious architect Innigo Jones, and written by Geo. Chapman. [1613?] (2 edns); ed J. Nichols, Progresses of James I vol 2, 1828.

The revenge of Bussy D'Ambois: a tragedie, as it hath beene often presented at the private play-house in the White-fryers. 1613; ed F. S. Boas 1905; Menston 1968 (facs).

Andromeda liberata: or the nuptials of Perseus and Andromeda. 1614.

Eugenia: or true nobilities trance for the most memorable death of William Lord Russell. 1614.

A free and offenceless justification of Andromeda liberata. 1614.

Homers Odysses. [1614?]. Bks 1–12.

Twenty-four bookes of Homers Odisses. [1615?]; ed R. Hooper 2 vols 1857; 2 vols 1897 (Temple Classics). Adds bks 13–24 to reissue of previous item.

The divine poem of Musaeus: first of all bookes, translated according to the originall. 1616; ed E. S. Donno, Elizabethan minor epics, 1963.

The whole works of Homer, prince of poetts, in his Iliads and Odysses. [1616] (re-issues edns of [1611], [1615?] with new general title-page), 1904, 4 vols Oxford 1930–1.

The Georgicks of Hesiod, translated elaborately out of the Greek. 1618.

Pro Vere autumni lachrymæ, inscribed to the immortal memorie of Sir Horatio Vere. 1622.

The crowne of all Homers workes, Batrachomyomachia or the battaile of frogs and mise, his hymn's and epigrams. [1624?], 1818; ed R. Hooper 1858; Oxford 1931.

A justification of a strange action of Nero in burying with a solemne funerall one of the cast hayres of his mistresse Poppæa; also a just reproofe of a Romane smell-feast: being the fifth satyre of Juvenall translated. 1629.

Caesar and Pompey: a Roman tragedy, declaring their warres, out of whose events is evicted this proposition, only a just man is a freeman. 1631 (some copies as The warres of Pompey and Caesar), 1652, 1653.

The tragedie of Chabot Admirall of France, as it was presented by her Majesties servants at the private house in Drury Lane, written by George Chapman and James Shirly. 1639; ed E. Lehman, Philadelphia 1906. A revision by Shirley of a play written by Chapman c. 1613.

For Hero and Leander, *begun by Marlowe and completed by Chapman, see col 1444, above. In addition to Munday's* Fedele and Fortunio, *col 1464, above, Shirley's* The ball, *col 1726, below,* Rollo Duke of Normandy: or the bloody brother *in the Beaumont and Fletcher canon, col 1712, below, Marston's* Histrio–mastix, *col 1691, below, Glapthorne's* Revenge for honour, *col 1744, below, and the anon* Masque of the twelve months, *the following anon*

plays, cols 1758, 1759, 1761, 1762, below, have been wholly or partially assigned to Chapman: Alphonsus Emperour of Germany, Charlemagne: or the distracted emperor, The second maiden's tragedy, Time's triumph, Two wise men and all the rest fools.

§2

Hazlitt, W. In his Lectures on the dramatic literature of the age of Elizabeth, 1818.

Lowell, J. R. In his Conversations on some of the old poets, Cambridge Mass 1845.

Bodenstedt, F. Chapman in seinem Verhältnis zu Shakespeare. Sh Jb 1 1865.

Swinburne, A. C. Chapman: a critical essay. 1875. Also as introd to Chapman's Works, ed R. H. Shepherd vol 2; rptd in his Age of Shakespeare, 1908.

Hart, H. C. Notes on Bullen's old plays: Sir Gyles Goosecappe. Academy 6 Oct 1888.

Koeppel, E. Quellenstudien zu den Dramen Chapmans, Philip Massingers und John Fords. Quellen und Forschungen 82 1897.

Cook, A. S. The source of two similes in the Revenge of Bussy D'Ambois. JEGP 1 1898.

Stiefel, A. L. Chapman und das italienische Drama. Sh Jb 35 1899.

Dobell, B. Newly discovered documents of the Elizabethan and Jacobean periods. Athenaeum 23 March–13 April 1901. On ms V.a.321, now in Folger Shakespeare Library, Washington.

Boas, F. S. The sources of the Conspiracy of Byron and the Revenge of Bussy D'Ambois. Athenaeum 10 Jan 1903.

—— In his An introduction to Stuart drama, Oxford 1946.

Acheson, A. Shakespeare and the rival poet, with sundry poetical pieces by Chapman bearing on the subject. 1903.

—— Shakespeare, Chapman and Sir Thomas More. 1931.

Lohff, A. Chapmans Ilias-Übersetzung. Berlin 1903.

Stoll, E. E. On the dates of some of Chapman's plays. MLN 20 1905.

Parrott, T. M. Notes on the text of Chapman's plays. Anglia 30 1907. On Alphonsus Emperour of Germany.

—— The date of Bussy D'Ambois. MLR 3 1908.

—— The text of the Conspiracy and tragedy of Charles Duke of Byron. MLR 4 1909.

Jusserand, J.-J. Ambassador La Boderie and the 'compositeur' of the Byron plays. MLR 6 1911.

Schoell, F. L. Chapman and the Italian neo-Latinists of the Quattrocento. MP 13 1915.

—— Les emprunts de Chapman à Marsile Ficin. Revue de Littérature Comparée 3 1923.

—— In his Etudes sur l'humanisme continental en Angleterre à la fin de la Renaissance, Paris 1926.

Robertson, J. M. Shakespeare and Chapman: a thesis of Chapman's authorship of A lover's complaint and his origination of Timon of Athens. 1917.

Ferguson, A. S. The plays of Chapman. MLR 13 1918, 15 1920.

—— The tragedy of Chabot: III.ii.147–68. MLR 23 1928.

Bullen, A. H. In his Elizabethans, 1924.

Spens, J. Chapman's ethical thought. E & S 11 1925.

Thorn-Drury, G. George Chapman. RES 1 1925.

Brettle, R. E. Eastward ho: bibliography and circumstances of production. Library 4th ser 9 1928.

Solve, N. D. Stuart politics in Chapman's Tragedy of Chabot. Ann Arbor 1928.

Allen, P. Shakespeare and Chapman as topical dramatists. 1929.

—— The plays of Shakespeare and Chapman in relation to French history. 1933.

Williamson, G. In his Donne tradition, Cambridge Mass 1930.

Bensly, E. Chapman and epigrams attributed to Virgil. N & Q 21 May–4 June 1932.

Engel, C.-E. Les sources du Bussy D'Amboise de Chapman. Revue de Littérature Comparée 12 1932.

Janish, W. Die erste englische Übersetzung der Homerischen Hymnen. Mitteilungen des Vereins Klassischer Philologen in Wien 8 1933.

George Chapman. TLS 10 May 1934.

Ellis, H. Chapman, with illustrative passages. 1934; rptd in From Marlowe to Shaw, ed J. Gawsworth 1950.

Bartlett, P. Chapman's revisions in his Iliads. ELH 2 1935.

— Chapman and Phaer. MLN 56 1941.

— The heroes of Chapman's Homer. RES 17 1941.

— Stylistic devices in Chapman's Iliads. PMLA 57 1942.

— Ovid's banquet of sense? N & Q 2 Feb 1952.

Craig, H. Ethics in the Jacobean drama: the case of Chapman. In Essays in dramatic literature: the T. M. Parrott presentation volume, Princeton 1935.

Jump, J. D. The anonymous masque in ms Egerton 1994. RES 11 1935. On Time's triumph.

Kennedy, C. W. Political theory in the plays of Chapman. In Essays in dramatic literature: the T. M. Parrott presentation volume, Princeton 1935.

Kreider, P. V. Elizabethan comic character conventions as revealed in the comedies of Chapman. Ann Arbor 1935.

Smith, J. George Chapman. Scrutiny 3-4 1934-6.

Ellis-Fermor, U. The Jacobean drama. 1936, 1958 (rev).

Loane, G. G. Queries from Chapman's Iliad. N & Q 10 Oct 1936.

— Queries from Chapman's Odyssey. N & Q 7 Nov 1936.

— The text of Chapman's Homer. TLS 18 April 1936.

— Chapman and Holofernes. N & Q 2 Jan 1937. See also M. H. Dodds 17 April 1937.

— Chapman's Homer. Cornhill Mag Nov 1937.

— Chapman's method. TLS 24 July 1937.

— Misprints in Chapman's Homer. N & Q 4-25 Dec 1937, 21 May, 5 Nov 1938.

— Notes on Chapman's plays. MLR 33 1938, 38 1943.

— Chapman and Scapula. N & Q 10 June 1939.

— Some notes on Chapman's poems. N & Q 7 Nov, 5 Dec 1942.

Sisson, C. J. Lost plays of Shakespeare's age. Cambridge 1936. On Chapman's lost play The old joiner of Aldgate.

— and R. Butman. Chapman 1612-22: some new facts. MLR 46 1951.

Spencer, T. In his Death and Elizabethan tragedy, Cambridge Mass 1936.

Weevers, T. H. Coornhert's and Chapman's Odysseys: an early and a late Renaissance Homer. E Studies 18 1936. Coornhert's Dutch trn of the Odyssey 1-12, 1561 compared with Chapman's.

Bottrall, M. Chapman's defence of difficulty in poetry. New Criterion 16 1937.

Bowers, F. T. The date of Revenge for honour. MLN 52 1937. Reply by C. L. Shaver 53 1938.

— In his Elizabethan revenge tragedy, Princeton 1940.

Gilbert, A. H. Chapman's fortune with winged hands. MLN 52 1937, 54 1939.

Greg, W. W. A proof-sheet of 1606. Library 4th ser 17 1937. On text of Monsieur D'Olive.

— A fragment from Henslowe's Diary. Library 4th ser 19 1938. See also J. Q. Adams 20 1939.

— The copyright of Hero and Leander. Library 4th ser 24 1944.

M., M. Andromeda's rescue. More Books 13 1938.

Howarth, R. G. The date of Bussy D'Ambois. N & Q 8 July 1939.

— Notes on Chapman. N & Q 15 Feb 1947.

Pogrell, N. von. Die philosophisch-poetische Entwicklung Chapmans. Hamburg 1939.

Smalley, D. The ethical bias of Chapman's Homer. SP 36 1939.

Battenhouse, R. W. The shadow of night: an interpretation. SP 38 1941.

— Chapman and the nature of man. ELH 12 1945.

Perkinson, R. H. Nature and the tragic hero in Chapman's Bussy plays. MLQ 3 1942.

— The body as a triangular structure in Spenser and Chapman. MLN 64 1949.

Robertson, J. Some additional poems of Chapman. Library 4th ser 22 1942.

— The early life of Chapman. MLR 40 1945.

Crundell, H. W. Chapman and the Grevilles. N & Q 28 Aug 1943, 17 Nov 1945. On dedication of the Widow's tears.

Simpson, P. The problem of authorship of Eastward ho. PMLA 59 1944. Credits Chapman with the whole or parts of II.ii, III.i-iii, IV.i and IV.iv.

Gordon, D. J. Chapman's use of Cartari in the fifth sestiad of Hero and Leander. MLR 39 1944.

— Chapman's Hero and Leander. Eng Miscellany (Rome) 5 1954.

— Le masque memorable de Chapman. In Fêtes de la Renaissance, ed J. Jacquot, Paris 1956.

Stein, A. Sonnet structure in Chapman's blank verse. MLN 59 1944.

Higgins, M. H. Chapman's Senecal man. RES 21 1945.

— The development of the Senecal man: Chapman's Bussy D'Ambois and some precursors. RES 23 1947.

Sharpe, R. B. Jonson's Execration and Chapman's Invective: their place in their authors' rivalry. SP 42 1945.

Eccles, M. Chapman's early years. SP 43 1946.

Muir, E. Royal man: notes on the tragedies of Chapman. Orion 2 1946; rptd in his Essays on literature and society, 1949, 1965 (rev).

Parr, J. The Duke of Byron's malignant Caput Algol. SP 43 1946; rptd in his Tamburlaine's malady and other essays, Tuscaloosa 1953.

Bradbrook, M. C. Chapman and Webster. MLR 42 1947.

— In her Growth and structure of Elizabethan comedy, 1955.

Prior, M. In his Language of tragedy, New York 1947.

Peery, W. Eastward ho and A woman is a weathercock. MLN 62 1947.

Martin, L. C. Lucan—Marlowe—?Chapman. RES 24 1948.

Ure, P. Some differences between Senecan and Elizabethan tragedy. Durham Univ Jnl 9 1948.

— The main outline of Chapman's Byron. SP 47 1950.

— A note on 'opinion' in Daniel, Greville and Chapman. MLR 46 1951.

— The date of the revision of Bussy D'Ambois. N & Q 5 Jan 1952.

— Chapman's Tragedy of Bussy D'Ambois: problems of the revised quarto. MLR 48 1953.

— Chapman as translator and tragic playwright. In The age of Shakespeare, ed B. Ford 1955 (Pelican).

— The widow of Ephesus: some reflections on an international theme. Durham Univ Jnl 18 1956.

— Chapman's use of North's Plutarch in Caesar and Pompey. RES new ser 9 1958.

— Chapman's Tragedy of Byron IV.ii.291-5. MLR 54 1959.

— Chapman's tragedies. In Jacobean theatre, ed J. R. Brown and B. Harris 1960.

E., S. Y. Chapman's All fools. N & Q 4 Sept 1948, 8 Jan, 10 Dec 1949. Reply by J. G. McManaway 27 Nov 1948. On the dedication.

Adams, H. H. Cyril Tourneur on revenge. JEGP 48 1949. On influence of Revenge of Bussy D'Ambois.

McCollom, W. G. The tragic hero and Bussy D'Ambois. UTQ 18 1949.

Wieler, J. W. Chapman: the effect of Stoicism upon his tragedies. New York 1949.

Haydn, H. In his Counter-Renaissance, New York 1950.

Muir, K. A Chapman masque? TLS 15 Dec 1950. Replies by M. Dean-Smith 29 Dec 1950, 26 Jan 1951. On Masque of the twelve months.

Schrickx, W. Notes on the so-called Collier forgery of the dedication to All fools. Revue Belge 28 1950.
— Chapman's borrowings from Natali Conti. E Studies 32 1951.
— Mythological patterns in Chapman's Bussy D'Ambois: their interpretative value. Revue des Langues Vivantes 18 1952.
Fay, H. C. Chapman's materials for his translation of Homer. RES new ser 2 1951.
— Chapman's translation of Homer's Iliad. Greece 21 1952.
— Chapman's text corrections in his Iliads. Library 5th ser 7 1952.
— Critical marks in a copy of Chapman's Twelve books of Homers Iliades. Library 5th ser 8 1953.
— Poetry, pedantry, and life in Chapman's Iliads. RES new ser 4 1953.
Jacquot, J. Chapman: sa vie, sa poésie, son théâtre, sa pensée. Paris 1951.
— Buddy D'Ambois and Chapman's conception of tragedy. In English studies today: 2nd series, ed G. A. Bonnard, Berne 1961.
Sturman, B. The 1641 edition of Bussy D'Ambois. HLQ 14 1951.
Burton, K. M. The political tragedies of Chapman and Jonson. EC 2 1952.
Haddakin, L. A note on Chapman and two medieval English jurists. MLR 47 1952.
— Chapman's use of Irigen's Contra Celsum in the Tragedy of Caesar and Pompey. N & Q April 1953.
Lewis, C. S. Hero and Leander. Proc Br Acad 38 1952; rptd in his Selected literary essays, Cambridge 1969.
Smith, H. In his Elizabethan poetry, Cambridge Mass 1952.
Leech, C. The atheist's tragedy as a dramatic comment on Chapman's Bussy plays. JEGP 52 1953.
Brown, J. R. Chapman's Caesar and Pompey: an unperformed play? MLR 49 1954.
Doran, M. In her Endeavors of art, Madison 1954.
Fusillo, R. J. On the date of Sir Gyles Goosecap. N & Q Aug 1954.
Hunter, G. K. Henry IV and the Elizabethan two-part play. RES new ser 5 1954. On the Byron plays.
Rees, E. The tragedies of Chapman: Renaissance ethics in action. Cambridge Mass 1954.
— Chapman's Blind beggar and the Marlovian hero. JEGP 57 1958.
Heninger, S. K. The Tempestatis praesagia in Chapman's Eugenia. MLN 70 1955.
— Chapman's plagiarism of Poliziano's Rusticus. MLN 73 1958.
— In his A handbook of Renaissance meterology, Durham NC 1960.
Lord, G. Homeric Renaissance: the Odyssey of Chapman. New Haven 1956.
Rickey, M. E. Chapman and Crashaw. N & Q Nov 1956.
Williamson, M. L. Matter of more mirth. Renaissance Papers 1956. On Widow's tears.
Wilson, E. E. The genesis of the Revenge of Bussy D'Ambois. MLN 71 1956.
Pagnini, M. Forme e motivi nelle poesie e nelle tragedie di Chapman. Florence 1957.
Schwartz, E. Seneca, Homer and Bussy D'Ambois. JEGP 56 1957.
— The dates and order of Chapman's tragedies. MP 57 1959. Reply by R. Ornstein 59 1961.
— Chapman's Renaissance man: Byron reconsidered. JEGP 58 1959.
— The date of Chapman's Byron plays. MP 58 1961.
— The date of Bussy D'Ambois. MP 59 1961.
— A neglected play by Chapman. SP 58 1961. On Caesar and Pompey.
— Sir George Buc's authority as licenser for the press. Shakespeare Quart 12 1961. On printing of the Byron plays.

Forker, C. R. A midsummer night's dream and Chapman's Homer. N & Q Dec 1958.
Gerber, R. Übermensch und Treue: zur umstrittenen Entwicklung von Chapmans Drama. Anglia 76 1958.
Lever, J. W. Chapman and Shakespeare. N & Q March 1958.
Sühnel, R. Homer und die englische Humanität: Chapmans und Popes Übersetzungskunst im Rahmen der humanistischen Tradition. Tübingen 1958.
Kaufman, H. A. The blind beggar of Alexandria: a reappraisal. PQ 38 1959.
Ribner, I. Character and theme in Bussy D'Ambois. ELH 26 1959.
— The meaning of Chapman's Tragedy of Chabot. MLR 55 1960.
— In his Jacobean tragedy: the quest for moral order, 1962.
Ornstein, R. In his Moral vision of Jacobean tragedy, Madison 1960.
— The dates of Chapman's tragedies, once more. MP 59 1961.
Schoenbaum, S. The deformed mistress theme and Chapman's Gentleman usher. N & Q Jan 1960.
— The widow's tears and the other Chapman. HLQ 23 1960.
Barber, C. L. The ambivalence of Bussy D'Ambois. REL 2 1961.
Hoy, C. The shares of Fletcher and his collaborators in the Beaumont and Fletcher canon, pt 6. SB 14 1961. On Chapman's share in Rollo Duke of Normandy.
Ingledew, J. E. The date of composition of Caesar and Pompey. RES new ser 12 1961.
— Chapman's use of Lucan in Caesar and Pompey. RES new ser 13 1962.
Kermode, F. The banquet of sense. Bull John Rylands Lib 44 1961; rptd in his Shakespeare, Spenser, Donne, 1971.
Weidner, H. M. The dramatic uses of Homeric idealism: the significance of theme and design in the Gentleman usher. ELH 28 1961.
— Homer and the fallen world: focus of satire in the Widow's tears. JEGP 62 1963.
Nicoll, A. The dramatic portrait of Chapman. PQ 41 1962. Chapman identified with Bellamont in Dekker and Webster's Northward ho.
Waith, E. M. In his Herculean hero in Marlowe, Chapman, Shakespeare and Dryden, 1962.
Jones, M. and G. Wickham. The stage furnishings of the Tragedy of Charles Duke of Biron. Theatre Notebook 16 1962.
Røstvig, M.-S. The hidden sense and other essays. Oslo 1963. On number symbolism in Chapman's poems.
Wilkes, G. A. Chapman's lost play, The fount of new fashions. JEGP 62 1963. The fount identified with Sir Giles Goosecap.
Yamada, A. Bibliographical studies of Monsieur D'Olive 1606. Stud in Eng Lit (Tokyo) Eng no 1963.
— Bibliographical studies of the Gentleman usher (1606). Shakespeare Stud (Tokyo) 2 1963.
— The printing of sheet B in the W. A. Clark library copy of Monsieur D'Olive 1606. Jnl Faculty of Arts & Sciences, Shinshu Univ (Japan) 13 1963.
— Press-variants and emendations in Monsieur D'Olive. Ibid.
— Bibliographical studies of All fools (1605). Shakespeare Stud (Tokyo) 3 1964.
— Bibliographical studies of May-day 1611. Jnl Faculty of Arts & Sciences, Shinshu Univ (Japan) 15 1965.
— Bibliographical studies of the Widow's tears 1612. Shakespeare Stud (Tokyo) 4 1965.
— Bibliographical studies of An humorous day's mirth 1599. Shakespeare Stud (Tokyo) 5 1966.
— A proof-sheet in An humorous day's mirth 1599. Library 5th ser 21 1966.

— Bibliographical studies of the Blind beggar of Alexandria 1598. Shakespeare Stud (Tokyo) 6 1967.

— Bibliographical studies of the Memorable mask of the Middle Temple and Lincoln's Inn 1613. Shakespeare Stud (Tokyo) 7 1968.

Gabel, J. B. The original version of Chapman's Tragedy of Byron. JEGP 63 1964.

— Some notable errors in Parrott's edition of Chapman's Byron plays. PBSA 58 1964.

— The date of Chapman's Conspiracy and tragedy of Byron. MP 66 1969.

Reese, J. E. Unity in Chapman's Masque of the Middle Temple and Lincoln's Inn. Stud in Eng Lit 1500–1900 4 1964.

— Keats and others on Chapman's Homer. Cithara 4 1965.

Tomlinson, T. B. In his A study of Elizabethan and Jacobean tragedy, Cambridge 1964.

Herring, T. Chapman and an aspect of modern criticism. Renaissance Drama 8 1965.

Kennedy, E. D. James I and Chapman's Byron plays. JEGP 64 1965.

Phinny, E. Continental humanists and Chapman's Iliads. Stud in Renaissance 12 1965.

Walter, J. H. 'In a little room': Shakespeare and Chapman. N & Q March 1965.

Adams, R. P. Critical myths and Chapman's original Bussy D'Ambois. Renaissance Drama 9 1966.

Brodwin, L. L. Authorship of the Second maiden's tragedy: a reconsideration of the manuscript attribution to Chapman. SP 63 1966.

Crawley, D. The effect of Shirley's hand on Chapman's The tragedy of Chabot Admiral of France. SP 63 1966.

— Decision and character in the Tragedy of Caesar and Pompey. Stud in Eng Lit 1500–1900 7 1967.

Decap, R. Bussy D'Ambois, héros tragique: sur le Bussy D'Amboise de Chapman. In Hommage à Paul Dottin, Caliban 3 1966.

Kostić, V. Marlowe's Hero and Leander and Chapman's continuation. In Renaissance and modern essays presented to V. de Sola Pinto, 1966.

McDonald, C. O. In his Rhetoric of tragedy: form in Stuart drama, Amherst 1966.

MacLure, M. Chapman: a critical study. Toronto 1966.

Waddington, R. B. Chapman's Andromeda liberata: mythology and meaning. PMLA 81 1966.

— Prometheus and Hercules: the dialectic of Bussy D'Ambois. ELH 34 1967.

— Chapman and Persius: the epigraph to Ovid's banquet of sence. RES new ser 19 1968.

Bement, P. The imagery of darkness and of light in Bussy D'Ambois. SP 64 1967.

Eade, C. Some English Iliads: Chapman to Dryden. Arion 6 1967.

Hibbard, G. R. Chapman: tragedy and the providential view of history. Shakespeare Survey 20 1967.

— Goodness and greatness: an essay on the tragedies of Jonson and Chapman. Renaissance & Modern Stud 11 1967.

LaHood, M. J. Chapman's stoicism. Lock Haven (Penn) Rev 9 1967.

Margeson, J. M. R. In his Origins of English tragedy, Oxford 1967.

Spivack, C. George Chapman. New York 1967.

Bawcutt, N. W. Chapman's Friar Camolet. N & Q July 1968.

McPherson, D. C. Chapman's adaptations of new comedy. Eng Miscellany (Rome) 19 1968.

Myers, J. P. This curious frame: Chapman's Ovid's banquet of sense. SP 65 1968.

Smith, J. H. The genesis of the Strozza subplot in the Gentleman usher. PMLA 83 1968.

Stagg, L. C. Characterization through nature imagery in the tragedies of Chapman. Ball State College (Indiana) Forum 9 1968.

— An index to the figurative language of Chapman's tragedies. Charlottesville 1970.

Aggeler, G. The unity of Chapman's The revenge of Bussy D'Ambois. Pacific Coast Philology 4 1969.

Cannon, C. K. Chapman on the unity of style and meaning. JEGP 68 1969.

Freehafer, J. The contention for Bussy D'Ambois 1622–41. Theatre Notebook 23 1969.

Homan, S. R. Chapman and Marlowe: the paradoxical hero and the divided response. JEGP 68 1969.

Orange, L. E. Bussy D'Ambois: the web of pretense. Southern Quart (Univ of Southern Mississippi) 8 1969.

Parsons, R. D. Chapman's letter to Mr Sares: a Hamlet parallel. N & Q April 1969.

Presson, R. K. Wrestling with this world: a view of Chapman. PMLA 84 1969.

Sprinchorn, E. 'Wrapt in a canapie'. Theatre Notebook 24 1969. Tamyra's 'canapie' in Bussy D'Ambois.

Viebrock, H. 'Thus': das demonstrative Adverb als verbales Signal für klimatische dramatische Gesten, aufgezeigt an Beispielen aus dem v Akt von Chapmans Bussy D'Ambois. In Festschrift Rudolf Stamm, Berne 1969.

Bergson, A. The ironic tragedies of Marston and Chapman: notes on Jacobean tragic form. JEGP 69 1970.

Lewalski, B. K. Hero's name—and namesake—in Much ado about nothing. Eng Lang Notes 7 1970. Chapman's trn of Musaeus's Hero and Leander.

Ribner, R. M. The compasse of this curious frame: Chapman's Ovids banquet of sence and the emblematic tradition. Stud in Renaissance 17 1970.

Hogan, A. P. Thematic unity in Monsieur D'Olive. Stud in Eng Lit 1500–1900 11 1971.

Horwich, R. Hamlet and Eastward ho. Ibid.

Lever, J. W. In his Tragedy of state, 1971.

THOMAS MIDDLETON
1580–1627

Bibliographies

Tannenbaum, S. A. Middleton: a concise bibliography. New York 1940.

Donovan, D. Elizabethan bibliographies supplements 1: Middleton 1939–65. 1967.

Collections

Works. Ed A. Dyce 5 vols 1840.

Works. Ed A. H. Bullen 8 vols 1885–6.

Thomas Middleton. Vol 1, ed A. C. Swinburne 1887 (A trick to catch the old one, The changeling, A chaste maid in Cheapside, Women beware women, The Spanish gipsy); vol 2, ed H. Ellis 1890 (The roaring girl, The witch, A fair quarrel, The mayor of Queenborough, The widow) (Mermaid ser).

Thomas Middleton. Ed M. W. Sampson 1915. Contains Michaelmas term, A trick to catch the old one, A fair quarrel, The changeling.

§1

The wisdome of Solomon paraphrased. 1597.

Micro-cynicon: sixe snarling satyres, by T.M. 1599, 1842.

The ghost of Lucrece, by T.M. 1600; ed J. Q. Adams 1937 (facs).

Blurt master-constable: or the Spaniards night-walke, as it hath bin sundry times privately acted by the children of Paules. 1602 (anon); rptd W. R. Chetwood, A select collection of old plays, Dublin 1750. Or by Dekker?

The ant and the nightingale: or Father Hubburds tales, by T.M. 1604, 1604 (as Father Hubburds tales). Anon.

The blacke booke, by T.M. 1604.

The honest whore, pt 1. 1604. With Dekker; see col 1674, below.

The magnificent entertainment. 1604. To this Middleton contributed only the speech of Zeal; *see under Dekker, col 1674, below.*

Michaelmas terme, as it hath been sundry times acted by the children of Paules. 1607, 1630 (both edns anon); ed R. Levin 1966 (Regents ser).

The phoenix, as it hath beene sundry times acted by the children of Paules, and presented before his Majestie. 1607, 1630 (both edns anon).

The familie of love, acted by the children of his Majesties revells. 1608. Anon.

A mad world, my masters, as it hath bin lately in action by the children of Paules, composed by T.M. 1608, 1640; ed R. Dodsley, A select collection of old plays vol 5, 1744; ed I. Reed, Dodsley vol 5, 1780; Ancient British drama vol 2, 1810; ed J. P. Collier, Dodsley vol 5, 1825; ed S. Henning 1965 (Regents ser).

A tricke to catch the old-one, as it hath beene lately acted by the children of Paules. 1608 (anon), 1608-9 ('as it hath beene often in action both at Paules and the Black-fryers, presented before his Majestie on New-Yeares Night last, composde by T.M.'), 1616; ed C. W. Dilke, Old English plays vol 5, 1814; rptd Old English drama vol 3, 1830; ed W. A. Neilson, Chief Elizabethan dramatists, 1911; ed H. Spencer, Elizabethan plays, 1933; ed C. R. Baskervill, Elizabethan and Stuart plays, 1934; ed C. Barber 1968; ed G. J. Watson 1968 (New Mermaid ser).

Your five gallants, as it hath beene often in action at the Blackfriers. [1608?].

Sir Robert Sherley, sent ambassadour in the name of the King of Persia to Sigismond the third, King of Poland, his royal entertainment. 1609.

The roaring girle: or Moll Cut-purse, as it hath lately beene acted on the Fortune-stage by the Prince his players, written by T. Middleton and T. Dekkar. 1611; ed I. Reed, Dodsley vol 6, 1780; Ancient British drama vol 2, 1810; ed J. P. Collier, Dodsley vol 6, 1825; ed R. H. Shepherd, Dramatic works of Dekker, 1873; TFT 1914; ed F. T. Bowers, Dramatic works of Dekker, Cambridge 1958.

The manner of his Lordships entertainment on Michaelmas day last at that most famous and admired worke of the running streame from Amwell Head into the cesterne neere Islington, by T.M. 1613, 1613 (appended to reissue of Triumphs of truth, below); ed J. Nichols, Progresses of James I vol 2, 1828.

The triumphs of truth: a solemnity at the establishment of Sir Thomas Middleton, Knight, in the honorable office of Lord Mayor of London. 1613, 1613 (with Running-stream entertainment); ed J. Nichols, Progresses of James I vol 2, 1828.

Civitatis amor, the cities love: an entertainment by water at Chelsey and Whitehall. 1616; ed J. Nichols, Progresses of James I vol 3, 1828.

A faire quarrell, as it was acted before the King and divers times publikely by the Prince his Highnes servants, written by Thomas Middleton and William Rowley gentl. 1617, 1617 ('with new additions of Mr Chaughs and Trimtrams roaring and the bawds song'), 1622.

The tryumphs of honour and industry: a solemnity at establishment of G. Bowles, Lord Mayor. 1617.

The peace-maker: or Great Brittaines blessing. 1618.

The Inner-Temple masque: or masque of heroes, presented as an entertainment for many worthy ladies by gentlemen of the same ancient and noble house. 1619; ed R. C. Bald, A book of masques in honour of Allardyce Nicoll, Cambridge 1967.

The triumphs of love and antiquity: an honourable solemnitie at the establishment of Sir W. Cockayn, Lord Mayor. 1619; ed J. Nichols, Progresses of James I vol 3, 1828.

The mariage of the Old and New Testament. 1620 (dedication signed by Tho. Middleton, chronologer for the honourable citie of London), 1627 (as Gods parliament house: or the marriage of the Old and New testament).

A courtly masque: the device called the World tost at tennis, as it hath beene divers times presented to the contentment of many noble and worthy spectators by the Prince his servants, invented and set downe by Tho. Middleton and William Rowley gent. 1620.

Honorable entertainments, compos'de for the service of this noble cittie. 1621; ed R. C. Bald and F. P. Wilson 1953 (Malone Soc).

The sun in Aries: a noble solemnity at the establishment of Ed. Barkham, Lord Mayor. 1621.

An invention performed for the service of the Right Honorable Edward Barkham, Lord Mayor of the cittie of London. 1622. Ms in Conway Papers in Public Record Office (State Papers Domestic, James I, cxxix, article 53).

The triumphs of honor and virtue: a noble solemnitie at the establishment of P. Proby, Lord Mayor. 1622; ed J. L. Pearson, Shakespeare Society's Papers 2, Publications 29 1845.

The triumphs of integrity: a noble solemnity at the establishment of M. Lumley, Lord Mayor. 1623.

A game at chaess as it was acted nine days to gether at the Globe on the Banks side. [1625] (3 undated edns, the 2nd reissued with date 1625) (anon); ed R. C. Bald, Cambridge 1929; ed C. F. T. Brooke and N. B. Paradise, English drama, 1933; ed J. W. Harper 1966 (New Mermaid ser). Mss: (1) BM ms Lansdowne 690; (2) Bodley ms Malone 25; (3) Trinity College, Cambridge ms O.2.66; (4) Huntington Lib ms EL 34 B. 17; (5) Folger Shakespeare Lib ms V.a.231; (6) Folger Shakespeare Lib ms V.a.342.

The triumphs of health and prosperity: a noble solemnity at the inauguration of Cuthbert Hacket, Lord Mayor. 1626.

A chast mayd in Cheape-side: a pleasant conceited comedy never before printed, as it hath beene often acted at the Swan on the Banke-side by the Lady Elizabeth her servants. 1630; ed A. Brissenden 1968 (New Mermaid ser); ed R. B. Parker 1969 (Revels ser); Menston 1969 (facs); ed C. Barber 1969.

The widdow: a comedie, as it was acted at the private house in Black-fryers by his late Majesties servants, written by Ben Johnson, John Fletcher, Tho. Middleton gent. 1652; Ancient British drama vol 3, 1810; ed J. P. Collier, Dodsley vol 12, 1827. Principally if not entirely by Middleton.

The changeling, as it was acted at the privat house in Drury-Lane, and Salisbury Court, written by Thomas Midelton and William Rowley gent. 1653, 1668; ed C. W. Dilke, Old English plays vol 4, 1815; ed W. A. Neilson, Chief Elizabethan dramatists, 1911; ed C. F. T. Brooke and N. B. Paradise, English drama, 1933; ed H. Spencer, Elizabethan plays 1933; ed C. R. Baskervill, Elizabethan and Stuart plays, 1934; ed N. W. Bawcutt 1958 (Revels ser); ed P. Thompson 1964 (New Mermaid ser); ed M. W. Black 1966; ed G. W. Williams 1966 (Regents ser).

The Spanish gipsie, as it was acted at the privat house in Drury-Lane, and Salisbury Court, written by Thomas Midelton and William Rowley, gent. 1653, 1661; ed C. W. Dilke, Old English plays vol 4, 1815; ed E. C. Morris, Boston 1908; ed H. B. Clarke, Gayley vol 3, 1914.

The excellent comedy called the Old law: or a new way to please you, by Phil. Massinger, Tho. Middleton, William Rowley, acted before the King and Queene at Salisbury House and at severall other places. 1656. *Also included in collections of Massinger, col 1703, below.*

No wit (help) like a womans: a comedy. 1657. Rev Shirley: *see col 1727, below.*

Two new plays: viz More dissemblers besides women, a comedy: Women beware women, a tragedy. 1657. More dissemblers ed C. W. Dilke, Old English plays vol 4, 1815; Women beware women ed C. W. Dilke, Old English plays vol 5, 1815; Old English drama vol 3, 1830; ed R. Gill 1968 (Mermaid ser).

The Mayor of Quinborough: a comedy, as it hath been often acted at Black-fryars by his Majesties servants. 1661, 1661; ed I. Reed, Dodsley vol 11, 1780; Ancient British drama vol 3, 1810; ed J. P. Collier, Dodsley vol 11, 1826; ed R. C. Bald 1938 (as Hengist, King of Kent: or the Mayor of Queenborough). Mss: (1) Folger Shakespeare Lib ms J.b.6; (2) ms in Library of the Duke of Portland, Welbeck Abbey.

Any thing for a quiet life: a comedy, formerly acted at Black-fryers by his late Majesties servants. 1662; ed F. L. Lucas, Works of Webster vol 4, 1927.

A tragi-coomodie called the Witch, long since acted by his Majesties servants at the Black-friers. 1778 (first ptd from ms discovered by I. Reed, now Bodley ms Malone 12); Ancient British drama vol 3, 1810; ed L. Drees and H. de Vocht, Louvain 1945; ed W. W. Greg and F. P. Wilson 1950 (Malone Soc).

In addition to The nice valour *and* Wit at several weapons *in the Beaumont and Fletcher canon, col 1713, below and Tourneur's* The revenger's tragedy, *col 1695, below, the following anon plays, cols 1758, 1761, below have been wholly or partially ascribed to Middleton:* The bloody banquet, The Puritan, The second maiden's tragedy.

§ 2

Hazlitt, W. In his Lectures on the dramatic literature of the age of Elizabeth, 1818.

Holthausen, F. Zu Middletons No wit no help like a woman's. Anglia 12 1889.

Wiggin, P. G. An inquiry into the authorship of the Middleton-Rowley plays. Boston 1897.

Morris, E. C. On the date and composition of the Old law. PMLA 17 1902.
— The allegory in A game at chesse. E Studien 38 1907.

Baker, G. P. A new source of the Changeling. Jnl of Comparative Lit 1 1903.

Baxmann, E. Middletons Lustspiel The widow und Boccaccios Il Decamerone III.3 und II.2. Halle 1904.

Jung, H. Das Verhältnis Middletons zu Shakspere. Leipzig 1904.

Christ, K. Quellenstudien zu den Dramen Middletons. Strasbourg 1905.

Swinburne, A. C. In his Age of Shakespeare, 1908.

Ristine, F. H. In his English tragicomedy: its origin and history, New York 1910.

Symons, A. Middleton and Rowley. CHEL vol 6 1910; rptd in his Studies in the Elizabethan drama, 1919.

Oliphant, E. H. C. Problems of authorship in Elizabethan dramatic literature. MP 8 1911. Suggests Middleton as author of Second maiden's tragedy.
— The bloodie banquet: a Dekker-Middleton play. TLS 17 Dec 1925.
— The authorship of the Revenger's tragedy. SP 23 1926. Attributes to Middleton.
— In his Plays of Beaumont and Fletcher, New Haven 1927.

Withington, R. The Lord Mayor's show for 1623. PMLA 30 1915.
— In his English pageantry, 2 vols Cambridge Mass 1918-20.

Grossman, R. In his Spanien und das elizabethanische Drama, Hamburg 1920.

Bradford, G. The women of Middleton and Webster. Sewanee Rev 29 1921.

Lawrence, W. J. Early substantive masques. TLS 8 Dec 1921.

Sykes, H. D. In his Sidelights on Elizabethan drama, 1924.
— Middleton's early non-dramatic works. N & Q 20 June 1925.

Lloyd, B. A minor source of the Changeling. MLR 19 1924.

Dunkel, W. D. The dramatic technique of Middleton in his comedies of London life. Chicago 1925.
— The authorship of Anything for a quiet life. PMLA 43 1928.
— The authorship of the Puritan. PMLA 45 1930.
— The authorship of the Revenger's tragedy. PMLA 46 1931.
— Did not Rowley merely revise Middleton? PMLA 48 1933.

Bullock, H. B. Middleton and the fashion in playmaking. PMLA 42 1927.

Hillebrand, H. N. Middleton's The viper's brood. MLN 42 1927.

Welsford, E. In her Court masque, 1927.

Buckingham, E. L. Campion's Art of English poesie and Middleton's Chaste maid in Cheapside. PMLA 43 1928.

Eliot, T. S. In his For Lancelot Andrewes, 1928; rptd in his Selected essays, 1932, and Elizabethan essays, 1934.

Wagner, B. M. New allusions to A game at chesse. PMLA 44 1929.

Bald, R. C. A new manuscript of Middleton's Game at chesse. MLR 25 1930.
— Assembled texts. Library 4th ser 12 1931. A game at chess.
— Middleton's civic employments. MP 31 1933.
— The sources of Middleton's city comedies. JEGP 33 1934.
— The chronology of Middleton's plays. MLR 32 1937.
— An early version of Middleton's Game at chesse. MLR 38 1943.
— The foul papers of a revision. Library 4th ser 26 1945. Your five gallants.

Eccles, M. Middleton's birth and education. RES 7 1931.
— Middleton a poett. SP 54 1957.

Tannenbaum, S. A. A Middleton forgery. PQ 12 1933. Reply by B. M. Wagner 14 1935.

Dowling, M. A note on Moll Cutpurse: The roaring girl. RES 10 1934.

Hoole, W. S. Middleton's use of imprese in Your five gallants. SP 31 1934.

Bradbrook, M. C. In her Themes and conventions of Elizabethan tragedy, Cambridge 1935.
— Lucrece and Othello. TLS 27 Oct 1950.
— In her Growth and structure of Elizabethan comedy, 1955.

Christian, M. G. Middleton's acquaintance with the Merrie conceited jests of George Peele. PMLA 50 1935.
— Non-dramatic sources for the rogues in Middleton's plays. Baltimore 1936.
— An autobiographical note by Middleton. N & Q 8 Oct 1938.
— Middleton's residence at Oxford. MLN 61 1946.
— A sidelight on the family history of Middleton. SP 44 1947.

Empson, W. In his Some versions of pastoral, 1935. On Changeling.

Moore, J. R. The contemporary significance of Middleton's Game at chesse. PMLA 50 1935.

Ellis-Fermor, U. M. In her Jacobean drama, 1936, 1958 (rev).

Spencer, T. In his Death and Elizabethan tragedy, Cambridge Mass 1936.

Bowers, F. T. Middleton's Fair quarrel and the duelling code. JEGP 36 1937.
— In his Elizabethan revenge tragedy, Princeton 1940.

Knights, L. C. In his Drama and society in the age of Jonson, 1937.

Seaton, E. Richard Galis and the witches of Windsor. Library 4th ser 18 1937. The old law, v.1.

Simpson, P. Women beware women. MLR 33 1938.

Fisher, M. Notes on the sources of some incidents in Middleton's London plays. RES 15 1939.
— Bronstrops: a note on A fair quarrell. MLR 35 1940.

Maxwell, B. The old law. In his Studies in Beaumont, Fletcher and Massinger, Chapel Hill 1939.

—— The date of Women beware women. PQ 22 1943.

—— Michaelmas term. PQ 22 1943.

—— A note on the date of the Family of love with a query on the Porter's Hall theatre. In Elizabethan studies in honor of G. F. Reynolds, Boulder 1945.

—— The phoenix. In J. Q. Adams memorial studies, Washington 1948.

—— Twenty good nights: the Knight of the burning pestle and Middleton's Family of love. MLN 63 1948. Reply by W. J. Olive, SP 47 1950.

—— Your five gallants. PQ 30 1951. IV.i–ii should precede III.i.

Gordon, D. J. No wit, no help like a woman's and Della Porta's La sorella. RES 17 1941.

Stoll, E. E. Heroes and villains: Shakespeare, Middleton, Byron, Dickens. RES 18 1942.

Gilbert, A. H. The prosperous wittol in Giovanni Battista Modio and Middleton. SP 41 1944.

Barker, R. H. The authorship of the Second maiden's tragedy and the Revenger's tragedy. Shakespeare Assoc Bull 20 1945.

—— Middleton. New York 1958.

Mathews, E. G. The murdered substitute tale. MLQ 6 1945.

Muir, K. Swinburne on Middleton TLS 24 Feb 1945. Emendations in Phoenix and Michaelmas term.

Akrigg, G. P. V. Middleton: an allusion to the Shakespeare First Folio. Shakespeare Assoc Bull 21 1946.

Boas, F. S. In his An introduction to Stuart drama, Oxford 1946.

Price, G. R. The shares of Middleton and Dekker in a collaborated play. Papers of Michigan Acad 30 1946.

—— The early editions of the Ant and the nightingale. PBSA 43 1949.

—— The first edition of A faire quarrell. Library 5th ser 4 1949.

—— Medical men in A faire quarrell. Bull History of Medicine 24 1950.

—— Compositors' methods with two quartos reprinted by Augustine Mathewes. PBSA 44 1950. A faire quarrell, Q2.

—— The authorship and the manuscript of the Old law. HLQ 16 1953.

—— The Huntington ms of A game at chesse. HLQ 17 1953.

—— The first edition of Your five gallants and of Michaelmas term. Library 5th ser 8 1953.

—— The manuscript and the quarto of the Roaring girl. Library 5th ser 11 1956.

—— The quartos of the Spanish gypsy and their relation to the Changeling. PBSA 52 1958.

—— The Latin oration in A game at chess. HLQ 23 1960.

—— Setting by formes in the first edition of the Phoenix. PBSA 56 1962.

—— Dividing the copy for Michaelmas term. PBSA 60 1966.

—— The early editions of A trick to catch the old one. Library 5th ser 22 1967.

Teagarden, L. J. The Dekker–Middleton problem in Michaelmas term. SE 26 1947.

Dodson, D. Middleton's Livia. PQ 27 1948.

—— Blurt, master constable. N & Q Feb 1959.

Eberle, G. J. Dekker's part in the Familie of love. In J. Q. Adams memorial studies, Washington 1948.

—— The composition and printing of A mad world, my masters. SB 3 1951.

Gardner, H. Milton's Satan and the theme of damnation in Elizabethan tragedy. E & S ('English Studies') new ser 1 1948. Discusses Changeling.

Wilson, E. M. and O. Turner. The Spanish protest against A game at chess. MLR 44 1949.

Reed, R. R. A factual interpretation of the Changeling's madhouse scenes. N & Q 10 June 1950.

Johansson, B. Religion and superstition in the plays of

Jonson and Middleton. Essays & Studies on Eng Lang & Lit (Upsala) 7 1950.

—— Law and lawyers in Elizabethan England as evidenced in the plays of Jonson and Middleton. Stockholm 1967.

Schoenbaum, S. Hengist, King of Kent and sexual preoccupation in Jacobean drama. PQ 29 1950.

—— The revenger's tragedy and Middleton's moral outlook. N & Q 6 Jan 1951.

—— Middleton's share in the Honest whore, pts 1 and 2. N & Q 5 Jan 1952.

—— Middleton's tragedies. New York 1955.

—— Middleton's tragi-comedies. MP 54 1956.

—— A chaste maid in Cheapside and Middleton's city comedy. In Studies in the English Renaissance drama in memory of K. J. Holzknecht, New York 1959.

—— A new Middleton record. MLR 55 1960.

—— Blurt, master constable: a possible authorship clue. Renaissance News 13 1960.

Olive, W. J. Imitation of Shakespeare in the Family of love. PQ 29 1950.

Falk, S. Plautus' Persa and A trick to catch the old one. MLN 66 1951.

Reeves, J. D. Middleton and Lily's Grammar: some parallels. N & Q 16 Feb 1952.

Engelberg, E. A Middleton–Rowley dispute. N & Q Aug 1953.

—— Tragic blindness in the Changeling and Women beware women. MLQ 23 1962.

McCullen, J. T. The use of parlor and tavern games in Elizabethan and early Stuart drama. MLQ 14 1953. Discusses Michaelmas term, Your five gallants, Women beware women, A game at chess.

Bullough, G. The game at chesse: how it struck a contemporary. MLR 49 1954.

Doran, M. In her Endeavors of art, Madison 1954.

Holzknecht, K. J. The dramatic structure of the Changeling. Renaissance Papers 1954.

Phialas, P. G. An unpublished letter about A game at chess. MLN 69 1954.

—— Middleton's early contact with the law. SP 52 1955.

Bawcutt, N. W. The changeling: a source for the subplot. N & Q June 1955.

—— Middleton's The phoenix as a royal play. N & Q July 1956.

Ewbank (Ekeblad), I.-S. A textual note on the Changeling. N & Q April 1955.

—— The tenant of Wildfell Hall and Women beware women. N & Q Dec 1963.

—— Realism and morality in Women beware women. E & S new ser 22 1969.

Jump, J. D. Middleton's tragicomedies. In The age of Shakespeare, ed B. Ford 1955 (Pelican).

Cutts, J. P. The original music to the Witch. Shakespeare Quart 7 1956.

Barber, C. L. A rare use of the word 'honour' as a criterion of Middleton's authorship. E Studies 38 1957.

Hibbard, G. R. The tragedies of Middleton and the decadence of the drama. Renaissance & Modern Stud 1 1957.

Power, W. Middleton vs King James I. N & Q Dec 1957.

—— The phoenix, Raleigh and King James. N & Q Feb 1958. Reply by D. B. Dodson, Oct 1958.

—— Double, double. N & Q Jan 1959. The roaring girl and Anything for a quiet life.

—— Middleton's way with names. N & Q Jan–May 1960.

Williamson, M. L. Middleton's workmanship and the authorship of the Puritan. N & Q Feb 1957.

—— Blurt, master constable, III.iii and the Batchelars banquet. N & Q Dec 1957.

—— The phoenix: Middleton's comedy de regimine principum. Renaissance News 10 1957.

Baker, D. C. Metaphor in Swift's A tale of a tub and Middleton's The family of love. N & Q March 1958.

Sabol, A. J. Two songs with accompaniment for an Elizabethan choirboy play. Stud in Renaissance 5 1958.

Music for the song 'what meat eats the Spaniard' in Blurt, master constable.

— Ravenscroft's Melismata and the children of Paul's. Renaissance News 12 1959. Contains first 2 lines of a lyric intended to be sung in A trick to catch the old one.

Dunlap, R. James I, Bacon, Middleton and the making of the Peacemaker. In Studies in the English Renaissance drama in memory of J. K. Holzknecht, New York 1959.

Ribner, I. Middleton's Women beware women: poetic imagery and the moral vision. Tulane Stud in Eng 9 1959.

— In his Jacobean tragedy: the quest for moral order, 1962.

Taylor, A. Proverbs and proverbial phrases in the plays of Middleton. Southern Folklore Quart 23 1959.

Hoy, C. The shares of Fletcher and his collaborators in the Beaumont and Fletcher canon, pt 5. SB 13 1960. Middleton's share in Nice valour and Wit at several weapons.

Ornstein, R. In his Moral vision of Jacobean tragedy, Madison 1960.

Parker, R. B. Middleton's experiments with comedy and judgment. In Jacobean theatre, ed J. R. Brown and B. Harris 1960.

Ricks, C. The moral and poetic structure of the Changeling. EC 10 1960.

— Word-play in Women beware women. RES new ser 12 1961.

Brooks, J. B. Middleton's step-father and the captain of the Phoenix. N & Q Oct 1961.

Cope, J. I. The date of Women beware women. MLN 76 1961.

Henslowe's Diary. Ed R. A. Foakes and R. T. Rickert, Cambridge 1961.

Lawrence, R. G. A bibliographical study of the Changeling. Library 5th ser 16 1961.

Levin, R. Littera canina in Romeo and Juliet and Michaelmas term. N & Q Sept 1962.

— The lady and her horsekeeper: Middleton or Rowley? N & Q Aug 1963. See also S. W. Wells, Jan 1960; replies by editors, Aug 1966, June 1967, and J. H. P. Pafford, Oct 1966.

— Dekker's back-door'd Italian and Middleton's Hebrew pen. N & Q Sept 1963. See also R. K. Turner, Jan 1960.

— The three quarrels of A fair quarrel. SP 61 1964.

— The Dampit scenes in A trick to catch the old one. MLQ 25 1964.

— Proverbial phrases in the titles of Middleton's plays. Southern Folklore Quart 28 1964.

— The four plots of A chaste maid in Cheapside. RES new ser 16 1965.

— Middleton's way with names in A chaste maid in Cheapside. N & Q March 1965.

— Name puns in the Family of love. N & Q Sept 1965.

— 'The ass in compound': a lost pun in Middleton, Ford and Jonson. Eng Lang Notes 4 1966.

— The family of lust and the Family of love. Stud in Eng Lit 1500–1900 6 1966.

Southall, R. A. A missing source-book for A game at chesse. N & Q April 1962. Reply by R. Pineas, Sept 1965.

Tomlinson, T. B. Poetic naturalism: the Changeling. JEGP 63 1964.

— In his A study of Elizabethan and Jacobean tragedy, Cambridge 1964.

Bains, Y. S. Middleton's Blurt, master constable as a burlesque on love. In Essays presented to Amy G. Stock, Jaipur 1965.

Chatterji, R. Theme, imagery and unity in A chaste maid in Cheapside. Renaissance Drama 8 1965.

— Unity and disparity: Michaelmas term. Stud in Eng Lit 1500–1900 8 1968.

Gross, A. G. Middleton's Your five gallants: the fifth act. PQ 44 1965.

Huddlestone, E. L. The Spanish gipsy and La gitanilla: an unnoticed borrowing. N & Q March 1965.

Dessen, A. C. Middleton's The phoenix and the allegorical tradition. Stud in Eng Lit 1500–1900 6 1966.

George, D. Weather-wise's almanac and the date of No wit no help like a woman's. N & Q Aug 1966.

— The problem of Middleton's The witch and its sources. N & Q June 1967.

— Middleton at Oxford. MLR 65 1970.

— Middleton's sources: a survey. N & Q Jan 1971.

Krook, D. Tragedy and satire: Middleton's Women beware women. In Studies in English language and literature, ed A. Shalvi and A. A. Mendilow, Jerusalem 1966.

Mehl, D. In his Elizabethan dumb show, Cambridge Mass 1966.

Ure, P. Patient madman and honest whore: the Middleton-Dekker oxymoron. E & S new ser 19 1966.

Aggeler, G. Irony and honour in Jacobean tragedy. Humanities Assoc Bull (Canada) 18 1967.

Farr, D. M. The changeling. MLR 62 1967.

Kehler, D. Rings and jewels in the Changeling. Eng Lang Notes 5 1967.

Bry, A. Middleton et le public des 'city comedies'. In Dramaturgie et société, ed J. Jacquot, Paris 1968.

Burlebach, F. M. Theme and structure in the Spanish gipsy. Humanities Assoc Bull (Canada) 19 1968.

Davidson, C. The phoenix: Middleton's didactic comedy. Papers on Lang & Lit 4 1968.

— Middleton and the family of love. Eng Miscellany (Rome) 20 1969.

Frost, D. L. In his School of Shakespeare, Cambridge 1968.

Gibbons, B. In his Jacobean city comedy: a study of satiric plays by Jonson, Marston and Middleton, 1968.

Stafford, T. J. Middleton's debt to Chaucer in the Changeling. Bull Rocky Mountain Modern Lang Assoc 22 1968.

Berlin, N. The 'finger' image and relationship of character in the Changeling. Eng Stud in Africa 12 1969.

Hallett, C. A. Middleton's Allwit: the urban cynic. MLQ 30 1969.

— Volpone as the source of the sickroom scheme in Middleton's Mad world. N & Q Jan 1971.

— Penitent Brothel, the succubus and Parsons' Resolution: a reappraisal of Penitent's position in Middleton's canon. SP 69 1972.

Holmes, D. M. Middleton's Blurt, master-constable: or the Spaniard's night-walk. MLR 64 1969.

— The art of Middleton: a critical study. Oxford 1970.

Marotti, A. F. Fertility and comic form in A chaste maid in Cheapside. Comparative Drama 3 1969.

— The method in the madness of A mad world, my masters. Tennessee Stud in Lit 15 1970.

Slights, W. W. The trickster-hero and Middleton's A mad world, my masters. Comparative Drama 3 1969.

Jordan, R. Myth and psychology in the Changeling. Renaissance Drama new ser 3 1970.

Soens, A. L. Lawyers, collusions and cudgels: Middleton's Anything for a quiet life 1.i.220–221. Eng Lang Notes 7 1970.

Stagg, L. C. An index to the figurative language of Middleton's tragedies. Charlottesville 1970.

Williams, R. I. Machiavelli's Mandragola, Touchwood senior and the comedy of A chaste maid in Cheapside. Stud in Eng Lit 1500–1900 10 1970.

Holdsworth, R. V. A fair quarrel: an unnoticed borrowing. N & Q Jan 1971.

Kaplan, J. H. The feast day of Middleton's Loyola. N & Q Jan 1971.

Lake, D. J. The revenger's tragedy: internal evidence for Tourneur's authorship negated. N & Q Dec 1971.

Levine, R. T. Rare use of 'since' in Middleton's The widow and A chaste maid. N & Q Dec 1971.

BEN JONSON
1572?–1637

Bibliographies

Tannenbaum, S. A. Jonson: a concise bibliography. New York 1938; Supplement, New York 1947.

Steensma, R. C. Jonson: a checklist of editions, biography and criticism 1947–64. Research Opportunities in Renaissance Drama 9 1966.

Guffey, G. R. Elizabethan bibliographies supplements III: Jonson 1947–65. 1968.

Collections

The workes of Benjamin Jonson. 1616. Contains Every man in his humour, Every man out of his humour, Cynthia's revels, Poetaster, Sejanus, Volpone, Epicoene, Alchemist, Catiline, Epigrammes, Forrest, and entertainments and masques listed below to Mercurie vindicated.

The workes of Benjamin Jonson. 1640. The first vol reprints 1616, above. The 2nd (individual title-pages of which are variously dated 1631, 1640, 1641) contains Bartholomew fayre, Divell is an asse, Staple of newes, Magnetick lady, A tale of a tub, Sad shepherd, Underwood, Mortimer his fall, Horace his art of poetrie, English grammar, Timber, Execration against Vulcan, and entertainments and masques listed below from Christmas his masque, omitting An entertainment at the Blackfriars.

The works of Ben Jonson. 1692 (adds New inne, Leges convivales), 1716–17.

Four select plays: Epicoene, Volpone, Catiline, Alchemist [with Shadwell's Timon of Athens]. Advertised in Post-boy 16 March 1710.

Ben Johnson's plays in two volumes. 2 vols Dublin 1729. Volpone, Catiline, Bartholomew fair, Sejanus, Epicoene, Every man in and out of his humour, Alchemist.

The three celebrated plays of Ben Johnson. 1732 (Volpone, Alchemist, Epicoene), 1739 (with Bartholomew fair).

The favourite and celebrated comedies of Johnson. 1738. Volpone, Alchemist, Epicoene, Bartholomew fair.

Plays. Glasgow 1752. Volpone, Alchemist, Epicoene.

Works. Ed P. Whalley 7 vols 1756 (adds Case is altered).

Poems. Ed R. Anderson, Edinburgh 1793.

Poems. Ed A. Chalmers 1810.

Works. Ed W. Gifford 9 vols 1816; rptd F. Cunningham 3 vols 1871 (with corrections), 9 vols 1875.

The progresses, processions and magnificent festivities of King James the First. Ed J. Nichols 4 vols 1828. Reprints all the masques and entertainments.

Works. Ed 'Barry Cornwall' (B. W. Procter) 1838.

Poems. Ed R. Bell 1856.

Plays and poems. Ed H. Morley 1885. Alchemist, Volpone, Epicoene, Sad shepherd.

Dramatic works and lyrics. Ed J. A. Symonds 1886. Selection.

Masques and entertainments. Ed H. Morley 1890. Omits entertainments at Welbeck, Bolsover and Blackfriars.

Ben Jonson. Ed B. Nicholson, introd by C. H. Herford 3 vols 1893–4 (Mermaid ser). Contains Every man in and out of his humour, Poetaster, Bartholomew fair, Cynthia's revels, Sejanus, Volpone, Epicoene, Alchemist.

English masques. Ed H. A. Evans 1897. Contains Haddington masque, Masque of Queens, Oberon, Golden age restored, Lovers made men, News from the new world, Masque of augurs, Pan's anniversary, Neptune's triumph, Fortunate isles.

Ben Jonsons Dramen nach der Folio 1616. Ed W. Bang 2 pts Bang vol 7, 1905–8. Contains Every man in and out of his humour, Cynthia's revels, Poetaster, Sejanus, Volpone, and first half of Epicoene.

Works. Ed H. C. Hart 2 vols 1906. Incomplete.

Complete plays. Ed F. E. Schelling 2 vols 1910 (EL).

Works. Ed C. H. Herford, P. and E. M. Simpson 11 vols Oxford 1925–52. Standard edn of complete works.

Poems. Ed H. H. Hudson, New York 1936 (fac); ed B. H. Newdigate, Oxford 1936.

Selected works. Ed H. Levin, New York 1938.

Five plays. Oxford 1953 (WC). Contains Every man in his humour, Sejanus, Volpone, Alchemist, Bartholomew fair.

Poems. Ed G. B. Johnston 1954 (ML).

Poems. Ed J. Hollander, New York 1961.

Poems. Ed W. B. Hunter, New York 1963.

Complete masques. Ed S. Orgel, New Haven 1969.

Literary criticism. Ed J. D. Redwine 1970. Selection.

§ I
(in probable order of composition)

A tale of a tub. 1640 (licensed 7 May 1633, original version written c. 1596–7); ed H. Scherer, Bang vol 39, 1913; ed F. M. Snell, New York 1915.

The case is alterd, as it hath beene sundry times acted by the children of the Blacke-friers. 1609, 1609 (original version written c. 1597–8); ed W. E. Selin, New Haven 1917.

Every man in his humour, as it hath beene sundry times publickly acted by the Right Honorable the Lord Chamberlaine his servants. 1601 (acted 1598), 1616 (rev); 4° text of 1601 ed C. Grabau, Sh Jb 38 1902; ed W. W. Greg, Bang vol 10, 1905; folio text of 1616 ed W. Scott, Modern British drama vol 3, 1811; ed H. B. Wheatley 1877; ed W. M. Dixon 1901; ed H. Maas, Rostock 1901; ed W. A. Neilson, Chief Elizabethan dramatists, 1911; ed C. H. Herford, Gayley vol 2, 1913; ed P. Simpson, Oxford 1919; ed R. S. Knox 1923; ed G. B. Harrison 1926; ed C. F. T. Brooke and N. B. Paradise, English drama 1933; ed H. Spencer, Elizabethan plays 1933; ed C. R. Baskervill, Elizabethan and Stuart plays, 1934; ed A. Sale 1941, 1949 (rev); ed M. Seymour-Smith 1967 (New Mermaid ser); ed G. B. Jackson, New Haven 1969. Parallel texts of 4° and folio versions ed H. H. Carter, New Haven 1921; ed J. W. Lever 1971 (Regents ser).

The comicall satyre of Every man out of his humor, as it was first composed by the author B.J. 1600 (3 4° edns) (acted 1599), 1616 (rev); first 4° text ed W. W. Greg and F. P. Wilson 1921 (Malone Soc); 2nd–3rd 4° texts ed W. Bang and Greg, Bang vols 16–17 1907.

The fountaine of selfe-love: or Cynthias revels, as it hath beene sundry times privately acted in the Black-friers by the children of her Majesties chappell. 1601 (acted 1600), 1616 (rev); 4° text of 1601 ed W. Bang and L. Krebs, Bang vol 22, 1908; folio text of 1616 ed A. C. Judson, New York 1912.

Poems. In R. Chester, Love's martyr, 1601; ed A. B. Grosart 1878 (New Shakspere Soc); ed B. H. Newdigate, The phoenix and the turtle, Oxford 1937.

Poetaster: or the arraignment, as it hath beene sundry times privately acted in the Blacke friers by the children of her Majesties chappell. 1602 (acted 1601), 1616 (rev); 4° text of 1602 ed H. de Vocht, Louvain 1934; folio text of 1616 ed H. S. Mallory, New York 1905; ed J. H. Penniman, Boston 1913.

Sejanus his fall. 1605 (acted 1603), 1616 (rev); 4° text of 1605 ed H. de Vocht, Louvain 1935; folio text of 1616 ed W. D. Briggs, Boston 1911; ed W. A. Neilson, Chief Elizabethan dramatists, 1911; ed C. R. Baskervill, Elizabethan and Stuart plays, 1934; ed J. A. Barish, New Haven 1965; ed W. Bolton 1966 (New Mermaid ser).

Part of King James his royall and magnificent entertainment [on his state-entry into London 15 March 1604]; also a briefe panegyre of his Majesties first and well auspicated entrance to his High Court of Parliament [19 March 1604], with other additions [Entertainment of the Queen and Prince at Althrope 25 June 1603]. 1604, 1616.

A private entertainment of the King and Queen at High-gate. 1616 (presented 1 May 1604). The Penates.

Eastward hoe. 1605. With Chapman and Marston; *see under Chapman, col 1638, above.*

Volpone: or the foxe. 1607 (acted 1605), 1616, 1709; 4° text of 1607 ed V. O'Sullivan 1898; ed H. de Vocht, Louvain 1937; Menston 1968 (facs); folio text of 1616 ed W. Scott, Modern British drama vol 3, 1811; Old English drama vol 1, 1830; ed H. B. Wilkins, Paris 1906; ed W. A. Neilson, Chief Elizabethan dramatists, 1911; ed J. D. Rea, New Haven 1919; ed F. E. Schelling, Typical Elizabethan plays, New York 1926; ed C. F. T. Brooke and N. B. Paradise, English drama, 1933; ed H. Spencer, Elizabethan plays, 1933; ed C. R. Baskervill, Elizabethan and Stuart plays, 1934; ed A. Sale 1951; ed J. A. Barish, New York 1958; ed A. B. Kernan, New Haven 1962; ed J. B. Bamborough 1964; ed D. Cook 1967; ed P. Brockbank 1968 (New Mermaid ser); ed J. L. Halio 1968; tr Italian, 1943; French, 1946.

The characters of two royall masques, the one of black-nesse, the other of beautie. 1608 (performed respectively 6 Jan 1605, 10 Jan 1608), 1616. A ms of The masque of blackness is in BM ms Royal 17B.XXXI; rptd by J. P. Collier, Five Court masques, 1848 (Shakespeare Soc), and in Herford and Simpson edn of Jonson vol 7, pp. 195–201.

Hymenaei. 1606 (performed 5 Jan 1606), 1616.

The entertainment of the two Kings of Great Britaine and Denmarke at Theobalds. 1616 (presented 24 July 1606). BM ms Egerton 2877, f. 162b (speech of Eumone, Dice and Irene).

An entertainment of King James and Queene Anne at Theobalds. 1616 (presented 22 May 1607).

The description of the masque celebrating the marriage of John, Lord Ramsey, Viscount Haddington. 1608 (performed 9 Feb 1608), 1616; ed F. E. Schelling, Typical Elizabethan plays, New York 1926; ed C. R. Baskervill, Elizabethan and Stuart plays, 1934. Entitled by Gifford The hue and cry after Cupid.

The masque of Queenes. 1609 (performed 2 Feb 1609), 1616. BM ms Royal 18A.XLV; ed J. P. Collier, Five Court masques, 1848 (Shakespeare Soc); ed G. Chapman 1930 (facs, with Inigo Jones's designs).

Epicoene: or the silent woman. 1616 (acted 1609), 1620, 1709; Old English drama vol 3, 1830; ed A. Henry, New York 1906; ed C. M. Gayley vol 2, 1913; ed C. F. T. Brooke and N. B. Paradise, English drama, 1933; ed L. A. Beaurline 1966 (Regents ser).

The speeches at Prince Henries barriers. 1616 (performed 6 Jan 1610).

The alchemist. 1612 (acted 1610), 1616, 1709; 4° text of 1612, 1927 (facs); folio text of 1616 ed W. Scott, Modern British drama vol 3, 1811; ed C. M. Hathaway, New York 1903; ed F. E. Schelling, Boston 1903; ed W. A. Neilson, Chief Elizabethan dramatists, 1911; ed G. A. Smithson, Gayley vol 2, 1913; ed C. F. T. Brooke and N. B. Paradise, English drama, 1933; ed H. Spencer, Elizabethan plays, 1933; ed C. R. Baskervill, Elizabethan and Stuart plays, 1934; ed G. E. Bentley, New York 1947; ed R. J. L. Kingsford, Cambridge 1948; ed H. de Vocht, Louvain 1950; ed D. Brown 1966 (New Mermaid ser); ed J. Bamborough 1967; ed F. H. Mares 1967 (Revels ser); ed J. B. Steane, Cambridge 1967; ed S. Musgrove 1968; tr Italian, 1948.

Oberon: the Faery Prince. 1616 (performed 1 Jan 1611); ed R. Hosley, A book of masques in honour of Allardyce Nicoll, Cambridge 1967.

Love freed from ignorance and folly. 1616 (performed 3 Feb 1611); ed N. Sanders, A book of masques in honour of Allardyce Nicoll, Cambridge 1967.

Catiline his conspiracy. 1611 (acted 1611), 1616, 1635, 1635, 1669, 1674, 1739; ed L. H. Harris, New Haven 1916; ed W. Bolton and J. F. Gardner 1972 (Regents ser).

Love restored. 1616 (performed 6 Jan 1612).

Epigrammes. 1616 (S.R. 15 May 1612).

The Irish masque. 1616 (performed 29 Dec 1613, 3 Jan 1614).

A challenge at tilt. 1616 (performed 1 Jan 1614).

Bartholomew fayre. 1631, 1640 (acted 31 Oct 1614), 1739; ed C. S. Alden, New York 1904; ed H. Spencer, Eliza-bethan plays 1933; ed E. A. Horsman 1960 (Revels ser); ed E. M. Waith, New Haven 1963; ed M. Hussey 1964 (New Mermaid ser); ed E. B. Partridge 1964 (Regents ser).

The golden age restored. 1616 (performed presumably on 6, 8 Jan 1615).

Mercurie vindicated from the alchemists. 1616 (performed presumably on 1, 6 Jan 1616).

The forrest. 1616.

The Divell is an asse. 1631, 1640 (acted 1616), 1641, 1669; ed W. S. Johnson, New York 1905; ed M. Hussey 1967.

Christmas his masque. 1641 (performed 1616). Mss: (1) Folger Lib ms J.a.1; (2) Bodley ms Rawlinson poetry 160, ff. 173–4 (song of Christmas only); (3) BM ms Harley 4955, ff. 46–7 (song of Christmas only).

The vision of delight. 1641 (performed 6, 19 Jan 1617). BM ms Harley 4955, ff. 40–1 (fragment).

Lovers made men: a masque presented in the house of the Honorable the Lord Haye. 1617 (performed 22 Feb 1617), 1641; ed S. Wells, A book of masques in honour of Allardyce Nicoll, Cambridge 1967.

Pleasure reconciled to virtue. 1641 (performed 6 Jan 1618); ed R. A. Foakes, A book of masques in honour of Allardyce Nicoll, Cambridge 1967. Ms in Duke of Devonshire's collection at Chatsworth.

For the honour of Wales. 1641 (performed 18 Feb 1618).

Newes from the new world discover'd in the moone. 1641 (performed 17 Jan, 29 Feb 1620).

An entertainment at the Blackfriars (performed at christening of Charles Cavendish, May 1620). BM ms Harley 4955, ff.48–52; rptd Monthly Mag Feb 1816.

Pans anniversarie: or the shepherds holy-day. 1641 (performed 19 June 1620).

The gypsies metamorphos'd. 1640, 1640 (with extensive addns), 1641 (performed 3, 5 Aug, Sept 1621); ed G. W. Cole, New York 1931; ed C. F. T. Brooke and N. B. Paradise, English drama, 1933; ed W. W. Greg 1952. Mss: (1) Huntington Lib ms HM 741; (2) BM ms Harley 4955, ff. 2–30; (3) ms (fragment) in Conway papers in Public Record Office (State Papers Domestic, James I, CXXII, article 58); (4) Bodley ms Tanner 306, f. 252 (fragment); (5) Bodley ms Rawlinson poetry 172, f. 78 (fragment).

The masque of augures. [1622] (performed 6 Jan, 5 or 6 May 1622), 1641 (rev).

Time vindicated to himselfe and to his honors. [1623] (performed 19 Jan 1623), 1641.

Neptunes triumph for the returne of Albion. [1624] (planned for performance 6 Jan 1624), 1641.

The masque of owles. 1641 (performed 19 Aug 1624).

The fortunate isles and their union. [1625] (performed 9 Jan 1625), 1641. A revision of Neptunes triumph.

The staple of newes. 1631, 1640 (acted 1625); ed De Winter, New York 1905.

The new inne: or the light heart. 1631 (acted 1629), 1692; ed G. B. Tennant, New York 1908.

Loves triumph through Callipolis. 1630 (for 1631) (performed 9 Jan 1631), 1641.

Chloridia. [1631] (performed 22 Feb 1631), 1641.

The magnetick lady: or humors reconcild. 1640 (acted 1632); ed H. W. Peck, New York 1914.

The Kings entertainment at Welbeck. 1641 (presented 31 May 1633). BM ms Harley 4955, ff. 194–8.

Loves wel-come at Bolsover. 1641 (performed 30 July 1634). BM ms Harley 4955, ff. 199–202.

The sad shepherd: or a tale of Robin Hood. 1641 (3 acts only); ed F. G. Waldron 1783 (with continuation); ed W. W. Greg, Bang vol 11, 1905 (with Waldron's continuation); ed F. E. Schelling, Typical Elizabethan plays, New York 1926; ed L. J. Potts, Cambridge 1929; ed C. R. Baskervill, Elizabethan and Stuart plays, 1934; ed and completed A. Porter, New York 1944.

The under-wood. 1640, Cambridge 1905.

Mortimer his fall. 1640 (one scene only).

Horace his art of poetrie. 1640. Variant versions ptd in 12° and in folio collection; the 12° text rptd E. H. Blakeney 1928.

The English grammar. 1640; ed A. V. Waite 1909; ed S. Gibson 1928.

Timber: or discoveries made upon men and matter. 1641; ed H. Morley 1892; ed F. E. Schelling 1892; ed I. Gollancz 1898; ed M. Castelain, Paris [1906]; ed G. B. Harrison 1923; ed R. S. Walker, Syracuse NY 1953.

Execration against Vulcan, with divers epigrams. 1640 (edns in 4°, 12° and in folio collection).

Leges convivales. 1692.

For occasional poems not ptd in the folios, see Herford and Simpson vol 8, pp. 359–423.

Jonson has been connected with 2 plays in the Beaumont and Fletcher canon: Rollo Duke of Normandy: or the bloody brother, *col 1712, below, and* Love's pilgrimage, *col 1709, below. The title-page ascription to him (with Middleton and Fletcher) of* The widow *is generally rejected: see under Middleton, col 1648, above.*

Letters and Memoirs

Letters. Works vol 1, ed C. H. Herford and P. Simpson, Oxford 1925.

Dobell, B. Newly discovered documents of the Elizabethan and Jacobean periods. Athenaeum 30 March, 13 April 1901. 3 letters, now in ms v.a.321 in Folger Shakespeare Lib.

Simpson, P. Jonson and Cecilia Bulstrode. TLS 6 March 1930. One letter.

Heads of a conversation betwixt Ben Johnson and William Drummond. In Drummond's Works, Edinburgh 1711; ed D. Laing, Archaeologica scotica vol 4, 1833; 1842 (Shakespeare Soc); rptd in Gifford's Jonson vol 3, ed F. Cunningham 1871; ed P. Sidney 1906; ed G. B. Harrison 1923; ed R. F. Patterson 1923; ed C. H. Herford and P. Simpson, Works vol 1, Oxford 1925.

§2

Dekker, Thomas. Satiromastix: or the untrussing of the humorous poet. 1602.

Taylor, John. A funeral elegy upon the death of B. Jonson, poet. 1637.

Jonsonus virbius: or the memory of Ben Jonson revived by the friends of the Muses. Ed B. Duppa 1638.

Davenant, Sir William. To Doctor Duppa: an acknowledgment for his collection in honour of Ben Johnson's memory. In his Madagascar with other poems, 1638.

Fuller, Thomas. In his History of the worthies of England [Westminster, p. 243], 1662; ed J. Nichols, vol 2, 1811.

Dryden, John. Examen of the Silent woman. In his Of dramatick poesie: an essay, 1668.

Aubrey, John. Lives. 1813; ed A. Clark, Oxford 1898; ed C. H. Herford and P. Simpson in Ben Jonson, Works vol 1, Oxford 1925.

Upton, J. Remarks on three plays of Jonson. 1749. Volpone, Epicoene, Alchemist.

Chetwood, W. R. Memoirs of the life and writings of Ben Jonson. Dublin 1756.

Gilchrist, O. G. An examination of the charges of Jonson's enmity towards Shakespeare. 1808.

— A letter to W. Gifford. 1811.

Hazlitt, W. In his Lectures on the dramatic literature of the age of Elizabeth, 1818.

— On Shakespeare and Jonson. In his Lectures on the English comic writers, 1819.

Baudissin, W. von. Jonson und seine Schule. 2 vols Leipzig 1836.

Coleridge, S. T. Notes on Jonson. In his Literary remains vol 1, 1836.

Schmidt, A. Essay on the life and dramatic writings of Jonson. Danzig 1847.

[Cartwright, R.] Shakespeare and Jonson: dramatic versus wit combats. 1864.

Buff, A. The quarto edition of Every man in his humour. E Studien 1 1877.

Saegelken, C. Jonsons Römerdramen. Bremen 1880.

Nicholson, B. On the dates of the two versions of Every man in his humour. Antiquary 6 1882.

Symonds, J. A. Ben Jonson. 1886.

Holthausen, F. Die Quelle von Jonsons Volpone. Anglia 12 1889.

Swinburne, A. C. A study of Ben Jonson. 1889.

Hoffschulte, H. Ueber Jonsons ältere Lustspiele. Münster 1894.

Koeppel, E. Quellenstudien zu den Dramen Jonsons, Marstons und Beaumont und Fletchers. Erlangen 1895.

— Jonsons Wirkung auf zeitgenössische Dramatiker. Heidelberg 1906.

Simpson, P. Field and Jonson. N & Q 19 Oct 1895.

— Tanquam explorator: Jonson's method in the Discoveries. MLR 2 1907.

— and C. F. Bell. Designs by Inigo Jones for masques and plays at Court. 1924.

Simpson, P. The genuineness of the Drummond conversations. RES 2 1926.

— Jonson on Chapman. TLS 3 March 1932.

— The Jonson exhibition. Bodleian Lib Record 8 1937.

— Jonson and the Devil Tavern. MLR 34 1939.

— The problem of authorship of Eastward ho. PMLA 59 1944.

— The art of Jonson. E & S 30 1944; rptd in his Studies in Elizabethan drama, Oxford 1955.

— The castle of the rosy cross: Jonson and Theophilus Schweighardt. MLR 41 1946.

— Beaumont's verse-letter to Jonson. MLR 46 1951.

— A Westminster schoolboy and Jonson. TLS 27 Nov 1953.

Penniman, J. H. The war of the theatres. Boston 1897.

Grossmann, H. Jonson als Kritiker. Berlin 1898.

Reinsch, H. Jonsons Poetik und seine Beziehungen zu Horaz. Naumburg 1898.

Schelling, F. E. Jonson and the classical school. Baltimore 1898.

Woodbridge, E. Studies in Jonson's comedies. 1898.

Small, R. A. The stage-quarrel between Jonson and the so-called poetasters. Breslau 1899.

Hofmiller, J. Die ersten sechs Masken Jonsons in ihrem Verhältnis zur antiken Literatur. Freising 1901.

Hollstein, E. Verhältnis von Jonsons Devil is an ass und John Wilsons Belphegor zu Machiavellis Novelle vom Belfagor. Halle 1901.

Lumley, E. P. The influence of Plautus on the comedies of Jonson. 1901.

Stanger, H. Der Einfluss Jonsons auf Ludwig Tieck. Studien zur Vergleichenden Litteraturgeschichte 1–2 1901–2.

Brotanek, R. In his Die englischen Maskenspiele, Vienna 1902.

Herpich, C. A. Shakespeare and Jonson: did they quarrel? N & Q 12 April 1902.

Hart, H. C. Gabriel Harvey, Marston, Jonson and Nashe. N & Q 14 March, 11 April, 2 May, 27 June, 29 Aug, 3, 31 Oct, 21 Nov, 19 Dec 1903, 14 May 1904.

— 'The captain' in Fletcher and Jonson. N & Q 3 Sept 1904.

Adams, J. Q. The sources of Volpone. MP 2 1904.

— The sources of News from the new world discovered in the moon. MLN 21 1906.

— The bones of Jonson. SP 16 1919.

— Eastward hoe and its satire against the Scots. SP 28 1931.

Aronstein, P. Shakespeare und Jonson. E Studien 34 1904.
— Jonson. Heidelberg 1906.
— Fletchers Love's pilgrimage und Jonsons The new inn. E Studien 43 1911.
Sarrazin, G. Nym und Jonson. Sh Jb 40 1904.
Crawford, C. Jonson and the Bloody brother. Sh Jb 41 1905.
— Jonson's method of composing verse. In Collectanea vol 1, Stratford 1906.
— Jonson's Case is altered: its date. N & Q 16 Jan 1909.
Garnet, R. Jonson's probable authorship of scene 2, act 4, of Fletcher's The bloody brother. MP 2 1905.
Spingarn, J. E. The sources of Jonson's Discoveries. MP 2 1905.
Vogt, A. Catiline und ihre Quellen. Halle 1905.
Bang, W. Jonson und Castigliones Cortegiano. E Studien 36 1906.
Greg, W. W. Jonson's Staple of news. MLR 1 1906.
— In his Pastoral poetry and pastoral drama, 1906.
— The riddle of Jonson's chronology. Library 4th ser 6 1929.
— Some notes on Jonson's works. RES 2 1926.
— Jonson's masques: points of editorial principle and practice. RES 18 1942. Reply by E. M. Simpson, ibid.
— Shakespeare and Jonson. RES 22 1946.
Castelain, M. Jonson: l'homme et l'oeuvre. Paris 1907.
— Shakespeare et Jonson. Revue Germanique 3 1907.
Jusserand, J. J. Jonson's views on Shakespeare's art. In Shakespeare Head edn of Shakespeare vol 10, Stratford 1907.
Nason, A. H. Heralds and heraldry in Jonson's plays, masques and entertainments. New York 1907.
Baskervill, C. R. The sources of Jonson's Masque of Christmas and Love's welcome at Welbeck. MP 6 1908.
— English elements in Jonson's early comedy. Texas Univ Bull no 178 1911.
Birck, P. Literarische Anspielungen in den Werken Jonsons. Strasbourg 1908.
Herford, C. H. Jonson and the Cardinal Duperron. MLR 4 1908.
Smith, K. F. On the source of Jonson's song 'Still to be neat'. Amer Jnl of Philology 29 1908.
Chambers, E. K. Jonson and the Isle of dogs. MLR 4 1909.
Reyher, P. In his Les masques anglais, Paris 1909.
Kittredge, G. L. King James I and the Devil is an ass. MP 9 1911.
Briggs, W. D. The influence of Jonson's tragedy in the 17th century. Anglia 35 1912.
— Notes on Underwoods 30 and on the New inn. MP 10 1913.
— Studies in Jonson 1–5. Anglia 37–9 1913–16.
— On certain incidents in Jonson's life. MP 11 1914.
— Jonson's third ode to himself. Athenaeum 13 June 1914.
— Recovered lines of Jonson. MLN 29 1914. The conclusion of Forest 12.
— Source-material for Jonson's plays. MLN 31 1916. Alchemist, Bartholomew fair, Catiline, Devil is an ass, Epicoene.
— Source-material for Jonson's Epigrams and Forest. Classical Philology 11 1916.
— Cynthia's revels. In [Ewald] Flügel memorial volume, Stanford 1916.
— Source-material for Jonson's Underwoods and miscellaneous poems. MP 15 1917.
— The birth-date of Jonson. MLN 33 1918.
Kerr, M. The influence of Jonson on English comedy. Philadelphia 1912.
Sullivan, M. In his Court masques of James I, 1913.
Snell, F. M. The date of Jonson's Tale of a tub. MLN 30 1915.
Stonex, A. B. The sources of the Staple of news. PMLA 30 1915.

Graves, T. S. Jonson's Epicoene and Lady Arabella Stuart. MP 14 1917.
— Jonson in the jest books. In [J. M.] Manly anniversary studies, New York 1923.
Clark, D. L. The requirements of a poet. MP 16 1918. On sources of Timber 130.
Harris, L. H. Local color in Catiline and historical accuracy of the play. Classical Philology 14 1919.
— Lucan's Pharsalia and Catiline. MLN 34 1919.
— Three notes on Jonson. MP 17 1920.
Smith, G. G. Jonson. 1919 (EML).
Eliot, T. S. In his Sacred wood, 1920; rptd in his Selected essays, 1932, and Elizabethan essays, 1934.
Bradley, J. F. and J. Q. Adams. The Jonson allusion-book 1597–1700. New Haven 1922.
Swaen, A. E. H. Two notes on Jonson's Tale of a tub. Neophilologus 7 1922.
Huxley, A. In his On the margin, 1923.
Keller, W. Shakespeare, Jonson und die Folio von 1623. Sh Jb 59–60 1924.
— Jonson and Shakespeare. Sh Jb 73 1937.
Enders, J. F. A note on Jonson's Staple of news. MLN 40 1925.
Gollancz, I. Jonson's Ode to the phoenix and the turtle. TLS 8 Oct 1925.
— Jonson and the Elizabethan Tacitus. TLS 10 May 1928. Replies by P. Simpson 14 June; I. Gollancz 21 June; M. J. Ryan 19 July 1928.
Dunn, E. C. Jonson's art. Northampton Mass 1925.
Pottle, F. A. The staple of news. MLN 40 1925.
Stainer, C. L. Jonson and Drummond, their conversations: a few remarks on an 18th-century forgery. Oxford 1925. See F. P. Hett, The memoirs of Sir Robert Sibbald, Oxford 1932.
Fischer, W. Tieck als Jonson-Philologe. Sh Jb 62 1926.
Welsford, E. In her Court masque, 1927.
Allen, P. Shakespeare, Jonson and Wilkins as borrowers. 1928.
Gray, A. How Shakespeare 'purged' Jonson. Cambridge 1928.
Brown, H. Jonson and Rabelais. MLN 44 1929.
Evans, W. In his Jonson and Elizabethan music, Lancaster Pa 1929.
Knowlton, E. C. The plots of Jonson. MLN 44 1929.
Lindsey, E. S. The music in Jonson's plays. Ibid.
Marckwardt, A. H. A fashionable expression: its st atus in Poetaster and Satiromastix. Ibid.
Osborn, L. B. Jonson and Hoskyns. TLS 1 May 1930.
Warren, A. Pope and Jonson. MLN 45 1930.
Campbell, O. J. The relation of Epicoene to Aretino's Il marescalco. PMLA 46 1931.
— The dramatic construction of Poetaster. Huntington Lib Bull no 9 1936.
— Comicall satyre and Shakespeare's Troilus and Cressida. San Marino 1938.
Howell, A. C. A note on Jonson's literary methods. SP 28 1931.
Johnston, G. B. Notes on Jonson's Execration upon Vulcan. MLN 46 1931.
— Notes on Jonson. TLS 7 Feb 1935.
— Ben Jonson: poet. Cambridge Mass 1945.
— Scott and Jonson. N & Q 25 Nov 1950.
— An epistle mendicant by Jonson. N & Q Nov 1954.
— Jonson's Perseus upon Pegasus. RES new ser 6 1955. Reply by J. D. Reeves, ibid.
— An apocryphal Jonsonian epigram. N & Q Dec 1958.
Linklater, E. Jonson and King James: a biography and a portrait. 1931.
Maxwell, B. The date of Love's pilgrimage and its relation to the New inn. SP 28 1931.
Shamberg, R. S. The critic in Jonson's plays. Pittsburgh Univ Bull 28 1931.
van Draat, P. F. Sheridan's Rivals and Jonson's Every man in his humour. Neophilologus 18 1933.

Mueschke, P. and J. Fleisher. Jonsonian elements in the comic underplot of Twelfth night. PMLA 48 1933.

Tillotson, G. Othello and the Alchemist at Oxford in 1610. TLS 6 July 1933. Replies by F. S. Boas 31 Aug 1933 and M. Summers 7 Sept 1933.

van Dam, B. A. P. A prompt-book text of the Alchemist [1791] and its important lesson. Neophilologus 19 1934.

Gebhardt, E. R. Jonson's appreciation of Chaucer as evidenced in the English grammar. MLN 49 1934.

Howarth, R. G. The Alchemist and Epicoene. TLS 3 May 1934.

Nethercot, A. H. Milton, Jonson and the young Cowley. MLN 49 1934.

Palmer, J. Ben Jonson. 1934.

Pfeffer, K. Das elisabethanische Sprichwort bei Jonson. Giessen 1933.

Walker, R. S. Jonson's lyric poetry. Criterion 13 1934.

Allen, H. E. Dicing fly and the Alchemist. TLS 27 June, 1 Aug 1935.

Knights, L. C. Tradition and Jonson. Scrutiny 4 1935.
— Drama and society in the age of Jonson. 1937.
— Ben Jonson, dramatist. In The age of Shakespeare, ed B. Ford 1955 (Pelican).

Newdigate, B. H. Jonson's Underwood. TLS 7 Feb 1935. The correct title.

Noyes, R. G. Jonson on the English stage 1660–1776. Cambridge Mass 1935.
— Jonson's masques in the 18th century. SP 33 1936.
— A manuscript Restoration prologue for Volpone. MLN 52 1937.

ten Hoor, G. J. Jonson's reception in Germany. PQ 14 1935.

Bowers, F. T. Dekker and Jonson. TLS 12 Sept 1936.
— Jonson the actor. SP 34 1937.
— Jonson, Thomas Randolph and the Drinking academy. N & Q 4 Sept 1937.

Brulé, A. Sur Ben Jonson. Revue Anglo-américaine 13 1936.

Eccles, M. Jonson's marriage. RES 12 1936.
— Memorandums of the immortal Ben. MLN 51 1936.
— Jonson and the spies. RES 13 1937.

Ellis-Fermor, U. M. In her Jacobean drama, 1936, 1958 (rev).

Hankins, J. E. Jonson's Ode on Morison and Seneca's Epistulae morales. MLN 51 1936.

de Selincourt, B. Jonson, poet of justice and truth. Observer 21 June 1936.

Shillinglaw, A. T. Hobbes and Jonson. TLS 18 April 1936.
— New light on Jonson's Discoveries. E Studien 71 1937.

Snuggs, H. L. Fynes Moryson and Jonson's Puntarvolo. MLN 51 1936.
— The comic humours: a new interpretation. PMLA 62 1947.
— The source of Jonson's definition of comedy. MLN 65 1950.

The triumph of Jonson: tests of poetic magic. TLS 4 July 1936.

Avery, E. L. Jonson in the provinces. N & Q 2 Oct 1937.

Ben Jonson, poet: the social background of the plays. TLS 5 June 1937.

Ben Jonson the poet: his hold on reality. TLS 28 Nov 1937.

D., G. Ancestry of Jonson. Observer 22 Aug 1937.

Evans, B. I. Jonson and the economists. Observer 8 Aug 1937.

McKennen, W. Critical theory and poetic practice in Jonson. 1937.

Praz, M. L'Italia di Jonson. Rivista Italiana del Dramma 1937; rptd in his Machiavelli in Inghilterra ed altri saggi, Rome 1942; tr in his Flaming heart: essays in the relations between Italian and English literature, New York 1958.

Short, R. W. Was Lady Bedford the phoenix? TLS 13 Feb 1937. Reply by B. H. Newdigate 20 Feb 1937.

Snodgrass, A. E. Rare Ben Jonson. Cornhill Mag Aug 1937.

Stuart Court masques: 'a noble and lovely scene'. TLS 20 Nov 1937.

Ulrich, E. Die Musik in Jonsons Maskenspielen und Entertainments. Sh Jb 73 1937.

de Vocht, H. Comments on the text of Every man out of his humour. Louvain 1937.
— Comments on the text of Cynthia's revels. Louvain 1950.
— Studies on the texts of Poetaster and Sejanus. Louvain 1958.

White, F. C. O rare Ben Jonson. N & Q 9 Oct 1937. Reply by M. H. Dodds 23 Oct 1937.

Firth, C. H. Jonson and Raleigh's History of the world. In his Essays historical and literary, Oxford 1938.

Jonson in the years of his decline: Bartholomew fayre and its successors. TLS 23 April 1938.

King, A. H. 'Swell mee a bowle': notes on Jonson's Poetaster III.i.8–12. Studia Neophilologica 11 1938.
— The language of satirized characters in Poetaster: a socio-stylistic analysis 1597–1602. Lund Stud in Eng 10 1941.
— A note on the Virgil translation in Poetaster v.ii. E Studies 23 1941.

Levin, H. Jonson, Stow and Drummond. MLN 53 1938.
— Jonson's metempsychosis. PQ 22 1943.
— Two magian comedies: the Tempest and the Alchemist. Shakespeare Survey 22 1969.

Nicoll, A. In his Stuart masques and the Renaissance stage, 1938.

Simpson, E. M. Jonson's A new-yeares-gift. RES 14 1938.
— Jonson and Donne: a problem of authorship. RES 15 1939. Underwood 38–41.
— Jonson and Dickens: a study in the comic genius of London. E & S 29 1943.

Wells, H. W. Jonson: patriarch of speech study. Shakespeare Assoc Bull 13 1938.

Wheeler, C. F. Classical mythology in the plays, masques and poems of Jonson. Princeton 1938.

Wilson, E. Morose Ben Jonson. In his Triple thinkers, New York 1938, 1948 (rev).

Allen, D. C. Jonson and the hieroglyphics. PQ 18 1939.

Brown, J. L. Bodin et Jonson. Revue de Littérature Comparée 20 1939.

Eliot, S. A. The Lord Chamberlain's company as portrayed in Every man out of his humour. Smith College Stud in Modern Lang 21 1939.

Graham, C. B. Jonson allusions in Restoration comedy. RES 15 1939.
— The Jonsonian tradition in the comedies of John Dennis. MLN 56 1941.

McEuen, K. A. Classical influence upon the tribe of Ben. Cedar Rapids Iowa 1939.
— Jonson and Juvenal. RES 21 1945.

Neumann, J. H. Notes on Jonson's English. PMLA 54 1939.

Rendall, G. H. Jonson and the first folio editions of Shakespeare's plays. Colchester 1939.

Vincent, H. P. Jonson allusions. N & Q 8 July 1939.

Boughner, D. C. Clizia and Epicoene. PQ 19 1940.
— Jonson's use of Lipsius in Sejanus. MLN 73 1958.
— 'Rhodig' and Sejanus. N & Q July 1958.
— Juvenal, Horace and Sejanus. MLN 75 1960.
— Sejanus and Machiavelli. Stud in Eng Lit 1500–1900 1 1961.
— Lewkenor and Volpone. N & Q April 1962.
— The Devil's disciple: Jonson's debt to Machiavelli. New York 1968.
— Jonsonian structure in the Tempest. Shakespeare Quart 21 1970.

Funke, O. Jonson's English grammar. Anglia 64 1940.

Grubbs, H. A. An early French adaptation of an Elizabethan comedy: J.-B. Rousseau as an imitator of Jonson. MLN 55 1940.

Leech, C. Caroline echoes of the Alchemist. RES 16 1940.

Perkinson, R. H. Volpone and the reputation of Venetian justice. MLR 35 1940.

Symons, J. Jonson as a social realist: Bartholomew fair. Southern Rev 6 1940.

Kuethe, J. L. Mechanical features of a 17th-century submarine. MLN 56 1941. *See also* E. Emery 57 1942.

Parrott, T. M. Comedy in the Court masque: a study of Jonson's contribution. PQ 20 1941; rptd in Renaissance studies in honor of Hardin Craig, Stanford 1941.

Proebstef, L. The progress in the comedies of Jonson from classicism to pure realism. 1941.

Ransom, J. C. The new criticism. Norfolk Conn 1941.

Sewell, S. W. The relation between the Merry wives and Every man in. Shakespeare Assoc Bull 16 1941.

Wilson, F. P. Jonson and Ralph Crane. TLS 8 Nov 1941.

Bentley, G. E. 17th-century allusions to Jonson. HLQ 5 1942.

—— Shakespeare and Jonson: their reputations in the 17th century compared. 2 vols Chicago 1945.

Bervailler, M. Influencias italianas en las comedias de Jonson. Filosofia y Letras (Mexico) 1942.

Duncan, E. H. The alchemy in Mercury vindicated. SP 39 1942.

—— Jonson's use of Arnald of Villa Nova's Rosarium. PQ 21 1942.

—— Jonson's Alchemist and the literature of alchemy. PMLA 61 1946.

Kallich, M. Unity of time in Every man in his humour and Cynthia's revels. MLN 57 1942.

Maas, P. Notes on the text of Jonson's masques. RES 18 1942.

Berringer, R. W. Cynthia's revels and the war of the theatres. PQ 22 1943.

Esdaile, K. A. Jonson and the Devil Tavern. E & S 29 1943.

Gilbert, A. H. The function of the masques in Cynthia's revels. PQ 22 1943.

—— The Italian names in Every man out of his humour. SP 44 1947.

—— Jonson and Drummond or Gil on the King's senses. MLN 62 1947. *See also* C. F. Main 74 1959.

—— The symbolic persons in the masques of Jonson. Durham NC 1948.

—— The eavesdroppers in Sejanus. MLN 69 1954.

Gordon, D. J. The imagery of the Masque of blackness and the Masque of beautie. Jnl Warburg & Courtauld Inst 6 1943.

—— Hymenaei: Jonson's masque of union. Jnl Warburg & Courtauld Inst 8 1945.

—— Jonson's Haddington masque: the story and the fable. MLR 42 1947.

—— Poet and architect: the intellectual setting of the quarrel between Jonson and Inigo Jones. Jnl Warburg & Courtauld Inst 12 1949.

Harrison, T. P. Jonson's The sad shepherd and Spenser. MLN 58 1943.

Reynolds, G. F. The dramatic quality of Jonson's masques. PQ 22 1943.

Talbert, E. W. The classical mythology and the structure of Cynthia's revels. PQ 22 1943.

—— New light on Jonson's workmanship. SP 40 1943.

—— The purpose and technique of Poetaster. SP 42 1945.

—— The interpretation of Jonson's courtly spectacles. PMLA 61 1946.

—— Current scholarly works and the 'erudition' of Jonson's Masque of augurs. SP 44 1947.

McIlwraith, A. K. The press corrections in Jonson's The King's entertainment. Library 4th ser 24 1944.

Williams, W. M. The influence of Catiline upon John Oldham's Satyrs upon the Jesuits. ELH 11 1944.

Putney, R. What praise to give? Jonson vs Stoll. PQ 23 1944.

—— Jonson's poetic comedy. PQ 41 1962.

—— This so subtile sport: some aspects of Jonson's Epigrams. Univ of Colorado Stud in Lang & Lit 10 1966.

Parr, J. Non-alchemical pseudo-science in the Alchemist. PQ 24 1945; rptd in his Tamburlaine's malady and other essays, Tuscaloosa 1953.

—— A note on the Staple of news. MLN 60 1945.

Sharpe, R. B. Jonson's Execration and Chapman's Invective: their place in their authors' rivalry. SP 42 1945.

John, L. C. Jonson's Epigram 114 to Mistress Philip Sidney. JEGP 45 1946.

—— Jonson's To Sir William Sidney on his birthday. MLR 52 1957.

Nash, R. Milton, Jonson and Tiberius. Classical Philology 41 1946.

—— The comic intent of Volpone. SP 44 1947.

—— The parting scene in Poetaster IV. ix. PQ 31 1952.

—— Jonson's tragic poems. SP 55 1958.

Peery, W. The influence of Jonson on Nathan Field. SP 43 1946.

—— Eastward ho and A woman is a weathercock. MLN 62 1947.

Baum, H. W. The satiric and the didactic in Jonson's comedies. Chapel Hill 1947.

Ben Jonson's poems. TLS 5 July 1947.

Duffy, E. M. T. Jonson's debt to Renaissance scholarship in Sejanus and Catiline. MLR 42 1947.

Gray, H. D. The Chamberlain's men and the Poetaster. MLR 42 1947. Reply by P. Simpson 43 1948.

—— Shakespeare or Heminge? MLR 45 1950. Reply by P. Simpson, ibid. On identification of Aesop in Poetaster.

Lodge, O. A Ben Jonson puzzle. TLS 13 Sept 1947.

McGalliard, J. C. Chaucerian comedy: the Merchant's tale, Jonson and Molière. PQ 25 1947.

Prior, M. E. In his Language of tragedy, New York 1947.

Stroud, T. A. Jonson and Father Thomas Wright. ELH 14 1947.

Townsend, F. L. Apologie for Bartholomew fayre: the art of Jonson's comedies. New York 1947.

—— Jonson's 'censure' of Rutter's Shepheard's holy-day. MP 44 1947.

D., A. The genesis of Jonson's Epicoene. N & Q 7 Feb 1948.

Sackton, A. H. Rhetoric as a dramatic language in Jonson. New York 1948.

—— The rhymed couplet in Jonson's plays. SE 30 1951.

Sisson, C. J. A topical reference in the Alchemist. In J. Q. Adams memorial studies, Washington 1948.

—— Jonson of Gresham College. TLS 21 Sept 1951. *See also* G. B. Johnston 23 Dec 1951.

Keast, W. R. Some 17th-century allusions to Shakespeare and Jonson. N & Q 29 Oct 1949.

Potts, L. J. Jonson and the 17th century. E & S ('English Studies') new ser 2 1949.

Wilson, J. D. Jonson and Julius Caesar. Shakespeare Survey 2 1949.

Aylward, J. D. The inimitable Bobadill. N & Q 7–21 Jan 1950. Reply by K. T. Butler 4 March 1950.

—— Volpone at Drury Lane. N & Q 15 April 1950.

Bredvold, L. I. The rise of English classicism. Comparative Lit 2 1950.

Johansson, B. Religion and superstition in the plays of Jonson and Middleton. Essays & Stud on Eng Lang & Lit (Upsala) 7 1950.

—— Law and lawyers in Elizabethan England as evidenced in the plays of Jonson and Middleton. Stockholm 1967.

Haydn, H. In his Counter-Renaissance, New York 1950.

Reed, R. R. Jonson's pioneering in sentimental comedy. N & Q 24 June 1950.

Scheve, D. A. Volpone and traditional fox lore. RES new ser 1 1950.

Shaaber, M. A. The unclean birds in the Alchemist. MLN 65 1950.

Shapiro, I. A. The Mermaid club. MLR 45 1950.

Simonini, R. C. Jonson and John Florio. N & Q 25 Nov 1950.

Smith, H. 'No cloudie stuffe to puzzle intellect'. Shakespeare Quart 1 1950.

Bachrach, A. G. H. Sir Constantyn Huygens and Jonson. Neophilologus 25 1951.

Bryant, J. A. The nature of the conflict in Sejanus. Vanderbilt Univ Stud in the Humanities 1 1951.

— The significance of Jonson's first requirement for tragedy: truth of argument. SP 49 1952.

— Catiline and the nature of Jonson's tragic fable. PMLA 69 1954.

— Jonson's revision of Every man in his humour. SP 59 1962.

— Jonson's satirist out of his humour. Ball State College (Indiana) Forum 3 1962.

Honig, E. Sejanus and Coriolanus: a study in alienation. MLQ 12 1951.

Hussey, M. An oath in the Alchemist. N & Q 29 Sept 1951.

— Ananias the deacon: a study of religion in the Alchemist. English 9 1953.

McCullen, J. T. Conference with the Queen of fairies: a study of Jonson's workmanship in the Alchemist. Studia Neophilologica 23 1951.

Waith, E. M. The poet's morals in Poetaster. MLQ 12 1951.

— The staging of Bartholomew fair. Stud in Eng Lit 1500–1900 2 1962.

— A misprint in Bartholomew fair. N & Q March 1963.

Walker, R. S. Literary criticism in Jonson's Conversations with Drummond. English 8 1952.

— Jonson's Discoveries: a new analysis. E & S new ser 5 1952.

Burton, K. M. The political tragedies of Chapman and Jonson. EC 2 1952.

Cutts, J. P. William Lawes' writing for the theatre and the Court. Library 5th ser 7 1952. On setting for the first song from Entertainment at Welbeck in BM additional ms 31,432.

— Original music to Browne's Inner Temple masque and other Jacobean masque music. N & Q May 1954. On settings for songs from Oberon and Love freed.

— Jonson's The vision of delight. N & Q Feb 1956.

— Le rôle de la musique dans les masques de Ben Jonson et notamment dans Oberon. In Fêtes de la Renaissance, ed J. Jacquot, Paris 1956.

— Volpone's song: a note on the source and Jonson's translation. N & Q May 1958.

— Robert Johnson and the Court masque. Music & Letters 41 1960. Composer of music to Jonson's masques.

— 'When were the senses in such order plac'd?' Comparative Drama 4 1970. Love's welcome at Bolsover.

Enright, D. J. Poetic satire and satire in verse: a consideration of Jonson and Massinger. Scrutiny 18 1952.

McNeal, T. H. Every man out of his humour and Shakespeare's sonnets. N & Q 30 Aug 1952.

Maxwell, J. C. Comic mispunctuation in Every man in his humour. E Studies 33 1952.

Nosworthy, J. M. The case is altered. JEGP 51 1952.

Olive, W. J. Sejanus and Hamlet. In A tribute to G. C. Taylor, Chapel Hill 1952.

— A Chaucer allusion in Bartholomew fair. MLQ 13 1952.

Thompson, W. L. The source of the flower passage in Lycidas. N & Q 1 March 1952. Pan's anniversary.

Thomson, P. The literature of patronage. EC 2 1952.

Barish, J. A. The double plot in Volpone. MP 51 1953.

— Ovid, Juvenal and the Silent woman. PMLA 71 1956.

— Baroque prose in the theatre: Ben Jonson. PMLA 73 1958.

— Bartholomew fair and its puppets. MLQ 20 1959.

— Ben Jonson and the language of prose comedy. Cambridge Mass 1960.

Chute, M. Ben Jonson of Westminster. New York 1953.

Emslie, M. Three early settings of Jonson. N & Q Nov 1953.

Enck, J. J. The case is altered: initial comedy of humours. SP 50 1953.

— Jonson and the comic truth. Madison 1957.

— The peace of the poetomachia. PMLA 77 1962.

Partridge, A. C. Studies in the syntax of Jonson's plays. Cambridge 1953.

— The accidence of Jonson's plays, masques and entertainments. Cambridge 1953.

Seronsy, C. C. A Skeltonic passage in Jonson. N & Q Jan 1953.

— Sir Politic Would-be in Laputa. Eng Lang Notes 1 1963.

Withington, E. Nicholas Briot and Jonson's commendation of Joseph Rutter. N & Q April 1953.

Doran, M. In her Endeavors of art, Madison 1954.

Furniss, W. T. The annotation of Jonson's Masque of Queenes. RES new ser 5 1954.

— Jonson's antimasques. Renaissance News 7 1954.

— Jonson, Camden and the Black Prince's plumes. MLN 69 1954. Camden's Remaines and Jonson's Prince Henries barriers.

— Jonson's masques. In his Three studies in the Renaissance: Sidney, Jonson, Milton, New Haven 1958.

Goodman, P. Comic plots: the Alchemist. In his Structure of literature, Chicago 1954.

Main, C. F. Two items in the Jonson apocrypha. N & Q June 1954.

— Jonson and an unknown poet on the King's senses. MLN 74 1959.

Main, W. W. Insula fortunata in Every man out of his humour. N & Q May 1954.

Potts, A. F. Cynthia's revels, Poetaster and Troilus and Cressida. Shakespeare Quart 5 1954.

Sawin, L. The earliest use of 'autumnal'. MLN 69 1954. Epicoene 1.i.85.

Thayer, C. G. Jonson, Markham and Shakespeare. N & Q Nov 1954. Bartholomew fair IV.v.21–7.

— Theme and structure in the Alchemist. ELH 26 1959.

— Ben Jonson: studies in the plays. Norman Oklahoma 1963.

Weld, J. S. Christian comedy: Volpone. SP 51 1954.

Blanshard, R. A. Carew and Jonson. SP 52 1955.

Bradbrook, M. C. In her Growth and structure of Elizabethan comedy, 1955.

Cunningham, D. The Jonsonian masque as a literary form. ELH 22 1955.

Heffner, R. L. Unifying symbols in the comedy of Jonson. Eng Inst Essays 1954.

Moore, R. S. Some notes on the courtly love system in the New inn. In Essays in honor of W. C. Curry, Nashville 1955.

Partridge, E. B. The allusiveness of Epicoene. ELH 22 1955.

— A crux in the New inne. MLN 71 1956.

— The symbolism of clothes in Jonson's last plays. JEGP 56 1957.

— The broken compass: a study of the major comedies of Jonson. 1958.

— Jonson: the makings of the dramatist 1595–1602. In Elizabethan theatre, ed J. R. Brown and B. Harris 1966.

Phelps, G. Ben Jonson's poetry. In The age of Shakespeare, ed B. Ford 1955 (Pelican).

Sirluck, E. Shakespeare and Jonson among the pamphleteers of the first civil war: some unreported 17th-century allusions. MP 53 1955.

Ornstein, R. Volpone and Renaissance psychology. N & Q Nov 1956.

— In his Moral vision of Jacobean tragedy, Madison 1960.

— Shakespearian and Jonsonian comedy. Shakespeare Survey 22 1969.

Bacon, W. A. The magnetic field: the structure of Jonson's comedies. HLQ 19 1956.

Draper, R. P. The golden age and Volpone's address to his gold. N & Q May 1956.

Ekeblad, I.-S. A note on Hymenaei. N & Q Dec 1956.

Graziani, R. I. C. Chloridia: fame and her attendants. RES new ser 7 1956.

Hibbard, G. R. The country house poem of the seventeenth century. Jnl Warburg & Courtauld Inst 19 1956; rptd in Essential articles for the study of Alexander Pope, ed M. Mack, Hamden Conn 1964.

—— Goodness and greatness: an essay on the tragedies of Jonson and Chapman. Renaissance & Modern Stud 11 1967.

Peter, J. In his Complaint and satire in early English literature, Oxford 1956.

Wickham, G. Contribution de Jonson et de Dekker aux fêtes du couronnement de Jacques 1ᵉʳ. In Les fêtes de la Renaissance, ed J. Jacquot, Paris 1956.

Bradbrook, F. W. John Donne and Jonson. N & Q April 1957.

Cope, J. I. Volpone and the authorship of Eastward hoe. MLN 72 1957.

—— Jonson on the Christ's College dons. MLN 74 1959.

—— Jonson's reading of Spenser: the genesis of a poem. Eng Miscellany (Rome) 10 1959.

—— The date of Middleton's Women beware women. MLN 76 1961. Jonson's Hymenaei dates Middleton's play.

—— Bartholomew fair as blasphemy. Renaissance Drama 8 1965.

Hays, H. R. Satire and identification: an introduction to Jonson. Kenyon Rev 19 1957.

McGinnis, P. J. Jonson's Discoveries. N & Q April 1957.

—— Jonson on Savile's Tacitus. Classical Jnl 55 1959.

Musgrove, S. Shakespeare and Jonson. Auckland 1957.

Osborn, J. M. Jonson and the eccentric Lord Stanhope. TLS 4 Jan 1957.

Van Deusen, M. Criticism and Jonson's To Celia. EC 7 1957.

Cubeta, P. M. A celebration of Charis: an evaluation of Jonsonian poetic strategy. ELH 25 1958.

—— Jonson's religious lyrics. JEGP 62 1963.

—— A Jonsonian ideal: To Penshurst. PQ 42 1963.

Kirschbaum, L. Jonson, Seneca and Mortimer. In Studies in honor of J. Wilcox, Detroit 1958.

Rosenberg, M. On the dating of Othello. E Studies 39 1958. Othello influenced by Jonson's Masque of blackness.

Sabol, A. J. A newly discovered contemporary song setting for Cynthia's revels. N & Q Sept 1958.

—— Songs and dances for the Stuart masque. Providence 1959.

—— Two unpublished stage songs for the 'aery of children'. Renaissance News 13 1960. Music for the lyric 'O that joy so soone should waste' in Cynthia's revels.

—— A score for Lovers made men, the music adapted and arranged from compositions by Nicholas Lanier, Alphonso Ferrabosco and their contemporaries. Providence 1963.

Bamborough, J. B. Ben Jonson. 1959 (Br Council pamphlet).

—— The early life of Jonson. TLS 8 April 1960.

—— Joyce and Jonson. REL 2 1961.

—— Ben Jonson. 1970.

Everett, B. Jonson's A vision of beauty. CQ 1 1959.

Fitton Brown, A. D. Drink to me, Celia. MLR 54 1959.

Gerritsen, J. Stansby and Jonson produce a folio. E Studies 40 1959.

Goldberg, S. L. Folly into crime: the catastrophe of Volpone. MLQ 20 1959.

Kernan, A. In his Cankered muse: satire of the English Renaissance, New Haven 1959.

Sternfeld, F. W. Song in Jonson's comedy: a gloss on Volpone. In Studies in the English Renaissance drama in memory of K. J. Holzknecht, New York 1959.

Taylor, D. Clarendon and Jonson as witness for the Earl of Pembroke's character. Ibid.

Armstrong, W. A. Jonson and Jacobean stagecraft. In Jacobean theatre, ed J. R. Brown and B. Harris 1960.

Brown, A. Citizen comedy and domestic drama. Ibid.

Cloudsley, A. Volpone in Germany. Twentieth Century July 1960. On the première of Francis Burt's operatic adaptation.

Hill, G. The world's proportion: Jonson's dramatic poetry in Sejanus and Catiline. In Jacobean theatre, ed J. R. Brown and B. Harris 1960.

McElroy, D. D. The artificial sea in Jonson's Masque of blacknesse. N & Q Nov 1960.

—— The falling curtain in Jonson's Masque of blackness. N & Q May 1960.

Murray, W. A. Jonson and Dr Mayerne. TLS 2 Sept 1960.

Redding, D. C. A note on Jonson attribution. N & Q Feb 1960.

Reiman, D. H. Marston, Jonson and the Spanish tragedy additions. N & Q Sept 1960.

Fieler, F. B. The impact of Bacon and the new science upon Jonson's critical thought in Timber. Renaissance Papers 1961.

Hoy, C. The shares of Fletcher and his collaborators in the Beaumont and Fletcher canon, pt 6. SB 14 1961. Jonson's share in Rollo Duke of Normandy.

—— The pleasures and the perils of deception. In his Hyacinth room, 1964.

Redwine, J. D. Beyond psychology: the moral basis of Jonson's theory of humour characterization. ELH 28 1961.

Ricks, C. Sejanus and dismemberment. MLN 76 1961.

Robinson, J. E. Bartholomew fair: comedy of vapours. Stud in Eng Lit 1500–1900 1 1961.

Schlösser, A. Jonson's Roman plays. Kwartnalnik Neofilologiczny (Warsaw) 8 1961.

Huntley, F. L. Jonson and Anthony Munday: or the Case is altered, altered again. PQ 41 1962.

McKenzie, J. Jonson's Elizabeth L.H. N & Q June 1962.

Phialas, P. G. Comic truth in Shakespeare and Jonson. South Atlantic Quart 62 1963.

Rackin, P. Poetry without paradox: Jonson's hymne to Cynthia. Criticism 4 1962.

Savage, J. E. Ben Jonson in Ben Jonson's plays. Univ of Mississippi Stud in Eng 3 1962.

—— Some antecedents of the puppet play in Bartholomew fair. Univ of Mississippi Stud in Eng 7 1966.

—— Jonson and Shakespeare 1623–6. Univ of Mississippi Stud in Eng 10 1969.

Trimpi, W. Jonson's poems: a study of the plain style. Stanford 1962.

Babb, H. S. The epitaph on Elizabeth L.H. and Jonson's style. JEGP 62 1963.

Davison, P. H. Volpone and the old comedy. MLQ 24 1963.

Hart, J. Jonson's good society. Modern Age 7 1963. To Penshurst.

Sprague, A. C. The alchemist on the stage. Theatre Notebook 17 1963.

Stein, A. Plain style, plain criticism, plain dealing and Ben Jonson. ELH 30 1963.

Dessen, A. C. Volpone and the late morality tradition. MLQ 25 1964.

—— The alchemist: Jonson's 'estates' play. Renaissance Drama 7 1964.

—— Jonson's Knave of clubs and the Play of the cards. MLR 62 1967.

—— Jonson's moral comedy. Evanston 1971.

De Villiers, J. I. Jonson's tragedies. E Studies 45 1964.

Maclean, H. Jonson's poems: notes on the ordered society. In Essays presented to A. S. P. Woodhouse, Toronto 1964.

Meier, T. The naming of characters in Jonson's comedies. Eng Stud in Africa 7 1964.

Tomlinson, T. B. In his A study of Elizabethan and Jacobean tragedy, Cambridge 1964.

Watson, T. L. The detractor-backbiter: Iago and the tradition. Texas Stud in Lit & Lang 5 1964. On Every man out of his humour.

Arnold, J. The double plot in Volpone: a note on Jonsonian dramatic structure. Seventeenth-Century News 23 1965.

— Lovewit's triumph and Jonsonial morality: a reading of the Alchemist. Criticism 11 1969.

Barker, J. R. A pendant to Drummond of Hawthornden's Conversations. RES new ser 16 1965.

Hutchison, B. Jonson's 'Let me be what I am': an apology in disguise. Eng Lang Notes 2 1965.

Knoll, R. E. Jonson's plays: an introduction. Lincoln Nebraska 1965.

Kranidas, T. Possible revisions or additions in Epicoene. Anglia 83 1965.

La Regina, G. Jonson e la sua fortuna nel Seicento. Eng Miscellany (Rome) 16 1965.

Levin, R. The staple of news, the society of jeerers and canters' college. PQ 44 1965.

— The structure of Bartholomew fair. PMLA 80 1965.

Meagher, J. C. Method and meaning in Jonson's masques. Notre Dame Ind 1965.

O'Connor, D. Jonson's A hymne to God the father. N & Q Oct 1965.

Orgel, S. The Jonsonian masque. Cambridge Mass 1965.

— To make boards to speak: Inigo Jones's stage and the Jonsonian masque. Renaissance Drama 1 1968.

South, M. H. Animal imagery in Volpone. Tennessee Stud in Lit 10 1965.

Beaurline, L. A. The selective principle in Jonson's shorter poems. Criticism 8 1966.

— Jonson and the illusion of completeness. PMLA 84 1969. Replies by E. J. Jensen and Beaurline 86 1971.

Echeruo, M. J. C. The conscience of politics and Catiline. Stud in Eng Lit 1500–1900 6 1966.

Gottwald, M. Jonson's theory of comedy. Germanica Wratislaviensia (Wroclaw) 10 1966.

Hawkins, H. The idea of a theater in the New inn. Renaissance Drama 9 1966.

— Jonson's use of traditional dream theory in the Vision of delight. MP 64 1967.

— Folly, incurable disease and Volpone. Stud in Eng Lit 1500–1900 8 1968.

Miller, J. Volpone: a study of dramatic ambiguity. In Studies in English language and literature, ed A. Shalvi and A. A. Mendilow, Jerusalem 1966.

Champion, L. S. Jonson's dotages: a reconsideration of the late plays. Lexington Kentucky 1967.

— The magnetic lady: the close of Jonson's circle. Southern Humanities Rev 2 1968.

De Luna, B. N. Jonson's Romish plot: a study of Catiline and its historical context. Oxford 1967.

Donaldson, I. A martyrs resolution: Jonson's Epicoene. RES new ser 18 1967.

— Jonson's tortoise. RES new ser 19 1968.

— The world upside-down: comedy from Jonson to Fielding. Oxford 1970.

— Volpone: quick and dead. EC 21 1971.

Freeman, A. The earliest allusion to Volpone. N & Q June 1967.

Hayashi, T. Jonson and Shakespeare: their relationship and mutual criticism. East-West Rev (Kyoto, Japan) 3 1967.

Jones, R. C. The satirist's retirement in Jonson's apologetical dialogue. ELH 34 1967.

Jones-Davies, M.-T. Inigo Jones, Ben Jonson et le masque. Paris 1967.

Mills, L. L. A clarification of Broker's use of 'a perfect sanguine' in the Staple of news. N & Q June 1967.

Papajewski, H. Jonsons Laudatio auf Shakespeare: Kategorien des literarischen Urteils in der Renaissance. Poetica (Munich) 1 1967.

Salingar, L. G. Farce and fashion in the Silent woman. E & S new ser 20 1967.

Skelton, R. The masterpoet and the multiple tradition: the poetry of Jonson. Style (Univ of Arkansas) 1 1967.

Stagg, L. C. Index to the figurative language of Jonson's tragedies. Charlottesville 1967.

Bennett, J. W. Benson's alleged piracy of Shakespeare's sonnets and of some of Jonson's works. SB 21 1968.

Blissett, W. The venter tripartite in the Alchemist. Stud in Eng Lit 1500–1900 8 1968.

Dircks, R. J. Garrick and gentleman: two interpretations of Abel Drugger. Restoration & 18th-century Theatre Research 7 1968.

Empson, W. Volpone. Hudson Rev 21 1968.

— The alchemist. Hudson Rev 22 1969.

French, J. T. Jonson: his aesthetic of relief. Texas Stud in Lit & Lang 10 1968.

Gianakaris, C. J. Identifying ethical values in Volpone. HLQ 32 1968.

Gibbons, B. In his Jacobean city comedy: a study of satiric plays by Jonson, Marston and Middleton, 1968.

Houck, J. K. An unidentified borrowing in Discoveries. N & Q Oct 1968.

Jackson, G. B. Vision and judgment in Jonson's drama. New Haven 1968.

Janicka, I. Jonson's Staple of news: sources and traditional devices. Kwartnalnik Neofilologiczny (Warsaw) 15 1968.

McMillin, S. Jonson's early entertainments: new information from Hatfield House. Renaissance Drama new ser 1 1968.

Parfitt, G. A. E. The poetry of Jonson. EC 18 1968.

— Ethical thought and Jonson's poetry. Stud in Eng Lit 1500–1900 9 1969.

Parsons, D. S. J. The odes of Drayton and Jonson. Queen's Quart 75 1968.

Potter, J. M. Old comedy in Bartholomew fair. Criticism 10 1968.

Scoufos, A. L. Nashe, Jonson and the Oldcastle problem. MP 65 1968.

Stevenson, W. Shakespeare's hand in the Spanish tragedy 1602. Stud in Eng Lit 1500–1900 8 1968. Rejects Jonson's authorship of addns.

Wilson, G. E. Jonson's use of the Bible and the great chain of being in To Penshurst. Stud in Eng Lit 1500–1900 8 1968.

Calder, D. G. The meaning of 'imitation' in Jonson's Discoveries. Neuphilologische Mitteilungen 70 1969.

Doughtie, E. Ferrabosco and Jonson's The houre-glass. Renaissance Quart 22 1969.

Greenfield, T. N. In her Induction in Elizabethan drama, Eugene 1969.

Gum, C. The Aristophanic comedies of Jonson. Hague 1969.

Jones, M. Sir Epicure Mammon: a study in spiritual fornication. Renaissance Quart 22 1969.

Leggatt, A. The suicide of Volpone. UTQ 39 1969.

Litt, D. E. Unity of theme in Volpone. BNYPL 1969.

Ross, T. W. Expenses for Jonson's The masque of beauty. Bull Rocky Mountain Modern Lang Assoc 23 1969.

Spanos, W. V. The real toad in the Jonsonian garden: resonance in the nondramatic poetry. JEGP 68 1969.

Warren, M. J. The location of Catiline iii.490–754. PQ 48 1969.

Wykes, D. Jonson's 'chaste booke': the Epigrammes. Renaissance & Modern Stud 13 1969.

Anderson, M. A. The successful unity of Epicoene. Stud in Eng Lit 1500–1900 10 1970.

Craik, T. W. Volpone's young Antinous. N & Q June 1970.

Dale, L. Jonson's sick society. Bull Rocky Mountain Modern Lang Assoc 24 1970.

Dorenkamp, A. G. Jonson's Catiline: history as the trying faculty. SP 67 1970.

Duncan, D. A guide to the New inn. EC 20 1970.

Freehafer, J. Leonard Digges, Jonson and the beginning of Shakespeare idolatry. Shakespeare Quart 21 1970.

Greene, T. M. Jonson and the centered self. Stud in Eng Lit 1500–1900 10 1970.

Hallett, C. A. The satanic nature of Volpone. PQ 49 1970.

Kaplan, J. H. Dramatic and moral energy in Bartholomew fair. Renaissance Drama new ser 3 1970.

Kay, W. D. The shaping of Jonson's career: a re-examination of facts and problems. MP 67 1970.

Marotti, A. F. The self-reflexive art of Jonson's Sejanus. Texas Stud in Lit & Lang 12 1970.

Parker, R. B. The themes and staging of Bartholomew fair. UTQ 39 1970.

Slights, W. W. Epicoene and the prose paradox. PQ 49 1970.

Summers, J. H. The heritage of Donne and Jonson. UTQ 39 1970.

Boddy, M. A reading in Oberon. N & Q Jan 1971.

Chan, M. Cynthias revels and music for a choir school: Christ Church ms Mus. 439. Stud in Renaissance 18 1971.

Evans, K. W. Sejanus and the ideal prince tradition. Stud in Eng Lit 1500–1900 11 1971.

Hamilton, G. D. Irony and fortune in Sejanus. Ibid.

Horwich, R. Hamlet and Eastward ho. Ibid.

Lever, J. W. In his Tragedy of state, 1971.

McFarland, R. E. Jonson's Magnetic lady and the reception of Gilbert's De magnete. Stud in Eng Lit 1500–1900 11 1971.

Rathmell, J. C. A. Jonson, Lord Lisle and Penshurst. Eng Literary Renaissance 1 1971.

Thron, E. M. Jonson's Cynthia's revels: multiplicity and unity. Stud in Eng Lit 1500–1900 11 1971.

THOMAS DEKKER
1572?–1632

Bibliographies

Tannenbaum, S. A. Dekker: a concise bibliography. New York 1939; Supplement, New York 1945.

Donovan, D. G. Elizabethan bibliographies supplements II: Dekker 1945–65. 1967.

Collections

Dramatic works. Ed R. H. Shepherd 4 vols 1873.

Non-dramatic works. Ed A. B. Grosart 5 vols 1884–6 (Huth Lib). Vol 1, Cannaans calamitie (now attributed to Deloney), Wonderfull yeare, Batchelars banquet (no longer attributed to Dekker; see F. P. Wilson, Three notes on Dekker, MLR 15 1920); vol 2, Seven deadly sinnes, Newes from hell, Double pp, Guls horne-booke, Jests to make you merie; vol 3, Dekker his dreame, Belman of London, Lanthorne and candle-light, A strange horse-race; vol 4, Dead terme, Worke for armourours, Ravens almanacke, A rod for runawayes; vol 5, Foure birds of Noahs arke.

Thomas Dekker. Ed E. Rhys 1887 (Mermaid ser). Contains Shoemakers' holiday, Honest whore 2 pts, Old Fortunatus, Witch of Edmonton.

Dramatic works. Ed F. T. Bowers 4 vols Cambridge 1953–61, 1964–6 (vols 2–3 rptd with corrections) (standard edn); C. Hoy, Commentary, 2 vols Cambridge 1974.

Thomas Dekker. Ed E. D. Pendry 1968. Contains Wonderful year, Gull's horn-book, Penny-wise, English villainies discovered by lantern and candlelight, and selections from Raven's almanac and A knight's conjuring.

§I

The pleasant comedie of old Fortunatus, as it was plaied before the Queenes Majestie this Christmas by the Right Honourable the Earle of Nottingham, Lord High Admirall of England his servants. 1600 (anon); ed C. W. Dilke, Old English plays vol 3, 1814; ed H. Scherer,

Erlangen 1901; ed O. Smeaton 1904; ed F. E. Schelling, Typical Elizabethan plays, 1926.

The shomakers holiday: or the gentle craft, with the humorous life of Simon Eyre, shoomaker and Lord Mayor of London, as it was acted before the Queenes most excellent Majestie on New-Yeares Day at night last by the Right Honourable the Earle of Notingham, Lord High Admirall of England his servants. 1600 (anon), 1610, 1618, 1624, 1631, 1657; ed H. Fritsche, Thorn 1862; ed K. Warnke and L. Proescholdt, Halle 1886; ed H. M. Fitzgibbon, Famous Elizabethan plays, 1890; ed W. A. Neilson, Chief Elizabethan dramatists, 1911; ed A. F. Lange, Gayley vol 3, 1914; ed C. B. Wheeler, Six plays by contemporaries of Shakespeare, 1915; ed G. B. Harrison 1927; ed G. N. Pocock 1927; ed W. T. Williams 1927; ed W. J. Halliday 1927; ed H. C. Schweikert, Early English plays, 1928; ed G. A. Sheldon 1928; ed J. R. Sutherland, Oxford 1928; ed C. F. T. Brooke and N. B. Paradise, English drama, 1933; ed H. Spencer, Elizabethan plays, 1933; ed C. R. Baskervill, Elizabethan and Stuart plays, 1934; ed A. K. McIlwraith, Five Elizabethan comedies, Oxford 1934 (WC); ed J. B. Steane, Cambridge 1965; ed P. C. Davies 1968; tr French, 1955.

Satiro-mastix: or the untrussing of the humorous poet, as it hath bin presented publikely by the Right Honorable the Lord Chamberlaine his servants, and privately by the children of Paules. 1602; ed T. Hawkins, Origin of the English drama vol 3, 1773; ed H. Scherer, Bang vol 20, 1907; ed J. H. Penniman, Boston 1913.

Patient Grissil. 1603. With Chettle and Houghton; see under Chettle, col 1461, above.

The wonderfull yeare: wherein is shewed the picture of London lying sicke of the plague. 1603 (anon); 2 further edns before 1607; ed J. Morgan, Phoenix britannicus, 1731; ed G. B. Harrison 1924; ed F. P. Wilson, The plague pamphlets of Dekker, Oxford 1925; ed G. R. Hibbard, Three Elizabethan pamphlets, 1952.

Newes from Graves-end, sent to Nobody. 1604 (anon); ed F. P. Wilson, The plague pamphlets of Dekker, Oxford 1925.

The meeting of gallants at an ordinarie: or the walkes in Powles. 1604 (anon); ed J. O. Halliwell (-Phillipps) 1841 (Percy Soc); ed F. P. Wilson, The plague pamphlets of Dekker, Oxford 1925.

The honest whore, with the humours of the patient man and the longing wife. 1604, 1604 (as The converted curtezan), 1605, 1615 (some copies dated 1616), 1635; ed R. Dodsley, A select collection of old plays vol 3, 1744; ed I. Reed, Dodsley vol 3, 1780; Ancient British drama vol i, 1810; ed J. P. Collier, Dodsley vol 3, 1825; ed A. Dyce, Middleton's Works vol 3, 1840; ed W. A. Neilson, Chief Elizabethan dramatists, 1911; ed H. Spencer, Elizabethan plays, 1933; ed C. R. Baskervill, Elizabethan and Stuart plays, 1934. With Middleton.

The magnificent entertainment given to King James, Queene Anne his wife, and Henry Frederick the Prince upon the day of his Majesties tryumphant passage from the Tower through his honourable citie and chamber of London, being the 15 of March 1603, as well by the English as by the strangers, with the speeches and songes delivered in the severall pageants. 1604, 1604, Edinburgh 1604; ed R. Edwards, A collection of tracts from the Somers-collections, 1795; rptd in Somers tracts vol 3, 1810; ed J. Nichols, Progresses of James I vol 1, 1828. The speech of Zeal was by Middleton. Jonson's contribution to the Coronation Entertainment was separately ptd; see col 1656, above.

The double pp: a Papist in armes, bearing ten severall sheilds, encountred by the Protestant at ten severall weapons, a Jesuite marching before them. 1606. Anon.

Newes from Hell, brought by the Divells carrier. 1606, 1607 (rev as A knights conjuring: done in earnest, discovered in jest); ed E. F. Rimbault 1842 (Percy Soc) (1607 text).

The seven deadly sinnes of London, drawne in seven severall coaches through the seven severall gates of the citie, bringing the plague with them. 1606; ed J.P. Collier, Illustrations of old English literature vol 2, 1866; ed E. Arber 1879; Cambridge 1905; ed H. F. B. Brett-Smith, Oxford 1922.

Jests to make you merie, with the conjuring up of Cock Watt, the walking spirit of Newgate, to tell tales, unto which is added the miserie of a prison and a prisoner, and a paradox in praise of serjeants; written by T.D. and George Wilkins. 1607.

North-ward hoe, sundry times acted by the children of Paules, by Thomas Decker and John Webster. 1607; ed A. Dyce, Webster's Works, 1830, 1859 (rev); ed W. Hazlitt, Webster's Dramatic works, 1857; TFT 1914.

The famous history of Sir Thomas Wyat, with the coronation of Queen Mary, and the coming in of King Philip, as it was plaied by the Queens Majesties servants, written by Thomas Dickers and John Webster. 1607, 1612; ed A. Dyce, Webster's Works, 1830, 1859 (rev); ed W. Hazlitt, Webster's Dramatic works, 1857; ed W. J. Blew, Two old plays by Dekker and Heywood, 1876; TFT 1914.

West-ward hoe, as it hath beene divers times acted by the children of Paules, written by Tho. Decker and John Webster. 1607; ed A. Dyce, Webster's Works, 1830, 1859 (rev); ed W. Hazlitt, Webster's Dramatic works, 1857; TFT 1914.

The whore of Babylon, as it was acted by the Princes servants. 1607.

The dead tearme, or Westminsters complaint for long vacations and short termes, written in manner of a dialogue betweene the two cityes London and Westminster. 1608.

The belman of London, bringing to light the most notorious villanies that are now practised in the kingdome. 1608 (4 edns with slight changes) (anon), 1616, 1640; ed O. Smeaton 1904. Mainly a cento compiled from pamphlets on beggars and coney-catchers by Awdely, Harman, Greene and Rowlands.

Lanthorne and candle-light: or the bellmans second nights walke, in which hee brings to light a broode of more strange villanies then ever were till this yeare discovered. 1608, 1609 ('the second edition, newly corrected and amended'); 1612 (with many addns and some omissions as O per se o, or a new cryer of lanthorne and candle-light, being an addition or lengthening of the bell-mans second night-walke), 1616 (with new chs on prisons as Villanies discovered by lanthorne and candle-light, and the helpe of a new cryer called O per se o), 1620 (with slight addns), 1632 (with addns and omissions as English villanies six severall times prest to death by the printers), 1638 (as English Villanies seven severall times prest to death by the printers), 1648 (as English villanies eight severall times prest to death by the printers); ed O. Smeaton 1904.

Foure birds of Noahs arke: viz 1, the dove; 2, the eagle; 3, the pellican; 4, the phoenix. 1609; ed F. P. Wilson, Stratford 1924.

The guls horne-book. 1609; ed J. Nott, Bristol 1812; ed J. O. Halliwell (-Phillipps) 1862; ed C. Hindley 1872; ed G. Saintsbury 1892; ed R. B. McKerrow 1904; ed O. Smeaton 1904; Menston 1969 (facs). A satire on the Jacobean gallant. The early chs are indebted to Frederick Dedekind, Grobianus, 1549, tr R.F. as The schoole of slovenrie: or Cato turnd wrong side outward, 1605.

The ravens almanacke foretelling of a plague, famine and civill warre that shall happen this present yeare. 1609.

Worke for armorours, or the peace is broken: open warres likely to happin this yeare. 1609.

The roaring girl. 1611. With Middleton; see col 1647, above.

If this be not a good play the Divel is in it: a new play as it hath bin lately acted by the Queenes Majesties servants at the Red Bull. 1612 (as If it be not good the Divel is in it).

Troia-nova triumphans, London triumphing: or the solemne, magnificent and memorable receiving of that worthy gentleman, Sir John Swinerton knight, into the citty of London after his returne from taking the oath of mayoralty at Westminster on the morrow next after Simon and Judes day. 1612; ed F. W. Fairhold, Lord Mayors' pageants vol 2, 1844; rptd R. T. D. Sayle, Lord Mayors' pageants of the Merchant Taylors, 1931.

A strange horse-race, at the end of which comes in the catch-poles masque, and after that the bankrouts banquet, which done, the Divell, falling sicke, makes his last will and testament this present yeare. 1613.

The artillery garden: a poem dedicated to the honour of all those gentlemen who there practize military discipline. 1616; ed F. P. Wilson, Oxford 1952. The only known extant copy is in library of Univ of Göttingen.

Dekker his dreame, in which, beeing rapt with a poeticall enthusiasme, the great volumes of Heaven and Hell to him were opened, in which he read many wonderfull things. 1620; ed J. O. Halliwell (-Phillipps) 1860.

The virgin martyr. 1622. With Massinger; see col 1704, below.

A rod for run-awayes, Gods tokens of his feareful judgements, sundry wayes pronounced upon this city and on severall persons, both flying from it and staying in it. 1625, 1625 (with addns and omissions); ed F. P. Wilson, The plague pamphlets of Dekker, Oxford 1925.

Brittania's honor, brightly shining in severall magnificent shewes or pageants to celebrate the solemnity of the Right Honorable Richard Deane at his inauguration into the mayoralty of the honourable citty of London. 1628.

Warres, warres, warres. 1628. A verse pamphlet in praise of war and of the officers of the Artillery Garden.

Londons tempe: or the feild of happines, in which feild are planted severall trees of magnificence, state and bewty to celebrate the solemnity of the Right Honorable James Campbell at his inauguration into the honorable office of praetorship or mayoralty of London. [1629]; ed F. W. Fairholt, Lord Mayors' pageants vol 10, 1843.

London looke backe at that yeare of yeares 1625, and looke forward upon this yeare 1630; written not to terrifie, but to comfort. 1630 (anon); ed F. P. Wilson, The plague pamphlets of Dekker, Oxford 1925.

The blacke rod and the white rod, justice and mercie, striking and sparing London. 1630; ed F. P. Wilson, ibid.

The second part of the honest whore, with the humors of the patient man, the impatient wife, the honest whore perswaded by strong arguments to turne curtizan againe, her brave refuting those arguments, and lastly the comicall passages of an Italian Bridewell, where the scaene ends. 1630; ed R. Dodsley, A select collection of old plays vol 3, 1744; ed I. Reed, Dodsley vol 3, 1780; Ancient British drama vol 1, 1810; ed J. P. Collier, Dodsley vol 3, 1825; ed A. Dyce, Middleton's Works vol 3, 1840; ed W. A. Neilson, Chief Elizabethan dramatists, 1911; ed E. H. C. Oliphant, Shakespeare and his fellow dramatists vol 1, 1929; ed H. Spencer, Elizabethan plays, 1933.

A tragi-comedy called Match mee in London, as it hath beene often presented, first at the Bull in St Johns-street, and lately at the private-house in Drury-Lane called the Phoenix. 1631.

Penny-wise pound-foolish: or a Bristow diamond set in two rings and both crack'd. 1631 (anon); ed W. Bang, Bang vol 23, 1908. A version with English and Italian settings of the old story A pennyworth of wit.

The noble Spanish souldier, or a contract broken, justly reveng'd: a tragedy. 1634 (as The noble souldier, attributed to S. Rowley); ed A. H. Bullen, A collection of old English plays vol 1, 1882; TFT 1913.

The wonder of a kingdome. 1636; ed C. W. Dilke, Old English plays vol 3, 1814.

The sun's darling, a moral masque, as it hath been often presented at Whitehall by their Majesties servants, and after at the Cock-pit in Drury Lane, with great applause, written by John Ford and Tho. Decker gent. 1656. Included in collected edns of Ford; *see col 1721, below.*

Lust's dominion: or the lascivious Queen. 1657; ed C. W. Dilke, Old English plays vol 1, 1814; ed W. Oxberry, Old English drama, 1818, rptd in Dramatic works of Marlowe, 1827; ed G. Robinson, Works of Marlow vol 3, 1826; ed W. C. Hazlitt, Dodsley vol 14, 1875; ed J. Le G. Brereton, Louvain 1931.

The witch of Edmonton: a known true story composed into a tragi-comedy by divers well-esteemed poets: William Rowley, Thomas Dekker, John Ford etc, acted by the Princes servants often at the Cock-Pit in Drury-lane, once at Court. 1658; ed C. R. Baskervill, Elizabethan and Stuart plays, 1934. Included in collections of Ford; *see col 1722, below.*

The Welsh embassador. Ms Cardiff Public Lib; ed H. Littledale and W. W. Greg 1920 (Malone Soc).

Dekker's share in The book of Sir Thomas More *has been identified as Hand E in BM ms Harley 7368; it is rptd in* Dramatic works vol 1, ed Bowers. *Dekker has been suggested as the sole or partial author of Middleton's* Blurt master constable, *col 1646, above, and of the following anon plays:* The bloodie banquet, Charlemagne: or the distracted emperor, The merry devill of Edmonton, The telltale, The London prodigall; *his work has also been traced in the anon* Captaine Thomas Stukeley *and anon* The weakest goeth to the wall. *For the attribution to Dekker of the pamphlet* Looke up and see wonders, 1628, see F. P. Wilson, *The plague pamphlets of Dekker, Oxford 1925, p. 249. 19 verse passages attributed to Dekker are ptd in* England's Parnassus, 1600. *Dekker also wrote dedicatory verses to Anthony Munday in* The third and last part of Palmerin of England, 1602, *and in* A true and admirable historie of a mayden of consolens, 1603; to Stephen Harrison in *The archs of triumph erected in honor of the high and mighty Prince James, 1604; to John Taylor the Water Poet in* Taylors Urania: or his heavenly Muse, 1615; to Richard Brome in *The northerne lasse: a comoedie, 1632. The songs in the 1632 edn of Lyly's plays, col 1423, above have been assigned to Dekker. For the attribution to Dekker of 6 'characters' in the 9th impression (1616) of the Overbury collection, see W. J. Paylor, MLR 31 1936.*

§2

Hazlitt, W. In his Lectures on the dramatic literature of the age of Elizabeth, 1818.

Corser, T. In his Collectanea anglo-poetica, 1873 (Chetham Soc).

Herford, C. H. In his Studies in the literary relations of England and Germany in the 16th century, Cambridge 1886. For Grobianus, The guls horne-booke and the Fortunatus legend.

Hart, H. C. Notes on Bullen's old plays: the Noble Spanish souldier. Academy 1 Sept 1888.

Kupka, P. Über den dramatischen Vers Dekkers. Halle 1893.

Penniman, J. H. The war of the theatres. Boston 1897.

Small, R. A. The stage-quarrel between Jonson and the so-called poetasters. Breslau 1899. On Satiro-mastix.

Bang, W. Dekker-Studien. E Studien 28 1900.

Peterson, J. M. The Dorothea legend: its earliest records, Middle English version, and influence on Massinger's Virgin martyr. Heidelberg 1901.

Bielefeld, F. The witch of Edmonton by Rowley, Dekker, Ford: eine Quellenuntersuchung. Halle 1904.

Rühl, E. Grobianus in England. Berlin 1904.

Greg, W. W. The authorship of the songs in Lyly's plays. MLR 1 1905. Suggests Dekker as author, but *see* R. W. Bond, RES 6–7 1930–1. *See also* W. J. Lawrence,

The problem of Lyly's songs, TLS 20 Dec 1923; J. R. Moore, The songs in Lyly's plays, PMLA 42 1927; G. K. Hunter, John Lyly; the humanist as courtier, 1962 (appendix, pp. 367–72).

—— (ed). Henslowe papers: being documents supplementary to Henslowe's diary. 1907. Contains 2 letters to Edward Alleyn; facs of one in English literary autographs, ed W. W. Greg 1925.

—— Dramatic documents from the Elizabethan playhouses. 1931.

—— A fragment from Henslowe's diary. Library 4th ser 19 1938. *See also* J. Q. Adams 20 1939.

Stoll, E. E. The influence of Jonson on Dekker. MLN 21 1906.

Swinburne, A. C. In his Age of Shakespeare, 1908.

Pierce, F. E. The collaboration of Webster and Dekker. New Haven 1909.

—— The collaboration of Dekker and Ford. Anglia 36 1912.

Ristine, F. H. In his English tragicomedy: its origin and history, New York 1910.

Scheffler, W. Dekker als Dramatiker. Leipzig 1910.

Hunt, M. L. Thomas Dekker. New York 1911.

—— Geffray Mynshul and Dekker. JEGP 11 1912.

Mann, F. O. T. Deloney's works. Oxford 1912. Introd on the authorship of Canaans calamitie.

Aydelotte, F. In his Elizabethan rogues and vagabonds, Oxford 1913. On sources of Dekker's rogue pamphlets.

Wilson, F. P. Three notes on Dekker. MLR 15 1920.

—— The batchelars banquet. Oxford 1929. Introd on authorship of this adaptation of Les quinze joyes de mariage.

—— Dekker, Segar and some others. HLQ 18 1955. On Segar's Blazon of a Papist, the probable source of Double pp.

Ovaa, W. A. Dekker and the Virgin Mary. E Studies 3 1921.

Sykes, H. D. Massinger and Dekker's The virgin martyr. N & Q 28 Jan–4 Feb 1922.

—— In his Sidelights on Elizabethan drama, 1924. On authorship of Lust's dominion.

—— The authorship of the Witch of Edmonton. N & Q 18–25 Dec 1926.

Bullen, A. H. In his Elizabethans, 1924.

Gregg, K. L. Dekker: a study in economic and social backgrounds. Seattle 1924.

Law, R. A. The shoemakers' holiday and Romeo and Juliet. SP 21 1924.

Bradford, G. The women of Dekker. Sewanee Rev 33 1925.

Golding, S. R. The parliament of bees. RES 3 1927. On relation of Day's play to Wonder of a kingdom and Noble Spanish soldier.

Lawrence, W. J. The origin of the substantive theatre masque. In his Pre-restoration stage studies, 1927. On Sun's darling.

—— Dekker's theatrical allusiveness. TLS 30 Jan 1937. Reply by H. W. Crundell 13 Feb 1937.

Lloyd, B. The noble soldier and the Welsh embassador. RES 3 1927.

—— The authorship of the Welsh embassador. RES 21 1945.

Sisson, C. J. Keep the widow waking: a lost play by Dekker. Library 4th ser 8 1927; expanded in his Lost plays of Shakespeare's age, Cambridge 1936. *See also* G. B. Harrison, Library 4th ser 10 1930.

Chandler, W. K. The sources of the characters in the Shoemakers' holiday. MP 27 1929.

—— The topography of the Shoemakers' holiday. SP 26 1929.

Potter, R. Three Jacobean devil plays. SP 28 1931. On If this be not a good play the Devil is in it.

Bowers, F. T. The stabbing of a portrait in Elizabethan tragedy. MLN 47 1932.

—— Dekker and Jonson. TLS 12 Sept 1936.

— Dekker, Robert Wilson and the Shoemakers' holiday. MLN 64 1949.

— Essex's rebellion and Old Fortunatus. RES new ser 3 1952.

Fluchère, H. Dekker et le drame bourgeois. Cahiers du Sud 20 1933.

Dowling, M. A note on Moll Cutpurse, 'the roaring girl'. RES 10 1934.

Russell, H. K. Tudor and Stuart dramatizations of the doctrines of natural and moral philosophy. SP 31 1934. On Sun's darling.

Thieme, H. Zur Verfasserfrage des Dekkerschen Stückes Old Fortunatus. Leipzig 1934.

Boyce, B. A Restoration 'improvement' of Dekker. MLN 50 1935. A knight's conjuring.

Craig, H. In his Enchanged glass: the Renaissance mind in English literature, New York 1936.

Ellis-Fermor, U. M. In her Jacobean drama, 1936, 1958 (rev).

Paylor, W. J. Dekker and the Overburian characters. MLR 31 1936.

Spencer, T. In his Death and Elizabethan tragedy, Cambridge Mass 1936.

Knights, L. C. In his Drama and society in the age of Jonson, 1937.

Sackville-West, E. The significance of the Witch of Edmonton. New Criterion 17 1937.

Halstead, W. L. Dekker's Phaethon. N & Q 26 Nov 1938.

— Collaboration on Patient Grissel. PQ 18 1939.

— Note on the text of the Famous history of Sir Thomas Wyatt. MLN 54 1939.

— Note on Old Fortunatus. MLN 54 1939.

— Dekker's arrest by the Chamberlain's Men. N & Q 21 Jan 1939.

— Dating and holograph evidence in the Whore of Babylon. N & Q 18 Jan 1941.

— New source influence on the Shoemakers' holiday. MLN 56 1941.

— Surviving original materials in Old Fortunatus. N & Q 17 Jan 1942.

— Dekker's Cupid and Psyche and Thomas Heywood. ELH 11 1944.

Adams, J. Q. Hill's list of early plays in ms. Library 4th ser 20 1939.

— Another fragment from Henslowe's Diary. Ibid.

Adkins, M. G. M. Puritanism in the plays and pamphlets of Dekker. SE 19 1939.

Eccles, M. Dekker: burial place. N & Q 26 Aug 1939.

Reynolds, G. F. Aims of a popular Elizabethan dramatist. PQ 20 1941.

Child, H. Dekker and the underdog. TLS 31 May 1941; rptd in his Essays and reflections, 1948.

Adams, H. H. In his English domestic or homiletic tragedy, New York 1943.

Boas, F. S. In his An introduction to Stuart drama, Oxford 1946.

Price, G. R. The shares of Middleton and Dekker in a collaborated play. Papers of Michigan Acad 30 1946.

— Thomas Dekker. New York 1969.

Davenport, A. Westward hoe and Hall's Virgidemiae. N & Q 5 April 1947.

Shaw, P. The position of Dekker in Jacobean prison literature. PMLA 62 1947.

— Sir Thomas Wyat and the scenario of Lady Jane. MLQ 13 1952.

Teagarden, L. J. The Dekker–Middleton problem in Michaelmas term. SE 24 1947.

Eberle, G. J. Dekker's part in the Familie of love. In J. Q. Adams memorial studies, Washington 1948.

George, J. Four notes on the text of Dekker's Shoemakers' holiday. N & Q 30 April 1949.

Peery, W. The noble soldier and the Parliament of bees. SP 48 1951.

Schoenbaum, S. Middleton's share in the Honest whore pts 1 and 2. N & Q 5 Jan 1952.

Seronsy, C. D. Dekker and Falstaff. Shakespeare Quart 4 1953.

Wadsworth, F. W. The relationship of Lust's dominion and John Mason's The Turke. ELH 30 1953.

Wright, H. G. Some 16th- and 17th-century writers on the plague. E & S new ser 6 1953.

Doran, M. In her Endeavours of art, Madison 1954.

Howarth, R. G. Dekker not a merchant taylor. N & Q Feb 1954.

Lawlis, M. E. Another look at Simon Eyre's will. N & Q Jan 1954.

Miller, E. H. Samuel Rid's borrowings from Robert Greene. N & Q June 1954. Censure of Dekker in Martin Mark-all.

— Dekker: hack writer. N & Q April 1955. On sources of his exposures of roguery.

Bradbrook, M. C. In her Growth and structure of Elizabethan comedy, 1955.

Harder, K. B. The names of Dekker's devils. Names 3 1955. On Newes from hell.

Thornton, G. E. The social and moral philosophy of Dekker. Emporia Research Stud no 4 1955.

McDiarmid, M. P. The stage quarrel in Wily beguiled. N & Q Sept 1956.

Manifold, J. S. In his Music in English drama from Shakespeare to Purcell, 1956.

Thompson, P. The old way and the new way in Dekker and Massinger. MLR 51 1956.

Wickham, G. Contribution de Jonson et de Dekker aux fêtes du couronnement de Jacques 1er. In Fêtes de la Renaissance, ed J. Jacquot, Paris 1956.

Cross, G. More's Historie of Kyng Richarde the Third and Lust's dominion. N & Q May 1957.

— The vocabulary of Lust's dominion. Neuphilologische Mitteilungen 59 1958.

— The authorship of Lust's dominion. SP 55 1958. On Marston as a collaborator.

Manheim, L. M. The King in Dekker's The shoemakers' holiday. N & Q Oct 1957.

— The thematic structure of Dekker's Honest whore pt 2. Stud in Eng Lit 1500–1900 5 1965.

— The construction of the Shoemakers' holiday. Stud in Eng Lit 1500–1900 10 1970.

Ribner, I. In his English history play in the age of Shakespeare, Princeton 1957.

Ruoff, J. E. Dekker's dedication to Match me in London. N & Q Jan 1957.

Jones-Davies, M.-T. Un peintre de la vie londonienne: Dekker. 2 vols Paris 1958.

Martin, M. F. Stow's Annals and the Famous history of Sir Thomas Wyatt. MLR 53 1958.

Maugeri, A. Studi su Dekker. Messina 1958.

Maxwell, B. Conjectures on the London prodigal. In Studies in honor of T. W. Baldwin, Urbana 1958. Suggests Dekker as author.

Dodson, D. B. Allusions to the gunpowder plot in the Whore of Babylon. N & Q July–Aug 1959.

Harbage, A. The mystery of Perkin Warbeck. In Studies in the English Renaissance drama in memory of K. J. Holzknecht, New York 1959.

Brown, A. Citizen comedy and domestic drama. In Jacobean theatre, ed J. R. Brown and B. Harris 1960.

Greene, D. M. The Welsh characters in Patient Grissil. Boston Univ Stud in Eng 4 1960.

Novarr, D. Dekker's gentle craft and the Lord Mayor of London. MP 57 1960.

Turner, R. K. Dekker's 'back-door'd Italian': Honest whore pt 1, 11.i.355. N & Q Jan 1960. Reply by R. Levin, Sept 1963.

Evans, G. B. Dryden's Mac Flecknoe and Satiromastix. MLN 76 1961.

Henslowe's Diary. Ed R. A. Foakes and R. T. Rickert, Cambridge 1961.

Toliver, H. E. The shoemakers' holiday: theme and image. Boston Univ Stud in Eng 5 1961.

Ashton, J. W. Dekker's use of folklore in Old Fortunatus, If this be not a good play, and the Witch of Edmonton. PQ 41 1962.

Enck, J. J. The peace of the poetomachia. PMLA 77 1962.

Freeman, A. An emendation in Dekker. N & Q Sept 1962. If this be not a good play 1.i.28.

— The date of If this be not a good play the Devil is in it. PQ 44 1965.

Murray, P. B. The collaboration of Dekker and Webster in Northward ho and Westward ho. PBSA 56 1962.

Nicoll, A. The dramatic portrait of George Chapman. PQ 41 1962. Chapman identified with Bellamont in Northward ho.

Fischer, U. C. Un dramma martirologico barocco: The virgin martyr di Massinger. Siculorum Gymnasium 16 1963.

Hoeniger, F. D. Dekker, the restoration of St Paul's and J. P. Collier the forger. Renaissance News 16 1963. Argues for the authenticity of Paul his temple triumphant, attributed to Dekker in ms v.a.160 in the Folger Lib, with text of the poem.

Clubb, L. G. The virgin martyr and the tragedia sacra. Renaissance Drama 7 1964.

Best, M. R. A note on the songs in Lyly's plays. N & Q March 1965.

Bose, T. The date of the Welsh embassador. Indian Jnl of Eng Stud 6 1965.

Homan, S. R. Doctor Faustus, Old Fortunatus and the morality plays. MLQ 26 1965.

— Dekker as collaborator in Perkin Warbeck. Eng Lang Notes 3 1965.

— A looking-glass for London and England: the source of If it be not a good play the Devil is in it. N & Q Aug 1966.

— Shakespeare and Dekker as keys to Ford's 'Tis pity she's a whore. Stud in Eng Lit 1500-1900 7 1967.

Jones, E. Othello's countrymen. 1965. On Lust's dominion.

Pineas, R. The whore of Babylon and Paradise lost. Eng Lang Notes 2 1965.

Berlin, N. Dekker: a partial reappraisal. Stud in Eng Lit 1500-1900 6 1966.

— The base string: the underworld in Elizabethan drama. Rutherford NJ 1968.

Hale, D. G. Dekker and the body politic. Neuphilologische Mitteilungen 67 1966.

Lobzowska, M. Conventional and original elements in Dekker's non-dramatic prose satire. Kwartalnik Neofilologiczny (Warsaw) 13 1966.

Ure, P. Patient madman and honest whore: the Middleton-Dekker oxymoron. E & S new ser 19 1966.

Brodwin, L. L. The domestic tragedy of Frank Thorney in the Witch of Edmonton. Stud in Eng Lit 1500-1900 7 1967.

Keyishian, H. Dekker's whore and Marston's courtesan. Eng Lang Notes 4 1967.

Bergeron, D. M. Harrison, Jonson and Dekker: the magnificent entertainment for King James. Jnl Warburg & Courtauld Inst 31 1968.

— Dekker's Lord Mayors' shows. E. Studies 51 1970.

Burelbach, F. M. War and peace in the shoemakers' holiday. Tennessee Stud in Lit 13 1968.

Rhodes, E. L. 'Me thinks this stage shews like a tennis court.' In Papers of Southeast Renaissance Conference, Durham NC 1968. On staging of Lust's dominion.

Conover, J. Dekker: an analysis of dramatic structure. Hague 1969.

Greenfield, T. N. In her Induction in Elizabethan drama, Eugene 1969.

Kaplan, J. H. Virtue's holiday: Dekker and Simon Eyre. Renaissance Drama new ser 2 1969.

McClure, D. S. Versification and Master Hammon in the Shoemakers' holiday. In Studies in the humanities, Indiana Pa 1969.

Ayres, P. J. The revision of Lust's dominion. N & Q June 1970.

McMillin, S. The book of Sir Thomas More: a theatrical view. MP 68 1970.

Kinney, A. F. Dekker's Twelfth Night. UTQ 41 1971. On Shoemakers' holiday.

THOMAS HEYWOOD
1574?-1641

Bibliographies

Clark, A. M. A bibliography of Thomas Heywood. Proc Oxford Bibl Soc 1 1925.

Tannenbaum, S. A. Thomas Heywood: a concise bibliography. New York 1939.

Donovan, D. G. Elizabethan bibliographies supplements 11: Thomas Heywood 1938-65. 1967.

Collections

Dramatic works. Ed J. P. Collier and B. Field 2 vols 1841-51 (Shakespeare Soc). Contains Edward IV 2 pts; If you know not me 2 pts: Fair maid of the exchange; A woman killed with kindness; Golden age; Silver age; Fair maid of the west 2 pts; Royal King and the loyal subject; Fortune by land and sea.

Dramatic works. Ed R. H. Shepherd 6 vols 1874. Contains all the plays and Lord Mayors' shows listed below except How a man may choose a good wife, Captives, Londini artium, Londini emporia. Includes Fair maid of the exchange, no longer attributed to Heywood (see col 1759, below).

Thomas Heywood. Ed A. W. Verity 1888 (Mermaid ser). Contains A woman killed with kindness; Fair maid of the west pt 1; English traveller; Wise woman of Hogsdon; Rape of Lucrece.

§ 1

Oenone and Paris. 1594; ed J. Q. Adams, Washington 1943; ed E. S. Donno, Elizabethan minor epics, New York 1963.

The first and second partes of King Edward the Fourth: containing his mery pastime with the Tanner of Tamwoorth, as also his love to fayre Mistresse Shoare, as it hath divers times been publiquely played by the Right Honorable the Earle of Derby his servants. 1599 (anon), 1600, 1605, 1613, 1619, 1626; ed S. de Ricci 1922 (facs).

A pleasant conceited comedie wherein is shewed how a man may chuse a good wife from a bad, as it hath bene sundry times acted by the Earle of Worcesters servants. 1602 (anon), 1605, 1608, 1614, 1621, 1630, 1634; ed C. Baldwin, Old English drama vol 1, 1825; ed W. C. Hazlitt, Dodsley vol 9, 1875; ed A. E. H. Swaen, Bang vol 35, 1912; TFT 1912.

If you know not me, you know no bodie: or the troubles of Queen Elizabeth. 1605 (anon), 1606, 1608, 1610, 1613, 1623, 1632, 1639; ed W. J. Blew, Two old plays by Dekker and Heywood, 1876; ed M. Doran 1935 (Malone Soc).

The second part of If you know not me, you know no bodie, with the building of the Royall Exchange, and the famous victorie of Queene Elizabeth in the yeare 1588. 1606 (anon), 1609 (as The second part of Queene Elizabeths troubles, Doctor Paries treasons, with the humors of Hobson and Tawney-cote), 1623, 1633; ed M. Doran 1935 (Malone Soc).

A woman kilde with kindnesse. 1607, 1617 ('The third edition, as it hath beene often times acted by the Queenes Majest. servants') (no 2nd edn known); ed R. Dodsley, A select collection of old plays vol 4, 1744; ed I. Reed, Dodsley vol 7, 1780; Ancient British drama vol 2, 1810; ed J. P. Collier, Dodsley vol 7, 1825; ed J. S. Keltie, Works of the British dramatists, 1870; ed A. W. Ward 1897; ed F. J. Cox, Old English plays,

1907; ed W. A. Neilson, Chief Elizabethan dramatists 1911; ed K. L. Bates, Boston 1917; ed C. F. T. Brooke and N. B. Paradise, English drama, 1933; ed H. Spencer, Elizabethan plays, 1933; ed C. R. Baskervill, Elizabethan and Stuart plays, 1934; ed R. Van Fossen 1961 (Revels ser).

The rape of Lucrece: a true Roman tragedie, with the severall songes in their apt places by Valerius, the merrie lord amongst the Roman peeres, acted by her Majesties servants at the Red Bull neere Clarkenwell. 1608, 1609, 1614, 1630, 1638 ('revised, and sundry songs before omitted, now inserted in their right places'); ed C. Baldwin, Old English drama vol 1, 1825; ed A. Holaday, Urbana 1950.

The two most worthy and notable histories which remaine unmained to posterity, viz, the conspiracie of Cateline undertaken against the government of the senate of Rome, and the warre which Jugurth for many yeares maintained against the same state, both written by C. C. Salustius. 1608 (anon); ed C. Whibley 1924 (Tudor trns).

Troia britanica, or Great Britaines Troy. 1609. Extracts in The passionate pilgrim, 1612, and Poems written by Wil. Shakespeare gent, 1640.

The golden age, or the lives of Jupiter and Saturne, with the defining of the heathen gods, as it hath beene sundry times acted at the Red Bull by the Queenes Majesties servants. 1611 (certain copies read 'deifying' for 'defining' in the title).

An apology for actors, containing three briefe treatises: 1, their antiquity; 2, their ancient dignity; 3, the true use of their quality. 1612, [1658] (as The actors vindication); rptd Somers tracts vol 1, 1750; ed W. Scott, Somers tracts vol 3, 1810; ed J. P. Collier, Shakespeare Soc 1841; ed E. K. Chambers (condensed in Elizabethan stage vol 4, 1923).

The brazen age, the first act containing the death of the centaure Nessus, the second the tragedy of Meleager, the third the tragedy of Jason and Medea, the fourth Vulcans net, the fifth the labours and death of Hercules. 1613.

A funerall elegie upon the death of Henry Prince of Wales. 1613 (ptd in Three elegies on the most lamented death of Prince Henrie).

A marriage triumphe in memorie of the happie nuptials betwixt the high and mightie Prince Count Palatine and the most excellent Princesse the Lady Elizabeth. 1613; ed J. P. Collier, Percy Soc 1842; ed E. M. Goldsmid, Aungervyle Soc 1884.

The silver age, including the love of Jupiter to Alcmena, the birth of Hercules, and the rape of Proserpine, concluding with the arraignement of the moone. 1613. BM ms Egerton 1994, ff. 74a–95a includes Calisto or The escapes of Jupiter, made up of scenes from The golden and silver ages.

The foure prentises of London, with the conquest of Jerusalem, as it hath bene diverse times acted at the Red Bull by the Queenes Majesties servants. 1615, 1632; ed I. Reed, Dodsley vol 6, 1780; Ancient British drama vol 3, 1810; ed J. P. Collier, Dodsley vol 6, 1825.

Γυναικεῖον: or nine bookes of various history concerning women, inscribed by the names of the nine Muses. 1624, 1657 (as The generall historie of women).

Publii Ovidii Nasonis de arte amandi: or the art of love. nd. Other edns under various titles nd (2 edns), 1650, 1662?, 1667, 1672, 1677, 1682, 1705.

A funeral elegie upon King James. 1625.

Englands Elizabeth: her life and troubles during her minoritie from the cradle to the crowne. 1631, Cambridge 1632, 1641; rptd Harleian miscellany vol 10, 1808.

The fair maid of the west: or a girle worth gold, the first part as it was lately acted before the King and Queen by the Queens Majesties comedians, written by T. H. 1631; ed K. L. Bates, Boston 1917; ed R. K. Turner 1967 (Regents ser).

The fair maid of the west: the second part. 1631; ed R. K. Turner 1967 (Regents ser).

Londons jus honorarium, exprest in sundry triumphs, pagiants and shews at the initiation or entrance of the Right Honourable George Whitmore into the mayoralty. 1631.

The iron age: contayning the rape of Hellen, the siege of Troy, the combate betwixt Hector and Ajax, Hector and Troilus slayne by Achilles, Achilles slaine by Paris, Ajax and Ulisses contend for the armour of Achilles, the death of Ajax etc. 1632.

The second part of the iron age: which contayneth the death of Penthesilea, Paris, Priam and Hecuba; the burning of Troy; the deaths of Agamemnon, Menelaus, Clitemnestra, Hellena, Orestes, Egistus, Pillades, King Diomen, Pyrhus, Cethus, Synon, Thersites etc. 1632.

Londini artium & scicentiarum scaturigo: or Londons fountaine of arts and sciences, exprest at the initiation of the Right Honorable Nicholas Raynton into the mayorty. 1632; ed A. M. Clark, Theatre miscellany, Oxford 1953 (Luttrell Soc).

The English traveller, as it hath beene publikely acted at the Cock-pit in Drury-lane by her Majesties servants. 1633; ed C. W. Dilke, Old English plays vol 6, 1815.

Londini emporia: or Londons mercatura at the inauguration of the Right Honorable Ralph Freeman into the mayorty. 1633; ed A. M. Clark, Theatre miscellany, Oxford 1953 (Luttrell Soc).

The late Lancashire witches: a well received comedy lately acted at the Globe on the Banke-side by the Kings Majesties actors, written by Thom. Heywood and Richard Brome. 1634; rptd L. Tieck, Shakespeares Vorschule vol 1, 1823; ed J. O. Halliwell (-Phillipps) 1853.

A pleasant comedy called A mayden-head well lost, as it hath beene publickly acted at the Cocke-pit in Drury-Lane by her Majesties servants. 1634; rptd C. Baldwin, Old English drama vol 2, 1824.

The hierarchie of the blessed angells. 1635.

Londini sinus salutis: or Londons harbour of health and happinesse at the initiation of the Right Honourable Christopher Clethrowe into the mayoralty. 1635.

Philocothonista: or the drunkard opened, dissected and anatomized. 1635.

The wonder of this age: or the picture of a man living who is one hundred and fifty two yeeres old and upward, this 12th day of November. 1635. Anon.

A challenge for beautie, as it hath beene sundry times acted by the Kings Majesties servants at the Blacke-friers, and at the Globe on the Banke-side. 1636; ed C. W. Dilke, Old English plays vol 6, 1815.

Loves maistresse: or the Queens masque, as it was three times presented before their two excellent Majesties within the space of eight dayes in the presence of sundry forraigne ambassadors; publikely acted by the Queens comoedians at the Phoenix in Drury-lane. 1636, 1640, 1640 (for 1661?); ed T. Wilkins 1792; ed C. Baldwin, Old English drama vol 2, 1825; ed E. M. Goldsmid, Bibliotheca curiosa, Edinburgh 1886; ed H. M. Blake 1910.

The new-yeeres gift presented at Court from the Lady Parvula to the Lord Minimus (commonly called Little Jefferie) her Majesties servant, with a letter written by Microphilus. 1636 (signed T.H.), 1638.

The three wonders of this age. 1636.

A true discourse of the two infamous upstart prophets, Richard Farnham Weaver of White-Chappell, and John Bull Weaver of Saint Butolphs Algate, now prisoners, as also of Margaret Tennis now prisoner, written by T.H. 1636.

A curtaine lecture as it is read by a countrey farmers wife to her good man, by a countrey gentlewoman or lady to her esquire or knight, by a souldiers wife to her captain or lieutenant, by a citizens or tradesmans wife to her husband, by a Court lady to her Lord, concluding with an imitable lecture read by a queene to her soveraigne Lord and King. 1637. Signed T.H.

Londini speculum: or Londons mirror at the initiation of the Right Honorable Richand Fenn into the mayrolty. 1637.

The phoenix of these late times: or the life of Mr Henry Welby esq. 1637, 1637.

Pleasant dialogues and dramma's, selected out of Lucian, Erasmus, Textor, Ovid etc. 1637; ed W. Bang, Bang vol 3, 1903. R. H. Shepherd includes most of Pleasant dialogues and dramas in Dramatic works vol 6, 1874.

The royall King and the loyall subject, as it hath beene acted by the Queenes Majesties servants. 1637; ed C. W. Dilke, Old English plays vol 6, 1815; ed K. W. Tibbals, Philadelphia 1906.

A true description of his Majesties royall ship built this yeare 1637 at Wooll-witch in Kent. 1637, 1638 (with addns). An extract rptd in The common-wealths great ship commonly called the Soveraigne of the Seas, 1653.

Porta pietatis: or the port or harbour of piety at the initiation of the Right Honourable Sir Maurice Abbot knight into the mayoralty. 1638; ed F. W. Fairholt, Lord mayors' pageants, 1843–4 (Percy Soc).

The wise-woman of Hogsdon: a comedie. 1638.

The life and death of Queene Elizabeth, written in heroicall verse. 1639. Anon.

Londini status pacatus: or Londons peacable estate at the innitiation of the Right Honourable Henry Garway into the mayoralty. 1639.

A true relation of the lives and deaths of the two most famous English pyrats, Purser and Clinton, who lived in the reigne of Queene Elizabeth. 1639. Anon.

The exemplary lives and memorable acts of nine the most worthy women of the world: three Jewes, three Gentiles, three Christians; written by the author of the history of women. 1640.

The black box of Roome opened, from whence are revealed the damnable blcody plots, practises and behaviour of Jesuites, priests, papists and other recusants in generall. 1641. Anon.

Brightmans predictions and prophecies. 1641. Anon.

A dialogue or accidental discourse betwixt Mr Alderman Abell and Richard Kilvert, the two maine projectors for wine, and also Alderman Abels wife etc. 1641. Anon.

The life of Merlin, sirnamed Ambrosius, his prophesies and predictions interpreted; being a chronographicall history of all the kings from Brute to the reigne of our royall soveraigne King Charles. 1641, 1651 (as Merlins prophesies and predictions interpreted). An extract rptd in Seven severall strange prophesies, 1642; Nine notable prophesies, 1644; and Twelve strange prophesies, nd.

Machiavels ghost, as he lately appeared to his deare sons, the moderne projectors. 1641 (anon), 1641 (as Machiavel, as he lately appeared). An extract rptd in Hogs caracter of a projector, 1642 etc.

A new plot discovered, practised by an assembly of Papists for the deliverance of William Waller, alias Walker, alias Ward, alias Slater, a Jesuite which was hang'd, drawn and quartered, revealed by John Hodgskins a porter, by a letter. 1641. Anon.

The rat-trap: or the Jesuites taken in their owne net etc. 1641. Anon.

Reader, here you'l plainly see judgement perverted by these three: a priest, a judge, a patentee. 1641.

A revelation of Mr Brightmans revelation, in a dialogue betweene a minister of the gospell, and a citizen of London, whereby it is manifest that Mr Brightman was a true prophet. 1641. Anon.

Fortune by land and sea: a tragi-comedy, as it was acted by the Queens servants, written by Tho. Haywood and William Rowly. 1655; ed J. E. Walker, Boston 1899.

The famo[us] and remarkable hist[ory of] Sir Richard Whittingto[n, three] times Lord Mayor of Lon[don], written by T.H. 1656, 1678, [1680?].

The captives: or the lost recovered. BM ms Egerton 1994, ff. 52ª–73ª; ed A. H. Bullen, Old English plays vol 4, 1885; ed A. C. Judson, New Haven 1921; ed A. Brown 1953 (Malone Soc).

Heywood's share in The book of Sir Thomas More *has been identified as Hand B in BM ms Harley 7368. He has been connected as collaborator or reviser with the following anon plays:* Captain Thomas Stukeley; *and* Dick of Devonshire, The trial of chivalry, Nobody and somebody, The fair maid of the exchange, A Yorkshire tragedy, *cols 1759–62, below; and with Dekker and Webster's* Sir Thomas Wyatt, *col 1675, above; Webster's* Appius and Virginia, *and Webster and W. Rowley's* A cure for a cuckold, *cols 1698–9, below; Wilkins's* Miseries of enforced marriage, *col 1757, below; H. Shirley's* The martyred soldier, *below; Marlowe's* Jew of Malta, *col 1445, above; and Shakespeare's* Pericles, *col 1553, above.*

§2

Hazlitt, W. In his Lectures on the dramatic literature of the age of Elizabeth, 1818.

Fairholt, F. W. Lord Mayors' pageants. 1843–4 (Percy Soc). Reprints 1638 pageant with descriptions of those for 1632–3.

Gosse, E. In his Seventeenth-century studies, 1883.

— In his Jacobean poets, 1894.

— In his Books on the table, 1921.

Marshall, F. A woman killed with kindness. Theatre 1 April 1887.

Hart, H. C. Notes on Bullen's old plays: the Captives. Academy 13 Oct 1888.

Swinburne, A. C. The historical and classical plays of Heywood. Nineteenth Century April 1895.

— The romantic and contemporary plays of Heywood. Nineteenth Century Sept 1895. Both rptd in his Age of Shakespeare, 1908.

Sprenger, R. Kleine Bemerkungen: Thomas Heywood. E Studien 19 1894.

Kittredge, G. L. Notes on Elizabethan plays. JEGP 2 1899. On Captives.

van Dam, B. A. P. and C. Stoffel. The fifth act of Heywood's Queen Elizabeth: second part. Sh Jb 38 1902.

Kämpfer, O. Das Verhältnis von Heywoods The royal King and the loyal subject zu Painters Palace of pleasure. Halle 1903.

Bolte, J. Eine Hamburger Aufführung von Nobody and somebody. Sh Jb 41 1905.

Brereton, J. Le G. Notes on the text of Heywood. In his Elizabethan drama: notes and studies, Sydney 1906.

Grierson, H. J. C. In his First half of the 17th century, Edinburgh 1906.

Budig, W. Untersuchungen über Jane Shore. Rostock 1908.

Thomas, D. L. On the play Pericles. E Studien 38 1908.

Baskervill, C. R. The sources and analogues of How a man may choose a good wife from a bad. PMLA 24 1909.

Hibbard, L. A. The authorship and date of the Fayre maide of the exchange. MP 7 1910.

Ristine, F. H. In his English tragicomedy: its origin and history, New York 1910.

Martin, R. G. A new source for A woman killed with kindness. E Studien 43 1911.

— Is the Late Lancashire witches a revision? MP 13 1915.

— Notes on Heywood's Ages. MLN 33 1918.

— A new specimen of the revenge play. MP 16 1918.

— A critical study of Heywood's Gunaikeion. SP 20 1923.

— The sources of If you know not me you know nobody pt 1. MLN 39 1924.

Oliphant, E. H. C. Problems of authorship in Elizabethan dramatic literature. MP 8 1911.

Adams, J. Q. Heywood and How a man may choose a good wife from a bad. E Studien 45 1912.

— Shakespeare, Heywood and the classics. MLN 34 1919.

Andrews, C. E. The authorship of the Late Lancashire witches. MLN 28 1913; rptd in his Richard Brome: a study of his life and works, New Haven 1913.

Aronstein, P. Thomas Heywood. Anglia 37 1913.

—— Die Verfasserschaft des Dramas The fair maid of the exchange. E Studien 45 1912.

Brooke, R. The authorship of the later Appius and Virginia. MLR 8 1913; shortened in his John Webster and the Elizabethan drama, 1916.

Gilbert, A. H. Heywood's debt to Plautus. JEGP 12 1913.

Tatlock, J. S. P. The siege of Troy in Elizabethan literature, especially in Shakespeare and Heywood. PMLA 30 1915.

Winkler, A. Heywoods A woman killed with kindness und das Ehebruchsdrama seiner Zeit. Leipzig 1915.

Frost, M. M. Heywood's indebtedness to Stow. MLR 11 1916.

Jewell, R. Heywood's The fair maid of the west. In Studies in English drama: first series, ed A. Gaw, New York 1917.

Clark, A. M. The authorship of Appius and Virginia. MLR 16 1921.

—— Heywood as a critic. MLN 37 1922.

—— Heywood's Art of love lost and found. Library 4th ser 3 1922.

—— Lydgate's Troy book. TLS 2 Oct 1924.

—— A Marlowe mystification. TLS 16 July 1925.

—— Thomas Heywood: playwright and miscellanist. Oxford 1931.

Velte, M. The bourgeois elements in the dramas of Heywood. Mysore 1922.

Sykes, H. D. In his Sidelights on Elizabethan drama, 1924.

—— Heywood's authorship of King Edward IV. N & Q 12 Sept 1925.

Gray, H. D. Heywood's Pericles revised by Shakespeare. PMLA 40 1925.

—— Appius and Virginia by Webster and Heywood. SP 23 1926.

Greg, W. W. The escapes of Jupiter: an autograph play of Thomas Heywood. Palaestra 148 1925.

—— In his English literary autographs 1550–1650 pt 1: dramatists, 1925.

—— In his Dramatic documents from the Elizabethan playhouses, 1931.

Lloyd, B. Thomas Heywood and the NED. TLS 4 March 1926.

Wright, L. B. The male friendship cult in Heywood's plays. MLN 42 1927.

—— Heywood and the popularising of history. MLN 43 1928.

—— Notes on Heywood's later reputation. RES 4 1928.

—— In his Middle-class culture in Elizabethan England, Chapel Hill 1935.

Cromwell, O. Thomas Heywood: a study in the Elizabethan drama of everyday life. New Haven 1928.

Giordano-Orsini, G. N. The copy for If you know not me you know nobodie pt 1. TLS 4 Dec 1930.

—— Heywood's play on the Troubles of Queen Elizabeth. Library 4th ser 14 1933.

Rice, W. G. The Moroccan episode in the Fair maid of the west. PQ 9 1930.

Rouse, C. A. Was Heywood a servant of the Earl of Southampton? PMLA 45 1930.

Bescou, Y. Heywood et le problème de l'adultère. Revue Anglo-américaine 9 1931.

—— Heywood et la sorcellerie. Revue de l'Enseignement des Langues Vivantes 49 1932.

—— Heywood et la bourgeoisie de la Renaissance. Revue de l'Enseignement des Langues Vivantes 52 1933.

—— La place de Heywood dans le théâtre de son époque. Revue de l'Enseignement des Langues Vivantes 55 1938.

Eliot, T. S. Thomas Heywood. TLS 30 July 1931; rptd in his Selected essays, 1932, and Elizabethan essays, 1934.

Martin, M. T. If you know not me and the Famous historie of Sir Thomas Wyatt. Library 4th ser 13 1932.

Fosca, F. Mesure de Heywood. Cahiers de Sud 10 1933.

Craig, H. In his Enchanted glass: the Renaissance mind in English literature, New York 1936.

Galinsky, H. Die Familie im Drama von Thomas Heywood. Breslau 1936.

Spencer, T. In his Death and Elizabethan tragedy, Cambridge Mass 1936.

Knights, L. C. In his Drama and society in the age of Jonson, 1937.

Patterson, M. The origin of the main plot of A woman killed with kindness. SE 17 1937.

Smith, H. D. A woman killed with kindness. PMLA 53 1938.

Bush, D. William Painter and Heywood. MLN 54 1939.

Sisson, C. J. Notes on early Stuart tragedy. MLR 37 1942.

Adams, H. H. In his English domestic or homiletic tragedy, New York 1943.

Halstead, W. L. Dekker's Cupid and Psyche and Heywood. ELH 11 1944.

Brooke, C. F. T. The royal Fletcher and the loyal Heywood. In Elizabethan studies in honor of G. F. Reynolds, Boulder 1945.

Holaday, A. Robert Browne and the date of Heywood's Lucrece. JEGP 44 1945.

—— Heywood's Troia britannica and the Ages. JEGP 45 1946.

—— Heywood and the Puritans. JEGP 49 1950.

—— Heywood and the Low Countries. MLN 56 1951.

Boas, F. S. In his An introduction to Stuart drama, Oxford 1946.

—— Thomas Heywood. 1950.

McManaway, J. G. Latin title-page mottoes as a clue to dramatic authorship. Library 4th ser 26 1946. On authorship of Dick of Devonshire.

Townsend, F. L. The artistry of Heywood's double plots. PQ 25 1946.

Prior, M. E. In his Language of tragedy, New York 1947.

Burke, J. Archbishop Abbot's tomb at Guildford: problems in early Caroline iconography. Jnl Warburg & Courtauld Inst 12 1949. Iconography of tomb derives not from Spenser but from Heywood's iconographic programme for the Sovereign of the Seas.

Ure, P. Marriage and domestic drama in Heywood and Ford. E Studies 32 1951.

Harbage, A. In his Shakespeare and the rival traditions, New York 1952.

Doran, M. In her Endeavors of art, Madison 1954.

Grivelet, M. Th' untun'd kennel: notes sur Heywood et le théâtre sous Charles Ier. Etudes Anglaises 7 1954.

—— Heywood et le drame domestique élisabéthain. Paris 1957.

—— The simplicity of Heywood. Shakespeare Survey 14 1961.

Bradbrook, M. C. In her Growth and structure of Elizabethan comedy, 1955.

Brown, A. Two notes on Heywood. MLR 50 1955.

—— Citizen comedy and domestic drama. In Jacobean theatre, ed J. R. Brown and B. Harris 1960.

—— Heywood's dramatic art. In Essays on Shakespeare and the Elizabethan drama in honor of Hardin Craig, Columbia Missouri 1962.

Herrick, M. T. In his Tragicomedy: its origins and development in Italy, France and England, Urbana 1955.

Reeves, J. D. Perseus and the flying horse in Peele and Heywood. RES new ser 6 1955.

Roberts, W. E. Ballad themes in the Fair maid of the west. Jnl of Amer Folklore 68 1955.

Bowen, H. E. Heywood: teacher of tradition. Renaissance Papers 1956.

Nosworthy, J. M. Hand B in Sir Thomas More. Library 5th ser 11 1956. Against ascription to Heywood.

Ribner, I. In his English history play in the age of Shakespeare, Princeton 1957.

—— In his Jacobean tragedy, 1962.

Schanzer, E. Milton's fall of Mulciber and Troia britannica. N & Q Sept 1957.

—— Heywood's Ages and Shakespeare. RES new ser 11 1960.

Johnston, G. B. The lute speech in A woman killed with kindness. N & Q Dec 1958.

McNeir, W. F. Heywood's sources for the main plot of A woman killed with kindness. In Studies in the English Renaissance drama in memory of K. J. Holzknecht, New York 1959.

Spacks, P. M. Honor and perception in A woman killed with kindness. MLQ 20 1959.

Patrides, C. A. Heywood and literary piracy. PQ 39 1960.

Cutts, J. P. Heywood's The gentry to the King's head in the Rape of Lucrece and John Wilson's setting. N & Q Oct 1961.

Hooper, A. G. A woman killed with kindness. Eng Stud in Africa 4 1961.

Rabkin, N. Dramatic deception in Heywood's The English traveller. Stud in Eng Lit 1500–1900 1 1961.

—— The double plot: notes on the history of a convention. Renaissance Drama 7 1964.

Burns, F. D. A. Heywood and the Annalia dubrensia 1636. N & Q Feb 1962.

Berry, L. E. A note on A woman killed with kindness. MLR 58 1963.

Cook, D. A woman killed with kindness: an unshakespearian tragedy. E Studies 45 1964.

Coursen, H. R. The subplot of A woman killed with kindness. Eng Lang Notes 2 1965.

Forker, C. R. Shakespeare's histories and If you know not me you know nobody. Neuphilologische Mitteilungen 66 1965.

Greer, D. Heywood's parody of a lyric by Campion. N & Q Sept 1965.

Jones, E. Othello's countrymen. 1965. For Fair maid of the west.

McDermott, J. J. Henryson's Testament of Cresseid and A woman killed with kindness. Renaissance Quart 20 1967.

Stagg, L. C. An index to the figurative language of Heywood's tragedies. Charlottesville 1967.

Low, A. Heywood's authorship of the Captives. N & Q July 1968.

Wiemann, R. Le déclin de la scène indivisible élisabéthaine; Beaumont, Fletcher et Heywood. In Dramaturgie et société, ed J. Jacquot, Paris 1968.

Bergeron, D. Two compositors in Heywood's London ius honorarium 1631. SB 22 1969.

Briggs, K. M. Heywood's Hierarchie of the blessed angells. Folklore 80 1969.

Canuteson, J. The theme of forgiveness in the plot and subplot of A woman killed with kindness. Renaissance Drama new ser 2 1969.

Greenfield, T. N. In her Induction in Elizabethan drama, Eugene 1969.

Herndl, G. C. The high design: English Renaissance tragedy and the natural law. Lexington Kentucky 1970.

Lake, D. J. The Pericles candidates: Heywood, Rowley, Wilkins. N & Q April 1970.

Sturgess, K. M. The early quartos of A woman killed with kindness. Library 5th ser 25 1970.

JOHN MARSTON
1576–1634

Bibliographies

Tannenbaum, S. A. Marston: a concise bibliography. New York 1940.

Pennel, C. A. and W. P. Williams. Elizabethan bibliographies supplements IV: Marston 1939–65. 1968.

Collections

The workes of Mr John Marston: being tragedies and comedies collected into one volume. Ed W. Sheares 1633, 1633 (as Tragedies and comedies). Contains Antonio and Mellida, Antonio's revenge, Wonder of women or the tragedy of Sophonisba, What you will, Fawne, Dutch courtezan.

Works. Ed J. O. Halliwell (-Phillipps) 3 vols 1856. Omits Histrio-mastix and Jack Drum's entertainment.

Poems. Ed A. B. Grosart, Manchester 1879.

Works. Ed A. H. Bullen 3 vols 1887. Omits Histrio-mastix and Jack Drum's entertainment.

Plays. Ed H. H. Wood 3 vols Edinburgh 1934–9.

Poems. Ed A. Davenport, Liverpool 1961.

§ 1

The metamorphosis of Pigmalions image and certaine satyres. 1598 (as by William Kinsayder); rptd J.C., Alcilia 1613, 1619, 1628; ed J. Bowle, Miscellaneous pieces of poesie, 1764; Waltham St Lawrence 1926; ed E. S. Donno, Elizabethan minor epics, New York 1963.

The scourge of villanie: three bookes of satyres. 1598 (as by William Kinsayder), 1599 (2 edns, with Satyra nova); ed J. Bowle, Miscellaneous pieces of poesie, 1764; ed G. B. Harrison 1925.

Jacke Drums entertainment: or the comedie of Pasquill and Katherine, as it hath bene sundry times plaide by the children of Powles. 1601, 1616, 1618; ed R. Simpson, The school of Shakespeare vol 2, 1878; TFT 1912.

Poems. In R. Chester, Love's martyr, 1601; ed A. B. Grosart 1878 (New Shakspere Soc); ed B. H. Newdigate, The phoenix and the turtle, Oxford 1937.

The history of Antonio and Mellida: the first part, as it hath beene sundry times acted by the children of Paules, written by J.M. 1602; ed C. W. Dilke, Old English plays vol 2, 1814; ed W. W. Greg 1921 (Malone Soc); ed G. K. Hunter 1965 (Regents ser).

Antonios revenge: the second part, as it hath beene sundry times acted by the children of Paules, written by J.M. 1602; ed C. W. Dilke, Old English plays vol 2, 1814; ed W. W. Greg 1921 (Malone Soc); ed G. K. Hunter 1965 (Regents ser).

The malcontent. 1604 (3 edns, the last 'with the additions played by the Kings Majesties servants, written by Jhon Webster'); ed R. Dodsley, A select collection of old plays vol 4, 1744; ed I. Reed, Dodsley vol 4, 1780; Ancient British drama vol 2, 1810; ed J. P. Collier, Dodsley vol 4, 1825; ed W. A. Neilson, Chief Elizabethan dramatists, 1911; ed C. F. T. Brooke and N. B. Paradise, English drama, 1933; ed G. B. Harrison 1933; ed H. Spencer, Elizabethan plays, 1933; ed C. R. Baskervill, Elizabethan and Stuart plays, 1934; ed M. L. Wine 1964 (Regents ser); ed B. Harris 1967 (New Mermaid ser). Also included in some edns of Webster; see col 1698, below.

The Dutch courtezan, as it was playd in the Blacke-friars by the children of her Majesties revels. 1605; ed H. R. Walley and J. H. Wilson, Early 17th-century plays, 1930; ed M. L. Wine 1965 (Regents ser); ed P. Davison 1968.

Eastward hoe. 1605. With Chapman and Jonson; see under Chapman, col 1638, above.

Parasitaster: or the fawne, as it hath bene divers times presented at the Black friars by the children of the Queenes Majesties revels. 1606 (2 edns, the 2nd 'corrected of many faults which by reason of the author's absence were let slip in the first edition'); ed C. W. Dilke, Old English plays vol 2, 1814; ed G. A. Smith 1965 (Regents ser).

The wonder of women: or the tragedie of Sophonisba, as it hath beene sundry times acted at the Blacke friars. 1606, 1606.

The argument of the spectacle presented to the sacred Majestys of Great Brittan and Denmark as they passed through London [31 July 1606]. BM Royal ms 18 A xxxi; ed A. Davenport, Poems of Marston, Liverpool 1961.

What you will. 1607; ed C. W. Dilke, Old English plays vol 2, 1814.

The honorable Lorde and Lady of Huntingdons entertainement of theire right noble mother Alice, Countesse Dowager of Darby the first night of her Honors arrivall att the house of Ashby [Aug 1607]. Mss: (1) Huntington Lib ms EL 34 B. 9; (2) BM ms Sloane 848, f. 9 (fragment); ed A. Davenport, Poems of Marston, Liverpool 1961. Extracts in Works of Milton vol 5, ed H. J. Todd 1801, and Progresses of James I vol 2, ed J. Nichols 1828.

Histrio-mastix: or the player whipt. 1610; ed R. Simpson, The school of Shakespeare vol 2, 1878; TFT 1912.

The insatiate Countesse: a tragedie, acted at Whitefryers. 1613, 1616, 1631 (2 issues, one as 'written by William Barksteed'). Probably a fragment by Marston written up by Barksted.

§2

Hazlitt, W. In his Lectures on the dramatic literature of the age of Elizabeth, 1818.

Scholten, W. von. Metrische Untersuchungen zu Marstons Trauerspielen. Halle 1886.

Aronstein, P. Marston als Dramatiker. E Studien 20–1 1893.

Deighton, K. Marston's works: conjectural readings. 1893.

Koeppel, E. Quellenstudien zu den Draman Ben Jonsons, Marstons und Beaumont und Fletchers. Erlangen 1895.

Small, R. A. The authorship and date of the Insatiate Countess. Harvard Stud 5 1896.

— The stage-quarrel between Jonson and the so-called poetasters. Breslau 1899. See also H. C. Hart, N & Q 14 March, 11 April, 2 May 1903.

Penniman, J. H. In his War of the theatres, Boston 1897.

Wurzbach, W. von. John Marston. Sh Jb 33 1897.

Winckler, C. Marstons literarische Anfänge. Breslau 1903.

— Marstons Erstlingswerke und ihre Beziehungen zu Shakespeare. E Studien 33 1904.

Brereton, J. Le G. Notes on the text of Marston. E Studien 33 1904.

— In his Elizabethan drama, Sydney 1909; rptd in his Writings on Elizabethan drama, Melbourne 1948.

Holthausen, F. Die Quellen von Marstons What you will. Sh Jb 41 1905.

Hoppe, F. F. Histriomastix-Studien. Breslau 1906.

Stoll, E. E. Shakspere, Marston and the malcontent type. MP 3 1906.

— The date of the Malcontent: a rejoinder. RES 11 1935.

Swinburne, A. C. In his Age of Shakespeare, 1908.

Crawford, C. In his Collectanea: 2nd series, Stratford 1907.

Ristine, F. H. In his English tragicomedy: its origin and history, New York 1910.

Lockert, L. Marston, Webster and the decline of the Elizabethan drama. Sewanee Rev 27 1915.

Allen, M. S. The satire of Marston. Columbus 1920.

Beckwith, E. A. On the Hall-Marston controversy. JEGP 25 1926.

Brettle, R. E. Bibliographical notes on some Marston quartos and early collected editions. Library 4th ser 8 1927, 12 1931.

— Marston, dramatist, at Oxford. RES 3 1927.

— Marston, dramatist: some new facts about his life. MLR 22 1927.

— Marston born in Oxfordshire. Ibid.

— The 'poet Marston' letter to Sir Gervase Clifton 1607. RES 4 1928.

— Marston bibliography: a correction. Library 4th ser 15 1934.

— Notes on Marston. RES new ser 13 1962.

— Everard Guilpin and Marston. RES new ser 16 1965.

— Marston and the Duke of Buckingham 1627–8. N & Q Sept 1967.

Flood, W. H. G. A Marston letter. RES 4 1928.

Praz, M. Machiavelli and the Elizabethans. Proc Br Acad 14 1928; rev in his Flaming heart: essays in the relations between Italian and English literature, New York 1958.

— In his Studi sul concettismo, Florence 1946; tr as Studies in seventeenth-century imagery, 2 vols 1939–47 (Warburg Inst), 1 vol Rome 1964 (enlarged).

Upton, A. W. Allusions to James I and his Court in Marston's Fawn and Beaumont's Woman hater. PMLA 44 1929.

Adams, J. Q. Eastward hoe and its satire against the Scots. SP 28 1931.

Davenport, A. Some notes on references to Joseph Hall in Marston's satires. RES 9 1933.

— The quarrel of the satirists. MLR 37 1942.

Walley, H. R. The dates of Hamlet and the Malcontent. RES 9 1933. Reply by E. E. Stoll 11 1935.

Eliot, T. S. John Marston. TLS 26 July 1934; rptd in his Elizabethan essays, 1934.

Spencer, T. John Marston. Criterion 13 1934.

— In his Death and Elizabethan tragedy, Cambridge Mass 1936.

Bradbrook, M. C. In her Themes and conventions of Elizabethan tragedy, Cambridge 1935.

Craig, H. In his Enchanted glass, New York 1936.

Ellis-Fermor, U. M. In her Jacobean drama, 1936, 1958 (rev).

Crundell, H. W. Marston's Drusus. TLS 30 Oct 1937.

Eidson, J. O. Senecan elements in Antonio and Mellida and a Marston note. MLN 52 1937.

Farmer, A. J. The source de Eastward ho: Rabelais. Etudes Anglaises 1 1937.

Campbell, O. J. Comicall satyre and Shakespeare's Troilus and Cressida. San Marino 1938.

Howarth, R. G. Dipsas in Lyly and Marston. N & Q 9 July 1938.

— John Marston. N & Q 22 Nov 1952.

McGinn, D. J. A new date for Antonio's revenge. PMLA 53 1938.

Tilley, M. P. Lamb, Marston and du Bartas. MLN 53 1938.

Bowers, F. T. In his Elizabethan revenge tragedy, Princeton 1940.

Halstead, W. L. An explanation for the two editions of Marston's Fawne. SP 40 1943.

Stein, A. The second English satirist. MLR 38 1943.

Higgins, M. The convention of the stoic hero as handled by Marston. MLR 39 1944.

Simpson, P. The problem of authorship of Eastward ho! PMLA 59 1944. Credits Marston with the original idea, Act 1 etc.

Boas, F. S. In his An introduction to Stuart drama, 1946.

Hughes, L. and A. H. Scouten. Some theatrical adaptations of a picaresque tale. SE 26 1946.

Peery, W. Eastward ho! and A woman is a weathercock. MLN 62 1947.

Levin, H. An echo from the Spanish tragedy. MLN 64 1949.

Ure, P. Marston's Sophonisba: a reconsideration. Durham Univ Jnl 10 1949.

Haydn, H. In his Counter-Renaissance, New York 1950.

Peter, J. D. Marston's plays. Scrutiny 17 1950.

— Marston's use of Seneca. N & Q April 1954.

— In his Complaint and satire in early English literature, Oxford 1956.

Wilcox, J. Informal publication of late 16th-century verse satire. HLQ 13 1950.

McNeir, W. F. Marston versus Davies and Terpsichore. PQ 30 1951.

Jackson, J. L. Sources of the sub-plot of the Dutch courtezan. PQ 31 1952.

Pellegrini, G. Il teatro di Marston. Pisa 1952.

Schoenbaum, S. The precarious balance of Marston. PMLA 67 1952.

Schrickx, W. The portraiture of Gabriel Harvey in the Parnassus plays and Marston. Neophilologus 36 1952.

Zall, P. M. Marston: moralist. ELH 20 1953.

Cross, G. Some notes on the vocabulary of Marston. N & Q Oct 1954, Jan–Feb, May, Aug, Oct–Nov 1955, Aug, Nov 1956, Feb, May, July, Dec 1957, Jan, March, May 1958, March, April, July–Aug, Oct 1959, April 1960, April, Aug, Oct 1961, Aug 1963.

—— Manningham's libel on Marston. N & Q Sept 1956. Replies by S. Race, Feb, June 1957; G. Jenkins, June 1957.

—— Ovid metamorphosed: Marston, Webster, and N. Lee. N & Q June, Dec 1956.

—— The date of Antonio and Mellida. MLN 72 1957.

—— An unrecognized poem by Marston. MLQ 19 1958.

—— The authorship of Lust's dominion. SP 55 1958. Suggests Marston as collaborator.

—— 'The way of all flesh'. N & Q June 1958. On occurrence of the phrase in Dutch courtezan and Westward ho.

—— The date of the Malcontent once more. PQ 39 1960.

—— Marston, Montaigne and morality: the Dutch courtezan reconsidered. ELH 27 1960.

—— Marston's Metamorphosis of Pigmalions image: a mockepyllion. Etudes Anglaises 13 1960.

—— The retrograde genius of Marston. REL 2 1961.

—— Tilley's Dictionary of proverbs in English, H348, and Antonio and Mellida. N & Q April 1961.

Doran, M. In her Endeavors of art, Madison 1954.

Kiefer, C. Music and the Malcontent. SP 51 1954.

Axelrad, A. J. Un malcontent Elizabéthain: Marston. Paris 1955.

Herrick, M. T. In his Tragicomedy, Urbana 1955.

Maxwell, J. C. The relation of Macbeth to Sophonisba. N & Q Sept 1955.

—— A reading in Marston. N & Q May 1961. Fawne I.ii.310. Reply by G. Smith, Oct 1961.

—— An echo of Tacitus in Marston. N & Q Jan 1971. Fawne I.ii. 319–23.

Ingram, R. W. The use of music in the plays of Marston. Music & Letters 37 1956.

—— Marston: old or new Elizabethan. Humanities Assoc Bull 17 1966.

Presson, R. K. Marston's Dutch courtezan: the study of an attitude in adaptation. JEGP 55 1956.

O'Connor, J. J. The chief source of Marston's Dutch courtezan. SP 54 1957.

George, J. Marston in the Trumbull correspondence. N & Q May 1957.

Kernan, A. Marston's play Histriomastix. MLQ 19 1958.

—— In his Cankered Muse: satire of the English Renaissance, New Haven 1959.

Smith, J. H., L. D. Pizer and E. K. Kaufman. Hamlet, Antonio's revenge and the ur-Hamlet. Shakespeare Quart 9 1958.

Turner, R. K. The composition of the Insatiate Countess, Q2. SB 12 1959.

Harris, B. Men like satyrs. In Elizabethan poetry, ed J. R. Brown and Harris 1960.

Hunter, G. K. English folly and Italian vice: the moral landscape of Marston. In Jacobean theatre, ed J. R. Brown and B. Harris 1960.

—— The spoken dirge in Kyd, Marston and Shakespeare. N & Q April 1964.

Ornstein, R. In his Moral vision of Jacobean tragedy, Madison 1960.

Reiman, D. H. Marston, Jonson and the Spanish tragedy additions. N & Q Sept 1960.

Sabol, A. J. Two unpublished stage songs for the 'aery of children'. Renaissance News 13 1960. Music for Francischina's song in Dutch courtezan.

Taylor, A. Proverbs and proverbial phrases in the plays of Marston. Southern Folklore Quart 24 1960.

Caputi, A. Marston: satirist. Ithaca 1961.

Korninger, S. Marston und die Bedeutung des Malcontent. In Festschrift Theodor Spira, Heidelberg 1961.

Finkelpearl, P. J. Henry Walley of the Stationers' Company and Marston. PBSA 56 1962.

—— Donne and Everard Gilpin: additions, corrections and conjectures. RES new ser 14 1963.

—— From Petrarch to Ovid: metamorphoses in Marston's Metamorphosis of Pigmalions image. ELH 32 1965.

—— Marston's Histrio-mastix as an Inns of Court play: a hypothesis. HLQ 29 1966.

—— The use of the Middle Temple's Christmas revels in the Fawne. SP 64 1967.

—— Marston of the Middle Temple: an Elizabethan dramatist in his social setting. Cambridge Mass 1969.

Foakes, R. A. Marston's fantastical plays: Antonio and Mellida and Antonio's revenge. PQ 41 1962.

Dent, R. W. Ovid, Marlowe and the Insatiate Countess. N & Q Sept 1963.

Kilby, J. A. 'Drinking Danes' in Shakespeare and Marston. Ibid.

Orrell, J. The sources of the Wonder of women or the tragedie of Sophonisba. N & Q March 1963.

Hoy, C. In his Hyacinth room: an investigation into the nature of comedy, tragedy and tragicomedy, 1964.

Tomlinson, T. B. In his A study of Elizabethan and Jacobean tragedy, Cambridge 1964.

Davis, G. R. The characterization of Mamon in Jack Drum's entertainment. Eng Lang Notes 3 1965.

Jones, E. Othello's countrymen. 1965. On Sophonisba.

Mehl, D. In his Elizabethan dumb show, Cambridge Mass 1966.

McDonald, C. O. In his Rhetoric of tragedy: form in Stuart drama, Amherst 1966.

Jensen, E. J. Hall and Marston: the role of the satirist. Satire Newsletter 4 1967.

—— Theme and imagery in the Malcontent. Stud in Eng Lit 1500–1900 10 1970.

Keyishian, H. Dekker's whore and Marston's courtesan. Eng Lang Notes 4 1967.

Frost, D. L. In his School of Shakespeare, Cambridge 1968.

Gibbons, B. Jacobean city comedy: a study of satiric plays by Jonson, Marston and Middleton. 1968.

Berland, E. The function of irony in Antonio and Mellida. SP 66 1969.

Greenfield, T. N. In her Induction in Elizabethan drama, Eugene 1969.

Gunby, D. C. The third quarto of the Malcontent: Marston's additions and their effects. AUMLA 31 1969.

Kaplan, J. Marston's Fawn: a saturnalian satire. Stud in Eng Lit 1500–1900 9 1969.

Bergson, A. The ironic tragedies of Marston and Chapman. JEGP 69 1970.

Andrews, M. C. Jack Drum's entertainment as burlesque. Renaissance Quart 24 1971.

Geckle, G. L. Fortune in the Malcontent. PMLA 86 1971.

Horwich, R. Hamlet and Eastward ho. Stud in Eng Lit 1500–1900 11 1971.

O'Neill, D. G. The commencement of Marston's career as a dramatist. RES new ser 22 1971.

Schäfer, J. Huarte: a Marston source. N & Q Jan 1971. Fawn II.i.147–58.

CYRIL TOURNEUR
1575?–1626

Bibliographies

Tannenbaum, S. A. and D. R. Tourneur: a concise bibliography. New York 1946.

Donovan, D. G. Elizabethan bibliographies supplements II: Tourneur 1945–65. 1967.

Collections

Plays and poems. Ed J. C. Collins 2 vols 1878.

Webster and Tourneur. Ed J. A. Symonds 1888 (Mermaid ser). Contains Atheist's tragedy, Revenger's tragedy.

Complete works. Ed A. Nicoll 1930.

§1

The transformed metamorphosis. 1600.

The revengers tragaedie, as it hath beene sundry times acted by the Kings Majesties servants. 1607 (some copies dated 1608) (anon); ed R. Dodsley, A select collection of old plays vol 4, 1744; ed I. Reed, Dodsley vol 4, 1780; Ancient British drama vol 2, 1810; ed J. P. Collier, Dodsley vol 4, 1825; ed W. C. Hazlitt, Dodsley vol 10, 1876; ed A. H. Thorndike, Elizabethan minor dramatists, New York 1916; ed E. H. C. Oliphant, Shakespeare and his fellow dramatists, New York 1929; ed G. H. W. Rylands, Elizabethan tragedy, 1933; ed G. B. Harrison 1934; ed H. Fluchère, Paris 1960; ed R. C. Harrier, An anthology of Jacobean drama, New York 1963; ed R. A. Foakes 1966 (Revels ser); ed L. J. Ross 1966 (Regents ser); ed B. Gibbons 1967 (New Mermaid ser).

A funerall poeme upon the death of Sir Francis Vere, knight. 1609. Anon.

The atheist's tragedie: or the honest man's revenge, as in divers places it hath often beene acted. 1611 (some copies dated 1612); ed I. Ribner 1964 (Revels ser).

A griefe on the death of Prince Henrie. In Three elegies on the most lamented death of Prince Henrie, 1613.

The character of Robert Earle of Salesburye. Mss: (1) BM Harley ms 36, ff. 495-7; (2) Public Record Office (S. P. Dom James I. lxix no 59); (3) ms in possession of Col and Mrs Clifton of Clifton Hall, Nottingham; (4) Burley ms now or formerly preserved at Burley-on-the-Hill; (5) the Mostyn copy, calendered by the Historical Mss Commission (Report IV, appendix p. 361); rptd in Nicoll's edn of Tourneur's Works.

Tourneur has been assigned a share in the anon Charlemagne: or the distracted Emperor, *col 1759, below, in the anon* Second maiden's tragedy, *col 1761, below, and in* The honest man's fortune *in Beaumont and Fletcher canon, col 1713, below.*

§2

Thorndike, A. H. Hamlet and contemporary revenge plays. PMLA 17 1902.

Stoll, E. E. John Webster. Boston 1905. Pp. 105-16; appendix 1.

Swinburne, A. C. In his Age of Shakespeare, 1908.

Schücking, L. L. Eine Anleihe Shakespeares bei Tourneur. E Studien 50 1917.

Wenzel, P. Tourneurs Stellung in der Geschichte des englischen Dramas. Breslau 1918.

Sykes, H. D. The revenger's tragedy; The second maiden's tragedy. N & Q Sept 1919.

Oliphant, E. H. C. The authorship of the Revenger's tragedy. SP 23 1926. Attributes to Middleton.

—— In his Plays of Beaumont and Fletcher, New Haven 1927.

—— Tourneur and Mr T. S. Eliot. SP 32 1935.

Eliot, T. S. Cyril Tourneur. TLS 13 Nov 1930 (anon). Replies by E. H. C. Oliphant 18 Dec 1930; Eliot 1 Jan 1931; E. H. C. Oliphant 5 Feb 1931; B. M. Wagner 23 April 1931; J. R. Sutherland 16 April 1931; F. L. Jones 18 June 1931. Rptd in his Selected essays, 1932, and in his Elizabethan essays, 1934.

Dunkel, W. The authorship of the Revenger's tragedy. PMLA 46 1931.

Tannenbaum, S. A. A Tourneur mystification. MLN 47 1932.

Bradbrook, M. C. In her Themes and conventions of Elizabethan tragedy, Cambridge 1935.

Ellis-Fermor, U. M. The imagery of the Revengers tragedie and the Atheists tragedie. MLR 30 1935.

—— In her Jacobean drama, 1936, 1958 (rev).

Lockert, L. The greatest of Elizabethan melodramas. In Essays in dramatic literature: the T. M. Parrott presentation volume, Princeton 1935.

Spencer, T. In his Death and Elizabethan tragedy, Cambridge Mass 1936.

Napier, C. S. The revenger's tragedy. TLS 13 March 1937. Reply by E. M. Waith, MLN 57 1942.

Pym, D. A theory on the identification of Mavortio. N & Q 19 March 1938. *See also* J. D. Peter 18 Sept 1948. On Transformed metamorphosis.

Salingar, L. G. The revenger's tragedy and the morality tradition. Scrutiny 6 1938.

—— Tourneur and the tragedy of revenge. In The age of Shakespeare, ed B. Ford 1955 (Pelican).

—— The revenger's tragedy: some possible sources. MLR 60 1965.

Mincoff, M. K. The authorship of the Revenger's tragedy. Studia Historica-philologica Serdicensia (Sofia) 2 1939.

Bowers, F. T. In his Elizabethan revenge tragedy, Princeton 1940.

Cameron, K. N. Tourneur and the Transformed metamorphosis. RES 16 1940.

Jenkins, H. Cyril Tourneur. RES 17 1941.

Higgins, M. H. The influence of Calvinistic thought in Tourneur's Atheist's tragedy. RES 19 1943.

—— The development of the Senecal man. RES 23 1947.

Barker, R. H. The authorship of the Second maiden's tragedy and the Revenger's tragedy. Shakespeare Assoc Bull 20 1945.

—— Thomas Middleton. New York 1958.

Tompkins, J. M. S. Tourneur and the stars. RES 22 1946.

Prior, M. E. In his Language of tragedy, New York 1947.

Adams, H. H. Tourneur on revenge. JEGP 48 1949.

Maxwell, J. C. Two notes on the Revenger's tragedy. MLR 44 1949.

—— The atheist's tragedy 1792 and 1794. N & Q June 1970.

Feldman, A. B. Cyril Tourneur. TLS 5 Aug 1949, 18 Aug 1950.

Schoenbaum, S. The revenger's tragedy: a neglected source. N & Q 5 Aug 1950.

—— The revenger's tragedy and Middleton's moral outlook. N & Q 6 Jan 1951. Suggests Middleton as author; but *see* his Internal evidence and Elizabethan dramatic authorship, Evanston 1966.

—— The revenger's tragedy: Jacobean dance of death. MLQ 15 1954.

—— Middleton's tragedies: a critical study. New York 1955.

McCullen, J. T. Madness and the isolation of characters in Elizabethan and early Stuart drama. SP 48 1951. On Atheist's tragedy.

Gerritsen, J. The honest man's fortune: a critical edition of ms Dyce 9 (1625). Groningen 1952. Introd attributes play to Fletcher, Massinger, Field and Tourneur.

Quennell, P. C. In his Singular preference, 1952.

Foakes, R. A. On the authorship of the Revenger's tragedy. MLR 48 1953.

Leech, C. The atheist's tragedy as a dramatic comment on Chapman's Bussy plays. JEGP 52 1953.

Doran, M. In her Endeavours of art, Madison 1954.

Ornstein, R. The atheist's tragedy and Renaissance naturalism. SP 51 1954.

—— The ethical design of the Revenger's tragedy. ELH 21 1954.

—— The atheist's tragedy and T. Beard's account of Marlowe's death. N & Q July 1955.

—— In his Moral vision of Jacobean tragedy, Madison 1960.

Cope, J. I. Tourneur's Atheist's tragedy and the jig of 'Singing Simpkin'. MLN 70 1955.

Ekeblad, I.-S. A note on the Revenger's tragedy. N & Q March 1955.

—— An approach to Tourneur's imagery. MLR 54 1959.

—— On the authorship of the Revenger's tragedy. E Studies
41 1960.

Wadsworth, F. W. The authorship of the Revenger's
tragedy. MLR 50 1955.

Peter, J. In his Complaint and satire in early English
literature, Oxford 1956.

—— The revenger's tragedy reconsidered. EC 6 1956.
Replies by T. W. Craik and Peter, ibid.

Bawcutt, N. W. The revenger's tragedy and the Medici
family. N & Q May 1957.

Hamilton, A. C. Spenser and Tourneur's Transformed
metamorphosis. RES new ser 8 1957.

Hoy, C. The shares of Fletcher and his collaborators in
the Beaumont and Fletcher canon pt 4. SB 12 1959.
Tourneur's collaboration in Honest man's fortune
rejected.

—— In his Hyacinth room, 1964.

Hunter, G. K. A source for the Revenger's tragedy. RES
new ser 10 1959.

Legouis, P. Réflexions sur la recherche des sources à
propos de la Tragédie du vengeur. Etudes Anglaises
12 1959.

Lisca, P. The revenger's tragedy: a study in irony. PQ 38
1959.

Price, G. R. The authorship and the bibliography of the
Revenger's tragedy. Library 5th ser 15 1960.

Tomlinson, T. B. The morality of revenge: Tourneur's
critics. EC 10 1960.

—— In his A study of Elizabethan and Jacobean tragedy,
Cambridge 1964.

Murray, P. B. The authorship of the Revenger's tragedy.
PBSA 56 1962.

—— A study of Tourneur. Philadelphia 1964.

Nicoll, A. The revenger's tragedy and the virtue of
anonymity. In Essays on Shakespeare and Elizabethan
drama in honor of Hardin Craig, Columbia Missouri
1962.

Ribner, I. In his Jacobean tragedy, 1962.

Love, G. A. Morality and style in the Atheist's tragedy.
Humanities Assoc Bull (Canada) 1964.

Levin, R. The subplot of the Atheist's tragedy. HLQ 29
1965.

McDonald, C. O. The rhetoric of tragedy: form in Stuart
drama. Amherst 1966.

Frost, D. L. In his School of Shakespeare, Cambridge
1968.

Kelly, M. The dramaturgy of Tourneur's trial scene.
Cithara 8 1968.

Kaufmann, R. J. Theodicy, tragedy and the psalmist:
Tourneur's Atheist's tragedy. Comparative Drama 3
1969.

Herndl, G. In his High design: English Renaissance
tragedy and the natural law, Lexington Kentucky
1970.

Stagg, L. C. An index to the figurative language of Tourneur's tragedies. Charlottesville 1970.

Sternlicht, S. Tourneur's imagery and the Revenger's
tragedy. Papers on Lang & Lit 6 1970.

Lake, D. J. The revenger's tragedy: internal evidence for
Tourneur's authorship negated. N & Q Dec 1971.

Lever, J. W. In his Tragedy of state, 1971.

JOHN WEBSTER
c. 1580–c. 1634

Bibliographies

Tannenbaum, S. A. Webster: a concise bibliography. New
York 1941.

Donovan, D. Elizabethan bibliographies supplements 1:
Webster 1940–65. 1967.

Collections

Works. Ed A. Dyce 4 vols 1830, 1 vol 1857 (rev).

Dramatic works. Ed W. C. Hazlitt 4 vols 1857, 1897.

Webster and Tourneur. Ed J. A. Symonds 1888 (Mermaid ser). Contains White Devil, Duchess of Malfi.

Works. Ed F. L. Lucas 4 vols 1927.

§1

North-ward hoe. 1607. With Dekker; see col 1675,
above.

The famous history of Sir Thomas Wyat. 1607. With
Dekker; see col 1675, above.

West-ward hoe. 1607. With Dekker; see col 1675, above.

The White Divel: or the tragedy of Paulo Giordano
Ursini, Duke of Brachiano, with the life and death of
Vittoria Corombona the famous Venetian curtizan,
acted by the Queenes Majesties servants. 1612, 1631,
1665, 1672; ed R. Dodsley, A select collection of old
plays vol 3, 1744; ed I. Reed, Dodsley vol 6, 1780;
Ancient British drama vol 3, 1810; ed J. P. Collier,
Dodsley vol 6, 1825; ed M. W. Sampson, Boston 1904;
ed A. H. Thorndike, New York 1912; ed C. B. Wheeler,
Six plays by contemporaries of Shakespeare, 1915;
ed E. H. C. Oliphant, Shakespeare and his fellow
dramatists, New York 1929; ed H. R. Walley and J. H.
Wilson, Early 17th-century plays, New York 1930;
ed G. B. Harrison 1933; ed G. H. Rylands, Elizabethan
tragedy, 1933; ed H. Spencer, Elizabethan plays, 1933;
ed J. R. Brown 1960 (Revels ser); ed E. Brennan 1966
(New Mermaid ser); ed J. R. Mulryne 1969 (Regents
ser); ed C. Hart 1970.

A monumental columne erected to the living memory of
the ever-glorious Henry, late Prince of Wales. In Three
elegies on the most lamented death of Prince Henrie,
1613.

New characters (drawne to the life) of severall persons
in several qualities. 1615. Anon. At end of 6th
impression of Overbury's Characters.

The Devils law case: or when women goe to law the Devill
is full of business, a new tragecomoedy, the true and
perfect copie from the originall as it was approovedly
well acted by her Majesties servants. 1623; ed F. Shirley
1972 (Regents ser).

The tragedy of the Dutchesse of Malfy, as it was presented
privately at the Blackfriers and publiquely at the Globe
by the Kings Majesties servants: the perfect and exact
coppy with diverse things printed that the length of the
play would not beare in the presentment. 1623, 1640,
[c. 1664] ('as it was acted by his late Majesties s[er]vants
at Black fryers with great applause, thirty years since,
and now acted by his Highnesse the Duke of York's
servants'), 1678, 1708; Ancient British drama vol 3,
1810; ed C. E. Vaughan 1896; ed M. W. Sampson,
Boston 1904; ed W. A. Neilson, Chief Elizabethan
dramatists, 1911; ed A. H. Thorndike, New York 1912;
ed F. Allen 1921; ed C. F. T. Brooke and N. P. Paradise,
English drama, 1933; ed C. R. Baskervill, Elizabethan
and Stuart plays, 1934; ed G. H. Rylands and C. Williams 1945; ed A. K. McIlwraith, Five Stuart tragedies,
Oxford 1953 (WC); ed J. R. Brown 1964 (Revels ser);
Menston 1968 (facs).

Monuments of honor, celebrated in the honorable city of
London at the sole munificent charge and expences of
the right worthy and worshipfull fraternity of the
eminent Merchant-Taylors at the confirmation of John
Gore in the high office of his Majesties lieutenant over
this his royall chamber. 1624; ed R. T. D. Sayle,
Lord Mayors' pageants of the Merchant Taylors'
Company in the 15th, 16th and 17th centuries, 1931.

Appius and Virginia: a tragedy. 1654, 1654, 1655, 1659,
1679; ed I. Reed, Dodsley vol 6, 1780; ed C. W. Dilke,
Old English plays vol 5, 1815; ed A. H. Thorndike,
New York 1912. With Heywood?

A cure for a cuckold: a pleasant comedy, as it hath been several times acted with great applause, written by John Webster and William Rowley. 1661, 1661, adapted S. Spring-Rice, Oxford 1885 (the main plot alone, as Love's graduate). With Heywood?

Webster's work has been connected with Middleton's Anything for a quiet life, *col 1649, above.* The fair maid of the inn *in Beaumont and Fletcher canon col 1713, below, and the anon* The weakest goeth to the wall. *The ascription to him on the title-page of* The Thracian wonder, *col 1761, below, is generally rejected.*

§2

Hazlitt, W. In his Lectures on the dramatic literature of the age of Elizabeth, 1818.

Easy, B. Webster's Devil's law case: its date. N & Q 19 Sept 1863.

Gnoli, D. Vittoria Accoramboni. Florence 1870.

Gosse, E. In his Seventeenth-century studies, 1883.

Kiesow, K. Die verschiedenen Bearbeitungen der Novelle von der Herzogin von Amalfi des Bandello in der Literatur des XVI und XVII Jahrhunderts. Anglia 17 1895.

Lauschke, J. Websters Tragödie Appius and Virginia: eine Quellenstudie. Potsdam 1899.

Stoll, E. E. John Webster. Boston 1905.

Morellini, D. Giovanna d'Aragona, Duchessa d'Amalfi. Cesena 1906.

Crawford, C. Collectanea: 1st and 2nd series. Stratford 1906–7. Articles on Webster's borrowings from Sidney, Montaigne et al.

Simpson, P. An allusion in Webster. MLR 2 1907. White Devil III.ii.129–39.

Tischner, F. Die Verfasserschaft der Webster–Rowley-dramen. Marburg 1907.

Krusius, P. Eine Untersuchung der Sprache Websters. Halle 1908.

Swinburne, A. C. In his Age of Shakespeare, 1908.

Pierce, F. E. The collaboration of Webster and Dekker. New Haven 1909.

Briggs, W. D. The influence of Jonson's tragedy in the 17th century. Anglia 35 1912.

Brooke, R. The authorship of the later Appius and Virginia. MLR 8 1913.

— Webster and the Elizabethan drama. 1916.

Sykes, H. D. An attempt to determine the date of Webster's Appius and Virginia. N & Q 24–31 May, 14 June, 26 July 1913.

— Webster's share in A cure for a cuckold. N & Q 16–23 May, 6–13 June 1914.

— Was Webster a contributor to Overbury's Characters? N & Q 24 April–15 May 1915.

— In his Sidelights on Elizabethan drama, 1924.

Bourgeois, A. F. The probable date of the Devils law case. N & Q 18 July 1914.

Lockert, L. Marston, Webster and the decline of the Elizabethan drama. Sewanee Rev 27 1915.

Archer, W. The Duchess of Malfi. Nineteenth Century Jan 1920.

Bradford, G. The women of Middleton and Webster. Sewanee Rev 29 1921.

Clark, A. M. The authorship of Appius and Virginia. MLR 16 1921.

— In his Thomas Heywood, Oxford 1931. On Appius and Virginia.

Olivero, F. La Duchessa di Amalfi di Webster. Rivista d'Italia March 1925; rptd in Studi britannici, Turin 1931.

Gray, H. D. Appius and Virginia by Heywood and Webster. SP 24 1927.

— A cure for a cuckold by Heywood, Rowley and Webster. MLR 22 1927.

Haworth, P. In his English hymns and ballads and other studies in popular literature, Oxford 1927.

Hendy, E. W. Webster: playwright and naturalist. Nineteenth Century Jan 1928.

Praz, M. Machiavelli and the Elizabethans. Proc Br Acad 14 1928; rev in his Flaming heart: essays in the relations between Italian and English literature, New York 1958.

— In his Studies in seventeenth-century imagery, 2 vols 1939–47 (Warburg Inst), 1 vol Rome 1964 (rev).

— Il dramma elisabettiano: Webster-Ford. Rome 1946.

— The Duchess of Malfi. TLS 18 June 1954.

— Webster and the Maid's tragedy. E Studies 37 1956.

Wagner, B. M. New verses by Webster. MLN 46 1931.

Hayakawa, S. I. A note on the madmen's scene in the Duchess of Malfi. PMLA 47 1932.

Summers, M. Webster and Cardano. N & Q 10 Dec 1932.

Howarth, R. G. John Webster. TLS 2 Nov 1933.

— Webster's burial. N & Q March 1954.

— Webster's Vincentio Lauriola. N & Q March 1955.

— Two notes on Webster. N & Q Sept 1962.

— Webster: property-owner? N & Q June 1965.

— Webster's Guise. N & Q Aug 1966.

— A commendatory sonnet by Webster. Eng Stud in Africa 9 1966.

— Webster's Appius and Virginia. PQ 46 1967.

— The model-source of Webster's A monumental columne. Eng Stud in Africa 11 1968.

— Two notes on Webster. MLR 63 1968.

Edwards, W. A. In Determinations, ed F. R. Leavis 1934.

Bradbrook, M. C. In her Themes and conventions of Elizabethan tragedy, Cambridge 1935.

— Two notes upon Webster. MLR 42 1947. On fate and chance in the Duchess of Malfi; Chapman and Webster.

Ellis-Fermor, U. M. In her Jacobean drama, 1936, 1958 (rev).

Glen, E. Webster and Lavater. TLS 11 April 1936.

Spencer, T. In his Death and Elizabethan tragedy, Cambridge Mass 1936.

Anderson, M. L. Hardy's debt to Webster in the Return of the native. MLN 54 1939.

— Webster's debt to Guazzo. SP 36 1939.

Halstead, W. L. Note on the text of the Famous history of Sir Thomas Wyatt. MLN 54 1939.

Smith, J. The tragedy of blood. Scrutiny 8 1939.

Bax, C. The life of the White Devil. 1940.

Bowers, F. T. In his Elizabethan revenge tragedy, Princeton 1940.

Reynolds, G. F. The staging of Elizabethan plays at the Red Bull theatre 1605–25. New York 1940.

Parr, J. The horoscope in the Duchess of Malfi. PMLA 60 1945; rptd in his Tamburlaine's malady and other essays, Tuscaloosa 1953.

Joseph, B. Lewis Theobald and Webster. Comparative Lit Stud 17–18 1945.

Boas, F. S. In his An introduction to Stuart drama, Oxford 1946.

Morgan, F. C. A deed of gift 1624 and Webster. N & Q 15 Nov 1947.

Prior, M. E. In his Language of tragedy, New York 1947.

Reed, A. W. Erasmus and Webster. TLS 14 June 1947.

Webster's women. TLS 1 Feb 1947.

Cecil, D. In his Poets and story-tellers, 1949.

Jack, I. The case of Webster. Scrutiny 16 1949.

Akrigg, G. P. V. Oaths in the White Devil and the Duchess of Malfi. N & Q 27 May 1950.

— Webster's 'devil in crystal'. N & Q Feb 1954.

— Webster and the Book of homilies. N & Q June 1959.

Dent, R. W. Webster's debt to William Alexander. MLN 65 1950.

— Webster and Nicolas de Montreux. PQ 35 1956.

— Webster's borrowing. Berkeley 1960.

— The White Devil or Vittoria Corombona? Renaissance Drama 9 1966.

Leech, C. Shakespeare's tragedies and other studies in 17th-century drama. 1950.

— Webster: a critical study. 1951.

— An addendum on Webster's Duchess. PQ 37 1958. A reply to articles by F. W. Wadsworth and M. Seiden 35 1956.

— Webster: the Duchess of Malfi. 1963.

Brown, J. R. On the dating of the White Devil and the Duchess of Malfi. PQ 31 1952.

— The printing of Webster's plays. SB 6 1954, 8 1956, 15 1962.

— The date of the Devil's law case. N & Q March 1958.

Baldini, G. Webster e il linguaggio della tragedia. Rome 1953.

Doran, M. In her Endeavors of art, Madison 1954.

Bogard, T. The tragic satire of Webster. Berkeley 1955.

Ekeblad, I.-S. Webster's 'wanton boyes'. N & Q July 1955.

— Storm imagery in Appius and Virginia. N & Q Jan 1956.

— Webster's constructional rhythm. ELH 24 1957.

— The 'impure art' of Webster. RES new ser 9 1958.

Price, H. T. The function of imagery in Webster. PMLA 70 1955.

Sypher, W. In his Four stages of Renaissance style, New York 1955.

Cross, G. A note on the White Devil. N & Q March 1956.

— Ovid metamorphosed: Marston, Webster and N. Lee. N & Q June, Dec 1956.

— Webster and Marston: a note on the White Devil v.iii.106. N & Q Sept 1960.

Lucas, F. L. The Duchess of Malfi iv.ii.207–9. TLS 13 July 1956.

Seiden, M. Two notes on Appius and Virginia. PQ 35 1956. Reply by C. Leech 37 1958.

Thomas, S. Webster and Nashe. N & Q Jan 1956.

Todd, F. M. Webster and Cervantes. MLR 51 1956.

Wadsworth, F. W. Webster's Duchess of Malfi in the light of some contemporary ideas on marriage and re-marriage. PQ 35 1956. Reply by C. Leech 37 1958.

— Some nineteenth-century revivals of the Duchess of Malfi. Theatre Survey 8 1967.

Blau, H. Language and structure in poetic drama. MLQ 18 1957.

Boklund, G. The sources of the White Devil. Cambridge Mass 1957.

— The Duchess of Malfi: sources, themes, characters. Cambridge Mass 1962.

Gross, S. L. A note on Webster's tragic attitude. N & Q Sept 1957.

Hunter, G. K. Notes on Webster's tragedies. N & Q Feb 1957.

Padgett, L. E. An entry from Guevara in Webster's commonplace-book? N & Q April 1957.

Thayer, C. G. The ambiguity of Bosola. SP 54 1957.

Davies, C. W. The structure of the Duchess of Malfi. English 12 1958.

Larkin, D. I. Hooker and Webster. N & Q Oct 1958.

Emslie, McD. Motives in Malfi. EC 9 1959.

Kernan, A. In his Cankered Muse: satire of the English Renaissance, New Haven 1959.

Layman, B. J. The equilibrium of opposites in the White Devil: a reinterpretation. PMLA 74 1959.

Whitman, R. F. Webster's Duchess of Malfi. N & Q May 1959.

Freeman, A. A note on the White Devil iii.iii.72–7. N & Q Nov 1960.

— The White Devil i.ii.295: an emendation. N & Q March 1963.

Hoy, C. The shares of Fletcher and his collaborators in the Beaumont and Fletcher canon, pt 5. SB 13 1960. On Webster's share in Fair maid of the inn.

Mulryne, J. R. The White Devil and the Duchess of Malfi. In Jacobean theatre, ed J. R. Brown and B. Harris 1960.

Ornstein, R. In his Moral vision of Jacobean tragedy, Madison 1960.

Franklin, H. B. The trial scene of the White Devil examined in terms of Renaissance rhetoric. Stud in Eng Lit 1500–1900 1 1961.

Henslowe's Diary. Ed R. A. Foakes and R. T. Rickert, Cambridge 1961.

Jenkins, H. The tragedy of revenge in Shakespeare and Webster. Shakespeare Survey 14 1961.

Ribner, I. Webster's Italian tragedies. Tulane Drama Rev 5 1961.

— In his Jacobean tragedy, 1962.

Calderwood, J. L. The Duchess of Malfi: styles of ceremony. EC 12 1962.

Hurt, J. R. Inverted rituals in the White Devil. JEGP 61 1962.

Murray, P. B. The collaboration of Dekker and Webster in Northward ho and Westward ho. PBSA 56 1962.

— A study of Webster. Hague 1970.

Brennan, E. The relationship between brother and sister in the plays of Webster. MLR 58 1963.

Lagarde, F. Les emprunts de Webster. Etudes Anglaises 16 1963.

— John Webster. Toulouse 1968.

Vernon, P. F. The Duchess of Malfi's guilt. N & Q Sept 1963.

Allison, A. W. Ethical themes in the Duchess of Malfi. Stud in Eng Lit 1500–1900 4 1964.

Luecke, J. M. The Duchess of Malfi: comic and satiric confusion in a tragedy. Ibid.

Riewald, R. G. Shakespeare burlesque in the Duchess of Malfi. E Studies (suppl) 45 1964.

Scott-Kilvert, I. John Webster. 1964 (Br Council pamphlet).

Tomlinson, T. B. In his A study of Elizabethan and Jacobean tragedy, Cambridge 1964.

Benjamin, E. B. Patterns of morality in the White Devil. E Studies 46 1965.

Brückl, O. Sir Philip Sidney's Arcadia as a source for the Duchess of Malfi. Eng Stud in Africa 8 1965.

Cunningham, J. E. In his Elizabethan and early Stuart drama, 1965.

Jones, E. Othello's countrymen. 1965. On White Devil.

Ridley, M. R. In his Second thoughts: more studies in literature, 1965.

Sensabaugh, G. F. Tragic effect in the White Devil. Stud in Eng Lit 1500–1900 5 1965.

Gill, R. 'Quaintly done': a reading of the White Devil. E & S new ser 19 1966.

Gunby, D. C. Further borrowings by Webster? N & Q Aug 1966.

— The Devil's law-case: an interpretation. MLR 63 1968.

— Webster: another borrowing from Jonson's Sejanus? N & Q June 1970.

McDonald, C. O. In his Rhetoric of tragedy: form in Stuart drama, Amherst 1966.

Mehl, D. In his Elizabethan dumb show, Cambridge Mass 1966.

Moonschein, H. A note on the White Devil. N & Q Aug 1966. On Guazzo as a source for v.i.230.

Moore, D. D. Webster and his critics 1617–1964. Baton Rouge 1966.

Ure, P. Another debt to Sir William Alexander. N & Q Aug 1966. The Alexandrean tragedy v.i.2575–8 as source for Duchess of Malfi v.iv.54.

Aggeler, G. Irony and honour in Jacobean tragedy. Humanities Assoc Bull (Canada) 18 1967.

Driscoll, J. P. Integrity of life in the Duchess of Malfi. Drama Survey 6 1967.

Fieler, F. B. The eight madmen in the Duchess of Malfi. Stud in Eng Lit 1500–1900 7 1967.

Savage, J. E. An unpublished epigram, possibly by Webster. Univ of Mississippi Stud in Eng 8 1967.

Stagg, L. C. An index to the figurative language of Webster's tragedies. Charlottesville 1967.

Forker, C. R. Two notes on Webster and Anthony Munday: unpublished entries in the records of the Merchant Taylors. Eng Lang Notes 6 1968.
—— A possible source for the ceremony of the Cardinal's arming in the Duchess of Malfi. Anglia 87 1969.
—— 'Wit's descant on any plain song': the prose characters of Webster. MLQ 30 1969.
Frost, D. L. In his School of Shakespeare, Cambridge 1968.
Hart, C. Wild-fire, St Anthony's fire and the White Devil. N & Q Oct 1968.
—— Press-variants in the Duchess of Malfi and the White Devil. N & Q Aug 1969.
Stevenson, W. Shakespeare's hand in the Spanish tragedy 1602. Stud in Eng Lit 1500–1900 8 1968.
Cook, D. The extreme situation: a study of Webster's tragedies. Komos 2 1969.
Davison, R. A. Webster's moral view re-examined. Moderne Språk (Stockholm) 63 1969.
Gianetti, L. D. A contemporary view of the Duchess of Malfi. Comparative Drama 3 1969.
Greenfield, T. N. In her Induction in Elizabethan drama, Eugene 1969.
Thornton, R. K. The Cardinal's rake in the Duchess of Malfi. N & Q Aug 1969.
Herndl, G. C. In his High design: English Renaissance tragedy and the natural law, Lexington Kentucky 1970.
Lever, J. W. In his Tragedy of state, 1971.

PHILIP MASSINGER
1583–1640

Bibliographies
Tannenbaum, S. A. Massinger: a concise bibliography. New York 1938.
Pennel, C. A. and W. P. Williams. Elizabethan bibliographies supplements VIII: Massinger 1937–65. 1968.

Collections
Dramatic works. Ed T. Coxeter 4 vols 1759, 1761 (with introd by G. Colman).
Dramatick works. Ed J. M. Mason 4 vols 1779 (with introds by T. Davies and G. Colman).
Plays. Ed W. Gifford 4 vols 1805 (adds Parliament of love), 1813 (rev; the standard edn). With essay on the dramatic writings of Massinger by J. Ferriar.
Dramatic works of Massinger and Ford. Ed H. Coleridge 1840, 1848, 1851.
Plays. Ed F. Cunningham 1871. From the text of Gifford, above, adding Believe as you list.
Philip Massinger. Ed A. Symons 2 vols 1887–9 (Mermaid ser). Contains Duke of Milan, A new way to pay old debts, Great Duke of Florence, Maid of honour, City madam, Roman actor, Fatal dowry, Guardian, Virgin martyr, Believe as you list.
Philip Massinger. Ed L. A. Sherman, New York 1912. Contains Roman actor, Maid of honour, A new way to pay old debts, Believe as you list.
Poems. Ed D. S. Lawless, Muncie Ind 1968.

§1
The copie of a letter written upon occasion to the Earle of Pembrooke Lord Chamberlaine [c. 1615–23]. Ms: Trinity College, Dublin ms G.2.21, ff. 554–7; ed A. B. Grosart, E Studien 26 1899; ed P. Simpson, Athenaeum 8 Sept 1906; ed A. H. Cruickshank, Philip Massinger, Oxford 1920.
A newyeares guift presented to my lady and mistress the then Lady Katherine Stanhop, now Countesse of Chesterfeild [c. 1615–23]. Ms: Trinity College, Dublin ms G. 2. 21, ff. 557–9; ed A. B. Grosart, E Studien 26 1899; ed P. Simpson, Athenaeum 8 Sept 1906; ed A. H. Cruickshank, Philip Massinger, Oxford 1920.

Sir John van Olden Barnavelt. 1619. With Fletcher; see col 1713, below.
The virgin martir: a tragedie, as it hath bin divers times publickely acted by the servants of his Majesties revels, written by Phillip Messenger and Thomas Decker. 1622, 1622, 1631, 1651, 1661; ed J. S. Keltie, Works of the British dramatists, 1827; ed F. T. Bowers, Dekker's Dramatic works vol 3, Cambridge 1958.
The Duke of Millaine: a tragædie, as it hath beene often acted by his Majesties servants at the Blacke Friers. 1623, 1638; ed T. Dibdin, London theatre, 1816; ed T. W. Baldwin, Lancaster Pa 1918.
To my honorable freinde Sir Frances Foljambe knight and baronet. Autograph inscription in Dyce copy of Duke of Milan, 1623, in Victoria and Albert Museum. Ed W. Gifford, Massinger's Plays, 1813 (2nd edn); Handbook of the Dyce and Forster collections, 1880 (facs).
The bond-man: an antient storie, as it hath been often acted at the Cock-pit in Drury-lane by the most excellent Princesse the Lady Elizabeth her servants. 1624, 1638; Modern British drama vol 1, 1804; ed B. T. Spencer, Princeton 1932.
Londons lamentable estate in any great visitation [1625?]. Ms: Bodley ms Rawlinson poetry 61, ff. 71^r–76^r; ed H. W. Garrod, Genius loci and other essays, Oxford 1950. See F. P. Wilson, Library 4th ser 7 1927.
The virgins character [c. 1625–30]. Ms: BM ms Harley 6918, ff. 52^r–54^r; ed A. K. McIlwraith, RES 4 1928.
The Roman actor: a tragedie, as it hath divers times beene acted at the private play-house in the Black-friers by the Kings Majesties servants. 1629; ed W. L. Sandidge, Princeton 1929; ed A. K. McIlwraith, Five Stuart tragedies, Oxford 1953 (WC).
The picture: a tragæcomedie, as it was often presented at the Globe and Blacke-friers play-houses by the Kings Majesties servants. 1630; ed R. Dodsley, A select collection of old plays vol 8, 1744.
The renegado: a tragæcomedie, as it hath beene often acted by the Queenes Majesties servants at the private play-house in Drurye-Lane. 1630. Ms: Bodley Rawlinson poetry 20 (a Restoration adaptation).
The Emperour of the East: a tragæ-comœdie, the scæne Constantinople, as it hath bene divers times acted at the Black-friers and Globe play-houses by the Kings Majesties servants. 1632.
The fatall dowry: a tragedy, as it hath beene often acted at the private house in Blackefryers by his Majesties servants, written by P.M. and N.F. 1632; Modern British drama vol 1, 1804; ed C. L. Lockert, Lancaster Pa 1918; ed T. A. Dunn 1969. With Nathan Field.
The maid of honour, as it hath beene often presented at the Phoenix in Drurie-Lane by the Queenes Majesties servants. 1632; Cumberland's British theatre, 1829; ed E. A. W. Bryne 1927; ed C. R. Baskervill, Elizabethan and Stuart plays, 1934.
A new way to pay old debts: a comœdie, as it hath beene often acted at the Phoenix in Drury-Lane by the Queenes Majesties servants. 1633; ed R. Dodsley, A select collection of old plays vol 8, 1744; Modern British drama vol 1, 1804; ed N. Deighton 1893; ed C. Stronach 1904; ed W. A. Neilson, Chief Elizabethan dramatists, 1911; ed B. Matthews, Gayley vol 3, 1914; ed A. H. Cruickshank, Oxford 1926; ed C. F. T. Brooke and N. B. Paradise, English drama, 1933; ed H. Spencer, Elizabethan plays, 1933; ed C. R. Baskervill, Elizabethan and Stuart plays, 1934; ed M. St C. Byrne 1949; ed T. W. Craik 1964 (New Mermaid ser).
Sero, sed serio: to the Right Honourable my most singular good lord and patron Philip Earle of Pembrooke and Montgomerye, uppon the deplorable and untimely death of his sonne Charles [1635]. Ms: BM P. 28,875, Royal 18 A. xx, ff. 1^r–4^r; ed T. Coxeter, Massinger's Dramatic works, 1759 etc.
The great Duke of Florence: a comicall historie, as it hath beene often presented by her Majesties servants at the

Phoenix in Drurie Lane. 1636; ed J. M. Stochholm, Baltimore 1933.

The unnaturall combat: a tragedie, the scaene Marsellis, as it was presented by the Kings Majesties servants at the Globe. 1639; ed R. Dodsley, A select collection of old plays vol 8, 1744; ed R. S. Telfer, Princeton 1932.

Three new plays, viz:
> The bashful lover: a tragi-comedy, as it hath been often acted at the private-house in Black-friers by his late Majesties servants. 1655.
>
> The guardian: a comical-history, as it hath been often acted at the private-house in Black-friars by his late Majesties servants. 1655; ed R. Dodsley, A select collection of old plays vol 8, 1744.
>
> A very woman, or the Prince of Tarent: a tragi-comedy, as it hath been often acted at the private-house in Black-friars by his late Majesties servants. 1655. With Fletcher. Never printed before. 1655.

The old law. 1656. With Middleton and Rowley; *see under Middleton, col 1648, above.*

The city-madam: a comedie, as it was acted at the private house in Black Friers. 1658 (some copies dated 1659); ed R. Dodsley, A select collection of old plays vol 8, 1744; ed R. Kirk, Princeton 1934; ed T. W. Craik 1964 (New Mermaid ser); ed C. Hoy 1964 (Regents ser).

To his sonne, upon his Minerva. Date uncertain; prefixed to James Smith, The innovation of Penelope and Ylysses in Wit restor'd in severall select poems, 1658. Rptd T. Coxeter, Massinger's Dramatic works, 1759 etc.

Believe as you list. BM ms Egerton 2828; ed T. C. Croker 1849 (Percy Soc); TFT 1907; ed C. J. Sisson 1927 (Malone Soc).

The parliament of love. Victoria and Albert Museum ms Dyce 39 (imperfect); ed K. M. Lea 1928 (Malone Soc).

Massinger has a share in the following plays in the Beaumont and Fletcher canon, col 1709, below: Beggars' bush, Custom of the country, Double marriage, Elder brother, Fair maid of the inn, False one, Honest man's fortune, Knight of Malta, Little French lawyer, Lovers' progress, Love's cure, Prophetess, Queen of Corinth, Rollo Duke of Normandy or the bloody brother, Sea voyage, Spanish curate, Thierry and Theodoret. *See C. Hoy*, The shares of Fletcher and his collaborators in the Beaumont and Fletcher canon, *SB 8–9 1956–7, 11–15 1958–62. Massinger contributed commendatory verses to J. Shirley,* The gratefull servant, *1630; rptd in collections of Massinger and Shirley.*

§2

Hazlitt, W. In his Lectures on the dramatic literature of the age of Elizabeth, 1818.

Addis, J. Massinger and Molière. N & Q 28 Oct 1865. On Emperor of the East and Le malade imaginaire.

Fleay, F. G. On metrical tests as applied to dramatic poetry. Trans New Shakspere Soc 1 1874. Fletcher, Beaumont, Massinger.

Gardiner, S. R. The political element in Massinger. Contemporary Rev Aug 1876; rptd Trans New Shakspere Soc 1 1876.

Phelan, J. Philip Massinger. Anglia 2 1879.

Stephen, L. In his Hours in a library: third series, 1879.

Boyle, R. On Beaumont, Fletcher and Massinger. E Studien 5 1882, 7–10 1884–7.

Swinburne, A. C. Philip Massinger. Fortnightly Rev July 1889; rptd in his Contemporaries of Shakespeare, 1919.

Oliphant, E. H. C. The works of Beaumont and Fletcher. E Studien 14–16 1890–2.

—— Shakespeare's plays: an examination. MLR 3–4 1908–9.

—— The plays of Beaumont and Fletcher. New Haven 1927.

—— The plays of Beaumont and Fletcher: some additional notes. PQ 9 1930.

Lowell, J. R. Massinger and Ford. In his Latest literary essays and addresses, 1891.

Adams, F. 'Aery': curious misinterpretation. N & Q 23 July 1892. The maid of honour.

Koeppel, E. Quellenstudien zu den Dramen George Chapmans, Massingers und John Fords. Quellen und Forschungen 82 1897.

Wurzbach, W. von. Philip Massinger. Sh Jb 35–6 1899–1900.

Raebel, K. Massingers drama The maid of honour in seinem Verhältnis zu Painters Palace of pleasure. Halle 1901.

W[arner], G. F. An autograph play of Massinger. Athenaeum 19 Jan 1901. Believe as you list.

Morris, E. C. On the date and composition of the Old law. PMLA 17 1902.

Shands, H. A. Massingers The great Duke of Florence und seine Quellen. Halle 1902.

Gerhardt, E. P. Massingers The Duke of Milan und seine Quellen. Halle 1905.

Heckmann, T. Massingers The renegado und seine spanischen Quellen. Halle 1905.

Merle, A. Massingers The picture und Painter II. 28. Halle 1905.

Beck, C. Massinger, The fatall dowry: Einleitung zu einer neuen Ausgabe. Erlangen 1906.

Greg, W. W. Henslowe papers: being documents supplementary to Henslowe's diary. 1907.

—— Autograph corrections in the Duke of Milan. Library 4th ser 4 1923.

—— More Massinger corrections. Library 4th ser 5 1924. *See also* A. H. Cruickshank, ibid.

—— Another note [on Believe as you list]. Library 4th ser 12 1931.

—— In his Dramatic documents from the Elizabethan playhouses, 1931.

Ristine, F. H. In his English tragicomedy: its origin and history, New York 1910.

Briggs, W. D. The influence of Jonson's tragedy in the 17th century. Anglia 35 1912.

Sykes, H. D. A source of Massinger's Parliament of love. N & Q 8 Aug 1914.

—— Elizabethan and Jacobean plays: suggested textual emendations. N & Q Oct 1917. The Roman actor I.ii.38.

—— In his Sidelights on Elizabethan drama, 1924.

Farnham, W. Colloquial contractions in Beaumont, Fletcher, Massinger and Shakespeare as a test of authorship. PMLA 31 1916.

Perott, J. de. Über eine anno 1587 erschienene heute aber gänzlich vergessene Novelle als Quelle von Massingers A very woman. Anglia 39 1916.

Stratton, C. The Cenci story in literature and in fact. In Studies in English drama: first series, ed A. Gaw, Philadelphia 1917.

Symons, A. In his Studies in the Elizabethan drama, 1919.

Cruickshank, A. H. Philip Massinger. Oxford 1920.

—— Massinger and the Two noble kinsmen. Oxford 1922.

—— Massinger corrections. Library 4th ser 5 1924.

Eliot, T. S. In his Sacred wood, 1920; rptd in his Selected essays, 1932, and in his Elizabethan essays, 1934.

Lockert, L. A scene in the Fatal dowry. MLN 35 1920.

Thorn-Drury, G. A little ark. 1921. Contains a biographical poem addressed to Massinger by Henerie Parker.

Frijlinck, W. P. Preface to her edn of Sir John van Olden Barnavelt, Amsterdam 1922.

Lister, J. T. A comparison of two works of Cervantes with a play by Massinger. Hispania 5 1922. The fatal dowry.

Massinger and the Inns of Court mission. Spectator 18 Feb 1922. The great Duke of Florence.

Turner, W. J. A new way to pay old debts at the Old Vic. Spectator 25 Nov 1922.

Chelli, M. Le drame de Massinger. Lyons 1923.

— Etude sur la collaboration de Massinger avec Fletcher et son groupe. Paris 1926.

Makkink, H. J. Massinger and Fletcher: a comparison. Rotterdam 1927.

Tannenbaum, S. A. Corrections to the text of Believe as you list. PMLA 42 1927.

McIlwraith, A. K. Patrons of the City-madam. Bodleian Quart Record 5 1928.

— Did Massinger revise the Emperour of the East? RES 5 1929.

— An allusion in Massinger. RES 6 1930. The bondman.

— Some bibliographical notes on Massinger. Library 4th ser 11 1930.

— Pen-and-ink corrections in books of the 17th century. RES 7 1931. The city-madam.

— On the date of A new way to pay old debts. MLR 28 1933.

— A further patron of the City-madam. Bodleian Quart Record 8 1935.

— The printer's copy for the City-madam. MLN 50 1935.

— Marginalia on press-corrections in books of the early 17th century. Library 5th ser 4 1950. The bondman.

— The manuscript corrections in Massinger's plays. Library 5th ser 6 1951.

Garrod, H. W. In his Profession of poetry, Oxford 1929.

Lawrence, W. J. The renegado. TLS 24 Oct 1929. Late 17th-century adaptation in ms.

— A misunderstood topical masque metaphor in Massinger. RES 6 1930. The bondman.

— Massinger's punctuation. Criterion 11 1932; rptd in his Those nut-cracking Elizabethans, 1935.

Rice, W. Source of William Cartwright's The royall slave. MLN 45 1930. The bondman.

— The sources of the Renegado. PQ 11 1932.

Ball, R. H. Massinger and the house of Pembroke. MLN 46 1931.

— Sir Giles Mompesson and Sir Giles Overreach. In Essays in dramatic literature: the T. M. Parrott presentation volume, Princeton 1935.

— The amazing career of Sir Giles Overreach. 1939.

Steiner, A. Massinger's The picture, Bandello and Hungary. MLN 46 1931.

Eccles, M. Arthur Massinger. TLS 16 July 1931.

Jones, F. A. An experiment with Massinger's verse. PMLA 47 1932.

Spencer, B. T. In Seventeenth-century studies, ed R. Shafer, Princeton 1933.

McManaway, J. G. Massinger and the Restoration drama. ELH 1 1934.

Bradbrook, M. C. In her Themes and conventions of Elizabethan tragedy, Cambridge 1935.

Ward, C. E. Massinger and Dryden. ELH 2 1935.

Harbage, A. In his Cavalier drama, New York 1936.

Evans, G. B. Note on Fletcher and Massinger's Little French lawyer. MLN 52 1937.

Knights, L. C. In his Drama and society in the age of Jonson, 1937.

Maxwell, B. In his Studies in Beaumont, Fletcher and Massinger, Chapel Hill 1939.

Bowers, F. T. In his Elizabethan revenge tragedy, Princeton 1940.

Massinger: a master of plot and tragicomedy. TLS 16 March 1940. Reply by C. Leech 23 March 1940.

Boas, F. S. In his An introduction to Stuart drama, Oxford 1946.

Kermode, J. F. A note on the history of the Fatal dowry in the 18th century. N & Q 3 May 1947.

Waith, E. M. The sources of the Double marriage by Fletcher and Massinger. MLN 64 1969.

— In his Pattern of tragicomedy in Beaumont and Fletcher, New Haven 1952.

— Controversia in the English drama: Medwall and Massinger. PMLA 68 1953.

Leech, C. Shakespeare's tragedies and other studies in 17th-century drama. 1950.

Gray, J. E. The source of the Emperour of the East. RES new ser 1 1950.

— Still more Massinger corrections. Library 5th ser 5 1950. See also A. K. McIlwraith 5th ser 6 1951.

Phialas, P. G. Massinger and the commedia dell' arte. MLN 65 1950.

— The sources of Massinger's Emperour of the East. PMLA 65 1950.

McCullen, J. T. Madness and the isolation of characters in Elizabethan and early Stuart drama. SP 48 1951. On A new way to pay old debts.

Martin, L. C. Marvell, Massinger and Sidney. RES new ser 2 1951.

Clark, D. B. An 18th-century adaptation of Massinger. MLQ 13 1952.

Enright, D. J. Poetic satire and satire in verse: a consideration of Jonson and Massinger. Scrutiny 18 1952.

— Elizabethan and Jacobean comedy. In The age of Shakespeare, ed B. Ford 1955 (Pelican).

Gerritsen, J. The honest man's fortune: a critical edition of ms Dyce 9 (1625). Groningen 1952. Introd attributing the play to Fletcher, Massinger, Field and Tourneur.

Quennell, P. In his Singular preference, 1952.

Blayney, G. H. Massinger's reference to the Calverley story. N & Q Jan 1954. The guardian.

Lyons, J. O. Massinger's imagery. Renaissance Papers 1955.

Salingar, L. G. The decline of tragedy. In The age of Shakespeare, ed B. Ford 1955 (Pelican).

Hoy, C. The shares of Fletcher and his collaborators in the Beaumont and Fletcher canon. SB 8–9 1956–7, 11–15 1958–62.

— Verbal formulae in the plays of Massinger. SP 56 1959.

Thompson, P. The old way and the new way in Dekker and Massinger. MLR 51 1956.

Dunn, T. A. Massinger: the man and the playwright. Edinburgh 1957.

Lawless, D. S. Anne Massinger and Thomas Crompton. N & Q Oct 1957, June, Dec 1958.

— Massinger, Smith, Horner and Selden. N & Q Feb 1957.

— Arthur Massinger of London. N & Q Jan 1960.

— Massinger and his associates. Muncie Ind 1967.

— The parents of Massinger. N & Q July 1968.

— The burial of Massinger. N & Q Jan 1971.

Bowers, R. H. A note on Massinger's New way to pay old debts. MLR 53 1958.

Evans, G. L. The unnatural combat. N & Q March 1958.

Gibson, C. A. Massinger's use of his sources for the Roman actor. AUMLA no 15 1961.

— Massinger's 'composite mistresses'. AUMLA no 29 1968.

— 'Behind the arras' in the Renegado. N & Q Aug 1969.

— Massinger's London merchant and the date of the City madam. MLR 65 1970.

Edwards, P. Massinger the censor. In Essays on Shakespeare and Elizabethan drama in honor of Hardin Craig, Columbia Missouri 1962.

— The sources of the Bondman. RES new ser 15 1964.

Davison, P. R. The theme and structure of the Roman actor. AUMLA no 19 1963.

Clubb, L. G. The virgin martyr and the tragedia sacra. Renaissance Drama 7 1964.

Cunningham, J. E. In his Elizabethan and early Stuart drama, 1965.

Gill, R. 'Necessities of state': Massinger's Believe as you list. E Studies 46 1965.

— Collaboration and revision in Massinger's A very woman. RES new ser 18 1967.

Bennett, A. L. The early editions of Massinger's plays. Papers on Eng Lang & Lit 1 1965.

— The moral tone of Massinger's dramas. Papers on Eng Lang & Lit 2 1966.

Gross, A. Contemporary politics in Massinger. Stud in Eng Lit 1500–1900 6 1966.

— Social change and Massinger. Stud in Eng Lit 1500–1900 7 1967.

Mullany, P. F. Religion in the Maid of honour. Renaissance Drama new ser 2 1969.

FRANCIS BEAUMONT
1585?–1616
and
JOHN FLETCHER
1579–1625

Bibliographies

Tannenbaum, S. A. Beaumont and Fletcher: a concise bibliography. New York 1938; Supplement, New York 1946.

Pennell, C. A. and W. P. Williams. Elizabethan bibliographies supplements VIII: Francis Beaumont, John Fletcher 1937–65. 1968.

Collections

Comedies and tragedies written by Francis Beaumont and John Fletcher, gentlemen, never printed before, and now published by the authors originall copies. 1647. Contains Mad lover, Spanish curat, Little French lawyer, Custome of the countrey, Noble gentleman, Captaine, Beggars bush, Coxcombe, False one, Chances, Loyal subject, Laws of Candy, Lovers progress, Island Princesse, Humorous lieutenant, Nice valour or the passionate mad-man, M. Francis Beaumonts letter to Ben Johnson, Maid in the mill, Prophetesse, Tragedie of Bonduca, Sea voyage, Double marriage, Pilgrim, Knight of Malta, Womans prize or the tamer tamed, Loves cure or the martial maid, Honest mans fortune, Queene of Corinth, Women pleas'd, A wife for a moneth, Wit at severall weapons, Tragedie of Valentinian, Faire maide of the inne, Loves pilgrimage, Maske of the gentlemen of Grayes-Inne and the Inner-Temple at the marriage of the Prince and Princesse Palatine of the Rhene, Four plays or morall representations in one.

The 34 plays included above were all previously unptd. Masque of the Inner Temple and Gray's Inn had been ptd c. 1613. Wild-goose chase was omitted because the copy had gone astray. When recovered, it was ptd separately in folio 1652.

Fifty comedies and tragedies written by Francis Beaumont and John Fletcher, gent, published by the authors original copies, the songs to each play being added. 1679. Reprints the contents of 1647, above and adds the following plays: Maids tragedy, Philaster, A King and no King, Scornful lady, Elder brother, Wit without money, Faithful shepherdess, Rule a wife and have a wife, Monsieur Thomas, Bloody brother or Rollo a tragedy, Wild-goose chase, Knight of the burning pestle, Night-walker, Cupids revenge, Two noble kinsmen, Tragedy of Thierry and Theodoret, Woman hater. The edn contains 52 plays, including erroneously Shirley's Coronation, with Masque of the Inner Temple and Gray's Inn.

Works. [Ed G. Langbaine] 7 vols 1711.

Works, collated with all the former editions and corrected, with notes, by the late Mr Theobald, Mr Seward and Mr Sympson. 10 vols 1750.

Dramatic works. [Ed G. Colman the elder] 10 vols 1778.

Dramatic works of Ben Jonson and Beaumont and Fletcher, the latter from the text and with the notes of G. Colman. 4 vols 1811.

Works. Ed H. Weber 14 vols 1812. Adds Faithful friends.

Works. Ed G. Darley 2 vols 1840. Text of Weber, above, with addns in Humorous lieutenant from Dyce's Demetrius and Enanthe, 1830.

Works. Ed A. Dyce 11 vols 1843–6.

Beaumont et Fletcher. Tr French by Ernest Lafond, Paris 1865. Contains Two noble kinsmen, Valentinian, Rollo, Little French lawyer.

Works: variorum edition. Ed A. H. Bullen et al 1904–12. To have been completed in 12 vols of which only 4 were pbd. Vol 1 contains Maid's tragedy, ed P. A. Daniel; Philaster, ed Daniel; A King and no King, ed R. W. Bond; Scornful lady, ed Bond; Custom of the country, ed Bond; vol 2: Elder brother, ed W. W. Greg; Spanish curate, ed R. B. McKerrow; Wit without money, ed McKerrow; Beggars' bush, ed Daniel; Humorous lieutenant, ed Bond; vol 3, Faithful shepherdess, ed Greg; Mad lover, ed Bond; Loyal subject, ed J. Masefield; Rule a wife and have a wife, ed Bond; Laws of Candy, ed E. K. Chambers; vol 4: False one, ed M. Luce; Little French lawyer, ed C. Brett; Valentinian, ed R. G. Martin; Monsieur Thomas, ed Martin; Chances, ed Chambers.

Ten plays. Ed J. St Loe Strachey 2 vols 1904 (Mermaid ser). Vol 1 contains Maid's tragedy, Philaster, Wild-goose chase, Thierry and Theodoret, Knight of the burning pestle; vol 2 contains a King and no King, Bonduca, Spanish curate, Faithful shepherdess, Valentinian.

Beaumont and Fletcher. Ed A. Glover and A. R. Waller 10 vols Cambridge 1905–12. Rptd from folio of 1679, with collation of all previously ptd texts.

Select plays. Ed G. P. Baker 1911 (EL). Contains Knight of the burning pestle, Maid's tragedy, A King and no King, Faithful shepherdess, Wild-goose chase, Bonduca.

The dramatic works in the Beaumont and Fletcher canon. Ed F. T. Bowers et al, Cambridge 1966–. In progress; 2 vols of a projected 10 have appeared. Vol 1 contains Knight of the burning pestle, ed C. Hoy; Masque of the Inner Temple and Gray's Inn, ed Bowers; Woman hater, ed G. W. Williams; Coxcomb, ed I. B. Cauthen; Philaster, ed R. K. Turner; Captain, ed L. A. Beaurline; vol 2: Maid's tragedy, ed Turner; A King and no King, ed Williams; Cupid's revenge, ed Bowers; Scornful lady, ed Hoy; Love's pilgrimage, ed Beaurline.

§1

Salmasis and Hermaphroditus. 1602 (anon); 1847 (Shakespeare Soc); ed E. S. Donno, Elizabethan minor epics, 1963; ed N. Alexander, Elizabethan narrative verse, 1968. By Beaumont.

The woman hater, as it hath beene lately acted by the children of Paules. 1607 (anon); 1648 ('as it hath beene acted by his Majesties servants, written by John Fletcher gent'), 1649 (as The woman hater, or the hungry courtier: a comedy written by Francis Beaumont and John Fletcher, gent).

The faithfull shepheardesse, by John Fletcher. [1609?]. 1629, 1634, 1656, 1665; ed F. W. Moorman 1896; ed W. A. Neilson, Chief Elizabethan dramatists, 1911; ed C. R. Baskervill, Elizabethan and Stuart plays, 1934.

The knight of the burning pestle. 1613 (anon), 1635 ('as it is now acted by her Majesties servants at the private house in Drury Lane, written by Francis Beaumont and John Fletcher'), 1635, [presumably ptd in the early 1650's]; ed F. W. Moorman 1898; ed H. S. Murch, New Haven 1908; ed R. M. Alden, Boston 1910; ed W. T. Williams 1924; ed G. B. Harrison 1926; ed M. J. Sargeaunt 1928; ed J. K. Peel 1929; ed C. F. T. Brooke and N. B. Paradise, English drama, 1933; ed H. Spencer, Elizabethan plays, 1933; ed C. R. Baskervill, Elizabethan and Stuart plays, 1934; ed J. Doebler 1967, (Regents ser); ed A. Gurr 1968.

The masque of the Inner Temple and Grayes Inne presented before his Majestie, the Queenes Majestie, the Prince, Count Palatine and the Lady Elizabeth their Highnesses in the Banqueting House at White-hall on Saturday the twentieth day of Februarie 1612 [i.e. 1613]. [1613] (with variant title-pages, attributed to 'Francis Beamont' on the original, removed on the cancel; see F. T. Bowers's edn in Dramatic works vol 1, Cambridge 1966, p. 113); in Beaumont's Poems, 1653; ed J. Nichols, Progresses of James I vol 2, 1828.

Cupids revenge, as it hath beene divers times acted by the children of her Majesties revels, by John Fletcher. 1615, 1630 ('written by Fran. Beaumont and Jo. Fletcher'), 1635.

The scornful ladie: a comedie, as it was acted by the children of her Majesties revels in the Blacke Fryers, written by Fra. Beaumont and Jo. Fletcher, gent. 1616, 1625, 1630, 1635, 1639, 1651 (3 edns bearing this date, of which 2 are falsely dated; see C. Hoy's edn in Dramatic works vol 2, Cambridge 1970, pp. 452-3), 1677, 1691, [1711?], 1717.

Certain elegies done by sundrie excellent wits (Fr. Beau., M. Dr., N.H.) with satyres and epigrames. 1618, 1843.

A King and no King, acted at the Globe by his Majesties servants, written by Francis Beaumont and John Fletcher. 1619, 1625, 1631, 1639, 1655, 1661, 1676, 1693; ed R. M. Alden, Boston 1910; ed H. R. Walley and J. H. Wilson, Early 17th-century plays, 1930; ed R. K. Turner 1963 (Regents ser).

The maides tragedy, as it hath beene divers times acted at the Blacke-friers by the Kings Majesties servants. 1619 (anon), 1622, 1630 ('written by Francis Beaumont and John Fletcher'), 1638, 1641, 1650 (for 1660?), 1661, 1686, 1704, 1717; ed A. H. Thorndike, Boston 1906; ed W. A. Neilson, Chief Elizabethan dramatists, 1911; ed F. E. Schelling, Masterpieces of the English drama, 1912; ed C. F. T. Brooke and N. B. Paradise, English drama, 1933; ed H. Spencer, Elizabethan plays, 1933; ed C. R. Baskervill, Elizabethan and Stuart plays, 1934; ed A. K. McIlwraith, Five Stuart tragedies, Oxford 1953 (WC); ed H. Norland 1968 (Regents ser); ed A. Gurr 1969.

Phylaster: or love lyes a bleeding, acted at the Globe by his Majesties servants, written by Francis Baymont and John Fletcher, gent. 1620, 1622, 1628, 1634, 1639, 1652, [c. 1661] (falsely dated 1652), [after 1661], 1687, 1717; ed F. S. Boas 1898; ed A. H. Thorndike, Boston 1906; ed W. A. Neilson, Chief Elizabethan dramatists, 1911; ed F. E. Schelling, Masterpieces of the English drama, 1912; ed C. F. T. Brooke and N. B. Paradise, English drama, 1933; ed H. Spencer, Elizabethan plays, 1933; ed C. R. Baskervill, Elizabethan and Stuart plays, 1934 ed A. Gurr 1969 (Revels ser).

The tragedy of Thierry King of France and his brother Theodoret, as it was diverse times acted at the Blacke-friers by the Kings Majesties servants. 1621 (anon), 1648 ('written by John Fletcher'), 1649 ('written by Francis Beamont and John Fletcher').

Henry VIII. In Shakespeare folio of 1623; for later edns see under Shakespeare, col 1550, above.

The two noble kinsmen, presented at the Blackfriers by the Kings Majesties servants, written by the memorable worthies of their time, Mr John Fletcher and Mr William Shakespeare, gent. 1634; ed H. Littledale 1876 (New Shakspere Soc); ed C. H. Herford 1897; TFT 1910; ed G. L. Kittredge, Complete works of Shakespeare, 1936, 1969 (rev I. Ribner); ed C. Leech, New York 1966; ed G. R. Proudfoot 1970 (Regents ser). Also included in collections of the Shakespeare Apocrypha, col 1551, above.

The elder brother: a comedie, acted at the Blacke Friers by his Majesties servants, written by John Fletcher gent. 1637, 1637 (presumably ptd 1661), 1651 ('written by Francis Beaumont and John Fletcher'; some copies dated 1650), 1661, 1678; ed W. H. Draper 1916 ('with slight alterations and abridgement'). BM ms Egerton 1994, ff. 2-30.

The bloody brother: a tragedy, by B.J.F. 1639, Oxford 1640 (as The tragoedy of Rollo Duke of Normandy, acted by his Majesties servants, written by John Fletcher, gent), 1686 (as Rollo, Duke of Normandy: or the bloody brother, by John Fletcher, gent), 1718 ('by Mr Francis Beaumont and Mr John Fletcher'); ed J. D. Jump, Liverpool 1948.

Monsieur Thomas: a comedy, acted at the private house in Blacke Fryers, the author John Fletcher, gent. 1639, [c. 1661] (as Fathers own son).

Wit with-out money: a comedie, as it hath beene presented at the private house in Drurie Lane by her Majesties servants, written by Francis Beaumont and John Fletcher, gent. 1639, 1661, [c. 1708] ('with alterations and amendments by some persons of quality'), 1718 (the unaltered play).

Poems, by Francis Beaumont. 1640 (containing Salmacis and Hermaphroditus, Remedie of love, Elegy to Lady Markham and other poems, some certainly not by Beaumont), 1653 (with addns), 1660 (as Poems: the golden remains of Frances Beaumont and John Fletcher).

The night-walker, or the little theife: a comedy, as it was presented by her Majesties servants at the private house in Drury Lane, written by John Fletcher, gent. 1640, 1661. Rev James Shirley.

Rule a wife and have a wife: a comoedy, acted by his Majesties servants, written by John Fletcher, gent. Oxford 1640, London 1697, 1717 etc; ed G. Saintsbury, Gayley vol 3, 1914. For the numerous 18th- and early 19th-century edns, and the alterations by Garrick, Kemble and others, see introd to R. W. Bond's edn in Variorum vol 3, pp. 366-8.

The wild-goose chase: a comedie, as it hath been acted with singular applause at the Black-friers, being the noble, last, and onely remaines of those incomparable dramatists, Francis Beaumont and John Fletcher, gent. 1652; ed W. A. Neilson, Chief Elizabethan dramatists, 1911; ed H. R. Walley and J. H. Wilson, Early 17th-century plays, 1930; ed H. Spencer, Elizabethan plays, 1933; ed G. E. Bentley, The development of English drama, 1950.

The beggars bush, written by Francis Beaumont and John Fletcher, gentlemen. 1661, 1661, [1706?] (as The royal merchant, altered by H.N. [Henry Norris?]), 1717 (the unaltered play). For the later 18th- and early 19th-century alterations of the play by T. Hull and D. Kinnaird, see introd to P. A. Daniel's edn in Variorum vol 2, pp. 344-5. The unaltered play ed C. F. T. Brooke and N. B. Paradise, English drama, 1933; ed J. Dorenkamp, Hague 1967 (see C. Hoy, Stud in Eng Lit 1500-1900 8 1968). Ms: Folger Lib J.b.5.

The island Princess, or the generous Portugal: a comedy, as it is acted at the Theatre Royal by his Majesties servants, with the alterations and new additional scenes. 1669 (altered anon), 1687 (altered by N. Tate), 1699 ('Made into an opera, as it is performed at the Theatre Royal, all the musical entertainments and the greatest part of the play new and written by Mr Motteux'), 1717 (the unaltered play); ed C. F. T. Brooke and N. B. Paradise, English drama 1933 (Fletcher's original play).

The chances: a comedy, as it was acted at the Theater Royal, corrected and altered by a person of honour [George Villiers, 2nd Duke of Buckingham]. 1682, 1692 (another edn of Buckingham's alteration), 1705 (altered by Buckingham), 1718 (the unaltered play), 1773 (altered by Garrick).

Valentinian: a tragedy, as 'tis alter'd by the late Earl of Rochester, and acted at the Theatre-Royal. 1685, 1717 (the unaltered play).

The prophetess: or the history of Dioclesian, written by Francis Beaumont and John Fletcher, with alterations and additions after the manner of an opera. 1690, 1690, 1719.

The humorous lieutenant, or generous enemies: a comedy, as it is now acted by his Majesties servants at the

Theatre-Royal in Drury-Lane. 1697, 1717. Ms: Brogyntyn 42 in the library of Lord Harlech, as Demetrius and Enanthe; ed A. Dyce 1830; ed M. Cook and F. P. Wilson 1951 (Malone Soc).

A wife for a month. 1697 (rev T. Scott as The unhappy kindness, or a fruitless revenge: a tragedy), 1717 (the unaltered play).

The pilgrim: a comedy, as it is acted at the Theatre-Royal in Drury-Lane, written originally by Mr Fletcher, and now very much alter'd, with several additions, likewise a prologue, epilogue, dialogue and masque written by the late great poet Mr Dryden just before his death. 1700 (2 issues; alterations by Vanbrugh), 1718 (the unaltered play).

The loyal subject: or the faithful general. 1706 (2 issues, one undated), 1706 (altered as The faithful general, written by a young lady (M.N.], 1717 (the unaltered play).

The custom of the country. 1717.

Bonduca. 1718. Ms: BM additional 36,758; ed W. W. Greg 1951 (Malone Soc).

Love's cure: or the martial maid. 1718.

The maid in the mill. 1718.

The Spanish curate. 1718.

Wit at several weapons. 1718.

The tragedy of Sir John van Olden Barnavelt. BM additional ms 18,653; ed A. H. Bullen, Old English plays vol 2, 1883; ed W. P. Frijlinck, Amsterdam 1922. By Fletcher and Massinger.

Verses by Frances Beaumont. TLS 15 Sept 1921.

The faire maide of the inne. Ed F. L. Lucas, Webster's Works vol 4, 1927.

Songs and lyrics from the plays of Beaumont and Fletcher with contemporary musical settings. Ed E. H. Fellowes 1928.

The honest mans fortune. Victoria and Albert Museum ms Dyce 9 (1625); ed J. Gerritsen, Groningen 1952.

The woman's prize: or the tamer tamed. Ed G. B. Ferguson, Hague 1966. Ms: Folger Lib J.b.3.

For Fletcher's share in A very woman, *see Massinger, col 1705, above. The inclusion of the anon* The faithful friends *in the Beaumont and Fletcher canon is now generally rejected (see col 1759, below), as is the title-page ascription to Fletcher (with Middleton and Jonson) of* The widow *(see Middleton, col 1648, above).*

§2

Dryden, J. In his Of dramatick poesie: an essay, 1668.
— Preface to An evening's love, 1671.
— The grounds of criticism in tragedy. Preface to Troilus and Cressida, 1679.
Mason, J. M. Comments on the plays of Beaumont and Fletcher. 1798.
Hazlitt, W. In his Lectures on the dramatic literature of the age of Elizabeth, 1818.
Hickson, S. The shares of Shakespeare and Fletcher in the Two noble kinsmen. Westminster Rev 92 1847; rptd in Trans New Shakspere Soc 1 1874.
Salmacis and Hermaphroditus not by Beaumont. Shakespeare Soc Papers 3 1847.
Spedding, J. On the several shares of Shakespeare and Fletcher in Henry VIII. GM Aug 1850; rptd in Trans New Shakspere Soc 1 1874.
Keightley, T. Fletcher's Custom of the country. N & Q 5 Jan 1861.
Fleay, F. G. On metrical tests as applied to dramatic poetry pt 2: Fletcher, Beaumont and Massinger. Trans New Shakespeare Soc 1 1874.
— Chronology of the plays of Fletcher and Massinger. E Studien 9 1886.
Swinburne, A. C. Beaumont and Fletcher. Encyclopaedia britannica 1875 (9th edn); rptd in his Studies in prose and poetry, 1894.

— The earlier plays of Beaumont and Fletcher. Eng Rev May 1910.
Boyle, R. Beaumont, Fletcher and Massinger. E Studien 5 1882, 7–10 1884–7.
— Shakespeare und die beiden Vettern. E Studien 4 1881.
Macaulay, G. C. Beaumont: a critical study. 1883.
Symonds, J. A. Some notes on Fletcher's Valentinian. Fortnightly Rev Sept 1886.
Hart, H. C. Notes on Bullen's Old plays: Sir John Barneveldt. Academy 15 Sept 1888.
— The Captain in Fletcher and Ben Jonson. N & Q 3 Sept 1904. The fair maid of the inn.
Oliphant, E. H. C. The works of Beaumont and Fletcher. E Studien 14–16 1890–2.
— The plays of Beaumont and Fletcher: an attempt to determine their respective shares and the shares of others. New Haven 1927.
— The plays of Beaumont and Fletcher: some additional notes. PQ 9 1930.
— Three Beaumont and Fletcher plays. RES 12 1936.
Bahlsen, L. Spanische Quellen der dramatischen Litteratur besonders Englands zu Shakespeares Zeit. Zeitschrift für Vergleichende Litteratur 6 1893. The maid in the mill and A wife for a month.
Koeppel, E. Quellen-studien zu den Dramen Ben Jonsons, John Marstons, und Beaumont und Fletchers. Erlangen 1895.
Stiefel, A. J. Die Nachahmung spanischer Komödien in England unter den ersten Stuarts. Archiv 99 1897.
— Über die Quelle von Fletchers Island Princess. Archiv 103 1899.
— Zur Quellenfrage von Fletchers Monsieur Thomas. E Studien 36 1906.
Stoye, M. Das Verhältnis von Cibbers Tragödie Caesar in Egypt zu Fletchers The false one. Halle 1897.
Leonhardt, B. Die Textvarianten von Rule a wife and have a wife. Anglia 24 1901.
Thorndike, A. H. The influence of Beaumont and Fletcher on Shakespeare. Worcester Mass 1901.
Rosenbach, A. S. N. The curious impertinent in English dramatic literature. MLN 17 1902.
Blühm, E. Über The knight of Malta und seine Quellen. Halle 1903.
Kiepert, W. Fletchers Women pleased und seine Quellen. Halle 1903.
Crawford, C. Ben Jonson and the Bloody brother. Sh Jb 41 1905.
Garnett, R. Ben Jonson's probable authorship of scene 2, act 4 of Fletcher's Bloody brother. MP 2 1905.
Hatcher, O. L. Fletcher: a study in dramatic method. Chicago 1905.
— The sources of Monsieur Thomas. Anglia 30 1907.
Klein, E. Fletchers The Spanish curate und seine Quellen. Halle 1905.
Tupper, J. The relation of the heroic play to the romances of Beaumont and Fletcher. PMLA 20 1905.
Bensly, E. Burton and Fletcher. N & Q 15 Dec 1906, 5 March 1910.
De Perrott, J. Beaumont and Fletcher and the Mirrour of knighthood. MLN 22 1907.
Aronstein, P. Die Moral des Beaumont-Fletcherschen Dramas. Anglia 31 1908.
— Fletchers Love's pilgrimage und Ben Jonsons The new inn. E Studien 43 1911.
Bradford, G. An unnoted Elizabethan source. Nation (New York) 10 Dec 1908. The humorous lieutenant.
Thompson, E. N. S. Elizabethan dramatic co-operation. E Studien 40 1908.
Brereton, J. Le G. Notes on some plays of Beaumont and Fletcher. In his Elizabethan drama: notes and studies, Sydney 1909.
Chambers, E. K. The date of Fletcher's The chances. MLR 4 1909. Replies by G. C. Macaulay and Chambers 5 1910.

Schwarz, H. F. One of the sources of the Queen of Corinth. MLN 24 1909.

Jacobi, G. A. Zur Quellenfrage von Fletchers The sea voyage. Anglia 33 1910.

Ristine, F. H. In his English tragicomedy: its origin and history, New York 1910.

Briggs, W. D. The influence of Jonson's tragedy in the 17th century. Anglia 35 1912.

— First song in the Beggar's bush. MLN 39 1924.

Ulrich, O. Die pseudohistorischen Dramen Beaumonts und Fletchers Thierry and Theodoret, Valentinian, The prophetess und The false one und ihre Quellen. Strasbourg 1913.

Case, R. H. Beaumont and Fletcher. Quart Rev 220 1914.

Gayley, C. M. Beaumont the dramatist. New York 1914.

Farnham, W. Colloquial contractions in Beaumont, Fletcher, Massinger and Shakespeare as a test of authorship. PMLA 31 1916.

Heldt, W. Fletcher's Wild-goose chase and Farquhar's Inconstant. Neophilologus 3 1917.

Symons, A. In his Studies in Elizabethan drama, 1919. On Henry VIII.

Greg, W. W. The printing of the Beaumont and Fletcher folio of 1647. Library 4th ser 2 1921.

— Nathan Field and the Beaumont and Fletcher folio of 1679. RES 3 1927.

— In his Dramatic documents from the Elizabethan playhouses, 1931.

Vogt, G. M. The wife of Bath's tale, Women pleased and La fée Urgele: a study in the transformation of folk-lore themes in drama. MLN 37 1922.

Chew, S. C. Lycidas and the play of Barnavelt. MLN 38 1923.

Maxwell, B. Fletcher and Henry VIII. In [J. M.] Manly anniversary studies in language and literature, Chicago 1923.

— The hungry knave in the Beaumont and Fletcher plays. PQ 5 1926.

— The date of Love's pilgrimage and its relation to the New inn. SP 28 1931.

— Notes towards dating Wit without money. PQ 12 1933.

— The date of the Pilgrim. PQ 13 1934.

— The woman's prize. MP 32 1935.

— The date of the Night-walker. MLN 50 1935.

— Studies in Beaumont, Fletcher and Massinger. Chapel Hill 1939.

— The source of the principal plot of the Fair maid of the inn. MLN 59 1944.

— Twenty good nights: the Knight of the burning pestle and Middleton's Family of love. MLN 63 1948. Reply by W. J. Olive, SP 47 1950.

Lindsey, E. S. The music of the songs in Fletcher's plays. SP 21 1924.

— The original music for the Knight of the burning pestle. SP 26 1929.

Schutt, J. H. Philaster considered as a work of literary art. E Studies 6 1924.

Sykes, H. D. In his Sidelights on Elizabethan drama, 1924. John Fletcher. TLS 20 Aug 1925.

Chelli, M. Etude sur la collaboration de Massinger avec Fletcher et son groupe. Paris 1926.

Harrison, T. P. A probable source of Philaster. PMLA 41 1926.

Jeffrey, V. M. Italian influence in Fletcher's Faithful shepherdess. MLR 21 1926.

Sprague, A. C. Beaumont and Fletcher on the Restoration stage. Cambridge Mass 1926.

Fenton, F. L. The authorship of Acts 3 and 4 of the Queen of Corinth. MLN 42 1927.

Makkink, H. J. Massinger and Fletcher: a comparison. Rotterdam 1927.

Brinkley, R. F. Nathan Field: the actor-playwright. New Haven 1928.

Lloyd, B. The juggling captain in the Fair maid of the inn. TLS 12 Jan 1928.

Wells, W. The bloody brother. N & Q 7 Jan 1928.

Wilson, J. H. The influence of Beaumont and Fletcher on Restoration drama. Columbus 1928.

Tannenbaum, S. A. A hitherto unpublished Fletcher autograph. JEGP 28 1929.

— The Fletcher holograph. PQ 13 1934. Replies by W. W. Greg 14 1935 and Tannenbaum 15 1936.

Upton, A. W. Allusions to James I and his Court in Marston's Fawn and Beaumont's Woman hater. PMLA 44 1929.

Ward, C. E. Note on Beaumont and Fletcher's Coxcomb. PQ 9 1930.

Hiscock, W. G. The prophetess. TLS 26 March 1931.

Warren, A. Pope's index to Beaumont and Fletcher. MLN 46 1931.

Elson, J. J. (ed). The wits or sport upon sport. Ithaca 1932.

Ault, N. A memento for mortalitie. TLS 12 Jan 1933. On the tombs in Westminster Abbey not by Beaumont.

Koszul, A. Beaumont et Fletcher et le baroque. Cahiers du Sud 10 1933.

Bond, R. W. On six plays in Beaumont and Fletcher, 1679. RES 11 1935. Comments by E. H. C. Oliphant 12 1936.

Bradbrook, M. C. In her Themes and conventions of Elizabethan tragedy, Cambridge 1935.

Lawrence, W. J. In his Those nut-cracking Elizabethans, 1935.

McKeithan, D. M. Bullen's Beaumont and Fletcher. TLS 7 Feb 1935. On the incomplete variorum edn of 1904–12.

— The debt to Shakespeare in the Beaumont and Fletcher plays. Austin 1938.

— Shakespearian echoes in the Florimel plot of Fletcher and Rowley's The maid in the mill. PQ 17 1938.

Ellis-Fermor, U. M. In her Jacobean drama, 1936, 1958 (rev).

Simpson, P. King Charles I as a dramatic critic. Bodleian Quart Record 8 1936; rptd in his Studies in Elizabethan drama, Oxford 1955.

— Beaumont's verse-letter to Ben Jonson. MLR 46 1951.

Spencer, T. In his Death and Elizabethan tragedy, Cambridge Mass 1936.

— The two noble kinsmen. MP 36 1939.

Evans, G. B. Note on Fletcher and Massinger's Little French lawyer. MLN 52 1937.

Bald, R. C. Bibliographical studies in the Beaumont and Fletcher folio of 1647. Trans Bibl Soc (suppl) 13 1938.

Kempling, W. B. The faithful shepherdess. TLS 22 Jan 1938.

Bowers, F. T. In his Elizabethan revenge tragedy, Princeton 1940.

— A bibliographical history of the Fletcher-Betterton play The prophetess 1690. Library 5th ser 16 1961.

Eccles, M. Beaumont's Grammar lecture. RES 16 1940.

Wasserman, E. R. The source of Motherwell's Melancholye. MLN 55 1940. The nice valour.

Mizener, A. The high design of A King and no King. MP 38 1941.

Powell, W. C. A note on the stage history of Love's pilgrimage and the Chances. MLN 56 1941.

Waith, E. M. Characterization in Fletcher's tragicomedies. RES 19 1943.

— A tragi-comedy of humours: Fletcher's The loyal subject. MLQ 6 1945.

— The sources of the Double marriage by Fletcher and Massinger. MLN 64 1949.

— Fletcher and the art of declamation. PMLA 66 1951.

— The pattern of tragicomedy in Beaumont and Fletcher. New Haven 1952.

Grant, R. P. Cervantes' El casamiento enganoso and Fletcher's Rule a wife and have a wife. Hispanic Rev 12 1944.

Brooke, C. F. T. The royal Fletcher and the loyal Heywood. In Elizabethan studies in honor of G. F. Reynolds, Boulder 1945.

Adkins, M. G. M. The citizens in Philaster. SP 43 1946.

Boas, F. S. In his An introduction to Stuart drama, Oxford 1946.

Maxwell, J. C. A dramatic echo of an Overburian character. N & Q 28 June 1947. The elder brother.

Mincoff, M. In his Baroque literature in England, Sofia 1947.

— The social background of Beaumont and Fletcher. Eng Miscellany (Rome) 1 1950.

— The authorship of the Two noble kinsmen. E Studies 33 1952.

— Henry VIII and Fletcher. Shakespeare Quart 12 1961.

— Fletcher's early tragedies. Renaissance Drama 7 1964.

— The faithful shepherdess: a Fletcherian experiment. Renaissance Drama 9 1966.

— Shakespeare, Fletcher and baroque tragedy. Shakespeare Survey 20 1967.

Pelligrini, G. Introduzione a Beaumont e Fletcher. Rivista di Letterature Moderne 2 1947.

Prior, M. E. In his Language of tragedy, New York 1947.

Savage, J. E. Philaster and Sidney's Arcadia. ELH 14 1947.

— The date of Cupid's revenge. ELH 15 1948.

— The gaping wounds in the text of Philaster. PQ 28 1949.

— The effects of revision in Wit at several weapons. Univ of Mississippi Stud in Eng 1 1960.

Wallis, L. B. Fletcher, Beaumont and company: entertainers to the Jacobean gentry. New York 1947.

Child, H. In his Essays and reflections, 1948.

Rulfs, D. J. Beaumont and Fletcher on the London stage 1776–1833. PMLA 63 1948.

Wilson, E. M. Did Fletcher read Spanish? PQ 27 1948.

— Rule a wife and have a wife and El sagaz estacio. RES 24 1948.

Gerritsen, J. The printing of the Beaumont and Fletcher folio of 1647. Library 5th ser 3 1949.

— The honest man's fortune: a critical edition of ms Dyce 9 (1625). Groningen 1952. Introd attributes play to Fletcher, Massinger, Field and Tourneur.

Partridge, A. C. The problem of Henry VIII reopened. Cambridge 1949.

Sherbo, A. Fletcher's 'in flagrante delicto'. N & Q 5 March 1949.

— The knight of Malta and Boccaccio's Filocolo. E Studies 33 1952.

Leech, C. In his Shakespeare's tragedies and other studies in 17th-century drama, 1950.

— The dramatic style of Fletcher. In English studies today: 2nd series, ed G. A. Bonnard, Berne 1961.

— The Fletcher plays. 1962.

Toynbee, M. R. Le capitaine Bessus. TLS 14 July 1950.

Abend, M. Moslem generosity and Beaumont and Fletcher. N & Q 6 Jan 1951.

— Shakespeare's influences in Beaumont and Fletcher. N & Q 21 June, 16 Aug 1952, May 1953.

McCullen, J. T. Madness and the isolation of characters in Elizabethan and early Stuart drama. SP 48 1951. Nice valour, Noble gentleman, Mad lover.

Cutts, J. P. William Lawes' writing for the theatre and the court. Library 5th ser 7 1952. Setting in BM additional ms 31,432 for the song Lovers rejoice from Cupid's revenge.

— Music and the Mad lover. Stud in Renaissance 8 1961.

— Shakespeare's song and masque hand in the Two noble kinsmen. Eng Miscellany 18 1967.

Danby, J. F. In his Poets on fortune's hill: studies in Sidney, Shakespeare, Beaumont and Fletcher, 1952.

Wilson, H. S. Philaster and Cymbeline. Eng Inst Essays 1951.

Oras, A. Extra monosyllables in Henry VIII and the problem of authorship. JEGP 52 1953.

Doran, M. In her Endeavors of art, Madison 1954.

Herrick, M. T. In his Tragicomedy: its origin and development in Italy, France and England, Urbana 1955.

Salingar, L. G. The decline of tragedy. In The age of Shakespeare, ed B. Ford 1955 (Pelican).

Stevenson, A. The case of the decapitated cast or the Nightwalker at Smock Alley. Shakespeare Quart 6 1955.

Appleton, W. W. Beaumont and Fletcher: a critical study. 1956.

Beecham, T. John Fletcher. Oxford 1956 (Romanes lecture).

Feldman, A. B. The yellow malady: short studies of five tragedies of jealousy. Lit & Psychology 6 1956.

Hoy, C. The shares of Fletcher and his collaborators in the Beaumont and Fletcher canon. SB 8–9 1956–7, 11–15 1958–62.

— Renaissance and Restoration dramatic plotting. Renaissance Drama 9 1966.

Praz, M. John Webster and the Maid's tragedy. E Studies 37 1956.

Brossman, S. W. Dryden's Cleomenes and Fletcher's Bonduca. N & Q Feb 1957.

Masefield, J. Beaumont and Fletcher. Atlantic Monthly June 1957.

Ribner, I. In his English history play in the age of Shakespeare, Princeton 1957.

Taylor, A. Proverbial comparisons in the plays of Beaumont and Fletcher. Jnl of Amer Folklore 70 1957.

— Proverbial phrases in the plays of Beaumont and Fletcher. Tennessee Folklore Soc Bull 23 1957.

— Proverbs in the plays of Beaumont and Fletcher. Southern Folklore Quart 24 1960.

Muir, K. Shakespeare's hand in the Two noble kinsmen. Shakespeare Survey 11 1958.

Law, R. A. The double authorship of Henry VIII. SP 56 1959.

Sabol, A. J. Songs and dances for the Stuart masque: an edition of 63 items of music for the English Court masque from 1604 to 1641. Providence 1959. Music for Beaumont's Masque of the gentlemen of Gray's Inn and the Inner Temple.

Edwards, P. The danger not the death: the art of Fletcher. In Jacobean theatre, ed J. R. Brown and B. Harris 1960.

— On the design of the Two noble kinsmen. REL 5 1964.

Ornstein, R. In his Moral vision of Jacobean tragedy, Madison 1960.

Howarth, W. D. Cervantes and Fletcher: a theme with variations. MLR 56 1961.

Turner, R. K. Notes on the text of Thierry and Theodoret Q1. SB 14 1961.

— The morality of A King and no King. Renaissance Papers 1961.

— The printers and the Beaumont and Fletcher folio of 1647. SB 20 1967.

Erickson, M. E. A review of scholarship dealing with the problem of a Spanish source for Love's cure. In Studies in comparative literature, ed W. F. McNeir, Baton Rouge 1962.

Mehl, D. Beaumont und Fletchers The faithful friends. Anglia 80 1962.

Davison, P. The serious concerns of Philaster. ELH 30 1963.

Leimberg, I. Das Spiel mit der dramatischen Illusion in The knight of the burning pestle. Anglia 81 1963.

Pritchard, A. Puritan charges against Beaumont and Fletcher. TLS 2 July 1964.

Rabkin, N. The double plot: notes on the history of a convention. Renaissance Drama 7 1964.

Tomlinson, T. B. In his A study of Elizabethan and Jacobean tragedy, Cambridge 1964.

Bertram, P. Shakespeare and the Two noble kinsmen. New Brunswick NJ 1965. See also C. Hoy, MP 67 1969.

Cunningham, J. E. In his Elizabethan and early Stuart drama, 1965.

Doebler, J. The knight of the burning pestle and the prodigal son plays. Stud in Eng Lit 1500–1900 5 1965.

Jones, E. In his Othello's countrymen, 1965. On Knight of Malta.

Aggeler, G. Irony and honour in Jacobean tragedy. Humanities Assoc Bull (Canada) 18 1967.

Fletcher, I. Beaumont and Fletcher. 1967 (Br Council pamphlet).

Gill, R. Collaboration and revision in Massinger's A very woman. RES new ser 18 1967.

Steiger, K. P. 'May a man be caught with faces?': the convention of heart and face in Fletcher and Rowley's The maid in the mill. E & S new ser 20 1967.

Eddy, D. M. Melville's response to Beaumont and Fletcher: a new source for the Encantadas. Amer Lit 40 1968.

Frost, D. L. In his School of Shakespeare, Cambridge 1968.

Ingram, R. W. Patterns of music and action in Fletcherian drama. In Music in English Renaissance drama, ed J. H. Long, Lexington Kentucky 1968.

Weimann, R. Le déclin de la scène indivisible élisabéthaine: Beaumont, Fletcher et Heywood. In Dramaturgie et société, ed J. Jacquot, Paris 1968.

Willson, R. F. Beaumont and the Noble gentleman. E Studies 49 1968.

Finkelpearl, P. J. The authorship of Salmacis and Hermaphroditus. N & Q Oct 1969.

— Beaumont, Fletcher, and Beaumont and Fletcher: some distinctions. Eng Literary Renaissance 1 1971.

Freehafer, J. Cardenio by Shakespeare and Fletcher. PMLA 84 1969.

— A textual crux in the Two noble kinsmen. Eng Lang Notes 7 1970.

Greenfield, T. N. In her Induction in Elizabethan drama, Eugene 1969.

Henning, S. The printers and the Beaumont and Fletcher folio of 1647. SB 22 1969.

Herndl, G. C. In his High design: English Renaissance tragedy and the natural law, Lexington Kentucky 1970.

Neill, M. 'The simetry which gives a poem grace': masque, imagery and the fancy of the Maid's tragedy. Renaissance Drama new ser 3 1970.

Gabler, H. W. Cupid's revenge (Q1) and its compositors. SB 24 1971.

— John Beale's compositors in A King and no King. Ibid.

WILLIAM ROWLEY
1585?–1626

Collections

The Spanish gipsie and All's lost by lust. Ed E. C. Morris, Boston 1908.

All's lost by lust and A shoemaker a gentleman. Ed C. W. Stork, Philadelphia 1910.

§1

The travailes of the three English brothers. 1607. With Day and Wilkins; see under Day, col 1462, above.

A search for money: or the lamentable complaint for the losse of the wandring knight Mounsieur l'Argent, or come along with me, I know thou lovest money. 1609, 1840 (Percy Soc).

A faire quarrell. 1617. With Middleton; see col 1647, above.

The world tost at tennis. 1620. With Middleton; see cols 1647–8, above.

A new wonder, a woman never vext: a pleasant conceited comedy, sundry times acted, never before printed. 1632; ed C. W. Dilke, Old English plays vol 5, 1815; ed W. C. Hazlitt, Dodsley vol 12, 1875.

A match at midnight: a pleasant comœdie, as it hath been acted by the children of the revells, written by W.R. 1633; ed R. Dodsley, A select collection of old plays vol 6, 1744; ed I. Reed, Dodsley vol 7, 1780; Ancient British drama vol 2, 1810; ed J. P. Collier, Dodsley vol 7, 1825; ed W. C. Hazlitt, Dodsley vol 13, 1875.

A tragedy called All's lost by lust, divers times acted by the Lady Elizabeths servants and now lately by her Majesties servants at the Phoenix in Drury Lane. 1633.

A merrie and pleasant comedy never before printed called A shoomaker a gentleman, as it hath beene sundry times acted at the Red Bull and other theatres, by W.R. gentleman. 1638.

The maid in the mill. 1647. With Fletcher; see col 1709, above.

The changeling. 1653. With Middleton: see col 1648, above.

The Spanish gipsie. 1653. With Middleton; see col 1648, above.

Fortune by land and sea. 1655. With Heywood; see col 1683, above.

The old law. 1656. With Middleton and Massinger; see col 1648, above.

The witch of Edmonton. 1658. With Dekker and Ford; see col 1677, above.

A cure for a cuckold. 1661. With Webster; see col 1699, above.

The birth of Merlin: or the childe hath found his father. written by William Shakespeare and William Rowley, 1662; ed T. E. Jacob 1889; TFT 1910. Also included in collections of the Shakespeare Apocrypha; col 1551, above.

Rowley has been suggested as partial author with Middleton of Wit at several weapons *in the Beaumont and Fletcher canon. The ascription to him on the title-page of* The Thracian wonder, col 1761, below *is generally rejected. Rowley wrote a series of verses on the death of Prince Henry included in* John Taylor's Great Britain all in black, 1612, *and* W. Drummond's Mausoleum: or the choicest flowres of the epitaphs written on the death of Prince Henrie, Edinburgh 1613. *He wrote commendatory verses for* John Taylor's Nipping or snipping of abuses, 1614, *and for* Webster's Duchess of Malfi, 1623.

§2

See also under Middleton, col 1649, above.

Howe, F. A. The authorship of the Birth of Merlin. MP 4 1906.

Tischner, F. Die Verfasserschaft der Webster-Rowley Dramen. Marburg 1907.

Swinburne, A. C. In his Age of Shakespeare, 1908.

Thompson, E. N. S. Elizabethan dramatic collaboration. E Studien 11 1908.

Symons, A. Middleton and Rowley. CHEL vol 6 1910; rptd in his Studies in the Elizabethan drama, 1919.

Sykes, H. D. In his Sidelights on Elizabethan drama, 1924.

Gray, H. D. A cure for a cuckold. MLR 22 1927.

Oliphant, E. H. C. The plays of Beaumont and Fletcher. New Haven 1927.

Dickson, M. J. William Rowley. TLS 28 March 1929.

Sisson, C. J. In his Lost plays of Shakespeare's age, Cambridge 1936.

Sackville-West, E. The significance of the Witch of Edmonton. New Criterion 17 1938.

Bowers, F. T. In his Elizabethan revenge tragedy, Princeton 1940.

Robb, D. M. The canon of Rowley's plays. MLR 45 1950.

Wells, S. W. William Rowley and the Golden legend. N & Q April 1959.

— The lady and the stable groome. N & Q Jan 1960. Rowley as a collaborator in Wit at several weapons.

— Some stage directions in A shoomaker a gentleman. N & Q Sept 1960.

Hoy, C. The shares of Fletcher and his collaborators in the Beaumont and Fletcher canon pt 5. SB 13 1960. Rowley's share in Maid in the mill and Wit at several weapons.

Shapiro, I. A. Tityre-tu and the date of Rowley's Woman never vext. RES new ser 11 1960.

Jones, E. Othello's countrymen. 1965. On All's lost by lust.

Steiger, K. P. 'May a man be caught with faces?': the convention of heart and face in Fletcher and Rowley's The maid in the mill. E & S new ser 20 1967.

JOHN FORD
1586?–1639?

Bibliographies

Tannenbaum, S. A. Ford: a concise bibliography. New York 1941.

Pennel, C. A. and W. P. Williams. Elizabethan bibliographies supplements VIII: Ford 1940–65. 1968.

Collections

Dramatic works. Ed H. Weber 2 vols Edinburgh 1811.

Dramatic works [with Fame's memorial]. Ed W. Gifford 2 vols 1827; rev A. Dyce 3 vols 1869, 1895.

Dramatic works of Massinger and Ford. Ed H. Coleridge 1840.

John Ford. Ed H. Ellis 1888 (Mermaid ser). Contains Lover's melancholy, 'Tis pity she's a whore, Broken heart, Love's sacrifice, Perkin Warbeck.

Dramatic works. Ed W. Bang and H. de Vocht, Bang vol 23, 1908, new ser vol 1, 1927.

§1

Fames memoriall: or the Earle of Devonshire deceased, with his honourable life, peacefull end and solemne funerall. 1606; [ed S. E. Brydges], Lee Priory 1810.

Honor triumphant: or the peeres challenge by armes defensible at tilt, turney and barriers in honor of all faire ladies, and in defence of these foure positions following: 1, Knights in ladies service have no freewill; 2, Beauty is the mainteiner of valour; 3, Faire lady was never false; 4, Perfect lovers are onely wise, mainteined by arguments; also the monarches meeting: or the King of Denmarkes welcome into England. 1606, 1843 (Shakespeare Soc).

A line of life, pointing at the immortalitie of a vertuous name. 1620, 1843 (Shakespeare Soc).

The lovers melancholy, acted at the private house in the Blacke Friers, and publikely at the Globe by the Kings Majesties servants. 1629.

The broken heart: a tragedy, acted by the Kings Majesties servants at the private house in the Black-friers, Fide Honor. 1633; ed C. Scollard, New York 1895; ed O. Smeaton 1906; ed W. A. Neilson, Chief Elizabethan dramatists, 1911; ed S. P. Sherman, Boston 1915; ed E. H. C. Oliphant, Shakespeare and his fellow dramatists, New York 1929; ed C. F. T. Brooke and N. B. Paradise, English drama, 1933; ed H. Spencer, Elizabethan plays, 1933; ed C. R. Baskervill, Elizabethan and Stuart plays, 1934; ed B. Morris 1965 (New Mermaid ser); ed D. Anderson 1968 (Regents ser). Fide Honor is an anagram for Iohn Forde.

Loves sacrifice: a tragedie acted by the Queenes Majesties servants at the Phoenix in Drury-lane. 1633.

Tis pitty shee's a whore, acted by the Queenes Majesties servants at the Phoenix in Drury-Lane. 1633; ed R. Dodsley, A select collection of old plays vol 5, 1744; ed I. Reed, Dodsley vol 8, 1780; tr French by M. Maeterlinck 1895 (as Annabella); ed S. P. Sherman, Boston 1915; tr French by G. Pillement 1925; ed G. H. W. Rylands, Elizabethan tragedy, 1933; ed A. K. McIlwraith, Five Stuart tragedies, Oxford 1953 (WC); ed N. W. Bawcutt 1966 (Regents ser); ed B. Morris 1969 (New Mermaid ser).

The chronicle historie of Perkin Warbeck: a strange truth, acted (some-times) by the Queenes Majesties servants at the Phoenix in Drurie lane, Fide Honor. 1634, 1714; ed J. P. Pickburn and J. Le G. Brereton 1896; ed M. C. Struble, Seattle 1926; ed C. R. Baskervill, Elizabethan

and Stuart plays, 1934; ed D. Anderson 1965 (Regents ser); ed P. Ure 1968 (Revels ser).

The fancies chast and noble, presented by the Queenes Majesties servants at the Phoenix in Drury-lane, Fide Honor. 1638.

The ladies triall, acted by both their Majesties servants at the private house in Drury Lane, Fide Honor. 1639.

The Queen, or the excellency of her sex: an excellent old play found out by a person of honour, and given to the publisher Alexander Goughe. 1653 (anon); ed W. Bang, Bang vol 13 1906. Ford's authorship of the play is accepted; *see* Bentley, III. 457–8.

The sun's darling. 1656. With Dekker; *see col 1677, above.*

The witch of Edmonton. 1658. With Dekker and W. Rowley; *see col 1677, above.*

A share has been claimed for Ford in The laws of candy *and* The fair maid of the inn *in the Beaumont and Fletcher canon, col 1709, above, in Dekker's Welsh embassador, col 1677, above, and in Middleton and Rowley's* The Spanish gipsy, *col 1648, above. Ford wrote commendatory verses for Barnaby Barnes's* Four books of office, *1606;* Overbury's *The wife, 1616; Henry Cockeram's English dictionary, 1623; Webster's* Duchess of Malfi, *1623; Shirley's* The wedding, *1629; Massinger's* The Roman actor, *1629; Brome's* The northern lass, *1632; Massinger's* The great Duke of Florence, *1636; and* Jonsonus virbius, *1638.*

§2

Lamb, C. In his Specimens of English dramatic poets, 1808.

Hazlitt, W. In his Lectures on the dramatic literature of the age of Elizabeth, 1818.

Lowell, J. R. In his Conversations on some of the old poets, Cambridge Mass 1845.

Wolff, M. Ford: ein Nachahmer Shakespeares. Heidelberg 1880.

Hannemann, H. L. E. Metrische Untersuchungen zu Ford. Halle 1886.

Swinburne, A. C. In his Essays and studies, 1888.

Bouchier, J. Ford: Francois Coppée. N & Q 1 Aug 1891.

Gehler, V. Das Verhältnis von Fords Perkin Warbec zu Bacons Henry VII. Halle 1895.

Koeppel, E. Quellen-Studien zu den Dramen George Chapmans, Philip Massingers und Fords. Quellen und Forschungen 82 1897.

— Fords Chronicle history of Perkin Warbeck und Thomas Gainsfords History of Warbeck. Anglia Beiblatt 22 1911.

Bang, W. Ford und Parthenios von Nikaia. E Studien 36 1906.

Sherman, S. P. Ford's contribution to the decadence of the drama. Bang vol 23, 1908.

— Stella and the Broken heart. PMLA 24 1909.

— A new play by Ford. MLN 23 1909. The Queene.

Brereton, J. Le G. The sources of Perkin Warbeck. Anglia 34 1911.

Pierce, F. E. The collaboration of Dekker and Ford. Anglia 36 1912.

Baskervill, C. R. Bandello and the Broken heart. MLN 28 1913.

Sykes, H. D. In his Sidelights on Elizabethan drama, 1924.

— Ford, the author of the Spanish gipsy. MLR 19 1924.

— The authorship of the Witch of Edmonton. N & Q 18–25 Dec 1926.

Lloyd, B. An inedited ms of Ford's Fame's memorial. RES 1 1925.

— An unprinted poem by Ford (?). Ibid.

— The authorship of the Welsh embassador. RES 21 1945. Claims Ford as Dekker's collaborator.

Struble, M. C. The indebtedness of Perkin Warbeck to Gainsford. Anglia 49 1925.

Woolf, V. Notes on an Elizabethan play. TLS 5 March 1925; rptd in her Common reader, 1925.

Lawrence, W. J. The origin of the substantive theatre masque. In his Pre-Restoration stage studies, 1927. On Sun's darling.

Eliot, T. S. John Ford. TLS 5 May 1932; rptd in his Selected essays, 1932, and Elizabethan essays, 1934.

Sargeaunt, M. J. Ford at the Middle Temple. RES 8 1932.

— Writings ascribed to Ford by Joseph Hunter in Chorus Vatum. RES 10 1934.

— John Ford. Oxford 1935.

Cochnower, M. E. In Seventeenth-century studies, ed R. Shafer, Princeton 1933.

Russell, H. K. Tudor and Stuart dramatizations of the doctrines of natural and moral philosophy. SP 31 1934. For Sun's darling.

Bradbrook, M. C. In her Themes and conventions of Elizabethan tragedy, Cambridge 1935.

Babb, L. Abnormal psychology in Perkin Warbeck. MLN 51 1936.

Ellis-Fermor, U. M. In her Jacobean drama, 1936, 1958 (rev).

Sensabaugh, G. F. Burton's influence on the Lover's melancholy. SP 33 1936.

— Ford's tragedy of love-melancholy. E Studien 83 1939.

— Ford and platonic love in the Court. SP 36 1939.

— Ford and Elizabethan tragedy. PQ 20 1941.

— The tragic muse of Ford. Stanford 1944.

— Ford revisited. Stud in Eng Lit 1500–1900 4 1964.

Spencer, T. In his Death and Elizabethan tragedy, Cambridge Mass 1936.

Ewing, S. B. Burton, Ford and Andromana. PMLA 54 1939.

— Burtonian melancholy in the plays of Ford. Princeton 1940.

Bowers, F. T. In his Elizabethan revenge tragedy, Princeton 1940.

Harbage, A. Elizabethan-Restoration palimpsest. MLR 35 1940. Suggests Sir Robert Howard's The great favourite, 1668 was based on a ms play by Ford; confirmed by F. G. Sensabaugh, MLQ 3 1942, but see Bentley III.458–9, V.1062–4.

— The mystery of Perkin Warbeck. In Studies in the English Renaissance drama in memory of K. J. Holzknecht, New York 1959. Suggests Dekker as a collaborator in the play.

Adams, H. H. English domestic or homiletic tragedy 1575 to 1642. New York 1943.

Parrott, T. M. A note on Ford. MLN 58 1943.

Boas, F. S. In his An introduction to Stuart drama, Oxford 1946.

Praz, M. Il dramma elisabettiano: Webster-Ford. Rome 1946.

Wilcox, J. On reading Ford. Shakespeare Assoc Bull 21 1946.

Prior, M. E. In his Language of tragedy, New York 1947.

Bacon, W. A. The literary reputation of Ford. HLQ 11 1948.

Leech, C. Shakespeare's tragedies and other studies in 17th-century drama. 1950.

— Ford and the drama of his time. 1957.

— A projected restoration performance of the Lover's melancholy? MLR 56 1961.

— John Ford. 1964 (Br Council pamphlet).

Ure, P. Cult and initiates in Love's sacrifice. MLQ 11 1950.

— Marriage and the domestic drama in Heywood and Ford. E Studies 32 1951.

— A pointer to the date of Perkin Warbeck. N & Q June 1970.

Davril, R. Ford and La Cerda's Inés de Castro. MLN 66 1951.

— Ford et les Caractères overburiens. Etudes Anglaises 6 1953.

— Le drame de Ford. Paris 1954.

— Shakespeare and Ford. Sh Jb 94 1958.

McCullen, J. T. Madness and the isolation of characters in Elizabethan and early Stuart drama. SP 48 1951.

Cutts, J. P. William Lawes' writing for the theatre and the Court. Library 5th ser 7 1952. Settings in BM additional ms 31,432 for songs from Lady's trial.

Quennell, P. C. In his Singular preference, 1952.

Doran, M. In her Endeavours of art, Madison 1954.

Carrère, F. La tragédie espagnole de Thomas Kyd et Le coeur brisé de Ford. Etudes Anglaises 8 1955.

O'Connor, J. A lost play of Perkin Warbeck. MLN 70 1955.

— William Warner and Ford's Perkin Warbeck. N & Q June 1955.

Oliver, H. J. The problem of Ford. 1955.

Salingar, L. G. The decline of tragedy. In The age of Shakespeare, ed B. Ford 1955 (Pelican).

Cecil, D. In his Fine art of reading, 1957.

Howarth, R. G. John Ford. N & Q June 1957.

Ribner, I. In his English history play in the age of Shakespeare, Princeton 1957.

— 'By nature's light': the morality of 'Tis pity she's a whore. Tulane Stud in Eng 10 1960.

— In his Jacobean tragedy, 1962.

Blayney, G. H. Convention, plot and structure in the Broken heart. MP 56 1958.

Carsaniga, G. M. The 'truth' in the Broken heart. Comparative Lit 10 1958. See also F. M. Burelbach. N & Q June 1967.

Anderson, D. K. Kingship in Perkin Warbeck. ELH 27 1960.

— The heart and the banquet: imagery in 'Tis pity and the Broken heart. Stud in Eng Lit 1500–1900 2 1962.

— Richard II and Perkin Warbeck. Shakespeare Quart 13 1962.

— The date and handwriting of a ms copy of Perkin Warbeck. N & Q Sept 1963. Reply by M. Crum, March 1965.

Hoy, C. 'Ignorance in knowledge': Marlowe's Faustus and Ford's Giovanni. MP 57 1960.

— The shares of Fletcher and his collaborators in the Beaumont and Fletcher canon pt 5. SB 13 1960. Ford's share in Laws of Candy and Fair maid of the inn.

— Renaissance and Restoration dramatic plotting. Renaissance Drama 9 1966. On Love's sacrifice.

Kaufmann, R. J. Ford's tragic perspective. Texas Stud in Lit & Lang 1 1960.

— Ford's waste land: the Broken heart. Renaissance Drama new ser 3 1970.

Ornstein, R. In his Moral vision of Jacobean tragedy, Madison 1960.

McDonald, C. O. The design of the Broken heart. SP 59 1962.

— In his Rhetoric of tragedy: form in Stuart drama, Amherst 1966.

Novarr, D. 'Gray dissimulation': Ford and Milton. PQ 41 1962.

Sutton, J. Ford's use of Burton's imagery. N & Q Nov 1963.

— Platonic love in the Fancies chaste and noble. Stud in Eng Lit 1500–1900 7 1967.

Brissenden, A. Impediments to love: a theme in Ford. Renaissance Drama 7 1964.

Tomlinson, T. B. In his A study of Elizabethan and Jacobean tragedy, Cambridge 1964.

Weathers, W. Perkin Warbeck: a 17th-century psychological play. Stud in Eng Lit 1500–1900 4 1964.

Cunningham, J. E. In his Elizabethan and early Stuart drama, 1965.

Ravignani, D. Ford e Burton: riesame di un rapporto. Eng Miscellany (Rome) 17 1966.

Sasayama, T. A note on decadence in Ford's tragedies. Stud in Eng Lit (Tokyo) 1966.

Bawcutt, N. W. Seneca and Ford's 'Tis pity she's a whore. N & Q June 1967.

Homan, S. R. Shakespeare and Dekker as keys to 'Tis pity she's a whore. Stud in Eng Lit 1500–1900 7 1967.

Davison, P. La dramaturgie en Angleterre à la veille de la guerre civile: Ford et la comédie. In Dramaturgie et société, ed J. Jacquot, Paris 1968.

Frost, D. L. In his School of Shakespeare, Cambridge 1968.

Neill, M. Ford and Gainsford: an unnoticed borrowing. N & Q July 1968.

Orbison, T. The date of the Queen. Ibid.

Stavig, M. Ford and the traditional moral order. Madison 1968.

Findley, R. R. Macklin's 1748 adaptation of the Lover's melancholy. Restoration & 18th-century Theatre Research 8 1969.

Jordan, R. Calantha's dance in the Broken heart. N & Q Aug 1969.

McMaster, J. Love, lust and sham: structural pattern in the plays of Ford. Renaissance Drama new ser 2 1969.

Pellizzi, G. The speech of Ithocles on ambition in the Broken heart. Eng Miscellany (Rome) 20 1969.

Putt, S. G. The modernity of Ford. English 18 1969.

Reinecke, G. F. Ford's 'missing' Raleigh passage. Eng Lang Notes 6 1969. A line of life.

Barish, J. A. Perkin Warbeck as anti-history. EC 20 1970.

Burbridge, R. T. The moral vision of the Broken heart. Stud in Eng Lit 1500–1900 10 1970.

Herndl, G. C. The high design: English Renaissance tragedy and the natural law. Lexington Kentucky 1970.

Maxwell, J. C. A neglected emendation in Perkin Warbeck [v.iii.105]. N & Q June 1970.

Gibson, C. A. The date of the Broken heart. N & Q Dec 1971.

Monsarrat, G. D. Ford's authorship of Christes bloodie sweat. Eng Lang Notes 9 1971.

JAMES SHIRLEY
1596–1666

Bibliographies

Tannenbaum, S. A. and D. R. Shirley: a concise bibliography. New York 1946.

Pennel, C. A. and W. P. Williams. Elizabethan bibliographies supplements VIII: Shirley 1945–65. 1968.

Collections

Dramatic works and poems. Ed W. Gifford and A. Dyce 6 vols 1833.

James Shirley. Ed E. Gosse 1888 (Mermaid ser). Contains Witty fair one, Traitor, Hyde Park, Lady of pleasure, Cardinal, Triumph of peace.

§ 1

The wedding, as it was lately acted by her Majesties servants at the Phenix in Drury-Lane. 1629, 1633, 1660; ed A. S. Knowland, Six Caroline plays, Oxford 1962 (WC).

The gratefull servant: a comedie, as it was lately presented at the private house in Drury-Lane by her Majesties servants. 1630, 1637, [1662?].

The schoole of complement, as it was acted by her Majesties servants at the private house in Drury Lane, by J.S. 1631, 1637, 1667 (as Love tricks: or the school of complements, as it is now acted by his Royal Highnesse the Duke of York's servants at the theatre in Little Lincolns-Inne Fields).

Changes, or love in a maze: a comedie, as it was presented at the private house in Salisbury Court by the company of his Majesties revels. 1632.

A contention for honour and riches, by J.S. 1633.

The wittie faire one: a comedie, as it was presented at the private house in Drury Lane by her Majesties servants. 1633.

The bird in a cage: a comedie, as it hath beene presented at the Phoenix in Drury-Lane. 1633; ed R. Dodsley, A select collection of old plays vol 9, 1744; ed I. Reed, Dodsley vol 8, 1780; Ancient British drama vol 1, 1810.

The triumph of peace: a masque presented by the foure honourable houses or Innes of Court before the King and Queenes Majesties in the Banqueting-house at White Hall, February the third 1633 [i.e. 1634]. 1633 (3 edns, the 3rd re-issued with a new speech by Genius); ed H. A. Evans, English masques, 1897; ed C. Leech, A book of masques in honour of Allardyce Nicoll, Cambridge 1967.

The traytor: a tragedie, acted by her Majesties servants. 1635, 1692 ('with alterations, amendments and additions, as it is now acted at the Theatre Royal by their Majesties servants, written by Mr Rivers'); ed E. H. C. Oliphant, English dramatists other than Shakespeare, New York 1931; ed J. S. Carter 1965 (Regents ser).

Hide Parke: a comedie, as it was presented by her Majesties servants at the private house in Drury Lane. 1637.

The gamester, as it was presented by her Majesties servants at the private house in Drury-Lane. 1637; ed R. Dodsley, A select collection of old plays vol 9, 1744; ed I. Reed, Dodsley vol 9, 1780; Ancient British drama vol 2, 1810.

The young admirall, as it was presented by her Majesties servants at the private house in Drury Lane. 1637.

The example, as it was presented by her Majesties' servants at the private house in Drury-Lane. 1637.

The lady of pleasure: a comedie, as it was acted by her Majesties servants at the private house in Drury Lane. 1637; ed W. A. Neilson, Chief Elizabethan dramatists, 1911; ed H. Spencer, Elizabethan plays, 1933; ed C. R. Baskervill, Elizabethan and Stuart plays, 1934; ed A. S. Knowland, Six Caroline plays, Oxford 1962 (WC).

The Dukes mistris, as it was presented by her Majesties servants at the private house in Drury-Lane. 1638.

The royall master, as it was acted in the new theater in Dublin, and before the Right Honorable the Lord Deputie of Ireland in the Castle. 1638; ed A. W. Ward, Gayley vol 3, 1914; tr German, 1911.

The ball: a comedy, as it was presented by her Majesties servants at the private house in Drury Lane, written by George Chapman and James Shirly. 1639; rptd in collections of Chapman, col 1637, above, but the title-page ascription to him is now rejected; see Bentley v.1076–9.

The maides revenge: a tragedy, as it hath beene acted at the private house in Drury Lane by her Majesties servants. 1639.

Loves crueltie: a tragedy, as it was presented by her Majesties servants at the private house in Drury Lane. 1640.

The opportunitie: a comedy, as it was presented by her Majesties servants at the private house in Drury Lane. 1640.

The coronation: a comedy, as it was presented by her Majesties servants at the private house in Drury Lane, written by John Fletcher, gent. 1640, 1679 (in 2nd Beaumont and Fletcher folio). Licensed to Shirley 6 Feb 1635 and claimed by him in 1653.

The constant maid: a comedy. 1640, 1661 (as Love will finde out the way: an excellent comedy, by T.B.), 1667 (as The constant maid: or love will finde out the way, a comedy by J. S.).

St Patrick for Ireland: the first part. 1640; ed W. R. Chetwood, A select collection of old plays, 1750. No 2nd pt is known.

The humorous courtier: a comedy, as it hath been presented at the private house in Drury-Lane. 1640.

A pastorall called the Arcadia, acted by her Majesties servants at the Phoenix in Drury Lane. 1640.

Poems. 1646 (1, Verses on various subjects; 2, Narcissus: or the self lover; 3, Several prologues and epilogues; 4, The triumph of beautie); ed R. L. Armstrong, New

York 1941; Narcissus ed E. S. Donno, Elizabethan minor epics, 1963.

The triumph of beautie, as it was personated by some young gentlemen for whom it was intended at a private recreation. 1646. Appended to Poems.

Via ad latinam linguam complanata: the way made plain to the Latin tongue, the rules composed in English and Latine verse for the greater delight and benefit of learners. 1649, 1651 (as Grammatica anglo-latina).

Six new plays, viz:

The brothers: a comedie, as it was acted at the private house in Black Fryers. 1652.

The doubtful heir: a tragi-comedie, as it was acted at the private house in Black-friers. 1652.

The imposture: a tragi-comedie, as it was acted at the private house in Black Fryers. 1652.

The Cardinal: a tragedie, as it was acted at the private house in Black Fryers. 1652; ed W. A. Neilson, Chief Elizabethan dramatists, 1911; ed H. R. Walley and J. H. Wilson, Early 17th-century plays, 1930; ed C. F. T. Brooke and N. B. Paradise, English drama, 1933; ed C. R. Baskervill, Elizabethan and Stuart plays, 1934; ed C. R. Forker, Bloomington 1964.

The sisters: a comedie, as it was acted at the private house in Black Fryers. 1652.

The Court secret: a tragi-comedy, never acted but prepared for the scene at Black-friers. 1653. Worcester College, Oxford ms 120.

All written by James Shirley. 1653.

Cupid and Death: a masque, as it was presented before his Excellencie the Embassadour of Portugal upon the 26 of March 1653, written by J.S. 1653, 1659 (as Cupid and Death, a private entertainment, represented with scenes and musick, vocall and instrumentall, written by J.S.) (2 issues); ed E. J. Dent, Musica britannica vol 2, 1951; ed B. A. Harris, A book of masques in honour of Allardyce Nicoll, Cambridge 1967. Mss: (1) BM additional ms 17,799 (music only); (2) BM additional ms 17,800; (3) Huntington Lib ms HM 601.

The polititian: a tragedy, presented at Salisbury Court by her Majesties servants. 1655 (2 issues, one 8°, the other 4°).

The gentleman of Venice: a tragi-comedie, presented at the private house in Salisbury Court by her Majesties servants. 1655 (2 issues, one 8°, the other 4°).

The rudiments of grammar: the rules composed in English verse for the greater benefit and delight of young beginners. 1656, 1660 (enlarged as Manductio: or a leading of children by the hand through the principles of grammar).

Honoria and Mammon. [1658] (with the Contention of Ajax and Ulisses), nd, 1659. Honoria and Mammon is an altered and enlarged version of A contention for honour and riches.

The contention of Ajax and Ulysses for the armor of Achilles, as it was nobly represented by young gentlemen of quality at a private entertainment of some persons of honour. [1658] (with Honoria and Mammon), nd, 1659.

The true impartial history and wars of the kingdom of Ireland. 1693. Epistle to reader signed J.S.

A little ark containing sundry pieces of 17th-century verse. Ed G. Thorn-Drury 1921. Contains An ode upon the happy return of King Charles II to his long wishing nation, May 29 1660, by James Shirley gent.

The following plays survive in texts rev Shirley: Chapman's The tragedie of Chabot Admirall of France, *col 1639, above, Middleton's* No wit no (help) like a woman's, *col 1648, above, Fletcher's* The night-walker, *col 1712, above. It is likely that he aided the Duke of Newcastle in the latter's* Country captain, *col 1736, below. Andromana, or the merchant's wife was licensed as 'by Iam: Shirley' on 19 May 1660 and ptd 1660 as by J.S. but*

the identification with Shirley is generally rejected, as is the attribution of The Prince of prigs' revels, *1651 ('written by J.S.'), cols 1758, 1760–1, below. It has been suggested that Lewis Theobald's* Double falsehood, *1728, was based upon a lost ms play by Shirley, but there is no evidence for this.*

§2

Life and writings of Shirley. Quart Rev 49 1833.

Fleay, F. G. Annals of the careers of James and Henry Shirley. Anglia 8 1885.

Stiefel, A. L. Die Nachahmung spanischer Komödien in England unter den ersten Stuarts. Romanische Forschungen 5 1890.

Swinburne, A. C. James Shirley. Fortnightly Rev 1 April 1890; rptd in his Contemporaries of Shakespeare, 1919.

Nissen, P. Shirley: ein Beitrag zur englischen Litteraturgeschichte. Hamburg 1901.

Ritter, O. Shirley's Amor und Tod. E Studien 32 1903.

Greg, W. W. In his Pastoral poetry and pastoral drama, 1906.

— The triumph of peace: a bibliographer's nightmare. Library 5th ser 1 1947.

Baskervill, C. R. The source of the main plot of Love tricks. MLN 24 1909.

Reyher, P. Les masques anglais. Paris 1909.

Ristine, F. H. In his English tragicomedy: its origin and history, New York 1910.

Schipper, J. Shirley: sein Leben und seine Werke, nebst einer Übersetzung seines Dramas The royal master. Vienna 1911.

Forsythe, R. S. The relations of Shirley's plays to the Elizabethan drama. New York 1914.

Parlin, H. T. Shirley's comedies of London life. Univ of Texas Bull no 371 1914.

Schelling, F. E. Shirley and the last of the old drama. In his English drama, 1914.

Nason, A. H. Shirley, dramatist: a biographical and critical study. New York 1915.

Summers, M. A Restoration prompt-book [of the Sisters]. TLS 24 June 1920; rptd in his Essays in petto, 1928. See also E. A. Langhans, Theatre Annual 14 1956.

Baugh, A. C. Some new facts about Shirley. MLR 17 1922.

— Further facts about Shirley. RES 7 1931.

Lynch, K. M. The social mode of Restoration comedy. New York 1926.

Welsford, E. In her Court masque, 1927.

Radtke, S. J. Shirley: his Catholic philosophy of life. Washington 1929.

Clark, W. S. The relation of Shirley's prologue to Orrery's The general. RES 6 1930.

Howarth, R. G. A ms of Shirley's Court secret. RES 7–8 1931–2.

— Some unpublished poems of Shirley. RES 9 1933.

— Cupid and Death. TLS 15 Nov 1934.

Green, A. W. The Inns of Court and early English drama. 1931.

Elson, J. J. (ed). The wits or sport upon sport. Ithaca 1932.

MacMullan, H. The sources of St Patrick for Ireland. PMLA 48 1933.

— A note on source-studies of St Patrick for Ireland. PMLA 51 1936.

Bradbrook, M. C. In her Themes and conventions of Elizabethan tragedy, Cambridge 1935.

Gregory, G. M. Two studies in Shirley. Durham NC 1935.

Harbage, A. In his Cavalier drama, New York 1936.

— The wedding and the marriage of Sir Kenelm Digby. PQ 16 1937.

— The authorship of the dramatic Arcadia. MP 35 1938.

Huberman, E. Bibliographical note on the Polititian. Library 4th ser 18 1938 See also R. J. Fehrenbach, The printing of the Polititian, SB 24 1971.

Bentley, G. E. Shirley and a group of unnoted poems on the wedding of Thomas Stanley. HLQ 2 1939.

Bowers, F. T. In his Elizabethan revenge tragedy, Princeton 1940.

Miles, T. Place-realism in a group of Caroline plays. RES 18 1942. On Hyde Park.

Stevenson, A. H. Shirley and the actors at the first Irish theatre. MP 40 1942.

— Shirley's years in Ireland. RES 20 1944.

— Shirley's publishers: the partnership of Crooke and Cook. Library 4th ser 25 1945.

— Shirley's dedications and the date of his return to England. MLN 61 1946.

— New uses of watermarks as bibliographical evidence. SB 1 1948.

— The case of the decapitated cast: or the Night-walker at Smock Alley. Shakespeare Quart 6 1955.

Boas, F. S. In his An introduction to Stuart drama, Oxford 1946.

Scott, F. R. Teg: the stage Irishman. MLR 42 1947. On Hyde Park.

Ure, P. The 'deformed mistress' theme and the platonic convention. N & Q 26 June 1948.

Leech, C. In his Shakespeare's tragedies and other studies in 17th-century drama, 1950.

Scherrer, G. F. Shirleys Nachruhm. Zürich 1951.

Cutts, J. R. William Lawes' writing for the theatre and the Court. Library 5th ser 7 1952. Settings in BM additional ms 31,432 for songs from Triumph of peace and Cardinal, and for Shirley's poem To his mistress.

— Seventeenth-century songs and lyrics in Edinburgh University Library Music ms Dc.1.69. Musica Disciplina 13 1959. A single voice part for Song 7 from Triumph of peace.

Gerber, R. Shirley: Dramatiker der Dekadenz. Berne 1952.

— Shirleys Komödiendialog und die Welt am Hyde Park. Sh Jb 95 1959.

Sensabaugh, G. F. Platonic love in the Lady of pleasure. In A tribute to G. C. Taylor, Chapel Hill 1952.

Enright, D. J. Elizabethan and Jacobean comedy. In The age of Shakespeare, ed B. Ford 1955 (Pelican).

Reed, R. A. Shirley and the sentimental comedy. Anglia 73 1955.

Feil, J. P. Shirley's years of service. RES new ser 8 1957.

Hoy, C. The shares of Fletcher and his collaborators in the Beaumont and Fletcher canon pt 4. SB 12 1959. Shirley's revision of Fletcher's Night-walker.

Morillo, M. 'Frier Sherley': Shirley and Mercurius Britanicus. N & Q Sept 1960.

— Sherley's preferment and the Court of Charles I. Stud in Eng Lit 1500–1900 1 1961.

Taylor, A. M. Shirley and Mr Vincent Cane the Franciscan. N & Q Jan 1960.

Salmon, V. Shirley and some problems of 17th-century grammar. Archiv 197 1961.

Bas, G. Shirley: pasteur dans le Hertfordshire. Etudes Anglaises 15 1962.

— Shirley et 'Th' untun'd kennell': une petitie guerre des théâtres vers 1630. Etudes Anglaises 16 1963.

Riemer, A. P. A source for the Traitor. RES new ser 14 1963.

— Shirley's revisions and the date of the Constant maid. RES new ser 17 1966.

King, T. J. Shirley's Coronation and Love will find out the way: erroneous title-pages. SB 18 1965.

Lefkowitz, M. The Longleat papers of Bulstrode Whitelocke: new light on Shirley's Triumph of peace. Jnl Amer Musicological Soc 18 1965.

Manley, F. The death of Hernando in Shirley's Cardinal. N & Q Sept 1965.

Crawley, D. The effect of Shirley's hand on Chapman's The tragedy of Chabot. SP 63 1966.

McGrath, J. Shirley's uses of language. Stud in Eng Lit 1500–1900 6 1966.

Morton, R. Deception and social dislocation: an aspect of Shirley's drama. Renaissance Drama 9 1966.

Sabol, A. J. New documents on the Triumph of peace. Music & Letters 47 1966.

Davis, J. L. The sons of Ben: Jonsonian comedy in Caroline England. Detroit 1967.

Levin, R. The triple plot of Hyde Park. MLR 62 1967.

Wertheim, A. The presentation of St Patrick for Ireland at the first Irish playhouse. N & Q June 1967.

Crinò, A. M. Shirley: drammaturgo di corte. Verona 1968.

Frost, D. L. In his School of Shakespeare, Cambridge 1968.

Ochester, E. F. A source for the Contention of Ajax and Ulysses. N & Q June 1970.

C. H.

XI. MINOR JACOBEAN AND CAROLINE DRAMA
(1603–60)

ROBERT ARMIN
1565?–1610

§ 1

Foole upon foole. 1599, 1605. Anon; enlarged below.

Quips upon questions. 1600, 1601, 1602; ed F. Ouvry 1875. See col 1082, above.

A nest of ninnies. 1608 (enlarged version of Foole upon foole, above), 1842 (Shakespeare Soc).

Phantasma the Italian tailor and his boy. 1609.

The history of the two maids of More-clacke, with the life and simple maner of John in the hospitall, played by the children of the Kings Majesties revels. 1609; ed A. B. Grosart, Works of Robert Armin, actor, Blackburn 1880; TFT 1913.

§ 2

Gray, A. K. Armine the foole. PMLA 42 1927.

Murry, J. M. A fellow of Shakespeare: Armin. New Adelphi March 1928.

Herring, R. The whale has a wide mouth. Life & Letters 36 1943.

Dudley, O. H. T. John in the hospital. TLS 17 June 1949.

Williams, P. The compositor of the 'Pied Bull' Lear. SB 1 1949.

Felver, C. S. Armin, Shakespeare's fool: a biographical essay. Kent State Univ Bull 49 1961.

BARNABE BARNES
1570?–1609

§ 1

Parthenophil and Parthenope. 1593; ed A. B. Grosart, Occasional issues, 1875.

The Divils charter: a tragædie conteining the life and death of Pope Alexander the Sixt, as it was laide before the Kings Majestie upon Candlemasse night last by his Majesties servants. 1607, 1607; ed R. B. McKerrow, Bang vol 6, 1904; TFT 1913.

§2

Knight, J. Barnabe Barnes. Athenaeum 20 Aug 1904.
Swaen, A. E. H., G. C. M. Smith and R. B. McKerrow. Notes on the Devil's charter. MLR 1 1906.
—— Notes on the Devil's charter. MLR 2 1907.
Bayley, A. R. N & Q 12 April 1924.
Eccles, M. In Thomas Lodge and other Elizabethans, ed C. J. Sisson, Cambridge Mass 1933.
Fellheimer, J. Barnes' use of Geoffrey Fenton's Historie of Guicciardin. MLN 57 1942.
Dodds, M. H. Barnabe Barnes. Archaeologia Aeliana 4th ser 24 1946.
See also under Sonnet, *col 1078, above.*

ROBERT BARON
1630–58

§1

'ΕΡΩΤΟΠΑΙΓΝΙΟΝ: or the Cyprian academy. 1647 (some copies dated 1648). A romance incorporating the masque Deorum dona, and the pastoral Gripsius and Hegio: or the passionate lovers, each ptd with a separate title-page.
An apologie for Paris for rejecting of Juno and Pallas, and presenting of Ate's golden ball to Venus. 1649. Prose dialogue.
Mirza: a tragedie, really acted in Persia in the last age; the author R.B. [1655].
See also col 1298, above.

§2

Smith, G. C. M. Robert Baron. N & Q 3–24 Jan, 14 March 1914.
Beck, E. Barons Leben und Werke. Strasbourg 1915.
Slagle, K. C. Baron: Cavalier poet. N & Q 12 Oct 1935.
Forker, C. R. Baron's use of Webster, Shakespeare and other Elizabethans. Anglia 83 1965.

LORDING BARRY
(wrongly designated David, Lord Barry and Lodowick Barry)
1580–1629

§1

Ram-Alley, or merrie-trickes: a comedy divers times here-to-fore acted by the children of the Kings revels, written by Lo Barrey. 1611, 1611, 1636; ed I. Reed, Dodsley vol 5, 1780; Ancient British drama vol 2, 1810; ed J. P. Collier, Dodsley vol 5, 1825; ed W. C. Hazlitt, Dodsley vol 10, 1875; TFT 1913; ed C. E. Jones, Louvain 1952.

§2

Adams, J. Q. Lordinge (alias Lodowick) Barry. MP 9 1912.
Lawrence, W. J. The mystery of Barry. SP 14 1917.
Ewen, C. L'E. Lording Barry: dramatist. N & Q 12 Feb 1938.
—— Lording Barry: poet and pirate. 1938.

SIMON BAYLIE
fl. 1620–40

The wizard. Durham Cathedral Lib ms Hunter 77; BM additional ms 10,306; ed H. de Vocht, Louvain 1930.

DAUBRIDGCOURT BELCHIER
c. 1581–1621

Hans Beer-Pot his invisible comedie of See me and see me not, acted in the Low Countries by an honest company of health-drinkers. 1618.

SIR WILLIAM BERKELEY
1606?–77

§1

The lost lady: a tragycomedy. 1638, 1638 (some copies dated 1639); ed R. Dodsley, A select collection of old plays vol 10, 1744; ed W. C. Hazlitt, Dodsley vol 12, 1875. Folger Lib ms J.b.4 (last 298 lines missing).

§2

Bald, R. C. Berkeley's The lost lady. Library 4th ser 17 1937.
Cutts, J. P. William Lawes' writing for the theatre and the Court. Library 5th ser 7 1952. Setting in BM additional ms 31,432 for song beginning Where did you borrow that last sigh, from the Lost lady.

LADY ELIZABETH BRACKLEY
and LADY JANE CAVENDISH
collaborated c. 1645

The concealed fansyes. Bodley ms Rawlinson Poetry 16; ed N. C. Star, PMLA 46 1931. The ms contains a 2nd piece by the same authors called A pastorall.

ANTHONY BREWER
fl. 1617?

§1

The love-sick King: an English tragical history, with the life and death of Cartesmunda, the fair nun of Winchester, written by Anth. Brewer, gent. 1655; ed W. R. Chetwood, A select collection of old plays, 1750; ed A. E. H. Swaen, Bang vol 18, 1907.

§2

Swaen, A. E. H. The date of Brewer's Love-sick King. MLR 4 1908.
Dodds, M. H. Edmond Ironside and the love-sick King. MLR 19 1924.
Dent, R. W. The love-sick King: Turk turned Dane. MLR 56 1961.

THOMAS BREWER
fl. 1623

A knot of fools. 1624, 1658. A semi-dramatic satire in dialogue.

ALEXANDER BROME
1620–66

See col 1301, above.

RICHARD BROME
1590?–1652 or 1653

Collections
Dramatic works. Ed R. H. Shepherd 3 vols 1873.

§ 1

The northern lasse: a comoedie, as it hath beene often acted at the Globe and Black-fryers by his Majesties servants. 1632, 1663, 1684, 1706, 1717.

The late Lancashire witches. 1634. With Heywood; see col 1684, above.

The sparagus garden: a comedie, acted in the yeare 1635 by the then company of revels at Salisbury Court. 1640.

The antipodes: a comedie, acted in the yeare 1638 by the Queenes Majesties servants at Salisbury Court in Fleetstreet. 1640; ed G. P. Baker, Gayley vol 3 1914; ed A. S. Knowland, Six Caroline plays, Oxford 1962 (WC); ed A. Haaker 1966 (Regents ser).

A joviall crew: or the merry beggars, presented in a comedie at the Cock-pit in Drury Lane in the yeer 1641. 1652, 1661, 1684; ed R. Dodsley, A select collection of old plays vol 6, 1744; ed I. Reed, Dodsley vol 10, 1780; Ancient British drama vol 3, 1810; ed J. P. Collier, Dodsley vol 10, 1826; ed A. Haaker 1968 (Regents ser).

Five new playes, viz:
A mad couple well match'd. 1653; ed A. S. Knowland, Six Caroline plays, Oxford 1962 (WC).
The novella: a comedie, acted at the Black-friers by his Majesties servants, anno 1632. 1653.
The Court begger: a comedie, acted at the Cock-pit by his Majesties servants, anno 1632. 1653.
The city wit, or the woman wears the breeches: a comedy. 1653.
The damoiselle, or the new ordinary: a comedy. 1653. By Richard Brome. 1653.

The Queenes exchange: a comedy, acted at the Black-friers by his Majesties servants. 1657, 1661 (as The royall exchange).

Five new plays, viz:
The English moor: or the mock-marriage, a comedy as it was often acted by her Majesties servants. 1658 (some copies dated 1659). Ms: Lichfield Cathedral Lib.
The love-sick Court, or the ambitious politique: a comedy. 1658.
The weeding of the Covent-Garden, or the Middlesex-Justice of Peace: a facetious comedy. 1658.
The new academy: or the new exchange. 1658.
The Queen and concubine: a comedie. 1659.
By Richard Brome. 1659.

§ 2

Nicholson, B. The date of Northward ho, A chaste maid and the Northern lass. N & Q 19 April 1873. Reply by F. G. Stephens 10 May 1873.
— Brome's Queene's exchange 1657 and Royal exchange 1661. N & Q 16 Feb 1889.
Symonds, J. A. Academy 21 March 1874. Review of Dramatic works of Brome.
Faust, E. K. R. Brome: ein Beitrag zur Geschichte der englischen Litteratur. Halle 1887.
Swinburne, A. C. Brome. Fortnightly Rev April 1892; rptd in his Contemporaries of Shakespeare, 1919.
Koeppel, E. The Queen and concubine. Quellen und Forschungen 82 1897.
Allen, H. F. A study of the comedies of Brome, especially as representative of dramatic decadence. 1912.
Andrews, C. E. Brome: a study of his life and works. New Haven 1913.

Martin, R. G. Is the Late Lancashire witches a revision? MP 13 1915.
Thaler, A. Was Brome an actor? MLN 36 1921.
Aronstein, P. In his Das englische Renaissance-Drama, Leipzig 1929.
Sharpe, R. B. The source of Brome's The novella. SP 30 1933.
Harbage, A. In his Cavalier drama, New York 1936.
Guardia, C. E. Brome as a follower of Ben Jonson. Bull Louisiana State Univ 31 1939.
Miles, T. Place-realism in a group of Caroline plays. RES 18 1942. For Weeding of the Covent-Garden and Sparagus garden.
Davis, J. L. Brome's neglected contribution to comic theory. SP 40 1943.
— The sons of Ben: Jonsonian comedy in Caroline England. Detroit 1967.
Cook, E. The plays of Brome. More Books 22 1947.
Leech, C. In his Shakespeare's tragedies and other studies in 17th-century drama, 1950.
Field, H. The early quartos of Brome's Northern lasse. PBSA 54 1960.
Kaufmann, R. J. Suckling and Davenant satirized by Brome. MLR 55 1960.
— Brome: Caroline playwright. New York 1961.
Crowther, J. W. The literary history of A joviall crew. In Studies in English Renaissance literature, ed W. F. McNeir, Baton Rouge 1962.
Cutts, J. The anonymous masque-like entertainment in Egerton ms 1994 and Brome. Comparative Drama 1 1967.
Freehafter, J. Brome, Suckling and Davenant's theatre project of 1639. Texas Stud in Lit & Lang 10 1968.
Donaldson, I. In his World upside-down: comedy from Jonson to Fielding, Oxford 1970. On Antipodes.

WILLIAM BROWNE OF TAVISTOCK
1590?–1645?

For Browne's Inner Temple masque, see col 1195, above.

HENRY BURKHEAD
fl. 1640–5

A tragedy of Cola's furie: or Lirenda's miserie, written by Henry Burkhead. 1645.
Burkhead has been suggested as the author of the anon The female rebellion; see col 1759, below.

HENRY BURNELL
fl. 1641

Landgartha: a tragie-comedy, as it was presented in the new theater in Dublin, being an ancient story, written by H.B. 1641.

THOMAS CAMPION
1567–1620

For Campion's masques, see col 1069, above.

THOMAS CAREW
1595?–1640

For Carew's masque Coelum britannicum, see col 1207, above.

LODOWICK CARLELL
1601 or 1602-1675

§1

The deserving favorite, as it was lately acted first before the Kings Majestie, and since publikely at the Black-friers by his Majesties servants. 1629, 1659; ed C. H. Gray 1905, below.

Arviragus and Philicia, as it was acted at the private house in Black-fryers by his Majesties servants: the first and second part. 1639. Mss: (1) Bodley ms English miscellany d. 11; (2) Petworth House ms owned by Lord Leconfield; *see* J. E. Ruoff, A 'lost' manuscript of Carlell's Arviragus and Philicia, N & Q Jan 1955.

The passionate lovers: a tragi-comedy, the first and second parts, twice presented before the King and Queens Majesties at Somerset-House, and very often at the private house in Black-friars by his late Majesties servants. 1655 (2 issues, one 8°, the other 4°).

Two new playes, viz: 1. The fool would be a favourit, or the discreet lover; 2, Osmund the great Turk: or the noble servant, as they have been often acted by the Queen's Majesty's servants. 1657; ed A. Nicholl 1926.

Heraclius, Emperour of the East: a tragedy, written in French by Monsieur de Corneille, englished by Lodowick Carlell esq. 1664.

§2

Gray, C. H. Carliell: his life, a discussion of his plays and the Deserving favourite, a tragi-comedy. Chicago 1905.

Harbage, A. In his Cavalier drama, New York 1936.

Mills, L. J. One soul in bodies twain. 1937.

Ruoff, J. E. A 'lost' manuscript of Carlell's Arviragus and Philicia. N & Q Jan 1955. Reply by M. Toynbee and Sir Gyles Isham, May 1955.

— The dating of Carlell's Passionate lovers. N & Q Feb 1956.

— Carlell after 1660. N & Q Jan 1957.

Duncan-Jones, E. E. The two Osmund plays. N & Q April 1961.

GEORGE CARTWRIGHT
fl. 1650

The heroick-lover: or the infanta of Spaine. 1661. According to dedication to Charles II, 'penn'd many years ago'.

WILLIAM CARTWRIGHT
1611-43

See col 1302, below.

LADY ELIZABETH CARY
1586-1639

The tragedy of Mariam, written by that truly noble Ladie E.C. 1613, 1613; ed A. C. Dunstan and W. W. Greg 1914 (Malone Soc). Written 1602-5. *See* A. C. Dunstan, Examination of two English dramas: the Tragedy of Mariam by Elizabeth Cary and the True tragedy of Herod and Antipater by Markham and Sampson, Königsberg 1908.

HENRY CARY,
VISCOUNT FALKLAND
1634-63

§1

The marriage night. 1664; ed R. Dodsley, A select collection of old plays vol 10, 1744; ed W. C. Hazlitt, Dodsley vol 15, 1876.

§2

Bowers, F. T. In his Elizabethan revenge tragedy, Princeton 1940. Henry confused with George Cary.

Rothstein, E. In his Restoration tragedy, Madison 1967.

MARGARET CAVENDISH,
DUCHESS OF NEWCASTLE
1623-73

§1

Playes written by the thrice noble, illustrious and excellent Princess the Lady Marchioness of Newcastle. 1622. Contains the following plays, all unacted: Loves adventures (2 pts); Several wits: the wise wit, the wild wit, the cholerick wit, the humble wit; Youths glory and deaths banquet (2 pts); The lady contemplation (2 pts); Wits cabal (2 pts); The unnatural tragedie; The publick wooing; The matrimonial trouble (2 pts); Natures three daughters, beauty, love and wit (2 pts); The religious; The comical hash; Bell in campo (2 pts); The apocriphal ladies; The female academy.

Plays never before printed. 1668. Contains the following plays, all unacted: The social be companions, or the female wits; The presence; The bridals; The convent of pleasure; and fragments.

§2

Perry, H. T. E. The first Duchess of Newcastle and her husband as figures in literary history. Cambridge Mass 1921.

Grant, D. Margaret the First: a biography of Margaret Cavendish Duchess of Newcastle. 1957.

For the Duchess's non-dramatic works, see col 1303 above.

WILLIAM CAVENDISH,
1st DUKE OF NEWCASTLE
1592-1676

§1

The country captaine: a comoedye, lately presented by his Majesties servants at the Blackfryers. In The country captaine, and the Varietie: two comedies written by a person of honor, Hague 1649. BM ms Harley 7650; ed A. H. Bullen and attributed to James Shirley as Captain Underwit, Old English plays vol 2, 1883. *For the view that Shirley may have aided in the authorship, see Bentley III. 148.*

The varietie: a comoedy, lately presented by his Majesties servants at the Black-friers. In Country captaine, and the Varietie, above.

Sir Martin Mar-all: or the feign'd innocence. 1668. With Dryden.

The humorous lovers: a comedy, acted by his Royal Highnes's servants. 1677. BM ms Harley 7367, article I.

A pleasant and merry humour of a rogue. Ms in lib of Duke of Portland, Welbeck Abbey; ed F. Needham, Welbeck miscellany no 1, 1933.

The triumphant widow: or the medley of humours. 1677. An elaboration of A pleasant and merry humour of a rogue, above. With Shadwell.

§2

Perry, H. T. E. The first Duchess of Newcastle and her husband as figures in literary history. Boston 1918.
Mandach, A. de. Molière et la comédie de moeurs en Angleterre. Neuchâtel 1946.
Moore, F. H. The nobler pleasure. Chapel Hill 1963.

ROBERT CHAMBERLAIN
1607–c. 1640

A new book of mistakes. 1637.
Nocturnal lucubrations. 1638.
Conceits, clinches, flashes and whimzies, newly studied. 1639, 1640 (enlarged as Jocabella: or a cabinet of mistakes).
The swaggering damsell: a comedy, written by R.C. 1640.

WILLIAM CHAMBERLAYNE
1619–89

See col 1304, above.

JOHN CLAVELL
1601–43

§1

A recantation of an ill led life: or a discoverie of the high-way law, with vehement dissuasions of all (in that kind) offenders. 1628, 1628, 1634.
The soddered citizen. Ms in private collection of Lt-Col E. G. Troyte-Bullock, Zeals House, Mere, Wilts; ed J. H. P. Pafford and W. W. Greg 1936 (Malone Soc). The play dates from c. 1630.

§2

Lawless, D. S. and J. H. P. Pafford. Clavell: highwayman, author and quack doctor. N & Q Jan 1957.

SIR ASTON COKAYNE
1608–84

Collections

Small poems of divers sorts. 1658 (contains The obstinate lady, Trappolin and A masque), 1658 (as A chain of golden poems) (some copies dated 1659), 1662 (as Poems with the Tragedy of Ovid added), 1662, 1669 (as Choice poems of several sorts).
Dramatic works. Ed J. Maidment and W. H. Logan, Edinburgh 1874.
Poems. Ed A. E. Cockayne 1877.
Dramen. Ed H. Spaemann, Münster 1923.

§1

The obstinate lady: a new comedy never formerly published; the scene London. 1657, 1658 (in Small poems), 1658 (in A chain of golden poems), 1662 (in Poems), 1662, 1669 (in Choice poems).
A masque presented at Bretbie in Darbyshire on twelfth-night 1639. 1658 (in Small poems), 1658 (in A chain of golden poems), 1662 (in Poems), 1662, 1669 (in Choice poems).
Trappolin creduto principe: or Trappolin suppos'd a Prince, an Italian trage-comedy, the scene part of Italy. 1658 (in Small poems), 1658 (in A chain of golden

poems), 1662 (in Poems), 1662, 1669 (in Choice poems).
The tragedy of Ovid. 1662 (in Poems), 1662, 1669 (in Choice poems).

§2

Lea, K. M. Cokayne and the commedia dell'arte. MLR 23 1928.
Burns, M. The devil of a Duke. TLS 18 July 1929.
Kaufman, H. A. Trappolin supposed a Prince and Measure for measure. MLQ 18 1957.

JOHN COOKE
fl. 1612

Greene's Tu quoque: or the cittie gallant, as it hath beene divers times acted by the Queenes Majesties servants, written by Jo. Cooke, gent. 1614, 1622, [after 21 May 1628]; ed R. Dodsley, A select collection of old plays vol 3, 1744; ed I. Reed, Dodsley vol 7, 1780; Ancient British drama vol 2, 1810; ed J. P. Collier, Dodsley vol 7, 1825; ed W. C. Hazlitt, Dodsley vol 11, 1875; TFT 1913.

ABRAHAM COWLEY
1618–67

See col 1219, above.

ROBERT COX
1604?–55?

Actaeon and Diana, with a pastorall story of the nymph Oenone, followed by the severall conceited humors of Bumpkin the huntsman, Hobbinall the shepheard, Singing Simpkin, and John Swabber the seaman. [1655], 1656 (with the additional 'droll' Simpleton the smith) rptd in part in The wits: or sport upon sport pt 1, 1662, 1672; pt 2, 1673 (2 issues, one 4°, the other 8°); rptd W. R. Chetwood, A select collection of old plays, 1750; ed J. J. Elson, Ithaca 1932 (with 3 drolls by Cox not included in Wits). See H. E. Rollins, Contribution to the history of the English Commonwealth drama, SP 18 1921, 20 1923; TLS 3–10, 24 Aug 1922.

ROBERT DABORNE
d. 1628

§1

A Christian turn'd Turke: or the tragicall lives and deaths of the two famous pirates, Ward and Dansiker, as it hath been publickly acted. 1621; ed A. E. H. Swaen, Anglia 20 1898.
The poor-mans comfort: a tragi-comedy, as it was divers times acted at the Cock-pit in Drury Lane with great applause. 1655; ed A. R. H. Swaen, Anglia 21 1899. BM ms Egerton 1995, ff. 268–93; ed K. Palmer 1955 (Malone Soc).

§2

Greg, W. W. (ed). In Henslowe papers: being documents supplementary to Henslowe's Diary, 1907.
Boas, F. S. In his Shakespeare and the universities, 1923.
Flood, W. H. G. Fennor and Daborne at Youghal in 1618. MLR 20 1925.
Oliphant, E. H. C. In his Plays of Beaumont and Fletcher, New Haven 1927.
Bacon, W. A. The source of the Poor man's comfort. MLN 57 1942. Warner's Syrinx.

McManaway, J. G. Additional notes on 'the great Danseker'. MLR 47 1952. 2 edns of 1609 newsbook about the pirates Ward and Danseker.

Henslowe's Diary. Ed R. A. Foakes and R. T. Rickert, Cambridge 1961.

Maxwell, B. Notes on Daborne's extant plays. PQ 50 1971.

SIR WILLIAM DAVENANT
1606–68

See col 1208, above.

ROBERT DAVENPORT
fl. 1624–40

Collections

Works. Ed A. H. Bullen, Old English plays, new ser vol 3, 1890.

§1

A dialogue between polity and piety [c. 1635]. Folger Lib ms v.a.313.

A pleasant and witty comedy called A new tricke to cheat the Divell, written by R.D. gent. 1639.

King John and Matilda: a tragedy, as it was acted by her Majesties servants at the Cock-pit in Drury-lane. 1655, 1662; ed W. A. Armstrong, Elizabethan historical plays, Oxford 1965 (WC).

The city-night-cap, or crede quod habes & habes: a tragi-comedy, as it was acted by her Majesties servants at the Phoenix in Drury Lane. 1661; ed R. Dodsley, A select collection of old plays vol 9, 1744; ed I. Reed, Dodsley vol 11, 1780; Ancient British drama vol 3, 1810; ed J. P. Collier, Dodsley vol 11, 1827; ed W. C. Hazlitt, Dodsley vol 13, 1875.

§2

Retrospective Rev 4 1821.

Swinburne, A. C. In his Contemporaries of Shakespeare, 1919.

Jordan, J. C. The city night-cap and Greene's Philomela. MLN 36 1921. *See also* J. S. Dean, Borrowings from Philomela in the City-night-cap, N & Q Aug 1966.

Eckhardt, E. Davenports Lustspiel A new trick to cheat the devil. Anglia 59 1935.

McManaway, J. G. Ms of Davenport's Policy without piety: John Withorn, Sir John Kaye. N & Q 25 April 1936.

— Latin title-page mottoes as a clue to dramatic authorship. Library 4th ser 26 1946. Suggests Davenport as the author of anon Dick of Devonshire, generally attributed to Heywood, and of anon Bloody banquet. *See also* McManaway's introd to his edn of Dick of Devonshire, 1955 (Malone Soc).

Harbage, A. Elizabethan-Restoration palimpsest. MLR 35 1940.

Olive, W. J. Shakespeare parody in A new tricke to cheat the Divell. MLN 66 1951.

Ribner, I. In his English history play in the age of Shakespeare, Princeton 1957.

Maxwell, J. C. Notes on King John and Matilda. N & Q June 1967.

SIR JOHN DENHAM
1615–69

See col 1217, above.

SIR WILLIAM DENNY
1603?–76

The sheepheard's holiday. BM additional ms 34,065; ed W. C. Hazlitt, Huth's Inedited poetical miscellanies 1584–1700, 1870.

GEORGE GERBIER D'OUVILLY

The false favourite disgrac'd and the reward of loyalty: a tragi-comedy, never acted. 1657, 1657.

THOMAS DRUE
fl. 1623

§1

The life of the Duchess of Suffolke. 1631.

The anon Bloody banquet *has been attributed to Drue: see col 1758, below.*

§2

Lawrence, W. J. Found: a missing Jacobean dramatist. TLS 23 March 1922, 12 July 1923.

Neill, J. K. Drue's Dutches of Suffolke and the succession. MLN 48 1933.

Oliver, L. M. Drue's Duchess of Suffolk: a Protestant drama. SB 3 1951.

MILDMAY FANE,
EARL OF WESTMORLAND
1602–66

§1

Raguaillo D'Oceano: this show was written and prepared to be acted in anno 1640. BM additional ms 34,221, ff. 107^{v}–23^{r}; ed C. Leach, Louvain 1938.

Candia restaurata presented in a shew at Apthorpe the 12th of February 1640 [i.e. 1641] to the lord and lady of that place by some of their owne children and famely. Mss: (1) Huntington Lib ms HM 771; (2) BM additional ms 34,221, ff. 1^{v}–18^{v}; ed C. Leech, Louvain 1938.

The change: a showe written in December 1642. BM additional ms 34,221, ff. 50^{r}–68^{v}.

Tymes trick upon the cards, prepared to be represented at Apthorpe by the youth and servantes their the 22th of February 1641 [i.e. 1642]. BM additional ms 34,221, ff. 19^{v}–49.^{v}

Virtues triumph: this comedy was writt in anno 1644. BM additional ms 34,221, ff. 69^{v}–106^{v}.

Don Phoebo's triumph. [1645]. Huntington Lib ms HM 770.

Otia sacra. 1648 (priv ptd). Poems.

De pugna animi. [1650]. BM additional ms 34,221, ff. 124^{v}–47^{r}.

Of the art of well governing a people. Tr from Italian; incomplete. BM additional ms 34,251.

Autobiography. In Latin; c. 1662. BM additional ms 34,220.

Poems. Ed A. B. Grosart, Manchester 1879.

Fugitive verses. *See* Historical Mss Commission, Earl of Westmorland mss: 10th report, 1885.

A seventeenth-century poem: It well becomes ye glory of ye press. Life & Letters 51 1946.

§2

Harbage, A. An unnoted Caroline dramatist. SP 31 1934.

Leech, C. A 'drame of ease'. TLS 11 Jan 1936.

Withington, E. The 'fugitive poetry' of Mildmay Fane. Harvard Lib Bull 9 1955.
— Mildmay Fane's political satire. Harvard Lib Bull 11 1957.

SIR RICHARD FANSHAWE
1608–66

§1

Il pastor fido, the faithful shepherd: a pastorall written in Italian by Baptista Guarini, and now newly translated. 1647 (anon), 1648 ('with an addition of divers other poems'), 1664, 1676, 1692, 1736; ed W. F. Staton and W. E. Simeone, Oxford 1964.
Selected parts of Horace, prince of lyricks, concluding with a piece out of Ausonius and another out of Virgil, now newly put into English. 1652.
The Lusiad: or Portugals historicall poem. 1655; ed J. D. M. Ford, Cambridge Mass 1940; ed G. Bullough 1963. Tr from Camoens.
La fida pastora [i.e. Fletcher's Faithful shepherdess]: comoedia pastoralis, autore F.F. Anglo-Britanno; adduntur nonnulla varii argumenti carmina ab eodem. 1658.
Querer por solo querer, To love only for love sake: a dramatick romance by Antonio de Mendoza, paraphrased in English anno 1654. 1670, 1671. BM additional ms 32,133.
Original letters of his Excellency Sir Richard Fanshawe during his embassies in Spain and Portugal. 2 vols 1702–24.
Memoirs of Lady Fanshawe, to which are added extracts from the correspondence of Fanshawe. Ed H. Nicholas 1829; ed B. Marshall 1905; ed E. J. Fanshawe 1907.
Historical Mss Commission. The mss of J. M. Heathcote of Conington Castle. Ed S. C. Lomas, Norwich 1899. Includes Fanshawe's correspondence.
The fourth book of Vergil's Aeneid. Ed A. L. Irvine, Oxford 1929.
Shorter poems and translations. Ed N. W. Bawcutt, Liverpool 1964.

§2

Mackail, J. W. Sir Richard Fanshawe. Trans Royal Soc Lit 1909; rptd in his Studies of English poets, 1926.
Harbage, A. Fanshawe and Hobbes's Leviathan. TLS 30 June 1932.
Ford, J. D. M. The first translator of the Lusiades of Camoens. Annual Bull Modern Humanities Research Assoc 17 1938.
Simeone, W. E. A letter from Fanshawe to John Evelyn. N & Q 21 July 1951.
— A probable antecedent of Marvell's Horatian ode. N & Q 19 July 1952.
Bullough, G. Fanshawe and Guarini. In Studies in English language and literature presented to K. Brunner, Vienna and Stuttgart 1958.
Hunter, G. K. Pope's imitation of Fanshawe. N & Q May 1959.
Buxton, J. In his A tradition of poetry, 1967.

NATHAN FIELD
1587–1619 or 1620

Collections
Plays. Ed W. Peery, Austin 1950.

§1

A woman is a weather-cocke: a new comedy, as it was acted before the King in White-hall, and divers times privately at the White-friers, by the children of her Majesties revels. 1612; rptd T. White, Old English drama vol 2, 1830; ed J. P. Collier, Five old plays, 1833; ed W. C. Hazlitt, Dodsley vol 11, 1875; ed A. W. Verity, Nero and other plays, 1888 (Mermaid ser).
Amends for ladies: a comedie, as it was acted at the Blacke-fryers, both by the Princes servants, and the Lady Elizabeths. 1618, 1618 (as Amends for ladies, with the humour of roring: a comedie), 1639 (Amends for ladies, with the merry prankes of Moll Cut-Purse, or the humour of roaring: a comedy full of honest mirth and wit); rptd T. White, Old English drama vol 2, 1830; ed J. P. Collier, Five old plays, 1833; ed W. C. Hazlitt, Dodsley vol 11, 1875; ed A. W. Verity, Nero and other plays, 1888 (Mermaid ser).
The fatall dowry: a tragedy, written by P.M. and N.F. 1632. With Massinger, col 1704, above.
Four plays or moral representations in one. 1647. With Fletcher; see Beaumont and Fletcher, col 1709, above.
The honest man's fortune. 1647. With Fletcher and Massinger; see under Beaumont and Fletcher, col 1709, above.
The knight of Malta. 1647. With Fletcher and Massinger: see under Beaumont and Fletcher, col 1709, above.
The Queen of Corinth. 1647. With Fletcher and Massinger; see under Beaumont and Fletcher, col 1709, above.

§2

Halliwell(-Phillipps), J. O. The remonstrance of Field addressed to a preacher in Southwark who had been arraigning against the players at the Globe theatre in the year 1616, now first edited from the original manuscript. 1865; rptd in his Illustrations of the life of Shakespeare, 1874.
Beck, C. Philip Massinger, The fatall dowry: Einleitung zu einer neuen Ausgabe. Erlangen 1906.
Fischer, H. Fields Komödie Amends for ladies. Kiel 1907.
Greg, W. W. (ed). In his Henslowe papers: being documents supplementary to Henslowe's Diary, 1907.
— Field and the Beaumont and Fletcher folio of 1679. RES 3 1927.
Sykes, H. D. Field's work in the Beaumont and Fletcher plays. N & Q 19 Feb–12 March 1921; rptd in his Sidelights on Elizabethan drama, 1924.
Chelli, M. Etude sur la collaboration de Massinger avec Fletcher et son groupe. Paris 1926.
Brinkley, R. F. Nathan and Nathaniel Field. MLN 42 1927.
— Field: the actor-playwright. New Haven 1928.
Oliphant, E. H. C. The plays of Beaumont and Fletcher. New Haven 1927.
— MLN 42–3 1927–8. On F. L. Fenton.
Lawrence, W. J. A puzzling point in A woman is a weathercock. TLS 12 July 1928.
Aronstein, P. In his Das englische Renaissance-Drama, Leipzig 1929.
Peery, W. The curious impertinent in Amends for ladies. Hispanic Rev 14 1946.
— The influence of Jonson on Field. SP 43 1946.
— Field's dates. MLR 41 1946.
— The portrayal of woman in the comedies of Field. Shakespeare Assoc Bull 21 1946.
— Note on a commonplace: the three souls. PQ 25 1946.
— Eastward ho! and A woman is a weather-cocke. MLN 62 1947.
— Nineteenth-century editorial practice as illustrated in the descent of the text of Field. SE 1947.
— Shakespeare and Field. Neophilologus 34 1950.
Scott, F. R. Teg the stage Irishman. MLR 42 1947. Amends for ladies.
Verhasselt, E. A biography of Field: dramatist and actor. Revue Belge 25 1947.
Gerritsen, J. (ed). The honest man's fortune. Groningen 1952. Introd attributing the play to Fletcher, Massinger, Tourneur and Field.

Blayney, G. H. Field's parody of a murder play. N & Q Jan 1955.
—— Field and the Faerie Queene. N & Q Feb 1955
Hoy, C. The shares of Fletcher and his collaborators in the Beaumont and Fletcher canon pt 4. SB 12 1959. Field's share in Four plays in one, Honest man's fortune, Knight of Malta, and Queen of Corinth.

THOMAS FORDE
fl. 1647–1661
See col 2050, below.

SIR RALPH FREEMAN
c. 1590–1667

§ 1

L. A. Seneca, the philosopher, his booke of consolation to Marcia, translated into an English poem. 1635.
Imperiale, a tragedie. 1639, 1640, 1655. BM ms Egerton 2948.
Lucius Annaeus Seneca, the philosopher, his booke of the shortnesse of life, translated into an English poem. 1662 ('second edn').

§ 2

Gumm, C. C. Sir Ralph Freeman's Imperiale. In Studies in English drama: first series, ed A. Gaw, New York 1917.
Richards, K. The sources of Freeman's Imperiale. Studia Neophilologica 40 1968.

HENRY GLAPTHORNE
1610–after 1643

Collections
Plays and poems. Ed R. H. Shepherd 2 vols 1874.

§ 1

Argalus and Pathenia, as it hath been acted at the Court before their Majesties, and at the private-house in Drury-Lane, by their Majesties servants. 1639.
Poems. 1639.
The tragedy of Albertus Wallenstein, late Duke of Fridland and generall to the Emperor Ferdinand the Second, acted at the Globe on the Banke-side by his Majesties servants. 1639 (some copies dated 1640); rptd C. Baldwin, Old English drama vol 2, 1825.
The Hollander: a comedy written 1635, and now printed as it was then acted at the Cock-pit in Drury lane by their Majesties servants and at the Court before both their Majesties. 1640.
The ladies priviledge, as it was acted at the Cock-pit in Drury-lane, and before their Majesties at White-Hall twice, by their Majesties servants. 1640; rptd C. Baldwin, Old English drama vol 2, 1825.
Wit in a constable: a comedy written 1639, and now printed as it was lately acted at the Cock-pit in Drury lane by their Majesties servants. 1640.
His Majesties gracious answer to the message sent from the honourable citie of London concerning peace. 1643.
White-Hall: a poem written 1642, with Elegies on the Right Honourable Francis Earl of Bedford and Henry Earle of Manchester, Lord Privy Seale, both deceased during this present session of Parliament; with an anniversarie on the timelesse death of Mrs Anne Kirk, wife to the truly Noble Geo. Kirk, gentleman of the robes and of his Majesties bed chamber, drowned unfortunately passing London Bridge, July 7 1641. 1643.

Revenge for honour: a tragedie, by George Chapman. 1654, 1654, 1659. Included in some collections of Chapman, col 1637 above, though the ascription to him is generally rejected; *see* Bentley IV.489–93.
The lady mother. BM ms Egerton 1994, ff. 212–45; ed A. H. Bullen, Old English plays vol 2, 1883; ed A. Brown 1959 (Malone Soc).

§ 2

Retrospective Rev 10 1824.
Zwickert, M. Henry Glapthorne. 1881.
Nicholson, B. Glapthorne's Albertus Wallenstein, editions 1639, 1640. N & Q 16 Feb 1889.
Koeppel, E. Die Chapman zugeschriebene Tragödie Revenge for honour. Beiblatt zur Anglia 18 1907.
Thomas, D. L. Authorship of Revenge for honour. MP 5 1908.
—— Concerning Wit in a constable. JEGP 14 1915.
Adams, J. Q. Some notes on Glapthorne's Wit in a constable. JEGP 13 1914.
Cosulich, G. Revenge for honour and Othello. MLN 29 1914.
Sykes, H. D. Revenge for honour: Glapthorne's play attributed to Chapman. N & Q 20 May 1916.
—— Glapthorne's play: the Lady mother. N & Q 29 Dec 1923.
Beckingham, C. F. Othello and Revenge for honour. RES 11 1935.
Walter, J. H. Henry Glapthorne. TLS 19 Sept 1936.
—— Revenge for honour: date, authorship and sources. RES 13 1937. Reply by F. T. Bowers 14 1938.
—— Wit in a constable: censorship and revision. MLR 34 1939.
Bowers, F. T. The date of Revenge for honour. MLN 52 1937. Reply by C. L. Shaver 53 1938.
Leech, C. In his Shakespeare's tragedies and other studies in seventeenth-century drama, 1950.
Cutts, J. P. William Lowe's writing for the theatre and the Court. Library 5th ser 7 1952. Setting in BM additional ms 31,432 for song beginning Love's a child from Argalus and Parthenia.
Davis, J. L. The sons of Ben: Jonsonian comedy in Caroline England.

THOMAS GOFFE
c. 1591–1629

§ 1

The raging Turke, or Bajazet the Second: a tragedie written by Thomas Goffe of Christ-Church in Oxford, and acted by the students of the same house. 1631.
The couragious Turke, or Amurath the First: a tragedie written by Thomas Goffe, Master of Arts and student of Christ-Church in Oxford, and acted by the students of the same house. 1632. Mss: (1) The tragedy of Amurath third tyrant of the Turkes, ms in lib of John Leicester-Warren, Tabley House, Knutsford Cheshire (Historical Mss Commission: first report, appendix 1, 1870); (2), Harvard Univ ms Thr 10.1, ff. 57–71 (an actor's part).
The tragedy of Orestes, written by Thomas Goffe, Master of Arts and student of Christs Church in Oxford, and acted by the students of the same house. 1633.
Three excellent tragoedies, viz the Raging Turk, the Couragious Turk and the Tragoedie of Orestes: the second edition, carefully corrected by a friend of the author. 1656.
The careles shepherdess: a tragi-comedy, acted before the King and Queen, and at Salisbury-Court, written by T.G. Mr of Arts. 1656.

§2

Briggs, W. D. The influence of Jonson's tragedy in the seventeenth century. Anglia 35 1912.

Lawrence, W. J. Goffe's The careless shepherdess. MLR 14 1919.

—— The authorship of the Careless shepherdess. TLS July 24 1924.

Thaler, A. Goffe's Praeludium. MLN 36 1921.

Harbage, A. Notes on manuscript plays. TLS 20 June 1936.

O'Donnell, N. F. Shakespeare, Marston and the university: the sources of Goffe's Orestes. SP 50 1953.

—— The authorship of the Careless shepherdess. PQ 33 1954. Attributes to John Gough instead of Thomas Goffe.

—— A lost Jacobean Phoenissae. MLN 69 1954.

Cutts, J. P. Goffe's The courageous Turke. N & Q Aug 1955.

FRANCIS GOLDSMITH
1613-55

Hugo Grotius his Sophompaneas, or Joseph: a tragedy. 1652.

ROBERT GOMERSALL
1602?-44?

See col 1309, above.

JOHN GOUGH
c. 1610-61

The strange discovery: a tragi-comedy. 1640. *See* N. F. O'Donnell, PQ 33 1954, for the suggestion that Gough, not Thomas Goffe, is the author of Careless shepherdess.

WILLIAM HABINGTON
1605-54

See col 1208, above.

SAMUEL HARDING
1616 or 1618-99?

Sicily and Naples, or the fatall union: a tragoedy, by S.H. 1640.

WILLIAM HAWKINS
1602?-37

Apollo shroving composed for the schollars of the Free-schoole of Hadleigh in Suffolke, and acted by them on Shrove-tuesday, being the sixt of February 1626 [i.e. 1627]. [c. 1627] (anon); ed H. G. Rhoads, Philadelphia 1936.

Hawkins also pbd several collections of Latin verse.

WILLIAM HEMINGES
1602-before 1653

§1

The fatal contract: a French tragedy, as it was acted by her Majesties servants. 1653, 1654, 1661, 1687 (as The eunuch: a tragedy).

The Jewes tragedy: or their fatal and final overthrow by Vespatian and Titus his son, agreeable to the authentick and famous history of Josephus. 1662; ed H. A. Cohn, Bang vol 40, 1913.

The time poets. Ed J. J. Parry, JEGP 19 1920.

William Hemminge's Elegy on Randolph's finger. Ed G. C. Moore Smith, Oxford 1923.

§2

Junge, O. The fatal contract, a French tragedy by William Hemings: kritische Neuausgabe mit Einleitung und Anmerkungen. Strasbourg 1912. Introd for an edn.

Adams, J. Q. Heminge and Shakespeare. MP 12 1914.

Heming's Time poets. TLS 24 May 1923.

Bowers, F. T. In his Elizabethan revenge tragedy, Princeton 1940.

FRANCIS JACQUES
fl. 1642

§1

The Queen of Corsica: a tragedy written by Fran: Jaques anno dom: 1642. BM ms Lansdowne 807, ff. 2-28.

§2

Leech, C. Jaques: author of the Queene of Corsica. Durham Univ Jnl 8 1947.

JOHN JONES
fl. 1635

Adrasta, or the womans spleene and loves conquest: a tragi-comedie, never acted. 1635.

THOMAS JORDAN
c. 1620-85?

§1

Poetical varieties. 1637. For Jordan's numerous later books of verse, *see* D. G. Wing, Short-title catalogue 1641-1700.

Cupid his coronation in a mask as it was presented at the Spittle diverse tymes by masters and yong ladyes that were theyre scholers, in the year 1654. Bodley ms Rawlinson B. 165 ff. 190-13.

Fancy's festivals: a masque, as it hath been privately presented by many civil persons of quality, and now at their requests newly printed. 1657, nd. A dramatic medley incorporating Cupid his coronation.

The walks of Islington and Hogsdon, with the humours of Woodstreet-Compter: a comedy, as it was publikely acted 19. days together. 1657, nd (as Tricks of youth: or the walks of Islington and Hogsdon, with the humours of Woodstreet-Compter).

Bacchus' festival, or a new medley: being a musical representation at the entertainment of his Excellency the Lord General Monk at Vintners' Hall, 12 April [1660]. 1660.

A new droll, or the counter-scuffle: the second part. 1663.

Money is an asse: a comedy. 1668, nd (as Wealth outwitted: or money's an ass).

Jordan wrote the Lord Mayors' pageants every year from 1671 to 1684. He has been suggested as author of the anon The wasp; see col 1762, below. For his prose pamphlets see Wing, Short-title catalogue.

§2

Lord Mayor's pageants. Ed F. W. Fairholt 1843-4 (Percy Soc.).

Thorn-Drury, G. Jordan's Money is an ass. RES 1 1925.

Baskervill, C. R. In his Elizabethan jig, 1929.
Gourlay, J. J. Thomas Jordan. TLS 17 Aug 1933.
—— A Caroline play, The wasp. TLS 5 June 1943.
Leech, C. Jordan's interregnum masques. TLS 12 April
1934. *See also* P. A. Scholes 14 June, C. Leech 28 June
1934.
Stevenson, A. H. James Shirley and the actors at the first
Irish theatre. MP 40 1942.
Eisley, R. C. God and the soldier. N & Q 10 May 1952.
Howarth, R. G. A poem by Carew? N & Q 22 Nov 1952.
Pinsent, P. A. Plagiarism by Jordan. N & Q Sept 1967.

HENRY KILLIGREW
1613–1700

§ 1

The conspiracy: a tragedy, as it was intended for the
nuptialls of the Lord Charles Herbert and the Lady
Villers. 1638, 1653 (as Pallantus and Eudora: a
tragoedia).

§ 2

Neimeyer, C. Killigrew and the Duke of Buckingham.
RES 12 1936.

THOMAS KILLIGREW
1612–83

§ 1

The prisoners: a tragae-comedy, as it was presented at the
Phoenix in Drury-Lane by her Majesties servants. 1640
(separate title-page in 12° edn of Prisoners and Claracilla; the joint title-page is dated 1641).
Claracilla: a tragae-comedy, as it was presented at the
Phoenix in Drury-Lane by her Majesties servants. 1641
(separate title-page in 12° of 1641). Ms: Castle Howard
lib.
Comedies and tragedies. 1644. Includes, each with
separate title-page and all dated 1663 except the last,
which is dated 1664: (1) The Princess, or love at first
sight: a tragi-comedy; (2) The parsons wedding: a
comedy; (3) The pilgrim: a tragedy; (4) The first part
of Cicilia and Clorinda: or love in arms; (5) The second
part of Cicilia and Clorinda; (6) Thomaso, or the
wanderer: a comedy; (7) The second part of Thomaso;
(8) The first part of Bellamira her dream: or the love
of shadows; (9) The second part of Bellamira her dream;
(10) Claricilla; (11) The prisoners. The parson's wedding
ed R. Dodsley, A select collection of old plays vol 9,
1744; ed I. Reed, Dodsley vol 11, 1780; Ancient British
drama vol 3, 1810; ed J. P. Collier, Dodsley vol 11,
1827; ed W. C. Hazlitt, Dodsley vol 14, 1875; ed M.
Summers, Restoration comedies, 1921; ed A. S. Knowland, Six Caroline plays, Oxford 1962 (WC). A ms text
of the 2 pts of Cicilia and Clorinda in Folger Lib ms
v.b.208–9.

§ 2

Ristine, F. H. In his English tragicomedy, New York
1910.
Hotson, L. In his Commonwealth and Restoration stage,
Cambridge Mass 1928.
Harbage, A. Killigrew, Cavalier dramatist. Philadelphia
1930.
Summers, M. In his Playhouse of Pepys, 1935.
Boas, F. S. Killigrew's Claracilla. TLS 18 March 1944.
Van Lennep, W. Killigrew prepares his plays for produc-
tion. In J. Q. Adams memorial studies, Washington
1948.
Stoye, J. W. The whereabouts of Thomas Killigrew
1639–41. RES 25 1949.

Keast, W. R. Killigrew's use of Donne in the Parson's
wedding. MLR 45 1950.
Wertheim, A. Fraternity and the catches in two Restoration theater productions. Jnl Catch Soc of America
1 1969. On Killigrew's Princess and Fletcher's Knight
of Malta.

JOHN KIRKE
fl. 1629–42?

§ 1

The seven champions of Christendome, acted at the Cocke-
pit and at the Red-Bull in St Johns Streete, written by
J.K. 1638; rptd T. White, Old English drama vol 3,
1830; ed G. E. Dawson, Western Reserve Univ Bull 32
1929.

§ 2

Lawrence, W. J. Kirke: the Caroline actor-dramatist.
SP 21 1924.

R. KIRKHAM

Alfrede or right reinthron'd: being a tragicomedie. 1659.
Bodley ms Rawlinson poetry 80.

RALPH KNEVET
1600–71

§ 1

Στρατιωτικόν: or a discourse of militarie discipline.
1628.
Rhodon and Iris: a pastorall, as it was presented at the
florists feast in Norwich, May 3 1631. 1631.
Funerall elegies consecrated to the immortal memory of
the Lady Katherine Paston. 1637.
A gallery to the temple: lyricall poemes upon sacred
occasions. BM ms additional 27,447; ed G. Pellegrini,
Pisa 1954.
See also col 1313, above.

§ 2

Smith, H. Pastoral influence in the English drama. PMLA
12 1897.
Laidler, J. A history of pastoral drama in England until
1700. E Studien 35 1905.
Greg, W. W. In his Pastoral poetry and pastoral drama,
1906.
Millican, C. B. Knevet: author of the 'supplement' to
Spenser's Faerie Queene. RES 14 1938; rptd 1938.
Charles, A. M. The ms of Knevet's Gallery to the temple.
N & Q May 1959.
Merchant, W. M. Knevet of Norfolk: poet of Civill warre.
E & S new ser 13 1960.

SIR WILLIAM LOWER
c. 1600–62

§ 1

The phaenix in her flames: a tragedy. 1639.
Polyeuctes, or the martyr. 1655. Tr from Corneille.
Horatius: a Roman tragedie. 1656. Tr from Corneille.
The enchanted lovers: a pastoral. Hague 1658, London
1659, 1661; in Three new playes, 1661; ed W. B. Gates,
Dramatic works and trns of Lower, Philadelphia 1932.
Folger Lib ms J.b.2 (adapted and combined with
Davenport's City night cap).

The noble ingratitude: a pastoral tragi-comedy. Hague 1659, London 1661; in Three new plays, 1661. Tr from Quinault.
The amourous fantasme: a tragi-comedy. Hague 1660, London 1661; in Three new plays, 1661. Tr from Quinault.
Don Japhet of Armenia. Bm additional ms 28,723. Tr from Scarron.
The three Dorothies: or Jodelet boxed. Ms formerly in collection at Skeffington Hall. Tr from Scarron.

§ 2

Gates, W. B. Dramatic works and translations of Lower. Philadelphia 1932.

JAMES MABBE
1572-1642?

§ 1

The Spanish bawd, represented in Celestina: or the tragicke-comedy of Calisto and Melibea. 1631, 1634 (with 3rd edn of Mabbe's trn of M. Aleman, The rogue: or the life of Guzman de Alfarache); ed J. Fitzmaurice-Kelly 1894; ed H. W. Allen 1908; 1923 (tr from de Rojas). Ms, probably of this play, reported at Alnwick Castle, Historical Mss Commission 3, 119.
For Mabbe's non-dramatic trns, see cols 2179, 2183, below.

§ 2

Houck, H. P. Mabbe's pagination of the Celestina. PMLA 54 1939.
Secord, A. W. I.M. of the first folio Shakespeare and other Mabbe problems. JEGP 47 1948.
Pierce, F. Mabbe and La espanola inglesa. Revue de Littérature Comparée 23 1949.

LEWIS MACHIN
fl. 1608

See col 2011, below.

COSMO MANUCHE
fl. 1642-64

§ 1

The just general: a tragi-comedy. 1652.
The bastard: a tragedy. 1652. Anon. Usually assigned to Manuche, probably in error.
The loyal lovers: a tragi-comedy. 1652.
The feast. Ms Worcester College, Oxford.
The banish'd shepheardess. Huntington Lib ms EL 8395.
Another ms of Feast and of Banish'd shepheardess, together with the mss of the following otherwise unknown plays of Manuche, were once reported to be in Lord Northampton's lib at Castle Abbey: Agamemnon, The captives, Lenotius King of Cyprus, The mandrake, Mariamni, and an unnamed comedy (actor: Hermenigildus) and tragedy (actors: Macrinus, Papinianus and Ardentius).

§ 2

Ristine, F. H. In his English tragicomedy, New York 1910.
Wagner, B. M. Ms plays of the seventeenth century. TLS 4 Oct 1934.
Watkin-Jones, A. Seventeenth-century plays. TLS 15 Nov 1934.
Harbage, A. In his Cavalier drama, New York 1936.

GERVASE MARKHAM
1568?-1637

See col 1126, above.

SHAKERLEY MARMION
1602-39

Collections
Dramatic works. Ed J. Maidment and W. H. Logan 1875.

§ 1

Hollands leaguer: an excellent comedy, as it hath bin lately and often acted by the high and mighty Prince Charles his servants at the private house in Salisbury Court. 1632.
A fine companion, acted before the King and Queene at White-Hall, and sundrie times at the private house in Salisbury Court by the Prince his servants. 1633.
A morall poem intituled the legend of Cupid and Psyche 1637, 1638, 1666; ed S. W. Singer 1820; ed A. J. Nearing, Philadelphia 1944.
The antiquary: a comedy, acted by her Majesties servants at the Cock-Pit. 1641; ed R. Dodsley, A select collection of old plays vol 7, 1744; ed I. Reed, Dodsley vol 10, 1780; Ancient British drama vol 3, 1810; ed J. P. Collier, Dodsley vol 10, 1826; ed W. C. Hazlitt, Dodsley vol 13, 1875.

§ 2

Kerr, M. In her Influence of Ben Jonson on English comedy, Philadelphia 1912.
Jones, F. L. Echoes of Shakespere in later Elizabethan drama. PMLA 45 1930.
Simpson, P. Ben Jonson and the Devil Tavern. MLR 34 1939.
Miles, T. Place-realism in a group of Caroline plays. RES 18 1942.
Maxwell, S. An addition to the first idyll of Moschus in Imitations to the year 1800. Amer Jnl of Philology 64 1943.
—— A misprint in Holland's leaguer. MLR 39 1944.
Leech, C. In his Shakespeare's tragedies and other studies in seventeenth-century drama, 1950.
Cope, J. I. Marmion and Pope's Rape of the lock. MLN 72 1957.
Davis, J. L. In his Sons of Ben: Jonsonian comedy in Caroline England, Detroit 1967.

JOHN MASON
b. 1581

§ 1

The Turke: a worthie tragedie, as it hath bene divers times acted by the children of his Majestics revels. 1610, 1632 (as An excellent tragedy of Mulleasses the Turke, and Borgias governour of Florence); ed J. Q. Adams, Bang vol 37, 1913.

§ 2

Smith, G. C. M. Mason and Edward Sharpham. MLR 8 1913.
Bowers, F. T. In his Elizabethan revenge tragedy, Princeton 1940.
Wadsworth, F. W. The relationship of Lust's dominion and Mason's The Turke. ELH 20 1953.

JOHN MASON
fl. 1647

§1

Princeps rhetoricus: or Πιλομαχια, the combat of caps 1648. Extracts of an academic play performed by the boys of Mason's school at Camberwell, Surrey, 21 Dec 1647.

§2

Northrup, S. C. On a school play of 1648. E Studien 45 1912.

THOMAS MAY
c. 1595–1650

§1

The heire: an excellent comedie, as it was lately acted by the company of the revels. 1622, 1633; ed R. Dodsley, A select collection of old plays vol 7, 1744; ed I. Reed, Dodsley vol 8, 1780; Ancient British drama vol 1, 1810; ed J. P. Collier, Dodsley vol 8, 1825; ed W. C. Hazlitt, Dodsley vol 11, 1875.
The tragedy of Antigone, the Theban Princesse. 1631.
The tragedie of Cleopatra Queen of Ægypt. 1639, 1654 (singly and bound with Julia Agrippina as Two tragedies). Acted 1626. BM ms Royal 18 c. vii.
The tragedie of Julia Agrippina, Empresse of Rome. 1639, 1654 (singly and bound with Cleopatra as Two tragedies); ed F. E. Schmid, Bang vol 43, 1914.
The old couple: a comedy. 1658; ed R. Dodsley, A select collection of old plays vol 7, 1744; ed I Reed, Dodsley vol 10, 1780; Ancient British drama vol 3, 1810; ed J. P. Collier, Dodsley vol 10, 1826; ed W. C. Hazlitt, Dodsley vol 12, 1875.

§2

Strube, H. S. Centlivres Lustspiel The stolen heiress und sein Verhältnis zu The heir von May; nebst Anhang: May und Shakespeare. Halle 1900.
Wolf, H. May's Tragedy of Cleopatra. Strasbourg 1904.
Briggs, W. D. The influence of Jonson's tragedy in the seventeenth century. Anglia 35 1912.
Chester, A. G. May: man of letters. Philadelphia 1932.
—— Dryden and May. TLS 19 July 1934.
Wagner, B. M. Ms plays of the seventeenth century. TLS 4 Oct 1934.
Wilkinson, C. H. A note on May. RES 11 1935.
Bruère, R. T. The Latin and English versions of May's Supplementum Lucani. Classical Philology 44 1949.
Smith, H. 'No cloudie stuffe to puzzle intellect'. Shakespeare Quart 1 1950.
Davies, H. N. Dryden's All for love and May's Cleopatra. N & Q April 1965.
Barry, J. W. May's Cleopatra. Discourse 11 1968.
The ms of May's Latin tragedy Julius Caesar *has been several times reported but is now lost; for May's trns and his historical and political works, see col 2244, below.*

JASPER MAYNE
1604–72

§1

The citye match: a comoedye, presented to the King and Queene at White-Hall, acted since at Black-friers by his Majesties servants. Oxford 1639, 1658 (in Two plays, 4°), 1659 (8°); ed R. Dodsley. A select collection of old plays vol 10, 1774; ed I. Reed, Dodsley vol 9, 1780; Ancient British drama vol 2, 1810; ed J. P. Collier, Dodsley vol 9, 1825; ed W. C. Hazlitt, Dodsley vol 13, 1875.

The amorous warre: a tragi-comoedy. 1648, 1658 (in Two plays), 1659 (4°), 1659 (8°).
For Mayne's sermons see col 1995, below.

§2

Abell, E. T. A note on Mayne. Report & Trans of Devonshire Assoc for Advancement of Science, Lit & Art 57 1925.
Greg, W. W. The printing of Mayne's plays. Oxford Bibl Soc Proc & Papers 1 1927.
Davis, J. L. In his Sons of Ben: Jonsonian comedy in Caroline England, Detroit 1967.

THOMAS MERITON
b. 1638

The wandring lover, a tragy-comedie; being acted severall times privately at sundry places by the author and his friends, by T.M. 1658.
Love and war: a tragedy. 1658.

WALTER MONTAGU
1603?–77

The shepheard's paradise: a comedy, privately acted before the late King Charles by the Queen's Majesty and ladies of honour. 1659 (some copies erroneously dated 1629). Mss: (1) BM ms Sloane 3649; (2) BM ms Stowe 976; (3) BM additional ms 41,617; (4) Folger Lib ms v.b.203; (5) Folger Lib ms v.b.204.

WALTER MOUNTFORT
fl. 1613–35

The lanchinge of the Mary, written by W.M. gent in his returne from East India, anno 1632: or the seamans honest wyfe. BM ms Egerton 1994, ff. 317–49; ed J. H. Walter 1933 (Malone Soc).

THOMAS NABBES
c. 1605–41

Collections

Plays, maskes, epigrams, elegies and epithalamiums. 1639. A 'nonce collection' made up of copies of original edns of Microcosmus, Hannibal and Scipio, Covent Garden, Spring's glory, Tottenham Court, Unfortunate mother, Bride.
Works. Ed A. H. Bullen, Old English plays new ser vols 1–2, 1887.

§1

Hannibal and Scipio: an historicall tragedy, acted in the yeare 1635 by the Queenes Majesties servants at their private house in Drury Lane. 1637.
Microcosmus: a morall maske, presented at the private house in Salisbury Court, and heere set down according to the intention of the authour. 1637; ed R. Dodsley, A select collection of old plays vol 5, 1744; ed I. Reed, Dodsley vol 9, 1780; Ancient British drama vol 2, 1810; ed J. P. Collier, Dodsley vol 9, 1925.
Covent Garden: a pleasant comedie, acted in the yeare 1632 by the Queenes Majesties servants. 1638, 1639.
A presentation intended for the Prince his Highnesse on his birth-day the 29 of May, 1638, annually celebrated. 1638, 1639 (with Springs glorie).
The springs glorie, vindicating love by temperance against the tenent: sine Cerere & Baccho friget Venus; moralized in a maske, with other poems, epigrams, elegies

and epithalamiums. 1638, 1639 (with A presentation for the Prince); ed J. R. Brown, A book of masques in honour of Allardyce Nicoll, Cambridge 1967.

Totenham Court: a pleasant comedie, acted in theye are 1633 at the private house in Salisbury-Court. 1638, 1639.

The bride: a comedie, acted in the yeere 1638 at the private house in Drury-lane by their Majesties servants. In Plays, maskes, 1639; 1640 (separately).

The unfortunate mother: a tragedie, never acted, but set downe according to the intention of the author. In Plays, maskes, 1639; 1640 (separately).

§ 2

Moore, C. The dramatic works of Nabbes. Menasha 1918.

Swinburne, A. C. In his Contemporaries of Shakespeare, 1919.

Lawrence, W. J. Early substantive masques. TLS 8 Dec 1921.

—— The origin of the substantive theatre masque. In his Pre-Restoration stage studies, 1927.

Koch, J. Nabbes: ein zu wenig beachteter Dichter. Anglia 47 1923.

—— Echte und 'unechte' Masken. E Studien 58 1924.

Welsford, E. In her Court masque, 1927.

Russell, H. K. Tudor and Stuart dramatizations of the doctrines of natural and moral philosophy. SP 31 1934.

Miles, T. Place-realism in a group of Caroline plays. RES 18 1942. On Covent Garden and Tottenham Court.

Cutts, J. P. Nabbes's Hannibal and Scipio. Eng Miscellany (Rome) 14 1963.

Davis, J. L. In his Sons of Ben: Jonsonian comedy in Caroline England, Detroit 1967.

Vince, R. W. Nabbes's Hannibal and Scipio: sources and theme. Stud in Eng Lit 1500–1900 11 1971.

THOMAS NEWMAN

The two first comedies of Terence called Andria and the Eunuch newly Englished, fitted for schollers private action in their schooles. 1627.

WILLIAM PEAPS

Love in it's extasie, or the large prerogative: a kind of royall pastorall written long since by a gentleman student at Æton. 1649.

EDMUND PRESTWICH

Hippolytus. 1651. A rimed trn from Seneca.

The ascription to Prestwich of the anon The Hectors: or the false challenge is now rejected; see col 1759, below.

FRANCIS QUARLES
1592–1644

See col 1199, above.

THOMAS RAWLINS
c. 1618–70

The rebellion: a tragedy, as it was acted ninedayes together, and divers times since by his Majesties company of revells. 1640, 1652; Ancient British drama vol 3, 1810; ed W. C. Hazlitt, Dodsley vol 14, 1875.

HENRY REYNOLDS
1563?–1635?

Torquato Tasso's Aminta englisht; to this is added Ariadne's complaint in imitation of Anguillara. 1628.

NATHANIEL RICHARDS
1612?–54?

See col 1317, above.

WILLIAM RIDER

The twins: a tragi-comedy, acted at the private house at Salisbury-Court. 1655.

JOSEPH RUTTER
fl. 1633–40

The shepheards holy-day: a pastorall tragi-comaedie, acted before both their Majesties at White-Hall by the Queenes servants; with an elegie on the death of the most noble lady, the Lady Venetia Digby. 1635; ed W. C. Hazlitt, Dodsley vol 12, 1875. See F. L. Townsend, Ben Jonson's censure of Rutter's Shepheards Holy-day, MP 44 1947; E. Withington, Nicholas Briot and Jonson's commendation of Rutter, N & Q April 1953.

The Cid: a tragicomedy, out of French made English, and acted before their Majesties at Court and on the Cockpit stage in Drury-lane by the servants to both their Majesties. 1637 (for 1638), 1650 ('the second edn corrected and amended'). From Corneille.

The second part of the Cid. 1640. Tr from Desfontaines, La vraie suite de Cid.

WILLIAM SAMPSON
c. 1600

§ 1

The true tragedy of Herod and Antipater, with the death of faire Marriam, according to Josephus, the learned and famous Jewe, as it hath beene of late divers times publiquely acted at the Red Bull by the company of his Majesties revels, written by Gervase Markham and William Sampson, gentlemen. 1622.

The vow breaker: or the faire maide of Clifton, in Nottinghamshire, as it hath beene divers times acted by severall companies. 1636; ed H. Wallrath, Bang vol 42, 1914.

Virtus post funera vivit: or honour triumphing over death. 1636.

§ 2

Godfrey, J. T. Sampson: a seventeenth-century poet and dramatist. 1894.

Dunstan, A. C. Examination of two English dramas: the Tragedy of Mariam by Elizabeth Carew, and the True tragedy of Herod and Antipater by Markham and Sampson. Königsberg 1908.

Silbermann, A. M. Untersuchungen über die Quellen des Dramas The true tragedy of Herod and Antipater von Markham and Sampson. Würzburg 1928.

Tomlinson, W. E. Der Herodes-charakter im englischen Drama. Palaestra 195 1934.

Tillotson, K. Samson's Vow-breaker and the lost Henslowe play Black Batman of the north. MLR 35 1940.

Valency, M. J. The tragedies of Herod and Mariamne. New York 1940.

Scragg, L. Shakespearian influence in Herod and Antipater. N & Q July 1968.

GEORGE SANDYS
1578–1644

See col 1186, above.

LEWIS SHARPE
fl. 1640

The noble stranger, as it was acted at the private house in Salisbury Court by her Majesties servants, the author L.S. 1640.

EDWARD SHARPHAM
1576–1608

§1

The fleire, as it hath beene often played in the Blackefryers by the children of the revells. 1607, 1610, 1615, 1631; ed H. Nibbe, Bang vol 36, 1912.

Cupids whirligig, as it hath bene sundry times acted by the children of the Kings Majesties revels. 1607, 1611, 1616, 1630; ed A. Nicoll 1926.

§2

Smith, G. C. M. Edward Sharpham. N & Q 11 July 1908.
—— John Mason and Sharpham. MLR 8 1913.

Sampson, M. W. The plays of Sharpham. In Studies in language and literature in celebration of the seventieth birthday of J. M. Hart, New York 1910.

Leech, C. The plays of Sharpham. RES 11 1935.

SIR EDWARD SHERBURNE
1618–1702

See vol 2 col 484, below.

HENRY SHIRLEY
c. 1594–1627

§1

The martyr'd souldier, as it was sundry times acted at the private house in Drury lane, and at other publicke theaters, by the Queenes Majesties servants. 1638; ed A. H. Bullen, Old English plays vol 1, 1882.

§2

Hart, H. C. Notes on Bullen's old plays: the Martyred souldier. Academy 1 Sept 1888.

Clark, A. M. In his Thomas Heywood: playwright and miscellanist, 1931. Suggests Heywood as collaborator or revisor of Martyr'd soldier.

Cutts, J. P. Henry Shirley's The martyred soldier. Renaissance News 12 1959.

JONATHAN SIDNAM
fl. 1630

Filli di Sciro, or Phillis of Scyros: an excellent pastorall, written in Italian by C. Guidubaldo de' Bonarelli, and translated into English by J.S. gent. 1655, 1655.

Il pastor fido, or the faithfull sheapheard: an excellent pastorall written in Italian by Battista Guarini and translated into English by Jonathan Sidnam esq; anno 1630. BM additional ms 29,493.

W[ENTWORTH?] SMITH
fl. 1601–15

The Hector of Germaine, or the Palsgrave, Prime Elector: a new play, an honourable hystorie, as it hath beene publikely acted at the Red Bull and at the Curtayne by a companie of young men of this citie, made by W. Smith, with new additions. 1615; ed L. W. Payne, Philadelphia 1906.

JOHN STEPHENS
fl. 1611–17

Cinthia's revenge: or Maenanders extasie. 1613, 1613. *See* P. Simpson, The authorship and original issue of Cinthia's revenge, MLR 2 1907.

SIR JOHN SUCKLING
1609–42

See col 1213, above.

GILBERT SWINHOE
fl. 1658

The tragedy of the unhappy fair Irene. 1658.

ROBERT TAILOR
fl. 1613–15

§1

The hogge hath lost his pearle: a comedy, divers times publikely acted by certaine London prentices. 1614; ed R. Dodsley, A select collection of old plays vol 3, 1744; ed I. Reed, Dodsley vol 6, 1780; Ancient British drama vol 3, 1810; ed J. P. Collier, Dodsley vol 6, 1825; ed W. C. Hazlitt, Dodsley vol 11, 1875.

§2

Albright, E. N. A stage cartoon of the mayor of London in 1613. In The [J. M.] Manly anniversary studies, Chicago 1923.

SIR GILBERT TALBOT
fl. 1657

Filli di Sciro. Mss: (1) BM additional ms 12,128; (2) Bodley ms Rawlinson poetry 130. Tr from Bonarelli.

JOHN TATHAM
c. 1610?–after 1664

Collections

The fancies theater. 1640, 1657 (as The mirrour of fancies).

Ostella: or the faction. 1650.

Dramatic works. Ed J. Maidment and W. H. Logan, Edinburgh 1879.

§1

Love crowns the end: a pastorall presented by the schollees of Bingham in the county of Nottingham in the yeare 1632. In Fancies theatre, 1640, 1657.

The distracted state: a tragedy, written in the year 1641, by J.T. gent. 1651.

The Scots figgaries, or a knot of knaves: a comedy. 1652, 1652 (some copies dated 1653).

The rump, or the mirrour of the late times: a new comedy acted many times with great applause at the private house in Dorset-Court. 1660, 1661 ('The second impression, corrected with many additions').

Tatham wrote the London civic pageants for Lord Mayors' shows and other occasions from 1657 to 1664.

AURELIAN TOWNS(H)END
1583?–1643?

Albions triumph. 1631; Tempe restored, 1631. 2 masques with Inigo Jones, both ed E. K. Chambers, Oxford 1912. *see col 1323, above.*

CHRISTOPHER WASE
1625?–90

Electra of Sophocles, presented to her Highnesse the Lady Elizabeth, with an epilogue shewing the parallel in two poems, the Return and the Restauration, by C.W. Hague 1649.

GEORGE WILKINS
fl. 1604–08

§ 1

Three miseries of Barbary: plague, famine, civill warre. [1606?].

Jests to make you merie. 1607. With Dekker, *col 1675, above.*

The miseries of inforst mariage, as it is now playd by his Majesties servants. 1607, 1611, 1629, 1637; ed I. Reed, Dodsley vol 5, 1780; Ancient British drama vol 2, 1810; ed J. P. Collier, Dodsley vol 5, 1825; ed W. C. Hazlitt, Dodsley vol 9, 1874; TFT 1913; ed G. H. Blayney 1964 (Malone Soc).

The travailes of the three English brothers. 1607. With Day and Rowley; *see Day, col 1462, above.*

The painfull adventures of Pericles Prince of Tyre. 1608; ed T. Mommsen, Oldenburg 1857; ed K. Muir, Liverpool 1953.

§ 2

Boyle, R. On Wilkins' share in the play called Shakspere's Pericles. New Shakespeare Soc Trans pt 2 1880–5.

Sykes, H. D. In his Sidelights on Shakespeare, 1919.

Golding, S. R. Day and Wilkins as collaborators. N & Q 12–19 June 1926.

Appen, P. In his Shakespeare, Wilkins and Jonson as borrowers. 1928.

Clark, A. M. In his Thomas Heywood: playwright and miscellanist, Oxford 1931.

Spiker, S. Wilkins and the authorship of Pericles. SP 30 1933.

Hastings, W. T. Exit George Wilkins. Shakespeare Assoc Bull 11 1936.

Borrish, M. E. Day's Law tricks and Wilkins. MP 34 1937.

Dickson, G. B. The identity of Wilkins. Shakespeare Assoc Bull 14 1939.

Blayney, G. H. Wilkins and the identity of W. Calverley's guardian. N & Q Aug 1953. *See also* B. Maxwell, Oct 1953.

—— Wardship in English drama 1600–50. SP 53 1956.

—— Wilkins's revisions in the Miseries of inforst mariage. JEGP 56 1957.

—— The enforcement of marriage in English drama 1600–50. PQ 38 1959.

Maxwell, B. In his Studies in the Shakespeare apocrypha, New York 1956.

Krueger, R. Ms evidence for dates of Wilkins's Three miseries of Barbary and E. Grymston's Miscelanea. Library 5th ser 16 1961.

The first 2 acts of Shakespeare's Pericles, col 1553, above, and the anon The Yorkshire tragedy, col 1762, below, have been attributed to Wilkins, and he has been suggested as a collaborator in Day's Law-tricke, col 1462, above.

LEONARD WILLAN
fl. 1649–70

Astraea, or true love's myrrour: a pastoral. 1651.

Orgula, or the fatall error: a tragedy composed by L.W. 1658.

See M. L. Birkett, Five minor poets, *TLS 29 Sept 1932. For Willan's version of Aesop, see col 2165, below.*

ARTHUR WILSON
1595–1652

§ 1

The inconstant lady: or better late than never [c. 1630]. Mss: (1) Bodley ms Rawlinson poetry 9; (2) Bodley ms Rawlinson poetry 128; (3) Folger Lib ms J.b.1; ed P. Bliss, Oxford 1814.

The Swisser [1631]. BM additional ms 36,759; ed A. Feuillerat, Paris 1904.

The corporal [c. 1632]. Mss: (1) Bodley ms Rawlinson poetry 9, fol 45ʳ (title and dramatis personae only); (2) Bodley ms Douce C.2 (a late seventeenth- or early eighteenth-century transcript of act I and 125 lines of act II); (3) Victoria and Albert Museum, Forster ms 638 (2 non-consecutive leaves).

§ 2

Wilson, A. Observations of God's providence in the tract of my life. Ed F. Peck in Desiderata curiosa, 1732; rptd in P. Bliss's edn of Inconstant lady, Oxford 1814.

Arthur Wilson's play The Swisser. Athenaeum 14 Feb 1903.

Wagner, B. M. Manuscript plays of the seventeenth century. TLS 4 Oct 1934.

Bald, R. C. The inconstant lady. Library 4th ser 18 1938.

For Wilson's non-dramatic works, see col 2241, below.

ANONYMOUS PLAYS

The tragedy of Alphonsus Emperour of Germany as it hath been very often acted with great applause at the privat house in Black-friers by his late Majesties servants, by George Chapman gent. 1654; ed K. Elze, Leipzig 1867; ed H. F. Schwarz, New York 1913. Also included in collections of Chapman, col 1637, above, though almost certainly not his. Bentley v.1285–8.

Andromana: or the merchant's wife; the scaene, Iberia; by J.S. 1660; ed R. Dodsley, A select collection of old plays vol 11, 1744; ed I. Reed, Dodsley vol 11, 1780; ed W. C. Hazlitt, Dodsley vol 14, 1875. Bentley v.1034–5; *see* M. C. Andrews, The sources of Andromana, RES new ser 19 1968.

The bloodie banquet: a tragedie, by T.D. 1639; TFT 1914; ed S. Schoenbaum 1962 (Malone Soc). *See* W. Bacon's edn of W. Warner, Pan his Syrinx, 1950, for source of play; and Bentley III.282–4, for its attribution to Thomas Drue.

The famous tragedie of King Charles I, basely butchered. 1649, 1649 (2nd edn apparently dating from c. 1660).

The tragedy of that famous Roman oratour Marcus Tullius Cicero. 1651. Bentley v.1370–1.

The tragedie of Claudius Tiberius Nero, Rome's greatest tyrant, truly represented out of the purest records of those times. 1607, 1607; TFT 1913; ed W. W. Greg, 1914 (Malone Soc).

Charlemagne: or the distracted emperor. BM ms Egerton 1994, ff. 119–36; ed A. H. Bullen, Old English plays, vol 3, 1884; ed F. L. Schoell, Princeton 1920; ed J. H. Walter 1937 (Malone Soc). See F. L. Schoell, Un drame élisabéthain anonyme: Charlemagne, Revue Germanique 8 1912; F. S. Boas, Shakespeare and the universities, 1923.

The costlie whore: a comicall historie, acted by the companie of the revels. 1633; ed A. H. Bullen, Old English plays vol 4, 1885. Bentley v.1312–14. See H. C. Hart, Notes on Bullen's old plays: the Costlie whore, Academy 13 Oct 1888.

The Cyprian conqueror: or the faithless relict. BM ms Sloane 3709. Bentley v.1316–17.

Dick of Devonshire. BM ms Egerton 1994 ff. 30–32; ed A. H. Bullen, Old English plays vol 2, 1883; ed J. G. and M. R. McManaway 1955 (Malone Soc) (attributing to Robert Davenport). See H. C. Hart, Notes on Bullen's old plays: Dick of Devonshire, Academy 15 Sept 1888.

The disloyal favourite: or the tragedy of Mettellus. Bodley ms Rawlinson D. 1361, ff. 285–306.

Every woman in her humor. 1609; ed A. H. Bullen, Old English plays vol 4, 1885; TFT 1913. See H. C. Hart, Notes on Bullen's old plays: Everie woman in her humor, Academy 13 Oct 1888; J. Q. Adams, Every woman in her humour and the Dumb knight, MP 10 1913; J. P. Cutts, Everie woman in her humour, Renaissance News 18 1965.

The extravagant sheepherd: a pastorall comedie; englished by T.R. 1654. Tr from Thomas Corneille.

The faire maide of Bristow, as it was plaide at Hampton before the King and Queenes most excellent Majesties. 1605; ed A. H. Quinn, Philadelphia 1902; TFT 1912. See Sh Jb 31 1895 for a German trn by L. Tieck, ed J. Bolte. See also J. Le G. Brereton, Notes on the Fair maid of Bristowe, MLR 3 1907.

The fayre mayde of the exchange, with the pleasaunt humours of the cripple of Fanchurch. 1607, 1625, 1637; ed B. Field 1845 (Shakespeare Soc); ed R. H. Shepherd Dramatic works of Heywood, 1874; ed P. H. Davison and A. Brown 1963 (Malone Soc).

The fairy knight: or Oberon the second. Folger Lib ms V.a.128; ed F. T. Bowers 1942. Bentley v.1328–30.

The faithful friends. Victoria and Albert Museum, Dyce ms 10; in the Weber (1812) and Dyce (1843–6) edns of Beaumont and Fletcher.

The fatal maryage: or a second Lucreatya. BM ms Egerton 1994, ff. 137–60; ed S. B. Younghughes and H. Jenkins 1959 (Malone Soc).

The female rebellion. Mss: (1) Bodley ms Tanner 466; (2) Glasgow Univ ms Hunterian 635. Ed A. Smith, Glasgow 1872. Bentley III.95–6.

The argument of the pastorall of Florimene, with the description of the scoenes and intermedii, presented before the Kings Majesty in the hall at Whitehall the 21 of December. 1635. Bentley v.1333–4.

[Ghismonda]. BM additional ms 34,312. An untitled tragedy of the 17th century, variously called Ghismonda, and Tancred and Ghismonda. Ed H. G. Wright, Manchester 1933. Bentley v.1340–2.

The ghost, or the woman wears the breeches: a comedy written in the year 1640. 1653. Bentley v.1342.

The gossips braule, or the women weare the breeches: a mock comedy. 1655. Bentley v.1344.

The governor: a tragicomedy. [1656]. BM additional ms 10,419. Bentley III.465–8.

The hectors, or the false challenge: a comedy written in the year 1655. 1656.

The tragical history, admirable atchievments and various events of Guy, Earl of Warwick: a tragedy acted very frequently by his late Majesties servants, written by B. J. 1661. Bentley v.1347–8.

The honest lawyer, acted by the Queenes Majesties servants, written by S.S. 1616; TFT 1914.

The King and Queenes entertainment at Richmond after their departure from Oxford, in a masque presented by the most illustrious Prince, Prince Charles, Sept 12 1636. Oxford 1636; ed W. Bang and R. Brotanek, Bang vol 2, 1903. Bentley v.1357–60.

The knave in graine, new vampt: a witty comedy, acted at the Fortune many dayes together; written by J.D. gent. 1640; ed R. C. Bald 1961 (Malone Soc). Bentley III.187–90.

Lady Alimony, or the alimony lady: an excellent pleasant new comedy duly authorized, daily acted and frequently followed. 1659; ed W. C. Hazlitt, Dodsley vol 14, 1875. Bentley v.1361–3. See also K. R. Richards, The anonymous Lady Alimony: a reconsideration, Archiv 205 1968.

The London chaunticleres: a witty comoedy, full of various and delightful mirth, often acted with great applause and never before published. 1659; ed W. C. Hazlitt, Dodsley vol 12, 1875. Bentley v.1364–5.

The London prodigall. 1605. See under Shakespeare, col 1556 above.

Loves changelings change. BM ms Egerton 1994. Bentley v.1367.

Love's victorie. Huntington Lib ms HM 600. Ed J. O. Halliwell (-Phillipps), A brief description of the ancient and modern mss preserved in the Public Library, Plymouth 1853 (extracts comprising nearly one-third of the play). Bentley v.1368–9.

The marriage broker: or the pander, by M.W. In Gratiae theatrales: or a choice ternary of English plays,]composed upon especial occasions by several ingenious persons, 1662. A collection of 3 plays, including Haughton's Grim the collier of Croyden; and Thorney Abbey. All appear to be old plays, with texts sophisticated.

The merry Devill of Edmonton, as it hathe beene sundry times acted by his Majesties servants at the Globe. 1608, 1612, 1617, 1626, 1631, 1655; ed I. Reed, Dodsley vol 5, 1780; Ancient British drama vol 2, 1810; ed J. P. Collier, Dodsley vol 5, 1825; ed W. C. Hazlitt, Dodsley vol 10, 1875; ed H. Walker 1897; TFT 1911; ed J. M. Manly, Gayley vol 2, 1913; ed W. A. Abrams, Durham NC 1941. Also included in the Shakespeare apocrypha collections, col 1551, above, to whom the play was assigned in the Stationers' register entry for 1653.

Nebuchadnezzars fierie furnace. BM ms Harley 7578. Ed M. Rösler, Bang vol 12, 1936.

The tragedy of Nero, newly written. 1624, 1633, 1676 (as Piso's conspiracy, with alterations). BM ms Egerton 1994. Ed A. H. Bullen, Old English plays vol 1, 1882; ed H. P. Horne, Nero and other plays, 1888 (Mermaid ser). Bentley v.1379–82. See H. C. Hart, Notes on Bullen's old plays: Tragedy of Nero, Academy 1 Sept 1888.

No-body and some-body, with the true chronicle historie of Elydure, who was fortunately three severall times crowned King of England: the true coppy thereof, as it hath beene acted by the Queens Majesties servants. [1606]; ed A. Smith 1877; ed R. Simpson, School of Shakespeare vol 1, 1878; TFT 1911; ed F. Bischoff, Niemand und jemand in Graz in Jahre 1608, Mitteilungen des Historischen Vereins für Steiermark 47 1899; tr German, Englische Comedien und Tragedien, 1620; L. Tieck, ed J. Bolte, Sh Jb 29 1894. See G. Calmann, The picture of nobody: an iconographical study, Jnl Warburg & Courtauld Inst 23 1960.

The partiall law. Folger Lib ms v.a. 165. Ed B. Dobell 1908. Bentley v.1388–9.

Pelopidarum secunda. BM ms Harley 5110. A tragedy in English acted at Winchester College. Bentley v.1393–4.

An excellent comedy called the Prince of Priggs revels: or the practises of that grand thief Captain James Hind, relating divers of his pranks and exploits, never here-tofore published by any; repleat with various conceits and Tarltonian mirth, suitable to the subject; written by J.S. 1651. Bentley v.1035-6.

The Puritaine: or the widdow of Watling-streete. 1607. *See under Shakespeare, col 1556, above.*

The rebellion of Naples: or the tragedy of Massenello commonly so called, but rightly Tomaso Aniello di Malfa, Generall of the Neopolitans, written by a gentleman who was an eye-witness where this was really acted upon that bloudy stage, the streets of Naples 1647. 1649. Bentley iii.8-9.

The second maiden's tragedy. BM ms Lansdown 807. Ed C. Baldwin, Old English drama vol i, 1824; ed R. H. Shepherd, Chapman's Works vol 3, 1875; ed W. C. Hazlitt, Dodsley vol 10, 1875; ed W. W. Greg 1909 (Malone Soc). *See* W. Nicholson, MLN 27 1912; S. Schoenbaum, Middleton's tragedies, New York 1955; R. Levin, The double plot of the Second maiden's tragedy, Stud in Eng Lit 1500–1900 3 1963.

Swetnam, the woman-hater, arraigned by women: a new comedie, acted at the Red Bull by the late Queenes servants. 1620; ed A. B. Grosart 1880; TFT 1914; ed C. Crandall, Purdue 1969. Bentley v.1416–8.

The telltale. Dulwich College ms xx. Ed R. A. Foakes and J. C. Gibson 1960 (Malone Soc). Bentley v.1418–19. *See also* A. Freeman, The authorship of the Tell-tale, JEGP 62 1963; K. L. Wheelen, A critical view of the Telltale, Emporia State Research Stud 15 1966.

Thorny-Abbey, or the London-maid: a tragedy, by T.W. 1662. In Gratiae theatrales; *see* Marriage broker, above. *See* E. H. C. Oliphant, MP 8 1910.

The Thracian wonder: a comical history, as it hath been several times acted, written by John Webster and William Rowley. 1661; ed C. W. Dilke, Old English plays vol 6, 1815; ed W. C. Hazlitt, Dramatic works of Webster, 1857. Issued with A cure for a cuckold (*see* Webster, col 1699, above) as Two new playes. The ascription to both Webster and Rowley is generally rejected. *See* Chambers iv.45.

Time's triumph. BM ms Egerton 1994. An untitled dramatic allegory dated 5 Aug 1643, variously called Time's triumph, Juno in Arcadia, Juno's pastoral: or the bonds of peace, Sight and search. Bentley v.1419–21.

Titus: or the palm of Christian courage to be exhibited by the scholars of the society of Jesus at Kilkenny AD 1644. Waterford 1644.

The true tragi-comedie formarly acted at Court and now revived by ane eie witnes. BM additional ms 25,348. A treatment of the divorce of Robert Carr and Lady Frances Howard; written c. 1654. Bentley v.1424–5.

The history of the tryall of chevalry, with the life and death of Cavaliero Dicke Bowyer, as it hath bin lately acted by the Right Honourable the Earle of Darby his servants. 1605, 1605; ed A. H. Bullen, Old English plays vol 3, 1884; TFT 1912. *See* C. R. Baskervill, Sidney's Arcadia and the Trial of Chivalry, MP 10 1912; F. L. Jones, PMLA 41 1925. Chambers iv 50–1.

A pleasant comedie called the Two merry milke-maids: or the best words weare the garland, as it was acted before the King by the companie of the revels, by I.C. 1620, 1620, 1661; TFT 1914. Bentley iii.101–4.

The two noble ladies and the converted conjurer. BM ms Egerton 1994. Ed R. G. Rhoads 1930 (Malone Soc). Bentley v.1426–7.

Two wise men and all the rest fooles: or a comicall morall censuring the follies of this age, as it hath beene diverse times acted. 1619; ed R. H. Shepherd, Works of Chapman, 1874–5, 1889; TFT 1913. Bentley v.1428–9.

Tyranicall-government anatomized, or a discourse concerning evil-councellors: being the life and death of John the Baptist. 1643; ed J. T. T. Brown, George Buchanan: Glasgow quatercentenary studies, Glasgow 1907. Tr from Buchanan's Baptistes.

The valiant Scot, by J.W. gent. 1637. Bentley v.1233–6.

The valiant Welshman: or the true chronicle history of the life and valiant deedes of Caradoc the great, King of Cambria, now called Wales, as it hath beene sundry times acted by the Prince of Wales his servants, written by R.A. gent. 1615, 1663; ed V. Kreb, Munich 1902; TFT 1913. *See* S. Lloyd, The authorship of the Valiant Welshman, N & Q 27 Sept 1952 (attributing play to Robert Anton).

The wasp. Alnwick Castle, Northumberland, ms 507. Bentley v.1433–4.

The whimsies of Senor Hidalgo: or the masculine bride. BM ms Harley 5152. Bentley v.1436–7.

The white Ethiopian. BM ms Harley 7313. Bentley v.1439–40.

Wine, beere, and ale, together by the eares: a dialogue, written first in Dutch by Gallobelgicus, and faithfully translated out of the originall copies by Mercurius Brittannicus, for the benefite of his nation. 1629, 1630 (enlarged as Wine, beere, ale and tobacco, contending for superiority), 1658; ed J. O. Halliwell(-Phillipps) 1854; ed J. H. Hanford, SP 12 1915. Ms: Univ of Edinburgh ms Laing iii.493. Bentley v.1442–4. Not a trn but an original interlude.

A pleasant comoedie wherein is merily shewen the wit of a woman. 1604; TFT 1912; ed W. W. Greg 1913 (Malone Soc). *See* J. Morgan, Towards a textual study of the Wit of a woman, Emporia State Research Stud 15 1966.

Wit's triumvirate: or the philosopher. BM additional ms 45,865. *See* S. Schoenbaum, Wit's triumvirate: a Caroline comedy recovered, Stud in Eng Lit 1500–1900 4 1964.

The world's idol, Plutus: a comedy written in Greek by Aristophanes, translated by H.H.B. together with his notes and a short discourse upon it. 1659.

[Xamolxis and Perindo]. BM additional ms 29,496. An untitled pastoral, probably late 17th-century.

A Yorkshire tragedy. 1608. *See under Shakespeare, col 1556, above.*

C. H.

XII. UNIVERSITY PLAYS (1500–1642)

In this section the term university includes the London Inns of Court.

(1) GENERAL STUDIES

The Latin plays acted before the University of Cambridge. Retrospective Rev 12 1825.

Courtney, W. L. Oxford plays down to the Restoration. N & Q 11 Dec 1886.

Plummer, C. Elizabethan Oxford: reprints of rare tracts. 1887 (Oxford Historical Soc).

Lee, M. L. Narcissus. A Twelfe Night merriment. 1893. Introd contains list of Oxford plays.

Evans, H. A. English masques. 1897.

Churchill, G. B. and W. Keller. Die lateinischen Universitäts-Dramen Englands in der Zeit der Königin Elizabeth. Sh Jb 34 1898.

Greg, W. W. Pastoral poetry and pastoral drama. 1906.

Gofflot, L. V. Le théâtre au collège du Moyen Age à nos jours. Paris 1907.

Moore Smith, G. C. Notes on some English university plays. MLR 3 1908.

—— Plays performed in Cambridge colleges before 1585. In Fasciculus J. W. Clark dictatus, 1909.

—— Latin plays acted at Cambridge. MLR 6 1911.

—— The academic drama at Cambridge: extracts from college records. In Malone Society collections vol 2, 1923.

—— College plays performed in the University of Cambridge. Cambridge 1923.

Boas, F. S. University plays. CHEL vol 6 1910.

—— University drama in the Tudor age. 1914.

—— Shakespeare and the universities. [1923].

—— Introduction to Tudor drama. Oxford 1933.

—— Introduction to Stuart drama. Oxford 1946.

Boas, F. S. and W. W. Greg. James I at Oxford in 1605. In Malone Society collections vol 1, 1909.

Cunliffe, J. W. Early English tragedy. CHEL vol 5 1910.

Morgan, L. B. The Latin university drama. Sh Jb 47 1911. Supplements Churchill and Keller, above, with account of 13 plays, though some do not seem to be of Oxford or Cambridge origin.

Campbell, L. B. Scenes and machines on the English stage during the Renaissance. Cambridge 1923.

Simpson, P. and C. F. Bell. Designs by Inigo Jones for masques and plays at Court. Oxford 1924.

Reed, A. W. Early Tudor drama. 1926.

Welsford, E. The Court masque. Cambridge 1927.

Green, A. W. The Inns of Court and early English drama. New Haven 1931.

Nicoll, A. Stuart masques and the Renaissance stage. 1937.

Frost, S. T. Revels in the Inns of Court. Res Judicatae 2 1939.

Eccles, M. Francis Beaumont's grammar lecture. RES 16 1940. Christmas revels at Inner Temple.

Davis, J. L. The case for comedy in Caroline theatrical apologetics. PMLA 58 1943.

Brooke, C. F. T. Latin drama in Renaissance England. ELH 13 1946.

Hiscock, W. G. Christ Church plays. In his Christ Church miscellany, Oxford 1946. Productions by George Peele 1583.

Young, G. M. Shakespeare and the Termers. Proc Br Acad 1946; rptd in his Today and yesterday, 1948. On Inns of Court audiences.

Carpenter, N. C. Musicians in early university drama. N & Q 28 Oct 1950.

Rossiter, A. P. English drama from early times to the Elizabethans. 1950.

Schoeck, R. Sir Thomas More and Lincoln's Inn revels. PQ 29 1950.

—— Satire of Wolsey in Heywood's Play of love. N & Q 17 March 1951. Reply by D. S. Bland 24 Nov 1951; by Schoeck 24 May 1952.

—— Early Tudor drama and the Inns of Court. Amer Soc for Theatre Research News Letter 2 1957.

Bland, D. S. Interludes in fifteenth-century revels at Furnival's Inn. RES new ser 3 1952.

Bentley, G. E. Jacobean and Caroline stage. 7 vols Oxford 1941–68.

Alton, R. E. The academic drama at Oxford. In Malone Society collections vol 5, 1959.

Mills, L. J. The acting in university comedy of early seventeenth-century England. In Studies in the English Renaissance drama in memory of Karl J. Holzknecht, New York 1959.

Clemen, W. English tragedy before Shakespeare. 1961.

Cunningham, J. P. Dancing in the Inns of Court. 1965.

Mehl, D. The Elizabethan dumb show. 1965.

Baugh, A. C. A fifteenth-century dramatic performance at the Inns of Court. Tennessee Stud in Lit 11 1966.

S[pencer], T. J. B. and S. W. W[ells]. A book of masques in honour of Allardyce Nicoll. Cambridge 1967.

Finkelpearl, P. J. John Marston of the Middle Temple. Cambridge Mass 1969.

Wilson, F. P. The English drama 1485–1585. Oxford 1969 (OHEL).

(2) PLAYS

*English and Latin plays, either ptd or in mss still extant. Lost plays are not included, except in a few cases of special import-
ance. For other lost plays, and plays dating after 1642, see G. C. Moore Smith, College plays, Cambridge 1923.*

WILLIAM ALABASTER
1568–1640

§ 1

Roxana. 1632, 1632. Mss: Trinity College Cambridge R.17.10; Univ Lib Cambridge Ff.11.9; Lambeth Palace 838; Emmanuel College Cambridge III.1.17. Synopsis, Sh Jb 34 1898.

§ 2

Dobell, B. The sonnets of Alabaster. Athenaeum 26 Dec 1903. *See also cols 1080, 1295 above.*

THOMAS ATKINSON
1600–39

Homo. Ms: BM Harley 6925.

FRANCIS BEAUMONT
1585?–1616

Masque of the Inner Temple and Grayes Inne. [1613], 1653 (with omissions), 1679; ed J. Nichols, Progresses of James I vol 2, 1828; ed H. A. Evans, English masques, 1897; ed A. Glover and A. R.

Waller, Works of Beaumont and Fletcher vol 10, Cambridge 1912; ed F. T. Bowers, Dramatic works in the Beaumont and Fletcher canon vol 1, Cambridge 1966; ed P. Edwards, A book of masques in honour of Allardyce Nicoll, Cambridge 1967.

HENRY BELLAMY
b. 1604

Iphis. Ms: Bodley Latin miscellaneous 1.17.

SAMUEL BERNARD
1591–1657

Andronicus Comnenus. Ms: BM Sloane 1767. *See* Sh Jb 34 1898, 47 1911.

JOHN BLENCOWE
b. 1609

§ 1

Mercurius. Ms: St John's College Oxford.

§ 2

Boas, F. S. Recently recovered mss at St John's College Oxford. MLR 11 1916.

SAMUEL BROOKE
d. 1632

Adelphe. Mss: Trinity College Cambridge R.3.9; R.10.4.
Melanthe. 1615; ed J. S. G. Bolton 1928. Ms: Folger Lib;
see B. M. Wagner, TLS 11 July 1935.
Scyros. Mss: Trinity College Cambridge R.6.3 (1612):
R.3.37; R.10.4; R.17.10; O.3.4; Emmanuel College
Cambridge III.117; Univ Lib Cambridge Ee.V.16;
Shipdham Church Thetford.

WILLIAM BROWNE
1591–1643?

§1

The Inner Temple masque. 1772 (presented 1615; also
called Ulysses and Circe); ed W. Thompson and T.
Davies, Works of Browne, 1772; ed W. C. Hazlitt,
Whole works of Browne, 1868; G. Goodwin, Poems of
Browne vol 2, 1894; ed G. Jones 1954.

§2

Cutts, J. P. Original music to Browne's Inner Temple
masque, and other Jacobean masque music. N & Q
May 1954.

ROBERT BURTON
1577–1670

See col 2219, below.

WILLIAM CARTWRIGHT
1611–43
Collections

Comedies, tragi-comedies, with other poems. 1651.
Includes The lady errant, The royall slave ('the third
edition'), The ordinary, The Siedge or Love's convert.
Plays and poems. Ed G. B. Evans, Madison 1951.

§1

The royall slave. Oxford 1639, 1640. Ms: BM additional
41,616.
The ordinary. Rptd Dodsley, and Ancient British drama
vol 3.

§2

Rice, W. G. Sources of Cartwright's Royal slave. MLN
45 1930.
Evans, W. M. To Splendora. PMLA 54 1939.
Danton, J. P. Cartwright and his Comedies, tragi-
comedies, with other poems 1651. Lib Quart 12 1942.
Evans, G. B. Comedies, tragi-comedies, with other poems:
a bibliographical study. Library 4th ser 23 1943.
Ruoff, J. E. Cartwright's human sacrifice scene in the
Royal slave. N & Q July 1957.
See also col 1990, below.

GEORGE CHAPMAN
1559?–1634
Bibliographies

Yamada, A. Chapman: a checklist of editions, biography
and criticism 1946–65. Research Opportunities in
Renaissance Drama 10 1967.

§1

Memorable maske of the Middle Temple and Lyncolns
Inne. [1613]; ed J. Nichols, Progresses of James I

vol 2, 1828; ed R. H. Shepherd, Works of Chapman:
plays, 1875; ed T. M. Parrott, Plays and poems of
Chapman: the comedies, 1914; ed G. B. Evans, Plays
of Chapman: the comedies, Urbana 1970.

§2

Jacquot, J. George Chapman. Paris 1951.
Dean-Smith, M. A Chapman masque. TLS 26 Jan 1951.
Reese, J. E. Unity in Chapman's Masque of the Middle
Temple and Lincoln's Inn. Stud in Eng Lit 1500–1900
4 1964.
Maclure, M. George Chapman. Toronto 1966.
See also col 1637, above.

JOHN CHRISTOPHERSON
d. 1558

Ἰεφθάτ. Ed F. H. Fobes and W. O. Sypherd, Newark
Del 1928 (with trn). Mss: Trinity College Cambridge
O.1.37; St John's College Cambridge 284.
Iephthe. Latin version of above. Ms: Bodley Tanner
466; *see* B. M. Wagner, TLS 26 Sept 1929; F. S. Boas,
TLS 30 Jan 1930.

ABRAHAM COWLEY
1618–67

See col 1219, above.

JOSEPH CROWTHER

[Cephalus and Procris]. Ms: St John's College Oxford.
See F. S. Boas, Recently recovered mss at St John's
College, Oxford, MLR 11 1916.

AQUILA CRUSO
fl. 1614–18

Euribates Pseudomagus. Ms: Emmanuel College Cambridge III.1.17. *See* Sh Jb 34 1898.

SAMUEL DANIEL
1562–1619

See col 1061, above.

SIR WILLIAM DAVENANT
1606–68

§1

The triumphs of the Prince d'Amour. 1635 (Middle
Temple masque); rptd Works, 1673; ed J. Maidment
and W. H. Logan, Dramatic works of Davenant,
Edinburgh 1872–4.

§2

Harbage, A. Davenant. Philadelphia 1935.
Marchant, E. C. Sir William Davenant. Oxford 1936.
Nethercot, A. H. Sir William Davenant. Chicago 1938.
See also col 1208, above.

RICHARD EDWARDS
1524–66

See col 1415, above.

JASPER FISHER

Fuimus Troes Ænid 2: the true Trojans. 1633; rptd Hazlitt's Dodsley vol 12.

PHINEAS FLETCHER
1586–1650

Sicelides a piscatory. 1631. *See col 1188, above.*

EDWARD FORSET
1553–1630

§ 1

Pedantius: comoedia. 1631; ed G. C. Moore Smith, Bang vol 8, 1905. Mss: Caius College Cambridge 62; Trinity College Cambridge R.17(9), a copy of Caius ms. *See* Sh Jb 34 1898.

§ 2

Moore Smith, G. C. Notes on some English university plays. MLR 3 1908.
— TLS 10 Oct 1918.

ABRAHAM FRAUNCE
fl. 1582–1633

See col 1106, above.

WILLIAM GAGER
1555–1632

§ 1

Dido. Performed 1583. Mss: Christ Church Oxford; BM additional 22,583 (imperfect). On BM mss *see* Sh Jb 34 1898. BM ms also ptd in A. Dyce, Works of Christopher Marlowe, 1853.
Meleager tragoedia nova. Oxford 1592. Performed 1582. *See* Sh Jb 34 1898.
Oedipus. MS: BM additional 22,583 (imperfect). *See* Sh Jb 34 1898.
Panniculus Hippolyto Senecae tragoediae assutus. 1591. Ptd as appendix to Meleager.
Ulysses redux: tragoedia nova. Oxford [1592]. *See* Sh Jb 34 1898.

§ 2

Boas, F. S. A defence of Oxford plays and players. Fortnightly Rev Aug 1907. On Gager's controversy with Dr John Rainolds.
Young, K. Gager's defence of the academic stage. Trans Wisconsin Acad 18 1916.
Brooke, C. F. T. Gager to Queen Elizabeth. SP 29 1932.
— Gager's Pyramis. Trans Connecticut Acad of Arts & Sciences 32 1936.
— Some pre-Armada propagandist poetry in English 1585–6. Proc Amer Philosophical Soc 135 1941.
— Latin drama in Renaissance England. ELH 13 1946.
— Life and times of Gager. Proc Amer Philosophical Soc 95 1951.
Williams, F. B. Gager's will. TLS 18 April 1936. Replies by J. B. Whitmore 25 April 1936, M. E. Slater 2 May 1936.
Bowers, R. M. Gager's Oedipus. SP 44 1949.

GEORGE GASCOIGNE
1542?–77

§ 1

Supposes. In A hundreth sundrie flowres, [1573] (performed at Gray's Inn 1566); 1575; Pleasantest works, 1587; rptd T. Hawkins, Origin of English drama, Oxford 1773; ed F. J. Child, Four old plays, Cambridge Mass 1848; ed W. C. Hazlitt, Complete poems, 1869; Supposes and Jocasta, ed J. W. Cunliffe 1906, and Works, 2 vols Cambridge 1907–10; ed R. W. Bond, Early plays from the Italian, Oxford 1911; ed J. Q. Adams, Chief pre-Shakespearean dramas, [1924]; ed C. R. Baskerville, V. B. Heltzel and A. H. Nethercot, Elizabethan and Stuart plays, New York [1934]; ed F. S. Boas, Five pre-Shakespearean comedies, Oxford 1934 (WC).

§ 2

Schelling, F. E. Life and writings of Gascoigne. Boston 1893.
Prouty, C. T. George Gascoigne. New York 1942.

GEORGE GASCOIGNE and FRANCIS KINWELMERSHE
fl. 1557–80?

Jocasta. In A hundredth sundrie flowres, [1573] (performed at Gray's Inn 1566); 1575 (?), 1587; ed F. J. Child, Four old plays, Cambridge Mass 1848; ed J. W. Cunliffe, Supposes and Jocasta, 1906, and Early English classical tragedies, Oxford 1912.

THOMAS GOFFE
c. 1591–1629

See col 1744, above.

WILLIAM GOLDINGHAM
d. 1589

Herodes. Ms: Univ Lib Cambridge Mm.1.24. *See* Sh Jb 34 1898.

GRAY'S INN

Gesta Grayorum. 1688 (performed Christmas 1594–5). Contains Masque of Proteus by Francis Davison (BM Harleian 541); ed J. Nichols, Progresses of Elizabeth, 1923; ed B. Brown, Law Sports at Gray's Inn, New York 1921; ed W. W. Greg 1914 (Malone Soc); ed D. S. Bland, Liverpool 1968.
Masque of flowers. 1614 (performed 1613); ed J. Nichols, Progresses of Elizabeth, 1823; ed A. W. à Beckett 1887; ed H. A. Evans, English masques, 1897. Ms: Gray's Inn Lib.
Masque of Mountebankes [performed 1617]. Ed J. P. Collier and P. Cunningham, Inigo Jones and five Court masques, 1848. Mss: Gray's Inn Lib; BM additional 5956; Bodley Ashmole 36–7; Huntington Lib HM 21.
Gesta Grayorum pt 2. Fragment of performance 1617–18. No connection with performance of 1594. Ed J. Nichols, Progresses of James I, 1828. Includes Masque of Mountebankes, above.
See G. E. Bentley, Jacobean and Caroline stage vol 5, Oxford 1956 (on Masque of Mountebankes); S. Orgel, The Jonsonian masque, Cambridge Mass 1965 (on Masque of Proteus).

NICHOLAS GRIMALD
1519?–62?

See col 1110, above.

MATTHEW GWYNNE
1558?–1627

Nero tragoedia nova. 1603, 1603, 1639. *See* Sh Jb 34 1898.
Vertumnus sive annus recurrens. 1607. Performed 1605.

JOHN HACKET
1592–1670

Loiola. 1648. Mss: Trinity College Cambridge R.17.9, R.17.10 (imperfect); Durham Cathedral Hunter mss (4° 26.1); Shipdham Church Thetford.

PETER HAUSTED
d. 1645

§1

The rival friends: a comoedie. 1632; ed L. J. Mills, Bloomington 1951.
Senile odium: comoedia. 1633; ed and tr L. J. Mills, Bloomington 1949. Ms: Longleat Lib.

§2

Mills, L. J. Peter Hausted. Bloomington 1945.
— Hausted's Elegy on Colonel Robert Arden. N & Q 30 Sept 1950.
Elmer, P. The death of Hausted. N & Q 7 Jan 1950.

WALTER HAWKESWORTH
d. 1606

Labyrinthus: comoedia. 1636. Performed 1622. Mss: Univ Lib Cambridge Ee.v.16; Trinity College Cambridge R.3.6, R.3.9; St John's College Cambridge J.8; Lambeth 836; Bodley Douce 43, 315; Shipdham Church, Thetford. *See* Sh Jb 34 1898.
Leander. Performed 1598, 1602. Mss: Trinity College Cambridge R.3.9; BM Sloane 1762; St John's College Cambridge J.8; Emmanuel College Cambridge I.2.30; Bodley Rawlinson miscellany 341; Univ Lib Cambridge Ee.v.16; Lambeth 838 (imperfect); Shipdham Church, Thetford. *See* Sh Jb 34 1898.

BARTEN HOLYDAY
1593–1661

§1

Τεχνογαμια: or the marriages of the arts: a comedie. 1618, 1630. (performed 1618); ed M. J. C. Cavanaugh, Washington 1942.

§2

Warton, T. History of English poetry: an unpublished continuation. Ed R. M. Baine, Los Angeles 1953 (Augustan Reprint Soc).
Nichols, J. In his Progresses of James I vol 4, 1828, pp. 1109–12.

THOMAS HUGHES
fl. 1587

§1

The misfortunes of Arthur. In Certain devises and shewes presented to her Majestie by the gentlemen of Grayes-Inne, 1587; rptd Hazlitt's Dodsley; ed J. P. Collier, Five old plays, 1828; ed H. C. Grumbine, Berlin 1900; TFT 1911; ed J. W. Cunliffe, Early English classical tragedies, Oxford 1912.

§2

Waller, E. A possible interpretation of the Misfortunes of Arthur. JEGP 1925.
Reese, G. Political import of the Misfortunes of Arthur. RES 21 1945.
Maxwell, J. C. Lucan's first translator. N & Q 29 Nov 1947.
— Seneca in The misfortunes of Arthur. N & Q May 1960.
Armstrong, W. A. Topicality of the Misfortunes of Arthur. N & Q Sept 1955.
— Elizabethan themes in the Misfortunes of Arthur. RES new ser 7 1956.
Dilke, O. A. W. Thomas Hughes, plagiarist. N & Q March 1963.
Ramel, J. Biographical notes on the authors of the Misfortunes of Arthur 1588. N & Q Dec 1967.
Logan, G. M. Hughes' use of Lucan in the Misfortunes of Arthur. RES new ser 20 1969.

LEONARD HUTTEN
1557?–1632

Bellum grammaticale: tragico-comoedia. 1635; ed A. Hume, Edinburgh 1658, 1698; ed R. Spencer 1726, 1729; ed J. Bolte, Andrea Guarnas Bellum grammaticale und seine Nachahmungen, Berlin 1908. *See* Sh Jb 34 1898.

INNER TEMPLE

Revels of 1561. In Gerard Legh, Accedens of armorie, 1562 etc. A selective account. *See* R. J. Schoeck, Gerard Legh, herald, N & Q April 1955 (reply by H. S. London, June 1955); D. S. Bland, Pegasus at the Inner Temple, N & Q Jan 1969; Arthur Broke, Gerard Legh and the Inner Temple, N & Q Dec 1969; M. Axton, Robert Dudley and the Inner Temple, Historical Jnl 13 1970.

WILLIAM JOHNSON
1534–1614

Valetudinarium. Performed 1637. Mss: Emmanuel College Cambridge 1.2.32; Univ Lib Cambridge Dd.III.73; St John's College Cambridge S, 59 (imperfect).

THOMAS LEGGE
1535–1607

§1

Richardus Tertius [performed 1579–80]. 1844 (Shakespeare Soc); Hazlitt-Collier, Shakespeare's library vol 2, 1875. Mss: Univ Lib Cambridge Mm.IV.40; Caius College Cambridge 62; Emmanuel College Cambridge 1.3.19; Clare College Cambridge Kk.3.12; Bodley Tanner 306 (first act only); BM Harley 2412, 6926. *See* Sh Jb 34 1898.

§2

Churchill, G. B. Richard III bis Shakespeare. Palaestra 10 1900.

Moore Smith, G. C. Notes on some English university plays. MLR 3 1908.

Lordi, R. J. The relationship of Richardus Tertius to the main Richard III plays. Boston Univ Stud in Eng 5 1961.

JASPER MAYNE
1604–72

See col *1751*, above.

ROBERT MEAD
1616–53

The combat of love and friendship. 1654.

PETER MEASE
fl. 1618–27

§1

Adrastus parentans sive Vindicta: tragoedia. Ms: BM additional 10,417.

§2

Moore Smith, G. C. Notes on some English university plays. MLR 3 1908.

WILLIAM MEWE
fl. 1620–50

Pseudomagia. Mss: Emmanuel College Cambridge I.3.16; Trinity College Cambridge R.17.10.

MIDDLE TEMPLE

Le Prince d'Amour. 1660. Performed 1599? See J. A. Manning, Memorials of Sir Benjamin Rudyerd, 1841 (life of author, or part-author, of Le Prince d'Amour); P. J. Finkelpearl, Sir John Davies and the 'Price d'Amour', N & Q Aug 1963.

THOMAS MIDDLETON
1580–1627

§1

The Inner-Temple masque: or masque of heroes. 1619; ed A. Dyce, Works, 1840; ed A. H. Bullen, Works, 1885. See also col *1647*, above.

§2

Barker, R. H. Thomas Middleton. 1958.

THOMAS NEALE
1614–46

The warde: a tragicomedy [performed 1637]. Ed J. A. Mitchell, Philadelphia 1937. Ms: Bodley Rawlinson Poetry 79 (contains several works by Neale 1637–44).

THOMAS NORTON
1532–84
and
THOMAS SACKVILLE
1536–1608

§1

The tragedie of Gorboduc. 1565 (performed at Inner Temple 1561), [1570?] (as Ferrex and Porrex), 1590; Dodsley; ed T. Hawkins, Origin of English drama, Oxford 1773; ed W. D. Cooper 1847 (Shakespeare Soc); ed R. W. Sackville-West, Works of Sackvill, 1859; ed L. T. Smith, Heilbronn 1883; Manly; ed J. S. Farmer, Dramatic writings of Richard Edwards, Norton and Sackville, 1906; TFT 1908; ed H. A. Watt, Madison 1910; ed A. Thorndyke, Minor Elizabethan drama, 1910; ed J. W. Cunliffe, Early English classical tragedies, Oxford 1912; ed J. Q. Adams, Chief pre-Shakespearean Dramas, [1924]; ed C. R. Baskervill, V. B. Heltzel and A. H. Nethercot, Elizabethan and Stuart plays, New York [1934]; A. K. McIlwraith, Five Shakespearean tragedies, Oxford 1938 (WC).

§2

Schmidt, H. Seneca's influence upon Gorboduc. MLN 2 1887.

Koeppel, E. Beiträge zur Geschichte des elisabethanischen Dramas. E Studien 16 1892.

Small, S. A. The political import of the Norton half of Gorboduc. PMLA 44 1931.

Baker, H. Induction to tragedy. Baton Rouge 1939.

Reese, G. C. The question of the succession in Elizabethan drama. SE 22 1942.

Herrick, M. T. Senecan influence in Gorboduc. In Studies in honor of A. M. Drummond, New York 1944.

Prior, M. E. In his Language of tragedy, New York 1947.

Swart, J. Thomas Sackville. Groningen 1949.

Johnson, S. F. Gorboduc and Howell, his devises 1581. N & Q 13 Oct 1951.

Peters, R. A. Gorboduc and Grafton's Chronicle. N & Q 22 Aug 1957.

De Mendonça, B. H. C. The influence of Gorboduc on King Lear. Shakespeare Survey 13 1960.

Bacquet, P. L'influence de Sénèque sur Gorboduc. Etudes Anglaises 14 1961.

— Structure et valeur dramatiques de Gorboduc. Filoski Pregled (Belgrade) 1–2 1964.

— L'imitation de Sénèque dans Gorboduc. In J. Jacquot and M. Oddon, Les tragédies de Sénèque et le théâtre de la Renaissance, Paris 1964.

— Contribution à l'étude de Sackville. Die Neueren Sprachen 13 1964.

— Le Moyen Âge anglais et les idées morales de Sackville. Bulletin de la Faculté des Lettres de Strasbourg 42 1964.

— Un contemporain d'Elizabeth I: Sackville. Geneva 1966.

Turner, R. Y. Pathos and the Gorboduc tradition. HLQ 25 1962.

Cauthen, I. B. Gorboduc, Ferrex and Porrex: the first two quartos. SB 15 1963.

Talbert, E. W. The political import and the first two audiences of Gorboduc. In Studies in honor of De Witt T. Starnes, Austin 1967.

PHILIP PARSONS
1595–1653

Atalanta. Ms BM Harley 6924.

THOMAS RANDOLPH
1605–36

Bibliographies
Tannenbaum, S. A. and D. R. Thomas Randolph. New York 1947.

Collections
Poems with the Muses looking-glasse and Amyntas. 1638, 1640, 1664 (5th edn); rptd Dodsley; Ancient British drama vol 2.

Poetical and dramatic works. Ed W. C. Hazlitt 2 vols 1875.

§1
Aristippus: or the joviall philosopher. 1630 (3 edns), 1631, 1635? Added to 4th edn of Poems, above. Ms: BM Sloane 2531 (variants from ptd text).

The jealous lovers: a comedie. Cambridge 1632, 1634, 1640 (also in 1640 edn of Poems).

Hey for honesty, down with knavery, augmented and published by F.J. 1651. Adaptation of Aristophanes' Plutus.

The drinking academy. Ed H. E. Rollins, PMLA 39 1924; ed Rollins and S. A. Tannenbaum, Cambridge Mass 1930. G. C. Moore Smith, RES 6 1930, assigns to Robert Baron, but see Rollins, PMLA 46 1931. Ms: Huntington Lib HM 91.

Cornelianum dolium: comoedia. 1638. Drafted by Randolph and completed by Richard Braithwait?

§2
Greg, W. W. In his Pastoral poetry and pastoral drama, 1906.

Kottas, K. Randolph: sein Leben und seine Werke. Vienna 1909.

Moore Smith, G. C. The canon of Randolph's dramatic works. RES 1 1925.

—— Thomas Randolph. Proc Br Acad 23 1927.

Day, C. L. Randolph's part in the authorship of Hey for honesty. PMLA 41 1926.

—— New poems by Randolph. RES 8 1932.

Bowers, F. T. Ben Jonson, Randolph and the Drinking Academy. N & Q 4 Sept 1937.

—— Problems in Randolph's Drinking Academy and its manuscript. HLQ 1 1938.

—— Mariot's two editions of Randolph's Aristippus. Library 4th ser 20 1940.

—— A possible Randolph holograph. Ibid.

—— Randolph's Salting. MP 39 1942.

Dunlap, R. Some unpublished verses by Randolph. MLN 39 1942.

Bentley, G. E. Randolph's Praeludium and the Salisbury Court theatre. In J. Q. Adams memorial studies, Washington 1948.

J. RICKETS
fl. 1625–33

Byrsa Basiliea. Performed 1569–70. Ms: Bodley Tanner 209. See Sh Jb 34 1898.

GEORGE RUGGLE
1575–1622

§1
Ignoramus: comoedia. 1630, 1630 (2nd edn), 1659 1668, 1707, 1731, Dublin 1736, London 1737; ed J. S. Hawkins 1787. Mss: Bodley Douce 43; Tanner 306; BM Harley 6869 (imperfect), 7042, folio 245 (cast only).

Ignoramus: a comedy. 1662. Tr into English by R. C[oddington].

An English prologue and epilogue to Ignoramus, by George Dyer. Cambridge 1797.

The English lawyer: a comedy acted at the Royal Theatre, written by Edward Ravenscroft. 1678.

§2
Mullinger, J. B. In his University of Cambridge vol 2, Cambridge 1884. Analysis of plot of Ignoramus.

Wagner, B. M. John Rhodes and Ignoramus. RES 5 1929.

JOHN SADLER
1615–74

Masquerade du ciel. 1640.

GEORGE SALTERNE
b. 1658

Tomumbeius sive sultanici in Aegypto inperii eversio: tragoedia. Ms: Bodley Rawlinson Poetry 75. See Sh Jb 34 1898.

JOSEPH SIMEON or SIMONS
1594–1671

Fratrum concordia saeva seu Zeno. Rome 1648.

Leo Armenus sive impietas punita. With Zeno, above, in J. Simonis, Tragoedia quinque, Liège 1657, London 1680, 1697.

Mss of both plays, Univ Lib Cambridge Ii.VI.35; Zeno only, BM Harley 5024; St John's College Cambridge.

THOMAS SNELLING
b. 1614

Thibaldus. Oxford 1640, 1650 (as Pharamus). See J. Bolte, Die Oxforder Tragödie Thibaldus, Sh Jb 27 1892.

THOMAS SPARROWE
fl. 1630–3

Confessor. Ms: Bodley Rawlinson Poetry 77. See G. C. Moore Smith, Notes on some English university plays, MLR 3 1908.

WILLIAM STEVENSON?
fl. 1553

Gammer Gurton's nedle. 1575. See col 1417, above.

WILLIAM STRODE
1602–45

The floating island: a tragi-comedy. 1655 (performed at Oxford 1636); ed B. Dobell, Poetical works of Strode, 1907; ed E. G. Hoffsten, St Louis 1908.

EDMUND STUB
§1

Fraus honesta: comoedia. 1632. Performed at Cambridge 1618. Mss: Trinity College Cambridge R.17.9 and R.17.10; Emmanuel College Cambridge III.1.17; BM Harley 2296.

§2

Moore Smith, G. C. Notes on some English university plays. MLR 3 1908.

THOMAS TOMKIS
d. 1634?

§1

Lingua: or the combat of the tongue and the five senses. 1607, 1617, 1622, 1657, nd; rptd Dodsley; Collier-Dodsley; Hazlitt's Dodsley; TFT 1913.
Albumazar [comedy presented at Cambridge 1614]. 1615, 1615, 1634, 1634 ('newly revised and corrected by a speciall hand'), 1688; rptd Ancient British drama; Hazlitt's Dodsley; ed H. G. Dick, Berkeley 1944.

§2

Moore Smith, G. C. Some notes on English university plays. MLR 3 1908. On Lingua.
Boas, F. S. Macbeth and Lingua. MLR 4 1909.
Tilley, M. P. The comedy Lingua and Du Bartas La sepmaine. MLN 42 1927.
— The comedy Lingua and Sir John Davies's Nosce teipsum. MLN 44 1929.
Dick, H. G. The lover in a cask: a tale of a tub. Italica 18 1941.
— Presentation copy of Tomkis's Albumazor. N & Q 6 Jan 1941.
Mander, G. P. Thomas Tomkis. TLS 31 March 1945.

NICHOLAS UDALL
1505–56

See col 1414, above.

SIR FRANCIS VERNEY
1583–1615

The tragedye of Antiope. Ms: Bodley English Poetry 3.5. See G. C. Moore Smith, Notes on some English university plays, MLR 3 1908.

THOMAS VINCENT
d. 1663

§1

Paria. 1648. Performed at Cambridge 1627. Ms: Emmanuel College Cambridge 1.3.16.

§2

Odinga, T. Vincent's Paria. E Studies 16 1892.
Moore Smith, G. C. College plays. 1923.

ROBERT WARD
fl. 1623–42

Fucus Histriomastix. Ed G. C. Moore Smith 1909. Mss: Lambeth Palace 838; Bodley Rawlinson Poetry 21.

NATHANIEL WIBOURNE
d. 1613

Machiavellus. Ms: Bodley Douce 234 (imperfect). Dated 9 Dec 1597. Attribution to Wibourne in Douce's handwriting. See Sh Jb 34 1898.

GEORGE WILDE
1610–65

Eumorphus sive Cupido adultus: comoedia. Performed at Oxford 1634. Ms: BM additional 14,047.
Love's hospitall. Performed at Oxford 1636. Ms: BM additional 14,047.
The converted robber: a pastorall. Performed at Oxford 1637. Ms: BM additional 14,047. Attributed to Wilde because included with other 2 plays, above.

ROBERT WILMOT, HENRY NOEL, R. STAFFORD, G. AL. and CHRISTOPHER HATTON

§1

The tragedie of Tancred and Gismund. 1591, 1592. Performed at the Inner Temple. Rptd Dodsley; Hazlitt's Dodsley; Brandl; TFT: ed J. W. Cunliffe, Early English classical tragedies, Oxford 1912.

§2

Cunliffe, J. W. Gismund of Salerne. PMLA 21 1906.
Klein, D. According to the decorum of these daies. PMLA 33 1918.
Habicht, W. Die Nutrix-Szenen in Gismond of Salerne und Tancred and Gismund. Anglia 81 1936.
Murray, J. Tancred and Gismund. RES 14 1938.
Griffin, E. G. Gismund of Salerne: a critical appreciation. REL 4 1963.

RALPH WORSELEY
d. 1590

§1

Synedrii. Latin verse tragedy, written 1553–4. Ms: Trinity College Cambridge O.3.25. Also contains Synedrium, an imperfect version in Latin prose.

§2

Boas, F. S. University drama in the Tudor age. 1914. Appendix 2.

CHRISTOPHER WREN
1591–1658

ΦΥΣΙ-ΠΟΝΟ-ΜΑΧΙΑ. Latin comedy. Ms: Bodley 30.

RICHARD ZOUCHE
1590–1661

The sophister: a comedy. 1639. Ms: BM Harley 6869 (as Fallacy: or the troubles of the great Hermenia, dated 1531, different from ptd version).

ANONYMOUS PLAYS

[Absalon]. Ms: BM Stowe 957. *See* Sh Jb 34 1898; F. S. Boas, University drama in the Tudor age, 1914 (appendix 1).

The tragedy of Amurath. Performed at Oxford 1618. Historical Mss Commission Report vol 1, p. 49.

Andronicus: a tragedy. 1661. Printer's preface states play 'was born some eighteen years since in Oxford'.

Antonius Bassianus Caracalla. Latin tragedy. Ms: Bodley Rawlinson C.590. *See* Sh Jb 34 1898.

A merrie dialogue betweene Band, Cuffe and Ruffe. 1615, 1661, 1615 (as Exchange ware at the second hand) (with introductory dialogue). Performed at Cambridge. Rptd T. Park, Harleian miscellany vol 10, 1813; ed J. O. Halliwell(-Phillipps), Contributions to early English literature, 1849; ed C. Hindley, Miscellanea antiqua anglicana vol 2, 1871. Ms: BM additional 23,723.

The barriers. Ed D. S. Bland, Guildhall Miscellany 6 1956. Performance by the 4 Inns of Court 1616. Ms: Guildhall, London 4160.

The birthe of Hercules. Ed M. W. Wallace 1903; ed R. W. Bond 1910 (Malone Soc).

The tragedie of Caesar's revenge. nd (performed at Oxford); rptd as The tragedie of Caesar and Pompey, 1607; F. S. Boas 1911 (Malone Soc); ed W. Mühlfeld, Sh Jb 47–8 1911–12. *See* T. M. Parrot, The academic tragedy of Caesar and Pompey, MLR 5 1910.

[The Christmas prince]. Performed at Oxford 1607. Ms: St John's College Oxford. Includes following plays of unknown authorship: Ara fortunae; Saturnalia; Philomela; Time's complaint; The seven dayes of the weeke; Philomathes; Ira seu Tumulus fortunae; Periander. Narrative part of ms and The seven dayes ptd in Miscellanea antiqua anglicana vol 1, 1816, as The Christmas prince. Ed F. S. Boas and W. W. Greg 1923 (Malone Soc).

Schelling, F. E. The Queen's progress. 1904.

Harbage, A. The authorship of the Christmas prince. MLN 50 1935.

Cancer: comoedia. 1648. With Loiola, Stoicus Vapulaus and Paria. Ms: Folger Lib, Washington. *See* G. C. Moore Smith, College plays, 1923.

Club law. nd (performed at Cambridge c. 1599); ed G. C. Moore Smith 1907. Ms: St John's College Cambridge S.62 (imperfect). *See* W. W. Greg, MLR 4 1909.

Clytophon. Latin comedy. Ms: Emmanuel College Cambridge III.1.17. *See* Sh Jb 34 1898.

Fatum Vortigerni. Ms: BM Lansdowne 723. *See* Sh Jb 1898; W. H. McCabe, TLS 15 Aug 1935 (by Thomas Carleton, acted at Douay 1619).

Fraus Pia. Latin comedy. Ms: BM Sloane 1855. *See* G. C. Moore Smith, Notes on some English university plays, MLR 3 1908.

Grobiana's nuptialls. Performed at Oxford. Ms: Bodley 30.

Hispanus. Performed at Cambridge 1586. Ms: Bodley Douce 234. *See* Sh Jb 34 1898.

Hymeneus. nd (performed at Cambridge 1579); ed G. C. Moore Smith 1908. Mss: Caius College Cambridge 62; St John's College Cambridge S. 45. *See* Sh Jb 34 1898.

[Jovis et Junonis nuptiae]. Latin mythological play. Ms: Trinity College Cambridge R.10.4, lacks title-page.

Laelia. Ed G. C. Moore Smith, Cambridge 1910. Ms: Lambeth Palace 838. *See* Sh Jb 34 1898; G. C. Moore Smith, The Cambridge play Laelia, MLR 6 1911, 23 1928.

Mercurius rusticans. Latin comedy. Ms: Bodley Wood D. 18.

Microcosmus. Latin Cambridge play. Ms: Trinity College Cambridge R.10.4. *See* G. C. Moore Smith, College plays, 1923.

Narcissus: a Twelve Night merriment. Performed at Oxford 1602. Ed M. L. Lee 1893. Ms: Bodley Rawlinson Poetry 212. *See* C. H. Collister, Narcissus plays distinguished, MLN 20 1905.

Nottola. Latin comedy. Ms: Bodley Douce 47.

[The Parnassus plays]. The pilgrimage to Parnassus, with the two parts of the return from Parnassus: three comedies performed in St John's College Cambridge AD MDXCVII–MDCI. Ed W. D. Macray 1886; TFT 1912; ed J. B. Leishman 1949.

The returne from Parnassus: or the scourge of simony. 1606, 1606; ed T. Hawkins, Origin of the British drama vol 3, Oxford 1773; Ancient British drama; Hazlitt's Dodsley; ed E. Arber 1880; ed O. Smeaton 1905; TFT 1912. Mss: Bodley Rawlinson D 398, no 72; Folger Lib 448.12.

Bullen, A. H. The works of John Day. 1881. Introd.

Mullinger, J. B. In his University of Cambridge vol 1, 1884.

Hales, J. W. Academy 19 March 1887. On Macray, above.

—— Three English comedies. Macmillan's Mag May 1887.

Fleay, F. G. In his Biographical chronicle of the English drama, 2 vols 1891.

Sarrazin, G. Thomas Kyd und sein Kreis. Berlin 1892.

Ward, A. W. In his History of English dramatic literature vol 2, 1899.

Moore Smith, G. C. The Parnassus plays. MLR 10 1915.

Golding, S. R. The Parnassus plays. N & Q 19 Nov 1927.

Northam J. The Parnassus plays. TLS 24 Feb 1950.

Thomas, S. and M. L. Reyburn. A note on Owen Gwyn and the return from Parnassus pt 2. PMLA 76 1961.

Parthenia: comaedia pastoralis. Ms: Emmanuel College Cambridge I.3.16. *See* Sh Jb 34 1898.

Pastor Fidus. Pastoral tragi-comedy. Mss: Univ Lib Cambridge Ff.II.9; Trinity College Cambridge R.3.27. *See* Sh Jb 34 1898; W. W. Greg, Pastoral poetry and pastoral drama, 1906.

Pathomacia: or the battell of affections. 1630. Ms: BM Harley 6869; Bodley English Miscellany 3. 5 (imperfect). *See* G. C. Moore Smith, Notes on some English university plays, MLR 3 1908.

Perfidus Hetruscus. Ms: Bodley Rawlinson C.787. *See* Sh Jb 34 1898.

[Psyche et filii ejus]. Latin allegorical play. Ms: Bodley Rawlinson Poetry 171. *See* G. C. Moore Smith, Notes on some English university plays, MLR 3 1908.

Romeus et Julietta. Ms: BM Sloane 1775. *See* H. de W. Fuller, Romeo and Juliette, MP 4 1907.

Sapientia Salomonis. Tragi-comedy. Performed at Cambridge 1565–6. Ms: BM additional 20,061 (performed at Westminster School). *See* Sh Jb 34 1898.

Senilis Amor. Ed and tr L. J. Mills, Bloomington 1952. Ms: Bodley Rawlinson Poetry 9 (imperfect), dated 1635. L. B. Morgan, Sh Jb 47 1911, suggests author is Peter Hausted; rejected by Mills.

Sylvanus. Latin comedy. Performed at Cambridge 1596. Ms: Bodley Douce 234. *See* Sh Jb 34 1898.

Solymannidae tragoedia. Performed 1581. Ms: BM Lansdowne 723. *See* Sh Jb 1898.

Stoicus Vapulans. 1648. Allegorical comedy. Performed at Cambridge 1618.

Susenbrotus comoedia. Performed at Cambridge 1615. Mss: Bodley Rawlinson Poetry 195; Earl of Ellesmere. with title of Fortunia. *See* G. C. Moore Smith, College plays, 1923.

Timon. nd. Ed A. Dyce 1842 (Shakespeare Soc). Ms: Victoria & Albert Museum Dyce 52. *See* C. F. T. Brooke, Tudor drama, 1911; G. A. Bonnard, Note sur les sources de Timon of Athens, Etudes Anglaises 7

1954; M. C. Bradbrook, The comedy of Timon, Renaissance Drama 9 1966, and The tragic pageant of Timon of Athens, Cambridge 1966.

Wily beguilde. 1606, 1623, 1630, 1635, [?]; ed T. Hawkins, Origin of the English drama vol 3, Oxford 1773; Hazlitt's Dosley; ed W. W. Greg 1912 (Malone Soc); TFT 1912.

Boas, F. S. Works of Thomas Kyd. 1901. Introd.

Sarrazin, G. Thomas Kyd und sein Kreis. 1892.

Baldwin, M. Wily beguiled. SP 19 1922.

Maxwell, B. The two angry women of Abington and Wily beguiled. PQ 20 1941.

Krzyzanowski, J. Some conjectural remarks of Elizabethan dramatists. N & Q 22 June 1947, 16 Sept 1950.

Worke for cutlers. 1615. Comedy. Performed at Cambridge. Rptd T. Park, Harleian miscellany vol 10, 1813; ed C. Hindley, Miscellanea antiqua anglicana vol 2, 1872; ed A. F. Sieveking 1904.

Zelotypus. Performed at Cambridge 1606. Mss: Emmanuel College Cambridge III.i.17; Trinity College Cambridge R.3.9. See Sh Jb 34 1898; G. C. Moore Smith, Notes on some early English university plays, MLR 3 1908.

D. S. B.

4. RELIGION

I. HUMANISTS AND REFORMERS

Linacre, Erasmus, Colet, More, Tindale, Gardiner, Latimer, Cheke, Coverdale, Cranmer,
Lupset, Fish, Elyot, Ridley, Parker, Caius, Ponet, Ascham, Lever, Wilson, Fulke

For a more detailed bibliographical survey, especially of the minor figures, see H. Gough, A general index to the publications
of the Parker Society, *1855 (Parker Soc); for more recent pbns, especially on the Continent, see bibliography in P. Meissner,*
England im Zeitalter von Humanismus, Renaissance und Reformation, *1952, and in V. de S. Pinto,* The English
Renaissance, *1966, below.*

GENERAL STUDIES

Seebohm, F. The Oxford reformers of 1498: Colet, More,
Erasmus. 1867, 1869 (enlarged).
Dixon, R. W. History of the Church of England. 6 vols
1878–1902.
Morley, H. English writers. Vol 7, 1891. Bibliographies.
Einstein, L. The Italian Renaissance in England. New
York 1902.
— Tudor ideals. New York 1921.
Gairdner, J. A history of the English Church in the 16th
century. 1902.
— Lollardry and the Reformation. 4 vols 1908–13.
Hale, E. E. Ideas on rhetoric in the sixteenth century.
PMLA 18 1903.
Gasquet, F. A. The bibliography of some devotional books
printed by the earliest English printers. Trans Bibl Soc 7
1904.
Frere, W. H. A history of the English Church 1558–1625.
1904.
Opus epistolarum Des. Erasmi Roterodami. Ed P. S.
and H. M. Allen and H. W. Garrod 11 vols Oxford
1906–47.
Moore, J. L. Tudor-Stuart views on the English language.
Halle 1910.
Allen, P. S. Some sixteenth-century manuscript letter-
books. Trans Bibl Soc 12 1913.
— The age of Erasmus. Oxford 1914.
Berdan, J. M. Early Tudor poetry 1485–1547. New York
1920.
Taylor, H. O. Thought and expression in the sixteenth
century. 2 vols New York 1920–1, 1962.
Kelso, R. The doctrine of the English gentleman. Urbana
1929.
Janelle, P. L'Angleterre catholique à la veille du schisme.
Paris 1935.
Schirmer, W. F. Der englische Humanismus. Neuphilo-
logische Monatsschrift 7 1936.
Meissner, P. Renaissance und Humanismus im Rahmen
der national-englischen Kulturidee. Sh Jb 73 1937
— England im Zeitalter von Humanismus, Renaissance
und Reformation. Heidelberg 1952.
Bush, D. Tudor humanism and Henry VIII. UTQ 7 1938.
— The Renaissance and English humanism. Toronto 1939.
Pinto, V. de S. The English Renaissance 1510–1688. 1938,
1951 (rev), 1966 (rev). With bibliography.
Tilley, A. Greek studies in England in the early sixteenth
century. EHR 53 1938.
Hutson, H. H. John Leland's list of early English
humanists. HLQ 2 1939.
— The epigram in the English Renaissance. Princeton
1947.
Rebora, P. Aspetti dell'umanesimo in Inghilterra.
Rinascita 2 1939.
Tuve, R. Ancients, Moderns and Saxons. ELH 6 1939.
On the study of Anglo-Saxon for purposes of religious
polemic.
Baumer, F. le van. The early Tudor theory of kingship.
New Haven 1940.

Collins, J. B. Christian mysticism in the Elizabethan age.
Baltimore 1940.
Williams, R. R. Religion and the English vernacular: a
historical study 1526–53. 1940.
Wright, L. B. The significance of religious writings in the
English Renaissance. JHI 1 1940.
Hyma, A. The continental origins of English humanism.
HLQ 4 1941.
Williams, A. L. The two matters: classical and Christian in
the Renaissance. SP 38 1941.
— The common expositor: an account of the commen-
taries on Genesis 1537–1633. Chapel Hill 1948.
Jones, R. F. The moral sense of simplicity. In Studies in
honor of F. W. Shipley, St Louis 1942. On reaction
against eloquence in writing.
White, H. C. Some continuing traditions in English
devotional literature. PMLA 57 1942.
— Social criticism in popular religious literature of the
sixteenth century. New York 1944.
— Sixteenth-century English devotional literature. In
J. Q. Adams memorial studies, Washington 1948.
— The Tudor books of private devotion. Madison 1951.
— Tudor books of saints and martyrs. Madison 1963.
Zeeveld, W. G. Social equalitarianism in a Tudor crisis.
JHI 7 1946. The Pilgrimage of grace.
— Foundations of Tudor policy. Cambridge Mass 1948.
Barker, E. The connection of the Renaissance and the
Reformation. In his Traditions of civility, Cambridge
1948.
Castelli, A. Note sull'umanesimo in Inghilterra. Milan
[1949].
Hexter, J. H. The education of the aristocracy in the
Renaissance. Jnl Modern History 22 1950; rptd in his
Reappraisals in history, New York 1963.
Southern, A. C. Elizabethan recusant prose 1559–82.
1950.
Surtz, E. L. 'Oxford reformers' and scholasticism. SP 47
1950.
Bennett, H. S. English books and readers 1475–1557.
Cambridge 1952, 1969 (rev).
Jayne, S. Ficino and the Platonism of the English Renais-
ance. Comparative Lit 4 1952.
Siegel, P. N. English humanism and the new Tudor
aristocracy. JHI 13 1952.
Borinski, L. Das politische Denken des englischen
Humanismus. Studium Generale 6 1953.
Butterworth, C. C. The English primers 1529–45.
Philadelphia 1953.
Cassirer, E. The Platonic Renaissance in England. Edin-
burgh 1953. Tr from German, Leipzig 1932.
Smith, L. B. Tudor prelates and politics. Princeton
1953.
Caspari, F. Humanism and the social order in Tudor
England. Chicago 1954.
Hale, J. R. England and the Italian Renaissance. 1954.
Lewis, C. S. English literature in the sixteenth century
excluding drama. Oxford 1954 (OHEL).

Loane, M. L. Masters of the English Reformation. 1954.

Parks, G. B. The English traveler to Italy vol 1: the Middle Ages (to 1525). Rome 1954.

Chester, A. G. The 'new learning': a semantic note. Stud in Renaissance 2 1955.

Kaegi, W. The transformation of the spirit in the Renaissance. In Spirit and nature: papers from the Eranos yearbooks vol i, 1955.

Howell, W. S. Logic and rhetoric in England 1500–1700. Princeton 1956.

Nugent, E. M. The thought and culture of the English Renaissance: an anthology of Tudor prose 1481–1555. Cambridge 1956.

Rupp, E. G. Six makers of English religion 1500–1700. 1957.

Dugmore, C. W. The mass and the English reformers. 1958.

Maclure, M. The Paul's cross sermons 1534–1642. Toronto 1958.

Porter, H. C. Reformation and reaction in Tudor Cambridge. Cambridge 1958.

Clarke, M. L. Classical education in Britain 1500–1900. Cambridge 1959.

Hogrefe, P. The Sir Thomas More circle. Urbana 1959.

Mason, H. A. Humanism and poetry in the early Tudor period. 1959.

Ong, W. J. Latin language study as a Renaissance puberty rite. SP 56 1959.

— Tudor writings on rhetoric. Stud in Renaissance 15 1968. On influence of Cicero, Erasmus and Ramus.

Ferguson, A. B. The Indian summer of English chivalry. Durham NC 1960.

— The articulate citizen and the English Renaissance. Durham NC 1965.

Gilbert, N. W. Renaissance concepts of method. New York 1960.

Greenslade, S. L. The English reformers and the Fathers of the Church. Oxford 1960.

Jungmann, E. Die politische Rhetorik in der englischen Renaissance. Britannica et Americana 5 1960.

Knox, D. B. The doctrine of faith in the reign of Henry VIII. 1961.

Lehmberg, S. E. English humanists, the Reformation and the problem of counsel. Archiv für Reformationsgeschichte 52 1961.

Adams, R. P. The better part of valor: More, Erasmus, Colet and Vives on humanism, war and peace 1496–1535. Seattle 1962.

McLuhan, H. M. The Gutenberg galaxy. Toronto 1962.

Blench, J. W. Preaching in England in the late fifteenth and sixteenth centuries 1450–c. 1600. Oxford 1964.

Clebsch, W. A. England's earliest Protestants 1520–35. New Haven 1964.

Loades, D. M. The press under the early Tudors: censorship and sedition. Trans Cambridge Bibl Soc 4 1964.

— The Oxford martyrs. 1970.

Bluhm, H. S. Martin Luther: creative translator. St Louis 1965. On Tindale and Coverdale.

Charlton, K. Education in Renaissance England. 1965.

Hughes, P. E. Theology of the English reformers. 1965.

McConica, J. K. English humanists and Reformation politics. Oxford 1965.

Parker, T. H. L. (ed). English reformers. 1966.

Simon, J. Education and society in Tudor England. Cambridge 1966.

Pace, R. De fructu qui ex doctrina percipitur 1517. Ed and tr F. Manley and R. S. Sylvester, New York 1967.

Bowker, M. The secular clergy in the diocese of Lincoln 1495–1520. Cambridge 1968.

Heninger, S. K. Tudor literature of the physical sciences. HLQ 32 1969.

O'Malley, C. D. Tudor medicine and biology. HLQ 32 1969. Includes Caius, Linacre and Elyot.

Coogan, R. Petrarch's Trionfi and the English Renaissance. SP 67 1970.

— Petrarch's Latin prose and the English Renaissance. SP 68 1971.

Masek, R. Humanistic interests in the early Tudor episcopate. Church History 39 1970.

Whitney, R. D. J. The Tudor Commonwealth 1529–59. 1970.

McLean, A. Humanism and the rise of science in Tudor England. 1972.

JOHN FISHER
1469–1535

See col 1923, below.

THOMAS LINACRE
1460?–1524

§1

Linacri progymnasmata. [1510?]. A Latin grammar written for Colet's school but not adopted. First surviving edn 1519?

De emendata structura latini sermonis libri sex. 1524, Paris 1527, Basle 1530, Paris 1532 (2nd edn), 1540; ed P. Melanchthon 1543; Lyons 1539, 1544, 1548, Paris 1550, Venice 1557, Lyons 1559, Menston 1968 (facs of 1524).

Rudimenta grammatices diligenter castigata denuo. [1523?], [1525], Menston 1971 (facs of 1525); tr G. Buchanan, Paris 1533, Lyons 1539, Paris 1540, 1545, Lyons 1548, Paris 1550, Lyons 1552, Paris 1556.

For Linacre's trns and edns of Greek and Latin scientific works see H. Morley, English writers *vol 7 1891 p. 323, and col 2365, below.*

§2

Johnson, J. N. The life of Linacre. Ed R. Graves 2 vols 1835.

Payne, J. F. Galen, De temperamentis [ed Linacre]. 1881 (facs). Introd contains important corrections and addns to Johnson, above.

Burrows, M. Linacre's catalogue of books belonging to Grocyn, with a memoir of Grocyn. Collectanea Oxford Historical Soc 2 1890.

Blach, S. Die Schriftsprache in der Londoner Paulsschule (bei Colet, Lily, Linacre, Grocyn). Halberstadt 1905.

Osler, W. Thomas Linacre. Cambridge 1908.

Williamson, R. T. English physicians of the past. Newcastle 1923.

Fulton, J. F. Early medical humanists: Leonicenus, Linacre and Thomas Elyot. New England Jnl of Medicine 205 1934.

Mitchell, R. J. Thomas Linacre in Italy. EHR 50 1935.

Weiss, R. Letters of Linacre. TLS 26 Sept 1936. Unpbd letter to P. Machiavelli.

— Notes on Linacre. Studi e Testi 124 1946.

— Un allievo [Linacre]. In Il Poliziano e il suo tempo: atti del IV Convegno Internazionale di Studi sul Rinascimento, Florence 1957.

Thornton, J. L. Andrew Boorde's Dyetary of helth and its attribution to Linacre. Library 5th ser 2 1948.

Parks, G. B. The English traveller to Italy. Vol 1, 1954. Corrects facts of Linacre's stay in Italy.

Himsworth, H. The integration of medicine: the endeavour of Linacre. Br Medical Jnl 23 July 1955.

Sharpe, W. D. Linacre: an English physician scholar of the Renaissance. Bull History of Medicine 34 1960.

Brown, T. J. English scientific autographs: Linacre. Book Collector 13 1964.

Cameron, R. Linacre at the portal to scientific medicine. Br Medical Jnl 5 Sept 1964.

Clark, G. N. A history of the Royal College of Physicians of London. Vol 1, 1964. Ch 3.

O'Malley, C. D. English medical humanists: Linacre and Caius. Lawrence Kansas 1965.

— Tudor medicine and biology. HLQ 32 1969.

Marc'hadour, G. Thomas More and Linacre. Moreana 4 1967.

Watson, C. J. Linacre and Locke: pillars of medical humanism. California Medicine 107 1967.

Bennett, J. W. John Morer's will: Linacre and Sellyng's Greek teaching. Stud in Renaissance 15 1968.

DESIDERIUS ERASMUS
1469?–1536

This is not a bibliography of Erasmus, but of Erasmus in England. For further information see Répertoire des œuvres d'Erasme, *3 vols Ghent 1893 (Bibliotheca Erasmiana);* Bibliographie des oeuvres d'Erasme, *7 vols Ghent 1897–1908 (Bibliotheca Erasmiana); J.-C. Margolin,* Douze années de bibliographie érasmienne 1950–61, *Paris 1963;* Quatorze années de bibliographie érasmienne 1936–49, *Paris 1969; E. J. Devereux,* English translations of Erasmus to 1700, *Oxford 1968.*

Collections

Opera omnia. Ed J. LeClerc 10 vols Leyden 1703–6.

Ferguson, W. K. Erasmi opuscula. Hague 1933.

§1
Latin Works Printed in England

Libellus de octo partium orationis. 1513.

Familiarum colloquiorum formulae. 1519, 1520, 1571.

Christiani hominis institutum. [1520?], 1520, 1555.

Libellus de conscribendis epistolis. Cambridge 1521.

Disticha moralia titulo, Catonis cum scholiis auctis Erasmi. [1525?], 1532, 1561, 1571 (Latin and Greek), 1572 (Latin and Greek), 1577, 1580, 1592.

De copia, cum scholiis marginalibus C. Hegendorphii. 1528; commentarijs M. Veltkirchij, 1556, 1569, 1573.

Epitome colloquiorum Erasmi. 1557, 1602, 1608, Cambridge 1634.

De ratione studii. Edinburgh 1579, Aberdeen 1623, Edinburgh 1632, 1640.

Dicta sapientium e Graecis. Edinburgh 1580, 1620, 1639.

Parabolae sive similia. [1587?].

Moriae encomium. Oxford 1633.

English Translations to 1640
Colloquies

The earliest English translations of Erasmus' Colloquia 1536–66. Ed H. de Vocht, Louvain 1928. Important introd and A mery dialogue; Two dyaloges; A dialoge or communication; One dialogue or colloquye.

Earliest English translation of Erasmus's Diversoria. Louvain 1928.

The dyalogue called Funus [trn of 1534]; A very pleasaunt and fruitful diologe called the Epicure [trn of 1545]. Ed R. R. Allen, Chicago 1969.

The dyaloge called Funus. 1534.

A dialoge or communication of two persons intituled the pylgremage of pure devotyon. [1540?].

A very pleasaunt and fruitful diologe called the epicure. Tr P. Gerrard 1545.

Two dyalogues: one called Polyphemus, the other dysposyng of thinges and names. Tr E. Becke, Canterbury [1550].

A mery dialogue, declarying the propertyes of shrowde shrewes and honest wyves. Tr J. Rastell? 1557, 1557.

One dialogue: or colloquyc (entituled Diversoria). Tr E. H[ake?] 1566, Amsterdam 1970 (facs).

A very mery and pleasaunt historie: a coniuration or spirite. Tr T. Johnson 1567.

A modest meane to mariage. Tr N. L[eigh] 1568.

Seven dialogues both pithie and profitable. Tr W. B[urton] 1606 (also issued as Utile dulce), 1606.

Pleasant dialogues and drammas. Tr T. Heywood 1637.

Other Writings

A devout treatise upon the pater noster. [Tr M. Roper] [1526?], [1531?].

De immensa Dei misericordia: a sermon. [Tr G. Hervet] [1526?], [1531?], 1533, 1547.

The sayenges of the wyse men of Grece. Tr T. Berthelet [1527?].

An exhortation to the diligent studye of scripture. [Tr W. Roy?], [Antwerp] 1529, [1534?], [1534?], [1548?].

Taverner, R. (tr). A ryght frutefull epystle in laude of matrymony. [1531?].

—— (tr and ed). Commonplaces of Scripture ordrely set forth. 1538.

—— (tr and ed). The garden of wysdom. 1539, [c. 1545] ('newly recognised and augmented'), [c. 1547], [c. 1550], [1556?]; The second booke, 1539, [1542?], [c. 1547], [c. 1550], [1556?].

—— (tr and ed). Proverbes or adagies; also added Mimi Publiani. 1539; With newe additions of Latyn proverbes as of Englysshe [but without Mimi Publiani], 1545, 1550, 1552, 1552, 1569, Gainesville 1956 (facs of 1569), Amsterdam 1969 (facs of 1539).

—— (tr and ed). Flores aliquot sententiarum ex variis collecti scriptoribus. 1540, 1547, 1550, [1556?]. Latin and English.

—— (tr). An introduction to a Christian concord. 1545 (no known copy).

—— Catonis disticha moralia cum annotationibus R. Taverneri. 1540 (Latin and English), 1553, 1555, 1561 (Latin only), 1562 (Latin and English). Includes Mimi Publiani, Flores aliquot sententiarum.

Practica Plutarche. [c. 1531].

A treatise perswadynge a man patientlye to suffre the deth of his frende. [1531?], [1545?] (in The table of Ceres).

De civilitate morum puerilium: a lytell book of good maners for chyldren. Tr R. Whytyngton 1532, 1534, 1540, 1554, 1554 (Latin and English), 1578 (Latin only).

De contemptu mundi. Tr T. Paynell [1532?], 1533, Gainesville 1967 (facs).

An epystell unto Christofer Bysshop of Basyle concernyng the forbedinge of eatynge of flesshe. [1533?], [1534?].

A sermon. [1533?]. On the marriage at Cana.

Bellum Erasmi, translated into Englyshe. 1533.

A booke called in Latyn Enchiridion and in Englysshe the Manuell of the Christen knyght. [Tr W. Tindale?] 1533, 1534 (as Enchiridion militis christiani, newly corrected) 1538, 1538, 1541, 1544, 1544, 1548, [1551?], 1576, 1576; tr T. Artour [1561?]; 1905 (from 1533), Amsterdam 1969 (facs of 1533). *See* J. A. Gee, Tindale and the 1533 English Enchiridion of Erasmus, PMLA 49 1934. *See also* Coverdale's Abridgement 1545, below.

An exhortacyon to the study of readynge the Gospell. [1534?], [1534?], [1548].

A playne and godly exposytion of the commune crede and of the X commaundementes. Tr W. Marshall [1534], [1534].

The dialoge betwene Julius, Genius and Saynt Peter. [1534?], 1535.

A lytle treatise of the maner of confession. [1535?].

The paraphrase of Erasmi upon the epistle of Paule unto Titus. Tr L. Cox [1535?].

A declamacion in the prayse and commendation of phisyke. [c. 1535].

An epistle concernynge the veryte of the sacrament of Christes body. [1536].

[A sermon of the chylde Jesus]. [1536?]. Copy in BM without title-page; also Detroit Public Lib.

An exposicyon of the xv psalme. 1537. De puritate ecclesiae christianae.

The comparation of a vyrgin and a martyr. Tr T. Paynell 1537, Gainesville 1970 (facs).

Preparation to deathe. 1538, 1543.

Apophthegmes: that is to saie, prompte saiynges. Tr N. Udall 1542, 1564, Boston Lincs 1877, Amsterdam 1969 (facs of 1542).

The precepts of Plutarche. Tr J. Hales 1543.

A scorneful image of monstrus shape of a marvelous strange fygure called Sileni Alcibiadis. [1543?].

The governaunce of good helthe, Erasmus beynge interpretoure. [c. 1545], [c. 1555]. From Plutarch.

Coverdale, M. A shorte recapitulacion of Erasmus Enchiridion. [Antwerp] 1545.

Preceptes of Cato with annotacions of Erasmus. Tr R. Burrant 1545.

Sage and prudente saiynges: wyse saiynges of Publius. Tr R. Burrant [1545]. Dicta sapientium and Mimi publiani.

The first tome of the paraphrase of the Newe testament. Tr N. Udall 1548; The seconde tome, tr M. Coverdale and J. Olde 1549.

The praise of folie. Tr Sir T. Chaloner 1549, [1557?], 1577; ed C. H. Miller 1965 (EETS).

A treatise of schemes and tropes; whereunto is added a declamation that chyldren should be well and gently broughte up in learnynge. Tr R. Sherry [1550], Gainesville 1961 (facs).

The censure and judgement of Erasmus: whyther dyvorsemente stondeth with the lawe of God. Tr N. Lesse [1550?].

A comfortable exhortation agaynst the chaunces of death. 1553.

An epistle to perswade a young jentleman to mariage. In T. Wilson, Arte of rhetorique, 1553.

Howe one may take profite of his enemies. [c. 1553]. From Plutarch.

The epistle sente unto Conradus Pelicanus concerning the blessed sacrament. 1554.

The complaint of peace. Tr T. Paynell 1559, New York 1946 (with facs).

The civilitie of childehode, translated oute of Frenche by T. Paynell. 1560.

A godly boke to be exercised by all Christes souldiers. 1561. Abridgement of Enchiridion, above.

A touchstone for this time present. Tr E. Hake 1574. From De pueris ad virtutem instituendis.

Erasmus in his Chiliades. Tr Timothy Kendall, Flowers of epigrammes, 1577.

Adagia in Latine and English. [Tr B. Robertson] 1621, Aberdeen 1622.

Letters

The epistles of Erasmus to his fifty-first year. Ed F. M. Nichols 3 vols 1901–18. English trns.

Opus epistolarum Des. Erasmi Roterodami. Ed P. S. and H. M. Allen and H. W. Garrod 11 vols Oxford 1906–47; Index, 1958.

Erasmus and Cambridge: the Cambridge letters of Erasmus. Tr D. F. S. Thomson, introd, commentary and notes by H. C. Porter, Toronto 1963, 1970 (rev).

Erasmus and Fisher: their correspondence 1511–24. Ed and tr French by J. Rouschausse, Paris 1968.

§2

Jortin, J. The life of Erasmus. 2 vols 1758–60.

Seebohm, F. The Oxford reformers of 1498: Colet, More, Erasmus. 1867, 1869 (enlarged).

Drummond, R. B. Erasmus: his life and character. 2 vols 1873.

Froude, J. A. Life and letters of Erasmus. 1894.

Allen, P. S. The age of Erasmus. 1904.

— Erasmus's services to learning. Proc Br Acad 11 1925.

— Erasmus: lectures and wayfaring sketches. Oxford 1934.

Bang, W. and H. de Vocht. Klassiker und Humanisten: John Lyly und Erasmus. E Studien 36 1906.

de Vocht, H. De invloed van Erasmus op de engelsche tooneel-literatur der xvie en xviie eeuwen 1: Shakespeare Jest Books—Lyly. Ghent 1908.

Savage, J. H. The first visit of Erasmus to England. PMLA 37 1922.

Bauer, K. Johann Colet und Erasmus. Festschrift für H. Schubert, Leipzig 1929.

Starnes, D. T. A heroic poem on the death of More. SE 9 1929. On Carmen heroicum.

Pfeiffer, R. Humanitas erasmiana. Leipzig 1931.

Thomson, J. A. K. Erasmus in England. Vorträge der Bibliothek Warburg 1931.

Baskervill, C. R. Taverner's Garden of wisdom and the Apophthegmata of Erasmus. SP 29 1932.

Gee, J. A. Tyndale and Erasmus's Enchiridion. PMLA 49 1934.

— Hervet's English translation, with its glossary, of Erasmus's De immensa Dei misericordia. PQ 15 1936.

— Margaret Roper's English version of Erasmus' Precatio dominica. RES 13 1937.

— Berthelet's Latin-English publication of the Apophthegmata. SP 35 1938.

Delcourt, M. L'amitié d'Erasme et de More. Bulletin de l'Association G. Budé no 50 1936.

Erasmus in praise of England. TLS 11 July 1936. Replies by H. R. Creswick 18 July, H.W.D. 8 Aug 1936.

Hyma, A. Erasmus and the Oxford reformers 1493–1503. Hague 1936; 1503–19, Archief voor Kerkgeschiedenis 38 1951.

Cowell, H. J. Erasmus's personal and literary associations with England. Huguenot Soc Proc 15 1936.

— Erasmus and his English friends. Essays by Divers Hands 20 1943.

Kluge, O. Erasmus Beziehungen zu Frankreich und England. Neuphilologische Monatsschrift 7 1936.

Rowse, A. L. Erasmus and England. Spectator 10 July 1936.

Rüegg, A. Erasmus Lob der Torheit und Thomas Mores Utopie. In Gedenkschrift zum 400 Todestage des Erasmus, Basle 1936.

Giese, R. Erasmus' knowledge of the vernacular languages. Romanic Rev 28 1937.

Ulback, E. Erasmus and his writings. Bibliotheca Sacra 94 1937. Influence of Oxford and Colet.

Mackail, J. W. Erasmus on war. In his Studies in humanism, 1938. Especially on Henry VIII and his wars.

Exner, H. Der Einfluss des Erasmus auf die englische Bildungsidee. Berlin 1939.

Matthes, H. C. Francis Meres und Erasmus. Anglia 63 1939.

Thompson, C. R. The translations of Lucian by Erasmus and More. Ithaca 1940.

— Erasmus, More and the conjuration of spirits. Moreana 6 1969.

— Erasmus and Tudor England. Actes du Congrès Erasme. Amsterdam 1971.

Hudson, H. H. Current English translations of the Praise of folly. In Renaissance studies in honor of Hardin Craig, Stanford 1941.

Campbell, W. E. Erasmus in England. Dublin Rev 211 1942.

— Erasmus, Tyndale and More. 1949.

Phillips, M. M. Erasmus and propaganda: a study of the translations of Erasmus in English and French. MLR 37 1942.

— Erasmus and the northern Renaissance. 1949.

Mozley, J. F. The English Enchiridion of Erasmus 1533. RES 20 1944. On evidence of Tindale's authorship.

White, O. B. Richard Taverner's interpretation of Erasmus in Proverbes or adagies. PMLA 59 1944.

Adams, R. P. Designs by More and Erasmus for a new social order. SP 42 1945.

— Erasmus' ideas of his role as a social critic c. 1480–1500. Renaissance News 11 1958.

— The better part of valor. Seattle 1962.

Moholi, J. English-Hungarian connections in the circle of Erasmus. History 32 1947.

Buchner, K. Die Freundschaft zwischen Hutten und Erasmus: Brief des Erasmus an Ulrich von Hutten über Thomas Morus. Munich 1948.

Castelli, A. Note sull'umanesimo in Inghilterra. Milan [1949]. On friendship of Erasmus and More family, the 'anglica fata' of Erasmus and his connections with English humanism.

Garrod, H. W. Erasmus and his English patrons. 1949.

Rooy, N. de. Utopia gewonnen en verloren: de tragedie van Thomas Morus en Erasmus. Hague 1950.

Schram, R. H. John of Garland and Erasmus on the principle of synonymy. SE 30 1951. On background to De copia.

Marcel, R. Les 'découvertes' d'Erasme en Angleterre. Bibliothèque d'Humanisme et Renaissance 14 1952.

Butterworth, C. C. Erasmus and Bilney and Foxe. BNYPL Dec 1953.

Hallam, G. W. An Ascham borrowing from Erasmus. N & Q March 1955.

Pizzi, C. Un amico di Erasmo, l'umanista Andrea Ammonio 1478–1517. Florence 1956.

Crossett, J. More and Lucian. MLN 72 1957.

Marc'hadour, G. Erasmus englished by Margaret More. Clergy Rev 43 1958.

— Saint Thomas More: son portrait par Erasme. Namur 1962.

— L'univers de Thomas More. Paris 1963.

— More, Erasme et l'exégèse médiévale. Moreana 1 1964.

— Erasmus' paraphrase of the Pater Noster 1523 with its English translation 1524. Moreana 2 1965.

Samuel, I. The brood of Folly. N & Q Oct 1958.

Muir, K. Shakespeare among the commonplaces. RES new ser 10 1959.

Nurse, P. Le Cymbalum mundi en Angleterre. Bibliothèque d'Humanisme et Renaissance 21 1959.

Pineas, R. Erasmus and More: some contrasting theological opinions. Renaissance News 13 1960.

Allison, A. F. and H. M. Nixon. Three sixteenth-century English translations of Erasmus. BM Quart 23 1961. Funus 1534, An Epystell unto Christopher Bysshop of Basyle c. 1530–6, Julius c. 1533–5.

Devereux, E. J. The English editions of Erasmus' Catechismus. Library 5th ser 17 1962.

— Some lost English translations of Erasmus. Ibid. Corrections and addns 19 1964.

— Richard Taverner's translations of Erasmus. Library 5th ser 19 1964.

— English translators of Erasmus 1522–57. In Editing sixteenth-century texts, ed R. J. Schoeck, Toronto 1966.

— An English glossary by Gentian Hervet. Moreana 4 1967. On Hervet's glossary to his trn of De misericordia.

— The publication of the English paraphrases of Erasmus. Bull John Rylands Lib 51 1969.

— Tudor uses of Erasmus on the Eucharist. Archiv für Reformationsgeschichte 62 1971.

Krodel, G. G. Luther, Erasmus and Henry VIII. Archiv für Reformationsgeschichte 53 1962.

Rieger, J. H. Erasmus, Colet and the schoolboy Jesus. Stud in Renaissance 9 1962.

Sowards, J. K. Erasmus in England 1509–14. Bull Univ of Wichita 37 1962.

— The two lost years of Erasmus. Stud in Renaissance 9 1962.

— Thomas More, Erasmus and Julius II. Moreana 6 1969.

Kaiser, W. Praisers of Folly: Erasmus, Rabelais, Shakespeare. Cambridge Mass 1963.

Schirmer, W. F. Der englische Frühhumanismus: ein Beitrag zur englischen Literaturgeschichte des 15 Jahrhunderts. Tübingen 1963. Supplants 1931 edn.

Thomson, D. F. S. and H. C. Porter. Erasmus and Cambridge. Toronto 1963, 1970 (rev).

Geraldine, Sr M. Erasmus and the tradition of paradox. SP 61 1964.

Porter, H. C. The nose of wax: scripture and the spirit from Erasmus to Milton. Trans Royal Historical Soc 14 1964.

Bietenholz, P. G. Erasmus' view of More. Moreana 2 1965.

McConica, J. K. English humanists and Reformation politics. Oxford 1965.

Reynolds, E. E. Thomas More and Erasmus. 1965.

Bainton, R. H. The Paraphrases of Erasmus. Archiv für Reformationsgeschichte 57 1966.

Garanderie, M. M. de la. Le féminisme de Thomas More et d'Erasme. Moreana 3 1966.

Nierynck, M. Erasmus en Thomas More. Vlaandeven 15 1966.

Colie, R. L. Some notes on Burton's Erasmus. Renaissance Quart 20 1967.

Nauwelaerts, M. A. Un ami anversois de More et d'Erasme: Petrus Aegidius. Moreana 4 1967.

Starr, G. A. Antedatings from Nicholas Udall's translation of Erasmus's Apoppthegmes. N & Q Dec 1967.

Green, C. and A. B. Whittingham. Excavations at Walsingham Priory, Norfolk 1961. Archaeological Jnl 125 1968.

Haugard, W. P. Katherine Parr: religious convictions. Renaissance Quart 22 1969.

Rossi, S. Profilo dell'umanesimo enriciano: Erasmo e Thomas More. In Richerchi sull'umanesimo e sul Rinascimento in Inghilterra, Milan 1969.

Kleinhans, R. G. Erasmus' Ecclesiastes and the Church of England. Historical Mag of Protestant Episcopal Church 39 1970.

Remy-Dumoulin, Y. Le portrait de More par Erasme. In Hommages à Marie Delcourt, Brussels 1970.

Yost, J. K. Taverner's use of Erasmus and the protestantization of English humanism. Renaissance Quart 23 1970.

— German Protestant humanism and the early English Reformation: Taverner and official translation. Bibliothèque d'Humanisme et Renaissance 32 1970.

Parker, D. H. J. F. Mozley's The English Enchiridion of Erasmus 1533: some qualifications. N & Q June 1971.

Russell, J. G. The conference at Calais and Bruges in 1521. Jnl Inst of Historical Research 44 1971. On humanist search for general peace.

Stenger, G. The Praise of folly and its parerga. Mediaevalia et Humanistica new ser 2 1971.

JOHN COLET
1467?–1519

For a bibliography see Jayne, below.

§I

Oratio habita ad clerum in convocatione anno 1511. [1511–12]; tr Thomas Lupset? [1530?], [1531?]; ed J. H. Lupton, Life of Colet, 1887.

Libellus de constructione. 1513, [Cambridge? 1521?], London 1531, 1533, 1539, 1540 (enlarged and rev). Also attributed to W. Lily and Erasmus.

Joannis Coleti aeditio una cum quibusdam G. Lilij Grammatices rudimentis [in English]. Antwerp 1527, 1533, 1534, 153[5], 1536, 1537, 1539, Menston 1971 (facs of 1527). Colet's initial catechism and the source for Erasmus' Christiani hominis institutum. Also

London [1527?], 1529 (ptd by Wolsey for Ipswich grammar school), 1534, [1534?]. Extract ptd by R. Redman c. 1540 as De nominibus heteroclitis.

The vij petycions of the pater noster by Jhon Collet Deane of Powels. [Antwerp? c. 1530?].

A ryght frutefull monycion concerning the ordre of a good Chrysten mannes lyfe. 1534, 1534, 1563, 1577, 1582.

Opus de sacramentis ecclesiae. Ed J. H. Lupton 1867.

Two treatises on Hierarchies of Dionysius. Ed and tr J. H. Lupton 1869.

An exposition of St Paul's epistle to the Romans. Ed and tr J. H. Lupton 1873.

An exposition of St Paul's first epistle to the Corinthians. Ed and tr J. H. Lupton 1874.

Letters to Radulphus on the Mosaic account of the creation. Ed and tr J. H. Lupton 1876. Also includes shorter works by or attributed to Colet.

§2

Erasmus, D. The lives of Jehan Vitrier and Colet. Ed and tr J. H. Lupton 1883.

Knight, S. The life of Dr Colet. 1724, Oxford 1823.

Seebohm, F. The Oxford reformers of 1498: Colet, More, Erasmus. 1867, 1869 (enlarged).

Lupton, J. H. Life of Colet. 1887.

—— The influence of Colet upon the reformation of the English Church. 1893.

Simpson, W. S. On a newly-discovered ms containing statutes compiled by Colet for the government of the clergy in St Paul's cathedral. Archaeologia 52 1890.

Allen, P. S. Colet and Warham. EHR 17 1902.

Black, S. Die Schriftsprache in der Londoner Paulsschule (bei Colet, Lily, Linacre, Grocyn). Halberstadt 1905.

Bauer, K. Colet und Erasmus. In Festschrift für Hans von Schubert, Leipzig 1929.

Marriott, J. A. R. Life of Colet. 1933.

Ferguson, W. K. An unpublished letter of Colet. Amer Historical Rev 39 1934. Letter to Urswick from Rome 1 April 1493.

Nelson, W. The friendship of More and Colet: an early document. MLQ 1 1940.

MacKenzie, K. C. Colet of Oxford. Dalhousie Rev 21 1941.

Campbell, W. E. Colet: Dean of St Paul's. Dublin Rev April 1946.

Grossman, F. Holbein, Torrigiano and some portraits of Colet. Jnl Warburg & Courtauld Inst 13 1950.

Miles, L. W. Protestant Colet and Catholic More: a study of contrast in the use of Platonism. Anglican Theological Rev 33 1951.

—— Fishers with Platonic nets: study of Plato in the religious thought of Colet, More and Erasmus. Hanover Ind 1957.

—— Colet and the Platonic tradition. 1962.

—— Platonism and Christian doctrine: the revival of interest in Colet. Philosophical Forum 21 1964.

—— Colet: an appreciation. Moreana 6 1969.

Rice, E. F. Colet and the annihilation of the natural. Harvard Theological Rev 45 1952.

Duhamel, P. A. The Oxford lectures of Colet. JHI 14 1953.

Clebsch, W. Colet and the Reformation. Anglican Theological Rev 37 1955.

Hunt, E. W. Colet and his theology. 1956.

Parsons, D. J. Colet's stature as an exegete. Anglican Theological Rev 40 1958.

Rieger, J. H. Erasmus, Colet and the schoolboy Jesus. Stud in Renaissance 9 1962.

Jayne, S. Colet and Marsilio Ficino. Oxford 1963.

Porter, H. C. The gloomy dean and the law. In Essays in memory of Norman Sykes, 1966.

Marc'hadour, G. Le doyen Colet. Moreana 6 1969.

Meulon, H. Lettre de More à Colet, Londres 23 oct 1504. Ibid.

Peters, R. Colet's knowledge and use of patristics. Ibid.

Santinello, G. Tre meditazioni umanistiche sulla passione. In his Studi sull'umanesimo europeo: Cusano e Petrarca, Lefebvre, Erasmo, Colet, Moro. Padua 1969.

Jarrott, C. A. L. On Corpus ms 355, Colet in Romanos et in Genesim. Trans Cambridge Bibl Soc 5 1970.

SIR THOMAS MORE
1478–1535
Bibliographies

Gibson, R. W. and J. M. Patrick. More: a preliminary bibliography of his works and of Moreana to 1750. New Haven 1961. See Book Collector 11 1962; TLS 13 April, 11 May 1962; Library 5th ser 18 1963.

Reynolds, E. E. More: a bibliographical study. 1965.

Sullivan, F. and M. P. Moreana: materials for the study of More. 4 vols Los Angeles 1964–8; Index, 1971. Annotated bibliography of modern studies. See F. Sullivan, More: a first bibliographical notebook, Inglewood Cal 1953.

A handlist of printed books in Guildhall Library by or relating to More. Guildhall Miscellany 4 1972.

Articles on recent More scholarship are listed below under appropriate headings. See also the journal Moreana; a complete listing of its contents is not attempted here. For collections see under Latin Works, English Works, below.

§1
The Utopia
Latin Text

Libellus vere aureus de optimo reip. statu, deque nova insula Utopiae cura P. Aegidii nunc primum editus. [Louvain 1516], Paris [1517?], Basle 1518, 1518, Leeds 1966 (facs of 1516). The Latin text accompanies Lupton's and Sampson's edns of Robinson's trn, below.

Utopia. Ed M. Delcourt, Paris 1936.

Utopia. Ed E. Surtz and J. H. Hexter. In Yale edn of Works of More vol 4, New Haven 1965.

Ralph Robinson's Translation

A fruteful and pleasaunt work of the newe yle called Utopia, translated into Englyshe by Raphe Robynson. 1551, 1556, 1597, 1624, 1639; ed T. F. Dibdin 1808; ed E. Arber 1869; ed J. R. Lumby 1897; ed J. H. Lupton, Oxford 1895 (with Latin text and additional trns); ed G. Sampson and A. Guthkelch 1910 (with Latin text and bibliography); ed P. E. Hallett 1937. For misrepresentations in Robinson see J. Binder, MLN 62 1947. Finely ptd edns: Kelmscott Press 1893 (foreword by William Morris), Ashendene Press 1906; Golden Cockerel Press 1929 (introd by A. W. Reed). Facs: Amsterdam 1969 (1551), Menston 1970 (1556).

Other Translations

[Burnet, G.] Utopia: written in Latin by Sir Thomas More. 1684; ed H. Morley 1885; ed S. Lee 1906 (with the poems).

[Cayley, Sir A.] Memoirs of Sir Thomas More; with a new translation of his Utopia, History of King Richard III and Latin poems. 2 vols 1808.

Also tr V. Paget 1909, G. C. Richards 1923. For earlier trns into other languages see Guthkelch's bibliography, above, pp. 435–6; R. E. Peggram, The first French and English translations of Utopia, MLR 35 1940; R. W. Gibson, Preliminary bibliography, above.

Fiore, T. L'Utopia. Bari 1942.

Bartolozzi, R. L'Utopia. [Rome] 1945.

Maleina, A. I. Utopiya. Moscow 1947.

Ogden, H. V. S. Utopia. New York 1949.

Rooy, N. de. In his Utopia gewonnen en verloren, Hague 1950.

Ryba, B. Utopie. Prague 1950.

1951 (EL) (rev) (with A dialogue of comfort).

Voltes, P. M. Utopia. Buenos Aires 1952.

Surtz, E. In Selected works, New Haven 1964.

Marshall, P. K. Utopia: a new translation. New York 1965.

Turner, P. Utopia. 1965 (Pelican).

Stouvenel, V. L'Utopie. Paris 1965, 1966 (rev).

Surtz, E. and J. H. Hexter (ed). Utopia. Vol 4 of Complete works, New Haven 1965. *See* A. B. Ferguson, The Yale edition of More's Utopia, JHI 29 1968.

Delcourt, M. L'Utopie. Brussels 1966.

Screech, M. A. (ed). La description de l'isle d'Utopie. New York 1967 (facs of Paris 1550).

Foss, O. Om den bedste statsforfatning og om den nyeø Utopia [from Yale edn]. Copenhagen 1968.

Sawada, A. Utopia. Tokyo 1968.

Studies

Beger, L. Morus und Plato: ein Beitrag zur Geschichte des Humanismus. Zeitschrift für die Gesamte Staatswissenschaft 35 1879. Early study of More's sources.

Kautsky, K. More und seine Utopia, mit historischer Einleitung. Stuttgart 1890; tr 1927, New York 1959 (with foreword by R. Ames).

Dudok, G. More and his Utopia. Amsterdam 1923.

Reed, A. W. More. In Social and political ideas of the Renaissance and Reformation, ed F. J. C. Hearnshaw 1925.

Chambers, R. W. The saga and myth of More. Proc Br Acad 12 1926.

Dermenghem, G. E. Morus et les Utopistes de la Renaissance. Paris 1927.

Brockhaus, H. Die Utopia-schrift des Morus. Leipzig 1929.

Campbell, W. E. More's Utopia and his social teaching. 1930.

—— Utopia. In The King's good servant, ed R. O'Sullivan, Oxford 1948.

Freund, M. Zur Deutung der Utopia des Morus. Historische Zeitschrift 142 1930.

Brandt, C. D. J. More and his Utopia. Utrecht 1932.

Carmichael, M. The Utopia: its doctrine of the common life. Dublin Rev 191 1932.

Jevons, H. S. Contemporary models of More. TLS 2 Nov 1935.

Delcourt, M. Le pouvoir du roi dans l'Utopie. In Mélanges offerts à Abel Lefranc, Paris 1936.

—— Utopiana. Latomus 25 1966.

Fyfe, W. H. Tacitus' Germania and More's Utopia. Trans & Proc Royal Soc of Canada 30 1936.

Rüegg, A. Erasmus Lob der Torheit und Mores Utopie. In Gedenkschrift zum 400 Todestage des Erasmus, Basle 1936.

O'Sullivan, R. The social life and theories of More. Dublin Rev 199 1936.

Zavala, S. La Utopia de Moro en la Nueva España y otros estudios. Mexico City 1937.

—— The American Utopia of the sixteenth century. HLQ 10 1947; rptd as More in New Spain, Cambridge 1955. On More's influence on Quiroga and his plans for New Spain.

—— L'Utopie réalisée: More au Mexique. Annales 3 1948.

Parks, G. B. Utopia and geography. JEGP 37 1938.

Ritter, G. Machtstaat und Utopie: vom Streit um die Dämonie der Macht seit Machiavelli und Morus. Munich 1940; tr and rcv as The corrupting influence of power, 1952.

Adams, R. P. The philosophic unity of Utopia. SP 38 1941.

—— Designs by More and Erasmus for a new social order. SP 42 1945.

—— The social responsibilities of science in Utopia, New Atlantis and after. JHI 10 1949.

—— The better part of valor: More, Erasmus, Colet and Vives on humanism, war and peace 1496–1535. Seattle 1962.

Brie, F. Machtpolitik und Krieg in der Utopie des More. Historisches Jahrbuch 61 1941.

Dupont, V. L'Utopie et le roman utopique dans la littérature anglaise. Paris 1941.

Gee, J. A. Tunstall's copy of the first edition of Utopia. Yale Univ Lib Gazette 15 1941.

Donner, H. W. Introduction to Utopia. 1945.

Bloch, E. Freiheit und Ordnung: Abriss der Sozial-Utopien. New York [1946].

Morgan, A. E. Nowhere was somewhere. Chapel Hill 1946. On parallels with Peru under the Incas.

Grace, W. J. The conception of society in Utopia. Thought 22 1947.

Ames, R. Citizen More and his Utopia. Princeton 1949.

Battaglia, F. Saggi sull'Utopia. Bologna 1949.

Surtz, E. Epicurus in Utopia. ELH 16 1949.

—— More and Communism. PMLA 64 1949.

—— The defence of pleasure in Utopia. SP 46 1949.

—— Logic in Utopia. PQ 29 1950.

—— Interpretations of Utopia. Catholic Historical Rev 38 1952.

—— More and the great books. PQ 32 1953. On Greek books in Utopia.

—— More and his Utopian embassy of 1515. Catholic Historical Rev 39 1953.

—— The link between pleasure and Communism in Utopia. MLN 70 1955.

—— The setting for More's plea for Greek in Utopia. PQ 35 1956.

—— The praise of wisdom. Chicago 1957.

—— The praise of pleasure. Cambridge Mass 1957.

—— More's apologia pro Utopia sua. MLQ 19 1958.

—— Illustrations in the Yale Utopia. Moreana 3 1966.

—— Sources, parallels and influences: supplementary to the Yale Utopia. Ibid.

—— Aspects of More's Latin style in Utopia. Stud in Renaissance 14 1967.

Jones, R. O. Some notes on Utopia in Spain. MLR 45 1950.

—— El Thomás Moro de Fernando de Herrera. Boletín de la Real Academia Española 30 1950.

Rooy, N. de. Utopia gewonnen en verloren: de tragedie van More en Erasmus. Hague 1950.

Ruyer, R. L'Utopie et les Utopies. Paris 1950.

Sanderlin, G. The meaning of Utopia. College Eng Nov 1950.

Fuz, J. K. Welfare economics in English Utopias. Hague 1952.

Hexter, J. H. More's Utopia: the biography of an idea. Princeton 1952.

—— The loom of language: Il Principe and Utopia. Amer Historical Rev 69 1964.

—— Utopia and Geneva. In Action and conviction in early modern Europe, ed T. K. Rabb and J. E. Siegel, Princeton 1969.

Mannheim, K. Ideologie und Utopie. Frankfurt 1952.

Sowards, J. K. Some factors in the re-evaluation of More's Utopia. North-west Missouri State College Stud 25 1952.

Möbus, G. Macht und Menschlichkeit in der Utopia. Berlin 1953.

—— Politik des Heiligen: Geist und Gesetz der Utopia. Berlin 1953.

Villasenor, R. Luciano, Moro y el utopismo de Vasco de Quiroga. Cuadernos Americanos 68 1953.

Schoeck, R. J. Levels of word-play and figurative signification in Utopia. N & Q Dec 1954.

—— More, Plutarch and King Agis: Spartan history and the meaning of Utopia. PQ 35 1956.

—— The intellectual milieu of Utopia: some notes. Moreana 1 1964.

—— A nursery of correct and useful institutions: Utopia as a dialogue. Moreana 6 1969.

Duhamel, A. Medievalism of Utopia. SP 52 1955.

Françon, M. Historical background of Utopia. Modern Langs Jnl 39 1955.

Fueyo, J. Tomás Moro y el utopismo político. Revista de Estudios Politicos 56 1956.

Miles, L. The Platonic sources of Utopia's minimum religion. Renaissance News 9 1956.

Marsh, T. N. The first Bishop of Utopia: an attempt at identification. N & Q Jan 1957. Dr Rowland Philips?

Coles, P. The interpretation of Utopia. Hibbert Jnl 56 1958.

Rudnianski, S. Utopiści angielscy o wychowaniu (The ideas of English Utopians on education). In Materialy do studiów pedagogicznych (Warsaw) vol 4, 1958.

Harbison, E. H. Machiavelli's Prince and More's Utopia. In Facets of the Renaissance, ed W. H. Werkmeister, Los Angeles 1959.

Boewe, C. Human nature in Utopia. Personalist 41 1960.

Crossett, J. Two notes on Utopia. N & Q Oct 1960. More and Herodotus; an omission in Robynson's trn bk 2 ch 4.

Herbrüggen, H. S. Utopie und anti-Utopie. Beiträge zur Englischen Philologie 43 1960.

Bevington, D. M. The dialogue in Utopia: two sides to the question. SP 58 1961.

Liljegren, S. B. Studies on the origin and early tradition of English Utopian fiction. Essays & Stud on Eng Lang & Lit (Upsala and Copenhagen) no 23 1961.

Simmonds, J. D. More's use of names in Book II of Utopia. Die Neueren Sprachen 6 1961.

Traugott, J. A voyage to Nowhere with More and Jonathan Swift: Utopia and the Voyage to the Houyhnhnms. Sewanee Rev 69 1961.

Abbundo, V. Tommaso Moro: saggio. Naples 1962. Appendix with first Italian trn of Utopia 1548.

Armytage, W. H. G. Heavens below: Utopian experiments in England 1560–1960. 1962.

Avineri, S. War and slavery in Utopia. International Rev of Social History (Assen) 7 1962.

Bernstein, M. Nouvelles lumières sur l'Utopie de More. Bibliothèque d'Humanisme et Renaissance 24 1962.

Derrett, J. D. M. More and Joseph the Indian. Royal Asiatic Soc Jnl pt i 1962. See his More's Utopia and Indians in Europe, Moreana 2 1965.

—— More's lands and the law of fraud. Ibid.

—— Gemistus Plethon, the Essenes and Utopia. Bibliothèque d'Humanisme et Renaissance 27 1965.

—— The Utopian alphabet. Moreana 3 1966.

Spens, W. de. Les royaumes d'Utopie. La Table Ronde 168–70 1962.

Allen, P. R. Utopia and european humanism: the function of the prefatory letters and verses. Stud in Renaissance 10 1963.

Bierman, J. Science and society in the New Atlantis and other Renaissance Utopias. PMLA 78 1963.

Cassidy, V. The voyages of an island. Speculum 38 1963.

Elliott, R. C. The shape of Utopia. ELH 30 1963.

Heiserman, A. R. Satire in Utopia. PMLA 78 1963.

Manzalaoui, M. More's reference to the Syrians in Utopia bk I. N & Q Aug 1963.

—— Reflexions on Liljegren's Studies of English Utopian fiction. Moreana 1 1964.

Martinez Estrada, E. El Nuevo Mundo, la Isla de Utopia y la Isla de Cuba. Cuadernos Americanos 127 1963.

Mucchielli, R. L'Utopie de Morus. In Les Utopies à la Renaissance, Brussels and Paris 1963.

Nomad, M. Political heretics: Plato to Mao. Ann Arbor 1963. Includes commentary on Utopia.

Saulnier, V. L. L'Utopie en France: Morus et Rabelais. In Les Utopies à la Renaissance, Brussels and Paris 1963.

Eliade, M. Paradis et Utopie. Eranos Jahrbuch (Zürich) 1964.

Gallagher, L. (ed). More's Utopia and its critics. Chicago 1964.

Mölk, U. Philologische Bemerkungen zu Morus Utopia. Anglia 82 1964.

Pineas, R. Utopia and Protestant polemics. Renaissance News 17 1964.

Berger, H. The Renaissance imagination: second world and green world. Centennial Rev 9 1965.

Cappelletti, A. J. Moro y su utopia. Nordeste (Resistencia) 7 1965.

Gleason, J. B. Sun-worship in Utopia: le soleil à la Renaissance. Paris and Brussels 1965.

López Estrada, F. La primera versión española de la Utopia de Moro, por Jerónimo Antonio de Meninilla (1637). In Collected studies in honour of Américo Castro's 80th year, Oxford 1965.

—— Queredo y la Utopia de Moro. In Actas del Segundo Congreso Internacional de Hispanistas, Nijmegen 1967.

Rops, D. More: planiste de l'Utopie. Moreana 2 1965.

Secretan, P. L'Utopie comme symbole. Cahiers Internationaux de Symbolisme 8 1965.

Silva Herzog, J. La Utopia de Tomás Moro. Cuadernos Americanos 141 1965.

Van der Wal, G. A. Motieven in Morus' Utopia. Tijdschrift voor Filosofie 27 1965.

Beumer, J. Lässt sich die Utopia ökumenisch deuten? Theologie und Philosophie 41 1966.

Erzgräber, W. Zur Utopia des Morus. In Literatur-Kultur-Gesellschaft in England und Amerika: Aspekte und Forschungsbeiträge Friedrich Schubel, Frankfurt 1966.

Manuel, F. E. (ed). Utopias and Utopian thought. Boston 1966.

Miller, C. H. The English translation in the Yale Utopia: some corrections. Moreana 3 1966.

Monsuez, R. Le Latin de More dans Utopia. Annales Publiées par la Faculté des Lettres de Toulouse 2 1966.

Nipperdey, T. Die Utopia des Morus und der Beginn der Neuzeit. In Die moderne Demokratie und ihr Recht: Festschrift für Gerhard Leibholz vol 1, Tübingen 1966.

Parker, T. M. More's Utopia. In Essays in memory of Norman Sykes, 1966.

Quiros, J. M. Community in Utopia. Filologia Moderna (Madrid) 6 1966.

Bataillon, M. Don Vasco de Quiroga, Utopien. Moreana 4 1967.

Böckenförde, E. W. Die Entstehung des Staates als Vorgang der Säkularisation. In Säkularisation und Utopie: Festschrift Ernst Forsthoff, Stuttgart 1967.

Brugmans, H. Morus' Utopia en verder. Moreana 4 1967.

Dorsch, T. S. More and Lucian: an interpretation of Utopia. Archiv 203 1967.

Frackowiak, M. Poglady ekonomiczne Tomasza More. Poznan 1967. On More's economic ideas.

Kronenberg, M. E. Some notes on the first edition of the Utopia. Moreana 4 1967.

Merlaud, A. L'Utopie: une bouteille à la mer. Moreana 4 1967.

Neirynck, M. M. Over More en zijn Utopia, verschenen te Leuven in December 1516. Revue de l'Université Catholique de Louvain 2 1967.

Padberg, R. Der Sinn der Utopie des Morus: Fragen der politischen Verantwortung des Christen am Vorabend der Reformation. Theologie und Glaube 57 1967.

Sawada, P. A. Biblioteka Lenina in Moscow and More's Utopia. Moreana 4 1967.

—— Hermann Oncken and Utopia. Ibid.

—— Toward the definition of Utopia. Moreana 8 1971.

Servier, J. Histoire de l'Utopie. Paris 1967.

Skinner, Q. Utopia. Past & Present 38 1967. Review of recent research.

Süssmuth, H. Studien zur Utopia des Morus. Münster 1967. With extensive bibliographical survey of current literature on Utopias.

Togeby, L. Utopia: om Mores stadig aktuelle samfundssatire med saerligt sideblik til Johan Fjord Jensen. Danks Udsyn 47 1967.

—— Utopia (et radioforedrag, en inledning til Mores Utopia). Copenhagen [1968].

Zandvoort, R. W. On translating Utopia. Moreana 4 1967.

Babelon, J. L'Utopie. In Humanisme actif: mélanges offerts à Julien Cain vol 1, Paris 1968.

Bucci, O. Il segreto dell'Utopia: Israele è l'archetipo di Utopia. Renovatio 3 1968.

Davis, N. Z. Réné Choppin on Utopia. Moreana 5 1968.

Gatto, L. C. Suicide and Utopian philosophy. Baltimore State Univ Forum 9 1968.

Nelson, W. Twentieth-century interpretations of Utopia. Englewood Cliffs NJ 1968. Kautsky, R. W. Chambers, Conner, Ritter, Ames, Hexter, C. S. Lewis, Surtz, Barker, A. W. Reed, Cassirer etc.

Quinzio, S. Utopia ed escatologia. Renovatio 3 1968.

Sylvester, R. S. Si Hythlodaeo credimus: vision and revision in Utopia. Soundings 51 1968.

Wartburg, W. von. Die Utopia des Morus: Versuch einer Deutung. In Discordia concors: Festgabe für Edgar Bonjour vol 1, Basle and Stuttgart 1968.

Graziani, R. Non-Utopian euthanasia: an Italian report c. 1554. Renaissance Quart 22 1969.

Johnson, R. S. Utopia: ideal and illusion. New Haven 1969.

McCutcheon, E. More, Raphael Hythlodaeus and the Angel Raphael. Stud in Eng Lit 1500–1900 9 1969.

—— Denying the contrary; More's use of litotes. Moreana 8 1971.

Minatur, J. More's Utopia and Kerala. Moreana 6 1969.

Ossinovsky, I. N. Utopia in Russia. Ibid.

Stevens, R. G. The new republic in More's Utopia. Political Science Quart 84 1969.

Davis, J. C. More, Morton and the politics of accommodation. Jnl of Br Stud 9 1970.

McKinnon, D. G. Marginal glosses in More's Utopia. Renaissance Papers 1970.

Seeber, H. U. Wandlungen der Form in der literarischen Utopie. Göppingen 1970.

—— Hythloday as preacher and a debt to Macrobius. Moreana 8 1971.

Allen, W. Hythloday and the root of all evil. Moreana 8 1971.

Bertagnoni, M. Discordia concors: Utopia e il Dialogo del conforto. Ibid.

Bleich, D. More's Utopia: confessional modes. Amer Imago 28 1971.

Coogan, R. Nunc vivo ut volo. Moreana 8 1971. On scholarship about Hythloday.

Guy, A. Vives socialiste et l'Utopie de More. Ibid.

Halkin, L.-E. Mithra dans l'Utopie. Ibid.

Johnson, R. S. The argument for reform in Utopia. Ibid.

Jones, J. P. Plato's Philebus and the philosophy of pleasure in Utopia. Ibid.

Khanna, L. C. The case for open-mindedness in the commonwealth. Ibid.

Lacombe, M. M. La sagesse d'epicure dans l'Utopie de More. Ibid.

Park, J. W. Utopian economics of More. Amer Jnl of Economics & Sociology 30 1971.

Peters, R. Utopia and More's orthodoxy. Moreana 8 1971.

Prévost, A. L'Utopie: le genre littéraire. Ibid.

Quattrocki, E. Injustice, not councilorship, the theme of Utopia bk 1. Ibid.

Samaan, A. B. Utopia and Utopian novels 1516–1949: a preliminary bibliography. Ibid.

Latin Works

Collections

Lucubrationes. Basle 1563. A collection of Latin works already pbd separately, with letters on More's life, character and death.

Omnia opera. Louvain 1565, 1566. First appearance of Latin text of More's History of King Richard III. *See* Yale edn vol 2, ed R. S. Sylvester, New Haven 1963, below.

Opera omnia latina. Frankfurt 1689, London 1963. Based on the earlier collections with additional elogia.

Separate Works

Luciani compluria opuscula ab Erasmo & Thoma Moro in latinorum linguam traducta. [Paris 1506], 1514, Venice 1516 (with addns by Erasmus), 1517, Basle 1528. More was responsible for Cynicus, Menippus (Necromantia), Philopseudes, Tyrannicida with the Declamatio Mori de eodem.

Epigrammata pleraque e Graecis versa. Basle 1518, 1520; ed J. H[aviland] 1638.

Epistola ad Germanum Brixium. 1520. Answer to G. Brixii Antimorus, Paris 1520.

Eruditissimi viri Ferdinandi Baravelli opus elegans quo repellit Lutheri calumnias. 1523, 1523 (as Eruditissimi viri G. Rossei opus). Rosseus was More's pseudonym. *See* Thomas Morus in Lutherum, in Louvain edn of Latin works, 1565; Responsio ad Lutherum, ed J. M. Headley 2 pts New Haven 1969.

Epistola ad academiam Oxon. Ed R. James, Oxford 1633. Reproving the University for neglect of Greek.

Modern Editions and Translations

Atkins, S. H. Certain of More's Epigrams translated by Stanihurst. MLR 26 1931.

History of the Passion, translated from the Latin by his grand-daughter Mistress Mary Basset. Ed P. E. Hallett 1941.

Scott-Craig, T. S. K. More's 1518 letter to the University of Oxford. Renaissance News 1 1948.

Latin epigrams. Ed and tr L. Bradner and C. A. Lynch, Chicago 1953.

A translation of More's Responsio ad Lutherum. Ed G. J. Donnelly, Washington 1962.

Lynch, C. A. Translations of some of the Latin epigrams of More. Classical Folia 16 1962.

The history of King Richard III. Ed R. S. Sylvester, New Haven 1963. Includes edns of both Latin and English versions.

Responsio ad Lutherum. Ed J. M. Headley, English trn by Sr Scholastica Mandeville, 2 pts New Haven 1969 (Latin and English).

English Works

Collections

The workes of Sir Thomas More wrytten by him in the Englysh tonge. Ed William Rastell 1557; ed W. E. Campbell, with introd by R. W. Chambers and notes and introds by A. W. Reed 2 vols 1931 (facs with modernized texts).

The wisdom and wit of blessed Thomas More: being extracts from such of his works as were written in English. Ed T. E. Brigett 1892.

Selections from his English works and from the lives by Erasmus and Roper. Ed P. S. and H. M. Allen, Oxford 1924.

English prayers and treatise on the Holy Eucharist. Ed P. E. Hallett 1938.

Prayers made by More while he was prisoner in the Tower of London. Ed E. F. Rogers, Madison 1952.

Ecrits de prison, précédés de la vie de More par William Roper. Tr P. Leyris, Paris 1953.

Textes traduits et présentés par G. Marc'hadour. Namur 1962. Letter to Dorp; Supplication of souls.

Complete works. Ed. R. S. Sylvester et al 14 vols New Haven 1963–.

Selected works. Ed E. Surtz, New Haven 1964.

The essential More. Ed J. J. Greene and J. P. Dolan 1967.

Preghiere della torre, con una lettera di Erasmo da Rotterdam. Tr M. Bertagnoni, Brescia 1968.

Separate Works

The lyfe of Johan Picus Erle of Myrandula (Here begin xii rulys). [1510?] (J. Rastell), c. 1525 (de Worde); ed J. M. Rigg 1890 (from de Worde).

A mery jest how the sergeant would lerne to play the frere. [1516?] (Julian Notary).

The supplycacyon of soulys, agaynst the supplycacyon of beggars. [1529], [1529] (W. Rastell). An answer to Simon Fish. A transcript from Black Letter by E. Morris 1970 (with text of S. Fish, The supplication of beggars 1528), Amsterdam 1971 (facs).

A dyaloge of Syr Thomas More of ymages, praying to sayntys, othere thynges touchyng the pestylent sect of Luther and Tyndale. 1529 (J. Rastell), 1530 (W. Rastell, 'newly oversene'). See W. Tindale, An answere unto Mores dialoge, [1530], 1850 (Parker Soc).

The confutacyon of Tyndales answere. 1532 (W. Rastell) (bks i–iii); Complete works, ed F. Sullivan, Los Angeles 1957–8 (facs in part).

The second parte of the confutacion of Tyndales answere. 1533 (W. Rastell).

The debellacyon of Salem and Bizance. 1533 (W. Rastell).

The apologye of Syr T. More knyght. 1533 (W. Rastell); ed A. I. Taft 1930 (EETS); Amsterdam 1970 (facs of 1533).

A letter of Syr Tho. More knyght impugnynge the erronyouse wrytyng of J. Fryth. 1533 (W. Rastell).

Syr Thomas Mores answere to the fyrst parte of the poysoned booke which [Tindale] hath named the Souper of the Lorde. 1534 (W. Rastell).

The boke of the fayre gentylwoman Lady Fortune. [c. 1540] (R. Wyer). 'Tho. Mo.'

A dialoge of comfort against tribulacion. 1553 (Tottell); Antwerp 1573; ed P. E. Hallett 1937; ed M. Stevens 1951; ed L. Miles, Bloomington 1966; Menston 1970 (facs of 1573).

Versions of More's History of King Richard III originally appeared in the chronicles of Hardyng and Hall. There are modern edns by S. W. Singer 1821; J. R. Lumby 1883 (with omissions); R. S. Sylvester, New Haven 1964 (vol 2 of Yale edn of Works); P. Kendall 1965 (Folio Soc) (with Horace Walpole's Historic doubts); tr Italian, 1964. On authorship see Yale edn.

The four last things. Ed D. O'Connor 1935.

A new prayer of More. Ed A. G. Dickens, Church Quart Rev 124 1937. In ms book compiled by Robert Parkyn.

New corn from an old field: More's treatise upon the Passion. Ed M. Thecla, Catholic World 164 1947.

The More Circle

Rastell, John (1470?–1536). Of gentylnes and nobylyte a dyaloge. [1529?]. Anon. For the plays assigned to Rastell, see col 1412, above; for his activities as law printer, compiler of law books and controversialist, see A. W. Reed, Early Tudor drama, 1926.

—— The pastyme of people: the cronycles of dyvers realmys. [1530?]; ed T. F. Didbin 1811. A history of England with remarkable woodcuts.

—— A newe boke of purgatory. 1530, 1530.

Frith, John. A disputacion of purgatorye whiche answereth unto Sir Thomas More. [Antwerp 1531?], [London 1537?].

—— A boke made by J.F. prisoner in the tower of London. Münster 1533.

Smythe, Walter, Twelve merry jests of the widow Edith. 1525 (J. Rastell); ed W. C. Hazlitt, Shakespeare jest-books vol 3, 1864. References to More household.

Tindale, William. The souper of the Lorde, wheryn incidently M. Moris letter agenst J. Frythe is confuted. Antwerp 1533. Anon.

Roy, William. Rede me and be nott wrothe. [1528], [1546]; ed E. Arber 1871. See A. Koszul, Was Bishop William Barlowe friar Jerome Barlowe?, RES 4 1928.

Literae virorum eruditorum ad F. Craneveldium 1522–8. Ed H. de Vocht, Louvain 1928.

Secondary literature on the More circle is included under §2, below.

Letters, Diaries etc

Thomas Morus Eduardo Leo. [1519?]. 1 May 1519 answering Lee's criticism of Erasmus's New testament.

Die Briefe des heiligen Thomas More aus dem Gefängnisse. Ed and tr K. Schmidthüs, Freiburg 1938.

Correspondence. Ed E. F. Rogers, Princeton 1947.

Selected letters. Ed E. F. Rogers, New Haven 1961.

Neue Briefe mit einer Einführung in die epistolographische Tradition. Ed H. S. Herbrüggen, Münster 1966.

Venti lettere. Ed A. Castelli, Rome 1966.

Prayer book. Ed L. L. Martz and R. S. Sylvester, New Haven 1969.

§2

Lives

For the Tudor lives see R. W. Chambers, Proc Br Acad 12 1926.

Harpsfield, N. The life and death of Sir Thomas Moore. Ed E. V. Hitchcock 1932 (EETS) (from mss). Includes The continuity of English prose, a Life of Harpsfield and notes, all by R. W. Chambers; appendixes contain biographical fragments.

Stapleton, T. Tres Thomae. Douai 1588; tr P. E. Hallett 1928 (St Thomas, Thomas à Becket, More); Vita Thomae Mori, Frankfurt 1689, Frankfurt 1964 (facs) (see H. S. Herbrüggen, Renaissance News 18 1965); The life and illustrious martyrdom of More, tr P. Hallett, ed E. E. Reynolds, New York 1966.

Roper, W. The mirrour of vertue in wordly greatnes: or the life of More. Paris 1626; ed E. V. Hitchcock 1935 (EETS); ed J. M. Cline, New York 1950; ed R. S. Sylvester and D. P. Harding, New Haven 1962 (with Cavendish's Life of Wolsey); ed E. E. Reynolds 1963 (with Harpsfield's life) (EL); Menston 1970 (facs of 1626); tr Italian, 1963, 1968.

Ba., Ro. Ed C. Wordsworth, Ecclesiastical biography vol 2, 1810 (from mss); ed E. V. Hitchcock, P. E. Hallett and A. W. Reed 1950 (EETS).

More, Cresacre. The life and death of More, written by M.T.M. [Paris 1631?]; ed J. Hunter 1828, Menston 1971 (facs).

Mackintosh, Sir J. In Lardner's cabinet cyclopaedia, 1830.

Seebohm, F. The Oxford reformers of 1498: Colet, More, Erasmus. 1867, 1869 (enlarged).

Bridgett, T. E. Life and writings of blessed More. 1891.

Hutton, W. H. Sir Thomas More. 1895.

Bremond, H. Le bienheureux Thomas More. Paris 1904; tr 1904.

Chesterton, G. K. In The English way, ed M. Ward 1933.

Hollis, C. St Thomas More. 1934.

Routh, E. M. G. More and his friends. 1934.

Sargent, D. Thomas More. 1934.

Chambers, R. W. Thomas More. 1935. See R. Stamm, Die Morus-Biographie von Chambers und ihre Auswirkung, Theologische Zeitschrift 7 1951.

Delcourt, J. Deux saints anglais: Fisher et More. Paris 1935.

Erb, A. Morus und Fisher. Freiburg 1935.

Kapfinger, H. Morus und Fisher: Märtyrer der Wahrheit. Bamberg 1935.

O'Connell, J. R. Saint Thomas More. 1935.

Cecil, A. Portrait of More. 1936.

Zeyde, M. H. van der. More. Amsterdam 1941.

Maynard, T. Humanist as hero: life of More. New York 1947.

Morawska, H. Tomasz More. Kielce 1947.

Campbell, W. E. Erasmus, Tyndale and More. 1949.

Heidingsfelder, G. More: Leben und Bedeutung des grossen Humanisten mit einer Auswahl aus seinen Schriften. Nuremberg 1950.

Paul, L. Sir Thomas More. 1953.

Reynolds, E. E. Saint Thomas More. 1953.

— Sir Thomas More. 1965.

— More and Erasmus. 1965.

— The field is won: the life and death of More. 1968.

Farrow, J. N. V. The story of More. New York 1954.

Bolt, R. Man for all seasons: a play in two acts. 1961.

Vásquez de Prada, A. Sir Thomas Moro, Lord Canciller de Inglaterra. Madrid 1962.

Marc'hadour, G. L'univers de More: chronologie critique de More, Erasme et leur époque 1477–1536. Paris 1963.

— More: ou la sage folie. Paris 1971.

Basset, B. Born for friendship: the spirit of More. 1965.

Küng, H. Freiheit in der Welt: More. Zürich 1965.

Guinness, G. More: collection of contemporary documents. 1968.

For the play The book of Sir Thomas Moore, *see col 1551, above. For works containing references to More see Guthkelch's bibliography*, Utopia, *1910 pp. 429–31; R.W. Gibson*, Preliminary bibliography §8.

Studies

Bruce, J. Inedited documents relating to the imprisonment and condemnation of More. Archaeologia 27 1838. Petition on More's behalf and indictment, from ms Arundel 152.

Hutton, W. H. The religious writings of More. EHR 4 1889.

Ganss, H. G. More and the persecution of heretics. Amer Catholic Quart 25 1900.

Emkes, M. A. Das Erziehungsideal bei More, Elyot, Ascham und Lyly. Marburg 1904.

Delcourt, J. La langue de More d'après ses oeuvres anglaises. Paris 1914.

— Some aspects of More's English. E & S 21 1936.

— A propos du ive centenaire et de la canonisation de More. Revue Anglo-américaine 13 1936.

— More: some new aspects, Catholic World 148 1939.

— More and France. Traditio 5 1947.

Reed, A. W. The editor of More's English works, William Rastell. Library 4th ser 4 1924.

Brooks, E. St J. Link with Peter Heylyn and More. N & Q 19 Feb 1927. Reply by A. Pulling 12 March 1927.

Sisson, C. More and North Mimms. RES 5 1929.

The fame of blessed Thomas More. Ed R. W. Chambers 1929. Essays by R. Knox, G. K. Chesterton et al.

Starnes, D. T. A heroic poem on the death of More. SE 9 1929. On Carmen heroicum.

Hogrefe, P. More's connections with the Roper family. PMLA 48 1933.

— John More's translations. PBSA 49 1955.

— The More circle. Urbana 1959.

— More and Doctors Commons. Moreana 4 1967.

Beck, E. More and the law. Dublin Rev 197 1935.

Bodleian Library, Oxford University. An exhibition in commemoration of the canonization of More: catalogue. Oxford 1935.

Coulton, G. G. The faith of More. Quart Rev 265 1935.

Doyle-Davidson, W. A. G. The earlier English works of More. E Studies 17 1935.

Hollis, C. More: European. Studies 24 1935.

Janelle, P. Humanisme et unité chrétienne: Fisher et More. Etudes 223 1935.

Luca, G. de. Moro 'beato martire'. Nuova Antologia 70 1935. On More and Machiavelli.

O'Connell, J. R. More as citizen. Dublin Rev 197 1935.

Delcourt, M. L'amitié d'Erasme et de More entre 1520 et 1535. Bulletin de L'Association G. Budé no 50 1936.

— Recherches sur More: la tradition continentale et la tradition anglaise. Humanisme et Renaissance 3 1936.

Kuckhoff, J. Morus und Erasmus. Stimmen der Zeit 130 1936.

O'Sullivan, R. The social life and theories of More. Dublin Rev 199 1936.

— (ed). The King's good servant. Oxford 1948. Papers mainly on legal questions suggested by the life and work of More.

— (ed). Under God and the law. Oxford 1949.

O'Sullivan, R. More and Lincoln's Inn. Catholic Lawyer 3 1957.

Wilby, N. M. More and the refugees in Flanders. Dublin Rev 199 1936.

Brie, F. More der Heitere. E Studien 71 1937.

Chambers, R. W. The place of More in English literature and history. 1937, New York 1964 (rev).

Grosse, F. Um die Toleranz Mores. Neue Jahrbücher für Deutsche Wissenschaft 13 1937.

Pyle, F. More's verse rhythms. TLS 30 Jan 1937.

Sargent, D. The trial of More. Catholic Historical Rev 22 1937.

Castelli, A. Un poemetto inedito del secolo xvi in onore di Moro. Aevum (Milan) 12 1938. By Zanobio Ceffino of Florence 11 May 1536.

— Note sull'umanesimo in Inghilterra. Milan [1949]. On Dialogue of comfort, More and Oxford, and More's defence of the Encomium moriae.

— I due 19 maggio o l'ultimo scherzo di Moro. Moreana 4 1967.

Glunz, H. H. Shakespeare und Morus. Bochum 1938.

Atkinson, A. Tyndale and More: a literary battle. Churchman Jan–March 1939.

Nelson, W. The friendship of More and Colet: an early document. MLQ 1 1940.

— More: grammarian and orator. PMLA 58 1943.

Thompson, C. R. The translations of Lucian by Erasmus and More. Ithaca 1940.

Zeeveld, W. G. A Tudor defense of Richard III. PMLA 55 1940.

Hutchinson, F. E. More as a translator of the Bible. RES 17 1941.

Sullivan, F. A lesson from More. Historical Bull 20 1941.

Dean, L. Literary problems in More's Richard III. PMLA 58 1943.

Hendriks, O. St Thomas Morus: de kerk vóór het evangelie. Studia Catholica (Nijmegen) 19 1943.

— De aantrekkingskracht van More. Katholick Cultureel Tijdschrift Streven (Amsterdam and Louvain) 7 1954.

Smelser, M. Political philosophy of More. In Saint Louis studies in honor of St Thomas Aquinas vol 1, 1943.

Leechman, D. John Rastell and the Indians. Queen's Quart 51 1944. On report of new world.

Campbell, W. E. More's Supplication of souls. Dublin Rev 216 1945.

Pirard, P. More: humaniste, chancelier et martyr. Paris 1946.

Rogers, E. F. More's letter to Bugenhagen. Modern Churchman 35 1946.

Thecla, M. More and the Catena aurea. MLN 61 1946. His use of the book in prison.

— More's Treatise upon the Passion. Catholic World 164 1947.

Visser, F. T. A syntax of the English language of More. 3 vols Louvain 1946–56.

Larkin, J. F. The status of scholarship on More. Amer Ecclesiastical Rev 117 1947.

MacNalty, A. S. More as public health reformer. Jnl Royal Inst of Public Health 10 1947.

— More as student of medicine and public health reformer. In Science, medicine and history: essays on the evolution of scientific thought and medical practice written in honour of Charles Singer, Oxford 1954.

— Shakespeare and More. E & S new ser 12 1959.

Paul, F. Holbein and portraits of the More family. Apollo 46 1947.

de Vocht, H. Acta Thomae Mori: history of the reports of his trial and death with an unedited contemporary narrative. Louvain 1947.

Büchner, K. Die Freundschaft zwischen Hutten und Erasmus: Brief des Erasmus an Ulrich von Hutten über Morus. Munich 1948.

Saboł, A. J. An English source for one of More's Latin epigrams. MLN 63 1948.

Scott-Craig, T. S. K. More's 1518 letter to the University of Oxford. Renaissance News 1 1948. Trn of 1633 edn.

Bowers, F. T. Printing evidence in de Worde's edition of the Life of John Picus by More. PBSA 43 1949.

Greyerz, H. von. Über Thomas Morus (Forschungs-bericht). Schweizer Beiträge zur Allgemeine Geschichte (Arrau) 7 1949.

Kan, A. H. De correspondentie van More. Tijdschrift voor Geschiedenis (Groningen) 62 1949.

Schoeck, R. J. Was More a Roman lawyer? N & Q 14 May 1949.

— Two notes on Margaret Gigs Clement. N & Q 10 Dec 1949. See 24 June 1950.

— More and Lincoln's Inn revels. PQ 29 1950.

— More, Erasmus and the Devil. N & Q 21 July 1951.

— Anthony Bonvisi, the Heywoods and the Ropers. N & Q 26 April 1952.

— William Rastell and the protonotaries: a link in the story of the Rastells, Ropers and Heywoods. N & Q 13 Sept 1952.

— Another Renaissance biography of More. E Studies 34 1953. Account of Bishop A. M. Graziani 1537–1611.

— More's schooldays. TLS 18 Dec 1953. Cites evidence that More studied under Nicholas Holt at St Anthony's school. See also J. O'Leary 4 Dec 1953, 1 Jan 1954; R. S. Stanier 1 Jan 1954, L. Paul 25 Dec 1953.

— More, the Devil and Cardinal Morton: a note on 16th-century name devices. N & Q May 1954.

— The meaning of ex officio in the sixteenth century. N & Q Oct 1960.

— More's use of Aulus Gellius' Noctes atticae. Renaissance News 13 1960.

— The use of Chrysostom: Christopher St German and More in 1533. Harvard Theological Rev 54 1961.

— The Cronica cronicarum of More and Tudor historians. Bull Inst Historical Research 35 1962.

— More: humanist and lawyer. UTQ 34 1964.

— Lord Acton's views of More. Moreana 3 1966.

— On the letters of More. Moreana 4 1967.

— More and the Italian heritage of early Tudor humanism. In Actes du Quatrième Congrès International de Philosophie Médiévale, Montreal and Paris 1969.

— More's Dialogue of comfort and the problem of the real grand Turk. Eng Miscellany (Rome) 20 1969.

Vian, N. S. More fra la saga e il mito. In Miscellanea P. Paschini (Rome) vol 2, 1949.

Howarth, R. G. Hopkins and More. N & Q 30 Sept 1950.

Rooy, N. de. Utopia gewonnen en verloren: de tragedie van More en Erasmus. Antwerp 1950.

Rubertis, A. de. Per la tradizione degli amori degli angeli di Morre. Bolletino Storico Pisano 19 1950.

Donner, H. W. The Emperor and Sir Thomas Elyot. RES new ser 2 1951. On the authenticity of the story of the Emperor and More's death.

— More's Treatise on the four last things and the gothicism of the transalpine Renaissance. Eng Miscellany (Rome) 3 1952.

Miles, L. W. Protestant Colet and Catholic More: a study of contrast in the use of Platonism. Anglican Theological Rev 33 1951.

Hastings, M. More's ancestry. TLS 12 Sept 1952.

Huber, P. J. V. Traditionsfestigkeit und Traditionskritik bei Morus. Basle 1953.

Surtz, E. More and the great books. PQ 32 1953.

— John Fisher and the scholastics. SP 55 1958. Includes account of More's views.

— Richard Pace's sketch of More. JEGP 57 1958.

— More's friendship with Fisher. Moreana 4 1967.

Brunner, K. Expanded verbal forms in early modern English. E Studies 36 1955.

Schuster, Sr M. F. Philosophy of life and prose style in More's Richard III and Francis Bacon's Henry VII. PMLA 70 1955.

Dart, J. L. C. Thomas Becket and More: were they both martyrs? Church Quart Rev 157 1956.

Falke, R. More-ismo velut Plato. Bulletin de l'Association G. Budé 4th ser 2 1956.

Lehmberg, S. E. More's Life of Pico. Stud in Renaissance 3 1956.

Malloch, A. E. The techniques and function of the Renaissance paradox. SP 53 1956. On Donne, More and Montaigne.

Marc'hadour, G. More aux Etats-Unis. Etudes Anglaises 9 1956. On More scholarship.

— More. Month 29 1963.

— More, Erasme et l'exégèse médiévale. Moreana 1 1964.

— Supplique de Dame Alice More au Chancelier Dudley 1538? Ibid.

— More: les arcanes d'un nom. Moreana 1–2 1964–5.

— A godley meditation. Moreana 2 1965. On More's autograph marginalia in Book of hours, Paris 1530; see letter by E. Birchenough and reply, ibid.

— More: patron des libres-penseurs? Ibid.

— Another signature. Moreana 3 1966. In Kent archives.

— Three Tudor editors of More. In Editing sixteenth-century texts, ed R. J. Schoeck, Toronto 1966. Richard Tottel, William Rastell, John Fowler.

— Translating More and translator More. Moreana 3 1966.

— More's English works: toward a census and an anatomy. Moreana 4 1967.

— More and Thomas Linacre. Moreana 4 1967.

— With a coal. Ibid. Reply to L. Miles, PQ 45 1966.

— Hugh Latimer and More. Moreana 5 1968.

— The Bible in the works of More. 2 vols Nieuwkoop 1969–72.

— More et la Bible: la place des livres saints dans son apologétique et sa spiritualité. Paris 1969.

— More vu par Erasme. Angers 1969.

Cross, G. More's Historie of Kyng Rycharde the Third and Lusts's Dominion. N & Q May 1957.

Crossett, J. More and Lucian. MLN 72 1957.

— More and Seneca. PQ 40 1961.

Harbison, E. H. The intellectual as social reformer: Machiavelli and More. Rice Inst Pamphlet 44 1957; rptd in his Christianity and history, Princeton 1964.

Parmiter, G. de C. The indictment of More. Downside Rev 75 1957.

— More and the oath. Downside Rev 78 1960.

— Tudor indictment illustrated by the indictment of More. Recusant History 6 1961.

Fletcher, H. The earliest (?) printing of More's two epigrams to John Holt. In Studies in honor of T. W. Baldwin, Urbana 1958.

Marsh, T. N. Humor and invective in early Tudor polemic prose. Rice Inst Pamphlet 44 1958.

Sullivan, F. More. TLS 26 Dec 1958. 'Three hitherto unnoticed facts' concerning More's life and work; also TLS 9 Jan 1959.

— The letter of the law of a Christian Socrates. Moreana 4 1967.

Adams, R. P. Bold bawdry and open manslaughter: the English new humanist attack on medieval romance. HLQ 23 1959. More, Erasmus, Colet and Vives.

Flesseman-van Leer, E. The controversy about Scripture and tradition between More and William Tyndale. Nederlands Archief voor Kerkgeschiedenis 43 1959.

— The controversy about ecclesiology between More and Tyndale. Nederlands Archief voor Kerkgeschiedenis 44 1960.

Bell, P. I. The trial of More. Month 23 1960.

Black, J. B. The literary survival of More. Culture (Quebec) 21 1960.

Derrett, J. D. M. Neglected versions of the contemporary account of the trial of More. Bull Inst of Historical Research 33 1960. With reconstructed text of the account.

—— The 'new' document on More's trial. Moreana 1 1964.
—— The trial of More. EHR 79 1964.
—— More's attainder and Dame Alice's predicament. Moreana 2 1965.
—— More's conveyance of his lands and the law of fraud. Ibid.
—— Two dicta of More's and a correction. Ibid.
—— More and the nun of Kent. Moreana 4 1967.
—— More and the legislation of the corporation of London. Guildhall Miscellany 2 1968.
Fisher, B. English spiritual writers xiii: More. Clergy Rev 45 1960.
Gage, J. England in the Italian Renaissance. History Today 10 1960. On reputation of Reginald Pole, More.
Pineas, R. Erasmus and More: some contrasting theological opinions. Renaissance News 13 1960.
—— More's use of the dialogue form as a weapon of religious controversy. Stud in Renaissance 7 1960.
—— More's controversy with Christopher Saint-German. Stud in Eng Lit 1500–1900 1 1961.
—— More's use of humor as a weapon of religious controversy. SP 58 1961.
—— More versus Tyndale: a study of controversial technique. MLQ 24 1963.
—— Tyndale's accusation of forgery against More. Amer N & Q 3 1965. Tindale's claim that More wrote Barlow's Dialogue.
—— Polemical exemplum in sixteenth-century religious controversy. Bibliothèque d'Humanisme et Renaissance 28 1966. Polemical use of exempla by More and Tindale.
—— More's controversy with Simon Fish. Stud in Eng Lit 1500–1900 7 1967.
—— More and Tudor polemics. Bloomington 1968.
Reynolds, E. E. Margaret Roper: eldest daughter of More. [1960].
—— The trial of More. 1964.
—— An unnoticed document. Moreana 1 1964. An account in the State Papers of the conversation between More and Sir Richard Rich 12 Jan 1535.
—— More, Coverdale and Cromwell. Moreana 3 1966.
—— Which More? a retraction. Moreana 4 1967. On statement that More was appointed to Commission of Peace for Hampshire.
—— Relict of Sir John. Moreana 5 1968. Identification of Dame Alice More.
'Plaidy, Jean' (E. Burford). Meg Roper: daughter of More. 1961.
Hexter, J. H. More: on the margins of modernity. Jnl of Br Stud 1 1961.
—— The loom of language and the fabric of imperatives: the case of Il Principe and Utopia. Amer Historical Rev 60 1964.
Jarrot, C. The vocation of More. Amer Benedictine Rev 12 1961.
McAleer, J. More and his detractors. Month 26 July 1961. Mainly on charge that More persecuted heretics. See L. Miles, Persecution and the Dialogue of comfort, below.
Newell, V. His own good daughter. New York 1961.
Bradner, L. and C. A. Lynch. On More: an epitaph of uncertain origin. Renaissance News 15 1962.
Sylvester, R. S. More and the Further I go the More behind. N & Q Oct 1962. On More's 2 allusions to the ballad.
—— John Constable's poems to More. PQ 42 1963.
—— The man for all seasons again: Robert Whittington's verses to More. HLQ 26 1963.
—— More: humanist in action. In Medieval and Renaissance studies, ed O. B. Hardison jr, Chapel Hill 1966.
—— A part of his own: More's literary personality in his early works. Moreana 4 1967.
Thrupp, S. L. (ed). Millenial dreams in action. Hague 1962.
Watkins, D. R. The More project. Yale Univ Lib Gazette 36 1962.

Bullough, G. More in Valencia: a holograph ms of the Latin Passion. Tablet 21 Dec 1963.
Herbrüggen, H. S. Das More Project der Yale University. Archiv 200 1963.
—— Some new letters of More: diplomacy on the Continent. Tablet 218 1964.
—— A letter of Dr Johann Eck to More. Moreana 2 1965.
—— More's dates. TLS 20 Jan 1966. On accepting the Chancellorship.
—— Ein unbekannter Brief an More. Moreana 4 1967.
—— Mores Fortuna-Verse: ein Beitrag zur Lösung einiger Probleme. In Lebende Antike: Symposion für Rudolf Sühnel, Berlin 1967.
—— A prayer-book of More. TLS 15 Jan 1970. A ms prayer-book possibly in use in the More family.
Morison, S. The likeness of More. Ed and supplemented by N. Barber 1963.
Oakley, F. More, St German, Gerson and pseudo-Chrysostom on Matthew 21.12. N & Q Aug 1963.
Pupals, E. Humanismo y heroísmo del canciller Tomás Moro. Atlántida 1 1963.
White, H. C. Tudor books of saints and martyrs. Madison 1963. On 4 Tudor lives of More.
Blackburn, E. John More's A sermon of the aulter. Moreana 1 1964.
—— The Christian empire of Prester John: Goes' account and John More's English version. Moreana 4 1967.
Egretier, Sr N.-M. More: le meilleur des Anglais. Moreana 1 1964.
Eldredge, L. (tr). Latin poetry of the Renaissance. Antioch Rev 24 1964. Includes several epigrams of More.
McConica, J. K. The recusant reputation of More. Report of Canadian Catholic Historical Assoc (Ottawa) 30 1964; rev in his English humanists and Reformation politics, Oxford 1965.
Meulon, H. Présence de More. Moreana 1 1964.
—— Le sens d'une vie. Moreana 2 1965.
—— La docilité chez More. Moreana 3 1966.
—— Une intaille antique: More 1520. Ibid.
—— More à Cambrai. Moreana 4 1967; Notes 5 1968.
—— La dévotion chez More. Moreana 5 1968.
—— Lettre de More à Colet 23 Oct 1504. Moreana 6 1969. French trn and edn.
—— More, homme d'action: le défenseur de la cité. Ibid.
—— Un poème inédit de More? Ibid. In a 1508 edn of Fisher's Treatise concernynge the fruytfull saynges of David.
—— La pensée du ciel chez More. Moreana 7 1970.
—— Un sermon entendu par More: l'Oraison de la paix. Ibid. In Cambrai Cathedral 5 Aug 1529.
Miles, L. More: disenchanted saint. In Literature and society, ed B. Slate, Lincoln Nebraska 1964.
—— More's sources. N & Q Oct 1964. On exact identification of works by writers named by More in Dialogue of comfort.
—— Boethius and More's Dialogue of comfort. Eng Lang Notes 3 1965.
—— Patristic comforters in More's Dialogue of comfort. Moreana 2 1965.
—— Persecution and the Dialogue of comfort: a fresh look at the charges against More. Jnl of Br Stud 5 1965.
—— The Dialogue of comfort and More's execution: some comments on literary purpose. MLR 61 1966.
—— The literary artistry of More. SE 6 1966. On Dialogue of comfort.
—— More's Dialogue of comfort as a first draft. SP 63 1966.
—— With a coal? the composition of More's Dialogue of comfort. PQ 45 1966.
Mölk, U. Philologische Bemerkungen zu Mores Utopia. Anglia 82 1964.
Rigobello, A. Attualità di Tomaso Moro. Humanitas 14 1964.

Rulli, G. Tommaso Moro e alcune recenti valutazioni. Civiltà Cattolica 115 1964.

Schmitt, C. B. Who read Gianfrancesco Pico della Mirandola? Stud in Renaissance 11 1964.

Trapp, J. B. Suavius olet: a bronze medal of More and its motto. Moreana 1 1964.

— The Abate Picinelli, Domenico Regi and More: a postscript. Moreana 2 1965. On motto Suavius olet.

— Dame Christian Colet and More. Moreana 4 1967.

— The holograph of More's expositio passionis: a postscript. Moreana 5 1968.

Welti, M. A propos des premières collections d'écrits de More. Moreana 1 1964.

Bietenholtz, P. G. Erasmus' view of More. Moreana 2 1965.

— A Protestant presentation of More in 1581. Moreana 4 1967.

Cavanaugh, J. R. The Saint Stephen motif in More's thought. Moreana 2 1965.

Cooper, Sr M. S. More and the letter to Martin Dorp. Ibid.

Gabrieli, V. I dialoghi di Tommaso Moro. Cultura (Milan) 3 1965.

— Giovanni Pico and More. Moreana 4 1967.

Gilmore, M. More's translation of Gianfrancesco Pico's biography. In L'opera e il pensiero di G. Pico della Mirandola nella storia dell' umanesimo vol 2, Florence 1965.

Goulder, L. More's London. Critic 24 1965.

López Estrada, F. Santo Tomás Moro en España y en la América Hispana. Moreana 2 1965.

— La difusión por España de las noticias sobre el proceso y la muerte de Santo Tomás Moro. In Homenaje al Dr D. Emilio Alarcos Garcia vol 2, Valladolid 1965–7.

— Tomás Moro y el Brocense 1525–1601. Moreana 4 1967.

Manzalaoui, M. Syria in the Dialogue of comfort. Moreana 2 1965.

Barker, A. E. Clavis Moreana: the Yale edition of More. JEGP 65 1966.

Birchenough, E. and J., and G. Marc'hadour. More's appointment as Chancellor and his resignation. Moreana 3 1966.

Brugmans, H. More: humaniste européen. Revue Nouvelle 44 1966.

Byron, B. The fourth count of More's indictment. Moreana 3 1966.

Garanderie, M. M. de la. Le féminisme de More et d'Erasme. Ibid.

— La correspondance de Guillaume Budé et More. Moreana 5 1968.

— Sur la publication de l'épitaphe de More. Ibid.

Hoeniger, F. D. Three amusing references to More in Peter Heylyn. Moreana 3 1966.

Marie-Claire, Sr et al. Erasmus et Margareta Ropera. Ibid.

Neirynck, M. Erasmus en More. Vlaandeven 15 1966.

O'Grady, W. A note on Busleyden's letter to More. Moreana 3 1966.

Rogers, E. F. Margaret of Austria's gifts to Tunstal, More and Hacket after the Ladies peace. Ibid.

Wilson, J. B. An analogue of transcendentalism. JHI 27 1966. The More circle as a source of ideas for Transcendentalists.

Gruffyd, R. G. A prayer of More in Welsh 1587. Moreana 4 1967.

Headley, J. More against Luther: on laws and the magistrate. Ibid.

— Thomas Murner, More and the first expression of More's ecclesiology. Stud in Renaissance 14 1967.

— More and Luther's revolt. Archiv für Reformationsgeschichte 60 1969.

Marius, R. The pseudonymous patristic text in More's Confutation. Moreana 4 1967.

— More and the early Church Fathers. Traditio 24 1968.

Martz, L. The design of More's Dialogue of comfort. Moreana 4 1967.

— and R. S. Sylvester. More's Prayer book. Yale Univ Lib Gazette 43 1968.

Miller, C. H. The holograph of More's Expositio passionis. Moreana 4 1967.

— A Vatican ms containing three brief works by More. Ibid. On Barberini Latin 2567.

Nauwelaerts, M. A. Petrus Aegidius. Ibid. Friend to More and Erasmus.

Richards, H. Thomas Stapleton. Jnl of Ecclesiastical History 18 1967.

Telle, E. Trois contes érasmiques et une note sur More. Moreana 4 1967.

— More, Theotimus et l'ivresse. Moreana 6 1969.

Ward, A. Speculation on More's use of Hysychius. PQ 46 1967.

— Some remarks on Gold. Moreana 5 1968.

Zeeveld, W. G. Apology for an execution. Moreana 4 1967.

Bergamaschi, A. Grandeur et limites d'une conscience chrétienne: More. Etudes Franciscaines 17 1968.

Crawford, C. W. Thomas Stapleton and More's letter to Bugenhagen. Moreana 5 1968.

Elton, G. R. More and the opposition to Henry VIII. Bull Inst of Historical Research 41 1968.

Gabrieli, V. Giovanni Pico et More. La Cultura 6 1968.

Hastings, M. The ancestry of More. Guildhall Miscellany 2 1968.

Heath, T. G. Another look at More's Richard. Moreana 5 1968.

Holahan, S. L. More's epigrams on Henry Abyngdon. Ibid.

Jacques, J. Le détachement à l'école de More. Ibid.

Lassalle, J.-P. Quelques hypothèses sur More et la tradition. Ibid.

Meyer, C. S. More and the Wittenberg Lutherans. Concordia Theological Monthly April 1968.

Moser, F. de M. Tomás More e o teatro. Brotéria (Lisbon) 86 1968.

Peebles, B. M. More in the Clavis calendaria. Moreana 5 1968.

Coogan, R. Petrarch and More's concept of fortune. Italica 46 1969.

— Petrarch and More. Moreana 6 1969.

Fines, J. An unnoticed tract of the Tyndale-More dispute? Bull Inst of Historical Research 42 1969. Letter pbd 1586.

Graaf, B. de. More's Choriambicum de vita suavi. Moreana 6 1969.

Kuhn, J. The function of Psalm 90 in More's Dialogue of comfort. Ibid.

Maguire, J. Roper's Life of More: the working method of a Tudor biographer. Ibid.

Major, J. R. Renaissance monarchy as seen by Erasmus, More, Seyssel and Machiavelli. In Action and conviction in early modern Europe, ed T. K. Rabb and J. E. Seigel, Princeton 1969.

Nédoncelle, M. L'humour d'Erasme et l'humour de More. Scrinium Erasmianum 2 1969.

Prévost, A. More et la crise de la pensée européenne. [Tours 1969].

Rossi, S. Profilo dell 'umanesimo Enriciano: Erasmo et More. In Richerche sull 'umanesimo e sul Rinascimento in Inghilterra, Milan 1969.

Santinello, G. Tre meditazioni umanistiche sulla passione. In his Studi sull'umanesimo europeo: Cusano e Petrarca, Lefebvre, Erasmo, Colet, Moro, Padua 1969. On Colet, Erasmus and More.

Sowards, J. K. More, Erasmus and Julius II. Moreana 6 1969.

Szmydtowa, Z. Erazm z Rotterdamu, Tomasz Morus, Piotr Tomicki. Przeglad Humanistyczny (Warsaw) 13 1969.

Watanabé, K. More et Rabelais. Trans Japan Acad 27 1969.

Mason, D. E. and R. J. Schoeck. On More's Dialogue concerning heresies 1529. Moreana 7 1970. On More's attitude to Hunne affair.

Murray, F. G. Feminine spirituality in the More household. Ibid.

Ossinovsky, I. Rare editions of More's works in libraries of USSR. Ibid.

Reiter, R. E. On the genre of More's Richard III. Ibid.

Remy-Dumoulin, Y. Le portrait de More par Erasme. In Hommages à Marie Delcourt, Brussels 1970.

Wheeler, T. An Italian account of More's trial and execution. Moreana 7 1970. By Nicholas Schomberg 12 Aug 1535.

— More in Italy 1535–1700. Ibid.

Williams, F. B. Some More allusions. Ibid. In English writers 1525–1646.

Hitchcock, J. More and Tyndale's controversy over revelation: a test of the McLuhan hypothesis. Jnl Amer Acad of Religion 39 1971.

Haas, S. W. Simon Fish, Tyndale and More's Lutheran conspiracy. Jnl of Ecclesiastical History 23 1972.

WILLIAM TINDALE
1494?–1536
Collections

The whole works of W. Tyndall, J. Frith and Doct. Barnes. 2 vols 1572. Preface by Foxe.

Work. Ed G. E. Duffield, Appleford 1964.

§1

A compendious introduccion unto the pistle to the Romayns. [Worms 1520] (anon), London 1564.

The obedience of a Christen man. [Antwerp] 1528, 1535 ('diligently corrected'), 1537 ('diligently corrected'), [London 1537?], [1548], [1548?], [1548?], 1561, Menston 1970 (facs of 1528).

The parable of the wicked mannon. [Antwerp] 1528, 1528, Southwark 1536, [London] '1528' (for 1537?) ('lately corrected'), 1547, [1548] ('lately corrected'), 1549, [1561?].

An answere unto Sir T. Mores dialoge. [Antwerp 1530?].

The examinacion of Master William Thorpe; The examinacion of Syr J. Oldcastell. [Antwerp 1530]. Ed Tindale.

The practyse of prelates, whether the Kynges grace may be separated from hys Quene. [Antwerp] 1530, 1548, [1549?].

The exposition of the fyrste epistle of Seynt Jhon by W.T. [Antwerp] 1531, ed T. H. L. Parker, Library of Christian classics, 1966; Of the fyrste, seconde and thyrde epistles [second and third are trns of Bullinger], Southwark [1537?], 1538.

The praier and complaynte of the ploweman unto Christe. [Antwerp 1531?], [London c. 1532]. Ed Tindale.

An exposicion upon the v, vi, vii chapters of Mathew. [Antwerp? 1533?] (by W.T.), [London 1536?], [1536?], [1537?], [1548] ('newly set furth'), [1549?] ('and corrected').

A fruitefull and godly treatise expressing the right institution of the sacraments. [1533?]. First surviving copy as A briefe declaration, [1548?].

The souper of the Lorde. [Antwerp?] '1533' (for 1546?) (anon), [London] '1533' [1547?], '1533' [1547?], '1533' (for 1547?).

The testament of W. Tracie esquier, expounded. Antwerp 1535. By Tindale and J. Frith.

A pathway into the holy scripture. [1536?] (anon), [1536?], 1564.

Tyndale's expositions and Practice of prelates. Ed H. Walter 1849 (Parker Soc).

An answer to More's Dialogue: the Supper of the Lord, and Wm Tracy's testament expounded. Ed H. Walter 1850 (Parker Soc).

Doctrinal treatises and introductions to different portions of the holy scriptures. Ed H. Walter 1858 (Parker Soc). Contains Parable of the wicked mammon, Obedience of a Christian man.

For Tindale's biblical trns see col 1829, below. See also under Erasmus and More, above.

§2

Demaus, R. Tyndale: a biography. 1871, 1886 (rev R. Lovett).

Frédériq, P. La fin de Tyndale brûlé à Vilvorde en 1536. In Mélanges d'histoire offerts à M. Charles Bémont, Paris 1913.

Gee, J. A. Tindale and the 1533 Enchiridion of Erasmus. PMLA 49 1934.

Reed, A. W. In K. Garvin (ed), The great Tudors, 1935.

Chambers, R. W. Tyndale and our Bible: the English prose tradition. TLS 3 Oct 1936; rptd in his Man's unconquerable mind, 1939.

Guppy, H. Tindale: scholar and martyr. Bull John Rylands Lib 20 1936.

Haslehurst, R. S. T. William Tyndale. Nineteenth Century Oct 1936.

— Tyndale the translator. Church Quart Rev 123 1937.

Knappen, M. M. Tindale: first English Puritan. Church History 22 1936.

Likeman, H. William Tyndale. Cornhill Mag Nov 1936.

Thomas, A. The life and martyrdom of Tyndale. Essays by Divers Hands 15 1936.

Bailey, J. W. Tyndale and the New testament. Crozer Quart 14 1937.

Gray, L. F. Tyndale: translator, scholar and martyr. Hibbert Jnl 35 1937.

Mozley, J. F. William Tyndale. 1937.

— Tyndale's Supper of the Lord. N & Q 21 Nov 1942.

— The English Enchiridion of Erasmus 1533. RES 20 1944. On evidence of Tindale's authorship.

— The Supper of the Lord: Tyndale or Joye? Moreana 3 1966.

Greenslade, S. L. The work of Tindale, with an essay on Tindale and the English language by G. D. Bone. 1938.

Atkinson, A. Tyndale and More: a literary battle. Churchman 53 1939.

Coates, J. R. Tyndale's influence on English literature. In Tyndale commemoration volume, ed R. M. Wilson 1939.

M., M. Tyndale's Parable of the wicked mammon. More Books Oct 1941.

Moholi, J. English–Hungarian connections in the humanist circle of Erasmus. History 32 1947.

Campbell, W. E. Erasmus, Tyndale and More. 1949.

Weigle, L. A. The English New testament from Tyndale to the Revised standard version. 1950.

Trinterud, L. J. The origins of Puritanism. Church History 20 1951.

— A reappraisal of Tyndale's debt to Luther. Church History 31 1962.

Morris, C. Political thought in England: Tyndale to Hooker. Oxford 1953 (Home Univ Lib).

Rupp, G. Six makers of English religion 1500–1700. 1957.

Bluhm, H. Luther and the first printed English Bible: Epistle to the Galatians. Anglican Theological Rev 40 1958. On debt to Luther.

Marsh, T. N. Humor and invective in early Tudor polemic prose. Rice Inst Pamphlet 44 1958.

Flesseman-van Leer, E. The controversy about scripture and tradition between More and Tyndale. Nederlands Archief voor Kerkgeschiedenis 43 1959.

— The controversy about ecclesiology between More and Tyndale. Nederlands Archief voor Kerkgeschiedenis 44 1960.

Thompson, W. D. J. C. Who wrote the Supper of the Lord? Harvard Theological Rev 53 1960. Advocates authorship of George Joye rather than Tindale.

Clebsch, W. A. More evidence that George Joye wrote the Souper of the Lorde. Harvard Theological Rev 55 1962.
— England's earliest Protestants 1520–35. New Haven 1964.
— Tyndale's influence on John Bale's polemical use of history. Archiv für Reformationsgeschichte 53 1962.
— Tyndale's polemical use of the scriptures. Nederlands Archief voor Kerkgeschiedenis 45 1962.
— Tyndale's use of history as a weapon of religious controversy. Harvard Theological Rev 55 1962.
Møller, J. G. The beginnings of Puritan covenant theology. Jnl of Ecclesiastical History 14 1963. Traced from Tindale rather than Cranmer.
Pineas, R. Tyndale: controversialist. SP 60 1963.
— Tyndale's accusation of forgery against More. Amer N & Q 3 1965.
— Polemical exemplum in sixteenth-century religious controversy. Bibliothèque d'Humanisme et Renaissance 28 1966. On polemical use of exempla by More and Tyndale.
Maveety, S. R. Doctrine in Tyndale's New testament: translation as a tendentious art. Stud in Eng Lit 1500–1900 6 1966.
Karpman, D. M. Tyndale's response to the hebraic tradition. Stud in Renaissance 14 1967.
Fimes, J. An unnoticed tract of the Tyndale-More dispute? Bull Inst of Historical Research 42 1969.
Williams, C. H. William Tyndale. 1969.
Yost, J. K. Tyndale's use of the Fathers: a note on his connections to northern humanism. Moreana 6 1969.
— Tyndale and the Renaissance humanist origins of the English via media. Nederlands Archief voor Kerkgeschiedenis 41 1971.
Davis, N. Tyndale's English of controversy. 1971.
Hitchcock, J. More and Tyndale's controversy over revelation: a test of the McLuhan hypothesis. Jnl of Amer Acad of Religion 39 1971.
Haas, S. W. Simon Fish, Tyndale and More's Lutheran. Jnl of Ecclesiastical History 23 1972.

STEPHEN GARDINER
1483?–1555
Bibliographies

Muller, J. A. In his Gardiner and the Tudor reaction, 1926.

§1

Stephani Winton. episcopi de vera obedientia oratio. 1535, [Wesel?] 1553; tr 1553, 1553; ed B. A. Heywood 1870; Leeds 1966 (facs of 1553).
Stephani Winton. Ad Bucerum de impudenti eiusdem pseudologia conquestio. Louvain 1544, Cologne 1545.
The rescuyunge of the Romische fox: otherwyse called the examination of the hunted devised by Steven Gardiner. [Bonn 1545]. Pseudonym W. Wraghton; prints and answers Gardiner's Examination of the hunter, which apparently circulated only in ms.
Stephani Winton. ad Martinum Bucerum epistola. Louvain 1546, Ingolstadt 1546.
A declaration of such true articles as George Joye hath gone about to confute. 1546, 1546.
A detection of the Devils sophistrie, wherwith he robbeth the unlearned people, of the true byleef, in the sacrament of the aulter. 1546, 1546.
Theyr dedes in effect my lyfe wolde haue. [London 1548?]. 2 poems, the first signed Stephen Wynton, the 2nd in reply signed H.S.
An explication and assertion of the true catholique fayth, touchyng the moost blessed sacrament of the aulter. [Rouen] 1551; rptd in Cranmer's reply, An answer.
Confutatio cavillationum quibus sacrosanctum eucharistiae sacramentum ab impiis capernaitis impeti solet, authore Marco Antonio Constantio theologo lovaniensi.

Paris 1552 (anon), Louvain 1554 (under Gardiner's name). Reply to Cranmer.
An admonishion to the Bishoppes of Winchester, London and others. [London] 1553.
The communication betwene my Lord Chauncelor and judge Hales. [London 1553]. Anon.
Exetasis testimoniorum quae M. Bucerus ex sanctis patribus non sancte edidit. Louvain 1554.
A traictise declaryng that the pretensed marriage of priests is no marriage. 1554. Attributed to Gardiner.
Concio habita dominica prima adventus. Rome 1555. Latin trn by Nicholas Harpsfield.
De pronunciatione linguae graecae et latinae. Basle 1555. Ptd with Cheke's treatise by C. S. Curio.
Responsio venerabilium sacerdotum Henrici Ioliffi & Roberti Ionson ad articulos Ioannis Hoperi una cum confutationibus Hoperi et replicationibus Stephani Gardineri. Antwerp 1564. Mostly by Gardiner.
Obedience in Church and State: three political tracts by Gardiner. Ed P. Janelle, Cambridge 1930. Prints from ms a tract on Fisher's execution 1535 and an answer to Bucer 1541; and reprints De vera obedientia, 1535 and English trn of 1553.

Letters etc

Letters. Ed J. A. Muller, Cambridge 1933.
Registra Stephani Gardiner et Johannis Poynet episcoporum wintoniensium 1531–47, 1551–2. Ed H. Chitty 1930 (Canterbury & York Soc).

§2

Gairdner, J. In W. E. Collins (ed), Typical English churchmen, 2 vols 1902.
Muller, J. A. Gardiner and the Tudor reaction. 1926.
Janelle, P. La controverse entre Etienne Gardiner et Martin Bucer sur la discipline ecclésiastique 1541–8. Revue des Sciences Religieuses 7 1927.
— An unpublished poem on Gardiner. Bull Inst of Historical Research 6 1928.
— L'Angleterre catholique à la veille du schisme. Paris 1935. Mainly on Gardiner.
Pontifex, D. Stephen Gardiner. Downside Rev 52 1934.
Morris, C. In his Political thought in England: Tyndale to Hooker, Oxford 1953 (Home Univ Lib).
Thomson, G. S. Background for a Bishop. In Studies presented to Sir Hilary Jenkinson, Oxford 1957.

HUGH LATIMER
1492?–1555
Collections

The sermons of Master Latimer. 2 vols 1758. With life.
Sermons of Latimer arranged, with life. Ed J. Watkins 2 vols 1824.
Sermons. Ed G. E. Corrie 1844 (Parker Soc).
Sermons and remains. Ed G. E. Corrie 1845 (Parker Soc).
Sermons. Ed H. C. Beeching [1906].
Selected sermons. Ed A. G. Chester, Charlottesville 1968.

§1

Concio quam habuit pater H. Latimer in conventu spiritualium. Southwark [1537], 1592 (as Oratio apud totum ecclesiasticorum conventum); tr 1537, 1537.
A notable sermon [on the plough] of Maister Latemer, preached in the shroudes at Paules Churche. 1548, [1548], [1548]; ed E. Arber 1868.
The fyrste sermon of mayster Latimer, preached before the Kinges Majestie at Westminster. [1549] (4 edns); ed E. Arber 1869.
The seconde [third, fourth, fifth, sixth, seventh] sermon preached before the Kynges Majestie. [1549] (3 edns), 1562 (as The seven sermons).

A most faithfull sermon preached before the Kynges Majestye. [1550], [1553?].

A sermon preached at Stamford. [1550?].

Sermons made before Katherine, Duches of Suffolke. Ed A. Bernher 1552, 1562.

Twenty-seven sermons preached by Latimer. 1562. Preface by T. Solme.

Frutefull sermons newly imprinted. 3 pts 1571-2, 1575, 1578, 1584, 1596, 1607, 1635. 38 sermons.

Seven sermons made upon the Lordes Prayer. 1572.

§2

Becon, T. The jewel of joye. [1553]. On Latimer's preaching.

Demaus, R. Latimer: a biography. 1869, 1881 (rev).

Carlyle, R. W. and A. J. Hugh Latimer. 1900.

Ryle, J. C. Bishops Latimer and Ridley. 1925.

Hastings, E. T. A sixteenth-century manuscript translation of Latimer's first sermon before Edward. PMLA 60 1945.

Gray, C. M. Latimer and the sixteenth century. Cambridge Mass 1950.

Chester, A. G. Latimer at Cambridge. Crozier Quart 28 1951.

— Milton, Latimer and the Lord Admiral. MLQ 14 1953.

— Latimer: apostle to the English. Philadelphia 1954.

Darby, H. S. Hugh Latimer. 1953.

Marchant, G. J. C. Latimer's candle. Evangelical Quart 28 1956.

Owst, G. R. In his Literature and pulpit in medieval England, Oxford 1961.

Thomas, G. L. Latimer: preacher ad populum. Quart Jnl of Speech 51 1965.

Anderson, F. D. Dispositio in the preaching of Latimer. Speech Monographs 35 1968.

Janton, P. L'éloquence et la rhétorique dans les sermons de Latimer. Paris 1968.

Marc'hadour, G. Latimer and Thomas More. Moreana 5 1968.

Yost, J. K. Latimer's reform programme 1529-36 and the intellectual origins of the Anglican via media. Anglican Theological Rev 53 1971.

SIR JOHN CHEKE
1514-57

§1

D. Ioannis Chrysostomi homiliae duae. 1543 (Latin and Greek), 1543. English trn of the second and of discourse on Job and Abraham, 'made out of Greke into Latin by master Cheke' by T. Chaloner, 1544, 1553.

D. Ioannia Chrysostomi de providentia Dei ac de fato orationes sex. 1545 (Latin trn).

The hurt of sedicion. 1549, 1549, 1549, 1569 ('newly perused and printed', running title, The true subiect to the rebell), 1576. Anon. Ptd in Holinshed's Chronicles, 1587, and by G. Langbaine with life of Cheke, Oxford 1641; Menston 1971 (facs of 1549).

De obitu doctissimi Buceri epistolae duae; item epigrammata varia. 1551, Basle 1587. First letter by Cheke to P. M. Vermigli, 2nd by N. Carr to Cheke. 2 letters also in C. Hubertus, Historia vera de vita Buceri, Strasbourg 1562.

Defensio verae et catholicae doctrinae de sacramento corporis et sanguinis Christi. 1553, Emden 1557, 1557. Latin trn from Cranmer's English.

Leonis imperatoris De bellico apparatu liber e graeco in latinum conversus I. Checo interp. Basle 1554, 1595.

De pronuntiatione graecae potissimum linguae disputationes cum Stephano Wintoniensi. Basle 1555, Menston 1968 (facs).

Reformatio legum ecclesiasticarum. 1571, 1640, 1641. Anon trn by Cheke with W. Haddon.

A treatise of superstition. In Strype, Life 1705. Trn by W. Elstob from Latin ms.

For Cheke's biblical trn see col 1842, below; prose ed H. Craik, English prose selections, 1893.

§2

Strype, J. Life of Cheke. 1705, Oxford 1821.

Baker, T. History of St John's College. Ed J. E. B. Mayor, Cambridge 1869.

Hale, E. E. Ideas on rhetoric in the sixteenth century. PMLA 18 1903.

Nathan, W. L. Cheke und der englische Humanismus. Bonn 1928.

Meritt, H. The vocabulary of Cheke's partial version of the Gospels. JEGP 39 1940.

Davies, H. S. Cheke and the translation of the Bible. E & S new ser 5 1952.

See also T. W. Baldwin, Shakspere's small Latine and lesse Greeke, Urbana 1944; C. S. Lewis, English literature in the sixteenth century, Oxford 1954; J. K. McConica, English humanists and Reformation politics, Oxford 1965; W. K. Jordan, Edward VI, 1968-.

MILES COVERDALE
1488-1568

§1

Goostly psalmes. [1536?].

A confutacion of that treatise which one J. Standish made agaynst D. Barnes. [Zürich 1541?].

The order that the Churche in Denmarke doth use. [1549?].

Certain most godly letters of such true saintes as gaue their lyves. 1564; ed E. Bickersteth 1837. Preface only by Coverdale.

Memorials. Ed J. J. Lowndes 1838.

Writings. Ed G. Pearson 1844 (Parker Soc).

Remains. Ed G. Pearson 1846 (Parker Soc).

For Coverdale's trn of the Bible see col 1832, below. For his other trns see under Erasmus, above; Satires on women, col 2031, below; Calvin, col 2183, below.

§2

Swearingen, G. F. Die englische Schriftsprache bei Coverdale. Weimar 1904.

Althoff, E. Coverdales Goostly psalmes und das deutsche Kirchenlied. Bochum 1935.

Guppy, H. Coverdale and the English Bible 1488-1568. Bull John Rylands Lib 19 1935.

Willoughby, H. R. Hans Holbein and the Coverdale Bible borders of 1535 and 1539-40. Anglican Theological Rev 24 1942.

Smothers, E. R. The Coverdale translation of Psalm LXXXIV. Harvard Theological Rev 38 1945.

Mozley, J. F. Miles Coverdale. N & Q April 1953. Reply by W. H. Welby, July 1953.

— Coverdale and his Bibles. 1953.

Dickinson, A. E. F. The first chorale book in England. Durham Univ Jnl 49 1957. Music of Coverdale's Ghostly psalms and spiritual songs.

Mennie, D. M. The first reception of Luther's hymns in England. Ibid. On Coverdale's hymnal c. 1536.

Bluhm, H. Luther and the first printed English Bible: Epistle to the Galatians. Anglican Theological Rev 40 1958. On debt to Luther's trn.

Beer, B. L. A note on Queen Catherine Parr's almoner. HLQ 25 1962. Not Coverdale but George Day; correction to C. F. Hoffman, HLQ 23 1960.

Robertson, J. Miles Coverdale. N & Q April 1963. On Coverdale's last years from records of Clothworkers' Company.

Reynolds, E. E. More, Coverdale and Cromwell. Moreana 3 1966.

THOMAS CRANMER
1489–1556
Collections

Remains. Ed H. Jenkyns 4 vols Oxford 1833.

Writings and Disputations relative to the sacrament of the Lord's supper. Ed J. E. Cox 1844–6 (Parker Soc). With life.

Miscellaneous writings and letters. Ed J. E. Cox 1846 (Parker Soc).

Selected writings. Ed C. S. Meyer 1961. With bibliography.

The work of Cranmer. Ed G. E. Duffield, Appleford 1964.

§1

Catechismus: that is to say, a shorte instruction into Christian religion. 1548 (3 edns). Tr from J. Jonas.

A defence of the true and catholike doctrine of the sacrament. 1550 (3 edns); tr French, 1552; tr Latin by Sir John Cheke 1553; [Emden] 1557 (rev); ed C. H. H. Wright 1907.

An answer unto a crafty and sophistical cavillation devised by Stephen Gardiner. 1551, 1580 ('revised and corrected by the Archbyshop').

An answere against the false calumniacion of Richarde Smyth. [1551?].

All the submyssyons and recantations of Cranmer. 1556 (first 4 in English, last 2 in Latin).

The copy of certain lettres sent to the Quene. [Emden 1556?].

The recantation of Cranmer translated out of Latin. [1556]. Original Latin is 5th recantation, above.

A confucation of vnwritten verities. Tr E.P. [Wesel? 1557?], 1582.

Reformatio legum ecclesiasticarum [anon]. Ed J. Foxe etc, tr W. Haddon and Sir John Cheke 1571, 1640.

Recantacyons. Ed Lord Houghton and J. Gairdner 1885 (Philobiblon Soc).

Cranmer's first litany. Ed J. E. Hunt, New York 1939.

§2

Strype, J. In his Memorials, 1694.

Nichols, J. G. Narratives of the days of the Reformation, with two contemporary biographies of Cranmer. Camden Soc 77 1859. Material not used by either Foxe or Strype.

Dixon, R. W. History of the Church of England. 6 vols 1884–1902. Full treatment of Cranmer.

Bailey, A. A legal view of Cranmer's execution. EHR 7 1892.

Mason, A. J. Thomas Cranmer. 1898.

Pollard, A. F. Cranmer and the English Reformation. 1904.

Brightman, F. E. The litany under Henry VIII. EHR 24 1909.

Legg, J. W. Cranmer's liturgical projects. 1915.

Wilson, J. M. The visitations and injunctions of Cardinal Wolsey and Cranmer to the priory of Worcester. Worcester 1924. See EHR 40 1925.

Smyth, C. H. Cranmer and the Reformation under Edward VI. Cambridge 1926. See C. Hopf, Martin Bucer and the English Reformation, Oxford 1946.

Deane, A. C. Life of Cranmer. 1927.

Belloc, H. Cranmer. 1931.

Styron, A. The three pelicans: Cranmer and the Tudor juggernaut. New York 1932.

Roberts, R. E. In The great Tudors, ed K. Garvin 1935.

Baskerville, G. A sister of Cranmer. EHR 51 1936.

Jenkins, C. Life and times of Cranmer. Canterbury 1936.

Willoughby, H. R. The first authorized English Bible and the Cranmer preface. Chicago 1942. With facs of preface.

Baumer, F. le van. The Church of England and the common corps of Christendom. Jnl of Modern History 16 1944. Also on More and Gardiner.

Symonds, H. E. Cranmer and the Edwardine prayer books. Theology 49 1946.

Timms, G. B. Dixit Cranmer. Church Quart Rev 143 1947. Reply by G. Dix, Dixit Cranmer et non timuit 145–6 1948.

Darby, H. S. Cranmer's first prayer-book. London Quart 18 1949.

1519 Prayer book: Language and liturgy. TLS 12 March 1949.

Osborn, R. R. Holy Communion in the Church of England. 1949. Mainly on Cranmer and his eucharistic writings.

Richardson, C. C. Zwingli and Cranmer on the eucharist. Evanston 1949.

Shepherd, M. H. The prayer book and the Bible. Anglican Theological Rev 31 1949. Mainly on Cranmer.

— The eucharistic lectionary. Anglican Theological Rev 32 1950. On Cranmer's revision of the traditional proper lessons.

Hutchinson, F. E. Cranmer and the English Reformation. 1951.

DuBoulay, F. R. H. Cranmer and the Canterbury temporalities. EHR 67 1952.

Micklewright, F. H. A. The concluding blessing in the eucharistic rite. N & Q 19 Jan 1952.

Bourne, E. C. E. Cranmer and the liturgy of 1552. Church Quart Rev 155 1954.

Bromiley, G. W. Cranmer, Archbishop and martyr. 1955.

— Cranmer, theologian. 1956.

— In B. A. Gerrish, Reformers in profile, Philadelphia 1967.

Jayne, S. and F. R. Johnson. The Lumley library. 1956. Started by Cranmer.

Maynard, T. The life of Cranmer. Chicago 1956.

Meyer, C. S. Cranmer's legacy. Concordia Theological Monthly 27 1956.

Ratclif, E. C. The liturgical work of Cranmer. Jnl of Ecclesiastical History 7 1956.

— The prayer of Chrysostom: note on Cranmer's rendering. Anglican Theological Rev 42 1960.

Rice, H. A. L. Thomas Cranmer. History Today 6 1956.

Ridler, A. The trial of Cranmer: a play. 1956.

Sykes, N. Thomas Cranmer. 1956.

Rupp, E. G. Six makers of English religion 1500–1700. 1957.

Dugmore, C. W. The mass and the English reformers. 1958. See T. M. Parker, Jnl of Theological Stud 12 1961.

Neilson, C. A. Twelve Reformation heroes. Glasgow 1960.

Brooks, P. Cranmer studies in the wake of the quatercentenary. Historical Mag of Protestant Episcopal Church 31 1962. Review of recent scholarship.

— Cranmer's doctrine of the eucharist. 1965.

Ridley, J. G. Thomas Cranmer. Oxford 1962.

Nijenhuis, W. Sporen van een Lutherse avondmaalsleer bij Cranmer. Nederlands Archief voor Kerkgeschiedenis 45 1963.

Woodhouse, H. F. The character of Cranmer. Anglican Theological Rev 45 1963.

McGee, E. K. Cranmer and nominalism. Harvard Theological Rev 57 1964. Replies by W. J. Courtenay, ibid, and McGee 59 1966.

Selwyn, D. G. A neglected edition of Cranmer's catechism. Jnl of Theological Stud 15 1964.

Devereux, J. A. Reformed doctrine in the collects of the first Book of common prayer. Harvard Theological Rev 58 1965.
— The primers and the prayer book collects. HLQ 32 1969.
— The collects of the first Book of common prayer as works of translation. SP 66 1969.
Smith, L. B. Henry VIII and Protestantism. Amer Historical Rev 71 1966. On Cranmer and the last religious settlements of the reign.
Beesley, A. Peter Martyr Vermigli's Adhortatio ad coenum Domini mysticam: an unpublished source of the Book of common prayer. Jnl of Ecclesiastical History 19 1968.
Fletcher, J. M. and J. Fines. Nicholas Harpsfield's note of Cranmer's recantation. Trans Cambridge Bibl Soc 4 1968.
Haugaard, W. P. The English Litany from Henry to Elizabeth. Anglican Theological Rev 51 1969.
Wayne, D. B. Behind Cranmer's offertory rubrics: the offering of the people in the Mass before the Reformation. Ibid.
Forman, J. P. Cranmer, Tudor diplomacy and primitive discipline. Sixteenth-century Essays & Stud (St Louis) 2 1971.
Shepard, R. F. Cranmer's Prayer books and the redemptive process. Anglican Theological Rev 53 1971.
Wellington, J. E. The Litany in Cranmer and Donne. SP 68 1971.

THOMAS LUPSET
1495–1530

The sermon of Doctor Colete made to the convocacion at Paulis. [1531?]. The anon trn is probably by Lupset.
A treatise of charite. 1533 (anon), 1535, 1539.
A compendious and a very fruteful treatyse, teachynge the waye of dyenge well. 1534, 1541.
Here be gathered counsailes of Saynct Isodorie. 1534, 1539, 1544.
An exhortation to yonge men, perswadinge them to walke in the pathe way that leadeth to honeste and goodnes. 1535, 1538, 1544.
A sermon of saint Chrysostome, translated into Englishe. 1542.
Workes. 1546, 1560.
The life and works of Lupset, with a critical text of the original treatises [2nd–4th items above] and the letters. Ed J. A. Gee, New Haven 1928. With bibliography and canon of Lupset's works, and other writings that have been ascribed to him.
Starkey, T. A dialogue between Reginald Pole and Lupset. Ed J. M. Cowper 1871 (as England in the reign of King Henry the Eighth) (EETS); ed K. M. Burton 1948 (preface by E. M. W. Tillyard).

SIMON FISH
d. 1531

§1

A supplicacyon for the beggers. [ptd abroad 1528–9?] (anon); ed F. J. Furnivall 1871 (EETS); ed E. Arber, Birmingham 1878.
The summe of the holye Scripture and ordynance of Christen teachyng. [Antwerp] 1529, London [1535?], [1536?], [1540], [1547], 1548, [1550?]. Tr from Dutch.
A supplication of the poore commons, whereunto is added the Supplication of beggars. 2 pts [1546].

§2

Pineas, R. Thomas More's controversy with Fish. Stud in Eng Lit 1500–1900 7 1967.
Haas, S. W. Fish, Tyndale and More's Lutheran conspiracy. Jnl of Ecclesiastical History 23 1972.

SIR THOMAS ELYOT
1499?–1546
Collections

Four political treatises: The doctrinal of princes; Pasquil the playne; The banquette of sapience: The image of governance. Gainesville 1967.

§1

Papyrii gemini eleatis hermathena: seu de eloquentia victoria. Cambridge 1522. By Elyot?
The education or bringinge up of children. [Before 1530], [1532?], [1550?]; ed R. D. Pepper, Gainesville 1966 (in Four Tudor books on education), Amsterdam 1969 (facs).
The boke named the governour. 1531, 1537, 1544, 1546, 1553, 1557, 1565, 1580; ed H. S. Croft 2 vols 1880 (with introd on life and works); ed F. Watson 1907; ed S. E. Lehmberg 1962 (facs of 1531).
How one may take profyte of his enmyes. [1531?] (anon). Tr from Plutarch.
A dialoge betwene Lucian and Diogenes of life. [1532?].
Pasquil the playne: a dialogue on talkativeness and silence. 1532, 1533, 1540. Anon.
Of the knowledge which maketh a wise man. 1533, [after 1548?]; ed E. J. Howard, Oxford Ohio 1946.
The doctrinal of princes. [1533?], [c. 1550]. Tr from Isocrates.
A swete and devoute sermon of holy Saynte Ciprian of the mortalitie of man; [with] The rules of a Christian lyfe made by Picus Earle of Mirandula. 1534, 1539. Trns: Sermon, [1556], Rules, Rouen 1585, [English secret press] 1615.
The dictionary of Syr Thomas Elyot [Latin and English]. 1538, 1542 (as Bibliotheca Elyotae), 1545; rev and 'inriched' by T. Cooper 1548, 1552, 1559; Menston 1970 (facs of 1538).
The Castel of Helth. [1536–9], 1539 ('and augmented'), 1541, 1541, 1541 ('corrected') (for 1544?), 1547, [1550?], [1559?], [1560?], 1561, 1572, 1576, 1580, 1587, 1595, 1610; New York 1937 (facs of 1541 with title-page and preface to 1536–9).
The bankette of sapience. 1539 ('newly augmented'), 1542, 1545, 1545, 1557, 1564.
The defence of good women. [1540], 1545; ed E. J. Howard, Oxford Ohio 1940.
The image of governance compiled of the actes of Alexander Severus. 1541, 1544, 1544, 1549, 1549, 1556.
A preservatiue agaynste deth. 1545.

§2

Hale, E. E. Ideas on rhetoric in the sixteenth century. PMLA 18 1903.
Emkes, M. A. Das Erziehungsideal bei More, Elyot, Ascham und Lyly. Marburg 1904.
Benndorf, C. Die englische Pädagogik im 16 Jahrhundert: Elyot, Ascham und Mulcaster. Vienna 1905.
Schroeder, K. Platonismus in der englischen Renaissance vor und bei Eliot, nebst Neudruck von Eliots Disputacion Platonike 1533. Berlin 1920.
Hogrefe, P. Elyot and the Boke called Cortigiano in Ytalion. MP 27 1930. Quotes letter from Bonner to Cromwell on influence of the Courtier.
— Elyot's intention in the opening chapters of the Governour. SP 60 1963.
— Life and times of Elyot. Ames Iowa 1967.
Pollard, A. F. Sir Thomas More and Elyot. TLS 17 July 1930.
Starnes, D. T. Elyot and the Sayings of philosophers. SE 13 1933.
— Thomas Cooper and the Bibliotheca Eliotae. SE 30 1951.
— Elyot and the Lanquet-Cooper chronicle. SE 34 1955.

—— Elyot redivivus. SE 36 1957. On Workes of armorie 1572 by J. Bossewell.

Fulton, J. F. Early medical humanists: Leonicenus, Linacre and Elyot. New England Jnl of Medicine 205 1934.

Heltzel, V. B. Breton, Elyot and the Court of honour. MLN 53 1938.

Schlotter, J. Elyots Governour in seinem Verhältnis zu Francesco Patrici. Freiburg 1938.

Warren, L. C. Humanistic doctrines of the Prince from Petrarch to Elyot. Chicago 1939.

—— Patrizi's De regno et regis institutione and the plan of Elyot's Governour. JEGP 49 1950.

Pace, G. B. Elyot against poetry. MLN 56 1941.

Howard, E. J. Elyot on the turning of the earth. PQ 21 1942.

—— Some words in Of the knowledge which maketh a wise man. MLN 58 1943.

Richards, G. R. B. The Castle of Health. More Books Feb 1945.

Wortham, J. Elyot and the translation of prose. HLQ 11 1948.

Sargent, R. M. Elyot and the integrity of the Two gentlemen of Verona. PMLA 65 1950.

Butt, J. A plea for more English dictionaries. Durham Univ Jnl 12 1951. On Elyot's use of language.

Donner, H. W. The Emperor and Elyot. RES new ser 2 1951. On authenticity of the story of the Emperor and More's death.

Lascelles, M. Elyot and the legend of Alexander Severus. RES new ser 2 1951.

Schoeck, R. J. Rhetoric and law in sixteenth-century England. SP 50 1953.

Bühler, C. F. Diogenes and the Boke named the Governour. MLN 69 1954.

Caspari, F. Humanism and the social order in Tudor England. Chicago 1954.

Sledd, J. Nowell's Vocabularium saxonicum and the Elyot-Cooper tradition. SP 51 1954.

Maxwell, J. C. [Shakespeare's] Julius Caesar and Elyot's Governour. N & Q April 1956.

Lehmberg, S. E. Elyot and the English Reformation. Archiv für Reformationsgeschichte 48 1957.

—— Elyot: Tudor humanist. Austin 1960.

Bouck, C. W. On the identity of Papyrius Geminus Eleates. Trans Cambridge Bibl Soc 2 1958.

Major, J. M. The moralization of the dance in Elyot's Governour. Stud in Renaissance 5 1958.

—— Elyot and Renaissance humanism. Lincoln Nebraska 1964.

Ammann, R. E. Die Verbalsyntax in Elyots Governour mit vergleichenden Beispielen aus Aschams Schoolemaster. Aarau 1961.

Holmes, E. The significance of Elyot's revision of the Governour. RES new ser 12 1961.

Brooks, H. F. Shakespeare and the Governour. Shakespeare Quart 14 1963.

Ferguson, A. B. The articulate citizen and the English Renaissance. Durham NC 1965.

Rydén, M. Relative constructions in early sixteenth-century English, with special reference to Elyot. Upsala 1966.

NICHOLAS RIDLEY
1500?–55

Collections

Works. Ed H. Christmas 1841 (Parker Soc).

§1

A brief declaracion of the Lordes supper. [Emden] 1555, [no place] 1559, London 1586; ed H. C. G. Moule 1895.

Certein godly, learned and comfortable conferences betwene Ridley and H. Latimer. [Emden] 1556, 1556, [Strasbourg 1556] (with A treatise agaynst transsubstantiation), London 1574 (newly againe imprinted).

A frendly farewel which master Ridley did write unto all his true louers and frendes in God, a little before that he suffred. [Ed J. Foxe] 1559 ('newly set forth').

A pituous lamentation of the miserable estate of the Churche of Christ in Englande, in the time of the late revolt from the gospel. 1566, 1566.

Praefatio et protestatio habita Aprilis 20 1555. [c. 1580]; tr and ed G. Ironside, Oxford 1688; 1792 (Latin).

The way to peace amongst all Protestants: being a letter of reconciliation sent by Bp Ridley to Bp Hooper with some observations upon it by Sam Johnson. 1688, 1703, 1846.

§2

Merrill, L. R. The life and poems of Nicholas Grimald. New Haven 1925. Introd.

Ryle, J. C. Bishops Latimer and Ridley. 1925.

Bromiley, G. W. Ridley: scholar, Bishop, theologian, martyr. [1950].

Ridley, J. G. Ridley: a biography. 1957.

Hutchins, C. H. Ridley: English reformer, theologian and martyr. Evangelical Quart 41 1969.

MATTHEW PARKER
1504–75

§1

How we ought to take the death of the godly: a sermon made in Cambrydge at the buriall of M. Bucer. [1551?]; tr T. Newton [1587] (tr from an abridged Latin version ptd abroad).

An admonition to all suche as shall intende to enter the state of matrimonye. 1560, [c. 1560], [c. 1560], 1563, 1571, 1594, [c. 1600] [c. 1600], [1605?], 1620, Oxford [c. 1630], London 1639.

Concio in funere Buceri habita. Latin trn in C. Hubertus, Historia de vita Buceri, Strasbourg 1562.

A briefe examination of a certaine declaration. [1566?]. Attributed to Parker.

The whole psalter translated into English metre. [1567?] (with four-part settings by T. Tallis). See col. 1902, below.

De antiquitate britannicae ecclesiae cantuariensis, cum archiepiscopis ejusdem 70. 1572–4 (anon), 1605; ed S. Drake 1729; tr [Zürich] 1574.

The life off the 70 Archbishopp off Canterbury englished. [Zürich] 1574.

Registrum Matthei Parker 1559–75. Ed W. H. Frere 1907–35 (Canterbury & York Soc).

Parker also translated the canons and decrees of the Council of Trent, wrote preface to the anon Defence of priestes mariages, [1567?] and notes to the next edn [1567?], edited a sermon of Aelfric's, the Anglo-Saxon version of the Gospels, and the following chroniclers: Asser, Matthew of Westminster, Matthew Paris, Thomas Walsingham.

Letters

Correspondence. Ed J. Bruce and T. T. Perowne 1853 (Parker Soc).

§2

Strype, J. Life and acts of Parker. 1711, Oxford 1821.

Freeman, E. A. Archbishop Parker. In his Historical essays, 1892.

Kennedy, W. P. M. Life of Archbishop Parker. 1908.

Davis, E. J. Archbishop Parker's register. EHR 34 1919.

Pearce, E. C. Matthew Parker. Library 6 1925.

Rope, H. E. G. Parker's witness against continuity. 1931.

Thompson, B. M. H. The consecration of Archbishop Parker. 1934.

Greg, W. W. Books and bookmen in the correspondence of Parker. Library 4th ser 16 1935.

Stead, M. T. In The great Tudors, ed K. Garvin 1935.
Perry, E. W. Under four Tudors. 1940. *See* C. S. Carter, The real Matthew Parker, Church Quart Rev 136 1943.
Darby, H. S. Parker. London Quart 6th ser 10 1941.
Flower, R. William Salesbury, Richard Davies and Archbishop Parker. Jnl Nat Lib of Wales 2 1942.
Whitebrook, J. C. The consecration of Parker. 1945.
— The consecration of Parker. N & Q 12 Jan, 4 May, 18 May, 7 Sept, 21 Sept 1946.
Shirley, F. J. Elizabeth's first Archbishop: a reply to Whitebrook. 1948.
Williams, G. Bishop Sulien, Bishop Richard Davies and Parker. Jnl Nat Lib of Wales 5 1948.
Pennington, E. L. The episcopal succession during the English Reformation. 1952.
Wright, C. E. Monastic libraries and Anglo-Saxon studies: Parker and his circle. Trans Cambridge Bibl Soc 1 1953.
Kearley, D. A. and B. C. Weber. An unpublished letter of Parker [17 Aug 1563]. Historical Mag of Protestant Episcopal Church 24 1955.
Taylor, J. Henry Wharton and the Lambeth ms of the Flores historiarum. N & Q June 1956. On Wharton's collation of Parker's edn 1570.
Nixon, H. M. A binding for Parker c. 1574. Book Collector 6 1957.
— A binding by the Macdurnan Gospels binder c. 1570. Book Collector 18 1969.
Bennett, H. R. Matthew Parker. Anglican Theological Rev 42 1960.
Brook, V. J. K. A life of Parker. Oxford 1962.
Daeley, J. I. Pluralism in the diocese of Canterbury during the administration of Parker 1559–75. Jnl of Ecclesiastical History 18 1967.
Murphy, M. Religious polemics in the genesis of Old English studies. HLQ 32 1969.

JOHN CAIUS
1510–73
Collections

Ioannis Caii opera aliquot et versiones. Louvain 1556.
Works. Ed E. S. Roberts, Cambridge 1912. With memoir by John Venn.

§1

De medendi methodo. Basle 1544.
A boke or counseill against the disease called the sweate. 1552 (Latin and English); rptd in J. C. F. Hecker, The epidemics of the Middle Ages, 1844; ed A. Malloch, New York 1937 (facs of 1552).
De antiquitate cantabrigiensis academiae libri duo. 1568, 1574. On 1574 *see* Library 3rd ser 7 1927.
De canibus britannicis liber unus; De rariorum animalium et stirpium historia; De libris propriis. 3 pts 1570. Pt I tr A. Fleming as Of English dogges, 1576, Amsterdam 1969 (facs).
De pronunciatione Graecae & Latine linguae cum scriptione noua libellus. 1574; tr J. B. Gabel, Leeds 1968 (with facs of 1574).
Historia cantabrigiensis academiae liber. 1574.
Caius also edited and translated Galen's works into Latin; see col 2366, below.

§2

Venn, J. Annals of Gonville and Caius College. Cambridge 1904.
Albion, G. Caius of Cambridge. Clergy Rev 16 1939.
Brown, W. L. Caius and the revival of learning. Proc Royal Soc of Medicine 35 1942.
Raven, C. E. English naturalists from Neckham to Ray. 1947.
Smith-Dampier, J. L. East Anglian worthies. Oxford 1949.
O'Malley, C. D. The relations of Caius with Andreas Vesalius. Jnl History of Medicine 10 1955.

— English medical humanists: Thomas Linacre and Caius. Lawrence Kansas 1965.
Wohlfarth, P. Dr Caius, a French physician. Sudhoffs Archiv 40 1956. With bibliography.
Barber-Lomax, J. W. De canibus britannicis. Jnl of Small Animal Practice 1 1960.
Clark, G. N. In his A history of the Royal College of Physicians of London vol 1, 1964. Chs 6–7.
Cule, J. A note on Hugo Glyn and the statute banning Welshmen from Gonville and Caius. Jnl Nat Lib of Wales 16 1969.
McNair, Lord. Why is the doctor in the Merry wives of Windsor called Caius? Medical History 13 1969.

JOHN PONET or POYNET
1514?–56

§1

A defence for mariage of priestes. 1549, [1567?].
A tragoedie or dialoge of the unjuste primacie of the Bishop of Rome. 1549; ed C. E. Plumptre 1899. Tr from Bernardino Ochino.
A notable sermon concerninge the ryght use of the Lordes supper. 1550.
Catechismus brevis. 1553; tr in Library of Christian classics, 1966. Probably compiled by Ponet.
The humble and unfained confession of certain poore banished men. [Wesel] 1554. Attributed to Ponet.
An apologie fully aunsweringe a blasphemose book by D. Steph. Gardiner. Strasbourg 1555, 1556.
A shorte treatise of politike power. [Strasbourg] 1556, [Paris?] 1639, Menston 1970 (facs).
Diallacticon. [Strasbourg] 1557.
Registra Stephani Gardiner et Johannis Poynet. Ed H. Chitty 1930 (Canterbury & York Soc).

§2

Hudson, W. S. Ponet: advocate of limited monarchy. Chicago 1942. Biography, with facs of A shorte treatise.
Garrett, C. M. Ponet and the confession of the banished ministers. Church Quart Rev 137 1944.

ROGER ASCHAM
1515–68

Bibliographies

Tannenbaum, S. A. and D. R. Ascham: a concise bibliography. New York 1946; suppl 1946–66 by R. C. Johnson, 1968.

Collections

English works. Ed J. Bennet 1761; rev J. G. Cochrane 1815.
Whole works. Ed J. A. Giles 4 vols in 3 1864–5.
English works: Toxophilus; Report of the affaires of Germany; The scholemaster. Ed W. A. Wright, Cambridge 1904.

§1

Toxophilus: the schole of shootinge conteyned in two bookes. 1545, 1571 ('newlye perused'), 1589; ed J. Walters, Wrexham 1788; ed E. Arber, Birmingham 1868; Wakefield 1968 (facs of 1788), Amsterdam 1969 (facs of 1545), Menston 1971 (facs of 1545).
A report and discourse of the affaires and state of Germany. [1570?].
The scholemaster: or plaine and perfite way of teachyng children the Latin tong. 1570, 1571, 1571, 1579, 1589; ed J. Upton 1711, 1743 (rev); ed J. E. B. Mayor 1863; ed E. Arber, Birmingham 1869; ed J. Holzamer, Vienna 1881; ed D. C. Whimster 1934; ed L. V. Ryan, Ithaca

1967; Menston 1967 (facs of 1570), Amsterdam 1968 (facs of 1570).

Apologia pro caena dominica; themata; expositiones in epistolas theologicas; cui accesserunt Pauli ad Titum & Philemonem. Ed E. Grant 1577.

Letters

Familiarium epistolarum libri tres. [1576], 1578 (rev), 1581, 1590, Hanover 1602; ed E. G[rant], Hanover 1610; ed W. Elstob, Oxford 1703.

§2

Katterfeld, A. Ascham: sein Leben und seine Werke. Strasbourg 1879.

Quick, R. H. In his Essays on educational reformers, 1888.

Fischer, T. A. Drei Studien zur englischen Literatur-geschichte. Gotha 1892.

Emkes, M. A. Das Erziehungsideal bei More, Elyot, Ascham und Lyly. Marburg 1904.

Benndorf, C. Die englische Pädagogik im 16 Jahrhundert: Elyot, Ascham und Mulcaster. Vienna 1905.

Hettler, A. Ascham: sein Stil und seine Beziehung zur Antike. Elberfeld 1915.

Radford, L. B. Roger Ascham. Quart Rev 256 1931.

Parks, G. B. The first draft of Ascham's Scholemaster. HLQ 1 1938.

Rosenzweig, S. Ascham's Scholemaster and Spenser's February eclogue. Shakespeare Assoc Bull 15 1940.

Maxwell, J. C. English anti-Machiavellianism before Gentillet. N & Q April 1954.

Rope, H. E. G. The 'Italianate' Englishman. Month 11 1954.

Hallam, G. W. An Ascham borrowing from Erasmus. N & Q March 1955.

Braham, L. Johnson's edition of Ascham. N & Q Aug 1956.

— Ascham and the Regius Professorships. N & Q Sept 1956.

Reaney, P. H. Ascham, Margaret Rampston and Salisbury Hall. N & Q Aug 1957.

Staton, W. F., jr. The character of style in Elizabethan prose. JEGP 57 1958.

— Ascham's theory of history writing. SP 56 1959.

Ryan, L. V. Ascham's Toxophilus in heroic verse. HLQ 22 1959.

— Roger Ascham. Stanford 1963.

Ammann, R. E. Die Verbalsyntax in Elyots Governour mit vergleichenden Beispielen aus Aschams Schoolemaster. Aarau 1961.

Hornát, J. Lyly's Anatomy of wit and Ascham's Scholemaster. Prague 1961.

Klein, K. L. Rhetorik und Dichtungslehre in der elisabethanischen Zeit. In Festschrift zum 75 Geburtstag von Theodor Spira, Heidelberg 1961.

Parks, G. B. The first Italianate Englishman. Stud in Renaissance 8 1961.

Smith, C. I. Some ideas on education before Locke. JHI 23 1962.

Miller, W. E. Double translation in English humanistic education. Stud in Renaissance 10 1963.

Test, G. A. Archer's feathers in Chaucer and Ascham. Amer N & Q 2 1964.

Watson, T. A humanist's 'trew imitation': Thomas Watson's Absalom, a critical edition and translation. Ed J. H. Smith, Urbana 1964. On Ascham see introd.

Smith, J. H. Ascham's troubled years. JEGP 65 1966.

Rott, J. and R. Faerber. Un Anglais à Strasbourg: John Hales, Ascham et Jean Sturm. Etudes Anglaises 21 1968.

Greene, T. M. Ascham: the perfect end of shooting. ELH 36 1969. On Scholemaster.

Giddey, E. Notes sur le style de Ascham. In Mélanges d'historie offerts à Henri Meylan, Geneva 1970.

THOMAS LEVER
1521–77

A meditacion upon the Lordes prayer. [1551], [1551].

A treatise of the right way from danger of synne nowe newly augmented. 1571, 1575.
For sermons, see col 1943, below.

THOMAS WILSON
1524?–81

§1

The rule of reason: conteining the arte of logique set forthe in Englishe. 1551, 1552, 1553, 1563, 1567, 1580, Amsterdam 1970 (facs of 1551).

Vita et obitus duorum fratrum Hen. et Car. Brandoni. 1551, nd. With Walter Haddon.

The arte of rhetorique for the use of all suche as are studious of eloquence sette forth in Englische. 1553, 1560 ('newlie sette forthe again'), 1562, 1563, 1567, 1580, 1584, 1585; ed G. H. Mair, Oxford 1909 (from 1560); Gainesville 1962 (facs of 1553), Amsterdam 1969 (facs of 1553).

Oratio habita Pataviae in mortem Domini Edowardi Courtenai 1556. In Strype, Ecclesiastical memorials vol 3, 1721.

The three orations of Demosthenes in favour of the Olynthians with fower orations against King Philip of Macedonie, englished by T. Wylson. 1570, Amsterdam 1968 (facs).

A discourse upon usurye. 1572, 1584; ed R. H. Tawney 1925.

A treatise of England's perils. 1578; ed A. J. Schmidt, Archiv für Reformationsgeschichte 46 1955.

§2

Hale, E. E. Ideas on rhetoric in the sixteenth century. PMLA 18 1903.

Reed, A. W. Nicholas Udall and Wilson. RES 1 1925.

Wagner, R. H. The text and editions of Wilson's Arte of rhetorique. MLN 44 1929.

— Wilson and his sources. Quart Jnl of Speech 15 1929.

— Wilson's speech against usury. Quart Jnl of Speech 38 1952.

— Wilson's Arte of rhetorique. Speech Monographs 27 1960.

Englehardt, G. J. The relation of Sherry's Treatise of schemes and tropes to Wilson's Arte of rhetorique. PMLA 62 1947.

Kuiper, G. Wilson's Rule of reason 1551 en het continentale humanisme. De Nieuwe Taalgids 46 1953.

Schoeck, R. J. Rhetoric and law in sixteenth-century England. SP 50 1953.

Peterson, D. L. A probable source for Shakespeare's sonnett CXXIX. Shakespeare Quart 5 1954.

Anderson, D. M. Wilson's translation of Montemayor's Diana. RES new ser 7 1956. BM additional ms 18,638.

Schmidt, A. J. A household inventory 1581. Proc Amer Philosophical Soc 101 1957.

— Wilson: Tudor scholar and statesman. HLQ 20 1957.

— Wilson and the Tudor commonwealth: an essay in civic humanism. HLQ 23 1960.

— A humanist describes and prescribes: Wilson and medicine. Bull History of Medicine 34 1960.

Sowton, I. Hidden persuaders as a means of literary grace: sixteenth-century poetics and rhetoric in England. UTQ 32 1963.

McNally, J. R. Prima pars dialecticae. Renaissance Quart 21 1968.

WILLIAM FULKE
1537–89

§ 1

Antiprognosticon contra inutiles astrologorum praedictiones. 1560; tr W. Painter, 1560 (whereunto is added a shorte treatise for the better subversion of that fained arte).

A goodly gallerye with a most pleasant prospect, into the garden of naturall contemplation. 1563, 1602, 1634 (2nd edn), 1639 (3rd edn).

The most noble auncient and learned playe, called the Philosophers game, 1563 (with Ralph Lever). *See* E. Rosenberg, Leicester, 1955.

A sermon preached at Hampton Court 12 Nov 1570. 1570, 1571, 1572, 1574, 1579, 1580.

A confutation of a popishe libelle. 1571, 1573, 1574.

Οὐρανομαχία: hoc est astrologorum ludus. 1571, 1572.

In sacram diui Ioannis Apocalypsim praelectiones. 1573; tr 1573.

A comfortable sermon of faith, preached 1573. 1574, [1574?], 1578, 1586, 1611 ('newly corrected').

A sermon preached on 17 March at S. Alpheges. 1577; tr Latin by John Foxe, De Christo gratis justificante, 1583.

Two treatises written against the Papistes. 1577; 2nd treatise also issued separately with rev preface as An answer of a true Christian, 1577.

A commentarie upon Josue. 1578. Tr from Calvin, sometimes attributed to Fulke.

Gulielmi Fulconis Angli, ad epistolam Stanislai Hosii responsio. 1578.

Μετρομαχία: sive ludus geometricus. 1578.

Ad Thomae Stapletoni controversiarum cavillationes responsio. 1579.

D. Hoskins, D. Sanders, a. M. Rastel overthrowne. 1579.

A godly sermon preached 26 Februarie 1580. [1580?], [1580?]. Anon.

A retentive to stay good Christians. 1580. Includes 2nd work, A discovery of the daungerous rocke, ed R. Gibbings 1848 (Parker Soc).

T. Stapleton and Martiall confuted. 1580; ed R. Gibbings 1848 (Parker Soc).

A briefe confutation of a popish discourse by J. Howlet. 1581.

A rejoynder to Bristows replie. 1581.

A sermon preached upon Sunday the twelfth of March. 1581.

A defense of the sincere and true translations of the holie scriptures into the English tong; whereunto is added a briefe confutation. 1583, 1617, 1633; ed C. H. Hartshorne 1843 (Parker Soc).

Epistle to the reader. In Jean de Serres, A godlie commentarie upon Ecclesiastes 1585 (tr John Stockwood).

A briefe and plaine declaration concerning the desires of all those faithfull ministers that seeke for the reformation of the Church of England. 1584. Sometimes attributed to Fulke, ed John Field. Rptd in L. Trinterud, Elizabethan Puritanism, 1971.

De successione ecclesiastica contra T. Stapletoni. 1584.

A treatise against the Defense of the censure. 1586. Includes 2 treatises by Fulke.

The text of the New testament translated by the Papists at Rhemes, with a confutation. 1589, 1601 ('perused and enlarged'), 1617, 1633.

[Greenham, R.?]. A true reporte of a conference betwixt Doctour Fulke a. the Papists at Wisbiche Castle. 1581; Downside Rev 54 1936.

Nowell, A. and W. Day. A true report of the Disputation had in the Tower. 1583. Includes account of Fulke's conferences with Campion, 1588, reported by John Field.

§ 2

Wren, M. Life. In Thomas Hearne, Collections vol 4, Oxford 1898.

Allen, D. C. The star-crossed Renaissance. New York 1941. On Fulke's scientific writings.

Porter, H. C. In his Reformation and reaction in Tudor Cambridge, Cambridge 1958.

Heninger, S. K. A handbook of Renaissance meteorology. Durham NC 1960.

— Tudor literature of the physical sciences. HLQ 32 1969.

J. K. M.

II. THE ENGLISH BIBLE

DMH A. S. Herbert, Historical catalogue of printed editions of the English Bible 1525–1961, 1968 (rev and expanded from T. H. Darlow and H. F. Moule, 1903)

(1) BIBLIOGRAPHIES

[Ames, J.] A list of various editions of the Bible and parts thereof, in English, from the year 1526 to 1776, much enlarged and improved [by M. C. Tutet, A. C. Ducarel et al]. 1776, 1778 (rev); enlarged and improved by C. Cruttwell in introd to his edn of Holy Bible, 3 vols Bath 1785, 5 vols 1790 (DMH 1302); continued to 1797 in introd to J. Hewlett's edn of Holy Bible, 3 vols 1812 (DMH 1564); to 1812 in Hewlett, Commentaries and annotations on the holy scriptures, 5 vols 1816; the 1778 edn continued to 1792 in Newcome, An historical view, Dublin 1792, below, continued to 1816 in Lewis, A complete history, 1818 (3rd edn), below; rev to 1611 in Anderson, Annals, below, 1845, New York 1849 (abridged), London 1862 (rev). On authorship of original edns *see* J. Nichols, Literary anecdotes of the eighteenth century vol 6 1812 pp. 390–1, and Cotton, pp. x–xii, below.

Cotton, H. A list of editions of the Bible and parts thereof in English, from the year MDV to MDCCCXX, with an appendix containing specimens of translations and bibliographical descriptions. Oxford 1821, 1852 (as Editions to MDCCCL).

Orme, W. Bibliotheca biblica: a select list of books on sacred literature. Edinburgh 1824.

Horne, T. H. A manual of biblical bibliography: comprising a catalogue, methodically arranged, of the principal editions and versions of the holy scriptures. 1839. A reissue with new title of part of Horne, An introduction to the critical study and knowledge of the holy scriptures, 1818, 1869 (12th edn); the bibliography of English trns appeared only in 7th edn 1834, 8th edn 1839 (vol 2, pt 2 in both), and 9th edn 1846 (vol 5).

Parker, J. W. Bibles, Testaments, Books of common prayer and Proper lessons, printed at the Cambridge University Press. [Cambridge 1839]. A catalogue with specimens.

Wilson, L. Bibles, Testaments, Psalms and other books of the holy scriptures in English, in the collection of Lea Wilson. 1845.

O'Callaghan, E. B. A list of editions of the holy scriptures and parts thereof, printed in America previous to 1860. Albany 1861, Detroit 1966. From 1661.

Loftie, W. J. A century of Bibles: or the Authorised version from 1611 to 1711; to which is added W. Kilburne's tract 1659 [below], with lists of Bibles in the British Museum and other libraries. 1872.

Stevens, H. The Bibles in the Caxton Exhibition 1877: or a bibliographical description of nearly one thousand representative Bibles in various languages. 1878.

Lovett, R. The English Bible in the John Rylands Library 1525–1640. 1899.

Darlow, T. H. and H. F. Moule. Historical catalogue of the printed editions of holy scripture in the library of the British and Foreign Bible Society. 2 vols in 4 1903–11, New York 1963, London 1968 (rev A. S. Herbert) (vol 1). Earlier less detailed catalogues of this collections were pbd 1822, 1832, 1857 (by G. Bullen) and 1901 (English Bibles to 1640, by H. F. M[oule]). Vol 1 (English), 1903, superseded by DMH.

Milligan, G. Notes on the Euing Collection of Bibles in Glasgow University Library. Records of Glasgow Bibl Soc 4 1915.

Rumball-Petre, E. A. R. Rare Bibles: an introduction for collectors and a descriptive checklist. New York 1938, 1954 (rev), 1963.

Kronenberg, M. E. with W. Nijhoff. Nederlandsche bibliographie van 1500 tot 1540 vol 2. Hague 1940. Includes, pp. 127–143, 26 edns ptd in Netherlands, all in DMH except no 2492.

Hills, M. T. The English Bible in America: a bibliography of editions of the Bible and the New testament published in America 1777–1957. New York 1961.

Pullen, G. E. Catalogue of the Bible collections in the Old Library at St Mary's, Oscott c. 1472–c. 1850. Sutton Coldfield 1971.

Useful illustr guides to Bible exhibitions have been pbd by British and Foreign Bible Soc (1611–1961), by D. G. Dance and W. J. Bradnock, 1961; BM (1611–1911), by A. W. Pollard et al, 1911, 1927; see also A. R. Habershon, The Bible and the British Museum, 1909; Glasgow Univ Lib (by G. Milligan: 1611–1911, 1911; 1525, 1925); John Rylands Lib (1904, 1907, 1911, 1925, 1935; all by H. Guppy, the first 3 anon); Preston Public Lib (1611–1911, 1911); Sunderland Public Lib (1611–1911, 1911); Washington Cathedral (In the beginning was the word, 1965), Wigan Public Lib (1538–1938, [1938]), Yale Univ Lib (1611–1911, 1911) etc. Some General Studies, below, contain lists of Bible edns.

Periodical bibliographies

Elenchus bibliographicus biblicus. Suppl to Biblica (Rome) 1– 1920–. Regularly includes a section Versio anglica; valuable from 46 1965; suppl in Verbum Domini (Rome) 39– 1960–.

Society for Old Testament Study. Book list (Bristol) 1–1936–. Well annotated; includes sections on Text and versions. Vols 1–11 1946–56 collected as H. H. Rowley (ed), Eleven years of Bible bibliography, Indian Hills Colorado 1957, and 12–21 1957–66 as G. W. Anderson (ed), A decade of Bible bibliography, Oxford 1967.

Internationale Zeitschriftenschau für Bibelwissenschaft und Grenzgebiete, International review of biblical studies, Revue internationale des études bibliques. Stuttgart (vol 1), Düsseldorf (from vol 2), 1– 1951–.

(2) CONCORDANCES, DICTIONARIES ETC

See Orme pp. 118–120, above; Horne 1839 pp. 432–3, above; A. G. Kennedy, A bibliography of writings on the English language to 1922, Cambridge Mass 1927 pp. 246–9; R. C. Alston, A bibliography of the English language to 1800 vol 3, pt 2, Leeds 1971 pp. 6–32.

[Gibson (Gybson), T.] The concordance of the New Testament. 1535. Tyndale's trn; variously attributed to Tyndale and Coverdale.

[Gramelin, M.] A table of the pryncypall matters conteyned in the Byble, in wych the readers may fynde and practyse many commune places. Prefixed to Matthew Bible, 1537. Tr, probably by J. Rogers, from the Indice des principales matières contenues en la Bible, in P. R. Olivetan's French Bible, Neuchâtel 1535.

[Marbeck, J.] A concordance: that is to saie a worke wherein by the ordre of the letters of the ABC ye maie redely finde any worde conteigned in the whole Bible. 1550. Matthew version.

Bullinger, H., L. Jude, C. Pellicane. A briefe and compendiouse table, in a maner of a concordaunce of the whole Bible, as amply as doeth the great concordaunce [Marbeck]. Tr W. Lynne 1550, 1563. Tr from German concordance, Ein kurtzer Zeiger der fürnemsten Hystorien, unnd gemeinsten Artickeln des Alten und Neüwen Testaments, prefixed to some edns of Zürich Bible from 1531 (Darlow and Moule 4196).

H[errey], R. F. (R. Harrison). Two right profitable and fruitfull concordances: the first conteyning the interpretation of the Hebrue, Caldean, Greeke and Latin, wordes and names; the seconde comprehending all such other principall words and matters. [1580] etc. Ptd separately, and with most 4° edns of Geneva Bible till 1622.

W[ilcox], T. A concordance or table conteyning the principall both wordes and matters in the Newe testament. 1579 (Dr Williams's Lib only). Geneva trn.

Knight, W. A concordance axiomaticall. 1610. Geneva trn.

Allen, R. Concordances of the holy Proverbs of King Salomon and of his like sentences in Ecclesiastes. 1612.

Wilson, T. A Christian dictionarie. 1612, 1616, 1622; ed J. Bagwell [1628–40], 1647, 1654 (as A complete Christian dictionary) (London Dutch Church only); ed A. Symson (Simson) 1655, 1661, 1678.

[Cotton, C.] The Christians concordance: containing the most materiall words in the New testament. 1622.
—— A concordance to all the bookes of the Old testament. 1627. Both Authorized version.

Cotton, C. A complete concordance to the Bible of the last translation. 1631, 1631, 1635 (as A large concordance), 1635 (rev H.T., unauthorized), 1638; rev S. Newman as A large and complete concordance, 1643, 1650 (2nd edn, under Newman's name alone), 1658, Cambridge 1662 (as A concordance), 1672 (as An exact concordance), 1682, 1698, London 1720 (as The Cambridge concordance), 1889 (as A concordance, from 1672). Authorized version; the basis of principal later concordances.

[Downame, J.] A briefe concordance to the Bible of the last translation. 1630, 1630, 1631, 1632 (as A concordance), 1633, [1633?] (2 edns),]1634?] (As A concordance), 1639 (enlarged), 1642 (as A briefe concordance), 1646, 1652, 1652, 1654, 1659, 1663, 1671, 1671, 1688, 1689, 1690, 1726 (3 edns), 1732, 1739, 1745, 1752, 1757, 1762, 1767, 1773, Edinburgh 1774, Trenton 1790. Authorized version; considerably shorter than concordances of Cotton, above, by whose assigns 1632–9 were pbd; ptd in various formats to be bound up with Bibles.

Leigh, E. Critica sacra: observations on all the radices or primitive Hebrew words of the Old testament in order alphabeticall. 1641, 1642; Critica sacra: or philologicall and theologicall observations upon all the Greek words of the New testament in order alphabeticall, 1639, 1646; Critica sacra, in two parts [the 2 works combined], 1650 (3rd edn), 1662, 1664.

B[elke], T. An epitome of sacred scripture digested into severall heades. 1644.

Bernard, R. Thesaurus biblicus: seu promptuarium sacrum. 1644, 1661 (rev W. Retchforde).

[Hart, J.] The fort-royal of the scriptures: or the vade-mecum concordance. Ptd London, pbd Edinburgh 1649, Edinburgh 1649, London 1652, 1655, 1656, 1732 (rptd from 1649).

W[ickens], R. A compleat and perfect concordance of the English Bible. Oxford 1655.

Bennet, R. A theological concordance of the synonymous terms in the holy scriptures. 1657.

C[ockaine], T. A Greek English lexicon: containing the derivations and various significations of all the words in the New testament. 1658; An English Greek lexicon, containing the derivations and various significations of all the words in the New testament, 1661. The latter mainly by J. Caryl, with Cockaine, R. Venning, W. Dell, M. Barker, W. Adderley, M. Mead, H. Jessey.

Chadwell, W. A profitable and well grounded concordance: wherein may be found the chiefest words contained in the scriptures. 1660, 1663.

(3) COLLECTIONS

A collation of the sacred scriptures; with a historical account of all the English versions, and also an account of the more ancient mss and editions, and memoirs of the principal translators by C. Roger. Dundee 1847. Old testament: Rogers-Matthew 1537, Bishops' 1572 and 1575, Geneva 1579, Authorized version 1611; New testament: Wyclif c. 1380, Rogers-Matthew 1537, Rheims 1582, Geneva 1560, Authorized version 1611, Wakefield 1795. Extracts from each ch in parallel (DMH 1867).

The English hexapla, exhibiting the six important English translations of the New testament scriptures [ed S. Bagster]; preceded by an historical account of the English translations [by S. P. Tregelles]. 1841, [1848?] (with Tregelles's introd replaced by another by J. Stoughton), [1872?] (with another new introd). Wyclif c. 1380 (rev Purvey 1394), Tindale 1534, Great 1539, Geneva 1557, Rheims 1582, Authorized version 1613-11; with Greek after J. M. A. Scholz 1830-6 (DMH 1840).

The holy gospel (the Acts, the Epistles and the Revelation): a comparison of the text as it is given in the Protestant and Roman Catholic versions in the English language in use in America, with a brief account of the origin of the several versions by F. J. Firth. 2 vols New York [1911-12]. Douai 1582, Authorized version 1611, Revised version 1881, American standard version 1901.

The New testament octapla: eight English versions of the New testament in the King James tradition. Ed L. A. Weigle, New York [1962]. Tindale 1535, Coverdale (Great) 1540, Geneva 1562, Bishops' 1620, Rheims 1582, Authorized version 1873, American standard version 1901, Revised standard version 1960 (DMH 2328 note).

The Genesis octapla. Ed L. A. Weigle, New York 1965. Tindale, Great Bible, Geneva, Bishops', Douai, Authorized version, American standard version, Revised standard version.

The New testament from twenty-six [English] translations. Ed C. Vaughan, Grand Rapids 1967. Complete Authorized version with selections from 20th-century versions.

(4) THE BIBLES

Minor trns are separately listed cols 1841–2, below. For separate edns of the Psalms see cols 1895–1914, below.

WILLIAM TINDALE
1494?–1536

Bibliographies

Fry, F. A bibliographical description of the editions of the New testament, Tyndale's version. 1878.

§1

(a) New testament (with help from W. Roy): [Cologne 1525] (DMH 1: fragment only, to Matthew xxii.12; ed E. Arber 1871 (facs), ed A. W. Pollard 1926 (facs): DMH 1988, 2224; see H. F. Moule, Library 4th ser 7 1927), [Worms] 1526 (DMH 2: 2 incomplete copies, at Bristol Baptist College and St Paul's Cathedral; ed G. Offor 1831, ed J. P. Dabney, Andover Mass 1837, ed F. Fry, Bristol 1862 (facs), ed J. Bosworth and G. Waring, The Gothic and Anglo-Saxon gospels in parallel columns with the versions of Wycliffe and Tyndale, 1865, 1874; DMH 1816, 1821, 1936); Antwerp 1526, [1530?] (Cambridge history of the Bible vol 3 p. 143), 1534 (rev) (DMH 13; in The English hexapla 1841 etc and separately ed N. H. Wallis, Cambridge 1938), 1535 (4 edns, the 'G.H.' [Godfrid van der Haghen] edn rev: DMH 15-16 and Kronenberg 1492; in Matthew's Bible, 1537-51, below, and The New testament octapla 1962), [Antwerp] 1536 (3 4° edns, the 'Mole', the 'Blank Stone' and the 'Engraver's Mark' edns, and 4 8°, one 16°: DMH 19-26), [London] 1536 (folio, the first New testament ptd in England: DMH 27), 1538, 1548 (DMH 36, 37; each with Latin of Erasmus), 1548 (3 edns: DMH 68-70), [1548-] 1549 (DMH 77);

London [Antwerp?] 1549 (3 edns, 2 with Latin of Erasmus: DMH 78, 79, 83), 1550 (DMH 88, with Latin of Erasmus), [Zürich] 1550 ('tr Miles Coverdal': DMH 90), [1550?] (DMH 91), 1551 (2 edns: DMH 96-7; also with Taverner's Old testament: DMH 93).

(b) Tyndale's New testament rev George Joye without Tyndale's authority: Antwerp 1534, 1535 (DMH 12, 17).

(c) Tyndale's New testament rev Richard Jugge: [1552?] (2 edns: DMH 99-100), 1553 (2 edns: DMH 104-5), [1561?] (5 edns: 111-15), [1566?] (DMH 121).

(d) Pentateuch, with help from Coverdale: 'Malborrow' [Antwerp] 1530 (5 pts: DMH 4), [Antwerp] 1534 (Genesis rev, the rest a reissue: DMH 8), 1537-51 in Matthew's Bible, below; the 1530 edn ed J. I. Mombert 1884, re-ed F. F. Bruce 1967; Genesis in The Genesis octapla, 1965.

(e) Jonah: [Antwerp 1531] (DMH 6); ed F. Fry, Bristol 1863 (facs); ed D. Daiches 1937 (with Authorized version).

(f) The liturgical 'Epistles' from the Old testament: first ptd as appendix to Tindale's 1534 New testament (DMH 13); ed N. H. Wallis, Cambridge 1938.

(g) Joshua-II Chronicles: in Matthew's Bible, 1537-51, below.

§2

See also col 1809, above.

More, Sir T. A dyaloge concerning heresies. 1529, 1530-1, 1927; in Workes, 1557.

— The confutacyon of Tyndale's answere. 2 pts 1532-3; in Workes, 1557 (book 9 first ptd in 1557).

— The apologye. 1533; in Workes, 1557; ed A. I. Taft 1930 (EETS).

Tindale, W. An answere unto Sir T. Mores dialoge. [Antwerp? 1530]; ed H. Walter, Cambridge 1850 (Parker Soc).

Joye, G. An apologye to satisfye W. Tindale, of hys New testament. 1535 (Cambridge Univ Lib only); ed E. Arber, Birmingham 1882, 1883.

H., A., et al. Comparison between the New testaments of Tyndale and Luther. Christian Observer Dec 1836.

M[askell], W. A collation of Tyndale's version with the Authorized version of the New testament. 1846.

Walter, H. (ed). Doctrinal treatises and introductions to different portions of the holy scriptures; Expositions and notes on sundry portions of the holy scriptures. 2 vols Cambridge 1848–50 (Parker Soc).

Demaus, R. William Tindale. [1871], 1886 (rev R. Lovett).

Fry, F. A list of most of the words noticed, exhibiting the peculiar orthography used in the Newe testament by Willyam Tindale MD and XXXV. [1871].

Bradshaw, H. Godfried van der Haghen (G.H.), the publisher of Tindale's own last edition of the New testament in 1534–5. Bibliographer Dec 1881; rptd in his Collected papers, Cambridge 1889.

Cheney, J. L. The sources of Tindale's New testament. Anglia 6 1883.

Pocock, N. The last New testament of the reign of Edward VI 1553. 3 pts Athenæum 5–26 June 1886. On Tindale-Jugge.

—— The Tyndale Testament of 1535. Athenæum 8 Jan 1887.

Roberts, R. Tyndale's Testament. Athenæum 14 Sept 1889.

Smith, G. B. Tyndale, and his translation of the English Bible. [1896].

Duff, E. G. Adrian Kempe van Bouckhout and the quarto New testament of 1536. Library 2nd ser 7 1906. On Mole edn.

—— A short account of Tyndale's Pentateuch, 'Marburg' 1530. [1910?].

Slater, J. R. The sources of Tyndale's version of the Pentateuch. 1906.

Steele, R. Hans Luft of Marburg: a contribution to the study of Tyndale. Library 3rd ser 2 1911. On Antwerp as place of printing.

Kronenberg, M. E. De geheimzinnige drukkers Adam Anonymus te Basel en Hans Luft te Marburg outmaskerd 1526–35. Het Boek 8 1919. Identifies printer of 1530 and 1534 Pentateuchs as Johannes Hoochstraten of Antwerp.

—— Notes on English printing in the Low Countries 1491–1540. Library 4th ser 9 1929.

Gruber, L. F. The truth about the so-called Luther's Testament in English, Tyndale's New testament. Lutheran Church Rev Oct 1916, April–May 1917; rptd St Paul Minnesota 1917; rev as The first English New testament and Luther: the real extent to which Tyndale was dependent upon Luther as a translator, Burlington Iowa 1928.

Guppy, H. Tindale and the earlier translators of the Bible into English. Bull John Rylands Lib 9 1925.

—— Tindale: scholar and martyr. Bull John Rylands Lib 20 1936.

Wood, H. G. Tyndale's place in English literature. Lib Assoc Record 2nd ser 3 1925.

Mozley, J. F. Tyndale's knowledge of Hebrew. [1935].

—— William Tyndale. 1937. The standard work.

Chambers, R. W. Tyndale and our Bible: the English prose tradition. TLS 3 Oct 1936; rptd in his Man's unconquerable mind, 1939.

Bailey, J. W. Tyndale and the New testament. Crozer Quart 14 1937.

Gray, L. F. Tyndale: translator, scholar and martyr. Hibbert Jnl 35 1937.

Haslehurst, R. S. T. Tyndale the translator. Church Quart Rev 123 1937.

Gray, C. Tyndale and the English Bible. [1938].

Greenslade, S. L. (ed). The work of Tindale. 1938. Includes G. D. Bone, Tindale and the English language.

Wilson, R. M. (ed). Tyndale commemoration volume, reproducing substantial parts of Tyndale's revised Testament of 1534. 1939. Includes J. F. Mozley, The life of Tyndale, and J. R. Coates, Tyndale's influence on English literature.

Hatfield, J. T. The Hanseatic League and the King James Bible. Amer-German Rev 11 1945; rptd Evangelical Quart 20 1948. On support of German merchants in London for Tindale.

Campbell, W. E. Erasmus, Tyndale and More. 1949.

Bluhm, H. Luther and the first printed English Bible: Epistle to the Galatians. Anglican Theological Rev 40 1958. On Tindale's and Coverdale's debt to Luther.

Flesseman-van Leer, E. The controversy about scripture and tradition between More and Tyndale. Nederlands Archief voor Kerkgeschiedenis 43 1959.

Trinterud, L. J. A reappraisal of Tyndale's debt to Luther. Church History 31 1962.

Pineas, R. More versus Tyndale: a study of controversial technique. MLQ 24 1963.

Maveety, S. R. Doctrine in Tyndale's New testament: translation as a tendentious art. Stud in Eng Lit 1500–1900 6 1966.

Karpman, D. M. Tyndale's response to the Hebrew tradition. Stud in Renaissance 14 1965.

Williams, C. H. William Tyndale. 1969.

GEORGE JOY
1495?–1553

§1

(a) Psalter 1530 and 1534, 2 different prose trns: see col 1897, below.

(b) Isaiah: [Antwerp] 1531 (DMH 5: Cambridge Univ Lib and Bodley only).

(c) Proverbs, Ecclesiastes: [Antwerp 1532–3] (a lost edn presumed: Mozley, Coverdale p. 50; Butterworth and Chester, Joye pp. 135–43); London [1534–5] (DMH 10: one copy in private ownership).

(d) New testament rev from Tindale, 1534; see col 1830, above.

(e) Jeremiah, Lamentations, Song of Moses (Exodus xv. 1–18): [Antwerp] 1534 (DMH 11).

(f) The liturgical 'Epistles' from Old testament, appended to 2nd edn of (d) above, 1535.

(g) Daniel: Geneva 1545 (The exposicion of Daniel, including 197 out of 357 verses), London 1550, 1550.

§2

Joye, G. An apologye to satisfye W. Tindale of hys New testament. 1535, 1882, 1883.

Pollard, A. W. Recent English purchases at the British Museum. Library 2nd ser 6 1905.

Steele, R. Notes on English books printed abroad 1525–8. Trans Bibl Soc 11 1912.

Butterworth, C. C. In his Literary lineage of the King James Bible, Philadelphia 1941.

—— The English primers 1529–45: their publication and connection with the English Bible. Philadelphia 1953.

—— and A. G. Chester. George Joye 1495?–1553: a chapter in the history of the English Bible and the English Reformation. Philadelphia 1962.

MILES COVERDALE
1488–1568

Collections

Writings and translations. Ed G. Pearson 2 vols Cambridge 1844–6 (Parker Soc).

§ 1

(a) Psalms (paraphrase) 1534: *col 1897, below.*
(b) Ecclesiastes: with Psalms 1535 (*col 1897, below*).
(c) Bible: The first 'Bug' Bible (Psalms xci.5), this rendering followed by Taverner and Matthew versions; also the first 'Treacle' Bible (Jeremiah viii. 22), followed in the Bishops' Bible. [Cologne or Marburg, not Zürich] 1535 (DMH 18; rptd S. Bagster 1838, 1847), Southwark 1537 (2 edns, the earliest English Bibles ptd in England: DMH 32–3), [ptd Zürich, pbd London] 1550 (DMH 84); [ptd Zürich, pbd London] 1553 (DMH 101).
(d) New testament: [Southwark? 1537?] (4 edns: DMH 40–3), Southwark 1538 (2 edns, both with Latin of Erasmus: DMH 37–8), ptd Paris, pbd London 1538 (with Latin of Erasmus: DMH 39), Antwerp 1539 (DMH 48), London 1549 (rev after Tindale: DMH 80).
(e) Proverbs, Ecclesiastes, Wisdom, Ecclesiasticus, The Story of Bel (The Books of Solomon): Southwark 1537 (St Paul's Cathedral Lib only: Mozley, Coverdale p. 327).
(f) Joshua; with annotations probably by Lancelot Ridley: [London? 1538?] (DMH 35: New York Public Lib only).
(g) Psalms (metrical) 1539: *col 1897, below.*
(h) Psalms (prose) 1540: *col 1897, below.*
(j) The 'Great Bible', rev Coverdale from 'Matthew' version, below.

§ 2

See also col 1814, above.

Lowndes, J. J. Memorials of Coverdale. 1838.
Botfield, B. Some account of the first English Bible. [1856?].
Fry, F. The Bible of Coverdale MDXXXV. 1867.
Swearingen, G. F. Die englische Schriftsprache bei Coverdale; mit einem Anhang über ihre weitere Entwicklung in den Bibelübersetzungen bis zu der Authorized version 1611. Weimar 1904.
Moule, H. F. The Coverdale Bible of 1535. Library 3rd ser 2 1911.
Richards, G. C. Coverdale and the cursus. Church Quart Rev 110 1930.
Sheppard, L. A. The printers of the Coverdale Bible, 1535. Library 4th ser 16 1936.
Willoughby, H. R. Current errors concerning the Coverdale Bible. Jnl of Biblical Lit 55 1936. With census of copies of all edns.
— Hans Holbein and the Coverdale Bible borders of 1535 and 1539–40. Anglican Theological Rev 24 1942.
Mozley, J. F. Coverdale and his Bibles. 1953. The standard work.
Bluhm, H. Luther and the first printed English Bible: Epistle to the Galatians. Anglican Theological Rev 40 1958. On Tindale's and Coverdale's debt to Luther.
Robertson, J. Miles Coverdale. N & Q April 1963.
Tarr, J. C. What caused the delay in printing the first Bible in English? Black Art 2 1963.

JOHN ROGERS
1500?–55

The so-called 'Matthew' Bible ed Rogers under the (probable) pseudonym Thomas Matthew, adopting Tindale's Penta-teuch (1530), Joshua–II Chronicles (here first ptd), New testament (1535, 'G.H.' edn), Coverdale's Ezra-Malachi and Apocrypha, Rogers translating the Prayer of Manasses after the French of P. R. Olivetan (1535).

§ 1

(a) Bible: [ptd Antwerp, pbd London] 1537 (DMH 34), London 1549 (2 edns, one rev and ed E. Becke, called

the 'Wife-beater's Bible' from a note to 1 Peter iii. 2: DMH 74–5), 1551 (6 versions: DMH 92 A–F). Selections in Roger's Collation 1847, above.
(b) New testament: [London] 1538 (DMH 44).

§ 2

Whitley, W. T. Thomas Matthew of Colchester and Matthew's Bible of 1537. 3 pts Essex Rev 43 1934. An incorrect identification of T. Matthew.
— Thomas Matthew of Colchester and his Bible of 1537. Essex Rev 56 1947.
Hutson, H. H. and H. R. Willoughby. Decisive data on Thomas Matthew problems; a census of extant Matthew Bibles. Jnl of Bible & Religion 6 1938.
Knowles, M. D. Notes on a Bible of Evesham Abbey. EHR 79 1964. A Matthew Bible.

RICHARD TAVERNER
1505?–75

§ 1

(a) Bible: 1539 (DMH 45). Rev from 'Matthew', above.
(b) New testament: 1539 (2 edns: DMH 49, 50).
(c) Liturgical Epistles and Gospels: 1540–[1545?] (6 edns).
(d) Old testament: 1549–51 (5 'parts': DMH 94, 81, 86–7, 82, the last containing the earliest English version of III Maccabees, but *see* (e) below), 1551 (with Tindale's New testament to constitute a Bible, ed E. Becke: DMH 93).
(e) III Maccabees: in W. Lynne (ed and tr), A briefe and compendiouse table in a maner of a concordaunce, 1550, 1563. Claims to be pbd before DMH 82, 1549, as (d) above.

§ 2

Hutson, H. H. and H. R. Willoughby. The ignored Taverner Bible of 1539. Crozer Quart 16 1939.

GREAT BIBLE

Rev Coverdale from 'Matthew' Bible above; 1539 sometimes called after Thomas Cromwell under whose patronage Coverdale worked, 1540 after Thomas Cranmer, who contributed a prologue to the rev edns of 1540 etc.

§ 1

(a) Bible: [Paris and] London 1539 (DMH 46); rev T. Cranmer 1540 (3 edns: DMH 52–4), 1541 (4 edns: DMH 60–3), 1549 (DMH 76), 1550 (DMH 85), 1552 (DMH 98), 1553 (2 edns: DMH 102–3), 1561 (DMH 110), 1562 (2 edns, one Rouen: DMH 117, 119), [1566?] (DMH 120), 1568 (DMH 122), 1569 (3 edns: DMH 127–9). Genesis in The Genesis octapla, 1965.
(b) New testament: 1539 (DMH 51), 1540 (2 edns: DMH 58–9), 1546 (DMH 64), 1547 (DMH 65), 1548 (DMH 71), Worcester 1548 (2 edns: DMH 95 note), London 1548–9 (with Erasmus' paraphrase, 2 vols, 2 edns: DMH 72–3), 1550 (DMH 89), Worcester 1550–1 (2 or 3 edns: DMH 95), 1551–2 (as 1548–9: DMH 73 note); in The English hexapla, 1841 etc; The New testament octapla, 1962.
(c) Proverbs, Ecclesiastes, Song of Solomon, Wisdom, Ecclesiasticus: 1540 (DMH 57), [1544?], [1546?], [1547?], 1550, 1551, 1551.
(d) Psalter: *see col 1897, below.*
(e) Liturgical Epistles and Gospels: 1540, 1550, 1551, 1553 (7 edns in all).

§2

Cranmer's Bible 1540. Book-Lore 2 1885.

Plomer, H. R. Anthony Marler and the Great Bible. Library 3rd ser 1 1910.

Fry, F. A description of the Great Bible 1539 and the six editions of Cranmer's Bible 1540 and 1541 etc. 1865.

Guppy, H. The royal injunctions of 1536 and 1538 and the Great Bible 1539 to 1541. Bull John Rylands Lib 22 1938.

Sheppard, L. A. A vellum copy of the Great Bible 1539. Jnl Nat Lib of Wales 1 1939.

Willoughby, H. R. The first authorized English Bible and the Cranmer preface. Chicago 1942.

GENEVA BIBLE

Tr W. Whittingham (1524?–79), with Coverdale, Christopher Goodman (1520–1603), William Cole (d. 1600), Anthony Gilby (d. 1585), Thomas Sampson (1517?–89) et al; the Old testament substantially rev from Great Bible. The earliest English New testament and Bible ptd in Roman type and with verse divisions. Called the 'Breeches' Bible from the trn of Genesis iii. 7, taken from Wyclif.

§1

(a) New testament, mostly tr Whittingham:
  (i) Geneva 1557 (DMH 106); [1842] (facs); in The English hexapla, 1841 etc.
  (ii) a different trn: Geneva 1560, London 1575, 1575–6, 1583, 1618–19 (DMH 109, 141, 147, 178, 371); in The New testament octapla, 1962.
  (iii) rev Laurence Tomson; more Calvinist than before: 1576, 1577, 1577, 1578, 1580 (3 edns), 1582, 1583 (rev) (DMH 146, 152–3, 156, 166–8, 175, 180); edns ptd at London most years till 1603 (DMH 189, 192–3, 196, 203–4, 213, 216–7, 231, 239–40, 242, 246, 260, 279), with edns ptd at Cambridge [1590?] (DMH 207) and Dort [pbd Edinburgh] 1601, 1603 (DMH 267, 278), London 1609, 1609, 1611, 1613, [1613?], 1615 (DMH 299, 299A, 311, 327, 329, 346).
  (iv) Tomson's revision with the commentary on Revelation tr from du Jon, below: 1602, 1610, 1616 (DMH 172, 305, 351).
(b) Psalms 1557: *see col 1903, below.*
(c) Bible:
  (i) with the 1560 New testament (above): Geneva 1560 (DMH 107; ed L. E. Berry, Madison 1969 (facs)), 1561–2 (DMH 116: the 'Whig' Bible, from Matthew v.9), 1568–70 (DMH 130), London 1576, ptd there almost every year till 1615, c. 64 edns (DMH 143–4, 148–9, 154, 159–161, 164–5, 170–1, 173–4, 179, 182–4, 187, 190–1, 195, 197, 199–201, 206, 211–12, 215, 219–23, 229, 234, 236, 243, 247, 256–7, 263, 269–70, 273, 276–7, 280–1, 286–7, 290, 293–4, 296, 303–4, 308, 330, 340–1) with edns pbd at Edinburgh 1576–9 (the 'Bassandyne' Bible, the earliest ptd in Scotland: DMH 158), Cambridge 1591 (the earliest ptd there: DMH 208), and Dort [pbd Edinburgh] 1601 (DMH 264); London 1610–11 called the 'Judas' Bible from John vi.67 (DMH 307); in Roger's Collation 1847, above; Genesis in The Genesis octapla, 1965.
  (ii) with Tomson's New testament: 1587, 1590, 1591–2, 1594, 1595, 1597, 1598, 1600, 1602, 1610 (DMH 194, 205, 210, 218, 225–6, 235, 244, 262, 268, 301).
  (iii) with Tomson's New testament and the du Jon-Barbar Apocalypse, 1592 (col 1886, below); without the Apocrypha: 'London' (Amsterdam, Dort '1599' [1616–33] (at least 8 edns: DMH 248–55), London 1603, 1603, 1606, 1607, 1608, 1609

(DMH 274–5, 285, 289, 295, 298), Edinburgh 1610 (DMH 302), London 1610–11, 1611–12, 1615, 1616 (DMH 306, 312, 342, 348), Amsterdam 1633, 1640, 1644 (DMH 473, 545, 579).

(d) Job, Psalms, Proverbs, Ecclesiastes, Song of Solomon ('The third part of the Bible'); in 1616 replaced by Authorized version: 1580, 1583, 1614 (DMH 169, 181, 336).

§2

Fry, F. Standard edition of the English New testament of the Genevan version. Jnl of Sacred Lit 33 (4th ser 4) 1864; also separately, 1864.

Green, M. A. E. (ed). The life of Mr William Whittingham. 1870.

Pocock, N. Saturday Rev 25 Sept, 6, 27 Nov 1880.

— Some notices of the Genevan Bible. 8 pts Bibliographer 2–5 1882–4.

Dobson, W. T. History of the Bassandyne Bible, the first printed in Scotland. Edinburgh 1887.

Mansergh, J. F. The Geneva Bible. Athenæum 31 Aug 1889. Replies by J. R. Dore 21 Sept, Mansergh 28 Sept, Dore 5 Oct 1889.

D[ore], J. R. The Geneva folio Bible. Library 1st ser 4 1892.

Colligan, J. H. The honourable William Whittingham of Chester. Chester 1934.

— William Whittingham and his contemporaries. Manchester [1941].

Eason, C. The Genevan Bible: notes on its production and distribution. Dublin 1937.

Craig, H. The Geneva Bible as a political document. Pacific Historical Rev 7 1938.

Johnson, A. F. J. F. Stam, Amsterdam and English Bibles. Library 5th ser 9 1954; rptd in his Selected essays, ed P. H. Muir 1971.

Morison, S. The Geneva Bible. 1955.

Hall, B. The Genevan version of the English Bible. 1957.

Oudersluys, R. C. Celebrating the Geneva Bible. Reformed Rev 10 1957.

Clark, F. M. Early Geneva Bibles in the University of Texas library. Texas Quart 1959. Edns of 1560, 1581, 1583, 1588, 1597, 1602.

Metzger, B. M. The Geneva Bible of 1560, Theology Today 17 1961.

— The influence of Codex Bezae upon the Geneva Bible of 1560. New Testament Stud 8 1962; rptd in New Testament Tools & Stud 8 1968.

Meyer, C. S. The Geneva Bible. Concordia Theological Monthly 32 1961.

Ryrie, C. C. Calvinistic emphases in the Geneva and Bishops' Bible. Bibliotheca Sacra 122 1965.

Lupton, L. A history of the Geneva Bible. 7 vols 1966–.

— Conrad Badius. Evangelical Quart 39 1967. With a table of Geneva Bibles.

BISHOPS' BIBLE

Rev from Great Bible by Matthew Parker et al.

§1

(a) Bible: 1568, 1569 (DMH 125–6), 1572 (rev, mainly in New testament, by Giles Lawrence; Psalms in both Coverdale's Great Bible and Prayer Book and Bishops' versions; the 'Leda' Bible, from initial at beginning of Hebrews: DMH 132), [1573?] (Psalms in Coverdale's Great Bible and Prayer Book version only, and in all subsequent edns except 1585: DMH 135), 1574–8 (14 edns, 9 in 1575: DMH 137, 139–40, 145, 150–1, 155), 1584 (2 edns: DMH 185–6), 1585 (Psalms in Bishops' version, the only edn thus since 1572: DMH 188), 1588, 1591, 1595, 1602 (DMH 198, 209, 227, 271), [not 1606: DMH 271 note]; in Roger's Collation 1847, above; Genesis in The Genesis octapla, 1965.

(b) New testament:
  (i) 1568 (2 edns: DMH 123-4), [1573-7?] (rev as in
      1572 Bible; 3 edns: DMH 133-4, 136), 1575,
      [1578?], 1579, 1581, 1582 (DMH 142, 157, 163,
      172, 176), 1595, 1596, 1597, 1598, 1600 (DMH 228,
      232, 241, 245, 259), 1605 (3 edns), 1606, 1608
      (DMH 282-4, 288, 297), 1613, 1613-14, 1615, 1617,
      1617-19, 1618, nd (2 edns) (DMH 328, 337-8,
      344, 356-8); in The New testament octapla, 1962.
  (ii) Bishops' and Rheims versions parallel, ed W.
      Fulke, below: 1589, 1601, 1601, 1617, 1617, 1633
      (DMH 202, 265-6, 359-60, 480).
(c) Gospels, with the Anglo-Saxon, ed John Foxe for M.
    Parker: 1571 (DMH 131).

§2

Martin, G. A discoverie of the manifold corruptions of
  the holy scriptures by the heretikes of our daies, specially
  the English sectaries. Rheims 1582; rptd in Fulke.
Fulke, W. A defense of the sincere and true translations
  of the holie scriptures into the English tong, against
  Gregorie Martin. 1583, 1617, 1617, 1633; ed C. H.
  Hartshorne, Cambridge 1843 (Parker Soc).
Whitaker, W. Disputatic de sacra scriptura. Cambridge
  1588, Herborn 1590, 1600; in Opera theologica, ed A.
  Assheton 2 vols Geneva 1610; tr W. Fitzgerald, Cam-
  bridge 1849 (Parker Soc).
Broughton, H. An epistle to the learned nobilitie of
  England touching translating the Bible. Middleburg
  1597.
Pocock, N. The Bishops' Bible. 4 pts Bibliographer Jan-
  April 1882.
— The Bishops' Bible of 1568, 1572 and 1602. Athenæum
  25 Feb 1888.
Dore, J. R. Notes on the last edition of the Bishops' New
  testament. Book-Lore March 1885.
Clair, C. The Bishops' Bible 1568. Gutenberg-Jahrbuch
  1962.
Ryrie, C. C. Calvinistic emphases in the Geneva and
  Bishops' Bible. Bibliotheca Sacra 122 1965.

RHEIMS-DOUAI BIBLE

*Roman Catholic; tr Gregory Martin (d. 1582), rev William
Allen (1532-94) and Richard Bristow (1538-81).*

Bibliographies
See Cotton, Rhemes and Doway, 1855, *below.*
Shea, J. D. G. A bibliographical account of Catholic
  Bibles, testaments and other portions of scripture,
  translated from the Vulgate and printed in the United
  States. New York 1859. From 1790. Rptd from New
  York Freeman's Jnl and Catholic Register.

§1

(a) New testament:
  (i) Rheims 1582 (DMH 177), Antwerp 1600, 1621,
      (DMH 158, 382), 1630 (Pope p. 271), [Rouen?]
      1633 (DMH 479), [Douai or London] 1738 (5th
      edn) (perhaps ed R. Challoner and F. Blyth: DMH
      1041), Liverpool 1788 (6th edn), 1789, New York
      1834 (Cotton p. 169); in Roger's Collation 1847,
      above; The English hexapla, 1841 etc, Firth's Holy
      Gospel, 1911-12, and New testament octapla, 1962.
  (ii) Rheims and Bishops' versions parallel, ed W.
      Fulke: 1589-1633, above.
  (iii) rev Robert Witham (d. 1738): [Douai] 2 vols 1730
      (with notes: DMH 1009, Cambridge history of
      Bible p. 367); the notes rptd in the Manchester
      Bible, 1813 (DMH 1579).
  (iv) rev Richard Challoner (1691-1781): [Dublin?]
      1749 (DMH 1086; rptd London 1815, 1818, 1823,

1825, Dublin 1826, 1834, 1835, 1837, 1840, 1850:
Cotton p. 169), [Dublin?] 1750 (2nd edn) (DMH
1090; also as vol 5 of 1750 Bible; rptd 1818, Dublin
1820, 1825 etc: Cotton p. 169), [Dublin?] 2 vols
1752, 1 vol 1764 (also as vol 5 of 1763 Bible) (3rd-
5th edns), London 1772 (DMH 1099, 1156, 1224),
Edinburgh 1797 (from 1764 edn: DMH 1422; also
as vol 5 of 1796-7 Bible); many subsequent revisions and reprints from that of B. MacMahon,
Dublin 1783 (often called after J. T. Troy, who
sanctioned the work: DMH 1292, 1538), Philadelphia 1805 (Hills no 126, DMH 1343 note) etc.
(b) Old testament:
  (i) 2 vols Douai 1609-10, [Rouen] 1635 (both as The
      holy Bible, to be accompanied by the New testa-
      ments of 1582-1600 and 1633: DMH 300, 499);
      Genesis in The Genesis octapla, 1965.
  (ii) rev R. Challoner: 4 vols [Dublin?] 1750, 1763,
      Edinburgh 1796 (all as The holy Bible, to be
      accompanied by the New testaments of 1750, 1764,
      1797: DMH 1089, 1156, 1408).
(c) Bible:
  (i) 3 vols Rheims or Antwerp-Douai 1582 or 1600-
      1609-10, [Rouen] 1633-5.
  (ii) rev R. Challoner 5 vols [Dublin?] 1750, 1763-4
      (a and b above), 2 vols Philadelphia 1790 (DMH
      1343), 5 vols Edinburgh 1796-7 (Old testament
      4 vols 1796, New testament 1 vol 1797: DMH 1408,
      1422), 1805, Dublin 1811, Liverpool 1816-17
      (Cotton p. 169).
  (iii) many subsequent revisions and reprints from those
      of B. MacMahon, Dublin 1791 (often called after
      J. T. Troy, who sanctioned the work: DMH 1538
      note), Philadelphia 1805 (Hills no 120, DMH 1343
      note), Manchester 1811-13 (ed G. L. Haydock:
      DMH 1579) etc.

§2

Martin, G. A discoverie of the manifold corruptions of the
  holy scriptures by the heretikes of our daies, specially
  the English sectaries. Rheims 1582.
Fulke, W. A defense of the sincere and true translations of
  the holie scriptures into the English tong, against G.
  Martin. 1583, 1617, 1617, 1633; ed C. H. Hartshorne,
  Cambridge 1843 (Parker Soc). Incorporates the whole
  of Martin's text, answered paragraph by paragraph.
Whitaker, W. Ad Nicolai Sanderi demonstrationes quadraginta, in octavo libro Visibilis monarchiae positas,
  quibus Romanum Pontificem non esse Antichristum
  docere instituit, responsio. 1583.
— An answere to a certeine booke by W. Rainolds
  entitled A refutation. Cambridge and London 1585
  (3 edns), Cambridge 1590; tr Latin by H. Jackson,
  Oppenheim 1612.
Rainolds, W. A refutation of sundry reprehensions by
  which M. Whitaker laboureth to deface the late English
  translation, and Catholike annotations of the New
  testament. Paris 1583.
Bilson, T. The true difference betweene Christian subjection and unchristian rebellion, against the Jesuits
  sophismes, notwithstanding the vaine shew made in
  their late Rhemish testament. Oxford 1585, London
  1586, Oxford 1595.
B[ulkeley], E. (tr.) An answere to ten frivolous reasons,
  set down by the Rhemish Jesuits and Papists in their
  preface before the New testament. 1588.
Cartwright, T. Σὺν θεῷ ἐν Χριστῷ: the answere to the
  preface of the Rhemish Testament. Edinburgh 1602.
— A confutation of the Rhemists translation, glosses
  and annotations on the New testament. [Leyden]
  1618.
Bernard, R. Rhemes against Rome: or the remooving of
  the gagg of the new gospell, and rightly placing it in
  the mouthes of the Romists, by the Rhemists; in their
  English translation of the scriptures. 1626.

Barnard, J. The life and death of Richard Challoner. 1784, 1793.

[Cotton, H.] Notes on the preface to the Rhemish testament [printed in Dublin, 1813]. Dublin 1817.

Hamilton, G. Observations on the present state of the Catholic English Bible, showing that it has never been edited on any uniform plan. 1825, Dublin 1826; A second letter, on the present state of the English Roman Catholic Bible, Dublin 1826.

A brief history of the versions of the Bible of the Anglo-Roman churches. Dublin 1830.

MacGhee, R. J. The complete notes on the Doway Bible and Rhemish Testament, extracted from the quarto editions of 1816 and 1818. 1837.

G[ratet]-D[uplessis, P. A.] Notice sur une traduction de l'Ecriture Sainte désignée ordinairement sous le titre de Bible de Douai et Nouveau testament de Reims. 1841.

'Phoenix'. Archbishop Murray's Douay and Rhemish Bible and the Bordeaux New testament, examined in four letters. 1850.

Cotton, H. Rhemes and Doway: an attempt to shew what has been done by Roman Catholics for the diffusion of the holy scriptures in English. Oxford 1855. With a bibliography of edns 1582-1854.

Collette, C. H. The Authorized version as compared with the Douay and Rhemish versions vindicated from the charge of corruption. 1891.

Carleton, J. G. The part of Rheims in the making of the English Bible. Oxford 1902.

Williams, J. M. Roman Catholic and Protestant Bibles compared. New York 1905.

Burton, E. H. The life and times of Bishop Challoner. 2 vols 1909.

Eason, C. The circulation of the Douay Bible in Ireland. Dublin 1931.

H[iggins], D. L. The Douay Bible: being remarks on what is said by authority in regard to it. [1931].

Trappes-Lomax, M. Bishop Challoner. [1936].

Pope, H. English versions of the Bible. Rev S. Bullough, London and St Louis 1952. Inaccurate, but with new material on the Rheims-Douai Bibles. First pbd as 2 articles in Library 4th ser 20-1 1940-1.

Morisony, S. The writings of Challoner. [1945?].

Richard Challoner 1691-1781: his life, times, works, influence etc. Westminster 1946. By various authors; one essay, Challoner and the Douay version, rptd as ch 4 of R. A. Knox, On englishing the Bible, 1949.

Maveety, S. R. The glossary in the Rheims New testament of 1582. JEGP 61 1962.

Marmion, J. P. Gregory Martin: the origins and influence of his criticisms. Scripture 20 1968.

AUTHORIZED VERSION

Bibliographies

L[enox], J. The early editions of King James' Bible in folio. [1861].

Fry, F. A description of the Great Bible 1539, also of the edition in large folio of the Authorized version printed in 1611, 1613, 1617, 1634, 1640. 1865.

Scrivener, F. H. A. The Authorized edition of the English Bible 1611: its subsequent reprints and modern representatives. Cambridge 1884.

§1

(a) Bible: 1611 (the Great 'He' Bible, from Ruth iii. 15: DMH 309; rptd Oxford 1833, together with Revised version, as The parallel Bible, 1885, ed W. A. Wright 5 vols Cambridge 1909, ed A. W. Pollard, Oxford 1911 (2 edns, one a facs: DMH 1792, 2040, 2166)); 1611-13 (the Great 'She' Bible, from Ruth iii. 15, or 'Judas' Bible, from Matthew xxvi. 36: DMH 319); 1612-60 London edns every year, often several in different for-

mats (DMH 313-671), including the 'Revenge' Bible from Romans xii. 17, 1613, the 'Wicked' Bible, from Exodus xx. 14, 1631, the 'Forgotten Sins' Bible, from Luke vii. 47, 1638, the 'More Sea' Bible, from Revelation xxi. 1, 1641, and the 'Unrighteous' Bible, from 1 Corinthians vi. 9, 1653 (DMH 322, 444, 529-32, 553-5, 635-7), and edns ptd at Amsterdam 1625, 1638 [1656?], 1644, 1645 (DMH 399, 529-32, 582, 584, 586, 588, 599?; also Canne's edns listed below), Cambridge 1629, 1630, 1631, 1633, 1635, 1637, 1637-8, 1638, 1639, 1639-40, 1645, 1645-6, 1647?, 1648, 1657, 1659, 1660 (DMH 424, 432-3, 438, 474, 497, 513-14, 520-1, 540, 544, 585, 587, 589, 599?; 612-16, 656-7, 666, 668), Edinburgh 1633, 1636-7, 1637, 1638, 1648-9 (DMH 476, 510-12, 522, 618); edns of Cambridge 1629 and especially 1638 rev, the latter by S. Ward et al, remaining the standard text till rev F. S. Paris and H. Therold, Cambridge 1762, and rev B. Blayney, Oxford 1769 (DMH 424, 520, 1142, 1194); many other edns since 1661.

Scrivener, F. H. A. (ed). The Cambridge paragraph Bible of the Authorized English version, with the text revised by a collation of its early and other principal editions and a critical introduction prefixed. Cambridge 1873. Selections in Roger's Collation 1847, above.

Authorized version text with Geneva notes ed J. Canne, Amsterdam 1642, 1642-3, 1644?, 1647, 1662, 1664, 1672, 1679, 1683, London 1698, [ptd Amsterdam] pbd London 1700, [Amsterdam?] 1707-8, 1715, 1720?, Edinburgh 1727, 1747, 1754, 2 vols 1764-6 (as The pulpit and family Bible); tr Welsh, Trefecca 1790, Caermarthen 1812 (DMH 564, 571, 601, 680, 688, 708, 778, 782, 848, 859, 897, 936, 987, 1080, 1106, 1173).

The translators' preface separately rptd 1870, Oxford [1870], London [1880], [1911]; ed E. J. Goodspeed, Chicago 1935 (title varies).

(b) New testament: 1611 (DMH 310; rptd in The New testament hexapla 1841 etc; Firth's Holy gospel [etc] 1911-12, and The New testament octapla, 1962, and, together with the Revised version, as The parallel New testament, Oxford and Cambridge 1882 etc: DMH 1840, 2025), 1612-60 (London edns most years, often several in different formats: DMH 318-652), Edinburgh 1619, 1628, 1631, 1633, 1635, 1636, 1640, 1642, 1643, 1647 (DMH 373, 420, 457, 481, 496, 506, 508, 549, 568-9, 575, 603), Aberdeen 1631 (DMH 456), Cambridge 1628 (DMH 421-2); ed C. Hoole, parallel with Beza's Latin, 1659 (DMH 667) etc.

(c) Job, Psalms, Proverbs, Ecclesiastes, Song of Solomon ('The third part of the Bible'); replacing a similar Geneva collection: 1616, 1626, 1632, 1638 (DMH 350, 404, 470, 523), Edinburgh 1642 (DMH 570).

§2

Barlow, W. The summe and substance of the conference at Hampton Court. 1604, 1605, 1625, 1638; ed J. Dunton, Phenix, 2 vols 1707-8: reissued as A collection of choice, scarce and valuable tracts, 2 vols 1721.

Broughton, H. A censure of the late translation for our churches. [Middleburg 1612?].

Gell, R. An essay towards the amendment of the last English translation of the Bible. 1659.

McClure, A. W. The translators revived: a biographical memoir of the authors of the English version of the holy Bible. New York 1853.

Tagart, E. Two discourses on the history of the Authorized version. 1856.

Gilman, E. W. Early editions of the Authorized version of the English Bible. Bibliotheca Sacra 16 1859.

King James folio editions of the Authorized version of the English Bible. Historical Mag 5 1861.

Paul, C. K. Chapter headings in the Authorized version of the English Bible. Theological Rev 6 1869.

Smith, W. E. A study of the Great 'She' Bible 1613 or 1611. Library 1st ser 2 1890.

Hart, H. On the red printing in the 1611 Bible. Library 3rd ser 2 1911. Reply by R. B. McKerrow, ibid.

Strachan, L. R. M. An historic Bible at Heidelberg. Library 3rd ser 2 1911. On Authorized version 1612.

Gruber, L. F. The version of 1611: propriety of calling it Authorized version or King James's version. [1914].

Hatfield, J. T. The Hanseatic League and the King James Bible. Amer-German Rev 11 1945; rptd Evangelical Quart 20 1948. On support of German merchants in London for Tindale.

Willoughby, E. E. The making of the King James Bible. Los Angeles 1956.

Handover, P. M. The 'Wicked' Bible [1631] and the King's printing house, Black Friars. Times House Jnl Dec 1958.

Parker, P. In praise of 1611. Anglican Theological Rev 46 1964.

Allen, W. John Bois' notes. Renaissance News 19 1966. On Corpus Christi College Oxford ms 312, on the final revision of the Authorized version.

— (tr and ed). Translating for King James: notes made by a translator [J. Bois] of King James's Bible. 1970.

Marmion, J. P. Gregory Martin: the origins and influence of his criticisms. Scripture 20 1968.

THEODORE HAAK

1605–90

The complete text of the Bible, tr at the request of the West-minster Assembly of Divines 1645 from the Dutch annotated edn authorized by the States General at the Synod of Dort 1618–19, ed J. Bogermann, W. Baudart, G. Bucerus, A. Thysius, A. Walaeus, F. Hommius and J. Rolandus, and pbd Leyden 1636–7, with annotations in brackets in the text. See A. F. Mitchell and J. Struthers (ed), Minutes of the sessions of the Westminster Assembly, Edinburgh 1874, pp. 132–3, and S. W. Carruthers, The everyday work of the Westminster Assembly, Philadelphia 1943, p. 192.

§ 1

The Dutch annotations upon the whole Bible. 2 vols 1657 (DMH 659).

§ 2

Chambers, T. W. The States Bible of Holland. Reformed Quart Rev 27 1880.

Bruin, C. C. de. De Statenbijbel en zijn voorgangers. Leyden 1937.

Nederlands Bijbelgenootschap. De Statenvertaling 1637–1937. Haarlem 1937. Essays by several authors.

MINOR VERSIONS

For the Golden legend, Westminster 1483 etc, W. Caxton's extended trn of a French version of the Legenda aurea of Jacobus de Voragine, into which Caxton inserts the Bible histories, including much of the Pentateuch and the Gospels, see col 531, above. For English versions of the Lord's Prayer, the Ten Commandments, and the Beatitudes 1500–26, see DMH p. xxxi.

Sir Thomas More

1478–1535

§ 1

Miscellaneous passages tr incidentally in his writings, 1522–34.

(a) De quatuor novissimis: or the four last things 1522. In Workes, 1557; ed D. O'Connor 1903, 1935; in English works vol 1, ed W. E. Campbell 1931.

(b) A dialoge of comfort against tribulacion. 1553 (written 1534); in Workes, 1557; separately Antwerp 1573, London 1847; 1910 (EL) (with Utopia), 1951 (rev); ed P. E. Hallett 1937; ed M. Stevens 1951; extracts ed H. S. Bowden 1915 (Crumbs of comfort).

(c) A treatice to receave the blessed body of our Lorde 1534. In Workes, 1557.

(d) A treatice upon the passion of Chryste 1534. In Workes, 1557.

§ 2

See col 1792, above.

Chambers, R. W. In his On the continuity of English prose from Alfred to More and his school. Introd to N. Harpsfield, The life and death of Sr Thomas Moore, ed E. V. Hitchcock 1932 (EETS).

Hutchinson, F. E. More as a translator of the Bible. RES 17 1941.

Marc'hadour, G. More et la Bible. Paris 1969.

— The Bible in the works of More. 2 vols Nieuwkoop 1969–72.

Sir John Cheke

1514–57

§ 1

Matthew and Mark i, tr c. 1550 (ms at Corpus Christi College, Cambridge). Ed J. Goodwin 1843 (DMH 1847).

§ 2

Meritt, H. The vocabulary of Cheke's partial version of the Gospels. JEGP 39 1940.

Davies, H. S. Cheke and the translation of the Bible. E & S new ser 5 1952.

Henry Ainsworth

1571–1623?

(a) Psalms 1612. See col 1908, below.

(b) Pentateuch, with notes (Annotations upon the five books of Moses): [ptd Amsterdam, pbd London] 1622 (with Psalms; 2 edns: DMH 385), 1626–7, 1639 (both with Psalms and Song of Songs).

   (i) Genesis [Amsterdam] 1616, 1621, 1622 etc (in (b)).

   (ii) Exodus: [Amsterdam] 1617, 1622, 1622 etc (in (b)).

   (iii) Leviticus: [Amsterdam] 1618, 1622 etc (in (b)).

   (iv) Numbers: [Amsterdam] 1619, 1622 etc (in (b)).

   (v) Deuteronomy: no place 1619, 1622 etc (in (b)).

(c) Song of Songs, with notes: [Amsterdam?] 1623, 1626–7, 1639 (both in (b)).

Soldiers' Pocket Bible

Extracts

§ 1

(a) The souldiers pocket Bible. 1643 (DMH 577); ed G. Livermore, Cambridge Mass 1861 (facs), ed G. Livermore, New York 1861 (modernized: 5 edns); ed F. Fry 1862 (facs: DMH 1938); 1894 (facs); ed Viscount Wolseley, Boston and London 1895; New York 1898, 1917; in Willoughby, Soldiers' Bibles, 1944, below. From Geneva version.

(b) The Christian soldiers penny Bible. 1693; ed F. Fry 1862 (facs) (DMH 830, 1939). From Authorized version.

§ 2

Willoughby, H. R. Soldiers' Bibles through three centuries. Chicago 1944. Includes reprint of (a).

EPITOMES AND EXTRACTS

Incipiunt exempla sacre scripture ex utroque testamento. St Albans 1481.

Storys and prophesis out of the holy scriptur. Antwerp 1536.

Artopoeus (Becker), P. The divisyon of the places of the lawe and of the gospell, gathered owt of the hooly scriptures. [Tr J. Bradford] 1548.

Viret, P. A notable collection of places of the sacred scriptures, which make to the declaratyon of the Lordes prayer, translated oute of Frenche by A. Scoloker. 1548.

Paynell, T. The piththy and moost notable sayinges of al scripture. 1550, [1552?].

Shepery (Shepreve), J. Summa et synopsis Novi testamenti distichis ducentis sexaginta, quae totidem capitibus respondent, comprehensa. Ed J. Parkhurst, Strasbourg [1556?], London 1560 (?) (both edns doubtful); ed L. Humfrey, Oxford 1586; in [W. Smyth], Gemma Fabri, 1598; in [J. Shaw], Biblii summula, 1621, 1623.

Samuel, W. An abridgement of all the canonical books of the Olde testament, written in Sternholds meter. 1569.

B[roughton], H. Textes of scripture, chayning the holy chronicle untyll the sunne lost his lyght. 1591, [1600?].

Drayton, M. The harmonie of the Church: containing the spirituall songes and holy hymnes, of godly men, patriarckes and prophetes: now newlie reduced into sundrie kinds of English meetre. 1591, 1610; ed A. Dyce 1843 (Percy Soc); ed J. P. Collier 1856 (Roxburghe Club); in Works vol 3, ed R. Hooper 1876; in Works vol 1, ed J. W. Hebel Oxford 1931–41, 1961. Verse trns of Song of Solomon (complete) and 19 shorter passages from Old testament and Apocrypha; not in other edns of Drayton.

Clapham, H. A briefe of the Bible's history, drawne first into English poesie, and then illustrated by apt annotations: wherto is added a synopsis of the Bible's doctrine. [Edinburgh] 1596, London 1603, 1608, 1639.

Hill, R. The contents of scripture: containing the sum of every booke and chapter of the Old and New testament; gathered from Tremellius, Junius, Beza, Piscator and others, translated by R. Hill; (pt 2) The consent of the foure Evangelists: or the life of Christ, collected by C.I. and placed before his Harmony; englished. 1596. Pt 2 extracted and tr from C. Jansen, Commentariorum in suam concordiam, ac totam historiam evangelicam partes IIII, Louvain 1572, 1576, Paris 1586, Mainz 1612.

[Smyth, W.] Gemma Fabri: qua sacri Biblii margaritæ fere omnes continentur. 1598.

B[entley], J. The harmonie of holie scriptures, with the severall sentences of sundry learned and worthy writers. 1600.

Perkins, W. A digest or harmony of the bookes of the Old and New testament. In Works vol 2, 1608–31.

Guild, W. The harmony of all the prophets. In Moses unvailed, 1619–20, 1623, 1626, '2658' [1658], Edinburgh 1684, London 1701, 1755; in A paraphrase on the book of Job, 1716.

[Shaw, J.] Biblii summula. 1621, 1623.

Wastell, S. A true Christians daily delight: being the summe of every chapter of the Old and New testaments, set downe alphabetically, in English verse. 1623; Old testament rewritten and New testament rptd in Microbiblion: or the Bibles epitome in verse, 2 pts 1629.

Cartwright, T. Harmonia evangelica, commentario analytico, metaphrastico, practico, illustrata: antehuc diversis voluminibus edita, nunc summa industria in unum corpus redacta, summariis aucta, & à mendis repurgata. Amsterdam 1627, Amsterdam and Leyden 1647.

Bernard, R. The Bibles abstract and epitome. 1642.

B[rowne], E. Rules for kings, and good counsell for subjects: being a collection of certaine places of holy scripture, directing the one to governe, and the other to obey. 1642.

HARMONIES ETC

Bible

Broughton, H. A concent of scripture. [1590]; in Workes ed J. Lightfoot 1662; tr Latin by J. Genius, Hanau 1602, Frankfurt 1606.

— An epistle to the umpires touching the Concent of scripture. [1591]; A defence of the booke called A concent of scripture, [Middleburg] 1609.

Usher, J. The annals of the world: containing the history of the Old and New testaments. 1658. From Annales veteris testamenti (— novi testamenti), 2 pts 1650–4, 1 vol Paris 1673, 2 pts Bremen 1686; in Whole works, ed C. R. Elrington and J. H. Todd 17 vols Dublin 1847–64.

Old Testament

Lightfoot, J. The harmony, chronicle and order of the Old testament; also a second part of the harmony of the four evangelists. 1647; in Works ed G. Bright and J. Strype 2 vols 1684; Opera omnia, ed J. Texelius 2 vols Rotterdam 1686; ed J. Leusden 3 vols Utrecht 1699; Whole works, ed J. R. Pitman 13 vols 1822–5; The Old testament, arranged in historical and chronological order, on the basis of Lightfoot's Chronicle, by G. Townsend, 2 vols 1821. An earlier version in Rules for a student of the holy scriptures, in Some genuine remains, ed J. Strype 1700.

Gospels

Becon, T. Christ's chronicle: containing briefly in a most godly and pleasant order whatsoever is written at large in the Gospels. In Worckes vol 3, 1563; in Prayers and other pieces, ed J. Ayre, Cambridge 1844 (Parker Soc).

Cope, A. Syntaxis historiae evangelicae. Louvain 1572; as Historiae evangelieae unitas, Douai 1603.

[Calvin, J.] A harmonie upon the three evangelists, Matthew, Mark and Luke, with the commentarie of J. Calvine; translated out of Latine by E. P[agit]; whereunto is also added a commentarie upon the evangelist S. John [with the text], by the same author, translated by C. Fetherstone. 1584, 1610. From Harmonia ex tribus evangelistis composita, adiuncto seorsum Iohanne, cum Joh. Calvini commentariis, [Geneva] 1555, Geneva 1595.

Holland, R. The holie history of our Lord Jesus Christs nativitie, life, resurrection and ascension: gathered into English meeter. 1594.

Rollock, R. Lectures upon the history of the passion, resurrection, and ascension of Christ: beginning at the eighteenth chapter of the Gospell, according to S. John, and from the 16 verse of the 19 chapter thereof, containing a perfect harmonie of all the foure evangelists. Edinburgh 1616.

Hiud, J. The storie of stories, or the life of Christ, according to the foure holy evangelists; with a harmonie of them. 1632.

Garthwait, H. Μονοτέσσαρον: the evangelicall harmonie, reducing the foure evangelists into one continued context. Cambridge 1634.

[Ferrar, N., et al]. The actions and doctrine and other passages touching Jesus Christ, as they are related by the foure evangelists, reduced into one complete bodie of historie. [Little Gidding 1630?] (Harvard Univ Lib), [1631?] (Bodley), [1635?] (BM), [1636?] (BM). Individual paste-ups of Authorized version. See J. E. Acland-Troyte, afterwards Acland, An account of the harmonies contrived by Nicholas Ferrar, Archæologia 51 1888, and Little Gidding and its inmates, with an account of the harmonies designed and constructed by N. Ferrar, 1903; C. L. Craig, The earliest Little Gidding concordance, Harvard Lib Bull 1 1947.

Lightfoot, J. The harmony of the four evangelists. 3 pts 1644, 1647 (as pt 2 of The harmony of the Old testament), 1650; as The harmony, chronicles, and order of the New testament, 1655; in Works 1684 etc, as above. An earlier version, to a year before Christ's death, is in The order of the evangelists, in Rules for a student of the holy scriptures, in Some genuine remains, ed J. Strype 1700.

Torshell, S. A designe about disposing the Bible into an harmony. 1647.

RECONCILIATIONS OF SEEMING 'CONTRADICTIONS'

See T. H. Horne, A catalogue of the library of Queens' College *vol 1, Cambridge 1827*.

Broke, A. (tr) The agreement of sondry places of scripture, seeming in shew to jarre, serving instead of commentaryes, not onely for these, but others lyke, translated out of French. 1563.

Sharp (Scharpius), J. Symphonia prophetarum, et apostolorum, in qua ordine chronologico loci sacræ scripturæ, specie tenus contradicentes, conciliantur. Geneva 1625, 1639, 1653, 1670.

Streat, W. The dividing of the hooff: or seeming contradictions throughout sacred scriptures distinguished, resolved and applied. 1654.

T[haddeus], J. The reconciler of the Bible: wherein above two thousand seeming contradictions throughout the Old and New testament are fully and plainly reconciled. 1655-6, 1662.

(5) STUDIES

A compendious olde treatyse, shewynge, howe that we ought to have the scripture in Englysshe. 'Marlborough' [Antwerp] 1530, London 1530 (as A proper dyaloge betwene a gentillman and a husbandman).

Standish, J. A. A discourse wherein is debated whether the scripture should be in English. 1554, 1555.

Whitaker, W. Disputatio de sacra scriptura, contra R. Bellarminum & T. Stapletonum. Cambridge 1588, Herborn 1590, 1600; in Opera theologica, ed A. Assheton 2 vols Geneva 1610; tr W. Fitzgerald, Cambridge 1849 (Parker Soc).

Broughton, H. An epistle to the learned nobilitie of England touching translating the Bible. Middelburg 1597; in Works, 1662.

W(h)etenhall, E. Scripture authentick and faith certain: a discourse which may serve for an answer to divers late aspersions on the integrity of originals, and validity of our modern translations. 1686.

Johnson, A. An historical account of the several English translations of the Bible, and the opposition they met with from the Church of Rome. 1730; in R. Watson (ed), A collection of theological tracts vol 3, Cambridge 1785, London 1791.

Lewis, J. A history of the several translations of the H. Bible and N. testament into English. 1731 (prefixed to the earliest ptd edn of the Wycliffite New testament); separately as A complete history, 1739, 1818.

Newcome, W. An historical view of the English biblical translations. Dublin 1792.

Marsh, H. A history of the translations which have been made of the scriptures, from the earliest to the present age, throughout Europe, Asia, Africa and America. 1812. An attack on British and Foreign Bible Soc, pbd as appendix to Marsh's An inquiry into the consequences of neglecting to give the Prayer book with the Bible, Cambridge 1812; for replies, counterblasts etc see BM catalogue under Marsh.

[Holmes, A.] An historical sketch of the English translations of the Bible. [Boston 1815].

Todd, H. J. A vindication of our authorized translation and translators of the Bible, and of preceding English versions authoritatively commended to the notice of those translators. 1819, Malton 1834 (as An authentic account of our authorized translation of the holy Bible, and of the translators), London 1835, 1842.

A plea for the Protestant canon of scripture, with the history of the translations of the English Bible and Apocrypha at the period of the Reformation. 1825.

A brief history of the versions of the Bible of the English and Roman churches. Dublin 1830.

Anderson, C. The annals of the English Bible. 2 vols 1845, 1 vol 1862(rev); abridged by S. I. Prime, New York 1849.

Conant, H. O'B. C. The English Bible. New York 1856, London 1859, New York [1881] (rev T. J. Conant as The popular history of the translation of the holy scriptures into the English tongue).

Westcott, B. F. A general view of the history of the English Bible. 1868, 1872, 1905 (rev W. A. Wright).

Blunt, J. H. A plain account of the English Bible, from the earliest times of its translation to the present day. 1870.

Walden, T. Our English Bible and its ancestors. Philadelphia [1871].

Dore, J. R. Old Bibles: or an account of the various versions of the English Bible. 1876, 1888 (rev).

— Some recently discovered early printed copies of the English Bible. Academy 7 May 1892.

Eadie, J. The English Bible: an external and critical history of the various English translations. 2 vols 1876.

Moulton, W. F. The history of the English Bible. 1878, [1884], [1887], [1911] (rev J. H. and W. F. Moulton jr); abridged by A. W. Harrison 1937.

Stoughton, J. Our English Bible: its translations and translators. [1878]. Rewritten from introd to The English hexapla, [1848?] (2nd edn above).

Davidson, R. T. Authorization of the English Bible. Macmillan's Mag Oct 1881.

Condit, B. History of the English Bible, extending from the earliest Saxon translations to the present Anglo-American revision. New York 1882, [1896?] (rev).

Woollcombe, H. The English Bible and its versions. [1882].

Mombert, J. I. English versions of the Bible: a handbook. New York and London 1883, 1906 (rev), 1907 (rev), 1911, 1931. Some edns as A handbook of the English versions of the Bible.

Schaff, P. A companion to the Greek Testament and the English versions. London and New York 1883, 1888 (rev).

Cameron, H. P. History of the English Bible. 1885, Paisley 1916.

Smyth, J. P. How we got our Bible. [1885], 1899 (rev), [1938] (rev).

Edgar, A. The Bibles of England. Paisley and London 1889.

Talbot, R. T. Our Bible: how it has come to us. 1893.

Lovett, R. The printed English Bible 1525–1885. [1894].

— The English Bible in the John Rylands Library 1525–1640. 1899.

Pattison, T. H. The history of the English Bible. London and Philadelphia 1894.

Kenyon, F. G. Our Bible and the ancient manuscripts: being a history of the text and its translations. 1895, [1911] (rev), 1939 (rev), 1958 (rev A. W. Adams). Includes ch on English ptd Bible.

— The story of the Bible. 1936.

Milligan, G. The English Bible: a sketch of its history. 1895.

— The New testament and its transmission. 1932.

Ayres, S. G. and C. F. Sitterly. The history of the English Bible studied by the library method. New York [1898].

Hoare, H. W. The English Bible, Wyclif to Coverdale. Nineteenth Century April 1898; rptd Eclectic Mag 131 1898.
— The English Bible from Henry VIII to James I. Nineteenth Century April–May 1899.
— The evolution of the English Bible. 1901, 1902 (rev), 1911 (rev as Our English Bible).
Purey-Cust, A. P. Diversity in English versions of holy scripture: its use and abuse. York 1899.
Owen, G. L. Notes on the history and text of our early English Bible, and of its translation into Welsh. 1901.
Barker, H. English Bible versions, with special reference to the Vulgate, the Douay Bible and the Authorized and Revised versions. New York 1907.
Price, I. M. The ancestry of our English Bible: an account of manuscripts, texts and versions. Philadelphia 1907, New York 1934 (rev), 1949 (rev W. A. Irwin and A. P. Wikgren), 1956 (rev).
Heaton, W. J. Our own English Bible: its translators and their work. 3 vols 1905–13. Vol 1 (the ms period), 1905; 2, The Bible of the Reformation (Tyndale to Coverdale), 1910; 3, The puritan Bible and other contemporaneous Protestant versions (Cheke to the Authorized version), 1913.
MacComb, S. The making of the English Bible. 1910.
Bevan, J. O. Our English Bible: the history of its development 1611–1911. 1911.
Brown, J. The history of the English Bible. Cambridge 1911.
Canton, W. The Bible and the English people. 1911, 1914 (rev as The Bible and the Anglo-Saxon people).
Girdlestone, R. B. Our English Bible: how we got it. 1911.
Leonard, G. H. The Authorized version of the English Bible. [1911] (Bristol Univ, Historical Pbns 1).
Margoliouth, G. The story of the English Bible. [1911].
Muir, W. Our grand old Bible: being the story of the Authorized version. 1911.
Payne, J. D. The English Bible: an historical survey from the dawn of English history to the present day. 1911.
Pells, S. F. Lectures on the texts of the Bible and our English translations. 1911.
— The Church's ancient Bible: the Septuagint, the Old Latin, the Latin Vulgate, the Bible in the Book of common prayer and the English Bibles. Hove [1924].
Pollard, A. W. Records of the English Bible: the documents relating to the translation and publication of the Bible in English 1525–1611. Oxford 1911.
MacAfee, C. B. The greatest English classic: a study of the King James version of the Bible. 1912.
Scott, W. The story of our English Bible. Glasgow [1916] (3rd edn).
Penniman, J. H. A book about the English Bible. New York 1919.
Guppy, H. A brief sketch of the history of the transmission of the Bible down to the Revised English version of 1881–95. Manchester 1926. First bpd as introd to John Rylands Library exhibition catalogue, 1925.
Baikie, J. The English Bible and its story. 1928.
Pope, H. The Catholic Church and the Bible. New York 1928.
— A brief history of the English versions of the New testament first published at Rheims in 1582, continued down to the present day. 2 pts Library 4th ser 21 1940; rev S. Bullough as English versions of the Bible, St Louis and London 1952.
Wild, L. H. The romance of the English Bible: a history of the translation of the Bible into English. Garden City NY 1929.
National Commemoration Committee, USA. Commemoration of four hundred years of the printed English Bible 1535–1935. New York 1935. 5 pamphlets.
Storr, V. F. The story of the English Bible. [1937].
— (ed). The English Bible. 1938. Essays by H. H. Henson, J. R. Lowes, W. M. Dixon, A. Clutton-Brock, A. T. Quiller-Couch.

Whitley, W. T. The English Bible under the Tudor sovereigns. 1937.
Inge, W. R. et al. Our English Bible. 1938.
Leishman, T. L. Our ageless Bible: from early manuscripts to modern versions. Boston 1939, New York 1960 (rev).
Robinson, H. W. (ed). The Bible in its ancient and English versions. Oxford 1940, 1954 (rev). See chs 6–7 by J. Isaacs.
Butterworth, C. C. The literary lineage of the King James Bible 1340–1611. Philadelphia 1941.
Grierson, H. J. C. The English Bible. 1943; rptd in W. J. Turner (ed), Impressions of English literature, 1944, New York 1945 (as Romance of English literature).
Newgass, E. The English Bible in retrospect. Steyning 1943.
— The everlasting gospel: a panorama of the English Bible. 1950, Bushey Heath 1964 (rev as A panorama of the English Bible).
— An outline of Anglo-American Bible history. 1958.
Cowell, H. J. The coming of the English Bible: biographical notes concerning J. Wycliffe, W. Tindale, M. Coverdale and others. 1944.
Weigle, L. A. The English New testament from Tyndale to the Revised standard version. Nashville and New York 1949, Edinburgh 1950.
May, H. G. Our English Bible in the making. Philadelphia 1952.
Herklots, H. G. G. Back to the Bible: a literary pilgrimage. 1954, 1957 (as How our Bible came to us), 1959 (rev).
The Bible: historical, social and literary aspects. Times (suppl) June 1954. Includes J. F. Mozley, Translations before the Authorized version; anon, The Geneva Bible: literary achievement of the English Protestants; N. Sykes, The origins of the Authorized version.
Clair, C. Word abiding: the story of the English Bible. [1955].
Thompson, C. R. The Bible in English 1525–1611. Washington 1958.
MacGregor, J. G. The Bible in the making. Philadelphia 1959.
Bruce, F. F. The English Bible. 1961, 1970 (rev).
— The Authorized version and others. International Rev of Missions 50 1961.
The 350th anniversary of the Authorized version: a special supplement. Times 27 March 1961. Articles by G. W. Anderson, W. O. Chadwick, F. D. Coggan, C. W. Dugmore et al.
Coggan, F. D. The English Bible. 1963 (Br Council pamphlet).
— Word and world. 1971.
Greenslade, S. L. (ed). The Cambridge history of the Bible [vol 3]: the West from the Reformation to the present day. Cambridge 1963. Includes Greenslade, English versions of the Bible 1525–1611; L. A. Weigle, English versions since 1611; M. H. Black, The printed Bible.

Influences on Translations

Daiches, D. The King James version of the English Bible, with special reference to the Hebrew tradition. Chicago 1941.
Flack, E. E. Luthers Einfluss auf die englische Bibelübersetzung. Zeitschrift für Systematische Theologie 24 1955.
Schwartz, W. Principles and problems of biblical translation: some Reformation controversies and their background. Cambridge 1955. On continental versions and background to English trns.
Blume, F. E. Luther and our English Bible translations. Wisconsin Lutheran Quart 62 1965.
Nix, W. E. Theological presuppositions and sixteenth-century English Bible translation. Bibliotheca Sacra 124 1967.

Printing and Publishing

[Sparke, M.] Scintilla: or a light broken into darke warehouses, with observations upon the monopolists of seaven severall patents and two charters, practised and performed, by a mistory of some printers, sleeping stationers, and combining book-sellers. 1641; rptd in E. Arber, A transcript of the registers of the Company of Stationers vol 4, 1877, in Darlow and Moule vol 1, 1903, and in DMH. On prices of Bibles and Bible trade.
— A second beacon fired by Scintilla: wherein is remembred the former actings of the Papists in their secret plots and wicked designes to set up Popery by introducing pictures to the holy Bible. 1652. See DMH 476.
Errors in printing the English Bible. Congregational Mag 6 1823.
Lee, J. Memorial for the Bible Societies in Scotland. Edinburgh 1824; Remarks on the complaint of his Majesty's printers against the Bible Societies, 1824; Additional memorial, 1826; Index [by W. J. Couper], Records of Glasgow Bibl Soc 4 1918.
Curtis, T. The existing monopoly, an inadequate protection of the Authorised version. 1833. See E. Cardwell, Oxford Bibles: Mr Curtis' misrepresentations exposed, Oxford 1833; T. Turton, The text of the English Bible as now printed by the Universities considered, Cambridge 1833.
'Crito'. On the italic readings of the English Bibles. Christian Observer Feb 1839.
Thomson, A. (of Coldstream). The Bible monopoly inconsistent with Bible circulation. 1840.
Thomson, A. (of Hawick). The Bible printing patent: shall it be renewed? 1859.
Schneffer, C. F. Marginal readings of the New testament. Bibliotheca Sacra 26 1869.
Tedder, H. R. The Barkers and the early history of the Bible-patent. Lib Chron 2 1885, 4 1887.
Kingdon, J. A. Incidents in the lives of T. Poyntz and R. Grafton, who suffered loss and incurred danger in common with Tyndal, Coverdale and Rogers, in bringing out the Bible in the vulgar tongue. 1895.
— Richard Grafton: a sequel. 1901.
Elliot, H. R. Curious facts about the printing etc of the most popular book in the world. Century Mag 46 1904.
Cambridge University Press. 300 years of printing the Authorized version of the holy Bible at Cambridge 1629–1929. Cambridge 1929.
Miles, F. J. The world's best seller and why? commemorating the quarto centenary of the setting up in English parish churches of the English Bible 1538. [1937].
Wikgren, A. P. The use of marginal notes in the English Bible. Crozer Quart 27 1950.
Waite, H. E. Printing and circulating the Bible in Great Britain. Gutenberg-Jahrbuch 1954. From Tyndale to modern times.
Strachan, J. Early Bible illustrations. Cambridge 1957.
Vogel, P. H. Niederländische und englische Bibeldrücke des 15 und 16 Jahrhunderts. Libri 8 1958.
Handover, P. M. Printing in London. 1960. Ch 3, The Bible patent.
Black, M. H. The evolution of a book-form: the octavo Bible from manuscript to the Geneva version. Library 5th ser 16 1961.
Specht, W. E. The use of italics in English versions of the New testament. Cambridge Mass 1968 (Andover Univ Seminary Stud 6).

The English Bible as Literature

MacCulloch, J. M. Literary characteristics of the holy scriptures. Greenock 1845.
Halsey, L. J. The literary attractions of the Bible: or a plea for the word of God, considered as a classic. New York 1858.

Whitman, W. The Bible as poetry. Critic 3 1883; rptd in collections of Whitman's prose works.
Jones, P. L. The poetry of the Bible in its relation to exegesis. Baptist Rev 8 1886.
Bowen, F. A layman's study of the English Bible, considered in its literary and secular aspect. New York 1885.
Moulton, R. G. The literary study of the Bible. Boston 1895.
— A. B. Bruce et al. The Bible as literature. Cambridge Mass 1899 (for 1898).
Moffatt, J. Literary illustrations of Ecclesiastes, the book of Daniel. Expositor 6th ser 10–11 1904–5.
Gardiner, J. H. The Bible as English literature. 1906.
Innes (formerly Royds), K. E. The Bible as literature. 1930.
Dinsmore, C. A. The English Bible as literature. 1931.
Baroway, I. The Bible as poetry in the English Renaissance. JEGP 32 1933.
— The accentual theory of Hebrew prosody: a further study in renaissance interpretation of biblical form. ELH 17 1950.
Blakeney, E. H. The English Bible as literature. Theology June 1938.
Sypherd, W. O. The literature of the English Bible. New York 1938.
Henn, T. R. The Bible in relation to the study of English literature today. Hermathena 100 1965.
— The Bible as literature. 1970.
MacGregor, J. G. A literary history of the Bible from the Middle Ages to the present day. Nashville and New York 1968.

Influence of the English Bible

Petty (later Fitz-Maurice), W. T., Earl of Kerry. An essay upon the influence of the translation of the Bible upon English literature. 1830.
Eaton, T. R. Shakespeare and the Bible. 1858.
Wordsworth, C. On Shakspeare's knowledge and use of the Bible. 1864.
Bullock, C. Shakspeare's debt to the Bible; with memorial illustrations. [1879].
Dickson, N. The Bible in Waverley, or Sir Walter Scott's use of the sacred scriptures. Edinburgh 1884.
Burgess, W. The Bible in Shakspeare. Chicago and Winona Lake 1903.
Ellwanger, W. D. The Bible as a source of style. Critic 43 1903.
Carter, T. Shakespeare and holy scripture, with the version he used. 1905.
Taylor, A. The Bible and English life. [1911].
Dobschütz, E. A. A. O. A. von. The influence of the Bible on civilisation. New York 1914.
Moffatt, J. The Bible in Scots literature. [1924].
Landrum, G. W. Spenser's use of the Bible and his alleged puritanism. PMLA 41 1926.
Fletcher, H. F. The use of the Bible in Milton's prose. Urbana 1929.
Coleman, E. D. The Bible in English drama: an annotated list of plays. BNYPL Jan–March 1931.
Baroway, I. The imagery of Spenser and the Song of songs. JEGP 33 1934.
Noble, R. S. H. Shakespeare's biblical knowledge and use of the Book of common prayer. 1935.
Anderson, D. The Bible in seventeenth-century Scottish life and literature. 1936.
Ackermann, C. The Bible in Shakespeare. Columbus 1938.
Chavasse, C. M. The English Bible in English history. [1938].
Conklin, G. N. Biblical criticism and heresy in Milton. New York 1949.
Lewis, C. S. The literary impact of the Authorised version. 1950; rptd in his They asked for a paper, 1962, and Selected literary essays, Cambridge 1969.

Coleman, H. Shakespeare and the Bible. New York 1955.

Jack, J. H. Macbeth, King James, and the Bible. ELH 22 1955.

Macht, D. I. Biblical allusion in Shakespeare's The tempest in the light of Hebrew exegesis. Jewish Forum Aug 1955.

Siegel, P. N. Echoes of the Bible story in Macbeth. N & Q April 1955.

Sims, J. H. Biblical allusion in Shakespeare's comedies. Forsyth Georgia 1960.

— The Bible in Milton's epics. Gainesville 1962.

— Dramatic uses of biblical allusions in Marlowe and Shakespeare. Gainesville 1966.

Lewalski, B. K. Biblical allusion and allegory in the Merchant of Venice. Shakespeare Quart 13 1962.

MacCallum, H. R. Milton and figurative interpretation of the Bible. UTQ 31 1962.

Language of Translations

Cotton, H. A short explanation of obsolete words in our version of the Bible. 1832.

Jameson, J. A glossary of the obsolete and unusual words and phrases of the holy scriptures in the Authorized English version. 1850.

Booker, J. Obsolete words and phrases in the Bible and Apocrypha and also in the Prayer book, familiarly explained. Dublin 1853, 1856 (rev as A scripture and Prayer book glossary).

Marsh, G. P. The English Bible. Lecture 28 in his Lectures on the English language, New York 1860; ed W. Smith 1862; ser 1, New York 1885 (rev).

Trimmer, K. Motes upon crystal: or obsolete words of the Authorized version of the holy Bible, critically and chronologically considered. 1864.

Trench, R. C. Synonyms of the New testament. Cambridge 1854, London 1865 (rev); tr French, 1869.

Davies, T. L. O. Bible English: chapters on old and disused expressions in the Authorized version of the scriptures and the Book of common prayer. 1875.

Alexander, W. L. Old English words in the Bible. Catholic Presbyterian 4 1880.

Lumby, J. R. A glossary of difficult, ambiguous or obsolete Bible words. [1880], [1880] (as Glossary of Bible words, now difficult or obsolete, explained and illustrated, in The Queen's printers of the holy Bible, aids to the student); pbd separately and in T. K. Cheyne (ed), The Sunday School centenary Bible, 1880; also as Glossary of Bible words, selected from the larger work, in Aids to Bible students, [1880].

Mayhew, A. L. A select glossary of Bible words; also a glossary of important words and phrases in the Prayer book. 2 pts [1891].

Montefiore, C. G. Catalogue of metaphors of the English Bible. Jewish Quart Rev 3 1891.

Cook, A. S. The Bible and English prose style: selections and comments. Boston 1892.

Clapperton, J. A. Pitfalls in Bible English. 1899.

König, F. E. Stilistik, Rhetorik, Poetik in Bezug auf die biblische Litteratur. Leipzig 1900.

Rosenau, W. Hebraisms in the Authorized version of the Bible. Baltimore 1902.

Grainger, J. M. Studies in the syntax of the King James version. SP 2 1907.

Daddow, W. B. Buried pictures in our English version of the Bible. [1911]. On metaphors.

Deutschbein, M. Der rhythmische Charakter der neuenglischen Bibelübersetzung von 1611. E Studien 70 1935.

Olsen, M. E. The prose of our King James version: its origin and course of development. Washington 1947.

Cooper, L. Certain rhythms in the English Bible, with illustrations from the Psalms, Ecclesiastes and the Lord's Prayer. Ithaca 1952.

Beer, J. B. The language of the New testament. Manchester Literary & Philosophical Soc Proc 105 1963. From Wyclif to New English Bible.

Metzger, A. Moderne englische Bibelübersetzungen und die Authorized version: vergleichende Untersuchung von I Kor. 13 unter philologischen und literarischen Gesichtspunkten. Studien zur Englischen Philologie new ser 6 1964.

Elliott, M. E. The language of the King James Bible: a glossary explaining its words and expressions. Garden City NY 1967.

Translations of Individual Books

Hurdis, J. Select critical remarks on the English version [of 1611] of the first ten chapters of Genesis. 1793.

Howorth, H. H. The origin and authority of the biblical canon in the Anglican Church. Jnl of Theological Stud 8 1907. On history of Apocrypha in English versions.

Cleaveland, E. W. A study of Tindale's Genesis compared with the Genesis of Coverdale and of the Authorized version. New York 1911.

Kyes, D. H. The literary style of the prophetic books of the English Bible. Boston [1919].

Errors in Translation

Kilburne, W. Dangerous errors in several late printed Bibles to the great scandal and corruption of sound and true religion. Finsbury 1659; rptd in Loftie, A century of Bibles, 1872.

W[ard], T. The errata to the Protestant Bible: or the truth of their English translations examined. 1688, 1737, Dublin 1807, Philadelphia 1824, Dublin 1841. See R. Ryan, An analysis of Ward's Errata, Dublin 1808; R. Grier, An answer to Ward's Errata, 1812.

Lookup, J. The erroneous translations in the vulgar versions of the scriptures detected in several instances taken from the original. 1739, 1740.

Lindsey, T. A list of the false readings of the scriptures and the mistranslations of the English Bible. 1790.

Winstanley, C. A vindication of certain passages in the common English version of the New testament. 1805.

Wemyss, T. Biblical gleanings: or a collection of passages of scripture that have been generally considered to be mistranslated in the received English version, with proposed corrections. York 1816.

Newman, S. Emendations of the Authorised version of the Old testament. 1839.

Sharpe, S. Critical notes on the Authorised version of the New testament. 1856.

Stuart, C. E. Textual criticism of the New testament for English Bible students: being a comparison of the Authorised version with the critical [Greek] texts of Griesbach, Schulz etc. [1862].

Stifler, J. M. Mistranslation of the Greek article in the King James's version. Baptist Rev 1 1879.

Murray, J. H. A help for English readers to understand mistranslated passages in our Bible. 1881.

Jannaris, A. N. Misreadings and misrenderings in the New testament. Expositor 5th ser 8–10 1898–9.

Wilkinson, B. G. Our authorized Bible vindicated. Washington 1930.

Hills, E. F. The King James version defended: a Christian view of the New testament manuscripts. Des Moines 1956.

Proposals for Revision

[Lecène, C.] An essay for a new translation of the Bible: wherein is shewn from reason, and the authority of the best commentators, interpreters and critics, that there is a necessity for a new translation. [Tr] by H. R[oss] 2 pts 1702–17, 1727. Tr from Projet d'une nouvelle version françoise de la Bible, Rotterdam 1698, Hague 1705, Amsterdam 1722 (as Nouvelle critique de toutes les versions de la Bible en françois).

The reasons for revising by authority our present version of the Bible, briefly stated and impartially considered. Cambridge 1788.

Symonds, J. Observations upon the expediency of revising the present English version of the four Gospels and of the Acts of the apostles. Cambridge 1789; Of the Epistles in the New testament, Cambridge 1794.

Bellamy, J. General preface and introd. In his trn of Bible [Genesis–Proverbs iii. 8 only], 1818 (DMH 1675). *See* virulent review and reply by Bellamy, Quart Rev 19 1818; A critical examination of the objections made to the new translation, 1820; Replies to the Quarterly Reviewer [23 1820] on the new translation, 1820; Reply to Samuel Lee on the new translation, 1820.

Burges (later Lamb), J. B. Reasons in favour of a new translation of the holy scriptures. 1819. Supports Bellamy, above.

Todd, H. J. A vindication of our authorized translation and translators of the Bible, and of preceding English versions authoritatively commended to the notice of those translators. 1819, Malton 1834 (as An authentic account of our authorized translation of the holy Bible, and of the translators), London 1835, 1842.

Hurwith, H. Vindiciæ Hebraicæ. or a defence of the Hebrew scriptures, occasioned by the recent strictures of Mr J. Bellamy, and in confutation of his attacks on all preceding translations. 1820.

[Laurence, R.] Remarks upon the critical principles, and the practical application of those principles, adopted by writers who have at various periods recommended a new translation of the Bible as expedient and necessary. Oxford 1820.

Whittaker, J. W. An historical and critical enquiry into the interpretation of the Hebrew scriptures, with remarks on Mr Bellamy's new translation. Cambridge 1819; Supplement, 1820.

Lee, S. A letter to Mr J. Bellamy on his new translation of the Bible, with some strictures on a tract entitled Remarks. Cambridge 1821. *See* R. Laurence, A reply to Some strictures of S. Lee, Oxford 1821; Lee, A vindication of certain strictures, in answer to A reply, Cambridge 1822.

Scholefield, J. Hints for an improved translation of the

New testament. Cambridge 1832, 1836 (rev), 1849 (with appendix).

Craik, H. Improved renderings of those passages in the English version of the New testament, which are capable of being more correctly translated. 1836.

Cumming, J. Bible revision and translation: an argument for holding fast what we have. 1856, [1857].

Iliff, F. A plea for a revisal of the Bible translation of 1611. Sunderland 1856.

Malan, S. C. A vindication of the Authorised version of the English Bible, from charges brought against it by recent writers. 1856.

[Abbott, T. K.] Revision of the Authorized version: the English Bible, and our duty with regard to it. 1857, Dublin 1871 (as The English Bible: a plea for revision).

Biber, G. E. A plea for an edition of the Authorized version with explanatory and emendatory marginal readings. 1857. *See* Will the version by the five clergymen help Dr Biber?: or an examination of Dr Biber's plan, 1857 (anon).

Burgess, H. Revision of translations of the holy scriptures: an argument against objectors. 1857. Rptd from Jnl of Sacred Lit.

Day, H. T. A letter to Lord Palmerston for a revision of the authorised translation of the holy scriptures. 1857.

— A second letter. 1857.

— Bible and ritual revision: a plea for the revision of the Authorized version of the holy scriptures. 1858.

MacCaul, A. Reasons for holding fast the Authorized English version of the Bible. 1857.

Trench, R. C. On the Authorized version of the New testament, in connexion with some recent proposals for its revision. 1858, 1859 (new).

Tomlin, J. Improved renderings and explanations of many important and difficult passages in the authorised translation of the scriptures. Liverpool 1865.

Fox, H. C. On the revision of the Authorised version of the scriptures, with an account of the revision now in progress. 1875.

(6) COMMENTARIES ETC

On the theory and practice of the commentators see the bibliographies in R. M. Grant, The Bible in the church, New York 1948, London 1965 (rev as A short history of the interpretation of the Bible); J. D. Smart, The interpretation of scripture, 1961, and The Cambridge history of the Bible vol 3, 1963.

Bibliographies

James, T. Catalogus expositorum S. Scripturæ iuxta ordinem voluminum utriusque Testamenti dispositus. In his Catalogus librorum bibliothecæ publicæ in academia oxoniensi, Oxford 1605, 1635 (enlarged by J. Verneuil as Catalogus interpretum S. Scripturæ); apparently pbd as pt 2 of J. Rouse, Appendix ad catalogum librorum in Bibliotheca Bodleiana, 1635. An intermediate Catalogus expositorum qui vel in omnes, vel in aliquot, vel in singulos Bibliorum libros scripserunt, in James's Ecloga oxonio-cantabrigiensis pt 2, 1600 lists only medieval commentators preserved in ms.

V[erneuil], J. A nomenclator of such tracts and sermons as have beene printed or translated into English upon any place of holy scripture. Oxford 1637, 1642 (much enlarged).

[Crowe, W.] An exact collection or catalogue of our English writers on the Old and New testament, either in whole or in part. 1663, 1668 (much enlarged as The catalogue); Elenchus scriptorum in sacram scripturam tam græcorum, quam latinorum, 1672. Arranged in Bible order, by verses; the Elenchus is a distinct work, listing British and foreign commentaries in Latin and Greek.

Kempen, M. Charismatum sacrorum trias: sive bibliotheca Anglorum theologica. Königsberg 1677.

Orme, W. Bibliotheca biblica. Edinburgh 1824.

Horne, T. H. A manual of biblical bibliography. 1839.

Darling, J. Cyclopædia bibliographica: a library manual of theological and general literature. 2 vols [1851–]9. Vol 1, analytical, bibliographical and biographical, 1851–4; 2, holy scriptures, 1857–9.

Spurgeon, C. H. Commenting and commentaries: two lectures, with a catalogue of biblical commentaries and expositions. 1876, 1969. Critical.

Gillett, C. R. Catalogue of the McAlpin Collection of British history and theology (in the Union Theological Seminary New York). 5 vols New York 1927–30. Gives full titles and collations of most of the commentaries; arranged chronologically 1501–1700, with alphabetical index in vol 5.

Collections

Walton, B. (ed). Biblia sacra polyglotta. 6 vols 1657, '1657' (for 1660) (reissued with dedication to Charles II), 1 vol in 2 1669 (with text in Hebrew, Samaritan, Chaldee, Greek, Syriac, Arabic, Ethiopian, Persian and Latin, by E. Castell, J. Lightfoot et al, accompanied by Castell's Lexicon heptaglotton), 2 vols 1686. *See* J. Owen, Of the divine originall, in some considerations on the late Biblia polyglotta, Oxford 1659 (pt 2, Pro sacris scripturis, 1658); Walton, The considerator considered, 1659, and as vol 2 of H. J. Todd, Memoirs of the life and writings of B. Walton, 2 vols 1821; Walton, In Biblia polyglotta prolegomena, cd J. A. Dathe, Leipzig 1777, ed F. Wrangham 2 vols Cambridge 1828; T. F. Dibdin, An introduction to the knowledge of editions of the classics vol 1, 1827 (4th edn); L. Bodenheimer, Das Lied Mosis: eine wissenschaftliche Vergleichung der auf diesen Pentateuch-Abschnitt in der Walton'schen Polyglotte enthaltenen Uebertragungen, Crefeld 1856, continued as Der Segen Mosis, 1860.

Pearson, J., A. Scattergood, F. Gouldman, R. Pearson (ed). Critici sacri: sive doctissimorum virorum in Ss. Biblia annotationes & tractatus. 9 vols 1660; ed N. Gürtler 7 vols Frankfurt 1695, 9 vols Amsterdam 1698; suppl 2 vols 1700–1, another as Thesaurus novus theologicus-philologicus 2 vols 1732. In Latin; contains a few English commentators.

Poole (Pole), M. (ed). Synopsis criticorum aliorumque S. Scripturæ interpretum. 5 vols 1669–76, Frankfurt 1679; ed J. Leusden 5 vols Utrecht 1684–6; ed J. H. Maius, Frankfurt 1694; ed J. G. Pritz (Pritius) 1712. In Latin; contains a few English commentators. See Poole et al, Annotations upon the holy Bible, 2 vols 1683–5, 1688, 1696, 1700, 4 vols Edinburgh 1800, 3 vols 1840, 1852.

Richmond, L. (ed). The fathers of the English Church: or a selection from the writings of the reformers and early Protestant divines of the Church of England. 8 vols 1807–12. List of contents in Darling, Cyclopædia bibliographica vol 1, 1859 cols 2551–2.

Bradley, C. (ed). Select British divines. 28 vols 1821–7. Copy at Trinity College, Dublin.

Hughes, T. S. (ed). A series of the most esteemed divines of the Church of England, with a life of each author. 22 vols 1830–2. Vols 1–5, T. Sherlock; 6–12, I. Barrow; 13–17, J. Taylor; 18–20, J. Hall; 21, W. S. Powell and J. Fawcett; 22, S. Ogden.

The Parker Society, instituted for the publication of the works of the early writers of the reformed English Church. Publications, 53 vols Cambridge 1841–53; General index by H. Gough, 1855. List in W. T. Lowndes, The bibliographer's manual of English literature vol 4, ed H. G. Bohn 1864, 1875 (appendix pp. 55–8).

Library of Anglo-Catholic theology. 79 vols in 87 Oxford 1841–55. List in Lowndes, 1875 above, pp. 376–7.

Nichol's series of commentaries of the puritan period. Edinburgh (afterwards London) 1863–8.

Bible

Extensive notes are in edns of Geneva Bible (puritan, 1560–1644, above; the notes ed T. Webster and accompanied by Authorized version, 1810: DMH 1532), the Rheims-Douai Bible (Roman Catholic, 1582 etc, above), Canne's edns of the Authorized version (puritan, 1642 etc, above), and the Dutch Annotations (puritan, 1657, above).

Calvin, J. Opera. 9 vols Geneva 1563–1617, Amsterdam 1667–71; ed W. Baum, E. Cunitz, E. Reuss 59 vols in 42 Brunswick 1863–1900 (Corpus reformatorum vols 29–87); tr as 22 commentaries in 52 vols Edinburgh 1843–56 (Calvin Trn Soc) (list in Lowndes, 1875, above, pp. 112–13); rearranged as Commentaries, Grand Rapids 1948–; tr German, Auslegung der heiligen Schrift, Neukirchen 1951–; tr French, Commentaires sur l'Ancien testament, Paris 1962–. The 16th- and 17th-century English trns of Calvin's commentaries are listed individually below; see F. A. G. Tholuck, The merits of Calvin as an interpreter of the holy scriptures, tr L. Wood 1845, 1854 (with Calvin's commentary on Joshua); Commentaries, selected and tr J. Haroutunian and L. P. Smith, Philadelphia and London 1958 (arranged by topic).

Tindale, W. Expositions and notes on sundry portions of the holy scripture. Ed H. Walter, Cambridge 1849 (Parker Soc).

Estey, G. Certaine godly and learned expositions upon divers parts of scripture. 2 pts 1603.

Boys, J. An exposition of all the principall scriptures used in our English liturgie. 1609, 1610, 1611; in his Workes, 1622, 1629, 1638.

Luther, M. [Werke]. 12 vols Wittenberg 1539–59, 1565–1603; with 7 Latin vols 1545–57, 1561–83; 8 vols Jena 1555–61 (German), 1572–81, 1585–1613; with 4 Latin vols 1556–8, 1564–70; ed J. J. Greiff 22 vols Leipzig 1728–34; ed J. G. Walch 24 vols Halle 1740–53 (German and Latin); ed J. K. Irmischer et al 67 vols Erlangen 1826–57 (German), 26 vols 1862–85, with 28 Latin vols 1829–86; ed G. Stöckhardt et al 24 vols St Louis 1880–1910 (from Walch); ed J. K. F. Knaake et al, Weimar 1883– (with bibliography prefixed to each work); trn ed J. J. Pelikan 30 vols St Louis 1955–. Individual commentaries tr into English 1500–1660 are separately listed below; see Pelikan, Luther the expositor, St Louis 1959.

Hall, J. Contemplations upon the principall passages of the holie storie (the Old testament). 21 books in 8 vols 1612–26; Contemplations [New testament]: the first booke, 1634; The residue of the contemplations upon the principal passages of the history of the New testament [bk 4], 1634; the New testament complete as Contemplations upon the remarkable passages in the life of the Holy Jesus, 1679; Contemplations on the history of the New testament, ed W. Dodd 2 vols 1759. As Contemplations on the Old and New testament, in C. Bradley (ed), Select British divines vols 12–14, [1824?]; as Contemplations on the historical passages of the Old and New testaments, 3 vols Edinburgh 1770, ed J. Pratt 2 vols 1808, 3 vols 1824, ed T. S. Hughes 3 vols 1831–2, ed R. Wardlaw 2 vols Glasgow 1834, ed J. Hamilton, Edinburgh 1838, 1844, ed C. Wordsworth [1871]; tr Dutch, Amsterdam 1642; German, 2 vols 1665–6, 3 vols 1672–9, 1 vol 1699; Contemplations on the Old testament in his Works [vol 1] as A recollection of such treatises as have been heretofore severally published and are now revised, 1614, 1615, 2 pts 1617, 1620–1, as Works 1625, 1627–8, 1628, 1633, 1634, 1647, 1648; Contemplations on the New testament in his Works vol 2 1633, 1634; the complete Contemplations in his Works vols 1–2 ed J. Pratt 1808, ed P. Hall, Oxford 1837, ed P. Wynter 1863.

— A plaine and familiar explication, by way of paraphrase, of all the hard texts of the whole divine scripture of the Old and New testament. 1633 (sometimes treated as vol 4 to accompany his 3-vol Works, above); in his Works tr 3–4 1808, 1837, 1863.

Fuller, N. Miscellaneorum theologicorum, quibus non modo scripturæ divinæ, sed et aliorum classicorum auctorum plurima monumenta explicantur, atque illustrantur, libri tres. Heidelberg 1612; accessit liber quartus, Oxford 1616, London 1617; Miscellaneorum sacrorum libri duo, quintus & sextus, Leyden 1622; Miscellaneorum theologicorum libri sex, Strasbourg 1650; in J. Pearson (ed), Critici sacri vol 8 1660, vol 9 Amsterdam 1698.

Mayer, J. A commentary upon the whole of the Old testament, added to that upon the New testament. 7 vols 1631–53: vol 1 [Pentateuch], 1653; 2, Many commentaries in one [the historical books], 1647; 3, A commentary upon the holy writings of Job, David and Solomon, 1653; 4, A commentary upon all the prophets both great and small, 1652; 5–7 (see Mayer, cols 1873–4, below.)

Gordon, J. Commentaria in sacra Biblia. 3 vols Paris 1636.

Sandys, G. A paraphrase upon the divine poems (Iob, Psalmes, Ecclesiastes, Lamentations: a paraphrase upon the songs collected out of the Old and New testaments). 1637–8, 1648, 1676; Selections from the metrical paraphrases, ed H. J. Todd 1839. The Psalms and songs previously pbd 1636 (col 1911, below); see F. T. Bowers and R. B. Davis, George Sandys: a bibliographical catalogue of printed editions in England to 1700, BNYPL April–June 1950.

Diodati, G. Pious annotations upon the holy Bible. Tr R.G. 1642, 1643, 1648 (as Pious and learned annotations), 1651, 1664. From Annotationes in Biblia, Geneva 1607.

Annotations upon all the books of the Old and New testament. 1645, 2 vols 1651, 1657; Additional annotations 1658. By J. Downame, J. Ley, W. Gouge, M. Casaubon, F. Taylor, E. Reynolds, T. Gataker, D. Featley, J. Reading, J. Richardson et al; pbd for Westminster Assembly, hence known as the Assembly's Annotations, or as the English Annotations, in distinction to Haak's Dutch Annotations of 1657; see T. Gataker, His vindication of the Annotations (on Jeremiah x.2), 1653, and Richardson, below.

Gregory, J. Notes and observations upon some passages of scripture. Oxford 1646, London 1650, 1665, 1671, 1684; in his Opuscula, 1650, and his Works 2 pts 1664-5, 1671, 1683-4; tr Latin by R. Stokes in J. Pearson (ed), Critici sacri vol 9, 1660, Amsterdam 1698.

Roberts, F. Clavis bibliorum: the key of the Bible. 1648, 1649, Edinburgh 1649, London 1664, 1665, 2 pts 1674-5. The 3rd-4th edns include a metrical trn of all the Psalms.

Trapp, J. Annotations (A commentary or exposition) upon the Old and New testaments. 5 vols: 1 (first edn as A clavis upon the Pentateuch, 1650): Pentateuch, Joshua, Judges, Ruth, Samuel, Kings, Chronicles, 1662 (2nd edn); 2, Ezra, Nehemiah, Esther, Job, Psalms, 1657; 3 (first edn as Salomonis πανάρετος: or a commentarie upon the books of Proverbs, Ecclesiastes and the Song of songs, 1650), 2 pts 1660 (2nd edn with same contents with 4 major prophets); 4, Twelve minor prophets, 1654; 5, New testament (see Trapp, col 1874, below); Commentary on the Old and New testaments, ed H. Martin, W. Webster and A. B. Grosart 5 vols 1867-8.

[Bogerman, J., W. Baudart, G. Bucerus, A. Thysius, A. Walaeus, F. Hommius and J. Rolandus]. The Dutch annotations upon the whole Bible, as ordered by the Synod of Dort 1618 and published [i.e. tr] in English by T. Haak. 2 vols 1657. See col 1841, above.

Doughty, J. Analecta sacra: sive excursus philologici super diversis S. Scripturæ locis. 2 pts 1658-60.

Old Testament

Cooper, T. A briefe exposition of such chapters of the Olde testament, as usually are redde in the Church. 1573.

Jackson, A. A help for the understanding of the holy scripture: containing certain short notes of exposition upon the five books of Moses; 2, Annotations upon the remaining historicall part of the Old testament; 3, Annotations upon the five books, immediately following the historicall part of the Old testament, commonly called the five doctrinall or poeticall books, to wit, the book of Job, the Psalms, the Proverbs, Ecclesiastes and the Song of Solomon; 4, Annotations upon the whole book of Isaiah. Vols 1-2, Cambridge 1643-6; vols 3-4, London 1658-82.

[Scattergood, A. (ed)]. Annotations in Vetus testamentum, et in epistolam ad Ephesios. Cambridge 1653, [ed J. Rhenferd], Franecker 1704, Leyden 1722. Sometimes attributed to Archbishop John Williams, in whose library the anon ms was found.

Richardson, J. Choice observations and explanations upon the Old testament, additionals to the large annotations made by some of the Assembly of Divines [1645, 1651 etc]. 1655, 1657. Commonly joined with Leigh's New testament, 1657.

Leigh, E. Annotations on five poetical books of the Old testament: viz Job, Psalmes, Proverbs, Ecclesiastes and Canticles. 1657.

Pentateuch

Babington, G. Comfortable notes upon the five books of Moses. In Workes, [ed M. Smith] 1615, 1622, 1637.

Genesis, Exodus, Leviticus previously pbd separately, below.

A[insworth], H. Annotations upon the five books of Moses and the booke of Psalmes. 6 pts 1622 (reissues of earlier separate pts), 7 pts 1626-7 (with Song of songs), 1639; tr Dutch, 1690; German, 1692.

Taylor, F. (tr). Targum Hierosolymitanum in quinque libros legis, e lingua chaldaica in latinam conversum. 1649.

Trapp, J. A clavis to the Bible: or a comment upon the Pentateuch or five books of Moses. 1650, 1662 (expanded).

Lightfoot, J. Collatio Pentateuchi hebraici cum samaritico. In B. Walton (ed), Biblia sacra polyglotta vol 6, 1657, '1657' (for 1660).

Genesis

Colet, J. Letters to Radulphus on the Mosaic account of the creation. Ed and tr J. H. Lupton 1876, Ridgewood NJ 1966. On Genesis 1. See C. A. L. Jarrott, On Corpus ms 355, Colet in Romanos et in Genesim, Trans Cambridge Bibl Soc 5 1970.

Calvin, J. A commentarie upon the first booke of Moses called Genesis, translated out of Latine by T. Tymme. 1578 (with the text); ed J. King 2 vols Edinburgh 1847-50 (from Latin and French) (Calvin Trn Soc, with text in a new Latin version and the Authorized version), Grand Rapids 1948, London 1965. From In primum Mosis librum, qui Genesis vulgo dicitur, commentarius, [Geneva] 1554, ed E. Hengstenberg 2 vols Berlin 1838; Mosis libri v, cum commentariis: Genesis seorsum, reliqui quatuor in formam harmoniæ digesti, Geneva 1563, 1573 (as Commentarii in quinque libros Mosis), 1583, 1595 (with Joshua); in Opera omnia vol 1, Geneva 1617, Amsterdam 1667; Commentaire sur le premier livre de Moyse, dit Genèse, Geneva 1554; Commentaires sur les cinq livres de Moyse, 1564, [Heidelberg] 1602; Latin and French in his Opera vol 23, Brunswick 1882.

Hunnis, W. A hyve full of hunnye: contayning the firste booke of Moses called Genesis, turned into English meetre. 1578.

Babington, G. Certaine plaine, briefe and comfortable notes upon everie chapter of Genesis. 1592, 1596 (enlarged); in his Workes, 1615, 1622, 1637.

Clapham, H. Bibliotheca theologica: or a librarye theological. Amsterdam 1597. An analysis of Genesis 1-14.

Gibbens, N. Questions and disputations concerning the holy scripture wherein are contained expositions of the most difficult places: the first part of the first tome. 1601, 1602. Chs 1-14; no more pbd.

Willet, A. Hexapla in Genesin: that is, a sixfold commentarie upon Genesis. Cambridge 1605, 2 vols 1608, 1632-3; in Hexapla in Genesin & Exodum, 1633 ('4th edn').

A[insworth], H. Annotations upon Genesis. [Amsterdam] 1616, 1621; rptd in his Pentateuch, 1622-39, above.

Ross, A. The first book of questions and answeres upon Genesis [chs 1-6]. 1620; The second booke [chs 7-14], 1622; The first and second booke, 1622; 1626 (as An exposition on the fourteene first chapters of Genesis).

W., H. A meditation upon the xxth chapter of Genesis. 1631; rptd in Sir W. Ralegh, Instructions to his sonne and to posteritie, Edinburgh 1634.

Lightfoot, J. A few and new, observations upon the booke of Genesis. 1642; in his Works vol 1, 1684 etc.

— Annotationes Talmudicæ in Genesin. In his Works, 1684, etc.

Cartwright, C. Electa thargumico-rabbinica; sive annotationes in Genesin. 1648, 1653, 1658; in J. Pearson (ed), Critici sacri vol 1, 1660, Amsterdam 1698.

Needler, B. Expository notes, with practical observations, towards the opening of the five first chapters of the first book of Moses, Genesis. 1655.

White, J. A commentary upon the three first chapters of Genesis. 1656.

Andrewes, L. (?) [106 sermons on Genesis 1–4] in
'Αποσπάσματα sacra: or a collection of posthumous and
orphan lectures. 1657. Excluded, as of doubtful authenticity, from his Works, ed J. P. Wilson and J. Bliss 11
vols 1841–54 (Lib of Anglo-Catholic Theology); see
Minor works etc p. lxxvii.

Exodus

Babington, G. Comfortable notes upon the bookes of
Exodus and Leviticus. 2 pts 1604; in his Workes, 1615,
1622, 1637.
Willet, A. Hexapla in Exodum: that is, a sixfold com-
mentary. 2 pts 1608, 2 vols 1633; in Hexapla in Genesin
& Exodum, 1633 (4th edn of Genesis).
A[insworth], H. Annotations upon Exodus. [Amsterdam]
1617, London 1622; in his Pentateuch, 1622–39.
Jackson, T. (d. 1640). A paraphrase upon the eleven first
chapters of Exodus, with usefull annotations, observa-
tions, and parallels. In his Works pt 2, 1653, vol 3 1673,
vol 9 Oxford 1844.
Lightfoot, J. An handfull of gleanings out of the book of
Exodus. 1643; in his Works vol 1, 1684 etc.
Cartwright, C. Electra thargumico-rabbinica: sive anno-
tationes in Exodum. 1653, 1658.

Leviticus

Babington, G. Comfortable notes upon the bookes of
Exodus and Leviticus. 1604 etc. See Exodus, above.
Ainsworth, H. Annotations upon Leviticus. [Amsterdam]
1618; in his Pentateuch, 1622–39.
Willet, A. Hexapla in Leviticum: that is, a six-fold commentarie, 1631.
Weemes, J. An exposition of the first and second tables
of the morall law. 2 vols 1632; in An exposition of the
lawes of Moses: viz morall, ceremoniall, judiciall, 1632,
and in his Workes, 3 vols 1633.

Numbers

Bale, J. The apology agaynste a ranke papyst: a brefe expo-
sycyon also upon the xxx chaptre of Numeri. [1550–5?].
Attersoll, W. The pathway to Canaan: or an exposition
upon the xx and xxi chapters of the booke of Numbers.
1609; A continuation of the exposition of the booke of
Numbers, or the historie of Balek the king and Balaam
the false prophet: or an exposition uppon the xxij,
xxiij, xxiiij and xxv chapters of the booke of Numbers,
1610; A commentarie upon the fourth booke of Moses,
called Numbers, 1618. The 2 earlier works are incorporated, with slight revision, in the last.
Babington, G. Comfortable notes upon Numbers. In his
Workes 1615, 1622, 1637.
Ainsworth, H. Annotations upon Numbers. [Amsterdam]
1619; in his Pentateuch, 1622–39.

Deuteronomy

Calvin, J. The sermons upon Deuteronomie. Ed D.
Raguenier, tr A. Golding 1583. For the Latin and French
edns of Calvin's commentary on Pentateuch see above;
in Opera vols 25–9, Brunswick 1882–5; also Sermones
sur Deuteronome, Geneva 1567; Commentaries on the
four last books of Moses, arranged in the form of a
harmony, tr C. W. Bingham 4 vols Edinburgh 1852–5
(Calvin Trn Soc), Grand Rapids 1950.
Babington, G. Comfortable notes upon Deuteronomy.
In his Workes, 1615, 1622, 1637.
Ainsworth, H. Annotations upon Deuteronomie. [Am-
sterdam?] 1619; in his Pentateuch, 1622–39.

Joshua

Calvin, J. A commentarie upon the booke of Josue. Tr
W. F[ulke?] 1578. With the text; from In librum Iosue
brevis commentarius, Geneva 1564, 1575, and with
Pentateuch, 1595 above; Commentaires sur le livre de
Josué, 1564, 1565, Lyons 1565; in his Opera vol 25,
Brunswick 1882; Commentaries on the book of Joshua,

tr H. Beveridge, Edinburgh 1854 (Calvin Trn Soc),
Grand Rapids 1949.
B[urton], H. Israels fast: or a meditation upon the
seventh chapter of Joshuah. 1628, La Rochelle 1628.

Judges

Vermigli, P. M. (Peter Martyr). Most fruitfull and
learned commentaries (upon Judges). 1564. From In
librum Iudicum commentarij, Zürich 1561, 1565, 1571,
1582, Heidelberg 1609.
Rogers, R. A commentary upon the whole booke of
Judges. 1615.

Ruth

Lavater, L. The book of Ruth, expounded in 28 sermons,
translated by E. Pagitt. 1586. From Liber Ruth
homiliis xxviii expositus, Zürich 1578, Heidelberg 1601.
Topsell, E. The reward of religion: delivered in sundrie
lectures upon the booke of Ruth. 1596, 1597, 1601, 1613
(corrected and augmented).
Bernard, R. Ruths recompence: or a commentarie upon
the booke of Ruth. 1628, Edinburgh 1865 (Nichol's
Commentaries) (with Fuller's Ruth).
Fuller, T. A comment on Ruth [chs 1–2]. 1654, Edinburgh 1865 (Nichol's Commentaries) (with Bernard's
Ruth); ed W. Nichols 1868 (Nichol's Commentaries)
(with Fuller's Jonah).

I and II Samuel

Willet, A. An harmonie upon the first booke of Samuel.
Cambridge 1607, 1614; An harmonie upon the second
booke of Samuel, 1614.
Guild, W. The throne of David: or an exposition of the
second of Samuell. [Ed J. Owens], Oxford 1659.

Chronicles

James VI and I. Ane meditatioun upon the xxv, xxvi,
xxvii, xxviii and xxix verses of the xv chap. of the first
buke of the Chronicles of the Kings. Edinburgh 1589,
London 1603; in his Workes, ed J. Montagu 1616; tr
Latin, Opera ed J. Montagu 1619, Frankfurt 1689.

Nehemiah

Pilkington, J. A godlie exposition upon certeine chapters
of Nehemiah. Cambridge 1585; in his Works, ed J.
Scholefield, Cambridge 1842 (Parker Soc). On i–v. 5.

Esther

Brenz (Brentius), J. A right godly and learned discourse
upon the booke of Ester, translated by J. Stockwood.
1584. From In epistolam Pauli ad Philemonem, et in
historiam Esther commentarioli, Schwäbisch Hall 1543,
Frankfurt 1543, 1544, 1559; in Explicationes epistolarum
Pauli ad Galatas, Philippenses, Philemonem, & in
historiam Esther, 1566, 1570; Esther in Opera vol 2,
Tübingen 1576; tr German by J. Spangenberg, Mans-
feld 1551.
Merlin, P. A most plaine and profitable exposition of the
booke of Ester, delivered in 26 sermons. Tr 1599. From
Sermons sur le livre d'Esther, La Rochelle 1591, Geneva
1594; Homeliæ sex et viginti in librum Esteræ, ex
Gallicis Latinæ factæ, Geneva 1593.
Cooper, T. The churches deliverance: contayning meditations and short notes uppon the booke of Hester. 1609,
1628.
Taylor, F. Targum prius et posterius in Esteram, nunc
primum urbe donatum, & in linguam latinam translatum.
1655.

Job

Calvin, J. Sermons upon the booke of Job, translated out
of French by A. Golding. 1574, 1579–80, 1580, 1584.
From Sermons sur le livre de Job, Geneva 1563, 1569,
1611; In librum Iob conciones, ed T. Beza 1593; in his
Opera vol 33, Brunswick 1887.

Bèze, T. de. Job expounded partly in manner of a commentary, partly in manner of a paraphrase, translated out of Latine. Ptd Cambridge, pbd London [1589?]. From Iobus partim commentariis partim paraphrasi illustratus; cui additus est Ecclesiastes, Solomonis concio paraphrasticè explicata, Geneva 1589, London 1589.

Adamson, P. (d. 1592). Paraphrasis poetica Jobi, Threnorum Jeremiæ. In Poemata sacra, ed T. Wilson 1619; in W. Lauder (ed), Poetarum scotorum musæ sacræ vol 2, Edinburgh 1739, 1740.

Holland, H. The Christian exercise of fasting; hereunto are added some meditations on 1, 2 Job. 2 pts 1596.

Humphreys, R. The conflict of Job, by way of dialogue: being a paraphrase on the book of Job. 1607.

Broughton, H. Job. To the King: a Colon-Agrippina studie of one moneth for the metricall translation, but of many yeres, for Ebrew difficulties. 1610; in his Works, ed J. Lightfoot 1662.

Quarles, F. Job militant with meditations, divine and moral. 1624; in his Divine poems, 1630 etc.

Young, P. (ed). Catena Græcorum patrum in beatum Job, collectore Niceta. 1637. In Greek, with Latin trn by Young; an 11th-century compilation; in B. Walton (ed), Biblia sacra polyglotta vol 6, 1657 (for 1660).

Abbot, G. The whole book of Job paraphrased, or made easie for any to understand. 1640.

Caryl, J. An exposition with practicall observations upon the three first chapters of the booke of Job. 1643, 1644, 1647 (York Univ Lib), 1664, 1669, 1676; chs 4–7, 1645, 1648, 1656; chs 8–10, 1647, 1649, 1669; chs 11–14, 1652, 1670; chs 15–17, 1650, 1653, 1671; chs 18–21, 1653, 1658; chs 22–6, 1655, 1659; chs 27–9, 1657, 1670; chs 30–1, 1659; chs 32–4, 1661, 1669; chs 35–7, 1664; chs 38–42 (being the five last chapters), 1666; An abridgment of Caryl's exposition, Edinburgh 1836.

Scnault, J. F. A paraphrase upon Job, written in French, translated into English. 1648, 1657 (as The pattern of patience, in the example of holy Job: a paraphrase upon the whole book). From Paraphrases sur Job, Paris 1637, 1664, 1667 (9th edn), Rouen 1667, Paris 1668.

Manley, T. The affliction and deliverance of the saints: or the whole booke of Job, composed into English heroicall verse, metaphrastically. 1652.

Duport, J. Θρηνοθρίαμβος: sive liber Iob græco carmine redditus. Cambridge 1637, 1653, 1653. With a Latin prose version.

Durham, J. Exposition of Job. 1659, Glasgow 1759.

Psalms

Where double numbers of psalms are given (e.g. 30/31) the lower number is that of Latin and Roman Catholic versions, the higher that of English Protestant trns; where one number only is given it is the latter.

Fisher, J. This treatise concernynge the fruytfull saynges of Davyd the Kynge and prophete in the seven penytencyall psalmes, devyded in seven sermons. 1508, 1509, 1510, [1515?], 1525, 1529, 1555; in his Opera omnia, Würzburg 1597 (Latin trn by J. Fen), and English works pt 1, ed J. E. B. Mayor 1876 (EETS), 1935.

[Aretino, P.] A paraphrase upon the seaven penitentiall psalmes of the kingly prophet, translated out of Italian by J. H[awkins]. [Douai] 1635 (Allison & Rogers 758). From I sette salmi de la penitentia di David, Venice 1534, 1536, 1540, [1560?]; tr French, Lyons 1540, Paris 1605 (another trn); formerly attributed to Savonarola.

Savonarola, G. [Expositions or meditations on psalms 30/31, 50/51, 79/80]. A meditacyon upon the psalme of In te domine speraui [31]. [1536?]; An exposicyon (after the maner of a contemplacyon) upon the li psalme, Paris 1538 (2 edns, Latin and English), London 1539, [1540?] (4 edns, some as An exposicyon after the maner of a contemplation, upon the Psalme called Miserere

mei deus pt 2, A meditation uppon the Psalme of In te domine speraui), [1558] (An exposition after the maner of a contemplacion uppon the li psalme, called Miserere mei deus, pt 2 A godly exposycion uppon the xxx Psalme In te domine speraui, An other meditacion uppon the lxxx Psalme of David Qui regis Israeli intende); A pithie exposition upon the 51 psalme, also a godly meditation upon the 31 psalme, newly augmented by A. Fleming 1578. Probably tr from Latin versions, variously entitled Expositio or Meditatio etc, pbd on the Continent, mostly in Italy, separately, in various combinations and in larger collections, from 1496 (psalm 80), [1498?] (51) and [1498–9?] (31) in many edns before the English trns and in a few later; also available to the English translators in foreign vernacular versions, Italian [1497?] (31), [1498–9?] (51), [1495?] (80), German 1522 (31), 1498 (51), 1542 (80), Spanish 1547 (31), [1495?] (51), 1547 (80); Dutch [1516?] (51); later English trns of 31 (anon as Sorrow and hope, 1894), 31 and 51 by E. H. Perowne 1900.

Luther, M. A very excellent and swete exposition upon the xxii psalme. Tr M. Coverdale, Southwark 1537, 1538 (with A sermon out of the 91st Psalme, by A. Osiander). With the text; from Der xxii Psalm ausgelegt, Wittenberg [1536]; in various edns of Luther's works to Weimar vol 51, 1914; Osiander's Wie und wohin ein Christ die grausamen Plag der Pestilentz fliehen soll: ein Predig, aus dem 91 Psalm, Nuremberg 1533, 1543, 1562; Coverdale's trn as How and whither a Christen man ought to flye the horrible plage of the pestilence: a sermon out of the Psalme Qui habitat in adjutoris altissimi [psalm 91. 1–8], Southwark 1537, [1564].

— A commentarie upon the fiftene psalmes, called Psalmi graduum, that is, psalmes of degrees [120–34], translated out of Latine by H. Bull. 1577, 1615, 1637, Lewes 1823. With the text; from Enarrationes in psalmos graduum, ex prælectionibus collectæ et editæ per V. Theodorum, Strasbourg 1540, 1542; Ausslegung D. M. Luther's über die funfzehen Psalmen der Lieder im höhern Chor, verteuscht durch C. Hedio, 1541; in various edns of Luther's works, Latin and German, from Wittenberg vol 3 1549 (Latin) and 8 1556 (German) to Weimar vol 40 pt 3 1930.

— An exposition upon the 130 psalme. Tr T. Potter 1577. From Der cxxx Psalm von D. Mar. Luth. in lateinischer Sprach ausgelegt, und jtzt verdeudscht, durch Georg Major, Wittenberg 1539.

Campensis (van den Campen), J. A paraphrasis upon al the psalmes of David, translated out of Latyne [by M. Coverdale]. [Antwerp 1535], London 1539 (DMH 14). From Psalmorum omnium juxta hebraicam paraphrastica interpretatio, Nuremberg 1532, Lyons 1533, 1534, Paris 1534, Strasbourg 1545; tr Dutch, Delft 1534, Leyden 1537, Campen 1566; tr French, Lyons 1542, Antwerp 1556; tr German, Augsburg 1534.

Sampson, R. In priores quinquaginta psalmos Dauiticos, familiaris explanatio. 1539; Explanationis psalmorum secunda pars [51–100], 1548.

Taverner, R. An epitome of the psalmes: or briefe meditations upon the same, with diverse other most Christian prayers, translated. 1539.

Cope, Sir A. A godly meditacion upon xx select psalmes of David. 1547; ed W. H. Cope 1848. Psalms 1, 6, 12–13, 23, 32, 49, 51, 73, 84, 90, 102–4, 116, 121, 130, 138–9, 146.

Calvin, J. A short declaration upon the 87 psalme. In Foure godlye sermons, [tr R. Horne] 1561; in Foure sermons, [tr J. Feilde] 1579. From Briève exposition du psaume 87; tr Latin in Homiliae sive conciones vii, Geneva 1556, Opera vol 32, Brunswick 1887; tr French, Œuvres françoises, Paris 1842.

— Thre notable sermones upon psalme 46. Tr W. Warde 1562, 1568.

— The psalmes of David and others, with J. Calvins commentaries. Tr A. Golding 2 pts 1571; A commentary on the psalms of David, based on Golding's translation 3 vols 1840; tr J. Anderson, J. McLean and G. McCrie 5 vols Edinburgh 1845–9 (Calvin Trn Soc), Grand Rapids 1949; psalm 19 rptd in Cotton 363. From In librum Psalmorum commentarius, [Geneva] 1557, Basle 1563, Geneva 1564, 1578, 1590, 1610, ed A. Tholuck 2 vols Berlin 1836; tr French, [Paris] 1558, 1561 (rev), [Geneva] 1563, 2 vols Paris 1859; in Opera omnia vol 3, Amsterdam 1667, vols 31–2 Brunswick 1887; tr Welsh, Aberrhondda 1828; Latin and French, ed H. Expert, Paris 1902. Preached 1552, 1555.

— Two and twentie sermons, in which is handled the hundred and nineteenth psalme. Tr T. S[tocker] 1580. From Vingtdeux sermons, auxquels est exposé le pseaume centdixneufième, Geneva 1554, 1562; in Opera vol 32, Brunswick 1887. Preached 1553.

Hooper, J. An exposition upon the 23 psalme. [Ed H. Bull] 1562; incorporated in Certeine comfortable expositions upon the xxiii, lxii, lxxiii and lxxvii psalmes, [ed Bull] 1580, 1583; in Richmond's Fathers of the English Church vol 5, 1810; in Later writings of Hooper ed C. Nevinson, Cambridge 1852 (Parker Soc).

The boke of psalmes, wherein are contayned prayers, translated faithfully according to the Ebrewe, with brief and apt annotations in the margent. 1576. Geneva version.

Bèze, T. de. The psalmes of David, truely opened and explaned by paraphrasis. Tr A. Gilby 1580, 1581, 1590. From Psalmorum Dauidis et aliorum prophetarum libri quinque, argumento & latina paraphrasi illustrati, ac etiam vario carmine genere, latine expressi, Geneva 1579, 1580, Antwerp and London 1581, Geneva 1581 (2nd edn); also with some edns of Buchanan's Latin metrical version, below; Les pseaumes de David et les cantiques de la Bible, avec les argumens et la paraphrase de T. de Besze, traduits de latin, 1581.

— Christian meditations upon eight psalmes, translated out of French by J. S[tubs]. 1582, [1583?]. Psalms 1, 6, 32, 38, 51, 102, 130, 143 (the penitential psalms) in prose.

— Right godlie psalmes to be said of Queene Elizabeth especiallie upon the 17 daie of November, parapharastically explaned and opened by T. Beza. In T. Bentley (ed), The monument of matrones vol 1 pt 3, 1582. Psalms 18 and 118 in a prose trn, apparently new.

— The psalter or psalmes of David, pointed; also a briefe table declaring the true use of everie psalme, made by T. Beza. 1600, 1606. The table is based on the arguments prefixed to each psalm in the Latin version by Beza, above.

Strigel (Strigelius), V. [Psalms 1–21] Part of the harmony of King Davids harp, containing the first xxi psalmes, briefly and learnedly expounded. 1582; [22–'35' i.e. 34] A proceeding in the harmonie of King Davids harpe, [1591]; ['34–45', i.e. 35–44] A second proceeding, [1593]; [45–61] A third proceeding, 1595; [62–7] A fourth proceeding, 1596; [68–72] A fift proceeding, 1598 (all tr R. Robinson). From Ὑπομνήματα in omnes psalmos Davidis, Leipzig 1563, 1567, 1573.

Gentili, S. Paraphrasis aliquot Psalmorum Davidis, carmine heroico. 1581; In xxv Davidis Psalmos epicæ paraphrases, 1584; in Opera omnia 8 vols Naples 1763–9.

— Psalmi sexti epica paraphrasis. In H. Doneau (Donellus), Opuscula postuma, Hanau 1604.

W[ilcox], T. A right godly and learned exposition upon the whole book of psalmes. 1586, 1591; in his Works, [ed J. Burges] 4 pts 1624.

Regius (Rhegius), U. The solace of Sion and joy of Jerusalem, being a godly exposition of the lxxxvii psalme, translated into English by R. Robinson. 1587, 1591, 1594. From Commentariolus in psalmum 87 (1536), in his Opera, Nuremberg 1562.

Turnbull, R. An exposition upon the canonicall epistle of Saint James (Saint Jude; The xv Psalme). 3 pts 1591, 1592, 1606.

Mornay, P. de. Meditations upon the 101 psalme. Tr T. Wilcox 1599. From Meditationes in psalmos et alia scripturæ loca; see his Meditations chrestiennes sur les pseaumes vi, xxv, xxx & xxxii; plus sur le pseaume cxxxvii par P. de Pelisson, La Rochelle 1586.

Gheeraerts (Gerardus), A., called Hyperius. A speciall treatise of Gods providence, with an exposition of the 107 psalme, tr J. L[udham] [1600?], 1602. From De providentia Dei, et consolationibus, contra omnis generis pericula ab ea petendis, cum enarratione psalmi 107, in his Opuscula theologica pt 2, Basle 1571.

Rollock, R. In selectos aliquot psalmos Davidis commentarius. Geneva 1599, 1610; An exposition upon some select psalmes of David, translated out of Latine by C. L[umisden], Edinburgh 1600. Psalms 3, 6, 16, 23, 32, 39, 42, 49, 51, 62, 65, 84, 116, 130, 137.

Willet, A. Ecclesia triumphans: that is, the joy of the English church, for the coronation of Prince James, with a briefe exposition of the 122 Psalme, and fit application to the time. Cambridge 1603, 1614.

Downame, G. Lectures on the xv psalme. 1604.

Temple, Sir W. A logicall analysis of twentie select psalmes. 1605; Analysis logica triginta psalmorum, 1611. Psalms 1–2, 16, 27, 34, 37, 39, 49–51, 73, 84, 90–1, 94, 103–4, 107, 116, 139; Geneva trn.

V., G. D. Holy meditations upon seaven penitentiall psalmes. 1612.

Bois, J. An exposition of the last psalme in a sermon at Pauls crosse. 1613, 1615; An exposition of the proper psalms used in our English liturgie, 1615, 1616, 1616–17; in his Works, 1622, 1629, 1638.

Cowper, W. Good newes from Canaan: or an exposition on the 51 psalme. 1613; A holy alphabet for Sion's scholars; by way of commentary upon the whole cxix psalme. 1613; both in his Works, 1623, 1626, 1628–9.

Horne, R. The Christian governour in the commonwealth, and private families. 1614 (on psalm 101); The shield of the righteous: or the ninety first psalme, expounded, 1625.

Dyke, D. Certaine comfortable sermons upon the 124 psalme. 1616, 1617, 1635; in his Workes, 2 pts 1633–5.

Smith, S. Davids blessed man: or a short exposition upon the first psalme. 1614, 1617, 1635, 1642, 1658, 1675, 1682; with W. Gouge, The saints sacrifice, and T. Pierson, Excellent encouragements, Edinburgh 1868 (Nichol's Commentaries); Davids repentance: or a plaine and familiar exposition of the 51 psalme, 1614, 1620, 1623, 1625, 1640, 1655, 1660, 1667, 1682, 1691, 1694, 1718, 1735, 1745, 1754; The chiefe shepheard: or an exposition upon the xxiii psalme, 1625; Moses his prayer: or an exposition of the nintieth psalme, 1656.

B[ernard], R. and R. A[lleine?]. Davids musick: or psalmes [1–3] unfolded logically, expounded paraphrastically. 1616.

[Hieron, S.] Davids penitentiall psalme opened: in thirtie severall lectures [on psalm 51]. Cambridge 1617; in his Sermons, 1620; Workes, 2 vols [1620?]; Sermons (vol 2: Workes), 1624–5; Workes, 2 vols 1628–9, [1634–5].

Taylor, T. Davids learning: or the way to true happinesse, in a commentary upon the 32 psalme. 1617, 1618, 1659; in his Works, 1653, 1659.

Day, J. Day's descant on Davids psalmes [1–8]: or a commentary upon the psalter, as it is usually read throughout the yeare, at morning, and evening prayer: and first, of the first eight psalmes, appointed to be read, the first day of the moneth. Oxford 1620.

Bradshaw, W. A meditation of mans mortalitie: containing an exposition of the ninetieth psalme. Ed T. Gataker 1621.

Hallewill, G. King David's vow for reformation, delivered in twelve sermons upon psalm 101. 1621, 1622.

Hayward, Sir J. Davids teares. 1622–3 (2 edns), 1623, 1632, 1636. Commentaries on psalms 6, 32 and 130.

Simson, A. A sacred septenarie on the seven psalmes of repentance. 1623 (2nd impression), 1638.

Gouge, W. The saints sacrifice: or a commentarie on the cxvi psalme. 1632, Edinburgh 1868 (with S. Smith, David's blessed man, and T. Pierson, Excellent encouragements) (Nichol's Commentaries).

Fletcher, P. The way to blessednes: a treatise on the first psalme. 1632.

Reynolds, E. An explication of the hundred and tenth psalm. 1632, 1635, 1642, 1654, 1656, 1837; in his Workes, 1658, 1678–9; ed A. Chalmers 6 vols 1826 (vol 2).

Ames, W. Lectiones in CL (omnes) psalmos Davidis. Amsterdam 1635, London 1647; in his Workes, 1643; Opera quæ latinè scripsit omnia, ed M. Nethenus 5 vols Amsterdam 1658.

Hildersam, A. CLII lectures upon psalme LI. 1635, 1642, 1662; tr Hungarian, 1672.

Baker, Sir R. Meditations and disquisitions upon the first psalme of David. 1638, 1640; Meditations and disquisitions upon the one and fiftieth psalme, 1638; Meditations and disquisitions upon the seven psalmes of David, commonly called the penitentiall psalmes, viz. the 6, 32, 38, 51, 102, 130 and 143 and upon the three last psalmes, 1639; Meditations and disquisitions upon seven consolatorie psalmes, viz. the 23, 27, 30, 34, 84, 103 and 116, 1640; Meditations and disquisitions upon the first psalm, the penitential psalms, and seven consolatory psalms, ed A. B. Grosart 1882; tr German, Frankfurt 1688.

Vicars, J. Decapla in psalmos: sive commentarius ex decem linguis; viz. Hebr. Arab. Syriac. Chald. Rabbin. Græc. Rom. Ital. Hispan. Gallic. 1639, 1655. Specimens of the psalms in the 10 languages, with the vulgate text.

Bythner, V. Lyra prophetica Davidis regis: sive analysis critico-practica psalmorum. 1644, 1650, 1653, 1654, 1664, 1679; tr T. Dee, Dublin 1836, 1847.

Foord, J. Expositio libri psalmorum. 1646.

Pierson, T. Excellent encouragements against afflictions [on psalms 27, 84–5, 87]. 1647; Edinburgh 1868 (Nichol's Commentaries) (with W. Gouge, The saints sacrifice, and S. Smith, Davids blessed man).

Abbot, G. The whole book of psalms paraphrased: or made easier for any to understand. 1650, 1651 (as Brief notes upon the whole book of psalms). With the Authorized version text.

Dickson, D. A brief explication of the first fifty psalms. 1653, 1655; A briefe explication of the other fifty psalmes, from ps. 50 to ps. 100, 1653, 1655; A briefe explication of the last fifty psalmes, from ps. 100 to the end, 1654, 1655; The psalms of David in metre: newly translated [the Scottish version of 1650], together with the annotations of D. Dickson, Edinburgh 1748, Glasgow 1761, 1767; The explications of all the psalms, ed R. Woodrow 2 vols Glasgow 1834.

Hammond, H. A paraphrase and annotations upon the books of the psalms. [1653?], 1659, 1683; in his Workes vol 4, ed W. Fulman 1684; ed T. Branckner 2 vols Oxford 1850.

Kellison, M. A devout paraphrase on the 50th psalme. Paris 1655.

Llanvaedonon, W. A brief exposition upon the second psalme. 1655.

Cartwright, C. A practical and polemical commentary or exposition on the whole fifteenth psalm. 1658.

Hall, T. The beauty of magistracy: in an exposition of the 82 psalm. 1660.

Price, J. Annotationes in psalmorum librum. In Commentarii in varios Novi testamenti libros, 1660; in J. Pearson (ed), Critici sacri vol 5, 1660, Amsterdam 1698.

Proverbs

Holkot, R. In prouerbia Salomonis explanationes. Paris 1510, 1515.

[Hall, J.] Certayne chapters of the proverbes of Salomon wyth other chapters of the holy scripture and certayne psalmes of David, drawen into metre. [1550?]. Formerly wrongly attributed to Thomas Sternhold.

Baynes, R. In Prouerbia Salomonis tres libri commentariorum. Paris 1555.

Cop (Cope), M. A godly and learned exposition upon the proverbes of Solomon, written in French and translated by M. O[utred]. 1580. From Sur les proverbes de Salomon: exposition familière, Geneva 1556.

W[ilcox], T. A short, yet sound commentarie; on the proverbs of Salomon. 1589, 1597; in his Works, 4 pts 1624.

M[uffett], P. A commentarie upon the proverbes of Salomon. 1592, 1596, Edinburgh 1868 (Nichol's Commentaries) (with Cotton's Ecclesiastes and Song of Solomon).

A[llen], R. An alphabet of the holy proverbs of King Salomon, specially from the beginning of the tenth chapter to the end of the booke. 1596; Concordances of the holy proverbs of King Salomon, Ecclesiastes, 1612.

Cleaver, R. A plaine and familiar exposition of the 1st and 2nd chapters of the proverbs of Solomon. 1614; J. Dod and R. Cleaver, 9th and 10th chapters, 1606, 1608, 1612; 11th and 12th, 1607, 1608, 1612; 13th and 14th, 1608, 1609, 1615, 1631; 15th, 16th and 17th, 1609, 1611; 18th, 19th and 20th, 1610, 1611; Dod and W. Hinde, Bathshebaes instructions to her son Lemuel: containing a fruitfull and plane exposition of the last chapter [31] of the proverbs, 1614; Cleaver, A briefe explanation of the whole book of the proverbs of Salomon, 1615.

Hall, J. Salomons divine arts, drawne out of his proverbs and Ecclesiastes, with a paraphrase upon the Song of songs. 1609; tr French, 1632; in various edns of his Works, 1614–1863.

E[gerton], S. Indecorum: or a brief treatise upon one of Solomon's proverbs chap. 11.22. 1613.

Cartwright, T. Commentarii succincti & dilucidi in proverbia Salomonis. Leyden 1617, Amsterdam 1638, 1663.

Jermin, M. Paraphrasticall meditations, by way of commentarie, upon the proverbs of Solomon. 1638.

Taylor, F. An exposition with practicall observations upon the three first chapters of the Proverbs. 1655; The 4, 5, 6, 7, 8, 9 chapters, 1657.

Hammond, H. (d. 1660). [A paraphrase and annotation]. In his Workes vol 4, ed W. Fulman 1684. On chs 1–10.

Ecclesiastes

Sherwood, R. Liber hebræorum concionatoris: seu Ecclesiastes, nuper ad veritatem hebraicam recognitus, cum annotationibus. Antwerp 1523.

Pace, R. Præfatio in Ecclesiasten recognitum ad hebraicam veritatem. [1530?].

Wakefield, R. Paraphrasis in librum Koheleth. [1530?].

Luther, M. An exposition of Salomons booke, called Ecclesiastes. 1573. From Ecclesiastes Salomonis cum annotationibus M. Lutheri, 1532; Ecclesiastes Salomonis enarratus in schola Wittenbergensi, Frankfurt 1548; Le livre de l'Ecclésiaste, familièrement expliqué, Geneva 1557; in edns of Luther's works to Weimar vol 20, 1898.

Serres (Serranus), J. de. A godlie and learned commentarie upon Ecclesiastes. Tr J. Stockwood 1585. From Commentarius in Solomonis Ecclesiasten, Geneva 1580.

Gifford, G. Eight sermons upon the first foure chapters, and part of the fift, of Ecclesastes. 1589.

Bèze, T. de. Ecclesiastes: or the preacher, with a paraphrase or short exposition, translated out of Latin. Cambridge [1593?]. From Ecclesiastes Solomonis, concio paraphrasi illustrata, Geneva 1588; Iobus partim commentarijs partim paraphrasi illustratus; cui additus est Ecclesiastes, Solomonis concio, paraphrasticè explicata, Geneva 1589, London 1589.

L[ok], H. Ecclesiastes, otherwise called the Preacher, compendiously abridged, and also paraphrastically dilated in English poesie. 2 pts 1597.

Cartwright, T. In librum Salomonis, qui inscribitur Ecclesiastes. 1604; as Metaphrasis et homiliæ, Marburg 1604, Amsterdam 1632, 1647, 1663.

Broughton, H. A comment upon Coheleth or Ecclesiastes. 1605; in Works, ed J. Lightfoot 4 vols 1662.

Hall, J. Salomons divine arts, drawne out of his proverbs and Ecclesiastes, with a paraphrase upon the Song of songs. 1609 etc.

Granger, T. A familiar exposition or commentarie on Ecclesiastes. 1621.

Pemble, W. Salomon's recantation and repentance: or the booke of Ecclesiastes briefly and fully explained. 1627, 1628, 1632; in his Workes, 1635 ('3rd', i.e. first edn), Oxford 1658 ('4th', i.e. 2nd edn).

Jermin, M. A commentary upon Ecclesiastes. 1639.

Quarles, F. Solomons recantation, entitled Ecclesiastes, paraphrased, with a soliloquie or meditation upon every chapter. 1645, 1645, 1648.

Cotton, J. A briefe exposition with practicall observations upon the whole book of Ecclesiastes. Ed A. Tuckney 1654, 1657, Edinburgh 1868 (Nichol's Commentaries) (with Cotton's Song of Solomon and Muffett's Proverbs).

Nisbet, A. (d.c. 1658). An exposition, with practical observations. Edinburgh 1694.

Song of Solomon

Holkot, R. In Cantica canticorum. Venice 1509.

Baldwin, W. The canticles or balades of Solomon, phraselyke declared in Englyshe metres. 1549. With a prose version.

Smith, J. A mistical devise of the spirituall and godly love, newly set forth in verse. [Ed J. Wharton] 1575. A paraphrase on chs 5–6.

Andrewes, B. Certaine verie worthie sermons, upon the fifth chapter of the Songe of Solomon. 1583, 1595.

W[ilcox], T. An exposition uppon the booke of the Canticles. 1585; in Works, 4 pts 1624.

Bèze, T. de. Sermons upon the three first chapters of the Canticle of canticles, translated out of French by J. Harmar. Oxford 1587. From Sermons sur les trois premiers chapitres du Cantique des cantiques, de Salomon, [Geneva] 1586, 1615; In Canticum canticorum Solomonis homiliæ, ex gallicis latinæ factæ, 1587, and in his Poemata varia, 1599.

[Fenner, D.] The Song of songs, translated into Englishe meeter and interpreted by a short commentarie. Middelburg 1587, 1594.

Brucioli, A. A commentary upon the Canticle of canticles, translated by T. James. 1598. From Annotationi sopra Proverbii di Salomo, Venice 1533.

Gifford, G. Fifteene sermons upon the Song of Solomon. 1598, 1600, 1612, 1620.

Clapham, H. The Song of songs: the first part [ch i] (second and third parts [ch ii.1–7, 8–17]) expounded. 1602; Three partes of Salomon his Song of songs expounded, 1603 [chs i–ii]; The fourth and fifth parts of Salomons Songe of Songs expounded, 1606.

James, T. Concordantiæ sanctorum patrum, hoc est libri canticorum per patres universos tam græcos quam latinos expositio. Oxford 1607.

Hall, J. An open and plaine paraphrase, upon the Song of songs. In Salomons divine arts, 1609; in edns of his Works, 1614 etc; tr French, 1632.

Dove, J. The conversion of Salomon: commentaries upon the whole booke of Canticles. 1613.

Thargum, hoc est paraphrasis in Canticum canticorum. 1614.

[Finch, Sir H.] An exposition of the Song of Solomon. Ed W. Gouge 1615.

A[ylett] or A[rgall], R. The Song of songs metaphrased in English heroiks. 1621.

Ainsworth, H. Solomons Song of songs in English metre, with annotations. [Amsterdam?] 1623; in his Pentateuch, 1626–7, 1639, 1641, 1662. With a prose trn slightly altered from the Authorized version.

Hildersam, A. (d. 1632). The Canticles: or Song of Solomon paraphrased. 1672.

Sherlock, P. Anteloquia in Salomonis Canticorum canticum, ethica pariter & historica. Lyons 1633, 3 vols 1637–40, Venice 1639–41.

Young, P. (ed). Expositio in Canticum canticorum Gilberti Folioti [d. 1188]. 1638.

Sibbes, R. Bowels opened: or a discovery of the neere and deere love, union and communion betwixt Christ and the Church, in divers sermons on Canticles 4, 5, and 6. 1639, 1641; in his Works vol 3, Aberdeen 1809, 1812; ed A. B. Grosart vol 2, Edinburgh 1862.

Alsted, J. H. See Daniel, below.

Sandys, G. A paraphrase upon the Song of Solomon. 1641, 1642. In verse.

Cotton, J. A briefe exposition of the whole book of Canticles. 1642, 1648; A brief exposition with practical observations upon the whole book of Canticles, ed A. Tuckney 1655, Edinburgh 1868 (with Cotton's Ecclesiastes and Muffett's Proverbs) (Nichol's Commentaries) (a different work).

Brightman, T. A commentary on the Canticles. 1644; in his Workes, 1644.

Robotham, J. An exposition on the whole book of Solomons Song. 1651, 1652.

Homes, N. A commentary literal or historical, and mystical or spiritual, on the whole book of Canticles. In his Works, 1652.

Slater, S. Epithalamium: or Solomons Song, digested into meeter. 1653. With the Authorized version in the margin.

The Song of Solomon in meeter, as Psalm 25. 1653. With the Authorized version in the margin.

Spirituall hymnes by way of paraphrase upon the whole book of Canticles. In The disciples of gathered churches, 1654.

Knollys, H. An exposition of the first chapter of the Song of Solomon. 1656.

Guild, W. Love's entercours between the lamb and his bride, Christ and his Church: or a clear explication and application of the Song of Solomon. 1657–8.

Isaiah

Calvin, J. A commentary upon the prophecie of Isaiah, translated out of French by C. C[otton]. 1609. From Commentaires sur le prophète Isaie, ed and tr from the Latin by N. des Gallars, Geneva 1552, 1572; Commentarii in Isaiam prophetam, Geneva 1551, 1559, 1570, 1583, 1617; in his Opera vol 5, Amsterdam 1667, vol 36 Brunswick 1888; tr W. Pringle 4 vols Edinburgh 1850–3 (Calvin Trn Soc), Grand Rapids 1948.

Rogers, N. A strange vineyard in Palæstina: in an exposition of Isaiahs parabolical song of the Beloved, discovered. 1623, 1632 (as The wild vine). On Isaiah v. 1–7.

Barford, J. Paraphrastical meditations upon Isaiah 55. 1649.

Day, W. An exposition of the book of the prophet Isaiah. 1654.

Aspinall, W. Thunder from heaven against backsliders and apostates of the times, in some meditations on the 24 chapter of Isaiah. 1655.

The prophets Malachy and Isaiah prophecying to the saints and professors of this generation, by a wel-wisher to the kingdome of our Lord Jesus. 1656.

Jeremiah

Calvin, J. Two and twenty lectures upon the five first chapters of Jeremiah [tr from the French by C. Cotton]. 1620. From Leçons ou commentaires et expositions, tant sur les Revelations que sur les Lamentations du prophéte Jérémie, tr Lyons 1565; Prælectiones in librum prophetiarum Heremiæ, et Lamentationes, ed J. Budé and C. Jonville, Geneva 1563, 1576, 1589; in his Opera vol 6, Amsterdam 1667, vols 37–9 Brunswick 1888–9; Commentaries on the book of the prophet Jeremiah and the Lamentations, tr J. Owen 5 vols Edinburgh 1850–5 (Calvin Trn Soc), Grand Rapids 1950.

Lamentations

Drant, T. The waylings of the prophet Hieremiah, done into English verse. In A medicinable morall: that is, the two bookes of Horace his satyres englyshed, 1566.

Fetherstone, C. Lamentations in prose and meter, with apt notes. 1587.

Adamson, P. (d. 1592). Paraphrasis poetica Jobi, Threnorum Jeremiæ. In his Poemata sacra, ed T.Wilson 1619; in W. Lauder (ed), Poetarum scotorum musæ sacræ vol 2, Edinburgh 1739, 1740.

[Udall, J.] A commentarie upon the Lamentations of Jeremy. 1593, 1595, 1599, 1608, 1637.

Broughton, H. The Lamentations of Jeremy, translated with explications. [Amsterdam?] 1606, 1608; in his Works, ed J. Lightfoot 4 vols 1662.

D[od], J., and R. C[leaver]. Two sermons on the third of the Lamentations of Jeremie. 1608, 1610, 1618.

Meditations upon the Lamentations of Jeremy, translated out of French by A. J[enkinson]. 1609.

Hull, J. An exposition upon a part of the Lamentations of Jeremie. 1618 (on i.1–6); Lectures upon the Lamentations of Jeremiah, 1620.

Quarles, F. Sions elegies, wept by Jeremie the prophet and periphras'd [in verse]. 1624–5; in his Divine poems 1630, 1633.

The Lamentations of the prophet Jeremiah paraphras'd, suitable to the exigencies of these times. 1647. Royalist.

Quarles, J. The Lamentations of Jeremiah. In his Fons lachrymarum, 1648, 1649, 1655, 1677.

Taylor, F. [Hebrew] sive Jeremiæ vatis lamentationes. 1651.

The Lamentations of Jeremiah in meeter. 1652.

Swift, D. Zion's sufferings: an exposition of Lamentations v. 1654.

Ezekiel

Greenhill, W. Exposition of the prophecy of Ezekiel. 5 vols 1645–62: chs 1–5, 1645, [1649], 1650; 6–13, 1649; 14–19, 1651; 20–9, 1658; 30–48, 1662; ed J. Shearman 1839; Edinburgh 1863 (Nichol's Commentaries).

Daniel

Joye, G. The exposicion of Daniel the prophete, gathered oute of Philip Melanchton, Johan Ecolampadius, Chonrade Pellicane and out of Iohan Draconite etc. 'Geneva' (for Antwerp) 1545, London 1550, 1550.

Calvin, J. Commentaries upon the prophet Daniell. Tr A. G[olding] 1570. From Prælectiones in librum prophetiarum Danielis, ed J. Budé and C. Jonville, Geneva 1561, Lyons 1571, Geneva 1591, La Rochelle 1609; in his Opera vol 8, Amsterdam 1667, vols 41–2 Brunswick 1890; Leçons sur le livre des prophéties de Daniel, Geneva 1562 (tr from Latin); Quarante sept sermons sur les huict derniers chapitres de Daniel, La Rochelle 1565; Commentaries on the book of the prophet Daniel, tr T. Myers 2 vols Edinburgh 1852–3 (Calvin Trn Soc), Grand Rapids 1948, London 1966.

Rollock, R. In librum Danielis prophetæ commentarius. Edinburgh 1591, Heidelberg 1594, Geneva 1598, 1610.

[Broughton, H.] Daniel his Chaldic visions and his Ebrew: both translated and expounded. 1596, 1597; Daniel, with a briefe explication, Hanau 1607; tr Latin by J. Boreel, Basle 1599; in his Works, ed J. Lightfoot 4 vols 1662.

Willet, A. Hexapla in Danielem: that is, a six-fold commentarie. 1610.

Alsted, J. H. The beloved city: or the saints reign on earth a thousand years. 1643. From Diatribe de mille annis apocalypticis Danielis & Iohannis, Frankfurt 1627,

London 1627, Frankfurt 1630; tr German by S. Francke, 1630.

— Trifolium propheticum, id est Canticum canticorum Salomonis, Prophetia Danielis, Apocalypsis Johannis, explicata. Herborn Nassau 1640; The worlds proceeding woes and succeeding joyes, or the triple presage, 1642.

Huit, E. The whole prophecie of Daniel explained, by a paraphrase, analysis and briefe comment. 1643, 1644.

Brightman, T. A most comfortable exposition of the last and most difficult part of the prophecie of Daniel. In his Workes, 1644. With the text of xi. 26–xii. 13.

Parker, T. The visions and prophecies of Daniel expounded. 1646.

Clavis apocalyptica: or a prophetical key, by which the great mysteries in the Revelation of St John, and the prophet Daniel, are opened. Tr S. Hartlib 1651.

Tillinghast, J. Generation-work: [pt 2] an exposition of Rev. 16; [pt 3] an exposition of the 11, 12, and 14 chapters of the Revelations; to which is added A key to unlock the mysticall numbers of Daniel and the Revelations. Pt 2, 1654, 1655; pt 3, 1655.

More, J. A trumpet sounded, or the great mystery of the two little horns unfolded: being as a candle set up in the dark lanthorn of Daniel. 1654.

Minor Prophets

Lively, E. Annotations in quinq; priores ex minoribus prophetis. 1587; in J. Pearson (ed), Critici sacri vol 4, 1660, Amsterdam 1698.

Daneau (Danaeus), L. A fruitfull commentarie upon the twelve small prophets. Tr J. Stockwood, Cambridge 1594. From Commentarius in Joelem, Amos, Micham, Habacuc, Sophoniam, Haggæum, Zachariam et Malachiam, Geneva 1578; Commentariorum in prophetas minores tomus primus (secundus), 2 vols Geneva 1586, 1594.

Trapp, J. A commentary: or exposition upon the xii minor prophets. 1654.

Hutcheson, G. A briefe exposition of the xii small prophets. 3 vols 1654–5, 1 vol 1657.

Stokes, D. A paraphrasticall explication of the twelve minor prophets. 1659.

Hosea

Downame, J. Lectures upon the foure first chapters of Hosea. 1608.

Smith, S. An exposition upon the sixt chapter of the prophesie of Hosea. 1616.

Sibbes, R. The returning backslider: or a commentary upon the whole xiiii chapter of the prophecy of the prophet Hosea. 1638–9, 1641, 1650; in his Works, ed A. B. Grosart vol 2, Edinburgh 1862 (Nichol's Standard divines).

Burroughs, J. An exposition of the prophecie of Hosea. 4 vols 1643–51 etc: chs 1–3, 1643, 1652; 4–7, 1650; 8–10, 1650; (4–10, 1650); 11–13, 1651; (8–13, 1654); completed with ch 14 by T. Hall and E. Reynolds 1837; ed J. Sherman 1843, Edinburgh 1863, 1865 (Nichol's Commentaries).

Reynolds, E. Israels petition in time of trouble: a sermon. 1642, '1649' (for 1645) (as The first sermon upon Hosea, chap. 14, vers. 1, 2); in Israel's prayer in time of trouble: or an explication of the 14th chapt. of the prophet Hosea, in seven sermons, 1645, 1649, 1658, 1831, 1846; in his Works 1658, 2 vols 1678–9, [ed J. R. Pitman] 6 vols 1826 (vol 3); Select works, 1824 (Bradley's Select British divines 28); Select meditations: being portions from sermons upon Hosea, ed C. Smalley 1838

Joel

Walther (Gualtherus), R. The homilies or familiar sermons upon the prophet Joel, translated from Latine by J. Ludham. 1582. From In prophetas duodecim, quos vocant minores, homiliae, Zürich 1563, 1566, 1572, 1577, 1582, 1592.

Udall, J. The true remedie against famine and warres: five sermons upon the first chapter of the prophesie of Joel. 1586.

Bunny, E. A necessarie admonition out of the prophet Joel. 1588 (Lambeth Palace Lib only).

Topsell, E. Times lamentation: or an exposition on the prophet Joel. 1599, 1613.

Amos

Benefield, S. A commentary or exposition upon the first chapter of the prophecy of Amos, delivered in xxi sermons. Oxford 1613, London 1629; tr Latin, Oppenheim 1615; A commentarie or exposition upon the second chapter of the prophecie of Amos, in twenty-one sermons, 1620; A commentary or exposition upon the third chapter of the prophecie of Amos, in seventeen sermons, 1628, 1629; 1629 (the 3 together as A commentary upon the three first chapters of Amos).

Hall, T. An exposition, by way of supplement [to Benefield], on the fourth, fifth, sixth, seventh, eighth and ninth chapters of Amos. 1661.

Obadiah

Pilkington, J. An exposition upon Abdyas. [1562]; Aggeus and Abdias prophetes, both at large declared, 1562; in his Works, ed J. Scholefield, Cambridge 1842 (Parker Soc).

Walther (Gualtherus), R. Certaine godlie homilies or sermons upon the prophets Abdias and Jonas: conteyning a most fruitfull exposition. Tr R. Norton 1573. From In prophetas duodecim, quos vocant minores, homiliae, Zürich 1563, 1566, 1572, 1577, 1582, 1592.

Rainolds, J. A sermon upon part of the prophecie of Obadiah. 1584; The prophecie of Obadiah opened and applyed in sundry sermons, ed W. Hinds, Oxford 1613; Edinburgh 1864 (with Rainolds's Haggai and King's Jonah) (Nichol's Commentaries).

Ellis, J. Bellum in Idumæos: seu propheta Obadias commentario illustratus. 1641.

The dammee cavalliers warning piece, in a view on the prophecy of the prophet Obadiah. 1643.

Marbury, E. A brief commentarie or exposition upon Obadiah. 1649[-50]; Edinburgh 1865 (with Marbury's Habakkuk) (Nichol's Commentaries).

Hutcheson, G. A brief exposition of the prophecies of Obadiah. 1654, 1654.

Jonah

Hooper, J. An oversight and deliberacion upon the holy prophete Jonas. 1550, [1560].

Brenz (Brentius), J. Newes from Ninive to Englande, brought by the prophete Jonas: plainly published in the godly and learned exposition, translated out of Latine by T. Tymme. 1570. From Explicationes Ionæ prophetæ, Frankfurt 1566; in his Opera vol 4, Tübingen 1580.

Walther, R. See under Obadiah, above.

Calvin, J. The lectures or daily sermons upon the prophet Jonas. Tr N. B[axter]. 1578, 1580. From Prælectiones in duodecim prophetas, quas vocant, minores, Geneva 1559, 1567, 1581, 1610; Leçons et expositions familières sur les douze petis prophètes, traduites en françois, 1560, Lyons 1563, Geneva 1565; in his Opera vols 42–4 Brunswick 1890; Commentaries on the twelve minor prophets tr J. Owen 5 vols Edinburgh 1846–9 (Calvin Trn Soc), Grand Rapids 1950. 2 distinct commentaries.

King, J. Lectures upon Jonas, delivered in 1594. Oxford 1597, 1599, 1600, London 1611, 1611, 1618; Edinburgh 1864 (with Rainolds on Obadiah and Haggai) (Nichol's Commentaries).

Abbot, G. An exposition upon the prophet Jonah. 1600, 1613; ed G. Webster 2 vols 1845; Edinburgh 1847.

Quarles, F. A feast for wormes, set forth in a poeme of the history of Jonah. 1620, 1626; in his Divine poems, 1630

etc; Complete works, ed A. B. Grosart 3 vols 1880–1. A paraphrase.

Fuller, T. Notes upon Jonah. In his A collection of sermons, 1656–7; ed W. Nichols, Edinburgh 1868 (with Fuller's Ruth) (Nichol's Commentaries).

Micah

Gilby, A. A commentarye upon the prophet Mycha. 1551.

Habakkuk

Marbury, E. A commentarie or exposition upon the prophecie of Habakkuk. 1643, 1650, 1652; Edinburgh 1865 (with Marbury's Obadiah) (Nichol's Commentaries).

[Stokes, D.] A paraphrasticall explication of the prophecie of Habakkuk. Oxford 1646.

Zephaniah

Walther (Gualtherus), R. The sermons upon the prophet Zephaniah. Tr M. Wilton 1580. From In prophetas duodecim, quos vocant minores, homiliae, Zürich 1563, 1566, 1572, 1577, 1582, 1592.

Perkins, W. Exhortation to repentance out of Zephaniah. 1605 (Cambridge Univ Lib); as A faithfull and plaine exposition upon the two first verses of the second chapter of Zephaniah, 1606 (3rd impression), 1609; in his Works 3 vols 1608–9, 1612–13, 1616–18, 1626, 1631, 1635 (vol 3).

Haggai

[Pilkington, J.] Aggeus the prophete declared by a large commentarye. 1560; Aggeus and Abdias prophetes, both at large declared, 1562; in his Works, ed J. Scholefield, Cambridge 1842 (Parker Soc).

Grynaeus, J. J. Haggeus, the prophet, where-unto is added a most plentifull commentary, gathered out of the publique lectures, translated out of Latin by C. Fetherstone. 1586. From Haggæus propheta, in quem accessit commentarius ex Grynæi prælectionibus collectus, Geneva 1581.

Rainolds, J. The prophesie of Haggai interpreted and applyed in sundry sermons. [Ed W. Hinde and E. Leigh] 1649 (for 1648); Edinburgh 1864 (with Rainolds's Obadiah and King's Jonah) (Nichol's Commentaries).

Hutcheson, G. A brief exposition of the prophecies of Haggai. 1654.

Zechariah

Pemble, W. A short and sweete exposition upon the first nine chapters of Zachary. [Ed R. Capel] 1629; in his Workes, 1635 ('3rd', i.e. first edn), Oxford 1658 ('4th', i.e. 2nd edn).

Malachi

Stock, R. A learned and very usefull commentary upon the whole prophesie of Malachy; whereunto is added an exercitation upon the same prophesie of Malachy, by S. Torshel. 2 pts 1641; Edinburgh 1865 (Nichol's Commentaries).

Sclater, W. A brief and plain commentary upon the whole prophecie of Malachy. 1650.

The prophets Malachy and Isaiah prophecying to the saints and professors of this generation, by a wel-wisher to the kingdome of our Lord Jesus. 1656.

Apocrypha

Broughton, H. Principall positions for groundes of the holy Bible, positions historique; and of the Apocrypha, Tobit particularly handled, Judith severally handled. 1609; in his Works, ed J. Lightfoot 4 vols 1662.

Rainolds, J. Censura librorum Apocryphorum Veteris testamenti. Oppenheim 1611.

Esdras

A pretie new enterlude both pithie and pleasant of the story of Kyng Daryus: beinge taken out of the third and fourth chapter of the thyrd booke of Esdras. 1565, 1577, 1860, 1906.

L., T. Babylon is fallen: or a prophesie that had lain hid above two thousand years. 1597, 1610 (as A prophesie that hath lyen hid), 1614; Babilon is fallen, 1620, 1651 (Babylon); in A voyce out of the wildernes crying = Πολυπενθεος θρηνῳδια, the mourners song, 1651. On II Esdras xi; apparently from a German or Latin original pbd 1595.

Tobit

Touchet (later Davies, later Douglas), Lady E. Tobit's book. 1652.

Wisdom

Holkot, R. Opus super Sapientiam Salomonis. [Cologne c. 1479], [no place] 1480, Speyer 1483, [Paris] 1489 (as Super librum sapientie), Basle 1489, Reutlingen 1489, Hagenau 1494, Venice 1500 (as Praelectiones CCXII in librum sapientiae), Basle 1506, Venice 1509, Paris 1511, 1518, [Basle] 1586.

Middleton, T. The Wisdom of Solomon paraphrased. 1596, 1597.

Ecclesiasticus

Holkot, R. Expositio super septem priora capita libri Ecclesiastici. Venice 1509.

New Testament

Extensive notes are included in the edns of the Rheims New testament (Roman Catholic, 1582 etc) and W. Fulke, Confutations thereof, 1589.

The epistles and gospelles, with a brief postil upon the same. (Postilles or homilies upon the epistles and gospels). Ed R. Taverner 1540. Great Bible version.

Erasmus, D. The first (seconde) tome or volume of the paraphrase upon the Newe testament. 2 vols 1548–9, 1551–2. Great Bible text: from Paraphrasis in Novum testamentum, Basle 1524 (Gospels and Acts only), 2 vols 1540 (complete), Paris 1540, Basle 1541, 1556, 1557; ed J. Clericus and J. F. S. Augustin 3 vols Berlin 1778–80; in his Opera omnia vol 7, Basle 1540; ed J. Clericus vol 7, Leyden 1706. The Latin paraphrases on many separate books also pbd individually. *See* H. J. Cowell, The four chained books (including Erasmus's Paraphrases), 1938.

Calvin, J. Commentaire sur le Nouveau testament. Geneva 1561, 4 vols Paris 1854–5; ed J. Foltz 4 vols Toulouse 1891–4; In Novum testamentum commentarii, ed A. Tholuck 7 vols Berlin 1833–4, 2 vols Brunswick 1891–2; Calvin's Commentaries [tr], ed D. W. and T. F. Torrance, Edinburgh 1959–. English trns of individual books are listed separately below. *See* T. H. L. Parker, Calvin's New testament commentaries, 1971.

Becon, T. A new postil conteinyng most godly and learned sermons upon all the Sonday Gospelles. 2 pts 1566. Great Bible version.

Bridges, J. Sacro-sanctum Novum testamentum in hexametros versus translatum. 1604.

Bois, J. An exposition of the dominical epistles and gospels in our English liturgie. 1610, 1611–13, 1615–16, 1638; An exposition of the festivall epistles and gospels, 1613, 1614–15; both in his Workes, 1622, 1629, 1638; Veteris interpretis cum Beza aliisque recentioribus collatio in quatuor Evangeliis & Apostolorum Actis, 1655.

Mayer, J. A commentarie upon the New testament. 3 vols 1631. Vol 1 (first edn as A treasury of ecclesiasticall expositions, upon the difficult and doubtful places of the scriptures, throughout the Gospels and the Acts of the Apostles, 1622), A commentary upon the foure evangelists and the Acts of the apostles; 2, A commentarie upon all the Epistles of the Apostle Paul; 3 (first edn as Ecclesiastica interpretatio: or the exposi-

tions upon the difficult and doubtfull passages of the seven epistles called Catholike, and the Revelation, 1627), A commentarie upon the seven smaller Epistles, called Catholike, and the booke of the Revelation. Also forming vols 5–7 of Mayer's commentary on the Bible, above.

Trapp, J. A commentary or exposition upon the four evangelists and the Acts of the apostles. 3 pts 1646–7; A commentary or exposition upon all the epistles, and the Revelation, 2 pts 1647; 1656 (2nd edn as A commentary or exposition upon all the books of the New testament) (also forming vol 5 of Trapp's commentary on the Bible, above); A commentary on the New testament, ed W. Webster 1865.

Leigh, E. Annotations upon all the New testament, philologicall and theologicall. 1650; In universum Novum testamentum annotationes, tr T. Arnoldi, Leipzig 1732. Commonly associated with Richardson's Old testament, 1655.

Hammond, H. A paraphrase, and annotations upon all the books of the New testament. 1653, 1659, 1671, 1675 (as Workes, ed W. Fulman 4 vols 1674–84 vol 3), 1681, 1689, 1702, 4 vols Oxford 1845; tr Latin, 1699, 1714; Dutch, 17 vols 1740–7. *See* J. Le Clerc, A supplement to Dr Hammond's Paraphrase and annotations on the New testament, 1699.

Lightfoot, J. Horæ hebraicæ et talmudicæ. 6 vols 1658–78: Matthew, Cambridge 1658; Mark, 1663; Luke, Cambridge and London 1674, 1674; John, 1671; I Corinthians, Cambridge 1664, Paris 1677, Amsterdam 1677, ed J. B. Carpzov, Leipzig 1679; Acts and part of Romans, ed R. Kidder 1678, Paris 1679; Acts, Rom., I Cor., ed Carpzov, Leipzig 1679; Gospels, ed Carpzov 1675, 1684; Gospels, Acts, Rom., I Cor., ed R. Gandell 4 vols Oxford 1859; completed for the New testament in C. Schöttgen, Horæ hebraicæ et talmudicæ in Novum testamentum, quibus horæ J. Lightfooti supplentur, 2 vols Dresden 1733–42; in Works, ed and tr G. Bright and J. Strype 2 vols 1684, ed J. R. Pitman 13 vols 1822–5 (vols 8, 11–12); ed J. Leusden 2 vols Rotterdam 1686 (in Latin), 3 vols Frankfurt 1699.

Knatchbull, Sir N. Animadversiones in libros Novi testamenti paradoxæ orthodoxæ. 1659, 1672, Oxford 1676, 1677; in J. Doughty (ed), Analecta sacra, Amsterdam 1694; in N. Gürtler (ed), Supplementum [to J. Pearson's Critici sacri] 2 vols Frankfurt 1700–1; tr as Annotations upon some difficult texts in all the books of the New testament, Cambridge 1693.

Price, J. Commentarii in varios Novi testamenti libros. 1660; in J. Pearson (ed), Critici sacri vol 5, 1660, Amsterdam 1698.

Gospels

Bullinger, H. The summe of the four evangelistes comprehending both the course of the historie, and also the severall points of doctrine set foorth in the same. Tr J. Tomkys 1582. Trn of ch summaries of Bullinger's commentaries on the 4 gospels, pbd in In sacrosanctum evangelium secundum Matthæum (Marcum, Lucam, Ioannem) commentariorum libri: Matthew, Zürich 1542, 1554; Mark, 1545, 1554; Luke, 1546, 1548, 1557; John, 1543, 1548, 1556.

Rollock, R. Lectures upon the history of the passion, resurrection and ascension of our Lord Jesus Christ. Edinburgh 1616; in his Select works vol 2, ed W. M. Gunn 1849. On John xviii.1–xxi.25 and the parallel passages in other 3 gospels.

Stapleton, T. Promptuarium morale super evangelia dominicalia totius anni, pars hyemalis. Antwerp 1591, 1593, Paris 1602, 1606, Antwerp 1613, Cologne 1615, Paris 1617, Cologne 1620, Paris 1627; pars æstivalis, Antwerp 1591, 1593, Venice 1593, 1594, Paris 1606, Mainz 1610, Antwerp 1613, Cologne 1620, Paris 1627; Promptuarium catholicum in evangelia dominicalia totius anni, Cologne 1592, 1602, Paris 1606, 1617,

Cologne 1624; Promptuarium catholicum in evangelia ferialia totius quadragesimae, Cologne 1594, Paris 1606, 1615, Cologne 1624; Promptuarium catholicum in evangelia festorum totius anni, Cologne 1592, 1594, Antwerp 1608; all in his Opera vol 4, Paris 1620.

—— Antidota evangelica contra horum temporum haereses, in quibus quatuor evangeliorum illi textus explicantur, quibus haeretici hodie (maxime Calvinus et Beza) uti solent. Lyons 1595, Antwerp 1595; in his Opera vol 3, Paris 1620.

Cartwright, T. Commentaria practica in totam historiam evangelicam, ex quatuor evangelistis harmonice concinnatam. 3 vols [Leyden?] 1630; incorporated in Harmonia evangelica, Amsterdam and Leyden 1647.

Boyd, Z. (d. 1653). The four evangels: a paraphrase in verse. Unpbd; ms in Glasgow Univ Lib.

Matthew

[Tindale, W.] An exposicion uppon the v, vi, vii chapters of Mathew. [Antwerp 1530?], [London 1530?], London 1548, [1550?]; in his Whole workes 2 vols 1572-3; in T. Russell (ed), Works of the English and Scottish reformers vol 2, 1829; in his Expositions and notes on sundry portions of the holy scriptures, ed H. Walter, Cambridge 1849 (Parker Soc); in The work of Tyndale, ed G. E. Duffield, Appleford 1964; extracts in L. Richmond (ed), Father of the English church vol 1, 1807.

Marlorat, A. A catholike and ecclesiasticall exposition of the holy Gospell after S. Mathewe, translated out of Latine by T. Tymme. 1570. From Novi testamenti catholica expositio ecclesiastica, 2 vols [Geneva] 1561, 1564, 1570, 1585, 1593, Heidelberg 1605; Le Nouveau testament, avec annotations par A. Marlorat, Geneva and Lyons 1563, Paris 1567; tr Dutch (from French), [Emden?] 1567, 1568, Leyden 1579, Delft 1598.

Trigge, F. Analysis capitis vicesimi quarti evangelii secundum Matthæum. Oxford 1591.

Philips, E. Certaine godly and learned sermons. 1605, 1607. 15 sermons on Matthew 1-4 etc.

Perkins, W. A godly and learned exposition of Christ's Sermon in the Mount. Cambridge 1608, 1611; in his Works, 1608-35. On chs 5-7.

Sympson, W. A full and profitable interpretation of all the proper names within the genealogie of Jesus Christ, as set forth in the first chapter of S. Matthewe. Cambridge 1619.

James VI and I. A meditation upon the 27, 28, 29 verses of the xxvii chapter of S. Matthew. 1620; in his Workes, ed J. Montagu '1616' (for 1620) (2nd edn); Meditatio in cap. xxvii Evangelii S. Matth. 27, 28, 29, 1620; in his Opera, ed J. Montagu, '1619' [1620?], Frankfurt 1689.

Ward, R. Theologicall questions, dogmaticall observations and evangelicall esays, upon the gospel of Jesus Christ according to St Matthew. 1640.

Price, J. Matthæus ex sacra pagina, sanctis patribus, illustratus. Paris 1646; in Commentarii in varios Novi testamenti libros, 1660, and in J. Pearson (ed), Critici sacri vol 5, 1660, Amsterdam 1698.

Dickson, D. A brief exposition of the evangel of Jesus Christ according to Matthew. Ptd Glasgow, pbd Edinburgh 1647, London 1647, 1651.

White, T. Πανθεολογία: or the summe of practical divinity practiz'd in the wilderness: being observations upon the fourth, fifth, sixth and seventh chapters of St Matthew. 1653-4.

Blackwood, C. Exposition and sermons upon the ten first chapters of the gospel according to Matthew. 1659.

Burroughs, J. Four books on the eleventh of Matthew. 1659; The second (third and fourth) book on Matth. 11. 29, 1659.

Penington, I. An exposition on Christs sermon, as it is related in the fifth, sixth and seventh chapters of Matthews Gospel. In his Expositions, with observations sometimes, on severall scriptures pt 1, 1656.

Mark

Marlorat, A. A catholike and ecclesiasticall exposition of the holy gospel after S. Marke and Luke, translated out of Latine by T. Timme. 2 pts 1583. Latin original 1561, etc; see Matthew, above.

Petter, G. A learned, pious and practical commentary upon the gospel according to St Mark. 1641, 2 vols 1661.

Luke

Marlorat, A. 1583. See Mark, above.

Benefield, S. Eight sermons publikely preached in the university of Oxford on Luke and James. Oxford 1614.

John

Luther, M. A ryght notable sermon upon the twentieth chapter of Johan. [Tr R. Argentine], Ipswich 1548.

Brenz (Brentius), J. A verye fruitful exposicion upon the syxte chapter of Saynte John, divided into x homelies or sermons. Tr R. Shirrye 1550. Extracted from Evangelion quod inscribitur, secundum Ioannem, usque ad historiam de Lazaro [chs 1-11] octuaginta duobus homiliis explicatum, Schwäbisch Hall 1545, Frankfurt 1549; Evangelii secundum Ioannem undecim posteriora capita [chs 11-21] sexaginta nouem homiliis explicata, Schwäbisch Hall 1548, septuaginta duobus homiliis, Frankfurt 1549; [chs 1-21] Centum quinquaginta quatuor homiliis 2 vols 1551, 1554, 1559, 1569, 1570; in his Opera vol 6, Tübingen 1584.

—— In D. Iohannis evangelium exegesis. Hagenau 1527, 1528, 1529, 1530, 1532, 1534, Frankfurt 1542, Schwäbisch Hall 1543; in his Opera vol 6, Tübingen 1584; tr German by H. Gast, Hagenau 1539.

Traheron, B. An exposition of a part of S. Johannes gospel made in sondrie readings in the English congregation. [Wesel?] 1557, 1558.

Marlorat, A. A catholike and ecclesiasticall exposition of the holy gospell after S. John, translated out of Latin by T. Tymme. 1575. Latin original 1561 etc; see Matthew, above.

Calvin, J. The holy gospel of Iesus Christ, according to John, with the commentary, translated out of Latine by C. Fetherstone. Pt 2 of A harmonie upon the three evangelists, tr E. P[agit] 1584, 1610. From In euangelium secundum Iohannem commentarius, [Geneva] 1553; Commentaire sur l'evangile selon sainct Jen, 1553; in Opera vol 47, Brunswick 1892; Commentary on the gospel according to St John, tr W. Pringle 2 vols Edinburgh 1846-7 (Calvin Trn Soc), Grand Rapids 1949; Pringle's trn rev T. H. L. Parker 2 vols Edinburgh 1959-61.

Rollock, R. In evangelium secundum S. Iohannem commentarius. Geneva 1599, 1608.

—— Five-and-twentie lectures, upon the last sermon of Jesus Christ with his disciples [John 14-17]. Edinburgh 1619.

Willet, A. Thesaurus ecclesie, set forth in the 17 chapter of the Gospel of S. John. Cambridge 1604.

Dyke, D. Six evangelical histories contained in the 2d, 3d and 4th chapters of St John's gospel, opened and handled. 1617; in his Workes 2 pts 1633-5.

Hildersam, A. Lectures upon the fourth of John. 1629, 1632 (as CVIII lectures), 1647, 1656.

[Gouge, W.] An exposition of the whole fifth chapter of S. Johns gospell. Ed W. Pemble 2 pts 1630, 1631 (pt 1). Pt 2 is on Ephesians v. 22-4, vi. 4, 5, 9-15.

Trapp, J. A brief commentary or exposition upon the Gospel according to St John. 1646; also as part of Trapp's commentary on the New testament, above.

Burgesse, A. CXLV sermons upon the 17th chapter of John. 1656.

Hutcheson, G. An exposition of the gospel of Jesus Christ according to John. 1657, 1841.

Newton, G. An exposition with notes on the 17th chapter
of John. 1660; Edinburgh 1867 (Nichol's Commentaries).

Acts

Tye, C. The Actes of the apostles, translated into English
metre. 1553. With music.
Walther (Gualtherus), R. An hundred, threescore and
fiftene homeleyes or sermons uppon the Actes of the
apostles. Tr J. Bridges 1572. From In Acta apostolorum per divum Lucam descripta, homiliæ clxxv,
Zürich 1557, Lyons 1562, Zürich 1562, 1569, 1586.
Calvin, J. The commentaries upon the Actes of the apostles,
translated out of Latine by C. Fetherstone. 1585; rev
H. Beveridge 2 vols Edinburgh 1843 (Calvin Trn Soc).
From Commentariorum in Acta apostolorum liber prior,
Geneva 1552, 1560; liber posterior, 1554; libri duo,
1554, 1560–1, 1563, 1564, 1573, 1584, 1609; ed A.
Tholuck, Berlin 1833; Commentaires sur les Actes des
apostres, 2 vols Geneva 1552–4, 1562, Paris 1854; in
Opera vol 48, Brunswick 1892; Commentary upon the
Acts of the apostles, Grand Rapids 1949; tr J. W. Fraser
and W. J. G. McDonald 2 vols Edinburgh 1965–6;
tr Dutch by J. Florianus, ed G. Wielenga 2 vols Kampen
1899–1900.
Stapleton, T. Antidota apostolica contra nostri temporis
hæreses. In Acta apostolorum to[mus] primus. Antwerp 1591, 1595, Lyons 1596; in his Opera vol 3, Paris
1620.
Malcolm, J. Commentarius in apostolorum Acta. Middelburg 1615.
Lightfoot, J. A commentary upon the first twelve chapters
of the Acts of the apostles. 1645; in his Works 2 vols
1684, Whole works vol 8, ed J. R. Pitman 1825.
Price, J. Acta apostolorum ex sacra pagina, sanctis patribus
græcisque ac latinis gentium scriptoribus illustrata.
Paris 1647; in Commentarii in varios Novi testamenti
libros, 1660, and in J. Pearson (ed), Critici sacri vol 5,
1660, Amsterdam 1698.

Epistles

Calvin, J. Commentarii in quatuor Pauli epistolas, ad
Galatas, ad Ephesios, ad Philippenses, ad Colossenses.
Geneva 1548; Commentarii in epistolas canonicas, 1551,
1554, 1558; Commentarii in omnes Pauli apostoli
epistolas, atque etiam in epistolam ad Hebraeos, 1551,
1556, 1557, ed A. Tholuck, Halle 1831; Commentarii
in omnes Pauli apostoli epistolas, atque in epistolam ad
Hebraeos, item in canonicas 2 pts Geneva 1556, 1557,
1565, [1572?], 1579, 1580, 1600, 1617; Commentarii
in epistolas catholicas, Geneva 1551 (Latin and French,)
ed A. Tholuck, Halle 1832; Commentarii in omnes
Novi testamenti epistolas, ed A. Tholuck, Halle and
Berlin 1834; Commentaires sur quatre épistres de S.
Paul, Geneva 1548; Commentaires sur les épistres
canoniques, [Geneva] 1556, 1560, 1562; Commentaires
sur les épistres de S. Paul et les épistres canoniques,
Lyons 1563; Commentaires sur les épistres de l'apostre
St Paul, et aussi sur l'épistre aux Hébreux, item sur les
épistres canoniques, Geneva 1557, 1560, 1561, 1562,
1565, 1572, 1580, 1600, 1617; Uitleginge over de brieven
von Paulus, Amsterdam 1616; Uitleginge op alle send-
briefe der apostelen, 1617; in Opera vols 49–55, Brunswick 1892–6; Commentaries on the catholic epistles,
tr J. Owen, Edinburgh 1855 (Calvin Trn Soc), Grand
Rapids 1948.
Rollock, R. Certaine sermons upon severall places of the
epistles of Paul. Edinburgh 1599.
Dickson, D. Expositio analytica omnium apostolicarum
epistolarum. Glasgow 1645, 1647; An exposition of all
St Pauls epistles, 1659.
Dale, J. The analysis of all the epistles of the New testament. Oxford 1652, 1657.

Romans

Colet, J. Enarratio in epistolam S. Pauli ad Romanos: an
exposition of St Paul's epistle to the Romans [c. 1497];
ed and tr J. H. Lupton 1873, Ridgewood NJ 1965;
Epistolæ B. Pauli ad Romanos expositio; exposition of
St Paul's epistle to the Romans, in Opuscula quædam
theologica, ed J. H. Lupton 1876, Ridgewood NJ 1966.
See C. A. L. Jarrott, On Corpus ms 355, Colet in
Romanos et in Genesim, Trans Cambridge Bibl Soc 5
1970.
Tindale, W. A compendious introduction unto the pistle
to the Romayns. [Worms 1520].
Sampson, R. In D. Pauli epistolam ad Romanos, atque in
priorem ad Corinthios explanatio. 1546.
Hooper, J. Godly and most necessary annotations in the
xiij chapyter to the Romaynes. Worcester 1551; in
his Later writings, ed C. Nevinson, Cambridge 1852
(Parker Soc).
Vermigli, P. M. (Peter Martyr). Most learned and fruitfull
commentaries upon the epistle of S. Paul to the Romanes.
Tr H. Billingsley 1568. From In epistolam S. Pauli ad
Romanos commentarii doctissimi, Basle 1558, 1560,
1570, Heidelberg 1612.
Corro, A. del. A theological dialogue, wherin the epistle
of S. Paul to the Romanes is expounded. 1575. From
Dialogus theologicus, quo epistola D. Pauli apostoli ad
Romanos explanatur, 1574, 1581.
Calvin, J. A commentarie upon the epistle of Saint Paul
to the Romanes, translated out of Latine by C. Rosdell.
1583; ed H. Beveridge, Edinburgh 1844 (Calvin Trn
Soc). From Commentarii in epistolam Pauli ad Romanos,
Strasbourg 1540, Halle 1831, Berlin 1834, 1864; for
further Latin edns, 1551 etc, see above; Commentaire
sur l'épistre aux Romains, Geneva 1550; tr J. Gibson,
London 1834, Philadelphia 1836; tr J. Owen, Edinburgh
1849 (Calvin Trn Soc), Grand Rapids 1948; tr R.
Mackenzie, Edinburgh 1960 (with Thessalonians); tr
German, Frankfurt 1837, Neukirchen 1961–2 (with
Corinthians).
Wilcox, T. A Christian exposition upon Romans. 1587
(Folger Lib only).
Luther, M. A methodicall preface before the epistle to the
Romanes. Tr W.W. [1590–4?], 1632. From Vorrede
auf die Epistel S. Pauli an die Römer, in Luther's
German trn of the New testament 1522; in edns of
Luther's works to the Weimar Bibel vol 7, 1931; tr
Latin by J. Jonas, Præfatio methodica in epistolam
Pauli ad Romanos 1524, in Luther's rev Vulgate 1529,
and the Weimar Bibel vol 5 1914.
Stapleton, T. Antidota apostolica in epistolam Pauli ad
Romanos. Antwerp 1591, 1595, Lyons 1596; in his
Opera vol 3, Paris 1620.
Rollock, R. Analysis dialectica in epistolam ad Romanos.
Edinburgh 1593, 1594, Geneva 1596, 1608.
Powel, G. Prodromus: a logicall resolution of the 1 chap.
of the epistle unto the Romanes. Oxford 1602.
Draxe, T. The worldes resurrection: a familiar commentary
upon the eleventh chapter of Saint Paul to the Romaines.
1608.
Cowper, W. Three heavenly treatises upon the eight chapter
to the Romanes [verses 1–17, 17–30, 31–9]. 1609, 1612;
as Heaven opened, 1611 (the first treatise only), 1613
(complete), 1615–16, 1619, 1631–2, 1632; in his Workes
1623, 1626, 1628–9 (2nd edn).
Sclater, W. A key to the key of scripture, or an exposition
with notes, upon the epistle to the Romanes: the three
first chapters. 1611, 1629; An exposition with notes,
on the whole fourth chapter, 1650.
[Willet, A.] Hexapla: that is, a six-fold commentarie upon
the most divine epistle of the holy apostle S. Paul to the
Romanes. Cambridge 1611, 1620.
Wilson, T. A commentarie upon the most divine epistle
of S. Paul to the Romanes. 1614, 1620, 1627 (2nd edn),
1653 (3rd edn).

Elton, E. Complaint of a sanctified sinner answered: or an explanation of the seventh chapter of the epistle to the Romans. 1618, 1622; The triumph of a true Christian described: or an explanation of the eight[h] chapter, 1623; The great mystery of godlinesse opened: being an exposition upon the whole ninth chapter, 1653 (as pt 3 of the following); Three excellent and pious treatises, viz in sundry sermons, upon the whole seventh, eight[h], and ninth chapters. 1653.

Parr, E. A plaine exposition upon the whole 8, 9, 10, 11 chapters of the epistle of Saint Paul to the Romanes. 1618; chs 8–12, 1620 (2nd edn), 1620; chs 13–16, 1622; in his Workes, 1632 ('3rd', i.e. first edn), 1651 ('4th', i.e. 2nd edn) (on i. 1–ii. 2, viii–xvi).

Stoughton, T. The Christians sacrifice: or a logicall and theologicall exposition of the two first verses of the twelfth to the Romanes. 1622.

Sutton, T. Lectures upon the eleventh chapter to the Romans. [Ed J. Downame] 1632.

Ferme, C. Analysis logica in epistolam Apostoli Pauli ad Romanos. Edinburgh 1651.

Binning, H. (d. 1653). The sinners sanctuary, in fourty sermons, upon Romans chap. 8. Edinburgh 1670; in his Works vols 1–2, 1839.

Goodwin, J. An exposition of the ninth chapter of the epistle to the Romans. 1653.

I-II Corinthians

Colet, J. Enarratio in primam epistolam S. Pauli ad Corinthios: an exposition of St Paul's first epistle to the Corinthians [c. 1496]. Ed and tr J. H. Lupton 1874, Ridgewood NJ 1965.

Roy, W. (?). An exposition into the seventh chapter of the first pistle to the Corinthians. In D. Erasmus, An exhortation to the diligent studye of scripture, [tr W. Roy?], [Antwerp] 1529, London [1540?].

Sampson, R. 1546. See Romans, above.

Calvin, J. A commentarie upon S. Paules epistles to the Corinthians, translated out of Latine by T. Tymme. 1577. From Commentarii in priorem epistolam Pauli ad Corinthios, Strasbourg 1546; in secundam, Geneva 1548; Commentaire sur la premiere (seconde) epistre aux Corinthiens 2 vols Geneva 1547; tr J. Pringle 2 vols Edinburgh 1848–9 (Calvin Trn Soc), Grand Rapids 1948; tr J. W. Fraser and T. A. Smail 2 vols Edinburgh 1960–4 (with Timothy, Titus and Philemon); tr German, Neukirchen 1961–2 (with Romans).

Morton, T. Prioris Corinthiacæ epistolæ expositio quædam. 1596.

Bird, S. The lectures upon the 8 and 9 chapters of the second epistle to the Corinthians. Cambridge 1598.

Rollock, R. In utramque ad Corinthios, cum notis J. Piscatoris. Herborn 1600, Jena 1602.

Stapleton, T. Antidota evengelica in duas epistolas ad Corinthios. Antwerp 1600; in his Opera vol 3, Paris 1620.

Sclater, W. Utriusque epistolæ ad Corinthios explicatio analytica. Oxford 1633.

Sibbes, R. A learned commentary upon the first chapter of the second epistle to the Corinthians. 1655; ch 4, 1656; both in his Works vols 3–4, ed A. B. Grosart 1863–4 (Nichol's Standard divines).

Galatians

Luther, M. A commentarie upon the epistle of S. Paul to the Galathians, translated out of Latine. 1575, 1577, 1580, 1588, 1603, 1615, 1616, 1635, 1644, 1741, 1760, 1774, Wigan 1791, Chester 1796, 2 vols Lewes 1807; ed E. Middleton 1807, 1810, Edinburgh 1822, London 1839, 1845, 1864; ed J. P. Fallowes [1939]; [ed P. S. Watson] 1953; An abstract of a commentarie [upon] the Galachians, [tr E. Ferrers] [1642]. From In epistolam S. Pauli ad Galatas commentarius, ex prælectione [delivered 1531], ed G. Rörer, Wittenberg 1535, Hagenau 1535, Wittenberg 1538, Frankfurt 1543, 1546, 1563, ed J. C. Irmischer 3 pts Erlangen 1843–4, ed

K. Haas, Der ungefälschte Luther vol 2, Stuttgart 1881, in Werke vol 40, Weimar 1911–14; tr German, Frankfurt 1714, 1717, Halle 1737, Culm 1846, Berlin 1856; French, Geneva 1560, Antwerp 1583; Swedish, Upsala 1775. Different from work with similar title pbd Leipzig 1519, Basle 1523, Wittenberg 1523, Strasbourg 1523, 1524, Basle 1525; tr German, Wittenberg 1525, Basle 1525; and in edns of Luther's Opera, Latin and German, from Wittenberg vol 5 1554 (Latin) and 1 1539 (German) to Weimar 2 1884, and from a 3rd, much shorter, delivered 1516, ed H. V. Schubert, Heidelberg 1918, in Weimar 57 1939.

Calvin, J. A commentarie upon the epistle to the Galatians. Tr R. V[aux] 1581; Sermons upon the epistle to the Galathians, tr A. Golding, with Golding's trn of most of Paul's epistle, 1574. For the Latin edns, 1548 etc, see above; Sermons sur l'épistre de S. Paul aux Galatiens, Geneva 1563; Commentaries on the epistles to Galatians and Ephesians, tr W. Pringle, Edinburgh 1841, 1854 (Calvin Trn Soc), Grand Rapids 1948; tr T. H. L. Parker, Edinburgh 1965 (with Ephesians, Philippians, Colossians).

Rollock, R. Analysis logica in epistolam Pauli apostoli ad Galatas. [Ed H. Charteris] 1602, Herborn 1603, Geneva 1610.

Perkins, W. A commentarie on the five first chapters of the epistle to the Galatians. Cambridge 1604; continued with a supplement upon the sixt chapter, by R. Cudworth, 1617; in edns of his Works (first as A golden chaine, Cambridge 1600), 3 vols 1603–35.

Torshell, S. The three questions of free iustification, explicated in a briefe comment on St Paul to the Galatians [ii. 16–iii. 26]. 1632.

[Crell, J.] The iustification of a sinner: being the maine argument of the epistle to the Galatians. [Tr T. Lushington] 1650. From Commentarius in epistolam Pauli apostoli ad Galatas, ed J. Schlichting, Racow 1628; in his Opera omnia exegetica 3 vols 'Eleutheropolis' (Amsterdam) 1656.

Fergusson, J. A brief exposition of the epistles of Paul to the Galatians and Ephesians. 1656, 1659, Edinburgh 1659, London 1841.

Ephesians

Ridley, L. A commentary in Englyshe upon Saynte Paules epystle to the Ephesyans. [1540]; in Richmond's Fathers of the English Church vol 2, 1880.

Calvin, J. The sermons upon the epistle too the Ephesians. Tr A. Golding 1577; Sermons sur l'épistre aux Ephésiens, Geneva 1562; tr T. H. L. Parker, Edinburgh 1965 (with Galatians, Philippians, Colossians). For Latin edns 1548 etc see Epistles, above; for English trns 1841 etc see Galatians, above.

Hemmingsen (Hemmingius), N. The epistle of the blessed apostle Saint Paule to the Ephesians, faithfullie expounded, translated out of Latin by A. Fleming. 1581. From Commentarius in epistolam Pauli ad Ephesios, 1576; Commentaria in omnes epistolas, Leipzig 1572, Frankfurt 1579, Strasbourg 1586.

St John Chrysostom. An exposition upon the epistle of S. Paule the apostle to the Ephesians, truely and faithfully translated out of Greeke. 1581. From Εἰς πάσας τὰς Παύλου ἐπιστολὰς ἑρμηνεία, Verona 1529; Greek and Latin, Heidelberg 1596; De laudibus Pauli, super epistolas Pauli expositiones, tr Latin by L. Bernardus, [no place] [1505?]; Enarrationes in Pauli epistolas, ed D. Erasmus, Basle 1536; Commentary on the epistle to the Galatians and homilies on the epistle to the Ephesians, tr W. J. Copeland, Oxford 1840, 1879 (rev H. Walford) (Library of Fathers 6); Homilies on Galatians, Ephesians etc, ed P. Schaff, New York 1889 (trn), 1894 (Nicene and Post-Nicene Fathers 1st ser 13); in Opera græce vol 3, ed H. Savile [and J. Bois] Eton 1612, Opera (Greek and Latin), ed B. de Montfaucon, 13 vols Paris 1738 etc, vol 11 1860 (Patrologia graeca 62).

Rollock, R. In epistolam Pauli apostoli ad Ephesios commentarius. Edinburgh 1590, Geneva 1592, 1593, 1606.

Bayne, P. A commentarie upon the first chapter of the epistle of Saint Paul, written to the Ephesians. 1618, 1643; An entire commentary upon the whole epistle of the apostle Paul to the Ephesians, 1643, 1645, 1647, 1658 (5th edn as A commentary), Edinburgh 1865 (as An entire commentary) (Nichol's Commentaries).

Gouge, W. Of domesticall duties [on Ephesians v. 21–vi. 9]. 1622, 1626 (as Works vol 1, 1627); 1634.

— Πανοπλία τοῦ Θεοῦ: the whole armour of God [on Ephesians vi. 10–20]. 1616, 1619; 1627 (as Works vol 2).

— An exposition on part of the fifth and sixth chapters of the Ephesians [v. 22–4, vi. 4, 5, 9–15, different from preceding]. 2 pts 1630 (as pt 2 of An exposition of the whole fifth chapter of S. John's gospell), 1631.

Boyd (Bodius), R. In epistolam Pauli apostoli ad Ephesios prælectiones supra CC. 1652, Geneva 1660.

[Scattergood, A. (ed)]. Annotationes in Vetus testamentum, et in epistolam ad Ephesios. Cambridge 1653; [ed J. Rhenferd]. Franecker 1704, Leyden 1722. Sometimes attributed to Archbishop J. Williams, in whose library the anon ms was found.

Fergusson, J. A brief exposition of the epistles of Paul to the Galatians and Ephesians. 1656, 1659, Edinburgh 1659, London 1841.

Philippians

Ridley, L. An exposytion in Englyshe upon the epistyll of Saynt Paule to the Philippians. Canterbury [1550?]; in Richmond's Fathers of the English Church vol 2, 1808.

Calvin, J. A commentarie uppon the epistle to the Philippians, translated out of Latine by W. B[ecket]. 1584. For the Latin edns, 1548 etc, see Epistles above; Exposition of the epistles of Paul to the Philippians and Colossians, by Calvin and G. C. Storr, tr R. Johnston, Edinburgh 1852; Commentary on St Paul's epistles to the Philippians, Colossians and Thessalonians, tr J. Pringle 1851 (Calvin Trn Soc), Grand Rapids 1948; tr T. H. L. Parker, Edinburgh 1965 (with Galatians, Ephesians, Colossians).

Airey, H. Lectures upon the whole epistle of St Paul to the Philippians. Ed C. P[otter] 1618; Edinburgh 1864 (Nichol's Commentaries) (with Cartwright on Colossians).

Sibbes, R. An exposition of the third chapter of the epistle of St Paul to the Philippians (An exposition of part of the second chapter). Ed J. G[oodwin?] 2 pts 1639, 1647; in his Works vol 5, ed A. B. Grosart 1864 (Nichol's Standard divines).

Fergusson, J. A brief exposition of the epistles of Paul to the Philippians and to the Colossians. Edinburgh 1656, London 1841.

Colossians

Ridley, L. An exposicion in Englishe upon the epistle of S. Paule, to the Colossians. 1548.

Calvin, J. A commentarie upon the epistle to the Colossians. Tr R. V[aux] [1581?]. For Latin edns 1548 etc see Epistles, above; for other English edns see Philippians, above.

Rollock, R. Commentarius in epistolam Pauli ad Colossenses. [Ed H. Charteris], Edinburgh 1600, Geneva 1602; Lectures upon the epistles of Paul to the Colossians, [ed H. Holland] 1603.

Dod, J. (?) A profitable metaphrase upon the epistle of Paul to the Colossians. In Dod and R. Cleaver, Ten sermons tending chiefly to the fitting of men for the worthy receiving of the Lords Supper. 1609, 1610, 1620, 1621, 1628, 1632, 1634, 1661.

Cartwright, T. A commentary upon the epistle of Saint Paule written to the Colossians. 1612; Edinburgh 1864 (Nichol's Commentaries) (with Airey on Philippians).

Byfield, N. An exposition upon the epistle to the Colossians. 3 pts 1615, 1617, 1627, 1628, 1649, Edinburgh 1869 (Nichol's Commentaries).

Elton, E. An exposition of the epistle of St Paule to the Colossians. 1615, 1620, 1637.

Davenant, J. Expositio epistolæ ad Colossenses. Cambridge 1627, 1630, 1639, Amsterdam 1646, Groningen 1655; tr J. Allport 2 vols 1821–2.

Bayne, P. A commentarie upon the first and second chapters of Saint Paul to the Colossians. 2 pts 1634, 1635.

Fergusson, J. A brief exposition of the epistles of Paul to the Philippians and to the Colossians. Edinburgh 1656, London 1841.

I–II Thessalonians

Bullinger, H. Commentary upon the seconde epistle to the Thessalonians. Southwark 1538. From In omnes apostolicas epistolas XIIII et VII canonicas, commentarii, Zürich 1537, 1539, 1544, 1558; Commentarii in omnes Pauli epistolas, ad Hebræos, omnes epistolas canonicas, 1562, 1582.

Jewel, J. An exposition upon the two epistles of the apostle Saint Paule to the Thessalonians. [Ed J. Garbrand] 1583, 1584, 1594; in his Works, 4 pts 1609, 1611; in Richmond's Fathers of the English Church vol 7, 1811; ed P. Hall 1841.

Tymme, T. The figure of Antichriste disciphered by a Catholike: a catholike and divine exposition of the second epistle of Paul to the Thessalonians. 1586.

Rollock, R. In epistolam Pauli apostoli ad Thessalonicenses priorem (posteriorem) commentarius. 2 pts Edinburgh 1598; In utramque epistolam ad Thessalonicenses commentarius, necnon analysis epistolæ ad Philemonem, Herborn 1601; Lectures upon the first and second epistles of Paul to the Thessalonians, ed H. Charteris and W. Arthur, Edinburgh 1606.

Sclater, W. An exposition with notes upon the first epistle to the Thessalonians. 1619; second epistle, 1627, 1629, 1632; first and second epistles, 2 vols 1627, 1627–9, 1630, 1630–2, 1638.

Bradshaw, W. A plaine and pithy exposition of the second epistle to the Thessalonians. Ed T. Gataker 1620.

Jackson, T. A brief and plaine, yet orthodoxall and methodicall exposition upon S. Pauls second epistle, written to the Thessalonians. 1621.

Squire, J. A plaine exposition upon the first part of the second chapter of Saint Paul his second epistle to the Thessalonians. 1630.

I–II Timothy

Calvin, J. Sermons on the epistles to Timothie and Titus, translated out of French by L. T[omson]. 1579. From Sermons sur les deux épistres de sainct Paul à Timothée et sur l'épistre à Tite, Geneva 1561, 1563; in his Opera vols 53–4, Brunswick 1895. A distinct work from Calvin's Commentarii in utramque Pauli epistolam ad Timotheum, Geneva 1548 etc; tr French, 1548; tr English by J. Pringle, Edinburgh 1855 (Calvin Trn Soc), Grand Rapids 1948, and by T. A. Smail, Edinburgh 1964.

Barlow, J. An exposition of the second epistle of the apostle Paul to Timothy: the first chapter. 1625; An exposition of the first and second chapters of the latter episte [sic] to Timothie, 4 pts 1632.

Hall, T. A practical and polemical commentary: or exposition upon the third and fourth chapters of the latter epistle of Saint Paul to Timothy. 1658. Suppl to Barlow, above.

Titus

Erasmus, D. The paraphrase upon the Epistle of Saint Paule unto his discyple Titus. Tr [L. Cox] [1535?]. From Paraphrases in omnes epistolas Pauli, Mainz 1522, Paris 1523; also included in edns of paraphrase on New testament, 1540 etc.

Calvin, J. Sermons on the epistles to Timothie and Titus, translated out of French by L. T[omson]. For French original, 1561 etc, *see above*. A distinct work from his Commentarii in epistolam ad Titum, Geneva 1550; Commentaire sur l'épistre à Tite, 1550.

Taylor, T. A commentarie upon the epistle of Saint Paul written to Titus. Cambridge 1612, 1619, London 1658; in his Works, 1653, 1659.

Philemon

[Fenner, D. A logical analysis of the epistle to Philemon]. In Fenner's trn of O. Talon's (A. Talaeus's) Rhetorica, as The artes of logike and rethorike, [Middelburg] 1584, 1588, in P. Ramus et al, A compendium of the art of logick and rhetorick, 1651, and in M. Joseph, Shakespeare's use of the arts of language, New York 1949.

Rollock, R. Analysis epistolæ Pauli ad Philemonem. In his In utramque epistolam ad Thessalonicenses commentarius, Herborn 1601.

Attersoll, W. A commentarie upon the epistle of Saint Paule to Philemon. 1612, 1633.

Dyke, D. Two treatises: the one, a most fruitfull exposition upon Philemon; the other, the schoole of affliction. Ed J. Dyke 2 pts 1618, 1633; in his Workes, 2 pts 1633–5.

Jones, W. A commentarie upon the epistles of Saint Paul to Philemon, and to the Hebrewes, together with a compendious explication of the second and third epistles of Saint John. 1635, 1636.

Hebrews

Dering, E. A lecture or exposition upon a part of the v chapter of the epistle to the Hebrues. 1573, 1574, 1583; XXVII lectures: or readings upon part of the epistle written to the Hebrues [chs 1–6], 1576, 1577, 1578, 1583, 1590; in his Workes, 2 pts 1590, 3 pts 1597, 1614.

Bird, S. The lectures upon the II chapter of the epistle unto the Hebrewes, and upon the 38 psalme. Cambridge 1598.

Calvin, J. A commentarie on the whole epistle to the Hebrewes, translated out of French [by C. Cotton]. 1605. From Commentarii in epistolam ad Hebræos, Geneva 1549; Commentaire sur l'épistre aux Ebrieux, Geneva 1549; for the other Latin edns, 1551 etc, and French edns, 1561 etc, *see* Epistles, *above*; in his Opera vol 55, Brunswick 1896; Commentary on the epistle to the Hebrews, tr anon 1841, tr J. Owen, Edinburgh 1853 (Calvin Trn Soc), Grand Rapids 1948, 1949; tr W. B. Johnston, Edinburgh 1963 (with I–II Peter).

Rollock, R. Analysis logica in epistolam ad Hebræos [completed and ed H. Charteris]. Edinburgh 1605, Geneva 1605.

Broughton, H. A petition to the King to hasten allowance for Ebrew institution of Ebrewes. [1608].

Perkins, W. A cloud of faithfull witnesses: or a commentary upon the eleventh chapter to the Hebrewes. 1607 (Pembroke College Cambridge), 1608, 1622; in edns of his Works (first as A golden chaine, Cambridge 1600), 3 vols 1603–35.

Dickson, D. A short explanation of the epistle of Paul to the Hebrewes. Aberdeen 1635, Dublin 1637, Cambridge 1649, London 1839.

Jones, W. A commentarie upon the epistles of Saint Paul to Philemon, and to the Hebrewes. 1635, 1636.

[Crell, J.] The expiation of a sinner, in a commentary upon the epistle to the Hebrewes. Tr G.M. (T. Lushington) 1646. From Commentarius in epistolam ad Hebræos, ed J. Schlichting, Racow 1634; in his Opera omnia exegetica, 3 vols 'Eleutheropolis' (Amsterdam) 1656. Lushington's version criticized as Socinian by R. Porter, God incarnate, 1655.

Gouge, W. A learned and very useful commentary on the whole epistle to the Hebrewes. 4 pts 1655, 3 vols Edinburgh 1866–7 (Nichol's Commentaries).

James

An exposicyon upon a pece of Saint James epistle. 1536. Ch 2, 'D' to the end.

Hemmingsen (Hemmingius), N. A learned and fruitefull commentarie upon the epistle of James the apostle, translated by W. G[ace]. 1577. From Commentarius in epistolam Pauli ad Jacobum, 1577 (Folger Lib only); Commentaria in omnes epistolas, Leipzig 1572, Frankfurt 1579, Strasbourg 1586.

Gifford, G. A godlie zealous and profitable sermon upon the second chapter of St James. 1582, 1583.

Morgan, J. A short analysis of a part of the second chapter of S. James, with a briefe confutation of the Rhemistes annotations. 1588.

Turnbull, R. An exposition upon the canonicall epistle of Saint James (Saint Jude, The xv Psalme). 3 pts 1591, 1592, 1606.

Benefield, S. Eight sermons publikely preached in the University of Oxford on Luke and James. Oxford 1614.

Est (East), W. The right rule of a religious life, in certaine lectures upon the first chapter of the epistle of S. James. 1616.

Mayer, J. Praxis theologica: or the epistle of St James resolved, expounded and preached upon. 1629.

Manton, T. A practical commentary: or an exposition with notes on the epistle of James. 1651, 1652–3, 1657; ed J. Sherman 1840 (with Jenkyn on Jude), 1842, 1858; abridged T. M. Macdonogh 1843–4.

Gorton, S. Saltmarsh returned from the dead: or the resurrection of James the apostle, appearing in his fifth chapter. 1655.

I–II Peter

Alley, W. Exposition of 1 Peter. In his Πτωχομυσεῖον: the poore man's librarie, 1560.

Colet, J. Enarratio in primam B. Petri epistolam. In his Opuscula quædam theologica, ed J. H. Lupton 1876, Ridgewood NJ 1966. Authorship doubtful.

Luther, M. A commentarie upon the two epistles generall of Sainct Peter and that of Saint Jude. Tr T. Newton 1581. From Epistel S. Petri gepredigt und ausgelegt, Wittenberg 1522, 1523, [Augsburg] 1523, and Die andere Epistel S. Petri und eine S. Judas gepredigt und ausgelegt, Wittenberg 1523, 1524; in his Works vols 12, 14, Weimar 1891–5.

Hull, J. Saint Peter's prophesie of these last daies. 1610, 1611.

Byfield, N. Sermons upon the first chapter of the first epistle generall of Peter. 1617; A commentary: or sermons upon the second chapter of the first epistle of Saint Peter, [ed W. Gouge] 1623; Sermons upon the ten first verses of the third chapter of the first epistle of S. Peter, ed W. Gouge 1626; A commentary upon the three first chapters of the first epistle of Peter, [ed W. Gouge] 3 pts 1636–7.

Denison, S. An exposition upon the first chapter of the second epistle of Peter. 1622.

Ames, W. Vtriusque epistolæ D. Petri explicatio analytica. Amsterdam 1625, 1628, 1635, London 1647; in his Opera quæ latine scripsit omnia, ed M. Nethenus 5 vols Amsterdam 1658; An analyticall exposition of both the epistles of the apostle Peter, 1641, and in his Workes, 1643.

Pocock, E. (ed). Epistolæ quatuor, Petri secunda, Johannis secunda & tertia, & Judæ una; ex Bibliothecæ Bodleianæ examplari charactere hebræo, versione latina, notisque quibusdam insignitæ. Leyden 1630. In Syriac, Greek and Latin.

Simson (Symson), A. An exposition upon the second epistle generall of Saint Peter. 1632.

Adams, T. A commentary or, exposition upon the divine second epistle generall, written by St Peter. 1633; ed J. Sherman 1839; in his Works, ed J. Angus 3 vols Edinburgh 1861–2 (Nichol's Standard divines).

Mede, J. A paraphrase and exposition of the prophesie of Saint Peter, described in the third chapter of his second epistle. 1642, 1649, 1650, 1652; in his Works, 1648, 1664, 1667, 1672, 1677.

Rogers, J. A godly and fruitful exposition upon all the first epistle of Peter. Ed S. Simpson 1650.

Nisbet, A. A brief exposition of the first and second epistles generall of Peter. Edinburgh 1658, London 1658.

I–III John

T[indale], W. The exposition of the fyrste epistle of seynt Jhon. [Antwerp] 1531; The exposition of the epistles of St Jhon, Southwark 1538; in his Whole workes, 2 vols 1572–3; in T. Russell (ed), Works of the English and Scottish reformers vol 2, 1829; in his Expositions and notes, ed H. Walter, Cambridge 1849 (Parker Soc); extracts in Richmonds, Fathers of the English Church vol 1, 1807.

Marlorat, A. A catholike and ecclesiastical exposition uppon the twoo last epistles of John. Tr [1578?]; also as part of J. Calvin, The lectures or daily sermons on the prophet Jonas, 1578, 1580. For Latin original 1561 see Matthew, above.

Calvin, J. The comentaries upon the first epistle of Sainct Jhon and upon the epistle of Jude. Tr W.H. [c. 1580]. For other Latin, French and later English versions see Epistles, above; also Commentaire sur l'épistre canonique de S. Jean, Geneva 1551.

Perkins, W. A case of conscience [the text of 1 John and Psalm 15 with a commentary]. 1592, Edinburgh 1592, London 1595, Cambridge 1604 (pt 1 only), 1606, 1608, 1611, 1619, 1628, 1632, 1635, 1636; in a golden chaine, Cambridge 1600, and edns of his Works, 1603–35.

Pocock, E. (ed). 1630. See 1–11 Peter, above.

Jones, W. 1635 etc. See Philemon, above.

Roberts, F. Believer's evidences for eternal life, collected out of 1 John. 1649.

Binning, H. (d. 1653). Fellowship with God: or twenty-eight sermons on 1 John i and ii. 1–3. In his Works vol 2, 1839; 1833 (Religious Tract Soc).

Cotton, J. A practical commentary: or an exposition, with observations, upon the first epistle generall of John. [Ed C. Scott] 1656, 1658.

Hardy, N. The first general epistle of St John, unfolded and applied. 2 pts 1656–9; Edinburgh 1865 (Nichol's Commentaries). Chs 1–2 only.

Pennington, I. An exposition on the first epistle of John: pt 4 of Expositions, with observations sometimes, on severall scriptures. 4 pts 1656.

Jude

[Ridley, L.] An exposition in the epistell of Jude. 1538, [1549?]; in Richmond's Fathers of the English Church vol 2, 1808.

Calvin, J. [c. 1580]; see 1–III John, above. Exposition sur l'épistre de sainct Iudas, Geneva 1542; Commentaire sur l'épistre canonique de S. Jude, 1551.

Luther, M. 1581. See 1–11 Peter, above.

Turnbull, R. 1591 etc. See James, above.

[Willet, A.] A catholicon, gathered out of the catholike epistle of S. Jude, briefly expounded. Cambridge 1602.

Perkins, W. A godly and learned exposition upon the whole epistle of Jude. Ed T. Taylor 1606 (2 edns, one probably as appendix to his Works, 1605), 1607 (Bodley), and in his Works 1608–35.

Pocock, E. (ed). 1630. See 1–11 Peter, above.

Otes, S. An explanation of the generall epistle of Saint Jude. 1633.

Jenkyn, W. An exposition of the epistle of Jude: first part. 1652–3, 1653, 1656 (2nd edn); pt 2, 1654, 1656; ed J. Sherman 1839; 1840 (with Manton on James), 1849, 1858; Edinburgh 1863 (with Daillé's Philippians and Colossians) (Nichol's Commentaries).

Manton, T. A practical commentary: or an exposition with notes on the epistle of Jude. 1657–8, 1662.

Revelation

Bale, J. The image of bothe churches after the Revelacion of Sainct John. 3 pts [1548?], 1550, [1550?], [1551?], 1570; pt 2, [1550?]; in his Select works, ed H. Christmas, Cambridge 1849 (Parker Soc).

Traheron, B. An exposition of the 4 chap. of S. Joans Revelation made in sondrie readings before his countre men in Germanie. [Zürich?] 1557–8, London 1573, 1577, 1583.

Bullinger, H. A hundred sermons upon the Apocalips. [Tr J. Daws] 1561, 1573. From In Apocalypsim conciones centum, Basle 1557, 1559, 1570; tr German by L. Lavater, Zürich 1587; Cent sermons sur l'Apocalypse, Geneva 1558, 1564, Lyons 1564, Geneva 1565.

Fulke, W. In sacram diui Ioannis Apocalypsin prælectiones. 1573; Prælections upon the Revelation of St John, tr G. Gyffard 1573.

Marlorat, A. A catholike exposition upon the Revelation of Sainct John. [Tr A. Golding] 1574. For Latin original 1561 see Matthew, above. See F. Buckley, Note on Marlorat's Exposition of the Revelation of St John, 1574, [1941].

Brocardo, G. The reveled Revelation. [Tr S. Batman?] 1582; The revelation of S. John reveled, tr J. Sanford 1582, 1610. From In Apocalypsim interpretatio et paraphrasis, Leyden 1580, 1610.

Foxe, J. Eicasmi, seu meditationes in sacram Apocalypsin. 1587, Geneva 1596.

James VI and I. Ane fruitfull meditation: containing ane plaine and facill expositioun of the vii, viii, ix and x versis of the 20 chapter of the Revelatioun. Edinburgh 1588, London 1603; tr French, 1589; the English in his Workes, and J. Montagu 1616 (with A paraphrase upon the Revelation of the Apostle S. John); both tr Latin in his Opera, ed J. Montagu 1619, Frankfurt 1689.

H[ellwis], E. A marvell deciphered. 1589. An exposition of ch 12.

Napier, J. A plaine discovery of the whole Revelation of Saint John. Edinburgh 1593, 1594, 1611, 1645; Napiers narration: or an epitome of his booke on the Revelation, 1641.

Du Jon (Junius), F. Apocalypsis: a briefe and learned commentarie upon the Revelation of Saint John. [Tr L. Tomson?] 1592, 1594 (as The Revelation of Saint John, with a briefe and learned commentarie), 1600; included in some edns of the Geneva Bible and New testament, '1599', 1603–44 (DMH 214, 224, 261). With Beza's notes as in the Geneva Bibles from 1557–60 onwards; from Apocalypsis S. Joannis apostoli et evangelistæ, methodica analysi argumentorum, notisque brevibus illustrata, Heidelberg 1591, 1599, Basle 1599, in edns of the Beza-Tremellius-Junius Latin Bible from 3rd edn Hanau 1596, and in Junius's Opera theologica vol 1, Geneva 1607, 1613.

—— The Apocalyps, or Revelation of S. John, with a briefe and methodicall exposition. Tr T. B[arbar], Cambridge 1596 (DMH 233). From Apocalypse ou Revelation de S. Jean, avec une briefve et methodique exposition, [Geneva] 1592, 1598; much longer than Junius's earlier Latin commentary. See F. W. Cuno, Franciscus Junius der ältere, Amsterdam 1891.

Gifford, G. Sermons upon the whole booke of the Revelation. 1596, 1599.

Foord, J. Apocalypsis Jesu Christi revelata. 1597.

Dent, A. The ruine of Rome: or an exposition upon the whole Revelation. 1603, 1607, 1611, 1622, 1628, 1631, 1633, 1644, 1650, 1656.

Perkins, W. Lectures upon the three first chapters of the Revelation. Ed R. Hill 1604; ed T. Pierson 1606 (as A godly and learned exposition or commentarie upon the three first chapters of the Revelation) (probably as appendix to his Works, 1605); 1607 (3rd edn); in his Works 1608–35 etc.

Broughton, H. A revelation of the holy Apocalyps. [Amsterdam?] 1610; A petition to the King, for authority and allowance to expound the Apocalyps in Hebrew and Greek, [Middelburg] 1611; in his Works, ed J. Lightfoot 4 vols 1662.

Brightman, T. A revelation of the Apocalyps. Amsterdam 1611; A revelation of the Revelation, 1615; Leyden 1616 (as The Revelation of S. John illustrated), Amsterdam 1644, London 1644; in his Workes, 1644. From Apocalypsis analysi et scholiis illustrata, Frankfurt 1609.

Forbes, P. An exquisite commentarie upon the Revelation of Saint John. 1613, Middelburg 1614 (as An learned commentarie); Commentarius in Apocalypsin, Amsterdam 1646.

Bernard, R. A key of knowledge for the opening of the secret mysteries of St Johns revelation. 1617.

Cowper, W. Pathmos: or a commentary on the Revelation of Saint John [chs 4–7]. 1619; 3 pts [chs 4–7, 8–11, 12–16] in his Workes, 1623, 1626, 1628–9 (2nd edn).

Mason, T. A revelation of the Revelation. 1619.

Wilkinson, J. An exposition of the 13 chapter of Revelation. Amsterdam 1619; in C. Burrage, The early English dissenters vol 1, Cambridge 1912.

A plaine explanation of the whole Revelation of Saint John. 1622.

L., T. An exposition of the xi, xii and xiii chapters of the Revellation. [no place] 1623; rptd in A voyce out of the wilderness crying, 1651.

Mayer, J. 1627 etc. See New testament, above.

Mede, J. Clavis apocalyptica. Cambridge 1627, 1632 (with pt 2, In sancti Joannis Apocalypsin commentarius, nunc primum typis editus), 1649; tr R. More as The key of the Revelation, 1643, 1650; tr R. B. Cooper 1833; in his Works, 1648, 1664, 1667, 1672, 1677. See R. Hayter, The meaning of the Revelation, in which the synchronisms of Mr Joseph Mede are called in question, 1675, 1676; A review and defence of Mr Mede's exposition of the four first vials, 1720 (anon); S. Johnson,

An explanation of scripture prophecies: observations on Mr Mede's Clavis apocalyptica, 1742; J. Leifchild, A help to the private reading of the scriptures, including an analysis of Mr Mede's scheme of the Apocalypse, [1829]; R. Graves, Analysis of the Revelations, chiefly founded on the commentaries of J. Mede, 1854.

Burton, H. The seven vials: or a briefe and plaine exposition upon the 15 and 16 chapters of the Revelation. 1628.

Cotton, J. The pouring out of the seven vials: or an exposition of the 16th chapter of the Revelation. 2 pts 1642, 1645; An exposition of the thirteenth chapter of the Revelation, [ed T. Allen] 1655, 1656.

Alsted, J. H. 1643 etc. See Daniel, above.

Paré (Pareus), D. A commentary upon the divine Revelation. Tr E. Arnold, Amsterdam 1644. From Commentarius in divinam Apocalypsin S. Johannis, Heidelberg 1618, 1622.

Trapp, J. 1647 etc. See New testament, above.

[Hall, J.] The Revelation unrevealed: concerning the thousand yeares reigne of the saints with Christ upon earth. 1650; in his Works vol 3 1662, vol 8 1808, 1837, 1862.

Holland, H. An exposition: or a short, but full, plaine and perfect epitome of the most choice commentaries upon the Revelation of Saint John. 1650.

Clavis apocalyptica. 1651. See Daniel, above.

[Strong, W.] Clavis apocalyptica ad incudem revocata. [1653].

Tillinghast, J. 1653 etc. See Daniel, above.

Guild, W. The sealed book opened: or a clear explication of the prophecies of the Revelation. 1656.

Durham, J. A commentarie upon the book of the Revelation. Ed J. Carstairs, Edinburgh 1658, London 1658, Amsterdam 1660, Edinburgh 1680, Glasgow 1680, 1739, 1764, 1788, Falkirk 1799.

Hicks, W. Ἀποκάλυψις Ἀποκαλύψεως: or the Revelation revealed: being a practical exposition on the Revelation of St John [chs 1–3]. 1659, 1661.

C. B. L. B.

III. THE PRAYER BOOK

Bibliographies

List of printed books, according to the ancient usages of the Anglican Church. 1850.

Frère, E. Des livres de liturgie des églises d'Angleterre (Salisbury, York, Hereford), imprimés à Rouen dans les xve et xvie siècles: étude, suivie du catalogue de ces impressions. Rouen 1867.

Hoskins, E. Horæ beatæ Mariæ virginis: or Sarum and York primers, with kindred books. 1901.

Lacombe, P. Livres d'heures imprimés au xve et au xvie siècle conservés dans les bibliothèques publiques de Paris: catalogue. Paris 1907, Nieuwkoop 1963.

Bohatta, H. Bibliographie der Livres d'heures, horae BMV des xv und xvi Jahrhunderts. Vienna 1909, 1924 (rev).

Cowan, W. A bibliography of the Book of common order and Psalm book of the Church of Scotland 1556–1644. Edinburgh 1913 (Edinburgh Bibl Soc). Rev and expanded from the Society's Hand list of editions of the psalms, old Scottish version, 1891.

Church of Scotland, Committee on Public Worship and Aids to Devotion. Draft of a catalogue of books on psalters, hymns and hymnology in National Library of Scotland, Aberdeen University Library, New College Library, Edinburgh, Trinity College Library, Glasgow. Edinburgh 1939.

British Museum. Catalogue of an exhibition commemorating the four hundredth anniversary of the introduction of the Book of common prayer. 1949.

Adams, H. M. Tables for identifying the edition of imperfect copies of the Book of common prayer 1600–40; pt I, quarto editions 1611–39. Trans Cambridge Bibl Soc 1 1953. No more pbd.

Page, J. R. A descriptive catalogue of the Book of common prayer and related material in the collection of J. R. Page. Los Angeles 1955.

Allison, A. F. and D. M. Rogers. A catalogue of Catholic books in English printed abroad or secretly in England 1558–1640. Biographical Stud 3 1956.

Collections

L'Estrange, H. The alliance of divine offices. Oxford 1659, 1690, 1699, 1846 (Lib of Anglo-Catholic Theology). Contains texts of 1549 and 1637.

The two Books of common prayer, set forth in the reign of Edward VI, compared. [Ed E. Cardwell], Oxford 1838, 1841, London 1852.

The two liturgies 1549–52, the Primer 1553, the catechism and articles, set forth by Edward VI. Ed J. Ketley, Cambridge 1844 (Parker Soc).

Liturgiæ britannicæ: or the several editions of the common prayer, from its compilation to the last revision together with the liturgy set forth for the use of the Church of

Scotland, arranged to show their respective variations by W. Keeling. 1842, 1851.

The liturgical services of the time of Queen Elizabeth. Ed W. K. Clay, Cambridge 1851 (Parker Soc). Prayer book 1559, Godley prayers, The ordinal 1559, New calendar etc.

Reprints of early editions of the common prayer book, from Edward VI to Charles II etc. Ed W. Pickering 7 vols 1844. 1, 1549; 2, 1552; 3, 1559; 4, 1604; 5, 1637; 6, 1662; 7, 1844.

The ancient liturgy of the Church of England according to the uses of Sarum, Bangor, York and Hereford, and the modern Roman liturgy arranged in parallel columns, by W. Maskell. 1844, 1846, Oxford 1882 (rev).

Monumenta ritualia ecclesiæ anglicanæ: occasional offices of the Church of England according to the ancient use of Salisbury, the Prymer in English, and other prayers and forms. Ed W. Maskell 3 vols 1846–7.

Reliquiæ liturgicæ: documents connected with the liturgy of the Church of England. Ed P. Hall 5 vols Bath 1847. 1, A booke of the forme of common praycr, 4th edn Middelburgh 1602; 2, 1637; 3, Directory for public worship, 1644; 4, The Savoy liturgy, 1661; 5, Book of common prayer for the episcopal church of New York etc, Philadelphia 1786.

Fragmenta liturgica: documents illustrative of the liturgy of the Church of England. Ed P. Hall 7 vols 1847, Bath 1848. List of contents 1644–1844, in Lowndes iii. 1957.

Burton, J. Three primers put forth in the reign of Henry VIII. Oxford 1834, 1848, 1858. Joye 1535, Hilsey 1539, Henry VIII 1545.

Private prayers, put forth by authority during the reign of Queen Elizabeth. Ed W. K. Clay, Cambridge 1851 (Parker Soc). Primer 1559, Orarium 1569, Preces privatae 1564, Christian prayers 1578, Litany 1544.

Breviary
The generall rubriques of the breviarie, put into English. St Omer 1617.

Primers

[Sarum]. Thys prymer in Englyshe and in Laten is newly translatyd after the Laten texte. Rouen 1536, London [1537?], Rouen 1537, Paris 1537, Rouen 1538 (5 edns), Paris 1538, 1538, London 1538, [1540?] (2 edns), 1541, 1541, 1542 (4 edns), 1543, 1543, 1544; An uniforme and catholyke prymer in Latin and Englishe, 1555; The primer in english ('Queen Mary's book'), 1555 (3 edns), Rouen 1555 (4 edns), 1556 (3 edns) London 1556, 1556, 1557, 1557, 1558 (4 edns). A few Latin edns from 1527 had parts in English.

[Sarum children's primer]. The primer in English for children, after the use of Sarum. [1537?], [1539?], 1556.

[The first reformed primer, called W. Marshall's; probably tr G. Joye]. Englyshe, with certeyn prayers and godly meditations for all that understonde not the Latyne tongue. [1534–5]; A godly prymer in Englysshe, newly corrected, 1535 (4 edns), 1536, [1537?] (2 edns), [1539?].

[Mixed primers, partly Sarum and partly Marshall's]. This prymer of Salysbery use bothe in Englyshe and in Laten is set out a longe without any serchyng. 1536, 1540.

[Bishop J. Hilsey's reformed primer]. The manual of prayers, or the prymer, in Englysh and Laten. 1539 (3 edns, one a selection for children), 1540, [1543?].

[Henry VIII's reformed primer]. The primer, set foorth by the Kynges Majestie and his clergie. 1545 (7 edns), 1546 (5 edns).

[Edward VI's primer, similar to Henry VIII's, above]. The primer set forth by the Kinges Majestie and his clergie. 1547, 1547, 1548[–9], 1549, [1550?], 1551, 1552.

[Primer of Edward VI in accordance with 1552 Prayer book]. A prymmer: or boke of private prayer nedeful to be used for al faythfull Christianes. 1553 (3 edns),

1560, 1560, [1564?], [1566?], [1568?], [1580?], [1670?], [1685?], 1758, 1764, 1766, 1769, 1772, 1775, 1777, 1783; ed H. Walter 1825.

[Elizabeth's primer, similar to Henry VIII's and Edward VI's, above]. The primer set forth at large, with many godly and devoute prayers. 1559, [1560?], 1564, 1568, 1573, 1575.

['Reformed' Roman primer, from the Latin revision Rome 1571; some edns in Latin and English, some in English alone]. The primer: or office of the Blessed Virgin Marie. Antwerp 1599, 1604, Douai 1614, Mechlin 1615, St Omer 1616, [England] 1617, St Omer 1621, Douai 1623, Rouen 1630, St Omer 1631, [no place] 1632, 'Rouen' (for St Omer?) 1632, 1633, 1633, Antwerp 1650, 1658, St Omer 1673, Antwerp 1685, London 1720, 1736–7, 1750, Cork 1789, Dublin [1803?], 1804, 1814, [1815?], 1817, 1818, 1832, Mechlin 1844, Dublin 1867; The primer more ample, Rouen 1669, 1684, 1700, 1701.

Edward VI's First Prayer Book

§ 1

The booke of common praier and administration of the sacramentes. 1549 (9 edns), Worcester 1549, 1549, London 1550 (with music by J. Marbeck), Dublin 1551, London 1551; 1910 (EL).

§ 2

Dix, M. Lectures on the first Prayer book of King Edward VI. 1881.

Preparations for the first Prayer book of Edward VI. Church Quart Rev 35 1893.

Bowles, C. W. J. The Prayer book of 1549. Churchman new ser 63 1949.

Brookes, T. H. The first Prayer-book of Edward VI. Contemporary Rev June 1949.

Darby, H. S. Cranmer's first Prayer book. London Quart 174 1949.

Hegarty, W. J. The fourth centenary of the first Book of common prayer. Irish Ecclesiastical Record 5th ser 72 1949.

Morris, C. The Book of common prayer 1549 [and revisions]. Printing Rev 51 1949.

1549 Prayer book: language and the liturgy. TLS 12 March 1949.

Devereux, J. A. Reformed doctrine in the collects of the first Book of common prayer. Harvard Theological Rev 58 1965.

— The collects of the first Book of common prayer as works of translation. SP 66 1969.

Calvinist Prayer Books

§ 1

The forme of common praiers used in the churches of Geneva. 1550; The forme of prayers and ministration of the sacraments, used in the English congregation at Geneva and approved by John Calvyn, Geneva 1556; 1557 (bound with prose psalter) (Cambridge Univ Lib), 1558, 1561 (3 edns), Edinburgh 1562 (transitional between Genevan and Scottish orders; for subsequent Scottish revisions see below); A forme of prayers to be used in private houses, 1570 (in 3rd edn of Geneva Bible); A booke of the forme of common prayers, administration of the sacraments, agreable to the use of the reformed churches, [1584] (separately), Middelburg 1586, 1587, 1602, London 1643; tr Latin, Ratio et forma publice orandi Deum, Geneva 1556.

§ 2

Colligan, J. H. The Geneva service book of 1555. Manchester [1931].

Maxwell, W. D. John Knox's Genevan service book of 1556. Edinburgh 1931. With text in Latin and English.

Lupton, L. F. A history of the Geneva Bible 2: reform. 1969.

Edward VI's Second Prayer Book

§1

The booke of common prayer. 1552 (9 edns), Worcester 1552, London 1553 (4 edns); 1910 (EL).

§2

Preparations for the second Prayer book of Edward VI. Church Quart Rev 37 1894.

Bourne, E. C. E. Cranmer and the liturgy of 1552. Church Quart Rev 37 1894.

Queen Elizabeth's Prayer Book

The booke of common prayer and administration of the sacramentes. 1559 (5 edns), 1560, 1560, 1562, 1564, 1566, [Rouen?] 1566, London 1567, 1570, 1570, 1571, 1572, 1573, 1574, [1575], [1575], [1576], 1580 (3 edns), 1585, [1585], 1587, 1588, 1589, 1590, [1590], 1592, 1592, [1595], [1595], 1596, 1596, 1597, 1599, 1600, 1603.

Scottish Book of Common Order

The forme of prayers and ministration of the sacraments used in the English churche at Geneva. Edinburgh 1562; approved and received by the Churche of Scotland, 1564–5, 1565, [Geneva?] 1566, Edinburgh 1571, 1575, [Geneva?] 1584, London 1587, 1587, Middelburg 1594, Edinburgh 1595–6, [Middelburg 1599], Edinburgh 1599–1602, Dort 1601, Middelburg 1602, Edinburgh 1611, 1611, 1615, 1617, 1622, Aberdeen 1629, 1633, Edinburgh 1634, 1635, 1640 (3 edns, all incomplete); tr Gaelic, Edinburgh 1567.

Jacobean Prayer Book

1603[–4], 1604 (3 edns), 1605, 1605, 1606, 1606, 1607, 1608, 1609, [1610?], 1611, 1611, [1612?], 1613, 1613–14, 1613–14, 1614, 1614, 1615 (4 edns), 1616 (4 edns), 1617, 1618, 1619, 1619, 1619–20, 1620 (3 edns), 1621, 1621, 1622, 1622, 1623, 1623, 1624, 1625, 1625, 1626, 1626, 1627 (4 edns), 1628 (5 edns), 1629 (3 edns), Cambridge 1629, 1630, London 1630 (4 edns), 1631, 1631, 1632 (5 edns), 1632–3, 1632–3, 1633 (3 edns), Edinburgh 1633, London 1633–4, 1633–4, 1634, Edinburgh 1634, 1634, Cambridge 1635, London 1635, 1636, 1636, 1637, 1637, Cambridge 1637, Dublin 1637, London 1638 (4 edns), Cambridge 1638, 1638, London 1638–9, 1639 (7 edns), London 1640, 1640, Cambridge 1640, London 1641, 1642, 1645, 1660 (4 edns), Cambridge 1660, London 1661, 1661.

The 1604 Prayer book is a slight revision of Queen Elizabeth's, above; also called the Hampton Court book.

Scottish Prayer Book

§1

The booke of common prayer for the use of the Church of Scotland. Edinburgh 1636–7 ('Laud's Book', 3 edns); The new booke of common prayer, according to the forme of the Kirke of Scotland, 1644, Edinburgh 1712.

§2

Donaldson, G. The making of the Scottish Prayer-book of 1637. Edinburgh 1954.

Directory for Public Worship

1644 (2 edns) etc. Compulsory 1645–60.

Baxter's Proposed Savoy Liturgy

The reformation of the liturgy, as it was presented to the bishops by the divines appointed by his Majesties Commission [the Savoy Conference], to treat of the alteration to it [by R. Baxter]. In Baxter, A petition for peace, 1661; in E. Calamy, The history of nonconformity, 1704; in P. Hall, Reliquiæ liturgicæ vol 4, 1847.

Charles II's Prayer Book

The book of common prayer and administration of the sacraments. 1662 ('Sealed Book', 2 edns), Cambridge 1662, 1662, 1663, London 1663, 1663, 1665, Cambridge 1666, London 1667, Dublin 1668, London 1669, Cambridge 1670, London 1671, Cambridge 1673, Oxford 1675, Cambridge 1675, 1676, London 1676, 1678, Oxford 1679, Cambridge 1679, London 1680, 1680, Dublin 1680, Oxford 1680, 1681, 1682, 1683, London 1683, Cambridge 1683, Oxford 1684, 1685, 1686, 1687, London 1687, 1687, 1688, Oxford 1688, 1691, London 1692, 1693, Oxford 1693, Cambridge 1694, London 1695, Cambridge 1696, Oxford 1696, 1697, 1698, 1699, 1700, Dublin 1700 etc; with an exposition and preface by J. Fludger (Fludyer), 1735, 1739; illustrated and explained by L. Howard, 1761; with preface and notes by J. Reeves, 1801, 1802, 1804, 1807; with introd and notes by R. Warner, Bath 1806; with notes by Sir J. Bayley, 1813, 1816, 1824; with notes explanatory, practical, and historical, by R. Mant, Oxford 1820, 1822, 1825, 1836, London 1840, 1850; illustrated so as to show its various modifications, by W. K. Clay, 1841; annotated, by J. H. Blunt, 1866; ed A. P. Stanley 1870.

William and Mary's Proposed Prayer Book

The revised liturgy. 1689; Being the Book of common prayer [1683–6] interleaved with the alterations proposed by the Royal Commissioners, ed J. Taylor 1855; A copy of the alterations in the Book of common prayer, prepared by the Royal Commissioners for the revision of the liturgy in 1689, printed by order [1854] of the House of Commons, 1856.

Polyglot

The book of common prayer in eight languages: namely English, French, Italian, German, Spanish, Greek, ancient and modern, Latin. 1821, 1825, [1866].

Translations

See W. T. *Lowndes*, The bibliographer's manual of English literature, *ed. H. G. Bohn, vol 3, 1864, 1875, cols 1946–7.*

The following first appeared before 1662:

Dutch: Rotterdam 1645 (from English and Latin edns of 1574 and 1575), rev A. Duez and B. Hoefnagel, London 1704; with the English, Amsterdam 1711, Dordrecht 1728, Amsterdam 1838, London 1853.

French: tr F. Philippe, Paris 1553, London 1616 (version of 1662); tr J. Durel, London 1667, 1678, 1683, 1688, 1689, 1695, Amsterdam 1700; at least 40 edns 1702–1886; London 1938, 1954.

Greek and Latin: London 1553, 1562, 1569.

Greek: tr E. Petilius 1638; version of 1662 tr J. Duport, Cambridge 1665, London 1818, 1820, 1923.

Irish: tr W. Daniel, Dublin 1608, 1825, 1856.

Latin: [1549] by A. Ales, Leipzig 1551, rptd in M. Bucer, Scripta anglicana, Basle 1577; rev W. Haddon, [1560?], rptd in W. K. Clay (ed), Liturgical services, Cambridge 1847 (Parker Soc); [1569], 1571–2, 1574, 1594, 1604, 1848; in verse, tr R. Gilpin 1657; version of 1662, tr J. Durel 1669, 1670, 1680, 1685, 1687, 1690, 1696, 1703; tr T. Parsell 1706 and 6 more edns to 1759; ed E. Harwood 1791, 1800, 1826, 1840; tr W. Bright and P. G. Medd 1865, 1868–9, 1872, 1877, 1902.

Spanish: [1612?], 1613, 1616; tr T. Carrascon, Augusta

Trinobantum [i.e. London 1623]; tr F. A. de Alvarado, 1707, 1715, 1839, 1852, 1864, 1905.

Welsh: tr R. Davies and W. Salesbury, 1567, 1586, 1599, 1621, 1630, 1634, 1664, 1678; 18 edns 1708–1899; ed M. Richards and G. Williams, Cardiff 1953, 1967.

Concordances

Green, J. B. A concordance to the liturgy: or Book of common prayer etc, according to the use of the United Church of England and Ireland. 1851. Excludes Psalms; poor on rubrics and some other sections.

[Parker, J.] A concordance and index to the rubrics etc in the first Prayer-book of Edward VI compared with the successive revisions of the Book of common prayer. Oxford 1877, 1883 (rev). Covers the rubrics to the Prayer books of 1549, 1552, 1559, 1604, 1637, 1662.

Studies

Whittingham, W. A brieff discours off the troubles begonne at Franckford in Germany AD 1554, abowte the Booke of common prayer to thende of Q. Maries reigne. [Zürich?] 1574, 1575, 1642; ed J. Petheram 1846; in [J. Dunton (ed)], Phenix vol 2, 1708, reissued as a collection of choice, scarce, and valuable tracts vol 2, 1721.

An explanation of the terms, order and usefulness, of the liturgy of the Church of England, by way of question and answer. 1602.

Hutton, T. Reasons for refusall of subscription to the Booke of common praier, with an amswere [sic]. Ptd Oxford pbd London 1605, pt 2 London 1606. Replies: The removoall of certaine imputations laid upon the ministers by T. H[utton], [Middelburg] 1606; S. Hieron, A defence of the ministers reasons for refusall of subscription, 3 pts [no place] 1607–8.

A survey of the Booke of common prayer, by way of 197 queres. 1606, 1610 (rev).

Fisher, A. A defence of the liturgie of the Church of England, in a dialogue. 1630.

The triall of the English liturgie. 1637.

Certaine grievances, etc for the satisfaction of those that do clamour and revile them that labour to have the Common prayer reformed. 1640.

B[aillie], R. A parallel, or briefe comparison of the liturgie with the masse-book, the breviarie, the ceremoniall, and other Romish ritualls. 1641, 1661. Reply by L. Womock, Beaten oyle for the lamps, 1641.

A copie of the proceedings of some worthy and learned divines, appointed by the Lords; together with considerations upon the Common prayer book. 1641.

W., I. Certaine reasons why the Booke of common-prayer being corrected, should continue. 1641.

LIX exceptions against the Booke of common prayer. 1644.

Sparrow, A. A rationale upon the Book of common prayer. 1655, 1657, 1661, 1664, 1668, 1672, 1676, 1684, 1704; ed S. Downes 1722, 1722; ed J. H. Newman, Oxford 1839, 1843, 1852. The edns of 1722 include Downes, The lives of the compilers of the liturgy.

Taylor, J. A collection of offices, or forms of prayer in cases ordinary and extraordinary, together with a large preface in vindication of the liturgy of the Church of England. 1658, 1690; the preface also prefixed to the posthumous 3rd edn of An apology for authorized and set forms of liturgie, and ptd with this in his Works, ed R. Heber 15 vols 1822, 1828, 1839 vol 7, ed C. F. Eden 10 vols 1847–54 vol 5.

The common prayer book unmasked by divers ministers. 1660.

Powell, V. Common-prayer-book no divine service. 1660, 1661 (3 edns).

[Baxter, R.] An account of all the proceedings of the Commissioners appointed by his Majesty for the review and amendment of the Book of common prayer. 1661, 1661.

Gauden, J. Considerations touching the liturgy of the Church of England. 1661. Replies by T. Bolde, Rhetorick restrained, '1660'; H.D.M.A., A discovery of the weakness, 1661; O.F., The liturgical considerator considered, 1661.

[Pearse, E.] The conformists plea for the nonconformists. 1682.

Nicholls, W. The Book of common prayer, paraphras'd. 1709, 1716.

—— A comment on the Book of common-prayer. 1710, 1712; Supplement, 1711.

Reasons for restoring some prayers and directions as they stand in the communion service of the first English reform'd liturgy of Edward VI. 1717; No reason to alter the present liturgy on account of prayers for the dead, 1717; A defence of the Reasons, being a reply to No reason, 1718; No sufficient reason: a dialogue in vindication of our present liturgy, 2 pts 1718–19; A vindication of the Reasons and Defence, 1719; A reply to the Vindication; A further defence: being an answer to A reply, 1720.

Sharp, T. The rubric in the Book of common prayer, considered. 1753, 1787, Oxford 1834, 1853.

Palmer, W. Origines liturgicæ. 2 vols Oxford 1832, 1836, 1839, London 1845. See W. Beal, Analysis, Cambridge 1850.

Cardwell, E. A history of conferences and other proceedings connected with the revision of the Book of common prayer from 1558 to 1690. Oxford 1840, 1842, 1849 (rev).

Brogden, J. Illustrations of the liturgy and ritual of the united Church of England and Ireland: being sermons and discourses from the seventeenth century. 3 vols 1842.

Lathbury, T. A history of the convocation of the Church of England. 1842.

—— A history of the Book of common prayer. 1858, 1859.

Clay, W. K. An historical sketch of the Prayer book. 1849.

Procter, F. A history of the Book of common prayer. 1855, 1880 (rev), 1889 (rev); rev and rewritten by W. H. Frere as A new history, 1901, 1902 (rev), 1905 (rev). Standard.

Duke, E. Explanation of some of the words in the Book of common prayer. [1868].

Dowden, J. Literary aspects of revision of the Book of common prayer. Contemporary Rev Sept 1871.

Facsimile of the black-letter Prayer-book containing manuscript alterations and additions made in the year 1661. 1871. The Convocation book.

Jacobson, W. (ed). Fragmentary illustrations of the history of the Book of common praycr. 1874. Contains items by Sanderson, M. Wren et al.

Davies, T. L. O. Bible English: chapters on old and disused expressions in the Book of common prayer. 1875.

Daniel, E. The Prayer-book: its history, language and contents. 1877, 1901 (20th edn, rev).

Parker, J. An introduction to the history of the successive revisions of the Book of common prayer. Oxford 1877.

Selbourne, Lord. Notes on some passages in the liturgical history of the reformed English church. 1878.

Luckock, H. M. Studies in the history of the Book of common prayer. 1882.

Marshall, C. and W. W. The Latin Prayer book of Charles II: or an account of the Liturgia of Dean Durel, together with a reprint and translation of the catechism therein contained. Oxford 1882.

Gibson, F. Standard editions of the Book of common prayer. Church Rev 45 1885.

Quaritch, B. A short sketch of liturgical history and literature, illustrated by examples. 1887.

Facsimile of the original manuscript of the Book of common prayer. 1891. The Annexed book.

Deviations of modern editions of the Prayer book from the text of the Sealed book: report of the Committee of the Lower House of Convocation of the Province of York. 1892.

Dixon, B. H. The Bible and the Prayer book: mistranslations, mutilations. [1895?].

Tomlinson, J. T. The Prayer book, Articles and Homilies. 1897.

Pullan, L. The history of the Book of common prayer. Oxford 1900.

Fleming, W. The first and second Books of common prayer. Amer Catholic Quart 26 1901.

Thomas, D. R. The life and work of Bishop Davies and William Salesbury, with an account of some early translations into Welsh of the Holy scriptures and the Prayer book. 1902.

Cooper, J. (ed). The Book of common prayer for the use of the Church of Scotland. Edinburgh 1904.

Brightman, F. E. The litany under Henry VIII. EHR 24 1909.

— The English rite. 2 vols 1915.

Legg, J. W. English orders for consecrating churches. 1911.

— Cranmer's liturgical projects. 1915.

Osmond, P. H. A life of John Cosin. 1913.

Dugmore, C. W. Eucharistic doctrine in England from Hooker to Waterland. 1942.

Morison, S. English liturgical books. Cambridge 1942.

Symonds, H. E. Cranmer and the Edwardine Prayer books. Theology June–July 1946.

Pepper, G. W. An analytical index to the Book of common prayer and a brief account of its evolution. [1948].

B[ühler], C. F. The four hundredth anniversary of the Book of common prayer. New York [1949]. On an exhibition at Pierpont Morgan Lib.

Gerrard, J. F. Notable editions of the Prayer book. 1949.

Ratcliff, E. C. The booke of common prayer of the Church of England: its making and revisions 1549–1661. 1949.

— The liturgical work of Cranmer. Jnl of Ecclesiastical History 7 1956.

Warman, F. S. G. Our Prayer book: the story of four hundred years. 1949.

Malone, K. Our literary heritage and the Book of common prayer. [1950].

Donaldson, G. The making of the Scottish Prayer-book of 1637. Edinburgh 1954.

Cuming, G. J. The making of the Durham book. Jnl of Ecclesiastical History 6 1955.

— (ed). The Durham book: being the first draft of the revision of the Book of common prayer in 1661. Oxford 1961.

Grisbrooke, W. J. (ed). Anglican liturgies of the seventeenth and eighteenth centuries. 1958.

Scheele, M. S., and D. H. Turner. The Book of common prayer 1662. BM Quart 25 1962.

Berry, C. L. '. . . and all the Royal Family': since the reign of James I members of the royal house have been variously prayed for in the services of the Church of England. History Today April 1966.

Morgan, P. Some bibliographical aspects of the Scottish Prayer book of 1637. Bibliotheck 5 1967.

Beesley, A. An unpublished source of the Book of common prayer: Peter Martyr Vermigli's Adhortatio ad Coenam Domini mysticam. Jnl of Ecclesiastical History 19 1968.

Devereux, J. A. The primers and the Prayer book collects. HLQ 32 1968.

King, P. The reasons for the abolition of the Book of common prayer in 1645. Jnl of Ecclesiastical History 21 1970.

C. B. L. B.

IV. VERSIONS OF THE PSALMS

Complete and partial versions, metrical and prose, trns and paraphrases, liturgical and non-liturgical, pbd separately or in larger works other than Bibles and Prayer books, above.

References

Aston   [W. H. Aston, Baron (ed)], Select psalms in verse, with critical remarks by [R.] Lowth and others, 1811.

Cotton   H. Cotton, Editions of the Bible and parts thereof in English, Oxford 1852 (2nd edn).

Holland   J. Holland, The psalmists of Britain: records, biographical and literary, with specimens, 2 vols 1843.

Farr   E. Farr (ed), Select poetry, chiefly devotional, of the reign of Queen Elizabeth, 2 pts Cambridge 1845 (Parker Soc).

Farr 3   E. Farr (ed), Select poetry, chiefly sacred, of the reign of James I, Cambridge 1847.

Latham   [H. Latham (ed)], Anthologia Davidica, 1846 (with list of metrical versions, and specimens).

Glass   H. A. Glass, The story of the psalters: a history of the metrical versions of Great Britain and America, from 1549 to 1885, 1888.

Julian   J. Julian, A dictionary of hymnology, 1892, 2 vols 1907 (rev), 1925.

Steele   R. Steele, The earliest English music printing: a description and bibliography of English printed music to the close of the sixteenth century, 1903 (Bibl Soc).

Brooke   W. T. Brooke, Old English psalmody, from the accession of Edward VI to the restoration of Charles II 1547–1660, 1916 (with specimens).

BUCOEM   British union-catalogue of early music, ed E. B. Schnapper 2 vols 1957.

Aldis   H. G. Aldis, A list of books printed in Scotland before 1700, Edinburgh 1904 (Edinburgh Bibl Soc), 1970 (rev).

(1) BIBLIOGRAPHIES

See also references above.

Lowndes, W. T. In The bibliographer's manual of English literature, rev H. G. Bohn, vol 3 1864, 1875.

Cowan, W. A bibliography of the Book of common order and Psalm book of the Church of Scotland 1556–1644. Edinburgh 1913 (Edinburgh Bibl Soc). Rev and expanded from the Society's Hand list of editions of the psalms, old Scottish version, 1891.

(2) COLLECTIONS

See also references above.

The hexaplar psalter: being the book of psalms in six English versions. Ed W. A. Wright, Cambridge 1911.

Coverdale 1535, Great Bible 1539, Geneva 1560, Bishops 1568, Authorized version 1611, Revised version 1885.

(3) VERSIONS

George Joye (1495?–1553). The psalter of David in Englishe purely and faithfully translated after the texte of ffeline. 'Argentine' (for Antwerp) 1530, London [1532–4] (DMH 3, 7). Prose; under the pseudonym Johan Aleph; from the Latin of 'Aretius Felinus' i.e. Martin Bucer, Strasbourg 1529; psalm 19 rptd in Cotton.

— Davids psalter diligently translated by G. Joye. [Antwerp] 1534, London [1541–2?] (DMH 9). Prose; a different trn from above; from the Latin of Felix Pratensis, Venice 1515, Hagenau 1522, Lyons 1530, Strasbourg 1545; psalm 19 rptd in Cotton.

Miles Coverdale (1488–1568). A paraphrasis upon al the psalmes of David, made by Johannes Campensis and translated out off Latyne into Englishe. [Antwerp] 1534 (Cambridge history of the Bible p. 148), [Antwerp] 1535, London 1539 (DMH 14). Prose paraphrase, from Latin of J. van Kampen (Campensis), Enchiridion psalmorum, Paris 1532, Paris and London 1534 etc.

— The psalter or booke of the psalmes; wher unto are added other devoute praiers. [1540?], 1540 (with Latin) 1548, [1550?] (DMH 55–6). Prose; extracted from Coverdale's Bible, 1535.

— A very excellent and swete exposition upon the two and twentye [i.e. 23] psalme, translated out of hye Almayne [of M. Luther] in to Englyshe. Southwark 1537, 1538; rptd in Cotton. Prose; from Luther's Warhafftig Widerlegung, der grossen Verfelschung der judischen Lehrer, des 22 Psalm, Nuremberg 1536, Wittenberg [1536] etc.

— The psalter or psalmes of David corrected and poynted. 1549, [1549], Worcester 1549, Canterbury 1549, 1550, London [1553?], 1566, 1570, 1571, 1572, 1574, 1575, 1576, 1577, [1579]?, [1583], 1594, 1598, 1600, 1604, 1606, 1615, 1617, 1618, 1620, 1624, 1634, 1635 (DMH 162 etc); ed F. Wormald 1930. Great Bible version, 1539; used in the Book of common prayer, 1549, 1558, 1662.

— Goostly psalmes. [1536?] (DMH 47; Steele 13). Metrical trn, with music from various German metrical versions, of 13 psalms, 2 (50 and 127) in 2 trns: psalms 2, 11 [12], 13 [14], 24 [25], 45 [46], 50 [51], 66 [67] 123 [124], 127 [128], 129 [130], 132 [133], 136 [137], 146 [147]: psalm 137 rptd in Cotton, psalm 50 in Holland. 3rd and 5th rptd in G. Pearson (ed), Coverdale's Remains, Cambridge 1846 (Parker Soc); 2nd and 4th in The hexaplar psalter, 1911; 2nd, 4th and most of 5th in E. Clapton (ed), Coverdale's Bible: our Prayer book psalter, 1934.

Mitchell, A. F. The Wedderburns and their work. Edinburgh 1867.

— (ed). A compendious book of godly and spiritual songs. Edinburgh 1897 (STS).

Herford, C. H. Coverdale's Spiritual songs and the German Kirchenlied. Academy 31 May 1884. Replies by J. Mearns 21 June (also in Julian pp. 442–3) and Mitchell 28 June.

— Studies on the literary relations of England and Germany in the sixteenth century. Cambridge 1886.

Althoff, E. Myles Coverdale's Goostly Psalmes and spirituall Songes und das deutsche Kirchenlied. Bochum 1935. Mostly tr from Luther.

Willoughby, H. R. (ed). The Coverdale psalter and the quatro-centenary of the printed English Bible. Chicago 1935. Facs of 2nd psalter, with census of copies of all edns of Coverdale's Bible.

Smethers, E. R. The Coverdale translation of Psalm lxxxiv. Harvard Theological Rev 38 1945.

Dickinson, A. E. F. The first chorale book in England. Durham Univ Jnl 49 1957. The Spiritual songs.

Mennie, D. M. The first reception of Luther's hymns in England. Ibid. Dates the Spiritual songs 1536–8.

Thomas Becon (1512–67). The hundred and fiftene psalme, Credidi propter, with a fruitefull exposition and godly declaration. In Davids harpe ful of most delectable armony, newely stringed and set in tune, 1542; in his Worckes vol 1, 1564; in his Early works, ed J. Ayre, Cambridge 1843 (Parker Soc). Psalm 116.10–19 in prose, under pseudonym T. Basille.

— Confortable epistle. Strasbourg 1554; in his Worckes vol 3, 1563; in Prayers and other pieces, ed J. Ayre, Cambridge 1844 (Parker Soc). Contains psalms 103 and 112 in verse; from the German.

— Metrical trn of psalms 117 and 134, in the appendix to Sternhold and Hopkins 1560 etc, below; psalm 134 in Brooke.

Sir Thomas Smith (1513–77). Certaigne psalmes or songues of David, translated into Englishe meter. In BM Royal ms 17 A. xvii. Psalms 30, 40, 54, 70, 85, 102, 119, 142, 144–5, 152; ed B. Danielsson, Stockholm Stud in Eng 12 1963; psalm 54 in Holland.

Sir Thomas Wyatt (1503?–42). Certayne psalmes commonly called thee vii penytentiall psalmes, drawen into englyshe meter. [Ed J. Harington] 1549, [1550?]; in edns of Wyatt's works, 1717 etc, R. Hughey, The Arundel Harington manuscript of Tudor poetry vol 1, Columbus 1960, and Collected poems, ed K. A. Muir and P. Thomson, Liverpool 1969; psalm 51 in Cotton, 102 in Holland, 130 in Brooke. The penitential psalms (6, 32, 38, 51, 102, 130, 143) and psalm 37; principally from parallel Latin trns of J. van Kampen (Campensis) and U. Zwingli in Enchiridion psalmorum, Lyons 1533, using also P. Aretino's Italian paraphrase, Venice 1536, Joye's English prose psalter of 1530, the Latin vulgate and Coverdale's Great Bible, 1539; trn generally regarded as made in 1542, but dated 1540 or earlier by K. A. Muir, Life and letters of Wyatt, Liverpool 1963 pp. 174–5.

Mason, H. A. Wyatt and the psalms. TLS 27 Feb– 6 March 1953.

John Wedderburn (1500?–56). Psalmes of David with uther new pleasand ballatis translatit out of Enchiridion psalmorum. Pt 4 of Ane compendious buik of godlie psalmes and spirituall sangis, Edinburgh [1567–8], 1578, 1600, [1621] (Aldis 55, 148, 327, 570); ed D. Laing, Edinburgh 1868 (from edn of 1578); ed A. F. Mitchell, Edinburgh 1897 (STS) (from edn of 1567–8). Metrical version of 22 psalms (2, 12–13, 15, 23, 31, 33, 37, 51, 64, 67, 73, 79, 83, 91, 114–15, 124, 128, 130, 137, 145), ed and probably tr J. Wedderburn, vicar of Dundee, perhaps assisted by his brother Robert (1510?–57?), from the German; tr 1539–43 (Julian) or 1549 (Mitchell). Known as Dundee psalms.

Mitchell, A. F. The Wedderburns and their work. Edinburgh 1867.

Queen Elizabeth I (1533–1603). Metrical trn of psalm '13' [14], in her trn of A godly medytacyon of the Christen sowle, by Margaret d'Angoulême, Queen of Navarre, ed J. Bale 1548; only verse one in edn of [1568–70?]; ed P. Ames 1897; indexed but not found in T. Bentley (ed), The monument of matrones vol 1 pt 2, 1582; in

T. Park (ed), A catalogue of the royal and noble authors of England by H. Walpole vol 1, 1806; in Holland, Farr, and Cotton. Tr 1544.

John Bale (1495–1563). Metrical trn of psalm 54 in The first examinacyon of Anne Askewe, Marburg 1546, London [1585?]; in his Select works, ed H. Christmas, Cambridge 1849 (Parker Soc).

— Metrical trn of psalms 23 and 130 in An expostulation or complaynte agaynste the blasphemyes of a franticke papyst of Hamshyre, [1552?].

Sir John Croke (d. 1554). Thirteen psalms, and the first chapter of Ecclesiastes, translated into English verse, Ed A. Croke and P. Bliss 1844 (Percy Soc). Psalms 6, 13, 19, 31.1–6, 32, 38, 43, 51, 91, 102, 130, 139, 143. Tr by 1547.

Henry Howard, Earl of Surrey (1517–47). Metrical trn of psalms 31, 51, 88 in T. Sternhold, or rather J. Hall, Certayne chapters of the proverbes, [1549?] (later edns under Hall's name contain different psalms). Psalms 55, 73, 88 in J. Harington, Nugae antiquae vol 2, ed T. Park 1804. The 3 are ptd in edns of Surrey's works, 1807–8, 1815–16 etc, R. Hughey (ed), The Arundel Harington manuscript of Tudor poetry vol 1, Columbus 1960, Poems, ed E. Jones, Oxford 1964. Psalm 88 in Holland. Principally from Latin paraphrase of J. van Kampen (Campensis) in Enchiridion psalmorum, Paris 1532 etc.

Huttar, C. A. Poems by Surrey and others in a printed miscellany circa 1550. Eng Miscellany (Rome) 16 1965.

Mason, H. A. The first two printed texts of Surrey's poems. TLS 4 June 1971.

Luke Shepherd (fl. 1548–54). J. Bale, Scriptorum illustrium Brytannie catalogus vol 2, 1559 p. 109, followed by T. Warton, History of English poetry vol 4, ed W. C. Hazlitt 1871 p. 233, says he translated some psalms into metre; nothing survives.

Robert Crowley (Crole) (1518?–88). The psalter of David newely translated into Englysh metre. Holborn 1549 (BUCOEM 817; Steele 16). First complete English metrical version, from the Latin of Leo Juda et al, Biblia sacrosancta, Zürich 1543, 1543–4, 1544, Paris 1545, Salamanca 1584–5 etc; with music in 4 pts; psalm 19 rptd in Cotton, psalm 112 in Holland.

Sternhold and Hopkins, the 'Old Version'. See Holland 1 91–144, with psalm 9 (Sternhold), 37 (Whittingham), 84 (Hopkins), 125 (Kethe, Wisdom), 132 ('Mardley' or rather Marckant), 136 ('Churchyard' or rather Craig), 146 (Norton), 149 (Pullain); Farr xlvi–li, 480–99, with psalms 18, 103 (Sternhold), 84 (Hopkins), 147 (Norton), 51 (Whittingham), 125 (Kethe, Wisdom), 149 (Pullain), 145 ('Mardley' or rather Marckant); psalms 23, 35, 100, 104 (rev) in Latham; psalm 19 (1549, 1551, 1556, 1564) in Cotton; see Glass 65–6; Julian 857–66, 1538–41.

Long the standard Anglican metrical psalter; by Thomas Sternhold (d. 1549), John Hopkins (d. 1570), William Whittingham (1524?–79), John Pullain (1517–65), Thomas Norton (1532–84), William Kethe (d. 1608?), John Marckant (not Mardley), Robert Wisdom (d. 1568), John Craig (1512–1600) (not Thomas Churchyard (1520–64)) and T. Becon (1512–67); after 1696 known as the 'Old Version' in distinction from Tate and Brady's 'New Version'.

Church of England

Certayne psalmes chosen out of the psalter of David, and drawen into English metre. [1547–8?] (19 psalms, all by Sternhold: 1–5, 20, 25, 28 (misprinted '27'), 29 ('19'), 32, 34 ('33'), 41, 49, 73, 78, 103, 120, 123 ('122'), 128 ('138'): DMH 66); Al such psalmes of David as T. Sternholde did draw into English metre, 1549, (37 psalms by Sternhold, 19 as before, with 6–17, 19, 21, 43–4, 63, 68, and 7 by Hopkins: 30, 33, 42, 52, 79, 82, 146); total 44); [1550?], 1551 (3 edns), 1553, 1553.

Church of Geneva

One and fiftie psalmes of David in English metre [pt 2 of The forme of prayers, and ministration of the sacraments, used at Geneva]. Geneva 1556 (44 as before, rev Whittingham, with 7 by Whittingham [23, 51, 114–15, 130, 133, 137], total 51; the first edn with music, adapted from that ed and composed by Bourgeois for the French psalter of C. Marot and T. de Bèze, 1552–54; BUCOEM 817); Psalmes [pt 2 of The forme of prayers], 1558 (51 as before, with 9 by Whittingham [37, 50, 67, 71, 119, 121, 124, 127, 129], and 2 by Pullain [148–9], total 62).

Church of England

Psalmes of David. 1560 (62 as before, with 2 by Wisdom [67, 125], one anon [95], 2 by Becon in an appendix [117, 134], total 67; 42 tunes: BUCOEM 817; Steele 36), 1561 (67 as before, the anon 95 being moved to the appendix, omitting Wisdom's 67 and Whittingham's 67 and 71, and adding 3 by Sternhold [18, 22–3], 14 by Hopkins [24, 26–7, 31, 62, 64–7, 69–72, 74], one by Norton [75], and one by Kethe [100], total 83; 40 tunes: Steele 38).

Church of Geneva

Foure score and seven psalmes [separately and in The forme of prayers]. [London or Geneva] 1561 (62 as 1558, with 25 by Kethe [27, 36, 47, 54, 58, 62, 70, 85, 88, 90–1, 94, 100–1, 104, 107, 111–13, 122, 125–6, 134, 138, 142], total 87; 62 tunes: Steele 37).

Complete edns:

The whole book of psalmes. Ed Hopkins 1562 (40 psalms by Sternhold: 19 first in 1547–8, 18 in 1549, 3 in 1561; 60 by Hopkins: 7 in 1549, 14 in 1561, 39 in 1562 [35–6, 38–40, 45–8, 50, 54–61, 76–7, 80–1, 83–99]; 10 by Whittingham: 5 of 7 from 1556 [51, 114, 130, 133, 137], and 5 of 9 from 1558 [37, 119, 121, 124, 127]; 26 by Norton: one in 1561, 25 in 1562 [51, 53, 101–2, 105–6, 108–10, 115–17, 129, 136, 138–45, 147, 149–50]; 4 by Marckant: 118, 131–2, 135, first in 1562; 9 by Kethe, from his 25 in 1561: 104, 107, 111–13, 122, 125–6, 134; one by Pullain: 148 from 1558, omitting 149, an anon psalm 100, and the anon 95 and 2 by Becon [1560] in appendix; total 150 psalms in 154 versions; with 65 tunes: DMH 118; BUCOEM 817; Steele 40); 291 edns 1563–1640 [London, except for 11 Cambridge edns 1628–38 and 7 undated Amsterdam edns c. 1630–3] (1563–4 restoring Whittingham's psalm 50, Kethe's 100 and Wisdom's 125; 1565 restoring Whittingham's 23; 1581 adding Craig's 136 from the Scottish psalter: 287 edns in BUCOEM 817–827; 80 edns 1563–1600 in Steele among 41–196), over 200 edns 1641–1700, at least 275 edns 1701–1852 (BM).

1601 (with Geneva version, parallel or in the margin), 1603, 1605, 1613, 1615, 1617, 1623, 1628, 1628, 1631.

1635 (with the Prayer book prose version, Coverdale 1539).

With music:

(i) *The standard music accompanying nearly all edns of Sternhold and Hopkins began with 51 tunes to the 51 psalms in the Geneva edn of 1556, increased in stages to 65 tunes in the first complete edn of 1562; of these 65, 10 are from that of 1556, 13 from 1560, 7 from 1561, the remaining 35 new; many are derived from the music partly adapted and partly composed by Louis Bourgeois for the French psalter of C. Marot and T. de Bèze, 1542–62, a few from German sources; the French sources are conveniently described in Grove's Dictionary of music, 5th edn 9 vols 1954, article Bourgeois, the English tunes article Psalter; the principal edns 1556–1677 etc are listed in BUCOEM 817–28.*

(ii) *The 65 tunes of 1562 supplemented by 30 more and furnished with multiple settings, in all 141: 81 by W. Parsons, 27 by T. Causton, 17 by J. Hake, 11 by R. Brimle,*

4 by N. Southerton; to accompany Sternhold and Hopkins, only the opening words of each psalm being given, for musicians, in 4 pt-books: The whole psalmes in foure partes, which may be song to al musicall instrumentes, *1563, 165* (BUCOEM 817; Steele 41). *Contains 59 psalms in 60 versions: 1, 3, 6, 14, 18, 21–2, 25, 30, 35, 41–4, 46, 49, 50 (2 versions), 51–2, 59, 61, 63, 68–9, 72, 77–8, 81, 86, 88, 92–3, 100, 103–4, 111, 113–14, 119–22, 124–6, 128, 130–1, 133–7, 139, 141, 143, 145–8.*

(iii) William Damon (Daman), The psalmes of David in English meter with notes of foure partes, *1579 (ed J. Bull and E. Hake, without Damon's knowledge), 1591 (2 versions, one with tunes in the medius, the other in the tenor; ed W. Swayne, probably after Damon's death)* (BUCOEM 250; Steele 74, 128–9; *each edn in 4 pt-books).*

(iv) John Cosyn, Sixty psalms in metre. *In* Musike of six, and five parts, made upon the common tunes used in singing of the psalms, *4 pts 1585* (BUCOEM 226, Steele 97).

(v) The whole booke of psalmes, with their wonted tunes, composed into foure parts, compiled by (x) sundry authors. *1592, 1594 [1598?], 1604, 1611* (BUCOEM 819–21; Steele 135, 140, 164); *rptd 1844 (Musical Antiquarian Soc). Settings composed by J. Farmer (17), G. Kirbye (12), R. Allison (10), G. Farnaby (9), E. Blancks (7), J. Dowland (5), W. Cobbold (5), E. Hooper (4), E. Johnson (3), M. Cavendish (1); ed T. Este.*

(vi) Richard Alison, The psalmes of David in meter, the plaine song beeing the common tunne to be sung and plaide upon the lute, orpharyon, citterne or base violl, *1599* (BUCOEM 820, Steele 178).

(vii) Thomas Ravenscroft, The whole booke of psalmes, composed into four parts by sundry authors, *1621, 1633* (BUCOEM 876, *with ten 18th-century revisions and selections). 105 settings, 28 from earlier collections, 69 by 8 additional composers: Ravenscroft (55), J. Milton (3), T. Tomkins, J. Tomkins, S. Stubbs (2 each), R. Palmer, W. Harrison, W. Carnfield or Cranford, J. Ward, M. Pierson (one each). The music rptd 1845.*

Barton, W. A view of many errors and some gross absurdities in the old translation of the psalms in English metre. 1655.

Beveridge, W. A defence of the book of psalms collected into English metre by Thomas Sternhold, John Hopkins and others. 1710.

Todd, H. J. Observations upon the metrical version of the psalms, made by Sternhold, Hopkins and others. 1822.

Cowan, W. Ravenscroft's Whole book of psalmes 1621. Edinburgh Bibl Soc Pbns 6 1906.

John Hall (1529?–66?). The proverbs of Salomon, three chapters of Ecclesiastes and certayn psalmes of David, drawen into metre. [1549?]. Contains 5 psalms (34, 54, 112, 114–15); the only copy is incomplete at the end.

— Certayne chapters taken out of the proverbes of Salomon etc. [1548–9]. Contains 9 psalms: '21' [i.e. 24], 33, 53, 64, 111–13, 114 (unnumbered), 144.

— The Courte of Vertu: contaynynge many holy songes, sonettes, psalmes and ballettes. 1565 (BUCOEM 817; Steele 49; contains 12 psalms: 25, 34, 54, 65, 112–15, 130, 137, 140, 145). Psalm 115 in Holland and Farr. *The 2nd follows numbering of the Vulgate, while 1549 and 1565 follow the English style; for 3 psalms in the earlier edn of 1549 see the Earl of Surrey, above.*

Lady Elizabeth Fane. Certaine psalmes of godly meditation in number 21, with a 102 proverbs. 1550. No known copy: A Maunsell, The catalogue of English printed books, 1595, p. 85, followed by T. Tanner, Bibliotheca britannico-hibernica, 1748 p. 273, and J. Ames, Typographical antiquities, 1749 p. 271, etc; *see also* G. Ballard, Memoirs of several ladies of Great Britain, 1752 p. 119.

William Hunnis (d. 1597). Certayne psalmes chosen out of the psalter of David and drawen furth into Englysh meter. 1550. Psalms 51, 56–7, 113, 117, 147; supplementary to Sternhold and Hopkins 1549; 51 rptd in Cotton and Farr.

— Seven sobs of a sorrowfull soule for sinne: comprehending those seven psalmes called pœnitentiall, reduced into meeter. 1583, 1587, 1589, 1597, 1600, 1604, 1609, 1615, 1618, 1629. (BUCOEM 516; Steele 86, 108, 122, 162). Psalms 6, 32, 38, 51 (different from above), 102, 130, 143; with 7 tunes; psalm 6 rptd in Holland and Farr.

Stopes, C. C. Hunnis and the revels of the Chapel Royal. Materialien zur Kunde des älteren englischen Dramas 29 1910.

William Forrest (fl. 1530–81). Certayne psalmes of Davyd in meeatre, added to maister Sternholdis and others. 1551. Not ptd, except psalm 47 in Holland; 49 psalms: (Vulgate-Douai numbering) 6–20, 22–3, 25, 30, 32, 35, 37, 42, 45–7, 50, 53, 55–6, 59–60, 65–6, 69, 71, 74, 85, 87, 92, 94–7, 100, 112, 129, 148, 150 in BM Royal ms 17 A. xxi; Roman Catholic.

Francis Segar (Seager) (fl. 1549–63). Certayne psalmes select out of the psalter of David, and drawen into Englyshe metre. 1553 (BUCOEM 909; Steele 18). 20 psalms: 31, 43, 51, 64, 70, 88, 112, 120, 130, 138, 140–9, ptd as 19; with two 4-pt settings, possibly by Christopher Tye; psalm 112 rptd in Cotton, 140 in Holland.

John Knox (1505–72). A percel of the VI psalme expoundet. [Wesel 1554] (running title), [abroad 1556?] (as An exposition uppon the syxt psalme); ed A. Fleming 1580 (as A fort for the afflicted); in his Works vol 3, ed D. Laing, Edinburgh 1854.

Matthew Parker (1504–75). The whole psalter translated into English metre. [1567?] (BUCOEM 817; Steele 53). With 8 4-pt tunes by T. Tallis; completed in 1555; anon; authorship established by acrostic at psalm 119; incorrectly attributed to John Keeper or Keper by A. Wood, Athenae oxonienses, 1721 (2nd edn) I. 181, corrected in P. Bliss's edn, 1813 I. 416–18. Psalms 1–8 rptd in Clerical & Scholastic Monthly Note Book 1 1851; 19 in Cotton; 23 in Sir J. Hawkins, A general history of music vol 3, 1776 p. 504; 92, 110 in Farr; 129 in Holland; 146 in Aston.

George Buchanan (1506–82). [Latin metrical versions of 18 psalms]. In Davidis psalmi aliquot latino carmine expressi a quatuor poetis, ed H. Estienne, [Paris] 1556; [entire psalter as] Psalmorum Davidis paraphrasis poetica, authore G. Buchanano, psalmi aliquot [6: 1, 2, 6, 15, 18, 104] à Th. B[eza] versi, [Paris 1564–5], 1566, Strasbourg 1566, Antwerp 1566, 1567, Strasbourg 1568, 1571, 1572, Strasbourg 1572, [no place] 1572, Paris 1575, Strasbourg 1575. Some of Buchanan's versions in Psalmorum Davidis aliquot metaphrasis græca I. Serrani, [Paris] 1575; Buchanan's complete psalter, Antwerp 1576, Strasbourg 1578, Lyons 1579 (psalms 1–41 set to music), Geneva 1579, London 1580, Paris 1580; parallel with Beza's version in Psalmorum Davidis libri quinque duplici poetica metaphrasi, Morgiis 1581; Buchanan's version, Antwerp 1582, London 1583; ed with music by N. Chytraeus (Kochhoff), Frankfurt 1585, Cologne 1586, Herborn 1586, 1588, Antwerp 1588, Herborn 1590, Geneva 1590, 1591, Leyden 1591, Herborn 1592, London 1592; parallel with Beza's version, Geneva 1593, 1594; Buchanan's version, Leyden 1595; ed Chytraeus, Herborn 1595, Wittemberg 1595, Siegen [Wittenberg] 1597, Herborn 1600, Leyden 1600, Châlons 1601, Leyden 1603, Frankfurt 1605, [Leyden] 1609, Herborn 1610, Edinburgh 1611, 1615, Herborn 1616, Amsterdam 1618, Herborn 1619, London 1620 (Ecphrasis, ed A. Yule), Leyden 1621, Edinburgh 1621, Herborn 1624, 1637, 1646, London 1647–8, Amsterdam 1650, Herborn 1656, London 1660, Herborn 1664, Aberdeen 1672, Glasgow

1684, Amsterdam 1688, Edinburgh 1694, 1695–9, Herborn 1703, Stendaliae 1710, Edinburgh 1716, Basle 1721, Edinburgh 1725, Paris 1729, Edinburgh 1730, 1732, 1737, London 1742, Glasgow 1750, Edinburgh 1762, 1764, Glasgow 1765, London 1775, Edinburgh 1786, Glasgow 1790, Edinburgh 1793, Glasgow 1797, Edinburgh 1807, 1812, 1815, 1825, 1882; tr T. Cradock 1754 (English verse); select psalms tr J. Fanch 1764; complete trn into English prose by A. Waddel, with Latin, Edinburgh 1772, London 1775, Edinburgh 1786, Glasgow 1797; English only, Edinburgh 1816, 1825 etc; tr J. Eadie, Glasgow 1836 (English verse); with an Italian verse trn, Milan 1833. For these edns and additional selections etc *see* D. Murray in George Buchanan: Glasgow quatercentenary studies 1906, ed G. Neilson, Glasgow 1907 pp. 407–30.

Miles Hogarde (Huggarde) (fl. 1548–57). A short treatise in meter upon the cxxix psalme of David called De profundis. 1557. Psalm 130 (E. Arber, A transcript of the Registers of the Company of Stationers 1554–1640 vol 4, 1894 p. 16); ptd book, if ever actually pbd, not known to survive; Hogarde's metrical paraphrase in BM ms additional 15,233 ff. 57v–58r.

The Geneva psalms. [Prose, probably by Anthony Gilby, based on Calvin's commentaries, 1557, and Sternhold and Hopkins]. [Geneva] 1557. Copies in Bodley and Cambridge Univ Lib.

—— [A different prose trn; the same as in 1560 Geneva Bible, above]. Geneva 1559, London 1576; ptd parallel with 10 edns of Sternhold and Hopkins, 1601–31, above; in The hexaplar psalter, 1911.

William Kethe (Keith) (d. 1608?). Psalme of David XCIII (XCIIII) turned to metre. In J. Knox, The appellation from the cruell sentence, Geneva 1558; in Knox, Works vol 4, ed D. Laing, Edinburgh 1855.

—— [Metrical versions of 25 psalms, 27, 36, 47, 54, 58, 62, 70, 85, 88, 90–1, 94, 100–1, 104, 107, 111–13, 122, 125–6, 134, 138, 142]. In Geneva psalter, 1561 etc and Scottish psalter 1564–5 etc. 9 psalms (between 104 and 134) are adopted in the English Sternhold and Hopkins 1562 and constantly thereafter. Psalm 100 (All people that on earth do dwell) added in Sternhold and Hopkins 1564 appendix, 1565 text, and thence in all English and Scottish (including 1650) edns; in many hymnals from the mid-18th century, e.g. Hymns ancient and modern, 1009 no 316; versions of 1565 and 1578, ptd in Knox's Works vol 6, Edinburgh 1895. Psalm 104 (My soul, praise the Lord) is adopted in some modern hymnals, e.g. B. H. Kennedy, Hymnologia christiana, 1863 no 1023 (altered).

John Craig (1512–1600). Verse trns of 15 psalms (24, 56, 75, 102, 105, 108, 110, 117–18, 132, 140–1, 143, 145) in Scottish psalter of 1564–5 below and subsequent edns; 3 (136, 143, 145), considerably altered, repeated in the Scottish psalter of 1650; 136 added as alternative to 1581 and later edns of Sternhold and Hopkins under misprinted initials T.C. (formerly identified as Thomas Churchyard); psalm 110 ptd in Blackwood's Mag April–May 1818 and Holland; 24 (1565) and 145 (1578) in D. Laing (ed), The works of J. Knox vol 6, Edinburgh 1895.

Robert Pont (Kylpont, Kynpont) (1524–1606). Verse trns of 6 psalms (57, 59, 76, 80–1, 83) in the Scottish psalter of 1564–5, below and subsequent edns: he was probably one of the compilers of this psalter, and in 1601 the General Assembly of the Kirk of Scotland ordered from him a revision which he never accomplished; 76 ptd in Blackwood's Mag April–May 1818; 57 (versions of 1565 and 1578) in D. Laing (ed), Works of John Knox vol 6, Edinburgh 1895; 96 in Holland.

First Scottish Psalter. Ed John Knox and, specially after 1575, rev Robert Pont, above; the standard Presbyterian psalter till 1650; mainly derived from Sternhold and Hopkins but with divergences in texts and tunes. Adopts all 87 versions from the Anglo-German psalter

of 1561, above (37 by Sternhold, 7 by Hopkins, 16 by Whittingham, 2 by Pullain, 25 by Kethe), 42 more from Sternhold and Hopkins 1562 (2 by Sternhold (18, 22), 30 by Hopkins (26, 31, 35, 38–40, 45–6, 48, 55, 60–1, 64–6, 69, 72, 74, 77, 84, 86–7, 89, 92–3, 95–9), 8 by Norton (53, 106, 109, 116, 139, 144, 147, 150), 2 by Marckant (131, 135)), and adds 15 by John Craig, above, and 6 by Pont, above. The psalms, sometimes separately, sometimes with Book of common order; most edns contain music; from 1602 (?) many edns contain also the Geneva prose trn; title varies: The whole psalmes of David in English meter, in The forme of prayers, and ministration of the sacraments, used in the English church at Geneva, approved and received by the Church of Scotland, Edinburgh 1564–5, 1565, [Geneva?] 1566, Edinburgh 1571; The CL psalmes of David in English metre, with the forme of prayers etc, 1575, 1584, 1587, London 1587, Middelburg 1594, Edinburgh 1595–6, Middelburg 1596, [1599], Edinburgh 1599–1602, ptd Dort and pbd Edinburgh 1601, Middelburg 1602, Edinburgh 1603, [1603–11], 1607, 1611, 1614, 1615, 1616, 1617, 1618, 1621, 1622, 1625, Aberdeen 1625, 1626, 1629, Edinburgh 1630, 1632, Aberdeen 1632, 1633, Edinburgh 1633, 1634, 1635, 1636–7, 1640, 1641, 1642, 1643, 1644 (BUCOEM 818–27; Steele 42, 46, 65, 106, 145, 153; Aldis pp. 135 Forme of prayers, and 145 and 171 Psalms].

Livingston, N. The Scottish metrical psalter of AD 1635, reprinted in full and illustrated with dissertations, titles and facsimiles. Glasgow 1864; ed R. R. Terry 1935.

Laing, D. An account of the Scottish Psalter of AD 1566. Proc Soc of Antiquaries of Scotland 7 1871.

MacMeeken, J. W. History of the Scottish metrical psalms. Glasgow 1872.

Barclay, H. Notes on the psalm book, especially on the Scotch metrical version. Edinburgh 1877.

Cowan, W. and J. Love. The music of the church hymnary and the psalter in metre: its sources and composers. Edinburgh 1901.

Williams, G. The Scottish psalms in metre. 1906.

Gilchrist, A. G. Psalm-versions and French tunes in the Scottish psalter of 1564. Records of Scottish Church History Soc 5 1935.

Terry, R. R. A forgotten psalter. In his A forgotten psalter and other essays, Oxford 1929. On edn of Aberdeen 1623.

Fulton, A. The 1633 and 1635 editions of the old Scottish psalm book. Manchester 1935.

Farmer, H. G. In his A history of music in Scotland, 1947.

Patrick, M. In his Four centuries of Scottish psalmody, Oxford 1949.

Donaldson, R. An early imprint of Andro Hart. Bibliotheck 4 1963. Psalmes in prose and metre 1607.

John Coxe (Cockis) (fl. 1565–72). The comentarye or exposition of Wolfegang Musculus upon the li psalme, newely translated [by Coxe?] out of Latine into Englishe. 1565 (St Paul's Cathedral Lib); tr J. Stockwood (d. 1610) 1586. Prose; extracted from Enarrationes in totum psalterium Davidis regis, 2 vols Basle 1551 etc.

John Pits (Pitts, Pyttes) (fl. 1566). Metrical trn of psalms 67 and 100 in A poore mannes benevolence to the afflicted Church, 1566.

Alexander Scott (1525?–84?). [Metrical trn of psalms 1 and 50 [51]; ptd from Bannatyne ms in Nat Lib of Scotland]. In Poems, ed D. Laing, Edinburgh 1821; ed W. Mackean, Paisley 1887 (modernized); Glasgow 1882; ed A. K. Donald 1902 (EETS); ed A. Scott, Edinburgh 1952; psalm 51 in Holland.

William Samuel (fl. 1550–69). An abridgement of all the canonical books of the Olde testament, written in Sternholds meter. 1569. Includes an 8-line metrical summary of each psalm. Psalm 19 in Farr.

George Gascoigne (1542–77). [Metrical trn of psalm 130]. In A hundreth sundrie flowres, bounde up in one small posie, [1572–3], 1575 (as The posies corrected and augmented), 1587 (as Whole woorkes), 1587 (as The pleasauntest workes); Complete works vol 1, ed J. W. Cunliffe 1907; A hundreth sundrie flowres, ed B. M. Ward 1926; ed C. T. Prouty, Columbia Missouri 1942; Menston 1970 (facs). Psalm 130 in Aston, Holland and Farr.

Christopher Carlile (d. 1588). The psalms of David in English, with annotations. 1573. Prose; not ptd; Cambridge Univ Lib ms Ff.5.6.

G.C. [Metrical paraphrases of 4 psalms: 4, 5, 8, 10]. In A piteous platforme of an oppressed mynde set downe by the extreme surmyzes of sundrye distressed meditations, [1576–7].

Thomas Rogers (d. 1616). A golden chaine, taken out of the rich treasure house: the psalmes of King David; also the pretious pearles of King Salomon. 1579, 1587. A cento from the Geneva trn of Psalms and Proverbs.

Scipione Gentili (Gentile) (1563–1616). Paraphrasis aliquot psalmorum Davidis, carmine heroico. 1581, 1584 (as In xxv Davidis psalmos epicæ paraphrases). Psalms 8, 11, 18, 20, 46, 48, 50, 61, 65, 74–5, 84, 87, 93, 102, 104, 106, 113–14, 118, 126, 133, 137, 147–8.

Thomas Bentley (?). Psalme 121. In The monument of matrones vol 3 pt 5, ed Bentley 1582. Prose trn, apparently new.

Richard Stanyhurst (Stanihurst) (1547–1618). [Metrical trn of psalms 1–4]. In his trn of Thee first foure bookes of Virgil his Aeneis, Leyden 1582, London 1583, 1620; ed J. M[aidment], Edinburgh 1836; ed E. Arber, English scholar's library vol 10, 1880, 1895; ed D. van der Haar, Amsterdam 1933. Psalm 2 rptd in Cotton and Holland.

King James VI and I (1566–1625). The CIII psalm, translated out of Tremellius. In his Essayes of a prentise in the divine art of poesie, Edinburgh 1584, 1585 etc. In verse.
— [Metrical trn of 30 psalms: 1–7, 9–21, 29, 47, 100, 104, 125, 128, 131, 133, 148, 150]. BM Royal ms 18 B. xvi (autograph); rev and completed by Sir W. Alexander and ptd 1631 etc, below. Psalm 29 in Holland and Farr. Both in Poems vol 2, ed J. Craigie 1958 (STS).

William Byrd (Bird) (1543?–1623). [Metrical trn of psalms 12–13, 15, 112, 119 (2 sections only), 123, 130, with 6 and 55 in Sternhold and Hopkins version]. In Psalmes, sonets and songs of sadnes and pietie, made into musicke of five parts, 5 pts 1588, [1599?] (BUCOEM 147; Steele 113). Psalms 13 and 15 in Farr. The date of 2nd edn corrected from [1589–90?] by H. K. Andrews, Printed sources of W. Byrd, Psalmes, sonets and songs, Music & Letters 44 1963.

Richard Robinson (fl. 1569–89). [Metrical trn of psalm 6]. In A golden mirrour, 1589; ed T. Corser, Manchester 1851 (Chetham Soc); Farr.

Abraham Fraunce (d. c. 1633). [Metrical trn of Certeine psalmes: 1, 6, 8, 29, 38, 50, 73, 104]. In The Countesse of Pembrokes Emanuell, 1591; in A. B. Grosart (ed), Miscellanies of the Fuller worthies' library vol 3, 1872. Psalm 8 rptd in Cotton 364, 73 in Holland and Farr.

Edmund Spenser (1552–99). [Metrical trn of the seven penitential psalms mentioned, with Spenser's lost trns of Ecclesiastes and the Song of Solomon, in the printer's preface to Spenser's Complaints, 1591; lost]. See T. Palgrave, Minor poems of Spenser, in A. B. Grosart's edn of Spenser's Works 9 vols 1882 4 (vol 4 pp. xcvii–c); Works vol 8, Minor poems 2 Baltimore 1947.

Edmund Sheafe (fl. 1592). Metrical trn of the psalms, c. 1592. Unpbd autograph ms in Bodley ms Rawlinson poetry 112.

Henry Lok (Lock) (1553?–1608?). Sundry psalms of David, translated into verse. 1594; in Ecclesiastes, otherwise called the preacher, 1597. Psalms 27, 71, 119, 121, 130; 121 rptd in Cotton and Farr, 27 in Holland and Farr.

Michael Cosowarth (Cosworth) (fl. 1600). Metrical trn of selected psalms in BM ms Harley 6906; unpbd except psalm 30 in Holland and Farr.

Some Latin metrical psalms. In Songes of sundrye natures, whereof somme ar divine, some are madrigalles, and the rest spalmes [sic] and hymnes in Latin composed for 5 and 6 voyces and one for 8 voyces, by Nathanaell Patrick. Licensed to Thomas Este, 22 Oct 1597 (E. Arber, A transcript of the registers of the Company of Stationers 1554–1640, vol 3 1876 p. 93; Steele 51*). Perhaps never ptd.

Sir William Vaughan (c. 1575–1641). Paraphrasis in aliquot psalmos selectiores. In Ἐρωτοπαίγνιον pium: continens Canticum canticorum Salomonis et psalmos aliquot selectiores, 2 pts 1597–8. Latin metrical paraphrases of psalms 8–9, 24, 27, 30, 40, 48.

Sir Philip Sidney (1554–86) and his sister Mary Herbert Countess of Pembroke (1555–1621). Metrical; psalms 1–43 by Sidney (probably tr c. 1585), 44–150 by the Countess (c. 1590–9); mainly from Les CL pseaumes mis en rime françoise par C. Marot et T. de Bèze, 1562, using also the Prayer book prose version from Coverdale's Great Bible 1539, Geneva Bible 1560, Bishops' Bible 1568 and Bèze's Latin metrical paraphrase 1580.
The psalmes of David, translated into divers and sundry kinds of verse, begun by Sir P. Sidney and finished by the Countess of Pembroke. [Ed S. W. Singer] 1823; Complete works vol 3, ed A. Feuillerat, Cambridge 1923 (1–43); Poems, ed W. A. Ringler, Oxford 1962 (1–43); ed J. C. A. Rathmell, Garden City NY 1963 (1–150).
Psalm 137 in Guardian no 18, 1 April 1713; 137 in Sidney's Works vol 3 1725; 51, 69, 104, 112, 117, 120, 137 in Sir J. Harington, Nugae antiquae vol 2, 1775, ed T. Park 1804 (psalms 112, 137); 93 and 137 in T. Zouch, Memoirs of the life and writings of Sidney, York 1809 (2nd edn); 93, 100, 127 in Zouch's Works vol 2, ed F. Wrangham 1820; much of 44–5, 62, 78, 81, 90, 119, 137 in N. Drake, Mornings in spring vol 1, 1828; 68, 75, 114, 122 in Sidneiana, ed S. Butler 1837; 44, 65, 93, 96, 139 in England's antiphon, ed G. Macdonald 1868; 69 in J. Hannah, The courtly poets from Raleigh to Montrose, 1870; 14–15 in J. Ruskin, Fors clavigera 2, letter 23, 1872, in Ruskin's Works vol 27, 1907; 1–20, 25–31, 33–5, 41–2, 44, 49–50, 53–5, 58, 62, 65, 69, 71–5, 78, 80, 83, 85, 89, 101 with notes in Ruskin, Rock honeycomb: broken pieces of Sidney's psalter, Bibliotheca Pastorum 2 1877, in Ruskin's Works vol 31, 1907; 93 and 110 in Brooke 48–50; 23 in D. Brown (ed), Selected poems from George Herbert, with a few representative poems by his contemporaries, 1960.
Donne, J. Upon the translation of the psalmes by Sydney and the Countess of Pembroke his sister. In Poems, 1635 etc; in Rathmell, above.
Nicholson, B. The Sidneian Psalms. Athenaeum 16 July 1881.
Young, F. C. B. Mary Sidney, Countess of Pembroke. 1912. See pp. 135–9.
Rathmell, J. C. A. Hopkins, Ruskin and the Sidney Psalter. London Mag Sept 1959.
England, M. W. Sidney and François Perrot de Méssières: their verse versions of the Psalms. BNYPL Jan–Feb 1971.

Sir John Harington (1560–1612). 'The psalmes put into verse' in Bodley ms Douce 361. Psalms 24, 112, 137 ptd in Nugae antiquae vol 2, ed T. Park 1804; 112 and 137 in Farr; 112 in Brooke. All 150 psalms.

Charles Lumisden (c. 1560–1630). An exposition upon some select psalms of David, written by Robert Rollock, and translated out of Latine. Edinburgh 1600. Prose trn of 15 psalms (3, 6, 16, 23, 32, 39, 42, 49, 51, 62, 65, 84, 116, 130, 137); tr from In selectos aliquot psalmos Davidis commentarius, Edinburgh 1599, 1610.

Richard Rowlands alias Verstegan (fl. 1565–1620). Odes in imitation of the seaven penitential psalms. [Antwerp] 1601. Psalms 6, 32, 38, 51, 102, 130, 143; 32 in Holland; '129' [130] in Cotton.
Fitzmaurice-Kelly, J. New Rev July 1897.

Joseph Bryan. Metrical trn c. 1602 of 22 psalms (1, 3, 6, 8, 23, 26, 28, 54, 56, 65, 70, 93, 107.23–31, 112–14, 124, 127, 133, 137, 142, 146) in BM ms Harley 6930, transcribed by Ralph Crane in Harley 3357 and (by the same, 1626) Bodley ms Rawlinson poetry 61; psalms 133, 146 in Aston; 142 in Holland; 54, 127, 142 in Farr; psalms 28 and 65, the latter under T. Carew's name, in G. Fletcher, Christ's victory and triumph, ed W. T. Brooke 1888; 15 psalms unpbd. On Harley 3357 see F. P. Wilson, Library 4th ser 7 1926.

Christopher Davison. Metrical trn c. 1602 of psalms 15 and 125 in BM ms Harley 6930, transcribed in Harley 3357 and Bodley ms Rawlinson poetry 61; psalms 15 and 125 in F. Davison, Poetical rhapsody vol 3, ed S. E. Brydges, Lee Priory 1817; vol 2 ed N. H. Nicolas 1826 (psalms from this edn also separately); vol 2 ed A. H. Bullen 1891 (psalm 15 only, also in Holland); 15 and 125, the latter misattributed to F. Davison, in Farr; 15 and 125 in G. Fletcher, Christ's victory and triumph, ed W. T. Brooke 1888; 125 in Brooke 1916. On Harley 3357 see F. P. Wilson, above.

Francis Davison (c. 1575–c. 1621). Metrical trn c. 1602 of 16 psalms in 18 versions (1. 2–4, 6, 13, 23 (3 versions), 30, 43, 73. 1–5, 79, 86, 123, 130–1, 133, 137, 142) in BM ms Harley 6930 (probably autograph; psalms 43, 123, 128 anon), transcribed in Harley 3357 (all attributed to F. Davison) and Bodley ms Rawlinson poetry 61; all except 43, 123 and 128 in Poetical rhapsody vol 3, ed Brydges (above) and Nicolas's edn vol 2 1826; 6, 13 and 23 (one version) in Bullen's edn vol 2 1891; all 18 versions in G. Fletcher, Christ's victory and triumph, ed W. T. Brooke 1888; 13, 23, 43, 73, 86, 123, 130, 132, 137, 142 in Farr; 131 in Brooke 1916 (dating the collection after 1613). On Harley 3357 see F. P. Wilson, above.

Richard Gipps. Metrical trn c. 1602 of psalms 1 and 6 in BM ms Harley 6930, transcribed in Harley 3357 and Bodley ms Rawlinson poetry 61; psalm 1 in G. Fletcher, Christ's victory and triumph, ed W. T. Brooke 1888; 6 in Holland and Farr. On Harley 3357 see F. P. Wilson, above.

Henry Dod (1550?–1630?). Certaine psalmes of David reduced into English meter. 1603. Psalms 104, 111, 120, 122, 124–6, 130; with prose in the margin.

—— Al the psalmes of David with certeine songes and canticles, nowe faithfully reduced into easie meeter. 1620. With prose in the margin; 127 in Holland and Farr; 19 in Cotton; extracts from 1, 18, 23 in T. Corser, Collectanea anglo-poetica 5, 1873 (Chetham Soc).

Elizabeth Grymeston (Grimston) née Barney (c. 1565–1603). Odes in imitation of the seven pœnitentiall psalms, in seven severall kinde of verse. In Miscelanea, meditations, memoratives, 1604, [1606?], [1608?], [1610?]; psalm 51 in Farr.

Alexander Montgomerie (1556?–1610?). The mindes melodie: contayning certayne psalmes applyed to a new and pleasant tune. Edinburgh 1605 (Aldis 389). 15 psalms: 1, 4, 6, 8, 15, 19, 23, 43, 57, 91, 101, 117, 121, 125, 128; in Poems, ed D. Laing and D. Irving, Edinburgh 1821; ed J. Cranstoun and G. Stevenson vol 1 1887 (STS) (also trns of psalms 1 [rev], 2, 36 as Devotional poems); 19 in Cotton; 1 and 23 in A. Ramsay, The ever green vol 2, Edinburgh 1724 etc, and in Montgomerie's Poetical works, Glasgow 1754.

Joseph Hall (1574–1656). Some fewe of Davids psalms metraphrased, for a taste of the rest. Pt 2 of Holy observations, 1607, 1609; in edns of Works vol 1, 1614–48; Complete poems, ed A. B. Grosart, Manchester 1879. Psalms 1–10; in metre; 7 rptd in Holland and Latham; 8 in Cotton; 4 in Brooke.

Henry Ainsworth (1571–1623?). The book of psalmes englished, both in prose and metre, with annotations. Amsterdam 1612 (with music: DMH 317, BUCOEM 821), 1617–18 (as Annotations upon the book of psalmes) (BUCOEM 822); in Annotations upon the five books of Moses and the booke of psalmes, 1622, 1622, 1626–7, 1639 (DMH 385); The booke of psalmnes, Amsterdam 1644 (BUCOEM 827), Glasgow 1843; The booke of psalmes in English metre, [Amsterdam?] 1632 (with music; metrical version only: BUCOEM 825), Rotterdam 1638. The music is derived partly from Sternhold and Hopkins 1562 etc, partly from Dutch psalter c. 1558, which was musically identical with French psalter of 1551–4; the standard psalter of the Independents, popular in New England 1620–98; 19 in Cotton (verse and prose).
Axon, W. E. A. and R. Ainsworth: the puritan commentator. Trans Lancashire & Cheshire Antiquarian Soc 6 1889.
Pratt, W. S. Music of the pilgrims. Boston 1921. Includes Ainsworth's 39 tunes.
Scholes, P. A. In his Puritans and music in England and New England, Oxford 1934.

George Chapman (1559–1634). Petrarchs seven penitentiall psalmes, paraphrastically translated. 1612; in his Works vol 2, ed A. C. Swinburne and R. H. Shepherd 1875; Poems, ed P. B. Bartlett, New York 1944. From Petrarch's Septem psalmi poenitantiales 1355, [Bruges 1477–81] and at least 17 other edns separately and in collections before date of trn.

John Davies of Hereford (1565?–1618). The dolefull dove: or Davids 7 penitentiall psalmes, paraphrastically turned into verse. In The Muses sacrifice: or divine meditations, 1612; in his Works vol 2, ed A. B. Grosart 1878.

Sir William Leighton (fl. 1603–14). Seven psalmes of Davids repentance. In The teares of lamentations of a sorrowfull sowle, 1613, 1614 (with music: BUCOEM 608). The 7 penitential psalms in verse.

Sir David Murray (1567–1629). A paraphrase of the civ psalme. Edinburgh 1615 (Aldis 478); in his Poems 1823; Blackwood's Mag April–May 1818.

Sir Edwin Sandys (1561–1629). Sacred hymns: consisting of fifti select psalms of David and others, paraphrastically turned into English verse. 1615 (BUCOEM 993). Psalms 1–2, 8, 15–17, 19–22, 25, 32, 34, 36–7, 40, 42, 44–5, 49–51, 67–9, 73, 79, 82, 84, 90, 92, 94, 100–1, 103–4, 107, 110–12, 118–19, 122, 128, 130, 137, 139, 141, 145–6; 5-pt music by Robert Tailour to psalms 8, 16, 19, 21, 42, 84, 90, 94, 103, 112, 130, 137. 128 in Holland and Farr 3. 19 in Cotton; 134 in Brooke.

Sir Thomas Hope. Latin metrical paraphrase of the psalms, 1617, in ms in Nat Lib of Scotland; psalm 104 in Poetarum Scotorum musæ sacræ vol 2, ed W. Lauder, Edinburgh 1739, 1740.

George Eglishem (Eglisham) (fl. 1618–42). Latin metrical version of psalm 104 in Duellum poeticum: contendentibus, Georgio Eglisemmio & Georgio Buchanano pro dignitate paraphraseos psalmi centesimi quarti, 1618(–19); in Octupla, ed A. Symson, Edinburgh 1696 (Aldis 3586); in Poetarum Scotorum musæ sacræ vol 2, ed W. Lauder 1739, 1740. With Buchanan's version.

George Wither (Wyther, Withers) (1588–1667). A preparation to the psalter. 1619, 1884 (Spenser Soc). Includes much of the trns, later rev, of psalms 8, 18–19, 104, 107, 148; 57 in Aston, Holland and Farr 3; 148 in Brooke.

—— Exercises upon the first psalme, both in prose and verse. 1620, 1882 (Spenser Soc).

—— The psalmes of David, translated into lyrick-verse. [Netherlands] 1632, 2 vols 1881 (Spenser Soc); psalms 1–2, 6, 10, 17–18, 24, 29, 48–9, 75, 77, 89, 91, 93, 98, 115, 126, 131, 137, 143, 150 in Latham; 150 in Brooke; 137 in N. Drake, Mornings in spring vol 1, 1828.

Thomas Carew (Carey) (1595?–1640). Metrical trn of 9 psalms (1, 2, 51, 91, 104, 113–14, 119 (part), 137); all except 1 and 137 in Bodley ms Don.b.9; all except ps

119 in Bodley ms Ashmole 38; psalm 91 in BM ms Harley 3357 and Bodley ms Rawlinson poetry 61 (1626); 104 in BM ms Egerton 2877 (c. 1622) and additional 22,118; Certaine psalmes of David translated into English verse by T. Carew, licensed to be ptd by T. Walkley, 27 June 1640 (E. Arber, Transcript of the registers of the Company of Stationers 1554–1640, vol 4, 1877 p. 514) but apparently not pbd (the psalms are not in Carew's Poems 1640); 137 in P. Bliss (ed), A. Wood's Athenae oxonienses vol 2, 1815 (3rd edn) and hence in Carew's Poems [ed T. Maitland] Edinburgh 1824; all 9 psalms in Poems, ed W. C. Hazlitt 1870, ed J. W. Ebsworth 1893, ed R. Dunlap, Oxford 1949; in R. G. Howarth (ed), Minor poets of the seventeenth century 1931 (EL); psalm 91 in G. Fletcher, Christ's victory and triumph, ed W. T. Brooke 1888 (the version of 65 there given under Carew's name is by J. Bryan, above). Psalm 137 set to music for 5 voices by Henry Lawes (autograph ms, BM additional 31,434), ptd in his Select psalmes of a new translation, 1655.

John Milton (1608–74). Metrical paraphrases of psalms 114 and 136, made at age 15, influenced by G. Buchanan's Latin paraphrases; ptd in his Poems in English and Latin, 1645; psalm 136, Let us with a gladsome mind, adapted for many hymnals; Nine of the psalms done into metre, 1648 (psalms 80–8); 1–8, done into verse, 1653; [Psalm 114 in Greek metre], in Poemata, 1645. All 20 psalms in Poems in English and Latin, 1673 (2nd edn, etc; 2 vols Oxford 1952–5, 1 vol 1958, 1961.
Boddy, M. Milton's translation of the psalms 80–8. MP 64 1966.

Sir John Davies (1570–1626). [Metrical 'metaphrase' c. 1624 of psalms 1–50, 67, 91, 95, 100, 103, 150]. In his Works vol 1, ed A. B. Grosart 1869.

Francis Bacon, Lord Verulam (1561–1626). Translation of certaine psalmes into English verse. 1625; in his Works, 5 vols 1765 etc; in A. B. Grosart, Fuller worthies miscellanies vol 1, 1870. 7 psalms: 1, 12, 90, 104, 126, 137, 149; 137 in Cotton.

S.P.L. One and forty divine odes englished, set to King Davids princely harpe (An assay: or Buchanan his paraphrase on the first twentie psalm of David, translated). 1627.

Alexander Top (fl. 1597–1629). The book of prayses, called the psalmes: the keyes and holly things of David, translated out of the Hebrew, according to the letter, and the mystery of them; opened in proper arguments upon every psalme. Amsterdam 1629. Prose trn.

William Slatyer (Slater) (1587–1647). Psalmes or songes of Sion, turned into the language and set to the tunes of a strange land, intended for Christmas carols. [1630–4], 1642. With music; 35 psalms: 1, 6, 8, 11, 13, 15–16, 19, 23, 42–3, 47–8, 52, 57, 60–1, 63, 65, 84, 87, 93, 97, 99, 101, 108, 110, 114, 117, 121, 124, 126, 130, 137, 150; also psalms 1 and 128 in Latin and Greek verse. Psalm 101 in Holland.

— The psalmes of David, in four languages and in four parts, set to the tunes of our Church. 1643, 1652 (BUCOEM 909–10). With music; psalms 1–22; Hebrew, Greek, Latin, English.

Sir William Alexander, Earl of Stirling (1567?–1640). The psalmes of King David, translated by King James. Oxford 1631 (DMH 452), [London?] 1631, London 1636 (rev), [1637?], 1637 (BUCOEM 826); in The book of common-prayer for the use of the Church of Scotland, Edinburgh 1712. Revision and completion of King James's ms version of 30 psalms, above; in 1627 Alexander was given the right of exclusive pbn for 31 years and in 1634 all other psalters were prohibited in Scotland, but opposition brought about a revision in 1636, reissued with Laud's service book, above, then a General Assembly at Glasgow in 1638 which rescinded the privilege and prohibition; psalm 19 in Cotton.

[Calderwood, D. (?)] Reasons against the reception of King James's metaphrase of the psalms. 1631; rptd

in Bannatyne miscellany vol 1, ed Sir W. Scott and D. Laing, Edinburgh 1827. Includes psalms 1 and 148 (part) from King James's ms, and 1 and 8 from the edns of 1631 and 1636.

John Vicars (1580/2?–1652). Divers of Davids psalmes, according to the French forme and metre. In Englands hallelu-jah: or Great Brittaines gratefull retribution for Gods gratious benediction, with divers of Davids psalmes, according to the French metre and measures, 1631. 19 psalms: 1–6, 8, 10, 15, 23, 51–3, 55–6, 101, 103, 105, 107, 123, 'paraphrased by way of thanksgiving for our great deliverances from the Papists pouder-plot'; from the French psalter of 1551–62 by C. Marot and T. de Bèze; 23 and 123 in Cotton.

[Thomas Harper (ed) (fl. 1604–56).] All the French psalm tunes with English words, accorded to the verses and tunes generaly used in the reformed churches of France and Germany. 1632, [1650] (BUCOEM 825, 827; Julian 935). Words and music from the French psalter of 1551–62 by C. Marot and T. de Bèze.

John Donne (1572–1631). [Metrical trn of psalm 137]. In his Poems, 1633 etc.

Phineas Fletcher (1582–1650). Certain of the royal prophets psalmes metaphrased. In his Purple island, Cambridge 1633; in Poetical works, Edinburgh 1793, Poems 1810; ed A. B. Grosart 4 vols 1869. Psalms 1, 42, 63, 127, 130, 137.

George Herbert (1593–1633). [Metrical trn of psalm 23]. In his Temple: sacred poems and private ejaculations, Cambridge 1633 etc; Works, ed F. E. Hutchinson, Oxford 1941. Also in Playford, below (BUCOEM 790). Metrical trn of psalms 1–7, 'supposed to be' by Herbert. In J. Playford, Psalms and hymns in solemn musick, 1671.
Steese, P. Herbert and Crashaw: two paraphrases of the twenty-third psalm. Jnl of Bible & Religion 33 1965.
Freer, C. Music for a King: Herbert's style and the metrical psalms. Baltimore 1971.

Arthur Johnston (1587–1641). [Latin metrical version of the seven penitential psalms: 6, 32, 38, 51, 102, 130, 143]. In Canticum Salomonis paraphraste A. Jonstono, 1633.
— Paraphrasis poetica psalmorum Davidis. Aberdeen 1637, London 1657 (Aldis 889); in his Poemata, Middelburg 1642; ed D. van Hoogstraten, Amsterdam 1706; psalms 1–50 in Poetarum scotorum musæ sacræ vol 1, ed W. Lauder, Edinburgh 1739, 1740; the complete Paraphrasis ed W. Benson 1740 (with Authorized version), 1741 (2 edns, one with Latin notes), 1742 (2 edns, one with Latin notes and one with Greek trn of J. Duport), 1743 (with Authorized version); in Musae latinae Aberdonenses vol 3, ed W. D. Geddes and W. K. Leask 1910 (New Spalding Club); psalm 104, from the edn of 1637, in Octupla, ed A. Symson, Edinburgh 1696; 18 psalms (13, 15, 43, 54, 67, 70, 93, 100, 117, 120, 123–5, 127, 131, 133–4, 150) in Davidis selecti psalmi, ed H. B. Wilson 1809.
Scots Mag 2 1740.
[Love, J.] A letter to a gentleman in Edinburgh, wherein the proposal made to the late General Assembly for having Dr Johnston's paraphrase of the psalms taught in the schools is considered; Buchanan is vindicated and critical remarks upon the Doctor's paraphrase are offered. Edinburgh 1740.
Lauder, W. Calumny display'd, or Pseudo-Philo-Buchananus couch'd: being a reply to an impudent libel, entituled A letter. Edinburgh 1740.
Love, J. A second letter to a gentleman. Edinburgh 1740–1.
Lauder, W. Calumny display'd. Pts 2–3, Edinburgh 1741.
Benson, W. A prefatory discourse to a new edition of the psalms of David translated into Latin verse by A. Johnston, containing a comparison betwixt

Johnston and Buchanan. 1741, 1741 (with The conclusion of the prefatory discourse).

Ruddiman, T. A vindication of G. Buchanan's paraphrase of the book of psalms, from the objections rais'd against it by Benson. Edinburgh 1745.

George Sandys (1578–1644). A paraphrase upon the psalmes of David, and upon the hymnes dispersed throughout the Old and New testaments. 1636, 1637 (in A paraphrase upon the divine poems, set to new tunes [by H. Lawes]), 1637–8, 1648, 1676, York 1789 (with music ed M. Camidge as Psalmody for a single voice), London 1790 (BUCOEM 603–4); psalms 8, 91, 121 and pts of psalms 17, 26, 28, 90, 103–4, 130, 137, 139, 148 in Selections from the metrical paraphrases, ed H. J. Todd 1839. In verse: psalm 133 set to music by W. King, Poems of [A.] Cowley and others, Oxford 1668 (BUCOEM 571); psalms 90 and 114 ptd in Blackwood's Mag April–May 1818; 28, 34, 59, 66, 68, 74, 92, 99, 110, 118, 122, 129, 148 in Latham; 66 (part), 92, 123 in G. Macdonald (ed), England's antiphon 1868; 40–1, 115, 125, all adapted, in B. H. Kennedy, The psalter, 1860 and Hymnologia christiana, 1863.

[Richard Brathwayte (Brathwait) (1588?–1673)]. The psalmes of David the King and prophet and of other holy prophets, paraphras'd in English: conferred with the Hebrew veritie, set forth by B. Arias Montanus, together with the Latin, Greek Septuagint, and Chaldee paraphrase. 1638; psalms 107, 133, 137 in Brathwayte's Barnabæ itinerarium vol 1, ed J. Haslewood 1820 (9th edn); psalms 18 (part), 23, 137 in T. Corser, Collectanea anglo-poetica vol 2, 1861 (Chetham Soc). In verse; by R.B., sometimes identified as Robert Burnaby, Robert Baillie (1599–1662), or Sir Richard Baker (1568–1645). From Biblia sacra, Hebraice, Chaldaice, Græce & Latine, ed B. Arias Montanus 8 vols Antwerp 1569–73, 6 pts 1584, [Geneva] 1609, 6 vols [Leyden] 1610–15, 7 pts Geneva 1619, Leipzig 1657 etc; and other sources.

Francis Rous (Rouse) (1579–1659). The booke of psalmes in English meeter. Rotterdam 1638 (anon), London 1641, 1643 (rev as The psalmes of David in English meeter), 1646 (rev, with Authorized version in the margin). In 1643–5, with the authority of the Commons, this trn was approved by the Westminster Assembly, which in 1646 ordered its exclusive use; it was one of the principal sources for the Scottish psalter of 1650 and the New England psalter of 1651: psalm 19 (1641 and 1646 versions) in Cotton.

Sir William Mure (More, Muir) (1594–1657). Some psalmes translated and presented. Psalms 1–51 and 100–50 in his Works, vol 2, ed W. Tough 1898 (STS). In verse; composed 1622–39; psalms 52–99 lost; one of the versions ordered to be used for the Scottish psalter of 1650; psalms 15, 23, 122 also in Mure's The historie and descent of the house of Rowallane, ed W. Muir, Glasgow 1825.

Sir Henry Wotton (1568–1639). [Metrical trn of psalm 104]. In Reliquiæ Wottonianæ, 1651, 1654, 1672, 1685; in J. Hannah, The courtly poets from Raleigh to Montrose, 1870; Brooke.

'Bay Psalm Book'. The whole booke of psalmes faithfully translated into English metre. [Cambridge Mass] 1640; ed John Cotton and Thomas Shepard 1647; Cambridge Mass 1651 (3rd edn rev Henry Dunster, Richard Lyon(s) et al, using Rous, as The psalms, hymns, and spiritual songs; 'The New England Psalm Book'), [c. 1664], [1665] (5th edn as The whole book of psalms), London 1671, 1680, 1694; Boston 1695, 1697, London 1697; Boston 1698 (first edn with music) etc; c. 27 edns alleged for 1640–50, over 100 altogether (70 in America) ptd at Boston (the last in 1773), London (18 edns, the last in 1754), Edinburgh (22 Scottish edns, the last in 1759) etc; rev Thomas Prince, Boston 1758. Facsimiles of the 1st edn [ed N. B. Shurtleff] 1862; ed W. Eames, New York 1903; ed Z. Haraszti, Chicago 1956, below. Psalm 1 (rev 1650) rptd in I. Thomas,

History of printing in America, 2 vols Worcester Mass 1810, Albany NY 1874, and hence in Cotton 373; psalm 19 (1640) in Cotton 371–2; 66 (1755) in Latham. By John Cotton, Thomas Shepard, Richard Mather, John Eliot, John Wilson (probably psalms 69, 72, 74, 86, 89, 118, 148); Peter Bulkeley, probably 29, 90; Francis Quarles (source versions of 16, 25, 51, 88, 113, 137: these rptd in A. B. Grosart, Complete works of F. Quarles vol 1 1880).

Cotton, J. Singing of psalmes: a gospel ordinance. 1647, 1650.

[Eames, W.] List of editions of the Bay Psalm Book or New England version of the psalms. New York 1885.

Roden, R. F. The Cambridge press 1638–92: a history of the first printing press in English America, together with a bibliographical list of the issues of the press. New York 1905.

Scholes, P. A. In his Puritans and music in England and New England, Oxford 1934.

Foote, H. W. An account of the Bay Psalm Book. New York 1940.

—— The Bay Psalm Book and Harvard hymnody. Harvard Theological Rev 33 1940.

Holmes, T. J. The minor Mathers. Cambridge Mass 1940. Pp. 82–104 describe 67 edns 1640–1759.

MacDougall, H. C. Early New England psalmody. Brattleboro 1940.

Jantz, H. S. The first century of New England verse. Proc Amer Antiquarian Soc 1944.

Winship, G. P. The Cambridge [Mass] press 1638–92: a reexamination of the evidence concerning the Bay Psalm Book. Philadelphia 1945.

Haraszti, Z. The enigma of the Bay Psalm Book. Chicago 1956. Reassigns authorship as above; with facs of first edn as companion vol.

Sir John Spelman (1594–1643) (ed). Psalterium Davidis latino-saxonicum vetus. 1640.

Henry Clifford, 5th Earl of Cumberland (1591–1643). Poeticall translations of some psalmes. In Bodley ms Rawlinson poetry 95. 16 psalms: 1, 8, 35, 38, 51, 65, 73, 93, 103–4, 107, 113–14, 121 (2 versions), 125, 131; psalm 38 ptd in A. Wood, Athenae oxonienses vol 3, ed P. Bliss 1818.

Mercurius Davidicus: or a patterne of loyall devotion used in the King's army before and after battell. Oxford 1634 (for 1643). Extracts, freely adapted, with references.

William Barton (1598/1603–78). The book of psalms in metre, with musicall notes. 1644, 1645, 1646(?), 1654, 1655(?), 1672(?), 1682, 1691, 1692, 1696, Dublin [c. 1698], London 1705, Dublin 1706, [c. 1708] (BUCOEM 827–9). The 1646 edn is said to have been approved by the Lords but rejected by Westminster Assembly: psalms 11, 45, 61, 65, 70, 101, 123 rptd in Latham.

—— The choice and flower of the old psalmes, collected by John Hopkins and others and now revised and emended by W. Barton. 1645. With music.

—— Psalms and hymns composed for the public thanksgiving, October 24 1651. 1651. Psalms 46, 48, 76, 135, mostly adapted from 1644, above.

—— Four centuries of select hymns, 1668 (unauthorized; the 3rd–4th centuries are based on the psalms); Two centuries of select hymns collected out of the psalms, 1672; Six centuries of select hymns and spiritual songs (The three last centuries of select hymns collected out of the psalms of David [rev and expanded from the edn of 1668]), ed E. Barton 1688.

Zachary Boyd (1585–1653). The psalmes of David in meeter, with the prose interlined. 1644 (?), Glasgow 1646, 1646, 1648 (rev). (Aldis 1215.5, 1216, 1311). In 1647 named by the General Assembly of Kirk of Scotland as one of versions to be used as a basis for new Scottish psalter 1650. Psalm 138 in Holland.

Francis Roberts (1609–75). The book of hymnes of praises:

viz the (fourth) book of psalms [90–106], translated immediately out of the Hebrew, and analytically expounded. 1644 (Corpus Christi College, Oxford), [1648?] (Cambridge Univ Lib); The whole book of psalms, in Clavis bibliorum, the key to the Bible, 1665 (3rd edn), 1674. Not in first and 2nd edns, 1648, 1649, 1664; metrical. Psalm 22 in Holland.

Richard Crashaw (1613?–49). [Metrical trns of psalms 23 and 137]. In his Steps to the temple: sacred poems, 1646 etc.

—— [Latin metrical trn of part of psalm 1 in Bodley ms Tanner 465]. In his Works vol 2, ed A. B. Grosart 1873.

Steese, P. Herbert and Crashaw: two paraphrases of the twenty-third psalm. Jnl of Bible & Religion 33 1965.

John White of Dorchester (1574–1648). Davids psalms in metre, agreeable to the Hebrew, to be sung in usuall tunes. 1655. From the Latin of J. I. Tremellius, using the Authorized version. Psalm 52 in Holland.

Second Scottish psalter. The psalms of David in meeter, newly translated and diligently compared with the original text and former translations; more plain, smooth and agreeable to the text than any heretofore; allowed by the authority of the General Assembly of the Kirk of Scotland. Edinburgh 1650, 1651, 1653, 1655, 1656, 1658, 1659 (Aldis 1418–23.5, 1449.5–50, 1464.5–7, 1483, 1524–6, 1554–5, 1582, 1613.5); 18 further edns ptd at Edinburgh 1661–99 (Aldis pp. 145, 171), at least 44 18th-century edns, 79 19th-century edns, 21 edns 1900–39. Compiled by a committee of 4 (John Adamson d. 1653 for psalms 1–40, Thomas Crawford d. 1662 for 41–80, John Row 1598?–1672? for 81–120, John Nevey c. 1606–72 for 121–150) appointed in 1647; based on first Scottish psalter 1564–5, Rous 1646, Boyd 1646 and Mure 1639, with some use of Alexander 1636 and Barton 1644; their draft, submitted in 1648, was further rev by a committee of 6 appointed in 1649 (James Hamilton d. 1666, John Smith d. 1667, Hugh MacKail d. 1660, Robert Traill 1603–78, George Hutcheson 1614–74, Robert Lowrie c. 1606–78); standard in Scotland till 20th century.

See also the first Scottish psalter 1564–5, above.

Ferguson, G. The Scottish psalter 1650. Choir June 1950.

Henry Vaughan (1622–95). [Metrical trn of psalm 121]. In his Silex scintillans: or sacred poems pt 1, 1650; psalms 65 and 104 in pt 2, 1655; Works ed L. C. Martin 2 vols Oxford 1914; psalm 121 in Brooke.

Thomas 3rd Baron Fairfax (1612–71). [Metrical trn of the psalms 1651]. In his Imployment of my solitude. 2 autograph mss in Bodley, Fairfax 38 and 40 (rev); psalm 137 in Cotton; 18 in C. R. Markham, A life of the great Lord Fairfax, 1870.

Henry King (1592–1669). The psalms of David, from the new translation of the Bible, turned into meeter. 1651, 1654, 1671; 15 psalms in J. Playford, Psalms and hymns in solemn musick, 1671; psalms 4, 24, 27 (part), 30, 46, 50 (part), 51, 80 (part), 102, 127, 130–1, 139 (part) in his Poems and psalms, ed J. Hannah 1843; 30, 46 in Aston; 26 in Holland; 30, 102 in Latham; 19 in Cotton; 46 in Brooke; 130 in his Poems, ed M. Crum, Oxford 1965.

Abraham Cowley (1618–67). [Metrical trn of psalm 114]. In his Davideis: a sacred poem of the troubles of David [book 1, section 42]. In his Poems, 1656 etc; English writings, ed A. R. Waller 2 vols Cambridge 1905–6.

Richard Baxter (1615–91). A paraphrasc on the psalms of David. Ed M. Sylvester 1692. Probably written late in 1650's and rev 1691. Psalm 53 in Holland.

Francis Knollys (b. 1627?). Metrical trns of paraphrases of selected psalms 1660. Psalms 1, 8, 11, 14–15, 23–4, 29, 30, 37, 42–3, 50, 57–8, 60, 68, 73–4, 79, 88, 93, 96–7, 101, 107, 114, 117, 119 pts 11–14, 123–4, 126–8, 130–1, 137, 139, 148. Unpbd; autograph ms in Bodley ms Rawlinson poetry 60.

Concordances

P., B. The parish-clerks vade mecum: or an alphabetical concordance of the most material words and sentences in the book of singing psalms. 1694. Sternhold and Hopkins.

Girdlestone, C. A concordance to the psalms of David, according to the version in the Book of common prayer. 1834, [1864] (rev).

Concordance to the metrical psalms and paraphrases. Edinburgh 1856. Church of Scotland version.

J., II. A concordance to the prayer-book version of the psalms. 1857.

A concordance to the book of psalms in the Authorized version; together with a concordance to the psalter to the Book of common prayer. 2 pts New York [1877].

Studies

A brief and full account of Mr Tate's and Mr Brady's new version of the psalms, by a true son of the Church in England. 1698.

Miller, J. Our hymns: their authors and origin. 1866, 1869 (as Singers and songs of the Church).

Swinburne, C. A. Sacred and Shakespearian affinities: being analogies between the writings of the psalmists and of Shakespeare. 1890.

Vaganay, H. Les traductions du psautier en vers latin au xvie siècle. Fribourg 1898.

Stopes, C. C. The metrical psalms and the Court of Venus. Athenaeum 24 June 1899; rev in her Shakespeare's industry, 1916.

Prothero, R. E. (Baron Ernle). The psalms in human life. 1903.

Young, T. The metrical psalms and paraphrases: a short sketch of their history, with biographical notes of their authors. 1909.

Riese, T. Die englische Psalmdichtung im sechzehnten Jahrhundert. Münster 1937.

Reuter, O. A study of the French words in the earliest complete English prose psalter. Helsinki 1938.

Rohr-Sauer, P. von. English metrical psalms from 1600 to 1660. Freiburg 1938.

Pratt, W. S. The music of the French psalter of 1562. New York 1939. Ch 10.

Hawkins, J. E. Lear and the psalmist. MLN 61 1946.

Smith, H. English metrical psalms in the sixteenth century and their literary significance. HLQ 9 1946.

Stubbings, G. W. The twenty-third psalm. Choir Jan 1951. Some metrical versions.

—— The 104th psalm. Choir May 1951. Some metrical versions.

Frost, M. English and Scottish psalm and hymn tunes c. 1543–1677. 1953.

Gaertner, J. A. Latin verse translations of the psalms 1500–1620. Harvard Theological Rev 49 1956.

C. B. L. B.

V. SERMONS AND DEVOTIONAL WRITINGS

ECCLESIASTICAL BACKGROUND AND HISTORY OF PREACHING

General Studies

Maunsell, A. The first part of the catalogue of English printed books which concerneth divinitie. 1595.

Verheiden, J. Praestantium aliquot theologorum effigies. Hague 1602, Middelburg 1636; tr D. Lupton, History of the moderne Protestant divines, 1637 (selection).

Holland, H. Herwologia anglica. [1620]; tr Lupton, ibid (selection).

Hook, W. F. Ecclesiastical biography. 8 vols 1852.

Broadus, J. A. Lectures on the history of preaching. 1876.

Dixon, R. W. History of the Church of England. 6 vols 1878–1902. Gives special attention to preachers.

Rothe, R. Geschichte der Predigt. Bremen 1881.

Blaikie, W. G. The preachers of Scotland from the sixth to the nineteenth century. 1888.

Ker, J. Lectures on the history of preaching. 1888.

Hering, H. Geschichte der Predigt. Berlin 1897.

Dargan, E. C. A history of preaching. 2 vols 1905–13.

Hutchinson, F. E. The English pulpit from Fisher to Donne. CHEL vol 4 1911.

Mitchell, W. F. English pulpit oratory from Andrewes to Tillotson. 1932. With bibliography.

Kapp, R. Können wir aus der englischen Predigt volks-typologische Rückschlüsse ziehen? Anglia 60 1936.

Smyth, C. H. E. The art of preaching: a practical survey of preaching in the Church of England 747–1939. 1940.

Brilioth, Y. T. Landmarks in the history of preaching. 1950.

Caplan, H. and H. M. King. Pulpit eloquence: a list of doctrinal and historical studies in English. Speech Monographs 22 1955.

Allison, A. F. and D. M. Rogers. A catalogue of Catholic books printed abroad or secretly in England 1558–1640. Pt 1, Bognor Regis 1956.

Howell, W. S. Logic and rhetoric in England 1500–1700. Princeton 1956.

Pollard, W. English sermons. 1963 (Br Council pamphlet).

Ong, W. J. Oral residue in Tudor prose style. PMLA 80 1965.

Hirsch, R. Surgant's list of recommended books for preachers 1502–3. Renaissance Quart 20 1967.

Chandos, J. (ed). In God's name: examples of preaching in England from the Act of Supremacy to the Act of Uniformity 1534–1662. 1970.

For ME sermons see col 481, above.

The Reformation

Haweis, J. O. Sketches of the Reformation, taken from the contemporary pulpit. 1844.

Coleridge, S. T. Notes on English divines. Ed D. Coleridge 2 vols 1853.

Tulloch, J. Leaders of the Reformation. 1859, 1883 (enlarged).

Taylor, R. W. The Scottish pulpit from the Reformation. 1887.

White, F. O. Lives of the Elizabethan bishops. 1898.

Brown, J. Puritan preaching in England. 1900.

Frere, W. H. The English Church in the reigns of Elizabeth and James I. 1904.

Wordsworth, C. and H. Littlehales. The old service books of the English Church. 1904.

Mosher, J. A. The exemplum in the early religious and didactic literature of England. New York 1911.

Krapp, G. P. In his Rise of English literary prose, New York 1915.

Bishop, E. Liturgica historica: liturgy and religious life of the Western Church. Oxford 1918.

Allen, J. W. A history of political thought in the 16th century. 1928.

Chambers, R. W. The continuity of English prose from Alfred to More. In N. Harpsfield, Life of Sir Thomas More, 1932 (EETS).

White, H. C. English devotional literature (prose) 1600–40. Madison 1931.

— Some continuing traditions in English devotional literature. PMLA 57 1942.

— Sixteenth-century English devotional literature. In J. Q. Adams memorial studies, Washington 1948.

— The Tudor books of private devotion. Madison 1951.

— Tudor books of saints and martyrs. Madison 1963.

Polman, P. L'élément historique dans la controverse religieuse du xvie siècle. Gembloux 1932.

Owst, G. R. Literature and pulpit in medieval England. Cambridge 1933, Oxford 1961 (with addns).

Haller, W. The rise of Puritanism: or the way to the new Jerusalem as set forth in pulpit and press from Thomas Cartwright to John Lilburne and John Milton 1570–1643. New York 1938.

Brooke, C. F. T. Queen Elizabeth's prayers. HLQ 2 1939.

Collins, J. B. Christian mysticism in the Elizabethan age with its background in mystical methodology. Baltimore 1940.

Herr, A. F. The Elizabethan sermon: a survey and a bibliography. Philadelphia 1940.

Wright, L. B. The significance of religious writings in the English Renaissance. JHI 1 1940.

Donovan, M. and A. R. Vidler. The homilies. Theology 43 1941.

Dowdell, V. L. Aristotle and Anglican religious thought. Ithaca 1942.

O'Connor, M. C. The art of dying well: the development of the ars moriendi. New York 1942.

Davies, H. The worship of the English Puritans. 1948.

— Worship and theology in England from Cranmer to Hooker 1534–1603. Princeton 1970. With bibliography.

Hennig, J. Primer versions of liturgical prayers. MLR 39 1944.

Seuert, A. The place of Allen, Campion and Parsons in the development of English prose. RES 20 1944.

Fryckberg, M. Pirates in the pews. Historical Mag of Protestant Episcopal Church 26 1947.

Koller, K. The Puritan preacher's contribution to fiction. HLQ 11 1948.

Thomas, S. A note on the reporting of Elizabethan sermons. Library 5th ser 3 1948.

Butterworth, C. C. Early primers for the use of children. PBSA 43 1949.

— The term 'Lord's Prayer' instead of 'Pater noster'. Lib Chron 18 1952.

— The English primers 1529–45: their publication and connection with the English Bible and the Reformation in England. Philadelphia 1953.

Langston, B. Essex and the art of dying. HLQ 13 1950.

Jorgensen, P. A. Moral guidance and religious encouragement for the Elizabethan soldier. HLQ 13 1950.

Southern, A. C. Elizabethan recusant prose 1559–80. 1950.

Smith, L. B. Tudor prelates and politics. Princeton 1953.

Abel, D. The Elizabethan archbishops. History Today 6 1956.

Mozley, J. F. The Marian martyrs. London Quart 180 1955.

Hart, A. T. The country clergy in Elizabethan and Stuart times 1558–1660. 1958.

Porter, H. C. Reformation and reaction in Tudor Cambridge. Cambridge 1958.

Brown, W. J. Life of Rowland Taylor. 1959.

Clarke, F. Eucharistic sacrifice and the Reformation. 1960.

George, C. H. and K. The Protestant mind of the English Reformation. Princeton 1961.

Owen, H. G. Lectures and lectureships in Tudor London. Church Quart Rev 162 1961.

—— Tradition and reform: ecclesiastical controversy in an Elizabethan London parish. Guildhall Miscellany 2 1961.

—— A nursery of Elizabethan nonconformity 1567–72. Jnl of Ecclesiastical History 17 1966.

Smith, E. O., jr. The royal mystique and the Elizabethan liturgy. Historical Mag of Protestant Episcopal Church 21 1962.

—— The doctrine of the prince and the Elizabethan episcopal sermon 1559–1609. Anglican Theological Rev 25 1963.

—— The Elizabethan doctrine of the prince as reflected in the sermons of the episcopacy. HLQ 28 1964.

Thornton, M. English spirituality. 1963.

Blench, J. W. Preaching in England in the late 15th and 16th centuries. Oxford 1964.

Clebsch, W. A. England's earliest Protestants. New Haven 1964.

Dickens, A. G. The English Reformation. 1964.

Hill, G. The sermons of John Watson, canon of Aberdeen. Innes Rev 15 1964.

Trimble, W. R. The Catholic laity in Elizabethan England 1558–1603. Cambridge Mass 1964.

Bossy, J. Henri IV, the Appellants and the Jesuits. Recusant History 8 1965.

Cross, M. C. The 3rd Earl of Huntingdon and trials of Catholics in the north 1581–95. Recusant History 8 1965.

Kelly, M. The submission of the clergy. Trans of Royal Historical Soc 15 1965.

Loades, D. M. The enforcement of reaction 1553–8. Jnl of Ecclesiastical History 16 1965.

Morgan, I. The godly preachers of the Elizabethan Church. 1965.

Roberts, J. R. (ed). A critical anthology of English recusant devotional prose 1558–1603. Pittsburgh 1965.

Robinson, H. W. Politics and preaching in the English Reformation. Bibliotheca Sacra 122 1965.

Kelly, F. L. Prayer in 16th-century England. Gainesville 1966.

Booty, J. E. Preparation for the Lord's Supper in Elizabethan England. Anglican Theological Rev 49 1967.

Dugmore, C. W. Some recent aids to Reformation studies. Jnl of Ecclesiastical History 18 1967.

Meyer, A. O. England und die Katholische Kirche unter Elisabeth und den Stuarts. Rome 1911; tr 1916, ed J. Bossy 1967.

Methods of Preaching

Erasmus, D. Desiderii Erasmi Roterodami Ecclesiastae: sive de ratione concionandi libri quatuor. Basle 1535; ed F. A. Klein, Leipzig 1820; tr 1797.

Hemminge (Hemmingsen), N. The preacher: or methode of preaching. 1574.

de la Ramée, P. The logike of P. Ramus, newly translated by M. R. MacIlmenius. 1574.

Polanus, A. De concionum sacrarum methodo. Basle 1574.

Gerardus, A. (Hyperius). The practis of preaching. Tr J. Ludham 1577.

Luis de Granada. Ecclesiasticae rhetoricae, sive de ratione concionandi: libri sex. Cologne 1582.

Osiander, L. De ratione concionandi. Tübingen 1582.

Gybson, T. A fruitful sermon, preached at Occham in Rutland. 1583.

Wilson, T. The arte of rhetorique. 1585; ed G. H. Mair, Oxford 1909.

Perkins, W. Prophetica: sive de sacra ratione concionandi. 1592; tr 1606; The art of prophesying, Works vol 3, 1631.

Sutcliffe, M. De recta studii theologici ratione. 1602.

LANCELOT ANDREWES
Bishop of Winchester
1555–1626

Chambers, D. D. C. A catalogue of the library of Bishop Andrewes. Trans Cambridge Bibl Soc 5 1970.

Collections

Scala coeli: nineteene sermons concerning prayer. 1611.

Sermons. Pt 1, 1618; pts 2–3, 1618; pt 4, 1620.

xcvi sermons. Ed W. Laud and J. Buckeridge 1629, 1631, 1632 (another issue with altered date), 1632, 1635 (with alphabetical table), 1641, 1661; ed J. P. Wilson 5 vols 1841–3.

Opuscula quaedam posthuma. 1629. Includes Latin sermons.

The moral law expounded whereunto is annexed nineteene sermons upon prayer; also seven sermons upon our Saviours tentations. 1642.

Seventeen sermons. Ed C. Daubeny 1821.

Sixteen sermons chiefly concerning fasts and festivals. Ed M. A. Davis 1831.

Works. Ed J. P. Wilson and J. Bliss 11 vols Oxford 1841–54 (Lib of Anglo-Catholic Theology).

Selections from the sermons. 1865; ed J. S. Utterton 1867.

Seventeen sermons on the Nativity. 1887, 1898.

Sermons, selected. Ed G. M. Story, Oxford 1967.

§1
Sermons

The wonderfull combate betweene Christ and Satan, opened in seven sermons. 1592 (anon), 1627.

The copie of the sermon preached on Good Friday [6 April 1604]. 1604, 1610, 1640.

A sermon before the King concerning the right and power of calling assemblies [28 Sept 1606]. 1606, 1610; tr Latin, 1608; Dutch, 1610.

Concio coram Jacobo rege. [abroad?] 1608.

Concio Latine habita coram regia majestate, quinto Augusti 1606. 1610.

A sermon preached before his Majestie the fifth of August last. 1610.

A sermon preached Monday 25 December 1609. 1610.

A sermon preached Tuesday 25 December 1610. 1610, [1611?].

Two sermons preached before the King's Majestie, Christmas Day 1609. 1610, 1610.

A sermon on Easter day. 1611, 1611.

A sermon on Easter day. 1614.

A sermon on Easter day. 1618.

A sermon preached the fifth of November 1617. 1618.

A sermon on Easter day. 1620.

Sermon of the pestilence, preached 1603. 1636.

Sacrilege a snare: a sermon ad clerum, translated from Latin. 1646.

Of justification in Christ's name: a sermon preached 23 November 1600. 1740, 1765, 1846.

On the pillars of government. 1823.

Of convocation. In J. Brodgen, Catholic safeguards vol 3, 1851.

The duty of a nation and its members in time of war, preached before Elizabeth at Richmond. 1854.

Of being doers of the word. 1858 (Bishops Tracts no 2).

Two sermons concerning the Resurrection. Cambridge 1932.

Devotions

See F. E. Brightman, The preces privatae, 1903, pp. xiii–xxv, for detailed description of the mss and ptd texts.

I. Isaacson's version

Institutiones piae: or directions to pray. Ed H. Isaacson 1630, 1633, 1640, 1684 (7th edn); ed W. H. Hale 1839.
Holy devotions. 1655.
The true Church of England-man's companion in the closet collected from the writings of Archbishop Laud, Bishop Andrewes and others. 1749. Source of Andrewes's work is Institutiones piae.

II. Original versions

Verus christianus. Ed D. Stokes, Oxford 1668. First appearance of Preces, selections only.
Preces privatae, graece et latine. Ed J. Lamphire 1675 (first comprehensive edn); rev Patris Lanc. Andrewes, Preces privatae graece et latine, Oxford 1675, 1680; Editio tertia et emendatior [P. Hall], 1828, ed J. Barrow 1853 (Lib of Anglo-Catholic Theology), ed F. Meyrick 3 pts 1865–73; ed P. Hall 1828 (Preces privatae quotidianae); ed P. G. Medd 1892 (as The Greek devotions); ed H. Veale 1895, 1899.

III. Translations

(a) Moseley–Drake

The private devotions. Tr from the Greek, ed H. Moseley 1647. See Private prayers, above.
A manual of the private devotions, translated out of a fair Greek ms by R. D[rake]. 1648, 1670, 1674, 1682, 1692. This differs considerably from preceding. Drake set out to correct the erroneous impression he considered Moseley to have made. The same text pbd as A manual of directions for the sick, tr from Greek ms by R. D[rake] 1648, 1670, 1682, 1692, 1853 (with corrections in Churchman's Lib); ed J. Bliss 1854 (Lib of Anglo-Catholic Theology); 1855 (selections in A manual of private devotions, Churchman's Lib) etc.

(b) Stanhope

Private prayers for every day in the week. Tr G. Stanhope 1730, 1778, 1808, 1818, 1826, 1832 (includes A manual of directions for the sick) etc. 2nd edn etc as The devotions of Bishop Andrewes.
Private devotions. Tr P. Hall 1830, 1839. A new version of Stanhope, above.
Prayers and offices of private devotion. Ed B. Bouchier 1834. Abridged from Stanhope, above.

(c) Newman–Neale

The Greek devotions of Bishop Andrewes. Tr J. H. Newman 1840 (78th Tract for the Times), Oxford 1842 (nearly all of Preces pt 1). Completed J. M. Neale, Private devotions of Bishop Andrewes translated from the Latin, 1844. 2 sections later combined.
Private devotions. Ed (from J. H. Newman and J. M. Neale) E. Venables 1883, 1885 (rev from Scriptural texts).
Private devotions of Bishop Andrewes, selected and arranged with variations adapted to general use. Ed J. E. Kempe 1897 (from Newman and Neale), New York 1950 (facs).
Private prayers. Ed H. Martin 1957.
See also J. Burns (ed), A litany and prayers of the Holy Communion, 1844; J. W. H. M[olyneux], Private prayers for members of the Church of England selected from the devotions of Bishop Andrewes, 1866, 1883; The mantle of prayer: a book of devotions compiled chiefly from those of Bishop Andrewes, 1881.

(d) Brightman

The preces privatae. Tr F. E. Brightman 1903, New York 1961 (with T. S. Eliot, For Lancelot Andrewes 1928).
The preces privatae: selections from the translation of F. E. Brightman. Ed A. Burn 1908, 1949.

(e) Other translations

A manual of devotions. Ed A. Bettesworth 1700 (2nd edn).
Private prayers. Tr E. Bickersteth 1839. A new trn of pts 1–2.
The private devotions newly done into English by P. G. Medd. 1899.

IV. Miscellany

The moral law expounded. 1642. See Collections, above.
Εὐχαι ἰδιαι καθημεριναι ἐκδιδοντος φριδερικου Μερρικου. [1867].
Manual. Ed H. P. Liddon 1869–70, 1874, 1883; ed F. E. Brightman 1909.
Whyte, A. Lancelot Andrewes and his private devotions: a biography, a transcript and an interpretation. Edinburgh 1896.
An horology. Ed A. Gurney 1897.
Brief passages from his sermons and devotions. 1907.
Devotions. Ed T. S. Kepler, Cleveland 1957.

Other Works

Quaestiones, nunquid per ius divinum, magistratui liceat, a reo iusiurandum exigere? 1593.
Tortura torti. 1609; ed F. Meyrick 1872 (excerpts as De primatu sedis Romanae argumenta); tr 1877, 1884.
Responsio ad apologiam Cardinalis Bellarmini contra praefationem monitoriam Jacobi R. 1610.
Fides catholica antiqua revindicata in ecclesia anglicana. Ed F. Meyrick 1872. Excerpts from Responsio.
Stricturae: or a brief answer to Cardinal Perrons reply to King James. 1629 (pt of pt 2 of Opuscula quaedam posthuma).
A patterne of catechisticall doctrine. 1630, 1641, 1641, 1650, 1675.
A summarie view. Oxford 1641, 1641 (as Certain briefe treatises), 1661 (as The form of church government in N. Bernard, Clavi Trabales, pt 4).
Of episcopacy. 1647.
Of the right of tithes (Theologica determinatio de decimus). 1647, 1842 (as A dissertation upon tithes, ed C. E. Harles).
Reverendissimi Lanceloti Wintoniensis de synodo ablatis a D. Whitakero Articulis judicium. Pt 4 of Articuli Lambethani, 1651.
A defence of the thirty-nine articles of the Church of England with the judgment of Bishop Andrews. 1700, 1710. Trn of Reverendissimi, above.
A learned discourse of ceremonies. 1653.
Αποσπασματα sacra: posthumous and orphan lectures. 1657. By Andrewes?
The form of a consecration of a church. 1659, 1672, 1688, 1703 (rev). Form of consecration of a churchyard 1898 (after the 1659 service which is of 1620).

§2

Becanus, M. Controversis anglicana de potestate Pontificis et Regis contra Lancellottum. 1613.
—— Refutatio Torturae torti. 1610.
Capello, M. A. F. M. A. Capelli adversus primatum ecclesiasticum regis Angliae liber in quo Jacobi et ejus eleemosynarij [Andrewes] confutantur scripta. 1610.
Burhil, R. Pro Tortura Torti contra M. Becanus responsio. 1611.

— De potestate regis et usurpatione papali pro Tortura Torti. 1613.

Eudaemon-Joannes, A. Parallelus Torti ac Tortoris ejus L. Cicestrensis. 1611.

Thomson, R. Elenchus refutationis [by M. Becanus] Torturae Torti. 1611.

Collins, S. Increpatio Andreae Eudaemono-Iohannis Iesuitae pro anstite Eliensi. 1612.

— Epphata to F.T.; or, the defence of the Bishop of Elie concerning his answer to Cardinall Bellarmines Apologie. 1617.

T., F. An adjoynder to the supplement of Father Robert Persons. 1613.

Fitz-Herbert, T. The Obmutesce of Fitzherbert T. to the Epphata of D. Collins. 1621.

Buckeridge, J. A sermon preached at the funeral of the right honorable and reverend Father in God Lancelot. 1629.

Isaacson, H. An exact narration of the life and death of Lancelot Andrewes. 1650, 1650; in Abel redevivus, 1651, 1817, 1829.

Fell, afterwards Fox, M. The examination and tryall of M. Fell and G. Fox, also something in answer to Bishop L. Andrewes sermon concerning swearing. 1664.

Hoadly, B. The plain account compared with the account given by Dr L. Andrewes [of Lord's Supper]. 1736.

Daubeny, C. Anti-Radicalism. 1821.

Kirby, W. Seven sermons on our Lord's temptation, grounded upon those of Bishop Andrewes. 1829.

Mozley, J. B. Sermons of Lancelot Andrewes. Br Critic 31 1842.

Teale, W. H. In his Lives of the English divines, 1844, 1849.

Russell, A. T. Memoirs of the life and works of Bishop Andrewes. Cambridge 1860, 1863. See his Life of Bishop Andrewes, Christian Observer 60 1860.

Gibson, R. C. The Lord's prayer, collated chiefly from Bishop Andrewes' sermons on the Lord's prayer. 1875.

Church, R. W. In his Masters in English theology, 1877.

North, J. H. Andrewes, the Catholic preacher. 1878.

F., E. Of the power of absolution. 1880.

Norton, P. Seven lamps of fire. 1892.

Ottley, R. L. Lancelot Andrewes. 1894.

Bayfield-Roberts, G. Lancelot Andrewes. Revue Anglo-romaine 3 1896.

Frere, W. H. Andrewes as a representative of Anglican principles. Church Historical Soc Pbns 44 1898.

Wood, M. S. The story of a saintly Bishop's life: Andrewes. 1898.

Nairne, A. Lancelot Andrewes. Revue Internationale de Théologie 26 1899.

Coats, R. H. Andrewes and John Bunyan. Hibbert Jnl 9 1910.

Macleane, D. Andrewes and the reaction. 1910.

Swete, H. B. Two Cambridge divines of the seventeenth century. 1913. On Andrewes and John Pearson.

Eliot, T. S. In his For Lancelot Andrewes, 1928.

Barker, F. E. Crashaw and Andrewes. TLS 21 Aug 1937.

Williamson, H. R. In his Four Stuart portraits, 1949.

Blackstone, B. Some notes on Andrewes. Theology 53 1950.

Higham, F. Lancelot Andrewes. 1952.

Reidy, M. F. Bishop Andrewes: Jacobean Court preacher. Chicago 1955.

Welsby, P. A. Lancelot Andrewes. 1958. With bibliography.

Wilson, F. P. In his Seventeenth-century prose, Cambridge 1960.

Bishop, J. G. Andrewes, Bishop of Chichester 1605–9. Chichester 1963.

Lancia, M. Il linguaggio dei sermoni di Andrewes. Eng Miscellany (Rome) 16 1965.

Webber, J. Celebration of word and world in Andrewes' style. JEGP 64 1965.

McCutcheon, E. Andrewes' Preces privatae: a journey through time. SP 65 1968.

Stanwood, P. G. Patristic and contemporary borrowing in the Caroline divines. Renaissance Quart 23 1970.

RICHARD BANCROFT
Archbishop of Canterbury
1544–1610

§1

A sermon preached at Paules Crosse [9 Feb 1588]. 1588, 1588, 1588 (with addns), 1636, 1637, 1709.

Daungerous positions and proceedings. 1593 (anon), 1640, 1641, 1712; ed R. G. Usher 1905 (Camden Soc).

A survay of the pretended holy discipline. 1593 (anon), 1663, 1663.

Tracts ascribed to Bancroft. Ed A. Peel (from a ms in Lib of St John's College, Cambridge), Cambridge 1953.

§2

[Penry, J.] A briefe discovery of the untruthes and slanders contained in a sermon [8 Feb 1588] by D. Bancroft. [London? 1588].

D. Bancrofts rashness in rayling against the Church of Scotland, noted in answer to a letter of a worthy person of England. 1590.

Articles to be enquired of within the Diocese of London, in the visitation of Richard, Bishop of London. 1601.

Articles to be enquired of in the generall visitation of Richard, Bishop of London. 1604.

Articles in the first metropoliticall visitation of Richard, Archbishop of Canterbury. 1605.

Certaine demandes with their grounds drawne out of holy writ [presented to Bancroft]. 1605.

The judgment and doctrine of the clergy of the Church of England concerning one special branch of the King's prerogative, viz in dispensing with the penal laws, assented to by the Lords Arch-bishops Bancroft, Laud etc. [1687].

Usher, R. G. The reconstruction of the English Church. 2 vols New York 1910.

Donaldson, G. The attitude of Whitgift and Bancroft to the Scottish Church. Trans Royal Historical Soc ser 4 24 1942.

Babbage, S. S. Puritanism and Bancroft. 1962.

Cargill Thompson, W. D. J. Reconsideration of Bancroft's Paul's Cross sermon of 9 February 1588/9. Jnl of Ecclesiastical History 20 1969.

THOMAS BECON
1512–67

Collections

The worckes of Becon whiche he hath hytherto made and published. 3 vols 1560–4; ed J. Ayre 3 vols Cambridge 1843–4 (Parker Soc).

§1

Davids harpe ful of [h]armony, by T. Basille [pseudonym]. 1542. 114th Psalm.

The true defence of peace. 1542.

The floure of godly prayers. 1551.

The pomander of prayer. 1558 (anon) etc; 5 edns by 1578. Another book with this title ptd W. de Worde 1530.

The relikes of Rome. [1560?], 1563.

The syck mans salue. 1561 etc, 15 edns by 1632.

A new postil conteinyng sermons upon all the Sonday gospelles. 2 vols 1566, 1567.

§2

Bailey, D. S. Becon and the Reformation of the Church of England. 1952.
Newell, A. G. Becon and literary studies. Evangelical Quart 33 1961.
Pineas, R. Becon as a religious controversialist. Nederlands Archif vour Kerkegeschiedenis 46 1965.
— Polemical technique in the works of Becon. Moreana 5 1968.

JOHN COLET
1467?–1519
See col 1790 above.

JOHN DONNE
Dean of St Paul's
1572–1631
See col 1169, above.

SIR THOMAS ELYOT
1490?–1546
See col 1818, above.

JOHN FISHER
Bishop of Rochester
1469–1535

Mss, especially of correspondence, are in BM, Cambridge Univ Lib, St John's College Cambridge and Public Records Office.

Collections

Opera quae hactenus inveniri potuerunt omnia. Würzburg 1597, Farnborough 1967 (facs); tr R. Bayne and ed J. E. B. Mayor 1876 (EETS).

§1

This treatise concernynge the fruytfull saynges of Davyd in the seven penytencyal psalmes. 1508, 1509, 1509, 1509, 1510, [1516?], [1518?], 1525, 1529, 1555, 1714; ed J. E. B. Mayor 1876 (EETS); ed K. Vaughan 1888 (as Sermons on the seven penitential psalms); ed J. S. Phillimore 2 vols 1914 (as Commentary on the seven penitential psalms), 1915 (Catholic Lib vols 14, 16). *See* Fisher's ms Latin commentary on the Psalms, Public Record Office SP 2/R, 28–277.
Here after foloweth a mornynge remembraunce had at the moneth mynde of Margarete Countesse of Rychemonde. [1509]; ed T. Baker 1708; ed J. Hymers, Cambridge 1840; ed J. E. B. Mayor 1876 (EETS); ed C. R. Ashbee 1906.
This sermon folowynge was compyled and sayd in the cathedrall chyrche of Saynt Poule, the body beynge present of the moost famouse prynce Kynge Henry the vii, the x daye of Maye mcccccix. 1509. Another edn 'enprinted the fyrst yere of the regyne of Henry the viij', [1509].
Eversio munitionis quam Jodocus Clichtobeus erigere moliebatur adversus unicam Magdalenam per Joannem Roffensis ecclesiae episcopum. Louvain [1519].
Reverendi patris J.F. confutatio secundae disceptationis per J. Fabrum Stapulensem habitae. Paris 1519, 1519. These 2 works were Fisher's answer to Faber and van Clichtove on the identity of Mary Magdalen.
The sermon of Johan the Bysshop of Rochester [on John 15.26] made agayn the pernicyous doctryn of M. Luuther [12 May 1521]. [1521?, 1521?]. Another edn as The

sermon of John the Bysshop of Rochester made again the pernicious doctryn of M. Luther, [1528?], 1554, 1556; tr Latin by R. Pace, Cambridge 1521, Ditchling 1935 (rptd from first edn).
Convulsio calumniarum U. Veleni. Antwerp 1522, 1698.
Apologia S. Hessi adversus Roffensem Episcopum. [1523].
Von dem hochgelehrten und geistlichen Bischoff Johannes von Roffa. Strasbourg 1523, 1524.
Defensio Regie assertionis [of Henry VIII] contra Babylonice captivitate [of M. Luther] per D. D. Johannem Roffensem Episcopu. Cologne 1525, 1525, 1562.
Sacri sacerdotij defensio contra Lutherum jamprimum evulgata. Cologne 1525, 1525, Münster 1925 (Corpus Catholicorum no 9); tr P. E. Hallett 1935.
Was die christelichen Alten von der Beycht haben gehalten. Dresden 1525.
De veritate corporis et sanguinis Christi in Eucharistia adversus J. Oecolanpadium. Cologne 1527, 1527; tr German, 1528.
A sermon had at Paulis upon quinquagesom Sonday [11 Feb 1525] concernynge certayne hereticks. [1526?]. This sermon is sometimes confused with The sermon agayn the pernicyous doctryn of Martin Luuther [1521]. It is not included in any modern edn. The BM copy (c.536.15) has several corrections, made in a contemporary hand, not Fisher's, but perhaps at his instance. *See* G. J. Gray, Fisher's sermon against Luther, 1912.
De causa matrimonii serenissimi Regis Angliae liber [Henry VIII with Catherine of Arragon]. [Alcalá 1530], [Compluti] 1530.
Here after ensueth two fruytfull sermons. 1532. Both on Matthew 5.20.
A spiritual consolation written by J. Fisher to hys sister Elizabeth. [1535]; ed D. O'Connor 1903, 1935; tr French, 1875.
Psalmi seu precationes ex variis Scripturae lacis collectae. Cologne [1525?], 1544, 1544, 1555, 1568, London 1554, 1572. Attributed to Fisher.
Reverendi patris D.J.F. opusculum de fiducia et misericordia Dei. Cologne 1556.
Tractatus de orando deum. Douai 1576; tr as A godlie treatisse declaryng the benefits of prayer, 1560, 1576, 1577.
A treatise of prayer. Tr R.A.B[att?], Paris 1640; ed a monk of Fort-Augustus 1887; 1969 (facs).
A position and testimony against all swearing. [1692?].
Oratio habita coram illustrissimo Rege Henrico Septimo Cantabrigiae AD 1506. 1770; rptd in J. Lewis, Life of Dr John Fisher vol 2, 1855.

Letters

Erasmus, D. The epistles of Erasmus. Ed F. M. Nichols 3 vols 1901–18.
— Opus epistolarum Des. Erasmi Roterodami. Ed P. S. Allen 12 vols Oxford 1906–58.
Gray, G. J. Letters of Bishop Fisher 1521–3. Library 3rd ser 4 1913.
Thomson, D. F. S. and H. C. Porter. Erasmus and Cambridge: the Cambridge letters of Erasmus. Toronto 1963, 1970 (rev).
Rouschausse, J. (ed). Erasmus and Fisher: their correspondence 1511–24. Paris 1968. Latin text with English trn.

§2

Frith, J. A disputacion of Purgatorye: the thyrde boke maketh answere unto my lorde of Rochester. [1533?], [1535?].
Bayly, T. [R. Hall]. Life and death of that renowned John Fisher, Bishop of Rochester. 1655, Dublin 1835 (7th edn).
Bruce, J. Observations on the circumstances which occasioned the death of Fisher. Archæologia 25 1834.
Histoire de Jean Fisher. Lille 1855 (2nd edn).

Lewis, J. Life of Dr John Fisher. Ed T. H. Turner 2 vols 1855.

Mayor, J. E. B. (ed). Early statutes of the College of St John the Evangelist. Cambridge 1859.

Kerker, M. Fisher: sein Leben und Wirken. Tübingen 1860.

Pocock, N. Records of the Reformation: the divorce 1527–33. Oxford 1870.

Mullinger, J. B. The University of Cambridge from the earliest times to the Royal Injunctions of 1535. Cambridge 1873.

Cooke, R. Catholic memories of the tower of London; with an appendix containing Bishop Fisher's spiritual consolation to his sister written in the tower on the eve of his martyrdom. 1875.

Baumstark, R. John Fisher. Freiburg 1879.

Haeghen, F. van der. In his Bibliotheca belgica ser 1 vol 4 no C428, Ghent 1880–90.

Rome, Church of. Westmonasterien. Beatificationis Jo. Card. Fisher positio super introductione causae. 1881.

— Westmonasterien. Concessiones et approbationis officii in honorem beatorum martyrum Angliae. [1931].

Rye, W. B. The ancient episcopal palace at Rochester and Bishop Fisher. 1886.

Bridgett, T. E. Life of Bl. John Fisher. 1888.

Cologan, W. H. Blessed John Fisher and the royal supremacy. [1890].

Ortroy, F. van. Vie du bienheureux martyr Jean Fisher: texte anglais et traduction latine du xvie siècle, annotés. Brussels 1893 (once attributed to R. Hall); Analecta Bollandiana 10 1891, 12 1893, ed R. Bayne 1921 (EETS).

Fischer-Treuenfeld, R. Lord Johan Fyssher. 1894.

Mason, A. J. In his Lectures on Colet, Fisher and More, 1895.

Camm, B. Martyrs under Henry VIII. In Lives of the English martyrs vol 1, 1904.

Bayne, R. The life of Fisher, transcribed from ms Harleian 6382. 1921 (EETS). See van Ortroy, above.

Blessed John Fisher and Blessed Thomas More. Venerabile (English College in Rome) 3 1926–8.

Muller, J. A. In his Stephen Gardiner and the Tudor reaction, New York 1926.

Rackham, H. (ed). Early statutes of Christ's College, Cambridge. Cambridge 1927.

Wilby, N. M. The story of Blessed John Fisher. 1929.

Constant, G. Westmonasterien. Canonizationis Johannis Card. Fisher. 1934 (La Réforme en Angleterre vol 1).

Benians, E. A. John Fisher. Cambridge 1935.

Delcourt, J. In his Deux saints anglais, Paris 1935.

Evennett, H. O. B. Fisher and Cambridge. Clergy Rev 9 1935.

Fisher and More. TLS 30 May 1935.

Janelle, P. L'Angleterre catholique à la veille du schisme. Paris 1935.

Kapfinger, H. Morus und Fisher: Martyren der Wahrheit. Bamberg 1935.

Laffan, R. G. D. Fisher and Cambridge. Dublin Rev 197 1935.

Llanos y Tottiglia, F. de. El divorcio de Catalina de Aragón: San Juan Fisher y Santo Tomás Moro. Madrid 1935.

McNabb, V. J. Saint John Fisher. 1935.

Parkinson, H. J. Fisher, defender of the unity of Christendom. [1935].

Rope, H. E. G. Fisher and More. 1935.

Smith, R. L. Fisher and More: two English saints. 1935.

— St John Fisher. 1945.

Underhill, F. Fisher: Bishop of Rochester and Cardinal. [1935].

Heynck, V. Der hl. John Fisher: skotische Reulehre. Franziskanische Studien 25 1938.

McCann, P. A valiant Bishop against a ruthless King. St Louis 1938.

Court of King's Bench. Beatorum martyrum Iohannis Card. Fisher et Thomas Mori causae iudicales et sententiae capitales nunc primum ex originalibus asservatis in Tabulario Nationali Angliae editae. 1944.

Hughes, P. In his Reformation in England vol 1, 1950, 1963 (rev).

Duggan, G. H. The Church in the writings of St John Fisher. 1953.

Reynolds, E. E. Saint John Fisher. 1955.

— A portrait of St John Fisher. Moreana 1 1964.

Porter, H. C. In his Reformation and reaction in Tudor Cambridge, Cambridge 1958.

Surtz, E. Fisher and the scholastics. SP 55 1958.

— More's friendship with Fisher. Moreana 4 1967.

— The works and days of John Fisher. Cambridge Mass 1967. Detailed study with extensive notes and references.

— Fisher and the nature of man. Moreana 6 1969.

Dickens, A. G. Lollards and Protestants in the diocese of York 1509–58. 1959.

— In his English Reformation, 1964.

Ridley, J. In his Thomas Cranmer, Oxford 1962.

Rouschausse, J. Discours, traité de la prière, écrits de prison. Ed J. Rouschausse, Collège Écrits des Saints, Namur 1964.

— Une nouvelle biographie de saint John Fisher. Moreana 6 1969.

Kelly, M. The submission of the clergy. Trans Royal Historical Soc 5th ser 15 1965.

Lawler, T. M. C. Some parallels between Walter Hilton's Scale of perfection and St John Fisher's Penitential psalms. Moreana 8 1966.

Manzelli, D. M. Recirca della verità nella chiesa. Memoriale tradotto [da Confutatio assertionis lutheranae] e presentato da Dino M. Manzelli. Sotto il Monte 1966 (Antro di Studi Ecumenici).

Macklem, M. God have mercy: the life of John Fisher of Rochester. Ottawa 1967. Includes bibliography of a number of ptd and ms sources.

Cameron, R. M. Attack on the biblical work of Lefevre d'Etaples 1514–21. Church History 38 1969.

Jagu, A. L'assertionis Lutheranae confutatio de John Fisher. Moreana 6 1969.

Dougherty, T. M. Fisher and the 16th-century eucharistic controversy. Moreana 6 1969.

Trapp, J. B. A seventeenth-century eulogy of St John Fisher. Moreana 6 1969.

RICHARD HOOKER
1554–1600

See col 1949, below.

JOHN HOOPER
Bishop of Worcester
d. 1555

Collections

Early writings. Ed S. Carr, Cambridge 1843 (Parker Soc).

Later writings. Ed C. Nevison, Cambridge 1852 (Parker Soc).

§ I

A declaration of Christe. Zürich 1547.

A declaration of the ten holy commaundementes. Zürich 1548.

A funerall oratyon made the xiiij day Januarij. 1549.

A lesson of the incarnation of Christe. 1549, 1549, 1550.

An oversight and deliberation upon the prophete Jonas. 1550.

Godly and most necessary annotations in ye xiii chapyter to the Romaynes. 1551.

A godly confession and protestacion of the Christian fayth. [1551?].
An homelye to be read in the tyme of pestylence. 1553.
The wordes of Maister Hooper at his death. 1559.
An exposition upon the 23 psalmes. 1562.
Certeine comfortable expositions upon the xxiii, lxii, lxxiii and lxxvii psalmes. 1580.
A briefe and cleare confession of the Christian faith. Issued as part of J. Baker, Lectures, 1581 etc.

§2

Gairdner, J. Bishop Hooper's visitation of Gloucester. EHR 19 1904.
Price, F. D. Gloucester diocese under Bishop Hooper 1551–3. Trans Bristol & Gloucestershire Archaeological Soc 60 1938.
West, W. M. S. Hooper and the origins of Puritanism. Baptist Quart Rev 15–16 1954–5.
Opie, J. Anglicizing of John Hooper. Archiv für Reformationsgeschichte 59 1968.
Ross, D. S. Hooper's alleged authorship of A brief and clear confession of the Christian faith. Church History 39 1970.

JOHN JEWEL
Bishop of Salisbury
1522–71

Collections

Seven godly sermons never before imprinted. 1607.
[Featley, D.] Works, and a briefe discourse of his life. 4 pts 1609, 1611.
Works. Ed J. Ayre 4 vols Cambridge 1845–50 (Parker Soc).
Works. Ed R. W. Jelf 8 vols Oxford 1848.

§1

The copie of a sermon pronounced at Paules Crosse the second Sondaye before Easter 1560. [1560]. Jewel's challenge was first given in a sermon at Paul's Cross 26 Nov 1559; it was repeated in substance in a Court sermon 17 March 1560, and at Paul's Cross again 31 March. It was ptd 'as nere as the authour could call it to remembraunce' on 10 May, as above. The ensuing controversy led to Jewel's Apologia ecclesiae anglicanae, 1562.
An apologie or aunswer in defence of the Church of England. [Tr Ann, Lady Bacon] 1562; ed J. E. Booty, Ithaca 1963 (Folger Lib); Menston 1969 (facs).
[Cooper, T.] An apologie of private masse spredde abroade in writyng against the offer made in certain sermons by the Byshop of Salesburie, with an answere. 1562.
A replie unto M. Hardinges answeare to the sermon on I Cor. xi. 23. 1565.
A defence of the Apologie of the Churche of Englande: an answeare to a certain booke by M. Hardinge. 1567.
A viewe of a seditious bul sent into Englande 1569. 1582.
Certaine sermons preached before the Queenes Maiestie and at Paules crosse. 1583.
An exposition upon the two epistles to the Thessalonians. 1583, 1584, 1594.
A sermon made in Latine in Oxenforde. [1586?].

§2

Southgate, W. M. Jewel and the problem of doctrinal authority. Cambridge Mass 1962.
Woodhouse, H. F. Jewel's Apology. Theology 65 1962.
Booty, J. E. Jewel as apologist of the Church of England. 1965.
Crofts, R. A. Defense of the Elizabethan Church: Jewel, Hooker and James I. Anglican Theological Rev 54 1972.

JOHN KNOX
1505–72

Collections

Writings of the Rev John Knox. [1830?] (Religious Tract Soc).
The history of the reformation of religion in Scotland to which are appended several other pieces of his writing; including the first book of discipline, complete, and his dispute with the Abbot of Crossraguel; with a memoir by W. McGavin. Glasgow 1831.
Works. Ed D. Laing 6 vols 1846–64.
The history of the Reformation, with which are included Knox's confession and the book of discipline. Rev and ed C. Lennox 1905.

§1

An admonition that the faithful Christians in London, Newcastel, Barwycke and others, may avoid Gods vengeance. [Antwerp?] 1554.
A confession and declaration of praiers. 1554; Upon the death of King Edward VI. Rome (for London) 1554.
A faythfull admonition unto the professours of Gods truthe in England. [Zürich] 1554.
A godly letter sent too the fayethfull in London, Newcastell etc; A confession and declaration of praiers etc. 2 pts Rome (for London) 1554; pt 2, 1581.
The copie of a letter, sent to the ladye Mary dowagire, Regent of Scotland etc. [Geneva? 1556], Geneva 1558 (nowe augmented by the authour).
The appellation of J. Knoxe from the cruell sentence pronounced against him by the false bishoppes and clergey of Scotland. Geneva 1558. An admonition by A. Gilby.
The first blast of the trumpet against the monstrous regiment of women. [Geneva] 1558, [Edinburgh? 1687?], London 1878, 1880.
The copie of an epistle sent unto the inhabitants of Newcastle and Barwike; in the ende whereof is added A brief exhortation to England. 2 pts Geneva 1559, 1560.
An answer to a great nomber of blasphemous cavillations. [Geneva] 1560, 1581.
Heir followeth the coppie of the ressoning betwix the Abbote of Crossraguell and J. Knox. Edinburgh 1563, 1812.
A sermon [on Isaiah 26.13] preached in the publique audience of church of Edenbrough, 19 August 1565. [Edinburgh] 1566.
To his loving brethren. [Edinburgh] 1571.
An answer to a letter of a Jesuit named Tyrie, be Johne Knox. St Andrews 1572.
A fort for the afflicted. 1580.
Exposition upon the fourth of Mathew. [1583].
The first booke of the history of the reformation of religioun within the realme of Scotland. 1587 (with bks 2–3); The historie of the reformation of the Church of Scotland, ed D.B[uchanan] 1644, Edinburgh 1644, London 1681, Edinburgh 1732, 1790, 2 vols 1816, 1 vol Glasgow 1831; ed R. S. Walker 1940 (selection); ed W. C. Dickinson 2 vols New York 1949, Edinburgh 1950.
The first booke of discipline, drawn up by J. Knox. Vol 2, 1719 (Church of Scotland Collections of Official Documents).
Knox's judgment on the true nature of Christian worship. 1842.
The source and bounds of kingly power. In H. C. Fish, History of the Repository of pulpit eloquence vol 2, 1857.

§2

Winzet, N. The last blast of the trompet of Godis worde aganis the usurpit auctoritie of Johne Knox. Edinburgh 1562.

Tyrie, J. The refutation of ane answer made by Schir Johne Knox. Paris 1573.

Briegerus, J. Flores Calvinistici Ioannis Knoxij. Naples 1585.

The rise and growth of fanaticism, with an extract of the life of that pretended reformer, John Knox. 1715.

McCrie, T. The life of Knox with an appendix of letters [by Knox]. Edinburgh 1812, 1813, 1818, 1839, 1905.

Dens, P. A letter showing that Knox and our Protestant reformers have all sanctioned the intolerant principles ascribed to P. Dens. 1836.

Lorimer, P. Precursors of Knox: Patrick Hamilton. Edinburgh 1857.

— Knox and the Church of England. 1875.

Laing, D. Documents connected with Knox as a notary. Proc Soc of Antiquaries of Scotland 3 1858.

Richardson, J. On the present state of the question Where was Knox born? Ibid.

Moncrieff, J. The influence of Knox and the Scottish reformers on England. 1860.

Brandes, F. H. John Knox. 1862.

Candlish, R. S. Knox and his devout imagination. 1872.

Rogers, C. In his Genealogical memoirs, 1879.

Barbour, R. W. In his Evangelical succession, Edinburgh 1883.

Taylor, M. C. John Knox. 1883.

Miller, P. Knox and his manse. Proc Soc of Antiquaries of Scotland 25 1891; see also 27 1893.

Wilson, D. Supplementary notes on Knox's house. Proc Soc of Antiquaries of Scotland 25 1891.

Brown, P. H. John Knox. 1895.

— Knox and his times. 1905.

Andrew, A. Knox: the hero of the Scottish Reformation. [1896].

Miller, R. Where did Knox live in Edinburgh? Proc Soc of Antiquaries of Scotland 33 1899.

'Harland, Marion' (M. V. Hawes). John Knox. 1900.

Hurault, E. Knox et ses relations avec les églises réformées du continent. Cahors 1902.

Stather, J. Knox: his ideas and ideals. 1904.

Cowan, H. John Knox. 1905.

Fleming, D. H. The date of Knox's birth. Bookman (London) 1905.

— The influence of Knox. Scottish Historical Rev 2 1905.

Innes, A. T. John Knox. 1905.

Lang, A. Knox and the Reformation. 1905, Port Washington NY 1967.

— Knox as historian. Scottish Historical Rev 2 1905.

Macmillan, D. Knox: a biography. 1905.

Mezger, A. Knox et ses rapports avec Calvin. Montauban 1905.

Miller, E. Knox: the hero of the Scottish Reformation. [1905].

Sprotte, A. O. Sprachgebrauch bei Knox. 1906.

Hart, A. B. Knox as a man of the world. Amer Historical Rev 13 1908.

Leishman, J. F. A son of Knox. Glasgow 1909.

Paul, J. B. Clerical life in Scotland in the sixteenth century. Scottish Historical Rev 17 1920.

Barbe, L. A. The story of Knox. Glasgow 1921.

Muir, E. Knox: portrait of a Calvinist. 1929.

Maxwell, W. D. Knox's Genevan service book. Edinburgh 1931.

Borgeaud, C. Le vrai portrait de Knox. Bulletin de la Société de l'Histoire du Protestantisme Français 84 1935.

Pearce, G. R. John Knox. 1936.

Percy, E. John Knox. 1937.

Niven, W. D. Knox and the Scottish Reformation. 1938.

Gray, J. R. The political theory of Knox. Church History 8 1939.

'Preedy, George R.' (G. M. V. Campbell). The life of Knox. 1940.

MacDougall, D. The Queen sends for Knox: the story of Knox the great reformer. [1942].

MacRae, J. John Knox. 1946.

Watt, H. Knox in controversy. 1950.

Mackie, J. D. John Knox. 1951 (Historical Assoc pamphlet).

Read, D. H. C. John Knox. Theology 55 1952.

Burns, J. H. Knox and Bullinger. Scottish Historical Rev 34 1955.

The ordination of Knox: a symposium. Innes Rev 6 1955.

Anderson, W. J. Knox as registrar. Innes Rev 7 1956.

McHardy, J. The priesthood of Knox. Ibid.

MacGregor, G. The thundering Scot. 1958.

Donaldson, G. 'Flitting Fri', the Beggars' Summons and Knox's sermon at Perth. Scottish Historical Rev 39 1960.

— In his Scottish Reformation, Cambridge 1960.

Whitley, E. Plain Mr Knox. 1960.

McEwen, J. S. The faith of Knox. 1961.

Reid, W. S. Knox's attitude to the English Reformation. Westminster Theological Jnl 26 1963.

Lee, M. Knox and his history. Scottish Historical Rev 45 1966.

Stempel, D. Knox and Milton's two-handed engine. Eng Lang Notes 3 1966.

Janton, P. Knox: l'homme et l'oeuvre. Paris 1967.

Ridley, J. John Knox. Oxford 1968 (with detailed bibliography).

HUGH LATIMER
1485?–1555

See col 1812, above.

SIR THOMAS MORE
1478–1535

See col 1792, above.

MATTHEW PARKER
Archbishop of Canterbury
1504–75

See col 1820, above.

ROBERT PARSONS SJ
1546–1610

§1

The firste parte of the booke of the Christian exercise appertayning to resolution. Rouen 1582, [Rouen?] 1585 (with addns as A Christian directorie, guiding men to their salvation, commonly called the resolution, with reproofe of the falsified edition published by E. Buny). Edmund Bunny in 1584 edited a Protestant version of which there were many edns; see H. Thurston, Catholic writers and Elizabethan readers, Month Dec 1894, and 'N. Doleman', A conference about the next succession to the crowne of Ingland, 2 pts [Antwerp?] 1594.

§2

The judgment of a Catholicke English-man living in banishment for his religion. 1608; ed W. T. Costello, Gainesville 1957 (facs).

Taunton, E. L. In his History of the Jesuits in England 1580–1773, Philadelphia 1901. The appendix contains summaries of the Main writings of Parsons.

Strathmann, E. A. Parsons: essay on atheism. In J. Q. Adams memorial studies, Washington 1948.

Hicks, L. Father Persons SJ and the seminaries in Spain. Month March, May–June 1931, July–Sept 1931.

— Sir Robert Cecil, Father Persons and the succession 1600–1. Archivum Historicum Societatis Jesu 24 1955.

—— Father Robert Persons SJ and the book of succession. Recusant History 4 1956.

Meadows, D. In his Elizabethan quintet, 1956.

Clancy, T. H. Notes on Persons's Memorial for the Reformation of England 1596. Recusant History 5 1959.

—— Papist pamphleteers: the Allen-Persons party and the political thought of the counter-Reformation in England 1572–1615. Chicago 1964.

Driscoll, J. P. The seconde parte: another Protestant version of Robert Persons's Christian directorie. HLQ 25 1962.

Parish, J. E. Parsons and the English Counter-Reformation. Rice Univ Stud 52 1966.

WILLIAM PERKINS
1558–1602
Collections

A golden chaine: or the description of theologie [with 12 other treatises]. 13 pts Cambridge 1600 ('newly corrected according to his own copies'), 18 pts Cambridge 1603 (with 5 additional treatises), 1 vol Cambridge 1605 (enlarged), 3 vols Cambridge 1608, 1609 (vol 3), 1612–13 etc.

Perkins: English puritanist. Ed T. F. Merrill, Nieuwkoop 1966. Prints Perkins' A discourse of conscience 1596 and The whole treatise of the cases of conscience 1606.

The works of Perkins. Ed I. Breward, Abingdon 1971.

§1

A treatise tending unto a declaration whether a man be in the estate of damnation. [1588?].

The foundation of Christian religion. 1590, 1638 (13th edn), Hamburg 1688 (with J. Wallis, Grammatica linguae anglicanae).

Armilla aurea. Cambridge 1590, [1591?], 1592.

A golden chaine: or the description of theologie, containing the order of the causes of saluation and damnation according to Gods word. 1591, 1612 (5th edn).

An exposition of the Lords prayer. 1592.

A direction for the government of the tongue. Cambridge 1593.

Two treatises: 1, Of repentance; 2, Of the combat of the flesh and spirit. Cambridge 1593.

An exposition of the symbole or creed of the apostles. Cambridge 1595.

A salve for a sicke man. Cambridge 1595, 1632 (5th edn).

A declaration of the true manner of knowing Christ crucified. Cambridge 1596.

A discourse of conscience. [Cambridge] 1596.

A reformed Catholike. Cambridge 1598; tr German, 1602.

How to live and that well. Cambridge 1601, 1611, 1615.

A commentarie on the five first chapters of the Epistle to the Galatians. Cambridge 1604.

The first part of the cases of conscience. Cambridge 1604.

Lectures upon the three first chapters of the Revelation. 1604.

Of the calling of the ministerie. 2 pts 1605.

A Christian and plaine treatise of pre-destination. 1606.

A faithfull and plaine exposition upon the first two verses of the second chapter of Zephaniah. 1606.

A godly and learned exposition upon the whole epistle of Jude. 1606.

The whole treatise of the cases of conscience. Cambridge 1606, 1636 (7th edn); tr German, 1690.

A cloud of faithfull witnesses: a commentary on Hebrews 11. 1608.

A discourse of the damned art of witchcraft. Cambridge 1608.

A godly and learned exposition of Christ's sermon in the mount. Cambridge 1608.

Christian oeconomie: or a short survey of the right manner of ordering a familie according to the Scriptures. 1609.

A graine of musterd-seede. [Cambridge] 1611.

Deaths knell: or the sicke mans passing-bell. 1628.

§2

Bishop, W. A reformation of a Catholike deformed: M. W. Perkins. [London?] 1604.

Baarsel, J. J. von. William Perkins. Hague 1912.

Wright, L. B. Perkins: Elizabethan apostle of practical divinity. HLQ 3 1940.

Hill, C. Puritans and the poor. Past & Present 2 1952.

Sisson, R. A. Perkins: apologist for the Elizabethan Church of England. MLR 47 1952.

Mosse, G. L. The holy pretence: a study in Christianity and reason of state from Perkins to John Winthrop. Oxford 1957.

Porter, H. C. In his Reformation and reaction in Tudor Cambridge, Cambridge 1958.

Breward, I. Perkins and the ideal of the ministry in the Elizabethan church. Reformed Theological Rev 24 1965.

—— The significance of Perkins. Jnl of Religious History 4 1967.

—— Perkins and the origins of reformed casuistry. Evangelical Quart 40 1968.

Malone, M. T. The doctrine of predestination in the thought of Perkins and Hooker. Texas Stud in Lit & Lang 12 1970.

JOHN RAINOLDS (or REYNOLDS)
1549–1607
Collections

The prophecie of Obadiah opened and applyed in sundry sermons preached by J. Rainolds. Ed W. Hinde, Oxford 1613.

V. Cl. D. J. Rainoldi Orationes duodecim, cum aliis quibusdam opusculis; edjecta est oratio funebris in obitu ejusdem habita a M. I. Wake. Oxford 1614, 1619, 1628.

§1

A sermon upon part of the prophesie of Obadiah. 1584.

The summe of the conference betwene J. Rainoldes and J. Hart touching the head and faith of the Church. 1584, 1588, 1598, 1609; tr Latin, 1610.

A sermon upon part of the eighteenth psalm preached in the Universitie of Oxford. Oxford 1586, 1613.

An answere to a sermon preached the 17 of April 1608 by G. Downame. 2 pts 1609. Anon.

A defence of the judgment of the reformed churches (touching adultery and remarriage). 1609, 1610.

The discovery of the man of sinne: sermons by J. R[ainolds]; published by W. H[inde]. Oxford 1614.

The prophesie of Haggai interpreted in sundry sermons. never before printed. 1649.

§2

Bryant, J. H. Reynolds of Exeter and his canon. Library 5th ser 15 1960, 18 1963.

—— Reynolds of Exeter's Love's laurell garland: an unpublished romance. Manuscripta 8 1964.

HENRY SMITH
1550–91
Collections

The sermons gathered into one volume. 1592; ed T. Fuller 1657 (with memoir), 1675, 2 vols 1866–7.

Works. Ed T. Smith, Edinburgh 2 vols 1866–7.
A selection of the sermons. Ed J. Brown, Cambridge 1908.

§ 1

The examination of usurie in two sermons, taken by characterie, and after examined. 1591. With a short preface, signed Thine H.S. These and other sermons of Smith were ptd in the author's lifetime, or immediately after his death; and for over 30 years after his death there were many edns of his sermons, singly, in small sets and in collections. On the use of shorthand for taking down sermons (the case with most of Smith's) *see* F. Watson, The English grammar schools, 1908.

§ 2

White, H. C. In her Social criticism in popular religious literature in the sixteenth century, New York 1944.
Lievsay, G. L. Silver-tongued Smith: paragon of Elizabethan preachers. HLQ 11 1948.

ROBERT SOUTHWELL sj
c. 1561–95

Bibliographies

McDonald, J. H. Poems and prose writings of Southwell SJ. Oxford 1937 (Roxburghe Club).
Allison, A. F. and D. M. Rogers. A catalogue of Catholic books in English printed abroad or secretly in England 1558–1640. Biographical Stud 3 1956.
For poetical works see col 1059, above.

Collections

Prose works. Ed W. J. Walter 1828.
Poetical works. Ed A. B. Grosart 1872; ed J. H. McDonald and N. P. Brown, Oxford 1967.
Spiritual exercises and devotions. Ed J. M. de Buck, tr P. E. Hallett 1931.

§ 1

An epistle of comfort to the reverend priestes. Secretly ptd in England 1587–8 (*see* Allison and Rogers, Catalogue of Catholic books no 781), Paris nd (anon), 1605 [place?] (anon), [St Omer] 1616; ed M. Waugh 1965.
An epistle of a religious priest unto his father. [London? 1596–7]. Ptd anon as pt 2 of A short rule of good life, below; ed J. W. Trotman, The triumphs over death, 1914 below. *See* Allison and Rogers no 787.
Marie Magdalens funerall teares. 1591, 1592, 1594, 1602, 1609; ed W. Tooke 1772; rptd 1823.
The triumphs over death: or, a consolatorie epistle. 1595, 1596, 1596; ed S. E. Brydges, Archaica vol 1, 1815, ed J. W. Trotman 1914 (includes several letters) (from mss).
An humble supplication to her Majestie. 1595; ed R. C. Bald, Cambridge 1953.
A short rule of good life, newly set forth according to the author's direction before his death. [London? 1596–7], [1598?], St Omer 1622 (all anon); ed N. P. Brown, Charlottesville 1972 (as Two letters and short rules of a good life). *See* Allison and Rogers no 787.
A foure-fold meditation: of the foure last things. 1606. Anon. Probably by Philip Howard, Earl of Arundel.
Hundred meditations on the love of God. Ed J. Morris 1873 (from Stonyhurst ms). Tr from Diego de Estella. Anon. Unlikely to be by Southwell, as Morris claims.

§ 2

Thurston, H. Catholic writers and Elizabethan readers. Month Feb–March 1895.
Pollen, J. H. (ed). Unpublished letters relating to the English martyrs 1584–1603. Pbns of Catholic Record

Soc 5 1908. Letters, with account of Southwell's execution.
Mascaró, J. Diégo de Estella and Southwell. TLS 20–7 Nov 1930.
Of Father Southwell's coming to live with her [Countess of Arundel and her household], transcribed from the ms at Arundel Castle by M. A. Tierney. Ed C. A. Newdigate, Month March 1931. *See* Lives of Philip Howard, Earl of Arundel, and of Anne Dacres his wife (1857), from same mss.
Foley, H. (ed). Records of the English province of the Society of Jesus. 1st ser vol i, 1877. Pp. 301–87.
Janelle, P. Southwell the writer. Clermont-Ferrand 1935.
Mangam, C. R. Southwell and the Council of Trent. Revue Anglo-américaine 12 1935.
Devlin, C. Southwell and the Mar-Prelates: the date of the Epistle of comfort. Month Feb 1948.
— The patriotism of Southwell. Month Dec 1953.
— The life of Southwell, poet and martyr. 1956.
Dwyer, J. J. Robert Southwell. Month July 1956.
Moseley, D. H. Blessed Robert Southwell. New York 1957.
Parish, J. E. An Englishman who collaborated with the Spanish Armada. Rice Inst Pamphlets 44 1957.
White, H. C. The contemplative element in Southwell. Catholic Historical Rev 48 1962.
— Southwell: metaphysical and baroque. MP 61 1964.
Kanasaki, T. From Southwell to Donne. Stud in Eng Lit (Tokyo) 39 1963.
Loomis, R. The Barrett version of Southwell's Short rule of good life. Recusant History 7 1964.
Brown, N. P. The structure of Southwell's Saint Peter's complaint. MLR 61 1966.
Schten, C. A. Southwell's Christ's bloody sweat: a meditation on the Mass. Eng Miscellany (Rome) 20 1969.

JOHN WHITGIFT
Archbishop of Canterbury
1530?–1604

Collections

Works. Ed J. Ayre 3 vols Cambridge 1851–3 (Parker Soc).

§ 1

An answere to a certen libel intituled An admonition to the Parliament [by J. Field and T. Wilcox]. 1572, 1572, 1573 (rev).
The defense of the aunswere to the Admonition. 1574.
A godlie sermon preached before the Queenes Maiestie. 1574, 1714.
A most godly and learned sermon, preached at Pauls Crosse. 1589.

§ 2

Paule, G. Life of Whitgift. 1612, 1699.
Strype, J. The life and acts of Whitgift. 1718, 3 vols Oxford 1822.
Donaldson, G. The attitude of Whitgift and Bancroft to the Scottish Church. Trans Royal Historical Soc ser 4, 24 1942.
McGinn, D. J. The Admonition controversy. New Brunswick NJ 1949.
Hill, C. Economic problems of the Church from Archbishop Whitgift to the Long Parliament. Oxford 1956.
Brook, V. J. K. Whitgift and the English church. 1957.
Porter, H. C. The Anglicanism of Archbishop Whitgift. Historical Mag of Protestant Episcopal Church 31 1962.
Collinson, P. The 'Nott conformyte' of the young Whitgift. Jnl of Ecclesiastical History 15 1964.
New, J. F. H. The Whitgift-Cartwright controversy. Archiv für Reformationsgeschichte 2 1968.

OTHER WRITERS

JOHN ALCOCK
Bishop of Ely
1430–1500

[Spousage of a virgin to Christ] Desponsacio virginis Xristo. [c. 1496].
Mons perfectionis: the hylle of perfeccyon. 1497, [1498], 1501.
Gallicantus in sinodo apud Bernwell. [1498].
[Sermon for a boy bishop] In die innocencium. nd, nd.
Sermo: Qui habet aures audiendi. nd, nd.

ANONYMOUS

The abbaye of the Holy Ghost. [c. 1496], [c. 1500]; ed F. J. H. Jenkinson, Cambridge 1907 (facs).
Certain sermons appointed by the Queen's Majesty to be declared and read by all parsons, vicars and curates, every Sunday and holiday in their churches. Ed G. E. Corrie, Cambridge 1850.
Horae Beatae Mariae Virginis or Sarum and York primers with kindred books and primers of the reformed Roman use. Ed E. Hoskins 1901.
The lives of women saints. Ed C. Horstmann 1886 (EETS) (from ms compiled c. 1610–15).
Ortulus animae: the garden of the soule. 1530. See L. A. Sheppard, The hortulus animae in English 1530, Library 5th ser 6 1951.
A pathway to penitence. 1591. See W. A. Mardslen, A pathway to penitence [1591], BM Quart 13 1939.
Prayers of the Byble. 1535. See C. C. Butterworth, Robert Redman's Prayers of the Byble, Library 5th ser 3 1948.
The tretyse of love. Ed J. H. Fisher 1951 (EETS).
The viniard of devotion. 1599. See E. F. Bosanquet, Three little Tudor books, Library 4th ser 14 1934.

GERVASE BABINGTON
1550–1610

A briefe conference betwixt mans frailtie and faith. 1583, 1584, 1590, 1596, 1602.
Workes. 5 pts 1615, 1615, 1622, 1637.

HENRY BARROW
d. 1593

Collections
Writings 1587–90. Ed L. H. Carlson 1962.
Writings of John Greenwood and Barrow 1591–3. Ed L. H. Carlson 1970.

§1

A true description out of the word of God of the visible Church. 1589, [1610?]. Anon.
A briefe discoverie of the false Church. [place?] 1590.
The examinations of H. Barrow, J. Greenwood and J. Penrie, penned by the prisoners themselves before their deathe. [place? 1593].

§2

Carlson, L. H. The rise of Elizabethan separatism. Rice Inst Pamphlet 46 1960.

LEWIS BAYLY
Bishop of Bangor
1565–1631

§1

The practise of pietie. 1613 (3rd edn, earlier edns not traced), 1640 (45th edn); ed G. Webster 1842; tr French 1625; German, 1629; Welsh, 1630; Polish, 1647.

§2

Bailey, J. E. [Life and work]. Papers of Manchester Literary Club 9 1883.

THOMAS BETSON
fl. 1500

Here begynneth a right profytable treatyse to dyspose men to be vertuously occupied. [c. 1500]; ed. F. Jenkinson, Cambridge 1905 (facs).

THOMAS BILSON
Bishop of Winchester
1547–1616

§1

The true difference betw. Christian subjection and unchristian rebellion. Oxford 1585, 1586, 1595.
A compendious discourse proving episcopacy to be of divine institution. 1593.
The perpetual government of Christes Church. 1593, 1611; ed R. Eden, Oxford 1842; tr Latin, 1611.

§2

Challen, W. H. Thomas Bilson, Bishop of Winchester: his family and their connections. Proc Hants Field Club 19 1956.
Lamont, W. M. The rise and fall of Bishop Bilson. Jnl of Br Stud 5 1966.

JOHN BOYS
Dean of Canterbury
1571–1625

Collections
Workes. 5 pts 1622, 1629, 1638.
Remaines, containing sundry sermons. 1631.

§1

An exposition of the dominicall epistles and gospels. 1610, 1611, 1612, 1613, 1615–16, 1638.
An exposition of the festivall epistles and gospels. 1613, 1615.
An exposition of the last psalme in a sermon at Paul's crosse. 1613, 1615.
An exposition of the proper psalms. 1615, 1616, 1616, 1617.

JOHN BRADFORD
1510?–55

§1

A sermon of repentaunce. [1553], 1619, 1623, 1631.
The complaynt of veritie. 1559.
A godlye medytacyon. 1559.

All the examinations of John Bradford. 1561.
Godlie meditations upon the Lordes prayer. 1562.
Godly meditations uppon the ten commaundementes. 1567, 1578.
Two notable sermons, the one of repentaunce and the other of the Lordes supper. 1574, 1581, 1599, 1617.
Bradfords beades, contayning godly meditations. 1597.
A worthy sermon upon the Lords supper. 1621.

§2

Loane, M. L. In his Pioneers of the Reformation in England, 1964.

THOMAS BRINTON (or BRUNTON)
Bishop of Rochester
d. 1389

§1

Sermons. Ed M. A. Devlin 2 vols 1954 (Camden Soc).

§2

Devlin, M. A. Bishop Brunton and his sermons. Speculum 14 1939.

HUGH BROUGHTON
1549–1612
Collections

Sundry works. [1591–2?].
The works of the great Albionean divine. Ed J. Lightfoot 4 vols 1662.

§1

An apologie in briefe assertions defending that our Lord died in the time foretold to Daniel. 1592.
Daniel his Chaldie visions and his Ebrew. 1596, 1597.
An epistle to the learned nobilitie of England touching translating the Bible. Middelburg 1597.
Declaration of generall corruption of religion wrought by D. Bilson. [Middelburg] 1603, 1604.
An exposition upon the Lord's Prayer, compared with the decalogue. [1603?]. Preached at Ostlands, 13 Aug 1603.
An advertisement of corruption in our handling of religion. [Middelburg] 1604, [Amsterdam?] 1605.
Daniel with a brief explication. Hanover 1607.
A petition to the Lords to examine the religion and cariage of D. Ban[croft]. [no place] 1608.
A defence of the book entitled a Concent of Scriptures. [Middelburg] 1609.
A revelation of the holy apocalyps. [Amsterdam?] 1610 (with extended Explication), [Middelburg] 1610.
A declaration unto the lordes: of the Jewes desire for Ebrew explication of our Greeke gospell. [no place] 1611.
A censure of the late translation [of the Bible] for our churches. [Middelburg? 1612?].

ROBERT BROWNE
1550?–1633?
Collections

The writings of Robert Harrison and Browne. Ed A. Peel and L. H. Carlson 1953.

§1

A booke which sheweth the life and manners of all true Christians. Middelburg 1582.
An answere to Master Cartwright his letter for joyning with the English Church. [1583].

§2

Carlson, L. H. The rise of Elizabethan separatism. Rice Inst Pamphlet 46 1960.

ROBERT BRUCE
1554–1631

Sermons upon the Sacrament of the Lords Supper: preached in the Kirk of Edinburgh. Edinburgh [1590?]; ed T. F. Torrance, Richmond Va 1958.
Sermons preached in the Kirk of Edinburgh. Edinburgh 1591.
The way to true peace and rest, delivered at Edinborough in xvi sermons. 1617. An English rendering of the 2 preceding volumes, which are in Scottish.
Sermons, reprinted from the original editions of 1590 and 1591, with collections for his Life by R. Woodrow. Ed W. Cunningham 1843 (Woodrow Soc).
Sermons on the Sacrament done into English, with a biography. Ed J. Laidlaw 1901.

HENRY BULL
d. 1575?

Christian praiers and holie meditations, gathered by H. B. 1566, 1596 (6th edn), Cambridge 1842 (Parker Soc).

NICHOLAS BYFIELD
1579–1622

The signes: or an essay concerning the assurance of Gods love and mans salvation. 1614.
An exposition upon the epistle to the Colossians. 3 pts 1615.
Sermons upon the first chapter of the first epistle generall of Peter. 1617.
The cure of the feare of death. 1618.
Directions for the private reading of the Scriptures. 1618 (2nd edn), 1626.
The paterne of wholsome words. 1618.
The marrow of the oracles of God. 1620, 1640 (11th edn).
A commentary: or sermons upon the second chapter of the first epistle of Peter. 1623.
The principall grounds of Christian religion. 1625.
Sermons upon the ten first verses of the third chapter of the first epistle of Peter. 1626.
The beginning of the doctrine of Christ. 1630.
A commentary upon the three first chapters of the first epistle of Peter. 1636–7, 3 pts 1637.
The spiritual touchstone. 1637.

CATHERINE PARR
Queen of England
1512–48

§1

Prayers stirryng the mynd unto heavenly medytacions. 1545, 1559 (11th edn).

§2

Haugaard, W. P. Katherine Parr: the religious convictions of a Renaissance Queen. Renaissance Quart 22 1969.

THOMAS COLE
d. 1571

A sermon at Maydstone, the fyrste Sonday in Lent. 1553.
A sermon before the Queene, March 1 1564. 1564.

WILLIAM COWPER
Bishop of Galloway
1568–1619

Collections
Workes. 1623, 1626, 1629.

§ 1

The triumph of a Christian: 1, Jacobs wrestling; 2, The conduit of comfort; 3, Preparative for the Lord's Supper. 3 pts 1608.
Three heavenly treatises upon the eighth chapter to the Romans. 1609, 1612.
The anatomie of a Christian man. 1611.
Heaven opened, newly amended and enlarged. 1611. No 1 of Three heavenly treatises, above.
A most comfortable and Christian dialogue betweene the Lord and the soule. 1611 (2nd edn).
Two sermons preached in Scotland before the King. 1618.
The life and death of W. Cowper; whereunto is added a resolution, penned by himselfe. 1619.

RICHARD DAY
1552–1607?

§ 1

Christian prayers and meditations in English. 1569.
A booke of Christian prayers, collected out of the auncient writers. 1578, 1581, 1590, 1608. Included in Private prayers put forth by authority during the reign of Queen Elizabeth, ed W. K. Clay, Cambridge 1851 (Parker Soc). Based on a book of prayers ptd by his father, John Day, in 1569.

§ 2

Chew, S. C. The iconography of A book of Christian prayers 1578, illustrated. HLQ 8 1945.
Oliver, L. M. The procession of virtues in A booke of Christian prayers. Harvard Lib Bull 6 1952.

JOHN DENNISON
d. 1629

A three-fold resolution verie necessarie to salvation. 1608.
The Christian petitioner: a sermon. 1611.
The sinne against the Holy Ghost plainly described. 1611.
The heavenly banquet: or the doctrine of the Lords supper. 1619.
Foure sermons: the blessednesse of peace-makers etc. 1620.
The Christian's care for the soules safety. 1621.
De confessionis auricularis vanitate, adversus Cardinalis Bellarmini sophismata. Oxford 1621.
Heavens joy: a sermon. 1623.
The sinners acquittance: 3 sermons. 1624, 1634.

ARTHUR DENT
d. 1607

§ 1

A sermon of repentaunce: a verie godly sermon. 1583, 1583, 1587; 20 edns by 1638.
A plaine exposition of the articles of our faith. 1594, 1609, 1616.
The plaine mans path-way to heaven. 1601, 1629 (20th edn), 1648 (27th edn), 1682 (31st edn).
The ruine of Rome: or an exposition upon the whole revelation. 1603, 1607, 1611, 1633, 1644, 1650, 1656.

A pastime for parents contayning the grounds of Christian religion. 1606, 1606, 1609, 1637.
Christes miracles, delivered in a sermon. 1608.
The opening of heaven gates. 1610.
A learned and fruitful exposition upon the Lord's Prayer. 1611, 1613.
The hand-maid of repentance: or a short treatise of restitution. 1614.

§ 2

Hussey, M. Arthur Dent, Rector of South Shoebury. Essex Rev 39 1948.
— Arthur Dent's Plaine man's pathway to heaven. MLR 44 1949.

EDWARD DERING
1540?–76

Collections
Maister Derings workes. 1590. Two godly sermons 1586 and xxvii lectures 1576.
Workes. 3 pts 1597, 1614.

§ 1

Godly private praiers for householders to meditate upon, and to say in their families. 1576 (anon), 1580, 1581, [1585?], [1590], 1615.
A sermon preached before the Quenes Majestie the 25 Februarie, anno 1569. [1570?] etc; 1603 (12th edn).
A sermon preached at the tower of London the eleventh day of December 1569. [1570?] (3 edns anon), 1584, 1589.
A shorte catechisme for househoulders, with prayers to the same adjoyning. 1582, 1631 (13th edn).

§ 2

Collinson, P. A mirror of Elizabethan Puritanism: the life and letters of Godly Master Dering. 1964.

THOMAS DRANT
d. 1578?

Two sermons preached, the one at St Maries Spittle on Tuesday in Easter week 1570, and the other at the court at Windsor Jan 8 1569. [1570?].
A sermon concerning almes giving, preached at S. Maries Spittle. [1572?].
Three godly and learned sermons. 1584.

ROGER EDGEWORTH
d. 1560

§ 1

Sermons very fruitfull, godly and learned. 1557.

§ 2

Blench, J. W. John Longland and Edgeworth: two forgotten preachers of the early sixteenth century. RES new ser 5 1954.

RICHARD FIELD
1561–1616

§ 1

A learned sermon. 1604.
Of the church: five bookes. 1606–10, 1628, 1635; ed J. S. Brewer 1843 (from 3rd edn), 4 vols Oxford 1847–52.

§ 2

Field, N. Some short memorials. 1717.

RICHARD FITZJAMES
Bishop of London
d. 1522

Sermo die lune in ebdomada Pasche. [c. 1495]; ed F. J. H. Jenkinson, Cambridge 1907 (facs).

BERNARD GILPIN
1517–83

§ 1

A sermon preached in the Court at Greenwich the firste Sonday after the Epiphanie [1552]. 1581, 1630, 1636, 1752 (in Life of Gilpin).

§ 2

Lightfoot, J. B. Leaders in the northern Church. 1890.

WILLIAM GOUGE
1578–1653
Collections

Workes. 2 vols 1627.

§ 1

An exposition of the Song of Solomon. 1615.
A short catechisme. 1615.
Πανοπλία τοῦ θεοῦ: the whole-armor of God. 1616, 1619.
Of domesticall duties. 1622, 1626, 1634.
The dignities of chivalrie. 1626.
A guide to goe to God. 1626, 1636.
An exposition of the whole fifth chapter of S. John's gospell. 2 pts 1630 (anon), 1631 (signed).
God's three arrows: plague, famine, sword. 5 pts 1631 (2nd edn).
The saints sacrifice. 1632.
A recovery from apostacy set out in a sermon. 1639.

RICHARD GREENHAM
Archbishop of Canterbury
1535?–94?
Collections

The works, examined, corrected, and published [by H. Holland]. 4 pts 1599.

§ 1

A fruitful and godly sermon. Edinburgh 1595.
A most sweet and assured comfort. 1595.
Two learned and godly sermons. 1595.
Godly instructions for the due examination and direction of all men. [1599].
Παραμύθιον: two treatises of the comforting of an afflicted conscience. 1598.
Short rules sent to a gentlewoman. 1621.

JOHN GREENWOOD
d. 1593
Collections

Writings 1587–90, with the joint writings of Henry Barrow and Greenwood 1587–90. Ed L. H. Carlson 1962.
Writings of Greenwood and Henry Barrow 1591–3. Ed L. H. Carlson 1970.

§ 1

An answere to G. Giffords pretended defence of read praiers. 1590, [abroad?] 1640.
M. Some laid open in his coulers. [1590?].

§ 2

Carlson, L. H. The rise of Elizabethan separatism. Rice Inst Pamphlet 46 1960.

EDMUND GRINDAL
Archbishop of Canterbury
1519?–83

§ 1

A sermon at the funeral solemnitie of Ferdinandus the late Emperour. 1564; rptd in Remains, ed W. Nicholson, Cambridge 1843 (Parker Soc); tr Latin, 1564.

§ 2

Strype, J. The history of the life and acts of Grindal. 1710.
Whitebrooke, J. C. Grindal, Foxe and Wendelin. N & Q 28 Aug 1942.
Mozley, J. F. Grindal and Foxe. N & Q 23 July 1949.
Arundale, R. L. Grindal and the northern province. Church Quart Rev 160 1959.
Lehmberg, S. E. (ed). Archbishop Grindal and the prophesyings. Historical Mag of Protestant Episcopal Church 34 1965.

JOHN HARPSFIELD
1516–78

Concio habita coram Patribus et clero in ecclesia Paulina Londini 26 Octobris 1553. 1553.
A notable and learned sermon or homilie, made upon Saint Andrewes daye last paste [1556]. 1556.

ROBERT HARRISON
d. 1585?

The writings of Harrison and Robert Browne. Ed A. Peel and L. H. Carlson 1953.

ROGER HUTCHINSON
d. 1555
Collections

Works. Ed J. Bruce, Cambridge 1842 (Parker Soc).

§ 1

The image of God: or laie mans booke. 1550, 1560, 1560, 1573, 1580 ('newly corrected').
A faithful declaration of Christes holy supper in three sermons preached at Eaton Colledge. 1552, 1560.

JOHN KING
Bishop of London
1559?–1621

§ 1

Lectures upon Jonas 1594. Oxford 1597, 1599, 1600, 1611, 1611, 1618; ed A. B. Grosart, Edinburgh 1864.

The fourth sermon preached at Hampton Court on Tuesday the last of September. Oxford 1606.
A sermon preached the 5th of November 1607. Oxford 1607.
A sermon preached at Whitehall 5 November 1608. Oxford 1608.
A sermon preached at St Maries at Oxford. Oxford 1608.
A sermon preached at the funeral of John [Piers] Archbp of Yorke 1594. 1611.
A sermon preached at Yorke 1595. 1618.
A sermon of publicke thanks-giving for the happie recoverie of his Majestie. 1619.
A sermon at Paules Crosse on behalfe of Paules church. 1620.

§ 2

Muschet, G. The Bishop of London his legacy. [St Omer] 1623.
Davidson, A. The conversion of Bishop King. Recusant History 9 1968.

THOMAS LEVER
1521–77

A fruitfull sermon made in Poules churche at London in the shroudes the seconde daye of February. 1550.
A sermon preached at Pauls Crosse 14 December 1550.
A sermon preached the thyrd Sonday in Lent before the Kynges Majestie. 1550, [1550].
A sermon preached the fourth Sundaye in Lente before the Kynges Majestie. 1550, [1550].
A meditacion upon the Lordes prayer. [1551], [1551].
Three fruitfull sermons 1550: now newlie perused by the aucthour. 1572; ed E. Arber 1870, 1895.
A treatise of the right way from danger of sinne. 1575.

JOHN LONGLAND
Bishop of Lincoln
1473–1547

§ I

Conciones exposituae in psalmum xxxviii, anno 1520. [1521?].
Sermones [on Psalms 6, 21, 101]. [1521?].
J. Longlondi, Dei gratia Lincolniensis Episcopi, tres conciones. [Tr T. Caius?] [1527?]. Includes Quinque sermones. The Conciones were delivered in 1519, 1525, and 1527; the 5 sermons, delivered in English in Lent 1517, are here in a Latin trn, probably by Thomas Caius. According to DNB the sermons were ptd by Pynson in 1517, but no copy can be traced. See S. R. Maitland, Early printed books at Lambeth, 1843, pp. 230–2, 243.
Exposito concionalis quinti psalmi poenitentialis. [1532?].
A sermon spoken before the Kynge at Grenwiche uppon Good Fryday. 1536.
A sermond made befor the Kynge at Rychemunte, uppon Good Fryday MCCCCXXXVI. [1535?]. The date of delivery is inconsistent with that of the preceding entry, and W. G. Hiscock, TLS 31 Dec 1931, gives reasons for assigning this sermon to 1535. Copy in Trinity College, Cambridge.
A sermonde made before the Kynge at Greenwich. 1538, [1538?].

§ 2

Blench, J. W. Longland and Roger Edgeworth: two forgotten preachers of the early sixteenth century. RES new ser 5 1954.

THOMAS LUPSET
1498?–1530
See col 1817, above.

JOHN NORDEN
1548–1625

A pensive mans practise. 1584, [1640?] (12th edn).
A progresse of pietie. 1596, Cambridge 1847 (Parker Soc).
A pathway to patience. 1626.
See also col 1130, above.

JOHN OVERALL
Bishop of Norwich
1560–1619

§ I

Bishop Overall's convocation book MDCVI. 1690 (pbd by Archbishop Sancroft before his sequestration in 3 bks, transcribed from Overall's mss of the convocations of 1603–10), Oxford 1844 (Lib of Anglo-Catholic Theology).

§ 2

Porter, H. C. In his Reformation and reaction in Tudor Cambridge, Cambridge 1958.

THOMAS PLAYFERE
1561?–1609
Collections

Ten sermons by that eloquent divine of famous memory, Thomas Playfere. Cambridge 1610 (9 sermons only), 1612 (as Nine sermons), 1621; also issued in Whole sermons, 1623, 1633.
The whole sermons gathered into one volume. 3 pts 1623, 1633 (6th edn).

§ I

A most excellent and heavenly sermon upon the 23 chapter of the gospell of S. Luke. 1595 (anon), 1596 (as The meane in mourning, with the Pathway to perfection), 1597, 1607, 1611, 1616.
The pathway to perfection: a sermon [preached 1593]. 1596 (with The meane in mourning), 1597, 1607, 1611, 1616.
The power of praier: a sermon [preached Aug 1596]. Cambridge [1596], 1603, 1611, 1617.
Heart's delight: a sermon [preached at Paul's Cross 1593]. Cambridge 1603, 1611, 1617, 1633. Heart's delight was issued with The power of praier and The sickmans couch, 1611, 1617, 1633.
The sickmans couch: a sermon [preached 12 March 1604]. Cambridge 1605, 1611, 1617.
Caesaris superscriptio. 1606.
Sufficit: sive de misericordia Dei [preached 1603 in Cambridge]. 1607.
A funerall sermon, preached in S. Maries, 10 May 1665. Cambridge 1609.
A sermon preached before the King's Majestie at Drayton the sixth day of August 1605. Cambridge 1609. Includes A sermon preached the 27 Aug 1605, A funerall sermon preached 10 May 1605, A sermon preached 1609. The first sermon was also issued separately.

RICHARD ROGERS
1551?–1618

A garden of spiritual flowers, planted by Ri. Ro[gers], Will. Per[kins] etc. 1609, 1638 (9th edn).
Certaine sermons. 1612.
Two Elizabethan Puritan diaries [by Rogers and Samuel Ward]. Ed M. M. Knappen, Chicago 1933 (Amer Soc of Church History).

THOMAS ROGERS
d. 1616

§ I

Of the imitation of Christ: three bookes, translated. 1580 etc; many edns to 1640.
A pretious booke of heavenlie meditations, called a private talke of the soule with God, written, as some think, by S. Augustine. 1581. From 1592 usually ptd with Imitation of Christ.
Saint Augustines praiers in the English tong; whereunto is annexed Saint Augustines Psalter translated. 1581. Supposititious works of St Augustine.
Soliloquium Animae, the sole-talke of the soule. 1592. From Thomas à Kempis.
See also col 1905, above.

§ 2

Williams, F. B. Rogers on Raleigh's atheism. N & Q Oct 1968.

ROBERT ROLLOCK
1555?–99

Collections
Select works, with the life H. Charteris. Ed W. M. Gunn 2 vols 1844–9 (Woodrow Soc).

§ I

Certaine sermons upon severall places of the epistles of Paul. 1599.
An exposition upon some select psalmes of David. 1600.
Lectures upon the epistle of Paul to the Colossians. 1603.
A treatise of Gods effectual calling. Tr H. Holland 1603.
Lectures upon the first and second epistles of Paul to the Thessalonians. Edinburgh 1606.
Certaine sermons upon severall texts of Scripture. Edinburgh 1616.
Lectures upon the history of the passion of Christ. Edinburgh 1616.
Five and twenty lectures upon the last sermon of our Lord. Edinburgh 1619.

NICHOLAS SANDERS (or SANDER)
1530?–81

§ I

The supper of our Lord. Louvain 1565.
The rocke of the Churche. Louvain 1567.
A treatise of the images of Christ and of his saints. Louvain 1567.
A briefe treatise of usurie. Louvain 1568.

§ 2

Veech, T. M. Dr Nicholas Sanders and the English Reformation 1530–81. Louvain 1936.
Southern, A. C. In his Elizabethan recusant prose, 1950.

EDWIN SANDYS
Archbishop of York
1516?–88

§ I

Sermons. 1585, 1616; ed J. Ayre, Cambridge 1941 (Parker Soc).

§ 2

Ellis, I. P. Archbishop Sandys and the usurers. Jnl of Ecclesiastical History 21 1970.

SIMON THE ANCHORITE

The fruyte of redempcyon, compyled in Englysshe. 1514, 1517, 1530, 1532.

THOMAS STAPLETON
1535–98

Collections
Opera omnia. 4 vols Paris 1620.

§ I

The history of the Church of Englande by Venerable Bede. Tr Thomas Stapleton, Antwerp 1565, St Omer 1622, 1626; ed P. Hereford, Oxford 1930.
A fortresse of the faith. Antwerp 1566, St Omer 1625.
A returne of untruthes upon M. Jewelles replie. Antwerp 1566.
A counterblast to M. Hornes veyne blaste against M. Fekenham. Louvain 1567.
Orationes sex: tres funebres, dogmaticae tres. Antwerp 1576.
Principiorum fidei doctrinalium demonstratio methodica. Paris 1578, 1579, 1581, 1582.
Speculum pravitatis haereticae. Douai 1580.
Universa justificationis doctrina hodie controversa. Paris 1582.
Tres Thomae [St Thomas the Apostle, St Thomas of Canterbury, St Thomas More]. Douay 1588, Cologne 1612. The Life of More is rptd separately and as a preface to More's collected Latin works, Graz 1689, tr P. Hallett, The life and illustrious martyrdom of Sir Thomas More, 1928, ed E. E. Reynolds, New York 1966.
Promptuarium catholicum ad instructionem concionatorum contra haereticos nostri temporis. Lyons 1591.
Apologia pro Rege Philippo II Hispaniae. Constance [1592].
Authoritatis ecclesiasticae circa S. Scriptuarum approbationem defensio. Antwerp 1592.
Antidota apostolica contra nostri temporis haereses. Antwerp 1595, Lyons 1596.
Vere admiranda: seu de magnitudine romanae ecclesiae. Antwerp 1599.

§ 2

Southern, A. C. In his Elizabethan recusant prose, 1950.
O'Connell, M. R. Stapleton and the Counter Reformation. New Haven 1964.
Richards, M. Thomas Stapleton. Jnl of Ecclesiastical History 18 1967.
Seybold, M. Glaube und Rechtfertigung bei Stapleton. Paderborn 1967.
Crawford, C. W. Stapleton and More's letter to Bugenhagen. Moreana 5 1968, 7 1970.

CHRISTOPHER SUTTON
1565?–1629

Disce mori. 1600, 1626 (9th edn); ed J.H.N[ewman] 1839.
Godly meditations upon the most holy sacrament. 1601, 1635 (5th edn); ed J.H.N[ewman] 1838.
Disce vivere. 1602, 1634 (8th edn); ed J. H N[ewman] 1839.

CUTHBERT TUNSTALL
Bishop of Durham
1474–1559

§1

A sermon of Cuthbert Bysshop of Duresme upon Palme Sondaye before Kynge Henry the viii. 1539.
De veritate corporis et sanguinis Domini nostri Iesu Christi in Eucharistia. Paris 1554.
Certaine godly and devout prayers. 1558.

§2

Quinn, E. Bishop Tunstall's treatise on the Holy Eucharist. Downside Rev 51 1933.
Sturge, C. Tunstall: churchman, scholar, administrator. 1938.
Butterworth, C. C. Bishop Tunstall and the English Hortulus. Lib Chron 16 1950.
Forster, A. Bishop Tunstall's priests. Recusant History 9 1968.

JOHN UDALL
1560?–92

§1

Amendment of life: three sermons. 1584, 1588.
Obedience to the gospell: two sermons. 1584, 1588.
Peter's fall: two sermons. 1584, [1590?].
The combate betwixt Christ and the Devill: foure sermons. [1588?].
A demonstration of the trueth of that discipline which Christe hath prescribed. [1588] (anon); ed E. Arber 1880.
The state of the Church of Englande, laide open in a conference between Diotrephes, a Byshop, Tertullus, a Papist etc. [1588] (anon); ed E. Arber 1879.
The true remedie against famine and warres: five sermons. [1588].
A new discovery of old pontificall practices. 1643.

§2

Emerson, E. H. Udall and the Puritan sermon. Quart Jnl of Speech 44 1958.

SAMUEL WARD
1571?–1643
Collections

A collection of such sermons as have been written by S. Ward. 9 pts 1627–8, 1636.

§1

Balm from Gilead to recover conscience. 1616, 1617, 1618, 1622, 1626.
The happinesse of practice. 1621, 1622, 1627.
The life of faith. 1621, 1621, 1622, 1625, 1627.

Two Elizabeth Puritan diaries [by Richard Rogers and Ward]. Ed M. M. Knappen, Chicago 1933 (Amer Soc of Church History).

§2

Parkander, D. J. Puritan eloquence: the sermons of Ward of Ipswich. Anglican Theological Rev 41 1959.

THOMAS WATSON
Bishop of Lincoln
1513–84

§1

Two notable sermons before the Quene concernynge the reall presence. 1554.
Holsome and Catholyke doctryne concerninge the seven sacraments in shorte sermons 10 February 1558. 1558, 1558, (a surreptitious edn same month with another on 7 June); ed T. E. Bridgett 1876 (modernized).
Absalom. Ed J. H. Smith, Urbana 1964 (as A humanist's 'trew imitation').
A body of divinity. 1965.

§2

Steuert, D. H. The English prose style of Watson, Bishop of Lincoln. MLR 41 1946.
Clubb, L. G. Gabriel Harvey and the two Thomas Watsons. Renaissance News 19 1966. On Watson the poet and Watson the Bishop of Lincoln.

RICHARD WHITFORDE OR WHYTFORD
fl. 1495–1555?

§1

The Psalter of Jesus. 1529, [1545?], Antwerp 1575, 1583 etc (some edns ptd at Douai); ed W. Raynal 1872, 1908. Attributed to Whitforde, it is also found at the end of a Salisbury Primer, ptd Y. Bonhomme, from a ms of the 15th century. Preface signed H.G[ough], 1885. Also written apparently without knowledge of H.G.'s tract; see S. H. Sole, Jesu's Psalter: what it was at its origin, 1888.
A werke for householders. 1530, 1533, 1537.
A werke of preparation: a werke for householders. 1531, nd.
The folowynge of Cryste. Bks 1–3, [1531?], bk 4, [1532?], [1535?] etc. Based on trn of Thomas à Kempis by W. Atkynson 1503–4.
The pype, or tonne, of the lyfe of perfection. 1532. See S. R. Maitland, Early printed books at Lambeth, 1843, p. 193. See also col 2274, below.

§2

Francis, F. C. Three unrecorded English books of the sixteenth century. Library 4th ser 17 1937.
Klein, E. J. The imitation of Christ: from the first edition. New York 1941.
Peters, W. A. M. Whitford and St Ignatius' visit to England. Archivum Historicum Societatis Jesu 25 1956.

JOHN WOLLTON
Bishop of Exeter
1535?–94

An armourr of proufe. 1576.
The Christian manuell. 1576, Cambridge 1851 (Parker Soc).
A newe anatomie of whole man. 1576.
Of the conscience. 1576.
The castell of Christians beseeged and defended. 1577.
A treatise of the immortalitie of the soule. 1596.

P. G. S.

VI. RICHARD HOOKER
1554-1600

Manuscripts

The fullest account of extant mss and of changes in the text of succeeding edns, and the best discussion of the last 3 bks of the Polity, *are in Keble's edn of Hooker's Works, 1888 (rev). This is supplemented by F. Paget's introd to the* Fifth *book, 1907 (rev), by Houk's edn of bk 8 1931, and by Sisson,* Judicious marriage of Hooker, *1940. Letters and other mss of Hooker at Corpus Christi College, Oxford, are catalogued in H. O. Coxe,* Catalogue of Oxford mss *pt 2, 1852. The only autograph of Hooker,* A sermon of pride, *is in Trinity College, Dublin.*

Simpson, P. In his Proof-reading by English authors of the 16th and 17th centuries, 1927. On 'unrivalled' ms of bk 5 in Bodley.

Bibliographies

Hill, W. S. Hooker: a descriptive bibliography of the early editions 1593-1724. Cleveland 1970.

Collections

Works. Ed J. Gauden 1662. With life.
Works, with life by I. Walton. 1666 (2nd edn), 1676, 1682, 1705, Dublin 1721, London 1723, 1724 (re-issue of Dublin edn with signature A reset), Oxford 1793, 1807, London 1822.
Works. Ed W. S. Dobson 2 vols 1825.
Works. Ed B. Hanbury 3 vols 1830. Excerpts Christian letter [1599] and reprints Covel's Defence [1603].
Works. Ed J. Keble 3 vols Oxford 1836, 1841, 1845, 1850, 1863, 1874, 1875, 1890; rev R. W. Church and F. Paget, Oxford 1888 (with much unpbd supplementary matter), New York 1967.
Of the laws of ecclesiastical polity. 2 vols 1907 (EL), 1954 (rev C. Morris). Based on Keble, above.

§ I
Polity

Of the lawes of ecclesiastical politie: eyght bookes. [1593]. Entered at Stationers' Hall, 8 bks, 29 Jan 1593. Gives headings of 8 bks, but contains only preface and bks 1-4.
The fift booke. 1596. The last book of the Polity to appear in Hooker's lifetime. Bodley ms additional C.165, with corrections in Hooker's hand, was used by printers for bk 5. *See* Simpson, above.
Books i-v. 1604. Though styled 2nd edn, strictly a 2nd edn of preface and 1-4 only; bk 5 unchanged from 1597, and vol not continuously paged.
Books i-v. 1611. 3rd edn of preface and 1-4, 2nd of 5.
Books i-v. 1617 (first state, 4th edn of preface and 1-4, 3rd edn of 5), 1618 (2nd state, preface and 1-5 as before, pt 1; Certayne tractates, pt 2).
Books i-v. 1622 (5th cdn of preface, bks 1-4, 4th edn of bk 5, 2nd collected edn of Tractates).
Books i v. 1631-2 (first state, 2nd edn of preface, bks 1-4, issued with 5th edn bk 5, 3rd collected edn of Tractates), 1631-2 (2nd state, 6th edn of preface, bks 1-4, 5th edn of bk 5, 3rd collected edn of Tractates).
Books i-v. In Certain divine tractates 1638-9 (7th edn of preface and bks 1-4, 6th edn of bk 5, 5th collected edn of Tractates, 4th of 1635-6).
Books i-v. Menston 1969 (facs of 1593).
A discovery of the causes of these contentions concerning Church-government, out of the fragments of Richard Hooker. In Certain briefe treatises concerning the government of the Church, Oxford 1641. This composite volume was probably prepared by, or under direction of, Archbishop Ussher. Keble, who prints A discovery as appendix 2 to bk 8 of Polity, is doubtful if it is Hooker's.

The dangers of new discipline discovered [chs 8 and 9 of the preface, part of ch 79 of bk 5]. 1642.
The sixth and eighth books according to the most authentique copies. 1648 (first issue first state, 'London, printed by Richard Bishop, and are to be sold by John Crook, 1648'), 1648 (2nd state with cancel title, 'London, printed in the year 1648'), 1648 (3rd state, with cancel title, 'London, printed by Richard Bishop, 1648'), 1651 (2nd issue, with cancel title, 'London, printed by R.B. to be sold by George Badger, 1651').
Mr Hookers judgment of the Kings power in matters of religion. In Nicholas Bernard, Clavi trabales, 1661. The editor of the composite vol, formerly Ussher's chaplain, ptd Mr Hookers judgment from mss that had belonged to the Archbishop. It includes pts of bk 8 which had not appeared in the version of 1648 and 1651, but which are represented, although with variations of wording and order, in Gauden's edn of 1662, below.
Works. Ed J. Gauden 1661-2. First complete edn of all 8 books of the Polity; includes bk 7 for the first time and adds 8 unpbd folio pages to the end of bk 8 except for some passages included in Nicholas Bernard, Clavi trabales, 1661.
Works. Ed J. Keble 1836. Bk 8 ptd from a fuller and better arranged ms (120, Trinity College, Dublin). Keble also detached the last 2 pages of bk 8, as ptd by Gauden and subsequent editors, because he believed them to be misplaced, and ptd them as appendix 2, 'Supposed fragments of a sermon on civil obedience'. He also questioned whether bk 6, although in his judgement Hooker's, belonged to the Polity, because its contents did not correspond closely with Hooker's description of bk 6 in the 1593 edn or with the Notes on bk 6 supplied to Hooker by his former pupils, George Cranmer and Sir Edwin Sandys (ptd in Keble's edn; ms at Corpus Christi College, Oxford).
Book i, with introduction and glossary by R. W. Church. 1868, 1868, 1873, 1896.
Book v, with Prolegomena and appendices by R. Bayne. 1902. Bayne reprints the Christian letter as well as Hooker's ms replies, first ptd by Keble, above.
Book viii. Ed R. A. Houk, New York 1931 (from Trinity College Dublin ms 120).

Sermons and Tractates

A learned and comfortable sermon of the certaintie of faith. Oxford 1612. On Habakkuk 1, 4, first pt.
A learned discourse of justification. Oxford 1612, 1613. On Habakkuk 1, 4, 2nd pt.
The answere to a supplication preferred by Mr Walter Travers to the Privie Counsell. Oxford 1612. On the connection of Travers's appeal to the Privy Council with Hooker's 2 preceding sermons; *see* Walton's Life.
A learned sermon of the nature of pride. Oxford 1612. On Habakkuk 2, 4. Keble ptd for first time a large addn to this sermon from Trinity College, Dublin ms 121.
A remedie against sorrow and feare, delivered in a funerall sermon. Oxford 1612.
Two sermons upon part of S. Judes epistle. Oxford 1614. If these are his, Keble thinks they are a very early work, but Paget (p. 327) gives reasons against an early date. All the above items were ed Henry Jackson, under the supervision of John Spenser, President of Corpus Christi College, Oxford. On their genuineness, *see* Sisson pp. 109-111.
A sermon of Richard Hooker found in the study of Bishop Andrews. Appendix to Walton, Life of Dr Sanderson, 1678.

§2

See also bibliography on Marprelate Controversy, below.

Contemporary Criticism (*in alphabetical order*)

[Bacon, F.] Considerations touching the better pacification of the Church. 1604 (3 edns), 1640, 1689.

Bacon, F. An advertisement touching the controversies of the Church. 1640. Written in 1589. Paget (p. 157) thinks that Hooker saw this in ms.

Bancroft, R. A sermon preached at Paul's Crosse the 9th of Februarie 1588. 1588, 1636.

— Daungerous positions under pretence of reformation. 1593 (anon), 1640; ed R. G. Usher 1905 (Camden Soc).

— A survay of the pretended holy discipline. 1593. Anon.

Bilson, T. The perpetual governement of Christes church. 1593, 1610; tr Latin, 1611 (enlarged); ed R. Eden, Oxford 1842.

Bridges, J. A defence of the government established in the Church of Englande. 1587.

Buchanan, G. De jure regni apud Scotos. Edinburgh 1579, London 1580; tr 1689.

Cosin, R. An apologie of and for sundrie proceedings by jurisdiction ecclesiasticall. 1591, 1593.

— Conspiracie for pretended reformation. 1592.

— Ecclesiae anglicanae politeia in tabulas digesta. 1604, 1634.

[Cartwright, T.] A seconde admonition to the Parliament. [Wandsworth 1572], [Leipzig] 1617. For the first Admonition, see Field and Wilcox, below.

— A replye to an answere made of M. Doctor Whitegift. [Wandsworth c. 1574].

— The second replie agaynst Maister Whitgiftes second answere, by T.C. [Zürich] 1575.

— The rest of the second replie. [no place] 1577.

— A brief apologie against M. Sutcliffe. Middelburg 1596.

— A Christian letter of certaine English Protestants unto Mr R. Hoo. [Middelburg 1599]. Hooker ptd no answer to this attack on the Polity, but Keble ptd in 1836 extensive fragments of an intended answer from Trinity College, Dublin ms 121, as well as annotations in Hooker's hand in a copy of A Christian letter at Corpus Christi College, Oxford.

Covell, W. A. A just and temperate defence of the five books of Ecclesiastical policie against a letter of certain English Protestants. 1603; rptd in Hanbury's edn of Works, above.

Cranmer, G. Concerning the new church discipline: a letter to R.H. [no place] 1642. Written in 1598? *See* H. Craig, JHI 5 1944, who argues for earlier date. Commonly ptd after Walton's Life in edns of Hooker.

[Fenner, D.] A defence of the godlie ministers against the slaunders of D. Bridges. [Middelburg] 1587.

[Field, J. and Thomas Wilcox?]. An admonition to the Parliament. [Wandsworth 1572, 1572].

[Fulke, W.] A declaration: containing the desires of all those ministers that seek discipline and reformation. 1584. B. Brook, Lives of the Puritans vol 1, p. 388, says that this work was by Fulke, though Fenner's name is prefixed.

Helwys, T. A short declaration of the mistery of iniquity. [Amsterdam?] 1612, 1935 (facs).

Jewel, J. Apologia ecclesiae anglicanae. 1562; tr 1562, ed J. E. Booty, Ithaca 1963, Menston 1969 (facs).

Orders and dealings in the church of Northampton (drawn up 5 June 1571). In State papers domestic vol 73, p. 388. Ptd in Strype's Annals of the Reformation.

Querimonia ecclesiae. 1592.

[Sandys, E.] A relation of the state of religion. 1605 (3 edns). Ptd without author's permission; burnt 7 Nov 1605 by order of the High Commission, perhaps at Sandys's request. Copies with author's autograph correc-

tions in BM and Bodley. From BM corrected copy a new edn, under the title Europae speculum: or a view or survey of the state of religion, was ptd Hague 1629, 1631 etc. The Hague imprint may be false since the printer, Michael Sparkes, was a well known Puritan.

Saravia, H. De diversis ministrorum gradibus. 1590; tr 1591.

— Defensio tractationis de diversis gradibus. 1594.

Sutcliffe, M. A treatise of ecclesiasticall discipline. 1590, 1591.

— De presbyterio. 1591.

— The examination of T. Cartwright's late apologie. 1596.

Travers, W. Ecclesiasticae disciplinae explicatio. La Rochelle 1574 (anon), tr probably by T. Cartwright as A full and plaine declaration of ecclesiasticall discipline, [Zürich] 1574, Geneva 1580.

— A defence of the ecclesiastical discipline, against a replie of Maister Bridges. 1588. Anon.

— A supplication made to the Privy Counsel. Oxford 1612. Commonly ptd in edns of Hooker.

Whitgift, J. An answere to a certain libel intituled An admonition to the Parliament. 1572, 1573 ('augmented').

— The defense of the aunswere to the admonition. 1574.

Later Criticism

Hudson, S. A vindication of the essence and unity of the Church Catholike visible in answer to Mr Hooker. 1650.

Firmin, G. A sober reply to the sober answer of Mr Cawdrey, to the question of Mr Hooker concerning the baptisme of infants. 1653.

Fuller, T. Church-history of Britain. 1655. IX vii 49–63.

Gauden, J. Life. In his edn of Hooker's Works, 1662.

Walton, I. The life of Mr Rich Hooker. 1665. Prefixed to most edns of Hooker from 1666, and included in Walton's Lives from 1670.

Baxter, R. A Christian directory. 1673.

Wood, A. In his Athenae oxonienses, 2 vols 1691–2.

Considerations on the explication of the doctrine of the Trinity by Mr Hooker in A second collection of tracts. 10 pts [1693] (unpbd ms notes).

Collier, J. An ecclesiastical history of Great Britain, chiefly of England. Vol 1, 1708; vol 2, 1714; 9 vols 1840, 1852.

Hoadly, B. The original of civil government discussed. 1709, 1710 (with A defense of Mr Hooker's judgment).

Strype, J. Annals of the Reformation. 2 pts 1709–8. Enlarged in succeeding edns up to 1737.

— The life and acts of John Whitgift. 2 pts 1717–18. Both works, together with other collections of Strype, were rptd at Oxford, with a general index, 21 vols 1812–28.

Swift, J. Tatler no 230 1710.

Collinson, J. An analysis of Hooker's 8th book of Ecclesiastical polity. 1810.

Landor, W. S. Lord Bacon and Hooker. In Imaginary conversations, ed T. E. Welby, Works vol 4, 1927.

Keble, J. Editor's preface. In his edn of Works, 1836. Walton's Life is included, with many corrections and addns.

Wordsworth, C. In his Christian institutes, 4 vols 1837.

D'Israeli, I. In his Amenities of literature, 1841.

Hallam, H. In his Constitutional history of England, 3 vols Paris 1851. *See* I, iv.

Cardwell, E. (ed). Documentary annals of the reformed Church of England. 2 vols Oxford 1844.

Cattermole, R. In his Literature of the Church of England vol 1, 1844.

A brief vindication of Jewel, Hooker, Ussher, Taylor and Pearson. Cambridge 1850. Anon.

Richardson, J. A letter to the Rev W. Goode, with a comment on the famous passage from Hooker. 1850.

Coleridge, S. T. In his Notes on English divines, ed D. Coleridge 2 vols 1853. *See* Coleridge on the seventeenth century, ed R. F. Brinkley, Durham NC 1955, where the Coleridge notes on Hooker are gathered.

MacLean, J. (ed). The life and times of Sir Peter Carew, by John Hooker. 1857. On Irish residence of Hooker's father, Carew's steward.

Sack, K. H. Hooker von den Gesetzen des Kirchenregiments. Heidelberg 1868.

Ruskin, J. In his Modern painters vol 2, 1869.

Hunt, J. In his Religious thought in England from the Reformation vol 1, 1870.

Rémusat, C. F. M. de. In his Histoire de la philosophie en Angleterre, Paris 1875.

Barry, A. In his Masters of English theology, 1877.

Fowler, T. In his History of Corpus Christi College [Oxford], Oxford 1893.

Hunt, T. W. Hooker: the Elizabethan ecclesiastic. Homiletic Rev 28 1894.

Paget, F. An introduction to the fifth book. Oxford 1899, 1907. The results of Paget's recension of Keble in 1888.

Bidder, H. J. 'The wise-woman of Tekoah' [a sermon]: a plea for comprehension with a note upon Hooker's view of the national church. Oxford 1900.

Dowden, E. In his Puritan and Anglican, 1900.

Seabury, W. J. Paget on Hooker's fifth book. Church Eclectic 27 1900.

Mason, A. J. In his Typical English Churchmen, 1902.

Nash, H. S. A statesman of the English Church. Amer Jnl of Theology 7 1903.

Figgis, J. N. Political thought in the sixteenth century. In Cambridge modern history vol 3, Cambridge 1904.
— Studies of political thought from Gerson to Grotius. Cambridge 1907, 1916 (rev).

Dale, R. W. In his History of English Congregationalism, ed A. W. W. Dale 1907.

Staley, V. Richard Hooker. 1907.

Galante, A. La teoria delle relazioni fra lo stato e la chiesa. In Festschrift Emil Friedberg, Leipzig 1908.

Foakes-Jackson, F. J. CHEL vol 3 1909.

Usher, R. G. In his Reconstruction of the English Church, 2 vols 1910.

Saintsbury, G. In his History of English prose ryhthm, 1912.

Bernard, J. H. The father of Hooker. Irish Church Quart 6 1913.

Krapp, G. P. In his Rise of English literary prose, New York 1915.

Taylor, H. O. In his Thought and expression in the 16th century vol 2, New York 1920.

Murray, R. H. Hooker and his teaching. 1924.
— In his Political consequences of the Reformation, 1926.

Thornton, L. S. Hooker: a study of his theology. 1924.

Sykes, N. In The social and political ideas of some great thinkers of the 16th and 17th centuries, ed F. J. C. Hearnshaw 1926.
— The Church of England and non-episcopal churches in the 16th and 17th centuries. Theology, Occasional Papers new ser 2 1948.
— Old priest and new presbyter. Cambridge 1956.
— In his English religious tradition, 1961.

Allen, J. W. In his History of political thought in the sixteenth century, 1928.

Pauck, W. Das Reich Gottes auf Erden: eine Untersuchung zur englischen Staatskirche des 16 Jahrhunderts. Berlin 1928.

Dimond, S. G. Hooker and the twentieth century. Church Quart Rev 108 1929.

Shirley, F. J. J. Hooker and the Jesuits. Church Quart Rev 113 1931.
— Hooker and contemporary political ideas. 1949.

Bull, G. What did Locke borrow from Hooker? Thought 8 1932.

d'Entrèves, A. P. Hooker e Locke. In Studi filosofico-giuridici, dedicati a Giorgio Del Vecchio, Modena 1931.
— Hooker: contributo alla teoria e alla storia del diritto naturale. Turin 1932.
— The medieval contribution to political thought: Aquinas, Marsilius of Padua, Hooker. Oxford 1939.

— In his Natural law, Oxford 1951.

Dibdin, L. In his Establishment in England, 1932.

Schöffler, H. Die Anfänge des Puritanismus: Versuch einer Deutung der englischen Reformation. Leipzig 1932.

Michaelis, G. Hooker als politischer Denker. Berlin 1933.

Morris, C. In The great Tudors, ed K. Garvin 1935.

Previté-Orton, C. W. Marsilius of Padua. Proc Br Acad 21 1935. On connections with Hooker.

Craig, H. In his Enchanted glass, New York 1936.
— Of the Laws of ecclesiastical polity: first form. JHI 5 1944.

Looten, C. Un avocat de l'église anglicane: Hooker. Revue d'Histoire Ecclésiastique 33 1937.

Garret, C. H. The Marian exiles 1553–9: a study in the origins of Elizabethan Puritanism. Cambridge 1938.

Boughner, D. C. Notes on Hooker's prose. RES 15 1939.

Knappen, M. M. In his Tudor Puritanism, Chicago 1939, 1965.

Whitney, E. A. Erastianism and divine right. HLQ 2 1939.

Jackson, S. R. Hooker: an approach to the Renaissance. Manitoba Arts Rev 2 1940.

Koenen, J. Die Busslehre Hookers: der Versuch einer anglikanischen Bussdisziplin. Freiburg 1940.

Sisson, C. J. The judicious marriage of Mr Hooker and the birth of the Laws of ecclesiastical polity. Cambridge 1940.

Thompson, J. V. P. Supreme governor: a study of Elizabethan ecclesiastical policy and circumstance. 1940.

Thompson, E. N. S. Hooker among the controversialists. PQ 20 1941.

Yoder, S. A. Disposition in Hooker's Laws of ecclesiastical polity. Quart Jnl of Speech 27 1941.

Bevenot, M. The Catholicism of Hooker. Hibbert Jnl 41 1942.

Dugmore, C. W. Eucharistic doctrine in England from Hooker to Waterland. 1942.
— The Mass and the English reformers. 1959.

Percy, H. C. Hooker and Izaak Walton. Hibbert Jnl 41 1942.

Ryan, C. J. The Jacobean oath of allegiance and English lay Catholics. Catholic Historical Rev 28 1942.

Marshall, J. S. Hooker and the Anglo-Saxon ideal. Sewanee Rev 52 1944.
— Hooker's theory of church and state. Anglican Theological Rev 27 1945.
— Hooker's doctrine of God. Anglican Theological Rev 29 1947.
— Hooker and the origins of American constitutionalism. In Origins of the natural law tradition, ed A. L. Harding, Dallas 1954.
— Hooker's theology of common prayer: the 5th book of the Polity paraphrased and expanded into a commentary on the prayer book. Sewanee 1956.
— Freedom and authority in classical Anglicanism. Anglican Theological Rev 45 1963.
— Hooker and the Anglican tradition. 1963.

Carter, C. S. Richard Hooker. Church Quart Rev 139 1945.
— In his Great churchmen, 1947.

Strathmann, E. A. Ralegh and the Catholic polemists. HLQ 8 1945.

Davies, E. T. The political ideas of Hooker. 1946.
— In his Episcopacy and the royal supremacy, Oxford 1950.

Hooker in the modern world. TLS 11 May 1946.

Northrop, F. S. C. Hooker and Aristotle. In his Meeting of east and west, New York 1946.

Dirksen, C. F. A critical analysis of Hooker's theory of the relation of church and state. South Bend Indiana 1947.

Dunkin, P. S. Two notes on Hooker. PBSA 41 1947. Windet's use of a particular ornament favours 1593 dating of Polity bks 1–4.

Gautier, C. D. Verdensorden og Evangelium i Hookers theologi. In Festckrift til Jens Noerregaard, Copenhagen 1947.

Hecht, D. and G. L. Mosse. Liturgical uniformity and absolutism in the 16th century. Anglican Theological Rev 29 1947.

M., M. A Puritan challenge to Hooker. More Books 22 1947.

Rupp, E. G. In his Studies in the making of the English Protestant tradition, Cambridge 1947.

Green, V. H. H. In his From St Augustine to William Temple, 1948.

Pamp, F. E. Walton's redaction of Hooker. Church History 17 1948.

Carré, M. H. In his Phases of thought in England, Oxford 1949.

Cremeans, C. D. In his Reception of Calvinistic thought in England, Urbana 1949.

Davies, J. G. Hooker and the rites of burial. Theology 52 1949.

Cragg, G. R. In his From Puritanism to the age of reason, 1950.

Johnson, A. F. The exiled English church at Amsterdam and its press. Library 5th ser 5 1950.

Trinterud, L. J. The origins of Puritanism. Church History 20 1951.

Wilmer, R. H. Hooker on authority. Anglican Theological Rev 33 1951.

Kearney, H. F. Hooker: a reconstruction. Cambridge Jnl Feb 1952.

Munz, P. The place of Hooker in the history of thought. 1952.

Pennington, E. L. The episcopal succession during the Elizabethan Reformation. New York 1952.

Schuetz, P. Hooker: der grundlegende Theologe des Anglikanismus. Göttingen 1952.

Woodhouse, A. S. P. Religion and some foundations of English democracy. Philosophical Rev 61 1952.

Addison, J. T. Early Anglican thought. Historical Mag of Protestant Episcopal Church 12 1953.

Bromiley, G. W. In his Baptism and the Anglican reformers, 1953.

Smith, L. B. In his Tudor prelates and politics, Princeton 1953.

Wolin, S. S. Hooker and English conservatism. Western Political Quart 6 1953.

Woodhouse, H. F. The authenticity of Hooker's Book vii. Church History 22 1953.

—— In his Doctrine of the church in Anglican theology 1574–1603, 1954.

—— Permanent features of Hooker's Polity. Anglican Theological Rev 42 1960.

Hughes, P. In his Reformation in England vol 3, 1954.

—— In his Theology of the English reformers, 1965.

Reardon, B. M. G. Hooker's Apology for Anglicanism. Hibbert Jnl 52 1954.

Richard Hooker. TLS 30 April 1954.

Flesseman-van Leer, E. Hooker: Anglicanisme en Protestantisme. Kerk en Theologie 6 1955.

Abel, D. The Elizabethan archbishops. History Today Oct 1956.

Hill, C. In his Economic problems of the Church from Archbishop Whitgift to the Long Parliament, New York 1956.

Stueber, M. S. The balanced diction of Hooker's Polity. PMLA 71 1956.

Keen, R. Inventory of Richard Hooker 1601. Archaeologia Cantiana (Kent Archaeological Soc) 70 1956.

Jenssen, D. E. Das Licht der Vernunft in der Theologie Hookers. In Festgabe für R. Hermann, Berlin 1957.

Novarr, D. The making of Walton's Lives. Ithaca 1958.

Friedrich, C. J. Sir Thomas Smith and Hooker. In his Philosophy of law in historical perspective, Chicago 1958.

Lamont, W. M. Episcopacy and a godly discipline 1641–6. Jnl of Ecclesiastical History 10 1959.

Facio Moreno, A. Dos notas en torno a la idea de derecho natural en Locke. Revista de Estudios Politicos 190 1960.

Greenslade, S. L. In his English reformers and the Fathers of the Church, 1960.

Cross, W. O. The doctrine of the church in Tudor and Caroline writings. Historical Mag of Protestant Episcopal Church 12 1961.

Chiasson, E. J. Swift's clothes philosophy in the Tale and Hooker's concept of law. SP 59 1962.

Congar, Y. In Catholicisme vol 5, ed G. Jacquement, Paris 1962.

de Lara, D. Hooker's concept of law. Anglican Theological Rev 44 1962.

Hillerdal, G. Reason and revelation in Hooker. Lund 1962.

Hoopes, R. Right reason in the English Renaissance. Cambridge Mass 1962.

Knox, S. J. Walter Travers: paragon of Elizabethan Puritanism. 1962.

Orr, R. Chillingworth versus Hooker: a criticism of natural law theory. Jnl of Religious History (Sydney) 2 1962.

Smith, E. Hooker at Salisbury. TLS 30 March 1962.

Southgate, W. M. In his John Jewel and the problem of doctrinal authority, Cambridge Mass 1962. Compares rationalism of Jewel and Hooker.

Grislis, E. Hooker's image of man. Durham NC 1963.

—— Hooker's method of theological inquiry. Anglican Theological Rev 45 1963.

—— The role of consensus in Hooker's method of theological inquiry. In The heritage of Christian thought: essays in honor of Robert Lowry Calhoun, New York 1965.

McGrade, A. S. The coherence of Hooker's Polity: the books on power. JHI 24 1963.

—— The public and the religious in Hooker's Polity. Church History 37 1968.

Parris, J. R. Hooker's doctrine of the Eucharist. Scottish Jnl of Theology 16 1963.

Patrides, C. A. The universal and publike manuscript of commonplaces. Neophilologus 47 1963. On John Dove as plagiarist of Hooker.

Ross, M. M. Ruskin, Hooker and 'the Christian theoria'. In Essays in English literature, ed M. MacLure and F. W. Watt, Toronto 1964.

Willey, B. In his English moralists, 1964.

Faulkner, R. K. Reason and revelation in Hooker's ethics. Amer Political Science Rev 59 1965.

Hurstfield, J. (ed). In his Reformation crisis, 1965.

McAdoo, H. R. In his Spirit of Anglicanism, New York 1965.

Allison, C. F. In his Rise of moralism: the proclamation of the Gospel from Hooker to Baxter, 1966.

Booty, J. E. Quest for the historical Hooker. Churchman 80 1966.

Field, G. C. Donne and Hooker. Anglican Theological Rev 48 1966.

Morrel, G. Hooker: theologian of the English Reformation. Christianity Today 10 1966.

Parker, T. H. (ed). In his English reformers, 1966.

Pollard, A. Richard Hooker. 1966 (Br Council pamphlet).

Schmidt, M. Die Rechtfertigungslehre bei Hooker in Geist und Geschichte der Reformation. In Festgabe an Hans Rückert, Berlin 1966.

Sparkes, A. W. Begging the question. JHI 27 1966. On origin of the term in Cartwright and Hooker.

Oberman, H. A. In his Forerunners of the Reformation, New York 1967.

Surlis, P. Natural law in Hooker. Irish Theological Quart 35 1968.

Tooley, M. J. Political thought and the theory and practice of toleration. In New Cambridge modern history vol 3, Cambridge 1968.

Allan, V. Hooker and the Utopians. E Studies 51 1970.

Hill, W. S. Hooker's Preface, chapters viii and ix. N & Q Dec 1969.

— The authority of Hooker's style. SP 67 1970.

— Hooker's Polity: the problem of the 'three last books'. HLQ 34 1971.

— (ed). Hooker: essays preliminary to an edition of his works. Cleveland 1972.

— Doctrine and polity in Hooker's Laws. Eng Literary Renaissance 2 1972.

Cohen, E. Z. The visible solemnity: ceremony and order in Shakespeare and Hooker. Texas Stud in Lit & Lang 12 1970.

Little, D. In his Religion, order and law, Oxford 1970.

Malone, M. T. The doctrine of predestination in the thought of William Perkins and Hooker. Anglican Theological Rev 52 1970.

Urban, L. A revolution in English moral theology. Anglican Theological Rev 53 1971.

Williams, R. R. Hooker on Church and State report. Churchman 85 1971.

Crofts, R. A. Defense of the Elizabethan Church: Jewel, Hooker and James I. Anglican Theological Rev 54 1972.

Stanwood, P. G. and L. Yeandle. Hooker's use of Thomas More. Moreana 35 1972.

P. G. S.

VII. THE MARPRELATE CONTROVERSY

For mss see Bibliographies, below. For mss relating to Udall, Penry and Waldegrave after their flight to the north, see Pierce, *John Penry, 1923 and Pearson. Many contemporary Puritan papers are in A. Peel's edn of* Seconde parte of a register, *1915.*

Bibliographies

The best bibliographies are in W. Pierce, Historical introduction to the Marprelate Tracts, 1908 and The Marprelate tracts, 1911. On related literature, see E. Arber, Introductory sketch to the Martin Marprelate controversy, 1879. For the history of the Presbyterian movement whose left wing is represented by Marprelate, for information regarding original documents and for an account of the Puritan press etc see A. F. Scott Pearson, Thomas Cartwright and Elizabethan Puritanism, 1925. D. J. McGinn, John Penry and the Marprelate controversy, 1966 includes an extensive bibliography.

§ 1

The Marprelate Tracts

The Epistle

Oh read over D. John Bridges, for it is a worthy worke: or an epitome of the fyrste booke of that right worshipfull volume, written against the Puritanes, in the defence of the noble cleargie, by as worshipfull a prieste, John Bridges, Presbyter, priest or elder, doctor of divillitie, and Deane of Sarum; wherein the arguments of the Puritans are wisely prevented, that when they come to answere M. Doctor, they must needes say something that hath bene spoken; by the reverend and worthie Martin Marprelate gentleman, and dedicated to the Confocationhouse; the Epitome is not yet published: in the meanetime, let them be content with this learned Epistle; printed oversea, in Europe, within two furlongs of a bounsing priest, at the cost and charges of M. Marprelate, gentleman. [1588] (secretly ptd by Waldegrave, East Molesey, October); ed J. Petheram 1842; ed E. Arber 1880; ed W. Pierce 1911.

The Epitome

Oh read over [as in Epistle, above]: by the reverend and worthie Martin Marprelate gentleman, and dedicated by a second epistle to the terrible priests; printed on the other hand of some of the priests. [1588] (secretly ptd by Waldegrave, Fawsley); ed J. Petheram 1843; ed W. Pierce 1911.

The Mineralls

Certaine minerall and metaphisicall schoolpoints, to be defended by the reverende bishop and the rest of my cleargie masters of the Convocation house, against bothe the universities, and al the reformed Churches in Christendome. [1589] (broadside secretly ptd by Waldegrave at Coventry before 20 Feb 1589); ed W. Pierce 1911.

Hay any worke for Cooper

Hay any worke for Cooper: or a briefe pistle directed by way of an hublication to the reverende byshopps, counselling them, if they will needs be barrelled up, for feare of smelling in the nostrels of her Majestie and the State, that they would use the advise of reverend Martin, for the providing of their Cooper; penned and compiled by Martin the Metropolitane; printed in Europe, not farre from some of the Bounsing Priestes. [1589] (secretly ptd by Waldegrave at White Friars Coventry, March) 1641 (as Reformation no enemie), 1642 (under proper title); ed J. Petheram 1845; ed W. Pierce 1911.

Martin Junior or Theses Martinianae

Theses Martinianae: that is, certaine demonstrative conclusions, sette downe and collected (as it should seeme) by that famous and renowned Clarke, the reverend Martin Marprelate the great; published and set foorth as an after-birth of the noble gentleman himselfe, by a prety stripling of his, Martin Junior, and dedicated by him to his good neame and nuncka, Maister John Kankerbury; printed by the assignes of Martin Junior. [1589] (secretly ptd by John Hodgkins at the Priory, Wolston July); ed W. Pierce 1911.

Martin Senior or the just censure

The just censure and reproofe of Martin Junior: wherein the rash and undiscreete headines of the foolish youth, is sharply mette with, and the boy hath his lesson taught, him, I warrant you, by his reverend and elder brother, Martin Senior, sonne and heir unto the renowned Martin Marprelate the Great. [1589] (secretly ptd by John Hodgkins at the Priory, Wolston July); ed W. Pierce 1911.

Protestatyon

The protestatyon of Martin Marprelat: wherein not with standing the surprizing of the printer, he maketh it known unto the world that he feareth, neither proud priest, Anti-christian Pope, tiranous prellate not godlesse catercap; but defiethe all the race of them by these presents and offereth conditionally, as is farthere expressed hearin by open disputation to apear in the defence of his caus aginst them and theirs; published by the worthie gentleman D. Martin marprelat D. in all the faculties primat and metropolitan. [1589] (after seizure of main Puritan press and arrest of Hodgkins and his assistants at Manchester this tract was secretly and very imperfectly ptd probably in Sept 1589 at Wolston?); ed W. Pierce 1911.

Contemporary Writings

[Fulke, W.] A briefe and plaine declaration concerning the desires of all those faithfull ministers, that have and do seeke for the discipline and reformation of the Church of Englande, which may serve for a just apologie against the false accusations and slanders of their adversaries. 1584. Written 1573 and pbd, without author's knowledge or sanction, by the Puritans, who added a preface and gave it running headline A learned discourse of ecclesiasticall government. It was generally referred to as A learned discourse. It must be distinguished from A full and plaine declaration, [1574], with which it has been confused.

A commission sente to the Pope, Cardynales, Bishops, Friers, Monkes, with all the rable of that viperous generation by the highe and mighty Prince and King Sathanas, the Devil of Hell. 1586.

Bridges, J. A defence of the government established in the Church of Englande for ecclesiasticall matters: contayning an answere unto a treatise called the Learned discourse of eccl. government, otherwise intituled A briefe and plaine declaration etc; comprehending likewise an answer to the arguments in a treatise named the Judgement of a most reverend and learned man from beyond the seas. 1587. The book against which the first Marprelate tracts were directed.

Fenner, D. A defence of the godlie ministers against the slaunders of D. Bridges, contayned in his answere to the preface before the discourse of ecclesiasticall governement, with a declaration of the bishops proceding against them. 1587. The preface vindicated is that placed by the Puritans before Fulke's Briefe and plaine declaration or A learned discourse. According to reprint in A parte of a register, this Defence was written by Fenner 'a moneth before his death'. Probably ptd by Schilders, Middelburg.

Penry, J. A treatise containing the aequity of an humble supplication which is to be exhibited unto hir gracious Majesty and this High Court of Parliament in the behalfe of the countrey of Wales, that some order may be taken for the preaching of the Gospell among those people. Oxford 1587; ed A. J. Grieve 1905 (Congregational Historical Soc).

—— Th'appellation of John Penri unto the Highe Court of Parliament from the bad and injurious dealing of th'Archb. of Canterb. and other his colleagues of the High Commission: wherin the complainant, humbly submitting himselfe and his cause unto the determination of this honorable assembly; craveth nothing els, but either release from trouble and persecution or just tryall. [1589]. Dedication dated 7 March. Secretly ptd, probably by Waldegrave.

—— A briefe discovery of the untruthes and slanders (against the true governement of the Church of Christ): contained in a sermon, preached the 8 of Februarie 1588 by D. Bancroft, and since that time, set forth in print, with additions by the said authour. [1590]. Probably ptd by Waldegrave in Edinburgh.

—— Notebook 1593. Ed A. Peel 1944 (Royal Historical Soc).

—— Three treatises concerning Wales. Ed D. Williams, Cardiff 1960.

Udall, J. The state of the Church of Englande, laide open in a conference betweene Diotrephes a Bishop, Tertullus a papist, Demetrius an usurer, Pandocheus an In-Keeper, and Paule a preacher of the word of God. [1588] (secretly ptd by Waldegrave, April); ed E. Arber, A parte of a register c. 1592, 1879.

—— A demonstration of the trueth of that discipline which Christe hath prescribed in his worde for the government of his Church, in all times and places, untill the ende of the worlde. [1588] (secretly ptd by Waldegrave on Marprelate press at East Molesey, about August); ed E. Arber, A parte of a register c. 1592, 1880.

[Travers, W.] A defence of the ecclesiasticall discipline ordayned of God to be used in his Church, against a replie of Maister Bridges to a brief and plain declaration of it which was printed in 1584; which replie he termeth A defence of the government established in the Church of Englande, for ecclesiasticall matters. 1588. Probably ptd by Schilders, Middelburg. See J. D. Wilson, Trans Bibl Soc 11 1912.

Bancroft, R. A sermon preached at Paules Crosse the 9 of Februarie, being the first Sunday in the Parleament, anno 1588. 1588, 1588. Entered at Stationers' Hall 3 March 1589; rptd Bibliotheca scriptorum ecclesiae anglicanae 1709.

—— Daungerous positions and proceedings, published and practised within this iland of Brytaine and under pretence of reformation, and for the Presbiteriall discipline. 1593.

—— A survey of the pretended holy discipline. 1593.

—— Tracts ascribed to Richard Bancroft. Ed A. Peel, Cambridge 1953.

C., T. [Thomas Cooper, Bishop of Winchester]. An admonition to the people of England: wherein are answered, not onely the slaunderous untruethes, reprochfully uttered by Martin the Libeller, but also many other crimes by some of his broode, objected generally against all bishops, and the chiefe of the cleargie, purposely to deface and discredite the present state of the Church. 1589 (3 edns); ed J. Petheram 1847; ed E. Arber 1882.

A dialogue, wherein is laid open the tyrannicall dealing of L. Bishopps against Gods children; with certaine points of doctrine, wherein they approve themselves (according to D. Bridges his judgement) to be truely the bishops of the Divell. [1589] (probably ptd on Waldegrave's press shortly after April), 1643 (as The character of a Puritan and his gallimaufrey of the antichristian clergie; prepared with D. Bridges sawce for the present time to feed on, by the worthy gentleman D. Martin Mar-Prelat).

Mar-Martin. I know not why a fruitelesse lye in print. [1589?].

Mar-Martine.

> I know not why a trueth in rime set out
> Maie not as well mar Martine and his mates,
> As shamelesse lies in prose-books cast about
> Marpriests, and prelates, and subvert whole states.
> For where truth builds, and lying overthroes,
> One truth in rime, is worth ten lies in prose.

7 pp. of doggerel priv ptd c. May 1589; partly rptd among Doubtful works *in* Works of John Lyly vol 3, *ed R. W. Bond, Oxford 1902.*

Marre Mar-Martin: or Marre-Martins medling, in a manner misliked:

> Martins vaine prose, Marre-Martin doth mislike,
> Reason (forsooth) for Martin seekes debate:
> Marre-Martin will not so; yet doth his patience strike,
> Last verse, first prose, conclude in one selfe hate:
> Both maintaine strife, unfitting Englands state.
> Martin, Marre-Martin, Barrow joyned with Browne
> Shew zeale: yet strive to pull Religion downe.

Priv ptd probably in London, c. June 1589; rptd S. E. Brydges, Censura literaria *vol 2, 1805–9, article 73.*

Anti-Martinus: sive Monitio cujusdam Londonensis, ad Adolescentes utriusque Academiae, contra personatum quendam rabulam, qui se Anglicè Martin Marprelat Hoc est, Martinum Μαστιγάρχον ἢ μισάρχον, vocat. 1589. Signed at end, Totus Vester A.L. Entered at Stationers' Hall 3 July 1589.

A counter-cuffe given to Martin Junior by the venturous, hardie, and renowned Pasquill of England, Cavaliero: from the unpriviledged Presse of Ass-ignes of Martin Junior. 1589, 1589 (priv ptd Aug 1589); rptd Nashe's Works vol 1, ed A. B. Grosart 1883 (Huth Lib); ed R. B. McKerrow, Works vol 1, 1904. By Nashe?

Martins months minde, that is A certaine report, and true description of the death and funeralls, of olde Martin Marreprelate, the great makebate of England and father of the factious. 1589. Priv ptd London c. Aug 1589, rptd Nashe's Works vol i, ed A. B. Grosart 1883. It has been suggested that the author of this was also the author of An almond for a parrat, but was not Pasquil.

Rythmes against Martin Marre-Prelate. [1589]. M. Some laid open in his colours: wherein the indifferent reader may easily see, howe wretchedly and loosely he hath handeled the cause against M. Penri; done by an Oxford man, to his friend in Cambridge. [1589] (secretly ptd by Waldegrave c. Aug, the last page signed I.G.). By Job Throkmorton?

A whip for an ape: or Martin displaied. [1589] (priv ptd c. Oct); also pbd from same type as Rythmes against Martin Marre-Prelate. Ascribed to John Lyly. Rptd I. D'Israeli, Quarrels of authors vol 3, 1814; in Bibliographical miscellany no 5, 20 March 1854; Lyly's Works vol 3, ed R. W. Bond, Oxford 1902.

[Nashe, T.?]. The returne of the renowned cavaliero Pasquill of England, from the other side of the seas, and his meeting with Marforius at London upon the Royall Exchange: my breath be so hote that I burne my mouth, suppose I was printed by Pepper Allie. 1589. Dated at end '20 Octobris', rptd Nashe's Works vol 1, ed A. B. Grosart 1883; ed R. B. McKerrow, Works vol 1, 1904.

— An almond for a parrat: or Cutbert Curry-knaves almes, fit for the knave Martin and the rest of those impudent Beggers, imprinted at a place, not farre from a place, by the assignes of Signior Some-body and are to be sold at his shoppe in Trouble-knave Street, at the signe of the Standish. [1590] (priv ptd); ed J. Petheram 1846; ed R. B. McKerrow, Works of Thomas Nashe vol 3, 1905.

— The firste parte of Pasquils apologie. 1590 (priv ptd). Dated at end, 2 July. A reply to Penry, A treatise wherein is manifestlie proved, that reformation and those that sincerely favor the same, are unjustly charged to be enemies unto hir Majestie, and the state, which was ptd by Waldegrave in Scotland c. April 1590, rptd Nashe's Works vol 1, ed A. B. Grosart 1883; ed R. B. McKerrow, Works vol 1, 1904.

[Lyly, J.] Pappe with a hatchet, alias a figge for my God sonne; imprinted by John Anoke, and John Astile, for the Baylive of Withernam, cum privilegio perennitatis, and are to bee sold at the signe of the crab tree cudgell in Twackcoate Lane. [1589] (priv ptd c. Nov); ed J. Petheram 1844; ed G. Saintsbury, Elizabethan and Jacobean pamphlets, 1892; ed R. W. Bond, Lyly's Works vol 3, Oxford 1902.

A myrror for Martinists, and all other schismatiques, which in these daungerous daies doe breake the godlie unitie, and disturbe the Christian peace of the Church. 1590. Entered at Stationers' Hall 22 Dec 1589.

Wright, L. A friendly admonition to Martine Marprelate and his mates. 1590. Entered at Stationers' Hall 19 Jan.

Plaine Percevall the peace-maker of England, sweetly indevoring with his blunt persuasions to botch up a reconciliation between Mar-ton and Mar-tother; compiled by lawful art. [1590]; ed J. Petheram 1860. The authorship has been ascribed to one of the Harvey brothers.

[Harvey, R.] A theologicall discourse of the Lamb of God and his enemies. 1590.

A petition directed to her most excellent Majestie, wherein is delivered: 1, A meane howe to compound the civill dissension in the Church of England: 2, A proofe that they who write for Reformation, doe not offend against the stat. of 23 Eliz. 101, and therefore till matters bee compounded, deserve more favour. [c. 1591]. Probably written by a lawyer.

A parte of a register: contayninge sundrie memorable matters, written by divers godly and learned in our time, which stande for and desire the reformation of our Church, in discipline and ceremonies, according to the pure worde of God, and the lawe of our lande. [c. 1592]. Schilders, Middelburg, has been suspected

as the printer, but Bancroft thought the work was imported from Scotland.

Sutcliffe, M. An answere to a certaine libel supplicatorie, or rather diffamatory, and also to certaine calumnious articles and interrogatories, both printed and scattered in secret corners, to the slaunder of the ecclesiasticall state, and put forth under the name and title of A petition directed to her Majestie. 1592. Dedicatory epistle dated 20 Dec.

— An answere unto a certaine calumnious letter published by M. Job Throkmorton, entituled A defence against the slaunders of M. Sutcliffe, wherein the vanitie both of the defence of himselfe and the accusation of others is manifestly declared. 1595.

Harvey, G. An advertisement for Papp-Hatchett. Dated 5 Nov 1589, but pbd as second book of Pierces supererogation, 1593; ed S. E. Brydges, Archaica vol 2, 1815; ed A. B. Grosart, Harvey's Works vol 2, 1884 (Huth Lib).

Throkmorton, J. The defence of Job Throkmorton against the slaunders of Maister Sutcliffe, taken out of a copye of his owne hande as it was written to an honorable personage. 1594. Throkmorton denies that he is Martin Marprelate. Probably ptd by Schilders, Middelburg.

Bacon, F. An advertisement touching the controversies of the Church of England. In Francis Bacon, Resuscitatio, 1657; ed J. Spedding, Works, 1857–74; ed E. Arber, Introductory sketch, 1879.

Cartwright, T. Cartwrightiana. Ed A. Peel and L. H. Carlson 1951 (from mss).

§2

Burnet, G. History of the Reformation of the Church of England. 2 pts 1679–81; ed N. Pocock 7 vols Oxford 1865; Menston 1969–70 (facs).

Strype, J. Annals of the Reformation. 2 pts 1709–8, 4 vols 1725–31 (complete), 4 vols in 7 Oxford 1824, 1965.

— Life of John Whitgift. 2 pts 1718, Oxford 1822.

Dodd, C. The church history of England from 1500–1688. 3 vols Brussels 1737–42; ed M. A. Tierney 5 vols 1839–43.

Brook, B. The lives of the Puritans. 3 vols 1813.

d'Israeli, I. Quarrels of authors. 3 vols 1814.

Neal, D. The history of the Puritans. 3 vols 1837.

Petheram, J. Reprints of the Epistle, the Epitome, Hay any worke, Pappe with a hatchet, An almond for a parrat, An admonition to the people of England, Plaine Percevall. 1842–7.

Maskell, W. History of the Martin Marprelate controversy. 1845.

Arber, E. An introductory sketch to the Martin Marprelate controversy. 1878. Reprints Diotrephes, Demonstration of discipline, Epistle, Admonition to the people of England.

Dexter, H. M. The Congregationalism of the last three hundred years, as seen in its literature. New York 1880.

Grosart, A. B. (ed). The works of Thomas Nashe. 1883.

— (ed). The works of Gabriel Harvey. 1884.

Saintsbury, G. Elizabethan and Jacobean pamphlets. 1892.

Allnutt, W. H. The Marprelate press 1588–9. Bibliographica 2 1896.

Bond, R. W. (ed). Complete works of John Lyly. 3 vols Oxford 1902.

Lee, S. The last years of Elizabeth. In The Cambridge modern history vol 3, Cambridge 1904. See also DNB on Penry, Throkmorton, Udall, Waldegrave.

Frere, W. H. The English Church in the reigns of Elizabeth and James I. 1904.

— and C. E. Douglas (ed). Puritan manifestoes. 1954.

McKerrow, R. B. (ed). The works of Thomas Nashe. 5 vols 1904–10, Oxford 1958.

Wilson, J. D. A date in the Marprelate controversy. Library 2nd ser 8 1907.

—— The Marprelate controversy. CHEL vol 3 1909.
—— Richard Schilders and the English Puritans. Trans Bibl Soc 11 1912.
—— Martin Marprelate and Shakespeare's Fluellen. 1912. *See also* Library 3rd ser 3 1912.
Pierce, W. An historical introduction to the Marprelate tracts. 1908.
—— The Marprelate tracts. 1911.
—— John Penry: his life, times and writings. 1923.
Henson, H. H. Puritanism in England. 1912.
Burrage, C. John Penry. Oxford 1913.
Mason, A. J. The Church of England and episcopacy. 1914.
Peel, A. (ed). The seconde parte of a register. 2 vols Cambridge 1915.
Bonnard, G. La controverse de Martin Marprelate. Geneva 1916.
Pearson, A. F. S. Thomas Cartwright and Elizabethan Puritanism. Cambridge 1925.
—— Church and state: political aspects of sixteenth-century Puritanism. Cambridge 1928.
McCorkle, J. N. Note concerning Mistress Crane and the Martin Marprelate controversy. Library 2nd ser 12 1931.
Stearns, R. P. Congregationalism in the Dutch Netherlands: the rise and fall of the English Congregational classis 1621–35. Chicago 1940.
M., M. Answer to a Puritan manifesto. More Books 16 1941.
McGinn, D. J. The real Martin Marprelate. PMLA 58 1943.
—— A perplexing date in the Marprelate controversy. SP 41 1944.
—— Nashe's share in the Marprelate controversy. PMLA 59 1944.
—— The admonition controversy. New Brunswick NJ 1949.
—— John Penry and the Martin Marprelate controversy. New Brunswick NJ 1966. Identifies Penry with the anon Martin.
Wilson, H. S. Gabriel Harvey's orations on rhetoric. ELH 12 1945.
Johnson, A. F. Books printed at Heidelberg for Thomas Cartwright. Library 5th ser 2 1947.
Davies, D. H. The worship of the English Puritans. Westminster Md 1948.
Summersgill, F. L. The influence of the Marprelate controversy upon the style of Thomas Nashe. SP 48 1951.
Holden, W. P. Anti-Puritan satire 1572–1642. New Haven 1954.

Whale, J. S. The Protestant tradition. New York 1955.
Calder, I. M. (ed). Activities of the Puritan faction of the Church of England 1625–33. 1957.
Sutherland, J. In his English satire, Cambridge 1958.
Coolidge, J. S. Martin Marprelate, Marvell and Decorum personae as a satirical theme. PMLA 74 1959.
—— The Pauline renaissance in England. Oxford 1970.
Haller, W. Foxe's Book of Martyrs and the elect nation. 1963.
Clebsch, W. A. England's earliest Protestants 1520–55. New Haven 1964.
Dickens, A. G. In his English Reformation, 1964.
—— The Marprelate tracts 1588–9. Leeds 1967 (facs).
Hilkested, C. In his Society and Puritanism in pre-revolutionary England, New York 1964.
Knappen, M. M. In his Tudor Puritanism, 1965.
Ruhr, J. von. Covenant and assurance in early English Puritanism. Church History 34 1965.
Anselment, R. A. Martin Marprelate: a new source for Dryden's fable of the martin and the swallows. RES new ser 17 1966.
—— Rhetoric and the dramatic satire of Martin Marprelate. Stud in Eng Lit 1500–1900 10 1970.
Breen, T. H. The non-existent controversy: Puritan and Anglican attitudes on work and wealth 1600–40. Church History 35 1966.
Cragg, G. R. The collapse of militant Puritanism. Modern Eng Church History 40 1966.
Wolzer, M. The revolution of the saints. 1966.
Booty, J. E. The expulsion of John Sanderson: trouble in an Elizabethan university. Historical Mag of Protestant Episcopal Church 36 1967.
Collinson, P. In his Elizabethan Puritan movement, Berkeley 1967.
Nuttall, G. F. The Puritan spirit: essays and addresses. 1967.
New, J. F. H. The Whitgift-Cartwright controversy. Archiv für Reformationsgeschichte 2 1968.
Oakley, F. Jacobean radical theology: the absolute and ordinary powers of the King. JHI 29 1968.
Grant, L. T. Seventeenth-century Puritan catechetical writings. Princeton Seminary Bull 62 1969. Bibliography.
Johnson, J. T. English Puritan thought on the ends of marriage. Jnl of Ecclesiastical History 20 1969.
Rutman, D. B. American Puritanism. Philadelphia 1970. A bibliographical essay, especially on English origins.

P. G. S.

VIII. THE CAROLINE DIVINES (1620–60)

GENERAL STUDIES

For works on preaching see col 1915, above.

Fuller, T. Abel redivivus: the lives and deaths of the moderne divines. 1651, 1652.
—— The church-history of Britain. 1655.
Heylyn, P. Cyprianus anglicus. 1668.
Moulin, L. du. A short and true account of the several advances the Church of England hath made towards Rome. 1680.
Hacket, J. Scrinia reserata. 1693.
Calamy, E. An abridgement of Mr Baxter's history of his life and times; with an account of many others of those worthy ministers who were ejected at the Restoration. 1702, 2 vols 1713; A continuation of the account, 2 vols 1727; rev S. Palmer 2 vols 1775, 3 vols 1802 (as The Nonconformist's memorial); A. G. Matthews, Calamy revised, Oxford 1934.

Collier, J. An ecclesiastical history of Great Britain. 2 vols 1708–14, 9 vols 1840, 1852.
Walker, J. An attempt towards recovering an account of the numbers and sufferings of the clergy. 1714; A. G. Matthews, Walker revised, Oxford 1948. *See also* G. B. Tatham, Dr John Walker and the sufferings of the clergy, 1911.
LeNeve, J. Fasti ecclesiae anglicanae. 1716, 3 vols Oxford 1854, 1969 (rev)–. Pt 1, St Paul's, London 1541–1857.
Neal, D. The history of the Puritans 1517–1688. 4 vols 1732–8, 5 vols 1793–7.
Crosby, T. The history of the English Baptists. 4 vols 1738.
Bloom, J. H. Pulpit oratory in the time of James the First. 1831.

Cattermole, R. Literature of the Church of England. 2 vols 1844.

D'Ewes, S. Autobiography and correspondence. Ed J. O. Halliwell-Phillipps 2 vols 1845.

Teale, W. H. Lives of the English divines. 1846.

Coleridge, S. T. Notes on English divines. Ed D. Coleridge 2 vols 1853; Coleridge on the seventeenth century, ed R. F. Brinkley, Durham NC 1955.

Diary of John Manningham. Ed J. Bruce 1868 (Camden Soc).

Hunt, J. Religious thought in England to the end of the 18th century. 3 vols 1870–3.

Tulloch, J. Rational theology and Christian philosophy in England in the seventeenth century. 2 vols Edinburgh 1872.

Barclay, R. The inner life of the religious societies of the Commonwealth. 1867.

Drysdale, A. H. History of the Presbyterians in England. 1889.

Wakeman, H. O. The Church and the Puritans 1570–1660. 1889.

Schickler, F. de. Les églises du refuge en Angleterre. 3 vols Paris 1892.

Makower, F. The constitutional history of the Church of England. 1895.

Brown, J. Puritan preaching in England. 1900.

Dowden, E. Puritan and Anglican. 1900.

Shaw, W. A. A history of the English Church 1640–60. 2 vols 1900.

Campagnac, E. T. The Cambridge Platonists. Oxford 1901.

Usher, R. G. Reconstruction of the English Church. 2 vols 1910.

Hutton, W. H. The English Church from the accession of Charles I to the death of Anne. 1903, 1913 (rev).

— Caroline divines. CHEL vol 7 1911.

Braithwaite, W. C. The beginnings of Quakerism 1647–60. 1912.

Tatham, G. A. B. Puritans in power [1640–60]. 1913.

Bremond, H. Histoire littéraire du sentiment religieux en France. 11 vols Paris 1920–36; tr 3 vols 1928–36.

Henson, H. H. Studies in English religion in the 17th century. New York 1923.

— Selected English sermons. Oxford 1939 (WC).

Powicke, F. J. The Cambridge Platonists. 1926.

Richardson, C. F. English preachers and preaching 1640–70. New York 1928.

Grierson, H. J. C. Cross currents in English literature of the seventeenth century. 1929.

Jones, R. F. The attack on pulpit eloquence in the Restoration. JEGP 30 1931; rptd in his The seventeenth century, Stanford 1951.

— Spiritual reformers in the 16th and 17th centuries. Boston 1959.

White, H. C. English devotional literature [prose] 1600–40. Madison 1931.

Schneider, H. W. The Puritan mind. 1931.

Cassirer, E. Die platonische Renaissance in England und die Schule von Cambridge. Leipzig 1932; tr 1954.

Jones, R. M. Mysticism and democracy in the English commonwealth. 1932.

Jordan, W. K. The development of religious toleration in England. 4 vols Cambridge Mass 1932–40. Vols 2–4 on 1603–60.

Liturgy and worship. Ed W. K. L. Clarke 1932.

Mâle, E. L'art religieux après le concile de Trente. Paris 1932.

Mitchell, W. F. English pulpit oratory from Andrewes to Tillotson. 1932. Bibliography pp. 401–73.

Davies, G. Arminian versus Puritan in England c. 1620–40. Huntington Lib Bull no 5 1934.

— In his Early Stuarts 1603–60, Oxford 1937 (Oxford History of England), 1959 (rev).

— English political sermons 1603–40. HLQ 3 1939.

Tracts on liberty in the Puritan Revolution 1638–47. Ed W. Haller 3 vols New York 1934.

Willey, B. The seventeenth-century background. 1934.

More, P. E. and F. L. Cross (ed). Anglicanism: the thought and practice of the Church of England illustrated from the religious literature of the seventeenth century. 1935.

Mathew, D. Catholicism in England 1535–1935. 1936.

Poppers, H. Der religiöse Ursprung des modernen englischen Freiheits- und Staats-Ideals: die Geschichtsgestaltung des Independentismus. Prague 1936.

Struck, W. Der Einfluss Jacob Boehmes auf die englische Literatur des 17 Jahrhunderts. Berlin 1936.

Harrison, A. H. W. Arminianism. 1937.

Lyon, T. The theory of religious liberty in England 1603–39. Cambridge 1937.

Allen, J. W. English political thought 1603–60. Vol 1, 1603–44, 1938. Chs on Montague, Mainwaring, Sibthorpe.

Magee, B. The English Recusants. 1938.

Puritanism and liberty: being the army debates 1647–9. Ed A. S. P. Woodhouse 1938.

Kirby, E. W. Sermons before the Commons 1640–2. Amer Historical Rev 44 1939.

Smyth, C. H. E. The art of preaching. 1940, 1944 (rev).

Witte, H. Die Ansichten Jakobs I von England über Kirche und Staat. Berlin 1940.

Addleshaw, G. W. O. The High Church tradition: a study in the liturgical thought of the 17th century. 1941.

Hughes, P. Rome and the Counter-Reformation in England. 1942.

McNeill, J. T. Casuistry in the Puritan age. Religion in Life 12 1943.

Krapp, R. M. Liberal Anglicanism 1643–7. Ridgefield Conn 1944.

Leveller manifestoes of the Puritan Revolution. Ed D. M. Wolfe 1944.

McAdoo, H. R. The structure of Caroline moral theology. Theology 48 1945.

— The structure of Caroline moral theology: an investigation of principles. 1949.

— The spirit of Anglicanism. New York 1965.

— The Carolines under criticism. Theology 72 1969.

Maclean, J. F. The influence of the Puritan clergy on the House of Commons 1625–9. Church History 14 1945.

Bush, D. English literature in the earlier seventeenth century 1600–60. Oxford 1945 (OHEL), 1962 (corrected). Ch 10.

Nuttall, G. F. The Holy Spirit in Puritan faith and experience. Oxford 1946.

— Visible saints. Oxford 1957.

— The Puritan spirit. 1967.

Randall, H. W. The rise and fall of a martyrology: sermons on Charles I. HLQ 10 1947.

Calder, I. M. A seventeenth-century attempt to purify the Anglican Church. Amer Historical Rev 53 1948.

— (ed). Activities of the Puritan faction in the Church of England 1625–33. 1957.

Davies, H. The worship of the English Puritans. Westminster Md 1948.

Hudson, W. S. Mystical religion in the Puritan Commonwealth. Jnl of Religion 28 1948.

Johnson, G. A. From seeker to finder: a study in the 17th-century English spiritualism before the Quakers. Church History 17 1948.

Ryan, J. K. The reputation of St Thomas Aquinas among the English Protestant thinkers of the 17th century. New Scholasticism 22 1948.

Harris, V. All coherence gone. Chicago 1949.

Ryan, C. J. Theories of church-state relationships in 17th-century England. Historical Bull 27 1949.

Wood, T. The 17th-century English casuists on betting and gambling. Church Quart Rev 149 1949.

— English casuistical divinity in the 17th century. 1952.

— 17th-century moralists and the marital relationship. Trivium 1 1966. On Taylor, Andrewes, Hall.

Brilioth, Y. T. Landmarks in the history of preaching. 1950.

Knox, R. A. Enthusiasm. Oxford 1950.

Stedmond, J. M. English prose of the 17th century. Dalhousie Rev 30 1950.

Stratford, E. W. King Charles the martyr. 1950.

West, F. H. Nottinghamshire parson in the 17th century [William Sampson, b. 1632]. Church Quart Rev 151 1950.

Bosher, R. S. The making of the Restoration: the influence of the Laudians 1649–62. 1951.

Nédoncelle, M. Trois aspects du problème anglo-catholique au 17e siècle. Paris 1951. On John Barnes, Obadiah Walker and Christopher Davenport.

Williamson, G. The Senecan amble. Chicago 1951.

Bailey, S. William Forbes, first Bishop of Edinburgh: the spirit of Anglicanism. Church Quart Rev 153 1952.

Fisch, H. The Puritans and the reform of prose style. ELH 19 1952.

Baker, H. The wars of truth: studies in the decay of Christian humanism in the earlier seventeenth century. Cambridge 1952.

Addison, J. T. Early Anglican thought 1559–1667. Historical Mag of Protestant Episcopal Church 22 1953.

Frere, W. H. and C. E. Douglas. Puritan manifestoes: a study of the origin of the Puritan revolt. 1953.

George, C. H. A social interpretation of English Puritanism. Jnl of Modern History 25 1953.

— Puritanism as history and historiography. Past & Present 41 1968.

Mason, S. F. Science and religion in 17th-century England. Past & Present 3 1953.

Notestein, W. The English people on the eve of colonization 1603–30. 1954.

Carré, M. H. The new philosophy and the divines. Church Quart Rev 156 1955.

Haller, W. Liberty and reformation in the Puritan Revolution. New York 1955.

May, G. L. (ed). Wings of an eagle: an anthology of Caroline preachers. 1955.

Owst, G. R. Sermon as literature. London Quart 180 1955.

Simpson, A. Puritanism in old and new England. Chicago 1955.

Hardacre, P. H. The Royalists during the Puritan Revolution. Hague 1956.

Hill, C. Economic problems of the Church from Archbishop Whitgift to the Long Parliament. Oxford 1956.

— The century of revolution 1603–1714. 1961.

Huntley, F. L. Heads for an essay on the seventeenth-century funeral sermon in England. Anglican Theological Rev 38 1956.

Wilkinson, J. T. The pastor in the seventeenth century. London Quart 181 1956.

Wakefield, G. S. Puritan devotion. 1957.

Costello, W. The scholastic curriculum at early seventeenth-century Cambridge. Cambridge Mass 1958.

Grisbrooke, W. J. Anglican liturgies of the 17th and 18th centuries. 1958.

MacLure, M. The Paul's Cross sermons 1534–1642. Toronto 1958.

Peck, A. L. Anglicanism and episcopacy. 1958.

Westfall, R. S. Science and religion in seventeenth-century England. New Haven 1958.

Curtis, M. H. Oxford and Cambridge in transition 1558–1642. Oxford 1959.

— Hampton Court conference and its aftermath. History 46 1961.

— The alienated intellectuals of early Stuart England. Past & Present 23 1962.

Cooper, B. G. Millenary preachers 1645–7. London Quart 185 1960.

Marchant, R. A. The Puritans and the Church Courts in the diocese of York 1560–1642. 1960.

Saveson, J. E. Differing reactions to Descartes among the Cambridge Platonists. JHI 31 1960.

Wilson, F. P. In his Seventeenth-century prose, Cambridge 1960.

Janelle, P. English devotional literature in the 16th and 17th centuries. In English studies today: series 2, ed G. A. Bonnard, Berne 1961. On Parsons, Andrewes, Cosin, Laud, Stafford's Femall glory [1635].

Stranks, C. J. Anglican devotion. 1961.

Cuming, G. J. The grand debate [the Savoy conference 1661]. Church Quart Rev 163 1962.

— A history of Anglican liturgy. 1969.

Havran, M. J. The Catholics in Caroline England. 1962.

Murray, I. (ed). Sermons of the great ejection. 1962.

Hart, A. T. Four Archbishops of Canterbury [Parker, Laud, Sancroft, Tillotson]. Modern Churchman 6 1963.

Huelin, G. The delight of the English nation: William Juxon 1582–1663. Church Quart Rev 164 1963.

Lamont, W. M. Marginal Prynne 1660–9. 1963.

Knox, R. B. A Caroline trio: Ussher, Laud and Williams. Church Quart Rev 164 1963.

Pollard, A. English sermons. 1963 (Br Council pamphlet).

Barbour, H. The Quakers in Puritan England. New Haven 1964.

Green, V. H. H. Religion at Oxford and Cambridge. 1964.

Bussby, F. George Morley: Caroline divine. Church Quart Rev 165 1964.

— An Anglican in exile. Church Quart Rev 166 1965. On George Morley 1649–60.

New, J. F. H. Anglican and Puritan: the basis of their opposition. Stanford 1964.

Parker, T. M. Arminianism and Laudianism in seventeenth-century England. Stud in Church History 1 1964.

Stanwood, P. G. A portrait of Stuart orthodoxy. Church Quart Rev 165 1964. On Joseph Beaumont 1616–99.

— Patristic and contemporary borrowing in the Caroline divines. Renaissance Quart 23 1970.

Flindall, R. P. Theological reading in the seventeenth century. Church Quart Rev 166 1965.

Allison, C. F. The rise of moralism: the proclamation of the Gospel from Hooker to Baxter. 1966.

Snapp, H. F. The protestation of the twelve bishops in 1641. Historical Mag of Protestant Episcopal Church 35 1966.

— Church and state relations in early Caroline England. Jnl of Church & State 9 1967.

Freeman, A. 'The fatal vesper' and 'The doleful evensong': claim-jumping in 1623. Library 5th ser 22 1967.

Höltgen, K. J. and J. Horden. Arthur Warwick: the author of Spare minutes [2nd edn, 1634]. Library 5th ser 22 1967.

Ritz, J.-G. Saint François de Sales et l'église anglicane du 17e siècle. Revue Savoisienne 1967 (numéro spécial).

Spalding, J. C. Sermons before Parliament 1640–9 as a public Puritan diary. Church History 36 1967.

Trevor-Roper, H. R. Religion, the Reformation and social change. 1967. Includes Fast sermons before Long Parliament.

Wood, P. A. The spirit and the candle: a study of the Cambridge Platonists. Historical Mag of Protestant Episcopal Church 36 1967.

Allen, J. B. The style and content of Baptist sermons in 17th-century England. Furman Stud 15 1968.

Cragg, G. R. (ed). The Cambridge Platonists. New York 1968. An anthology of selections from various writers, Whichcote, More et al.

Bridenbaugh, C. Vexed and troubled Englishmen 1590–1642. New York 1968.

Emerson, E. H. (ed). English Puritanism from John Hooper to John Milton. Durham NC 1968. An anthology.

King, P. The episcopate during the Civil Wars 1642–9. EHR 83 1968.

— The reasons for the abolition of the Book of common prayer in 1645. Jnl of Ecclesiastical History 21 1970.

Weatherby, H. L. The encircling gloom: Newman's departure from the Caroline tradition. Victorian Stud 12 1968. Especially on Hooker, Andrewes, Hammond, Cosin, Laud.

Beckwith, R. T. Methodism and the Mass. Churchman 83 1969.

Cave, T. C. Devotional poetry in France c. 1570–1613. Cambridge 1969. Devotional tradition and literature, with reference to the funeral sermon.

Lamont, W. M. Godly rule: politics and religion 1603–60. 1969.

Ossory, The Bishop of (H. R. McAdoo). The Carolines under criticism. Theology 72 1969.

Patrides, C. A. (ed). The Cambridge Platonists. 1969. Sermons and other selections of Whichcote, Cudworth, Smith and More, with introd and notes.

Stewart, B. S. Cult of the royal martyr. Church History 38 1969.

Wilson, J. F. Pulpit in Parliament. Princeton 1969.

Owen, D. M. The records of the Established Church in England excluding parochial records. 1970. An archival guide.

Seaver, P. S. The Puritan lectureships. Stanford 1970.

Macfarlane, A. The family life of Ralph Josselin, a seventeenth-century clergyman. Cambridge 1970.

— Witchcraft in Tudor and Stuart England. 1970.

Slights, C. Ingenious piety: Anglican casuistry of the seventeenth century. Harvard Theological Rev 63 1970.

Welsby, P. A. (ed). Sermons and society: an Anglican anthology. Baltimore 1970.

Thomas, K. Religion and the decline of magic. 1971.

Contemporary Treatises on Preaching

Askew, E. Brotherly reconcilement, with An apologie of the use of fathers and secular learning in sermons. 1605.

Hierion, S. The preacher's plea. 1605.

Keckermann, B. Rhetoricae ecclesiasticae. Hanover 1606 (3rd edn).

Bernard, R. The faithfull shepherd. 1621.

James, R. A sermon delivered in Oxford concerning the apostles preaching and ours. 1630.

Wilkins, J. Ecclesiastes: or a discourse concerning the gift of preaching as it falls under the rules of art. 1646 etc; 7 edns by 1679.

Chappell, W. Methodus concionandi. 1648; tr 1656 (as The preacher: or the art and method of preaching).

Bowles, O. De pastore evangelico tractatus. 1649.

Prideaux, J. Scholasticae theologiae syntagma mneminicum. Oxford 1651, 1660.

Hall, T. Vindiciae literarum: the schools guarded. 1654, 1655.

Wright, A. Five sermons, in five several styles or waies of preaching. 1656. Includes 2 genuine sermons by Andrewes and Hall, and 3 parodies—of Mayne and Cartwright, of the Presbyterians, and of the Independents.

Price, W. Ars concionandi. Amsterdam 1657.

Eachard, J. The grounds and occasions of the contempt of the clergy. 1670 etc; 9 edns by 1685; ed E. Arber 1883.

Arderne, J. Directions concerning the matter and stile of sermons. 1671; ed J. Mackay, Oxford 1952 (Luttrell Soc).

Glanvill, J. An essay concerning preaching, written for the direction of a young divine. 1678.

— A seasonable defence of preaching, and the plain way of it. 1678.

Manningham, J. Diary 1602–3. 1868 (Camden Soc).

GEORGE ABBOT

Archbishop of Canterbury
1562–1633

Bibliographies

Christophers, R. A. A bibliography of George Abbot, Archbishop of Canterbury. Charlottesville 1966.

§1

Questiones sex totidem praelectionibus in schola theologica oxoniae, pro forma habitis, discussae et discuptate anno 1597, in quibus e sacra scriptura et patribus, quid statuendum sit definitur. 1598.

A brief description of the whole world. 1599. *See col 2119, below.*

An exposition on the prophet Jonah, in certain sermons preached at St Mary's church in Oxford. 1600.

A sermon preached at Westminster, May 26 1608, at the funeral solemnities of the Right Hon Thomas Earl of Dorset. 1608.

Account, written by Dr George Abbot, Archbishop of Canterbury, with the speech he intended to have made, and King James's letter to him [Essex divorce]. 1613; rptd in W. Cobbett, Complete collection of state trials vol 2, 1809.

A treatise of the perpetual visibility and the succession of the true Church in all ages. 1624.

Archbishop Abbot in his narrative [concerning his sequestration]. 1627; rptd in J. Rushworth, Historical collections vol 1, 1721 and in W. Cobbett, Complete collection of state trials vol 2, 1809.

§2

A short apology for Archbishop Abbot, touching the death of Peter Hawkins, by an unknown hand. 1621; rptd in English works of Sir Henry Spelman, ed E. Gibson 1727.

Spelman, H. An answer to the foregoing apology [touching the death of Peter Hawkins]. 1621; rptd in English works of Sir Henry Spelman, ed E. Gibson 1727.

Onslow, A. The character of Archbishop Abbot upon reading Lord Clarendon's account of him. 1723.

Abbot, J. T. An apology for Dr George Abbot, Lord Archbishop of Canterbury, as touching some stricture on his memory. 1863.

Welsby, P. A. Abbot: the unwanted Archbishop. 1962.

THOMAS ADAMS
c. 1583–c. 1660

Collections

The divells banket. 1614. 6 sermons.

A divine herball. 1616. 5 sermons.

Workes: being the summe of his sermons. 1629; ed J. Angus 3 vols Edinburgh 1861–2; ed J. Brown, Cambridge 1909 (selection).

§1

The gallants burden. 1612, 1614, 1616.

Heaven and earth reconcil'd. 1613.

The white devil: or the hypocrite uncased. 1613, 1613, 1615.

The blacke devill or the apostate, with the Wolf worrying the lambes and the Spirituall navigator. 3 pts 1615.

England's sickness. 1615. 2 sermons.

Mysticall bedlam. 1615. 2 sermons.

Diseases of the soule: a discourse. 1616.

The sacrifice of thankefulnesse. 1616.

The souldiers honour. 1617.

The happiness of the church. 1618.

The barren tree: a sermon. 1623.

The temple. 1624.

A commentary upon the second epistle by St Peter. 1633.

God's anger and man's comfort. 1652[3]. 2 sermons.

§2

Mulder, W. Style and the man: Adams, prose Shakespeare of Puritan divines. Harvard Theological Rev 48 1958.

Dent, R. W. In his John Webster's borrowing, Berkeley 1960.

RICHARD BAXTER
1615–91

Bibliographies

For a complete catalogue of Baxter's books, see his Compassionate counsel to all young men, *1691 (2nd edn).*

Grosart, A. B. Annotated list of the writings of Baxter. [Edinburgh] 1868 (in his edn of Baxter, What we must do to be saved).

Matthews, A. G. The works of Baxter: an annotated list. 1932. Rev from Congregational Historical Soc Trans 11 1932.

Nuttall, G. F. A transcript of Baxter's library catalogue. Jnl of Ecclesiastical History 2 1951.

— The manuscript of the Reliquiae Baxteriana. Dr Williams's Lib Occasional Paper 1 1954.

— In his Richard Baxter, 1966.

Rogers, T. The Baxter treatises: a catalogue of the Baxter papers (other than letters) in Dr Williams's Library. Dr Williams's Library Occasional Paper 8 1959. The library contains the largest collection of Baxter's letters and other mss.

Collections

The practical works of the late reverend and pious Mr Richard Baxter, with a preface giving some account of the author. 4 vols 1707; ed W. Orme 23 vols 1830, 1833; 4 vols 1838, 1845–7, 1854.

§ 1

The following list gives only Baxter's most familiar or important works and omits many of the numerous controversial and occasional books pbd in his own lifetime. For a complete list of works, longer than that of any other Caroline divine, see Bibliographies; also cols 1892, 1914, above.

Aphorismes of justification, with their explication annexed; published especially for the use of the Church of Kidderminster in Worcestershire. 1640 (for 1649), 1655; ptd by J. Wesley, Newcastle 1745 (extract); 1831 (17th edn).

The saints everlasting rest: or a treatise of the blessed state of the saints in their enjoyment of God in glory. 4 pts 1650, 1659 (8th edn rev author), 1677 (11th edn rev author), 2 pts 1814 (13th edn, to which is added The dying thoughts of the Rev R. Baxter); ed W. Young 1907; ed J. T. Wilkinson [1962] (abridged); tr Dutch, 1677.

Apology against the modest exceptions of Mr T. Blake. 1654, 1654.

A sermon of judgement. 1655.

Gildas Salvianus: the first part, i.e. The reformed pastor; shewing the nature of the pastoral work, especially in private instruction and catechizing. 1656; abridged S. Palmer 1808; 1841 (from 1656 edn with appendix); ed J. Wilkinson 1939.

A call to the unconverted to turn and live. 1658, 1669 (13th edn); many later edns, many trns.

The crucifying of the world, by the cross of Christ; with a preface to the nobles, gentlemen and all the rich, directing them how they may be richer. 1658; ed J. Baillie 1861.

The life of faith, as it is the evidence of things unseen: a sermon preached—contractedly—before the King at Whitehall upon July the 22nd 1660. 1660, 1670.

A sermon of repentance, preached before the honourable House of Commons at their late solemn fast for the settling of these nations, April 30 1660. 1660.

A treatise of death, the last enemy to be destroyed: part of it was preached at the funerals of Elizabeth the late wife of Mr Joseph Baker. 1660.

Now or never: the holy, serious, diligent believer justified, encouraged, excited and directed, and the opposers and neglecters convinced by the light of Scripture and reason. 1662, 1689.

The divine life, in three treatises: the first, Of the knowledge of God; the second, Of walking with God; the third, Of co[n]versing with God in solitude. 1664, 1824.

The cure of church-divisions: or directions for weak Christians, to keep them from being dividers or troublers of the Church; with some directions to the pastors how to deal with such Christians. 1670.

A Christian directory: or a summ of practical theologie and cases of conscience. 4 pts 1673, 1678; ed J. Tawney 1925.

The poor man's family book: 1, teaching him how to become a true Christian; 2, how to live as a Christian; 3, how to die as a Christian; in plain familiar conferences between a teacher and a learner. 2 pts 1674.

Richard Baxter's Catholick theologie: plain, pure, peaceable, for pacification of the dogmatical word-warriours, in three books. 4 pts 1675. 3rd bk never pbd.

A sermon preached at the funeral of Mr Henry Stubbs. *See* T. Vincent, The death of ministers improved, 1678.

Church-history of the government of Bishops and their Councils abbreviated. 1680.

A sermon preached at the funeral of Mr John Corbet, with his true and exemplary character. [1680].

A breviate of the life of Margaret, the daughter of Francis Charlton and wife of Richard Baxter. 1681; ed J. Wilkinson 1928.

Compassionate counsel to all young men: especially 1, London-apprentices; 11, students of divinity, physick and law: 111, the sons of magistrates and rich men. 1681, 1691 (2nd edn with complete catalogue of his books).

Poetical fragments: heart-imployment with God and it self; the concordant discord of a broken-healed heart. 1681, 1689, 1699, 1700 (with Additions to the poetical-fragments), 1821.

The poor husbandman's advocate to rich racking land-lords. 1691; ed F. J. Powicke, Bull John Rylands Lib 10 1926. Baxter's last treatise.

Reliquiae Baxterianae: or Mr Richard Baxter's narrative of the most memorable passages in his life and times. Ed M. Sylvester 1696; abridged J. M. L. Thomas 1925 (EL). *See also col 1914, above.*

Letters

[Letter from R. Baxter to Richard Allestree 20 Dec 1679]. *See* R. Warner, Original letters from Baxter and Matthew Prior, with biographical illustrations. 1817.

Some unpublished correspondence of the Reverend Baxter and the Reverend John Eliot, the apostle of the American Indians 1656–1682. Ed F. J. Powicke, Bull John Rylands Lib 15 1931.

§ 2

C., J. Some arguments to prove the certaine salvation of the christened infants of ungodly parents, dying before actual sin, with an enquiry into Mr Baxter's doctrine of particular churches, and terms of church unity, and detection thereof as faulty. 1680.

Stillingfleet, E. The unreasonableness of separation: the second part, with special remarks on the life and actions of Mr R. Baxter. 1682.

Glanvil, J. Mr J. Glanvil's full vindication of the late reverend, pious and learned Mr Richard Baxter. [1691].

Bates, W. A funeral-sermon for the reverend divine Mr Richard Baxter, with an account of his life. 1692.

Sylvester, M. Elisha's cry after Elijah's God, consider'd with reference to the decease of Richard Baxter. 1696.

Calamy, E. An abridgement of Mr Baxter's history of his life and times. 1702, 2 vols 1713; rev S. Palmer 3 vols 1802–3; ed A. G. Matthews, Calamy revised, Oxford 1834, 1937.

Daubeny, C. A brief confutation of the Rev Mr Daubeny's strictures on Mr Richard Baxter, in the appendix to his guide to the Church. 1801.

Ryle, J. C. The Bishop, the pastor and the preacher, in three biographical lectures. 1854. Bishop Latimer; Baxter and his times; George Whitefield.

Tulloch, J. In his English Puritanism and its leaders, 1826.

Boyle, G. D. Richard Baxter. 1883.

Davies, J. H. The life of Baxter. 1887.

Gordon, A. Heads of English Unitarian history; with appended lectures on Baxter and Priestley. 1895.

Grosart, A. B. In his Representative Nonconformists, 1899.

Eayrs, G. Baxter and the revival of preaching and pastoral service. 1912.

Powicke, F. J. A Puritan idyll: or the Rev Baxter's love story. 1917.

—— Story and significance of the Rev Baxter's Saints' everlasting rest. 1920.

—— A life of the Reverend Baxter. 2 vols 1924.

—— Baxter and the Countess of Balcarres. 1925.

—— The Reverend Baxter under the Cross 1622–91. 1927.

—— An episode in the ministry of the Reverend Henry Newcombe and his connexion with the Reverend Baxter. 1929.

Cave, T. John Baskerville, Baxter and Kidderminster parish church. 1923.

Haden, W. H. Baxter: the man and his work. London Quart 164 1939.

Morgan, I. The non-conformity of Baxter. 1946.

Carter, C. S. Richard Baxter. [1948].

Dearing, V. A. Baxter's Saints' everlasting rest. Harvard Lib Bull 2 1948.

Kemp, C. F. A pastoral triumph: the story of Baxter and his ministry at Kidderminster. New York 1948.

Wood, T. Baxter's The reformed pastor. Theology 52 1949.

Nuttall, G. F. Baxter's correspondence: a preliminary survey. Jnl of Ecclesiastical History 1 1950.

—— Baxter and Philip Doddridge. 1951.

—— Presbyterians and Independents. Presbyterian Historical Jnl 10 1952.

—— Baxter's Apology [1654]: its occasion and composition. Jnl of Ecclesiastical History 4 1953.

Nuttall, G. F. The manuscript of Reliquiae Baxterianae. 1954.

—— Richard Baxter. 1966. Includes list of Baxter's works.

Wiley, M. L. In her Subtle knot, Cambridge Mass 1952.

Packer, J. I. Great pastors. Theology 56 1953.

Martin, H. Puritanism and Baxter. 1954.

Martz, L. L. The poetry of meditation. New Haven 1954, 1962 (rev). Ch 4.

Bottrall, M. In her Every man a phoenix, 1958.

Schlatter, R. Baxter and Puritan politics. New Brunswick NJ 1958. Includes selections from Baxter's political writings.

Abernathy, G. R. Baxter and the Cromwellian church. HLQ 24 1961.

DePauley, W. C. Baxter surveyed. Church Quart Rev 164 1963.

Rooy, S. H. In his Theology of missions in the Puritan tradition, Delft 1965.

Webber, J. In her Eloquent 'I', Madison 1968.

MacGillivray, R. Baxter: a Puritan in the provinces. Dalhousie Rev 49 1969.

Watkins, O. C. In his Puritan experience, 1972. On Reliquiae.

WILLIAM CHILLINGWORTH
1602–43
Collections

Works. 1704, 1719 (7th edn), 1727, 1742 (with life by T. Birch), 2 vols Dublin 1752, 3 vols 1820, Oxford 1838.

§1

The religion of Protestants a safe way to salvation. Oxford 1637, 1638, 1664, 1674, 1684, 1687, 3 vols 1820, 1838, 2 vols 1839.

§2

Des Maizeaux, P. Historical and critical account. 1725.

Plumptre, E. H. In Masters in English theology, ed A. Barry 1877.

Weber, K. In his Lucius Cary, 2nd Viscount Falkland, New York 1940. Ch 5.

William Chillingworth. TLS 29 Jan 1944.

Waller, J. William Chillingworth. Jnl of Ecclesiastical History 6 1955.

Orr, R. R. Reason and authority. Oxford 1967.

See also Francis Cheynell, col 1990, below.

JOHN COSIN
Bishop of Durham
1595–1672
Collections

Works. Ed J. Sansom 5 vols Oxford 1843–55 (Lib of Anglo-Catholic Theology). The autograph ms of Cosin's English sermons, ptd in Works vol 1, 1843, is in Durham Cathedral Chapter Library, A.IV.31.

§1

A collection of private devotions. 1627 (3 edns), 1635, 1638, 1655, 1664, 1672 (all anon), 1676 (signed); ed P. G. Stanwood, Oxford 1967 (text of first edn, with introd and commentary).

A forme of prayer, used in the King's chappel [in Paris] on Tuesdayes. 1649. BM copy with ms addns.

A scholastical history of the canon of the Holy Scriptures. 1657, 1672, 1683.

Argument proving that adultery works a dissolution of the marriage. [1665].

Historia transubstantiationis papalis [written 1655]. 1675; tr 1676, 1679, 1834; ed J. S. Brewer 1840; ed J. Brogden, Catholic Safeguards vol 2, 1846; Liverpool 1864 (as The history of Popish transubstantiation); both works rptd in Works vol 4, 1851.

The Right Reverend Doctor John Cosin his opinion for communicating rather with Geneva than Rome. 1684. Written as a letter to R. Watson, 19 June 1646.

Regni Angliae religio catholica [written c. 1652]. In T. Smith, 1707 below; ed W. Wekett 1729 (as Regni Angliae sub imperio serenissime); ed F. Meyrick 1853; tr 1870; Italian, 1854; Greek, [1856]; French, 1857; German, 1888 (2nd edn).

Letters

Correspondence. Ed G. Ornsby 2 vols Durham 1868–72 (Surtees Soc nos 52, 55); ed J. C. Hodgson, Northumbrian documents pt 2, Durham 1918 (Surtees Soc no 131). *See also* Works vol 4, 1851. Most of the original letters are in Cosin's Lib, Durham Univ.

Stanwood, P. G. and A. I. Doyle. Cosin's correspondence. Trans Cambridge Bibl Soc 5 1969.

§2

Burton, H. A tryall of Private devotions. 1628.

Prynne, W. A briefe survay and censure of Mr Cozens his couzening Devotions. 1628.

Smart, P. The vanitie and downe-fall of superstitious popish ceremonies. 1628.

The articles or charge exhibited in Parliament against D. Cozens of Durham. 1641.

The doctors last will and testament. [London?] 1641. Satiric attack.

Finch, J. The coppy of a letter sent from John Lord Finch, late Lord Keeper, to his friend Dr Cozens. 1641.

Rous, F. Mr Rouse his speech before the Lords at the transmission of Dr Cossens March 16 1640. 1641.

Mercurius ecclesiasticus. 1645. Anon; satirical verses.

Vane, T. An answer to a libell. Paris 1646.

Sancroft, W. A sermon preached in S. Peter's Westminster at the consecration [of Cosin]. 1660.

du Moulin, L. Vindiciae ecclesiae anglicanus. [Leyden] 1661.

Basire, I. The dead man's real speech. 1673. The funeral sermon by Cosin's chaplain 29 April 1672.

Smith, T. Vita Joannis Cosini. In Vitae quorundam eruditissimorum et illustrium virorum, 1707.

Osmond, P. H. A life of Cosin. 1913.

Bosher, R. S. In his Making of the Restoration settlement, 1951. Ch 2.

Porter, H. B., jr. Cosin's Hours of prayer: a liturgical review. Theology 56 1953.

Jasper, R. C. D. Some notes on the early life of Cosin. Bishoprick (Durham diocesan mag) 30 1954.

Hanson, L. W. Cosin's Collection of private devotions 1627. Library 5th ser 13 1958.

The Durham book. Ed G. J. Cuming 1961.

Stanwood, P. G. Cosin as homilist. Anglican Theological Rev 47 1965.

Mueller, J. M. A borrowing of Donne's Christmas sermon of 1621. HLQ 30 1967. Cosin borrowed extensively from Donne in his sermon for Christmas 1651 on John 1. 9–10.

Gilby, C. W. and A. I. Doyle. Durham bishops: Cosin. In Northern Notes 1970.

O'Connor, D. Southwell's and Cosin's English versions of the Lauda Sion Salvatorem of St Thomas Aquinas. N & Q Nov 1970. Cosin's borrowing in Moeoniae 1595.

Cornforth, J. Auckland Castle, Co. Durham. Country Life 27 Jan–10 Feb 1972. On Cosin's architectural changes in 1660's.

NICHOLAS FERRAR
1593–1637
Manuscripts

BM additional mss 34,657–9, 3 folio vols of the Story books or religious exercises of Little Gidding, Huntingdonshire.
  Collection for the history of the memory of Little Gidding by Francis Peck, ms vol in Clare College Cambridge.
  Ms letters in Magdalene College Cambridge.
  These and other mss described in Blackstone's edn, below.

§1

Hygiasticon by Leonard Lessius [Louvain 1613]. Cambridge 1634. Tr Ferrar.

Acta apostolorum. [1635?].

Actions and doctrine and other passages touching our Lord Jesus Christ. [1635].

Harmonies. [1636?]. This and the preceding 2 items, now in BM, were compiled by Ferrar and his family at Little Gidding, being cuttings from other books.

The hundred and ten considerations of Signior John Valdesso [Basle 1550]. Oxford 1638, [London 1906]. Trn and introd by Ferrar, notes by George Herbert.

The story books of Little Gidding: being the religious dialogues recited in the great room 1631–2. Ed E. C. Sharland 1899.

The Ferrar papers. Ed B. Blackstone, Cambridge 1938.

Chronicles of Little Gidding. Ed A. L. Maycock 1954.

Conversations at Little Gidding: on the retirement of Charles V; on the austere life. Ed A. M. Williams, Cambridge 1970.

§2

The Arminian nunnery [1641]. Ed M. Hussey, Church Quart Rev 148 1949.

Peckard, P. Memoirs of the life of Mr Nicholas Ferrar. Cambridge 1790, London 1852 (abridged).

McDonogh, T. M. (ed). Brief memoirs of Nicholas Ferrar, chiefly collected from a narrative by Dr Francis Turner [from BM additional ms 34,656: the draft of the extracts by Turner, Christian Mag 2 1761]. Bristol 1829, London 1837.

Mayor, J. E. B. (ed). Ferrar: two lives by his brother John and by Doctor Jebb. Cambridge 1855.

Shorthouse, J. H. John Inglesant. 1880 (priv ptd), 1881.

Acland-Troyte, J. E. (later Acland). An account of the harmonies of Ferrar. Archæologia 51 1888.

— Little Gidding and its inmates in the time of Charles I. 1903.

Carter, T. T. Ferrar: his household and his friends. 1892.

Davenport, C. Little Gidding bindings. Bibliographica 2 1896.

— Three recently discovered bindings with Little Gidding stamps. Library 1st ser 1 1900.

Skipton, H. P. K. The life and times of Ferrar. 1907.

Collett, H. Little Gidding and its founder. 1925.

Beachcroft, T. O. Ferrar and George Herbert. Criterion 11 1932.

Blackstone, B. Story books of Little Gidding: wine and poetry. TLS 21 March 1936.

— Discord at Little Gidding. TLS 1 Aug 1936.

Maycock, A. L. Ferrar of Little Gidding. 1938. With bibliography.

— Little Gidding discovery. TLS 27 Jan 1966. On BM additional ms 34,659.

Eliot, T. S. Little Gidding. 1942; rptd in Four quartets, New York 1943.

Craig, C. L. The earliest Little Gidding concordance. Harvard Lib Bull 1 1947.

— Nicholas Ferrar junior: a linguist of Little Gidding. 1950.

Kirchberger, C. A. Link with Little Gidding. Theology 52 1949.

Williams, G. W. Richard Crashaw and the Little Gidding bookbinders. N & Q Jan 1956.

Smyth, C. Little Gidding and Leighton Bromswold. Church Quart Rev 165 1964.

THOMAS FULLER
1608–61

See col 2233, below.

JOHN GAUDEN
Bishop of Exeter
1605–62
Collections

Three sermons preached upon severall publike occasions. 1642.

§1

The love of truth and peace. 1641, 1641. Sermon before House of Commons.

Certaine scruples and doubts of conscience. [1645].

Εἰκὼν Βασιλική: the pourtraicture of his sacred Majestie. 1648 etc (all anon); ed P. A. Knachel, Ithaca 1966. Once attributed to Charles I; probably written with Gauden.

The religious and loyal protestation. 1648 (for 1649).

Funerals made cordials. 1658. Funeral sermon for Robert Rich.

Ἱερὰ δάκρυα: ecclesiae anglicanae suspiria; the tears. 1659.

A sermon preached in the Temple-Chappel, at the funeral of Dr Brownrig. 1660.

Μεγαλεία θεοῦ: Gods great demonstrations. 1660. Sermon before House of Commons.

Anti-Baal-Berith: or the binding of the Covenant and all Covenanters to their good behaviors. 1661.

Considerations touching the liturgy. 1661.

Edited works of Richard Hooker with life, 1662. See Hooker, above.

§ 2

Madan, F. F. A new bibliography of the Eikon basilike of King Charles the First, with a note on the authorship. Oxford Bibl Soc Pbns new ser 3 1950.

Trevor-Roper, H. R. Eikon basiliké: the problem of the King's book. History Today Sept 1951.

Beecham, H. A. Gauden and the authorship of Eikon basilike. Library 5th ser 20 1965.

Greene, D. G. A note on Eikon basilike. N & Q May 1972.

JOSEPH HALL
Bishop of Norwich
1574–1656

Collections

A recollection of such treatises as have been heretofore severally published. 1615(–14), 1617, 1621.

Works. 1 vol 1625, 2 vols 1628(–7), 1633, 1634, 3 vols 1662 (vol 1 1634, 1647, 1648: vol 2 1634, 1648), 1 vol in 2 pts 1714 (pt 2 with separate title-page 1708); ed J. Pratt 10 vols Oxford 1808; ed P. Hall 12 vols Oxford 1837–9; ed P. Wynter 10 vols Oxford 1863.

The shaking of the olive-tree: remaining works. 1659, 1660 (with 14 of the sermons not before pbd, the first 10 tr French 1664).

Extracts from various devotional writings. Ed J. Riland, Birmingham 1784.

Selections. Ed B. Montagu 1807.

Sacred aphorisms, selected. Ed R. B. Exton 1823.

Select tracts. 1824.

Devotions, sacred aphorisms and religious table-talk. Ed J. W. Morris 1867.

Complete poems. Ed A. B. Grosart, Manchester 1879.

Collected poems. Ed A. Davenport, Liverpool 1949.

§ 1

Sermons

See above: A recollection, Works, Shaking of the olive-tree.

Pharisaisme and Christianity [1 May 1608]. 1608, 1608, 1609, 1614, 1627, 1642.

The Passion sermon [14 April 1609]. 1609, 1614, 1627, 1642.

An holy panegyricke [24 March 1613]. 1613, 1627, 1642.

The righteous mammon: an hospitall sermon. 1618.

A sermon preached before his Majestie at Thebalds [15 Sept 1622]. 1622.

The great imposter [2 Feb 1623]. 1623, 1628, 1643.

The best bargaine [Theobalds 21 Sept 1623]. 1623.

A sermon preached at the reconcilement of the chappell of Exeter [St Stephen's day 1623]. 1624, 1627.

The true peace-maker [19 Sept 1624]. 1624, 1627.

Columba Noae olivum adferens jactatissimae Christi arcae. 1624; ed F. Meyrick 1874; tr Joseph Hall, Works, 1625 etc.

A sermon of publique thanksgiving for the wonderfull mitigation of the late mortalitie [Whitehall 29 Jan 1625]. 1626.

Westminster on the public fast [5 April 1628] and To H.M. before the fast [30 March 1628], Whitehall. 1628. 2 sermons pbd together as One of the sermons preacht at Westminster, on the day of the publike fast.

One of the sermons preacht to the Lords on Ash Wednesday, Feb 18. 1629.

The hypocrite [28 Feb 1629]. 1630.

Exeter—at the consecration of a new burial place, on St Bart's day 24 Aug 1637. 1637 (with The remedy of prophaneness).

The character of man [1 March 1634]. 1635.

A sermon preach't to his Majesty, Aug 8. 1641.

Other Works

Virgidemiarum: sixe books. 1598; pt 1, 1598, 1602; pt 2, 1599; Oxford 1753, [1808]; ed S. W. Singer, Chiswick 1824 (as Satires; *see col 1112, above*); Certaine worthy ms poems, 1597 (sometimes regarded as pt 3 of Virgidemiarum).

The anathomie of sin. 1603, 1608 (as Two guides to a good life). Attributed to Hall.

The Kings prophecie: or weeping joy. 1603; ed W. E. Buckley 1882 (Roxburghe Club).

Meditations and vowes divine and morall. 1605, 1606, 1607, 1609 (with Characters of vertues and vices), 1616, 1621, 1851; ed C. Sayle 1901; tr French, 1614.

Mundus alter et idem [signed Mercurius Brittanicus]. Frankfurt [1605?], Hanover 1607; ed W. Knight, Frankfurt [1640?], Utrecht 1643, Munich 1664; ed H. J. Anderson 1908; tr J. Healey [1609?]; tr Healey and ed H. Brown, Cambridge Mass 1937; ed H. Morley, Ideal commonwealths, 1885 (fragment); tr German, 1613, 1704. *See* E. A. Petherick, On the authorship and translations of Mundus alter et idem 1605, GM July 1896. W. W. Greg, English literary autographs vol 3, 1932, considers the first edn ptd in London.

Occasionall meditations. 1630, 1631, 1633, 1851; Meditations for Sundays and holydays, 1856.

Heaven upon earth. 1606, 1606, 1607, 1621 (with Meditations and vowes); tr German, 1632.

The arte of divine meditation. 1606, 1607, 1609, 1621 (with Meditations and vowes).

Holy observations. 1607, 1609, 1621 (with Meditations and vowes). All edns include Some fewe of David's psalmes metaphrased, which was not pbd separately.

Characters of vertues and vices. 1608, 1608, 1609, 1621 (with Meditations and vowes), 1691; ed R. Kirk, New Brunswick NJ 1948; versified by Nahum Tate 1691; tr French, 1610, 1619, 1634; tr German, 1628, 1652, 1685, 1696.

Epistles. Vols 1–2, 1608; vol 3, 1611; vol 3 pt 2, 1610; ed W. H. Hale 1846; tr French, 1633.

Salomon's divine arts (with paraphrase of the Song of songs). 1609.

The peace of Rome [with No peace with Rome]. 1609, 1844 (with A serious dissuasive from Poperie, tr French 1629), 1852.

A common apologie of the Church of England. 1610.

Contemplations upon the principall passages of the holy storie. Vol 1, 1612, 1617; vol 2, 1614, 1617, 1661; vol 3, 1615, 1617; vol 4, 1618; vol 5, 1620; vol 6, 1622; vol 7, 1623; Contemplations upon the historicall part of the Old testament: eighth and last volume, 1626. Pbd as Contemplations on the historical passages of the Old and New testaments, 3 vols 1824 (Select British divines 12–14); ed T. S. Hughes 3 vols 1831–2; ed R. Wardlaw 2 vols Glasgow 1834–5; ed C. Wordsworth 1871; tr Dutch, 1642; German, 1665, 1666, 3 vols 1672–4–9, 1699.

Polemices sacrae pars prior: Roma irreconciliabilis. 1611, 1612.

A recollection of such treatises as have bene heretofore severally published and are now revised. 1614, 1615, 1617, 1621 (augmented).

Quo vadis? a just censure of travell as it is commonly undertaken by the gentlemen of our nation. 1617, 1617; tr French, 1628. *See* Bishop Hall's sayings concerning travellers, 1674.

The honor of the married clergie mayntayned. 1620.

The olde religion. 1627, 1628, 1630, 1636, 1686; tr German, 1662.

An answer to Pope Urban his inurbanitie. 1629.

The reconciler. 1629.

Occasionall meditations. 1630, 1631, 1633, 1851; Meditations for Sundays and holydays, 1856.

A plaine and familiar explication of the Old and New testament. 1632.

An explication by way of paraphrase of all the hard texts in the Old and New testament. 1633.

Propositiones catholicae. 1633 (anon); tr as Certaine Catholicke propositions, 1633.

The residue of the contemplation upon the New testament, with sermons. 1634.

Joseph Halli αὐτοσχεδιάσματα. 1635.

The remedy of prophanenesse. 1637, 1638.

Certaine irrefragable propositions. 1639.

An humble remonstrance to the High Court of Parliament. 1640, 1640; A defence of the humble remonstrance, 1641.

Christian moderation. 1640.

Episcopacie by divine right. 1640, 1640.

A letter sent to an honourable gentleman, in way of satisfaction. 1641.

Answer to the tedious vindication. 1641.

A short answer to the tedious vindication of Smectymnuus. 1641.

A survay of that foolish, seditious, scandalous, prophane libell. 1641.

Osculum pacis. 1641.

A letter lately sent by a reverend Bishop [Hall] from the Tower. 1642, 1642.

A modest confutation. 1642.

The lawfulness and unlawfulness of an oath. [Oxford?] 1643.

A modest offer of some meet considerations. [Oxford] 1644, 1660.

The devout soul. 1644, 1650, 1658.

The peace-maker. 1645, 1647.

The remedy of discontentment. 1645, 1652, 1684.

The balme of Gilead. 1646, 1650, 1652, 1655, 1660; tr German, 1662, 1663, 1663.

Three tractates. 1646.

Christ mysticall. 1647.

Satans fiery darts quenched. 1647.

The breathings of the devout soul. 1648.

Pax terris. 1648.

Select thoughts: one century. 1648, 1654, 1682.

Of resolutions and decisions of divers practicall cases. 1649, 1650, 1654, 1652, 1659.

Χειροθεσία: or the apostolique institution. 1649 (for 1659).

The revelation unrevealed. 1650.

Susurrium cum Deo. 1651, 1651, 1659, 1659.

Holy raptures. 1652, 1653.

The great mysterie of godliness. 1652, 1659, 1847.

The holy order. 1654; tr German, 1683.

An apologeticall letter to a person of quality. 1655.

A letter concerning Christmasse. 1659.

The invisible world. 1659.

Divers treatises: third tome. 1662.

Psicittacorum regis. 1669.

Contemplations upon the remarkable passages in the life of holy Jesus. 1679.

Episcopal admonition. 1681.

Bishop Hall's hard measure. 1647, 1710.

§2

Milton, John. An apology against a pamphlet A modest confutation of the animadversions upon the remonstrant against Smectymnuus. 1641. *See col 1241, above.*

Whitefoote, J. Ἰσραὴλ ἀγχίθανης: deaths alarum, a funeral sermon preached at St Peters in Norwich, Sept 30 1656 for Joseph Hall. 1656.

Jones, J. Bishop Hall: his life and times. 1826.

Wardlaw, R. Introductory essay [to Contemplations]. [Glasgow 1831].

Hone, R. B. The lives of N. Ridley, Hall and the Hon Robert Boyle. 1837.

Oliver, G. In his Lives of the Bishops of Exeter, 1861.

Lewis, G. A life of Hall. 1886.

Schulze, K. Die Satiren Halls. Berlin 1910.

Waterhouse, G. In his Literary relations of England and Germany in the seventeenth century, 1914.

Salyer, S. M. Renaissance influences in Hall's Mundus. PQ 6 1927.

Vančura, Z. Usečný styl v anglické próze sedemnáctého století. Časopis pro Moderní Filogii 18 1932.

Davenport, A. Some notes on references to Hall in Marston's Satires. RES 9 1933.

Ketton-Cremer, R. W. In his A Norfolk gallery, 1948.

Smith, P. A. Bishop Hall: our English Seneca. PMLA 63 1948.

— The limits of Hall's Senecanism. Proc of Leed Philological Soc 6 1950.

Fisch, H. Bishop Hall's Meditations. RES 25 1949.

Chew, A. Hall and John Milton. ELH 17 1950.

Kinloch, T. F. The life and works of Hall. 1951.

Hall, J. H. Hall, the English Seneca and champion of episcopacy. Historical Mag of Protestant Episcopal Church 21 1952.

MacKinnon, M. H. M. Sir John Harington and Bishop Hall. PQ 37 1958.

Erskine-Hill, H. H. Edmund Waller and Samuel Butler: two poetic debts to Hall's Occasionall meditations. N & Q April 1965.

Stout, G. D., jr. Sterne's borrowings from Hall's Quo vadis? ELN 2 1965.

Dewar, M. W. Bishop Joseph Hall. Churchman 80 1966; rev as An ecumenical Calvinist churchman, Evangelical Quart 40 1968.

Jensen, E. J. Hall and Marston: the role of the satirist. Satire News Letter 4 1967.

Kirk, R. A seventeenth-century controversy: extremism vs moderation. Texas Stud in Lit & Lang 9 1967.

HENRY HAMMOND
1605–60

Collections

XIX sermons preached on several occasions by the reverend and learned Henry Hammond. 1664, 1675.

Workes. Ed W. Fulman 4 vols 1684–9.

Miscellaneous theological works. Ed N. Pocock 3 vols Oxford 1847–50 (Lib of Anglo-Catholic Theology).

§1

A practical catechism. Oxford 1644, 1646.

To the Right Honourable the Lord Fairfax and his council of war, the humble address of Henry Hammond [15 Jan 1648]. 1649.

The Christian's obligations to peace and charity; with 9 sermons more. 1649, 1652 ('corrected').

Of the reasonableness of Christian religion. 1650.

A paraphrase and annotations upon the New testament. 1653, 1671, 1675, 1702, 4 vols Oxford 1845.

Of schisme: a defence of the Church of England against the exceptions of the Romanists. 1653.

A vindication of the dissertations concerning episcopacy from the answers or exceptions offered against them by the London ministers in their Ius divinum ministerii evangelici. 1654.

Of fundamentals, schisme and heresie. 1654.

Some profitable directions both for priest and people, in two sermons preached before the evil times. 1657.

A paraphrase and annotations upon the books of the psalms. 1659, 2 vols Oxford 1850.

The daily practice of piety; also devotions and prayers in time of captivity. 1660.

Spiritual sacrifice: or devotion and prayers. 1660.

§2

Fell, J. Life of Hammond. 1661, 1662; in Works vol 1, 1684, 1847.

Packer, J. W. The transformation of Anglicanism 1643–60, with special reference to Hammond. Manchester 1969. With detailed bibliography.

GEORGE HERBERT
1593–1633

See col 1201, above.

HENRY KING
Bishop of Chichester
1592–1669

§1

A sermon preached at Paul's Crosse, the 25 of November 1621: upon occasion of that false and scandalous Report (lately printed) touching the supposed apostasie of the right Reverend Father in God, John King, late Lord Bishop of London. 1621.

David's Enlargement. In Two sermons upon the Act Sunday, being the 10th of July 1625, Oxford 1625.

A sermon of deliverance: preached at the Spittle on Easter Monday 1626. 1626.

Two sermons preached at White-Hall in Lent, March 3 1625 and February 20 1626. 1627.

An exposition upon the Lords Prayer delivered in certaine sermons in the Cathedrall Church of St Paul. 1628, 1634.

A sermon preached at St Pauls March 27 1640: being the anniversary of his Majesties happy inauguration to his crowne. 1640.

A sermon preached before the King's most excellent Majesty at Oxford. Oxford 1643.

A sermon preached at White-Hall on the 29th of May 1661: being the happy day of his Majesties inauguration and birth. 1661, 1713.

A sermon preached at the funeral of the Rt Reverend Father in God Bryan, Lord Bp of Winchester, April 24 1662. 1662.

A sermon preached at Lewis in the diocese of Chichester, by the Lord Bp of Chichester, at his visitation held there, October 8 1662. 1663.

A sermon preached the 30th of January at White-Hall 1664: being the anniversary commemoration of K. Charles the I, martyred on that day. 1665.

For King's poems, see cols 1199, 1913, above.

§2

Mason, L. Life and works of King. Trans Connecticut Acad 18 1913.

Berman, R. King and the seventeenth century. 1964.

Crum, M. In her edn of Poems of King, Oxford 1965. Includes Life.

WILLIAM LAUD
Archbishop of Canterbury
1574–1645

Collections

Seven sermons preached upon severall occasions. 1651.

The second volume of the remains of William Laud. Ed H. and E. Wharton 1700.

Works. Ed W. Scott and J. Bliss 7 vols in 9 Oxford 1847–60 (Lib of Anglo-Catholic Theology).

§1

A sermon preached before his Majestie at Wansted. 1621.

A sermon preached at Whitehall on the 24 of March 1621. 1622.

A sermon preached before his Majestie [on Psalm 75, 2–3]. 1625.

A sermon preached on Munday, the sixt of February, at the opening of the Parliament at Westminster [on Psalm 122, 3–5]. 1625.

A sermon preached before his Majestie on the fifth of July at the solemn fast. 1626.

A sermon preached on Munday, the 17th of March, at Westminster. 1628.

A speech delivered in the starr-chamber, at the censure of J. Bastwick. 1637 (3 edns).

A relation of the conference betweene W. Laud and Mr Fisher, the Jesuite. 1639, 1639, 1673, 1686; ed C. H. Simpkinson 1901.

The Archbishop of Canterbury's speech: or his funeral sermon preacht by himself on the scaffold on Tower-Hill, on Friday the 10 of January 1644; all faithfully written by John Hinde. 1644, 1660; rptd Harleian miscellany vol 8, 1744, 1808. Another version, first ptd Oxford 1644, is rptd in Somers tracts vol 4, 1809.

A summarie of devotions. 1667.

The history of the troubles and tryal of William Laud, wrote by himself. [Ed H. Wharton] 1695, 1700 (with some of Laud's other writings).

§2

H[oyle], J[oshua]. Jehojadahs justice against Mattan, Baal's priest, preacht upon the occasion of a speech utter'd upon Tower-Hill. 1645. An arraignment of Laud.

Prynne, W. Canterburie's Doome. 1646.

Heylin, P. Cyprianus anglicus. 1668.

Papers relating to Archbishop Laud's visitation. In Historical Mss Commission 4th report pt 1, 1874.

Mozley, J. B. In his Lectures and theological papers, 1883.

Hutton, W. H. William Laud. 1895.

Cooper, J. The book of Common Prayer commonly known as Laud's liturgy 1637. Edinburgh 1904.

Duncan-Jones, A. S. Archbishop Laud. 1927.

Coffin, R. P. T. William Laud. New York 1930.

Trevor-Roper, H. R. Archbishop Laud. 1940.

Moorman, J. R. H. In commemoration of Archbishop Laud, executed on Tower Hill, January 19 1645. Bull John Rylands Lib 29 1944.

Ballard, A. W. Laud: a vindication. Church Quart Rev 141 1945.

The benevolent chancellor: Laud at Oxford. TLS 27 Oct 1945. Replies by W. H. Lowry 3 Nov 1945 and M. Beza 24 Nov 1945.

Costin, W. C. William Laud. 1945.

Watt, H. In his Recalling the Scottish covenants, New York 1946.

Bourne, E. C. E. The Anglicanism of Laud. 1947.

Micklewright, F. H. A. The authorship of the Scottish liturgy of 1637. N & Q 11 Dec 1948, 5 March, 16 April, 20 Aug 1949. Replies by A.C.E. 5 March, 1 Oct 1949.

Addison, J. T. Laud, prelate and champion of order. Historical Mag of Protestant Episcopal Church 21 1952.

Kellaway, W. Two letters of Laud. Jnl of Ecclesiastical History 5 1954.

Williams, F. B., jr. The Laudian imprimatur. Library 5th ser 15 1960.

Bell, E. G. W. Two unprinted letters of Archbishop Laud. Bodleian Lib Record 7 1961.

Rhodes, D. E. The authorship of the Life and death of Laud 1645. Library 5th ser 16 1961. E.W. on title-page was Ezekias Woodward 1590-1675.

Lamont, W. M. Macaulay, the Archbishop and the Civil War. History Today Nov 1964.

Echlin, E. P. Was Laud's liturgy wholly Laud's? Historical Mag of Protestant Episcopal Church 32 1968.

Carter, H. Archbishop Laud and scandalous books from Holland. In Studia bibliographica in honorem Herman de la Fontaine Verney, Amsterdam 1968.

King, P. Reasons for the abolition of the Book of common prayer in 1645. Jnl of Ecclesiastical History 21 1970.

Campbell, J. The quarrel over the Communion table. Historical Mag of Protestant Episcopal Church 40 1971.

HENRY MORE
1614-87

See col 2334, below.

WILLIAM SANCROFT
Archbishop of Canterbury
1617-93

Collections

Occasional sermons; with some remarks of his life and conversation, in a letter to a friend. 1694, 1703.

§1

Modern policies. 1652, 1653, 1657 (7th edn), 1690.

A sermon preached in S. Peter's Westminster, on the first Sunday in Advent. 1660. At Cosin's consecration.

A sermon preach'd November 13th 1678. 1678.

Letters

Familiar letters to Sir Henry North, to which is prefixed some account of his life and character. 1757.

§2

D'Oyly, G. The life of Sancroft. 1821.
The Durham book. Ed G. J. Cuming 1961.

ROBERT SANDERSON
Bishop of Lincoln
1587-1663

Collections

Works. Ed W. Jacobson 6 vols Oxford 1854.

§1

Two sermons preached at Boston. 1622.

Ten sermons. 1627, 1632 (enlarged as Twelve sermons), 1637 (enlarged as Twelve sermons; whereunto are added two sermons more), 1656 (enlarged as Twenty sermons), 1657 (rptd from 1637 edn as Fourteen sermons), 1671 (enlarged as 34 sermons), 1674, 1681 (enlarged as 35 sermons, with Walton's life), 1686, 1689; ed R. Montgomery 2 vols 1841.

Two sermons preached at Paules-Crosse. 1628.

Two sermons. 1635.

De juramenti. 1647, 1661, 1670 etc; tr as De juramento: seven lectures, 1655.

A resolution of conscience. 1649.

A sermon preached at Newport, October 1648. 1653.

Several cases of conscience. 1660.

Episcopacy. 1661, 1673, 1678, 1683.

Five causes of conscience. 1666, 1667 (enlarged as Eight cases of conscience), 1674 (enlarged as Nine cases of conscience), 1685; tr Latin as Casus conscientiae, Cambridge 1688.

De obligatione conscientiae. 1660, 1661, 1670 etc; tr as Ten lectures on the obligation of humane conscience, 1660; ed W. Whewell, Cambridge 1851; ed and tr C. Wordsworth, Lincoln 1877. Lectures given 1647.

Ad clerum: a sermon [1641]. Oxford 1670.

Bishop Sanderson's judgement concerning submission. 1678.

Judicium universitatis oxoniensis. 1682; tr as Reasons of the present judgement of the University of Oxford, 1647, 1647.

A discourse concerning the Church. 1688.

A preservative against schism and rebellion. 3 vols 1722. Includes trns of De juramenti and De obligatione conscientiae, above; Reasons of the present judgement of the University of Oxford, above.

For Sanderson's philosophical works see col 2331, below.

§2

Walton, I. The life of Dr Sanderson. 1678.

Walker, G. G. Bishop Sanderson on conscience. 1911.

Lewis, G. In his English theologians, 1924.

Wood, T. A great English casuist. Church Quart Rev 147 1948.

Novarr, D. The making of Walton's lives. Ithaca 1958. Ch 11.

Kelly, K. T. Conscience: dictator or guide? 1967. On Sanderson's moral theology.

Slights, C. Ingenious piety. Harvard Theological Rev 63 1970.

JEREMY TAYLOR
Bishop of Down and Connor
1613-67

Bibliographies

Gathorne-Hardy, R. In Golden grove, ed L. P. Smith, Oxford 1930. See also Gathorne-Hardy's notes and articles, under §2, below.

— and W. P. Williams. A bibliography of the writings of Taylor to 1700. Dekalb Ill 1971.

Collections

Twenty-eight sermons preached at Golden Grove together with a discourse of the office ministeriall. 1651, 1654, 1668.

Twenty-five sermons preached at Golden Grove. 1653, 1655, 1668, 1673.

Ἐνιαυτός: a course of sermons for all the Sundays of the year. 1653, 1655, 1668, 1673, 1678 (all enlarged).

The righteous evangelicall described: the Christian's conquest over the body of sin; Fides formata: or faith working by love, in three sermons. 1663, Dublin 1663.

Ἑβδομάς ἐμβολιμαῖος: a supplement to the Ἐνιαυτος, or course of sermons for the whole year, being seven sermons preached since the Restoration. 1663.

Δεκάς ἐμβολιμαῖος: a supplement to the Ἐνιαυτος, being ten sermons preached since the Restoration. 1667, 1673, 1678.

Whole works. Ed R. Heber 15 vols 1822 (with life); rev C. P. Eden 10 vols 1847-54.

Poems and verse-translations. Ed A. B. Grosart 1870.

The golden grove: selected passages from the sermons and writings. Ed L. P. Smith, Oxford 1930.

§1

A sermon preached in Saint Maries church in Oxford, upon the anniversary of the gunpowder-treason. Oxford 1638.

Of the sacred order and offices of episcopacy, by divine institution, apostolicall tradition and Catholike practice. Oxford 1642, London 1647.

A discourse concerning prayer ex tempore or by pretence of the Spirit. 1646 (anon), 1647, 1649 (enlarged as An apology for authorised and set forms of liturgie).

A new and easie institution of grammar. 1647. With William Wyatt.

Θεολογία ἐκλεκτική: a discourse of the liberty of prophesying. 1647.

Treatises of 1, The liberty of prophesying; 2, Prayer ex tempore; 3, Episcopacie; together with a sermon preached at Oxon. 1648, 1650.

An apology for authorized and set forms of liturgie. 1649.

The great exemplar of sanctity and holy life according to Christian institution. 1649, 1653, 1657, 1667 etc.

A funerall sermon, preached at the obsequies of the right honorable and most vertuous lady the Lady Frances, Countesse of Carbery. 1650.

The rule and exercises of holy living. 1650, 1651, 1651, 1654, 1656, 1660, 1663, 1668 etc; ed A. R. Waller 2 vols 1900; ed T. S. Kepler 1956.

Clerus domini. 1651, 1655, 1668, 1672.

The rule and exercises of holy dying. 1651, 1652, 1655, 1658, 1663, 1666, 1668 etc; ed A. R. Waller 1900. Holy living and Holy dying are commonly bound together from 1658 on, and treated explicitly as one vol from 1676.

A short catechism for the institution of young persons in the Christian religion; to which is added An explication of the apostolicall Creed. 1652.

A discourse of baptisme: its institution and efficacy upon all believers. 1652, 1653.

Two discourses: 1, Of baptisme; 2, Of prayer ex tempore. 1652, 1653.

Rules and advices to the clergy of the diocese of Down and Connor. 1653, Dublin 1661, London 1661, 1663.

The real presence and spirituall of Christ in the Blessed Sacrament. 1654.

The golden grove: or a manuall of daily prayers and letanies, fitted to the dayes of the weeke. 1655, 1659 (4th edn), 1680 (12th edn), 1703 (21st edn) etc.

Unum necessarium: or the doctrine and practice of repentance. 1655.

An answere to a letter written by the R.R. 1656.

Deus justificatus: two discourses of original sin. 1656.

A further explication of the doctrine of original sin. 1656.

A discourse of the nature, offices and measures of friendship. 1657, 1657 (as The measures and offices of friendship), 1662, 1671, 1675, 1684, 1920.

Σύμβολον Ἠθικο-πολεμικόν: or a collection of polemical and moral discourses. 1657, 1674 (3rd edn enlarged).

A collection of offices or forms of prayers in cases ordinary and extraordinary. 1658, 1690.

A sermon preached at the funerall of Sr George Dalston. 1658.

B. Taylor's opuscula: the measures of friendship, with additional tracts. 1658, 1675, 1678, 1684.

The worthy communicant or a discourse of the nature, effects and blessings consequent to the worthy receiving of the Lords Supper. 1660, 1661, 1667, 1671, 1674, 1683, 1686, 1689, 1695.

Ductor dubitantium: or the rule of conscience in all her general measures. 2 vols 1660, 1671, 1676, 1696; abridged R. Bancroft 2 vols 1725.

A sermon preached, May 8 1661. 1661.

A sermon preached at the consecration of two archbishops and ten bishops in the cathedral in Dublin. Dublin 1661, 1663.

A sermon preached at the opening of the Parliament in Ireland. 1661.

Via intelligentiae: a sermon preached to the university of Dublin. 1662.

A sermon preached in Christ-Church, Dublin: at the funeral of the Archbishop of Armagh; with a narrative of his whole life. Dublin 1663, 1663, 1663 ('enlarged').

Χρίσις τελειωτική: a discourse of Confirmation. Dublin 1663, 1664.

A choice manual. 1664.

A dissuasive from Popery to the people of Ireland. Dublin 1664, 1664, London 1664, 1668 (enlarged), 1686.

The second part of the dissuasive from Popery, in vindication of the first part. 1667.

Antiquitates christianae. 1675, 1678, 1684 (7th edn).

Christ's yoke an easy yoke, and yet the gate to heaven a strait gate, in two excellent sermons. 1675.

Toleration tolerated. 1687, 1688?

On the reverence due to the altar. Ed J. Barrow, Oxford 1848.

§2

Rust, G. A funeral sermon, preached August 13th 1667. 1668, 1670; rptd in Works, ed Heber and Eden 1822, 1847.

Wilmott, R. A. Taylor: his predecessors, contemporaries and successors. 1846.

Farrar, F. W. Jeremy Taylor. 1877.

May, E. H. A dissertation of the life, theology and times of Taylor. 1892.

Gosse, E. Jeremy Taylor. 1904 (EML).

Worley, G. Taylor: a sketch of his life and times. 1904.

Brown, W. J. Jeremy Taylor. 1925.

Nicolson, M. H. New material on Taylor. PQ 8 1930.

Gathorne-Hardy, R. Taylor: undescribed first editions. TLS 15 Sept 1932.

—— Montaigne among the English. TLS 13 Sept 1947.

—— Taylor's annotations. TLS 20 Sept 1947.

—— Some notes on the bibliography of Taylor. Library 5th ser 2–3 1947–8.

—— Taylor and Christian consolations. TLS 20 April 1951.

de Beer, E. S. Taylor in 1653. N & Q 11 Jan 1936.

Mackenzie, E. H. Golden grove. TLS 20 Nov 1937.

Steffan, T. G. Taylor's criticism of abstract speculation. SE 1940.

Stranks, C. J. Jeremy Taylor. Church Quart Rev 131 1940.

—— The life and writings of Taylor. 1952.

Antoine, M. S. The rhetoric of Taylor's prose: ornament of the Sunday sermons. Washington 1946.

Bentley, G. B. Taylor's Ductor dubitantium. Theology 50 1947.

Brinkley, R. F. Coleridge's criticism of Taylor. HLQ 13 1950.

Hoopes, R. G. Voluntarism in Taylor and the Platonic tradition. HLQ 13 1950.

Greenslade, B. D. Taylor in 1655. N & Q 17 March 1951.

Addison, J. T. Taylor: preacher and pastor. Historical Mag of Protestant Episcopal Church 21 1952.

Brown, W. J. Taylor's sermons. TLS 11 Jan 1952.

Wiley, M. L. In her Subtle knot, 1952.

Williamson, H. R. Jeremy Taylor. 1952.

Wood, T. English casuistical divinity during the 17th century, with special reference to Taylor. 1952.

Elmen, P. Taylor and the fall of man. MLQ 14 1953.

—— Fame of Taylor. Anglican Theological Rev 44 1962.

Hopkirk, D. S. Seventeenth-century classic: Taylor's The liberty of prophesying. Reformed Theological Rev 14 1955.

King, J. R. Certain aspects of Taylor's prose style. E Studies 37 1956.

—— In his Studies in six 17th-century writers, Athens Ohio 1966.

Bolton, F. R. The Caroline tradition of the Church of Ireland, with particular reference to Taylor. 1958.

Perkins, E. B. Taylor on gambling. London Quart 184 1959.

Hughes, H. T. The piety of Taylor. 1960.

Nossen, R. Taylor: 17th-century theologian. Anglican Theological Rev 42 1960.

Peterson, R. A. Taylor's theology of worship. Anglican Theological Rev 46 1964.

—— Taylor on conscience and law. Anglican Theological Rev 48 1966.

Jaekle, C. R. Some reflections on the meaning of illness for Taylor. Historical Mag of Protestant Episcopal Church 34 1965.

Greiffenhagen, M. Skepsis und Naturrecht in der Theologie Taylors. Hamburg 1967.

McAdoo, H. R. Jeremy Taylor 1667–1967. Hermathena 107 1968.

Blewett, W. E. The affinity of the religious opinions of Taylor and Francis Bacon. Historical Mag of Protestant Episcopal Church 38 1969.

Clert-Rolland, L. Taylor et la tolérance religieuse au xviie siècle. Revue d'Histoire et de Philosophie Religieuse (Strasbourg) 49 1969.

Welcher, J. K. John Evelyn to Taylor 27 April 1656. N & Q Oct 1969.

Beaty, N. L. The craft of dying: a study in the literary tradition of the ars moriendi in England. New Haven 1970.

Huntley, F. L. Taylor and the great rebellion. Ann Arbor 1970.

Slights, C. Ingenious piety. Harvard Theological Rev 63 1970.

Day, W. G. Forbidden embraces: Taylor's Holy dying. N & Q Aug 1971.

JAMES USSHER
Archbishop of Armagh
1581–1656

The largest collection of Ussher's mss is in Trinity College, Dublin. See W. O'Sullivan, Hermathena 88 1856.

Collections

Eighteen sermons preached in Oxford 1640. 1659, 1660, 1660.

Twenty sermons. 1678.

Whole works. Ed C. R. Elrington and J. H. Todd 17 vols Dublin 1847–64.

§1

The soveraignes power and the subjects duty: a sermon at Christ Church. Oxford 1644.

The rights of primogeniture, or the excellency of royall authority: a sermon before his Majesty upon the anniversary of his birthday. 1648.

For Ussher's other writings, see Index.

§2

Parr, R. The life of Ussher, late Lord Archbishop of Armagh. 1686. Contains 323 letters to or from Ussher.

Wright, W. B. The Ussher memoirs. Dublin 1889.

Carr, J. A. The life and times of Ussher, Archbishop of Armagh. 1895.

Arneke, H. In his Kirchengeschichte und Rechtsgeschichte, Halle 1937.

Bolton, F. R. Archbishop Ussher's scheme of church government. Theology 50 1948.

Hudson, W. M. Archbishop Ussher quotes Taliesin. N & Q 5 Aug 1950.

Knox, R. B. Ussher and the church of Ireland. Church Quart Rev 161 1960.

—— Archbishop Ussher and his circle. London Quart 178 1962.

—— James Ussher Archbishop of Armagh. Cardiff 1967.

Windsor, G. Reunion views of Archbishop Ussher and his circle. Churchman 77 1963.

Fraser, J. G. Documents from a Samaritan genizah in Damascus. Palestine Exploration Quart 103 1971.

Barnard, T. C. The purchase of Archbishop Ussher's library in 1657. Long Room (Dublin) 2 1972.

BENJAMIN WHICHCOTE
1609–83

See col 2342, below.

MATTHEW WREN
Bishop of Ely
1585–1667

Manuscripts

For Wren's mss see Common-place book, 2 vols in Pembroke College Library, Cambridge, and an extensive scriptural commentary in Peterhouse Library, Cambridge.

Bibliographies

Walker, T. A. In his A Peterhouse bibliography, Cambridge 1924.

§1

A sermon preached before the Kings Majestie. 1627.

Bishops Wren's petition to the Parliament. 1642.

Considerations on Mr Harrington's Commonwealth. 1657. *See col 2339, below.*

Increpatio Bar Jesu: sive polemicae. 1660.

Monarchy asserted. Oxford 1659, 1660.

An abandoning of the Scottish covenant. 1662.

§2

Wrens anatomy. 1641. Anon.

The wrens-nest defil'd. 1641, 1641. Anon.

Perrot, J. A wren in the burning-bush. 1660.

The Durham book. Ed G. J. Cuming 1961.

Jukes, H. A. Bishop Matthew Wren and the non-conforming ministers of the diocese of Norwich. Historical Stud 11 1968.

King, P. Bishop Wren and the suppression of the Norwich lecturers. Ibid.

—— The episcopate during the Civil Wars 1642–9. EHR 83 1968. On Wren's fate.

OTHER WRITERS

DAVID (AUGUSTIN) BAKER
1575–1641

Collections

Sancta sophia: or directions for the prayer of contemplation, extracted out of more than 40 treatises by Augustin Baker and methodically digested by Serenus Cressy. 2 vols Douai 1657; ed J. N. Sweeney 1876; 1932 (rev as Holy wisdom).

§1

The confessions of Augustin Baker. Ed J. McCann 1922.
The cloud of unknowing and other treatises by an English mystic of the fourteenth century, with a commentary on the Cloud by Augustin Baker. Ed J. McCann 1924.
A spirituall life in a secular state: being an addition to the abridgement of a spirituall life. 1927.

§2

Sweeney, J. N. The life and spirit of Father Augustine Baker. 1861.
McCann, J. and H. Connolly (ed). Memorials of Father Augustine Baker. Pbns of Catholic Record Soc 33 1933.
Salvin, P. and S. Cressy. The life of Father Augustin Baker. Ed J. McCann 1933. With bibliography.
Cowley, P. Father Augustine Baker and the sources of Sancta Sophia. Theology 37 1938.
Renaudin, P. Quatre mystiques anglais. Paris 1945.
Watkin, E. I. In his Poets and mystics, 1953.
Knowles, D. In his English mystical tradition, 1961.
Haynes, R. Augustine Baker. Month March 1961.
Low, A. Augustine Baker. New York [1970].

ROBERT BOLTON
1572–1631

Collections

Workes. 1641.

§1

A discourse about the state of true happinesse. 1611, 1638 (7th edn).
Mr Boltons last and learned worke Of the last four things; with his life [by E. Bagshawe]. 1632, 1639 (4th edn).

JOHN BRAMHALL
1594–1663

See col 2337, below.

RALPH BROWNRIG or BROWNRIGG
Bishop of Exeter
1592–1659

Collections

Fourty sermons. 1661, 2 vols 1664–5 (with Twenty-five sermons), 1674 (as Sixty-five sermons), 1685.
Twenty-five sermons. 1664, 1674 (with Fourty sermons, above).

§1

Repentance and prayer. 1660.
A sermon on the 5th of November. 1660.

HENRY BURTON
1578–1648

Israel's fast: or a meditation upon Joshua 7, 6. 1628, 1628.
The seven vials: or a briefe and plaine exposition upon Revelation. 1628.
A tryall of private devotions. 1628. Burton and William Prynne represent an extreme Puritan reaction to John Cosin's Devotions, 1627; *see under Cosin, above.*
For God, and the King: the summe of two sermons. 1636, 1636.
A most godly sermon shewing the necessity of self-denyall and humiliation, in regard of the present plague. 1641.
England's bondage and hope of deliverance. 1641. Sermon before Parliament.

EDMUND CALAMY
1600–66

The noblemans patterne. 1643, 1643. Sermon before House of Lords.
An indictment against England because of her selfe-murdering divisions. 1645. Sermon.
Englands antidote against the plague of Civil Warre. 1645. Sermon.
The godly mans ark. 1657.
The fixed saint held forth in a farewell sermon. 1662, 1662 (with the final sermons of other prominent non-Conformists, Baxter, Case, Jacomb, Manton, Watson et al as An exact collection of farewell sermons).
Eli trembling for fear of the ark. Oxford 1663. Calamy was committed to Newgate for preaching this sermon.

WILLIAM CARTWRIGHT
1611–43

§1

An offspring of mercy issuing out of the womb of cruelty: a passion sermon preached at Christ's Church in Oxford. 1652.

§2

Goffin, R. C. The life and poems of Cartwright. Cambridge 1918.

FRANCIS CHEYNELL
1608–65

Sion's memento, and Gods alarum. 1643. Sermon before House of Commons.
Chillingworthi novissima: or the sicknesse, heresy, death and buriall of William Chillingworth. 1644.
The man of honour described. 1645. Sermon before Parliament.

HUGH PAULIN (SERENUS) CRESSY
1605–74

Exomologesis: or a faithful narrative of the conversion into Catholique unity of Hugh Paulin de Cressy. Paris 1647, 1653, 1659, [no place] 1679.
The church history of Brittany from the beginning of Christianity to the Norman Conquest. [Rouen] 1668.

RALPH CUDWORTH
1617–88

See col 2336, below.

NATHANAEL CULVERWEL
d. 1651?

See col 2338, below.

WILLIAM DELL
d. 1664

Collections
Several sermons and discourses. 1652, 1709, 2 vols 1817.

§1
The building and glory of the truely Christian and spiritual church. 1646. Sermon before Fairfax and his officers at Marston.
Right reformation. 1646. Sermon before House of Commons.
The stumbling stone: wherein the university is reproved by the Word of God. 1653. Sermon in answer to Sydrach Simpson.

§2
Solt, L. F. Dell: New Model Army chaplain. Church Quart Rev 155 1954.

GEORGE DOWNAME
Bishop of Derry
d. 1634

§1
Two sermons, the one commending the ministerie; the other defending the office of bishops. 2 pts 1608.
An abstract of the duties commanded in the law of God. 1620.
The Christian arte of thriving. 1620. Sermon.
The covenant of grace: or an exposition upon Luke 1. 73–5. Dublin 1631.
A godly and learned treatise of prayer. [Cambridge 1640.

§2
Dredge, J. I. Dr George Downame. Manchester 1881.

BRIAN DUPPA
Bishop of Winchester
1588–1662

Private forms of prayer. Oxford 1645.
Angels rejoicing. 1648.
The soules soliloquie. 1648.
Two prayers, one for the safety of his Majesties person. 1648.
A guide for the penitent. 1660.
Holy rules and helps: second part. 1673.

Letters
The correspondence of Duppa and Sir Justinian Isham 1650–60. Ed G. Isham, Pbns of Northants Record Soc 17 1955.

THOMAS EDWARDS
1595–1645
Gangraena: or a catalogue and discovery of many of the errours of the sectaries of this time. 3 pts 1646 (3 edns).

PATRICK FORBES
Bishop of Aberdeen
1564–1635

An exquisite commentary upon the Revelation of St John. 1613.
A defence of the lawful calling of the ministers of reformed churches. 1614.
See also col 2459, below.

MARK FRANK
1613–64

LI sermons. 1672; ed W.H.M. 2 vols Oxford 1849 (Lib of Anglo-Catholic Theology).

GODFREY GOODMAN
Bishop of Gloucester
1583–1656

§1
The fall of man. 1616, 1618.
The creatures praysing God: or the religion of dumbe creatures. 1622, 1624. Anon.
The two great mysteries of Christian religion. 1653.
Beawty in raggs, or divine phancies putt into broken verse: poems. Ed R. J. Roberts, Reading 1958.

§2
Gundry, D. W. Godfrey Goodman, Bishop of Gloucester. Church Quart Rev 144–5 1947.
Soden, G. I. Godfrey Goodman, Bishop of Gloucester. 1953.
Hepburn, R. W. Goodman: nature vilified. Cambridge Jnl April 1954. On Goodman's Fall of man.

PETER GUNNING
Bishop of Ely
1613–84

§1
A contention for truth in two several publique disputations betweene Mr Gunning and Mr Denne in the church of St Clement-Denes. 1638.
Schism unmasked: or a late conference between Mr Peter Gunning and Mr John Pierson on the one part and two disputants of the Romish persuasion on the other. Paris 1658.
The Paschal or Lent fast, apostolical and perpetual; with an appendix containing an answer to the objections of the Presbyterians against the fast of Lent. 1662; ed C. P. Eden, Oxford 1845 (Lib of Anglo-Catholic Theology).

§2
Jukes, H. A. L. Gunning: scholar, churchman, controversialist. Stud in Church History 1 1964.
— Gunning and the Worcestershire argument. Modern Churchman new ser 7 1964.

GEORGE HAKEWILL
1578–1649

Bibliographies

Dredge, J. I. A few sheaves of Devon bibliography: the second sheaf. 1890.

§ 1

The vanitie of the eie. Oxford 1608, 1608, 1615, 1633.
King David's vow for reformation: delivered in twelve sermons before the Prince. 1621.
A comparison between the dayes of Purim and that of the powder treason. Oxford 1626.
An apologie or declaration of the power and providence of God. Oxford 1627, 1630, 2 pts 1635.
A sermon preached at Barnstaple. 1632.

§ 2

Hepburn, R. W. Hakewill: the virility of nature. JHI 16 1955.

JOHN HALES
Bishop of Norwich
1584–1656

§ 1

Golden remaines of the ever memorable Mr John Hales. 1659, [1659], 1673 (enlarged), 1677, 1688.
Sermons preached at Eton. 1660, 1673.
Several tracts. 1677, 1716 (enlarged).
Works. Ed D. Dalrymple 3 vols Glasgow 1765.

§ 2

Elson, J. H. Hales of Eton. New York 1948.
Murray, J. J. Hales on history. HLQ 19 1955.

THOMAS HALL
1610?–65

The pulpit guarded. 1651, 1651, 1652.
The beauty of holiness. 1653, 1655.
Vindiciae literarum: the schools guarded. 1654, 1655.
Funebra florae: the downfall of Maygames. 1660, 1661.

NATHANIEL HARDY
1618–70

Collections

Several sermons. 1653, 1658.

§ 1

Justice triumphing: or the spoylers spoyled, laid forth in a gratulatory sermon for the glorious delivery from the barbarous powder plot. 1646, 1647, 1648, 1656.
A divine prospective: representing the just man's peacefull end, in a funeral sermon on Sir John Gay. 1649, 1654, 1660.
Love and fear, the inseparable twins of a blest matrimony, characterized in a sermon occasioned by the late nuptials between Wm Christmas and Elizabeth Adams. 1653, 1658.

Lamentation, mourning and woe, sighed forth in a sermon preached the next Lord's day after the dismal fire in the city of London. 1666.

HENRY HAWKINS
1577–1646

See col 1329, above.

ARTHUR HILDERSHAM
1563–1632

Lectures upon the fourth of John. 1629, 1632 ('corrected and enlarged' as CVIII lectures), 1647.

BARTEN HOLYDAY
1593–1661

Motives to a good life, in ten sermons. Oxford 1657.
A survey of the world in ten books. Oxford 1661. Poem.
For Holyday's Τεχνογαμία, see col 1769, above; for his trns from Horace and Persius cols 2171, 2174, below.

NATHANIEL INGELO
1621?–83

The perfection, authority and credibility of the holy scriptures. 1659, 1659. Sermon before Cambirdge Univ.
Bentivolio and Urania. 1660, 1660, 1673, 1682. An allegorical and religious romance.

THOMAS JACKSON
1579–1640

Collections

Divine sermons. Oxford 1637.
A collection of the works. Ed B. O[ley] 3 pts 1653–7, 3 vols 1673, 12 vols Oxford 1844.

§ 1

Nazareth and Bethlehem, and mankind's comfort: two sermons. Oxford 1617.

ROBERT LEIGHTON
Archbishop of Glasgow
1611–84

§ 1

Sermons published after his death from his papers. 1692.
Expository works and other remains revised by Philip Doddridge. 2 vols Edinburgh 1748.
Remains: consisting of all the unpublished pieces left by him to the diocese of Dunblane, with his life by G. Jerment. 1814.
Genuine works; to which is prefixed the life of the author by E. Middleton. 4 vols 1819.
Whole works. Ed W. West 6 vols 1869–75; ed J. N. Pearson, New York 1874.

§ 2

Tulloch, J. In his Scottish divines 1505–1872, Edinburgh 1883.

Butler, D. Life and letters of Leighton. 1903.
Knox, E. A. Leighton, Archbishop of Glasgow. 1930.
Davidson, G. W. H. The library of Leighton. Historical Mag of Protestant Episcopal Church 28 1959.

CHRISTOPHER LOVE
1618–51

Collections

Grace, the truth and growth thereof: the summe and substance of fifteen sermons. 1652, 1652, 1653, 1654, 1657, 1670, 1677.
A treatise of effectual calling and election, in 16 sermons. 1653.
The combate between the flesh and spirit, being the summe and substance of 27 sermons, to which is added the Christians' directory in 15 sermons. 2 pts 1654, 1658.

§1

England's distemper, set forth in a sermon preacht on the first day of the treaty. 1645, 1651.
Heaven's glory, hell's terror: or two treatises. 2 pts 1653, 1655, 1658, 1671.

STEPHEN MARSHALL
1594?–1655

Collections

Works. 1661.

§1

A peace offering to God: a sermon preached to the House of Commons at their publique thanksgiving for the peace. 1641.
A sermon preached Nov 17 1640. 1641, 1645.
Reformation and desolation: or a sermon preached to the House of Commons. 1642.
A sacred panegyrick: or a sermon of thanksgiving preached to the two Houses of Parliament. 1644.
A sermon on the baptizing of infants. 1644, 1645.
Θρηνωδια: a sermon. 1644.
Θρηνωδια: the churches lamentation. 1644, 1644.
A sacred record to be made of God's mercies to Sion: a thanksgiving sermon preached to the two Houses of Parliament June 19 1645, being the day of their publick thanksgiving for the victory in Naseby-field. [1645].
A sermon preached Aug 12 1647. 1647.
A sermon preached January 26 1647. 1647 (for 1648).
A thanksgiving sermon. 1648.
A sermon preached Easter Monday April 1652. |1652, 1653.
Smectymnuus redivivus. 1654.
The power of the civil magistrate in matters of religion vindicated in a sermon preached before Parliament. 1657.

JASPER MAYNE
1604–72

A sermon concerning unity and agreement preached at Carfax Church in Oxford. 1646, 1647.
A sermon against false prophets, preached in Oxford, shortly after the surrender of that garrison. 1646.
A late printed sermon against false prophets, vindicated by letter, from the causeless aspersions of Mr Francis Cheynell. 1647.
The amorous warre. 1648, 1659, 1659.
A sermon against schisme. 1652.
Certaine sermons and letters. 1653.
A sermon preached at the consecration of Herbert [Croft], Lord Bishop of Hereford. 1662.
For Mayne's plays see col 1751, above.

ROGER MAYNWARING
Bishop of St David's
1590–1653

§1

Religion and allegiance: in two sermons. 1627.

§2

Snapp, H. F. The impeachment of Maynwaring. HLQ 30 1967.

JOHN MOORE
1595?–1657

The crying sin of England not caring for the poor, wherein inclosure is arraigned: being two sermons. 1653.

DAME GERTRUDE MORE
1606–33

§1

The holy practises of a devine lover: or the sainctly ideots devotions. Paris 1657; ed H. L. Fox 1909.

§2

Collins, H. Life of Dame Gertrude More. 1877.

GEORGE MORLEY
Bishop of Winchester
1597–1684

Collections

Several treatises, written upon several occasions. 1683.

§1

A modest advertisement concerning the present controversie about church government. 1641.
A sermon preached at the magnificent Coronation of Charles the II. 1661, 1661.
Epistola ad virum clarissimum D. Cornelium Triglandium. 1663.

THOMAS MORTON
Bishop of Durham
1564–1659

§1

Salomon; whereunto is annexed another treatise of the right constitution of a church. 2 pts 1596.
Apologia catholica. 1605–6.
An exact discoverie of Romish doctrine in the case of a conspiracie and rebellion. 1605.
A Catholike appeale for Protestants. 1609, 1610.
The grand imposture of the (now) Church of Rome. [1626?], 1628.
Of the institution of the sacrament of the blessed bodie and blood of Christ. 2 pts 1631, 1635.
A sermon preached in the cathedral church of Durham. 1639, Newcastle 1639.
The necessity of Christian subjection. Oxford [1643].

§2

Barwick, J. Ἰερονιχης [with life]. 1660. Funeral sermon and memoir.

Mayor, J. E. B. Materials for the life of Morton. Communications of Cambridge Antiquarian Soc 3 1879 (pt 1 1864–5).

RICHARD MOUNTAGUE
(or MONTAGU)
Bishop of Chichester
1577–1641

A gagg for the new gospell? no, a new gagg for an old goose: an answer to a late abridger of Controversies [M. Kellison?]. 1624.

Appello Caesarem: a just appeale from two unjust informers. 1625.

The acts and monuments of the Church. 1642.

Letters

Correspondence of John Cosin vol i. Ed G. Ornsby 2 vols Durham 1868–72 (Surtees Soc nos 52, 55).

See also cols 2297–9, above.

JOHN OWEN
1616–83

Collections

A complete collection of the sermons. [Ed J. Asty] 1721.

Works. Ed T. Russell 28 vols 1826. Includes W. Orme, Memoirs of the life, writings and religious connexions of Owen, 1820. Vol 3 rptd 1966 (Banner of Truth).

§1

Ουρανων Ομρανια, the shaking and translating of heaven and earth: a sermon preached to the House of Commons. 1649.

§2

Wilterdink, J. B. Owen en ziyn invloed op Jeremias de Decker en Revins. Tijdschrift voor Ned. Taal en Letterkunde 76 1959.

HERBERT PALMER
1601–47

The glasse of God's providence. 1644. Sermon before Parliament.

Memorials of godlinesse and Christianitie. 3 pts 1644, 1670 (10th edn); ed A. B. Grosart, Edinburgh 1865. Pt 2 is sometimes incorrectly ascribed to Francis Bacon.

The duty and honour of church-restorers. 1646. Sermon before the House of Commons.

JOHN PEARSON
Bishop of Chester
1613–86

Collections

Opera posthuma. 1688.

Minor theological works. Ed E. Churton 2 vols Oxford 1844.

Five lectures on the Acts of the Apostles. Ed J. R. Crowfoot, Cambridge 1851.

§1

An exposition of the Creed. 1659; at least 8 edns by 1704; ed T. Chevallier and R. Sinker, Cambridge 1882.

Vindiciae epistolarum S. Ignatii. 1672; ed E. Churton 2 vols Oxford 1852.

Pearson also wrote prefaces for Meric Casaubon's edn of Hierocles, 1655, and The golden remains of John Hales, 1659.

HUGH PETER(S)
1598–1660

§1

God's doings and man's duty. 1646 (3 edns). Sermon before Parliament.

A sermon preached before his death. 1660.

§2

Patrick, J. M. Peter: a study in Puritanism. Univ Buffalo Stud 5 1946.

—— The arrest of Peter. HLQ 19 1956.

Stearns, R. P. Peter and his biographers. Bostonian Soc Annual Proc 1935.

—— The strenuous Puritan: Peter. Urbana 1954.

—— 'Peter was a wit'. Proc Amer Antiquarian Soc 77 1967.

THOMAS PIERCE (or PEIRSE)
1622–91

Collections

A collection of sermons. 1671, 1671.

§1

A third and fourth part of Pegasus. 1648.

A correct copy of some notes concerning God's decrees. 1655, 1657, 1658, 1671, 1672.

The sinner impleaded in his own court. 1656, 1660, 1670, 1679.

The divine philanthropie. 1657, 1658.

The divine purity. 1657, 1659.

The Christian's rescue. 1658.

The self-defender exemplified. 1658.

Αυτοκατακρισις: or self-condemnation. 1658.

Εαυτοντιμωρούμενος: or the self-revenger. 1658.

Φιλαλληλια: or the grand characteristick. 1658, 1658.

Εμψυχον νεκρον: or the lifelessness of life. 1659.

The new discoverer discovered. 1659.

England's season. 1660.

An impartial inquiry into the nature of sin. 1660.

Concio synodica ad clerum Anglicanum. 1661.

The primitive rule of Reformation. 1663, 1663 (8th edn); rptd in Collection of sermons, 1671; tr French, 1663.

A true account of the proceedings. 1663.

The signal diagnostick. 1670, 1679.

A decad of caveats. 1679.

A seasonable caveat. 1679.

A vindication of the King's sovereign rights. 1683.

Pacificatorium orthodoxae theologiae corpusculum. 1683, 1685.

The law and equity of the gospel. 1686.

A prophylactick from disloyalty. 1688.

Death considered as a door to a life of glory. 1690?

JOHN PRESTON
1587–1628

§ I

The breast-plate of faith and love in 18 sermons. 1630, 1630, 1634 (4th edn), 1651 (6th edn).
Sermons preached before his Majestie, and upon other special occasions. 1630, 1630, 1631, 1634, 1637.
Life eternall: or a treatise of the knowledge of the divine essence, delivered in 18 sermons. 1631, 1631, 1632, 1634.
Foure godly and learned treatises. 1633 (3rd edn), 1636.
Remaines. 1634. Judas's repentance: Saints' spirituall strength; Paul's conversion.
An abridgement of Dr Preston's works. 1648.

§ 2

Morgan, I. Prince Charles's Puritan chaplain. 1957.
Maclean, J. F. Puritan relations with Buckingham. HLQ 21 1958.

WILLIAM PRYNNE
1600–69
See col 2224, below.

EDWARD REYNOLDS
Bishop of Norwich
1599–1676

Collections

An explication of the fourteenth chapter of the prophet Hosea, in several sermons. 1658.
Workes. 1658, 1679.
Divers sermons preached. 1659.
Twenty sermons. 1660.
Whole works. [Ed J. R. Pitman] 6 vols 1826 (with Life by R. Chalmers).

§ I

Meditations on the holy sacrament of the Lord's last supper. 1638.
The sinfulnesse of sinne. 1639 (4th edn).
A treatise of the passions. 1647.
The comfort and crown of great actions. 1658. Sermon before the East India Company.
A sermon touching the use of humane learning, preached at the funeral of John Langley, late school-master at Paul's School in London. 1658.
A sermon preached before the Peers November 7 1666, being a day of solemn humiliation for the continuing pestilence. 1666.

JOHN SALTMARSH
c. 1610–47

§ I

Poemata sacra, latine et anglice scripta. Cambridge 1636.
Holy discoveries and flames. 1640, 1811.
Dawnings of light. 1645.
The fountains of free grace opened. 1645.
Perfume against the sulpherous stinke of the snuffe of the light for smoak. 1646.
Reasons for unitie, peace, and love. 1646; extracts in D. M. Wolfe, Milton in the Puritan revolution, New York 1941.
The smoke in the temple. 1646 (3 edns).
Sparkles of glory, or some beams of the Morning-star. 1647, 1811, 1847.

§ 2

Jordan, W. K. Sectarian thought and its relation to the development of religious toleration 1640–60. HLQ 3 1940.
Solt, L. F. Saltmarsh: New Model Army chaplain. Jnl of Ecclesiastical History 2 1951.

GILBERT SHELDON
Archbishop of Canterbury
1598–1677

§ I

David's deliverance and thanksgiving: a sermon preached before the King, being the day of solemn thanksgiving for the happy return of his Majesty. 1660.
The dignity of kingship asserted. 1660.
Monarchy triumphing over traiterous republicans. 1661.

§ 2

Higham, F. A note on Sheldon. Jnl of Eng History 14 1962.

ROBERT SHELFORD
1563–1627

Lectures or readings upon Proverbs 22.6. 1602.
Five pious and learned discourses. 1635.

RICHARD SIBBES
1577–1635

Collections

Complete works. 1809, 1812; ed A. B. Grosart 7 vols 1862–4.

§ I

The saints cordials. 1629, 1637. Anon.
The bruised reed and smoaking flax: some sermons. 1630, 1638 (6th edn).
Bowels opened: or a discovery of the neare and deare love, union and communion betwixt Christ and the Church; delivered in divers sermons. 1632, 1639, 1641.
Light from heaven, in foure treatises. 1638.
An exposition of the third chapter of the epistle of St Paul to the Philippians [and other sermons]. 1639, 1647.
Beames of divine light breaking forth from several places of holy scripture, in 21 sermons. 1639.
The glorious feast of the gospel in divers sermons. 1650.

§ 2

Hudson, R. F. Sibbes's theory and practice of persuasion. Quart Jnl of Speech 44 1958.
Rooy, S. H. In his Theology of missions in the Puritan tradition, Delft 1965.

ROBERT SIBTHORPE
d. 1662

A counter-plea to an apostate's pardon. 1618.
Apostolike obedience. 1627.

JOHN SMITH
1618–52

See col 2340, below.

WILLIAM SPURSTOW
1605–66

England's patterne and duty in its monthly fasts. 1643. Sermon before Parliament.
England's eminent judgments. 1644. Sermon before House of Lords 5 Nov 1644.
Death and grave no bar to believers happinesse. 1656. Funeral sermon for Lady Vyner.

PETER STERRY
1613–72

§ 1

The spirit convincing of sinne. 1645, 1646. Sermon before House of Commons.
The clouds in which Christ comes. 1648. Sermon before House of Commons.
The teachings of Christ in the soul. 1648. Sermon before House of Lords.
The comings forth of Christ opened in a sermon before Parliament for the victories obtained in Ireland. 1650.
England's deliverance from the northern presbytery: a thanksgiving sermon. 1652. Before Parliament.
The way of God with his people in these nations: a thanksgiving sermon for the victory over the Spaniards. 1657. Before House of Lords.
The true way of uniting the people of God in these nations. 1660. Sermon.
A discourse of the freedom of the will. 1675.
The rise, race, and royalty of the kingdom of God in the soul of man opened in several sermons. 1683.
The appearance of God to man in the gospel. 1710.

§ 2

Pinto, V. de S. Sterry and his unpublished writings. RES 6 1930.
—— Sterry: a biographical and critical study with passages selected from his writings. Cambridge 1934.
—— Sterry: Platonist and Puritan. Cambridge 1934.

RICHARD STEWARD
1593?–1651

Collections

Three sermons. 1656, 1658.
Golden remains: or three sermons. 1661.

§ 1

Catholique divinity: or the most solid and sententious expressions of the primitive doctors. 1657.
A discourse of episcopacy and sacrilege by way of letter, written in 1646. 1683.

§ 2

Pocock, N. Life of Steward. 1908.

EDWARD STILLINGFLEET
1635–99

See vol 2 cols 271, 849f.

WILLIAM STRODE
1602–45

Collections

Poetical works. Ed B. Dobell 1907. Includes Floating island, 1655.

§ 1

A sermon concerning death. Oxford 1644.
A sermon concerning swearing. Oxford 1644.
A sermon preached at a visitation held at Lynn in Norfolk. 1660.

THOMAS TAYLOR
1576–1633

Collections

A mappe of Rome, preached in five sermons on occasion of the gunpowder treason. 1619, 1620, 1634.
Works. 1653, 1659.

§ 1

A man in Christ: or a new creature; to which is added a treatise, containing meditations from the creatures. 1628, 1629 ('corrected'), 1632, 1635.

HERBERT THORNDIKE
1598–1672

Collections

Theological works. 6 vols Oxford 1844–56 (Lib of Anglo-Catholic Theology). Includes 8 pieces left in ms. Vols 3–6 ed A. W. Haddan; life and bibliography in vol 6.

§ 1

Epitome lexici hebraici, rabinici et arabici. 1635.
Of the government of churches: a discourse pointing at the primitive form. Cambridge 1641, 1649; ed D. Lewis 1841.
Of religious assemblies and the public service of God. Cambridge 1642.
A discourse of the right of the church in a Christian state. 1649.
A letter concerning the present state of religion amongst us. 1656.
An epilogue to the tragedy of the Church of England. 1659.
The due way of composing the differences on foot. 1660, 1662, 1687.
Just weights and measures. 1662, 1662 (with Due way, above), 1687.
A discourse of the forebearance of the penalties, which a due reformation requires. 1670.
De ratione ac jure finiendi controversias ecclesiae disputatio. 1670.

JOHN TOMBES
1603?–76

Fermentum Pharisaeorum. 1643. Sermon.
Jehovah Jireh: or God's providence in delivering the godly, opened in two sermons in Bristol of thanksgiving for the deliverance of that citie from the invasion without, and the plot of the malignants within. 1643.
Anthropolatria: or the sinne of glorifying in eminent ministers of the gospel. 1645. Sermon.

JOHN WALLIS
1616–1703

§ 1

Theological discourses [and sermons]. 2 pts 1692.
For Wallis's other writings see col 2336, below.

§ 2

Scott, J. F. Mathematical work of Wallis. 1938.

BRIAN WALTON
Bishop of Chester
1600–61

§ 1

B. Waltoni introductio ad lectionem linguarum orientalium.
1655, 1655, 1821.
The considerator considered. 1659. A reply to John Owen.

§ 2

Todd, H. J. Memoirs of the life and writings of Walton.
2 vols 1821.
Barnes, W. E. In Studies in memory of A. W. Ward,
Cambridge 1924.

SETH WARD
Bishop of Salisbury
1617–89

§ 1

Vindiciae academiarum. Oxford 1654.
Against resistance of lawful powers: a sermon. 1661.
The Christian's victory over death: a sermon at the funeral
of the Duke of Albemarle. 1670.
A sermon against the Anti-Scripturists; also another
concerning infidelity, preached at White-Hall. 2 pts
1670.
An apology for the mysteries of the gospel: a sermon. 1673.

§ 2

Pope, W. Life of Seth, Lord Bishop of Salisbury. 1697;
ed J. B. Bamborough, Oxford 1961 (Luttrell Soc).
Fletcher, J. M. J. Ward, Bishop of Salisbury 1667–89.
Wiltshire Archaeological & Natural History Mag 49
1940.

BENJAMIN WHICHCOTE
1609–83
See col 2342, below.

JOHN WILKINS
1614–72

Collections

Sermons preached upon several occasions before the King
at Whitehall. 1677, 1680, 1682 (with preface by Tillotson), 1701.
Mathematical and philosophical works, with a short life
of the author. 1708, 2 vols 1802.

§ 1

The discovery of a world in the moone. 1638 (anon), 2 pts
1640.
Mercury: or the secret messenger. 1641, 1694.
Ecclesiastes: or a discourse concerning the gift of preaching
as it falls under the rules of art. 1646, 1647, 1651, 1656,
1659, 1669, 1679.
Mathematicall magick, in two books. 1648, 1680.
A discourse concerning the beauty of providence in all the
rugged passages of it. 1649, 1704 (7th edn).
A discourse concerning the gift of prayer. 1653, 1704
(8th edn); tr French, 1665.
An essay towards a real character and a philosophical
language. 1668. *See* O. Funke, Zum Weltsprachen-
problem in England im 17 Jahrhundert, Heidelberg 1929.
Of the principles and duties of natural religion. [Ed I.
Ibbotson] 2 pts 1675, 1722–3 (8th edn). Preface by
Tillotson.

§ 2

Henderson, P. A. The life and times of Wilkins. 1910.
Hogben, L. Dangerous thoughts. 1939.
Christensen, F. Wilkins and the Royal Society's reform of
prose style. MLQ 7 1946.
Funke, O. On the sources of Wilkins' Philosophical
language, 1668. E Studies 40 1959.
Linsky, S. S. Wilkins' linguistic views. Zeitschrift für
Anglistik und Amerikanistik (East Berlin) 14 1966.
Shapiro, B. J. Wilkins 1614–72: an intellectual biography.
Berkeley 1969.

JOHN WILLIAMS
Archbishop of York
1582–1650

§ 1

A sermon of apparell. 1620.
Great Britain's Salomon: a sermon. 1625.
Perseverentia sanctorum: a sermon. 1628.
A sermon preached before the Lords. 1628.
The holy table, name and thing, more anciently, properly
and literally used under the New testament, than that
of an altar: written by a minister in Lincolnshire in
answer to D. Coal [or rather to P. Heylyn, A coale from
the altar]. 1637 (3 edns).

Letters

Letters of Archbishop Williams. Ed J. E. B. Mayor,
Communications of Cambridge Antiquarian Soc 2–3
1864–79.
The unpublished correspondence between Archbishop
Williams and the Marquis of Oxford. Archaeologia
Cambrensis 3rd ser 15 1869.

§ 2

Hacket, J. Scrinia reserata. 1693.
Philips, A. The life of Williams. Cambridge 1700.
Abridged from Hacket, above.
Roberts, R. O. Mitre and musket. 1938. With biblio-
graphy.

JOHN WORTHINGTON
1618–71

Bibliographies

Christie, R. C. Bibliography. Chetham Soc new ser 13 1888.
Copinger, W. A. On the English translations of the
Imitatio Christi. Bibliographiana 3 1900.

Collections

Select discourses. 1725, 1826.

§ 1

The Christian's pattern. 1654. A trn of Thomas à Kempis.

Ὑποτύπωσις ὑγιαινόν τῶν λόγων: a form of sound words, or a Scripture catechism, shewing what a Christian is to believe and practise in order to salvation. 1673 etc; 7 edns by 1733.

The great duty of self-resignation to the divine will. 1675, 1689, Bristol 1823.

The doctrines of the Resurrection and the reward to come, considered as the grand motives to an holy life. 1690.

Charitas evangelica: a discourse of Christian love. 1691.

Forms of prayer for a family. 1693, 1721.

Letters

Miscellanies, also a collection of epistles; with the author's character by Archbishop Tillotson. 1704.

Diary and correspondence of Worthington. Ed J. Crossley 2 vols 1847–86 (Chetham Soc).

P. G. S.

5. POPULAR AND MISCELLANEOUS PROSE

I. PAMPHLETEERS AND MISCELLANEOUS WRITERS

BARNABY RICH
1542–1617

§ 1

A right exelent and pleasaunt dialogue, betwene Mercury and an English souldier. [1574].

Allarme to England, foreshewing what perilles are procured where the people live without regarde of martiall lawe. 1578, 1578, 1625 (as Vox militis, adapted by G. Marcelline).

Riche his farewell to militarie profession. 1581, 1583, 1594 (rev), 1606 (rev); ed J. P. Collier, Eight novels employed by English dramatic poets, 1846 (Shakespeare Soc); ed T. M. Cranfill, Austin 1959. Apolonius and Silla ed J. Boswell, Plays and poems of Shakespeare vol 11, 1821; ed J. P. Collier, Shakespeare's library vol 2, [1843]; ed H. Morley 1889 (with Twelfth night); ed H. H. Furness, New variorum vol 13, 1901 (with Twelfe night); ed M. Luce 1912; ed E. J. O'Brien, Elizabethan tales, 1937; ed G. Bullough, Narrative and dramatic sources of Shakespeare vol 2, 1958; ed M. Lawlis, Elizabethan prose fiction, New York 1968; ed T. J. B. Spencer, Elizabethan love stories, 1968 (Pelican). Phylotus and Emelia ed J. W. Mackenzie, Edinburgh 1835 (with Philotus). Two brethren and their wives ed G. Bullough, Narrative and dramatic sources vol 2, 1958.

The straunge and wonderfull adventures of Don Simonides. 1581.

The true report of a late practise enterprised by a Papist with a yong maiden in Wales. 1582.

The second tome of the travailes and adventures of Don Simonides. 1584.

A path-way to military practise. 1587.

The adventures of Brusanus, Prince of Hungaria. 1592.

A martial conference, pleasantly discoursed betweene two souldiers, the one Captaine Skil, the other Captaine Pill. 1598 (title-page only).

A souldiers wishe to Britons welfare. 1604. Also issued as The fruites of long experience.

Faultes, faults and nothing else but faultes. 1606; ed M. H. Wolf, Gainesville 1965 (facs).

A short survey of Ireland truely discovering who hath armed that people with disobedience. 1069 (for 1609).

Roome for a gentleman: or the second part of Faultes, collected for the true meridian of Dublin. 1609.

A new description of Ireland, wherein is described the disposition of the Irish. 1610, 1624 (as A new Irish prognostication, anon).

A true and a kinde excuse written in defence of that booke intituled A newe description of Irelande. 1612.

A Catholicke conference betweene Syr Tady MacMareall a popish priest and Patricke Plaine. 1612.

The excellency of good women. 1613.

Opinion diefied, discovering the ingins, traps and traynes that are set to catch opinion. 1613.

The honestie of this age. 1614, 1615, 1615, 1616, Edinburgh [1616?]; ed P. Cunningham 1844 (Percy Soc).

My ladies looking glasse, wherein may be discerned a wise man from a foole. 1616.

The Irish hubbub: or the English hue and crie. 1617, 1617 (rev), 1618, 1622.

Remembrances of the state of Ireland 1612. Ed C. L. Falkiner, Proc Royal Irish Acad 26 1906.

Rych's Anothomy of Ireland [1615], with an account of the author. Ed E. M. Hinton, PMLA 55 1940.

§ 2

Anders, H. R. D. In his Shakespeare's books, Berlin 1904.

Baskervill, C. R. The source of the main plot of Shirley's Love tricks. MLN 24 1909.

— Source and analogues of How a man may choose a good wife from a bad. PMLA 24 1909.

Becker, G. The adventures of Don Simonides: ein Roman und seine Quelle. Archiv 131 1913.

Forsythe, R. S. In his Relations of Shirley's plays to the Elizabethan drama, New York 1914.

Starnes, D. T. Riche's Sappho Duke of Mantona. SP 30 1933.

Hinton, E. M. In his Ireland through Tudor eyes, Philadelphia 1935.

Bruce, D. H. The merry wives and Two brethren. SP 39 1942.

Webb, H. J. Riche: sixteenth-century military critic. JEGP 42 1943.

Cranfill, T. M. Rich's Sappho and the Weakest goeth to the wall. SE 1946.

— Rich and King James. ELH 16 1949.

— Rich: an Elizabethan reviser at work. SP 46 1949.

— and D. H. Bruce. Rich: a short biography. Austin 1953.

Jorgensen, P. A. Rich: soldier, suitor and honest critic of women. Shakespeare Quart 7 1956.

Lievsay, J. L. A word about Rich. JEGP 55 1956.

Ferrara, F. Riche: difensore del soldato inglese e autore di A larum for London. Eng Miscellany (Rome) 8 1957.

NICHOLAS BRETON

See col 1027, above.

GABRIEL HARVEY
1550–1631

Bibliographies

McKerrow, R. B. In Works of Nashe vol 5 appendix A, 1910.

Collections

Works. Ed A. B. Grosart 3 vols 1884–5 (Huth Lib).

§ 1

Ode natalitia: vel opus eius feriae in memoriam P. Rami. 1575. Signed A.P.S., i.e. Aulae Pembr. socius?

Gabrielis Harveii Ciceronianus: vel oratio. 1577; ed H. S. Wilson, tr C. A. Forbes, Lincoln Nebraska 1945.

Gabrielis Harveii rhetor: vel duorum dierum oratio. 1577.

Gabrielis Harveii Valdinatis; Smithus; vel musarum lachrymae pro obitu Thomae Smithi. 1578.

Gabrielis Harveii gratulationum Valdinensium libri quatuor. 1578.

Three proper and wittie familiar letters. 1580; ed J. Haslewood, Ancient critical essays vol 2, 1815; ed E. de Selincourt, Poetical works of Edmund Spenser, Oxford 1912.

Crispinus Joannes. Lexicon graecolatinum. 1581. Orations by 'G.H.'.

Three letters and certaine sonnets, especially touching Robert Greene. 1592, 1592 (with 4th letter as Foure letters), 1592; ed S. E. Brydges, Archaica vol 2, 1815; ed J. P. Collier [1870]; ed G. B. Harrison, Edinburgh 1923; Menston 1969 (facs of 3rd edn).

Pierces supererogation: or a new prayse of the old asse. 1593; ed S. E. Brydges, Archaica vol 2, 1815; ed J. P. Collier [1870]; Menston 1970 (facs of 1593).

A new letter of notable contents. 1593 (with Pierces supererogation?); ed S. E. Brydges, Archaica vol 2, 1815; ed J. P. Collier [1870]; Menston 1970 (facs of 1593).

The trimming of Thomas Nashe gentleman, by the high-tituled patron Don Richardo de Medico campo. 1597; ed J. P. Collier [1870]; ed C. Hindley, The old book collector's miscellany vol 1, 1871. By Harvey?

Letter-book. Ed E. J. L. Scott 1884 (Camden Soc). See G. C. Moore Smith, N & Q 8 April 1911; J. W. Bennett, MP 29 1931; E. M. Albright, ibid.

Marginalia. Ed G. C. Moore Smith, Stratford 1913. See C. Ruutz-Rees, PMLA 25 1910; F. Marcham, The prototype of Shylock, Harrow Weald 1927; S. A. Tannenbaum, MLR 25 1930; G. C. Moore Smith and W. A. Jackson, MLR 28–30 1933–5; C. Camden, PQ 13 1934; C. B. Bourland, HLQ 4 1940; W. L. Godshalk, MLR 59 1964; F. D. Hoeniger, Shakespeare Quart 17 1966. See also col 2309, below.

§2

D'Israeli, I. In his Calamities of authors vol 2, 1812.

Morley, H. In his Clement Marot and other studies vol 2, 1871.

Moore Smith, G. C. In Bang's Materialien vol 8, Louvain 1905.

McKerrow, R. B. In Works of Thomas Nashe, 1910.

Berli, H. Harvey: der Dichterfreund und Kritiker. Zürich 1913.

Moore, H. Harvey's references to Marlowe. SP 23 1926.

Sanders, C. Robert Greene and the Harveys. Indiana Univ Stud 18 1931.

Orsini, N. In his Studii sul rinascimento italiano in Inghilterra, Florence 1937.

Wilson, H. S. Harvey's orations on rhetoric. ELH 12 1945.
—— Harvey's method of annotating his books. Harvard Lib Bull 2 1948.
—— The humanism of Harvey. In J. Q. Adams memorial studies, Washington 1948.

Oppel, H. Gabriel Harvey. Sh Jb 82–3 1948.

Hendrickson, G. L. Elizabethan quantitative hexameters. PQ 28 1949.

Ribner, I. Harvey in Chancery 1608. RES new ser 2 1951.

Duhamel, P. A. The Ciceronianism of Harvey. SP 49 1952.

Schrickx, W. The portraiture of Harvey in the Parnassus plays and John Marston. Neophilologus 36 1952.
—— Shakespeare's early contemporaries. Antwerp 1956.

Perkins, D. Issues and motivations in the Nashe-Harvey quarrel. PQ 39 1960.

Hibbard, G. R. In his Thomas Nashe, 1962.

Ball, B. W. George Peele's Huanebango: a caricature of Harvey. Renaissance Papers 1968.

Harlow, C. G. Did Harvey read Nashe's Christ's tears? N & Q Dec 1969.

McPherson, D. C. Aretino and the Harvey-Nashe quarrel. PMLA 84 1969.

Snare, G. Satire, logic and rhetoric in Harvey's earthquake letter to Spenser. Tulane Stud in Eng 18 1970.

THOMAS LODGE
See col 1434, above.

ROBERT GREENE
See col 1437, above.

HENRY CHETTLE
See col 1461, above.

SIR JOHN HARINGTON
1560–1612

§1

Orlando furioso in English heroical verse. 1591, 1607, 1634 (rev, with The most elegant epigrams, 1633); ed R. Gottfried, Bloomington 1963 (selection). See col 1113, above.

A new discourse of a stale subject, called the Metamorphosis of Ajax, written by Misacmos to his friend Philostilpnos. 1596, 1596, 1596, 1596. Each contains 2 appendices also issued separately: An anatomie of the metamorpho-sed Ajax, by T. C. [i.e. Thomas Combe the illustrator], 1596, [1596]; An apologie, [1596] (anon), [1596] (3 edns); ed S. W. Singer, Chiswick 1814 (with Ulysses upon Ajax, below); ed P. Warlock and J. Lindsay 1927 (with an anatomie); ed E. S. Donno 1962.

Ulysses upon Ajax, written by Misadiaboles to his friend Philaretes. 1596 (anon; probably not by Harington), 1596; ed S. W. Singer, Chiswick 1814 (with A new discourse, An anatomie, An apologie, above).

The Englishmans docter: or the schoole of Salerne. Tr 1607 (anon), 1608, 1609, Edinburgh 1613 (as Conservandae bonae valetudinis praecepta), London 1617 (under first title, with addn by H. Ronsovius), 1624; ed A. Croke, Oxford 1830; ed F. R. Packard and F. H. Garrison, New York 1920, London 1922; Salerno 1953.

C., I. Alcilia, Philoparthens loving folly. 1613 (2nd edn). With epigrammes by Sir J. H[arington].

Epigrams both pleasant and serious. 1615, 1615. Partly rptd in following.

The most elegant and witty epigrams of Sir J. Harington. 4 bks 1618 (with some Epigrams, 1615, above), 1625, 1633 (also with Orlando, 1634, above); ed N. E. McClure, Philadelphia 1926; Menston 1970 (facs of 1618).

A briefe view of the state of the Church of England. 1653, 1779 (in Nugae, below). Harington's title was A supplie or addicion to the Catalogue of bishops to the year 1608.

Nugae antiquae: a miscellaneous collection of original papers. Ed Henry Harington 2 vols 1769–75, 3 vols 1779, 1792; ed T. Park 2 vols 1804.

A short view of the state of Ireland written in 1605. Ed W. D. Macray, Oxford 1879.

A tract on the succession to the Crown (AD 1602) by Sir John Harington. Ed C. R. Markham 1880 (Roxburghe Club).

The letters and epigrams of Sir John Harington together with the Prayse of private life [and bibliography]. Ed N. E. McClure, Philadelphia 1930. See also M. H. M. MacKinnon, PQ 37 1958.

The Arundel Harington manuscript of Tudor poetry. Ed R. Hughey 2 vols Columbus 1960.

§2

Raleigh, W. In his Some authors, Oxford 1923.
Kirwood, A. E. M. The metamorphosis of Ajax and its sequels. Library 4th ser 12 1931.

Hughey, R. The Harington manuscript at Arundel Castle and related documents. Library 4th ser 15 1935.

Rich, T. Harington and Ariosto: a study in Elizabethan verse translation. New Haven 1940.

Schmutzler, K. E. Harington's metrical paraphrases of the seven penitential psalms: three manuscript versions. PBSA 53 1959.

Lea, K. M. Harington's folly. In Elizabethan and Jacobean studies presented to F. P. Wilson, Oxford 1959. On Harington as translator.

Nelson, T. G. A. Harington: a mistaken attribution. N & Q Dec 1969.

— Harington as a critic of Sir Philip Sidney. SP 67 1970.

THOMAS NASHE

See col 1456, above.

GERVASE MARKHAM
1568?–1637

Bibliographies
Poynter, F. N. L. A bibliography of Markham. Oxford 1962 (Oxford Bibl Soc).

§I

A discsource of horsmanshippe. 1593, 1595 (enlarged as How to chuse, ride, traine and diet horses), 1596, 1597, 1599, 1606 (enlarged), 1615 (abridged in Countrey contentments), 1616 (abridged in Cheape and good husbandry), 1639 (abridged in The complete farrier); ed T. Harris, Markham's masterpiece, [1883?] (as The complete jockey); ed H. J. Schonfield 1933.

The gentlemans academie: or the booke of S. Albans by Juliana Barnes. 1595.

The most honorable tragedie of Sir Richard Grinvile, knight. 1595; ed E. Arber, The last fight of the Revenge at sea, 1871; ed E. Goldsmid, The last fight of the Revenge, Edinburgh 1886.

The poem of poems, or Sions Muse: contayning the divine song of King Salomon. [1596].

Devoreux: vertues teares for the losse of King Henry III of Fraunce. 1597. From the French.

A health to the gentlemanly profession of servingmen. 1598; ed W. C. Hazlitt, Inedited tracts, 1868; ed A. V. Judges, Oxford 1931 (facs). Attributed to Markham.

The teares of the beloved: or the lamentation of Saint John. 1600 (by J.M.); ed A. B. Grosart, Miscellanies vol 2, 1871.

Marie Magdalens lamentations. 1601, 1604; ed A. B. Grosart, ibid. Attributed to Markham.

A most exact discourse, how to trayne and teach horses to amble. 1605.

Cavelarice: or the English horseman. 8 bks 1607, 1617.

The shape and porportion of a perfit horse. 1607 (probably issued with Cavelarice, above).

The English Arcadia, alluding his beginning from Sir Philip Sydnes ending. 2 pts 1607–13 (by G.M.).

Rodomonths infernall: or the divell conquered; Ariostos conclusions of the marriage of Rogero with Bradamanth. 1607. From the French.

The dumbe knight: a historicall comedy acted sundry times by the Children of his Majesties Revelles. 1608, 1633; ed R. Dodsley, Collection of old plays vol 6, 1744; rev I. Reed vol 4, 1780; rev J. P. Collier vol 4, 1825; rev W. C. Hazlitt vol 10, 1875; ed Sir Walter Scott, Ancient British drama vol 2, 1810. With Lewis Machin.

The famous whore: or noble curtizan Paulina, mistress unto Cardinall Hypolito of Est. 1609; ed F. Ouvry 1868.

A cure for all diseases in horses. 2 bks 1610, 1616 (as Markhams method).

Markhams maister-peece: or what doth a horse-man lacke. 1610, 1615, 1623, 1631 (for 1630), 1636, 1643, 1651, 1656, 1662, 1668, 1675, 1681, 1683, 1688, 1694; ed T. Harris [1883?]; tr French, 1666. *See* Markhams faithfull farrier, below.

The most famous and renowned historie of Mervine, sonne to Oger the Dane. 2 pts 1612. Tr from French by J. M[arkham]?

Hobsons horse-load of letters: or a president for epistles. Bk 1, 1613 (by G.M.); 2 bks 1617.

The English husbandman. Bk 1, 1613; bk 2, 1614 (with appendix, The pleasures of princes); 2 bks 1635. Pleasures of princes rptd 1631 with Country contentments in A way to get wealth; ed H. G. Hutchinson, The art of angling, 1927; ed J. M. French, Three books on fishing 1599–1659, Gainesville 1962 (in part).

Cheape and good husbandry for the well-ordering of all beasts and fowles. 1614, [1616?] (abridged in Markhams method), 1616 (including abridgement of A discource of horsmanshippe, 1606), 1623 (in A way to get wealth, below).

Countrey contentments. 1615. Bk 1, The whole art of riding great horses, including abridgement of A discource of horsmanshippe, rptd, with The pleasures of princes from English husbandman, above, as Country contentments: or the husbandman's recreations, in A way to get wealth, 1631 etc below. Bk 2, The English huswife rptd as Country contentments: or the English huswife, in A way to get wealth, 1623 etc below, and as The English house-wife; ed Constance, Countess De la Warr 1907 (in part).

A schoole for young souldiers. [1615] (anon), 1616.

Maison rustique: or the countrey farme, by Charles Stevens and John Liebault, translated by Richard Surflet; reviewed, corrected and augmented by Gervase Markham. 1616.

Markhams method or epitome. [1616?] (abridgement of Cheape and good husbandry, 1614, above), 1616, 1623, 1628, 1630, 1633, 1641, 1650, 1671, 1684.

The horsemans honour. 1620. By Markham?

Markhams farwell to husbandry. 1620, 1623 etc (in A way to get wealth).

Hungers prevention: or the whole arte of fowling. 1621, 1655.

Verus pater: or a bundell of truths. 1622. Probably not by Markham.

A second part to the mothers blessing: or a cure against misfortunes. 1622. Nicholas Breton and Dorothy Leigh both wrote a Mothers blessing.

The true tragedy of Herod and Antipater, with the death of faire Marriam, as it hath beene acted at the Red Bull, by Gervase Markham and William Sampson. 1622.

Certaine excellent and new invented knots and mazes, for plots for gardens. 1623. Sometimes attributed to Markham.

Honour in his perfection: Henry Earle of Oxenford, Henry Earle of Southampton, Robert Earle of Essex, Robert Bartue, Lord Willoughby of Eresby. 1624 (by G.M.).

The inrichment of the Weald of Kent. 1625 (anon), 1631 etc (in A way to get wealth).

The souldiers accidence. 1625 (by G.M.), 1635, 1639 (in The souldiers exercise, below).

The souldiers grammar. Pt 1, 1626; pt 2, 1627; 2 pts 1639 (in The souldiers exercise, below).

The description of that ever to be famed knight, Sir John Burgh. 1628.

Markhams faithfull farrier. 1629 (from Markhams maisterpeece, 1610, above), 1630, 1631, 1635, 1636, 1638, 1640, 1647, 1656, 1661, 1687.

A way to get wealth. 1623 (with Markhams farwell to husbandry, 1620, above; Cheape and good husbandry, 1623; Country contentments: or the English huswife, 1623; William Lawson, A new orchard and garden, 1623 augmented), 1625 (with Markhams farwell to husbandry, 1625), 1631 (Cheape and good husbandry,

1631; Country contentments: or the husbandmans recreations, 1631; The English house-wife, 1631; The inrichment of the Weald of Kent, 1631; Markhams farwell to husbandry, 1631; William Lawson, A new orchard and garden, 1631), 1638 (with later edns of same items), 1648 (for 1649), 1653, 1657, 1660, 1660, 1668, 1676, 1683, 1695.

Heresbatch, Conrade. The whole art of husbandrie. Tr Barnaby Googe 1631 (enlarged by Markham).

The art of archerie. 1634.

The complete farriar. 1639. Abridged from A discource of horsmanshippe, 1606.

The souldiers exercise. 1639 (with The souldiers accidence and The souldiers grammar), 1643 (3rd edn).

The perfect horseman: or the experienc'd secrets of Mr Markham's fifty years practice. 1655 (abridged from Cavelarice, above), 1656, 1660, 1668, 1671, 1680, 1684.

§2

Markham, D. F. A history of the Markham family. 1854, 2 vols 1913 (with many addns and corrections by C. R. Markham, as Markham memorials).

Dunstan, A. C. Examination of two English dramas by Elizabeth Carew and by Markham. Königsberg 1908.

Wallace, C. W. Markham, dramatist. Sh Jb 46 1910.

Adams, J. Q. Every woman in her humour and the Dumb knight. MP 10 1913.

Smith, F. In his Early history of veterinary literature vol 1, 1919.

Lyon, J. H. H. A study of the Newe metamorphosis. New York 1919. By Markham?

Silbermann, A. M. Untersuchungen über die Quellen des Dramas The true tragedy of Herod and Antipater. Wittenberg [1929].

Crow, J. Marlowe yields to Jervis Markham. TLS 4 Jan 1947. See also TLS 11–18 Jan, 8 Feb, 21 June, 5 July 1947. On authorship of I walkt alongst a streame.

Gittings, R. Shakespeare's rival. 1960.

Poynter, F. N. L. Gervase Markham. E & S new ser 15 1962.

THOMAS DEKKER

See col 1673, above.

SAMUEL ROWLANDS
1570?–1630?

Collections

Complete works. Ed E. Gosse and S. J. H. Herrtage 3 vols Glasgow 1880 (Hunterian Club). Omits A theater of delightfull recreation, Bride; includes spurious Martin Mark-All. Ave Caesar was added separately to the works in 1886, and the contents page cancelled.

The four knaves. Ed E. F. Rimbault 1842 (Percy Soc). Includes Knave of clubbes, Knave of harts, More knaves yet?

Uncollected poems 1604?–17. Ed F. O. Waage, Gainesville 1970. Includes Humors ordinarie, A theater of delightfull recreation, Humor, antique faces, and Bride.

§1

The betraying of Christ: Judas in despaire. 1598.

The letting of humors blood in the head-vaine. 1600, 1600, 1600, [1605?] (as Humors ordinarie), 1607 (with addns), 1610, 1611 (as The letting of humours blood), 1613; ed Sir Walter Scott, Edinburgh 1814; ed F. O. Waage, Uncollected poems, Gainesville 1970 (facs of Humors ordinarie).

Tis merrie when gossips meete. 1602, 1609 (pt of A whole crew of kind gossips), [1613?] ('enlarged'), 1619 (as Well met gossip), 1627, 1673, Chiswick 1818.

Ave Caesar: God save the King. 1603; ed W. C. Hazlitt, Fugitive poetical tracts ser 2, 1875.

Looke to it, for Ile stabbe ye. 1604, 1604; ed E. V. Utterson, [Ryde] 1841.

Humors antique faces. 1605 (by E.M.); ed F. O. Waage, Uncollected poems, Gainesville 1970 (facs).

Hell's broke loose. 1605. By Rowlands?

A theater of delightfull recreation. 1605; ed F. O. Waage, Uncollected poems, Gainesville 1970 (facs).

A terrible battell betweene time and death. [1606?].

Diogines lanthorne. 1607, 1608, [1608?], 1628 (for 1608?), 1628, 1631, 1634, 1659.

Democritus: or Doctor Merry-Man his medicines against melancholy humors. [1607], 1609 (as Doctor Merrie-Man: or nothing but mirth), 1614 (title-page only), 1616, 1618, 1619, 1623, 1627, 1642, 1657, 1671, 1681.

Humors looking-glasse. 1608 (mainly from Humors antique faces and Humors ordinarie, 1607); ed J. P. Collier 1870.

The famous historie of Guy Earle of Warwick. 1609, [c. 1620], [c. 1625], 1632, 1635, 1649, 1654, 1667, [1680?], [1680?], [1699?].

A whole crew of kind gossips all met to be merry. 1609 (with Tis merrie when gossips meete), 1613 ('inlarged' as A crew of kind gossips), 1663 (in A crew of kind London gossips), 1684.

The knave of clubbes. 1609 (non-extant first edn A merry meeting: or 'tis merry when knaves meet, 1600), 1611, 161[2?], 1612, 1612, 1613; ed E. V. Utterson, [Ryde] 1841; ed E. F. Rimbault, The four knaves, 1843 (Percy Soc).

The knave of harts: haile fellow well met. 1612 (anon), 1613; ed E. V. Utterson, [Ryde] 1840; ed E. F. Rimbault, The four knaves, 1843 (Percy Soc).

More knaves yet? the knaves of spades and diamonds. [1613], [1613?] (with addns); ed E. V. Utterson, [Ryde] 1841; ed E. F. Rimbault, The four knaves, 1843 (Percy Soc).

Sir Thomas Overbury: or the poysoned knights complaint. [1614?].

A fooles bolt is soone shott. 1614.

The melancholie knight. 1615, 1615 (title-page only); ed E. V. Utterson, [Ryde] 1841.

The bride. 1617; ed A. C. Potter, Boston 1905; ed F. O. Waage, Uncollected poems, Gainesville 1970 (facs).

A sacred memorie of the miracles wrought by Jesus Christ. 1618.

The nigt-raven. 1620, 1634; ed E. V. Utterson, [Ryde] 1841.

A paire of spy-knaves. [1620?].

Good newes and bad newes. 1622; ed E. V. Utterson, [Ryde] 1841.

Heavens glory, seeke it; hearts vanitie, flye it; Hells horror, fere it. 1628 (with M. Sparke?), 1639 (as A most excellent treatise containing the way to seek Heavens glory), 1657 (as Time well improved).

§2

Gosse, E. In his Seventeenth-century studies, 1883. Rptd from his edn of Complete works.

Davenport, A. Rowlands and Thomas Lodge. N & Q 2 Jan 1943.

George, T. Rowlands's The betraying of Christ and Guevara's The mount of Calvarie: an example of Elizabethan plagiarism. N & Q Dec 1967.

JOHN TAYLOR
1580–1653

Bibliographies

Johnston, W. The thumb bibles of Taylor. Aberdeen 1910 (priv ptd); Pbns Edinburgh Bibl Soc 9 1913.

Stone, W. M. The Verbum sempiternum of Taylor. Amer Collector 5 1927.

Collections

All the workes of John Taylor the water-poet: beeing sixty and three in number, with sundry new additions, corrected, revised. 1630, 3 pts 1868–9 (Spenser Soc).

Works of John Taylor the water poet not included in the folio volume of 1630. 5 pts 1870–8 (Spenser Soc).

The old book collector's miscellany. Ed C. Hindley 4 vols 1871–3. Vol 1 has 6, vol 2 7, vol 3 6, vol 4 2 pieces by Taylor.

Works. Ed C. Hindley 1872. 21 pieces and bibliography.

Early prose and poetical works. 1888. 13 pieces.

§ I

Great Britaine, all in blacke for the incomparable losse of Henry, our late worthy Prince. 1612.

The sculler, rowing from Tiber to Thames. 1612, 1614 (as Taylors water-worke).

Laugh and be fat: or a commentary upon the Odcombyan banket. [1612].

The eighth wonder of the world: or Coriats escape from his supposed drowning; with his peregrination through the Turkish territories. 1613.

Odcombs complaint: or Coriats funerall epicedium. 1613.

Heavens blessing, and earths joy: or a true relation of the al-beloved mariage of Fredericke and Elizabeth. 2 pts 1613; ed Sir W. Scott, Somers tracts vol 3, 1809; ed J. Nichols, Progresses of James I vol 2, 1828.

The nipping or snipping of abuses; with a proclamation concerning tobacco. 1614.

Verbum sempiternae. 2 pts 1614, 1616 (corrected, as Verbum sempiternum), 1627, 1631, Aberdeen 1670, London 1678 (as The epitome of the Bible), 1693 (with title of 2nd edn), [1693], [1700?], 1720, 1818 (from 1693), 1849 (from [1700?]), New York [1889] (from 1720, as The thumb bible), Aberdeen 1908 (from 1614).

[The watermens suit, concerning players]. [1614?] (anon); rptd 'Basil Brown' (Isabelle Brown), Supposed caricature of the Droeshout portrait of Shakespeare, New York 1911.

Faire and fowle weather. 1615.

Taylors Urania: or his heavenly Muse; with a briefe narration of the thirteene sieges of Jerusalem. 1615.

Taylors revenge: or the rymer William Fennor firkt. 1615.

A cast over the water given gratis to William Fennor, the rimer. 1615.

The booke of martyrs: 1616, 1617 (anon), 1627, [1631?], 1633, 1635, 1639.

The Dolphins danger and deliverance: being a ship of 220 tunne. 1617.

Three weekes, three daies and three houres observations and travel from London to Hamburgh. 1617; ed C. Hindley 1873.

Jack a Lent: his beginning and entertainment. [1617?], 1620.

Master Thomas Coriat to his friends in England. 1618. Anon; satirical verses signed J.T.

A briefe remembrance of all the English monarchs from the Normans Conquest. 1618, 1618, 1621, 1622, 1622 (advertisement).

The pennyles pilgrimage: or the money-lesse perambulation of John Taylor from London to Edenborough. 1618.

A kicksey winsey: or a lerry come-twang, where-in John Taylor hath satyrically suited his bad debters for his returne from Scotland. 1619, 1624 (as The scourge of basenesse).

An English-mans love to Bohemia: farewell to that honorable expedition. 1620.

Fill gut and pinch belly. 1620. Not by Taylor?

The life and death of the Virgin Mary. 1620, 1622.

The praise of hemp-seed; with the voyage of Mr Roger Bird and the writer hereof in a boat of brown-paper from London to Quinborough in Kent. 1620, [1623].

Taylor his travels from London to Prague. 1620, 1621 (rev).

The Muses mourning: or funerall sonnets for the death of John Moray. [c. 1620].

The colde tearme: or the metamorphosis of the River of Thames. [1621]. Anon; by Taylor?

A shilling: or the travailes of twelve-pence. [1621], 1635 (as The travels of twelve-pence).

Superbiae flagellum: or the whip of pride against aspersions upon poets. 1621.

Taylors goose, describing the wilde goose. 1621.

Taylors motto: et habeo, et careo, et curo. 1621, [1621].

The unnaturall father: or the cruell murther committed by one John Rowse. 1621 (anon); ed C. Hindley 1873.

The subjects joy for the Parliament. [1621].

The praise, antiquity and commodity of beggery, beggers and begging. 1621.

An arrant thiefe; with a comparison betweene a thiefe and a booke. 1622, 1625, 1635.

A common whore with all these graces grac'd. 1622, 1622, 1625, 1635.

The great O Toole. 1622, 1623 (with A verry merry wherry-ferry-voyage, as O Toole the great).

A memorial of all the English monarchs. 1622, 1630 (expanded).

Sir Gregory Nonsence his newes from no place. 1622; ed C. Hindley 1873.

Taylors farewell to the Tower-bottles. 1622.

A verry merry wherry-ferry voyage: or Yorke by sea from London by John Taylor and Job Pennell. 1622, 1623 (with O Toole the great); ed C. Hindley 1873.

The water-cormorant his complaint. 1622.

Honour conceal'd strangely reveal'd: or the worthy praise of Archibald Armstrong. 1623.

The praise and vertue of a jayle and jaylers. 1623.

The world runnes on wheeles. 1623, 1635.

A new discovery by sea with a wherry from London to Salisbury. 1623; ed C. Hindley 1873.

Prince Charles his welcome from Spaine. 1623; ed Sir Walter Scott, Somers Tracts vol 2, 1809.

The praise of cleane linnen. 1624, 1624.

Taylors pastorall: or the noble antiquitie of shepheards. 1624.

True loving sorow upon the funerall of Lewis Steward Duke of Richmond and Linox. 1624.

For the sacred memoriall of Charles Howard, Earle of Nottingham. 1625. Anon.

A living sadnes in duty consecrated to the memory of our late soveraigne James. [1625].

The fearefull summer: or Londons calamity. Oxford 1625, Oxford (for London) 1625, London 1636.

Christian admonitions. Oxford 1625 (as pt of The fearefull summer, above), [London c. 1630] (separately).

A warning for swearers. Oxford 1625 (as pt of The fearefull summer, above), Oxford (for London) 1625, London 1626 (separately).

A funerall elegie in memory of Lancelot, Bishop of Winchester. 1626.

Wit and mirth. 1626, 1628, 1629, 1635 (abridged); ed W. C. Hazlitt, Shakespeare jest-books vol 3, 1864.

An armado or navye of 103 ships and other vessels who have the art to sayle by land as well as by sea, morrally rigd, mand, munitioned. 1627, 1635.

A famous fight at sea: foure English ships in the Gulfe of Persia. 1627.

A dog of war: or the travels of Drunkard, the famous curre. [1628?], 1927.

The churches deliverances. 1630.

A meditation on the passion. 1630.

The great eater of Kent: or part of the exploits of Nicholas Wood. 1630; ed C. Hindley 1873.

The needles excellency. 1631, 1634, 1636, 1640. The praise of the needle, and Certaine sonnets.

The complaint of Christmas and the teares of twelfetyde. 1631.

Taylor on Thame Isis: or the description of the Thame and Isis. 1632.

The triumphs of fame and honour at the inauguration of R. Parkhurst into the office of Lord Maior. 1634.

A bawd. 1635.

The olde old very olde man: or the age and long life of Thomas Par. 1635, 1635 (with Postscript), [1700?]; Harleian miscellany, 1744 etc; ed J. Caulfield, Curious tracts, 1794; ed C. Hindley 1873; tr Dutch, 1636.

The coaches overthrow. [1636]. Anon.

A brave, memorable and dangerous sea-fight foughten neere the road of Tittawan in Barbary. 1636.

The honorable and memorable foundations of divers cities within ten shires; also a relation of the wine tavernes. 1636.

Taylors travels and circular perambulation of London and Westminster. 1636.

A funerall elegie in memory of Benjamin Jonson. 1637. Anon.

The phoenix of these late times. 1637, 1637. Anon; testimonial verses.

The carriers cosmographie: or a briefe relation of the innes in and neere London. 1637, [c. 1660] (abridged as A brief director); ed E. W. Ashbee, Occasional facsimile reprints, 1869; ed E. Arber, English garner vol 1, 1877.

Drinke and welcome: or the historie of the drinks in use now, by Haldricke van Speagle, translated. 1637; ed E. W. Ashbee, Occasional facsimile reprints, 1871.

Stripping, whipping and pumping: or the five mad shavers of Drury-lane. 1638.

A sad and deplorable loving elegy to the memory of M. Richard Wyan. [1638].

Taylors feast, contayning twenty-seaven dishes. 1638.

Bull, beare and horse. 1638.

Newes and strange newes from St Christophers of a hurry-cano; whereunto is added the accident at Withicombe in Devon. 1638; ed C. H. Wilkinson, Two tracts, 1946. By Taylor?

Make-peace, Mary. Divers crabtree lectures: the severall languages that shrews read. 1639.

A juniper lecture; with the description of all sorts of women: second impression. 1639, 1652.

A most horrible, terrible, tollerable, termagant satyre. [1639].

Part of this summers travels: or news from Hell, Hull and Hallifax etc. [1639]; ed C. Hindley 1873.

Most curious Mercurius Britannicus. [164-?]. By Taylor?

Differing worships, or the oddes betweene some knights service and Gods: or Tom Nash his ghost, the old Martin queller. 1640.

Tattlewell, Mary. The womens sharp revenge: or an answer to Sir Seldome Sober. 1640. By Taylor?

A valorous and perillous sea-fight. 1640, 1640 (as A brave and valiant sea-fight upon the coast of Cornewall).

The complaint of M. Tenter-hooke the projector and Sir Thomas Dodger the patentee. 1641.

The Irish footman's poetry: or George the runner against Henry the Walker, in defence of John the swimmer. 1641 (anon; by Taylor?); ed W. C. Hazlitt, Fugitive tracts ser 2, 1875.

A pedlar and a Romish priest. 1641, 1699 (rev as A dialogue between a pedler and a popish priest).

A swarme of sectaries. 1641.

A reply as true as steele to An answer to A swarme of sectaries. 1641.

The discovery of a swarme of seperatists. 1641. By Taylor?

The Hellish parliament: being a counter-parliament to this in England. 1641.

The liar. 1641. Anon.

Religions enemies. 1641, 1641. By Taylor?

The Pope's benediction. 1641. By Taylor?

A letter from Rhoan in France. 1641. By Taylor?

The Brownists conventicle. 1641. By Taylor?

The Brownists synagogue[s]: or a late discovery of their conventicles. 1641. By Taylor?

Englands comfort and Londons joy expressed in the royall entertainment of King Charles at his returne from Scotland. 1641.

John Taylors last voyage with a scullers boate from London to Hereford. 1641.

New preachers new. [1641], 1821.

Lucifers lacky or the Devils new creature: being the true character of a dissembling Brownist. 1641. By Taylor?

The answer to the rattle-heads. 1641[2]. By Taylor?

A tale in a tub: or a tub lecture by My-heele Mendsoale, an inspired Brownist. 1641[2] ('by J.T.'), 1642.

To the right honorable assembly of the House of Commons, the petition of the watermen. 1642.

The aprentices advice to the XII bishops. 1642.

A delicate, dainty, damnable dialogue between the Devill and a Jesuite. 1642.

Cornu-copia. 1642. By Taylor?

Religions lotterie. 1642. By Taylor?

St Hillaries teares shed upon all professions. 1642, 1642; ed Harleian Miscellany vol 2, 1809. By Taylor?

Short compendious. 1642. By Taylor?

A three-fold discourse betweene three neighbours, Aldgate, Bishopsgate and John Heyden. 1642; ed E. W. Ashbee, Occasional facsimile reprints, 1871. By Taylor?

Heads of all fashions. 1642 (by J.M.); ed E. W. Ashbee, Occasional facsimile reprints, 1871.

Mad fashions, od fashions, all out of fashions. 1642; ed E. W. Ashbee, Occasional facsimile reprints, 1871; ed C. Hindley 1873; 1955 (Roxburghe Club of San Francisco).

A plea for prerogative, by Thorny Aylo, alias John Tayler. 1642.

An apology for private preaching. [1642] ('by T.J.'), 1642.

An honest answer to the late Apologie for private preaching. [1642] ('by T.J.').

A cluster of coxcombes: the donatists, publicans, disciplinarians, anabaptists and Brownists. 1642.

The Devil turn'd round-head. [1642]. Anon.

Grand Plutoes remonstrance. 1642. By Taylor?

An humble desired union betweene prerogative and priviledge. 1642.

John Taylors manifestation and just vindication against Josua Church. 1642.

A seasonable lecture disburthened from Henry Walker, taken in short writing by Thorny Ailo. 1642.

The whole life and progresse of Henry Walker. 1642; ed C. Hindley 1873.

A full and compleat answer against the writer of A tale in a tub, by Thorny Ailo, annagram. 1642.

A Puritane set forth in his lively colours: or K. James his description of a Puritan [from Basilicon doron], whereunto is added the round-heads character with the character of an holy sister. 1642 (3 characters). By Taylor?

A description of the round-head and rattle head. 1642. By Taylor?

The divisions of the Church of England crept in. 1642. By Taylor?

The anatomy of the separatists alias Brownists. 1642. By Taylor?

The diseases of the times. [1642]. By Taylor?

Rare physick for the church sick of an ague. 1642 (for 1643).

Truth's triumph in the gracious preservation of the King. [Oxford] 1643.

The conversion, confession, contrition of a rebellious round-head. 1643.

An intercepted letter sent to London from a spie at Oxford. 1643.

A letter sent to London from a spie at Oxford, by Thorny Ailo. Oxford 1643.

A preter-pluperfect spick and span new nocturnall. [Oxford] 1643.

The noble cavalier caracterised, and a rebellious caviller cauterised. [Oxford? 1643].

A dialogue between a Brownist and a schismatick. 1643. By Taylor?

Some small and simple reasons, delivered in a hollow-tree, by Aminadab Blower, against the liturgy. [Oxford 1643]; Harleian miscellany vol 7, 1744 etc. By Taylor?

Tom Tel-troths come. 1643. By Taylor?

Love one another: a tub lecture preached at Watford in Hartfordshire at a coventicle by John Alexander, a joyner. [1643]. Anon.

Mercurius Aquaticus: or the water-poets answer to Mercurius Britanicus. [Oxford] 1644.

Mad verse, sad verse, glad verse and bad verse. [Oxford 1644].

Ad populum. 1644.

John Taylor being yet unhanged sends greeting to John Booker. [Oxford] 1644.

Mercurius Infernalis: or orderlesse orders by a committee of the Divell. [Oxford] 1644.

No Mercurius Aulicus; with the pretended besiedging of Oxford, also the breaking of Booker. [Oxford] 1644.

Crop-eare curried: or Tom Nash his ghost declaring the pruining of Prinnes two last parricidicall pamphlets. [Oxford] 1644 (for 1645).

The generall complaint of the Commons. [Oxford 1645] ('by Jo-Ta.').

The causes of the diseases of this kingdom. [Oxford] 1645.

Aqua-Musae: or Cacafogo, cacadaemon, Captain George Wither wrung in the withers. [Oxford 1644] (for 1645).

Rebells anathematized. Oxford 1645.

A most learned speech by Miles Corbet, revised. [Oxford 1645].

Oxford besiedged, surprised, taken. [Oxford] 1645 ('by Io-Ta.').

A briefe relation of the idiotismes of Miles Corbet, by Antho. Roily. 1646.

A letter sent to George Wither. 1646 (signed Alethe-graphus [= Taylor?]); ed B[rook] P[ulham] 1834.

The complaint of Christmas. [Oxford 1646].

A recommendation to Mercurius Morbicus. 1647. Anon; by Taylor?

The world turn'd upside down. 1647.

The Kings most excellent majesties wellcome to Hampton Court. 1647; ed C. Hindley 1871.

A fresh whip. 1647. By Taylor?

Westminster fayre, newly proclaimed. 1647. By Taylor?

The fooles of fate: or the unravelling of the parliament and army. 1648. By Taylor?

A brown dozen of drunkards. 1648. By Taylor?

ΊΠΠ-ΑΝΘΡΩΠΟΣ: or an ironicall expostulation for the horse of the Lord Mayor of London. 1648. Anon.

The wonder of a kingdome. 1648.

Tailors travels from London to the Isle of Wight. 1648; ed J. O. Halliwell (-Phillipps), Literature of sixteenth and seventeenth centuries illustrated, 1851.

Mercurius Nonsensicus. [London?] 1648. By Taylor?

Mercurius Melancholicus. 1648. By Martin Parker and Taylor?

Mercurius Melancholicus for King Charles the Second. 1649. By Taylor?

Winstanley, G. The true levellers standard advanced. 1649. Preface by Taylor.

The number and names of all the Kings of England and Scotland. 1649, 1650.

John Taylors wanderings to see the wonders of the west. 1649; ed E. W. Ashbee 1869 (facs); ed C. Hindley 1873.

Taylors arithmeticke. [1650?], 1650, 1653.

A late weary merry voyage from London to Gravesend to Cambridge. 1650.

Mercurius Pacificus. [1650]. Anon; probably by Taylor.

Alterations strange. 1651.

Epigrammes; besides two new made satyres. 1651.

Ale ale-vated into the ale-titude: or a learned oration before a civill assembly of ale-drinkers between Paddington and Hogsdon. 1651, 1652, 1653, 1656.

Ranters of both sexes. 1651.

Nonsence upon sence. [1651].

Christmas in and out. 1652, 1653.

The impartialist satyre that ever was seen. 1652 (anon), 1653.

Misselanies. 1652.

News from tenebris. 1652.

The names of all the dukes, marquesses etc dead or living since Elizabeth. 1652, 1653.

A short relation of a long journey round Wales. [1653]; ed J. O. Halliwell(-Phillips) 1852; ed C. Hindley 1873.

The certain travailes of an uncertain journey. [1654]; ed C. Hindley 1873; ed J. B. Caldecott, Sussex Archaeological Collections 81 1940 (in part).

The essence of nonsense upon sence. [1654].

A dreadful battle between a Taylor and a louse. 2 pts [1655?].

The trayters perspective-glass. 1622. By Taylor?

The suddaine turne of ffortunes wheale. [1631]; ed J. O. Halliwell (-Phillipps), Contributions to early English literature, 1849 (from ms).

§2

Lohmann, F. Taylor the water-poet: sein Leben und seine Werke nach der Folio von 1630. Dülmen 1911.

Thorp, Willard. John Taylor, water poet. Texas Rev 8 1922.

Rushforth, M. Two Taylor manuscripts at Leonard Lichfield's press. Library 4th ser 11 1931.

Taylor, E. G. R. Taylor the water-poet and the transport problems of the early Stuart period. Scottish Geographical Mag 49 1933.

Notestein, W. In his Four worthies, 1956.

Kendall, Lyle H. Taylor's piracy of the Pack-mans paternoster. PBSA 57 1963. In A pedlar and a Romish priest.

RICHARD BRATHWAIT
1588?–1673

§1

The golden fleece; whereto bee annexed two elogies, Narcissus change and Aesons dotage. 1611.

The poets willowe: or the passionate shepheard. 1614.

The prodigals teares: or his fare-well to vanity. 1614.

The schollers medley: or an intermixt discourse upon historicall and poeticall relations. 1614, 1638 (as A survey of history: or a nursery for gentry), 1651 (as History surveyed in a brief epitomy), 1652.

A strappado for the Divell: epigrams and satyres, by Μισοσυκος. 2 pts 1615 (pt 2: Loves labyrinth: or the true lovers knot); ed J. W. Ebsworth, Boston 1878.

Disputatio inauguralis: jus potandi exponet Blasius Multibibus. [Leipzig?] 1616, 1617, 1626, 1627, [1630?], 1688; tr German, 1616; tr 2 pts 1617 (as A solemne joviall disputation briefely shadowing the law of drinking) (pt 2: The smoaking age, with the life and death of tobacco, dedicated by Eucapnus Nepenthiacus); The law of drinking, ed W. B. Hooker and M. H. Tillit, New Haven 1903; The smoaking age, 1703 (abridged).

Remains after death: divers memorable observances upon discourse of epitaphs, by R.B. (Musophilus) 1618. In Patrick Hannay, A happy husband, 1619.

The description of a good wife: or a rare one amongst women, by R.B. (Musophilus). In Patrick Hannay, A happy husband, 1619.

Buenting, H. Itinerarium totius sacrae scripturae: or the travels of the patriarchs, prophets etc, done into English by R.B. [Brathwait?]. 1619, 1623, 1629, 1636.

A new spring shadowed in sundry pithie poems, by Musophilus. 1619.

Essaies upon the five senses, with a pithie one upon detraction. 1620, 1625 (for 1635) (rev and enlarged); ed S. E. Brydges, Archaica vol 2, 1815.

The shepheards tales. Pt 1, 1621, 1623 (for 1621) (with Natures embassie), 1626; pt 2, 1621 (in Natures embassie).

Natures embassie: or the wilde-mans measures. 5 pts 1621, 1623 (for 1621) (as and with The shepherds tales, above), 1626 (as and with The shepherds tales revised and revived); ed J. W. Ebsworth, Boston 1877; ed S. E. Brydges as Brathwayte's odes: or Philomel's tears, Lee Priory Kent 1815 (extracts).

Times curtaine drawne: or the anatomie of vanitie. 2 pts 1621 (pt 2: Panedone: or health from Helicon).

Querela clientis; medela patientis. [c. 1625?].

The English gentleman: sundry excellent rules. 1630, 1633 (rev and enlarged), 1641 (with The English gentlewoman, below), 1652 (as Times treasury), 1655, 1656.

The English gentlewoman drawne out to the full body. 1631, 1641 (with The English gentleman, above).

Whimzies: or a new cast of characters, by Clitus-Alexandrinus. 2 pts 1631 (pt 2: A cater-character throwne out of a box); ed J. O. Halliwell (-Phillipps) 1859.

Novissima tuba. 1632, 1658 (with Lignum vitae); tr John Vicars as The last trumpet: or a six-fold Christian dialogue, 1635.

A strange metamorphosis of man, transformed into a wildernesse. 1634 (anon; by Brathwait?); ed D. C. Allen, Baltimore 1949.

Anniversaries upon his Panarete, Mrs Brathwait. 1634. Anon.

Anniversaries upon his Panarete: the second yeeres annivers. 1635. Anon.

Raglands Niobe: or Eliza's elegie. 1635.

The Arcadian Princess: or the triumph of justice, by Mariano Silesio. 1635.

The fatall nuptiall: or mournefull marriage, the drowning of 47 persons. 1636. Anon.

Barnabae itinerarium, Mirtili & Faustuli nominibus insignitum. [c. 1636] (Latin version of first 2 pts only), 4 pts [1638] (as Barnabees journall under the names of Mirtilus and Faustulus, shadowed, by Corymbaeus), 1805; ed J. H[aslewood] 1818 (with bibliography), 1822; rev W. C. Hazlitt 1876; ed D. B. Thomas 1933.

R[andolph], T. Cornelianum dolium: comoedia lepidissima. 1638. Ed Brathwait?

A spirituall spicerie: sundrie sweet tractates. 1638.

The psalmes of David and of other holy prophets paraphras'd, by R.B. 1638. *See col 1911, above.*

An epitome of all the lives of the Kings of France, translated by R.B. 1639.

Ar't asleepe husband? a boulster lecture, by Philogenes Panedonius. 1640.

The two Lancashire lovers: or the excellent history of Philocles and Doriclea, by Musaeus Palatinus. 1640.

A paraphrase upon the Lords prayer. 1641. By Brathwait?

The penitent pilgrim. 1641; rptd 1847; ed G. E. Watts 1897 (abridged).

Astraea's tears: upon the death of Sir R. Hulton. 2 pts 1641. Anon. Pt 2: Panaretees triumph.

Mercurius Britannicus judicialis. [1641?], [1641?]; Latin text ed Sir Walter Scott, Somers tracts vol 5, 1809; tr 1641, 1641, 1641 (with addns), 1641.

The Devills white boyes. 1644. By Brathwait?

A mustur roll of the evill angels, by R.B. gent. 1655 (also as Capitall hereticks), 1659.

Lignum vitae. 1658 (with Novissima tuba).

An excellent piece of concepted poesy. 1658. By Brathwait?

The honest ghost: or a voice from the vault, by Parthenius Osiander and Polymorphus Simianus. 1658. Anon.

Panthalia: or the royal romance, by Castalion Pomerano [Brathwait?]. 1659.

To his Majesty upon his happy arrivall in our late discomposed Albion. 1660.

The chimneys scuffle. 1662. Anon.

Tragi-comoedia, cui in titulum inscribitur regicidium. 2 pts 1665.

The captive-captain: or the restrain'd cavalier. 1665 (signed R.B.).

A comment upon the two tales of Chaucer, the Miller's tale and the Wife of Bath, by R.B. 1665; ed C. F. E. Spurgeon 1901 (Chaucer Soc).

The history of moderation, by Hesychius Pamphilus. 1669, 1683 (as The trimmer).

Some rules and orders for the government of the house of an Earle. In R. Triphook, Miscellanea antiqua anglicana, 1821 (from Jacobean ms).

§2

Cowper, H. S. Notes on Braithwaite of Burneside. Trans Cumberland & Westmorland Antiquarian & Archaeological Soc 22 1922.

Black, M. W. Brathwait: an account of his life and works. Philadelphia 1928. With bibliography.

Boyce, B. History and fiction in Panthalia: or the royal romance. JEGP 57 1958.

E. D. P.

II. MINOR POPULAR LITERATURE

Tracts – Pamphlets – Jest-books – Burlesques – Broadside Ballads etc

(1) BIBLIOGRAPHIES

Beloe, W. Anecdotes of literature and scarce books. 6 vols 1807–12.

Ames, J. and W. Herbert. Typographical antiquities. Ed T. F. Dibdin 4 vols 1810–19.

Collier, J. P. A bibliographical and critical account of the rarest books in the English language. 2 vols 1865.

Hazlitt, W. C. Handbook to the popular, poetical and dramatic literature of Great Britain. 1867. Bibliographical collections and notes, with suppls, general index etc 1876–1903.

Brooks, H. F. Rump songs: an index with notes. Proc Oxford Bibl Soc 5 1940.

Frank, J. Hobbled Pegasus: a descriptive bibliography of minor English poetry 1641–60. Albuquerque 1968.

(2) COLLECTIONS OF TRACTS

The Harleian miscellany: a collection of scarce, curious and entertaining pamphlets and tracts. Ed W. Oldys 8 vols 1744–6; ed T. Park 10 vols 1808–13.

Collection of scarce and valuable tracts. 16 vols 1748–52; ed Sir W. Scott 13 vols 1809–15. Somers tracts.

Brydges, S. E. Archaica: containing a reprint of scarce old English prose tracts. 2 vols 1815.

Triphook, R. Miscellanea antiqua anglicana. 7 pts 1816.

Utterson, E. V. Select pieces of early popular poetry. 2 vols 1817.

Halliwell (-Phillipps), J. O. Contributions to early English literature. 6 pts 1849.

—— The literature of the sixteenth and seventeenth centuries illustrated by reprints of very rare tracts. 1851.

Collier, J. P. Illustrations of early English popular literature. 2 vols 1863–4.

—— Illustrations of old English literature. 3 vols 1866.

Hazlitt, W. C. Remains of the early popular poetry of England. 4 vols 1864–6.

—— Fugitive tracts written in verse. 2 sers 1875.

Ashbee, E. W. Occasional facsimile reprints. 1868–72.

Hindley, C. Miscellanea antiqua anglicana: the old book collector's miscellany. 3 vols 1871–3.

Arber, E. An English garner. 8 vols 1877–90; ed T. Seccombe 12 vols 1903–4.

Edmonds, C. The Isham reprints. 2 vols 1895.

Harrison, G. B. The Bodley head quartos. 15 vols 1923 (for 1922)–6.

(3) GENERAL STUDIES

Sheavyn, P. The literary profession in the Elizabethan age. Manchester 1909; rev J. W. Saunders 1967.

Miller, E. The professional writer in Elizabethan England: a study of nondramatic literature. Cambridge Mass 1959.

Baumgartner, P. R. From medieval fool to Renaissance rogue: Cock Lorelles bote and the literary tradition. Annuale Mediaevale 4 1963.

(4) GENERAL SOCIAL SATIRES

Cocke Lorelles bote. [1506–10], [1519?], 1817 (Roxburghe Club); [ed J. Maidment], Edinburgh 1841; ed E. F. Rimbault 1842 (Percy Soc); [ed J. P. Edmond], Aberdeen 1884.

Colin Blowbols testament. [c. 1508]; ed J. O. Halliwell (-Phillipps), Nugae poeticae, 1844 (from ms); ed W. C. Hazlitt, Early English popular poetry vol 1, 1864.

A treatyse of a galaunt. [1510?], [1520?], [1522?] (with addns), [1521?] (extract); ed J. O. Halliwell (-Phillipps) 1860; ed W. C. Hazlitt, Early English popular poetry vol 3, 1864; ed E. W. Ashbee 1871 (facs).

Brinkelow, Henry. The lamentacion of a Christian against the citie of London, by R. Mors. [Bonn? 1542], [Antwerp?] 1545 (anon), [London?] 1548 (anon); ed J. M. Cowper 1874 (EETS).

—— The com-playnt of Roderyck Mors for the redresse of certen wicked lawes. [Strasbourg? 1542?], [London 1548?], [London 1548?], [London? 1560?], [London 1642] (extract, as The true coppy); ed J. M. Cowper 1874 (EETS).

The wyll of the Devyll. [1548?], [1577?], [1577?], [Edinburgh c. 1835]; ed J. P. Collier, Illustrations of early English popular literature vol 1, 1863; ed F. J. Furnivall 1871.

Borde, Andrew. The fyrst boke of the introduction of knowledge. [1555?], [1562?]; ed F. J. Furnivall 1870 (EETS).

Hill, Thomas. The shaking of the sheets or the dance of death. nd; ed W. Chappell, Popular music of the olden time vol 1, 1855.

[Rogers, John?]. The glasse of godly love. [1569]; ed F. J. Furnivall 1876 (with Tell-Trothes new yeares gift) (New Shakspere Soc).

Hake, Edward. A touchestone for this time present. 1574. Tr from Erasmus, Libellus novus et elegans de pueris.

—— Newes out of Powles churchyarde. [1579]; ed C. Edmonds 1872.

—— An oration conteyning an expostulation. [1587].

—— Of golds kingdome and this unhelping age. 1604.

Northbrooke, John. Spiritus est vicarius Christi in terra: a treatise wherein dicing, dauncing, vaine plaies or enterluds are reproved. [1577?], 1579; ed J. P. Collier 1843 (Shakespeare Soc).

Gosson, Stephen. The s[c]hoole of abuse: conteining a plesaunt invective against poets, pipers, plaiers, jesters and such like caterpillers of a commonwelth. 1579,

1579, 1587; ed J. P. Collier 1841 (Shakespeare Soc); ed E. Arber 1868. See A. F. Kinney, Gosson's art of argumentation, SE 7 1967.

[Walker, Gilbert]. A manifest detection of dice-play. [1580?]; ed J. O. Halliwell (-Phillipps) 1850 (Percy Soc); ed A. V. Judges, Elizabethan underworld, 1930.

Salter, Thomas. A contention betweene three bretheren, that is to say the whoremonger, the drunkarde and the dice-player. 1580, 1581, 1608. Tr from Philippus Beroaldus.

W[ilcox], T. A glasse for gamesters. 1581.

Stafford, W. A compendious or briefe examination of certayne ordinary complaints. 1581, 1581, 1581; ed F. D. Matthew and F. J. Furnivall 1876 (New Shakspere Soc).

Stubbes, Philip. The anatomie of abuses. 1583, 1583 (augmented), 1584–5 (rev), 1595 (rev); pt 2, 1583; pt 1, ed W. B. D. D. Turnbull 1836; ed J. P. Collier [1870]; 2 pts ed F. J. Furnivall 1877–82 (New Shakspere Soc). See T. P. Pearson, The composition and development of Phillip Stubbes's Anatomie of abuses, MLR 56 1961.

[Newton, T.] True and Christian friendshippe. 1586. Tr from Lambert Daneau. Includes A treatise touching dyce-play and prophane gaming.

R[ankins], W. The English ape, the Italian imitation, the foote-steppes of Fraunce. 1588.

Tarltons newes out of Purgatorie. 1590, [c. 1600], 1630; ed J. O. Halliwell (-Phillipps) 1844 (Shakespeare Soc).

Tell-Trothes new yeares gift and the passionate morrice. 1593; ed F. J. Furnivall 1876 (New Shakspere Soc).

B[anchieri], A[driano]. The noblenesse of the asse, by A.B. 1595.

Pleasant quippes for upstart newfangled gentlewomen. 1595 (anon), 1596; rptd C. Clark 1847; ed W. C. Hazlitt, Remains of the early popular poetry of England vol 4, 1866; ed E. J. Howard, Oxford Ohio 1942. By Stephen Gosson?

Covell, W. Polimanteia: or the meanes to judge of the fall of a commonwealth; whereunto is added a letter from England to Cambridge, Oxford, Innes of Court. Cambridge 1595. Letter rptd A. B. Grosart, Elizabethan England, Manchester 1881.

'Dando, John' and 'Harry Runt'. Maroccus extaticus: or Bankes bay horse in a trance. 1595; ed E. F. Rimbault, Early English poetry 1844 (Percy Soc).

The hospitall of incurable fooles. 1600. Tr from T. Garzoni.

Lane, John. Tom Tel-Troths message and his pens complaint. 1600; ed F. J. Furnivall 1876 (with Tell-Trothes new yeares gift) (New Shakspere Soc).

[Dekker, Thomas?]. The meeting of gallants at an ordinarie: or the walkes in Powles. 1604; ed J. O. Halliwell(-Phillips) 1841 (Percy Soc); ed F. P. Wilson, The plague pamphlets of Thomas Dekker, Oxford 1925.

Pimlyco: or runne Red-Cap. 1609; ed A. H. Bullen, Antient drolleries vol 2, Oxford 1890.

Rowley, William. A search for money: or the lamentable complaint for the losse of the wandring knight, Moun-sieur l'Argent. 1609, 1840 (Percy Soc).

J[ohnson], R[ichard]. Looke on me, London: I am an honest Englishman ripping up the bowels of mischiefe, lurking in thy sub-urbs and precincts. 1613; ed J. P. Collier, Illustrations of early English popular literature vol 2, 1864.

Cary, Walter. The present state of England expressed in this paradox: our fathers were very rich with little and wee poore with much. 1626; rptd Harleian miscellany vol 3, 1809.

Prynne, W. Healthes sicknesse: or a discourse proving the drinking of healthes to be sinfull. 1628, 1628 (corrected).
— The unlovelinesse of love-lockes. 1628, 1628.

Powell, T. Tom of all trades: or the plaine path-way to preferment. 1631; ed F. J. Furnivall 1876 (with Tell-Trothes new yeares gift) (New Shakspere Soc).

Lupton, Donald. London and the countrey carbonadoed. 1632. See col 2045, below.

The hunting of the hare; with her last wyll and testament. [1635?], [1640?], [1648?].

Peacham, Henry. The worth of a peny: or a caution to keep money. 1641, 1647, 1664, 1667, 1669, 1677, 1687, 1695; ed E. Arber, An English garner vol 6, 1883; ed A. Lang, Social England illustrated, 1903.

Hall, Thomas. Comarum ἀκοσμια: the loathsomnesse of long haire. 1654.

(5) JEST-BOOKS, COMIC DIALOGUES, BURLESQUES, MOCK PROGNOSTICATIONS, DROLLERIES ETC

Bibliographies

Esdaile, A. A list of English tales and prose romances printed before 1740. 2 pts 1912 (Bibl Soc).

Zall, P. M. English prose jestbooks in the Huntington Library: a chronological checklist 1535?–1799. Shake-spearean Research & Opportunities no 4 1969.

Collections

Facetiae. Ed T. Park 2 vols 1817.

Thoms, W. J. Early prose romances. 3 vols 1827–8, 1858 (rev), [1907] (rev).

Hazlitt, W. C. Shakespeare jest-books. 3 vols 1864.

Ashton, J. Humour, wit and satire of the seventeenth century. 1883.

Morley, H. Early prose romances. 1889; rptd in Thoms [1907], above.

Zall, P. M. A hundred merry tales and other English jestbooks of the fifteenth and sixteenth centuries. Lincoln Nebraska 1963.

— A nest of ninnies and other English jestbooks of the seventeenth century. Lincoln Nebraska 1970. Mainly selections.

§I

Howe Howleglas deseyved a wynedrawer in Lubeke. [Antwerp c. 1519?] (fragment); ed F. W. D. Brie, Eulenspiegel in England, Berlin 1903. See A merye jest [1555?], below.

[The parson of Kalenborowe]. [Antwerp c. 1520] (frag-ment); ed E. Schröder, Jahrbuch des Vereins für Niederdeutsche Sprachforschung 13 1887. From the German.

Smith, Walter. Twelve merry gestys of one called Edyth. 1525 (fragments), 1573; ed W. C. Hazlitt, Shakespeare jest-books vol 3, 1864.

A C mery talys. [1526?] (imperfect), 1526 (rev); ed S. W. Singer, Shakspeare's jest book, Chiswick 1815 (fragments), 1845; ed W. C. Hazlitt, Shakespeare jest-books vol 1, 1864; ed H. Oesterley 1866 (complete text); ed W. C. Hazlitt 1887 (facs of complete text); ed P. M. Zall 1963. From the Italian.

Tales and quicke answeres very mery and pleasant to rede. [1532?], 1567 (enlarged as Merry tales); ed S. W. Singer, Shakspeare's jest book, Chiswick 1814 (from [1532?]) with 1567 addns); ed S. W. Singer, The hundred merry tales, 1831 (from 1567); 1845 (from [1532?], with A hundred merry tales, above, as Shak-speare's merry tales); ed W. C. Hazlitt, Shakespeare jest-books vol 1, 1864 (1567 text); ed H. Oesterley,

Shakespeare's jest book, 1866 (from 1567); ed P. M. Zall, A hundred merry tales, Lincoln Nebraska 1963 (from [1532?]).

D[ernyll?], J. or W. W. A mery pronosticacion. 1544 (anon), [1577] (rev and augmented), 1623 (as A new and merrie prognostication).

Barnes,——. The treatyse answerynge the Boke of Berdes. [1548?]; ed F. J. Furnivall 1870 (EETS). Reply to a lost tract by Andrew Borde.

[Copland, William?]. A merye jest of a man that was called Howleglas. [1555?], [1560?], [1565?]; ed K. Mackenzie 1860; ed F. Ouvry 1867; ed P. M. Zall, A hundred merry tales, Lincoln Nebraska 1963 (first edn, with omissions). See Howe Howleglas [c. 1519?], above.

Bullein, William. A dialogue wherin is a goodly regimente against the fever pestilence. 1564, 1573, 1578; ed M. and A. H. Bullen 1888 (EETS). See W. S. Mitchell, Bullein: Elizabethan physician and author, Medical History 3 1959.

B[orde?], A[ndrew?]. Merie tales of the mad men of Gotam. [c. 1565], 1630, [1690?]; ed J. O. Halliwell (-Phillipps) 1840; ed W. C. Hazlitt, Shakespeare jest-books vol 3, 1864; ed S. J. Kahrl, Evanston 1965 (from newly discovered first edn).

Skelton, John. Merie tales. [1567]; ed A. Dyce, Poetical works, 1843; ed W. C. Hazlitt, Shakespeare jest-books vol 2, 1864; ed P. M. Zall 1963.

The jestes of Skogyn. [c. 1570], 1626 (as The first and best part of Scoggins jests, gathered by A. Boord), [1690?]. Pt 2, 1613 (as Scoggins jestes). Pt 1 ed W. C. Hazlitt, Shakespeare jest-books vol 2, 1864.

Sanforde, James. The garden of pleasure: contayninge most pleasante tales worthy deeds and witty sayings. 1573, 1576 (as Houres of recreation). Tr from Ludovico Guicciardini.

Des Périers, Jean. The mirrour of mirth. 1583, 1592; ed J. W. Hassell, Columbia SC 1959. Tr by T.D. See J. W. Hassell, An Elizabethan translation of the tales of Des Périers, SP 52 1955.

F[ist[on], W. The welspring of wittie conceites. 1584. Tr from Italian.

The cobler of Caunterburie. 1590, 1608, 1614 (as The merry tales), 1630 (as The tincker of Turvey); ed J. O. Halliwell (-Phillipps) 1844 (Shakespeare Soc); ed F. Ouvry 1862; ed C. C. Mish, Short fiction of the seven-teenth century, New York 1963 (from 1630).

Ferris, Richard. The most dangerous and memorable adventure of R. Ferris, who undertooke to rowe by sea to Bristowe. 1590; ed J. P. Collier, Illustrations of early

English popular literature vol 2, 1864; ed A. Lang, Social England illustrated, 1903.

Smell-knave, Simon. The fearefull and lamentable effects of two comets which shall appeare in 1591. [1590?].

Foulweather, Adam. A wonderfull, strange and miraculous prognostication for this year 1591. [1591], [1591] (corrected). See H. Brown, MLR 13 1933.

Copley, Anthony. Wits, fittes and fancies. 2 pts 1595, 1614 (anon), 1614. After Melchor de Santa Cruz de Dueñas' Floresta española.

Barckley, Sir Richard. A discourse of the felicitie of man: or his summum bonum. 1598.

[Armin, Robert]. Quips upon questions: or a clownes conceite. 1600. As by C. de C. Snuffe.

— Foole upon foole: or sixe sortes of sottes, [by] Clonnico de Curtanio Snuffe. 1600, 1605, 1608 (with addns as A nest of ninnies); ed J. P. Collier, Fools and jesters, 1842 (Shakespeare Soc) (from 3rd edn); ed P. M. Zall 1963 (from 3rd edn).

See also Works, ed A. B. Grosart, Blackburn 1880.

B[reton], N[icholas]. Pasquils passe and passeth not. 1600.

Kemp, William. Kemps nine daies wonder, performed in a daunce from London to Norwich. 1600; ed A. Dyce 1840 (Camden Soc); ed A. Lang, Social England illustrated, 1903; ed G. B. Harrison 1923; ed A. C. Ward, A miscellany of tracts, 1927.

[Corrozet, Gilles]. Memorable conceits of divers noble and famous personages. 1602.

Jacke of Dover, his quest of inquirie. 1604, 1615 (as Jacke of Dovers merrie tales); ed T. Wright 1842 (Percy Soc); ed W. C. Hazlitt, Shakespeare jest-books vol 2, 1864. From the Italian. The penniless parliament of threadbare poets not rptd with Jacke of Dover but rptd separately 1608, 1649; Harleian miscellany vol 1, 1744; ed C. Hindley, Old book collector's miscellany vol 1, 1871. The penniless parliament plagiarises Simon Smell-knave, above.

Pasquils jests, mixed with Mother Bunches merriments. 1604, 1609 (corrected with new addns), 1629, [1632?], 1635, [1650?]; ed W. C. Hazlitt, Shakespeare jest-books vol 3, 1864.

[Dekker, Thomas?]. Newes from Graves end. 1604; ed F. P. Wilson, The plague pamphlets of Thomas Dekker, Oxford 1925.

— The ravevens [i.e. ravens] almanacke. 1609, 1609, 1609.

— and George Wilkins. Jests to make you merie. 1607.

Eavesdropper, Adam. Platoes cap cast at this yeare 1604. 1604.

M[iddleton], T[homas]. The ant and the nightingale: or Father Hubburds tales. 1604, 1604 (augmented as Father Hubburds tales).

Terilo, William. A piece of Friar Bacons brazen-heads prophesie. 1604; ed J. O. Halliwell (-Phillips) 1844 (Percy Soc).

Newes from Rome, also certaine prophecies of a jew called Cabel Shilock. 1606.

Nixon, Anthony. The blacke yeare. 1606.

Merrie conceited jests of George Peale. 1607, [1620?], 1627, 1627, 1657, 1671; ed W. C. Hazlitt, Shakespeare jest-books vol 2, 1864; ed C. Hindley 1869.

Dobsons drie bobbes: sonne and heire to Skoggin. 1607; ed E. Schulz, Die englischen Schwankbücher bis herab zu Dobson's Drie Bobs (1607), Berlin 1912; ed E. A. Horsman, Oxford 1955. See B. Colgrave, Durham Univ Jnl new ser 12 1951.

Johnson, Richard. The pleasant conceites of old Hobson the merry Londoner. 1607, 1610 (enlarged), 1634, 1640; ed J. O. Halliwell (-Phillips) 1843 (Percy Soc); ed W. C. Hazlitt, Shakespeare jest-books vol 3, 1864.

— The pleasant walkes of Moore-fields. 1607; ed J. P. Collier, Illustrations of early English popular literature vol 2, 1864.

— The history of Tom Thumbe, by R[ichard?] J[ohnson?]. 1621; ed C. F. Bühler, Evanston 1965.

Certaine conceyts and jeasts. In Michael Scott, The philosophers banquet, 1609, 1614 ('inlarged'), 1633 (rev). Tr by W.B. from Mensa philosophica, also attributed to Theobaldus Anguilbertus and tr T[homas?] T[wyne?] as The schoolemaster: or teacher of table philosophie, 1576, 1583. Certaine conceyts ed W. C. Hazlitt, Shakespeare jest-books vol 3, 1864.

Tarltons jests. 1611, 1613, 1638; ed J. O. Halliwell (-Phillips) 1844 (Shakespeare Soc); ed W. C. Hazlitt, Shakespeare jest-books vol 2, 1864; ed E. W. Ashbee [1876?] (facs).

Cobbes prophecies. 1614; ed A. H. Bullen, Antient drolleries vol 1, Oxford 1890.

W[illet], R[owland]. Merry jests, concerning popes, monks and friers. 1617. Tr from N.S.

The owles almanacke. 1618, 1618; ed D. C. Allen, Baltimore 1943.

A helpe to discourse. 1619, 1620, 1621, 1623, 1627, 1628, 1629, 1630, 1631, 1635, 1636, 1638, 1640, 1648, 1654, 1663. Sometimes attributed to W[illiam] B[asse] and E. P[hilips].

[Fennor, William?]. Pasquils palinodia and his progresse to the taverne. 1619; ed J. P. Collier, Illustrations of old English literature vol 1, 1866.

Westward for smelts: or the waterman's fare of mad merry western wenches whose tales are sweet and will much content you, written by kinde Kit of Kingstone. 1620; ed J. O. Halliwell (-Phillips) 1848 (Percy Soc).

The historie of Frier Rush. 1620, 1626, 1629 (title-page only), 1659, 1810; ed W. J. Thoms, Early prose romances vol 1, 1828; ed H. Morley, Early prose romances, 1889; ed D. Senior, Some old English worthies, 1912.

The life and pranks of Long Meg of Westminster. 1620, 1635, 1636; ed R. Triphook, Miscellanea antiqua anglicana, 1816 (from 1635); ed C. Hindley, The old book collector's miscellany vol 2, 1872; ed C. C. Mish, Short fiction of the seventeenth century, New York 1963 (from 1620).

Vox graculi: or Jacke Dawes prognostication. 1622.

Painter, William. Chaucer new painted. [1623].

Bacon, Francis. Apophthegmes new and old. 1625, 1626.

H., L. Gratiae ludentes: jests from the universities. 1628 (for 1638?).

Robin Good-Fellow his mad prankes and merry jestes. 2 pts 1628, 1639; ed J. P. Collier 1841 (Percy Soc); ed J. O. Halliwell (-Phillips), Illustrations of fairy mythology, 1845 (Shakespeare Soc); ed W. C. Hazlitt, Fairy mythology of Shakespeare, 1875.

Taylor, John. Wit and mirth. 1629, 1635 (abridged); ed W. C. Hazlitt, Shakespeare jest-books vol 3, 1864.

— Taylors feast. 1638.

— Bull, beare and horse. 1638.

A banquet of jests: or change of cheare. 1630, [1632?], 1634 (4th edn with addns), 1636, 1639 (with addns); pt 2, 1633, 1636.

A pleasant history of the life and death of Will Summers. 1637, 1676; ed J. Caulfield 1794.

A new booke of mistakes. 1637. Anon; attributed to Robert Chamberlain.

The booke of bulls: baited with two centuries of bold jests, collected by A.S. 1638. Anon; attributed to Robert Chamberlain.

[Chamberlain, Robert]. Conceits, clinches, flashes and whimzies. 1639, 1640 (enlarged as Jocabella: or a cabinet of conceits); ed J. O. Halliwell (-Phillips) 1860; ed W. C. Hazlitt, Shakespeare jest-books vol 3, 1864.

S., S. Paradoxes or encomions in the praise of being lowsey, treachery, nothing, beggary. 1653.

Cox, R. Actaeon and Diana. [1655?], 1656.

M[ennes], J[ohn]. Musarum deliciae. 1655, 1656.

— Wit and drollery. 1656; ed E.M.1661, 1682.

— Wit restor'd. 1658.

[Gayton, E.] Wit revived. 1656, 1674.

[Phillipps, John]. Sportive wit. 1656.

— Choyce drollery. 1656; ed J. W. Ebsworth, Boston 1876.
[Wright, Abraham]. Parnassus biceps. 1656; ed G. Thorn-Drury 1927.
Here's Jack in a box, that will conjure the fox. 1656.
Mirth in abundance. 1659.
The hangmans joy. [1660].
F[ord], E. Fair play in the lottery. [1660].
[Armstrong, Archibald]. A choice banquet of witty jests. 1660, 1665.
R[owlands], S[amuel]. A crew of kind London gossips, to which is added wit and drollery. 1663, 1684.
The sack-full of newes. 1673; ed J. O. Halliwell (-Phillipps) 1861; ed W. C. Hazlitt, Shakespeare jest-books vol 2, 1864; ed M. Lawlis, Elizabethan prose fiction, New York 1968. From Italian.

§2

Herford, C. H. Studies in the literary relations of England and Germany in the sixteenth century. Cambridge 1886.

Clouston, W. A. The book of noodles: stories of simpletons, or fools and their follies. 1888.
Brie, F. W. D. Eulenspiegel in England. Berlin 1903.
de Vocht, Henry. De invloed van Erasmus op de engelsche tooneelliteratuur der xvie en xviie eeuwen: 1, Shakespeare jest-books—Lyly. Ghent 1908.
Schulz, E. Die englischen Schwankbücher bis 1607. Berlin 1912.
Field, J. E. The myth of the pent cuckoo: a study in folklore. 1913. About the wisemen of Gotham.
Wilson, F. P. Some English mock-prognostications. Library 4th ser 19 1939; rev in his Shakespearian and other studies, Oxford 1969.
— The English jestbooks of the sixteenth and early seventeenth centuries. HLQ 2 1939; rev ibid.
Smith, C. C. The seventeenth-century drolleries. Harvard Lib Bull 6 1952.
Kahrl, S. J. The medieval origins of the sixteenth-century English jest-books. Stud in Renaissance 13 1966.

(6) QUOTATIONS, MAXIMS, PROVERBS, ADAGES

Collections and Bibliographies

Case, A. E. A bibliography of English poetical miscellanies 1521–1750. Oxford 1935 (Oxford Bibl Soc).
The Oxford dictionary of English proverbs. Ed W. G. Smith, Oxford 1935, 1948 (rev); rev F. P. Wilson, Oxford 1970.
Tilley, M. P. A dictionary of proverbs in England in the seventeenth and eighteenth centuries. Ann Arbor 1950.
Wilson, F. P. English proverbs and dictionaries of proverbs. Library 4th ser 26 1946.
— English proverbs. Bodleian Lib Record 2 1941–9.
Whiting, B. J. and H. W. Proverbs, sentences and proverbial phrases from English writings mainly before 1500. Cambridge Mass 1968.

§1

Taverner, Richard. The garden of wysdom. Bk 1, 1539, 1539, [1540?] (augmented); bk 2, 1539; 2 bks nd, [1550?], [1556?]. See C. R. Baskervill, SP 29 1932.
— Proverbes or adagies. 2 pts 1539, 1545 (with addns), 1550, 1552, 1569. From Erasmus.
Udall, Nicholas. Apophthegmes. 1542, 1564. From Erasmus.
— Floures for Latine spekynge. 1533, 1538, 1560, 1575 (with J. Higgins), 1581. From Terence.
Coverdale, M. A shorte recapitulacion or abrigement of Erasmus Enchiridion. [Antwerp?] 1545.
Heywood, John. A dialogue conteinyng the nomber in effect of all the proverbes in the Englishe tongue. 1546, 1550, 1556, 1561; ed R. E. Habenicht, Berkeley and Los Angeles 1963.
Baldwin, William. A treatise of morall phylosophie: contaynyng the sayinges of the wyse. 2 pts 1547, 1550, [1552?], [c. 1555] (with addns by Baldwin), [c. 1555] (with addns by T. Paulfreymann), 1557 (with further addns by Paulfreymann), 1564 (with further addns by Paulfreymann), 1567 (with further addns by Paulfreymann), 1571, 1575, 1579 (with further addns by Paulfreymann), 1584, 1587, 1591, 1596, 1600, 1605, 1610, [c. 1620] (with further addns by Paulfreymann), [c. 1620], [c. 1635], [c. 1640], 1651; ed E. Arber, The sayings of the wise, 1907 (from c. 1555); ed R. H. Bowers, Gainesville 1967 (from c. 1620).
Blage, Thomas. A schole of wise conceytes. 1569, 1572.
Florio, John. Florio his firste fruites. [1578?].
— Second frutes. 1591; ed R. C. Simonini, Gainesville 1953 (facs).
Crewe, Thomas. The nosegay of morall philosophie. 1580. From Gabriel Meurier.

R[obson], S[imon]. The choise of change. 1585, 1585, 1585, 1585, 1585, 1585, 1598, 1598, 1636 (selected as The figure of three: or a patterne of good counsell).
Fletcher, A. Certaine very proper and most profitable similes. [1595].
Bodenham, John. Politeuphuia: wits commonwealth. 1597, 1598 (corrected and augmented), 1598 (corrected and augmented), 1608, [1608?], [after 1612], [c. 1615], [1620?], [1626?], [1628?], [1630?], [c. 1640], 1641, 1647, 1650, 1653, 1655, 1661, 1663, 1667, 1669, 1671, 1674, 1678, 1684, 1688, 1699. Compiled for Bodenham by Nicholas Ling. See J. W. Hebel, Nicholas Ling and Englands Helicon, Library 4th ser 5 1925; D. T. Starnes, Sir Thomas Elyot and the Sayings of the philosophers, SE 13 1933, The French academie and Wits commonwealth, PQ 13 1934; F. B. Williams, Bodenham, SP 31 1934.
— Bel-vedere: or the garden of the Muses. Ed A. M[unday?] 1600, 1610. See C. Crawford, F. Studien 43 1911; D. T. Starnes, Some sources of Wits theatre of the little world (1599) and Bodenham's Belvedere (1600), PQ 30 1951; C. T. Wright, Anthony Mundy and the Bodenham miscellanies, PQ 40 1961. See also under Politeuphuia, above.
Meres, F. Palladis tamia: wits treasury. 1598; Poetrie, ed D. C. Allen, Urbana 1933.
Allott, R. Wits theater of the little world. 1599. See Bodenham, above.
— Englands Parnassus: or the choysest flowers of our moderne poets. 1600; rptd 1814 in Heliconia 1815; ed J. P. Collier, Seven English poetical miscellanies [vol 6], [1867]; Menston 1970 (facs).
Cawdrey, Robert. A treasurie or store-house of similies. 1600, 1609.
[Wrednott, William]. Palladis palatium. 1604.
Breton, Nicholas. Wits private wealth. 1607, 1611, 1612, 1613, 1615, 1629, 1639, 1642, 1670.
— Crossing of proverbs: crosse-answeres and crosse-humours. Pt 1, 1616, 1631; pt 2, 1616, 1632, [after 1640: 1676?] (with addns); ed A. B. Grosart 1879.
— The figure of foure: or a handfull of sweet flowers. Pt 1, 1631; pt 2, 1626, 1636, 1653, 1654; ed A. B. Grosart 1879.
See Nicholas Breton, col 1027, above.
Camden, William. Remaines concerning Britaine. 1614 (2nd edn), 1623, 1629, 1636, 1657 (3 edns), 1674; ed T. Moule and M. A. Lower 1870.
Draxe, Thomas. Bibliotheca scholastica instructissima: or a treasurie of ancient adagies and sententious proverbs. 1616, 1633, 1654.

Robinson (Robertson), Bartholomew. Adagia in Latine and English. 1621, 1622. From Erasmus.

Leycester, John. Enchiridion, seu fasciculus adagiorum selectissimorum: or a manuall of the choysest adagies. 1623. From Erasmus.

Clarke, John. Paroemiologia anglo-latina: or proverbs English and Latin. 1639.

H[erbert], G[eorge]. Outlandish proverbs. 1640 (also issued as Witts recreations pt 2), 1651 (as Jacula prudentum); Facetiae vol 2, 1817.

Fergusson, David. Scottish proverbs. Edinburgh 1641; ed E. Beveridge 1924 (STS).

P[arker], M[artin]. The figure of five. [1645?].
— The figure of seven. 1647.

The country-mans new common-wealth. 1647.

N., D. The figure of six. 1652, 1654.

'Democritus Secundus'. Comes facundus in via: the fellow-traveller through city and country. 1658, 1658

(as The fellow-traveller). By N. Mendicus Hodiernus (Henricus Edmundson?).

Phillips, Edward. The mysteries of love and eloquence. 1658, 1685 (3rd edn), 1699 (as The beau's academy).

Spencer, John. Καινα και Παλαια: things new and old, or a storehouse of similies, sentences etc. 1658.

Howell, James. Παροιμιογραφία: proverbs or old sayed sawes and adages. 1659, 1660 (in Lexicon tetraglotton) (3 edns).

R., N. Proverbs English, French, Dutch, Italian and Spanish. 1659. By Nathaniel Richards?

Letters and exercises of the Elizabethan schoolmaster John Conybeare. Ed F. C. Conybeare 1905.

§2

Crane, W. G. Wit and rhetoric in the Renaissance. New York 1937.

(7) RIDDLES

The demaundes joyous. 1511; ed C. H. Hartshorne, Ancient metrical tales, 1829; ed J. Timbs, The literary world, 1839.

The boke of a hundred riddles. [1530?] (one leaf).

Delectable demaundes and pleasaunt questions. [1566], 1596. Tr from Alain Chartier by W. Painter.

The riddles of Heraclitus and Democritus. 1598.

The booke of meery riddles. 1629, 1660, 1672; ed J. O. Halliwell (-Phillipps), The literature of the sixteenth and seventeenth centuries, 1866.

(8) TRACTS AND SATIRES ON WOMEN AND MARRIAGE

Bibliographies

[Gay, Jules]. Bibliographie des principaux ouvrages relatifs à l'amour, aux femmes, au mariage. Rev J. Lemonnyer 4 vols Paris 1893–1900.

Utley, F. L. The crooked rib: an analytical index to the argument about women in English and Scots literature to the end of the year 1568. Columbus 1944.

§1

Walter, William. The spectacle of lovers: a lytell controvers dyalogue bytwene love and councell. [1520?].

The boke of mayd Emelyn. [1525]; ed G. Isted 1820 (Roxburghe Club); ed E. F. Rimbault, Ancient poetical tracts, 1842 (Percy Soc); ed W. C. Hazlitt, Early popular poetry of England vol 4, 1866.

An interlocucyon with an argument betwyxt man and woman. [1525?]. From the French.

The payne and sorowe of evyll maryage. [c. 1530]; ed J. P. Collier 1840 (Percy Soc); ed W. C. Hazlitt, Early popular poetry of England vol 4, 1866. Tr from Golias de conjuge non ducenda.

[Copland, Robert]. The complaynte of them that ben to soone maryed. 1535. From the French.
— The complaynte of them that ben to late maryed. [1506?], [1518?]; ed J. P. Collier, Illustrations of early English popular literature vol 1, 1863. From the French.
— Jyl of Braintfords testament. [1560?], [1561?]; ed F. J. Furnivall 1871.
— The seven sorowes that women have when theyr husbandes be deade. [1565?].
  See F. C. Francis, Copland: sixteenth-century printer and translator, Glasgow 1961.

Elyot, Sir Thomas. The defence of good women. 1540, 1545.

Coverdale, Miles. The Christen state of matrimonye. [Antwerp] 1541, London 1542 (as The golden boke of Christen matrimonye), 1543 (The Christen state), 1543, 1546 (for 1543?), 1552, 1575. Tr from Heinrich Bullinger.

Gosynhill, Edward. The prayse of all women, called mulierum pean. [1542?], [1560?].

— The vertuous scholehous of ungracious women [1550?]. Anon; from the German.
— A dialogue betwene the comen secretary and jelowsy touchynge the unstablenes of harlottes. [1530?], [1556?]; ed J. P. Collier 1844 (facs); ed C. Hindley, Old book collector's miscellany vol 1, 1871. Not by Gosynhill?

Vaughan, Robert. A dialogue defensyve for women. 1542.

Heywood, John. A dialogue conteinyng the nomber in effect of all the proverbes in the Englishe tongue. 1546, 1550, 1556, 1561; ed R. E. Habenicht, Berkeley and Los Angeles 1963.

Bansley, Charles. A treatyse shewing the pryde of women. [c. 1550]; ed J. P. Collier [1841]; ed W. C. Hazlitt, The early popular poetry of England vol 4, 1866.

The deceyte of women to the instruction and ensample of all men, yonge and olde. [1557?] (newly corrected), [1558?]; ed F. Brie, Archiv 156 1929.

Knox, John. The first blast of the trumpet against the monstruous regiment of women. [Geneva] 1558; ed E. Arber, The English scholars library vol 2, 1878.

A lyttle treatyse called the image of idlenesse: matters moved betwene Walter Wedlocke and Bawdin Bacheler. [1559], 1574 (corrected and augmented).

More, Edward. A lytle and bryefe treatyse called the defence of women made agaynst the Schole-howse of women. 1560; ed E. V. Utterson, Select pieces of early popular poetry vol 2, 1817.

The proude wyves pater noster. 1560; ed E. V. Utterson, Select pieces of early popular poetry vol 2, 1817; ed W. C. Hazlitt, Early popular poetry of England vol 4, 1866.

The scole house of women. 1541 (for 1561), 1560, 1572; ed E. V. Utterson, Select pieces of early popular poetry vol 2, 1817; ed W. C. Hazlitt, Early popular poetry of England vol 4, 1866. Not by Gosynhill?

Evans, Lewis. A new balet entituled howe to wyve well. [1561]; ed J. P. Collier, Old ballads, 1840 (Percy Soc).

T., T. W. A mery balade, how a wife entreated her husband to have her owne wyll. [1568]; rptd in A collection of seventy-nine black-letter ballads, 1867.

Pyrrye, C. The praise and dispraise of women. [1569].

Tusser, Thomas. Dialogue betweene two bachelers. In A hundreth good pointes of husbandrie, 1570; ed W. Payne and S. J. Herrtage 1878 (English Dialect Soc).

A merry jeste of a shrewde and curste wyfe lapped in morrelles skin. [1580?]; ed E. V. Utterson, Select pieces of early popular poetry vol 2, 1817; [ed J. P. Collier] 1844 (Shakespeare Soc); ed W. C. Hazlitt, Early popular poetry of England vol 4, 1866.

Pleasant quippes for upstart newfangled gentlewomen. 1595 (anon), 1596; ed J. P. Collier 1841 (expurgated); rptd [E. F. Rimbault] 1841; rptd C. Clark 1847; ed W. C. Hazlitt, Early popular poetry of England vol 4, 1866; ed E. J. Howard, Oxford Ohio 1942. By Stephen Gosson?

[Tofte, Robert?]. The batchelors banquet. 1603; ed F. P. Wilson 1929.

Heale, William, An apologie for womenkinde. 1605.

The parlament of women. 1640, 1646, 1647 (as A parliament of ladies), 1656 (under first title).

H., I. A strange wonder. 1642.

Strong, James. Joanereidos. 1645, 1674.

Neville, Henry. The parliament of ladies. 1647, 1647, 1647 (as The ladies parliament), 1752 (Somers tracts), 1768, 1811 (Somers tracts: another version).

— The ladies a second time assembled in parliament. 1647.

— An exact diurnall of the parliament of ladyes. 1647. Perhaps by Neville.

— Newes from the New Exchange: or the commonwealth of ladies. 1650.

The city-dames petition in the behalfe of the Cavaliers. 1647.

The Divell a married man: or the Divell hath met with his match. [1647]. Tr from Machiavelli.

Hey hoe for a husband: or the parliament of maides. 1647.

Women will have their will. 1648.

A dialogue between Mistris Macquerella, a suburb bawd, Mrs Scolapendra, a noted curtezan, and Mr Pimpinello an usher etc, pitifully bemoaning the tenour of the act now in force against adultery and fornication. 1650.

G[erbier], C[harles]. Elogium heroinum. 1651.

Fleetwood, E. The glory of women. 1652. Tr from H. C. Agrippa. Another trn by Hugh Crompton, 1652.

A brief anatomie of women. 1653.

The citie matrons. 1654.

The gossips braule. 1655.

[Thorowgood, G.] Pray be not angry: or the womens new law, with their several votes, orders, rules and precepts to the London prentices. 1656.

Now or never: or a new parliament of women assembled. 1656.

An invective against the pride of women. 1657.

Blake, William. The yellow book. 1656, 1658, 1659.

— The trial of the ladies. 1656, 1658 (as A new trial of the ladies).

The crafty whore. 1658.

Philalethes, Mercurius. Select city quaeries. 1660.

The taming of a shrew. Ed J. Ritson, Ancient songs and ballads vol 2, 1829. Caroline?

(9) ROGUE PAMPHLETS AND PRISON TRACTS ETC

Bibliographies

Hazlitt, W. C. A tentative catalogue of our prison-literature. Bibliographer 6 1884.

Gable, J. H. Bibliography of Robin Hood. Lincoln Nebraska 1939.

Collections

The rogues and vagabonds of Shakspere's youth. Ed E. Viles and F. J. Furnivall 1869 (EETS), 1880 (New Shakspere Soc).

The Elizabethan underworld: a collection of Tudor and early Stuart tracts and ballads. Ed A. V. Judges 1930.

§ I

Robin Hood

[The knightly tale of Golagros and Gawane]. 1508; ed D. Laing, Edinburgh 1827; rptd G. Stevenson, Pieces from the Makculloch and the Gray mss, 1918 (STS) (in part).

Jones, Robert. A musicall dreame: or the fourth booke of ayres. 1609. Contains In Sherwood livde stout Robin Hood; ed [J. Ritson], Robin Hood vol 2, 1795; ed J. M. Gutch, A lytell geste of Robin Hode vol 2, 1847.

Renowned Robin Hood: or his famous archery truly related before Queen Katherine. [c. 1628?], [1635?]; rptd in The Roxburghe ballads vol 2, Hertford 1871–99. See also 3 versions of Robin Hood and Queen Katherine; ed T. Evans, Old ballads vol 1, 1777; ed Ritson vol 2, 1795; ed Gutch vol 2, 1847; ed Child vol 3, [1883–98] (with following); tr German, 1864.

The famous battell betweene Robin Hood and the curtall fryer. [c. 1630], [1670–80], [1672?]; ed Evans vols 1–2, 1777–1810; ed Ritson vol 2, 1795; ed Gutch vol 2, 1847; ed F. J. Child, The English and Scottish popular ballads vol 3, [1883–98]; tr German, 1864.

The noble fisherman: or Robin Hood's preferment, shewing how he won a prize on the sea. [1631], [c. 1631], [c. 1648–63], [1670–82], [1680?]; ed Ritson vol 2, 1795; ed Evans, vol 1, 1777; ed Gutch vol 2, 1847; ed Child vol 3, [1883–98]; tr German, 1864.

Parker, Martin. A true tale of Robbin Hood. [1632?],

[1632?], 1686, Newcastle [1800?], Coventry [1820?], Manchester [1843?]; ed Ritson vol 2, 1795; ed Gutch vol 2, 1847; ed Child vol 3, [1883–98].

A. 1500–1640

Copland, Robert. The hye way to the spyttell hous. [1536?]; ed E. V. Utterson, Select pieces of early popular poetry vol 2, 1817; ed W. C. Hazlitt, Early popular poetry of England vol 4, 1866; ed A. V. Judges 1930. After Robert de Balzac. See col 2366, below.

[Awdely, John?]. The fraternitie of vacabondes. 1565, 1575, 1603; ed E. Viles and F. J. Furnivall 1869 (EETS); ed A. V. Judges 1930.

Harman, Thomas. A caveat for commen cursetors. 1567, 1567, 1573, 1592 (as The groundworke of conny-catching), 1814; ed E. Viles and F. J. Furnivall 1869 (EETS); ed A. V. Judges 1930.

[Walker, Gilbert?]. A manifest detection of dice-play. [1580?]; ed J. O. Halliwell (-Phillipps) 1850 (Percy Soc); ed A. V. Judges 1930.

Greene, Robert. The blacke bookes messenger: the life and death of Ned Browne. 1592. Initialled R.G.

— A disputation betweene a hee conny-catcher and a shee conny-catcher. 1592, 1615 (as Theeves falling out), 1617, 1621, 1638.

— A notable discovery of coosenage. [1591], 1591, 1591, 1592; pt 2, 1591, 1592; pt 3, 1592, 1592.

The defence of conny-catching. 1592, 1592, 1859; ed G. B. Harrison 1924. See T. P. Pearson, N & Q April 1959; I. A. Shapiro, An unsuspected earlier edition of the Defence of conny-catching, Library 5th ser 18 1963.

R., B. Greenes newes both from heaven and hell. 1593; ed R. B. McKerrow, Stratford 1911.

Hutton, Luke. The blacke dogge of Newgate. [1596], 1612 (augmented as The discovery of a London monster), 1638; ed A. V. Judges 1930.

— Luke Huttons lamentation. 1598, [c. 1635?], [1670–82]; ed J. P. Collier, Early English poetry vol 1, 1840; ed C. Hindley, Curiosities of street literature, 1871; rptd in Roxburghe ballads vol 8, 1897; ed A. V. Judges 1930. See M. A. Shaaber, Luke Hutton's repentance, Lib Chron 21 1955.

S[harpham ?], E. The discoverie of the knights of the poste. 1597.

Mihil Mumchance his discoverie of the art of cheating in false dyce play. 1597.

A newe ballade shewinge the cruell robberies of Phillip Collins alias Osburne commenlye called Phillip of the West. [1597?]; ed A. Clark, The Shirburn ballads, Oxford 1907.

Greenes ghost haunting conie-catchers. 1602, 1626; ed J. O. Halliwell (-Phillipps) 1860. See E. D. McDonald, An example of plagiarism among Elizabethan pamphleteers, Indiana Univ Stud 1 1911.

M[iddleton], T[homas]. The blacke booke. 1604.

The life and death of Gamaliell Ratsey, a famous thief. [1605]; ed J. P. Collier, Illustrations of old English literature vol 3, 1866; ed S. H. Atkins 1935 (with Ratseis ghost) (Shakespeare Assoc). See J. J. O'Connor, On the authorship of the Ratsey pamphlets, PQ 30 1951.

Ratseis ghost: or the second part of his madde pranks. [1605]; ed H. B. Charlton, Manchester 1933 (facs).

Dobsons drie bobbes. 1607; ed E. Schulz, Die englischen Schwankbücher bis herab zu Dobsons Drie Bobs (1607), Berlin 1912; ed E. A. Horsman, Oxford 1955. See B. Colgrave, Durham Univ Jnl new ser 12 1951.

Dekker, Thomas. The belman of London. 1608 (anon), 1608, 1608, 1616, 1640.

—— Lantherne and candle-light: or the bell-mans second nights walke. 1608, 1609 (corrected), 1612 (with addns, as O per se O), 1616 (as Villainies discovered), 1620 (corrected and enlarged), 1632 (as English villainies), 1638, 1648.
See P. Shaw, The position of Thomas Dekker in Jacobean prison literature, PMLA 62 1947.

R[id], S. Martin Mark-All: beadle of Bridewell. 1610; ed A. V. Judges 1930.

—— The art of jugling. 1612, 1614.

The madde pranckes of merry Moll of the Banckside. 1610.

The life, apprehensio[n], arraignement and execution of Charles Courtney. 1612.

The severall notorious and lewd cousonages of John West and Alice West. 1613.

Fennor, William. The compters common-wealth. 1617, 1619 (as The miseries of a jaile), 1629 (as A true description of the lawes of a compter); ed A. V. Judges 1930.

Mynshul, Geffray. Certaine characters and essayes of prison and prisoners. 1618, 1618 (as Essayes and characters of a prison and prisoners), 1638 (with addns), Edinburgh 1821 (from 2nd edn). See col 2044, below.

S[peed], R[obert]. The counter-scuffle. 1621 (anon), 1623 (augmented), [1626?], 1628, 1635, 1637, 1647, 1648, 1651, 1653, 1658, 1664, 1667, 1670, 1680, 1684, 1693, 1693.

Harris, A. The Oeconomy of the Fleete: or an apological answeare. [1621]. Ed A. Jessopp 1879 (Camden Soc).

Taylor, John. The praise and vertue of a jayle and jaylers. 1623.

Wither, George. The schollers purgatory. [1625?]. See J. A. Langford, Prison books and their authors, 1861.

Clavell, John. A recantation of an ill led life: or a discoverie of the high-way law. 1628, 1628 (with addns), 1634 (with addns). See D. S. Lawless and J. H. P. Pafford, John Clavell 1603–42: highwayman, author and quack doctor, N & Q Jan 1957.

Another bloody murther comitted neere Ware. [1633]; ed W. Chappell, The Roxburghe ballads vol 3, 1880.

Wickins, Nathan. Wood Street Compter's plea for its prisoner. 1638.

B. 1640–60

Tracts on Prisons and Administration of Law

L., W. The courts of justice corrected and amended: or the corrupt lawyer untrust, lash'd and quasht. 1642.

Bagwell, William. The distressed merchant and the prisoners comfort in distresse. 1645.

A looking-glasse for all proud, ambitious, covetous and corrupt lawyers. 1646.

Robins, Robert. A whip for the Marshalls Court. 1648, [1648].

P., Theophilus. Salus populi desperately ill of a languishing consumption. 1648.

Jones, John. The crie of bloud. 1651, 1651, 1653.

—— Every mans case: or lawyers routed. 1652.

March, John. Amicus reipublicae. 1651.

Leach, Edmund. The down-fall of the unjust lawyers. 1652 (for 1653).

Miscellanea magna: the second century. 1653. Satirical misinterpretations of lawyer's Latin.

Multum in parvo: or a summary narrative on behalfe of prisoners captived for debt. 1653.

Rogers, John. Sagrir: or doomes-day drawing nigh with thunder and lightening to lawyers. 1654, 1654.

A new case put to an old lawyer. 1656.

Cole, William. A rod for the lawyers, who are hereby declared to be the grand robbers and deceivers of the nation. 1659, 1659.

Pryor, William. The out-cries of the poor, oppressed and imprisoned. 1659.

Adis, Henry. A fannaticks letter sent out of the dungeon of the Gate-House Prison of Westminster. 1660.

Rogue pamphlets and burlesques

I am a brave padder: the high-way Hector. [1640–60].

Frogges of Egypt: or the catterpillars of the commonwealth truly dissected and laid open. 1641.

True description of the birth, education, life and death of the notorious highway-man William Ward, alias Walker, alias Waller, alias Slaughter. 1641.

Wonderful strange newes from Woodstreet Counter. 1642, 1642.

Hinds elder brother, or the master thief discovered: being a relation of the life of Major Thomas Knowls. 1651.

A pill to purge melancholy: or merry newes from Newgate. 1652.

B., J. The knight errant: being a witty, notable and true relation of the strange adventures of Sir William Hart. 1652.

Gayton, Edmund. Pleasant notes upon Don Quixot. 1654.

—— Wil Bagnal's ghost. 1655.

S., E. The witty rogue arraigned, condemned and executed: or the history of that incomparable thief Richard Hainam. 1656.

The Devil's cabinet broke open: or a new discovery of the high-way thieves. 1658.

The catterpillars of this nation anatomized. 1659.

James Hind

F[idge], G[eorge]. Hind's ramble. 1651.

—— The English Gusman: or the history of that unparallel'd thief James Hind. 1652, [1652?] (abridged as Wit for money).

The pleasant and delightful history of Captain Hind. 1651.

The true and perfect relation of the taking of Captain James Hind. 1651.

The last will and testament of James Hynd. 1651.

The trial of Captain James Hind. [1651].

We have brought our hogs to a fair market: or strange newes from Newgate of Captain James Hind. 1651 (for 1652).

A pill to purge melancholy: or merry newes from Newgate of Captain James Hind. 1652.

No jest like a true jest: the merry life and mad exploits of Captain James Hind. [1657], [1670?], 1674, 1680; ed G. Smeeton 1817.

§2

Ashton, J. The Fleet: its rivers, prison and marriages. 1888.

Chandler, F. W. The literature of roguery. 2 vols Boston 1907. With bibliography.

Aydelotte, F. Elizabethan rogues and vagabonds. Oxford 1913.

Humphreys, A. L. The highwayman and his chap-book. N & Q 4 May 1940.

Lievsay, J. L. Newgate penitents. HLQ 7 1944.

Baumgartner, P. R. From medieval fool to Renaissance rogue: Cock Lorelles Bote and the literary tradition. Annuale Medievale 4 1963.

Dobb, C. London's prisons. Shakespeare Survey 17 1964.

McPeek, J. A. S. The black book of knaves and unthrifts in Shakespeare and other Renaissance authors. Storrs Conn 1969.

(10) TOBACCO PAMPHLETS

Bibliographies

Bragge, W. Bibliotheca nicotiana: a catalogue of books about tobacco. Birmingham 1880.

Potter, A. C. Some early books on tobacco. Harvard Lib Notes 3 1936.

Brooks, J. E. Tobacco: its history illustrated by the books, manuscripts and engravings in the library of George Arents. 5 vols New York 1937–52. Vol 1 covers 1507–1615, vol 2 1615–98. See also S. A. Dickson, Tobacco: a catalogue of the books, manuscripts and engravings acquired since 1942, 9 pts New York 1958–68.

§ I

Frampton, John. Joyfull newes out of the newe founde worlde. 1577 (also as The three bookes written in the Spanishe tonge), 1580 (with addns), 1925. Tr from Nicolas Monardes.

C[hute], A[nthony]. Tabaco: the distinct and severall opinions of the phisitions. 1595; ed F. P. Wilson, Oxford 1961. See R. J. Kane, Chute, Thomas Nashe and the first English work on tobacco, RES 7 1931.

Buttes, Henry. Dyets dry dinner. 1599.

A new and short defense of tobacco. 1602.

[Beaumont, Sir John]. The metamorphosis of tobacco. 1602; ed J. P. Collier, Illustrations of early English literature vol 1, 1863.

H. J. (Philaretes). Work for chimny-sweepers: or a warning for tabacconists. 1602, 1602; ed S. H. Atkins, Oxford 1936. See R. J. Kane, Hall and Work for chimny-sweepers, PMLA 51 1936.

A defence of tabacco, with a friendly answer to Worke for chimny-sweepers. 1602. By R. Marbecke?

King James I. A counter-blaste to tobacco. 1604 (anon), 1616 (in Workes); ed J. Hancock 1672 (also in Two broad-sides), 1676 (adapted by Hancock as the Touch-stone or trial of tobacco); ed E. Arber 1869 (with The essayes of a prentise); ed C. Hindley, Old book collector's miscellany vol 1, 1871; ed E. M. Goldsmid, Bibliotheca curiosa, Edinburgh 1885; ed R. S. Rait, A royal rhetorician, 1900; ed C. H. McIlwain, Cambridge Mass 1918 (in Workes); 1954 (separately); tr Latin, 1619 (as Misocapnus), 1644, 1644, 1689.

G[ardiner], E[dmund]. The triall of tabacco. 1610, 1611 (as Phisicall and approved medicines), 1624.

Perfuming of tobacco and the great abuse committed in it. 1611.

Barclay, William. Nepenthes: or the vertues of tabacco. Edinburgh 1614, London 1841 (Spalding Club).

T., C. An advice how to plant tobacco in England. 1615.

Deacon, John. Tobacco tortured: or the filthie fume of tobacco refined. 1616.

Sylvester, Joshua. Tobacco battered and the pipes shattered by a volley of holy shot. [1617–20].

Rich, Barnaby, The Irish hubbub: or the English hue and crie. 1617, 1617 (rev), 1618, 1622.

Brathwait, Richard. The smoaking age: or the man in the mist. 1617 (in A solemne joviall disputation), 1703 (abridged).

Bretnor, T. Opiologia: or a treatise concerning opium. 1618. Tr from Angelo Sala.

Bennett, Edward. A treatise touching the inconveniences that tobacco hath brought into this land. [1620?].

Venner, Tobias. A briefe and accurate treatise concerning the taking of the fume of tobacco. 1621.

Thorius, Raphael. Hymns tabaci. 1626, 1651.

The tryumph of tobacco over sack and ale. 1640.

§ 2

Fairholt, F. W. Tobacco: its history and associations. 1859.

Dickson, S. A. Panacea or precious bane: tobacco in sixteenth-century literature. New York 1954.

Mackenzie, Compton. Sublime tobacco. 1957.

(11) MORAL AND POLITICAL TRACTS AND PAMPHLETS

Bibliographies

Rump: or an exact collection of the choycest poems and songs relating to the late times from anno 1639 to anno 1661. 1662.

Wright, T. Political ballads published in England during the Commonwealth. 1841 (Percy Soc).

— History of grotesque and caricature. 1865.

Catalogue of the pamphlets, books, newspapers and manuscripts relating to the Civil War, the Commonwealth and Restoration, collected by George Thomason 1640–61. 1908.

Previté-Orton, C. W. Political satire in English poetry. Cambridge 1910.

Brooks, H. F. Rump songs: an index with notes. Proc Oxford Bibl Soc 5 1940.

Dahl, F. A bibliography of English corantos and periodical newsbooks 1620–42. 1952 (Bibl Soc).

Wolfe, D. M. Unsigned pamphlets of Richard Overton 1641–9. HLQ 21 1958.

Collections and Selections

Furnivall, F. J. Ballads from manuscripts. 2 vols 1868–73.

Haller, W. Tracts on liberty in the Puritan revolution 1638–47. 3 vols New York 1933.

— and G. Davies. The Leveller tracts 1647–53. New York 1944.

Woodhouse, A. S. P. Puritanism and liberty. 1938.

Wolfe, D. M. Leveller manifestoes of the Puritan revolution. New York 1944.

'Orwell, George' and R. Reynolds. British pamphleteers vol 1: from the sixteenth century to the French Revolution. 1948.

§ I

A. 1500–1640

Vox populi vox dei [1515–20]. Ed W. C. Hazlitt, Early English popular poetry vol 3, 1864.

[Copland, Robert]. The hye way to the spyttell hous. [1536?]; ed W. C. Hazlitt, Early English popular poetry vol 4, 1864; ed A. V. Judges, The Elizabethan under-world, 1930. Adapted from the French.

Crowley, Robert. An informacion and peticion agaynst the oppressours of the pore commons. [1548], [1548].
—— The voyce of the laste trumpet. 1549, 1549.
—— One and thyrtye epigrammes. 1550, 1573 (as 33 epigrams).
—— The way to wealth. 1550.
—— Pleasure and payne, heaven and hell. 1551.
—— Select works. Ed J. M. Cowper 1872 (EETS). Includes all the above.
[The booke in meeter of Robin Conscience]. [1560?], [after 1584] (corrected); ed J. O. Halliwell (-Phillipps), Contributions to English literature, 1849; ed W. C. Hazlitt, Early English popular poetry vol 3, 1864.
Newes come from Hell of love unto usurers. 1565.
Mosse, Miles. The arraignment and conviction of usurie. 1595.
Usurie araigned and condemned. 1625.

Commonwealth Literature

Armstrong, Clement. Howe to reforme the realme. [c. 1535]; ed R. H. Tawney and Eileen Power, Tudor economic documents vol 3, 1924.
—— A treatise concerninge the staple. [c. 1519–35]; ed Tawney and Power, ibid. See S. T. Bindoff, Armstrong and his treatises of the commonweal, Economic History Rev 14 1945.
Morison, Richard. A remedy for sedition. 1536 (anon), 1536; ed E. M. Cox 1933.
Starkey, Thomas. A dialogue between Cardinal Pole and Thomas Lupset. [c. 1538?]; ed J. M. Cowper 1871 (EETS); ed K. M. Burton 1948.
Policies to reduce this realme of Englande unto a prosperous wealthe and estate. 1549; ed Tawney and Power vol 3, 1924.
[Smith, Thomas?]. Discourse of the commonweal. [1549?]; ed E. Lamond, Cambridge 1893; ed M. Dewar, Charlottesville 1969. See E. Hughes, The authorship, Bull John Rylands Lib 21 1937.
Pyers plowmans exhortation unto the lordes, knightes and burgoysses of the parlyamenthouse. [1550?].

B. The Civil War

Gerrard Winstanley (1609?–76)

Works. Ed G. H. Sabine, Ithaca 1941.
Selections from his works. Ed L. Hamilton 1944.
  Petegorsky, D. W. Left-wing democracy in the English Civil War: the social philosophy of Winstanley. 1940.
  Hudson, W. S. Economic and social thought of Winstanley. Jnl of Modern History 18 1946.
  Hardacre, P. H. Winstanley in 1650. HLQ 22 1959.
  Vann, R. T. The later life of Winstanley. JHI 26 1965.

Satires on Political Characters

A description of the passage of Thomas late Earle of Strafford over the river of Styx. 1641. By Richard Overton?
A dialogue or rather a parley betweene Prince Ruperts dogge whose name is Puddle, and Tobies dog whose name is Pepper. 1643.
A true and strange relation of a boy who was entertained by the Devill about Crediton. 1645.
Blacke Tom his speech to the House. 1647. On Fairfax.
White-Hall Fayre: or who buyes good penniworths of Barkstead. 1648.
The world in a maize: or Olivers ghost. 1659.
Nelson, Abraham. A perfect description of Antichrist and his false prophet, Cromwell and John Presbiter, written in 1654. 1660.
H., T. Haslerig and Vain: or a dialogue between them in the Tower of London. [1660].
Hugh Peters his last will and testament. [1660].
The pretended saint and a prophane libertine. 1660. Robert Tichborne and Henry Marten.
A rope for Pol: or a hue and cry after Marchemont Nedham, the late scurrulous news-writer. 1660.

B., F. The character of Sr Arthur Haslerig. [1661].
The knavish merchant. [1661]. Against Richard Neave, for Thomas Crocker.

Mock Testaments

The late will and testament of the Doctors Commons. 1641. By Richard Overton?
P., R. A true inventory of the goods and chattels of superstition. 1642.
B., J. The last will and testament of superstition. 1642.
The last will and testament of P. Rupert. 1645; of Charing Crosse, 1646, ed E. W. Ashbee 1872 (facs); of Sir John Presbyter, 1647 (by Richard Overton?); of Sir James Independent, 1647; of Tom Fairfax, 1648; of Richard Brandon, 1649; of Philip Herbert Earl of Pembroke who dyed of foole-age, 1650 (by M. Oldisworth); of James Hynd, 1651.
Mercurius Democritus his last will and testament. 1652.

Pamphlets on King Charles

The Kings cabinet opened: or certain packets of secret letters and papers written with the Kings own hand and taken in his cabinet at Nasby-Field, June 14 1645. 1645; rptd Harleian miscellany vol 7, 1811. See R. E. Maddison, The Kings cabinet opened: a case study in pamphlet history, N & Q Jan 1966.
Symmons, Edward. A vindication of King Charles. 1648 (for 1647).
Howell, J. The instruments of a King. 1648.
Wotton, Sir H. A panegyrick of King Charles. [1649?], 1649.
Quarles, John. Regale lectum miseriae. 1649, 1649, 1649, 1658, 1659, 1660, 1679.
The confession of Richard Brandon. 1649.
B[rome], R[ichard]. Lachrymae musarum. 1649, 1650.
[Philipps, Fabian]. King Charles the First no man of blood but a martyr for his people. 1649, 1660.
A dialogue: or a dispute between the late hangman [R. Brandon] and death. 1649.
[Cleveland, John]. Majestas intemerata. 1649, 1689.
The princely pellican. 1649.
The none-such Charles. 1651.
Wood, Adam. A new conference between the ghosts of King Charles and Oliver Cromwell. 1659.

Tracts against Christmas

Taylor, John. The complaint of Christmas. [Oxford 1646].
H., T. A ha! Christmas. 1647.
Y[ounge], R[obert]. A touch-stone to try whether we be Christians in name onely or Christians indeed. 1648.
Palmer, George. The lawfulness of the celebration of Christ's birthday debated. 1649.
Reading, John. Christmas revived. [1660].

Tracts on Past History

Cotton, Sir Robert. The troublesome life and raigne of King Henry the Third. 1642.
Brinkelow, Henry. The true coppy of the complaint of Roderyck Mors. [1642].
Chamberlayne, E. The present warre parallel'd: or a briefe relation of the five yeares civil warres of Henry the Third. 1647, 1660 (as The late war).
W[alker], G[eorge]. Anglo-tyrannus. 1650.

Exposures and Reflections arising out of the War

Jordan, Thomas. A diurnall of dangers. [1642].
Newes, true newes, laudable newes, citie newes, Court news, countrey newes. 1642, 1679.
A remonstrance of Londons occurrences. [1642], 1642, [1643].
Edwards, Thomas. Gangraena. 3 pts 1646 (3 edns), 1646, 1646.
A fresh whip for all scandalous lyers [i.e. the Diurnall-writer and the Perfect occurrence writer]. 1647.
Mercurius anti Mercurius. [1648].
Forde, Thomas. Lusus fortunae. 1649.

The hue and cry after those rambling protonotaries of the times, Mercurius Electicus, Britanicus, Melancholicus and Aulicus. 1651.

Peace Pamphlets

Maddison, Sir Ralph. England looking in and out. 1640.

Morton, Thomas. England warning-piece. 1642.

Prynne, W. A soveraign antidote to prevent, appease and determine our unnaturall civill warres and dissentions. 1642, 1642.

The virgins complaint for the losse of their sweet-hearts by these present wars, and keeping their virginities against their wills. 1642 (for 1643), [1642], 1646, [c. 1664].

Taylor, John. The causes of the diseases of this kingdom. [Oxford] 1645.

Study to be quiet. 1647.

Jennings, Theodore. The right way to peace. 1647.

Levitt, William. The Samaritans box newly opened. 1647.

Herbert, Sir Percy. Certaine conceptions. 1650, 1651, 1652.

Homes, Nathaniel. Plain dealing. 1652, 1652.

A cure for the state. [1654], 1659.

Shaaber, M. A. Some forerunners of the newspaper in England 1476–1622. Philadelphia 1929.

White, H. C. Social criticism in popular religious literature of the sixteenth century. New York 1944.

Ferguson, A. B. Renaissance realism in the Commonwealth literature of early Tudor England. JHI 16 1955.

—— The articulate citizen and the English Renaissance. Durham NC 1965.

Morton, A. L. The place of Lilburne, Overton and Walwyn in the tradition of English prose. Zeitschrift für Anglistik und Amerikanistik 1 1958.

Frank, J. The beginnings of the English newspaper 1620–60. Cambridge Mass 1961.

Abernethy, F. A. Popular literature and social protest 1485–1558. In Studies in English Renaissance literature, ed W. F. McNeir, Baton Rouge 1962.

Clancy, T. H. Papist pamphleteers: the Allen-Persons party and the political thought of the Counter-Reformation in England 1572–1615. Chicago 1964.

(12) BROADSIDE BALLADS

Reprints and Catalogues

The Harleian miscellany. Ed W. Oldys 8 vols 1744–6; ed T. Park 10 vols 1808–13.

Collier, J. P. Old ballads. 1840 (Percy Soc).

—— A book of Roxburghe ballads. 1847.

—— Broadside black-letter ballads printed in the sixteenth and seventeenth centuries. 1868.

—— Twenty-five old ballads. 1869.

See G. E. Dawson, Authenticity and attribution of written matter, Eng Inst Annual 1942; S. Race, Collier and his fabrications, N & Q 11 Nov 1950, Sept 1953.

Wright, T. Political ballads published in England during the Commonwealth. 1841 (Percy Soc).

—— Songs and ballads. 1860.

Deloney, Thomas. The garland of good will. 1631; ed J. H. Dixon 1851 (Percy Soc).

—— Works. Ed F. O. Mann, Oxford 1912.

Chappell, W. Popular music of the olden time. 2 vols 1855–9, 1893.

—— and J. W. Ebsworth. The Roxburghe ballads. 9 vols Hertford 1869–99 (Ballad Soc). See C. M. Simpson, Ebsworth and the Roxburghe ballads, Jnl of Amer Folklore 61 1948.

Halliwell (-Phillipps), J. O. A catalogue of an unique collection of ancient broadside ballads. 1856.

Wilkins, W. W. Political ballads of the seventeenth and eighteenth centuries. 2 vols 1860.

Mackay, C. Cavalier songs and ballads 1642–84. 1863.

Lemon, R. Catalogue of a collection of broadsides. 1866 (Soc of Antiquaries).

A collection of seventy-nine black-letter ballads and broadsides printed in the reign of Queen Elizabeth between the years 1559 and 1597. 1867, Detroit 1968.

Huth, Henry. Ancient ballads and broadsides published in England in the sixteenth century. 1867 (Philobiblon Soc).

Morfill, W. R. Ballads from manuscripts. 1873 (Ballad Soc).

Bibliotheca Lindesiana: catalogue of a collection of English ballads. 1890.

Clark, Andrew. The Shirburn ballads 1585–1616. 1907.

Fortescue, G. K. Catalogue of the pamphlets collected by George Thomason 1640–61. 2 vols 1908.

Catalogue of the fifty manuscripts and printed books bequeathed by A. H. Huth. 1912.

Collmann, H. L. Ballads and broadsides, chiefly of the Elizabethan period, now at Britwell Court. 1912 (Roxburghe Club).

Rollins, H. E. Old English ballads 1553–1625, chiefly from manuscripts. Cambridge 1920.

—— A Pepysian garland 1595–1639. Cambridge 1922.

—— Cavalier and Puritan 1640–60. New York 1923.

—— The pack of Autolycus: or strange and terrible news as told in broadside ballads of the years 1624–93. Cambridge Mass 1927.

Robinson, Clement. A handful of pleasant delights. [c. 1575], 1584 (with addns); ed H. E. Rollins, Cambridge Mass 1924; ed A. Kershaw 1927.

Draper, J. W. A century of broadside elegies. 1928.

The battle of Nieuport. Ed D. C. Collins 1935 (facs).

Hodgson, N. H. The murder of Nicholas Turberville: two Elizabethan ballads. MLR 33 1938.

Good newes from Virginia 1623. William & Mary Quart 3rd ser 1948.

Goldstein, L. M. An account of the Faustus ballad. Library 5th ser 16 1961.

Sanderson, J. L. The rebellion and 'flight of the Earls' in verse. TLS 17 March 1961.

I., R. The history of Tom Thumbe. Ed C. F. Bühler, Evanston 1965.

Simpson, C. M. The British broadside ballad and its music. New Brunswick NJ 1966.

History and Criticism

Sievers, R. Thomas Deloney: eine Studie über Balladenlitteratur der Shakspere-Zeit. Weimar 1903.

Firth, C. H. The ballad history of the reigns of King Henry VII and Henry VIII. Trans Royal Historical Soc 2–3 1908–9.

Esdaile, A. Autolycus' pack. Quart Rev 218 1913.

—— The British Museum: the collections. In The uses of libraries, ed E. A. Baker 1927.

Rollins, H. E. The black-letter broadside ballad. PMLA 34 1919.

—— Martin Parker. MP 16 1919.

—— William Elderton, Elizabethan actor and balladwriter. SP 17 1920.

—— An analytical index of the ballad-entries in the registers of the Company of Stationers. Chapel Hill 1924.

Dormer, E. W. Gray of Reading: a sixteenth-century controversialist and ballad-writer. Reading 1923.

Shaaber, M. A. Some forerunners of the newspaper in England 1476–1622. Philadelphia 1929.

Hamer, D. References to Chevy Chase 1548–1765. N & Q 6th May 1933.

—— Editions of Chevy Chase. N & Q 3 June 1933.

Baker, H. C. Classical material in broadside ballads 1550–1625. PMLA 54 1939.

Humphreys, A. L. The highwayman and his chap-book. N & Q 4 May 1940.

Pinto, V. de S. The street ballad and English poetry. Politics & Letters 1 1947.

Chester, A. G. The authorship and provenance of a political ballad of the reign of Henry VIII. N & Q 13 May 1950.

Hodgart, M. J. C. The ballads. 1950.

Elderton, W. William Elderton, ballad-writer. Genealogists' Mag 11 1953. *See also* M. H. Dodds in A history of Northumberland vol 14, Newcastle 1935.

McAleer, J. J. Ballads on the Spanish Armada. Texas Stud in Lit & Lang 4 1963.

Fowler, D. C. A literary history of the popular ballad. Durham NC 1968.

Long, J. H. The ballad medley and the fool. SP 67 1970.

(13) JIGS

Sievers, R. Thomas Deloney: eine Studie über Balladen-litteratur der Shakspere-Zeit. Weimar 1903.

Baskervill, C. R. The Elizabethan jig and related song drama. Chicago 1929.

E. D. P.

III. CHARACTER-BOOKS AND ESSAYS

(1) CHARACTER-BOOKS

Bibliographies

Murphy, G. A bibliography of English character-books 1608–1700. Oxford 1925.

Greenough, C. N. A bibliography of the Theophrastan character in English. Cambridge Mass 1947.

Selections

Halliwell (-Phillipps), J. O. Books of characters. 1857.

A book of characters. Edinburgh 1865, 1869 (as The mirror of character).

Morley, H. Character writings of the seventeenth century. 1891.

Aldington, R. A book of 'characters'. [1924].

Murphy, G. A cabinet of characters. Oxford 1925.

Rouse, W. H. D. A book of characters. 1930.

Bowman, I. A theatre of natures: some 17th-century character writings. 1955.

§ I

Hall, Joseph. Characters of vertues and vices. 1608 (24 characters), 1608, 1608, 1621 (as Meditations and vowes, and Characters of vertues and vices); rptd in his Works 1625, 1628, 1634, 1647, 1648, 1808, 1837, 1863; tr French, 1610, 1619, 1634; versified by Nahum Tate as Characters of virtue and vice, 1691.

H[eywood], T[homas]. Troia britannica. 1609 (one character).

— A true discourse of the two prophets. 1636 (one character).

— Machiavel as he lately appeared to his deare sons the moderne projectors. 1641 (also pt issued as Machiavels ghost; one character and 10 short sketches of particular projectors), 1642 (extract, as Hogs caracter of a projector).

Overbury, Thomas. A wife now the widow of Sir Thomas Overburye; whereunto are added many witty characters. 1614 (2nd edn of A wife, 1614, adding 21 characters), 1614 (30 characters), 1614 (31 characters), 1614, 1615 (as New and choise characters; 73 characters, 32 of them by John Webster), 1616 (as Sir Thomas Overburie his wife, with new elegies upon his (now knowne) untimely death; whereunto are annexed new newes and characters; 72 characters), 1616 (72 characters), 1616 (81 characters), 1618, 1622 (82 characters including John Donne's A dunce, rptd with A Scot, in Paradoxes, problems, essayes, characters, 1652), [Dublin] 1626, 1627, 1628, 1630, 1632, 1638, 1655, 1664; 1756 (in Miscellaneous works in verse and prose); ed E. F. Rimbault, Miscellaneous works in prose and verse, 1856

(from 1616); ed W. J. Paylor, Oxford 1936; ed J. E. Savage, Gainesville 1968 (facs of 1616, as The conceited newes).

See C. E. Gough, The life and characters of Overbury, Norwich 1909; W. J. Paylor, Thomas Dekker and the 'Overburian' characters, MLR 31 1936; The editions of the 'Overburian' characters, Library 4th ser 17 1936; C. R. Forker, 'Wit's descant on any plain song': the prose characters of John Webster, MLQ 30 1969.

Brathwait, Richard. A strappado for the Divell. 1615 (3 characters).

— Essaies upon the five senses. 1620 (2 characters).

— The English gentleman. 1630 (one character).

— The English gentlewoman. 1631 (6 characters).

— Whimzies: or a new cast of characters. 1631 (28 characters); ed J. O. Halliwell (-Phillipps) 1859.

— A strange metamorphosis of man, transformed into a wildernesse, deciphered in characters. 1634 (anon; 40 characters); ed D. C. Allen, Baltimore 1949. Sometimes attributed to Brathwait.

See Richard Brathwait, col 1336, above.

Breton, Nicholas. Characters upon essaies morall and divine. 1615 (16 characters); ed S. E. Brydges, Archaica vol 1, 1815.

— The good and the badde: or descriptions of the worthies and unworthies of this age. 1616 (50 characters), 1643 (as England's selected characters; 28 characters, 5 new); ed S. E. Brydges, Archaica vol 1, 1815.

— Fantasticks: serving for a perpetuall prognostication. 1626 (38 characters); M. Stevenson, The twelve moneths, 1661 (12 characters from Fantasticks, 1626, adapted); ed B. Rhys 1927.

Stephens, John. Satyrical essayes characters and others: or accurate and quick descriptions fitted to the life of their subjects. 1615 (43 characters), 1615 (as Essayes and characters ironicall and instructive; 50 characters), 1627 (as The errors of men personated in sundry essaies), 1631 (as New essayes and characters).

[Mynshul, Geffray]. Certaine characters and essayes of prison and prisoners: compiled by Novus Homo a prisoner in the Kings Bench. 1618 (signed Yarffeg Llahsnym; 7 characters, 9 essays), 1618 (as Essayes and characters of a prison and prisoners; signed G. Mynshul; 8 characters, 2 of them new), 1638 (enlarged), Edinburgh 1821 (from 2nd edn).

P[arrot], H[enry]. Cures for the itch: characters, epigrams, epitaphs, by H.P. 1626 (13 characters).

Earle, John. Micro-cosmographie: or a peece of the world discovered in essayes and characters, newly composed for the northerne parts of this kingdome. 1628 (anon:

54 characters), 1628, 1628, 1628, 1629 (77 characters), 1630, 1633 (78 characters), 1638, 1650 (54 characters), 1650 (71 characters), 1650, 1660, 1664 (78 characters), 1669; ed P. Bliss 1811; ed E. Arber 1868; ed H. Morley 1889; ed A. S. West, Cambridge 1897; ed S. T. Irwin, Bristol 1897; ed W. H. D. Rouse 1899; Cambridge 1903, London 1904 (for 1903); ed G. Murphy 1928; ed H. Osborne 1933. Selections: A true description of the pot-companion poet; also a character of the swilbole cook, 1642; The character of a tavern, 1675; A gallery of portraits, Dublin 1813 (32 portraits adapted from Earle); A book of characters, selected from the writings of Overbury, Earle and Butler, Edinburgh 1865 (67 characters from Earle), 1869 (as The mirror of character); Menston 1966 (ms facs); tr Latin, 1654 (52 characters), 1662, 1669; tr French, 1671 (94 characters, 52 from Earle).

M., R. Micrologia: characters or essayes of persons, trades and places offered to the city and country, by R.M. 1629 (16 characters).

L[enton], F[rancis]. Characterismi: or Lentons leasures, expressed in essayes and characters. 1631 (41 characters), 1632 (as Spare time), 1636 (as Lentons leisures described in divers moderne characters), 1640 (as A piece of the world painted in proper colours), 1653 (as Lentons characters: or witty and ingenious descriptions of severall professions, presented to all judicious readers), 1663 (as Characters: or wit and the world in their proper colours).
See L. S. Willis, Lenton: Queen's poet, *Philadelphia 1931, which reprints* Characterismi.

Saltonstall, Wye. Picturae loquentes: or pictures drawne forth in characters. 1631 (26 characters), 1635 (38 characters); ed C. H. Wilkinson, Oxford 1946 (Luttrell Soc).

Lupton, Donald. London and the countrey carbonadoed and quartred into severall characters. 1632 (36 characters), Edinburgh 1883 (Aungervyle Soc).
— The quacking mountebanck: or the Jesuite turn'd Quaker. 1655. Character of a Quaker.

J[ordan], T[homas]. Pictures of passions, fancies and affections, poetically deciphered in variety of characters. 1641 (19 characters), [1641].

Browne, Humphry. A map of the microcosme: or a morall description of man, newly compiled into essayes. 1642 (19 characters).

Fuller, Thomas. The holy state; the profane state. Cambridge 1642 (51 characters), 1648, 1652, 1663, 1840, 1844 (9 characters and Lives omitted); The marvellous wisdom and quaint conceits of Fuller, abridged by A. L. J. Gosset 1893.

[Palmer, Herbert]. The upright Protestant. 1643 (one character), 1645 (as The character of a believing Christian), 1648 (as A believing Christian, in Remaines of Francis Lord Verulam).

Cleveland, John. The character of a London diurnall. Oxford 1644 (for 1645), 1644 (for 1645), 1644 (for 1645), 1647 (17 poems), 1647 (18 poems), 1647 (20 poems), 1647, 1647 (21 poems), 1647 (22 poems), 1647 (23 poems), 1651 etc (in Poems), 1677 (in Clievelandi vindiciae: or Clieveland's genuine poems etc), 1657 (in Works), 1699.
— The character of a moderate intelligencer; with some select poems by J.C. [1647] (2 characters).
— The character of a country committee-man. 1649, 1651 etc (in Poems), 1677 (in Clievelandi vindiciae), 1687 (in Works), 1699.
— A character of a diurnal-maker, by J.C. 1654 (for 1653), 1654, 1654 etc (in Poems), 1677 (in Clievelandi vindiciae), 1687 (in Works), 1699.
— The Puritan. 1659 (in J. Cleaveland revived), 1660, 1662, 1668, 1687 (in Works), 1699.
See *John Cleveland, col 1304, above.*

F[ord], T[homas]. The times anatomiz'd in severall characters. 1647 (30 characters).

A fresh whip for all scandalous lyers: or a true description of the two eminent pamphliteers or squib-tellers of this kingdome. 1647 (2 characters).

Flecknoe, Richard. Miscellania: or poems of all sorts, with divers other pieces. 1653 (4 characters).
— Enigmaticall characters, all taken to the life from severall persons, humours and dispositions. 1658 (69 characters), 1665 (as Fifty-five enigmatical characters), 1665 (as Sixty-nine enigmatical characters; with 69 characters as in 1658), 1665 (as Richard Flecknoe's Ænigmatical characters; 78 characters, 22 new).
— Heroick portraits with other miscellary pieces. 1660 (4 portraits, 15 characters); rptd in Richard Flecknoe, Ænigmatical characters, 1665, and in A collection, 1673.
— A farrago of several pieces. 1666 (7 characters).
— A collection of the choicest epigrams and characters of Richard Flecknoe. 1673 (63 characters, 19 new), 1677 (as Seventy-eight characters of so many vertuous and vitious persons. 63 characters, 2 new).
See *vol 2 col 764.*

Controversial Characters

The true character of an untrue Bishop. 1641.

Lucifers lacky or the Devils new creature: being the true character of a dissembling Brownist. 1641. By John Taylor?

The lively character of the malignant partie. 1642 (6 characters).

A Puritane set forth in his lively colours: or K. James his description of a Puritan [from Basilicon doron], whereunto is added the round-heads character with the character of an holy sister. 1642 (3 characters). By John Taylor?

T., G. Roger the Canterburian: or the character of a prelaticall man. 1642.

A description of the round-head and rattle head. 1642 (3 characters). By John Taylor?

The anatomy of the separatists alias Brownists. 1642. By John Taylor?

[May, Thomas]. The character of a right malignant. 1644 (for 1645).

A character of an antimalignant. 1645.

A new anatomie: or character of a Christian or round-head. 1645.

The true character of Mercurius Aulicus. 1645.

The character of an Oxford-incendiary. [1645]; rptd Harleian miscellany vol 5, 1810.

Geree, John. The character of an old English Puritane or non-conformist. 1646, 1646, 1649, 1659, 1660 (as A vindication of Calvin), [1670?] (as The character of an old English Protestant), 1672, 1673 (as The character of the sober non-conformist); ed M. Hussey, Church Quart Rev 148 1949.

The character of an agitator. 1647.

A recommendation to Mercurius Morbicus, together with a fair character upon his worth. 1647. By John Taylor?

An agitator anotomiz'd. 1648.

The character of a phanatique. 1660.

A breife description or character of the religion and manners of the phanatiques. 1660.

The character of a presbyter. 1660.

Books with Characters

M., W. The man in the moone, telling strange fortunes: or the English fortune-teller. 1609 (13 characters), 1640 (adapted as The wandering-jew, telling fortunes to Englishmen, 1640; 18 characters, 6 from Man in the moone).

Adams, Thomas. Mystical Bedlam: or the world of madmen. 1615 (20 characters), 1629 (in Workes), 1861.
— Diseases of the soule. 1616 (19 characters), 1629 (in Workes), 1861.

H[eath], J[ohn]. The house of correction: or certain satyricall epigrams, together with a few characters, called Par pari. 1619 (9 characters).

Habington, William. Castara. 1635 (2nd edn; 3 characters), 1640 (4 characters); ed A. Chalmers, Works of the English poets vol 6, 1810 (from 1640); ed C. A. Elton, [Bristol] 1812; ed. R. Southey 1831; ed E. Arber 1870; Poems, ed K. Allott 1948.

North, Dudley, Baron North. A forest of varieties. 1645 (11 characters), 1659 (as A forest promiscuous; 12 characters).

Wortley, Francis. Characters and elegies. 1646 (14 characters).

Herbert, George. Herbert's remains. 1652, 1671, 1675, 1701, Menston 1970 (facs of 1652).

Gayton, E. Wil Bagnal's ghost in his perambulation of the prisons of London. 1655 (4 characters).

[Sprigg, William]. Philosophicall essayes. [Oxford] 1657 (6 characters).

Osborne, Francis. A miscellany of sundry essayes, paradoxes and characters. 1659 (4 characters), 1659.

Ellis, Clement. The gentile sinner: or England's brave gentleman characterized. Oxford 1660 (29 characters), 1661, 1664, 1668, 1672, 1679, 1690.

§2

Baldwin, E. C. The character books of the seventeenth century in relation to the development of the novel. Bull Western Reserve Univ Oct 1900.

Gordon, G. S. Theophrastus and his imitators. In his English literature and the classics, Oxford 1912.

Smith, D. N. The character. In his Characters from the histories and memoirs of the seventeenth century, Oxford 1918.

Thompson, E. N. S. Character books. In his Literary bypaths of the Renaissance, New Haven 1924.

—— Character-books and familiar letters. In his Seventeenth-century English essay, Iowa City [1927].

Clausen, W. The beginnings of English character-writing in the early seventeenth century. PQ 25 1946.

Boyce, B. The Theophrastan character in England to 1642. Cambridge Mass 1947.

(2) ESSAYS

§1

Heron, Haly. A newe discourse of morall philosophie. 1579. See V. B. Heltzel, Heron: Elizabethan essayist and euphuist, HLQ 16 1952.

D[aunce?], E[dward]. The prayse of nothing. 1585. See R. M. Sargent, The authorship of the Prayse of nothing, Library 4th ser 12 1932.

Paulet, William, Marquis of Winchester. The Lord Marques idlenes. 1586, 1587. See S. Thomas, The Lord Marquess' idleness: the first English book of essays, SP 45 1948.

Churchyard, Thomas. A sparke of frendship and warme goodwill. 1588; rptd Harleian miscellany vol 2, 1809.

Segar, William. The booke of honor and armes. 1590.

Remedies against discontentment, drawen into severall discourses, by Anonymus. 1596.

Bacon, Francis. Essayes. 1597 etc.

—— Apophthegmes new and old. 1625, 1626 1674 (as A collection). See col 2324, below.

Tyro, T. Tyros roring Megge. 1598.

Greenham, Richard. Works. Ed H. H[olland] 1599, 1599, 1600 (2nd pt), 1601 (both pts), 1605, 1612.

King James I. Βασιλικὸν Δῶρον, devided into three bookes. Edinburgh 1599. Anon; see col 1905, above.

Cornwallis, Sir William. Essayes. Pt 1, 1600; pt 2, 1601; 1610 (both pts 'newly enlarged', with Discourses upon Seneca, 1632 (for 1631) ('newly corrected' by H[enry] O[lney]); Essayes 1600–10, ed D. C. Allen, Baltimore 1946.

—— Discourses upon Seneca the tragedian. 1601.

—— Essayes: or rather encomions, prayses of sadnesse. 1616, 1616 (in following).

—— Essayes of certaine paradoxes. 1616 (anon), 1617 (with Essayes: or rather encomions).

See P. B. Whitt, New light on Cornwallis the essayist, RES 8 1932; R. E. Bennett, Cornwallis's use of Montaigne, PMLA 48 1933. Harvard Stud 13 1931 prints 4 ms paradoxes.

Johnson, Robert. Essaies: or rather imperfect offers. 1601, 1607, 1613, 1638 (as Johnsons essayes).

H[ynd?], J[ohn?]. The mirrour of worldly fame. 1603; rptd Harleian miscellany vol 2, 1809.

Digges, Thomas and Dudley. Foure paradoxes or politique discourses. 1604.

Grymeston, Elizabeth. Miscelanea, meditations, memoratives. 1604, [1606?] (enlarged), [1608?], [1618?].

Hall, Joseph. Meditations and vowes, divine and morall. 1605, 1606 (2 pts), 1606, 1607 (enlarged), 1609, 1616, 1621 (with Caracters of vertues and vices).

—— Contemplations upon the principall passages of the holie storie. 1612 (first vol in 4 bks), 1614 (2nd vol in 4 bks), 1615 (3rd vol in 3 bks), 1617 (in A recollection of treatises), 1618 (4th vol), 1620 (5th vol), 1622 (6th vol), 1623 (7th vol in 2 bks: Contemplations upon the historie of the Old testament), 1626 (8th vol), 1634 (in Complete works).

—— Occasionall meditations. 1630.

Rich, Barnaby. Faultes, faults and nothing else but faultes. 1606.

Walkington, Thomas. The optick glasse of humors. 1607, Oxford [1631?], London 1639, 1664, 1664.

Breton, Nicholas. Divine considerations of the soule. 1608.

—— Characters upon essaies morall and divine. 1615.

T[uvill], D[aniel]. Essaies politicke morall. 1608.

—— Essayes, morall and theologicall. 1609, 1629 (as Vade mecum), 1631, 1638.

—— The dove and the serpent. 1614.

—— Asylum veneris or a sanctuary for ladies. 1616.

—— Christian purposes and resolutions. 1622. See J. L. Lievsay, Tuvill's resolves, SP 46 1949.

See also J. L. Lievsay, Tuvill's advancement of Bacon's learning, HLQ 9 1945.

Stafford, Anthony. Meditations and resolutions, moral, divine, politicall. 1612.

T[uke], T[homas]. New essayes: meditations and vowes. 1614.

Stephens, John. Satyrical essayes characters and others. 1615.

R[ous], F[rancis]. Meditations of instruction, of exhortation, of reprofe. 1616.

Gainsford, Thomas. The rich cabinet, furnished with varietie of excellent discriptions, exquisite charracters, witty discourses, and delightfull histories, disgested alphabetically into common places. 1616.

[Mynshul, Geffray]. Certaine characters and essayes of prison and prisoners. 1618.

Brathwait, Richard. Essaies upon the five senses. 1620.

[Brydges, Grey, Baron Chandos]. Horae subsecivae: observations and discourses. 1620.

Mason, William. A handful of essaies. 1621.

Felltham, Owen. Resolves, divine, morall, politicall. [1623?], 1628 (with addns), 1628 (addns only), 1628 (complete), 1631, 1634, 1636, 1642, 1647, 1661, 1661 (with addns), 1670, 1677, 1696; ed J. Cumming 1806; ed O. Smeaton 1904. See F. S. Tupper, New facts regarding Felltham, MLN 54 1939; J. Robertson, The use made of Felltham's Resolves: a study in plagiarism, MLR 39 1944; R. F. Kennedy, Words from Felltham, N & Q Jan 1971.

Donne, John. Devotions upon emergent occasions. 1624, 1624, 1626 (for 1627), 1634, 1638.
— Essayes in divinity, interwoven with meditations and prayers. 1651.
— Paradoxes, problemes, essayes, characters, with Ignatius his conclave. 1652, 1652.
See col 1169, above.
Robinson, John. Observations divine and morall. 1625, 1628 (as New essayes), 1638 (as Essayes).
Henshaw, Joseph. Horae succisivae: or spare-houres of meditations. 1631 (2nd edn), 1632, 1635, 1640.
Ralegh, Walter. Instructions to his sonne and to posterity. 1632, 1632, 1633, 1633, 1634, 1636.
— The Prince: or maxims of state. 1642.
Culverwel, Ezekiel. Time well spent in sacred meditations, divine observations, heavenly exhortations. 1634, 1635.
Warwick, Arthur. Spare minutes: or resolved meditations. 2 pts 1634 (2nd edn corrected and enlarged), 1635 (rev), 1635, 1636, 1637, 1640, 1641, 1680; ed W. J. Loftie 1881. *See* K. J. Höltgen and J. Horden, Warwick 1603/4–33: the author of Spare minutes, Library 5th ser 21 1966.
Austin, William. Devotionis Augustinianae flamma: or certaine devout, godly and learned meditations. 1635, 1637.
Person, David. Varieties: or a surveigh of rare and excellent matters. 1635.
Peacham, Henry. The truth of our times, revealed out of one mans experience by way of essay. 1638; ed R. R. Cawley, New York 1942 (facs).
— The valley of varietie: or discourse fitting for the times. 1638.
Quarles, Francis. Enchyridion. 1640, 1641, 1644, 1646, 1654, 1658, 1664, 1667, 1670; Observations concerning princes, 1642 (collected from Enchyridion).
— Boanerges and Barnabas: or judgement and mercy for afflicted soules. Pt 1, 1646, 1646; pt 2, 1644, 1646, 1646; 2 pts 1657, 1667, 1671, 1674, 1679.
Jonson, Ben. Timber: or discoveries. 1641 (in Works vol 2). *See col 1655, above.*
Fuller, Thomas. The holy state, the profane state. Cambridge 1642.
— Good thoughts in bad times. Exeter 1645.
— Good thoughts in worse times. 1647.
— Mixt contemplations in better times. 1660.
See col 2233, below.
Palmer, Herbert. Memorials of godlinesse and Christianitie. 1644, 1645, 1655 (5th edn), 1657 (7th edn), 1670 (10th edn), 1681; rptd in Bacon's Remaines, 1648 (in part); ed A. B. Grosart, Edinburgh 1865 (complete).
Howell, James. Epistolae Ho-Elianae: familiar letters domestic and forren. 4 vols 1645, 1650, 1655, 1673, 1678, 1688. *See col 2225, below.*
[North, Dudley, Baron North]. A forest of varieties. 1645.
Hall, John (1627–56). Horae vacivae: or essays. 1646.
— Paradoxes by J. de la Salle. 1650, 1653, 1656 (as Paradoxes by John Hall).

Montagu, Walter. Miscellanea spiritualia: or devout essaies. 2 pts 1648–54.
F[orde], T[homas]. Lusus fortunae: the play of fortune, continually acted by the severall creatures on the stage of the world. 1649.
— Virtus rediviva: a panegyricke on our late King Charles the I, with severall other pieces from the same pen. 1660, 1661. Contains, with separate pagination and title-pages but continuous signatures, the following pieces, variously dated 1660 and 1661 and 'By Tho. Forde': (1) Virtus rediviva, (2) A theatre of wits, ancient and modern, represented in a collection of apothegmes, (3) Faenestra in pectore: or familiar letters, (4) Love's labyrinth: or the royal shepherdess, a tragicomedie, (5) Fragmenta poetica: or poetical diversions. The 5 pieces were also issued separately. *See* J. Q. Adams, Forde's Love's labyrinth, in Studies in language and literature in celebration of James Morgan Hart, New York 1910.
Herbert, Sir Percy. Certaine conceptions or considerations upon the strange change of peoples dispositions and actions in these latter times. 1650, 1651, 1652.
Cottoni posthuma. 1651, 1672, 1679. Sir Robert Bruce Cotton's remains, ed James Howell, attributing essays to Sir Philip Sidney and Sir Francis Walsingham.
Harflete, Henry. A banquet of essayes. 1653.
S., S. Paradoxes: or encomions. 1653.
[Master, William]. Λογοι εὔκαιροι: essayes. 1654.
Whitlock, Richard. ΖΩΟΤΟΜΙΑ: or observations. 1654. *See* G. Williamson, Whitlock: learning's apologist, PQ 15 1936.
Wotton, Sir Henry. Aphorisms of education. 1654 (in Reliquiae Wottonianae, 2nd edn). *See col 1325, above.*
C[ulpeper], T[homas]. Morall discourses and essayes. 1655.
[King, Philip]. The surfeit to ABC. 1656.
Osborne, Francis. Advice to a son. Oxford 1656, 1656, 1656, 1656, 1656, 1658; pt 2, 1658.
— A miscellany of sundry essayes. 1659, 1659.
[Sprigg, William]. Philosophicall essayes. [Oxford] 1657.
H., J. Two essays of love and marriage. 1657.
Witty apophthegms. 1658. By King James, King Charles, Worcester, Bacon, More.
Heath, Robert. Paradoxical assertions. 1659. For his Clarastella, *see col 1336, above.*
T[ubbe], H[enry]. Meditations divine and morall. 1659.
Ashley, Robert. Of honour. [1596]; ed V. B. Heltzel, San Marino 1947. *See* V. B. Heltzel, Ashley: Elizabethan man of letters, HLQ 10 1947.

§2

MacDonald, W. L. Beginnings of the English essay. Toronto 1914.
Thompson, E. N. S. The seventeenth-century English essay. Iowa City [1927].

E. D. P.

IV. PROSE FICTION

(1) BIBLIOGRAPHIES

Esdaile, A. A list of English tales and prose romances printed before 1740. 1912 (Bibl Soc).
Rolfe, F. On the bibliography of seventeenth-century prose fiction. PMLA 49 1934.
Mish, C. C. English prose fiction 1600–1700. Charlottesville 1952, 1967 (rev).

O'Dell, Sterg. A chronological list of prose fiction in English 1475–1640. Cambridge Mass 1954.
Bell, I. F. and D. Baird. The English novel 1578–1956: a checklist of twentieth-century criticism. Denver 1959.

(2) COLLECTIONS

Early prose romances. Ed W. J. Thoms 3 vols 1827–8, 1858 (rev), [1907] (rev).

Shakespeare's library: a collection of the romances, novels, poems and histories, used by Shakespeare as the foundation of his dramas. Ed J. P. Collier 2 vols [1843], 1850; rev W. C. Hazlitt 6 vols 1875.

Shakespeare jest-books. Ed W. C. Hazlitt 3 vols 1864.

Fairy tales, legends and romances illustrating Shakespeare and other early English writers. Ed W. C. Hazlitt 1875.

Early prose romances. Ed H. Morley 1889; rptd in Thoms, above, [1907].

Some old English worthies. Ed D. Senior 1912.

Shorter novels vol 1: Elizabethan and Jacobean. Ed G. Saintsbury and P. Henderson 1929.

Elizabethan tales. Ed E. J. O'Brien 1937.

Elizabethan fiction. Ed R. Ashley and E. H. Moseley, New York 1953.

The descent of Euphues: three Elizabethan romance stories. Ed J. Winny, Cambridge 1957.

The counterfeit lady unveiled and other criminal fiction of seventeenth-century England. Ed S. Peterson, Garden City NY 1961.

A hundred merry tales and other English jestbooks of the fifteenth and sixteenth centuries. Ed P. M. Zall, Lincoln Nebraska 1963.

Short fiction of the seventeenth century. Ed C. C. Mish, New York 1963.

Elizabethan prose fiction. Ed M. Lawlis, New York 1968.

Elizabethan love stories. Ed T. J. B. Spencer 1968 (Pelican).

A nest of ninnies and other English jestbooks of the seventeenth century. Ed P. M. Zall, Lincoln Nebraska 1970.

(3) FICTION

The deceyte of women. [1557?] (newly corrected), [1558?]; ed F. Brie, Archiv 156 1929.

A lyttle treatyse called the image of idlenesse: matters moved betwene Walter Wedlocke and Bawdin Bacheler. [1559], 1574 (corrected and augmented).

B[orde?], A[ndrew?]. Merie tales of the mad men of Gotam. [c. 1565], 1630, [1690?]; ed J. O. Halliwell (-Phillipps) 1840; ed W. C. Hazlitt, Shakespeare jest-books vol 3, 1864; ed S. J. Kahrl, Evanston 1965 (newly discovered first edn).

Painter, William. The palace of pleasure: pleasaunt histories and excellent novelles. 1566, 1569, 1575 (corrected and augmented); Second tome, 1567, [1580?] (agayn corrected and encreased); [ed J. Haslewood] 1813; ed J. Jacobs 3 vols 1890; ed H. Miles 4 vols 1929. See D. Bush, The classical tales in Painter's Palace of pleasure, JEGP 23 1924; H. G. Wright, The indebtedness of Painter's translations from Boccaccio to the French version of le Maçon, MLR 46 1951.

Fenton, G. See under Bandello, col 2181, below.

Tilney, Edmund. A briefe and pleasant discourse of duties in mariage called the flower of friendshippe. 1568, 1568, 1571, 1577.

Baldwin, William. A marvelous hystory intitulede beware the cat. 1570, 1584, 1652 (fragment); ed W. P. Holden, New London Conn 1963.

[Gascoigne, George]. A pleasant discourse of the adventures of master F.I. [1573] (in A hundreth sundrie flowres), 1575 (augmented, rev and transferred to an Italian setting), 1587 (as Whole woorkes), 1587 (as Pleasauntest workes); ed B. M. Ward 1926; ed C. T. Prouty, Columbia Missouri 1942; ed R. Ashley and E. M. Moseley, Elizabethan fiction, New York 1953; ed M. Lawlis, Elizabethan prose fiction, New York 1968. See L. Bradner, The first English novel, PMLA 45 1930, Point of view in Gascoigne's fiction, Stud in Short Fiction 3 1965; C. T. Prouty, Elizabethan fiction, in Studies in honor of A. H. R. Fairchild, Columbia Missouri 1946; R. P. Adams, Gascoigne's Master F.J. as original fiction, PMLA 73 1958; F. B. Fieler, Gascoigne's use of courtly love conventions in the Adventures, Stud in Short Fiction 1 1963; R. A. Lanham, Narrative structure in Gascoigne's F.J., Stud in Short Fiction 4 1966; A. Anderau, Gascoigne's The adventures, Swiss Stud in Eng 57 1966; C. W. Smith, Structural and thematic unity in Gascoigne's The adventures, Papers in Lang & Lit 2 1966; M. R. Rohr, Gascoigne and 'my master Chaucer', JEGP 67 1968.

— The pleasant tale of Hemetes the hermite. 1579 (as by Abraham Fleming in A paradoxe proving baldnesse better than bushie haire), 1585 (in The Queen Majesty's entertainment), 1587 (in Whole works), 1587.

Rich, Barnaby. A right exelent and pleasaunt dialogue, betwene Mercury and an English souldier. [1574].

— Riche his farewell to militarie profession. 1581, 1583, 1594 (rev), 1606 (rev).

— The straunge and wonderfull adventures of Don Simonides. 1581.

— The second tome of the travailes and adventures of Don Simonides. 1584.

— The adventures of Brusanus, Prince of Hungaria. 1592.

Pettie, George. A petite pallace of Pettie his pleasure: many pretie histories. [1576?], [1578?], [c. 1585], [c. 1590], 1608, 1613; ed I. Gollancz 2 vols 1908; ed H. Miles 4 vols 1930; ed H. Hartman, Oxford 1938. See D. Bush, JEGP 27 1928; C. J. Vincent, Pettie and Greene, MLN 54 1939; J. Swart, Lyly and Pettie, E Studies 23 1941.

Whetstone, George. The rocke of regard. 1576.

— An heptameron of civill discourses: the Christmasse exercise of sundrie gentlemen and gentlewomen. 1582, 1593 (as Aurelia). See C. T. Prouty, Elizabethan fiction: Whetstone's Rinaldo and Giletta and Grange's The golden Aphroditis in Studies in honor of A. H. R. Fairchild, Columbia Missouri 1946.

Grange, John. The golden Aphroditis. 1577; ed H. E. Rollins, New York 1939 (facs). See H. E. Rollins, Harvard Stud 16 1934; M. P. Tilley, Borrowings in Grange's Golden Aphroditis, MLN 53 1938. See Whetstone, above.

Lyly, John. Euphues: the anatomy of wyt. [1578].

— Euphues and his England. 1580.

C., H. The forrest of fancy: pleasant histories. 1579. See col 1089, above.

Gosson, Stephen. The ephemerides of Phialo. 1579, 1586.

Gifford, Humphrey. A posie of gilloflowers. 1580; ed F. J. H. Darton 1933. See col 1107, above.

Munday, Anthony. Zelauto: the fountaine of fame. 1580.

Saker, Austin. Narbonus: the laberynth of libertie. 2 vols 1580.

Greene, Robert. Mamillia: a mirrour or looking-glasse for the ladies of Englande. 1583, 1593 (The second part of the triumph of Pallas).

— Arbasto: the anatomie of fortune. 1584.

— Gwydonius: the carde of fancie. 1584. See R. W. Dent, Greene's Gwydonius: a study in Elizabethan plagiarism, HLQ 24 1961.

— Morando the tritameron of love. Pt 1, 1584; 2 pts 1587.

— The myrrour of modestie, by R.G. 1584.

— Planetomachia. 1585.

— Euphues his censure to Philautus. 1587.

— Penelopes web. [1587].

— Pandosto: the triumph of time. 1588.

— Perimedes the blacke-smith. 1588.

— Ciceronis amor: Tullies love. 1589.

— The Spanish masquerado. 1589.

— Menaphon Camilla's alarum to slumbering Euphues. 1589, 1599, [1605?], 1610 (as Greenes arcadia), 1616.

— Greenes farewell to folly. 1591.

— The blacke bookes messenger: the life and death of Ned Browne, by R.G. 1592.

— Greenes never too late. 1590.

— Greenes mourning garment. 1590.

— Philomela: the Lady Fitzwaters nightingale. 1592.

— Greenes groats-worth of witte. 1592.

— Greenes Orpharion: a musicall concorde of pleasant histories. 1599.

— Alcida Greenes metamorphosis. 1617.

Melbancke, Brian. Philotimus: the warre betwixt nature and fortune. 1582 (for 1583). See H. E. Rollins, Notes on Brian Melbancke's Philotimus, SP ex ser 1 1929; Notes on the sources of Melbancke's Philotimus, Harvard Stud 18 1935, Thomas Deloney and Melbancke: notes on sources, Harvard Stud 19 1936; M. P. Tilley, Further borrowings from poems in Philotimus, SP 27 1930.

Averell, William. A dyall for dainty darlings. 1584, 1590 (expanded as Foure notable histories).

Lodge, Thomas. An alarum against usurers: the delectable historie of Forbonius and Prisceria. 1584.

— Rosalynde: Euphues golden legacie. 1590.

— The famous, true and historicall life of Robert second Duke of Normandy, by T.L.G. 1591.

— Euphues shadow: the battaile of the sences. 1592.

— The life and death of William Longbeard. 1593. See J. Hornát, An old Bohemian legend in Elizabethan literature, Philologica Pragensia 7 1964.

— A Margarite of America. 1596.

See A. Walker, The reading of an Elizabethan, RES 8 1932.

Warner, William. Pan his syrinx or pipe: seven tragical and comicall arguments. [1584], 1597 (newly perused and amended).

C., W. The adventures of Ladie Egeria. [1585?].

Tarltons newes out of Purgatorie. 1590, [c. 1600], 1630; ed J. O. Halliwell (-Phillipps) 1844 (Shakespeare Soc).

The cobler of Caunterburie: or an invective against Tarltons newes out of Purgatorie. 1590, 1608, 1614 (as The merry tales), 1630 (as The tincker of Turvey); ed J. O. Halliwell (-Phillipps) 1844 (Shakespeare Soc); ed F. Ouvry 1862; ed C. C. Mish, Short fiction of the seventeenth century, New York 1963 (from 1630).

Roberts, Henry. A defiance to fortune proclaimed by Andrugio, noble Duke of Saxony: the honorable warres of Galastino, Duke of Millaine. 1590.

— Pheander the mayden knight. 1595, 1617 (4th edn, enlarged), 1661; adapted as Marianus: or loves heroick champion, 1641.

— Honours conquest: the famous hystorie of Edward of Lancaster, with the famous victories performed by the Knight of the Unconquered Castel. 1598.

— Haigh for Devonshire: sixe gallant marchants of Devonshire. 1600, 1612. See L. B. Wright, Robarts: patriotic propagandist and novelist, SP 29 1932.

Sidney, Sir Philip. The Countesse of Pembrokes Arcadia. 1590. See col 1047, above.

M., Jo. Philippes Venus: sundrye fine and wittie arguments of the gods and goddesses for the expelling of wanton Venus. 1591.

Fraunce, Abraham. The third part of the Countesse of Pembrokes Yvychurch, entituled Amintas dale: the most conceited tales of the pagan gods. 1592.

Johnson, Richard. The nine worthies of London. 1592; rptd Harleian miscellany vol 8, 1811.

— The most famous history of the seaven champions of Christendome. Pt 1, 1596; pt 2, 1597; 1608 (both pts), [1616], [1626], [1639?], [after 1640?], [1660], 1670, 1675, 1676, 1680, [1680], 1686, 1687, 1696; pt 3,

1686, 1689, 1694; abridged 1661, 1675, 1679; rptd R. Kennedy, Portland Oregon 1967 (facs of 18th-century edn).

— The most pleasant history of Tom a Lincolne. 1631 (6th impression), 1635, 1655, 1668, 1682, 1682; abridged [1695]; ed W. J. Thoms, Early prose romances vol 2, 1828 etc.

— The pleasant conceites of old Hobson the merry Londoner. 1607, 1610 (enlarged), 1634, 1640; ed J. O. Halliwell (-Phillipps) 1843 (Percy Soc); ed W. C. Hazlitt, Shakespeare jest-books vol 3, 1864.

— The history of Tom Thumbe, by R[ichard?] J[ohnson?]. 1621; ed C. F. Bühler, Evanston 1965.

C[hettle], H[enry]. Kind-harts dreame. [1593].

— Piers Plainnes seaven yeres prentiship. 1595.

D[ickenson], J[ohn]. Arisbas, Euphues amidst his slumbers: or Cupids journey to Hell. 1594.

— Greene in conceipt new raised from his grave to write the tragique historie of faire Valeria of London. 1598.

Nashe, Thomas. The unfortunate traveller: or the life of Jacke Wilton. 1594.

Forde, Emanuel. The most pleasant historie of Ornatus and Artesia. [1595?], 1607, 1619, 1634, 1650, 1662, 1669, 1683; abridged [1688?], [1694?] [c. 1700]; ed P. Henderson, Shorter novels, Jacobean and Restoration, 1930.

— Parismus, the renoumed Prince of Bohemia. 1598, 1599 (pt 2: Parismenos), 1604 (both pts), 1608, 1615, 1630, 1636, 1649, 1657, 1661, 1663, 1664 (pt 1 only), 1665 (pt 2 only), 1671-2 (pt 1), 1672 (pt 2), 1677 (complete), 1681, 1684, 1689, 1696; abridged [c. 1660], 1677, 1683, 1699, [1700?]; ed R. B. Johnson, The birth of romance, 1928 (extracts).

— The famous historie of Montelyon, knight of the oracle. 1633, 1640, 1661, 1663, 1668, 1673, 1677, 1680, 1687, 1695, 1697.

Parry, Robert. Moderatus: the most delectable and famous historie of the blacke knight. 1595.

M., C. The first part of the nature of a woman. 1596; The second part of the history, 1596. Attributed to C. Middleton, below.

Breton, Nicholas. The miseries of Mavillia. 1597 (in The wil of wit), 1599, 1606 (corrected).

— The strange fortunes of two excellent princes. 1600.

— Grimellos fortunes. 1604.

See col 1027, above.

Middleton, Christopher. The famous historie of Chinon of England; with the worthy achievment of Sir Lancelot du Lake and Sir Tristram du Lions. 1597; ed W. E. Mead 1925 (EETS).

Deloney, Thomas. The gentle craft. Pt 2, [c. 1598] (fragment), 1639 (newly corrected and augmented), 1660; Pt 1, 1627, 1637, 164[0], 1648 (with pictures), 1652, 1660, [1670], 1672, 1674, [1675?], 1676, 1678, [1680?], [1685], [1690?], 1696; ed A. F. Lange, Berlin 1903; ed W. H. D. Rouse 1926; pt 1 ed W. J. Halliday, Oxford 1928. Sequel by L.P., The most pleasant history of Bovinian, 1656.

— The pleasant history of John Winchcomb, Jack of Newberie. 1619 (8th edn), 1626 (10th edn), 1630, 1633, 1637, 1672, [1690?], [1700?]; abridged 1684; ed J. O. Halliwell (-Phillipps) 1859; ed R. Sievers, Deloney, Weimar 1903; ed W. H. D. Rouse 1920; ed G. Saintsbury, Shorter novels vol 1, 1929; ed R. Ashley and E. M. Moseley, Elizabethan fiction, New York 1953.

— Thomas of Reading: or the sixe worthy yeomen of the west. 1612 (4th edn), 1623, 1632, 1636, 1672, 1690, 1690 (abridged); rptd Edinburgh 1812 (from 1632); ed W. J. Thoms, Early prose romances vol 1, 1827; ed C. Aldrich and L. S. Kirtland, New York 1903; ed D. Senior, Some old English worthies, 1912; ed W. H. D. Rouse 1920; ed G. Saintsbury, Shorter novels vol 1, 1929; ed M. Lawlis, Elizabethan prose fiction, New York 1968; Menston 1969 (facs of 1612).

—— Works. Ed F. O. Mann, Oxford 1912; Novels, ed M. E. Lawlis, Bloomington 1961.

See R. Sievers, Deloney: eine Studie über Balladen-litteratur der Shakspere-Zeit, Weimar 1903; A. Chevalley, Deloney: le roman des métiers au temps de Shakespeare, Paris 1926; H. E. Rollins, Deloney's Euphuistic learning and the Forest, PMLA 50 1935, Deloney's sources for Euphuistic learning, PMLA 51 1936, Deloney and Melbancke: notes on sources, Harvard Stud 19 1936; G. W. Kuehn, Deloney: two notes, MLN 52 1937, The novels of Deloney a source for 'climate of opinion' in sixteenth-century economic history, Jnl of Political Economy 48 1940; R. Kapp, Deloney, The gentle craft: eine hagiologische Untersuchung, Anglia 62 1938; O. Reuter, Some aspects of Deloney's prose style, Neuphilologische Mitteilungen 40 1939; M. E. Hablützel, Die Bildwelt Deloneys, Berne 1946; T. Dahl, An inquiry into aspects of the language of Deloney, Copenhagen 1951; E. D. Mackerness, Deloney and the virtuous proletariat, Cambridge Jnl Oct 1951; R. G. Howarth, Two Elizabethan writers of fiction, Thomas Nashe and Deloney, Cape Town 1956; F. Dall'Ara, Drappieri della vecchia Inghilterra, Rome 1956; W. E. Roberts, Folklore in the novels of Deloney, in Studies in folklore in honor of Stith Thompson, ed W. E. Richmond, Bloomington 1957; M. E. Lawlis, Apology for the middle class: the dramatic novels of Deloney, Bloomington 1960; C. Lapart, La promotion du travail à l'époque élisabéthaine, vue à travers les romans de Deloney, Caliban 2 1966; K.-M. Pätzold, Deloneys Thomas of Reading und das Jest-book The pinder of Wakefield, Neuphilologische Mitteilungen 72 1971.

Kittowe, Robert. Loves load-starre. 1600. *See* J. D. Hurrell, Boston Univ Stud in Eng 1 1956.

The heroicall adventures of the knight of the sea, Prince Oceander. 1600.

Armin, Robert. Foole upon foole: or six sortes of sottes, [by] Clonnico de Curtanio Snuffe. 1600, 1605, 1608 (with addns as A nest of ninnies); ed J. P. Collier, Fools and jesters, 1842 (Shakespeare Soc) (from 1608); ed A. B. Grosart, Manchester 1880 (from 1605); ed P. M. Zall 1963 (from 1608).

G., R. The famous historie of Albions Queene. 1600, 1601.

[Corrozet, Gilles]. Memorable conceits of divers noble and famous personages. 1602.

Dekker, Thomas. The wonderfull yeare. 1603.

—— Newes from hell. 1606, 1607 (as A knights conjuring).

—— and George Wilkins. Jests to make you merie. 1607. *See col 1673, above.*

The thrie tailes of the thrie priests of Peblis. Edinburgh 1603; ed D. Laing, Edinburgh 1826; ed C. B. Gunn, Selkirk 1894; ed T. D. Robb, Edinburgh 1920 (Scottish Text Soc).

Pasquils jests, mixed with Mother Bunches merriments. 1604, 1609 (corrected with new addns), 1629, [1632?], 1635, [1650?]; ed W. C. Hazlitt, Shakespeare jest-books vol 3, 1864.

H[ind], J[ohn]. The most excellent historie of Lysimachus and Varrona. 1604.

—— Eliosto libidinoso: described in two bookes wherein their imminent dangers are declared guiding their life by affection. 1606.

Jacke of Dover. His quest of inquirie. 1604, 1615 (as Jacke of Dovers merry tales).

The first and second part of the history of the famous Evordanus Prince of Denmark; with the strange adventures of Iago Prince of Saxonie; and of both theyr severall fortunes in love. 1605.

Dobsons drie bobbes: sonne and heire to Skoggin. 1607; ed E. Schulz, Die englischen Schwankbücher bis herab zu Dobsons Drie Bobs (1607), Berlin 1912; ed E. A. Horsman, Oxford 1955. *See* B. Colgrave, Durham Univ Jnl new ser 12 1951.

Peele, George. The merrie conceited jests of George Peale. 1607, [1620?], 1627, 1627, 1657, 1671; ed W. C. Hazlitt, Shakespeare jest-books vol 2, 1864; ed C. Hindley 1869.

Markham, Gervase. The English Arcadia, alluding his beginning from Sir Philip Sydnes ending. 1607.

—— The second and last part of the first booke of the English Arcadia. 1613.

Bettie, W. The historie of Titana and Theseus. 1608, 1636. *See* J. S. Weld, PQ 26 1947. On dependence on Greene's Pandosto.

Wilkins, George. The painfull adventures of Pericles Prince of Tyre: being the true history of the play of Pericles, as it was lately presented. 1608; ed T. Mommsen, Oldenburg 1857; ed K. Muir, Liverpool 1953.

The famous and renowned history of Morindos a King of Spain who maryed with Miracola a Spanish witch. 1609; ed C. C. Mish, Short fiction of the seventeenth century, New York 1963.

Tarlton, Richard. Tarltons jests, drawn into three parts. 1611, 1613, 1638; ed J. O. Halliwell (-Phillipps) 1844 (Shakespeare Soc); ed W. C. Hazlitt, Shakespeare jest-books vol 2, 1864; ed E. W. Ashbee [1876?] (facs).

Anton, Robert. Moriomachia. 1613; ed G. Becker, Archiv 122 1909; ed C. C. Mish, Short fiction of the seventeenth century, New York 1963.

Gainsford, Thomas. The historie of Trebizond. 1616.

The famous history of George Lord Faukonbridge bastard son to Richard Cordelion King of England. 1616, 1635.

C., W. The first part of the renowned historie of Fragosa King of Aragon. 2 pts 1618, 1646, 1656, 1663.

Westward for smelts: or the water-mans fare of mad-merry western wenches, written by Kinde Kit of Kingstone. 1620; ed J. O. Halliwell(-Phillipps) 1848 (Percy Soc).

The life and pranks of Long Meg of Westminster. 1620, 1635, 1636; ed R. Triphook, Miscellanea antiqua anglicana, 1816 (from 1635); ed C. Hindley, The old book collector's miscellany vol 2, 1872; ed C. C. Mish, Short fiction of the seventeenth century, New York 1963 (from 1620).

Reynolds, John. The triumphs of Gods revenge against murther, in thirty severall tragicall histories. Bk 1, 1621, 1629; bk 2, 1622; bk 3, 1623; bks 1-6, 1635 (for 1634), 1639, 1657, 1662, 1663, 1670, 1679 (enlarged), 1682, 1685 (abridged as The glory of God's revenge), 1686, 1687, 1688 (as God's revenge). Pirated as Blood for blood, 1661; tr Dutch, 1664.

—— The flower of fidelitie: the various adventures of three foraign princes. 1650, 1654, 1655, 1660. *See* J. H. Bryant, Reynolds of Exeter and his canon, Library 5th ser 15 1960.

Wroth, Lady Mary. The Countesse of Mountgomeries Urania. 1621.

B[eling], R[ichard]. A sixth booke to the Countesse of Pembrokes Arcadia. Dublin 1624, London 1627 (for 1628), 1633, 1638, 1655, 1662, 1674. *See under Sidney, col 1047, above.*

Bacon, Francis. The new Atlantis. 1626. *See col 2324, below.*

B[ernard], R[ichard]. The Isle of Man: or the legall proceeding in Man-shire against sinne. 1626, 1627, 1627 (4th edn 'much enlarged'), 1628, 1630 (7th edn), 1632, 1634, 1635 (10th edn), 1640, 1648, 1658, 1659, 1668, 1674, 1676, 1677, 1683; ed R. Edwards, Bristol 1803; rptd London 1834; ed D. F. Jarman 1851 (as Sin apprehended). *See* J. I. Dredge, The writings of Bernard: a bibliography, Horncastle 1890; M. Müller, The Isle of Man 1626: eine literargeschichtliche Untersuchung, Markneukirchen 1933.

The famous historie of Fryer Bacon. 1627, 1629, [1640], 1661, 1666, 1679, 1683; ed W. G. Thoms, Early prose romances vol 1, 1828; ed H. Morley, Early prose romances, 1889; ed D. Senior, Some old English worthies, 1912.

Robin Good-Fellow his mad prankes. 2 pts 1628, 1639. *See col 2028, above.*

Mainwaringe, M. Vienna: noe art can cure this hart. [1628], [1632?], 1650. Reworking of old romance of Paris and Vienne.

Brewer, T. The life and death of the merry devill of Edmonton. 1631, 1819; ed W. A. Abrams, Durham NC 1942 (with the play).

The pinder of Wakefield: being the merry history of George a Greene. 1632; ed E. A. Horsman, Liverpool 1956. A different version, printed 1706, ed W. J. Thoms, Early prose romances vol 2, 1827–8; ed D. Senior, Some old English worthies, 1912. See K.-M. Pätzold, Deloneys Thomas of Reading und das Jestbook The pinder of Wakefield, Neuphilologische Mitteilungen 72 1971.

Goodman, Nicholas. Hollands leaguer: or an historical discourse of the life and actions of Dona Britanica Hollandia. 1632; ed D. S. Barnard, Hague 1970.

Cacoethes leaden legacy: or his schoole of ill manners. [1634].

A pleasant history of the life and death of Will Summers. 1637, 1676; ed J. Caulfield 1794.

Godwin, Francis. The man in the moone: or a discourse of a voyage thither by D. Gonsales. 1638 (anon), 1657 (with Nuncius inanimatus, 1629); ed G. McColley, Northampton Mass 1937; rptd F.C.M., Hereford 1959; ed C. C. Mish, Short fiction of the seventeenth century, New York 1963 (from 1657); tr from the Latin by E[dward?] M[ahon?]; tr French, 1648; Dutch, 1651; German, 1659. Abridged versions ed N. Crouch, View of the English acquisitions in the East Indies, 1686; rptd Harleian miscellany vol 8, 1811 (as A view of St Helena); ed E. Hönncher, The voyage of Domingo Gonzales to the world of the moon, Anglia 10 1888. See H. W. Lawton, Bishop Godwin's Man in the moone, RES 7 1931; G. McColley, The date of Godwin's Domingo Gonsales, MP 35 1937, The pseudonyms of Francis Godwin, PQ 16 1937; M. H. Nicolson, Cosmic voyages, ELH 7 1940, Voyages to the moon, New York 1948; G. Negley and J. M. Patrick, The quest for utopia, New York 1952; W. H. van Seters, De Nederlandse uitgaven, Het Boek 31 1953; H. N. Davies, Bishop Godwin's 'lunatique language', Jnl of Warburg & Courtauld Inst 30 1967; J. R. Knowlson, A note on Bishop Godwin's Man in the moone: the East Indies trade route and a 'language' of musical notes, MP 65 1968.

Rivers, George. The heroinae: or the lives of Arria, Paulina, Lucrecia, Dido, Theutilla, Cypriana, Arctaphila. 1639.

S., J. Clidamas: or the Sicilian tale. 1639.

Brathwait, Richard. Ar't asleepe husband? 1640.
— The two Lancashire lovers. 1640.
— The penitent pilgrim. 1641.

H[owell], J[ames]. Δενδρολογία: Dodona's grove, or the vocall forrest. 1640, 1644, Cambridge 1645, [1649]; pt 2, 1650. See also col 2225, below.

The pleasant history of Cawwood the rooke: or the assembly of birds. 1640, 1656, 1683; ed C. C. Mish, Short fiction of the seventeenth century, New York 1963.

C., S. The famous and delectable history of Cleocreton and Cloryana. [1640?].

Johnson, John. The academy of love, describing the folly of younge men and the fallacy of women. 1641.

Baron, Robert. ΈΡΩΤΟΠΑΙΓΝΙΟΝ: or the Cyprian academy. 1647, 1648.
— An apologie for Paris for rejecting of Juno and Pallas. 1649.

Neville, Henry. The parliament of ladies: or divers remarkable passages of ladies in Spring-Garden in parliament assembled. 1647, 1647, 1647 (as The ladies' parliament), 1752 (Somers tracts), 1768, 1811 (Somers tracts; another version).
— The ladies a second time assembled in parliament. 1647.
— Newes from the New Exchange: or the commonwealth of ladies. 1650.

Bayly, Thomas. Herba parietis, or the wall-flower as it grew out of the prison of Newgate: being a history partly true. 1650, 1679 (as The wall-flower).

Sheppard, Samuel. The loves of Amandus and Sophronia. 1650.

Beware the beare: the strange but pleasing history of Balbulo and Rosina. 1650.

The famous history of stout Stukley. [c. 1650].

The merry Oxford knight: or the pleasant intrigues of Sir Humphrey Frollicksome. [c. 1650?].

Boyle, Roger, Earl of Orrery. Parthenissa. 2 pts Waterford 1651; pt 1 (bks 1–6), 1654; pt 3 (bks 1–4), 1656; pt 3 (bks 5–8), 1669, 1676 (complete). See C. W. Miller, A bibliographical study, SB 2 1949; K. M. Lynch, Roger Boyle, Knoxville 1965.

Charleton, Walter. The Ephesian and Cimmerian matrons. [1651?], 1668 (partly rptd from 1659, below), 1694 (in Three choice novels). The Cimmerian matron, 'by P.M.', ed C. C. Mish, Restoration prose fiction 1666–1700, Lincoln Nebraska 1970; this is probably not by Charleton.
— The Ephesian matron. 1659; tr Latin, 1665 (as Matrona Ephesia).

The pleasant and delightful history of Captain Hind. 1651.

F[idge], G[eorge]. Hind's ramble. 1651.
— The English Gusman: or the history of that unparallel'd thief James Hind. 1652, [1652?] (abridged as Wit for money).

W[eamys], A[nna]. A continuation of Sir Philip Sydney's Arcadia. 1651, 1690.

Cloria and Narcissus. 2 vols 1653–4, 1661 (complete).

Triana: or a threefold romanza of Mariana Paduana Sabina. 1654, 1664 (wrongly ascribed to Thomas Fuller).

Crouch, H[umphrey]. A new and pleasant history of unfortunate Hodg of the south. 1655.

P[rice], L[aurence]. The witch of the woodlands. 1655, [1670?], [1677?], [c. 1684?].

[Sales, Sir W.]. Theophania: or severall modern histories. 1655.

Cavendish, Margaret, Duchess of Newcastle. Natures pictures. 1656, 1671. See D. Grant, Margaret the First, 1957.

Heywood, Thomas. The famous and remarkable history of Sir Richard Whittington. 1656, [167?], 1678, [c. 1680].

Harrington, James. The common-wealth of Oceana. 1656, 1656, 1658; ed H. Morley 1887; ed S. B. Liljegren, Lund 1924. See col 2339, below.

[Holland, Samuel]. Don Zara del Fogo: a mock-romance. 1656 (also as Wit and fancy in a maze), 1660 (as Romancio-mastrix).

P., L. The most pleasant history of Bovinian: being an addition to Crispine and Crispianus [i.e. Deloney's Gentle craft]. 1656. By Laurence Price?

M., T. The life of a satyrical puppy called Nim. 1657. Probably not by Thomas May.

'Pomerano, Castalion'. Panthalia: or the royal romance. 1659. Probably not by Brathwait or Howell. See B. Boyce, History and fiction in Panthalia, JEGP 57 1958.

(4) STUDIES

Warton, Thomas. The history of English poetry. 4 vols 1774–81; rev W. C. Hazlitt 4 vols 1871.

Ashton, J. Romances of chivalry. 1887.

Jusserand, J. J. Le roman au temps de Shakespeare. Paris 1887; tr 1890, 1899 (enlarged).

Koeppel, E. Studien zur Geschichte der italienischen Novelle in der englischen Litteratur des sechzehnten Jahrhunderts. Quellen und Forschungen 70 1892.

Raleigh, W. The English novel. 1894, 1929 (rev).

Chandler, F. W. Romances of roguery. Pt 1, Picaresque novel in Spain, New York 1899.

— The literature of roguery. 2 vols Boston 1907.

Canby, H. S. The short story in English. New York 1909.

Morgan, C. E. The rise of the novel of manners: a study of English prose fiction between 1600 and 1740. New York 1911.

Tieje, A. J. The expressed aim of the long prose fiction from 1579 to 1740. JEGP 11 1912.

— The critical heritage of fiction in 1579. E Studien 47 1913.

— The theory of characterization in prose fiction prior to 1740. Minneapolis 1916.

Wolff, S. L. The Greek romances in Elizabethan prose fiction. New York 1912.

Long, P. W. From Troilus to Euphues. In G. L. Kittredge anniversary papers, Boston 1913.

Prÿs, J. Der Staatsroman des 16 und 17 Jahrhunderts. Würzburg 1913.

Scott, M. A. Elizabethan translations from the Italian. New York 1916.

Savage, H. J. Italian influence in English fiction. PMLA 32 1917.

Thomas, H. Spanish and Portuguese romances of chivalry. Cambridge 1920.

Prothero, R. E., Baron Ernle. Tudor novels and romances. Nineteenth Century July, Dec 1922.

— The light reading of our ancestors. 1927.

Baker, E. A. The history of the English novel vol 2: The Elizabethan age and after. 1929.

Hoops, R. Der Begriff Romance in der mittelenglischen und frühneuenglischen Literatur. Heidelberg 1929.

Haviland, T. P. The roman de longue haleine on English soil. Philadelphia 1931.

Wright, L. B. Middle-class culture in Elizabethan England. Chapel Hill 1935.

Pruvost, R. Matteo Bandello and Elizabethan fiction. Paris 1937.

Wilson, F. P. The English jestbooks of the sixteenth and early seventeenth century. HLQ 2 1939; rev in his Shakespearian and other studies, Oxford 1969.

MacCarthy, B. G. Women writers: their contribution to the English novel 1621–1744. Cork 1944.

Parks, G. B. Before Euphues. In J. Q. Adams memorial studies, Washington 1948.

Miller, E. H. The professional writer in Elizabethan England. Cambridge Mass 1959.

Randall, D. B. J. The golden tapestry: a critical survey of non-chivalric Spanish fiction in English translation 1543–1657. Durham NC 1963.

Schlauch, M. Antecedents of the English novel 1400–1600. 1963.

— English short fiction in the 15th and 16th centuries. Stud in Short Fiction 3 1966.

Mish, C. C. English short fiction in the seventeenth century. Stud in Short Fiction 6 1969.

Davis, W. R. Idea and act in Elizabethan fiction. Princeton 1969.

O'Connor, J. J. Amadis de Gaule and its influence on Elizabethan literature. New Brunswick NJ 1970.

(5) TRANSLATIONS INTO ENGLISH

Translations of Works of Known Authorship

ACHILLES TATIUS

See col 2165, below.

MATEO ALEMÁN

See col 2179, below.

BARTHÉLÉMI ANEAU

[Hammon, J. ?]. 'Αλέκτωρ the cock: the first part of the historie of the valorous squire Alector. 1590.

APULEIUS

See col 2166, below.

LUCA ASSARINO

B., J. La stratonica: or the unfortunate Queen. 1651.

VITAL D'AUDIGUIER

D., W. A tragi-comicall history of Lisander and Calista. 1627, 1635, 1652.

B[arwick], W. Love and valour: celebrated in the person of the author by the name of Adraste. 1638.

BANDELLO

See col 2181, below.

JOHN BARCLAY

See col 2300, below.

FRANÇOIS DE BELLEFOREST

The hystorie of Hamblet. 1608; ed J. P. Collier, Shakespeare's library vol 1, [1843]; ed H. Morley, Early prose romances, 1889; ed I. Gollancz, The sources of Hamlet, 1926.

BIDPAI

See col 2181, below.

GIOVANNI FRANCESCO BIONDI

Hayward, Ja[mes]. Eromena: or love and revenge. 1632.

— Donzella desterrada: or the banish'd virgin. 1635.

G[entilis], R[obert]. Coralbo: a new romance. 1655.

BOCCACCIO

See col 2182, below.

FRANCOIS LE METEL DE BOISROBERT

G., W. The Indian history of Anaxander and Orazia. 1657. By William Duncomb?

JEAN PIERRE CAMUS

Du Verger, S[usan] and T. Brugis. Admirable events, together with morall relations. 1639.
—— Diotrephe: or an historie of valentines. 1641.
Wright, James. The loving enemie. 1650, 1667.
—— Nature's paradox, or the innocent impostor: a pleasant Polonian history originally intituled Iphigenes. 1652.
Jennings, John. Elise: or innocencie guilty. 1655.

FRANCESCO CARMENI

Nissena, englished by an honorable anti-Socordist. 1652, 1653.

JEAN DE CARTIGNY

Goodyear, William. The voyage of the wandering knight. 1581, 1584, 1607, [1615?], [1626?], 1650, 1661, 1670, 1687 (as The conviction of worldly-vanity); ed D. A. Evans, Seattle 1951.

RENÉ DE CERIZIERS

T[asborough], J[ohn]. Innocency acknowledg'd in the life and death of S. Genovefa Countesse Palatin of Trevers. Ghent 1645.
Lower, Sir William. The innocent lady. 1654, 1674.
—— The innocent lord, or the divine providence: the incomparable history of Joseph. 1655.
—— The triumphant lady. 1656.

CERVANTES

See col 2183, below.

GONZALO CESPEDES Y MANESES

Digges, Leonard. Gerardo the unfortunate Spaniard: or a patterne for lascivious lovers. 1622, 1653.

CHRISTINE DU CASTEL

[Anslay, B.] The boke of the cyte of ladyes. 1521.
W[yer], R. The C. historyes of Troye. [1540?].

FRANCESCO COLONNA

D[allington], R. Hypnerotomachia: the strife of love in a dreame. 1592; ed A. Lang 1891.

GUIDO DELLE COLONNE

Paynell, Thomas. The faythfull and true storye of the destruction of Troye. 1553.

CYRANO DE BERGERAC

See col 2184, below.

JEAN DESMARETS DE SAINT-SORLIN

Ariana. 1636, 1641.

JEAN BONAVENTURE DES PÉRIERS

D., T. The mirrour of mirth. 1583, 1592; ed J. W. Hassell, Columbia SC 1959. See J. W. Hassell, An Elizabethan translation of the tales of Des Périers, SP 52 1955.

HENRI ESTIENNE

C[arew?], R. A world of wonders. 1607, Edinburgh 1608.

JUAN DE FLORES

The historie of Aurelio and of Isabell, doughter of the Kinge of Schotlande; nyeuley translatede in foure langagies, Frenche, Italien, Spanishe and Inglishe. Antwerp 1556, Brussels 1608.
A paire of turtle doves: or the tragicall history of Bellora and Fidelio. 1606. Tr Robert Greene?
See B. Matulka, The novels of Juan de Flores and their European diffusion, New York 1931.

CARLOS GARCIA

M[elvin], W[illiam]. The sonne of the rogue: or the politick theefe. 1638, 1650 (as Lavernae: or the Spanish gipsy), 1657 (as Guzman, Hinde and Hannam outstript), 1659 (as A scourge for a den of thieves). From the French of Vital d'Audiguier.

GIOVANNI BATTISTA GIRALDI (CINTHIO)

See col 2185, below.

JEAN OGIER DE GOMBAULD

Hurst, Richard. Endimion: an excellent fancy. 1639.

MARIN LE ROY, SIEUR DE GOMBERVILLE

Browne, William. The history of Polexander, in five bookes. 1647, 1648.

SIMON GOULART

Grimeston, Edward. Admirable and memorable histories containing the wonders of our time. 1607.

LODOVICO GUICCIARDINI

See col 2187, below.

JOSEPH HALL

H[ealey], J[ohn]. The discovery of a new world: or a description of the South Indies. [1609?]; ed H. Brown, Cambridge Mass 1937.

HELIODORUS

See col 2169, below.

GAUTIER DE COSTES DE LA CALPRENEDE

See col 2187, below.

OLIVIER DE LA MARCHE

Lewkenor, Lewis. The resolved gentleman, translated out of Spanishe. 1594. From the version of Hernando de Acuña.

FRANCISCO DE LAS COVERAS (FRANCISCO DE QUINTANA)

The history of Don Fenise. 1651. From the French.

LONGUS

See col 2172, below.

GIOVANNI FRANCESCO LOREDANO

Cokaine, Sir Aston. Dianea. 1654.
S., J. The life of Adam. 1659.

LUCIAN

See col 2172, below.

MACHIAVELLI

The Divell a married man. [1647].

MARGUERITE DE NAVARRE

The Queene of Navarres tales: verie pleasant discourses of fortunate lovers. 1597.
Codrington, Robert. Heptameron: or the history of the fortunate lovers. 1654.

ETIENNE DE MAISONNEUVE

Jennynges, M. The gallant, delectable and pleasaunt hystorie of Gerileon of Englande. 1578.
M[unday], A. Gerileon of England: the second part. 1592.

PEDRO MEXÍA

Fortescue, Thomas. The foreste: or collection of histories dooen out of Frenche. 1571, [1576]. From the French of Claude Gruget.

JUAN PEREZ DE MONTALVÁN

S[tanley], T[homas]. Aurora and the Prince, [with] Oronta the Cyprian virgin, by Sigr Girolamo Preti. 1647, 1650.
P[hillips], E[dward]. The illustrious shepherdess; The imperious brother. 2 pts 1656.

JORGE DE MONTEMAYOR

See col 2189, below.

NICOLAS DE MONTREUX

T[ofte], R[obert]. Honours academie: or the famous pastorall of the faire shepheardesse Julietta. 1610.

SIR THOMAS MORE

See col 1792, above.

DIEGO ORTUÑEZ DE CALAHORRA

See col 2190, below.

ENEA SILVIO PICCOLOMINI (AENEAS SILVIUS)

The goodli history of the Ladye Lucres of Scene in Tuskane. [1515?] (fragment), [1553?], 1560, 1567; ed H. H. Gibbs 1873 (with The hystorie of the moste noble knight Plasidas) (Roxburghe Club); 1596 (another trn as The historie of Euryalus); 1639 (another trn by Charles Allen; ed C. C. Mish, Short fiction of the seventeenth century, New York 1963.

PLUTARCH

Sanford, James. The amorous and tragicall tales of Plutarch; whereunto is annexed the hystorie of Cariclea and Theogenes, and the sayings of the Greeke philosophers. 1567.

FRANCISCO DE QUEVEDO Y VILLEGAS

C[roshawe], R[ichard]. Visions: or Hels kingdome and the worlds follies and abuses. 1640; tr R[oger] L[Estrange] 1667 etc.
Messervy, Edward. Hell reformed. 1641.
The life and adventures of Buscon the witty Spaniard; to which is added the provident knight. 1657, 1669/70, 1670.

RABELAIS

See col 2192, below.

DIEGO HERNANDEZ DE SAN PEDRO

See col 2187, below.

GILBERT SAULNIER, SIEUR DU VERDIER

The love and armes of the Greeke princes: or the romant of romants. 3 pts 1640.

MADELEINE DE SCUDERY

See col 2192, below.

MARIANO SILESIO

Brathwait, Richard. The Arcadian Princesse: or the triumph of justice. 1635.

CHARLES SOREL

[Davies, John]. The extravagant shepherd: the anti-romance: or the history of the shepherd Lysis. 1653, 1654, 1660.
The comical history of Francion. 1655, 1661 (as The most delightful and pleasant history).

JOSÉ TEIXEIRA

The strangest adventure that ever happened: a discourse concerning the King of Portugall Dom Sebastion. 1601.

HONORE D'URFE

See col 2194, below.

LOPE DE VEGA

The pilgrime of Casteele. 1621, 1623.

Translations of Anonymous Works

Robert the Devyll. [1500?], [1510?] (fragment), [1517?]; ed W. J. Thoms, Early prose romances vol 1, 1827; ed H. Morley, Early prose romances 1889. From the French.

Watson, Henry. The hystory of the two valyaunte brethren Valentyne and Orson, sonnes unto the Emperour of Grece. [c. 1503–5] (fragment), [c. 1548–58] (imperfect), [1565?], 1637 (abridged), 1649, 1671, [1675?], 1682, 1685, 1688, 1694, [169?]; new abridgement by Laurence Price 1673, 1683; ed A. Dickson 1937 (EETS). From the French.

— The hystorye of Olyver of Castylle, and of the fayre Helayne doughter unto the Kynge of Englande. 1518; ed R. E. Graves 1898 (Roxburghe Club). From the French.

The noble hystory of Kynge Ponthus of Galyce and lytell Brytayne. [1505?], [c. 1510], 1511.

The dystruccyon of Jherusalem by Vaspazyan and Tytus. [1508?], [1513?], 1528.

[Copland, Robert]. Kynge Appolyn of Thyre. 1510; ed E. W. Ashbee 1870 (facs). From the French.

— The hystory of the noble Helyas knyght of the swanne. 1512, [1565?]; ed W. J. Thoms, Early prose romances vol 3, 1827. From the French.

[Joseph of Arimathea]. A treatyse taken out of a boke whiche somtyme Theodosius the Emperour founde, of Joseph of Armathy. [1511?].

Gesta Romanorum. [1517?], 1557, 1595 (rev R. Robinson), 1600 (for 1599), 16[02] (imperfect, with addn), [c. 1605] (imperfect), 1610 (with addn), [c. 1620], [c. 1630], [c. 1640], 1648, 1650, 1662, 1663, 1668, 1672, 1672, 1681, 1682, 1689, 1696, 1698; abridged 1698; ed S. J. H. Herrtage 1879 (EETS).

A lyttell story that was of a trwethe done in the lande of Gelders of a mayde that was named Mary of Nemmegen that was the Dyvels paramoure. Antwerp [1518?]; ed H. M. Ayres and A. J. Barnouw, Cambridge Mass 1932 (facs). *See* M. Schlauch, Mary of Nijmeghen (the female Faust) in an English prose version of the early Tudor period, Philologica Pragensia 6 1963.

This mater treateth of a merchauntes wyfe that afterwarde went lyke a man and was called Frederyke of Jennen. Antwerp 1518, [London? 1520?], [London 1560?].

Virgilius. This boke treath of the lyfe of Virgilius and of his deth and many mervayles that he dyd in his lyfe tyme. Antwerp [1518?], [1561?]; ed W. J. Thoms, Early prose romances vol 2, 1828; ed H. Morley, Early prose romances, 1889. *See* J. W. Spargo, Virgil the necromancer, Cambridge Mass 1934.

Celestina. *See Barley, below and col 2183, below.*

The dialoges of creatures moralysed. [Antwerp 1530?]. From the Latin.

Bourchier, John, Baron Berners. The boke of Huon of Burdeuxe. [c. 1534], 1601 (3rd edn, corrected, as The ancient historie); ed S. Lee 3 pts 1882–7 (EETS); ed R. Steele 1895.

— Arthur of Brytayn: the hystory of Arthur of lytell Brytayne. [1560?], [1582]; ed E. V. Utterson 1814. From the French.

[Copland, William?]. A merye jest of a man called Howleglas. [1555?], [1560?], [1565?]. *See* F. Brie, Eulenspiegel in England, Berlin 1903. *And see col 2026, above.*

Amadis of Gaul. *See col 2179, below.*

S[mythe], R[obert]. Straunge, lamentable and tragicall hystories. 1577. From the French.

W[otton], H[enry]. A courtlie controversie of Cupids cautels: five tragicall histories. 1578. From the French.

Lazarillo de Tormes. *See col 2187, below.*

Munday, Anthony. Palmerin d'Oliva. Pt 1, 1588, 1615; 2 pts 1597, 1616, 1637, 1653.

— The famous, pleasant and variable historie of Palladine of England. 1588, 1664, [1700?]. From the French of Claude Colet.

— The honorable historie of Palmendos. 1589, 1653, 1663. From F. de Moraes.

— Primaleon of Greece. Pt 1, 1595; pt 2, 1596; 3 pts 1619.

— The no lesse rare historie of Palmerin of England. Pt 1, 1609; 2 pts 1596, 1616, 1639, 1664; pt 3, 1602. Abridged 1685, 1691. From F. de Moraes.

See M. Patchell, The Palmerin romances in Elizabethan prose fiction, New York 1947.

F., P. The historie of the damnable life and deserved death of Doctor John Faustus. 1592, 1608, 1610, 1618, 1636, 1648, 1664, 1682, [1687?], [1696?]; abridged [c. 1685], [c. 1690], [c. 1696]; rptd 1827 (from 1636); ed W. J. Thoms, Early prose romances vol 3, 1827–8 (with The second report of Doctor Faustus, 1594, 1594); ed W. Rose [1925]; ed B. Ashmore 1948 (with Marlowe's play).

Twine, L. The historie of painfull adventures. [1594?], 1607; ed J. P. Collier, Shakespeare's library vol 1, [1843]. *See* Copland, 1510, above.

G[oodwine], T[homas] P[ope]. The moste pleasaunt historye of Blanchardine sonne to the King of Friz; and the faire Lady Eglantine. 2 vols 1596, 1597. From the French.

[Barley, William?]. The delightful history of Celestina the Faire, daughter to the King of Thessalie. 1596. From the French version of Primaleon.

A., L. The honour of chivalrie: the most famous historie of Prince Don Bellianis. 1598, 1650, 1663, 1664 (pt 2), 1671 (2 pts), 1672 (pt 3), 1673 (3 pts), 1678 (pt 1), 1683 (3 pts). From the Italian.

C[hambers], R[obert]. Palestina. 'Florence' (London?) 1600.

M., J. The most famous and renowned historie of that woorthie and illustrous knight Mervine, sonne to Oger the Dane. 1612. From the French. By Gervase Markham?

W[illet], R[owland]. Merry jests concerning popes, monkes and friers, written first in Italian by N.S. and thence translated into French by G.I. and now into English. 1617.

The ancient, true and admirable history of patient Grisel. 1619 (from the French), [1630?] (as The true history), 1663, 1674, 1682 (as The true and admirable history); [1640?] (tr from Italian, adapted from a ballad probably by Deloney, as The pleasant and sweet history), 1686. Both versions rptd J. P. Collier 1842 (Percy Soc); first version ed G. L. Gomme and H. B. Wheatley 1885 (Villon Soc); 2nd ed J. E. Masters, Bristol 1939.

The historie of Frier Rush. 1620, 1626, 1629 (title-page only), 1659, 1810; ed W. J. Thoms, Early prose romances vol 1, 1828; ed H. Morley, Early prose romances 1889; ed D. Senior, Some old English worthies, 1912.

The true history of the tragicke loves of Hipolito and Isabella Neapolitans. 1628, 1633. From [Meslier?], Les amours tragiques d'Hypolite et Isabelle, Paris 1610.

H[awkins], Sir T. A Saxon historie of the admirable adventures of Clodoaldus and his three children. 1634. From the French of N.C.

Godwin, Paul. Histoire des larrons: or the history of theeves. 1638. From the French, probably of François de Calvi.

Hart, Alexander. The tragi-comicall history of Alexto and Angelica. 1640; ed C. C. Mish, Short fiction of the seventeenth century, New York 1963.

G., T. The right pleasant and variable tragicall historie of Fortunatus. 1640, 1676, 1682; [1650?] (another trn, as The history of the birth, travels, strange adventures and death of Fortunatus), 1682. Abridged [c. 1685] (as The most excellent and delightful history). From the Dutch.

C., R. The troublesome and hard adventures in love, written in Spanish by Michael Cervants. 1652. Not from Cervantes. See D. B. J. Randall, The troublesome and hard adventures in love: an English addition to the bibliography of Diana, Bull of Hispanic Stud 38 1961.

Choice novels and amorous tales written by the most refined wits of Italy. 1652.

Kirkman, Francis. The loves and adventures of Clerio and Lozia. 1652. From the French.

The fortunate, the deceived and the unfortunate lovers. 1683 (2nd edn?), 1685 (in English and French). One tale ed J. O. Halliwell (-Phillipps), The first sketch of Shakespeare's Merry wives, 1842 (Shakespeare Soc). From the Italian.

E. D. P.

V. NEWS-SHEETS AND NEWSBOOKS

From the earliest days of printing, pamphlets, ballads and broadsides were issued containing news of domestic or foreign affairs. These vary greatly in reliability, but all bear witness to a growing interest in news of events at home and abroad.

No periodical pbns were established in England until the 1620s. Those that then emerged, as a development from the occasional coranto, were restricted by government decree to publishing foreign news. Nevertheless, individual pamphlets and broadsides on domestic affairs continued to be pbd and became the predecessors of that spate of ephemeral news pamphlets occasioned by the Civil War and encouraged by the collapse of government controls over the press.

In this section an attempt has been made to list a representative selection of separate pamphlets, broadsides and ballads on current events from the 1480s to the 1640s, and to set out the various series of periodical pbns in the last 20 years of that period. Periodical pbn has been interpreted as the publisher's intention to issue parts of a series at intervals of not more than one month.

The separate news pamphlets issued after 1640 are too numerous to list: for that period only the news-sheets and newsbooks of ostensibly frequent and regular pbn have been listed. Details of the separate pamphlets will be found in bibliographies listed under (6), notably in the Catalogue of the Thomason Tracts.

(1) Bibliographies and general studies to 1640; (2) Pamphlets on domestic affairs to 1640; (3) Pamphlets on affairs abroad to 1640; (4) Unnumbered newsbooks 1620-2; (5) Numbered newsbooks 1622-41; (6) Bibliographies and general studies (including contemporary accounts) 1640-59; (7) Journalists, printers and publishers after 1640; (8) Newsbooks 1641-59.

(1) BIBLIOGRAPHIES AND GENERAL STUDIES TO 1640

Morgan, J. Phoenix britannicus. 2 vols 1732.

Park, T. (ed). Harleian miscellany: or a collection of scarce curious and entertaining tracts found in the late Earl of Oxford's library. 10 vols 1808-13.

Scott, Sir Walter. Collection of scarce and valuable tracts selected from public as well as private libraries, particularly that of the late Lord Somers. 13 vols 1809-15.

Ames, J. Typographical antiquities (with additions by W. Herbert and T. F. Dibdin). 4 vols 1810-19.

Timperley, C. H. Encyclopaedia of literary and typographical anecdote. 1842.

Andrews, A. The history of British journalism. 2 vols 1859.

Lemon, R. Catalogue of a collection of printed broadsides in the possession of the Society of Antiquaries. 1866.

Hazlitt, W. C. Hand-book to the popular, poetical and dramatic literature of Great Britain. 1867.

— Collections and notes 1867-76. 4 sers 1876-1903.

Hart, W. H. Index expurgatorius anglicanus. 5 pts 1872-8.

Arber, E. A transcript of the registers of the Company of Stationers 1554-1640. 5 vols 1875-94.

Paterson, J. The liberty of the press, speech and public worship. 1880.

Stephen, J. F. A history of the criminal law of England. 3 vols 1883.

British Museum. Catalogue of books in English to the year 1640 3 vols 1885.

Bourne, H. R. F. English newspapers. 2 vols 1887.

Bücher, C. Industrial evolution. Tr S. M. Wickett, New York 1901.

Firth, C. H. (ed). Stuart tracts 1603-93. 1903.

— The ballad history of the reigns of Henry VII and Henry VIII. Trans Royal Historical Soc 2 1908.

— The ballad history of the reigns of the later Tudors. Trans Royal Historical Soc 3 1909.

— Ballad history of the reign of James I. Trans Royal Historical Soc 5 1911.

— Ballads and broadsides. In his Essays historical and literary, Oxford 1938, 1968 (corrected).

Pollard, A. F. (ed). Tudor tracts. 1903.

Duff, E. G. A century of the English book trade. 1905.

Putnam, G. H. The censorship of the Church of Rome. 2 vols New York 1907.

Williams, J. B. (J. G. Muddiman). A history of English journalism to the foundation of the Gazette. 1908.

— The beginnings of English journalism. CHEL vol 7 1911.

— The earliest English corantos. Library 3rd ser 4 1913.

— Tercentenary handlist of English and Welsh newspapers, magazines and reviews. 1920, 1966. See also N & Q 29 Jan-26 Feb, 26 March 1921, 11-18 March 1922.

McKerrow, R. B. (ed). A dictionary of printers and booksellers 1557-1640. 1910.

— Booksellers, printers and the stationers' trade. In Shakespeare's England, 2 vols Oxford 1916.

Notestein, W. A history of witchcraft in England from 1558 to 1718. Washington 1911.

— and F. H. Relf. Commons debates for 1629. Minneapolis 1921.

Barwick, G. F. Corantos. Library 3rd ser 4 1913.

Esdaile, A. Autolycus' pack; the ballad journalism of the sixteenth century. Quart Rev 218 1913.

Pollard, A. W. Shakespeare's fight with the pirates. Cambridge 1917.

McIlwain, C. H. (ed). The political works of James I. Cambridge Mass 1918.

Rollins, H. E. The black-letter broadside ballads. PMLA 34 1919.

— Old English ballads. Cambridge 1920.

—— A Pepysian garland. Cambridge 1922.
—— Cavalier and puritan. New York 1923.
—— An analytical index to the ballad entries 1557–1709 in the registers of the Company of Stationers of London. SP 21 1924.
—— The pack of Autolycus. Cambridge Mass 1927.
—— The Pepys ballads. 8 vols Cambridge Mass 1929–32.
Bloom, J. H. English tracts, pamphlets and printed sheets: a bibliography. Vol 1, Suffolk; vol 2, Leicestershire, Staffordshire, Warwickshire, Worcestershire. 1922–3 (all pbd).
Salmon, L. M. The newspaper and authority. New York 1923.
Reed, A. W. Early Tudor drama. [1926].
Albright, E. M. Dramatic publication in England 1580–1640. New York 1927.
Crane, R. S. and F. B. Kaye. A census of British newspapers and periodicals 1620–1800. Chapel Hill 1927, 1967.
Harlow, A. F. Old post bags. New York 1928.
Harrison, G. B. An Elizabethan journal. 1928; A second Elizabethan journal, 1931; A last Elizabethan journal, 1933.
Shaaber, M. A. Some forerunners of the newspaper in England 1476–1622. Philadelphia 1929.
—— The history of the first English newspaper. SP 29 1932.
Morison, S. The English newspaper. Cambridge 1932.
—— The origins of the newspaper. 1954.
Stewart, A. Catalogue of an exhibition illustrating the history of the English newspaper from the library of the Press Club. 1932.
—— The evolution of the English newspaper from its origins to the present day. 2 vols 1935–46.
Clyde, W. M. The struggle for the freedom of the press from Caxton to Cromwell. 1934.
Milford, R. T. and D. M. Sutherland. A catalogue of English newspapers and periodicals in the Bodleian library 1622–1800. Proc Oxford Bibl Soc 4 1936.
Collins, D. C. Handlist of news pamphlets 1590–1610. 1943.
Dahl, F. Dutch corantos 1618–1650. Hague 1946.
—— Amsterdam: cradle of English newspapers. Library 5th ser 4 1949.
—— A bibliography of English corantos and periodical news-books 1620–1642. 1952.
Weed, K. K. and R. P. Bond. Studies in British newspapers and periodicals from their beginning to 1800: a bibliography. Chapel Hill 1946.
Oates, J. C. T. The trewe encountre: a pamphlet on Flodden Field. Trans Cambridge Bibl Soc 1 1950.

Skelton, R. A. Pieter van den Keere. Library 5th ser 5 1950.
Stewart, R. British newspapers and periodicals 1632–1800: a descriptive catalogue of a collection at the University of Texas. Austin 1950.
Bennett, H. S. English books and readers 1475–1557. Cambridge 1952; English books and readers 1558–1603, Cambridge 1965; English books and readers 1603–40, Cambridge 1970.
Siebert, F. S. Freedom of the press in England 1476–1776. Urbana 1952.
Simpson, P. The official control of Tudor and Stuart printing. In his Studies in Elizabethan drama, Oxford 1955.
Allison, A. F. and D. M. Rogers. A catalogue of Catholic books in English printed abroad or secretly in England 1558–1640. 2 pts Bognor Regis 1956.
Lievsay, J. L. William Barley, Elizabethan printer and bookseller. SB 8 1956.
Jackson, W. A. (ed). Records of the court of the Stationers' Company 1602–40. 1957.
—— Robert Waldegrave and the books he printed or published in 1603. Library 5th ser 13 1958.
Rostenberg, L. Nathaniel Butter and Nicholas Bourne, first 'Masters of the Staple'. Library 5th ser 12 1957.
—— Literary, political, scientific, religious and legal publishing printing and bookselling in England 1551–1700. 2 vols New York 1965.
—— The minority press and the English Crown 1558–1625. Nieuwkoop 1971.
Johnson, A. F. The 'Cloppenburg' press 1640, 1641. Library 5th ser 13 1958.
Salmon, J. H. M. The French religious wars in English political thought. Oxford 1959.
Frank, J. The beginnings of the English newspaper. Cambridge Mass 1961.
Greg, W. W. Licensers for the press to 1640. Oxford 1962.
Loades, D. M. The press under the early Tudors. Trans Cambridge Bibl Soc 4 1964.
Parker, J. Books to build an Empire: a bibliographical history of English overseas interests to 1620. Amsterdam 1965.
Simmons, J. Publications of 1623. Library 5th ser 21 1966.
Bridenbaugh, C. Vexed and troubled Englishmen 1590–1642. Oxford 1968.
Breslow, M. A. A mirror of England: English puritan views of foreign nations 1618–40. Cambridge Mass 1970.

(2) PAMPHLETS ON DOMESTIC AFFAIRS TO 1640

The promisse of matrimonie. [1485?].
The traduction and mariage of the Princesse Kateryne [of Aragon]. [1501].
The solempnities and triumphes doon at the spousells of the Kyng's doughter. [1508].
Hereafter ensue the trewe encountre or batayle lately don betwene Englande and Scotlande. [1513].
[Lyly, William]. Of the tryumphe and the uses that Charles themperour and the Kyng of England were saluted with passyng through London. [1522].
The determinations of the universities of Italy and Fraunce that it is so unlefull for a man to marie his brothers wyfe that the Pope hath no power to dispence therwith. [1531].
The noble tryumphaunt coronation of Quene Anne. [1533].
Answere made by the Kynges Hyghnes to the petitions of the rebelles in Yorkeshire. 1536.
A protestation made for the Kynge of Englande [on Council at Mantua]. 1537.

The enquirie and verdite of the quest panneld of the death of R. Hune. [1539?].
The copye of the submissyon of Oneyll. [1542].
A declaration conteynyng the just causes of this present warre with the Scottis. 1542.
The late expedicion in Scotlande under the Erle of Hertforde. 1544.
Patten, William. The expedicion into Scotlande of the Duke of Soomerset. 1548.
A message sent by the Kynges Maiestie to certain of his people assembled in Devonshire. 1549.
The communication betwene my Lord Chauncelor and Judge Hales. [Rouen 1553].
The saying of John late Duke of Northumberlande upon the scaffolde. [1553].
Proctor, John. The historie of Wyates rebellion. 1554.
Elder, John. The copie of a letter sent in to Scotlande of the arivall and marryage of Philippe Prynce of Spaine to Marye Quene of England. [1555].

The copye of the wordes that Lorde Sturton spake at his death as his confession. 1557.

The passage of our most drad soveraigne lady Quene Elyzabeth to Westminster the daye before her coronacion. 1558.

Marckant, John. The purgacion of the Lord Wentworth concerning the crime layde to his charge. 1559.

[Pilkington, James]. The true report of the burnyng of the steple and churche of Poules in London. 1561.

D., John. A discription of a monstrous chylde borne at Chychester. 1562.

A declaration of the Quenes Majestie: conteyning the causes which have constrayned her to arme certaine of her subjectes. 1562.

The description of a monstrous pig farrowed at Hamsted. 1562.

The true reporte of a monstrous childe borne at Muche Horkeslye. [1562].

The true discription of two monsterous chyldren borne at Herne in Kent. [1565].

Philip, John. The examination and confession of certaine wytches at Chelmsford. 1566.

The forme and shape of a monstrous child borne at Maydstone. 1568.

Granger, Timothy. A most true and marveilous straunge wonder of 17 monstrous fisshes taken in Suffolke. [1568].

Of the endes and deathes of two prisoners lately pressed to death in Newgate. [1569].

R., C. The true discription of this marveilous straunge fishe. 1569.

Seres, William. An aunswere to the proclamation of the rebels in the north. 1569.

The confessioun of maister J. Kello. Edinburgh 1570.

Davie, Sampson. The end and confession of T. Norton and C. Norton, dyed 27 May 1570. 1570.

Knell, T[homas]. A declaration of such tempestious fluddes as hath been in divers places of England. 1570.

Kyrkh[am], W. Joyfull newes for true subjectes to God and the crowne. 1570.

Partridge, I. The ende and confession of John Felton. [1570].

The severall confessions of Thomas Norton and Christopher Norton. 1570.

Tarlton, Richard. A very lamentable and woful discours of the fierce fluds in Bedfordshire. 1570.

A copie of a letter to a frende concernyng D. Story. [1571].

A declaration of the lyfe and death of John Story. 1571.

The copie of a letter concernyng the credit of the late published detection of the doynges of the ladie Marie of Scotland. [1572].

G[olding] A[rthur]. A briefe discourse of the late murther of George Saunders. 1573.

S., D. A true reporte of an horrible murther doen by Jhon Kynnestar. 1573.

The confession and declaration of Robert Sharpe of the familie of love. 1575.

La[neham], Ro[bert]. A letter whearin part of the entertainment untoo the Queen at Killingwoorth Castl. is signified. [1575].

Fleming, Abraham. A straunge and terrible wunder wrought in the parish church of Bongay. [1577].

Ga[rter], Ber[nard]. The joyfull receyving of the Queenes Majestie into Norwiche. 1578.

Churchyard, Thomas. A moste true reporte of James Fitz Morrice death. [1579?].

A detection of damnable driftes practized by three witches arraigned at Chelmsforde. [1579].

E[lderton], W[illiam]. A newe ballade declaryng the shootyng of the gunne at the courte. [1579].

Newe newes contaynyng a shorte rehersall of the late enterprise of certaine rebelles of Ireland. 1579.

A true report of the message of hir Majestie to the place where T. Appeltree should have suffered. 1579.

Shakelton, Francis. A blazyng starre or burnyng beacon seene the 10 of October laste. 1580.

Ellyot, George. A very true report of the apprehension of Edmond Campion. 1581.

Goldwel, Henry. A briefe declaration of the shews performed before the French ambassadours. [1581].

M., A. The true reporte of the success which God gave unto our English souldiours in Ireland. [1581].

M[unday], A[nthony]. A breefe discourse of the taking of Edmund Campion and divers other papistes in Barkeshire. 1581.

S., M. The araignment and execution of a traitour named Everalde Ducket alias Hauns. 1581.

A true report of the death of martyrdome of M. Campion, Jesuite. [Douai 1581].

[Allen, William]. A briefe historie of the glorious martyrdom of xii reverend priests. 1582.

Munday, Anthony. A breefe and true reporte of the execution of certaine traytours at Tiborne. 1582.

A particular declaration of the traiterous affection borne against her Majesty by Edmund Campion, Jesuite. 1582.

W., W. A true and just recorde of all the witches at S. Oses Essex. 1582.

B., R. The severall executions and confessions of John Slade and John Bodye. [1583].

A briefe discourse of two most cruell murthers committed in Worcestershire. 1583.

The execution of justice in England against certaine stirrers of sedition. 1583.

Saxey, Samuel. A straunge and wonderfull example of the iudgement of God vpon two adulterous persons. [1583?].

A true report of the late apprehension of John Nicols. Rheims 1583.

Churchyard, Thomas. A scourge for rebels. 1584.

A discovery of the treasons practised by F. Throckmorton. 1584.

Harrington, Richard. A famous dittie of the ioyful receaving of the Queens Maiestie by the citizens of London. 1584.

Stubbes, Philip. The intended treason of doctor Parrie. 1584.

Lamentable n[ewes] from the towne of Darnton in Durham. 1585.

The life and end of Thomas Awfeeld and Thomas Webley. [1585].

The Queenes Majesties entertainment at Woodstock. 1585.

Studley, Christopher. Treason pretended against the King of Scots. 1585.

A true and plaine declaration of the treasons practised by W. Parry. [1585].

A true and summarie reporte of the Earle of Northumberlands treasons. [1585].

The true copie of a letter from the Queens Maiesty to the Lord Mayor of London. 1586.

The Scottish Queens burial at Peterborough. [1587].

A briefe treatise discovering the offences of the late 14 traitors. 1588.

Certaine aduertisements out of Ireland concerning the losses to the Spanish nauie. 1588.

The copie of a letter sent out of England to don Bernardin Mendoza ambassadour in France for Spaine declaring the state of England. 1588.

A true report of the inditement and execution of John Weldon, William Hartley and Robert Sutton. 1588.

The apprehension and confession of three notorious witches at Chelmsford. [1589].

The most dangerous and memorable adventure of Richard Ferris from Tower wharfe in a small wherry boate to Bristowe. 1590.

A true recitall touching the death of Thomas Bales a seminarie priest. 1590.

The araignment examination and judgement of A. Cosbye who murdered the Lord Burke. 1591.

Newes from Scotland of Doctor Fian a notable sorcerer. [1591].

Speeches deliuered to her Maiesty this last progresse. Oxford [1592].

The most strange discouerie of the three witches of Warboys. 1593.

A true reportarie of the baptisme of Frederik Henry, Prince of Scotland. Edinburgh [1594?].

A most horrible murther committed at Mayfield in Sussex. 1595.

A declaration of the causes mouing the Queenes Maiestie to send a nauy to the seas. 1596.

Chapman, John. A most true report of the mouing and sinking of ground at Westram in Kent. 1597.

Darrell, John. A brief narration of the possession of W. Sommers. 1598.

The true lamentable discourse of the burning of Tiuerton. 1598.

A true discourse of a cruell fact committed by a gentle-woman towardes her husband. 1599.

Darrell, John. A true narration of the vexation by the devil of 7 persons in Lancashire. 1600.

The Earle of Gowries conspiracie against the Kings Majestie of Scotland. 1600, 1603.

W., G. Newes out of Cheshire of the new found well. 1600.

[Bacon, Francis]. A declaration of the treasons by Robert late Earle of Essex. 1601.

Her Majesties most princelie answere delivered on the last day of November. 1601.

A living remembrance of master Robert Rogers leather-seller of London deceased. [1601].

A strange report of sixe witches. 1601.

E., I. A letter from a souldier in Ireland touching the victorie of her Majesties forces. 1602.

An apologie of the Earle of Essex against those which tax him to be the hinderer of peace. 1603.

Chettle, Henry. Englandes mourning garment in memorie of Elizabeth to which is added the manner of her funerall. 1603.

The manner of the murther of W. Storre. Oxford 1603.

P[etowe], H[enry]. Elizabetha quasi vivens, Elizas funerall. 1603.

The true narration of the entertainment of his Majestie from Edenbrough till London. 1603.

The Kings Majesties speach in Parliament. 1604.

The copie of his Majesties letter sent the 26 of June 1604 signifying his pleasure to the Commons House of Parliament. 1604.

[Daniel, Samuel]. The true description of a royall masque. 1604.

[Dekker, Thomas]. The magnificent entertainment given to King James upon his passage through London. 1604.

Dugdale, Gilbert. The time triumphant declaringe the arival of King James into England. 1604.

— A true discourse of the practises of Elizabeth Caldwell on the parson of T. Caldwell. 1604.

Sir Francis Bacon his apologie in certaine imputations concerning the late Earle of Essex. 1604.

To the King's Majestie: the humble petition of two and twenty preachers in London and the suburbs thereof. [1604].

Hamond, Th[omas]. The late commotion of certaine Papists in Herefordshire. 1605.

His Majesties speach in this last session of Parliament. 1605.

The life and death of Gamaliell Ratsey a famous theefe. [1605].

Two most unnaturall and bloodie murthers. 1605.

A faithfull report of proceedings anent the assemblie at Aberdeen 2 July 1605. 1606.

The horrible murther of a young boy. 1606.

A true and perfect relation of the proceedings against Garnet and his confederates. 1606.

W., T. The araignement and execution of the late traytors. 1606.

His Majesties speech to Parliament the last day of March. [1607].

Jones, William. Gods warning to his people of England by the great overflowing of the waters or floudes. 1607.

Nixon, Anthony. The three English brothers. 1607.

A true report of the araignment of a popish priest named Robert Drewrie. 1607.

Two horrible murders done in Lincolnshire by two husbands. 1607.

The apprehension and execution of Elizabeth Abbot for a cruell murther. 1608.

Newes from Lough-foyle in Ireland. 1608.

The over-throw of an Irish rebell, Sir Carey Adoughertie. 1608.

Two monstrous births in Devon and Plymouth. 1608.

The woefull wast and spoile done by a fire in S. Edmonds-bury. 1608.

The arraignment and execution of E. Sudlow at West Chester. [1609].

The Kings Majesties speach to the Lords and Commons the xxj of March 1609.

The order and solemnitie of the creation of Prince Henrie Prince of Wales. 1610.

A record of some worthy proceedings in the Howse of Commons in the late Parliament. [Amsterdam?] 1611.

Chapman, George. An epicede or funerall song on the death of Henry Prince of Wales. 1612.

The life and execution of C. Courtney. 1612.

Wofull newes from the west-parts of England. 1612.

[Campion, Thomas]. A relation of the late royall enter-tainment given by the lord Knowles. 1613.

The last terrible tempestious windes and weather. 1613.

Leigh, William. Strange news of a monster borne at Adlington in Lancashire. 1613.

The marriage of the two great princes Fredericke Count Palatine and the Lady Elizabeth. 1613.

Potts, Thomas. The wonderfull discoverie of witches in Lancaster. 1613.

The Charterhouse with the last will and testament of Thomas Sutton. 1614.

A horrible murder committed at Putney 21 Aprill last upon E. Hall. 1614.

Lamentable newes out of Lincolnshire of the overflowing of waters. 1614.

The lieutenant of the Tower his speech and repentance at the time of his death. [1615].

His Majesties speach in the Starre-Chamber the xx of June. [1616].

I., N. A true relation of the murther committed by J. Bartram upon Sir J. Tyndal. 1616.

The just downfall of Weston, M. Turner and Franklin for the murder of Sir Tho: Overbury. [1616].

Middleton, Tho[mas]. Civitatis amor. The cities love: an entertainment by water at the receiving of Charles to bee created Prince of Wales. 1616.

Platte, T. Anne Wallens lamentations for the murthering of her husband. [1616].

Hay, John. A speach delivered to the Kings Majestie at his entrie into Edinburgh. 1617.

A true relation of a murder committed upon Sir J. Tindall. 1617.

A declaration of the demeanor of Sir Walter Raleigh. 1618.

Newes from Perin in Cornwall of a murther. 1618.

To the Kings most excellent Majestie, the humble petition and information of Sir Lewis Stucley touching Sir Walter Raleigh. 1618.

Damnable practises of three Lincoln-shire witches. 1619.

Gainsford, Th[omas]. The true exemplary and remark-able history of the Earle of Tirone. 1619.

Goodcole, Henry. The wonderfull discoverie of E. Sawyer a witch. 1621.

His Majesties speach in the Upper House of Parliament 26 March 1621. 1621.

The wonderfull battell of starelings fought at Corke in Ireland. 1622.

The cryes of the dead or the late murther in South-warke. [1625].

The last will and testament of J. Kendricke draper of London. 1625.

A declaration of the true causes which moved his Majestie to assemble and dissolve the Parliament. 1626.

A briefe and true relation of the murther of T. Scott. 1628.

The copies of two speeches in Parliament. 1628.

His Majesties declaration of the causes which moved him to dissolve the last Parliament. 1628.

Sir Benjamin Rudierd his speech in behalfe of the clergie. 1628.

The articles of peace agreed upon betwixt Great Britaine and France. 1629.

Taylor, John. The great eater of Kent. 1630.

[Drummond, W.?]. The entertainment of the high and mighty monarch Charles into his auncient city of Edinburgh. 1633.

A true relation of a barbarous murder committed by Enoch ap Evan. 1633.

B[edford] Th[omas]. A true and certaine relation of a strange birth at Stone-house. 1635.

H[eywood], T[homas]. A true discourse of the two infamous upstart prophets Richard Farnham and John Bull. 1636.

The arivall and intertainements of the embassador from the Emperor of Morocco. 1637.

A briefe relation of certain passages in the Starre-Chamber June 14. 1637.

Heywood, Thomas. A true description of his Majesties royall ship built this yeare. 1637, 1638 (with addns).

The protestation of the noblemen ministers and commons at the Mercate Crosse of Edinburgh. [Edinburgh] 1638.

A true relation of those sad accidents which happened in the parish church of Withycombe. 1638.

The protestation of the Generall Assembly of the Kirke of Scotland. Edinburgh 1639.

Articles exhibited in Parliament against William Laud Archbishop of Canterbury. 1640.

A certaine relation of the hog-faced gentlewoman. 1640.

The demands and behaviour of the rebels in Scotland. 1640.

His Majesties declaration concerning his proceedings with his subjects of Scotland. 1640.

Lenthall, William. Mr Speaker his speech to his Majestie in Parliament. 1640.

A list of the colonels as also the names of ships, captaines and lieutenants that are now set forth under the command of the Earle of Northumberland. [1640].

Mr St John's speech to the Lords concerning ship-money. 1640.

Bloody newes from Norwich: or a relation of a bloody attempt of the Papists to consume the city by fire. 1641.

The confession of a papist priest who was hanged at Tiburne. 1641.

An exact relation of a battell fought by the Lord Moore against the rebels in Ireland. 1641.

The last and best newes from Ireland, 3 to 17 November. 1641.

Mr Speakers speech with his Majesties speech to Parliament at the passing of the bill for tonnage and poundage. 1641.

Murther murther or a bloody relation how Anne Hamton murthered her husband. 1641.

The marine mercury or a true relation of the strange appearance of a man-fish in the river Thames. 1642.

(3) PAMPHLETS ON AFFAIRS ABROAD TO 1640

[Caorsin, Gulielmus]. [The siege of Rhodes]. Tr Johan Kay [1482?].

Sex que elegantissime epistole quarum tris a Sixto Quarto ad Venetiarum ducem totidemque ab ipso duce conscripte sunt. [1483].

Of the new landes founde by the messengers of the Kynge of Portyngale. [Antwerp 1520?].

This horryble monster is cast of a sowe in Eestlande in Pruse. [1531].

The maner of the tryumphe at Caleys and Bulleyn. [1532].

The tryumphant vyctory of the imperyall mageste agaynst the Turkes. 1532.

The actes of the disputacion in the cowncell of the Empyre at Regenspurg. [Antwerp?] 1542.

Hevy newes of an horryble earthquake in Sharbaria. [1542]

Vyllagon, Nicholas. A lamentable and piteous treatise of themperour Charles V and his army. 1542.

The supplicacion that the nobles and comons of Osteryke made unto Kyng Ferdinandus. [1543?].

Newes concernynge the general councell holden at Trydent. [1549].

Esquillus, Publius. Wonderfull news of the death of Paule the III; englyshed by W. B. [1552].

A warnyng for Englande conteynyng the horrible practises of the Kyng of Spayne in the kyngdome of Naples. 1555.

The copie of the publication of the trewse made betwene Kynge Henry second, themperour and the Kyng of Ingland. [1556].

The actes of the ambassage passed at Naumburg. [1561].

The destruction and sacke cruelly committed by the Duke of Guyse in the toune of Vassy. 1562.

The great wonders that are chaunced in the realme of Naples. 1566.

An edict of the French King: conteining a prohibition of al exercise of any other religion then of the Catholique, the Apostolique and the Romaine. Louvain 1568.

A true declaration of the voyadge of M. John Haukins to Guynea and the West Indies. 1569.

A coppie of the letter sent from Ferrara. [1571?].

Letters sent from Venice anno 1571. [1571?].

Veramund, Ernest [i.e. François Hotman]. A true and plaine report of the furious outrages of Fraunce. [London?] 1573.

Whittingham, William. A brieff discours off the troubles begonne at Franckford AD 1554. [Zürich?] 1574.

A true rehersall of the victory which the defenders of the trueth have had against the heape of ye Albanists. 1573.

Gilbert, Sir Humphrey. A discourse of a discoverie for a new passage to Cataia. 1576.

[Gascoigne, George]. The spoyle of Antwerpe. [1577?].

The strange and marveilous newes lately come from Chyna. [1577?].

C., W. The true reporte of the skirmish fought betwene the States of Flaunders and Don Joan. [1578?].

Churchyard, Thomas. A lamentable and pitifull description of the wofull warres in Flaunders. 1578.

A request presented to the Kyng of Spayn by the inhabitantes of the Lowe Countreyes protesting that they will live according to the reformation of the gospell. [1578?].

A dolorous discourse of a most terrible battel fought in Barbarie. [1579].

Churchyard, Thomas. The miserie of Flaunders, calamitie of Fraunce misfortune of Portugall. [1579].

— A plaine or moste true report of a daungerous service by English men and other worthy souldiours for the takyng of Macklin. 1580.

Newes from Antwerp the 10 day of August 1580. [1580?].

A briefe discourse of the assault committed upon William Prince of Orange. 1582.

Lingham, John. A true relation of all suche Englishe captaines and lieuetenants as have been slaine in the Lowe Countries. 1584.

Newes out of Germanie of a cruell murderer. [1584].

P., G. The true report of the death of William of Nassawe. Middelburg 1584.

A declaration of the causes mooving the Queene of England to give aide to the people in the Lowe Countries. 1585.

Mote, Humphrey. The Primrose of London with her valiant adventure on the Spanish coast. 1585.

M., W. A true discourse of the late battaile fought betweene our En[g]lishmen and the Prince of Parma. 1585.

A true report of the taking of Marseilles. [1585].

D., T. A briefe report of the militarie services done in the Low Countries by the Erle of Leicester. 1587.

Haslop, Henry. Newes out of the coast of Spaine. 1587.

D[eloney], T[homas]. A joyfull new ballad declaring the happie obtaining of the great galleazzo. 1588.

Orders set downe by the Duke of Medina, General of the Kings fleet to be observed in the voyage towards England. 1588.

A true and perfect discourse of accidents in Italie. 1588.

A treu discourse of the armie which the King of Spaine caused to bee assembled against England. 1588.

B., I. The copy of a letter lately written by a Spanishe gentleman to his friend in England. [abroad] 1589.

Bigges, Walter. A summarie and true discourse of Sir Francis Drakes West Indian voyage. 1589.

de M., D. F. R. An answer to the untruthes published in Spaine in glorie of their supposed victorie against our English navie. 1589.

A true coppie of a discourse written by a gentleman employed in the late voyage of Spaine and Portingale. 1589.

The whole and true discourse of the enterprises against Henry de Valois. 1589.

A breife and true report of the proceedings of the Earle of Leycester for the reliefe of Sluce. 1590.

Credible reports from France and Flanders. 1590.

News from Rome, Spayne, Palermo etc. 1590.

Articles concerning the yeilding of Grenoble. 1591.

The honorable actions of Edward Gleinham against the Spaniards and the Holy League in foure sundrie fightes. 1591.

A journall or briefe report of the late service in Britaigne by the Prince de Dombes. 1591.

Newes from Sir Roger Williams. 1591.

Newes lately come from France. 1591.

A particuler of the yeelding uppe of Zutphen and the beleagering of Deventer. 1951.

[Ralegh, Sir Walter]. A report of the truth of a fight betwixt the Revenge and an armada of the King of Spaine. 1591.

The true coppie of a letter written from the leager by Arnheim. 1591.

A true discourse of an overthrow given to the army of the Leaguers in Provence. 1591.

True newes from one of Sir Fraunces Veres companie. 1591.

The true reporte of the service in Britanie, performed by Sir John Norreys. 1591.

The valiant and most laudable fight in the straights by the Centurion against five Spanish gallies. 1591.

News out of France on the first of March. 1592.

A relation of the King of Spaines receiving in Valliodolid and in the Inglish college of the same towne in August 1592. [abroad ?] 1592.

The sea-mans triumph, declaring the takinge of the great carrick lately brought to Dartmouth. 1592.

A true declaration of the streight siedge laide to Steenwich. 1592.

Articles accorded for the truce generall in France. 1593.

The copy of a letter written by the Lord of Themines. 1593.

Newes from Spayne and Holland conteyning an information of Inglish affayres in Spayne. [abroad ?] 1593.

Newes from Brest: a diurnal of al that Sir John Norreis hath doone. 1594.

R[oberts] H[enry]. Newes from the Levane seas. 1594.

— Lancaster his allarums in Brasill. [1595].

— The most royall and honourable entertainement of Christiern the fourth. 1606.

Strange signes seene in the aire about the citie of Rosenburg. 1594.

Newes from Rome, Venice and Vienna touching the present proceedinges of the Turkes against the Christians. 1595.

Monings, Edward. The Landgrave of Hessen his receiving of her Majesties embassador. 1596.

A discourse of the ouerthrowe given to the King of Spaines armie. 1597.

Newes from divers countries as from Spaine, Antwerpe, Collin, Venice, Rome. 1597.

A most strange and wonderfull herring taken on 26 no 1597 neere unto Drenton, Norway. 1598.

A briefe and true declaration of the sicknesse and death of the King of Spaine. 1599.

A briefe discourse of the cruell dealings of the Spanyards in Gulick and Cleve. 1599.

The happy entrance of the Queene of Spaine in the citty of Ferrara. 1599.

A strange and miraculous accident happened in the cittie of Purmerent. 1599.

A true report and description of the taking of the iland of St Maries. 1599.

The battaile fought betweene Count Maurice and Albertus, Archduke. 1600.

An extract translated out of the French copie and taken out of the registers of the French Kings Privie Councell. [1600 ?].

A true credible report of a great fight at sea between certaine ships of England and five ships of warre of the King of Spaines. [1600].

A true report of a famous victorie by the Black Galley of Dort. 1600.

Newes from Ostend of the oppugnation. 1601.

A true discourse of the occurrences in the warres of Savoy. 1601.

A copie of the articles granted to the governour of Grave. 1602.

C., W. Copie of a letter lately sent from the campe before Grave. 1602.

Extremities urging Sir Fra. Veare to offer the late antiparle with the Arch-duke Albertus. 1602.

Mansel, Sir Robert. A true report of the service done upon certaine gallies passing through the narrow seas. 1602.

[Teixeira, José]. The true historie of the adventures of Don Sebastian King of Portugall. 1602.

A letter written to the East Indian marchants in London: containing the estate of the East Indian fleete. 1603.

A true reporte of three accidents lately happened at Pernaw. 1603.

Newes from Graues-end sent to nobody. 1604.

A declaration of the lordes and states of Hungarie. 1605.

A true report of the overthrow given unto the Spaniards in Bergen-op-Zoom. 1605.

Russell, William. The reporte of a bloudie massacre in the city of Mosco. 1607.

Strange fearful and true newes which hapned at Carlstadt in Croatia. [1606].

A declaration of the archdukes of Brabant. 1607.

Smith, John. A true relation of such occurrences as hath hapned in Virginia. 1608.

Newes from sea of two notorious pyrats, Ward and Danseker. 1609.

Newes out of Cleave-land. 1610.

A publike declaration made by the united protestant Princes Electors. 1610.

The terrible and deserved death of Francis Ravilliack for the murther of the French King. 1610.

News from Spaine. The King of Spaine's edict for the expulsion of Moores. 1611.

Newes from Francfort concerning the election of the Emperor Matthias. 1612.

Newes out of Germanie. 1612.

The great victory which God hath given unto eight Holland shippes. 1613.

Late newes out of Barbary. 1613.

A true declaration of the arrivall of Cornelius Haga ambassador for the United Netherlands at Constantinople. 1613.

Brereton, Henry. Newes of the present miseries of Rushia. 1614.

Newes from Gulick and Cleve. 1615.

Remonstrances made by the Kings Majesties ambassadour unto the French King. 1615.

A true relation of the treasons attempted against foure townes in the Netherlands. 1615.

Miraculous newes from the cittie of Holdt. 1616.

[Roberts, Henry]. A true relation of a fight performed by two small shippes of London against six great galles of Tunes. [1616].

A fight at sea famously fought by the Dolphin of London. 1617.

A relation of the late entertainment of the Lord Roos his Majesties embassador to the King of Spaine. 1617.

A true report of a mighty sea-monster. 1617.

Newes from France or a relation of a fearfull accident. 1618.

News from Italy. 1618.

The speech of Sir Dudley Carleton ambassador for the King of Great Britaine made in the Estates generall of the Low Countries. 1618.

A briefe relation of the persecution lately made against the Catholike Christians in Japonia. [St Omer] 1619.

Harrison, John. A short relation of the departure of Prince Frederick from Heydelberg towards Prague. Dordrecht 1619.

News from Bohemia: an apologie made by the states of Bohemia. 1619.

The true description of the execution of justice upon Sir John van Olden Barnevelt. 1619.

A most true relation of the late proceedings in Bohemia, Germany etc. Dort 1620.

The present state of the affaires betwixt the Emperor and the King of Bohemia. [London?] 1620.

A relation containing the manner of the election and coronation of Ferdinand the Emperour in Francford. 1620.

[Scott, Thomas]. Vox populi: or newes from Spayne. [Gorcum?] 1620. A forgery.

The true copies of sundrie letters concerning the affaires of Bohemia. 1620.

B[utton], J. Algiers voyage in a journall. 1621.

The certaine and true newes from Germany and Poland. 1621.

Certaine letters declaring in part the passage of affaires in the Palatinate. 1621.

A declaration set forth by the Protestants in France. La Rochelle 1621.

M., A. A relation of the passages of our English companies since their first departure to Germanie. 1621.

Newes from Poland, the Turks formidable threatening of Europe. 1621.

True copies of the insolent letter written by the great Turke for denouncing of warre against Poland. 1621.

A true relation of the bloody execution of some chief statesmen in Prague. 1621.

A courante of newes from the East India. 1622.

The famous and wonderful recoverie of the Exchange from the Turkish pirates. 1622.

A journall or daily register of the siege of Berghen-up-Zoome. 1622.

A relation strange and true of a ship of Bristol named the Jacob taken by the Turkish pirats. 1622.

A second courante of newes from the East India. 1622.

The true relation of that worthy sea fight in the Persian Gulph. 1622.

La Peña, Juan Antonio de. A relation of the royall festivities at Madrid to honour the espousall of the Prince of Wales with the Infanta Maria. 1623.

A true relation and journall of the entertainment given to Prince Charles by the King of Spaine at Madrid. 1623.

[Du Mats de Montmartin, Esau]. An admirable discovery of an horrible attempt, slaunderously fathered upon those of Rochell. 1624.

A true relation of the unjust and barbarous proceedings against the English at Amboyna in the East-Indies by the Neatherlandish governour. 1624.

W[inslow], E[dward]. Good news from New-England. 1624.

A journall and relation of the action which Edward Lord Cecil did undertake upon the coast of Spaine. 1625.

A true discourse of the contract and mariage of Charles, King of Great Britaine and the Lady Henrietta of Burbon. 1625.

Peeke, Richard. Three to one: being an English Spanish combat with an English quarter staffe against three Spanish rapiers. [1626].

A journall of all the proceedings of the Duke of Buckingham in the Isle of Ree. 6 nos Aug–Nov 1627.

Taylor, John. A famous fight at sea. 1627.

Robson, Charles. Newes from Aleppo. 1628.

Articles of peace in a treaty at Madrit. 1630.

Pellham, Edward. Gods power and providence, shewed in the preservation of eight Englishmen left in Green-land. 1631. See col 2128, below.

The great and famous battel of Lutzen. 1633.

Crowne, William. A true relation of the travels of Thomas Lord Howard, ambassadour to Ferdinando, Emperour of Germanie. 1637. See col 2128 below.

Hexham, Henry. A true and brief relation of the famous siege of Breda. 1637.

Bruton, William. Newes from the East Indies. 1638.

The invasions of Germanie. 1638.

Parker, Martin. A true and terrible narration of a horrible earthquake in Calabria. 1638.

Sad news from the seas being a relation of the losse of the Merchant Royall. 1641.

A true and perfect relation of the victorie gained by Philip King of Spaine against Lewis the French King. 1641.

(4) UNNUMBERED NEWSBOOKS 1620–2

During these years a number of corantos were issued, some of which, because of the similarity of title or of the identity of the publisher, may be seen as the true forerunners of the numbered newsbooks which began to appear in 1622. These are listed here in chronological order of the first known issue.

The new tydings out of Italie are not yet com. Amsterdam for Petrus Keerius 2 Dec 1620.

Corrant out of Italy, Germany etc. Amsterdam for Petrus Keerius 23 Dec 1620; 4 Jan 1921; 21 Jan; 31 March; 9 April; 25 May; 20 June; 5 July; 9 July; 15 July; 9 Aug; 6 Sept; 12 Sept (2 edns); 18 Sept.

Courante or newes from Italy and Germany. Amsterdam (Broer Jansz) 9 April 1621; 22 April; 6 June; 25 June; 3 July; 9 July; 20 July; 2 Aug.

News from the Low Countries. Altmore [Alkmaar?] 29 July 1621.

Corrant or newes from Italie, Germanie, France and other places. [Alkmaar?] 6 Aug 1621.

Corante: or newes from Italy, Germany, Hungaria, Polonia, France and Dutchland. Hague 10 Aug 1621.

Corante: or newes from Italy, Germany, Hungarie, Spaine and France. N[athaniel] B[utter] (or possibly Nicholas Bourne) 24 Sept 1621; 30 Sept; 2 Oct; 6 Oct; 9 Oct; 11 Oct; 22 Oct.

Newes from Turkie and Poland. Hague (Jan or Feb) 1622.

Newes from the Palatinate. Hague (March) 1622.

More newes from the Palatinate. (March) 1622.

Good newes for the King of Bohemia. 17 April 1622.

The King of Bohemia's welcome to Count Mansfield. (April) 1622.

Three great overthrowes one in the Palatinate against Monsieur Tilley. 4 May 1622.

[no title extant, text begins] It is certified from Palermo in Sicilia that Don Francisco di Castro. (Nicholas Bourne and Thomas Archer) May 1622.

Weekely newes from Italy, Germanie, Hungaria, Bohemia, the Palatinate, France and the Low Countries. Bourne & Archer 23 May 1622.

A true relation of all such battailes as have beene fought in the Palatinate since the Kings arrivall there. Bourne & Archer (24 May) 1622.

Weekly newes from Italy, Germanie, Hungaria, Bohemia, the Palatinate, France and the Low Countries. Bourne & Archer 30 May 1622.

More newes from the Palatinate. N[athaniel] Butter & W[illiam] Sheffard 3 June 1622 (another edn 5 June).

Good newes from Alsasia and the Palatinate. Bourne & Archer 5 June 1622.

The true copie of a letter sent from Franckfort. Bourne & Archer 14 June 1622.

Weekely newes from Italy, Germanie, Hungaria, Bohemia, the Palatinate and the Low Countries. Nathaniel Newbery & William Sheffard 18 June 1622.

A letter sent from Maynhem concerning the late defeate given the Duke of Brunswicke by Monsieur Tilley. Butter 20 June 1622.

The true copies of two especiall letters verbatim sent from the Palatinate by Sir F.N. Bourne & Archer 21 June 1622.

The late proceedings in all troubled parts of Christendome. Bourne & Archer 25 June 1622.

A continuation of the warres. Bourne & Archer 3 July 1622.

The safe arrivall of Christian Duke of Brunswick unto the King of Bohemiah. Bourne & Archer 3 July 1622.

A true relation of the murther of Osman the great Turke. Butter 4 July 1622.

A true relation of the proceedings of the Bavarian and Spanish forces before the city of Heydelburgh. Bourne & Archer 11 July 1622.

The strangling and death of the great Turke, and his two sonnes. Bourne & Archer 15 July 1622.

The relation of all the last passages of the warres in the Palatinate. Newbery & Sheffard 18 July 1622.

In this weekly newes is related the great difference or unlikelihood of agreement betweene the Emperour and Bethlem Gabor. Bourne & Archer 19 July 1622.

The surprisall of two imperial townes by Count Mansfield and the Duke of Brunswick. Bourne & Archer 19 July 1622.

A continuation of more newes from the Palatinate. Bourne & Archer 26 July 1622.

A true, plaine and compendious discourse of the besieging of Bergen Up Zome. Bourne & Archer 26 July 1622.

The certaine newes of this present weeke. Butter 2 Aug 1622.

A remonstration of the French subjects professing the reformed religion unto the French King. Bourne & Archer 2 Aug 1622.

The post of the prince, which advises us the taking of Steen Bergh. Bourne & Archer 13 Aug 1622.

The entertainment of Count Mansfield, and the Duke of Brunswick into the service and pay of the Duke of Bulloygne. Bourne & Archer 19 Aug 1622.

The certaine newes of this present weeke. Butter 23 Aug 1622.

Mansfeilds arrivall in the Dukedome of Brabant. Bourne & Archer 27 Aug 1622.

Two great battailes very lately fought. Bourne & Archer 2 Sept 1622.

Newes from sundry places, both forraine and domestique. Butter 4 Sept 1622.

Count Mansfields proceedings since the last battaile. Bourne & Archer 9 Sept 1622.

A relation of many memorable passages from Rome, Italy, Spaine, France, Germany, the Low Countries, the Palatinate and other places. Butter Downes & Sheffard 14 Sept 1622.

The newes which now arrive from divers parts. Butter & Sheffard 20 Sept 1622.

Newes from most parts of Christendome. Butter & Sheffard 25 Sept 1622.

A relation of letters, and other advertisements of newes. Butter & Archer 27 Sept 1622.

A true relation of the affaires of Europe. Butter & Bourne 4 Oct 1622.

(5) NUMBERED NEWSBOOKS 1622–41

From Oct 1622 onwards, with various interruptions, series of numbered newsbooks were pbd. At first there was no regular pattern in the titles and it may be difficult to be certain where a particular newsbook should be placed. The arrangement adopted here follows that devised by F. Dahl.

In addn to the 13 sers which Dahl identified there are a few newsbooks issued by Thomas Archer 1624–8, after he had left the syndicate responsible for the early series: there is some evidence that in 1627 Ralph Mabb issued a Currant of newes of which no copies are extant; in 1633 when the printing of newsbooks in England was forbidden, a small number of newsbooks in English were ptd in Amsterdam. None of these items has been listed here, but details will be found in Dahl's Bibliography.

(a) First Series Oct 1622–Oct 1623

This series was issued by a syndicate and not all the publishers were associated with each issue. Nathaniel Butter, Nicholas Bourne, Bartholomew Downes, William Sheffard and Thomas Archer were all involved. In these short title entries for this and subsequent series the surnames only of the publishers have been ptd. The date and number allocated to each issue are, generally, the dates and numbers which appear in the first line of the titles of these newsbooks, but occasionally this information appears elsewhere on the title-page.

Some issues of these series have not survived. Issues which are not extant but to which there is some reliable contemporary reference have been noted within brackets.

A relation of the late occurrents which have happened in Christendome. no 1 Butter & Bourne 15 Oct 1622.

A continuation of the affaires of the Low-countries and the Palatinate. no 2 Butter & Downes 15 Oct 1622.

A relation of the weekely occurences of newes out of Bohemia. no 3 Butter Downes & Sheffard 22 Oct 1622.

A continuation of the weekly newes from Bohemia. no 4 Butter Bourne & Archer 30 Oct 1622 (another issue, same date, for Butter & Downes).

A continuation of the newes of this present weeke. no 5 Downes & Archer 5 Nov 1622.

A coranto, relating divers particulars concerning the newes. no 6 Butter Bourne & Sheffard 7 Nov 1622.

A continuation of the newes of this present weeke. no 7 Butter Bourne & Sheffard 16 Nov 1622.

The continuation of the former newes. no 8 Butter Downes & Archer 21 Nov 1622.

Briefe abstracts out of diverse letters of trust. no 9 Butter Bourne & Sheffard 28 Nov 1622.

[no 10 18 Dec 1622] ? Butter & Bourne.

[no 11] ? Butter & Downes 8 Jan 1623.

[no 12 before 18 Jan 1623].

Weekely newes: containing the imprisonment of the cardinall Clossell. no 14 Butter Bourne & Downes 20 Jan 1623.

Weekely newes: containing the late proceedings in the Grisons countrey. no 15 Butter Bourne & Downes 28 Jan 1623.

Weekely newes: containing the propositions of the ambassador of the Emperor at Wolffenbuttel. no 16 Butter Bourne & Sheffard 30 Jan 1623 (another issue, 31 Jan 1623).

A new survey of the affaires of Europe. [no 17] Butter Downes & Archer 6 Feb 1623.

Weekely newes: containing these particulars: a proclamation by the States etc. no 18 Butter Bourne & Sheffard 11 Feb 1623.

A relation of the late horrible treason, intended against the Prince of Orange. no 19 Butter Downes & Archer 19 Feb 1623.

The newes of forraine partes, lately received. no 20 Butter Bourne & Sheffard 28 Feb 1623.

A proclamation by the states of the province of Utrecht against certaine others of the conspirators. no 21 Butter Bourne & Archer 7 March 1623.

The sentence and execution done upon the bodies of certaine persons being convicted for the horrible conspiracie against the Prince of Orange. no 22 Butter & Sheffard 7 March 1623.

Weekly newes: containing the great treason lately attempted against Bethlem Gabor. no 23 Butter Bourne & Archer 14 March 1623.

Weekly newes, from forraine parts. no 24 Butter Bourne & Sheffard 31 March 1623.

A relation of the last newes from severall parts of the world. no 25 Butter Bourne & Archer 8 April 1623.

The continuation of our former newes from Aprill the 8 untill the 17. no 26 Butter Bourne & Archer 17 April 1623.

The continuation of our weekely newes. no 27 Butter & Bourne 21 April 1623.

The continuation of our former newes. no 28 Butter Bourne & Archer 24 April 1623.

The continuation of our weekely newes. no 29 Butter & Sheffard 2 May 1623.

A relation of the Duke of Brunswicks march to encounter with Monsieur Tilley. no 30 Butter Bourne & Archer 7 May 1623.

The newes of this present weeke: relating the late encounter of the Duke of Brunswicke with Don Gonsales. no 31 Butter Bourne & Sheffard 12 May 1623.

The last newes. no 32 Butter & Sheffard 17 May 1623.

A relation of Count Mansfeilds last proceedings. no 33 Butter Bourne & Sheffard 26 May 1623.

The last newes: containing the arrivall of Bethlem Gabor. no 34 Butter & Archer 30 May 1623.

More newes of the affaires of the world. no 35 Butter & Archer 10 June 1623.

The affaires of the world for this present weeke. no 36 Butter & Bourne 16 June 1623.

More newes: containing the troubles in the Empire upon the comming of Bethlem Gabor. no 37 Butter & Archer 26 June 1623.

The relation of our last newes: containing the Emperours composition offered to Bethlem Gabor. no 38 Butter & Archer 4 July 1623.

The last newes continued. no 39 Butter & Sheffard 10 July 1623.

The weekely newes continued: relating the Hungars invasion of Austria and Niclaesburgh. no 40 Butter & Bourne 18 July 1623.

More newes of the Duke of Brunswick. no 41 Butter & Sheffard 22 July 1623.

More newes of the good successe of the Duke of Brunswicke. no 42 Butter & Bourne 29 July 1623.

Our last weekly newes: declaring what hath last hapned in the Empire betweene the Emperor and the princes. no 44 Butter & Bourne 21 Aug 1623.

More newes for this present weeke. no 45 Butter & Sheffard 27 Aug 1623.

More newes from Europe. no 46 Butter & Archer 29 Aug 1623.

Our last weekely newes: relating the continuance of the reports of the comming downe of the Turkes. no 46 Butter & Sheffard 5 Sept 1623.

Our last weekely newes: relating the proceedings betwixt the Emperour and Bethlem Gabor. no 47 Butter & Bourne 12 Sept 1623.

Weekely newes: relating the continuance of the reports concerning the comming on of Bethlem Gabor. no 48 Butter & Sheffard 17 Sept 1623.

More newes for this present weeke: relating the last businesse betwixt the Emperour and Bethlem Gabor. no 49 Butter & Sheffard 24 Sept 1623.

Our last newes: containing a relation of the last proceedings betwixt the Emperour, Bethlem Gabor and other princes. no 50 2 Oct 1623.

(b) Second Series Oct 1623–Dec 1624

This series was issued by a syndicate including Thomas Archer, Nicholas Bourne, Nathaniel Butter, Nathaniel Newbery and William Sheffard.

Our last weekely newes: containing the invasion of Bethlem Gabor and of the Marques of Jagerendorp. no 1 Butter & Archer 11 Oct 1623.

A most true relation: contayning the great invasion made by Bethlem Gabor. no 2 Butter & Sheffard 28 Oct 1623.

The wonderfull resignation of Mustapha, and the advancing of Amarath. no 3 Butter & Bourne 11 Nov 1623.

The affaires of Italy, with the crowning and inauguration of the new Pope Barbarino. no 4 Butter 20 Nov 1623 (no 5 not extant).

First from Constantinople shewing the establishing of princely Amurath. no 6 Butter & Bourne 2 Dec 1623.

Weekely newes from Germanie and other places of Europe. no 7 Butter & Bourne 13 Dec 1623 (no 8 not extant).

The newes and affaires of Europe. no 9 Butter & Bourne 7 Jan 1624.

The newes and affaires of Europe. no 10 Butter & Sheffard 15 Jan 1624 (nos 11–13 not extant).

The affaires and generall businesse of Europe more particularly. no 14 Butter 24 Feb 1624 (no 15 not extant).

The newes and affaires of Europe more particularly. no 16 Butter & Bourne 6 March 1624.

Newes of Europe with the severall particulars of each countrey. no 17 Butter & Sheffard 12 March 1624.

Newes from Europe; with the particular accidents. no 18 Butter 19 March 1624 (no 19 not extant).

Extraordinary newes containing many admirable, strange, joyfull and pitifull accidents and passages. no 20 Butter 7 April 1624.

The newes of Europe with all such particular accidents as have chanced in severall provinces. no 21 Butter & Bourne 20 April 1624 (nos 22–3 not extant).

A true relation of the newes of this present weeke. no 24 Butter & Bourne 12 May 1624 (nos 25–9 not extant).

Late newes or true relations. no 30 Butter & Bourne 3 July 1624.

A true and particuler relation of the taking of Todos los Sanctos in Brasiel, by the Hollanders. no 31 Butter 1 Sept 1624.

The continuation of the weekely newes. no 32 Butter Bourne Newbery & Sheffard 11 Sept 1624.

The continuation of the weekly newes. no 33 Butter & Bourne 16 Sept 1624.

A continuation of the weekly newes. no 34 (publishers unknown) 22 Sept 1624 (no 35 not extant).

The continuation of the weekely newes. no 36 Butter & Bourne 5 Oct 1624 (no 37 not extant).

The newes of this present weeke continued. no 38 Butter & Bourne. 20 Oct 1624 (nos 39–40 not extant).

The continuation of our weekely newes. no 41 Butter & Bourne 15 Nov 1624.

The continuation of our weekely newes. no 42 Butter & Bourne 22 Nov 1624.

The continuation of our weekely newes. no 43 Butter & Bourne 4 Dec 1624 (4 subsequent issues noted in the Stationers' Register, but no copies extant).

(c) Third Series Dec 1624–Jan 1626

This is the first series to have complete uniformity in the title of all extant copies. All numbers were issued without the names of the publishers, simply 'for Mercurius Britannicus', but are attributed to Nicholas Bourne and Nathaniel Butter. Issues not extant are shown within square brackets.

[The continuation of our weekly newes. no 1 30 Dec 1624]; no 2 5 Jan 1625; [no 3 13 Jan]; no 4 21 Jan; [no 5 27 Jan]; no 6 1 Feb; no 7 8 Feb; [no 9 nd; no 10 24 Feb]; no 11 2 March; [nos 12–14 nd; no 15 29 March]; no 16 7 April; no 17 14 April; no 18 21 April; no 19 27 April; no 20 5 May [no 21 12 May]; no 22 19 May; no 23 24 May; no 24 30 May; [nos 25–6 nd; no 27 21 June]; no 28 28 June; [nos 29–39 nd; no 40 Nov?; nos 41–7 nd; no 48 11 Jan 1626]; no 49 18 Jan 1626.

(d) Fourth Series Jan/Feb 1626–Jan 1627

Very few copies of numbers in this series have survived. It seems to have retained the title and general style of the third series, above.

[The continuation of our weekely newes. nos 1–11 nd; no 12 17 May 1626]; no 13 23 May; [no 14 nd; no 15 9 June]; no 16 14 June; [nos 17–19 nd; no 20 27 June; nos 21–5 nd]; no 26 24 Aug; [nos 27–40 nd; no 41 6 Dec]; no 42 8 Dec; [nos 43–50 nd].

(e) Fifth Series Jan/Feb 1627–Feb 1628

Very few copies of this series have survived. It began with the same style and title as the third and fourth series, above but 'for Mercurius Britannicus' was dropped from the title during the year. The series is attributed to Nicholas Bourne and Nathaniel Butter.

[The continuation of our weekly newes nos 1–24 nd]; no 25 1 Aug 1627; [nos 26–31 nd]; no 32 12 Sept; [nos 33–9 nd]; A true report of all the speciall passages of note lately happened in the Ile of Ree no 40 Butter 1 Nov; [nos 41–6 nd]; The further continuation of our weekely newes no 47 Butter 25 Jan 1628; [nos 49–50 nd].

(f) Sixth Series Feb/March 1628–Dec 1629

This series seems to have continued the general title of the previous 3 series. Pbn was shared by Nicholas Bourne and Nathaniel Butter.

[The continuation of our weekely newes. nos 1–18 nd]; no 19 28 Oct 1628; [nos 20–1 nd]; no 22 19 Nov; [nos 23–30 nd; no 31 24 April 1629]; Newes of certaine commands lately given by the French King concerning the interteinment of the English, no 32 5 May; [no 33 18 May]; no 34 4 June; [nos 35–9 nd; no 40 18 Aug]; no 41 25 Aug; [nos 42–50 nd].

(g) Seventh Series Dec? 1629/Jan 1630–Nov 1631

This series follows the general pattern of the preceding, but there are occasional variations in the titles. It was again issued by Bourne and Butter.

[The continuation of our weekly newes. nos 1–7 nd; no 8 4 June 1630]; The continuation of the most remarkable occurrences of newes, no 9 16 July?; [nos 10–13 nd; no 14 1 Oct]; no 15 12 Oct; [nos 16–21 nd]; (no 22) A relation of the King of Sweden his happie and incomparable successe, 18 Feb; no 23 14 March; no 24 The copie of a letter written from Hambrough, 7 April; no 25 The continuation of our weekly avisoes, 18 April; no 26 The solemnity of the marriage of the Emperours sonne, 3 May; no 27 The continuation of our forreigne newes, 9 May; no 28 (title as no 27) 16 May; no? A relation of that which hath passed in France since the 6 of February nd (nos 39–30 nd, but *see* previous entry); no 31 The continuation of our weekly newes from forraine parts, 25 June; [no 32 nd; no 33 22 July]; no 34 4 Aug; no 35 The continuation of our forreine occurrences 20 Aug; [no 36 20 Aug]; no 37 The continuation of our forraine avisoes, 2 Sept; [no 38 9 Sept]; no 39 The continuation of our forreine newes, 19 Sept; [no 40 28 Sept]; no 41 The continuation of our weekely newes, 3 Oct; no '43' (for 42) 6 Oct; no 43 The continuation of our newes from forraigne parts 13 Oct; no 44 The continuation of our late avisoes 20 Oct; [no 45 29 Oct]; no 46 9 Nov; no 47 10 Nov; no 48 19 Nov; no 49 22 Nov; no 50 29 Nov.

(h) Eighth Series Nov 1631–Oct 1632

These newsbooks were pbd more frequently than those in the preceding series, sometimes more than one on the same day. There are still variations in the titles, but after no 13 the title is generally: The continuation of our forraine avisoes. The series was pbd by Bourne & Butter.

The continuation of our weekely intelligence. no 1 29 Nov 1631; no 2 The continuation of our forraine newes, 8 Dec; no 3 The continuation of our weekely newes, 17 Dec; [no 4 nd]; no 5 2 Jan 1632; no 6 The continuation of our weekely avisoes, 12 Jan; [no 7 19 Jan]; no 8 The continuation of our forraine avisoes, 24 Jan; no 9 The continuation of our forraine newes, 30 Jan; no 10 The continuation of our forraine intelligence, 8 Feb [no 11 13 Feb; no 12 24 Feb]; no 13 The continuation of our forraine avisoes (this becomes regular title) 27 Feb; no 14 6 March; no 15 15 March; no 16 24 March; no 17 9 April; no 18 14 April; no 19 24 April; no 20 28 April; no 21 4 May; no 22 4 May; no 23 12 May; no 24 16 May; no 25 28 May; no 26 6 June; no 27 9 June; [no 28 16 June]; no 29 23 June; [no 30 27 June; no 31 30 June]; no 32 The continuation of our weekely avisoes, 6 July; [no 33 14 July]; no 34 (weekely avisoes) 19 July; no 35 (weekely avisoes) 25 July; no 36 (weekely avisoes) 30 July; no 37 (weekely avisoes) 3 Aug; no 38 Advice given unto the States of the Low-Countries, 3 Aug; no 39 (weekely avisoes) 13 Aug; no 40 (weekely avisoes) 23 Aug; no 41 (weekely avisoes) 30 Aug; no 42 (weekely avisoes) 1 Sept; no 42 The continuation of our Swedish intelligence, 1 Sept; no 43 The continuation of our Swedish and French with some Low-Country newes, 4 Sept; no 44 (to no 49 title reverts to Forraine avisoes) 12 Sept; no 45 19 Sept; no 46 22 Sept; no 47 26 Sept; no 48 3 Oct; no 49 (weekely newes) 10 Oct; no 50 (forraine avisoes) 12 Oct 1632.

(i) Ninth Series Oct 1632

Only one issue of this projected series was pbd before the Star Chamber decree of 17 Oct 1632, forbidding the pbn of newsbooks.

Journall of all the principall passages of that late famous siege and taking of the citie of Mastricht by the Prince of Orange. no 1 Butter & Bourne 16 Oct 1632.

(j) Tenth Series Dec 1638–July 1639

This series was issued by Bourne & Butter after they received Letters Patent on 20 Dec 1638 authorizing them to recommence pbn of newsbooks. The pagination is continuous. From Feb 1639 the newsbooks generally carry the title: Ordinary weekly corant from . . . The place of origin of the news varied (in the following entries it is given within round brackets) and more than one number in the series was occasionally pbd on the same day, with news from a different source.

An abstract of some speciall forreigne occurrences brought down to the weekly newes, of the 20 of December. no 1 20 Dec 1638; [nos 2–5 not extant]; no 6 From Norimberg. Ordinary avisoes: 1 Jan 1639; no 7 Ordinary weekly currantoes from Frankford 1 Jan; no 8 Ordinary weekly currantoes from Holland 1 Jan; no 9 The articles and other circumstances and particulars of the taking of Brisack by the Duke of Weymar 1 Jan; no 10 The weekly curranto from Norimberg 9 Jan; no 11 The continuation of the Frankford curranto by the last post 9 Jan; [nos 12–15 not extant]; no 16 The weekly curranto from Norimberg 18 Jan; no 17 The weekly curranto from Frankford 18 Jan; [nos 18–20 not extant]; no 21 Ordinarie weekely currantos from Norimberg 1 Feb; no 22 (Franckford) 1 Feb; no 23 (Holland) 1 Feb; [nos 24–8 not extant]; no 29 (Norimberg) 17 Feb; no 30 (Frankford) 17 Feb; no 31 (Holland) 18 Feb; [nos 32–4 not extant]; no 35 (Norimberg) 1 March; no 36 (Franckford) 1 March; no 37 (Holland) 1 March; no 38 (Norimberg) 12 March; no 39 (Frankford) 12 March; no 40 (Holland) 12 March; [nos 41–6 not extant]; no 47 (Norimberg) 3 April; no 48 (Frankford) 3 April; no 49 (Holland) 3 April; [nos 50–63 not extant]; no 64 Extractes of private letters from Germany, France etc 13 May; no 65 (Norrimberg) 13 May; no 66 (Franckford) 13 May; no 67 (Holland) 13 May; no 68 (Norimberg) 22 May; no 69 (Franckford) 21 May; no 70 (Holland) 22 May; no 71 A true and particular relation of the battell fought neare Kemnitz, 22 or 27 May; no 72 (Holland) 27 May; no 73 (Frankford) 27 May; no 74 (Norimberg) 27 May; [nos 75–83 not extant]; no 84 The Norimberg curranto of this week, 21 June; [no 85 not extant]; no 86 The curranto this weeke from Holland 21 June 1639.

(k) Eleventh Series July/Aug 1639–March 1640

The title of each issue in this series is preceded by the words Century 2: otherwise in general the style is the same as in tenth series, above.

[nos 1–39 not extant]; no 40 The curranto of this week from Holland 18 Oct 1639; no 41 An extraordinary curranto: wherein is related the late sea-fight betwixt the Spaniards and the Hollanders, 18 Oct; [nos 42–85 not extant]; no 86 (title as no 40 but Norimberg) 12 Feb; no 87 (Franckford) 11 Feb; no 88 (Holland) 11 Feb; [no 89 not extant]; no 90 (Franckford) 22 Feb; no 91 (Franckford) 22 Feb; no 92 (Holland) 22 Feb; no 93 (Norimberg) 24 Feb; no 94 (Frankeford) 24 Feb; no 95 (Holland) 24 Feb; [no later issues extant].

(l) Twelfth Series March 1640–Jan/Feb 1641

Newsbooks in this series bear the legend Century 3. The style of title for the first 19 issues is the same as that of the preceding series. After no 20, when Nathaniel Butter was probably the sole publisher, there is less uniformity of title.

[nos 1–7 not extant]; no 8 The curranto for this weeke from Norimberg, 25 March 1640; no 9 (Franckford) 24 March; no 10 (Holland) 25 March; no 11 A true narration of a late sea-fight betwixt 15 men of warre of Dunkerke and one man of warre of Sealand, 27 March; no 12 (Norimberg) 31 March; no 13 (Franckford) 31 March; no 14 (Holland) 31 March; no 15 (Norimberg) 10 April; no 16 A true and fearefull pronouncing of warre against the Roman Imperiall Majesty, 10 April; no 17 (Holland) 10 April; no 18 (Franckford) 20 April; no 19 (Holland) 20 April; no 20 The news for this week from Norimberg, Frankford and Holland, 23 April; [nos 21–6 not extant]; no 27 Newes of this present weeke from Germany, Italy and Spaine, 6 June; [no 28] A true relation of a late very famous sea-fight, made betwixt the Spaniard and the Hollander in Brasil, 12 June; [nos 29–30 not extant]; no 31 Newes of this present weeke from severall places, 27 June; [nos 32–45 not extant]; no 46 The continuation of our last two weeks printed newes from forraigne parts, 4 Dec; no 47 The continuation of the forraine avisoes, 10 Dec; no 48 The continuation of the forraine occurrents for 5 weekes last past, 11 Jan 1641; no 49 The continuation of the forraine avisoes for two weekes last past, 23 Jan; [no later issues extant].

(m) Thirteenth Series Feb–Sept 1641

In this, the last recognizable series of newsbooks, there is again little continuity in style or title, although most issues bear the words Cent. 4. The series was issued by Nathaniel Butter.

The forraine aviso's continued. no 1 2 Feb 1641; [nos 2–5 not extant]; no 6 The forraigne weekely avisoes continued March ?; [nos 7–8 not extant]; no 9 From Hamborough, From Wolfenbutle, From Caments 8 April; no 10 The continuation of our weekely avisoes, 10 April; no 11 The continuation of our weekely avisoes, 19 April; no 12 The continuation of our weekely avisoes, 19 April; [nos 13–15 not extant]; no 16 The continuation of our weekely avisoes, 12 May; no 17 From Rome, From Hamborough 2, 21 May; [nos 18–20 not extant]; no 21 The continuation of our weekely newes, 10 June; [no 22] Extraordinary avisoes of foreine matters, 18 June; [no 23] The forraine avisoes for the last week past, 30 June; no 24 Received this weeke extraordinary newes from Germany, 10 July; [nos 25–29 not extant]; no 30 The Imperialists have victualled Wolffenbuttle but have not recovered the damme, 4 Sept; [no 31 not extant]; no 32 The continuation of our weekely avisoes, 23 Sept 1641; [no later issues extant].

During 1642 a small number of newsbooks were issued by Nathaniel Butter, and although it seems clear from editorial comment that he intended to continue publishing periodical newsbooks, those that survive give no indication that they constitute part of any recognizable series.

(6) BIBLIOGRAPHIES AND GENERAL STUDIES 1641–59
(*including contemporary accounts*)

Old newes newly revived. [June] 1641.
A presse full of pamphlets. [April] 1642.
J[ordan], T[homas]. A diurnial of dangers. [14 Aug] 1642.
A remonstrance of Londons occurrences. [31 Jan] 1643.
[Parker, Henry]. Humble remonstrance of the Company of

Stationers. [April] 1643; ed E. Arber, Transcript of the registers of the Company of Stationers vol 1, 1875.
A copy of a letter written by Mr Stephen Marshall. [17 May 1643].
A letter from Mercurius Civicus to Mercurius Rusticus. Oxford [25 Aug] 1643.

[Featley, Daniel]. Sacra nemesis, the Levites scourge. [1 Aug] 1644.

M[ilton], J[ohn]. Areopagitica. [24 Nov] 1644.

[Cleveland, John]. The character of a London diurnall. [Oxford Jan] 1645.

[Wither, George]. The great assizes holden in Parnassus by Apollo. [11 Feb] 1645.

A character of the new Oxford libeller in answer to his character of a London diurnall. [11 Feb] 1645.

The Oxford character of a London diurnall examined and answered. [31 March] 1645.

[Pecke, Samuel]. A full answer to a scandalous pamphlet intituled A character of a London diurnall. [10 April] 1645.

[Taylor, John]. Rebels anathematized and anatomized. Oxford [25 May] 1645.

The Cavaliers diurnall written by adventure. [31 March 1647].

[Cleveland, John]. A character of a moderate intelligencer. [29 April] 1647.

A true diurnall with some perfect occurrences, weekly and moderate intelligence. [31 May] 1647.

A fresh whip for all scandalous lyers. [9 Sept] 1647.

Mercurius Diabolicus. [29 Sept] 1647.

Welcome, most welcome newes. [15 Oct] 1647.

Hinc illae lacrimae. [23 Dec] 1647.

Loyalty speaks truth. [10 Jan] 1648.

[Harris, John]. Mercurius anti-mercurius communicating all humours, conditions, forgeries and lies. [4 April] 1648.

A muzzle for Cerberus and his three whelps. [20 June] 1648.

Hermes straticus. 17 Aug 1648.

[Hackluyt, John? or John Harris]. Mercurius anti-mercurius. no 1, 19 Sept–no 3, 2 Oct 1648.

[Howell, James]. A trance. [11 Dec] 1648.

The hue and cry after those rambling protonotaries of the times, Mercurius Elencticus, Britanicus, Melancholicus and Aulicus. [7 Feb] 1651.

[Sheppard, Samuel]. Mercurius Mastix. no 1, 27 Aug 1652.

S[heppard] S[amuel]. The weepers. [13 Sept] 1652.

[Cleveland, John]. A character of a diurnall maker. [28 Nov] 1653.

A collection of the state papers of John Thurloe. Ed T. Birch 7 vols 1742.

Journals of the House of Commons. 2–7 [1742].

Journals of the House of Lords. 4–10 [1771].

Chalmers, G. The life of Thomas Ruddiman. 1794. Chronological list of civil war newspapers in appendix 6.

Nichols, J. Literary anecdotes of the eighteenth century. 9 vols 1812–16.

Wright, T. Political ballads published in England during the Commonwealth. 1841 (Percy Soc).

Timperley, C. H. An encyclopaedia of literary and typographical anecdote. 1842.

Hunt, F. K. The fourth estate: contributions towards a history of newspapers and of the liberty of the press. 2 vols 1850.

Andrews, A. The history of British journalism. 2 vols 1859.

Hart, W. H. Index expurgatorius anglicanus. 5 pts 1872–8.

Calendar of state papers, domestic series: the Commonwealth 1649–60. Ed M. A. E. Green 13 vols 1875 6.

Bullen, G. and W. Rayner. Caxton celebration catalogue. 1877. See also N & Q 28 July 1877.

Paterson, J. The liberty of the press, speech and public worship. 1880.

Calendar of state papers, domestic series: Charles I 1641–9. Vols 17–23, ed W. D. Hamilton 1882–97.

Jackson, M. The pictorial press. 1885.

Bourne, H. R. F. English newspapers. 2 vols 1887.

Plomer, H. R. Notices of printers and printing in the state papers. Bibliographica 2 1896.

British Museum catalogue of printed books: periodical publications. 1899–1900, 1963.

[Edmond, J. P.] Bibliotheca Lindesiana. In Collations and notes no 5, Aberdeen 1901.

'Williams, J. B.' (J. G. Muddiman). The newsbooks and letters of news of the Restoration. EHR 23 1908.

— A history of English journalism to the foundation of the Gazette. 1908.

— The beginnings of English journalism. CHEL vol 7 1911.

— Tercentenary handlist of English and Welsh newspapers, magazines and reviews. 1920, 1966. See also N & Q 29 Jan, 5, 26 Feb, 26 March 1921, 11–18 March 1922.

British Museum. Catalogue of the Thomason tracts. 2 vols 1908. See also L. Spencer, 1958.

Acts and ordinances of the Interregnum. Ed C. H. Firth and R. S. Rait 3 vols 1911.

Escott, T. H. S. Masters of English journalism. 1911.

Madan, F. In his Oxford books vol 2, Oxford 1912.

A transcript of the registers of the Stationers' Company 1641–1708. Ed G. E. Briscoe Eyre (and H. R. Plomer) 3 vols 1912–13.

Yale University. A list of newspapers in the Yale University library. New Haven 1916.

Notestein, W. and F. H. Relf. Commons debates for 1629. Minneapolis 1921.

McCutcheon, R. P. The beginning of book reviewing in English periodicals. PMLA 37 1922.

Rollins, H. E. Cavalier and puritan. New York 1923.

Griffiths, R. H. Some unrecorded newsbooks. TLS 11 Dec 1924.

Thompson, E. N. S. War journalism of the seventeenth century. In Literary bypaths of the Renaissance, New Haven 1924.

Manwaring, G. E. Journalism in the days of the commonwealth. Edinburgh Rev 244 1926.

Crane, R. S. and F. B. Kaye. A census of British newspapers and periodicals 1620–1800. Chapel Hill 1927, 1967.

Gabler, A. J. Check list of English newspapers and periodicals before 1801 in the Huntington library. Huntington Lib Bull 2 1931.

Morison, S. The English newspaper. Cambridge 1932.

— The origins of the newspaper. 1954.

Stewart, A. Catalogue of an exhibition illustrating the history of the English newspaper from the library of the Press Club. 1932.

— The evolution of the English newspaper from its origins to the present day. 2 vols 1935–46.

Richardson, H. The old English newspaper. 1933.

Clyde, W. M. The struggle for the freedom of the press from Caxton to Cromwell. St Andrews 1934.

Milford, R. T. and D. M. Sutherland. A catalogue of English newspapers and periodicals in the Bodleian library 1622–1800. Proc Oxford Bibl Soc 4 1936.

Abbot, W. C. The writings and speeches of Oliver Cromwell. 4 vols Cambridge Mass 1937–47.

— The first newspapermen. Proc Mass Historical Soc 66. Boston 1942.

Bruner, H. M. Catalogue of English pamphlets in the Sutro library. Pt 2, San Francisco 1941.

French, J. M. Seventeenth century English newsbooks. Jnl Rutgers Univ Lib 7 1943.

— The life records of John Milton. 5 vols New Brunswick 1949–58.

Weed, K. K. and R. P. Bond. Studies in British newspapers and periodicals from their beginning to 1800: a bibliography. Chapel Hill 1946.

Stewart, R. British newspapers and periodicals 1632–1800: a descriptive catalogue of a collection at the University of Texas. Austin 1950.

Berg, V. Holdings of seventeenth- and eighteenth-century English newspapers in the University of Illinois library. Coranto 2 (Urbana) 1950.

Herd, H. The march of journalism. 1952.
Siebert, F. S. Freedom of the press in England 1476–1776. Urbana 1952, 1965.
Dahl, F. A bibliography of English corantos and periodical publications 1620–42. 1952.
Stewart, J. D. et al. British union catalogue of periodicals. 4 vols 1955–8.
Guildhall, London. A complete list of the seventeenth-century newspapers in the Guildhall library. Guildhall Miscellany 8 1957.
Blagden, C. The Stationers' Company in the Civil War period. Library 5th ser 13 1958.
Spencer, L. The professional and literary connexions of George Thomason. Ibid.

—— The politics of George Thomason. Library 5th ser 14 1959.
Frank, J. The beginnings of the English newspaper 1620–60. Cambridge Mass 1961.
—— Hobbled Pegasus: a descriptive bibliography of minor English poetry 1641–60. Albuquerque 1968. On verse in newsbooks.
[Gemmell, J.] The Mitchell library, Glasgow: catalogue of periodicals. Glasgow 1962.
Freitag, R. S. Union list of serials: a bibliography. Washington 1964.
Titus, E. B. Union list of serials in libraries of the United States and Canada. 5 vols New York 1965.

(7) JOURNALISTS, PRINTERS AND PUBLISHERS AFTER 1640

Wood, A. Athenae oxonienses. Ed P. Bliss 4 vols 1813–20.
Aubrey, J. Brief lives. Ed A. Clark 2 vols Oxford 1898.
Plomer, H. R. A dictionary of booksellers and printers 1641–67. 1907 (Bibl Soc).

Individual Journalists etc

Simeon Ashe (A continuation of true intelligence 1644)
[Barwick, John]. Querela cantabrigiensis. Oxford [1 April] 1646.
Thomas Audley (Mercurius Britanicus 1643–4)
[Taylor, J.] Mercurius aquaticus. Oxford [18 Jan] 1644.
Mercurius anti-Britanicus. [Oxford Aug] 1645.
Mercurius diutinus. 20–7 Jan 1647.
Sir John Berkenhead (Mercurius Aulicus 1643–5).
The recantation of Mercurius Aulicus. [14 March] 1644.
The true character of Mercurius Aulicus. 1645.
Thomas, P. W. Sir John Berkenhead 1617–79. Oxford 1969.
Nicholas Bourne (Le Mercure anglois 1644–8; Generall news from all parts of Christendome 1646)
Dahl, F. A bibliography of English corantos and periodical newsbooks 1620–42. 1952 (Bibl Soc).
Rostenberg, L. Nathaniel Butter and Nicholas Bourne, first 'Masters of the Staple'. Library 5th ser 12 1957.
Edward Bowles (A faithful relation of the Scottish army 1644)
Calamy, E. The nonconformist's memorial vol 3. Ed S. Palmer 1803.
Nathaniel Butter (Heads of severall proceedings 1641–2; The passages in Parliament 1642)
See Nicholas Bourne, above.
John Cleveland (Mercurius Pragmaticus 1647)
A character of the new Oxford libeller. [11 Feb] 1645.
Lake, J. Clievelandi vindiciae. 1677.
Percy, T. Biographia britannica vol 3. 1784.
Poems. Ed B. Morris and E. Withington. Oxford 1967.
John Dillingham (Parliament scout, 1643–5; Moderate intelligencer, 1645–9; Moderate messenger, 1653)
The copy of a letter written from Northampton. [6 Feb] 1646.
Weekly intelligencer. 22 Feb–1 March 1653.
William Dugard (Nouvelles ordinaires 1650–?)
William Dugard: pedagogue and printer to the Commonwealth. PBSA 52 1958.
Walter Frost (A brief relation 1649)
Mercurius Elencticus. 5 Nov 1649.
Frank, J. The levellers. Cambridge Mass 1955.
John Hackluyt (Mercurius Melancholicus 1647–8 etc)
Mercurius Melancholicus no 2. 2 June 1649. Counterfeit attributed to John Taylor.
John Hall (Mercurius Brittanicus 1648 etc)
Mercurius Elencticus nos 27–9, 34. May–July 1648.
D[avies], J[ohn]. Memoir in Hierocles upon the golden verses of Pythagoras. Tr John Hall 1657.
Croston, A. K. Introd to John Hall, The advancement of learning (1649). Liverpool 1953.

John Harris (Mercurius Militaris 1648 etc)
Mercurius impartialis. 5–12 Dec 1648.
Mercurius fumigosus. 30 Nov, 13 Dec 1654.
The speech of Major John Harris at the place of execution. [Sept] 1660.
John Milton (Mercurius Politicus 1650–2)
Williams, J. B. (J. G. Muddiman). Milton: journalist. Oxford & Cambridge Rev 18 1912.
French, J. M. Milton, Needham and Mercurius Politicus. SP 33 1936.
Beller, E. A. Milton and Mercurius Politicus. HLQ 5 1942.
Henry Muddiman (Parliamentary intelligencer 1659)
Muddiman, J. G. The King's journalist. 1923.
Marchamont Needham (Mercurius Britanicus 1644–6 etc)
[Taylor, John]. Rebells anathematized and anatomized. Oxford [25 May] 1645.
Mercurius anti-britanicus: or the second part of the King's cabinet vindicated. [Oxford Aug] 1645.
Wortley, Sir Francis. Characters and elegies. 1646.
Match me these two. [29 July] 1647.
[Cleveland, John]. The committee man's complaint. [26 Aug] 1647.
—— The poor committee man's accompt. [26 Aug] 1647.
—— The character of Mercurius Politicus. [14 Aug] 1650.
—— The second character of Mercurius Politicus. [23 Oct] 1650.
Kilburne, W. A new year's gift for Mercurius Politicus. [29 Dec] 1959.
The downefall of Mercurius Britannicus—Pragmaticus—Politicus. [9 April 1660].
A dialogue between Thomas Scot and Marchamont Needham. [1660].
[L'Estrange, Sir Roger]. A rope for pol. [7 Sept] 1660.
Wright, T. Political ballads. 1841.
Samuel Pecke (A perfect diurnal 1642–55 etc)
A fresh whip for all scandalous lyers. [9 Sept] 1647.
John Rushworth (London post 1647 etc)
Man in the moon. 24 Oct 1649.
John Saltmarsh (Perfect occurrences 1646)
Fuller, T. The history of the worthies of England. 1662.
Samuel Sheppard (Mercurius Pragmaticus 1647 etc)
The Metropolitan Nuncio. 3 June 1649.
Rollins, H. E. Samuel Sheppard and his praise of poets. SP 24 1927.
George Smith (Scottish Dove 1643–6)
The Scottish Dove sent out the last time. [25 Dec] 1646.
John Streater (Observations upon Aristotle 1654)
Secret reasons of state. [23 May] 1659.
John Taylor (Mercurius Melancholicus (counterfeit) 1647 etc)
Hindley, C. Introd to Taylor's Works, 1872.
Henry Walker (Perfect Occurrences 1647–9 etc)
[Taylor, John]. The whole life and progress of Henry Walker the ironmonger. 1642; ed C. Hindley, Old book collectors' miscellany vol 3, 1873.

A fresh whip for all scandalous lyers. [7 Sept] 1647.

A recommendation to Mercurius Morbicus. [6 Oct] 1647.

Wood, A. Athenae oxonienses vol 2. Ed P. Bliss 1815.

Williams, J. B. (J. G. Muddiman). Henry Walker, journalist of the Commonwealth. Nineteenth Century March 1903.

Sirluck, E. To your tents, O Israel: a lost pamphlet. HLQ 19 1955.

Sir George Wharton (Mercurius Elencticus 1647-9) [Hall, John]. The late story of Mr William Lilly. [2 Feb] 1648.

(8) NEWSBOOKS 1641-59

For the purpose of the following list a newsbook is defined as a pamphlet containing current news or comment, issued or intended to be issued periodically. The presence of a serial number ptd on the pamphlet is accepted as evidence of intention to issue periodically. Sometimes a single pamphlet has sequels which develop into a numbered series (e.g. 19 Aug 1642); and in such cases the pamphlets at the beginning, though unnumbered and with varying titles, have been included if clearly part of one series. The pamphlets of Irish news in 1642, though often listed as newsbooks, have been omitted from this list as not falling within the scope of the definition. In no case has the title only of a pamphlet been taken as a criterion of its being a newsbook.

Of many of the entries in this list there exist different forms under the same title and date. These are usually called counterfeits; but they fall into 3 distinct classes: (i) where the same title, numbering, text and imprint have been set up differently throughout, it has been referred to as a reprint; most reprints have the names of 2 printers in the imprint, and presumably arose from the double setting up required to print a large edn in a short time; (ii) where the same title and imprint occur with a different text, it has been referred to as a counterfeit; their object was often political; in the present list the use of this term has been restricted to this form of variant; (iii) where the title is the same, but the text and the imprint differ, it has been referred to as an imitation. Only one case has so far been noticed in which the same title and text are found with a different imprint (A continuation of the true diurnall of passages in Parliament, no 2 24 Jan 1642, sold by Stationers). When alterations have been made in what is the same setting of type, it has been referred to as an issue.

'Ptd', 'pbd' have been added to distinguish different forms or series of similar titles. They are intended to identify the particular piece listed, and they refer to the imprint thereon whether false or not. Where adequate evidence is known to the compiler of this list, authorship has been indicated without qualification; but the phrase 'attributed to' has been used in the absence of such knowledge. A few attributions have been suggested with the phrase 'perhaps by'. All newsbooks, with the exception of 2 noted in 1654, were issued in small 4°. An asterisk has been used to distinguish entries which derive solely from bibliographies and of which no extant copy has been traced. Numbers, dates or imprints not ptd on the newsbooks themselves have been enclosed in square brackets.

All dates are recorded in the new style irrespective of that ptd on the newsbook. The dates given are the days of issue in so far as they are ascertainable. The run of a periodical in this list is not dated from the earliest date mentioned in the text of the earliest issue, but from the latest date in the earliest issue to the latest date in the last. Where the news mentioned has taken place in London, the latest date is assumed to be that of the issue of the newsbook. Where the latest date concerns an event outside London, or where there is no date at all, the ms dates of the Thomason Collection or other contemporary notes have been supplied within square brackets.

It is not always simple to decide if one paper is a continuation of another, or to judge how far the identity of a newsbook may survive a change of title or printer or suspension for varying periods. In general it has been considered more accurate to adopt in this list a more conservative attitude than that of BM General Catalogue and most previous bibliographies. To mitigate the misconceptions arising from this, cross-references have been added. Under the date on which any title first appears in this list there have been noted the dates of all similar titles, supposed continuations, revivals, imitations or counterfeits. Under the date of each subsequent appearance of the same title is noted the date of its earliest appearance together with the dates of its immediate predecessor or continuation and any counterfeits of this particular series that are separately entered.

The heads of severall proceedings in this present Parliament. [no 1] 29 Nov 1641. [Continued as] The heads of severall proceedings in both Houses of Parliament, [no 2] 6 Dec; [no 3 not extant]; [continued as] Diurnall occurrences: or the heads of severall proceedings in both Houses of Parliament. [no 4] 20 Dec 1641-[no 9] 24 Jan 1642; no 4 31 Jan-no 6 14 Feb 1642. The subtitle varies slightly, that of 31 Jan reading 'or the last weekes proceedings in both Houses of Parliament'. All pbd John Thomas, but 20 Dec with T.B. (Thomas Bates) and 3-10 Jan with Nathaniel Butter. *See* 20 Dec 1641, 17 Jan, 23 May 1642.

The diurnall: or the heads of all the proceedings in Parliament. [no 1] 13 Dec-[no 3] 26 Dec 1641. No 1 pbd J.W. and T.B.; nos 2-3 pbd John Wright.

The diurnall occurrances: or the heads of proceedings in Parliament. [no 1] 20 Dec 1641. [Pbd T. Bates and F. Coules (2 issues)]. *See* 29 Nov 1641, 17 Jan 1642.

Diurnal occurrances, touching the dayly proceedings in Parliament. [no 1] 25 Dec 1641; [no 2] 3 Jan; [no 3] 10 Jan 1642. [no 1 no imprint; nos 2-3 pbd John Hammond; no 2 rptd Edinburgh 1642].

Diurnall occurrences in Parliament. [no 1] 2 Jan; [no 2] 10 Jan; [no 3] 17 Jan 1642. [no 1, no imprint; nos 2-3 pbd William Cooke.] *See* 17 Jan, 6 June 1642.

The passages in Parliament. [no 1] 10 Jan 1642. [Pbd Nathaniel Butter].

Diurnal occurrences: or the heads of proceedings in both Houses of Parliament. [no 1 not extant]; [no 2] 17 Jan-no 6 14 Feb 1642. [Pbd John Greensmith]. *See* 29 Nov, 20 Dec 1641.

The diurnall occurrances in Parliament. [no 1] 17 Jan; no 2 24 Jan-no 6 14 Feb 1642. [Pbd F. Coules and T. Banks]. *See* 20 Dec 1641; 2 Jan, 6 June 1642.

A true diurnall of the last weeks passages in Parliament. no 1 17 Jan 1642; [continued as] A continuation of the true diurnall of passages in Parliament, no 2 24 Jan-no 11 28 March 1642. [nos 1-2 pbd Humphrey Blunden; nos 3-11 no imprint. There is a counterfeit of no 11]. *See* 24 Jan, 31 Jan, 28 Feb 1642.

Griffith, R. H. The second English newspaper. TLS 4 Dec 1924.

The diurnal occurrences: or proceedings in the Parliament the last weeke. [no 1] 17 Jan 1642; [no 2 not extant]; [continued as] A true diurnall occurrences: or proceedings in the Parliament this last weeke, no 3 31 Jan 1642. [no 1 pbd John Burroughes; no 3 pbd F.L. and George Thompson]. *See* 7 Feb, 21 March 1642.

A true diurnall: or the passages in Parliament. no 2 24 Jan 1642[-?]; [perhaps continued as] A true diurnall of the passages in Parliament, [?-]; no 10 21 March; [no 11 28 March 1642]. [no 2 pbd Humphrey Tuckey; no 10 no imprint). *See* 17 Jan, 24 Jan, 31 Jan, 28 Feb, 14 March, 28 March 1642.

A continuation of the true diurnall of passages in Parliament. [no 2] 24 Jan 1642[-?]. [Pbd George Hutton]. *See* 17 Jan, 24 Jan, 28 Feb 1642.

A continuation of the true diurnall of passages in Parliament. no 2 24 Jan 1642[-?]. 'Sold by Stationers'. This has the same text as no 2 of A true diurnall, above (no 1 17 Jan 1642).

A true diurnall of the last weeks passage in both Houses of Parliament. no 2 24 Jan 1642[-?]. No imprint. *See* 17 Jan, 21 Jan, 28 Feb, 14 March 1642.

A true diurnall of the last weekes passages in Parliament. no 3 31 Jan 1642. [Pbd John Wright]. *See* 17 Jan, 24 Jan, 28 Feb, 14 March 1642.

A perfect diurnall of the passages in Parliament. [no 1] 31 Jan–no 12 4 April 1642. [nos [1]–[8] have neither number nor imprint; nos 9–12 pbd William Cook. There are 2 settings of same text for nos 9 (misnumbered 7) and 11. By Samuel Pecke]. *See* 20 June, 11 July, 23 July, 1 Aug, 29 Aug, 12 Sept 1642 (2), 3 July 1643, 16 July, 17 Dec 1649, 22 July 1650, 8 May 1654, 21 Feb 1660.

The true diurnal occurrances: or the heads of the proceedings of both Houses of Parliament. [no 1] 7 Feb; [no 2] 14 Feb 1642. [Pbd John Hammond. no 1 by R.P.; no 2 by J[ohn] B[ond]]. *See* 17 Jan, 28 March 1642.

A continuation of the true diurnall of all the passages in Parliament. no 7 28 Feb–no 11 28 March 1642. [no imprint; imitation of no 10 (pbd R. Wood); counterfeit of no 11 with different text]. *See* 17 Jan 1642 etc.

A continuation of the true diurnall occurrences in Parliament. no 3 7 March 1642 [?–no 11 28 March 1642] [no imprint]. *See* 17 Jan 1642 etc.

A continuation of the true diurnall of proceedings in Parliament. no 9 14 March; no 10 21 March [no 11 28 March 1642]. No imprint.

A true diurnal of the passages in Parliament. [no 1] 14 March; [no 2] 21 March; [no 3? 28 March 1642]. No imprint. *See* 24 Jan 1642.

A continuation of the true diurnall occurrences and passages in both Houses of Parliament. no 10 21 March; no 11 28 March 1642. No imprint. *See* 17 Jan, 7 Feb, 7 March 1642.

*A continuation of the weekly occurrences in Parliament [no ?] 23 May 1642.

*Remarkeable occurrences from the High Court of Parliament. [no?] 23 May 1642; [probably continued as] The heads of all the proceedings in both Houses of Parliament, [no?] 30 May 1642 [-?]. [Pbd J. Smith and A. Coe]. *See* 29 Nov 1641.

Some special passages from London, Westminster, Yorke [etc]. no 2 24 May; no 3 31 May; no 1 2 June–no 11 9 Aug 1642. Towns mentioned in the title vary; it is probable there are 2 different sers running under this title. no 1 pbd Thomas Baker; no 10 (Aug 1) pbd R.O[ulton] and G.D[exter]. *See* 16 Aug 1642.

Diurnall ocurrences in Parliament. [no 1] 6 June; no 2 13 June; [no 3] 20 June; [no 4] 25 June 1642. [Pbd F. Coles and T. Banks; imitations of nos 1–3 without no or imprint].

Remarkeable passages in Parliament. [no 1] 6 June 1642. *See* 12 Sept 1642, 2 Nov 1643.

A perfect diurnall of the passages in Parliament. no 1 20 June–no 9 15 Aug 1642. [nos 1–3 'London printed'; nos 4–6 pbd William Cooke; nos 7–9 pbd William Cooke 'at Furnifalls Inne Gate'. By Samuel Pecke]. *See* 31 Jan 1642 etc. 8 distinct sers under this title in 1642 are listed separately in their chronological places, but 14 imitations of single nos have been grouped together in the next entry.

A perfect diurnall of the passages in Parliament [imitations]. [unnumbered] 11 July 1642 (pbd William Rodgers); [unnumbered] 18 July (pbd Robert Williamson); [unnumbered] 19 July (no imprint); [unnumbered] 25 July (pbd John Thomas); [unnumbered] 25 July (2 issues pbd J.G. and R.W.); no 7 1 Aug (pbd John Jonson); no 9 15 Aug (ptd Thomas Fawcet for T.C.); no 14 19 Sept (pbd Walt Cook and Robert Woodner); no 14 19 Sept; no 15 26 Sept (both pbd Walt Cook and Robert Woody); no 17 [thus for 16] 3 Oct (pbd William Cookes); no 18 [thus for 17] 10 Oct (pbd Walter Cooke and Robert Wood); no 17 [thus for 20] 31 Oct 1642 (pbd T.F. for Wil Cooke).

A perfect diurnall of the passages in Parliament. [unnumbered] 11 July 1642; [unnumbered] 25 July; [unnumbered] 1 Aug; no 8 8 Aug; no 9 15 Aug 1642. [First 4 nos pbd William Cook; nos 8–9 pbd William Cook 'at Furnivals Inne']. *See* 31 Jan, 20 June 1642.

A true and perfect diurnall of all the chiefe passages in Lancashire. no 1 9 July 1642 (Pbd T.U.].

A current. [?] 12 July 1642[-?].

A perfect diurnall of the passages in Parliament. no 6 25 July–no 9 15 Aug 1642. [Pbd Thomas Cook]. *See* 31 Jan, 20 June 1642.

A diurnall and particular of the last weekes daily occurrents. [no 1] [26] July [1642]. [Pbd D.C.].

A perfect diurnall of the passages in Parliament. [unnumbered] 1 Aug; no 8 8 Aug 1642–no 54 19 June 1643. [The first] no and no 8 pbd Robert Wood: from no 9 on, pbd Walter Cook and Robert Wood, but spelling of first name varies on nos 9–12. Later ptd R. Austin and A. Coe for Walter Cook and Robert Wood and sold by T. Bates. Counterfeits of no 14 19 Sept and no 19 24 Oct–no 26 12 Dec 1642. Reprints of nos 29, 31, 2, 16 Jan 1643. *See* 31 Jan, 20 June 1642.

A continuation of the true diurnall of passages in Parliament. no 1 15 Aug 1642. [Pbd T. Paine and M. Simmons]. *See* 17 Jan 1642 etc.

An exact and true diurnall of the proceedings in Parliament [no 1] 15 Aug–[no 4] 5 Sept 1642. [Pbd W. Cooke, except [no 2] pbd Thomas Cooke].

Some speciall and considerable passages from London, Westminster [etc]. no 1 16 Aug 1642; [continued as] Some speciall passages from divers parts etc, no 2 23 Aug 1642; [continued as] Speciall passages and certain informations from severall places. no 3 30 Aug 1642–no 44 13 June 1643. [Pbd Humphrey Blunden. There is an imitation of no 2 23 Aug and counterfeits of nos 19–20 20 and 27 Dec 1642]. *See* 24 May, 13 Sept 1642, 19 July 1643. *See* also Mercurius Civicus, 8 June 1643.

A true relation of certaine speciall and remarkable passages. [no 1] 19 Aug 1642; [continued as] Certaine speciall and remarkable passages from both Houses of Parliament, [no 2] 23 Aug; [no 3] 26 Aug 1642; [continued as] A continuation of certaine speciall and remarkable passages, no 4 30 Aug 1642–no 59 13 Oct 1643 [-?]. [no 1 pbd F. Leach; no 2 on, pbd F. Leach and F. Coles. Came out twice a week, with 2 exceptions, till 2nd week in Oct 1642. By Samuel Pecke]. *See* 8 Oct, 14 Oct (twice), 11 Nov, 24 Nov 1642, 5 Jan, 10 July 1644, 26 Sept 1645, 9 June 1647.

A perfect diurnall of the passages in Parliament. no 11 29 Aug–no 15 3 Oct 1642. [Pbd Will Cooke. There is a reprint of no 13 12 Sept 1642]. *See* 31 Jan, 20 June 1642.

A true and perfect diurnall of the passages in Parliament. no 11 [6 Sept 1642]. [Pbd H. Blundell].

Remarkable passages, or a perfect diurnall of the weekly proceedings in both Houses of Parliament. no 1 12 Sept 1642. [Pbd M. Walbank and J.W.]. *See* 6 June 1642, 8 Nov 1643.

A perfect diurnall of the passages in Parliament. [All unnumbered]. 12 Sept 1642 (pbd William Cooke); 19 Sept (pbd Robert Wood, Wil Cooke); 26 Sept; [3 Oct]; 10 Oct (both pbd Wil Cooke); 17 Oct 1642 (pbd William Cooke at Furnivals Inne). *See* 31 Jan, 20 June 1642.

A perfect diurnall of the passages in Parliament. no 13 12 Sept 1642–no 53 19 June 1643. [Ptd F. Leach and I. Okes, pbd F. Coles. There are reprints of no 16 3 Oct; no 18 17 Oct; no 27 19 Dec 1642; no 32 23 Jan 1643; no 36 20 Feb; and no 37 27 Feb 1643. By Samuel Pecke]. *See* 31 Jan, 20 June 1642.

Quotidian occurrences in and about London. [unnumbered] 12 Sept 1642.

Englands memorable accidents. [no 1 12 Sept]; [no 2] 19 Sept 1642–no 19 16 Jan 1643. [Pbd Stephen Bowtell].

Speciall passages and certain informations. no 1 13 Sept 1642. [Ptd R. Austin and A. Coe]. *See* 16 Aug 1642.

A continuation of our weekly intelligence from his Majesties army. [unnumbered] 16 Sept 1642.

A perfect relation: or summarie. no 1 19 Sept; no 2 12 Oct 1642. [Ptd F. Coles].

A continuation of true and special passages. [unnumbered]. 29 Sept 1642. [Pbd William Cook].

Certain speciall and remarkable passages of the proceedings in both Houses of Parliament. [no 1] 6 Oct 1642. [Pbd T.B.]. *See* 19 Aug 1642.

A continuation of certaine speciall and remarkable passages. no 13 8 Oct; no 14 12 Oct; no 15 14 Oct 1642–no 52 16 June; [no 53 23 June 1643]. [The first 3 nos pbd Robert Wood; from no 21 1 Dec 1642 on, pbd Walter Cooke and Robert Wood]. *See* 19 Aug 1642.

Weekly intelligence from severall parts of this kingdome. [no 1] 11 Oct; [no 2] 18 Oct 1642. [Pbd R. Howes].

A continuation of certaine speciall and remarkable passages. no 15 14 Oct 1642. [Pbd John Wright]. *See* 19 Aug 1642.

A continuation of certaine speciall and remarkable passages. no 1 14 Oct 1642. [Pbd Marke Walbank]. *See* 19 Aug 1642.

A collection of speciall passages. [unnumbered] 2 Nov 1642. [Pbd F. Coles].

A continuation of certaine speciall and remarkable passages. [all unnumbered] 11 Nov, 18 Nov, 24 Nov 1642. [Pbd John White]. *See* 19 Aug, 14 Oct 1642.

A continuation of certaine speciall and remarkable passages [unnumbered] 24 Nov 1642 [Pbd I. Coule]. *See* 19 Aug 1642.

A grand diurnall of the passages in Parliament. no 1 28 Nov 1642 (Pbd J. Field).

A continuation of the most remarkable passages in both Houses of Parliament, by G.H. [no 1] 3 Dec 1642. [Ptd R. Herne].

The kingdomes weekly intelligencer sent abroad to prevent misinformation. [no 1] 3 Jan 1643–[no 332] 9 Oct 1649. [nos 187–98 omitted]. Counterfeits: no 24 [thus for 4] 24 Jan 1643; no 22 6 June; no 23 13 June 1643; [unnumbered] 13 June 1643 (pbd Peter Cole). Attributed to Richard Collings.

The Oxford diurnall communicating the intelligence and affaires of the court to the rest of the kingdome. no 1 7 Jan 1643. [Oxford].

Mercurius Aulicus, communicating the intelligence and affaires of the Court to the rest of the kingdome. [no 1] 8 Jan 1643–[no 118] 7 Sept 1645. [Oxford. With some interruptions after no 99 24 Nov 1644. By Sir John Berkenhead, but by Peter Heylin in Aug–Sept 1643 and June 1644. Counterfeit: [no 40] 7 Oct 1643].

Mercurius Aulicus [etc *London reprints*]. [no 2] 14 Jan 1643–[no 8] 25 Feb; [no 10] 11 March; [no 40] 7 Oct 1643; [no 53] 6 Jan 1644–[no 57] 3 Feb; [no 64] 23 March; [no 70] 4 May; [no 72] 18 May; [no 75] 8 June; [no 80] 13 July; [no 84] 10 Aug; [no 88] 7 Sept; [no 94] 19 Oct; [no 96] 2 Nov; [no 98] 16 Nov; [no 99] 23 Nov 1644. [Several of these have different text from the corresponding nos ptd at Oxford]. *See* 3 Feb 1648, 7 Aug 1648, 21 Aug 1649, 20 March 1654.

Mercurius Aulicus, a diurnall communicating the intelligence and affaires of the Court to the rest of the kingdome: the earliest regular English newspaper, edited, printed and published in Oxford during the siege 1643–5. Ed F. J. Varley, Oxford 1948. A selection.

A letter from a minister in his excellence his army by way of prevention to Mercurius Aulicus and his complices. [18 April] 1643. Perhaps by Edward Bowles.

A copy of a letter written by Mr Stephen Marshall. [17 May] 1643.

An antidote against the malignant influence of Mercurius (surnamed) Aulicus. 2 Sept 1643.

An answer to Mercurius Aulicus. [c. 15 Dec] 1643.

Anti-Aulicus. [no 1 6 Feb 1644]; [no 2 8 Feb 1644].

The recantation of Mercurius Aulicus: or Berkinhead's complaint. [14 March] 1644.

Mercurius Aulico-Mastix: or the whipping Mercury. no 1 12 April 1644.

[Cheynell, Francis]. Aulicus his dream. [15 May] 1644 (twice).

Ruperts sumpter and private cabinet rifled. [19 July] 1644].

The true character of Mercurius Aulicus. 1645.

News from Smith the Oxford jaylor with the arraignment of Mercurius Aulicus. [5 Feb] 1645.

A whip for an ape: or Aulicus his whelp worm'd. [29 Aug] 1645.

Certaine informations. no 1 23 Jan 1643–no 57 21 Feb 1644. By William Ingler.

The daily intelligencer of Court, city and countrey. no 1 30 Jan 1643.

Mercurius Civicus. London's intelligencer: or truth really imparted. no 1 11 May 1643–no 183 10 Dec 1646. Attributed to Richard Collings.

[Berkenhead, Sir John]. A letter from Mercurius Civicus to Mercurius Rusticus. Oxford [25 Aug] 1643.

Plomer, H. R. An analysis of the civil war newspaper Mercurius Civicus. Library 3rd ser 6 1905.

Mercurius Rusticus: or the countries complaint. [no 1] 20 May 1643–no 21 16 March 1644. [Oxford. Issued irregularly; rptd 1647 (as Angliae Ruina), 1685, 1723, 1732. By Bruno Ryves]. *See* 26 Oct 1643, 12 Nov 1647.

A coranto from beyond the sea. no 1 9 June 1643.

The Parliaments scouts discovery. no 1 16 June 1643. Attributed to John Dillingham.

The Parliament scout communicating his intelligence to the kingdome. no 1 27 June; no 2 6 July 1643–no 85 30 Jan 1645. [By John Dillingham].

A perfect diurnall of some passages in Parliament and from other parts of this kingdom. no 1 3 July 1643–no 323 8 Oct; no 324 12 Nov 1649. [Pbd F. Coles and Laurence Blaicklock. There are reprints of practically the whole series; and a counterfeit of no 161 31 Aug 1646, and probably others. By Samuel Pecke]. *See* 31 Jan 1642.

A perfect diurnall of some passages in Parliament 1643–9. Ed P. Radin, California State Lib (Sutro Branch) Occasional Papers Eng ser 2 1939.

A weekly accompt: or perfect diurnall. no 1 10 July 1643. Attributed to Daniel Border. [Pbd Robert Wood and John Greensmith]. *See* 3 Aug, 6 Sept 1643, 25 May, 1 June 1659.

Wednesday's Mercury: or speciall passages and certain informations. no 1 19 July 1643; [continued as] The speciall passages continued, no 2 22 July; no 3 28 July; [continued as] Wednesday's Mercury: or the speciall passages and certain informations, no 4 2 Aug 1643. [Ptd T.P[aine] and M.S[immons]]. *See* 16 Aug 1642.

A weekly accompt of certain special and remarkable passages from both Houses of Parliament. no [1] 3 Aug 1643. [Ptd Bernard Alsop]. *See* 10 July 1643.

Mercurius Britanicus communicating the affaires of Great Britaine. no 1 29 Aug 1643–no 130 18 May 1646. [None issued 9–30 Sept 1644. Counterfeits; no 27 18 March–no 29 1 April 1644, and probably others. nos 1–51 by Thomas Audley; nos 52–130 by Marchamont Needham]. *See* 24 June 1647, 7 April, 23 May 1648, 4 May 1649, 26 July 1652, 23 May 1653.

[Featley, D.] Britanicus Vapulans. *See* 4 Nov 1643, below.

[Taylor, John]. Mercurius Aquaticus: or the water poet's answer to all that shall be written by Mercurius Britanicus. [18 Jan] 1644. This pamphlet involved Taylor in a lengthy controversy with John Booker.

[Prynne, W.] A checke to Britanicus. [14 Feb] 1644.

[? Needham, M. or J. Saltmarsh]. A check to the checker of Britanicus. [24 Feb] 1644.

Ruperts sumpter and private cabinet rifled by way of dialogue between Mercurius Britannicus and Mercurius Aulicus. [20 July] 1644.

[Berkenhead, Sir John]. Mercurius Anti-Britannicus. [Oxford 4 Aug 1645].

Mercurius Britannicus his apologie to all well-affected people. [11 Aug] 1645.

[Berkenhead, Sir John]. Mercurius Anti-Britannicus; or part of the King's cabinet vindicated from the aspersions of Mercurius Britannicus. [Oxford 11 Aug] 1645.

Aulicus his hue and cry sent forth after Britanicus. [13 Aug] 1645. Attributed to Francis Cheynell.

[Berkenhead, Sir John]. Mercurius Anti-Britannicus; or the second part of the King's cabinet vindicated. [18? Aug 1645].

[Wortley, Sir Francis]. Britannicus his blessing; Britanicus his welcome. Cambridge [17 Jan] 1646; rptd as Mercurius Britanicus his welcome to hell; with the devill's blessing to Britanicus, [25 Feb] 1647; also rptd in Wortley's Characters and elegies, [15 July] 1646.

Mercurius Britannicus his vision: being a reply to a pamphlet termed Britanicus his welcome to hell. [25 March] 1647. Attributed to Marchamont Needham.

The weekly account. no 1 6 Sept 1643–no 17 29 April 1647; [continued as] The perfect weekly account, no 18 5 May 1647–no 52 28 Dec 1647; no 1 5 June 1648. There may have been 2 sers running May–June 1647 and there is a new series numbering each January. Ptd B. Alsop. Attributed to Daniel Border. See 10 July 1643, 29 March 1648, 17 July 1650.

The true informer: continuing a collection of the most speciall and observable passages. no 1 [23 Sept 1643]–no 67 22 Feb 1645. Attributed to Henry Whalley. See 26 April 1645, 28 Aug 1651, 6 Jan 1654.

New Christian uses upon the weekly true passages. no 1 7 Oct 1643. Attributed to George Smith.

The Scottish Mercury. [unnumbered] [13 Oct 1643]. [By George Smith].

The Scotch intelligencer, relating the weekly news from Scotland, the court and other places. [no 1] 17 Oct; [no 2] 25 Oct 1643.

The Scotish dove sent out and returning. no 1 20 Oct 1643–no 161 26 Nov 1646; [continued as] The Scotish dove sent out the last time, [1 no 25 Dec 1646]. [By George Smith].

Mercurius Rusticus: or a countrey messenger. [no 1] [26 Oct 1643]. [By George Wither]. See 20 May 1643.

The Welch Mercury, communicating remarkable intelligence and true news. no 1 28 Oct–no 3 11 Nov 1643[–?]; [probably continued as] The British Mercury: or the Welch diurnall [?–]; no 6 3 Dec 1643[–?]. [Ptd W. Ley and G. Lindsay]. See 11 Feb 1644.

Mercurius Cambro-Britannus, the British Mercury or the Welch diurnall. [no 1 30 Oct]–no 4 20 Nov 1643–no 8 24 Jan 1644. [Ptd B. Alsop. None issued 5 Dec 1643–13 Jan 1644].

The compleate intelligencer and resolver. [no 1] 2 Nov; no 2 7 Nov–no 5 28 Nov 1643. Attributed to George Smith.

Informator Rusticus: or the country intelligencer. no 1 3 Nov 1643. Attributed to Henry Walker.

Britanicus Vapulans: or the whipping of poor British Mercury by Mercurius Urbanus, younger brother to Aulicus. no 1 4 Nov 1643; [continued as] Mercurius Urbanus, [no 2] 9 Nov 1643; [no 3 nd]. Attributed to Daniel Featley.

Remarkable passages. no 1 8 Nov–no 8 29 Dec 1643. [Pbd A. Coe]. See 6 June 1642.

The kingdomes weekly post with his packet of letters, publishing his message to the city and the countrey. no 1 9 Nov 1643–no 10 10 Jan 1644. Attributed to John Rushworth. See 15 Oct 1645, 5 Jan 1648.

A continuation of certain speciall and remarkable passages. no 1 5 Jan–no 18 2 May 1644. [Ptd F.C[oules] for F. Leach. By Samuel Pecke]. See 19 Aug 1642.

Occurrences of certain speciall and remarkable passages. [no 1 5 Jan]; no 2 12 Jan–no 21 24 May 1644; [continued as] Perfect occurrences of Parliament, no 22 31 May 1644–[3rd ser] no 10 6 March 1646; [continued as] Perfect occurrences of both Houses of Parliament, no 11 13 March 1646–no 53 1 Jan 1647; [continued as] Perfect occurrences of every dayes journall in Parliament, no 1 8 Jan 1647–no 145 12 Oct 1649. [Pbd Andrew Coe, Jane Coe. Attributed to John Saltmarsh to 1646. From 8 Jan 1647 by Henry Walker]. See 6 Feb 1654.

Mercurius &c. [no 1] 17 Jan; no 2 6 Feb 1644; [continued as] Mercurius Veridicus, no 3 13 Feb–no 11 10 April 1644. See 19 April 1645, 21 April 1648.

The spie: communicating intelligence from Oxford. no 1 30 Jan–no 22 25 June 1644. [By Durant Hotham].

Anti-Aulicus. [no 1] [6 Feb]; [no 2] [8 Feb 1644].

Mercurius Anglicus: or a post from the north. no 1 7 Feb, no 2 20 Feb 1644. [Pbd T.B.] See 3 Aug 1648, 1 Oct 1650.

A perfect tiurnall: or Welch post. [no 1?] 11 Feb 1644. See 28 Oct 1643.

A faithfull relation of the late occurrences and proceedings of the Scotish army. [no 1] 21 Feb 1644[–?]; [continued as] The late proceedings of the Scottish army, [–?]; no 4 21 March 1644[–?]; [continued as] Intelligence from the Scottish army, no 6 14 April 1644; [continued as] Extract of letters, no 7 30 April 1644; [continued as] Intelligence from the south borders of Scotland, no 8 13 May 1644. [Pbd R. Bostock and S. Gellibrand. By Edward Bowles].

The military scribe. no 1 27 Feb–no 6 2 April 1644.

Britains remembrancer of the most remarkable passages in both kingdomes. no 1 19 March–no 3 2 April 1644.

Mercurius Aulico-Mastix: or the whipping Mercury. no 1 12 April 1644. [Ptd G. Bishop].

A true and perfect journall of the warres in England. no 1 16 April; no 2 30 April 1644.

The weekly news from forraigne parts beyond the seas. no 1 1 May; no 2 6 May; no 3 13 May 1644.

The flying post. no 1 10 May 1644.

A particular relation of the successes of the Earl of Manchesters army. [no 1] 6 [10] May 1644; [continued as] A continuation of true intelligence from the Earl of Manchester's army, no 2 1[4] June 1644; [continued as] A particular relation of the most remarkable occurrences from the united forces in the north, no 3 10 [13] June 1644; [continued as] A continuation of true intelligence from the Earl of Manchesters army, no 4 17 [21] June–no 7 16 [20] Aug 1644. [Pbd Thomas Underhill. By Simeon Ashe and William Good].

Cheife heads of each dayes proceedings in Parliament. [no 1] 15 May 1644.

An exact diurnall. no 1 22 May 1644; [continued as] A diary: or an exact journal, no 2 31 May–no 88 22 Jan 1646; no 1 29 Jan–no 6 5 March 1646. See 17 July 1647, 29 Sept 1651.

Le Mercure anglois. no 1 [7 June]; no 2 13 June; no 3 10 July 1644–no 63 13 Nov 1645; no 1 20 Nov 1645–no 65 15 April 1647; [?–] No 4 29 July 1647–no 73 14 Dec 1648 [–?]. Attributed to John Cotgrave. [Pbd Nicholas Bourne].

The Court Mercurie: communicating the most remarkable passages of the Kings armie. no 1 2 July–no 15 16 Oct 1644. Attributed to John Cotgrave.

A continuation of certain speciall and remarkable passages. no 1 10 July–no 4 1 Aug 1644. [Perhaps by Samuel Pecke]. See 19 Aug 1642.

The London post. no 1 6 Aug 1644–no 30 [31] 8 April 1645. Attributed to John Rushworth and Gilbert Mabbott. See 31 Dec 1646.

*The countrey messenger: or the faithfull foot post. no 1 20 Sept 1644.

The countrey foot-post. no 1 2 Oct 1644; [continued as] The countrey messenger, no 2 11 Oct 1644. Attributed to John Rushworth.

Perfect passages of each dayes proceedings in Parliament. no 1 23 Oct 1644–no 71 4 March 1646. Attributed to Henry Walker. *See* 5 July 1650.

Januaries account. [no 1] [? 1 Feb 1645]; [continued as] The monthly account, no 2 [1 March 1645]; [continued as] The general account, [no 3] [31 March 1645]. [Monthly. Pbd Richard Harper].

The moderate intelligencer impartially communicating martiall affaires to the kingdome of England. no 1 6 March 1645–no 237 4 Oct 1649. [By John Dillingham]. *See* 29 June 1648, 24 May, 5 June 1649, 8 Dec 1652, 26 April, 9 May 1653, 23 Feb 1654.

The weekely post-master. no 1 15 April–no 4 6 May 1645.

Mercurius Veridicus: or true informations. no 1 19 April 1645–no 35 6 Jan 1646; no [3] 17 Jan–no 10 7 March 1646. *See* 17 Jan 1644.

A perfect declaration. no 1 26 April 1645; [continued as] The true informer containing a perfect collection of the proceedings in Parliament, no 2 3 May 1645–no 45 7 March 1646. Attributed to Henry Whalley. *See* 23 Sept 1643.

The Parliaments post. no 1 13 May–no 21 7 Oct 1645.

The exchange intelligencer. no 1 15 May–no 8 18 July 1645.

Mr Peters report from the army. no 1 26 July 1645. Ptd Jane Coe.

Heads of some notes of the citie scout. no 4 19 Aug–no 10 30 Sept 1645; [continued as] The city scout; no 11 7 Oct–no 16 11 Nov 1645.

Mercurius Anti-Britannicus [Oxford]. [no 1] [4 Aug]–[no 3] [18 Aug 1645].

A continuation of certaine speciall and remarkable passages. no 1 26 Sept 1645–no 24 6 March 1646. [By Samuel Pecke]. *See* 19 Aug 1642.

The kingdomes weekly post. [no 1] 15 Oct–[no 10] 16 Dec 1645. Attributed to John Harris. *See* 9 Nov 1643.

A packet of letters from Sir Thomas Fairfax his quarters. no 1 30 Oct 1645. *See* 26 June 1646, 18 March 1648.

The kingdomes scout. no 1 2 Dec–no 3 16 Dec 1645.

Mercurius Academicus [Oxford]. [no 1] 20 Dec 1645–[no 14] 21 March 1646. Attributed to Richard Little or Thomas Swadlin. *See* 15 April 1648.

The citties weekly post. [no 1] 22 Dec 1645–no 11 3 March 1646.

The phoenix of Europe or the forraine intelligencer. no 1 16 Jan 1646. [By W. Pendred].

The moderate messenger. no 1 3 Feb–no 4 3 March 1646. *See* 23 Feb 1647, 30 April 1649, 7 Feb 1653.

An exact and true collection of the weekly passages. [no 1] [26 Feb]; [no 2] [March? 1646].

The westerne informer. no 1 7 March 1646.

Generall news from all parts of Christendome. no 1 12 May; no 2 26 May 1646 [no 4? Pbd Nicholas Bourne].

The packet of letters. [no 1] 26 June 1646. [Pbd Thomas Bates]. *See* 30 Oct 1645, 18 March 1648.

Papers sent from the Scotts quarters. no 1 14 Oct 1646; [continued as] A continuation of papers [etc], no 2 28 Oct 1646; [continued as] A continuation of a journall of passages of the Parliament and other papers [etc]; no 3 5 Nov–no 6 26 Nov 1646. [By Samuel Pecke; suppls to A perfect diurnal].

The military actions of Europe. no 1 27 Oct; no 2 2 Nov 1646.

Mercurius Candidus. no 1 20 Nov 1646[–?]. Attributed to John Harris. *See* 28 Jan 1647.

Diutinus Britanicus. no 1 2 Dec; no 2 8 Dec 1646; [continued as] Mercurius Diutinus (not Britanicus), no 3 16 Dec 1646; [continued as] Mercurius Diutinus, no 4 23 Dec 1646–no 11 10 Feb 1647. [By Thomas Audley].

The London post. no 1 31 Dec 1646–no 9 26 Feb 1647. Attributed to John Rushworth and Gilbert Mabbott. *See* 6 Aug 1644.

England's remembrancer of London's integritie. no 1 [19 Jan]; no 2 [11 Feb 1647].

Mercurius Candidus. no 1 28 Jan 1647. Attributed to Samuel Pecke.

The moderate messenger. no 22 23 Feb 1647. [Only number].

A continuation of certaine speciall and remarkable passages. [no 1] 9 June–no 13 17 Sept 1647. [By Samuel Pecke]. *See* 19 Aug 1642.

Mercurius Britanicus. no 1 24 June–no 3 8 July 1647. [Ptd B.W.].

The armies post. no 1 8 July 1647.

A diarie or an exact journall of the proceedings of the treaty betwixt the Parliament and the army. no 1 17 July–no 3 29 July 1647. *See* 22 May 1644.

A perfect summary of chiefe passages in Parliament. [no 1] 26 July–no 11 6 Oct 1647. Attributed to Henry Walker. *See* 19 Feb, 9 Oct 1648, 29 Jan 1649.

The moderne intelligencer. no 1 19 Aug–no 7 30 Sept 1647. *See* 3 Sept 1651.

Mercurius Melancholicus. [no 1] nd; no 2 11 Sept 1647–no 59 8 Oct 1648. [By John Hackluyt]. There is a reprint of no 1.

Mercurius Melancholicus. [counterfeits]. no 1 11 Sept 1647; no 2 11/17 Sept; no 3 11/18 Sept; no 4 25 Sept (2 issues); no 45 23 July 1648 (2 issues)–no 52 21 Aug 1648, except no 47 17 July; no 58–62 (in one number) 21 Nov 1648. Attributed to Martin Parker and John Taylor. *See* 28 July 1648, 1 Jan 1649, 31 May 1649, and Mercurius Anti-Melancholicus, below, 24 Sept 1647.

Mercurius Morbicus: or newes from Westminster and other parts. no 1, 2, 3 (one number) [20 Sept]; no 4 27 Sept 1647. [By Henry Walker].
A recommendation to Mercurius Morbicus. [6 Oct] 1647. Attributed to John Taylor or Martin Parker.

Mercurius Pragmaticus communicating intelligence from all parts. no 1 21 Sept 1647–no 28 28 March 1648; no 1 4 April 1648–[no 53] 8 May 1649. [By John Cleveland and Samuel Sheppard; in 1648 by Marchamont Needham]. *See* 24 April, 17 Sept 1649, 10 June 1651, 25 May, 6 July 1652, 25 May 1653, 30 Aug 1658, 20 June, 6 Sept, 30 Dec 1659.

Mercurius Pragmaticus [reprints]. [1st ser] no 6 26 Oct 1647; no 7; no 10; no 11; no 16 3 Jan 1648; [2nd ser] no 7 16 May 1648.

Mercurius Pragmaticus [counterfeits]. [1st ser] no 2 28 Sept; no 9; no 10; no 11 30 Nov 1647; no 18 18 Jan 1648; [2nd ser] no 7 16 May; no 19 8 Aug 1648; no 20 15 Aug; no 20 12 Sept 1648–no 22; no 23 [for 24]; no 24 [for 25]; no 38; no 39; no 43; [no 51]; [no 52] 1 May 1649. *See* Mercurius Anti-Pragmaticus, below, 19 Oct 1647.

Mercurius Anti-Melancholicus. no 1 24 Sept 1647.

Mercurius Clericus: or newes from Syon communicated to all who love (and seek) the peace of Jerusalem. no 1 24 Sept 1647.

Mercurius Clericus or newes from the assembly of their last III years in the holy convocation at Westminster. no 1 [25 Sept 1647].

Mercurius Medicus or a soveraigne salve for these sick times. no 1 [11 Oct]; no 2 22 Oct 1647. [By Henry Walker].

Mercurius Anti-Pragmaticus. no 1 19 Oct 1647–no 19 3 Feb 1648.

Mercurius Elencticus communicating the unparallell'd proceedings at Westminster. [no 1] 5 Nov 1647–no 59 9 Jan 1649. [By Sir George Wharton and Samuel Sheppard. There are counterfeits of no 36 2 Aug and of no 46 11 Oct 1648.] *See* 7 Feb, 13 Feb, 28 Feb, 11 April, 1 May, 7 May 1649, 22 April 1650, 10 June 1651, 25 May, 6 July 1652.

Mercurius Populus. no 1 11 Nov 1647.

Mercurius Rusticus. no 1 [12 Nov]–no 5 10 Dec 1647. *See* 20 May 1643.

Mercurius Bellicus. no 1 22 Nov 1647–no 27 26 July 1648. [Suspended from 29 Nov 1647–14 Feb 1648. By Sir John Berkenhead].
For details of a quasi-periodical of the same name in 1643, see H. H. Weber, The Mercurius Bellicus of 1643, N & Q 18 Nov 1933.

Mercurius Vapulans. [no 1] [27 Nov 1647]; no 2 nd.

The kingdom's weekly post. no 1 5 Jan–no 10 9 March 1648. Attributed to Daniel Border.

Heads of chiefe passages in Parliament. no 1 12 Jan–no 3 26 Jan 1648; [continued as] Kingdoms weekly account of heads of chiefe passages in Parliament, no 4 2 Feb–no 11 22 March 1648. Attributed to Henry Whalley.

Mercurius Dogmaticus. no 1 13 Jan–no 4 3 Feb 1648. Attributed to Samuel Sheppard.

Mercurius Aulicus againe communicating intelligence from all parts. no 1 3 Feb–no 15 18 May 1648. [nos 7–9, 10–12, 10–13, and 12–14 each formed one number. Attributed to Samuel Sheppard]. *See* 8 Jan 1643.

A perfect summarie of chiefe passages in Parliament. no 1 19 Feb 1648. *See* 26 July 1647.

Packets of letters. no 1 18 March–no 37 28 Nov 1648. [Irregular: suppls to Perfect occurrences. By Henry Walker]. *See* 30 Oct 1645.

Westminster projects: or the mystery of Darby House discovered. [no 1] [23] March 1648; [continued as] Tricks of state: or more Westminster projects, [no 2] 18 April 1648; [–?]; [continued as] Windsor projects and Westminster practices, [no 4] [15 May 1648]; [continued as] Westminster projects: or the mystery of iniquity of Darby-House discovered, no 5 [6 June]; no 6 [23 June] 1648. [nos 1–2 possibly by Marchamont Needham].

Mercurius Insanus Insanissimus. [no 1, ?]; no 2 [27 March]; no 3 [17 April 1648]–no 7 nd.

The perfect weekly account. no 1 29 March 1648–[unnumbered] 10 Oct 1649. [By 'B.D.']. *See* 6 Sept 1643.

Mercurius Brittanicus communicating his most remarkable intelligence unto the kingdome. no 1 7 April 1648. [no imprint. By John Hall]. *See* 29 Aug 1643, 23 May 1648.

Mercurius Critticus. no 1 13 April–no 3 4 May 1648. Attributed to John Crouch.

Mercurius Academicus. no 1 15 April 1648. Attributed to Thomas Swadlin. *See* 20 Dec 1645.

Mercurius Anti-Mercurius. [no 1] 4 April; [no 2] but ptd no 1 19 Sept; no 3 2 Oct 1648. Attributed to John Harris.

Mercurius Veridicus communicating intelligence from all parts of Great Britaine. no 1 21 April–no 3 8 May 1648. *See* 17 Jan 1644.

Mercurius Militaris communicating intelligence from the saints dissembled at Westminster. no 1 28 April 1648. *See* 10 Oct 1648, 24 April, 29 May 1649.

Mercurius Urbanicus: or newes from London and Westminster. [unnumbered] 9 May 1648.

Mercurius Gallicus. no 3 [12 May 1648].

Mercurius Poeticus. [no 1] 13 May 1648. *See* 1 March 1654.

Mercurius Publicus communicating emergent occurrences. no 1 [15 May]–no 3 29 May 1648.

The parliament-kite or the tell tale bird. no 1 15 May–no 15 31 Aug 1648. Attributed to Samuel Sheppard.

Mercurius Britanicus alive again. no 1 16 May 1648; [continued as] Mercurius Britanicus giving a perfect accompt, no 2 23 May–no 12 1 Aug 1648; [continued as] Mercurius Britanicus stating the affairs, no 13 16 Aug 1648. *See* 29 Aug 1643.

Mercurius Honestus: or newes from Westminster. no 1 [19 May] 1648; no 2 [25 May 1648].

Mercurius Censorius. no 1 1 June–no 3 20 June 1648. Attributed to John Hall.

Mercurius Domesticus. no 1 [5 June 1648].

New news, strange news, true news. [no 1] [15] June 1648.

Mercurius Psitacus: or the parroting Mercury. no 1 12 June–no 9 7 Aug 1648.

The Parliaments vulture. no 1 22 June 1648.

A perfect diary of passages of the Kings army. [no 1] [26 June 1648].

The moderate communicating martial affaires to the kingdome of England. no 171 29 June–no 173 13 July 1648; no 1 18 July 1648–no 63 25 Sept 1649. Attributed to Gilbert Mabbott. *See* 6 March 1645.

The Parliaments scriche owle. no 1 [29 June]–no 3 14 July 1648.

A wonder: a Mercury without a lye in's mouth. [no 1] [6 July 1648].

Mercurius Scoticus. no 1 [19 July 1648]. Attributed to Sir George Wharton. *See* 30 Sept 1651.

Mercurius Melancholicus: or newes from Westminster and the head quarters. no 1 28 July 1648. Attributed to John Crouch. *See* 11 Sept 1647.

The royall diurnall. no 1 31 July–no 5 29 Aug 1648. Attributed to Samuel Sheppard. *See* 25 Feb 1650.

Mercurius Anglicus. no 1 3 Aug 1648. *See* 7 Feb 1644.

Mercurius Aulicus communicating intelligence from all parts of the kingdome. [no 1] [7 Aug]–no 4 [28 Aug 1648]. Attributed to Samuel Sheppard. *See* 8 Jan 1643.

Mercurius Aquaticus. [no 1] 11 Aug 1648. Attributed to John Taylor.

The Colchester spie. no 1 [11 Aug]; no 2 17 Aug; [no 3 28 Aug] 1648. [2 issues of no 1].

Hermes Straticus: or a scourge for Elencticus. no 1 17 Aug 1648.

Mercurius Fidelicus. no 1 24 Aug; no 2 31 Aug 1648.

The Parliament porter: or the door keeper of the House of Commons. no 1 4 Sept–no 4 25 Sept 1648.

Mercurius Catholicus. no 1 [15 Sept]; no 2 11 Dec 1648. Attributed to Thomas Budd.

The treaty traverst. no 1 26 Sept 1648.

Mercurio Volpone: or the fox. no 1 5 Oct; no 2 12 Oct 1648.

A perfect summary. [no 1] 9 Oct 1648. *See* 26 July 1647.

Mercurius Militaris: or the armies scout. no 1 10 Oct–no 5 21 Nov 1648. Attributed to John Harris. *See* 8 Nov 1648, 28 April 1648.

The true informer or monthly Mercury: being the certain intelligence of Mercurius Militaris. no 1 [7 Oct] 8 Nov 1648. [Monthly].

Mercurius Pacificus. [no 1] [8 Nov 1648]. Attributed to John Taylor. *See* 24 May 1649.

Martin nonsence his collections. no 1 27 Nov 1648.

A declaration collected out of the journals of both Houses of Parliament. no 1 6 Dec–no 3 20 Dec 1648; [continued as] Heads of a diarie, no 4 27 Dec 1648–no 6 9 Jan 1649. [By Henry Walker].

*Passages concerning the King, the army, city and kingdom. no 1 6 Dec 1648.

Mercurius Impartialis: or an answer to that treasonable pamphlet Mercurius Militaris, together with the moderate. no 1 12 Dec 1648. Attributed to Sir George Wharton.

Mercurius Melancholicus communicating the generall affaires of the kingdome. no 1 1 Jan–no 3 12 Jan 1649. Attributed to John Hackluyt. *See* 11 Sept 1647, 28 July 1648, 31 May 1649.

A perfect narrative of the whole proceedings of the High Court of Justice in the tryal of the King. no 1 23 Jan 1649; [continued as] A continuation of the narrative [etc], no 2 25 Jan; no 3 29 Jan 1649. There is a reprint of no 2.

The armies modest intelligencer. [no 1] 26 Jan–no 3 8 Feb 1649; [continued as] The armies weekly intelligencer, no 4 15 Feb; no 5 22 Feb 1649.

A perfect summary of exact passages. no 1 29 Jan–no 9 26 March 1649; [continued as] A perfect summary of an exact diarye, no 10 3 April–no 27 1 Oct 1649. Attributed to Theodore Jennings. no 9 is entitled A perfect collection [etc]; no 22 reverts to the original form. *See* 26 July 1647.

The kingdomes faithfull scout. no 1 2 Feb 1649; [continued as] The kingdomes faithfull and impartiall scout, no 2 9 Feb-no 37 12 Oct 1649. Attributed to Daniel Border. no 5 reverts to the style of no 1.

Mercurius Elencticus communicating the unparallell'd proceedings at Westminster. no 1 7 Feb 1649. Attributed to Sir George Wharton. See 5 Nov 1647, 13, 28 Feb 1649.

Mercurius Elencticus communicating the unparallell'd proceedings at Westminster. no 56 13 Feb 1649. See preceding.

Mercurius Elencticus communicating intelligence from all parts. no 69 28 Feb 1649. See preceding.

The impartiall intelligencer. no 1 7 March-no 29 19 Sept 1649.

A modest narrative of intelligence fitted for the Republique of England and Ireland. no 1 7 April-no 25 22 Sept 1649.

Mercurius Elencticus communicating the unparallell'd proceedings of the rebells at Westminster. no 1 11 April 1649. Attributed to Samuel Sheppard. See 5 Nov 1647, 7, 13, 28 Feb, 1, 7 May 1649.

The man in the moone discovering a world of knavery under the sunne. [no 1] 16 April 1649-no 56 5 June 1650. [By John Crouch].

Mercurius Philo-Monarchicus. no 1 17 April; [unnumbered] 21 May 1649.

Continued heads of perfect passages. no 1 20 April-no 5 18 May 1649. [Pbd A. Coe].

Mercurius Pragmaticus (for King Charles II). 2 pts no 1 24 April 1649-no 53 28 May 1650. Attributed to Marchamont Needham. Counterfeits: no 4 15 May 1649-no 10 26 June; no 14 24 July 1649. Attributed to John Cleveland. See 21 Sept 1647, 17 Sept 1649.

Mercurius Militaris or the people's scout. no 1 24 April-no 3 [8 May 1649]. There is a reprint of no 2. Attributed to John Harris. See 28 April 1648.

England's moderate messenger. no 1 30 April-no 11 9 July 1649; [continued as] The moderate messenger, no 12 16 July-no 22 24 Sept 1649. Attributed to Daniel Border. See 3 Feb 1646.

Mercurius Elencticus communicating the unparalell'd proceedings of the rebbells at Westminster. no 1 1 May-no 27 5 Nov 1649. See 5 Nov 1647, 11 April, 7 May 1649.

Mercurius Brittanicus communicating intelligence from all parts, and handling the humours and conceits of Mercurius Pragmaticus. no 1 4 May-no 7 5 June 1649. Attributed to Gilbert Mabbott. See 29 Aug 1643.

Mercurius Elencticus (for King Charls II) communicating intelligence from all parts: pars [2]. no 1 7 May 1649. See 5 Nov 1647, 24 April, 1 May 1649.

A moderate intelligence impartially communicating martial affairs to the kingdom of England. no 1 24 May; no 2 31 May 1649. [Pbd Robert White]. See 6 March 1645.

Mercurius Pacificus. no 1 25 May; no 2 31 May 1649. Attributed to John Taylor. See 8 Nov 1648.

Mercurius Republicus. no 1 29 May 1649.

Mercurius Militaris: or times only truth-teller. no 1 29 May 1649; [continued as] The metropolitan nuncio, no 1 6 June; no 3 13 June 1649. Attributed to John Hackluyt. See 28 April 1648.

Mercurius Melancholicus for King Charls the Second. no 1 31 May; no 2 7 June 1649. Attributed to John Taylor. See 11 Sept 1647.

Mercurius Verax or truth appearing after seaven yeares banishment. [no 1] [4 June 1649].

*The moderate intelligencer. no 1 5 June 1649[-?]. Attributed to John Dillingham. See 6 March 1645.

The moderate Mercury. no 1 21 June; no 2 28 June 1649.

A perfect diurnall of passages in Parliament. no 1 16 July; no 2 23 July 1649. [Pbd Robert Wood. Imitations of the paper started on 3 July 1643]. See 31 Jan 1642.

A Tuesdaies journall. no 1 24 July-no 4 21 Aug 1649. [By Henry Walker].

Mercurius Carolinus. no 1 26 July 1649.

The armies painfull-messenger. no 1 2 Aug 1649.

Great Britaines paine-full messenger affording true notice of all affaires. no 1 16 Aug-no 3 30 Aug 1649. Attributed to A. Ford.

Mercurius Aulicus (for King Charls II). [no 1] 21 Aug-no 3 4 Sept 1649. See 8 Jan 1643.

Mercurius Hybernicus. no 1 6 Sept 1649.

Mercurius Pragmaticus for King Charls II. no 1 17 Sept 1649; no 2 24 Sept 1649[-?]. See 21 Sept 1647, 24 April 1649.

A briefe relation of some affaires and transactions civill and military, both forraigne and domestique. no 1 2 Oct 1649-no 56 1 Oct; no 57 22 Oct 1650. [By Walter Frost].

Severall proceedings in Parliament. no 1 9 Oct 1649-no 186 21 April 1653; [continued as] Severall proceedings of state affaires, no 187 28 April 1653-no 261 28 Sept 1654; [continued as] Severall proceedings of Parliament, no 262 5 Oct 1654-no 278 25 Jan 1655; [continued as] Several proceedings of state affaires, no 279 1 Feb-no 282 22 Feb 1655; [continued as] Perfect proceedings of state affaires, no 283 1 March-no 313 27 Sept 1655. [By Henry Scobell and Henry Walker]. See 26 July 1653.

A very full and particular relation. no 6 [31 Oct 1649]. [Pbd M. Simmons. Suppl to A briefe relation].

A perfect and more particular relation. no 2 [19 Nov 1649]. [Pbd F. Leach].

A perfect diurnall of some passages and proceedings of and in relation to the armies. no 1 17 Dec 1649-no 302 24 Sept 1655. [By John Rushworth and Samuel Pecke. Counterfeits: no 138 2 Aug-no 140 16 Aug 1652]. See 31 Jan 1642.

The royall diurnall (for King Charls II). no 1 25 Feb-no 7 15 April; no 1 22 April; no 2 30 April 1650. See 31 July 1648.

Mercurius Elenticus (for King Charles the II). no 1 22 April-no 7 3 June 1650. See 5 Nov 1647.

Mercurius Politicus comprising the summ of all intelligence. no 1 13 June 1650-no 615 12 April 1660. Attributed to John Hall and Marchamont Needham till Jan 1653; by M. Needham till end except 13 May-16 Aug 1659, when it is by John Canne. Supervised by John Milton till Jan 1653; by John Thurloe Feb 1653-May 1659].

[Cleveland, John?]. The character of Mercurius Politicus. [14 Aug] 1650.

— The second character of Mercurius Politicus. [23 Oct] 1650.

Webster, John. The picture of Mercurius Politicus. [12 Oct 1653].

Nouvelles ordinaires de Londres. [no 1 June? 1650]-no 186 22 Jan-no 229 5 Nov 1654; [probably suspended 1661-2]-no 567 3 May 1663[-?]. Attributed to Jean de l'Ecluse in 1663 but possibly by William Dugard.

Alger, J. G. A French newspaper in London 1650-8. N & Q 11 April 1896.

Bastide, C. The Anglo-French entente in the seventeenth century. 1914.

The impartial scout. no 53 28 June 1650-no 66 27 Sept 1653. Attributed to Daniel Border.

Perfect passages of every daies intelligence. no 1 5 July 1650-no 80 31 Dec 1652; [continued as] The moderate publisher of every dayes intelligence, no 81 21 Jan-no 94 22 April 1653; no 140 29 April-no 149 9 Sept 1653. [Ptd J. Clowes. Counterfeit: no 83 28 Jan 1653 (ptd E. Neile). By Henry Walker]. See 16 Oct 1644, 31 Oct 1651, 14 Oct 1653, 20 Jan 1654.

The perfect weekly account. [no 59] 17 July-no 70 26 Sept 1650. [Ptd B. Alsop]. Attributed to Daniel Border. See 6 Sept 1643, 29 March 1648.

A perfect diurnal of some passages of Parliament. no 324 22 July; no 325 29 July 1650. [Ptd W. Hunt for F. Coales, L. Chapman and L. Blaiklock. Imitations of the periodical started 17 Dec 1649]. See 31 Jan 1642.

The weekly intelligencer of the commonwealth. no 1 23 July 1650–[2nd ser no 6] 25 Sept 1655. Attributed to Richard Collings. *See* 10 May, 26 July 1659.

True intelligence from the head quarters. no 1 23 July– no 3 7 Aug 1650.

The best and most perfect intelligencer. no 1 8 Aug 1650. Attributed to William Huby.

Mercurius Anglicus. no 1 1 Oct 1650. Attributed to Henry Walker. *See* 7 Feb 1644.

The faithfull scout. no 1 3 Jan 1651–no 102 31 Dec 1652; no 103 11 Feb–no 108 18 March 1653[–?]; [continued as] The armies scout, [?–] no 114 30 April–[no 119] 3 June 1653; [continued as] The faithfull scout, no 115 10 June 1653–no 246 28 Sept 1655. [Ptd Robert Wood]. Attributed to Daniel Border. *See* 29 April 1659.

A perfect account of the daily intelligence. [no 1 15 Jan 1651]–no 3 29 Jan 1653–no 246 26 Sept 1655. 'By B.D.'.

Mercurius Pragmaticus revived and from the shades of his retirement return'd again. no 1 10 June 1651 [continued as] Mercurius Elencticus, no 2 17 June–no 4 1 July 1651; [continued as] Mercurius Scommaticus, no 1 8 July 1651. Attributed to Samuel Sheppard. *See* 21 Sept, 5 Nov 1647.

Several letters from Scotland. no 1 15 [23] July 1651. [Ptd F. Neile].

The armies intelligencer. no 1 5 Aug 1651.

The true informer. no 1 28 Aug 1651. [Pbd F.N.] *See* 23 Sept 1643.

The modern intelligencer. no 5 3 Sept 1651. Attributed to Henry Walker. *See* 19 Aug 1647.

The diary. no 1 29 Sept–no 6 3 Nov 1651. [Ptd Bernard Alsop]. *See* 22 May 1644.

Mercurius Scoticus: or the royal messenger. no 2 30 Sept 1651. Attributed to Francis Nelson. *See* 19 July 1648.

Perfect particulars of every daies intelligence. no 39 31 Oct 1651. [Ptd F. Neile. An imitation of Perfect passages]. *See* 5 July 1650.

The French intelligencer. no 1 25 Nov 1651–no 26 18 May 1652. [Ptd Robert Wood]. Attributed to Daniel Border.

Mercurius Bellonius. no 1 4 Feb–no 5 3 March 1652. [Ptd J.C.]. Attributed to John Crouch.

The Dutch spy. no 1 24 March–no 3 7 April 1652. Attributed to Daniel Border.

Mercurius Democritus: or a true and perfect nocturnall communicating wonderfull news of the world in the moon. no 1 8 April–no 21 25 Aug 1652; [continued as] The laughing Mercury, no 22 8 Sept–no 30 3 Nov 1652; [continued as] Mercurius Democritus, no 31 10 Nov 1652–no 81 9 Nov 1653. [By John Crouch]. *See* 25 Jan 1654, 3 May 1659.

Mercurius Democritus his last will and testament. [16 Sept] 1652.

Newes from tenebris: or preterpluperfect nocturnall or night worke. 1652. Attributed to John Taylor.

A hue and cry after Mercurius Democritus and the wandering whore. 1662.

Mercurius Phreneticus. no 2 [8 April]–no 4 [22 April 1652]. Attributed to Samuel Sheppard. *See* 19 July 1652.

Mercurius Zeteticus. [no 1] [22 April 1652].

The French occurrences. no 1 17 May 1652–no 40 3 Jan 1653. [Pbd George Horton]. Attributed to Daniel Border.

Mercurius Pragmaticus. no 1 25 May–no 6 30 June 1652. Attributed to Samuel Sheppard. *See* 21 Sept 1647, 6 July 1652.

Mercurius Heraclitus. no 1 28 June–no 3 12 July 1652. [Pbd J.C. and D.W. By John Crouch].

Mercurius Pragmaticus. no 1 6 July 1652. [By Marchamont Needham]. *See* 21 Sept 1647, 25 May 1652.

Mercurius Phreneticus. no 1 19 July 1652. Attributed to Samuel Sheppard.

Mercurius Britannicus. no 1 26 July–no 23 28 Dec 1652. [The first 5 nos by Marchamont Needham. There is a counterfeit of no 21 14 Dec. Pbd Robert Wood].

Mercurius Cinicus: or a true and perfect intelligence. no 1 11 Aug 1652.

Mercurius Mastix, faithfully lashing all scouts, Mercuries, posts, spys and others who cheat the commonwealth. no 1 27 Aug 1652. [By Samuel Sheppard].

*The Dutch intelligencer. no 1 8 Sept 1652.

The flying eagle. no 1 4 Dec 1652–no 5 1 Jan 1653. [Ptd T. Fawcet for A.P.].

The moderate intelligencer. no 166 8 Dec–no 169 29 Dec 1652. [Pbd Robert Wood]. Attributed to John Dillingham. *See* 5 June 1649, 26 April 1653.

The moderate messenger. no 1 7 Feb–no [5] 14 March 1653. [Pbd George Horton].

The faithful post. no 89 1 April–no 93 29 April 1653; no 131 6 May–no 140 8 July 1653; no 120 15 July–no 126 2 Sept 1653. [During April and May pbd G. Horton; 3 June pbd R. Eeles; 10–24 June pbd T.L.; 8 July–2 Sept pbd R.E. An offshoot from The faithfull scout].

The faithfull post [counterfeits]. no 116 14 June–no 123 2 Aug 1653. [5, 12 July, no imprint; the rest pbd G. Horton]. *See* 3 Jan 1651, 9 Nov 1653, 11 Jan 1654.

Moderate occurrences. no 1 5 April–no 9 31 May 1653. [Pbd George Horton].

The moderate intelligencer. no 175 26 April 1653. [Ptd Robert Wood].

The moderate intelligencer. no 1 9 May–no 17 29 Aug 1653. *See* 6 March 1645, 23 Feb 1654.

Mercurius Britannicus. no 2 23 May–no 10 20 June 1653. [Pbd George Horton].

Mercurius Pragmaticus. no 1 25 May–no 8 13 July 1653. [Ptd Matthew Mede]. *See* 21 Sept 1647.

The daily proceedings. [no 1] [17 June 1653].

Mercurius Rhadamanthus. [no 1] [27 June]–no 5 25 July 1653.

The true and perfect Dutch diurnall. no 1 3 July; no 2 26 July 1653. [Pbd Tho. Lock]. *See* 10 Jan 1654.

Severall proceedings of Parliament. no 1 26 July–no 21 13 Dec 1653. [Ptd John Field].

The loyal messenger. no 1 10 Aug 1653. [Pbd George Horton].

The newes or the ful particulars of the last fight. no 1 12 Aug 1653.

The moderate publisher of every dayes intelligence. no [1] 14 Oct 1653–no 12 13 Jan 1654. [Pbd J.C[lowes] and T.W.]. *See* 5 July 1650, 20 Jan 1654.

Great Brittain's post. no 136 9 Nov (ptd R. Wood); no 151 21 Dec; no 152 28 Dec 1653. [Pbd G. Horton]. *See* 1 April 1653, 11 Jan 1654.

The true informer. no 1 6 Jan; [no 2] 13 Jan 1654; [continued as] The true and perfect informer, [no 3] 20 Jan 1654. [Ptd T. Lock]. *See* 23 Sept 1643.

The true and perfect Dutch diurnall. no 3 10 Jan 1654–no 15 22 May 1654. [Ptd T. Lock]. *See* 3 July 1653.

The politique post. [unnumbered] 11 Jan 1654; [continued as] The grand politique post, no 127 17 Jan; no 127 24 Jan; no 164 15 Feb; no 172 11 April 1654; [continued as] The weekly post, no 174 18 April 1654–no 245 17 Sept 1655. [Pbd G. Horton]. Attributed to Daniel Border. *See* 1 April, 9 Nov 1653, 10 May 1659.

The moderate publisher of every dayes intelligence. no 1 20 Jan 1654; [continued as] Certain passages of every dayes intelligence, no 2 27 Jan 1654–[3rd ser] no 4 28 Sept 1655. [Ptd F. Neile]. Attributed to Henry Walker. *See* 5 July 1650, 14 Oct 1653.

Mercurius Democritus. no 82 25 Jan–no 86 22 Feb 1654. [Pbd George Horton; J. Crouch and T.W.]. *See* 8 April 1652.

The loyal intelligencer. no 73 30 Jan 1654. [Pbd G. Horton].

The politique informer. no 1 30 Jan; no 2 6 Feb 1654. [Ptd R. Wood].

Perfect occurrences. no 1 6 Feb–no 5 23 June 1654.

The moderate intelligencer. no 165 23 Feb–no 177 10 May 1654. [Pbd G. Horton. Counterfeits: no 171 5 April;

no 172 12 April; no 174 26 April 1654 (all ptd R. Wood)]. *See* 6 March 1645, 9 May 1654.

Mercurius Poeticus. [no 1 1 March]; no 2 8 March[–no 5 29 March 1654]. Attributed to Marchamont Needham.

Mercurius Nullus: or the invisible nuncio. [no 1] [13 March] 1654; [no 2] [20 March] 1654.

Mercurius Aulicus. no 1 20 March–no 3 3 April 1654. *See* 8 Jan 1643.

The loyal messenger or newes from Whitehall. no 4 10 April 1654. [Pbd R. Moon. Probably by John Streater].

Observations historical, political and philosophical upon Aristotle's first book of political government, together with a narrative of state-affaires in England, Scotland and Ireland. no 1 11 April–no 11 4 July 1654. [Pbd R. Moon; folio. By John Streater].

Perfect diurnall occurrences of certain military affairs. no 1 8 May 1654; [continued as] A perfect diurnall: or occurrences of certain military affairs, no 2 15 May–no 28 30 Oct 1654. *See* 31 Jan 1642.

Perfect and impartial intelligence together with a politick commentary on the life of Caius Julius Caesar. no 1 [16 May]–no 3 2 June 1654. [Pbd R. Moon. Perhaps by John Streater].

The weekly abstract. no 1 3 June–no 3 19 June 1654. Folio.

Mercurius Fumigosus. no 1 7 June 1654–no 70 3 Oct 1655. [By John Crouch].

Mercurius Jocosus or the merrie Mercurye. [no 1] 21 July–[no 3] 4 Aug 1654. Attributed to Thomas Lock.

The observator, with a summary of intelligence. no 1 31 Oct; no 2 7 Nov 1654. [By Marchamont Needham].

The publick intelligencer. no 1 8 Oct 1655–no 225 9 April 1660. [By Marchamont Needham except 13 May–16 Aug 1659 when it was by John Canne; under the supervision of John Thurloe until May 1659].

The publick adviser. no 1 26 May–no 19 28 Sept 1657. [By Marchamont Needham. The first paper devoted entirely to advertizing].

[Needham, Marchamont]. The office of publick advice newly set up. [14 May] 1657.

The weekly information from the office of intelligence. no 1 20 July 1657. [By Oliver Williams. Also an advertizing paper].

[Williams, Oliver]. A prohibition to all persons who have set up any offices called by the names of addresses, publique advice or intelligence in London. [26 May] 1657.

Mercurius Pragmaticus. no 1 30 Aug 1658. [?–6 Sept 1659]. *See* 21 Sept 1647.

The faithful scout. no 1 29 April–no 11 9 July 1659; [continued as] The national scout, no 12 16 July 1659; [continued as] The loyall scout, [unnumbered] 22 July 1659–no 36 6 Jan 1660–?–no 78 17 June 1660. [Pbd G. Horton]. Attributed to Daniel Border. *See* 3 Jan 1651.

Mercurius Democritus communicating faithfully the affairs both in city and countrey. no 2 3 May 1659; [perhaps continued as] Mercurius Democritus or a perfect nocturnall, no 1 10 May–no 13 16 Aug 1659. [By John Crouch]. *See* 8 April 1652.

The weekly post. no 1 10 May 1659–no 42 21 Feb 1660[–?]. [Pbd G. Horton]. Attributed to Daniel Border. *See* 11 Jan 1654.

The weekly intelligencer of the commonwealth. no 1 10 May–no 30 6 Dec 1659[–?]. Attributed to R. Collings. *See* 23 July 1650.

The moderate informer. [no 1] 19 May; [no 2] 25 May 1659. Attributed to Marchamont Needham.

*The weekly account, on the establishment of a free state. no 1 25 May 1659. *See* 6 Sept 1643.

The weekly account faithfully representing the most remarkable passages in Parliament. no 1 1 June 1659. [Ptd E. Alsop]. *See* 6 Sept 1643.

Mercurius Pragmaticus. [unnumbered] [20 June 1659]. *See* 2 Sept 1647.

A particular advice from the office of intelligence. no 1 30 June–no 51 30 Dec 1659; [continued as] An exact accompt of the daily proceedings in Parliament, no 53 6 Jan–no 104 6 July 1660[–?]. [After the first few issues numbered consecutively with Occurrences from foreign parts. By Oliver Williams et al].

Occurrences from foreign parts. no 1 5 July 1659–no 88 18 May 1660[–?]. [After the first few issues numbered consecutively with A particular advice. By Oliver Williams et al].

*The weekly intelligencer of the commonwealth. no 1 26 July 1659. *See* 23 July 1650, 10 May 1659.

Mercurius Pragmaticus communicating his weekly intelligence. no 1 6 Sept 1659. [Pbd H. Marsh]. *See* 21 Sept 1647, 30 Aug 1658.

The parliamentary intelligencer. no 1 26 Dec 1659–no 53 31 Dec 1660; [continued as] The kingdomes intelligencer, no 1 7 Jan 1661–31 Aug 1663. [New series–number each year. By Henry Muddiman and Giles Dury].

*The loyall scout. no 1 26 Dec 1659.

Mercurius Pragmaticus impartially communicating the true state of affairs. no 2 30 Dec 1659. *See* 21 Sept 1647, 6 Sept 1659.

R. E. M.

VI. TRAVEL

(1) BIBLIOGRAPHIES

Catalogue of books of voyages and travels. In John Pinkerton, A collection of voyages and travels vol 17, 1814.

Tiele, P. A. Mémoire bibliographique sur les journaux des navigateurs néerlandais et sur les anciennes éditions hollandaises des journaux de navigateurs étrangers. Amsterdam 1867.

Upcott, W. A bibliographical account of the principal works relating to English topography. 3 vols 1818.

Sabin, Joseph. Bibliotheca americana: a dictionary of books relating to America. New York 1872–.

Amat di San Filippo, Pietro. Bibliografia dei viaggiatori italiani. Rome 1874.

— Biografia dei viaggiatori italiani colla bibliografia delle loro opere. Vol 1 of Studi bibliografici e biografici sulla storia della geografia in Italia, Rome 1875, Florence 1875.

Anderson, J. P. The book of British topography. 1881.

Roehricht, R. Bibliotheca geographica Palaestine. Berlin 1890.

Fordham, H. G. Studies in carto-bibliography, British and French, and in the bibliography of itineraries and road books. 1914.

— The road books and itineraries of Great Britain 1570–1850. Cambridge 1916, 1924 (rev and enlarged).

— The road books and itineraries of Ireland 1647–1850. Dublin 1923.

Scott, M. A. Elizabethan translations from the Italian. PMLA 14 1899; Boston 1916.

A catalogue of books relating to the discovery and early history of North and South America forming a part of the library of E. D. Church. Ed G. W. Cole 5 vols New York 1907.

Bourgeois, E. and L. André. Les sources de l'histoire de France. Pt 3 vol 1, Paris 1913.

Mitchell, A. and C. G. Cash. A contribution to the bibliography of Scottish topography. 2 vols Edinburgh 1917 (Scottish Historical Soc).

Forster, W. A guide to the India Office Records 1600–1858. 1919.

Atkinson, G. La littérature géographique française de la Renaissance [to 1610]. Paris 1927.

Davies, G. Bibliography of British history: Stuart period. Oxford 1928, 1971 (rev).

Manwaring, G. E. Bibliography of British naval history. 1930.

Read, C. Bibliography of British history: Tudor period 1485–1603. Oxford 1933, 1959 (rev).

Sabin, J. Bibliotheca americana. 29 vols New York 1872–1936. Completed by W. Eames and R. W. G. Vail.

Cox, E. G. A reference guide to the literature of travel [in English]. 3 vols Seattle 1935–49. Lists with descriptions and bibliography the narratives in English of travellers of all nations before 1800. Vol 1, The Old World; 2, The New World; 3, Britain.

Fussell, G. E. The exploration of England: a select bibliography of travel and topography 1570–1815. 1936.

McCain, R. English travellers in Italy during the Renaissance. Bull of Bibliography 19 1948.

Warner, O. English maritime writings: Hakluyt to Cook. 1958.

Encyclopaedia of world travel. New York and Toronto 1961, 1967 (rev).

Pritchard, A. From these uncouth shores: 17th-century literature of Newfoundland. Canadian Lit no 14 1962.

Berry, L. E. Giles Fletcher the elder: a bibliography. Trans Cambridge Bibl Soc 3 1963.

Parker, J. Books to build an empire. Amsterdam 1966.

Skelton, R. A. County atlases of the British Isles 1579–1850: a bibliography. Vol 1, 1579-1703, 1970.

(2) COLLECTIONS AND HISTORIES

d'Anghiera, Pietro Martire. The decades of the newe worlde of West India: conteyning the navigations and conquestes of the Spanyardes, translated into Englysshe by Rycharde Eden. 1555; ed E. Arber, The first three English books on America, Birmingham 1885. In part from De orbe novo decades, Alcala 1516, and De nuper repertis insulis, Basle 1521; and from other sources concerning both East and West Indies.
—— The history of travayle in the West and East Indies, and other countreys lying eyther way, towardes the fruitfull and rych Moluccaes; newly set in order, augmented and finished by Richarde Willes. 1577. Adding to Peter Martyr a large pt 2 from other sources.
—— De orbe novo Petri Martyris Anglerii decades octo, labore & industria Richardi Hakluyti. Paris 1587. 2nd edn of the complete work, originally Alcala 1530.
—— De orbe novo: or the historie of the West Indies, contayning the acts and adventures of the Spanyardes; whereof three have been formerly translated into English by Richard Eden, whereunto the other five are newly added by M[ichael] Lok. 1612, [1625], 1628; rptd in Hakluyt's collection of early voyages vol 5, 1809–12; rptd in A selection of curious rare and early voyages, 1812.

Hakluyt, Richard. Divers voyages touching the discoverie of America. 1582. See Voyages to America, below.
—— The principall navigations, voiages and discoveries of the English nation, made by sea or over land, to the most remote and farthest distant quarters of the earth. 1589; rptd as The principal navigations, voiages, traffiques and discoveries, 3 vols 1598–1600; rptd as Hakluyt's collection of the early voyages, travels and discoveries of the English nation, 5 vols 1809–12; rptd as Principal navigations of the English nation, 16 vols Edinburgh 1884–90, 12 vols Glasgow 1903–5 (Hakluyt Soc); rptd as Hakluyt's voyages, 8 vols 1908 (EL); rptd Salem Mass and Cambridge 1965 (Hakluyt Soc and Peabody Museum); New York 1969 (facs of 1903–5). Referred to as Hakluyt, below.

Galvam, Antonio. The discoveries of the world from their first originall unto the yeere of our Lord 1555; briefly written in the Portugall tongue by Antonie Galvano, corrected, quoted and now published in English by Richard Hakluyt. 1601; rptd in Harleian voyages vol 2, 1745, 1747; rptd in J. S. Clarke, The progress of maritime discovery, from the earliest period to the close of the 18th century vol 1, 1803; rptd in A selection of curious, rare and early voyages, 1812; ed C. R. D. Bethune 1862 (Hakluyt Soc), Amsterdam and New York 1969 (facs of 1601). From the Tratado de todos os descrobimentos, Lisbon 1563.

Purchas, Samuel. Hakluytus posthumus or Purchas his pilgrimes: contayning a history of the world, in sea voyages and lande travells, by Englishmen and others. 4 vols 1625, 20 vols Glasgow 1905–7 (Hakluyt Soc); tr Dutch, 1655 (in part). Referred to as Purchas, below.

Ramusio, Giovanni Battista. Primo volume delle navigationi e viaggi. Venice 1550, 1554, 1563, 1588, 1606, 1613; Secondo volume, Venice 1559, 1574, 1583, 1606; Terzo volume, Venice 1556, 1565, 1606; ed R. A. Skelton and G. B. Parks, Mundus novus ser 1 vols 2–4, Amsterdam 1967.

de Bry, Theodore. Collectiones peregrinationum in Indiam orientalem et Indiam occidentalem, xxv partibus comprehensae. Frankfurt 1590–1634 etc. In Latin and German. America pt 1 pbd in English and French, Frankfurt 1590. Work referred to as De Bry, below.

Hulsius, Levinus. Sammlung von sechs und zwanzig Schiffahrten in verschiedene fremde lande. Nuremberg etc 1598–1650. In German and Latin. Referred to as Hulsius, below.

Churchill, Awnsham and John. A collection of voyages and travels, some now first printed from original manuscripts. 6 vols 1704–32, 1732, 1644–6; vols 7–8, 1747; 8 vols 1752. Referred to as Churchill, below.

Harris, John. Navigantium atque itinerantium bibliotheca: or a compleat collection of voyages and travels. 2 vols 1705, 1744–8, 1764. Referred to as Harris, below.

van der Aa, Pieter. Verzameling der gedenkwaardigste reysen naar Oost en West Indies. 28 vols Leyden 1706–7, 8 vols Leyden 1727. Referred to as Van der Aa, below.

Oldys, William. The Harleian miscellany: a collection of scarce, curious and entertaining pamphlets and tracts, selected from the library of Edward Harley, second Earl of Oxford. 8 vols 1744–6; ed T. Park 10 vols 1808–13, 12 vols 1808–11. Referred to as Harleian miscellany below.

Osborne, Thomas. A collection of voyages and travels, consisting of authentic writers in our own tongue: compiled from the late Earl of Oxford. 2 vols 1745, 1747. Referred to as Harleian voyages, below.

Astley, Thomas. A new general collection of voyages and travels: consisting of the most esteemed relations which have been hitherto published in any language. 4 vols 1745–7; tr German as J. J. Schwabe, Allgemeine Historie der Reisen vol 1–7, Leipzig 1747–74; French, as Abbé Prévost, Histoire des voyages, 20 vols Paris 1746–89, 25 vols Amsterdam 1747–89. Referred to as Astley, Schwabe and Prévost, below.

Callander, John. Terra Australis cognita: or voyages to the Terra Australis or Southern Hemisphere during the sixteenth, seventeenth and eighteenth centuries. 3 vols Edinburgh 1766–8. Referred to as Callander, below.

Dalrymple, Alexander. A collection of voyages chiefly in the southern Atlantick ocean. 1775. Referred to as Dalrymple, below.

Pinkerton, John. A general collection of the best and most interesting voyages and travels in all parts of the world. 17 vols 1808–14. Referred to as Pinkerton, below.

Kerr, Robert. A general history and collection of voyages and travels, arranged in systematic order: forming a complete history of the origin and progress of navigation, discovery and commerce, by sea and land, from the earliest ages to the present time. 18 vols Edinburgh and London 1811–24. Referred to as Kerr, below.

A selection of curious, rare and early voyages and histories of interesting discoveries, chiefly published by Hakluyt, or at his suggestion, but not included in his celebrated compilation. Ed R. H. Evans 1812.

Force, Peter. Tracts and other papers, relating principally to the origin, settlement and the progress of the colonies in North America. 4 vols Washington 1836–46, 2 vols Rochester and New York 1898–9 (in part as American colonial tracts). Referred to as Force, Tracts, below.

Hakluyt Society publications. 1847–.

Arber, E. An English garner. 8 vols 1877–97, 12 vols 1903–4. In 2nd edn most of the relevant pieces are grouped together as Voyages and travels, ed C. R. Beazley 2 vols 1903, 1965. Referred to as Arber, below.

Payne, E. J. Voyages of the Elizabethan seamen: select narratives from the principal navigations of Hakluyt. 2 vols Oxford 1880. Referred to as Payne, below.

Navy Records Society publications. 1896–.

Danvers, F. C. and W. Foster. Letters received by the East India Company from its servants in the East 1602–17. 6 vols 1896–1902.

Hakluyt's English voyages, selected. Ed E. E. Speight 1905.

Original narratives of early American history. Ed J. F. Jameson 18 vols New York 1906–17, 1959. Referred to as Original narratives, below.

Massachusetts Historical Society: Americana series, photos at reproductions. Boston 1919–. Referred to as Americana ser, below.

The Broadway travellers. Ed E. D. Ross and E. Power 26 vols 1926–37.

Argonaut Press classics of travel and exploration. Ed N. M. Penzer 1926–38.

A selection of the Principal voyages, traffiques and discoveries of the English nation. Ed L. Irving 1926.

Hakluyt, Richard. Voyages and documents. Ed J. Hampden 1958.

They told Mr Hakluyt: being a selection of tales and other matter taken from Richard Hakluyt's The principal navigations. Ed F. Knight 1964.

Hakluyt's voyages; the principal navigations, selected. Ed I. R. Blacker 1965.

March of America facsimile reprint series. Ann Arbor 1966.

The English experience: its record in early printed books published in facsimile. Amsterdam and New York 1968–.

The Tudor venturers. Ed J. Hampden 1970 (Folio Soc). Selected from Hakluyt, above.

(3) GENERAL STUDIES

Peschel, O. F. Geschichte des Zeitalters der Entdeckungen. Stuttgart 1858.

Ruge, Sophus. Geschichte des Zeitalters der Entdeckungen. Berlin 1881.

Winsor, J. Narrative and critical history of America. 8 vols Boston 1886–9.

— Cartier to Frontenac: geographical discoveries in the interior of North America. Boston 1894.

The dawn of British trade to the East Indies as recorded in the court minutes of the East India Company 1599–1603. 1886.

Gravière, J. de la. Les Anglais et les Hollandais dans les mers polaires et dans la mer des Indes. 2 vols Paris 1890.

Corbett, J. S. Drake and the Tudor navy. 2 vols 1898, 1898–9.

— The successors of Drake. 1900.

— England in the Mediterranean 1603–1713. 2 vols 1904.

Hunter, W. W. A history of British India. 2 vols 1899–1900.

Underhill, J. G. Spanish literature in the England of the Tudors. New York 1899.

Einstein, L. The Italian Renaissance in England. New York 1902.

Errera, C. L'epoca delle grandi scoperte geografiche [to 1522]. Milan 1902, 1910, 1926 (both rev and enlarged).

Gunther, S. Das Zeitalter der Entdeckungen. Leipzig 1902.

The Cambridge modern history. Ed A. W. Ward et al 13 vols Cambridge 1902–11. Vol 1, ch 1, E. J. Payne, The age of discovery; ch 2, E. J. Payne, The New World; vol 4 ch 25, H. E. Egerton, The transference of colonial power to the United Provinces and England.

The new Cambridge modern history. Ed G. N. Clark et al, Cambridge 1957–. Vol 1 ch 2, H. C. Darby, The face of Europe on the eve of the great discoveries; ch 15, H. V. Livermore and J. H. Parry, The New World; ch 16, E. E. Rich, Expansion as a concern of all Europe; vol 2 ch 19, J. H. Parry, The New World; ch 20, I. A. Macgregor, Europe and the East; vol 3, ch 17, J. H. Parry and J. B. Harrison, Colonial development and international rivalries outside Europe; vol 5, ch 14, Rich, Europe and North America; ch 15, J. Regla, Spain and her empire; ch 16, V. M. Godinho, Portugal and her empire; ch 17, Europe and Asia, (1) J. B. Harrison, The European connection with Asia, (2) C. D. Cowan, The English and Dutch East India Companies; ch 25, W. Philipp, Russia: the beginning of westernization.

Hugues, L. Cronologia delle scoperte e delle esplorazioni geografiche dall'anno 1492 a tutto il secolo xix. Milan 1903.

Bohme, M. Die grossen Reisesammlungen des 16 Jahrhunderts und ihre Bedeutung. Strasbourg 1904.

Raleigh, W. The English voyages of the 16th century. Glasgow 1906. Also in Hakluyt's voyages vol 12, Glasgow 1905 (Hakluyt Soc).

Ker, W. P. The Elizabethan voyagers. TLS 12 July 1907; rptd in his Collected essays vol 1, 1925.

Robinson, C. N. and J. Leyland. The literature of the sea, from the origins to Hakluyt. CHEL vol 4 1909.

— Seafaring and travel. Ibid.

Scott, W. R. The constitution and finance of English, Scottish and Irish joint-stock companies to 1720. 3 vols Cambridge 1910–12.

Bates, E. S. Touring in 1600. 1911.

Heawood, E. A history of geographical discovery in the 17th and 18th centuries. Cambridge 1912.

Williamson, J. A. Maritime enterprise 1485–1558. Oxford 1913.

Howard, C. English travellers of the Renaissance. 1914.

Shakespeare's England vol 1. Oxford 1916. Ch 5, L. G. Carr Laughton, The navy: ships and sailors; ch 6, J. D. Rogers, Voyages and exploration: geography: maps; ch 7, Charles Hughes, Land travel.

Cambridge history of American literature vol 1. Ed W. P. Trent et al 1918, 1961. Ch 1, G. P. Winship, Travellers and explorers 1583–1763; ch 2, J. S. Bassett, The historians 1607–1783.

Gillespie, J. E. The influence of overseas expansion on England to 1700. New York 1920.

Markham, C. R. The lands of silence: a history of Arctic and Antarctic exploration. Cambridge 1921.

Mutschmann, H. Studies concerning the origin of Paradise lost [in Hakluyt]. Acta et Commentationes Universitatis Dorpatensis 5 1924.

Adair, E. R. William Thomas: a forgotten clerk of the Privy Council. In Tudor studies, 1924 (London Univ).

Parkes, J. Travel in England in the 17th century. 1925.

Hall, D. G. Early English intercourse with Burma 1587–1743. 1928, 1968 (enlarged).

Parks, G. B. Richard Hakluyt and the English voyages. New York 1928 (Amer Geographical Soc).

— Frobisher's third voyage 1578. Huntington Lib Bull no 7 1935.

— John Evelyn and the art of travel. HLQ 10 1947.

— Travel as education. In R. F. Jones et al, The seventeenth century, Stanford 1951.

— The English traveller to Italy vol 1: the Middle Ages (to 1525). Rome 1954.

Cambridge history of the British Empire vol 1. Ed J. Holland Rose et al 1929. Ch 2, J. A. Williamson, England and the opening of the Atlantic; ch 3, A. P. Newton, The beginnings of English colonization 1569–1618; ch 4, J. H. Rose, Sea power 1580–1660; ch 5, A. P. Newton, The great emigration 1618–48.

Taylor, E. G. R. Tudor geography 1485–1583. 1930.

— Samuel Purchas. Geographical Jnl 75 1930.

— Late Tudor and early Stuart geography 1583–1650. 1934.

— The original writings and correspondence of the two Richard Hakluyts. 2 vols 1936.

de Beer, G. R. Early travellers in the Alps. 1930.

Locke, J. C. (ed). The first Englishman in India. 1930.

Baker, J. N. L. A history of geographical exploration and discovery. 1931.

The great age of discovery. Ed A. P. Newton 1932.

Rice, W. G. Early English travellers to Greece and the Levant. In Essays and studies by members of the English Department, Ann Arbor 1933.

Grey, C. The Merchant Venturers of London: a record of far eastern trade and piracy during the 17th century. 1932.

Gillespie, J. E. A history of geographical discovery 1400–1900. New York 1933.

Judson, A. C. Spenser in southern Ireland. Bloomington 1933.

Pioneer histories:

Brebner, J. B. The explorers of North America 1492–1806. 1933.

Foster, W. England's quest of eastern trade. 1933.

Newton, A. P. The European nations in the West Indies 1493–1688. 1933.

Beaglehole, J. C. The discovery and exploration of the Pacific 1934, 1947 (rev).

Williamson, J. A. The age of Drake. 1938.

Wilkinson, H. The adventures of Bermuda: a history of the island to 1684. 1933.

Wood, A. C. History of the Levant Company. Oxford 1935.

Flower, R. E. Laurence Nowell and the discovery of England in Tudor times. 1935.

de Beer, E. S. George Sandys' account of Campania. Library 4th ser 17 1937.

— Robert Langton's Pylgrymage. Library 5th ser 10 1955.

Rowse, A. L. Sir Richard Grenville of the Revenge. 1937.

Williamson, J. A. The ocean in English history. Oxford 1941, 1949 (rev).

— Hawkins of Plymouth. 1949.

Penrose, B. Urbane travellers 1591–1635. Philadelphia 1942.

— Travel and discovery in the Renaissance 1420–1620. Cambridge Mass 1952.

— Tudor and early Stuart voyaging. Washington 1962 (Folger Lib).

Wright, L. B. The noble savage of Madagascar in 1640. JHI 4 1943. On Walter Hamond, A paradox, 1640.

— Religion and empire. Chapel Hill 1943.

Jones, H. M. The literature of Virginia in the 17th century. Memoirs of Amer Acad of Arts & Sciences 19 pt 2 1946, 1968 (with S. B. Walcutt).

— The colonial impulse: an analysis of the 'promotion' literature of colonization. Proc Amer Philosophical Soc 90 1946.

Quinn, D. B. Raleigh and the British empire. 1947.

Letts, M. Sir John Mandeville: the man and his book. 1949.

Wood, H. J. Exploration and discovery. 1951.

Wright, I. A. (ed). Further English voyages to Spanish America. 1583–94. 1951 (Hakluyt Soc).

Stoye, J. W. English traveller abroad 1606–67: their influence in English society and politics. 1952.

Mitchell, R. J. Robert Langton's Pylgrymage. Library 5th ser 8 1953.

Bennett, J. W. The rediscovery of Sir John Mandeville. New York 1954.

Davis, R. B. George Sandys: poet-adventurer. New York 1955.

Fedden, R. English travellers in the Near East. 1958.

Moir, E. A. L. The early English antiquaries. History Today 17 1958.

Anderson, M. S. Britain's discovery of Russia. 1958.

Dorsch, T. S. Two English antiquaries: John Leland and John Stow. E & S new ser 12 1959.

Strauss, G. The image of Germany in the 16th century. Germanic Rev 34 1959.

Lamar, V. A. Travel and roads in England. Washington 1960.

Parry, J. H. The age of reconnaissance. 1962.

Kenny, A. Anthony Mundy in Rome. Recusant History 6 1962.

Edelen, G. William Harrison. Stud in Renaissance 9 1962.

Marsh, T. N. An unpublished Hakluyt manuscript? New Eng Quart 35 1962.

Strachan, M. The life and adventures of Thomas Coryate. Oxford 1962.

Moir, E. The discovery of Britain: the English tourist 1540–1840. 1964.

Prasad, R. C. Early English travellers in India: a study in the travel literature of the Elizabethan and Jacobean periods. Delhi 1965.

Culliford, S. G. William Strachey. Charlottesville 1965.

Rae, T. Scotland in the time of Shakespeare. New York 1965.

Quinn, D. B. The Elizabethans and the Irish. Ithaca 1966 (Folger Lib).

— North American discovery circa 1000–1612. 1971.

Weslager, C. A. The English on the Delaware 1610–82. Brunswick NJ 1967.

Reed, R. B. Richard Eden: an early English capitalist. Serif 4 1967.

Trease, G. The grand tour 1618–1860. 1967.

Lach, D. F. China in the eyes of Europe in the 16th century; India in the eyes of Europe in the 16th century; Japan in the eyes of Europe in the 16th century; SE Asia in the eyes of Europe in the 16th century. Chicago 1968. With bibliographies.

Barr, P. Foreign devils: Westerners in the Far East from the sixteenth century to the present day. 1970 (Pelican).

Breslow, M. A. A mirror of England: English puritan views of foreign nations 1618–40. Cambridge Mass 1970.

Crone, G. R. and A. Kendall. The voyages of discovery. 1970.

Henley, P. Spenser in Ireland. Grosse Pointe Michigan 1970.

Kollek, T. and M. Pearlman. Pilgrims to the Holy Land: the story of pilgrimage through the ages. 1970.

Ziff, L. The literature of America: colonial period. New York 1970.

Cross, A. Russia under western eyes 1517–1825. 1971.

Cumming, W. P., R. A. Skelton and D. B. Quinn. The discovery of North America. 1971.

Morison, S. E. The European discovery of America: the northern voyages. Oxford 1971.

Sauer, C. O. Sixteenth-century North America: the land and the people as seen by the Europeans. Berkeley 1971.

Barker, N. In fair Verona: English travellers in Italy and their accounts of the city from the Middle Ages to modern times. 1972 (Pelican).

Literary Influences

'Lee, Vernon' (V. Paget). The Italy of the Elizabethan dramatists. In her Euphorion, 2 vols 1884, 1 vol 1885 (rev).

Elze, T. Venezianische Skizzen zu Shakespeare. Munich 1899.

Hume, M. Spanish influence on English literature. 1905.

Naval songs and ballads. Ed C. H. Firth 1908 (Navy Records Soc).

Robinson, C. N. and J. Leyland. The British tar in fact and fiction. 1909.

Whall, W. B. Shakespeare's sea terms explained. Bristol 1910.

Wann, L. The oriental in Elizabethan drama. MP 12 1914.

Brie, F. Imperialistische Strömungen in der englischen Literatur. Halle 1916. Also Anglia 40 1916.

Gilbert, A. H. A geographical dictionary of Milton. New Haven 1919.

— Pierre Davity: his geography and its use by Milton. Geographical Rev 7 1919.

Thompson, E. N. S. Milton's knowledge of geography. SP 16 1919.

Grossmann, R. Spanien und das elisabethanische Drama. Hamburg 1920.

Whitney, L. Spenser's use of the literature of travel in the Faerie Queene. MP 19 1921.

— Did Shakespeare know Leo Africanus? PMLA 37 1922.

Cawley, R. R. Warner and the voyagers. MP 20 1922.

— Drayton and the voyagers. PMLA 38 1923.

— Shakespeare's use of the voyagers in the Tempest. PMLA 41 1926.

— George Gascoigne and the siege of Famagusta. MLN 43 1928.

— The voyagers and Elizabethan drama. Boston 1938.

— Unpathed waters: studies in the influence of the voyagers on Elizabethan literature. Princeton 1940.

— Milton and the literature of travel. Princeton 1951.

Atkinson, Geoffroy. Les relations de voyages du dix-septième siècle et l'évolution des idées. Paris [1924].

Hughes, W. J. Wales and the Welsh in English literature from Shakespeare to Scott. 1924.

Seaton, E. Marlowe's map. E & S 10 1924.

— Fresh sources for Marlowe. RES 5 1929.

Sugden, E. H. A topographical dictionary to the works of Shakespeare and his fellow dramatists. Manchester 1925.

Sencourt, R. India in English literature. 1926.

Treneer, A. The sea in English literature, from Beowulf to Donne. 1926.

Magnus, L. English literature in its foreign relations. 1927.

Hull, V. E. N. The English and Welsh topographical sources of Polyolbion. Cambridge Mass 1930.

Watson, H. F. The sailor in English fiction and drama 1550–1800. New York 1931.

Chew, S. C. The crescent and the rose: Islam and England during the Renaissance. New York 1937.

Jones, H. M. The image of the New World. In Elizabethan studies in honor of G. F. Reynolds, Boulder 1945.

McCam, F. T. English discovery of America to 1585. New York 1952.

Colie, R. L. Marvell's Bermudas and the Puritan paradise. Renaissance News 10 1957.

Legris, M. The English countryside in Harrison's Description of England. Renaissance Papers 1957.

Friedrich, G. The genesis of Michael Drayton's ode To the Virginian voyage. MLN 72 1957.

Sasek, L. A. The literary temper of the English Puritans. Louisiana State Univ Stud Humanities ser no 9 1961.

Lindsay, R. O. Richard Hakluyt and Of the Russe common wealth. PBSA 57 1963.

Lytton Sells, A. The paradise of travellers: the Italian influence on Englishmen in the 17th century. 1964.

Davies, D. W. Dutch influences on English culture 1558–1625. New York 1964.

Jones, E. Othello's countrymen: the African in English Renaissance drama. 1965.

Arthos, J. Milton and the Italian cities. New York 1968.

Berry, L. E. Giles Fletcher the elder and Milton's A brief history of Moscovia. RES new ser 11 1960.

— Richard Hakluyt and Turberville's poems on Russia. PBSA 61 1967.

(4) GENERAL

Bartholomaeus Anglicus. De proprietatibus rerum. [Cologne 1470] etc. No Latin edns in England.

— Bartholomeus de proprietatibus rerum. [Tr John de Trevisa], [Westminster 1495], 1535; rptd as Batman uppon Bartholome his booke De proprietatibus rerum, 1582 (with addns by Stephen Batman); rptd New York 1935 (facs of ms in private hands).

[Gauthier or Gossouin de Metz]. The mirrour of the world or thymage of the same. [1481], [1490], [1529]; ed O. H. Prior 1913 (EETS). Written c. 1245. Tr William Caxton from Image du Monde.

Higden, Ranulf. Mappa mundi or description of the world [bk 1 of the Polychronicon, tr John de Trevisa 1377]. 1482, 1495, 1527; rptd New York 1931 (facs). BM Cotton ms Tiberius D vii. Latin original ed C. Babington, 9 vols 1865–86 (facs) (Rolls ser). See Description of British Isles, below.

Diadochus, Proclus. De sphaera: sive circulis coelestibus libellus. Pbd with Latin trn by Thomas Linacre, Venice 1499, Leipzig [1500], Vienna 1511, Paris 1534 etc.

— The descripcion of the Sphere or frame of the worlde, englysshed by me Wyllym Salysburye. [1550].

— Procli Sphaera. Ed John Bainbridge 1620. Greek and Latin.

Barlow, Roger. A brief summe of geographie. Ed E. G. R. Taylor 1932 (Hakluyt Soc). 1541. BM Royal ms. 18B xxviii. Tr from Martin Fernandez de Enciso, Suma de geographia, Seville 1519, 1530, 1546.

Munster, Sebastian. A treatyse of the newe India, with other new founde landes and ilandes, as well eastwarde and westwarde, translated out of Latin into English, by Rycharde Eden. 1553; ed E. Arber, The first three English books on America, Birmingham 1885. From portions of Cosmographia universalis, bk 5, Basle 1550 etc.

— A briefe collection and compendious extract of straunge and memorable thinges gathered out of the Cosmographye of Sebastian Munster. 1572, 1574. Anon compilation.

Boemus, Joannes. The discription of the contrey of Aphrique, the fyrst part of the worlde, translated out of Frenche into Englyshe by Wyllyam Prat. 1554. From the first bk of the Repertorium Librorium trium de omnium gentium ritibus, Augsburg 1520, later as Omnium gentium mores, leges & ritus; French edns, 1540, 1542, 1547.

— The fardle of facions conteining the auncient maners, customes and lawes, of the peoples enhabiting the two partes of the earth, called Affrike and Asie. 1555; rptd Hakluyt's collection of early voyages vol 5, 1809–12; rptd A selection of curious, rare and early voyages, 1912; rptd E. and G. Goldsmid, Edinburgh 1888; Amsterdam and New York 1970 (facs of 1555). Tr William Watreman.

— A discoverie of the countries of Tartaria, Scithia and Cataya, by the North-East; with the manners, fashions and orders which are used in those countries, set foorth by John Frampton. 1580. From Boemus via Francisco Thamara, El libro de las costumbres de todas las gentes del mundo, Antwerp 1556.

— The manners, lawes and customes of all nations. 1611. Tr complete E. Aston, with other material.

Cuningham, William. The cosmographical glasse: conteinyng the principles of cosmographie, geographie, hydrographie or navigation. 1559, Amsterdam and New York 1968 (facs).

Plinius Secundus, Gaius. A summarie of the antiquities and wonders of the worlde, abstracted out of the sixtene first bookes of Plinie, translated oute of French by I.A. [1556]; rptd as The secrets and wonders of the world, 1585, 1587. From Pierre de Changy, Paris 1559.

— The historie of the world, commonly called the naturall historie of C. Plinius Secundus, translated into English by Philemon Holland. 2 vols 1601, 1634, 1635; ed P. Turner, Carbondale 1962 (abridged).

Periegetes, Dionysius. The surveye of the world, or situation of the earth so muche as is inhabited; now englished by Thomas Twine. 1572, Cambridge 1633. Greek edn, Eton [1607]; Latin commentary by William Hill, 1658.

Buchanan, George. De sphaera fragmentum. In Franciscanus et Fratres, [Geneva] 1584, 1585.

— Sphaera: Georgii Buchanani Scoti quinque libris descripta. Herborn 1586, 1587, 1617; rptd in Franciscanus et Fratres, [no place] 1594; Heidelberg 1594, 1597, 1604, 1609; rptd in Poemata omnia, Edinburgh 1615, Leyden 1621, Saumur 1621, Leyden 1628, Amsterdam 1641, 1657, 1665, 1676, Edinburgh 1677, 1686, Amsterdam 1687; in Opera omnia, Edinburgh 1715, Leyden 1725; tr J. R. Naiden, Philadelphia 1952 (from Herborn 1586).

Mela, Pomponius. The worke of Pomponius Mela the cosmographer concerning the situation of the world, translated out of Latine by Arthur Golding. 1585, 1590 (combined with next item).

Solinus, Julius. The excellent and pleasant worke of Julius Solinus polyhistor, translated out of Latin into English, by Arthur Golding. 1587, 1590 (combined with preceding item as The rare and singular worke of Pomponius Mela); ed G. Kish, Gainesville 1955 (facs).

Saluste, Guillaume de, Seigneur du Bartas. The colonies of Bartas; with the commentary of S.G.S. Tr William Lisle 1598; rptd in his Part of Du Bartas, 1625 (English and French); rptd in Foure bookes of Dubartas, 1637 (English and French); tr Joshua Sylvester in The second weeke: or childhood of the world, 1598; New York 1931 (facs); tr Sylvester in Bartas his devine weekes and workes, 1605, 1608, 1611, 1613, 1621, 1633, 1641; rptd Waukesha 1908; tr Thomas Winter, The second day of the first week, 1603.

The theatre of the earth: containing very short and compendious descriptions of all countries, gathered out of the chiefest cosmographers, both ancient and modern, and disposed in alphabetical order. 1599, 1601.

[Abbot, George]. A briefe description of the whole worlde: wherein is particularly described all the monarchies, empires and kingdomes of the same. 1599, 1600, 1605, 1608, 1617, 1620, 1624, 1634, 1636, 1642, 1656, 1644, Amsterdam and New York 1970 (facs of 1599).

Botero, Giovanni. The travellers breviat: or a historicall description of the most famous kingdomes in the world. 1601; rptd as The worlde: or an historicall description, 1601; rptd as An historicall description, 1603; rptd as

Relations of the most famous kingdomes, 1608, 1611, 1616, 1630; Amsterdam and New York 1699 (facs of 1601), tr Robert Johnson from Le relazioni universali, Rome 1592 etc.

— A treatise: concerning the causes of the magnificencie and greatnes of cities, done into English by Robert Peterson. 1606. From the Tre libri delle cause della grandezza delle citta, Ferrara 1589 etc.

— The cause of the greatnesse of cities. 1635. Tr Sir T. Hawkins from the same.

Ortelius, Abraham. Abraham Ortelius his epitome of the theater of the worlde. 1603, [1610]. From the Latin, Epitome, Antwerp 1589 etc.

— Theatrum orbis terrarum Abrahami Orteli, Antverp, geographi regii: the theatre of the whole world. 1606; ed R. A. Skelton, Amsterdam 1968. From the Latin, Antwerp 1570 etc.

Stafforde, Robert. A geographicall and anthologicall description of all the empires and kingdomes, both of continents and ilands in this terrestriall globe. 1607, 1618, 1618, 1634.

Zouche, Richard. The dove: or passages of cosmography. 1613; ed R. Walker, Oxford 1839. Verse.

Purchas, Samuel. Purchas his pilgrimage: or relations of the world and the religions observed in all ages and places discovered. 1613, 1614, 1617, 1626.

Brerewood, Edward. Enquiries touching the diversity of languages and religions through the cheife parts of the world. 1614, 1622; rptd Purchas, above; 1635, 1674; tr French, 1640, 1663; Latin, 1650, 1659.

d'Avity, Pierre. The estates, empires and principallities of the world: represented by ye description of countries, maners of inhabitants; translated out of French by E[dward] Grimstone. 1615. From Les empires, royaumes, estats et principautez du monde, Paris 1614 etc.

Heylyn, Peter. Microcosmus or a little description of the great world: a treatise historicall, geographicall, politicall, theologicall. Oxford 1621, 1625, 1627, 1629, 1631, 1633, 1636, 1639. Enlarged in next item.

— Cosmographie in four bookes contayning the chorographie and historie of the whole world, and all the principall kingdomes, provinces, seas and isles thereof. 1652, 1657, 1666, 1668–9, 1669, 1670, 1674, 1677, 1682, 1703.

Carpenter, Nathanael. Geography delineated forth in two bookes: containing the sphaericall and topicall parts thereof. Oxford 1625, 1635.

Pemble, William. A briefe introduction to geography containing a description of the grounds and generall part thereof. Oxford 1630, 1635; rptd in Workes of W. Pemble, 1635; Oxford 1658; rptd in Workes, Oxford 1659, 1669, 1675, 1685.

Speed, John. A prospect of the most famous parts of the world viz Asia, Affrica, Europe, America. 1631, 1646, 1662, 1668; rptd with The theatre of Great Britain, 1676.

Mercator, Gerard. Historia mundi, or Mercators atlas: containing his cosmographicall description of the fabricke and figure of the world, englished by W. S[altonstall]. 1635, 1637, 1639. Original Latin, Düsseldorf 1595 etc.

— Atlas or a geographicke description of the regions, countries and kingdomes of the worlde. 2 vols Amsterdam 1636, 1638, 1641; ed R. A. Skelton, Amsterdam 1968 (facs of 1636). Tr Henry Hexham.

Pagitt, Ephraim. Christianographie: or the description of the multitude and sundry sorts of Christians in the world not subject to the Pope. 1635, 1636, 1640, 1674.

— A relation of the Christians in the world. 1639.

Roberts, Lewes. The merchants mappe of commerce: wherein the universal manner and matter of trade is compendiously handled. 1638, 1671, 1677, 1677, 1700.

Bertius, Petrus. Breviarium totius orbis terrarum. In Tractatus duo mathematici, Oxford 1651, 1663; rptd Philippi Cluverii introductionis in universam geographiam, Oxford 1657, below. First pbd Leyden 1624.

Siculus, Diodorus. The history of Diodorus Siculus: containing all that is most memorable and of greatest antiquity in the first ages of the world until the war of Troy, done into English by H[enry] C[ogan]. 1653.

Ross, Alexander. Πανσεέβεια: or a view of all religions in the world, with the several church-governments, from the creation, to these times; together with a discovery of all known heresies, in all ages and places. 1653, 1655, 1658, 1659, 1664, 1672, 1673, 1675, 1683, 1696, [1780]; tr Dutch, 1663, 1671; French, 1666, 1669; German, 1667, 1701, 1717.

Campanella, Tommaso. A discourse touching the Spanish monarchy, wherein we have a politicall glasse, representing each particular country. 1654; rptd as Advice to the King of Spaine, [1660]. Tr Edmund Chilmead from the De monarchia hispanica discursus, Amsterdam 1640 etc.

Clarke, Samuel. A geographicall description of all the countries in the knowne world as also of the chiefest cittyes, famousest structures, greatest ruins, strangest fountaines. 1657, 1671, 1689.

Cluverius, Philippus. Introductionis in universam geographiam, tam veterem quam novam: libri vi; accessit P. Bertii Breviarium orbis terrarum. Oxford 1657; tr as An introduction into geography, both ancient and moderne, Oxford 1657. First pbd Leyden, 1624.

Fage, Robert, A description of the whole worlde, with some general rules touching the use of the globe, wherein is contained the situation of several countries. 1658.

P., R. A geographicall description of the world: describing Europe, Asia, Africa and America; with all its kingdoms, countries and common-wealths. Appended to Dionysius Petavius, The history of the world: or an account of time, 1659.

Porter, Thomas. A compendious view or cosmographical, and geographical description of the whole world, wherein is shewed the situation of the several countries and islands. 1659.

(5) EUROPE AND THE MEDITERRANEAN

Travels and Voyages

Informacion for pylgrymes unto the holy londe. [1498], 1515, 1524, Edinburgh 1824 (Roxburghe Club); ed E. G. Duff 1893 (facs). Partly from William Wey, Itineraries to Jerusalem, [c. 1460], Edinburgh 1857 (Roxburghe Club).

The pylgrymage of Sir Richarde Guylforde [1506–7] towardes Jherusalem. 1511; ed H. Ellis 1851 (Camden Soc).

Torkyngton, Rychard. The pylgrymage of Sir Rychard Torkyngton, person of Mulberton in Norffolke, and how he went towardys Jherusalem. Ed W. J. Loftie 1884. In 1517–18. BM additional ms 28,561–2.

Langton, Robert. The pylgrimage of M. Robert Langton, clerke to Saynt James in Compostell. 1522; ed E. M. Blackie, Cambridge Mass 1924.

Durand de Villegagnon, Nicolas. A lamentable and piteous treatise, wherin is contayned not onely the high enterprise and valiauntnes of th'emperour Charles the V and his army (in his voyage made to the towne of Argier in Affrique, agaynst the Turckes) but also the myserable chaunces of wynde and wether. 1542; rptd Harleian miscellany vol 4, 1808–13. From Caroli V Imperatoris expeditio in Africam et Argieriam, Paris 1542 etc.

Leland, John. The laboriouse journey and serche of Johan Leylande, for Englandes antiquitees, geven of him as a newe yeares gyfte [1546] to Kynge Henry, with declaracyons enlarged by Johan Bale. 1549, 1722, 1772, 1895, 1906 etc (with next item vol 1).

— [The itinerary of John Leland c. 1540]. Ed T. Hearne 9 vols Oxford 1710–17, 1745–54, 1768–9; ed H. Moody, Winchester 1868 (in part); ed J. E. Jackson, Devizes [1875] (in part); ed W. George, Bristol 1879 (in part); ed L. Toulmin Smith 5 vols 1906–10, Arundel Sussex 1964, Carbondale 1965; ed R. P. Chope, Early tours of Devon and Cornwall, Exeter 1918 (in part), Newton Abbot 1967; ed R. Douch, Southampton 1540–1956: visitors' descriptions, Southampton 1961.

The journey of the Queen's ambassadors unto Rome, anno 1555. In Philip Yorke, Lorde Hardwicke, Miscellaneous state papers vol 1, 1778. BM Harley ms 252 folios 49–73.

Hoby, Sir Thomas. The booke of the travaile and lief of me Thomas Hoby. Ed E. Powell, Camden miscellany vol 10, 1902. Travels on the Continent 1547–55, written by 1564. BM Egerton ms 2148.

An excellent discourse of Jhon Fox an Inglish-man who delivered 266 Christians [from the galleys]. 1579, 1589, 1599 (in Hakluyt); ed E. Arber vol 1, 1877, vol 1, 1903.

No known copy of 1579; formerly ascribed to Anthony Mundy, as well as the following item, an elaboration.

The admirable deliverance of 266 Christians by John Reynard Englishman from the captivitie of the Turkes. 1608; rptd Harleian miscellany vol 1, 1808; rptd Hakluyt's Collection of the early voyages, travels and discoveries of the English nation vol 2, 1809.

Mundy, Anthony. The English Romayne life, discovering the lives of the Englishmen at Roome. 1582, 1590; rptd Harleian miscellany vol 7, 1808–13; ed G. B. Harrison 1925.

Cambrensis, Giraldus. Itinerarium Cambriae: seu laboriosae Baldvini Cantuar Archiepiscopi per Walliam legationis descriptio; in Pontici virunnii Britannicae historiae libri sex, per Davidum Povelum. 1585; ed R. C. H. Hoare 1804. Also in Gulielmi Camdeni, Anglica hibernica, normannica, cambrica a veteribus scripta, Frankfurt 1602, 1603.

— Cambriae descriptio. 1585 (as above), 1602 and 1603 (as above).

— Topographia hiberniae: sive de mirabilibus Hiberniae. In Camden, 1602 and 1603 above. All in Opera, 7 vols 1861–91; tr 1806, 1863.

More, Humphrey. The Primrose of London with eher valiant adventure on the Spanish coast, truely published by Humphrey More. 1585, 1871; tr Dutch, 1585.

Nicolay, Nicolas de, Seigneur d'Arfeuille. The navigations, peregrinations and voyages made into Turkie, translated out of the French by T. Washington the younger. 1585; rptd Churchill vol 7, 1752 etc; rptd Harleian voyages vol 1, 1745, 1747; Amsterdam and New York 1968 (facs of 1585). From Les quatre premiers livres des navigations et pérégrinations orientales, Lyons 1568 etc.

Pigafetta, Marc-Antonio. Itinerario di Marc Antonio Pigafetta, gentil'huomo Vincentino [from Vienna to Constantinople and return 1567–8]. 1585.

Turbervile, George. Tragicall tales translated by Turbervile out of sundrie Italians, with some other broken pamphlettes and epistles sent to certaine his frends in England, at his being in Moscovia 1569. 1587, Edinburgh 1837; ed L. E. Berry and R. O. Crummey, Rude and barbarous kingdom, Madison 1969. The letters and pamphlets appended to Tragicall tales were ptd 1598 (in Hakluyt); ed E. R. Grahame, The archer and the steppe, [1860].

Haslop, Henry. Newes out of the coast of Spaine: the true report of the honourable service for England, perfourmed by Sir Frauncis Drake upon Cales; and also since that in Cape S. Vincent and Cape Saker, 1587.

Leng, Robert. The true discription of the last voiage [1587] of that worthy Captayne, Sir Frauncis Drake, Knight, with his service done against the Spanyardes. Ed C. Hopper, Camden miscellany vol 5, 1863 (from ms).

Saunders, Thomas. A true discription and breefe discourse of a most lamentable voiage, made latelie [1584–5] to Tripolie in Barbarie, in a ship named the Jesus; set foorth by Thomas Saunders, one of those captives. 1587, 1589, 1599 (in Hakluyt); ed E. Arber vol 3 1877–97, vol 1 1903–4.

Cavendish, Harrie. His journey to and from Constantinople [overland 1589] by Fox his servant. Ed A. C. Wood 1940 (Camden Soc) (from ms).

[Wingfield, Anthony]. A true coppie of a discourse written by a gentleman employed in the late voyage of Spain and Portingale. 1589, 1599 (in Hakluyt); ed Purchas; ed J. P. Collier 1870; tr Latin as Ephemeris expeditionis Norreysii & Draki in Lusitaniam, 1589, as Brevis et fida narratio, Frankfurt 1590, in Narrationes duae, Nuremberg 1590; tr German, [1590].

Ferris, Richard. The most dangerous and memorable adventure of R. Ferris, who undertooke to rowe by sea to Bristowe. 1590; ed J. P. Collier, Illustrations of early English popular literature vol 2, 1864; ed E. Arber vol 6, 1883; ed A. Lang 1903.

Ubaldino, Petruccio. A discourse concerninge the Spanish fleete invadinge Englande in the yeare 1588 and overthrowne by her Maties: navie; written in Italian by Petruccio Ubaldini and translated for A. Ryther. 1590, 1740; rptd Harleian miscellany vol 1, 1808–13 etc; ed J. K. Laughton 1894 (Navy Records Soc) (from BM Cotton Julius F x fols 111–17); rptd with a contemporary volume of drawings by Robert Adams 1919 (Roxburghe Club); ed G. P. B. Naish 1952 (Navy Records Soc) (tr from BM Royal 14 A x). Ubaldino's original ms is BM Royal 14 A x. Its original English form is BM Cotton Julius F x fol 111–17.

Webbe, Edward. The rare and most wonderful thinges which Edward Webbe an Englishman borne, hath seen and passed in his troublesome travailes in the landes of Jewrie, Egipt, Grecia, Russia and in the land of Prester John. 1590, 1590, [1592], [1600]; ed E. Arber, English reprints no 5, 1869, 1895; Mr Ashbee's Occasional facs reprints no 10, 1869 (facs); ed E. Goldsmid, Edinburgh 1885; ed E. Arber 1889.

Horsey, Sir Jerome. A relacion or memoriall abstracted owt of Sir Jerom Horsey his travells, imploiments, services and negociacions [in Russia 1573–91]. Extract 1598 (in Hakluyt); extract in Purchas; ed E. A. Bond 1856 (Hakluyt Soc); ed L. E. Berry and R. O. Crummey, Rude and barbarous kingdom: Russia in the accounts of 16th-century English voyagers, Madison 1969.

[Ralegh, Sir Walter]. A report of the truth of the fight about the Iles of Acores this last Sommer; betwixt the Revenge, one of her Majesties shippes, and an armada of the King of Spaine. 1591, 1599 (in Hakluyt); ed Astley vol 1, 1745–7; rptd Somers tracts vol 1, 1751, 1809; rptd 1757; rptd Harleian miscellany vol 10, 1808–13 etc; ed Pinkerton vol 1, 1808; rptd in Hakluyt's Collection of the early voyages vol 2, 1809–12; ed E. Arber 1871, 1895; Boston 1902, 1908; ed H. Newbolt 1908; 1915 (facs); Leeds 1967 (facs); Amsterdam and New York 1969 (facs of 1591); tr German by J. J. Schwabe, Allgemeine Historie der Reisen vol 1, Leipzig 1747; French by Abbé Prévost, Histoire des voyages vol 1, Paris 1746.

Seall, Francis. A treatise of my Lord Comberlans shippes voyage (in anno 1592) and of theyr takynge of the great carracte. Ed C. L. Kingsford, Naval miscellany vol 2, 1912 (Navy Records Soc). BM Harley ms 540 fols 111–14.

The sea-mans triumph: declaring the honourable actions of such gentleman captaines and sailers as were at the taking of the great carrick. 1592; rptd in Mr Ashbee's Occasional facs reprints, 1872 (facs).

R., H. Newes from the Levane seas: discribing the many perrilous events of Edward Glenham esquire [in a privateering voyage]. 1594; ed J. P. Collier, Illustrations of early English popular literature vol 1, 1866.

Hasleton, Richard. Strange and wonderfull things happened to Richard Hasleton in his ten yeares travailes in many forraine countries [1582–3 in slavery to the Moors]. 1595; ed E. Arber vol 8 1896, vol 2 1903.

Markham, Gervase. The most honorable tragedie of Sir Richard Grinvile, knight. 1595; ed E. Arber, English reprints, 1871; ed E. Goldsmid, Edinburgh 1883. Verse.

Spelman, William. A dialogue or confabulation betwen two travellers, which treateth of ther hard adventures in the tyme of ther travell through dyvers kingdomes and contries [in Europe]. Ed J. E. L. Pickering 1896 (Roxburghe Club). Written c. 1595.

Warner, William. Albions England: a continued historie of the same kingdome, from the originals of the first inhabitants thereof. 1596, 1597, 1602, 1612; ed A. Chalmers, The works of the English poets vol 4, 1810. The first 3 edns 1586, 1589, 1592 do not include the 11th–12th bks, which contain the Russia voyage narratives as derived from Hakluyt.

Slingsby, Sir William. The voyage to Calis in Andaluzia, faithfully related by Sr W. Slyngisbye employed in that service, AD 1596. Ed J. S. Corbett 1902 (Navy Records Soc). Alnwick ms.

Wright, Edward. The voyage of the Right Ho. George Earle of 1599, Cumberland to the Azores. In his Certaine errors in navigation, 1599, 1599 (in Hakluyt), 1610; rptd Harleian voyages vol 2, 1745, 1747; ed Pinkerton vol 1; ed E. Arber vol 3 1877–97, vol 2 1903–4.

A true report and description of the taking of the iland of St Maries 1599. 1600. Tr from Dutch.

A true report of a great fight at sea between certaine ships belonging to sundrye merchants of England and five well approved ships of warre of the King of Spaines. [1600].

Dallam, Thomas. [The diary of Master Thomas Dallam 1599–1600 of a voyage to Constantinople]. Ed J. T. Bent, Early voyages and travels in the Levant, 1893 (Hakluyt Soc).

Kemp, William. Kemps nine daies wonder, performed in a daunce from London to Norwich. 1600, 1840 (Camden Soc); rptd Mr Ashbee's Occasional facs reprints, 1876; ed E. Arber vol 7, 1883, 1903; ed E. Goldsmid, Edinburgh 1884 (from ms); ed G. B. Harrison, London and New York 1923, 1966.

A true discourse of the late voyage made by the right worshipfull Sir Thomas Sherley the younger, knight. 1602. Unique copy in BM; see R. A. Skelton, BM Quart 22 1960.

A briefe discourse of the memorable voyage to Portugall, anno 1589, by Sir John Norice and Sir Francis Drake. In A true discourse historicall of the succeeding Governours in the Netherlands, 1602. Tr T. Churchyard and R. Robinson from E. van Meteren's Historiae belgicae.

[Timberlake, Henry]. A true and strange discourse of the travailes of two English pilgrimes: what admirable accidents befell them in their journey to Jerusalem, Gaza, Grand Cayro, Alexandria and other places. 1603, 1608, 1609, 1611, 1612, 1616, 1620, 1631; rptd in R. B., Two journeys to Jerusalem, 1683, 1685, 1715, 1759; rptd Harleian miscellany vol 1, 1744 etc; rptd in R. B., Memorable remarks, 1786; rptd in Richard Burton, Judaeorum memorabilia, Bristol 1796.

Sanderson, John. [The travels of John Sanderson in the Levant 1584–1602]. Partly in Purchas; ed W. Foster 1931 (Hakluyt Soc). Written by 1604. BM Lansdowne ms 241.

Sir Thomas Smithes voiage and entertainment in Rushia, with the tragicall ends of two Emperors and one Empresse. 1605.

Tresswell, Robert. A relation of such things as were observed to happen in the journey of Charles Earle of Nottingham Ambassadour to the King of Spaine. 1605; rptd Harleian miscellany vol 2, 1808–13 etc; rptd Somers tracts vol 2, 1752, 1809.

N., A. A true relation of the travels of M. Bush, a gentleman: who made a pynace in which hee past by ayre, land and water from Lamborne to London. 1608.

Barker, Andrew. A true and certaine report of the beginning, proceedings, overthrowes and now present estate of Captaine Ward and Danseker, the two late famous pirates. 1609.

[Biddulph, William]. The travels of certaine Englishmen into Africa, Asia, Troy, Bythinia, Thracia and to the Blacke Sea [and Palestine 1600–8]. 1609, 1612; rptd Purchas; rptd Churchill vol 7, 1747 etc; rptd Harleian voyages vol 1, 1745 etc; Amsterdam and New York 1968 (facs of 1609).

[Veer, Gerrit de]. The true and perfect description of three voyages by the ships of Holland and Zeland, on the north sides of Norway, Muscovia and Tartaria. 1609; rptd Purchas (abridged); rptd Harris vol 1, 1705; rptd Harleian voyages vol 2, 1745 etc; rptd in A selection of curious, rare and early voyages, 1812; ed C. T. Beke 1853 (Hakluyt Soc); ed K. Beynen 1876 (Hakluyt Soc); Amsterdam and New York 1970 (facs of 1609). Tr William Phillip from the Waerachtige beschrijvinghe van drie seylagien, Amsterdam 1598.

Coryat, Thomas. Coryats crudities, hastily gobled up in five moneths travells. 1611; rptd Purchas; 3 vols 1776, 2 vols Glasgow 1905. See also Voyages to Asia.

A true declaration of the arrival of Cornelius Haga (with others that accompanied him) ambassador for the General States of the United Netherlands, at the great city of Constantinople, faithfully translated out of the Dutch copy. 1613; rptd Harleian miscellany vol 8, 1746 etc.

[Fotherbie, Robert]. A short discourse of a voyage made 1613 to the late discovered countrye of Greenland [= Spitzbergen], and a briefe discription of the same countrie. Archaeologia Americana 4 1860; ed C. R. Markham, The voyages of William Baffin 1881 (Hakluyt Soc). From ms in Library of Amer Antiquarian Soc, Worcester Mass.

Davies, William. A true relation of the travailes and most miserable captivitie of William Davies, barber-surgion of London, under the Duke of Florence. 1614; rptd Harleian voyages vol 1, 1745, 1747.

Sandys, George. A relation of a journey begun an. dom. 1610: foure bookes containing a description of the Turkish Empire, of Aegypt, of the holy land, of the remote parts of Italy, and ilands adjoyning. 1615, 1621; extract in Purchas, 1627, 1632, 1637; as Sandys travailes, 1652, 1658, 1670, 1673; extract in Harris vol 2, 1705 etc; rptd 1864; tr Dutch, 1653, 1654, 1654, 1659, 1665; German, 1669.

R., H. A true relation of a most worthy and notable fight [June 1616] by two small shippes of the citie of London, the Vineyard and the Unicorne, against six great gallies of Tunes in the Straights. [1616].

Moryson, Fynes. A itinerary written by Fynes Moryson gent: containing his ten yeers travell through the twelve dominions of Germany, Bohmerland, Switzerland, Netherland, Denmarke, Poland, Italy, Turky, France, England, Scotland and Ireland. 1617, Dublin 1735 (section on Ireland); ed H. Morley 1890 (section on Ireland); ed C. Hughes, Shakespeare's Europe 1903, 1967 (pt 4); 4 vols Glasgow 1907–8 (complete).

Taylor, John. Three weekes, three daies and three houres observation and travel from London to Hamburgh. 1617; rptd in Workes, 1630; in Workes, Manchester 1869 (Spenser Soc); ed C. Hindley, Works, 1872; rptd in Early prose and poetical works, 1888.

— A fight at sea famously fought by the Dolphin of London, against five of the Turkes men of warre and a

satty 1616. 1617; in Workes, 1630; rptd Workes, Manchester 1869 (Spenser Soc); ed E. Arber vol 2 1879, 1903.

— The pennyles pilgrimage: or the moneylesse perambulation of John Taylor, on foot from London to Edenborough. 1618; in Workes, 1630; rptd Workes, Manchester 1869 (Spenser Soc); ed C. Hindley, Works, 1872; rptd Early prose and poetical works, 1888.

— Taylor his travels: from the citty of London in England to the citty of Prague in Bohemia. 1620; in Workes, 1630; Workes, Manchester 1869 (Spenser Soc).

— The voyage of Mr Roger Bird and the writer hereof, in a boat of browne-paper, from London to Quinborough in Kent. In The praise of hemp-seed, 1620; rptd in Workes, 1630; in Workes, Manchester 1869 (Spenser Soc).

— A verry merry wherry-ferry-voyage: or Yorke for my money. 1622; in Workes, 1630; in Workes, Manchester 1869; ed C. Hindley, Works, 1872; in Early prose and poetical works, 1888.

— Prince Charles his welcome from Spaine, and the relation of such townes as are scituate in the wayes to take post-horse at from London to Dover, and from Callice to Madrid. 1623; in Workes, 1630; rptd Somers tracts vol 2, 1809; Workes, Manchester 1869.

— A new discovery by sea, with a wherry from London to Salisbury. 1623; in Workes, 1630; in Workes, Manchester 1869; ed C. Hindley, Works, 1872; in Early prose and poetical works, 1888.

— A famous fight at sea. 1627; in Workes, 1630; in Workes, Manchester 1869. See Voyages to Asia, below.

— Taylor on Thame Isis; or the description of the two famous rivers of Thame and Isis. 1632; rptd in Works not included in the folio volume vol 1, Manchester 1870 (Spenser Soc).

— A brave and memorable and dangerous sea fight foughten neere the road of Tittawan in Barbary. [1636].

— Taylors travels and circular perambulation of the famous cities of London and Westminster. 1636; rptd in Workes not included in the folio volume vol 2, Manchester 1873 (Spenser Soc).

— The honorable and memorable foundations, erections, raisings and ruines of divers cities within ten shires; also a relation of the wine tavernes. 1636, 1636; rptd in Works not included in the folio volume vol 4, Manchester 1877 (Spenser Soc); rptd 1889.

— The carriers cosmographie: or a briefe relation of the innes, in and neere London, where the carriers doe usually come. 1637; rptd in Works not included in the folio volume vol 2, Manchester 1873; rptd Mr Ashbee's Occasional facs reprints, 1869; ed E. Arber vol 1, 1877, vol 1, 1903.

— Part of this summers travels: or news from Hell, Hull and Hallifax. [1639]; rptd in Works not included in the folio volume vol 1, Manchester 1870; C. Hindley, Works, 1872; rptd Early prose and poetical works, 1888.

— A valorous and perillous sea-fight, fought with three Turkish ships, pirats or men of warre, on the coast of Cornewall by the good ship named the Elizabeth of Plimmoth. 1640; rptd as A brave and valiant sea fight, 1640; rptd Works not included vol 4, Manchester 1877.

— John Taylors last voyage and adventure, performed with a scullers boate, from London to Oxford, Gloucester and Hereford. 1641; rptd Works not included vol 2, Manchester 1873.

— Tailors travels, from London to the Isle of Wight. 1648; ed J. O. Halliwell (-Phillipps), Literature of the 16th and 17th centuries illustrated, 1851; rptd in Works not included vol 4, Manchester 1877.

— John Taylors wandering to see the wonders of the west: how he travelled from London to Lands end and home againe. 1649, 1670; rptd Mr Ashbee's Occasional facs reprints, 1869; rptd Works not included vol 1, Manchester 1870; ed C. Hindley 1872.

—— A late weary merry voyage from London to Gravesend, to Cambridge. 1650.

—— A short relation of a long journey made round or ovall by encompassing the principalitie of Wales. 1653; ed J. O. Halliwell(-Phillipps) 1859; rptd Works not included vol 1, Manchester 1870; ed C. Hindley 1872.

—— The certain travailes of an uncertain journey [in Sussex and Kent]. 1653; ed C. Hindley 1872; rptd Works not included vol 2, Manchester 1873.

Bernard, Richard. The fabulous foundation of the Popedome; thereunto is added a chronologicall description of Paules peregrination with Peters travells, and the reasons why he could not be at Rome. Oxford 1619.

Buenting, Heinrich. Itinerarium totius sacrae scripturae: or the travels of the Holy Patriarchs, Prophets, Judges, Kings, our Saviour Christ and his Apostles, done into English by R.B. 1619, 1623, 1629, 1636, 1705. From the German original, Helmstadt 1581 etc.

B[utton], J. Algiers voyage in a journall: or briefe reportory of all occurrents hapning in the fleet of ships sent out against the pirates of Algiers. 1621; rptd Purchas; ed E. P. Statham, History of the family of Maunsell vol 1, 1917. From PRO SP Dom, Jas I 122, no 106.

Rawlins, John. The famous and wonderfull recoverie of a ship of Bristoll called the Exchange from the Turkish pirates of Argier. 1622; rptd Purchas; rptd Arber vol 4, 1877, 1903.

Wynne, Sir Richard. [Relation of the journey of Prince Charles to Madrid, 1623]. Ed T. Hearne, Historia Ricardi II, 1729; ed J. O. Halliwell (-Phillipps), Autobiography of Sir Simonds D'Ewes vol 2, 1845.

Monson, Sir William. [The Naval Tracts, in six books. Books 1 and 2 relating to naval voyages to date of first writing 1624]. Megalopsychy, 1682 (in part, as A true and exact account of the wars with Spain in the reign of Queen Elizabeth); Churchill vol 3, 1704–32 etc (complete); ed M. Oppenheim 1902–14 (Navy Records Soc) (from ms).

Glanville, Sir John. A relation touching the fleete and armie of King Charles, sett forth in the first year of his Highnes raigne [to Cadiz]. Ed A. B. Grosart 1883 (Camden Soc), 1965. From Eliot ms, written 1625.

Cecil, Edward, Viscount Wimbledon. A journall and relation of the action which Edward Lord Cecyl did undertake upon the coast of Spaine. 1626, 1627; Amsterdam and New York 1968 (facs of 1626); tr German, 1628.

—— [A defence of his action against the charge by the Earl of Essex and others]. In Sir Richard Granville, Two original journals, 1724.

A true relation of a brave English stratagem practised lately upon a sea-towne in Galizia by an English ship alone of 30 tonne. 1626; ed E. Arber vol 1, 1877, 1903.

Granville, Sir Richard. A journal of the expedition to the Isle of Rhee in France, anno 1627. In Two original journals, 1724.

A relation of a brave and resolute sea-fight, made by Sir Kenelam Digby on the Bay of Scandarone, with certaine galegasses and galeasses, belonging to the States of Venice. In Articles of agreement made betweene the French King and those of Rochell, 1628.

Digby, Sir Kenelm. [Journal of a voyage into the Mediterranean 1628]. Ed J. Bruce 1868 (Camden Soc) (from ms).

Robson, Charles. Newes from Aleppo: a letter [concerning his voyage] by Charles Robson, preacher to the company of our English merchants at Aleppo. 1628.

Cooper, Capt Dawtrey. [A sea-diary of the La Rochelle expedition of 1628]. Ed S. I. Bruce, Three sea journals of Stuart times, 1936.

Wadsworth, James. The English Spanish pilgrime: or a new discoverie of Spanish popery, and Jesuiticall stratagems. 1629, 1630, 1630; Amsterdam and New York 1970 (facs of 1629). Travels in Spain, France and Flanders.

—— Further observations of the English Spanish pilgrime, concerning Spaine. 1630, 1630.

—— The present estate of Spayne: or a true relation of some remarkable things touching the Court and government of Spayne. 1630, 1630.

Pellham, Edward. Gods power and providence, shewed in the miraculous preservation and deliverance of eight Englishmen, left by mischance in Green-land [= Spitzbergen], anno 1630. 1631; rptd Churchill vol 4, 1704–32 etc; ed A. White 1855 (Hakluyt Soc).

Mundy, Peter. [The travels of Peter Mundy to Spain and Turkey 1617–28; in S. England 1635; in England and Wales 1639; to Danzig and Archangel 1639–47]. Written as Relations 1–2, 20, 31, 31–5 of the Itinerarium Mundii, first draft completed 1634; ed R. C. Temple 1907–24 (Hakluyt Soc). BM Harley ms 2286, copied and continued in Bodley ms Rawlinson A 315. See Voyages to Asia, below.

A relation of a short survey of 26 counties [north from Norwich], observed in a seven weeks journey begun 1634, by a Captain and a Lieutenant, and an Ancient. Newcastle 1847 (in part); ed L. G. Wickham Legg 1904 (complete), Camden miscellany 1936; in R. P. Chope, Early tours in Devon and Cornwall, Exeter 1918 (in part), Newton Abbot 1967; in R. Douch, Southampton 1540–1956: visitors' descriptions, Southampton 1961 (extract).

Brereton, Sir William. The journal of Sir William Brereton, 1634 [to Holland]. In Chetham Society remains vol 1, 1844.

—— The journal of Sir William Brereton, 1635 [to northern England, Scotland, norther Ireland]. In Chetham Society remains vol 1, 1844; ed M. A. Richardson, Newcastle 1847–9 (facs).

Blount, Henry. A voyage into the Levant: a briefe relation of a journey, lately performed [1634–6] from England by the way of Venice, into Dalmatia, Sclavonia, Bosnah, Hangary, Macedonia, Thessaly, Thrace, Rhodes and Egypt. 1636, 1637, 1638, 1650, 1664, 1669, 1671; rptd Churchill vol 1, 1747 etc; rptd Harleian voyages vol 1, 1745, 1747; rptd Pinkerton vol 10 1811; tr Dutch 1707; German, 1687.

Poyntz, Sydnam. A true relation of these German warres from Mansfield's going out of England which was in the yeare (1624) untill this last yeare 1636. Ed A. T. S. Goodrick 1908 (Camden Soc). Bibliothèque Nationale ms, Fonds Anglais 55.

Crowne, William. A true relation of all the remarkable places and passages observed in the travels of Thomas Lord Howard, ambassadour extraordinary to his sacred Majesty Ferdinand the Emperour of Germanie, anno domini 1636. 1637, 1871 (Camden Soc); ed F. C. Springell, Connoisseur and diplomat, 1963; Amsterdam and New York 1971 (facs of 1637).

Monro, Robert. Monro his expedition with the worthy Scots regiment levied in August 1626 for his Majesties service of Denmark. 2 pts 1637.

Dunton, John. A true journall of the Sally fleet, with the proceedings of the voyage; whereunto is annexed a list of Sally captives names and places where they dwell. 1637; rptd Harleian voyages vol 2, 1745, 1747; rptd Churchill vol 8, 1752.

Mayeres, Randulph. Mayeres his travels: containing a true recapitulation of all the remarkable passages which befell in the authors peregrinations and voyages. [1638]. Military and naval. Partly in verse.

Carteret, Sir George. [The Barbary voyage of 1638]. Ed B. Penrose, Philadelphia 1929 (from ms).

Aston, John. [The journal of John Aston to Scotland 1639]. Ed J. Crawford Hodgson 1910 (Surtees Soc).

Two famous sea-fights lately made betwixt the fleetes of the King of Spaine and the fleets of the Hollanders: the one in the West-Indyes; the other betwixt Callis and Gravelin. 1639.

Carve, Thomas. Itinerarium R.D. Thomae Carve Tipperariensis; Sacellani maioris in legione streniussimi domini Colonelli D. Walteri Deveroux. Mainz 1639, 1640, 1641, Speyer 1646; ed M. Kerney 1859; tr German 1640.

Drunken Barnby's four journies to the north of England, in Latin and English metre. 1640.

Knight, Francis. A relation of seaven yeares slaverie under the Turkes of Argeire, suffered by an English captive merchant. 1640, 1640; rptd Harleian voyages vol 2, 1745, 1747.

Sad news from the seas: being a relation of the losse of that good ship the Merchant Royall, which was cast away ten leagues from the Lands end. 1641.

Joyfull newes from sea: or good tidings from my Lord of Warwicke, of his encounter with some Spanish ships [off Ireland], with the happy successe he obtained thereby. 1642.

Newes from Sally: of a strange delivery of foure English captives [taken on a return voyage from La Rochelle] from the slavery of the Turkes. 1642; ed J. A. Foster, Ingram Pa 1939.

Edward, Baron Herbert of Cherbury. The life of Edward Lord Herbert of Cherbury [including his continental travels 1608-24, written c. 1643]. Strawberry Hill 1765, London 1770, Dublin 1771, London 1778, 1792, 1824, 1826, 1827, 1830, 1853, Boston 1877, London 1877; ed S. Lee 1886, 1906; ed W. H. Dircks 1888; 1904; ed W. H. D. Rouse 1912; ed C. H. Herford, Newtown Montgomeryshire 1928.

— Expeditio in Ream insulam, anno 1630. Ed T. Baldwin 1656; rptd as The expedition to the Isle of Rhe, 1860 (Philobiblon Soc) (from ms).

Evelyn, John. Memoirs illustrative of the life and writings of John Evelyn comprising his diary [with account of his travels in the Low Countries 1641 and in France, Italy and Switzerland, 1643-7]. Ed W. Bray 2 vols 1818 etc; ed H. B. Wheatley 1879, 1906; ed A. Dobson 1904; ed E. S. de Beer 6 vols Oxford 1955, 1 vol 1959 (OSA).

Raymond, John. An itinerary, contayning a voyage he made through Italy in the years 1646 and 1647, illustrated with divers figures of antiquities. 1648.

The Common-Wealths great ship commonly called the Soveraigne of the Seas, built in the yeare 1637; with all the fights we have had with the Hollander, since the engagement of Lieutenant-Admirall Trompe neer Dover, against the English fleet under the command of Generall Blake. 1653.

Flecknoe, Richard. A relation of ten years travells in Europe, Asia, Affrique and America [1652-4], all by way of letters occasionally written to divers noble personages. [1654], 1665.

Hane, Joachim. A short relacion of the severall wonderfull passages which I did meete withall in my jorney into France [1653-4]. Ed C. H. Firth as The journal of Joachim Hane, Oxford 1896.

Whitelocke, Bulstrode. [A journal of the Swedish Embassy in the years 1653 and 1654]. Ed C. Morton 2 vols 1772; ed H. Reeve 2 vols 1885.

Weale, John. Perfect journal of my voyage to Ligorne 1654. Ed J. R. Powell 1952 (Navy Records Soc) (from ms).

Brett, Samuel. A narrative of the proceedings of a great council of Jews, assembled in the Plain of Ageda in Hungaria; also a relation of some other observations in his travels beyond the seas. 1655; in Nathaniel Crouch, A journey to Jerusalem, 1666; rptd in T.H., Two journeys to Jerusalem, 1683; rptd in R.B., Two journeys, 1685, 1715, 1759; rptd Phenix vol 1, 1707 etc; rptd Robert Clayton, Bishop of Killala, A dissertation on Prophecy, 1749; rptd in R.B., Memorable remarks upon the Jewish nation, 1786; ed N. H. Keene 1795; rptd in Richard Burton, Judaeorum memorabilia, 1796; rptd Harleian miscellany vol 1, 1744, 1753, 1808, vol 6, 1810; rptd 1876.

Penn, Sir William. [Journals of various naval services

1644-55 and later]. Ed Granville Penn, Memorials of Sir William Penn, 2 vols 1833.

A briefe relation or remonstrance of the injurious proceedings and inhumane cruelties of the Turks [of Alexandria], perpetrated on the commander and company of the ship Lewis of London. [1657].

Blake, Robert. Letters [1644-57]. Ed J. R. Powell 1937 (Navy Records Soc) (from ms).

Bispham, Thomas. Iter australe, a reginensibus oxon. anno 1658 expeditum. [Oxford 1658]. Latin verse on a journey in southern England.

Reresby, Sir John, Bart. [Travels to Italy 1654-8]. In The travels and memoirs, 1813, 1904; ed A. Browning 1936.

Mortoft, Francis. Francis Mortoft his book: being his travels through France and Italy 1658-9. Ed M. Letts 1925 (Hakluyt Soc). BM Sloane ms 2142.

Iter Carolinum: being a succinct relation of the necessitated marches, retreats and sufferings of his Majesty Charles the I [1641-8], collected by a daily attendant. 1660; rptd Somers tracts vol 2, 1751, vol 5 1809; rptd Collecteana curiosa vol 2, 1781; ed H. S. Crowe, Royalist revelations and the truth about Charles I, 1922.

Ghiselin de Busbecq, Ogier. Omnia quae extant. Oxford 1660; rptd with Georgievitz 1570 (see below); tr 1694 (in part), 1744, Glasgow 1761, Oxford 1927; tr C. E. Forster 2 vols 1881 (complete).

The British Isles

Bede. Historiae ecclesiasticae gentis Anglorum libri v. [Strasbourg 1475] etc; rptd in Opera omnia, Basle 8 vols 1563 etc; ed A. Wheloc, Cambridge 1643, 2 vols 1644. 1722 etc.

— History of the Church of Englande. [Tr T. Stapleton], Antwerp 1565, St Omer 1622, 1626 etc; ed P. Hereford, Oxford 1930, London 1935; Amsterdam and New York 1970 (facs of 1565).

Higden, Ranulf. Therfor I entende to sette in this booke the discripcion of this said Ile of Britayne. 1480, 1498; also as bk 1 of Polychronicon, 1482, 1495, 1527; appended to This present cronycle of Englonde, 1497, 1502, 1504, 1510, 1515, 1515, 1520, 1528; tr John Trevisa 1377. Polychronicon rptd New York 1931 (facs); Amsterdam and New York 1971 (facs of 1481). BM Cotton ms Tiberius D vii; Trevisa trn.

Major, John. De Britanniae descriptione. In Historia majoris Britanniae, tam Angliae quam Scotiae bk 1, Paris 1521, Edinburgh 1740; tr A. Constable 1892 (Scottish Historical Soc).

Boethius, Hector. Scotorum regni descriptio. In his Scotorum historiae a prima gentis origine, [Paris 1526], Paris 1575; tr John Bellenden, Heir beginnis the hystory and croniklis of Scotland, Edinburgh [1540?]; ed T. Maitland, Works of John Bellenden vols 1-2, Edinburgh 1822; tr 'out of the Scotish' by William Harrison, The description of Scotlande, in Raphael Holinshed, The firste volume of the chronicles of England, 1577, 1587, 1805, 1807; tr Italian by Petruccio Ubaldino, Descrittione del regno di Scotia, Antwerp (or London) 1588.

Ben, John. Descriptio insularum Orchadiarum, anno 1529, per me Joannem Ben ibidem Colentem. In G. Barry, History of the Orkney Islands, Edinburgh 1805, 1808, Kirkwall 1867; rptd 1908 (Scottish Historical Soc).

Caesar, Gaius Julius. Julius Caesars commentaryes, newly translated owte of Laten in to Englyshe [by John Tiptoft], as much as concernyth thys realm of England. 1530.

— The eyght bookes of C. Julius Caesar conteyning his martiall exploytes in the realme of Gallia. 1565, 1578, 1590. Tr Arthur Golding.

— C. Julii Caesaris Commentarii. 1585, 1590, 1601.

— Observations upon Caesars comentaries. 1609, [1609]. Ed and tr C. Edmundes.

— The commentaries of C. Julius Caesar. 1655, 1677, 1695, 1719. Tr C. Edmundes.

Vergil, Polydore. De divisione Britanniae. In his Anglicae historiae libri xxvi, Basle 1534, 1546, 2 vols Ghent 1556–7; in libri xxvii, Basle 1555, 1556, 1557, 1570, 2 vols Douay 1603, Leyden 1651; tr 1846 (Camden Soc), 1950; Menston 1972 (facs of 1555).

Borde, Andrew. The peregrination of Doctor Boarde. Ed T. Hearne, De vita et gestis Henrici II vol 2, Oxford 1735. Written c. 1542.

[Lindsay, Alexander]. La navigation du Roy d'Escosse Jaques cinquiesme autour de son royaume [1546]. Paris 1583. A routier tr Nicolas de Nicolay; retr in Miscellanea antiqua, 1710, Miscellanea scotica vol 3, Glasgow 1819.

Monro, Sir Donald. A description of the Westerne Isles of Scotland by Mr Donald Monro, quho travelled through maney of them in anno 1549. Edinburgh 1774, 1805; Miscellanea scotica vol 2, Glasgow 1884; 1884; rptd 1908 (Scottish Historical Soc).

[Edward Walshe, Conjectures concerning the state of Ireland [1552]]. Ed D. B. Quinn, Irish Historical Stud 5 1947.

Bale, John. Descriptiones Angliae, Scotiae, Hyberniae. In his Illustrium majoris Brytanniae scriptorum, 1548, 1549, Basle 1557–9. Compiled from Paulus Jovius, George Lily, John Leland and Polydore Virgil.

Talbot, Robert. Annotationes in eam partem itinerarii Antonini quae ad Britanniam pertinet. Ed T. Hearne, Oxford 1712 etc (with Leland's Itinerary). Written c. 1558.

B., J., Gentleman. A letter sent by J.B. gentleman unto his very frende Mayster R.C. Esquire, wherin is contained a large discourse of the peopling & inhabiting the cuntrie called the Ardes and other adjacent in the north of Ireland. [1572].

Llwyd, Humphrey. Commentarioli Brittanicae descriptionis fragmentum. Cologne 1572; ed Moses Williams 1731; tr Thomas Twyne as The breviary of Britayne, 1573; rptd in J. Lewis, The history of Great Britain, 1729.

— De Mona druidum insula. In Sir John Pryce, Historiae Brytanniae defensio, 1573; in Ortelius, Parergon, Antwerp 1579 etc; 1731 (with preceding); tr in Ortelius, Theatre of the whole world, 1606.

— A description of Cambria. In The history of Cambria now called Wales, 1584, 1697, 1774, 1811, Merthyr 1812, Shrewsbury 1832.

Erdeswicke, Sampson. Certaine verie rare observations of the north countrie. 1574, Newcastle 1848. Attributed to Erdeswicke; BM Harley ms 473.

— A survey of Staffordshire: containing the antiquities of that county. 1717, 1723; ed S. Shaw, The history of Staffordshire, 1798; ed T. Horwood 1820, 1844. Written 1591–1603; entered Stationers' register 1656–7.

Saxton, Christopher S. An atlas of England and Wales: the maps of Christopher Saxton 1574–9. Ed E. Lynam 1937.

Hooker, John. The description of the cittie of Excester, collected and gathered by John Vowel alias Hooker. [1576], Exeter 1765, 1775, 1919 (Devon & Cornwall Record Soc).

Lambard, William. A perambulation of Kent: conteining the description, hystorie and customes of that shyre. 1576, 1576, 1596, [1640], 1656, Chatham 1826; ed R. Church, Bath 1970 (facs).

— Dictionarium Angliae topographicum et historicum. 1730. Compiled c. 1577.

Harrison, William. An historicall description of the islande of Britayne. In Raphael Holinshed, The firste volume of the chronicles of England, 1577, 1587, 1805, 1807 etc; ed F. J. Furnivall, Harrison's description of England in Shakespere's youth, 1877–81, 1966 (with 2nd–3rd bks of his Description of Britsine, ed from first 2 edns of Holinshed's Chronicle); ed G. Edelen, Ithaca 1968 (Folger Lib) (based on 1587 edn of Holinshed collated with Furnivall's edn of Harrison).

Stanyhurst, Richard. A treatise conteining a plaine and perfect description of Ireland, compiled by Richard Stanihurst. In Raphael Holinshed, Chronicles vol 2, 1577, 1586, 1805, 1807 etc.

— De rebus in Hibernia gestis, libri quattuor. Antwerp 1584. Bk 1 is descriptive.

Leslie, John. Regionum et insularum Scotiae descriptio. In De origine, moribus et rebus gestis Scotorum, Rome 1578; Amsterdam 1675; rptd in S. Jebb, De vita Mariae Reginae vol 1, 1725; tr in James Dalrymple, The historie of Scotland, 1596, 1888 (STS).

Merrick, Rice. Morganiae archaiographia [c. 1578]. Ed T. Phillipps, A book of Glamorganshire antiquities, Middle Hill 1825, London 1887. From ms at the Queen's College, Oxford.

Derricke, John. The image of Irelande, with a discourse of Woodkarne, wherin is most lively expressed the nature and qualitie of the saied wilde Irish Woodkarne. 1581; rptd Somers tracts vol 1, 1809; ed J. Small, Edinburgh 1883 (facs).

Buchanan, George. [A description of Scotland]. In Rerum scoticarum historia, Edinburgh 1582, 1583, Frankfurt 1584, 1594, 1624, Utrecht 1668, 1697, Edinburgh 1700, 1727, Aberdeen 1762; pbd also in Elzevir Respublica Scotiae, Leyden 1627; tr as The history of Scotland, 1690 etc; tr Spanish in J. Blaeu, Atlas major vol 4, Amsterdam 1659; tr French in J. Blaeu, Le grand atlas vol 6, Amsterdam 1667.

Smith, Sir Thomas. De republica Anglorum: the maner of government or policie of the realme of England. 1583, 1584, 1589 (as The Commonwelth of England), 1594, 1601, 1609, 1612, 1621, 1633, 1635, 1640, 1691; ed L. Alston and F. W. Maitland, Cambridge 1906; Amsterdam and New York 1970 (facs of 1583); tr Latin, [1610], 1625, 1630, 1641; Dutch, 1673 (in part); German, 1688.

Smith, William. The Vale-Royall of England: or the County Palatine of Chester [written 1585]. 1656; ed and expanded by G. Ormerod, History of the County Palatine vol 1, 1819, 1882.

— The particuler description of England, with the portratures of certaine of the chieffest citties and townes. Ed H. B. Wheatley and E. W. Ashbee 1879. Written 1588. BM Sloane ms 2596.

Cambrensis, Giraldus. See Voyages in Europe, 1585, above.

Camden, William. Britannia: sive florentissimorum regnorum Angliae, Scotiae, Hiberniae chorographica descriptio. 2 pts 1586, 1 vol 1587, Frankfurt 1590, London 1590, 1594, 1600, 1607, Frankfurt 1616; rptd in Epitomen contracta a R. Vitellio, Amsterdam 1617, 1639; tr Philemon Holland as Britain: or a chorographicall description, 1610, 1637, 1695, 2 vols 1722, 1753, 1772; ed R. Gough 3 vols 1789, 1806; ed S. Piggott and G. Walters, Newton Abbot 1971 (facs of 1695); abridged as The abridgement of Camdens Britannia, 1626, 2 vols 1701.

— Remaines of a greater worke concerning Britaine: but especially England and the inhabitants thereof. 1605, 1614, 1623, 1629, 1636, 1637, 1657, 1674, 1856, 1870.

Churchyard, Thomas. The worthines of Wales: wherein are more than a thousand severall things rehearsed. 1587, 1776, Manchester 1876 (Spenser Soc).

Payne, Robert. A briefe description of Ireland, made in this year 1589 by Robert Payne unto xxv of his partners. 1589, 1590, Dublin 1841 (Irish Archaeological Soc).

Norden, John. Speculum Britanniae: the first parte an historicall, chorographicall discription of Middlesex. 1593, 1637, 1723; rptd in part as Notes on London and Westminster 1592 by J. Norden from his Description of Middlesex, ptd W. B. Rye in England as seen by foreigners in the days of Elizabeth and James I, 1865.

— Essex discribed by Jo. Norden [1594]. Ed H. Ellis 1840 (Camden Soc). Hatfield ms.

— Norden's preparative to his Speculum Britanniae, intended a reconciliation of sundrie propositions by divers persons tended. 1596, 1723 (with the description of Middlesex and Hartfordshire).

— Speculi Britanniae pars: the description of Hartford-shire. 1598, 1723 (with above), Ware 1903; Amsterdam and New York 1971 (facs of 1598).

— Speculi Britanniae pars altera: or a delineation of Northamptonshire. [1610], 1720.

— England: an intended guyde for English travailers, shewing in generall how far one citie and many shire townes in England are distant from other. 1625, 1635, 1643, [1677], 1680.

— Speculi Britanniae pars: a topographical and choro-graphical description of Cornwall. 1728.

— The chorography of Norfolk: an historicall and choro-graphicall description of Norffolk. Ed C. M. Hood 1938. Ed from ms. Formerly attributed to Thomas Beckham.

[Monipennie, John]. Description of whole Scotland, with all the iles and names thereof. In his Certaine matters composed together, Edinburgh [1594], [1597], 1603; rptd Somers tracts vol 3, 1809.

— A true description and division of the whole realme of Scotland. In Abridgement or summarie of the Scots chronicles, 1612, 1612, Edinburgh 1633, 1650, 1662, 1671, 1756; in Miscellanea scotica vol 1, 1818; Glasgow 1671, 1820.

Stow, John. A survay of London: contayning the originall antiquity, increase, modern estate and description of that citie. 1598, 1599, 1603, 1618, 1633, 2 vols 1720, 1734-5, 1753, 1754-5; ed W. J. Thoms 1842, 1876; ed H. Morley 1890, 1893, [1908]; ed C. L. Kingsford 3 vols Oxford 1908-27; ed H. B. Wheatley 1912 (EL), 1956 (rev).

[A discourse of Ireland c. 1599]. Ed D. B. Quinn, Proc Royal Irish Acad 47 1942.

Dymmok, John. A treatise of Ireland. Ed R. Butler 1843 (Irish Archaeological Soc). c. 1600. BM Harley ms 1291.

[Coryat, George]. Descriptio Angliae, et descriptio Londini: two poems in Latin verse. Written c. 1600.

Carew, Richard. The survey of Cornwall. 1602; ed H. C. (P. des Maizeaux) 1723, 1769; ed T. Tonkin and F. Baron de Dunstanville 1811; ed F. E. Holliday 1953; Amsterdam and New York 1969 (facs).

Harington, Sir John. A short view of Ireland written in anno 1605. Ed W. D. Macray, Anecdota bodleiana vol 1, Oxford 1879.

Rich, Barnaby. A new description of Ireland: wherein is described the disposition of the Irish whereunto they are inclined. 1610.

Speed, John. The theatre of the empire of Great Britain: presenting an exact geography of the kingdomes of England, Scotland, Ireland and iles adjoyning. 1611, 1614, 1615, [1623], 1623, 1627, 1646, 1650, 1676 (with A prospect of the most famous parts of the world); The Countie Palatine of Chester, in C. Hulbert, Cheshire antiquities, 1838 (in part); History of the Isle of Man [extract of 1627], Manx Soc vol 18, Douglas 1859 etc (in part); Speed's England: a coloured facsimile of the maps and text from the Theatre 1611, ed J. Arlott 1953 (in part); ed J. E. Rawnsley, Wakefield 1970 (facs of pt 2 of 1676).

— A description of England and Wales. Bound sheets as taken from Theatre, above, each county dated 1615.

— England, Wales, Scotland and Ireland described and abridged from a farr larger voulume. [1620], 1627 (3 issues), 1666; ed E. G. R. Taylor as An atlas of Tudor England and Wales from Speed's pocket atlas of 1627, 1951.

Drayton, Michael. Poly-Olbion. [1612]; rptd as Poly-Olbion: or a chorographicall description of this renowned Isle of Great Britaine, 1613, 1622; rptd Works, 1748, 1753; ed R. Anderson, Poets of Great Britain vol 3, 1793; ed A. Chalmers, English poets vol 4, 1810; ed

Southey, Select works of British poets, 1831; 1856 (Roxburghe Club); rptd Works, 1876; rptd Manchester 1889 (Spenser Soc); ed J. W. Hebel, Works vol 4, 1933, Oxford 1962; ed J. Buxton 1953 (abridged).

Gentleman, Tobias. Englands way to win wealth and to employ ships and mariners; and also a discourse of the sea-coast townes of England, and the most fit and com-modious places and harbours that we have for Busses, by Tobias Gentleman, fisherman and mariner. 1614, 1660; Harleian miscellany vol 3, 1744, 1808; ed E. Arber vol 4, 1877, 1903.

Thornes, Edward. Encomium Salopiae: or the descrip-tion of the pleasant situation of the ancient and famous towne of Shrowesbury. 1615. Verse.

Gainsford, Thomas. The glory of England: or a true description of many excellent prerogatives and remark-able blessings, whereby she triumpheth over all the nations of the world. 1618, 1619, 1620, 1622; rptd in D. B. Quinn, The Elizabethans and the Irish, Ithaca 1966 (Folger Lib) (in part).

Manship, Henry, the younger. [The history of Great Yarmouth, written 1619]. Ed C. J. Palmer, Great Yarmouth 1854 (from ms).

[Taylor, John]. The cold tearme, or the frozen age: or the metamorphosis of the river of Thames. 1621.

Burton, William. The description of Leicester Shire: containing matters of antiquitye, historye, armorye and genealogy. [1622], Lynn 1777; J. Nichols, The history of the County of Leicester, 1795.

Laet, Joannes de. Respublica sive status regni Scotiae et Hiberniae. Leyden 1627. From Buchanan, Camden, Boethius, Morrison, Giraldus, Stanihurst.

— Angliae chorographica descriptio. In Thomae Smithi Angli de republica Anglorum, Leydem 1630. From Camden, Speed, Barclay, Lambard.

Ane description of certaine pairts of the highlands of Scotland [c. 1630]. Ed A. Mitchell, Edinburgh 1906 (Scottish Historical Soc) (from ms).

Dodridge, Sir John. The history of the ancient and moderne estate of the principality of Wales, Dutchy of Cornewall and Earldom of Chester. 1630, 1714.

Bedwell, Wilhelm. A briefe description of the towne of Tottenham High-Crosse in Middlesex. 1631, 1718; ed W. Robinson, The history and antiquities of the parish of Tottenham High Cross, 1818; ed W. J. Roe, Ancient Tottenham, 1950.

Campion, Edmund. [A description of Ireland: 7 chs of] The historie of Ireland. Ed Sir James Ware, Dublin 1633, Amsterdam and New York 1971 (facs); rptd in Ancient Irish histories, Dublin 1809, Port Washington 1970 (facs); ed R. B. Gottfried, New York 1940 (facs); ed A. F. Vossen, Two bokes of the histories of Ireland, Assen 1963 (from Bodley ms Jones 6).

Spenser, Edmund. A view of the present state of Ireland. Ed Sir James Ware, The historie of Ireland, Dublin 1633, above; Dublin 1763; in Ancient Irish histories, Dublin 1809, Port Washington 1970 (facs); in A collec-tion of tracts and treatises illustrative of the political state of Ireland vol 1, 1860 etc; ed H. Morley, Ireland under Elizabeth and James I, 1890; ed W. L. Renwick 1934 (from ms 188,221 Caius College, Cambridge).

Stafford, Sir Thomas. Pacata Hibernia, Ireland appeased and reduced: or an historie of the late warres of Ireland, especially within the province of Mounster under the government of Sir George Carew [1599-1602]. 1633, 2 vols Dublin 1810; ed S. O'Grady 2 vols 1896.

A direction for the English traviller, by which he shall be inabled to coast about all England and Wales. 1633, 1636, 1643; rptd as A book of the names of all parishes, market towns etc in England and Wales, 1657, 1662, 1668, 1677, Amsterdam and New York 1969 (facs of 1636).

Somner, William. The antiquities of Canterbury: or a survey of that ancient citie with the suburbs and cathedrall. 1640, 1703.

Peacham, Henry. The art of living in London: or a caution how gentlemen, countreymen and strangers, thrown by occasion of businesse, should dispose of themselves in the thriftiest way, not onely in the city, but in all other populous places. 1642; Harleian miscellany vol 9, 1808 etc; ed V. B. Heltzel, Ithaca 1962 (Folger Lib).

N., G. A geographicall description of the kingdom of Ireland, according to the 5 provinces, and 32 counties. 1642.

[Pont, Timothy]. Noates and observations of dyvers parts of the Hielands and isles of Scotland. Ed A. Mitchell, Edinburgh 1907 (Scottish Historical Soc). Written c. 1644.

Butcher, Richard. The survey and antiquities of the towne of Stamford in the county of Lincolne. 1646, 1717; ed F. Peck, Academia tertia anglicana, 1727.

Ireland or a booke; together with an exact mappe of the most principall townes great and small in the said Kingdome. 1647.

Buchanan, David. Provinciae Edinburgenae descriptio. Ed A. Mitchell 1907 (Scottish Historical Soc). Written c. 1647.

Gordon, James. Abredoniae utriusque descriptio. Aberdeen 1842 (Spalding Club); ed A. Mitchell 1907 (Scottish Historical Soc). Written c. 1647.

[Weldon, Sir Anthony]. Terrible newes from Scotland. 1647; rptd as A perfect description of the people and country of Scotland, 1649, 1659; rptd Abbotsford Club miscellany vol 1, 1837. Written 1617, BM Lansdowne ms 973; wrongly ascribed to James Howell.

Woodhouse, John. A guide for strangers in the kingdome of Ireland; wherein the high-wayes and roads from all the sea townes, market parishes, great or small is truely set down. 1647.

— The map of Ireland, with the exact dimensions of the provinces, with the names of all the townes and places great and small alphabetically set downe. 1653.

G[ray], W. Chorographia: or a survey of Newcastle upon Tine; as also A relation of the County of Northumberland. 1649, Newcastle 1649; rptd Harleian miscellany vol 3, 1744, 1808; 1813 (Newcastle Soc of Antiquaries), 1819; ed T. M. Richardson, Antiquities of the Border Counties, Edinburgh 1818; Newcastle 1883, 1970 (facs).

Boate, Gerard. Irelands naturall history: being a true and ample description of its situation, greatness, shape and nature; published by Samuell Hartlib. 1652, 1657, Dublin 1726, 1755; rptd A collection of tracts illustrative of the natural history of Ireland vol 1, 1860; tr French, 1666.

Ware, Sir James. De Hibernia & antiquitatibus ejus disquisitiones. 1654, 1658; tr in The antiquities and history of Ireland, 1704 (separate title-page Dublin 1705); rptd in Whole works of Sir James Ware vol 2, Dublin 1746; rptd in A collection of tracts vol 1, Dublin 1860.

Porter, Thomas. A new booke of mapps: being a ready guide or direction for any stranger, or other, who is to travel in England, Scotland and Ireland. 1655.

Villare anglicum: or a view of the townes of England; collected by the appointment of Sir Henry Spelman knight. 1656, 1678; rptd Works, 1698, 1727. A gazetteer.

Dugdale, Sir William. Antiquities of Warwickshire illustrated, beautified with maps, prospects and portraictures. 1656, 2 vols 1730, 1 vol Coventry 1765, Warwick 1786, Coventry 1817 (in part).

Tucker, Thomas. Report on the settlement of the revenue of Excise and Customs in Scotland 1656. Ed J. A. Murray, Edinburgh 1825 (Bannatyne Club); rptd Scottish Burgh Records Soc Miscellany, Edinburgh 1881.

Howell, James. Londinopolis: an historical discourse or perlustration of the city of London. 1657, [1660].

Kilburne, Richard. A brief survey of the county of Kent, viz the names of the parishes in the same. 1657. A 11 epitome of following.

— A topographie or survey of the county of Kent. 1659.

Franck, Richard. Northern memoirs, calculated for the meridian of Scotland, wherein most of the cities, citadels, sea-ports are described; writ in the year 1658. 1694; ed Sir W. Scott, Edinburgh 1821.

Burton, William. A commentary on Antoninus his itinerary: or journies of the Romane empire, so far as it concerneth Britain. 1658.

Hawkins, Richard. A discourse of the nationall excellencies of England. 1658.

[Evelyn, John]. A character of England, as it was lately presented in a letter to a noble man of France. 1659, 1659; rptd Harleian miscellany vol 10, 1808–13 etc; Somers tracts vol 7, 1812; rptd in Miscellaneous writings, 1825.

Leigh, Edward. England described: or the several counties and shires thereof briefly handled, to set forth the glory of this nation. 1659.

Philipott, John. Villare Cantianium, or Kent surveyed and illustrated: being an exact description of all the parishes, burroughs, villages and mannors. 1659, 1664, Lynn 1776.

Childrey, J. Britannia Baconica: or the natural rarities of England, Scotland and Wales, according as they are to be found in every shire. 1660, 1661, 1662; tr French, 1667, 1667.

Europe and the Mediterranean Countries

Caorsin, Gulielmus. The siege of the noble and invyncyble cytee of Rhodes [in 1480]. [1482]; ed H. W. Fincham 1926; Amsterdam and New York 1970 (facs). Tr John Kay from the Obsidionis Rhodie urbis descriptio, Rome [1480].

The copy of a carete, composynge the circuet of the worlde and the compace of every yland. In The customs of London, otherwise called Arnold's Chronicle, [1503], [1521], 1811; separately as Mappa Mundi: otherwyse called the compasse and cyrcuet of the worlde, [1536]; in, The compost of Ptholomeus, The rutter of the dystaunces from one porte or countree to another, [1535] (2nd edn) (in part).

Garcie, Pierre. The rutter of the sea with the havens, rodes, soundings, kennings, windes, floods and ebbes. 1528, 1536, [1555], [1555], 1557 (with A rutter of the northe by R. Proude), [1565], 1573; ed D. W. Waters, New Haven 1967 (facs of 1557).

Ramberti, Benedetto. The order of the great Turkes Courte, of his menne of warre, and of all hys conquestes, with the summe of Mahumetes doctryne, translated oute of French. 1524 (for 1542). From the Libri tre delle cose de Turchi, Venice 1539 etc.

Jovius, Paulus. A shorte treatise upon the Turkes chronicles compyled by Paulus Jovius, drawen oute of the Italyen tong in to Latyne and translated out of Latyne into Englysh by Peter Ashton. 1546. From the Commentarii delle cose de Turchi, Venice [1531] etc; tr Latin, 1537 etc.

Borde, Andrew. The fyrst boke of the introduction of knowledge, the whych dothe teache a man to know the usage and fashion of all maner of countreys. [1548], 1555, [1562]; ed W. Upcott 1814; ed F. J. Furnivall 1870 (EETS).

Thomas, William. The historie of Italie: a boke excedyng profitable to be redde. 1549, 1561; ed A. D'Aubant, Works, 1774; ed G. B. Parks, Ithaca 1963 (Folger Lib) (abridged).

Munster, Sebastian. The description of Swedland, Gotland and Finland, the auncient estate of theyr kynges, the most horrible and incredible tiranny of the second Christiirn, Kyng of Denmarke; collected and gathered chieflye out of Sebastian Mounster, by George North. 1561; ed M. W. S. Swan, New York 1946 (facs). From the Cosmographia, Basle 1550 etc. *See* General Descriptions, 1553 above.

Cambini, Andrea. Two very notable commentaries, the one of the originall of the Turcks and empire of the house of Ottomano, written by Andrewe Cambini, and thother of the warres of the Turcke against George Scanderbeg; translated oute of the Italian into Englishe by John Shute. 1562. From the Libro della origine de Turchi, Florence 1529 etc and Francesco Sansovino, Dell'historia universale dell'origine de Turchi, Venice 1560–1.

Polybius. The hystories of the most famous and worthy cronographer Polybius, englished by C. W[atson]. 1568.
— The history of Polybius the Megalopolitan, translated into English by Edward Grimeston. 1633, 1634, 1634.

Georgievitz, Bartholomaeus. The ofspring of the house of Ottomano, and officers pertaining to the great Turkes court; whereunto is added Bartholomeus Georgieviz Epistome, of the customes, rytes, ceremonies and religion of the Turkes, englished by Hugh Gough. [1570]. From the De origine imperii Turcorum, Wittenberg 1562, including the De moribus, condictionibus et nequicia Turcorum, Rome [1480] etc.
— De Turcorum moribus epitome. In A. Gislenii Busbequii quae extant omnia, 1660.

Martinengo, Nestore. The true report of all the successe of Famagosta, a citie in Cyprus, englished out of Italian by William Malim. 1572, 1599 (in Hakluyt), 1810. From L'assedio e presa di Famagosta, Verona 1572.

Turlerus, Hieronymus. The traveller of Jerome Turler, devided into two bookes: the first of the maner, and order of traveiling oversea; the second comprehending an excellent description of the most delicious realme of Naples in Italy. 1575; ed D. E. Baughan, Gainesville 1951 (facs). From De peregrinatione et agro neapolitano, Strasbourg 1574.

Rowlands, Richard. The post of the world: wherein is contayned the antiquities and originall of the most famous cities in Europe; with their trade and traficke; with their wayes and distance of myles. 1576. From an unidentified German source.

Herodotus. The famous hystory of Herodotus: conteyning the discourse of dyvers countreys. 1584; ed A. Lang as Euterpe: being the second book of the famous history of Herodotus englished by B.R. 1584 (in part), 1888; ed L. Whibley 1924. Bks 1–2 tr B.R.
— Herodoti historiarum liber primus. Oxford 1591.

Caesar, Gaius Julius. *See* British Isles, 1530 above.

The safegard of sailers and great rutter: contayning the courses, dystances, deapths, soundings, flouds and ebbes, with the marks for the entring of sundry harboroughs, translated out of Dutch into English by Robert Norman Hydrographer. 1584, 1587, 1590, 1600; augmented by E. Wright 1605, 1612, 1640, 1671.

Florio, John. A letter lately written from Rome by an Italian gentleman, wherein is declared the state of Rome, newely translated out of Italian into English by I[ohn] F[lorio]. 1585.

Wagenaer, Lucas Jansen. The mariners mirrour: wherin may playnly be seen the courses, heights, distances, depths, soundings, flouds and ebs, set forth in divers exact sea-charts, and now fitted with necessarie additions for the use of Englishmen by Anthony Ashley. 1588; ed R. A. Skelton, Amsterdam 1966. From the Spieghel der zeevaert, Amsterdam 1584 etc.

Daunce, Edward. A briefe discourse of the Spanish state. [1590], Amsterdam and New York 1968 (facs).

Fletcher, Giles. Of the Russe common wealth: or maner of government by the Russe Emperour, with the manners and fashions of the people of that countrey. 1591; 1598 (part in Hakluyt); rptd Purchas; rptd as The history of Russia, 1643, 1656, 1657; rptd Harris vol 1, 1705; rptd in Hakluyt's collection of the early voyages vol 1, 1809; ed E. A. Bond 1856 (Hakluyt Soc); ed L. E. Berry, English works, Madison 1964; ed A. J. Schmidt, Ithaca

1966 (Folger Lib); ed R. Pipes and J. V. A. Fine 1966 (facs); ed L. E. Berry and R. O. Crummey, Rude and barbarous kingdom, Madison 1969.

[Eliot, John]. The survay or topographical description of France; with a new mappe helping greatly for the surveying of every particular country, cittye, fortresse, river, mountaine and forrest. 1592, 1593.

Guicciardini, Lodovico. The description of the Low Countreys and of the provinces thereof, fathered into an epitome out of the Historie of Guicciardini. 1593. Tr Thomas Danett from the Descrittione di tutti i Paesi Bassi, Antwerp 1567 etc.

Van Adrichom, Christian. A briefe description of Hierusalem and of the suburbs therof. 1595, 1654, York 1666; Amsterdam and New York 1969 (facs of 1595). Tr Thomas Tymme from the Jerusalem et suburbarum descriptio, Cologne 1584 etc.

Lonicerus, Philippus. The policy of the Turkish empire, the first booke: containing the state and summe of the Turkes religion. 1597. Adapted by an anon translator from the Chronicorum Turcicorum tomus primus, Frankfurt 1578.

Tacitus, Publius Cornelius. The description of Germanie. In The Annales of Cornelius Tacitus, 1598, 1604, 1612, 1622, 1640. Tr R. Grenewey.

Contarini, Gasparo. The common-wealth and government of Venice, translated out of Italian by Lewes Lewknor esquire. 1599. From the Italian version, Venice 1544 etc, of De magistratibus et republica Venetorum, Paris 1543 etc.

The Mahumetane of Turkish historie, containing three bookes: translated by Raffe Carr. 1600. From various sources.

Conestaggio, Girolamo. The historie of the uniting of the kingdom of Portugall to the crowne of Castill: containing the last warres of the Portugals: the description of Portugall: of the East Indies, the Isles of Terceres and other dependencies. 1600. Tr for Edward Blunt from the Dell'unione dei regno di Portogallo, Genoa 1585 etc.

Marlianus, Joannes Bartholomaeus. A summarie collected by John Bartholomew Marlianus, touching the topographie of Rome in ancient time. In The Romane historie written by T. Livius, tr Philemon Holland 1600, 1659. From Epitome 1552 etc of Antiquae Romae topographia, Rome 1534.

Josephus, Flavius. The famous and memorable works of Josephus, a man of much honour and learning among the Jewes, faithfully translated out of the Latin and French, by Tho[mas] Lodge. 1602, 1609, 1620, 1632, 1632, 1640, 1655–6, 1670.

Knolles, Richard. The generall historie of the Turkes, from the first beginning of that nation, faithfully collected out of the best histories. 1603, 1610, 1621, 1631, 1638, 3 vols 1687–1700, 2 vols 1701.

Soranzo, Lazzaro. The Ottoman of Lazaro Soranzo, wherein is delivered as well a report of the might and power of Mahamet the third as also a true description of divers peoples, countries, cities and voyages: translated out of Italian into English by Abraham Hartwell. 1603. From L'Ottomano, Ferrara 1599 etc.

Dallington, Sir Robert. The view of Fraunce. 1604 (unauthorized), 1936 (facs) (Shakespeare Assoc).
— A method for travell, shewed by taking the view of France, as it stoode in the yeare of our Lord 1598. [1605].
— A survey of the Great Dukes state of Tuscany in the yeare of our Lord 1596. 1605, 1605.

[Sandys, Sir Edwin]. A relation of the state of religion, and with what hopes and policies it hath beene framed and is maintained in the severall states of these westerne parts of the world. 1605 (3 edns, all unauthorized).
— Europae speculum: or a view or survey of the state of religion. Hague 1629, London 1632, 1632, 1637, 1638, 1673, 1687; tr Italian, 1625; French, 1626; Dutch, 1675. Written 1599.

Sherley, Sir Thomas. Discours of the Turks [1606]. Ed E. D. Ross 1936 (Camden Soc) (from ms).

B., J., merchant. The merchants avizo: verie necessarie for their sons and servants, when they first send them beyond the seas, as to Spaine and Portingale or other countries. 1589, 1590, 1591, 1607, 1616, 1640; ed P. McGrath, Cambridge Mass 1957; Amsterdam and New York 1969 (facs of 1607).

Marcellinus, Ammianus. The Roman historie: containing such acts and occurrents as passed under Constantius, Julianus and Valens, done by Philemon Holland. 1609.

C., Ro. A true historicall discourse of Muley Hamets rising to three kingdomes of Moruccoes with a view of Moorish customs. 1609; rptd Purchas (in part); ed H. de Castries, Les sources inédites de l'histoire du Maroc, Archives de l'Angleterre vol 2, 1925.

Carew, Sir George. A relation of the state of France, with the characters of Henry IV and the principal persons of that Court, drawn up by Sir George Carew upon his return from his embassy there in 1609. Ed T. Birch, An historical view of the negotiations between the courts of England, France and Brussels, 1749.

Le Petit, Jean François. The Low-Country common wealth: contayninge an exact discription of the eight United Provinces now made free, translated out of French by Ed Grimeston. 1609, Amsterdam and New York 1969 (facs). From La grande chronique ancienne et moderne, de Hollande etc, Dordrecht 1601.

A true description and direction of what is most worthy to be seen in all Italy. In Harleian miscellany vol 5, 1808–13 etc. From ms written c. 1610.

Blaeu, Willem Janszoon. The light of navigation: wherein are declared and pourtrayed all the coasts and havens of the west, north and east seas. Amsterdam 1612, 1620, 1622; ed R. A. Skelton, Amsterdam [1964]. From Het licht der zeevaert, Amsterdam 1608 etc.

— The sea-mirrour: containing a briefe instruction in the art of navigation and a description of the easterne, northerne and westerne navigation. Amsterdam 1625, 1643–4. From the Zeespiegel, Amsterdam 1623 etc.

Fougasses, Thomas de. The generall historie of the magnificent state of Venice: from the first foundation thereof untill this present; englished by W. Shute. 2 vols 1612. From the Histoire générale de Venise, Paris 1608.

Barclay, John. Icon animorum. 1614, Paris 1614, 1617, Strasbourg 1623 (with Euphormion), Frankfurt 1625, Leyden 1625, Milan 1664, Frankfurt 1668, 1675, Dresden 1680, Leipzig 1733, Augsburg 1774; tr T[homas M[ay], The mirrour of mindes: or Barclay's Icon animorum, 1631, 1633; tr French, 1623, 1625, 1625; German, 1649, 1660, 1784, 1821, 1902.

Godwyn, Thomas. Romanae historiae anthologia: an English exposition of the Romane antiquities. Oxford 1614, 1616, 1620, 1623, 1625, 1628, 1631, 1633, 1638, 1642, London 1648, 1655, 1658, 1661, 1668, 1671, 1671, 1674, 1680, 1685, 1686, 1689, 1695, 1696.

— Synopsis antiquitatum hebraicarum, ad explicationem utriusque testamenti valde necessaria. Oxford 1616; tr 1625, 1626, 1628, 1631, 1634, 1641, 1655, 1662, 1667, 1671, 1672, 1672, 1678; expanded as Moses and Aaron: civil and ecclesiastical rites used by the ancient Hebrewes, 1685; tr Latin from English, 1698, 1710, 1710, 2 vols 1723–4; in B. Ugolinus, Thesaurus antiquitatum vol 3, Venice 1744.

[Bon, Ottavio]. A description of the Grand Signors seraglio: or Turkish Emperours court. Pbd Purchas; ed John Greaves 1650, 1653; in Miscellaneous workes of John Greaves vol 2, 1737. Pbd as by Robert Withers, actually tr by him from Italian ms.

Overbury, Sir Thomas. His observations in his travailes upon the state of the XVII Provinces as they stood 1609. 1626, 1651 (as Observations upon the United Provinces) rptd Harleian miscellany vol 8, 1746 etc; Harleian voyages vol 1, 1745, 1747; rptd in Miscellaneous works,

1856; ed E. Arber vol 4, 1882, 1903; Amsterdam and New York 1969 (facs of 1626); tr French, 1853.

Richardson, Gabriel. Of the state of Europe XIIII bookes: containing the historie and relation of the many provinces hereof. Oxford 1627.

A short survey of the kingdome of Sweden containing a briefe description of all the provinces of this whole dominion. 1632. From Dutch.

Rous, Francis. Archaeologiae attica libri tres: three bookes of the atticke antiquities: containing the description of the citties glory, government, division of the people and townes. Oxford 1637, London 1645, Oxford 1649, 1654 (enlarged to 7 bks), 1658; [ed Zachariah Bogan], Oxford 1662, 1667, 1670, 1671, 1675, London 1685.

Colom, Jacob. The first book of the fierie sea-columne: wherein The description of whole North-sea? Amsterdam 1639, 1644, 1649 (as The new fierie sea-colomne). From De vyerighe colom, Amsterdam 1632 etc.

Fuller, Thomas. The historie of the holy warre [1095–1294]. Cambridge 1639, 1640, 1647, 1651, London 1840.

— A pisgah-sight of Palestine and the confines thereof, with the History of the Old and New testament acted thereon. 1650, 1652, 1689, 1869.

The European mercury: describing the highwayes and stages from place to place, through the most remarkable parts of Christendom. 1641. Tr from the Italian by James Wadsworth.

Ussher, James. A geographicall and historicall disquisition touching the Lydian or Proconsular Asia; and the seven metropoliticall churches contained therein. In Certaine briefe treatises written by divine learned men concerning the ancient and moderne government of the church, Oxford 1641, 1643; rptd Harleian voyages vol 1, 1745, 1747; rptd in Works, Dublin 1847–64; tr Latin, 1687, in Opuscula duo, 1688, Bremen 1701.

Howell, James. Instructions for forreine travell: showing by what cours, and in what compasse of time, one may take an exact survey of the kingdomes and states of Christendome. 1642, 1652; ed E. Arber, English reprints, 1869.

— Epistolae Ho-Elianae: familiar letters domestic and forren. 1645, 1650, 1655, 1673, 1678, 1688, 1705, 1713, 1726, 1737, Aberdeen 1753, London 1754; ed J. Jacobs 1890, 2 vols 1892; ed W. H. Bennett 2 vols 1890; ed O. Smeaton 3 vols 1903; ed A. Repplier, Boston 1907; New York 1928 (in part).

— SPQV: a survey of the signorie of Venice, of her admired policy, and method of government. 1651.

— Brief description of Asia and the Holy Land. In his trn of Josephus, The wonderful and most deplorable history of the latter times of the Jews, 1652, 1653, 1662, 1669, 1684, 1699.

— A German diet: or the ballance of Europe wherein the power and weakness of all the kingdoms and states of Christendom are impartially poizd. 1653.

— Parthenopoeia; Londinopolis. See 1654, 1657, below.

[Felltham, Owen]. Three moneths observations of the Low-Countries, especially Holland: containing A brief description of the country, customes, religion, manners and dispositions of the people. 1648, 1652. Pirated edns of the next item.

— A brief character of the Low-Countries under the states: being three weeks observation of the vices and vertues of the inhabitants. 1652, 1660; in his Resolves, 1661, 1662, 1770.

The Alcoran of Mahomet, translated out of Arabique into French by the Sieur Du Ryer, and newly englished. 1649, 1649, 1688; rptd in A complete history of the Turks, 1719.

Grotius, Hugo. A treatise of the antiquity of the commonwealth of the Battavers which is now the Hollanders, translated out of both the Latin and Dutch into English, by Tho. Woods. 1649. From the Liber de antiquitate reipublicae Bativicae, Leyden 1610 etc; tr Dutch, 1641.

A book and map of all Europe, with the names of all the towns of note in that known quarter of the world. 1650.

Milton, John. A brief history of Moscovia, and of other less-known countries lying eastward of Russia as far as Cathay. 1682 etc. *See under Milton, col 1243, above.* Written c. 1650. Ed R. R. Cawley, Milton's literary craftsmanship, Princeton 1941.

Modena, Leon. The history of the rites, customs and manner of life of the present Jews throughout the world; translated by Edmund Chilmead. 1650; rptd as The history of the present Jews, 1707. From the Historia de gli riti hebraici, Paris 1637 etc.

The land of Canaan as it was possessed by the twelve tribes, the promised land or whole Palestina. 1652.

Bentivoglio, Guido. Historicall relations of the United Provinces of Flanders, written originally in Italian by Cardinall Bentivoglio, and now rendred into English by Henry Earle of Monmouth. 1652. From the Relationi fatte in tempo delle sue nuntiature di Fiandra, Cologne 1629 etc.

E[velyn], J[ohn]. The state of France, as it stood in the ixth yeer of this present monarch Lewis XIIII, written to a friend by J.E. 1652; rptd in his Miscellaneous writings, 1825.

Khojah Effendi (Sa'd al-Din Ibn Hasanjan). The reign of Sultan Orchan Second King of the Turks [1325–59], translated out of Hojah Effendi, an eminent Turkish historian, by William Seaman. 1652. From the Latin version, Annales sultanorum, of J. Leunclavius, Frankfurt 1588.

Cunaeus, Petrus. Of the common-wealth of the Hebrews, translated by C.B. 1653. From the De republica Hebraeorum libri III, Leyden 1631 etc.

Procopius. The history of the warres of the Emperour Justinian in eight books, englished by Henry Holcroft, Knight. 1653.

A description and plat of the sea-coasts of England, from London, all along the coasts to the Orchades; as also all those parts over against us. 1653. A routier.

Lunadoro, Girolamo and Martinelli, Fioravante. The Court of Rome: wherein is sett forth the whole government thereof and a direction for such as shall travell to Rome; translated out of Italian into English by H[enry] C[ogan]. 1654. From the Relatione della Corte di Roma, Rome 1635 etc and the Roma ricercata nel suo sito, Rome 1644 etc; respectively.

Mazzella, Scipione. Parthenopoeia: or the history of the most noble and renowned kingdom of Naples; the first part by Scipio Mazzella, made English by Mr Samson Lennard; The second part compil'd by James Howell. 1654. From the Descrittione del regno di Napoli, Naples 1586 etc.

Heylyn, Peter. France painted to the life, by a learned and impartial hand. 1656, 1657, 1673, 1679. Unauthorized edns of the following.

— A full relation of two journeys: the one [1625] into the main-land of France; the other [1629] into some of the adjacent ilands. 1656. Written as observations rather than narrative.

[Osborne, Francis]. Political reflections upon the government of the Turks etc, by the author of the late advice to a son. Oxford 1656; rptd in Works, 1673 etc.

Lupton, Donald. Flanders: or an exact and compendious description of that fair, great and fat countrey of Flanders. 1658.

[Chaloner]. A true and exact relation of the strange finding out of Moses his tombe in a valley neere unto Mount Nilso Palestina etc. 1657, Oxford 1958 (Luttrell Soc).

Magnus, Olaus. A compendious history of the Goths, Swedes and Vandals, and other northern nations. 1658. From the Historia de gentibus septentrionalibus, Rome 1555 etc.

Morland, Samuel. The history of the evangelical churches of the valleys of Piemont: containing a most exact geographical description of the place. 1658.

A character of France: to which is added Gallus Castratus: or an answer to a late slanderous pamphlet called the Character of England. 1659.

The character of Italy: or the Italian anatomiz'd by an English chyrurgion. 1660.

The character of Spain: or an epitome of their virtues and vices. 1660.

Moore, Andrew. A compendious history of the Turks: containing an exact account of the originall of that people; the rise of the Ottoman family. 1660 (for 1659).

Schottus, Franciscus. Italy in its original glory, ruine and revival: being an exact survey of the whole geography and history of that famous country. 1660. Tr Edmund Warcupp from the Itinerarii Italiae rerumque Romanarum libri tres, Antwerp 1660 etc; and the Itinerario, Padua 1629 etc.

(6) AFRICA AND ASIA

Voyages to Farther Africa and Asia

'Mandeville, Sir John'. Here endeth the boke of John Maundvyle, Knight of wayes to Jerusalem and of marveylys of ynde. [1496], 1499, 1503, [1510], 1568, [1582], 1612, 1618, 1625, 1632, [1640], 1650, 1657, 1670, 1677, 1677, 1684, 1696, 1704, 1705, [1710], 1722, 1725, 1727, [1730–5], [1745–50], [c. 1750], [c. 1780], [c. 1785], 1839; ed T. Wright, Early travels in Palestine, 1848, 1866; ed E. Matzner 1869, 1883; ed G. Munro, New York 1886; ed J. Ashton 1887; ed G. F. Warner 1889 (Roxburghe Club); ed A. Lanyard and J. W. Redway, New York 1898; ed A. W. Pollard 1900 etc (from ms); ed P. Hamelius 1919–23 (EETS); San Francisco 1928, London 1928 (EL); 1932 (from 1568 edn); ed M. Letts 1953 (Hakluyt Soc) (from ms); ed M. C. Seymour 1963 (EETS) (from Bodley ms collated with BM ms Royal 13 E ix).

Springer, Balthazar. Of the newe landes and of ye people founde by the messengers of the Kynge of Portyngale named Emanuel. [Antwerp 1509]; ed E. Arber, The first three English books on America, Birmingham 1885. The first part of a pamphlet ptd by John of Doesborowe, also containing: Of the x dyvers nacyons crystened: of Pope John and his landes. Springer's narrative

in German, Augsburg [1508]; in Flemish, Antwerp 1508.

Goes, Damianus de. The legacye or embassate of Prester John unto Emanuell, Kynge of Portyngale. 1533. Tr John More from the Legatio, Antwerp 1532.

Barbaro, Giosafatte. [Travels to Tana and Persia 1436–52 and 1471]. Ed Lord Stanley of Alderley 1873 (Hakluyt Soc). Tr William Thomas c. 1550 from Viaggi fatti da Venezia, Venice 1543 etc. BM Royal ms 17 C x.

[Thomas Windham to Barbary and Guinea 1551–6: accounts from Eden, Hakluyt and documents]. Ed J. W. Blake, Europeans in West Africa 1450–1560, 1942 (Hakluyt Soc).

Escalante, Bernardino de. A discourse of the navigation which the Portugales doe make to the realmes and provinces of the East partes of the world, translated out of Spanish by John Frampton. 1579; rptd Harleian voyages vol 2, 1745, 1747. From the Discurso de la navigacion, Seville 1577.

Polo, Marco. The most noble and famous travels of Marcus Paulus, one of the nobilitie of the state of Venice, into the East partes of the world, as Armenia, Persia, Arabia, Tartary, with many other kingdoms and provinces. 1579; ed N. M. Penzer 1929, 1937. From the Spanish, Cosmographia breve, Seville 1503 etc. Other

English versions in Purchas; Harris vol 1, 1705 etc;
Pinkerton vol 7; by W. Marsden 1818 etc; by H. Murray,
Edinburgh 1844 etc; by H. Yule 1871 etc; by A. Ricci
1931.

Lopes de Castanheda, Fernao. The first booke of the
historie of the discoverie and conquest of the East
Indias, enterprized by the Portingales, in their daungerous navigations. 1582. Tr Nicholas Lichfield from
Historia do descobrimento bk 1, Coimbra 1551.

Madox, Richard. [The official journal of the voyage of
Capt Edward Fenton to Sierra Leone and Brazil
1582-3]. Ed E. G. R. Taylor, The troublesome voyage
of Capt Edward Fenton, 1582-3, 1959 (Hakluyt Soc).
BM Cotton ms Otho E viii, fols 130-43, 173.

— [Extracts from Madox's diary concerning the voyage].
Ed E. G. R. Taylor 1959 (Hakluyt Soc). BM Cotton
ms, App xlvii, and Titus B viii, fol 179-221.

Fenton, Edward. Sea journal. Ed E. G. R. Taylor 1959
(Hakluyt Soc). Magdelene College Cambridge, Pepys
ms 2133.

Walker, John. [Extracts from his diary of the same
voyage]. Ed E. G. R. Taylor 1959 (Hakluyt Soc). BM
Cotton ms Otho E viii fols 202-23, 160-4.

Jeffery, Peter. [Narrative of same voyage June 1583].
Ed E. G. R. Taylor 1959 (Hakluyt Soc). BM Cotton ms
Otho E viii fol 186-7.

Hawkins, William. [Narrative of same voyage 6 July
1583]. Ed E. G. R. Taylor 1959 (Hakluyt Soc). BM
Cotton ms Otho E viii fol 224-8.

Gonzalez de Mendoza, Juan. L'historia del gran regno
della China, composta primieramente in ispagnuolo, e
poi fatta vulgare da Francesco Avanzi. 'Vinegia'
(London) 1587.

— The historie of the great and mightie kingdome of
China, and the situation therof: to gither with the great
riches, huge citties, politike governement and rare
inventions in the same, translated out of Spanish by
R[obert] Parke. 1588; ed G. T. Staunton 1853-4
(Hakluyt Soc). From the Historia del gran regno de la
China, Rome 1585 etc.

Federici, Cesare. The voyage and travaile [1563-81]: of
M. Caesar Frederick, merchant of Venice, into the East
India, the Indies and beyond the Indies. 1588; 1599
(in Hakluyt); rptd Purchas; Amsterdam and New York
1971 (facs of 1588). Tr Thomas Hickok from the
Viaggio nell'India orientale, Venice 1587.

Pigafetta, Filippo. A report of the kingdome of Congo, a
region of Africa, and of the countries that border rounde
about the same; translated out of Italian by Abraham
Hartwell. 1597; rptd Purchas; rptd Harleian voyages
vol 2, 1745, 1747; rptd Churchill vol 8, 1752; Amsterdam
and New York 1970 (facs of 1597). Retrn by Margarete
Hutchinson, 1881, Westport Conn 1969. From
Relatione de reame di Congo, Rome 1591.

Van Linschoten, Jan Huighen. John Huighen van
Linschoten his Discours of voyages into ye Easte and
Weste Indies. 1598; rptd Purchas (in part); ed A. C.
Burnell and P. A. Tiele 1885 (Hakluyt Soc); ed E.
Arber, vol 3 1877, vol 2 1903. Tr William Phillip from
the Itinerario, Amsterdam 1596.

The description of a voyage made by certaine ships of
Holland [1595-7] into the East Indies; translated out
of Dutch into English by W[illiam] P[hillip]. 1598;
rptd Harleian voyages vol 2, 1745, 1747; rptd Hakluyt's
collection of the early voyages vol 2, 1809-12; rptd A
selection of curious, rare and early voyages, 1812. From
the Verhael vande reyse, Middleburg 1597.

Geritszoon, Cornelius. An addition to the sea journal or
navigation of the Hollanders unto Java, compiled by
Cornelius Geraldson. 1598; rptd Harleian voyages vol 2,
1745, 1747; Amsterdam and New York 1968 (facs of
1598). From the Appendix of te by- voechsel achter
tJournael vande reyse, Middelburg 1598.

A true report of the gainefull, prosperous and speedy
voiage [1598-9] to Java in the East Indies, performed
by a fleete of eight ships of Amsterdam. [1599]; rptd
Hakluyt's collection of the early voyages vol 5, 1809-12;
rptd A selection of curious, rare and early voyages, 1812.
From an unidentified Dutch original.

The conquest of the Grand Canaries, made this last
summer by three-score and thirteene saile of [Dutch]
shippes; with the taking of a towne in the Isle of
Gomera. 1599; rptd Hakluyt's collection of the early
voyages vol 5, 1809-12; rptd A selection of curious, rare
and early voyages, 1812.

Jonghe, Ellert de. The true and perfect declaration of the
mighty army by sea under the conduct of Peter Vander
Does. 1600; rptd A selection of curious, rare and early
voyages, 1812. From the Waerachtigh verhael vande
machtighe Scheeps-Armade, Amsterdam 1600.

A true report of Sir Anthony Shierlies journey overland to
Venice, from thence by sea to Antioch, Aleppo and
Babilon, and soe to Casbine in Persia; reported by two
gentlemen, who have followed him in the same. 1600;
ed E. D. Ross, Sir Anthony Sherley and his Persian
adventure, 1933.

The journall or dayly register, contayning a true manifestation and historicall declaration of the voyage, accomplished by eight shippes of Amsterdam [to the East
Indies 1598-1600]. 1601; rptd Hakluyt's collection of
the early voyages vol 5, 1809-12. Tr William Walker
from the Journael ofte dagh-register, Amsterdam 1600.

Parry, William. A new and large discourse of the travels
of Sir Anthony Sherley Knight, by sea and over land,
to the Persian empire, written by William Parry,
gentleman, who accompanied Sir Anthony. 1601; rptd
in Purchas (in part); ed J. P. Collier, Illustrations of
early English popular literature vol 2, 1864; ed E. D.
Ross, Sir Anthony Sherley and his Persian adventure,
1933.

A true and large discourse of the voyage of the whole
fleete of ships set forth the 20 of April 1601 by the
Governours and Assistants of the East Indian Merchants
in London, to the East Indies. 1603; ed W. Forster,
The voyages of Sir James Lancaster, 1940 (Hakluyt Soc).

A true and perfect relation of the newes sent from Amsterdam concerning the fight of five Dutch shippes in the
East Indies, against the Portugall fleete. 1603; ed B.
Penrose, Sea fights in the East Indies, Cambridge Mass
1931.

The last East-Indian voyage: containing much varietie of
the state of the severall kingdomes where they have
traded, begun by one of the voyage. 1606; ed J. B.
Corney 1855 (Hakluyt Soc); ed W. Foster, The voyage
of Sir Henry Middleton to the Moluccas 1943 (Hakluyt Soc); Amsterdam and New York 1971 (facs of
1606).

Scott, Edmund. A exact discourse of the subtilties,
fashions, pollicies, religion and ceremonies of the East
Indians as well Chyneses as Javans: whereunto is added
a briefe description of Java Major. 1606; rptd Purchas;
rptd Harris vol 1, 1705 etc; rptd Harleian voyages vol 1,
1745, 1747; ed W. Foster 1943 (Hakluyt Soc).

[Nixon, Anthony]. The three English brothers: Sir
Thomas Sherley his travels; Sir Anthony Sherley his
embassage to the Christian princes; Master Robert
Sherley his wars against the Turkes, with his marriage
to the Emperour of Persia his neece. 1607.

Manwaring, George. A true discourse of Sir Anthony
Sherley's travels into Persia, what accidents did happen
in the waye, with the businesse he was employed in
from the Sophi. In The three brothers, 1825; ed E. D.
Ross, Sir Anthony Sherley, 1933. From ms written
c. 1607.

An historicall and true discourse of a voyage made by the
Admiral Cornelis Mateleif into the East Indies [1605-8].
1608; ed B. Penrose, Sea fights in the East Indies,
Cambridge Mass 1931. From the Breeder Verhael
van tghene dan Admirael Cornelis Matelief, Rotterdam
1608.

[Middleton, Thomas]. Sir Robert Sherley, sent ambassadour, in the name of the King of Persia, to Sigismond the Third, King of Poland and Swecia. 1609; rptd Harleian miscellany vol 5, 1808-13 etc.

Cartwright, John. The preachers travels: wherein is set downe a true journall to the confines of the East Indies, through the great countreyes of Syria, Mesopotamia, Armenia, Media, Hircania and Parthia. 1611; rptd Purchas (in part); 1647; rptd Harleian voyages vol 1, 1745, 1747; tr Dutch, Van der Aa.

Coverte, Robert. A true and almost incredible report of an Englishman that (being cast away in the good ship called the Assention in Cambaya) travelled by land throw many unknowne kingdomes and cities. 1612, 1614, 1631; rptd Harleian voyages vol 2, 1745, 1747; ed B. Penrose, Philadelphia 1931; Amsterdam and New York 1971 (facs of 1606); tr German, Hulsius pt 15, 1617, 1648, De Bry, Eastern voyages pt 11, 1618, 1628, Schwabe vol 1, 1747-74; tr Latin, De Bry, Eastern voyages pt 11, 1619; Dutch, Van der Aa.

Sherley, Sir Anthony. Sir Antony Sherley his relation of his travels into Persia: the dangers and distresses which befell him in his passage, both by sea and land, and his strange and unexpected deliverances. 1613; rptd Purchas (abridged); Harleian miscellany vol 10, 1808-13; tr Dutch, Van der Aa.

The great victory which God hath given unto eight Holland shippes in their passage toward the East Indies against 17 great Spanish shippes, translated out of the Dutch copie. Middelburg 1613.

Saris, John. The voyage of Captain John Saris from Java to Japan 1613. Ed É. M. Satow 1900 (Hakluyt Soc). From India Office ms, Marine Record 14. Account ptd in Purchas, rptd Harris vol 1, 1705; Astley vol 1, 1745 etc; ed R. Kerr, A general history and collection vol 9, 1813.

Lithgow, William. A most delectable and true discourse of an admired and painefull peregrination from Scotland to the most famous kingdomes in Europe, Asia and Affrike. 1614, 1616, 1623; rptd Purchas (in part); rptd as The totall discourse of the rare adventures and painefull peregrinations of long nineteene years travayles, 1632, 1640, 1682, 1692, Edinburgh 1770, Leith 1814, Glasgow 1906, 1928 (abridged), Amsterdam and New York 1971 (facs of 1614); tr Dutch, 1652, 1656, 1659.

Best, Thomas. The voyage of Thomas Best to the East Indies 1612-14. Ed W. Foster 1934 (Hakluyt Soc).

Floris, Peter. Peter Floris his voyage to the East Indies in the Globe 1611-15 [contemporary trn of his journal]. Ed W. H. Moreland 1934 (Hakluyt Soc).

The voyage of Nicholas Downton to the East Indies 1614-15. Ed W. Foster 1939 (Hakluyt Soc). Extracts from Downton's journals and letters, with Christopher Farewell's East-India Colation, below.

Feynes de Monfart, Henri de. A exact and curious survey of all the East Indies, even to Canton the chiefe cittie of China: all duly performed [1608-12] by land, newly translated out of the travailers manuscript. 1615; rptd Somers tracts vol 1, 1751, vol 3 1809; tr French, 1630 etc.

Withington, Nicholas. A briefe discoverye of some things best worth noteinge in the travells [1612-16] of Nicholas Withington, a factor in the East Indiase. In A journey by John Cockburn, 1735, 1740, [1742], 1794, 1810; ed W. Foster, Early travels in India, 1916. Abridged in Purchas.

Coryat, Thomas. Thomas Coriate traveller for the English wits: greeting from the Court of the Great Mogul. 1616, 1616, London [1810] (facs), Amsterdam and New York 1968 (facs). Later edns with the next item.

— Mr Thomas Coriat to his friends in England sendeth greeting: from Agra 1616. 1618; rptd Workes of John Taylor, 1630; rptd Works vol 3, 1776; ed W. Foster, Early travels in India, 1926.

Letters received by the East India Company from its servants in the East 1602-17. Ed F. C. Danvers and W. Foster 6 vols 1896-1902. Including many accounts of voyages; letters after 1617 ptd in Calendar form.

Jourdain, John. A journall kept by John Jourdain in a voiage for the East Indies sett fourth by the Honourable Companie [1608-17]. Ed W. Foster 1905 (Hakluyt Soc). BM Sloane ms 858.

Adams, William. Letters from Japan 1611-17. Ed T. Rundall 1850 (Hakluyt Soc); ed D. B. W. Sladen and N. Lorimer, More queer things about Japan, 1904. From India Office ms.

— The log-book of William Adams 1614-19. Ed C. J. Purnell, Trans Japan Soc 13 1916.

Saris, Edward. Journals of Edward Saris, Japan to Cochin-China 1617-18. Ed C. J. Purnell, ibid. From India Office, Marine Records xxvi.

Roe, Sir Thomas. The embassy of Sir Thomas Roe to India 1615-19. Ed W. Foster 2 vols 1899 (Hakluyt Soc); ed W. Foster, Oxford 1926 (rev and abridged). Ms diary and letters, BM additional ms 6115, 19,277. Abridgements in Purchas, Churchill, Harris, Pinkerton; in Dutch, Amsterdam 1656; in French, M. Thevenot, Divers voyages vol 1, 1663, Prevost vol 13; in German, Schwabe vol 11.

Cocks, Richard. The diary of Richard Cocks, capemerchant in the English factory in Japan 1615-22. Ed E. M. Thompson 1883 (Hakluyt Soc), 2 vols Tokyo 1899. BM additional ms 31,300-1.

A true relation without all exception, of strange and admirable accidents which lately happened in the Kingdome of the great Magor or Magull, written and certified by eye-witnesses. 1622; rptd Harleian miscellany vol 1, 1744 etc. Relating to the voyage of 1618.

The true relation of that worthy sea fight which two of the East India shipps had with 4 Portugals in the Persian Gulph; with the lamentable death of Captain Andrew Shilling. 1622; ed B. Penrose, Sea fights in the East Indies, Cambridge Mass 1931.

Jobson, Richard. The golden trade: or a discovery of the river Gambra and the golden trade of the Aethiopians. 1623; rptd Purchas (abridged); Astley vol 2, 1745-7; Harleian voyages vol 2, 1745, 1747; ed C. G. Kingsley, Teignmouth 1904; 1932; ed C. G. Kingsley 1968; Amsterdam and New York 1968 (facs of 1623).

Xenophon. The historie of Xenophon: containing the ascent of Cyrus into the higher countries; wherein is described the admirable journey of ten thousand Grecians from Asia the Lesse into the territories of Babylon, and their retrait from thence into Greece, translated by Joh. Bingham. 1623.

Taylor, John. A famous fight at sea: where foure English ships under Captain John Weddell, and foure Dutch ships, fought three dayes in the Gulph of Persia against 8 Portugall gallions, and 32 frigots [in 1625]. 1627; rptd in Workes, 1630; Manchester 1869 (Spenser Soc); ed B. Penrose, Sea fights in the East Indies, Cambridge Mass 1931.

Stodart, Robert. Journal [of voyage to Persia with Sir Dodmore Cotton 1628-9]. Ed E. D. Ross 1935 (from ms).

Two memorable relations: the former, a relation of some late conflicts betwcen the Portugals and the English at Surat. 1631; ed B. Penrose, Sea fights in the East Indies, Cambridge Mass 1931.

F[arewell], C[hristopher]. An East-India colation: or a discourse of travels collected by the author in a voyage he made unto the East-Indies. 1633; ed W. Foster, The voyage of Nicholas Downton, 1939 (Hakluyt Soc); Amsterdam and New York 1971 (facs of 1633).

H[erbert], Sir T[homas]. A relation of some yeares travaile [1627-30], into Afrique and the greater Asia, especially the territories of the Persian monarchie. 1634, 1638, 1639, 1665, 1677; rptd Harris vol 1, 1705 etc (abridged); ed W. Foster 1928 (abridged); Amsterdam and New

York 1971 (facs of 1634); tr Flemish, 1658; French, 1663.

Mundy, Peter. A briefe relation of certaine journeies and voyages into Fraunce, Spaine, Turkey and East India [relations iv–xix of Indian voyages 1628–34]. Ed R. C. Temple 1914 (Hakluyt Soc). Written by 1634, BM Harley ms 2286; copied 1639 and later in Bodley Rawlinson ms A 315.

—— Itinerarium mundii: that is a memoriall of sundry relations of certaine voiages journeies ettc [relations xxi–xxx of Indian voyage 1636–8]. Ed R. C. Temple 2 pts 1919 (Hakluyt Soc). From Rawlinson ms A 315, copied 1639 and continued later.

—— Itinerarium mundii [relation of the last East Indian voyage 1655–6]. Ed R. C. Temple 1936 (Hakluyt Soc).

Bruton, William. Newes from the East-Indies: or a voyage [1633] to Bengalla one of the greatest kingdomes under the Great Mogull. 1638; rptd Harleian voyages vol 2, 1745, 1747; rptd in Hakluyt's collection of the early voyages vol 5, 1809–12; rptd A selection of curious, rare and early voyages, 1812.

A terrible sea-fight [at Goa]. 1640; ed B. Penrose, Sea fights in the East Indies, Cambridge Mass 1931.

A most execrable and barbarous murder done by an East-Indian devil, or a native of Java-Major, in the road of Bantam, aboard an English ship [in 1641]. 1642.

Mendes Pinto, Fernao. The voyages and adventures of Fernand Mendez Pinto, a Portugall: during his travels for the space of one and twenty years in the kingdoms of Ethiopia, China, Tartaria, Conchinchina, Calaminham, Siam, Pegu, Japan and a great part of the East Indies, done into English by H[enry] C[ogan]. 1653, 1663, 1692; ed A. Vambery 1891 (abridged); ed C. D. Ley, The furthest East 1537–8, 1947 (chs 25–46 of The voyages and adventures). From the Peregrinacao, Madrid 1614 etc. Passage ptd in Purchas.

Camoens, Luis de. The Lusiad: or Portugals historicall poem, written in the Portingall language by Luis de Camoens, and now newly put into English by Richard Fanshaw. 1655; ed J. D. M. Ford, Cambridge Mass 1940. From Os Lusiadas, Lisbon 1572 etc.

Terry, Edward. A voyage to East-India [1615–19], within that rich and most spacious empire of the Great Mogol; observed by Edward Terry, then chaplain to the Right Honorable Sr Thomas Row, Knight. 1655; rptd in The travels of Pietro della Valle, 1665; 1777; ed W. Foster, Early travels in India, 1926.

Stayner, Sir Richard. A true relation of the destroying of the Spanish shipps at the Isle of Tenariff, the 20th Aprill 1657, from the first intelligence we had of them as we lay before Cales. Ed C. H. Firth 1912 (Navy Records Soc). BM additional ms 32,093 fol 372.

Le Blanc, Vincent. The world surveyed: or the famous voyages and travailes of Vincent le Blanc, or White of Marseilles, who from the age of fourteen years, to threescore and eighteen, travelled through most parts of the world; rendred into English by F[rancis] B[rooke]. 1660. From Les voyages fameux, Paris 1648 etc.

Farther Africa and Asia

Haiton of Armenia. Here begynneth a lytell cronycle [of Asia]. [1530]. From Les fleurs des hystoyres de la terre dorient, Paris [1515] etc. Part in Purchas, retr from Ramusio's Viaggi.

The strange and marveilous newes lately come from the great Kingdome of Chyna, translated out of the Castlyn tongue by T. N[icholas]. [1577].

[Nichols, Thomas]. A pleasant description of the fortunate ilandes called the Ilands of Canaria, with their straunge fruits and commodities. 1583; rptd Hakluyt 1599; rptd Astley vol 2, 1745–7; tr German, Schwabe vol 2.

Minadoi, Giovanni Tommaso. The history of the warres betweene the Turkes and the Persians. 1595. Tr Abraham Hartwell from the Historia della guerra fra Turchi e Persiani, Venice 1588 etc.

Agatharchides. Excerpta quaedam ex Agatharchide de rubro Mari. In Agatharchidis et Memnonis historicorum, quae supersunt; omnia e graeco iam recens in latinum traducta: per Rich. Brettum, Oxford 1597. Greek and Latin.

Memnon de statu Heracl. poticae (excerpta quaedam). Oxford 1597, above.

Duc Bec-Crispin, Jean. The historie of the great Emperour Tamerlan, drawn from the auncient monuments of the Arabians; newly translated out of Franch by H. M. 1597; in Purchas (in part). From the Histoire du grand Empereur Tamerlanes, Rouen 1595.

Johannes Leo Africanus. A geographical historie of Africa, written in Arabicke and Italian by John Leo a More; before which is prefixed a generall description of Africa; translated and collected by John Pory. 1600; in Purchas (in part); Harris vol 1, 1705 etc; rptd in Hakluyt's collection of early voyages vol 5, 1809–12; ed R. Brown 3 vols 1896 (Hakluyt Soc), 1963; Amsterdam and New York 1969 (facs of 1600). From the Descrittione dell'Africa in Ramusio vol 1, 1550 etc.

Houtman, Frederik de. Dialogues in the English and Malaiane languages: or certain common formes of speech, first written in Latin, Malaian and Madagascar tongues, by Gotardus Arthusius, translated into the English tongue by Augustine Spalding. 1614. Ultimately from the Spraecke ende woord-boeck, Amsterdam 1603 etc.

B[edwell], W[illiam]. The Arabian trudgman: that is, certaine Arabicke termes, as names of places, titles of honour, dignitie etc oft used by writers. 1615.

Lord, Henry. A display of two forraigne sects in the East Indies vizt: the sect of the Banians of the ancient natives of India and the sect of the Persees. 1630; rptd Churchill vol 6, 1704–32 etc; Pinkerton vol 8; tr French, 1667, 1723.

Borri, Cristoforo. Cochin-China: containing many admirable rarities and singularities of that countrey; extracted out of an Italian relation and published by Robert Ashley. 1633; retr Churchill vol 2, 1704–32 etc; Pinkerton vol 9; Amsterdam and New York 1971 (facs of 1633). From the first pt of the Relatione della Nuova Missione, Rome 1631.

Baudier, Michel. The history of the imperiall estate of the Grand Seigneurs: their habitations, lives, titles, qualities, exercises, workes; translated out of French by E[dward] G[rimeston]. 1635. From the Histoire générale du serrail et de la cour du grand Seigneur; ensemble l'histoire de la cour du Roy de la Chine, Paris 1624 etc.

Hamond, Wa[lter]. A paradox: prooving that the inhabitants of the isle called Madagascar, or St Laurence (in temporall things) are the happiest people in the world. 1640; part rptd Harleian miscellany vol 1, 1744 etc.

—— Madagascar, the richest and most fruitfull island in the world: wherein the temperature of the clymate, the nature of the inhabitants and the facility and benefit of a plantation by our people there, are compendiously described. 1643.

The East-India trade: a true narration of divers parts in East-India; of the commodities, and trade one kingdome holdeth with another; whereby it appeareth how much profit this nation is deprived by restraint of trade to those parts. [1641].

Boothby, Richard. A breife discovery or description of the most famous island of Madagascar or St Laurence in Asia neare unto East-India. 1646; rptd Harleian voyages vol 2 1745, 1747; rptd Churchill 1752.

Greaves, John. Pyramidographia: or a description of the pyramids in Aegypt. 1646; rptd Churchill vol 2, 1704–32; tr French, in M. Thevenot, Relations, 1663.

—— A description of the Grand Signors seraglio. 1650, 1653. Ed John Gresves, as by Robert Withers: see Europe, 1625, above.

—— Chorasmiae, et Mawaralnahrae, hoc est regionum extra fluvium Oxum descriptio, ex tabulis Abulfedae Ismaelis. 1650; rptd with further material in J. Hudson, Geographiae veteris scriptores graeci minores vol 3, 1698; 1711. Persian text, with Latin version.

—— Binae tubulae geographicae, una Nassir Eddini Persae, altera Ulug Beigi Tatari. 1652. Persian texts with Latin version.

Waldegrave, Powle. A answer to Mr Boothbies book, of the description of the island of Madagascar, in vindication of the Honorable Society of merchants trading to East-India. 1649.

Hunt, Robert. The island of Assada, neere Madagascar impartially defined: being a discription of the situation, fertility and people therein inhabiting. [1650].

Pocock, Edward. Specimen historiae Arabum: sive Gregorii Abul Farajii de origine & moribus Arabum succincta narratio. 1650, Oxford 1806. Brief text, Arabic and Latin, with lengthy notes.

—— The nature of the drink Kauhi or coffee, and the berry of which it is made; described by an Arabian phisitian. 1659. Arabic and English text, 4 pages.

D[arell], J[ohn]. Strange news from th'Indies: or East-India passages further discovered. 1652.

[Clarke, Samuel]. The life of Tamerlane the Great, with his wars against the Great Duke of Moso, the King of China, Bajazet the Great Turk. 1653.

Martini, Martinus. Bellum tartaricum: or the conquest of the Empire of China, by the invasion of the Tartars, who in these last seven years have wholly subdued that vast Empire. 1654, 1655 (with next item). From De bello tartarico, Antwerp 1654.

Semmedo, Alvaro. The history of that great and renowned monarchy of China: wherein all the particular provinces are accurately described, now put in English by a person of quality. 1655. From the Imperio de la China, in Portuguese, Madrid 1642, via the Italian, Rome 1643.

(7) AMERICA

Voyages to America

The voyage of the Barbara to Brazil, anno 1540. Ed R. G. Marsden 1912 (Navy Records Soc) (in Naval miscellany vol 2). From High Court of Admiralty Oyer et Terminer 34: The examinacyon of George Mone etc.

Ribaut, Jean. The whole and true discovery of Terra Florida (englished the Florishing lande), never founde out before the last yere 1562. 1563, 1582 (in Hakluyt's Divers voyages); rptd in Historical collections of Louisiana and Florida, New York 1875; ed H. P. Biggar, EHR 32 1917 (from Sloane ms 3644); ed J. Thurber, Pbns Florida State Historical Soc 7 1927 (facs); tr Dutch, Van der Aa.

[Le Challeux, Nicholas]. A true and perfect description of the last voyage or navigation, attempted by Capitaine John Rybaut into Terra Florida, this yeare past 1565. [1566]; rptd Americana Ser 1920; tr S. Lorant, The New World, New York 1946, 1954. From the Discours de l'histoire de la Floride, Dieppe 1566 etc.

Thevet, André. The new found worlde, or Antarctike: wherein is contained wonderful and strange things, as well of humaine creatures, as beastes. 1568, Amsterdam and New York 1971 (facs). Tr from Les singularitez de la France Antarctique, Paris 1558 etc.

Hawkins, Sir John. A true declaration of the troublesome voyadge of M. John Haukins to the parties of Guynea and the West Indies. 1569, 1589, 1600 (in Hakluyt); ed E. Arber vol 5 1877, vol 1 1903; ed C. R. Markham 1878 (Hakluyt Soc); rptd Payne; ed H. S. Burrage, Original narratives, 1906, 1959; Americana ser 1921; ed G. R. G. Conway, Mexico City 1926 (facs).

An account of Hawkins' third slaving voyage 1569. Ed J. A. Williamson, Sir John Hawkins, 1927. BM Cotton ms Otho E viii folios 17–41.

An account of Frobisher's first voyage 1576. Ed R. Collinson 1867 (Hakluyt Soc). BM Cotton ms Otho E viii folio 47.

Settle, Dionyse. A true reporte of the laste voyage into the west and northwest regions etc 1577, worthily atchieved by Capteine Frobisher. 1577, 1577, 1589, 1600 (in Hakluyt); rptd Pinkerton vol 12; Providence 1868 (facs); Americana ser 1925; ed V. Stefansson, Three voyages of Martin Frobisher, 2 vols 1938; Amsterdam and New York 1969 (facs of 1577); tr French, 1578; German and Latin, 1580; Latin, 1675; Italian, 1582; Dutch, Van der Aa 1707.

[Best, George]. A true discourse of the late voyages of discoverie, for the finding of a passage to Cathaya, by the northweast, under the conduct of Martin Frobisher Generall. 1578, 1600 (in Hakluyt); rptd Pinkerton vol 12; ed R. Collinson 1867 (Hakluyt Soc); ed V. Stefans-

son, Frobisher; tr Dutch, [1640], 1678, Van der Aa; German, 1679; French, J. F. Bernard, Recueil de voiages au nord, Amsterdam 1715, 1720, 1731.

Churchyarde, Thomas. A prayse, and reporte of Maister Martyne Forboishers [second] voyage to Meta Incognita. 1578; rptd Americana ser 1921.

Ellis, Thomas. A true report of the third and last voyage into Meta Incognita, atchieved by the worthie Capteine, M. Martine Frobisher esquire, anno 1578; written by Thomas Ellis sailer and one of the companie. [1578], 1589, 1600 (in Hakluyt); rptd Pinkerton vol 12; Americana ser 1922; ed V. Stefansson, Frobisher; tr Dutch, Van der Aa.

Sellman, Edward. An account of Frobisher's third voyage 1578. Ed R. Collinson 1867 (Hakluyt Soc) (from ms).

Lopez de Gomara, Francisco. The pleasant historie of the conquest of the Weast India, now called New Spayne, atchieved by the worthy Prince Hernando Cortes; translated out of the Spanish tongue by T[homas] N[icholas]. 1578, 1596; rptd Purchas (in part); ed H. I. Priestley, New York 1940 (facs). From Historia general de las Indias, Saragossa 1552 etc.

Cartier, Jacques. A shorte and briefe narration of the two navigations and discoveries [1534–5] to the north-weast partes called Newe France, turned into English by John Florio. 1580, 1600 (in Hakluyt); rptd Churchill vol 4; Pinkerton vol 12; Kerr; rptd March of America vol 10, Ann Arbor 1966 (facs); rptd D. B. Quinn with Hakluyt's Divers voyages, 2 vols in Mundus Novus 1st ser vol 1, Amsterdam 1967 (facs). Florio's trn from Ramusio's Viaggi, vol 3 1556 etc; tr H. P. Biggar, Ottawa 1924.

Cooke, John. For Fraunses Drake, Knight, sone to Sir [Edmund] Drake, vickar of Upchurche, in Kent, anno dni 1577. Ed W. S. W. Vaux 1854 (Hakluyt Soc); ed R. C. Temple, The world encompassed, 1926. A ms account of part of the Voyage of circumnavigation, BM Harley 540 fol 93.

Fletcher, Francis. The first part of the second voiage about the world attempted continued and happily accomplished with the tyme of 3 years by Mr Ffrancis Drake; written and faithfully layed downe by Ffrancis Fletcher. Ed R. C. Temple, The world encompassed, 1926. BM Sloane ms 61. This is the basis of the younger Drake's narrative, The world encompassed 1628, below. Other narratives in Hakluyt.

Zarate, Augustin de. The strange and delectable history of the discoverie and conquest of the provinces of Peru, in the South Sea; translated out of the Spanish tongue, by T[homas] Nicholas. 1581; ed D. B. Thomas 1933. From Historia del descumbrimiento y conquista del Peru, Antwerp 1555 etc.

Ingram, David. Relation, in travelling by land from the Bay of Mexico [1568–82] [ms BM Sloane 1477]. 1589, 1600 (in Hakluyt); ed P. C. J. Weston, Documents connected with the history of South Carolina, 1856 (from original ms); Arber vol 5 1882, vol 1 1903 (from Hakluyt); ed E. de Golyer as The journey of three Englishmen across Texas, El Paso 1947 (from Hakluyt); rptd in March of America vol 14, Ann Arbor 1966 (from Hakluyt) (facs).

H[akluyt], R[ichard]. Divers voyages touching the discoverie of America and the ilands adjacent unto the same, made first of all by our Englishmen, and afterward by the Frenchmen and Britons. 1582; ed J. W. Jones 1850 (Hakluyt Soc); rptd in March of America vol 5, Ann Arbor 1966 (facs); ed D. B. Quinn, Mundus novus 1st ser vol 1, Amsterdam 1967 (facs). Most items rptd in the Principal navigations vol 3, 1600.

Carleill, Captain [Christopher]. A discourse upon the entended voyage to the nethermost partes of America. [1583], 1589, 1600 (in Hakluyt); rptd Americana ser 1923; ed D. B. Quinn, The voyages and colonizing enterprises of Sir Humphrey Gilbert 1940 (Hakluyt Soc) (collated with PRO SP/12/155, 87, 88).

P[eckham], [Sir] G[eorge]. A true reporte of the late discoveries and possession, taken in the right of the Crowne of England, of the New-found Landes; by Sir Humfrey Gilbert. 1583, 1589, 1600 (in Hakluyt); rptd Mag Amer History 68 1920; Americana ser 1927; ed D. B. Quinn, Sir Humphrey Gilbert, 1940 (Hakluyt Soc); Amsterdam and New York 1971 (facs of 1583).

The discourse and description of the voyage of Sir Frawncis Drake and Mr Captaine Frobisher, set forward 1585 [to the West Indies]. Ed J. S. Corbett 1898 (Navy Records Soc). BM Royal ms 7 C xvi, art 36.

Espejo, Antonio de. El viaje que hizo Antonio de Espejo [1583] en neuvo Mexico; impressa en Madrid anno de 1586, y de neuvo en Paris en mesmo anno a la costa de Richardo Hakluyt. Paris 1586. Extracted from Mendoza's China, Madrid 1586. Hakluyt was probably responsible also for French trn by Martin Basanier, Paris 1586. Tr A.F. as New Mexico: otherwise the voiage of Anthony of Espeio, 1587; rptd Americana ser 1921; ed F. W. Hodge, New York 1928. The narrative was also included in Parke's English trn of Mendoza's China, 1588 (see Asia, above), though not in Italian trn of 1587. Another trn, presumably by Hakluyt, Principal navigations vol 3, 1600. Tr H. E. Bolton, Original narratives, 1916 (from ms).

Laudonnière, René de. L'histoire notable de la Floride située es Indes Occidentales, contenant les trois voyages faits en icelle par certains capitaines & pilotes françois [1562–5]. Paris 1586 etc (discovered and pbd by Hakluyt, ed Martin Basanier); tr R[ichard] H[akluyt] as A notable historie containing foure voyages made by certayne French captaynes unto Florida, 1587, 1600 (in Principal navigations); ed B. Franklin, Historical collections of Louisiana and Florida, New York 1869; ed W. A. Courtenay, The genesis of South Carolina 1562-1670, Columbia SC 1907; ed T. R. Adams, New York 1964 (facs); tr German, De Bry pt 14, 1631; Dutch, Van der Aa.

Greepe, Thomas. The true and perfecte newes of the woorthy and valiaunt exploytes, performed and doone by that valiant Knight Syr Fraucis Drake, not onely at Sancto Domingo and Carthagena, but also now at Cales. [1587]; rptd Americana ser 1924; ed D. W. Waters, Americanum nauticum no 3, Hartford 1955 (facs). Verse.

Cates, Thomas. A summarie and true discourse of Sir Frances Drakes West Indian voyage. 1589, 1589, 1600 (in Hakluyt); in Sir Francis Drake revived, 1653 (1626 below); in A selection of curious, rare and early voyages, 1812; rptd Payne; tr Latin, 1588, 1590 (in Narrationes duae, with account of Portugal voyage); French, 1588; German, 1589. Begun by Walter Biggs, continued by Lieutenant Cripps, 'published' by Thomas Cates.

Hortop, Job. The rare travailes of Job Hortop an Englishman: wherin is declared the dangers he escaped in his voiage to Gynnie [and Mexico, with Hawkins 1569]. 1591, 1591, 1600 (in Hakluyt); rptd Arber vol 5, 1877, vol 1 1903; Americana ser 1925; ed G. R. G. Conway, Mexico City 1928 (facs).

R[oberts], H[enry]. Our Ladys retorne to England, accompanied with Saint Frances and the Good Jesus of Viona in Portugal who, comming from Brasell, arrived at Clovelly. 1592.

—— Lancaster his allarums, honorable assaultes and supprising of block-houses in Brasill. [1595]; ed W. Foster, The voyages of Sir James Lancaster 1940 (Hakluyt Soc).

Wyatt, Captain. An account of Robert Dudley's voyage to the West Indies 1594. Ed G. F. Warner 1899 (Hakluyt Soc). From BM Sloane ms 858.

Kendall, Abram. [An account of the same]. Ed G. F. Warner 1899 (Hakluyt Soc). First ptd in Italian in Robert Dudley, Arcano del mare, Florence 1646, 1661; retr for English edn.

[Hawkins, Sir Richard]. Treslado de una carta ed R. Hauquines, escrita en el puerto de Perico 1594 para embiar a su padre. [Seville 1595]. Retr J. A. Williamson in following.

—— The observations of Sir Richard Hawkins Knight, in his voiage into the South Sea, anno domini 1593. 1622; rptd Purchas; rptd Harris vol 1, 1705, etc; ed C. R. D. Bethune 1847 (Hakluyt Soc); ed C. R. Markham 1878 (Hakluyt Soc); ed J. A. Williamson 1934; Amsterdam and New York 1968 (facs of 1622).

The seaventh voyadge of the Right Honnorable the Earle of Cumberland to the West Indies in the years of Our Lord 1593 and 1594. Ed K. R. Andrews, English privateering voyages to the West Indies 1588-95, 1959 (Hakluyt Soc). From ms in Appleby Castle.

Maynarde, Thomas. Sir Francis Drake his voyage 1595. In Sir Francis Drake revived, 1653 (1626 below); ed W. D. Cooley 1849 (Hakluyt Soc); ed K. R. Andrews, The last voyage of Drake and Hawkins, 1972 (Hakluyt Soc). BM additional ms 5209.

Troughton, John. Journal of the last voyage of Drake and Hawkins 1595. In Purchas; ed K. R. Andrews 1972 (Hakluyt Soc). PRO SP 12/257 no 48.

Austyn, John. The confession of John Austyn of London, marryner, taken the xxvth daye of Marche 1595, whoe was one of the late compaynye of Sir Francis Drake and Sir John Hawkins, kneightes, taken before George Baron, depute to James Bagge, Maior of Plymmouthe; endorsed 25 March 1596. Ed K. R. Andrews 1972 (Hakluyt Soc). PRO SP 12/256 no 111.

Baskerville, Sir Thomas. Discourse [of the last voyage of Drake and Hawkins]. 1596; ed K. R. Andrews 1972 (Hakluyt Soc). BM Harley ms 4762 folios 70-4.

Savile, Henry. A libell of Spanish lies, found at the sacke of Cales, discoursing the fight in the West Indies, and of the death of Sir Francis Drake, with an answere briefely confuting the Spanish lies and a short relation of the fight according to truth. 1596, 1600 (in Hakluyt); ed K. R. Andrews 1972 (Hakluyt Soc). Original Spanish text in Museo Naval Madrid, Navarrete ms V no 11 folios 81-3.

Ralegh, Sir Walter. The discoverie of the large, rich and bewtiful empyre of Guiana, with a relation of the great and golden citie of Manoa (which the Spanyards call El Dorado). 1596 (3 edns), 1600 (in Hakluyt); ed T. Birch, Works of Sir Walter Raleigh vol 2, 1751; ed A. Cayley, Life of Sir Walter Raleigh vol 1, 1805; in History of the world, Edinburgh 1820; in Works vol 8, Oxford 1829; ed R. H. Schomburgk 1848 (Hakluyt Soc); rptd Payne; ed H. Morley 1887; ed W. H. D. Rouse 1905; ed V. T. Harlow 1928; Leeds 1967 (facs); Amsterdam and New York 1968 (facs); tr German, in Hulsius pt 5, 1598, 1599, 1601, 1603, 1612, in Schwabe, 1747; Dutch, 1598, 1605, 1617, 1644, and in Van der Aa; Latin, in

Hulsius pt 5, 1599, De Bry pt 8, 1599, 1625; French, in Voyages de F. Coreal, 1722, and in Recueil de voyages dans l'Amérique méridionale vol 1, Amsterdam 1738.
— Of the voyage for Guiana. In The history of the world, 1820; ed Schomburgk 1848 (Hakluyt Soc); ed Harlow, 1928. BM Sloane ms 1133.
— [Journal of the second voyage to Guiana 1618]. Ed R. H. Schomburk 1848 (Hakluyt Soc); ed H. Morley 1887; ed V. T. Harlow 1932. BM Cotton ms Titus B VIII, folios 162–75.
— Sir Walter Rawleigh his apologie for his voyage to Guiana. In Judicious and select essayes and observations, 1650, 1667; in An abridgment of Sir Walter Raleigh's History of the world, 1700, 1702; in T. Birch, Works vol 2, 1751; in A. Cayley, Life vol 2, 1805, 1806; in History of the world vol 6, 1820; in Works vol 8, Oxford 1829; ed V. T. Harlow 1932.
Keymis, Lawrence. A relation of the second voyage to Guiana, performed and written in the yeare 1596. 1596, 1600 (in Hakluyt); Amsterdam and New York 1968 (facs of 1596); tr Latin, De Bry pt 8 1599, 1625; Dutch 1605, 1619; German, in Schwabe vol 16, 1747; French, 1722 (with Ralegh, The discoverie), 1738.
Ercilla y Zuniga, Alonso de. The historie of Araucana, written in verse: translated out of the Spanishe into Englishe prose allmost to the ende of the 16: canto [c. 1600]. Ed F. W. Pierce, Manchester 1964. Lambeth Palace Lib ms 688. Tr George Carew, Earl of Totnes.
Brierton, John. A briefe and true relation of the discoverie of the north part of Virginia, made this present yeare 1602 by Captaine Bartholomew Gilbert; written by M. John Brereton one of the voyage. 1602, 1602 (augmented); rptd Collections Massachusetts Historical Soc ser 3 vol 8, 1843 (2nd issue); ed L. S. Livingston, New York 1903 (facs of first issue); ed G. P. Winship, Sailors' narratives of voyages along the New England coast, Boston 1905 (2nd issue); ed H. S. Burrage, Original narratives, 1906 (first issue), 1959; rptd in March of America vol 16, Ann Arbor 1966 (facs of 1602).
Rosier, James. A true relation of the most prosperous voyage made this present yeere 1605, by Captaine George Waymouth, in the discovery of the land of Virginia. 1605; rptd Purchas (in part); ed G. Prince, Bath Maine 1860; ed H. S. Burrage, Portland Maine 1887 (Gorges Soc); ed G. P. Winship, Sailors narratives; ed H. S. Burrage, Original narratives, 1906, 1959.
Hall, James. A report to King Christian IV on the Danish expedition to Greenland under Captain John Cunningham 1605. Ed C. C. A. Gosch 1897 (Hakluyt Soc). BM Royal ms 17 A XLVIII.
A relatyon of the discovery of our river from James Forte into the maine, made by Capt Christofer Newport [May–June 1607]. Ed E. E. Hale, Archaeologia americana vol 4, Boston 1860; ed E. Arber, Works of Captain John Smith, Birmingham 1884; 2 vols 1895, Edinburgh 1910; ed P. L. Barbour, The Jamestown voyages under the first charter 1606–9, 2 vols 1969 (Hakluyt Soc). PRO State Papers Colonial, America 1, 15.
A breif discription of the people [of Virginia c. 1607]. Ed E. E. Hale, Archaeologia americana vol 4, Boston 1860; ed E. Arber, Smith's works, 1884 etc; ed P. L. Barbour 1969 (Hakluyt Soc). PRO CO/1/1 folios 55–6.
The discription of the now discovered river and country of Virginia, with the liklyhood of ensuing ritches, by Englands ayd and industry c. 1607. Ed E. E. Hale, Archaeologia, 1860; ed E. Arber, Smith's works, 1884 etc; ed P. L. Barbour 1969 (Hakluyt Soc). PRO CO/1/1 folios 53–5.
Copie of a letter from Virginia dated 22th of June 1607 the Councell their, to the Councell of Virginia here in England. Ed E. D. Neill, Early settlement of Virginia and Virginiola, Minneapolis 1878; ed P. L. Barbour 1969 (Hakluyt Soc). Northumberland Papers, Syon House ms folio 263.

[Davies, James]. The relation of a voyage unto New England began from the Lizard, the first of June 1607, by Captn Popham and Captn Gilbert. Ed B. F. de Costa, Cambridge Mass 1880; ed H. O. Thayer, Portland Maine 1892 (Gorges Soc); ed G. P. Winship, Sailors' narratives, Boston 1905; ed H. S. Burrage, Original narratives, 1906 (from Lambeth ms).
Nicholl, John. An houre glasse of indian newes: or A true and tragicall discourse, shewing the most lamentable miseries indured by 67 Englishmen, which were sent for a supply to the planting in Guiana in the yeare 1605. 1607; rptd Purchas (abridged); Americana ser 1925.
Smith, Captain John. A true relation of such occurrences and accidents of noate as hath hapned in Virginia since the first planting of that collony. 1608, Richmond Virginia 1845; ed C. Deane, Boston 1866; ed E. Arber, Smith's works, 1884 etc; ed L. G. Tyler, Original narratives, 1907 etc; ed P. L. Barbour 1969 (Hakluyt Soc).
— A map of Virginia, with a description of the countrey, the commodities, people, government and religion. Oxford 1612; in Smith's Generall historie, 1624; rptd Purchas (abridged); ed E. Arber, Smith's works, 1884 etc; ed L. G. Tyler, Original narratives, 1907 etc; ed B. C. MacCary, Jamestown 1957; ed P. L. Barbour 1969 (Hakluyt Soc).
— A description of New England: or the observations and discoveries of Captain John Smith in the north of America 1614; with the success of sixe ships that went 1615. 1616; rptd Collections of Massachusetts Historical Soc 3rd ser 6 1837; Force, Tracts vol 2, 1836–46; ed C. Deane, Boston 1865; ed E. Arber, Smith's works, 1884 etc; ed G. P. Winship, Sailors narratives, 1905; tr Latin, Dr Bry pt 10, 1619; German, Hulsius pt 14, 1617, 1628, De Bry pt 10, 1618.
— New Englands trials: declaring the successe of 26 ships employed thether within these sixe yeares; with the benefit of that countrey by sea and land. 1620, 1622; Force, Tracts vol 2, 1836–46, 1897–9 (from 2nd edn); ed C. Deane, Cambridge Mass 1867 (from 2nd edn); ed C. Deane, Cambridge Mass 1873 (from first edn); ed E. Arber, Smith's works, 1884 etc; Amsterdam and New York 1971 (facs of 1620).
— The generall historie of Virginia, New England and the Summer Isles. 1624, 1625, 1626, 1627, 1631, 1632; rptd Pinkerton vol 13; ed E. Arber, Smith's works, 1884 etc; rptd Glasgow 1907 (with The travels); ed L. G. Tyler, Original narratives, 1907 etc (in part); A. Smith, Virginia 1584–1607, 1957 (in part).
— The true travels, adventures and observations of Captaine John Smith, in Europe, Asia, Affrica and America, from anno domini 1593 to 1629; together with a continuation of his generall history. 1630; rptd Churchill vol 2; ed J. H. Rice, Richmond Virginia 1819; ed E. Arber, Smith's works, 1884 etc; rptd Glasgow 1907 (with Generall historie); Amsterdam and New York 1968 (facs); tr Dutch, Van der Aa.
— Advertisements for the unexperienced planters of New-England, or any where; with the yearely proceedings of this country in fishing and planting, since the yeare 1614. 1631; rptd Collections of Massachusetts Historical Soc 3rd ser 3 1833; ed C. Deane, Boston 1865; ed E. Arber, Smith's works, 1884 etc; ed L. B. Wright, Newes from the new-world, San Marino 1946; Amsterdam and New York 1971 (facs).
[Wingfield, Edward-Maria]. Here followeth what happened in James Towne, in Virginia, after Captayne Newports departure for Engliund [in 1607]. 1845; ed C. Deane, Archaeologia americana vol 4, Boston 1860; ed E. Arber, Smith's works, 1884 etc; ed P. L. Barbour 1969 (Hakluyt Soc).
Letter of Peter Winne [Wynne] to Sir John Egerton [from Virginia] Nov 26 1608. Ed C. M. Andrews, The colonial period of American history vol 1, New Haven 1934;

ed L. B. Wright, Newes from the new-world, San Marino 1946; ed P. L. Barbour 1969 (Hakluyt Soc).

Spelman, Henry. Henry Spelmans relation of Virginea 1609. Ed J. F. Hunnewell 1872; ed E. Arber, Smith's works, 1884 etc.

J[ohnson], R[obert]. Nova Britannia: offring most excellent fruites by planting in Virginia. 1609; rptd Force, Tracts vol 1, 1836, 1897; ed J. Sabin, New York 1867; Amsterdam and New York 1969 (facs).

—— The new life of Virginea, declaring the former successe and present estate of that plantation: being the second part of Nova britannia. 1612; rptd Collections of Massachusetts Historical Soc 2nd ser 8 1826; rptd Force, Tracts vol 1, 1836, 1897.

Elvas, A gentleman of. Virginia richly valued, by the description of the maine land of Florida, her next neighbour, out of the foure yeers discoverie of Don Ferdinando de Soto, translated out of Portuguese by Richard Hakluyt. 1609; as The worthye and famous history, of the conquest of Terra Florida, 1611; rptd Purchas (abridged); in Hakluyt's collection of the early voyages, travels and discoveries of the English nation vol 5, 1812; in a selection of curious, rare and early voyages, 1812; rptd Force, Tracts vol 4, 1845; ed W. B. Rye 1851 (Hakluyt Soc); in March of America vol 12, Ann Arbor 1966 (facs).

West, Thomas, Lord de la Warr. [A letter to the patentees in England relative to the voyage of 1610]. Ed R. H. Major 1849 (Hakluyt Soc). BM Harley ms 7009 folio 58.

—— The relation of the Right Honourable the Lord De-la-Warre, Lord Governour and Captaine Generall of the colonie planted in Virginea. 1611; rptd Purchas; 1858; New York 1867 (facs); ed A. Brown, Genesis of the United States vol 1, Boston 1890; ed L. G. Lyon, Original narratives, 1907 etc.

[Jourdan, Silvester]. A discovery of the Barmudas, otherwise called the Ile of Divels, by Sir Thomas Gates, Sir George Sommers and Captayne Newport. 1610, 1613 (as A plaine description of the Barmudas); in Hakluyt's collection of the early voyages vol 5 1812; rptd A selection of curious, rare and early voyages, 1812; rptd Force, Tracts vol 3, 1836-46; rptd Edinburgh 1884 (Aungervyle Soc) (from 1610); ed J. Q. Adams, New York 1940 (facs); ed L. B. Wright, A voyage to Virginia in 1609, Charlottesville 1964 (from 1610); Amsterdam and New York 1971 (facs of 1613).

Rich, R[ichard]. Newes from Virginia: the lost flocke triumphant; with the happy arrival of Sr Thomas Gates into Virginia; with the maner of their distresse in the Iland of Devils (otherwise called Bermoothawes). 1610; ed J. O. Halliwell(-Phillipps) 1865, 1874; ed E. D. Neill, Early settlement of Virginia, Minneapolis 1878; Mag of Amer History 1883; in A. Brown, Genesis of the United States vol 1, Boston 1890; ed W. F. Craven, New York 1940 (facs); Amsterdam and New York 1970 (facs). Verse.

A true and sincere declaration of the purpose and ends of the Plantation begun in Virginia, of the degrees which it hath received, and meanes by which it hath been advanced, and the resolution and conclusion of his Majestie's Council of that Colony; set forth by the authority of the Governors and Councellors. 1610; ed A. Brown, Genesis vol 1, Boston 1890.

A true declaration of the estate of the colonie in Virginia, with a confutation of such scandalous reports as have tended to the disgrace of so worthy an enterprise; published by advise and direction of the Councell of Virginia. 1610; rptd Force, Tracts vol 3, 1844.

Dale, Sir Thomas. [A report on Virginia in a letter to Lord Salisbury 17 Aug 1611]. Ed A. Brown, Genesis vol 1, Boston 1890. PRO SP Col America, I. 26.

Gatonbe, John. A voyage into the North-West Passage, undertaken in the year 1612 by Captain James Hall. Churchill vol 6, 1732 etc; rptd in C. R. Markham, The

voyages of William Baffin, 1881 (Hakluyt Soc) (in part); ed C. C. A. Gosch 1897 (Hakluyt Soc).

Strachey, William. The historie of travaile into Virginia Britannia: expressing the cosmographie and comodities of the country. In Purchas (in part); ed R. H. Major 1849 (Hakluyt Soc); ed L. B. Wright and V. Freund 1953 (Hakluyt Soc). c. 1612. BM Sloane ms 1622, Bodley Ashmole ms 1758, used for 1849 edn. For 1953 edn Princeton ms used in collation with the 2 preceding mss.

Harcourt, Robert. A relation of a voyage to Guiana: describing the climat, scituation, fertilitie, provisions and commodities of that country. 1613, 1626; rptd Purchas (abridged); rptd Harleian miscellany vol 6, 1808-13 (from 1613); ed C. A. Harris 1928 (Hakluyt Soc).

Whitaker, Alexander. Good newes from Virginia; wherein also is a narration of the present state of that country and of our colonies there. 1613; rptd Purchas; New York 1936 (facs).

Baffin, William. A true relation of such thinges as happened during the voyage of 1615. Ed T. Rundall 1849 (Hakluyt Soc); ed C. R. Markham 1881 (Hakluyt Soc). BM additional ms 12,206.

Hamor, Ralph. A true discourse of the present estate of Virginia, and the successe of the affaires there till the 18 of June 1614. 1615, rptd Albany NY 1860; ed A. L. Rowse, Richmond Virginia 1957; Amsterdam and New York 1971 (facs of 1615).

Hughes, Lewis. A letter sent into England from the Summer Ilands. 1615; rptd Americana ser 1926.

—— A plaine and true relation of the goodnes of God towards the Sommer Ilands. 1621; rptd Americana ser 1926.

Rolfe, John. A true relation of the state of Virginia 1616. Virginia Historical Register 1 1848; ed New Haven 1951 (from ms) (facs). BM Royal ms 18. A. xi.

Fernandez de Quiros, Pedro. Terra Australis incognita: or a new southerne discoverie, containing a fifth part of the world; lately found out by Ferdinand de Quir. 1617; rptd Purchas; [1723]; ed J. Callander, Terra Australis cognita vol 2, Edinburgh 1766; Amsterdam and New York 1970 (facs). From the Spanish petition of 1610, Seville. Several other trns.

M., R. Newes of Sr Walter Rauleigh; with the true description of Guiana, sent from a gentleman of his fleet 1617. 1618; rptd Force, Tracts vol 3, 1836-46; ed V. T. Harlow 1932 (in part).

Pory, John. [Three letters describing Plymouth colony in the early years 1619 and 1622]. Letter to Sir Dudley Carleton 30 Sept 1619. In Collections of Massachusetts Historical Soc 4th ser 9; ed L. G. Tyler, Original narratives, 1907 etc; ed L. B. Wright, The Elizabethan's America, 1965. PRO ms.

—— [Two letters c. 1622, one to the Earl of Southampton, the other to Sir Francis Wyatt]. Ed C. Burrage, John Pory's lost description of Plymouth colony, Boston 1918; ed S. V. James, Three visitors to early Plymouth, Plymouth Mass 1963. From ms in Carter Brown Lib.

The relation of a wonderfull voiage made by William Cornelison Schouten of Horne: shewing how south from the straights of Magelan, he sayled round about the world. 1619; rptd Purchas; ed J. Callander, Terra Australis vol 2, Edinburgh 1766-8; ed A. Dalrymple, A collection of voyages chiefly in the southern Atlantick ocean vol 2, 1775; ed J. H. Moore, A new collection of voyages vol 1, [1778]; tr William Phillip from the Journael ofte beschryvinge, Amsterdam 1618.

Whitbourne, Richard. A discourse and discovery of New-Found-Land, with many reasons to proove how worthy and beneficiall a plantation may there be made. 1620, 1622, 1623; in Purchas (in part); tr German, Dr Bry pt 13, 1628, Hulsius pt 20, 1629; Latin, Hulsius pt 20, 1629.

— A discourse containing a loving invitation for the advancement of his Majesties most hopefull plantation in the New-Found Land. 1622, 1622, 1622 (with preceding work), 1623 (with preceding work); ed M. Carroll, The seal and herring fishcries of Newfoundland, Montreal 1873.

Winne, Edward. A letter to Sir George Calvert, from Feryland in Newfoundland. 1621, 1622, 1622 (with Whitbourne's Loving invitation, 2nd issue), 1622 (with Whitbourne's Discourse and discovery), 1623 (with Whitbourne's Discourse and discovery).

C., M. A true relation of a wonderfull sea-fight betweene two great and well appointed Spanish ships, and a small English ship [off Guadelope]. 1621, Amsterdam 1621 (abridged as A notable and wonderfull sea-fight).

A briefe relation of the discovery and plantation of New England and of sundry accidents therein occurring, from [1607 to 1622]. 1622; rptd Purchas; rptd Collections of Massachusetts Historical Soc vol 8, 1819, 1826; ed J. P. Baxter, Boston 1890 (Prince Soc).

[Bradford, William and Edward Winslow]. A relation or journal of the beginning and proceedings of the English plantation setled at Plimouth in New England. [Ed G. Mourt and often entitled Mourt's relation] 1622; rptd Purchas (abridged); rptd Collections of Massachusetts Historical Soc 1st ser 8, 1792 etc. Purchas version; rptd Collections 2nd ser 9 1832 (from original ms); ed A. Young, Chronicles of the Pilgrim Fathers, Boston 1841; rptd G. B. Cheever, New York 1848-9, Glasgow 1849; ed H. M. Dexter, Boston 1865; ed E. Arber, The story of the Pilgrim Fathers, 1897; ed T. Besterman, The Pilgrim Fathers: a journal of their coming in the Mayflower, 1939; rptd as Homes in the wilderness, New York 1939; ed S. E. Morison, New York 1952; ed D. B. Heath, New York 1963; in March of America, Ann Arbor 1966 (facs).

Butler, Nathaniel. The historye of the Bermudaes or Summer Islands [1609-22]. Ed J. H. Lefroy 1882 (Hakluyt Soc). BM Sloane ms 750.

Norwood, Richard. Insularum de la Bermuda detectio [c. 1622]. Ed C. Burrage, John Pory's lost description of Plymouth, Boston 1918.

— The journal. Ed W. F. Craven and W. B. Hayward, New York 1945 (facs).

Altham, Emmanuel. [4 letters describing Plymouth colony in its early years 1623 to 1625].

[Letters to Sir Edward Altham, 1623, 1624 and 1625]. Ed S. V. James, Three visitors to early Plymouth, Plymouth Mass 1963. From a private collection. First pbd by S. V. James.

— [Letter to James Sherley 1624]. Ed J. F. Jameson, Proc of Massachusetts Historical Soc 44 1911; ed S. V. James, Three visitors, Plymouth Mass 1963. PRO Adm. Court Misc. bundle 1142.

A true relation of that which lately hapned to the great Spanish fleet and galeons of Terra Firma in America; with many strange deliveries of Captaines and souldiers in the tempest, faithfully translated out of the Spanish originall. 1623; rptd Americana ser 1923.

W[inslow], E[dward]. Good newes from New England: or a true relation of things very remarkable at the plantation of Plimouth in New England [1621-3]. 1624, 1624; rptd Purchas (abridged); rptd Collections of Massachusetts Historical Soc 1st ser 8 1792 etc; ed A. Young, Chronicles of the Pilgrim Fathers, Boston 1841; ed E. Arber, The story of the Pilgrim Fathers, 1897; rptd [1910] (EL).

A true relation of the fleete which went under the Admirall Jaquis Le Hermite [1623-6] through the Straights of Magellane towards the coasts of Peru and the towne of Lima in the West-Indies. 1625. From the Waerachtigh verhael van het succes van de vlote, Amsterdam 1625.

B[aers?], J[an]. A plaine and true relation of the going forth of a Holland fleete 1623, to the coast of Brasile; with the taking in of Salvedoe; and also the base delivery

up of the said towne, by I.B. that hath ben an eye and eare-witnesse. Rotterdam 1626.

Sir Francis Drake revid'd, calling upon this dull or effeminate age to follow his noble steps for gold and silver. 1626, 1628, 1653 (below); ed E. Arber, vol 5 1882, vol 1 1903; ed I. A. Wright, Documents concerning English voyages to the Spanish Main 1569-80, 1932 (Hakluyt Soc); ed J. D. Upcott, Three voyages of Drake, [1936]. An account, by Philip Nichols et al, of the Panama voyage 1572, rev and ed Drake with dedication to Elizabeth I, 1592-3.

Drake, Sir Francis. The world encompassed by Sir Francis Drake: being his next voyage to that to Nombre de Dios. 1628, 1635, 1653 (in next item); rptd Hariclian voyages vol 2, 1745 etc; ed W. S. W. Vaux 1854 (Hakluyt Soc); ed R. C. Temple 1926; ed G. E. Hollingsworth 1933; ed J. D. Upcott, Three voyages, [1936]; Amsterdam and New York 1969 (facs of 1628).

— Sir Francis Drake revived: being a summary and true relation of foure severall voyages. 1653, 1682 (abridged as The voyages of the ever renowned Sr Francis Drake into the West Indies); condensed as a chap-book of 24 pp, The voyages and travels of that renowned Captain etc, [1690]. Includes Sir Francis Drake reviv'd, 1626; The world encompassed, 1628; T. Cates, A summarie and true discourse, 1589; T. Maynarde, A full relation of another voyadge into the West-Indies, 1595.

Levett, Christopher. A voyage into New England begun in 1623 and ended in 1624. 1624, 1628; rptd Collections of Massachusetts Historical Soc 3rd ser 8 1843; rptd Collections of Maine Historical Soc vol 2, 1847, 1902; ed J. P. Baxter, Portland Maine 1893 (Gorges Soc); ed G. P. Winship, Sailor's narratives, 1905.

A true relation of the vanquishing of the towne Olinda, cituated in the capitania of Phernambuco: through the renowned and valiant sea-man Henry C. Lonck, for the licensed West-India Company. Amsterdam 1630.

[Higginson, Francis]. New-Englands plantation: or a short and true description of the commodities as dis-commodities of that countrey. 1630 (3 edns); rptd Collections of Massachusetts Historical Soc 1st ser 1 1792, 1806; rptd Force, Tracts vol 1, 1836 etc (in part); rptd Salem Mass 1908 (Essex Book & Print Club); rptd New York 1930 (New England Soc); Amsterdam and New York 1970 (facs).

— A true relacion of the last voyage to New England, declaring all circumstances with the manner of the passage we had by sea. Ed T. Hutchinson, Boston 1769; rptd A. Young, Chronicles of the first planters of the colony of Massachusetts Bay, 1846; rptd Boston 1865 (Prince Soc); rptd Salem Mass 1908 (Essex Book & Print Club); ed E. L. Smith, Boston 1921.

Dudley, Thomas. [Letter to the Countess of Lincoln, 28 March 1631, giving an account of his voyage]. In Massachusetts: or the first planters, Boston 1696; rptd Collections of Massachusetts Historical Soc 8 1802; rptd from ms collections of New Hampshire Historical Soc vol 4, 1834; rptd Force, Tracts vol 2, 1838 etc; rptd A. Young in Chronicles of Massachusetts Bay, Boston 1846.

Colt, Sir Henry, The voyage of Sr Henrye Colt Knight to the ilands of the Antilleas in the shipp called the Alexander. Ed V. T. Harlow 1925 (Hakluyt Soc). A letter from St Christophers, 1631, ms in Cambridge Univ Lib.

White, Father Andrew. Declaratio coloniae: a declaration of the colony of the Lord Baltimore in Maryland 1632. Tr N. C. Brooks, Force, Tracts vol 4, 1836-46 etc; Latin text ed and tr by J. H. Converse, Baltimore 1874 (Maryland Historical Soc); rptd C. C. Hall, Original narratives, 1910 etc. Ms in Archives of Society of Jesus, Rome.

— A relation of the successfull beginnings of the Lord Baltemores plantation in Maryland: being an extract of certaine letters written from thence. 1634; ed J. G. Shea, Baltimore 1865; Calvert Papers no 3, Baltimore 1899 (Maryland Historical Soc); rptd C. C. Hall, Original narratives, 1910 etc. English version of next item.

—— Relatio itineris in Marylandiam 1634. Tr N. C. Brooks, Force, Tracts vol 4, 1836–46 etc. Brooks trn rev and rptd Woodstock letters, 1872; Latin text ed and tr J. H. Converse, Baltimore 1874–5 (Maryland Historical Soc). Ms in Archives of Society of Jesus, Rome.

James, Thomas. The strange and dangerous voyage of Captaine Thomas James, in his intended discovery of the Northwest Passage; with an appendix concerning longitude by Master Henry Gellibrand. 1633, 1740; rptd Churchill vol 2, 1704–32 etc; rptd Harris vol 1, 1705 etc; rptd The world displayed vol 10, 1773; rptd 1807; ed R. M. Christy 1894 (Hakluyt Soc); rptd R. B. Bodilly 1928 (abridged); Amsterdam and New York 1968 (facs of 1633).

Yong, Captain Thomas. A breife relation of a voyage lately made by me since my departure from Virginia, upon a discovery [up the Delaware river]. Ed P. C. J. Weston, Documents connected with the history of S. Carolina, 1856; rptd Collections of Massachusetts Historical Soc 4th ser 9 1871; rptd Maryland Historical Soc 1876; rptd A. C. Myers, Original narratives, 1912, 1959. Ms in Virginia State Lib, a letter to Sir Francis Windebanke, Secretary of State, from Jamestown 1634.

A relation of Maryland; together with a map of the countrey, the conditions of plantation. 1635; ed J. Sabin, New York 1865; ed C. C. Hall, Original narratives, 1910 etc.

Fox, Luke. North-west Fox: or Fox from the Northwest Passage, beginning with King Arthur. 1635; ed R. M. Christy 2 pts 1894 (Hakluyt Soc).

Mather, Richard. A voyage to New England 1635. Ed A. Young, Chronicles of Massachusetts Bay, Boston 1846; rptd Collections of Dorchester Antiquarian and Historical Soc, Boston 1850.

Thatcher, Anthony. A relation of a shipwreck on the New England coast 1635. Ed A. Young, Chronicles of Massachusetts Bay, Boston 1846.

Jackson, William. A briefe journall: or a succinct and true relation of the most remarkable passages observed in that voyage undertaken by Captaine William Jackson to the Westerne Indies or continent of America [1642–5]. Ed V. T. Harlow, Camden miscellany vol 13, 1924.

Bradford, William. [History of Plymouth plantation 1606–46]. Partial reprint of Nath. Morton's copy of Bradford's History in A. Young, Chronicles of the Pilgrim Fathers, Boston 1841; rptd Collections of Massachusetts Historical Soc 4th ser 3 1856; ed J. A. Doyle 1896; Boston 1898 (facs); rptd from ms with a report of the proceedings incident to the return of the ms to Massachusetts, 1901; ed W. T. Davis, Original narratives, 1908 etc; ed W. C. Ford, Boston 1912; ed H. Wish, New York 1962; ed S. E. Morison, New York 1963.

The case of Mainwaring, Hawes, Payne and others, concerning a depredation made [in 1637] by the Spanish-West-India fleete, upon the ship Elizabeth: restitution sought in Spayne, justice denied and justice petitioned of Parliament. 1646.

Gage, Thomas. The English-American his travail by sea and land [1625–37]: or a new survey of the West India's. 1648, 1655, 1677, 1699, 1702, 1711; ed A. P. Newton, 1928; ed E. S. Thompson, Norman Oklahoma 1958; tr French, 1663, 1672, 1677, 1680, 1695, 1699, 1720, 1721, 1722; Dutch, 1682, 1700; German, 1693.

Winthrop, John. A journal of the transactions and occurrences in Massachusetts 1630–49. Hartford Conn 1790; ed J. Savage 2 vols Boston 1825–6, 1853; ed J. K. Hosmer, Original narratives, 2 vols 1908, 1959.

Norwood, Colonel. A voyage to Virginia. 1649. In Churchill vol 6, 1732 etc; rptd Force, Tracts vol 3, 1836–46 etc.

Bland, Edward. The discovery of New Brittaine, begun 1650, from Fort Henry to the fals of Blandina, first river in New Brittaine. 1651; ed J. Sabin, New York 1873; ed A. S. Salley, Original narratives, 1911; ed C. W. Alvord and L. Bidgood, The first explorations of the Trans-Allegheny region, Cleveland 1912; rptd Americana ser 1923; rptd W. L. Clements, Ann Arbor 1954 (facs); rptd March of America, Ann Arbor 1966 (facs).

Johnson, Edward. A history of New-England, from the English planting in the yeere 1628 until the yeere 1652. 1654, 1654; rptd in Gorges, America painted to the life, 1659 (below); rptd Collections of Massachusetts Historical Soc 2nd ser 1814–19; ed W. F. Poole, Andover Mass 1867; ed J. F. Jameson as The wonderworking providence, Original narratives, 2 vols 1910 etc.

Yeardley, Francis. A letter to John Farrar esq of excursions into Carolina 1654. Thurloe State Papers vol 2, 1742; ed A. S. Salley, Original narratives, 1911.

Penn, Sir William. [Journals relating to the West Indies expedition 1654–5]. In G. Penn, Memorials of Sir William Penn, 2 vols 1833.

A great and wonderful victory obtained by the English forces under General Pen and General Venables against the French and others in the West Indies. 1655 (3 April).

Three great and bloody fights between the English and the French: the first by Gen. Pen and Gen. Venables against St Christophers; the second neer St Mallows; the third near the Isle of Majorica, by Gen. Blake. 1655 (10 April).

Daniell, J. [A letter from Jamaica 3 June 1655]. Thurloe State Papers vol 3, 1742. An account of the West Indies naval voyage.

A dialogue containing a compendious discourse concerning the present designe in the West Indies. 1655 (20 Sept).

S., I. A brief and perfect journal of the late proceedings and successe of the English army in the West-Indies, continued until June the 24th. 1655; By I.S. an eye witnesse, 1655 (19 Dec); rptd Harleian miscellany vol 3, 1744, 1808.

Venables, General Robert. [A narrative by General Venables of his expedition to the island of Jamaica and the conquest thereof]. In Interesting tracts relating to the island of Jamaica, St Jago de la Vega 1800; ed C. H. Firth 1900 (Camden Soc). From BM additional ms 11,410 and 12,429.

A true narrative of the late success of the fleet of this Commonwealth against the King of Spains West-India fleet. 1656.

An attempt on the island of Jamaica, and taking the town of St Jago de la viga 1655; with a true narrative of the late successe against the King of Spains West India fleet. 1657. In a Book of the continuation of forreign passages.

[Doyley, Edward]. A narrative of the great success God hath been pleased to give his Highness forces in Jamaica, as it was communicated in a letter from the Governor of Jamaica. 1658; rptd Americana ser, 1942.

Gorges, [Sir] Ferdinando. America painted to the life: the true history of the Spaniards proceedings, as also of the original undertakings of the advancement of plantations into those parts. 1658, 1659, 1659. Pt 2, A brief narration of the originall undertakings, by Sir Ferdinando Gorges, rptd in Collections of Massachusetts Historical Soc 3rd ser 6 1837; rptd in Collections of Maine Historical Soc, 1847; ed J. P. Baxter, Boston 1890 (Prince Soc). Pt 3, America painted to the life, in Edward Johnson, The history of New-England 1654 (above).

Rivers, Marcellus and Oxenbridge Foyle. Englands slavery or Barbados merchandize: represented in a Petition to the high and honourable Court of Parliament. 1659. On voyage of 1656.

America

Gilbert, Sir Humfrey. A discourse of a discoverie for a new passage to Cataia. 1576, 1589, 1600 (in Hakluyt); rptd in Hakluyt's collection of early voyages vol 3, 1809; ed H. Morley 1886; ed C. Slafter, Boston 1903 (Prince Soc); ed D. B. Quinn, Sir Humphrey Gilbert 1940 (Hakluyt Soc); Amsterdam and New York 1968 (facs of 1576).

Monardes, Nicholas. Joyfull newes out of the newe founde worlde, wherein is declared the rare and singular vertues of diverse and sundrie hearbes, trees, oyles, plantes and stones, englished by John Frampton. 1577 (in part), 1580 (complete), 1596 (complete); ed S. Gaselee, Tudor translations, 2 vols 1925; Amsterdam and New York 1970 (facs of 1577). From Historia medicinal de las cosas de nuestras Indias Occidentales, Seville 1574 etc.

Parkhurst, Anthony. Letter to Richard Hakluyt [the elder] containing notes concerning Newfoundland 1577-8. In E. G. R. Taylor, The original writings and correspondence of the two Richard Hakluyts, 2 vols 1935 (Hakluyt Soc). BM Lansdowne ms 100 no 10.

Fernandez de Enciso, Martin. A briefe description of the portes, creekes, bayes and havens of the Weast India, translated out of the Castill tongue by John Frampton. 1578. From the Suma de geographia, Seville 1519 etc; see Roger Barlow 1541, above.

Hakluyt, Richard. A discourse of the commodity of the taking of the Straight of Magellanno. In E. G. R. Taylor, The original writings and correspondence, 2 vols 1935 (Hakluyt Soc). PRO SP Dom Elizabeth I, 229 no 97.

Las Casas, Bartolome de. The Spanish colonie: or a briefe chronicle of the acts and gestes of the Spaniardes in the West Indies translated into English by M.M.S. 1583; rptd Purchas (abridged); rptd in March of America vol 8, Ann Arbor 1966 (facs).

— The tears of the Indians. 1656, Stanford [1953] (facs). Another trn by John Phillips.

Hakluyt, Richard. A particular discourse concerning the great necessitie and manifolde comodyties that are like to growe to this realme of Englande by the westerne discoveries lately attempted, written 1584. Ed L. Woods and C. Deane, Collections of Maine Historical Soc 2nd ser 1877; ed E. G. R. Taylor, Original writings and correspondence, 1935 (Hakluyt Soc). Ms in New York Public Lib; less complete copy in PRO. SP Dom Elizabeth I, 195 no 127.

Hariot, Thomas. A briefe and true report of the new found land of Virginia, discovered by the English colony there seated. 1588; rptd in De Bry, America pt 1, Frankfurt 1590; rptd 1589, 1600 (in Hakluyt); rptd Pinkerton vol 12, 1808-14; rptd J. Sabin, New York 1871 (facs); ed I. N. Tarbox, Boston 1884 (Prince Soc); rptd Manchester 1888 (facs); ed B. Quaritch, Narratives of the discovery of America no 4, 1893 (De Bry edn); ed H. Stevens 1900; rptd Bibliographer (New York) 1902; ed L. S. Livingston, New York 1903; ed R. G. Adams, Ann Arbor 1931; rptd in S. Lorant, The new world, New York 1946; rptd 1951 (facs); ed D. B. Quinn, The Roanoke voyages, 1955 (Hakluyt Soc); rptd in L. B. Wright, The Elizabethan's America, 1965 (in part); rptd in March of America vol 15, Ann Arbor 1966 (facs); Amsterdam and New York 1971 (facs of 1588); tr Latin, De Bry pt 1, 1590, 1608, 1634; French, De Bry pt 1, 1590; German, Dr Bry pt 1, 1590, 1600, 1620; in M. Dresser, Historien und Bericht von dem Königreich China, 1597.

Davis, John. The worldes hydrographical discription, whereby appeares that from England there is a short and speedie passage into the South Seas. 1595; rptd in Hakluyt's collection of early voyages vol 4, 1811; rptd in A selection of curious, rare and early voyages, 1812; ed A. H. Markham 1880 (Hakluyt Soc); rptd Americana ser 1925.

[Antonelli], Baptista. A relation of the ports, harbours, forts and cities in the West Indies which have bene surveied, edified, finished, made and mended, with those which have bene builded, in a certaine survey by the King of Spaine his direction and commandement; written by Baptista Antonio, surveyour in those parts for the said King, anno 1587. 1600 (in Hakluyt); ed K. R. Andrews 1972 (Hakluyt Soc).

Acosta, Jose de. The naturall and morall historie of the East and West Indies. 1604; rptd Purchas (in part); rptd Harris, 1705 etc; ed C. R. Markham 1880 (Hakluyt Soc); tr Edward Grimstone from the Historia natural y moral de las Indias, Seville 1590 etc.

Lescarbot, Marc. Nova Francia: or the description of that part of New France which is one continent with Virginia, described in the three late voyages and plantation made by Monsieur de Monts; translated out of French into English by P[ierre] E[rondelle]. 1609, [1624]; rptd Harleian voyages vol 2, 1745, 1747; ed H. P. Biggar 1928. The descriptive portions of the Histoire de la Nouvelle-France, Paris 1609. Complete re-trn by W. L. Grant, Toronto 1907-14 (Champlain Soc).

[Digges, Sir Dudley]. Fata mihi totum mea sunt agitanda per orbem. 1611; rptd as Of the circumference of the Earth: or a treatise of the North-east [west] passage, 1612.

Mason, John. A briefe discourse of the Newfoundland, with the situation, temperature, and commodities thereof. Edinburgh 1620; ed D. Laing 1867 (Bannatyne Club); ed J. W. Dean, Boston 1887 (Prince Soc); rptd Americana ser 2 1938.

More excellent observations of the estate and affaires of Holland, in a discourse shewing how necessarie it is to trade into the West Indies; faithfully translated out of the Dutch. 1622.

Waterhouse, Edward. A declaration of the state of the colony and affaires in Virginia; with a relation of the barbarous massacre, and a treatise annexed, written by Henry Briggs, of the north west passage to the South Sea through the continent of Virginia, and by Fretum Hudson. 1622, Amsterdam and New York 1970 (facs). Briggs treatise rptd in Purchas.

C., T. A short discourse of the New-Found-Land: contayning diverse reasons and inducements for the planting of that countrey. Dublin 1623.

Alexander, Sir William. An encouragement to colonies. 1624, 1625; rptd as The mapp and description of New-England, 1630; rptd 1867 (Bannatyne Club); ed E. F. Slafter, Boston 1873 (Prince Soc); Amsterdam and New York 1968 (facs of 1624).

Eburne, Richard. A plaine path-way to plantations; with certaine motives for a present plantation in New-found land above the rest. 1624; ed L. B. Wright, Ithaca 1962 (Folger Lib).

[Gordon, Sir Robert]. Encouragements for such as shall intention to bee under-takers in the new plantation of Cape Briton, now New Galloway in America, by mee Lochinvar. Edinburgh 1625; rptd 1867 (Bannatyne Club).

Hagthorpe, John. Englands-Exchequer: or a discourse of the sea and navigation with some things concerning plantations. 1625.

Morrell, William. New England: or a briefe enarration of the ayre, earth, water, fish and fowles of that country, in Latine and English verse. 1625; rptd Collections of Massachusetts Historical Soc 1 1792, 1806, 1859; ed J. F. Hunnewell, Boston 1895.

[Vaughan, William]. Cambrensium Caroleia, quibus precepta necessaria ad rempublicam intexuntur: ex australissima novae terrae plaga. 1625; American ser 1926. Verse.

— The golden fleece, under which are discouvered the wayes to get wealth, transported from Cambrioll Colchios. 1626.

Breefe notes of the river Amazones and of the coast of Guiana. 1627; rptd Americana ser 1920. 3 copies in PRO CO 1/4 nos 5, 6, 7. Based on ms by Roger North.

H[ayman], R[obert]. Quodlibets, lately come over from New Britaniola, Old-Newfound-Land: epigrams and other small parcels. 1628. Verse.

[White, John]. The planters plea: or the grounds of plantations examined; together with a manifestation of the causes mooving such as have lately undertaken a plantation in New-England. 1630; rptd Force, Tracts vol 2, 1836–46 etc.

D., I. A publication of Guianas plantation newly undertaken by the Earle of Barkshire and company for that most famous river of Amazones in America. 1632; rptd Harleian miscellany vol 10, 1808–13 etc.

Wood, William. New Englands prospect: a true, lively and experimentall description of that part of America commonly called New England. 1634, 1635, 1639; ed C. Deane, Boston 1865 (Prince Soc); ed H. W. Boynton, Boston 1898; Amsterdam and New York 1968 (facs of 1634).

Morton, Thomas. New English Canaan or New Canaan: containing an abstract of New England. Amsterdam 1637; rptd Force, Tracts vol 2, 1836–46 etc; ed C. F. Adams, Boston 1883; Amsterdam and New York 1969 (facs of 1637).

Vincent, Philip. A true relation of the late battell fought in New England, between the English and the salvages; with the present state of things there. 1637, 1638, 1638; rptd in Collections of Massachusetts Historical Soc 3rd ser 6 1837; ed C. Orr, History of the Pequot war, Cleveland 1897.

Taylor, John. Newes and strange newes from St Christophers of a tempestuous spirit, which is called by the Indians a hurricano, which hapneth in many of those islands of America or the West-Indies, as it did in August last the 5, 1638; ed C. H. Wilkinson, Oxford 1946 (Roxburghe Club).

Underhill, John. Newes from America: or a new and experimentall discoverie of New England; also a discovery of Queenapoick, Agu-wom, Hudsons river, Long Island. 1638; rptd Collections of Massachusetts Historical Soc 3rd ser 6 1837; ed C. Orr, History of the Pequot war, Cleveland 1897; ed D. H. Underhill, [Brooklyn] 1902; Amsterdam and New York 1971 (facs of 1638).

Colmenero de Ledesma, Antonio. A curious treatise of the nature and quality of chocolate. 1640, [1652], 1685. From the Curioso tratado del Chocolate, Madrid 1631 etc; tr D. Diego de Vades-forte or James Wadsworth.

Evelin, Robert. A direction for adventurers, and the true description of the healthiest, pleasantest and richest plantation of new Albion, in North Virginia, with a letter from Mayster Robert Evelin. 1641; in Beauchamp Plantagenet, 1648 (below); rptd Force, Tracts vol 2, 1836–46 etc; rptd Americana ser 1922.

Lechford, Thomas. Plain dealing, or newes from New-England: a short view of New-Englands present government, both ecclesiasticall and civill. 1642; rptd as New-Englands advice to Old-England, 1644; rptd Collections of Massachusetts Historical Soc 3rd ser 3 1833; ed J. H. Trumbull, Boston 1867.

Certain inducements to well minded people to transport themselves, or some servants or agents for them into the West Indies, for the propagating of the Gospel and increase of trade. [1643]; ed J. Sabin, New York 1865.

Williams, Roger. A key into the language of America: or an help to the language of the natives, in that part of America called New England; together with brief observations of the customs, manners and worship. [1643]; rptd Collections of Massachusetts Historical Soc 3 1794, 1810, 5 1798, 1816, 1835; rptd Collections of Rhode Island Historical Soc 1827 (from Bodley ms); ed J. H. Trumbull, Boston 1866.

Castell, William. A short discoverie of the coasts and continent of America, from the Equinoctiall northward, and of the adjacent isles. 1644, 1644; rptd Harleian voyages vol 2, 1745 etc; rptd Collections of New York Historical Soc 2nd ser 3 1857 (in part).

Good news from New England, with an exact relation of the first planting that countrey; with the names of the severall towns, and who be preachers to them. 1648; rptd Collections of Massachusetts Historical Soc 4th ser 1 1852. Mainly verse.

A perfect description of Virginia: being a full and true relation of the present state of the plantation sent from Virginia. 1649; rptd Collections of Massachusetts Historical Soc 2nd ser 9 1832 etc; rptd Force, Tracts vol 2, 1836 etc.

[Plantagenet, Beauchamp]. A description of the province of New Albion and a direction for adventurers with small stock to get two for one. 1648; rptd Force, Tracts vol 2, 1836 etc; rptd G. D. Scull, The Evelyns in America, Oxford 1881. The Direction taken from Robert Evelin, 1641 above.

Bullock, William. Virginia impartially examined and left to publick view. 1649; rptd Force, Tracts vol 3, 1836–46 etc.

W[illiams], E[dward]. Virgo triumphans: or Virginia richly and truly valued, more especially the south part thereof, viz the fertile Carolana. 1650, 1650; rptd Force, Tracts vol 3, 1836–46 etc.

— Virginias discovery of silke-wormes, with their benefit, and the implanting of Mulberry trees; also the dressing and keeping of vines for the rich trade of making wines there. 1650 (with preceding item).

Thorowgood, Tho[mas]. Jewes in America: or probabilities that the Americans are of that race; with earnest desires for effectuall endeavors to make them Christian. 1650; rptd as Digitus Dei, 1652.

— Jews in America: or probabilities that those Indians are judaical, made more probable. 1660.

Gardyner, George. A description of the New World: or America islands and continent, and by what people those regions are now inhabited and what places are there desolate. 1651.

Woodnoth, Arthur. A short collection of the most remarkable passages from the originall to the dissolution of the Virginia Company. 1651.

L'Estrange, Sir Hamon. Americans no Jewes: or impossibilities that the Americans are of that race. 1652.

[Peake, Thomas]. America: or an exact description of the West-Indies, more especially of those provinces which are under the dominion of the King of Spain, faithfully represented by N.N. gent. 1655.

Hammond, John. Leah and Rachel, or the two fruitfull sisters Virginia and Maryland: their present condition impartially stated and related. 1656; rptd Force, Tracts vol 3, 1836–46 etc; ed C. C. Hall, Original narratives, 1910 etc.

Ligon, Richard. A true and exact history of the island of Barbados, illustrated with a mapp of the Island. 1657, 1673, Kingston Jamaica [1949] (abridged); tr French, Recueil de divers voyages fait en Afrique et en l'Amérique, 1674.

A true description of Jamaica, with the fertility, commodities and healthfulness of the place, as also the towns, havens, creeks, promontories and the circuit of the whole island. 1657.

Gardener, Lion. [A relation of the Pequot warres, written 1660]. In Collections of Massachusetts Historical Soc 3 1833; rptd Cincinnati 1860; rptd C. C. Gardiner, The papers and biography of Lion Gardiner, St Louis 1883, and in Lion Gardiner and his descendants, St Louis 1890; rptd C. Orr, History of the Pequot war 1897; rptd Hartford Conn 1901 (Acorn Club).

Gerbier, Sir Balthazar. A sommary description, manifesting that greater profits are to bee done in the hott then in the could parts off the coast off America. Amsterdam 1660.
— Advertysement for men inclyned to plantacions in America. Rotterdam 1660, Amsterdam 1660 (with preceding item).

Maverick, Samuel. A briefe discription of New England [1660] and the severall townes therein, together with the present government thereof. Ed J. W. Dean, Boston 1885.

J. L.

VII. TRANSLATIONS INTO ENGLISH

Translations from Greek and Latin classics; Translations from medieval and contemporary authors; Bibliographies and criticism.

In the following lists trns of poetry are in verse and of prose in prose unless otherwise stated. With the exception of versions of short poems and occasional passages they are largely complete for the authors selected. See also Literary Relations with the Continent, col 833, above.

(1) TRANSLATIONS FROM GREEK AND LATIN CLASSICS

Achilles Tatius

B[urton], W[illiam]. The most delectable and pleasaunt history of Clitophon and Leucippe. 1597, Oxford 1638; ed S. Gaselee and H. F. B. Brett-Smith, Oxford 1923.
H[odges], A[nthony]. The loves of Clitophon and Leucippe: a most elegant history. Oxford 1638.

Aelian

Fleming, Abraham. Claudius: a registre of hystories, delivered in Englyshe (as well according to the Greeke text as Latine). 1576.
B[ingham], J[ohn]. Aelianus Tacticus. The Tactiks of Aelian. [1616]; [Pt 2], 1629, 1631.

Aesop

Bullokar, William. Æsopź fablz in tru ortŏgraphy with grammar-nótz. 1585; ed M. Plessow, Berlin 1906.
Sturtevant, Simon. The Etymologist of Æsops Fables, containing the construing of his Latine fables into English; also the Etymologist of Phaedrus fables, containing the construing of Phaedrus into English, verbatim, both very necessarie helps for young schollers. 1602.
[Brinsley, J.] Esops fables translated for the grammar-schoole. 1624. First ptd with Pueriles confabulatiunculae, 1617.
A., R. The fabulist metamorphosed, and mythologized: or the fables of Esop, translated into English verse, and moralized. 1634.
B[arret], W. The fables of Aesop, with his whole life; translated into English verse and moralliz'd, as also emblematically illustrated with pictures. 1639.
Aesop's fables [45] with the fables of Phaedrus [31, i.e. bk 1] moralized, translated verbatim [from G. H. Goudanus], published by H.D. 1646.
Willan, Leonard. The Phrygian fabulist; or the fables of Aesop [231]; moraliz'd. 1650. Verse.
Ogilby, J[ohn]. The fables of Aesop paraphras'd in verse. 1651.
Aesops fables [213] with their moralls, in prose and verse grammatically translated. 1651.
[Shirley, James]. Introductorium anglo-latino-graecum: complectens Colloquia familiaria, Aesopi fabulas, et Luciani selectiores Mortuorum dialogos. 1656.

Anacreon

Stanley, Thomas. Anacreon, Bion, Moschus; Kisses by Secundus; Cupid crucified by Ausonius; Venus vigils. 1651; rptd Sir S. E. Brydges, 1815. Anacreon only rptd A. H. Bullen 1893. Ed G. M. Crump, Oxford 1962.

Appian

B., W. An auncient historie and exquisite chronicle of the Romanes warres, with a continuation from the death of Sextus Pompeius till the overthrow of Antonie and Cleopatra. 2 pts 1578. [Pt 2 only by W.B.]. Ed E. Schanzer, Shakespeare's Appian, Liverpool 1956 (selections).

Apuleius

Adlington, William. The xi bookes of the golden asse, conteininge the Metamorphosie of Lucius Apuleius with the Mariage of Cupide and Psiches. 1566, 1571, 1582, 1596, 1639; ed A. Lang 1887; ed C. Whibley 1893 (Tudor Translations); ed T. Seccombe 1913; ed E. B. Osborn 1923; ed F. J. H. Darton 1924; ed W. H. D. Rouse 1929 (selections); ed L. MacNeice 1946.

Aristophanes

B., H. B. The world's idol, or Plutus the god of wealth. 1659.

Aristotle

[Wilkinson, John]. The ethiques. 1547. From the Italian compendium of B. Latini.
The problemes of Aristotle, with other philosophers and physitions, wherein are contayned divers questions, with their answers, touching the estate of mans bodie. 1595, Edinburgh 1595, 1597, 1607.
D., I. Aristotle's politiques, or discourses of government. 1598. From the French of Loys le Roy, called Regius.
[Hobbes, Thomas]. A briefe of the art of rhetorique. 1637, 1651.
H. R. Palmer, List of English editions and translations of Greek and Latin classics printed before 1641, 1911, includes as trns, besides a medical appendix by Thomas Hyll, [1550?], Thomas Wilson's Arte of rhetorique, 1553, and various books on logic by Rollo MacIlmaine 1574, M. [Thomas] Blundevile, 1599, Anthony Wotton, 1626, R. F[age], 1632. P. Ramus's name appears on all the title-pages in 2nd group except Blundevile's.

Marcus Aurelius

Casaubon, M[eric]. Marcus Aurelius Antoninus the Roman Emperor, his meditations concerning himselfe; with notes. 1634, 1635; ed W. H. D. Rouse 1898 (as The golden book of Marcus Aurelius), 1900, 1906 (EL).

Ausonius

Kendall, Timothy. Epigrams. In Flowers of epigrammes, 1577.
Beaumont, Sir John. The sixteenth idyll. In Bosworth-field, 1629.
Stanley, Thomas. Europa [by Moschus]; Cupid crucified [by Ausonius, Latin and English]; Venus vigils. 1649, 1651; ed S. E. Brydges 1815; Poems and translations, ed G. M. Crump, Oxford 1962.
See also Turbervile under Greek Anthology and Fanshawe under Horace.

Bion

See under Anacreon, above.

Caesar

[Tiptoft, John (Earl of Worcester)]. Julius Cesars commentaryes as much as concernyth thys realm of England. 1530. English and Latin in parallel columns. Printer W. Rastell?

Golding, Arthur. The eyght bookes of Caius Julius Caesar: conteyning his martiall exploytes in Gallia and the countries bordering. 1565, 1578, 1590.

Edmondes, Sir Clement. Commentaries. In Observations upon the five first bookes of Cæsars Commentaries, 1600, 1604 (with 6th and 7th bks), 1609 (with Civil wars bks 1–3), 1655.

C[ruso], T. The complete captain: or an abbridgement of Cesars warres, with observations; written by the Duke of Rohan. Cambridge 1640. Appendix.

Dionysius Cato

Taverner, Richard. Catonis disticha moralia ex castigatione D. Erasmi una cum annotationibus & scholiis Richardi Taverneri anglico idiomate conscriptis. 1540, 1553, 1562, 1572, 1580, 1592, 1620. Latin and English.

[Burrant, Robert]. Preceptes of Cato the Sage, with annotacions of D. Erasmus. 1545 (no copy extant?), 1553, 1560.

Cato construed: first doen in Laten and Frenche by Maturinus Corderius and now englished to the comforte of all young schollers. 1577 (no copy extant?), 1584.

Bullokar, William. The short senteňcez of the wýz Cato. Pt 2 of Aeşopź fablź in tru ortŏgraphy, 1585. Separate title-page.

[Brinsley, John]. Cato (concerning the precepts of common life) translated grammatically. 1612, 1622.

P[enkethman], J[ohn]. A handful of honesty: or Cato in English verse. 1623, 1624.

Baker, Sir Richard. Cato variegatus: or Catoes morall distichs, translated and paraphras'd with variations of expressing, in English verse. 1636.

Hoole, Charles. 1, Catonis disticha de moribus; 2, Dicta insignia septem sapientium Graeciae; 3, Mimi Publiani, sive Senecae proverbia, anglo-latina. 1659.

Cebes

[Poyntz, Sir Francis]. The tables of Cebes the philosopher. [c. 1530], 1560.

See also under Epictetus, below.

Cicero

Whittington, Robert. The thre bookes of Tullyes Offyces bothe in Latyne tongue and in Englysshe. 1534, 1540.

—— Tullius de senectute, bothe in latyn and Englysshe tonge. [1535?].

—— The paradox of Marcus Tullius Cicero. 1540.

Harrington, John. The booke of freendeship. 1550, 1562, 1904; ed W. H. D. Rouse 1907.

Grimald, Nicholas. M. Tullius Ciceroe's thre boks of dueties, to Marcus his sonne. 1553, 1556, 1558, 1568, 1574, 1583, 1588, 1590, 1596, [1600?], 1610. Latin and English.

Sherry, Richard. A treatise of schemes and tropes. 1550. Includes Ad Herennium, traditionally attributed to Cicero.

—— The oration which Cicero made to Cesar of Marcus Marcellus. In Treatise of the figures of grammer and rhetorike, 1555.

G[ylby], G[oddred]. An epistle: or letter of exhortation to Quintus. 1561.

Dolman, John. Those fyve questions which Marke Tullye Cicero disputed in his manor of Tusculanum. 1561.

[Newton, Thomas]. The booke of M. T. Cicero entituled Paradoxa Stoicorum, whereunto is annexed Scipio hys dreame. 1569; Scipio's dream, ed W. H. D. Rouse 1907.

[——] The worthye booke of old age. 1569; ed W. H. D. Rouse 1907.

—— Fowre several treatises of M. Tullius Cicero, conteyninge Discourses of frendshippe; Old age; Paradoxes and Scipio his dreame. 1577.

W., T. A certaine draught taken out of Ciceroes Epistles for the exercise of children in the Latin speache. 1575. Latin and English.

Fleming, Abraham. Select epistles. In Panoplie of epistles, 1576.

The Latine grammar [of Ramus] whereunto is joyned a grammatical analysis uppon an epistle of Tullie. Cambridge 1585.

[Haine, William?]. Certain epistles of Tully verbally translated. 1611.

[Brinsley, John]. The first booke of Tullies offices translated grammatically. 1616, 1631.

[Webbe, Joseph]. The familiar epistles of M. T. Cicero englished and conferred with the French, Italian and other translations. [1620].

S., E. G. Scipio's dreame: or the Statesman's extasie. 1627.

Austin, William. Cato major: or the book of old age. 1648.

See also under P. de Mornay, col 2189, below.

Claudian

Digges, Leonard. The rape of Proserpine, translated into English verse. 1617, 1628. Ed H. H. Huxley, Liverpool 1959.

Beaumont, Sir John. Epigrams, in Bosworth-field, 1629.

Quintus Curtius

Brende, John. The historie of Quintus Curtius, conteyning the actes of the greate Alexander. 1553, 1561, 1570, 1584, 1592, 1602, 1614.

Dares Phrygius

[Lydgate, John]. The hystorye sege and dystruccyon of Troye. 1513, 1555.

Paynell, Thomas. The faythfull and true storye of the destruction of Troye. 1553.

Demosthenes

Wilson, Thomas. The three orations of Demosthenes in favour of the Olynthians, with those his fower orations against King Philip of Macedonie. Demosthenes's lyfe is set foorth and gathered out of Plutarch, Lucian, Suidas and others. 1570.

G[okin], T[homas]. The first oration against Philip of Macedon. 1623.

Diodorus Siculus

Skelton, John [from Poggio's Latin]. Ed F. M. Salter and H. L. R. Edwards 2 vols 1956–7.

Stocker, Thomas. A righte noble history of the successors of Alexander, taken out of Diodorus Siculus [bk 18] and Plutarch. 1569. From French.

C[ogan], H[enry]. The history of Diodorus Siculus. 1653.

Dionysius Periegetes

Twyne, Thomas. The surveye of the world, or situation of the earth. 1572.

Epictetus

Sandford, James. The manuell of Epictetus, translated out of Greeke into French, and now into English; hereunto are annexed the apothegs. 1567.

Healey, John. Epictetus his manuall, and Cebes his table. 1610, 1616 (adds Theophrastus his morall characters), 1636; Theophrastus, ed W. H. D. Rouse 1899 (Temple Classics).

Euclid

Billingsley, Sir Henry. The elements of geometrie of Euclide, with a very fruitfull preface made by M[aster] J[ohn] Dee. 1570.

Eunapius Sardianus

The lyves of phylosophers and oratours. [1579]. From the Latin of H. Junius Hornamus.

Euripides

Gascoigne, George and Francis Kinwelmersh. Jocasta: a tragedie written in Greeke by Euripides; translated and digested into Acte by George Gascoygne and Francis Kinwelmershe, of Grayes Inne, and there by them presented, 1566. From the Italian adaptation of the Phoenissae by Lodovico Dolce. *For edns see under Gascoigne, col 1025, above.*

Lumley, Jane, Lady. Iphigenia at Aulis. Ed H. Child 1909 (Malone Soc) (from c. 1555 ms).

Eutropius

Haward, Nicholas. A briefe Chronicle, where in are described shortlye the originall and successive estate of the Romaine weale publique. 1564.

Florus

[Bolton, Edmund]. The Roman histories of Lucius Julius Florus. [1618 or 1619], [1621?], 1636, 1658 (corrected, amended, and with annotations by M. Casaubon). *See also Holland under Livy, below.*

Frontinus

Morison, [Sir] Richard. The stratagemes, sleyghtes and policies of warre. 1539.

Galen

Gale, Thomas. Certain workes of Galens called Methodus medendi. 1586.
Other translators cited by H. R. Palmer are R. Copland, [1542], W. Turner, [1568], G. Baker, 1574, J. Jones, 1574, P. English, 1656.

Greek Anthology

Turbervile, George. Epitaphes, epigrams, songs and sonets. 1567, 1570; ed J. P. Collier [1867]. *See* H. B. Lathrop, MLN 43 1928, for pieces from the anthology.
Kendall, Timothy. Out of Greek epigrammes. In Flowers of epigrammes, 1577. 61 trns.

Heliodorus

Underdowne, Thomas. An Æthiopian historie. [1569?], 1587, 1606, 1622 (rev W. Barrett); ed C. Whibley 1895 (Tudor Translations); rev F. A. Wright 1923; ed G. Saintsbury 1924. From the Latin of S. Warszewicki.
Fraunce, Abraham. The beginning of Heliodorus his Æthiopicall history in English hexameters. In The Countesse of Pembrokes Yvychurch, 1591. From Underdowne.
Lisle, William. The faire Æthiopian. 1631, 1638. Verse. *See also Sandford under Plutarch, below.*

Herodian

Smyth, Nicholas. The history of Herodian translated into Latin by Angelus Politianus and into Englyshe by Nicholas Smyth. [1550?].
M[axwell], J[ames]. Herodian of Alexandria his history of twenty Roman Caesars and Emperors. 1629, 1635.
Stapylton, C. B. Herodian of Alexandria his imperiall history of twenty Roman Caesars and Emperours of his time, converted into an heroick poem. 1652.
Pts of Herodian and Suetonius were adapted in Mirror for magistrates; *see D. Bush, SP 22 1925.*

Herodotus

R[ich?], B[arnaby?]. The famous hystory of Herodotus, conteyning the discourse of dyvers countreys, the succession of theyr kyngs, devided into nine bookes, entituled with the names of the nine Muses. 1584; ed A. Lang 1888 (bk 2 only); ed L. Whibley 1925 (Tudor Translations) (bks 1-2 only).

Hesiod

Chapman, George. The Georgicks of Hesiod, translated elaborately out of the Greek. 1618; ed R. H. Shepherd, Works of Chapman vol 3, 1875.

Hippocrates

Llwyd, Humphrey. The aphorismes of Hypocrates redacted to a certayne order. In trn of Petrus Hispanus (Pope John XXI), The treasury of healthe, [1550?], [1550?], 1558, 1585.
H., S. The whole aphorismes of Hippocrates. 1610.
Lowe, Peter. The presages of divine Hippocrates. 1612, 1634.
Other trns [1530?], 1599.

Homer

Hall, Arthur. Ten books of Homers Iliades, translated out of French. 1581.
Fraunce, Abraham. Selected passages. In Arcadian rhetorike, 1588.
Colse, Peter. Penelopes complaint: or a mirrour for wanton minions, written in English verse. 1596; ed A. B. Grosart, Manchester 1880. A free adaptation and paraphrase of some passages.
Chapman, George. Seaven bookes of the Iliades of Homere, prince of poets, translated according to the Greeke in judgement of his best Commentaries. 1598. The bks are 1-2, 7-11.
— Achilles shield, translated as the other seven bookes of Homer, out of his eighteenth booke of Iliades. 1598.
— Homer, prince of poets, translated according to the Greeke in twelve bookes of his Iliads. [1610? (re-issued 1611); ed W. C. Taylor 2 vols 1843; ed H. Morley 1884.
— The Iliads of Homer, prince of poets, never before in any languag truely translated, with a comment upon some of his chiefe places. [1611], 1612. The first complete edn of Chapman's Iliad.
— The whole works of Homer, prince of poetts, in his Iliads and Odysses. [c. 1612], [1616?]; ed R. Hooper, 4 vols 1857; ed R. H. Shepherd 1871; rptd 2 vols Oxford 1931; ed A. Nicoll 2 vols, New York 1957.
— Homers Odysses [bks 1-12]. [1614?].
— Homers Odysses [bks 1-24]. [1615?].
— The crowne of all Homers workes, Batrachomyomachia or the battaile of frogs and mise, his hymn's and epigrams. [1624?]; ed S. W. Singer 1818; ed R. Hooper 1858; rptd 1904.
F[owldes], W[illiam]. The strange, wonderfull and bloudy battell betweene frogs and mise; paraphrastically done into English heroycall verse. 1603, 1634; ed F. Wild, Vienna 1918. A freely expanded paraphrase.
Grantham, Thomas. The first [part of the second and the third] booke of Homer's Iliads. 1660.
Ogilby, John. Homer his Iliads. 1660.

Horace

Evans, Lewis. The fyrste twoo satars or poyses of Horace. [1565].
— The second poesye of Horace. [1565].
Drant, Thomas. A medicinable morall, that is, the two bookes of Horace his satyres, englyshed accordyng to the prescription of Saint Hierome. 1566. On priority of Drant's or Evans's trn *see* O. L. Jiriczek, Sh Jb 55 1919.
— Horace his art of poetrie, pistles and satyrs, englished. 1567. Drant's prefaces and portions of text rptd by O. L. Jiriczek, Sh Jb 47 1911, 55 1919.
Webbe, William. Passages from the epistles. In A discourse of English poetrie, 1586; ed J. Haslewood, Ancient critical essays upon English poets and poësy vol 2, 1815.
[Ashmore, John]. Certain selected odes of Horace. 1621.
H[awkins], Sir T[homas]. Odes [and four epodes] contayning much morallity and sweetnesse, selected and

translated. 1625, 1631, 1635 (Latin and English), 1638 (Latin and English), 1652.

Beaumont, Sir John. Sixth satire of the second book, 29th ode of the third book and second epode. In Bosworth-field, 1629.

Rider, Henry. All the odes and epodes, translated into English verse. 1638.

Jonson, Ben. Q. Horatius Flaccus his art of poetry englished. 1640; ed E. H. Blakeney 1928 (in Horace on the art of poetry).

S[mith], J[ohn]. The lyrick poet: odes and satyres. 1649. Selections.

[Fanshawe, Sir Richard]. Selected parts of Horace, prince of lyricks, concluding with a piece out of Ausonius and another out of Virgil [pt of Georgics bk 3]. 1652. Latin and English.

[Holyday, Barten]. All Horace his lyrics or his four books of odes and his book of epodes. 1653. Based on Hawkins's version.

Isocrates

Elyot, Sir Thomas. The doctrinall of princes. [1534], [1534], [1548?]. The Ad Nicoclem.

[Bury, John]. Paranesis: or admonytion to Demonicus; whereto is annexed [Benedict Burgh's trn, 1484, of] Cato in olde Englysh meter. 1557 (colophon 1558).

Fleming, Abraham. The extract of epistles out of Isocrates. In Panoplie of epistles, 1576.

Forrest, Thomas. A perfite looking glasse of all estates: in three orations of morall instructions, translated into Lataine by Hieronimus Wulfius. 1580.

[Brinsley, John]. Admonition to Demonicus. In Cato translated grammatically, 1622.

Barnes, Thomas. Archidamus: or the councell of warre. 1624.

Josephus

Lodge, Tho[mas]. The famous and memorable workes of Josephus, faithfully translated out of the Latin and French. 1602, 1609, 1620, 1632, 1632, 1640, 1655-6.

Markham, Gervase and William Sampson. The true tragedie of Herod and Antipas. 1622, 1622. Based on Josephus, bks 14-15.

Juvenal

B[arksted?], W. That which seemes best is worst, exprest in a paraphrastical transcript of Juvenals tenth satyre, with Virginias death. 1617.

Beaumont, Sir John. Satire 10. In Bosworth-field, 1629.

Chapman, George. A justification of a strange action of Nero [etc]; also a just reproofe of a Romane smell-feast, being the fifth satyre of Juvenall. 1629; ed R. H. Shepherd, Works of Chapman vol 3, 1875.

Biddle, John. The two first satyrs of Juvenal. In Virgil's Bucolicks englished, 1634.

[Stapleton, Sir Robert]. The first six bookes of Juvenal. Oxford 1644.

—— Juvenal's sixteen satyrs: or a survey of the manners and actions of mankind, with arguments, marginall notes and annotations. 1647, 1660 (as Mores hominum).

Vaughan, Henry. The tenth satyre of Iuvenal englished. In his Poems, 1646.

Livy

Bellenden, John. The first five books of the Roman history. Ed [T. Maitland], Edinburgh 1822 (from ms c. 1533); ed W. A. Craigie 1901 (STS).

Cope, Sir Anthony. The historie of two the most noble captaines of the worlde, Anniball and Scipio, translated into Englishe out of Titus Livius and other authores. 1544, 1548, 1561, 1590.

Wilson, Thomas. The hystorie of P. Sulpitius Consull. 2 pp. prefixed to his trn of Demosthenes, The three orations, 1570.

P[iot], L[azarus]. Selections. In The orator [tr from A. Sylvain, i.e. A. van den Busche]: handling a hundred severall discourses; some of the arguments drawne from Titus Livius, 1596.

Holland, Philemon. The Romane historie written by Titus Livius of Padua; also the breviaries of L. Florus. 1600, 1659.

Longinus

H[all], J[ohn]. Περὶ ὕψους: or Dionysius Longinus of the height of eloquence. 1652.

Longus

Day, Angel. Daphnis and Chloe excellently describing the weight of affection [etc], finished in a pastorall termed the Shepeards holidaie. 1587; ed J. Jacobs 1890 (from the French of J. Amyot).

Thornley, George. Daphnis and Chloe: a sweet and pleasant pastorall romance for young ladies. 1657, 1893; ed G. Saintsbury 1923.

Lucan

Marlowe, Christopher. Lucans first booke, translated line for line. 1600; ed C. F. T. Brooke, Works of Marlowe, Oxford 1910.

Gorges, Sir Arthur. Lucans Pharsalia, translated into English, whereunto is annexed the life of the authour. 1614.

M[ay], T[homas]. Lucan's Pharsalia. 1626 (bks 1-3), 1627 (complete), 1631, 1635, 1650, 1659.

Beaumont, Sir John. Selections. In Bosworth-field, 1629.

Lucian

A dialog of the poet Lucyan, fer his fantesye faynyd for a mery pastyme; interlocutores Menippus and Philonides. [1530?]. 'Johannes Rastell me fieri fecit'. The Necromantia.

[Elyot, Sir Thomas]. A dialogue betwene Lucian and Diogenes of the life harde and sharpe and of the lyfe tendre and delicate. nd.

Fletcher, Giles. Doris and Galatea. In Licia, 1593.

Hickes, Francis. Certaine select dialogues of Lucian, together with his true historie. Oxford 1634, 1925; The true historie, ed C. Whibley 1894; ed J. S. Phillimore 1927.

Heywood, T[homas]. Pleasant dialogues and dramma's selected out of Lucian, Erasmus, Textor, Ovid etc. 1637; ed W. Bang, Louvain 1903 (Materialien vol 3).

See also Shirley under Æsop, above.

Lucretius

Evelyn, J[ohn]. An essay on the first book of T. Lucretius Carus De rerum natura, interpreted and made English verse. 1656.

Ammianus Marcellinus

Holland, Philemon. The Romane historie. 1609.

Martial

Martial to himselfe, treating of worldly blessedness, in Latin, English and Walsch. 1571. Bk 10.

Kendall, Timothy, Epigrammes out of Martial. In Flowers of epigrammes, 1577.

May, Thomas. Selected epigrams of Martial. 1629.

Fletcher, R. Ex otio negotium: or Martial his epigrams. 1656. Selection.

Pecke, Thomas. Libellus de spectaculis: or an account of the most memorable monuments of the Romane glory. 1659. General title-page, Parnassi puerperium [etc].

Parts of bk 1 tr Sir Edward Sherburne, Salmacis, 1651. The Earl of Surrey translated epigram 47; see H. H. Hudson, MLN 38 1923.

Pomponius Mela

Golding, Arthur. The worke of Pomponius Mela the cosmographer, concerninge the situation of the world. 1585, 1590 ('whereunto is added that learned worke of Julius Solinus Polyhistor').

Moschus

See under Ausonius, above.

Musaeus

Marlowe, Christopher and George Chapman. Hero and Leander. 1598, 1598, 1600, 1606, 1629, 1637. First 2 sestiads by Marlowe, continuation by Chapman.

Chapman, George. The divine poem of Musaeus. 1616.

Stapleton, Sir Robert. Ἐρωτοπαίγνιον: the loves of Hero and Leander, written by Musaeus. Oxford 1645, 1647 (rev with annotations as Musaeus on the loves of Hero and Leander; includes Leander's letter to Hero, and her answer, taken out of Ovid).

Onosander

Whitehorne, Peter. Onosandro Platonico, of the Generall Captaine, and of his office. 1563. From the Italian of Fabio Cotta.

Ovid

The flores of Ovide De arte amandi, with theyr Englysshe afore them and two alphabete tablys. 1513. Latin and English.

H[owell?], T[homas?]. The fable of Ovid treting of Narcissus, translated into Englysh mytre. 1560.

Peend, Thomas. The pleasant fable of Hermaphroditus and Salmacis. 1565.

Golding, Arthur. The fyrst fower bookes of P. Ovidius Nasos worke, intitled Metamorphosis, translated into Englishe meter. 1565.

—— The xv bookes of P. Ovidius Naso, entytuled Metamorphosis, translated into English meeter. 1567, 1575, 1584, 1587, 1593, 1603, 1612; cd W. H. D. Rouse 1904; ed J. F. Nims, New York 1965.

Turbervile, George. The heroycall epistles of the learned poet Publius Ovidius Naso, in Englishe verse; with Aulus [Angelus] Sabinus aunsweres to certaine of the same. 1567, [1569], [1570?], [1580?], 1600, [1605]; ed F. S. Boas 1928.

Helen's epistle to Paris is in John Lyly, Euphues; see M. P. Tilley, MLN 45 1930.

[Underdowne, Thomas]. Ovid his invective against Ibis, translated into English meeter. 1569, 1577.

[Churchyard, Thomas]. The thre first bookes of Ovids De tristibus. [1572], 1578, 1580, 1816 (Roxburghe Club).

Marlow[e], C[hristopher]. Certaine of Ovids elegies. 'Middelburg' [1590?].

—— All Ovids elegies: 3 bookes; epigrams by [Sir] J[ohn] D[avies]. 'Middelburg' [c. 1597], [1600?], [1635?], [1640?]; rptd 1925.

L., F. Ovid his remedie of love, translated and intituled to the youth of England. 1600.

[Beaumont, Francis]. Salmacis and Hermaphroditus. 1602; rptd 1847 (Shakespeare Soc).

Heywood, Thomas. Troia britanica: or Great Britaines Troy. 1609. Passages from Heroides, De arte amandi, De remedio amoris.

—— Publii Ovidii Nasonis de arte amandi: or the art of love. [1612], Amsterdam [1635?], [1640?] (Heywood's trn appropriated by H. Austin). See A. M. Clark, Library 4th ser 3 1922.

—— Two dramas: Jupiter and Io, and Apollo and Daphne [tr from or founded on 2 stories in Metamorphoses]. In Pleasant dialogues and drammas, 1637; ed W. Bang, Louvain 1903 (Materialien vol 3).

A[ustin], H. The scourge of Venus: or the wanton lady, with the rare birth of Adonis. 1613, 1614, 1614, 1620; ed A. B. Grosart 1876. Myrrha and Cinyras, Metamorphoses bk 10.

B[rinsley], J[ohn]. Ovid's Metamorphosis translated grammatically and also according to the propriety of our English tongue, as farre as Grammar and the verse will well beare. 1618, 1656. Bk 1, fables 1–9.

Overbury, Sir Thomas. The first and second part of the remedy of love. 1620.

S[andys], G[eorge]. Ovid's Metamorphosis englished. 1626, 1628, 1638, 1656.

—— Ovid's Metamorphosis englished, mythologiz'd and represented in figures: an essay to the translation of Virgil's Aeneis. Oxford 1632, 1640; ed K. T. Hulley and S. T. Vandersall, Lincoln Nebraska 1970.

Gresham, James. The picture of incest, lively portraicted in the historie of Cinyras and Myrrha. 1626; ed A. B. Grosart, Manchester 1876.

Hatton, Richard. Ovid's Walnuttree transplanted. 1627.

R[eynolds], H[enry]. The tale of Narcissus briefly mythologised. In Mythomystes, 1632.

S[altonstall], W[ye]. Ovids Tristia containinge five bookes of mournfull elegies. 1633, 1637.

—— Ovids Heroicall epistles. 1636, 1639.

—— Ovid de Ponto, containing foure books of elegies. 1639, 1640.

[Carpenter, John]. Ovids Remedy of love, directing lovers how they may by reason suppresse the passion of love. 1636.

Sherburne, John. Ovids Heroicall epistles. 1639.

Catlin, Zachary. Publ Ovid, De tristibus: or mournefull elegies, in five bookes. 1639.

Gower, John. Ovids Festivalls: or Romane calendar, translated into English verse equinumerally. 1640.

[Hall, Thomas]. Wisdom's conquest: or an explanation and grammaticall translation of the thirteenth book of Ovid's Metamorphoses. 1651.

—— Phaeton's folly, or the dounfal of pride: a translation of the second book of Ovid's Metamorphosis, paraphrastically and grammatically as a supplement to Mr Brinslyes translation of the first book. 1655; An essay on the first elegy of Ovid's De tristibus, 1655.

Jones, John. Ovid's Invective or curse against Ibis. Oxford 1658.

See also Stapleton under Musaeus, above.

Persius

Holyday, Barten. Aulus Persius Flaccus his satires. Oxford 1616, 1617, London 1617, 1635, 1650.

Beaumont, Sir John. The second satire of Persius. In Bosworth-field, 1629.

Pervigilium Veneris

See under Ausonius, above.

Petronius

Fanshawe, Sir Richard. Bellum civile. Ed J. P. Sullivan, Arion 5 1966.

Plato

Spenser, Edw. [Edmund?]. Axiochus: a most excellent dialogue by Plato the phylosopher, concerning the shortnesse and uncertainty of this life, with the contrary ends of the good and wicked. 1592; ed F. M. Padelford, Baltimore 1934.

See also under Philippe de Mornay, below.

Plautus

A new enterlued for chyldren to playe, named Jacke Jugeler. An imitation of Amphitruo. *For edns see col 1420, above.*

W[arner], W[illiam]. Menæcmi: a pleasant comedie. 1595; ed W. C. H[azlitt], Shakespeare's library vol 5, 1875; ed W. H. D. Rouse 1911.

Pliny the Elder

A[lday?], J[ohn?]. A summarie of the antiquities, and wonders of the worlde, abstracted out of the sixtene first bookes of Plinie, translated oute of French. [1566], 1585, 1587 (as The secrets and wonders of the world). From the French version of P. de Changy.

Holland, Philemon. The historie of the world, commonly called the naturall historie. 2 vols 1601, 1634, 1635.

Pliny the Younger

Fleming, Abraham. Extract of epistles out of C. Plinius and others. In Panoplie of epistles, 1576.

Stapleton, Sir Robert. Pliny's Panegyricke: publike thankes to the Emperour Trajan. Oxford 1644.

Plutarch

Wyatt, Sir Thomas. Tho. Wyatis translatyon of Plutarches boke of the quyete of mynde. [1528]; ed C. R. Baskervill, Cambridge Mass 1931 (facs).

The governaunce of good helthe, Erasmus beynge interpretoure. [1530?].

Practica Plutarche the excellent phylosopher. [1530?]. Extracts; medical prescriptions.

[Elyot, Sir Thomas?]. Howe one may take profite of his enmyes. [1533?], [1550?] (with the Tables of Cebes).

Elyot, Sir Thomas. The education or bringinge up of children. [1535?].

[Hales, John]. The preceptes of the excellent clerke and grave philosopher Plutarche for the preservation of good healthe. 1543.

Sandford, James. The amorous and tragicall tales of Plutarch; whereunto is annexed the hystorie of Cariclea and Theagenes and the sayings of the Greeke philosophers. 1567.

Grant, Edward. A president for parentes translated and partly augmented by Ed Grant. 1571, Cambridge 1595.

North, Sir Thomas. The lives of the noble Grecians and Romanes, translated into French by J. Amyot. 1579, 1595, 1603, 1612, 1631, 1657; Shakespeare's Plutarch, ed W. W. Skeat, Oxford 1875; ed G. Wyndham 6 vols 1895 (Tudor Translations); ed C. F. T. Brooke 2 vols 1909, 8 vols Oxford 1928, 5 vols 1929–30; Shakespeare's Plutarch, ed T. J. B. Spencer 1964 (Penguin).

Lives of Epaminondas and Philip of Macedon etc 1602, incorporated in 1603 and subsequent edns, which contain also more lives from Æmylius Probus.

Blundeville, Thomas. Three morall treatises: the learned prince; the fruites of foes; the port of rest. 1580.

Clapham, John. A philosophical treatise concerning the quietness of the mind. 1589. From the French of Amyot.

Inimicus amicus: an excellent treatise shewing how a man may reape profit by his enemy. 1601.

Holland, Philemon. The philosophie, commonlie called the morals. 1603, 1657; ed J. Jacobs 1888; ed F. B. Jevons 1892; ed E. H. Blakeney [1911] (EL) (in part).

See also under Cebes and Diodorus Siculus, above, and Queen Elizabeth's englishings of Boethius, Plutarch etc, ed C. Pemberton 1899 (EETS); Poems of Queen Elizabeth I, ed L. Bradner, Providence 1964.

Polybius

W[atson], C[hristopher]. The hystories of the most famous and worthy Cronographer Polybius. 1568. Bk 1 only.

Grimstone, Edward. The history of Polybius the Megalopolitan according to the Greeke originall. 1633, 1634, 1634.

[Ralegh, Sir Walter]. A notable and memorable story of the cruel war between the Carthaginians and their own mercenaries, gathered out of Polybius and other authors. 1647. From History of the world bk 5 ch 2.

Pompeius Trogus

See under Trogus, below.

Proclus

Salesbury, William. The description of the sphere or frame of the worlde. [1550]. From Latin version of Thomas Linacre.

Publilius Syrus

See Dionysius Cato, above.

Sallust

Barclay, Alexander. Here begynneth the famous cronycle of the warre gaainst Jugurth. [1520?], [1520?]; rptd with Thomas Paynell's trn of C. Felicius, The conspiracie of Catiline, 2 vols 1557.

[Heywood, Thomas]. The two most worthy and notable histories, viz the conspiracie of Cateline and the warre which Jugurth for many yeares maintained. 1608; ed C. Whibley 1924 (Tudor Translations).

[Crosse, William]. The workes of Caius Crispus Salustius. 1629.

Seneca

Whittington, Robert. L. A. Senecae ad Gallionem de remediis fortuitorum: the remedyes agaynst all casuall chaunces; Dialogus inter sensum et rationem: a dialogue between sensualyte and reason. 1547 (Latin and English); ed R. G. Palmer, Seneca's De remediis fortuitorum and the Elizabethans, Chicago 1953.

Heywood, Jasper. The sixt tragedie of the most grave and prudent author, Lucius Anneus Seneca, entituled Troas. 1559, 1559, [1560?].

— The seconde tragedie of Seneca entituled Thyestes. 1560.

— Lucii Annei Senecæ tragedia prima qui inscribitur Hercules Furens: the first tragedie of Lucius Anneus Seneca, intituled Hercules Furens. 1561. Latin and English.

Heywood's 3 trns were ed H. de Vocht, Louvain 1913 (W. Bang's Materialien vol 41). On Troas see W. W. Greg, Library 4th ser 11 1930.

Neville, Alexander. The lamentable tragedie of Œdipus the sonne of Laius. 1563.

Studley, John. The eyght tragedie of Seneca, entituled Agamemnon. 1566.

— The seventh tragedie of Seneca, entitled Medea. 1566; Studley's Agamemnon and Medea ed E. M. Spearing, Louvain 1913 (W. Bang's Materialien vol 38).

N[uce], T[homas]. The ninth tragedie of Lucius Anneus Seneca, called Octavia. [1566].

Haward, Nicolas. The line of liberalitie dulie directing the wel bestowing of benefits and reprehending the comonlie used vice of ingratitude [bks 1–3 only]. 1569. *See* H. H. Davis, HLQ 24 1961; K. Soerenson 29 1966. Haward used French trn by S. Accaurrat.

A[ggas?], E[dward?]. [Selections from the philosophical works]. [1577?]. Bound with P. de Mornay, Excellent discours de la vie et de la mort, 1581. *See* M. St C. Byrne, Library 3rd ser 4 1924.

Golding, Arthur. The woorke of the excellent philosopher Lucius Annæus Seneca concerning benefyting. 1578.

Newton, Thomas et al. Seneca his tenne tragedies, translated [by J. Heywood, A. Neville, J. Studley, T. Nuce and T. Nenton]. 1581; ed T. S. Eliot 2 vols 1927 (Tudor Translations).

Lodge, Thomas. The workes of Lucius Annæus Seneca, both morrall and naturall. 1614, 1620, 1632. With a life of Seneca by J. Lipsius.

— On benefits. Ed W. H. D. Rouse 1899 (Temple Classics).

'Philophrastes' (Sir Ralph Freeman). Lucius Annæus Seneca, the philosopher, his booke of consolation to Marcia, translated into an English poem. 1635.

[Freeman, Sir Ralph]. Lucius Annæus Seneca, the philosopher: his booke of the shortnesse of life, translated into an English poem. 1636, 1663.

S[herburne], [Sir] E[dward]. Medea: a tragedie. 1648.

— Seneca's answer to Lucilius his Quære: why good men suffer misfortunes, seeing there is a Divine Providence, translated into English verse. 1648.

Prestwich, Edmund. Hippolitus, translated out of Seneca, with other poems of the same author. 1651.

P[ordage], S[amuel]. Troades englished (with comments annexed). 1660.

See also under P. de Mornay, col 2189 below.

Sophocles

W[ase], C[hristopher]. Electra. 2 pts Hague 1649.

Statius

S[tephens], T[homas]. An essay upon Statius: or the five first books of P. Papinius Statius his Thebais. 1648. *See* J.M., GM Jan 1850; A. Sparke, N & Q 23 April 1927.

Howard, Sir Robert. Achilleis. In his Poems, 1660.

Suetonius

Holland, Philemon. The historie of twelve Caesars. 1606; ed C. Whibley 1899 (Tudor Translations); ed J. H. Freese [1923]. *See also under Herodian, above.*

Tacitus

[Savile, Sir Henry]. The ende of Nero and beginning of Galba: fower bookes of the histories of Cornelius Tacitus; the life of Agricola. Oxford 1591, 1598, 1604, 1612, 1622, 1640.

[Grenewey, Richard]. The annales of Cornelius Tacitus: the description of Germanie. 1598, 1604, 1612, 1622, 1640. Pbd as pt 2 of Savile's trn, above.

Terence

[Rastell, John?]. Terens in Englysh: Andria. [1520?]. English with Latin in margin.

Udall, Nicholas. Floures for Latine spekynge selected and gathered out of Terence. 1533, 1538, 1560.

Udall, Nicholas and J[ohn] Higgins. Flowers or eloquent phrases of the Latine speach gathered out of al the sixe comœdies of Terence: whereof those of the first thre were selected by Nicolas Udall, and those of the latter three by J. Higgins. 1575, 1581.

Kyffin, Maurice. Andria: the first comœdie of Terence. 1588.

B[ernard], R[ichard]. Terence in English. Cambridge 1598, 1607, 1614, 1629, 1641. Latin and English; each edn 'much amended'.

Newman, Thomas. The two first comedies of Terence called Andria and the Eunuch fitted for schollers private action in their schooles. 1627.

Webbe, [George]. The first comedy of Pub. Terentius called Andria: or the woman of Andros; English and Latine, claused for such as would write or speake the pure language of this author, especially after the method of Dr Webbe. 1629.

— The second comedie of Pub. Terentius called Eunuchus; English and Latine, the uses whereof the reader may finde in the epistle before the first comedie. 1629.

Theocritus

Sixe idillia: that is, sixe small or petty poems. Oxford 1588, 1922; ed E. Arber, English garner vol 8, 1896, and in A. H. Bullen, Some longer Elizabethan poems, 1903. *See* O. L. Jiriczek, Sh Jb 55 1919.

Bradshaw, Thomas. The shepherds starre, now of late merveilous orient in the East. 1591. A paraphrase of 3rd idyll of Theocritus, in dialogue.

Sherburne, Sir Edward. The Syracusians (idyll 15), The shepheard (20), The pastorall wooing (27), The penitent murderer (Εἰς νεκρὸν Ἀδωνιν). In Poems and translations, 1651; The Coraces: or Hieron (16), in Poems by several hands and on several occasions, collected by N. Tate, 1685.

Theophrastus

See under Epictetus, above.

Thucydides

Nicolls, Thomas. The hystory writtone by Thucidides the Athenyan. 1550. From the French of C. de Seyssel. History, translated into Englishe. 1607.

Hobbes, Thomas. Eight bookes of the Peloponnesian warre. 1629, 1634; ed Sir W. Molesworth and W. B. Whittaker 1845; The funeral oration, 1929; ed D. Greene 2 vols Ann Arbor 1959.

Trogus Pompeius

[Norton, Thomas]. Orations of Arsanes agaynst Philip the trecherous Kyng of Macedone. [1560?]. First and 3rd oration from Justin's Epitome.

Golding, Arthur. Thabridgment of the histories of Trogus and Pompeius, collected and wrytten by Justine. 1564, 1570 ('corrected'), 1578.

W[ilkins], G[eorge]. The historie of Justine; whereunto is added a briefe collection of the lives and manners of all the Emperours unto Rudulphus now raigning. 1606.

Codrington, Robert. The history of Justine, taken out of the four and forty books of Trogus Pompeius. 1654.

Vegetius

Sadler, John. The four bookes of Flavius Vegetius Renatus of martiall policye. 1572.

Virgil

Howard, Henry (Earl of Surrey). Certain bokes [i.e. 2 and 4] of Virgiles Æneis turned into English meter. 1557, 1814 (Roxburghe Club); ed F. M. Padelford, Poems of Surrey, Seattle 1920; ed H. Hartman, Oxford 1933 (bk 4 only); ed F. H. Ridley, Berkeley 1963; ed E. L. Jones, Oxford 1964.

Phaer, Thomas. The seven first bookes of the Eneidos of Virgill, converted in Englishe meter. 1558.

— The nyne fyrst bookes of the Eneidos with so much of the tenthe booke as coulde be founde. 1562.

Phaer, Thomas and Thomas Twyne. The whole xii bookes of the Æneidos of Virgill, whereof the first ix and part of the tenth were converted into English meeter by Thomas Phaer, and the residue supplied by Thomas Twyne; there is added Virgils life out of Donatus. 1573, 1584 (adds as 13th bk the suppl tr Twyne of Maphaeus Vegius), 1596, 1600, 1607, 1620.

Fleming, Abraham. The Bucolikes drawne into Englishe verse for verse. 1575.

F[leming], A[braham]. The Bucoliks of Publius Virgilius Maro; together with his Georgiks conteyning foure bookes. 1589.

Stanyhurst, Richard. The first foure bookes of Virgil his Aeneis translated intoo English heroicall verse. Leyden 1582, 1583, 1600; ed E. Arber 1880.

[Fraunce, Abraham?]. The lamentation of Corydon, for the love of Alexis, verse for verse out of Latine. In The lawiers logike, 1588, and in The Countesse of Pembrokes Yvychurch, 1591.

Spenser, Edmund. Virgils gnat. In Complaints, 1591.

[Brinsley, John]. Virgils Eclogues, with his booke de Apibus. 1620, 1633.

Wroth, Sir Thomas. The destruction of Troy: or the acts of Aeneas, translated out of the second booke of the Aeneads, Latine and English; also a centurie of epigrams and a motto upon the Creede. 1620.

Didos death [Æneid bk 4], translated by one that hath no name. 1622.

P[enkethman], J[ohn]. The epigrams of P. Virgilius Maro and others. 1624.

L[isle], W[illiam]. Virgils Eclogues translated into English. 1628.

May, Tho[mas]. Virgil's Georgicks englished. 1628.

Beaumont, Sir John. Translations from Virgil's fourth eclogue. In Bosworth-field, 1629.

Vicars, John. The xii Aeneids of Virgil translated into English deca-syllables. 1632.

Sandys, George. The first booke of Virgils Æneis. In Ovid's Metamorphosis, Oxford 1632, London 1640.

Biddle, John. Virgil's Bucolicks englished; whereunto is added the translation of the two first satyrs of Juvenal. 1634.

Stapleton, Sir Robert. Dido and Aeneas: the fourth booke of Virgils Aeneis now englished. [1634].

[Denham, Sir John]. The destruction of Troy: an essay upon the second book of Virgils Æneis. 1656; rptd in Denham's Works, 1668 etc; ed T. H. Banks, New Haven 1928.

Ogilby, John. The works of Publius Virgilius Maro. 1649, 1650, 1654.

Fanshawe, Sir Richard. The fourth book of the Aeneid on the loves of Dido and Aeneas done into English. 1652; ed A. L. Irvine, Oxford 1924. Spenserian stanzas.

Harington, Sir John. An essay upon two of Virgil's eclogues and two books of his Aeneis. 1658. Eclogues 1 and 9, Aeneid bks 1–2.

—— Virgil's Aeneis. 1659. Bks 3–6.

[Howard, Sir Robert]. The fourth book of Virgill: of the loves of Dido and Aeneas. In Poems, 1660.

See also Fanshawe under Horace, above. For Gavin Douglas's version of the Aeneid see col 662, above.

Xenophon

Hervet, Gentian [and Thomas Lupset]. Xenophons treatise of householde. 1532, 1537, 1544, [after 1547], 1557, 1573.

Barker, William. The bookes of Xenophon: contayning the discipline, schole and education of Cyrus. [1553?] (6 bks), 1567 ('the viii bookes').

Bingham, John. The historie of Xenophon: containing the ascent of Cyrus into the higher countries and retrait from thence. 1623.

Holland, Philemon. Cyrupaedia. The institution and life of Cyrus. 1632, 1936.

On the anon trn of Hiero attributed to Queen Elizabeth I see L. Bradner, Jnl Warburg & Courtauld Inst 27 1964. See also under Grisone, below.

(2) TRANSLATIONS FROM MEDIEVAL AND CONTEMPORARY AUTHORS

Æneas Silvius

See E. S. Piccolomini, below.

Cornelius Agrippa

Clapham, David. The commendation of matrimony. 1540, 1545.

—— A treatise of the nobilitie of woman kynde. 1542.

Barker, William. The nobility of women. Ed R. W. Bond 2 vols 1904–5 (Roxburghe Club) (from 1559 ms). From Lodovico Domenichi, but based on Agrippa.

San[ford], Ja[mes]. Henrie Cornelius Agrippa, of the vanitie and uncertaintie of artes and sciences. 1569, 1675.

F[reake?], J. Three books of occult philosophy. 1651; ed W. F. Whitehead, Chicago 1898.

C., H. (Henry Care or Hugh Crompton?). The glory of women, translated into prose but now turned into English heroicall verse. 1652.

Fleetwood, Edward. The glory of women. 1652.

Turner, Robert. Henry Cornelius Agrippa his fourth book of occult philosophy. 1655. With several other works on magic.

Leon Battista Alberti

Hecatonphila: the art of love or love discovered in an hundred severall kinds. 1598.

Mateo Alemán

[Mabbe, James]. The rogue: or the life of Guzman de Alfarache. 1622, 1623, 2 pts Oxford 1630, 3 pts 1634, 2 pts 1656; ed J. Fitzmaurice-Kelly 4 vols 1924 (Tudor Translations).

Alessio (Girolamo Ruscelli?)

Ward, William. The secretes of the reverende mayster Alexis of Piemount: conteinyng remedies agaynst diseases. Pt 1, 1558, 1559, 1562, 1568, 1580, 1615; pt 2, 1560, 1563, [1568?], [1580], 1614; pt 3, 1562, 1566, 1578, 1614. From French.

Androse, Richard. A verye excellent booke: the fourth and finall booke of secretes. 1569, 1578, 1614.

Amadis of Gaul

Paynell, Thomas. The treasurie of Amadis of Fraunce. [1567 or 1573?]. On identity of the translator see H. Salter and A. F. Pollard, TLS 12, 26 Feb, 12 March 1931.

[Munday, Anthony]. The first book of Amadis of Gaule. [1590–2?]; The second booke of Amadis de Gaula, 1595. 4 pts 1619–8. Bk 2 of the trn is by Lazarus Piot, but it is uncertain whether Lazarus Piot, or Pyott, was merely a

pseudonym of Munday's; see M. St C. Byrne, Anthony Munday and his books, Library 4th ser 1 1921.

Kirkman, Francis. The famous and renowned history of Amadis de Gaula: being the sixt part never before published. [1652].

Aretino

See L. Bruni, below.

Ariosto

Gascoigne, George. Supposes: a comedie. In A hundreth sundrie flowres, [1573]; rptd in The posies of Gascoygne, 1575; Whole woorkes of Gascoygne, 1587; ed J. W. Cunliffe, Cambridge 1907; ed R. W. Bond, Early plays from the Italian, Oxford 1911. Performed at Gray's Inn, 1566.

Harington, Sir John. Orlando Furioso in English heroical verse. 1591, 1607, 1634 (with Harington's epigrams); ed G. Hough 1962; ed R. McNulty, Oxford 1972; Selections, ed R. Gottfried, Bloomington 1963.

T[ofte], R[obert]. Two tales translated out of Ariosto. 1597.

—— Ariosto's satyres, in seven famous discourses, by Gervis Markham [really Tofte]. 1608, 1611.

5 nos of Musica transalpina, 1588, are trns of stanzas in Orlando Furioso. See E. G. Ainsworth, RES 7 1931.

Saint Augustine

Paynell, Thomas. Twelve sermons. nd.

Bodius, H. Certein places gathered out of S. Austens boke intituled De essentia divinitatis. 1548.

Conway, W. A woorke concernyng adulterous mariages. 1550.

Lesse, Nicholas. A worke of the predestination of saints: item, of the vertue of perseveraunce to thend. 1550.

Scory, John. Two bokes of the noble doctor and B. S. Augustine of the predestinacion of saintes, thother perseveraunce unto thende. [Emden 1556?].

Certaine select prayers, gathered out of S. Augustines Meditations; also his manuell or booke of the contemplation of Christ. 1574, 1575, 1577, 1585, 1586.

Rogers, Thomas. A pretious booke of heavenlie meditations; whereunto is annexed Saint Augustines psalter. 1581, 1600, 1612, 1616, 1629, 1640.

—— A right Christian treatise entituled S. Augustines praiers. 1581, 1591, 1600, 1604.

H[ealey], J[ohn]. St Augustine, Of the citie of God. 1610, 1620.

[Matthew, Sir Tobie]. The confessions of the incomparable doctour S. Augustine. [St Omer] 1620, 1638.

Batt, Antony. A heavenly treasure of comfortable meditations and prayers. 1624.

[Floyd, John]. The meditations. Paris 1631.

Watts, William. Saint Augustines Confessions. 1631, Paris 1638.

The kernell or extract of the historicall part of S. Augustins Confessions. Paris 1638.

[Woodhead, Abraham]. The life of S. Augustine: the first part, written by himself in the first ten books of his Confessions. 1660.

Luis de Ávila y Zúñiga

[Wilkinson, John]. The comentaries of Don Lewes de Avela and Suniga which treateth of the great wars in Germany, made by Charles the Fifth. 1555.

Francis Bacon

See col 2324, below.

Jean Louis Guez de Balzac

T[irwhyt], W[illiam]. The letters of Monsieur de Balzac. 1634, 1638.

Baker, Sir Richard. New epistles of Monsieur de Balzac: being the second and third volumes. 2 vols 1638.

— Letters of Mounseur de Balzac: 1, 2, 3, and 4th parts, now collected into one volume. 1654 (engraved title, 1655). Includes 3 previous items.

G., H. The Prince. 1648.

Balzac's remaines: or his last letters. 1658.

W., R. Aristippus, or M. de Balsac's masterpiece: being a discourse concerning the Court. 1659.

Bandello

Br[oke], Ar[thur]. The tragicall historye of Romeus and Juliet, written in Italian by Bandell. 1562; ed J. J. Munro 1908. A poem, through the French version of Boiastuau 1559.

Fenton, Sir Geoffrey. Certaine tragicall discourses written oute of Frenche and Latin. 1567, 1579; ed R. L. Douglas 1898 (Tudor Translations); ed R. L. Douglas and H. Harris 1924. From Belleforest's and Boiastuau's French version.

[Achelly], T[homas]. Violenta and Didaco, translated into English meter. 1576.

The French Bandello, a selection: the original text of four of Belleforest's Histoires tragiques. Tr Geoffrey Fenton and William Painter, anno 1567. Ed F. S. Hook, Missouri Univ Stud 22 1948.

See also under Boccaccio, below.

John Barclay

Long, Kingsmill. Barclay his Argenis translated out of Latine. 1625, 1636. The verses tr Thomas May.

Le Grys, Sir Robert and Thomas May. John Barclay his Argenis translated, the prose by Sir Robert Le Grys and the verses by Thomas May. 1629.

M[ay], Th[omas]. The mirrour of mindes. 2 pts 1631, 1633.

[Man, Judith]. An epitome of the history of faire Argenis and Polyarchus put into French by N. Coeffeteau. 1640.

See also col 2300, below.

Bede

Stapleton, Thomas. The history of the Church of Englande, translated out of Latin. Antwerp 1565, St Omer 1622, 1626; ed P. Hereford, Oxford 1930.

Beza

G[olding], A[rthur]. A tragedie of Abrahams sacrifice. 1577; ed M. W. Wallace, Toronto 1906.

Among the translators of various others of Beza's works were R[obert] F[yll], T. W[ilcox], I.S., J. Fielde, T. S[tocker], A. Gilbie, A. Golding, J. Stockwood, [J. Penry].

Bidpai

North, Sir Thomas. The moral philosophie of Doni: drawne out of the auncient writers, first compiled in the Indian tongue, and now englished out of the Italian. 1570, 1601; ed J. Jacobs 1888.

Boccaccio

Elyot, Sir Thomas. The boke named the Governour. 1531. *For edns see col 1818, above.* Bk 2 ch 12 is a trn of Boccaccio's Titus and Gisippus.

C., T. A pleasant and delightful history of Galesus, Cymon and Iphigenia. [1560?]

G[rantham], H. A pleasant disport of divers noble personages entitled Philocopo. [1566?], 1571, 1587; ed E. Hutton 1927. *See* H. G. Wright, MLR 36 1941, for Grantham's authorship.

T., C. A notable historye of Nastagio and Traversari. 1569. In verse.

[Young, Bartholomew]. Amorous Fiammetta, done into English by B. Giovano del M. Temp. 1587; ed E. Hutton 1926; ed K. H. Josling 1929.

The Decameron: containing an hundred pleasant novels. 2 vols 1620; 1625 (vol 1 only, as The modell of wit preserved to posterity by John Boccaccio), 1634; 2 pts 1657-5; ed E. Hutton 4 vols 1909 (Tudor Translations). The first complete trn.

Parker, Henry. Forty-six lives, translated from De claris mulieribus. Ed H. G. Wright 1943 (EETS). First pbd Literary Museum 1792, ed F. G. Waldron.

Boccaccio and Bandello

Turbervile, George. Tragical tales, translated by Turbervile, in time of his troubles. 1576, Edinburgh 1837. 7 by Boccaccio, 2 by Bandello.

Versions of Boccaccio's tales may be found in other collections, such as Painter's Palace of pleasure and H.C.'s Forest of fancy, [1579].

Boccalini

[Florio, John and William Vaughan]. The new-found politicke. 1626. *See* M. W. Croll, MLN 34 1919.

[Carey], Henry (Earl of Monmouth). I ragguagli di Parnasso: or advertisements from Parnassus, in two centuries, with the politick touch-stone. 1656.

Jacob Boehme

For trns of Boehme's writings, see col 877, above.

Boethius

Walton, J. The boke of comfort called in Latin Boetius de consolatione philosophiae. 1525.

Colvile, George. Boetius de consolationae philosophiae: the boke of Boecius, called the comforte of philosophye. 1556; ed E. B. Bax 1897. Latin and English.

T., J. Five bookes, of philosophicall comfort. 1609; ed H. F. Stewart and E. K. Rand 1918 (Loeb Lib).

M., S. E. Boethius de consolatione anglo-latine expressus per S.M.E. [for S.E.M.]. 1654. Contains the life of Boethius from P. Bertius and J. M. Rota. On the identity of the translator (probably Edward Spencer), *see* W. E. Houghton, RES 7 1931.

See also Queen Elizabeth's englishings of Boethius, Plutarch etc, *ed C. Pemberton 1899 (EETS); ed L. Bradner, Providence 1953.*

Boiardo

T[ofte], R[obert]. Orlando innamorato: the three first bookes done into English heroicall verse. 1598.

Leonardo Bruni (Aretino)

Golding, A[rthur]. The historie of Leonard Aretino, concerning the warres betwene the Imperialles and Gothes for the possession of Italy. 1563.

John Caius

Fleming, Abraham. Of Englishe dogges. 1576; ed E. Arber, An English garner pt 3, 1880; ed E. S. Roberts, Works of Caius, Cambridge 1912.

Calvin

[Coverdale, Miles]. A fayrhful and moste godly treatyse concernynge the Sacrament. [1549?], nd, nd.

N[orton], T[homas]. The institution of Christian religion. 1561, 1562, 1574, 1578, 1580, 1582, 1587, 1599, 1611, 1634.

Fetherstone, Christopher. An abridgement of the Institution of Christian religion, by W. Lawne. Edinburgh 1585, [Edinburgh?] 1586, 1587.

Among the translators of others of Calvin's works were G. G[ylby], H. Holland, T. Tymme, [W. Fulke?], C. Cotton, E. P[aget], C. Rosdell, R. V[aux], N.B., W.H., T. Stocker, A. Golding, [R.G.], T. Broke, J. Fielde, L. T[homson], [A.L.], J. H[armer], W. Warde, A. M[unday], S. Wythers, W. Hucke, R. Horne, Edward Duke of Somerset.

Camden

See col 2213, below.

Camoens

Fanshawe, Sir Richard. The Lusiad: or Portugals historicall poem. 1655; ed G. Bullough 1963.

Girolamo Cardano

Bedingfield, Thomas. Cardanus comforte. 1573, 1576 ('corrected and augmented').

Giovanni Della Casa

Peterson, Robert. Galateo of Maister John Della Casa. 1576; ed H. J. Reid 1892; ed J. E. Spingarn, Boston 1914.

H[awkins], F[rancis]. Youth's behavior or decency in conversation among men. 1646 (4th edn), 1651, 1654. An epitome of the Galateo. *See* M. P. Tilley, Romanic Rev 9 1918.

Mathias Casimir

See col 855, above.

Castiglione

Hoby, [Sir] Thomas. The courtyer. 1561, 1577, 1588, 1603; ed W. Raleigh 1900 (Tudor Translations); ed W. H. D. Rouse [1928] (EL).

Girolamo Cataneo

G[rantham?], H[enry?]. Most briefe tables to knowe redily how many ranckes of footemen armed with corslettes,' as unarmed, go to the making of a just battayle. 1574, [1588]. With Machiavelli, Arte of warre.

Celestina

[Rastell, John]. A new comodye in Englysh in maner of an enterlude [of Calisto and Melebea]. [c. 1527], 1908 (Malone Soc); ed H. W. Allen 1923 (with Mabbe's trn of Celestina). An adaptation of a section of Celestina.

[Mabbe, James]. The Spanish bawd, represented in Celestina: or the tragicke-comedy of Calisto and Melibea. 1631; ed J. Fitzmaurice-Kelly 1894 (Tudor Translations); ed H. W. Allen 1923.

See also Barley, col 2066, above.

Cervantes

[Shelton, Thomas]. The history of the valorous and wittie knight-errant Don Quixote of the Mancha. Pt 1, 1612, [1620?]; pt 2, 1620, 1652. Both pts ed J. Fitzmaurice-Kelly 4 vols 1896 (Tudor Translations); ed F. J. H. Darton 2 vols 1923.

The travels of Persiles and Sigismunda. 1619. Dedication signed M.L.

[Mabbe, James]. Exemplarie novells. 1640, 1654 (as Delight in severall shapes), 1928 (as The Spanish ladie and other stories).

Alain Chartier

Delectable demaundes and pleasaunt questions, with their several aunswers in matters of love. [1566], 1596.

Cinthio

See G. B. Giraldi, below.

Matthieu Coignet

Hoby, Sir Edward. Politique discourses upon trueth and lying. 1586.

Guido delle Colonne

[Lydgate, John]. The hystorye sege and dystruccyon of Troye. 1513.

—— The auncient historie and onely trewe cronicle of the warres. 1555.

Paynell, Thomas. The faythfull and true storye of the destruction of Troye. 1553.

Philippe de Comines

[Danett, Thomas]. The historie of Philip de Commines. 1596, 1601, 1614; ed C. Whibley 2 vols 1897 (Tudor Translations).

Girolamo Conestaggio

[Blount, Edward]. The historie of the uniting of the Kingdom of Portugall to the Crowne of Castill. 1600.

Casparo Contarini

Lewkenor, Sir Lewis. The common-wealth and government of Venice. 1599.

Pierre Corneille

Rutter, Joseph. The Cid: a tragicomedy. 1637.

Lower, Sir William. Polyeuctes: or the martyr. 1655.

—— Horatius: a Roman tragedie. 1656.

Claudio Corte

[Bedingfield, Thomas]. The art of riding. 1584.

Martín Cortés

Eden, Richard. The arte of navigation. 1561, 1572, 1579, 1584, 1589, 1596 (corrected and augmented by John Tapp), 1609, 1615.

Cyrano de Bergerac

Satyrical characters and handsome descriptions in letters written to severall persons of quality. 1658.

St Serf, Sir Thomas. Σεληναρχία: or the government of the world in the moon. 1659; ed C. H. Page, New York 1899.

Friedrich Dedekind

F., R. The schoole of Slovenrie: or Cato turned wrong side outward. 1605, Berlin 1904.

Descartes

A discourse of a method for the well guiding of reason. 1649.

The passions of the soule, in three books. 1650.

[Brouncker, William, Viscount]. Renatus Des-Cartes excellent compendium of musick. 1653.

Philippe Desportes

M[arkham], G[ervase]. Rodomonths infernall: or the Divell conquered; Ariostos conclusions paraphrastically translated. [1607].

Du Bartas

See Saluste du Bartas, below.

Guillaume du Bellay

Ive, Paul. Instructions for the warres. 1589.

Joachim du Bellay

Trns from Du Bellay by Edmund Spenser appear in Van der Noodt's Theatre, 1569, and in his own Complaints, *1591, as* Visions of Bellay *and* Ruines of Rome.

Erasmus

For English trns from Erasmus see col 1785, above.

Alonso de Ercilla y Zúñiga

[Carew, George]. The history of Araucana, written in verse by Don Alonso de Ercilla, translated out of the Spanishe into Englishe prose, allmost to the ende of the 16: canto. Ed F. W. Pierce, Manchester 1964.

Henri Estienne

A mervaylous discourse upon the lyfe, deedes and behaviour of Katherine de Medicis. 'Heydelberge' (for London?) 1575, Cracow 1576.
N[orth], G[eorge]. The stage of Popish toyes, compiled by G.N. 1581.
C[arew?], R. A world of wonders. 1607, Edinburgh 1608.

Froissart

Bourchier, John (Baron Berners). The first [second] volume of Sir Johan Froyssart of the cronycles of England, Fraunce, Spayne. 2 vols 1523–5, [1545]; ed W. P. Ker 6 vols 1901–3 (Tudor Translations), 8 vols Oxford 1927–8. *See* G. Schleich, Archiv 166 1934.
Golding, Pe[te]r. An epitome of Froissard compiled by J. Sleydane. 1608, 1611.

Federico Furio Ceriol

Blundeville, Thomas. A very briefe and profitable treatise declaring howe many counsells a prince ought to have. [1570].

Giovanni Battista Gelli

Iden, Henry. Circes. 1557, [1558–9].
Barker, William. The fearful fancies of the Florentine cooper. 1568, 1599.

Innocent Gentillet

Bowes, Sir Jerome. An apology or defence for Christians of Fraunce which are of the Evangelicall religion. 1579.
Patrick, Simon. A discourse upon the meanes of wel governing a kingdome against Nicholas Machiavell. 1602, 1608.

Conrad Gesner

Morwyng, Peter. The treasure of Evonymus: conteyninge the wonderfull hid secretes of nature. [1559], 1565.
Baker, George. The newe jewell of health. 1576.
—— The practise of the new and old phisicke. 1599.
Topsell, Edward. The historie of the foure-footid beastes. 1607, 1658.

Giovanni Battista Giraldi (Cinthio)

[Bryskett, Lodowick]. A discourse of civill life. 1606. An adaptation.
Trns and adaptations of various tales from Gli hecatommithi *of Cinthio appear in the Elizabethan story books by Barnabe Rich, George Whetstone, Brian Melbancke et al.*

Reginaldus Gonsalvius Montanus

[Skinner, Vincent]. A discovery and playne declaration of sundry subtill practises of the Holy Inquisition of Spayne. 1568, 1569, 1625.

Pope Gregory I

Lyfe of S. Gregorys mother. 1515, [Canterbury 1549?].
W[oodewarde], P[hilippe]. The dialogues of S. Gregorie. Paris 1608; ed E. G. Gardner 1911.
The second booke of the dialogues. 1638.

Pierre Gringoire (Vaudemont)

Barclay, Alexander. The castell of labour. Paris [1503?], [1505?], 1506, 1506; ed A. W. Pollard 1905 (Roxburghe Club).

Federico Grisone

[Blundeville, Thomas]. A newe booke: containing the arte of ryding and breakinge greate horses. [1560?]. Adapted and abridged.
Astley, John. The art of riding out of Xenophon and Gryson verie expert and excellent horsemen. 1584.

Hugo Grotius

See col 848, above.

Giovanni Battista Guarini

[Dymock, Edward]. Il Pastor fido: or the faithfull shepheard. 1602, 1633.
Sidnam, Jonathan. The faithfull sheapheard. Written 1630; BM additional ms 29,493.
Fanshawe, Sir Richard. Il Pastor fido: the faithfull shepheard, with an addition of divers other poems. 1648. Separate title-page of Pastor fido dated 1647; ed W. F. Staton and W. E. Simeone, Oxford 1964.

Stefano Guazzo

Pettie, George. The civile conversation of M. Steeven Guazzo. 1581 (3 bks from the French of G. Chappuys 1586; adds bk 4, tr from Italian by Bartholomew Young); ed E. Sullivan 2 vols 1925 (Tudor Translations ser 2).

Antonio de Guevara

Bourchier, John (Baron Berners). The golden boke of Marcus Aurelius. 1534; 12 more edns 1535–86; ed J. M. G. Olivares, Berlin 1916. From French version of René Bertaut.
Briant, Sir Francis. A dispraise of the life of a courtier. 1548, 1575 (as A looking-glasse for the Courte).
North, Sir Thomas. The diall of princes. 1557, 2 pts 1568 (rev with bk 4, The favoured courtier), 1582, 1619; ed K. N. Colville 1919 (selections, with introd and bibliography). From French of Bertaut.
Hellowes, Edward. Familiar epistles of Sir Antonie Guevara. 1574, 1577, 1584.
—— A chronicle, conteyning the lives of tenne Emperours of Rome. 1577.
—— A booke of the invention of the arte of navigation. 1578.
Fenton, Sir Geoffrey. Golden epistles, gathered, as wel out of the remaynder of Guevaraes woorkes, as other authours Latin, French and Italian. 1575, 1577, 1582. Suppl to Hellowes, above; all but 2 from Guevara through the French.
The Mount of Calvarie. 1595, 1618; pt 2, 1597.
Vaughan, Henry. The praise and happiness of the countrie-life. In Olor Iscanus, 1651 (abridged).
Painter's Palace of pleasure *vol 2, novels 12–14 correspond to Guevara's* Letters *bk 2 30–4, 1. 63, 2. 26.*

Francesco Guicciardini

Fenton, Sir Geoffrey. The historie of Guicciardin: conteining the warres of Italie. 1579, 1599, 1618.
A briefe collection of all the notable things in the hystorie of Guicchiardine. 1591.
I., W. Two discourses which are wanting in the thirde and fourth bookes of his historie. 1595. Italian, French and English.
[Dallington, Sir Robert]. Aphorismes civill and militarie exemplified out of the first quarterne of F. Guicciardini. 1613, 1629.
P., P. Choice proverbs and dialogues in Italian and English; also delightfull stories and apothegms taken out of Guicciardine. 1660.
See P. Guicciardini, La storia guicciardiniana nelle traduzioni inglesi, *Florence 1951.*

Lodovico Guicciardini

Sanford, John. The garden of pleasure. 1573, 1576.
[Danett, Thomas]. The description of the low Countreys, gathered into an epitome out of the historie of Guicchardini. 1593.

Diego Hernandez de San Pedro

Bourchier, John (Baron Berners). The castell of love. [1540?] (fragment), [1549?], [1560?]. From a French version. See W. G. Crane, PMLA 49 1934.
'Hollyband, Claudius' (i.e. Claude Desainliens). The pretie and wittie historie of Arnalt and Lucenda. 1575, 1597, 1608. From the Italian version of Bartolomeo Miraffi.
L[awrence], L[eonard]. A small treatise betwixt Arnalte and Lucenda, turn'd into English verse. 1639.

Juan de Dios Huarte Navarro

C[arew], R[ichard]. Examen de ingenios: the examination of mens wits. 1594, 1596, 1604, 1616.

Huon of Bordeaux

Bourchier, John (Baron Berners). The boke of Huon of Burdeux. [1534?], 1601 (3rd edn); ed S. Lee 3 pts 1882–7 (EETS).

Jaques Hurault

Golding, Arthur. Politicke, moral and martial discourses. 1595.

Joannes de Mediolano

Paynell, Thomas. Regimen sanitatis Salerni. 1528, 1530, 1535, 1541, 1557, 1575, 1597, 1617, 1634.
Harington, Sir John. The Englishmans doctor: or the schoole of Salerne. 1607, 1608, 1609, 1617, 1624; ed F. R. Packard and F. H. Garrison 1922.

Pope John XXI (Petrus Hispanus)

Llwyd, Humphrey. The treasuri of helth: contaynynge many profytable medicines. [1550?], 1558, 1585.

Gautier de Costes de la Calprenède

[Digby, George (Earl of Bristol)]. Cassandra: the fam'd romance rendered into English by an honorable person. 1652. Bks 1–3.
Loveday, R[obert] et al. Hymen's Praeludia: or love's masterpiece, being the first part of Cleopatra. Cléopâtre pts 1–3 tr R. Loveday 1652–5; pts 4–7 tr J[ohn] C[oles] 1656–8; pt 8 tr J[ames] W[ebb] 1658; pts 11–12 tr J[ohn] D[avies] 1659.
Cleopatra a new romance, now englished by a gent. of the Inner Temple. 1652.
Cotterell, Sir Charles. Cassandra the fam'd, now rendred into English. 1667. First edn c. 1653?.

François de la Noue

A[ggas], E[dward]. The politicke and militarie discourses of the Lord de la Noue. 1587.
[Munday, Anthony]. The declaration of the Lord de la Noue, upon his taking arms for the defence of Sedan and Jametz. 1589.
A discourse upon the declaration published by the Lord de Noue. 1589. English and French.

Pierre de la Primaudaye

B[owes], T[homas]. The French Academie, wherin is discoursed the institution of manners. 1586, 1589, 1594, 1602, 1614; pt 2, 1594, 1605.
Dolman, Richard. The third volume of the French Academy. 1601; The whole in 4 bks, 1618 (bk 4 tr W.P.).

Lazarillo de Tormes

Rowland, David. The pleasant history of Lazarillo de Tormes. 1586, 1596, 1624, 1639; ed J. E. V. Crofts, Oxford 1924. Entered Stationers' Register 1569.

P., W. [William Phiston or Fiston?]. The most pleasaunt and delectable histoire of Lazarillo de Tormes: the second parte. 1596.
J. de Luna, Pursuit of the historie of Lazarillo de Tormes, was tr T. W. Calkley 1622, 1631.

John Leland

Robinson, Richard. A learned and true assertion of the life, actes and death of Prince Arthure, King of Great Brittaine. 1582; ed W. E. Mead 1925 (EETS).

Giovanni Paolo Lomazzo

H[aydocke], R[ichard]. A tracte containing the artes of curious paintinge, carvinge, buildinge. Oxford 1598.

Luis de Granada

[Hopkins, Richard]. Of prayer and meditation. Paris 1582, Rouen 1584, London 1592, 1599, 1602, Douai 1612, London 1623, 1633.
— A memoriall of a Christian life. Rouen 1586, 1599, Douai 1612, St Omer 1625.
Meres, Francis. Grenadas devotion. 1598. Anon.
— Granadas spirituall and heavenlie exercises. 1598, Edinburgh 1600.
— The sinners guyde. 1598, 1614.
[Gibbons, Richard]. Of prayer and meditation, abridged and translated. Louvain 1599.
— A spirituall doctrine: conteining a rule to live wel. Louvain 1599, St Omer 1630.
An excellent treatise of consideration and prayer. 1601. Also issued with some edns of Of prayer and meditation, above.
L[odge], T[homas]. The flowers of Lodowicke of Granado: the first part. 1601. From Michael ab Isselt, Flores Lodovici Granatensis.
A paradise of prayers. 1633 (4th edn).

Luther

The chiefe and pryncypall articles of the Christen faythe with other thre very profitable bokes. 1548.
A commentarie of M. Doctor Martin Luther upon Galatians, translated for the unlearned. 1575, 1577, 1580, 1588, 1603, 1615, 1616, 1635, 1644.
Bull, Henry. A commentarie upon the fifteen psalmes, called Psalmi gradum. 1577, 1615, 1637.
G[ace], W[illiam]. Special and chosen sermons. 1578, 1581.
Bell, James. A treatise touching the libertie of a Christian. 1579, 1636.
Other translators of Luther's writings were T. Newton, 'Eusebius Pamphilus', W. Lynne, J. Fox, W. W., R. Argentine, M. Coverdale, E. Ferrers, H. Bell; many trns unsigned.

Machiavelli

Whitehorne, Peter. The arte of warre, set forthe in Englishe. 2 pts 1560–2, 3 pts 1574, 1588; ed H. Cust 2 vols 1905 (Tudor Translations) (with Bedingfield's trn of The Florentine historie and Dacres's trn of Prince).
B[edingfield], Thomas. The Florentine historie. 1595.
D[acres], E[dward]. Machiavels discourses upon the first decade of T. Livius. 1636.
— Nicholas Machiavel's Prince; also the life of Castruccio Castracani of Lucca, and the meanes Duke Valentine us'd to put to death Vitellozzo Vitelli. 1640.
The Divell a married man: or the Divell hath met with his match. [1647].
The Prince: an Elizabethan translation. Ed H. Craig, Chapel Hill 1944. From anon ms.

Mantuan

See B. Spagnuoli, below.

Pedro de Medina

Frampton, John. The arte of navigation. 1581, 1595.

Melanchthon

Taverner, Richard. Apologie of Melanchon who defendeth the aforesaid confessyon of the Germans. [1536?].

Beauchamp, Lewis. A very godly defense defending the mariage of preistes sent unto the Kyng of England Henry the Aight. [Ipswich 1541].

A newe work concerning both partes of the sacrament to be receyved of the lay peple. 1543, [1546?] (3 edns).

Joye, George. The exposicion of Daniel the prophete. Geneva 1545.

C[respin], J. The epistle of P. Melancton made unto Kynge Henry the Eyght for the revokinge of the six artycles. 1547.

Lesse, Nicholas. The justification of man by faith only. 1548.

Rogers, John. A waying and considering of the interim. 1548.

G[oodale], J[ohn]. A civile nosegay wherein is contayned not onylye the offyce and dewty of all magistrates and judges but of all subjectes. [1550?].

Bradford, John. A godly treatyse of prayer. [1553?].

Brooke, John. Of two wonderful popish monsters. 1579.

R[obinson], R[ichard]. A godly and learned assertion in defence of the true Church. 1580.

Other translators from Melanchthon include John Bale and J. Bradforde.

Bernardino de Mendoza

Hoby, Sir Edward. Theorique and practise of warre. 1597.

Pedro Mexía

Fortescue, Thomas. The foreste: or collection of histories. 1571, [1576]. From French version of Claude Gruget.

N[ewton?], T[homas?]. A delectable dialogue concerning phisicke and phisitions. 1580.

T[raheron], W[illiam]. The historie of all the Romane emperors. 1604, 1623 (as The Imperial historie, with continuation by E. Grimeston).

[Milles, Thomas]. The treasurie of auncient and moderne times: containing the learned collections, judicious readings and memorable observations, translated out of Pedro Mexia and M. Francesco Sansocino, etc. 1613.

—— Ἀρχαιο-πλοῦτος: containing ten following bookes to the former Treasurie. 1619.

B[aildon], J[ohn?]. The rarities of the world, touching the beginning of kingdomes and common-wealths. 1651. Selected from Silva de varia lecio 1540.

Giovanni Tommaso Minadoi

Hartwell, Abraham. The history of the warres betweene the Turkes and the Persians. 1595.

Montaigne

Florio, John. The essayes or morall, politike and militarie discourses of Lo: Michaell de Montaigne. 1603, 1613, 1632 (with Index); ed G. Saintsbury 6 vols 1892–3 (Tudor Translations); ed A. R. Waller 6 vols 1897; ed D. MacCarthy 3 vols 1928; ed J. I. M. Stewart 2 vols 1931.

Jorge de Montemayor

Googe, Barnabe. Eglogs, epytaphes and sonettes. 1563. 5th and 6th eclogues borrowed from Diana.

Young, Bartholomew. Diana. 1598; ed J. M. Kennedy, Oxford 1969; also tr Sir Thomas Wilson (1560?–1629) in BM additional ms 18,638.

Sir Thomas More

See col 1792, above.

Philippe de Mornay

A[ggas], E[dward]. The defence of death. 1576, 1577.

—— On the truth of the Christian religion. 1576.

F[ield], J[ohn]. A notable treatise of the Church. 1579, 1580, 1581, 1606.

Sidney, Sir Philip and Arthur Golding. A woorke concerning the trewnesse of the Christian religion. 1587, 1592, 1604, 1617.

Sidney, later Herbert, Mary (Countess of Pembroke). Discourse of life and death; Antonius a tragedie written also in French by R. Garnier: both done in English by the Countesse of Pembroke. 1592, 1600, 1606, 1607; ed A. Luce, Weimar 1897.

Six excellent treatises of life and death. 1607. Contains also Plato's supposititious work, Axiochus, and selections from Cicero and Seneca.

Other translators of Mornay's writings were: R.S., I. V[erneuil?], S. Lennard, J. Healey, J. Bulteel, A. M[unday].

Remigio Nannini

T., W. Civil considerations upon many and sundry histories: containing rules and precepts for princes, commonwealths. 1601. From French of Gabriel Chappuys.

Francesco Negri de Bassano

Cheeke, Henry. A certayne tragedie entituled Freewyl. [1589].

Bernardino Ochino

[Argentine, Richard]. Sermons. Ipswich 1548.

Ponet, John. A tragoedie or dialoge of the unjuste usurped primacie of the Bishop of Rome. 1549; ed C. E. Plumptre 1899.

[Argentine, Richard and Anne Cooke (Lady Bacon)]. Certayne sermons. [1550?]. 25, 6 tr Argentine and 14 (also pbd separately) tr Anne Cooke.

C[ooke], A[nne], Lady Bacon. Sermons (to the number of 25) concerning the predestination and election of God. [1570?]. Anne Cooke also translated Bishop Jewel's Apologie, 1562.

Phiston [i.e. Fiston], William. Certain godly and very profitable sermons of faith, hope and charity. 1580.

A dialogue of polygamy rendered into English by a person of quality. 1657.

Diego Ortúñez de Calahorra

T[yler], M[argaret]. The mirrour of princely deedes and knighthood. [1578], [1580?], [1599?].

P., R. The second part of the first booke of the myrrour of knighthood. 1585, 1599; The third part of the first booke, [1586?], [1598 or 1599?].

Bks 4–9 of Mirrour, not by Ortúñez, were tr F.P. 1583, 1598, and L.A. 1598–1601.

Jeronimo Osorio da Fonseca

Shacklock, Richard. An epistle to Elizabeth, Quene of England. Antwerp 1565.

Fenn, John. A learned treatis wherein he confuteth a certayne aunswere made by M. W. Haddon. Louvain 1568.

Blandie, William. The five bookes of Hieronimus Osorius contayning a discussion of civill and Christian nobilitie. 1576.

John Owen

See col 2299, below.

Antonio dalla Paglia

G[olding?], A[rthur?]. The benefite that Christians receive by Jesus Christ crucified. 1573, [1575?], 1580, 1633, 1638.

Courtenay, Edward (Earl of Devonshire). The benefite of Christ's death. Ed C. Babington 1855 (from ms dated 1548).

Marcellus Palingenius, i.e. P. A. Manzolli

Googe, Barnabe. The zodiake of life. 1565, 1576 (rev), 1588. Bks 1–3, 1560; bks 1–6, 1561.

Paracelsus
See col 850, above.

Pascal
Les provinciales: or the mysteries of Jesuitisme discover'd in certain letters. 1657, 1658.

Petrarch
Parker, Henry (Baron Morley). The tryumphes of Fraunces Petrarcke. c. 1553?, 1887 (Roxburghe Club); ed D. D. Carnicelli, Cambridge Mass 1971.
Twyne, Thomas. Phisicke against fortune, as well prosperous as adverse. 1579.
Spenser, Edmund. Petrarches visions [Standomi un giorno solo, alla fenestra]. In his Complaints, 1591. *See also* sonnets in Van der Noodt's Theatre, 1569.
Chapman, George. Petrarch's seven penetentiall psalmes. 1612.
Hume, Anna. The triumphs of love, chastitie, death. Edinburgh 1644.
See G. Watson, The English Petrarchans: a critical bibliography of the Canzoniere, *1967 (Warburg Inst).*

Philibert de Vienne
North, George. The philosopher of the Court. 1575.

Joannes Philippson (Sleidanus)
Daus, John. A famous cronicle of oure time. 1560.
Wythers, Stephen. A briefe chronicle of the foure principall empyres. 1563.
The key of historie: abridgement of the foure chief monarchies. 1627, 1631, 1635.
Mock majesty: or the siege of Munster: a true story of King John Becock and his companions the Anabaptists. 1644. A trn of part of Sleidan's Commentaries.
H[ughes], W[illiam]. Munster and Abingdon, or the open rebellion there and unhappy tumult here. Oxford 1657. The part on Münster tr from bk 10 of Sleidanus's Commentaries.
See also under Froissart, above.

Enea Silvio Piccolomini (Pope Pius II, known as Æneas Silvius)
The goodlie history of the Ladye Lucres of scene in Tuskane. [1550?], 1560, 1567; rptd in The hystorie of the most noble knight Plasidas, 1873 (Roxburghe Club).
Braunche, William. The most excellent historie of Euryalus and Lucresia. 1596.
Aleyn, Charles. The historie of Eurialus and Lucretia. 1639, 1875 (Roxburghe Club).

E. S. Piccolomini and Baptista Spagnuoli (Mantuan)
Barclay, Alexander. The eglogs of Alexander Barclay, the first thre out of Miserie curialium. [c. 1515] (3 edns), [1521?], [1521], 1870 (Spenser Soc). Much adaptation. The first 3, from Æneas Silvius, rptd in De curialium miseriis epistola, ed W. P. Mustard, Baltimore 1928; ed B. White 1928 (EETS). For Barclay's use of Mantuan's eglogues *see* Mantuanus, ed W. P. Mustard, Baltimore 1911.

Giovanni Pico della Mirandola
See col 850, above.

Marco Polo
[Frampton, John]. The most noble and famous travels of Marcus Paulus into the east partes of the world. 1579; ed N. M. Penzer 1929. From the Spanish version. Another trn in Samuel Purchas, Hakluytus posthumus, 1625, Glasgow 1905–7 (Hakluyt Soc).

Primaleon
[Munday, Anthony]. Primaleon of Greece: first booke. 1595; Second booke, 1596; 3 pts 1619.

Francisco de Quevedo y Villegas
See col 2064, above.

Les Quinze Joyes de Mariage
[Copland, Robert]. The fyftene joyes of maryage. 1509.
[Tofte, Robert]. The batchelars banquet. 1603, 1604. 1626, 1631; ed F. P. Wilson, Oxford 1929.

Rabelais
Urquhart, Sir Thomas. The first [second] book of the works of Mr Francis Rabelais. 2 vols 1653; ed J. L. May 2 vols 1927. Completed by Peter Motteux 1708.
John Eliot, Ortho-epia gallica, *1593, contains translated extracts from Rabelais. See H. Brown*, Rabelais in English literature, *Cambridge Mass 1933.*

Pierre de la Ramée (Ramus)
See under Aristotle and col 851, above.

Annibale Romei
K[epers], J[ohn]. The courtiers academie. [1598].

Guillaume de Saluste du Bartas
James I, King. Uranie. In Essays of a prentise in the divine art of poesie, Edinburgh 1584, 1585.
—— The furies. Part of Semaine 2, jour 1, in His majesties poeticall exercises at vacant houres, 1591.
Hudson, Thomas. The historie of Judith. 1584; rptd in Sylvester's trn, 1608, below.
Sylvester, Joshua. A canticle of the victorie obteined by Henrie the Fourth, at Ivry. 1590, 1615.
—— Bartas his devine weekes and workes. 1605, 1608, 1611, 1613, 1621, 1633, 1641. Pts appeared 1592, 1595, 1598, 1606, 1607.
Winter, Thomas. The second day of the first weeke. 1603. Anon.
—— The third dayes creation done verse for verse. 1604.
Lisle, William. Foure bookes of Dubartas in French and English. 1637. Pts appeared 1595, 1598, 1625.
For a list of trns from Du Bartas 1584–1641 see A. H. Upham, French influence in English literature, *New York 1909. See also A. L. Prescott*, Renaissance News 19 *1966 on an unpbd trn by Robert Barret.*

Francesco Sansovino
Hichcock, Robert. The quintescence of wit. 1590.
See also under Mexia, above.

Paolo Sarpi
A full and satisfactorie answer to the late unadvised Bull against Venice. 1606.
An apology or apologiticall answere made unto Cardinall Bellarmine. 1607.
Brent, [Sir] N[athaniel]. The historie of the Councel of Trent. 1620, 1629, 1640.
B[edell], W[illiam]. The free [true] school of warre. 1625.
P[otter], C[hristopher]. The history of the quarrels of Pope Paul V with the state of Venice. 1626.
Gentilis, Robert. The history of the Inquisition. 1639.
Roe, Sir Thomas. The reasons of the resolution taken in the Valteline. In The cruell subtilty of ambitioin discovered, [1650?].

Madeleine de Scudéry
Cogan, Henry. Ibrahim: or the illustrious Bassa. 1652. The whole work.
G., F. Artamenes or the Grand Cyrus. 5 vols 1653–5.
[Wolley, Edward]. Curia politiae: or the apologies of severall princes. 1654.
B., T. A triumphant arch erected and consecrated to the glory of the feminine sex. 1654, 1656.
[Davies, John and George Havers]. Clelia. 5 vols 1656–61. Pts 1–3 tr Davies, pts 4–5 tr Havers.

Johannes Secundus
See under Anacreon, above.

Jean de Serres
Timms, Thomas. The thre parts of commentaries of the civill warres of Fraunce. 1574; The fourth parte, 1576.
Golding, Arthur. The lyfe of the most godly capteine Jasper Colignie Shatilion. 1576.
Stockwood, John. A godlie and learned commentarie upon Ecclesiastes. 1585.
Grimeston, Edward. A general inventorie of the history of France unto 1598. 1607, 1611 ('continued unto this present'), 1624 ('continued unto 1622'). *See* F. S. Boas, MP 3 1906.

Sleidanus
See J. Philippson, above.

Baptista Spagnuoli (Mantuan)
Bale, John. A lamentable complaynte of Baptista Mantuanus. [1560?].
Turbervile, George. The eglogs of the poet B. Mantuan. 1567, 1572.
Harvey, Tho[mas]. The bucolicks of Baptist Mantuan in ten eclogues. 1656.
See also under Piccolomini, above.

Niccoló Tartaglia
Lucar, Cyprian. Three books of coloquies concerning the arte of shooting in great and small peeces of artillerie. 1588.

Tasso
K[yd], T[homas]. The houscholders philosophie. 1588.
Fraunce, Abraham. The affectionate life and unfortunate death of Phillis and Amyntas. In The Countesse of Pembrokes Yvychurch, 1591.
C[arew], R[ichard]. Godfrey of Bulloigne or the recouerie of Hierusalem: an heroicall poeme. 1594; ed A. B. Grosart, Manchester 1881. 5 cantos, Italian and English.
Fairfax, Edward. Godfrey of Bulloigne: or the recouerie of Jerusalem. 1600, 1624.
[Reynolds, Henry]. Torquato Tassos Aminta englisht. 1628.
Dancer, John. Aminta: the famous pastoral, translated in English verse. 1660.
Thomas Watson's Latin Amyntas, the indebtedness of which to Tasso has been exaggerated, was tr Abraham Fraunce 1587, 1588, 1589, 1596.

Till Eulenspiegel
[Andrewe, Lawrence?] Tyll Howleglas. Antwerp [c. 1510] (fragment).

[Copland, William?] A merye jest of a man called Howleglas, and of many marvelous thinges and jestes that he did in his lyffe. [1528?], [1530?], [c. 1559–63]. *See* F. W. D. Brie, Eulenspiegel in England, Berlin 1903.

Antonio de Torquemada
[Walker, Ferdinand]. The Spanish Mandevile of miracles. 1600, 1618.

Honoré d'Urfé
The history of Astrea: the first part. 1620.
D[avies], J[ohn]. Astrea: a romance, translated by a person of quality. 3 vols 1657–8.

Francisco de Valdés
Thorius, John. The sergeant major. 1590.

Crispin van de Pass
Hortus floridus: the first book contayning a very lively and true description of the flowers. [1615]; ed E. S. Rohde 1928.

Pierre Viret
Scoloker, Anthony. A notable collection of places of the sacred scriptures. 1548.
Viret's other translators included T. Stocker, J. Brooke, J. Shute, T. S[hute], F.H.

Juan Luis Vives
Hyrde, Richard. The instruction of a Christen woman. [1529?], [1540?], 1541, 1547 (for 1541), 1557, 1585, 1592.
Morrison, [Sir] Richard. An introduction to wysedome. 1540, 1544, 1550, [1550?], 1564.
Paynell, Thomas. The office and duetie of an husband. [1553?].

Vincent Voiture
D[avies], J[ohn]. Letters of affaires, love and courtship, written to several persons of honour and quality. 2 pts 1657.

Ulrich Zwingli
The rekening and declaration of the faith of Huldrik Zwingly. Zürich 1543, 1548.
Argentine, Richard. Certeyne preceptes. 1548, 1550.
Dorset, T. The detection of the blasphemies for errours. 1548.
[Véron, Jean]. A short pathwaye to the ryghte and true understanding of the holye scriptures. Worcester 1550.
—— The ymage of both pastoures. 1550.
Cotsforde, Thomas. The accompt rekenynge and confession of the faith of Huldrik Zwinglius. Geneva 1555.
A briefe rehersal of the death of Christ. [1560?].

(3) BIBLIOGRAPHIES AND CRITICISM

Farmer, Richard. An essay on the learning of Shakespeare. 1767.
Warton, T. History of English poetry vol 3. 1781; ed W. C. Hazlitt, vol 4, 1871.
Steevens, G. Ancient translations from classic authors. In E. Malone, Prolegomena to Shakespeare, 1790.
Moss, J. W. A manual of classical bibliography. 2 vols 1825, 1837 (rev).
Herford, C. H. Studies in the literary relations of England and Germany in the sixteenth century. Cambridge 1886.
Schmidt, H. Richard Stanyhursts Übersetzung von Vergils Aeneide i–iv: ihr Verhältnis zum Original. Breslau [1887].
Koeppel, E. Die englischen Tasso-Übersetzungen des xvi Jahrhunderts. Anglia 11 1889.
—— Studien zur Geschichte der italienischen Novelle in der englischen Litteratur des sechzehnten Jahrhunderts. Quellen und Forschungen 70 1892.

Jusserand, J. J. The English novel in the time of Shakespeare. Tr 1890, 1899 (enlarged).
Cunliffe, J. W. The influence of Seneca on Elizabethan tragedy. 1893.
Chandler, F. W. Romances of roguery. Pt 1, New York 1899.
Underhill, J. G. Spanish literature in the England of the Tudors. New York 1899.
Einstein, L. The Italian Renaissance in England. New York 1902.
Voyages and travels. Ed C. R. Beazley 2 vols 1903 (Arber's English garner).
Bolle, W. Die gedruckten englischen Liederbücher bis 1600. Berlin 1903.
Brie, F. W. D. Eulenspiegel in England. Berlin 1903.
—— Die erste Übersetzung einer italienischen Novelle ins Englische durch Henry Parker, Lord Morley. Archiv

124 1907. Masuccio, Novellino 49; trn rptd from BM ms Royal 18 A lxii.

Carpenter, F. I. Thomas Watson's Italian madrigal englished. 1590. JEGP 2 1903.

Dieckow, F. A. F. John Florios Übersetzung der Essais Montaignes. Strasbourg 1903.

Fest, O. Über Surreys Virgilübersetzung. Berlin 1904.

Elizabethan critical essays. Ed G. Gregory Smith 2 vols Oxford 1904.

Whibley, C. In his Literary portraits, 1904. On Montaigne et al.

— Translators. CHEL vol 4, 1909.

Imelmann, R. Surreys Aeneis IV in ursprünglicher Gestalt. Sh Jb 41 1905.

Minor poets of the Caroline period. Ed G. Saintsbury 3 vols Oxford 1905-21.

Snell, F. J. The age of transition vol 2. 1905.

Greg, W. W. Pastoral poetry and pastoral drama. 1906.

Schelling, F. E. Elizabethan drama 1558-1642. 2 vols Boston 1908.

— English literature during the lifetime of Shakespeare. New York 1910.

Upham, A. H. The French influence in English literature from the accession of Elizabeth to the Restoration. New York 1908.

de Vocht, H. De invloed van Erasmus op de engelsche tooneelliteratuur der xvie en xviie eeuwen. Ghent 1908.

— The earliest English translations of Erasmus' colloquies, 1536-66. Louvain 1928. R. Pruvost, RES 5 1929, cites an English verse abridgment of De pueris instituendis.

Fehlauer, F. Die englischen Übersetzungen von Boethius De consolatione philosophiae. Berlin 1909. See also Boethius, ed H. F. Stewart and E. K. Rand 1918 (Loeb Lib).

Harris, W. J. The first printed translations into English of the great foreign classics. [1909].

Jockers, E. Die englischen Seneca-Übersetzer des 16 Jahrhunderts. Strasbourg 1909.

Fitzmaurice-Kelly, J. The relations between Spanish and English literature. Liverpool 1910.

Hatcher, O. L. Aims and methods of Elizabethan translators. E Studien 44 1910.

Kerlin, R. T. Theocritus in English literature. Lynchburg 1910.

Lee, S. The French Renaissance in England. 1910.

Schulze, K. Die Satiren Halls: ihre Abhängigkeit von den altrömischen Satirikern und ihre Realbeziehungen auf die Shakespearezeit. Berlin 1910.

Palmer, H. R. List of English editions and translations of Greek and Latin classics printed before 1641, with an introduction by V. Scholderer. 1911 (Bibl Soc).

Brenner, J. W. Phaers Virgilübersetzung in ihrem Verhältnis zum Original. Heidelberg 1912.

Esdaile, A. A list of English tales and prose romances printed before 1740. 1912 (Bibl Soc).

Spearing, E. M. The Elizabethan translations of Seneca's tragedies. Cambridge 1912.

Wolff, S. L. The Greek romances in Elizabethan prose fiction. New York 1912.

Perott, J. de. The Mirrour of knighthood. Romanic Rev 4 1913.

Bailey, M. L. Milton and Jakob Boehme. New York 1914. Especially ch 3: Boehme in England.

Cooper, C. B. Some Elizabethan opinions of the poetry and character of Ovid. Chicago 1915.

Koch, A. Die schottische Liviusübersetzung des John Bellenden. Königsberg 1915.

Scott, M. A. Elizabethan translations from the Italian. New York 1916. Suppl by C. R. Baskervill, MP 16 1919; J. de Perott, Romanic Rev 9 1918.

Foster, F. M. K. English translations from the Greek. New York 1918. Addns and corrections for Homer by D. Bush, PMLA 41 1926.

Willcock, G. D. A hitherto uncollated version of Surrey's translation of the fourth book of the Aeneid. MLR 14-15 1919-20, 17 1922.

Wright, H. G. Life and works of Arthur Hall of Grantham. Manchester 1919.

Amos, F. R. Early theories of translation. New York 1920.

Berdan, J. M. Early Tudor poetry. New York 1920.

Thomas, H. Spanish and Portuguese romances of chivalry. Cambridge 1920.

— Three translators of Gongora and other Spanish poets during the seventeenth century. Revue Hispanique 48 1920. Thomas Stanley, Sir Richard Fanshawe, Philip Ayres; English and Spanish texts.

— English translations of Portuguese books before 1640. Library ser 7 4th 1923. See also C. Estorrinho, Portugal and Brazil: an introduction, ed H. V. Livermore, Oxford 1953.

— The English translations of Guevara's works. In Estudios in memoriam de Adolfo Bonilla vol 2, Madrid 1930.

— The English translation of Quevedo's La vida del Buscón. Revue Hispanique 81 1933.

Chambrun, C. (Longworth). Giovanni Florio: un apôtre de la Renaissance en Angleterre. Paris 1921.

Morgan, B. Q. A bibliography of German literature in English translation. Madison 1922, Stanford 1938 (enlarged).

Colville, K. N. Fame's twilight. 1923. On Thomas North and John Barclay.

Modersohn, A. B. Cicero im englischen Geistesleben des 16 Jahrhunderts. Archiv 149 1923.

Specimens of Tudor translations from the classics. Ed O. L. Jiriczek, Heidelberg 1923.

Bush, D. The classical tales in Painter's Palace of pleasure. JEGP 23 1924.

— Musaeus in English verse. MLN 43 1928, 45 1930.

— Mythology and the Renaissance tradition in English poetry. Minneapolis 1932.

Duckett, E. S. Catullus in English poetry. Northampton Mass 1925.

Hayes, G. R. Anthony Munday's Romances of chivalry. Library 4th ser 6-7 1925-6.

Merrill, L. R. Life and poems of Nicholas Grimald. New Haven 1925. See also H. H. Hudson, Grimald's translations from Beza, MLN 39 1924.

Pompen, A. The English versions of the Ship of fools. 1925.

Praz, M. Stanley, Sherburne and Ayres as translators and imitators of Italian, Spanish and French poets. MLR 1925.

Whipple, T. K. Martial and the English epigram from Sir Thomas Wyatt to Ben Jonson. Berkeley 1925. Suppl by H. B. Lathrop, MLN 43 1928.

Harrison, T. P. Bartholomew Yong, translator. MLR 21 1926.

Schoell, F. Etudes sur l'humanisme continental en Angleterre à la fin de la Renaissance. Paris 1926.

Wilder, M. L. Jonson's indebtedness to Latin authors, shown chiefly in his non-dramatic poems. Ithaca 1926.

Conley, C. H. The first English translators of the classics. New Haven 1927.

Hasselkuss, H. K. Der Petrarkismus in der Sprache der englischen Sonettdichter der Renaissance. Münster 1927.

Nixon, P. Martial and the modern epigram. New York 1927.

Prothero, R. E. (Baron Ernle). The light reading of our ancestors. 1927.

Emperor, J. B. The Catullian influence in English lyric poetry circa 1600-50. Columbia Missouri 1928.

Turner, C. Anthony Munday: an Elizabethan man of letters. Berkeley 1928.

Spanish short stories of the sixteenth century in contemporary translations. Ed J. B. Trend, Oxford 1928 (WC).

Dodge, R. E. N. The text of the Gerusalemme liberata in the versions of Carew and Fairfax. PMLA 44 1929. *See also* W. L. Bullock 45 1930.

Scott, J. G. Les sonnets élisabéthains: les sources et l'apport personnel. Paris 1929.

McClure, N. E. The letters and epigrams of Sir John Harington. Philadelphia 1930. Martial.

Smith, F. S. The classics in translation. 1930.

Matthiessen, F. O. Translation: an Elizabethan art. Cambridge Mass 1931.

Chester, A. G. Thomas May: man of letters 1595–1650. Philadelphia 1932.

Gates, W. B. The dramatic works and translations of Sir William Lower. Philadelphia 1932.

Koszul, A. L'offrande d'un traducteur: notes sur l'anglais de John Florio. Revue Anglo-américaine 19 1932.

Wright, L. B. Translations for the English middle class. Library 4th ser 13 1932.

Brown, H. Rabelais in English literature. Cambridge Mass 1933.

Lathrop, H. B. Translations from the classics into English 1477–1620. Madison 1933.

Pruvost, R. Le Daphnis et Chloe d'Angel Day 1587. Revue Anglo-américaine 10 1933.

Van der Haar, D. Richard Stonyhurst's Aeneis. Amsterdam 1933.

Yates, F. A. John Florio. Cambridge 1934.

Bourne, J. A. Some English translations of seventeenth-century Spanish novels. MLR 31 1936.

Wright, H. G. The first English translations of the Decameron. MLR 31 1936.

— The Elizabethan translation of the Questione d'amore in the Filocolo. MLR 36 1941.

— The indebtedness of Painter's translations from Boccaccio in the Palace of pleasure to the French version of le Maçon. MLR 46 1951.

Gee, J. A. Margaret Roper's English version of Erasmus' Precatio dominica. RES 13 1937.

Golding, L. T. An Elizabethan Puritan: Arthur Golding. New York 1937.

Orsini, N. Elizabethan ms translations of Machiavelli's Prince. Jnl Warburg & Courtauld Inst 1 1937.

— Le traduzioni elisabettiane inedite di Machiavelli. In his Studii sul rinascimento italiano in Inghilterra, Florence 1937.

Davis, H. John Brende: soldier and translator. HLQ 1 1938.

Koller, K. Two Elizabethan expressions of the idea of mutability. SP 35 1938. On Robert Ashely's trn of Louis Le Roy 1594.

Anthéunis, L. Un refugié anglais traducteur de Louis de Grenade: Richard Hopkins. Revue d'Histoire Ecclésiastique 35 1939.

Clements, A. F. (ed). Tudor translations: an anthology. Oxford 1940.

Gottfried, R. B. Geoffrey Fenton's Historie of Guicciardin. Bloomington 1940.

Rich, T. Harington and Ariosto: a study in Elizabethan verse translation. New Haven 1940.

Workman, S. K. Fifteenth-century translation as an influence on English prose. Princeton 1940.

Hudson, H. H. Current English translations of the Praise of folly. PQ 20 1941.

Knowles, E. B. The first and second editions of Shelton's Don Quixote [1612, 1620]. Hispanic Rev 9 1941.

— Some textual peculiarities of the first English Don Quixote. PBSA 37 1943.

Webb, H. J. The Elizabethan translation of Vegetius' De re militari. MLN 56 1941.

— English translations of Caesar's Commentaries in the sixteenth century. PQ 28 1949.

Fellheimer, J. Barnabe Barnes' use of Geoffrey Fenton's Historie of Guicciardin. MLN 57 1942.

— Notes on Geoffrey Fenton's minor translations. PQ 22 1943.

— Geoffrey Fenton's History of Guicciardin and Holinshed's Chronicles of 1587. MLQ 6 1945.

— Hellowes' and Fenton's translation of Guevara's Epístolas familiares. SP 44 1947.

Phillips, M. M. Erasmus and propaganda: a study of the translations of Erasmus in English and French. MLR 37 1942.

Fucilla, J. G. Petrarchan translations in British periodicals. Bull of Bibliography 18 1943.

Pellegrini, A. M. Giordano Bruno on translations. ELH 10 1943.

Pane, R. U. English translations from the Spanish 1484–1943: a bibliography. New Brunswick NJ 1944. *See also* E. G. Mathews, JEGP 44 1945.

Munsterberg, M. The Decameron in English [1620]. More Books 19 1944.

Fairfax's Tasso. TLS 11 March 1944.

Buell, L. M. Arthur Golding and the earthquake of 1580. PQ 24 1945.

Strathmann, E. The 1595 translation of Du Bartas' First day. HLQ 8 1945.

Riddlebough, G. B. Queen Elizabeth's translation of Boethius' De consolatione philosophiae. JEGP 45 1946.

Farrar, C. P. and A. P. Evans. Bibliography of English translations from medieval sources. New York 1946.

Tappert, T. G. On the translation of Martin Luther's works. Lutheran Church Quart 19 1947.

Bell, C. G. Edward Fairfax, a natural son. MLN 62 1947.

— A history of Fairfax criticism. Ibid.

Boas, F. S. Ovid and the Elizabethans. 1947.

Fellheimer, J. Hellowes' and Fenton's translations of Guevara's Epístolas familiares. SP 44 1947.

Flenley, R. The first English translation of Champlain. Canadian Historical Rev 28 1947. On Grimston's General inventorie of the history of France 1607.

Maxwell, J. C. Lucan's first translator. N & Q 29 Nov 1947. On Thomas Hughes's Misfortunes of Arthur 3. 3.

Grierson, H. J. C. Verse translation, with special reference to translation from Latin. Oxford 1948; rptd in his Criticism and creation, 1949.

Martin, L. C. Lucan–Marlowe–?Chapman. RES 24 1948.

McManaway, J. G. The first five bookes of Ovids Metamorphosis 1621. SB 1 1949.

Wortham, J. Sir Thomas Elyot and the translation of prose. HLQ 11 1948.

— Arthur Golding and the translation of prose. HLQ 12 1949.

Tatlock, J. S. P. The legendary history of Britain: Geoffrey of Monmouth's Historia regum Britanniae and its early vernacular versions. Berkeley 1950.

Tucker, J. E. John Davies of Kidwelly: translator from the French. PBSA 44 1950. With bibliography.

Fay, H. C. Chapman's Materials for his translation of Homer. RES new ser 2 1951.

Marquardt, W. F. The first English translators of Trajano Boccalini's Ragguagli di Parnasso: a study of literary relationships. HLQ 15 1951.

Simonsen, V. L. Joshua Sylvester's English translation of Du Bartas' La première semaine. Orbis Litterarum 8 1952.

Brodersen, G. L. Seventeenth-century translations of Juvenal. Phoenix 7 1953.

Fay, H. C. Poetry, pedantry and life in Chapman's Iliads. RES new ser 4 1953.

Jones, R. F. The triumph of the English language: a survey of opinions concerning the vernacular from the introduction of printing to the Restoration. Stanford 1953.

Russell, P. E. A Stuart Hispanist: James Mabbe. Bull of Hispanic Stud 30 1953.

Wright, H. G. The first English translation of the Decameron 1620. Upsala 1953. Translator probably John Florio.

Bolgar, R. R. The translations of the Greek and Roman classical authors before 1600. In his Classical heritage and its beneficiaries, Cambridge 1954. *See also* H. Nørgaard, RES new ser 9 1958.

Barzanò, G. Le prime due traduzioni inglesi dell'Aminta. Studi Tassiani 5 1955.

Davis, R. B. The translation of Ovid's Metamorphoses. In his George Sandys: poet-adventurer, 1955.

—— In re George Sandys' Ovid. SB 8 1956.

Hassell, J. W. An Elizabethan translation of the Tales of Des Périers: the mirror of mirth 1583 and 1592. SP 52 1955. By T[homas?] D[eloney]?

Rees, D. G. Sir Thomas Wyatt's translations from Petrarch. Comparative Lit 7 1955.

Anderson, D. M. Sir Thomas Wilson's translation of Montemayor's Diana. RES new ser 7 1956.

Lord, G. deF. Homeric renaissance: the Odyssey of George Chapman. 1956.

Parks, G. B. William Barker: Tudor translator. PBSA 51 1957.

Roe, F. C. Sir Thomas Urquhart and Rabelais. Oxford 1957.

Wright, H. G. Boccaccio in England from Chaucer to Tennyson. 1957.

Gasquet, E. S. Machiavelli's Discourses: a forgotten English translation. N & Q April 1958.

George, J. Thomas Shelton, translator, in 1612–14. Bull of Hispanic Stud 35 1958.

Jacobsen, E. Translation, a traditional craft: an introductory sketch with a study of Marlowe's Elegies. Copenhagen 1958.

Knowles, E. B. Thomas Shelton: translator of Don Quixote. Stud in Renaissance 5 1958.

Sühnel, R. Homer und die englische Humanität: Chapmans und Popes Übersetzungskunst. Tübingen 1958.

Wilson, E. M. and E. R. Vincent. Thomas Stanley's translations and borrowings from Spanish and Italian poems. Revue de Littérature Comparée 32 1958.

Brault, G. J. English translations of the Celestina in the sixteenth century. Hispanic Rev 28 1960.

Hietsch, O. Die Petrarcaübersetzungen Sir Thomas Wyatts. Vienna 1960.

Hughey, R. (ed). The Arundel Harington manuscript of Tudor poetry. 2 vols Columbus 1960. Trn of Petrarch's Trionfo dell'eternità attributed to Elizabeth I.

Sørensen, K. Thomas Lodge's translation of Seneca's De beneficiis compared with Arthur Golding's version. Copenhagen 1960.

—— Thomas Lodge's Seneca. Archiv 199 1963.

Whiting, B. J. Sir Richard Baker's Cato variegatus 1636. In Humaniora: essays honoring Archer Taylor, New York 1960.

Winny, J. (ed). Elizabethan prose translation. Cambridge 1960.

Eames, M. John Ogilby and his Aesop. BNYPL Feb 1961.

Lievsay, J. L. A pair of traitors. In his Stefano Guazzo

and the English Renaissance 1575–1675, Chapel Hill 1961. On trns of Pettie and Young.

Van Beeck, F. J. (ed). The poems and translations of Sir Edward Sherburne 1616–1702 excluding Seneca and Manilius. Assen 1961.

Thomson, P. Sir Thomas Wyatt: classical philology and English humanism. HLQ 25 1962.

—— Wyatt and his background. 1964.

Muir, K. A. Wyatt's poetry: translations. In his Life and letters of Sir Thomas Wyatt, Liverpool 1963.

Neri, N. Il Pastor fido in Inghilterra con il testo della traduzione secentesca di Sir Richard Fanshawe. Turin 1963.

Sprott, S. E. Ralegh's Sceptic and the Elizabethan translation of Sextus Empiricus. PQ 42 1963.

Bawcutt, N. W. (ed). Sir Richard Fanshawe: shorter poems and translations. Liverpool 1964.

Steane, J. B. The first book of Lucan; Ovid's Elegies. In his Marlowe, Cambridge 1964.

Whitfield, J. H. Sir Richard Fanshawe and the Faithfull shepherd. Italian Stud 19 1964.

Bennett, H. S. Translations and translators. In his English books and readers 1558 to 1603, Cambridge 1965.

—— In his English books and readers 1475 to 1557, Cambridge 1969 (2nd edn). With Appendix: Trial list of translations printed between 1475–1600. *See Ebel, below.*

—— In his English books and readers 1603 to 1640, Cambridge 1970.

Guss, D. L. Wyatt's Petrarchism. HLQ 29 1965.

Lacalle, G. M. A manuscript version of Mabbe's Celestina. Revue de Littérature Comparée 39 1965.

Phinney, E. Continental humanists and Chapman's Iliads. Stud in Renaissance 12 1965.

MacLure, M. Homer: the minor translations. In his George Chapman, Toronto 1966.

Ebel, J. G. A numerical survey of Elizabethan translations. Library 5th ser 22 1967.

Watson, G. The English Petrarchans: a critical bibliography of the Canzoniere. 1967 (Warburg Inst).

Kidde, C. A. Rabelais in English: Urquhardt and Kimes. N & Q March 1968.

Parks, G. B. and R. Z. Temple. The literatures of the world in English translation: a bibliography. Vol 1, The Greek and Latin literatures, New York 1968; vol 3, The romance literatures, New York 1970.

Robinson, F. G. A note on the Sidney-Golding translation of Philippe de Mornay's De la vérité de la religion chrestienne. Harvard Lib Bull 17 1969.

Real, H. J. Die Geschichte der Lukrez-Übersetzung in England bis 1682. In his Untersuchungen zur Lukrez-Übersetzung von Thomas Creech, Bad Homburg 1970. On Lucy Hutchinson and John Evelyn.

E. J. K.

6. HISTORY, PHILOSOPHY, SCIENCE AND OTHER FORMS OF LEARNING

I. HISTORIANS, BIOGRAPHERS AND ANTIQUARIES

A. GENERAL WORKS

Hendrichs, D. Geschichte der englischen Autobiographie von Chaucer bis Milton. Leipzig 1925.

Schütt, M. Die englische Biographik der Tudor-Zeit. Hamburg 1930.

Stauffer, D. English biography before 1700. Cambridge Mass 1930.

Walters, H. B. Some English antiquaries. Essays by Divers Hands new ser 12 1933.

— The English antiquaries of the sixteenth, seventeenth and eighteenth centuries. 1934.

Major, J. C. The role of personal memoirs in English biography and the novel. Philadelphia 1935.

Flower, R. Laurence Nowell and the discovery of England in Tudor times. Proc Br Acad 21 1936.

Arneke, H. Kirchengeschichte und Rechtsgeschichte in England von der Reformation bis zum frühen 18 Jahrhundert. Halle 1937.

Barnes, H. E. A history of historical writing. Norman Oklahoma 1937.

Butt, J. The facilities for antiquarian research in the seventeenth century. E & S 24 1938.

Campbell, L. B. The use of historical patterns in the reign of Elizabeth. HLQ 1 1938.

Douglas, D. English scholars 1660–1730. 1939, 1951 (rev).

Dick, H. G. (ed). Thomas Blundeville's The true order and methode of writing and reading hystories 1574. HLQ 3 1940. A reprint.

Thompson, J. W. A history of historical writing. 2 vols New York 1942.

Macdonald, H. The law and defamatory biographies in the seventeenth century. RES 20 1944.

Bates, B. W. Literary portraiture in the historical narrative of the Renaissance. New York 1945.

Nearing, H. J. English historical poetry 1599–1641. Philadelphia 1945.

Ullman, B. L. Leonardo Bruni and humanistic historiography. 1946.

Dean, L. F. Tudor theories of history writing. Ann Arbor 1947.

Kendrick, T. D. British antiquity. 1950.

Matthews, W. British diaries: an annotated bibliography of British diaries written between 1442 and 1942. Berkeley 1950.

— British autobiographies: an annotated bibliography of British autobiographies published or written before 1951. Berkeley 1955.

Trimble, W. R. Early Tudor historiography 1485–1548. JHI 11 1950.

Kliger, S. The Goths in England. Cambridge Mass 1952.

Burford, A. H. History and biography: the Renaissance distinction. In A tribute to G. C. Taylor, Chapel Hill 1952.

Stenton, D. M. The pipe rolls and the historians 1660–1883. Cambridge Historical Jnl 10 1952.

Shumaker, W. English autobiography: its emergence, materials and form. Berkeley 1954.

Fox, L. (ed). English historical scholarship in the sixteenth and seventeenth centuries. Oxford 1956 (Dugdale Soc).

Evans, J. History of the Society of Antiquaries. 1956.

Pocock, J. G. A. The ancient constitution and the feudal law: English historical thought in the 17th century. Cambridge 1957.

Moir, E. A. L. The early English antiquaries. History Today Nov 1958.

Gottfried, R. B. Antiquarians at work. Renaissance News 11 1958. On Sir John Price and Lambarde.

Schoeck, R. J. Early Anglo-Saxon and legal scholarship in the Renaissance. Stud in Renaissance 5 1958. On Nowell, Lambard, Spelman, Simonds D'Ewes.

— The Cronica cronicarum of Sir Thomas More and Tudor historians. Bull Inst of Historical Research 35 1962.

Staton, W. F., jr. Ascham's theory of history writing. SP 56 1959.

Anglo, S. The 'British history' in early Tudor propaganda. Bull John Rylands Lib 44 1961. On Geoffrey of Monmouth.

Fussner, F. S. The historical revolution: English historical thought 1580–1640. New York 1962.

— Tudor history and historians. New York 1970.

Kirkwood, J. J. Bacon's Henry VII: a model of a theory of historiography. Renaissance Papers 1965.

Ferguson, A. B. Reginald Pecock and the Renaissance sense of history. Stud in Renaissance 13 1966.

Levy, F. J. Tudor historical thought. San Marino 1967.

Baker, H. The race of time: three lectures on Renaissance historiography. Toronto 1967.

Delany, P. British autobiography in the seventeenth century. 1969.

For useful brief annotations on the 16th-century chronicles see C. Read, Bibliography of British history: Tudor period, Oxford 1959 (rev).

B. 1500-58

(1) HALL AND LELAND

EDWARD HALL
d. 1547

§1

The union of the two noble and illustrate [illustre] famelies of Lancastre and York. 1548, 1550, [1560?], with some sheets ptd in 1547; [ed H. Ellis] 1809, New York 1965; Henry VIII, ed C. Whibley 2 vols 1904.

§2

Tanner, T. Bibliotheca britannico-hibernica. 1748.

Brewer, J. S. The reign of Henry VIII. Ed J. Gairdner 2 vols 1884.

Smith, R. M. The date and authorship of Hall's Chronicle. JEGP 17 1918.

Pollard, A. F. Hall's will and chronicle. Bull Inst of Historical Research 9 1932.

— A lawsuit over Hall's will. Bull Inst of Historical Research 11 1933.

Pollard, G. The bibliographical history of Hall's Chronicle. Bull Inst of Historical Research 9 1932.

Begg, E. Shakespeare's debt to Hall and Holinshed in Richard III. SP 32 1935.

Zeeveld, W. G. The influence of Hall of Shakespeare's English historical plays. ELH 3 1936.

Wolf, E. Halle's union of Lancastre and Yorke and its place among English Americana. PBSA 33 1939.

Keen, A. A short account of the recently discovered copy of Hall's Union of the noble houses of Lancaster and York, notable for its ms additions. Bull John Rylands Lib 24 1940.

— Hall and Shakespeare. TLS 26 April, 29 Nov 1947. Replies by J. Crow 10 May, D. Hay 17 May, W. J. F. Hutcheson 24 May, A. P. Rossiter 31 May 1947.

JOHN LELAND
1506-52

§1

Assertio inclytissimi Arturii regis Britanniae. 1544; tr R. Robinson 1582 (as A learned and true assertion of the life of prince Arthure); ed W. E. Mead 1925 (EETS) (appended to C. Middleton, The famous historie of Chinon of England, with Robinson's trn).

The laboryouse journey and serche of Johan Leylande, geven of hym as a newe yeares gyfte to Kynge Henry the VIII. 1549, 1596 (in R. Brooke, A discoverie of certaine errours), 1631 (in J. Weever, Funerall monuments), 1710 (in Itinerary ed T. Hearne vol 1), Oxford 1722, 1772 (in W. Huddesford, Lives of Leland etc); ed W. A. Copinger, Manchester 1895.

The itinerary of John Leland the antiquary. Ed T. Hearne 9 vols Oxford 1710-12, 1744-5, 1770; ed L. Toulmin Smith 11 pts in 5 vols 1906-10; 5 vols Carbondale [1964] (foreword by T. Kendrick).

§2

Bale, J. The laboryouse journey. 1549. Preface.

Huddesford, W. The lives of those eminent antiquaries John Leland, Thomas Hearne and Anthony à Wood. Ed W. Huddesford 2 vols Oxford 1772. Life of Leland by Huddesford.

Burton, Edward (attributed). Life of Leland, with notes and bibliography. 1896.

Smith, L. T. Introd to Itinerary vol 1, 1907.

Hudson, H. H. Leland's lists of mss in Lincolnshire monasteries. EHR 54 1939.

Skeat, T. C. Two 'lost' works by Leland. EHR 65 1950.

Dorsch, T. S. Two English antiquaries: Leland and Stow. E & S new ser 12 1959.

Hutton, J. S. Leland's Laudatio pacis [1546]. SP 58 1961.

(2) MINOR HISTORIANS

ROBERT FABYAN
d. 1513

[Begin] Prima pars cronecarum. 2 vols 1516 (anon), 1533, 1542 (2 issues, expurgated), 1559 (with continuation by another hand to 15 Jan 1559, another issue continued to 8 May 1559); ed H. Ellis 1811 (as The new chronicles of England and France).

RICHARD ARNOLD
d. 1521?

[Begin] In this booke is conteyned the names of the baylifs, custos, mairs and sherefs of the cite of London. [Antwerp 1503?], [Antwerp c. 1515], [Southwark 1525?]; [ed F. Douce] 1811 (as The customs of London, otherwise called Arnold's chronicle).

POLYDORE VERGIL
1470?-1555?

§1

De inventoribus rerum. Venice 1499, Paris 1500, Strasbourg 1509, Basle 1521 etc. Many 16th-century edns and trns.

Polydori Vergilii urbinatis anglicae historiae libri xxvi. Basle 1534, 1546, 1555 (continued to 1538), 1556, 2 vols Ghent 1556-7, 1 vol Basle 1570, Leyden 1651; ed and tr H. Ellis 1844 (Camden Soc) (as Three bookes of Polydore Vergil's English history: comprising the reigns of Henry VI, Edward IV and Richard III); Polydore Vergil's English history: containing the first eight books, comprising the period prior to the Norman Conquest, ed H. Ellis 1846 (Camden Soc); ed and tr D. Hay 1950 (Camden Soc, Royal Historical Soc).

An abridgement of the notable woorke of Polydore Vergil. Tr T. Langley 1546, 1546, 1551, [c. 1560]; ed W. A. Hammond, New York 1868.

§2

Ferguson, J. Notes on the work of Vergil De inventoribus rerum. Isis 17 1933.

Hay, D. The ms of Vergil's Anglica historia [c. 1512-13]. EHR 54 1939.

— The life of Vergil. Jnl Warburg & Courtauld Inst 12 1949.

— Vergil: Renaissance historian and man of letters. Oxford 1952. With a list of letters.

Koebner, R. Henry VIII, Constantine and Vergil. Bull Inst of Historical Research 26 1953.

Starnes, D. T. Tyrwhitt's copy of Vergil's De inventoribus rerum. Texas Stud in Lit & Lang 7 1965.

Clough, C. H. Frederigo Veterani, Vergil's Anglica historia and Castiglione's Epistola ad Henricum Angliae regum. EHR 82 1967.

CHARLES WRIOTHESLEY
1508?–62

A chronicle of England during the reigns of the Tudors. Ed W. D. Hamilton 2 vols 1875–7 (Camden Soc).

NICHOLAS HARPSFIELD
1519?–75

A treatise on the pretended divorce between Henry VIII and Catherine of Aragon. Ed N. Pocock 1878 (Camden Soc).
Life of Sir Thomas More. Ed Lord Acton 1877 (in part, with historical portion of A treatise); ed R. W. Chambers and E. V. Hitchcock 1932 (EETS) (as The Tudor lives of Sir Thomas More. For criticism see More, col 1792, above.

THOMAS LANQUET or LANKET
1521–45
§1

An epitome of cronicles continued to the reigne of Edwarde the Sixt by T. Cooper. 1569 (for 1549), 1559 (to the reigne of Quene Elizabeth, by R. Crowley), 1560 (Coopers chronicle unto the late death of Queene Marie), 1565, 1565.

§2

Tolbert, J. M. The argument of Shakespeare's Lucrece: its sources and authorship. SE 29 1950. Prefatory Argument not by Shakespeare; Lanquet in Coopers' Chronicle one main source.

WILLIAM PATTEN
1521?–84

The expedicion into Scotlande of the most woorthely fortunate Prince Edward, Duke of Somerset, 30 June 2 Edward VI. 1548; ed J. G. Dalyell, Edinburgh 1798 (as Fragments of Scotish history); ed E. Arber 1880 (English garner vol 3), 1903 (Tudor Tracts).
The historie of Wyates rebellion. 1554, 1555, 1809 (in vol 3 of Antiquarian repertory, ed P. Grose, Thomas Astle et al, 4 vols 1807–9).

LONDON AND OTHER TOWN CHRONICLES

Chronicles of London. Ed C. L. Kingsford, Oxford 1905.
Six town chronicles of England. Ed R. Flenley, Oxford 1911. Introd on town chronicles and bibliography.
The chronicle of Calais in the reigns of Henry VII and Henry VIII. Ed J. G. Nichols 1846 (Camden Soc).
A London chronicle during the reigns of Henry VII and Henry VIII. Ed C. Hopper, Camden Miscellany 4 1859.
Chronicle of the Grey Friars of London. Ed J. G. Nichols 1852 (Camden Soc).
The great chronicle of London. Ed A. H. Thomas and I. D. Thornley 1939.
Dickens, A. G. The register or chronicle of Butley Priory, Suffolk 1510–35. Winchester 1951.

ANONYMOUS AND MISCELLANEOUS

The chronicle of Queen Jane, and of two years of Queen Mary, written by a resident in the Tower of London. Ed J. G. Nichols 1850 (Camden Soc).
Narratives of the days of the Reformation, chiefly drawn from the mss of John Foxe the martyrologist; with two contemporary biographies of Archbishop Cranmer. Ed J. G. Nichols 1859 (Camden Soc).

(3) MINOR BIOGRAPHERS

WILLIAM ROPER
1496–1578

The mirrour of vertue in worldly greatnes: or the life of Syr T. More. Paris [St Omer] 1626; ed T. Hearne, [Oxford] 1716, Cambridge 1879; ed J. Lewis 1720 (from better ms), 1731, Dublin 1765, 1835; ed S. W. Singer 1817, 1822; ed E. Rhys [1890]; ed I. Gollancz 1902, 1903, 1910 (Bohn's Lib); ed E. V. Hitchcock 1935 (EETS); ed J. M. Cline, New York 1950. For criticism see More, col 1792, above.

GEORGE CAVENDISH
1500–61
§1

Life of Cardinal Wolsey. 1641 (as The negotiations of Thomas Woolsey), 1667, 1706, 1742 (in J. Grove, History of Cardinal Wolsey), 1745 (Harleian miscellany vol 5); ed J. Grove 1761 (more accurate version), 1810 (Harleian miscellany rev T. Park vol 5); ed C. Wordsworth 1810 (Ecclesiastical biography vol 1) (from ms), 1818, 1837, 1853; ed S. W. Singer 2 vols 1825, 1827, 1855 (Morley's Universal Lib); ed J. Holmes 1852; ed E.H. 1855; ed F. S. Ellis 1893 (Kelmscott Press); 1899 (Temple Classics); Chipping Campden 1930; ed R. S. Sylvester 1959 (EETS); ed R. Lockyer 1962.
Two early Tudor lives. Ed R. S. Sylvester and D. P. Harding, New Haven 1962. With Roper's Life of More.

§2

Steuart, H. Cavendish's Life of Wolsey. Downside Rev 57 1939.
Wiley, P. L. Renaissance exploitation of Cavendish's Life of Wolsey. SP 43 1946.
Steiner, F. G. A note on Cavendish's Life of Wolsey. English 9 1952.
Sylvester, R. S. Cavendish's Life of Wolsey: the artistry of a Tudor biographer. SP 57 1960.

C. 1558–1603

(1) FOXE, PARKER, HOLINSHED AND STOW

JOHN FOXE
1516–87
§1

Commentarii rerum in ecclesia gestarum: liber primus. Strasbourg 1554, 1564 (as Chronicon ecclesiae continens historiam rerum).

Rerum in ecclesia gestarum commentarii. 2 pts Basle 1559–63.

Actes and monuments. 1563, 2 vols 1570, 1576, 1583, 1596, 1610, 3 vols 1631–2, 1641, 1684; ed S. R. Cattley 8 vols 1837–41 (dissertation by G. Townsend); rev M. H. Seymour 1838; rev G. Townsend 8 vols 1843–9; rev J. Pratt 8 vols [1877] (with introd by J. Stoughton). An abridgement of the Acts and monumentes by T. Bright. 1589.

Foxe's Book of martyrs. Ed F. A. Williamson 1965 (abridged).

Μαρτυρολογία ἀλφαβετική: or an alphabetical martyrology. 1677.

Proposals for printing the Book of martyrs. [1683].

For trns and minor works see Mozley, below.

§2

Day, R. Preface to trn of Foxe's Christus triumphans, 1579.

Life. Prefixed to vol 2 of 1641 edn of Actes and monuments and attributed to Foxe's son Samuel.

Maitland, S. R. A review of Foxe's History of the Waldenses. 1837.

—— Six letters on Foxe's Acts and monuments. 1837.

—— Twelve letters on Foxe's Acts and monuments. 1841.

—— Notes on the contributions of G. Townsend to the new edition of Foxe's Martyrology. 8 pts 1841–2.

—— Remarks on Cattley's defense of his edition of Foxe's Martyrology. 1842.

Winter, W. Biographical notes on Foxe. 1876.

Bauer, W. E. Foxe's book of Martyrs. Church History 3 1934.

Mozley, J. F. Foxe and his book. 1940, New York 1970. With a list of Foxe's minor works.

—— George Joy and Foxe. TLS 21 Sept 1940.

Brooks, E. St J. Foxe and Shipton. TLS 21 Sept 1940.

Whitebrook, J. C. Grindal, Foxe and Wendelin. N & Q 29 Aug 1942.

Oliver, L. M. The seventh edition of Foxe's Acts and monuments. PBSA 37 1943.

—— Rowley, Foxe and the Faustus additions. MLN 60 1945.

—— Single page imposition in Foxe's Acts and monuments 1570. Library 5th ser 1 1946. Details and corrections by P. S. Dunkin 2 1947.

—— Foxe and the drama New custom. HLQ 10 1947.

—— Foxe and the Conflict of conscience [by N. Woodes]. RES 25 1949.

Haller, W. Foxe and the Puritan revolution. In Seventeenth-century studies by R. F. Jones et al, Stanford 1951.

—— Foxe's Book of martyrs and the elect nation. 1963, New York 1963 (as The elect nation: the meaning and relevance of Foxe's Book of martyrs).

White, H. C. In her Tudor books of saints and martyrs, Madison 1963. Chs 5–6.

MATTHEW PARKER
1504–75
§1

De antiquitate Britanniae ecclesiae et privilegiis ecclesiae cantuariensis. [Lambeth] 1572[–4] (anon), Hanover 1605 (imperfect); ed S. Drake 1729.

Parker also edited:

Elegans, illustris et facilis rerum praesertim britannicarum narratio, quam Matthaeus westmonasteriensis Flores historiarum scripsit. 2 pts [London] 1567, 1570 (as Flores historiarum per Matthaeum westmonasteriensem collecti).

Matthaei Paris historia major. 1571.

Aelfredi regis res gestae ab Asserio conscriptae. 1574.

Historia brevis Thomae Walsingham et ypodigma Neustriae. 1574.

See also col 1820, above.

§2

Strype, J. The life and acts of Parker. 1711, 3 vols Oxford 1821.

Perry, E. W. Under four Tudors: the story of Parker. 1940.

Danby, H. S. Matthew Parker. London Quart 166 1941.

Carter, C. S. The real Parker. Church Quart Rev 126 1943.

Whitebrook, J. C. The consecration of Parker. 1945.

Shirley, F. J. Elizabeth's first Archbishop. 1948. A reply to Whitebrook, above; see also review of Whitebrook in N & Q 7 Nov 1945, and controversy 17 Nov 1945–8 Feb 1947 on date and 17th-century citation of Fabyan.

Wright, C. E. The dispersal of the monastic libraries and the beginnings of Anglo-Saxon studies: Parker and his circle, a preliminary study. Trans Cambridge Bibl Soc 1 1949–53.

Brook, V. J. K. The life of Archbishop Parker. 1962.

RAPHAEL HOLINSHED
d. 1580?
§1

The firste [laste] volume of the chronicles of Englande, Scotlande and Irelande. 4 pts 1577, 3 vols 1587, 6 vols 1807–8. The Privy Council ordered the excision of 8 ll. in vol 2 and 26 ll. in vol 3; some of these were replaced by new leaves. BM has all the original ll. among its copies. For 18th-century reprints of castrations *see* Masten, 1958, below.

Boswell-Stone, W. G. Shakespeare's Holinshed: the chronicle and the historical plays compared. 1896, 1907, New York 1966 (Shakespeare Lib).

Holinshed's chronicle as used in Shakespeare's plays. Ed A. and J. Nicoll 1927 (EL).

§2

Courtenay, T. P. Commentaries on the historical plays of Shakespeare. 2 vols 1840.

Brownfield, C. The Holinshed family. TLS 19 Sept 1936.

—— Holinshed and his editors. TLS 7 Aug 1937.

Schelling, F. E. Holinshed's chronicles. Lib Chron 5 1937.

Dodson, S. C. The Northumberland of Shakespeare and Holinshed. SE 19 1939.

—— Holinshed's sources for the prognostications about the years 1583 and 1588. Isis 38 1947.

—— Abraham Fleming: writer and editor. SE 34 1955. On editor of 1587 Holinshed.

Smith, R. M. Spenser, Holinshed and the Leabhar Gabhàla. JEGP 43 1944.

Fellheimer, J. Fenton's Historie of Guiccardin and Holinshed's Chronicles of 1587. MLQ 6 1945.

Stibbs, J. H. Raleigh and Holinshed. MLR 44 1949.

Masten, K. I. Three eighteenth-century reprints of the castrated sheets in Holinshed's Chronicle. Library 5th ser 13 1958.

Benbow, R. M. The providential theory of historical causation in Holinshed's Chronicles: 1577 and 1587. Texas Stud in Lit & Lang 1 1960.

Miller, W. E. Abraham Fleming: editor of Shakespeare's Holinshed. Ibid.

Edelen, G. William Harrison 1535–93. Stud in Renaissance 9 1962.

JOHN STOW
1525–1605

§1

The workes of Geoffrey Chaucer, with divers addicions which were never in print before. 1561. The notes on Chaucer and list of Lydgate's works were also ptd in T. Speght's edn of Chaucer, 1598 and 1602.

A summarie of English chronicles. 1565, 1566, [1570], [1573], [1574], [1575], 1590.

The summarie of Englyshe chronicles abridged. 1566, [1567], [1573], [1579], 1584, [1587], 1598, 1598, 1604; continued by E.H[owes] [1607], 1611, 1618.

The chronicles of England from Brute unto this present year 1580. [1580], [1592] (as The Annales of England until 1592), [1600], [1601], [1605] (with addns probably by G. Eld); continued by E. Howes 1615 (with an appendix on the universities of Oxford, Cambridge and London by Sir G. Buck), 1631.

The Summary grows from 8º to 4º to folio, ending as the Annals; the Abridgement grows from 16º to 8º. Each edn differs to some extent from the rest, but in general each abridgement is adapted and brought up to date from the most recent large version.

A survey of London. 1598, 1599 (with variants), 1603; rev A.M[unday] 1618; rev A.M[unday], D.D[yson] et al 1633 (one reissue after 1640); ed J. Strype 2 vols 1720, 1754–5; ed A gentleman of the Inner Temple 2 vols 1753; ed W. J. Thoms 1842, 1876; ed H. Morley 1889 (Carisbrooke Lib), 1893; ed C. L. Kingsford 2 vols Oxford 1908 (standard edn with bibliography); ed H. B. Wheatley [1912] (EL), [1960] (rev).

Three fifteenth-century chronicles (from Stow). Ed J. Gairdner 1880 (Camden Soc).

Two London chronicles from the collections of Stow. Ed H. L. Kingsford, Camden Miscellany 12 1910.

§2

Bonner, A. Stow and his Survey. London & Middlesex Archaeological Soc Trans new ser 8 1938.

Nichols, J. F. Stow memorial lecture. Ibid.

Bryant, J. A. Stow's continuator and the Defense of Brute. MLR 45 1950.

Martin, M. F. Stow's Annals and the Famous historie of Sir Thomas Wyat. MLR 53 1958.

(2) MINOR HISTORIANS

RICHARD GRAFTON
1507–73

A abridgement of the chronicles of England. 1563 (for Feb 1562, variant colophon dated 1563), 1564, 1570, 1572.

A manuell of the chronicles of England to this yere 1565. [1565].

A chronicle at large, unto the first yere of Q. Elizabeth. 2 vols 1569 (title-page to vol 2 dated 1568); [ed H. Ellis] 2 vols 1809.

[Begin] Salutem in Christo. Good men and evill delite in contraryes. [1571] (4 edns). On the imprisonment of the Duke of Norfolk, signed R.G. Attributed to Grafton.

Grafton also wrote the continuation from the reign of Edward IV in J. Hardyng's Chronicle, 1543.

JOHN CLAPHAM
b. 1566

The historie of England: the first booke. 1602 (by 'Philomathes'), 1606 (enlarged as The historie of Great Britannie).

Elizabeth of England. Ed E.P. and C. Read, Philadelphia 1951. From ms entitled Certain observations concerning the life and reign of Queen Elizabeth.

HUMPHREY LLWYD
1527–68

Commentarioli britannicae descriptionis fragmentum. Cologne 1572; ed Moses Williams 1731 (with De Mona, below); tr T. Twyne 1573 (as The breviary of Britayn); ed J. Lewis 1729 (as The history of Great Britain).

Angliae regni florentissimi nova descriptio. [ptd abroad] 1573.

De Mona druidum insula. 1573 (in Sir John Price, Historiae brytannicae defensio), Antwerp 1579 (in A. Ortelius, Theatrum orbis terrarum, parergon); ed Moses Williams 1723, 1731 (with Commentariolum); tr 1606 (in A. Ortelius, Theatre of the whole world).

The historie of Cambria now called Wales. 1584 (trn of Brut y Twysogion, erroneously attributed to Caradoc of Llancarfan, with addns and corrections by David Powel and a Description of Cambria by Sir John Price); ed and enlarged W. Wynne 1697; ed R. Llwyd, Shrewsbury 1832.

WILLIAM LAMBARD
1536–1601

§1

'Αρχαιονομία: sive de priscis Anglorum legibus libri. 1568; ed A. Whelock 2 vols Cambridge 1644 (with Bede's Historia ecclesiastica).

A perambulation of Kent. 1576, 1596 (with addns), [1640?], 1656 (reissue of previous edn with cancel title-page), Chatham 1826 (from 1596 edn with life of Lambard).

Eirenarcha: or the office of the justices of peace. 1581, 1582 (2 edns and another issue with colophon dated 1583), 1588, 1591 (1588 edn with new prelims), 1592, 1594, 1599 etc.

The duties of constables, borsholders, tithing-men. 1582, 1582, 1583, 1584, 1587 (enlarged), 1591, 1594, 1599, 1601 etc.

Archion: or a commentary upon the High Courts of Justice in England. 1635, 1635; ed C. W. McIlwain and P. H. Ward, Cambridge Mass 1957 (as Archeion).

Dictionarium Angliae topographicum et historicum. 1730. Written c. 1577.

§2

Putnam, B. H. The earliest form of Lambard's Eirenarcha and a Kent wage visitation of 1563. EHR 41 1926.

Caldiero, F. Shakespeare's signature in Lambard's 'Αρχιανομία [sic]. N & Q 21 April 1945.

Heltzel, V. B. Sir Thomas Egerton and Lambard. HLQ 11 1948.

Dunkel, W. D. Lambard's friendship with Ralph Rokeby. N & Q 26 April 1952.

— Lambarde, Elizabethan jurist. New Brunswick NJ [1965].

Read, C. Lambard's Ephemeris 1580–8. HLQ 15 1952.
—— (ed). Lambard and local government. Ithaca 1962.
Ward, P. L. Lambard's Collection on Chancery. Harvard Lib Bull 7 1953.

SIR THOMAS SMITH
1513–77

Many mss, both of works and letters, are in BM, Public Record Office and elsewhere.

Collections
Literary and linguistic works. 1542, 1549, 1568. Pt 1 ed B. Danielsson, Stockholm [1963].

§ 1
De republica Anglorum: the maner of government of England. 1583, 1584, 1589 (as The commonwealth of England), 1594, 1601, 1609, 1612, 1621, 1633, 1635, 1640, 1691; ed L. Alston and F. W. Maitland, Cambridge 1906; Menston 1970 (facs of 1583); tr Latin, [1610], 1625, 1630, 1641; Dutch, 1673 (in part); German, 1688.
An old mould to cast new lawes. [Oxford] 1643.
A discourse of the commonweal of the realm of England. Ed E. Lamond 1892, 1929; ed M. Dewar, Charlottesville 1969 (Folger Lib). Attributed to Smith.

§ 2
[Strype, John]. The life of the learned Sir Thomas Smith. 1698, 1820 (rev).
Nichols, J. G. Some additions to the biography of Smith. Archaeologia 38 1860.
Hughes, E. The authorship of the Discourse of the commonweal. Bull John Rylands Lib 21 1937.
Quinn, D. B. Smith and the beginnings of English colonial theory. Proc Amer Philosophical Soc 89 1945.
Dewar, M. Smith: a Tudor intellectual in office. 1964.

NICHOLAS SANDERS
1530?–81

De origine ac progressu schismatis anglicani, editus et auctus per Edouardum Rishtonum. Cologne 1585, Rome 1586, Ingoldstadt 1588, Cologne 1610, 1628; tr French, 1587, 1676, 1678, 1715; German, 1594; ed and tr D. Lewis 1877.

DAVID POWELL
1552?–98

§ 1
The historie of Cambria. 1584. *See under Humphrey Llwyd, above.*
Pontici Virunnii britannicae libri sex. 1585. With Itinerarium and Descriptio Cambriae of Giraldus Cambrensis and De britannica historia recte intelligendi epistola.

§ 2
Lloyd, J. E. Powel's Historie 1584. Archaeologia Cambrensis 97 1943.
—— and V. Scholderer. Powel's Historie 1584. Nat Lib of Wales Jnl 1944.

RICHARD CAREW of Anthony
1555–1620

Godfrey of Bulloigne or the recouverie of Hierusalem, translated into English by R.C. esquire: and now the first part containing five cantos imprinted in both languages. 1594; ed A. B. Grosart, Manchester 1881.
Examen de ingenios: the examination of mens wits by John Huarte, translated out of the Spanish tongue by M. Camillo Camilli, englished by R.C. esquire. 1594 (variant issues), 1596, 1604, 1616; ed C. Rogers, Gainesville 1959.
A herrings tayle: contayning a poeticall fiction of divers matters worthy the reading. 1598. Anon, attributed to Carew chiefly on the evidence of West Country words, many of which appear elsewhere only in the Survey.
The survey of Cornwall. 1602; ed H.C. (P. des Maizeaux) 1723, 1769 (with The excellencie of the English tongue); ed T. Tonkin and Francis Bacon de Dunstanville 1811; ed F. E. Halliday 1953 (with sketch of life).
The excellencie of the English tongue by R.C. of Anthony esquire, to W.C. In 2nd and later edns of William Camden, Remaines, 1614, 1623 etc, 1870; ed Des Maizeaux 1723 (with Survey), 1869; ed G. G. Smith, Elizabethan critical essays vol 2, Oxford 1904 (from ms).
The trn of Henri Estienne, A world of wonders, 1607, is also attributed to Carew.

SAMPSON ERDESWICKE
d. 1603

A survey of Staffordshire. 1717 (poor text), 1723, 1798–1801 (with S. Shaw, History of Staffordshire); ed T. Harwood, Westminster 1820, 1844.
The true use of armorie, by William Wyrley. 1592, 1853. Attributed to Erdeswick by Dugdale, denied by Wood.

EDMUND SPENSER
1552–99

See col 1029, above.

JOHN NORDEN
1548–1625?

§ 1
Speculum Britanniae: the first parte an historicall, chorographicall discription of Middlesex. 1593, 1637, 1723.
Norden's preparative to his Speculum Britanniae. 1596, 1723 (with Middlesex and Hartfordshire).
Speculi Britanniae pars: the description of Hartfordshire. [1598], 1723 (with above), Ware 1903 (with biography).
Speculi pars altera: or a delineation of Northamptonshire. 1720.
Speculi Britanniae pars: an historical and chorographical description of Essex. 1594; ed H. Ellis 1840 (Camden Soc).
Speculi Britanniae pars: a description of Cornwall. 1728.
The surveyors dialogue. 1607, 1610, 1618, 1738; ed J. W. Papworth, Detached essays 6 1853 (Archaeological Pbns Soc).
A description of the honor of Winsor. Maps and abstracts of portions of ms in R. R. Tighe and J. E. Davis, Annals of Windsor, 2 vols 1858.
England: an intended guyde for English travailers. 1625, 1635, 1636, 1643 (as A direction for the English traviller).
Vicissitudo rerum: an elegiacall poeme. 1600, 1601 (one issue with cancel title-page A store-house of varieties); ed D. C. Collins, New York 1931 (Shakespeare Assoc facs).
The chorography of Norfolk. Ed I. Hood, Norwich 1938. Formerly attributed to T. Beckham.

§ 2
Gerish, W. B. John Norden. 1903.
Pollard, A. W. The unity of Norden. Library 3rd ser 7 1927.

(3) MINOR BIOGRAPHERS AND AUTOBIOGRAPHERS

The life of Fisher, once attributed to R. Hall. Ed F. van Ortroy, Analecta Bollandina 10, 12 1891, 1893; ed R. Bayne 1921 (EETS).

THOMAS STAPLETON
1535-98

§ 1

The history of the Church of Englande, compiled by Venerable Bede, Englishman, translated out of Latin. Antwerp 1565, St Omer 1622, 1626; ed P. Hereford, Oxford 1935.
Tres Thomae. Douay 1588, Cologne 1612. Lives of St Thomas the Apostle, St Thomas of Canterbury and Thomas More. The life of More ptd separately at Frankfort 1689, 1964 (facs), Graz [1689] and as preface to Latin Works 1565; tr P. E. Hallett 1928.
The life and illustrious martyrdom of Sir Thomas More. Tr P. Hallett, ed E. E. Reynolds, New York 1966.

§ 2

Paul, L. Sir Thomas More's schooldays. TLS 25 Dec 1953. Reply to J. O'Leary 4 Dec 1953.

O'Connell, M. R. Stapleton and the Counter Reformation. New Haven 1964.
Crawford, C. W. Stapleton and More's letter to Bugenhagen. Moreana 5 1968, 7 1970.
Richards, M. Thomas Stapleton. Jnl of Ecclesiastical History 18 1967.

DAVID MOYSIE
fl. 1590

Memoirs of the affairs of Scotland 1577-1603. Edinburgh 1755, 1830 (Bannatyne Club).

SIR FRANCIS VERE
1560-1609

The commentaries: being diverse pieces of service wherein he had command. Ed W. Dillingham, Cambridge 1657, 1672; ed E. Arber in English garner vol 7, 1883.

D. 1603-60

(1) CAMDEN, RALEGH, BURTON, WALTON, PRYNNE, HOWELL, WHITELOCKE, SIR THOMAS BROWNE, FULLER, URQUHART

WILLIAM CAMDEN
1551-1623

§ 1

Britannia sive florentissimorum regnorum Angliae, Scotiae, Hiberniae chorographica descriptio. 1586, 1587, Frankfurt 1590, London 1590, 1594, 1600, 1607 (with addns in successive edns), 1616 etc; tr P. Holland 1610, 1637; ed E. Gibson 1695, 2 vols 1722, 1753; ed G. Scott 1772 (with corrections); ed R. Gough 3 vols 1789, 4 vols 1806, 1 vol Menston 1970 (facs of 1695).
Remaines of a greater worke concerning Britaine. 2 pts 1605, 1614, 1623, 1629 (all initialled M.N.); ed J. Philipot 1636, 1637 (variant with altered date) etc, 1870.
Annales rerum anglicarum et hibernicarum regnante Elizabetha. Pt 1 (to 1589), 1615, 1616; pts 1–2 (to 1603), Leyden 1625; pt 2, 1627, Leyden 1639, Amsterdam 1677; ed T. Hearne 3 vols [Oxford] 1717; tr French 1624 (pt 1), 1627 (pts 1–2); tr A. Darcie 1625 (pt 1 from French); T. Browne 1629 (pt 2); R. N[orton] 1630 pts 1–2), 1635. Later English edns 1675, 1688 and in White Kennett, Complete history vol 2, 1706; ed W. T. Macaffrey 1970 (selection).
Regni regis Jacobi I annalium apparatus; Memorabilia de seipso. Both in T. Smith, V. Cl. Gulielmi Camdeni epistolae 1691; tr of the first with omissions in White Kennett, above.
Anglica, normannica, hibernica, cambrica a veteribus scripta. Ed W. Camden, Frankfurt 1602, 1603.
The abridgement of Camden's Britannia, with the maps. 1626.
Discourse concerning the prerogative of the crown, printed from ms by F. S. Fussner. Proc Amer Philological Soc 101 1957.

§ 2

Brooke, R. A. A discoverie of certaine errours in Britannia, [1596].
Wheare, D. Parentatio historica. In Camdeni insignia. Oxford 1624.
Fuller, T. In his Holy state, profane state, Cambridge 1642.
Smith, T. Camdeni epistolae. 1691.
Bolton, E. Hypercritica. 1722.
Gottfried, R. B. The early development of the section on Ireland in Camden's Britannia. ELH 10 1943.
Powicke, M. Camden. E & S 'English Studies' new ser 1 1948.
Van Norden, L. Peiresc and the English scholars. HLQ 12 1949.
— Celtic antiquarianism in the Curious diseases. In Essays dedicated to L. B. Campbell, Berkeley 1950.
Piggott, S. Camden and the Britannia. Proc Br Acad 37 1951.
Kliger, S. In his Goths in England, Cambridge Mass 1952.
Levy, F. J. The making of Camden's Britannia. Bibliothèque d'Humanisme et Renaissance 26 1964.

SIR WALTER RALEGH
1554-1618

Bibliographies

Brushfield, T. N. A bibliography of Raleigh. Plymouth 1886, 1908 (enlarged).
E[ames], W. A bibliography of Raleigh. New York 1886.

Collections

Judicious and select essayes and observations upon the first invention of shipping; the misery of invasive warre; the navy royall and sea-service; with his Apologie for his voyage to Guiana. 1650, 1667.

Maxims of state. 1650, 1651 (both with Instructions to his son; his son's advice to his father), 1656 (with all items of Remains, below, except 10).

Sir Walter Raleigh's sceptick. 1651 (with items 4–5, 7–9 of Remains, below).

Remains of Sir Walter Raleigh. 1657, 1661, 1664, 1669, 1675, 1681, 1702 (with new letters). From 1661 with 10 items: 1, Maxims of state; 2, Advice to his son; his son's advice to his father; 3, The sceptick; 4, Observations concerning the magnificence of cities; 5, The seat of government; 6, Observations touching trade with the Hollander; 7, Letters; 8, Verses; 9, Speech before he was beheaded; 10, The prerogative of parliaments. 1657 omits item 10; some textual repetition in 1661, 1664, 1669; Prerogative of parliaments part of continuous pagination from 1675.

Three discourses: 1, Of a war with Spain; 2, Of the original cause of war; 3, Of ecclesiastical power, published by Philip Ralegh esq his only grandson. 1702. The ch On unnatural war pbd here for the first time.

Works, political, commercial and philosophical; together with his letters and poems. Ed T. Birch 2 vols 1751 (with a life). Omits several minor works and History of the world.

Works. 8 vols Oxford 1829, New York 1965. With lives by W. Oldys and T. Birch.

Selections from the History of the world, letters etc. Ed G. E. Hadow, Oxford 1917.

Selected prose and poetry. Ed A. M. C. Latham 1965.

§ 1

Historical

The history of the world. 1614 (anon), 1617, 1621 (dated 1617; variant with date corrected), 1621, 1628, 1634, 1652, 1652, 1666, 1671, 1676, 1677, 1687, 1736, Edinburgh 1820 (with other pieces). Until 1652 engraved title-pages keep the date 1614.

An abridgement of Sir Walter Raleigh's History of the world; to which is added his Premonition to princes. [Ed L. Echard] 1698 (with variants).

An abridgement [etc], second edition with some genuine remains: 1, Of the first invention of shipping; 2, A relation of the action at Cadiz; 3, A dialogue between a Jesuite and a recusant; 4, An apology for his voyage to Guiana; publish'd by Philip Raleigh. 1700, 1702.

Naval and Military

A report of the fight about the iles of the Açores. 1591 (anon), Leeds 1967 (facs); rptd in Hakluyt, Voyages vol 2, 1599; in Somers tracts vol 1, 1751, 1809; ed E. Arber 1871 (with other tracts); ed E. Goldsmid, Edinburgh 1886 (with other documents).

The discoverie of the large, rich and bewtiful empyre of Guiana. 1596 (3 edns), Cleveland 1966 (facs), Leeds 1967 (facs), New York 1968 (facs); rptd in Hakluyt's Voyages vol 3, 1600; tr Latin, 1599; German, 1599, 1601, 1603, 1612, 1633; Dutch, 1598, 1706; Spanish, 1947; Russian, 1963; ed R. H. Schomburgk 1848 (Hakluyt Soc); ed V. T. Harlow 1928 (with Spanish documents). See col 2152, above.

Orders to the fleet. 1617. Licensed 17 March 1618. No ptd copy extant; see News of Sir Walter Rauleigh, 1618; ptd from ms in Works, 1751, 1829, 1905 (Navy Records Soc).

Sir Walter Rawleigh his apologie for his voyage to Guiana. 1650.

A discourse of the originall and fundamentall cause of natural warre with the mysery of invasive warre. 1650.

A military discourse. 1734.

Arguments to manifest the advantages of a good fleet, added to Sir Clement Edmons's Observations on landing forces for invasion. 1759. An extract from History of the world, above.

Political and Philosophical

The prerogative of parlaments [sic; variant with reset title-page]. Hamburg (for London) 1628, Middelburg (from London) 1628 (3 edns), [London] 1640; rptd in Somers tracts vol 4, 1850, vol 3, 1809; Harleian miscellany vol 5, 1744, 1808.

Sir Walter Raleigh's instructions to his sonne and to posterity. 1632, 1632, 1633, 1633, Edinburgh 1634, London 1636, 1728; ed C. Whibley 1927; Manteo NC 1939; ed L. B. Wright, Ithaca 1962 (with Burghley's Precepts and Osborne's Advice) (Folger Documents).

The prince: or maxims of state. 1642; rptd in Somers tracts vol 3, 1809.

The interest of England with regard to foreign alliances explained in two discourses: 1, Concerning a match between the Lady Elizabeth and the Prince of Piemont; 2, Touching a marriage between Prince Henry of England and a daughter of Savoy. 1750.

A treatise of the soule. In Works, 1829.

Poems

For ascriptions and the first appearance of individual poems see Latham, below.

Poems. Ed S. E. Bridges, Lee Priory 1813, 1814.

Poems by Wotton, Raleigh and others. Ed J. Hannah 1845.

The poems of Raleigh, Wotton and other courtly poets. Ed J. Hannah 1870, 1892, 1910.

Poems. Ed A. M. C. Latham 1929, 1951 (ML).

Silver poets of the sixteenth century. Ed G. Bullett 1947 (EL). Includes all his finished poems and the Ocean.

Seddon, G. A new poem from ms. Illustr London News 28 Feb 1953.

Doubtful Attributions

Tubus historicus: an historical perspective discovering the empires of the world. 1636.

The life and death of Mahomat. 1637.

Observations concerning the Royall Navy. 1650. Attributed to Gorges by H. E. Sandison in her Arthur Gorges, New York 1928.

Observations touching trade with the Hollander. 1653 (with variants). By John Kymer?

The cabinet-council. 1658, 1661, 1692, 1697. By Thomas Bedingfield? See E. A. Strathmann, TLS 1956, below.

An introduction to a breviary of the history of England. 1693. By Samuel Daniel? See R. B. Gottfried, SP 53 1956, below.

A discourse of sea-ports. 1700, 1701 (as An essay on ways to maintain the honour of England).

A military discourse. 1754. See E. A. Strathmann, TLS 1956, below.

A discourse of tenures which were before the Conquest. Ed J. Gutch, Collectanea curiosa vol 1, 1761. See E. A. Strathmann, HLQ 1957, below.

For other doubtful attributions see P. Lefranc, Ralegh: écrivain, below.

Lost Works?

Treatise of the West Indies. See Dedication to Discovery of Guiana, above.

Discourse how war may be made against Spain and the Indies. See Three discourses, above.

Treatise on the art of war by sea. See History of the world, above, bk 5, pt 2.

Of mines and trials of minerals. See Wood, Athenae oxonienses vol 2, 1692.

Of the present state of Spain. See Wood, ibid.

Letters

Edwards, E. The life of Raleigh, together with his letters. 2 vols 1868.

§ 2

Newes of Sr Walter Rauleigh; with the true description of Guiana. 1618, Boston 1940 (facs).

A declaration of the demeanor and cariage of Sir Walter Ralegh which occasioned his Majestie to proceed in doing justice upon him. 1618 (with variants); rptd in Harleian miscellany vol 3, 1745.

Naunton, Sir R. In his Fragmenta regalia, 1641; ed E. Arber 1895.

The arraignement and conviction of Sr Walter Rawleigh on the 17 of November 1603. 1648.

Ross, A. Some animadversions upon Raleigh's History of the world. [1653].

Winstanley, W. In his England's Worthies, 1660.

Fuller, T. In his Worthies, 1662.

Lloyd, D. In his State worthies, 1670.

Shirley, J. The life of the valiant and learned Sir Walter Ralegh. 1677.

Wood, A. In his Athenae oxonienses, 2 vols 1691–2.

Prince, J. In his Worthies of Devon, 1701.

Oldys, W. The life of Ralegh. Prefixed to History of the world, 1736, and Works 1829.

Birch, T. Life. Prefixed to Works, 1751, 1829.

Cayley, A. The life of Ralegh. 2 vols 1805, 1806 (rev).

Aubrey, J. In his Brief lives, 1813; ed O. L. Dick 1949.

Tytler, P. F. Life. Edinburgh 1833.

St John, J. A. Life. 2 vols 1868. Spanish documents.

Hennessy, J. P. Raleigh in Ireland. 1883.

Tarbox, I. N. Raleigh and his colony in America. Boston 1884 (Prince Soc), New York [1967].

Buff, A. Who is author of Some observations touching trade with the Hollander. E Studien 1 1887.

Brushfield, T. N. Raleghana. 8 pts [Plymouth 1896–1907]. Rptd from Trans of Devonshire Assoc 28–39.

Gosse, E. Raleigh. 1886.

— Raleigh's Cynthia. Athenaeum 9 Jan 1886.

Stebbing, W. Ralegh: a biography. Oxford 1891, 1899 (with new bibliography).

Hume, M. A. S. Sir Walter Raleigh. 1897, New York 1926. Spanish documents.

Rodd, R. Sir Walter Raleigh. 1904 (English Men of Action).

Thoreau, H. D. Sir Walter Raleigh, lately discovered among his unpublished journals and edited by H. A. Metcalf. Boston 1905 (Bibliophile Soc).

Firth, C. H. Raleigh's History of the world. Proc Br Acad 8 1918; rptd in Essays literary and historical, Oxford 1938.

Kempner, N. Raleghs staatstheoretische Schriften: die Einführung des Machiavellismus in England. Leipzig 1928.

Waldman, M. Sir Walter Raleigh. 1928.

Harlow, V. T. Raleigh's last voyage. 1932.

Ustick, W. L. Advice to a son: a type of xviith-century conduct book. SP 29 1932.

Sorenson, F. Ralegh's library. N & Q 10 Feb 1934. Replies by W. Jaggard 24 Feb, M. 31 March 1934.

— Ralegh's marriage. SP 33 1936.

Beau, J. La religion de Ralegh. Revue Anglo-américaine 11 1934.

Anthony, I. Ralegh and his world. New York 1934.

Sandison, H. E. Ralegh's orders once more. Mariner's Mirror 20 1934.

Thompson, E. J. Ralegh: the last of the Elizabethans. 1935.

Ralegh's prose. TLS 31 Jan 1935.

Bradbrook, M. C. The school of night: a study in the literary relationships of Ralegh. Cambridge 1936.

Heltzel, V. B. Ralegh's 'Even such is time'. Huntington Lib Bull no 10 1936.

Konetzke, R. Ralegh und die geistesgeschichtlichen Grundlagen des englischen Imperialismus. Neuphilologische Monatsschrift 7 1936.

Whiting, G. W. Sicily in Ortelius and in Ralegh. TLS 11 July 1936.

Williamson, J. B. Ralegh and his trial. 1936.

McNeir, W. F. Raymundus and Ralegh. TLS 4 Dec 1937.

Latham, A. M. C. Ralegh's letters. TLS 4 Feb 1938.

— Ralegh's farewell letter to his wife in 1603: a question of authenticity. E & S 25 1939.

— Ralegh's gold mine: new light on the last Guiana voyage. E & S new ser 4 1951.

— A birth-date for Ralegh [1554]. Etudes Anglaises 9 1956.

— Ralegh's Instructions to his sonne. In Elizabethan and Jacobean studies presented to F. P. Wilson, Oxford 1959.

— Ralegh. 1964 (Br Council pamphlet).

— Ralegh's will. RES new ser 22 1971. Recently discovered will of 1597.

French, J. M. Raleigh, Frobisher and the Great Carack of Spain. N & Q 7 May 1938.

Brooke, C. F. T. Ralegh as poet and philosopher. ELH 5 1938; rptd in his Essays in Shakespeare and other Elizabethans, New Haven 1948.

Buchan, A. M. Ralegh's Cynthia: facts or legend. MLQ 1 1940.

Strathmann, E. A. The history of the world and Ralegh's skepticism. HLQ 3 1940.

— Ralegh on natural philosophy. MLQ 1 1940.

— An epitaph attributed to Ralegh. MLN 40 1945.

— Ralegh and the Catholic polemists. HLQ 8 1945.

— John Dee as Ralegh's 'conjuror'. HLQ 10 1947.

— Ralegh: a study in Elizabethan skepticism. New York 1951.

— A note on the Ralegh canon. TLS 13 April 1956. Against Ralegh's authorship of Cabinet-council, ed John Milton 1658.

— Ralegh's Discourse of tenures and Sir Roger Owen. HLQ 20 1957. Not by Ralegh.

Bennett, J. W. Early texts of two of Ralegh's poems from a Huntington Library ms. HLQ 4 1941.

Clark, E. G. Ralegh and Marlowe: a study in Elizabethan fustian. New York 1941.

Stapleton, L. Halifax and Raleigh. JHI 2 1941.

Quinn, D. B. Ralegh and the British Empire. 1947.

Starkey, L. G. and P. Ropp. The printing of A declaration of the demeanor and cariage of Sir Walter Ralegh 1618. Library 5th ser 3 1948.

Luciani, V. Ralegh's Discourse of tenures. Tulane Law Rev 22 1947.

— Ralegh's Discourses of war and Machiavelli's Discorsi. MP 46 1949.

— Ralegh's Cabinet-council and Guicciardini's Aphorisms. SP 46 1949.

— Ralegh's Discourse on the Savoyan matches and Machiavelli's Istorie fiorentine. Italica 29 1952.

Stibbs, J. R. Ralegh and Holinshed. MLR 44 1949.

Shirley, J. W. Ralegh's Guiana finances. HLQ 13 1950.

Bowers, R. H. Ralegh's last speech: the 'elms' document. RES new ser 2 1951.

Jacquot, J. L'élément platonique dans l'Histoire du monde. In Mélanges offerts à H. Chamard, Paris 1951.

Ralegh's 'Hellish verses' and the Tragicall reigne of Selimus. MLR 48 1953.

Thorpe, W. A. 'Even such is time'. TLS 12 Oct 1951. Reply by H. G. Carter 2 Nov 1951.

Williamson, H. R. Sir Walter Raleigh. 1951.

Edwards, P. Sir Walter Ralegh. 1953.

Quinn, D. B. The Roanoke voyages 1584–90. 2 vols 1955 (Hakluyt Soc).

Lefranc, P. Un inédit de Ralegh sur la conduite de la guerre 1596–7. Etudes Anglaises 8 1955.

— A miscellany of Ralegh material. N & Q Jan 1957.

— Un inédit de Ralegh sur la succession. Etudes Anglaises 13 1960.

— Ralegh in 1596 and 1603: three unprinted letters in the Huntington Library. HLQ 29 1966.

— Ralegh, écrivain: l'oeuvre et les idées. Paris 1968.

Gottfried, R. B. The authorship of A breviary of the history of England. SP 53 1956.

Popkin, R. H. A manuscript of Ralegh's Scepticke. PQ 36 1957.

Wallace, W. M. Sir Walter Raleigh. Princeton 1959.

Oakeshott, W. The Queen and the poet. 1960.

— Ralegh's library. Library 5th ser 23 1968. Description and list.

Davie, D. A reading of the Ocean's love to Cynthia. In Elizabethan poetry, ed J. R. Brown and B. Harris 1960.

Ure, P. The poetry of Ralegh. REL 1 1960.

Gullans, C. B. Raleigh and Ayton: the disputed authorship of Wrong not sweete empresse of my heart. SB 13 1961.

Rowse, A. L. Ralegh and the Throckmortons. 1962, New York 1962 (as Ralegh: his family and private life).

Williams, N. L. Sir Walter Raleigh. 1962.

Sprott, S. E. Ralegh's Sceptic and the Elizabethan translation of Sextus Empiricus. PQ 42 1963.

Racin, J., jr. The early editions of the History of the world. SB 17 1964.

Hill, C. In his Intellectual origins of the English Revolution, Oxford 1965.

Adamson, J. H. and H. F. Folland. The shepherd of the ocean. 1969.

Bishop, C. J. Raleigh satirized by Harington and Davies. RES new ser 22 1971.

ROBERT BURTON
1577–1640

Bibliographies

Jordan-Smith, P. Bibliographia Burtoniana: a study of Burton's Anatomy of melancholy with a bibliography of Burton's writings. Stanford 1931.

— and M. Mulhauser. Burton's Anatomy of melancholy and Burtoniana: a checklist. Claremont Cal 1959.

Donovan, D. G. Sir Thomas Browne 1924–66; Robert Burton 1924–66. 1968.

§1

The anatomy of melancholy, what it is; with all the kindes, causes, symptomes, prognostickes and several cures of it: in three maine partitions with their several sections, members and subsections, philosophically, medicinally, historically opened and cut up, by Democritus Junior. Oxford 1621, 1624, 1628 (with engraved title-page, Latin elegiacs, Democritus Junior ad librum suum and the Author's abstract of melancholy), 1632 (with argument of frontispiece), Oxford, Edinburgh and London 1638, Oxford and London 1651 or 1652 (all edns after 1621 with substantial alterations and addns), London 1660, 1676; [ed Stephen Jones] 2 vols 1800 etc; 2 vols Philadelphia 1836; 1845 (with trns of many Latin quotations); 3 vols Cambridge Mass 1861; ed A. R. Shilleto, introd by A. H. Bullen 3 vols 1893, 1896, 1904, 1923 etc; 2 vols 1925 (Nonesuch Press, illustr E. M. Kauffer, without marginal notes); ed Floyd Dell and P. Jordan-Smith 2 vols New York 1927, 1 vol 1930 (without marginal notes, with trns of all Latin); ed H. Jackson 3 vols 1932 (EL).

Melancholy, drawn chiefly from Burton's Anatomy. 1801, 1824, 1827, 1865, 1881.

Burton the anatomist: being extracts from the Anatomy of melancholy. Ed G. C. F. Mead and R. C. Clift with preface by W. H. D. Rouse 1925.

The anatomy of melancholy. Ed L. Babb, East Lansing 1965. Selection.

Philosophaster, comoedia; poemata adhuc sparsim edita, nunc in unum collecta. Ed W. E. Buckley, Hertford 1862 (Roxburghe Club). The poems had already appeared in Academiae oxoniensis pietas, Oxford 1603; Musa hospitalis ecclesiae Christi, Oxford 1605; Justa oxoniensum [in memory of Prince Henry], 1612; Death repealed: verses on Lord Bayning, Oxford 1638; and similar collections. Buckley omits the elegiacs to Frances Holyoake pbd in Rider's Dictionarie, 1613.

Philosophaster; with an English translation [and] Burton's minor writings in prose and verse. Ed P. Jordan-Smith, Stanford 1931.

Early Imitations

Ferrand, J. Ἐρωτομανία: or a treatise discoursing of the essence causes and cure of love. Oxford 1640.

Greenwood, William. Ἀπογραφή στοργῆς: or a description of the passion of love. 1657.

§2

Burton, W. A description of Leicester Shire. [1622], Lynn 1777; and in Nichols, The history and antiquities of the county of Leicester, below.

Lluelyn, Martin. Elegie: on the death of Master R.B. In Men-miracles with other poems, Oxford 1646.

Fuller, T. In his Worthies, 1662.

Hearne, T. Remarks and collections. 1885– (Oxford Historical Soc). 21 May 1711, 2 Aug 1713, 23–8 Jan 1734.

Ferriar, John. In his Illustrations of Sterne, 1798, 2 vols 1812.

Nichols, J. The history and antiquities of the county of Leicester. 8 vols 1795–1815. Vols 3–4.

[W. L. Collins]. Burton's Anatomy of melancholy. Blackwood's Mag Sept 1861.

Macray, W. D. In his Annals of the Bodleian Library, 1890. On Burton's library.

Brown, T. E. Robert Burton. New Rev 13 1895.

Bensly, E. Burton's Anatomy of melancholy. N & Q 8, 21 March, 4, 25 April, 6 June, 4, 25 July, 20 Aug, 17 Oct, 7 Nov, 5 Dec 1903; 16 Jan, 21 Feb, 21 March, 9 April, 13 Aug, 17 Sept, 3 Dec 1904; 18 March, 8 July, 30 Dec 1905; 24 Feb, 25 Aug 1906; 9 Feb, 9 March 1907; 14 Nov 1908. Identification of passages from earlier authors.

— Burton and Fletcher. N & Q 15 Dec 1906.

— A hitherto unknown source of Montaigne and Burton. Athenaeum 5 Sept 1908. See also 6–13 June.

— Burton and Jaques Ferrand. N & Q 10 April 1909.

— Theodorus Prodromus, Barclay and Burton. N & Q 6 Feb 1909.

— The title of Burton's Anatomy of melancholy. MLR 4 1909.

— Grunnius in Burton's Anatomy. N & Q 5 Aug 1933.

— Burton in the eighteenth century. N & Q 1 Feb 1936.

Dieckow, F. John Florios englische Übersetzung der Essais Montaignes und Lord Bacons; Ben Jonsons und Burtons Verhältnis zu Montaigne. Strasbourg 1903.

Lake, B. A general introduction to Charles Lamb, together with a special study of his relation to Burton. Leipzig 1903.

Whibley, C. In his Literary portraits, 1904.

Aitken, P. H. The cypher of Burton's signature solved. Athenaeum 24 Aug 1912.

Osler, W. Burton's Anatomy of melancholy. Yale Rev new ser 3 1914.

— Burton: the man, his book, his library. Proc Oxford Bibl Soc 1 1926.

Lowes, J. L. The loveres maladye of hereos. MP 11 1914.

Murry, J. M. In his Countries of the mind: 1st ser, 1922.

Duff, E. G. The fifth edition of Burton's Anatomy of melancholy. Library 4th ser 4 1924.

Madan, F. et al. Oxford Bibl Soc 1 1922–6. Contributions on Burton by F. Madan, W. Osler, E. G. Duff, E. Bensly, S. Gibson, F. D. R. Nedham; with list of Burton's books in Bodley and Christ Church.

Hughes, M. Y. Burton on Spenser. PMLA 61 1926.

Cajori, F. Burton's horoscope and the date of his birth. Popular Astronomy 36 1928.

Jackson, H. Burton his book. Book Collector's Quart 1 1931.

Williamson, G. Mutability, decay and seventeenth-century melancholy. ELH 2 1935.

Sensabough, G. F. Burton's influence on Ford's The lovers melancholy. SP 33 1936.

Miller, J. L. A discussion of Burton's Anatomy. Annals of Medical History new ser 8 1936.

Gottlieb, H. J. Burton's knowledge of English poetry. New York 1937.

Taeusch, H. W. Democritus Junior anatomizes melancholy. Cleveland 1937.

Ewing, S. B. Burton, Ford and Andromana. PMLA 54 1939.

— Burtonian melancholy in the plays of Ford. Princeton 1940.

Cawley, R. R. Burton, Bacon and Sandys. MLN 56 1941.

Evans, B., with G. J. Mohr. The psychiatry of Burton. New York 1944.

Patrick, J. M. Burton's utopianism. PQ 27 1948.

Mueller, W. R. Burton's economic and political views. HLQ 11 1948.

— Burton's frontispiece. PMLA 64 1949.

— The anatomy of Burton's England. Berkeley 1952.

— Burton's 'satyricall preface'. MLQ 15 1954.

Prawer, S. Burton's Anatomy of melancholy. Cambridge Jnl Aug 1948.

Babb, L. In his Elizabethan malady: a study of melancholy in English literature from 1580 to 1642, East Lansing 1951.

— Sanity in Bedlam: a study of Burton's Anatomy of melancholy. East Lansing 1959.

Browne, R. M. Burton and the new cosmology. MLQ 13 1952.

Bamborough, J. B. In his Little world of man, 1952.

Roberts, K. S. and N. P. Sacks. Dom Duarte and Burton: 'two men of melancholy'. Jnl History of Medicine 9 1954.

Lievsay, J. L. Burton's De consolatione. South Atlantic Quart 60 1956.

Wilson, F. P. In his Seventeenth-century prose, Cambridge 1960.

Skeat, T. C. A letter by Burton. BM Quart 22 1960. Almost the only extant example of his handwriting.

Simon, J. R. L'anatomie de la mélancolie. Études Anglaises 15 1962. On text in modern edns.

— Burton et l'Anatomie de la mélancolie. Paris 1964.

Mesnard, P. L'Utopie de Burton. In Les utopies à la Renaissance: colloque internationale (Avril 1961), Brussels 1963.

Hodgen, M. M. In her Early anthropology in the sixteenth and seventeenth centuries, Philadelphia 1964.

Höltgen, K. J. Die astrologischen Zeichen in Burtons Anatomy of melancholy. Anglia 82 1965.

— Synoptische Tabellen in der medizinischen Literatur und die Logik Agricolas und Ramus. Sudhoffs Archiv für Geschichte der Medizin und der Naturwissen-schaften 49 1965.

Colie, R. In her Paradoxia epidemica: the Renaissance structure of paradox, Princeton 1966.

— Some notes on Burton's Erasmus. Renaissance Quart 20 1967.

Donovan, D. G. A note on the text of the Anatomy of melancholy. PBSA 60 1966.

— Two corrected-forme readings in the 1632 The anatomy of melancholy. Book Collector 15 1966.

King, J. R. The genesis of Burton's Anatomy of melancholy. In his Studies in six seventeenth-century writers, Athens Ohio 1966.

Webber, J. In her Eloquent I: style and self in seventeenth-century prose, Madison 1968.

Heventhal, C., jr. Burton's Anatomy of melancholy in America. PBSA 63 1969.

IZAAK WALTON
1593–1683

Bibliographies etc

Westwood, T. The chronicle of the Compleat angler. 1864; rptd with addns in Marston's edn of the Compleat angler, 1888.

Wood, A. A. A bibliography of the Complete angler. New York 1900.

Butt, J. E. A bibliography of Walton's Lives. Proc Oxford Bibl Soc 2 1930. See also bibliographical notes in Compleat Walton, ed G. L. Keynes 1929 (Nonesuch Press).

Oliver, P. A new chronicle of the Compleat angler. New York 1936. Lists edns to date.

Collections

The complete angler and lives. Ed A. W. Pollard 1901.

Waltoniana. Ed R. H. Shepherd 1878. Most of Walton's remains in prose and verse.

The compleat Walton. Ed G. L. Keynes 1929 (Nonesuch Press).

§I

The life and death of Dr Donne. 1640 (in LXXX sermons by John Donne), 1658 (much enlarged as The life of John Donne); [ed T. E. Tomlins] 1852, 1865. See Lives, below.

The life of Sir Henry Wotton. 1651 (in Reliquiae Wotton-ianae), 1654 (ibid with addns and alterations), 1672 (ibid, with further addns and alterations), 1685. See Lives, below.

The compleat angler: or the contemplative man's recreation. 1653 (rptd 1810, 1876 etc), 1655 (much enlarged), 1661 (with alterations), 1664, 1668, 1676 (as The universal angler, made so by three books of fishing; alterations in Walton's part, 2nd bk by Charles Cotton, 3rd by R. Venables); ed Moses Browne 1750; ed John Hawkins 1760; ed John Major 1823; ed H. Nicolas 2 vols 1836; [ed G. W. Bethune], New York 1847; ed R. B. Marston 2 vols 1889; ed A. Lang 1896 (Walton only), 1906 (EL); tr German, 1859; Danish, 1943; Swedish, [1945]; French, 1963 (in part), 1964. Most edns after 1676 have included Cotton but not Venables, but the 1676 text of Walton alone has often been rptd. Over 300 edns, including many reprints of important or popular edns, have been pbd.

The life of Mr Rich. Hooker. 1665, 1666 (with addns and alterations, in Works of Mr Richard Hooker), 1676, 1682, 1705, 1723; ed J. Keble, Oxford 1836 (in Works of Hooker vol 1). See Lives, below.

The life of Mr George Herbert. 1670, 1674 (with alterations, in Temple, with which it has often been rptd; ed V. de Sola Pinto 1951 (in his English biography in the seventeenth century). See Lives, below.

The life of Dr Sanderson (with some short tracts or cases of conscience by Sanderson, and a sermon of Hooker). 1678, 1681 (with addns and alterations in XXXV sermons by Sanderson), 1686, 1689; ed W. Jacobson, Oxford 1854 (in Works of Sanderson vol 6).

The lives of Dr John Donne, Sir Henry Wotton, Mr Richard Hooker, Mr George Herbert. 1670, Menston 1969 (facs) (with addns and alterations in first 3 lives, 2nd pbn of life of Herbert), 1675 (with addns or alterations in lives of Donne, Herbert, Hooker); ed T. Zouch, York 1796 etc (with life of Sanderson); ed A. H. Bullen 1884 (Bohn's Lib); ed H. Morley 1888 (without Sanderson); ed A. Dobson 2 vols 1898 (Temple Classics); ed G. Saintsbury, Oxford 1927 (WC) etc.

Love and truth. 1680. Anon. Attributed to Walton by Archbishop Sancroft, supported by modern critics.

§2

Franck, R. Northern memoirs. 1694; ed Sir Walter Scott, Edinburgh 1821. Apparently written 1658.

Marston, R. B. Walton and some earlier writers on fish and fishing. 1894. *See also* introd to his edn of Compleat angler 1888.

Beeching, H. C. In his Religio laici, 1902.

'Martin, Stapleton' (J. S. Walton). Walton and his friends. 1903, 1904 (rev).

Stauffer, D. A. In his English biography before 1700, Cambridge Mass 1930.

Butt, J. E. Walton's copy of Pembroke and Ruddier's poems. Bodleian Quart Record 7 1933.

— Walton's methods in biography. E & S 19 1934.

— Walton's collections for Fulman's life of John Hales. MLR 29 1934.

— Biography in the hands of Walton, Johnson and Boswell. Los Angeles 1966.

Frechtman, B. Walton: fragments of letters. N & Q 30 Nov 1935.

Schneider, R. Idyll und Tragödie (die Angler). Deutsche Rundschau 47 1936.

— Das stille England: Walton. Die Literatur 39 1936.

Swaen, A. E. H. Walton's 'bockerel', 'bockeret'. MLR 31 1936.

Bennett, R. E. Walton's use of Donne's letters. PQ 16 1937.

McElderry, B. R. Walton's Lives and Gillman's Life of Coleridge. PMLA 52 1937.

Coon, A. M. The family of Walton. TLS 15 May 1937.

— Walton's mother. TLS 25 Dec 1937.

— Walton's occupation and residence. N & Q 18 Feb 1939.

— Walton's second marriage. N & Q 29 April 1939.

— Walton's 'prochein amy'. MLN 54 1939.

— Walton's 'honest Nat and R. Roe'. N & Q 20 April, 28 Sept 1940. Replies by W. J. Carlton 25 May, 28 Dec 1940.

— Walton and Edmund Carew. N & Q 27 April 1940.

— Walton as stationer? MLN 56 1941.

Sisson, C. J. In his Judicious marriage of Mr Hooker and the birth of the Laws of ecclesiastical polity, Cambridge 1940. Against Walton's interpretation.

Brooke, T. The Lambert Walton-Cotton collection. Yale Univ Lib Gazette 17 1943.

Percy, M. C. Hooker and Walton. Hibbert Jnl 41 1943.

Haight, G. S. The author of the Address in Quarles' Shepheards oracles. MLN 49 1944.

Oliver, H. J. Walton's prose style. RES 21 1945.

— The composition and revisions of the Compleat angler. MLR 42 1947.

— Walton as the author of Love and truth and Thealma and Clearchus. RES 25 1949.

Pamp, F. E. Walton's redaction of Hooker. Church History 17 1948.

Novarr, D. Walton, Bishop Morley and Love and truth. RES new ser 2 1951.

— The making of Walton's Lives. Ithaca 1958.

Wing, D. W. Walton. TLS 13 July 1951.

Greenslade, B. D. The compleat angler and the sequestered clergy. RES new ser 5 1954.

Bottrall, M. Izaak Walton. 1955.

Goldman, M. S. Walton and the Arte of angling 1577. In Studies in honor of T. W. Baldwin, Urbana 1958.

French, J. M. Introd to Three books on fishing 1599-1659 associated with the Compleat angler, Gainesville 1962.

Cooper, J. R. The art of the Compleat angler. Durham NC 1968.

WILLIAM PRYNNE
1600–69

Bibliographies etc

Sparke, M. A catalogue of printed books written by Prynne. 1643. 31 items.

— An exact catalogue. 1660. 160 items.

Wood, A. In his Athenae oxonienses, 2 vols 1691-2.

Gardiner, S. R. Documents relating to the proceedings against Prynne (with an unfinished biographical preface and a list of Prynne's works by J. Bruce). 1877 (Camden Soc).

Green, E. Bibliotheca Somersetiensis. Taunton 1902.

Kirby, E. W. In his Prynne: a study in Puritanism, Cambridge Mass 1931.

Fry, M. A. and G. Davies. Prynne in the Huntington Library. HLQ 20 1957. Over 200 entries, with annotation on issues, reissues under different titles etc.

Collections

The works of William Prynne of Swainswick esquire since his last imprisonment. 1655. 6 works.

§1

A selection; for full list see Fry and Davies, above.

The Church of Englands old antithesis to new Arminianisme. 1629, 1630 (with large addns as Anti-Arminianisme).

Histrio-mastix: the players scourge or actors tragædie. 1633; tr Dutch, 1639.

Newes from Ipswich: discovering certaine late detestable practises of some domineering lordly prelates. Ipswich (for London, Edinburgh) 1636 (4 edns), London 1641; tr Dutch, 1637. By 'Matthew White'.

The unbishoping of Timothy and Titus. [Amsterdam] 1636, London 1660, 1661, 1661. Initialled A.B.C.

A breviate of the prelates intollerable usurpations. 2 pts [Amsterdam] 1637 (called 3rd edn much enlarged). Sparke, above, refers to 2 edns of 1635. By 'W. Huntley'.

A catalogue of such testimonies as evidence bishops and presbyters to be both one. 1637, 1641, 1645, 1647. Anon.

The antipathie of the lordly English prelacie both to regall monarchy and civill unity. 2 pts 1641.

An humble remonstrance against the tax of ship-money. 1641 (anon), 1643.

A soveraigne antidote to prevent, appease and determine our unnaturall and destructive civil wars. 1642 (3 edns). Anon.

The soveraigne power of parliaments and kingdomes. 4 pts 1643. Anon. 2 edns of pt 1, enlarged from The treachery and disloyalty of papists to their soveraignes, 1642.

The popish royall favourite: or a full discovery of his Majesties extraordinary favour to notorious Papists. 1643 (with variants).

The opening of the great seale of England. 1643; rptd in Somers tracts vol 4, ed Sir Walter Scott 1810.

A breviate of the life of William Laud. 1644.

Hidden workes of darkenes brought to publike light: or a necessary introduction to the history of the Archbishop of Canterburies triall. 1645.

Canterburies doome: or the first part of a compleat history of the tryall, condemnation, execution of William Laud. 1646.

The levellers levelled to the very ground. 1647.

Irenarches redivivus: or a brief collection of sundry statutes concerning the dis-commissioning of Justices of Peace. 1648.

A breife memento to the present unparliamentary junto touching their present intentions to depose and execute Charles Steward. 1648 (3 edns), 1649; tr Latin and Dutch.

Mr Pryn's last and finall declaration to the Commons it is high treason, to compasse or imagine the deposition or death of our soveraign lord King Charles. 1648.

A plea for the Lords: or a vindication of the judiciary and legislative powere of the Lords. 1648, 1649, 1658 (much enlarged), 1659, 1675.

The first part of a historical collection of the ancient parliaments of England from 673 till 1216. 1649.

A legall vindication of the liberties of England, against illegall taxes. 1649, 1649, 1660.

A seasonable, legal and historicall vindication of the good, old, fundamental liberties of all English freemen. 3 pts 1654-7, 1679; pts 1-2, 1655; pt 3 (as Historiarchos), 1659.

A new discovery of free-state tyranny: containing four letters to Mr John Bradshaw and his associates at White-Hall. 1655.

The Quakers unmasked and clearly detected to be but the spawn of Romish frogs. 1655, 1655 (enlarged), 1664.

A short demurrer to the Jewes long discontinued remitter into England. 2 pts 1656, 1656 (pt 1 enlarged).

A new discovery of some Romish emissaries, Quakers. 1656, 1658 (with new title-page).

A summary collection of the principal fundamental rights liberties and proprieties of all English freemen. 1656, 1656, 1658 (enlarged as Demophilos: or the assertor of the peoples liberty).

An exact abridgement of the records in the Tower of London, collected by Sir Robert Cotton, revised by William Prynne. 1657, 1679, 1689.

The first [second, fourth] part of a brief register, kalendar and survey of parliamentary writs. 4 pts 1659-64 (pt 3 as Brevia parliamentaria rediviva).

Mr Pryns letter and proposal to our gracious lord and soveraign King. 1660.

The signal loyalty and devotion of Gods true saints towards their Kings. 2 pts 1660; ed C. Wordsworth 1892 (in part) (Bradshaw Soc).

An exact chronological vindication of our [British, Roman etc] Kings supreme ecclesiastical jurisdiction. 3 vols 1665-8; vol 3 rptd 1670 as The history of King John, King Henry III and King Edward I; rptd as Antiquae constitutiones regni Angliae, 1672 (index 1675). Unique copy of 4th vol, without title-page but captioned An exact chronological history of the Popes intollerable usurpations, is in Library of Lincoln's Inn, London. Usually called Prynne's Records.

Aurum reginae: or a compendious tractate of records in the Tower concerning Queen-gold. 1668. Usually bound with an additional appendix, also 1668.

Brief animadversions on the fourth part of the Institutes of the lawes of England, compiled by Sir Edward Cooke. 1669.

§2

For many contemporary pamphlet attacks on Prynne see Bibliographies, above.

Kirby, E. W. Prynne: a study in Puritanism. Cambridge Mass 1931.

Hill, C. and E. Dell (ed). In their Good old cause, 1949.

Hurst, G. B. In his Lincoln's Inn essays, 1949.

Lamont, W. M. Prynne: 'the mountainous ice' of Puritanism. History Today March 1961.

— Marginal Prynne. 1963.

— Prynne, Burton and the Puritan triumph. HLQ 27 1964.

JAMES HOWELL
1594?-1666

Bibliographies etc

Parthenopoeia. 1654. With catalogue of his works.

Londinopolis. 1657. With catalogue of his works.

Wood, A. In his Athenae oxonienses, 2 vols 1691-2.

Vann, W. H. Notes on the writings of Howell. Waco 1924. An annotated bibliography.

§1

Δενδρολογία: Dodona's grove, or the vocall forrest. 1640, 1644 (with Parables reflecting upon the times, and England's teares for the present warres), Cambridge 1645, [1649] (with England's teares and The pre-eminence of Parlement); pt 2, 1650; pt 1 tr Latin, 1646, French, 1641, 1648.
A ms of Δενδρολογία (to this present epoch 1638) is in the Harvard Univ Library; it is dedicated to Wentworth.

The vote: or a poeme royall, presented to his Majestie for a New-Yeares gift. 1642, 1647 (in Epistolae vol 2), 1654 (in Some minor works).

Instructions for forreine travell. 1642, 1650 (enlarged); ed E. Arber, English reprints, 1869.

The true informer who discovereth the chief causes of the said distempers in Great Brittany. Oxford 1643, [London] 1643 (both anon), 1661 (in Divers historicall discourses).

A discourse: or parly, continued betwixt Patricius and Peregrine touching the civill wars of England and Ireland. 1643 (by J.H.), 1664 (in Divers discourses).

Parables reflecting upon the times. 'Paris' (for London) 1643 (anon), 1644 (with Dodona's grove), 1661 (in Divers discourses as apologs or fables mythologiz'd).

Mercurius hibernicus: or a discourse of the late insurrection in Ireland. Bristol 1644 (2 anon edns), 1661 (in Divers discourses as Of the land of Ire).

The preheminence and pedigree of Parlement. 1644 (by J.H.), 1644 (with England's teares), 1645 and 1649 (with Dodona's grove), 1661 (in Divers discourses as A vindication of his Majesty), 1677; rptd in Harleian miscellany vols 1, 6, ed T. Park 1808-10; rptd in Somers tracts vol 5, 1809; ed F. Masères, Occasional essays on various subjects, 1809.

England's teares for the present wars. 1644, 1644 (with The preheminence of Parliament), 1644, 1645 and 1649 (with Dodona's grove); rptd in Harleian miscellany vol 8, 1811; rptd in Somers tracts vol 5, 1811; tr Latin, 1646; Dutch, 1649.

Epistolae Ho-Elianae: familiar letters domestic and forren, by J.H. Vol 1, 1645; vol 2, 1647; vols 1-3, 1650; 1655 (collected with vol 4), 1673 etc (many edns to 1754); ed W. H. Bennett 1890; ed J. Jacobs 2 vols 1890-2 (standard edn); ed O. J. Smeaton 3 vols 1902 (Temple Classics); ed A. Repplier, Boston 1907.

Lustra Ludovici: or the life of Lewis XIII. 1646.

A letter to the Earle of Pembrooke concerning the times. 1647 (anon), 1654 (in Some minor works), 1661 (in Divers discourses).

Down-right dealing: or the despised Protestant speaking plain English. 1647. Initialled J.H.; attributed to Howell.

Bella scot-anglica: a brief of all the battles 'twixt England and Scotland. 1648 (anon), 1654 (in Some minor works).

The instruments of a King: or a short discourse of the sword, the sceptre, the crowne. 1648, 1654 (in Some minor works), 1661 (in Divers discourses as The sway of the sword).

A Venice looking-glass: or a letter written from London to Rome, touching these present distempers. 1648 (by J.B.C.), 1654 (in Some minor works), 1661 (in Divers discourses as An Italian prospective).

A winter dreame. [London] 1649 (anon), 1654 (in Some minor works), 1661 (in Divers discourses as A nocturnal progress); rptd in Harleian Miscellany vol 7, 1811.

A trance: or newes from Hell. 1649, 1654 (in Some minor works as Mercurius Acheronticus).

An inquisition after blood; to the Parliament and to the army. 1649 (anon), 1654 (in Some minor works), 1661 (with minor changes in Divers discourses as A glance upon the ile of Wight).

S.P.Q.V. A survey of the Signorie of Venice. 1651.

The vision: or a dialog between the soul and the bodie. 1651 (for 1652).

A German diet: or the ballance of Europe. 1653.

Ah, ha; tumulus, thalamus: two counter-poems. 1653 (by J.H.), 1654 (in Some minor works).

Some of Mr Howell's minor works. 1654. 9 titles separately paginated, some with new prelims.

An admonition to my Lord Protector and his council of their present danger. 1654 (by J.H.). Attributed to Howell, but doubtful.

Some sober inspections made into the cariage and consults of the late-long-parlement. 1655, 1656, 1658, 1660 (as Philanglus: some sober inspections). All edns by J.H.

Londinopolis; an historicall discourse or perlustration of the City of London and Westminster. 1657. With catalogue of Howell's writings.

A discours of the empire and of the election of a King of the Romans. 1658, 1659.

Παροιμιογραφία: proverbs or old sayed sawes and adages in English, Italian, French and Spanish, whereunto the British are added. 1659, 1659 (in A particular vocabulary), 1660 (in Lexicon tetraglotton).

A particular vocabulary of nomenclature in English, Italian, French and Spanish of the proper terms belonging to several arts and sciences, to recreations, to common professions and callings. 1659, 1660 (in Lexicon tetraglotton).

Lexicon tetraglotton: an English-French-Italian-Spanish dictionary. 1660, 1660.

England's joy, expressed to the Lord General Monck. 1660. Initialled J.H. Attributed to Howell by C. Hazlitt; doubtful.

Θηρολογία: the parley of beasts. 1660.

A late letter from Florence touching these present distempers of England. 1660, 1661 (in Divers discourses as Advice sent from the prime statesmen of Florence).

Divers historicall discourses of the late popular insurrections in Great Britain and Ireland: the first tome [all pbd]. 1661-42 (variant title-page Twelve several treatises).

A cordial for the cavaliers. 1661. Initialled J.H. Attributed to Howell from next entry, in which it is rptd, and from R. L'Estrange, Caveat, 1661.

Som sober inspections made into those ingredients that went to the composition of a late cordial. 1661.

A brief account of the royal matches since the year 800 which the Kings of England have made to this present 1662. 1662. Initialled J.H. Attributed to Howell, but improbably.

A new English grammar for forreners to learn English. 1662 (with a Spanish grammar etc and a discourse on travel in Spain and Portugal).

Poems on several choice and various subjects. Ed P[ayne] F[isher] 1663, 1664 (as Poems upon divers emergent occasions; variant title-page).

Προεδρία Βασιλική: a discourse concerning the precedency of Kings (with a distinct treatise of ambassadors). 1664. Initialled J.H.; tr Latin, 1664, [1668] (with new title-page).

A discours of Dunkirk. 1664, 1664 (with addns probably by J. H. Donke, both edns anon). Attributed.

Editions

Cotgrave's French and English dictionary. 1650, 1660, 1673.

Cottoni posthuma. 1651, 1672, 1679; ed E. Goldsmid, Edinburgh 1884-7.

Parthenopœia: or the history of Naples. 1654. Pt 1 tr from Italian of S. Mazzella by S. Leonard; pt 2 compiled by Howell from various Italian writers.

Finetti Philoxenis some choice observations of Sr John Finett. 1656.

Translations

St Paul's late progress upon earth, about a divorce 'twixt Christ and the Church of Rome. 1644. From Italian of Ferrante Pallavacino.

An exact historie of the revolution in Naples. 2 pts 1650-2 (pt 2 The second part of Masaniello), 1663-4, 1663-79. From the Italian of Alessandro Giraffi.

The process and pleadings in the Court of Spain upon the death of Antonie Ascham. 1651; rptd in Harleian miscellany vol 4, 1809.

The wonderful and most deplorable history of the latter times of the Jews, written first in Hebrew. 1652, 1653, 1662, 1669, 1684, 1699.

The nuptialls of Peleus and Thetis. 1654.

See also Vann, above, for other attributions.

§2

Warner, G. F. Two letters of Howell. EHR 9 1894.

Jürgens, G. Die Epistolae Ho-Elianae. Marburg 1901.

Bensly, E. James Howell. Aberystwyth Stud 3-6 1922-4, 8-9 1926-7.

Mensel, E. H. Howell as practical linguist. JEGP 25 1926.

Hirst, V. M. The authenticity of Howell's Familiar letters. MLR 54 1959.

BULSTRODE WHITELOCKE
1605-75
§1

Speech. 1642.

Three speeches made. 1659. One by Whitelocke.

Monarchy asserted. 1660, 1679. Anon.

Memorials of the English affairs: from the beginning of the reign of King Charles the first to King Charles the Second his happy restauration. 1682 (initialled B.W.), 1732 (with addns), 4 vols Oxford 1853.

Essays ecclesiastical and civil; to which is subjoined a treatise of the work of the sessions of the peace. 1706.

Memorials of English affairs, from the suppos'd expedition of Brute to the end of the reign of James the First; with some account of his [Whitelocke's] life and writings by W. Penn, and a preface by J. Welwood. 1709.

Notes upon the Kings writt for choosing members of Parlement XIII Car. II. Ed C. Morton 2 vols 1766.

A journal of the Swedish ambassy, in the years 1653 and 1654. Ed C. Morton 2 vols 1772; ed H. Reeve 2 vols 1855; tr Swebish, 1777.

Annals of his life. 1860. Extracts in R. H. Whitelocke, Life, below.

§2

Mr Lord Whitlock's reports on Machiavel. 1659. A satirical pamphlet.

Oldmixon, J. Clarendon and Whitlock compar'd. 1727.

Clarendon and Whitlock farther compar'd: or a discovery of mistakes by Oldmixon. 1739.

Norton, C. Preface to his edn of Swedish ambassy, 1772; rptd in Reeve's edn 1855.

Whitelocke, R. H. Memoirs, biographical and historical, of Whitelock. 1860.

SIR THOMAS BROWNE
1605-82

None of the 17th-century mss of Religio medici are autograph, nor are there known autograph versions of Browne's principal works. But BM has mss of some of the minor works and much note-book material, some unpbd. There are also mss in Bodley, Norwich etc.

Bibliographies

Keynes, G. L. A bibliography of Browne. Cambridge 1924, Oxford 1968 (rev and enlarged). Original edns, criticism to date, imitations and forerunners.

Leroy, O. A French bibliography of Browne. 1931.
Donovan, D. G. Browne 1924–66; Burton 1924–66. 1968. Recent edns and criticism.

Collections

The works of the learned Sr Thomas Browne: containing 1, Enquiries into vulgar and common errors; 2, Religio medici, with annotations and observations upon it; 3, Hydriotaphia: or urn-burial, together with the Garden of Cyrus; 4, Certain miscellany tracts. 1686; tr Dutch, 1688.
Works, including life and correspondence. Ed S. Wilkin 4 vols 1835–6, 3 vols 1852 (with omissions) (Bohn's Lib).
Works. Ed C. Sayle 3 vols 1904–7 (vol 3 Edinburgh), Edinburgh 1912.
Works. Ed G. L. Keynes 6 vols 1928–31, 4 vols 1964 (rev and enlarged; the text of Religio medici based on that of V. Sanna, of Hydriotaphia and Garden of Cyrus on that of J. Carter, the Latin writings tr W. R. Le Fanu). Vols 5–6 of Works 1928 (Miscellaneous writings, Letters) reissued 1946.

Selections

Tracts by Browne. Ed J[ames] C[rossley], Edinburgh and London 1822. Hydriotaphia, A letter to a friend, Musaeum clausum.
Miscellaneous works. Ed A. Young, Cambridge Mass 1831. Religio medici, Hydriotaphia, A letter to a friend, a few brief selections from Pseudodoxia epidemica.
Religio medici; to which is added Hydriotaphia. Ed J. A. St John 1838, 1841, 1845 (with Christian morals), 1848.
Religio medici, its sequel Christian morals, with resemblant passages from Cowper's Task and a verbal index. Ed J. Peace 1844.
Religio medici, together with A letter to a friend and Christian morals. Ed H. Gardiner 1845.
Religio medici, A letter to a friend, Christian morals, Urn burial and other papers. Ed J. T. Fields, Boston 1862.
Religio medici, Hydriotaphia and A letter to a friend. Ed J. W. Willis Bund 1869.
Religio medici, A letter to a friend, Christian morals. Ed W. A. Greenhill 1881, 1885 (rev).
Religio medici, Urn burial, Christian morals and other essays [A letter to a friend, On dreams]. Ed J. A. Symonds 1886.
Religio medici and other essays [Christian morals, A letter to a friend, Hydriotaphia]. Ed L. Roberts 1892, 1898 (rev), [1905] (Museum edn with new unsigned introd).
Religio medici, Hydriotaphia. Ed W. A. Greenhill and U. Holme 1896 (Temple Classics).
Religio medici, Urn burial and Christian morals. 1904. Introd signed G.B.M.; also includes A letter to a friend.
Religio medici and other essays [Hydriotaphia, Brampton urns, On dreams]. 1906.
Religio medici and other writings [Hydriotaphia, Brampton urns, A letter to a friend, The garden of Cyrus, Christian morals]. Ed C. H. Herford 1906 (EL); ed F. L. Huntley, New York 1951; ed H. Sutherland 1962 (EL); ed M. R. Ridley 1966 (EL).
Religio medici and other works (Religio medici, Hydriotaphia, The garden of Cyrus, A letter to a friend with ms version, Christian morals). Ed L. C. Martin, Oxford 1964.
The prose of Browne (Religio medici, Hydriotaphia, The garden of Cyrus, A letter to a friend, Christian morals, with selections from Pseudodoxia epidemica, Miscellany tracts and ms notebooks and letters). Ed N. J. Endicott, New York 1967.
Selected writings (Religio medici, A letter to a friend, Hydriotaphia, The garden of Cyrus, and selections from Christian morals, Pseudodoxia epidemica, Miscellany tracts and mss). Ed G. L. Keynes 1968.

§1

Religio medici. 1642 (2 anon unauthorized edns), 1643 (with addns and corrections), 1645, 1645, 1656 (with annotations by Thomas Keck included in later 17th-century edns), 1659, 1659 (with other works and Digby's Observations, included also in later 17th-century edns), 1669, 1672 (with Pseudodoxia), 1678, 1682, 1686 (in Works), 1736, 1736, 1738, 1754; ed T. Chapman, Oxford 1831; ed W. A. Greenhill 1881 (with Christian morals); ed Greenhill 1883 (facs of 1642); Oxford 1909 (facs of 1643); ed W. Murison, Cambridge 1922; ed J.-J. Denonain, Cambridge 1953, 1955 (without apparatus criticus); ed Denonain from Pembroke College Oxford ms, Algiers 1958; ed V. Sanna 2 vols Cagliari 1958 (the most complete apparatus criticus, with Italian trn); Menston 1968 (facs of 1643); tr Latin, 1644, 1644, 1650, 1652 (with annotations by L.N. M.E.M. [L. N. von Moltke], 1665 (some copies dated 1652), 1677, 1692, 1743; tr Dutch, 1665, 1683, 1688 (in Alle de werken); French, 1668, 1947; Italian, 1931, 1958 (in Sanna, above); Swedish, 1948; Japanese, 1963 (World's essays on life vol 4).
Pseudodoxia epidemica: or enquiries into very many received tenents and commonly presumed truths. 1646, 1650, 1658, 1658 (with Hydriotaphia and Garden of Cyrus, below), 1659 (reissue of 1658 folio with Religio, above, Hydriotaphia, Garden of Cyrus), 1669 (with Hydriotaphia and Garden of Cyrus), 1672 (with Religio), 1686 (in Works); tr Dutch, 1668, 1688 (in Alle de werken); German, 1680; French, 2 vols 1733 (3 edns), (unsold sheets) 1738, 1741, 1753; Italian (from French) 1737, 1743, 1754.
Hydriotaphia, urne-buriall: or a discourse of the sepulchrall urnes lately found in Norfolk; together with the Garden of Cyrus: or the quincunciall lozenge, or network plantations of the ancients, artificially, naturally, mystically considered. 1658, 1658, 1659 and 1669 (with other works), 1686 (in Works); 1736 (with Brampton urns, Of artificial hills, and 3 chs of Garden of Cyrus); ed J. Evans 1893; ed W. A. Greenhill 1896; ed W. Murison, Cambridge 1922; 1927 (facs); ed J. Carter, illustr J. Nash 1932, 1958 (without marginal notes and illustrations); tr French, 1929 (ch 5); Italian, 1931 (with Religio). From 1736 to 1896 Garden of Cyrus was not ptd with Hydriotaphia except in Works.
Certain miscellany tracts. 1683 (first issue), 1684, 1686 (in Works); tr Dutch, 1688 (in Alle de werken).
A letter to a friend upon occasion of the death of his intimate friend. 1690, 1712 (in Posthumous works); ed H. Macdonald 1924.
Posthumous works of the learned Sir Thomas Browne, printed from his original manuscripts: viz 1, Repertorium: or the antiquities of the cathedral church of Norwich; 2, An account of some urnes &c found at Brampton in Norfolk anno 1667; 3, Letters between Sir William Dugdale and Sir Tho. Browne; 4, Miscellanies, to which is prefix'd his life. 1712 (with variants), 1722, 1723. Includes also A letter to a friend and J. Whitefoot, Minutes for a life, as well as fragments and one piece not by Browne.
Christian morals. Ed J. Jeffery, Cambridge 1716, Halle 1723, London 1756 (with life by Samuel Johnson), 1761; 1863; Cambridge 1904; ed S. C. Roberts, Cambridge 1927.
Notes and letters on the natural history of Norfolk, more especially on the birds and fishes, from the mss of Sir Thomas Browne. Ed T. Southwell 1902.

§2

For many brief early references see Keynes, above.

Digby, Sir Kenelm. Observations upon Religio medici. 1643 (2 issues), 1644 (2 issues), 1659. From 1669 ptd with Religio.

Ross, A. Medicus medicatus. 1645.
—— Arcana microcosmi. 1651.
Robinson, J. Endoxa. 1656; tr 1658.
Whitefoot, J. Minutes for a life of Browne. In Posthumous works, 1712.
Birch, T. Life of Browne. In A general dictionary historical and critical, 1735.
Heister, E. F. In his Apologia pro medicis, Amsterdam 1736.
Johnson, Samuel. Life. Prefixed to Christian morals, 1756.
Hazlitt, W. In his Lectures chiefly on the dramatic literature of the age of Elizabeth, 1820.
Coleridge, S. T. In his Literary remains, 2 vols 1836. *See also* Miscellaneous criticism, ed T. M. Raysor, Cambridge Mass 1936, and Coleridge on the seventeenth century, ed R. F. Brinkley, Durham NC 1952.
Wilkin, S. Memoir. In his Works vol 1, 1836.
Stephen, L. In his Hours in a library: ser 2, 1876.
Pater, W. In his Appreciations, 1889.
Dowden, E. In his Puritan and Anglican, 1900.
Williams, C. The pedigree of Browne. 1902.
—— A bibliography of the Religio medici. 1905.
Gosse, E. Sir Thomas Browne. 1905 (EML).
Osler, W. In his An Alabama student, 1908.
Schonack, W. Browne's Religio medici. 1911.
Strachey, L. In his Books and characters, 1922.
Tildesley, M. L. Browne: his skull, portraits and ancestry. 1923.
Howell, A. C. Browne and seventeenth-century scientific thought. SP 22 1925.
—— A note on Browne's knowledge of languages. SP 22 1925.
—— Browne and the Elizabethans. SP 28 1931.
—— John Dunton and an imitation of the Religio medici. SP 29 1932.
—— Browne as wit and humorist. SP 42 1945.
'Sencourt, Robert' (R. E. G. George). In his Outflying philosophy, 1925.
Dunn, W. P. Browne: a study in religious philosophy. Menasha 1926, Minneapolis 1950 (rev).
Tempest, N. R. Rhythm in the prose of Browne. RES 3 1927.
Ashton, A. J. Browne en famille. Eng Rev 43–4 1926–7.
Praz, M. Sir Thomas Browne. E Studies 11 1929.
—— In his Studi e svaghi inglesi, Florence 1937.
Tyler, D. A review of the interpretation of Browne's part in a witch trial of 1664. Anglia 54 1930.
Leroy, O. Le chevalier Thomas Browne. Paris 1931.
Olivero, F. In his Studi britannici, Turin 1931.
Needham, J. In his Great amphibium, 1931.
Thaler, A. Browne and the Elizabethans. SP 28 1931.
Cawley, R. R. Browne and his reading. PMLA 48 1933.
Kane, R. J. James Crossley, Browne and the Fragment on mummies. RES 9 1933.
Loiseau, J. Browne: écrivain 'métaphysique'. Revue Anglo-américaine 10 1933.
Piccoli, R. Browne: poesia e vita spirituale. Bari 1934.
Barnes, W. H. Browne's Hydriotaphia with a reference to adipocera. Isis 20 1934.
Blau, J. L. Browne's interest in cabalism. PMLA 49 1934.
Chalmers, G. K. Hieroglyphs and Browne. Virginia Quart Rev 11 1935.
—— Three terms of the corpuscularian philosophy. MP 33 1936.
—— Browne, true scientist. Osiris 2 1936.
—— The lodestone and the understanding of science in seventeenth-century England. Philosophy of Science 4 1937.
—— 'That universal and publick manuscript'. Virginia Quart Rev 26 1950.
Buchinger, H. Beiträge zur Erkenntnis des individuellen Moments im Wortschatz der Religio medici. Borna 1936.
Finch, J. S. Musaeum clausum. TLS 13 Nov 1937.

—— A newly discovered Urn burial. Library 4th ser 19 1939.
—— An author-corrected Urne buriall. TLS 16 March 1940. Reply by J. Carter 11 May 1940.
—— Early drafts of the Garden of Cyrus. PMLA 55 1940.
—— Browne and the quincunx. SP 37 1940.
—— Browne: early biographical notices and the disposition of his library and manuscripts. SB 2 1949.
—— The Norfolk persuaders of Browne: a variant copy of the 1712 Posthumous works. Princeton Univ Lib Chron 11 1950.
—— Browne: a doctor's life of science and faith. New York 1950.
Iseman, J. S. A perfect sympathy: Charles Lamb and Browne. Cambridge Mass 1937.
Parker, E. L. The cursus in Browne. PMLA 53 1938.
Carter, J. Browne's autograph corrections. Library 4th ser 19 1939.
—— Browne's Urne buriall. Library 5th ser 2 1947.
—— 'The iniquity of oblivion foil'd'. Book Collector 15 1966.
Cline, J. M. In Five studies in literature, ed B. H. Bronson, Berkeley 1940.
Houghton, W. E. The English virtuoso in the seventeenth century. JHI 3 1942.
Bischoff, D. Browne als Stilkünstler. Heidelberg 1943.
Ziegler, D. K. In divided and distinguished worlds: rhetoric in the writings of Browne. Cambridge Mass 1943.
Oppenheimer, J. M. John Hunter, Browne and the experimental method. Bull History of Medicine 21 1947.
Raven, C. E. In his English naturalists, Neckham to Ray, Cambridge 1947.
Williams, A. In his Common expositor: an account of the commentaries on Genesis 1527–1633, Chapel Hill 1948.
Cook, E. The first edition of Religio medici. Harvard Lib Bull 2 1948.
Wiley, M. L. Browne and the genesis of paradox. JHI 9 1948; rptd in her Subtle knot: creative scepticism in seventeenth-century England, 1952.
Merton, E. S. Browne's scientific quest. Jnl History of Medicine 3 1948.
—— Science and imagination in Browne. 1949.
—— Browne's interpretation of dreams. PQ 28 1949.
—— Browne's embryological theory. Jnl History of Medicine 5 1950.
—— Browne as zoologist. Osiris 9 1950.
—— Browne's theories of respiration and combustion. Osiris 10 1952.
—— The botany of Browne. Isis 47 1956.
—— Microcosm, epitome and seed: some seventeenth-century analogies. History of Ideas News Letter 3 1957.
—— Browne on astronomy. History of Ideas News Letter 4 1958.
—— Old and new physiology in Browne. Isis 57 1966.
Heideman, M. A. Hydriotaphia and the Garden of Cyrus: a paradox and a cosmic vision. UTQ 19 1950.
Huntley, F. L. Browne, Harvey and the metaphor of the circle. Bull History of Medicine 25 1951.
—— The occasion and date of Browne's A letter to a friend. MP 48 1951.
—— Browne and the metaphor of the circle. JHI 14 1953.
—— Browne: the relationship of Urn burial and the Garden of Cyrus. SP 52 1956.
—— Browne: a biographical and critical study. Ann Arbor 1962.
Warren, A. The style of Browne. Kenyon Rev 13 1951.
Moran, B. Browne's reading on the Turks. N & Q 30 Aug–13 Sept 1952.
Colie, R. Browne's 'entertainment' in xviith century Holland. Neophilologus 36 1952. Dutch criticism.
—— In her Paradoxia epidemica: the Renaissance tradition of paradox, Princeton 1966.
Bottrall, M. In her Every man a phoenix: studies in seventeenth-century autobiography, 1958.

Moloney, M. F. Metre and cursus in Browne's prose. JEGP 58 1959.

Endicott, N. J. Browne as 'orphan'. UTQ 30 1961.
— Browne, Montpellier and the tract of languages. TLS 24 Aug 1962. Comment by D. E. Rhodes 7 Sept 1962.
— Some aspects of self revelation and self portraiture in Religio medici. In Essays presented to A. S. P. Woodhouse, Toronto 1964.
— Browne's A letter to a friend. UTQ 36 1966.
— Browne's A letter to a friend. TLS 15 Sept 1967. Replies by K. J. Höltgen 20 Oct, F. L. Huntley 9 Feb 1968.

Denonain, J.-J. La personnalité de Browne. Paris 1959.

Whallon, W. Hebraic synonymy in Browne. ELH 28 1961.

Bennett, J. Browne: a man of achievement in literature. Cambridge 1962.

Zolla, E. Musica e cabala in Browne. Eng Miscellany (Rome) 16 1965.

Cawley, R. R., and G. Yost. Studies in Browne. Eugene Oregon 1965.

Shaaber, M. A. A crux in Religio medici. Eng Lang Notes 3 1966. 'Atomist' perhaps misprint for 'Adamist' or 'Adamite'.

Nathanson, L. The strategy of truth: a study of Browne. Chicago 1967.

Mackenzie, N. Browne as a man of learning: a discussion of Urn burial and the Garden of Cyrus. Eng Stud in Africa 10 1967.

Webber, J. In her Eloquent I: style and self in seventeenth-century prose, Madison 1968.

THOMAS FULLER
1608–61

Bibliographies etc

Bailey, J. E. In his Life of Fuller, 1874, and his edn of Collected sermons, 2 vols 1891.

Gibson, S. A bibliography of the works of Fuller. Proc Oxford Bibl Soc 4 1935. Addns and corrections, new ser 1 1927; *see also* TLS 13 June 1936.

Collections

Pulpit sparks: being 19 sermons of that godly and popular divine Fuller. Ed M. J. Fuller 1886.

Collected sermons. Ed J. E. Bailey and W. E. Axon 2 vols 1891.

Wise words and quaint counsels. Ed A. Jessopp, Oxford 1892.

Fuller's thoughts. Ed A. R. Waller 1902.

Selections, with [excerpts from] essays by Charles Lamb, J. Crossley, L. Stephen et al. Ed E. K. Broadus, Oxford 1928.

§ I

David's hainous sin, heartie repentance, heavy punishment. 1631, Edinburgh 1868 (in Poems and translations), 1869.

The historie of the holy warre. Cambridge 1639, 1640, 1647, 1647, 1651, London 1840.

Joseph's partly-coloured coat. 1640 (2 issues), 1867.

The holy state; the profane state. Cambridge 1642, 1648 (enlarged), London 1652, 1663; [ed A. Young], Cambridge Mass 1831; 1840; cd J. Nichols 1841; ed M. G. Walten 2 vols New York 1938 (with Andronicus 1648) (facs).

A fast sermon preached on Innocents day. 1642, 1654 (with A sermon preached at the collegiat church of St Peter).

A sermon on the day of his Majesty's inauguration. 1643, 1643, 1654.

A sermon of reformation. 1643, 1643 (with Truth maintained); ed J. E. Bailey 1875.

Truth maintained. Oxford 1643, 1643.

Jacob's vow: a sermon preached before his Majesty. Oxford 1644.

Good thoughts in bad times. Exeter 1645, London 1645, 1646.

Feare of losing the old light. 1646.

Andronicus: or the unfortunate politician. 1646 (3 issues), 1648 etc (in Profane state, above), 1649; tr Dutch, 1659.

The cause and cure of a wounded conscience. 1647, 1649, 1810, 1812, 1815.

Good thoughts in worse times. 1647.

Good thoughts in bad times, together with good thoughts in worse times. 1649, 1649, 1652, 1657, 1659, 1665, 1669, 1680, Oxford 1810, 1830, 1831, 1841 (with Mixt contemplations), 1863.

A sermon of assurance. 1647, 1648.

A sermon of contentment. 1648. Initialled T.F.

The just man's funeral. 1649, 1652, 1660, (in The house of mourning), 1672.

A pisgah-sight of Palestine. 1650, 1658, 1662, 1869.

Abel redivus: or the dead yet speaking. 1651 (several variants), 1652; ed J. W. Nichols 2 vols 1867. Preface and some lives by Fuller.

A comment on the eleven first verses of the fourth chapter of S. Matthew's gospel in 12 sermons. 1652.

Perfection and peace: delivered in a sermon. 1653 (2 issues).

The infants advocate: or circumcision on Jewish children and baptisme [on] Christian. 1653.

Two sermons. 1654.

A comment on Ruth, together with Two sermons. 1654, 1865.

A triple reconciler. 1654 (2 issues).

Ephemeris parliamentaria. 1654, 1658, 1660. Preface.

Life out of death: a sermon. 1655.

The church-history of Britain; with the history of the university of Cambridge and the history of Waltham Abbey in Essex. 1655 (one issue 1656); ed J. Nichols 3 vols 1837 etc; ed J. S. Brewer 6 vols 1845.

Antheologia: or the speech of flowers. 1655. Anon; attributed.

A collection of sermons, together with Notes upon Jonah. 1656, 1657.

The best name on earth, together with several other sermons lately preached. 1657, 1659 (2 issues).

A sermon preached at St Clemens Danes at the funeral of Mr George Heycock. 1657, 1660 (as The righteous man's service to his generation, in The house of mourning), 1672.

The sovereigns prerogative. 1657, 1658 (both anon), 1660.

The appeal of injured innocence. 1659.

Sermons of Mr Henry Smith. 1657, 1675. A brief life of Smith.

An alarum to the counties of England and Wales. 1660.

A happy handful. 1660. Anon. Title and dedication probably by Fuller.

A panegyrick to his Majesty on his happy return. 1660.

Mixt contemplations in better times. 1660, 1830 etc (with Good thoughts in bad times and Good thoughts in worse times).

Andronicus: a tragedy. 1661. Verse play attributed to Fuller; see J. O. Wood, below.

The history of the worthies of England. 1662 (2 issues), 1684 (abridged by George Sandys as Anglorum speculum, several issues); ed J. Nichols 2 vols 1811; ed P. A. Nuttall 3 vols 1840, New York 1965; ed J. Freeman 1952 (abridged). An index pbd in 1744 is sometimes bound up with 1662.

Poems and translations in verse. Ed A. B. Grosart, Edinburgh 1868.

For works to which Fuller contributed see Gibson, above.

§2

The life of that reverend divine and learned historian Dr Thomas Fuller. 1661, 1662, Oxford 1662 (all anon); rptd in Brewer's edn of the Church-history, Oxford 1845, and in Broadus, above.

Lamb, Charles. Specimens from the writings of Fuller. Reflector 4 1811; rptd in Works, 2 vols 1818.

Coleridge, S. T. In Literary remains, ed H. N. Coleridge 4 vols 1836-9, and Notes on English divines ed D. Coleridge 2 vols 1853; see also Miscellaneous criticism, ed T. M. Raysor, Cambridge Mass 1936, and Coleridge on the seventeenth century, ed R. F. Brinkley, Durham NC 1952.

Crossley, J. Fuller's Holy and profane states. Retrospective Rev 3 1821.

Russell, A. T. Memorials of the life and works of Fuller. 1844.

Rogers, H. An essay on the life and genius of Fuller. 1856.

Stephen, L. Cornhill Mag Jan 1872.

Bailey, J. E. The life of Fuller, with notices of his books, his kinsmen and his friends. 1874.

Fuller, M. J. The life, times and writings of Fuller. 2 vols 1884.

Tovey, D. C. In his Reviews and essays in English literature, 1897. On Fuller's sermons.

Minchin, H. C. Glimpses of Fuller. Fortnightly Rev July 1908.

Thompson, E. N. S. In his Literary bypaths of the Renaissance, New Haven 1924.

Kellett, E. E. Thomas Fuller. London Quart Rev 145 1926; rptd in his Reconsiderations, Cambridge 1928.

Stauffer, D. In his English biography before 1700, Cambridge Mass 1930.

Lyman, D. B. The great Tom Fuller. Berkeley 1935.

Arneke, H. In his Kirchengeschichte und Rechtsgeschichte in England von der Reformation bis zum frühen 18 Jahrhundert. Halle 1937.

Buckingham, C. F. Parallel passages in Bacon and Fuller. RES 13 1937.

Houghton, W. E. The formation of Fuller's Holy and profane states. Cambridge Mass 1938.

Whiting, B. J. Pepys, Fuller and an Archbishop. Harvard Theological Rev 38 1945.

Addison, W. Worthy Dr Fuller. 1951.

Novarr, D. Walton and Fuller. TLS 10 Aug 1951.

Roberts, S. C. Fuller: a seventeenth-century worthy. Manchester 1953; rptd in his Doctor Johnson and others, 1958.

Wood, J. O. Fuller's Oxford interlude. HLQ 17 1954. On authorship of Andronicus 1661.

Resnick, R. B. Fuller's pulpit wit. Xavier Univ Stud 4 1965.

Woodward, D. H. Fuller, the Protestant divines and Plagiary yet speaking. Trans Cambridge Bibl Soc 1965.

— Fuller, William Dugard and the pseudonymous life of Sidney 1655. PBSA 62 1968. Attributes life of Sidney in 1655 Arcadia to Fuller.

SIR THOMAS URQUHART
1611–60

Collections

Tracts of the learned and celebrated antiquarian Urquhart. [Ed D. Herd], Edinburgh 1774, 1782.

The works of Urquhart. [Ed G. Maitland], Edinburgh 1834 (Maitland Club).

Selections from Urquhart. Ed J. Purves, Edinburgh 1942 (Saltire Soc).

§1

Epigrams: divine and moral. 1641, 1646.

The trissotetras: or a most exquisite table for resolving all manner of triangles. 1645, 1650 (as The most easy and exact manner of resolving all sorts of triangles).

Εκσκυβαλαμρον: or the discovery of a most exquisite jewel, found in the kennel of Worcester-streets, anno 1651. 1652. By 'Christianus Presbyteriomastix'.

Παντοχρονοχανον: or a peculiar promptuary of time, wherein is displayed a most exact directory for all particular chronologies, in what family soever: and that by deducing the true pedigree of the Urquharts, in the house of Cromartie, since the creation of the world until 1650. 1652.

Logopandecteison: or an introduction to the universal language. 1653.

The first book of the works of Mr Francis Rabelais, doctor in physick, now faithfully translated into English. 1653, 1654 (both anon); The second book, 1653 (by S.T.U.C.), 1664; The third book, 1693.

The works of F. Rabelais MD, done out of French by Sir Tho Urchard Kt and others. 5 vols 1694. P. A. Motteux edited the 3rd bk of Urquhart's trn, revised the first 2, and himself translated bks 4-5. The 5 bks (including the 1693 vol) constituted the Works.

The whole works of F. Rabelais MD, done out of French by Sr Thomas Urchard Kt, Mr Motteux and others. 2 vols 1708; ed J. Ozell 5 vols 1737; ed T. Martin, Edinburgh 1838; ed A. Wallis 5 vols 1897; ed C. Whibley 3 vols 1900 (Tudor Translations); ed A. J. Knock and C. R. Wilson 2 vols New York 1931.

The history of the admirable Crichton (from 'Εκσκυβαλαυρον 1652]. Retrospective Rev 6 1822; ed H. Miles 1927 (as The life and death of the admirable Crichtoun).

A challenge from Urquhart. Ed C. H. Wilkinson, Oxford 1948 (Luttrell Soc).

§2

Irving, D. In his Lives of Scottish writers, 2 vols Edinburgh 1839.

Miller, H. In his Scenes and legends of the north of Scotland, 1850.

Whibley, C. Sir Thomas Urquhart. New Rev 17 1897; rptd in his Studies in frankness, 1910.

Brown, H. In his Rabelais in English literature, Cambridge Mass 1933.

Roe, F. C. Urquhart and Rabelais. 1957.

(2) MINOR HISTORIANS

FRANCIS BACON, VISCOUNT ST ALBANS
1561–1626

See col 2324, below.

SAMUEL DANIEL
1562–1619

Bibliographies

Sellers, H. A bibliography of the works of Daniel. Proc Oxford Bibl Soc 2 1927-30.

Tannenbaum, S. A. A concise bibliography of Daniel. New York 1942.

§1

The first fowre books of the civile warres betweene the two houses of Lancaster and Yorke [also the fifth book]. 1595 (2 edns of 5th book), 1599 (in Poeticall essayes, one issue as The civill wars of England); bks 1-6, 1601 (in Works); complete text with bks 7-8 as The civile warres betweene the howses of Lancaster and Yorke corrected and continued, 1609; ed L. Michel, New Haven 1958.

The first part of the historie of England [to end of Stephen]. 1612, 1613; The collection of the historie of England [to end of Edward III], [1618], 1621, 1626, 1634; 2 pts (with continuation from Edward III by John Trussell), 1650, 1685, 1706 (in White Kennett, Complete history vol 1).

§2

Eccles, M. Daniel in France and Italy. SP 34 1937.
Nearing, H., jr. In his English historical poetry 1599–1641, Philadelphia 1945.
McKisack, M. Daniel as historian. RES 23 1947.
Greer, C. A. Did Shakespeare use Daniel's Civil wars? N & Q 3 Feb 1951.
McManaway, J. G. Some bibliographical notes on Daniel's Civil wars. SB 4 1952.
Seronsy, C. C. Daniel's ms Civil wars with some previously unpublished stanzas. JEGP 52 1953.
—— The doctrine of cyclical recurrence and some related ideas in the works of Daniel. SP 54 1957.
Tillyard, E. M. W. In his English epic and its background, 1954.
Gottfried, R. B. Daniel's method of writing history. Stud in Renaissance 3 1956.
—— The authorship of A breviary of the history of England. SP 53 1956. Daniel, not Ralegh.
Blissett, W. Daniel's sense of the past. E Studies 38 1957.
Godshalk, W. L. Daniel's History. JEGP 63 1964.
Logan, G. M. Daniel's Civil wars and Lucan's Pharsalia. Stud in Eng Lit 1500–1900 11 1971.
See also col 1061, above.

SIR GEORGE CAREW
d. 1612 or 1613

§1

A relation of the state of France 1609. Ed T. Birch 1749 (in An historical view of the negotiations between the Courts of England, France and Brussels).
A relation of the state of Polonia and the United Provinces of that crown. Ed C. H. Talbot, Rome 1965.

§2

Mews, S. Ein englischer Gesandtschaftsbericht über den polnischen Staat. Leipzig 1936.

SIR JOHN DAVIES
1569–1626

A discoverie of the true causes why Ireland was never entirely subdued, until his Majesties raigne. 1612, 1613 (variant issue as A discoverie of the state of Ireland), Dublin 1644, London 1704 (in J. Ware, Antiquities of Ireland, 1705), 1747, Dublin 1761; ed G. Chalmers 1786, Dublin 1787 (in Historical tracts); ed A. B. Grosart 1869–76 (in Works); ed H. Morley 1890 (in Ireland under Elizabeth and James I).
Le primer report des cases resolves en les courts del roy en Ireland. Dublin 1615, London 1628, 1674; tr Dublin 1762, Edinburgh 1907 (English reports vol 80).
For poems and criticism see col 1071, above.

SIR JOHN HAYWARD
1564–1627

§1

The first part of the life and raigne of King Henrie the IIII. 1599, [1604–10?], [1610?], [c. 1625], [1638–9?] (these 4 edns dated 1599), 1639, 1642 (with Sir R. Cotton, Short view of the raign of Henry III).

An answer to the first part of a certaine conference [an answer to A conference about the next succession to the crowne of Ingland, by Parsons, Rowlands and others 1594]. 1603, 1683 (as The right of succession asserted).
A treatise of union of England and Scotland. 1604. By I.H.
A reporte of a discourse concerning supreme power in affaires of religion. 1606 (anon), 1607 (another issue, signed), 1624 (as Of supremacie in affaires of religion).
The lives of the III Normans, Kings of England. 1613; ed T. Park, Harleian miscellany vols 2, 9, 1809, 1812.
The life and raigne of King Edward the Sixt. 1630, 1636 (with the beginning of the reigne of Queene Elizabeth), 1706 (in White Kennett, Complete history vol 2).
Annals of the first four years of the reign of Queen Elizabeth. Ed J. Bruce 1840 (Camden Soc).

§2

Dowling, M. Hayward's troubles over his life of Henry IV. Library 4th ser 11 1930.
Jackson, W. A. Counterfeit printing in Jacobean times. Library 4th ser 15 1934.
Smith, G. The influence of Hayward and of Joshua Sylvester on Drummond's Cypress grove. PQ 26 1947.
Goldberg, S. L. Hayward, 'politic' historian. RES new ser 6 1955.
Benjamin, E. B. Hayward and Tacitus. RES new ser 8 1957.

WILLIAM FARMER
fl. 1614

Certaine chroniculary discourses, for the years of our Lord 1612–15. Dublin 1772 (in J. Lodge, Desiderata curiosa hibernica).
Annals of Ireland from the year 1594 to 1613. Ed C. L. Falkiner, EHR 22 1907.

JOHN SPEED
1552?–1629

§1

The theatre of the empire of Great Britaine: presenting an exact geography of England, Scotland, Ireland [etc]. 1611 (for 1612), 1615, 1623, 1627, 1627, 1646, 1650, 1676; tr Latin by P. Holland, 1616.
The history of Great Britaine. 1611, 1614, 1623, 1623, 1627, 1631 (variant 1632), 1650. A continuation of Theatre, above.
Speed's England: a coloured facsimile of the maps and text [of Theatre]. Ed J. Arlott 4 pts 1953–4.
An atlas of Tudor England and Wales: forty plates from Speed's pocket atlas of 1627. Ed E. G. R. Taylor 1951 (Penguin).

§2

Gardner, E. Speed's Theatre. TLS 6 Dec 1947.
Willoughby, E. E. A long use of a setting of type. SB 2 1950.
Bryant, J. A. Stow's continuator and the Defense of Brut. MLR 45 1950.

SIR WILLIAM MONSON
1569–1643

§1

Naval tracts. 1704 (in A. and J. Churchill, Collection of voyages vol 3); ed M. Oppenheim 5 vols 1902–14 (Navy Records Soc). An excerpt was ptd as A true and exact account of the wars with Spain in the reign of Queen Elizabeth, 1682.

§2

Abbott, W. C. A true Elizabethan. In his Conflicts with oblivion, Cambridge Mass 1924.

EDMUND BOLTON
1575?–after 1634

§1

The element of armories. 1610. First issue initialled E.B.
The Roman histories of Lucius Florus. Tr E.M.B. [1619], [1621?], 1636 (by 'Philanactophil').
Nero Caesar, or monarchie depraved. 1624 (by 'Philanactophil'), 1627 (with addns).
The cities advocate, in this case or question of honor and arms: whether apprenticeship extinguisheth gentry. 1629 (anon), 1674 (as The cities great concern in this case).
Hypercritica: or a rule of judgement for writing or reading our history's. Oxford 1722 (in Nicolai Triveti annalium continuatio), London 1815 (in Ancient critical essays upon English poets and poesy vol 2, ed J. Haslewood), Oxford 1908 (in Critical essays of the seventeenth century vol 2, ed J. E. Spingarn).

§2

Portal, E. M. The Academ Roial of King James I. Proc Br Acad 7 1916.

FRANCIS GODWIN,
Bishop of Hereford
1562–1633

§1

A catalogue of the bishops of England. 1601 (by F.G.), 1615 (with addns and A discourse concerning the first conversion of Britaine, and A discourse concerning such Englishmen as have been cardinals), [1625?] (one issue with cancel title-page The succession of the bishops of England); tr Latin by Godwin 2 pts 1616 (as De praesulibus Angliæ commentarius); 3rd pt, Ad commentarium appendix [1621–4]; ed and continued by W. Richardson, Cambridge 2 vols 1743.
Rerum anglicarum Henrico VIII, Edwardo VI et Maria regnantibus annales. 1616 (anon), 1628, 1653; tr M. Godwin 1630, 1676 (with Bacon, History of Henry VII); tr J. H[ughes] 1706 (in White Kennett, Complete history vol 2); tr French, 1647.
Catalogus episcoporum Bathoniensium et Wellensium, partly printed by T. Hearne. In John de Trokelowe, Annales Edwardi II, 1729, and John de Wethamstede, Chronicon, 2 vols Oxford 1732.
Nuncius inanimatus. Utopia (for London) 1629 (anon).
The man in the moone: or, a discourse of a voyage thither by D. Gonsales. 1638 (initialled E. M[ahon]), 1657 (with Nuncius inanimatus); ed G. McColley with Nuncius inanimatus (tr T. Smith), Northampton Mass 1937; tr French, 1648, 1666; German, 1659, 1660.

§2

Lawton, H. W. Bishop Godwin's Man in the moone. RES 7 1931.
Nicolson, M. H. A world in the moon. Northampton Mass 1936.
—— Cosmic voyages. ELH 7 1940.
McColley, G. The date of Godwin's Domingo Gonsales. MP 35 1937.
—— The pseudonyms of Godwin. PQ 16 1937.
—— The third edition of Godwin's The man in the moon. Library 4th ser 18 1937.

—— In his Literature and science, Chicago 1947. With extracts.
Merchant, W. M. Bishop Francis Godwin, historian and novelist. Jnl Historical Soc of Church in Wales 5 1955.

SIR GEORGE BUCK or BUC
d. 1623

§1

Δαφνίς πολυστέφανος: an eclogue treating of crownes and of garlandes. 1605, 1635 (much rev by Buck's great-nephew Sir George Buck as The great Plantagenet or a continued succession of that royall name from Henry the Second to our sacred sovereign King Charles).
The third universitie of England: or a treatise of the foundations of all the colledges, auncient schooles of priveledge and of houses of learning and liberal arts, within and about the most famous cittie of London. Appended to J. Stow, Annales, continued by E. Howes 1615.
The history of the life and reigne of Richard the Third. 1646 (rev Sir George Buck), 1647; rptd in White Kennett, Complete history vol 1, 1706.

§2

Eccles, M. Buc: Master of the Revels. In Thomas Lodge and other Elizabethans, ed C. J. Sisson, Cambridge 1933.

GEORGE, BARON CAREW and EARL OF TOTNES
1555–1629

Letters from Carew to Sir Thomas Roe. Ed J. MacLean 1860 (Camden Soc).
Carew translated French version of Irish poem by Maurice Regan, The history of Ireland, *and French account of Richard II's visit to Ireland in 1399, both pbd in W. Harris*, Hibernica, *1747. See also Sir Thomas Stafford, below.*

FYNES MORYSON
1566–1630

§1

An itinerary containing his ten yeares trave lthrough the twelve dominions of Germany, Bohmerland, Sweitzerland, Netherland, Denmarke, Poland, Italy, Turky, France, England, Scotland and Ireland, divided in 3 parts. 1617, 4 vols Glasgow 1907–8; part of a 4th pt ed C. Hughes 1903 (as Shakespeare's Europe), New York 1967; 2nd pt and part of 3rd pt Dublin 1735 (as An history of Ireland from 1599–1603); Irish pt in Ireland under Elizabeth and James the First, ed H. Morley 1890.

§2

Hughes, C. In his Shakespeare's Europe, 1903.
Whitebrook, J. C. Moryson, Bruno and Shakespeare. N & Q 10 Oct 1936.
Gottfried, R. B. The debt of Moryson to Spenser's View. PQ 17 1938.
Penrose, B. In his Urbane travellers, 1942.

GEORGE CARLETON,
Bishop of Chichester
1559–1628

§1

Tithes examined and proved to be due to the clergy by a divine right. 1606, 1611.

A thankefull remembrance of Gods mercy, in an historicall collection of the deliverance of the church and state of England from the beginning of Queene Elisabeth. 1624, 1625, 1627, 1630.

§ 2

Vita Bernardi Gilpini viri sanctissimi. 1628, 1681 (in Bates, Vitae selectorum aliquot virorum); [tr W. Freake] 1629 (2 issues), 1636 (4th edn, with his sermon preached before Edward VI), 1752, 1810 etc (in C. Wordsworth, Ecclesiastical biography vol 3).

JOHN SPOTTISWOODE,
Archbishop of St Andrews
1565–1639

The history of the Church of Scotland, beginning the year of our Lord 203 and continued to the end of the reign of James VI. 1655, 1677; ed M. Russell and M. Napier 3 vols Edinburgh 1847–51 (Spottiswoode Soc and Bannatyne Club).

SIR ROBERT NAUNTON
1563–1635

Fragmenta regalia. 1641, 1641, 1642, 1650, 1653 (better text, as Fragmenta regalia: or observations on the late Q. Elizabeth her times and favorites); ed J. Caulfield 1814 (1641 text); rptd from 1641 or 1653 text in various collections, including Harleian miscellany and Somers tracts; ed E. Arber 1870; ed A. C. Ward, Miscellany of tracts and pamphlets, 1927; tr French (in G. Leti, La vie d'Elizabeth vol 2, Amsterdam 1703); by J. Le Pelletier 1745; Italian (in G. Leti, Historia overo vita di Elisabetta, Amsterdam 1693).

SIR THOMAS STAFFORD
fl. 1633

Pacata Hibernia: Ireland appeased and reduced. 1633 (one issue dated 1634), 2 vols Dublin 1810; ed S. O'Grady 2 vols 1896. Based on mss bequeathed to Stafford by Carew.

THOMAS HOBBES
1588–1679
See col 2325, below.

ARTHUR WILSON
1595–1652

The history of Great Britain: being the life and reign of King James I. 1653, 1706 (in White Kennett, Complete history vol 2).
Observations of God's providence in the tract of my life. Ed F. Peck 1735 (in Desiderata curiosa vol 2); ed P. Bliss as appendix to Wilson's play The inconstant lady, 1814. See also col 1758, above.

DAVID CALDERWOOD
1575–1650

The true history of the Church of Scotland, from the beginning of the Reformation unto the end of the reigne of King James VI. [Edinburgh?] 1678, 1680, [Holland?] 1704 (for 1678); ed T. Thomson as The history of the Kirk of Scotland (with a life) 8 vols Edinburgh 1842–9 (Wodrow Soc).

JOHN TRUSSELL
fl. 1620–42

§ 1

A continuation of the collection of the history of England, beginning where S. Daniell ended. 1636, 1641.

§ 2

Nearing, H. 'Yorke in choller' and other unrecorded allusions to Richard II. N & Q 10 Aug 1946.

WALTER BALCANQUHALL
1586?–1645

A large declaration concerning the late tumults in Scotland, by the King. 1639. Attributed.

PETER HEYLYN
1599–1662

Bibliographies etc
Wood, A. In his Athenae oxonienses, 2 vols 1691–2.

Collections
Ecclesia vindicata: or the Church of England justified. 1657. 6 pts, all pbd already except 2nd pt of History of episcopacie.
Κειμήλια Ἐκκλησιαστικά: the historical and miscellaneous tracts of Peter Heylyn. 1681. The tracts in Ecclesia vindicata rptd with others also already pbd except A brief discourse asserting the bishops right of peerage; with a life by [G. Vernon]; rptd 1682 (with Vernon's name).

§ 1

Microcosmus: or a little description of the great world. Oxford 1621 (initialled P.H.), 1625, 1627, 1629, 1631, 1633, 1636, 1639 (misprinted 1939), London 1652 (enlarged as Cosmographie), 1657, 1666, [1668]–9, 1669, 1670, 1674, 1677, 1682; 4th bk, 1668; 4th bk pt 2, [1662].
The historie of that most famous saynt and souldier St George of Cappadocia. 1631, 1633.
Augustus: or an essay of those meanes and counsels, whereby the commonwealth of Rome was altered and reduced unto a monarchy. 1632 (anon), [1710]. Incorporated in Cosmographie, 1666 (3rd edn).
The history of the sabbath in two books. 1636, 1636, 1681 (in Historical and miscellaneous tracts).
A coale for the altar. 1636. Anon. On the placing of the communion table.
Antidotum Lincolniense: or an answer to a book entitled the Holy table [by John Williams]. 1637.
A briefe and moderate answer to the seditious and scandalous challenges of Henry Burton. 1637.
Πρωτολογία Anglorum: or a help to English history. 1641, 1642 (both by 'Robert Hall'), 1652 (as A help to English history), 1669, 1670, 1671, 1675, 1680, 1709, 1773, 1786.
A briefe relation of the remarkable occurrencies in the northerne parts. Oxford 1642[–3]. Anon.
A second, but more perfect relation of the great victory [of Lord Hopton, at Bodmin]. Oxford 1642. Anon.
The historie of episcopacie, by Theophilus Churchman. 2 pts 1642, 1657 (in Ecclesia vindicata), 1681 (in Historical and miscellaneous tracts).
Lord have mercie upon us. Oxford 1643. Anon. Attributed.
The rebells catechisme. 1643 (for 1644), Oxford 1643 (for 1644), [York?] 1644. By P.H.

A briefe relation of the death and sufferings of the L. Archbishop of Canterbury. Oxford 1644 (for 1645). Anon.

Parliaments power in lawes for religion. Oxford 1645 (anon), 1653 (as The way of reformation of the Church of England), 1657 (in Ecclesia vindicata).

The undeceiving of the people in the point of tithes. 1648 (for 1647) (by 'Ph Treleinie'), 1657 (in Ecclesia vindicata), 1708 (in G. Hickes, Three short treatises).

Theologia veterum: or the summe of Christian theology. 1654, 1673.

A full relation of two journeys: the one into the main-land of France, the other into some of the adjacent ilands. 1656.

France painted to the life by a learned and impartial hand. 1656, 1657, 1673, 1679. Pirated versions by R. Bignell of A full relation, above.

A survey of the estate of France. 1656.

Observations on the historie of the reign of King Charles published by H.L. [Estrange] esq. 1656, 1656. Anon. Heylyn disclaimed authorship of this in his Extraneus vapulans, below, but this is not accepted.

Extraneus vapulans. 1656. An attack on L'Estrange and Dr Bernard.

The stumbling block of disobedience and rebellion. 1658.

Respondet Petrus. 1658. Reply to N. Bernard and appendix in answer to R. Sanderson.

A short view of the life and reign of King Charles. 1658 (several issues, by P.H.); tr French, 1664.

Examen historicum. 2 pts 1659.

Certamen epistolare: or the letter combate managed by Peter Heylyn with Mr Baxter [et al]. 1659.

Bibliotheca regia: or the royal library. 1659. Anon; compilation attributed to Heylyn by Wood.

The parable of the tares expounded and applyed in ten sermons preached before his late Majesty K. Charles. 1659.

Historia quinqu-articularis: or a declaration. 1660, 1681 (in Historical and miscellaneous tracts).

Affairs of church and state in England during the life and first eight years of the reign of Queen Elizabeth. 1660 (in Ecclesia restaurata 1661, below).

Ecclesia restaurata: or the history of the Reformation. 1660-1, 1670, 1674; ed J. C. Robertson 2 vols 1849 (Ecclesiastical History Soc).

Cyprianus anglicus: or the history of the life and death of William [Laud] Archbishop of Canterbury. Ed H. Heylyn 1668, 1671, Dublin 1719.

Aerius redivivus: or the history of the Presbyterians. Oxford 1670, 1670, London 1672, 1969 (facs).

The voyage of France. 1673, 1679.

Memorial of Bishop Waynflete. Ed J. R. Bloxam 1851 (from ms) (Caxton Soc), New York 1967.

See Wood, above, for other attributions.

§2

Hakewill, G. A dissertation with Dr Heylyn touching the pretended sacrifice of the eucharist. 1641.

[Harrington, J.] The stumbling block of disobedience and rebellion cunningly imputed by P.H. unto Calvin, removed in a letter from I.H. 1658.

Fuller, T. The appeal of injured innocence in a controversie betwixt Dr Peter Heylyn and Thomas Fuller. 1659.

Hickman, H. A review of the Certamen epistolae. Oxford 1659.

—— Historia quinq-articularis: or animadversions on Dr Heylyns quinqarticular history. 1673.

Barnard, J. Theologo-historicus: or the true life of the most reverend divine and excellent historian Peter Heylyn. 1683.

Hudson, J. P. Heylyn's poetry notebook. BM Quart 34 1969.

Heylyn was attacked or criticized in various contemporary tracts and books.

SIR RICHARD BAKER
1568–1645

§1

A chronicle of the Kings of England from the time of the Romans government unto the raigne of our soveraigne lord King Charles. 1643, 1653, 1660 (continued to 1658), 1665, 1670, 1674, 1679, 1684, 1696, 1730, 1733 (each with continuations); abridgement 1684; tr Dutch, 1649.

Theatrum redivicum: or the theatre vindicated in answer to Mr Pryn's Histrio-mastix. 1662, 1670 (as Theatrum triumphans).

Baker also pbd trns from Latin, French and Italian.

§2

Blount, T. Animadversions upon Sr Richard Baker's Chronicle. Oxford 1672.

Whiting, B. J. Baker's Cato variegatus 1636. In W. D. Hand (ed), Humaniora, Locust Valley NY [1960].

THOMAS MAY
c. 1595–1650

§1

A discourse concerning the success of former Parliaments. [1642] (anon), 1644.

The character of a right malignant. [1644]. Anon. Attribution doubtful.

The Lord George Digby's Cabinet and Dr Goff's negotiations. 1646. Anon.

The history of the Parliament of England wich began November the third MDCXL, with a short and necessary view of some precedent yeares. 1647; ed F. Maseres 1812; Oxford 1854; tr French, 1823.

Historiae parliamenti Angliae breviarum tribus partibus explicitum. [1650], 1651 (by T.M.); tr as A breviary of the history of the Parliament of England, 1650, 1655, 1680; ed F. Maseres, Select tracts relating to the civil wars in England, 1815.

The changeable covenant. 1650. Anon; attribution doubtful.

For May's plays and trns see col 1751, above.

§2

Chester, A. G. May: man of letters. Philadelphia 1932.

JOSHUA SPRIGGE
1618–84

§1

The ancient bounds: or liberty of conscience tenderly stated. 1645. Anon; *see* Kiefer, below.

Anglia rediviva: England's recovery, being the history of the army under Sr Thomas Fairfax. 1647, Oxford 1854, ed H. T. Moore, Gainesville 1960 (facs).

Certain weighty considerations humbly tendered to the consideration of the members of the High Court of Justice for the trial of the King. 1648.

§2

Kiefer, B. The authorship of Ancient bounds: Joshua Sprigge not Francis Rous. Church History 22 1953.

NEHEMIAH WALLINGTON
1598–1658

Historical notes and meditations 1583–1649. Ed R. Webb, Historical notices of events occurring chiefly in the reign of Charles I, 2 vols 1869.

SIR EDWARD WALKER
1612–77

The order of the ceremonies used at the celebration of St George's feast at Windsor. 1671, 1674. Anon.

Historical discourses upon several occasions. [Ed H. Clopton] 1705, 1707 (as Historical collections).

A circumstantial account of the preparations for the coronation of Charles II, and a minute detail of that splendid ceremony. 1820.

HENRY GUTHRY, Bishop of Dunkeld
1600?–76

Memoirs: wherein the conspiracies and rebellion against Charles I are briefly and faithfully related. 1702, Glasgow 1747 (with addns), 1748 (with life by G. Crawfurd).

SIR HAMON L'ESTRANGE
1605–60

The reign of King Charles. 1655, 1656 (enlarged). By H.L.

The alliance of divine offices exhibiting all the liturgies of the Church of England since the Reformation. 1659, 1690, 1699, Oxford 1846 (Lib of Anglo-Catholic Theology).

WILLIAM LILLY
1602–81

Monarchy or no monarchy in England. 1651; ed F. Maseres, Select tracts, 1815 (with Several observations upon the life and death of Charles late King of England); rptd with addns as The true history of King James the first and King Charles the First, 1715; ed C. Burman, The lives of Elias Ashmole and Lilly, 1774.

History of his life and times. 1715; ed C. Burman 1774 (with Ashmole's life), 1822.

See also col 2358, below.

SIR RICHARD BELLINGS
d. 1677

The history of the Irish confederation and war in Ireland 1641–3. 1646–9; ed J. T. Gilbert 7 vols Dublin 1882–91; bks 2–3 (inaccurate text) ptd as Fragmentum historicum in J. Lodge, Desiderata curiosa hibernica vol 2, 1772.

GODFREY GOODMAN,
Bishop of Gloucester
1583–1656

§ 1

The fall of man: or the corruption of nature proved by the light of our natural reason. 1616 (2 issues), 1618, 1629 (as The fall of Adam from Paradice).

The creatures praysing God: or the religion of dumbe creatures. 1622 (by G.G.), 1624 (another issue).

The Court of King James the First. Ed J. S. Brewer 2 vols 1839; ed J. E. B. Mayor, Cambridge 1864 (Cambridge Antiquarian Soc).

§ 2

Hakewill, G. In his An apologie of the power and providence of God, 1635 (3rd edn).

Jones, R. F. In his Ancients and moderns, St Louis 1936.

Gundry, D. W. Goodman, Bishop of Gloucester. Church Quart Rev 144 1947.

Harris, V. I. In his All coherence gone, Chicago 1949.

Soden, G. I. Goodman, Bishop of Gloucester. 1953. With bibliography to 1949.

Hepburn, R. W. Goodman: nature vilified. Cambridge Jnl April 1954.

SIR WILLIAM SANDERSON
1586?–1676

§ 1

Aulicus coquinariae: or a vindication in answer to a pamphlet entituled the Court and character of King James [by Sir A. Weldon]. 1650 (anon); rptd in Secret history of the Court of James I, ed Sir Walter Scott 2 vols Edinburgh 1811.

A compleat history of the lives and reigns of Mary Queen of Scotland and of her son James the sixth in vindication against two scandalous authors [Weldon and Wilson]. 2 pts 1656–5.

An answer to a scurrilous pamphlet intituled Observations upon a compleat history of Mary Queen of Scotland and her son James. 1656.

A compleat history of the life and raigne of King Charles from his cradle to his grave. 1658.

Post haste: a reply to Dr Peter Heylyn's appendix. 1658.

Peter pursued: or Dr Heylyn overtaken, arrested and arraigned. 1658.

§ 2

Hard, F. Ideas from Bacon and Wotton in Sanderson's Graphice. SP 36 1939.

FRANCIS OSBORNE
1593–1659

Bibliographies

Madan, F. F. Some notes on the bibliography of Osborne. Oxford Bibl Soc Pbns new ser 4 1950–2. *See* especially for dubious imprints.

Collections

Works in four several tracts. 1673 ('7th edn'), 1682, 1689, 1701.

Miscellaneous works. 2 vols 1722; ed E. A. Parry 1896.

§ 1

A seasonable expostulation with the Netherlands, declaring their ingratitude to and the necessity of their agreement with the commonwealth of England. Oxford 1652 (2 edns anon), 1652.

A perswasive to a mutuall compliance under the present government: a plea for a free state compared with monarchy. Oxford 1652. By F.O.

Political reflections upon the government of the Turks; Nicolas Machiavel [etc]. 1656 (with variants), [Oxford] 1656 (both by F.O.), Oxford 1662.

The private Christians non ultra, by Philolaoclerus. Oxford 1656.

Advice to a son. Oxford 1656 (5 edns anon), Oxford (for London) 1658 (3 edns); pt 2, Oxford 1658 (3 edns with variants); ed E. A. Parry 1896; ed L. B. Wright, Ithaca [1962] (with Precepts of Lord Burghley and Ralegh's Instructions) (Folger Lib).

Historical memoires on the reigns of Queen Elizabeth and King James. London (for Oxford) 1658 (2 edns anon); ed Sir W. Scott, The secret history of the Court of James the First, 2 vols Edinburgh 1811.

A miscellany of sundry essayes, paradoxes [etc]. 1659, 1659; ed B. Fabian, Münster 1969 (facs).

§2

Betz, S. A. E. In Seventeenth-century studies: 2nd ser, ed R. Shafer, Princeton 1937.

ANONYMOUS

The secret history of the reign of James I. In Autobiography and correspondence of Sir Simonds D'Ewes, ed J. O. Halliwell (-Phillipps) 2 vols 1845.

The reign of Charles I. 1656.

(3) BIOGRAPHERS AND AUTOBIOGRAPHERS

JOHN GERARD
1564–1637

Narratio P. Johannis Gerardi de rebus a se in Anglia gestis. Tr and ed G. R. Kingdon 1886 (as During the persecution).

A narrative of the gunpowder plot. Ed J. Morris 1871, 1872 (in The condition of Catholics under James I), 1881 (as The life of Father John Gerard).

The autobiography of an Elizabethan. Tr P. Caraman 1951.

CRESACRE MORE
1572–1649

D.O.M.S. The life and death of Sir Thomas Moore, by M. T. M[ore, or rather C. More]. [Antwerp? 1631], 1642, 1726; ed J. Hunter 1828.

The life and death of Sir Thomas More. Ed J. L. Kennedy, Greenberg Pa 1941. Modernized text.

ROBERT CAREY,
EARL OF MONMOUTH
1560?–1639

Memoirs of the life of Robert Cary, written by himself. Ed John Earl of Corke and Orrery 1759; ed Sir Walter Scott, Edinburgh 1808 (with Naunton, Fragmenta regalia); ed G. H. Powell 1905; ed. F. H. Mares, Oxford 1972.

SYDENHAM (or SYDNAM) POYNTZ
fl. 1624–50

The vindication of Colonel General Poyntz against the false and malicious slanders secretly cast forth against him. 1645.

The vindication of Collonel General Points against the slanders cast forth against him by the army. 1648.

The relation of Sydnam Poyntz 1624–36. Ed A. T. S. Goodrick 1908 (Camden Soc). On Thirty Years' War; see col 2128, above.

PHINEAS PETT
1570–1647

Autobiography. Ed W. G. Perrin 1918 (Navy Records Soc).

SIR SIMONDS D'EWES
1602–50

§1

The journals of all the Parliaments during the reign of Queen Elizabeth. Ed P. Bowes 1682, 1693.

The autobiography and correspondence. Ed J. O.

Halliwell (-Phillipps) 2 vols 1845. Contains also The secret history of King James I, and Sir Richard Wynne, An account of the journey of the Prince's servants into Spain, 1623.

College life in the time of James [the First]. [Ed J. H. Marsden] 1851. Compiled from D'Ewes's unpbd diary.

Journal. Ed W. Notestein, New Haven 1923.

Journal, from the first recess of the Long Parliament to the withdrawal of King Charles from London. Ed W. H. Coates, New Haven 1942, New York 1970.

§2

Carré, M. H. A Puritan at Cambridge. History Today Oct 1963.

Watson, A. G. The library of D'Ewes. 1966 (BM Bicentenary Pbns).

ROBERT BLAIR
1593–1666

Memoirs of the life of Mr Robert Blair in two parts: the first part wrote by himself and the second by Mr William Row. 1754.

The life of Mr Robert Blair, minister of St Andrews: containing his autobiography 1593–1636, with supplement to life, and history of the times to 1680, by W. Row. Ed T. M'Crie, Edinburgh 1848 (Wodrow Soc).

ROBERT MONRO, Major-General
d. 1680

Monro his expedition with the worthy Scots regiment. 2 pts 1637.

A true relation of the proceedings of the Scottish armie now in Ireland, by three letters: the first sent from Monroe. 1642.

A letter of great consequence sent by Monro out of the Kingdom of Ireland concerning the state of the rebellion there; ordered by the Commons [to] be printed. 1643.

A full relation of the expedition of Monroe in the province of Uulster, by authority. 1644.

WILLIAM LAUD,
Archbishop of Canterbury
1573–1645

Collections

Works. Ed W. Scott and J. Bliss 7 vols in 9 Oxford 1847–60 (Lib of Anglo-Catholic Theology).

§1

Diary. In W. Prynne, A breviate of the life of W. Laud, 1644. Garbled text.

The history of the troubles and tryal of William Laud,

wrote by himself; to which is prefixed the diary of his own life. Ed H. Wharton 1695, 1700 (with addns).

An historical account of all material transactions relating to the University of Oxford [during Laud's Chancellorship]. In Remains vol 2, ed H. Wharton 1700.

Bell, E. G. W. Two unpublished letters of Archbishop Laud. Bodleian Lib Record 7 1961.

See also col 1982, above.

EDWARD WALSINGHAM
fl. 1643–54

Britannicae virtutis imago: or the life of Major Generall Smith. Oxford 1644.

Alter Britanniae heros: or the life of Sir Henry Gage. Oxford 1645.

The life of Sir John Digby. Ed G. Bernard, Camden Miscellany 12 1910.

JOSEPH HALL,
Bishop of Exeter and Norwich
1574–1656

Collections

Works. Ed J. Pratt 10 vols 1808; ed P. Hall 12 vols Oxford 1837–9; ed P. Wynter 10 vols Oxford 1863.

§ 1

An humble remonstrance to the High Court of Parliament by a dutiful son of the Church. 1640 (for 1641) (2 edns anon).

Hard measure. 1647, 1660 (in The shaking of the olive-tree), 1710.

Observations of some specialities of divine providence in the life of Joseph Hall. 1660 (with Hard measure, in The shaking of the olive-tree, above).

See also col 1977, above.

— ROE

Memoirs of some actions in which collonel John Birch was engaged [1642–6] written by his secretary [Rowe]. Ed J. and T. W. Webb, Military memoir of Colonel John Birch, 1873 (Camden Soc).

EDWARD HERBERT, 1st BARON HERBERT OF CHERBURY
1583–1648

§ 1

The life and raigne of King Henry the Eighth. 1649, 1672, 1682, 1706 (in White Kennett, Complete history vol 2).

Expeditio in Ream insulam. 1656. Latin version by T. Baldwin of The expedition to the Isle of Rhé, ed Earl of Powis 1860 (Philobiblon Soc) (from ms).

The life of Edward Lord Herbert of Cherbury, written by himself. Strawberry Hill 1764, London 1770, 1771, 1778, 1792, 1809, 1824 etc; in Lives of Lord Herbert of Cherbury and Thomas Elwood, with introductory essays by W. D. Howells, Boston 1877; ed S. Lee 1886, [1906] (rev); ed H. Dircks 1888; ed C. H. Herford, Newtown 1928.

§ 2

Blunden, E. In his Votive tablets, 1931.

Willey, B. Herbert of Cherbury: a spiritual Quixote of the seventeenth century. E Studies 27 1941.

Aaron, R. I. The autobiography of Herbert of Cherbury: the original manuscript material. MLR 36 1941.

Merchant, W. M. Lord Herbert and seventeenth-century historical writing. Trans Honourable Soc of Cymmrodorion 1956.

See also col 1311, above.

SIR ANTHONY WELDON
d. 1649?

The Court and character of King James. 1650, 1651 (whereunto is added the Court of King Charles); ed Sir Walter Scott, The secret history of the Court of James the First, 2 vols Edinburgh 1811; ed G. Smeeton, Smeeton's historical and biographical tracts, 2 vols 1820. Scott also reprints Sir William Sanderson's attack, Aulicus coquinariae, 1650.

RALPH, BARON HOPTON
1598–1652

§ 1

Bellum civile: Hopton's narrative of his campaign in the West 1642–4. Ed H. C. Healey 1902 (Somerset Records Soc).

§ 2

Edgar, F. T. R. Hopton: the King's man in the West 1642–52. Oxford 1968.

SIR KENELM DIGBY
1603–65

Bibliographies etc

Petersson, R. T. Appendix B. In his Sir Kenelm Digby, Cambridge Mass 1956.

Huston, E. G. Digby checklist. Los Angeles 1969 (priv ptd).

§ 1

Articles of agreement made between the French King and those of Rochell; also a relation of the brave sea-fight made by Sr Kenelam Digby. 1628 (with variants).

A coppy of 1, the letter sent by the Queene's Majestie concerning the collection of recusant mony for the Scottish warre; 2, the letter sent by Sir Kenelme Digby and Mr Montague concerning the contribution. 1641, 1641.

Sr Kenelme Digbyes honour maintained. 1641. Attributed.

Private memoirs of Sir Kenelm Digby, written by himself. Ed H. Nicolas 1827. Suppl (castrations) 1828, 1932 (in Bligh, below); ed V. Gabrieli, Rome 1968 (as Loose fantasies).

Journal of a voyage into the Mediterranean [1628]. Ed J. Bruce 1968 (Camden Soc).

See also col 2337, below.

§ 2

Aubrey, J. In his Lives, 1813.

Wood, A. In his Athenae oxonienses, 2 vols 1691–2.

T.L[ongueville]. The life of Digby, by one of his descendants. 1896.

Bligh, E. W. Digby and his Venetia. 1932.

Fulton, J. F. Digby: writer, bibliophile and protagonist of William Harvey. New York 1937.

Harbage, A. Shirley's The wedding and the marriage of Digby. PQ 16 1937.

Gabrieli, V. La missione di Digby alla corte de Innocenzo X. Eng Miscellany (Rome) 5 1954.

— A new Digby letter-book: In praise of Venetia. Jnl Nat Lib of Wales 9–10 1956–8.

—— Digby: un inglese italianato nell' età della Controriforma. Rome 1957.
Petersson, R. B. Sir Kenelm Digby. Cambridge Mass
1956.

SIR THOMAS HERBERT
1606–82

§1

A relation of some yeares travaile, begunne anno 1626 into
Afrique and the greater Asia. 1634 (with engraved title-
page A discription of the Persian monarchy), 1638, 1665,
1667; ed J. Harris, Navigantium atque itinerantium
bibliotheca vol 1, 1705; ed J. H. Moore, New and complete collection of voyages and travels vol 2, [1780?]; ed
W. Foster 1928 (abridged); tr Dutch, 1658; French, 1663.
Threnodia Carolina. 1678, 1702, 1711; ed G. Nicol 1813
(in Memoirs of the two last years of Charles I).

§2

Penrose, B. In his Urbane travellers, Philadelphia 1942.

SIR HUGH CHOLMLEY
1600–57

Memoirs addressed to his sons. 1787, 1870.
Some observations touching the Hothams. In State papers
collected by Edward, Earl of Clarendon vol 2, ed R.
Scrope, Oxford 1773.
Memorials touching the battle of York. Ed C. H. Firth,
Two accounts of the battle of Marston Moor, EHR 5
1890.
Memorialls tuching Scarbrough. Ed C. H. Firth, Sir
Hugh Cholmley's narrative of the siege of Scarborough
1644–5, EHR 32 1917.

SIR HENRY SLINGSBY
1602–58

The diary of Slingsby. Ed D. Parsons 1836. First pbd
abridged with autobiography of Captain John Hodgson as
Original memoirs written during the great Civil War,
[ed Sir Walter Scott], Edinburgh 1806.

JOHN ASHBURNHAM
1603–71

A letter written from Carisbrooke Castle to William
Lenthall. 1647.
A narrative of his attendance on King Charles the First.
2 vols 1830.

JOHN, BARON BERKELEY
1607–78

Memoirs. 1699, 1702; rptd in Harleian miscellany vol 9,
ed T. Park 1812; ed F. Maseres, Select tracts, 1815;
appendix to Ashburnham's Narrative, 1830.

SIR HENRY SPELMAN
1564–1641

Collections

The English works, together with his posthumous works
relating to the laws and antiquities of England [and] the
life of the author. Ed E. Gibson 1723, 2 pts 1727.

HENRY TOWNSHEND
fl. 1640–63

Diary of Henry Townshend of Elmley Lovett 1640–63.
Ed J. W. Willis Bund 4 pts 1915–20 (Worcestershire
Historical Soc).

SIR PHILIP MONCKTON
1620?–79

The Monckton papers. Ed E. Peacock, Philobiblon Soc
Miscellany 15 1877–84.

ANNE, LADY HALKETT
1622–99

§1

Autobiography. Ed J. G. Nichols 1875 (Camden Soc).

§2

Cumming, L. M. Anne, Lady Halkett. Blackwood's Mag
Nov 1924.

MARGARET CAVENDISH,
DUCHESS OF NEWCASTLE
1623–73

§1

A true relation of my birth, breeding and life. 1656 (in
Natures pictures drawn by fancies pencil), 1814; ed
M. A. Lower 1872 (with Life, below); ed E. Jenkins as
The Cavalier and his lady, 1872 (with selection); ed
C. H. Firth 1886 (with Life, below); 1915 (EL).
The life of William Cavendish, Duke of Newcastle. 1667,
1675. See above.
For other works see col 1736, above.

§2

Whibley, C. In his Essays in biography, 1913.
Perry, H. T. E. The first Duchess of Newcastle and her
husband as figures in literary history. Boston 1918.
Woolf, V. In her Common reader, 1925.
Turberville, A. S. In his A history of Welbeck Abbey and
its owners vol 1, 1938.
Meyer, G. D. In his Scientific lady in England 1650–1760,
Berkeley 1955.
Grant, D. Margaret the First. 1957.
Gagen, J. Honor and fame in the works of the Duchess of
Newcastle. SP 56 1959.

MEMOIRS OF CHARLES I

Memoirs of the two last years of King Charles I, by Sir
Tho. Herbert, Major Huntington, Col Edw. Coke and
Mr Hen. Firebrace [et al]. 1702, 1711; ed G. Nicol
1813.

(4) ANTIQUARIES

Reliquiae Spelmannianae: the posthumous works of Sir
H. Spelman relating to the laws and antiquities of
England. Ed E. Gibson with a life of the author, Oxford
1698.

§1

De non temerandis ecclesiis: a tracte of the rights and
respect due unto churches. 1613 (2 further issues

'enlarged'), Edinburgh 1616 (with epistle to the Bishops of the Church of Scotland), London 1616, Oxford 1646, 1668, London 1676.

Archeologus in modum glossarii. Pt 1, 1626; pts 1–2 as Glossarium archaiologicum ed C. Spelman 1664, 1687.

Consilia, decreta, leges, constitutiones in re ecclesiarum orbis britannici. Vol 1, 1639; vol 2, ed C. Spelman 1664.

The growth, propagation and condition of tenures by knight service. 1641.

De sepultura. 1641.

Tithes too hot to be touched. Ed J. Stephens 1646, 1647 (as The larger treatise concerning tithes).

An apology of the treatise de non temerandis ecclesiis; also his epistle to Richard Carew concerning tithes. Ed J. Stephens 1647.

Aspilogia. Ed E. Biss 1654.

Villare anglicum: or a view of the townes of England. 1656. By Spelman and R. Dodsworth.

Of the law terms. 1684.

The history and fate of sacrilege. 1698, 1846, 1853; ed C. F. S. Warren 1895; tr French 1698 (abridged), 1798; German, 1878.

§2

Powicke, M. Spelman and the Concilia. Proc Br Acad 16 1930.

Schuyler, R. L. The antiquaries and Spelman. Proc Amer Philosophical Soc 90 1946.

Van Norden, L. Peiresc and the English scholars. HLQ 12 1949.

—— Spelman on the chronology of the Elizabethan College of Antiquaries. HLQ 13 1950.

Cronne, H. A. In English historical scholarship in the sixteenth and seventeenth centuries, ed L. Fox 1956.

Wilson, J. S. Spelman and the Royal Commission on fees. In Studies presented to Sir Hilary Jenkinson, Oxford 1957.

THOMAS HABINGTON
1560–1647

The epistle of Gildas. [Tr T. Habington] 1638, 1652 (unsold sheets with new title-page).

The antiquities of the Cathedral Church of Worcester; to which are added Antiquities of Chichester and Lichfield. [Ed R. Rawlinson] 1717, 1723.

A survey of Worcestershire. Ed J. Amphlett 7 pts 1893–9 (Worcestershire Historical Soc).

WILLIAM SOMNER
1598–1669

The antiquities of Canterbury. 1640; ed N. Battely 1703.

Dictionarium saxonico-latino-anglicum. 2 pts Oxford 1659, 1 vol Oxford 1701 (with addns by T. Benson).

A treatise of gavelkind, both name and thing. 1660, 1726 (rev and much enlarged, with life by White Kennett).

Chartham news: or a brief relation of some strange bones there lately digged up. Ed J. Somner 1669; 1703 (in Antiquities of Canterbury).

A treatise of the Roman ports and forts in Kent. Ed J. Brome, Oxford 1693 (with notes by F. Gibson and a life of Somner by White Kennett).

SIR ROGER TWYSDEN
1597–1672

§1

The commoners liberty: or the English-mans birthright. 1648. Anon.

Historiae anglicanae scriptores X. 1652. Ed Twysden.

An historicall vindication of the Church of England in point of schism, as it stands separated from the Roman. 1657, 1675; [ed G. E. Corrie], Cambridge 1847.

Certaine considerations upon the government of England. Ed J. M. Kemble 1849 (Camden Soc).

An historicall narrative of the two Howses of Parliament and either of them, their committees and agents violent proceedings against Sir Roger Twysden. Ed L. B. L[arking] as Journal, Archaeologia Cantiana 1–4 1858–61.

§2

Twisden, J. R. Twysden. TLS 28 Feb 1935.

—— and C. H. Ward. The family of Twysden and Twisden: their history and archives. 1939.

Jessup, F. W. Sir Roger Twysden. 1965.

MATTHEW CARTER
b. 1625?

A most true relation of that as honourable as unfortunate expedition of Kent, Essex and Colchester. [London] 1650 (by 'M.C.'); ed P. Morant and T. Luffkin, Colchester [1750?] etc; also in King, Parliament and army: more particulars as related by M. Carter enlarged by W. Howard-Flanders, 1906.

Honor redivivus: or an analysis of honor and armory. 1655, 1660, 1669, 1673.

N. J. E.

II. LETTERS, DIARIES, AUTOBIOGRAPHIES AND BIOGRAPHIES

(1) LETTERS

General Studies

Albert, P. Le genre épistolaire chez les anciens, chez les modernes. Paris 1869.

Williams, H. English letters and letter writers. 1886.

Rannie, D. W. Letter writing as a form of literature. Oxford 1895.

Paul, H. The art of letter writing. Nineteenth Century July 1898.

Allen, P. S. Some sixteenth-century manuscript letter-books. Trans Bibl Soc 12 1913.

Thompson, E. N. S. In his Literary bypaths of the Renaissance, New Haven 1924. Ch 3.

Robertson, J. The art of letter writing during the sixteenth and seventeenth centuries. 1942.

Vulliamy, C. E. English letter-writers. 1945.

Irving, W. H. The providence of wit in the English letter writers. Durham NC 1955.

Davis, N. Style and stereotype in early English letters. Leeds Stud in Eng 1 1967.

Letters

(in alphabetical order)

Allen, P. S. (ed). Some letters of masters and scholars 1500–30. EHR 22 1907.

Allen, William. Some correspondence of 1579–85. Ed P. Ryan, Catholic Record Soc Miscellany 7 1911.

Arundel, Thomas Howard, Earl of. The life, correspondence and collections. Ed M. F. S. Hervey, Cambridge 1921.

Ascham, Roger. Familiarium epistolarum libri tres. Ed W. Elstob, Oxford 1703; Whole works, ed J. A. Giles 1865, 3 vols New York 1965. Latin correspondence (1539–68) in Giles edn tr M. A. Hatch, Ithaca 1948.

Ashmole, Elias. Diary with original letters. Ed C. Burman 1717, 1774, Reading 1925; Autobiographical and historical notes, his correspondence etc, ed C. H. Josten 5 vols Oxford 1966.

Bacon, Francis. Collected works with his letters and life. Ed J. Spedding et al 14 vols 1857–74.

Basire, Isaac. Correspondence 1634–75. Ed W. N. Darnell 1831.

Bateson, Mary (ed). Collection of original letters from the Bishops to the Privy Council 1564. Camden Soc Miscellany 9 1893.

Beaumonts of Yorkshire. Letters. Ed W. D. Macray 1884. 15th–17th centuries.

Birch, Thomas (compiler). The Court and times of James I: a series of historical and confidential letters. Ed R. F. Williams 2 vols 1849.

—— The life of Henry Prince of Wales. 1760. Includes letters 1595–1612.

Blundell, William. Letters to his friends 1620–98. Ed M. Blundell 1933.

Bodley, Sir Thomas. Letters to Thomas James. Ed G. W. Wheeler, Oxford 1926. 1599–1613.

Bowes, Robert. Correspondence. Ed J. Stevenson 1842 (Surtees Soc). 1577–83.

Bromley, G. (ed). Original royal letters 1619–65. 1787. Includes letters by Charles I, II, James II, Prince Rupert et al.

Browne, Sir Thomas. Selected correspondence. In Works vol 6, ed G. L. Keynes 1928, 1964 (vol 4).

Bryskett, Lodowick. The life and correspondence. Ed H. R. Plomer and T. P. Cross, Chicago 1927. Reprints letters March 1580–Aug 1581 and excerpts others.

Cabala sive scrinia sacra. 2 pts 1654, 1691. Covers the reigns of Henry VIII–Charles I and includes letters by Francis Bacon, William Cecil, Francis Walsingham et al.

Cambridge University. Letters and documents 1500–72. Ed J. Lamb 1838.

Cary, H. (ed). Memorials of the great civil war in England 1646–52. 2 vols 1842. Includes original letters.

Cecil, Sir Robert. Letters to Sir George Carew. Ed J. Maclean 1864 (Camden Soc). 1600–3.

Chamberlain, John. Letters. Ed S. Williams 1861 (Camden Soc); ed E. P. Statham 1921; ed N. E. McClure, Amer Philosophical Soc Memoirs 12 1939; ed E. M. Thomson, New York 1965.

Charles I. Letters to Queen Henrietta Maria in 1646. Ed J. Bruce 1856 (Camden Soc).

—— Correspondence with Sir Edward Nicholas. In John Evelyn, Diary, ed W. Bray and H. B. Wheatley vol 4 1879. Letters 1641–8.

Clare College. Letters and documents. Ed J. R. Wardale, Cambridge 1903.

Clifford, Lady Anne. Life, letters and work. Ed G. C. Williamson, Kendal 1922.

Conway, Anne Viscountess. Correspondence with Henry More and their friends 1642–84. Ed M. H. Nicolson, New Haven 1930.

Conybeare, John. Letters and exercises. Ed F. C. Conybeare 1905. Elizabethan schoolmaster in late 1500's.

Copley, Thomas. Letters to Elizabeth I and her ministers. Ed R. C. Christie 1897 (Roxburghe Club). Letters 1572–84.

Cornwallis, Jane, Lady. Private correspondence 1613–44. 1842.

Cosin, John. Correspondence. Ed G. Ormsby 2 vols 1869–72. (Surtees Soc). Letters 1616–71.

Coverdale, Myles (ed). Letters of the martyrs. 1564; ed E. Bickersteth 1837. Cranmer, Ridley, Hooper, Taylor et al.

Cowley, Abraham. Letters. Ed A. H. Nethercot, MLN 43 1928.

Cranmer, Thomas. Miscellaneous writings and letters. Ed J. E. Cox 1846 (Parker Soc). Documents 1534–56.

Cromwell, Oliver. Writings. Ed T. Carlyle 2 vols 1845; rev S. C. Lomas 2 vols 1904; ed R. B. Merriman 2 vols Oxford 1902; ed W. C. Abbott 4 vols Cambridge 1937–47. All edns include letters.

Daniel, Samuel. Panegyricke with certaine epistles. 1603. Letters to Egerton, Howard, Lady Anne Clifford et al.

Davenant, Charles. Letters. Ed G. Davies and M. Schofield, HLQ 4 1941.

Davison, William. Life. Ed N. H. Nicolas 1823. Many letters ptd in full.

Dee, John. Letter nine years since declaring his faithfulness to the Queen. 1605.

D'Ewes, Sir Simonds. Correspondence. Ed J. O. Halliwell 2 vols 1845. To 1649.

Digges, Dudley. The compleat ambassador. 1655. Correspondence 1570–3 and 1581 by Walsingham, Burghley et al, on the intended marriage of Elizabeth.

Donne, John. Letters from the Continent 1611–12. Ed R. E. Bennett, PQ 19 1940.

—— Selected letters. Ed E. Gosse 2 vols 1899; ed W. Milgate, Oxford 1967 (in Satires etc); ed E. Simpson, Oxford 1967 (in Selected prose).

Dryden, John. Letters of Dryden and to him. Ed C. E. Ward, Durham NC 1942.

Dugdale, Sir William. Life, diary and correspondence. Ed W. Hamper 1827.

Edmondes, Sir Thomas. A selection from the correspondence. Ed G. G. Butler 1913 (Roxburghe Club). Letters 1592–9.

Egerton papers from the time of Elizabeth and James I. Ed J. P. Collier 1840 (Camden Soc). Letters by members of Elizabeth's Privy Council.

Eliot, Sir John. Life. Ed J. Forster 2 vols 1864. Numerous letters from Eliot and Sir Ben Grenville.

Elizabeth I. Original letters of her times. Ed T. Wright 2 vols 1838.

—— A narrative of her girlhood in contemporary letters. Ed F. A. Mumby 1909. Letters 1533–59.

—— Letters. Ed G. B. Harrison 1935.

Ellis, H. (ed). Original letters. 3 sers 11 vols 1825–46. Each ser includes letters from before 1400 to after 1700.

—— Letters of eminent literary men of the sixteenth, seventeenth and eighteenth centuries. 1843 (Camden Soc).

Erasmus. Opus epistolarum. Ed P. S. and H. M. Allen 12 vols Oxford 1906–58.

Essex, Walter, Robert and Robert Devereux, 1st, 2nd and 3rd Earls of Essex. Lives and letters. Ed W. B. Devereux 2 vols 1853.

Essex, Robert Devereux, 2nd Earl of. Two excellent letters on travell. nd. One by Essex, the other by Sidney.

Evans, W. and T. (ed). Letters of the early Friends. Friends Lib 11 1847.

Evelyn, John. Memoirs and familiar letters 1642–1704. Ed W. Bray 2 vols 1818; ed H. B. Wheatley 3 vols 1906.

Fairfax correspondence. In Memoirs of the reign of Charles I, ed J. G. W. Johnson 2 vols 1848. To 1642.

Farington papers. Ed S. M. Ffarington 1856 (Chetham Soc). Letters and documents 1547–1688.

Ferrar papers. Ed B. Blackstone, Cambridge and New York 1938. Includes selection of family letters.

Fitzherbert, Thomas. Letters 1608–10. Ed L. Hicks, Catholic Record Soc Pbns 41 1948.

Fletcher, Giles. English works. Ed L. E. Berry, Madison 1964. Includes letters 1576–1609.

Foley, H. (ed). Records of the English Province of the Society of Jesus. 7 vols 1877–83. 16th–17th century documents with letters of Father Anthony Rivers.

Fox, George. Letters to William Dewsbury and others. Ed H. J. Cadbury, Jnl of Friends Historical Soc 1948 (suppl 22).

Fox, Richard. Letters 1486–1527. Ed P. S. and H. M. Allen, Oxford 1929.

Fugger news-letters. Ed V. von Klarwill 2 sers 1924–6. Trn; covers 1568–1605.

Gairdner, J. (ed). Letters illustrative of the reigns of Richard III and Henry VII. 2 vols 1873 (Rolls ser).

Gardiner, S. R. (ed). Letters and papers illustrating the relations between Charles II and Scotland in 1650. 1894 (Scottish Historical Soc).

Gawdy, Philip. Letters. Ed I. H. Jeayes 1906 (Roxburghe Club). Letters 1579–1616 to various members of his family.

Gresham, Sir Thomas. Life and times. Ed J. W. Burgon 2 vols 1839. Includes letters.

Grey, Lady Jane. Letters. Ed D. Geary, Ilfracombe 1951.

Hakluyt, Richard and Richard. Original writings and correspondence. Ed E. G. R. Taylor 2 vols 1935 (Hakluyt Soc).

Halliwell(-Phillipps), J. O. (ed). Letters illustrative of science in England from Elizabeth to Charles II. 1841 (Historical Soc of Science).

Hardwicke, Philip Yorke, 2nd Earl of. Hardwicke state papers 1501–1726. 2 vols 1778. Includes letters of Mary Stuart, Nicholas Throgmorton, E. Stafford et al.

Harington, H. (ed). Nugae antiquae: original papers written during the reigns of Henry VIII, Edward VI, Queen Mary, Elizabeth and James I. 2 vols 1769; ed T. Park 2 vols 1804.

Harington, Sir John. Letters and epigrams. Ed N. E. McClure, Philadelphia 1930.

Harley, Lady Brilliana. Letters. Ed T. T. Lewis 1854 (Camden Soc). Covers 1625–43.

Harvey, Gabriel. Letter-book. Ed E. J. L. Scott 1884 (Camden Soc). Covers 1573–80.

Hatton, Christopher Hatton, 1st Viscount. Correspondence of the Hatton family. Ed E. M. Thompson 1878 (Camden Soc). Chiefly letters to Christopher Hatton.

Hearne, T. (ed). Sylloge epistolarum a variis angliae principibus scriptarum. Oxford 1716. Letters mainly from Tudor period.

Henry VIII. Love letters to Anne Boleyn. Ed T. Hearne, Oxford 1720; ed G. A. Crapelet, Paris 1826; ed L. Black 1907, 1933 (rev); ed H. W. Trovillion 1933.
— Selected letters and documents. Ed M. St Clare Byrne 1936.
— State papers published under the authority of Henry VIII. 11 vols 1830–52.
— Letters and papers of the reign of Henry VIII 1509–47. Ed J. S. Brewer, J. Gairdner, R. H. Brodie 21 vols in 33 pts 1862–1910. Vol 1 rptd 1920, vol 1 addns 1929–32.

Herbert family. Epistolary curiosities. Ed R. Warner 2 vols in 1 Bath 1818. 17th–18th centuries.

Hoskyns, John. Life, letters and writings. Ed L. B. Osborn, Yale Stud in Eng 87 1937.

Howell, James. Epistolae Ho-Elianae. Ed J. Jacobs 1890, introd by A. Repplier 2 vols New York 1907. Familiar letters 1618–50.

Hutton, Matthew Correspondence. Ed J. Raine 1843 (Surtees Soc). Letters 1565–1638 of Hutton family.

Isham, G. (ed). Correspondence of Bishop Brian Duppa and Sir Justinian Isham 1650–60. Northamptonshire Records Soc 17 1955.

James IV. Letters 1505–13. Ed R. L. Mackie and Anne Spilman, Scottish Historical Soc 45 1953.

James V. Letters. Ed R. K. Hannay and D. Hay, Edinburgh 1954.

Jonson, Ben. Works. Ed C. H. Herford and P. Simpson 11 vols Oxford 1925–52. Vol 1 includes letters and Drummond correspondence 1605–31.

Knyvett letters 1620–44. Ed B. Schofield, Norfolk Records Soc 20 1949.

Laneham, Robert. Letter describing the entertainment of Queen Elizabeth at Kenilworth Castle in 1575. Ed F. J. Furnivall, New York 1907.

Locke, John. Lettres à ses amis Nicolas Thoynard, Phillippe van Limborch et Edward Clarke. Ed H. Ollion and T. J. De Boer, Hague 1912.
— Correspondence [with] Edward Clarke. Ed B. Rand, Oxford 1927.

Loseley manuscripts. Ed A. J. Kempe 1836. Contains miscellaneous letters by Donne, Walter Ralegh, James I et al.

Lupset, Thomas. Life, works, treatises and letters. Ed J. A. Gee, New Haven 1928.

Marvell, Andrew. Poems and letters. Ed H. M. Margoliouth 2 vols Oxford 1927. Vol 2 contains letters 1653–78.

Mary Queen of Scots. Letters. Ed A. Strickland 3 vols in 2 1843.

Mary Stuart. Letters. Ed and tr W. B. Turnbull 1845.

Matthew, Sir Tobie. Life. Ed A. H. Mathew and A. Calthrop 1907. Includes letters.

Milton, John. Letters of state to princes and republics of Europe 1649–59. Ed E. Phillips 1694.
— Private correspondence and academic exercises. Tr P. B. Tillyard, introd by E. M. W. Tillyard, Cambridge 1932.
— Complete prose works. Ed D. Bush et al 5 vols in 4 New Haven 1953–66. Each vol contains section of the total correspondence 1624–60.

Moorhouse, E. H. (ed). Letters of English seamen 1587–1808. 1910.

More, Sir Thomas. Correspondence. Ed W. E. Campbell 1924 (Catholic Lib); ed E. F. Rogers, Princeton 1947 (218 letters 1499–1535). A calendar of the correspondence by E. F. Rogers, EHR 37 1922.

Newcastle, Margaret Cavendish, Duchess of. Letters to her husband. Ed R. W. Goulding 1909.

Newdigate, Anne (Fitton), Lady. Gossip from a muniment-room. Ed A. E. Newdigate-Newdegate 1897, 1898. Chiefly the correspondence of Anne Fitton.

Nicholas, Sir Edward. Correspondence. Ed G. F. Warner 4 vols 1886–1920 (Camden Soc). Covers 1641–60.

Nickolls, J. (ed). Letters and papers addressed to Oliver Cromwell found among the collection of John Milton. 1743.

Ormerod, G. (ed). Epistolary relics of Lancashire and Cheshire antiquaries 1653–73. Chetham Soc Miscellany 1 1851. Letters from Dugdale, Sir Peter Leycester et al.

Osborne, Dorothy. Letters to Sir William Temple. Ed E. A. Parry 1888, 1903 (enlarged); ed G. C. Moore Smith, Oxford 1928 (from ms). Letters to her future husband 1652–4.

Oxinden letters 1607–42. Ed D. Gardiner 1933. Letters of Henry Oxinden and his circle.

Oxinden and Peyton letters 1642–70. Ed D. Gardiner 1937.

Parker, Matthew. Correspondence by and to him 1535–75. Ed J. Bruce and T. T. Perowne 1853 (Parker Soc).

Paston letters. Ed J. Gairdner 3 vols 1872–5, 4 vols 1901, 6 vols 1904 (expanded to include letters 1417–1509); A. D. Greenwood 1920 (selections); ed N. Davis, Oxford 1958 (selection 1426–84). See H. S. Bennett, The Pastons and their England, Cambridge 1922, 1932.

Paston, Lady Catherine. Correspondence 1603–27. Ed R. Hughey, Norfolk Records Soc Pbns 14 1941. Mainly addressed to her son William Paston.

Peck, Francis (ed). Desiderata curiosa. 2 vols 1732–5; ed T. Evans 2 vols 1779. Contains correspondence of Bishop Chaderton of Chester and other material of Elizabeth's reign.

Pepys, Samuel. Correspondence. Ed J. R. Tanner 2 vols 1926 (1679–1703), 1929 (1662–79); ed H. T. Heath, Oxford 1955 (1663–92).

Pole, Reginald. Epistolae Poli et aliorum ad se. Ed A. M. Quirini 5 vols Brescia 1744–57.

Porcacchi, T. (ed). Lettere di xiii huomini illustri. Venice 1565, [1580?]. On period of Henry VIII.

Porter, Endymion. Life and letters. Ed D. Townshend 1897.

Ralegh, Sir Walter. Works. Ed W. Oldys 8 vols 1829, New York 1964 (vol 8 includes intermittent letters 1583–1618); Life, ed E. Edwards 2 vols 1868 (letters interspersed).

Rand, B. (ed). Correspondence of George Berkeley and Sir John Percival. Cambridge 1914.

Rigaud, S. P. and S. J. (ed). Correspondence of scientific men of the seventeenth century. 2 vols Oxford 1841–62. Letters by Newton, Barrow, Wallis et al.

Rochester, John Wilmot, Earl of. Life, writings and private correspondence. Ed J. Prinz, Leipzig 1927.

Rochester-Savile letters 1671–80. Ed J. H. Wilson, Columbus 1941.

Rupert, Prince. Memoirs and private correspondence. Ed E. B. G. Warburton 3 vols 1849.

Sidney papers. Ed A. Collins 2 vols 1746. Letters and other material written and collected by Henry, Philip and Robert Sidney on state affairs, Court gossip etc.

Sidney, Sir Philip. Miscellaneous works and letters. Ed W. Gray, Oxford 1829, Boston 1860, 1893.
— Correspondence with Hubert Languet. Ed S. A. Pears 1845; ed W. A. Bradley, Boston 1912. Covers 1573–80.

Sitwell, G. (ed). Letters of the Sitwells and Sacheverells. 2 vols Scarborough 1900–1. Especially for George Sitwell.

Spenser, Edmund. Prose works. Ed R. Gottfried, Baltimore 1949 (includes letters).
— Three proper and wittie familiar letters. 1580. Portions ed G. G. Smith in Elizabethan critical essays vol 1, Oxford 1904.

Stuart, Lady Arabella. Life. Ed E. T. Bradley 2 vols 1889. Includes letters.

Symcotts, John. Letters of an English physician in the early seventeenth century. Ed F. G. Marcham, Isis 16 1931; ed F. N. L. Poynter and W. J. Bishop, Bedfordshire Historical Records Soc Pbns 31 1951 (with correspondence, case histories etc). A 17th-century doctor and his patients.

Tanner letters. Ed C. McNeill, Dublin 1943. On Irish affairs in 16th–17th centuries.

Totnes, George Carew, Earl of. Letters to Sir Thomas Roe. Ed J. Maclean 1860 (Camden Soc). Covers 1615–17.

Trevelyan papers. Ed J. P. Collier, W. C. and C. L. Trevelyan 1857–72 (Camden Soc). Covers c. 1318–1776.

Tusmore papers. Ed L. G. W. Legg, Oxfordshire Records Soc 20 1939. Transcripts of letters and other papers 1309–1806, mainly addressed to Fermor family of Tusmore.

Tytler, P. F. (ed). England under the reigns of Edward VI and Mary, illustrated in a series of letters. 2 vols 1839.

Verheyden, A. L. E. (ed). Une correspondance adressée par des familles protestantes des Pays-Bas à leurs coreligionnaires d'Angleterre. Bulletin de la Commission Royale d'Histoire 120 1955.

Verney family. Letters and papers. Ed J. Bruce 1853 (Camden Soc) (letters 1616–39); Memoirs, ed F. P. and M. M. Verney 4 vols 1892–6, 2 vols 1904 (rev), 1925 (covers 1642–96).

Wadham, Dorothy. Letters 1609–18. Ed R. B. Gardiner 1904.

Walsingham, Sir Francis. Seine Zeit. Ed K. Stählin, Heidelberg 1908. Includes letters.

Ward, B. M. (ed). The seventeenth Earl of Oxford. 1928. Prints many letters.

Wood, M. A. E. (ed). Letters of royal and illustrious ladies of Great Britain. 3 vols 1846. 12th–17th centuries.

Wotton, Sir Henry. Reliquiae Wottoniae. Ed I. Walton 1651, 1654, 1672, 1685. Collection of lives, letters, poems.
— Letters and dispatches 1617–20. Ed G. Tomline 1850 (Roxburghe Club); Life and letters, ed L. P. Smith 2 vols Oxford 1907.

Wren, Sir Christopher. Letters to John Fell. Ed W. D. Caroe, Oxford 1923.

Wright, T. (ed). Queen Elizabeth and her times. 2 vols 1838. Correspondence of Burghley, Leicester, Walsingham, Hatton et al.
— Three chapters of letters relating to the suppression of monasteries. 1843 (Camden Soc).

Wyatt, Sir Thomas. Life and letters. Ed K. Muir, Liverpool 1963.

Zurich letters. Ed and tr H. Robinson 3 sers 1842–7 (Parker Soc). On English Reformation 1531–1602.

(2) DIARIES

General Studies

Ponsonby, A. (ed). English diaries. 1923; More English diaries, 1927; Scottish and Irish diaries, 1927.

Fyfe, J. G. (ed). Scottish diaries and memoirs 1550–1746. Stirling 1928.

D'Oyley, E. (ed). English diaries. 1930; More English diaries, 1938. Selections from diaries 16th–19th centuries.

Aitken, J. English diaries of the 16th, 17th and 18th centuries. New York 1941.

O'Brien, K. English diaries and journals. 1943.

Matthews, W. (ed). British diaries: an annotated bibliography of British diaries written between 1442 and 1942. Los Angeles 1950, Gloucester Mass 1967.

Gräser, A. Das literarische Tagebuch: Studien über Elemente des Tagebuch als Kunstform. Saarbrücken 1955.

Willy, M. English diarists: Evelyn and Pepys. 1963.
— Three women diarists: Celia Fiennes, Dorothy Wordsworth, Katherine Mansfield. 1964.

Diaries

(in alphabetical order)

Anon. Public diary 1442–3. Journal of one of the suite of Thomas Bekington. Ed N. H. Nicholas 1828.

Anon. Prison diary 1580–5. In J. Bayley, The history and antiquities of the Tower of London vol 2, 1821.

Anon. Military journal 1588. In Historical Mss Commission report, Earl of Ancaster's mss, 1907.

Anon. Travel diary 1649–52. Ms Bodley Rawlinson collection D76.

Archer, Sir John. Legal diary 1658. Essex Rev 30 1922.

Ashmole, Elias. Memoirs by way of a diary. 1717 (with letters); The diary and will of Ashmole, ed R. T. Gunther, Oxford 1927; ed C. H. Josten 5 vols Oxford 1966 (in Autobiographical and historical notes).

Assheton, Nicholas. Country social diary 1617–18; The journal of Nicholas Assheton, ed F. R. Raines 1848 (Chetham Soc).

Ayshcombe, William. Social diary 1608–33. Historical Mss Commission 10th Report, appendix vi.

Baillie, Robert. Public diary 1637–62; The letters and journals of Robert Baillie, ed D. Laing 3 vols Edinburgh 1841–2; vol 4, 1867 (Bannatyne Club).

Bannatyne, Richard. Public diary 1570–73. In Journal of the transactions in Scotland, ed J. G. Dalyell, Edinburgh 1806.

Barlow, Edward. Sea diary 1659–1703. In Barlow's journal, ed B. Lubbock 2 vols 1934.

Bassompière, François de. Diplomatic diary Sept–Dec 1626. Memoirs of the Embassy of de Bassompière, tr G. W. Croker 1819.

Birrel, Robert. Public diary 1532–1605. In Diary of Birrel, Edinburgh 1798; Extracts from the diary, Edinburgh 1820.

Blundell, Capt William. Military diary 1660–80. In Crosby records, ed T. E. Gibson 1880.

Bourgoyne, Dr. Medical diary 1586–7. In The last days of Mary Stuart, ed S. Cowan 1907.

Brereton, Sir William. Travel diary 1634–5. In Travels in Holland, ed E. Hawkins 1844 (Chetham Soc).

— Travel diary June–Aug 1635. In North Country diaries, 1914 (Surtees Soc); ed P. H. Brown, Early travellers in Scotland, Edinburgh 1891.

Brodie, Alexander. Religious diary 1652–80. In The diary of Brodie, ed D. Laing, Aberdeen 1863.

Brownlow, Sir John. Country diaries and notebooks 1660–76. In Records of the Cust family ser 2, ed E. Cust 1909.

Bulkeley, Robert. Country diary 1630–6. Anglesey Antiquarian Soc Trans 1937.

Casaubon, Isaac. Study diary 1597–1614. In Ephemerides Isaaci Casauboni, ed J. Russell 2 vols Oxford 1850.

Charles II. Escape from Worcester. Ed W. Matthews, Los Angeles 1966. First-hand accounts by Charles et al.

Cork, Richard Boyle, 1st Earl of. Public diary 1611–43. In The Lismore papers 1st ser, ed A. B. Grosart 5 vols 1886.

Crosfield, Thomas. University diary 1626–54 (gap 1640–53); Diary of Crosfield, ed F. S. Boas, Oxford 1935.

Cuningham, Thomas. Public diary 1640–54. In The journal of Cuningham, ed E. J. Courthope, Edinburgh 1928.

Dee, Dr John. Astrologer's diary 1577–1601. In The private diary of Dee, ed J. O. Halliwell 1842 (Camden Soc).

D'Ewes, Sir Simonds. J. H. Marsden's College life in the time of James I, 1851, based upon his diary.

Douay College. Diaries 1598–1654. Ed E. H. Burton and T. L. Williams, Catholic Records Soc 10–11 1911.

Dowsing, William. Puritan diary 1643–4. In The journal of Dowsing, ed R. Loder, Woodbridge 1786; The rich man's duty, Woodbridge 1840; ed C. H. T. White, Ipswich 1885.

Drake, Nathan. Civil War diary 1644–5. 1860 (Surtees Soc).

Drummond, Sir William. Private diary 1657–9. In Miscellany of Scottish Historical Society 1941.

Dugard, Rev Thomas. Teacher's diary 1632–43. Ms BM additional mss 23,146.

Dugdale, Sir William. Antiquary's diary 1643–86. In The life, diary and correspondence of Dugdale, ed W. Hamper 1827; diary for 1656 in Athenaeum 3 Nov 1888.

Edward VI, King of England. Public diary 1549–52. In Literary remains of Edward VI, ed J. G. Nichols 1857; rptd 1884 (Clarendon Historical Reprints).

Evelyn, John. Memoirs [1640–1706] illustrative of the life and writings of Evelyn. Ed W. Bray 2 vols 1818; Diary and correspondence, ed J. Forster 4 vols 1850–2, re-ed A. Dobson 3 vols 1906; Diary, ed E. S. de Beer 6 vols Oxford 1955.

Eyre, Adam. Country diary 1646–9. In Yorkshire diaries, 1875 (Surtees Soc).

Fanshawe, Lady Anne. Memoirs. Ed H. C. Fanshawe 1829; ed B. Marshall 1905.

Forman, Simon. Astrologer's diary 1564–1602. In Autobiography and diary of Forman, ed J. O. Halliwell 1849.

Fox, George. Journal [1624–75]. Ed N. Penney 2 vols 1901, Cambridge 1911; ed J. L. Nickalls, Cambridge 1952.

Gershow, Frederic. Travel diary Sept–Oct 1602. Trans Royal Historical Soc 6 1892.

Gordon, Patrick. Military diary 1655–68. In Passages from the diary of Gordon, ed J. Robertson 1859 (Spalding Club).

Greene, John. EHR 43–4 1928–9. Legal diary 1635–59 (with gaps).

Greene, Thomas. Public diary 1614–17. In C. M. Ingleby, Shakespeare and the enclosure of common fields at Welcombe, 1885.

Hay, Andrew. Diary. Ed A. G. Reid, Edinburgh 1901. Private diary 1659–60.

Henry, Rev Philip. Diaries and letters. Ed M. H. Lee 1882. Religious diary 1650–84.

Henslowe, Philip. Diary. Ed J. P. Collier 1845 (Shakespeare Soc) (corrupt text); Henslowe's diary, ed W. W. Greg 1904, 1908; ed R. A. Foakes and R. T. Rickerts, Cambridge 1968. Theatre diary 1592–1603.

Hoby, Lady Margaret. Diary of Lady Hoby. Ed D. M. Meads 1930; extracts in Trans Royal Historical Soc 2 1908. Domestic diary 1599–1605.

Hope, Sir Thomas. A diary of the public correspondence. Edinburgh 1843 (Bannatyne Club); account and extracts in Scottish Historical Rev 3 1905–6. Public diary 1633–46.

Isham, Sir John. Diary. Ed W. Rye, Norwich 1875. Travel diary 1626.

Jaffray, Alexander. Diary 1833, 1834. Ed J. Barclay, Aberdeen 1856. Public diary 1649–50.

Josselin, Rev Ralph. Diary of Rev Josselin. Ed E. Hockliffe 1908 (Royal Historical Soc). Country diary 1644–81.

Lambarde, William. Genealogical memoranda relating to the Lambarde family. 1869 (priv ptd). Family diary 1504–88.

Lamont, John. Diary. Edinburgh 1830 (Maitland Club) (originally pbd 1810). Public diary 1649–71.

Laud, Rt Rev William. History of the troubles and trials 1695; rptd in his Works vol 3, Oxford 1847–60. Ecclesiastical diary 1592–1643.

Leicester, Robert Sidney, 2nd Earl of. Sydney papers. Ed R. W. Blencowe 1825. Public diary 1646–61.

Leslie, Rt Rev John. In Bannatyne Club miscellany, ed D. Laing vol 3, 1855. Public diary April–Oct 1571.

Luke, Sir Samuel. Journal. Ed I. G. Philip 3 vols 1950–3 (Oxfordshire Records Soc).

Machin, Henry. Diary of Machin. Ed J. G. Nichols 1848 (Camden Soc). Public diary 1550–63.

Maisse, André Hurault de. Diplomatic diary 1597–8. In The journal of De Maisse, tr G. B. Harrison 1931.

Manningham, John. Diary of Manningham. Ed J. Bruce 1868 (Camden Soc). Social diary 1602–3.

Melville, Rev James. Diary. Ed G. R. Kinloch, Edinburgh 1829; Autobiography and diary, ed R. Pitcairn, Edinburgh 1842; extracts in Fyfe, Scottish diaries, Stirling 1928. Public diary 1571–1610.

Mildmay, Lady Grace. Private diary and autobiography 1570–1617. Quart Rev 215 1911. Account and extracts.

Mildmay, Sir Humphrey. Country diary 1633–51. Ed P. L. Ralph, New Brunswick NJ 1947.

Milton, John. Life records. Ed J. French 5 vols New Brunswick NJ 1949–58.

Moore, Robert. Diarium historico poeticum. 1595.

Mordaunt, Elizabeth (Cary), Viscountess. Religious diary 1656–78; The private diarie, Duncairn 1856, 1861.

Oglander, Sir John. Country diary 1595–1648. In The Oglander memoirs, ed W. H. Long 1888; A Royalist's notebook, ed F. Bamford 1936.

Pembroke, Lady Anne Clifford, Countess of. Domestic diary 1616–19 with reminiscences from 1603; Memoirs illustrative of York 1847–8; Diary, ed V. Sackville-West 1923.

Pepys, Samuel. Private diary 1660–9; Memoirs, ed Richard Lord Braybrooke 2 vols 1825, 1828, 5 vols 1848–9, 1854; Diary and correspondence deciphered with additional notes, ed M. Bright 4 vols 1875–9; Diary, ed H. B. Wheatley 8 vols 1893–6; Diary: a new and complete transcription, ed R. C. Latham and W. Matthews 11 vols 1970–.

Powell, Walter. Private diary 1603–54. Diary. Ed J. A. Bradney, Bristol 1907.

Reresby, Sir John. Public diary 1654–89. Memoirs. Ed J. Cartwright 1875; ed A. Browning, Glasgow 1936 (best edn).

Rogers, Rev Richard. Religious diary Feb 1586/7. In Two Elizabethan Puritan diaries, ed M. M. Knappen, Chicago 1933.

Rous, Rev John. Public diary 1625–42 [intermittent]. In Diary, ed M. A. E. Green 1856 (Camden Soc).

Sanderson, Christopher. Family diary 1640–88. In Diary and pedigree, ed F. C. Beazley 1905.

Sandwich, Edward Montagu, 1st Earl of. Naval diaries 1659–65. In Journal, ed R. C. Anderson 1929 (Naval Records Soc).

Shaftesbury, Anthony Ashley Cooper, 1st Earl of. Public diary 1645–50. In Life vol 1, ed W. D. Christie 1871.

Slingsby, Sir Henry. Civil War diary 1638–48. In Diary, ed D. Parsons 1836.

Smith, Capt John. Travels and works. Ed E. Arber, introd A. G. Bradley 2 vols Edinburgh 1910.

Stodart, Robert. Travel diary 1628–9. In Journal, ed D. Ross 1935.

Townshend, Henry. Civil War diary 1640–3. In Diary, ed J. W. W. Bund 2 vols 1920.

Twysden, Sir Roger. Parliamentary affairs 1641–8. Ed L. B. Larking, Archaeologia Cantiana 1–4 1858.

Von Vendenheym, Hans Jacob Wurmsser. Travel diary March–May 1610. In England as seen by foreigners, ed W. B. Rye 1865.

Von Wedel, Lupold, of Pomerania. Travel diary 1584–5. In Trans Royal Historical Soc 9 1895.

Walsingham, Sir Francis. Public diary 1570–83. Camden Miscellany 6 1871.

Walton, Izaak. The compleat angler. 1653 etc; ed R. B. Marston 2 vols 1888.

Ward, Rev John. Private diary 1648–79. In Diary, ed C. Severn 1839.

Ward, Dr Samuel. Religious diary 1595–9 with some entries 1601, 1621, 1625, 1629. In Two Elizabethan Puritan diaries, ed M. M. Knappen, Chicago 1933.

Wariston, Lord, Sir Archibald Johnston. Public diaries 1632–60 with gaps. In Diary, 4 vols 1896–1940 (Scottish Historical Soc).

Whiteway, William. Public diary 1618–34. Antiquary 39 1903; Dorset Natural History & Antiquarian Field Club Proc 13 1892.

Wood, Anthony. Antiquarian diary 1657–95. In Life and times of Wood, ed A. Clark 5 vols Oxford 1891–1907.

Worthington, Dr John. University diary 1635–8. In Diary and correspondence, 3 vols 1847–86 (Chetham Soc).

(3) AUTOBIOGRAPHIES

General Studies

Calamy, Edward. An historical account of my own life. Ed J. T. Rutt 2 vols 1829. Introd contains a history of autobiography to 18th century.

Of autobiographies. Atlantic Monthly Dec 1906.

Burr, A. R. B. The autobiography. Boston and New York 1909.

Wohlfarth, P. Die Selbstbiographie als Formproblem. Berlin 1923.

Hendrichs, D. Geschichte der englischen Autobiographie von Chaucer bis Milton. Leipzig 1925.

Clark, A. M. Autobiography: its genesis and phases. Edinburgh 1935.

Uhlig, K. Die Autobiographie als erziehungswissenschaftliche Quelle. Hamburg 1936.

Bates, E. S. Inside out: an introduction to autobiography. 2 vols 1936–7, 1 vol New York 1937.

Misch, G. Geschichte der Autobiographie. 3 vols in 6 Berne 1949–62; tr 2 vols 1950.

Shumaker, W. English autobiography: its emergence, materials and form. Berkeley 1954.

Matthews, W. (ed). British autobiographies: an annotated bibliography of British autobiographies published or written before 1951. Los Angeles 1955, Hamden Conn 1968.

Reichenkron, G. (ed). Formen der Selbstdarstellung. Berlin 1956.

Bottrall, M. Every man a phoenix: studies in seventeenth-century autobiography. 1958.

Osborn, J. M. The beginnings of autobiography in England. Los Angeles 1959.

Diaz Arrieta, H. Historia de la biografía. Santiago Chile 1960.

Pascal, R. Design and truth in autobiography. 1960.

Delany, P. British autobiography in the seventeenth century. 1969.

Autobiographies
(in alphabetical order)

Allen, Hannah. Satan his methods and malice baffled. 1683.

Anglesey, Arthur Annesley, 1st Earl. Memoirs. 1693.

Ames, William. A declaration of the witness of God manifested in me from my youth. 1656.

Ashburnham, John. A narrative. 1830. Covers 1646–7.

Ashmole, Elias. Memoirs. Ed C. Burman 1717; ed R. T. Gunther, Oxford 1927; ed C. H. Josten 5 vols Oxford 1966.

Aubrey, John. Miscellanies. 1696. Preface with autobiographical details.

Bale, John. The vocacyon of Johan Bale to the Bishoprick of Ossorie. Rome 1553.

Bamfield, Col. Joseph. Apology. [Hague?] 1685.

Barnes, Ambrose. Memoirs of the life. Ed W. H. D. Longstaffe 1867 (Surtees Soc).

Baxter, Richard. Reliquiae Baxterianae: passages of his life and times. Ed M. Sylvester 1696; ed J. M. Lloyd Thomas 1931 (selection).

Berkeley of Stratton, John Berkeley, 1st Baron. Memoirs. 1699.

Bernardi, Major John. A short history. 1729.

Blair, Robert. Life. Ed T. M'Crie, Edinburgh 1898; Memoirs, Edinburgh 1754.

Blakhall, Gilbert. Brieffe narration. Aberdeen 1844. Covers 1631–49.

Blaugdone, Barbara. An account. 1691. Quaker's testimony.

Bodley, Sir Thomas. Life. Oxford 1647, 1913 (as Trecentale Bodleianum).

Boyle, Mary, Lady Warwick. Autobiography. Ed T. C. Croker 1848 (Percy Soc).

Boyle, Robert. An account of Philaretus during his minority. In Life of Boyle, ed T. Birch 1734.

Bramston, Sir John. Autobiography. Ed Lord Braybrooke 1845 (Camden Soc). On Restoration times.

Briggs, Thomas. An account of the travels and sufferings. 1685. Quaker.

Buchanan, George. Opera omnia. Edinburgh 1715.

Bunyan, John. Grace abounding. 1666; ed G. B. Harrison 1928; ed R. Sharrock, Oxford 1962 (OSA).

Burnet, Bishop Gilbert. Autobiography. In A supplement to Burnet's history of my own time, ed H. C. Foxcroft, Oxford 1902.

Burnyeat, John. The truth exalted. In Journal of the lives of William Caton and Burnyeat, 1691, 1839. Quaker.

Burrough, Edward. A true description. 1663. Quaker.

Burton, Henry. Narration of the life. 1643.

Camden, William. Memorabilia de se ipso. In Thomas Smith, Vita, 1691. His life to 1622.

Carleton, Capt George. Military memoirs. 1728; ed C. H. Hartmann 1929; ed A. W. Lawrence 1929. Soldier of fortune 1672–1713.

Castlehaven, James Touchet, 3rd Earl of. Memoirs of James Lord Audley. 1680. Covers 1642–51.

Caton, William. Journal of the life. 1689. Quaker 1652–64.

Chappell, William. Vita. In Desiderata curiosa, ed F. Peck 1735; Appendicis ad J. Lelandi collectanea, ed T. Hearne 1770. Written in 1640s.

Chomley, Sir Hugh. Memoirs. 1787. Civil War.

Clanricarde, Ulick de Burgh, Marquis of. Memoirs. 1722. Covers 1650–2.

Clarendon, Edward Hyde, 1st Earl of. An account of the life. Oxford 1759; sections in History of the rebellion, 3 vols Oxford 1702–4. Covers c. 1609–67.

Clavell, John. Recantation of an ill-led life. 1628.

Coppin, Richard. Truth's testimony. 1655.

Cork, Richard Boyle, 1st Earl of. The Lismore papers. Ed A. B. Grosart 5 vols 1886–8; True remembrances, Life of Boyle, ed T. Birch 1734.

Courthope, Sir George. Memoirs 1616–85. Ed S. C. Lomas 1907 (Camden Soc).

Cowper, William. Life and death. In Workes, 1629.

Coxere, Edward. Adventures by sea. Ed E. H. W. Meyerstein, New York 1946. 17th century.

Crab, Roger. The English hermit. 1655. Leveller.

[Croke, Charles]. Fortune's uncertainty by Rodolphus. 1667; ed I. M. Westcott, Oxford 1959.

Crook, John. A short history of the life. 1706. 17th-century Quaker.

Curwen, Alice. A relation of the labour, travail and suffering. 1608. Quaker.

Dalrymple, Sir James, Viscount Stair. Apology for himself. 1690, Edinburgh 1825 (Bannatyne Club).

Derby, James Stanley, 7th Earl of. An account of the main events of life to 1650. Ms copy at Chetham's Lib Manchester.

Dering, Sir Edward. Autobiographical notes 1598–1640. Ms in Bodley, Gough Kent 20.

D'Ewes, Sir Simonds. Autobiography. Ed J. O. Halliwell 1845. College life.

Digby, Sir Kenelm. Private memoirs. Ed N. H. Nicholas 1827. Passages expurgated in this edn are bound in some copies and ptd as appendix to E. W. Bligh, Sir Kenelm Digby and his Venetia, 1932.

Ellwood, Thomas. History of the life. 1714; ed G. C. Crump 1900.

Evans, Arise. An eccho to the voice from heaven. 1652.

Evelyn, John. Memoires for my grand-son. Ed G. L. Keynes, Oxford 1926.

Ewen, C. H. L. (ed). The golden chalice: a documented narrative of an Elizabethan pirate. Paignton 1939. On John Callice or Challis of Tintern.

Fanshawe, Lady Anne. Memoirs. Ed N. H. Nicholas 1829; ed H. C. Fanshawe 1907. 17th century.

Farnsworth, Richard. The heart opened by Christ. 1654. Quaker.

Flamsteed, John. An account of the Rev John Flamsteed, by Francis Baily 1835. Covers 1646–1716.

Forman, Simon. Autobiography and personal diary. Ed J. O. Halliwell 1849. 16th century.

Fox, George. A journal of the life. 1694; ed N. Penney, Cambridge 1911; ed J. L. Nickalls, Cambridge 1952. 17th-century Quaker.

Fox, Margaret. A brief collection of remarkable passages. 1710.

Fuller, William. The whole life. 1702. To 1691.

Gerard, Father John. Autobiography. Tr and ed G. R. Kingdon 1886; tr P. Caraman, New York 1952, London 1956. Written in Latin 1609.

Godfrey, Thomas. Autobiography and diary. Ed J. G. Nichols, Topographer and genealogist vol 2 1853. Early 17th century.

Green, Theophilus. Narrative of some passages of the life. 1702. Quaker.

Greene, Thomas. A declaration to the world of my travel and journey out of Aegypt into Canaan. 1659. Quaker.

Guise, Sir Christopher. Memoirs of the family of Guise. Ed G. Davies 1917. Written c. 1662–5.

Halkett, Lady Anne (Murray). Autobiography. Edinburgh 1701; ed J. G. Nichols 1875 (Camden Soc).

Hall, Rev Joseph. Autobiography. In Works vol 1, ed J. Pratt 1808.

Halyburton, Thomas. Memoirs of the life. Edinburgh 1715, Princeton 1833. From 1674.

Hamilton, Lady Margaret. A pairt of the life. Edinburgh 1827. Late 16th and early 17th century.

Hane, Joachim. Journal [1653–4]. Ed C. H. Firth, Oxford 1896.

Haselton, Richard. Strange and wonderful things. 1595. Experiences among Moors 1583–93.

Herbert of Cherbury, Edward Herbert, Baron. Life. Ed Horace Walpole, Strawberry Hill 1764; ed C. H. Herford 1928.

Herbert, George. Country parson. Ed H. C. Beeching, Oxford 1898, 1916. First pbd in Remains vol 1, 1652.

Heywood, Oliver. Autobiography and diaries. Ed J. H. Turner 4 vols Brighouse 1872–85. Later 17th century.

Hickey, William. Memoirs. Ed A. Spencer 4 vols 1919–25.

Hobbes, Thomas. Life. 1680; Vita in Opera quae latine scripsit vol 1, ed G. Molesworth 1839.

Hoby, Sir Thomas. A booke of the travaile and lief. Ed E. Powell, Camden Soc Miscellany 10 1902. Covers 1547–64.

Hodgson, Capt John. Autobiography. Ed W. Scott, Edinburgh 1806; ed J. H. Turner, Brighouse 1882. Later 17th century.

Holland, Hugh. To my mayden muse. Preface to his Pancharis. In Illustrations of old English literature vol 2, ed J. P. Collier 1866.

Howgill, Francis. The inheritance of Jacob discovered. 1656. Quaker.

Hutchinson, Lucy. Life. In Memoirs of the life of Colonel Hutchinson, 1806; ed C. H. Firth 2 vols 1885. 17th century.

James II, King of England. Memoirs. Tr A. L. Sells, Bloomington 1962. His compaigns as Duke of York 1652–60.

Jonson, Ben. Conversations with Drummond. Ed D. Laing 1842 (Shakespeare Soc); ed R. F. Patterson 1923.

Keimer, Samuel. Brand pluck'd from the burning. 1718.

Kidder, Richard. Life. Ed A. E. Robinson 1924 (Somerset Record Soc). Covers 1633–1703.

Kirkman, Francis. The unlucky citizen. 1673.

Knollys, Hanserd. Life and death. 1692.

Laud, William. History of the troubles and trial. 1695; in Works vol 3, Oxford 1847–60; Autobiography, Oxford 1839.

Lilly, William. History of his life. 1715, 1822. 17th century.

Lister, Joseph. Autobiography. Ed T. Wright 1842.

Livingstone, John. Autobiography. In Select biographies vol 1, ed W. K. Tweedie, Edinburgh 1845. To 1666.

Lucas, T. (ed). Memoirs of the lives, intrigues and comical adventures of the most famous gamesters and sharpers from the reigns of Charles II to Anne. 1714.

Ludlow, Edmund. Memoirs. 3 vols Vivay 1698–9; ed C. H. Firth 2 vols Oxford 1894. 17th century.

Lurting, Thomas. The fighting sailor. 1711. Covers 1646–66.

Macky, John. Memoirs of the Secret Services. 1733. During reigns of William III, Anne, George I.

Martindale, Adam. Life. Ed R. Parkinson 1845 (Chetham Soc). 17th century.

Matthew, Sir Tobie. True historical relation. Ed A. H. Mathew 1904. Begins 1605.

Mellidge, Anthony. A true relation. 1656. Quaker.

Melvill, Sir Andrew. Memoirs. 1918. Soldier-of-fortune 1650–80.

Melville, Sir James. Memoirs. Ed G. Scott 1683; ed A. F. Stewart, New York 1929. 16th century.

Monmouth, Robert Carey, Earl of. Memoirs. Ed John Earl of Cork and Orrery 1759; ed G. H. Powell 1905. To 1626.

More, Henry. Autobiography. In Opera omnia vol 1, 1679. Partially tr R. Ward, Life, 1710.

Moryson, Fynes. An itinerary. 1617. End of 16th century.

Muggleton, Lodowick. The acts of the witnesses of the spirit. 1699, 1764.

Newcastle, Margaret Cavendish, Duchess of. A true relation of the birth. In Nature's pictures, 1656; ed E. Bridges 1814. Appended to her Life of the Duke of Newcastle, ed C. H. Firth 1906; ed E. Rhys nd (EL).

Newcome, Henry. Autobiography. Ed R. Parkinson 2 vols 1852 (Chetham Soc). Covers 1627–95.

Nimmo, James. Autobiography of Scottish covenanter in the 17th century. Edinburgh Scottish Historical Soc 6 1887.

North, Roger. Autobiography. 1887. Later 17th century.

Ogilvie, John. Relatio incarcerationis. Douai 1615; tr C. J. Kerslake 1877.

Patrick, Rev Simon. Autobiography. Oxford 1839.

Peeke, Richard. Three to one. 1626.

Persons (or Parsons), Robert. Autobiography. 2 vols 1905–7 (Catholic Record Soc). In Elizabeth I's reign.

Peters, Hugh. A dying father's last legacy to an onely child. 1660.

Peters, John. A brief narration of the life. 1709. Quaker.

Pett, Phineas. Autobiography. Ed W. G. Perrin 1918 (Navy Record Soc). To 1638.

Powell, Vavasor. Life and death. 1671; ed T. Jackson, Library of Christian biography vol 12, 1840.

Poyntz, Sydnam. Relation. Ed S. Goodrick 1908 (Royal Historical Soc). Covers 1624–36.

Pringle, Walter. Memoirs. Edinburgh 1723; ed W. Wood, Edinburgh 1847. Mid 17th century.

Rawdon, Marmaduke. Life. Ed R. Davies 1863 (Camden Soc). 17th century.

Raymond, Thomas. Autobiography. In Memoirs of the family of Guise, ed G. Davies 1917 (Camden Soc). Mid 17th century.

Reresby, Sir John. Memoirs. 1734, Glasgow 1936 (best edn). Later 17th century.

Robinson, Matthew. Autobiography. In J. E. B. Mayor, Cambridge in the 17th century pt 2, Cambridge 1856.

Rofe, George. The righteousness of God to man. 1656. Quaker.

Salmon, Joseph. Heights in depths and depths in heights. 1651.

Shaftesbury, Anthony Ashley Cooper, 1st Earl of. Memoirs, letters and speeches. 1859. Contains fragment of autobiography 1621–39.

Sibbald, Sir Robert. Memoirs. Ed F. P. Hett 1932. Mid-17th century.

Smith, Capt John. The true travels. 1630; Works, 1884.

Stout, William. Memoirs of a seventeenth-century Quaker. Ed J. A. Frees, Friends' Quart Examiner 56 1922.

Symonds, Thomas. The voice of the just uttered. 1656. Quaker.

Thornton, Alice. Autobiography. Ed C. Jackson 1875 (Surtees Soc). Covers 1629–69.

Turner, Sir James. Memoirs. Ed I. Thomson, Edinburgh 1829. Covers 1632–70.

Veitch, William. Memoirs of Veitch and Bryson. Ed T. M'Crie, Edinburgh 1825. Later half of 17th century.

Vere, Sir Francis. Commentaries. 1657. Military memoirs.

Warwick, Mary Rich, 4th Countess of. Autobiography. Ed T. C. Croker 1848 (Percy Soc). 17th century.

Weston, Father William. Autobiography. In The troubles of our Catholic forefathers, by John Morris, 1875, continued in Catholic Record Soc Miscellany 1 1905; tr P. Caraman, New York 1955. On reign of Elizabeth I.

Whiston, William. Memoirs of the life. 1749. Late 17th century.

Whitelocke, Bulstrode. Annals of his life. BM additional mss 37,341–7; extracts in R. H. Whitelock, Life, 1860.

Whitelocke, Sir James. Liber familicus. 1858 (Camden Soc). Early 17th-century.

Whythorne, Thomas. Autobiography. Ed J. M. Osborn, Oxford 1961, 1962 (modernized). Later 16th century.

Wilson, Arthur. Observations of God's providence. In Desiderata curiosa vol 2, ed F. Peck 1735; ed P. Bliss, Oxford 1814. First half of 17th century.

Wood, Anthony. Life and times 1632–95. Early life of the 17th-century antiquary in BM ms Harley 5409. Ed A. Clark 5 vols Oxford 1889–1900.

[Woodcock, Thomas?]. Account of some remarkable passages in the life of a private gentleman. 1708. Ascribed to Defoe.

(4) BIOGRAPHIES

General Studies

Taylor, I. Beginnings of European biography. 1827.

Lee, S. Principles of biography. 1911.

Dunn, W. H. English biography. New York 1916.

Benson, A. C. The art of the biographer. Trans Royal Soc of Lit 6 1926.

Johnston, J. C. Biography: the literature of personality. New York 1927.

Nicolson, H. The development of English biography. 1927.

Schuett, M. Die englische Biographie der Tudor-Zeit. Hamburg 1930.

Stauffer, D. A. English biography before 1700. Cambridge Mass 1930.

Ludwig, E. Die Kunst der Biographie. Paris 1936.

Ortega, E. C. Historia de la biografía. Buenos Aires 1945.

Romein, J. M. De biografie: een inleiding. Amsterdam 1946.

Pinto, V. da S. Introduction to English biography in the seventeenth century. 1951.

Dresden, S. De structuur van de biografie. Hague 1956.

Edel, L. Literary biography. Toronto 1957.

Garraty, J. A. The nature of biography. 1957.

Clifford, J. L. (ed). Biography as an art: selected criticism 1560–1960. New York 1962.

Altick, R. D. Lives and letters: a history of literary biography in England and America. New York 1965.

Biographies
(in alphabetical order)

Alleine, Joseph. Life and death, by G. Newton, T. Alleine, R. Fairclough et al. [1668–72], 1673.

Andrews, Margaret. Life and death. 1680. Anon.

Anthoine, Nicholas. Account of the life and tryal of Anthoine, burnt for Judaism in 1632. Anon; rptd in Harleian miscellany vol 2.

Arminius, James. Life and death, by J.K. 1672.

Arthur, King. The most ancient and famous history. 1634. Anon.

Athanasius, St. The history of the life and actions, N.B. Catholick. 1664.

Aubrey, John. Brief lives. Ed A. Clark 2 vols Oxford 1898; ed O. L. Dick 1958.

Bacon, Francis. The life of the honourable author. Preface to Bacon, Resuscitatio, ed W. Rawley 1657.

Bacon, Nicholas. A remembraunce of the woorthie and well imployed life, by G. Whetstone. 1578.

Baker, Father Augustin. An account of the life. Probably by C. Gascoign 1663; Bodley ms Wood B4.

Bale, John. Illustrium majoris Britanniae scriptorum summarium in quinque centurias divisum. Ipswich 1548, Basle 1557–9 (expanded).

— Actes or unchaste examples of the Englysche votaryes. 1549.

— Index of British and other writers. Ed R. L. Poole, Oxford 1902.

Barksdale, Clement. Memorials of worthy persons, two decades. 1661; 3rd decade, 1662; 4th, 1663.

— A remembrancer of excellent men. 1670. On Protestant churchmen.

Barnes, Dr Robert. The whole workes of Tyndall, Firth and Barnes. 1573. Prefatory life by John Foxe.

Barrow, Isaac. Works. 4 vols 1683–7, 9 vols 1859. 1683 contains life of Barrow by A. Hill.

Barwick, John. The life of translated from Latin to English. 1724 (Latin life by P. Barwick 1721); ed G. F. Barwick 1903.

Bates, George (ed). The lives, actions and executions of the prime actors and principal contrivers of that horrid murder of Charles I. 1661.

Baxter, Margaret. A breviate of the life, by R. Baxter. 1681.

Beaton, David. The tragedy, by Sir David Lyndsay. 1546. Illustrates influence of Lydgate.

Becket, Thomas. Life. Ed J. C. Robertson 7 vols 1875 (Rolls Ser). Includes several pre-1200 lives.

— Life, by A.B. 1639.

— Tres Thomae, by T. Stapleton. Douai 1588.

— Life of in verse, by L. Wade 1497 (ms Bennet College Cambridge).

Bedell, Bishop William. True relation of the life and death of. Ed T. W. Jones 1872 (Camden Soc) (by his son William Bedell).

— Speculum episcoporum. Ed E. S. Shuckburgh, Cambridge 1902. By his son-in-law Alexander Clogie.

Bedford, Francis, Earl of. The life, death and devine vertues, by G. Whetstone. 1585.

Bedloe, Capt William. Life and death. 1681. Anon; defamatory.

Birch, Colonel John. Military memoir by Roe, his secretary. Ed J. and T. W. Webb 1873 (Camden Soc).

Blair, Robert. Life. 1663; ed T. McCrie 1848 (Wodrow Soc).

Blakman, John (ed). Collectarium mansuetudinum et bonorum morum regis Henrici vi. [1510?]; rptd T. Hearne 1732; rptd and tr M. R. James, Cambridge 1919.

Blood, Thomas. Remarks on the life and death. 1680.

Blount, Thomas Pope (ed). Censura celebriorum authorum. 1690.

— Characters and censures of the most considerable poets. 1694.

Bolton, Robert. Foure last things, with the life and death, by E. Bagshaw. 1633.

Bradwardine, Thomas. In Sir H. Savile, De causa Dei, 1618. Short Latin biography as preface.

Bramhall, John. Life, by J. Lymeric. Preface to Works, Dublin 1677.

Brathwait, Richard (ed). The schollers medley: or a discourse upon historicall and poeticall relations. 1614. Shows relation of history to biography.

— The lives of all the Roman emperors. 1636. From Caesar to Ferdinand II.

Brettergh, Katherin. Deaths advantage little regarded with the Christian life and godly death of, [by W. Harrison?]. 1601, 1617 (5th edn). Puritan.

Brice, Thomas (ed). A compendious register of the patient sufferings of the members of Jesus Christ and the cruelly burned within England from Edward VI to Elizabeth. 1559; rptd E. Arber, English garner vol 4, 1882.

Browne, Sir Thomas. [Character sketch]. In Posthumous works, ed J. Whitefoot 1712. Whitefoot first knew Browne c. 1637.

Buckland, Robert (ed). Lives of women saints of England. Ed C. Horstmann 1886 (EETS). Written c. 1610.

Burgh, Sir John. The description of and his unfortunate death, by R. Markham. 1628.

Cecil, William, Lord Burghley. The life of that great statesman. 1732. Written shortly after his death in 1598.

— The compleat statesman. Ed F. Peck, Desiderata curiosa, 1779.

Butler, Nathaniel. The penitent murderer [of John Knight], by R. Yearwood. 1657.

Campion, Edmund. Vita et martyrium, by J. Fenne. In Concertatio ecclesiae catholicae in Anglia, 1583.

Caraccioli, Galeaceo. The Italian convert, by W. Crashaw. 1635. Written before 1609.

Cavendish, William. Life, by Margaret Duchess of Newcastle. 1667; ed C. H. Firth 1886.

Chandos, John. The glorious life and honourable death, by W. Wyrley. In The true use of armorie, 1592.

Charles I, King of England. Eikon basilike by J. Gauden. 1648; Short view of the life and reign [by P. Heylyn?], 1658; The life and reigne, by J. Milton, 1651; The royal martyr, by R. Perrinchief, 1676; Compleat history of the life and raigne, by W. Sanderson, 1658; The life and actions, by Sir E. Walker in Historical discourses, 1705 (written 1655); Life and raigne, by L. Wood, 1659.

Charles II, King of England. An imperfect pourtaicture by W. Charleton. 1661; Eikon basilike by D. Lloyd, 1660; A character by G. Savile, 1750, ed W. Raleigh 1912; A character by S. Tuke or G. Morley, 1660.

Chaucer, Geoffrey. Life by T. Speght. In Preface to 1598 edn of Chaucer's poems.

Churchyard, Thomas (ed). A lamentable description of the warres in Flaunders since the last foure years of Charles V to 1578. 1578.

Clarendon, Edward Hyde, 1st Earl of (ed). The history of the rebellion and civil wars in England. 3 vols Oxford 1702–4; ed B. Bandinel 7 vols Oxford 1849; ed W. D. Macray 6 vols Oxford 1888.

Clark, Samuel (ed). Collection of the lives of ten eminent divines. 1662; The marrow of ecclesiastical history, 1675; Lives of sundry eminent persons, 1683.

Clitherow, Margaret. Vita & martyrium, by J. Mush 1612. Catholic life written 1586.

Colet, John. The life by Erasmus. Cambridge 1661. Tr T. Smith.

Collier, Jeremy (ed). The great historical, geographical, genealogical and poetical dictionary. 1694; later edns and vols 1701, 1705, 1721. Illustrates encyclopaedic tendency of late 17th century.

Cosin, Richard. Vita et obitus, by W. Barlow. 1598.

Cotton, John. The life and death, by J. Norton. 1658.

Cowley, Abraham. Account of the life and writings, by T. Sprat. Preface to Cowley's Works, 1668. Latin life as preface to edn of Cowley's Latin poems, 1668.

Cromwell, Oliver. The pourtaiture. 1658 (anon); Flagellum: or the life, death, birth and burial [by S. Tuke or J. Heath], 1663, 1665 (3rd edn); The history, by R. Burton, 1692; Historie and policie of the Lord Protector from his cradle to his tomb, by H. Dawbeny, 1659; Brief reflexions on his life, by R. Flecknoe, 1659; The perfect politician, by H. Fletcher, 1660; The history by J. Heath, 1663, rptd Harleian miscellany.

Cromwell, Thomas. The historie of the life and death, by M. Drayton. 1607; rptd in 1610 edn of Mirror for magistrates.

Cusack, George. The life and death of the great sea-robber. 1676. Anon.

Defamatory biography. *See* A handlist of printed books in the Wood collection, Bodley nos 365–73, and 424–8. A cat may look upon a king, 1652 (brief calumniatory lives of English kings from William to Charles II) (anon).

Deloney, Thomas (ed). The gentle craft shewing what famous men have been shoomakers in this land. 1648. Written 1597–1600.

Derby, James Stanley, Earl of. Private devotions and miscellanies. Ed F. R. Raines 3 vols 1867 (Chetham Soc).

Digby, Sir John. Hector britannicus. Ed G. Bernard 1910 (Camden Soc). Probably by E. Walsingham.

Donne, John. The life and death, by I. Walton. As preface to Donne, LXXX sermons, 1640.

Drake, Sir Francis. The life and death, by S. Clark. 1671; His honorable lifes commendation and his tragicall deathes lamentation by C. Fitz-Geffrey, 1596.

Drummond, William (ed). History of the lives and reigns of the five James's, Kings of Scotland. 1655, 1711.

Dudley, Lady Alice, Duchess. A mirrour of Christianity, by R. Boreman. 1669.

Dugdale, William (ed). Monasticon anglicanum. 3 vols 1655–73; Antiquities of Warwickshire, 1656.

Duppa, Brian. The author's life. Preface to The history of the Church of Scotland by J. Spotswood, 1655. Anti-Puritan.

Edward I and Edward II, Kings of England. Chronicles of the reigns. Ed W. Stubbs 2 vols 1882–3 (Rolls ser).

Edward II, King of England. History by Henry Cary, Lord Falkland. 1680, 1680 (expanded); History by Sir Robert Howard 1689 (also attributed to G. Savile); The deplorable life and death, by F. Hubert [?], 1628; Vita et mors, ed W. Stubbs 1883 (Rolls ser).

Edward III, King of England. Victorious reigne, by T. May, 1635. Verse.

Edward IV, King of England. Historie, by W. Habington. 1640.

Edward V, King of England. The pitifull life and unfortunate death, by T. More. 1641.

Edward VI, King of England. Literary remains. Ed J. G. Nichols 2 vols 1857 (Roxburghe Club); Annales of England containing the reigns of Henry VIII, Edward VI and Mary, by F. Godwin, 1630 (tr from Latin edn 1616).

Elizabeth I, Queen of England. The life and death of from the wombe to the tombe. 1639 (heroical verse) (anon); A collection of the felicities, by F. Bacon, written in Latin and pbd in trn in W. Rawley, Resuscitatio, 1657; The historie of the life and reigne, by T. Browne, 1629; Her life and troubles from the cradle to the Crowne by T. Heywood, 1631; Fragmenta regalia by R. Naunton 1641, rptd Harleian miscellany vol 2 1744; Historical memoires by F. Osborne, 1658.

Essex, Robert, Earl of. A parallel between Essex and Buckingham, by H. Wotton 1641.

Falkland, Lady Letice, Viscountess. Holy life and death, by J. Duncon. 1647, 1649, 1653; ed M. F. Howard 1908.

Farr, Richard. The cheating solliciter cheated. 1665.

Ferrar, Nicholas. Two lives by his brother John and by Dr Jebb. Ed J. E. B. Mayor, Cambridge 1855; The Ferrar papers, ed B. Blackstone, Cambridge 1938 (life of Nicholas by his brother John).

Firth, C. H. (ed). Stuart tracts 1603–93. 1903.

Fox, George (ed). Book of miracles. Ed J. H. Cadbury, Cambridge 1948.

Foxe, John (ed). Actes and monuments. 1554, 1563; ed J. Pratt 8 vols 1877 (4th edn). Narrative of the days of the Reformation, ed J. G. Nichols 1859 (Camden Soc).

Fuller, Thomas (ed). The history of the worthies of England. 1662; ed J. Nichols 2 vols 1811; ed P. A. Nuttall 3 vols 1840; ed J. Freeman 1952 (abridged).
— Life. 1661 (anon); An elegie upon Fuller, by J. Heath, 1661.

Gage, Sir Henry. Life of Gage, Governor of Oxford, by E. Walsingham. Oxford 1645.

Godolphin, Margaret. Life, by J. Evelyn. Ed S. Wilberforce 1847. Written 1678.

Grenville, Richard. The most honorable tragedie, by G. Markham. 1595. Verse.

Grosteste, Robert. Vita, by R. Bardney. In Wharton, Anglia sacra vol 2. Written 1503.

Hainam, Richard. History of that incomparable thief. 1656; The desperate life and deserved death, [c. 1656] (anon).

Hamilton, James and William, Dukes of Hamilton and Castleherald. Memoires by G. Burnet, 1677; Life and death of James by N. Needham, 1649.

Harpsfield, Nicholas. Historia anglicana ecclesiastica. 1622. Written c. 1575.

Henry III, King of England. Troublesome life and raigne. 1642 (anon); A short view, 1627 (anon); A brief survey, 1680.

Henry V, King of England. The first English life. Ed C. L. Kingsford, Oxford 1911 (anon); Acts, by P. Basset nd; Historia, by R. Redman, ed C. A. Cole 1858 (Rolls ser) (written 1536–44).

Henry VII, King of England. Historie of the raigne, by Francis Bacon. 1622.

Henry VIII, King of England. The life and raigne, by Edward Lord Cherbury. 1649, 1672, 1682, 1741; The flower of fame, by U. Fulwell 1575, rptd Harleian miscellany suppl 1813; Analyticall character, by J. Howell as preface to Cherbury, Henry VIII, 1649.

Herbert, George. Prefatory view of the life, by B. Oley. Preface to Herbert, Remains, 1652; Life by I. Walton, 1670.

Heywood, Thomas (ed). The general history of women. 1624, 1657; Exemplary lives and acts of nine the most worthy women of the world, 1640.

Holinshed, Raphael (ed). Chronicles of England, Scotlande and Ireland. 1577.

Hooker, Richard. Account of his holy life and happy death. 1662; Life by I. Walton, 1665 as preface to Works, 1666.

James I, King of England. *See* Drummond, above.

James II, King of England. Historical memoires. 1683 (anon); Original papers, ed J. Macpherson 2 vols 1775; Life, ed J. S. Clarke 2 vols 1816; Papers, 1925 (Roxburghe Club) (diplomatic reprint of original ms).

James, Thomas (ed). The Jesuits downefall with a life of Father Persons. 1612.

Jones, Henry. The bloody murtherer. 1672. Sensational.

Jonson, Ben. Ionsonus virbius. 1638. Various elegies pbd shortly after his death.

Knox, John. Last days, by R. Bannatyne. Ed D. H. Fleming 1913 (Knox Club) (written c. 1572); Life, by G. Buchanan as preface to History of the Church of Scotland, 1644.

Laud, William. A true relation of the birth and life. 1641 (anon); rptd Harleian miscellany vol 4; History of the life and death, by P. Heylyn, 1668; The history of the tryals and troubles, ed H. Wharton 1695.

Leland, John (ed). Commentarii de scriptoribus britannicis. Ed A. Hall, Oxford 1709. Written 1534–43.

Luther, Martin. Life and death, by T. Hayne. 1641.

Martyn, William (ed). Historie and lives of twentie Kings of England. 1615, 1628, 1638. Patriotic and popular.

Mary Stuart, Queen of Scotland. Compleat history of the lives and reigns of Mary Stuart and James VI, by W. Sanderson. 1656; The history of the life and death by W. Stranguage, 1624.

Milton, John. Account of his life, by E. Phillips. Preface to Letters of state written by Milton, 1694; Life by J. Toland as preface to Works, 1698; The earliest life, ed E. S. Parsons, 1902 (rptd from EHR); The early lives, ed H. Darbishire 1932.

More, Sir Thomas. [Short Latin life]. In Erasmus, Virorum, Frankfurt 1536; Life, by Nicholas Harpsfield, ed E. V. Hitchcock and R. W. Chambers 1931 (EETS); Life by W. Roper, Paris 1626, ed E. V. Hitchcock 1934 (EETS); ed R. S. Sylvester and D. P. Harding, New

Haven 1962; History of the reports of his trial and death, ed H. de Vocht, Louvain 1947.

Oldcastle, Sir John. Examinacyon and death by J. Bale. 1544; The life and death by J. Weever, 1601 (verse).

Pits, John (ed). Relationum historicarum de rebus anglicis. Paris 1619. Written from Catholic viewpoint against Bale.

Pole, Reginald. Vita, by A. Dudith. 1563. Tr from Italian of Becatelli.

Ralegh, Sir Walter. Life by J. Shirley. 1677.

Ratsey, Gamaliel. The life and death of a famous thief. 1605; rptd J. P. Collier 1866.

Rawdon, Marmaduke. Life. Ed R. Davis 1863 (Camden Soc). Anon.

Reynardson, Sir Abraham. Memoir of London during the great rebellion. Ed C. M. Clode 1892.

Richard II, King of England. The life and reign. 1680. Anon.

Richard III, King of England. The life and reigne, by G. Buck. 1646; History, by T. More, in Hall's Chronicle 1548 and in More's Works, 1557.

Rochester, John Wilmot, 2nd Earl of. Life and death by G. Burnet. 1680; Valentinian by one of his friends, 1685.

Sanderson, Robert. Life, by I. Walton. 1678.

Savage, Thomas. The wicked life and penitent death. [c. 1688] (anon); The murtherer turned true penitent, nd (anon).

Savile, Sir Henry (ed). Rerum anglicarum scriptores post Bedam praecipui. 1596.

Shaftesbury, Anthony Ashley Cooper, Earl of. Memoires of offered to the Protestant dissenters. 1683 (anon); Some memoirs, 1681 (anon).

Shore, Jane. In Mirror for magistrates, 1563 (verse life by T. Churchyard); Beawtie dishonoured by A. Chute 1593, rptd W. Budig, Untersuchungen über Jane Shore, Rostock 1908.

Sidney, Sir Henry. Epitaph of the life and death, by W. Griffith. 1591.

Sidney, Sir Philip. Life, by F. Greville. 1652; ed N. Smith, Oxford 1907; Life and death, by J. Phillips, 1587 (verse), rptd 1837 (Roxburghe Club); Life, death and true vertues, by G. Whetstone, 1587.

Smith, Major-General John. Famous actions, by E. Walsingham. Oxford 1644.

Spenser, Edmund. An account of his life. In his Works, 1679 (3rd folio).

Stanley, Thomas (ed). The history of philosophy. 1655. Contains lives of the ancient philosophers and defence of biography of thought.

Story, John. Lyfe and death of a Romish canonicall doctor. 1571; rptd Harleian miscellany vol 2.

Stubbes, Katherine. The Godly life and Christian death, by her husband P. Stubbes. 1592, 1626.

Taylor, Jeremy (ed). The life and death of Jesus Christ. 1649.

Taylor, John (ed). The booke of martyrs. 1617; Life and death of the Virgin Mary, 1620; The old old very old man Thomas Par, 1635; The whole life and progress of Henry Walker the iron-monger, 1642. See Taylor, Works, 1630, 3 vols 1868–9, ed C. Hindley 1872.

Usher, James. Life and death, by N. Bernard. 1656; ed T. Jackson 1837; Vita by W. Dillingham, 1700; The life with letters by R. Parr, 1686.

Walker, Elizabeth. Holy life. 1690, 1823.

Wallis, Ralph. The life and death of the cobler of Glocester. 1670. Witty libel, anon.

Walton, Izaak. Lives. 1670; ed A. H. Bullen 1884; ed A. Dobson 2 vols 1898; introd by G. Saintsbury 1927.

Walton, Izaak. Lives. Ed T. Zouch 1796, 1817 (3rd edn with good biography of Walton, pbd separately 1823).

Watson, John. English martyrologie. 1608.

Whitelocke, Bulstrode. Memorials of the English affairs from the reign of Charles I to Charles II. 1682, 4 vols 1853.

Whittingham, William. Life and death. Ed M. A. E. Green 1870 (Camden Soc). Written 1603.

Whytford, Richard. The martiloge. 1526. A trn.

Wilson, Arthur. The history of Great Britain: being the life and reign of James I. 1653.

Winstanley, William. England's worthies. 1660; The loyal martyrology, 1665.

Wolsey, Thomas. Negotiations, by G. Cavendish. 1641; ed H. Morley 1885; ed R. S. Sylvester and D. P. Harding, New Haven 1962. Verse life by T. Churchyard in Mirror for magistrates, 1563. Satire against, by W. Roy, Wesel 1546, rptd Harleian miscellany suppl; Life and death, by T. Storer, Oxford 1599, 1826 (with notes).

Wood, Anthony. Athenae oxonienses 1500–1690. 2 vols 1691–2; ed P. Bliss 6 vols 1813–20, Oxford 1848 (rev).

Wotton, Henry. Life, by I. Walton. As preface to Reliquiae Wottonianae, 1651.

W. M.

III. ECONOMICS AND POLITICS

(1) BIBLIOGRAPHIES

Clark, G. N. Bibliography of British history: Stuart period 1603–1714. Oxford 1928, 1970 (rev).

Encyclopedia of the social sciences. Ed E. R. A. Seligman 15 vols 1930–5.

Read, C. Bibliography of British history: Tudor period 1485–1603. Oxford 1933, 1959 (rev).

Levine, M. Tudor England 1485–1603. Cambridge 1968.

(2) GENERAL STUDIES

Tawney, R. H. The agrarian problem in the sixteenth century. 1912.

Heckscher, E. Mercantilism. 2 vols 1935, 1955 (rev).

Nef, J. U. Industry and government in France and England 1540–1640. Philadelphia 1940.

Clapham, J. A. A concise economic history of Britain from the earliest times to 1750. Cambridge 1949.

Supple, B. E. Commercial crisis and change in England 1600–1642. Cambridge 1959.

Ramsey, P. Tudor economic problems. 1963.

Laslett, P. The world we have lost. 1965, 1971 (rev).

Wilson, C. England's apprenticeship 1603–1763. 1965.

Kerridge, E. The agricultural revolution. 1967.

— Agrarian problems in the sixteenth century and after. 1969.

Hill, C. Reformation to industrial revolution: British economy and society 1530–1780. 1967.

Outhwaite, R. B. Inflation in Tudor and early Stuart England. 1969.

(3) SELECT DOCUMENTS

Bland, A. E., P. A. Brown and R. H. Tawney. English economic history: select documents. 1914.

Tawney, R. H. and E. Power. Tudor economic documents. 3 vols 1924.

Elton, G. R. The Tudor constitution. Cambridge 1960.

Kenyon, J. P. The Stuart constitution. Cambridge 1966.

Williams, C. H. English historical documents 1485–1558. 1967.

(4) CONTEMPORARY WRITINGS

Politics

Fortescue, J. De laudibus legum Angliae. [1546]; ed S. B. Chrimes, Cambridge 1942. Written in 1460s.

Dudley, E. The tree of commonwealth. Ed D. M. Brodie, Cambridge 1948. Written 1510.

Machiavelli, N. The prince. Tr 1640; written 1513; ms English versions in circulation in 16th century.

More, T. Utopia. Louvain 1516; tr R. Robinson 1551.

Starkey, T. A dialogue between Reginald Pole and Thomas Lupset. Ed K. M. Burton 1948. Written 1530s.

Goodman, C. How superior powers oght to be obeyd of their subjects. Geneva 1558.

Buchanan, G. Ane admonition direct to the trew lordis mantenaris of the Kingis graces authoritie. London and Stirling 1571.

Frere, W. H. and C. E. Douglas. Puritan manifestoes. 1907. Reprints 1572 admonitions to Parliament etc.

Harrison, W. The description of England. 1577; ed G. Edelen, Ithaca 1968.

Smith, T. De republica Anglorum: the maner of government of England. 1583, ed L. Alston, Cambridge 1906; A discourse of the commonweal of this realm of England, 1581, ed M. Dewar, Charlottesville 1969.

Parsons, R. A conference about the next succession to the crowne of Ingland. Antwerp 1594.

Spenser, E. A view of the present estate of Ireland. 1596; ed W. L. Renwick 1970.

Bacon, F. Essayes. 1597 etc; New Atlantis, 1627.

James I. The true lawe of free monarchies. Edinburgh 1598; Works, 1616.

Bodin, J. The six bookes of a commonweale. Tr R. Knolles 1606.

Cowell, J. The interpreter. Cambridge 1607.

Davies, J. A discoverie of the true causes why Ireland was never entirely subdued untill his Majesties raigne. 1612.

Camden, W. Annales rerum anglicarum et hibernicarum, regnante Elizabetha. 2 pts 1615–27.

Selden, J. The history of tithes. 1618.

Filmer, R. Patriarcha. 1680; ed P. Laslett, Oxford 1949. Written 1638.

Hooker, R. Of the lawes of ecclesiasticall politie, book VIII. 1648.

Milton, J. Of reformation touching church-discipline in England. 1641; The tenure of kings and magistrates, 1649.

Hobbes, T. Elementa philosophica de cive. Paris 1642; De corpore politico: or the elements of law, moral and politick, 1650; Leviathan, 1651; Behemoth: the history of the causes of the civil wars, 1682.

Charles I. The trial of Charles I. Ed R. Lockyer 1959 (material from T. Herbert and J. Rushworth).

Haller, W. (ed). Tracts on liberty in the Puritan revolution 1638–47. 3 vols New York 1934.

Haller, W. and G. Davies (ed). The Leveller tracts 1647–53. New York 1944.

Woodhouse, A. S. P. (ed). Puritanism and liberty: being the army debates 1647–9 from the Clarke mss, with supplementary documents. 1938.

Educational Theory

Colet, J. Statutes of St Paul's School c. 1518. In J. H. Lupton, A life of John Colet, 1887.

Elyot, T. The boke named the governour. 1531.

Ascham, R. The scholemaster. 1570.

Mulcaster, R. Positions wherein those circumstances be examined necessarie for the training up of children. 1581; The first part of the elementarie, which intreateth of right writing of our English tung, 1582.

Kempe, W. The education of children in learning. 1588.

Coote, E. The Englishe scholemaister. 1596.

Bacon, F. Of the proficience and advancement of learning. 1605.

Brinsley, J. Ludus literarius: or the grammar schoole. 1612; A consolation for our grammar schooles, 1622.

Milton, J. Of education. 1644.

Hartlib, S. Some proposals for the advancement of learning. Ed C. Webster, Cambridge 1970. Written in 1640s.

Hoole, C. A new discovery of the old art of teaching schoole. 1660.

Usury

Sanders, N. A briefe treatise of usurie. Louvain 1568.

Wilson, T. A discourse uppon usurye. 1572; ed R. H. Tawney 1925.

Lodge, T. An alarum against usurers. 1584; ed E. W. Gosse 1883.

Smith, H. The examination of usury, in two sermons. 1591.

Bell, T. The speculation of usurie. 1596.

A., T. The massacre of money. 1602.

Fenton, R. A treatise of usurie. 1611.

Filmer, R. Quaestio quodlibetica: or a discourse, whether it may bee lawfull to take use for money. 1653.

Colonies

Jensen, M. (ed). American colonial documents to 1776. 1955.

Wright, L. B. (ed). The Elizabethan's America: a collection of early reports by Englishmen on the new world. 1955.

—— and E. W. Fowler (ed). English colonisation of North America. 1968.

Hakluyt, R. The principall navigations, voiages and discoveries of the English nation. 1589, 3 vols 1598–1600.

Quinn, D. B. (ed). The voyages and colonising enterprises of Sir Humphrey Gilbert. 1940.

—— The Roanoke voyages 1584–90. 1955.

Las Casas, B. The Spanish colonie: or a briefe chronicle of the acts and gestes of the Spaniardes. 1583.

Brereton, J. A briefe and true relation of the discoverie of the north part of Virginia. 1602.

Benson, G. A sermon preached at Pauls Cross. 1609.

Crakanthorp, R. A sermon. 1609. Preached at Paul's Cross.

Gray, R. A good speed to Virginia. 1609.

Johnson, R. Nova Britannia, offring fruits by planting in Virginia. 1609; The new life of Virginea being the second part of Nova Britannia, 1612.

Price, D. Sauls prohibition staide: a sermon. 1609.

Symonds, W. Sermon preached at Whitechapel. 1609.

Crashaw, W. A sermon preached before the Lord Lawarre, Lord Governor of Virginia. 1610.

Rich, R. Newes from Virginia. 1610.

Strachey, W. The history of travel into Virginia Britania. 1849; ed L. B. Wright and V. Freund 1953. Written 1612.

Purchas, S. Purchas his pilgrimage. 1613; Purchas his pilgrims, 1625.

Whitaker, A. Good newes from Virginia. 1613.

Hamor, R. A true discourse of the present estate of Virginia. 1615.

Copeland, P. Virginias God be thanked. 1622.

Smith, J. The generall historie of Virginia, the Somer Iles and New England. 1624.

Bradford, W. Of Plymouth plantation. Ed S. E. Morison, New York 1952. *See col 2157, above.*

Eburne, R. A plaine path-way to plantations. 1624; ed L. B. Wright, Ithaca 1962.

Morton, T. New English Canaan. 1637.

Paupers, Rogues and Vagabonds

Salter, F. R. (ed). Some early tracts on poor relief. 1926.

Judges, A. V. (ed). The Elizabethan underworld: a collection of Tudor and early Stuart tracts and ballads. 1930.

Vives, J. L. De subventione pauperum. Bruges 1526.

Fish, S. A supplicacyon for the beggars. [1528–9].

Harman, T. A caveat or warning for commen cursetors. 1567; The fraternity of vacabondes, 1575.

Arth, H. Provision for the poore now in penurie. 1597.

Chamberlen, P. The poor mans advocate: or Englands samaritan. 1649.

Moore, J. The crying sin of England, not caring for the poor. 1653.

Agriculture and Fisheries

Fitzherbert, J. The boke of surveying. 1523; The boke of husbandry, 1523.

Benese, R. This boke sheweth the maner of measurynge of all maner of lande. 1537.

Tusser, T. A hundreth good pointes of husbandrie. 1557, 1573 etc (as Five hundreth points of good husbandry); ed E. V. Lucas 1931.

Scot, R. A perfite platforme of a hoppe garden. 1574.

Dee, J. General and rare memorials pertayning to the perfecte arte of navigation. 1577.

Heresbach, C. Four bookes of husbandry, newly englished by B. Googe. 1577.

Hitchcock, R. A pollitique platt, for the honour of the Prince. 1580.

Platt, H. The jewell house of art and nature. 1594.

Norden, J. The surveyors dialogue. 1607.

Gentleman, T. Englands way to win wealth, and to employ ships and mariners. 1614; ed E. Arber 1882.

Blith, W. The English improver: or a new survey of husbandry. 1649, 1652 (rev).

Burroughs, J. The soveraignty of the British seas, proved by records, history and the municipal lawes of this kingdom. 1651; ed T. C. Wade, Edinburgh 1920.

Dugdale, W. The history of imbanking and drayning of divers fenns and marshes. 1662.

Commerce

McCulloch, J. R. (ed). A select collection of early English tracts on commerce. 1856, Cambridge 1954.

Gresham, T. Memorandum for the understanding of the exchange. Ed R. de Roover, Cambridge Mass 1949.

Browne, J. The marchants avizo. 1589; ed P. McGrath, Cambridge Mass 1957.

Wheeler, J. A treatise of commerce. Middelburg and London 1601; ed G. B. Hotchkiss, New York 1931.

Malynes, G. de. A treatise of the canker of Englands commonwealth. 1601; Englands view, in the unmasking of two paradoxes, 1603; Consuetudo vel lex mercatoria: or the ancient lawe merchant, 1622.

Mun, T. A discourse of trade unto the East Indies. 1621; Englands treasure by foreign trade, 1664.

Roberts, L. The merchants mappe of commerce. 1638, 1677 (rev); The treasure of trafficke or a discourse of forraigne trade, 1641.

Violet, T. The advancement of merchandize. 1651.

H. C. P.

IV. LAW

(1) BIBLIOGRAPHIES

Fulbecke, W. A direction or preparative to the study of lawe. 1600, 1620, 1808; ed T. H. Stirling 1829 (2nd edn).

London, W. A. A catalogue of the most vendible books in England. 1657, 1658 (with suppl), 1660. Contains a section on common and civil law books.

Basset, Thomas. Catalogue of common and statute law books. 1671, 1672, 1673, 1682, 1684, 1685, 1686, 1694 (3rd edn), 1700, 1725, 1726.

Advocates, Faculty of. Catalogus bibliothecae juris. Edinburgh 1692, 3 vols 1742–1807; ed D. Irving 1831, 1851, 7 vols in 9 1863–79.

Middle Temple. Bibliotheca in ordinen juxta rerum naturam redacta ac digesta. 1700; Catalogus librorum bibliothecae ordine dictionarii dispositus, 1734, 1877 (with suppl), 1 vol 1880; ed C. E. A. Bedwell 3 vols 1914 (with suppl), 1925.

Worrall, John. Bibliotheca legum: or a new and complete list of all the common and statute law books. 1731, 1746 (6th edn). Numerous edns to 1782. Continued by Worrall and Brooke, below.

Worrall, John and Edward Brooke. Bibliotheca legum Angliae. Pt 1, A catalogue of the common and statute law books of this Realm; pt 2, containing a general account of the laws and Law-writers of England, 2 vols 1788 (with suppls 1792, 1794, 1800, 1806 by J. Clarke, 1808). Continuation by Clarke, below.

Inner Temple. Catalogue of the printed books and manuscripts. 1806, 1821, 1833, 1843.

Bridgman, R. W. A short view of legal bibliography: containing some critical observations on the authority of the reporters and other law writers. 1807.

Reed, W. Bibliotheca nova legum Angliae: or a complete catalogue of law books. 1809.

Clarke, John. Bibliotheca legum: or complete catalogue of the common and statute law books of the United Kingdom. [1810], 1819, 1824. Continuation of Worrall and Brooke, above.

Advocates, College of. Catalogue of the books in the library in Doctors Commons. 1818, 1827, 1848, 1856, 1858, 1861.

Lincoln's Inn. Catalogue of printed books in the library. 1835, 1859; suppls 1–5, 1862–81, suppl 6, 1890.

King's Inns, Dublin. Catalogue of the library. Edinburgh 1836 (with suppl); ed H. Connor 1846.

Law Society. Catalogue of the library. 1841, 1851, 1869, 1891; suppls, 1891, 1894, 1897, 1898, 1906.

Marvin, J. G. Legal bibliography or thesaurus of American, English, Irish and Scotch law books. Philadelphia 1847.

Wallace, J. W. The reporters. Philadelphia 1855 (3rd edn); ed F. F. Heard, Boston 1882 (4th edn).

Gray's Inn. Catalogue of books in the library of the honourable society. 1872; suppls, 1874, 1878, 1888, 1906.

Soule, C. C. The lawyer's reference manual of law books and citations. Boston 1883, 1884.
— Year book bibliography. Harvard Law Rev 14 1901.
Procurators, Faculty of. Catalogue of the books in the library. Glasgow 1887, 1903; with suppls, 1909, 1923.
Jones, L. A. An index to legal periodical literature [to 1899]. 2 vols Boston 1888–99. Continued by Chipman, below.
Incorporated Law Society of Ireland. Catalogue of the library. Ed S. W. Evan, Dublin 1895, 1909.
Encyclopedia of the laws of England. 12 vols 1897–8, 1904 (with suppl), 17 vols 1906–19, 5 vols 1938–40 (incomplete).
Jelf, E. A. Where to find your law: a discursive bibliographical essay upon the various divisions and subdivisions of the law of England. 1897, 1900, 1907. Continued by Where to look for your law, 1908, below.
Maitland, F. W. English law and the Renaissance. Cambridge 1901. Contains among the notes (pp. 90–4) lists of law books available 1550–1600.
Arber, E. The Term catalogues 1668–1709: contemporary bibliography of English literature. 3 vols 1903–6.
Steele, Robert. What fifteenth-century books are about. Law Library 1905.
Lincoln's Inn. Catalogue of pamphlets 1506–1700. 1908.
Where to look for your law. 1908, 1912, 1926, 1929, 1935, 1938, 1943, 1944, 1946, 1948, 1954, 1957, 1960, 1962. Contains lists of contemporary books in print, with prices. Continuation of Jelf, above.
Harvard University. Catalogue of the library of the law school. 2 vols Cambridge Mass 1909, 1967 (facs).
Index to legal periodicals. Chicago 1909–. In progress.
Fox, J. C. Handbook of English law reports, from the last quarter of the eighteenth century to 1865. 1913.
Maxwell, W. H. Complete list of British and colonial law reports and legal periodicals. 1913 (with suppl), 1920, 1937 (3rd edn).
Chipman, F. E. An index to legal periodical literature 1898–1922. 2 vols Boston 1919–24. Continuation of Jones, above.

Hicks, F. C. Materials and methods of legal research, with bibliographical manual. Rochester NY 1923, 1942 (3rd edn).
Holdsworth, Sir William. A history of English law vol 7. 1925, 1937. Contains short titles list of books 1668–1700.
— Sources and literature of English law. Oxford 1925.
Maxwell, W. H. and L. F. A bibliography of English law to 1932. 3 vols 1925–33; vol 4, A bibliography of Irish law to 1935, 1936; vol 5, A bibliography of Scottish law to 1936, 1937; vol 6, A bibliography of the laws of Australia, New Zealand, Fiji and the Western Pacific to 1938, 1938; vol 7, Bibliography of the law of the British colonies, protectorates, mandated territories, 1949; suppls, 1946, 1950, 1954, 7 vols 1955–64 (2nd edn).
Winfield, P. H. Chief sources of English legal history. Cambridge 1925.
Beale, J. H. A bibliography of early English law books [to 1600]. Cambridge Mass 1926, 1943 (with suppl by R. B. Anderson) (Ames Foundation).
Foreign Office. Catalogue of printed books in the library. 1926.
Cowley, J. D. A bibliography of abridgments, digests, dictionaries and indexes of English law to 1800. 1932 (Selden Soc).
Stair Society publications vol 1: introductory survey of the sources and literature of Scots law (by various authors). Edinburgh 1936.
Institute of Advanced Legal Studies. A survey of legal periodicals: union catalogue of holdings in British libraries. 1949, 1957, 1968.
Coke, Sir Edward. Catalogue of the library. Ed W. O. Hassell, New Haven 1950.
Institute of Advanced Legal Studies. A bibliographical guide to the law of the United Kingdom, the Channel Islands and the Isle of Man. 1956.
Nicholson, J. Register of manuscripts of year books extant. 1956 (Selden Soc). Includes list of ptd edns.
Plucknett, T. F. T. Early English legal literature. Cambridge 1958.
Bland, D. S. Bibliography of the Inns of Court. 1965 (Selden Soc).

(2) GENERAL STUDIES

Dugdale, Sir William. Origines juridiciales. 1666, 1671, 1680.
Reeves, John. History of English law to the death of Elizabeth. 5 vols 1814–29 (3rd edn); rev F. W. Finlason 3 vols 1869.
Crabb, G. History of the English law. 1829, Burlington 1831, London 1840.
Brunner, H. Die Entstehung der Schwurgerichte. Berlin 1871.
— Sources of the law of England: an historical introduction to the study of English law, from the German by W. Hastie. Edinburgh 1888.
— Geschichte der englischen Rechtsquellen im Grundriss, mit einem Anhang über die normanischen Rechtsquellen. Leipzig 1909.
Glasson, E. Histoire du droit et des institutions politiques, civiles et judiciaires de l'Angleterre. 6 vols Paris 1882–3.
Selden Society publications. 1888–. In progress. Includes Year Book series from vol 17 onwards.
Pollock, F. and F. W. Maitland. History of English law before the time of Edward I. 2 vols Cambridge 1895, 1898, 1969 (rev with bibliography).
Maitland, F. W. English law and the Renaissance. Cambridge 1901.
— Collected papers. Ed H. A. L. Fisher 3 vols Cambridge 1911.
— Selected essays. Ed H. D. Hazeltine [et al], Cambridge 1936.
Holdsworth, W. S. A history of English law. 16 vols 1903–66. Vols 13–16 ed A. L. Goodhart and H. G.

Hanbury. Various edns and reprints of vols 1–9 issued For bibliography see Law Quart Rev 69 1953.
— Some makers of English law. Cambridge 1938.
— Essays in law and history. Oxford 1946.
Liebermann, F. Die Gesetze der Angelsachsen. 3 vols Halle and Wörterbuch 1903–16. Vols 1–2 rptd 1935.
Pound, R. and T. F. T. Plucknett. Readings on the history and system of the common law. Rochester 1904, 1913, 1927. Plucknett was co-author of 1913 and 1927 edns only.
Pound, R. Interpretations of legal history. Cambridge 1923.
Select essays in Anglo-American legal history. 3 vols Cambridge Mass 1907–9.
Oxford studies in social and legal history. Ed P. Vinogradoff 9 vols Oxford 1909–27.
Jenks, E. Short history of English law. 1912, 1920, 1924, 1929, 1934 (with suppl ch), 1938, 1949.
Ames, J. B. Lectures on legal history and miscellaneous legal essays. Cambridge Mass 1913.
Essays in legal history. Ed P. Vinogradoff, Oxford 1913.
Cambridge studies in English legal history. Ed H. A. Holland and H. D. Hazeltine 17 vols Cambridge 1921–. Individual works by various authors. In progress.
Plucknett, T. F. T. A concise history of the common law. Rochester NY 1929, London 1936, 1940, 1948, 1956.
— Legislation of Edward I. Oxford 1949.
Fifoot, C. H. S. English law and its background. 1932.
— History and sources of the common law: tort and contract. 1949.

Potter, H. An historical introduction to English law and its institutions. 1932.

Levy-Ullman, H. The English legal tradition: its sources and history. 1935.

Stair Society publications. Edinburgh 1936–. In progress.

Goebel, J. Felony and misdemeanor: a study in the history of English criminal procedure. Vol 1 (all pbd), New York 1937.

Radcliffe, G. R. Y. and G. Cross. The English legal system. 1937.

Windeyer, W. I. Lectures on legal history. Sydney 1938.

A discourse upon the exposicion and understandinge of statutes, with Sir Thomas Egerton's additions. Ed S. E. Thorne, San Marino 1942.

Carter, A. T. A history of the English courts. 1899. 1944 (7th edn). Originally pbd as Outlines of English legal history.

Hanbury, H. C. English courts of law. 1944, 1967 (4th edn).

Hastings, M. The Court of Common Pleas in fifteenth-century England: a study of legal administration and procedure. Ithaca 1947.

Radzinowicz, L. A history of criminal law and its administration from 1750. Vols 1–4, 1948–68. In progress.

Prerogative regis: tertia lectura Roberti Constable de Lyncolnis Inne anno II H.7. Ed S. E. Thorne, New Haven 1949.

Costin, W. C. and J. C. Watson. The law and working of the Constitution: documents 1660–1914. 2 vols 1952, 1961–4 (rev).

Winfield, P. Select legal essays. 1952.

English historical documents c. 500–1914. Ed D. C. Douglas et al 13 vols 1953–. Vols 3, 13 not yet pbd.

Kiralfy, A. K. R. The English legal system. 1954, 1956, 1960 (with suppl), 1967.

Thorne, S. E. Readings and moots at the Inns of Court in the fifteenth century. Vol 1, 1955.

Ogilvie, B. The King's government and the common law 1471–1641. Oxford 1958.

Lyon, B. D. Constitutional and legal history of medieval England. New York [1960].

Cameron, J. R. Frederick William Maitland and the history of English law. Norman Oklahoma 1961.

Hand, G. J. English law in Ireland 1290–1324. Cambridge 1967.

Jones, W. The Elizabethan Court of Chancery. Oxford 1967.

Milsom, S. F. C. Historical foundations of the common law. 1969.

(3) INDIVIDUAL WRITERS
(in alphabetical order)

Articuli ad narrationes novas. 1525. Numerous edns to 1547.

Ashe, Thomas. Le promptuarie: ou repertory generall de les annales, et plusors autres livres del common ley d'Engleterre. 2 vols 1614.

Bacon, Sir Francis (Viscount St Albans). Collection of some principall rules and maximes of the common lawes of England. 1630.

— The elements of the common lawes of England: a double tract, one contayning rules and maximes of the common law, the other, use of the common law. 1630, 1635–6, 1639.

— The learned reading upon the Statute of Uses. 1642, 1785; ed W. H. Rowe 1806.

— Ordinances for the better administration of justice in the Chancery. 1623, 1640, 1642, 1656.

— The use of the law. 1629, 1630, 1635, 1636, 1639. Perhaps by Bacon.

— Works. Ed J. Spedding, R. L. Ellis and D. D. Heath 14 vols 1857–74 (with life and letters).

Bacon, Nathaniel. An historical discourse of the uniformity of the government of England. 2 pts 1647–51; pt 2, 1657; 2 pts 1672, 2 pts in 1 vol 1682, 1689, 1739, 1760. The 1672 and 1682 edns were ptd secretly.

Bekinsau, J. De supremo et absoluto regis imperio. 1546 (colophon date 1547), 1611.

Bracton, Henry de. De legibus et consuetudinibus Angliae. 1569, 1640; ed T. Twiss 6 vols 1878–83; ed G. E. Woodbine 4 vols New Haven 1915–42 (vols 5–6 projected but not issued); ed S. E. Thorne, Cambridge Mass vols 1–2, 1968. A revision of Woodbine projected in 5 vols. Vols 1–2 are a reprint of Woodbine.

Brooke, Sir Robert. Le graunde abridgement. 2 pts in 1 vol 1573, 1576, 1586.

— Reading upon the Statute of Limitations, 32 H.8. cap 2. 1647.

— The reading upon the Statute of Magna Carta, chap 16. 1641.

Brownlow, R. Brevia judicialia: or an exact collection of approved forms of judiciall writs in the Common Bench. 1662.

— Declarations and pleadings in English. Pt 1, 1652, 1653, 1659; pt 2, 1654; tr Latin, 1693.

— Writs judiciall: shewing the formes etc of all manner of executions in reall, personall and mixt actions. 1653.

Caesar, Julius. The ancient state, authority and proceedings of the Court of Requests. 1597.

Callis, Robert. The reading upon the statute of 23 H.8 cap 5 of sewers delivered at Gray's Inn. 1622, 1647, 1685, 1686, 1810 (with ms notes by Serjeant Hill), 1824.

Calthorpe, Charles. The relation betweene the lord of a manor and the coppyholder his tenant. 1635, 1650, 1650 (with Coke's Compleate copyholder).

Carta feodi. Parus libellus continens formaz multarum rerun pro-ut patet in Kalendario in fine in contento. [1506?]. Numerous edns to 1546.

Clayton, J. Topicks in the laws of England. 1646, 1647.

Coke, Sir Edward. A booke of entries. 1614, 1671.

— The compleate copyholder. 1630, 1641, 1644, 1650 (with suppl on copyhold and customary estates), 1668, 1673. Also included in his first pt of the Institutes, 1703, 1719, 1738, and in his Three law tracts, 1764.

— Declarations and other pleadings in the eleven parts of [his] Reports. Tr W. Hughes 1659.

— First part of the Institutes of the lawes of England: or commentarie upon Littleton. 1628 (considered very incorrect), 1629 (rev). 19 edns issued to 1832, of which the 18th, 1823, and 19th, 1832 are rptd from the 17th, 1823.

— A little treatise of bail and mainprize. 1635, 1637. Also included in his first pt of the Institutes, 1684, 1703, 1719 and 1735, and in his Three law tracts, 1764.

— Le reading sur lestatute de 27 E.I. appelle lestature de finibus levatis. 1662. Also in his first pt of the Institutes, 1684, 1703, 1719 and 1738, and in his Three law tracts, 1764.

Cowell, John. Institutiones juris anglicani. Cambridge 1605, 1630, London 1651 (tr W.G.), Oxford 1664, 1676.

— The interpreter: or booke containing the signification of words and termes mentioned in the lawe writers, or statutes. Cambridge 1607, 1637, 1658, 1672 (enlarged T. Manley), 1684 (2nd edn), 1701, 1707, 1727.

Crompton, Richard. L'authoritie et iurisdiction des courts de la Maiestie de la Roygne. 1594, 1637.

Dalton, Michael. Countrey justice. 1618. Numerous edns to 1746.

— Officium vicecomitum: or the office and authoritie of sherifs. 1623, 1662, 1670, 1682, 1700. Also abridged edns, 1628 and 1651.

De legato et absoluto principe perduellionis reo. Oxford 1587.

Doddridge, Sir John. A compleat parson: or a description of advowsons, or church-living. 1630, 1641.

—— The English lawyer, describing a method for the managing of the lawes of this land. 1631.

—— The lawyers light: or a true direction for the study of the law. 1629.

Duck, Sir Arthur. De usu et authoritate juris civilis Romanorum. 1653, 1654, 1679, 1689; tr in Ferriere, History of the Roman or civil law, 1724.

Egerton, Thomas. Certain observations concerning the office of Lord Chancellor. 1657. Perhaps by Egerton.

Finch, Sir Henry. Law: or discourse thereof. 1613, 1627, 1636, 1661, 1678, 1730 (with notes by Pickering), 1759.

—— Nomotechnia: un description del common leys d'Angleterre. 1613; tr 1759.

Fitzherbert, Sir Anthony. Diversite des courtz et leur jurisdictions. 1523, 1525, 1526, 1528, [1530?], 1533, 1535, 1543, [1545?]. Also ptd with Novae narrationes, 1561, and Natura brevium, 1534. Tr Hughes in various edns of Horne, Mirror of justices.

—— La graunde abridgement. 3 vols 1516, 3 vols in 1 1565, 1577, 1586.

—— La nouvelle natura brevium. 1534. Various edns to 1635; tr W. Hughes 1652, 1730 (7th edn with commentary by Hale), 1755, 2 vols 1794, Dublin 1793.

—— L'office de vicountes, baylifes, escheators, constables, coroners. 1583. Included in his L'Office et auctoryte des justyces de peas, 1584.

—— L'office et auctoryte des justyces de peas. 1583; Inlarge per [Richard] Crompton, 1583, [1584], [1587], 1593, 1594, 1606, 1617.

Fortescue, Sir John. De laudibus legum Angliae. [1546]; ed and tr J. Selden 1616 etc; tr S. B. Chrimes, Cambridge 1942.

Fulbecke, William. A direction or preparitive to the study of the lawe. 1600, 1620, 1808, 1829.

—— The pandects of the law of nations. 1602.

—— A parallele or conference of the civill, canon and common law of England. 2 pts 1601–2; pt 1, 1618.

Gentilis, Albericus. De jure belli. Oxford 1588, Hanover 1598, 1612; ed T. E. Holland, Oxford 1877 (from 1612); ed and tr J. C. Rolfe 2 vols Oxford 1933 (facs).

—— De legationibus. 1585, 1594, Hanover 1607; ed and tr G. J. Laing 2 vols New York 1924 (facs of 1594).

—— Hispanicae advocationis. Hanover 1613, Amsterdam 1661; ed and tr F. F. Abbott 2 vols New York 1921 (facs).

Glanville, Ralph de. Tractatus de legibus et consuetudinibus regni Anglie tempore Regis Henrici secundi compositus. [c. 1554], 1604, 1673, 1780; ed T. Twiss 1896 (Rolls ser); ed G. E. Woodbine, New Haven 1932.

Gregory, Arthur. L'abridgement des cases concernant les titles plus materiall pur les estudients & practiciones des leyes du royalme. 1599; tr W. Hughes 1663 (as Moot book: a survey of the general titles).

Hawke, Michael. The grounds of the lawes of England. 1657.

Herne, John. The pleader: containing perfect presidents and formes of declarations, pleadings [etc] in all kinds of actions. 1657.

Hobbes, Thomas. De corpore politico: or the elements of law, moral and politick. 1650, 1652, 1652; ed F. Tönnies 1889, Cambridge 1928.

Intrationum liber omnibus legum Anglie studiosis apprime necessarius in se complectens diversas formas placitorum. 1546.

Jones, John. The workes in reference to the putting all the law into English and reforming the abuses thereof. 1651.

Kitchin, John. Aucthoritie of al Justices of Peace. 1580–79, 1580, 1580, 1656, 1663.

—— Le Court Leete et Court Baron. [1579] (in Aucthoritie of al Justices of Peace, 1580), 1580, 1581, 1585, 1587, 1592, 1598, 1607, 1613, 1623.

—— Jurisdictions: or the lawful authority of Courts Leet, Courts Baron, Court of Marshalseyes, Court of Pypowder and ancient Demesne. 1651, 1653, 1656, 1657, 1663, 1675 (5th edn).

Lambard, William. Archion: or a commentary upon the High Courts of Justice. 1635. Another edn of 1635 entitled Archion: or discourse, ed T. Lambard is a more correct copy.

—— 'Αρχαιονομία: sive de priscis Anglorum legibus libri. 1568, Cambridge 1644 (with Bede, Historia ecclesiastica).

—— Duties of constables [etc]. 1582. Numerous edns to [1633].

—— Eirenarcha: or the office of the justices of peace. 1581. Numerous edns to 1619.

Littleton, Sir Thomas. Tenures. [c. 1481]. Numerous edns in French to 1639. First trn 1574.

Malynes, Gerard. Consuetudo vel lex mercatoria: or the ancient law merchant. 1622, 1629, 1636, 1656, 1685, 1686.

Manwood, John. A brefe collection of the lawes of the forests. [1592], 1598 (as Treatise and discourse of lawes of the forrest), 1615, 1665; ed W. Nelson 1717 (4th edn), 1741. Abridgements, 1697, 1721.

Meriton, George. Landlord's law. 1665, 1668, 1669, 1681, 1697.

Novae narrationes. [1496], [1515], 1591.

Perkins, John. A profitable booke [incipit perutilis tractatus]. 1528, 1532, 1541. Numerous edns to 1642 (1st trn); ed R. J. Greening 1827 (15th edn).

Phaer, Thomas. Boke of presidentes. 1543. Numerous edns to 1641.

Plowden, Edmund. Les Quaeres. [1620?]; tr 1662. Included in his Commentaries, 1654, 1779–61, 1816.

Powell, R. Antiquity, authority, uses and jurisdiction of the ancient courts of Leet. 1641, 1642, 1688.

Powell, T. Attourneys academy. 1623, 1630, 1647.

Prynne, William. A brief register, kalendar and survey of the several kinds, forms, of all parliamentary writs. 4 pts 1659–64.

—— A seasonable, legall and historicall vindication of the fundamentall liberties [and] laws of all English freemen. 3 pts 1654–7, 1655–7, 1659 (pt 3 as Historiarchos).

—— The soveraigne power of parliaments and kingdomes. 4 pts in 1 vol 1643.

Pulton, Ferdinando. An abstract of all the penal statutes. 1560, 1577, 1579, 1579, 1581, 1586, 1592, 1596, 1600.

—— Collections of sundrie statutes. 1618. Numerous edns to 1670.

—— De pace regis et regni: a treatise declaring which be the great and generall offences of the realme. 1609, 1610, 1615, 1623.

Rastell, John. Expositiones terminorum legum Anglorum. [1526?], 1527; tr W. Rastell 1563. Various edns to 1618; 1624 (as Les termes de la ley). Numerous edns to 1812.

Rastell, William. A colleccion of all the statutes from the begynning of Magna Carta unto the yere of our Lorde 1557. 1557, 1559, 1559, 1565. Numerous later edns to 1621.

—— A colleccion of entrees. 1566, 1574, 1596, 1670.

Registrum omnium brevium tam originalium quam judicialium. 1531, 1531, 1553, 1595, 1634, 1687.

Returna brevium. 1516, 1519. Numerous edns to 1552.

Ridley, Thomas. View of the civil and ecclesiastical law. 1607.

Saint-German, Christopher. Dyaloges in Englishe betwene a Doctour of Divinitie and a student in the lawes of England. First pbd as Dialogus de fundamentis legum Angliae et de conscientia, 1528. Numerous edns to 1886.

Scobell, Henry. A collection of acts and ordinances, 1640 to 1556.

Selden, John. Ad Fletam dissertatio. Appended to Fleta: seu commentarius juris anglicani, 1647, 1685, 1685; tr R. Kelham 1771; tr and ed D. Ogg, Cambridge 1925 (from 1647).

—— Brief discourse concerning the power of Peeres and Commons of Parliament in point of judicature. 1640, 1640, 1680, 1746, 1809, 1811.

—— Brief discourse touching the office of Lord Chancellor. Ed W. Dugdale 1671, 1672, 1677.

—— De jure naturali et gentium, iuxta disciplinam Ebraeorum. 1640, Strasbourg 1665, Leipzig 1665.

—— England's epinomis: original of ecclesiastical jurisdictions of testaments. In his Tracts, 1683.

—— The history of tythes. 1618. No known copy of first edn.

—— Jani Anglorum facies altera. 1610, 2 vols 1673, 1 vol 1681. Another edn in his Tracts, 1683.

—— Mare clausum. 1635, 1636, 1636, Hague 1636, Leyden 1636; tr 1652, 1663, Bratislava 1751.

—— Opera omnia. Ed D. Wilkins 3 vols 1726.

Sheppard, William. Epitome of all the common and statute laws of this nation in force. 1656, 1658.

—— The president of presidents: or one general president for common assurances by deeds. 1655 etc; ed T. W. Williams 1825.

—— Sure guide for his Majesty's Justices of Peace. 1649, 1652, 1663, 1669.

—— Touch-stone of common assurances. 1641, 1648, 1651, 2 vols in 1 1826 (8th edn). Perhaps by Sheppard.

—— Whole office of the country Justice of Peace. 2 pts in 1 vol 1650, 1652, 1652, 2 pts in 1 vol 1655–6 (enlarged).

Skene, J. De verborum significatione. Edinburgh 1597, Waldegrave 1599, London 1681.

Smith, Sir Thomas. De republica Anglorum. 1583. Numerous edns to 1685; ed L. Alston, Cambridge 1906 (preface by W. Maitland).

Somner, William. Treatise of gavelkind. 1660, 1663, 1726 (2nd edn).

Spelman, Sir Henry. Archaeologus: in modum glossarii. [Pt I], 1626, 1627; [pt 2], ed W. Dugdale 1664, 1687 (3rd edn).

—— Concilia, decreta, leges, constitutiones in re ecclesiarum orbis britannici. 2 vols 1639–64.

—— Spelmanni reliquiae. Ed E. Gibson, Oxford 1698, London 1723.

Staunford, Sir William. An exposition of the King's prerogative collected out of the great abridgement of Fitzherbert and other old writers. 1567, 1568, 1573, 1577, 1568–77, 1590, 1607.

—— Les plees del coron. 1557, 1560, 1567, 1567–57, 1568, 1574, 1583, 1607.

Style, William. Regestrum practicale: or the practical register, consisting of rules [etc] concerning the practice of the common law at Westminster. 1657, 1670, 1671, 1694, 1707 (4th edn). Continuation by J. Lilly, 2 pts 1710.

Sutcliffe, M. The practice, proceedings and lawes of armes, 1593.

Swinburne, Henry. A briefe treatise of testaments and last willes. 1590, 1611, 1633, 1635, 1640, 1677, 1728, 1743, 2 vols Dublin 1793, 3 vols 1803.

—— A treatise of spousals or matrimonial contracts. 1686, 1711.

Tabula libri assisarum. [London 1517?], 1555 (as The abridgement of the Book of Assizes).

Theloall, Simon. Le digest des briefes originals. 1579, 1687.

Wentworth, Thomas. The office and dutie of executors. 1641. Various edns to 1829. Ascribed to Sir John Doddridge. The first 2 edns were anon.

West, William. Symboleographia. 2 pts 1590–4. Various edns to 1647.

Wilkinson, John. A treatise concerning the office and authoritie of coroners and sherifs, together with [a] method for the keeping of a Court Leet, Court Baron and Hundred Court. 1618, 1620, 1628, 1638, 1641, 1651, 1652, 1657, 1675.

Wingate, Edmund. The body of the common law of England. 1655, 1655, 1662, 1662, 1678.

—— An exact abridgement of all statutes from Magna Charta until 1641. 1642, 1655, 1666, 1689 (8th edn continued to 1869 by J. Washington), 1700, 1704, 1708.

—— The exact constable, with his original and power in the offices of churchwardens [etc]. 1660, 1682 (6th edn).

—— Justice revived: being the whole office of a country Justice of the Peace. 1644, 1661.

—— Maximes of reason: or the reason of the common law of England. 1658.

—— Statuta pacis: or a perfect table of all the statutes which concerne the office of a justice of peace. 1641, 1644.

Zouche, Richard. Cases and questions resolved in the civil law. Oxford 1652.

—— Descriptio iuris et iudicii ecclesiastici. In his Elementa iurisprudentiae, 1636, and also in Mocket, Tractatus de politia ecclesiae anglicanae, 1683, 1705.

—— Descriptio iuris et iudicii fecialis. 1650, Oxford 1658, Hague 1659; ed T. E. Holland 2 vols Washington 1911 (with trn by J. L. Brierley).

—— Descriptio iuris et iudicii maritimi. Oxford 1640. Also in his Elementa iurisprudentiae, Amsterdam nd, 1652, Hague 1665.

—— Descriptio iuris et iudicii militaris. Oxford 1640. Also in his Elementa iurisprudentiae, Amsterdam nd, 1652, Hague 1665.

—— Descriptio iuris et iudicii sacri. 1640. In his Elementa iurisprudentiae, Amsterdam nd, 1652, Hague 1665.

—— Descriptio iuris et iudicii temporalis. In his Elementa iurisprudentiae, 1636, and also in Mocket, Tractatus de politia ecclesiae anglicanae, 1683, 1705.

—— Descriptio iuris et iudicii feudalis. Oxford 1634, 1640.

—— Elementa iurisprudentiae. Oxford 1629, 1629, 1636, Amsterdam nd, 1652, Hague 1665.

—— Specimen questionum iuris civilis. 1653, 1682.

W. W. S. B.

V. SCHOLARSHIP

General studies; Dictionaries; Contemporary works of general learning; Biblical scholarship; The Early Fathers and Schoolmen; Disputational learning; Ecclesiastical and theological learning; Latin, Greek.

This section is mainly concerned with the period 1590–1660. For the earlier years the section on Education, col 2381, below, should be consulted. See also Translations into English, col 2165, above.

(1) GENERAL STUDIES

Casaubon, Meric. Vindicatio patris. 1624; tr 1624 (as The vindication or defence of Isaac Casaubon).

Wase, Christopher. Considerations concerning Free Schools, as settled in England. 1678. On secondary schools in England from the Reformation.

Burnet, Gilbert. Life of Sir Matthew Hale. 1682.

Parr, R. Life of James Usher, late Lord Archbishop of Armagh. 1686. With 323 letters to or from Ussher.

Hacket, John. Scrinia reserata: a memorial offered to the

great deservings of John Williams (Archbishop of York). 2 vols 1693.

Morhof, D. G. Polyhistor literarius, philosophicus et practicus. Lübeck 1714.

Walker, John. Sufferings of the clergy in the late times of the Grand Rebellion. 1714.

Baillet, A. Jugemens des savans. 8 vols Paris 1722–30, Amsterdam 1725.

Ward, John. Lives of the professors of Gresham College. 1740.

Middleton, Erasmus. Biographia evangelica: or an historical account of the lives and deaths of the most eminent and evangelical authors or preachers both British and foreign, in the several denominations of Protestants from the beginning of the Reformation to the present time. 4 vols 1779–86.

Brüggemann, L. W. View of the English editions, translations and illustrations of the ancient Greek and Latin authors. Stettin 1797.

Calamy, Edmund. The Nonconformists' memorial. Ed S. Palmer 3 vols 1802–3.

Dibdin, T. F. An introduction to the knowledge of rare and valuable editions of the Greek and Roman classics. Gloucester 1802, 1804, 2 vols 1808, 1827 (all enlarged).

Aubrey, John. Lives. 1813; Brief lives, chiefly of contemporaries, ed A. Clark 2 vols Oxford 1898; ed O. L. Dick 1950.

Wood, A. Athenae oxonienses. Ed P. Bliss 4 vols 1813–20.

Todd, H. J. The polyglot Bible: memoirs and writings of the Rt Rev Brian Walton, Lord Bishop of Chester, with notices of his coadjutors in that illustrious work; of the cultivation of oriental learning in this country, preceding and during their time; and of the Authorised English version of the Bible. 2 vols 1821.

Basire, Isaac. Correspondence in the reigns of Charles I and Charles II and memoir. Ed W. N. Darnell 1831.

Cattermole, R. Literature of the Church of England. 2 vols 1844.

Parkinson, R. Life of Adam Martindale, written by himself. 1845 (Chetham Soc).

Worthington, John. Diary and correspondence. Ed J. Crossley and R. C. Christie 3 pts 1847–86 (Chetham Soc). Worthington edited Joseph Mead's works and his correspondence reflects learned life.

Weld, C. R. History of the Royal Society. 2 vols 1848.

Hamilton, W. Discussions on philosophy and literature, education and university reform. 1852, 1853 (enlarged). Contains history of logic pp. 118–76; history of University of Leyden pp. 373–9.

Heywood, J. and T. Wright. Cambridge University transactions during the Puritan controversies of the 16th and 17th centuries. 2 vols 1854.

Fell, John. Life of Sir Matthew Hale [with catalogue of books and mss pp. 95–8] and life of Henry Hammond. Oxford 1856.

Mayor, J. E. B. Autobiography of Matthew Robinson. 1856. Contains Matthew Poole's Model for the maintaining of students of choice abilities at the University and principally in order to the Ministry. 1648.

— Spain, Portugal, the Bible. Cambridge 1892. On relations of English and foreign reformers.

Smith, P. A. History of education for the English Bar. 1860.

Young, G. History of Greek literature in England from the earliest times to the end of the reign of James I. Cambridge 1862.

Cox, R. The literature of the Sabbath question. 2 vols 1865. With bibliography of works on the Sabbath.

Dircks, H. A biographical memoir of Samuel Hartlib, with bibliographical notices. 1865. For letters between Hartlib and Dr Worthington see Worthington's Diary ed J. Crossley and R. C. Christie 3 pts 1847–86 (Chetham Soc).

Mullinger, J. B. Cambridge characteristics in the 17th century. Cambridge 1867.

— The University of Cambridge from the Royal Injunctions of 1535 to the accession of Charles I. Cambridge 1884.

Quick, R. H. Essays on educational reformers. 1868.

Pattison, M. Isaac Casaubon. 1875, Oxford 1892. With sketches of scholarship in England and abroad.

— Essays. 2 sers Oxford 1889. In ser 1: The Stephenses, Joseph Scaliger, Calvin at Geneva; ser 2: Learning in the Church of England.

Wordsworth, C. Scholae academicae: some account of the studies at the English universities in the eighteenth century. 1877.

Beard, C. The Reformation of the 16th century in its relation to modern thought and knowledge. 1883 (Hibbert lectures).

Mitchell, A. F. The Westminster Assembly: its history and standards. 1883.

Christie, R. C. The old Church and school libraries of Lancashire. 1885 (Chetham Soc).

Child, G. W. Church and State under the Tudors. 1890. On influence of Geneva.

Schickler, F. de. Les églises du refuge en Angleterre. 3 vols Paris 1892.

Bowes, R. Catalogue of books printed at or relating to Cambridge. 1894.

Madan, F. The early Oxford Press '1468'–1640. Oxford 1895.

Power, D'A. William Harvey. 1897.

Underhill, J. G. Spanish literature in the England of the Tudors. New York 1899.

Payne, J. F. Thomas Sydenham. 1900.

St John, W. Contest for liberty of conscience in England. Chicago 1900. With bibliography.

Shaw, W. A. History of the English church during the Civil Wars and under the Commonwealth 1640–60. 2 vols 1900.

Walton, J. Early history of legal studies in England. 1900.

Begley, Walter. Nova Solyma: the ideal city, an anonymous romance in Latin 1648, with introduction, translation, literary essays and a bibliography. 2 vols 1902.

Crowoll, A. and W. Eames. Three centuries of English book trade bibliography. New York 1903.

Hathaway, C. M. The alchemist by Ben Jonson. New York 1903. With introd on alchemical learning.

Laurie, S. S. Studies in the history of educational opinion. Cambridge 1903.

Sandys, J. E. A history of classical scholarship from the revival of learning to the end of the 18th century in Italy, France, England and the Netherlands. 3 vols Cambridge 1903–8.

Dexter, H. M. and M. The England and Holland of the Pilgrims. Boston 1905. With index of Separatist literature and controversy.

Moore, N. The history of the study of medicine in the British Isles. Oxford 1908.

Birch, U. Anna van Schurman: artist, scholar, saint. 1909.

Watson, F. Scholars and scholarship 1600–60. CHEL vol 7 1911.

Re, A. del. Florio, Bruno and the Sidney circle. In his Secret of the Renaissance, Tokyo 1930.

Allison, T. Pioneers of English learning. Oxford 1932.

Greg, W. W. (ed). English literary autographs 1550–1650; supplement: scholars and archaeologists. Oxford 1932.

Twigg, O. M. Richard Creagh, Archbishop of Armagh 1515–85. Dublin Rev 191 1932.

Young, R. F. Comenius in England 1641–2. 1932.

Hayes, C. J. H. The significance of the Reformation in the light of contemporary scholarship. Catholic History Rev 17 1933.

Humbert, P. Un amateur: Pieresc 1580–1637. Paris 1933.

Tchemerzine, A. Bibliographie d'ouvrages sur les sciences et les arts édités aux xve et xvie siècles. Courbevoie (Seine) 1933.

Zamick, M. Edmund Castell. TLS 2 Nov 1933.

Denholm-Young, N. and E. Craster. Roger Dodsworth 1584–1654 and his circle. Bodleian Quart Record 7 1934.

Flower, R. Laurence Nowell and a recovered Anglo-Saxon poem. BM Quart 8 1934.

Lloyd, A. H. The early history of Christ's College, Cambridge. Cambridge 1934. A history of scholarship just before the Reformation.

Williams, F. B. John Bodenham, 'art's lover, learning's friend'. SP 31 1934.

— Thomas Rogers of Bryanston, an Elizabethan gentleman-of-letters. Harvard Stud & Notes in Philology 16 1934.

— Scholarly publication in Shakespeare's day: a leading case. In J. Q. Adams memorial studies, Washington 1948. On John Minsheu's Guide into the tongues, 1617.

Cooligan, J. H. The Hon William Whittingham of Chester (c. 1524–79). 1935. Whittingham was a member of Brasenose College, All Souls and Christ Church, Oxford, and Dean of Durham.

Crosfield, Thomas. The diary of Thomas Crosfield, MA, BD, Fellow of Queen's College, Oxford: selection. Ed F. S. Boas 1935.

Fraser-Harris, D. F. William Harvey's knowledge of literature: classical, medieval, Renaissance and contemporary. Proc Royal Soc of Medicine 27 1935.

Stimson, D. Comenius and the invisible college. Isis 23 1935.

White, B. An early Tudor grammarian. MLR 30 1935. Robert Whittinton.

Allen, H. B. Old books. Quart Jnl of Speech 22 1936. Rainolde's Foundacion of rhetorike.

Craig, H. The enchanted glass: the Elizabethan mind in literature. New York 1936.

Fiedler, H. G. A contemporary of Shakespeare's on phonetics and on the pronunciation of English and Latin. Oxford 1936. Robert Robinson.

Jones, R. F. Ancients and moderns: a study of the background to the battle of the books. St Louis 1936.

Lehnert, M. Die Grammatik des englischen Sprachmeisters John Wallis (1616–1703). Breslau 1936.

Williamson, G. Richard Whitlock, learning's apologist. PQ 15 1936.

Walker, W. F. Renaissance academies. Humberside 6 1937.

Wasserman, E. R. The scholarly origin of the Elizabethan revival. ELH 4 1937.

Austin, W. B. Claudius Hollyband: an Elizabethan schoolmaster. N & Q 30 Sept, 7 Oct 1939.

Tuve, R. Ancients, moderns and Saxons. ELH 6 1939.

Borish, M. E. A second version of John Day's Peregrinatio scholastica. MLN 55 1940.

Bourland, C. B. Gabriel Harvey and the modern languages. HLQ 4 1941.

Ashton, J. W. The fall of Icarus. PQ 20 1941. The ethics of learning.

Paton, J. L. The tercentenary of Comenius's visit to England 1592–1641. Bull John Rylands Lib 26 1941.

Needham, J. (ed). The teacher of nations: essays and addresses in commemoration of the visit to England of Comenius. Cambridge 1941.

Utley, F. L. Two seventeenth-century Anglo-Saxon poems. MLQ 3 1942. On William Retchford.

Brinsley, John. A consolation for our grammar schools. Ed T. C. Pollock 1943.

Johnson, F. R. Two Renaissance textbooks of rhetoric: Aphthonius' Progymnasmata and Rainfold's Foundacion of rhetorike. HLQ 6 1943.

Kristeller, P. O. The place of classical humanism in Renaissance thought. JHI 4 1943.

Spinka, M. Comenius: that incomparable Moravian. Chicago 1943.

William Chillingworth. TLS 29 Jan 1944. Reply by J. R. Wingfield-Digby 12 Feb 1944.

Richards, G. R. B. A seventeenth-century Master and his 'grammar schoole'. More Books 19 1944. John Brinsley's Ludus literarius 1627 edn.

Turnbull, G. H. Notes on John Drury's 'reformed librarie-keeper'. Library 5th ser 1 1946.

— Hartlib, Drury and Comenius: gleanings from Hartlib's papers. Liverpool 1947.

— The visit of Comenius to England in 1641. N & Q 31 March 1951. On the tract 'England's thankfulnesse' pbd Sept or Oct 1641 by Hartlib and possibly written by Drury.

— Hartlib's connection with Sir Francis Kynaston's Musaeum Minervae. N & Q 19 Jan 1952.

Weisinger, H. The study of the revival of learning from Bacon to Hallam. PQ 25 1946.

Hulbert, J. R. On the origin of the grammarian's rules for the use of 'shall' and 'will'. PMLA 62 1947.

Emery, C. John Wilkins' universal language. Isis 38 1948.

McKracken, G. E. Athanasius Kircher's universal polygraphy. Isis 39 1948.

Turner, A. Another seventeenth-century Anglo-Saxon poem. MLQ 9 1948. By Joseph Williamson.

DeJongh, W. F. J. Western language manuals of the Renaissance. Albuquerque 1949.

Goepp, P. H. Verstegan's 'most ancient Saxon words'. In Philologica: the [Kemp] Malone anniversary studies, Baltimore 1949. On Verstegan's Restitution of decayed intelligence concerning the English nation, 1605.

Kökeritz, H. John Hart and early standard English. Ibid.

Van Norden, L. Pieresc and the English scholars. HLQ 12 1949.

Craig, L. C. Nicholas Ferrar, junior: a linguist of Little Gidding. 1950.

Hudson, W. M. Archbishop Ussher quotes Taliesin. N & Q 5 Aug 1950.

— Ossian in English before Macpherson: [Meredith] Hammer's Chronicle of Ireland, 1633. SE 29 1950.

Nadeau, R. Thomas Farnaby: schoolmaster and rhetorician of the English Renaissance. Quart Jnl of Speech 36 1950.

John Rainolds, epigrammatist. Bodleian Lib Record 3 1950.

Sir Henry Savile. TLS 27 Jan 1950. As Warden of Merton College Oxford.

Tillyard, E. M. W. The Elizabethan world picture. 1950.

Woolf, H. B. John Cleveland's 'West Saxon poet'. PQ 30 1951. The poet may be Abraham Wheloc.

— A note on William Retchford. N & Q 5 Jan 1952. Retchford's Anglo-Saxon poem.

Wright, C. E. The dispersal of the monastic libraries and the beginnings of Anglo-Saxon studies: Matthew Parker and his circle, a preliminary study. Trans Cambridge Bible Soc 1 1951.

Bennett, H. S. A check-list of Robert Whittinton's grammar. Library 5th ser 7 1952.

Simonini, R. C. Italian scholarship in Renaissance England. Chapel Hill 1952.

— John Florio, scholar and humanist. In Tribute to G. C. Taylor, Chapel Hill 1952.

— The Italian pedagogy of Claudius Hollyband. SP 49 1952.

Brewer, D. S. Sixteenth-, seventeenth- and eighteenth-century references to the voyage of Ohthere (Ohtheriana IV). Anglia 71 1953. Laurence Nowell's lost transcript of the text.

Duhamel, P. A. The Oxford lectures of John Colet. JHI 14 1953.

Maddison, F., D. Styles and A. Wood. Sir William Dugdale 1605–86: a list of his printed works and of his portraits with notes on his life and the manuscript sources. Warwick 1953.

Schlatter, R. The higher learning in Puritan England. Historical Mag of Protestant Episcopal Church 23 1954.

Danielsson, B. John Hart's works on English orthography and pronunciation 1551, 1569, 1570. 2 pts Stockholm 1955–63.

DeMott, B. Comenius and the Real Character in England. PMLA 70 1955.
— The sources and development of John Wilkins' philosophical language. JEGP 57 1958.
Goldschmidt, E. P. The first Cambridge press in its European setting. Cambridge 1955.
Fox, L. (ed). English historical scholarship in the sixteenth and seventeenth centuries. 1956.
Jayne, S. R. Library catalogues of the English Renaissance. Berkeley 1956.
Murray, J. J. John Hales on history. HLQ 19 1956.
O'Sullivan, W. Ussher as a collector of manuscripts. Hermathena 88 1956.
Costello, W. T. The scholastic curriculum at early seventeenth-century Cambridge. Cambridge Mass 1958.
Schoeck, R. J. Early Anglo-Saxon studies and legal scholarship in the Renaissance. Stud in Renaissance 5 1958.
Wormald, F. and S. E. Wright (ed). The English library before 1700. 1958.
Clarke, M. L. Classical education in Britain 1500–1900. Cambridge 1959.
Curtis, M. H. Oxford and Cambridge in transition 1558–1642. Oxford 1959.
Ker, N. R. Oxford college libraries in the sixteenth century. Bodleian Lib Record 6 1959.
Lehmberg, S. E. Sir Thomas Elyot: Tudor humanist. Austin 1960.
Lievsay, J. L. Stefano Guazzo and the English Renaissance 1575–1675. Chapel Hill 1961.
Rosier, J. L. The sources and methods of Minsheu's Guide into the tongues. PQ 40 1961.
Roth, L. Hebraists and non-Hebraists of the seventeenth century. Jnl of Semitic Stud 6 1961.
Fussner, F. S. The historical revolution: English historical writing and thought 1580–1640. 1962.
Jones, R. F. The humanistic defence of learning in the mid-seventeenth century. In Reason and the imagination, ed J. A. Mazzeo, New York 1962.
Owen, A. L. The famous Druids: a survey of three centuries of English literature on the Druids. Oxford 1962.
Major, J. M. Sir Thomas Elyot and Renaissance humanism. Lincoln Nebraska 1964.
Alston, R. C. A bibliography of the English language from the invention of printing to the year 1800. 20 vols Leeds 1965–. Covers grammars, dictionaries, teaching, Latin, Greek.
Charlton, K. Education in Renaissance England. 1965.
Hill, C. Intellectual origins of the English Revolution. Oxford 1965.
Danielsson, B. and R. C. Alston (ed). The works of William Bullokar. Leeds 1966–.
Josten, C. H. (ed). Elias Ashmole 1617–92. 5 vols Oxford 1966.
Sadler, J. E. Comenius and the concept of universal education. 1966.
Simon, J. Education and society in Tudor England. Cambridge 1966.
Sommerlad, M. J. The continuation of Anthony Wood's Athenae oxonienses. Bodleian Lib Record 7 1966.
Mackenzie, N. Sir Thomas Browne as a man of learning. Eng Stud in Africa 10 1967.
Hattaway, M. Paradoxes of Solomon: learning in the English Renaissance. JHI 29 1968.
Kearney, H. F. Scholars and gentlemen: universities and society in pre-industrial Britain 1500–1700. 1970.
McKisack, M. Medieval history in the Tudor age. Oxford 1971.

On the Sabbath question see:

Levy, D. Der Sabbath in England: Wesen und Entwicklung des englischen Sonntags. Leipzig 1933.
Whitaker, W. B. Sunday in Tudor and Stuart times. 1933.

(2) DICTIONARIES

Cotgrave, R. A dictionaire of the French and English tongues: edition of 1611. Ed W. S. Woods, Columbia Missouri 1950.
Nowell, L. Vocabularium saxonicum. Ed A. H. Marckwardt, Ann Arbor 1952.

Authorities

Starnes, D. T. Bilingual dictionaries of Shakespeare's day. PMLA 52 1937.
— English dictionaries of the seventeenth century. SE 17 1937.
— 'The London vocabulary' and its antecedents. SE 19 1939.
— Literary features of Renaissance dictionaries. SP 37 1940.
— and G. E. Noyes. The English dictionary from Cawdrey to Johnson 1604–1755. Chapel Hill 1946.
— The poetic dictionary and the poet. Texas Univ Lib Chron 2 1946.
— Thomas Cooper's Thesaurus: a chapter in Renaissance lexicography. SE 28 1949.
— Renaissance dictionaries: English-Latin and Latin-English. Austin 1954.
— Sir Thomas Elyot and the Lanquet-Cooper chronicle. SE 34 1955.
— and E. W. Talbert. Classical myth and legend in Renaissance dictionaries. Chapel Hill 1955.
Starnes, D. T. John Florio reconsidered. Texas Stud in Lit & Lang 6 1965.
Noyes, G. E. Some interrelations of English dictionaries of the seventeenth century. PMLA 54 1939.
— The development of Cant lexicography in England 1566–1785. SP 38 1941.
— The first English dictionary, Cawdrey's 'Table alphabeticall'. MLN 58 1943.
Caldwell, R. A. An English Chaucer glossary. MLN 58 1943.
Marckwardt, A. H. Laurence Nowell's Vocabularium saxonicum and Somner's Dictioniarum. PQ 26 1947.
— An unnoted source of English dialect vocabulary. JEGP 46 1947. Nowell's Vocabularium.
Sledd, J. The English verses in the Huloet Higgins Dictionaire of 1572. MLN 63 1948.
— Nowell's Vocabularium saxonicum and the Elyot-Cooper-tradition. SP 51 1954.
Smalley, V. E. The sources of A dictionaire of the French and English tongues by Randle Cotgrave (1611): a study in Renaissance lexicography. Baltimore 1948.
Butt, J. A plea for more English dictionaries. Durham Univ Jnl 12 1951. Sir Thomas Elyot's neologisms etc.
Simonini, R. C. Italian-English language books of the Renaissance. Romanic Rev 42 1951.
Hulbert, J. R. Dictionaries British and American. 1955.
Wright, H. G. Thomas Speght as a lexicographer and annotator of Chaucer's works. E Studies 40 1959.
Rosier, J. L. The sources of John Joscelin's Old English-Latin dictionary. Anglia 78 1960.
— Lexical strata in Florio's New world of words. E Studies 44 1963.
Mary Joan, Sr. Minsheu's Guide into the tongues and Somner's Dictionarium. Mediaeval Stud 24 1962.
For English dictionaries see J. A. H. Murray, The evolution of English lexicography, Oxford 1900, and M. M. Mathews, A survey of English dictionaries, 1933. For contemporary books in divinity, history, physic and chirurgery, mathematics, common and civil law, Hebrew,

Latin and Greek, see William London's Catalogue, below. For the school text-books of the period see John Brinsley, Ludus literarius, 1612; and his Consolation for our grammar schools, 1622; and Charles Hoole, New discovery of the old art of teaching school, 1660, which gives a list of 300 school books, arranged for use in each of the 6 forms of a school. William London, Catalogue of the most vendible books, 1660, includes section on books useful for schools and scholars. For books used in grammar school teaching in all subjects see F. Watson, English grammar schools to 1660: their curriculum and practice, Cambridge 1908. For books of instruction, other than those used in the grammar school, see F. Watson, The beginnings of the teaching of modern subjects, 1909. For biographies of scholars see General dictionary: historical and critical, founded on Bayle, by J. P. Bernard, Thomas Birch etc, 10 vols 1735. For an account of rhetoric study see G. H. Mair, Introduction to reprint of Wilson's Art of rhetoric, Oxford 1909; B. Vickers, Classical rhetoric in English poetry, 1970.

(3) CONTEMPORARY WORKS OF GENERAL LEARNING
(in alphabetical order)

Brerewood, Edward. Enquiries touching the diversity of languages and religion through the chiefe parts of the world. 1614, 1622, 1674.

Brinsley, John. Ludus literarius, or the grammar schoole: shewing how to proceede from the first entrance into learning, to the highest perfection required in the grammar schools with ease, certainty and delight, both to masters and schollers; onely according to our common grammar, and ordinary classical authors etc. 1612, 1627; ed E. T. Campagnac, Liverpool 1917.

Clarke, John (headmaster of Lincoln Grammar School). Paroemiologia anglo-latina: or proverbs English and Latin; methodically disposed according to the common-place heads in Erasmus his Adages. 1639. The most complete collection of English proverbs was that of John Ray, the naturalist, A collection of English proverbs with short annotations, 1670, the preface to which gives an account of the previous English collections.

Clarke, Samuel. The marrow of ecclesiastical history with lives of 148 Fathers, schoolmen and modern divines. 1649, 1654 (enlarged), 1675.

Crowe, William. An exact collection or catalogue of our English writers on the Old and New testament. 1663. References to English commentators on every book of the Bible, and almost to every ch, and often to nearly every verse of a ch. Crow's book was followed by Bishop Wilkins's Catalogue 1668.

Drury, John. The reformed school. [1649?].

Estienne, Henri. The art of making devises: treating of hieroglyphicks, symboles, emblemes, aenigmas, sentences, parables, reverses of medals, arms, blazons, cimiers, cyphres and rebus, translated into English by Thomas Blount. 1650. The making of 'devices' involved some pictorial representation together with a symbolic meaning. When this is expressed in words it becomes an emblem. In the 16th and 17th centuries emblem-books were a recognised recreation to the scholar, and were used in schools as helps in phrase-making in both Latin and Greek prose and verse composition. Amongst the English emblem-writers were Geoffrey Whitney, Choice of emblems, 1586; Andrew Willet, 1598; Peacham's Minerva britannica, 1612; Francis Quarles, 1635; George Wither, 1635. The foreign emblem-writers, Alciati, Bocchius, Jovius, Maccius, quickened language study, especially Latin, by presenting the foreign languages along with pictures of what was described in words. On emblem literature see H. Green, Shakespeare and the emblem-writers, 1870, and cols 1327–34 above.

Habington, Thomas. The epistle of Gildas, entitled De excidio et conquestu Britanniae, translated into English. 1638.

Hales, John. Golden remains. 1659.

Harvey, William. Exercitatio anatomica de motu cordis et sanguinis in animalibus. 1628.

Heylyn, Peter. Cosmographie in four bookes, containing the horographie and historie of the whole world. 1652.

Hoole, Charles. A new discovery of the old art of teaching school. 1660; ed E. T. Campagnac, Liverpool 1913. This work, which contains the most complete school text-book bibliography, is extremely rare; rptd in Henry Barnard, English pedagogy ser 2, Hartford Conn 1876. The summarized list of about 300 school text books is given in A. F. Leach, Yorkshire schools, vol 2 of the Yorkshire Archaeological Soc Record Ser 33 1903.

Horne, Thomas. Manuductio in aedem Palladis, quâ utilissima methodus authores bonos legendi indigitatur. 1641. Perhaps the best book on contemporary methods of classical study in the early stages.

Howell, James. Lexicon tetraglotton [English, French, Italian, Spanish]. 1660. Howell pays great attention to the collection of proverbs in all these languages 'to take off the reproach which useth to be cast' upon the subject. Leigh Foelix Consortium, 1663, gives a list of collections in various languages. See also John Clarke, above, and Edward Leigh, below.

Junius, Franciscus [François Du Jon]. The painting of the Ancients, in three bookes: declaring by historicall observations and examples, the beginning, progresse and consummation of that most noble art, and how those ancient artificers attained to their still so much admired excellencie. 1638. Written first in Latin, Amsterdam 1637.
— Caedmonis monachi paraphrasis poetica Genesios. Amsterdam 1655. Gothicum glossarium, quo argentii codicis vocabula explicantur, 1664, and in 1665, an edn of the Moeso-Gothic text of Ulphilas; Quatuor DNIC evangeliorum versiones perantiquae duae, gothica scilicet [by Junius] et anglo-saxonica [by T. Marshall], Dordrecht 1665.

Leigh, Edward. Foelix consortium, or a fit conjunction of religion and learning: or learning the excellency and usefulness of it, the liberal arts, the chiefest languages, the universities and publick schools of several nations; particularising the men eminent for religion and learning divine or humane, among the Jews, Christians, ancient or modern writers, Protestants or Papists, characterising their persons, and giving judgment of their works. 1663.

London, William. A catalogue of the most vendible books in England, orderly and alphabetically digested; under the heads of divinity, history, physick and chyrurgery, law, arithmetick, geometry, astrologie, dialling, measuring land and timber, gageing, navigation, architecture, horsemanship, faulconry, merchandize, limning, military discipline, heraldry, fortification and fireworks, husbandry, gardening, romances, poems, playes etc, with Hebrew, Greek and Latin books, for schools and scholars, the like work never yet performed by any; varietas delectat. 1658; supplementary list 1660. Contains an epistle dedicatory to the gentry, ministers of the Gospel and others; of a peculiar choice to the wise, learned and studious in the northern counties of Northumberland, Bhpk [Bishopric] of Durham, Westmoreland and Cumberland.

Minsheu, John. Ἡγεμὼν εἰς τὰς γλώσσας: id est Ductor in linguas: the guide into tongues, cum illarum harmonia, et etymologiis, originationibus, rationibus et derivationibus, in omnibus his undecim linguis, viz 1 Anglica, 2 Cambro-britanica, 3 Belgica, 4 Germanica, 5 Gallica, 6 Italica, 7 Hispanica, 8 Lusitanica seu portugallica, 8 Latina, 10 Graeca, 11 Hebrea. 1617.

Somner, William. Dictionarium saxonico-latino-anglicum cum grammatica et glossario Aelfrici. Oxford 1659.

Spelman, Sir John. Psalterium Davidis Latino-Saxonicum vetus. 1640.

—— The life of King Alfred the Great. Ed T. Hearne, Oxford 1709. A Latin version by Christopher Wase, with a commentary by Obadiah Walker, pbd at Oxford 1678.

Ware, Sir James. De scriptoribus Hiberniae. Dublin 1639.

Hall, John. The advancement of learning. Ed A. K. Croston, Liverpool 1953 (facs).

Stanbridge, John. The Vulgaria of John Stanbridge and of Robert Whittinton. Ed B. White 1936.

(4) BIBLICAL SCHOLARSHIP

Walton, Brian (Bishop of Chester). Biblia sacra polyglotta, complectentia textus originales, hebraicum, cum Pentateucho samaritano, chaldaicum, graecum; versionumque antiquarum, samaritanae, graecae lxxii; interp., chaldaicae, syriacae, arabicae, aethiopicae, persicae, vulg. lat. quicquid comparari poterat, cum textum & versionum orientalium translationibus latinis ex vetutissimis mss undique conquisitis, optimisque exemplaribus impressis, summa fide collatis, cum apparatu, appendicibus, tabulis, variis lectionibus, etc. 6 vols 1657. The great triumph in oriental studies by English scholars of the period. The following appear to have assisted Brian Walton: Edmund Castell, Archbishop Ussher, Herbert Thorndike, Edward Pococke, John Lightfoot, Thomas Greaves, Abraham Whelock, Samuel Clarke (architypographus of the University of Oxford), Dudley Loftus, John Vicars, David Stokes, Thomas Smith, Thomas Hyde, Richard Heath, Alexander Huish, Thomas Pierce, Henry Hammond, Patrick Young, Archbishop Sheldon, Archbishop Sterne, Bishop Sanderson, Bishop Ferne, William Fuller, Bruno Ryves, Samuel Baker, Richard Drake, John Johnson, Meric Casaubon, John Selden, William Norris, Claude Hardie.

Pearson, John (Bishop of Chester) et al. Critici sacri: sive doctissimorum virorum in SS. Biblia annotationes et tractatus. Ed John Pearson, A. Scattergood, F. Gouldman and R. Pearson 9 vols 1660, 13 vols Amsterdam 1698–1732.

Poole, Matthew. Synopsis criticorum aliorumque S. Scripturae interpretum opera Matthaei Poli. 5 vols 1669–76. The 2 works above, the Critici sacri and the Synopsis, are the most learned collections of annotations and treatises on the Bible of the period; they include the work of both foreign and English scholars.

Commentaries in English on the Whole Bible

The Douay commentary. 1609.

Commentaries. Ed John Mayer 7 vols 1653.

The annotations of John Diodati. 1656.

The Dutch annotations. Tr Theodore Haak 2 vols 1657.

The English annotations. 2 vols 1657.

For commentaries on separate books of the Bible, see W. Crow, and cols 1858f., above.

Ainsworth, Henry. The booke of Psalmes, englished both in prose and metre. Amsterdam 1612.

—— Solomon's Song of songs in English metre. 1623.

Bois, John. Veteris interpretis cum Beza aliisque recentioribus collatio in quatuor Evangeliis et Apostolorum Actis: opus auspiciis Lanceloti [Andrewes] Wintoniensis Episcopi coeptum et profectum. 1655.

Burgess, Anthony. 145 expository sermons on the whole 17th chapter according to John. 1656.

Cosin, John (Bishop of Durham). A scholastical history of the Canon of the Holy Scripture. 1657.

Diodati, Giovanni. Pious annotations upon the Holy Bible. 1643.

Ferrar, Nicholas (of Little Gidding). The actions and doctrine and other passages concerning our Lord Jesus Christ, as they are related by the foure Evangelists, reduced into one complete body of historie. 1635. Compiled by Ferrar and his family.

Fuller, Nicholas. Miscellaneorum theologicorum, quibus non modo Scripturae Divinae, sed et aliorum classicorum auctorum plurima monumenta explicantur atque illustrantur. Oxford 1616.

Hildersham, Arthur. Lectures upon the Fourth of John. 1629, 1632.

—— CLII lectures upon Psalm II. 1635.

Leigh, Edward. Critica sacra in two parts: the first containing observations on all the radices or primitive Hebrew words of the Old testament; the second, Philologicall and theological observations upon all the Greek words of the New testament. 1650.

Lightfoot, John. On the canon of Scripture. 1652.

Mede (or Mead), Joseph. Clavis Apocalyptica ex innatis et insitis visionum characteribus eruta et demonstrata. Cambridge 1627.

—— The key of the Revelation searched and demonstrated out of the naturall and proper characters of the visions; translated by Richard More, with a Preface written by Dr Twisse. 1643.

Smith, Miles. Said to have written the Preface to the Authorized Version of the Bible, 1611.

Authorities

Williams, A. Commentaries on Genesis as a basis for hexameral material in the literature of the late Renaissance. SP 34 1937.

—— The common expositor: an account of the commentaries on Genesis 1527–1633. Chapel Hill 1948.

Lockwood, D. P. and R. H. Bainton. Classical and biblical scholarship in the age of the Renaissance and Reformation. Church History 10 1941.

Woolf, H. B. A note on William Retchford. N & Q 5 Jan 1952. Retchford tr David Dickinson's Exposition of the Pauline Epistles from the Latin, and enlarged R. Bernard's Thesaurus biblicus.

Hall, B. Biblical scholarship: editing and commentaries. In The Cambridge history of the Bible vol 2, ed S. L. Greenslade, Cambridge 1963.

(5) THE EARLY FATHERS AND SCHOOLMEN

Burton, William. Annotations to the first epistle of Clement the apostle to the Corinthians. 1647. Set forth in Latin by Patrick Young, 1633, from which this English trn was made 'to cure the many distracting schisms of the time'.

—— Clement the blessed Paul's fellow labourer in the Gospel, his first epistle to the Corinthians. 1650.

Bustus, Matthaeus. Joannis Metropolitani Euchaitensis versus iambici in principalium festorum pictas in tabulis historias atque alia varia compositi; nunc primum in lucem edita. Eton 1610.

Evelyn, John. The golden book of St Chrysostom, concerning the education of children translated into English by J[ohn] E[velyn] esq. 1659.

Harmar, John. Eclogae sententiarum et similitudinum e D. Chrysostomo decerptae, graec. et lat. cum annot. 1622.
— Lexicon, etymologicon graecum, junctim cum Scapula. 1637.
Healey, John. Of the citie of God with the learned comments of Jo. Lodovicus Vives, englished first by J.H. and now in this second edition compared with the Latin originall, and in very many places corrected and amended. 1620. First edn 1610.
Humphrey, R. Christian offices cristall glass, written by S. Ambrose. 1637.
Montagu, Richard (Bishop of Chichester). Sancti Gregorii Nazianzeni in Julianum invectivae duae, cum scholiis graecis nunc primum editis et eiusdem authoris non-nullis aliis; omnia ex bibliotheca clarissimi viri D. Henrici Savilii edidit R. M[ontagu]. Eton 1610.
— Nonni Panopolitani collectio et expositio historiarum fabularumque in Gregorii Nazianzeni orationes, sive steliteuticas duas adversus Julianum Augustum; graece, ex codice Bibl Vindobonensis edidit R. Montagu, cum Gregorii Nazianzeni utraque in Julianum invectiva. Eton 1610.
— Eusebii de demonstratione evangelica libri decem, omnia studio R. M. Latine facta, notis illustrata. 1628.
— Φωτίου ἐπιστολαί: Photii sanctissimi patriarchae Constantinopolitani epistolae Latine redditae et notis subinde illustratae. 1651.
— Sancti Justini apoligia prima pro Christianis; cum Tryphone Judaeo dialogus: subjunctis emendationibus et notis Montacutii. 1700.
Rutherford, Samuel (1600–61). Mentioned in Milton's poem On the new forcers of conscience; for his works see DNB.
Savile, Sir Henry. S. Joannis Chrysostomi opera graece. 8 vols Eton 1610–3.
Spencer, William. Origenis contra Celsum libri octo; eiusdem Philocalia; Gulielmus Spencerus utriusque

operis versionem recognovit, et annotationes adjecit. Cambridge 1658.
Ussher (or Usher), James. Polycarpi et Ignatii epistolae; graec lat cum de eorum dissertatione scriptis, deque apostolicis canonibus et constitutionibus Clementi tributis. Oxford 1644. Text with Latin trn.
— Historia dogmatica controversiae inter orthodoxos et pontificios de scripturis et sacris vernaculis nunc primum duae de pseudo-Dionysii scriptis et de epistola ad Laodicenos, ante hac ineditae. Ed Henry Wharton 1690.
Whelock, Abraham. Quatuor evangeliorum Domini Nostri Jesu Christi versio persica, syriacam et arabicam suavissime redolens: ad verba et mentem graeci textus fideliter et venuste concinnata. Codicibus tribus manuscriptis ex oriente in academias utrasque Anglorum perlatis, operose invicem diligenterque collatis. 1657.
Young, Patrick (Patricius Junius). Clementis ad Corinthios epistola prior: ex laceris reliquiis vetustissimi exemplaris bibliotecae regiae, eruit, lacunas explevit, latinè vertit et notis brevioribus illustravit Patricius Junius. Oxford 1633.
— Catena graecorum patrum in beatum Job collectore Niceta, Heracleae metropolita, ex duobus mss bibliothecae Bodleianae codicibus, graece nunc primum in lucem edita, et latine versa. Accessit ad calcem textus Jobi διχήρως, juxta veram et germanam Septuaginta Seniorum interpretationem, ex venerando Bibliothecae Regiae ms codice, et totius orbis antiquissimo ac praestantissimo. 1637.

Studies

Ker, N. R. Thomas James's Collation of Gregory, Cyprian and Ambrose. Bodleian Lib Record 4 1952.
Oulton, J. E. L. Ussher's work as a patristic scholar and Church historian. Hermathena 88 1956.
Greenslade, S. L. The English reformers and the Fathers of the Church. Oxford 1960.

(6) DISPUTATIONAL LEARNING

Chillingworth, William. The religion of Protestants a safe way to salvation: or an answer to a booke entituled Mercy and truth, or charity maintained by Catholiques, which pretends to prove the contrary. Oxford 1638. Based on John Daillé, a French divine.
Crakanthorp, Richard. Justinian the Emperor defended against Cardinal Baronius. 1616.
— Defensio Ecclesiae Anglicanae contra M. Anton de Dominis Archiep. Spalatensis injurias. 1625.
— Vigilius dormitans: Rome's seer overseene; wherein the exceeding frauds of Cardinall Baronius and Binius are clearly discovered; opus posthumum. 1631.
Featley, Daniel. Roma ruens. 1644. Against Rome; author of nearly 40 different works, chiefly controversial.
— The dippers dipt. 1644. Against the Baptists.

Montagu, Richard (Bishop of Chichester). Appello Caesarem. 1625.
Rainolds, John. De romanae ecclesiae idolatria. Oxford 1596.
Sutcliffe, Matthew. De missa papistica variisque synagogae Rom. circa eucharistiae sacramentum erroribus et corruptelis, adversus R. Bellarminum. 1603.
Twisse, William. Vindiciae gratiae, potestatis ac providentiae Dei. Amsterdam 1632.
For further contemporary books of disputational literature see William London's Catalogue, 1660 and cols 1781–2006, above.

Studies

Porter, H. C. The nose of wax: scripture and the spirit from Erasmus to Milton. Trans Royal Historical Soc 5th set 14 1964.

(7) ECCLESIASTICAL AND THEOLOGICAL LEARNING

Baronius, Caesar, Cardinal. Annales ecclesiastici. 12 vols Rome 1588–1609.
Bilson, Thomas (Bishop of Winchester). De perpetua ecclesiae Christi gubernatione. 1611.
Birckbek, Simon. The Protestants evidence taken out of good records, showing that for 1500 years next after Christ, divers worthy guides of Gods Church have taught as the Church of England now doth. 1634.
Casaubon, Isaac. De rebus sacris et ecclesiasticis exercitationes 16 ad Baronii prolegomena in Annales. 1614.
Casaubon, Meric. On credulity and incredulity in things natural, civil and divine. 1668. Further pt issued 1670.
Clarke, Samuel (minister of St Benetfink). The marrow of

ecclesiastical historie, contained in the lives of the Fathers and other learned men. 1650, 1675 (3rd edn).
Crakanthorp, Richard. De providentia Dei tractatus. Cambridge 1623.
Field, Richard. Of the Church. 4 bks 1606; 5th bk, 1610.
Hall, Joseph (Bishop of Norwich). Polemices sacrae pars prior: Roma irreconciliabilis. 1611.
Leigh, Edward. Treatise of divinity, in three books. 1646.
— System or body of divinity, in 10 books. 1654.
Mason, Francis. Vindiciae Ecclesiae Anglicanae: sive de legitimo ejusdem ministerio, id est, de episcoporum successione, consecratione, electione et confirmatione libri 5. Ed N. Brent 1625.

Montagu, Richard (Bishop of Chichester). Diatribae upon the first part of the late History of tithes. 1621. An attack on Selden's History of tithes.
— Analecta ecclesiasticarum exercitationum. 1622. In answer to the Annales ecclesiastici of Baronius.
— Apparatus ad origines ecclesiasticas, collectore R. Montacutio. Oxford 1635.
— R. Montacutii de originibus ecclesiasticis commentationum tomus primus. 1636.
— ΘΕΑΝΘΡΩΠΙΚΟΝ: seu de vita Jesu Christi originum ecclesiasticarum libri duo, accedit Graecorum versio et index utriusque partis. 1640[-36]. Bk 2 not pbd.
— The acts and monuments of the Church before Christ incarnate. 1642.

Pearson, John (Bishop of Chester). Exposition of the Creed. 1659.

Rainolds, William. Calvino-Turcismus. Antwerp 1597.

Saltonstall, Wye. Ecclesiastical histories of Eusebius. 1650. 5th edn of Meredith Hanmer's trn (1577), to which were added Eusebius's Four books concerning the life of the Emperor Constantine and 2 orations by W.S.

Savile, Sir Henry. Thomae Bradwardini, archiepiscopi olim Cantuariensis, de causa Dei contra Pelagium et de virtute causarum. 1618.

Simson, Archibald. Hieroglyphica animalium terrestrium, volatilium, natatilium, reptilium, insectorum, vegetivorum, metallorum, lapidum etc, quae in scripturis sacris inveniuntur et plurimorum aliorum, cum eorum interpretationibus etc. 2 vols Edinburgh 1622-4.

Ussher (or Usher), James. De ecclesiarum christianarum successione et statu. 1613.
— Britannicarum ecclesiarum antiquitates. Dublin 1639.
— Chronologia sacra. Oxford 1660. Completed at Ussher's request by Gerard Langbaine.
— De romanae ecclesiae symbolo apostolico vetere alliisque fidei formulis diatriba. 1647.
— Annales veteris et Novi testamenti. 2 vols 1650-4.
— De graeca septuaginta interpretum versione syntagma. 1655.
For list of unpbd ms works see R. Parr, Life of Ussher, 1686, pp. 106-8.

Whelock, Abraham. Bedae Historia ecclesiastica gentis Anglorum v libris latine, cum saxonica versione Alfredi Regis cumque notis Abr Wheloci: adiecta etiam Chronologia saxonica, sax lat. Cambridge 1643, 1644.

Young, Patrick (Patricius Junius). Gilberti Foliot Episcopi Londiniensis expositio in Canticum canticorum, una cum compendio Alcuini; nunc primum è bibliotheca regio in lucem prodiit, opera & studio Patricii Junii. 1638.

For further contemporary books on ecclesiastical and theological subjects, see sections on divinity in William London's Catalogue, 1660 and cols 1781-2006, above. For books on Cases of conscience, see under Conscience in Robert Watt, Bibliotheca britannica 4 vols Edinburgh 1824. Also G. Every, Dr Grabe and his manuscript, Jnl of Theological Stud 8 1957.

(8) LATIN LEARNING

JOHN OWEN
1564?–1622

§ I

Epigrammatum Joannis Owen cambro-britanni libri tres, ad illustrissimam D. Mariam Neville. 1606, 1606, 1607, 1612.

Epigrammatum Joannis Owen cambro-britanni ad excellentissimam D. Arbellam Stuart liber singularis. 1607.

Epigrammatum Joannis Owen oxoniensis, cambro-britanni, libri tres; ad Henricum principem Cambriae duo; ad Carolum Eboracensem unus. 1612.

Epigrammatum Joannis Owen cambro-britanni oxoniensis; ad tres Mecaenates, libri tres; ad Edwardum Noel equitem & baronetum, unus; ad Gulielmum Sidley equitem & baronetum, alter; ad Rogerum Owen equitem auratum, tertius. 1612.

Epigrammatum Joannis Owen libri decem. Leipzig 1615, Leyden 1628 etc; ed A. A. Renouard, Paris 1794; ed F. A. Ebert, Leipzig 1824.

Translations into English

Vicars, John. Epigrams of that most wittie and worthie epigrammatist Mr John Owen. 1619.

H[ayman], R[obert]. Quodlibets, lately come over from New Britaniola, Old Newfound-land, the first foure bookes being the authors owne: the rest translated out of Mr John Owen and other rare authors. 1628.

Harflete, Henry. A banquet of essays, fetcht out of famous Owen's confectionary. 1653. Essays on Ep 1, 2, with a trn.

Pecke, Thomas. Parnasi puerperium: or some wellwishes to ingenuity in the translation of six hundred of Owens epigrams. 1659.

Harvey, Thomas. John Owen's Latin epigrams, englished. 1677.

Trns of isolated epigrams are frequent. See, e.g. William Cowper, Poetical works, ed H. S. Milford, Oxford 1905 p. 563.

§ 2

Urban, E. Owenus und die deutschen Epigrammatiker des xvii Jahrhunderts. Berlin 1890.

Bensly, Edward. Robert Burton, John Barclay and Owen. CHEL vol 4 1909. Ch 13.
— Owen the epigrammatist. N & Q 9 Jan 1909.

JOHN BARCLAY
1582–1621

Bibliographies

Dukas, J. Etude bibliographique et littéraire sur le Satyricon de Barclay. Paris 1880.

Collignon, A. Notes historiques, littéraires et bibliographiques sur l'Argenis de Barclay. Paris 1902.
— Le portrait des esprits (icon animorum) de Barclay. Nancy 1906.

Becker, P. A. Johann Barclay 1582-1621. Zeitschrift für Vergleichende Litteraturgeschichte 15 1903.

Schmid, K. F. Barclays Argenis: eine literarhistorische Untersuchung: 1, Ausgaben der Argenis, ihrer Forsetzungen und Übersetzungen. Berlin 1904.

§ I

In P. Statii Papinii Thebaidos libros IIII commentarii. Pont-à-Mousson 1601.

Euphormionis Lusinini Satyricon. 1603 (no copies extant), Paris 1605 ('emendatum et auctum'); Euphormionis Lusinini Satyricon pars secunda, Paris 1607; Euphormionis Satyrici Apologia pro se, Paris 1610; Joannis Barclaii Icon Animorum, 1614. Both pts of Euphormio were rptd together with Apologia, with separate titles and pagination, [no place] 1610-11. These 3 with Icon animorum were rptd in the same way, [no place] 1616, also Strasbourg 1623 (with key), London 1624, Rouen 1628, Amsterdam 1628 etc; ed L. G. Bugnot, Leyden 1674.

Ad Jacobum I: carmen gratulatorium. Paris 1603.

Sylvae. 1606. Latin verses.

Johannis Barclaii Pietas. Paris 1612. A defence of his father against Cardinal Bellarmin.

Poemata. 1615.

Paraenesis ad sectarios. Rome 1617.

Joannis Barclaii Argenis. Paris 1621, 1622, 1623, 1624, 1625, Frankfurt 1626 (with Explicatio nominum), Leyden 1627 (with Discursus in Argeniden and Elenchus nominum), 1630 (with further Discursus) etc; ed L. G. Bugnot, Leyden 1659.

Carminum libri II cum lib. III ex Argenide. Cologne 1626.

Series patefacti divinitus parricidii in Regem Britanniae cogitati: nonis IXbribus MDCV. Amsterdam 1628 (appended to Euphormio, above) etc.

In Phaethonta Gallicium [i.e. Mancini]. Paris nd. Signed I.B.

Poematum libri duo. Oxford 1636.

Delitiae poetarum scotorum. 1637. Pt 1, pp. 76–136.

There are also verses by Barclay in W. Barclay's edn of Tacitus, Paris 1599, and a preface in W. Barclay, De potestate Papae, 1609.

Translations into English

For trns into languages other than English see Dukas and Schmid, above.

Long, Kingsmill. Barclay his Argenis: or the loves of Poliarchus and Argenis. 1625, 1636. Verses tr Thomas May.

Le Grys, Sir Robert and Thomas May. John Barclay his Argenis, the prose upon his Majesties command: by Sir Robert Le Grys Knight, and the verses by Thomas May esquire. 1629.

M[ay], Th[omas]. The mirrour of mindes. 2 pts 1631, 1633.

John Barclay his vindication of the intercession of saints, by a person of quality. 1688. Paraenesis ad haereticos bk 2, ch 7.

John Barclay his defence of the Eucharist, by a person of quality. 1688. Paraenesis ad haereticos bk 2 ch 11.

Jacob, John. The adventures of Poliarchus and Argenis. Dublin 1734. Abridgement; see E. Bensly, MLR 4 1909.

[Reeve, Clara]. The Phoenix: or the history of Polyarchus and Argenis. 4 vols 1772.

Turner, Paul. Euphormio's Satyricon. 1954. Pt 1 only.

A trn of Argenis by Ben Jonson was entered at Stationers' Hall 2 Oct 1623.

§2

For a summary of the original sources for Barclay's life and a list of later biographical studies see P. A. Becker, Zeitschrift für Vergleichende Literaturgeschichte 15 1903.

Dalrymple, D. (Lord Hailes). Sketch of the life of Barclay. 1786.

Coleridge, S. T. In his Literary remains vol 1, 1836.

Dukas, J. Etude bibliographique et littéraire sur le Satyricon de Barclay. Paris 1880.

Körting, H. Geschichte des französischen Romans im xvii Jahrhundert. 2 vols Leipzig 1885-7.

Urbain, C. Apropos de Barclay. Bulletin du Bibliophile 1891. Unpbd letters.

Collignon, A. Notes sur l'Euphormion de Barclay. Nancy 1901.

—— Notes historiques, littéraires et bibliographiques sur l'Argenis de Barclay. Paris 1902.

—— Le portrait des esprits (Icon animorum) de Barclay. Nancy 1906. Appendix C: Note complémentaire sur l'Argenis.

Becker, P. A. Johann Barclay. Zeitschrift für Vergleichende Literaturgeschichte 15 1903.

Schmid, K. F. Barclays Argenis, eine literarhistorische Untersuchung: 1, Ausgaben der Argenis, ihrer Fortsetzungen und Übersetzungen. Berlin 1904. Pp. 167-74, 17th- and 18th-century works on Argenis.

Bensly, E. Robert Burton, Barclay and John Owen. CHEL vol 4 1909. Ch 13.

Kettelhoit, P. Formanalyse der Barclay-Opitzschen Argenis. Bottrop 1934.

Bardino, L. L'Argenis di Barclay e il romanzo greco. Palermo 1940.

Langford, G. Barclay's Argenis: a seminal novel. SE 26 1947.

Fleming, D. A. Barclay: neo-Latinist at the Jacobean Court. Renaissance News 19 1966.

—— Barclay's Satyricon: the first satirical roman à clef. MP 65 1967.

OTHER LATINISTS

Bond, J. A. Quinti Horatii Flacci poemata, cum notis. 1606.

—— Persii Flacci satyrae. 1614. With notes.

Brinsley, John. For list of his school textbooks of classical authors see his Ludus literarius (1612), col 2276 above.

Busby, Richard. Juvenalis et Persii satirae in usum scholae Westmonasteriensis. 1656.

—— Martialis epigrammata in usum scholae Westmonasteriensis. 1661.

Casaubon, Isaac. Persii Flacci satirarum liber. 1647 (3rd edn with addns by Meric Casaubon).

Cogan, Thomas. Epistolarum familiarium Ciceronis epitome. Cambridge 1602.

Dempster, Thomas. Antiquitatum Romanarum corpus absolutissimum, in quo praeter ea, quae Joannes Rosinus delineaverat, infinita supplentur, mutantur, adduntur. 1613.

—— Nomenclatura scriptorum scotorum. Bologna 1619.

—— Apparatus ad historiam scoticam scriptorum scotorum nomenclatura. Bologna 1622.

Edmundson, Henry (d. 1659). Lingua linguarum: the natural language of languages; wherein it is desired and endeavoured that tongues may be brought to teach themselves and words may be best fancied, understood and remembered. 1658. In a vocabulary contrived and built upon analogy.

—— Homonyma et synonyma linguae latinae conjuncta et distincta. Oxford 1661.

Evelyn, John. Essay on first book of Lucretius de rerum natura with a metrical version and notes. 1656.

Farnaby, T. J. Juvenalis et A. Persii Flacci satyrae; cum annotationibus marginalibus. 1612.

—— Senecae tragoediae. 1613. With notes.

—— Martialis epigrammaton libri. 1615. With notes.

—— Lucani Pharsalia. 1618. With notes.

—— P. Virgilii Maronis opera notis admarginalibus illustrata a T.F. 1634.

Farnaby, Thomas and Meric Casaubon. P. Terentii Afri comoediae sex; ex recensione Heinsiana, cum adnotationibus T.F. in quatuor priores & Merici Casauboni Is. filii in duas posteriores. 1651.

[Gott, Samuel]. Novae Solymae libri sex. 1648, 1649 (as Nova Solyma); ed and tr W. Begley 2 vols 1902.

Gouldman, Francis. Dictionarium. 1664. A 'comprisal' of the Latin dictionaries of Thomas Thomas, John Rider (1589), Thomas and P. Holland (1615). In his preface Gouldman gives a history of Latin dictionaries in England from Elyot's dictionary (1538) to his own.

[Hall, Joseph]. Mundus alter et idem: anth Mercurio Britannico. Frankfort (for London?) [1605]; tr J. H[ealey] [1609?]; ed H. Brown, Cambridge Mass 1937.

Heath, John. Two centuries of epigrammes. 1610.

Holyoke, Francis. Dictionarium etymologicum latinum. 1633. In the final form, 1677-6, there are 3 pts, English-Latin, Latin-English, and a Dictionary of names. This was ed and enlarged by the compiler's son Thomas Holyoke, who claims that in the English-Latin pt there are 10,000 more words than in any previous dictionary.

Jackson, Henry. Added marginal notes and copious index to the De tradendis disciplinis of J. L. Vives, pt of the De disciplinis libri xii, Leyden 1612.

James, William. 'Had a chief hand' (Wood) in The English introduction to the Latin tongue for the use of the lower forms in Westminster School, 1659.

Jones, Basset. Herm'aelogium: or an essay at the rationality of the art of speaking as a supplement to Lillie's Grammer, philosophically, mythologically and emblematically offered. 1659.

Kynaston (or Kinaston), Sir Francis. Translation of first and second books of Chaucer's Troilus and Criseyde into Latin. Oxford 1635. Prefaced by 15 short Latin poems.

Leech, John. Epigrammatum libri quatuor. 1622.

Ogilby, John. P. Virgilii Maronis opera per J. Ogilvium edita. 1658. Illustr Hollar, Faithorne, Lombart et al.

Pengry, Moses. Cooper's Hill [by John Denham] latine redditum. 1676.

Rainolds, John. Oratio in laudem artis poeticae [c. 1572]. Ed W. Ringler, tr W. Allen, Princeton 1940.

Savile, Sir Henry. The ende of Nero and beginning of Galba; Four books of the Histories of Tacitus; The life of Agricola. Oxford 1591, 1612 (4th edn). Notes tr Latin by Is. Gruter and ptd Amsterdam 1649.

— A view of certain militar matters. 1591. In his trn of Tacitus.

Stapylton, Sir Robert. Juvenal's sixteen satyrs, with arguments, marginal notes and annotations clearing the obscure places out of the history, lawes and ceremonies of the Romans. 1647.

Stephens, Thomas. An essay upon Statius: or five books of his Thebais translated into English verse by T[homas] S[tephens]. 1648.

— Publii Papinii Statii Sylvarum libri v et duo Achilleidos, cum notis marginalibus. Cambridge 1651.

Stradling, Sir John. Epigrammatum libri quatuor. 1607.

— Two books of constancie written in Latin by Justus Lipsius: englished by Sir John Stradling. Ed R. Kirk, New Brunswick NJ 1939.

Thomas, Thomas [and Philemon Holland]. Dictionarium. 1615.

Weston, Elizabeth Jane. Parthenicon Elizabethae Joannae Westoniae virginis nobilissimae, poetriae florentissimae, linguarum plurimarum peritissimae: lib i, ii, iii. Prague [c. 1606]. With list of learned women from Deborah to Elizabeth Weston.

For Latin academic plays see col 1371, above.

Studies

Meier, H. et al (ed). Bibliography on the survival of the classics. Vols 1-2, 1934-8. Text of German edn of 1932-4, with English trn.

Fiedler, H. G. A contemporary of Shakespeare's on phonetics and on the pronunciation of English and Latin. Oxford 1936.

Gee, J. A. Berthelet's Latin-English publication of the Apophthegmata Graeciae sapientum and other sayings formerly edited by Erasmus. SP 35 1938.

Gilbert, A. H. Mock-accents in Renaissance and modern Latin. PMLA 54 1939.

Mann, W. Lateinische Dichtung in England vom Ausgang des Frühhumanismus bis zum Regierungsantritt Elisabeths. Halle 1939.

Newdigate, B. H. The English pronunciation of Latin AD 1529. N & Q 30th Sept 1939.

Pyles, T. Tempest in teapot: reform in Latin pronunciation. ELH 6 1939.

Bradner, L. Musae anglicanae: a history of Anglo-Latin poetry 1500-1925. New York 1940.

Allen, D. C. Latin literature. MLQ 2 1941. A bibliographical survey.

Lockwood, D. P. and R. H. Bainton. Classical and biblical scholarship in the age of the Renaissance and Reformation. Church History 10 1941.

Schoell, F. L. Une discipline négligée: la littérature latine de la Renaissance. Lettres d'Humanité 6 1947.

Dain, A. Medieval and Renaissance Latin translations and commentaries. Bulletin de l'Association Guillaume Budé no 7 1949.

Weinberg, B. Translations and commentaries of Longinus, On the sublime, to 1600: a bibliography. MP 47 1950.

— Translations and commentaries of Demetrius, On style, to 1600: a bibliography. PQ 30 1951.

Starnes, D. T. Richard Huoet's Abcedarium: a study in English-Latin lexicography. SP 48 1951.

Allen, C. G. The sources of Lily's Latin grammar: a review of the facts and some further suggestions. Library 5th ser 9 1954.

— Certayne brief rules and Lily's Latin grammar. Library 5th ser 14 1959.

Finlayson, C. P. An unpublished commentary by George Buchanan on Virgil. Trans Edinburgh Bibl Soc 3-4 1957.

Kristeller, P. O. Latin manuscript books before 1600: a list of the printed catalogues and unpublished inventories of extant collections. New York 1965 (3rd edn).

— Medieval and Renaissance Latin translations and commentaries. Scriptorium 6 1952.

— Iter italicum: a finding list of uncatalogued or incompletely catalogued humanistic manuscripts of the Renaissance in Italian and other libraries; 1, Italy, Agrigento to Novara, 1963; 2, Italy, Orvieto to Volterra, Vatican City 1967.

(9) GREEK LEARNING

Barrow, Isaac. Euclidis elementorum libri xv breviter demonstrati. Cambridge 1655; tr 1660.

Burton, William. A commentary on Antonius his itinerary or journies of the Romane Empire so far as it concerneth Britain. 1658.

Busby, Richard (headmaster of Westminster School). Graecae grammatices rudimenta. [c. 1660].

Camden, William. Institutio graecae grammatices compendiaria in usum Regiae Scholae Westmonasteriensis. 1597. The standard Greek grammar for the 17th century as Lily's Grammar was for Latin.

Casaubon, Isaac. For Works see list in Mark Pattison's Life of Casaubon, 1892, pp. 475ff.

Casaubon, Meric. Marci Antonini Imperatoris de seipso et ad seipsum libri xii; nunc Xylandri versionem locis plurimis emendavit, et novam fecit; in Antonini libros notas et emendationes adjecit Mericus Casaubonus. 1632.

— Marcus Aurelius Antonius the Roman Emperour his meditations concerning himself [in English]. 1634.

— De verborum usu et accuratae eorum cognitionis utilitate diatriba. 1647.

— De quatuor linguis commentationis pars prior quae de lingua Hebraica: et de lingua saxonica. 1650. Casaubon did not finish the Latin and Greek.

— Cebetis tabula gr. et lat. cum notis MC cum epicteto. Cambridge 1659.

— Notae et emendationes in Optatum Afrum Milevitani episcopum de schismate Donatistarum. 1631.

— De nupera Homeri editione lugduno-batavica Hackiana; cum latina versione et Didymi Scholiis; sed et Eustathio et locis aliquot insignioribus ad Odysseam pertinentibus [etc]. 1659.

Chilmead, Edmund. De musica antiquâ graecâ. Appended to Oxford edn of Aratus, ed J. Fell, Bishop of Oxford, 1672.

Done, John. The auncient history of the Septuagint, written in Greeke by Aristeus 1900 years since, concerning the first translation of the holy Bible by the 72 interpreters. 1633.

Downes, Andrew. Eratosthenes, hoc est, brevis et luculenta defensio Lysiae pro caede Eratosthenis, praelectionibus illustrata. Cambridge 1593.

— [Notes in Sir Henry Savile's edn of St Chrysostom vol 8, 1613.]

— Praelectiones in Philippicam de Pace Demosthenis. 1621.

— [Letters in Greek to Casaubon; Epistolae].

— [Greek verses on death of Dr Whittaker (St John's College)].

— [Greek and Latin verses on death of Prince Henry, 1612].

Duport, James (Regius Professor of Greek, Cambridge). Θρηνοθρίαμβος: sive liber Job graeco carmine redditus, autore J[acobo] D[uport]. Cambridge 1637.

— Σολόμων ἔμμετρος: sive tres libri Solomonis scilicet, Proverbia, Ecclesiastes, Cantica, graeco carmine donati per J.D. Cambridge 1646.

— Homeri poetarum omnium saeculorum facile principis gnomologia duplici parallelismo illustrata: uno ex locis S. Scripturae, quibus gnomae Homericae aut prope affines aut non prorsus absimiles; altero ex gentium scriptoribus; ubi citationes, parodiae, allusiones et denique loci paralleli, etc. Cambridge 1660.

— Βίβλος τῆς Δημοσίας Εὐχῆς. [1665]. The Book of common prayer in ancient Greek.

— Δαβίδης ἔμμετρος: sive metaphrasis libri Psalmorum. Cambridge 1666.

Everard, Dr John. Divine Pymander of Hermes Trismegistus translated into English. 1650.

Farnaby, Thomas. Tabulae graecae linguac. nd.

Gataker, Thomas. Marci Antonini Imperatoris de rebus suis, sive de eis quae ad se pertinere censebat, libri xii, locis haud paucis repurgati, suppleti, restituti: versione insuper Latina nova; lectionibus item variis, locisque parallelis, ad marginem adjectis; ac commentario perpetuo, explicati atque illustrati. Cambridge 1652. For other contributions to classical learning by Gataker, see his Cinnus: sive adversaria miscellanea, 1651, and his Posthuma, 1659.

Goulston, Theodore. Aristotelis de poetica liber, latine conversus, et analytica methodo illustratus. 1623.

Greaves, John and Samuel Foster. Lemmata Archimedis, apud Graecos et Latinos jam pridem desiderata, e vetusto codice manuscripto arabico a J.G. traducta, et cum Arabum scholiis publicata, edidit et suis animadversionibus illustravit S.F. 1659. For edns of other writings on Greek mathematicians by Englishmen of the period, see John Wallis, Opera mathematica vol 3, Oxford 1699.

Grimeston (or Grimston), Edward. The history of Polybius, translated into English by E.G. 1633.

H., S. The whole Aphorisms of Hippocrates translated into English. 1610.

Hall, John (of Gray's Inn). Hierocles upon the golden verses of Pythagoras englished by J.H. 1657.

Healey, John. Epictetus his manuall: and Cebes his table, out of the Greek originall. 1610.

Hodges, Anthony. Achilles Tatius: the loves of Clitophon and Leucippe englished by A.H. Oxford 1638.

Langbaine, Gerard. Dionysii Longini Rhetoris de grandi loquentia. 1636. Ed and tr Latin with notes by Langbaine. Longinus, Of the height of eloquence was tr John Hall 1652.

Price, John. Commentarii in varios Novi testamenti libros; annotationes in Psalmorum librum [etc]. 1660.

Rainolds, John. Plutarchi Chaeronensis: 1, de utilitate ex hostibus capienda; 2, de morbis animi et corporis; D. Johanne Rainoldo interprete. Oxford 1614.

Selden, John. Marmora Arundelliana: sive saxa graece incisa, ex venerandis priscae orientis gloriae ruderibus, auspiciis et impensis Ill. Thomae, Comitis Arundelliae etc vindicata et in aedibus ejus hortisque disposita; accedunt inscriptiones aliquot veteris Latii, ex ejusdem vetustatis thesauro selectae; publicavit et Commentariolos adjecit Joh. Seldenus. 1628. With Richard James and Patrick Young.

Shirley, James. Εἰσαγωγή: sive introductorium anglo-latino-graecum; complectens colloquia familiaria, Aesopi Fabulas, et Luciani selectiores mortuorum dialogos, in usum scholarum. 1656.

Stanley, Thomas. Anacreon; Bion; Moschus; Kisses by Secundus; Cupid crucified by Ausonius: Venus Vigills; translated into English with notes. 1651.

Stapylton, C. B. Herodian of Alexandria his imperiall history converted into an heroick poem. 1652.

Stapylton (or Stapleton), Sir Robert. Musaeus, on the loves of Hero and Leander [with annotations by Stapleton]. 1647.

Stubbe, Henry. Otium literarum, sive miscellanea quaedam poemata. Oxford 1656. Includes Deliciae poetarum anglicanorum in graecum translatae, 1656, 1658. Stubbe tr Greek from Randolph and Crashaw in Horae subsecivae, 1651.

Thornley (or Thorneley), George. Longus, Daphnis and Cloe, translated into English. 1657.

Ussher (or Usher), James. De graeca septuaginta interpretum versione syntagma; cum libri Estherae editione Origenicâ, & vetere graecâ alterâ, ex Arundelliana Bibliotheca nunc primum in lucem producta. 1655.

Wallis, John (Savilian Professor of Geometry at Oxford). Claudii Ptolemaei harmonicorum libri tres, ex codd mss undecim, nunc primum graece editi; J. Wallis recensuit, edidit, versione et notis illustravit et auctarium adjecit. Oxford 1682. First Greek text of the work, with Latin trn and an account of Greek music; also a collection of passages from ancient authors bearing on musical theory, some from mss copies.

W[ase], C[hristopher]. Electra of Sophocles. Hague 1649.

Winterton, Ralph. Poetae minores graeci: Hesiodus, Theocritus, Moschus, Bion Smyrn, Simmias Rhod, Musaeus, Theognis, Phocylides, Pythagoras, Solon, Tyrtaeus, Simonides, Rhianus, Linus, Callimachus, Evenus Par, Eratosthenes, Menecrates, Posidippus, Metrodorus, fragmenta quaedam Philemonis etc. Cambridge 1635.

Studies

Meier, H. et al (ed). Bibliography on the survival of the classics. Vols 1–2, 1934–8. Text of the German edn of 1932–4, with English trn.

Tilley, A. Greek studies in England in the early sixteenth century. EHR 53 1938.

Lockwood, D. P. and R. H. Bainton. Classical and biblical scholarship in the age of the Renaissance and Reformation. Church History 10 1941.

Thompson, C. R. Some Greek and Grecized words in Renaissance Latin. Amer Jnl of Philology 64 1942.

Bush, D. Classical and foreign relations. In his English literature in the earlier seventeenth century, Oxford 1945, 1962 (rev). Bibliography.

Breaden, R. P. The first book printed in Greek. BNYPL Oct 1947.

Patton, J. M. Medieval and Renaissance visitors to Greek lands: Turkish Athens. Princeton 1951.

Dellarida, G. L. George Strachan: memorials of a wandering scholar of the seventeenth century. Aberdeen 1956. With catalogue of his oriental mss.

Simpkins, D. M. Early editions of Euclid in England. Annals of Science 22 1966.

E. J. K.

VI. LITERARY CRITICISM

See also The Puritan Attack on the Stage, *col 1395, above, which deals both with attacks and apologies they provoked; and J. E. Spingarn's list of contemporary foreign critics, CHEL vol 7, ch 11.*

(1) BIBLIOGRAPHIES

Wallace, K. R. Books on rhetorical theory 1500–1700. In his Francis Bacon on communication and rhetoric, Chapel Hill 1943.

Williams, F. B. Index of dedications and commendatory verses in English books before 1641. 1961 (Bibl Soc).

(2) COLLECTIONS

Haslewood, J. Ancient critical essays upon English poets and poesy. 2 vols 1811–15. *Haslewood.*

Collins, J. C. Critical essays and literary fragments. 1903 (Arber's English garner).

Gregory Smith, G. Elizabethan critical essays. 2 vols Oxford 1904. A full and representative collection with detailed introd and commentary; still standard. *Gregory Smith.*

Spingarn, J. E. Critical essays of the seventeenth century. 3 vols Oxford 1908–9. A sequel to Gregory Smith, above, with similarly full introd etc. *Spingarn.*

Klein, D. Literary criticism from the Elizabethan dramatists. New York 1910.

Cowl, R. P. The theory of poetry in England. 1914.

Jones, E. D. English critical essays: sixteenth, seventeenth and eighteenth centuries. Oxford 1922 (WC).

Bradley, J. F. and J. Q. Adams. The Jonson allusion-book 1597–1700. New Haven 1923.

Chambers, E. K. The Elizabethan stage. 4 vols Oxford 1923. Appendix C, vol 4, prints extracts from documents of literary criticism. *Chambers.*

— William Shakespeare. 2 vols Oxford 1930. Vol 2, Appendix c, The Shakespeare-mythos.

Spurgeon, C. F. E. Five hundred years of Chaucer criticism and allusion. 3 vols Cambridge 1925.

Gebert, C. An anthology of Elizabethan dedications and prefaces. Philadelphia 1933.

Smith, J. H. and E. W. Parks. The great critics. New York 1932, 1939 (rev and enlarged).

Flower, D. The pursuit of poetry: letters about poetry written by English poets 1550–1930. 1939.

Bate, W. J. Criticism: the major texts. New York 1952, 1970 (enlarged).

Adams, H. Critical theory since Plato. New York 1971.

(3) INDIVIDUAL CRITICS

Full bibliographies of many of these writers, including biographical and critical studies, and details of certain modern edns of the more important works, will be found elsewhere in this volume; see index. Only critical works are listed here. References to the standard selections, e.g. Gregory Smith, are not given except in the case of works not readily available in modern edns and of passages not easily located.

LEONARD COX
fl. 1572

The arte or crafte of rhetoryke. [1524], 1532; ed F. I. Carpenter, Chicago 1899.

SIR THOMAS ELYOT
1499?–1546

The boke named the governour. 1531 etc; ed H. H. S. Croft 2 vols 1880. *See* especially bk 1, chs 10, 13.

ROGER ASCHAM
1515–68

Collections
English works. Ed W. A. Wright, Cambridge 1904.

§ 1

Toxophilus. 1545, 1571 ('newlye perused') etc; ed E. Arber, Birmingham 1868.

A report and discourse of the affaires and state of Germany. [1570?]. Written 1553. Preface.

The scholemaster. 1570 etc; ed L. V. Ryan, Ithaca 1967.

RICHARD SHERRY
1506–55

A treatise of schemes and tropes. [1550], 1555 (much rev, as A treatise of the figures of grammar and rhetorike), Gainesville 1961 (facs of 1550).

THOMAS WILSON
1525?–81

The arte of rhetorique. 1553 (for 1554), 1560 ('newlie sette forthe again') etc; ed G. H. Mair, Oxford 1909, Gainesville 1962 (facs of 1553).

WILLIAM BALDWIN
c. 1515–63

§ 1

A myrroure for magistrates. [1559], 1563, 1571, 1574–5 (with Higgins's addns), 1578, 1578 (with Blenerhasset's addns), 1587 etc; ed L. B. Campbell 2 vols Cambridge 1938–46. Ed Baldwin, and partly by him.

§ 2

Thaler, A. Literary criticism in A mirror for magistrates. JEGP 49 1950.

RICHARD RAINOLDE
1530?–1606

The foundacion of rhetorike. 1563; ed F. R. Johnson, New York 1945 (facs).

RICHARD EDWARDS
1523?–66

The excellent comedie of Damon and Pythias. 1571. Prologue, rptd in Chambers.

JOHN RAINOLDS
1549–1607

Oratio in laudem artis poeticae. [c. 1572]; ed W. Ringler, tr W. Allen, Princeton 1940.

RICHARD WILLES
fl. 1558–73

§1

Ricardi Willeii poematum liber. In suorum poemat. librum scholia, 1573; ed and tr A. D. S. Fowler, Oxford 1958 (Luttrell Soc). With 3 theses: De re poetica; De poeticae natura atque ortu; Poeticam esse praestantiorem caeteris artibus.

§2

Seaton, E. In her edn of Fraunce, Arcadian rhetorike, Oxford 1950 (Luttrell Soc).

GEORGE GASCOIGNE
1542?–77

Certayne notes of instruction concerning the making of verse or ryme in English. In his Posies, 1575; rptd in Gregory Smith.

HENRY PEACHAM the elder
fl. 1577

The garden of eloquence. 1577, 1593 ('corrected and augmented'), Gainesville 1954 (facs of 1593).

GABRIEL HARVEY
1550–1631

Collections

Letter-book. Ed E. J. L. Scott 1884 (Camden Soc).
Marginalia. Ed G. C. Moore Smith, Stratford 1913.

§1

Rhetor: vel duorum dierum oratio, de natura, arte et exercitatione rhetorica. 1577.
Ciceronianus. 1577; ed H. S. Wilson, tr C. A. Foster, Lincoln Nebraska 1945.
Two other, very commendable letters of the same mens writing [Harvey and Spenser]. 1580 etc (written before Three letters); ed R. Gottfried in Works of Spenser: the prose works, Baltimore 1949.
Three proper, and wittie, familiar letters. 1580 etc; ed R. Gottfried, above.
Foure letters and certaine sonnets, especially touching Robert Greene. 1592; ed G. B. Harrison 1922; Menston 1969 (facs of 1592).
Pierces supererogation. 1593. Selections in Gregory Smith.
A new letter of notable contents. 1593. Selections in Gregory Smith.

§2

Wilson, H. S. Harvey's orations on rhetoric. ELH 12 1945.
Snare, G. Satire, logic and rhetoric in Harvey's earthquake letter to Spenser. Tulane Stud in Eng 18 1970.
Stern, V. F. The Bibliotheca of Harvey. Renaissance Quart 25 1972.

GEORGE WHETSTONE
1544?–87?

The right excellent and famous historye of Promos and Cassandra. 1578. Epistle to William Fleetwood, rptd in Gregory Smith.
A touchstone for the time. 1584 (as an Addition to A mirour for magistrates of cyties).

STEPHEN GOSSON
1555–1624

The schoole of abuse. 1579, 1586; ed E. Arber, Birmingham 1868.

THOMAS LODGE
1558?–1625

[A defence of poetry, music, and stage plays]. [1579]; ed D. Laing 1853 (Shakespeare Soc); rptd in part in Gregory Smith.

'E.K.'

§1

Spenser, Edmund. The shepheardes calender. 1579. Epistle dedicatory and notes by 'E.K.'

§2

Stephenson, E. A. Some stylistic links between Spenser and E.K. Renaissance Papers 1956.
Maclean, H. Fulke Greville and 'E.K.' Eng Lang Notes 1 1963.
Nicolet, W. Another note on E.K. Amer N & Q 2 1964.

EDMUND SPENSER
1552?–99

§1

Spenser-Harvey correspondence. 1580. See under Harvey, above.
A letter of the authors [to Ralegh]. 1596 etc; ed F. M. Padelford, Works of Spenser: Faerie Queene bk 1, Baltimore 1932.

§2

Evans, R. O. Spenser's role in the controversy over quantitative verse. Neuphilologische Mitteilungen 57 1956.

SIR PHILIP SIDNEY
1554–86

§1

An apologie for poetrie [written 1581–3?]. 1595, 1595 (as A defence of poesie), 1598 (appended to Arcadia) etc; ed G. Shepherd 1965.

§2

Hamilton, A. C. Sidney's idea of the 'right poet'. Comparative Lit 9 1957.
Hallam, G. W. Sidney's supposed Ramism. Renaissance Papers 1963.
Roberts, M. The pill and the cherries: Sidney and the neo-classical tradition. EC 16 1966.
Barnes, C. The hidden persuader: the complex speaking voice of Sidney's Defence of poetry. PMLA 86 1971.

Kinney, A. F. Parody and its implications in Sidney's Defence of poesie. Stud in Eng Lit 1500–1900 12 1972.

Hardison, O. B., jr. The two voices of Sidney's Apology for poetry. Eng Literary Renaissance 2 1972.

RICHARD STANYHURST
1547–1618

The first foure bookes of Virgil his Aeneis. Leyden 1582; ed D. van der Haas 1933. Dedication and preface, rptd in part in Gregory Smith.

KING JAMES VI and I
1566–1625

§ 1

Ane schort treatise: conteining some reulis and cautelis to be observit and eschewit in Scottis poesie. Edinburgh 1584 (in The essayes of a prentise, in the divine art of poesie) etc; ed R. S. Rait 1900 (in A royal rhetorician); rptd in Gregory Smith.

§ 2

Jack, R. D. S. James VI and Renaissance poetic theory. English 16 1967.

WILLIAM TEMPLE
1555–1627

§ 1

Analysis tractationis de poesi contextae a nobilissimo viro Philippo Sidneio equite aurato. In De L'Isle and Dudley mss. Written c. 1586; unpbd.

§ 2

Thorne, J. P. A Ramistical commentary on Sidney's An apologie for poetrie. MP 54 1957.

ANGEL DAY
fl. 1586

The English secretorie. 1586, 1595 ('with the second part [formerly] left out'), 1599 (rev), Gainesville 1967 (facs of 1599), Menston 1968 (facs of 1586).

WILLIAM WEBBE
b. 1552?

A discourse of English poetrie. 1586; ed E. Arber 1870; rptd in Gregory Smith.

ABRAHAM FRAUNCE
fl. 1582–1633

The lawiers logike. 1588.

The Arcadian rhetorike. 1588; ed E. Seaton, Oxford 1950 (Luttrell Soc); Menston 1970 (facs of 1588).

THOMAS NASHE
1567–1601?

Collections

Works. Ed R. B. McKerrow 5 vols 1904–10, Oxford 1958.

§ 1

To the gentlemen students of both universities. Epistle prefixed to Greene, Menaphon, 1589 etc.

The anatomie of absurditie. 1589 etc. Selections in Gregory Smith.

Sidney, Sir Philip. Astrophel and Stella. 1591 etc. Preface.

Strange news. 1592 etc. Selections in Gregory Smith.

§ 2

Sackton, A. H. Nashe as an Elizabethan critic. SE 26 1947.

[GEORGE PUTTENHAM]
d. 1590

§ 1

The arte of English poesie. 1589; ed E. Arber, Birmingham 1869; ed G. D. Willcock and A. Walker, Cambridge 1936; Menston 1968 (facs). Probably by Puttenham.

§ 2

Rushton, W. L. Shakespeare and the Arte of English poesie. Liverpool 1909.

Ward, B. M. The authorship of the Arte of English poesie. RES 1 1925.

Knauf, D. M. Puttenham's theory of natural and artificial discourse. Speech Monographs 34 1967.

SIR JOHN HARINGTON
1560–1612

§ 1

A preface: or rather a briefe apologie of poetrie, and of the author and translator [prefixed to his trn of Orlando furioso]. 1591 etc; ed R. McNulty in his edn of Harington's trn, Oxford 1972; rptd in Gregory Smith.

Commentary on Orlando furioso. 1591 (with above).

§ 2

Nelson, T. G. A. Harington as a critic of Sir Philip Sidney. SP 67 1970.

GILES FLETCHER the elder
1549?–1611

Licia. 1593; ed A. B. Grosart, Miscellanies of the Fuller Worthies' Library vol 3, 1871. Preface To the reader.

RICHARD CAREW of Anthony
1555–1620

The excellencie of the English tongue [written c. 1595]. 1614 (in 2nd edn of Camden's Remains); ed Gregory Smith (from BM ms Cotton F. xi, f. 265).

GEORGE CHAPMAN
1559?–1634

§ 1

To Ma. Mathew Royden. Prefixed to Ovids banquet of sence, 1595.

To the reader. Prefixed to Seaven bookes of the Iliads, 1598; rptd in Gregory Smith.

To the Earle Marshall; To the understander. Prefixed to Achilles shield, 1598; rptd in Gregory Smith.

To the high borne prince of men, Henrie; To the reader. Epistle dedicatory and verses prefixed to the Iliads, [1609] etc.

The preface to the reader. In Iliads, [1611] etc.

To Robert, Earle of Somerset. Epistle dedicatory to the Odysseys, [1614] etc.

Andromeda liberata. 1614. Epistle to Earl and Countess of Somerset.

Justification of Andromeda Liberata. 1614.

Poems to the Iliads and Odysseys. Ed P. B. Bartlett, Poems of George Chapman, New York 1941.

§ 2

Cannon, C. K. Chapman on the unity of style and meaning. JEGP 68 1969.

FRANCIS BACON
1561–1626
Collections

Works. Ed J. Spedding et al 14 vols 1857–74.

Essays. Ed R. F. Jones, New York 1937. Includes Advancement of learning etc.

§ 1

Essayes. 1597, 1612 (enlarged), 1625 (enlarged) etc.

The twoo bookes: of the proficience and advancement of learning. 1605 etc; ed T. Case 1906.

De sapientia veterum. 1609; ed Spedding 1861 (in Works vol 6).

§ 2

Shorey, P. Bacon and Demosthenes. Classical Philology 2 1930.

Wallace, K. R. Bacon on communication and rhetoric. Chapel Hill 1943.

Harrison, J. L. Bacon's view of rhetoric, poetry and the imagination. HLQ 20 1957.

Kocher, P. H. Bacon on the drama. In Essays on Shakespeare and Elizabethan drama in honor of Hardin Craig, Columbia Missouri 1963.

Vickers, B. Bacon and Renaissance prose. Cambridge 1968.

THE BODENHAM SERIES

Aids to composition planned by John Bodenham (fl. 1600)

Politeuphia: wits commonwealth. Ed Nicholas Ling 1597 etc. A collection of 'sentences'.

Palladis Tamia: wits treasury. Ed Francis Meres 1598 etc; ed D. C. Allen, New York 1938 (facs). Similitudes or comparisons.

Wits theater of the little world. Ed Robert Allott 1599. Examples.

Belvedere: or the garden of the Muses. [Ed Anthony Mundy?] 1600, 1875 (Spenser Soc). Sentences, similitudes and examples in verse.

Englands Helicon. Ed Nicholas Ling 1600, 1614 (enlarged) etc; ed H. Macdonald 1925. Poems offered as models or sources.

SAMUEL DANIEL
1562–1619

Musophilus. 1599 (in The poeticall essayes) etc; ed R. Himelick, West Lafayette 1965.

A defence of ryme. [1603] etc; ed G. B. Harrison 1925 (with Campion, Observations); ed A. C. Sprague 1930 (with other pieces); rptd in Gregory Smith. *See Campion, below.*

Prefatory verses to Florio's Montaigne. 1603 etc.

THE PARNASSUS PLAYS
written 1598–1601

The three Parnassus plays. Ed J. B. Leishman 1949 (from ms).

JOHN HOSKYNS
1566–1638

§ 1

Directions for speech and style [written c. 1599]. Ed H. H. Hudson, Princeton 1936; ed L. B. Osborn 1937, below.

§ 2

Osborn, L. B. The life, letters, and writings of Hoskyns. New Haven 1937 (includes an edn of Directions).

FRANCIS THYNNE
1545?–1608

Animadversions [on Speght's Chaucer]. Written 1599; first ptd in H. J. Todd, Illustrations of the lives and writings of Gower and Chaucer, 1810; ed G. H. Kingsley 1865 (EETS), 1875 (rev F. J. Furnivall).

SIR WILLIAM VAUGHAN
1577–1641

The golden grove. 1600. Summarized in Gregory Smith.

FULKE GREVILLE
1554–1628

Caelica [written 1577–1600]. In Certaine learned and elegant workes of the Right Honorable Fulke, Lorde Brooke, 1633; ed G. Bullough, Poems and dramas of Fulke Greville, 2 vols 1939. Sonnets 66, 80.

Of humane learning [written 1603–6]. 1633, above; ed G. Bullough, above. Stanzas 107–15.

Life of Sir Philip Sidney [written c. 1611]. Ed 'P.B.' 1652; ed N. C. Smith, Oxford 1907.

THOMAS CAMPION
1567–1620

Observations in the art of English poesie. 1602; ed P. Vivian, Works, Oxford 1909; ed G. B. Harrison 1925 (with Daniel, Defence of ryme); ed W. R. Davis, Works, New York 1967. *Reply by Daniel, above.*

MICHAEL DRAYTON
1563–1631

§ 1

To the reader. In The barrons wars, 1603 etc. On stanza form.

To the reader. In Poems lyrick and pastorall, 1606 etc. On ode.

Epistle to Henry Reynolds esquire of poets and poesie. 1627 (in The battaile of Agincourt) etc.

§2

Grundy, J. Brave translunary things. MLR 59 1964. 'Clear' as a critical term in Drayton et al.

BEN JONSON
1572?–1637
Collections

Works. Ed C. H. Herford, P. and E. M. Simpson 11 vols Oxford 1925–52. Many of the prefaces, epistles, prologues and epilogues of Jonson's plays, as well as some poems and epigrams and passages in the plays, are critically important.

Literary criticism. Ed J. R. Redwine, Lincoln Nebraska 1970.

§1

Sejanus his fall. 1605 etc. Preface.

Volpone. 1607 etc. Epistle dedicatory.

To the memory of my beloved, the author Mr William Shakespeare. Verses prefixed to First Folio, 1623 etc.

Timber: or discoveries made upon men and matter [compiled c. 1623–35]. In Works vol 2, 1640 etc; ed Herford and Simpson, vol 8 1947 (text), vol 11 1952 (commentary); ed R. S. Walker, Syracuse NY 1953 (rearranged).

Conversations with Drummond. Edinburgh 1711 (in Drummond's Works); ed D. Laing 1842 (Shakespeare Soc) (from ms); ed R. F. Patterson 1923.

§2

McKennen, W. Critical theory and poetic practice in Jonson. 1937.

Sackton, A. H. Rhetoric as a dramatic language in Jonson. New York 1948.

Walker, R. S. Literary criticism in Jonson's conversations with Drummond. English 8 1951.

— Jonson's discoveries: a new analysis. E & S new ser 5 1952.

Barish, J. A. Jonson and the language of prose comedy. Cambridge Mass 1960.

Fieler, F. B. The impact of Bacon and the new science upon Jonson's critical thought in Timber. Renaissance Papers 1958–60.

Calder, D. G. The meaning of 'imitation' in Jonson's Discoveries. Neuphilologische Mitteilungen 70 1969.

JOHN FLETCHER
1579–1625

To the reader. Prefixed to The faithful shepherdess, [1609] etc. On tragi-comedy.

THOMAS HEYWOOD
1574?–1641

§1

An apology for actors. 1612, 1658 (as Actors vindication); rptd 1841 (Shakespeare Soc); rptd A. H. Gilbert, Literary criticism Plato to Dryden, New York 1940.

§2

Clarke, A. M. Heywood as a critic. MLN 37 1922.

JOHN WEBSTER
c. 1580–c. 1634

To the reader. Prefixed to The White Divel, 1612 etc. On practicability of critical laws.

RICHARD BRATHWAIT or BRATHWAYTE
1588?–1673

The schollers medley: or an intermixt discourse upon historicall and poeticall relations. [1614], 1638 (as A survey of history) (much enlarged).

A comment upon the two tales of Sir Jeffray Chaucer, knight [written c. 1615]. 1665; ed C. F. E. Spurgeon 1901 (Chaucer Soc), Cambridge 1925 (in Five hundred years of Chaucer criticism). On Miller's and Wife of Bath's tales.

ALEXANDER GIL
1565–1635

Logonomia anglica. 1619, Menston 1969 (facs).

GEORGE WITHER
1588–1667

A preparation to the psalter. 1619, 1884 (Spenser Soc). Chs 9–10.

The schollers purgatory. [1625].

EDMUND BOLTON
1575?–1633?

§1

Hypercritica: or a rule of judgement for writing or reading our history's [completed c. 1621]. In Anthony Hall, Nicolai Triveti annalium continuatio, Oxford 1722; rptd Haslewood, Spingarn.

§2

Steele, R. C. Edmund Bolton. Cambridge Rev 24 Feb 1923.

Blackburn, T. H. The date and evolution of Bolton's Hypercritica. SP 63 1966.

THOMAS VICARS
fl. 1621

Manuductio ad artem rhetoricam. 1621, 1628.

HENRY PEACHAM the younger
1576?–1643?

The compleat gentleman. 1622, 1634, 1661; ed G. S. Gordon, Oxford 1906; ed V. B. Heltzel, Ithaca 1962 (with other pieces by Peacham).

THOMAS FARNABY
1575–1647

Index rhetoricus cui adjiciuntur formulae oratoriae. 1625, 1633, [1634], 1640, 1646, 1654, 1659 etc.

GEORGE HAKEWILL
1578–1649

An apologie or declaration of the power and providence of God in the government of the world. 1627, 1630, 2 pts 1635. *See* especially bk 3 ch 8 section 3.

SIR KENELM DIGBY
1603–65

Observations on the 22 stanza in the 9th canto of the 2d book of Spencers Faery Queen. 1643. Written 1628.
Concerning Spencer. Ed E. W. Bligh (in Digby and his Venetia, 1932). Written c. 1630; BM additional ms 41,846.

HENRY REYNOLDS
1563?–1635?

Mythomystes, wherein a short survay is taken of the nature and value of true poesy and depth of the Ancients above our moderne poets. [1632]; rptd Spingarn.

SIR WILLIAM ALEXANDER
1567?–1640

Anacrisis: or a censure of some poets ancient and modern [written c. 1634]. Edinburgh 1711 (in Works of William Drummond of Hawthornden); rptd Spingarn.

JOHN BARTON

The art of rhetorick concisely and compleatly handled. 1634.

SIR JOHN SUCKLING
1609–42

A session of the poets [written 1637]. 1646 (in Fragmenta aurea); rptd Spingarn; ed L. A. Beaurline (in An editorial experiment, SB 16 1963) (from ms).

FRANCISCUS JUNIUS or DU JON
1589–1677

§1

The painting of the Ancients. 1638. *See* especially bk 1 ch 4, bk 3 ch 1.

§2

Spencer, T. J. B. Longinus in English criticism: influences before Milton. RES new ser 8 1957.

JOHN MILTON
1608–74

§1

The reason of church-government. 1641 etc. Critical sections rptd Spingarn.
An apology [for] Smectymnuus. 1642 etc. Critical sections rptd Spingarn.
Areopagitica. 1644 etc; ed J. W. Hales, Oxford 1939; ed M. Davies 1963 (with Of education).
Of education. [1644] etc; ed O. M. Ainsworth, New Haven 1928; ed M. Davies 1963, above. Critical sections rptd Spingarn.
The verse. Prefixed in 1668 to copies then remaining of the first edn of Paradise lost, 1667.

Of that sort of dramatic poem which is call'd tragedy. Prefixed to Samson Agonistes, 1671 etc.

§2

Langdon, I. Milton's theory of poetry. New Haven 1924.
Rajan, B. 'Simple, sensuous and passionate'. RES 21 1945.
Fletcher, H. F. The intellectual development of Milton. 2 vols Urbana 1956–61.
Koehler, G. S. Milton on 'numbers', 'quantity' and rime. SP 55 1958.
Scott, W. O. Ramism and Milton's concept of poetic fancy. PQ 42 1963.
Mueller, M. Sixteenth-century Italian criticism and Milton's theory of catharsis. Stud in Eng Lit 1500–1900 6 1966.
Major, J. M. Milton's view of rhetoric. SP 64 1967.
Samuel, I. Milton on comedy and satire. HLQ 35 1972.

ALEXANDER ROSS
1591–1654

Mel heliconium: or poeticall honey gathered out of the weeds of Parnassus. 1642.
Gnomologicon poëticum: hoc est, sententiae veterum poëtarum insigniores. 1647.
Mystagogus poeticus, or the Muses interpreter: explaining the historicall mysteries and mystical histories of the ancient Greek and Latine poets. 1647, 1648, 1653, 1664, 1675.

JAMES HOWELL
1594–1666

Epistolae Ho-Elianae. 4 vols 1645–55 etc; ed O. Smeaton 3 vols 1903 (Temple Classics).

ANONYMOUS

The great assises holden in Parnassus by Apollo and his assessours. 1645; rptd 1885 (Spenser Soc); ed H. Macdonald 1948.

JOHN WILKINS
1614–72

Ecclesiastes: or a discourse concerning the gift of preaching as it fals under the rules of art. 1646, 1647, 1651, 1653, 1659, 1679, 1695.

SIR JOHN DENHAM
1615–69

To Sir Richard Fanshawe upon his translation of Pastor fido. 1648 (in Fanshawe's Il pastor fido) etc; ed W. F. Staton and W. E. Simeone in their edn of Fanshawe's trn, Oxford 1964.

SAMUEL GOTT

Novae Solymae libri sex. 1648; tr and ed W. Begley 2 vols 1902. Numerous critical passages.

THOMAS STEPHENS

Troposchematologia: maximam partem ex indice rhetorico Farnabii deprompta; additis insuper anglicanis exemplis. 1648, 1660. Rhetorical formulae and examples in English couplets.

SIR WILLIAM DAVENANT
1606–68

§1

A discourse upon Gondibert, an heroick poem written by Sir W. D'Avenant, with an answer to it by Mr Hobbs. Paris 1650, London 1651 (in Gondibert); rptd Spingarn.

§2

Dowlin, C. M. Davenant's Gondibert: its preface and Hobbes' answer. Philadelphia 1934.

THOMAS HOBBES
1588–1679

§1

Answer of Mr Hobbes to Sr Will. D'Avenant's preface before Gondibert. Paris 1650 (with Davenant's preface), London 1651 (with Gondibert); rptd Spingarn.
To the Honourable Edward Howard esq on his intended impression of his poem of the British princes. Prefixed to Howard's British princes, 1669.
To the reader concerning the vertues of an heroique poem. Prefixed to his trn of the Odyssey, 1675; rptd Spingarn.

§2

Dowlin, C. M. See under Davenant, above.
Thorpe, C. D. The aesthetic theory of Hobbes, with special reference to his contribution to the psychological approach in English literary criticism. Ann Arbor 1940.
Nigh, D. J. Hobbes' relevance to dramatic theory. Xavier Univ Stud 5 1966.

SAMUEL SHEPPARD

§1

Epigrams; also the Socratick session, or the arraignment and conviction of Julius Scaliger. 1651.

§2

Rollins, H. E. Sheppard and his praise of poets. SP 24 1927.

THOMAS BLOUNT
1618–79

The academie of eloquence, containing a compleat English rhetorique. 1654, 1656 (with addns), 1663, 1663, 1670, 1683.

JOHN COLLOP

Poesis rediviva: or poesie reviv'd. 1656; ed C. Hilberry, Madison 1962. Epistle dedicatory and various poems.

ABRAHAM COWLEY
1618–67

§1

Poems: 4 parts, viz I, Miscellanies; II, The mistress; III, Pindarique odes; IV, Davideis. Preface and notes to Odes and Davideis. Preface rptd Spingarn.

§2

Nethercot, A. H. Cowley's Discourse concerning style. RES 2 1926.
Goldstein, H. D. Discordia concors, decorum and Cowley. E Studies 49 1968.
Korshin, P. J. The theoretical bases of Cowley's later poetry. SP 66 1969.

JOSHUA POOLE

The English Parnassus: or a helpe to English poesie. 1656, 1677. The preface, 'being a short illustration of English poesy', is signed J.D.

JOHN SMITH

The mysterie of rhetorique unvail'd. 1657, 1665, 1673, 1688.

(4) GENERAL STUDIES

Schelling, F. E. Poetic and verse criticism of the reign of Elizabeth. Philadelphia 1891.
Wylie, L. J. Studies in the evolution of English criticism. Boston 1894.
Hamelius, P. Die Kritik in der englischen Literatur des 17 und 18 Jahrhunderts. Leipzig 1897.
Gayley, C. M. and F. N. Scott. An introduction to the methods and materials of literary criticism. Boston 1899.
Spingarn, J. E. A history of literary criticism in the Renaissance. New York 1899, 1963 (with introd by B. Weinberg).
Saintsbury, G. History of criticism and literary taste in Europe. 3 vols Edinburgh 1900–4.
—— A history of English criticism. Edinburgh 1911.
Symmes, H. S. Les débuts de la critique dramatique en Angleterre jusqu'à la mort de Shakespeare. Paris 1903.
Upham, A. H. The French influence in English literature from the accession of Elizabeth to the Restoration. New York 1908.
Diede, O. Der Streit der Alten und der Modernen in der englischen Literatur-geschichte des 16 und 17 Jahrhunderts. Greifswald 1912.
Miller, G. M. The historical point of view in English criticism 1550–1770. Heidelberg 1913.

Borinski, K. Die Antike in Poetik und Kunsttheorie. Leipzig 1914.
Routh, J. The rise of classical English criticism to the death of Dryden. New Orleans 1915.
Croll, M. W. Attic prose in the seventeenth century. SP 18 1921; rptd in his Style, rhetoric and rhythm, ed J. M. Patrick et al, Princeton 1966.
—— Attic prose: Lipsius, Montaigne, Bacon. In F. E. Schelling anniversary papers, New York 1923, and with above.
Clark, D. L. Rhetoric and poetry in the Renaissance. New York 1922.
Willey, B. Tendencies in Renaissance literary theory. 1922.
—— The seventeenth-century background. 1934.
Thume, H. Beiträge zur Geschichte des Geniebegriffs in England. Halle 1927.
Vines, S. The course of English classicism. 1930.
Bateson, F. W. English poetry and the English language. Oxford 1934, 1973 (rev).
White, H. O. Plagiarism and imitation during the English Renaissance. Cambridge Mass 1935.
Gilbert, A. H. Logic in the Elizabethan drama. SP 32 1935.

Crane, W. G. Wit and rhetoric in the Renaissance: the formal basis of Elizabethan prose style. New York 1937.

Baldwin, C. S. Renaissance literary theory and practice. Ed D. L. Clark, New York 1939.

Sweeting, E. J. Early Tudor criticism, linguistic and literary. Oxford 1940.

Wilson, H. S. Some meanings of 'Nature' in Renaissance literary theory. JHI 2 1941.

Robertson, J. The art of letter writing: an essay on the hand-books published in the sixteenth and seventeenth centuries. Liverpool 1942.

Hall, V. Renaissance literary criticism: a study of its social content. New York 1945.

Taylor, A. Renaissance guides to books. Berkeley 1945.

Weisinger, H. The seventeenth-century reputation of the Elizabethans. MLQ 6 1945.

Craigie, W. A. The critique of pure English from Caxton to Smollett. Oxford 1946 (Soc for Pure Eng). With a reprint of Vindex anglicus, 1644.

Herrick, M. T. The fusion of Horatian and Aristotelian literary criticism 1531–55. Urbana 1946.

— Comic theory in the sixteenth century. Urbana 1950.

Stafford, J. The social status of Renaissance literary critics. SE 25 1946.

Atkins, J. W. H. English literary criticism: the Renascence. 1947; Seventeenth and eighteenth centuries, 1951.

Tuve, R. Elizabethan and metaphysical imagery. Chicago 1947.

Hyde, M. C. Playwriting for Elizabethans. New York 1950.

Wallerstein, R. C. Studies in seventeenth-century poetic. Madison 1950.

Allison, A. W. Poetry and rhetoric: in defense of Elizabethan criticism. Virginia Univ Stud 4 1951.

Baine, R. M. The first anthologies of English literary criticism, Warton to Haslewood. SB 3 1951.

Bloom, E. A. The allegorical principle. ELH 18 1951.

Joseph, B. L. Elizabethan acting. Oxford 1951.

Marquardt, W. F. The first English translation of Trajano Boccalini's Ragguagli di Parnasso. HLQ 15 1951. On Thomas Scott's Newes from Parnassus, 1622, and Sir William Vaughan's The new-found politicke, 1626.

Williamson, G. The Senecan amble: a study in prose form from Bacon to Collier. 1951.

Jones, R. F. The triumph of the English language: a survey of opinions concerning the vernacular from the introduction of printing to the Restoration. Stanford 1953.

Doran, M. Endeavours of art: a study of form in Elizabethan drama. Madison 1954.

Martz, L. L. The poetry of meditation. New Haven 1954, 1962 (rev).

Howell, W. S. Logic and rhetoric in England 1500–1700. Princeton 1956.

O'Brien, G. W. Renaissance poetics and the problem of power. Chicago 1956.

Smith, A. J. An examination of some claims for Ramism. RES new ser 7 1956.

Rossky, W. Imagination in the English Renaissance: psychology and poetic. Stud in Renaissance 5 1958.

Adams, R. P. Bold bawdry and open manslaughter: the English new humanist attack on medieval romance. HLQ 23 1959.

Clemen, W. H. English tragedy before Shakespeare. Tr 1961.

Knox, N. The word 'irony' and its context 1500–1755. Durham NC 1961.

Sowton, I. Hidden persuaders as a means of literary grace: sixteenth-century poetics and rhetoric in England. UTQ 32 1962.

Thompson, J. The founding of English meter. New York 1962.

Hamilton, K. G. The two harmonies: poetry and prose in the seventeenth century. Oxford 1963.

Hardison, O. B. The enduring monument: a study of the idea of praise in Renaissance theory and practice. Chapel Hill 1963.

Dundas, J. Allegory as a form of wit. Stud in Renaissance 11 1964.

Tayler, E. W. Nature and art in Renaissance literature. New York 1964.

Papajewski, H. An Lucanus sit poeta. Deutsche Vierteljahrsschrift für Literaturwissenschaft und Geistesgeschichte 40 1966. On relation of history and poetry in Renaissance theory.

Peterson, D. L. The English lyric from Wyatt to Donne: a study of the plain and eloquent styles. Princeton 1967.

Lanham, R. A. A handlist of rhetorical terms: a guide for students of English literature. Berkeley 1968.

Ong, W. J. Tudor writings on rhetoric. Stud in Renaissance 15 1968.

Mulder, J. R. The temple of the mind: education and literary taste in seventeenth-century England. New York 1969.

Patterson, A. Hermogenes and the Renaissance: seven ideas of style. Princeton 1970.

Vickers, B. Classical rhetoric in English poetry. 1970.

R. C.

VII. PHILOSOPHY

General Studies – Francis Bacon – Thomas Hobbes – Other philosophical writers

GENERAL STUDIES

Tulloch, J. English Puritanism and its leaders. 1861.

— Rational theology and Christian philosophy in England in the seventeenth century. 2 vols Edinburgh 1872–4.

Rémusat, C. de. Histoire de la philosophie en Angleterre depuis Bacon jusqu'à Locke. Paris 1875.

Sorley, W. R. In his A history of English philosophy, Cambridge 1920.

Lamprecht, S. Innate ideas in the Cambridge Platonists. Philosophical Rev 35 1926.

— The role of Descartes in seventeenth-century England. Stud in History of Ideas 3 1935.

Powicke, F. J. The Cambridge Platonists. 1926.

Nicolson, M. H. Christ's College and the Latitude-men. MP 27 1929.

— The early stage of Cartesianism in England. SP 26 1929.

Baker, J. T. An historical and critical examination of English space and time theories from Henry More to Bishop Berkeley. New York 1930.

Muirhead, J. H. The Platonic tradition in Anglo-Saxon philosophy. 1931.

Cassirer, E. Die Platonische Renaissance in England und die Schule von Cambridge. Leipzig tr 1932; Edinburgh 1953.

De Boer, J. The theory of knowledge of the Cambridge Platonists. Madras 1931.

Harrison, C. T. Bacon, Hobbes, Boyle and the ancient atomists. Harvard Stud 15 1933.

— The ancient atomists and English literature of the

seventeenth century. Harvard Stud in Classical Philology 45 1934.

Willey, B. The seventeenth-century background. 1934.

— In his English moralists, 1965.

Wolf, A. A history of science, technology and philosophy in the sixteenth and seventeenth centuries. 1935.

Jones, R. F. Ancients and Moderns: a study of the rise of the background of the Battle of the Books. St Louis 1936, 1961 (rev).

— et al. The seventeenth century. Stanford 1951.

Jones, R. F. The rhetoric of science in England of the 'mid-seventeenth century. In Restoration and eighteenth-century literature, ed C. Camden, Chicago 1963.

McColley, G. The seventeenth-century doctrine of a plurality of worlds. Annals of Science 1 1936.

Jones, L. The divine science: the aesthetic of some representative seventeenth-century English poets. New York 1940.

Broad, C. D. The new philosophy: Bruno to Descartes. Cambridge Historical Rev 8 1945.

Harris, V. All coherence gone. Chicago 1949.

Bush, D. Science and English poetry. New York 1950.

Cragg, G. R. From Puritanism to the age of reason. Cambridge 1950.

Rivaud, A. Histoire de la philosophie. Vol 3, Paris 1950.

Bethell, S. L. The cultural revolution of the seventeenth century. 1951.

Leroux, A. and A. Leroy. La philosophie anglaise classique. Paris 1951.

Wiley, M. L. The subtle knot: creative scepticism in seventeenth-century England. 1952.

Paul, L. In his English philosophers, 1953.

Howell, W. S. Logic and rhetoric in England 1500–1700. Princeton 1956.

McRae, R. The unity of the sciences: Bacon, Descartes and Leibniz. JHI 18 1957.

Colie, R. Light and enlightenment: a study of the Cambridge Platonists and the Dutch Arminians. Cambridge 1957.

Boas, G. In his Dominant themes of modern philosophy, New York 1957.

Saveson, J. E. Differing reactions to Descartes among the Cambridge Platonists. JHI 21 1960.

Hoopes, R. Right reason in the English Renaissance. Cambridge Mass 1962.

Leeuwen, H. G. van. The problem of certainty in English thought 1630–90. Hague 1963.

Hamilton, K. G. The two harmonies: poetry and prose in the seventeenth century. Oxford 1963. On Bacon, Digby, Hobbes, Wilson and others.

Fisch, H. Jerusalem and Albion: the Hebraic factor in seventeenth-century literature. 1964.

Greenleaf, W. H. Order, empiricism and politics. Oxford 1964. Especially chs 5, 10.

Hill, C. Intellectual origins of the English revolution. Oxford 1965. Ch 3 on Bacon.

Kargon, R. H. Atomism in England from Hariot to Newton. Oxford 1966.

Smith, C. S. The texture of matter as viewed by artisan, philosopher and scientist in the seventeenth and eighteenth centuries. In Atoms, blacksmiths and crystals: practical and theoretical views of the structure of matter, Los Angeles 1967.

Roberts, J. D. From Puritanism to Platonism in seventeenth-century England. Hague 1968.

Shugg, W. The Cartesian beast-machine in English literature 1663–1750. JHI 29 1968.

von Leyden, W. Seventeenth-century metaphysics. 1968.

FRANCIS BACON
Baron Verulam, Viscount St Albans
1561–1626

Bibliographies

Gibson, R. W. Bacon: a bibliography of his works and of Baconiana to the year 1750. Oxford 1950. *See also* F. H. Anderson, The philosophy of Bacon, Chicago 1948 ch 3.

Collections

Scripta in naturali et universali philosophia. Amsterdam 1653, 1685, 1699.

Opuscula varia posthuma: philosophica, civilia et theologica. Ed William Rawley 1658, Amsterdam 1663.

Philosophical works. Ed Peter Shaw 3 vols 1733, 1737.

Works. Ed Mr Mallet 4 vols 1740.

Works. Ed J. Spedding, R. L. Ellis and D. D. Heath 14 vols 1857–74.

The life and letters of Bacon, including all his occasional works. Ed J. Spedding 7 vols 1861–74.

Essays, Advancement of learning, New Atlantis and other pieces. Ed R. F. Jones, New York 1937.

The New Organon and related writings. Ed F. H. Anderson, New York 1960.

§ 1

Essayes. 1597, 1598, 1606. 10 essays. *See* below for enlargements.

The twoo bookes of Francis Bacon: of the proficience and advancement of learning, divine and humane. 1605, 1629, Oxford 1633.

De sapientia veterum. 1609; tr 1619, 1622 etc (as The wisdom of the Ancients).

The essays of Sir Francis Bacon. 1612, 1613, Edinburgh 1614, 1624. 38 essays.

Novum organum: summi Angliae cancellarii instauratio magna. 1620, Leyden 1645, 1650, Amsterdam 1660; ed T. Fowler, Oxford 1889.

Historia naturalis et experimentalis. 1622.

Historia vitae et mortis. 1623, Amsterdam 1663; tr W. Rawley 1638.

De augmentis scientiarum: tomus primus, de dignitate et augmentis scientiarum, libros IX. 1623, Paris 1624; tr Oxford 1640 (Of the advancement of learning), London 1674; ed W. A. Wright 1900.

The essays, civil and moral. 1625, 1629, 1632; ed G. Grigson, Oxford 1937. 58 essays.

Sylva sylvarum: or a natural history in ten centuries. 1626, 1627, 1628; tr Latin, Amsterdam 1648. Also contains an early version of New Atlantis.

Nova Atlantis. Utrecht 1643; tr 1659.

A number of other individual works were pbd for the first time in collections, above.

§ 2

Rawley, E. (ed). Memoriae Francisci Baconis de Verulamio Sacrum. 1626; ed and tr E. K. Rand, Boston 1904.

Clerke, G. De plenitudine mundi brevis et philosophica dissertatio in qua defenditur Cartesiana philosophia contra sententias Francisci Baconi. 1660.

Maistre, J. M. de. Examen de la philosophie de Bacon. Paris 1836.

Rémusat, C. de. Bacon: sa vie, son temps, sa philosophie et son influence jusqu'à nos jours. Paris 1857.

Whewell, W. The philosophy of discovery. 1860. Chs 15–16.

Fischer, K. Bacon und seine Schule. Heidelberg 1904.

Church, R. W. Bacon. 1884.

Villey, P. Montaigne et François Bacon. Paris 1913.

Broad, C. D. The philosophy of Bacon. Cambridge 1926.

Taylor, A. E. Francis Bacon. Proc Br Acad 12 1927.

White, W. H. Bacon, Gilbert and Harvey. 1927.

Frost, W. Bacon und die Naturphilosophie. Munich 1927.

Lemmi, C. G. The classical deities in Bacon. Baltimore 1933.

Gregory, J. Chemistry and alchemy in the natural philosophy of Bacon. Ambix 2 1938.

Anderson, F. H. Bacon on Platonism. UTQ 11 1942.

— The philosophy of Bacon. Chicago 1948.

— Bacon: his career and his thought. Los Angeles 1962.

Wallace, K. R. Bacon on communication and rhetoric. Chapel Hill 1943.

Cresson, A. Francis Bacon. Paris 1948.

Adams, R. P. The social responsibilities of science in Utopia, New Atlantis and after. JHI 10 1949.

Farrington, B. Bacon: philosopher of industrial science. New York 1949.

— Bacon: pioneer of planned science. 1963.

— The philosophy of Bacon: an essay on its development 1603-9. Liverpool 1964.

Schuhl, P. M. La pensée de Bacon. Paris 1949.

Boas, M. Bacon and Gilbert. JHI 12 1951. Reply by D. Roller, Isis 44 1953.

Ducasse, C. J. Bacon's philosophy of science. In Structure, method and meaning, ed P. Henle, New York 1951.

Prior, M. E. Bacon's man of science. JHI 15 1954.

Kocher, P. H. Bacon on the science of jurisprudence. JHI 18 1957.

Rossi, P. Bacone: dalla magia alla scienza. Bari 1957; tr 1968.

Crowther, J. G. Bacon: the first statesman of science. 1960.

Larsen, R. E. The Aristotelianism of Bacon's Novum organum. JHI 23 1962.

Bowen, C. D. Bacon: the temper of a man. 1963.

Burman, J. Science and society in the New Atlantis and other Renaissance utopias. PMLA 78 1963.

— The New Atlantis: Bacon's utopia of science. Papers on Lang & Lit 1966.

Righter, A. In The English mind: studies in the English moralists presented to Basil Willey, Cambridge 1964.

Davis, W. R. The imagery of Bacon's late work. MLQ 1965.

Mazzeo, J. A. In his Renaissance and revolution, New York 1965.

Wallace, K. B. Bacon on the nature of man. Urbana 1967.

Primack, M. Outline of a reinterpretation of Bacon's philosophy. Jnl History of Philosophy 5 1967.

Luxembourg, L. K. Bacon and Denis Diderot: philosophers of science. Copenhagen 1967.

Vickers, B. Bacon and Renaissance prose. Cambridge 1968.

White, H. B. Peace among the willows: the political philosophy of Bacon. Hague 1968.

— Bacon's Wisdom of the Ancients. Interpretation (New York) 1970.

THOMAS HOBBES
1588-1679

Bibliographies

Macdonald, H. and M. Hargreaves. Hobbes: a bibliography. 1952 (Cambridge Bibl Soc).

Mizuta, H. The list of works of and relating to Hobbes. Tokyo 1954.

Pacchi, R. Bibliographia Hobbesiana dal 1840 ad oggi. Rivista Critica di Storia della Filosofia 17 1962.

Collections

Opera philosophica. Amsterdam 1668.

A supplement to Mr Hobbes his works. 1675.

Tracts. 1681; 1682 (a 2nd collection).

Hobbes Tripos. In Three discourses of human nature, 1684 (3rd edn).

The moral and political works of Hobbes. 1750.

The English works. Ed W. Molesworth 11 vols 1839-45.

§ I

Eight books of the Peloponnesian war written by Thucydides. 1629, 1634, 1676, 1822, 1960.

De mirabilibus pecci carmen. [1636 or 1666?], 1675, 1678, 1683.

Objectiones ad Cartesii meditationes de prima philosophia. In R. Descartes, Meditationes, Amsterdam 1641.

Preface to Ballistica and Tractatus opticus. In M. Mersenne, Cogitata physico-mathematica, Paris 1644.

Elementorum philosophiae sectio tertia: de cive. Paris 1642, Amsterdam 1647, 1669; ed S. P. Lamprecht, New York 1949. Tr as Philosophical rudiments, below. 3rd section of philosophical treatise, followed by first and 2nd sections, De corpore and De homine, below.

An answer to A discourse upon Gondibert: an heroic poem written by Sir William Davenant. Paris 1650 (in Gondibert).

Human nature: or the fundamental elements of policie. 1650, 1651.

De corpore politico: or the elements of law, moral and politick. 1650, 1652. See col 2283, above.

Epistolica dissertatio de principiis justis et decori. Amsterdam 1651.

Philosophical rudiments concerning government and society. 1651, 1659. Trn of De cive, above.

Leviathan: or the matter, forme and power of a commonwealth. 1651; ed A. R. Waller, Cambridge 1904; ed W. G. Pogson Smith 1909, 1958; ed M. Oakeshott, Oxford 1947, New York 1960 (with introd by R. S. Peters); tr Latin, Amsterdam 1670.

A brief of the art of rhetoric. In A compendium of the art of logick and rhetoric, 1651.

Of libertie and necessitie. 1654, Manchester 1839; ed C. von Brockdorff, Kiel 1938.

The questions concerning liberty, necessity and chance. 1656.

Elementorum philosophiae: sectio prima, de corpore. 1655; tr 1656; ed C. von Brockdorff 1934.

Elementorum philosophiae: sectio secunda, de homine. 1658.

Στιγμαί Ἀγεωμετρίας, Ἀγροικίας Ἀντιπολιτείας, Ἀμαθείας: or marks of the absurd geometry of John Wallis. 1657.

Examinatio et emendatio mathematicae hodiernae qualis explicatur in libris Johannis Wallisii. 1660.

Dialogus physicus: sive de natura aeris. 1661. Reply by Boyle in An examen of Mr Thomas Hobbes his Dialogus, 1662.

Problemata physica. 1662; tr 1682.

Mr Hobbes considered in his loyalty, religion, reputation and manners. 1662, 1680.

De principiis et ratiocinatione geometrarum. 1666.

Quadratura circuli. 1669.

Rosetum geometricum cum censura brevi doctrinae Wallisianae de motu. 1671; tr 1682.

Three papers presented to the Royal Society against Dr Wallis. 1671.

Lux mathematica excussa collisionibus Johannis Wallisii et Thomae Hobbesii. 1672.

The travels of Ulysses. 1673.

Principia et problemata aliquot geometrica. 1674; tr 1682, 1727.

The Iliads and Odyssey of Homer. 1673, 1674, 1675, 1676. Tr Hobbes.

A letter about liberty and necessity. 1676.

Behemoth: or an epitome of the civil wars of England. 1679, 1680 (corrected); 1682; F. Tönnies 1889 (from ms).

An historical narration concerning heresie and the punishment thereof. 1680.

A dialogue between a philosopher and a student of the common laws of England. 1681.

Historia ecclesiastica carmine elegiaco concinnata. 1688; tr 1722.

The elements of law, natural and politic. Ed F. Tönnies 1889, Cambridge 1928. Written and circulated in 1640.

§2

Cumberland, R. De legibus naturae disquisitio in qua elementa philosophiae Hobbinnae refutantur. 1672.

Tönnies, F. Hobbes Leben und Lehre. Stuttgart 1896.
— Contributions à l'histoire de la pensée de Hobbes. Archives de Philosophie 12 1936.

Brandt, G. Hobbes: Grundlinien seiner Philosophie. Kiel 1895.

Köhler, M. Die Naturphilosophie von Hobbes und ihre Abhängigkeit von Bacon. Archiv für Geschichte der Philosophie 15 1902.

Balz, A. G. A. Idea and essence in the philosophies of Hobbes and Spinoza. 1918.

Nicolson, M. H. Milton and Hobbes. SP 23 1926.

Brandt, F. Hobbes's mechanical conception of nature. Paris 1928.

Bredvold, L. I. Dryden, Hobbes and the Royal Society. MP 25 1928.

Laird, J. Hobbes. 1934.

Brockdorff, C. von. Des Sir Charles Cavendish Bericht für Joachim Junguus über die Grundzuge der Hobbesschen Naturphilosophie. Societas Hobbesiana (Kiel) 3 1934.

Dowlin, C. M. Sir William Davenant's Gondibert, its preface and Hobbes's Answer. Philadelphia 1934.

Shillinglaw, A. T. Concerning the Latin and English texts of Hobbes' Leviathan. E Studien 69 1935.
— Hobbes and Ben Jonson. TLS 18 April 1936.

Archives de Philosophie 12 1936.

Strauss, L. Political philosophy of Hobbes. Tr Oxford 1936, Chicago 1952. The original ms pbd as Hobbes politische Wissenschaft, Neuwied 1965.
— In his Natural right and history, Chicago 1953.

Teeter, L. The dramatic use of Hobbes' political ideas. ELH 3 1936.

Taylor, A. E. The ethical doctrine of Hobbes. Philosophy 13 1938.

The autobiographies of Hobbes. Mind 48 1939.

Gooch, G. P. Hobbes. Proc Br Acad 25 1939.

Thorpe, C. D. The aesthetic doctrine of Hobbes. Michigan Univ Stud in Lang & Lit 18 1940.

Lamprecht, S. P. Hobbes and Hobbism. Amer Political Science Rev 34 1940.

Gotesky, R. Social sciences and the significance of Hobbes' conception of the law of nature. Ethics 50 1940.

Brown, H. The Mersenne correspondence: a lost letter by Hobbes. Isis 34 1941.

Aaron, R. I. A possible early draft of De corpore. Mind 54 1945.

Wolfe, D. M. Milton and Hobbes: a contrast in social temper. SP 41 1944.

Kallich, M. The association of ideas and critical theory: Hobbes, Locke and Addison. ELH 12 1945.

Schlatter, R. Hobbes and Thucydides. JHI 6 1945.

Cohen, I. B. A lost letter from Hobbes to Mersenne found. Harvard Lib Bull 1 1947.

Hardacre, P. A letter from Edmund Waller to Hobbes. HLQ 11 1948.

James, D. G. The life of reason: Hobbes, Locke, Bolingbroke. 1949.

de Beer, G. R. Some letters of Hobbes. Notes & Records of Royal Soc 7 1950.

Bowle, J. Hobbes and his critics. 1951.

Henry, N. H. Milton and Hobbes. SP 48 1951.

Jacquot, J. Leviathan et ses critiques anglais au xviie siècle. Thales 7 1951.
— Notes on an unpublished work of Hobbes. Notes & Records of Royal Soc 9 1952.
— Un document inédit. Thales 8 1952.

Ong, W. J. Hobbes and Talon's Ramist Rhetoric in English. Trans Cambridge Bibl Soc 1 1951.

Hervey, H. Hobbes and Descartes in the light of some unpublished letters. Osiris 10 1952.

Mintz, K. Hobbes, Galileo and the circle of perfection. Isis 43 1952.

Polin, R. Politique et philosophie chez Hobbes. Paris 1953.

Levy, A. Economic views of Hobbes. JHI 15 1954.

Mintz, S. I. A broadside attack on Hobbes. History of Ideas Newsletter 1 1955.
— The hunting of Leviathan: seventeenth-century reactions to the materialism and moral philosophy of Hobbes. Cambridge 1962. With extensive bibliography of 17th-century attacks on Hobbes.
— Hobbes on the law of heresy: a new manuscript. JHI 29 1968.

Watson, G. Hobbes and the metaphysical conceit. JHI 16 1955. Reply by T. M. Gang 17 1956.
— Dryden, Hobbes and the nimble spaniel. N & Q June 1963. Reply by H. N. Davies, Sept 1963.

Krook, D. Hobbes' doctrine of meaning and truth. Philosophy 31 1956.

Peters, R. Hobbes. 1956 (Pelican).

Warrender, H. The political philosophy of Hobbes: his theory of obligation. Oxford 1957.
— The place of God in Hobbes' philosophy. Political Stud 8 1960.
— Hobbes' conception of morality. Rivista Critica de Storia della Filosofia 17 1962.

Brown, S. M. Hobbes: the Taylor thesis. Philosophical Rev 68 1959.

Jessop, T. E. Thomas Hobbes. 1960 (Br Council pamphlet).

Engel, S. M. Hobbes' table of absurdity. Philosophical Rev 70 1961.
— Analogy and equivocation in Hobbes. Ibid.

Brown, K. C. Hobbes' grounds for belief in a deity. Philosophy 37 1962.
— Hobbes studies. Oxford 1965.

Macpherson, C. B. In his Theory of possessive individualism, Oxford 1962.

Oakeshott, M. The moral life in the writings of Hobbes. In his Rationalism in politics and other essays, 1962.

Raphael, D. D. Obligation and rights in Hobbes. Philosophy 37 1962. On Warrender, above, with reply from Warrender.

Mourgeon, J. La science du pouvoir total dans le Leviathan de Hobbes. Annales de la Faculté de Droit de Toulouse 11 1963.

Berlin, I. Hobbes, Locke and Professor Macpherson. Political Quart 35 1964.

Brett, R. L. In The English mind: studies in the English moralists presented to Basil Willey, Cambridge 1964.

Hood, F. C. The divine politics of Hobbes: an interpretation of Leviathan. Oxford 1964.

King, B. The significance of Dryden's State of innocence. Stud in Eng Lit 1500–1900 4 1964. Discusses Hobbes on freedom and necessity.

Skinner, Q. D. Hobbes' Leviathan. Historical Jnl 7 1964.
— Hobbes on sovereignty: an unknown discussion. Political Stud 13 1965.
— The ideological context of Hobbes' political thought. Historical Jnl 9 1966.
— Hobbes and the nature of the early Royal Society. Historical Jnl 12 1969.

Mayer-Tasch, P. C. Hobbes und das Widerstandsrecht. Tübingen 1965.

Watkins, J. W. N. Hobbes' system of ideas: a study of the political significance of philosophical theories. 1965.

Gert, B. Hobbes, mechanism and egoism. PQ 15 1965.
— Hobbes and psychological egoism. JHI 28 1967.

Mazzeo, J. A. In his Renaissance and revolution, New York 1965.

Black, J. The influence of Hobbes on Nahum Tate's King Lear. Stud in Eng Lit 1500–1900 6 1966.

Glover, W. B. Human nature and the state in Hobbes. Jnl History of Philosophy 4 1966.

Goldsmith, M. M. Hobbes' science of politics. New York 1966.

Olafson, F. Hobbes and the modern theory of natural law. JHI 4 1966.

Pitkin, H. In his Concept of representation, Berkeley 1967.

McNeilly, F. S. The anatomy of Leviathan. 1968.

Baumrin, B. (ed). Hobbes' Leviathan: interpretations and criticism. Belmont Cal 1969.

Förster, W. Thomas Hobbes und der Puritanismus. Berlin 1969. With extensive bibliography.

Gauthier, D. P. The logic of Leviathan. Oxford 1969.

Kosellech, A. and A. Schnur. Hobbes-Forschungen. Berlin 1969.

MacGillivray, R. A study of Hobbes's Behemoth. JHI 31 1970.

Wolin, S. S. Hobbes and the epic tradition of political theory. Los Angeles 1970.

OTHER PHILOSOPHICAL WRITERS

See also Religion, above, and Science, below. Cross-references are not entered for individual authors.

SIR THOMAS MORE
1478–1535

Bibliographies

Gibson, R. W. More: a preliminary bibliography of his works and of Moreana to the year 1750. New Haven 1961.

Collections

Complete works. Ed R. S. Sylvester et al 14 vols New Haven 1963–.

§ 1

Utopia. Louvain 1516; tr 1551.

§ 2

Kautsky, K. More and his Utopia (1888). Tr 1959.

Hexter, J. H. More's Utopia: the biography of an idea. Princeton 1952.

Surtz, E. The praise of wisdom: a commentary on the religious and moral problems and backgrounds of St Thomas More's Utopia. Chicago 1957.

Hogrefi, P. The More Circle. Urbana 1959.

Johnson, R. S. More's Utopia. New Haven 1969.

Sylvester, R. S. More: action and contemplation. New Haven 1972.

WILLIAM BALDWIN
c. 1515–63

§ 1

A treatise of morall phylosophie, containing the sayings of the wise. 1547.

§ 2

Camp, T. W. Another version of the Thinges that cause a quiet lyffe. MLN 52 1937.

Bühler, C. F. A survival from the Middle Ages: Baldwin's use of the Dictes and sayings. Speculum 23 1948.

THOMAS WILSON
1525?–81

The rule of reason, containing the arte of logique. 1551.

The arte of rhetorique 1553, 1560; ed G. H. Mair, Oxford 1909.

RALPH LEVER
d. 1585

The arte of reason, rightly termed witchcraft. 1573.

EVERARD DIGBY
1578–1606

Theoria analytica, viam ad Monarchiam scientiarum demonstrans, totius philosophiae et reliquarum scientiarum. 1579.

De duplici methodo libri duo, unicam P. Rami methodum refutantes. 1580.

De arte natandi. 1587; tr C. Middleton 1595.

SIR WILLIAM TEMPLE
1555–1628

Francisci Mildapetti Navarreni ad Everardum Digbeium anglum admonitio de unica P. Rami methodo rejectis ceteris retinenda. 1580.

Pro Mildapetti de unica methodo defensione contra Diplodophilum, commentatio. 1581, Frankfurt 1584.

P. Rami Dialecticae libri duo, scholiis G. Tenpelli cantabrigiensis illustrati. 1576, Cambridge 1584, Frankfurt 1591, 1595.

Jacobi Martini Scoti Dunkeldensis philosophiae professoris publici, in Academia Taurinensi. Cambridge 1584, Frankfurt 1591, 1595. Martin's book was first pbd Turin 1577. For Temple *see* J. Freudenthal, Beiträge zur Geschichte der Englischen Philosophie, Archiv fur Geschichte der Philosophie 5 1892.

JOHN CASE
d. 1600

§ 1

Summa veterum interpretum in universam dialecticam Aristotelis. 1584, Oxford 1592, Frankfurt 1593, Oxford 1598.

Speculum moralium questionum in universam ethicen Aristotelis. Oxford 1585, Frankfurt 1589, Oxford 1596.

Sphaera civitatis. Oxford 1588.

Reflexus speculi moralis. Oxford 1596.

Thesaurus oeconomiae. Oxford 1597.

Lapis philosophicus. Oxford 1599, London 1612.

Ancilla philosophiae. Oxford 1599.

§ 2

Starnes, D. T. Chaucer, John Lyly and Sphaera civitatis 1588. N & Q 8 Aug 1936.

JOHN SANDERSON
d. 1602

Institutionum dialecticarum libri quattuor. Antwerp 1598, Oxford 1594, 1602, 1609.

WILLIAM PERKINS
1558–1602

Armilla aurea. Cambridge 1590, [1591 ?], [1592].
The whole treatise of the cases of conscience. 1608, 1611, 1614.

SIR RICHARD BARCKLEY

A discourse of the felicitie of man: or his summum bonum. 1598, 1603; ed T. Heywood 1631.

SIR JOHN DAVIES
1569–1626

Nosce teipsum: this oracle expounded in two elegies, 1: Of humane knowledge; 2: Of the soule of man and the immortalitie thereof. 1599.
Complete poems. Ed A. B. Grosart 1869, 1876.

JOSEPH HALL
1574–1656

Characters of vertues and vices. 1608; ed R. Kirk, New Brunswick NJ 1948 (with Heaven upon earth).
Resolutions and decisions of diverse practicall cases of conscience. 1649.

JOHN SELDEN
1584–1654

§1

The duello or single combat. 1610.
De dis syris syntagmata II. 1617.
The historie of tithes. 1618.
De successionibus ad leges Ebraeorum. 1631, 1636.
Mare clausum seu de dominio maris. 1635, 1636, Hague 1636, Leyden 1636, Amsterdam 1636.
De jure naturali & gentium juxta disciplinam Ebraeorum. 1640, Leipzig 1665, Strasbourg 1665.
A brief discourse of the powers of the Peeres and Comons. 1640.
Table-talk. Ed R. Milward 1689; ed S. H. Reynolds, Oxford 1892; ed F. Pollock 1927 (Selden Soc) (from ms).
Opera omnia. Ed D. Wilkins 3 vols 1726. For Selden's legal works see col 2284, above.

§2

Table-talk. Ed F. Pollock 1927 (Selden Soc) (from ms). With a life by E. Fry, rptd from DNB.

ROBERT SANDERSON
1587–1663

Logicae artis compendium. Oxford 1615 (anon), 1618, 1631, 1664 (6th edn).
De juramenti promissorii obligatione praelectiones septem. 1646, 1647, 1670, 1686; tr 1655 ('by his Majesties speciall command').
De obligatione conscientiae praelectiones decem habitae. 1660, 1661, 1670 etc; ed W. Whewell, Cambridge 1851; ed and tr C. Wordsworth, Lincoln 1877.
Works. Ed W. Jacobson 6 vols Oxford 1854.

ROBERT FLUDD
1574–1637

§1

Utriusque cosmi majoris scilicet et minoris, metaphysica, physica. 2 vols Frankfurt 1617–21.
Medicina catholica: seu mysticum artis medicandi sacrarum. Frankfurt 1629–30.
Clavis philosophiae et alchymiae Fluddanae. Frankfurt 1633.
Philosophia moysaica. Gouda 1638; tr 1659.
Opera. Gouda 1638.
See also col 2363, below.

§2

Craven, J. B. Doctor Robert Fludd. Kirkwall 1902.
Josten, C. H. Truth's golden harrow: an unpublished alchemical treatise of Fludd. Ambix 3 1949.
—— Fludd's theory of geomancy and his experiences at Avignon. Jnl Warburg & Courtauld Inst 27 1964.
Hutin, S. Fludd: le Rosicrucien. Paris 1953.
Debus, A. G. Fludd and the circulation of the blood. Jnl History of Medicine 16 1961.
—— Fludd and the use of Gilbert's De magnete in the weapon-salve controversy. Jnl History of Medicine 19 1964.
—— The sun in the universe of Fludd. In Le soleil à la Renaissance: sciences et mythes, Brussels 1965.
—— In his English Paracelsians, 1965.
—— Renaissance chemistry and the work of Robert Fludd. In Alchemy and chemistry in the seventeenth century, W. A. Clark Memorial Library, Los Angeles 1966.
Keynes, G. L. Life of William Harvey. Oxford 1966. Contains discussion of Fludd's relations with Harvey.
Yates, F. A. In her Art of memory, 1966.
—— In her Theatre of the world, 1969.
Amman, P. J. The musical theory and philosophy of Fludd. Jnl Warburg & Courtauld Inst 30 1967.

RICHARD CRAKANTHORP
1567–1624

Introductio in metaphysicam. Oxford 1619.
Logicae libri quinque de praedicabilibus. 1622, Oxford 1677.
De providentia Dei tractatus. Cambridge 1623.

NATHANAEL CARPENTER
1589–1628?

§1

Philosophia libera. Frankfurt 1621, Oxford 1622, 1636.

§2

Howell, W. S. Carpenter's place in the controversy between dialectic and rhetoric. Speech Monographs 1 1934.

MARTIN FOTHERBY
1549?–1619

Atheomastix: clearing foure truthes against atheists and infidels. 1622.

EDWARD HERBERT, 1st BARON HERBERT OF CHERBURY
1583–1648

§ 1

De veritate. Paris 1624, 1633, 1636, London 1645; tr M. H. Carré, Bristol 1937.
De causis errorum. 1645, 1656.
De religione gentilium. Amsterdam 1663, 1700; tr 1705.
Religio laici. Ed H. G. Wright, MLR 28 1933; ed H. R. Hutcheson, New Haven 1944.

§ 2

Lechler, G. V. In his Geschichte des englischen Deismus, Stuttgart 1841.
Rémusat, C. de. Lord Herbert de Cherbury. Paris 1874.
Sorley, W. R. The philosophy of Lord Herbert of Cherbury. Mind 3 1894.
Lyttle, C. Herbert of Cherbury: apostle of ethical theism. Church History 4 1935.
Willey, B. Herbert of Cherbury: a spiritual Quixote of the seventeenth century. E & S 27 1941.
Aaron, R. I. The autobiography of Herbert of Cherbury: the original ms material. MLR 36 1941.
Hutcheson, H. R. Lord Herbert and the Deists. Jnl of Philosophy 43 1946.

GEORGE HAKEWILL
1578–1649

The vanitie of the eie. Oxford 1608.
An apologie or declaration of the power and providence of God in the government of the world. Oxford 1627, etc.

WILLIAM AMES
1576–1633

De conscientia et ejus jure vel casibus. Amsterdam 1630, 1631, Oxford 1659; tr 1639.
Disputatio theologica adversa metaphysicam. 1632.
Demonstratio logicae verae. 1632.

JOHN FLAVEL
1596–1617

Tractatus de demonstratione methodicus et polemicus. Oxford 1619.

MERIC CASAUBON
1599–1671

A treatise concerning enthusiasme as it is an effect of nature. 1655.
The credulity and incredulity in things natural, civil and divine. 1668.
A letter of Meric Casaubon to Peter du Moulin concerning natural experimental philosophy. Cambridge 1669.

ROBERT GREVILLE, 2nd BARON BROOKE
1608–43

The nature of truth. 1640.
A discourse opening the nature of that episcopacie which is exercised in England. 1641, 1642.

SAMUEL HARTLIB
c. 1600–62

§ 1

A description of the famous kingdome of Macaria. 1641.
Englands thankfulnesse: or an humble remembrance presented to Parliament. 1642.
The Parliaments reformation. 1646.

§ 2

Turnbull, G. H. Hartlib: a sketch of his life and his relations to J. A. Comenius. Oxford 1920.
—— Hartlib, Dury and Comenius. 1947.
—— Hartlib's influence on the early history of the Royal Society. Notes & Records of Royal Soc 10 1953.
Trevor-Roper, H. R. The three foreigners: the philosophers of the Puritan Revolution. In his Religion, the Reformation and social change, 1967.
Webster, C. (ed). Hartlib and the advancement of learning. Cambridge 1970. With long introd.

JOHN HALL
1627–56

An humble motion to the Parliament of England concerning the advancement of learning. 1649.

HENRY MORE
1614–87

Collections

Philosophical poems. Cambridge 1647; ed A. B. Grosart 1876, 1878; ed G. Bullough, Manchester 1931 (selection).
A collection of several philosophical writings. 1662, 1712.
Henrici Mori cantabrigiensis opera. 3 vols 1675–9.
Theological works. 1708.
Philosophical writings. Ed F. I. Mackinnon, New York 1925.

§ 1

Ψυχωδία platonica: or a Platonicall song of the soul, consisting of foure severall poems, by H. M. Cambridge 1642.
Democritus platonissans: or an essay upon the infinity of worlds out of Platonick principles. Cambridge 1646. In verse.
Observations upon [Thomas Vaughan's] Anthroposophia theomagica and Anima magica abscondita, by Alazonomastix Philalethes. 1650.
The second lash of Alazonomastix. Cambridge 1651. Rptd with the preceding in Enthusiasmus triumphatus, 1656, below.
An antidote against atheism: or an appeal to the natural faculties of the mind of man, whether there be not a God. 1652, 1653, 1655 ('corrected and enlarged; with an appendix').
Conjectura cabbalistica: or a conjectural essay of interpreting the mind of Moses. 1653.
Enthusiasmus triumphatus: or a discourse of the nature, causes, kinds and cure of Enthusiasme. 1656; ed M. V. de Porte, Los Angeles 1965.
The immortality of the soule, so farre forth as it is demonstrable from the knowledge of nature and the light of reason. 1659.
An explanation of the grand mystery of godliness: or a true and faithful representation of the everlasting gospel. 1660. 4 chs rptd 1681 as Tetractys anti-astrologica.
Free-Parliament proposed to tender consciences, and published for the use of the Members now elected, by Alazonomastix Philalethes. 1660.

A modest enquiry into the mystery of iniquity. 1664. Appended is The apology of Dr Henry More.

Enchiridion ethicum, praecipua moralis philosophiae rudimenta complectens, illustrata ut plurimum veterum monumentis, et ad probitatem vitae perpetuo accommodata. 1667, 1668, 1669, Amsterdam 1679, 1695, 1695, 1696, 1711. Partial English version by More himself in Joseph Glanvill, Sadducismus triumphatus, 1681; rptd separately 1690, New York 1930 (facs).

Divine dialogues, containing sundry disquisitions and instructions concerning the attributes of God and his providence in the world, collected and compiled by Franciscus Palaeopolitanus. 1668, 1713, 3 vols Glasgow 1743. Appended is A brief discourse of the true grounds of the certainty of faith.

Philosophiae teutonicae censura. 1670. A criticism of Boehme.

Enchiridion metaphysicum: sive de rebus incorporeis succincta & luculenta dissertatio. 1671 (signed H.M.). An attack on Descartes.

A brief reply to a late Answer to Dr Henry More his Antidote against idolatry. 1672. Includes reprint of An antidote against atheism, above.

Remarks upon two late ingenious discourses [by Sir Matthew Hale]. 1676.

Apocalypsis Apocalypseos: or the Revelation of St John the Divine unveiled, containing a brief exposition of the whole Book of the Apocalypse. 1680.

A plain and continued exposition of the several prophecies or divine visions of the Prophet Daniel. 1681.

An answer to several Remarks upon Dr Henry More his expositions of the Apocalypse and Daniel by S.E. 1684.

A briefe discourse of the real presence of the body and blood of Christ in the celebration of the Holy Eucharist. 1686.

Discourses on several texts of Scripture. Ed J. Worthington 1692.

Letters on several subjects. Ed E. Elys 1694.

A collection of aphorisms, in two parts. 1704.

Divine hymns. 1706.

More also contributed to Kabbala denudata vol i, ed C. K. de Rosenroth 1677, tr 1677, and Joseph Glanvill, Sadducismus triumphatus, 1681, as well as providing elaborate notes to Glanvill and George Rust, Two choice and useful treatises, 1682. His letters to John Norris are in Norris, The theory and regulation of love, Oxford 1688, and The diary and correspondence of Dr John Worthington, ed J. Crossley 1847–86 (Chetham Soc), includes his letters to Worthington. Other letters will be found in Richard Ward, Life, and Conway letters, ed M. H. Nicolson, New Haven 1930.

§2

'Eugenius Philalethes' (Thomas Vaughan). The manmouse taken in a trap. 1650.

Ward, Richard. The life of the learned and pious Dr Henry More. 1710; ed M. F. Howard 1711.

Benson, A. C. In his Essays, 1896.

Anderson, P. R. Science in defense of liberal religion: a study of More's attempt to link religion with science. New York 1933.

Cohen, L. D. Descartes and More on the beast-machine: a translation of their correspondence pertaining to animal automatism. Annals of Science 1 1936.

Baker, J. T. More and Kant. Philosophical Rev 46 1937.

Reimann, H. Mores Bedeutung für die Gegenwart. Basle 1941.

Lewis, C. S. Above the smoke and stir. TLS 14 July, 29 Sept 1945. Replies by B. A. Wright 4 Aug, 2 Oct 1945, and R. Eisler 22 Sept 1945.

Colby, F. L. Thomas Traherne and More. MLN 62 1947.

Greene, R. A. More and Robert Boyle on the spirit of nature. JHI 23 1962.

Lichtenstein, A. More: the rational theory of a Cambridge Platonist. Cambridge Mass 1962.

Hutin, S. More: essai sur la doctrine théosphique chez les Platoniciens de Cambridge. Hildesheim 1966.

Power, J. E. More and Isaac Newton on absolute space. JHI 31 1970.

Hayles, J. In his Waning of the Renaissance 1640–1740, Hague 1971.

RALPH CUDWORTH
1617–88

Collections
Works. Ed T. Birch 4 vols Oxford 1829.
Works. Ed J. Harrison 1849.

§1

A discourse concerning the true notion of the Lords Supper, by R.C. 1642, 1670, 1676.

The union of Christ and the Church, in a shadow, by R.C. 1642.

A sermon preached before the honourable House of Commons, March 31 1647. Cambridge 1647, New York 1930 (facs).

Dantur rationes boni et mali aeternae et indispensabiles. Cambridge 1651. In verse.

A sermon preached to the honourable Society of Lincolnes-Inne. 1664.

The true intellectual system of the universe: the first part, wherein all the reason and philosophy of atheism is confuted. 1678; ed T. Birch 1743, 4 vols 1829; ed J. Harrison 3 vols 1845; tr Latin by J. L. von Mosheim 2 vols Jena 1733 (with elaborate biographical and critical notes, tr in Harrison's edn), abridged by Thomas Wise 2 vols 1706.

A treatise concerning eternal and immutable morality. Ed E. Chandler 1731.

A treatise on freewill. Ed J. Allen 1838.

§2

Janet, P. Essai sur le médiateur plastique de Cudworth. Paris 1860.

Lowrey, C. E. The philosophy of Cudworth. 1884.

Scott, W. R. An introduction to Cudworth's Treatise concerning eternal and immutable morality. 1891.

Schmitz, K. J. Cudworth und der Platonismus. Bonn 1919.

Aspelin, G. Cudworth's interpretation of Greek philosophy. Gothenburg 1943.

Passmore, J. A. Cudworth: an interpretation. Cambridge 1951.

Stewart, H. L. Cudworth the 'Latitude man'. Personalist 32 1951.

Carré, M. H. Ralph Cudworth. Philosophical Quart 3 1953.

Gysi, L. Platonism and Cartesianism in the philosophy of Cudworth. Berne 1962.

Sailor, D. B. Cudworth and Descartes. JHI 23 1962.

Kemp, J. In his Reason, action and morality, 1964.

JOHN WALLIS
1616–1703

§1

Truth tried: or animadversions on a treatise published by Robert Lord Brook. 1643.

Johannis Wallisii elenchus geometriae Hobbianae. Oxford 1655.

Due correction for Mr Hobbes: or schoole discipline, for not saying his lessons right. Oxford 1656.

Hobbiani puncti dispunctio, in answer to M. Hobs's Στιγμαί. Oxford 1657.

Hobbius heauton-timorumenos. Oxford 1662.
Thomae Hobbes quadratura circuli confutata. Oxford 1669.

§2

Yule, G. L. John Wallis DD FRS. Notes & Records of Royal Soc 2 1939.

JOHN BRAMHALL
1594–1663

Works. 4 vols Dublin 1674–7, 5 vols Oxford 1842.

§1

The serpent salve: or a remedy for the biting of an aspe. 1644. A defence of monarchy and criticism of the view that all power is derived from the people.
A defence of the true liberty of human actions from antecedent and extrinsicall necessity. 1655.
Castigations of Mr Hobbes his last animadversions in the case concerning liberty and universal necessity; with an appendix concerning the catching of Leviathan or the great whale. 1658.

§2

Loewe, J. H. Bramhall und sein Verhältniss zu Thomas Hobbes. Prague 1887.
Sparrow-Simpson, W. J. Archbishop Bramhall. 1927.

SIR KENELM DIGBY
1603–65

§1

Two treatises, in the one of which the nature of bodies; in the other the nature of mans soule is looked into. Paris 1644, London 1645, 1658, 1665.
Of bodies, and of man's soul, to discover the immortality of reasonable souls; with two discourses of the powder of sympathy and of the vegetation of plants. 1669.

§2

Fulton, J. F. Digby: writer, bibliophile and protagonist of William Harvey. New York 1937.
Beall, C. B. Digby's Tuscan Virgil. MLN 57 1942.
Miles, W. Digby: alchemist, scholar, courtier and man of adventure. Chymia 2 1949.
Petersson, R. T. Sir Kenelm Digby. 1956.

ALEXANDER ROSS
1591–1654

The philosophicall touch-stone: or observations upon Sir K. Digbie's Discourses. 1645.
Arcana microcosmi. 1651, 1652.
Πανσέβεια: or a view of all religions in the world. 1653. See col 2121, above.
Leviathan drawn out with a hook: or animadversions on Mr Hobbes his Leviathan. 1653.

THOMAS WHITE
1593–1676

Institutionum peripateticarum ad mentem K. Digbaei pars theorica. Leyden 1646, London 1647; tr 1656.
The grounds of obedience and government. 1655.
Sciri: sive sceptices et scepticorum à jure disputationis exclusio. 1663.

SIR ROBERT FILMER
1588?–1669

Bibliographies
Laslett, P. Concise bibliography of the works of Filmer. In Patriarcha and other political works of Filmer, ed Laslett, Oxford 1949.

Collections
Patriarcha and other political works. Ed P. Laslett, Oxford 1949.

§1

The necessity of the absolute power of all kings. 1648, 1680.
The free-holders grand inquest. 1648, 1679, 1680.
The anarchy of a limited or mixed monarchy. 1648, 1679, 1680.
Observations upon Aristotles politiques touching forms of government. 1652.
Directions for obedience to governors. 1652.
Observations concerning the original of government. 1652.
An advertisement to the jury-men of England touching witches. 1653.
Patriarcha: or the natural power of kings. 1680, 1685.

§2

Bohun, E. A defence of Filmer against Algernon Sidney. 1684.
Allen, J. W. In Social and political ideas of the Augustan age, ed F. J. C. Hearnshaw 1928.
Laslett, P. Sir Robert Filmer. William & Mary Quart 4 1948.
Smith, C. I. Filmer and the Knolles translation of Bodin. Philosophical Quart 13 1963.

NATHANIEL CULVERWEL
d. 1651?

§1

Spiritual opticks. 1651.
An elegant and learned discourse of the light of nature. 1652, 1654, Oxford 1669.

§2

Scupholm, A. C. Culverwel: a Cambridge Platonist. Theology 38 1939.

SETH WARD
1617–89

A philosophical essay towards an eviction of the being and attributes of God. 1652.
Vindiciae academiarum. 1654.
In Thomae Hobbii philosophiam exercitatio epistolica. Oxford 1656.

JOHN PORDAGE
1607–81

Innocence appearing. 1655.
Theologia mystica. 1683.

THOMAS STANLEY the elder
1625–78

The history of philosophy: containing the lives, opinions, actions and discourses of the philosophers of every sect. 3 vols 1655–62, 1687, 1701; tr Latin, 1690.

JAMES HARRINGTON
1611–77

Collections

The Oceana and other works collected by John Toland. 1700, 1737 (with addns).

§1

The common-wealth of Oceana. 1656, 1658; ed H. Morley 1887; ed S. B. Liljegren, Lund 1924.
The prerogative of popular government. 2 pts 1657–8.
A discourse shewing that the spirit of Parliaments, with a Council in the interval, is not to be trusted for a settlement. 1659.
A discourse upon this saying 'the spirit of the nation is not yet to be trusted with liberty'. [1659].
The art of law-giving in III books. 1659.
Aphorisms political. [1659].
Political discourses: tending to the introduction of a free commonwealth in England. 1660.

§2

Russell-Smith, H. F. Harrington and his Oceana. Cambridge 1914.
Liljegren, S. B. Some notes on the name of Harrington's Oceana. In his Probleme der englischen Sprache und Kultur, Heidelberg 1925.
—— Harrington and Leibnitz. Studies in Eng Philology (Minneapolis) 1929.
Koebner, R. Oceana. E Studien 68 1934.
Tawney, R. H. Harrington's interpretation of his age. Proc Br Acad 27 1941.
Fink, Z. S. In his Classical republicans, Evanston 1945.
Polin, R. Economique et politique au xviie siècle: l'Oceana de Harrington. Revue Française de Science Politique 2 1952.
Bohatec, J. James Harrington. Philosophia Reformata 18 1953.
Blitzer, C. Political writings of Harrington. New York 1955.
—— An immortal commonwealth: the political thought of Harrington. New Haven 1960.
Watson, G. Harrington: a last apology for poetry. MLN 71 1956.
Pocock, J. G. A. Machiavelli, Harrington and English political ideologies in the eighteenth century. William & Mary Quart 22 1965.

GEORGE LAWSON
d. 1678

An examination of the political part of Mr Hobbs his Leviathan. 1657, 1663.

MATTHEW WREN
1585–1667

Considerations on Mr Harrington's Oceana. 1657.
Monarchy asserted in vindication of the Considerations upon Mr Harrington's Oceana. Oxford 1659, London 1660.

THOMAS PIERCE
1622–91

'Αὐτοκατακρισις, with occasional reflexions on Master Hobbs. 1658.

HENRY STUBBE
1632–76

Clamor, rixa. 1657. An attack on Hobbes.
The commonwealth of Oceana put into the ballance. 1660.
Campanella revived: or an inquiry into the history of the Royal Society. 1670.

JOHN SMITH
1618–52

§1

Select discourses, as also a sermon preached by Simon Patrick at the author's funeral; with a brief account of his life and death. Ed J. Worthington 1660, Cambridge 1673; ed D. Dalrymple, Edinburgh 1756; ed H. G. Williams, Cambridge 1859.

§2

Ryan, J. K. Smith: Platonist and mystic. New Scholasticism 20 1946.

ROBERT BOYLE
1627–91

Bibliographies

Fulton, J. F. A bibliography of Boyle. Oxford 1941, 1961 (rev).

Collections

Works. Ed T. Birch 5 vols 1744, 6 vols 1772.

§1

The sceptical chymist. 1661.
An examen of Mr T. Hobbes his Dialogus physicus. 1662.
Some considerations touching the usefulnesse of experimentall naturall philosophy. Oxford 1663.
The origine of forms and qualities. Oxford 1666, 1667.
The excellency of theology compared with philosophy. 1674.

§2

More, L. T. The life and works of Boyle. 1944.
Fisher, M. S. Boyle: devout naturalist. New York 1945.
Boas, M. The establishment of the mechanical philosophy. Osiris 10 1952.
—— Boyle and seventeenth-century chemistry. Cambridge 1958.
Appelbaum, W. Boyle and Hobbes: a reconsideration. JHI 25 1964.
Hall, M. B. Boyle on natural philosophy. Bloomington 1965.
King, L. S. Boyle as an amateur physician. In Medical investigation in seventeenth-century England, Los Angeles 1968.
Reti, L. Van Helmont, Boyle and the alkahest. In Some aspects of seventeenth-century medicine and science, Los Angeles 1969.

WILLIAM LUCY
1594–1677

Observations, censures and confutations of errcurs in Mr Hobbs his Leviathan. 1657, 1663.

THEOPHILUS GALE
1628-78

The Court of the Gentiles. 4 vols Oxford 1669-77.
Idea theologiae. 1673.
Philosophia generalis. 1676.

SAMUEL PARKER
1640-88

Tentamina physico-theologica de Deo. 1665.
A free and impartial censure of the Platonick philosophie.
Oxford 1666, 1667.
Disputationes de Deo et divina providentia. 1678.

THOMAS TENISON
1636-1715

§ 1

The creed of Mr Hobbes examined. 1670.

§ 2

Carpenter, C. Thomas Tenison. 1948.

ANTOINE LEGRAND
d. 1699

Philosophia veterum e mente Renati Descartes more
scholastico breviter digesta. 1671.
Institutio philosophiae secundum principia Renati Descartes. 1672, 1675 (3rd edn), 1680; tr R. Blome 1694.
An expansion of Philosophia veterum, above.
Apologia pro R. Des-Cartes contra Samuelum Parkerum.
1679, Nuremberg 1681.

JOHN EACHARD
1636?-97

Mr Hobbs's state of nature considered, in a dialogue
between Philautus and Timothy. 1672.
Some opinions of Mr Hobbs considered in a second dialogue
between Philautus and Timothy. 1673.

JOHN MILTON
1608-74

§ 1

Of education. 1644.
The readie and easie way to establish a free common-
wealth. 1660. On Harrington, above.
Artis logicae plenior institutio. 1672.

§ 2

Woodhouse, A. S. P. Milton, Puritanism and liberty.
UTQ 4 1934.

Williamson, G. Milton and the moralist heresy. SP 32
1935.
Saurat, D. Milton: man and thinker. 1944.
Barker, A. E. Milton and the Puritan dilemma. Toronto
1952.
Svendsen, K. Milton and science. Cambridge Mass
1956.
Curry, W. C. Milton's ontology, cosmogony and physics.
Lexington Kentucky 1957.
Fisher, P. F. Milton's logic. JHI 23 1962.
Huntley, J. F. Proairesis, Synteresis and the ethical
orientation of Milton's Of education. PQ 43 1964.
Sirluck, E. Milton's political thought: the first cycle.
MP 61 1964.
Fixler, M. Milton and the kingdoms of God. Evanston
1964.

EDWARD HYDE, EARL OF CLARENDON
1609-74

A brief view of the dangerous errors in Hobbes's Leviathan.
1676.

JOHN WHITEHALL

The Leviathan found out: or the answer to Mr Hobbes's
Leviathan. 1679.

JAMES TYRRELL
1642-1718

Patriarcha non monarcha. 1681.
A brief disquisition of the law of nature as also confutation
of Mr Hobbs's principles. 1692, 1701 (enlarged).

JOHN DOWEL

The Leviathan heretical: or refutation of a book of
[Hobbes] entituled the Historical narration of heresie.
Oxford 1683.

BENJAMIN WHICHCOTE
1609-83

Θεοφορούμενα Δόγματα: or some select notions of the
learned Benj. Whichcote DD, faithfully collected from
him by a pupil and particular friend. 1685.
Select sermons. 1698 (with preface by Shaftesbury); ed
W. Wishart, Edinburgh 1742.
Several discourses, examined and corrected by his own
notes. Ed J. Jeffery 4 vols 1701-7, Aberdeen 1751 (as
Works).
The true notion of peace in the Kingdom or Church of
Christ, stated in a sermon on the malignity of Popery.
Ed J. Jeffery 1717.
Moral and religious aphorisms, published by Dr Jeffery,
now republished with very large additions. Ed S. Salter
1753; ed W. R. Inge 1931.

J. W. Y.

VIII. SCIENCE

General works – Mathematics and physical sciences – Astronomy – Astrology – Geography and navigation – Alchemy and chemistry – Medicine – Anatomy, physiology and surgery – Botany and herbals – Zoology – Magic and witchcraft.

(1) GENERAL WORKS

Bibliographies

Poggendorff, J. C. Biographisch-literarisches Handwörterbuch zur Geschichte der exacten Naturwissenschaften. Leipzig-Berlin 1863–.

Ferguson, J. Bibliographical notes on the histories of inventions and books of secrets. 6 pts Glasgow 1883–96 (with suppls).

Isis. Washington 1913–. A quarterly containing an annual history-of-science bibliography.

Whitrow, M. (ed). Isis cumulative bibliography [1913–65]. 1972.

Zeitlinger, H. and H. C. Sotheran. Bibliotheca chemico-mathematica: catalogue of works in many tongues on exact and applied science. 5 vols 1921–37.

Francis, W. W. et al. Bibliotheca Osleriana: a catalogue of books illustrating the history of medicine and science. Oxford 1929, 1969 (rev).

Cushing, H. The Harvey Cushing collection of books and manuscripts. New York 1943.

Dudley, F. A. et al. The relations of literature and science: a selected bibliography 1930–49. Washington 1949.

Sarton, G. A guide to the history of science. Waltham Mass 1952.

Current work in the history of medicine. 1954– (Wellcome Historical Medical Lib).

Taylor, E. G. R. Mathematical practitioners of Tudor and Stuart England. Cambridge 1954, 1967.

Sallander, H. Bibliotheca Walleriana: books illustrating the history of medicine and science collected by Dr Erik Waller. Stockholm 1955.

Wightman, W. P. D. Science and the Renaissance. 2 vols Edinburgh 1962.

Bulletin signalétique: histoire des sciences et des techniques. Paris 1962–. A bibliography pbd by the Centre National de Recherche Scientifique.

Maddison, F. R. Early astronomical and scientific instruments: a brief survey of sources and modern studies. History of Science 2 1963.

Bibliography of the history of medicine. Bethesda 1965–. Annual bibliography by US Dept of Health, Education & Welfare.

Durling, R. J. A catalogue of sixteenth-century printed books in the National Library of Medicine. Bethesda 1967.

Schüling, H. Bibliographie der psychologischen Literatur des xvi Jahrhunderts. 1967.

Eales, N. B. The Cole library of early medicine and zoology: part I, 1477–1800. 1969.

Gillispie, C. C. et al. Dictionary of scientific biography. New York 1970–.

Schmitt, C. B. A critical survey and bibliography of studies on Renaissance Aristotelianism. Padua 1971.

Modern Studies

Whewell, W. The history of the inductive sciences. 3 vols 1837, 4 vols 1847–57, 3 vols 1857.

— The philosophy of the inductive sciences. 2 vols 1840, 1847 (enlarged), 3 vols 1858 (rev with new titles for each vol).

Halliwell(-Phillipps), J. O. Letters illustrative of the progress of science in England. 1841.

Rigaud, S. P. Correspondence of scientific men of the sixteenth and seventeenth centuries. 2 vols 1841.

De Morgan, A. A budget of paradoxes. 1872, 2 vols Chicago 1915, New York 1954.

Lasswitz, K. Geschichte der Atomistik vom Mittelalter bis Newton. 2 vols Hamburg-Leipzig 1890, 1926.

Miall, L. C. The early naturalists: their lives and work 1530–1789. 1912.

Duncan, C. S. The new science and English literature in the classical period. Menasha 1913.

Shakespeare's England. 2 vols Oxford 1916. Vol 1 chs xiv–xv.

Singer, C. (ed). Studies in the history and method of science. 2 vols Oxford 1917–21.

Singer, C. The story of living things. Oxford 1931, 1950, 1959 (rev as History of biology).

— A short history of science to the nineteenth century. Oxford 1941, 1969 (rev to 1900).

Jaeger, F. M. Cornelis Drebbel en zijne tijdgenooten. Groningen 1922.

Thorndike, L. A history of magic and experimental science. 8 vols London and New York 1923–58.

Gunther, R. T. Early science in Oxford. 15 vols Oxford 1923–67.

— Early science in Cambridge. Oxford 1937.

Burtt, E. A. Metaphysical foundations of modern physical sciences. New York 1924, 1932 (rev), 1954.

Whitehead, A. N. Science and the modern world. Cambridge 1926, 1927, 1938.

Ornstein, M. The role of scientific societies in the seventeenth century. Chicago 1928.

Nordenskiold, E. The history of biology. New York 1928, 1946. Tr from Swedish.

Nicolson, M. H. Conway letters. New Haven 1930.

— Newton demands the Muse. New York 1946.

— Science and imagination. New York 1962.

Bukharin, N. I. et al. Science at the cross-roads. 1931, 1971 (rev).

Clay, R. S. and T. H. Court. The history of the microscope. 1932.

Willey, B. The seventeenth-century background. 1934.

Wolf, A. A history of science, technology and philosophy in the 16th and 17th centuries. 2 vols 1935, 1950 (rev D. McKie).

Jones, R. F. Ancients and Moderns: a study of the rise of the scientific movement in seventeenth-century England. Berkeley 1936, St Louis 1961.

— et al. The seventeenth century. Stanford 1951.

Lovejoy, A. O. The great chain of being. Cambridge Mass 1936.

Strong, E. W. Procedures and metaphysics: a study in the philosophy of science in the sixteenth and seventeenth centuries. Berkeley 1936.

Clark, G. N. Science and social welfare in the age of Newton. Oxford 1937, 1970 (rev).

Coffin, C. M. John Donne and the new philosophy. New York 1937.

Johnson, F. R. Astronomical thought in Renaissance England. Baltimore 1937.

— Gresham College: precursor of the Royal Society. JHI 1 1940.

— Latin versus English: the sixteenth-century debate over scientific terminology. SP 41 1944.

Merton, R. K. Science in seventeenth-century England. Osiris 4 1938; New York 1970 (rev).

Houghton, W. E. The history of trades. JHI 2 1941.

— The English virtuoso in the seventeenth century. JHI 3 1942.

Raven, C. E. John Ray naturalist. Cambridge 1942, 1950 (rev).
— English naturalists from Neckam to Ray. Cambridge 1947.
— Natural religion and Christian theology. 2 vols Cambridge 1953.
Lenoble, R. Mersenne ou la naissance du mécanisme. Paris 1943.
Collingwood, R. G. The idea of nature. Oxford 1945.
Butterfield, H. The origins of modern science 1300–1800. 1949, 1957 (rev).
Callot, E. La renaissance des sciences de la vie au xvie siècle. Paris 1951.
Boas, M. The establishment of the mechanical philosophy. Osiris 10 1952.
— Robert Boyle and seventeenth-century chemistry. 1958.
— The scientific renaissance. 1962.
Crombie, A. C. Augustine to Galileo. 1952, 1961 (rev).
— (ed). Scientific change. 1963.
Daumas, M. Les instruments scientifiques aux xviie et xviiie siècles. Paris 1953; tr 1972.
Kocher, P. H. Science and religion in Elizabethan England. San Marino 1953.
Mason, S. F. A history of the sciences. 1953.
Underwood, E. A. (ed). Science medicine and history: essays written in honour of C. Singer. 2 vols Oxford 1953.
Hall, A. R. The scientific revolution 1500–1800. 1954.
— From Galileo to Newton. 1963.
Singer, C., E. J. Holmyard and A. R. Hall (ed). A history of technology. 5 vols Oxford 1954–8.
Sarton, G. Appreciation of ancient and medieval science in the Renaissance. Philadelphia 1956.
Wiener, P. P. and A. Noland (ed). Roots of scientific thought. New York 1957. Articles from JHI.
Hooykaas, R. Humanisme, science et réforme. Leyden 1958.
Westfall, R. S. Science and religion in seventeenth-century England. New Haven 1958.
Dijksterhuis, E. J. The mechanisation of the world picture. Tr Oxford 1961.
McRae, R. F. The problem of the unity of science: Bacon to Kant. Toronto 1961.
Hirst, D. Hidden riches: traditional symbolism from the Renaissance to Blake. 1964.
Garin, E. Scienza e vita civile nel Rinascimento italiano. Bari 1965.
Hill, C. The intellectual origins of the English revolution. Oxford 1965.
Kargon, R. H. Atomism in England from Hariot to Newton. Oxford 1966.
Michel, H. Scientific instruments in art and history. Tr 1967.
Singleton, C. S. (ed). Art science and history in the Renaissance. Baltimore 1967.
Lefranc, P. Sir Walter Ralegh: écrivain. Paris 1968.
Purver, M. Royal Society: concept and creation. 1968.
Rossi, P. Francis Bacon: from magic to science. 1968.
— Philosophy, technology and the arts in the early modern era. New York 1970.
Hoeniger, F. D. and J. F. M. Hoeniger. The development of natural history in Tudor England. Charlottesville 1969.
— The growth of natural history in Stuart England. Charlottesville 1969.
Maddison, R. E. W. The life of the Honourable Robert Boyle. 1969.
Turner, G. L'E. The history of optical instruments: a brief survey of sources and modern studies. History of Science 8 1969.
Stillwell, M. B. The awakening interest in science during the first century of printing. New York 1970.
Thomas, K. Religion and the decline of magic. 1971.

Matthias, P. (ed). Science and society 1600–1900. Cambridge 1972.
McLean, A. Humanism and the rise of science in Tudor England. 1972.
Wightman, W. P. D. Science in a Renaissance society. 1972.

Contemporary Treatises

Woodville (or Wydevile), Anthony, Earl Rivers (1442?–83). The dictes or sayengis of the philosophres. Westminster 1477, [1480?], [1489], 1528; ed W. Blades 1877 (facs). For sources see C. F. Bühler, The dicts and sayings of the philosophers, 1941 (EETS).
Caxton, William (1422?–91). The myrror of the worlde. [1481], [1490], [1529?]; ed O. H. Prior 1913 (EETS). From the French Image du monde.
Trevisa, John de (1326–1412). Bartholomeus de proprietatibus rerum. [Westminster 1495], 1535; ed Stephan Bateman as Batman uppon Bartholome his Booke de proprietatibus rerum, 1582. From Bartholomaeus Anglicus. Extracts in Medieval lore: Bartholomew Anglicus, ed R. R. Steele 1893.
Walter of Henley (fl. 1250). Boke of husbandry. 1510; ed F. H. Cripps-Day, The manor farm, 1931 (facs).
Rastell, John (1470–1536). A new interlude and a mery of the nature of the iiij elements. [1519].
Fitzherbert, John (1460–1531?). The boke of husbandry. [1523?], [1530?], [1533?], [1534?], [1535?], etc; ed W. W. Skeat 1882 (attributed to Anthony Fitzherbert by Skeat et al). On J. Fitzherbert's authorship, see E. Clarke, Trans Bibl Soc 3 1896.
Copland, William. The boke of secretes of the vertues of herbes, stones and certaine beastes. [1549], [1560?], [1570?], 1595, 1599 etc. From Albertus Magnus.
Tusser, Thomas. A hundreth good pointes of husbandrie. 1557, 1570, 1571, 1573 (as Five hundred points), 1573, 1573 etc.
Googe, Barnaby (1540–94). The zodiake of life. 1560, 1561, 1565, 1588. From Marcellus Palingenius Stellatus. Latin edn as Zodiacus vitae 1572, 1574, 1575 etc; ed R. Tuve, New York 1947 (facs). See F. Watson, The Zodiacus vitae: an old school book, 1908.
Dee, John (1527–1608). Monas hieroglyphica. Antwerp 1564, Frankfurt 1591; tr French, 1925; tr 1947, Ambix 12 1964.
— A briefe discourse apologeticall. 1599, 1603.
— Rogerii Baconis Angli epistolae de secretis operibus artis et naturae. Ed J. Dee, Hamburg 1618; tr T.M. as Frier Bacon his discovery of the miracles of art, nature and magick, 1659.
— A true and faithful relation of what passed for many years between Dr John Dee and some spirits. Ed Meric Casaubon 1659.
— The compendious rehearsal of John Dee. Ed T. Hearne, Johannis Glastoniensis chronica vol 2, 1726; ed J. Crossley 1851 (Chetham Miscellany 24).
— Private diary. Ed J. O. Halliwell (-Phillipps) 1842 (Camden Soc); ed J. E. Bailey 1880.
Smith, C. F. John Dee. 1909.
Hort, G. M. Dee: Elizabethan mystic and astrologer. 1922.
French, P. J. Dee: the world of an Elizabethan magus. 1972.
A[lday?], J[ohn?]. A summarie of the antiquities and wonders of the worlde out of the sixteene first bookes of Plinie. [1566], 1585 (as The secrets and wonders of the world), 1587. From French of P. de Changy.
San[ford], Ja[mes]. Henrie Cornelius Agrippa: of the vanitie and uncertaintie of artes and sciences. 1569, 1575. From H. C. Agrippa von Nettesheim.
Hill, Thomas (d. 1575?). The contemplation of mankinde. 1571.
— A contemplation of mysteries. [1571].
— A briefe and pleasaunt treatise entituled naturall and artificiall conclusions. 1581, 1584, 1586.

— A pleasant history. 1613.

The whole art and trade of husbandry. 1577, 1631. From Conrad Heresbach.

Frampton, John (fl. 1577–95). Joyfull newes out of the new founde world. 1577, 1577, 1580, 1596. From Nicholas Monardes.

E., R. A discourse of housbandrie. 1580; ed H. A. D. Neville 1951 (facs). From Prudenz Croiselat.

Physicorum libri x. 1581, 1590. By Sebastian Verro.

Compendium physices Aristoteleae. Ed L. Hyperius 1583.

Cooke, Francis. The principles of geometrie, astronomie and geographie. [1591]. From Georg Henisch.

Ashley, Anthony (1551–1627). Of the interchangeable course or variety of things in the whole world, from Louis le Roy. 1594.

Blundeville, Thomas (fl. 1560–1602). His exercises containing six treatises for young gentlemen. 1594, 1597 (expanded to 8 treatises), 1605–6, 1613, 1621–2, 1636, 1636–8.

Compendium librorum physicorum Aristotelis. Ed Johann L. Hauwenreuther 1594.

Johnson, Thomas. Cornucopiae: or divers secrets. 1594, 1596.

Platt, Sir Hugh (1552–1611?). The jewell house of art and nature. 1594, 1594; ed D.B. 1653.

— The new and admirable arte of setting of corne. 1600 (3 issues), 1601.

Jones, Philip. Certaine briefe and speciall instructions for gentlemen, merchants, students, souldiers, marriners. 1595. From Albertus Meierus.

A new book of good husbandry. 1599. From Janus Dubravius.

Allott, Robert. Wits theater of the little world. 1599, 1599.

Gilbert, William (1540–1603). De magnete, magneticisque corporibus et de magno magnete tellure. 1600, Stettin 1628, 1633, Frankfurt 1629, 1638; tr P. Fleury Mottelay 1893, New York 1958; tr for Gilbert Club with notes by S. P. Thompson 1900.

— De mundo nostro sublunari philosophia nova. Amsterdam 1651; ed S. Kelly 2 vols Amsterdam 1965 (facs).

Zilsel, E. The origins of Gilbert's scientific method. JHI 2 1941.

Roller, D. H. D. The De magnete of Gilbert. Amsterdam 1959.

Hesse, M. Gilbert and the historians. Br Jnl of Philosophy of Science 11 1960.

Holland, Philemon (1552–1637). The historie of the world, commonly called the naturall historie of C. Plinius secundus. 2 vols 1601, 1634–5.

Abraham Ortelius his epitome of the theater of the worlde. 1603, [1610].

The naturall and morall historie of the East and West Indies. 1604. From Joseph Acosta.

Theatrum orbis terrarum: the theatre of the whole world. 1606. From Ortelius.

Bacon, Francis. See col 2324, above.

Cuffe, Henry. The differences of the ages of mans life. 1607, 1633, 1640, 1653.

Hill, Nicolas (1570?–1610?). Philosophia Epicurea, Democritiana, Theophrastica propositer simpliciter non educta. Paris 1610, Geneva 1619.

Vaughan, Rowland. Most approved and long experienced water-workes. 1610.

Tymme, Thomas (1550?–1620). A dialogue philosophicall wherein natures closet is opened and the cause of all motion in nature shewed out of matter and forme. 1612.

Fludd, Robert (1574–1637). Utriusque cosmi maioris scilicet et minoris metaphysica, physica atque technia historia. Oppenheim 1617.

— Tomus secundus de supernaturali, naturali, praeternaturali et contranaturali microcosmi historia. Oppenheim 1619.

— Tomi secundi tractatus secundus: de praeternaturali utriusque mundi historia. Frankfurt 1621, 1624.

— Philosophia sacra & vere Christiana seu meteorologia cosmica. Frankfurt 1626.

— Summum bonum. Frankfurt 1629.

— Pulsus, seu nova et arcana pulsuum historia. [Frankfurt 1631?].

— Philosophia Moysaica. Gouda 1638; tr as Mosaicall philosophy: grounded upon the essentiall truth or eternal sapience, 1659.

Craven, J. B. Doctor Robert Fludd. Kirkwall 1902.

Hutin, S. Fludd le Rosicrucien. Paris 1953.

Carpenter, Nathanael (1589–1628?). Philosophia libera. Frankfurt 1621, Oxford 1622, 1636, 1637, 1675.

Widdowes, Daniel. Natural philosophy. 1621, 1631. From Adolphus Gulielmus Scribonius.

Morrell, William. New England: or a briefe enarration of the ayre, earth, water, fish and fowles of that country. 1625.

Hakewill, George (1578–1649). An apologie or declaration of the power and providence of God. Oxford 1627, 1630 (rev), 1635 (rev).

Idea philosophiae tum moralis, tum naturalis. 1631. By Franco Burgersdijck.

Epitome naturalis scientiae. 1632. By Daniel Sennert.

Joston, John (1603–75). Natura constantia. Amsterdam 1632; tr J. Rowland 1657.

Bate, John. The mysteryes of nature and art: conteined in foure several tretises. 1634, 1634, 1635, 1654.

Swan, John. Speculum mundi: or a glosse representing the face of the world. 1635, Cambridge 1643, 1665, 1670.

Kynaston, Sir Francis (1587–1642). The constitutions of the Museum Minervae. 1636.

Hartlib, Samuel (1600–62). Conatuum Comeniorum praeludia. Oxford 1637, 1639 (as Pansophia Prodromus); tr as A Reformation of schooles, 1642. From J. A. Comenius.

— Chymical, medicinal and chirurgical addresses made to Samuel Hartlib. 1655. Includes Robert Boyle's first pbd work.

Plattes, Gabriel (1600?–44). A discovery of subterraneall treasure. 1639, 1653, 1679, 1684.

— A discovery of infinite treasure. 1639, 1639, 1656 (as Practical husbandry improved).

— A description of the famous kingdome of Macaria. 1641. See C. Webster, Past & Present 1972.

— The profitable intelligencer communicating his knowledge for the generall good of the commonwealth. Ed S. Hartlib [1644].

Boate, Arnold (1606–53) and Gerard Boate (1604–50). Philosophia naturalis reformata: id est philosophiae Aristotelicae accurata examinatio et solida confutio. Dublin 1641.

De Caus, Isaac. Nouvelle invention de lever l'eau. 1644; tr J. Leak 1659, 1704 (rev).

Browne, Sir Thomas. See col 2228, above.

Digby, Sir Kenelm. See col 2250, above.

Ross, Alexander (1591–1654). Medicus medicatus: or the physicians religion cured. 1645.

— Arcana microcosmi: or the hid secrets of mans body with a refutation of Dr Browns vulgar errors. 1651, 1652 (rev with refutations of Bacon, Harvey, Comenius et al).

Wilkins, John (1614–72). Mathematicall magick. 1648, 1648, 1680, 1691.

Shapiro, B. Wilkins: an intellectual biography. Berkeley 1969.

Petty, Sir William (1623–87). The advice of W.P. to Mr Samuel Hartlib. 1648.

Fitzmaurice, Lord. The Petty papers. 2 vols 1927.

Strauss, E. Petty: portrait of a genius. 1954.

Keynes, G. L. A bibliography of Petty. Oxford 1971.

Gerbier, Sir Balthazar (1591?–1667). Lecture[s] concerning navigation, cosmographie, geographie, military architecture or fortification. 1649–50.

B[aildon], J[oshua]. The rarities of the world. 1651. From Pedro Mexia.
— The wonders of the world. 1656. From Pedro Mexia.
Naturall philosophie reformed by divine light. 1651. From J. A. Comenius.
Collier, Jeremy (elder). A patterne of universal knowledge. 1651, 1651. From J. A. Comenius.
Boate, Gerard. Irelands naturall history. Ed S. Hartlib 1652, 1657.
Charleton, Walter (1620–1707). The darkness of atheism refuted by the light of nature. 1652.
— Physiologia Epicuro-Gassendo-Charltoniana. 1654, New York 1966 (facs).
— The immortality of the human soul. 1657.
More, Henry. See col 2334, above.
Cavendish, Margaret, Duchess of Newcastle. See col 1303, above.
Webster, John (1610–82). Academiarum examen: an examination of the academies. 1654; ed A. G. Debus 1970 (as Science and education in the seventeenth century).
[War]d, [Set]h and [Joh]n [Wilkin]s. Vindiciae academiarum: the vindication of the academies. 1654; ed A. G. Debus 1970.
Hobbes, Thomas. See col 2325, above.
Evelyn, John (1620–1706). Essay on the first book of T. Lucretius Carus De rerum natura. 1656.
White, Thomas (1593–1676). Euclides physicus: sive de principiis naturae stoicheidea. 1657.
The secret miracles of nature in four books. 1658. From Levinus Lemnius, Occulta natura miracula.
Natural magick in xx bookes by John Baptist Porta. 1658, 1669, New York 1957 (facs).
Culpeper, Nicholas (1616–54). Thirteen books of natural philosophy. 1659, 1660, 1661. From Daniel Sennert.
Childrey, Joshua (1623–70). Britannia Baconiana: or the natural rarities of England, Scotland and Wales. 1660, 1661, 1662.

(2) MATHEMATICS AND PHYSICAL SCIENCES

Modern Studies

Montucla, J. F. Histoire des mathématiques. 4 vols Paris 1799.
De Morgan, A. Arithmetical books. 1847.
Cantor, M. Vorlesungen über Geschichte der Mathematik. 3 vols Leipzig 1880–1900, 1922.
Ball, W. W. R. History of the study of mathematics at Cambridge. Cambridge 1889.
— A short account of the history of mathematics. Cambridge 1893.
Cajori, F. History of physics. New York 1899, 1929, 1962.
— History of the logarithmic slide rule. New York 1909.
— History of mathematical notations. 2 vols New York 1928–9.
Kistner, A. Geschichte der Physik. 2 vols Leipzig 1906.
Smith, D. E. History of mathematics. 2 vols Boston 1923–5.
Karpinski, L. C. Biographical checklist of all works on trigonometry to 1700. Scripta Mathematica 12 1924.
Thomas-Stanford, C. Early editions of Euclid's Elements. 1926.
Yeldam, F. A. The story of reckoning in the Middle Ages. 1926.
Laue, M. von. Geschichte der Physik. Bonn 1947.
Thompson, A. J. Logarithmetica britannica. 2 vols Cambridge 1952.
Dugas, R. La mécanique au xviie siècle. Neuchâtel 1954; tr 1958.
Balmer, H. Beiträge zur Geschichte der Erkenntnis des Erdmagnetismus. Aarau 1956.
Scott, J. F. History of mathematics. 1958.
Boyer, C. B. The history of the calculus. New York 1959.
Hofmann, J. E. Geschichte der Mathematik. 3 vols Berlin 1963.
Middleton, W. E. K. The history of the barometer. Baltimore 1964.
Sabra, A. I. Theories of light from Descartes to Newton. 1967.
Clagett, M. The science of mechanics in the Middle Ages. Madison 1969.
Heninger, S. K. Tudor literature of the physical sciences. HLQ 32 1969.
Clulee, N. H. John Dee's mathematics. Ambix 18 1971.

Contemporary Treatises

Tunstall, Cuthbert (1474–1559). De arte supputandi libri quattuor. 1522, Paris 1529, 1538, Strasbourg 1551.
Recorde, Robert (1510–58). The grounde of artes teachynge the worke and practise of arithmetike. 1543, 1561 (rev J. Dee), 1575, 1582 (rev J. Mellis), 1590, 1596 etc.

Part in R. R. Steele, The earliest arithmetics in English, 1922 (EETS). See F. P. Barnard, The casting counter and casting board, Oxford 1916.
— The pathway to knowledg: containing the first principles of geometrie. 1551, 1574, 1602.
— The whetstone of witte, which is the seconde parte of arithmeticke. 1557.
Johnson, F. R. and S. V. Larkey. Recorde's mathematical teaching. Huntington Lib Bull no 7 1935.
Digges, Leonard (1510–58). A booke named Tectonicon: briefly shewing the exacte measurynge all manner lande. 1556, 1561, 1562, 1566, 1570, 1585, 1592 etc.
— A geometrical practise named pantometria. 1571, 1591; The Theodelitus, ed R. T. Gunther, Oxford 1927 (part of Pantometria).
— An arithmeticall militare treatise named Stratioticos. 1579, 1590 (rev).
Baker, Humphrey (fl. 1557–87). The rules and righte ample documents touching the use of the common almanacks. 1558. From Oronce Finée.
— The well sprynge of sciences whiche teacheth the perfecte woork and practise of arithmeticke. 1562, 1564, 1568, 1574, 1576, 1580, 1583, 1591, 1598, 1602 etc.
Buckley, William (d. 1570?). Arithmetica memorativa nunc primum in lucem edita. 1567, 1567 (with John Seton's Dialectica), 1572, 1574, 1577, 1584 etc.
Billingsley, Sir Henry (d. 1606). The elements of geometrie of the most auncient philosopher Euclide of Megara. 1570. Preface by John Dee.
Digges, Thomas (1543?–95). Alae seu scalae mathematicae, quibus visibilium remotissima coelorum theatra conscendi possit. 1573. Also edited the works of his father Leonard Digges under Astronomy, below.
Gray, Dionis. The store-house of brevite in woorkes of arithmetike. 1577.
Fulke, William (1537–89). Μετρομαχία: sive ludus geometricus. 1578.
Blagrave, John (1558?–1612). The mathematicall jewel. 1585.
— Baculum familiare: a booke of the making and use of a staffe. 1590.
— The art of dyalling in two parts. 1609.
Hood, Thomas (fl. 1577–96). A copie of the speache: made by the mathematicall lecturer. 1588. See F. R. Johnson, Hood's inaugural lecture, JHI 3 1942.
— The elements of geometrie. 1590. From Petrus Ramus.
— The use of both the globes, celestiall and terrestriall. 1592.
— The use of two mathematicall instruments, the crosse staffe and the Jacob's staffe. 1590, 1596.

—— The elements of arithmeticke. 1596. From Christian Urstisius.

—— The making and use of the geometricall instrument called a sector. [1598].

Masterson, Thomas. His first [second, third] booke of arithmeticke. 3 vols 1592–5, 1 vol 1634.

Fale, Thomas (fl. 1586–93). Horologiographia: the art of dialling. 1593, 1626, 1626, 1627, 1633, 1652.

Hill, Thomas (d. 1575?). The arte of vulgar arithmeticke. 1600.

Norton, Robert (fl. 1590–1635). A mathematicall appendix for mariners at sea and for chorographers and surveyors of land. 1604.

—— Disme: the art of tenths or decimall arithmeticke. 1608, 1614. From Simon Stevin.

Briggs, Henry (1561–1630). Tables for the improvement of navigation. 1610. Appended to E. Wright, Errors, 1610.

—— Logarithmorum chilias prima. 1617; tr as The first chiliad of logarithmes, [1623].

—— Elements. 1620. Euclid bks 1–6.

—— Arithmetica logarithmica: sive logarithmorum chiliades triginta. 1624; ed A. Vlacq, Gouda 1628; tr Gouda 1628; rev and tr 1631.

—— Trigonometria britannica. Ed H. Gellibrand, Gouda 1633; tr John Newton 1658.

Tapp, John (fl. 1596–1631). The pathway to knowledge: containing the whole art of arithmeticke. 1613, 1621. Based on N. Tartaglia and V. Mennher.

Bedwell, William (d. 1632). Trigonum architectonicum: or the carpenters rule explained. [1614?].

—— Mesolabium architectonicum: that is a most rare instrument for measuring. 1631, 1639.

—— Via regia ad geometriam: the way to geometry. 1636. From Petrus Ramus.

Handson, Raphe (fl. 1612–30). Trigonometrie: or the doctrine of triangles. 1614, 1614, [1630], 1631. From Bartholomaeus Pitiscus.

Napier (Naper), John (1550–1617). Mirifici logarithmorum canonis constructio. Edinburgh 1614; rptd F. Masere, Scriptores logarithmici, 1807; tr E. Wright 1616, 1618 (with appendix by W. Oughtred) and H. Filipowski, Edinburgh 1857.

—— Rhabdologia: seu numerationis per vergulas libri duo. Edinburgh 1617, Berlin 1623, Verona 1623; tr J. Daunsie 1627.

—— Mirifici logarithmorum canonis constructio. Ed H. Briggs, Edinburgh 1619, Leyden 1620; tr W. R. Macdonald, Edinburgh 1889.

—— De arte logistica. Ed M. Napier, Edinburgh 1839.

Napier, M. Memoires of Napier of Merchiston. Edinburgh 1834.

Hobson, E. W. Napier and the invention of logarithms. Cambridge 1914.

Knott, C. G. (ed). Napier tercentenary memorial volume. Edinburgh 1915.

Wright, Edward (1558–1615). A description of the admirable table of logarithms. Ed H. Briggs 1616, 1618.

—— A short treatise of dialling. 1614.

Speidell, John. A geometricall extraction: or a compendious collection of the chiefe and choyse problemes. 1616, 1617.

—— New logarithmes: the first invention whereof was by John Napair. 1619, 1624.

—— A briefe treatise of sphericall triangles. 1627.

—— An arithmeticall extraction. 1628.

Pratt, William (fl. 1616–24). An arithmeticall jewell; containing the use of a small table whereby is speedily wrought as well all arithmetic works in whole numbers. 1617, 1617.

Lyte, Henry. The art of tenths. 1619. Based on Simon Stevin.

Gunter, Edmund (1581–1626). Canon triangulorum: sive tabulae sinuum et tangentium artificialium. 1620, 1623; tr 1620, 1623, 1636.

—— De sectore & radio: the description and use of the sector. 1623 (5 issues), 1624, 1630, 1636.

—— A description and use of his Majestys dials in Whitehall garden. 1624.

—— Works. Ed H. Bond 1624; ed S. Foster 1636, 1653; ed W. Leybourne 1661, 1673, 1680.

Cajori, F. On the history of Gunther's scale and slide rule. Univ of California Pbns in Mathematics 1 1920.

Savile, Sir Henry (1549–1622). Praelectiones tresdecim in principium elementorum Euclidis Oxoniae habitae. Oxford 1621.

Foster, Samuel (d. 1652). The use of a quadrant. 1624, 1652, 1653 etc.

—— The art of dialling. 1638, 1675.

—— Posthuma Fosteri: the description of a ruler. Ed W. Wingate 1652.

—— Elliptical or azimuthal horologiography. Ed J. Twysden and E. Wingate 1654.

—— Miscellanies or mathematical lucubrations. Ed J. Twysden 1659.

—— Geometrical dyalling. Ed J. Collins 1659.

Ingpen, William. The secrets of numbers. 1624.

Wingate, Edmund (1596–1656). L'usage de la reigle de proportion en arithmétique. Paris 1624; tr 1626, 1628, 1645, 1658.

—— Arithmétique logarithmétique. Paris 1626.

—— Λογαριθμοτεχνία: or the construction of the logarithmeticall tables. 2 pts 1635 (2nd edn), 1648.

—— Arithmetique made easie. 1630, 1650, 1652, 1658 etc.

—— Ludus mathematicus: or the mathematical game. 1654, 1681.

Daunsie, John. A mathematicall manual: wherein is handled arithmetic, planometry, stereometry. 1627.

Delamain, Richard (fl. 1610–45). Grammelogia: or the mathematicall ring. 1630, [1633].

—— The making, description and use of a small portable instrument, a horizontal quadrant. 1632, [1639?].

Harriot, Thomas (1560?–1621). Artis analyticae praxis ad aequationes algebraicas nova methodo resolvendas. Ed W. Warner 1631.

Stevens, H. Thomas Harriot. 1900.

Scriba, C. J. Wallis and Harriot. Centaurus 10 1964.

Lohne, J. A. Harriot als Mathematiker. Centaurus 11 1965.

Norwood, Richard (1590–1675). Trigonometrie. 1631, 1634, 1651, 1656 etc.

—— A triangular canon logarithmicall. [1655?], 1679, 1698.

—— Norwoods Epitomy: being the application of the doctrine of triangles in certain problems. 1659, 1667, 1669 etc.

Oughtred, William (1575–1660). Arithmeticae in numeris et speciebus institutio, quasi clavis mathematicae. 1631, [1647?], 1648, Oxford 1652, 1667 etc; tr R. Wood 1647. See P. J. Wallis, Bibliotheck 5 1968.

—— The circles of proportion and the horizontall instrument. Tr W. Foster 1632, 1633 (enlarged), 1639, 1660.

—— Mathematicall recreations. 1633, 1653, 1674. From Jean Leurechon.

—— The new artificial gauging line or rod. 1633.

—— The description and use of the double horizontall dyall. 1636, 1653 (rev).

—— The solution of all spherical triangles. 1651.

—— Trigonometria. 1657; tr R. Stokes and A. Houghton 1657.

—— Opuscula mathematica. Oxford 1677.

Cajori, F. William Oughtred. Chicago 1916.

Gellibrand, Henry (1597–1636). Trigonometria Britannia. 1633; tr 1658.

—— Instituto trigonometricae. Gouda 1635; tr 1658.

Barton, William. Arithmeticke abreviated. 1634.

Pell, John (1611–85). Ideae mathematicae. [1634], [1639]; tr 1650, 1651 (suppl to J. Dury, Reformed school); ed P. J. Wallis, Durham Research Rev no 18 1967. Latin edns possibly lost.

Babington, John. A short treatise of geometrie. 1635.

Wybard (Wyberd), John (fl. 1630–74). Horologiographia nocturna. 1639.

— Tactometria: or geometry of regulars. 1650.

Leybourne, William (1626–1716). Panometria: or the whole art of surveying land. 1650.

— The compleat surveyor. 1653, 1657, 1674 etc.

— Arithmetick vulgar, decimal, instrumental and al-gebraical. 1657, 1659, 1660 etc.

Moore, Sir Jonas (1617–79). An arithmetick, discovering the secrets of that art. 1650, 1660 etc.

— Resolutio triplex cuisdam problematis a domino J. de Montfort propositi. 1658.

Rudd, Thomas. Practical geometry in two parts. 1650.

— Euclides elements of geometry: the first vi books. 1651. With preface by J. Dee.

Jagger, Robert. Artificial arithmetic in decimals. 1651.

Wren, Christopher (1642–1723). Horologiorum scioteri-corum. 1652 (appendix to Oughtred, Clavis mathe-maticae). See Wallis, below.

Ward, Seth (1617–89). Idea trigonometriae demonstratio: item praelectio de cometis. Oxford 1653–4.

— In Thomae Hobbii philosophiam exercitatio epistolica. Oxford 1656.

Newton, John (1622–78). Institutio mathematica. 1654, 1671.

— Tabulae mathematicae. 1654, 1660.

— Geometrical trigonometry. 1659.

— Mathematical elements in three parts. 1660.

Barrow, Isaac (1630–77). Euclidis elementorum libri xv. Cambridge 1655, 1657, 1659; tr 1660.

— Euclidis data succincte demonstrata. Cambridge 1657. 1659.

— Mathematical works. Ed W. Whewell 1860.
Osmond, P. H. Barrow: his life and times. 1944.

Hobbes, Thomas. See col 2325, above.

Wallis, John (1616–1703). Arithmetica infinitorum. Oxford 1656.

— Mathesis universalis: sive arithmeticum opus in-tegrum. Oxford 1657.

— (ed). Commercium epistolicum. 1658. Includes letters by Wren.

— Tractatus duo, prior de cycloide, posterior de cissoide. Oxford 1659 (with sections by Wren). Wallis also exchanged polemical mathematical pamphlets with Hobbes.
Scott, J. F. The mathematical work of Wallis. 1938.
Scriba, C. J. Studien zur Mathematik des Wallis. Wiesbaden 1966.

Willsford, Thomas. Willsfords arithmetick, naturall and artificiall. 1656.

— The scales of commerce and trade. 1660.

Collins, John (1625–83). An introduction to merchants accounts. 1656. Appendix to G. Malynes, Consuetudo.

— The description and use of a general quadrant. 1658.

— The sector on a quadrant. 1659.

— The marriners plain scale new plain'd. 1659.

White, Thomas (1593–1676). Exercitatio geometria de geometria indivisibilium. 1658.

(3) ASTRONOMY

Modern Studies

Delambre, J. Histoire de l'astronomie moderne. Paris 1821.

Grant, R. History of physical astronomy. 1852.

Houzeau, J. C. and A. Lancaster. Bibliographie générale de l'astronomie. 2 vols Brussels 1887–9, 1969 (rev D. Dewhirst).

Dreyer, J. L. E. History of planetary systems. Cambridge 1906, New York 1953.

Orchard, T. N. Milton's astronomy. 1913.

Zinner, E. Geschichte der Sternkunde. Berlin 1931.

Johnson, F. R. Astronomical thought in Renaissance England 1500–1645. Baltimore 1937.

Koyré, A. Etudes Galiléennes. Paris 1939.

— From the closed world to the infinite universe. Balti-more 1957.

Nicolson, M. H. Voyages to the moon. New York 1948.

— The breaking of the circle. Evanston 1950.

King, H. C. The history of the telescope. 1955.

Heninger, S. K. A handbook of Renaissance meteorology. Durham NC 1960.

Contemporary Treatises

Linacre, Thomas (1460?–1524). De sphaera. Venice 1499, Leipzig 1500, Paris [1500?], Reggio Calabria 1503 etc.

De astronomia. [1528?], [1536?], [after 1536]. Spurious Aristotle.

Hugo of Caumpden. The boke of demaundes: of the sayence of phylosophe and astronomye betwene Kynge Bactus and the philosopher Bydracke. [1536?].

Boorde, Andrew (1490?–1549). The pryncyples of astronomye in manner a prognosticacyon to the worldes end. [1548].

Salesbury, William (1520–1600). The descripcion of the sphere or frame of the worlde. [1550]. From Proclus.

Digges, Leonard (1510–58). A prognostication of right good effect. 1555, 1556 (as A prognostication ever-lasting), 1564, 1567, 1574; ed Thomas Digges 1576, 1578, 1583, 1585, 1592, 1596, 1605.

Johnson, F. R. Digges the Copernican system and the idea of the infinity of the universe in 1576. Hunting-ton Lib Bull no 5 1934.

Bosanquet, E. F. Digges and his books. Oxford Bibl Soc Proc & Papers 1 1926.

Recorde, Robert (1510–58). The castle of knowledge: containing the explication of the sphere both celestiall and materiall. 1556, 1596.

Field, John. Ephemeris anni 1557 currentis juxta Copernici et Reinholdi canones supputata. 1556.

Dee, John (1527–1608). Propaedeumata aphoristica de praestantioribus quibusdam naturae virtutibus. 1558, 1558, 1568.

— Parallaticae commentationis praxeosque nucleus quidam. Ed T. Digges 1573.

Baker, Humphrey (fl. 1557–87). The rules and righte ample documentes touching the use and practise of the common almanackes. 1558. From Oronce Finée.

Hill, Thomas (d. 1575?). A contemplation of mysteries containing the rare effectes and significations of certayne cometes. [1571].

— The schoole of skil. 1599.

Cheyne, James (d. 1602). De priore astronomiae parte: seu de sphaera. Douai 1575.

— De sphaera: seu globi coelestis fabrica. Douai 1575.

Fleming, Abraham (1552?–1607). A treatise of all blasing starres in general. 1577, 1618, 1618. From F. Nausea.

Twyne, Thomas (1543–1613). The wonderfull woork-manship of the world. 1578. From Lambert Daneau.

— A view of certain wonderful effects of the Comete in 1577. 1578. By T.T., possibly Twyne.

Shakelton, Francis. A blazyng starre or burning beacon, seen the 10 of October laste. 1580.

Bruno, Giordano (1548–1600). Le cena de la ceneri. 1584. Anon.

— Della causa, principio et una. Venice (for London) 1584.

— Del'infinito universo et mondi. Venice (for London) 1584.

Buchanan, George (1506–82). De sphaera. Geneva 1584, Paris 1585, London 1640.

Greene, Robert. Planetomachia. 1585.

Turnbull, Charles (1556–1608). A perfect and very easie treatise of the use of the celestial globe. 1585, 1597.

Hood, Thomas (fl. 1577–96). The use of the celestial globe in plano. 1590.

— The use of both the globes. 1592, 1595, 1596.

Molyneux, Emery (fl. 1587–1605). The globes celestiall and terrestriall set forth in plano. 1592.

Tanner, Robert. A brief treatise of the use of the globe celestiall and terrestriall. 1592, 1616 (rev), 1620.

Hartgyll, George. Calendaria: sive tabulae astronomicae universales. 1594; tr 1594.

Hues, Robert (1553–1632). Tractatus de globis et eorum usu. 1594, Heidelberg 1611; tr E. Chilmead as A learned treatise of globes, 1639.

Blagrave, John (1558?–1612). Astrolabium uranicum generale: a necessary and pleasaunt solace and recreation for navigators. 1596.

Middleton, Christopher. The historie of heaven: containing the poeticall fictions of all the starres in the firmament. 1596.

Norden, John (1548–1625?). Vicissitudo rerum. 1600, 1601; ed D. C. Collins 1932 (Shakespeare Assoc) (facs).

Oliver, Thomas. A new handling of the planisphere. 1601.

— De sophistismatum praestigiis cavendis admonitio. Cambridge 1604.

Blundeville, Thomas. The theoretiques of the seven planets, shewing all their diverse motions. 1602.

Torporley, Nathaniel (1564?–1632). Diclides coelometricae: seu valvae astronomicae universales. 1602.

Lydiat, Thomas (1572–1646). Praelectio astronomica de natura coeli. 1605.

— Tractatus de variis annorum formis. 1605.

— Defensio tractatus de variis annorum formis. 1607.

— Emendatio temporum, compendio facta ab initio mundi. 1609, 1613.

— Ad Cl. Vir. D. Henricum Savilium epistola astronomica. 1621.

— Numerus aureus e thesauro anni magni restauratore T. Lydiat. 1621.

Wright, Edward (1558–1615). The description and use of the sphaere. 1613, 1627.

Bainbridge, John (1582–1643). An astronomical description of the late comet from the 18 of November 1618. 1619, 1619.

— De sphaera. 1620. From Proclus.

— Astronomiae studiosis. Oxford 1622. Probably by Bainbridge.

Brerewood (Bryerwood), Edward (1565?–1613). Tractatus duo quorum primus de meteoris, secundus de oculo. Oxford 1631, 1637, 1659.

James I (1566–1625). Learned Tico Brahae his astronomical conjecture of the new and much admired * which appeared in the yeare 1572. 1632.

Gil, Alexander (1565–1635). The new starr of the north shining upon the victorious King of Sweden. 1632, 1632.

Ross, Alexander (1591–1654). Commentum de terrae motu circulari. 1634.

— The new planet no planet: or the earth no wandring star. 1646.

Godwin, Francis (1562–1633). The man in the moone: or a discourse of a voyage thither by D. Gonsales. 1638.

Wilkins, John (1614–72). The discovery of a new world in the moone. 1638 (anon), 1640 (rev).

— A discourse tending to prove that tis probable our earth is one of the planets. 1640.

Shapiro, B. J. Wilkins: an intellectual biography. Berkeley 1969.

Horrocks, Jeremiah (1617–41). Venus in sole visa. Danzig 1662 (appended to J. Hevelius, Mercurius in sole visus); tr A. P. Whatton 1859. Written 1639.

— Opera posthuma. Ed J. Wallis 1672.

Gell, Robert. Stella nova: or a new starre leading wise men unto Christ. 1649.

Gregory, John (1607–46). Gregorii posthuma: the description and use of the terrestrial globe. 1649.

Wing, Vincent (1619–68) and William Leybourne (1626–1716). Uranica practica: or practical astronomie. 1649.

— Ens fictum Shakerlaei. 1649.

— An ephemerides of caelestial motions 1652–8. 1652.

— Astronomia instaurata. 1656.

Jenner, Thomas. Antiquity and excellency of globes. 1653.

Shakerley, Jeremy (d. 1653). Tabulae britannicae: the doctrine of the sphere. 1653.

Ward, Seth (1617–89). Idea trigonometriae demonstratae; item praelectio de cometis; et inquisitio in Bullialdi astronomiae Philolaicae fundamenta. Oxford 1653–4.

— De cometis ubi de cometarum natura disseritur. Oxford 1653.

— Astronomia geometrica. 1656.

Moxon, Joseph. A tutor to astronomie and geographie. 1654, 1659. From W. J. Blaeu.

Bagwell, William. The mystery of astronomy. 1655, 1673.

Norwood, Richard (1590–1675). A table of the suns true place, right ascension and declination. 1656.

Willsford, Thomas (b. 1610). Astronomia: the sea compass, navigation and cosmography. [1656?].

— Natures secrets: or the admirable and wonderfull history of the generation of meteors. 1658.

See also Leonard and Thomas Digges, Thomas Hood, Thomas Fale, Samuel Foster and William Gilbert, above.

(4) ASTROLOGY

Modern Studies

Wilson, J. A complete dictionary of astrology. 1819, 1885 (rev).

Saxl, F. Verzeichnis astrologischer und mythologischer illustrierter Handschriften des Mittelalters. 2 pts Heidelberg 1915–27.

Bosanquet, E. F. English printed almanacks and prognostications: a bibliographical history to the year 1600. 1917. Addns, Library 4th ser 8 1928.

— English seventeenth-century almanacks. Library 4th ser 10 1930.

Wedel, T. O. The mediaeval attitude toward astrology. Yale Stud in Eng 1920; Hamden Conn 1968.

Boll, F. and C. Bezold. Sternglaube und Sterndeutung: die Geschichte und das Wesen der Astrologie. Leipzig 1926.

Campden, C. Elizabethan astrological medicine. Annals of Medical History new ser 2 1930.

— Astrology in Shakespeare's day. Isis 19 1932.

— Elizabethan almanacs and prognostications. Library 4th ser 12 1932.

Larkey, S. V. Astrology and politics in the first years of Elizabeth's reign. Bull History of Medicine 3 1935.

Sondheim, M. Shakespeare and the astrology of his time. Jnl Warburg Inst 2 1939.

Allen, D. C. The star-crossed Renaissance. Durham NC 1941.

Dick, H. G. (ed). Thomas Tomkis, Albumazar. Berkeley 1944.

Parr, J. Sources of the Renaissance Englishman's knowledge of astrology 1473–1625. In his Tamburlaine's malady and other essays, Tuscaloosa 1958.

Thomas, K. Religion and the decline of magic. 1971.

Contemporary Treatises

The compost of Ptolomeus prynce of astronomye. [1532?], [1535?], [1540?], [1635].

Borde, Andrew (1490?–1549). The pryncyples of astronomye in manner a prognosticacyon to the worldes end. [1547?].

The boke of knowledge of thinges unknowen apperteynynge to astronomye. [1550], [1553?], 1585, 1588, [1619], 1626, 1640. From Godfridus.

Ascham, Anthony (d. 1559). A litell treatyse of astronomy very necessary for physyke and surgerye. [1552].

Baker, Humphrey (fl. 1557–87). Introduction to judiciall astrologie. [1557?], 1587.

Withers, Fabian. Briefe introductions unto the arte of chiromancy, whereunto is also annexed as well the artificiall as naturall astrologie. 1558, 1558, 1575, 1598, 1615, 1633. From Joannes ab Indagine.

— A briefe and most easie introduction to astrologicall judgement of the starres. [1583?], 1591, 1598 (with G. C., Mathematicall physicke, below), 1653. From Claudius Dariot.

Fulke, William (1537–89). Antiprognosticon contra inutiles astrologorum praedictiones. 1560; tr W. Painter 1560, 1563, 1571 (as A goodly gallerye), 1602, 1634, 1639, 1640 etc.

— Οὐρανομαχία: hoc est astrologorum ludus. 1571, 1572.

G[ylby], G[eorge]. An admonicion against astrology judicialle and other curiosities that raigne now in the world. 1561. From Calvin.

Coxe, Francis. A short treatise declaringe the detestable wickednesse of magicall sciences. [1561].

— The unfained retraction of F. Coxe. 1561.

Warde, William. The most excellent profitable and pleasaunt booke to find the fatall destiny of everyman. [1562], 1578, 1592, 1626, 1630, 1634, 1637.

Maplet, John (d. 1592). The diall of destiny. 1581.

Harvey, John (1563?–92). An astrologicall addition to the late discourse upon the conjunction of Saturne and Jupiter. 1583. See Richard Harvey, below.

— A discoursive probleme concerning prophesies. 1588.

Harvey, Richard (d. 1623?). An astrological discourse upon the conjunction of Saturne and Jupiter. 1583, 1583. Parodied by Thomas Nashe.

Heth, Thomas. A manifest and apparent confutation of an astrological discourse. [1583]. Against Richard Harvey.

Howard, Henry. A defensative against the poyson of supposed prophesies. 1583, 1620.

P., W. Four great lyers: striving who shall win the silver whetstone. [1585].

Dick, H. G. The authorship of Four great lyers. Library 4th ser 19 1939.

Nashe, Thomas (1567–1601?). A wonderful strange and miraculous astrologicall prognostication. 1591.

The geomancie of maister Christopher Gatton. 1591, 1608. From the French.

Kelway, Thomas (1567–1601). A learned astronomical discourse of the judgement of nativities. 1593, 1593, 1642. From Auger Ferrier.

Covell, William (d. 1614?). Polimanteia: or the means lawfull and unlawfull to judge of the fall of a commonwealth. 1595, 1595.

C., G. (George Carleton? 1559–1628). A treatise of mathematicall physicke: or a brief introduction to physicke by judiciall astronomy. 1598.

Chamber, John (1546–1604). A treatise against judiciall astrologie. 1601.

Heydon, Sir Christopher (d. 1623). A defence of judiciall astrologie, in answer to a treatise lately published by M. John Chamber. Cambridge 1603.

— An astrological discourse with mathematical demonstrations. Ed N. Fiske 1650, 1650.

Wright, Thomas. A succinct philosophicall declaration of the nature of clymactericall yeeres. 1604.

Lydiat, Thomas (1572–1646). Praelectio astronomica de natura coeli. 1605.

Fage, John. Speculum aegrotorum: the sicke mens glasse. 1606, 1638.

M[elton], Sir John (d. 1640). Astrologaster: or the figure-caster; rather the arraignment of artlesse astrologers. 1620.

C[harleton], G[eorge] (1559–1628). Ἀστρολογο μανια, the madnesse of astrologers: or an examination of Sir Christopher Heydons booke. 1624, 1651.

Lilly, William (1602–81). Englands propheticall merline. 1644.

— A prophecy of the White King. 1644.

— The starry messenger. 1645.

— Christian astrology modestly treated in three books. 1647, 1659; ed 'Zadkiel' (J. M. Morrison) 1835.

— The worlds catastrophe. 1647. With section by E. Ashmole.

— Monarchy or no monarchy in England. 1651.

— An easie method whereby to judge the effects depending on eclipses. 1652.

Geree, John (1601?–49). Astrologo-mastix: or a discovery of the vanity and iniquity of judicial astrology. 1646.

Astrology theologised: wherein is set forth what astrology and the light of nature is. 1649. From Valentin Weigel's spurious work.

Homes, Nathaniel (1599–1678). Daemonologie and theologie. 1650.

Raunce, John. A brief declaration against judicial astrologie. 1650.

— Astrologia accusata pariter & condemnata: or the diabolical art of judicial astrologie. 1650.

Ramesey (Ramsay), William (1627–76?). A reply to the scandalous pamphlet by John Raunce. 1650.

— Lux veritatis: or Christian judiciall astrology vindicated, in answer to N. Holmes. 1651.

— Vox stellatum: or the voice of the starres. 1652.

— A short discourse of the eclipse of the sunne. 1652.

— Astrologia restaurata: an introduction to the knowledge of the stars. 1653, 1654, 1655.

Culpeper, Nicholas (1616–54). Semeiotica uranica. 1651, 1655, 1658, 1671.

— Catastrophe magnatum: or the fall of monarchie. 1652.

— Opus astrologicum. 1654.

Warren, Hardick. Magick and astrology vindicated from false aspersions. 1651.

Childrey, Joshua (1623–70). Indago astrologica: or brief and modest enquiry into some principal points of astrology. 1652.

'Philastrogus'. Lilies ape whipt. 1652.

Gadbury, John (1627–1704). Philastrogus knavery epitomised. 1652.

— Animal cornutum, wherein is contained a brief method of the grounds of astrology. 1654.

— Coelestis legatus. 1656.

— The doctrine of nativities. 1658.

— Νεόφυτος ἀστρολόγος: the novice-astrologer instructed. 1660.

— Natura prodigiorum: or a discourse touching the nature of prodigies. 1660.

— Nuncius astrologicus. 1660.

Rowland, William (d. 1659). A judiciall astrologie judicially condemned. 1652.

Vicars, John (1580?–1652). Against William Li-Lie alias Lillie. 1652.

Brayne, John. Astrology proved to be the old doctrine of daemons. 1653.

S[wadlin], T[homas]. Divinity no enemy to astrology. 1653.

Turner, Robert (fl. 1636–60). Astrological optics. [1655]. From Johannes Angelus.

— Astrological institutions. 1658.

Andrews, William. The astrological physitian. 1656.

Carpenter, Richard. Astrology proved harmless, useful, pious. 1657.

P., T. Astrological institutions: being a perfect isagoge to the whole astral science. 1658.

A[llen], J[ohn]. Several cases of conscience concerning astrologie, answered. 1659.

—— Judiciall astrologers totally routed. 1659.

The vanity of judiciary astrology, or divination by the stars. 1659, 1659. From P. Gassendi.

Atwell, George (1588?–1659). An apology for the defence of astrologie. 1660.

(5) GEOGRAPHY AND NAVIGATION

Modern Studies

Heawood, E. History of geographical discovery in the seventeenth and eighteenth centuries. 1912 (Cambridge Geographical ser).

Taylor, E. G. R. Tudor geography. 1930.

—— Late Tudor and early Stuart geography. 1935.

—— The mathematical practitioners of Tudor and Stuart England. Cambridge 1954.

—— and M. W. Richey. The geometrical seaman: a book of early nautical instruments. 1962.

Penrose, B. Travel and discovery in the Renaissance 1420–1620. Cambridge Mass 1952.

Waters, D. W. The art of navigation in England in Elizabethan and early Stuart times. 1958.

Quinn, D. B. Sailors and the sea. Shakespeare Survey 17 1964.

Richeson, A. W. English land measuring to 1800: instruments and practice. 1966.

Maddison, F. R. Medieval scientific instruments and the development of navigational instruments in the xvth and xvith centuries. Coimbra 1969.

Deacon, M. Scientists and the sea. 1971.

Contemporary Treatises

Fitzherbert, John (1460–1531?). Here begynneth a ryght frutefull mater: and hath to name the boke of surveying. [1523?], [1530?], [1540?] [1533?], [1534?], [1535?], etc. On authorship see col 2346, above.

Copland, Robert. The rutter of the see. 1528, 1536, 1541 (with R. Proude, A rutter of the northe), [1548?], [1555?], [1555?], [1557?], [1565?], [1573?]; ed D. Waters, The rutters of the sea, New Haven 1967 (facs).

Benese, Richard (d. 1546). This boke sheweth the maner of measuryng of all manner of landes. Ed T. Paynell [1537?], [1550?], [1563], [1565?].

Eden, Richard (1521?–76). A treatyse of the newe India, after the description of Sebastian Munster. 1553.

—— The decades of the new worlde of West India. 1555; rptd E. Arber, First three English books on America, 1885. From Pietro Martire d'Anghiera.

—— The arte of navigation. 1561, 1572, 1579, 1584, 1589; ed John Tapp 1596, 1609, 1615, 1630. From Martin Cortes.

—— A briefe collection gathered out of the cosmographie of Sebastian Munster. 1572, 1574.

—— A very necessarie and profitable book concerning navigation. [1578]. From Jean Taisnier.

Cunningham, William. The cosmographical glasse: conteinyng the pleasant principles of cosmographie, geographie, navigation. 1559.

Twyne, Thomas (1543–1613). The surveye of the world: or situation of the earth. 1572. From Dionysius Periegetes.

—— A short and pithy discourse concerning earthquakes. 1580; ed R. E. Ockenden, Oxford 1936.

Bourne, William (fl. 1565–88). A regiment for the sea. [1574], 1576, 1577, 1580 (with Five ways to Cathay), 1584, 1587; ed T. Hood 1592, 1596 etc; ed E. G. R. Taylor, Cambridge 1963.

—— A booke called the treasure for travellers. 1578.

—— Inventions or devises very necessary for all generalles. 1578.

Cheyne, James (d. 1602). De geographia libri duo. Douai 1576.

Dee, John (1527–1608). General and rare memorials pertaining to the perfect arte of navigation. 1577.

Leigh, Valentine (fl. 1560–90). The most profitable and commendable science of surveying. 1577.

Hellowes, Edward (fl. 1574–1600). A booke of the invention of the art of navigation. 1578. From Antonio de Guevara.

Golding, Arthur (1536?–1605?). A discourse upon the earthquake. 1580.

Frampton, John (fl. 1577–96). The arte of navigation. 1581, 1595. From Pedro de Medina.

Warsop, Edward. A discoverie of sundrie errors and faults daily committed by landemeaters. 1582.

Tanner, Robert. A mirror for mathematiques. 1587, 1587.

Ashley, Anthony (1551–1627). The mariners mirrour. [1588]. From Lucas J. Waghenaer.

Harriot, Thomas (1560?–1621). A brief and true report of the new found land of Virginia. 1588.

Blundeville, Thomas. A briefe discription of universal mappes and cardes. 1589.

—— A making, description and use of two most ingenious and necessary instruments for sea-men. 1602.

Lucar, Cyprian (1544–90?). A treatise named Lucar Solace. 1590.

Forman, Simon (1553–1611). The groundes of longitude; with an admonition to all those that are incredulous. 1591.

Davis, John (1552–1605). The seamans secrets wherein is taught three kindes of sayling. 1595, 1599, 1607, 1626, 1633, 1880 (Hakluyt Soc).

—— The worldes hydrographical description. 1595.

Agas, Ralph (1545–1621). A preparative for plotting of lands and tenementes for surveighs. 1596.

Abbot, George (1562–1633). A briefe description of the whole worlde. 1599, 1599, 1600, 1605, 1608, 1617, 1620, 1624, 1634, 1635, 1636.

Wright, Edward (1558–1615). Certaine errors in navigation. 1599, 1599, 1610 (with The whole art of navigation from Roderigo Zamorano); ed J. Moxon 1657.

—— The haven-finding arte by the latitude and variation. 1599; ed J. Moxon 1657.

Tapp, John (fl. 1596–1631). The seamans kalender. 1602, 1605, 1608, 1615, 1617, 1620, 1622, 1625, 1631; ed H. Bond 1648.

Polter, Richard (fl. 1578–1605). The pathway to perfect sayling. 1605; ed H. Bond 1644.

Norden, John (1548–1625?). The surveiors dialogue. 1607, 1610, 1610, 1618; ed J. W. Papworth 1853 (Architectural Pbn Soc, Detached Essays 6).

Pollard, A. W. The unity of Norden, surveyor and religious writer. Library 4th ser 7 1926.

Folkingham, William. Feudigraphia: the synopsis or epitome of surveying. 1610.

Hopton, Arthur (1588–1614). Speculum topographicum. 1611.

The light of navigation. Amsterdam 1612, 1620, 1622, Amsterdam 1965 (facs). From W. J. Blaeu.

Rathborne, Aaron (1572–1618). The surveyor in foure bookes. 1616.

Aspley, John. Speculum nauticum: a looking-glasse for sea-men. 1624, 1632, 1638, 1647, 1662.

Addison, Thomas. Arithmeticall navigation. 1625.

Carpenter, Nathanael (1589–1628?). Geography delineated forth in two bookes. Oxford 1625, 1635.

Hynmers, Richard. The sea mirrour, containing a brief instruction in the art of navigation. Amsterdam 1625.

Pemble, William (1592?–1623). A briefe introduction to geography. Oxford 1630, 1658, 1669, 1675, 1685.

The fierie sea columne. Amsterdam 1633, 1637. By Jacob Colom.

James, Thomas. Strange and dangerous voyage. 1633. With H. Gellibrand, Appendix concerning longtitude etc.

S[altonstall], W[ye]. Historia mundi or Mercators atlas. 1635, 1637, [1639?].

Saltonstall, Charles (fl. 1627–65). The navigator: shewing and explaining the famous art of navigation. 1636, 1642, [1660?].

Hexham, Henry (1585?–1650?). Atlas: or a geographical description of the world. 2 vols Amsterdam 1636, 1638, 1641. From G. Mercator.

Norwood, Richard (1590–1675). The seamans practice contayning a fundamentall problem in navigation. 1637, 1644, 1655, 1659, 1662 etc.

Dudley, Robert (1573–1649). Dell 'arcano del mare. Florence 1647.

Leybourn, William. See under Mathematics, above.

Phillippes, Henry (fl. 1648–77). The geometrical sea-man: or the art of navigation. 1652, 1657.

— The advancement of the art of navigation. 1657, 1685.

Eyre, John. The exact surveyor: or the whole art of surveying land. 1654.

Hubbard, Benjamin. Orthodoxall navigation: or the admirable and excellent art of arithmeticall great circle sailing. 1656.

Atwell, George (1588?–1659). The faithfull surveyor. 1658, 1662, 1665.

Fage, Robert. A description of the whole world. 1658.

Magnet and Compass

Hellmann, G. Neudrucke von Schriften und Karten über Meteorologie und Erdmagnetismus. 15 pts Berlin 1893–1904.

Mottelay, P. F. Bibliographical history of electricity and magnetism. 1922.

Eden, Richard (1521?–76). A very necessarie and profitable book concerning navigation. [1578]. From Jean Taisnier.

Norman, Robert (fl. 1560–96). The newe attractive: containing a short discourse of the magnes or lodestone. 1581, 1585; ed W. Borrough 1596; ed J. Tapp 1614; ed G. Hellmann, Berlin 1898.

— The safeguard for saylers: or great rutter. 1584, 1587, 1590, 1600 etc.

Borough, William (1537–98). A discours of the variation of the cumpas: or magneticall needle. 1581, 1585, 1592, 1596; ed J. Tapp 1614; ed G. Hellmann, Berlin 1893.

Barlow, William (1544–1625). The navigators supply. 1597.

— Magneticall advertisements: or observations and experiments concerning the nature and properties of the loadstone. 1616, 1618.

— A briefe discovery of the idle animadversions of M. Ridley. 1618.

Gilbert, William. See col 2347, above.

De Nautonnier, Guillaume. The mecographie of the lodestone. 1603.

Ridley, Mark (1560–1624). A short treatise of magneticall bodies and motions. 1613.

— Magnetical animadversions to certain magneticall advertisements lately published by William Barlow. 1617.

Wakely, Andrew (fl. 1631–65). The mariners compass rectified. 1633, 1664, 1694.

Gellibrand, Henry (1597–1636). A discourse mathematical on the variation of the magneticall needle. 1635.

Bond, Henry. Sea-mans kalendar with the discovery of the secret of longtitude. 1637, 1640, 1696.

Ward, Samuel (d. 1643). Magnetis reductorium theologiam tropologicum. 1637, 1639.

— Wonders of the loadstone. Tr Sir H. Grimston 1640.

(6) ALCHEMY AND CHEMISTRY

Modern Studies

Schmeider, K. C. Geschichte der Alchemie. Halle 1832, Munich 1927.

Hoefer, F. Histoire de la chémie. 2 vols Paris 1842–3, 1866–9.

Kopp, H. F. M. Geschichte der Chemie. Brunswick 1843–7, Leipzig 1931.

— Die Alchemie in älterer und neuerer Zeit. 2 vols Heidelberg 1886.

Ferguson, J. Bibliotheca chemica. 2 vols Glasgow 1906, 1954.

— Some English alchemical books. Jnl Alchemical Soc 2 1913.

Waite, A. E. The secret tradition in alchemy. 1926.

Singer, D. W. and A. Anderson. A catalogue of Latin and vernacular alchemical manuscripts in Gt Britain. 3 vols Brussels 1928–31.

Duveen, D. Bibliotheca alchemica et chemica. 1949.

Holmyard, E. J. Alchemy. Edinburgh 1957.

Pagel, W. Paracelsus. Basle and New York 1958.

Partington, J. R. A history of chemistry. Vol 2, 1961.

Debus, A. G. The English Paracelsians. 1965.

— The chemical dream of the Renaissance. Cambridge 1968.

Multauf, R. The origins of chemistry. 1968.

De Jong, H. M. E. 'Atalanta fugiens': sources of an alchemical book of emblems. Leyden 1969.

Contemporary Treatises

Norton, Thomas (fl. 1477). The ordinall of alchemy. 1652 (in E. Ashmole, Theatrum chemicum); ed J. Holmyard 1928.

Andrewe, Lawrence. The vertuose boke of distyllacyon.

1527, [1528?], [1530?]. From Heironymus von Braunschweig.

Bacon, Roger (1214?–94?). This boke doth treate all of the beste waters artyficialles. [1550?].

— The mirror of alchimy. 1597. Attributed to Simon of Cologne.

Kelly, Edward (1555–95). Works. In Ashmole, Theatrum chemicum, 1652.

Morwyng, Peter (1530?–73?). The treasure of Euonymus: conteyning the wonderfull hid secretes of nature. [1559], 1565. From Conrad Gesner.

Turner, William (1508–68). A booke of the natures and properties of the bathes in England as of other bathes in Germanye and Italye. Cologne 1562 (appendix to Turner's Herbal), 1568.

Jones, John. See under Medicine, below.

Muffett, Thomas (1553–1604). De jure et praestantia chymicorum medicamentorum. Frankfurt 1584. With Epistolae chymicae.

Chaloner, Sir Thomas (1561–1615). A shorte discourse of the most rare and excellent vertue of nitre. 1584.

Hester, John (d. 1593?). A hundred and fourtene experiments and cures of Paracelsus. [1587], 1596.

— A breefe answere of Josephus Quercetanus concerning the original and causes of mettalles. 1591. See also Johnson and Hester, below.

Ripley, George (d. 1490?). The compound of alchymy. 1591, 1652 (in Ashmole, Theatrum chemicum).

— Opera omnia chemica. Cassel 1649.

Russel, Thomas. Diacatholicon aureum: or a general powder of gold. 1602.

Tymme, Thomas (d. 1620). The practise of chymical and hermeticall physicke. 1605.

—— A dialogue philosophical wherein natures secret closet is opened. 1608.

Anthony, Francis (1550–1623). Medicinae chymicae et veri potabilis auri assertio. Cambridge 1610, Hamburg 1618.

—— Apologia veritatis illuscentis pro auro potabile. 1616; tr 1616, Hamburg 1618, 1684 (in Collectanea chymica), 1893.

Rawlins, Thomas. Admonitio de pseudo-chymicis in quo D. D. Antonii aurum potabile obiter refutatur. [1611].

Gwinne, Mathew (1558?–1627). Aurum non aurum, in assertorem chymicae Fra Anthoniam adversaria. 1611.

Sturtevant, Simon. Metallica: or how to neale and worke all kinde of mettle-oares. 1612; ed J. N. Bagnall 1855.

Rovenzon, John. A treatise of metallica, but not that which was published by Mr Simon Sturtevant. 1613; ed J. N. Bagnall 1855.

Willis, Timothy. Praepositiones tentationum: sive propaedeumata de vitis et faecunditate compositorum naturalium. 1615.

—— The search for causes containing a theosophicall investigation of the possibilitie of transmutatorie alchemie. 1616.

Geddé, Walter. A booke of sundry draughtes principally for the glaziers, whereunto is annexed how to anniel glas. 1615–16, 1898 (facs).

Venner, Tobias (1577–1660). Via recta ad vitam longam; also the true use of our famous bathes of Bathe. 1620, 1622, 1622, 1628, 1637, 1638, 1650, 1660.

—— Viae rectae ad vitam longam pars secunda. 1623.

A revelation of the secret spirit, declaring the most concealed secret of alchymie. 1623. From Johann Baptista Lambye.

Cotta, John (1575?–1650?). Cotta contra Antonium, manifesting Doctor Antonii his apologie for Aurum potabile to be false. Oxford 1623.

Deane, Edmund. Spadacrene anglica: or the English spaw fountain in the forest of Knaresboro. 1626, York 1649; ed A. Butler 1922.

Stanhope, Michael. Newes out of Yorkshire: or an account of a journey in the true discovery of a sovereigne mineral medicinal water. 1626, 1627.

—— Cures without care: or a summons to repare to the northerne spaw. 1632, 1649, 1654.

Malthus, Francis. A treatise of artificial fireworks. 1629.

Foster, William (1591–1643). Hoplocrisma-spongus: or a sponge to wipe away the weapon-salve. 1631, 1641.

Fludd, Robert (1574–1637). Dr Fludds answer to M. Foster: or the squeezing of Parson Fosters sponge. 1631, 1638.

—— Clavis philosophiae et alchymiae Fluddanae. Frankfurt 1633.

Josten, C. H. Truth's golden harrow: an unpublished alchemical treatise of Fludd. Ambix 3 1949.

Rowzee, Lodowick. The Queenes welles: the nature and vertues of Tunbridge water. 1632, 1670, 1671.

Evans, John. The universall medicine: or the vertues of the antimoniall cup. 1634, 1642.

Johnson, Thomas (1600–44). Mercurius botanicus, huic accessit de thermis Bathonicis. 1634, 1674, 1849.

Babington, John. Pyrotechnia: or a discourse of artificiall fireworks. 1635.

Jones, Basset. Lapis chymicus philosophorum. Oxford 1648.

Ashmole, Elias (1617–92) ('James Hasolle'). Fasciculus chemicus: or chymical collections. 1650. From Arthur Dee and Jean d'Espagnet.

—— Theatrum chemicum britannicum. 1652; ed A. G. Debus, New York 1967. A collection of English alchemical texts.

—— The way to bliss. 1658.

—— Autobiographical and historical notes, his correspondence etc. Ed C. H. Josten 5 vols Oxford 1966.

Vaughan, Thomas (1622–66) ('Eugenius Philalethes'). Anthroposophia theomagica: or a discourse of the nature of man. 1650.

—— Anima magica abscondita: or a discourse of the universall spirit of nature. 1650.

—— Magica adamica: or the antiquitie of magic. 1650.

—— The man-mouse taken in a trap. 1650.

—— Lumen de lumine. 1651; ed A. E. Waite 1910.

—— Aula lucis: or the house of light. 1652.

—— Euphrates or the waters of the East. 1655.

—— The chemists key to shut and to open. 1657.

—— The magical writings. Ed A. E. Waite 1888.

—— Works. Ed A. E. Waite 1919.

F[rench], J[ohn] (1616–57). A new light on alchymie. 1650. From Sendigovius, Paracelsus and Dorn.

—— The art of distillation. 1651, 1653–2, 1664, 1667. Based on H. von Braunschweig and J. R. Glauber.

—— A description of new philosophical furnaces. 1651. From J. R. Glauber.

—— The Yorkshire spaw. 1652, 1654.

J[ohnson], W[illiam] and J[ohn] H[ester]. Three exact pieces of Leonard Phioravant. 1652. Based on Hester's edn of Foravanti, Paracelsus etc.

Johnson, William. Lexicon chymicum. 1652, 1652–3, 1660. Based on Ruland.

Pinnell, Henry (1613–74). Five treatises of the philosophers stone. 1652. From Alphonso, Sawtre etc.

—— Philosophy reformed and improved in four profound tractates. 1657. From O. Croll, Paracelsus.

Parkhurst, Ferdinando. Medicine diastatica or sympatheticall mumie. 1653. From Paracelsus and A. Tentzel.

Culpeper, Nicholas (1616–54). Physical and chymical works composed by Geor. Phaedro. 1654, 1656.

Vaughan, Henry (1622–95). Hermetical physick: or the right way to preserve and restore health. 1655. From Heinrich Noll.

Holmes, E. Vaughan and the Hermetic philosophy. Oxford 1932.

'Eirenaeus Philoponos Philalethes'. The marrow of alchymie. 1654–5. Usually attributed to G. Starkey. R. S. Wilkinson, Ambix 12 1964, proposes John Winthrop jr; withdrawn 19 1972.

Turner, Robert (fl. 1636–60). Paracelsus of the supreme mysteries of nature. 1656.

—— Paracelsus of chymical transmutation, genealogy and generation of metals and minerals. 1657. From Paracelsus, Tentzel, Lull.

—— Sal, lumen & spiritus mundi philosophici: or the dawning of the day. 1657. From Clovis Hestlau.

Starkey, George (1627–65). Natures explication and Helmonts vindication. 1657, 1661.

—— Pyrotechny asserted and illustrated. 1658, 1696.

Wilkinson, R. S. Starkey: physician and alchemist. Ambix 11 1963.

His last will and testiment; 12 keys; the stone of the ancient wise men etc. 1657, 1670, 1671. From Basil Valentine.

Brown, Thomas. Natures cabinet unlocked: wherein is disclosed the natural causes of metals, stones, precious earths, juices, humors and spirits. 1657.

Digby, Sir Kenelm (1603–65). A late discourse touching the cure of wounds by the powder of sympathy. Tr R. White 1658, 1658, 1660, 1664.

Cheiragogia heliana: a manduction to the philosophers magical gold. 1659. From Raphael I. Eglinus.

H[arding], J[ohn] (c. 1600–65). Paracelsus his aurora and treasure of the philosophers. 1659.

—— Paracelsus his archidoxis together with his books of renovation and restauration. 1660, 1661, 1663.

—— The triumphal chariot of antimony. 1660, 1661; ed A. E. Waite, The Hermetic museum, 1893. From Basil Valentine.

Willis, Thomas (1621–75). Diatribe duae medicophilosophicae, prior de fermentatione, altera de febribus. 1659, 1660, 1662, 1677.

Wittie, Robert (1613–84). Scarbrough spaw: or a description of the nature and vertues of the spaw at Scarbrough. 1660.

(7) MEDICINE

Modern Studies

Daremberg, C. V. Histoire des sciences médicales. 2 vols Paris 1870.

Haeser, H. Geschichte der Medicin. 2 vols Jena 1875–81.

Munk, W. The roll of the Royal College of Physicians. 3 vols 1878.

Creighton, C. A history of epidemics in Britain. 2 vols Cambridge 1891–4, 1965 (rev).

Neuberger, M. and J. Pagel. Handbuch der Geschichte der Medizin. 3 vols Jena 1902–5.

Barrett, C. R. B. The history of the Society of Apothecaries of London. 1905.

Crawfurd, R. The King's evil. Oxford 1911.

Garrison, F. H. An introduction to the history of medicine. Philadelphia 1913, 1929 (rev and enlarged).

Mercier, C. A. Astrology in medicine. 1914.

Wilson, F. P. The plague in Shakespeare's London. Oxford 1927.

Singer, C. A short history of medicine. Oxford 1928, 1962 (rev E. A. Underwood).

Comrie, J. D. History of Scottish medicine. 2 vols 1932.

Dick, H. G. Students of physic and astrology. Jnl History of Medicine 1 1946.

Allen, P. Medical education in 17th-century England. Ibid.

Russell, K. F. Check list of medical books published in English before 1600. Bull History of Medicine 21 1947.

Poynter, F. N. L. and W. J. Bishop. A seventeenth-century doctor and his patients, John Symcotts. Streatley 1951 (Pbns of Bedfordshire Historical Soc).

Simpson, R. R. Shakespeare and medicine. Edinburgh 1959.

Copeman, W. S. C. Doctors and disease in Tudor times. 1960.

Durling, R. J. A chronological census of Renaissance editions and translations of Galen. Jnl Courtauld & Warburg Inst 24 1961.

Wall, C., H. C. Cameron and E. A. Underwood. History of the Company of Apothecaries. 1963.

Clark, G. and A. M. Cooke. History of the Royal College of Physicians. 3 vols 1964–72.

Dewhurst, K. Dr Thomas Sydenham. 1966.

O'Malley, C. D. (ed). The history of medical education. Berkeley 1970.

Shrewsbury, J. F. D. A history of bubonic plague in the British Isles. Cambridge 1970.

Wightman, W. P. D. The emergence of scientific medicine. Edinburgh 1971.

Contemporary Treatises

A litil boke the which traytied many gode thinges for the pestilence. [1486?], [1488?], [1490?], [1510?], [1520?], Manchester 1910 (facs). Extracts in D. W. Singer, Some plague tractates, Proc Royal Soc of Medicine 9 1916.

Caxton, William (1422?–91). In this tretyse that is cleped gouvernayle of helthe. 1489, [?] (de Worde); ed W. Blades 1858.

Linacre, Thomas (1460?–1524). De sanitate tuenda. Paris 1517, Venice 1623, Cologne 1526, Paris 1526, 1530, 1538, 1540, Tübingen 1541, Lyons 1548, 1549. From Galen.

— Methodus medendi. Paris 1519, 1526, Venice 1527, Paris 1529 etc. From Galen.

— Galeni Pergameni de temperamentis et de inequali intemperie libri tres. Cambridge 1521, Paris 1523, 1527, 1537, Basle 1538 etc; ed J. F. Payne 1881 (facs).

— Galeni Pergameni de pulsuum usu. [1522], Paris 1528, 1632, 1637 etc.

— Galeni Pergameni de symptomatum differentiis liber unus: ejusdem de symptomatum causis libri tres. 1522, 1524, Paris 1528.

— Galeni Pergameni de naturalibus facultatibus libri tres. 1523, Paris 1528, 1537, 1541, 1546, Antwerp 1547 etc.

Johnson, J. N. The life of Linacre. 2 1835.

Osler, W. Thomas Linacre. Cambridge 1908.

O'Malley, C. D. English medical humanists: Linacre and Caius. Lawrence Kansas 1965.

The seynge of uryns of all coloures. 1525, [1526?], [1540?], [1540?], [1541?], 1544, 1548, [1550?], 1552, [1555?], 1562.

A new boke of medecynes intytulyd the treasure of pore men. [1526?], 1539, 1539, 1540, 1540, 1544, [1546?], 1547, [1548?], 1551, 1556 etc.

The judycall of uryns. [1527?], [1527?].

Copland, Robert (fl. 1508–47). Secreta secretorum: the secrete of secretes of Aristotle. 1528, 1572. Spurious.

— The hye way to the spyttell hous. [1536?]; rptd in A. V. Judges, The Elizabethan underworld, 1930.

Paynell, Thomas (fl. 1528–68). Schola Salernitana: regimen sanitatis Salerni: this boke techyng al people to gouerne them in helthe. 1528, 1530, 1535, 1541, 1557, 1575, 1596.

— De morbo gallico. 1533, 1536 (as Of the wood called guaiacum), 1539, 1539, 1540. From Ulrich von Hutten.

— A moche profitable treatise against the pestilence. 1534.

Prognosticacion drawen out of the bookes of Ipocras, Avicen and other notable auctours of physycke. [1530?].

Elyot, Sir Thomas (1499?–1546). The castell of helth. [1536–9], 1539, 1541 (7 issues), [1544?], 1547, [1559?], [1560?], 1561, 1572, 1576, 1580, 1580, 1587, 1595, 1610, New York 1936 (facs).

Moulton, Thomas. The myrrour or glasse of helth. [1539?], [1539?], [1540?] (3 edns), [1541?], [1541?], [1545?], [1546?], [1546?], [1550?], [1550?], [1565?], [1580?], 1656.

Borde, Andrew (1490?–1549). The boke for to lerne a man to be wyse in buylding of his howse for the helth of body. [1540?].

— A compendyous regyment or a dyetary of helth made in Mountpyllior. [1542], [1547], 1562, 1564, 1576; ed F. J. Furnivall 1870 (EETS).

— A breviary of helthe. 1547, 1552, 1556, 1557, 1575, 1587, 1598. Extracts in Furnivall.

Poole, H. E. The wisdom of Boorde. Leicester 1936.

Hales, John. The precepts of Plutarch for the preservacion of good healthe. 1543.

Phayre, Thomas (1510?–60). The regiment of lyfe; whereunto is added a treatise of the pestilence. [1543?], 1544, 1546, 1550, 1553 etc. From Jehan Goeurot.

Caius, John (1510–73). De medendi methodo libri duo, ex Cl. Galeni & Jo. Baptistae Montani. Basle 1544, 1558.

— Cl. Galeni libri aliquot. Basle 1544.

— An introduction into phisycke. [1545?].

— De tuenda valetudine. Basle 1549. From Galen.

— A boke or counseill against the disease commonly called the sweate. 1552; rptd J. C. F. Hecker, Epidemics of the Middle Ages, 1844.

— Opera aliquot et versiones. Louvain 1556, 1721.

— Works. Ed E. S. Roberts, Cambridge 1912.

O'Malley, C. D. English medical humanists: Linacre and Caius. Lawrence Kansas 1965.

Langton, Christopher (1521–78). A very brefe orderly declaring the principal parts of phisick. [1547].

Recorde, Robert (1510–58). The urinal of physicke. 1547, 1548, 1567, 1599, 1665.

Llwyd (Lloyd), Humphrey (1527–68). The treasurie of

helthe: conteynyng many profitable medycines. [1550?], [1550?], 1558, 1585. From Pedro Julian Rebello, Pope John XXI.

—— A litel treatise conteyninge the jugement of urynes. 1553. From Johannes Vasseus.

Traheron, Bartholomew (1510?–58?). This lytell practyse of J. de Vigo in medycyne for the helth of the body of man. [1550?], [1552?], [1555?], 1562, 1564.

The governaunce of good helthe, Erasmus being interpretoure. [c. 1553]. From Plutarch.

Ward, William (1534–1604?). The secretes of the reverende Maister Alexis of Piedmont. 1558, 1559, 1562, 1563, 1568, 1580, 1615.

—— The seconde parte of the secretes. 1560, 1563, 1568, 1580, 1614.

—— The thyrde and last parte of the secretes. 1562, 1566, 1578, 1614.

—— The secretes. 1595 (complete). See Richard Androse, below.

Bullein, William (d. 1576). A newe boke intituled the governement of helthe. [1558], [1558], 1559, 1595.

—— Bulleins bulwarke of defence againste all sicknes. 1562, 1579.

—— A comfortable regiment and very wholsome order against the most perilous pleurisi. 1562.

—— A dialogue bothe pleasaunte and pietifull: wherein is a godly regimente against the fever pestilence. [1564], 1564, 1573, 1578; ed M. W. and A. H. Bullen 1888 (EETS).

—— A brief and short discourse of the vertue and operation of balsame. 1585.

See A. H. Bullen, Elizabethans, 1924.

Hollybush, John. A most excellent homish apothecarye. Cologne 1561. From Hieronymus von Braunschweig.

Newton, Thomas (1542?–1607). The touchstone of complexions. 1565, 1576, 1581, 1633.

—— A direction for the health of magistrates and students. 1574. From William Gratarolus.

—— A delectable dialogue concerning physick and phisitions. 1580. From Pedro Mexia.

—— Approved medicines and cordiall receipts. 1580.

Jones, John (fl. 1550–1600). The dyall for all agues. 1566.

—— A briefe discourse of the naturall beginning of all growing and living things; Galens booke of elements. 4 pts 1572–4.

—— The bathes of Bathe ayde. 1572.

—— The benefit of the auncient bathes of Buckstones. 1572.

—— The arte and science of preserving bodie and soule in healthe wisdom and catholike religion. 1579, 1579.

Androse, Richard. The fourthe and final booke of his secretes. 1569, 1578, 1614. From Alexis of Piedmont.

Baker, George (1540–1600). The composition or making of the most excellent and pretious oil called oleum magistrale. 1574.

—— The newe jewell of health. 1576, 1599 (as The practise of the new and old phisicke). From Conrad Gesner.

—— Guydos questions, newly corrected. 1679. From Guy de Chauliac.

Partridge, John. Galenes book as of elementes. 1574.

—— The arte and science of preserving bodie and soul. 1579.

—— The treasurie of commodious conceits and hidden secrets. 1584, 1584, 1586, 1591 (as The treasure of hidden secrets), 1600 etc.

—— The widdowes treasure plentifully furnished with sundry secrets. 1595, 1599, [1600?], 1631, 1639.

Brasbridge, Thomas. The poore mans jewell. 1578, 1578, 1579, 1580, 1592. From Benedictus Anglica.

C., T. An hospital for the diseased. 1578, 1579, [1585?] (3 issues), [1587], 1595, 1598, 1610, 1619, 1630, 1638. Sometimes attributed to T. Cartwright.

H[ill], T[homas]. A joyfull jeyell: contayning orders and preservatives for the plague. Ed J. Hester [1579]. From L. Fioravanti.

Bright, Timothie (1550–1615). A treatise wherein is declared the sufficiencie of English medicines for the cure of all diseases. 1580, 1580, 1615.

—— Medicinae therapeuticae. 1583.

—— In physicam G. A. Scribonii animadversiones. 1584, Frankfurt 1593.

—— A treatise of melancholie. 1586, 1586, 1613; ed H. Craig, New York 1939 (facs).

Carlton, W. J. Timothy Bright. 1911.

Keynes, G. L. Timothie Bright. 1962. With bibliography.

Hester, John (d. 1593). A compendium of the rationall secretes of L. Phioravante. 1582. From L. Fioravanti.

—— These oils, waters and other compositions are at Pauls Wharfe. [1585?].

—— The pearle of practise or practisers pearle, for physicke and chirurgerie. Ed J. Fourestier 1594.

—— The first part of the key of philosophie. 1596, 1633. From spurious Paracelsus.

Problemata. 1583; tr as The problems of Aristotle, 1595 etc. Spurious Aristotle.

Barrough, Philip. The method of phisicke. 1583, 1590, 1596, 1601 etc.

Coghan, Thomas (1545?–1607). The haven of health. 1584, 1588, 1589, 1596, 1605, 1612, 1636, 1636.

B[ostocke], R[obert]. The difference betweene the auncient phisicke and the latter phisicke. 1585.

Bayley, Walter (1529–92). A briefe treatise touching the preservation of the eie sight. 1586, [1586–7], Oxford 1602, 1616. From J. Fernel and J. Riolan the elder. See D'Arcy Power, Medico-Chirurgical Trans 90 1907. See under Vaughan, below.

Gale, Thomas. The whole worke of J. Vigo. 1586.

—— Certaine workes of Galen called Methodus medendi. 1586.

Levens, Peter. A right profitable booke for all diseases called the pathway to health. 1587, 1632, 1654, 1664.

Kellwaye, Simon. A defensative against the plague. 1593.

Present remedies against the plague. 1594, 1603; ed W. P. Barrett 1933 (Shakespeare Assoc) (facs).

Wateson, George (1544–87). A rich storehouse or treasury for the diseased. Ed A.T. 1596, 1607, 1612, 1616, 1630, 1631.

—— The cures of the diseased in remote regions. 1598, 1598; ed C. Singer, Oxford 1915.

Tooker, William (1558?–1621). Charisma seu donum sanationis. 1597.

Mosan (Mose), Jacob. Praxis medicinae universalis: or a generall practise of physicke. 1598, 1598, 1605, 1617. From C. Wurtzung.

Surphlet, Richard. A discourse of the preservation of the sight. 1599; ed S. V. Larkey 1938 (facs). From A. Dulaurens.

Vaughan, Sir William (1575?–1641). Naturall and artificall directions for health. 1600, 1602, 1602, 1611, 1612, 1617, 1626 (with Bayley's Preservation of eie sight). 1633.

—— The newlanders cure. 1630.

Herring, Francis (d. 1628). Preservatives from the plague. 1603, 1625, 1636.

—— A modest defence of the caveat given to the wearers of imprisoned amulets. 1604.

—— The anatomyes of the true physition. 1605. From J. Oberndorff.

Lodge, Thomas (1558?–1625). A treatise of the plague. 1603.

—— The poore mans talent. Ed E. Gosse, Complete works of Lodge, 1883.

Dekker, Thomas (1570?–1641?). The wonderfull yeare. 1603 (3 issues), rptd 1924.

—— The ravens almanacke foretelling of a plague, famine and civile warre. 1609, 1609.

—— A rod for run-awayes. 1625, 1625.

—— The plague pamphlets. Ed F. P. Wilson, Oxford 1926.

Jorden, Edward (1569–1632). A briefe discourse of a disease called the suffocation of the mother. 1603.
—— A discourse of natural bathes and minerall waters. 1631, 1632; ed T. Guidott 1669, 1673.
D., E. Rules for the preservation of health: a discorse of empericks. 1606.
Harington, Sir John (1560–1612). The Englishmans doctor: or the schoole of Salerne. 1607, 1608, 1609, 1617, 1624; ed F. R. Packard and F. H. Garrison 1920, New York 1970.
H., S. The whole aphorismes of Hippocrates. 1610.
Cotta, John (1575?–1650?). A short discoverie of the unobserved dangers of several sorts of ignorant and unconsiderable practisers of physicke. 1612, 1617, 1619, 1627.
Holland, Philemon (1552–1637). Regimen sanitatis Salerni: or the schoole of Salernes learned and judicious directorie. 1617, [1617?], 1620, 1634, 1635, 1649.
—— Pharmacopoea. 1639. From Brice Bauderon.
College of Physicians, London. Pharmacopoeia londinensis. 1618, 1618, 1627, 1739; ed G. Urdang, Madison 1944 (facs); tr N. Culpeper 1650, 1651; tr N. Culpeper 1653, 1654, 1661 etc.
—— Certain necessary directions. 1636.
Burton, Robert. *See col 2219, above.*
Hart, James. The arraignment of urines. 1623. From P. Forrestus.
—— The anatiome of urines. 1625, 1652.
—— ΚΛΙΝΙΚΗ: or the diet of the diseased. 1633.
Browne, Peter (1575–1624?). Pseudomedicorum anatomia. 1624.
Bradwell, Stephen. A watch-man for the pest. 1625.
—— Helps for suddain accidents endangering life. 1633.
—— Physick for the sicknesse commonly called the plague. 1636.
Taylor, John (1580–1653). The fearefull summer: or Londons calamitie. Oxford 1625, 1636; in Works, 1630; rptd 1868–9 (Spenser Soc).
Fludd, Robert (1574–1637). Medicina catholica: seu mysticum artis medicandi sacrarium. Frankfurt 1629.
—— Integrum morborum mysterium: sive medicinae catholicae tractatus secundus. Frankfurt 1631.
Primrose, James (1580–1659). Academia Monspeliensis descripta. 1631.
—— De vulgi in medicina erroribus. 1638; tr Robert Wittie 1651.
—— The antimoniall cup twice cast. Tr R. Wittie 1640.
Sadler, John. The sicke womans private looking-glasse. 1636.
—— Praxis medicorum: vel formula remediorum. 1637; tr R. Turner 1657.
W., T. The charitable physitian, shewing the manner to make and prepare all remedies. 1639. From P. Guibert.
Brugis, Thomas. The marrow of physicke. 1640, 1669.
Goulston, Theodore (1572–1632). C. Galeni opuscula varia. 1640.
Whistler, Daniel (1619–84). De morbo puerili Anglorum quem vocant The Rickets. Leyden 1645, 1684.
Boate, Arnold (1606–53). Observationes medicae de affectibus omissis. 1649, 1664.
Charleton, Walter (1620–1707). Deliramenta catarrhi: or the incongruities couched under the vulgar opinion of defluxions. 1650. From J. B. van Helmont.
—— Spiritus gorgonicus vi sua saxipara exutus. Leyden 1650.

—— A ternary of paradoxes. 1650, 1650. From J. B. van Helmont.
Rolleston, H. Charleton. Bull History of Medicine 8 1940.
Glisson, Francis (1597–1677). De rachitide sive morbo puerili qui vulgo The Rickets dicitur. 1650, 1655, 1660, 1671; tr P. Armin and N. Culpeper 1651, 1651, 1688.
Pemell, Robert. De morbis capitis. 1650.
—— Tractatus de simplicium medicamentorum facultatibus. 1652, 1652.
—— De morbis puerorum: or a treatise of the diseases of children. 1653.
Biggs, Noah. Mataeotechnia medicinae praxeωs: the vanity of the craft of physick. 1651.
Culpeper, Nicholas (1616–54). A directory for midwives. 1651, 1656.
—— Galens art of physick. 1652, 1662, 1671.
—— A new method of physick. 1654. From Simeon Partlicius.
—— Culpepers last legacy. 1655.
—— The practice of physick in seventeen several books. 1655, 1661, 1663, 1665, 1668, 1678. From Lazare Riviere.
—— Two books of physick. 1656, 1662, 1670, Edinburgh 1664. From Jean Prevot.
—— The idea of practical physick in twelve books. 1657. From J. Jonston.
—— Mr Culpepers treatise of aurum potabile. 1657.
—— A sure guide: or the best and nearest way to physick and chirurgery. 1657, 1671. From J. Riolan.
—— Culpepers school of physick. 1659, 1678, 1696.
See F. N. L. Poynter, Culpeper and his books, Jnl History of Medicine 17 1962.
Bennet, Christopher (1617–55). Theatri tabidorum vestibulum. 1654.
—— Tabidorum theatrum: sive pthisius, atrophiae et hecticae xenodochium. 1656; tr 1720.
See Thomas Muffett, below.
Irvine, Christopher. Anatomia sambuci: or the anatomie of the elder. 1655, 1677. From Martin Blochwitz.
—— Medicina magnetica: or the rare and wonderful art of curing by sympathy. 1656. From C. de Iryngio.
—— Ex viri dni J. Wallaei medica omnia. 1660.
Muffett, Thomas (1553–1604). Healths improvement corrected and enlarged by Christopher Bennett. 1655.
The compleat midwife's practice. 1656 (by T.C., I.D., M.S., T.B., practitioners).
D[ugard], W[illiam] (1606–62). Paracelsus his dispensatory and chirurgery. 1656.
Hall, John (1575–1635). Select observations on English bodies and cures both empiricall and historicall. Tr John Cook 1657, 1679, 1683.
Thompson, James. Helmont disguised: or the vulgar errors of impericall and unskilfull practisers of physick confuted. 1657.
Digby, Sir Kenelm (1603–65). Discours fait en une célèbre assemblée touchant la poudre de sympathie. Paris 1658; tr R. White as A late discourse touching the cure of wounds by the powder of sympathy, 1658, 1658, 1660, 1664.
Willis, Thomas (1621–75). Diatribe duae medicophilosophicae, prior de fermentatione altera de febribus. 1659, 1660, 1662, 1677.
Highmore, Nathaniel (1613–84). Exercitationes duae, quarum prior de passione hysterica, altera de affectione hypochondriaca. Oxford 1660.

(8) ANATOMY, PHYSIOLOGY AND SURGERY

Modern Studies

Douglas, J. Bibliographiae anatomicae specimen: sive catalogus omnium pene auctorum qui ab Hippocrate ad Harveum rem anatomicam ex professo. 1715.
Choulant, J. L. Geschichte und Bibliographie der anatomischen Abbildung. Leipzig 1852; tr Chicago 1920.
South, J. F. Memorials of the craft of surgery in England. Ed D'Arcy Power 1886.
Young, S. Annals of the barber surgeons of London. 1890.

MacAlister, A. The history of the study of anatomy at Cambridge. Cambridge 1891.

Foster, M. Lectures on the history of physiology during the sixteenth, seventeenth and eighteenth centuries. Cambridge 1901, 1924, New York 1970.

Power, D'A. The Elizabethan revival of surgery. 1902.

— The place of the Tudor surgeons in English literacy. Proc Royal Soc of Medicine 1927.

— Selected writings. Oxford 1931.

Rothschuh, K. E. Geschichte der Physiologie. Berlin 1953, Frankfurt 1965 (rev).

Russell, K. F. British anatomy 1525–1800: a bibliography. Melbourne 1963.

Poynter, F. N. L. Gideon Delaune and his family circle. 1965.

O'Malley, C. D. Tudor medicine and biology. HLQ 32 1968.

Herrlinger, R. Geschichte der medizinischen Abbildung bis um 1600. Munich 1967; tr 1970.

Hall, T. S. Ideas on heat and life. 2 vols Chicago 1969.

Contemporary Treatises

The noble experyence of the vertuous handyworke of surgeri. 1525. From Hieronymus von Braunschweig.

Edwardes, David (1502–42). De indiciis et praecognitionibus, opus apprime utile medicis: eiusdem in anatomicen introductio luculenta et brevis. 1532; ed C. D. O'Malley and K. F. Russell, Oxford 1961 (facs).

Jonas, Richard. The byrth of mankind. 1540, 1540. From E. Roesslin. For later edns see Thomas Raynalde, below.

Copland, Robert (fl. 1508–47). The questyonary of cyrurgiens. 1542; ed George Baker 1579 (with Guydos questions corrected). From Guy de Chauliac. See The chirurgie of Guy de Chauliac, ed M. S. Ogden 2 vols 1971– (EETS).

Traheron, Bartholomew (1510?–58?). The most excellent workes of chirurgerye made and set forth by maister J. Vignon. 1543, 1550, 1571, 1586. From J. de Vigo.

Raynalde, Thomas (fl. 1540–51). The byrth of mankinde, otherwyse named the womans booke. 1545, 1545, 1552, 1560, [1561?], [1564?], 1565, 1565, [1585?], 1598 etc.

Ballantyne, J. W. The byrth of mankynde: its author, editions and contents. 1907.

Power, D'A. The birth of mankind: a bibliographical study. Library 4th ser 8 1927.

Geminus, Thomas (1500?–70). Compendiosa totius anatomie delineatio. 1545. From Vesalius; for trns see Nicholas Udall, below.

Udall, Nicholas (c. 1505–56). Compendiosa totius anatomie delineatio. [1553], 1553, 1559 (enlarged), 1561; ed C. D. O'Malley 1959 (facs).

Larkey, S. V. The Vesalian compendium of Geminus and Udall's translation. Library 4th ser 13 1933.

Gale, Thomas (1507–87). Certaine workes of chirurgerie newlie compiled and published. 1563–4, 1586.

— The institution of chirurgerie. 1567. Continuation of above.

— Certaine workes of Galens called Methodus medendi, with a briefe declaration of the worthie art of medicine, office of a chirurgion. 1586. See D'A. Power, Br Jnl of Surgery 15 1928.

Halle, John (1529–68). A most excellent and learned woorke of chirurgerie; also against the beastly abusers both of chyrurgerie and physicke in our time. 1565, 1565; rptd 1842 (Percy Soc).

Bannister, John (1533?–1600). A needful new and necessarie treatise of chyrurgerie. 1575, 1633.

— The historie of man sucked from the sappe of the most approved anathomistes. 1578.

— A compendious chyrurgerie gathered and translated especially out of Wecker. 1585, 1585. From H. J. Wecker.

— An antidotarie chyrurgicall. 1589.

— The workes of that famous chyrurgion. 3 vols 1633, 1633.

Vicary, Thomas (1490?–1561). A profitable treatise of the anatomie of mans body. 1577; ed F. J. Furnivall 1887 (EETS).

— The Englishemans treasure: or treasor for Englishmen with the true anatomye of mans body. 1586, 1587, 1596, 1599 etc.

Power, D'A. The education of a surgeon under Vicary. Br Jnl of Surgery 9 1921.

Clowes, William (1544–1604). A short and profitable treatise touching the cure of the morbus gallicus. 1579, 1585; rptd in the next 2 books.

— A prooved practise for all young chirurgions concerning burnings with gunpowder. 1588, 1591, 1596 (as A profitable and necessarie boke of observations for all those that are burned with the flame of gunpowder), 1637; ed De Witt T. Starnes and C. D. Leake, New York 1945 (facs).

— A right frutefull and approved treatise for the cure of that maladay called in Latin Stuma. 1602.

— Select writings. Ed F. N. L. Poynter 1948.

Major, R. H. William Clowes. Annals of Medical History 4 1932.

Hester, John (d. 1593). A short discourse uppon chirurgerie. 1580, 1626 (rev R. Booth). From L. Fioravanti.

— The sclopoterie of J. Quercetanus or his books: containing the cure of wounds received by shot of gunne. 1590. From J. DuChesne.

Hunton, Antony. A worthy treatise of eyes. 1587–8, 1587–8 (with W. Bayley, Preservation of eie sight), 1622 (rev).

Read, John. A most excellent and compendious method of curing woundes in the head and other parts of the body. 1588. From F. Arceus.

Lowe, Peter (1550–1613?). An easie, certaine and perfect method to cure and prevent the Spanish sicknes. 1596.

— A discourse of the whole art of chirurgerie; with the presages of Hypocrates. 1597, 1612, 1634, 1654. From Canape.

Finlayson, J. Account of the life and works of Maister Lowe. Glasgow 1889.

Hobbes, Stephen. C. Shilander his chirurgerie. 1596. From Cornelius Schilander.

— Margarita chyrurgica: containing a compendious practise of chyrurgerie. 1610.

Child-birth: or the happy delivery of women. 1612, 1635. From Jacques Guillemeau.

Crooke, Helkiah (1576–1635). Μικροκοσμογραφία: a description of the body of man. 1615, 1615, 1616, 1618, 1631 (2nd edn), 1651.

— An explanation of the fashion and use of instruments of chirurgery. 1634. From A. Paré.

Harvey, William (1578–1657). Prelectiones anatomiae universalis. 1886 (autotype reproduction of BM ms dated 1616); tr C. D. O'Malley, F. N. L. Poynter and K. F. Russell as Lectures on the whole of anatomy, Berkeley 1961; ed G. Whitteridge, The anatomical lectures of Harvey, Edinburgh 1964 (parallel texts, Latin and English).

— Exercitatio anatomica de motu cordis et sanguinis in animalibus. Frankfurt 1628, Venice 1635, Leyden 1639, Padua 1643 (with Epistolae duae of J. Walaeus), Amsterdam 1645, Leyden 1647, Rotterdam 1647, 1654, 1660, London 1660 etc; Florence 1928 (facs of 1628), Canterbury 1894, Springfield Ill 1928, Mexico City 1936, Paris 1950; tr as The anatomical exercises concerning the motion of the heart and blood, 1653, 1673; ed G. L. Keynes 1928 (facs of 1653); tr K. J. Franklin, Oxford 1957 (with Latin-English texts).

— Exercitatio anatomica de circulatione sanguinis, ad J. Riolan. 1649, Cambridge 1649, Rotterdam 1649, Paris 1650; thereafter with edns of De motu cordis; tr as The anatomical exercises, 1653, 1673; tr K. J. Franklin, Oxford 1957 (with Latin-English texts).

—— Exercitationes de generatione animalium. 1651, Amsterdam 1651, 1651; tr as Anatomical exercitations concerning the generation of living creatures, 1653.

—— Opera omnia. 1766 (including letters); tr R. Willis 1847 (Sydenham Soc) (writings on circulation, generation and letters).

Curtis, J. G. Harvey's views on the use of the circulation of blood. New York 1915.

Keynes, G. L. A bibliography of the writings of Harvey. 1928.

—— The life of Harvey. Oxford 1966.

Pagel, W. Harvey's biological ideas. Basle and New York 1967.

Whitteridge, G. Harvey and the circulation of the blood. 1971.

Read, Alexander (1580–1641). Σωματογραφία ’Ανθρωπινή: or a description of the body of man. 1616, 1634. Based on Crooke's Microkosmos.

—— A manuall of the anatomy of the body of man. 1634, 1638, 1642, 1650, 1653, 1655, 1658.

A treatise of all the muscles of the whole bodie. 1637, 1650, 1659.

—— Workes. 1650, 1659.

—— The chirurgicall lectures of tumors and ulcers. 1632, 1635.

Menzies, W. Read: physician and surgeon. Library 4th ser 12 1931.

Woodall, John (1556?–1643). The surgions mate or a treatise discovering faithfully and plainely the contents of the surgions chest, with a briefe explanation of sal, sulphur and mercury. 1617, 1639, 1658.

—— Woodalls viaticum: the path-way to the surgions chest 1628, 1639.

—— The cure of the plague by antidote called aurum vitae. 1640, 1640.

Debus, A. G. Woodall: Paracelsian surgeon. Ambix 10 1962.

Keynes, G. L. Woodall, surgeon. Jnl Royal College of Physicians 2 1967.

Fludd, Robert (1574–1637). Anatomiae amphitheatrum effigie triplici. Frankfurt 1623.

Primrose, James (1580–1659). Exercitationes et animadversiones in librum de motu cordis et circulatione sanguinis. 1630.

—— Animadversiones in Iohannes Wallaei. Amsterdam 1640.

Johnson, Thomas (d. 1644). The workes of that famous chirurgion. 1634, 1649, 1665, 1678, 1691. Extracts in The apologie and treatise of Paré, ed G. L. Keynes, New York 1968. From A. Paré.

Drake, Roger (1608–69). Disputatio medica de circulatione naturali: seu cordis et sanguinis motu circulari. Leyden 1640.

—— Vindiciae contra animadversiones D. D. Primrosii. 1641.

Ent, George (1604–89). Apologia pro circulatione sanguinis: qua respondetur Aemilio Parisano medico Veneto. 1641, 1685 (rev).

Cooke, James (1614–93). Mellificium chirurgiae: or the marrow of many good authors. 1647, 1662, 1676 etc.

—— Supplementum chirurgiae: or the supplement to the marrow of chyrurgerie. 1647, 1655.

Cohen, R. A. Documents concerning Cooke, surgeon of Warwick. Medical History 1 1957.

Molins, William. Μικροτομια: or the anatomical administration of all the muscles of the humane body. 1648, 1676, 1680.

Brugis, Thomas. Vade mecum: or a companion for a chyrurgion. 1651, 1652, 1653, 1657, 1679, 1689.

Highmore, Nathaniel (1613–85). Corporis humani disquisitio anatomica: in qua sanguinis circulationem prosequutus est. Hague 1651.

Ross, Alexander (1591–1654). Arcana microcosmi: or the hid secrets of mans body disclosed. 1651, 1652 (rev).

De lacteis thoracis in homine brutisque. 1652; tr as The anatomical history of Thomas Bartholinus, 1653.

Culpeper, Nicholas (1615–54). The anatomy of the body of man. 1653, 1677. From J. Vesling.

—— A sure guide: or the best and nearest way to physick and chirurgery. 1657, 1671. From J. Riolan.

New anatomical experiments. 1653. From J. Pecquet.

Turner, Robert. Μικροκοσμος: a description of the little-world. 1654, 1654.

Glisson, Francis (1597–1677). Anatomia hepatis. 1654, Amsterdam 1659, 1665, Hague 1681.

D., N. The institutions or fundamentals of physick and chirurgery. 1656, 1658. From D. Sennert.

Wharton, Thomas (1614–73). Adenographia: sive glandularum totius corporis descriptio. 1656, Amsterdam 1659.

Charleton, Walter (1620–1707). Natural history of nutrition, life and voluntary motion. 1659 (shorter version of next item).

—— Oeconomia animalis: novis in medicia hypothesibus superstructa et mechanice explicata. 1659, 1666, 1669, Amsterdam 1659, Bologna 1675, Leyden 1678, 1678, Hague 1681.

Pell, John (1611–85). The coppy of a certain large act of Yonker Louis de Bils touching the skill of a better way of anatomy of mans body. 1659.

Winston, Thomas (1575–1655). Anatomy lectures at Gresham Colledge. 1659, 1664.

Jackson, Henry. Μικροκοσμογραφία: or a description of the little world or body of man. 1660, 1664. From B. da Carpi.

Larkey, S. V. and L. tum Suden. Jackson's English translation of Berengarius of Carpi's Isagoge breves. Isis 21 1934.

(9) BOTANY AND HERBALS

Modern Studies

Haller, A. von. Bibliotheca botanica. Zürich 1771–2.

Pulteney, R. Historical and biographical sketches of the progress of botany in England. 2 vols 1790.

Winkler, E. Geschichte der Botanik. Frankfurt 1854.

Jessen, K. F. W. Botanik der Gegenwart und Vorzeit in culturhistorischer Entwickelung. Leipzig 1864; rptd in Chronica botanica, Waltham Mass 1948.

Greene, E. L. Landmarks of botanical history prior to 1562. Washington 1909.

Arber, A. Herbals: their origin and evolution. Cambridge 1912.

—— Natural philosophy of plant form. Cambridge 1938.

Oliver, F. W. (ed). Makers of British botany. Cambridge 1913.

Barlow, H. M. Old English herbals 1525–1640. Proc Royal Soc of Medicine 1914.

Rhode, E. The old English herbals. 1922.

Gunther, R. T. Early British botanists and their gardens, based on unpublished writings of Goodyer, Tradescant and others. Oxford 1932.

—— The Greek herbal of Dioscorides englished by John Goodyer. Oxford 1933.

Blunt, W. The art of botanical illustration. 1950.

Nissen, C. Die botanische Buchillustrations. 2 vols Stuttgart 1951.

Quinby, J. Catalogue of botanical books in the collection of McM. M. Hunt vol 1. Pittsburgh 1958.

Allen, M. The tradescants. 1964.

Leighton, A. Early English gardens in New England. 1970.

Contemporary Treatises

Banches (Bankes), Richard. A newe mater the whiche sheweth and treateth of ye vertues and proprytes of herbes, the which is called an herball. 1525, 1526, [1530?] (as Macers herbal practysed by Doctor Lynacro), [1535?] (as A new herbal of Macer, translated by Robert Wyer), [1537?], [1539?], [1540?], [1541?], 1541, [1542?], 1546, ed William Copland [1547?], [1548?], [1550?]; (as A boke of the properties of herbes called an herball); ed Anthony Ascham 1550 (as A little herball of the properties of herbes); ed Walter Cary 1552, [1552?], [1560?]; ed S. V. Larkey and T. Pyles, New York 1941. Johnson, F. R. A newe herball of Macer and Bancke's Herball. Bull History of Medicine 15 1944.

The grete herball whiche geveth parfyt knowledge and understandyng of all maner of herbes. 1526, 1529, 1539, 1561. Trn of Le grand herbier.

Turner, William (1508–68). Libellus de re herbaria novus. 1538; ed B. D. Jackson 1877 (facs) (with biographical introd).

—— The names of herbes in Greke, Latin, Englishe, Duche and Frenche. 1548; ed J. Britten 1881 (English Dialect Soc); ed R. T. Stearn 1965 (Ray Soc).

—— A newe herball. 1551; Cologne 1562 (2nd pt); 1568 (pts 1–3).

—— A newe boke of the natures of all wines. 1568.

Harrison, T. P. Turner: naturalist and priest. SE 33 1954.

Hill, Thomas (d. 1575?). A most pleasaunt treatyse teachynge howe to dress a garden. [1558?], [1563], 1568 etc.

—— The gardeners labyrinth. 1577, 1578, 1586, 1594, 1608, 1651.

Moore, Philip. The hope of health: wherein is conteined a goodlie regiment of life and the goodly vertues of sondrie herbes. 1565.

Mascall, Leonard. A booke of the manner howe to plant all sortes of trees. 1575, 1582, 1592, 1596, 1656.

Frampton, John (fl. 1577–96). Joyfull newes out of the newe founde worlde. 1577, 1577, 1580 (rev), 1596; ed S. Gaselee 1925. From Nicholas Monardes.

Lyte, Henry (1529?–1607). A niewe herball: or historie of plantes. 1578, 1586, 1595, 1619. See W. Ram, below. From R. Dodoens.

Gerard, John (1545–1612). Catalogus arborum. 1596, 1599; ed B. D. Jackson 1876; 1962 (facs).

—— The herball or general historie of plantes. 1597, 1633 (much enlarged by Thomas Johnson), 1634, 1636.

The orchard and the garden. 1597, 1640, 1653, 1654. Later edns as The expert gardener.

Langham, William. The garden of health, conteyning the vertues and properties of simples and plants. 1579 (for 1597), 1633.

Gardiner, Richard. Profitable instructions for planting kitchin gardens. 1603.

Ram, W. Rams little Dodoen: a brief epitome of the new herbal abbridged by W. Ram. 1606.

Platt, Sir Hugh (1552–1611?). Floraes paradise beautified. 1608.

—— The garden of Eden. 1653, 1653, 1654, 1655, 1659, 1660, 1675, 1675. Augmented form of above, ed Charles Bellingham.

—— The second part of the Garden of Eden. 1660, 1675.

Standish, Arthur. New directions for the increasing of timber. 1613, 1614, 1615.

Lawson, William. A new orchard and garden: the country housewife's garden. 1618, 1623, 1626, 1631, 1638, 1648, 1656.

Johnson, Thomas (1600–44). Iter plantarum investigationis in agrum cantianum. 1629.

—— Descriptio itineris in agrum cantianum. 1632.

—— Mercurius botanicus sive plantarum gratia suscepti itineris anno 1634 descriptio. 3 pts 1634–41; tr W. Jenkyn Thomas, Bangor 1908.

—— Opuscula omnia botanica. Ed T. S. Ralph 1847.

Kew, H. W. and H. E. Powell. Johnson: botanist and royalist. 1932.

Parkinson, John (1567–1650). Paradisi in sole: or a garden of flowers. 1629, 1635, 1656; rptd 1904.

—— Theatrum botanicum: the theater of plants or an herball of large extent. 1640.

Markham, Gervase (1568–1636). The countrymans recreation. 1640, 1653, 1654.

Bobart, Jacob (1598–1679), et al. Catalogus plantarum horti medici oxoniensis. Oxford 1648, 1658 (rev).

Gunther, R. T. Oxford gardens. Oxford 1912.

Vines, S. H. and G. C. Druce. An account of the Morisonian Herbarium. Oxford 1914.

Blith, Walter (d. 1653). The English improver. 1649, 1652 (rev).

How, William (1620–56). Phytologia britannica. 1650.

—— Matthiae de l'Obel Stirpium illustrationes, plurimas elaborantes inauditas plantas subreptitiis Joh. Parkinsoni rapsodiis. 1655.

Weston, Sir Richard (1591–1652). A discourse of husbandrie used in Brabant. 1650, 1652.

Hartlib, Samuel (1600?–62) (ed). His legacy: experiments and secrets in reference to universall husbandry. 1651, 1652, 1655 (rev).

Culpeper, Nicholas (1616–54). The English physitian: or an astrologo-physical discourse of the vulgar herbs of this nation. 1652 (3 issues), 1653, 1661, 1695.

Austen, Ralph (d. 1676). A treatise of fruit trees. Oxford 1653, 1657, 1665 (rev).

—— Observations on some parts of Sir Francis Bacon's Naturall history as it concernes fruit-trees, fruits and flowers. Oxford 1658.

Coles, William (d. 1662). The art of simpling. 1656.

—— Adam in Eden: or natures paradise. 1657.

Beale, John (1603–83). Herefordshire orchards a pattern for all England. 1657.

Browne, Sir Thomas (1605–82). Hydrotaphia, together with the Garden of Cyrus. 1658, 1658, 1659 etc.

Merton, E. S. The botany of Browne. Isis 47 1956.

Lovell, Robert (1630?–90). Παμβοτανολογία: sive enchiridion botanicum, or a compleat herball. Oxford 1659, 1665.

Speed, Adolphus. Adam out of Eden. 1659.

Sharrock, Robert (1630–84). The history of the propagation and improvement of vegetables. Oxford 1660, 1672, 1694 (as An improvement in the art of gardening).

(10) ZOOLOGY

Modern Studies

Harting, J. E. The ornithology of Shakespeare. 1871, Chicago 1965.

—— Bibliotheca accipitraria. 1891.

Phipson, E. The animal lore of Shakespeare's time. 1883.

Westwood, T. and T. Satchell. Bibliotheca piscatoria. 1883.

Marston, R. B. Walton and some writers on fish and fishing. 1894.

Seager, H. W. Natural history in Shakespeare's time. 1896.

Dean, B., C. R. Eastman, E. W. Gudges and A. W. Henn. A bibliography of fishes. 3 vols New York 1916–23.

Cole, F. J. Early theories of sexual generation. Oxford 1930.

—— History of comparative anatomy from Aristotle to 1800. 1944.

Bilikeiewicz, T. Die Embryologie im Zeitalter des Barocks und des Rokoko. Leipzig 1932.

Needham, J. A history of embryology. Cambridge 1934.

Merton, E. S. Sir Thomas Browne as zoologist. Osiris 9 1950.

Nissen, C. Die illustrierten Vogelbücher. Stuttgart 1953.

Delaunay, P. La zoologie au seizième siècle. Paris 1962.

Contemporary Treatises

Book of hawking and huntyng. [St Albans 1486], 1496 (with Treatyse of fyshinge), 1561–2, [1563?], 1586 etc.

Turner, William (1508–68). Avium praecipuarum, quarum apud Plinium et Aristotelem mentio est, brevis et succincta historia. Cologne 1544; ed A. H. Evans as Turner on birds, Cambridge 1903.

— (ed). Dialogus de avibus et earum nominibus. Cologne 1544. From Gisbertus Longilius.

— Epistola Conrado Gesnero. Zürich 1558. In Gesner Historia animalium vol 4.

Wotton, Edward. De differentiis animalium. Paris 1552.

Maplet, John (d. 1592). A green forest: or a naturall historie. 1567; rptd 1930.

Hill, Thomas (d. 1575?). Profitable instructions for the ordering of bees. 1568, 1579, 1593. From Georgius Pictorius.

Caius, John (1510–73). De canibus britannicis. 1570; tr A. Fleming as Of English dogs, 1576; ed E. Arber, An English garner vol 3, 1880.

The arte of angling. 1577; ed C. E. Bentley, Princeton 1956.

A book of fishing with hooke and line. 1590. Attributed to L. Mascall.

Muffett, Thomas (1553–1604). The silkewormes and their flies. 1599.

— Insectorum sive minimorum animalium theatrum. 1634 (3 issues); tr as Theatre of insects, appended to Topsell, Historie of fourefootid beastes, 1658; ed W. Ley, New York 1967 (facs).

Geffe, N. The perfect use of silkewormes. 1607. From Olivier de Serres.

Topsell, Edward (d. 1638?). The historie of fourefootid beastes collected out of all the volumes of Conrad Gesner. 1607; ed J.R[owland] 1658 (with Muffett, Theatre of insects, above).

— The historie of serpents: or the second booke of living creatures. 1608. Extracts in M. St Clare Bryne, The Elizabethan zoo, 1926.

Harrison, T. P. John White and Topsell. Amsterdam 1964.

Butler, Charles (d. 1647). The feminine monarchie: or a treatise concerning bees. Oxford 1609, 1634 (with phonetic spelling), London 1623; tr Latin by Richard Richardson 1673.

Stallenge, William. Instruction for the increasing of mulberrie trees and breeding of silke-wormes. 1609, 1609.

Dennys, John. Secrets of angling. 1613.

Morrell, William. New England: or a briefe enarration of the ayre, earth, water, fish and fowles of that country. 1625.

Animalium quadrupedeum, avium delineationes: a book of beast, birds etc. [1628?], 1630.

Levett, John. The ordering of bees. 1634.

Barker, Thomas. The art of angling. 1651, 1653 etc.

Harvey, William (1587–1657). De generatione. 1651. See col 2372, above.

Highmore, Nathaniel (1613–85). The history of generation. 1651.

Hartlib, Samuel (1600?–62). A rare and new discovery for the feeding of silkworms. 1652, 1655 (as The reformed Virginian silk-worm).

— The reformed common-wealth of bees. 1655.

Walton, Izaak (1593–1683). The compleat angler. 1653, 1655 (rev). See col 2222, above.

B[ateson], T[homas]. Ζωολογία: or the history of animals as they are useful in physick and chirurgery. 1659. From J. Schroeder.

The fifth discourse concerning the spontaneous generation of live things. [1660?]. From D. Sennert.

(11) WITCHCRAFT AND MAGIC

Modern Studies

Pernety, A.-J. Dictionnaire mytho-hermétique. Paris 1787.

Cockayne. O. Leechdoms, wortcunning and starcraft in early England. 3 vols 1864.

Thiselton-Dyer, C. H. Folk lore of Shakespeare. 1884.

Sharpe, C. K. Historical account of the belief in witchcraft in Scotland. 1884.

Waite, A. E. The real history of the Rosicrucians. 1887.

Lea, C. H. A history of the Inquisition of the Middle Ages. 3 vols 1888.

Moore, G. H. Bibliographical notes on witchcraft. 1888.

Winsor, J. The literature of witchcraft in New England. Proc Amer Antiquarian Soc 1895.

Jaggard, W. Folklore, superstition and witchcraft in Shakespeare: a bibliography. 1897.

Ferguson, J. Bibliographical notes on the witchcraft literature of Scotland. Edinburgh 1897.

Craven, J. B. Count Michael Maier: his life and writings. Kirkwall 1910, 1968.

Notestein, W. A history of witchcraft in England from 1558 to 1781. 1911 (Amer Historical Assoc).

Caillet, A. L. Manuel bibliographique des sciences psychiques et occultes. 3 vols Paris 1912.

Murray, M. A. The witch-cult in western Europe. Oxford 1921.

Summers, M. The history of witchcraft and demonology. 1926.

— The geography of witchcraft. 1927.

Ewen, C. L'E. Witch-hunting and witch-trials. 1929.

— Witchcraft and demonianism. 1933.

— Witchcraft and Star-Chamber. 1938.

Kittridge, G. L. Witchcraft in old and new England. Cambridge Mass 1929.

Blau, J. L. The Christian interpretation of the Cabala in the Renaissance. New York 1944.

Corpus hermeticum. Ed A. J. Festugière and A. D. Nock 4 vols Paris 1945–54.

Koyré, A. Mystiques, spirituels, alchimistes. Paris 1955.

Howland, A. C. Materials toward a history of witchcraft collected by H. C. Lea. New York 1957.

Walker, D. P. Spiritual and demonic magic from Ficino to Campanella. 1958.

Secret, F. Les kabbalistes chrétiens de la Renaissance. Paris 1964.

Nauert, C. G. Agrippa and the crisis of Renaissance thought. Urbana 1965.

Trevor-Roper, H. R. The European witch-craze. In his Religion, the Reformation and social change, 1967.

MacFarlane, A. Witchcraft in Tudor and Stuart England. 1970.

Rosen, B. Witchcraft. 1969.

Contemporary Treatises

H[arrison], R[obert] (d. 1585?). Of ghostes and spirites walking by night. 1572, 1596; ed J. D. Wilson and M. Yardley 1929 (Shakespeare Assoc). From Lavater.

Brigges, Agnes. The disclosing of a late counterfeyted possession by devyl in two maydens. [1574].

Twyne, Thomas (1543–1613). A dialogue of witches. 1575. From Lambert Daneau.

Cooper, Margaret. A true and most dreadfull discourse of a woman possessed with the Devill. [1584], 1886.

Bruno, Giordano (1548–1600). La cena de le ceneri. 1584.
— De la causa principio et una. Venice (for London) 1584.
— Del infinito universo et mondi. Venice (for London) 1584.
— Spaccio de la bestia trionfante. 1584.
— Cabala del cavallo pegaseo. 1585.
Singer, D. W. Bruno: his life and thought. 1950.
Yates, F. A. Bruno and the hermetic tradition. 1964.
Scot, Reginald (1538?–99). This discoverie of witchcraft. 1584, 1651, 1665; rptd 1886; ed M. Summers 1930.
Gifford, George (d. 1620). A discourse of the subtill practises of devilles. 1587.
— A dialogue concerning witches and witchcrafts. 1593, 1603; rptd 1842 (Percy Soc).
Holland, Henry (d. 1604). A treatise against witchcraft. 1590.
— Spirituall preservatives against the pestilence. 1593.
The most strange discoverie of the three witches of Warboys. 1593.
Nashe, Thomas (1567–1601?). The terrors of the night: or a discourse of apparitions. 1594.
— Works. Ed R. B. McKerrow 5 vols 1904–10, Oxford 1958 (rev F. P. Wilson).
Darrell, John. A brief narration of the possession of W. Sommers. 1598.
James I (1566–1625). Daemonologie in forme of a dialogue. Edinburgh 1598, 1603; rptd 1924.
Harsnet, Samuel (1561–1631). A discovery of the fraudulent practises of J. Darell. 1599.
— A declaration of egregious popish impostors. 1603, 1604, 1605.
Jorden, Edward (1569–1632). A briefe discourse of a disease called the suffocation of the mother. 1603.
Perkins, William (1558–1602). A discourse of the damned art of witchcraft. 1608, 1610, 1629.
Mason, James. The anatomie of sorcerie. 1612.
Potts, Thomas. The wonderfull discoverie of witches in the countie of Lancaster. 1612–13; rptd 1838; ed J. Crossley 1845 (Chetham Soc); ed G. B. Harrison 1929.
Cotta, John (1575?–1650?). The triall of witchcraft: shewing the true methode of the discovery. 1616, 1624, 1625.
Fludd, Robert (1574–1637). Apologie compendiara fraternitatem de Rosea Cruce. Leyden 1616.
— Tractatus apologeticus integritatem societatis de rosea cruce defendens. Leyden 1617.
— Summum bonum, quod est verum magiae, cabalae, alchymiae, fratrum rosae crucis verorum, verae subjectum. Frankfurt 1629.
Roberts, Alexander. A treatise of witchcraft; with a true narration of the witchcrafts which Mary Smith did practise. 1616.
Cooper, Thomas. The mystery of witchcraft. 1617.
'Eirenaeus Orandus'. Exposition of the heiroglyphicall figures. 1624. From Nicholas Flammel.
Bernard, Richard (1568–1641). A guide to grand jury men. 1627, 1629, 1630.
Fairfax, Edward (d. 1635). A discourse of witchcraft. Philobiblon Soc Miscellany vol 5, 1858–9; rptd Harrogate 1882.

Davenport, John (1597–1670). The witches of Huntingdon: their examinations and confessions. 1646.
Gaule, John (fl. 1628–1660). Select cases of conscience touching witches and witchcraft. 1646. Anon.
— Πυς-μαντία: the mag-astro-mances or the magicall-astrologicall divines posed and puzzled. 1652, 1657 (as A collection of vision, apparitions), 1657.
— Occult philosophie. nd.
Hopkins, Mathew (d. 1647). The discovery of witches. 1647; ed M. Summers 1928.
Stearne, J. A confirmation and discovery of witchcraft. 1648.
Chilmead, Edmund. Unheard of curiosities concerning the talismanical sculpture of the Persians. 1650. From J. Gaffarel.
F[rench], J[ohn]. Three books of occult philosophy written by Henry Cornelius Agrippa. 1651, 1651; ed W. F. Whitehead, Chicago 1898. From H. C. Agrippa von Nettesheim.
Warren, Hardick. Magick and astrologie vindicated. 1651.
Carpenter, Agricola. Pseuchographia anthromagica: or a magicall description of the soul. 1652.
Vaughan, Thomas (1621/2–1666), 'Eugenius Philalethes'. The fame and confession of the fraternity of R.C. commonly of the rosie cross. 1652; ed F. N. Pryce, Margate 1923 (facs).
Filmer, Sir Robert (d. 1653). An advertisement to the jurymen of England touching witches. 1653.
Hegge, Robert. Lusus serius: a serious passe time. 1654. From Michael Maier.
Gardiner, R. Englands grievance discovered. 1655.
Heydon, John (1629–67?). Eugenius Theodidactas: the prophetical trumpeter sounding the allarum to England. 1655.
— A new method of rosie crucian physick. 1658.
— The rosie-crucian infallible axiomata. 1660.
Turner, Robert (fl. 1630–60). Henry Cornelius Agrippa his fourth book of occult philosophy. 1655.
— Ars notoria: The notory art of Solomon, shewing the cabalistical key of magical operations. 1657. From Apollonius etc.
Boulton, Samuel. Medicina magica tamen physica: magical but natural physick. 1656, 1656.
Bunworth, Richard. Ὁμοτροπία naturae: a physical discourse, exhibiting the cure of diseases by signature. 1656.
Hodges, Nathaniel and Thomas Hodges. Themis aurea: the laws of the fraternity of the rosie crosse. 1656. From Michael Maier.
Davies, John. The history of magick. 1657. From G. Naudaeus.
The secret miracles of nature: in four books. 1658. From Levinus Lemnius.
Casaubon, Meric. A true and fruitful relation of what passed for many years between Dr John Dee and some spirits. 1659.
W[illiams], W[illiam]. Occult physick. 1660.

C. W.

IX. EDUCATION

A. BIBLIOGRAPHIES AND GENERAL STUDIES (1) BIBLIOGRAPHIES ETC: *General*; *1500–1660*; (2) GENERAL STUDIES: *British Isles*; *University and professional*; (3) STUDIES 1500–1700.

B. PRIMARY SOURCES (1) TREATISES AND TRACTS: *Collections; European influence to 1558; Some English writings 1500–58; Some writings and translations 1558–1603, 1603–40, 1640–60*; (2) TEXTBOOKS AND TEACHING: *Elementary and English teaching for those not to learn Latin; Religious instruction; Manners, morals and behaviour; Order of teaching in the grammar school; Grammars, vocabularies and dictionaries for children; First reading books: colloquies; Some introductions to classical texts, editions and translations, some contemporary texts; Active language study: some vulgaria and rhetorical phrasebooks, collections of illustrative material, progymnasmata and rhetoric, letter writing; Greek, Hebrew, marginal studies; On university teaching and tutoring.* (3) AUTOBIOGRAPHY; CORRESPONDENCE, DESCRIPTION ETC: *Biographical collections; Advice to a son; Schemes for academies; Contemporary descriptions covering education*; (4) CLASSES OF DOCUMENTS BEARING ON EDUCATION.

C. SECONDARY SOURCES: (1) WRITERS, THEORIES AND PEDAGOGY 1500–1600, 1600–60; (2) EDUCATIONAL PRACTICE: *School, university and college, Inns of Court, other professional bodies, British students abroad, household upbringing in home and locality.*

A. BIBLIOGRAPHIES AND GENERAL STUDIES

(1) BIBLIOGRAPHIES ETC

See Introduction: Bibliographies, col 5, above, for historical bibliographies with sections on education, guides to the archives of universities and colleges, library catalogues etc.

General

de Morgan, A. Arithmetical books from the invention of printing to the present. 1847.

Monumenta Germaniae paedagogica. Schulordnungen, Schulbücher und pädagogische Miscellaneen aus den Landen deutscher Zunge. Ed K. Kehrbach 61 vols Berlin 1886–1934; Mitteilungen der Gesellschaft für Deutsche Erziehungs- und Schulgeschichte, 20 vols Berlin 1891–1920.

Buisson, F. Dictionnaire de la pédagogie. 4 vols Paris 1887, 1911 (rev).

Sonnenschein's Cyclopaedia of education. 1889.

Gray, J. C. General index to Hazlitt's handbook and bibliographical collections. Ed W. C. Hazlitt 1893. Includes schoolbooks.

Axon, W. E. A. Hornbooks and abc's. Manchester 1903.

Erman, W. and E. Horn. Bibliographie der deutschen Universitäten. Leipzig and Berlin 3 vols 1904–5.

Many continental universities have ptd matriculation registers.

Blanco y Sanchez, R. Bibliografia pedagógica de obras escrites o traducidas en Castellano. 5 vols Madrid 1907–12. On mss and books from 1299.

Monroe, P. Cyclopaedia of education. 4 vols New York 1911–13.

Watson, F. List of research and literary work on the subject of education. 1913. *See* W. H. G. Armytage, Foster Watson 1860–1929, Br Jnl of Educational Stud 10 1961.

—— Encyclopaedia and dictionary of education. 4 vols 1921.

Burnham, W. H. Bibliographies on educational subjects: history of education. Worcester Mass 1917 (Clark Univ Lib).

Cavassala, F. La pedagogia moderna: guida bibliografica 1, Dall'umanesimo al Comenius; 2, Metodi e scuole dalla controriforma al secolo xviii; 3, Scienza e morale del secolo xvii al xviii. Turin [1930–2].

Heal, A. English writing masters and their copy-books 1570–1800: biographical dictionary and bibliography. Cambridge 1931.

Quaritch, B. Catalogue (no 464) of early school books (1500–1900). 1932.

Brickman, W. W. Guide to research in educational history. New York 1949. With bibliographies.

Muirhead, A. The English at school. Cambridge 1949 (Nat Book League).

British Educational Index 1954– (Lib Assoc). On history of education.

Bailyn, B. Education in the forming of American society: bibliographical essay. Chapel Hill 1960.

Alt, R. Bilderatlas zur Schul- und Erziehungsgeschichte. 2 vols Berlin 1960; English texts, Berlin 1961.

Kelly, T. Select bibliography of adult education in Great Britain. 1962 (Inst of Adult Education), 1970 (rev).

Jacobs, P. M. Registers of the universities, colleges and schools of Great Britain and Ireland. 1964 (Inst of Historical Research).

Alston, R. C. Bibliography of the English language from the invention of printing to 1800. Leeds and Bradford 1965–.

Wallis, P. J. Histories of old schools (before 1700): revised list for England and Wales. Newcastle 1966.

Higson, C. W. J. Sources (to 1870) for the history of education, including schoolbooks, in libraries of institutes and schools of education. 1967 (Lib Assoc).

Widener Library Shelflist 17: education vol 2. Cambridge Mass 1968 (Harvard Univ Lib). In chronological order.

Cordeaux, E. H. and D. H. Merry. Bibliography of printed works relating to the University of Oxford. Oxford 1968.

Craigie, J. Bibliography of Scottish education before 1872. 1970.

Silver, H. and S. J. Teague. The history of British universities 1800–1906: a bibliography. 1970. Excludes Oxford and Cambridge.

Argles, M. British government publications in education during the nineteenth century. History of Education Soc Bull 5 1970.

Many commission reports include historical information.

1500–1660

Buisson, F. Répertoire des ouvrages pédagogiques du xvie siècle. Paris 1886 (Bibliothèques de Paris et des Départements), Nieuwkoop 1962.

Bibliotheca erasmiana: répertoire des oeuvres d'Erasme. Ghent 1893.

Watson, F. Curriculum and textbooks of English schools in the first half of the seventeenth century. Trans Bibl Soc 6 1903.

Littlefield, G. E. Early schools and school-books of New England. Boston 1904.

Murray, D. Some early grammars and other school books in use in Scotland. Proc Royal Philosophical Soc of Glasgow 36–7 1904–6.

Anderson, P. J. Collections towards a bibliography of the universities of Aberdeen. Edinburgh 1907.

Smith, D. E. Rara arithmetica, before 1601. 1908, 1939 (with addns).

Dix, E. R. McC. School books printed in Dublin from the earliest period to 1715. Bibl Soc of Ireland 3 1926.

Norton, A. O. Harvard text-books and reference books in the 17th century. Pbns Colonial Soc of Massachusetts 28 1935.

Noyes, G. Bibliography of courtesy and conduct books in seventeenth-century England. New Haven 1937.

Cant, R. G. The St Andrews university theses 1579–1747. Edinburgh Bibl Soc Trans 2 1938–45.

Heltzel, V. B. Check list of courtesy books in the Newberry Library. Chicago 1942.

Carillo, M. A. G. Los tratados sobre educación de principes siglos 16 y 17. Madrid 1948.

Gibson, R. W. Bibliography of Bacon and Baconiana to 1750. Oxford 1950.

Bennett, H. S. Handlist of publications by Wynkyn de Worde 1492–1535. In his English books and readers 1475–1557, Cambridge 1952, 1969 (rev).

See Book Production, col 957, above for Stationers' Company registers, booksellers' catalogues etc.

Ong, W. J. A Ramus and Talon inventory. Cambridge Mass 1955.

Margolin, J.-C. Douze années de bibliographie érasmienne. Paris. 1963.

Pilz, K. J. A. Comenius, die Ausgaben des Orbis sensualium pictus: eine Bibliographie. Nuremberg 1967.

Sonnino, L. A. A handbook of sixteenth-century rhetoric. 1968. For list of textbooks.

Among English libraries with special collections:

University of Nottingham. Handlist of the W. G. Briggs collection of early educational literature. 1966; suppl 1969.

University of Newcastle-upon-Tyne. Bainbrigg collection. Appleby school library, 17th-century, catalogue forthcoming.

University of Leeds. Collection of classical texts.

University of London. Quick collection: history of education.

Guildhall Library, London. London schools, including archives Christ's Hospital.

Fawcett Society, London. The education of girls.

For collections of school histories:

Department of Education and Science; University of Leeds Institute of Education; Paddington Public Libraries; Preston Public Library; Institute of Historical Research (school and college registers).

(2) GENERAL STUDIES

Quick, R. H. Essays on educational reformers. 1868, 1888 (rev).

Browning, O. History of educational theories. 1881.

Schmidt, K. A. et al. Geschichte der Erziehung. 6 vols Stuttgart 1884–1902.

Compayré, G. History of pedagogy. 1900.

Adamson, J. W. Short history of education. Cambridge 1919, 1930 (rev).

Boyd, W. History of western education. 1921, 1950 (rev).

Gal, R. Histoire de l'éducation. Paris 1948.

Bolgar, R. R. The classical heritage and its beneficiaries. Cambridge 1954.

Castle, E. B. Moral education in Christian times. 1958.

Ariès, P. L'enfant et la vie familiale sous l'ancien régime. Paris 1960; tr as Centuries of childhood, 1962.

Ulich, R. The education of nations: a comparison in historical perspective. Oxford 1961.

— A history of religious education: documents and interpretations from the Judaeo-Christian tradition. 1970.

Myers, E. D. Education in the perspective of history: concluding chapter A. J. Toynbee. 1963.

Cipolla, C. M. Literacy and development in the West. 1969.

The Church and academic learning. Ed G. J. Cuming, Leyden 1969.

Macdonald, S. History and philosophy of art education. 1970.

British Isles

Carlisle, N. Endowed grammar schools in England and Wales. 2 vols 1818.

[Hackett, M.] Brief account of cathedral and collegiate schools: their statutes and endowments. 1827.

Staunton, H. The great schools of England. 1865.

Wright, T. History of domestic manners and sentiments in England. 1871.

Grant, J. History of the burgh schools of Scotland. 1876.

Castle, E. Schools and masters of fence from the Middle Ages to the end of the eighteenth century. 1892.

de Montmorency, J. E. G. State intervention in English education to 1833. Cambridge 1902.

Strutt, J. Sports and pastimes of the people of England from the earliest period. 1801, 1903 (rev J. C. Cox).

Strong, J. History of secondary education in Scotland. Oxford 1909.

Dunlop, O. J. English apprenticeship and child labour. 1912.

Kerr, J. Scottish education, school and university, early times to 1908. Cambridge 1913.

Motter, T. H. V. The school drama in England. 1921.

Turner, D. M. History of science teaching in England. 1927.

Corcoran, T. Education systems in Ireland from the close of the Middle Ages. Dublin 1928.

Gardiner, D. English girlhood at school. Oxford 1929.

Jones, E. J. History of education in Wales. Wrexham 1931.

Darton, F. J. H. Children's books in England: five centuries of social life. Cambridge 1932, 1960 (rev).

Mason, J. E. Gentlefolk in the making: studies in the history of English courtesy literature 1531–1774. Philadelphia 1935.

Yeldham, F. A. Teaching of arithmetic through four hundred years. 1936.

Auchmuty, J. J. Irish education: an historical survey. Dublin 1937.

Jarman, T. L. Landmarks in the history of education. 1951, 1963 (rev).

Stenton, D. M. The English woman in history. 1957.

Clarke, M. L. Classical education in Britain 1500–1900. Cambridge 1959.

Lawson, J. Primary education in east Yorkshire 1560–1902. 1959 (East Yorks Local History Soc).

— A town grammar school through four centuries (Hull). Oxford 1963.

Boyd, W. Education in Ayrshire through seven centuries. 1961.

Kelly, T. History of adult education in Great Britain. Liverpool 1962, 1970 (rev).

— Early public libraries. 1966.

Deloney, V. T. H. The law relating to charities in Ireland. Dublin 1962.

Armytage, W. H. G. Four hundred years of English education. Cambridge 1964.

Bain, A. Education in Stirlingshire from the Reformation to 1872. 1965.

Thompson, S. D. Education in Hexham from 1294. 1965 (Northumberland Record Office).

Seaborne, M. Education: a visual history. 1966.

Simon, B. (ed). Education in Leicestershire 1540–1940. Leicester 1968. Essays.

Pinchbeck, I. and M. Hewitt. Children in English society. Vol 1, From Tudor times to the eighteenth century, 1969.

Jones, G. H. History of the law of charity 1532–1827. Cambridge 1969.

Smout, T. C. History of the Scottish people 1560–1830. 1969.

Cremin, L. A. American education. Vol 1, The colonial experience 1607–1783, New York 1970. With bibliographical essay.

University and Professional

Smith, P. A. History of education for the English bar. 1860.

Mullinger, H. B. History of the University of Cambridge from the earliest times to the close of the Platonist movement. 3 vols Cambridge 1875–1911.

Grant, A. University of Edinburgh during the first three hundred years. 2 vols 1884. *See* D. B. Horn, Short history, Edinburgh 1967.

Foster, J. Alumni oxonicnscs. 8 vols 1887–1902.

Clark, J. W. Endowments of the University of Cambridge. 1904.

Anderson, P. J. (ed). Studies in the history and development of the University of Aberdeen. Aberdeen 1906.

Venn, J. Entries to Cambridge colleges 1544–1906. 1908.

—— and J. A. Alumni cantabrigienses. 8 vols Cambridge 1922–7.

Coutts, J. History of the University of Glasgow 1451–1909. Glasgow 1909. *See* J. D. Mackie, Short history, Glasgow 1954.

Mallet, C. E. History of the University of Oxford. 3 vols 1924–7.

Morgan, A. Scottish university studies. Oxford 1933.

Howard, H. F. Finances of St John's College, Cambridge 1511–1906. 1935.

Trevelyan, G. M. Trinity College: an historical sketch. Cambridge 1943.

Hodgkin, R. H. Six centuries of an Oxford college. Oxford 1949. Queen's.

Maxwell, C. History of Trinity College, Dublin. Dublin 1946. Vol 1, 1591–1892.

Cant, R. G. University of St Andrews: a short history. Edinburgh 1946.

Oxford. Victoria county history: Oxfordshire vol 3, ed H. E. Salter and M. D. Lobel 1954.

Armytage, W. H. G. Civic universities. 1955.

Costin, W. C. St John's College, Oxford 1598–1860. Oxford 1958.

Cambridge. Victoria county history: Cambridgeshire vol 3, ed J. P. C. Roach 1959.

White, A. C. T. Story of army education 1643–1943. 1963.

Poynter, F. N. L. (ed). Evolution of medical education in Britain. 1966.

All Oxford and Cambridge colleges are covered in 2 sers pbd at the turn of the century: Oxford college histories; Cambridge college histories.

(3) STUDIES 1500–1700

Watson, F. The state and education under the Commonwealth. EHR 15 1900.

Adamson, J. W. Pioneers of modern education 1600–1700. Cambridge 1905.

Sandys, J. Education; scholarship. In Shakespeare's England vol 1, Oxford 1917.

Woodward, W. H. Studies in education during the Renaissance 1400–1600. Cambridge 1924.

James, M. Social problems and policy during the puritan revolution. 1930.

Wood, N. The Reformation and English education. 1931.

Morrison, S. E. Founding of Harvard College. Cambridge Mass 1935. European background.

Houghton, W. E. Formation of Thomas Fuller's Holy and profane state. Cambridge Mass 1938.

Knappen, M. M. Tudor puritanism. Chicago 1939.

Bush, D. The Renaissance and English humanism. Toronto 1939.

Conant, J. B. The advancement of learning during the puritan revolution. Proc Massachusetts Historical Soc 66 1936–41.

Turnbull, G. H. Hartlib, Dury and Comenius: gleanings from Hartlib's papers. 1947.

Mathew, D. Social structure of Caroline England. Oxford 1948.

Zeeveld, W. G. Foundations of Tudor policy. Cambridge Mass 1948.

Rowse, A. L. The England of Elizabeth: structure of society. 1950.

Hexter, J. H. Education of the aristocracy in the Renaissance. Jnl of Modern History 22 1950; rptd in his Reappraisals in history, 1961.

Vincent, W. A. L. The state and school education in England and Wales 1640–60. 1950.

Caspari, F. Humanism and the social order in Tudor England. Chicago 1954.

Ashley Smith, J. W. The birth of modern education: contribution of the dissenting academies 1660–1800. 1954. With bibliography.

Schlatter, R. B. The higher learning in puritan England. Historical Mag of Protestant Episcopal Church 23 1954.

Harbison, E. H. The Christian scholar in the age of the Reformation. New York 1956.

Garin, E. Educazione in Europa 1400–1600. Bari 1957.

Weiss, R. Learning and education in western Europe 1470–1520. In New Cambridge modern history vol 1, Cambridge 1957.

Hay, D. Schools and universities: intellectual tendencies. In New Cambridge modern history vol 2, Cambridge 1958.

Porter, H. C. Reformation and reaction in Tudor Cambridge. Cambridge 1958. With Cambridge bibliography.

Jordan, W. K. Philanthropy in England 1480–1640. 1959.

Curtis, M. H. Oxford and Cambridge in transition 1558–1642. Oxford 1959.

—— Education and apprenticeship. In A. Nicoll (ed), Shakespeare in his own age, Cambridge 1964.

Durkan, J. Education in the century of the Reformation. In D. McRoberts, (ed), Essays on the Scottish Reformation 1573–1625, Glasgow 1962.

Beales, A. C. F. Education under penalty: English Catholic education from the Reformation to the fall of James I. 1963.

Stone, L. The educational revolution in England 1560–1640. Past & Present 28 1964.

Charlton, K. Education in Renaissance England. 1965.

Hill, C. Intellectual origins of the English revolution. Oxford 1965.

Simon, J. Education and society in Tudor England. Cambridge 1966. With bibliography.

Mazzeo, J. A. Renaissance and revolution. 1967. Ch 1.

Bridenbaugh, C. Vexed and troubled Englishmen 1590–1642. Oxford 1968.

On Various Aspects, and Guides to Original Sources

Cooper, C. H. and T. Athenae cantabrigienses 1500–1611. 2 vols Cambridge 1858–61; Index and addns, 1913. With bibliographical information.

Watson, F. English grammar schools to 1660: their curriculum and practice. Cambridge 1908.

—— Beginning of the teaching of modern subjects in England. 1909.

Corcoran, T. Studies in the history of classical teaching 1500–1700. Dublin 1911.

Howard, C. English travellers at the Renaissance. 1914.

Powell, C. L. English domestic relations 1487–1653. New York 1917.

Lambley, K. Teaching and cultivation of the French language in England during Tudor and Stuart times. Manchester 1920.

Taylor, E. G. B. Tudor geography 1485–1583. 1920.

— Tudor and Stuart geography 1583–1650. 1934.

— Mathematical practitioners of Tudor and Stuart England. 1954.

— Mathematical practitioners of Hanoverian England. 1966.

Schoell, F. Etudes sur l'humanisme continental en Angleterre à la fin de la Renaissance. Paris 1926.

Kelso, R. Doctrine of the English gentleman in the sixteenth century. Urbana 1929. With bibliography to 1626.

— Doctrine of the lady of the Renaissance. Urbana 1956.

White, H. English devotional literature 1600–40. Madison 1931.

— Social criticism in popular religious literature of the sixteenth century. New York 1944.

— Tudor books of private devotion. Madison 1951.

— Tudor books of saints and martyrs. Madison 1963.

Plimpton, G. A. Education of Shakespeare illustrated from school books. 1933.

Wright, L. B. Middle class culture in Elizabethan England [to 1640]. Chapel Hill 1935.

— Language helps for the Elizabethan tradesman. JEGP 30 1931.

Jones, R. F. Ancients and moderns: rise of the scientific movement in the seventeenth century. St Louis 1936, 1961 (rev).

— Triumph of the English language: opinions concerning the vernacular 1480–1660. Oxford 1953.

Johnson, F. R. Astronomical thought in Renaissance England: scientific writings 1500–1645. Baltimore 1937.

Robertson, J. The art of letter writing: handbooks of the sixteenth and seventeenth centuries. Liverpool 1942.

Penrose, B. Urbane travellers 1591–1635. Philadelphia 1942.

— Tudor and early Stuart voyaging. Washington 1962.

Baldwin, T. W. William Shakspere's petty school. Urbana 1943.

— William Shakspere's 'small Latine and lesse Greeke'. 2 vols Urbana 1944.

Wallace, K. R. Francis Bacon on communication and rhetoric. Chapel Hill 1943. With bibliography on rhetorical theory 1500–1700.

Bush, D. English literature in the earlier seventeenth century. Oxford 1945 (OHEL), 1962 (rev).

Starnes, De Witt T. The English dictionary 1604–1755. Chapel Hill 1946.

— Renaissance dictionaries, English-Latin, Latin-English. Austin 1954.

— and E. W. Talbert. Classical myth and legend in Renaissance dictionaries. Chapel Hill 1956.

Clarke, D. L. Milton at St Paul's school: ancient rhetoric in English Renaissance education. 1948.

de Jongh, W. G. J. Western language manuals of the Renaissance. New Mexico Univ Pbns in Lang & Lit 1 1949.

Simonini, R. C. Italian-English language books of the Renaissance. Romanic Rev 42 1951.

Stoye, J. W. English travellers abroad 1604–67. 1952. Noblemen and their tutors.

Bamborough, J. B. The little world of man. 1952. On psychological doctrine.

Sledd, J. A note on the use of Renaissance dictionaries. MP 49 1952.

Bell, H. E. Introduction to the history and records of the Court of wards and liveries. Cambridge 1953.

Sloane, W. Children's books in England and America in the seventeenth century: history and checklist. New York 1955.

Howell, W. S. Logic and rhetoric in England 1500–1700. Princeton 1956.

Fletcher, H. F. Intellectual development of John Milton. 2 vols Urbana 1956–61.

Funke, O. Spanische Sprachbücher im elizabethanischen England. In Studies presented to K. Brunner, Vienna 1957.

Costello, W. J. The scholastic curriculum in early seventeenth-century Cambridge. Cambridge Mass 1958.

Waters, D. W. The art of navigation in England in Elizabethan and early Stuart times. 1958. With bibliography, for vocational training.

Campbell, L. Divine poetry and drama in sixteenth-century England. 1959.

Wightman, W. P. D. Science and the Renaissance. 2 vols Aberdeen 1962. On the university library.

Fussner, F. S. The historical revolution 1580–1640. 1962.

Blench, J. W. Preaching in England in the late fifteenth and sixteenth centuries. Oxford 1964. On rhetoric; with bibliography.

Arthos, J. Milton and the Italian cities. 1968.

B. PRIMARY SOURCES

(with special reference to upbringing of children and school curricula)

(1) TREATISES AND TRACTS

(including translations)

Collections

Watson, F. Notices of some early English writers on education 1480–1603. Washington 1902–6; A source book, ed R. D. Pepper, Gainesville 1967.

Rowland, E. (ed). A pedagogue's commonplace book: extracts from works of the 16th and 17th centuries. 1925.

Eby, F. (ed). Early Protestant educators: educational writings of Luther, Calvin and others. New York 1931.

Nugent, E. (ed). Thought and culture of the English Renaissance 1481–1555. Cambridge 1956.

Torrance, T. F. (ed). The school of faith: catechisms of the reformed church 1541–1648. 1959.

Wright, L. B. (ed). Advice to a son: precepts of Burghley, Raleigh, Francis Osborne. New York 1962.

Pepper, R. D. (ed). Four Tudor books on education. Gainesville 1966. Elyot, Education of children; Clement, Petie schole; Fenner, Art of logike; Kempe, Education of children in learning.

Debus, A. G. (ed). Science and education in the seventeenth century: the Webster-Ward debate. 1970.

Webster, C. (ed). Samuel Hartlib and the advancement of learning. Cambridge 1970.

European Influence to 1588

Erasmus, Desiderius. Enchiridion militis christiani. Antwerp 1503; tr R. Himelick, Bloomington 1963; [tr William Tindale?] 1533.

— De ratione studii. Paris 1511; tr W. H. Woodward, Erasmus on education, Cambridge 1904 (extracts).

—— Institutio principis christiani. Louvain 1516; tr L. K. Born, Education of a Christian Prince, New York 1936.

—— Paracelsis ad christianae philosophiae studium. Basle 1516; [tr William Roy?], An exhortation to the diligent study of scripture, 1529.

—— De civilitate morum puerilium. Basle 1526; tr Robert Whittinton, Good maners for children, 1532; tr Thomas Paynell, Civilitie of childhood, 1560 etc.

—— De pueris instituendis. Basle 1529; ed J.-C. Margolin 1966; tr W. H. Woodward, Erasmus on education, Cambridge 1904; tr Richard Sherry, That children be well and gently brought up in learning, 1550.

—— Lives of Vitrier and Colet. Ed and tr J. H. Lupton 1883.

—— Opus epistolarum. Ed P. S. and H. M. Allen 12 vols Oxford 1906–58.

Melanchthon, Phillip. De artibus liberalibus. Wittenberg 1517; in Werke vol 3, Humanistische Schriften, ed R. Nürnberger, Gütersloh 1961.

Melanchthoniana paedagogica. Ed K. Hartfelder, Leipzig 1892.

Luther, Martin. An die Radherrn aller Stedte deutsches Lands. Wittenberg 1521; in Luther on education, ed F. V. N. Painter, Philadelphia 1889.

Zwingli, Ulrich. The Christian education of boys. Zürich 1523. In Zwingli and Bullinger, ed G. Bromiley 1953; tr Richard Argentine, Ipswich 1548.

Vives, Juan Luis. Introductio ad sapientiam. Louvain 1524; ed and tr M. L. Tobriner, New York 1968; tr Richard Morison, An introduction to wysdome, 1540.

—— De ratione studii puerilis. Louvain 1524; ed and tr F. Watson, Vives and the Renaissance education of women, 1912.

—— De subventione pauperum. Bruges 1526; tr F. R. Salter, Early tracts on poor relief, 1926.

—— De tradendis disciplinis. Antwerp 1531; ed and tr F. Watson, Vives on education, Cambridge 1931.

—— Literae virorum eruditorum ad Franciscum Craneveldium. Ed H. de Vocht, Louvain 1928.

Castiglione, Baldassare. Il cortegiano. Venice 1528; ed B. Maier, Turin 1955; tr Thomas Hoby, The courtyer, 1561, 1928 (EL); tr Latin by Bartholomew Clarke, De curiali sive aulico, 1571 etc.

Guevara, Antonio de. Libro del emperador Marco Aurelio. Vallodolid 1529; tr Lord Berners, The golden book of Marcus Aurelius, 1534 (14 edns by 1600).

—— Relox de principes. Vallodolid 1529; tr Thomas North, The diall of princes, 1557. See Thomas Elyot, Image of governance: compiled of the actes and sentences of the most noble emperour Alexander Severus, 1540.

—— Epistolas familiares. Vallodolid 1539–47; tr Edward Hellowes, Familiar epistles, 1574 (in part); supplemented by Golden epistles, tr Geoffrey Fenton 1575.

—— Menosprecio de la corte y alabanza de Aldea. Vallodolid 1539; tr Francis Burrant, A dispraise of the life of a courtier, 1548, 1575 (with notes by Twyne); tr Henry Vaughan, The praise and happiness of country life, 1651.

Sadoleto, Jacopo. De liberis recte instituendis. Venice 1533; ed E. T. Campagnac and E. Forbes, Sadoleto on education, Oxford 1916.

Plutarch. De liberis educandis. Tr Sir T. Elyot 1525; tr from Latin of Xylander by Edward Grant, A president for parentes, 1571, 1581 (as De educatione puerorum, a school text). Extract in William Kempe, Education of children in learning, 1588. Tr Philemon Holland, Philosophie of Plutarchus, 1603; ed E. H. Blakeney 1911.

Calvin, John. Catechism. 1542; tr J. K. S. Reid, A plan for instructing children, in Theological treatises vol 22, 1954.

Bucer, Martin. De regno Christi ad Ed. VI (1548). Basle 1557; in Scripta anglicana, 1577.
Gilbert, A. H. Bucer on education. JEGP 18 1919. Extracts translated.

Sturm, Johannes. De literarum ludis recte aperiendis. Strasbourg 1538.

—— Epistolae duae de nobilitate anglicana. Strasbourg 1551; tr T[homas] B[rowne], Nobilitas literata: a ritch storehouse for gentlemen, 1570.

Bruto, Giammichele. La institutione di una fanciulla nata nobilmente; L'institution d'une fille de noble maison; traduite de langue tuscane en français. Antwerp 1555, 1954 (facs); tr W.P., The necessary, fit and convenient education of a young gentlewoman, 1598.

See Literary Relations with the Continent, col 833, above.

Some English Writings 1500–58

See also under individual authors.

Colet, John. Appendices to S. Knight, Life of Dr J. Colet, 1724. See J. H. Lupton, A life, 1887, 1909 (rev).

More, Thomas. Utopia. Louvain 1516; ed and tr E. Surtz and J. H. Hexter 1965.

Pace, Richard. De fructu. Basle 1517; ed and tr F. Manley and R. S. Sylvester, The benefit of a liberal education, New York 1967.

Lupset, Thomas. Exhortacion to yonge men. 1530; in J. A. Gee, Life and works of Lupset, New Haven 1928.

Elyot, Sir Thomas. The boke named the governour. 1531; ed S. E. Lehmberg 1962.

Starkey, Thomas. Dialogue between Pole and Lupset. Ed K. M. Burton 1948.

—— Life and letters. Ed S. J. Herrtage 1878 (EETS).

Cranmer, Thomas. Preface to the Great Bible. 1540; Miscellaneous writings, ed J. E. Cox, Cambridge 1846 (Parker Soc).

Phaire (Phaer), Thomas. The boke of children. 1544; ed A. V. Neale and H. R. S. Wallis 1955 (from 1553). First paediatric treatise.

Ascham, Roger. Toxophilus: the schole of shootinge. 1545; English works, ed W. A. Wright, Cambridge 1904.

Becon, Thomas. Catechism with other pieces written in the reign of Edward VI. Ed J. Ayre, Cambridge 1844; Works, 3 vols 1563–4. See also sermons of Latimer and Lever, writings of Crowley.

Wilson, Thomas. The arte of rhetorique, for all studious of eloquence. 1553; ed G. H. Mair, Oxford 1909 (from 1585).

Bonner, Edmund. An honest godly instruction for bringing up of children. 1555.

The institucion of a gentleman. 1555, 1839 (priv ptd G[eorge] S[oaper]).

Some Writings and Translations 1558–1603

Humfrey, Laurence. De ratione interpretandi authores. Basle 1559.

—— Optimates. Basle 1560; tr as The nobles, or of nobilitye: the original nature, dutyes, ryght and Christian instruction thereof, 1563.

Knox, John. The book of discipline. 1561; in his History of the Reformation in Scotland vol 2, ed W. C. Dickinson 1949.

Golding, Arthur. The eight books containing his martial exploytes in Gallia. 1565 (from Julius Caesar). Preface. Golding, L. T. An Elizabethan Puritan: Golding. New York 1937.

Gilbert, Sir Humphrey. Queen Elizabethe's academy. Ed F. J. Furnivall 1869 (EETS).

Ascham, Roger. The scholemaster. 1570; ed L. V. Ryan, Oxford 1968.

Dee, John. Preface to Henry Billingsley, Elements of geometrie of Euclid, 1570.

Hill, Thomas. The contemplation of mankind: the art of physiognomie. 1571. Recommended to schoolmasters.

Hake, Edward. A touchestone: a perfect rule for parents and schoolmasters. 1574.

Blundeville, Thomas. The true order and methode of writing and reading hystorie according to the precepts of F. Patrizio and Accontino Tridentio. 1574; ed H. G. Dick, HLQ 3 1940.

Gascoigne, George. The glasse of government. 1575. On grammar-school studies.

T[wyne], T[homas]. The schoolmaster: or teacher of table phylosophie. 1576.

Casa, Giovanni della. Il Galateo. Venice 1558; ed G. Tinarella, Milan 1954; tr R. S. Pine-Coffin 1958. Tr Robert Peterson 1576. Often rptd, retranslated, adapted.

Stockwood, John. A sermon wherein is proved that it is the part of all those that are fathers, householders and scholemaisters to instruct all those under their government. 1578.

—— A Bartholomew fairing: shewing children are not to marie without consent of parents. 1589.

Heron, Haly. Newe discourse of moral philosophie. 1579.

Battus, Bartholomew (Batty). The Christian man's closet: a large discourse of the godly training up of children. Tr W. Lowth 1581.

Mulcaster, Richard. Positions wherein those primitive circumstances are examined, necessarie for training up children. 1581, 1887, 1888.

—— The first part of the elementarie. 1582; ed E. T. Campagnac 1925.

Averell, W. A dyall for dainty darlings, a glasse for all disobedient sonnes, a mirrour for vertuous maydes. 1584; A mervailous combat of contrarietes, 1588. By a schoolmaster.

Fenner, Dudley. The artes of logike and rhetorike with examples for the practise of the same in the government of the family, prescribed in the world of God. Middleburg 1584.

de la Primaudaye, Peter. The French academie: the institution of manners and whatsoever concerneth the good and happy life of all estates and callings. Tr T[homas] B[owes] 1586–94 (pts 1–2), R. Dolman 1601 (pt 3), in full 1618 (pt 4 tr W.P.). First pbd Paris 1550. Anderson, R. L. A French source for John Davies of Hereford's system of psychology. PQ 6 1927.

Moffett, Thomas. Nobilis: or a view of the life and death of a Sidney. Ed V. B. Heltzel and H. H. Hudson, San Marino 1940 (with lesser lugubris).

Stapleton, Thomas. Tres Thomae. Douai 1588; tr P. E. Hallett, Life and martyrdom of Sir T. More, 1928.

Bright, Timothy. Characterie. 1588. On shorthand. Keynes, G. L. Dr T. Bright 1550–1616. 1962.

Kempe, William. The education of children in learning. 1588; in Four Tudor books, ed R. D. Pepper 1966.

B[rowne], J[ohn]. The marchants avizo necessarie for their sonnes when they first send them beyond the seas. 1591.

Johnson, Richard. The nine worthies of London explaining the honourable exercise of arms (to apprentices). 1592; in Harleian miscellany vol 8, 1811.

Leroy, Louis. De la vicissitude ou variété des choses en l'univers. Paris 1575; tr R[obert] A[shley], Of the interchangeable course: or variety of things in the whole world and the concurrence of armes and learning; moreover, whether we ought by our own inventions to augment the doctrine of the Ancients, 1594.

Gundersheimer, W. L. Life and works of Le Roy. 1966.

Huarte, Juan de. Examen de ingenios. Baeza 1575; translated into Italian and englished out of the Italian by Richard Carew, Examination of men's wits, 1594, New York 1959 (facs).

Iriarte, M. de. Juan de Huarte. Madrid 1939.

Bacon, Francis. Essayes. 1597 etc, 1625 (rev).

Greenham, Richard. Of the good education of children. In Works, ed H. Holland 1599. A sermon.

Daniel, Samuel. Musophilus: containing a generall defence of learning. In Poeticall essayes, 1599.

James VI of Scotland. Basilikon doron: or his Majesty's instructions to his dearest sonne. Edinburgh 1599; ed C. H. McIlwain 1908 (from 1616); ed P. A. Knachel, Ithaca 1966.

Perkins, William. A treatise of the vocations or callings of men and the right use thereof; Christian oeconomie: or the right manner of ordering a familie. In Theologicall works, 3 vols Cambridge 1608.

Montaigne, Michel. Essais. Paris 1588; tr John Florio, The essayes or morall, politike and militarie discourses of Lo. Michaell de Montaigne, 1603. Extract of essay 25 tr in S. Hartlib (ed), The true and readie way to learne the Latine tongue, 1654.

Some Writings and Translations 1603–60

Bacon, Francis. The proficience and advancement of learning, divine and humane. 1605, 1623 (rev as De dignitate et augmentis scientiarum); tr Gilbert Wats as The advancement of learning, 1640.

Cleland, James. Hero-paideia: or the institution of a young noble man. Oxford 1607, 1612 (as The instruction); ed M. Molyneux, New York 1948 (from 1607).

Hall, Joseph. A complaint of the miseducation of our gentry. In Works vol 6, ed P. Wynter 1863.

Dod, J. and R. Cleaver. A godlie forme of household government. 1612.

See also:

Dod, J. and W. Hinde. Bathesheba's instructions to her son. 1614.

The office of Christian parents. Cambridge 1616.

Gataker, T. David's instructor. 1620. Sermons at Tonbridge school.

Scot, P. A father's advice. 1620.

Leigh, Dorothy. The mother's blessing. 1621 (7th edn).

Gouge, W. Of domesticall duties. 1622.

Joceline, Elizabeth. The mother's legacy. 1624, 1894 (facs of 1632).

Brinsley, John. Ludus literarius: or the grammar school. 1612; ed E. T. Campagnac 1917 (from 1627).

—— A consolation for our grammar schooles (for the Virginia Co). 1622; ed T. C. Pollock, New York 1943 (facs).

Craven, W. F. The Virginia Company of London 1606–24. 1957.

Martyn, William. Youth's instruction. 1612.

Granger, Thomas. The generall theorike or true groundes of teaching. In his Syntagma grammatica, 1616.

Lubinus, Eilhard. Didactic, prefacing his edition of Novum testamentum. 1617; tr in True and readie way to learne the Latine tongue, ed S. Hartlib 1654.

Andreae, J. V. Christianopolis. Strasbourg 1619; ed F. E. Held 1916; tr John Hall, Modell of a Christian society, Cambridge 1647.

Morrice, Thomas. An apology for schoole-masters. 1619. On status of tutors.

Bacon, Francis. Novum organum. 1620; ed T. Fowler, Oxford 1878.

—— Sylva sylvarum: or a naturall historie. Ed William Rawley 1627. Includes the unfinished New Atlantis.

Webbe, Joseph. An appeale to truth, in the controversie betweene art and use, about the most expedient course in languages. 1622.

—— A petition to parliament in behalf of auncient and authentique authors. 1623.

Hornbye, William. Hornbyes hornbook. 1622.

Earle, John. Microcosmographie. 1628.

Bolton, Edmund. The cities advocate, in this case of honor and armes; whether apprenticeship extinguisheth gentry. 1629, 1674 (as The cities great concern).

Brathwait, Richard. The English gentleman. 1630; The English gentlewoman, 1631.

Buc, Sir George. The third universitie of England. In John Stow, Annals, ed E. How 1631.

Greville, Fulke, Lord Brooke. A treatie of humane learning. In Poems vol 1, ed G. Bullough 1939.

Ralegh, Sir Walter. Instructions to his son and to posterity. 1632.

—— The Prince: or maxims of state (for Prince Henry). In Remains, 1657.

Sermoneta, Cardinal (Enrico Caetani). Instructions for young gentlemen. Oxford 1633.

Kynaston, Sir Francis. Constitutions of the Musaeum Minervae. 1636.

Comenius, J. A. Conatuum Comeniarum praeludia. Oxford 1637, 1639 (rev as Pansophia prodromus); tr as A reformation of schooles, 1642.

Woodward, Hezekiah. A childes patrimony. 1640.

—— A gate to the sciences, opened by a naturall key: or a practical lecture on the great book of nature, whereby the child is enabled to read the creatures there. 1641.

Bignell, Henry. The son's portion: moral instructions for the education of youth in knowledge. 1640.

Howell, James. Instructions for forrein travel. 1642; ed E. Arber 1869.

Wotton, Sir Henry. A philosophical survey of education: aphorisms of education. Ed H. S. Kermode 1938.

Jonson, Ben. Timber: or discoveries of men. In Works vol 2, 1640; ed M. Castelain, Paris 1906. A commonplace book.

1640–60

Gauden, John. The love of truth and peace: sermon before the House of Commons. 1640.

Petition of the university of Oxford in behalfe of episcopacy and cathedrals. 1641; Answer to the petition, 1641.

Barrow, Henry. The pollution of universitie-learning. 1642.

The countrymans care and the citizens fear, in bringing up children in good education. 1641.

Hartlib, Samuel. Description of the famous kingdom of Macaria. 1641.

—— Englands thankfulnesse. 1642. In Samuel Hartlib, ed C. Webster 1970.

Harmar, Samuel. Vox populi: or Glostersheres desire. 1642. For schools.

New England's first fruits. 1643. In S. E. Morison, Founding of Harvard, 1935.

Milton, John. Of education: to Master Hartlib. 1644; ed G. H. Sabine, New York 1951.

Grantham, Thomas. Discourse in derision of teaching in free-schooles. 1644.

—— The threepenny cooks fat in the fire. 1650.

Lewis, John. Contemplations upon these times. 1646. For university in Wales.

Nuttall, G. F. Merioneth Historical & Record Soc Jnl 2 1954.

A good motion. 1646. Funds for schools.

Hartlib, Samuel. The Parliaments reformation. 1646. Education poor children.

A vindication of learning from unjust aspersions. 1646.

Wilkins, John. Ecclesiastes: a discourse concerning the gift of preaching. 1646.

—— Mathematicall magick. 1648.

Lodowyck, F. A common writing whereby two not understanding one the others language may communicate. 1646.

—— The groundwork for framing a new perfect language. 1652.

For the universal character, see below.

[Gott, S.] Nova Solyma: the ideal city. 1648; ed W. Begley 2 vols 1902.

Patrick, J. M. UTQ 8 1939.

Motives for the present founding of an university in London. 1647. In H. Gollancz, A contribution to the history of University College, London, 1930.

Gerbier, Sir Balthazar. The academie for forrain languages and all noble sciences and exercises. 1648.

—— A series of six lectures. 1650.

Cudworth, Ralph. Sermon preached before the House of Commons, March 31 1647. Cambridge 1647, New York 1930 (facs).

Dury, John. Considerations tending to the happy accomplishment of Englands reformation. 1647; A seasonable discourse, 1649.

—— The reformed school. 1650, 1651 (with The reformed librarie-keeper and John Pell: an idea of mathematicks).

P[etty], W[illiam]. Advice of W.P. to Mr Samuel Hartlib, for the advancement of some particular parts of learning. 1648; rptd in Harleian miscellany vol 6, 1810.

Snell, George. The right teaching of useful knowledge to fit scholars for some honest profession. 1649.

Hall, John. An humble motion to the Parliament of England concerning the advancement of learning. 1649; ed A. K. Croston, Liverpool 1953.

Hartlib, Samuel. Londons charitie stilling the poore orphans cry. 1649; Londons charity enlarged, 1650.

[Dymock, Cressy]. An essay for advancement of husbandry learning. 1651.

Peter, Hugh. Good work for a magistrate. 1651. On provincial universities.

Winstanley, George. The law of freedom in a platform. 1652; ed L. D. Hamilton, Selected works, 1944.

Whitlock, Richard. Observations on the present manners of the English. 1654.

Williamson, G. PQ 15 1936.

On the University controversy:

Hobbes, Thomas. Leviathan. 1651.

Dell, William. The stumbling stone. 1653; The tryal of spirits, The right reformation of learning, 1653; rptd in Selected works, 1773.

Webster, John. Academiarum examen. 1654.

Vindiciae academiarum. Oxford 1654. Answer to Webster, Hobbes and Dell by John Wilkins and Seth Ward.

See also Thomas Hall, Noah Biggs, Joseph Sedgwick, Edward Waterhouse, Robert Boreman, John Horne, George Kendall.

A catalogue of the names of members of the last Parliament, whereof those marked with a starre were for the godly learned ministry and universities. 1654.

Hartlib, S. (ed). The true and readie way to learn the Latin tongue. 1654.

Harrington, James. Commonwealth of Oceana. 1656; ed S. B. Liljegren, Heidelberg 1924.

Osborne, Francis. Advice to a son. 1656; ed E. A. Parry 1896.

Barrow, Humphrey. Relief of the poore and advancement of learning proposed. 1656. In Dublin.

B., J., gent. Heroick education or choice maximes for training up youth. 1657.

Reynolds, E. Sermon touching the use of humane learning. 1657. Funeral oration for John Langley.

Starkey, George. Nature's explication and Helmont's vindication. 1657.

Bacon, Francis. Letter to Sir Henry Saville touching helps for the intellectual powers. In Resuscitatio, ed W. Rawley 1657.

Poole, Matthew. Model for maintaining students of choice abilities at university. 1648 (for 1658); rptd in Autobiography of Matthew Robinson, ed J. E. B. Mayor, Cambridge 1856.

[Allestree, Richard]. The whole duty of man. 1658; The gentleman's calling, 1659; rptd in Works of the author of the whole duty of man, 2 vols 1704.

Comenius, J. A. Opera didactica omnia. Amsterdam 1658, 3 vols Prague 1957. See The great didactic, ed and tr M. W. Keatinge 1896, 1910 (rev).

—— The school of infancy. Tr D. Benham 1858; ed E. M. Eller, Chapel Hill 1956.

—— The analytical didactic. Ed V. Jelinek, Chicago 1943.

Comenius in England. Ed R. F. Young, Oxford 1932. Stimson, D. Isis 23 1935.

Cowley, Abraham. Proposition for the advancement of experimental knowledge (1658). In Works, ed T. Sprat 1668.

Evelyn, John. Golden book of St John Chrysostom on education of children. 1659.

Higford, William. Institutions: or advice to his grandson. 1658, 1660 (rev Clement Barksdale as Institution of a gentleman); rptd in Harleian miscellany vol 9, 1812.

Schurman, A. M. van De ingenii muliebris (1641); tr Clement Barksdale as Whether a maid may be a scholar, 1659.

Sundry things from several hands concerning the University of Oxford. 1659; rptd in Harleian miscellany vol 6, 1810.

The looking-glasse of Englands libertie really restored. 1659.

Cornelius, Peter. A way propounded to make the poor happy in a little commonwealth. 1659.

Milton, John. The readie and easie way to establish a free commonwealth. 1660.

Sprat, Thomas. History of the Royal Society. 1667; ed J. I. Cope and H. W. Jones, St Louis 1958.

Sprig, William. A modest plea for an equal commonwealth. 1659.

Catalogue of the Thomason tracts 1640–60. Ed G. K. Fortescue 2 vols 1908. Includes textbooks.

(2) TEXTBOOKS AND TEACHING

General

Brinsley, John. Ludus literarius: or the grammar school. 1612; ed E. T. Campagnac 1917 (from 1627, with bibliographical index).

— A consolation for our grammar schooles. 1622; ed T. C. Pollock, New York 1943 (facs).

Wekherlin's patent for school-books. 1631; rptd in Companion to Arber, ed W. W. Greg, Oxford 1967.

Hoole, Charles. An advertisement touching school-books translated. In Catonis disticha, 1659.

— A new discovery of the old art of teaching schoole in four small treatises. 1660; ed E. T. Campagnac 1913 (with bibliographical index).

Elementary and English Teaching for those not to learn Latin

Clement, Francis. School of spelling and the petty scholars precepts for writing, numeration and placing of counters. 1576, 1587 (as The petie schole); rptd in Four Tudor books, ed R. D. Pepper 1966.

Coote, Edmund. The English schoolmaster. 1596, 1641 (19th edn).

Hodges, Richard. A special help to orthographie. 1643.

— The English primrose. 1644; ed H. Kauter, Heidelberg 1930.

Robertson, George. Learnings foundation firmly laid in a method of teaching to read English. 1651.

Lloyd, Richard. An English grammar, teaching to read English rightly and write accordingly. 1653.

ABC both in Latyn and English: facsimile of the earliest extant English reading book. Ed E. S. Shuckburgh 1889.

An early 16th-century ABC in Latin after the use of Sarum. Ed W. H. Alnutt 1891 (priv ptd).

Bradshaw, H. Cambridge Antiquarian Communications 3 1875.

Anders, H. Library 4th ser 16 1935.

Alston, R. C. Spelling books and ABCs. 1966.

For reading books, see Religion and Manners, below.

de Beau Chesne, John and John Baildon. A newe booke of copies containing divers sorts of sundry hands. 1574; ed B. Wolpe 1959.

See Handwriting, above.

Recorde, Robert. Ground of artes, teachyng the practise of arithmetike. 1543 etc.

Kempe, William (Plymouth School). The art of arithmeticke in whole numbers and fractions. 1593. After Ramus.

Wingate, Edward. Mr Wingate's arithmetic, revised John Kersey with supplement by George Shelley, writing master of Christ's Hospital. 1630.

Religious Instruction

Three primers put forth in the reign of Henry VIII. Ed E. Burton, Oxford 1834.

Horae beatae Maria virginia: Sarum and York primers. Ed E. Hoskins 1901.

Butterworth, C. C. Early primers for children. PBSA 43 1949.

Colet, John. Institution of a Christian man. In his Rudimenta, 1510; tr Erasmus, Christiani hominis institutum, Basle 1518 (verse); tr as The godly and pious institution of a Christian man, 1557.

Erasmus. Concio de puero Jesu pronuntiata a puero in schola Coletica nuper instituta Londoni. Strasbourg 1514.

Cranmer, Thomas. Short introduction into Christian religion. 1548; ed E. Burton, Oxford 1829.

Ponet, John. Catechismus brevis christiane disciplinae summam continens omnibus ludimagistris authoritate regia commendatus. 1552.

Calvin, John. The catechisme: or maner to teache children the Christian religion. Geneva 1558, London 1563. With prayers.

Nowell, Alexander. Catechismus: sive prima institutio disciplinaque pietatis christiane latine explicata. 1570; tr Thomas Norton 1570; ed G. E. Corrie, Cambridge 1853. 3 graded versions.

Mulcaster, Richard. Catechismus Paulinus. 1599.

Shorter catechism of the Westminster Assembly. 1647; ed W. Carruthers 1897 (facs).

Larger catechism of the Westminster Assembly. 1648, 1865. See Catechesis religionis christianae compendiosior, in linguam graecam pariter et latinam traducta opera et studio Joannis Harmari. 1660.

Sternhold, T., J. Hopkins, W. Whittingham et al. The whole book of psalms, collected into English metre. 1598. See The psalms in Latin distichs by Helius Eobanus Hessus.

Paget, Eusebius. History of the Bible briefly collected by way of question and answer. 1613.

Shaw, John. Biblium summale. Tr Simon Wastell (Northampton School) as A true Christian's daily delight: being the sum of every chapter of the Old and New testament in English verse, 1623, 1629 (as Microbiblion), 1683 (as The divine art of memory: or the sum of the holy scriptures in acrostick verses).

Perkins, William. Foundations of the Christian religion gathered into six principles. 1591.

Bayly, Lewis. Practice of piety. 1613 (3rd edn).

Gouge, William. A short catechism. 1631.

Webbe, George. The practice of quietness, directing a Christian how to live quietly in this troublesome world. 1633 (6th edn).

Manners, Morals and Behaviour

Sulpitius, Johannes. De moribus puerorum: carmen elegiacum. 1515.

Erasmus. De civilitate morum puerilium. Basle 1526; tr Robert Whittinton as A lytell booke of good maners for chyldren, 1532; tr Thomas Paynell (from a French version) as The civilitie of childhood, 1560; tr William Fiston (from a French paraphrase) as The schoole of good manners, 1595 etc.

Seneca. Tr Robert Whittinton, The forme and rule of honest living, 1546; The myrrour or glasse of maners, 1547.

Mancinus, Dominicus. De quattuor virtutibus. Paris 1488; tr as The Englysshe of Mancyne upon the foure cardynale vertues (by a schoolmaster), 1520; tr Alexander Barclay, The mirror of good manners, 1523; tr George Turberville, The plain path to perfect virtue, 1568. *See* Simon Harward, Enchiridion morale: in quot virtutes quattuor cardinales ex clarissimis oratoribus et poetis graecis, latinis, italicis, hispanis, gallicisq. describuntur, 1596.

Seager, Francis. The schoole of vertue and book of good nurture, teaching children and youth their duties, with a brief declaration of the duties of each degree also certain prayers and graces by R[obert] C[rowley]; extracts (1557 edn) in The babees book, ed F. J. Furnivall 1868 (EETS).

Weste, Richard. The school of vertue, the second part: the high-way to good manners, dieting of children and brideling their appetites. 1619 (with Seager, above).

Guazzo, Stefano. La civil conversatione. Brescia 1574; tr (from French) G[eorge] P[ettie], Civile conversation 2 vols 1581–6; ed E. Sullivan 1925.

Vaughan, Sir William. The golden-grove moralised in three books. 1600, 1608 (rev).

Hall, Joseph. Characters of virtues and vices. 1608.

Quarles, Francis. Divine fancies. 1632; Emblems, 1635; Works, ed A. B. Grosart 3 vols 1880–1.

Herbert, George. The temple: sacred poems and private ejaculations. Cambridge 1633.

Hawkins, Francis. Youth's behaviour: or decency in conversation amongst men. 1646 (4th edn) (from French trn of Della Casa's Galateo).

See also Latin texts, including colloquies, e.g.

Hoole, Charles (ed). Cato's distichs concerning manners; excellent sayings of the seven wisemen of Greece; Seneca's proverbs: wherein little children may understandingly learn the rules of behaviour. 1659.

Order of Teaching in the Grammar School

Malim, William. Statuta, ordinationes et consuetudines scholae etonensis in ordinem digesta (1561). In Laws of Eton and Kings, ed T. Heywood and C. E. Wright 1850.

Course taken by the schoolmaster of Westminster for those of the 6th and 7th forms c. 1630. In F. Forshall, Westminster School, 1884. *See* R. R. Bolgar, Classical reading in Renaissance schools, Durham Research Rev 6 1955.

The school's probation, for the use of Merchant-Tailors school in London. 1652. In operation from 1606. Wilson, H. B. History of Merchant Taylors School vol 1. 1812.

The constant method of teaching in St Paul's school, London (by Thomas Gale, after 1672). In D. L. Clarke, Milton at St Pauls, New York 1948.

De collegio seu potius collegiata schola Wicchamica Wintoniensi (by Robert Mathew c. 1643). Tr W. J. Cook, About Winchester College, 1917.

Letters and exercises of the Elizabethan schoolmaster John Conybeare. Ed F. W. Conybeare 1905.

Apollo shroving, composed for the schollars of the free school of Hadleigh. [1627].

Latin verses etc by scholars of Manchester grammar school. 1640; ed A. A. Mumford, Chetham miscellany vol 4, 1921 (Chetham Soc).

Most textbooks came from continental presses. The following lists concentrate on standard texts pbd in England and trns or addns by English authors known to have been used in schools. See also Translations from the Latin, col 2165, below.

Grammars

For traditional texts, sometimes in use up to 1550, see col 629, above.

For the Magdalen College grammarians:

The Vulgaria of John Stanbridge and the Vulgaria of Robert Whittinton. Ed B. White 1932 (EETS). Pafort, E. A group of early Tudor school books. Library 4th ser 26 1946.

Bennett, H. S. Checklist of Whittinton's grammars. Library 5th ser 7 1952.

Stanier, R. S. Magdalen school: a history of Magdalen College school, Oxford 1940, 1958 (rev).

King's Grammar. A shorte introduction of grammar by William Lily. Ed V. K. Flynn, New York 1945 (facs of 1567).

Allen C. G. The sources of Lily's Latin grammar. Library 5th ser 9 1954.

Wolsey, Thomas. Rudimenta grammatices et docendi methodus. 1529. Preface, tr J. J. Phillipps, A compendious way of teaching, 1750 (4th edn).

Cox, Leonard. De octo partium constructione libellus emend. ab Erasmo cum scholiis Henr. Pirmoei et Leonardi Cox. 1540.

Some later aids involving progressive adaptation and trn of the official grammar:

Stockwood, John. First grammar of the English language: a plain and easie laying open of the rules of construction in the English accidence. 1590.

— Treatise of the figures at the end of the rules of construction construed for the weaker sort. 1609.

Certain grammar questions for the exercise of young schollers in the learning of the accidence. [1602?].

Leech, John. A book of grammar questions to help young scholars in the accidence and Lilie's verses, with four colloquies (fruit of 40 years teaching). 1628 (2nd edn).

Brinsley, John. The posing of the parts. 1615.

Smetius, Henricus. Systema prosodiae in gratiam studiosae juventutis. Cologne 1600, London 1615. Ptd with official grammar.

Hampton, Barnaby. Prosodia construed. [1639], 1697.

Animadversions on Lily's grammar: or Lily scanned. 1625.

See also Thomas Granger 1616, John Hewes 1624, John Danes 1631, William Haine 1642, John Brookbank 1660 etc.

Hoole, Charles. The common rudiments of Latin grammar usually taught in all schools. 1659.

Syms, Christopher. Introduction to teaching the Latin speech. Dublin 1634.

Among Comenian contributions from English schoolmasters:

Horne, Thomas (ed). J. A. Comenius, Janua linguarum reserata: the gate of tongues unlocked. 1636. Unauthorized edn by J. Anchoran 1631.

— W. Bathe, Janua linguarum. 1634 (from Salamanca 1611).

Corcoran, T. Studies in classical teaching. 1911.

Hayne, Thomas. Linguarum cognatio: seu de linguis in genere et de variarum linguarum harmonia dissertatio. 1639.

— Grammatices latinae compendium. 1640. Preface on history of the official grammar.

Woodward, Hezekiah. Vestibulum: or a manuduction towards a fair edifice. 1640.

— A light to grammar. 1641.

Brookbank, Joseph. Vestibulum novissimum linguae latinae, made English with a vestibulary grammar and English table. 1657.

Hoole, Charles (ed). J. A. Comenius visible world: orbis sensualium pictus. 1659 (from Nuremberg 1658); ed J. Bowen, Sydney 1967 (facs of 1672).

Among other texts recommended as aids in school before 1660:

Hawkins, John. A brief introduction to syntax, collected out of Nebrissa, with a concordance. 1631.

Poole, Joshua. The English accidence: or a short way for attaining Latin by help of the English. 1646, 1662 (rev as The youth's guide).

Lloyd, Richard. The Latine grammar. 1653, 1654 (as The schoolmasters auxiliaries, with English grammar).

Walker, William. Treatise of English particles. [1655], 1691 (10th edn).

Dugard, W. The English rudiments of the Latin tongue. 1656.

Busby, John. An English introduction to the Latin tongue. 1659.

Burles, Edward. Grammatica burlesa: or a new English grammar made easy for teacher and scholar. 1652.

Wharton, J. A new English grammar. 1655.

Vocabularies and Dictionaries for Children

Stanbridge, John. Vocabula. 1500, 1596 (rev Thomas Newton), 1630 (rev John Brinsley as Stanbrigii embrion relimatum).

Withals, John. A shorte dictionarie (Eng-Lat) for yonge beginners. 1553. See A dictionary in English and Latine: devised for the capacitie of children and young beginners, at first set forth by M. Withals, with phrases both rythmicall and proverbiall, recognized by Dr Evans [1574], after by Abr. Fleming [1586]; and then by William Clerk [1602]; and now at this last impression enlarged with an encrease of words, sentences, phrases, epigrams, histories, poeticall fictions and alphabeticall proverbs, 1634.

Huloet, Richard. Abecedarium anglico-latinum. 1552, 1572 (rev John Higgins).

Estienne, Robert. Dictionariolum puerorum tribus linguis latina, anglica, gallica scriptum, cui anglicam interpretationem Joannes Veron nunc primum adiecit. 1552.

Levins, Peter. Manipulus vocabulorum: a dictionarie of English and Latine wordes, the Englishe going before the Latine. 1570; ed H. B. Wheatley 1867 (EETS). Recommended for schoolchildren.

Willis, Thomas. Vestibulum linguae latinae: a dictionarie for children. 1651.

Dugard, William. Vestibulum linguae latinae [of Comenius], cum dictionario latino-anglico. 1656.

Hoole, Charles. Vocabularium parvum anglo-latinum: a little vocabulary. 1657.

Early dictionaries included some exercises:

Elyot, Thomas. Biblioteca Eliotae: Eliotis librarie or dictionarie. 1538, 1548 (rev Thomas Cooper, Descrybing the true significacions of wordes which were greatly amisse by over muche folowying of Calepine), 1565 (rev as Cooper's Thesaurus).

Baret, John. An alvearie or triple dictionary. 1573, 1574 (as A quadruple dictionary, newlie enriched with phrases, proverbs and divers lightsome observations of grammar).

See Dictionaries, col 2291, above.

First Reading Books: Colloquies

Erasmus. Opuscula aliquot Erasmo castigatore et interprete. Cologne 1514. Includes Cato, Seneca, Isocrates, Seven wise men of Greece, Colet's Institutum.

As examples of the adaptation of traditional texts:

Cato, Dionysius. Liber Cathonis pro pueris. 1512; ed and tr Richard Taverner, Catonis disticha moralia ex castigatione Erasmi anglico idiomate conscriptis, 1540; ed Robert Burrant, Precepts of Cato the sage, 1545 (with Erasmus notes); Distica de moribus nomine Catonis [with notes by J. Badius, Erasmus et al] ac denique latina et gallica Maturii Corderii interpretatione, Paris 1533; tr as Cato construed, newly englished, [1577], 1584; tr grammatically John Brinsley as Cato concerning the precepts of common life, 1612; tr John Penkethman as A handful of honesty, 1623; ed and tr Charles Hoole, Catonis disticha (with other dicta Eng-Lat), 1659. *See col 2167, above.*

Aesop. Aesopi Phrygis fabulae, iam recenter ex collatione optimorum exemplarium emendatius excusae. 1621, Cambridge 1633; tr (for young scholars) Simon Sturtevant 1602, John Brinsley 1617. See Mythologia ethica: or three centuries of Aesopian fables in English prose,

done from Aesop, Phaedrus, Camerarius, by P. Ayres 1689.

Hale, D. G. Library 5th ser 27 1972.

Cuhlmann, Leonhard. Sententiae pueriles. Leipzig 1544; tr John Brinsley 1612; ed and tr Charles Hoole 1658 (Latin-English).

Gallus, Evaldus. Confabulatiunculae pueriles. Tr John Brinsley as Children's dialogues, little conferences or talkings together, 1617; Claused after the manner of Dr [George] Webbe 1627 (with Aesop's fables); tr Charles Hoole 1659 (Latin-English).

Mosellanus, Petrus (P. Schade). Paedologia in puerorum usum conscripta: dialogi xxxvii. Leipzig 1518; tr R. F. Seybolt, Renaissance student life, Urbana 1927, London 1532 etc (with Dialogi puerilis of C. Hegendorff).

Erasmus. Colloquia familiaria. Basle 1522; ed and tr C. R. Thompson, Chicago 1965. See Epitome colloquiorum Erasmi in puerorum usus edita, 1602 etc.

Schottenius, Hermannus. Instructio prima puerorum per colloquia mutua. 1533.

Vives, Juan Luis. Colloquia: sive exercitatio linguae latinae. Bruges 1538; ed and tr F. Watson, Tudor schoolboy life, 1908.

Cordier, Mathurin. Colloquia scholastica. Lyons 1565; ed A. Arellanus, Philadelphia 1904; tr grammatically John Brinsley 1614; tr Charles Hoole 1657 (preface 1652); tr John Clarke (Hull School) 1718. For trns see S. Loggan, Select colloquies of M. Cordier, 1790; for full bibliography of trns J. Le Coultre, Maturin Cordier, Neuchâtel 1926.

Castellio, Sebastien (Châteillon). Colloquia sacra. Basle 1545, London 1573; tr as Sacred dialogues: the history of the Bible, 1715.

Posselius, Joannes (the younger). Familiarium colloquiorum libellus, accessit dialogus de ratione studiorum. Wittenberg 1601; tr Edmund Rive, Dialogues containing all the most useful words of the Latine tongue and a Latin oration on learning and teaching the Latine and Greek tongues, 1623.

Helvicus, Christopherus. Helvici colloquia ex Erasmo Rot., Ludovico Vives et Schottenio Hesso selecta. 1638. A standard school edn.

Some Introductions to Classical Texts, Editions and Translations

Terence. Terens in Englysh. [1520?]. Trn of Andria.

— Tr Nicholas Udall. Floures for Latin spekynge gathered out of Terence. 1533.

— Ed John Higgins. Flowers or eloquent phrases out of all the six comedies. 1575.

— Ed Richard Bernard. Terence in English. Cambridge 1598.

— Ed Thomas Newman. Andria and the Eunuch, fitted for scholars private action in their schools. 1627.

— Ed George Webbe. The first comedy, claused for such as would write or speak the pure language of this author. 1629.

Cicero, M. T. De officiis, de amicitia, senectute et paradoxis. Ed J. Badius et al, Lyons 1519 (with Erasmus's notes).

— Tr Robert Whittinton. The three books of Tully's offices. 1554 (Latin and English).

— Tr Nicholas Grimald. Cicero's three books of duties to Marcus his son. 1553.

— Tr Thomas Newton. Cicero's fowre books, friendship, old age, paradoxis, Scipio. 1577.

— Tr grammatically John Brinsley 1616. First bk of De officiis.

— Principia latine loquendi scribendique: sive selecta quaedam ex Ciceronis epistolis, adiecta interpretatione gallica. Ed M. Cordier, Geneva 1556; tr T.W., A very necessary and profitable entrance to the spekyng and writyng of the Latin tongue, 1575.

— Certain epistles of Tully verbally translated with a short treatise on the benefite of verball translation.

1611. Dedicated to the Merchant Tailors, by William Haine?

—— Calliepeia: or a rich storehouse of proper, choice and elegant Latin words and phrases, collected for the most part out of all Tully's works, by Thomas Drax. 1612.

—— Lessons and exercises out of Cicero, after the method of Dr [George] Webbe, lately privileged from his Majesty for 31 years. 1627.

Ovid. The flowers of Ovid De arte amandi with their English afore them (and two alphabet tables). 1513; Ovids Metamorphoses, translated by John Brinsley, grammatically and according to the propriety of our English tongue, as far as grammar and the verse will well bear, 1618 (bk 1); tr Thomas Hall, Phaetons folly, 1655 (bk 2).

Virgil. Virgils Eclogues, with his book on the ordering of bees. Tr John Brinsley 1620.

Plautus. A new interlude for children to play named Jacke Jugeler. 1563; ed W. H. Williams, Cambridge 1914.

—— Colloquia Plautina viginti. Ed Alexander Rosse 1646.

Two schoolmaster editors of classical texts:

Bond, John (Taunton School). Horace, Poemata. 1606, 1611 (with Epistolae), 1612 (with Juvenal and Persius).

Farnaby, Thomas (London). Persius and Juvenal, Satyrae. 1612.

—— Seneca, Tragoediae. 1613.

—— Martial, Epigrammatan. 1615.

—— Lucan, Pharsalia. 1618.

—— Virgil, Opera. 1634.

—— Ovid, Metamorphoses. 1637.

—— Terence, Comoediae. 1651 (a late edn).

Many edns of these textbooks.

Translations recommended for school use:

Ovid. Metamorphoses. Tr Arthur Golding in English metre 1567; tr George Sandys 1626.

—— De tristibus, tr Thomas Churchyard 1572.

—— Heroycall epistles. Tr George Turbervile into English verse 1567.

Virgil. Eclogues. Tr Abraham Fleming in English verse 1575, 1589 (with Georgics).

—— Aeneid. Tr Thomas Phaer and Thomas Twyne 1573.

Tacitus. Four books of the histories. Tr Sir Henry Savile, Oxford 1581.

Homer. Seaven bookes of the Iliades. Tr George Chapman 1598 (bks 1–2, 7–11), 1611 (complete).

Livy. The Roman history. Tr Philemon Holland 1600 (with Breviaries of L. Florus).

Caesar. Commentaries. Tr Sir Clement Edmonds 1609.

Lucan. Pharsalia. Tr Sir Arthur Gorges 1614.

Seneca. Works. Tr Thomas Lodge 1614.

Persius. Satires. Tr Barten Holyday, Oxford 1616.

Florus. The Roman histories. Tr Edmund Bolton 1618 (for 1619?).

Some contemporary texts:

Mantuanus (Baptista Spagnuoli). Bucolica seu adolescentia. Mantua 1495; ed W. P. Mustard, Baltimore 1911; ed Badius Ascensius, [Paris 1503], London 1569; tr George Turbervile, The eglogs of the poet Mantuan, 1567 (verse), ed D. Bush, New York 1957; tr Thomas Harvey 1656.

Fullonius, Gulielmus. De folio comedia, Acolasto titula inscripta. Hague 1529; tr John Palsgrave, The comedy of Acolastus, 1540, ed P. L. Carver 1937 (EETS).

Betuleius (Sixt Birck). Sapientia Solomonis. Ed and tr E. R. Payne, New Haven 1938. *See School and Prodigal son plays, col 1419, above.*

Palingenius, Marcellus (P. A. Manzolli). Zodiacus vitae, de hominis vita, studio ac moribus optime instituendis. Venice [1531?]; tr Barnabe Googe, The first syxe bokes of the moste Christian poet M.P. called the zodiac of life, 1560–5. Bks 1–3 1560, 4–6 1561, complete edn 1565.

Watson, F. The Zodiacus vitae. 1908.

More, Thomas. Latin epigrams. Ed L. Bradner and C. A. Lynch, Chicago 1953.

Buchanan, George. Psalmorum Davidis paraphrasis poetica. Strasbourg 1566, London 1572.

Grant, Edward. Ad adolescentulos latinae linguae studiosos, De vita et obitu Rogeri Aschami (with letters from Sturm, Osorius et al). Oxford 1573, London 1590.

Terentius Christianus: utpote comediis sacris transformatus; quo purissimi sermonis elegantia lingua exornat et politis moribus ac insigna pietate mentem imbuat. Cologne 1591, London 1595 (Comediae duae stylo conscriptae ad usum scholarium seorsim excusae).

Ocland, Christopher. Anglorum praelia ab anno domine 1327 ad annum 1558. 1580, 1582 (with Carmine summatim perstricta).

—— De pacatissimo Angliae statu imperante Elizabetha. 1582 (rev); tr John Sharrock 1585.

Owen, John (Warwick School). Epigrammata. 1606.

Bradner, L. Musae anglicanae. 1940.

Bacon, Francis. De sapientia veterum. 1609; tr Sir Arthur Gorges, The wisedome of the Ancients, 1619.

Godwin, Thomas. Romanae historiae anthologia: an English exposition of the Roman antiquities for the use of Abingdon school. Oxford 1614, 1631 (rev).

Ross, Alexander. Virgilius evangelizans. 1634.

—— Mystagogus poeticus: or the Muses interpreter. 1647, 1653 (rev with genealogy of the gods).

Active Language Study

Some Vulgaria and Phrasebooks

Whittinton, Robert. Vulgaria. 1519; rptd in John Clarke, Dux grammaticus, 1633.

Horman, William. Vulgaria. 1519; ed M. R. James 1926 (Roxburghe Club).

Erasmus. De duplici copia verborum ac rerum. 1512, London 1556, 1569 (with commentaries of C. Hegendorff and M. Veltkirchius); tr and ed M. B. King and H. D. Rix, On copia of words and ideas, Milwaukee 1963. Many derivatives, e.g. Joshua Poole, Practical rhetorick: or sentences varied according to rules of Erasmus De copia, 1663.

Mosellanus, Petrus. Tabulae de schematibus et tropis, in rhetoricae tabulae P. Melanchthonis. In Erasmi libellum duplici copia, Antwerp 1529, London 1572.

Manutius, Aldus (the younger). Phrases linguae latinae, in anglicum sermonem conversae. 1579, 1599 (rev).

Junius, Adrianus (de Jonghe). Tr J[ohn] Hig[g]ins, The nomenclator, or remembrancer: containing proper names and apt terms for all things under their convenient titles, with dictional index, 1585. First pbd 1555.

Lloyd, Hugh (Winchester 1580–7). Phrases elegantiores in usum scholae Winton. Oxford 1654.

Robinson, Hugh (Winchester 1613–27). Scholae Wintoniensis phrases lat. 1658.

Farnaby, Thomas. Phrases oratoriae elegantiores et poeticae. 1628 (8th edn).

Haine, William (Merchant Taylors 1599–1625). Henry's phrases: a very useful book to enable young scholars to make and speak eloquent Latin. 1653.

Clarke, John (Lincoln School). Phraseologia puerilis anglo-latina. 1638, 1650 (rev William Dugard).

Hermes anglo-latinus: or directions to speak Latin purely. 1639.

Willis, Thomas. Phraseologia anglo-latina: Anglicisms latinized. 1655; rptd in William Walker, Paroemiologia anglo-latina, 1672.

Collections of Illustrative Material

Erasmus. Adagiorum chiliades. Venice 1508, Basle 1515 (rev), 1533 (rev); ed and tr M. M. Phillips, The adages of Erasmus, Cambridge 1964; tr Richard Taverner, Proverbes or adagies, 1539, 1545 (enlarged); ed De Witt T. Starnes, New York 1956 (facs of 1569). *See*

John Clarke, Paroemiologia anglo-latina, disposed as Erasmus in his adages, 1639.

— Parabolae. 1513. *See* Conrad Lycosthenes, Parabolae, 1557, London 1635.

— Apophthegmatum ex optimis utriusque linguae scriptoribus. Basle 1531; tr Richard Taverner, Garden of wysdome, 1539; tr Nicholas Udall, Prompte quicke wittie sayings, 1542; ed R. Roberts, Boston 1877. *See* Conrad Lycosthenes, Apophthegmata, 1596; Sententiae Ciceronis, Demosthenis ac Terentii, dogmata philosophica, item apophthegmata [of Erasmus], 1614. A standard epitome.

Ravisius, Joannes ('Textor' d. 1524). Textoris dialogi: item epigrammata. 1581; Epithetorum liber; accesserunt synonima poetica, 1588; Epithetorum epitome: synonyma poetica, 1626 (with George Sabinus, De carminibus veterum).

Estienne, Charles. Dictionarium historicum, geographicum, poeticum. Geneva and Paris 1566; ed Nicholas Lloyd 1686.

Valerius Maximus. De factis dictisque memorabilibus. 1470; with commentary, J. Badius 1513, London 1612.

Epictetus. Epicteti stoici philosophi encheiridion: item Cebetis tabula. Ed J. Wolphius, Cologne 1595. *See* Epictetus manual, Cebes table, Theophrastus characters, tr John Healy 1616.

Carminum proverbialium totius humanae vitae statum breviter delineantium loci communes in gratiam juventutis selecti. 1577. By S.A.I.

Poetarum illustrium flores per O. Mirandulam collecti nunc repurgati a Theodore Pulmanno Cranebrugio. 1611. A standard epitome.

Szegedinus (Stephen de Kis). Tabulae analyticae, quibus exemplar illud sermonum de fide, charitate et patientia, quod olim prophetae, evangelistae, apostoli, litteris memoriaeque mandaverunt. 1593.

Pelegromius, Simon. Synonymorum sylva olim collecta et alphabeto flandrico illustrata. Antwerp 1555; Nunc autem e belgarum sermone in anglicanum transfusa per H.F., 1585, 1609.

Reusner, Nicholas (d. 1602). Symbolorum imperatoriorum liber. 1619 (4th edn); Symbola heroica, Oxford 1633.

Meres, Francis. Palladis tamia, Wits treasury: being the second part of Wits commonwealth. 1598, 1634 (as A treasurie of divine morall and phylosophicall similies and sentences, more particularly published for schools), 1636 (as Witts academy, chiefly for young schollers).
See Collections of maxims, below.

Progymnasmata and Rhetoric

Aphthonius of Antioch. Progymnasmata, partim a R. Agricola, partim a J. M. Cataneo latinitate donata. Ed R. Lorich 1540, London 1572; tr R. Nadeau, Speech Monographs 19 1952. Adapted by Richard Rainolde, The foundacion of rhetorike, 1563; ed F. R. Johnson, New York 1945.

Hermogenes, Progymnasmata. Tr C. S. Baldwin, Medieval rhetoric, New York 1928 (in part).

Susenbrotus, Johannes. Epitome troporum ac schematum et grammaticorum, ad authores tum prophanos tum sacros. [Zürich c. 1540], London 1570, 1621. *See* Henry Peacham, Garden of eloquence, 1577.
Brennan, J. X. Joannes Susenbrotus: a forgotten humanist. PMLA 75 1960.

Talaeus, Audomerus. Rhetorica. Paris 1543, London 1576, Edinburgh 1621.
Howell, W. S. Logic and rhetoric in England 1500–1700. Princeton 1956.
Ong, W. J. A Ramus and Talon inventory. Cambridge Mass 1958.

By English schoolmasters and tutors

Sherry, Richard (Magdalen College School). A system of schemes and tropes (with trn of Erasmus, De pueris); ed H. E. Hildebrandt, Gainesville 1961 (facs).

— Treatise of the figures of grammar and rhetoric. 1555. With trn of Cicero's oration to Caesar.

Brownswerd, John (Macclesfield). Progymansmata quaedam poetica. Ed Thomas Newton 1589.

Stockwood, John (Tonbridge). Progymnasma scholasticum. 1597.

— Disputatiuncularum grammaticalium, ad puerorum in scholis trivialibus exacuenda ingenia excogitatis. 1598.

Butler, Charles (Basingstoke School, Magdalen College). Rhetoricae libri duo, quorum prior de tropis et figuris, posterior de voce et gestu, praecipue in usum scholarum accuratius editi. Oxford 1598, 1629 (with Oratoria). After Ramus.

Willis, John. Mnemonica: sive ars reminiscendi. 1618; tr as The art of memory, 1621 (in part); Mnemonica: or the art of memory, 1661.
Yates, F. A. The art of memory. 1966.

Vicars, Thomas. Manaductio ad artem rhetoricam. 1618.

Farnaby, Thomas. Index rhetoricus. 1625, 1633 (rev), 1646 (as Index rhetoricus et oratoricus). *See* Thomas Stephens (Bury School), Troposchematologia, ex indice rhetorico Farnabii, 1648 (Latin and English).

— Index poeticus, poetes veteres et recentiores. 1634.

Clarke, John. Formulae oratoriae in usum scholarum. 1632 (4th edn).

— Dux poeticus. 1628.

Pemble, William. Enchiridion oratorum. Oxford 1633.

Hawkins, John. Particulae latinae orationes, collectae et confabulationibus digestae. 1635.

Rainolds, John. Orationes duodecim, cum aliis quibusdam opusculis. 1619; An excellent oration of John Rainolds, lecturer in Greek in Oxford, tr J[ohn] L[eycester] schoolmaster 1638. Cited as model orator.

Dugard, William. Rhetorices elementa. [1640], 1673 (7th edn).

Horne, Thomas. Rhetoricae compendium, latino-anglicè. 1651.

— Manaductio in aedem Palladis, qua utilissima methodus authores bonos legendi indigitatur. 1641.

Lloyd, Richard. Artis poeticae formula recens et dilucida. 1653.

Poole, Joshua. The English Parnassus: or a help to English poesy. 1657.

Letter Writing

Erasmus. De conscribendis epistolis. Cambridge 1521 (unauthorized), Basle 1522.

Brandolinus, Lippus. De ratione scribendi libri tres; adiecti sunt Joan. Ludovici Vives, Des. Erasmi Roterodami, Conradi Celtis, Christophori Hegendorphini, de conscribendis epistolis libelli. Basle 1549, London 1573.

Verepaeus, Simon. De epistolis latine conscribendis. Antwerp 1571, London 1592.

Macropedius, Georgius. Methodus de conscribendis epistolis; accessit C. Hegendorphini methodus. Dollingen 1565, London 1595.

Greek Studies

Clenard, Nicholas (Kleynaerts). Graecae linguae institutiones. Louvain 1530, London 1588 (rev Antesignanus, Sylburgius, H. Stephanus). With extracts from authors.

Lucian. Complures Luciani dialogi a D. Erasmo in latinum conversi. 1528.
Thompson, C. R. Translations of Lucian by Erasmus and More. Ithaca 1940.

Xenophon. Tr William Barker (Eton), The institution schole and education of Cyrus, 1567.
Parks, G. B. William Barker. PBSA 51 1957.

Demosthenes. Graecorum oratorum principis orationes lat. conversae, Nicholas Carr. 1571. Prefatory Latin verses by Malim, Mulcaster et al.

Whitaker, William. Catechismus: sive prima institutio, disciplina, pietatis christianae, graece et latine explicata.

1573. Trn of Nowell's 'middle' catechism. Catechismus parva tr 1578.

Grant, Edward. Graecae linguae spicilegium. 1575, 1597 (rev as Institutio graecae grammatices compendiaria in usum scholae westmonasteriensis), 1597. Compiled William Camden; the standard grammar.

Morelius, Gulielmus. Verborum latinorum cum graecis anglicisque conjunctorum locupletissimi commentarii. 1583.

Stockwood, John. Progymnasma scholasticum; epigrammatum graecorum [from H. Estienne, Anthologia] interpretatione explicatorum praxis grammatica. 1597. Greek interlined Latin.

Farnaby, Thomas. Florilegium epigrammatum graecorum eorumque latino versu a variis redditorum. 1629. By More, Erasmus, Lily, Robertson et al.

Franklin, Richard. Orthotonia: sive tractatus de tonis in lingua graecanica. 1630.

The first Greek text, after the catechism, was the New testament.

Berchetus, Tussanus. Versio et notae ad Stephani catechismum graecum cum alio catechismo compendiosiori. [1615], London 1656.

Pasor, Georg. Lexicon graeco-latinum in N. testamentum. Herborn 1632, London 1644.

Hoole, Charles (ed). Novum testamentum: omnia difficiliorum vocabulorum themata quae in G. Pasoris lexico grammatice resolvuntur. 1653.

Shirley, James. Introductorium anglo-latino-graecum: complectens colloquia familiara, Aesopi fabulas et Luciani selectiores dialogus. 1656.

Dugard, William (Merchant Tailors School). Rudimenta graecae linguae. 1656.

— Lexicon graeci testamenti alphabeticum. 1660.

— (ed). Luciani dialogorum selectorum libri duo. 1655.

— (ed). Casparus Seidelius, Manuale graecae linguae gnomologicum novum. 1665 (3rd edn).

Busby, Richard. Graecae grammatices rudimenta in usum scholae westmonasteriensis. [1647], 1663.

Hebrew Studies

Martinius, Petrus. Grammaticae hebraeae libri duo. Paris 1567. *See* J. Udall, Key of the holy tongue, wherein is contained the Hebrew grammar of Martinius, a practize upon [3] psalmes, a short dictionarie. 1593.

Buxtorf, Johannes (the elder). Epitome radicum hebraicarum et chaldaicarum. Basle 1607, London 1653; tr N. Gray 1627, J. Davis 1656.

Some Marginal Studies, Depending on Schoolmasters

Hollyband, Claudius (de Saintliens). The French schoolmaster. 1573.

— The French Littleton. 1576?; ed M. St Clair Byrne, Cambridge 1953 (from 1609).

— The flourie field of 4 languages, for learners of the Latin, French, English, but cheeflie of the Italian tongues. 1583.

Blundeville, Thomas. The true order and methode of wryting and reading hystories according to the precepts of F. Patrizio and Accontino Tridentio. 1574; ed H. G. Dick, HLQ 3 1940.

Florio, John. His first frutes. 1576.

— A world of wordes. 1598, 1611 (rev), 1659 (rev).

Primaudaye, Pierre de la. Tr T[homas] B[owes] et al, The French academie, 1586–94 (in part), 1618 (in full). A compendium.

Digges, Thomas. A geometrical practise named Pantometria. 1591.

Camden, William. Annales. 1615; tr R. Norton 1630.

Heylyn, Peter. Microcosmus. Oxford 1621.

Swan, John. Speculum mundi: or a glass representing the face of the world. 1635.

Ross, Alexander. The marrow of historie. 1650. Epitome of Ralegh's history.

On University Teaching and Tutoring

Crauford, Thomas. History of the University of Edinburgh from 1580 to 1646. Edinburgh 1808.

Melville, James. Autobiography and diary. Ed R. Pitcairn, Edinburgh 1842. On Glasgow 1571–1610.

Whitgift, John. Original papers. Ed S. R. Maitland, Br Mag 22–3 1847–8. Tutorial ledgers, Trinity College Cambridge.

Ascham, Roger. Whole works. Ed J. A. Giles 2 vols 1864. Includes correspondence.

Harvey, Gabriel. Letter-book 1572–80. Ed E. J. L. Scott 1884 (Camden Soc).

— Ciceronianus. Ed and tr H. S. Wilson and C. A. Forbes, Lincoln Nebraska 1945.

Ball, Thomas. Life of the renowned Dr Preston. Ed E. W. Harcourt, Oxford 1885.

Jewel, John. Oratio contra rhetoricam. Tr H. H. Hudson, Quart Jnl of Speech 14 1928.

Milton, John. Private correspondence and academic exercises. Ed and tr P. B. and E. M. W. Tillyard, Cambridge 1932.

Crosfield, Thomas. Diary. Ed F. S. Boas, Oxford 1935. Queen's College 1626–40.

Two Elizabethan puritan diaries by Richard Rogers and Samuel Ward. Ed M. M. Knappen 1933.

Duport, James. Rules to be observed by young pupils and schollers in the University. Ed G. M. Trevelyan, Undergraduate life under the Protectorate, Cambridge Rev 22 May 1943.

[Holdsworth, Richard?]. Directions for a student in the universitie. In H. F. Fletcher, Intellectual development of Milton vol 2, Urbana 1961.

'A library for younger schollers'. Ed A. de Jordy and H. F. Fletcher, Urbana 1961.

Jacobsen, E. JEGP 63 1964.

Erasmus. Cambridge letters. Ed H. C. Porter, Toronto 1963.

Letter book of Robert Joseph, scholar of Evesham and Gloucester College, Oxford 1530–3. Ed H. Aveling and W. A. Pantin, Oxford 1967 (for 1964).

Owen, John. Correspondence. Ed P. Toon 1970.

Some standard textbooks for students by English authors:

Linacre, Thomas. Rudimenta grammatices ex anglico sermone in latinum versa: interprete Georgio Buchanano Scoto. Paris 1533.

— De emendate structura Latini sermonis libri sex. 1524. Later edns rev Melanchthon and Camerarius.

Tunstall, Cuthbert. De arte supputandi. 1522.

Seton, John. Dialectica. 1545; ed Peter Carter 1546 (with William Buckley, Arithmetica memorativa), 1611.

Smith, Samuel. Aditus ad logicam. Oxford and London 1614.

Brerewood, Edward. Elementa logica in gratiam studiosae juventutis. Oxford and London 1614. Bound with above.

Sanderson, Robert. Logicae artis compendium. 1618 (2nd edn).

Crackenthorp, Richard. Introductio in metaphysicam. Oxford 1619.

Richardson, Alexander. The logician's schoolmaster. 1629. Based on Ramus.

Pemble, William. Enchiridion oratorum. Oxford 1633.

See pbns of university presses, college and university library catalogues, especially:

Jayne, S. Library catalogues of the English Renaissance. Berkeley and Los Angeles 1956. Includes student inventories.

Adams, H. M. Catalogue of books printed in Europe 1501–1600 in Cambridge libraries. 2 vols Cambridge 1967.

Edelman, H. PBSA 62 1968.

See Scholarship, col 2285, above.

(3) AUTOBIOGRAPHY, CORRESPONDENCE, DESCRIPTION ETC

(in alphabetical order)

Many autobiographies and letters describe educational experiences, among them:

Baker, Augustine. Memorials. Ed J. McCann and H. Connelly 1933 (Catholic Record Soc 33).

Bodley, Thomas. Life. Oxford 1647. In Harleian miscellany vol 4, 1809.

Boyle, Robert. An account of Philaretus during his minority. In R. E. W. Maddison, Life of Boyle, 1970.

Chatterton, Laurence. A memoir. Ed and tr E. S. Shuckburgh, Cambridge 1884.

d'Ewes, Simonds. Diary and correspondence. Ed J. O. Halliwell (-Phillipps) 2 vols 1845.

Evelyn, John. Early life and education. Ed H. Maynard Smith, Oxford 1930.

Hutchinson, Lucy. Life of Colonel Hutchinson. Ed C. H. Firth 2 vols 1885.

Josselin, Ralph. Diary 1616–83. Ed E. Hockliffe 1908 (Camden Soc).

Lilly, William. Life and times 1602–82, written to his friend Elias Ashmole. 1721, 1822.

Martindale, Adam. Life written by himself. Ed R. Parkinson 1845 (Chetham Soc).

Oxinden letters 1607–42. Oxinden and Peyton letters 1642–70. Ed D. Gardiner 1933–7.

Reminiscences of Oxford by Oxford men 1559–1850. Ed L. M. Quiller Couch 1892 (Oxford Historical Soc).

Rogers, R. and S. Ward. Two Elizabethan puritan diaries. Ed M. M. Knappen, Chicago 1935.

Sidney, Sir Philip. Correspondence with Hubert Languet. Ed S. A. Pears 1845.

Twyne, Brian. Some correspondence. Bodleian Lib Record 5 1929. At Oxford 1596–1613.

Verney family. Letters and papers to 1639. Ed J. Bruce 1853 (Camden Soc).

—— During the Civil War and Commonwealth. Ed F. P. and M. M. Verney 4 vols 1892–9.

Wallis, John. Account of some passages of his life. In Thomas Hearne, Works vol 3, Oxford 1725; ed C. J. Scriba, Notes & Records of Royal Soc 25 1970.

Whitelocke, James. Liber famelicus. Ed J. Bruce 1858 (Camden Soc).

Whythorne, Thomas. Autobiography. Ed J. M. Osborn, Oxford 1962 (modernized). By a music teacher.

Wood, Anthony. Life and times 1632–95 written by himself. Ed A. Clark 5 vols Oxford 1891–1900 (Oxford Historical Soc).

Worthington, John. Diary and correspondence. Ed J. Crossley 3 vols 1846–86 (Chetham Soc).

Advice to a Son

Advice to a son: precepts of Burghley, Raleigh, Francis Osborn. Ed L. B. Wright, New York 1962.

Burton, Edward. The father's legacy for his onely son. 1649.

Cavendish, William. Letter to Charles Prince of Wales under his tutelage. In Original letters ser 2 vol 3, ed H. Ellis 1825.

Delaune, H. Patrikon doron: or a legacie to his sons. 1651, 1657 (rev).

Eliot, John. Advice to his son. In Political treatise of government and letter book vol 1, ed A. B. Grosart 1882.

Percy, Henry, 9th Earl of Northumberland. Advice to his son 1609. Ed G. B. Harrison 1930.

Peter, Hugh. A dying father's last legacy to an only child. 1660.

Richardson, Elizabeth. A ladies legacie to her daughters. 1645.

Slingsby, Henry. Diary and correspondence. Ed D. Parsons 1836. A father's legacy.

Tipping, William. The father's counsel. 1644; rptd in Harleian miscellany vol 9, 1812.

Vaughan, Richard. Advice to his sonn. 1651; ed V. B. Heltzel, Huntington Lib Bull no 12 1938.

Wandesford, Christopher. A book of instructions (1641). Cambridge 1777.

Schemes for Academies

Bacon, Nicholas. A school for wards (1561). In E. Waterhous, Fortescutus illustratus, 1663.

Bolton, Edmund. Scheme for erecting a royal academy (1614?). Ed J. Hunter, Archaeologia 32 1847.

Prince Henry's plan. 1621. In Collectanea curiosa, ed J. Gutch 1781.

Scheme of a new college at Ripon in Yorks. 1604. In F. Peck, Desiderata curiosa, 1779.

The academ roial of King James I. Ed E. M. Portal, Proc Br Acad 7 1916.

Contemporary Descriptions covering Education

A relation of the island of England [c. 1500 by a Venetian]. Tr C. A. Sneyd 1847 (Camden Soc).

Discourse of the commonwealth of England (1549). Ed E. Lamond, Cambridge 1893; ed M. Dewar, Austin 1970. As by Sir Thomas Smith.

Harrison, William. Description of England (1577, 1587). Ed F. J. Furnivall 1877 (New Shakspere Soc).

Smith, Sir Thomas. De republica anglorum (1583). Ed J. Alston 1906.

Stow, John. Survey of London (1598). Ed J. Strype 2 vols 1720.

Wilson, Thomas. The state of England (c. 1600). Ed F. J. Fisher, Camden miscellany 16 1936 (Camden Soc).

Carey, W. The present state of England. 1627; in Harleian miscellany vol 3, 1808.

Biographical Collections

Lloyd, David. Statesmen and favourites of England since the Reformation. 1665.

Clarke, Samuel. Lives of ten eminent divines. 1662. For bibliography of later edns, W. Haller, Rise of puritanism 1570–1643, 1938.

Fuller, Thomas. History of the worthies of England. 1662; ed P. Nuttall 3 vols 1840.

Aubrey, John. Lives. 1813; Brief lives and other writings, ed A. Powell 1949.

Wood, Anthony. Athenae oxonienses. Ed P. Bliss 4 vols 1815–20.

(4) CLASSES OF DOCUMENT BEARING ON EDUCATION

Statutes

Acts of the Parliament and Privy Council of Scotland relative to establishing and maintaining schools 1494–1696. Edinburgh 1839.

Enactments in Parliament concerning the universities of Oxford and Cambridge, Winchester, Eton and West-minster 1364–1910. Ed L. Shadwell 4 vols 1911–12 (Oxford Historical Soc).

Ecclesiastical

Chantry certificates: short guides to records 6. Ed L. Snell, History 48 1963.

Episcopal licensing of schoolmasters in the diocese of

London 1627–85. Ed S. M. Wide and J. A. Morris, Guildhall Miscellany 2 1967.

Norwich subscription books 1637–80. Ed E. H. Carter 1937.

Lambeth churchwardens accounts 1540–1645. Ed C. Drew 2 vols 1940–50.

State of the Church in the reigns of Elizabeth and James I. Ed C. W. Foster 1926 (Lincoln Record Soc).

Tudor parish documents in the diocese of York. Ed J. S. Purvis 1948.

Visitation articles and injunctions of the Reformation. Ed W. H. Frere and W. M. Kennedy 1910 (Alcuin Club).

Apprenticeship, Poor Relief, Wardship

Calendar of the Bristol apprenticeship book 1532–42. 1949 (Bristol Record Soc).

Calendar of Southampton apprenticeship registers 1609–1740. Ed A. L. Merson, Southampton 1968.

Poor relief in Elizabethan Ipswich. Ed J. Webb 1966 (Suffolk Record Soc).

Sales of wards in Somerset 1603–41. Ed M. J. Hawkins 1965 (Somerset Record Soc).

Schools

Carlisle, N. Endowed grammar schools in England and Wales. 2 vols 1818. Many extracts from statutes. *See also* accounts in Victoria county history of England and histories of individual schools.

University and College

An exact copy of the last will and testament of Sir Thomas Gresham. 1724.

Oxford university statutes. Tr G. R. M. Ward 2 vols 1845–51.

Early Cambridge university and college statutes in English. Ed J. Heywood 1855.

Baker, Thomas. History of the College of St John, Cambridge. Ed J. E. B. Mayor 2 vols Cambridge 1869. With abstracts of correspondence.

Book of matriculations and degrees 1544–1659. Ed J. and J. A. Venn, Cambridge 1913.

Cambridge University transactions during the puritan controversies of the 16th and 17th centuries. Ed J. Heywood and T. Wright 2 vols 1854.

Cambridge documents illustrative of the history of the University 1500–72. Ed J. Lamb 1838.

Laudian code of statutes for Oxford University 1636. Ed J. Griffiths and C. L. Shadwell, Oxford 1888.

Letters patent of Elizabeth and James I addressed to the University of Cambridge with other documents. Ed J. W. Clark, Cambridge 1892.

Register of the visitors of the University of Oxford 1647–58. Ed M. Burrowes 1881 (Camden Soc).

The Restoration visitation of the University of Oxford and its colleges. Ed F. J. Varley, Camden Miscellany 18 1948 (Camden Soc).

See also:

Cordeaux, M. H. and D. H. Merry. Bibliography of printed works relating to the University of Oxford. Oxford 1968.

Peake, H. and C. P. Hall. Archives of the University of Cambridge. Cambridge 1962.

Craigie, J. Bibliography of Scottish education. 1970.

Jacobs, P. M. Registers of universities, colleges and schools in Great Britain and Ireland. 1964 (Inst of Historical Research).

C. SECONDARY SOURCES

(1) WRITERS, THEORIES AND PEDAGOGY

1500–1600

Klaehr, T. Leben und Werke Richard Mulcasters. Dresden 1863.

Seebohm, F. The Oxford reformers: Colet, Erasmus, More. 1867, 1869 (rev).

Schmidt, O. G. Petrus Mosellanus. Leipzig 1867.

Massebieau, L. Les colloques scolaires du seizième siècle. Paris 1878.

Katterfeld, A. Roger Ascham: sein Leben und seine Werke. Strasbourg 1879.

Arnstadt, F. A. Roger Ascham und seine Geistesverwandschaft mit Johannes Sturm. Plauen 1881.

Wagner, E. Luther als Pädagoge. Langensalza 1887.

Lupton, J. H. Life of Colet. 1887, 1909 (rev).

Hartfelder, K. Melanchthon als Praeceptor Germaniae. Berlin 1889.

Buisson, F. Sebastien Castellion. 2 vols Paris 1892.

Boemer, A. Die lateinischen Schülergespräche der Humanisten. 2 vols Berlin 1897–9.

Richard, J. W. Melanchthon: Protestant preceptor of Germany. New York 1898.

Merz, G. Die Schulwesen der deutschen Reformation. Heidelberg 1902.

Oliphant, L. Educational writings of Richard Mulcaster. Glasgow 1903. With extracts.

Emles, M. A. Das Erziehungsideal bei More, Ascham, Elyot, J. Lyly. Marburg 1904.

Benndorf, C. Die englische Pädagogik im 16 Jahrhundert. Vienna 1905. On Elyot, Ascham, Mulcaster.

Scott, I. Controversies over the imitation of Cicero and some phases of their influence on the schools of the Renaissance. New York 1910.

Siske, G. Willens- und Charakterbildung bei J. L. Vives. Langensalza 1911.

Watson, F. Religious refugees and English education. Proc Huguenot Soc of London 1911.

—— Vives, father of modern psychology. Psychological Rev 22 1915.

—— Vives: el gran Valencian. 1922.

Graves, F. P. Peter Ramus and the educational reformation of the sixteenth century. 1912.

Dittrich, P. Plautus und Terenz in Pädagogik und Schulwesen der deutschen Humanisten. Leipzig 1915.

Le Coultre, J. Mathurin Cordier. Neuchâtel 1926.

Dressler, B. Die Entwicklung der englischen Erziehung im 17 Jahrhundert. Leipzig 1927.

Conley, C. H. The first English translators of the classics. New Haven 1927.

Shackford, M. H. Plutarch in Renaissance England. Wellesley Mass 1929.

Thorndike, L. Essays in intellectual history. New York 1929. On Vives.

Fitzpatrick, E. A. (ed). St Ignatius Loyala and the Ratio studiorum. New York 1933.

Rückert, H. Die Stellung der Reformation zur mittelalterlichen Universität. Stuttgart 1933.

Allen, P. S. Erasmus: lectures and wayfaring sketches. Oxford 1934.

de Vocht, H. Vives and his visits to England. Monumenta Humanistica Lovaniensia 4 1934.

—— History of the Collegium Trilingue Lovaniense 1517–50. 4 vols Louvain 1951–5.

Martin, L. C. Henry Vaughan and the theme of infancy. In Seventeenth-century studies for Herbert Grierson, Oxford 1938.

Porteau, P. Montaigne et la vie pédagogique de son temps. Paris 1935.

Johnson, F. R. and S. V. Larkey. Robert Recorde's mathematical teaching and the anti-Aristotelian movement. Huntington Lib Bull no 7 1935.

Höpffner, E. Jean Sturm et l'enseignement supérieur des lettres à l'école de Strasbourg. In L'humanisme en Alsace, Paris 1939 (Association Budé).

Farrell, A. P. The Jesuit code of liberal education. Milwaukee 1938.

Urmenita, F. de. Doctrinas psicológicos y pedagógicos de Vives. Madrid 1949.

Sancipriano, M. Erasmo e Vives. Humanitas 5 1950.

— Il pensiero psicológico e morale di Vives. Florence 1958.

Colish, M. The mime of God: Vives on the nature of man. JHI 23 1962.

Sinz, W. The elaboration of Vives' treatises on the arts. Renaissance Stud 10 1963.

Phillips, M. M. Erasmus and the northern Renaissance. 1949.

Gambaro, A. Pedagogia di Erasmus. Il Saggiatore 1 1951.

Stevens, L. C. The actuality of Erasmus pedagogy. Kentucky Foreign Lang Quart 2 1955.

Salmon, V. A pioneer of the 'direct method' in the Erasmus circle. Latomus 19 1960.

Erasmus. Ed T. A. Dorey 1970.

Rebhorn, W. A. Erasmian education and the Convivium religiosum. SP 69 1972.

Bohatec, J. Budé et Calvin. Graz 1950.

Simonini, R. C. The Italian pedagogy of Claudius Hollyband. SP 49 1952.

Dibon, P. La philosophie néerlandaise au siècle d'or. Amsterdam 1954. On Burgersdijk.

Tusquets, J. Ramon Lull: pedagogo de la Christiandad. Madrid 1955.

Major, J. M. Sir Thomas Elyot and Renaissance humanism. 1957.

Surtz, E. The praise of pleasure: philosophy, education and communism in More's Utopia. Cambridge Mass 1957.

Hooykaas, R. Humanisme, science et réforme: Pierre de la Ramée 1515–72. Leyden 1958.

Ong, W. J. Ramus, method and the decay of dialogue. Cambridge Mass 1958.

— Latin language study as a Renaissance puberty rite. SP 56 1959.

Rice, E. F. The Renaissance idea of wisdom. 1958.

Hogrefe, P. The Sir Thomas More circle. Urbana 1959.

Lehmberg, S. E. Sir Thomas Elyot: Tudor humanist. Austin 1960.

Gilbert, N. W. Renaissance concepts of method. New York 1960.

Volpicelli, L. Il pensiero pedagogico della controriforma. Florence 1960.

Randall, J. H. The school of Padua and the emergence of modern science. Padua 1961.

Bertin, G. M. La pedagogia humanistica nei secoli xv e xvi. Milan 1961.

Lechner, J. M. Renaissance concepts of the commonplaces. New York 1962.

Hardison, O. B., jr. The enduring monument: the idea of praise in Renaissance literary theory and practice. Chapel Hill 1962.

Gilmore, M. P. Humanists and jurists: six studies in the Renaissance. Cambridge Mass 1963. On study of history.

Ryan, L. V. Roger Ascham. Oxford 1963.

Kohls, E. W. Die Schule bei Martin Bucer in ihrem Verhältnis zu Kirche und Obrigkeit. Heidelberg 1963.

O'Malley, C. D. English medical humanists: Thomas Linacre and John Caius. Lawrence Kansas 1965.

Sir Thomas More: neue Briefe mit einer Einführung in die epistolographische Tradition. Ed H. S. Herbrüggen, Münster 1966. Introd.

Croll, M. W. Style, rhetoric and rhythm: essays. Ed J. M. Patrick et al, Princeton 1966.

Chrisman, M. U. Strasbourg and the reform. New Haven 1967.

Breen, Q. Christianity and humanism. Ed N. P. Ross, Grand Rapids 1968.

Vasoli, C. La dialettica e la retorica dell'ūmanesimo: 'invenzione' a 'metodo' nella cultura del xv e xvi secolo. Milan 1968.

Bolgar, R. R. Humanism as a value system, with reference to Budé and Vives. In Humanism in France, ed A. H. T. Levi, Manchester 1970.

— Humanist education and its contribution to the Renaissance. In The changing curriculum, 1971 (History of Education Soc).

1600–60

Scougal, H. J. Pädagogische Schriften John Durys. Jena 1905.

Kvacala, J. J. A. Comenius der Erzieher. Leipzig 1914.

Turnbull, G. H. Samuel Hartlib: life and relation to Comenius. Oxford 1920.

— Hartlib, Dury and Comenius. 1947.

Young, R. F. Comenius and the Indians of New England. 1929.

Jones, R. F. Ancients and Moderns: the rise of the scientific movement in the seventeenth century. St Louis 1936, 1961 (rev).

— et al. The seventeenth century. Stanford 1951.

Wundt, M. Die deutsche Schulmetaphysik des 17 Jahrhunderts. Tübingen 1939.

Wallace, K. R. Francis Bacon on communication and rhetoric. Chapel Hill 1943.

Syfret, R. H. Origins of the Royal Society. Notes & Records of Royal Soc 5 1948. On Comenian group.

Nadeau, R. Thomas Farnaby: schoolmaster and rhetorician. Quart Jnl of Speech 36 1950.

Schlatter, R. B. The higher learning in puritan England. Historical Mag of Protestant Episcopal Church 23 1954.

Hodendorft, G. Die neue Lehrart: pädagogische Schriften Wolfgang Ratkes. Berlin 1957.

Schaller, K. Die Pädagogik des Comenius und die Anfänge des pädagogischen Realismus im 17 Jahrhundert. Heidelberg 1962, 1965 (rev).

Salmon, V. Joseph Webbe: language-teaching and the nature of meaning. Bibliothèque d'Humanisme et Renaissance 23 1961.

— Problems of language teaching; a discussion among Hartlib's friends. MLR 59 1964.

— Language-planning in seventeenth-century England. In In memory of J. R. Firth, 1966.

Brambora, J. Les problèmes actuels de la Coméniologie. Paedagogica Historica 7 1967. With bibliography.

Trevor-Roper, H. R. Three foreigners: the philosophers of the puritan revolution. In his Religion, the Reformation and social change, 1967. On Hartlib, Dury and Comenius.

O'Brien, J. J. Commonwealth schemes for the advancement of learning. Br Jnl of Educational Stud 16 1968.

Blekastad, M. Versuch eines Umrisses vom Leben, Werk und Schicksal des J. A. Komenský. Oslo and Prague 1969.

Greaves, R. L. The puritan revolution and educational thought. New Brunswick NJ 1969.

Simon, J. The Comenian educational reformers and the Royal Society. Acta Comeniana 26 1970.

Webster, C. Science and the challenge to the scholastic curriculum 1640–60. In The changing curriculum, 1971 (History of Education Soc).

(2) EDUCATIONAL PRACTICE

School

Allen, P. S. A sixteenth-century school. EHR 10 1895.

Barker, G. F. R. Memoir of Richard Busby 1606-95, with some account of Westminster School. 1895.

Masson, D. James Melvin, rector of the grammar school of Aberdeen. Aberdeen 1895.

Leach, A. F. English schools at the Reformation. 1896. Pt 2, Chantry certificates.

Stowe, A. M. English grammar schools in the reign of Queen Elizabeth. New York 1908.

Watson, F. English grammar schools to 1660: their curriculum and practice. Cambridge 1908.

Caine, C. Cardinal Wolsey's college, Ipswich. Br Archaeological Assoc Jnl new ser 20 1914.

Knight, L. S. Welsh independent grammar schools to 1600. Newtown 1916.

Sandys, J. Education. In Shakespeare's England vol 1, Oxford 1917.

O'Sullivan, M. D. The lay school at Galway in the 16th and 17th centuries. Jnl Galway Archaeological & Historical Soc 15 1931.

Brown, J. H. Elizabethan schooldays. Oxford 1933.

Plimpton, G. The education of Shakespeare illustrated from the school books of his day. 1933.

Seybolt, R. F. The public schools of colonial Boston. Cambridge Mass 1935.

Wallace, K. R. Rhetorical exercises in Tudor education. Quart Jnl of Speech 22 1936.

Price, H. T. Grammar and composition in the 16th and 17th centuries. JEGP 38 1939.

Schulz, H. C. The teaching of handwriting in Tudor and Stuart times. HLQ 6 1943.

Baldwin, T. W. William Shakspere's petty school. Urbana 1943.

— William Shakspere's 'small Latine and lesse Greeke'. 2 vols Urbana 1944.

Clarke, D. L. Milton at St Paul's school: a study of ancient rhetoric in English Renaissance education. New York 1948.

— Rise and fall of progymnasmata in 16th- and 17th-century grammar schools. Speech Monographs 19 1952.

Gray, J. King's College school in 1564. Proc Cambridge Antiquarian Soc 56-7 1952-3.

Nelson, W. The teaching of English in Tudor grammar schools. SP 49 1952.

Simon, B. Leicestershire schools 1625-40. Br Jnl Educational Stud 3 1955.

Fletcher, H. F. The intellectual development of John Milton vol 1: the beginnings through grammar school. Urbana 1956.

Thompson, C. R. Schools in Tudor England. Washington 1958 (Folger Lib).

Birley, R. Robert Boyle's headmaster at Eton: Robert Boyle at Eton. Notes & Records of Royal Soc 13-14 1958-9.

Lawson, J. A town grammar school through four centuries. Oxford 1963. On Hull.

Beales, A. C. F. Education under penalty: English Catholic education from the Reformation to the fall of James I. 1963.

Withrington, D. Schools in the presbytery of Haddington in the 17th century. Trans East Lothian Antiquarian Soc 9 1963.

Craig, H. The sixteenth-century grammar school in relation to the English Renaissance. E Studies 4 1966.

Wallis, P. J. The Newcastle Commonwealth Commissioners and Auckland School. Durham Research Rev 20 1968.

Spufford, M. Schooling of the peasantry in Cambridgeshire 1575-1700. Agricultural History Rev 18 (suppl) 1970.

For individual schools:

Wallis, P. J. Histories of old schools (before 1700): revised list for England and Wales. Newcastle 1966.

School and University

Clarke, M. L. Classical education in Britain 1500-1900. Cambridge 1959.

Jacobs, P. M. Registers of the universities, colleges and schools of Great Britain and Ireland. 1964 (Inst of Historical Research).

Charlton, K. Education in Renaissance England. 1965.

Simon, J. Education and society in Tudor England. Cambridge 1966.

Craigie, J. Bibliography of Scottish education before 1872. 1970.

University and College

Ward, J. Lives of the professors of Gresham College. 1740.

Mullinger, J. B. The University of Cambridge vols 2-3. Cambridge 1884-1911.

Mahaffy, J. P. An epoch in Irish history: Trinity College, Dublin 1559-1660. 1903.

Venn, J. Early collegiate life. Cambridge 1913.

Boas, F. S. University drama in the Tudor age. Oxford 1914. See also University plays, col 1761, above.

Mallet, C. E. History of the University of Oxford vol 2. 1924.

Mitchell, W. F. English pulpit oratory, from Andrewes to Tillotson. 1932.

Morison, S. E. Harvard College in the seventeenth century. 2 vols Cambridge Mass 1936.

Hudson, W. S. The Morison myth concerning the foundation of Harvard. Church History 8 1939.

Haller, W. The rise of puritanism 1570-1643. New York 1938.

Miller, P. The New England mind: the seventeenth century. Cambridge Mass 1939.

Johnson, F. R. Gresham College, precursor of the Royal Society. JHI 1 1940.

Jones, H. S. Foundation and history of the Camden chair (of history at Oxford). Oxoniensia 8-9 1943-4.

Brown, W. L. Some chapters in Cambridge medical history. Cambridge 1946.

Allen, P. Medical education in 17th-century England. Jnl History of Medicine 1 1946.

— Scientific studies in 17th-century English universities. JHI 10 1949.

Henderson, G. D. Founding of the Marischal College, Aberdeen 1593. Aberdeen 1947.

Turnbull, G. G. Oliver Cromwell's college at Durham. Durham Research Rev 3 1952.

— Peter Stahl, first public teacher of chemistry at Oxford. Annals of Science 9 1953.

Carpenter, N. C. The study of music at the University of Oxford in the Renaissance 1450-1600. Musical Quart 41 1955.

Costin, W. C. St John's College, Oxford 1598-1860. Oxford 1958.

Harrison, W. J. Life in Clare College 1658-1713. Cambridge 1958.

Porter, H. C. Reformation and reaction in Tudor Cambridge. Cambridge 1958. With bibliography.

Costello, W. J. The scholastic curriculum at early 17th-century Cambridge. Cambridge Mass 1958.

Thompson, C. R. Universities in Tudor England. Washington 1959 (Folger Lib).

Curtis, M. H. Oxford and Cambridge in transition 1558-1642. Oxford 1959.

Fletcher, H. F. The intellectual development of John Milton vol 2: Cambridge University. Urbana 1961.

Hill, C. Intellectual origins of the English revolution. Oxford 1959. Appendix.
—— The intellectual origins of the Royal Society: London or Oxford? Notes & Records of Royal Soc 23 1968.
Hall, R. and M. B. The intellectual origins of the Royal Society: London and Oxford. Ibid.
McConica, J. K. English humanists and Reformation politics. Oxford 1965.
Horn, D. B. Origins of the University of Edinburgh. Edinburgh Univ Jnl 22 1966.
Cordeaux, E. H. and D. H. Merry. Bibliography of printed works relating to the University of Oxford. Oxford 1968.
Leif, P. Textbooks on natural philosophy 1600–50. JHI 30 1969.
Kearney, H. Scholars and gentlemen: universities and society in pre-industrial Britain 1500–1700. 1970.

Inns of Court

Odgers, W. B. A sketch of the history of the four Inns of Court. In Essays in legal history, ed P. Vinogradoff, Oxford 1913.
Holdsworth, W. S. Disappearance of the educational system of the Inns of Court. Univ of Pennsylvania Law Rev 1921.
Brown, Basil. Law sports at Gray's Inn 1594, with reprint of Gesta Grayorum. New York 1921.
Symonds, E. M. The diary of John Greene 1635–57. EHR 43 1928.
Young, G. M. Shakespeare and the termers. Proc Br Acad 33 1947; rptd in his Today and yesterday, 1948.
Shoeck, R. J. Rhetoric and the law student in 16th-century England. SP 50 1953.
—— Law French: status of the scholarship. Kentucky Foreign Lang Quart 6 1959.
—— The libraries of common lawyers in Renaissance England. Manuscripta 6 1962.
Charlton, K. Liberal education and the inns of court in the 16th century. Br Jnl of Educational Stud 9 1960.
—— The professions in sixteenth-century England. Birmingham Historical Jnl 12 1969.
Gleason, J. H. The justices of the peace in England 1558–1640. Oxford 1969.
Finkelpearl, P. J. John Marston of the Middle Temple. Cambridge Mass 1969.
Knafla, L. A. Law studies of an Elizabethan student. HLQ 32 1969.
Prest, W. R. The Inns of Court under Elizabeth and the early Stuarts 1590–1640. 1972.

Other Professional Bodies

Sheavyn, P. The literary profession in the Elizabethan age. Manchester 1909, 1967 (rev J. W. Saunders).
Power, D'A. Education of a surgeon under Thomas Vicary. Br Jnl of Surgery 1921.
Woodfill, W. A. Musicians in English society from Elizabeth to Charles I. Princeton 1953.
Evans, J. History of the Society of Antiquaries. Oxford 1956.
Clarke, G. History of the Royal College of Physicians vol 1. Oxford 1964.
Thompson, F. M. L. Chartered surveyors. 1968.

British Students Abroad

Peacock, E. Index to English speaking students graduated at Leiden University. 1882.
Guilday, P. English Catholic refugees on the Continent 1558–1795 vol 1: colleges in the Low Countries. 1914.
Malloch, A. Finch and Barnes. 1917. Medical studies at Padua 1653–9.
Brown, H. R. F. Inglesi e Scozzesi all'università di Padova. Venice 1921.
Smith, R. W. I. English-speaking students of medicine at Leiden. Leyden 1932. Corrects Peacock, above.

Sieber, M. Die Universität Basel im 16 Jahrhundert und ihre englischen Besucher. Basler Zeitschrift 55 1956.
Dorsten, J. A. van. Poets, patrons and professors. Leyden 1962.

Household Upbringing and Travel

Einstein, I. The Italian Renaissance in England. 1902. On fencing masters.
Howard, C. English travellers at the Renaissance. 1914.
Jones, P. V. B. The household of a Tudor nobleman. 1918.
Thompson, E. N. S. Literary bypaths of the Renaissance. New Haven 1924. On courtesy books.
Ustick, W. L. Changing ideals of aristocratic character in seventeenth-century England. MP 30 1933.
—— Advice to a son: a type of seventeenth-century conduct book. SP 29 1932.
Thomson, G. S. Life in a noble household 1641–1700. 1937.
Kleineck, W. Englische Fürstenspiegel vom Policraticus Johannes von Salisbury bis zum Basilikon Doron König Jakobs I. Studien zur Englischen Philologie 90 1937.
Cameron, K. W. Authorship and sources of Gentelness and nobility. Raleigh NC 1941.
Houghton, W. E. The English virtuoso in the seventeenth century. JHI 3 1942.
Parks, G. B. Travel as education. In R. F. Jones et al, The seventeenth century, Stanford 1951.
Stoye, J. W. English travellers abroad 1604–67. 1952.
Bell, H. E. Introduction to the history and records of the court of wards and liveries. Cambridge 1953.
Hurstfield, J. The Queen's wards: wardship and marriage under Elizabeth I. 1958.
Apelt, W. Wandlungen des Gentlemanideals in der ersten Hälfte des 17 Jahrhunderts. Halle-Wittenberg 1959.
Brauer, G. The education of a gentleman and theories of gentlemanly education in England 1660–1775. New York 1959.
Ferguson, A. B. The Indian summer of English chivalry. Durham NC 1960.
Sells, A. L. The paradise of travellers: the Italian influence on Englishmen in the seventeenth century. 1964.
Stone, L. The crisis of the aristocracy 1558–1641. Oxford 1965. Pt 3.
Cross, C. The puritan Earl: Henry Hastings, third Earl of Huntingdon 1536–95. 1966. Ch 2, The godly household.
Thirsk, J. Younger sons in the seventeenth century. History 54 1969.
Cliffe, N. T. The Yorkshire gentry from the Reformation to the Civil War. 1969. Ch 4.

Upbringing in Home and Locality

Godfrey, E. Home life under the Stuarts. 1903.
Ware, S. L. The Elizabethan parish. Baltimore 1908.
Dunlop, O. J. English apprenticeship and child labour. 1912.
Seybolt, R. F. Apprenticeship education in colonial New England. New York 1917.
Powell, C. L. English domestic relations 1487–1653. New York 1917. On conduct books.
Trotter, E. Seventeenth-century life in the country parish. Cambridge 1919.
Clark, A. Working life of women in the seventeenth century. 1919.
Schücking, L. L. Die puritanische Familie. Leipzig 1929, 1961 (rev); tr 1969.
Darton, F. J. H. Children's books in England: five centuries of social life. Cambridge 1932, 1960 (rev).
Whitaker, W. B. Sunday in Tudor and Stuart times. 1933.
Wright, L. B. Middle class culture in Elizabethan England. Chapel Hill 1935. To 1640.
Schlatter, R. B. Social ideas of religious leaders 1660–88. Oxford 1940.
Campbell, M. The English yeoman under Elizabeth and the early Stuarts. New Haven 1942.

Morgan, E. S. The puritan family in seventeenth-century New England. New York 1944, 1966 (rev).

Camden, C. The Elizabethan woman 1540–1640. Houston 1952.

Bennett, H. S. English books and readers 1475–1660. 3 vols Cambridge 1952–71.

Sloane, W. Children's books in England and America in the seventeenth century: history and checklist. New York 1955.

Notestein, W. The English woman 1580–1650. In Studies in social history, ed J. H. Plumb 1955.

Davies, M. G. The enforcement of English apprenticeship 1563–1642. Cambridge Mass 1956.

MacCaffery, W. T. Exeter 1540–1640. Cambridge Mass 1958.

Jordan, W. K. The charities of London 1480–1660. 1960.
—— The charities of rural England. 1961.
—— Social institutions of Kent. Archaeologia Cantiana 75 1961.
—— Social institutions of Lancashire. 1962 (Chetham Soc).
—— Charitable institutions in the west of England. Philadelphia 1960 (Amer Philosophical Soc).

George, C. H. and K. The Protestant mind of the English Reformation 1570–1640. Princeton 1961. Ch 7, The family.

Burton, E. The Jacobeans at home. 1962.
—— The Elizabethans at home. 1963.

Hill, C. Society and puritanism in pre-revolutionary England. 1964.

Brailsford, D. Sport and society from Elizabeth to Anne. 1969.

Pinchbeck, I. and M. Hewitt. Children in English society vol 1. 1969.

See also:

Select bibliography of adult education in Great Britain. Ed T. Kelly 1962 (Inst of Adult Education), 1970 (rev).

Local history handlist. Ed F. W. Kuhlicke and F. G. Emmison 1965 (Historical Assoc), 1969 (rev).

Sources for the history of education in libraries of institutes and schools of education. Ed C. W. J. Higson 1967 (Lib Assoc).

J. S.

7. SCOTTISH LITERATURE

I. INTRODUCTION

In addition to the bibliographies listed below, the following sources of information should be borne in mind: the county histories of Scotland; the pbns of the Abbotsford, Bannatyne, Hunterian, Maitland and Spalding (3 sers) Clubs and the Scottish Text Society (STS); The Scottish Historical Rev, Glasgow 1903–28, Edinburgh 1947–65, Aberdeen 1966–; and Scottish N & Q, Aberdeen 1888–.

(1) BIBLIOGRAPHIES

Aldis, H. G. A list of books printed in Scotland before 1700. 1904 (Edinburgh Bibl Soc).

Terry, C. S. A catalogue of the publications of Scottish historical and kindred clubs and societies. Glasgow 1909.

Geddie, W. A bibliography of Middle-Scots poets. 1912 (STS).

Cowan, W. A bibliography of the Book of Common Order and Psalm Book of the Church of Scotland 1556–1664. Edinburgh 1913.

Maclean, D. Typhographia scoto-gadelica: books in the Gaelic of Scotland 1567 to 1914. Edinburgh 1915. Based on J. Reid, Bibliotheca scoto-celtica, Glasgow 1832.

Fasti ecclesiae scoticanae. 7 vols Edinburgh 1915–28. Contains bibliographies of church and parish histories.

Black, G. F. A list of works relating to Scotland. New York 1916.

Anderson, A. K. A short bibliography on Scottish history and literature. Glasgow 1922.

Johnstone, J. F. K. and A. W. Robertson. Bibliographia aberdoniensis. Vol 1, 1472–1640; vol 2, 1640–1700, Aberdeen 1929–30 (Third Spalding Club).

Stuart, M. Guide to works of reference on the history and genealogy of Scottish families. Edinburgh 1930.

Murray, D. Some old Scottish authors whose books were printed abroad. Glasgow 1921. Rptd from Trans of Glasgow Archaeological Soc new ser 7 1920.

Baxter, J. H. and C. J. Fordyce. Books published abroad by Scotsmen before 1700. Records of Glasgow Bibl Soc 11 1933.

Hancock, P. D. Bibliography of works relating to Scotland 1916–50. 2 pts Edinburgh 1959.

(2) GENERAL STUDIES

Irving, D. Lives of the Scotish poets, with dissertations on the literary history of Scotland. 2 vols Edinburgh 1804.

—— Lives of Scotish writers. 2 vols Edinburgh 1839.

—— History of Scotish poetry. Ed J. A. Carlyle, Edinburgh 1861.

Ross, J. M. Scottish history and literature to the period of the Reformation. Ed J. Brown, Glasgow 1884.

Walker, H. Three centuries of Scottish literature. 2 vols Glasgow 1893.

Henderson, T. F. Scottish vernacular literature. 1898, 1910.

Millar, J. H. Literary history of Scotland. 1903.

—— Scottish prose of the 17th and 18th centuries. Glasgow 1912.

Smith, G. G. Scottish literature. 1919.

Mill, A. J. Medieval plays in Scotland. Edinburgh 1928.

Mackenzie, A. M. An historical survey of Scottish literature to 1714. 1933.

—— (ed). Scottish pageant 1513–1625. Edinburgh 1948. An annotated anthology.

Power, W. Literature and oatmeal. 1935.

Speirs, J. The Scots literary tradition. 1940, 1962 (rev).

Whiting, B. J. Proverbs and proverbial sayings from Scottish writings before 1600. Mediaeval Stud 11–12 1950–1.

Kinsley, J. (ed). Scottish poetry: a critical survey. 1955.

Wittig, K. The Scottish tradition in literature. Edinburgh 1958.

Kenneth, Brother. Popular literature of the Scottish Reformation. Innes Rev 10 1959.

Ross, I. S. Verse translation at the Court of King James VI of Scotland. Texas Stud in Lit & Lang 4 1962.

—— Sonneteering in 16th-century Scotland. Texas Stud in Lit & Lang 6 1964.

Greene, R. L. The burden and the Scottish variant of the Corpus Christi carol. MÆ 33 1964.

Jack, R. D. S. Imitation in the Scottish sonnet. Comparative Lit 20 1968.

(3) CULTURAL AND SOCIAL BACKGROUND

The Universities

The following university histories are especially useful for the information, biographical and bibliographical, which they provide about their members.

Anderson, P. J. (ed). Studies in the history and development of the University of Aberdeen. 1906.

McCulloch, W. W. Viri illustres Universitatum Aberdonensium. Aberdeen 1923.

Votiva tabella: a memorial volume of St Andrews University. Glasgow 1911.

Broer, A. History of the University of Edinburgh. 3 vols Edinburgh 1830.

Neilson, G. (ed). Glasgow quatercentenary studies. Glasgow 1907.

Coutts, J. History of the University of Glasgow. Glasgow 1909.

Miscellaneous Aspects

Grant, J. History of the Burgh Schools of Scotland. Glasgow 1876.

Williams, A. M. The Scottish school of rhetoric. Glasgow 1897.

Leith, W. F. Pre-Reformation scholars in Scotland in the xvith century. Glasgow 1915. Bibliography. For criticism, see D. H. Fleming, A Jesuit's misconception of Scottish history, Edinburgh 1916.

Warrack, J. Domestic life in Scotland 1488–1688. 1920.

Grant, I. F. The social and economic development of Scotland before 1603. Edinburgh 1930.

Anderson, D. The Bible in seventeenth-century Scottish life. 1936.
Henderson, G. D. Religious life in seventeenth-century Scotland. Cambridge 1937.
Notestein, W. The Scot in history. New Haven 1946.
Scott-Moncrieff, G. Edinburgh. 1947.
Finlay, I. Art in Scotland. 1948.

Patrick, M. Four centuries of Scottish psalmody. Oxford 1949.
Farmer, H. G. A history of music in Scotland. 1948.
Mathew, D. Scotland under Charles I. 1955.
Mitchell, W. S. A history of Scottish bookbinding 1432–1650. Aberdeen Univ Stud 134. 1955.
McDonald, W. R. Scottish seventeenth-century almanacs. Bibliotheck 4 1964.

II. POETRY AND DRAMA

(1) GENERAL COLLECTIONS AND ANTHOLOGIES

Delitiae poetarum scotorum. Ed A. Johnston 2 vols Amsterdam 1637.
Watson's choice collection of comic and serious Scots poems. 3 pts Edinburgh 1706–11; rptd Glasgow 1869. *Watson.*
Poetarum scotorum musae sacrae. Ed W. Lauder, Edinburgh 1739.
Ancient Scotish poems. Ed J. Pinkerton 2 vols Edinburgh 1786. *Pinkerton.*
Campbell, Alexander. An introduction to the history of poetry in Scotland, from the beginning of the thirteenth century to the present time; together with a conversation on Scotish songs, to which are subjoined Sangs on the Lowlands of Scotland. Edinburgh 1798.
Scotish poems of the sixteenth century. Ed J. G. Dalyell 2 vols Edinburgh 1801.
Chronicle of Scottish poetry. Ed J. Sibbald 4 vols Edinburgh 1802. *Sibbald.*
Various pieces of fugitive Scottish poetry, principally of the seventeenth century. Ed D. Laing 2 sers 1825–53.
Scotish elegiac verses 1629–1729. Ed J. Maidment, Edinburgh 1842.
A book of Scotish pasquils 1568–1715. Ed J. Maidment, Edinburgh 1868.
The Sempill ballates. Ed T. G. Stevenson, Edinburgh 1872.

The poets and poetry of Scotland from the earliest to the present time. Ed J. G. Wilson 2 vols 1876.
Satirical poems of the time of the Reformation. Ed J. Cranstoun 3 vols 1884–93 (STS). *See* F. Wollmann, Über politisch-satirische Gedichte aus der Schott-Reformationzeit, Vienna 1898.
Musa latina aberdonensis. Ed W. D. Geddes and W. K. Leask 3 vols 1892–1910 (New Spalding Club).
Scottish poetry of the sixteenth century. Ed G. Eyre-Todd, Glasgow 1892.
Scottish poetry of the seventeenth century. Ed G. Eyre-Todd, Glasgow 1895.
The book of Scottish poetry. Ed G. Douglas 1911.
A St Andrews treasury of Scottish verse. Ed Mrs and Professor A. Lawson 1920.
A book of Scottish verse, selected by R. L. Mackie. Oxford 1934 (WC), 1967 (rev).
Scottish poetry from Barbour to James VI. Ed M. M. Gray 1936.
The golden treasury of Scottish poetry. Ed 'H. MacDiarmid' 1940.
A Scots anthology. Ed J. W. Oliver and J. C. Smith, Edinburgh 1949.
The Oxford book of Scottish verse. Ed J. MacQueen and T. Scott, Oxford 1966.
Late medieval Scots poetry: a selection from the makars and their heirs down to 1610. Ed T. Scott 1967.

(2) THE LATER SCOTTISH 'MAKARIS'

A. ARBUTHNOT
1538–93

See Pinkerton and the Maitland quarto manuscript, *ed W. A. Craigie 1920 (STS).*

JOHN BELLENDEN
1500–48?

The proheme to the translation of Boeces history, the proheme of the cosmographe and Address to Bellona and King Iames. In Bellenden, The croniklis of Scotland, Edinburgh 1535, 1821, 1941 (STS).
The proloug apoun the traductioun of Titus Livius be Maister Iohnne Ballantyne. In Bellenden, The first five books of the Roman history, Edinburgh 1822, 1901 (STS).
The benner of pietie. In The Bannatyne manuscript, ed J. B. Murdoch 1896 (Hunterian Club).
See G. Eyre-Todd, Scottish poetry of the sixteenth century, *Glasgow 1892. On the form of the surname see* Livy's History of Rome, translated into Scots by John Bellenden, *ed W. A. Craigie 1901 (STS).*

MARK ALEXANDER BOYD
1563–1601

Elegiae, epigrammata nonnulla illustriumque mulierum elogia. Bordeaux 1590.
Epistolae quindecim quibus totidem Ovidii respondet. Bordeaux 1590.
Epistolae, Heroides et hymni. Antwerp 1592.
Poemata. In Delitiae poetarum scotorum, ed A. Johnston, Amsterdam 1637.

JOHN BUREL
fl. 1590

Poems. Edinburgh [1595?]. Unique copy in BM wanting title. Contents: verse dedication, To the richt, high Lodwik, Duke of Lenox; verse preface; Pamphilus speakand luf [colophon, Heir endis the historie of Pamphilus], and The additioun of the translater; An application concerning our Kings Majesties persoun; The discriptioun of the Queens Majesties maist honorable entry into Edinburgh, 19 May 1590; The passage of the pilgremer, devidit into two pairts. The Discriptioun and the Passage of the pilgremer rptd in Watson pt 2, 1708; the Discriptioun rptd in Sibbald 3, 1803.

JOHN DAVIDSON, minister of
Prestonpans
1549?–1604

Ane answer to the tractive, set furth in the zeir of God 1558 be maister Quentin Kennedy, Commendator, abbote of Crossraguel, for the establisching of ane Christiane mannis conscience. Edinburgh 1563. Prose.

Ane dialog or mutuall talking betuix a clerk and a courteour, concerning foure parische kirks till ane minister, collectit out of thair mouthis, and put into verse by a young man quha did then forgather with thame in his jornay, as efter followis. Edinburgh 1573; ed J. Maidment, Edinburgh 1829; rptd in Satirical forms of the time of the Reformation, ed J. Cranstoun 1891 (STS).

Ane breif commendatioun of uprichtnes, in respect of the surenes of the same, to all that walk in it, amplifyit cheiflie be that notabill document of Godis michtie protectioun in preseruing his maist vpricht seruand and feruent messinger of Christs euangele, Johne Knox, set furth in Inglis meter. St Andrews 1573. Includes Ane schort discurs of the estaitis quha hes caus to deploir the deith of this excellent servand of God; rptd in T. McCrie, The life of John Knox, Edinburgh 1812 etc; Satirical poems of the time of the Reformation vol 1, ed J. Cranstoun 1891 (STS).

Dr Bancrofts rashnes in rayling against the Church of Scotland, noted in an answere to a letter of a worthy person of England, and some reasons rendred, why the answere thereunto hath not hitherto come forth, by I.D., a brother of the said Church of Scotland. Edinburgh 1590. Prose.

A memorial of the life & death of two worthye Christians, Robert Campbel of the Kinyeancleugh and his wife Elizabeth Campbel, in English meter. Edinburgh 1595.

Some helps for young schollers in Christianity. Edinburgh 1602; rptd as Mr John Davidson's catechism, ed W. Jameson, Edinburgh 1708 (to which is prefixed A discourse giving an account of the occasion of this impression, as also containing several things useful for determining of the episcopal controversy); rptd Scottish catechisms of the Reformation, ed H. Bonar 1866.

Poetical remains; with a biographical account of the author and various illustrative papers. Ed J. Maidment, Edinburgh 1829.

Rogers, C. Three Scottish reformers with their poetical remains and Mr Davidson's Helps for young scholars in Christianity. 1874.

See R. M. Gillon, John Davidson of Prestonpans, *1938* (*with bibliography*).

WILLIAM FOWLER
1560–1612

An answer to the calumnious letter and erroneous propositions of an apostat named M. Jo. Hammiltoun. Edinburgh 1581. Prose.

A funeral sonet, written vpon the death of the honorable and maist vertuous gentlewoman, Elizabeth Douuglas, spouse to M. Samuell Cobuurne, Laird of Temple-Hall. nd.

Sonet. Prefixed to James VI, Essayes of a prentise in the divine art of poesie, Edinburgh 1584.

Sonet. Prefixed to T. Hudson's Historie of Judith, Edinburgh 1584

Sonet, to the onely royal poet. Prefixed to James VI, Poeticall exercises at vacant houres, Edinburgh 1591.

Epitaphe upon the death of Sir John Seton of Barns, knight, ane of the lordes of our soveranes Privie Counsell and session. Edinburgh 1594.

A true reportarie of the most triumphant, and royal accomplishment of the baptisme of the most excellent, right high and mightie Prince, Frederik Henry; by the grace of God, Prince of Scotland, solemnized the 30 day of August 1594. Edinburgh [1594]. Prose.

A true accompt of the most triumphant, and royall accomplishment of the baptism of the most excellent, right high and mighty Prince Frederick Henry, by the grace of God, Prince of Scotland and now Prince of Wales, as it was solemnized to 30 day of August 1594. 1603; rptd in Somers' tracts vol 1, 1750, vol 2, 1809 (2nd edn); J. Nichols, Progresses of Queen Elizabeth vol 3, 1805; rptd Edinburgh 1687, rptd in R. Buchanan, Scotia rediviva vol 1, 1826, and Tracts illustrative of the traditionary and historical antiquities of Scotland, Edinburgh 1836, 1703, 1745, Leith 1764. Prose.

The works of William Fowler. Ed H. W. Meikle, J. Purves and J. Craigie 3 vols 1914–40 (STS). Vol 1, Verse, including unpbd version of Petrarch's Trionfi and unpbd sonnet-sequence The tarantula of love; vol 2, Prose, including unpbd trn of portion of Machiavelli's Il Principe. Extracts from Triumphs of Petrarch ptd in J. Leyden, Scottish descriptive poems, Edinburgh 1803.

See J. Purves, Fowler and Scoto-Italian cultural relations in the sixteenth century, *in* Works of William Fowler, ed Meikle; Purves and Craigie vol 3, above; R. D. S. Jack, Fowler and Italian literature, MLR 65 1970.

THOMAS HUDSON
fl. 1584–1610

See col 1119, above.

ALEXANDER HUME
1560?–1609

§1

Ane treatise of conscience. Edinburgh 1594.

A treatise of the felicitie, of the life to come. Edinburgh 1594.

Hymnes or sacred songs, wherein the right use of poesie may be espied; whereunto are added, the experience of the authors youth and certaine precepts serving to the practise of sanctification. Edinburgh 1599, 1832 (Bannatyne Club).

Of the day estivall: a poem. See J. Leyden, Scottish descriptive poetry, 1803; rptd in Poets and poetry of Scotland, ed J. G. Wilson 1876.

The practise of sanctification. Ed R. M. Fergusson, Paisley 1901.

§2

Fergusson, R. M. Hume: an early poet-pastor of Logie, and his intimates. Paisley 1899.

Lindsay, D. W. Of the day estivall: a textual note. Stud in Scottish Lit 4 1966.

SIR PATRICK HUME of Polwart
d. 1609

The Promine: contening the maner, place and time of the maist illuster King James the Sext, his first passing to the feildis. Edinburgh 1580; rptd in Select remains of the ancient popular poetry of Scotland, ed D. Laing, Edinburgh 1822, 1884, 1885; Early popular poetry of Scotland, ed W. C. Hazlett 1895. *See also* Alexander Montgomerie, *below.*

JAMES VI of Scotland
1566–1625

§1

The essayes of a prentise in the divine art of poesie. Edinburgh 1584, 1585; ed R. P. Gillies, Edinburgh 1814; ed E. Arber 1869, 1895.

His Majesties poeticall exercises at vacant houres. Edinburgh 1591; ed R. P. Gillies, Edinburgh 1818. Includes The Furies, Lepanto and La Lepanthe de James VI, Roy d'Ecosse, faicte françoise par le sieur du Bartas. La Lepanthe rptd with works of Du Bartas, La Rochelle 1591, Geneva 1598, 1601, 1608, 1615, 1616, 1632, Rouen 1599, 1602, 1608, 1610, 1623, Lyons 1603, 1606, Paris 1603, 1611, 1614; tr Dutch, 1593, nd, 1628; Latin, 1604, rptd in Delitiae poetarum scotorum, Amsterdam 1637; German, 1623, 1641.

His Majesties Lepanto: or heroical song. 1603.

Rait, Sir Robert S. Lusus regius. 1901. 10 poems and one prose piece from ms Bodley 165, and one prose piece from Bodley 166, mss unpbd.

New poems by James I of England, from a hitherto unpublished manuscript [BM add ms 24,195]. Ed A. F. Westcott, New York 1911.

Poems. Ed J. Craigie 2 vols 1955–8 (STS). With bibliography.

See also col 2472, below.

§2

Willson, D. H. King James VI and I. 1956.
Jack, R. D. S. James VI and Renaissance poetic theory. English 16 1967.

SIR WILLIAM KIRKCALDY
of Grange
d. 1573

Ane ballate of the captane of the castell. Ptd J. G. Dalyell in Scotish poems of the sixteenth century, Edinburgh 1801; rptd in R. Bannatyne, Memorials of transactions in Scotland 1569–73, ed E. R. Pitcairn 1836 (Bannatyne Club); The Sempill ballates, Edinburgh 1872; Satirical poems of the time of the Reformation, ed J. Cranstoun 1891 (STS). The authorship is sometimes ascribed to Robert Sempill. *See* J. Grant, Memoirs and adventures of Kirkcaldy, Edinburgh 1849; L. Barbé, Kirkcaldy of Grange, Edinburgh 1897.

WILLIAM LAUDER
1520?–73

Ane compendious and breue tractate concerning the office and dewtie of Kingis, spirituall pastoris and temporall jugis, laitlie compylit be William Lauder for the faithfull instruction of Kyngis and Prencis. [St Andrews?] 1556; rptd in P. Hall, Crypt, 1827; ed F. Hall 1864 (EETS).

Ane godlie tractate or mirrour, quhairintill may be easilie perceavit quho thay be that ar ingraftit in to Christ and quho ar nocht; declaring also the rewaird of the godlie and punyschement of the wekit. Edinburgh [1569?].

Ane prettie mirrour or conference, betuix the faithfull Protestant and the dissemblit false hypocreit, intto the quhilk may be easylie perceaved and knawin the one from the uther, compylit be William Lauder minister of the wourd of God for the instructioun, confort, and consolatioun of all faithfull professours. Edinburgh [1570?]. Includes Ane trew and breue sentencius discription of the nature of Scotland; twiching the interteinment of virtewus men that laketh ryches; and Ane

gude exempill be the butterflie, instructing men to hait all harlottrie.

Minor poems. Ed F. J. Furnivall 1870 (EETS), 1910 (rev).

SIR DAVID LINDSAY
1490?–1555

Bibliographies

Poetical works. Ed D. Laing 3 vols 1870. With bibliography.

Hamer, D. The bibliography of Lindsay. Library 3rd ser 10 1929.

Poetical works. Ed D. Hamer 4 vols 1931–6 (STS). With bibliography.

Collections

Poetical works. Ed G. Chalmers 3 vols 1806.
Works. Ed F. Hall, J. Small and J. A. H. Murray 5 pts 1865–71 (EETS), 1883 (pt i rev).
Poetical works. Ed D. Laing 2 vols 1871, 3 vols 1879.
Poetical works. Ed D. Hamer 4 vols 1931–6 (STS).
Poems. Ed M. Lindsay, Edinburgh 1948 (Saltire Soc). A selection.

§1

For lost early quartos of 7 poems ptd in Scotland, see D. Hamer's bibliographies, *above*.

The complaynte and testament of a popinjay which lyeth sore wounded and maye not dye, tyll every man hathe herd what he sayth. 1583. English trn.

The tragedy of the late moste reverende father David, by the mercie of God Cardinall and Archbishoppe of sainct Andrewes, and of the whole realme of Scotland primate, Legate and Chanceler and Administrator of the bishoprich of Merapois in Fraunce and Commendator perpetuall of the Abbay of Aberbrothok. In The tragicall death of David Beaton, [1548?] (by Robert Burrant?]. English trn.

Ane dialog betuix Experience and ane Courteour off the miserabill estait of the warld, compylit be Schir Dauid Lyndesay of the mont knycht, and is devidit in foure partis, as efter followis. [St Andrews? 1554?] (John Scot), Rouen 1558, 1558 (4° and 8°). To both French edns are added reprints of lost quartos of the Testament and Complaynt of our soverane lordis papyngo, the Dreme of Shir Dauid Lindsay, the Deploratioun of the deith of Quene Magdalene and the Tragedy of maister reverende fader Dauid Beaton. The Dialog separately rptd by John Scott, c. 1559–60. To unsold copies of the first edn, and to all copies of the 2nd edn of the Dialog were appended reprints by Scot of the Testament and complaynt of the papyngo, the Dreme, the Deploratioun, and the Complaynt of Sir David Lindsay.

A dialogue betweene Experience and a Courtier of the miserable estate of the worlde, first compiled in the Schottishe tongue, nowe newly corrected and made perfit Englishe. 1566 (with anglicized versions of the Tragedie of the late Cardinal Beaton, the Testament and complaynt of the papyngo and the Deploratioun of the deith of Queene Magdalene), 1575 (with 20 lines of the Complaynt and confession of Bagsche), 1581.

Dialogus eller en Samtale immellom forfarenhed, oc en Hofftienere om verdens elendige vaesen, begribus udir fire bøger om monarchier. Copenhagen 1591. Danish trn of Ane dialog, together with the Dreme, the Complaynt, the Testament and complaynt of the papyngo, the Tragedy of the late Cardinal Beaton and the Deploratioun.

The warkis of the famous and vorthie knicht Schir David Lyndesay of the Mont, alias Lyoun King of Armes, newly correctit, and vindicate from the former errouris quhairwith thay war befoir corruptit; and augmentit with sindrie warkis quhilk was not befoir imprentit. Edinburgh 1568 (re-issued 1569, 1571), 1574, 1579? (re-issued 1582), 1592, 1597 (preliminaries dated 1597 covering 2 edns), 1604, 1610, 1614, 1617, 1619, 1628, 1630, 1634, 1645?, 1648, 1670, 1709, 1714, 1716, 1720, 1776–7, Glasgow 1656, 1665, 1672, 1683, 1686, 1696, 1712, 2 vols 1754, 1 vol Belfast 1714.

The historie of ane nobil and wailzeand squyer William Meldrum, umquhyle Laird of Cleische and Bynnis. Edinburgh 1594 (rptd from lost edn c. 1579), 1610, 1634, 1683, Glasgow 1669, 1683, 1696, Aberdeen 1711; rptd Pinkerton 1; ed J. Kinsley 1959.

Ane satyre of the thrie estaitis, in commendation of vertew and vituperation of vyce. Edinburgh 1602; ed J. Sibbald, Edinburgh 1802.

The satire of the three estates: acting text by R. Kemp. Edinburgh 1948, London 1951.

Ane satire of the thrie estaitis. Ed J. Kinsley with essays by A. M. Mackenzie and I. Brown 1954.

A satire of the three estates. Ed M. P. McDiarmid 1967.

A supplication in contemplation [*sic*] of side tailes and muzzled faces. Edinburgh [1690?]. A broadside.

§2

Tytler, P. F. In his Lives of the Scottish worthies vol 3, 1843.

Lindsay, A. W. C. (Earl of Crawford and Balcarres). In his Lives of the Lindsays vol 1, 1849.

Knauff, G. Studien über Lindsay. Berlin 1885.

Aschenberg, H. Lyndsays Leben und Werke 1: sein Leben. Glasbach 1891 (all pbd).

Koeppel, E. Lyndsays Anspielungen auf mittelenglische Dichtungen. Archiv 107 1902.

Lange, A. Lyndesays Monarche und die Chronica Carionis. Giessen 1904.

Mill, Anna J. The influence of continental drama on Lyndsay's Satyre of the thrie estaitis. MLR 25 1930.

— Representations of Lyndsay's Satyre of the thrie estaitis. PMLA 47 1932. Corrections 48 1933.

— The original version of Lindsay's Satyre of the thrie estaitis. Stud in Scottish Lit 6 1968.

Murison, W. Sir David Lindsay. Cambridge 1938.

Houk, R. A. Versions of Lindsay's Satire of the three estates. PMLA 55 1940.

Miller, E. S. The christening of the Three estates. MLN 60 1945.

McLaine, A. H. Christis Kirk on the Grene and Lindsay's Satyre of the thrie estaitis. JEGP 56 1957.

Macdonald, A. A footnote on Lindsay. N & Q Oct 1960.

Dessen, A. C. The Estaitis morality play. SP 62 1965.

MacQueen, J. Ane satyre of the thrie estaitis. Stud in Scottish Lit 3 1966.

SIR JOHN MAITLAND of Thirlstane
1545?–1595

See Sir Richard Maitland of Lethington, below.

SIR RICHARD MAITLAND
of Lethington
1496–1582

Poems, with an appendix of selections from the poems of Sir John Maitland, Lord Thirlstane and of Thomas Maitland. Ed J. Bain 1830 (Maitland Club).

See Pinkerton, Sibbald; Maitland folio manuscript and the Maitland quarto manuscript, ed W. A. Craigie 1919–27 (STS), 1920.

ANDREW MELVILLE
1545–1622

Principis scoto-britannorum natalia. Hagae-Comitis 1594.

Poemata. In Delitiae poetarum scotorum, ed A. Johnston, Amsterdam 1637.

ELIZABETH MELVILLE, LADY
COLVILLE of Culross
b. 1571?

Ane godlie dreame, compylit in Scottis meter, be M.M. gentelwoman in Culross, at the requeist of her freindis. Edinburgh 1603, [1604?], 1620, 1644, 1692, 1718, Aberdeen 1644; rptd in Scottish metrical tales, ed D. Laing, Edinburgh 1826; Glasgow 1889; in Early popular poetry of Scotland, ed W. C. Hazlet 1895; in Poems of Alexander Hume, ed A. Lawson 1902 (STS). For doubts on the attribution of this poem *see* DNB.

JAMES MELVILLE, minister of Kilrenny
1556–1614

A morning vision: or poeme for the practise of piety, faith and repentance. Ptd with A spirituall propine, Edinburgh 1580.

The black bastel: or a lamentation in name of the Kirk of Scotland, composed by M. James Melvil, when he was confined at Berwick anno 1611; abridged by N. [i.e. D. Calderwood] 1634, Newcastle 1820; in Various pieces of fugitive Scottish poetry, ed D. Laing, Edinburgh 1823.

See also col 2451, below.

ALEXANDER MONTGOMERIE
1556?–1610?

§1

The cherrie and the slaye, composed into Scottis meeter. Edinburgh 1597 ('prented according to a copie corrected be the author himselfe'), 1615 (known only from reprint in Ramsay's Evergreen), 1636, 1675, 1680, 1682, 1691, Aberdeen 1645, Glasgow 1668, 1698, 1726, 1746, 1751, 1754, Belfast 1700, Kilmarnock 1782, Kirkcudbright 1842, Edinburgh 1885 (facs); ed H. H. Wood 1937.

The cherry and the sloe, corrected and modernised, by J. D. Edinburgh 1779, Aberdeen 1792, Kilmarnock 1817.

Cerasum et sylvestre prunum: opus poematicum, authore primo A. Montgomrio, nunc rursus auctum & in latinos versus translatum, per T.D.S.P.M.B.P.P. [i.e. Thomas Dempsterus, Scotus etc]. Ortenburgh 1631, Edinburgh 1696.

The mindes melodie: contayning certayne Psalmes of the kinglie prophete David, applyed to a new pleasant tune. Edinburgh 1605.

The flytting betwixt Montgomerie and Sir Patrick Hume of Polwart, newlie corrected and ammended. Edinburgh 1621, 1629, 1632, 1688, Glasgow 1665; rptd Watson 3 1711.

Poems. Ed J. Cranstoun 1887 (STS). Supplementary volume, ed G. Stevenson 1910 (STS).

A selection from his songs and poems. Ed H. M. Shire, 1960 (Saltire Soc).

§2

Hoffmann, O. Studien zu Montgomerie. Altenburg 1894.

Brotanek, R. Untersuchungen über das Leben und die Dichtungen Mongomeries. Vienna 1896.

Maclean, C. M. Alexander Scott, Montgomerie and Drummond of Hawthornden as lyric poets. 1915.

Ross, I. The form and matter of the Cherrie and the Slae. SE 37 1958.

Dilworth, M. New light on Montgomerie. Bibliotheck 4 1965.

—— The Latin translation of the Cherrie and the Slae. Stud in Scottish Lit 5 1968.

Shire, H. M. Montgomerie: the opposition of the Court to conscience. Stud in Scottish Lit 3 1966.

Jack, R. D. S. Montgomerie and the Pirates. Ibid.

PHILOTUS

Philotus: quhair in we may persave the greit inconveniences that fallis out in the mariage betweene age and youth. Edinburgh 1603, 1612; ed J. W. Mackenzie 1835 (Bannatyne Club); ed A. J. Mill, STS miscellany volume, 1933; rptd in Pinkerton 3 1792. An anon comedy, the plot taken from a tale in Barnaby Rich, Riche his farewell to militarie profession.

JOHN ROLLAND of Dalkeith
fl. 1575

Ane treatise Callit the court of Venus, devidit into four buikis, newlie compylit be Johne Rolland in Dalkeith. Edinburgh 1575; ed W. Gregor 1884 (STS).

The sevin seages translatit out of prois in Scottis meter be Johne Rolland in Dalkeith, with an moralitie efter everie doctouris tale and siclike efter the emprice tale. Edinburgh 1578, 1592-5, 1620, 1631; rptd Sibbald 3 1803; ed D. Laing 1837 (Bannatyne Club); ed G. F. Black 1932 (STS).

See G. Buchner, Die Historia septem sapientium, nebst einer Untersuching über die Quelle der Sevin seages des Johne Rolland, Erlangen 1889.

ALEXANDER SCOTT
1525?-84

Collections

Poems from a manuscript written in the year 1658 [Bannatyne ms]. Ed D. Laing, Edinburgh 1821.

Poems. Glasgow 1882.

Poems. Ed J. Cranstoun 1896 (STS).

Poems, edited from the Bannatyne ms and the Maitland ms. Ed A. K. Donald 1902 (EETS).

§1

Ramsay, A. The evergreen. 1724. 7 poems.

Dalrymple, D. (Lord Hailes). Ancient Scotish poems. 1770. 7 poems.

Sibbald 3. 15 poems.

A modernized version of some poems was pbd by W. Mackean, Paisley 1887.

§2

Maclean, C. M. In her Alexander Scott, Montgomerie and Drummond of Hawthornden as lyric poets, 1915.

ROBERT SEMPILL
fl. 1570

Heir followis an ballat declaring the nobill and gude inclination of our King. Edinburgh 1567; rptd in Satirical poems of the time of the Reformation, ed J. Cranstoun 1891 (STS). Broadside.

Heir followis the testament and tragedie of umquhile King Henrie Stewart of gude memorie. Edinburgh 1567; rptd in J. G. Dalyell, Scotish poems of the sixteenth century, Edinburgh 1801; rptd in Cranstoun vol 1, 1891. Broadside.

The complaynt of Scotland. [1567?]; rptd in Cranstoun, ibid. Broadside.

Heir followis ane exhortatioun to the lordis. Edinburgh 1567; rptd in Cranstoun, ibid. Broadside.

Ane exhortatioun derect to my Lord Regent and to the rest of the lordis accomplisis. 1567; rptd in Cranstoun, ibid. Broadside.

Ane declaration of the lordis iust quarrel. Edinburgh 1567; rptd in Dalyell, Scotish poems of the sixteenth century, Edinburgh 1801; rptd in Cranstoun, ibid. Broadside.

Ane ansuer maid to the sklanderaris that blasphemis the Regent and the rest of the lordis. [1567]; rptd in Cranstoun, ibid.

The Kingis complaynt. [1567]; rptd in Cranstoun, ibid. Broadside.

A rhime in defence of the Queen of Scots against the Earl of Murray xi° decembris 1568. In G. Chalmers, Life of Mary Queen of Scots vol 2, 1818; rptd in Cranstoun, ibid.

Followis the ballat maid upoun Margret Fleming, callit the Fleming bark in Edinburgh. [1568?]. In A. Ramsay, The evergreen, 1724; rptd in Sibbald vol 2, 1802; Cranstoun, ibid.

Heir followis the defence of Crissel Sandilandis ffor using hirself contrair the ten comandis: being in ward for playing of the loun with every ane geif hir half a croun etc. [1568?]. In A. Ramsay, The evergreen, 1724; rptd in Cranstoun, ibid.

Followis the ballat maid be Robert Semple of Jonet Reid, ane violet and ane quhyt: being slicht wemen of lyf and conversatioun, and tavernaris. [1568?]. In A. Ramsay, The evergreen, 1724; rptd in J. G. Dalyell, Scotish poems of the sixteenth century, 1801; Cranstoun, ibid.

Ane tragedie, in forme of ane diallog betwix honour, gude fame and the author heirof in a trance. Edinburgh 1570; rptd in J. G. Dalyell, Scotish poems of the sixteenth century, 1801; Cranstoun, ibid.

The deploratioun of the cruell murther of James Erle of Murray, umquhile Regent of Scotland; togidder with ane admonitioun to the Hammiltounis committaris thairof. Edinburgh 1570; rptd in Cranstoun, ibid. Broadside.

The Regentis tragedie ending with ane exhortatioun. Edinburgh 1570; rptd in Cranstoun, ibid. Broadside.

The exhortatioun to all plesand thingis quhairin man can haif delyte to withdraw plesure from mankynde, and to deploir the cruell murther of vmquhile my lord Regentis grace. Edinburgh 1570; rptd in Cranstoun, ibid. Broadside.

The cruikit liedis the blinde. Edinburgh 1570; rptd in Cranstoun, ibid. Broadside.

The poysonit schot. Edinburgh 1570; rptd in Cranstoun, ibid. Broadside.

The admonitioun to the lordis. Edinburgh 1570, Stirling 1570; rptd in Cranstoun, ibid. Broadside.

The tragicall end and death of the Lord James Regent of Scotland, lately set forth in Scottish. 1570. Broadside.

Maddeis lamentatioun. Edinburgh 1570; rptd in Cranstoun, ibid. Broadside.

Maddeis proclamatioun. [1570?]; rptd in Cranstoun, ibid. Broadside.

The spur to the lordis. 1570; rptd in Cranstoun, ibid. Broadside.

The bird in the cage. Edinburgh 1570; rptd in Cranstoun, ibid. Broadside.

The hailsome admonitioun etc. Edinburgh 1570; rptd in Cranstoun, ibid. Broadside.

The tressoun of Dunbartane. Edinburgh 1570; rptd Dumbarton 1860; rptd in Cranstoun, ibid. Broadside.

The exhortation to the lordis. Stirling 1571; rptd in Cranstoun, ibid. Broadside.

Ane exhortatioun to my lord Regentis grace. In Pinkerton, 1786; rptd in Poems of Sir Richard Maitland of Lethington, ed J. Pain 1830 (Maitland Club); in Cranstoun, ibid. The authorship is sometimes attributed to Sir John Maitland, Lord Thirlstane.

The Bischoppis lyfe and testament. Stirling 1571; rptd in Cranstoun, ibid. Broadside.

A lewd ballet. 1571; rptd in Cranstoun, ibid.

My lord Methwenis tragedie. St Andrews 1572; rptd in Cranstoun, ibid. Broadside.

Ane premonitioun to the barnis of Leith. St Andrews 1572; rptd in Cranstoun, ibid. Broadside.

The lamentatioun of the commounis of Scotland. St Andrews 1572; rptd in Cranstoun, ibid. Broadside.

The lamentatioun of Lady Scotland, compylit by hir self, speiking in maner of ane epistle, in the moneth of Marche, the 3eir of God 1572. St Andrews 1572; rptd in J. G. Dalyell, Scotish poems of the sixteenth century, Edinburgh 1801; Cranstoun, ibid.

Ane new ballet set out be ane fugitive Scottisman that fled out of Paris at this lait murther. St Andrews 1572; rptd in Ancient ballads and broadsides, published in England in the sixteenth century, 1867 (Philobiblon Soc); Cranstoun, ibid.

Ane complaint upon fortoun. Edinburgh [1581?]; rptd in Ancient ballads and broadsides, published in England in the sixteenth century, 1867 (Philobiblon Soc); Cranstoun, ibid.

Heir followis the legend of the Bischop of St Androis lyfe, callit Mr Patrik Adamsone, alias Cousteane. In J. G. Dalyell, Scotish poems of the sixteenth century, Edinburgh 1801; rptd Cranstoun, ibid.

The sege of the castel of Edinburgh. Edinburgh 1583, 1583, 1813 (facs); rptd in J. G. Dalyell, Scotish poems of the sixteenth century, Edinburgh 1801; Cranstoun, ibid.

The Sempill ballates: a series of historical, political and satirical Scotish poems ascribed to Robert Sempill 1567-83; to which are added poems by Sir James Semple of Beltrees 1598-1610, now for the first time printed. Edinburgh 1872.

SIR JAMES SEMPLE of Beltrees
1566-1625

Sacrilege sacredly handled, that is according to Scripture onely; for the use of all churches in generall, but more especially for those of North Britaine. 1619. Prose.

A pick-tooth for the Pope: or the pack-mans pater noster, set downe in a dialogue betwixt a pack-man and a priest, translated out of Dutch by S.I.S. and newly augmented by his son. Glasgow 1642, 1669, 1695, Edinburgh 1669, 1700; rptd in Poems of the Sempills of Beltrees, Edinburgh 1849; ed G. Eyre-Todd, Scottish poetry of the seventeenth century, Glasgow 1895.

For poems assigned to Semple see the Sempill ballates, *Edinburgh 1782.*

JOHN STEWART of Baldyneiss
c. 1540-c. 1600

§ 1

Poems. Ed T. Crockett 1913 (STS). Contains Ane abbregement of Roland furious translait out of Ariost, Rapsodies of the authors 3outhfull braine (66 sonnets), Ane schersing out of trew felicitie.

§ 2

Purves, J. The Abbregement of Roland furious. Italian Stud 3 1946.

McDiarmid, M. P. Notes on the poems of Stewart of Baldyneiss. RES 24 1948.

—— Stewart of Baldyneiss. Scottish Historical Rev 29 1950.

JOHN WEDDERBURN
1500?-56

The haill hundreth and fyftie Psalmes of David, in Inglis meter, be Thomas Sternholde; with utheris diveris poyetis, quhilk completis the haill Psalmes, as efter followis of the best interpretouris. Edinburgh 1567; ed A. F. Mitchell 1897 (STS) (as A compendious book of godly and spiritual songs, commonly known as the Gude and godlie ballatis). Bibliography.

Ane compendious buik of godlie psalmes and spirituall sangis, collectit furthe of sindrie partis of the Scripture, with diveris utheris ballatis changeit out of prophaine sangis in godlie sangis, for avoyding of sin and harlatrie; with augmentation of sindrie gude and godlie ballattis not contenit in the first editioun. Edinburgh [1567-8], 1578, 1600, [1621]; rptd J. G. Dalyell, Scotish poems of the sixteenth century, Edinburgh 1801; ed D. Laing, Edinburgh 1868.

A specimen of a book intituled Ane compendious booke of godly and spiritual sangs. Ed Sir David Dalrymple Lord Hailes, Edinburgh 1765.

The gude and godlie ballatis. Ed I. Ross 1940 (Saltire Soc). A selection from 1578 edn. Perhaps with his brothers John and Robert.

Mitchell, A. F. The Wedderburns and their work. Edinburgh 1867. *See also* C. E. Herford, Studies in the literary relations of England and Germany in the sixteenth century, Cambridge 1886; W. B. Warfield, Mitchell's Gude and godlie ballads, Presbyterian & Reformed Rev (New York) 10 1899.

(3) THE LATER POETS (1603-60)

HENRY ADAMSON
1581-1637

The Muses threnodie, or mirthfull mournings on the death of Master Gall: containing varietie of pleasant poeticall descriptions, morall instructions, historicall narrations and divine observations, with the most remarkable antiquities of Scotland, especially at Perth. Edinburgh 1638; ed J. Cant, Perth 1774; rptd in T. H. Marshall, The history of Perth, Perth 1849. The original edn etc contain another piece by Adamson, The inventarie of the gabions in M. George his cabinet.

JOHN ADAMSON
d. 1653

Τὰ τῶν Μουσῶν εἰσόδια: the Muses welcome to the most high and mighty Prince James by the grace of God King of Great Britaine etc at his M. happie returne to his old and native kingdome of Scotland, after xiiii years absence. Edinburgh 1618, 1618.

Τὰ τῶν Μουσῶν ἐξόδια: planctus, & vota Musarum in augustissimi monarchae Iacobi I, recessu e Scotia in Angliam, Augusti 4, anno 1617. Edinburgh 1618.

Musarum votum et vaticinium. Edinburgh 1620.

See also col 2453, below.

SIR WILLIAM ALEXANDER, EARL OF STIRLING
1567?-1640

See col 1080, above.

SIR ROBERT AYTON
1570-1638

See col 1297, above.

JOHN BARCLAY
1582–1621

See col 2300, above.

ALEXANDER CRAIG of Rosecraig
1567?–1627

The poeticall essayes of Alexander Craige, Scoto-Britane. 1604.
Amorose songes, sonets and elegies. 1606.
Poeticall recreations. Edinburgh 1609, Aberdeen 1623.
The pilgrime and the heremite. Aberdeen 1631.
Poetical works 1604–31, now first collected. Ed D. Laing 1873 (Hunterian Club).

WILLIAM DRUMMOND of Hawthornden
1585–1649

See col 1188, above.

ALEXANDER GARDYNE or GARDEN
1585?–1634?

A garden of grave and godlie flowres: sonets, elegies and epitaphs. Edinburgh 1609; ed J. W. K. Eyton 1845 (Abbotsford Club).
The lyf, doings and deathe of the right reverend and worthy prelat, William Elphinstone, be the divyne providence the 23 Bishop of Aberdene. Aberdeen 1619.
Characters and essayes. Aberdeen 1625.
A theatre of Scottish worthies. Aberdeen [1626?].
The theatre of the Scottish kings. Edinburgh 1709; ed J. W. K. Eyton 1845 (Abbotsford Club).
Poetical works. Ed D. Laing 1878 (Hunterian Club).

PATRICK GORDON
fl. 1614–50

Neptunus britannicus. 1614. On the death of Prince Henry etc.
The first booke of the famous historye of Penardo and Laissa, otherwayes callit the warres of love and ambition, doone in heroik verse. Dordrecht 1615.
The famous historie of the renouned and valiant Prince Robert, surnamed the Bruce, King of Scotland, in heroik verse. Dordrecht 1615, Edinburgh 1718, Glasgow 1753.
Gordon may be the author of A short abridgement of Britanes distemper, ed J. Dunn 1844 (Spalding Club).
See Scottish Historical Rev 1904.

SIMION GRAHAME
1579?–1614

The passionate sparke of a relenting minde. 1604; ed R. Jameson 1830 (Bannatyne Club).
The anatomie of humors. Edinburgh 1609; ed R. Jameson 1830 (Bannatyne Club).

PATRICK HANNAY

A happy husband: or directions for a maide to choose her mate; as also A wives behaviour towards her husband after marriage. 1619; ptd R. Braithwaite in Description of a good wife, 1619.
Two elegies on the late death of our soveraigne Queene Anne, with epitaphes. 1619, 1622.
Songs and sonnets. 1622.
Poetical works. Ed D. Laing, [Glasgow] 1875 (Hunterian Club).
See also col 1310, above.

ANNA HUME
fl. 1644

The triumphs of love, chastitie, death; translated out of Petrarch. Edinburgh 1644; rptd in The sonnets, triumphs and other poems of Petrarch, translated into English verse by various hands, 1859 (Bohn's Lib).

DAVID HUME of Godscroft
1560–1630

Daphn-Amaryllis. 1605.
Lusus poetici. 1605.
Regi suo, post bis septennium in patriam ex Anglia redeunti, Scotiae gratulatio. Edinburgh 1617; rptd in Jacobaea, below.
Poemata. Paris 1632, 1639.
Jacobaea. Paris 1639.
See also col 2468, below.

ARTHUR JOHNSTON
1587–1641

Bibliographies

Johnston, W. The bibliography and extant portraits of Arthur Johnston MD. Aberdeen 1895. Rptd from Scottish N & Q; rptd in Musa latina Aberdonensis 1 1892, below.

§1

Duellum pöeticum pro dignitate paraphraseos psalmi ciii. Edinburgh 1619, Paris 1619.
Onopordus furens. Paris 1620.
Querelae Saravictonis & Biomeae. 1620.
Nicrina ad heroas anglos. Heidelberg nd. According to the catalogue of the National Library of Scotland, the imprint is false and the volume was ptd in London by W. Stansby, whose ornament is on the title-page, before 1622.
In obitu Jacobi pacifici, Magnae Britanniae, Irlandiae et Franciae Regis elegia. 1625.
Elegiae duae: vna ad episcopum Abredonensem, de fratris obitu: altera de pace rupta inter Scotos & Gallos. Abcrdccn 1628.
Epigrammata. Aberdeen 1632.
Parerga. Aberdeen 1632.
Canticum Salomonis paraphraste Arturo Jonstone. 1633, Edinburgh 1709.
Musae querulae, de regis in Scotiam profectione: the Muses complaint of the Kings journey to Scotland. 1633. With verse trn by Sir Francis Kinaston.
Musae aulicae. 1635. With verse trn by Kynaston.
Paraphrasis poetica psalmorum Davidis; accesserunt ejusdem cantica evangelica, symbolum apostolorum, oratio dominica, decalogus. Aberdeen 1637, London 1657, 1741, 1742, 1740 (with verse trn), Amsterdam 1706; rptd with Canticum Salomonis in W. Lauder, Poetarum scotorum Musae sacrae, Edinburgh 1739.
Poemata omnia. Middelburgh 1642.
Epigrams upon the City of Aberdeen and Epigrams upon severall of the royall burghs in this kingdom; [both] englished by I.B. [John Barclay]. In ΦΙΛΟΠΟΛΙΤΕΙΟΥΣ [Barclay], Memorialls of the government of the royalburghs of Scotland, Aberdeen 1685; rptd in A. Skene, A succinct survey of the famous city of Aberdeen, Aberdeen 1833.
Musa latina Aberdonensis. Ed W. D. Geddes. Vol 1, Parerga; vol 2, Epigrammata, miscellanea, encomia urbium, 1892–5 (New Spalding Club).
See col 1910, above.

§2

Robb, T. D. Johnston in his poems. Scottish Historical Rev 10 1913.

JOHN KENNEDY
fl. 1620–30

The historie of Calanthrop and Lucilla. Edinburgh 1626, 1631.
A theological epitome or divine compend apparently manifesting Gods great love and mercie towards man. Edinburgh 1629.

GEORGE LAUDER
1600?–77?

The anatomie of the Romane clergie: or a discoverie of the abuses thereof, written in Latin by sundrie authors of their owne profession, and translated into English verse by G. L. 1623.
The souldiers wishe. Edinburgh 1628.
The Scottish souldier. Edinburgh 1629.
Wight. Edinburgh 1629; rptd in A. Boswell, Frondes caducae vol 5, Auchinleck 1818 (with The Scottish souldier).
Tears on the death of Evander, occasioned by the loss of Sir John Swynton. Hague 1630.
Aretophel: or a funeral elegy on the death of the Right Honourable Walter Earle of Buccleuch. Middelburgh 1634.
Caledonias covenant: or ane panegyrick to the world wherein is brieflie set doune the trew caus and occasioune of the present trubles of the Kingdome of Scotland. 1641; rptd in Scotish fugitive poetry of the seventeenth century, ed D. Laing, Edinburgh 1853.
Tweeds teares of joy to Charles, Great Brittains King. In Scotish fugitive poetry of the seventeenth century, ed D. Laing, Edinburgh 1853.
A horse: or a new-yeares-gift to Sir Philip Balfour. Middelburg 1646.
On the most horrid and terrible treason, the unparalelled parricide committed upon the sacred person of the most high and mighty Prince Charles etc. In Scotish fugitive poetry of the seventeenth century, ed D. Laing, Edinburgh 1853.
Damon: or a pastoral elegy, on the death of his honoured friend William Drummond of Hawthornden. In Works of William Drummond of Hawthornden, Edinburgh 1711; rptd in Poetical works of Drummond, ed L. E. Kastner 1913 (STS).
Lauder is also credited with Mars Belgicus: or the funeral elegy on Henry, Prince of Orange, Breda 1647, *and* Achilles Auriacus: or a funeral elegie on the death of William Prince of Orange, Breda 1650.

WILLIAM LITHGOW
1582–1645?

The pilgrims farewell to his native countrey of Scotland: wherein are contained in way of diallogue the joys and miseries of peregrination. Edinburgh 1618.
Scotlands teares, by William Lithgow, in his countreyes behalf. 1625; rptd in Perth Lib & Antiquarian Soc Trans 1 1827; in Various pieces of fugitive Scottish poetry, ed D. Laing, Edinburgh 1853; Perth 1881.
Scotlands welcome to her native sonne and soveraigne lord King Charles. Edinburgh 1633.
The gushing teares of godly sorrow: containing the causes, conditions and remedies of sin. Edinburgh 1640.
Poetical remains. Ed J. Maidment, Edinburgh 1863.

ANDREW MELVILLE
1546–1622

Στεφανίσκιον ad Scotiae regem, habitum in coronatione reginae. Edinburgh 1590; rptd in Papers relative to the Marriage of King James VI to Princess Anne of Denmark, 1828 (Bannatyne Club).
Principis Scoti-Britannorum natalia. Edinburgh 1594; Hague 1594.
Viri illustrissimi A. Melvini Musae et D. Adamsoni vita et palinodia. Edinburgh 1620. Adamson's Palinodia is in prose.
Poemata. In Delitiae poetarum scotorum, ed A. Johnston, Amsterdam 1637.

JAMES GRAHAM, 1st Marquis of
Montrose
1612–50

I'le never love thee more. nd. Broadside.
Seven poems. In Watson pt 3.
Montrose's poems. In Mark Napier, Montrose and the Covenanters vol 2, 1838.
Selected poems. Ed R. S. Rait 1901.
Poems. Ed J. L. Weir 1938.

SIR WILLIAM MURE of Rowallan
1594–1657

The Kings Majestie came to Hamilton on Monday the xviii July [1617]. In J. Adamson, The Muses welcome, Edinburgh 1618.
A spirituall hymne: or the sacrifice of a sinner to be offred upon the altar of a humbled heart to Christ our redeemer, inverted in English sapphicks from the Latine of that reverend, religious and learned divine, Mr Robert Boyd of Trochorege. Edinburgh 1628. Trn of Boyd, Hecatombe ad Christum servatorem, Edinburgh 1627; with A. Johnston, Delitiae poetarum scotorum, Amsterdam 1637; W. Lauder, Poetarum scotorum Musae sacrae, Edinburgh 1739; Works of Mure, 1898 (STS).
Doomesday containing hells horrour and heavens happinesse. Edinburgh 1628 (with A spirituall hymne).
The true crucifixe for true Catholickes. Edinburgh 1629.
The joy of teares or cordials of comfort, springing up in the region of sorrow. Ed C. Davies 1933 (STS). Anon.
A counter-buffe to Lysamachus Nicanor [John Corbet], calling himself a Jesuite, by Philopatris. 1640. Anon.
Reply to Corbet, Epistle congratulatorie to the Covenanters in Scotland, wherein is paralleled our sweet harmony and correspondency in divers materiall points of doctrine and practice, 1640.
Caledons complaint against infamous libells. [1641].
The cry of blood and of a broken covenant. Edinburgh 1650.
The historie and descent of the house of Rowallane. Glasgow 1825. Written in or shortly before 1657. Prose.
Works. Ed W. Tough 2 vols 1898 (STS). *See* col 1911, *above*.

SIR DAVID MURRAY of Gorthy
1567–1629

The tragicall death of Sophonisba. 1611.
Caelia. 1611 (with The tragicall death of Sophonisba).
A paraphrase of the CIV psalme. Edinburgh 1615.
The complaint of the shepheard Harpalus. [1625?]. Ballad.
Poems. Ed T. Kinnear, Edinburgh 1823 (Bannatyne Club).

ANDREW RAMSAY
1574–1659

Poemata sacra et miscellanea et epigrammata sacra. Edinburgh 1633; rptd in A. Johnston, Delitiae poetarum scotorum, Amsterdam 1637; W. Lauder, Delectus auctorum Miltono facem praelucentium vol 1, 1752.

(4) WRITERS IN LATIN

A considerable amount of Latin verse was written by Scottish scholars between 1500 and 1660; some has been noted above. See also L. Bradner, Musae anglicanae: a history of Anglo-Latin poetry 1500–1925, 1940, chs 5–6 and bibliography; Delitiae poetarum scotorum, ed A. Johnston, Amsterdam 1637, where the following authors are included: Patrick Adamson, Henry Anderson, Sir Robert Ayton, John Barclay, William Barclay, Mark Alexander Boyd, Robert Boyd, Sir Thomas Craig, George Crichton, Henry Danskin, Thomas Dempster, David Echlin, Peter Goldman, David Halkerston, David Hume, Arthur Johnston, John Johnston, David Kynloch, Andrew Melville, James Malcolm, Sir John Maitland, Thomas Maitland, Thomas Murray, Adam King, Thomas Reid, John Ross, Andrew Ramsay, Hercules Rollock, Alexander Ross, John Scot, Sir John Scot, Thomas Seggat, George Strachan, George Thomson, Florence Wilson, David Wedderburn; and Musa latina Aberdonensis vol 3, ed W. K. Leask 1910 (New Spalding Club), which contains the work of the following writers: William Aidie, William Barclay, William Blackhall, Robert Brown, Thomas Cargill, William Cargill, Thomas Dempster, Alexander Downy, Robert Downy, Patrick Dun, John Forbes, Alexander Garden, James Gordon, Robert Gordon, Patrick Jamieson, John Johnston, William Johnston, James Kennedy, John Kemp, John Ker, James Keythe, William Lauder, James Lawson, David Leech, John Leech, William Leslie, Andrew Massie, William Meston, Gilbert Middleton, John Ray, Thomas Reid, John Row, James Sandilands, George Strachan, John Vaus, David Wedderburn, William Wedderburn, Florence Wilson.

III. PROSE

(1) REFORMATION AND RENAISSANCE

The ch on the Anglican settlement and the Scottish Reformation by F. W. Maitland in vol 2 of the Cambridge Modern History (1903), is still the best short study, but the most coherent account on a substantial scale is W. L. Matheson, Politics and religion: a study of Scottish history from the Reformation to the Revolution, Glasgow 1902. Their bibliographies, together with those in P. Hume Brown, History of Scotland vols 1–2, Cambridge 1902–5, in W. C. Dickinson and G. Pryde, A new history of Scotland, 2 vols Edinburgh 1961–2, and in G. Donaldson, Scotland: James V–James VII, Edinburgh 1965, provide full information about the materials available.

ALEXANDER ALANE (ALESIUS)
1500–65

Epistola contra decretum quoddam episcoporum in Scotia, quod prohibet legere Novi testamenti libros lingua vernacula. 1533. No place or date on title-page, but at the end of the book the date MD.XXXIII is given. In C. H. and T. Cooper, Athenae cantabrigienses vol I, 1858, p. 239, Wittenberg is given as place of pbd: the same authors say that edns were ptd at Strasbourg in 1542 and 1543.

Of the auctorite of the Word of God against the Bishop of London. [Leipzig? 1537?]; tr Latin, 1542.

De restituendis scholis, oratio habita ab Alexandro Alesio in Academia Francofortiana ad Oderam. Frankfurt 1540, Leipzig 1541.

De auctore et utilitate psalmorum. 1542.

Ad Scotorum regem contra episcopos. Strasbourg 1542.

Cohortatio ad concordiam pietatis ac doctrinae Christianae defensionem. Leipzig 1544.

Pro Scotorum concordia. Leipzig 1544.

De argumento epistolae ad Romanos. Leipzig 1547.

In caput viii epistolae Pauli ad Romanos disputatio. Leipzig 1548.

Edinburgi regiae Scotorum urbis descriptio. In Sebastian Munster, Cosmographia, Basle 1550, 1572; rptd in Bannatyne Club miscellany vol 1, 1827; tr in G. Mackenzie, Lives and characters of the most eminent writers of the Scots nation vol 2, Edinburgh 1708; R. Chambers, Minor antiquities of Edinburgh, Edinburgh 1833, and P. Hume Brown, Scotland before 1700, Edinburgh 1893.

Epitome catechismi D. P. Melanchthonis cui addita est expositio symboli et Orationis Dominicae. 1550.

Responsio ad Cochlei calumnias. Leipzig 1551. An answer to Cochlaeus, An expediat laicis legere Novi testamenti libros lingua vernacula, 1533, which sought to refute Alesius's Epistola contra decretum episcoporum in Scotia, 1533, and which had been dedicated to James V.

Commentarius in evengelium Joannis. Basle 1553.

Responsio ad Iacobum V regem. Leipzig 1554.

The extant works of Alane number c. 30, and most deal with Biblical exegesis or theological and doctrinal controversy. Accounts of his life and lists of his writings will be found in C. H. and T. Cooper, above; in appendix I to The Scottish Reformation, ed A. F. Mitchell, Edinburgh 1900, and in DNB.

ANE DECLARATIOUN

Ane declaratioun of the just and necessar causis, moving us of the nobillitie of Scotland and uthers the Kingis Majesteis faithfull subjectis to repair to his Hienes presence, and to remane with him for resisting of the present daingers appearing to Goddis trew religioun and professouris thairof, and to his Hienes awin person estait & croun. Stirling 1582; ed J. Maidment, Edinburgh 1822.

ANE SCHORT CATHOLIK CONFESSION

Ane schort catholik confession of the heades of the religion now controuerted in Scotland answering against the heretical negative confession set furth be Johne Craig in his catechisme. In Catholic tractates of the time of the Reformation, ed T. G. Law 1901 (STS).

HENRY BALNAVES
1502–70

§ 1

The confession of faith: conteining how the troubled man shoulde seeke refuge at his God, thereto led by faith; with the declaration of the article of justification at length. Edinburgh 1548; rptd in Writings of Edward the Sixth, 1831.

§ 2

Rogers, C. In his Three Scottish reformers, 1874.

RICHARD BANNATYNE
d. 1635

Journal of the transactions in Scotland 1570–3. In J. G. Dalyell, Illustrations of Scottish history, Edinburgh 1806.
Memorials of transactions in Scotland AD MDLXIX–AD MXLXXIII. Ed E. R. Pitcairn 1836 (Bannatyne Club).
The last days of John Knox. Ed D. H. Fleming, Edinburgh 1913 (Knox Club).

JOHN BELLENDEN
c. 1500–c. 1548

§ I

Croniklis of Scotland with the cosmography and dyscription thairof, compilit by the noble clerk maister Hector Boece, chanoune of Aberdene, translatit laitly in our vulgar and common language be maister John Bellenden. Edinburgh [1540?]; ed T. Maitland, Edinburgh 1822. The Dyscription was ptd in an anglicized form in the first (1577) edn of Holinshed's Chronicles, and in every subsequent edn; see col 2130, above.
The first five books of the Roman history. Ed T. Maitland, Edinburgh 1822; ed W. A. Craigie 2 vols 1901 (STS).
The chronicles of Scotland of Hector Boece. Tr John Bellenden. Ed R. W. Chambers, E. C. Batho and H. W. Husbands 2 vols 1938–41 (STS). Vol 2 contains a life of Bellenden by E. A. Sheppard.

§ 2

Baumann, F. Livius, Bersuire und Bellenden: vergleichende Studien zu Bellendens Livius-Übersetzung. Leipzig 1905.
Chambers, R. W. and W. W. Seton. Bellenden's translation of the History of Hector Boece. Scottish Historical Rev 19 1922.

ROBERT BIRREL
fl. 1567–1605

The diarey of Robert Birrel: containing divers passages of staite and uthers memorable accidents, from the 1532 zeir of our redemptione till the beginning of the zeir 1605. In J. G. Dalzell, Fragments of Scotish history, Edinburgh 1798; Extracts, Edinburgh 1820.

ADAM BLACKWOOD
1539–1613

Adversus Georgii Buchanani dialogum de iure regni apud Scotos pro regibus apologia. Poitiers 1581, Paris 1588.
Martyre de la Royne d'Ecosse, douairiere de France, contenant le vray discours des traisons à elle faictes à la suscitation d'Elizabet angloise. Paris 1587 (with false imprint 'a Edimbourg'), 1588, 1589, 1590, Antwerp 1588, 1589; rptd in S. Jebb, De vita & rebus gestis Mariae Scotorum reginae, 1725. A piece entitled La mort de la Royne d'Ecosse douairiere de France, [Paris?] 1587, 1589, is sometimes attributed to Blackwood, but since it is not included in his Opera omnia it is almost certainly not his.
History of Mary Queen of Scots: a fragment translated from the original French of Adam Blackwood. 1834 (Maitland Club).

HECTOR BOECE or BOETHIUS
1465?–1536

§ I

Episcoporum Murthlacensium et Aberdonensium vitae. Paris 1522; rptd 1825 (Bannatyne Club); ed and tr J. Moir 1894 (New Spalding Club).
Scotorum historiae. Paris 1526, [1547?]. For Bellenden's trn, see above.
The book of the croniclis of Scotland: a metrical version of the History of Hector Boece by William Stewart. Ed W. B. Turnbull 3 vols 1858 (Rolls ser). Apparently undertaken by command of James V and completed c. 1535.
Mar Lodge Boece. Ed G. Watson 1946 (STS). Vol 1 only.

§ 2

Simpson, W. D. University of Aberdeen quatercentenary of the death of Hector Boece. Aberdeen 1937.

BOOK OF COMMON ORDER
Bibliographies

Cowan, W. Bibliography of the Book of common order of the Church of Scotland. Edinburgh Bibl Soc 1 1896.
— Bibliography of the Book of common order and Psalm book of the Church of Scotland. Edinburgh Bibl Soc 10 1913.

§ I

The form of prayers and ministrations of the Sacraments. Geneva 1556, 1561, [place?] 1561, 1584, Edinburgh 1562, 1564–5, 1568, 1575, [1578]; tr Latin, 1556; tr Gaelic, Edinburgh 1567.
The cl psalmes of David in meeter. 1587, Edinburgh 1594, 1595–6, 1599, 1603, 1611, 1614, 1615, 1617, [1620?], 1621–2, 1625, 1630, 1632, 1633, 1634, 1635, 1640, 1640–1, 1643, 1644, Middelburgh 1594, 1596, 1602, Dort 1601, Aberdeen 1625, 1626, 1629, 1632, 1633, 1634, 1638.

ROBERT BRUCE
1559–1631

§ I

Sermons upon the sacrament of the Lords Supper, preached in the Kirk of Edinburgh. Edinburgh [1590?]; anglicized as The mysterie of the Lords Supper, cleerely manifested in fiue sermons, 1614; ed J. Laidler, Edinburgh 1900; ed T. F. Torrance, Edinburgh 1958 (modernized, with 1614 title).
Sermons preached in the Kirk of Edinburgh, as they were received. Edinburgh 1591.
The way to true peace and rest, delivered at Edinborough in xvi sermons. 1614. Reprint of 1614, above with anglicized version of 1591.
Narrative concerning his troubles in the year M.DC. In Bannatyne Club miscellany vol 1, 1827.
Sermons by the Rev Robert Bruce. Ed W. Cunningham 1843 (Wodrow Soc).

§ 2

Macnicol, D. C. Master Robert Bruce, minister of the Kirk of Edinburgh. Edinburgh 1907.

GEORGE BUCHANAN
1506–82
Bibliographies

Murray, D. Catalogue of printed books, manuscripts, charters and other documents. In George Buchanan: Glasgow quatercentenary studies 1906, ed G. Neilson,

Glasgow 1907. An enlarged and rev form of the Catalogue prepared by Murray for the exhibition at Glasgow University Library in 1906 to mark the quatercentenary of Buchanan's birth. Both forms of the Catalogue are very fully annotated.

Anderson, J. M. The writings of Buchanan. In Buchanan: a memorial, ed D. A. Millar, St Andrews [1907].

Collections

Poemata omnia. Edinburgh 1615, 1659.

Poemata quae supersunt omnia. Leyden 1621, Edinburgh 1677, London 1686.

Poemata quae extant editio postrema. Leyden 1628, Amsterdam 1641, 1665, 1675, 1687, Edinburgh 1677.

Opera omnia, ad optimorum codicum fidem summo studio recognita et castigata curante Thoma Rudimanno. Edinburgh 1715.

Opera omnia cum indicibus memorabilium, et prefatione Petri Burmanni. Leyden 1725. A rev edn of Ruddiman, above.

Works of Buchanan in the Scottish language. Ed D. Webster, Edinburgh 1823.

Vernacular writings. Ed P. Hume Brown 1892 (STS).

§1

Rudimenta grammatices Thomae Linacri ex anglico sermone in latinum versa, interprete Georgio Buchanano. Paris 1533, 1536, 1537, 1540, 1545, 1546, 1550, 1556, Lyons 1539, 1541, 1544, 1548, 1552.

Medea Euripidis poetae tragici Georgio Buchanano Scoto interprete. Paris 1544.

Jephthes, sive votum: tragoedia; auctore Georgio Buchanano Scoto. Paris 1554, 1557, 1575, Orleans 1567, Glasgow 1775; tr French, 1573, 1587; Polish, 1587; Italian, 1600; German, 1604; tr English by W. Tait, Edinburgh 1750; C. C., Truro 1853; A. G. Mitchell, Paisley 1903.

Euripidis poetae tragici Alcestis Georgio Buchanano Scoto interprete. Paris 1556, 1557, Wittenberg 1581, Gotha 1776, Cambridge 1816, 1818, 1826, 1830, 1837, 1844.

De Caleto nuper ab Henrico II. Francorum rege invictiss, recepto Georgii Buchanani carmen. Paris 1558.

Psalmorum Davidis paraphrasis poetica, nunc primum edita, authore Georgio Buchanano, Scoto, poetarum nostri saeculi facilè principe. Paris [1564–5], 1566 etc, Strasbourg 1568. The Glasgow quatercentenary catalogue lists more than one hundred edns, the latest being pbd Milan 1833, as well as several selections and trns into various vernaculars. *See col 1902, above.*

Georgii Buchanani Scoti, franciscanus: varia eiusdem authoris poemata. [Paris?] 1566; tr French by F. Chrestien as Le cordelier: ou le saint François de George Buchanan, Geneva 1567, Sedan 1599.

Tragoediae selectae Aeschyli, Sophoclis, Euripidis cum duplici interpretatione. Paris 1567.

Georgii Buchanani Scoti, poetarum nostri saeculi facilè principis, Elegiarum liber I, Sylvarum liber I, Endecasyllabon lib. I. Paris 1567, 1579.

Opinion anent the Reformation of the Universities of St Androis. In D. Irving, Memoirs of the life and writings of Buchanan, Edinburgh 1817 (2nd edn); in Bannatyne miscellany vol 2, 1836; P. Hume Brown, Vernacular writings of Buchanan, 1892 (STS). Written c. 1567.

The chamaeleon: or the crafty statesman, describ'd in the character of Mr Maitland of Lethington, Secretary of Scotland. 1701, 1741, Glasgow 1818. From the original ms in the Cotton Library. The Cotton ms bears the date 1570. The print of 1701 took considerable liberties with the text; rptd 1741 (as Chamaeleon redivivus: or Nathaniel's character reversed).

Ane admonitioun direct to the trew Lordis, maintenaris of justice and obedience to the Kingis grace, M. G. B. Stirling 1571; rptd in Harleian miscellany vol 2, 1745; in Sir E. Brydges, Restituta vol 2, 1815; D. Irving, Memoirs of the life and writings of George Buchanan,

Edinburgh 1817 (2nd edn); in D. Calderwood, Historie of the Kirk of Scotland vol 2, 1843 (Wodrow Soc).

De Maria Scotorum regina, totaque ejus contra regem conjuratione, foedo cum Bothuelio adulterio, nefaria in maritum crudelitate et rabie, horrendo insuper et deterrimo ejusdem parracidio: plena et tragica plane historia. [London? 1571?]. Probably ptd by John Day in London before Nov 1571. The title was subsequently changed to Detectio Mariae reginae, 1725; tr French by P. Camuz, 'Edinburgh 1572'.

Ane detectioun of the duinges of Marie Quene of Scottes, touchand the murder of hir husband, and hir conspiracie, adulterie and pretensed mariage with the Erle Bothwell: and ane defence of the trew Lordis, mainteineris of the Kingis graces actioun and authoritie, translated out of the Latin. [London? 1571?]. Probably ptd by John Day at London in Nov 1571; it contains more than the original Latin and is now doubtfully regarded as having been made by Buchanan himself, 1571, St Andrews 1572, Edinburgh 1577, 1578, in Anderson's Collections relating to the History of Mary Queen of Scotland vol 1, Edinburgh 1727; tr French, 'Edinburgh' 1572, Antwerp 1578; 1651 (anglicized), 1689, 1721.

Baptistes: sive Calumnia, tragoedia, auctore Georgio Buchanano Scoto. 1578, Frankfurt 1578, 1579; tr French by R. Brisset, Tours 1589–90; tr P. de Brinon, Rouen 1613; tr Dutch, 1654; tr English by A. Gibb, Edinburgh 1870; by A. G. Mitchell, Paisley 1904; by A. Brown, Edinburgh 1906.

De jure regni apud Scotos: dialogus, authore Georgio Buchanano Scoto. Edinburgh 1579, 1580, 1581, Glasgow 1750; tr English by Philalethes 1680, 1689; by R. Macfarlan 1799, Edinburgh 1843; in The Presbyterian's armoury vol 3, Edinburgh 1846; tr Dutch, 1598, 1610; tr German, 1796, 1821.

Rerum scoticarum historia, auctore Georgio Buchanano Scoto. Edinburgh 1582, 1700, 1727, [Oberwesel] 1583, Frankfurt 1584, 1594, 1624, Amsterdam 1643, 1697, Utrecht 1668, Aberdeen 1762; tr 1690, 1722, 1733; by J. Watkins 1827, 1840; Edinburgh 1751, 1762, 1766, 1821, 1827–9, Glasgow 1799, 1827.

De sphaera. Herborn 1586, 1587. Begun about 1555 but never finished.

Georgii Buchanani Scoti Franciscanus et fratres: elegiarum liber I, Silvarum liber I, Hendecasyllabon liber I, Epigrammaton libri III, De sphaera fragmentum. [Geneva] 1594, 1597, Heidelberg 1609.

De prosodia libellus. Edinburgh 1595, 1621, 1660, 1689, 1694, 1699, 1708, Glasgow 1667, 1672.

Commentarius in vitam Georgii Buchanani, ab ipsomet scripta. Edinburgh 1702. Ptd in Bibliotheca calcographica illustrium virtute atque eruditione in tota Europa clarissimorum virorum, Frankfurt 1598. Written c. 1582 if of Buchanan's authorship, but this is now questioned.

Ad viros sui saeculi clarissimos eorumque ad eundem epistolae. 1711.

Medea et Alcestis, cum interpretatione latina Georgii Buchanani Scoti. In usum academicarum scoticarum, ed T. Ruddiman, Edinburgh 1722.

§2

[Love, John]. A vindication of Mr George Buchanan. Edinburgh 1749.

Irving, D. Memoirs of the life and writings of Buchanan. Edinburgh 1807, 1817 (rev).

Brown, P. H. Buchanan: humanist and reformer. Edinburgh 1890.

Henriquez, J. C. Buchanan in the Lisbon Inquisition: the records of his trial with a translation of some of the papers, and an introduction. Lisbon 1906.

Macmillan, D. Buchanan: a biography. Edinburgh 1906.

Buchanan: Glasgow quatercentenary studies 1906. Ed G. Neilson, Glasgow 1907.

Buchanan: a memorial 1506–1906. Ed D. A. Millar, St Andrews [1907]. By various hands.

Photographs of five documents connected with the imprisonment, trial, sentence and release of Buchanan by the Inquisition in Portugal, with descriptive letterpress by J. C. Guthrie. Edinburgh 1907.

Lebègue, R. Buchanan: son influence en France et en Portugal. Coimbra 1931.

Aitken, J. M. The trial of Buchanan before the Lisbon Inquisition. Edinburgh 1939.

Burns, J. H. Catholic critics of Buchanan. Innes Rev 1 1950.

Gatherer, W. A. The tyrannous reign of Mary Stewart. Edinburgh 1958. Trn, with editorial notes, of Buchanan's Rerum scoticarum historia bks 17–19.

Santos, D. M. G. Jorge Buchanan e o ambiente coimbrao de seculo xvi. Coimbra 1962.

Durkan, J. Buchanan: some French connections. Bibliotheck 4 1963.

MacNeill, D. The art and science of government among the Scots. Glasgow 1965.

Trevor-Roper, H. R. Buchanan and the ancient Scottish constitution. EHR suppl 3 1966.

NICOL BURNE
fl. 1580

The disputation concerning the controversit headdis of religion, halden in the realme of Scotland betwix the pretendit ministeris of the deformed Kirk of Scotland and Nicol Burne. Paris 1581; rptd in Catholic tractates of the time of the Reformation, ed T. G. Law 1901 (STS).

DAVID CHALMERS
1530–92

Discours de la legitime succession des femmes aux possessions de leurs parents et du gouvernement des femmes aux empires et royaumes. Paris 1579; rptd in S. Jebb, De vita et rebus gestis Mariae Scotorum reginae, 1725.

Histoire abrégée de tous les roys de France, Angleterre et Escosse, mise en ordre par forme d'armonie: contenant aussi en brief discours de l'ancienne alliance et mutuel secours entre la France et l'Escosse. Paris 1579.

La recherche des singularitez plus remarquables concernant l'estat d'Ecosse. Paris 1579.

WALTER CHEPMAN and
ANDREW MYLLAR

The Chepman and Myllar prints. Edinburgh 1508; ed D. Laing, Edinburgh 1827 (facs); ed G. Stevenson 1918 (STS); ed W. Beattie, Edinburgh 1950 (Edinburgh Bibl Soc) (facs).

WILLIAM CHISHOLM
d. 1629

Examen confessionis fidei Calvinianae quam Scotis omnibus Ministri Calviniani subscribendam et iurandum proponunt. Avignon 1601; tr French, 1603.

PATRICK COCKBURN
d. 1559

In dominicam orationem pia meditatio. St Andrews 1555.

JOHN COLVILLE
1542?–1605

The palinod of John Colvill, wherein he doth penitently recant his former proud offences, speciallie that treasonable discourse latelie made by him against the undoubted and undeniable title of his dread soveraigne lord King James the Sixt, unto the crowne of England, after decease of Her Majesty present. Edinburgh 1600, 1604 rptd in Original letters of Colville, ed D. Laing 1858 (Bannatyne Club).

Paraenesis Ioannis Colvilli Scoti (post quadraginta annorum errores in gremium sanctae catholicae Romanae ecclesiae quasi postliminio reuersi) ad suos tribulares & populares. Paris 1601.

The Paraenese or admonition of Io. Coluille (laitly returnit to the Catholique Roman religion, in vhilk he vas bapteisit and brocht up till he had full 14 years of age) unto his cuntrey men. Paris 1602; rptd in Original letters of Colville, ed D. Laing 1858 (Bannatyne Club). Trn of Paraenesis, above.

Oratio funebris exequiis Elizabethae nuper Angliae, Hiberniae, reginae destinata. Paris 1604.

Memoirs of the affairs of Scotland: containing a full and unpartial account of the revolution in that Kingdom begun in 1567. Ed D. Crawfurd 1706, Edinburgh 1753, 1767. A version of the Historie and life of King James the Sext, much expanded from other sources.

The historie and life of King James the Sext. Ed M. Laing 1804; ed T. Thomson 1825 (Bannatyne Club). The case for Colville's authorship was first set out by T. Thomson in Original letters of Colville, above.

Original letters 1582–1603, with a memoir of the author by David Laing. 1858 (Bannatyne Club).

COMPLAYNT OF SCOTLAND

The complaynt of Scotland, vyth ane exortatione to the three Estaitis, to be vigilante on the diffens of their public veil. Paris 1549; ed J. Leyden, Edinburgh 1801; ed J. A. H. Murray 1872 (EETS). See Critiques by D. Herd and others upon the new edition of the Complaint of Scotland, with observations in answer by the editor Dr J. Leyden, Edinburgh 1829. For the dependence of the author on Alain Chartier, see W. A. Neilson, JEGP 1 1897; for plagiarisms from St Gelais, W. A. Craigie, Modern Quart Lang & Lit 1 1898; for other literary influences, M. P. McDiarmid, The complaynt of Scotlande: Patrick Cockburn, Antonio de Guevara, Antonio de Fregoso, N & Q July–Aug 1959.

CRAFT OF DEYNG

Craft of Deyng, Wisdom of Solomon, The vertewis of the Mess. In Ratis raving, ed J. R. Lumby 1870 (EETS); rptd in Ratis raving, ed R. Girvan 1939 (STS).

JOHN CRAIG
1512?–1600

§ 1

A shorte summe of the whole catechisme. Edinburgh 1581, 1632, London 1583, 1584, 1589, 1597; ed T. G. Law, Edinburgh 1883. See H. Bonar, Catechisms of the Scottish Reformation, 1866.

Ane forme of examination before the Communion; approved by the General Assembly of the Kirk of Scotland and appointed to be used in families and schools. Edinburgh 1592, 1739, [London?] 1764. See also col 1903, above.

§ 2

Story, R. H. Dr John Craig. Edinburgh 1884.
[Walker, A.] John Craig. Aberdeen 1889.

JOHN DAVIDSON
1549?–1604

See col 2423, above.

DEVOTIONAL PIECES

Devotional pieces in verse and prose. Ed J. A. W. Bennett 1955 (STS).

DIURNAL OF REMARKABLE OCCURRENTS

A diurnal of remarkable occurrents that have passed within the country of Scotland since the death of King James the Fourth till the year M.D. LXXV, from a manuscript in the possession of Sir John Maxwell of Pollock, Baronet. Ed J. Thomson 1833 (Bannatyne & Maitland Clubs).

GEORGE EGLISHAM
1595?–1642

Duellum poeticum, contendentibus Georgio Eglisemmio, medico regio et Georgio Buchanano, regio praeceptore, pro dignitate paraphraseos Psalmi ciii. 1618; rptd in W. Lauder, Poetarum scotorum Musae sacrae vol 2, 1739. *See also col 2471, below.*

DAVID FERGUSSON
1523?–98

Ane answer to ane epistle written by R. Benedict, to Sir John Knox and the rest of his brethren ministers of the Word of God. Edinburgh 1563.
Ane sermon preichit befoir the Regent and nobilitie, in the Kirk of Leith, on Sonday the 13 of Januarie, anno do 1571. St Andrews 1572.
Tracts by David Fergusson, minister of Dunfermline. Ed J. Lee 1860 (Bannatyne Club). Reprints Ane answer and Ane sermon and Benedict's Epistola of 1561.
Scottish proverbs, gathered together by David Fergusson, sometime minister of Dunfermline, and put together ordine alphabetico when he departed this life. Edinburgh 1641, 1659, 1675, 1706, [London?] 1649, 1692, 1709, 1785, Glasgow 1667, 1716, 1799; ed E. Beveridge 1924 (STS).

WILLIAM FOWLER
1560–1612

See col 2423, above.

JOHN GAU or GALL
d. 1553

The richt vey to the kingdome of hevine. Malmo 1533; ed A. F. Mitchell 1888 (STS). Trn of a Danish tractate by Christiern Pedersen, Den rette vey till Himmeriges.

ARCHIBALD HAMILTON
d. 1593

De confusione Calvinianae sectae apud Scotos, ecclesiae nomen ridiculè usurpantis dialogus. Paris 1577. Answered by T. Smetoun.
Calvinianae confusionis demonstratio contra maledicam ministrorum Scotiae responsionem in duos divisa libros. Paris 1581. A rejoinder to T. Smetoun.

JOHN HAMILTON
Archbishop of St Andrews
1511?–71

The catechisme; that is to say, ane commone and Catholik instructioun of the Christin people in materis of our Catholik faith. St Andrews 1552, Edinburgh 1882 (facs); ed T. G. Law, Oxford 1884 (with preface by W. E. Gladstone).
Ane godlie exhortatioun made and sett forth be Johane, Archbishope of Sanctandrous. St Andrews 1559; rptd in Bannatyne miscellany vol 3, 1855; also with 1882 edn of the Catechisme, above. Known as the Twopenny Faith.

JOHN HAMILTON
d. 1610?

A facile traictise: contenand first ane infallible reul to discerne trew from fals religion; nixt, a declaration of the nature, number, vertew and effects of the sacraments; togider with certaine prayeres of devotion. Louvain 1590; rptd in Catholic tractates of the time of the Reformation, ed T. G. Law 1901 (STS).
Ane Catholik and facile traictise, drauin out of the halie scriptures to confirme the real and corporell praesence of Chrystis pretious bodie and blude in the sacrament of the alter. Paris 1581; rptd in Catholic tractates of the time of the Reformation, ed T. G. Law 1901 (STS).
Certane orthodox and Catholik conclusiones with thair probationes, quhilk Johne Hamelton proponis to the Calvinolatre ministeris in the deformit kirk in Scotland. Paris [1581?]; rptd in Catholic tractates of the time of the Reformation, ed T. G. Law 1901 (STS).

PATRICK HAMILTON
1504?–28

§ 1

A brief treatise of Mr Patrike Hamelton, called Patrikes places, translated into English by John Frith; with the epistle of the sayd Frith prefixed before the same. In J. Frith, A boke made by John Frith, prisoner in the Tower of London, Münster 1533; rptd in Foxe's Book of martyrs, 1563 etc; Knox's Historie of the Reformation in Scotland etc.
A brief history: containing an account of the life, martyrdom and articles of faith of the learned Mr Patrick Hamilton. Dundee 1792. The Articles of faith, i.e. Patrick's places, have been modernized.
Patrick's places: a treatise on the Law and the Gospel, written originally in Latin, by Patrick Hamilton, translated by John Frith. 1807; rptd in the Fathers of English Church vol 1, ed L. Richmond 1807; and in Writings of Edward the Sixth, 1831. No Latin original for Patrick's places has so far been found.

§ 2

Lawson, J. P. Life of Patrick Hamilton, Abbot of Ferme, the first Scottish martyr. Edinburgh 1828.
Lorimer, P. Patrick Hamilton. Edinburgh 1857.
Patrick Hamilton, first Scottish martyr of the Reformation: a composite biography by several authors. Ed A. Cameron, Edinburgh 1929.

GEORGE HAY
1530?–88

The confutation of the Abbote of Crosraguels masse. Edinburgh 1563.

GILBERT OF THE HAYE

Gilbert of the Haye's prose manuscript AD 1456. Ed J. H. Stevenson 2 vols 1901–14 (STS).

JOHN HAY
1546–1607

Certaine demandes concerning the Christian religion and discipline proposed to the ministers of the new pretended Kirk of Scotland. Paris 1580; rptd in Catholic tractates of the time of the Reformation, ed T. G. Law 1901 (STS); tr French, 1583, 1584, 1595; German, 1585.

JOHANNES DE IRLANDIA
1440–96?

§1

The meroure of wyssdome, composed for the use of James IV, King of Scots, AD 1490. Ed C. Macpherson and F. Quinn 2 vols 1926–65 (STS).

§2

Burns, J. H. John Ireland and the Meroure of wyssdome. Innes Rev 6 1955.

HISTORIE AND LIFE OF KING JAMES THE SEXT

The historie and life of King James the Sext: being the account of the affairs of Scotland from the year 1566, to the year 1596; with a short continuation to the year 1617. 1825 (Bannatyne Club). For another work with a similar title, see John Colville, above.

JOHN JONSONE
fl. 1535

An comfortable exhortation of oure mooste holy Christen faith and her frutes, written (unto the Christen bretherne in Scotland) after the poore worde of God. Antwerp 1535. The unique copy in BM lacks 7 of its 48 leaves.

QUINTIN KENNEDY, Abbot of Crossraguel
1520–64

Ane compendious tractive conforme to the scripturis of almychtie God, ressoun and authoritie: declaring the nerrest and the onlie way to establische the conscience of ane Christiane man. Edinburgh 1558.

Ane oratioune in favouris of all thais of the Congregatione, set furth be Master Quintine Kennedy. Edinburgh 1563; ed A. Boswall, Edinburgh 1812.

Heir followeth the coppie of the ressoning which was betuix the Abbote of Crosraguell and John Knox, in Mayboill, concerning the masse. Edinburgh 1563; ed A. Boswall, Edinburgh 1812.

Ane litil breif tracteit, prevand cleirlye the real body of Iesu Christ to be present in the sacrament of the altare. In Kuipers, below.

Campbell, D. The 'ressoning' betwixt John Knox and the Abbot of Crossraguell at Maybole, in 1562, concerning the Mass; with a preliminary essay and remarks on the controversy. Edinburgh 1851.

Kuipers, C. H. Kennedy: two eucharistic tracts. Nijmegen 1964. Prints Ane litil breif tracteitn and Ane compendius ressoning; includes the only reliable account of Kennedy's writings. Earlier accounts, based largely on the statements of Dempster and Mackenzie, are highly inaccurate. Ane compendius tractive, Ane oratioune and Heir followeth the coppie of the ressoning were all ptd by D. Laing in his edn of the Works of John Knox vol 6.

ADAM KING
fl. 1580–90

Ane catechisme of schort instruction of Christian religion drawen out of the scripturs and ancient doctours compyled be the godlie and lerned father Peter Canisius. Paris 1588; tr Welsh, 1611; rptd in Catholic tractates of the time of the Reformation, ed T. G. Law 1901 (STS).

In Iacobum sextum Scotorum regem, Angliae, Franciae et Hiberniae corona, iure hereditario donatum Panegyris. Edinburgh 1603. Verse.

JOHN KNOX
1513?–72

There is no bibliography of the writings by or about Knox, the nearest approach being in the BM catalogue, and it is fuller on the second category than on the first. Since writings about him are mainly interested in the man of action in his historical setting rather than as a writer, only a very brief selection is given here.

Collections

Select practical writings. Edinburgh 1845.

Works, collected and edited by D. Laing. 6 vols 1846–64; 1846 (Bannatyne Club) etc; 1846 (Wodrow Soc) etc. For criticism of this see J. Young, Review of Works of Knox, collected and edited by David Laing, Edinburgh 1864.

§1

A confession and declaration of praiers added thrunto by Jhon Knox, minister of Christes most sacred Evangely, upon the death of that moste verteous and most famous King Edward the VI Kynge of Englande. Rome (for London) 1554.

A faythfull admonition made by John Knox, unto the professours of Gods truthe in England. Zürich 1554.

An admonition or warning that the faithfull Christians in London, Newcastel Barwycke and others, may avoide Gods vengeaunce, both in thys life and in the life to come. Wittonburge (for Bremen?) 1554, 1558.

A godly letter sent to the fayethfull in London, Newcastell, Barwyke; and to all other within the realme of Englande, that love the cominge of oure Lorde Iesus. Rome (for London) 1554.

The copie of a letter sent to the ladye Mary dowagire, Regent of Scotland, by John Knox in the year 1556; there is also a notable sermon, made by the sayde John Knox, wherin is evidentlyr proved that the masse is and alwayes hath ben abhominable before God and idolatrye; scrutamini scripturas. [Geneva? 1556], Geneva 1558 (augmented).

The copie of an epistle sent unto the inhabitants of Newcastle and Barwike, in the ende whereof is added A brief exhortation to England for the spedie imbrasing of Christes gospel hertofore suppressed and banished. Geneva 1559, 1560.

The first blast of the trumpet against the monstruous regiment of women. [Geneva] 1558, [Edinburgh? 1687?]; ed E. Arber 1878.

The appellation of John Knoxe from the cruell and most injust sentence pronounced against him by the false bishoppes and clergie of Scotland. Geneva 1558.

An answer to a great nomber of blasphemous cavillations written by an Anabaptist, and adversarie to Gods eternal predestination and confuted by John Knox, minister of Gods Word in Scotland. [Geneva] 1560, London 1591.

Heir followis the coppie of the ressonong betuix the Abbote of Crosraguell [Quintin Kennedy] and J. Knox. Edinburgh 1563.

A sermon preached by Iohn Knox minister of Christ Iesus in the publique audience of the Church of Edenbrough, upon Sonday, the 19 of August 1565; for the which the said John Knox was inhibite from preaching for a season. 1566.

A sermon against the masse. [?].

To his loving brethren whome God ones gloriously gathered in the church of Edinburgh, and now ar dispersed for tryall of our faith. Stirling 1571.

An answer to a letter of a Iesuit named Tyrie. St Andrews 1572.

A brief discours off the troubles begonne at Franckford in Germany anno domini 1554 abowte the Booke of common praier and ceremonies. 1575.

A fort for the afflicted, in an exposition uppon the syxt psalme of David, wherein is declared hys crosse, complayntes and prayers. [London?] 1580.

Exposition upon the fourth of Matthew concerning the tentations of Christ. 1583.

A comfortable epistell sente to the afflicted church of Christ, exhorting them to beare his crosse with patience; wrytten by the man of God J. K. [?].

A most wholsome talke and communication betwixt the prentyse and the pryest touching the matter of auricular confession. [?].

A confutation of all such arguments as the Popes Catholykes doe bring for to prove the mutilate receavyng of the sacrament under one kynde. [?].

The historie of the reformatioun of religioun within the realme of Scotland. 1586 (imperfect); ed D. Buchanan 1644; Edinburgh 1644; ed M. Crawford, Edinburgh 1732, 1740, 1816; rev and ed C. Lennox 1905; ed R. S. Walker 1940 (Saltire Soc) (selections); ed W. C. Dickinson 2 vols 1949.

The liturgy of the Church of Scotland: or John Knox's Book of common order. Ed G. Cumming 1840; ed G. W. Sprott and T. Leishman, Edinburgh 1868.

Liturgy of the Church of Scotland since the Reformation. Ed S. A. Hurlburt, pt 2, Washington 1945.

§2

Smetoun, T. Ad virulentem A. Hamiltonii dialogum responsio; adjecta est vera historia extremae vitae et obitus J. Knoxii. Edinburgh 1579.

M'Crie, T. Life of Knox. Edinburgh 1817.

Lorimer, P. Knox and the Church of England. 1875.

Brown, P. H. Knox: a biography. 2 vols 1895.

M'Cunn, F. John Knox. 1895.

Fleming, J. H. Influence of Knox. Scottish Historical Rev 2 1905.

Innes, T. John Knox. Edinburgh 1905.

Lang, A. Knox and the Reformation. 1905.

—— Knox as historian. Scottish Historical Rev 2 1905.

Rait, R. S. John Knox. Fortnightly Rev 78 1905.

—— John Knox. Quart Rev 205 1906.

Hewat, K. In his Makers of the Scottish Church, Edinburgh 1920.

Muir, E. John Knox. 1929.

Percy, E. John Knox. 1937.

Watt, H. Knox in controversy. 1950.

Ridley, J. John Knox. 1968.

JOHN LESLIE, Bishop of Ross
1527–96

§1

A defence of the honour of the right high, mightye and noble Princesse Marie Quene of Scotland and Dowager of France, with a declaration aswell of her right, title and interest to the succession of the crowne of Englande, as that the regiment of women ys comformable to the lawe of God and nature. 1569.

A treatise concerning the defence of the honour of Marie Queene of Scotland; A treatise concerning the right of Marie of Scotland; A treatise that the regiment of women is conformable; made by Morgan Philippes, Bachelar of Divinitie [pseudonym]. 3 pts Liège 1571.

L'innocence de la tresillustre, tres-chaste et debonnaire princesse, Madame Marie Royne d'Ecosse. [Paris?] 1572.

Libri duo: quorum uno, piae afflicti animi consolationes, divinaque remedia; altero, animi tranquilli munimentum et conservatio continentur. Paris 1574.

Pro libertate impetrandi oratio ad serenissimam Elizabetham, Angliae regina. Paris 1574.

De origine, moribus et rebus gestis Scotorum: libri decem. Rome (for Amsterdam?) 1578, 1675.

De titulo et iure serenissimae principis Mariae Scotorum reginae, quo regni Angliae successorem sibi iustèvindicat, libellus. Rheims 1580; tr [Rheims] 1584; tr French, [1587]; Spanish, [1587]; rptd in S. Jebb, De vita et rebus gestis Mariae Scotorum reginae, 1725.

De illustrium foeminarum in republica administranda ac ferenda legibus auctoritate, libellus. Rheims 1580. Pt 2 of De titulo et iure, above.

Consolations divines et remèdes sovverains de l'esprit affligé, livre I. Et le rampart preservatif de l'esprit tranquille. Cologne 1583, Rouen 1590.

Harangue funèbre sur la mort de la Royne d'Escosse, traduite d'Escossois en françois par N. L. [Nicholas Loiseul]. [Paris? 1588?].

The history of Scotland from the death of King James I, in the year MCCCCXXXVI, to the year MDLXI, by John Lesley, Bishop of Ross. 1830 (Bannatyne Club).

The diary of John Lesly, Bishop of Ross, April 11–October 16 1571. In Bannatyne Club miscellany vol 3, 1855.

The historie of Scotland wrytten first in Latin by the most reverend and worthy Jhone Leslie Bishop of Rosse and translated by Father James Dalrymple. Ed E. G. Cody 2 vols 1888–95 (STS).

§2

The case of the Bishop of Ross, Resident of the Queen of Scots. In Somers tracts vol 1, ed Sir Walter Scott 1809.

Lockie, D. M. The political career of the Bishop of Ross. Univ of Birmingham Historical Jnl 4 1954.

DAVID LINDSAY, Bishop of Edinburgh
1575?–1641

De potestate principis aphorismi. Edinburgh 1617; tr Dutch, 1617.

A true narration of the proceedings in the General Assembly, holden at Perth, 25th Aug 1618; together with a just defence of the Articles therein concluded, against seditious pamphlets. 1621. Answered by D. Calderwood.

The reasons of a pastors resolution: touching the reverend receiving of the Holy Communion. 1619. Answered by D. Calderwood.

The heavenly chariot laid open. St Andrews 1622.

The godly mans chariot to heaven. 1625.

ROBERT LINDSAY of Pitscottie
1500?–65?

The history of Scotland; from 21 February 1436 to March 1565, in which are contained accounts of many remarkable passages altogether differing from our other historians, and many facts are related, either concealed by some or omitted by others, done from the most authentick and most correct manuscripts; to which is added a continuation, by another hand, till August 1604. Ed R. Fairbairn, Edinburgh 1728, 1778, Glasgow 1749; ed J. G. Dalyell 2 vols Edinburgh 1814.
The historie and croniclis of Scotland from the slaughter of King James the First to the ane thousande fyve hundreith thrie scoir fyftein eir, written and collected by Robert Lindesay of Pitscottie. Ed Æ. J. G. Mackay 3 vols 1899–1911 (STS).

JOHN MAJOR
1469–1450

Historia Majoris Britanniae. Paris 1521, Edinburgh 1740; tr A. Constable with a bibliography by T. G. Law, and a life of the author by Æ. J. G. Mackay 1892 (Scottish Historical Soc).

SIR JAMES MELVILLE of Halhill
1535–1617

The memoires of Sir James Melvil of Hal-hill: containing an impartial account of the most remarkable affairs of state during the last age, not mentioned by other historians; more particularly relating to the Kingdoms of England and Scotland, under the reigns of Queen Elizabeth, Mary Queen of Scots and King James; in all of which transactions the author was personally and publickly concern'd, now published from the original manuscript by George Scott Gent. 1583, Glasgow 1735, 1751, 1752; ed T. Thomson 1827 (Bannatyne Club) (from ms), 1922 (Abbey Classics); ed A. F. Steuart 1929; tr French, 1694, 1694, 1704, 1745.

JAMES MELVILLE, Minister of Kilrenny
1556–1614

Ane fruitful and comfortable exhortatioun anent death. Edinburgh 1597. Contains also The manner of the sicknesse and departure of Jean D'Albret Queen of Navarre, wherein every Christian may see and learne the practice of the former doctrine, that is the plaine and plesant passage, from this miserie to the life everlasting.
A spiritual propine of a pastour to his people. Edinburgh 1598.
Ad serenissimum Jacobum Primum Britanniarum Monarcham, ecclesiae scoticanae libellus supplex. 1645.
Diary 1556–1601. Ed T. Thomson 1829 (Bannatyne Club).
Autobiography and diary. Ed R. Pitcairn 1844 (Wodrow Soc).
The historie of the lyff of James Melvill. Ed J. G. Fyfe 1948 (Saltire Soc). Selections.

DAVID MOYSIE
fl. 1582–1603

Memoirs of the affairs of Scotland: containing an account of the most remarkable transactions in that Kingdom 1577–1603; together with a discourse of the conspiracy of the Earl of Gowrie. Edinburgh 1755; ed J. Dennistoun 1830 (Maitland & Bannatyne Clubs).

MURDOCH NISBET

The New testament in Scots c. 1520. Ed T. G. Law 3 vols 1901–5 (STS).

ROBERTUS RICHARDINUS or RICHARDSON
fl. 1530–43?

Exegesis in canonem divini Augustini. Paris 1530.
Commentary on the Rule of St Augustine. Ed G. G. Coulton 1935 (Scottish Historical Soc).

JOHN RUTHERFORD
1536?–77

Commentariorum de arte disserendi libri quatuor. Edinburgh 1577.

GILBERT SKENE
1522?–99

Ane breve descriptioun of the pest, quhairin the causis, signis and sum speciall preservatioun and cure thairof ar content. Edinburgh 1568. The earliest medical work ptd in Scotland.
Ane breif descriptioun of the qualiteis and effectis of the well of woman hill besyde Abirdene. Edinburgh 1580.
Both works rptd in Tracts by Gilbert Skene, ed W. P. Skene *1860 (Bannatyne Club)*.

THOMAS SMETOUN
1536–83

Ad virulentum Archibaldi Hamiltonii apostatae dialogum, de confusione Calvinianae sectae apud Scotos; adjecta est vera historia extremae vitae & obitus eximii ciri Ioan Knoxii ecclesiae scoticanae instauratoris fidelissimi. Edinburgh 1579.

SPECTAKLE OF LUF

The spectakle of luf, translated from the Latin by G. Myll [July 1492]. Ed D. Laing, Bannatyne Club miscellany vol 2, 1836.

GEORGE THOMSON
fl. 1594–1612

De antiquitate christiane e religionis apud Scotos. Douai 1594, Rome 1594; ed and tr H. D. G. Law. In Scottish Historical Society miscellany vol 2, 1904.
Ouverture de tous les secrets de l'apocalypse ou revelation de S. Iean, en deux traités, par Iean Napeir (c'est a dire Nonpareil) sieur de Merchiston, revue par lui mesme et mit en Francois par George Thomson Escossois. La Rochelle 1602, 1605, 1607.
Ἀνακεφαλαίωσις: sive de reductione regnorum Britanniae ad unum principem, poema. 1604.
Vindex veritatis: adversus Iustum Lipsium libri duo. Alkmaar 1606, 1606.
Le chasse de la beste Romaine. La Rochelle 1611, Geneva 1612.
La desroute de la chasse du loup cervier: ou réfutation du traicté du jeune, fait par René Le Courvaisier contre quelques passages par lui attaqués en la chasse de la beste romaine. La Rochelle 1612.

JAMES TYRIE
1543-97

§1

The refutation of ane answer made by schir Johne Knox to ane letter, send be James Tyrie, to his umquhyle brother, sett furth be James Tyrie. Paris 1573; rptd in Catholic tractates of the time of the Reformation, ed T. G. Law 1901 (STS).

§2

Law, T. G. Note on some writings attributed to Father James Tyrie SJ 1594-5. 1899 (Edinburgh Bibl Soc).

NINIAN WINZET
1518-92

Certane tractatis for reformatioun of doctryne and maneris, set furth at the desyre, and in the name of the afflictit Catholikis, of inferiour ordour of clergie, and layit men in Scotland be Ninian Winzet, ane Catholike preist born in Renfrew. Edinburgh 1562.
The last blast of the trompet of Godis worde aganis the usurpit auctoritie of Johne Knox and his Calviniane brether intrudit precheouris etc, put furth to the congregatioun of the Protestantis in Scotlande. Edinburgh 1652. Imperfect.
The buke of four scoir thre questions proponit to the precheouris of the Protestants in Scotland. Antwerp 1563, London 1580.
Vincentius Lirinensis, of the natioun of Gallis, for the antiquitie and veritie of the Catholik fayth, aganis the prophane novationis of al haereseis, neulie translatit into Scottis be Ninian Winzet a Catholik preist. Antwerp 1563.
Flagellum sectariorum, qui religionis praetextu seditiones iam in Caesarem, aut in alios orthodoxos principes excitare student; accessit Velitatio in Georgium Buchananum. Ingolstadt 1582.
Certane tractatis for reformation of doctryne and maneris in Scotland, MDLXII-MDLXIII. 1835 (Maitland Club). Includes also The last blast of the trumpet, The buke of four scoir three questions, Vincentius Lirinensis.
Certain tractates together with the book of four score three questions and a translation of Vincentius Lirinensis. Ed J. K. Hewison 2 vols 1888-90 (STS). First 2 of these pieces rptd in Bishop R. Keith, History of the affairs of Church and State in Scotland vol 1, Edinburgh 1735; 1850 (Spottiswoode Soc).

(2) THEOLOGY AND RELIGIOUS CONTROVERSY (1603-60)

THOMAS ABERNETHIE

Abjuration of Poperie, by Thomas Abernethie: sometime Jesuite, but now a penitent sinner and an unworthy member of the true reformed Church of God in Scotland. Edinburgh 1638.

JOHN ADAMSON
d. 1653

The travellers joy: or a sermon on the third verse of the second chapter of Solomons Song. 1623.
Στοιχείωσις eloquiorum Dei: sive methodus religionis christianiae catechetica. Edinburgh 1627, 1637.
Dioptra gloriae divinae: seu enarratio psalmi xix, et in eundem meditationes. Edinburgh 1637.

PATRICK ANDERSON SJ
1575-1624

The ground of the Catholike and Roman religion in the Word of God with the antiquity and continuance therof throughout all kingdomes and ages, collected out of divers conferences, discourses and disputes which M. Patricke Anderson had at severall tymes with sundry bishops and ministers of Scotland, at his last imprisonment in Edinburgh, for the Catholike faith. St Omer 1623.

ALEXANDER BAILLIE
1591?-1637

A true information of the unhallowed offspring, progresse and impoisoned fruits of our Scottish-Calvinian gospel and gospellers. Würzburg 1628.

ROBERT BAILLIE
1599-1662

Ladensium ΑΥΤΟΚΑΤΑΚΡΙΣΙΣ, the Canterburians self-conviction: or an evident demonstration of the avowed Arminianisme, Poperie and tyrannie of that faction, by their own fonfessions; with a post-script to the personate Jueuite Lysimachus Nicanor [John Corbet]. 1640, 1641. Anon. Answered in A brief examination of a certain pamphlet lately printed in Scotland and intituled Ladensium autocatacrisis, 1641?
A large supplement of the Canterburians self-conviction, opening to the world yet more of the wicked mysteries of that faction from their own writs. [London?] 1641. Anon.
A parallel or briefe comparison of the liturgie with the massebook, the breviarie, the ceremoniall and other Romish ritualls. 1641, 1661.
The antidote against Arminianisme. 1641.
Prelacie is misery: or the suppressing of prelaticall goverment and establishing of provintiall and nationall sinods, is a hopeful meanes to make a flourishing Church and a happie kingdom. [London?] 1641. Anon.
The unlawfulness and danger of limited prelacie: or perpetual precidencie in the Church brieflie discovered. [London?] 1641. Anon.
The life of William now lord Arch-bishop of Canterbury examined: wherein his principall actions or deviations in matters of doctrine and discipline (since he came to that sea of Canterbury) are traced and set down. 1643.
Satan the leader in chief to all who resist the preparation of Sion. 1643.
A dissuasive from the errours of the time, vindicated from the exceptions of Mr Cotton and Mr Tombes. 1645, 1646, 1655. Answered by John Cotton in The way of congregational churches cleared, 1648.
A review of the seditious pamphlet lately published in Holland by Dr Brambell, pretended Bishop of London-derry, entitled His faire warning against the Scots discipline. Delft 1645, Hague 1661; tr Dutch, 1651.
Errours and induration are the great sins and the great judgements of the time. 1645.
An historicall vindication of the Church of Scotland from the manifest base calumnies which the most malignant of the prelats did invent of old, and now lately have been published with great industry in two pamphlets at London [J. Maxwell, Issachars burthen; P. Adamson, Declaration made by King James in Scotland concerning church-government and presbyterie]. 1646.
Anabaptisme the true fountain of Independency, Brownisme, Antinomy, Familisme etc: or a second part of the dissuasive from the errours of the time. 1646.

Anabaptisme unsealed. 1647.
Catachesis elenctica errorum qui hodie vexant ecclesiam, in gratiam studiosae juventutis Academiae Glasguensis. 1654.

WALTER BALCANQUHAL
1586–1645

A large declaration concerning the late tumults in Scotland, from their first originalls. 1639.

WILLIAM BARCLAY
1570?–1630?

Iudicium de certamine G. Eglisemmi cum G. Buchanano, pro dignitate paraphraseos psalmi ciii. 1620.

ROBERT BARON
1593–1639

Philosophia theologiae ancillans. St Andrews 1621, Oxford 1641, 1658, Amsterdam 1649.
Disputatio theologica, de formali objecto fidei. Aberdeen 1627.
Ad Georgii Turnebulli tetragonismum pseudographicum apodixis catholica: sive apologie pro disputatione de formali objecto fidei. Aberdeen 1631.
Disputatio theologica de vero discrimine peccati mortalis et venialis. Aberdeen 1638, Amsterdam [1649], Oxford 1658.
Metaphysica generalis opus postumum. Leyden 1657, Oxford 1658, [1669?], Cambridge 1685.
See Studies in the history and development of the University of Aberdeen, ed P. J. Anderson 1906; D. Macmillan, Aberdeen doctors, 1909; W. E. McCulloch, Viri illustres Universitatum Aberdonensium, 1923.

HUGH BINNING
1627–53

A treatise of Christian love on John XIII, 35. Glasgow 1651 (lost), 1743.
The common principles of the Christian religion clearly proved and singularly improven. Glasgow 1659, 1660, 1663, 1666, 1667, 1728, Edinburgh 1671; tr Welsh, 1838.
The sinners sanctuary, in xl sermons, upon the eighth chapter of Romans, from the first verse to the sixteenth. Edinburgh 1670.
Heart-humiliation. Glasgow 1667, 1725, Edinburgh 1671.
Fellowship with God: or xxviii sermons on the 1 epistle of John chap 1 and 2. Edinburgh 1671, London [1833].
A usefull case of conscience learnedly and accurately discussed and resolved. [Edinburgh?] 1693, Kilmarnock 1783.
A treatise of Christian love. Edinburgh 1743.
Works. Edinburgh 1735 (with Life), Glasgow 1768 (with Life); ed J. Cochrane 3 vols Edinburgh 1839–40; ed M. Leishman, Edinburgh 1847.

ROBERT BOYD
1578–1627

Hecatombe christiana, hymnus ἑκατόνστροφος ad Christum servatorem. Edinburgh 1627, 1825; rptd in W. Lauder, Poetarum scotorum Musae sacrae vol 1, 1739; tr Sir W. Mure, Edinburgh 1628 (as A spirituall hymne).
In epistolam Pauli Apostili ad Ephesios praelectiones. 1652.

ZACHARY BOYD
1585?–1653

The last battell of the soule in death, carefullie digested for the comfort of the sicke. 2 vols Edinburgh 1629; ed G. Neil, Glasgow 1831.
The balme of Gileade prepared for the sicke. Edinburgh 1629.
Two orientall pearles, grace and glory. Edinburgh 1629, 1718.
A cordiall of comforts for a wearied soule. Edinburgh 1629.
Two sermons, for those who are to come to the Table of the Lord. Edinburgh 1629.
Rex pater patriae instar pelicani liberos suos fovere debet, ad Carolum regem oratio panegyrica. Edinburgh 1633.
A cleare form of catechising. Glasgow 1639.
Four letters of comforts for the deaths of the Earle of Haddingtoun, and of the Lord Boyd. Glasgow 1640; ed J. Small, Edinburgh 1878.
1, Crosses; 2, Comforts; 3, Counsels needfull to bee considered, and carefully to be laid up in the hearts of the godly, in these boysterous broiles and bloody times. Glasgow 1643.
The battell of Newburne, where the Scots armie obtained a notable victorie against the English Papists, Prelats, and Arminians, the 28 day of August 1640. Glasgow 1643; rptd in Fugitive Scotish poetry ser 2, ed D. Laing, Edinburgh 1853.
The garden of Zion: wherein the life and death of godly and wicked men in scriptures are to be seene. 2 vols Glasgow 1644. Verse.
The psalmes of David in meeter. Glasgow 1646 (3rd edn). *See col 1912, above.*
Spiritual songs: or holy poems. Edinburgh 1686.
Four poems from Zion's Flowers: or Christian poems for spiritual edification. Ed G. Neil, Glasgow 1855.

DAVID CALDERWOOD
1575?–1650

Protestation and treatise from Scotland. [place?] 1608.
De regimine ecclesiae scoticanae brevis relatio. [Leyden] 1618. Anon.
A solution of Dr Resolutus [David Lindsay] his resolution for kneeling. [place?] 1619. Anon.
Perth Assembly: containing 1, The proceedings thereof; 2, The proofe of the nullitie thereof etc. [Leyden] 1619. Anon.
A defence of our argument against kneeling in the act of receiving the Sacramentall bread and wine impugned by Mr Michelsone. [place?] 1620. Anon.
Parasynagma Perthense et Iuramentum ecclesiae Scoticanae. [St Andrews?] 1620. Anon.
The speach of the Kirk of Scotland to her beloved children. [Leyden] 1620. Anon.
A dialogue betwixt Cosmophilus and Theophilus anent the urging of new ceremonies upon the Kirk of Scotland. [place?] 1620. Anon.
The altar of Damascus: or the patern of the English heirarchie and church policie obtruded upon the Church of Scotland. [place?] 1621. Anon.
Quaeres concerning the state of the Church of Scotland. [place?] 1621, 1638. Anon.
The first and second booke of discipline, together with some Acts of the Generall Assemblies, clearing and confirming the same. [place?] 1621. Anon.
The course of conformitie. [place?] 1622. Anon.
Scoti τοῦ τυχόντος paraclesis contra D. Tileni Silesii paraenesin ad Scotos Genevensis disciplinae zelotas conscriptam. [Amsterdam?] 1622. Anon.
Calderwoods recantation: or a tripartite discourse, directed to such of the minstrie and others in Scotland, that refuse

conformitie to the Ordinances of the Church. 1622. A fabrication by Patrick Scot.

Reply to Dr Mortons general defence of three nocent ceremonies. [place?] 1622. Anon.

A reply to Dr Mortons particular defence of three nocent ceremonies. [place?] 1623. Anon.

Altare Damascenus: seu ecclesiae anglicanae politia, ecclesiae scoticanae obtrusa. Leyden 1623, 1708.

An exhortation of the particular kirks of Christ in Scotland to their sister kirk in England. [place?] 1624. Anon.

An epistle of a Christian brother exhorting another to keepe himselfe undefiled from the present corruptions brought in to the ministration of the Lords Supper. [place?] 1624. Anon.

A dispute upon communicating at our confused communions. [place?] 1624. Anon.

The pastor and the prelate: or reformation and conformitie shortly compared. [place?] 1628, Edinburgh 1692; rptd in The Presbyterian armoury vol 3, Edinburgh 1843. Anon.

A re-examination of the five articles enacted at Perth anno 1618. [place?] 1636. Anon.

The re-examination of two of the articles abridged: to wit, of the communicants gesture in the act of receiving, eating and drinking; and the observation of festivall dayes. [place?] 1636. Anon.

An answer to Mr J. Forbes of Corse, his peacable warning. [place?] 1638. Anon.

The true history of the Church of Scotland from the beginning of the Reformation, unto the end of the reigne of King James VI. 1678, 1680.

The history of the Kirk of Scotland. Ed T. Thomson 8 vols 1842–9 (Wodrow Soc).

JOHN CAMERON
1579?–1625

§1

Traité auquel sont examinez les préjugés de ceux de l'église romaine contre la religion réformée. La Rochelle 1616, 1618; tr Oxford 1626.

§2

Maury, G. B. Cameron: a Scottish Protestant theologian in France. Scottish Historical Rev 7 1910.

ANDREW CANT
1596–1664

The evil and danger of prelacy: a sermon preached at a general meeting in the Gray-fryars-Church of Edinburgh upon the 13th day of June 1638. Edinburgh 1649, 1720, Rotterdam 1682; rptd in A collection of several remarkable and valuable sermons, speeches and exhortations, Glasgow 1741 (with Glasgow sermon of 1638).

A sermon preached after the renovation of the National Covenant and celebration of the Lord's Supper at Glasgow, anno 1638. Edinburgh 1727, Glasgow [1730?].

The protestation of diverse ministers against the proceedings of the late Commission of the Church of Scotland; as also against the lawfulnesse of the present pretended Assembly. Leith 1651.

DAVID CHALMERS
d. 1650?

De Scotorum fortitudine, doctrina et pietate ac de ortu et progressu haeresis in regnis Scotiae et Angliae: libri quattuor. Paris 1631.

JOHN CORBET
1603–41

The ungirding of the Scottish armour: or an answer to the informations for defensive arms against the Kings Majestie drawn up at Edinburgh. Dublin 1639.

The epistle congratulatorie of Lysimachus Nicanor of the society of Jesu, to Covenanters in Scotland. 1640, Oxford 1684.

DAVID DICKSON
1583–1663

True Christian love, to be sung with any of the common tunes of the Psalms. Edinburgh 1634, 1655, 1718, 1751, 1754, Glasgow 1700, 1772.

A short explanation of the Epistle of Paul to the Hebrews. Aberdeen 1635, Dublin 1637, Cambridge 1649.

Expositio analytica amnium apostolicarum epistolarum. Glasgow 1645, 1647; tr W. Petchworth 1659.

A brief exposition of the evangel of Jesus Christ according to Matthew. Glasgow 1647, 1651 (3rd edn).

A brief explication of the Psalms. 3 pts 1653–5.

Therapeutica sacra: seu de curandis casibus conscientiae circa regenerationem per foederum divinorum prudentem applicationem libri tres. 1656, 1664, 1695, 1697; tr Dickson, Edinburgh 1695 (2nd edn), 1697.

An exposition of all St Paul's epistles. Edinburgh 1659.

The true comfort of a Christian: or food for a distressed soul. Edinburgh 1718.

Truth's victory over error, with life by R. Wodrow. Glasgow 1684, 1725, 1772, Kilmarnock 1787.

Select practical writings. Edinburgh 1845.

WILLIAM DOUGLAS
fl. 1619–50

Vindiciae veritatis: seu dissertatio theologica. Aberdeen 1655.

Academiarum vindiciae, in quibus novantium praejudicia contra academias etiam reformatas averruncantur, eorundemque institutio recta proponitur. Aberdeen 1659.

The stable trueths of the kirk require a sutable behaviour, holden forth by way of a sermon. Aberdeen 1660.

JAMES DURHAM
1622–58

Bibliographies

Christie, G. A bibliography of Durham. Edinburgh Bibl Soc 11 1921.

§1

A commentarie upon the book of the Revelation. Edinburgh 1658, 1680, London 1658, Amsterdam 1660, Glasgow 1680, 1739, 1764, 1788, Falkirk 1799.

The dying man's testament to the Church of Scotland: or a treatise concerning scandal. Edinburgh 1659, 1680, [1690?], London 1659, Glasgow 1740.

Clavis cantici: or an exposition of the Song of Solomon. Edinburgh 1668, 1723, 1724, London 1669, Utrecht 1681, Glasgow 1688, 1723, c. 1770, 1788, Peterhead 1840.

The law unsealed: or a practical exposition of the x commandments. 1675, Edinburgh 1676, 1703, 1715, 1735, 1782, 1802, Glasgow 1676, 1677, 1777, 1798, 1802.

The blessednesse of the death of these that die in the Lord, and more especially in ane evil time, excellently discoursed in seven very searching, but very sweet, sermons. [Glasgow] 1681, [Edinburgh?] 1682, Edinburgh 1684, 1713, Glasgow 1751, 1754, 1756.

Christ crucified: or the marrow of the gospel evidently holden forth in lxxii sermons on the whole 53 chapter of Isaiah. Edinburgh 1683, 1686, 1702, 1726, London 1723, Glasgow 1761, 1769, 1792.

The unsearchable riches of Christ, and of grace and glory, in fourteen sermons. Glasgow 1685, 1695, 1709, 1764, 1773, Edinburgh 1696, 1704, 1729, 1745, Falkirk 1786, Berwick 1794.

Heaven upon earth, brought down and holden forth in XXII very searching sermons. Edinburgh 1685, 1732.

The great gain of contenting godliness, commended in four sermons. Edinburgh 1685, 1777.

The great corruption of subtile self; discovered, and driven from its lurking holes, in seven sermons. Edinburgh 1686, Glasgow 1723.

JAMES FERGUSSON
1621–67

A brief exposition of the epistles of Paul to the Philippians and Colossians. Edinburgh 1656.

A brief exposition of the epistles of Paul to the Galatians and Ephesians. Edinburgh 1659.

A brief exposition of the epistles of Paul to the Thessalonians. 1674, Glasgow 1675.

A brief refutation of the errors of tolleration, Erastianism, independency and separation, delivered in some sermons preached from 1 Joh 4.1. Edinburgh 1692.

A brief exposition of the epistles of Paul to the Galatians, Ephesians, Philippians, Colossians and Thessalonians, reprinted from the original editions 1656–75. [1841].

A brief refutation of the doctrine of Erastianism, with prefatory note by R. S. Candlish. Cupar 1843.

JOHN FORBES
1593–1648

§1

Disputationes theologicae. Edinburgh 1620.

Irenicum amatoribus veritatis et pacis in ecclesia scoticana. Aberdeen 1629, 1636.

Gemitus ecclesiae scoticanae: sive tractatus de sacrilegio. Aberdeen 1631.

Theologiae moralis libri octavi. Aberdeen 1632.

A peaceable warning to the subjects in Scotland. Aberdeen 1638.

Instructiones historico-theologicae. Amsterdam 1645.

Opera omnia. 2 vols Amsterdam 1702–3.

Certaine records touching the estate of the Kirk in the years MDCV and MDCVI. Ed D. Laing 1846 (Wodrow Soc).

§2

Henderson, G. D. Forbes of Corse in exile. Aberdeen Univ Rev Nov 1928.

PATRICK FORBES
1564–1635

§1

An exquisite commentarie upon the Revelation of Saint John. 1613, Middelburgh 1614 (rev as A learned commentarie upon the Revelation of St John).

A defence of the lawful calling of the ministers of the reformed churches. Middelburg 1614.

A short discovery of their divers deceits. Middelburgh 1614.

Letter to a Romish recusant. Middelburgh 1614.

Eubulus: or a dialogue, wherein a rugged Romish ryme (inscrybed Catholicke questions to the Protestant) is confuted, and the questions thereof answered. Aberdeen 1627, 1638.

Funerals of a right reverend father in God, Patrick Forbes of Corse, Bishop of Aberdene. Aberdeen 1635; ed C. F. Shand 1845 (Spottiswoode Soc).

§2

Snow, W. G. S. The times, life and thought of Forbes, Bishop of Aberdeen 1618–35. 1952.

WILLIAM FORBES
1585–1634

Considerationes moderatae et pacificae controversarium de iustificatione, purgatorio, invocatione sanctorum, Christo mediatore et eucharistia. 1658, Frankfurt 1707; ed G. H. Forbes 2 vols Oxford 1850–6.

GEORGE GILLESPIE
1613–48

A dispute against the English-Popish ceremonies, obtruded upon the Church of Scotland. 1637, 1660, 1844. Anon.

Reasons for which the Service Book, urged upon Scotland, ought to be refused. Edinburgh 1638.

An assertion of the government of the Church of Scotland. Edinburgh 1641.

Certaine brief observations and antiquaeries: on Master Prin his twelve questions about church-government. 1644.

Wholsome severity reconciled with Christian liberty: or the true resolution of a present controversie concerning liberty of conscience. 1645. Anon.

Nihil respondes: or a discovery of the extream unsatisfactorinesse of Master Colemans peece. 1645, Edinburgh 1844.

Male audis: or an answer to Mr Coleman on his Male dicis. 1646, Edinburgh 1844.

Aarons rod blossoming: or the divine ordinance of church government vindicated. 1646.

cxl propositions concerning the ministrie. Edinburgh 1647, 1648, 1844.

A form for church government and ordination. 1647.

The humble representation of the Commission 28 Aprile 1648. Edinburgh 1648, London 1648.

An usefull case of conscience discussed and resolved: concerning associations and confederacies with idolaters, infidels, hereticks, or any other known enemies of truth and godlinesse. Edinburgh 1649, London 1649, Paisley 1791.

A treatise of miscellany questions: wherein many usefull questions and cases of conscience are discussed and resolved. Edinburgh 1649, 1844.

Causes of the Lords wrath. [place?] 1653.

The scriptural mode of administering and receiving the Lord's Supper, as laid down in a treatise of miscellany questions, printed in 1649. Newcastle 1816.

Works, now first collected, with memoir of his life and writings, by W. M. Hetherington. 2 vols Edinburgh 1843–6.

Notes of debates and proceedings of the Assembly of Divines and other Commissioners at Westminster. Ed D. Meek, Edinburgh 1846.

ANDREW GRAY
1633–56

The mystery of faith opened up. Glasgow 1659, 1668, 1740, 1749, London 1660, Edinburgh 1669, 1671, 1678, 1697, 1715.

Great and precious promises. Edinburgh 1663, 1671, 1676, 1697, 1715, Glasgow 1669, 1686, 1740, 1750.

Directions and instigations to the duty of prayer. Glasgow 1669, 1740, 1751, 1764, Edinburgh 1671, 1679, 1680, 1698, 1715.

The spiritual warfare: or some sermons concerning the nature of mortification. Edinburgh 1672, 1673, London 1693, 1697, Glasgow 1740, Aberdeen 1832.

The great satisfaction offered and tendered, in two sermons on Heb 2. 3. 1694.

Eleven communion sermons. Edinburgh 1718, Glasgow 1754.

The breathing of a soul after the enjoyment of God. Glasgow 1780.

The great importance of a suitable preparation for death: a sermon. Glasgow 1789.

Whole works. Glasgow 1762, Paisley 1769.

WILLIAM GUILD
1586–1657

A young mans inquisition or triall. 1608.

The new sacrifice of Christian incense: or the true entrie to the tree of life and gratious gate of glorious Paradise. 1608.

Levi his complaint: or the moane of the poore ministrie. Edinburgh 1617.

Moses unvailed: or those figures which served unto the patterne and shaddow of heavenly things, pointing out the Messiah Christ Jesus, briefly explained. 1619, 1623, 1658, Edinburgh 1684.

Issachars asse braying under a double burden: or the uniting of churches. Aberdeen 1622.

Three rare monuments of antiquitie: or Bertram, priest, a Frenchman, Of the bodie and blood of Chrust (written 800 yeares agoe), Aelfricus, Archbishop of Canterburie, an Englishman, his sermon of the sacrament (preached 627 years agoe), all stronglie convincing that grosse errour of transubstantiation; translated and compacted by William Guild. Aberdeen 1624.

Ignis fatuus: or the elf-fire of purgatorie. Aberdeen 1625.

Popish glorying in antiquitie turned to their shame. Aberdeen 1626, 1627.

A compend of the controversies of religion, wherein trueth is confirmed and errour convinced, by authoritie of Scripture. Aberdeen 1627.

Limbo's batterie: or an answere to a popish pamphlet of Christs descence to Hell. Aberdeen 1630.

The humble addresse both of church and poore, to the sacred Majestie of Great Britaines monarch, for a just redress of the uniting of churches, and the ruine of hospitalls. 3 pts Aberdeen 1633, London 1641. Anon.

A short treatise against the prophanation of the Lords day. Aberdeen 1637.

Trueth triumphant: or the late conversion of Francis Cupif, translated by William Guild DD. [place?] 1637.

An antidote against poperie: fit (God willing) to preserve and arme euerie one agaynst the seduction thereof. Aberdeen 1639.

To the nobilitie: a friendly and faythfull advice. Aberdeen 1639.

The old Roman Catholik, as at first he was taught by Paul; in opposition to the new Roman Catholik, as of latter he is taught by the Pope. Aberdeen 1649.

Isagoge catechetica. Aberdeen 1649.

Anti-Christ pointed and painted out in his true colours: or the Pope of Rome proved to bee that man of sinne foreprophesied in scripture. Aberdeen 1655.

The noveltie of popery. Aberdeen 1656.

The sealed book opened: or a cleer explication of the prophecies of Revelation. 1656.

An answer to a popish pamphlet, called the touch-stone of the reformed gospell. Aberdeen 1656.

Loves entercours between the Lamb and his Bride: or a clear exposition of the Song of Solomon. 1658.

The throne of David: or an exposition of the second of Samuell wherein is set downe the pattern of a pious and prudent prince, and a clear type of the Prince of Princes Christ Jesus. Oxford 1659.

See J. Shirrefs, An enquiry into the life, writings and character of Guild, Aberdeen 1799 (2nd edn).

JAMES GUTHRIE
1612–61

§1

The nullity of the pretended Assembly at Saint Andrews and Dundee. [Leith] 1652. Anon.

A treatise of ruling elders and deacons, in which these things which belong to the understanding of their office and duty are clearly and shortly set down. Edinburgh 1652, 1690, 1699. Anon.

A humble acknowledgement of the sins of the ministry of Scotland. [Edinburgh] 1653. Anon.

Protesters no subverters, and Presbyterie no Papacie. Edinburgh 1658. Answered anon in A review and examination of a pamphlet lately published bearing the title of Protesters no subverrters, and Presbyterie no Papacy, Edinburgh 1659.

Some considerations contributing unto the discoverie of the dangers that threaten religion and the work of the Reformation in the Church of Scotland. Edinburgh 1660.

The true and perfect speech of Mr James Guthrey late minister of Sterling as it was delivered by himself immediately before his execution on June 1 1661 at Edinbrough. [London] 1661.

A cry from the dead, or the ghost of the famous Mr James Guthrie appearing: being the last sermon he preached in the pulpit of Stirling, before his martyrdom at Edinburgh June 1661; to which is added his last speech upon the scaffold: his ten considerations anent the decay of religion. Glasgow 1738, 1795, Stirling 1824.

The great danger of backsliding and defection from covenanted Reformation-principles; to which is added his speech in vindication of the above principles delivered before the Parliament of Scotland. Edinburgh 1739.

The last speech and dying testimony of that bloom of the Church the Reverend Mr James Guthrie. Edinburgh 1783.

Lives of Alexander Henderson and James Guthrie, with specimens of their writings. Edinburgh 1846.

§2

Thomson, D. P. Guthrie: the Covenanting minister of Lauder and Stirling. Galashiels 1946.

ALEXANDER HENDERSON
1583?–1646

§1

The remonstrance of the nobility, barones, burgesses, ministers and commons, within the kingdome of Scotland: vindicating them and their proceedings from the crymes, wherewith they are charged by the late proclamation in England, Feb 27 1639. Edinburgh 1639; tr Dutch, 1639. Anon.

The unlawfulness and danger of limited prelacie, or perpetuall precidencie, briefly discovered. [place?] 1641; tr French in P. Grebner, Prédiction, Rouen 1650. Anon.

The government and order of the Church of Scotland. Edinburgh 1641, 1690.

Two speeches delivered before the subscribing of the Covenant, the 25 of September, the one by Mr Philip Nye; the other by Mr Alexander Henderson. Edinburgh 1643.

Reformation of Church government in Scotland, cleared from some mistakes and prejudices. Edinburgh 1644.

The papers which passed at Newcastle betwixt his sacred Majestie and Mr A. L. Henderson, concerning the change of church-government anno 1646. 1649.

Sermons, prayers and pulpit addresses. Ed R. T. Martin, Edinburgh 1867.

§2

Aiton, J. The life and times of Henderson. Edinburgh 1836.

M'Crie, T. Life of Henderson. Edinburgh 1845.

Lives of Henderson and James Guthrie, with specimens of their writings. Edinburgh 1846.

Thomson, J. P. Henderson the Covenanter. Edinburgh 1912.

Orr, R. L. Henderson: churchman and statesman. 1919.

Loane, M. L. In his Makers of religious freedom in the seventeenth century, 1960 (with bibliography).

PETER HEWAT
1567?-1645

The excellent points of Christian doctrine. Edinburgh 1621.

ARCHIBALD JOHNSTON, LORD WARRISTON
1611-63

Causes of the Lords wrath against Scotland, manifested in his sad late dispensation. 1651, 1653, 1732, Edinburgh 1844. Anon. Long attributed to James Guthrie.

WILLIAM LESLIE
d. 1654?

Vindiciae theologicae pro perseverantia sanctorum in gratia salvifica. Aberdeen 1627.

JOHN MAXWELL
1590?-1647

Episcopacy not abjured in his Majesties realm of Scotland. 1641, 1643.

An answer by letter to a gentleman who desired of a divine some reasons by which it might appear how inconsistent presbyteriall government is with monarchie. Oxford 1644, Bristol 1644.

Sacro-sancta regum majestas: or the sacred and royall prerogative of Christian kings. Oxford 1644, 1680, 1686. Answered by Samuel Rutherford in Lex, Rex.

The burthen of Issacher: or the tyrannicall power and practises of the presbyteriall government in Scotland. 1646, 1703 (as Presbytery displayed: or the holy discipline of the kirk declared), 1708 (as The burden of Issacher).

JOHN MICHAELSON
1570?-1640?

The lawfulness of kneeling in the act of receiving the sacrament of the Lords Supper. St Andrews 1620.

NATIONAL COVENANT

The confession of faith subscribed at first by the Kings Majestie and his houshold, in the year of God 1580; therafter, by persons of all rankes, in the yeare 1581; subscribed againe by all sorts of persons in the yeare 1590, and now subscribed in the yeare 1638 by us, noblemen, barrons, gentlemen, burgesses, ministers and commons. Edinburgh 1638.

General demands concerning the late Covenant, propounded by the ministers and professors of divinitie in Aberdene. Edinburgh 1638.

General demands concerning the late Covenant, propounded by the ministers and professors of divinitie in Aberdene. Aberdeen 1662.

ANDREW RAMSAY
1574-1659

A warning to come out of Babylon, in a sermon at the receiving of Mr Thomas Abernethie, sometime Jesuite, into the society of the truely reformed Church of Scotland. Edinburgh 1638.

ALEXANDER ROSS
1591-1654

See col 1317, above.

SAMUEL RUTHERFORD
1600-61

Bibliographies

Bisset, J. The bibliography of Rutherford. Glasgow Bibl Soc Records 6 1920.

§1

Christ and the doves heavenly salutation, with their conference together: or a sermon before the communion in Anwoth, anno 1630. [1630?], [Edinburgh?] 1729.

Christ's napkin: or a sermon preached in Kirkcudbright at the communion, May 12 1633. [place?] [1633?], Edinburgh 1734, Glasgow 1739, 1779, [1784?], 1798.

Exercitationes apologeticae adversus Jacobum Arminianum ejusque asseclas. Amsterdam 1636.

A peaceable and temperate plea for Pauls presbyterie in Scotland. 1642.

Lex, Rex, the law and the prince: a dispute for the just prerogative of King and people. 1644, 1682, Edinburgh 1644, Glasgow 1843. Written chiefly as a reply to Maxwell's Sacro-sancta regum majestas, Oxford 1644.

The due right of presbyteries. 1644.

Sermon before the House of Commons 1644. Edinburgh 1709, Cheltenham nd.

Sermon before the House of Lords 1645. Edinburgh 1709.

The tryal and triumph of faith. 1645, 1652, Edinburgh 1727, 1845, 1854, Glasgow 1743, 1827.

The divine right of church government and excommunication. 1646.

Christ dying and drawing sinners to himself. 1647, Edinburgh 1724, Glasgow 1803.

A survey of the spirituall Antichrist. 1648.

Disputatio scholastica de divina providentia. Edinburgh 1649, 1650, 1657.

A free disputation against pretended liberty of conscience. 1649, 1651.

The covenant of life opened: or a treatise of the covenant of grace. Edinburgh 1655.

A survey of the survey of that summe of church discipline preached by Mr Thomas Hooker. 1658.

Influences of the life of grace. 1659.

Joshua redivivus: or Mr Rutherfoords letters, now published for the use of all the people of God. 1664, Rotterdam 1664; ed A. A. Bonar 2 vols Edinburgh 1863.

Examen Arminianismi. Utrecht 1668.

The power and prevalence of faith and prayer. [place?] 1713.

Exhortations at a communion in Loddon. Edinburgh 1721, 1742, 1746, 1751, Falkirk 1742.

The cruel watchman. Glasgow 1738, London 1830.

A testimony to the work of reformation. [place?] 1738, 1784.

The Lamb's marriage. Glasgow 1776, Falkirk nd.

A collection of valuable sermons. Glasgow 1802; rptd with addns by A. A. Bonar, Glasgow 1876, 1877.

Quaint sermons. Ed A. A. Bonar 1885.

Ane catechisme: conteining the soume of the Christian religion. In A. F. Mitchell, Catechism of the Second Reformation, 1886.

Religious letters written to eminent individuals during the persecution in Scotland. Aberdeen nd.

Letters of Samuel Rutherford, with a sketch of his life and biographical notices of his correspondents. Ed A. A. Bonar, Edinburgh 1891, London 1894.

Selected letters. Ed H. Martin. 1957.

§ 2

Murray, T. Life of Samuel Rutherford. Edinburgh 1828.

Loane, M. L. In his Makers of religious freedom in the seventeenth century, 1960 (with bibliography).

ARCHIBALD SIMSON or SYMSON
1564?-1628

Christes testament unfolded: or seaven godlie and learned sermons on our Lords seaven last words, spoken on the crosse. Edinburgh 1620.

Heptameron, the seven dayes: that is, meditations and prayers upon the worke of the Lords creation. St Andrews 1621.

Samsons seaven lockes of haire: allegorically expounded and compared to the seaven spirituall vertues. St Andrews 1621.

Hieroglyphica animalium terrestrium, quae in scripturis sacris inveniuntur. 4 pts Edinburgh 1622-4.

A sacred septenarie: or a godly and fruitfull exposition on the seven psalmes of repentance. 1623, 1638.

ANDREW STRACHAN

Panegyricus inauguralis universitatis Aberdonensis. Aberdeen 1631.

Vindiciae cultus divini. Aberdeen 1634.

WILLIAM STRUTHER
1578?-1633

Scotlands warning, or a treatise of fasting: containing a declaration of the causes of the solemne fast, indyted to bee kept in all the churches of Scotland, the third and fourth Sundayes of this instant moneth of May anno 1628 and the weeke dayes betwixt them. Edinburgh 1628.

Christian observations and resolutions: I, centurie, with a resolution for death, written under the sentence of death, in the time of a painfull disease. Edinburgh 1628, London 1629; Christian observances and resolutions: II, centurie, Edinburgh 1629.

A looking glasse for princes and people, delivered in a sermon of thanksgiving for the birth of the hopeful Prince Charles, and since augmented with allegations and historicall remarks; together with a vindication of princes from popish tyranny. Edinburgh 1632.

A looking glasse for princes and popes: or a vindication of the sacred authoritie of princes, from the antichristian usurpation of the Popes. Edinburgh 1632.

Letter to the Earle of Airth, in Grievances given in by the ministers before the Parliament holden in June 1633. [Edinburgh] 1635. Written 28 Jan 1633.

True happines: or King Davids choice, begunne in a sermon and now digested into a treatise. Edinburgh 1633.

(3) HISTORIANS AND ANTIQUARIANS (1603-60)

ROBERT BAILLIE
1599-1662

Operis historici et chronologici libri duo, in quibus historia sacra & profana compendiose deducitur ex ipsis fontibus, à creatione mundi ad Constantium Magnum. Amsterdam 1663, 1668.

Letters and Journals: containing an important account of public transactions, civil, ecclesiastical and military in England and Scotland, from the beginning of the Civil Wars, in 1637 to the year 1662. 2 vols Edinburgh 1775.

Letters and journals. Ed D. Laing 3 vols 1841-2 (Bannatyne Club).

SIR WILLIAM BAILLIE of Lamington
fl. 1648

Vindication for his own part of Kilsyth and Preston. 1841-2 (Bannatyne Club).

WILLIAM BARCLAY
1546-1608

§ I

De regno et regali potestate adversus Buchananum, Brutum, Boucherium & reliquos Monarchomachos: libri sex. Paris 1600.

De rebus creditis et de jurejurando. Paris 1605.

De potestate papae: an & quatenus in reges & principes seculares ius & imperium habeat. Paris 1609, Pont-à-Mousson 1609, 1610, Frankfurt 1609, Hanau 1612, 1617, Amsterdam 1709; tr French, 1611; Cologne 1687; tr English, 1611. Answered by R. Bellarmine, Tractatus de potestate summi pontificis in rebus temporalibus, adversus Gulielmum Barclaium, Cologne 1611.

§ 2

Smith, D. B. William Barclay. Scottish Historical Rev 11-12 1914-15.

ROBERT BLAIR
1593-1666

See col 2248, above.

DAVID CALDERWOOD
1575?-1650

See col 2456, above.

GEORGE CON

De duplici statu religionis apud Scotos libri duo. Rome 1628.

Vita Mariae Stuartae Scotiae reginae, dotariae Galliae, Angliae & Hibernicae haeredis. Rome 1624; rptd in S. Jebb, De vita et rebus gestis Mariae Scotorum reginae, 1725.

SIR THOMAS CRAIG
1538–1608

§1

Epithalamium, quo Henrici Darleii et Mariae Scotorum reginae nuptias celebravit. Edinburgh 1565, 1821; rptd with English trn in F. Wrangham, Epithalamia tria Mariana, Chester 1837. Verse.
Ius feudale libris tribus comprehensum. Edinburgh 1655, 1732, 1934, London 1665, Leipzig 1716.
Scotlands soveraignty asserted: being a dispute concerning homage, against those who maintain that Scotland is a feu or fee-liege of England, and that therefore the King of Scotland owes homage to the King of England. 1695, Edinburgh 1698.
The right of succession to the Kingdom of England, in two books, against the sophisms of Parsons the Jesuite, who assumed the counterfeit name of Doleman; written originally in Latin above 100 years since, and now faithfully translated from the Latin [by G. Ridpath]. 1703.
De Unione regnorum Britanniae tractatus. Ed and tr C. S. Terry 1909 (Scottish Historical Soc).

§2

Tytler, P. F. An account of the life and writings of Craig of Riccarton. Edinburgh 1823.
Smith, D. B. Craig, feudalist. Scottish Historical Rev 12 1915.

THOMAS CRAUFURD
d. 1662

History of the University of Edinburgh from 1580 to 1646. Edinburgh 1808.
Notes and observations on Mr George Buchanan's History of Scotland. Edinburgh 1708.

JAMES GORDON
1615?–86

History of Scots affairs from 1637 to 1641. Ed J. Robertson and G. Grub 3 vols 1841 (Spalding Club).
Abredoniae utriusque descriptio. Ed C. Innes 1842 (Spalding Club). An inaccurate trn of the Latin ms of c. 1647 in National Library of Scotland, Edinburgh.

T. H.

The beautie of the remarkable yeare of grace 1638, the yeare of the Great Covenant of Scotland. Edinburgh 1638.

A. HOUSTON

L'Escosse françoise: discours des alliances commencées depuis l'an sept cents septante sept, & continuées iusques à present, entre les couronnes de France & d'Escosse. Paris 1608; rptd in Papers relative to the Royal Guard of Scottish Archers in France, 1835 (Maitland Club).

DAVID HUME of Godscroft
1560–1630

§1

Illustrissimi principis Henrici justa. 1613.
Apologia basilica: seu Machiavelli ingenium, examinatum in libro quem inscripsit Principem. Paris 1626.
The origine and descent of the most noble and illustrious familie and name of Douglas. [place?] c. 1633.
De unione insulae britannicae. [1604?], Paris 1639.
The history of the houses of Douglas and Angus, wherein are discovered the most memorable passages of the kingdom of Scotland from the year 767, to the reign of our late soveraign lord King James the Sixth. Edinburgh 1644, London 1648.
A generall history of Scotland, from the year 767, to the death of King James: containing the principal revolutions and trans-actions of Church and State; with politicall observations and reflections upon the same. 1657, 1820, Edinburgh 2 vols 1743. A reprint of 1644, above.
De familia Humia Wedderburnensi liber. Ed J. Miller 1839 (Abbotsford Club).

§2

Johnston, G. P. The first edition of Hume of Godscroft's History. Edinburgh Bibl Soc Pbns 4 1901.

ROBERT JOHNSTON
1567–1639

The history of Scotland, during the minority of King James VI, written in Latine by Robert Johnston, done into English by T. M. [Thomas Middleton]. 1646, 1648; rptd in Scotia rediviva vol 1, Edinburgh 1826; also in Tracts illustrative of the traditionary and historical antiquities of Scotland vol 1, Edinburgh 1836.
Historia rerum britannicarum, ut et multarum gallicarum, belgicarum et germanicarum, ab anno 1572–1628. Amsterdam 1655.

SIR JAMES MELVILLE of Halhill
1535–1617
See col 2457, above.

JAMES MELVILLE
1556–1614
See col 2457, above.

ROBERT MONTEITH
fl. 1621–60

Histoire des troubles de la Grande Bretagne 1633–46. Paris 1649.
See col 2474, below.

JOHN ROW
1568–1646

The history of the kirk in Scotland, from the year 1558 to August 1637, with a continuation to July 1639 by his son John Row. Ed D. Laing 1842 (Wodrow Soc); 1842 (Maitland Club). This history, though not ptd till 1842, apparently circulated widely in ms in the 17th century.

SIR JOHN SCOT of Scotstarvet
1585–1670

Schediasmata miscellanea. In John Scot of Scotstarvet, In serenissimi et invictissimi regis Iacobi sexti e Scotia sua decessum hodoeporicon, Edinburgh 1619. Verse.

The staggering state of the Scots statesmen for one hundred years, viz from 1550 to 1650. Edinburgh 1754, 1872 (with a memoir of the author and historical illustrations by C. Rogers).

Trew relation of the principall affaires concerning the state, with introductory notes by G. Neilson. Scottish Historical Rev 11–14 1914–17.

PATRICK SIMSON
1556–1618

§1

A short compend of the historie of the first ten persecutions moved against Christians. 5 pts Edinburgh 1613–16, 1 vol 1624, 1634.

The historie of the Church since the dayes of our Saviour Jesus Christ untill this present age. 1624.

Spiritual songs or holy poems; A garden of true delights. Edinburgh 1685.

The Song of Solomon, called the Song of songs, in English meter, fitted to be sung with any of the common tunes of the psalms. Glasgow 1701. Rptd from Spiritual songs, above.

§2

Couper, W. J. A Gorbals imprint of 1701, with notes on Patrick Simson's Spiritual songs. Glasgow Bibl Soc Records 6 1920.

JOHN SPALDING
fl. 1650

History of the troubles and memorable transactions in Scotland from the year 1625 to 1645. 2 vols Aberdeen 1792, 1828–9 (Bannatyne Club).

Memorialls of the trubles in Scotland and England AD 1624–AD 1645. Ed J. Stuart 2 vols 1850–1 (Spalding Club).

JOHN SPOTTISWODE
1565–1639

See col 2241, above.

A TRUE RELATION

§1

A true relation of the happy successes of his Majestys forces in Scotland under the conduct of the Lord James Marquiss of Montrose against the rebels there. [place?] [1644].

§2

Duncan, G. Some sidelights on the history of Montrose's campaign. Scottish Historical Rev 2 1905.

GEORGE WISHART
1599–1671

De rebus auspiciis serenissimi et potentissimi Caroli sub imperio illustrissimi Jacobi Montisrosarum Marchionis anno 1644 et duobus sequentibus praeclare gestis: commentarius. 1647.

The history of the Kings Majesties affairs in Scotland, under the conduct of the most honourable James Marques of Montrose, in the years, 1644. 1645, 1646. Hague 1647 (rev), 1660, London 1648, Amsterdam 1649.

Montrose redivivus: or the portraicture of James late Marquess of Montrose. 1652.

The complete history of the wars. [place?] 1660.

A complete history of the wars in Scotland under the conduct of the illustrious James Marquis of Montrose, in two parts: the 1st part describing the wars in the years 1644, 45, 46; the 2d part containing an account of the year 1647 to the year 1650 inclusive, this 2d part being never before published, is now first done into English, from the Latin; as also fifteen letters to Montrose. 1720.

Memoirs of the most renowned James Graham Marquis of Montrose, translated from the Latin of G. W.; to which are added sundry original letters. Edinburgh 1819; ed and tr A. D. Murdoch and H. F. M. Simpson 1893 (with Latin original).

(4) MISCELLANEOUS WRITERS (1603–60)

PATRICK ANDERSON
fl. 1618–35

The colde spring of Kinghorne Craig, his admirable and new tryed properties, so far foorth as yet are found true by experience. Edinburgh 1618.

The copie of a barons court, newly translated by Whatsyou-call him, clerk to the Court. Edinburgh [1640?], [1686?]; rptd as The picture of a Scottish baron's court: a dramatic poem, with original notes [by D. Webster], Edinburgh 1821.

Grana angelica: or the rare and singular vertues and uses of those angelick and innocent pills discovered and left to posterity, by Dr Patrick Anderson, late physician of Edinburgh. Edinburgh 1664, 1667, 1681.

WILLIAM BARCLAY
1570?–1630?

Nepenthes: or the vertues of tabacco. Edinburgh 1614; rptd with Callirhoe, below, in Spalding Club miscellany vol 1, 1841.

Callirhoe, the nymph of Aberdene resuscitat: what diseases may be cured by drinking of the well at Aberdene and what is the true use thereof. Edinburgh 1615, 1670; rptd with Nepenthes, above.

The nature of the new found well at Kinghorne Craig. Edinburgh 1618.

Sylvae tres. Edinburgh 1619. Latin verse.

ADAM BLACKWOOD
1539–1623

De coniunctione religionis et imperii libri duo. Paris 1575. When rptd in his Opera omnia, below a 3rd pt was added and a new title supplied, De vinculo religionis et imperii: libri tres.

Sanctarum precationum prooemia: seu mavis, eiaculationes animae ad orandum se praeparantis. Poitiers 1598. Prose and verse.

Inauguratio Jacobi Magnae Britanniae regis. Paris 1606.

In psalmum Davidis quinquagesimum, cuius initium est, Miserere mei Deus. Poitiers 1608.

Varia generis poemata. Poitiers 1609.

Opera omnia. Paris 1644.

HABAKKUK BYSSET
fl. 1582–1626

Rolment of courtis. Ed P. J. Hamilton-Grierson 3 vols 1920–6 (STS).

JAMES CARMICHAELL
1543?–1628

The James Carmichaell collection of proverbs in Scots. Ed M. L. Anderson, Edinburgh 1957.

THOMAS DEMPSTER
1579?–1625

See col 2302, above.

WILLIAM DOUGLAS
fl. 1619–50

Encourgements for the warres of France. Edinburgh 1627.
Grampius gratulation to K. Charles. [Edinburgh? 1633?]. Verse.
Oratio panegyrica ad ΕΙΖΟΔΙΑ potentissimi monarchae Caroli II. Aberdeen 1660.

GEORGE EGLISHAM
1595?–42

Accurata methodus erigendi thematis natalitii, in diebus criticis disquirendis. Edinburgh 1616.
Prodromus vindictae in ducem Buckinghamae, pro virulento caede potentissimi Magnae Britanniae regis Iacobi; necnon Marchionis Hamiltonii, ac aliorum virorum principum. [Delft?] 1626; tr German, 1626; Dutch, 1644.
The fore-runner of revenge. Frankfurt 1626, London 1642; rptd in Harleian miscellany vol 2, 1744; in Somers tracts vol 2, 1750; in Harleian miscellany vol 2, 1809; in Somers tracts vol 5, 1809. Tr from Prodromus vindictae, above.
A declaration to the Kingdome of England concerning the poysoning of King James of happy memorie. 1648. Shortened form of Fore-runner of revenge, above.

JOHN GORDON
1544–1619

Echo! dialogus de institutione principis ad Henricum Fridericum Stuardum, Britanniarum principis. Paris 1603.

PATRICK GORDON
1635–99

§1

Passages from the diary of General Patrick Gordon of Auchleuchries. Ed J. Robertson 1860 (Spalding Club).

§2

Mackay, A. General Patrick Gordon, of Auchleuchries, Cruden: the life story of a soldier of fortune. Peterhead 1915.

GILBERT GRAY
d. 1616

Oratio funebris. Edinburgh 1614.
He is sometimes credited with an Oratio de illustribus Scotiae scriptoribus, *Aberdeen 1623, but no copy is known to exist.*

WILLIAM HART

Ecloga Caledon ad potentissimum et felicissimum Iacobum primum Britanniae et Hiberniae regem. Paris 1605.

PETER HAY

A vision of Balaams asse. 1616.
An advertisement to the subjects of Scotland. Aberdeen 1627.

ALEXANDER HUME
c. 1560–c. 1630

A diduction of the true and catholik meaning of our Saviour his words, This is my bodie, in the institution of his laste supper. Edinburgh 1602.
Grammatica nova in usum juventutis scoticae ad methodum revocata. Edinburgh 1612.
Prima elementa grammaticæ in usum juventutis scoticae digesta. Edinburgh 1612.
Of the orthographie and congruitie of the Britan tongue: a treates, noe shorter then necessarie, for the schooles. Ed H. B. Wheatley 1865 (EETS).

JAMES VI, King of Scotland
1566–1625

§1

Ane fruitfull meditatioun contening ane plane and facill expositioun of the 7, 8, 9 and 10 versis of the 20 chap of the Reuelatioun in forme of ane sermone. Edinburgh 1588, London 1603; tr French, 1589; Latin, 1603; 1603.
Ane meditatioun upon the xxv, xxvi, xxvii, xxviii and xxix verses of the xv chapt of the first Book of the Chronicles of the Kings. Edinburgh 1589, London 1603.
Daemonologie, in forme of a dialogue, divided into three books. Edinburgh 1597, London 1603; ed G. B. Harrison 1924; Edinburgh 1966; tr Dutch, 1603; Latin, 1607.
The true lawe of free monarchies: or the reciprock and mutuall dutie betwixt a free King and his naturall subjectes. Edinburgh 1598, 1603, London 1642. The Advertisement to the Reader is signed C. φιλοπατρις. *See* Assertio, *below.*
Basilicon doron. Edinburgh 1599, 1603, London 1603, 1682; ed C. Edmonds 1887 (Roxburghe Club); ed J. Craigie 2 vols 1944–50 (STS); tr French, 1603, 1604, 1616, 1617, 1646, 1603, 1604, nd, 1603, Hanau 1604; tr Dutch, 1603; Latin, 1604, 1604, 1607, 1679, 1682, 1689; German, 1604, 1604; Welsh, 1604 (in part), 1931; Swedish, 1606.
A counterblaste to tobacco. 1604, 1672, 1871; ed E. Arber 1869; ed A. Hill 1954; rptd in A royal rhetorician, ed R. S. Rait 1900; tr Danish, 1958. A modernized version appeared in The old book collectors' miscellany vol 2, ed C. Handley 1872.
Workes. 1616, 1620. Prose writings only.
Opera. 1619, Frankfurt 1689.
Assertio juris monarchici in regno Scototum: seu de mutuis regis Scotiae, et subditorum eius officia, dissertatio politica. [place?] 1653. Latin version of True lawe of free monarchies, above.
Political works. Ed C. H. McIlwain 1918.

§2

Willson, D. H. King James VI and I. 1956.
See H. M. Chew in Social and political ideas of some great thinkers of the 16th and 17th centuries, *ed F. J. Hearnshaw 1926; D. H. Willson, James I and his literary assistants, HLQ 8 1945; J. Craigie, The Basilicon doron, Library 5th ser 3 1948; and col 2037, above.*

LACHRYMAE ACADEMIAE

Lachrymae academiae Marischallanae. Aberdeen 1623. Greek, Latin and English verses on the death of the founder of Marischal College, Aberdeen.

ANDREW LEECH (or LOAECHIUS)
fl. 1603–9

§1

Jovis arbitrium: sive ius hereditarium, Iacobo D. G. Primo huius nominis Angliae, sexto Scotorum regi, in Angliam, Franciam et Hyberniam divinitus collatum. 1603.

§2

Durkan, J. Leech: Scottish Latinist. Bibliotheck 4 1963.

DAVID LEECH
fl. 1628–53

Positiones philosophicae. Aberdeen 1634, 1635, 1636, 1638.
Philosophia illacrimans. Aberdeen 1637.
Parerga. 1657. Verse.

JOHN LEECH (or LEOCHAEUS)
fl. 1594–1616

Iani sperantis strena, calendis Ianuarii anno dom 1617. Edinburgh 1617.
Iani malefici strena, calendis Ianuarii anno dom 1617. Edinburgh 1617.
Nemo, Calendis Maii. Edinburgh 1617.
Lachrymae in augustissimi monarchae Iacobi I, recessu de patria sua in Anglorum fines. Edinburgh 1617.
Musae priores: sive poematum pars prior. 1620. Contains Eroticon, libri vi; Idyllia, sive eclogae; Epigrammata, libri iv; each paged separately.
Epigrammata libri quatuor: editio tertia. 1623.

WILLIAM LITHGOW
1582–1645?

A most delectable and true discourse of an admired and painefull peregrination from Scotland to the most famous kingdomes in Europe, Asia and Africa etc. 1614, 1770 (11th edn), Leith 1814, Falkirk 1825, Glasgow 1850?, 1906; tr Dutch, 1652, 1656, 1659.
A true and experimentall discourse upon this last siege of Breda. 1637.
A briefe and summarie discourse upon that lamentable and dreadful disaster at Dunglasse, anno 1640. Edinburgh [1640].
An experimentall and exact relation of that famous and renowned siege of Newcastle. Edinburgh 1645; rptd in Somers tracts vol 5, 1819; Newcastle 1820.

JAMES MAKGILL

Discours particulier d'Escosse, escrit par commandement et ordonnance de la royne douariere et regente, par messires Iacques Macgill, clerc du registre, et Iean Bellenden clerc de la iustice, xi ianvier M.D.LIX. 1824 (Bannatyne Club).

JOHN MAKLUIRE

The buckler of bodilie health, whereby health may be defended and sicknesse repelled. Edinburgh 1630.
Sanitatis semita. Edinburgh 1630.

ROBERT MONTEITH (or MENTET)
fl. 1621–60

Histoire des troubles de la Grande Bretagne: contenant ce qui s'y est passé, depuis l'année 1633 iusques à la fin de l'année 1646. Paris 1649, 1661.
Remonstrance très humble, faite au serenissime prince Charles II, roi de la Grande Bretagne, sur la conjoncture présente des affaires de sa Majesté. Paris 1652.
The history of the troubles of Great Britain, written in French by Robert Monteth of Salmonet, translated into English by Captain James Ogilvie. 1735.

JOHN NAPIER of Merchiston
1550–1617

See col 2351, above.

WILLIAM OGSTON
d. 1667

Oratio funebris. Aberdeen [1623].

DAVID PRIMROSE
fl. 1602–30

Scotlands complaint, upon the death of our late soveraigne King James of most happy memorie. Edinburgh 1625; ed J. Maidment, Edinburgh 1817.
An apologie for advocates, against some pages of M. Peter Hay of Naughton his Advertisement to Scotland; called the First blast of his trumpet, by which he would abase that approved order. Edinburgh 1628. Verse.
The treatise of the Sabbath and the Lords-day. 1636.

JOHN ROW
1598?–1672?

Hebraeae linguae institutiones, Χιλιάς hebraica: seu vocabularium continens praecipuas radices linguae hebraeae, numero 1,000. 2 pts Glasgow 1644. In 1646 the General Assembly of the Church of Scotland recommended to general use this work, the first of its kind ptd in Scotland.
Εὐχαριστία Βασιλική, ad illustrissimum monarchum Carolum II carmen. Aberdeen 1660.
For suppl to his father's history, see col 2468, above.

JAMES SIBBALD
1590?–1650?

Assertiones philosophicae. Aberdeen 1623.
Theses philosophicae. Aberdeen 1625, 1626.
Theses theologicae de primatu B. Petri. Aberdeen 1627.
Diverse select sermons. Aberdeen 1658.

SIR JOHN SKENE
1543?–1617

De verborum significatione: the exposition of the termes and difficil words conteined in the foure buikes of Regiam Majestatem and uthers, in the Acts of Parliament, infeftments and used in practique of this realm. Edinburgh 1597, 1618, London 1641.

Regiam Majestatem: Scotiae veteres leges et constitutiones, ex archivis publicis, et antiquis libris manuscriptis collectae. Edinburgh 1609; tr Edinburgh 1609, 1774. Now regarded as not properly belonging to Scotland at all, but based on the legal system of England. *See* J. Davidson, Observations on the Regiam Majestatem, Edinburgh 1792.

Skene's memorabilia scotica 1475–1612, and Revisals of Regiam Majestatem. Ed G. Neilson, Glasgow 1923. First pbd in Analecta scotica vol 2, ed T. G. Stevenson, Edinburgh 1837.

Regiam Majestatem and Quoniam Attachiamenta. Ed and tr T. M. Cooper 1947 (Stair Soc).

A SOLEMN WARNING

A solemn warning to all members of this Kirk, from the Commission of the General Assemblie, with an Act for censuring such as act, or comply with, the sectarian armie now infesting this Kingdom. Aberdeen 1651.

DAVID WEDDERBURN
1580–1646

In obitu summae spei Principis Henrici lessus. Edinburgh 1613. Verse.

Invictissimo et potentissimo monarchae Jacobo VI Scotiam suam revisenti συνευφραντήριον. Edinburgh 1617; rptd in Τὰ τῶν Μουσῶν εἰσόδια: the Muses welcome, ed T. Adamson, Edinburgh 1618.

Abredonia strata, sub obitum Jacobi VI. Aberdeen 1625.

A short introduction to grammar. Aberdeen 1632, 1637, Edinburgh 1700.

Vivat Rex: seu προσευκτικόν pro incolumitate serenissimi regis Caroli ejusque felice in Scotia inauguratione. Aberdeen 1633.

Institutiones grammaticae. Aberdeen 1634, 1633 (for 1635).

Meditationum campestrium: seu epigrammatum moralium, centuriae duae. Aberdeen 1643; Centuria tertia, Aberdeen 1644.

Sub obitum viri spectatissimi Georgii Jamesoni. Aberdeen [1644].

Persius enucleatus: sive commentarius in Persium, poetarum omnium difficilimum. Amsterdam 1664.

WILLIAM WELWOOD
fl. 1576–1613

The sea-law of Scotland. Edinburgh 1590; ed T. Callander Wade 1933 (in STS Miscellany). One of the earliest British treatises on maritime law.

(5) PROSE WRITINGS IN LATIN

Many prose works were composed in Latin by Scottish writers between 1500 and 1660, and some have been noted above. But most have been omitted since their authors spent much of their lives, and in particular their most productive years, out of Scotland; since their subjects had no relation to Scottish life or affairs; since the audience at which they were directed was a European and not a purely Scottish one; and since they were all ptd abroad, usually in France, the United Provinces or Germany.

J. C.

INDEX

to Volume 1, containing the names of primary authors, British and Irish, together with certain headings. Numerals refer to columns. Volume 5 will provide a more detailed index to the whole of New CBEL.